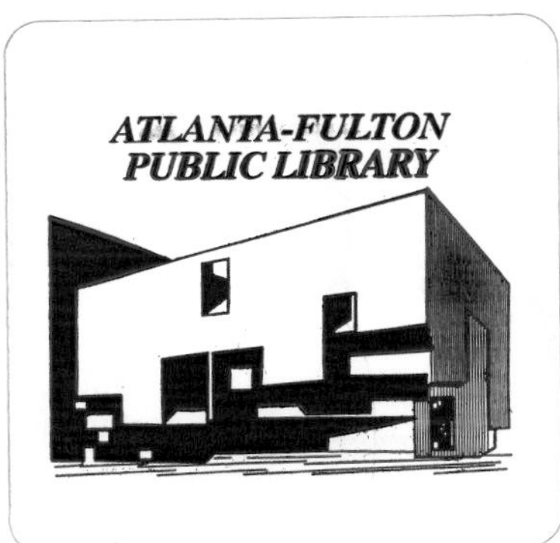
ATLANTA-FULTON
PUBLIC LIBRARY

PATTERSON'S

ELEMENTARY EDUCATION

2010 Edition
VOLUME XXII

edi

EDUCATIONAL DIRECTORIES INC.

Educational Directories Inc.
PO Box 68097
Schaumburg IL 60168-0097
(847) 891-1250 or (800) 357-6183
www.ediusa.com

First edition published 1989. Twenty Second edition 2010

ISBN 978-0-9821099-4-6
ISSN 1044-1417
Library of Congress Catalog Card Number: SN89-646629
Printed in the United States of America

CONTENTS

HOW TO USE THIS DIRECTORY

Patterson's ELEMENTARY EDUCATION (published annually since 1989) is the first, single-volume, comprehensive, national directory to elementary schools and the third in a series of school directories published by Educational Directories Inc. Patterson's AMERICAN EDUCATION (published annually since 1904) is THE standard directory to secondary schools; and Patterson's SCHOOLS CLASSIFIED (published annually since 1951) is the most comprehensive directory to post-secondary schools available. The three volumes combined fulfill the need for a single, systematized, comprehensive directory to our nation's schools from kindergarten through post-graduate studies.

Patterson's ELEMENTARY EDUCATION contains more than 12,000 public school districts, more than 66,000 public, private and Catholic elementary schools and more than 15,500 middle schools in an easy-to-use and consistent format. It is an invaluable resource for anyone involved in education or educational research. School registrars, guidance counselors, principals, superintendents, directors of admissions, financial aid officers, schools of education, public libraries, government agencies, armed forces and business people find it a welcome replacement for the multitude of other directories required for national coverage of our nation's school systems with their variation in size, content, format and publishing date.

One of the primary objectives of this directory is to make available the latest, most comprehensive information about elementary schools in a condensed and easily accessible format. Its general organization is geographical. Entries are arranged alphabetically, by state, then by community (post office) and then by District and School name. Each state begins with a listing of the officials in its Department of Education followed by the head of the State Board of Education. If a state has intermediate superintendents (a level of superintendent between the state superintendent of schools and the superintendents who actually supervise the schools) they appear in a table preceding the community listings. Community listings follow and include the community name, county name, community population, district name, total district student enrollment, the superintendent's name, address, telephone, fax number and website where available followed by a listing of the district schools, showing their enrollment, grade range and the principal's name, address, telephone number and fax number. A district may be responsible for schools in more than one community. To achieve consistency, the district office is listed in the community in which it is located. A cross-reference is provided to and from the schools of the district located in other communities.

A short line may appear at the end of the listing of public elementary schools. This line separates the public schools from the private and Catholic elementary schools located in the community. Private and Catholic school listings include their enrollment, grade range and the principal's name, address, telephone number and fax number. Please refer to page vi, "Guide to Editorial Style," for an example of how these elements work together to provide an easy-to-use format.

Schools Listed

Patterson's ELEMENTARY EDUCATION lists the following types of schools:

- **Kindergarten Schools**
- **Primary Schools** usually teach any combination of the first three elementary grades.
- **Intermediate Schools** usually teach any combination of grades four through six.
- **Elementary Schools** usually teach a combination of the first four to the first eight grades.
- **Middle Schools** usually teach any combination of grades five through eight.
- **K-12 Schools**

The following are included:

- All graded state approved public elementary schools.
- All graded elementary schools belonging to the National Catholic Education Association.
- All graded, regionally accredited, private elementary schools.
- Private elementary schools belonging to the member associations of the Council of American Private Education.

Non-graded, special education schools, and other non-traditional elementary schools are not listed.

Patterson's AMERICAN EDUCATION lists Junior High Schools, Junior-Senior High Schools, Senior High Schools, High Schools and K-12 Schools.

ABBREVIATIONS

AVC. . . Area Vocational Center
CCSD . . Community Consolidated School District
CDC . . Child Development Center
CESD . . Consolidated Elementary School District
CISD . . City Independent School District
CSD. . . City School District
CUSD . . Community Unit School District
ECC. . . Early Childhood Center
ECCSD . Elementary Community Consolidated School District
EHSD . . Elementary-High School District
ES . . . Elementary School
ESD. . . Elementary School District
EVD. . . Exempted Village District
HS . . . High School
HSD. . . High School District
IS . . . . Intermediate School
ISD . . . Independent School District
JESD . . Joint Elementary School District
JHS . . . Junior High School
JSD . . . Joint School District
JSHS . . Junior-Senior High School
JUESD . Joint Unified Elementary School District
JUHSD . Joint Unified High School District
JUNESD Joint Union Elementary School District
JUNHSD Joint Union High School District
JUSD . . Joint Unified School District
JVSD . . Joint Vocational School District
K . . . . Kindergarten
MS . . . Middle School
MSHS. . Middle School High School
PS . . . Primary School
RHSD. . Rural High School District
RISD . . Rural Independent School District
RSD. . . Reorganized School District
S . . . . School
SAD. . . School Administrative District
SC . . . School Corporation
SD . . . School District
SHS. . . Senior High School
SSD. . . Separate School District
UESD . . Unified Elementary School District
UFD. . . Union Free District
UHSD. . Unified High School District
UNESD . Union Elementary School District
UNHSD . Union High School District
UNSD. . Union School District
USD. . . Unified School District
Vo/Tech. Vocational/Technical

GUIDE TO EDITORIAL STYLE

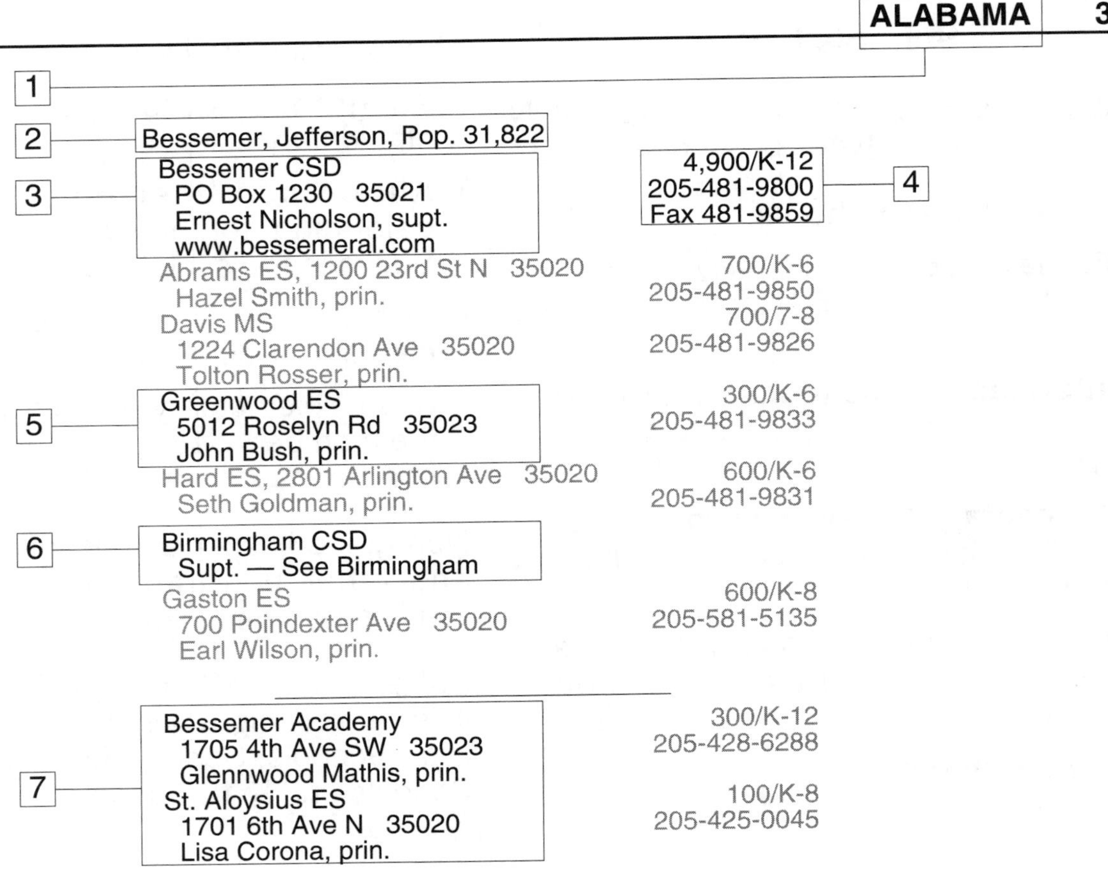

1. State.
2. City, county and city population.
3. Community school districts - school district name (refer to page v for abbreviations), address, superintendent's name and website.
4. Enrollment, grade range, phone number and fax number.
5. Community schools - school name, address and principal's name.
6. If the school district office is not located in this city, a cross-reference will show office location.
7. Private and Catholic elementary schools appear below a short line in the cities where they are located.

ELEMENTARY SCHOOL COUNTS BY STATE

State	Public						Private	Catholic	Total
	Districts	K-4	K-6	K-8	5-8	K-12			
Alabama	132	141	493	69	257	77	148	35	1,352
Alaska	53	7	134	16	35	185	28	5	463
Arizona	195	64	577	277	221	4	124	50	1,512
Arkansas	246	187	341	4	183	2	71	26	1,060
California	873	246	4,489	608	1,277	7	1,392	562	9,454
Colorado	178	44	812	51	271	8	166	50	1,580
Connecticut	158	126	412	76	194	1	83	116	1,166
Delaware	15	26	67	2	40	0	57	21	228
District Of Columbia	1	3	60	22	12	0	24	14	136
Florida	67	44	1,660	63	530	15	896	173	3,448
Georgia	179	104	1,148	11	474	6	320	35	2,277
Hawaii	1	1	167	5	35	6	75	26	316
Idaho	114	43	276	14	97	16	56	13	629
Illinois	769	481	1,236	680	774	2	445	433	4,820
Indiana	293	170	909	20	359	4	198	163	2,116
Iowa	361	175	527	14	285	3	73	104	1,542
Kansas	294	134	550	70	244	1	70	92	1,455
Kentucky	174	42	613	75	238	5	100	100	1,347
Louisiana	70	126	471	96	242	62	158	144	1,369
Maine	145	104	179	98	113	9	42	15	705
Maryland	24	35	758	67	230	1	221	128	1,464
Massachusetts	278	287	653	89	332	1	168	158	1,966
Michigan	551	342	1,280	97	597	30	489	215	3,601
Minnesota	333	134	631	32	218	18	190	191	1,747
Mississippi	149	132	281	37	192	40	110	25	966
Missouri	521	233	836	98	382	2	169	210	2,451
Montana	308	36	279	104	229	0	32	17	1,005
Nebraska	254	52	473	68	111	2	79	91	1,130
Nevada	17	13	322	17	91	7	74	11	552
New Hampshire	154	74	156	47	92	3	47	24	597
New Jersey	502	392	786	268	449	0	251	250	2,898
New Mexico	89	40	365	9	154	0	72	28	757
New York	682	429	1,803	179	807	78	587	537	5,102
North Carolina	115	108	1,148	76	471	3	338	39	2,298
North Dakota	175	14	207	40	35	3	14	23	511
Ohio	612	476	1,189	160	718	8	296	370	3,829
Oklahoma	532	136	516	288	292	2	70	30	1,866
Oregon	191	52	549	102	208	22	152	44	1,320
Pennsylvania	499	362	1,254	163	518	1	420	463	3,680
Rhode Island	35	34	147	1	54	1	32	37	341
South Carolina	85	88	521	15	262	2	142	28	1,143
South Dakota	157	23	213	88	158	1	29	25	694
Tennessee	135	200	602	178	311	19	249	48	1,742
Texas	1,029	788	3,142	88	1,609	114	549	231	7,550
Utah	40	13	488	4	50	2	53	12	662
Vermont	58	19	140	65	27	10	24	12	355
Virginia	132	91	1,073	9	348	2	265	63	1,983
Washington	295	79	975	55	329	21	311	81	2,146
West Virginia	55	99	310	38	123	2	49	25	701
Wisconsin	415	176	783	123	349	12	358	300	2,516
Wyoming	48	34	147	16	55	6	12	7	325
Total	12,788	7,259	37,148	4,892	15,682	826	10,378	5,900	94,873

ELEMENTARY SCHOOLS

ALABAMA

ALABAMA DEPARTMENT OF EDUCATION
PO Box 302101, Montgomery 36130-2101
Telephone 334-242-9700
Fax 334-242-9708
Website http://www.alsde.edu

State Superintendent of Education Joseph Morton

ALABAMA BOARD OF EDUCATION
PO Box 302101, Montgomery 36130-2101

President Governor Bob Riley

PUBLIC, PRIVATE AND CATHOLIC ELEMENTARY SCHOOLS

Abbeville, Henry, Pop. 2,963
Henry County SD 2,700/PK-12
300 N Trawick St 36310 334-585-2206
Dennis Coe, supt. Fax 585-2551
www.henrycountyboe.org/
Abbeville ES 500/K-5
100 Elm St 36310 334-585-3679
Beverly Clark, prin. Fax 585-1122
Abbeville MS 300/6-8
PO Box 547 36310 334-585-2185
Jill Barber, prin. Fax 585-1492
Other Schools – See Headland

Abbeville Christian Academy 300/K-12
PO Box 9 36310 334-585-5100
Barbara Lindsey, prin. Fax 555-5100

Adamsville, Jefferson, Pop. 4,845
Jefferson County SD
Supt. — See Birmingham
Adamsville ES 400/K-5
4600 Hazelwood Rd 35005 205-379-2400
Gayle Gober, prin. Fax 379-2445
Bottonfield MS 1,000/6-8
400 Hillcrest Rd 35005 205-379-2550
Dr. Jennifer Maye, prin. Fax 379-2553

Addison, Winston, Pop. 713
Winston County SD
Supt. — See Double Springs
Addison ES 400/K-6
PO Box 660 35540 256-747-1665
Ellan Oliver, prin. Fax 747-1654

Akron, Hale, Pop. 514
Hale County SD
Supt. — See Greensboro
Akron Community ES West 200/K-6
PO Box 48 35441 205-372-4246
Ruth Davis, prin. Fax 372-0003

Alabaster, Shelby, Pop. 27,517
Shelby County SD
Supt. — See Columbiana
Meadow View ES 1,000/K-3
2800 Smokey Rd 35007 205-682-5740
Jody Brewer, prin. Fax 682-5745
Thompson IS 900/4-5
10019 Highway 119 35007 205-682-5720
Ke'Andrea Jones, prin. Fax 682-5725
Thompson MS 1,400/6-8
1509 Kent Dairy Rd 35007 205-682-5710
Melissa Youngblood, prin. Fax 682-5715
Thompson Sixth Grade Center 100/6-6
10111 Highway 119 35007 205-682-5790
Brent Tolbert, prin.

Kingwood Christian Child Development Ctr 200/PK-PK
200 Harvest Way 35007 205-620-6720
Barbara Drackett, dir. Fax 564-0003
Kingwood Christian S 400/PK-12
1351 Royalty Dr 35007 205-663-3973
Margaret Pickett, prin. Fax 663-7145

Alberta, Wilcox
Wilcox County SD
Supt. — See Camden
ABC ES 200/PK-6
PO Box 129 36720 334-573-2550
Laurette Gibson, prin. Fax 573-9361

Albertville, Marshall, Pop. 18,615
Albertville CSD 3,700/K-12
107 W Main St 35950 256-891-1183
Dr. Frederic Ayer, supt. Fax 891-6303
www.albertk12.org
Alabama Avenue MS 600/7-8
600 E Alabama Ave 35950 256-878-2341
Michael Douglas, prin. Fax 891-6334
Albertville ES 1,300/1-4
1100 Horton Rd 35950 256-878-6611
Mona Sheets, prin. Fax 891-6390
Big Spring Lake K 400/K-K
257 Country Club Rd 35951 256-878-7922
Tracy Penney, prin. Fax 891-6386
Evans ES 600/5-6
901 W Mckinney Ave 35950 256-878-7698
Tim Tidmore, prin. Fax 891-7841

Marshall County SD
Supt. — See Guntersville
Asbury S 800/K-12
1990 Asbury Rd 35951 256-878-4068
Susan Collins, prin. Fax 878-5233

Marshall Christian Academy 50/PK-7
1631 Brashers Chapel Rd 35951 256-279-0192
Ed Rogers, admin. Fax 891-4160

Alexander City, Tallapoosa, Pop. 14,957
Alexander City SD 3,500/K-12
375 Lee St 35010 256-234-5074
Lou Ann Wagoner, supt. Fax 234-8649
www.alex.k12.al.us
Alexander City MS 500/7-8
359 State St 35010 256-234-8660
Tracy McGhee, prin. Fax 234-8659
Pearson ES 900/K-2
1240 Scott Rd 35010 256-234-8625
Ellen Martin, prin. Fax 234-8647
Radney ES 500/5-6
140 Alison Dr 35010 256-234-8636
Dr. Beverly Price, prin. Fax 234-8654
Stephens ES 600/3-4
851 Laurel St 35010 256-234-8631
Jose Reyes, prin. Fax 234-8653

Alexandria, Calhoun
Calhoun County SD
Supt. — See Anniston
Alexandria ES 800/K-5
PO Box 121 36250 256-741-4300
Sarah McClure, prin. Fax 820-7101

Aliceville, Pickens, Pop. 2,465
Pickens County SD
Supt. — See Carrollton
Aliceville ES 300/K-3
PO Box 430 35442 205-373-8722
Anissa Ball, prin. Fax 373-3337
Aliceville MS 200/4-6
1000 Columbus Rd NW 35442 205-373-6900
Johnny Johnson, prin. Fax 373-8296

Altoona, Etowah, Pop. 970
Etowah County SD
Supt. — See Gadsden
West End ES 500/K-6
6795 Highway 132 35952 205-589-6711
Andrea Collett, prin. Fax 589-6911

Andalusia, Covington, Pop. 8,691
Andalusia CSD 1,700/K-12
122 6th Ave 36420 334-222-3186
Dr. Beverly McAnulty, supt. Fax 222-8631
andalusia.al.schoolwebpages.com
Andalusia ES 900/K-5
1501 W Bypass 36420 334-222-1224
Patty Taylor, prin. Fax 427-7214
Andalusia MS 300/6-8
1201 C C Baker Ave, 334-222-6542
Ted Watson, prin. Fax 222-3875

Covington County SD 3,200/K-12
PO Box 460 36420 334-222-7571
Sharon Dye, supt. Fax 222-7573
www.cov.k12.al.us/
Pleasant Home S 500/K-12
12548 Falco Rd 36420 334-222-1315
Craig Nichols, prin. Fax 222-4415
Straughn ES 500/K-5
29324 Straughn School Rd, 334-427-1311
Bettye Anne Older, prin. Fax 427-1401
Straughn MS 300/6-8
29324 Straughn School Rd, 334-222-4090
Cassandra Scott, prin. Fax 222-4132
Other Schools – See Florala, Lockhart, Opp, Red Level

Anderson, Lauderdale, Pop. 348
Lauderdale County SD
Supt. — See Florence
Anderson S 200/K-9
201 Bayles St 35610 256-247-5673
Johnny Tidwell, prin. Fax 247-7985

Anniston, Calhoun, Pop. 23,741
Anniston CSD 2,500/K-12
PO Box 1500 36202 256-231-5000
Joan Frazier, supt. Fax 231-5073
www.annistonschools.com/
Anniston MS 600/6-8
4800 Mcclellan Blvd 36206 256-231-5020
Lywood Hawkins, prin. Fax 231-5024
Cobb ES 200/K-5
1325 Cobb Ave 36201 256-231-5030
Yolanda McCants, prin. Fax 231-5009
Constantine ES 200/K-5
1200 Johnson Ave 36201 256-231-5040
Marlon Jones, prin. Fax 231-5075
Golden Springs ES 200/K-5
100 Feary Dr 36207 256-231-5050
Betty Merriweather, prin. Fax 231-5052
Randolph Park ES 300/K-5
2200 W 17th St 36201 256-231-5080
Sandra Gunter, prin. Fax 231-5082
Tenth Street ES 400/K-5
1525 E 10th St 36207 256-231-5090
Dr. Sharron Morrow, prin. Fax 231-5044

Calhoun County SD 9,000/K-12
PO Box 2084 36202 256-741-7400
Judy Stiefel Ed.D., supt. Fax 237-5332
www.calhoun.k12.al.us
Saks ES 600/K-4
31 Watson St 36206 256-741-6800
Hector Baeza, prin. Fax 236-8181
Saks MS 400/5-7
32 Watson St 36206 256-741-6900
Wendy England, prin. Fax 236-9191
Wellborn ES 600/K-6
525 Cooper Cir 36201 256-741-7500
Douglas O'Dell, prin. Fax 236-3141
White Plains ES 500/K-4
5600 AL Highway 9 36207 256-741-7700
Andy Ward, prin. Fax 236-6008
White Plains MS 200/5-8
5800 AL Highway 9 36207 256-741-4700
Joseph Dyar, prin. Fax 238-1715
Other Schools – See Alexandria, Jacksonville, Ohatchee, Weaver

Oxford CSD
Supt. — See Oxford
Coldwater ES 400/K-4
530 Taylors Chapel Rd 36201 256-241-3870
Kenneth Gover, prin. Fax 236-6061
De Armanville ES 300/K-4
101 School Rd 36207 256-241-3918
Amy Copeland, prin. Fax 835-0121

Cornerstone Christian Academy 100/PK-12
2885 Choccolocco Rd 36207 256-236-1861
Sharon Cox, admin. Fax 236-1120
Donoho S 400/PK-12
2501 Henry Rd 36207 256-237-5477
Janice Hurd, pres. Fax 237-6474
Faith Christian S 300/PK-12
4100 Ronnaki Rd 36207 256-236-4499
Dr. Ben Character, hdmstr. Fax 236-4673
Sacred Heart S 200/PK-12
16 Morton Rd 36205 256-237-4231
Charlie Maniscalco, prin. Fax 237-2353

Arab, Marshall, Pop. 7,498
Arab CSD 2,500/PK-12
750 Arabian Dr NE 35016 256-586-6011
John Mullins, supt. Fax 586-6013
www.arabcityschools.org
Arab ES 600/3-5
241 8th Ave NE 35016 256-586-6085
Mike Shipp, prin. Fax 931-0427
Arab JHS 600/6-8
911 Old Cullman Rd SW 35016 256-586-6074
John Ingram, prin. Fax 586-1348

Arab PS 500/PK-2
121 Mimosa St NE 35016 256-586-6005
Leah Keith, prin. Fax 586-0616

Marshall County SD
Supt. — See Guntersville
Grassy ES 400/PK-5
2233 Shoal Creek Rd 35016 256-753-2246
Beverly Kirkland, prin. Fax 753-6630

Ardmore, Limestone, Pop. 1,106
Limestone County SD
Supt. — See Athens
Cedar Hill ES 500/K-5
27905 Cedar Hill Rd 35739 256-423-5950
Harold Johns, prin. Fax 423-5970

Ariton, Dale, Pop. 755
Dale County SD
Supt. — See Ozark
Ariton S 700/K-12
PO Box 750 36311 334-762-2371
Frank Brown, prin. Fax 762-2126

Arley, Winston, Pop. 321
Winston County SD
Supt. — See Double Springs
Meek ES 300/K-6
PO Box 260 35541 205-221-9425
Amy Hiller, prin. Fax 221-9425

Ashford, Houston, Pop. 1,932
Houston County SD
Supt. — See Dothan
Ashford ES 900/K-6
100 Barfield St 36312 334-899-5912
Mitchell Sellers, prin. Fax 899-4728

Ashford Academy 200/PK-12
1100 N Broadway St 36312 334-899-3286
Rebecca Baggett, hdmstr. Fax 899-7503

Ashland, Clay, Pop. 1,885
Clay County SD 2,100/K-12
PO Box 278 36251 256-354-5414
Ben Griffin, supt. Fax 354-5415
www.claycoboe.org/
Ashland ES 600/K-6
PO Box 128 36251 256-354-2567
Nina Hobdy, prin. Fax 354-2512
Other Schools – See Lineville

Ashville, Saint Clair, Pop. 2,429
Saint Clair County SD 7,600/PK-12
410 Roy Dr 35953 205-594-7131
Jenny Seals, supt. Fax 594-4441
www.stclaircountyschools.net
Ashville ES 500/K-4
33225 US Highway 231 35953 205-594-5242
Patti Johnson, prin. Fax 594-2239
Ashville MS 300/5-8
PO Box 340 35953 205-594-7044
Phillip Johnson, prin. Fax 594-2241
Other Schools – See Moody, Odenville, Ragland, Springville, Steele

Athens, Limestone, Pop. 20,972
Athens CSD 2,900/K-12
313 E Washington St 35611 256-233-6600
Dr. Orman Bridges, supt. Fax 233-6640
www.acs-k12.org
Athens ES 300/K-4
515 N Madison St 35611 256-233-6609
Ronnie Poole, prin. Fax 230-2861
Athens IS 400/5-6
1916 US Highway 72 W 35611 256-230-2880
Randall Murphy, prin. Fax 230-9593
Athens MS 400/7-8
601 S Clinton St 35611 256-233-6620
Mike Bishop, prin. Fax 233-6623
Brookhill ES 300/K-4
320 Brookhill Dr 35611 256-233-6603
Felicia Phillips, prin. Fax 230-2871
Cowart ES 300/K-4
1701 W Hobbs St 35611 256-233-6627
Janet Poole, prin. Fax 230-2884
Newman ES 300/K-4
517 Julian Newman St 35611 256-233-6630
Darin Aderholt, prin. Fax 230-2864

Limestone County SD 8,300/K-12
300 S Jefferson St 35611 256-232-5353
Barry Carroll Ed.D., supt. Fax 233-6461
www.lcsk12.org
Clements S 1,100/K-12
7730 US Highway 72 35611 256-729-6564
Donald Wilson, prin. Fax 729-1029
Johnson ES 300/K-5
21360 AL Highway 251 35613 256-233-6665
Casey Lewis, prin. Fax 233-6673
Owens ES 500/K-6
21465 AL Highway 99 35614 256-233-6669
Cleo Miller, prin. Fax 233-8025
Piney Chapel ES 200/K-6
20835 Elkton Rd 35614 256-233-6674
Bill Hardyman, prin. Fax 233-6697
Other Schools – See Ardmore, Elkmont, Harvest, Lester, Tanner

---

Athens Bible S 300/K-12
507 Hoffman St 35611 256-232-3525
Dr. Joseph Olson, prin. Fax 232-5417
Faith Christian Academy 200/PK-12
705 W Sanderfer Rd 35611 256-233-3778
Wayne Forsythe, admin. Fax 233-4550

Atmore, Escambia, Pop. 7,530
Escambia County SD
Supt. — See Brewton
Escambia County MS 600/5-8
PO Box 1236 36504 251-368-9105
Zickeyous Byrd, prin. Fax 368-0969
Moore ES 300/3-4
501 Beck St 36502 251-368-4245
David Nolin, prin. Fax 368-0244
Patterson ES 400/K-2
1102 W Craig St 36502 251-368-4860
Susan McKenzie, prin. Fax 368-0764

Escambia Academy 200/K-12
268 Cowpen Creek Rd 36502 251-368-2080
Betty Warren, hdmstr. Fax 368-1950

Attalla, Etowah, Pop. 6,474
Attalla CSD 1,700/PK-12
101 Case Ave SE 35954 256-538-8051
Danny Golden, supt. Fax 538-8388
www.attalla.k12.al.us
Curtiston PS 300/PK-2
300 Cullman Ave SW 35954 256-538-7266
Sheila Denson, prin. Fax 538-6064
Etowah MS 500/6-8
429 4th St SW 35954 256-538-3236
Jerald Cardin, prin. Fax 538-3232
Stowers Hill IS 300/3-5
404 9th Ave SW 35954 256-538-9261
Nancy Mitchell, prin. Fax 538-9261

Etowah County SD
Supt. — See Gadsden
Duck Springs ES 200/K-6
10180 Duck Springs Rd 35954 256-538-6301
Suzanne Nance, prin. Fax 538-0037
Ivalee ES 200/K-6
840 Gallant Rd 35954 256-538-9781
Eddie Vance, prin. Fax 538-0831

Auburn, Lee, Pop. 49,928
Auburn CSD 5,500/K-12
PO Box 3270 36831 334-887-2100
Dr. J. Terry Jenkins, supt. Fax 887-2107
auburnschools.org
Auburn Early Education Center 500/K-K
721 E University Dr 36830 334-887-4950
Janet Johnson, prin. Fax 887-2139
Dean Road ES 400/1-5
335 S Dean Rd 36830 334-887-4900
Jackie Greenwood, prin. Fax 887-0599
Drake MS 800/6-7
655 Spencer Ave 36832 334-887-1940
Debra Beebe, prin. Fax 887-5302
Ogletree ES 600/1-5
737 Ogletree Rd 36830 334-887-4920
Dr. Mary Martin-Smith, prin. Fax 826-1328
Richland ES 1-5
770 Yarbrough Farms Blvd 36832 334-887-1980
Debbie Smith, prin. Fax 502-2963
Woods ES 400/1-5
715 Sanders St 36830 334-887-4940
Deborah Brooks, prin. Fax 887-4172
Wrights Mill Road ES 400/1-5
807 Wrights Mill Rd 36830 334-887-1990
Lynda Tremaine, prin. Fax 887-4180
Yarbrough ES 500/1-5
1555 N Donahue Dr 36830 334-887-1970
Jeffrey Forster, prin. Fax 826-2516

Holy Trinity Day S 50/PK-K
100 Church Dr 36830 334-821-9838
Fax 887-9501
Lee-Scott Academy 600/PK-12
1601 Academy Dr 36830 334-821-2430
Don Roberts, hdmstr. Fax 821-0876

Autaugaville, Autauga, Pop. 865
Autauga County SD
Supt. — See Prattville
Autaugaville S 400/K-12
PO Box 99 36003 334-365-8329
James Davis, prin. Fax 365-8043

Baileyton, Cullman, Pop. 703
Cullman County SD
Supt. — See Cullman
Parkside S 400/K-8
12431 AL Highway 69 N 35019 256-796-5568
Chris Gambrill, prin. Fax 796-5507

Banks, Pike, Pop. 224
Pike County SD
Supt. — See Troy
Banks S 300/K-8
9769 N US Highway 29 36005 334-243-5514
Mark Head, prin. Fax 243-5984

Bay Minette, Baldwin, Pop. 7,808
Baldwin County SD 25,100/PK-12
2600 Hand Ave 36507 251-937-0306
Faron Hollinger Ed.D., supt. Fax 580-1856
www.bcbe.org
Bay Minette ES 600/PK-3
800 Blackburn Ave 36507 251-937-7651
Scott Langham, prin. Fax 937-6983
Bay Minette IS 300/4-6
600 Blackburn Ave 36507 251-580-0678
Albertnetta Hamilton, prin. Fax 937-0696
Bay Minette MS 600/7-8
1311 W 13th St 36507 251-580-2960
Tammie Fleming, prin. Fax 580-5120
Delta ES 300/PK-6
10251 Whitehouse Fork Road 36507 251-937-3657
Leah Ann Overstreet, prin. Fax 937-3637
Pine Grove ES 600/PK-6
43980 Pine Grove Rd 36507 251-937-0453
Martha Rabon, prin. Fax 580-4188
Other Schools – See Bon Secour, Daphne, Elberta, Fairhope, Foley, Gulf Shores, Loxley, Orange Beach, Perdido, Robertsdale, Silverhill, Spanish Fort, Stapleton, Summerdale

Bayou La Batre, Mobile, Pop. 2,725
Mobile County SD
Supt. — See Mobile
Alba MS 600/6-8
14180 S Wintzell Ave 36509 251-824-4134
James Gill, prin. Fax 824-1324

Bear Creek, Marion, Pop. 1,021
Marion County SD
Supt. — See Hamilton
Phillips ES 300/K-6
160 School Ave 35543 205-486-5062
David Pruitt, prin. Fax 486-5011

Beatrice, Monroe, Pop. 403
Monroe County SD
Supt. — See Monroeville
Beatrice ES 200/K-6
PO Box 68 36425 251-789-2575
Carol Brown, prin. Fax 789-2419

Berry, Fayette, Pop. 1,226
Fayette County SD
Supt. — See Fayette
Berry ES 300/PK-6
341 School Ave 35546 205-689-4464
Debbie Deavours, prin. Fax 689-4463

Bessemer, Jefferson, Pop. 28,641
Bessemer CSD 4,100/K-12
PO Box 1230 35021 205-432-3000
Michael Foster Ed.D., supt. Fax 432-3085
www.bessk12.org
Abrams ES 500/K-6
1200 23rd St N 35020 205-432-3100
Brenda Rumley, prin. Fax 432-3107
Davis MS 600/7-8
1224 Clarendon Ave 35020 205-432-3600
Albert Soles, prin. Fax 432-3607
Greenwood ES 400/K-6
5012 Roslyn Rd 35022 205-432-3200
Deborah Billups, prin. Fax 432-3207
Hard ES 400/K-6
2801 Arlington Ave 35020 205-432-3300
Barbara McCoy, prin. Fax 432-3307
Jonesboro ES 800/K-6
125 Owen Ave 35020 205-432-3400
Darryl Aikerson, prin. Fax 432-3466
Westhills ES 400/K-6
710 Glenn Rd 35022 205-432-3500
Mildred Posey, prin. Fax 432-3502

Jefferson County SD
Supt. — See Birmingham
Concord ES 300/K-5
6015 Warrior River Rd 35023 205-379-3150
David Foster, prin. Fax 379-3195
Greenwood ES 200/K-5
1219 School Rd SE 35022 205-379-3750
Dr. Dawn Kelley, prin. Fax 379-3751
Lipscomb ES 200/K-5
5605 10th St S 35020 205-379-4550
James Mcleod, prin. Fax 379-4571
Oak Grove ES 600/K-5
9000 Tiger Cub Trl 35023 205-379-2450
Charlene McMurry, prin. Fax 379-2495

Bessemer Classical S 50/K-3
1723 3rd Ave N 35020 205-451-5433
Jim Shaw, hdmstr.
Dunnam's Private S 200/PK-5
811 Glenn Rd 35022 205-425-4194
Flint Hill Christian S 400/PK-12
1630 Powder Plant Rd 35022 205-424-2675
Larry Pender, admin. Fax 424-3535
Rock Creek Academy 50/PK-12
901 Glaze Dr 35023 205-436-4867
Tammy Hope, prin. Fax 436-4867
St. Aloysius S 200/PK-8
751A Academy Dr 35022 205-425-0045
Dr. Bette Kersting-Bell, prin. Fax 425-0046

Billingsley, Autauga, Pop. 121
Autauga County SD
Supt. — See Prattville
Billingsley S 700/K-12
PO Box 118 36006 205-755-1629
Van Smith, prin. Fax 755-1633

Birmingham, Jefferson, Pop. 231,483
Birmingham CSD 26,200/PK-12
PO Box 10007 35202 205-231-4600
Barbara Allen, supt. Fax 231-4761
birmingham.schoolinsites.com/
Arrington MS 400/6-8
2101 Jefferson Ave SW 35211 205-231-1130
Mario Lumzy, prin. Fax 231-1133
Arthur ES 300/K-5
625 14th Ave NW 35215 205-231-5130
Sheila Wade, prin. Fax 231-5138
Avondale ES 400/K-5
4000 8th Ct S 35222 205-231-7130
Dr. Ann Curry, prin. Fax 231-7139
Barrett ES 500/K-5
7601 Division Ave 35206 205-231-8130
Wanda Birchfield, prin. Fax 231-8134
Brown ES 400/K-5
4811 Court J 35208 205-231-1190
Robbie Sullivan, prin. Fax 231-1193
Bush Magnet MS 500/6-8
1112 25th Street Ensley 35218 205-231-6000
Vanessa Byrd, prin. Fax 231-6007
Center Street MS 400/6-8
1832 Center Way S 35205 205-231-7190
Cassandra Fincher Fells, prin. Fax 231-7231

Central Park ES 700/K-5
4915 Avenue Q 35208 205-231-1250
Bettie Griggs, prin. Fax 231-1300
Councill ES 400/PK-5
1400 Avenue M 35218 205-231-6190
Steve Brown, prin. Fax 231-6943
EPIC ES 400/K-5
1000 10th Ave S 35205 205-231-7370
Victoria Stokes, prin. Fax 231-7419
Gaskins MS 500/6-8
200 Dalton Dr 35215 205-231-9200
Dr. Sherene Carpenter, prin. Fax 231-9253
Gaston S 300/K-8
5400 Oakwood St 35228 205-231-1310
Fred Stewart, prin. Fax 231-1368
Gate City ES 200/K-5
6910 Georgia Rd 35212 205-231-8310
Irene Hunter, prin. Fax 231-8309
Gibson ES 300/K-5
956 50th St N 35212 205-231-8370
Dr. Michael Curry, prin. Fax 231-8389
Glen Iris ES 700/K-5
1115 11th St S 35205 205-231-7440
Dr. Michael Wilson, prin. Fax 231-7443
Glenn MS 300/6-8
901 16th St W 35208 205-231-6370
Dr. Cleo Larry, prin. Fax 231-6954
Going Magnet ES 400/K-5
1015 N Martinwood Dr 35235 205-231-5310
Barbara Wells, prin. Fax 231-5352
Green Acres MS 500/6-8
2009 Avenue Q 35218 205-231-6740
Evelyn Baugh, prin. Fax 231-6786
Hemphill ES 400/PK-5
714 12th St SW 35211 205-231-7500
Dr. Gwendolyn Tilghman, prin. Fax 231-7499
Hill ES 200/K-5
507 3rd St N 35204 205-231-2190
Taylor Greene, prin. Fax 231-2226
Hudson S 500/K-8
3300 FL Shuttlesworth Dr 35207 205-231-3000
Jesse Daniel, prin. Fax 231-3072
Huffman Magnet MS 300/6-8
517 Huffman Rd 35215 205-231-5370
Milton Hopkins, prin. Fax 231-5426
Inglenook S 500/K-8
4120 Inglenook St 35217 205-231-3310
Donna Mitchell, prin. Fax 231-3338
Jackson ES 300/K-5
1401 16th Way SW 35211 205-231-7555
Millard Hicks, prin. Fax 231-7595
Jones Valley S 600/K-8
2000 31st St SW 35221 205-231-1062
Dr. Anthony McGraw, prin. Fax 231-1064
Kirby MS 300/6-8
1328 28th St N 35234 205-231-3370
Carolyn Denson, prin. Fax 231-3414
Lee ES 200/K-5
630 18th St SW 35211 205-231-1440
Dr. Elvirita Finley, prin. Fax 231-1437
Lewis ES 300/PK-5
2015 26th Ave N 35234 205-231-3440
Kathleen Lindsey, prin. Fax 231-3491
Minor ES 500/K-5
2425 Avenue S 35218 205-231-6555
Dr. Dave Porter, prin. Fax 231-6602
Mitchell MS 6-8
501 81st St S 35206 205-231-9400
Bettie Jones, prin. Fax 231-9464
North Birmingham ES 300/K-5
2620 35th Ave N 35207 205-231-3555
Jesse Watts, prin. Fax 231-3594
North Roebuck ES 500/K-5
300 Red Lane Rd 35215 205-231-5500
Irene O'Neil, prin. Fax 231-5535
Norwood ES 300/K-5
3136 Norwood Blvd 35234 205-231-3620
Errol Watts, prin. Fax 231-3661
Payne MS 400/6-8
1500 Daniel Payne Dr 35214 205-231-3190
Eddie Cauthen, prin. Fax 231-3236
Phillips Academy K-8
2316 7th Ave N 35203 205-231-9500
Mark Sullivan, prin. Fax 231-9580
Powderly ES 200/K-5
1901 20th St SW 35211 205-231-1500
Andrea Wallace, prin. Fax 231-1530
Price ES 300/K-5
532 28th St SW 35211 205-231-1555
Elaine Cooper-Young, prin. Fax 231-1559
Putnam Magnet MS 300/6-8
1757 Montclair Rd 35210 205-231-8680
Michael Scott, prin. Fax 231-8685
Robinson ES 500/K-5
8400 1st Ave S 35206 205-231-5555
Sandra Kindell, prin. Fax 231-5554
Smith MS 400/6-8
1124 Five Mile Rd 35215 205-231-5675
Charles Willis, prin. Fax 231-5899
South Hampton ES 600/K-5
565 Sheridan Rd 35214 205-231-6680
Cedric Tatum, prin. Fax 231-6683
Sun Valley ES 500/K-5
1010 18th Ave NW 35215 205-231-5740
Damita Pitts, prin. Fax 231-5747
Tuggle ES 300/K-5
412 12th Ct N 35204 205-231-2675
Johnnie Finkley, prin. Fax 231-2718
Washington S 300/K-8
901 9th Ave N 35204 205-231-2310
Linda Kimbrough, prin. Fax 231-2365
Wenonah ES 300/K-5
3008 Wilson Rd SW 35221 205-231-1800
Barbara Huntley, prin. Fax 231-1877
Whatley S 300/K-8
549 43rd St N 35222 205-231-3800
Tavis Hardin-Sloan, prin. Fax 231-3854

Wilkerson MS 300/6-8
116 11th Ct W 35204 205-231-2740
Constance Burnes, prin. Fax 231-2790
Wilson ES 300/K-5
1030 4th Ter W 35204 205-231-2800
Donnetta Brown, prin. Fax 231-2839
Wright Magnet ES 300/K-5
1212 Cheyenne Blvd 35215 205-231-5800
Susan Chalmers, prin. Fax 231-5836
Wylam ES 200/PK-5
1517 Hibernian St 35214 205-231-6800
Judith Ross, prin. Fax 231-6830

Hoover CSD
Supt. — See Hoover
Berry MS 1,000/6-8
4500 Jaguar Dr 35242 205-439-2000
Dr. Kathleen Wheaton, prin. Fax 439-2001
Deer Valley ES 700/K-5
4990 Ross Bridge Pkwy 35226 205-439-3300
Dr. Wayne Richardson, prin. Fax 439-3301

Jefferson County SD 35,700/K-12
2100 Richard Arrington Jr S 35209 205-379-2000
Dr. Phil Hammonds, supt. Fax 379-2311
www.jefcoed.com/
Center Point ES 700/K-2
4801 Indian Trl 35215 205-379-2900
Laura Rose, prin. Fax 379-2945
Chalkville ES 1,200/K-5
940 Chalkville School Rd 35215 205-379-2950
Rod Johnson, prin. Fax 856-6662
Crumly Chapel ES 400/K-5
2201 Pershing Rd 35214 205-379-3250
Harold Gray, prin. Fax 379-3295
Erwin ES 800/3-6
528 23rd Ave NW 35215 205-379-3350
Mike Barlow, prin. Fax 379-3395
Grantswood Community ES 300/K-2
5110 Grantswood Rd 35210 205-379-3700
Ann Tillman, prin. Fax 379-3745
Gresham ES 300/K-5
2650 Gresham Dr 35243 205-379-3830
Frances Finney, prin. Fax 379-3846
Hillview ES 300/K-5
1520 Cherry Ave 35214 205-379-4050
Jonetta Terry, prin. Fax 379-4095
Irondale MS 6-8
6200 Old Leeds Rd 35210 205-379-3800
Phyllis Montalto, prin. Fax 379-3845
Minor Community S 400/K-5
3006 Cora Ave 35224 205-379-4800
Marsha Clements, prin. Fax 379-4845
Other Schools – See Adamsville, Bessemer, Brighton, Clay, Dora, Fultondale, Gardendale, Graysville, Hueytown, Irondale, Kimberly, Mc Calla, Morris, Mount Olive, Pinson, Pleasant Grove, Quinton, Trussville, Warrior

Mountain Brook CSD
Supt. — See Mountain Brook
Crestline ES 700/K-6
3785 W Jackson Blvd 35213 205-871-8126
Michael Melvin, prin. Fax 877-8324

Shelby County SD
Supt. — See Columbiana
Inverness ES 600/K-3
5251 Valleydale Rd 35242 205-682-5240
Christine Hoffman, prin. Fax 682-5245
Mt. Laurel ES 600/K-5
1 Jefferson Pl 35242 205-682-7230
Angela Walker, prin. Fax 682-7235
Oak Mountain ES 800/K-3
5640 Cahaba Valley Rd 35242 205-682-5230
Jeanette Darby, prin. Fax 682-5235
Oak Mountain IS 800/4-5
5486 Caldwell Mill Rd 35242 205-682-5220
Dr. Linda Maxwell, prin. Fax 682-5225
Oak Mountain MS 1,300/6-8
5650 Cahaba Valley Rd 35242 205-682-5210
Larry Haynes, prin. Fax 682-5215
Riverchase MS 1,200/6-8
853 Willow Oak Dr 35244 205-682-5510
Charles Smith, prin. Fax 682-5515

Vestavia Hills CSD
Supt. — See Vestavia Hills
Vestavia Hills ES Cahaba Heights 300/K-6
4401 Dolly Ridge Rd 35243 205-402-5480
Dr. Kate Cox, prin. Fax 402-5480

Advent Episcopal Day S 300/PK-8
2019 6th Ave N 35203 205-252-2535
Una Battles, hdmstr. Fax 252-3023
Briarwood Christian S 800/PK-12
2204 Briarwood Way 35243 205-776-5800
Dr. Barrett Mosbacker, supt. Fax 776-5815
Bruno Montessori Academy 200/K-8
5509 Timber Hill Rd 35242 205-995-8709
Theresa Sprain, prin. Fax 995-0517
Central Park Christian S 200/K-12
1900 43rd St W 35208 205-786-4811
Cornerstone S of Alabama 200/PK-8
135 54th St N 35212 205-591-7600
Dr. Nita Thompson, dir. Fax 591-7656
Ephesus Academy 200/K-8
829 McMillon Ave SW 35211 205-786-2194
Michael Monette, prin. Fax 786-0857
Forestdale Baptist S 200/K-6
1400 Brisbane Ave 35214 205-798-1248
Janice Gibbons, prin. Fax 798-0413
Highlands S 300/PK-8
4901 Old Leeds Rd 35213 205-956-9731
Kathryn Barr, hdmstr. Fax 951-8127
Hilltop Montessori S 200/PK-8
6 Abbott Sq 35242 205-437-9343
Michele Scott, prin. Fax 437-9344

Holy Family S 200/PK-8
1916 19th Street Ensley 35218 205-780-5858
Chandra Farrier, prin. Fax 785-2666
Hoover Christian S 50/K-12
2113 Old Rocky Ridge Rd 35216 205-987-3376
Gaylan Herr, prin. Fax 987-4428
Integrity Christian Academy 200/PK-6
216 Roebuck Dr 35215 205-833-4416
Venandee Hennington, admin. Fax 833-4450
Miles Jewish Day S 100/K-8
4000 Montclair Rd 35213 205-879-1068
Bob Greenberg, hdmstr. Fax 879-6183
Our Lady of Fatima S 200/PK-8
630 1st St S 35205 205-251-8395
Velda Gilyot, prin. Fax 251-8393
Our Lady of Lourdes K 100/PK-K
980 Huffman Rd 35215 205-836-1218
Beth Abts, prin. Fax 836-5436
Our Lady of Sorrows Preschool 100/PK-PK
1703 29th Ct S 35209 205-380-2646
Lynne Stella, dir. Fax 380-2648
Our Lady of Sorrows S 400/K-8
1720 Oxmoor Rd 35209 205-879-3237
Mary Jane Dorn, prin. Fax 879-9332
Our Lady of the Valley S 500/PK-8
5510 Double Oak Ln 35242 205-991-5963
Sandra Roden, prin. Fax 995-1251
Parkway Christian Academy 400/PK-12
959 Huffman Rd 35215 205-833-2410
Michael Gallien, prin. Fax 833-4692
Pilgrim Lutheran S 50/PK-5
113 4th Ter N 35204 205-324-6470
Fax 324-6470
Redmont S 100/PK-8
1220 50th St S 35222 205-592-0541
Randy Brothers, admin. Fax 592-0596
St. Barnabas S 100/PK-8
7901 1st Ave N 35206 205-836-5385
Marilyn Coman, prin. Fax 833-0272
St. Francis Xavier Preschool PK-PK
2 Xavier Cir 35213 205-879-5596
Joy Mueller, prin. Fax 871-1674
St. Francis Xavier S 200/K-8
2 Xavier Cir 35213 205-871-1687
Nathan Wright, prin. Fax 871-1674
St. Peters Child Development Center 100/PK-PK
2061 Patton Chapel Rd 35216 205-822-9461
Susan Wilkens, prin. Fax 822-9451
St. Rose of Lima S 300/PK-8
1401 22nd St S 35205 205-933-0549
Sr. Mary Cebrowski, prin. Fax 933-0591
Sardis Christian S 100/K-8
1620 4th Ct W 35208 205-786-4379
Jimmie Swain, prin. Fax 780-5898
Webster Christian S 100/PK-8
2902 Pine Haven Dr 35223 205-871-2228
Lanford McCalley, hdmstr.
Williams Christian Academy 50/PK-12
8957 Glendale Dr 35206 205-453-8541
Linda Toodle, dir. Fax 453-8541

Blountsville, Blount, Pop. 1,923

Blount County SD
Supt. — See Oneonta
Blountsville ES 700/K-6
260 Page St 35031 205-429-2458
Kay Smallwood, prin. Fax 429-5540
Moore ES 700/K-6
3996 Susan Moore Rd 35031 205-466-5844
Helen Dunn, prin. Fax 466-3808

Boaz, Marshall, Pop. 7,893

Boaz CSD 2,200/PK-12
PO Box 721 35957 256-593-8180
Leland Dishman, supt. Fax 593-8181
www.boazk12.org/
Boaz ES 400/PK-1
362 Collier St 35957 256-593-3481
J. Randall Morton, prin. Fax 593-6738
Boaz IS 300/4-5
11 Newt Parker Dr 35957 256-593-9211
John Beck, prin. Fax 593-9388
Boaz MS 500/6-8
140 Newt Parker Dr 35957 256-593-0799
Ray Landers, prin. Fax 593-0729
Corley ES 400/2-3
505 Mount Vernon Rd 35957 256-593-3254
Jamie Burton, prin. Fax 593-7833

Etowah County SD
Supt. — See Gadsden
Carlisle ES 400/K-6
8025 US Highway 431 35956 256-593-4613
Donna Johnson, prin. Fax 593-4282
Whitesboro ES 300/K-6
5080 Leeth Gap Rd 35956 256-593-5406
Donald Graves, prin. Fax 593-5431

Boligee, Greene, Pop. 358

Greene County SD
Supt. — See Eutaw
Paramount S 400/K-8
PO Box 188 35443 205-336-8557
Dr. Harriett Lewis, prin. Fax 336-8571

Bon Secour, Baldwin

Baldwin County SD
Supt. — See Bay Minette
Swift Consolidated ES 200/PK-6
PO Box 7 36511 251-949-6422
Sandra Thorpe, prin. Fax 949-7015

Brantley, Crenshaw, Pop. 909

Crenshaw County SD
Supt. — See Luverne
Brantley S 600/PK-12
PO Box 86 36009 334-527-8879
Ashley Catrett, prin. Fax 527-3405

Bremen, Cullman
Cullman County SD
Supt. — See Cullman
Cold Springs ES 500/K-6
PO Box 120 35033 256-287-1247
Deborah Brown, prin. Fax 287-2775

Brent, Bibb, Pop. 4,129
Bibb County SD
Supt. — See Centreville
Brent ES 100/K-4
160 4th St 35034 205-926-4993
Dr. Cheryl Fondren, prin. Fax 926-5642

Brewton, Escambia, Pop. 5,373
Brewton CSD 1,300/K-12
811 Belleville Ave 36426 251-867-8400
Lynn Smith, supt. Fax 867-8403
www.brewtoncityschools.org/
Brewton ES 500/K-4
901 Douglas Ave 36426 251-867-8410
Saundra Ellis, prin. Fax 867-8408
Brewton MS 400/5-8
301 Liles Blvd 36426 251-867-8420
Douglas Prater, prin. Fax 867-8422

Escambia County SD 4,500/K-12
PO Box 307 36427 251-867-6251
William Hines, supt. Fax 867-6252
www.escambiak12.net
Pollard-McCall S 200/K-8
3975 Old Highway 31 36426 251-867-4070
Hugh White, prin. Fax 867-6387
Other Schools – See Atmore, East Brewton, Flomaton, Huxford

Bridgeport, Jackson, Pop. 2,693
Jackson County SD
Supt. — See Scottsboro
Bridgeport ES 300/K-4
1014 Jacobs Ave 35740 256-495-3147
Robert Downey, prin. Fax 495-3192
Bridgeport MS 200/5-8
620 Jacobs Ave 35740 256-495-2967
A.J. Buckner, prin. Fax 495-2850

Brighton, Jefferson, Pop. 3,416
Jefferson County SD
Supt. — See Birmingham
Brighton S 400/K-8
3400 Browns Cir 35020 205-379-2650
Margie Curry, prin. Fax 379-2695

Brilliant, Marion, Pop. 733
Marion County SD
Supt. — See Hamilton
Brilliant ES 200/K-6
10180 State Highway 129 35548 205-465-2323
Gracie Franks, prin. Fax 465-2473

Brookwood, Tuscaloosa, Pop. 1,466
Tuscaloosa County SD
Supt. — See Tuscaloosa
Brookwood ES 1,000/K-5
16049 Highway 216 35444 205-342-2668
Sally Wells, prin. Fax 342-2845

Brundidge, Pike, Pop. 2,327
Pike County SD
Supt. — See Troy
Pike County ES 400/K-6
186 Hillcrest Dr 36010 334-735-2683
Ken Bynum, prin. Fax 735-5660

Bryant, Jackson
Jackson County SD
Supt. — See Scottsboro
Bryant S 200/K-8
6645 AL Highway 73 35958 256-597-2203
Lloyd Ellison, prin. Fax 597-2851

Floral Crest SDA S 50/1-8
1228 County Road 89 35958 256-597-2582
Nancy Smith, prin.
Mountain View Christian Academy 100/PK-12
3665 AL Highway 73 35958 256-597-3467
Jonathan Aultman, prin. Fax 597-3467

Buhl, Tuscaloosa
Tuscaloosa County SD
Supt. — See Tuscaloosa
Buhl ES 200/K-5
11968 Buhl School Rd 35446 205-342-2640
Linda Lafoy, prin. Fax 333-3951

Butler, Choctaw, Pop. 1,780
Choctaw County SD 2,000/K-12
107 Tom Orr Dr 36904 205-459-3031
Glenda Moore, supt. Fax 459-3037
Choctaw ES 600/K-6
201 Tom Orr Dr 36904 205-459-3520
Arthur Longmire, prin. Fax 459-7406
Other Schools – See Gilbertown

Patrician Academy 300/K-12
901 S Mulberry Ave 36904 205-459-3605
Marcus Walters, prin. Fax 459-4802

Calera, Shelby, Pop. 6,707
Shelby County SD
Supt. — See Columbiana
Calera ES 800/K-5
855 10th St 35040 205-682-6120
Linda Chesler, prin. Fax 682-6125
Calera MS 6-8
8454 Highway 31 35040 205-682-6100
Brent Copes, prin. Fax 682-6145

Camden, Wilcox, Pop. 2,228
Wilcox County SD 2,200/PK-12
PO Box 160 36726 334-682-4716
Dr. Rosie Shamburger, supt. Fax 682-4179
www.wilcox.k12.al.us
Camden S of Arts & Technology 300/7-8
PO Box 698 36726 334-682-4514
Andre Saulsberry, prin. Fax 682-5934
Hobbs ES 500/PK-6
PO Box 578 36726 334-682-9310
Ora Colston, prin. Fax 682-9127
Other Schools – See Alberta, Pine Apple, Pine Hill

Wilcox Academy 300/K-12
PO Box 1149 36726 334-682-9619
Chris Burford, prin. Fax 682-2107

Camp Hill, Tallapoosa, Pop. 1,199
Tallapoosa County SD
Supt. — See Dadeville
Bell S 300/K-12
PO Box 490 36850 256-896-2865
Glenda Mennifee, prin. Fax 896-2661

Carbon Hill, Walker, Pop. 2,047
Walker County SD
Supt. — See Jasper
Carbon Hill S 600/K-8
283 Bulldog Blvd 35549 205-924-4101
Tanya Guin, prin. Fax 924-4199

Carrollton, Pickens, Pop. 956
Pickens County SD 3,100/K-12
PO Box 32 35447 205-367-2082
Dr. Leonard Duff, supt. Fax 367-8404
www.pcboe.org
Carrollton Unit ES 200/K-6
PO Box 320 35447 205-367-8152
Russell Smart, prin. Fax 367-8908
Other Schools – See Aliceville, Gordo, Reform

Pickens Academy 300/PK-12
225 Ray Bass Rd 35447 205-367-8144
Brach White, prin. Fax 367-1771

Castleberry, Conecuh, Pop. 560
Conecuh County SD
Supt. — See Evergreen
Conecuh County S 200/PK-8
2347 Cleveland Ave 36432 251-966-5411
Martha Hollinger, prin. Fax 966-2833

Cedar Bluff, Cherokee, Pop. 1,537
Cherokee County SD
Supt. — See Centre
Cedar Bluff S 600/K-12
3655 Old Highway 9 35959 256-779-6211
Bobby Mintz, prin. Fax 779-8328

Centre, Cherokee, Pop. 3,316
Cherokee County SD 4,200/PK-12
130 E Main St 35960 256-927-3362
Brian Johnson, supt. Fax 927-3399
www.cherokeek12.org/
Centre ES 800/K-5
725 E Main St 35960 256-927-3302
Dewayne Pierce, prin. Fax 927-4932
Centre MS 400/6-8
350 E Main St 35960 256-927-5656
Renee Williams, prin. Fax 927-4656
Cherokee County Preschool PK-PK
420 E Main St 35960 256-927-3322
Linda Prater, prin. Fax 927-3390
Other Schools – See Cedar Bluff, Gaylesville, Leesburg, Spring Garden

Centreville, Bibb, Pop. 2,507
Bibb County SD 2,900/K-12
157 SW Davidson Dr 35042 205-926-9881
Dr. Donald Elam, supt. Fax 926-5075
www.bibbed.org/
Centreville MS 500/5-8
1621 Montgomery Hwy 35042 205-926-9861
Earnie Cutts, prin. Fax 926-3917
Other Schools – See Brent, Randolph, West Blocton, Woodstock

Cahawba Christian Academy 100/PK-12
2415 Montevallo Rd 35042 205-926-4676

Chatom, Washington, Pop. 1,178
Washington County SD 3,600/K-12
PO Box 1359 36518 251-847-2401
Tim Savage, supt. Fax 847-3611
washingtoncounty.al.schoolwebpages.com
Chatom ES 400/K-4
PO Box 1209 36518 251-847-2946
Wayne Blackwell, prin. Fax 847-3903
Other Schools – See Fruitdale, Leroy, Mc Intosh, Millry

Chelsea, Shelby, Pop. 3,635
Shelby County SD
Supt. — See Columbiana
Chelsea IS 300/4-5
2315 Highway 39 35043 205-682-7220
Stephanie Herring, prin. Fax 682-7225
Chelsea MS 700/6-8
PO Box 600 35043 205-682-7210
Bill Harper, prin. Fax 682-7215
Chelsea Park ES 600/K-3
9000 Chelsea Park Trl 35043 205-682-6700
Dr. Jeanette Campisi-Snider, prin. Fax 682-6705

Cherokee, Colbert, Pop. 1,183
Colbert County SD
Supt. — See Tuscumbia
Cherokee ES 300/K-6
1305 North Pike 35616 256-359-6422
Pam Worsham, prin. Fax 359-6426

Chickasaw, Mobile, Pop. 6,000
Mobile County SD
Supt. — See Mobile
Chickasaw S of Math & Science 200/K-3
201 N Craft Hwy 36611 251-221-1105
Michelle Adams, prin. Fax 221-1107
Clark S of Math & Science 700/4-8
50 12th Ave 36611 251-221-2106
Dianne McWain, prin. Fax 221-2108
Hamilton ES 500/PK-5
80 Grant St 36611 251-221-1360
Laura Foster, prin. Fax 221-1363

Life Institute Christian S 50/K-12
351 S Craft Hwy 36611 251-456-2652
Dr. Henry Roberts, pres. Fax 456-2654

Childersburg, Talladega, Pop. 5,000
Talladega County SD
Supt. — See Talladega
Childersburg ES 300/K-4
235 Pinecrest Dr 35044 256-315-5525
Cyndi Brooks, prin. Fax 315-5535
Childersburg MS 500/5-8
800 4th St SE 35044 256-315-5505
Jena Jones, prin. Fax 315-5520
Watwood ES 400/K-4
3002 Limbaugh Blvd 35044 256-315-5460
Rhonda Sims, prin. Fax 315-5470

Citronelle, Mobile, Pop. 3,686
Mobile County SD
Supt. — See Mobile
Lott MS 500/6-8
17740 Celeste Rd 36522 251-221-2240
Richard Dickson, prin. Fax 221-2247
McDavid-Jones ES 1,000/PK-5
16250 US Highway 45 36522 251-221-1510
Rebecca Smyly, prin. Fax 221-1513

Clanton, Chilton, Pop. 8,336
Chilton County SD 7,500/PK-12
1705 Lay Dam Rd 35045 205-280-3000
Keith Moore, supt. Fax 755-6549
www.chilton.k12.al.us
Clanton ES 700/PK-2
1000 Cloverleaf Dr 35045 205-280-2730
Rebecca Threlkeld, prin. Fax 755-8483
Clanton IS 600/3-5
825 Temple Rd 35045 205-280-2790
Dennis Cobb, prin. Fax 280-2795
Clanton MS 700/6-8
835 Temple Rd 35045 205-280-2750
Don Finlayson, prin. Fax 755-2446
Other Schools – See Jemison, Maplesville, Thorsby, Verbena

Clay, Jefferson
Jefferson County SD
Supt. — See Birmingham
Clay ES 800/K-5
PO Box 127 35048 205-379-3000
Dr. Sharon Gallant, prin. Fax 379-3045

Clayton, Barbour, Pop. 1,402
Barbour County SD 1,200/PK-12
PO Box 429 36016 334-775-3453
Gary Quick, supt. Fax 775-7301
barbourschools.org
Barbour County PS 300/PK-2
PO Box 549 36016 334-775-3404
Fred Cooper, prin. Fax 775-9447
Other Schools – See Louisville

Cleveland, Blount, Pop. 1,363
Blount County SD
Supt. — See Oneonta
Cleveland ES 500/K-6
115 Stadium Dr 35049 205-274-2223
David Bradford, prin. Fax 274-2224

Coffeeville, Clarke, Pop. 354
Clarke County SD
Supt. — See Grove Hill
Coffeeville S 200/K-12
PO Box 130 36524 251-276-3227
Janice Richardson, prin. Fax 276-0349

Coker, Tuscaloosa, Pop. 789
Tuscaloosa County SD
Supt. — See Tuscaloosa
Westwood ES 400/K-5
11629 Westwood School Rd 35452 205-342-2666
Cindy Merrill, prin. Fax 339-1126

Collinsville, DeKalb, Pop. 1,667
De Kalb County SD
Supt. — See Rainsville
Collinsville S 700/K-12
PO Box 269 35961 256-524-2111
Donny Jones, prin. Fax 524-7526

Columbiana, Shelby, Pop. 3,664
Shelby County SD 25,700/K-12
PO Box 1910 35051 205-682-7000
Randy Fuller, supt. Fax 682-7005
www.shelbyed.k12.al.us
Columbiana MS 500/6-8
222 Joiner Town Rd 35051 205-682-6610
Christie Muehlbauer, prin. Fax 682-6615
Hill ES 600/K-5
201 Washington St 35051 205-682-6620
Betsy Hillman, prin. Fax 682-6625
Other Schools – See Alabaster, Birmingham, Calera, Chelsea, Helena, Maylene, Montevallo, Pelham, Shelby, Vincent, Wilsonville

Cornerstone Christian S 300/PK-12
24975 Highway 25 35051 205-669-7777
Laurie Porter, hdmstr. Fax 669-5283

Cordova, Walker, Pop. 2,336
Walker County SD
Supt. — See Jasper
Bankhead MS — 300/5-8
110 School St 35550 — 205-483-7245
Dr. Gypsy Stovall, prin. — Fax 483-7244
Cordova ES — 400/K-4
35 North St 35550 — 205-483-7666
Mike Scott, prin. — Fax 483-1026

Cottondale, Tuscaloosa
Tuscaloosa CSD
Supt. — See Tuscaloosa
Eastwood MS — 1,000/6-8
6314 Mary Harmon Bryant Dr 35453 — 205-759-3613
Dr. Bruce Prescott, prin. — Fax 759-3798

Tuscaloosa County SD
Supt. — See Tuscaloosa
Cottondale ES — 500/K-5
2301 Cottondale Ln 35453 — 205-342-2642
Cindy Montgomery, prin. — Fax 556-6979
Davis - Emerson MS — 400/6-8
1500 Bulldog Blvd 35453 — 205-342-2750
Dr. Walter Davie, prin. — Fax 633-1155

Tuscaloosa Christian S — 400/PK-12
PO Box 250 35453 — 205-553-4303
Dan Lancaster, prin. — Fax 553-4259

Cottonwood, Houston, Pop. 1,171
Houston County SD
Supt. — See Dothan
Cottonwood S — 700/K-12
663 Houston St 36320 — 334-691-2587
Judy Fowler, prin. — Fax 691-4200

Courtland, Lawrence, Pop. 765
Lawrence County SD
Supt. — See Moulton
Hubbard S — 300/K-12
12905 Jessie Jackson Pkwy 35618 — 256-637-3010
Thomas Jones, prin. — Fax 637-3006

Cropwell, Saint Clair
Pell City CSD
Supt. — See Pell City
Coosa Valley ES — 400/K-4
3609 Martin St S 35054 — 205-338-7713
Tammy Stewart, prin. — Fax 338-0694

Crossville, DeKalb, Pop. 1,449
De Kalb County SD
Supt. — See Rainsville
Crossville ES — 900/K-5
63 Justice St 35962 — 256-528-7859
Eddie Burke, prin. — Fax 528-5407

Cuba, Sumter, Pop. 334
Sumter County SD
Supt. — See Livingston
Kinterbish S — 200/K-8
5586 Kinterbish 10 36907 — 205-392-4559
Rita Bryant-Ertha, prin. — Fax 392-4566

Cullman, Cullman, Pop. 14,735
Cullman CSD — 2,700/K-12
301 1st St NE 35055 — 256-734-2233
Jan Harris Ed.D., supt. — Fax 737-9621
www.cullmancats.net
Cullman City PS — 400/K-1
900 Hoehn Dr 35055 — 256-775-0234
Tricia Culpepper, prin. — Fax 775-0238
Cullman MS — 500/7-8
800 2nd Ave NE 35055 — 256-734-7959
Lane Hill, prin. — Fax 734-7711
East ES — 500/2-6
608 4th Ave SE 35055 — 256-734-2232
David Wiggins, prin. — Fax 734-2241
West ES — 500/2-6
303 Rosemont Ave SW 35055 — 256-734-4271
Dr. Elton Bouldin, prin. — Fax 737-9378

Cullman County SD — 9,700/PK-12
PO Box 1590 35056 — 256-734-2933
L. Hank Allen, supt. — Fax 736-2402
www.ccboe.org/
Fairview ES — 600/K-5
700 Wesley Ave N 35058 — 256-796-6304
Jessica Johnson, prin. — Fax 796-0066
Fairview MS — 300/6-8
841 Welcome Rd 35058 — 256-796-0883
Dr. Susan Creel Patterson, prin. — Fax 796-0885
Good Hope ES — 300/3-5
210 Good Hope School Rd 35057 — 256-734-3824
Annette Creest, prin. — Fax 734-4985
Good Hope MS — 300/6-8
216 Good Hope School Rd 35057 — 256-734-9600
Wayne Weissend, prin. — Fax 734-9704
Good Hope PS — 400/PK-2
661 County Road 447 35057 — 256-734-0109
Janet Mattox, prin. — Fax 737-0680
Welti ES — 200/PK-6
8545 County Road 747 35055 — 256-734-4956
Brandon Payne, prin. — Fax 734-4855
West Point ES — 500/K-3
4300 County Road 1141 35057 — 256-775-6178
Shireen Coleman, prin. — Fax 734-5381
Other Schools – See Baileyton, Bremen, Garden City, Hanceville, Holly Pond, Logan, Vinemont

---

Cullman Christian S — 100/K-9
303 9th Ave SE 35055 — 256-734-0734
Roger Hood M.Ed., hdmstr. — Fax 734-0117
Sacred Heart S — 200/PK-8
112 2nd Ave SE 35055 — 256-734-4563
Eugene Houk, prin. — Fax 734-5882
St. Paul Lutheran S — 200/PK-6
510 3rd Ave SE 35055 — 256-734-6580
Robert Lange, prin. — Fax 734-6580

Dadeville, Tallapoosa, Pop. 3,145
Tallapoosa County SD — 3,200/K-12
125 N Broadnax St Rm 113 36853 — 256-825-1020
Philip Baker, supt. — Fax 825-1003
www.tallapoosak12.org/
Councill MS — 300/5-7
254 Leach St 36853 — 256-825-2846
Chris Hand, prin. — Fax 825-7473
Dadeville ES — 500/K-4
670 E Columbus St 36853 — 256-825-6811
Joe Ross, prin. — Fax 825-4068
Other Schools – See Camp Hill, New Site, Notasulga

Daleville, Dale, Pop. 4,545
Daleville CSD — 1,400/K-12
626 N Daleville Ave 36322 — 334-598-2456
Andrew Kelley, supt. — Fax 598-9006
www.daleville.k12.al.us
Daleville MS — 500/5-8
626 N Daleville Ave 36322 — 334-598-4463
Betty Flemming, prin. — Fax 598-9006
Windham ES — 500/K-4
626 N Daleville Ave 36322 — 334-598-4466
Christopher Mitten, prin. — Fax 598-4467

Danville, Morgan
Lawrence County SD
Supt. — See Moulton
Speake S — 300/K-8
6559 County Road 81 35619 — 256-974-9201
Dr. Tommy Whitlow, prin. — Fax 905-2483

Morgan County SD
Supt. — See Decatur
Danville MS — 400/5-8
5933 Highway 36 W 35619 — 256-773-7723
Gary Walker, prin. — Fax 773-7708
Danville-Neel ES — 500/PK-4
8688 Danville Rd 35619 — 256-773-7183
Glenn Lang, prin. — Fax 773-7718

Daphne, Baldwin, Pop. 18,581
Baldwin County SD
Supt. — See Bay Minette
Carroll IS — 300/4-6
1000 Main St 36526 — 251-626-0277
Dana Horst, prin. — Fax 626-0488
Daphne East ES — 600/K-5
26651 County Road 13 36526 — 251-626-1663
Rebecca Lundberg, prin. — Fax 625-2616
Daphne ES — 600/K-3
2307 Main St 36526 — 251-626-2424
Jan Palmer, prin. — Fax 626-6054
Daphne MS — 700/6-8
1 Jody Davis Cir 36526 — 251-626-2845
James Oliphant, prin. — Fax 626-0025

Bayside Academy — 800/PK-12
303 Dryer Ave 36526 — 251-338-6300
Thomas Johnson, prin. — Fax 338-6310
Christ the King S — 400/K-8
PO Box 1890 36526 — 251-626-1692
Maxwell Crain, prin. — Fax 626-9976

Dauphin Island, Mobile, Pop. 1,533
Mobile County SD
Supt. — See Mobile
Dauphin Island ES — 100/K-5
1501 Bienville Blvd 36528 — 251-861-3864
Katherine Gallop, prin. — Fax 861-8142

Deatsville, Elmore, Pop. 361
Autauga County SD
Supt. — See Prattville
Pine Level ES — 1,000/K-6
2040 US Highway 31 N 36022 — 334-358-2658
Cathy Loftin, prin. — Fax 358-2309

Elmore County SD
Supt. — See Wetumpka
Holtville ES — 600/PK-4
287 Whatley Dr 36022 — 334-569-3574
Mary Crapps, prin. — Fax 569-1016
Holtville MS — 500/5-8
655 Bulldog Ln 36022 — 334-569-3574
Jamey McGowin, prin. — Fax 569-3258

Decatur, Morgan, Pop. 54,909
Decatur CSD — 9,000/PK-12
302 4th Ave NE 35601 — 256-552-3000
Dr. Samuel Houston, supt. — Fax 552-3981
www.dcs.edu
Austinville ES — 400/PK-5
2320 Clara Ave SW 35601 — 256-552-3050
Beth Hales, prin. — Fax 552-4688
Banks-Caddell ES — 400/PK-5
211 Gordon Dr SE 35601 — 256-552-3040
Wanda Davis, prin. — Fax 552-4653
Brookhaven MS — 700/6-8
1302 5th Ave SW 35601 — 256-552-3045
Dr. Larry Collier, prin. — Fax 552-3047
Cedar Ridge MS — 800/6-8
2715 Danville Rd SW 35603 — 256-552-4622
Dr. Elizabeth Weinbaum, prin. — Fax 552-4623
Chestnut Grove ES — 500/K-5
3205 Cedarhurst Dr SW 35603 — 256-552-3092
Lauretta Teague, prin. — Fax 552-4646
Davis ES — 200/K-2
417 Monroe Dr NW 35601 — 256-552-3025
David Kross, prin. — Fax 552-4689
Eastwood ES — 300/PK-5
1802 26th Ave SE 35601 — 256-552-3043
Margaret Greer, prin. — Fax 552-4696
Harris ES — 500/K-5
1922 McAuliffe Dr SW 35603 — 256-552-3096
Hank Kimbrell, prin. — Fax 552-4659
Jackson ES — 200/K-5
1950 Park St SE 35601 — 256-552-3031
Rhonda Reece, prin. — Fax 552-4693
Nungester ES — 400/PK-5
726 Tammy St SW 35603 — 256-552-3079
Dr. Cheryl Bowman, prin. — Fax 552-4658
Oak Park MS — 600/6-8
1218 16th Ave SE 35601 — 256-552-3035
Dwight Satterfield, prin. — Fax 552-3082
Sheffield ES — 300/K-5
801 Wilson St NW 35601 — 256-552-3056
Rachel Poovey, prin. — Fax 552-4690
Somerville Road ES — 500/PK-5
910 Somerville Rd SE 35601 — 256-552-3033
Danna Jones, prin. — Fax 552-4692
West Decatur ES — 300/PK-5
708 Memorial Dr SW 35601 — 256-552-3027
Datie Priest, prin. — Fax 552-4694
Woodmeade ES — 300/PK-5
1400 19th Ave SW 35601 — 256-552-3023
Angie Whittington, prin. — Fax 552-4695

Morgan County SD — 7,400/PK-12
1325 Point Mallard Pkwy SE 35601 — 256-353-6442
Robert Balch, supt. — Fax 309-2187
www.morgank12.org
Priceville ES — 600/K-5
438 Cave Spring Rd 35603 — 256-341-9202
Anne Knowlton, prin. — Fax 341-0776
Priceville JHS — 300/6-8
317 Highway 67 S 35603 — 256-355-5104
Mary Speegle, prin. — Fax 355-5932
Other Schools – See Danville, Eva, Falkville, Hartselle, Joppa, Laceys Spring, Somerville, Trinity

---

Decatur Heritage Christian Academy — 300/PK-12
PO Box 5659 35601 — 256-351-4275
Scott Mayo, hdmstr. — Fax 355-4738
St. Ann S — 200/PK-8
3910A Spring Ave SW 35603 — 256-353-6543
Christine Wright, prin. — Fax 353-0705

Demopolis, Marengo, Pop. 7,555
Demopolis CSD — 2,500/PK-12
PO Box 759 36732 — 334-289-1670
Dr. L. Wayne Vickers, supt. — Fax 289-1689
www.demopoliscityschools.com
Demopolis MS — 600/6-8
300 E Pettus St 36732 — 334-289-4242
Clarence Jackson, prin. — Fax 289-2670
Jones ES — 500/3-5
715 E Jackson St 36732 — 334-289-0426
Dr. Tony Speegle, prin. — Fax 289-8456
Westside ES — 600/PK-2
1720 Mauvilla Dr 36732 — 334-289-0377
Connie Brown, prin. — Fax 289-0337

Marengo County SD
Supt. — See Linden
Essex S — 200/K-12
70 Essex Dr 36732 — 334-289-3504
Loretta McCoy, prin. — Fax 289-3591

Dixons Mills, Marengo
Marengo County SD
Supt. — See Linden
Marengo S — 400/K-12
212 Panther Dr 36736 — 334-992-2395
Tracy White, prin. — Fax 992-2197

Dora, Walker, Pop. 2,391
Jefferson County SD
Supt. — See Birmingham
Bagley S — 700/K-9
8581 Tate Mill Rd 35062 — 205-379-2500
Danny Conners, prin. — Fax 379-2545

Walker County SD
Supt. — See Jasper
Boyd S — 200/K-8
PO Box 697 35062 — 205-648-5912
Shirley Mitchell, prin. — Fax 648-5996

Dothan, Houston, Pop. 62,713
Dothan CSD — 8,900/K-12
500 Dusy St 36301 — 334-793-1397
Dr. Sam Nichols, supt. — Fax 794-2034
www.dothan.k12.al.us
Beverlye MS — 500/6-8
1025 S Beverlye Rd 36301 — 334-794-1432
James Larry Norris, prin. — Fax 792-0886
Carver S for Math Science & Technology — 700/6-8
1001 Webb Rd 36303 — 334-794-1440
Dr. James Kelley, prin. — Fax 794-1587
Cloverdale ES — 300/K-5
303 Rollins Ave 36301 — 334-794-1487
Aneta Walker, prin. — Fax 794-7451
Faine ES — 300/K-5
1901 Stringer St 36303 — 334-794-1455
Deloris Potter, prin. — Fax 671-7983
Girard ES — 300/K-5
522 Girard Ave 36303 — 334-794-1467
Glenda Sanders, prin. — Fax 794-1468
Girard MS — 400/6-8
600 Girard Ave 36303 — 334-794-1426
Greg Yance, prin. — Fax 794-6373
Grandview ES — 400/K-5
900 Sixth Ave 36301 — 334-794-1483
Todd Weeks, prin. — Fax 793-9012
Heard ES — 400/K-5
201 Daniel Cir 36301 — 334-794-1471
Peggy Maddox, prin. — Fax 792-6971
Hidden Lake ES — 500/K-5
1475 Prevatt Rd 36301 — 334-794-1491
Dr. Betty Armstrong, prin. — Fax 702-2997
Highlands ES — 500/K-5
1400 S Brannon Stand Rd 36305 — 334-794-1459
Vernell Paul, prin. — Fax 671-8163
Honeysuckle MS — 400/6-8
1665 Honeysuckle Rd 36305 — 334-794-1420
Patsy Slaughter, prin. — Fax 678-6546

Kelly Springs ES — 400/K-5
1124 Kelly Springs Rd 36303 — 334-983-6565
Sharon Kelley, prin. — Fax 983-5822

Landmark ES — 300/K-5
4130 Westgate Pkwy 36303 — 334-794-1479
Willie Brown, prin. — Fax 793-1180

Montana Street Academic Magnet S — 400/K-5
1001 Montana St 36303 — 334-794-1475
Beverly Sue Clark, prin. — Fax 794-1477

Selma Street ES — 400/K-5
1501 W Selma St 36301 — 334-794-1463
Charles Corbitt, prin. — Fax 794-1464

Houston County SD — 6,300/PK-12
404 W Washington St 36301 — 334-792-8331
Tim Pitchford, supt. — Fax 792-1016
hcboe.us/

Rehobeth ES — 900/PK-5
5631 County Road 203 36301 — 334-677-5153
Shirley Brewer, prin. — Fax 677-5947

Rehobeth MS — 500/6-8
5631 County Road 203 36301 — 334-677-5153
John Dixon, prin. — Fax 677-5947

Other Schools – See Ashford, Cottonwood, Newton, Webb

Emmanuel Christian S — 400/PK-12
178 Earline Rd 36305 — 334-792-0935
Mark Redmond, admin. — Fax 702-7410

Houston Academy — 600/PK-12
901 Buena Vista Dr 36303 — 334-794-4106
John O'Connell, hdmstr. — Fax 793-4053

Providence Christian S — 700/1-12
4847 Murphy Mill Rd 36303 — 334-702-8933
Emory Latta, hdmstr. — Fax 702-0700

St. Columba Pre School — 50/PK-K
2700 W Main St 36301 — 334-793-6742
Cathy Dedmon, prin. — Fax 792-2816

Trinity Lutheran S — 100/PK-PK
116 Luther Way 36301 — 334-793-6381
Kathy Jett, prin. — Fax 671-0086

Double Springs, Winston, Pop. 983

Winston County SD — 2,800/PK-12
PO Box 9 35553 — 205-489-5018
Sue Reed, supt. — Fax 489-3202
www.winstonk12.org

Double Springs ES — 400/PK-4
PO Box 550 35553 — 205-489-2190
Bobby Daniels, prin. — Fax 489-5159

Double Springs MS — 300/5-8
PO Box 669 35553 — 205-489-3813
Ben Aderholt, prin. — Fax 489-8832

Other Schools – See Addison, Arley, Lynn

Douglas, Marshall, Pop. 568

Marshall County SD
Supt. — See Guntersville

Douglas ES — 400/3-5
PO Box 299 35964 — 256-593-4420
Willard Moses, prin. — Fax 593-4423

Douglas MS — 400/6-8
PO Box 269 35964 — 256-593-1240
Larry Wilson, prin. — Fax 593-1259

Duncanville, Tuscaloosa

Tuscaloosa County SD
Supt. — See Tuscaloosa

Duncanville MS — 6-8
11205 Eagle Pkwy 35456 — 205-342-2830
Dottie Dockery, prin. — Fax 759-1998

Maxwell ES — 500/K-5
11370 Monticello Dr 35456 — 205-342-2656
Connie Clements, prin. — Fax 366-8625

Dutton, Jackson, Pop. 308

Jackson County SD
Supt. — See Scottsboro

Dutton S — 300/K-8
PO Box 38 35744 — 256-228-4265
John Kirby, prin. — Fax 228-3210

East Brewton, Escambia, Pop. 2,424

Escambia County SD
Supt. — See Brewton

Neal ES — 600/K-4
701 Williamson St 36426 — 251-867-7674
John Knott, prin. — Fax 809-2951

Neal MS — 500/5-8
703 Williamson St 36426 — 251-867-5035
Dennis Hadaway, prin. — Fax 867-5051

Eclectic, Elmore, Pop. 1,112

Elmore County SD
Supt. — See Wetumpka

Eclectic ES — 600/K-4
35 Harden St 36024 — 334-541-2291
Paula Flowers, prin. — Fax 541-3556

Eclectic MS — 500/5-8
170 S Ann St 36024 — 334-541-2131
Dane Hawk, prin. — Fax 541-3556

Eight Mile, See Prichard

Mobile County SD
Supt. — See Mobile

Collins-Rhodes ES — 300/PK-5
5110 Saint Stephens Rd 36613 — 251-221-1226
Hattie Alexander, prin. — Fax 221-1228

Indian Springs ES — 400/PK-5
4550 Highpoint Blvd 36613 — 251-221-1436
Rosalie Howley, prin. — Fax 221-1438

Elba, Coffee, Pop. 4,181

Coffee County SD — 2,000/PK-12
400 Reddoch Hill Rd 36323 — 334-897-5016
Dr. Linda Ingram, supt. — Fax 897-6207
www.coffeecountyschools.org

Other Schools – See Jack, Kinston, New Brockton

Elba CSD — 900/K-12
131 Tiger Dr 36323 — 334-897-2801
Danny Weeks, supt. — Fax 897-5601
www.elbaed.com

Elba ES — 400/K-6
145 Tiger Dr 36323 — 334-897-2814
LaKesha Brackins, prin. — Fax 897-2839

Elberta, Baldwin, Pop. 583

Baldwin County SD
Supt. — See Bay Minette

Elberta ES — 500/PK-3
25820 US Highway 98 36530 — 251-986-5888
Hope Zeanah, prin. — Fax 986-3664

Elberta MS — 600/4-8
13355 Main St 36530 — 251-986-8127
Jon Cardwell, prin. — Fax 986-7472

St. Benedict S — 200/PK-8
PO Box 819 36530 — 251-986-8143
Kendall McKee, prin. — Fax 986-8144

Elkmont, Limestone, Pop. 493

Limestone County SD
Supt. — See Athens

Elkmont S — 1,000/K-12
25630 Evans Ave 35620 — 256-732-4291
Mickey Glass, prin. — Fax 732-3418

Enterprise, Coffee, Pop. 22,892

Enterprise CSD — 5,600/PK-12
PO Box 311790 36331 — 334-347-9531
Dr. Jim Reese, supt. — Fax 347-5102
www.enterpriseschools.net/

College Street ES — 400/1-6
605 W College St 36330 — 334-347-6190
Twyla Pipkin, prin. — Fax 347-1146

Coppinville S — 500/7-7
301 N Ouida St 36330 — 334-347-2215
Angela Seals, prin. — Fax 347-7895

Enterprise Early Education Center — 100/PK-K
6500 Boll Weevil Cir 36330 — 334-393-9542
Waller Martin, prin. — Fax 393-9547

Harrand Creek ES — 300/1-6
216 Morgan Ln 36330 — 334-347-5383
Ronnie Retherford, prin. — Fax 347-0463

Hillcrest ES — 500/1-6
400 E Watts St 36330 — 334-347-6858
Hugh Williams, prin. — Fax 347-1322

Holly Hill ES — 600/1-6
201 Pineview Dr 36330 — 334-347-9700
Christie Mitten, prin. — Fax 347-0782

Pinedale ES — 500/1-6
207 Plaza Dr 36330 — 334-347-5460
Zel Thomas, prin. — Fax 347-0347

Rucker Boulevard ES — 400/1-6
209 Regency Dr 36330 — 334-347-3535
Jackie Dubose, prin. — Fax 347-0610

Enterprise Preparatory Academy — 200/PK-12
PO Box 310600 36331 — 334-308-0260
Bob Moore, hdmstr. — Fax 308-0264

Wiregrass Christian Academy — 100/PK-7
209 W College St 36330 — 334-393-8972
Joan Howell, prin. — Fax 393-1465

Eufaula, Barbour, Pop. 13,463

Eufaula CSD — 2,000/PK-12
333 State Docks Rd 36027 — 334-687-1100
Barry Sadler, supt. — Fax 687-1150
www.ecs.k12.al.us

Eufaula ES — 200/3-5
422 Sanford Ave 36027 — 334-687-1134
Reeivice Girtman, prin. — Fax 687-1136

Eufaula PS — 300/PK-2
520 Pump Station Rd 36027 — 334-687-1140
Suzann Tibbs, prin. — Fax 687-1142

Moorer MS — 700/6-8
101 Saint Francis Rd 36027 — 334-687-1130
Barbara Lee, prin. — Fax 687-1138

Lakeside S — 400/PK-12
1020 Lake Dr 36027 — 334-687-5748
Miranda Watson, hdmstr. — Fax 687-6306

Eutaw, Greene, Pop. 1,800

Greene County SD — 1,500/K-12
220 Main St 35462 — 205-372-4900
I. Atkins, supt. — Fax 372-3247
www.greene.k12.al.us

Carver MS — 400/4-8
PO Box 659 35462 — 205-372-4816
Garry Rice, prin. — Fax 372-4828

Eutaw PS — 300/K-3
PO Box 599 35462 — 205-372-1051
Betty Morrow, prin. — Fax 372-2568

Other Schools – See Boligee

Eva, Morgan, Pop. 494

Morgan County SD
Supt. — See Decatur

Eva S — 400/K-8
20 School Rd 35621 — 256-796-5141
Patrick Patterson, prin. — Fax 796-7108

Evergreen, Conecuh, Pop. 3,442

Conecuh County SD — 1,600/PK-12
100 Jackson St 36401 — 251-578-1752
Martha Hollinger, supt. — Fax 578-7061
www.conecuh.k12.al.us/

Evergreen ES — 300/PK-5
821 W Front St 36401 — 251-578-2576
Tonya Bozeman, prin. — Fax 578-7083

Lyeffion S — 200/PK-8
7575 Highway 83 36401 — 251-578-2800
Rita Nettles, prin. — Fax 578-5513

Marshall MS — 100/6-8
428 Reynolds Ave 36401 — 251-578-2866
Geneva Lyons, prin. — Fax 578-7067

Other Schools – See Castleberry, Repton

Sparta Academy — 300/PK-12
300 Pierce St 36401 — 251-578-2852
Wayne Hammonds, prin. — Fax 578-2878

Excel, Monroe, Pop. 601

Monroe County SD
Supt. — See Monroeville

Excel S — 1,000/K-12
PO Box 429 36439 — 251-765-2351
Kevin York, prin. — Fax 765-9153

Fairfield, Jefferson, Pop. 11,696

Fairfield CSD — 2,400/K-12
6405 Avenue D 35064 — 205-783-6850
Dr. Anthony Greene, supt. — Fax 783-6805
www.fairfield.k12.al.us

Donald ES — 400/K-5
715 Valley Rd 35064 — 205-783-6823
Corvetta Vann, prin. — Fax 783-6825

Forest Hills MS — 500/6-8
7000 Grasselli Rd 35064 — 205-783-6841
Walter Curry, prin. — Fax 783-6753

Glen Oaks ES — 300/K-5
1301 Highland Dr 35064 — 205-783-6837
Autumm Jeter, prin. — Fax 783-6763

Robinson ES — 300/K-5
301 61st St 35064 — 205-783-6827
Zenobia Odoms, prin. — Fax 783-6757

Mt. Pilgrim Christian Academy — 100/PK-5
143 Seminole Cir 35064 — 205-780-5096
Eleashia Roper, prin. — Fax 780-5098

Restoration Academy — 100/K-12
PO Box 30 35064 — 205-785-8805
Ben Sciacca, prin. — Fax 785-8870

St. Mary S — 100/PK-K
6124 Myron Massey Blvd 35064 — 205-923-5115
Shilisha Logan, prin. — Fax 923-5141

Fairhope, Baldwin, Pop. 15,391

Baldwin County SD
Supt. — See Bay Minette

Fairhope ES — 500/2-3
2 N Bishop Rd 36532 — 251-928-8400
Terry Beasley, prin. — Fax 928-9709

Fairhope IS — 500/4-5
1101 Fairhope Ave 36532 — 251-928-7841
Carol Broughton, prin. — Fax 990-2227

Fairhope K-1 Center — 400/K-1
100 S Church St 36532 — 251-928-7011
Patricia Carlton, prin. — Fax 990-2239

Fairhope MS — 700/6-8
2 Pirate Dr 36532 — 251-928-2573
Dr. Deadra Powe, prin. — Fax 990-0403

Newton ES — 600/K-6
9761 County Road 32 36532 — 251-990-3858
Suellen Brazil, prin. — Fax 990-9706

Bayshore Christian S — 100/K-7
23050 US Highway 98 36532 — 251-929-0011
Mark Cox, hdmstr. — Fax 928-0149

Falkville, Morgan, Pop. 1,177

Morgan County SD
Supt. — See Decatur

Falkville ES — 500/K-6
72 Clark Dr 35622 — 256-784-5249
Hank Summerford, prin. — Fax 784-9070

Fayette, Fayette, Pop. 4,761

Fayette County SD — 2,500/PK-12
PO Box 686 35555 — 205-932-4611
Reba Anderson, supt. — Fax 932-7246
www.fayette.k12.al.us

Fayette ES — 600/PK-4
509 2nd St NE 35555 — 205-932-3161
Sarah Newton, prin. — Fax 932-5285

Fayette MS — 500/5-8
418 3rd Ave NE 35555 — 205-932-7660
Rodney Hannah, prin. — Fax 932-7661

Hubbertville S — 400/PK-12
7360 County Road 49 35555 — 205-487-2845
Tim Dunavant, prin. — Fax 487-3375

Other Schools – See Berry

Five Points, Chambers, Pop. 144

Chambers County SD
Supt. — See Lafayette

Five Points S — 200/K-8
PO Box 98 36855 — 334-864-7615
Rhonda Givins, prin. — Fax 864-7612

Flat Rock, Jackson

Jackson County SD
Supt. — See Scottsboro

Flat Rock S — 100/K-8
788 County Road 326 35966 — 256-632-2323
Craig Robbins, prin. — Fax 632-6317

Flomaton, Escambia, Pop. 1,560

Escambia County SD
Supt. — See Brewton

Flomaton S — 400/K-8
1634 Poplar St 36441 — 251-296-5238
David Curran, prin. — Fax 296-3060

Florala, Covington, Pop. 1,893

Covington County SD
Supt. — See Andalusia

Florala City MS — 100/7-8
22975 7th Ave 36442 — 334-858-3642
Rodney Drish, prin. — Fax 858-7181

Florence, Lauderdale, Pop. 36,480

Florence CSD — 4,000/K-12
541 Riverview Dr 35630 — 256-768-3015
Dr. Kendy Behrends, supt. — Fax 768-3006
www.fcs.k12.al.us/

Florence MS 600/7-8
648 N Cherry St 35630 256-768-3100
William Griffin, prin. Fax 768-3105
Forest Hills ES 700/K-4
101 Stovall Dr 35633 256-768-2500
Anne Gipson, prin. Fax 768-2505
Harlan ES 400/K-4
2233 McBurney Dr 35630 256-768-2700
Dr. Shirley Coker, prin. Fax 768-2705
Hibbett S 500/5-6
1601 Appleby Blvd 35630 256-768-2800
Dr. Rose McGee, prin. Fax 768-2805
Weeden ES 400/K-4
400 Baldwin St 35630 256-768-2900
Chris Westbrook, prin. Fax 768-2905

Lauderdale County SD 8,800/K-12
PO Box 278 35631 256-760-1300
William Valentine, supt. Fax 766-5815
www.lcschools.org
Central S 1,300/K-12
3000 County Road 200 35633 256-764-2903
David Corl, prin. Fax 764-5409
Cloverdale S 200/K-9
12101 Highway 157 35633 256-764-4816
Kenneth Koss, prin. Fax 764-4816
Kilby Laboratory ES 100/K-6
PO Box 5035 35632 256-765-4303
Dr. Mary Maschal, prin. Fax 765-4167
Rogers S 1,300/K-12
300 Rogers Ln 35634 256-757-3106
Timothy Tubbs, prin. Fax 757-9625
Underwood ES 300/K-6
4725 Highway 157 35633 256-764-8939
Kevin Moore, prin. Fax 766-5044
Wilson S 1,300/K-12
7601 Highway 17 35634 256-764-8470
Gary Horton, prin. Fax 764-1304
Other Schools – See Anderson, Killen, Lexington, Rogersville, Waterloo

---

Mars Hill Bible S 600/K-12
698 Cox Creek Pkwy 35630 256-767-1203
Dr. Kenny Barfield, hdmstr. Fax 767-6304
Riverhill S 200/PK-9
2826 County Road 30 35634 256-764-8200
Cynthia Davis, prin. Fax 766-7006
St. Joseph S 200/PK-8
115 Plum St 35630 256-766-1923
Kelley Dewberry, prin. Fax 766-1713
Shoals Christian S 300/PK-12
301 Heathrow Dr 35633 256-767-7070
Thomas Hughes, hdmstr. Fax 766-5677

Foley, Baldwin, Pop. 11,419
Baldwin County SD
Supt. — See Bay Minette
Foley ES 700/PK-3
450 N Cedar St 36535 251-943-8861
Dr. William Lawrence, prin. Fax 943-1732
Foley IS 300/4-5
2000 S Cedar St 36535 251-943-1244
Lee Mansell, prin. Fax 970-2004
Foley MS 700/6-8
201 N Pine St 36535 251-943-1255
Branton Bailey, prin. Fax 943-8221
Magnolia ES 600/PK-6
1 Jaguar Loop 36535 251-965-6200
Pam Magee, prin. Fax 965-6221

St. Paul Lutheran S 50/PK-PK
400 N Alston St 36535 251-970-3769
Susan Taylor, prin.

Fort Deposit, Lowndes, Pop. 1,229
Lowndes County SD
Supt. — See Hayneville
Fort Deposit ES 300/K-5
PO Box 250 36032 334-227-8704
Darryl Arms, prin. Fax 227-4735
Lowndes County MS 200/6-8
PO Box 393 36032 334-227-4206
Marques Stewart, prin. Fax 227-4125

Fort Mitchell, Russell
Russell County SD
Supt. — See Phenix City
Mt. Olive ES 400/K-6
454 Highway 165 36856 334-855-4517
Bonnie Curry, prin. Fax 855-4544

St. Joseph Child Development Center PK-PK
1444 Highway 165 36856 334-855-3148
Debra Blanks, prin. Fax 855-3115

Fort Payne, DeKalb, Pop. 13,573
De Kalb County SD
Supt. — See Rainsville
Ruhuma S 200/K-8
3371 County Road 81 35967 256-845-3377
Hugh Taylor, prin. Fax 845-3377

Fort Payne CSD 2,900/PK-12
PO Box 681029 35968 256-845-0915
James Cunningham, supt. Fax 845-4962
www.ftpayk12.org
Fort Payne MS 900/5-8
4910 Martin Ave NE 35967 256-845-7501
Shane Byrd, prin. Fax 845-8292
Williams Avenue ES 400/3-4
1700 Williams Ave NE 35967 256-845-0626
Brian Jett, prin. Fax 845-0147
Wills Valley ES 800/PK-2
4111 Williams Ave NE 35967 256-845-3201
Cathy Jones, prin. Fax 845-2909

Fosters, Tuscaloosa
Tuscaloosa County SD
Supt. — See Tuscaloosa

Myrtlewood ES 200/K-5
14701 Gainsville Rd 35463 205-342-2658
Sheila Stromberg, prin. Fax 345-7259

Fruitdale, Washington
Washington County SD
Supt. — See Chatom
Fruitdale S 500/K-12
PO Box 448 36539 251-827-6655
Dr. Alfred Taylor, prin. Fax 827-6573

Fruithurst, Cleburne, Pop. 281
Cleburne County SD
Supt. — See Heflin
Fruithurst ES 200/K-6
222 School St 36262 256-579-2232
Christy Hiett, prin. Fax 579-2232

Fultondale, Jefferson, Pop. 6,853
Jefferson County SD
Supt. — See Birmingham
Fultondale ES 600/K-6
950 Central Ave 35068 205-379-3450
Cynthia Cornelius, prin. Fax 379-3495

Fyffe, DeKalb, Pop. 1,020
De Kalb County SD
Supt. — See Rainsville
Fyffe S 900/K-12
PO Box 7 35971 256-623-2116
Ricky Bryant, prin. Fax 623-4388

Gadsden, Etowah, Pop. 37,405
Etowah County SD 9,000/K-12
3200 W Meighan Blvd 35904 256-549-7578
Michael Bailey, supt. Fax 549-7582
www.ecboe.org/
Gaston S 600/K-12
4550 US Highway 411 35901 256-547-8828
Dr. Miria King-Garner, prin. Fax 543-7124
Highland S 300/K-8
3156 Tabor Rd 35904 256-546-7409
Teresa Lokey, prin. Fax 546-7158
Hokes Bluff ES 600/K-5
5375 Main St 35903 256-492-5571
Charles Gardner, prin. Fax 492-2513
Hokes Bluff MS 300/6-8
3121 Appalachian Hwy 35903 256-492-1963
Dr. Marguerite Early, prin. Fax 492-1950
Other Schools – See Altoona, Attalla, Boaz, Glencoe, Rainbow City, Southside

Gadsden CSD 6,000/K-12
PO Box 184 35902 256-543-3512
Dr. Ed Miller, supt. Fax 549-2950
www.gcs.k12.al.us
Adams ES 400/K-5
919 Raley St 35903 256-492-4952
Micah Cook, prin. Fax 492-3008
Brown ES 400/K-5
1231 Alcott Rd 35901 256-546-0011
Priscilla Yother, prin. Fax 546-6855
Donehoo ES 200/K-5
1109 E Broad St 35903 256-546-3604
Dr. Cynthia Woods, prin. Fax 547-9021
Floyd ES 400/K-5
601 Black Creek Rd 35904 256-546-0836
Nicole Chester, prin. Fax 546-9955
Gadsden MS 400/6-8
612 Tracy St 35901 256-547-6341
Joel Gulledge, prin. Fax 547-6323
Litchfield MS 300/6-8
1109 Hoke St 35903 256-492-6793
Kimberly Smith, prin. Fax 492-4010
Mitchell ES 400/K-5
1501 Noccalula Rd 35904 256-546-2711
Dr. Charlotte Berry, prin. Fax 549-2970
Sansom MS 500/6-8
2210 W Meighan Blvd 35904 256-546-4992
Ronald Mayes, prin. Fax 543-1060
Striplin ES 300/K-5
600 Cleveland Ave 35901 256-546-8616
Delsia Easley, prin. Fax 543-7905
Thompson ES 200/K-5
236 Goldenrod Ave 35901 256-546-7011
Yolando White, prin. Fax 546-7011
Walnut Park ES 400/K-5
3200 Walnut St 35904 256-546-4665
Nancy Croley, prin. Fax 546-9703

Coosa Christian S 400/K-12
2736 Wills Creek Rd 35904 256-547-1841
Fax 547-0045
Holy Comforter Episcopal Day S 100/PK-6
156 S 9th St 35901 256-546-9071
Laura McCartney, admin. Fax 546-7912
St. James S 100/PK-8
700 Albert Rains Blvd 35901 256-546-0132
John Parker, prin. Fax 546-0134

Garden City, Cullman, Pop. 587
Cullman County SD
Supt. — See Cullman
Garden City ES 100/K-6
PO Box 185 35070 256-352-5051
Susan Melton, prin. Fax 352-1924

Gardendale, Jefferson, Pop. 12,830
Jefferson County SD
Supt. — See Birmingham
Bragg MS 800/6-8
840 Ash Ave 35071 205-379-2600
Jeffrey Caufield, prin. Fax 379-2645
Gardendale ES 700/K-5
860 Bauers Ln 35071 205-379-3550
Ellen Andrews, prin. Fax 379-3595
Snow Rogers ES 200/K-5
2636 Snow Rogers Rd 35071 205-379-5400
Karen White, prin. Fax 379-5445

Gaylesville, Cherokee, Pop. 142
Cherokee County SD
Supt. — See Centre
Gaylesville S 400/PK-12
760 Trojan Way 35973 256-422-3401
Paul McWhorter, prin. Fax 422-3165

Geneva, Geneva, Pop. 4,379
Geneva CSD 1,300/K-12
511 Panther Dr 36340 334-684-1090
James Bixby, supt. Fax 684-3128
www.genevacity.schoolinsites.com
Geneva MS 300/6-8
501 Panther Dr 36340 334-684-6431
Danny Bedsole, prin. Fax 684-0476
Mulkey ES 600/K-5
800 W Meadow Ave 36340 334-684-2294
Virginia Hayes, prin. Fax 684-2543

Geneva County SD 2,700/K-12
PO Box 250 36340 334-684-5690
Danny Bedsole, supt. Fax 684-5601
genevacounty.schoolinsites.com/
Other Schools – See Hartford, Samson, Slocomb

Georgiana, Butler, Pop. 1,636
Butler County SD
Supt. — See Greenville
Butler County Magnet S 300/K-12
PO Box 680 36033 334-376-9130
Joseph Dean, prin. Fax 376-2956

Geraldine, DeKalb, Pop. 816
De Kalb County SD
Supt. — See Rainsville
Geraldine S 1,100/K-12
PO Box 157 35974 256-659-2142
Robert Richey, prin. Fax 659-4296

Gilbertown, Choctaw, Pop. 175
Choctaw County SD
Supt. — See Butler
Southern Choctaw ES 500/K-6
10935 Highway 17 36908 251-843-2461
Jacqui James, prin. Fax 843-4646

Glencoe, Etowah, Pop. 5,265
Etowah County SD
Supt. — See Gadsden
Glencoe ES 400/K-4
207 N College St 35905 256-492-4709
Tiffany Scott, prin. Fax 492-4704
Glencoe MS 400/5-8
809 Lonesome Bend Rd 35905 256-492-5627
Ginger Smith, prin. Fax 492-7076

Gordo, Pickens, Pop. 1,596
Pickens County SD
Supt. — See Carrollton
Gordo ES 600/K-6
535 4th St NW 35466 205-364-8480
Lisa Stamps, prin. Fax 364-0350

Goshen, Pike, Pop. 300
Pike County SD
Supt. — See Troy
Goshen ES 500/K-6
23 County Road 2238 36035 334-484-3442
Jackie Hall, prin. Fax 484-3009

Grand Bay, Mobile, Pop. 3,383
Mobile County SD
Supt. — See Mobile
Breitling ES 600/PK-5
8350 Grand Bay Wilmer Rd S 36541 251-865-0900
Cynthia Saliba, prin. Fax 865-0902
Castlen ES 600/K-5
9960 School House Rd 36541 251-865-6733
Pamela Adams, prin. Fax 865-0335
Grand Bay MS 700/6-8
12800 Cunningham Rd 36541 251-865-6511
Wade Whitney, prin. Fax 865-6182

Grant, Marshall, Pop. 677
Marshall County SD
Supt. — See Guntersville
Smith DAR ES 400/K-4
6077 Main St 35747 256-728-2226
Keith Buchanan, prin. Fax 728-8430
Smith DAR MS 400/5-8
6077 Main St 35747 256-728-5950
Susan Keller, prin. Fax 728-8447

Graysville, Jefferson, Pop. 2,452
Jefferson County SD
Supt. — See Birmingham
Brookville ES 300/K-5
4275 Brookville School Rd 35073 205-379-2700
Pam Tindal, prin. Fax 379-2745

Greensboro, Hale, Pop. 2,616
Hale County SD 3,200/PK-12
1115 Powers St 36744 334-624-8836
Joseph Stegall, supt. Fax 624-3415
www.halek12.org
Greensboro East ES 400/K-6
PO Box 167 36744 334-624-4005
Janet Gipson Sherrod, prin. Fax 624-0308
Greensboro West ES 500/PK-6
1801 South St 36744 334-624-8611
Stephanie Richey, prin. Fax 624-8644
Other Schools – See Akron, Moundville, Newbern

Southern Academy 300/K-12
407 College St 36744 334-624-8111
James Davis, prin. Fax 624-3778

Greenville, Butler, Pop. 7,104
Butler County SD 3,100/K-12
211 School Highlands Rd 36037 334-382-2665
Mike Looney, supt. Fax 382-8607
www.butlerco.k12.al.us

Greenville ES 400/3-4
102 Butler Cir 36037 334-382-8720
Dr. Tera Simmons, prin. Fax 382-2425
Greenville MS 800/5-8
300 Overlook Rd 36037 334-382-3450
Jai Hill, prin. Fax 382-0686
Parmer ES 600/K-2
100 Butler Cir 36037 334-382-8720
Catherine Sawicki, prin. Fax 382-2425
Other Schools – See Georgiana, Mc Kenzie

Fort Dale Academy 500/K-12
1100 Gamble St 36037 334-382-2606
David Brantley, prin. Fax 382-0912

Grove Hill, Clarke, Pop. 1,383
Clarke County SD 3,500/PK-12
PO Box 936 36451 251-275-3255
Woodie Pugh, supt. Fax 275-8061
www.clarkecountyschools.org/
Grove Hill ES 500/PK-4
PO Box 907 36451 251-275-3423
Kathy Spidle, prin. Fax 275-4887
Wilson Hall MS 400/5-8
PO Box 906 36451 251-275-8993
Larry Bagley, prin. Fax 275-4688
Other Schools – See Coffeeville, Jackson

Clarke Preparatory S 500/PK-12
20100 Highway 43 36451 251-275-8576
David Walker, prin. Fax 275-8579

Guin, Marion, Pop. 2,246
Marion County SD
Supt. — See Hamilton
Guin ES 300/PK-6
PO Box 10 35563 205-468-3433
Tracy Brown, prin. Fax 468-3575

Gulf Shores, Baldwin, Pop. 7,263
Baldwin County SD
Supt. — See Bay Minette
Gulf Shores ES 600/K-6
1600 E 3rd St 36542 251-968-7375
Julie Warlick, prin. Fax 968-7217
Gulf Shores MS 400/7-8
450 E 15th Ave 36542 251-968-8719
Phillip Fountain, prin. Fax 967-1577

Grace Christian Academy 100/PK-8
19470 County Road 6 36542 251-968-4352
Kathryn Grotefend, admin. Fax 968-5306

Guntersville, Marshall, Pop. 7,721
Guntersville CSD 1,900/K-12
PO Box 129 35976 256-582-3159
Andrew Lee, supt. Fax 582-6158
www.guntersvilleboe.com
Cherokee ES 400/3-5
3300 Highway 79 S 35976 256-582-3908
Bart Reeves, prin. Fax 582-3986
Guntersville ES 400/K-2
1800 Lusk St 35976 256-582-3364
Lou Ann Patton, prin. Fax 582-0892
Guntersville MS 500/6-8
901 Sunset Dr 35976 256-582-5182
Shirl Dollar, prin. Fax 582-4477

Marshall County SD 5,500/PK-12
12380 US Highway 431 35976 256-582-3171
Tim Nabors, supt. Fax 582-3178
www.marshallk12.org
Brindlee Mountain MS 300/6-8
1050 Scant City Rd 35976 256-753-2820
Barry Kirkland, prin. Fax 753-2802
Claysville S 300/PK-8
140 Claysville School Rd 35976 256-582-4444
Tim Isbill, prin. Fax 582-4454
Other Schools – See Albertville, Arab, Douglas, Grant, Horton, Union Grove

Gurley, Madison, Pop. 854
Madison County SD
Supt. — See Huntsville
Madison County S 400/K-8
173 Wood St 35748 256-776-9264
Becky Meador, prin. Fax 776-6676

Hackleburg, Marion, Pop. 1,475
Marion County SD
Supt. — See Hamilton
Hackleburg S 500/PK-12
PO Box 310 35564 205-935-3223
John Hardin, prin. Fax 935-8092

Haleyville, Winston, Pop. 4,159
Haleyville CSD 1,700/PK-12
2011 20th St 35565 205-486-9231
Dr. Clint Baggett, supt. Fax 486-8833
www.havc.k12.al.us
Haleyville ES 1,000/PK-6
2000 20th St 35565 205-486-3405
Russ O'Rear, prin. Fax 486-8960

Hamilton, Marion, Pop. 6,496
Marion County SD 3,700/PK-12
188 Winchester Dr 35570 205-921-9319
Ryan Hollingsworth, supt. Fax 921-7336
www.mcbe.net
Hamilton ES 700/K-4
784 10th Ave SW 35570 205-921-2145
Dr. Sherry Armstrong, prin. Fax 921-9857
Hamilton MS 500/5-8
400 Military St S 35570 205-921-7030
Steven Deavours, prin. Fax 921-3821
Other Schools – See Bear Creek, Brilliant, Guin, Hackleburg

Hampton, Madison
Huntsville CSD
Supt. — See Huntsville
Hampton Cove ES 900/K-5
261 Old Highway 431, 256-428-7180
Fillis McGhee, prin. Fax 428-7181
Hampton Cove MS 500/6-8
261 Old Highway 431, 256-428-8380
Dr. Debi Edwards, prin. Fax 428-8383

Hanceville, Cullman, Pop. 3,127
Cullman County SD
Supt. — See Cullman
Hanceville ES 500/K-5
799 Commercial St SE 35077 256-352-9196
Jeffrey Harper, prin. Fax 352-9221
Hanceville MS 300/6-8
805 Commercial St SE 35077 256-352-6175
Cynthia Roden, prin. Fax 352-9741

Hartford, Geneva, Pop. 2,372
Geneva County SD
Supt. — See Geneva
Geneva County ES 300/K-5
819 S 6th Ave 36344 334-588-2923
Rebecca Birdsong, prin. Fax 588-0553
Geneva County MS 200/6-8
301 Lily St 36344 334-588-2943
Mike Whitaker, prin. Fax 588-3650

Hartselle, Morgan, Pop. 13,080
Hartselle CSD 3,100/PK-12
305 College St NE 35640 256-773-5419
Dr. Mike Reed, supt. Fax 773-5433
www.hartselletigers.org
Barkley Bridge ES 400/K-5
2333 Barkley Bridge Rd SW 35640 256-773-1931
Susan Hayes, prin. Fax 773-4338
Burleson ES 400/K-5
1100 Bethel Rd NE 35640 256-773-2411
Sherry Calvert, prin. Fax 773-3643
Crestline ES 600/PK-5
600 Crestline Dr SW 35640 256-773-9967
Robin Varwig, prin. Fax 773-3255
Hartselle JHS 800/6-8
130 Petain St SW 35640 256-773-6094
Don Pouncey, prin. Fax 773-3499

Morgan County SD
Supt. — See Decatur
Sparkman S 300/K-8
72 Plainview St 35640 256-773-6458
Ron Moore, prin. Fax 751-1256

Harvest, Madison, Pop. 1,922
Limestone County SD
Supt. — See Athens
Creekside ES 900/K-5
16049 Sanderson Rd 35749 256-216-8702
Matthew Scott, prin. Fax 216-8704

Madison County SD
Supt. — See Huntsville
Endeavor ES 900/PK-5
1997 Old Railroad Bed Rd 35749 256-837-7475
Marilyn Hicks, prin. Fax 837-3063
Harvest ES 600/K-5
PO Box 360 35749 256-837-0379
Stephanie Burton, prin. Fax 890-0322

Hayden, Blount, Pop. 520
Blount County SD
Supt. — See Oneonta
Hayden ES 200/3-4
4111 State Highway 160 35079 205-647-6578
Shelley Vail-Smith, prin. Fax 647-1386
Hayden MS 5-7
310 2nd Ave 35079 205-647-3083
Kenneth Parker, prin. Fax 647-4462
Hayden PS 600/K-2
160 Brackin Ln 35079 205-647-2103
Linda Parker, prin. Fax 647-6520

Hayneville, Lowndes, Pop. 1,141
Lowndes County SD 2,100/K-12
PO Box 755 36040 334-548-2131
Dr. Daniel Boyd, supt. Fax 548-2161
www.lowndesboe.org/
Central ES 400/K-5
141 Main St 36040 334-563-7319
Mary Phelan-Jackson, prin. Fax 563-7347
Hayneville MS 300/6-8
PO Box 307 36040 334-548-2184
Bernard Mitchell, prin. Fax 548-5237
Jackson-Steele ES 200/K-5
570 Freedom Rd 36040 334-872-0758
Samita Jeter, prin. Fax 872-2923
Other Schools – See Fort Deposit

Hazel Green, Madison, Pop. 2,208
Madison County SD
Supt. — See Huntsville
Hazel Green ES 1,000/K-5
14250 Highway 231 431 N 35750 256-828-6109
Lorraine Boone, prin. Fax 828-0827
Meridianville MS 1,000/6-8
12975 Highway 231 431 N 35750 256-829-1165
Tom Highfield, prin. Fax 829-1104

Headland, Henry, Pop. 3,714
Henry County SD
Supt. — See Abbeville
Headland ES 800/PK-5
305 Mitchell St 36345 334-693-2330
Faye Shipes, prin. Fax 693-2151
Headland MS 400/6-8
1 Martin Luther King Dr 36345 334-693-3764
Rickey Allen, prin. Fax 693-9058

Heflin, Cleburne, Pop. 3,308
Cleburne County SD 2,500/K-12
93 Education St 36264 256-463-5624
David Easley, supt. Fax 463-5709
www.cleburneschools.net
Cleburne County ES 300/K-4
584 Evans Bridge Rd 36264 256-463-2654
Barbara Johnson, prin. Fax 463-5305
Cleburne County MS 300/5-7
661 Duke Dr 36264 256-463-2405
Emily Burke, prin. Fax 463-2482
Pleasant Grove ES 200/K-6
9855 Highway 9 36264 256-253-2146
Dr. Adam Dasinger, prin. Fax 253-2147
Other Schools – See Fruithurst, Ranburne

Helena, Shelby, Pop. 13,237
Shelby County SD
Supt. — See Columbiana
Helena ES 800/K-2
187 3rd St 35080 205-682-5540
Mary Cooper, prin. Fax 682-5545
Helena IS 700/3-5
3500 Highway 52 35080 205-682-5520
Wayne Williams, prin. Fax 682-5525
Helena MS 6-8
1299 Hillsboro Pkwy 35080 205-682-7000
Jenni Goulsby, prin. Fax 682-5305

Henagar, DeKalb, Pop. 2,507
De Kalb County SD
Supt. — See Rainsville
Henagar S 400/K-8
PO Box 69 35978 256-657-4483
Stevie Green, prin. Fax 657-4481

Higdon, Jackson
Jackson County SD
Supt. — See Scottsboro
North Sand Mountain S 700/K-12
PO Box 129 35979 256-597-2111
Chris Davis, prin. Fax 597-2505

Highland Home, Crenshaw
Crenshaw County SD
Supt. — See Luverne
Highland Home S 900/PK-12
18434 Montgomery Hwy 36041 334-537-4369
Joseph Eiland, prin. Fax 537-9805

Holly Pond, Cullman, Pop. 709
Cullman County SD
Supt. — See Cullman
Holly Pond ES 400/K-5
120 New Hope Rd 35083 256-796-0046
Karen Sparks, prin. Fax 796-5753
Holly Pond MS 200/6-8
91 Buckner Rd 35083 256-796-5898
Chuck Gambrill, prin. Fax 796-5753

Hollywood, Jackson, Pop. 929
Jackson County SD
Supt. — See Scottsboro
Hollywood S 200/K-8
6369 County Road 33 35752 256-574-2054
Paul Kennamer, prin. Fax 259-0331

Holt, Tuscaloosa, Pop. 4,125
Tuscaloosa County SD
Supt. — See Tuscaloosa
Holt ES 400/K-5
1001 Crescent Ridge Rd NE 35404 205-342-2650
Debbie Crawford, prin. Fax 507-0022

Homewood, Jefferson, Pop. 23,963
Homewood CSD 3,300/K-12
PO Box 59366 35259 205-870-4203
Dr. Bill Cleveland, supt. Fax 877-4544
www.homewood.k12.al.us
Edgewood ES 600/K-5
901 College Ave 35209 205-423-2400
Patricia Simpson, prin. Fax 423-2406
Hall Kent ES 500/K-5
213 Hall Ave 35209 205-423-2430
Carol Lord, prin. Fax 423-2432
Homewood MS 700/6-8
395 Mecca Ave 35209 205-870-0878
Martin Nalls, prin. Fax 877-4573
Shades Cahaba ES 600/K-5
3001 Independence Dr 35209 205-871-1113
Sue Grogan, prin. Fax 871-1186

Hoover, Jefferson, Pop. 67,469
Hoover CSD 11,400/K-12
2810 Metropolitan Way 35243 205-439-1015
Andy Craig, supt. Fax 439-1001
www.hoover.k12.al.us
Bluff Park ES 500/K-5
569 Park Ave 35226 205-439-2800
Dr. David Fancher, prin. Fax 439-2801
Bumpus MS 1,000/6-8
1730 Lake Cyrus Club Dr 35244 205-439-2200
Dr. Joy Brown, prin. Fax 439-2201
Green Valley ES 500/K-5
3200 Old Columbiana Rd 35226 205-439-2500
Jeff Singer, prin. Fax 439-2501
Greystone ES 700/K-5
300 Village St, Birmingham AL 35242 205-439-3200
Dr. Maurine Black, prin. Fax 439-3201
Gwin ES 600/K-5
1580 Patton Chapel Rd 35226 205-439-2600
Linda Joseph, prin. Fax 439-2601
Riverchase ES 600/K-5
1950 Old Montgomery Hwy 35244 205-439-3400
Dianne Baggett, prin. Fax 439-3401
Rocky Ridge ES 500/K-5
2876 Old Rocky Ridge Rd, Birmingham AL 35243
205-439-2900
Dr. Sonia Carrington, prin. Fax 439-2901

Shades Mountain ES 300/K-5
2250 Sumpter St 35226 205-439-3100
Juli Feltham, prin. Fax 439-3101
Simmons JHS 800/6-8
1575 Patton Chapel Rd 35226 205-439-2100
Brian Cain, prin. Fax 439-2101
South Shades Crest ES 700/K-5
3770 S Shades Crest Rd 35244 205-439-3000
Linda Gurosky, prin. Fax 439-3001
Trace Crossings ES 500/K-5
5454 Learning Ln 35244 205-439-2700
Dr. Dorothy Riley, prin. Fax 439-2701
Other Schools – See Birmingham

Prince of Peace S 400/PK-8
4650 Preserve Pkwy 35226 205-824-7886
Connie Angstadt, prin. Fax 824-2093
Shades Mountain Christian S 500/PK-12
2290 Old Tyler Rd 35226 205-978-6001
W. Laird Crump, hdmstr. Fax 978-9120

Hope Hull, Montgomery
Montgomery County SD
Supt. — See Montgomery
Pintlala ES 200/K-6
215 Federal Rd 36043 334-288-9523
Rodney Sellars, prin. Fax 288-4185

Hooper Academy 400/PK-12
380 Fischer Rd 36043 334-288-5980
Dr. John Niblett, prin. Fax 288-9171

Horton, Marshall
Marshall County SD
Supt. — See Guntersville
Sloman PS 500/PK-2
200 Bethleham Rd 35980 256-593-4912
Scott Bonds, prin. Fax 593-4874

Hueytown, Jefferson, Pop. 15,192
Jefferson County SD
Supt. — See Birmingham
Hueytown ES 900/K-5
112 Forest Rd 35023 205-379-4100
Stephanie Hendrix, prin. Fax 379-4145
Hueytown MS 800/6-8
701 Sunrise Blvd 35023 205-379-5150
Brett Kirkham, prin. Fax 379-5195
North Highland ES 400/K-5
2021 29th Ave N 35023 205-379-4950
Laura Moore, prin. Fax 379-4951

Huntsville, Madison, Pop. 166,313
Huntsville CSD 21,900/K-12
PO Box 1256 35807 256-428-6800
Dr. Ann Roy Moore, supt. Fax 428-6817
www.hsv.k12.al.us
Academy for Academics & Arts 400/K-8
2800 Poplar Ave NW 35816 256-428-7600
Wilbert Brown, prin. Fax 428-7601
Academy for Science & Foreign Language 500/K-8
3221 Mastin Lake Rd NW 35810 256-428-7000
Tammy Summerville, prin. Fax 428-7002
Blossomwood ES 500/K-5
1321 Woodmont Ave SE 35801 256-428-7020
Dr. Catherine Vasile, prin. Fax 428-7021
Chaffee ES 300/K-5
7900 Whittier Rd SW 35802 256-428-7040
Dr. Cecilia Bruton, prin. Fax 428-7047
Challenger ES 500/K-5
13555 Chaney Thompson Rd SE 35803
256-428-7060
Carol Costello, prin. Fax 428-7064
Challenger MS 600/6-8
13555 Chaney Thompson Rd SE 35803
256-428-7620
Edith Pickens, prin. Fax 428-7621
Chapman ES 300/K-5
2006 Reuben Dr NE 35811 256-428-7080
Peggy Harris, prin. Fax 428-7081
Chapman MS 300/6-8
2001 Reuben Dr NE 35811 256-428-7640
Dr. James Waters, prin. Fax 428-7641
Davis Hills MS 400/6-8
3221 Mastin Lake Rd NW 35810 256-428-7660
Bryon McGlathery, prin. Fax 428-7661
East Clinton ES 200/K-5
605 Clinton Ave E 35801 256-428-7140
Gwendolyn Foster, prin. Fax 428-7141
Farley ES 400/K-5
2900 Green Cove Rd SW 35803 256-428-7160
Donna White, prin. Fax 428-7165
Highlands ES 500/K-5
2500 Barney Ter NW 35810 256-428-7200
Michael Livingston, prin. Fax 428-7201
Huntsville MS 600/6-8
817 Adams St SE 35801 256-428-7700
Dr. Deborah Hargett, prin. Fax 428-7701
Jones Valley ES 500/K-5
4908 Garth Rd SE 35802 256-428-7220
Jeanne Greer, prin. Fax 428-7221
King ES 200/K-5
3112 Meridian St N 35811 256-428-7100
Dr. John Humphrey, prin. Fax 428-7101
Lakewood ES 400/K-5
3501 Kenwood Dr NW 35810 256-428-7240
Fred Barnes, prin. Fax 428-7241
Lincoln ES 200/K-5
1110 Meridian St N 35801 256-428-7260
Robert Jensen, prin. Fax 428-7261
McDonnell ES 400/K-5
4010 Binderton Pl SW 35805 256-428-7280
Allen Malone, prin. Fax 428-7281
Monte Sano ES 200/K-5
1107 Monte Sano Blvd SE 35801 256-428-7300
Brad Scott, prin. Fax 428-7301
Montview ES 300/K-5
2600 Garvin Rd NW 35810 256-428-7320
Dr. Kreslyn McGinnis, prin. Fax 428-7321
Morris ES 300/K-5
4801 Bob Wallace Ave SW 35805 256-428-7340
Tina Greer, prin. Fax 428-7341
Mountain Gap ES 400/K-5
821 Mountain Gap Rd SE 35803 256-428-7360
Nancy Murphree, prin. Fax 428-7361
Mountain Gap MS 400/6-8
821 Mountain Gap Rd SE 35803 256-428-7720
John Timlin, prin. Fax 428-7721
Providence S 800/K-8
10 Chalkstone St 35806 256-428-7125
Avis Waters-Maze, prin. Fax 428-7127
Ridgecrest ES 400/K-5
3505 Cerro Vista St SW 35805 256-428-7380
Dawn Williamson-Ashley, prin. Fax 428-7381
Rolling Hills ES 400/K-5
2901 Hilltop Ter NW 35810 256-428-7400
Helen Scott, prin. Fax 428-7401
University Place ES 300/K-5
4503 University Dr NW 35816 256-428-7440
Towana Davis, prin. Fax 428-7441
Weatherly Heights ES 600/K-5
1307 Cannstatt Dr SE 35803 256-428-7460
Teri Stokes, prin. Fax 428-7468
Westlawn MS 300/6-8
4217 9th Ave SW 35805 256-428-7760
Fraizier Barnes, prin. Fax 428-7761
West Mastin Lake ES 300/K-5
5308 Mastin Lake Rd NW 35810 256-428-7500
Diane Singletary King, prin. Fax 428-7501
White MS 500/6-8
4800 Sparkman Dr NW 35810 256-428-7680
Lynette Alexander, prin. Fax 428-7681
Whitesburg ES 400/K-5
6810 Whitesburg Dr S 35802 256-428-7520
Timothy Sutton, prin. Fax 428-7521
Whitesburg MS 600/6-8
107 Sanders Rd SW 35802 256-428-7780
Karen Nelson, prin. Fax 428-7781
Williams ES 200/K-5
155 Barren Fork Blvd SW 35824 256-428-7540
Lee McAllister, prin. Fax 428-7541
Williams MS 300/6-8
155A Barren Fork Blvd SW 35824 256-428-6800
Avis Williams, prin.
Other Schools – See Hampton

Madison County SD 18,700/PK-12
PO Box 226 35804 256-852-2557
Dr. Terry Davis, supt. Fax 852-2538
www.madison.k12.al.us
Central S 800/K-8
990 Ryland Pike 35811 256-852-5650
Alex Hughes, prin. Fax 852-0613
Monrovia ES 1,200/K-5
1030 Jeff Rd NW 35806 256-837-3628
Dr. Cheryl Davis, prin. Fax 837-9228
Monrovia MS 1,100/6-8
1216 Jeff Rd NW 35806 256-430-4499
Derrell Brown, prin. Fax 726-0230
Mt. Carmel ES 900/PK-5
335 Homer Nance Rd 35811 256-852-7187
Deborah Smith, prin. Fax 852-0039
Riverton ES 600/PK-5
2615 Winchester Rd NE 35811 256-746-9250
Pam Holden, prin. Fax 746-9252
Riverton MS 700/6-8
399 Homer Nance Rd 35811 256-859-3667
Todd Markham, prin. Fax 851-2610
Other Schools – See Gurley, Harvest, Hazel Green, Madison, Meridianville, New Hope, New Market, Owens Cross Roads, Toney

---

Country Day S 100/K-8
1699 Old Monrovia Rd NW 35806 256-837-5266
Sherri Naff, prin. Fax 722-3000
Grace Lutheran S 200/PK-8
3321 Memorial Pkwy SW 35801 256-881-0553
Dr. Ellen Brusick, prin. Fax 881-0563
Holy Family S 200/K-8
2300 Beasley Ave NW 35816 256-539-5221
Mary Tomaine, prin. Fax 533-0747
Holy Spirit S 400/K-8
619 Airport Rd SW 35802 256-881-4852
James Bell, prin. Fax 881-4904
Montessori S of Huntsville 100/PK-3
15975 Chaney Thompson Rd SE 35803
256-881-3790
Susan Borland, admin. Fax 881-3188
Oakwood Adventist Academy 200/K-12
7000 Adventist Blvd NW 35896 256-726-7010
Olivia Beverly, prin. Fax 726-7016
Providence Classical S 100/K-12
PO Box 22238 35814 256-852-8884
Pattie Steward, admin. Fax 852-8884
Randolph S 900/K-12
1005 Drake Ave SE 35802 256-881-1701
Dr. Byron Hulsey, hdmstr. Fax 881-1784
Union Chapel Christian Academy 100/K-8
315 Winchester Rd NE 35811 256-489-4728
Barbara Manning, admin. Fax 489-9025
Valley Fellowship Christian Academy 200/PK-12
3616 Holmes Ave NW 35816 256-533-5248
Patti Simon, prin. Fax 533-5253
Whitesburg Christian Academy 300/1-12
6806 Whitesburg Dr S 35802 256-704-5678
Gerald Porter, hdmstr. Fax 880-5304

Hurtsboro, Russell, Pop. 558
Russell County SD
Supt. — See Phenix City
Russell ES 200/K-6
733 Railroad St 36860 334-667-7471
Larry Screws, prin. Fax 667-7491

Huxford, Escambia
Escambia County SD
Supt. — See Brewton
Huxford ES 300/K-6
PO Box 10 36543 251-294-5475
Donna Silcox, prin. Fax 294-5858

Ider, DeKalb, Pop. 688
De Kalb County SD
Supt. — See Rainsville
Ider S 800/K-12
PO Box 127 35981 256-632-2302
Steven Street, prin. Fax 632-3481

Irondale, Jefferson, Pop. 9,531
Jefferson County SD
Supt. — See Birmingham
Irondale Community ES 300/3-5
225 16th St S 35210 205-379-4200
Dian Whatley, prin. Fax 379-4245

Irvington, Mobile
Mobile County SD
Supt. — See Mobile
Booth ES 500/PK-5
17001 Hurricane Blvd 36544 251-824-1740
Lisa Williams, prin. Fax 824-1762
Dixon ES 400/PK-5
8650 Four Mile Rd 36544 251-824-4314
Catherine Rogers, prin. Fax 824-7410
Haskew ES 700/K-5
7001 White Oak Dr 36544 251-221-1850
Susan White, prin. Fax 221-1855
Saint Elmo ES 500/K-6
8666 McDonald Rd 36544 251-957-6314
Deborah Fletcher, prin. Fax 957-3693

Jack, Coffee
Coffee County SD
Supt. — See Elba
Zion Chapel S 800/K-12
29256 Highway 87 36346 334-897-6275
Bob Hartwell, prin. Fax 897-5136

Jackson, Clarke, Pop. 5,285
Clarke County SD
Supt. — See Grove Hill
Gillmore ES 500/PK-2
PO Box 867 36545 251-246-2525
Shannon Odom, prin. Fax 246-4840
Jackson IS 500/3-5
2950 Highway 43 36545 251-246-1599
Gwendolyn Wheeler, prin. Fax 246-7208
Jackson MS 400/6-8
235 College Ave 36545 251-246-3597
Stuart Etheredge, prin. Fax 246-6017

Jackson Academy 200/K-12
PO Box 838 36545 251-246-5552
Rance Carr, prin. Fax 246-0202

Jacksonville, Calhoun, Pop. 8,862
Calhoun County SD
Supt. — See Anniston
Pleasant Valley ES 600/K-6
265 Mark Green Rd 36265 256-741-6600
Teresa Johnson, prin. Fax 782-0060

Jacksonville CSD 1,700/K-12
123 College St SW 36265 256-782-5682
Dr. Eric MacKey, supt. Fax 782-5685
www.jacksonville.k12.al.us
Stone ES 900/K-6
115 College St SW 36265 256-782-5191
Robert Phillips, prin. Fax 782-5978

Jacksonville Christian Academy 200/K-12
831 Alexandria Rd SW 36265 256-435-3333
Dr. Tommy Miller, prin. Fax 435-2059

Jasper, Walker, Pop. 14,088
Jasper CSD 2,700/PK-12
PO Box 500 35502 205-384-6880
Dr. Robert Sparkman, supt. Fax 387-5213
www.jasper.k12.al.us/
Maddox MS 600/6-8
1 Panther Trl 35501 205-384-3235
Patsy Stricklin, prin. Fax 387-5208
Memorial Park ES 500/K-5
800 10th Ave 35501 205-384-6461
Dr. Ann Jackson, prin. Fax 387-5219
Simmons ES 500/PK-5
1001 Viking Dr 35501 205-387-2535
James Clark, prin. Fax 387-5216
West Jasper ES 300/PK-5
1400 19th St W 35501 205-384-4311
Eric Smith, prin. Fax 387-5211

Walker County SD 8,300/PK-12
PO Box 311 35502 205-387-0555
Dr. Vonda Beaty, supt. Fax 384-0810
www.walkercountyschools.com/
Curry ES 500/K-4
85 Yellow Jacket Dr 35503 205-387-7845
Steve Rowe, prin. Fax 387-7871
Curry MS 400/5-8
115 Yellow Jacket Dr 35503 205-384-3441
David Hendon, prin. Fax 384-1110
Farmstead S 300/K-8
2760 Highway 195 35503 205-221-2001
Fax 221-2009
Valley S 600/PK-8
155 Valley School Rd 35504 205-483-9381
Tommy Kacharos, prin. Fax 483-9509
Other Schools – See Carbon Hill, Cordova, Dora, Nauvoo, Oakman, Parrish, Sipsey, Sumiton, Townley

Jemison, Chilton, Pop. 2,487
Chilton County SD
Supt. — See Clanton

Jemison ES 900/K-4
1495 County Road 44 35085 205-280-4820
Louise Pitts, prin. Fax 688-2812
Jemison MS 700/5-8
25125 US Highway 31 35085 205-280-4840
Mark Knight, prin. Fax 688-2302

Joppa, Morgan
Morgan County SD
Supt. — See Decatur
Ryan S 100/K-8
11001 Highway 67 S 35087 256-586-3785
David Estes, prin. Fax 586-1311

Killen, Lauderdale, Pop. 1,124
Lauderdale County SD
Supt. — See Florence
Brooks ES 900/K-6
100 School Ln 35645 256-757-2171
Jonathan Hatton, prin. Fax 757-1265

Kimberly, Jefferson, Pop. 2,321
Jefferson County SD
Supt. — See Birmingham
North Jefferson MS 600/6-8
8350 Warrior Kimberly Rd 35091 205-379-5500
Mary Blankenship, prin. Fax 379-5545

Kinston, Coffee, Pop. 612
Coffee County SD
Supt. — See Elba
Kinston S 500/K-12
201 College St 36453 334-565-3016
Terry Weeks, prin. Fax 565-3494

Laceys Spring, Morgan
Morgan County SD
Supt. — See Decatur
Laceys Spring S 400/K-8
48 School Rd 35754 256-881-4460
Paul Rogers, prin. Fax 881-1748

Lafayette, Chambers, Pop. 3,108
Chambers County SD 4,200/PK-12
202 1st Ave SE 36862 334-864-9343
Leonard Riley, supt. Fax 864-0119
www.chambersk12.org
Lafayette Eastside ES 400/PK-5
300 Avenue A SE 36862 334-864-8274
Sheree Core, prin. Fax 864-9018
Powell MS 200/6-8
621 1st St SE 36862 334-864-8876
Terry Reed, prin. Fax 864-8169
Other Schools – See Five Points, Lanett, Valley

Chambers Academy 200/K-12
15048 US Highway 431 36862 334-864-9852
Jim Childers, hdmstr. Fax 864-9691

Lanett, Chambers, Pop. 7,590
Chambers County SD
Supt. — See Lafayette
Huguley ES 400/PK-5
3011 S Phillips Rd 36863 334-576-2572
Nancy Maples, prin. Fax 576-7699

Lanett CSD 900/K-12
105 N Lanier Ave 36863 334-644-5900
Phillip Johnson, supt. Fax 644-3900
www.lanettcityschools.org
Lanett Central ES 500/K-6
200 S 8th Ave 36863 334-644-5915
Jamie Heard, prin. Fax 644-5926
Lanett JHS 100/7-8
1301 S 8th Ave 36863 334-644-5950
Joan Gilbert, prin. Fax 644-5964

Springwood S 300/PK-12
PO Box 1030 36863 334-644-2191
Dr. Theresa Williams, hdmstr. Fax 644-2194

Leeds, Jefferson, Pop. 11,053
Leeds CSD 1,400/K-12
PO Box 1083 35094 205-699-5437
Dr. Billy Pack, supt. Fax 699-6629
www.leedsk12.org/
Leeds ES 700/K-5
950 Ashville Rd 35094 205-699-4500
Michael McKee, prin. Fax 699-4504
Leeds MS 300/6-8
8404 Greenwave Dr 35094 205-699-4505
Elliot Harris, prin. Fax 699-4509

Leesburg, Cherokee, Pop. 820
Cherokee County SD
Supt. — See Centre
Sand Rock S 900/K-12
1950 Sand Rock Ave 35983 256-523-3564
Ben East, prin. Fax 523-3507

Leighton, Colbert, Pop. 835
Colbert County SD
Supt. — See Tuscumbia
Hatton ES 300/K-6
2130 Hatton School Rd 35646 256-446-5679
Jeff Cornelius, prin. Fax 446-8063
Leighton ES 300/K-6
8100 Old Highway 20 35646 256-446-8351
Sandy Thompson, prin. Fax 446-6668

Leroy, Washington
Washington County SD
Supt. — See Chatom
Leroy S 800/K-12
PO Box 40 36548 251-246-2000
Larry Massey, prin. Fax 246-2199

Lester, Limestone, Pop. 113
Limestone County SD
Supt. — See Athens

West Limestone S 1,000/K-12
10945 W School House Rd 35647 256-233-6687
Charlotte Craig, prin. Fax 233-8034

Lexington, Lauderdale, Pop. 830
Lauderdale County SD
Supt. — See Florence
Lexington S 900/K-12
101 School St 35648 256-229-6622
Willie Joiner, prin. Fax 229-6636

Lincoln, Talladega, Pop. 4,921
Talladega County SD
Supt. — See Talladega
Drew MS 300/7-8
450 Drew Ave 35096 256-315-5280
Dr. Rhonda Lee, prin. Fax 315-5290
Lincoln ES 600/K-6
79001 AL Highway 77 35096 256-315-5265
Donna Hudson, prin. Fax 315-5275

Linden, Marengo, Pop. 2,336
Linden CSD 500/K-12
PO Box 480609 36748 334-295-8802
Scott Collier, supt. Fax 295-8801
www.lindencity.org/
Austin JHS 100/6-8
PO Box 480699 36748 334-295-5378
Terry Gosa, prin. Fax 295-5376
Linden ES 200/K-5
PO Box 480579 36748 334-295-5860
Scott Collier, prin. Fax 295-5559

Marengo County SD 1,500/K-12
PO Box 480339 36748 334-295-4123
Luke Hallmark, supt. Fax 295-2259
marengocounty.schoolinsites.com
Other Schools – See Demopolis, Dixons Mills, Sweet Water, Thomaston

---

Marengo Academy 300/K-12
PO Box 480639 36748 334-295-4151
John Holley, prin. Fax 295-4159

Lineville, Clay, Pop. 2,389
Clay County SD
Supt. — See Ashland
Lineville ES 600/K-6
88584 Highway 9 36266 256-396-5320
Paul Thompson, prin. Fax 354-5335

Livingston, Sumter, Pop. 3,048
Sumter County SD 2,400/PK-12
PO Box 10 35470 205-652-9605
Dr. Fred Primm, supt. Fax 652-9641
www.sumter.k12.al.us
Livingston S 700/PK-8
PO Box 370 35470 205-652-2125
Milton Whitfield, prin. Fax 652-2174
Other Schools – See Cuba, Panola, York

Loachapoka, Lee, Pop. 162
Lee County SD
Supt. — See Opelika
Loachapoka ES 300/PK-6
PO Box 60 36865 334-887-8066
Mary Ross, prin. Fax 887-2948

Lockhart, Covington, Pop. 542
Covington County SD
Supt. — See Andalusia
Harlan ES 300/K-6
PO Box 267 36455 334-858-3866
Brent Zessin, prin. Fax 858-3295

Locust Fork, Blount, Pop. 1,136
Blount County SD
Supt. — See Oneonta
Locust Fork ES 600/K-6
155 School Rd 35097 205-681-9512
Mark Carter, prin. Fax 681-8479

Logan, Cullman
Cullman County SD
Supt. — See Cullman
Harmony S 300/K-8
4910 County Road 940 35098 256-747-1427
Mike Rodgers, prin. Fax 747-1043

Louisville, Barbour, Pop. 580
Barbour County SD
Supt. — See Clayton
Barbour County IS 300/3-5
PO Box 429 36048 334-266-5643
Jimmie Fryer, prin. Fax 266-5195
Barbour County MS 300/6-8
PO Box 459 36048 334-266-6151
Stacey Turvin, prin. Fax 226-5991

Dixie Academy 100/K-12
PO Box 67 36048 334-266-5311
James Partin, hdmstr. Fax 266-5090

Lower Peach Tree, Monroe
Monroe County SD
Supt. — See Monroeville
Monroe S 100/K-8
3366 County Road 49 36751 334-636-2032
Betty Madison, prin. Fax 636-0506

Lowndesboro, Lowndes, Pop. 135

Lowndes Academy 300/K-12
PO Box 99 36752 334-278-3366
Chuck Insinga, prin. Fax 278-4476

Loxley, Baldwin, Pop. 1,435
Baldwin County SD
Supt. — See Bay Minette

Loxley ES 400/PK-6
4999 County Road 49 36551 251-964-5334
Dr. De Ann Ramey, prin. Fax 964-7369

Luverne, Crenshaw, Pop. 2,668
Crenshaw County SD 2,500/PK-12
183 Votec Dr 36049 334-335-6519
Kathi Wallace, supt. Fax 335-6510
crenshawcounty.schoolinsites.com/
Luverne S 1,000/PK-12
194 First Ave 36049 334-335-3331
Charles Alford, prin. Fax 335-2241
Other Schools – See Brantley, Highland Home

Crenshaw Christian Academy 200/K-12
608 Country Club Dr 36049 334-335-5749
Angela Carpenter, prin. Fax 335-6422

Lynn, Winston, Pop. 719
Winston County SD
Supt. — See Double Springs
Lynn ES 300/K-7
531 E Main St 35575 205-893-5702
Sara Ritter, prin. Fax 893-2484

Mc Calla, Jefferson
Jefferson County SD
Supt. — See Birmingham
McAdory ES 1,000/K-5
6251 Eastern Valley Rd 35111 205-379-4650
Harold Jackson, prin. Fax 477-5848

Tuscaloosa County SD
Supt. — See Tuscaloosa
Lake View ES K-5
21610 Youngblood Pkwy 35111 205-342-2951
Martha Roop, prin. Fax 477-7696

Mc Intosh, Washington, Pop. 252
Washington County SD
Supt. — See Chatom
McIntosh ES 400/K-5
PO Box 357 36553 251-944-2481
Edna Billingsley, prin. Fax 944-2001

Mc Kenzie, Butler, Pop. 441
Butler County SD
Supt. — See Greenville
Mc Kenzie S 300/K-12
PO Box 158 36456 334-374-2711
J. Randy Williams, prin. Fax 374-8108

Madison, Madison, Pop. 35,893
Madison CSD 8,000/K-12
211 Celtic Dr 35758 256-464-8370
Dr. Dee Fowler, supt. Fax 774-0404
www.madisoncity.k12.al.us
Columbia ES 800/K-6
667 Balch Rd 35758 256-430-2751
Dennis James, prin. Fax 430-2794
Heritage ES 900/K-6
11775 County Line Rd 35758 256-772-2075
Dr. Lydia Davenport, prin. Fax 772-6580
Horizon ES 600/K-6
7855 Madison Pike 35758 256-464-3614
Fax 464-3689
Madison ES 400/K-6
17 College St 35758 256-772-9255
Theresia Mullen, prin. Fax 461-8300
Mill Creek ES, 665 Mill Rd 35758 K-6
Melanie Barkley, prin. 256-464-8370
Rainbow ES 900/K-6
50 Nance Rd 35758 256-824-8106
Dorinda White, prin. Fax 824-8110
West Madison ES 400/K-6
4976 Wall Triana Hwy 35758 256-837-1189
Dr. Daphne Patriece Jah, prin. Fax 837-1258

Madison County SD
Supt. — See Huntsville
Legacy ES PK-5
165 Pine Grove Rd 35757 256-562-0801
Dr. Claudia Styles, prin. Fax 562-0804

Madison Academy 700/K-12
325 Slaughter Rd 35758 256-971-1620
Robert Burton, hdmstr. Fax 971-1436
St. John the Baptist S 400/K-8
1057 Hughes Rd 35758 256-722-0772
Sherry Lewis, prin. Fax 722-0151
Westminster Christian Academy 300/PK-5
375 Mount Zion Rd 35757 256-705-8300
Craig Bouvier, hdmstr. Fax 705-8001

Maplesville, Chilton, Pop. 687
Chilton County SD
Supt. — See Clanton
Isabella S 800/K-12
11338 County Road 15 36750 205-280-2770
Ricky Porter, prin. Fax 755-8549
Maplesville S 500/K-12
1256 AL Highway 139 36750 334-366-2991
Maggie Hicks, prin. Fax 366-2531

Marbury, Autauga
Autauga County SD
Supt. — See Prattville
Marbury MS 6-8
210 County Road 20 E 36051 205-755-2118
Jason Wingate, prin. Fax 755-3168

Marion, Perry, Pop. 3,428
Perry County SD 2,000/K-12
PO Box 900 36756 334-683-6528
John Heard, supt. Fax 683-8427
www.perrycountyal.org/
Turner ES 600/K-6
901 Pegues Cir 36756 334-683-6622
Edwin Dial, prin. Fax 683-6647
Other Schools – See Uniontown

Maylene, Shelby
Shelby County SD
Supt. — See Columbiana
Creek View ES 1,000/K-3
8568 Highway 17 35114 205-682-5730
Joyce Dixon, prin. Fax 682-5735

Mentone, DeKalb, Pop. 472
De Kalb County SD
Supt. — See Rainsville
Moon Lake ES 100/K-6
PO Box 166 35984 256-634-4113
Brenda Wisner, prin. Fax 634-4113

Meridianville, Madison, Pop. 2,852
Madison County SD
Supt. — See Huntsville
Fanning ES 700/K-5
8861 Moores Mill Rd 35759 256-828-6592
Sherri Plant, prin. Fax 828-9732

Midfield, Jefferson, Pop. 5,319
Midfield CSD 1,200/K-12
417 Parkwood St 35228 205-923-2262
Dr. Douglas Ragland, supt. Fax 929-0585
www.midfield.k12.al.us/
Midfield ES 400/K-4
416 Parkwood St 35228 205-923-7727
Susan Harvill, prin. Fax 929-0594
Rutledge MS 400/5-8
1221 8th St 35228 205-780-8647
Nikita Williams, prin. Fax 780-3664

Midland City, Dale, Pop. 1,798
Dale County SD
Supt. — See Ozark
Midland City ES 400/K-4
PO Box 1110 36350 334-983-4591
Ben Baker, prin. Fax 983-1638

Midway, Bullock, Pop. 433
Bullock County SD
Supt. — See Union Springs
Merritt ES 100/K-6
PO Box 10 36053 334-529-3281
Annie Kimber, prin. Fax 529-3143

Millbrook, Elmore, Pop. 14,805
Elmore County SD
Supt. — See Wetumpka
Coosada ES 700/PK-2
5260 Airport Rd 36054 334-285-0273
Suzanne Goodin, prin. Fax 285-9231
Millbrook MS 1,300/5-8
4228 Chapman Rd 36054 334-285-2100
Rory McQueen, prin. Fax 285-2102
Robinson Springs ES 300/3-4
5720 Main St 36054 334-285-2115
Temeyra McElrath, prin. Fax 285-2116

Victory Baptist S 200/K-12
PO Box 1090 36054 334-285-5082
Dan Todd, prin. Fax 285-0203

Millport, Lamar, Pop. 1,062
Lamar County SD
Supt. — See Vernon
South Lamar S 500/K-12
300 Sls Rd 35576 205-662-4411
Ken Dawkins, prin. Fax 662-4544

Millry, Washington, Pop. 604
Washington County SD
Supt. — See Chatom
Millry S 600/K-12
PO Box 65 36558 251-846-2987
Larry Odom, prin. Fax 846-2986

Mobile, Mobile, Pop. 191,544
Mobile County SD 62,200/PK-12
PO Box 180069 36618 251-221-4000
Dr. Roy Nichols, supt. Fax 221-4399
www.mcpss.com
Austin ES 400/K-5
150 Provident Ln 36608 251-221-1015
Jacquelyn Zeigler, prin. Fax 221-1018
Brazier ES 300/PK-5
2161 Butler St 36617 251-221-1046
Veronica Coleman, prin. Fax 221-1048
Burns MS 1,000/6-8
6175 Girby Rd 36693 251-221-2025
John Adams, prin. Fax 221-2021
Calloway-Smith MS 600/6-8
350 N Lawrence St 36603 251-221-2042
Dorothy Robinson, prin. Fax 221-2041
Causey MS 1,500/6-8
2205 McFarland Rd 36695 251-221-2060
Mary Wood, prin. Fax 221-2062
Chastang MS 700/6-8
2800 Berkley Ave 36617 251-221-2081
Sonya Floyd, prin. Fax 221-2080
Collier ES 900/PK-5
601 Snow Rd N 36608 251-221-1120
Laveral Graf, prin. Fax 221-1123
Council Traditional ES 600/K-5
751 Wilkinson St 36603 251-221-1139
Maxine Wilson, prin. Fax 221-1140
Craighead ES 600/PK-5
1000 S Ann St 36605 251-221-1155
Tracey Hunter, prin. Fax 221-1151
Denton MS 700/6-8
3800 Pleasant Valley Rd 36609 251-221-2148
Joe Toomey, prin. Fax 221-2152
Dickson ES 900/K-5
4645 Bit and Spur Rd 36608 251-221-1180
Missy Nolen, prin. Fax 221-1185
Dodge ES 1,100/K-5
2615 Longleaf Dr 36693 251-221-1195
Dr. Suzanne Crist, prin. Fax 221-1197
Dunbar Magnet S 600/4-8
500 Saint Anthony St 36603 251-221-2160
Debra Smith, prin. Fax 221-2162
Eanes MS 800/6-8
1901 Hurtel St 36605 251-221-2189
Merrier Jackson, prin. Fax 221-2191
Eichold-Mertz ES 900/PK-5
2815 Government Blvd 36606 251-221-1210
Michelle Manzy, prin. Fax 221-1212
Fonde ES 700/PK-5
3956 Cottage Hill Rd 36609 251-221-1240
Rebecca Baker, prin. Fax 221-1243
Fonvielle ES 600/K-5
1 Magnum Pass 36618 251-221-1257
Judith Kearns, prin. Fax 221-1259
Forest Hill ES 500/K-5
4501 Moffett Rd 36618 251-221-1270
Joy Gould, prin. Fax 221-1271
Gilliard ES 900/PK-5
2757 Dauphin Island Pkwy 36605 251-221-1820
Laura Anderson, prin. Fax 221-1824
Griggs ES 600/PK-5
6001 Three Notch Rd 36619 251-221-1330
Stephanie Benson, prin. Fax 221-1335
Hall ES 500/PK-5
1108 Antwerp St 36605 251-221-1345
Agnes Tomlinson, prin. Fax 221-1348
Hillsdale MS 300/6-8
6301 Biloxi Ave 36608 251-221-2223
Lynda Allinder, prin. Fax 221-2221
Hollingers Island ES 300/K-5
2400 Hammock Rd 36605 251-221-1376
Shirley Thompson, prin. Fax 221-1375
Holloway ES 600/K-6
625 Stanton Rd 36617 251-221-1391
Iesha Williams, prin. Fax 221-1393
Howard ES 200/K-6
957 Dr Martin L King Jr Ave 36603 251-221-1406
Johnnita Bryant, prin. Fax 221-1410
Hutchens ES 900/K-5
10005 W Lake Rd 36695 251-221-1420
Dr. William Foster, prin. Fax 221-1425
Just 4 Preschool 300/PK-PK
2263 Saint Stephens Rd 36617 251-221-1450
Linda Blassingame, prin. Fax 221-1452
Leinkauf ES 500/K-5
1410 Monroe St 36604 251-221-1495
Twilla Hill, prin. Fax 221-1498
Maryvale ES 500/PK-5
1901 N Maryvale St 36605 251-221-1810
Katryna Ellis, prin. Fax 221-1812
Meadowlake ES 400/PK-5
8251 Three Notch Rd 36619 251-221-1529
Dr. Susan Smith, prin. Fax 221-1528
Morningside ES 400/K-5
2700 S Greenbrier Dr 36605 251-221-1540
Marva Carter, prin. Fax 221-1542
Old Shell Creative/Performing Art S 200/K-3
1706 Old Shell Rd 36604 251-221-1557
Karen Hilsee, prin. Fax 221-1559
Orchard ES 500/K-5
6400 Howells Ferry Rd 36618 251-221-1571
LaTunga Ransom, prin. Fax 221-1570
O'Rourke ES 900/K-5
1975 Leroy Stevens Rd 36695 251-221-1585
Cheryl Chapman, prin. Fax 221-1586
Phillips Preparatory S 800/6-8
3255 Old Shell Rd 36607 251-221-2287
Brenda Hartzog, prin. Fax 221-2285
Pillans MS 600/6-8
2051 Gatotkoco Dr 36605 251-221-2300
Kenneth Brown, prin. Fax 221-2314
Scarborough MS 600/6-8
1800 Phillips Ln 36618 251-221-2323
Charles Smith, prin. Fax 221-2321
Shepard ES 500/PK-5
3980 Burma Rd Ste B 36693 251-221-1645
Dr. Michelle Dumas, prin. Fax 221-1646
Spencer ES 300/PK-5
3160 Heather St 36607 251-221-1661
Diane Reynolds, prin. Fax 221-1660
Washington MS 400/6-8
1961 Andrews St 36617 251-221-2361
Reginald Wilson, prin. Fax 221-2364
Westlawn ES 500/K-5
3071 Ralston Rd 36606 251-221-1705
Lynda Finley, prin. Fax 221-1710
Will ES 500/PK-5
5750 Summit Ave 36608 251-221-1750
June Stanford, prin. Fax 221-1752
Woodcock ES 300/PK-5
261 Rickarby St 36606 251-221-1799
Teronda Smith, prin. Fax 221-1802
Other Schools – See Bayou La Batre, Chickasaw, Citronelle, Dauphin Island, Eight Mile, Grand Bay, Irvington, Mount Vernon, Prichard, Satsuma, Semmes, Theodore, Wilmer

---

Corpus Christi S 500/PK-8
6300 Mckenna Dr 36608 251-342-5474
Joan McMullen, prin. Fax 380-0325
Cottage Hill Baptist S 400/PK-8
4255 Cottage Hill Rd 36609 251-660-2427
Dr. Charles Lang, supt. Fax 660-0558
Covenant Christian S 200/PK-8
7150 Hitt Rd 36695 251-633-8055
Keith Currie, prin. Fax 633-5577
Emmanuel SDA S 50/1-8
2000 Dr Martin L King Jr 36617 251-478-1140
Faith Academy 1,700/K-12
8650 Tanner Williams Rd 36608 251-633-7267
Tim Skelton, hdmstr. Fax 633-9133
Government Street Baptist S 300/PK-8
3401 Government Blvd 36693 251-660-7444
Robert Murphy, prin. Fax 660-1097
Little Flower S 200/PK-8
2103 Government St 36606 251-479-5761
Clara Brunk, prin. Fax 450-3696
Mobile Christian S 700/K-12
5900 Cottage Hill Rd 36609 251-661-1613
David Pahman, hdmstr. Fax 661-1396
Mobile Jr. Academy 50/K-9
1900 Cody Rd S 36695 251-633-8638
Doug Carr, prin. Fax 633-8639
Most Pure Heart of Mary S 200/PK-8
310 Sengstak St 36603 251-432-5270
Sr. Nancy Crossen, prin. Fax 432-5271
Mt. Calvary Lutheran S 50/PK-6
1660 Dominick St 36605 251-471-4200
Fax 471-4200
Oak Park Christian S 100/PK-12
3321 Sollie Rd 36695 251-633-8045
Donna Dement, prin. Fax 639-8137
Revelation Baptist S 50/K-5
1711 Taylor Ln 36605 251-473-2555
Barbara Woods, prin. Fax 473-2727
St. Dominic S 500/PK-8
4160 Burma Rd 36693 251-661-5226
Martha Mundine, prin. Fax 660-2242
St. Ignatius S 500/PK-8
3650 Spring Hill Ave 36608 251-342-5442
Janet Murray, prin. Fax 344-0944
St. Luke's Episcopal S 500/PK-8
3975 Japonica Ln 36693 251-666-2991
Palmer Kennedy, hdmstr. Fax 666-2996
St. Mark United Methodist S 100/PK-5
439 Azalea Rd 36609 251-344-1490
St. Mary S 400/PK-8
107 N Lafayette St 36604 251-433-9904
Debbie Ollis, prin. Fax 438-9069
St. Paul's Episcopal S 1,300/PK-12
161 Dogwood Ln 36608 251-342-6700
Marty Lester, hdmstr. Fax 342-1844
St. Pius X S 400/PK-8
217 S Sage Ave 36606 251-473-5004
Lauren Alvarez, prin. Fax 473-5008
St. Vincent De Paul S 200/PK-8
6571 Larkspur Dr 36619 251-666-8022
Mary McLendon, prin. Fax 666-1296
Trinity Lutheran S 100/PK-8
2668 Berkley Ave 36617 251-456-7960
Bettye Brown, prin. Fax 456-7909
UMS Wright Prep S 1,200/K-12
65 Mobile St 36607 251-479-6551
Dr. Tony Havard, hdmstr. Fax 470-9050

Monroeville, Monroe, Pop. 6,690
Monroe County SD 4,100/PK-12
PO Box 967 36461 251-575-2168
Melanie Ryals, supt. Fax 575-5818
www.monroe.k12.al.us/
Monroeville ES 500/PK-2
297 S Mount Pleasant Ave 36460 251-743-3474
Anne Lambert, prin. Fax 575-3723
Monroeville JHS 500/6-8
201 York St 36460 251-575-4121
Rodney Lord, prin. Fax 575-2934
Monroeville MS 400/3-5
109 Pickens St 36460 251-575-3369
Darenell Payne, prin. Fax 743-3301
Other Schools – See Beatrice, Excel, Lower Peach Tree, Uriah

Monroe Academy 400/PK-12
4096 S Alabama Ave 36460 251-743-3932
Ronnie Williams, hdmstr. Fax 743-4267

Montevallo, Shelby, Pop. 5,092
Shelby County SD
Supt. — See Columbiana
Montevallo ES 700/K-5
171 Jeter Cir 35115 205-682-6420
Annie McClain, prin. Fax 682-6425
Montevallo MS 300/6-8
235 Samford St 35115 205-682-6410
Sheila Lewis, prin. Fax 682-6415

Shelby Academy 200/PK-12
9178 Highway 22 35115 205-668-2299
Steve Zaslofsky, hdmstr. Fax 668-1912

Montgomery, Montgomery, Pop. 200,127
Montgomery County SD 31,500/PK-12
PO Box 1991 36102 334-223-6700
John Dilworth, supt. Fax 269-3076
www.mps.k12.al.us
Baldwin Arts & Academics Magnet S 600/6-8
410 S McDonough St 36104 334-269-3870
Jannette Wright, prin. Fax 269-3918
Bear Exploration Center ES 500/K-5
2525 Churchill Dr 36111 334-284-8014
Elizabeth Hill, prin. Fax 284-8096
Blount ES 700/K-6
1650 Ray Thorington Rd 36117 334-244-0078
Mona Green, prin. Fax 244-0237
Brewbaker IS 600/4-6
4455 Brewbaker Dr 36116 334-284-8006
Fax 284-8067
Brewbaker PS 800/K-3
4445 Brewbaker Dr 36116 334-284-8005
Erika Tyler, prin. Fax 284-8035
Carver ES 600/K-5
3100 Mobile Dr 36108 334-269-3625
Cathey Hendricks, prin. Fax 269-2923
Catoma ES 200/K-5
1780 Mitchell Young Rd 36108 334-288-5799
Jason Bigham, prin. Fax 281-8232
Chisholm ES 800/K-6
307 E Vandiver Blvd 36110 334-269-3643
Laura Adams, prin. Fax 269-3645
Crump ES 500/K-6
3510 Woodley Rd 36116 334-284-8020
Randy Shaw, prin. Fax 284-8024

Dalraida ES 600/K-6
440 Dalraida Rd 36109 334-260-1007
Elise Keith, prin. Fax 260-1071
Dannelly ES 700/K-6
3425 Carter Hill Rd 36111 334-269-3657
Emily Little, prin. Fax 269-3655
Davis ES 500/K-6
3605 Rosa L Parks Ave 36105 334-269-3662
Ozella Ford, prin. Fax 241-5392
Dozier ES 400/K-6
200 Eastern Blvd 36117 334-260-1012
Cindy McKenzie, prin. Fax 260-1010
Fitzpatrick ES 600/K-6
4055 Fitzpatrick Blvd 36116 334-284-8044
Vera Thompson, prin. Fax 284-8045
Flowers ES 300/K-6
3510 Harrison Rd 36109 334-260-1015
Ethel Barnes, prin. Fax 260-1050
Floyd ES 500/K-6
630 Augusta Ave 36111 334-284-7120
Cheryl Coprich, prin. Fax 284-7117
Floyd MS for Math Science & Technology 600/6-8
3444 Le Bron Rd 36111 334-284-7130
Kim Pitts, prin. Fax 284-7125
Forest Avenue Magnet ES 700/K-5
1700 W 5th St 36106 334-269-3673
Jan Hill, prin. Fax 269-3963
Garrett ES 600/K-6
555 Mclemore Dr 36117 334-260-1090
Pam Morgan, prin. Fax 260-1092
Halcyon ES 700/K-6
1501 Parkview Dr S 36117 334-271-9000
Shirley Brooks, prin. Fax 271-9002
Harrison ES 400/K-6
164 E South Blvd 36105 334-284-8001
Emily Walker, prin. Fax 284-8063
Hayneville Road ES 400/K-5
3315 Hayneville Rd 36108 334-269-3681
Ronald Grace, prin. Fax 269-3679
Head ES 600/K-6
3950 Atlanta Hwy 36109 334-260-1025
Holly Thursby, prin. Fax 260-1054
Highland Avenue ES 400/K-6
2024 Highland Ave 36107 334-269-3690
Patricia Kornegay, prin. Fax 269-6151
Highland Gardens ES 600/K-6
2801 Willena Ave 36107 334-269-3685
Angela Kornegay James, prin. Fax 241-5329
Johnson ES 600/K-6
4550 Narrow Lane Rd 36116 334-284-8016
Jacquelyn Campbell, prin. Fax 284-8056
King ES 300/K-5
4655 Gateway Dr 36108 334-284-8080
Booker MacMillian, prin. Fax 284-8085
MacMillan International Academy 300/K-5
25 Covington St 36104 334-269-3752
Edward Drozdowski, prin. Fax 241-5364
McIntyre MS, 1220 Hugh St 36108 400/6-8
Edward McDonald, prin. 334-269-3755
McKee ES 600/K-6
4015 McInnis Dr 36116 334-284-7137
Lillian Sanders, prin. Fax 284-7569
Morningview ES 500/K-6
2849 Pelzer Ave 36109 334-260-1028
Kenyetta Miller, prin. Fax 260-1029
Morris ES 500/K-5
801 Hill St 36108 334-223-6920
Sophia Johnson, prin. Fax 241-5399
Nixon ES 600/PK-6
1000 Edgar D Nixon Ave 36104 334-269-3012
Dr. Regina Thompson, prin. Fax 269-3019
Paterson ES 300/K-6
1015 E Jefferson St 36104 334-269-3760
Dr. James Owens, prin. Fax 269-3989
Southlawn ES 400/K-5
5225 Patricia Ln 36108 334-284-8028
Janice Harvey, prin. Fax 284-8069
Southlawn MS 500/6-8
5333 Mobile Hwy 36108 334-284-8086
Ferlisa Ross, prin. Fax 284-8094
Vaughn Road ES 500/K-6
4407 Vaughn Rd 36106 334-260-1031
Brenda Lindsey, prin. Fax 260-1041
Wares Ferry Road ES 500/K-6
6425 Wares Ferry Rd 36117 334-260-1036
Marcus Roberts, prin. Fax 260-1035
Other Schools – See Hope Hull, Ramer

Alabama Christian Academy 1,000/K-12
4700 Wares Ferry Rd 36109 334-277-1985
Ronnie Sewell, prin. Fax 279-0604
Bethany Christian Academy 100/1-8
1765 Highland Ave 36107 334-264-2101
Victor Waller, prin. Fax 264-0513
Eastwood Christian S 300/K-12
1701 E Trinity Blvd 36106 334-272-8195
John Geiger, hdmstr. Fax 386-2399
Evangel Christian Academy 300/K-12
3975 Vaughn Rd 36106 334-272-3882
Rev. Victor Tubbs, prin. Fax 272-5662
Freedom Life Christian Academy 100/PK-12
221 W Fleming Rd 36105 334-284-1461
Annetta Tate, admin. Fax 281-1912
Green Gate S 100/PK-6
3265 McGehee Rd 36111 334-281-3300
Fax 286-4884
Holy Cross Episcopal S 200/PK-6
4400 Bell Rd 36116 334-395-8222
Melanie Kelley, prin. Fax 395-7280
Montgomery Academy 900/K-12
3240 Vaughn Rd 36106 334-272-8210
Archibald Douglas, hdmstr. Fax 277-3240
Montgomery Academy Lower S 300/K-4
1550 Perry Hill Rd 36106 334-272-8210
Archibald Douglas, hdmstr. Fax 270-1462
Montgomery Catholic Prep MS 200/7-8
5350 Vaughn Rd 36116 334-272-2465
Maria Nolen, prin. Fax 272-2330
Montgomery Catholic Prep - St. Bede 300/K-6
3860 Atlanta Hwy 36109 334-272-3033
Susan Duke, prin. Fax 272-9394
Montgomery SDA S 50/1-8
4233 Atlanta Hwy 36109 334-272-6437
Resurrection Catholic S 100/PK-8
2815 Forbes Dr 36110 334-265-4615
Sr. Gail Trippett, prin. Fax 265-7988
St. James S 1,100/PK-12
6010 Vaughn Rd 36116 334-277-8033
Melba Richardson, hdmstr. Fax 277-2542
Trinity Presbyterian S 1,000/K-12
1700 E Trinity Blvd 36106 334-213-2100
Robert Neu, hdmstr. Fax 213-2171

Moody, Saint Clair, Pop. 10,764
Saint Clair County SD
Supt. — See Ashville
Moody ES 700/PK-3
1006 HL Blocker Cir 35004 205-640-2180
Kathy Tice, prin. Fax 640-4971
Moody JHS 300/7-8
600 High School Dr 35004 205-640-2040
Ronald McFarling, prin. Fax 640-3036
Moody MS 500/4-6
1010 HL Blocker Cir 35004 205-640-2190
Debra Allred, prin. Fax 640-7903

Morris, Jefferson, Pop. 1,868
Jefferson County SD
Supt. — See Birmingham
Bryan ES 700/K-6
600 Kimberly Cut Off Rd 35116 205-379-2750
Debra Campbell, prin. Fax 379-2795

Moulton, Lawrence, Pop. 3,276
Lawrence County SD 5,000/K-12
14131 Market St 35650 256-905-2400
Heath Grimes, supt. Fax 905-2406
www.lawrenceal.org
Moulton ES 500/K-3
412 Main St 35650 256-905-2450
Paige Terry, prin. Fax 905-2480
Moulton MS 500/4-7
364 Main St 35650 256-905-2460
Gaylon Parker, prin. Fax 905-2481
Other Schools – See Courtland, Danville, Mount Hope, Town Creek, Trinity

Moundville, Hale, Pop. 2,188
Hale County SD
Supt. — See Greensboro
Moundville ES 500/K-6
537 Alabama Ave 35474 205-371-2679
Ronnie Garner, prin. Fax 371-4279

Mountain Brook, Jefferson, Pop. 20,821
Mountain Brook CSD 4,300/K-12
32 Vine St 35213 205-871-4608
Richard Barlow, supt. Fax 877-8303
www.mtnbrook.k12.al.us
Brookwood Forest ES 500/K-6
3701 S Brookwood Rd 35223 205-414-3700
Yvette Faught, prin. Fax 969-8121
Cherokee Bend ES 500/K-6
4400 Fair Oaks Dr, Birmingham AL 35213
205-871-3595
Betsy Bell, prin. Fax 877-8312
Mountain Brook ES 600/K-6
3020 Cambridge Rd 35223 205-871-8191
Belinda Treadwell, prin. Fax 877-8330
Other Schools – See Birmingham

Mount Hope, Lawrence
Lawrence County SD
Supt. — See Moulton
Mount Hope S 200/K-8
8455 County Road 23 35651 256-905-2470
Tony Rutherford, prin. Fax 905-2471

Mount Olive, Jefferson
Jefferson County SD
Supt. — See Birmingham
Mount Olive ES 400/K-5
1301 Brookside Rd 35117 205-379-4900
Judy Sullivan, prin. Fax 379-4945

Mount Vernon, Mobile, Pop. 819
Mobile County SD
Supt. — See Mobile
Belsaw-Mt. Vernon S 300/PK-8
PO Box 460 36560 251-221-1030
Renae Edmond, prin. Fax 221-1033
Calcedeaver ES 300/PK-6
20185 Richard Weaver Rd 36560 251-221-1092
Aimee Rainey, prin. Fax 221-1094

Munford, Talladega
Talladega County SD
Supt. — See Talladega
Munford ES 700/K-6
365 Cedars Rd 36268 256-315-5250
Rebecca Robinson, prin. Fax 315-5260

Muscle Shoals, Colbert, Pop. 12,523
Muscle Shoals CSD 2,700/PK-12
PO Box 2610 35662 256-389-2600
Jeff Wooten, supt. Fax 389-2605
www.mscs.k12.al.us
Highland Park ES 200/1-2
714 Elmhurst Ave 35661 256-389-2620
Hal Horton, prin. Fax 389-2625
Howell-Graves Preschool 200/PK-K
3201 Alabama Ave 35661 256-389-2630
Tim Morgan, prin. Fax 389-2632
McBride ES 600/3-5
1400 Avalon Ave 35661 256-389-2610
Brian Lindsey, prin. Fax 389-2613
Muscle Shoals MS 600/6-8
100 Trojan Dr 35661 256-389-2640
Mary Ann Stegall, prin. Fax 389-2647
Webster ES 200/1-2
200 Webster St 35661 256-389-2650
Dan Starkey, prin. Fax 389-2655

Nauvoo, Walker, Pop. 283
Walker County SD
Supt. — See Jasper
Lupton S 500/K-8
1110 Prospect Rd 35578 205-384-5838
Brenda McAdams, prin. Fax 387-0434

Newbern, Hale, Pop. 228
Hale County SD
Supt. — See Greensboro
Sunshine S 300/K-12
3125 County Road 10 36765 334-624-8747
Michael Ryans, prin. Fax 624-8781

New Brockton, Coffee, Pop. 1,236
Coffee County SD
Supt. — See Elba
New Brockton ES 400/PK-6
PO Box 489 36351 334-894-6152
Dale Kelley, prin. Fax 894-0058

New Hope, Madison, Pop. 2,671
Madison County SD
Supt. — See Huntsville
New Hope S 700/K-8
5300 Main Dr 35760 256-723-8879
Donnie Caves, prin. Fax 723-8563

New Market, Madison, Pop. 1,094
Madison County SD
Supt. — See Huntsville
New Market S 500/K-8
PO Box 217 35761 256-379-2751
Dr. Mark Minskey, prin. Fax 379-5170
Walnut Grove ES 200/K-5
1961 Joe Quick Rd 35761 256-828-4677
Barbara Maness, prin. Fax 828-8021

New Site, Tallapoosa, Pop. 828
Tallapoosa County SD
Supt. — See Dadeville
Horseshoe Bend S 800/K-12
10684 Highway 22 E 36256 256-329-9110
Casey Davis, prin. Fax 329-9119

Newton, Dale, Pop. 1,679
Dale County SD
Supt. — See Ozark
Newton ES 300/K-6
523 S College St 36352 334-299-3581
Mickey Teal, prin. Fax 299-6693

Houston County SD
Supt. — See Dothan
Wicksburg S 900/K-12
1172 S State Highway 123 36352 334-692-5549
Cheryl Smith, prin. Fax 692-3184

Northport, Tuscaloosa, Pop. 21,216
Tuscaloosa County SD
Supt. — See Tuscaloosa
Collins-Riverside MS 400/6-8
1400 3rd St 35476 205-342-2680
Bryant Williams, prin. Fax 752-8024
Crestmont ES 300/PK-5
2400 34th Ave 35476 205-342-2695
Katrina May, prin. Fax 339-1097
Echols MS 500/6-8
2701 Echols Ave 35476 205-342-2884
Nancy Terry, prin. Fax 339-1064
Faucett-Vestavia ES 500/K-5
1150 Vestavia Cir 35473 205-342-2646
Genea Monroe, prin. Fax 339-3072
Flatwoods ES 300/PK-5
3800 66th Ave 35473 205-342-2648
Tiffany Spencer, prin. Fax 333-5814
Huntington Place ES 700/K-5
11601 Huntington Pl 35475 205-342-2652
Debbie Benson, prin. Fax 336-8641
Matthews ES 400/K-5
1225 Rice Mine Rd 35476 205-342-2654
David Scott, prin. Fax 391-2169
Northport ES K-2
13695 Frankie Thomas Dr 35475 205-342-2862
Lucy Sellers, prin. Fax 333-3955
Northside MS 300/6-8
19130 Northside Rd 35475 205-342-2740
Gail Tunnell, prin. Fax 339-4680
Walker ES 700/K-5
13051 Northside Rd 35475 205-342-2664
Patricia Johnson, prin. Fax 333-5491
Wood MS 500/6-8
2300 26th Ave 35476 205-342-2690
Greg Hurst, prin. Fax 339-6642

Notasulga, Macon, Pop. 851
Macon County SD
Supt. — See Tuskegee
Notasulga S 400/K-12
PO Box 10 36866 334-257-3510
Brelinda Sullen, prin. Fax 257-4228

Tallapoosa County SD
Supt. — See Dadeville
Reeltown S 700/K-12
4085 AL Highway 120 36866 334-257-3784
Thomas Cochran, prin. Fax 257-3978

Oakman, Walker, Pop. 948
Walker County SD
Supt. — See Jasper
Oakman ES 500/K-6
PO Box 287 35579 205-622-3611
Dr. Dennis Willingham, prin. Fax 622-2322

Odenville, Saint Clair, Pop. 1,203
Saint Clair County SD
Supt. — See Ashville
Odenville ES 400/PK-2
420 Alabama St 35120 205-629-6406
Christa Urban, prin. Fax 629-6408
Odenville IS 3-5
PO Box 670 35120 205-629-2246
Joe Goble, prin. Fax 629-2249
Odenville MS 400/6-8
100 1st Ave 35120 205-629-2280
Debra Carroll, prin. Fax 620-2282

Ohatchee, Calhoun, Pop. 1,211
Calhoun County SD
Supt. — See Anniston
Ohatchee ES 600/K-6
365 J St 36271 256-741-4800
Natasha Scott, prin. Fax 892-2040

Oneonta, Blount, Pop. 6,537
Blount County SD 7,400/K-12
PO Box 578 35121 205-625-4102
James Carr, supt. Fax 625-4100
www.blountboe.net/
Appalachian S 700/K-12
350 County Highway 12 35121 205-274-9712
Mark Hitt, prin. Fax 274-9706
Other Schools – See Blountsville, Cleveland, Hayden, Locust Fork, Remlap

Oneonta CSD 1,400/K-12
27605 State Highway 75 35121 205-625-4106
Henry Housch, supt. Fax 274-2910
www.oneontacityschools.com
Oneonta City ES 800/K-6
27605 State Highway 75 35121 205-625-4108
Percy Parrish, prin. Fax 625-5509

Opelika, Lee, Pop. 23,804
Lee County SD 9,900/PK-12
100 S 6th St 36801 334-745-9770
Dr. Stephen Nowlin, supt. Fax 745-9822
www.lee.k12.al.us
Beauregard ES 900/PK-4
300 Lee Road 431 36804 334-745-2972
Steve Miller, prin. Fax 745-2287
Sanford MS 700/5-8
1500 Lee Road 11 36804 334-745-5023
Michelle Rutherford, prin. Fax 745-5685
Other Schools – See Loachapoka, Salem, Smiths, Smiths Station, Valley

Opelika CSD 4,200/PK-12
PO Box 2469 36803 334-745-9700
Dr. Mark Neighbors, supt. Fax 745-9706
www.opelikaschools.org
Carver PS 300/K-2
307 Carver Ave 36801 334-745-9712
Clarence Magee, prin. Fax 745-9722
Jeter PS 300/PK-2
700 Jeter Ave 36801 334-745-9723
William James, prin. Fax 745-9740
Morris Avenue IS 300/3-5
8 Morris Ave 36801 334-745-9734
Nino Mason, prin. Fax 745-9736
Northside ES 300/3-5
601 N 5th St 36801 334-745-9731
Dr. Chris Dark, prin. Fax 745-9755
Opelika MS 1,000/6-8
1206 Denson Dr 36801 334-745-9726
Farrell Seymore, prin. Fax 745-9730
Southview PS 300/K-2
2712 Marvyn Pkwy 36804 334-745-9711
Laura Hartley, prin. Fax 745-9741
West Forest IS 300/3-5
2801 Waverly Pkwy 36801 334-745-9737
Bradley Hunter, prin. Fax 745-9739

Russell County SD
Supt. — See Phenix City
Dixie ES 200/K-6
4914 US Highway 80 W 36804 334-298-0131
Dr. Charles Baker, prin. Fax 298-0166

Trinity Christian S 300/K-12
PO Box 311 36803 334-745-2464
Sharon Miller, prin. Fax 745-4856

Opp, Covington, Pop. 6,658
Covington County SD
Supt. — See Andalusia
Fleeta S 200/K-8
27463 County Road 30 36467 334-493-6772
Roger McLain, prin. Fax 493-9813

Opp CSD 1,400/PK-12
PO Box 840 36467 334-493-3173
Michael Smithart, supt. Fax 493-3060
oppcityschools.com/
Opp MS 400/5-8
303 E Stewart Ave 36467 334-493-6332
Aaron Hightower, prin. Fax 493-1120
South Highlands ES 500/PK-4
503 Brown St 36467 334-493-6031
Brett Kinsaul, prin. Fax 493-7082

Orange Beach, Baldwin, Pop. 5,055
Baldwin County SD
Supt. — See Bay Minette
Orange Beach ES 300/K-6
4900 S Wilson Blvd 36561 251-981-5662
Steve Baker, prin. Fax 981-5684

Orrville, Dallas, Pop. 214
Dallas County SD
Supt. — See Selma
Five Points ES 200/3-6
7333 County Road 33 36767 334-996-8383
Lou Ella Guthridge, prin. Fax 996-8383

Salem ES 200/K-2
3486 County Road 3 36767 334-996-8636
Melvin Brown, prin. Fax 996-3649

Owens Cross Roads, Madison, Pop. 1,313
Madison County SD
Supt. — See Huntsville
Owens Cross Roads ES 200/K-5
161 Wilson Mann Rd 35763 256-725-4233
Dr. Donna Goode, prin. Fax 725-2979

Big Cove Christian Academy 50/K-9
6354 Highway 431 S 35763 256-518-9642

Oxford, Calhoun, Pop. 19,981
Oxford CSD 3,900/PK-12
310 E 2nd St 36203 256-241-3140
Dr. Jeff Goodwin, supt. Fax 831-8620
www.oxford.k12.al.us/
Hanna ES 600/5-6
1111 Watson Dr 36203 256-241-3896
Shannon Stanley, prin. Fax 831-0389
Oxford ES 800/PK-4
1401 Caffey Dr 36203 256-241-3844
Debora Nelson, prin. Fax 831-1424
Oxford MS 700/7-8
1750 US Highway 78 W 36203 256-241-3816
Dr. Janice Campbell, prin. Fax 835-8813
Other Schools – See Anniston

Ozark, Dale, Pop. 14,833
Dale County SD 2,900/K-12
113 W Reynolds St 36360 334-774-2355
Phillip Parker, supt. Fax 774-3503
www.dalecountyboe.org/
Other Schools – See Ariton, Midland City, Newton, Pinckard, Skipperville

Ozark CSD, 1044 Andrews Ave 36360 2,600/K-12
Michael Lenhart, supt. 334-774-5197
www.ozarkcityschools.net
Lisenby ES 400/1-5
860 Faust Ave 36360 334-774-4919
Jaann Wells, prin. Fax 774-4960
Mixon ES 500/1-5
349 Sherril Ln 36360 334-774-4912
Donna Stark, prin. Fax 774-1402
Smith MS 600/6-8
994 Andrews Ave 36360 334-774-4913
Sylvia Malone, prin. Fax 774-2685
Thompkins ECC 200/K-K
271 Willa Cir 36360 334-774-4911
C. Eagerton, prin. Fax 774-3825

Panola, Sumter
Sumter County SD
Supt. — See Livingston
North Sumter S 200/K-8
PO Box 99 35477 205-455-2422
Elijah Bell, prin. Fax 455-2582

Parrish, Walker, Pop. 1,259
Walker County SD
Supt. — See Jasper
Parrish ES 300/K-6
PO Box 109 35580 205-686-5061
J.D. Williams, prin. Fax 686-7998

Pelham, Shelby, Pop. 19,450
Shelby County SD
Supt. — See Columbiana
Valley ES 700/K-2
310 Opportunity Dr 35124 205-682-5550
Debbie Scarbrough, prin. Fax 682-5555
Valley IS 600/3-5
2200 Highway 33 35124 205-682-5530
Dana Payne, prin. Fax 682-5535

Pell City, Saint Clair, Pop. 11,010
Pell City CSD 3,200/K-12
1000 Bruce Etheredge Pkwy 35128 205-884-4440
Dr. Bobby Hathcock, supt. Fax 814-1010
www.pellcityschools.net
Duran JHS 300/8-8
309 Williamson Dr 35125 205-338-2825
Fax 884-6502
Duran South JHS 50/7-7
813 16th St S 35128 205-884-7957
Cory O'Neal, prin. Fax 884-7959
Eden ES 500/K-4
412 Wolf Creek Rd N 35125 205-338-6930
Laurie Funderburg, prin. Fax 338-8613
Kennedy ES 500/K-4
250 Otis Perry Dr 35128 205-338-7896
Leah Stover Ed.D., prin. Fax 338-1659
Roberts ES 300/K-4
810 Martin St N 35125 205-338-7312
Karen Davis, prin. Fax 884-0936
Williams IS 5-6
2000 Hardwick Rd 35128 205-338-4949
Holly Costello, prin. Fax 338-4953
Other Schools – See Cropwell

Mountain View Christian Academy 50/1-8
925 Academy Cir 35128 205-640-5951
Victory Christian S 500/PK-12
PO Box 710 35125 205-338-2901
David Weir, prin. Fax 338-3916

Perdido, Baldwin
Baldwin County SD
Supt. — See Bay Minette
Perdido S 500/PK-8
PO Box 28 36562 251-937-8456
Richard Ford, prin. Fax 937-3073

Phenix City, Russell, Pop. 29,460
Phenix City SD 5,500/K-12
PO Box 460 36868 334-298-0534
Larry DiChiara, supt. Fax 298-6038
www.pcboe.net
Lakewood ES 600/K-5
3010 Silverlake Dr 36867 334-732-1173
Nicey Eller, prin. Fax 732-0866
Meadowlane ES 200/K-5
709 Meadowlane Dr 36869 334-298-2568
Marcus Dubose, prin. Fax 291-3008
Phenix City ES 500/K-5
2307 S Railroad St 36867 334-732-1160
David Jones, prin. Fax 732-1165
Phenix City IS 900/6-7
2401 S Railroad St 36867 334-298-8744
Joseph Blevins, prin. Fax 291-0824
Ridgecrest ES 700/K-5
1806 8th Pl S 36869 334-298-3004
Veatrice Thomas, prin. Fax 298-1763
Sherwood ES 400/K-5
706 Idle Hour Dr 36867 334-298-7097
Curtis Barber, prin. Fax 298-9429
South Girard S 400/8-8
521 Fontaine Rd 36869 334-298-2527
Reginald Sparks, prin. Fax 297-8274
Westview ES 300/K-5
1012 23rd St 36867 334-298-4507
Bonnie Burns, prin. Fax 298-7891

Russell County SD 3,500/K-12
PO Box 400 36868 334-298-8791
Dr. Yvette Richardson, supt. Fax 448-8825
www.russellcsd.net
Ladonia ES 500/K-5
9 Woodland Dr 36869 334-297-7313
Jason Hopper, prin. Fax 297-7563
Other Schools – See Fort Mitchell, Hurtsboro, Opelika, Seale

Mother Mary S 100/PK-8
318 Seale Rd 36869 334-298-6371
Sr. Cecelia Harrison, prin. Fax 298-7934
St. Patrick S 50/PK-8
3910 Lakewood Dr 36867 334-298-3408
Dominador Manio, prin. Fax 298-3352

Phil Campbell, Franklin, Pop. 1,050
Franklin County SD
Supt. — See Russellville
East Franklin S 200/K-9
1815 Highway 89 35581 256-331-2140
Gary Harris, prin. Fax 331-2144
Phil Campbell ES 400/K-6
PO Box 849 35581 256-331-2170
Jacqueline Ergle, prin. Fax 331-2171

Piedmont, Calhoun, Pop. 4,969
Piedmont CSD 1,000/K-12
502 W Hood St 36272 256-447-8831
Matthew Akin, supt. Fax 447-6486
www.piedmont.k12.al.us/
Piedmont ES 500/K-5
504 W Hood St 36272 256-447-7483
Chris Hanson, prin. Fax 447-8130
Piedmont MS 300/6-8
401 N Main St 36272 256-447-6165
Hugh McWhorter, prin. Fax 447-8070

Pinckard, Dale, Pop. 642
Dale County SD
Supt. — See Ozark
South Dale MS 400/5-8
PO Box D 36371 334-983-3077
Barbara Smith, prin. Fax 983-5882

Pine Apple, Wilcox, Pop. 304
Wilcox County SD
Supt. — See Camden
Watts ES 100/K-5
2544 County Road 59 36768 251-746-2415
Marshae Pelt, prin. Fax 746-2129

Pine Hill, Wilcox, Pop. 923
Wilcox County SD
Supt. — See Camden
Ervin ES 400/PK-6
PO Box 220 36769 334-963-4702
Richard Bryant, prin. Fax 963-9060

Pinson, Jefferson, Pop. 10,987
Jefferson County SD
Supt. — See Birmingham
Johnson ES 800/3-5
8300 Kermit Johnson Rd 35126 205-379-4350
Tom Waldrep, prin. Fax 379-4395
Pinson ES 800/K-2
4200 School Dr 35126 205-379-5050
Rosalie Ritchey, prin. Fax 379-5095
Rudd MS 900/6-8
4526 Rudd School Rd 35126 205-379-5300
Susan Whitehurst, prin. Fax 680-8124

Pisgah, Jackson, Pop. 702
Jackson County SD
Supt. — See Scottsboro
Pisgah S 600/K-12
60 Metcalf St 35765 256-451-3241
Mark Guffey, prin. Fax 451-3457
Rosalie S 300/K-8
162 County Road 355 35765 256-451-3616
Ricky Ragsdale, prin. Fax 451-3605

Plantersville, Dallas
Dallas County SD
Supt. — See Selma
Terry ES 100/K-6
70 Academy St 36758 334-366-2838
Susan Morgan, prin. Fax 366-5325

Pleasant Grove, Jefferson, Pop. 10,312
Jefferson County SD
Supt. — See Birmingham
Pleasant Grove ES 1,000/K-6
601 Park Rd 35127 205-379-5200
Jay Jacks, prin. Fax 379-5245

Prattville, Autauga, Pop. 30,043
Autauga County SD 9,400/K-12
153 W 4th St 36067 334-365-5706
Greg Faulkner, supt. Fax 361-3828
www.autaugacountyschool.org
Pratt ES 1,200/1-6
420 Harvest Loop 36066 334-361-6400
Norman Kleinschmidt, prin. Fax 358-2393
Prattville ES 600/3-4
134 Patrick St 36067 334-361-3885
Felissa Armistad, prin. Fax 361-3835
Prattville IS 600/5-6
1020 Honeysuckle Dr 36067 334-361-3880
Angela Landry, prin. Fax 361-3884
Prattville JHS 1,200/7-8
1089 Martin Luther King Dr 36067 334-365-6697
Spence Agee, prin. Fax 361-3870
Prattville K 500/K-K
338 1st St 36067 334-361-3890
Sue Riddle, prin. Fax 361-3891
Prattville PS 600/1-2
216 Wetumpka St 36067 334-365-6277
James Abraham, prin. Fax 365-0116
Other Schools – See Autaugaville, Billingsley, Deatsville, Marbury

---

Autauga Academy 200/K-12
497 Golson Rd 36067 334-365-4343
Gerald Carter, prin. Fax 365-7713
Prattville Christian Academy 500/PK-12
322 Old Farm Ln N 36066 334-285-0077
Jack Exum, prin. Fax 285-1777

Prichard, Mobile, Pop. 27,963
Mobile County SD
Supt. — See Mobile
Grant ES 400/PK-5
535 Easterling St 36610 251-221-1319
Kevlyn Trotter, prin. Fax 221-1315
Mobile County Training MS 400/6-8
800 Whitley St 36610 251-221-2267
Collins Woods, prin. Fax 221-2269
Robbins ES 600/PK-5
2416 W Main St 36610 251-221-1600
Marcelete Stewart, prin. Fax 221-1605
Whitley ES 300/PK-5
528 Capt Leon C Roberts St 36610 251-221-1737
Jaadaa Holcombe, prin. Fax 221-1736

Princeton, Jackson
Jackson County SD
Supt. — See Scottsboro
Paint Rock Valley S 100/K-12
PO Box 150 35766 256-776-2628
Laura Merritt, prin. Fax 776-0042

Quinton, Jefferson
Jefferson County SD
Supt. — See Birmingham
West Jefferson ES 200/K-6
4880 Freewill Dr 35130 205-379-5550
Brenda Cassady, prin. Fax 379-5595

Ragland, Saint Clair, Pop. 2,027
Saint Clair County SD
Supt. — See Ashville
Ragland S 600/K-12
1060 Main St 35131 205-472-2123
Hanley Hardy, prin. Fax 472-0086

Rainbow City, Etowah, Pop. 8,880
Etowah County SD
Supt. — See Gadsden
Jones ES 700/K-5
301 Lumbley Rd 35906 256-442-2900
Tanya Clark, prin. Fax 442-5060
Rainbow MS 700/6-8
454 Lumbley Rd 35906 256-442-1095
Tracy Cross, prin. Fax 442-1028

Westbrook Christian S 600/PK-12
100 Westminster Dr 35906 256-442-7457
Cynthia Greer, prin. Fax 442-7635

Rainsville, DeKalb, Pop. 4,782
De Kalb County SD 8,600/K-12
PO Box 1668 35986 256-638-6921
Charles Warren, supt. Fax 638-9720
www.dekalbk12.org
Plainview S 1,300/K-12
PO Box 469 35986 256-638-3510
Ronald Bell, prin. Fax 638-6274
Other Schools – See Collinsville, Crossville, Fort Payne, Fyffe, Geraldine, Henagar, Ider, Mentone, Sylvania, Valley Head

Ramer, Montgomery
Montgomery County SD
Supt. — See Montgomery
Dunbar-Ramer S 200/K-8
56 Naftel Ramer Rd 36069 334-562-3241
Dwight Brooks, prin. Fax 562-3134

Ranburne, Cleburne, Pop. 471
Cleburne County SD
Supt. — See Heflin
Ranburne ES 400/K-4
181 Young Dr 36273 256-568-9722
Timothy Ward, prin. Fax 568-2607

Randolph, Bibb
Bibb County SD
Supt. — See Centreville
Randolph ES 200/K-6
7259 Highway 36 36792 334-366-2897
Karen Peak, prin. Fax 366-5003

Red Bay, Franklin, Pop. 3,282
Franklin County SD
Supt. — See Russellville
Red Bay S 800/K-12
PO Box 1518 35582 256-331-2270
Kenny Sparks, prin. Fax 331-2275

Red Level, Covington, Pop. 550
Covington County SD
Supt. — See Andalusia
Red Level S 700/K-12
PO Box D 36474 334-469-5315
Johny Odom, prin. Fax 469-6192

Reform, Pickens, Pop. 1,858
Pickens County SD
Supt. — See Carrollton
Reform ES 400/K-6
815 7th Ave SW 35481 205-375-6351
Terry Sterling, prin. Fax 375-6777

Remlap, Blount
Blount County SD
Supt. — See Oneonta
Southeastern S 400/K-8
18770 State Highway 75 35133 205-681-3964
Michael Peoples, prin. Fax 681-3975

Repton, Conecuh, Pop. 265
Conecuh County SD
Supt. — See Evergreen
Repton S 200/PK-8
2340 Conaly St 36475 251-248-2960
John Ward, prin. Fax 578-2371

Roanoke, Randolph, Pop. 6,650
Roanoke CSD 1,500/K-12
PO Box 1367 36274 334-863-2628
Chuck Marcum, supt. Fax 863-2849
www.roanokecityschools.org/home.asp
Handley MS 600/4-8
PO Box 725 36274 334-863-4174
Greg Foster, prin. Fax 863-6129
Knight Enloe ES 500/K-3
PO Box 685 36274 334-863-2237
Dr. Kim Hendon, prin. Fax 863-6092

Robertsdale, Baldwin, Pop. 4,681
Baldwin County SD
Supt. — See Bay Minette
Central Baldwin MS 700/7-8
PO Box 930 36567 251-947-2327
Michael Vivar, prin. Fax 947-1949
Elsanor ES 300/PK-6
23440 US Highway 90 36567 251-947-5401
Susan Runnels, prin. Fax 947-4966
Robertsdale ES 800/PK-6
1 Cub Dr 36567 251-947-4003
Charles Downey, prin. Fax 947-1919
Rosinton ES 300/PK-6
19757 County Road 64 36567 251-964-5210
Dr. Theresa Harden, prin. Fax 964-4421

Central Christian S 300/PK-12
17395 State Highway 104 36567 251-947-5043
Tim Shelton, admin. Fax 947-2572
Faith Presbyterian Christian S 100/PK-12
PO Box 950 36567 251-947-1162
Tom Barnes, prin. Fax 947-5012
St. Patrick S 200/PK-8
PO Box 609 36567 251-947-7395
Sr. Margaret Harte, prin. Fax 947-3860

Rockford, Coosa, Pop. 405
Coosa County SD 1,400/K-12
PO Box 37 35136 256-377-4913
Dennis Sanford, supt. Fax 377-2385
coosaschools.k12.al.us/
Central ES Coosa County 500/K-4
RR 2 Box 66 35136 256-377-1456
Jennifer Gill, prin. Fax 377-1459
Central MS Coosa County 400/5-8
RR 2 Box 65 35136 256-377-1490
William Walker, prin. Fax 377-1493

Rock Mills, Randolph
Randolph County SD
Supt. — See Wedowee
Rock Mills S 200/K-8
415 County Road 75 36274 334-885-6823
Mary Kelly, prin. Fax 885-6806

Rogersville, Lauderdale, Pop. 1,186
Lauderdale County SD
Supt. — See Florence
Lauderdale County S 1,100/K-12
PO Box 220 35652 256-247-3414
James Stejskal, prin. Fax 247-3444

Russellville, Franklin, Pop. 8,793
Franklin County SD 3,100/K-12
PO Box 610 35653 256-332-1360
Bill Moss, supt. Fax 331-0069
www.franklin.k12.al.us/
Belgreen S 500/K-12
14220 Highway 187 35653 256-332-1376
Steve Pounders, prin. Fax 332-7209
Tharptown ES 300/K-6
145 Highway 80 35654 256-332-3404
David Hogan, prin. Fax 332-3402
Other Schools – See Phil Campbell, Red Bay, Vina

Russellville CSD 2,400/K-12
1945 Waterloo Rd 35653 256-331-2000
Dr. Wayne Ray, supt. Fax 332-7323
www.rcs.k12.al.us
Russellville ES 500/3-5
133 Chucky Mullins Memorial 35653 256-331-2123
Kristie Ezzell, prin. Fax 332-1880
Russellville MS 600/6-8
765 Summit St 35653 256-331-2120
Frankie Hammock, prin. Fax 332-8453
West ES 600/K-2
1340 Clay Ave 35653 256-331-2122
Ramona Robinson, prin. Fax 332-6124

Salem, Lee
Lee County SD
Supt. — See Opelika
Wacoochee JHS 1,000/7-8
125 Lee Road 254 36874 334-745-3062
Rick Harris, prin. Fax 745-3565

Samson, Geneva, Pop. 2,025
Geneva County SD
Supt. — See Geneva
Samson ES 400/K-6
505 N Johnson St 36477 334-898-7439
Donna Kirkpatrick, prin. Fax 898-2473
Samson MS 100/7-8
209 N Broad St 36477 334-898-1317
Danny Branch, prin. Fax 898-7576

Saraland, Mobile, Pop. 12,683
Saraland CSD 1,400/K-12
943 Saraland Blvd S 36571 251-375-5420
Paul Sousa, supt. Fax 375-5430
saralandcity.schoolinsites.com
Adams MS 900/6-8
401 Baldwin Rd 36571 251-679-9405
Dr. Stephen North, prin. Fax 679-9456
Saraland ES 500/K-5
229 McKeough Ave 36571 251-679-5739
Peggy Clements, prin. Fax 679-5749

North Mobile Christian S 300/K-8
1255 Industrial Pkwy 36571 251-679-3279
Michael Bell, prin. Fax 679-3273

Sardis, Dallas
Dallas County SD
Supt. — See Selma
Shiloh ES 200/K-6
6200 County Road 30 36775 334-874-8588
Carla Thompson, prin. Fax 874-8588

Satsuma, Mobile, Pop. 5,951
Mobile County SD
Supt. — See Mobile
Lee IS 600/3-5
251 Baker Rd 36572 251-221-1476
Joyce Mark, prin. Fax 221-1467
Lee PS 700/K-2
220 Baker Rd 36572 251-221-1466
Dana Price, prin. Fax 221-1473
North Mobile County MS 6-8
251 Baker Rd 36572 251-221-2000
Thomas Campbell, prin. Fax 221-2004

Satsuma Christian S 300/K-8
PO Box 610 36572 251-675-1295
Charnel Ettawil, prin. Fax 675-8363

Scottsboro, Jackson, Pop. 14,840
Jackson County SD 6,100/K-12
PO Box 490 35768 256-259-9500
Ken Harding, supt. Fax 259-0076
www.jackson.k12.al.us/
Skyline S 600/K-12
897 County Road 25 35768 256-587-6561
Chad Gorham, prin. Fax 587-6562
Other Schools – See Bridgeport, Bryant, Dutton, Flat Rock, Higdon, Hollywood, Pisgah, Princeton, Section, Stevenson, Woodville

Scottsboro CSD 2,600/K-12
305 S Scott St 35768 256-218-2100
Dr. Judith Berry, supt. Fax 218-2190
www.scottsboroschools.net
Brownwood ES 400/K-4
305 Bingham St 35768 256-218-2400
Steve Green, prin. Fax 218-2490
Caldwell ES 500/K-4
905 S Market St 35768 256-218-2500
Buddy Holt, prin. Fax 218-2590
Collins ES 400/5-6
102 Legion Dr 35768 256-218-2700
Lisa Duncan, prin. Fax 218-2790
Nelson ES 300/K-4
202 Ida Moody Rd 35769 256-218-2600
Carla Kimball, prin. Fax 218-2690
Scottsboro JHS 400/7-8
1601 Jefferson St 35768 256-218-2300
Hal Luse, prin. Fax 218-2390

Scottsboro Christian Academy 50/PK-12
9545 AL Highway 79 35768 256-259-5398
Debbie Johnson, admin. Fax 574-3639

Seale, Russell
Russell County SD
Supt. — See Phenix City
Oliver ES 400/K-6
77 Longview St 36875 334-855-3225
Brenda Coley, prin. Fax 855-3208
Russell County MS 600/7-8
4716 Old Seale Hwy 36875 334-855-4453
Dr. Mesha Ramsey, prin. Fax 855-4437

Section, Jackson, Pop. 763
Jackson County SD
Supt. — See Scottsboro
Macedonia S 200/K-8
196 County Road 49 35771 256-228-4483
Steven Paradise, prin. Fax 228-7083
Section S 600/K-12
PO Box 10 35771 256-228-6718
Steve Durham, prin. Fax 228-6252

Selma, Dallas, Pop. 19,401
Dallas County SD 4,300/K-12
PO Box 1056 36702 334-875-3440
Dr. Fannie Major-McKenzie, supt. Fax 876-4493
www.dallask12.org
Brantley ES 300/K-6
5585 Water Ave 36703 334-874-8185
Melissa Milligan, prin. Fax 874-6541
Craig ES 400/3-5
108 Craig Industrial Park 36701 334-875-7937
Tanya Miles, prin. Fax 875-7937
Southside PS 400/K-2
3104 Old Montgomery Rd 36703 334-874-9566
Melanie Wright, prin. Fax 874-8226
Tipton MS 300/7-8
2500 Tipton St 36701 334-872-8080
Hattie Shelton, prin. Fax 872-8008
Other Schools – See Orrville, Plantersville, Sardis, Valley Grande

Selma CSD 4,200/PK-12
PO Box 350 36702 334-874-1600
Dr. Austin Obasohan, supt. Fax 874-1604
www.selmacityschools.org
Byrd ES 200/K-5
625 Lapsley St 36701 334-874-1620
Marie Taylor, prin. Fax 874-1648
Cedar Park ES 200/PK-5
1101 Woodrow Ave 36701 334-874-1625
Logan Cowart, prin. Fax 874-1702
Clark ES 400/PK-5
405 Lawrence St 36703 334-874-1630
Jenise Hampton, prin. Fax 874-1711
Edgewood ES 400/PK-5
709 Highland Ave 36701 334-874-1640
Joe Peterson, prin. Fax 874-1641
Kingston ES 300/PK-5
2224 Selma Ave 36703 334-874-1635
Robert Carter, prin. Fax 874-1637
Knox ES 200/PK-5
1002 Mabry St 36701 334-874-1650
Joslyn Reddick, prin. Fax 876-4403
Meadowview ES 300/K-5
1816 Old Orrville Rd 36701 334-874-1655
Jeanne Brust, prin. Fax 874-1656
Payne ES 300/PK-5
1529 Franklin St 36703 334-874-1660
Bailey Dawson, prin. Fax 874-1662
School of Discovery Genesis Center 200/6-6
400 Washington St 36703 334-874-1670
Gerald Shirley, prin. Fax 874-1674
Selma MS CHAT Academy 600/7-8
1701 Summerfield Rd 36701 334-874-1675
Bertram Pickney, prin. Fax 874-1679

Central Christian Academy 100/1-12
1 Bell Rd 36701 334-877-1581
Meadowview Christian S 300/PK-12
1512 Old Orrville Rd 36701 334-872-8448
Dr. Michael Gaylor, prin. Fax 872-8443
Morgan Academy 600/K-12
PO Box 2650 36702 334-875-4464
Randy Skipper, prin. Fax 875-4465

Semmes, Mobile
Mobile County SD
Supt. — See Mobile
Allentown ES 800/K-5
10330 Howells Ferry Rd 36575 251-221-1000
Ashtiny Cleveland, prin. Fax 221-1003
Semmes ES 600/PK-5
10100 Blackwell Nursery S 36575 251-221-1631
Sharon Anderson, prin. Fax 221-1633
Semmes MS 1,500/6-8
4566 Ed George Rd 36575 251-221-2344
Brenda Shenesey, prin. Fax 221-2347

Sheffield, Colbert, Pop. 9,228
Sheffield CSD 1,200/PK-12
300 W 6th St 35660 256-383-0400
Richard Gardner, supt. Fax 386-5704
www.scs.k12.al.us/
Sheffield JHS 200/7-8
1803 E 30th St 35660 256-386-5735
Brezofski Anderson, prin. Fax 386-5706
Threadgill PS 300/PK-2
900 Annapolis Ave 35660 256-386-5720
Michael South, prin. Fax 386-5705
Willson ES 300/3-6
2200 E 31st St 35660 256-386-5730
Mary Napier, prin. Fax 386-5708

Shelby, Shelby
Shelby County SD
Supt. — See Columbiana
Shelby ES 200/K-5
19099 Highway 145 35143 205-682-6630
Karen Mitchell, prin. Fax 682-6635

Shorter, Macon, Pop. 337
Macon County SD
Supt. — See Tuskegee
Wolfe ES 200/K-6
4450 Cross Keys Rd 36075 334-727-1641
Mason McDade, prin. Fax 727-9958

Silverhill, Baldwin, Pop. 695
Baldwin County SD
Supt. — See Bay Minette
Silverhill ES 400/PK-6
PO Box 190 36576 251-945-5188
Catherine Rogers, prin. Fax 945-5116

Sipsey, Walker, Pop. 548
Walker County SD
Supt. — See Jasper
Sipsey S 300/PK-8
PO Box 30 35584 205-648-5083
Donnie Bridges, prin. Fax 648-5031

Skipperville, Dale
Dale County SD
Supt. — See Ozark
Long ES 400/K-6
2567 County Road 60 36374 334-774-0021
Lisa Welch, prin. Fax 774-0742

Slocomb, Geneva, Pop. 2,033
Geneva County SD
Supt. — See Geneva
Slocomb ES 600/K-5
108 S Hemby St 36375 334-886-2132
Rick Voss, prin. Fax 886-9842
Slocomb MS 300/6-8
591 S County Road 9 36375 334-886-2008
Max Whittaker, prin. Fax 886-9889

Smiths, Lee, Pop. 3,456
Lee County SD
Supt. — See Opelika
Smiths Station ES 900/2-3
171 Lee Road 728 36877 334-448-4422
Paul Kohler, prin. Fax 448-4499

Glenwood S 500/K-12
5801 Summerville Rd 36877 334-297-3614
Dr. Phillip Elder, prin. Fax 214-9027

Smiths Station, Lee, Pop. 4,477
Lee County SD
Supt. — See Opelika
Smiths Station IS 1,300/4-6
80 Lee Road 926 36877 334-298-8370
Kathie Ledbetter, prin. Fax 298-8474
Smiths Station PS 800/K-1
150 Lee Road 295 36877 334-298-6089
Kathy Henderson, prin. Fax 214-0361

Somerville, Morgan, Pop. 357
Morgan County SD
Supt. — See Decatur
Cotaco S 600/PK-8
100 Cotaco School Rd 35670 256-778-8154
Jimmy Scott, prin. Fax 778-8148
Union Hill S 400/K-8
2221 Union Hill Rd 35670 256-498-2431
Jeremy Childers, prin. Fax 498-3524

Southside, Calhoun, Pop. 7,838
Etowah County SD
Supt. — See Gadsden
Southside ES 600/K-5
2551 Highway 77 35907 256-442-1090
Jennifer Brunson, prin. Fax 442-1075

Spanish Fort, Baldwin, Pop. 5,642
Baldwin County SD
Supt. — See Bay Minette
Rockwell ES 700/K-5
10183 US Highway 31 36527 251-626-5528
Robert Owen, prin. Fax 621-7206
Spanish Fort ES 500/K-5
30900 State Highway 225 36527 251-626-9751
Rebecca Comer, prin. Fax 621-8018

Chi Alpha Academy 200/PK-12
PO Box 7547 36577 251-626-1379
Fax 626-1392

Spring Garden, Cherokee
Cherokee County SD
Supt. — See Centre
Spring Garden S 600/K-12
PO Box 31 36275 256-447-7045
Michael Welsh, prin. Fax 447-6947

Springville, Saint Clair, Pop. 3,054
Saint Clair County SD
Supt. — See Ashville
Springville ES 600/PK-4
75 Wilson St 35146 205-467-6550
Bobby Byrd, prin. Fax 467-2716
Springville MS 600/5-8
6691 US Highway 11 35146 205-467-2740
Virgil Winslett, prin. Fax 467-2742

Stapleton, Baldwin
Baldwin County SD
Supt. — See Bay Minette
Stapleton ES 200/K-6
35480 Harriot Ave 36578 251-937-2038
Charlotte Beasley, prin. Fax 580-2001

Steele, Saint Clair, Pop. 1,154
Saint Clair County SD
Supt. — See Ashville
Steele S 200/K-8
105 McHugh St 35987 256-538-5489
Judy Dixon, prin. Fax 538-5496

Stevenson, Jackson, Pop. 2,138
Jackson County SD
Supt. — See Scottsboro
Stevenson ES 300/K-4
930 Old Mount Carmel Rd 35772 256-437-2203
Dr. Linda Allen, prin. Fax 437-8372
Stevenson MS 300/5-8
701 Kentucky Ave 35772 256-437-2945
Dr. Dianne Brooks, prin. Fax 437-2747

Sulligent, Lamar, Pop. 2,033
Lamar County SD
Supt. — See Vernon
Sulligent S 800/K-12
PO Box 367 35586 205-698-9254
Craig Weeks, prin. Fax 698-8497

Sumiton, Walker, Pop. 2,582
Walker County SD
Supt. — See Jasper
Sumiton S 800/K-8
275 1st St N 35148 205-648-2390
Debbie Peake, prin. Fax 648-0183

Summerdale, Baldwin, Pop. 673
Baldwin County SD
Supt. — See Bay Minette
Summerdale S 500/PK-8
PO Box 9 36580 251-989-6850
Mark Pumphrey, prin. Fax 989-6611

Sweet Water, Marengo, Pop. 231
Marengo County SD
Supt. — See Linden
Sweet Water S 600/K-12
PO Box 127 36782 334-994-4263
Stan Stokley, prin. Fax 994-4686

Sycamore, Talladega
Talladega County SD
Supt. — See Talladega
Sycamore ES 200/K-4
18101 AL Highway 21 35149 256-315-5450
Melia Brashear, prin. Fax 315-5455

Sylacauga, Talladega, Pop. 12,956
Sylacauga CSD 2,400/K-12
605 W 4th St 35150 256-245-5256
Dr. Jane Cobia, supt. Fax 245-6665
www.sylacauga.k12.al.us
Indian Valley ES 600/K-2
1099 Oldfield Rd 35150 256-249-0397
Wanda Freels, prin. Fax 245-2699
Nichols-Lawson MS 500/6-8
1550 Talladega Hwy 35150 256-245-4376
Gerald Douglass, prin. Fax 245-4071
Pinecrest ES 600/3-5
615 Coaling Rd 35151 256-245-5700
Dan Deese, prin. Fax 245-2699

Talladega County SD
Supt. — See Talladega
Comer Memorial ES 700/K-6
803 Seminole Ave 35150 256-315-5430
Karen Culver, prin. Fax 315-5445
Fayetteville S 600/K-12
170 WW Averitte Dr 35151 256-315-5550
Dr. Patsy Lagen, prin. Fax 315-5575

Sylvania, DeKalb, Pop. 1,238
De Kalb County SD
Supt. — See Rainsville
Sylvania S 900/K-12
PO Box 390 35988 256-638-2030
Westley King, prin. Fax 638-7839

Talladega, Talladega, Pop. 17,149
Talladega CSD 2,600/K-12
501 South St E 35160 256-315-5600
Douglas Campbell, supt. Fax 315-5606
www.talladega-cs.net
Ellis JHS 400/7-8
414 Elm St 35160 256-315-5700
Scott Bailey, prin. Fax 315-5704
Graham ES 300/K-6
403 Cedar St 35160 256-315-5777
Melissa Howle-Dyer, prin. Fax 315-5781
Houston ES 300/K-6
1310 Ashland Hwy 35160 256-315-5800
Dr. Dolia Patterson, prin. Fax 315-5804
Northside-Henderson ES 200/K-6
400 Spring St N 35160 256-315-5855
Alicia Laros, prin. Fax 315-5859
Salter ES 200/K-6
106 Brecon Access Rd 35160 256-315-5822
Jenni Griffin, prin. Fax 315-5826
Young ES 300/K-6
200 E Damon Ave 35160 256-315-5888
Pattie Thomas, prin. Fax 315-5884

Talladega County SD 7,500/K-12
PO Box 887 35161 256-315-5100
Dr. Suzanne Lacey, supt. Fax 315-5126
www.tcboe.org
Stemley Road ES 500/K-6
2760 Stemley Bridge Rd 35160 256-315-5325
Judi Clark, prin. Fax 315-5335
Other Schools – See Childersburg, Lincoln, Munford, Sycamore, Sylacauga

Tallassee, Elmore, Pop. 5,032
Tallassee CSD 2,000/K-12
308 King St 36078 334-283-6864
Dr. James Jeffers, supt. Fax 283-4338
www.tcschools.com
Southside MS 600/5-8
901 EB Payne Sr Dr 36078 334-283-2151
Ron McDaniel, prin. Fax 283-3577
Tallassee ES 800/K-4
850 Friendship Rd 36078 334-283-5001
Wayne Pressley, prin. Fax 283-8661

Tanner, Limestone
Limestone County SD
Supt. — See Athens
Tanner S 800/K-12
12060 Sommers Rd 35671 256-233-6682
Billy Owens, prin. Fax 233-6449

Tarrant, Jefferson, Pop. 6,691
Tarrant CSD 1,000/PK-12
1318 Alabama St 35217 205-849-3700
Dr. Martha Rizzuto, supt. Fax 849-3728
www.tarrant.k12.al.us/
Tarrant City ES 400/PK-3
1269 Portland St 35217 205-841-7541
Dr. Shelly Mize, prin. Fax 849-3716
Tarrant City MS 200/4-6
1 Wildcat Dr 35217 205-849-0168
Judy Matthews, prin. Fax 849-1545

Theodore, Mobile, Pop. 6,509
Mobile County SD
Supt. — See Mobile
Burroughs ES 400/PK-5
6875 Burroughs Ln 36582 251-221-1077
Dr. Julia Nelson, prin. Fax 221-1076
Davis ES 500/PK-5
6900 Nan Gray Davis Rd 36582 251-221-1166
Eileen Mai, prin. Fax 221-1167
Hankins MS 1,100/6-8
5750 Katherine Hankins Dr 36582 251-221-2200
Cheryl Wittner, prin. Fax 221-2204

Magnolia Springs Baptist Academy 200/PK-8
6058 Theodore Dawes Rd 36582 251-653-0251
Bob Ramirez, prin. Fax 653-2668

Thomaston, Marengo, Pop. 375
Marengo County SD
Supt. — See Linden
Johnson S 300/K-12
PO Box 67 36783 334-627-3364
Lepolean Peterson, prin. Fax 627-3396

Thomasville, Clarke, Pop. 4,552
Thomasville CSD 1,600/K-12
PO Box 458 36784 334-636-9955
Dr. Vic Adkison, supt. Fax 636-4096
www.thomasvilleschools.org/
Thomasville ES 600/K-4
300 Quincy Ingram St 36784 334-636-0063
Adam Sealy, prin. Fax 636-0021
Thomasville MS 500/5-8
781 Gates Dr 36784 334-636-4928
Terry Norton, prin. Fax 636-4924

Thorsby, Chilton, Pop. 1,981
Chilton County SD
Supt. — See Clanton
Thorsby S 800/K-12
54 Opportunity Dr 35171 205-280-4880
Russ Bryan, prin. Fax 646-2197

Toney, Madison
Madison County SD
Supt. — See Huntsville
Madison Cross Roads ES 900/K-5
11548 Pulaski Pike 35773 256-828-4578
Mitzi Dennis, prin. Fax 828-8759
Sparkman MS 800/6-8
2697 Carters Gin Rd 35773 256-852-0112
Ronnie Blair, prin. Fax 852-4368

Town Creek, Lawrence, Pop. 1,209
Lawrence County SD
Supt. — See Moulton
Hatton ES 400/K-6
6536 County Road 236 35672 256-685-4000
Theresa Summers, prin. Fax 685-4004
Hazlewood S 200/K-8
PO Box 699 35672 256-685-4020
Gary Smith, prin. Fax 685-4008

Townley, Walker
Walker County SD
Supt. — See Jasper
Townley S 200/K-8
PO Box B 35587 205-924-8424
Karen Atkins, prin. Fax 924-8801

Toxey, Choctaw, Pop. 142

South Choctaw Academy 200/K-12
PO Box 160 36921 251-843-2426
Fax 843-2088

Trinity, Morgan, Pop. 1,842
Lawrence County SD
Supt. — See Moulton
East Lawrence ES 400/K-3
263 County Road 370 35673 256-905-2513
Dr. Jewell Satchel, prin. Fax 905-2522
East Lawrence MS 600/4-8
99 County Road 370 35673 256-905-2420
Cindy Praytor, prin. Fax 905-2477

Morgan County SD
Supt. — See Decatur
West Morgan ES 500/K-4
571 Old Highway 24 35673 256-350-8818
Earl Leonard, prin. Fax 350-8823

Troy, Pike, Pop. 13,935
Pike County SD 2,200/K-12
101 W Love St 36081 334-566-1850
Mark Bazzell, supt. Fax 566-2580
www.pikecountyschools.com
Other Schools – See Banks, Brundidge, Goshen

Troy CSD 2,400/K-12
PO Box 529 36081 334-566-3741
Dr. Linda Felton-Smith, supt. Fax 566-1425
www.troyschools.net
Henderson MS 500/6-8
PO Box 925 36081 334-566-5770
Chresal Threadgill, prin. Fax 566-3071
Troy ES 1,100/K-5
PO Box 708 36081 334-566-1444
Geoffrey Spann, prin. Fax 566-8142

Covenant Christian S 50/K-6
105 S George Wallace Dr 36081 334-566-0817
Laura Grice, admin. Fax 566-0878
Pike Liberal Arts S 400/K-12
PO Box 329 36081 334-566-2023
Ceil Sikes, hdmstr. Fax 670-2010

Trussville, Jefferson, Pop. 16,760
Jefferson County SD
Supt. — See Birmingham
Clay-Chalkville MS 1,100/6-8
6700 Trussville Clay Rd 35173 205-379-3100
Maurice Williams, prin. Fax 379-3145

Trussville City SD 4,100/PK-12
113 N Chalkville Rd 35173 205-228-3018
Dr. Suzanne Freeman, supt. Fax 228-3001
trussvillecityschools.com/
Hewitt-Trussville MS 900/6-8
5275 Trussville Clay Rd 35173 205-228-3700
Phyllis Faust, prin. Fax 228-3701
Paine IS 1,000/3-5
7600 Gadsden Hwy 35173 205-228-3300
Beth Bruno, prin. Fax 228-3301
Paine PS 1,000/PK-2
7500 Gadsden Hwy 35173 205-228-3200
Elizabeth H. Schmitt, prin. Fax 228-3201

Tuscaloosa, Tuscaloosa, Pop. 81,358
Tuscaloosa CSD 10,300/PK-12
PO Box 38991 35403 205-759-3560
Dr. Joyce Levey, supt. Fax 759-3711
www.tuscaloosacityschools.com
Alberta ES 500/K-5
2700 University Blvd E 35404 205-759-3564
Brenda Parker, prin. Fax 759-3753
Arcadia ES 400/K-5
3740 Arcadia Dr 35404 205-759-3567
Mary Jean Sutton, prin. Fax 759-3754
Central PS 300/PK-2
1510 Dinah Washington Ave 35401 205-759-3570
Portia Martin, prin. Fax 759-3755
King ES 400/3-5
2430 ML King Jr Blvd 35401 205-759-3619
Lisa Maddox, prin. Fax 759-3556
Northington ES 400/PK-5
1300 21st St E 35404 205-759-3622
Vertis Giles-Brown, prin. Fax 759-3761
Oakdale PS 200/PK-2
5001 25th St 35401 205-759-3626
Lucille Prewitt, prin. Fax 759-3762
Rock Quarry ES 500/K-5
2000 Rock Quarry Dr 35406 205-759-8347
Laura Jockisch, prin. Fax 759-8348
Rock Quarry MS 6-8
2000 Rock Quarry Dr 35406 205-759-3560
Brian Clayton, prin.
Skyland ES 600/K-5
408 Skyland Blvd E 35405 205-759-3638
Teresa McCollum, prin. Fax 759-3764
South ES K-5
315 McFarland Blvd E 35404 205-759-3560
Jami Mouchette, prin.
South MS 900/6-8
315 McFarland Blvd E 35404 205-759-3560
Clarence Sutton, prin.
University Place ES 500/PK-5
2000 1st Ave 35401 205-759-3664
Deron Cameron, prin. Fax 759-3768
University Place MS 6-8
2000 1st Ave 35401 205-759-3560
Becky Brown, prin.
Verner ES 600/K-5
2701 Northridge Rd 35406 205-759-3667
Elizabeth Curtis, prin. Fax 759-3769
Westlawn MS 500/6-8
1715 ML King Jr Blvd 35401 205-759-3673
Zachary Barnes, prin. Fax 759-3770
Woodland Forrest ES 700/K-5
6001 Hargrove Rd E 35405 205-759-3675
Wanda Fisher, prin. Fax 759-3771
Other Schools – See Cottondale

Tuscaloosa County SD 16,500/PK-12
PO Box 2568 35403 205-758-0411
Dr. Frank Costanzo, supt. Fax 758-2990
www.tcss.net/
Englewood ES 600/K-5
10300 Old Greensboro Rd 35405 205-342-2644
Jo Ann Bassett, prin. Fax 750-0579
Hillcrest MS 900/6-8
401 Hillcrest School Rd 35405 205-342-2820
C'Kimba Hobbs, prin. Fax 752-2467
Taylorville PS 700/K-2
350 Bobby Miller Pkwy 35405 205-342-2939
Dr. Steve Lamon, prin. Fax 759-3995
Other Schools – See Brookwood, Buhl, Coker, Cottondale, Duncanville, Fosters, Holt, Mc Calla, Northport, Vance

---

American Christian Academy 800/PK-12
2300 Veterans Memorial Pkwy 35404 205-553-5963
Dr. Dan Carden, hdmstr. Fax 553-5942
Holy Spirit S 400/PK-6
711 37th St E 35405 205-553-9630
Lisa Corona, prin. Fax 553-8880
Open Door Christian S 200/PK-12
1785 McFarland Blvd N 35406 205-349-4881
Daniel Habrial, admin. Fax 349-3246
Tuscaloosa Academy 400/PK-12
420 Rice Valley Rd N 35406 205-758-4462
Dr. George Elder, hdmstr. Fax 758-4418

Tuscumbia, Colbert, Pop. 8,170
Colbert County SD 2,800/K-12
1101 Highway 72 E 35674 256-386-8565
Billy Hudson, supt. Fax 381-9375
colbert.k12.al.us/
Colbert Heights ES 400/K-6
1551 Sunset Dr 35674 256-381-6132
Bob Montgomery, prin. Fax 389-9980
New Bethel ES 200/K-6
900 New Bethel Rd 35674 256-383-6471
Tom Windsor, prin. Fax 383-1098
Other Schools – See Cherokee, Leighton

Tuscumbia CSD 1,500/K-12
303 N Commons St E 35674 256-389-2900
Joe Walters Ed.D., supt. Fax 389-2903
www.tuscumbia.k12.al.us
Northside MS 400/6-8
598 N High St 35674 256-389-2920
Robert Mullen, prin. Fax 389-2921
Thompson IS 300/3-5
829 Frankfort Rd 35674 256-389-2930
Rene Thompson, prin. Fax 389-2931
Trenholm PS 300/K-2
601 Joe Wheeler Dr 35674 256-389-2940
Mary Smith, prin. Fax 389-2941

Covenant Christian S 300/PK-12
1900 Covenant Dr 35674 256-383-4436
Becky Odell, admin. Fax 381-4437

Tuskegee, Macon, Pop. 11,590
Macon County SD 3,200/PK-12
PO Box 830090 36083 334-727-1600
Dr. Gwendolyn Moore, supt. Fax 724-9990
www.maconk12.org
Carver ES 500/1-3
303 Union Springs Hwy 36083 334-727-2700
Melissa Williams, prin. Fax 727-5520
Tuskegee ES 300/4-5
202 E Price St 36083 334-727-3222
Joseph Asberry, prin. Fax 727-3703
Other Schools – See Notasulga, Shorter, Tuskegee Institute

Tuskegee Institute, See Tuskegee
Macon County SD
Supt. — See Tuskegee
Adams ECC 200/PK-K
1133 W Montgomery Rd 36088 334-727-5435
Mae Doris Williams, prin. Fax 727-0054
Tuskegee Institute MS 700/6-8
1809 Franklin Rd 36088 334-727-2580
Lonzo Bullie, prin. Fax 727-5089

St. Joseph S 100/PK-8
2009 W Montgomery Rd 36088 334-727-0620
Marjorie Reese, prin. Fax 727-0642

Union Grove, Marshall, Pop. 97
Marshall County SD
Supt. — See Guntersville
Union Grove ES 200/K-4
3685 Union Grove Rd 35175 256-753-2532
Tenna Anderton, prin. Fax 753-0021

Union Springs, Bullock, Pop. 3,443
Bullock County SD 1,700/K-12
PO Box 231 36089 334-738-2860
Keith Allen Stewart, supt. Fax 738-2802
bullock.k12.al.us/
South Highlands MS 500/4-7
PO Box 111 36089 334-738-2896
Julius Thomas, prin. Fax 738-5746
Union Springs ES 400/K-3
211 Conecuh Ave W 36089 334-738-2990
Willie Mitchell, prin. Fax 738-2923
Other Schools – See Midway

Uniontown, Perry, Pop. 1,520
Perry County SD
Supt. — See Marion
Uniontown ES 500/K-6
PO Box 649 36786 334-628-6318
Fred Moore, prin. Fax 683-6388

Uriah, Monroe
Monroe County SD
Supt. — See Monroeville
Blacksher S 600/PK-12
PO Box 430 36480 251-862-2130
Greg Shehan, prin. Fax 862-2808

Valley, Chambers, Pop. 9,000
Chambers County SD
Supt. — See Lafayette
Burns MS 800/6-8
292 Johnson St 36854 334-756-3567
Priscilla Holley, prin. Fax 756-7511
Fairfax ES 600/PK-5
502 Boulevard 36854 334-756-2966
Fran Groover, prin. Fax 756-4749
Harding-Shawmut ES 200/PK-5
3301 23rd Dr 36854 334-768-3474
Paul Sikes, prin. Fax 768-3475
Lafayette Lanier ES 200/K-5
6001 20th Ave 36854 334-756-3623
Victoria Leak, prin. Fax 756-4809

Lee County SD
Supt. — See Opelika
Beulah ES 700/PK-6
4747 Lee Road 270 36854 334-745-5028
Weldon Parkman, prin. Fax 745-2401

Valley Grande, Dallas
Dallas County SD
Supt. — See Selma
Martin MS 300/7-8
2863 County Road 81, 334-872-6417
Michael Blair, prin. Fax 875-4013
Valley Grande ES 500/K-6
2765 County Road 81, 334-872-7661
Sharon Streeter, prin. Fax 875-8834

Valley Head, DeKalb, Pop. 639
De Kalb County SD
Supt. — See Rainsville
Valley Head S 500/K-12
PO Box 145 35989 256-635-6228
William Monroe, prin. Fax 635-6229

Vance, Tuscaloosa, Pop. 555
Tuscaloosa County SD
Supt. — See Tuscaloosa
Brookwood MS 800/6-8
17021 Brookwood Pkwy 35490 205-342-2748
Mark Franks, prin. Fax 553-9910
Vance ES 500/K-5
PO Box 208 35490 205-342-2697
Karla Griffin, prin. Fax 553-9132

Verbena, Chilton
Chilton County SD
Supt. — See Clanton
Verbena S 500/K-12
202 County Road 510 36091 205-280-2820
Larry Raines, prin. Fax 755-0393

Vernon, Lamar, Pop. 1,984
Lamar County SD 2,400/K-12
PO Box 1379 35592 205-695-7615
Jeff Newman, supt. Fax 695-7678
www.lamarcountyschools.net
Vernon ES 300/K-3
PO Box 1349 35592 205-695-7717
Tracy Mixon, prin. Fax 695-8218
Other Schools – See Millport, Sulligent

Vestavia Hills, Jefferson, Pop. 31,022
Vestavia Hills CSD 5,800/K-12
PO Box 660826 35266 205-402-5100
Dr. Jamie Blair, supt. Fax 402-5134
www.vestavia.k12.al.us
Liberty Park ES 700/K-6
17051 Liberty Pkwy 35242 205-402-5400
Helen Holley, prin. Fax 402-5401
Liberty Park MS 6-8
17035 Liberty Pkwy 35242 205-402-5450
Kacy Pierce, prin. Fax 402-5450
Pizitz MS 1,200/6-8
2020 Pizitz Dr 35216 205-402-5350
David Miles, prin. Fax 402-5354
Vestavia Hills Central ES 600/4-5
1289 Montgomery Hwy 35216 205-402-5300
Marian Humphries, prin. Fax 402-5301
Vestavia Hills ES East 700/K-3
2109 Tyson Dr 35216 205-402-5200
Dr. Mark Richardson, prin. Fax 402-5211
Vestavia Hills ES West 600/K-3
1965 Merryvale Rd 35216 205-402-5151
Becky Patton, prin. Fax 402-5156
Other Schools – See Birmingham

Vina, Franklin, Pop. 398
Franklin County SD
Supt. — See Russellville
Vina S 300/K-12
8250 Highway 23 35593 256-331-2260
James Pharr, prin. Fax 351-4731

Vincent, Shelby, Pop. 1,950
Shelby County SD
Supt. — See Columbiana
Vincent ES 500/K-5
40800 Highway 25 35178 205-682-7320
Beverly Miller, prin. Fax 682-7325

Vinemont, Cullman
Cullman County SD
Supt. — See Cullman
Vinemont ES 500/K-5
PO Box 189 35179 256-734-0314
Dr. Jane Teeter, prin. Fax 737-3083
Vinemont MS 300/6-8
170 High School Rd 35179 256-739-1943
Michael Grantham, prin. Fax 737-1664
West Point IS 4-5
4541 County Road 1141 35179 256-734-8019
Shane Barnette, prin. Fax 739-0749
West Point MS 500/6-8
4545 County Road 1141 35179 256-734-5904
Clark Farley, prin. Fax 736-2354

Wadley, Randolph, Pop. 648
Randolph County SD
Supt. — See Wedowee
Wadley S 400/K-12
PO Box 49 36276 256-395-2286
Todd Wilson, prin. Fax 395-4488

Warrior, Jefferson, Pop. 3,037
Jefferson County SD
Supt. — See Birmingham
Corner S 1,000/K-12
10005 Corner School Rd 35180 205-379-3200
Ronald Cooper, prin. Fax 379-3245
Warrior ES 300/K-5
300 Montgomery St 35180 205-379-5500
Mike Frugoli, prin. Fax 379-5545

Waterloo, Lauderdale, Pop. 207
Lauderdale County SD
Supt. — See Florence
Waterloo S 300/K-12
PO Box 68 35677 256-766-3100
Ryan Harrison, prin. Fax 766-3194

Weaver, Calhoun, Pop. 2,555
Calhoun County SD
Supt. — See Anniston
Weaver ES 700/K-6
444 School Dr 36277 256-741-7100
Loretta Brown, prin. Fax 820-4101

Webb, Houston, Pop. 1,337
Houston County SD
Supt. — See Dothan
Webb ES 500/K-6
178 Depot St 36376 334-792-5744
Scott Beumer, prin. Fax 792-7967

Wedowee, Randolph, Pop. 824
Randolph County SD 2,300/K-12
PO Box 288 36278 256-357-4611
Paul Gay, supt. Fax 357-4844
www.randolph.k12.al.us/
Randolph County S 700/K-12
PO Box 490 36278 256-357-4751
Byron Nix, prin. Fax 357-2310
Wedowee MS 200/4-6
896 Woodland Ave W 36278 256-357-4636
Alan Robertson, prin. Fax 357-9576
Other Schools – See Rock Mills, Wadley, Woodland

New Hope S 50/PK-12
3500 County Road 56 36278 256-357-4968
James Harrington, admin. Fax 357-4968

West Blocton, Bibb, Pop. 1,418
Bibb County SD
Supt. — See Centreville
West Blocton ES 300/K-4
828 Cahaba River Dr 35184 205-938-9005
Karen Hubbard, prin. Fax 938-2653
West Blocton MS 500/5-8
4721 Truman Aldrich Pkwy 35184 205-938-2451
Duane McGee, prin. Fax 938-3261

Wetumpka, Elmore, Pop. 6,905
Elmore County SD 10,100/PK-12
PO Box 817 36092 334-567-1200
Jeffery Langham, supt. Fax 567-1405
www.elmoreco.com
Wetumpka ES 1,100/PK-3
510 Micanopy St 36092 334-567-4323
Kathy Willis, prin. Fax 567-1409
Wetumpka IS 800/4-6
1000 Micanopy St 36092 334-567-1413
Steve McKenzie, prin. Fax 567-1408
Wetumpka JHS 600/7-8
409 Alabama St 36092 334-567-1248
Bessie Robinson, prin. Fax 567-1407
Other Schools – See Deatsville, Eclectic, Millbrook

Wilmer, Mobile, Pop. 545
Mobile County SD
Supt. — See Mobile
Tanner Williams ES 300/K-5
13700 Tanner Williams Rd 36587 251-221-1675
Deborah Hess, prin. Fax 221-1678
Turner ES 500/K-5
8361 Lott Rd 36587 251-221-1285
Luann Rice, prin. Fax 221-1287
Wilmer ES 500/K-5
7456 Wilmer Georgetown Rd 36587 251-221-1780
Kathy Taylor, prin. Fax 221-1781

Wilsonville, Shelby, Pop. 1,742
Shelby County SD
Supt. — See Columbiana
Wilsonville ES 200/K-5
71 School St 35186 205-682-6640
Rosemary Liveoak, prin. Fax 682-6645

Winfield, Marion, Pop. 4,673
Winfield CSD 1,300/K-12
PO Box 70 35594 205-487-4255
Terrel Kirkpatrick, supt. Fax 487-4603
www.winfieldal.org/
Winfield ES 600/K-4
601 County Highway 14 35594 205-487-2305
Randy Thomley, prin. Fax 487-8907
Winfield MS 400/5-8
481 Apple Ave 35594 205-487-6901
Terri Miles, prin. Fax 487-6258

Woodland, Randolph, Pop. 208
Randolph County SD
Supt. — See Wedowee
Woodland S 800/K-12
PO Box 157 36280 256-449-2315
Rick Murphy, prin. Fax 449-2316

Woodstock, Bibb, Pop. 1,012
Bibb County SD
Supt. — See Centreville
Woodstock ES 300/K-4
19456 Eastern Valley Rd 35188 205-938-2028
Delores Garner, prin. Fax 938-2044

Woodville, Jackson, Pop. 755
Jackson County SD
Supt. — See Scottsboro
Woodville S 600/K-12
290 County Road 63 35776 256-776-2874
Bruce Maples, prin. Fax 776-4718

York, Sumter, Pop. 2,625
Sumter County SD
Supt. — See Livingston
York West End S 500/K-8
PO Box 127 36925 205-392-5901
Herman Wallace, prin. Fax 392-4700

Sumter Academy 200/K-12
181 Sumter Academy Rd 36925 205-392-5238
Paul Kirchharr, hdmstr. Fax 392-5239

ALASKA

ALASKA DEPARTMENT OF EDUCATION
PO Box 110500, Juneau 99811-0500
Telephone 907-465-2800
Fax 907-465-4165
Website http://www.eed.state.ak.us/

Commissioner of Education Larry LeDoux

ALASKA BOARD OF EDUCATION
PO Box 110500, Juneau 99811-0500

Chairperson Esther Cox

PUBLIC, PRIVATE AND CATHOLIC ELEMENTARY SCHOOLS

Adak, Aleutians West, Pop. 4,633
Aleutian Region SD
Supt. — See Anchorage
Adak S 50/K-12
100 Mechanic Dr 99546 907-592-3820
Julie Plummer, lead tchr. Fax 592-2249

Akhiok, Kodiak Island, Pop. 73
Kodiak Island Borough SD
Supt. — See Kodiak
Akhiok S 50/K-12
PO Box 5049 99615 907-836-2223
Rachel Hinman, lead tchr. Fax 836-2206

Akiachak, Bethel, Pop. 481
Yupiit SD 500/PK-12
PO Box 51190 99551 907-825-3600
Joseph Slats, supt. Fax 825-3655
www.yupiit.org/
Akiachak S 200/K-12
PO Box 51100 99551 907-825-3616
Allan Stockton, prin. Fax 825-3640
Other Schools – See Akiak, Tuluksak

Akiak, Bethel, Pop. 314
Yupiit SD
Supt. — See Akiachak
Akiak S 100/PK-12
PO Box 52049 99552 907-765-4600
Nancy Mazurek, prin. Fax 765-4642

Akutan, Aleutians East, Pop. 784
Aleutian East Borough SD
Supt. — See Sand Point
Akutan S 50/PK-12
PO Box 25 99553 907-698-2205
Arthur Woodard, prin. Fax 698-2216

Alakanuk, Wade Hampton, Pop. 697
Lower Yukon SD
Supt. — See Mountain Village
Alakanuk S 200/PK-12
PO Box 9 99554 907-238-3312
Peter Johnson, prin. Fax 238-3417

Aleknagik, Dillingham, Pop. 221
Southwest Region SD
Supt. — See Dillingham
Aleknagik S 50/K-8
PO Box 84 99555 907-842-5681
Jeffrey Ambrosier, lead tchr. Fax 842-1094

Allakaket, Yukon-Koyukuk, Pop. 92
Yukon-Koyukuk SD
Supt. — See Fairbanks
Allakaket S 50/PK-12
PO Box 69 99720 907-968-2205
Nancy Mason, prin. Fax 968-2250

Ambler, Northwest Arctic, Pop. 328
Northwest Arctic Borough SD
Supt. — See Kotzebue
Ambler S 100/PK-12
PO Box 109 99786 907-445-2154
Sherry McKenzie, prin. Fax 445-2159

Anaktuvuk Pass, North Slope, Pop. 262
North Slope Borough SD
Supt. — See Barrow
Nunamiut S 100/PK-12
PO Box 21029 99721 907-661-3226
Brian Freeman, prin. Fax 661-3402

Anchorage, Anchorage, Pop. 275,043
Aleutian Region SD 50/K-12
PO Box 92230 99509 907-277-2648
Joe Beckford, supt. Fax 277-2649
www.aleutregion.org
Other Schools – See Adak, Atka, Nikolski

Anchorage SD 47,200/PK-12
5530 E Northern Lights Blvd 99504 907-742-4000
Carol Comeau, supt. Fax 742-4318
www.asdk12.org
Abbott Loop ES 500/K-6
8427 Lake Otis Pkwy 99507 907-742-5400
Robin Pfannstiel, prin. Fax 742-5411
Airport Heights ES 300/PK-6
1510 Alder Dr 99508 907-742-4550
Mike Webb, prin. Fax 742-4570
Baxter ES 400/K-6
2991 Baxter Rd 99504 907-742-1750
Vicki Hodge, prin. Fax 742-1777
Bayshore ES 600/PK-6
10500 Bayshore Dr 99515 907-742-5360
Ben Hardwick, prin. Fax 742-5399
Bear Valley ES 500/K-6
15001 Mountain Air Dr 99516 907-742-5900
Linda Carlson, prin. Fax 742-5909
Begich MS 7-8
7440 Creekside Center Dr 99504 907-742-0500
Jeanne Fischer, prin. Fax 742-0510
Bowman ES 500/PK-6
11700 Gregory Rd 99516 907-742-5600
Darrell Vincek, prin. Fax 742-5611
Campbell ES 400/PK-6
7206 Rovenna St 99518 907-742-5560
Leroy Grant, prin. Fax 742-5575
Central MS of Science 500/7-8
1405 E St 99501 907-742-5100
Lisa Zelenkov, prin. Fax 742-5125
Chester Valley ES 300/PK-6
1751 Patterson St 99504 907-742-0335
Sharon Mitchell, prin. Fax 742-0350
Chinook ES 500/PK-6
3101 W 88th Ave 99502 907-742-6700
Jon Forbes, prin. Fax 742-6722
Chugach Optional ES 300/PK-6
1205 E St 99501 907-742-3730
Anne Salzer, prin. Fax 742-3747
Clark MS 800/7-8
150 Bragaw St 99508 907-742-4700
Cessilye Williams, prin. Fax 742-4756
College Gate ES 400/PK-6
3101 Sunflower St 99508 907-742-1500
Sue Liebner, prin. Fax 742-1515
Creekside Park ES 400/PK-6
7500 E 6th Ave 99504 907-742-1550
Robyn Rehmann, prin. Fax 742-1577
Denali S 400/PK-8
952 Cordova St 99501 907-742-4500
Brooke Hull, prin. Fax 742-4520
Fairview ES 400/PK-6
1327 Nelchina St 99501 907-742-7600
Roger LeBlanc, prin. Fax 742-7616
Goldenview MS 900/7-8
15800 Golden View Dr 99516 907-348-8626
Julie Maker, prin. Fax 742-8273
Government Hill ES 500/K-6
525 E Bluff Dr 99501 907-742-5000
Brian Singleton, prin. Fax 742-5015
Hanshew MS 900/7-8
10121 Lake Otis Pkwy 99507 907-349-1561
Sherry Ellers, prin. Fax 349-2835
Huffman ES 400/PK-6
12000 Lorraine St 99516 907-742-5650
Kris Bjornson, prin. Fax 742-5660
Inlet View ES 200/K-6
1219 N St 99501 907-742-7630
Kathy Iversen, prin. Fax 742-7650
Kasuun ES 500/PK-6
4000 E 68th Ave 99507 907-349-9444
Michael Day, prin. Fax 349-9402
Kincaid ES 500/PK-6
4900 Raspberry Rd 99502 907-245-5530
Mike Hanley, prin. Fax 245-5535
Klatt ES 400/PK-6
11900 Puma St 99515 907-742-5750
Debra Washington, prin. Fax 742-5757
Lake Hood ES 400/K-6
3601 W 40th Ave 99517 907-245-5521
Bonnie Whitney, prin. Fax 245-5528
Lake Otis ES 400/PK-6
3331 Lake Otis Pkwy 99508 907-742-7400
Dan Blanton, prin. Fax 742-7407
Mears MS 1,100/7-8
2700 W 100th Ave 99515 907-742-6400
Michael Perkins, prin. Fax 742-6444
Mountain View ES 400/K-6
4005 Mcphee Ave 99508 907-742-3900
Chris Woodward, prin. Fax 742-3911
Muldoon ES 400/PK-6
525 Cherry St 99504 907-742-1460
Ruth Dene, prin. Fax 742-1477
Northern Lights ABC S 600/K-8
2424 E Dowling Rd 99507 907-742-7500
Karen Wallace, prin. Fax 742-7530
North Star ES 400/PK-6
605 W Fireweed Ln 99503 907-742-3800
Cindy Bledsoe, prin. Fax 742-3822
Northwood ABC ES 300/PK-6
4807 Northwood Dr 99517 907-742-6800
Greg Balcao, prin. Fax 742-6822
Nunaka Valley ES 300/K-6
1905 Twining Dr 99504 907-742-0366
Jacqui Gorlick, prin. Fax 742-0393
Ocean View ES 500/PK-6
11911 Johns Rd 99515 907-742-5850
Maria Kreta-Dillon, prin. Fax 742-5885
O'Malley ES 300/PK-6
11100 Rockridge Dr 99516 907-742-5800
Leslie Walker, prin. Fax 742-5822
Ptarmigan ES 400/K-6
888 Edward St 99504 907-742-0400
Lori Cheek, prin. Fax 742-0425
Rabbit Creek ES 400/PK-6
13650 Lake Otis Pkwy 99516 907-742-5700
Mary Johnstone, prin. Fax 742-5711
Rogers Park ES 600/PK-6
1400 E Northern Lights Blvd 99508 907-742-4800
Brandon Locke, prin. Fax 742-4815
Romig MS 800/7-8
2500 Minnesota Dr 99503 907-742-5200
Sven Gustafson, prin. Fax 742-5252
Russian Jack ES 400/PK-6
4300 E 20th Ave 99508 907-742-1300
Sharon Story, prin. Fax 742-1341
Sand Lake ES 700/K-6
7500 Jewel Lake Rd 99502 907-243-2161
Patrick Garrity, prin. Fax 243-6025
Scenic Park ES 400/K-6
3933 Patterson St 99504 907-742-1650
Karen Pollard, prin. Fax 742-1677
Spring Hill ES 400/PK-6
9911 Lake Otis Pkwy 99507 907-742-5450
Lana Bailey, prin. Fax 742-5477
Susitna ES 600/PK-6
7500 Tyone Ct 99504 907-742-1400
Kim Bautista, prin. Fax 742-1418
Taku ES 400/PK-6
701 E 72nd Ave 99518 907-742-5940
Gale O'Connell-Smith, prin. Fax 742-5959
Trailside ES 500/PK-6
5151 Abbott Rd 99507 907-742-5500
Patrick Freeman, prin. Fax 742-5511
Tudor ES 600/PK-6
1666 Cache Dr 99507 907-742-1050
Michelle Prince, prin. Fax 742-1066
Turnagain ES 400/PK-6
3500 W Northern Lights Blvd 99517 907-742-7200
Meg Marman, prin. Fax 742-7207
Tyson ES 400/PK-6
2801 Richmond Ave 99508 907-742-8000
John Kito, prin. Fax 742-8008
Wendler MS 800/7-8
2905 Lake Otis Pkwy 99508 907-742-7300
Joel Roylance, prin. Fax 742-7307
Williwaw ES 400/K-6
1200 San Antonio St 99508 907-742-2000
Bonnie Goen, prin. Fax 742-2020
Willow Crest ES 400/K-6
1004 W Tudor Rd 99503 907-742-1000
Diane Hoffbauer, prin. Fax 742-1044
Wonder Park ES 400/K-6
5101 E 4th Ave 99508 907-337-1569
Mischelle Bain, prin. Fax 337-2046
Wood ES 500/PK-6
7001 Cranberry St 99502 907-742-6760
Jennifer Schmitz, prin. Fax 742-6779
Other Schools – See Chugiak, Eagle River, Elmendorf AFB, Fort Richardson, Girdwood

Chugach SD 200/PK-12
9312 Vanguard Dr Ste 100 99507 907-522-7400
Bob Crumley, supt. Fax 522-3399
www.chugachschools.com
Other Schools – See Chenega Bay, Tatitlek, Whittier

Anchorage Christian S 700/PK-12
6575 E Northern Lights Blvd 99504 907-337-9575
Tom Cobaugh, admin. Fax 338-3903
Anchorage Junior Academy 50/K-10
5511 OMalley Rd 99507 907-346-2164
Fax 346-1332
Anchorage Montessori S 200/PK-6
5001 Northwood Dr 99517 907-276-2240
Stephen O'Brien, prin. Fax 258-3552
Anchor Lutheran S 200/PK-8
8100 Arctic Blvd 99518 907-522-3636
Fax 522-3359
Aurora Waldorf S of Alaska 100/PK-8
3250 Baxter Rd 99504 907-333-9062
Fax 338-9362
Faith Lutheran S 100/K-8
5200 Lake Otis Pkwy 99507 907-563-3499
Bryan Schneck, prin. Fax 563-6057
Gateway S and Learning Center 50/K-12
PO Box 113149 99511 907-522-2240
Jon Meissner, dir. Fax 344-0304
Grace Christian S 700/K-12
12407 Pintail St 99516 907-868-1203
Nate Davis, supt. Fax 644-2261
Heritage Christian S 100/PK-12
9251 Lake Otis Pkwy 99507 907-349-8032
Mary Day, prin. Fax 349-8275
Pacific Northern Academy 100/PK-8
550 Bragaw St 99508 907-333-1080
Mark Niedermier, hdmstr. Fax 333-1652
St. Elizabeth Ann Seton S 200/K-6
2901 Huffman Rd 99516 907-345-3712
James Bailey, prin. Fax 345-2910

Anchor Point, Kenai Peninsula, Pop. 866
Kenai Peninsula Borough SD
Supt. — See Soldotna
Chapman S 100/K-8
PO Box 1109 99556 907-235-8671
Sharon Conley, prin. Fax 235-5460

Anderson, Denali, Pop. 324
Denali Borough SD
Supt. — See Healy
Anderson S 100/K-12
PO Box 3120 99744 907-582-2700
William Beaudoin, prin. Fax 582-2000

Angoon, Skagway-Hoonah-Angoon, Pop. 481
Chatham SD 200/K-12
PO Box 109 99820 907-788-3302
Fax 788-3252
www.chathamsd.org/
Angoon S 100/K-12
PO Box 209 99820 907-788-3811
Shane Hill, prin. Fax 788-3812
Other Schools – See Gustavus, Haines, Tenakee Springs

Aniak, Bethel, Pop. 581
Kuspuk SD 400/PK-12
PO Box 49 99557 907-675-4250
Brad Allen, supt. Fax 675-4305
www.kuspuk.org
Nicoli ES 100/PK-6
PO Box 29 99557 907-675-4363
John Fremin, prin. Fax 675-4247
Other Schools – See Chuathbaluk, Crooked Creek, Kalskag, Lower Kalskag, Red Devil, Sleetmute, Stony River

Anvik, Yukon-Koyukuk, Pop. 98
Iditarod Area SD
Supt. — See Mc Grath
Blackwell S 50/K-12
PO Box 90 99558 907-663-6348
Jolene Kinsland, prin. Fax 663-6349

Arctic Village, Yukon-Koyukuk, Pop. 96
Yukon Flats SD
Supt. — See Fort Yukon
Arctic Village S 50/PK-12
PO Box 22049 99722 907-587-5211
Fax 587-5210

Atka, Aleutians West, Pop. 81
Aleutian Region SD
Supt. — See Anchorage
Netsvetov S 50/K-12
PO Box 47050 99547 907-839-2210
Lynne Moore, lead tchr. Fax 839-2212

Atmautluak, Bethel, Pop. 258
Lower Kuskokwim SD
Supt. — See Bethel
Alexie Memorial S 100/PK-12
PO Box ATT 99559 907-553-5112
Michael Willyard, prin. Fax 553-5129

Atqasuk, North Slope, Pop. 212
North Slope Borough SD
Supt. — See Barrow
Meade River S 100/PK-12
General Delivery 99791 907-633-6315
Becky Crabtree, prin. Fax 633-6215

Barrow, North Slope, Pop. 4,218
North Slope Borough SD 1,800/PK-12
PO Box 169 99723 907-852-5311
Dr. Trent Blankenship, supt. Fax 852-9503
www.nsbsd.org/
Hopson Memorial MS 200/6-8
PO Box 509 99723 907-852-3880
Michael Seifert, prin. Fax 852-7794
Ipalook ES 600/PK-5
PO Box 450 99723 907-852-4711
Jennifer Litera, prin. Fax 852-4713
Other Schools – See Anaktuvuk Pass, Atqasuk, Kaktovik, Nuiqsut, Point Hope, Point Lay, Wainwright

Beaver, Yukon-Koyukuk, Pop. 103
Yukon Flats SD
Supt. — See Fort Yukon
Beaver S 50/PK-12
PO Box 24050 99724 907-628-6313
Charlene Fisher, prin. Fax 628-6615

Bethel, Bethel, Pop. 6,262
Lower Kuskokwim SD 3,900/PK-12
PO Box 305 99559 907-543-4800
Gary Baldwin, supt. Fax 543-4904
www.lksd.org
Kilbuck ES 300/3-6
PO Box 800 99559 907-543-4440
Gerry Kimsey-Shaw, prin. Fax 543-2533
Mikelnguut Elitnaurviat ES 300/K-2
PO Box 900 99559 907-543-2845
Josh Gill, prin. Fax 543-2429
Other Schools – See Atmautluak, Chefornak, Eek, Goodnews Bay, Kasigluk, Kipnuk, Kongiganak, Kwethluk, Kwigillingok, Mekoryuk, Napakiak, Napaskiak, Newtok, Nightmute, Nunapitchuk, Platinum, Quinhagak, Toksook Bay, Tuntutuliak, Tununak

Big Lake, Matanuska-Susitna, Pop. 1,477
Matanuska-Susitna Borough SD
Supt. — See Palmer
Big Lake ES 400/PK-6
PO Box 520049 99652 907-892-6019
Mark Vingoe, prin. Fax 892-6208
Houston MS 400/6-8
PO Box 520920 99652 907-892-9500
Andrew Murr, prin. Fax 892-9560

Brevig Mission, Nome, Pop. 278
Bering Strait SD
Supt. — See Unalakleet
Brevig Mission S 100/PK-12
General Delivery 99785 907-642-4021
Robin Gray, prin. Fax 642-4031

Buckland, Northwest Arctic, Pop. 430
Northwest Arctic Borough SD
Supt. — See Kotzebue
Buckland S 200/PK-12
PO Box 91 99727 907-494-2127
Terri Walker, prin. Fax 494-2106

Cantwell, Denali, Pop. 147
Denali Borough SD
Supt. — See Healy
Cantwell S 50/K-12
PO Box 29 99729 907-768-2372
Pete Hauschka, prin. Fax 768-2500

Central, Yukon-Koyukuk, Pop. 52
Yukon Flats SD
Supt. — See Fort Yukon
Central S 50/K-12
PO Box 30049 99730 907-520-5114
Jack Von Thaer, prin. Fax 520-5151

Chalkyitsik, Yukon-Koyukuk, Pop. 90
Yukon Flats SD
Supt. — See Fort Yukon
Chalkyitski S 50/PK-12
General Delivery 99788 907-848-8113
Margaret Waldrup, prin. Fax 848-8312

Chefornak, Bethel, Pop. 400
Lower Kuskokwim SD
Supt. — See Bethel
Chaptnquak S 200/PK-12
PO Box 50 99561 907-867-8700
Bruce Sheehan, prin. Fax 867-8727

Chenega Bay, Valdez-Cordova, Pop. 94
Chugach SD
Supt. — See Anchorage
Chenega Bay Community S 50/PK-12
PO Box 8030 99574 907-573-5123
Steve Grajewski, prin. Fax 573-5137

Chevak, Wade Hampton, Pop. 819
Kashunamiut SD 300/K-12
PO Box 345 99563 907-858-7713
Leslie Kramer, supt. Fax 858-7328
www.chevak.org/
Chevak S 300/K-12
PO Box 345 99563 907-858-7712
Delbert Lantz, prin. Fax 858-6150

Chignik, Lake and Peninsula, Pop. 67
Lake & Peninsula SD
Supt. — See King Salmon
Chignik Bay S 50/K-12
PO Box 9 99564 907-749-2213
Kary Hawkins, prin. Fax 749-2261

Chignik Lagoon, Lake and Peninsula, Pop. 53
Lake & Peninsula SD
Supt. — See King Salmon
Chignik Lagoon S 50/K-12
PO Box 50 99565 907-840-2210
Kary Hawkins, prin. Fax 840-2265

Chignik Lake, Lake and Peninsula, Pop. 133
Lake & Peninsula SD
Supt. — See King Salmon
Chignik Lake S 50/K-12
General Delivery 99548 907-845-2210
Mike Flanagan, prin. Fax 845-2254

Chiniak, Kodiak Island, Pop. 69
Kodiak Island Borough SD
Supt. — See Kodiak
Chiniak S 50/K-10
PO Box 5529 99615 907-486-8323
Fax 486-3185

Chuathbaluk, Bethel, Pop. 121
Kuspuk SD
Supt. — See Aniak
Crow Village Sam S 50/PK-12
PO Box CHU 99557 907-467-4229
Susan Hubbard, prin. Fax 467-4122

Chugiak, See Anchorage
Anchorage SD
Supt. — See Anchorage
Birchwood ABC S 300/PK-6
17010 Birchtree St 99567 907-742-3450
Dan Reed, prin. Fax 742-3495
Chugiak ES 500/PK-5
19932 Old Glenn Hwy 99567 907-742-3400
Susan Schmidt, prin. Fax 742-3411
Mirror Lake MS 700/6-8
22901 Lake Hill Dr 99567 907-742-3500
Scott Batchelder, prin. Fax 742-3545

Circle, Yukon-Koyukuk, Pop. 73
Yukon Flats SD
Supt. — See Fort Yukon
Circle S 50/PK-12
PO Box 49 99733 907-773-1250
Brian Rozell, prin. Fax 773-1259

Clarks Point, Dillingham, Pop. 58
Southwest Region SD
Supt. — See Dillingham
Clarks Point S 50/K-8
PO Box 29 99569 907-236-1218
Douglas Bushey, lead tchr. Fax 236-1285

Coffman Cove, Prince of Wales-Outer Ketchikan, Pop. 180
Southeast Island SD
Supt. — See Thorne Bay
Valentine S 50/K-12
PO Box 18002 99918 907-329-2244
Seth Darling, lead tchr. Fax 329-2210

Cold Bay, Aleutians East, Pop. 81
Aleutian East Borough SD
Supt. — See Sand Point
Cold Bay S 50/PK-12
PO Box 128 99571 907-532-2409
Ty DeVault, prin. Fax 532-2421

Cooper Landing, Kenai Peninsula, Pop. 243
Kenai Peninsula Borough SD
Supt. — See Soldotna
Cooper Landing S 50/K-8
PO Box 990 99572 907-595-1244
Jim Dawson, prin. Fax 595-1461

Copper Center, Valdez-Cordova, Pop. 449
Copper River SD
Supt. — See Glennallen
Copper Center ES 50/K-6
PO Box D 99573 907-822-3394
Byron Rice, prin. Fax 822-5843
Kenny Lake S 100/1-12
HC 60 Box 224 99573 907-822-3870
Sue Moore, lead tchr. Fax 822-3794

Cordova, Valdez-Cordova, Pop. 2,327
Cordova CSD 400/PK-12
PO Box 140 99574 907-424-3265
Jim Nygaard, supt. Fax 424-3271
cordovasd.org/
Mount Eccles ES 200/PK-6
PO Box 140 99574 907-424-3236
Frank Wicks, prin. Fax 424-3117

Craig, Prince of Wales-Outer Ketchikan, Pop. 1,217
Craig CSD 400/PK-12
PO Box 800 99921 907-826-3274
Jim Thomas, supt. Fax 826-3322
www.craigschools.com
Craig ES 100/PK-5
PO Box 800 99921 907-826-3274
Cassandra Bennett, prin. Fax 826-3322
Craig MS 100/6-8
PO Box 800 99921 907-826-3274
Cassandra Bennett, prin. Fax 826-3309

Southeast Island SD
Supt. — See Thorne Bay
Hollis S 50/K-12
PO Box 803 99921 907-530-7108
Julie Vasquez, lead tchr. Fax 530-7111

Crooked Creek, Bethel, Pop. 106
Kuspuk SD
Supt. — See Aniak
John S 50/PK-12
PO Box 20 99575 907-432-2205
Susan Hubbard, prin. Fax 432-2206

Deering, Northwest Arctic, Pop. 144
Northwest Arctic Borough SD
Supt. — See Kotzebue
Deering S 50/PK-12
PO Box 36009 99736 907-363-2121
Paul Clark, lead tchr. Fax 363-2128

Delta Junction, Southeast Fairbanks, Pop. 897
Delta-Greely SD 1,400/PK-12
PO Box 527 99737 907-895-4657
P.J. Ford Slack Ph.D., supt. Fax 895-4781
www.dgsd.k12.ak.us/
Delta Junction ES 400/PK-5
PO Box 647 99737 907-895-4696
Michelle Beito, prin. Fax 895-4051
Gerstle River S 50/PK-12
PO Box 527 99737 907-895-4655
Dr. Duncan Ware, prin. Fax 895-4246

Other Schools – See Fort Greely

Dillingham, Dillingham, Pop. 2,468
Dillingham CSD 500/PK-12
PO Box 170 99576 907-842-5223
Darlene Triplett, supt. Fax 842-5634
Dillingham ES 300/PK-5
PO Box 170 99576 907-842-5642
Marilyn Rosene, prin. Fax 842-4313

Southwest Region SD 700/K-12
PO Box 90 99576 907-842-5287
Jack Foster, supt. Fax 842-5428
dlg.swrsd.org/do/doHomePage.shtml
Other Schools – See Aleknagik, Clarks Point, Ekwok, Koliganek, Manokotak, New Stuyahok, Togiak, Twin Hills

---

Dillingham Adventist S 50/1-8
PO Box 969 99576 907-842-2496

Diomede, Nome, Pop. 147
Bering Strait SD
Supt. — See Unalakleet
Diomede S 50/PK-12
PO Box 7099 99762 907-686-3021
Sandra Quinn, prin. Fax 686-3022

Dot Lake, Southeast Fairbanks, Pop. 70
Alaska Gateway SD
Supt. — See Tok
Dot Lake S 50/K-12
PO Box 2280 99737 907-882-2663
Gordon Kron, prin. Fax 882-2112

Eagle, Southeast Fairbanks, Pop. 139
Alaska Gateway SD
Supt. — See Tok
Eagle Community S 50/K-12
PO Box 168 99738 907-547-2210
Ann Millard, prin. Fax 547-2302

Eagle River, See Anchorage
Anchorage SD
Supt. — See Anchorage
Alpenglow ES 500/PK-6
19201 Driftwood Bay Dr 99577 907-742-3300
Richard Toymil, prin. Fax 742-3348
Eagle River ES 400/PK-6
10900 Old Eagle River Rd 99577 907-742-3000
Nicole Ertischek, prin. Fax 742-3020
Fire Lake ES 300/PK-5
13801 Harry Mc Donald Rd 99577 907-742-3350
Lindsay Henry, prin. Fax 742-3366
Gruening MS 600/7-8
9601 Lee St 99577 907-742-3600
Bobby Jefts, prin. Fax 742-3666
Homestead ES 400/K-6
18001 Baronoff Ave 99577 907-742-3550
Barbara Nagengast, prin. Fax 742-3567
Ravenwood ES 400/PK-6
9500 Wren Cir 99577 907-742-3250
Audrey Chapman, prin. Fax 742-3260

Eagle River Christian S 100/K-12
10336 E Eagle River Loop Rd 99577 907-694-7331
Denny Archer, admin. Fax 694-7316

Eek, Bethel, Pop. 285
Lower Kuskokwim SD
Supt. — See Bethel
Eek S 100/PK-12
PO Box 50 99578 907-536-5228
Kip Layton, prin. Fax 536-5628

Egegik, Lake and Peninsula, Pop. 99
Lake & Peninsula SD
Supt. — See King Salmon
Egegik S 50/K-12
PO Box 10 99579 907-233-2210
Reta Doland, prin. Fax 233-2254

Eielson AFB, Fairbanks North Star, Pop. 5,251
Fairbanks-North Star Borough SD
Supt. — See Fairbanks
Anderson ES 400/PK-3
768 Kodiak St 99702 907-372-2167
Shari Merrick, prin. Fax 372-3437
Crawford ES 400/3-6
692 Ravens Way 99702 907-372-3306
Shirley Brazel, prin. Fax 372-3199

Ekwok, Dillingham, Pop. 130
Southwest Region SD
Supt. — See Dillingham
Nelson S 99580 50/K-8
Stan Dancer, lead tchr. 907-464-3344
Fax 464-3318

Elim, Nome, Pop. 316
Bering Strait SD
Supt. — See Unalakleet
Aniguiin S 100/PK-12
PO Box 29 99739 907-890-3041
Steve Petz, prin. Fax 890-3031

Elmendorf AFB, Anchorage
Anchorage SD
Supt. — See Anchorage
Aurora ES 400/PK-6
5085 10th St 99506 907-742-0300
Gary Webb, prin. Fax 742-0322
Mt. Spurr ES 300/PK-6
8414 Mcguire Ave 99506 907-742-0200
Helen Mullings, prin. Fax 742-0215
Orion ES 400/PK-6
5112 Arctic Warrior Dr 99506 907-742-0250
Ruth Tweto, prin. Fax 742-0265

Emmonak, Wade Hampton, Pop. 823
Lower Yukon SD
Supt. — See Mountain Village
Emmonak S 300/PK-12
General Delivery 99581 907-949-1248
William Sprott, prin. Fax 949-1148

Fairbanks, Fairbanks North Star, Pop. 31,324
Fairbanks-North Star Borough SD 14,400/PK-12
520 5th Ave 99701 907-452-2000
Dr. Nancy Wagner, supt. Fax 451-0541
www.northstar.k12.ak.us
Badger Road ES 600/PK-6
520 5th Ave 99701 907-488-0134
Dan File, prin. Fax 488-2045
Barnette Magnet S 400/K-8
1000 Barnette St 99701 907-456-6072
Kathie Weaver, prin. Fax 451-9602
Brown ES 500/K-6
520 5th Ave 99701 907-488-3200
Toni McFadden, prin. Fax 488-6208
Denali ES 400/PK-6
1042 Lathrop St 99701 907-452-2456
Tim Doran, prin. Fax 451-0792
Hunter ES 300/PK-6
1630 Gillam Way 99701 907-456-5775
Barbara Pile, prin. Fax 452-8891
Joy ES 400/PK-6
24 Margaret Ave 99701 907-456-5469
David Foshee, prin. Fax 456-1477
Ladd ES 400/PK-6
601 F St 99701 907-451-1700
Kathie Cook, prin. Fax 451-9137
Nordale ES 400/PK-6
397 Hamilton Ave 99701 907-452-2696
Barbara Burch, prin. Fax 456-5608
North Pole ES 500/PK-6
250 Snowman Ln 99705 907-488-2286
Kathy Beebe, prin. Fax 488-1232
Pearl Creek ES 400/PK-6
700 Auburn Dr 99709 907-479-4234
Kate LaPlaunt, prin. Fax 479-4025
Ryan MS 400/7-8
951 Airport Way 99701 907-452-4751
Heather Stewart, prin. Fax 451-8834
Salcha ES 100/K-6
520 5th Ave 99701 907-488-3267
Linda Kang, prin. Fax 488-5358
Smith MS 400/7-8
1401 Bainbridge Blvd 99701 907-458-7600
Sandy Kowalski, prin. Fax 458-7676
Tanana MS 500/7-8
600 Trainor Gate Rd 99701 907-452-8145
Edwina Strange, prin. Fax 456-2780
Two Rivers S 100/K-8
520 5th Ave 99701 907-488-6616
Dana Evans, prin. Fax 488-8487
University Park ES 500/PK-6
554 Loftus Rd 99709 907-479-6963
Kyra Aizstrauts, prin. Fax 479-6219
Weller ES 500/PK-6
520 5th Ave 99701 907-457-1629
Mary Carlson, prin. Fax 457-2663
Wien ES 500/PK-6
1501 Hampstead Ave 99701 907-451-7500
Leslie Campbell, prin. Fax 451-7564
Woodriver ES 500/PK-6
5000 Palo Verde Ave 99709 907-479-4211
Star Patterson, prin. Fax 479-5077
Other Schools – See Eielson AFB, Fort Wainwright, North Pole

Yukon-Koyukuk SD 300/PK-12
4762 Old Airport Way 99709 907-374-9400
Kerry Boyd, supt. Fax 374-9440
www.yksd.com
Other Schools – See Allakaket, Hughes, Huslia, Kaltag, Koyukuk, Manley Hot Springs, Minto, Nulato, Ruby

---

Fairhill Christian S 200/PK-12
101 City Lights Blvd 99712 907-457-2167
Marilyn Buchanan, prin. Fax 457-4382
Far North Christian S 100/PK-12
1110 20th Ave 99701 907-452-7979
Kevin Taylor, admin. Fax 452-5327
Golden Heart Christian S 50/1-8
PO Box 82997 99708 907-479-2904
Immaculate Conception S 300/PK-6
615 Monroe St 99701 907-456-4574
Amanda Angaiak, prin. Fax 456-7481
Open Arms - Zion Lutheran S 200/PK-K
2980 Davis Rd 99709 907-455-9466
Lenetta Colbert, dir. Fax 455-7208

False Pass, Aleutians East, Pop. 59
Aleutian East Borough SD
Supt. — See Sand Point
False Pass S 50/PK-12
PO Box 30 99583 907-548-2224
Ernest McKay, prin. Fax 548-2304

Fort Greely, Southeast Fairbanks, Pop. 1,147
Delta-Greely SD
Supt. — See Delta Junction
Ft. Greely S 200/6-8
Building 725, 907-869-3105
Patrick Mayer, prin. Fax 869-3382

Fort Richardson, Anchorage
Anchorage SD
Supt. — See Anchorage
Ursa Major ES 400/PK-6
454 Dyea Ave 99505 907-742-1600
Bobby Hinderliter, prin. Fax 742-1616
Ursa Minor ES 300/PK-6
336 Hoonah Ave 99505 907-428-1311
Wendy Brons, prin. Fax 428-1346

Fort Wainwright, Fairbanks North Star
Fairbanks-North Star Borough SD
Supt. — See Fairbanks
Arctic Light ES 500/PK-6
4167 Neely Rd 99703 907-356-2038
Bill Martin-Muth, prin. Fax 356-2189

Fort Yukon, Yukon-Koyukuk, Pop. 561
Yukon Flats SD 300/PK-12
PO Box 350 99740 907-662-2515
Bill Walz, supt. Fax 662-2519
www.yukonflats.net
Fort Yukon S 100/PK-12
PO Box 129 99740 907-662-2352
Doug Woods, prin. Fax 662-2958
Other Schools – See Arctic Village, Beaver, Central, Chalkyitsik, Circle, Stevens Village, Venetie

Fritz Creek, Kenai Peninsula, Pop. 1,426
Kenai Peninsula Borough SD
Supt. — See Soldotna
Kachemak Selo S 100/K-12
PO Box 15007 99603 907-235-5552
Randy Creamer, prin. Fax 235-5644
Voznesenka S 100/K-12
PO Box 15336 99603 907-235-8549
Alex Trout, prin. Fax 235-6086

Galena, Yukon-Koyukuk, Pop. 641
Galena CSD 100/PK-12
PO Box 299 99741 907-656-1205
Jim Smith, supt. Fax 656-2238
www.galenaalaska.org
Huntington ES 100/PK-6
PO Box 299 99741 907-656-1205
Chris Reitan, prin. Fax 656-1368

Gambell, Nome, Pop. 653
Bering Strait SD
Supt. — See Unalakleet
Gambell S 200/PK-12
PO Box 169 99742 907-985-5515
John Bruce, prin. Fax 985-5435

Girdwood, See Anchorage
Anchorage SD
Supt. — See Anchorage
Girdwood S 100/PK-8
PO Box 189 99587 907-742-5300
Kathy Recken, prin. Fax 742-5320

Glennallen, Valdez-Cordova, Pop. 451
Copper River SD 500/K-12
PO Box 108 99588 907-822-3234
Michael Johnson, supt. Fax 822-3949
www.crsd.k12.ak.us
Chistochina S 50/K-8
Mile 33 Tok Cutoff 99588 907-822-3854
Bob Snedigar, prin. Fax 822-3854
Glennallen ES 100/K-6
PO Box 108 99588 907-822-3232
Tammy VanWyhe, prin. Fax 822-8500
Other Schools – See Copper Center, Slana

Golovin, Nome, Pop. 145
Bering Strait SD
Supt. — See Unalakleet
Olson S 50/PK-12
PO Box 62040 99762 907-779-3021
Margaret Koegler, prin. Fax 779-3031

Goodnews Bay, Bethel, Pop. 234
Lower Kuskokwim SD
Supt. — See Bethel
Rocky Mountain S 100/PK-12
PO Box 153 99589 907-967-8213
Christopher Carmichael, prin. Fax 967-8228

Grayling, Yukon-Koyukuk, Pop. 184
Iditarod Area SD
Supt. — See Mc Grath
David-Louis Memorial S 50/K-12
PO Box 90 99590 907-453-5135
Matthew Brankman, prin. Fax 453-5165

Gustavus, Skagway-Hoonah-Angoon, Pop. 380
Chatham SD
Supt. — See Angoon
Gustavus S 50/K-12
PO Box 120 99826 907-697-2248
David McCourtney, prin. Fax 697-2378

Haines, Haines, Pop. 1,265
Chatham SD
Supt. — See Angoon
Klukwan S 50/K-12
PO Box 1409 99827 907-767-5551
Fax 767-5573

Haines Borough SD 300/PK-12
PO Box 1289 99827 907-766-6725
Michael Byer, supt. Fax 766-6794
glacierbears.hbsd.net/
Haines S 200/PK-8
PO Box 1289 99827 907-766-6700
Cheryl Stickler, prin. Fax 766-6791
Mosquito Lake S 50/K-8
PO Box 1289 99827 907-767-5527
Cheryl Stickler, prin. Fax 767-5527

Healy, Denali, Pop. 487
Denali Borough SD 600/K-12
PO Box 280 99743 907-683-2278
Kim Langton, supt. Fax 683-2514
denali.ak.schoolwebpages.com/
Tri-Valley S 200/K-12
PO Box 400 99743 907-683-2267
Robyn Taylor, prin. Fax 683-2632
Other Schools – See Anderson, Cantwell

Holy Cross, Yukon-Koyukuk, Pop. 215
Iditarod Area SD
Supt. — See Mc Grath
Holy Cross S 50/K-12
PO Box 210 99602 907-476-7131
Jeff Bader, prin. Fax 476-7161

Homer, Kenai Peninsula, Pop. 5,364
Kenai Peninsula Borough SD
Supt. — See Soldotna
Banks ES 200/K-2
1340 E End Rd 99603 907-226-1801
Benny Abraham, prin. Fax 235-8163
Homer MS 200/7-8
500 Sterling Hwy 99603 907-235-5700
Lisa Nissly, prin. Fax 235-5747
McNeil Canyon ES 100/K-6
52188 E End Rd 99603 907-235-8181
Peter Swanson, prin. Fax 235-8183
Razdolna S 50/K-12
PO Box 15098 99603 907-235-6870
Douglas Waclawski, prin. Fax 235-6485
West Homer ES 200/3-6
995 Soundview Ave 99603 907-235-5750
Charlie Walsworth, prin. Fax 235-2612

Hoonah, Skagway-Hoonah-Angoon, Pop. 751
Hoonah CSD 100/PK-12
PO Box 157 99829 907-945-3611
Steve Pine, supt. Fax 945-3492
Hoonah ES 100/PK-6
PO Box 157 99829 907-945-3613
Steve Pine, prin. Fax 945-3607

Hooper Bay, Wade Hampton, Pop. 1,085
Lower Yukon SD
Supt. — See Mountain Village
Hooper Bay S 300/PK-12
General Delivery 99604 907-758-4826
Scott Ballard, prin. Fax 758-4012

Hope, Kenai Peninsula, Pop. 161
Kenai Peninsula Borough SD
Supt. — See Soldotna
Hope S 50/K-12
PO Box 47 99605 907-782-3202
Jim Dawson, admin. Fax 782-3140

Hughes, Yukon-Koyukuk, Pop. 74
Yukon-Koyukuk SD
Supt. — See Fairbanks
Oldman S 50/K-12
PO Box 30 99745 907-889-2204
Bob Hawkins, prin. Fax 889-2220

Huslia, Yukon-Koyukuk, Pop. 277
Yukon-Koyukuk SD
Supt. — See Fairbanks
Huntington S 100/PK-12
PO Box 110 99746 907-829-2205
Doug Woods, prin. Fax 829-2270

Hydaburg, Prince of Wales-Outer Ketchikan, Pop. 351
Hydaburg CSD 100/K-12
PO Box 109 99922 907-285-3491
Don Johnson, supt. Fax 285-3391
Hydaburg S 100/K-12
PO Box 109 99922 907-285-3591
Don Johnson, prin. Fax 285-3391

Hyder, Prince of Wales-Outer Ketchikan, Pop. 99
Southeast Island SD
Supt. — See Thorne Bay
Hyder S 50/K-12
PO Box 110 99923 250-636-2100
Kathy Shirley, lead tchr. Fax 636-2112

Igiugig, Lake and Peninsula, Pop. 33
Lake & Peninsula SD
Supt. — See King Salmon
Igiugig S 50/K-12
PO Box 4010 99613 907-533-3220
Todd Washburn, prin. Fax 533-3221

Iliamna, Lake and Peninsula, Pop. 94
Lake & Peninsula SD
Supt. — See King Salmon
Newhalen S 100/K-12
PO Box 89 99606 907-571-1211
Adam Mokelke, prin. Fax 571-1466

Juneau, Juneau, Pop. 30,987
Juneau Borough SD 5,000/PK-12
10014 Crazy Horse Dr 99801 907-523-1700
Glenn Gelbrich, supt. Fax 523-1708
www.jsd.k12.ak.us
Auke Bay ES 300/K-5
10014 Crazy Horse Dr 99801 907-463-1775
Lori Hoover, prin. Fax 463-1751
Dryden MS 600/6-8
10014 Crazy Horse Dr 99801 907-463-1850
Tom Milliron, prin. Fax 463-1828
Gastineau ES 200/K-5
10014 Crazy Horse Dr 99801 907-463-1999
Angie Lunda, prin. Fax 463-1997
Glacier Valley ES 400/K-5
10014 Crazy Horse Dr 99801 907-780-1400
Ted Wilson, prin. Fax 780-1449
Harborview ES 400/PK-5
10014 Crazy Horse Dr 99801 907-523-1850
Dave Stollenberg, prin. Fax 523-1899
Heeni MS 600/6-8
10014 Crazy Horse Dr 99801 907-463-1899
Barb Mecum, prin. Fax 463-1877
Mendenhall River Community ES 400/PK-5
10014 Crazy Horse Dr 99801 907-463-1799
Patty Newman, prin. Fax 463-1777
Riverbend ES 400/PK-5
10014 Crazy Horse Dr 99801 907-463-1819
Carmen Katasse, prin. Fax 463-1792

Faith Community S 50/K-8
PO Box 33317 99803 907-790-2240
Heidi Boucher, admin.
Juneau SDA Christian S 50/1-8
4890 Glacier Hwy 99801 907-780-4336

Kake, Wrangell-Petersburg, Pop. 667
Kake CSD 100/K-12
PO Box 450 99830 907-785-3741
Eric Gebhart, supt. Fax 785-6439
www.kakeschools.com
Kake S 100/K-12
PO Box 450 99830 907-785-3741
Eric Gebhart, prin. Fax 785-6439

Kaktovik, North Slope, Pop. 272
North Slope Borough SD
Supt. — See Barrow
Kaveolook S 100/PK-12
PO Box 20 99747 907-640-6626
John Luhrs, prin. Fax 640-6718

Kalskag, Bethel, Pop. 186
Kuspuk SD
Supt. — See Aniak
Gregory ES 50/PK-1
PO Box 20 99607 907-471-2289
Greg Wohlman, prin. Fax 471-2326

Kaltag, Yukon-Koyukuk, Pop. 218
Yukon-Koyukuk SD
Supt. — See Fairbanks
Kaltag S 50/PK-12
PO Box 30 99748 907-534-2204
Colleen Stickman, prin. Fax 534-2227

Karluk, Kodiak Island, Pop. 71
Kodiak Island Borough SD
Supt. — See Kodiak
Karluk S 99608 300/K-12
Claudia Scotter, lead tchr. 907-241-2217
Fax 241-2207

Kasigluk, Bethel, Pop. 425
Lower Kuskokwim SD
Supt. — See Bethel
Akiuk Memorial S 100/PK-12
104 Village Rd 99609 907-477-6829
Carl Williams, prin. Fax 477-6314
Akula Elitnaurvik S 100/K-12
PO Box 79 99609 907-477-6615
Felicia Kleven, prin. Fax 477-6715

Kasilof, Kenai Peninsula, Pop. 383
Kenai Peninsula Borough SD
Supt. — See Soldotna
Tustumena ES 200/K-6
PO Box 749 99610 907-260-1345
Bob VanDerWege, prin. Fax 262-8477

Kenai, Kenai Peninsula, Pop. 7,464
Kenai Peninsula Borough SD
Supt. — See Soldotna
Kenai MS 400/6-8
201 N Tinker Ln 99611 907-283-1700
Paul Sorenson, prin. Fax 283-3180
Mountain View ES 200/K-5
315 Swires Rd 99611 907-283-8600
John Cook, prin. Fax 283-9340

Grace Lutheran S 50/K-8
PO Box 1683 99611 907-283-9551
Dennis Leckwee, prin. Fax 283-9551

Ketchikan, Ketchikan Gateway, Pop. 7,410
Ketchikan Gateway Borough SD 2,000/PK-12
333 Schoenbar Rd 99901 907-247-2142
Robert Boyle, supt. Fax 247-3822
www.kgbsd.org
Fawn Mountain ES 300/PK-6
400 Old Homestead Rd 99901 907-225-4741
Barbara Roberts, prin. Fax 247-4741
Houghtaling ES 400/PK-6
2940 Baranof Ave 99901 907-225-4128
Kurt Lindemann, prin. Fax 225-7925
Point Higgins ES 200/K-6
981 N Point Higgins Rd 99901 907-247-1500
Sheri Boehlert, prin. Fax 247-1558
Schoenbar MS 300/7-8
217 Schoenbar Rd 99901 907-225-5138
Bob Hewitt, prin. Fax 225-5761

Southeast Island SD
Supt. — See Thorne Bay
Edna Bay S K-12
PO Box EDB 99950 907-594-6110
Paul Haag, lead tchr. Fax 594-6111
Kasaan S 50/K-12
PO Box KXA 99950 907-530-7108
Kerrie Carl, lead tchr. Fax 530-7111
Naukati S 50/K-12
PO Box NKI 99950 907-629-4121
Evelyn Willburn, lead tchr. Fax 629-4122
Port Protection S 50/K-12
PO Box PPV 99950 907-489-2228
Paul Young, lead tchr. Fax 489-2260
Whale Pass S 50/K-12
PO Box WWP 99950 907-846-5320
Christine Cook, lead tchr. Fax 846-5319

Clover Pass Christian S 50/PK-8
105 N Point Higgins Rd 99901 907-247-2350
Tim Livingston, admin. Fax 247-0476
Holy Name S 100/PK-6
433 Jackson St 99901 907-225-2400
John Dickenson, prin. Fax 247-2121

Kiana, Northwest Arctic, Pop. 411
Northwest Arctic Borough SD
Supt. — See Kotzebue
Kiana S 100/PK-12
PO Box 190 99749 907-475-2115
Susan Johnson, prin. Fax 475-2120

King Cove, Aleutians East, Pop. 748
Aleutian East Borough SD
Supt. — See Sand Point
King Cove S 100/PK-12
PO Box 69 99612 907-497-2354
Ralph Lindquist, prin. Fax 497-2408

King Salmon, Bristol Bay, Pop. 696
Lake & Peninsula SD 400/K-12
PO Box 498 99613 907-246-4280
John Owens, supt. Fax 246-4473
www.lpsd.com
Other Schools – See Chignik, Chignik Lagoon, Chignik Lake, Egegik, Igiugig, Iliamna, Kokhanok, Levelock, Nondalton, Pedro Bay, Perryville, Pilot Point, Port Alsworth, Port Heiden

Kipnuk, Bethel, Pop. 470
Lower Kuskokwim SD
Supt. — See Bethel
Chief Paul Memorial S 200/PK-12
PO Box 19 99614 907-896-5011
Linae Sanger, prin. Fax 896-5428

Kivalina, Northwest Arctic, Pop. 399
Northwest Arctic Borough SD
Supt. — See Kotzebue
McQueen S 100/PK-12
General Delivery 99750 907-645-2125
Pauline Harvey, prin. Fax 645-2124

Klawock, Prince of Wales-Outer Ketchikan, Pop. 767
Klawock CSD 100/K-12
PO Box 9 99925 907-755-2228
Rich Carlson, supt. Fax 755-2320
www.klawockschool.com/
Klawock S 100/K-12
PO Box 9 99925 907-755-2220
Jim Holien, prin. Fax 755-2913

Kobuk, Northwest Arctic, Pop. 115
Northwest Arctic Borough SD
Supt. — See Kotzebue
Kobuk S 50/PK-12
PO Box 40 99751 907-948-2231
David Swift, lead tchr. Fax 948-2225

Kodiak, Kodiak Island, Pop. 6,273
Kodiak Island Borough SD 2,900/K-12
722 Mill Bay Rd 99615 907-481-6200
Stewart McDonald, supt. Fax 481-6218
www.kodiakschools.org
East ES 300/K-5
722 Mill Bay Rd 99615 907-481-6500
Paul Kubena, prin. Fax 486-9160
Kodiak MS 300/7-8
722 Mill Bay Rd 99615 907-481-2200
Steve Doerksen, prin. Fax 486-9061
Main ES 300/K-5
722 Mill Bay Rd 99615 907-486-2100
Nancy Moon, prin. Fax 486-2138
North Star ES 300/K-6
722 Mill Bay Rd 99615 907-481-2000
Deseree Wright, prin. Fax 486-9020
Peterson ES 300/K-6
722 Mill Bay Rd 99615 907-481-6400
Beth Cole, prin. Fax 487-2376
Other Schools – See Akhiok, Chiniak, Karluk, Larsen Bay, Old Harbor, Ouzinkie, Port Lions

---

Kodiak Christian S 100/PK-8
PO Box 49 99615 907-486-4905
Steve Steffensen, admin. Fax 486-2463
St. Marys S 100/K-8
2932 Mill Bay Rd 99615 907-486-3513
Joshua Lewis, prin. Fax 486-3117

Kokhanok, Lake and Peninsula, Pop. 152
Lake & Peninsula SD
Supt. — See King Salmon
Kokhanok S 50/K-12
General Delivery 99606 907-282-2210
Todd Washburn, prin. Fax 282-2247

Koliganek, Dillingham, Pop. 181
Southwest Region SD
Supt. — See Dillingham
Koliganek S 100/K-12
PO Box 5052 99576 907-596-3444
Joel Lovesee, prin. Fax 596-3484

Kongiganak, Bethel, Pop. 294
Lower Kuskokwim SD
Supt. — See Bethel
Kiunya Memorial S 100/PK-12
PO Box 5109, 907-557-5126
Daryl Daugaard, prin. Fax 557-5639

Kotlik, Wade Hampton, Pop. 635
Lower Yukon SD
Supt. — See Mountain Village
Kotlik S 200/PK-12
PO Box 20129 99620 907-899-4415
Harold Bollinger, prin. Fax 899-4515

Kotzebue, Northwest Arctic, Pop. 3,237
Northwest Arctic Borough SD 2,100/PK-12
PO Box 51 99752 907-442-3472
Norman Eck Ph.D., supt. Fax 442-2246
www.nwarctic.org/
Nelson ES 400/PK-7
PO Box 264 99752 907-442-3342
Linda Mason, prin. Fax 442-2142
Other Schools – See Ambler, Buckland, Deering, Kiana, Kivalina, Kobuk, Noatak, Noorvik, Selawik, Shungnak

Koyuk, Nome, Pop. 299
Bering Strait SD
Supt. — See Unalakleet
Koyuk-Malemute S 100/PK-12
PO Box 53009 99753 907-963-3021
Kim Hanisch, prin. Fax 963-2428

Koyukuk, Yukon-Koyukuk, Pop. 96
Yukon-Koyukuk SD
Supt. — See Fairbanks
Vernetti S 50/PK-12
PO Box 70 99754 907-927-2212
Josie Dayton, prin. Fax 927-2251

Kwethluk, Bethel, Pop. 726
Lower Kuskokwim SD
Supt. — See Bethel
Ket'acik Aap'alluk Memorial S 300/PK-12
PO Box 150 99621 907-757-6014
Kevin McCalla, prin. Fax 757-6013

Kwigillingok, Bethel, Pop. 278
Lower Kuskokwim SD
Supt. — See Bethel
Kwigillingok S 100/PK-12
PO Box 109 99622 907-588-8629
Walt Betz, prin. Fax 588-8613

Larsen Bay, Kodiak Island, Pop. 105
Kodiak Island Borough SD
Supt. — See Kodiak
Larsen Bay S 50/K-12
PO Box 70 99624 907-847-2252
Chuck Lawson, lead tchr. Fax 847-2260

Levelock, Lake and Peninsula, Pop. 105
Lake & Peninsula SD
Supt. — See King Salmon
Levelock S 50/K-12
PO Box 89 99625 907-287-3060
Todd Washburn, prin. Fax 287-3021

Lower Kalskag, Bethel, Pop. 272
Kuspuk SD
Supt. — See Aniak
Levi ES 100/2-6
General Delivery 99626 907-471-2318
Greg Wohlman, prin. Fax 471-2243

Mc Grath, Yukon-Koyukuk, Pop. 491
Iditarod Area SD 300/PK-12
PO Box 90 99627 907-524-3033
Joe Banghort, supt. Fax 524-3217
www.iditarodsd.org/
Lime Village S 50/K-12
PO Box 90 99627 907-524-3033
Karen Ladegard, prin. Fax 526-5225
Mc Grath S 100/K-12
PO Box 290 99627 907-524-3388
Joan O'Neal, prin. Fax 524-3751
Other Schools – See Anvik, Grayling, Holy Cross, Nikolai, Shageluk, Takotna

Manley Hot Springs, Yukon-Koyukuk, Pop. 96
Yukon-Koyukuk SD
Supt. — See Fairbanks
Manley Hart Springs Gladys Dart S 50/PK-12
PO Box 29 99756 907-672-3202
Marilyn Janke, prin. Fax 672-3201

Manokotak, Dillingham, Pop. 400
Southwest Region SD
Supt. — See Dillingham
Manokotak S 100/K-12
PO Box 30 99628 907-289-1013
Herman Gerving, prin. Fax 289-2050

Marshall, Wade Hampton, Pop. 374
Lower Yukon SD
Supt. — See Mountain Village
Marshall S 100/PK-12
PO Box 89 99585 907-679-6112
Grant Guy, prin. Fax 679-6637

Mekoryuk, Bethel, Pop. 213
Lower Kuskokwim SD
Supt. — See Bethel
Nuniwaarmiut S 50/PK-12
PO Box 49 99630 907-827-8415
Gary Stillwell, prin. Fax 827-8613

Mentasta Lake, Southeast Fairbanks, Pop. 96
Alaska Gateway SD
Supt. — See Tok
Mentasta Lake S 50/K-12
PO Box 6039 99780 907-291-2327
Diana Darby, prin. Fax 291-2325

Metlakatla, Prince of Wales-Outer Ketchikan, Pop. 1,407
Annette Islands SD 300/K-12
PO Box 7 99926 907-886-6332
Eugene Avey, supt. Fax 886-5130
aisd.k12.ak.us
Johnson ES 100/K-6
PO Box 7 99926 907-886-4121
John Hurley, prin. Fax 886-4120
Leask MS 50/7-8
PO Box 7 99926 907-886-6000
William McLeod, prin. Fax 886-5120

Minto, Yukon-Koyukuk, Pop. 218
Yukon-Koyukuk SD
Supt. — See Fairbanks
Minto S 50/PK-12
PO Box 81 99758 907-798-7212
Vicky Charlie, prin. Fax 798-7282

Moose Pass, Kenai Peninsula, Pop. 81
Kenai Peninsula Borough SD
Supt. — See Soldotna
Moose Pass S 50/K-8
PO Box 46 99631 907-288-3183
Wayne Young, prin. Fax 288-3607

Mountain Village, Wade Hampton, Pop. 808
Lower Yukon SD 2,000/PK-12
PO Box 32089 99632 907-591-2411
John Lamont, supt. Fax 591-2449
www.loweryukon.org/
Beans S 300/PK-12
PO Box 32105 99632 907-591-2819
Edna Apatiki, prin. Fax 591-2214
Other Schools – See Alakanuk, Emmonak, Hooper Bay, Kotlik, Marshall, Pilot Station, Russian Mission, Saint Marys, Scammon Bay, Sheldon Point

Naknek, Bristol Bay, Pop. 575
Bristol Bay Borough SD 200/K-12
PO Box 169 99633 907-246-4225
Jack Walsh, supt. Fax 246-6857
www.bbbsd.net
Naknek ES 100/K-6
PO Box 169 99633 907-246-4265
Trevor Townsend, prin. Fax 246-4447

Nanwalek, Kenai Peninsula
Kenai Peninsula Borough SD
Supt. — See Soldotna
Nanwalek S 100/K-12
PO Box 8007 99603 907-281-2210
Cheryl Schweigert, prin. Fax 281-2211

Napakiak, Bethel, Pop. 359
Lower Kuskokwim SD
Supt. — See Bethel
Miller Memorial S 100/PK-12
General Delivery 99634 907-589-2420
Bruce Kleven, prin. Fax 589-2515

Napaskiak, Bethel, Pop. 397
Lower Kuskokwim SD
Supt. — See Bethel
Qugcuun Memorial S 50/PK-12
PO Box 6199 99559 907-737-7214
Chris Meier, prin. Fax 737-7211
Williams S 200/K-12
PO Box 6089 99559 907-737-7212
Charlotte Calhoun, prin. Fax 737-7967

Nelson Lagoon, Aleutians East, Pop. 83
Aleutian East Borough SD
Supt. — See Sand Point
Nelson Lagoon S 50/PK-12
PO Box 19 99571 907-989-2225
Jim Wack, prin. Fax 989-2228

Nenana, Yukon-Koyukuk, Pop. 371
Nenana CSD 600/K-12
PO Box 10 99760 907-832-5464
Eric Gebhart, supt. Fax 832-5625
nenanasd.org
Nenana City S 200/K-12
PO Box 10 99760 907-832-5464
Joe Krause, prin. Fax 832-5625

New Stuyahok, Dillingham, Pop. 472
Southwest Region SD
Supt. — See Dillingham
Chief Blunka S 200/K-12
PO Box 29 99636 907-693-3144
Gene Anderson, prin. Fax 693-3163

Newtok, Bethel, Pop. 207
Lower Kuskokwim SD
Supt. — See Bethel
Ayaprun S 100/K-12
PO Box WWT 99559 907-237-2505
Grant Kashatok, prin. Fax 237-2506

Nightmute, Bethel, Pop. 211
Lower Kuskokwim SD
Supt. — See Bethel
Nightmute S 100/PK-12
General Delivery 99690 907-647-6313
Michael Thomas, prin. Fax 647-6227

Nikiski, Kenai Peninsula, Pop. 2,743
Kenai Peninsula Borough SD
Supt. — See Soldotna
Nikiski North Star ES 400/K-6
PO Box 8629 99635 907-776-2600
Lori Manion, prin. Fax 776-8423

Nikolaevsk, Kenai Peninsula, Pop. 371
Kenai Peninsula Borough SD
Supt. — See Soldotna
Nikolaevsk S 100/K-12
65478 Nikolaevsk Rd 99556 907-235-8972
Mike Sellers, prin. Fax 235-3617

Nikolai, Yukon-Koyukuk, Pop. 93
Iditarod Area SD
Supt. — See Mc Grath
Top of the Kuskokwim S 50/K-12
PO Box 9190 99691 907-293-2427
Denis Gardella, prin. Fax 293-2214

Nikolski, Aleutians West, Pop. 35
Aleutian Region SD
Supt. — See Anchorage
Nikolski S 50/K-12
100 Umnak Ln 99638 907-576-2200
Brent Nielsen, lead tchr. Fax 576-2230

Ninilchik, Kenai Peninsula, Pop. 456
Kenai Peninsula Borough SD
Supt. — See Soldotna
Ninilchik S 200/K-12
PO Box 39010 99639 907-567-3301
Terry Martin, prin. Fax 567-3504

Noatak, Northwest Arctic, Pop. 333
Northwest Arctic Borough SD
Supt. — See Kotzebue
Napaaqtugmiut S 200/PK-12
PO Box 49 99761 907-485-2153
Matthew Clark, prin. Fax 485-2150

Nome, Nome, Pop. 3,590
Nome SD 700/PK-12
PO Box 131 99762 907-443-2231
Rick Luthi, supt. Fax 443-5144
www.nomeschools.com
Nome ES 400/PK-6
PO Box 131 99762 907-443-5299
Carl White, prin. Fax 443-2850

Nome Adventist S 50/1-8
501 Round the Clock St 99762 907-443-5137
Fax 443-2968

Nondalton, Lake and Peninsula, Pop. 188
Lake & Peninsula SD
Supt. — See King Salmon
Nondalton S 50/K-12
100 School Rd 99640 907-294-2210
Ed Cox, prin. Fax 294-2265

Noorvik, Northwest Arctic, Pop. 672
Northwest Arctic Borough SD
Supt. — See Kotzebue
Aqqaluk / Noorvik S 200/PK-12
PO Box 165 99763 907-636-2178
Doyle Horton, prin. Fax 636-2160

North Pole, Fairbanks North Star, Pop. 1,778
Fairbanks-North Star Borough SD
Supt. — See Fairbanks
North Pole MS 500/6-8
300 E 8th Ave 99705 907-488-2271
Ernie Manzie, prin. Fax 488-9213

North Pole Christian S 100/PK-12
PO Box 55306 99705 907-488-0133
Ethan Gelineau, prin. Fax 488-8248

Northway, Southeast Fairbanks, Pop. 123
Alaska Gateway SD
Supt. — See Tok
Northway S 100/K-12
PO Box 519 99764 907-778-2287
Frank Cook, prin. Fax 778-2221

Nuiqsut, North Slope, Pop. 386
North Slope Borough SD
Supt. — See Barrow
Nuiqsut Trapper S 100/PK-12
PO Box 167 99789 907-480-6712
Bart Mwarey, prin. Fax 480-6621

Nulato, Yukon-Koyukuk, Pop. 318
Yukon-Koyukuk SD
Supt. — See Fairbanks
Demoski S 100/PK-12
PO Box 65029 99765 907-898-2204
Dan Reum, prin. Fax 898-2340

Nunapitchuk, Bethel, Pop. 474
Lower Kuskokwim SD
Supt. — See Bethel
Tobeluk Memorial S 200/K-12
PO Box 150 99641 907-527-5325
Gary Chadwell, prin. Fax 527-5610

Old Harbor, Kodiak Island, Pop. 217
Kodiak Island Borough SD
Supt. — See Kodiak
Old Harbor S 100/K-12
PO Box 49 99643 907-286-2213
Corrina Eaton, prin. Fax 286-2222

Ouzinkie, Kodiak Island, Pop. 206
Kodiak Island Borough SD
Supt. — See Kodiak
Ouzinkie S 50/K-12
PO Box 49 99644 907-680-2204
Jacob Parrett, prin. Fax 680-2288

Palmer, Matanuska-Susitna, Pop. 6,920
Matanuska-Susitna Borough SD 14,900/PK-12
501 N Gulkana St 99645 907-746-9255
George Troxel, supt. Fax 761-4076
www.matsuk12.us
Beryozava S, 501 N Gulkana St 99645 50/K-12
Margaret Brockman, prin. 907-746-9239
Butte ES 300/PK-5
4006 S Butte Rd 99645 907-745-4871
Dan Kitchen, prin. Fax 745-7720
Colony MS 700/6-8
9250 E Colony Schools Dr 99645 907-761-1500
Mary McMahon, prin. Fax 761-1592
Palmer MS 600/6-8
1159 S Chugach St 99645 907-761-4300
Gene Stone, prin. Fax 761-4372
Pioneer Peak ES 400/PK-5
1959 N Trunk Rd 99645 907-745-0157
Daniel Molina, prin. Fax 745-6113
Sherrod ES 400/3-5
561 N Gulkana St 99645 907-761-4100
Mark Hoffman, prin. Fax 761-4180
Swanson ES 500/PK-2
609 N Gulkana St 99645 907-745-3227
Mary Mayer, prin. Fax 745-1021
Other Schools – See Big Lake, Sutton, Talkeetna, Trapper Creek, Wasilla, Willow

---

Matanuska Valley SDA S 50/1-9
PO Box 3229 99645 907-745-2691

Pedro Bay, Lake and Peninsula, Pop. 42
Lake & Peninsula SD
Supt. — See King Salmon
Dena'ina S 50/K-12
General Delivery 99647 907-850-2207
Adam Mokelke, prin. Fax 850-2254

Pelican, Skagway-Hoonah-Angoon, Pop. 139
Pelican CSD 50/PK-12
PO Box 90 99832 907-735-2236
Connie Newman Ph.D., supt. Fax 735-2263
Pelican S 50/PK-12
PO Box 90 99832 907-735-2236
Connie Newman, prin. Fax 735-2263

Perryville, Lake and Peninsula, Pop. 108
Lake & Peninsula SD
Supt. — See King Salmon
Perryville S 50/K-12
PO Box 103 99648 907-853-2210
Kary Hawkins, prin. Fax 853-2267

Petersburg, Wrangell-Petersburg, Pop. 3,010
Petersburg CSD 600/K-12
PO Box 289 99833 907-772-4271
Dr. Gary Jacobsen, supt. Fax 772-4719
www.psgsd.k12.ak.us
Mitkof MS 100/6-8
PO Box 289 99833 907-772-3860
David Morris, prin. Fax 772-3617
Stedman ES 300/K-5
PO Box 289 99833 907-772-4786
Erica Kludt-Painter, prin. Fax 772-4334

Pilot Point, Lake and Peninsula, Pop. 85
Lake & Peninsula SD
Supt. — See King Salmon
Pilot Point S 50/K-12
PO Box 467 99649 907-797-2210
Mike Flanagan, prin. Fax 797-2267

Pilot Station, Wade Hampton, Pop. 590
Lower Yukon SD
Supt. — See Mountain Village
Pilot Station S 200/PK-12
PO Box 5090 99650 907-549-3212
David Sharstrom, prin. Fax 549-3335

Platinum, Bethel, Pop. 42
Lower Kuskokwim SD
Supt. — See Bethel
Arvig S 50/PK-12
PO Box 28 99651 907-979-8111
Sonya Rigg, prin. Fax 979-8213

Point Hope, North Slope, Pop. 704
North Slope Borough SD
Supt. — See Barrow
Tikigaq S 200/PK-12
PO Box 148 99766 907-368-2662
Darrell Richard, prin. Fax 368-2770

Point Lay, North Slope, Pop. 139
North Slope Borough SD
Supt. — See Barrow
Kali S 100/PK-12
PO Box 59077 99759 907-833-2311
Helen Eckelman, prin. Fax 833-2315

Port Alexander, Wrangell-Petersburg, Pop. 77
Southeast Island SD
Supt. — See Thorne Bay
Port Alexander S 50/K-12
PO Box 8170 99836 907-568-2205
Carolyn Barnes, lead tchr. Fax 568-2261

Port Alsworth, Lake and Peninsula, Pop. 55
Lake & Peninsula SD
Supt. — See King Salmon
Tanalian S 50/K-12
General Delivery 99653 907-781-2210
Ed Cox, prin. Fax 781-2254

Port Graham, Kenai Peninsula, Pop. 166
Kenai Peninsula Borough SD
Supt. — See Soldotna
Port Graham S 50/K-12
PO Box 5550 99603 907-284-2210
Steven Kenrick, prin. Fax 284-2213

Port Heiden, Lake and Peninsula, Pop. 101
Lake & Peninsula SD
Supt. — See King Salmon
Meshik S 50/K-12
General Delivery 99549 907-837-2210
Mike Flanagan, prin. Fax 837-2265

Port Lions, Kodiak Island, Pop. 234
Kodiak Island Borough SD
Supt. — See Kodiak
Port Lions S 50/K-12
PO Box 109 99550 907-454-2237
Kendra Bartz, prin. Fax 454-2377

Quinhagak, Bethel, Pop. 563
Lower Kuskokwim SD
Supt. — See Bethel
Kuinerrarmiut Elitnaurviat S 200/PK-12
General Delivery 99655 907-556-8628
Eric Pederson, prin. Fax 556-8228

Red Devil, Bethel, Pop. 53
Kuspuk SD
Supt. — See Aniak
Willis S 50/K-12
General Delivery 99656 907-447-3213
Susan Hubbard, prin. Fax 447-3214

Ruby, Yukon-Koyukuk, Pop. 178
Yukon-Koyukuk SD
Supt. — See Fairbanks
Kangas S 50/PK-12
PO Box 68110 99768 907-468-4465
Anne Titus, prin. Fax 468-4444

Russian Mission, Wade Hampton, Pop. 317
Lower Yukon SD
Supt. — See Mountain Village
Russian Mission S 100/PK-12
PO Box 90 99657 907-584-5615
Jason Moen, prin. Fax 584-5412

Saint George Island, Aleutians West, Pop. 59
Pribilof SD
Supt. — See Saint Paul Island
St. George S 50/PK-12
PO Box 959 99591 907-859-2228
Carol Randall, prin. Fax 859-2229

Saint Marys, Wade Hampton, Pop. 577
Lower Yukon SD
Supt. — See Mountain Village
Pitkas Point S 50/PK-12
PO Box 161 99658 907-438-2571
Cheryl Doyle, lead tchr. Fax 438-2948

Saint Mary's SD 200/PK-12
PO Box 9 99658 907-438-2411
David Herbert, supt. Fax 438-2735
www.smcsd.us
Saint Mary's S 200/PK-12
PO Box 9 99658 907-438-2411
Dewayne Bahnsen, prin. Fax 438-2735

Saint Michael, Nome, Pop. 366
Bering Strait SD
Supt. — See Unalakleet
Andrews S 100/PK-12
100 Baker St 99659 907-923-3041
Dan Eide, prin. Fax 923-3031

Saint Paul Island, Aleutians West, Pop. 400
Pribilof SD 100/PK-12
PO Box 905 99660 907-546-2221
Jamie Stacks, supt. Fax 546-2327
www.psd-k12.org
St. Paul S 100/PK-12
PO Box 905 99660 907-546-2221
Jamie Stacks, prin. Fax 546-2356
Other Schools – See Saint George Island

Sand Point, Aleutians East, Pop. 951
Aleutian East Borough SD 300/PK-12
PO Box 429 99661 907-383-5222
Dr. Phil Knight, supt. Fax 383-3496
www.aebsd.org
Sand Point S 100/PK-12
PO Box 269 99661 907-383-2393
Jeanne Perkins, prin. Fax 383-3833
Other Schools – See Akutan, Cold Bay, False Pass, King Cove, Nelson Lagoon

Savoonga, Nome, Pop. 648
Bering Strait SD
Supt. — See Unalakleet
Kingeekuk Memorial S 200/K-12
PO Box 200 99769 907-984-6811
Roxie Quick, prin. Fax 984-6413

Scammon Bay, Wade Hampton, Pop. 499
Lower Yukon SD
Supt. — See Mountain Village
Scammon Bay S 200/PK-12
General Delivery 99662 907-558-5312
Jim Cammon, prin. Fax 558-5320

Selawik, Northwest Arctic, Pop. 819
Northwest Arctic Borough SD
Supt. — See Kotzebue
Davis-Ramoth S 300/PK-12
PO Box 29 99770 907-484-2142
Remmel Grayson, prin. Fax 484-2127

Seldovia, Kenai Peninsula, Pop. 300
Kenai Peninsula Borough SD
Supt. — See Soldotna
English S 100/K-12
PO Box 171 99663 907-234-7616
Sheryl Hingley, prin. Fax 234-7884

Seward, Kenai Peninsula, Pop. 3,016
Kenai Peninsula Borough SD
Supt. — See Soldotna
Seward ES 300/K-6
PO Box 247 99664 907-224-3356
David Kingsland, prin. Fax 224-7077
Seward MS 100/7-8
PO Box 1149 99664 907-224-9000
Trevan Walker, prin. Fax 224-9001

Shageluk, Yukon-Koyukuk, Pop. 122
Iditarod Area SD
Supt. — See Mc Grath
Innoko River S 50/PK-12
PO Box 49 99665 907-473-8233
Bernard Grieves, prin. Fax 473-8268

Shaktoolik, Nome, Pop. 232
Bering Strait SD
Supt. — See Unalakleet
Shaktoolik S 50/PK-12
PO Box 40 99771 907-955-3021
Linda Goldeski, prin. Fax 955-3031

Sheldon Point, Wade Hampton, Pop. 121
Lower Yukon SD
Supt. — See Mountain Village
Sheldon Point S 100/PK-12
PO Box 32, Nunam Iqua AK 99666 907-498-4112
Mary Pipal, prin. Fax 498-4235

Shishmaref, Nome, Pop. 565
Bering Strait SD
Supt. — See Unalakleet
Shishmaref S 200/PK-12
1 Seaview Ln 99772 907-649-3021
Steve Sammons, prin. Fax 649-3031

Shungnak, Northwest Arctic, Pop. 272
Northwest Arctic Borough SD
Supt. — See Kotzebue
Shungnak S 100/PK-12
PO Box 79 99773 907-437-2151
Kitza Durkop, prin. Fax 437-2177

Sitka, Sitka, Pop. 8,986
Sitka SD 1,500/PK-12
300 Kostrometinoff St 99835 907-747-8622
Steve Bradshaw, supt. Fax 966-1260
www.ssd.k12.ak.us
Baranof ES 300/PK-2
305 Baranof St 99835 907-747-5825
Michelle Beach, prin. Fax 747-3049
Blatchley MS 400/6-8
601 Halibut Point Rd 99835 907-747-8672
Joe Robidou, prin. Fax 966-1460
Keet Gooshi Heen ES 400/2-5
307 Kashevaroff St 99835 907-747-8395
Beverly Hunter-Gillaspie, prin. Fax 966-1240

Sitka SDA S 50/1-8
1613 Halibut Point Rd 99835 907-747-8855

Skagway, Skagway-Hoonah-Angoon, Pop. 828
Skagway SD 100/K-12
PO Box 497 99840 907-983-2960
Dr. Michael Dickens, supt. Fax 983-2964
www.skagwayschool.org/
Skagway S 100/K-12
PO Box 497 99840 907-983-2960
Dr. Michael Dickens, prin. Fax 983-2964

Slana, Valdez-Cordova, Pop. 63
Copper River SD
Supt. — See Glennallen
Slana S 50/1-12
PO Box 870 99586 907-822-5868
Bob Snedigar, prin. Fax 822-3850

Sleetmute, Bethel, Pop. 106
Kuspuk SD
Supt. — See Aniak
Egnaty S 50/K-12
PO Box 69 99668 907-449-4216
Susan Hubbard, prin. Fax 449-4217

Soldotna, Kenai Peninsula, Pop. 4,087
Kenai Peninsula Borough SD 8,700/K-12
148 N Binkley St 99669 907-714-8888
Dr. Donna Peterson, supt. Fax 262-9645
www.kpbsd.k12.ak.us
Kalifornsky Beach ES 500/K-6
1049 E Poppy Ln 99669 907-260-1300
Melissa Stavola, prin. Fax 262-4096
Redoubt ES 400/K-6
486 W Redoubt Ave 99669 907-260-4300
John Pothast, prin. Fax 262-5815
Soldotna ES 200/K-6
162 E Park Ave 99669 907-260-5100
Carolyn Cannava, prin. Fax 262-4962
Soldotna MS 500/7-8
426 W Redoubt Ave 99669 907-260-2500
Sharon Moock, prin. Fax 262-7036
Other Schools – See Anchor Point, Cooper Landing, Fritz Creek, Homer, Hope, Kasilof, Kenai, Moose Pass, Nanwalek, Nikiski, Nikolaevsk, Ninilchik, Port Graham, Seldovia, Seward, Sterling, Tyonek

---

Cook Inlet Academy 200/PK-12
45872 Kalifornsky Beach Rd 99669 907-262-5101
Mary Rowley, admin. Fax 262-1541

Stebbins, Nome, Pop. 552
Bering Strait SD
Supt. — See Unalakleet
Tukurngailnguq S 200/K-12
General Delivery 99671 907-934-3041
Gerald Pickner, prin. Fax 934-3031

Sterling, Kenai Peninsula, Pop. 3,802
Kenai Peninsula Borough SD
Supt. — See Soldotna
Sterling ES 200/K-6
PO Box 89 99672 907-262-4944
Christine Ermold, prin. Fax 262-5128

Academy of Higher Learning 50/K-12
32930 Fair Game Ave Ofc 99672 907-260-7741
Catherine Gibson, prin. Fax 260-7741

Stevens Village, Yukon-Koyukuk, Pop. 102
Yukon Flats SD
Supt. — See Fort Yukon
Stevens Village S 50/PK-12
335 Bridge St 99774 907-478-7116
Eugenia Grammer, prin. Fax 478-7893

Stony River, Bethel, Pop. 51
Kuspuk SD
Supt. — See Aniak
Michael S 50/K-12
General Delivery 99557 907-537-3226
Susan Hubbard, prin. Fax 537-3237

Sutton, Matanuska-Susitna, Pop. 308
Matanuska-Susitna Borough SD
Supt. — See Palmer
Glacier View S 50/K-12
29170 W Glenn Hwy 99674 907-745-5122
Wendy Taylor, prin. Fax 746-5560
Sutton ES 100/K-6
PO Box 216 99674 907-745-6150
Katherine Ellsworth, prin. Fax 745-8425

Takotna, Yukon-Koyukuk, Pop. 38
Iditarod Area SD
Supt. — See Mc Grath
Takotna S 99675 50/K-12
Robert Absher, prin. 907-298-2115
Fax 298-2316

Talkeetna, Matanuska-Susitna, Pop. 250
Matanuska-Susitna Borough SD
Supt. — See Palmer
Talkeetna ES 100/K-6
PO Box 668 99676 907-733-2252
Jodi Picou, prin. Fax 733-1366

Tanacross, Southeast Fairbanks, Pop. 106
Alaska Gateway SD
Supt. — See Tok
Tanacross S 50/K-8
PO Box 76030 99776 907-883-4391
Peggy Charlie, prin. Fax 883-4390

Tanana, Yukon-Koyukuk, Pop. 290
Tanana CSD 100/K-12
PO Box 89 99777 907-366-7203
John Bania, coord. Fax 366-7201
Sommer S 100/K-12
PO Box 89 99777 907-366-7207
John Bania, prin. Fax 366-7201

Tatitlek, Valdez-Cordova, Pop. 119
Chugach SD
Supt. — See Anchorage
Tatitlek Community S 50/K-12
PO Box 167 99677 907-325-2252
Jed Palmer, prin. Fax 325-2299

Teller, Nome, Pop. 269
Bering Strait SD
Supt. — See Unalakleet
Isabell S 100/PK-12
100 Airport Ave 99778 907-642-3041
Jay Thomas, prin. Fax 642-3031

Tenakee Springs, Skagway-Hoonah-Angoon, Pop. 98
Chatham SD
Supt. — See Angoon
Tenakee Springs S 50/K-12
PO Box 62 99841 907-736-2204
Fax 736-2204

Thorne Bay, Prince of Wales-Outer Ketchikan, Pop. 503
Southeast Island SD 200/K-12
PO Box 19569 99919 907-828-8254
Lauren Burch, supt. Fax 828-8257
sisdschools.org/
Thorne Bay S 100/K-12
PO Box 19005 99919 907-828-3921
Sheila Nyquest, prin. Fax 828-3901
Other Schools – See Coffman Cove, Craig, Hyder, Ketchikan, Port Alexander

Togiak, Dillingham, Pop. 810
Southwest Region SD
Supt. — See Dillingham
Togiak S 200/K-12
PO Box 50 99678 907-493-5829
David Wick, prin. Fax 493-5933

Tok, Southeast Fairbanks, Pop. 935
Alaska Gateway SD 400/PK-12
PO Box 226 99780 907-883-5151
Todd Poage, admin. Fax 883-5154
www.agsd.us/
Tetlin S 50/PK-12
PO Box 277 99780 907-324-2104
Jane Broome, prin. Fax 324-2120
Tok S 200/K-12
PO Box 249 99780 907-883-5161
LeAnn Young, prin. Fax 883-5165
Other Schools – See Dot Lake, Eagle, Mentasta Lake, Northway, Tanacross

Toksook Bay, Bethel, Pop. 542
Lower Kuskokwim SD
Supt. — See Bethel
Nelson Island S 200/PK-12
General Delivery 99637 907-427-7815
Talbert Bentley, prin. Fax 427-7612

Trapper Creek, Matanuska-Susitna, Pop. 296
Matanuska-Susitna Borough SD
Supt. — See Palmer
Trapper Creek ES 50/K-7
PO Box 13108 99683 907-733-2298
Jodi Picou, prin. Fax 733-1370

Tuluksak, Bethel, Pop. 383
Yupiit SD
Supt. — See Akiachak
Tuluksak S 200/PK-12
PO Box 115 99679 907-695-5625
Mariah Thomas-Wolf, prin. Fax 695-5645

Tuntutuliak, Bethel, Pop. 300
Lower Kuskokwim SD
Supt. — See Bethel
Angapak Memorial S 100/PK-12
General Delivery 99680 907-256-2415
Frank Cook, prin. Fax 256-2527

Tununak, Bethel, Pop. 338
Lower Kuskokwim SD
Supt. — See Bethel
Albert Memorial S 100/K-12
PO Box 49 99681 907-652-6827
Brett Stirling, prin. Fax 652-6028

Twin Hills, Dillingham, Pop. 66
Southwest Region SD
Supt. — See Dillingham
Twin Hills S 50/K-8
PO Box TWA 99576 907-525-4915
Rodney Lindberg, prin. Fax 525-4216

Tyonek, Kenai Peninsula, Pop. 154
Kenai Peninsula Borough SD
Supt. — See Soldotna
Tebughna S 50/K-12
PO Box 82010 99682 907-583-2291
Sheryl Kaye, prin. Fax 583-2692

Unalakleet, Nome, Pop. 752
Bering Strait SD 1,700/PK-12
PO Box 225 99684 907-624-3611
Jim Hickerson, supt. Fax 624-3099
www.bssd.org
Unalakleet S 200/PK-12
PO Box 130 99684 907-624-3444
Ben Howard, prin. Fax 624-3388
Other Schools – See Brevig Mission, Diomede, Elim, Gambell, Golovin, Koyuk, Saint Michael, Savoonga, Shaktoolik, Shishmaref, Stebbins, Teller, Wales, White Mountain

Unalaska, Aleutians West, Pop. 4,347
Unalaska CSD 400/PK-12
PO Box 570 99685 907-581-3151
John Conwell, supt. Fax 581-3152
www.ucsd.net
Unalaska ES 200/PK-4
PO Box 570 99685 907-581-3979
Heather Jones, prin. Fax 581-3972

Valdez, Valdez-Cordova, Pop. 4,015
Valdez CSD 800/PK-12
PO Box 398 99686 907-835-4357
Dr. Lance Bowie, supt. Fax 835-4964
www.valdezcityschools.org/
Gilson JHS 100/7-8
PO Box 398 99686 907-835-2244
Rodney Morrison, prin. Fax 835-2540
Hutchens ES 400/PK-6
PO Box 398 99686 907-835-4728
Roz Strang, prin. Fax 835-2047

Venetie, Yukon-Koyukuk, Pop. 182
Yukon Flats SD
Supt. — See Fort Yukon
Venetie S 50/PK-12
PO Box 39 99781 907-849-8415
Odell Homer, prin. Fax 849-8630

Wainwright, North Slope, Pop. 507
North Slope Borough SD
Supt. — See Barrow
Alak S 200/PK-12
PO Box 10 99782 907-763-2541
Carla Seavey, prin. Fax 763-2550

Wales, Nome, Pop. 153
Bering Strait SD
Supt. — See Unalakleet
Wales S 50/PK-12
PO Box 490 99783 907-664-3021
Craig Probst, prin. Fax 664-3031

Wasilla, Matanuska-Susitna, Pop. 8,471
Matanuska-Susitna Borough SD
Supt. — See Palmer
Cottonwood Creek ES 500/PK-5
800 N Seward Meridian Pkwy 99654 907-376-7577
Lisa Vrvilo, prin. Fax 376-9194
Finger Lake ES 400/PK-5
PO Box 875910 99687 907-373-3242
Dave Nufer, prin. Fax 373-3649
Goose Bay ES 600/K-5
PO Box 877430 99687 907-352-6400
Brooke Kelly, prin. Fax 352-6480
Iditarod ES 400/PK-5
801 N Wasilla Fishhook Rd 99654 907-352-9100
Raymond Marshall, prin. Fax 352-9180
Knik ES 3-5
PO Box 877830 99687 907-352-0300
Traci Pedersen, prin. Fax 352-0380
Larson ES 400/K-5
2722 E Seldon Rd 99654 907-352-2300
Ann Marie Bill, prin. Fax 352-2345
Meadow Lakes ES 400/K-5
7362 W Parks Hwy Ste 824 99654 907-352-6100
Carl Chamblee, prin. Fax 352-6147
Shaw ES K-5
PO Box 875910 99687 907-352-0500
Karl Schleich, prin. Fax 352-0580
Snowshoe ES 500/K-6
2001 W Fairview Loop 99654 907-352-9500
Carol Boatman, prin. Fax 352-9560
Tanaina ES 400/PK-5
2550 N Lucille St 99654 907-352-9400
Thomas Lytle, prin. Fax 352-9481
Teeland MS 600/6-8
2788 N Seward Meridian Pkwy 99654 907-352-7500
Monica Goyette, prin. Fax 352-7585
Wasilla MS 800/6-8
650 E Bogard Rd 99654 907-352-5300
Amy Spargo, prin. Fax 352-5380

Cornerstone Christian S 100/K-12
4001 E Darrington Village 99654 907-357-9798
Karen Armstrong, prin. Fax 357-9799
Our Lady of the Valley S PK-8
260 E Nelson Ave 99654 907-376-0883
Suzanne Cyr, prin. Fax 376-0853
Wasilla Lake Christian S 200/K-12
2001 Palmer Wasilla Hwy 99654 907-373-6439
Christopher Wolfe, admin. Fax 373-6438

White Mountain, Nome, Pop. 205
Bering Strait SD
Supt. — See Unalakleet
White Mountain S 50/PK-12
PO Box 84069 99784 907-638-3041
Andy Haviland, prin. Fax 638-3031

Whittier, Valdez-Cordova, Pop. 172
Chugach SD
Supt. — See Anchorage
Whittier Community S 50/PK-12
PO Box 638 99693 907-472-2575
Stephanie Burgoon, prin. Fax 472-2409

Willow, Matanuska-Susitna, Pop. 285
Matanuska-Susitna Borough SD
Supt. — See Palmer
Willow ES 100/PK-6
PO Box 69 99688 907-495-6236
Sheela Hull, prin. Fax 495-6266

Wrangell, Wrangell-Petersburg, Pop. 2,117
Wrangell SD 400/K-12
PO Box 2319 99929 907-874-2347
Larry Wilson, supt. Fax 874-3137
www.wrangellschools.org
Evergreen ES 100/K-5
PO Box 736 99929 907-874-2321
Therese Ashton, prin. Fax 874-2621
Stikine MS 100/6-8
PO Box 1935 99929 907-874-3393
Monty Buness, prin. Fax 874-3149

Yakutat, Yakutat, Pop. 534
Yakutat SD 100/PK-12
PO Box 429 99689 907-784-3317
Howard Diamond, supt. Fax 784-3446
www.yakutatschools.org
Yakutat S 100/PK-12
PO Box 429 99689 907-784-3317
Howard Diamond, prin. Fax 784-3446

ARIZONA

ARIZONA DEPARTMENT OF EDUCATION
1535 W Jefferson St, Phoenix 85007-3280
Telephone 602-542-5393
Fax 602-542-5440
Website http://www.ade.az.gov/

Superintendent of Public Instruction Tom Horne

ARIZONA BOARD OF EDUCATION
1535 W Jefferson St, Phoenix 85007-3280

Director Vince Yanez

COUNTY SUPERINTENDENTS OF SCHOOLS

Apache County Office of Education
Dr. Pauline Begay, supt. 928-337-7539
PO Box 548, Saint Johns 85936 Fax 337-2033
www.acsbc.net/superintendent/

Cochise County Office of Education
Trudy Berry, supt. 520-432-8950
PO Box 208, Bisbee 85603 Fax 432-7136
www.cochise.az.gov/cochise_schools.aspx?id=462

Coconino County Office of Education
Cecilia Owen, supt. 928-679-8070
110 E Cherry Ave, Flagstaff 86001 Fax 679-8077
www.coconino.az.gov/schools.aspx

Gila County Office of Education
Dr. Linda O'Dell, supt. 928-402-8780
1400 E Ash St, Globe 85501 Fax 402-0038
www.gilacountyschools.org

Graham County Office of Education
Donna McGaughey, supt. 928-428-2880
921 W Thatcher Blvd Fax 428-8824
Safford 85546
www.graham.az.gov

Greenlee County Office of Education
Tom Powers, supt. 928-865-2822
PO Box 1595, Clifton 85533 Fax 865-4417
www.co.greenlee.az.us/School/SchoolHomePage.asp

Lapaz County Office of Education
Janice Shelton, supt. 928-669-6183
1112 S Joshua Ave Ste 205 Fax 669-4406
Parker 85344
www.lapazschools.org

Maricopa County Office of Education
Dr. Don Covey, supt. 602-506-3866
4041 N Central Ave, Phoenix 85012 Fax 506-3753
www.maricopa.gov/Schools/

Mohave County Office of Education
Michael File, supt. 928-753-0747
PO Box 7000, Kingman 86402 Fax 718-4958
www.mcss.k12.az.us/

Navajo County Office of Education
Linda Morrow, supt. 928-524-4204
PO Box 668, Holbrook 86025 Fax 524-4209
www.navajocountyaz.gov/schools/

Pima County Office of Education
Dr. Linda Arzoumanian, supt. 520-740-8451
130 W Congress St Fl 4 Fax 623-9308
Tucson 85701
www.schools.pima.gov/

Pinal County Office of Education
Orlenda Roberts, supt. 520-866-6565
PO Box 769, Florence Fax 866-4671
www.pinalcounty.org

Santa Cruz County Office of Education
Alfredo Velasquez, supt. 520-375-7940
2150 N Congress Dr Fax 375-7959
Nogales 85621
www.co.santa-cruz.az.us/schools/index.html

Yavapai County Office of Education
Tim Carter, supt. 928-771-3326
1015 Fair St Rm 324 Fax 771-3329
Prescott 86305
www.co.yavapai.az.us/Schools.aspx

Yuma County Office of Education
Thomas Tyree, supt. 928-373-1006
210 S 1st Ave, Yuma 85364 Fax 329-2008
www.co.yuma.az.us/schsup/

PUBLIC, PRIVATE AND CATHOLIC ELEMENTARY SCHOOLS

Aguila, Maricopa
Aguila ESD 63 200/K-8
PO Box 218 85320 928-685-2222
Donald German, supt. Fax 685-2433
Aguila S 200/K-8
PO Box 218 85320 928-685-2222
Donald German, prin. Fax 685-2433

Ajo, Pima, Pop. 2,919
Ajo USD 15 500/PK-12
PO Box 68 85321 520-387-5618
Robert Dooley Ed.D., supt. Fax 387-6545
ajoschools.org/
Ajo S 300/PK-8
PO Box 68 85321 520-387-7602
Fred Fout, prin. Fax 387-7603

Alpine, Apache
Alpine ESD 7 100/K-8
PO Box 170 85920 928-339-4570
Mike Cox, supt. Fax 339-1806
alpine.az.schoolwebpages.com
Alpine S 100/K-8
PO Box 170 85920 928-339-4570
Mike Cox, prin. Fax 339-1806

Amado, Pima
Sahuarita USD 30
Supt. — See Sahuarita
Sopori ES 200/K-5
5000 W Arivaca Rd 85645 520-398-2239
Desi Raulston, prin. Fax 398-2024

Anthem, Maricopa
Deer Valley USD 97
Supt. — See Phoenix
Anthem S 900/K-8
41020 N Freedom Way 85086 623-376-3700
Patrick Yennie, prin. Fax 376-3780

Cross of Christ Christian S 200/PK-5
39808 N Gavilan Peak Pkwy 85086 623-551-3454
Thomas Geyer, prin. Fax 551-4067

Apache Junction, Pinal, Pop. 32,297
Apache Junction USD 43 6,100/PK-12
1575 W Southern Ave Ste 3, 480-982-1110
Gregg Wyman, supt. Fax 982-6474
www.ajusd.org
Desert Shadows MS 700/6-8
801 W Southern Ave, 480-982-1110
Dotty Hunt, prin. Fax 983-4913
Desert Vista ES 700/K-5
3701 E Broadway Ave, 480-982-1110
Barb Sanchez, prin. Fax 288-0532
Four Peaks ES 400/K-5
1755 N Idaho Rd, 480-982-1110
Joyce Gingrich, prin. Fax 982-1708
Gold Canyon ES 500/K-5
5810 S Alameda Rd, 480-982-1110
Brenda Farris, prin. Fax 671-4324
Superstition Mountain ES 700/PK-5
550 S Ironwood Dr, 480-982-1110
Kendra Adams, prin. Fax 982-4978
Thunder Mountain MS 700/6-8
3700 E 16th Ave, 480-677-7550
Mark Blomgren, prin. Fax 671-1427
Other Schools – See Gold Canyon

Arizona City, Pinal, Pop. 1,940
Toltec ESD 22
Supt. — See Eloy
Toltec ES 700/PK-4
12115 W Benito Dr, 520-466-2450
Sylvia Mejia, prin. Fax 466-2499

Freedom Christian S 50/K-12
PO Box 2630, 520-510-8768
Diane Wiese, admin. Fax 494-8292

Arlington, Maricopa
Arlington ESD 47 300/K-8
9410 S 355th Ave 85322 623-386-2031
Chad Turner, supt. Fax 386-1627
arlingtonelem.org
Arlington S 300/K-8
9410 S 355th Ave 85322 623-386-2031
Chad Turner, prin. Fax 386-1627

Ash Fork, Yavapai
Ash Fork JUSD 31 300/K-12
PO Box 247 86320 928-637-2561
Jon Jones, admin. Fax 637-2623
www.afjusd.org/
Ash Fork ES 100/K-5
PO Box 247 86320 928-637-2561
Jon Jones, prin. Fax 637-2623
Ash Fork MS 100/6-8
PO Box 247 86320 928-637-2561
Jon Jones, prin. Fax 637-2623

Avondale, Maricopa, Pop. 66,706
Avondale ESD 44 6,100/PK-8
235 W Western Ave 85323 623-772-5000
Cathy Stafford, supt. Fax 772-5090
www.avondale.k12.az.us
Anderson S 800/K-8
45 S 3rd Ave 85323 623-772-5100
Randy Watkins, prin. Fax 772-5120
Coor S 1,200/K-8
1406 N Central Ave 85323 623-772-4400
Lori Goslar, prin. Fax 772-4420
Other Schools – See Goodyear

Litchfield ESD 79
Supt. — See Litchfield Park
Corte Sierra ES 800/PK-5
3300 N Santa Fe Trl, 623-547-1000
Chris Barnes, prin. Fax 935-2108
Rancho Santa Fe ES 700/PK-5
2150 W Rancho Santa Fe Blvd, 623-535-6500
Randy Dallas, prin. Fax 535-3072

Littleton ESD 65 4,300/PK-8
1252 S Avondale Blvd 85323 623-478-5600
Roger Freeman Ed.D., supt. Fax 478-5625
www.littletonaz.org
Collier S 900/K-8
350 S 118th Ave 85323 623-478-5900
Gioia Pitts, prin. Fax 478-5920
Littleton S 1,100/PK-8
1252 S Avondale Blvd 85323 623-478-5700
Dr. Juliet Mendez, prin. Fax 478-5720
Quentin S 1,000/K-8
11050 W Whyman Ave 85323 623-478-6000
Jazmin Pacheco, prin. Fax 478-6020
Other Schools – See Tolleson

Pendergast ESD 92
Supt. — See Phoenix
Canyon Breeze S 900/K-8
11675 W Encanto Blvd, 623-772-2610
Jeff Byrnes, prin. Fax 478-9912
Garden Lakes S 1,200/PK-8
10825 W Garden Lakes Pkwy, 623-772-2520
Harold Waltman, prin. Fax 877-9545
Rio Vista S 900/K-8
10237 W Encanto Blvd, 623-772-2670
Lee Ann Lawlor, prin. Fax 478-1972

St. Thomas Aquinas S 200/PK-8
13720 W Thomas Rd, 623-935-0945
Dr. James McDermott, prin. Fax 935-5044

Bagdad, Yavapai, Pop. 1,858
Bagdad USD 20 300/PK-12
PO Box 427 86321 928-633-4101
Rodney Wilhelm, supt. Fax 633-4345
Bagdad S 200/PK-8
PO Box 427 86321 928-633-2201
Tom Finnerty, prin. Fax 633-2541

Hillside ESD 35 50/K-8
HC 1 Box 3056 86321 928-442-3416
Camita de Ganahl, supt. Fax 442-9591
Hillside S 50/K-8
Main St 86321 928-442-3416
Carmita de Ganahl, lead tchr. Fax 442-9591

Bapchule, Pinal

St. Peter Indian Mission S 200/K-8
PO Box 10840, 520-315-3835
Sr. Martha Carpenter, prin. Fax 315-3963

Benson, Cochise, Pop. 4,934
Benson USD 9 1,000/PK-12
360 S Patagonia St 85602 520-586-2213
David Woodall, supt. Fax 586-2506
www.bensonsd.k12.az.us/
Benson ES 300/PK-4
360 S Patagonia St 85602 520-586-2213
Jomel Jansson, prin. Fax 586-2305
Benson MS 300/5-8
360 S Patagonia St 85602 520-586-2213
Shad Housley, prin. Fax 586-2253

Bisbee, Cochise, Pop. 6,177
Bisbee USD 2 1,000/PK-12
100 Old Douglas Rd 85603 520-432-5381
Dr. Gail McBride, supt. Fax 432-7622
www.busd.k12.az.us
Bisbee MS 200/4-6
100 Old Douglas Rd 85603 520-432-6100
Nancy Nicholson, prin. Fax 432-6139
Greenway PS 300/PK-3
100 Old Douglas Rd 85603 520-432-4361
Bruce Buffmire, prin. Fax 432-6121
Lowell JHS 100/7-8
100 Old Douglas Rd 85603 520-432-5391
Terri Romo, prin. Fax 432-6106

Black Canyon City, Yavapai, Pop. 1,811
Canon ESD 50 200/K-8
PO Box 89 85324 623-374-5588
Ron Hennings, supt. Fax 374-5046
www.canon50.com
Canon S 200/K-8
PO Box 89 85324 623-374-5588
Rick Barrett, prin. Fax 374-5045

Blue, Greenlee
Blue ESD 22 K-8
PO Box 80 85922 928-339-4346
Sally Hulsey, supt. Fax 339-4116
Blue S K-8
PO Box 80 85922 928-339-4346
Sally Hulsey, prin. Fax 339-4116

Bonita, Graham, Pop. 1,900
Bonita ESD 16 100/K-8
18008 S Fort Grant Rd 85643 928-828-3363
Ed Houser, supt. Fax 828-3422
www.bonita.k12.az.us
Bonita S 100/K-8
18008 S Fort Grant Rd 85643 928-828-3363
Ed Houser, prin. Fax 828-3422

Bouse, LaPaz
Bouse ESD 26 100/PK-8
PO Box S 85325 928-851-2213
Fax 851-2986
www.bouseschool.com/
Bouse S 100/PK-8
PO Box S 85325 928-851-2213
Kent Smith, lead tchr. Fax 851-2986

Bowie, Cochise
Bowie USD 14 100/K-12
PO Box 157 85605 520-847-2545
Patrick O'Donnell, supt. Fax 847-2546
www.bowieusd.k12.az.us
Bowie S 100/K-8
PO Box 157 85605 520-847-2545
Patrick O'Donnell, prin. Fax 847-2546

Buckeye, Maricopa, Pop. 9,619
Buckeye ESD 33 3,200/K-8
25555 W Durango St 85326 623-925-3400
Allen Steen, supt. Fax 386-6063
besd.k12.az.us
Bales S 700/K-8
25555 W Durango St 85326 623-847-8503
Fred Lugo, prin. Fax 327-0744
Buckeye MS 500/5-8
25555 W Durango St 85326 623-386-4487
Lorrese Roer, prin. Fax 386-7901
Buckeye PS 700/K-4
25555 W Durango St 85326 623-386-4487
Lorrese Roer, prin. Fax 386-7901
Inca S, 25555 W Durango St 85326 K-8
Corey Christiaens, prin. 623-925-3320
Jasinski S K-8
25555 W Durango St 85326 623-925-3100
Montessa Banning, prin. Fax 327-2708
Sundance S 1,400/K-8
25555 W Durango St 85326 623-847-8531
Tracy Casey, prin. Fax 386-6049
Westpark S 50/K-8
25555 W Durango St 85326 623-435-3282
Ruben Ruiz, prin. Fax 386-3398

Liberty ESD 25 2,800/PK-8
19871 W Fremont Rd 85326 623-474-6600
Dr. Andrew Rogers, supt. Fax 474-6629
www.liberty.k12.az.us
Freedom S 400/K-8
22150 W Sundance Pkwy 85326 623-327-2850
Kim Glenn, prin. Fax 327-2859
Liberty S 600/PK-8
19818 W US Highway 85 85326 623-327-2810
Nancy Bogart, prin. Fax 327-2819
Rainbow Valley S 700/K-8
19716 W Narramore Rd 85326 623-327-2830
Mike Cagle, prin. Fax 327-2839
Other Schools – See Goodyear

Litchfield ESD 79
Supt. — See Litchfield Park
Verrado ES 300/PK-5
20873 W Sunrise Ln, 623-547-1600
Molly Evans, prin. Fax 853-2314
Verrado MS 800/6-8
20880 W Main St, 623-547-1300
Kim Diaz, prin. Fax 853-2358

Saddle Mountain USD 90
Supt. — See Tonopah
Tartesso ES K-6
29677 W Indianola Ave, 623-474-5400
Carolyn Hardison, prin. Fax 474-5441

Wickenburg USD 9
Supt. — See Wickenburg
Festival Foothills ES K-5
26252 W Desert Vista Blvd, 928-501-6000
Marcia Hespen, prin. Fax 501-6010

Grace Fellowship Academy 100/K-8
1300 N Miller Rd 85326 623-393-8883
Sam Sacco, prin. Fax 393-8389

Bullhead City, Mohave, Pop. 39,101
Bullhead City ESD 15 3,900/PK-8
1004 Hancock Rd 86442 928-758-3961
William Allsbrooks, supt. Fax 758-4996
www.bullheadschools.com
Bullhead City JHS 700/6-8
1062 Hancock Rd 86442 928-758-3921
Pat Young, prin. Fax 758-7428
Coyote Canyon ES 700/PK-2
1820 Lakeside Dr 86442 928-758-4909
Dr. Carolyn Stewart, prin. Fax 758-8670
Desert Valley ES 700/3-5
1066 Marina Blvd 86442 928-758-6606
Cynthia Cochran, prin. Fax 758-5726
Diamondback ES 500/K-5
2550 Tesota Way 86442 928-758-6858
Jennifer Goodman, prin. Fax 758-5202
Fox Creek JHS 600/6-8
3101 Desert Sky Dr 86442 928-704-2500
Ronald Casey, prin. Fax 704-2504
Mountain View ES 300/K-5
2380 3rd St 86429 928-754-3203
Linda Anderson, prin. Fax 754-3852
Sunrise ES 300/K-5
2645 Landon Dr 86429 928-754-1815
Jennifer Flatten, prin. Fax 754-1820

Mohave Valley ESD 16
Supt. — See Mohave Valley
Camp Mohave ES 400/PK-6
1797 La Entrada Dr 86426 928-704-3600
David Berard, dir. Fax 704-3663
Fort Mojave ES 500/PK-6
1760 Joy Ln 86426 928-768-3986
Karen Reyer-Ferrand, prin. Fax 768-8075

Bylas, Graham, Pop. 1,219

Our Savior S 100/K-8
PO Box 18 85530 928-475-4448
Mark Moldenhauer, prin. Fax 475-4450

Cameron, Coconino, Pop. 493
Tuba City USD 15
Supt. — See Tuba City
Dzil Libei ES 86045 100/K-6
Sharlene Navaho, prin. 928-679-2243
Fax 679-2580

Camp Verde, Yavapai, Pop. 10,155
Camp Verde USD 28 1,600/PK-12
410 Camp Lincoln Rd 86322 928-567-8000
Jeff Van Handel Ph.D., supt. Fax 567-8004
www.campverdeschools.org
Camp Verde ES 700/PK-5
200 Camp Lincoln Rd 86322 928-567-8060
Debi Pottorff, prin. Fax 567-8063
Camp Verde MS 400/6-8
370 Camp Lincoln Rd 86322 928-567-8014
Dan Brown, prin. Fax 567-8022

Camp Verde United Christian S 100/K-8
PO Box 3126 86322 928-567-0415
Robin Showers, admin. Fax 567-9774

Carefree, Maricopa, Pop. 3,706

Our Lady of Joy S 100/PK-K
PO Box 1359 85377 480-595-6409
Deborah Allen, dir. Fax 437-1093

Casa Grande, Pinal, Pop. 32,855
Casa Grande ESD 4 6,600/PK-8
220 W Kortsen Rd, 520-836-2111
Frank Davidson, supt. Fax 426-3712
www.cgelem.k12.az.us
Cactus MS 1,100/6-8
1220 E Kortsen Rd, 520-421-3330
Deanna Smith-Stout, prin. Fax 421-7425
Casa Grande MS 1,100/6-8
300 W McMurray Blvd, 520-836-7310
Sylvia Trotter, prin. Fax 836-2399
Cholla ES 600/K-5
1180 E Kortsen Rd, 520-836-4719
Kathryn Steward, prin. Fax 836-1963
Cottonwood ES 600/K-5
1667 N Kadota Ave, 520-836-5601
Douglas Price, prin. Fax 836-1437
Desert Willow ES PK-5
2172 N Arizola Rd, 520-876-5397
Jennifer Murrieta, prin. Fax 876-0909
Evergreen ES 500/K-5
1000 N Amarillo St, 520-836-6694
Debbie John, prin. Fax 421-0423
Ironwood ES 700/K-5
1500 N Colorado St, 520-836-5086
Shirley Howell, prin. Fax 836-2203
McCartney Ranch ES PK-5
2631 N Brown Ave, 520-876-4235
Joanne Kramer, prin. Fax 876-4292
Mesquite ES 700/PK-5
129 N Arizola Rd, 520-836-7787
David Owen, prin. Fax 836-3289
Palo Verde ES 700/PK-5
40 N Roosevelt Ave, 520-421-1650
Daniel Garcia, prin. Fax 421-3013
Saguaro ES 600/K-5
1501 N Center Ave, 520-836-7661
Celie Downey-Foye, prin. Fax 836-1581
Villago MS 6-8
574 E Lakeside Pkwy, 520-423-0176
Jeffrey Lavender, prin. Fax 423-0177

Mary C. O'Brien Accommodation SD 90
Supt. — See Florence
O'Brien ES 100/K-6
PO Box 3125 85222 520-723-6700
Arlisa Crank-Townsend, prin. Fax 723-7232

St. Anthony of Padua S 300/PK-8
501 E 2nd St, 520-836-7247
Joseph Parzych, prin. Fax 836-7289

Cave Creek, Maricopa, Pop. 4,884
Cave Creek USD 93
Supt. — See Scottsdale
Desert Willow ES 600/PK-5
PO Box 426 85327 480-575-2800
Roger Hill, prin. Fax 419-7265
Horseshoe Trails ES 500/K-5
PO Box 426 85327 480-272-8500
Janiene Marlowe, prin. Fax 907-6643
Lone Mountain ES 600/K-5
PO Box 426 85327 480-437-3000
Nancy Shaver, prin. Fax 595-1312

Annunciation S 1-2
32648 N Cave Creek Rd 85331 480-595-0883
Dr. Sharon Pristash, prin. Fax 595-0886
Dynamite Montessori S 100/PK-6
29210 N 59th St 85331 480-563-5710
Paula Fabian-Leach, admin. Fax 515-4407

Chandler, Maricopa, Pop. 234,939
Chandler USD 80 35,400/PK-12
1525 W Frye Rd 85224 480-812-7000
Dr. Camille Casteel, supt. Fax 224-9128
ww2.chandler.k12.az.us/
Andersen ES 600/PK-6
1350 N Pennington Dr 85224 480-812-6000
Tony Smith, prin. Fax 812-6020
Andersen JHS 1,100/7-8
1255 N Dobson Rd 85224 480-883-5300
Jim Anderson, prin. Fax 883-5320
Basha ES 1,000/K-6
3535 S Basha Rd 85248 480-883-4400
Keith Falconer, prin. Fax 883-4420
Bogle JHS 1,100/7-8
1600 W Queen Creek Rd 85248 480-883-5500
Susie Avey, prin. Fax 883-5520
Bologna ES 800/K-6
1625 E Frye Rd 85225 480-883-4000
Jim Estes, prin. Fax 883-4020
Chandler Traditional JHS 6-7
191 W Oakland St 85225 480-224-3930
Don Shelley, prin.
Conley ES 800/K-6
500 S Arrowhead Dr 85224 480-812-6200
Erica Alexander, prin. Fax 812-6220
CTA Goodman Campus 500/PK-6
2600 W Knox Rd 85224 480-812-6900
Maureen Sniff, prin. Fax 812-6920
CTA Independence Campus 600/K-6
1405 W Lake Dr 85248 480-224-2700
Nancy Branch, prin. Fax 224-2720
CTA Liberty Campus 700/K-6
550 N Emmett Dr 85225 480-883-4900
Dr. Beth Ann Bader, prin. Fax 883-4920
Erie ES 500/K-6
1150 W Erie St 85224 480-812-6300
Leo Schlueter, prin. Fax 812-6320
Frye ES 800/K-6
801 E Frye Rd 85225 480-812-6400
Dr. Paul Ritz, prin. Fax 812-6420
Fulton ES 500/K-6
4750 S Sunland Dr 85248 480-224-3300
Susie Jayne, prin. Fax 224-3320
Galveston ES 900/K-6
661 E Galveston St 85225 480-812-6500
Mike Henderson, prin. Fax 812-6520
Haley ES PK-6
3401 S Layton Lakes Blvd, 480-224-3500
Pam Nephew, prin. Fax 224-3520
Hancock ES 700/K-6
2425 S Pleasant Dr, 480-883-5900
Connie Hull, prin. Fax 883-5920
Hartford Sylvia Encinas ES 700/PK-6
700 N Hartford St 85225 480-812-6700
Jim Tongring, prin. Fax 812-6720
Hull ES 1,100/K-6
2424 E Maren Dr 85249 480-883-4500
Cheryl Bromich, prin. Fax 883-4520
Humphrey ES 500/PK-6
125 S 132nd St 85225 480-812-6800
Luke Hickey, prin. Fax 812-6820
Jacobson ES 900/K-6
1515 NW Jacaranda Pkwy 85248 480-883-4100
Lynn Weed, prin. Fax 883-4120
Knox ES 500/K-6
700 W Orchid Ln 85225 480-812-6100
Ruth Michalscheck, prin. Fax 812-6120
Navarrete ES 1,100/K-6
6490 S Sun Groves Blvd 85249 480-883-4800
Sam Merrill, prin. Fax 883-4820

Ryan ES 1,000/K-6
4600 S Bright Angel Way 85249 480-224-3200
Diane Wells, prin. Fax 224-3220
Sanborn ES 900/K-6
700 N Superstition Blvd 85225 480-812-7300
Nel Capadona, prin. Fax 812-7320
San Marcos ES 500/K-6
451 W Frye Rd 85225 480-883-4200
Christine Sargent, prin. Fax 883-4220
Santan ES 1,000/K-6
1550 E Chandler Heights Rd 85249 480-883-4700
Heather Anguiano, prin. Fax 883-4620
Santan JHS 1,000/7-8
1550 E Chandler Heights Rd 85249 480-883-4600
Barbara Kowalinski, prin. Fax 883-4620
Shumway ES 600/K-6
1325 N Shumway Ave 85225 480-812-7400
Dr. Gary Londer, prin. Fax 812-7420
Tarwater ES 800/K-6
2300 S Gardner Dr, 480-883-4300
Jeff Hensley, prin. Fax 883-4320
Willis JHS 1,000/7-8
401 S McQueen Rd 85225 480-883-5700
Paul Bollard, prin. Fax 883-5720
Other Schools – See Gilbert, Queen Creek

Kyrene ESD 28
Supt. — See Tempe
Kyrene Aprende MS 1,000/6-8
777 N Desert Breeze Blvd E 85226 480-783-2200
Gerri Shaw, prin. Fax 940-0657
Kyrene de la Mirada ES 600/K-5
5500 W Galveston St 85226 480-783-2900
Donna Gallaher, prin. Fax 940-3560
Kyrene de la Paloma ES 600/K-5
5000 W Whitten St 85226 480-783-2700
Janet Tobias, prin. Fax 961-1745
Kyrene de las Brisas ES 700/PK-5
777 N Desert Breeze Blvd E 85226 480-783-2300
Christie Winkelmann, prin. Fax 940-5796
Kyrene del Cielo ES 700/PK-5
1350 N Lakeshore Dr 85226 480-783-2100
Mike Diegnan, prin. Fax 897-2986
Kyrene Del Pueblo MS 1,000/6-8
360 S Twelve Oaks Blvd 85226 480-783-2400
Jama Nacke, prin. Fax 961-4152
Kyrene del Sureno ES 400/K-5
3375 W Galveston St 85226 480-783-3000
Jim Strogen, prin. Fax 786-0848

Mesa USD 4
Supt. — See Mesa
Frost ES 500/K-6
1560 W Summit Pl 85224 480-472-3500
Jim Desmarchais, prin. Fax 472-3549
Jordan ES 600/PK-6
3320 N Carriage Ln 85224 480-472-3800
Mark Andrews, prin. Fax 472-3888
Pomeroy ES 500/K-6
1507 W Shawnee Dr 85224 480-472-3700
Rene Paschal, prin. Fax 472-3767
Sirrine ES 600/K-6
591 W Mesquite St 85225 480-472-3600
Greg Reid, prin. Fax 472-3666

Chandler Christian S 200/PK-6
301 N Hartford St 85225 480-963-0748
Ruth Zappe, admin. Fax 963-4322
CrossRoads Community S 100/K-8
2950 W Ray Rd 85224 480-722-1445
Barbara Cummings, admin. Fax 722-0770
St. Mary-Basha Catholic S 500/K-8
200 W Galveston St 85225 480-963-4951
Sr. Mary Norbert Long, prin. Fax 963-8959

Chinle, Apache, Pop. 5,059
Chinle USD 24 3,800/PK-12
PO Box 587 86503 928-674-9605
Jesus de la Garza, supt. Fax 674-9608
www.chinleusd.k12.az.us/
Canyon De Chelly S 600/1-3
PO Box 587 86503 928-674-9501
Moses Aruguete, prin. Fax 674-9557
Chinle ES 600/4-6
PO Box 587 86503 928-674-9503
Victor Benally, prin. Fax 674-9397
Chinle JHS 500/7-8
PO Box 587 86503 928-674-9505
Gloria Grant, prin. Fax 674-9424
Mesa View S 200/PK-K
PO Box 587 86503 928-674-9806
Lori Bitsui-Gray, prin. Fax 674-9899
Tsaile Public S, PO Box 587 86503 400/K-8
Florinda Jackson, prin. 928-674-9050
Other Schools – See Many Farms

Chinle SDA S 50/1-8
PO Box 2299 86503 928-674-3882

Chino Valley, Yavapai, Pop. 9,710
Chino Valley USD 51 2,800/PK-12
PO Box 225 86323 928-636-2458
Duane Noggle, supt. Fax 636-1434
www.cvsd.k12.az.us
Del Rio ES 700/PK-5
PO Box 225 86323 928-636-4414
Susan Clark, prin. Fax 636-6215
Heritage MS 700/6-8
PO Box 225 86323 928-636-4464
Scott Muir, prin. Fax 636-6214
Territorial ES 600/K-5
PO Box 225 86323 928-636-3842
Grant Turley, prin. Fax 636-0267

Clarkdale, Yavapai, Pop. 3,753
Clarkdale-Jerome SD 3 400/K-8
PO Box 248 86324 928-634-5035
Kathleen Fleenor, supt. Fax 639-0917
www.cjsd.k12.az.us

Clarkdale-Jerome S 400/K-8
PO Box 248 86324 928-634-7804
Kathleen Fleenor, prin. Fax 639-0917

Clifton, Greenlee, Pop. 2,265
Clifton USD 3 100/PK-12
PO Box 1567 85533 928-865-2752
Dr. Terry Bentley, supt. Fax 865-2792
Laugharn S 100/PK-8
PO Box 1567 85533 928-865-4917
Dr. Terry Bentley, prin. Fax 865-2792

Cochise, Cochise
Cochise ESD 26 100/K-8
PO Box 1088 85606 520-384-2540
Stephen Webb, supt. Fax 384-4836
www.cochiseschool.org
Cochise S 100/K-8
PO Box 1088 85606 520-384-2540
Stephen Webb, prin. Fax 384-4836

Colorado City, Mohave, Pop. 4,371
Colorado City USD 14 500/PK-12
PO Box 309 86021 928-279-7500
Carol Timpson, supt. Fax 279-7510
www.elcap.us
El Capitan S 500/PK-12
PO Box 309 86021 928-875-9000
Carol Timpson, prin. Fax 875-9098

Concho, Apache
Concho ESD 6 200/PK-8
PO Box 200 85924 928-337-4665
Barbara Berheim, admin. Fax 337-9354
www.conchoschool.net/
Concho S 200/PK-8
PO Box 200 85924 928-337-4665
Barbara Berheim, admin. Fax 337-2455

Congress, Yavapai
Congress ESD 100/K-8
PO Box 68 85332 928-427-9850
Toni Wayas, supt. Fax 427-9840
Congress S 100/K-8
PO Box 68 85332 928-427-9850
Toni Wayas, prin. Fax 427-9840

Coolidge, Pinal, Pop. 8,154
Coolidge USD 21 3,500/K-12
221 W Central Ave, 520-723-2040
Dr. Cecilia Johnson, admin. Fax 723-2442
www.coolidgeschools.org/
Heartland Ranch S K-8
1667 W Caroline St, 520-424-2100
Jessie Arroyos, prin. Fax 424-2110
Hohokam S 300/K-8
800 N 9th St, 520-723-2202
Macon Thompson, prin. Fax 723-2203
West S 1,100/K-8
460 S 7th St, 520-723-2702
Gerald Streit, prin. Fax 723-2707
Other Schools – See San Tan Valley

Cornville, Yavapai, Pop. 2,089
Cottonwood-Oak Creek ESD 6
Supt. — See Cottonwood
Oak Creek S 400/K-8
PO Box 310 86325 928-639-5109
Sherry Villas, prin. Fax 639-5108

Corona, Pima
Vail USD 20
Supt. — See Vail
Corona Foothills MS 500/6-8
16705 S Houghton Rd 85641 520-879-3500
Margaret Steuer, prin. Fax 879-3501

Cottonwood, Yavapai, Pop. 10,894
Cottonwood-Oak Creek ESD 6 2,500/PK-8
1 N Willard St 86326 928-634-2288
Barbara U'Ren, supt. Fax 634-2309
www.cocsd.k12.az.us
Bright ES 500/PK-2
1 N Willard St 86326 928-634-7039
Kathy Epperson, prin. Fax 639-8428
Cottonwood ES 500/3-5
1 N Willard St 86326 928-634-2191
Randy Koeppe, prin. Fax 639-0467
Cottonwood MS 700/6-8
1 N Willard St 86326 928-634-2231
Denise Kennedy, prin. Fax 634-2874
Tavasci ES 400/K-5
1 N Willard St 86326 928-649-8144
Sandra Huson, prin. Fax 649-8145
Other Schools – See Cornville

St. Joseph S PK-8
2715 E State Route 89A 86326 928-649-0624
Greg Kirkham, prin. Fax 649-1191
Verde Valley Adventist S 50/1-8
PO Box 1810 86326 928-634-7322
Verde Valley Christian S 200/PK-6
102 S Willard St 86326 928-634-8113
Henry Brown, admin. Fax 634-8278

Crown King, Yavapai
Crown King ESD 41 50/K-8
PO Box 188 86343 928-632-5207
Cheryl Franklin, lead tchr. Fax 632-5207
www.crownkingelementary.com/
Crown King S 50/K-8
PO Box 188 86343 928-632-5207
Cheryl Franklin, lead tchr. Fax 632-5207

Dateland, Yuma
Hyder ESD 16 200/K-8
PO Box 3001 85333 928-454-2242
John Koury, supt. Fax 454-2217
www.hyder-isd.org
Dateland S 200/K-8
PO Box 3001 85333 928-454-2242
Martha Jones, coord. Fax 454-2217

Sentinel ESD 71 50/K-8
53802 W US Hwy 80 E 85333 928-454-2474
Christopher Maynes, supt. Fax 454-2247
Sentinel S 50/K-8
53802 W US Hwy 80 E 85333 928-454-2474
Christopher Maynes, prin. Fax 454-2247

Dewey, Yavapai, Pop. 3,640
Humboldt USD 22
Supt. — See Prescott Valley
Bradshaw Mountain MS 600/6-8
12255 E Turquoise Cir 86327 928-759-4900
Brian Buchholtz, prin. Fax 759-4920

Dolan Springs, Mohave, Pop. 1,090
Kingman USD 20
Supt. — See Kingman
Mt. Tipton S 300/K-12
PO Box 248 86441 928-767-3350
Emma Weiss, prin. Fax 767-4330

Douglas, Cochise, Pop. 16,791
Apache ESD 42 50/K-8
PO Box 1119 85608 520-558-2364
Fax 558-2410
Apache S 50/K-8
PO Box 1119 85608 520-558-2364
Palma Hudson, lead tchr. Fax 558-2410

Douglas USD 27 4,300/PK-12
PO Box 1237 85608 520-364-2447
Earl Pettit, supt. Fax 364-7470
www.dusd.k12.az.us
Borane MS 400/6-8
PO Box 1237 85608 520-364-2461
Nick Schuerman, prin. Fax 364-5537
Carlson ES 400/K-5
PO Box 1237 85608 520-805-4400
Janice Gallagher, prin. Fax 364-6257
Clawson ES 400/K-5
PO Box 1237 85608 520-364-8466
Andrea Overman, prin. Fax 805-5531
Early Learning Center 200/PK-PK
PO Box 1237 85608 520-364-8473
Claudia Leon, prin. Fax 364-7470
Huber JHS 600/6-8
PO Box 1237 85608 520-364-2840
Martin Muecke, prin. Fax 364-2421
Marley ES 300/K-5
PO Box 1237 85608 520-364-3408
Claudia Leon, prin. Fax 805-5534
Stevenson ES 400/K-5
PO Box 1237 85608 520-364-2442
Rafael Ortiz, prin. Fax 364-7470
Other Schools – See Pirtleville

Lestonnac K 50/PK-K
1047 E 10th St 85607 520-364-3956
Rosa Delia Quintana, dir. Fax 364-1419
Loretto Catholic S 300/1-8
1200 E 14th St 85607 520-364-5754
Sr. Mary Marques, prin. Fax 364-7707

Duncan, Greenlee, Pop. 713
Duncan USD 2 500/K-12
PO Box 710 85534 928-359-2472
Eldon Merrell, supt. Fax 359-2807
duncan.k12.az.us
Duncan MS 200/3-8
PO Box 710 85534 928-359-2471
Cody Barlow, prin. Fax 359-1105
Duncan PS 100/K-2
PO Box 710 85534 928-359-2054
Cody Barlow, prin. Fax 359-2054

Eagar, Apache, Pop. 4,126
Round Valley USD 10
Supt. — See Springerville
Round Valley IS 300/3-5
165 S Brown 85925 928-333-6600
Darwin Rhoton, prin. Fax 333-6620
Round Valley MS 300/6-8
126 W 2nd St 85925 928-333-6700
John Allen, prin. Fax 333-5252

Ehrenberg, LaPaz, Pop. 1,226
Quartzsite ESD 4 300/K-8
PO Box 130 85334 928-923-7900
Jacque Price, supt. Fax 923-8908
www.qsd4.org
Ehrenberg S 200/K-8
PO Box 130 85334 928-923-7900
Jacque Price, prin. Fax 923-8908
Other Schools – See Quartzsite

Elfrida, Cochise
Elfrida ESD 12 200/PK-8
PO Box 328 85610 520-642-3428
Ron Aguallo, supt. Fax 642-3236
www.elfridaelem.org
Elfrida S 200/PK-8
PO Box 328 85610 520-642-3428
Ron Aguallo, prin. Fax 642-3236

Elgin, Santa Cruz
Sonoita ESD 25 100/K-8
HC 1 Box 36 85611 520-455-5514
Judy Neal, supt. Fax 455-5516
www.elgink12.com
Elgin S 100/K-8
HC 1 Box 36 85611 520-455-5514
Judy Neal, prin. Fax 455-5516

El Mirage, Maricopa, Pop. 22,171
Dysart USD 89
Supt. — See Surprise
Dysart S 1,100/K-8
12950 W Varney Rd 85335 623-876-7100
Patricia Buck, prin. Fax 876-7137
El Mirage S 1,100/K-8
13500 N El Mirage Rd 85335 623-876-7200
Dr. Joel Davidson, prin. Fax 876-7208

Public S 20 K-8
12701 N Main St 85335 623-523-8950
Andrea Willingham, prin. Fax 523-8961
Surprise S 1,100/K-8
12907 W Greenway Rd 85335 623-876-7400
Dr. David Dumon, prin. Fax 876-7411
Thompson Ranch S 700/K-8
11800 W Thompson Ranch Rd 85335 623-523-8400
Fran Sperling, prin. Fax 523-8411

Eloy, Pinal, Pop. 10,855
Eloy ESD 11 1,200/PK-8
1011 N Sunshine Blvd, 520-466-2100
Ruby James, supt. Fax 466-2101
www.eesd.k12.az.us/
Curiel Annex K 200/PK-K
1011 N Sunshine Blvd, 520-466-2110
Maria Wood, prin. Fax 466-2115
Curiel PS 400/1-3
1011 N Sunshine Blvd, 520-466-2120
Maria Wood, prin. Fax 466-2151
Eloy IS 400/4-6
1011 N Sunshine Blvd, 520-466-2130
Teresa Thorsen, prin. Fax 466-2114
Eloy JHS 300/7-8
1011 N Sunshine Blvd, 520-466-2140
Danny Rogers, prin. Fax 466-2150

Toltec ESD 22 1,200/PK-8
3315 N Toltec Rd 85131 520-466-2360
Dick Lesher, supt. Fax 466-2399
www.toltec.k12.az.us
Toltec MS 500/5-8
3315 N Toltec Rd, 520-466-2350
Dave Ascoli, prin. Fax 466-2399
Other Schools – See Arizona City

Flagstaff, Coconino, Pop. 57,391
Flagstaff USD 1 11,100/PK-12
3285 E Sparrow Ave 86004 928-527-6000
Dr. Kevin Brown, supt. Fax 527-6015
www.fusd1.org
Christensen ES 500/PK-6
4000 N Cummings St 86004 928-773-4140
Savino Ontiveros, prin. Fax 773-4138
Cromer ES 600/K-6
7150 Silver Saddle Rd 86004 928-773-4150
Kenneth Woolston, prin. Fax 526-8985
DeMiguel ES 600/K-6
3500 S Gillenwater Dr 86001 928-773-4000
Ninon Wilson, prin. Fax 773-4010
Flagstaff MS 700/7-8
755 N Bonito St 86001 928-773-8150
Steve Boadway, prin. Fax 773-8169
Killip ES 500/K-6
2300 E 6th Ave 86004 928-773-4080
Joseph Gutierrez, prin. Fax 773-4086
Kinsey ES 500/PK-6
1601 S Lone Tree Rd 86001 928-773-4060
Carolyn Hardy, prin. Fax 773-4070
Knoles ES 600/K-6
4005 E Butler Ave 86004 928-773-4120
Mary Walton, prin. Fax 773-4130
Leupp S 200/PK-8
3285 E Sparrow Ave 86004 928-686-6266
MaryJo Eldridge, prin. Fax 686-6246
Marshall ES 600/PK-6
850 N Bonito St 86001 928-773-4030
Stacie Zanzucchi, prin. Fax 773-4035
Mount Elden/Renaissance Magnet MS 700/7-8
3223 N 4th St 86004 928-773-8250
Rodney Johnson, prin. Fax 773-8269
Puente de Hozho Magnet S 400/K-6
3401 N 4th St 86004 928-773-4090
Dawn Trubakoff, prin. Fax 773-4100
Sechrist ES 500/K-6
2230 N Fort Valley Rd 86001 928-773-4020
John Albert, prin. Fax 773-4026
South Beaver ES 300/K-6
506 S Beaver St 86001 928-773-4050
Frank Garcia, admin. Fax 773-4048
Thomas ES 500/K-6
3330 E Lockett Rd 86004 928-773-4110
Tom Ziegler, prin. Fax 773-4108

Flagstaff Community Christian S 100/K-8
PO Box 30841 86003 928-522-5968
Eric Garland, admin.
Montessori S of Flagstaff 50/6-8
2212 E Cedar Ave 86004 928-774-1600
Marlane Spencer, prin. Fax 774-0424
Mt. Calvary S 100/PK-8
2605 N Fort Valley Rd 86001 928-774-8811
Kurt Mueller, prin. Fax 779-2352
Peace Lutheran S 100/PK-PK
3430 N 4th St 86004 928-526-9256
Fax 526-0260
San Francisco de Asis S 300/PK-8
320 N Humphreys St 86001 928-779-1337
Mary Malinoski, prin. Fax 774-1943

Florence, Pinal, Pop. 17,053
Florence USD 1 4,000/PK-12
PO Box 2850, 520-866-3500
Dr. Gary Nine, supt. Fax 868-2302
www.florenceusd.org/
Anthem S K-8
PO Box 2850, 520-723-6400
Kathy Brown, prin. Fax 723-0124
Florence S 900/PK-8
PO Box 2850, 520-866-3540
Manuel Hernandez, prin. Fax 868-2312
Other Schools – See Queen Creek

Mary C. O'Brien Accommodation SD 90 200/K-6
PO Box 769 85132 520-866-6565
Orlenda Roberts, supt. Fax 866-6890
www.pinalcountyschools.org
Other Schools – See Casa Grande

Fort Defiance, Apache, Pop. 4,489
Window Rock USD 8 2,400/K-12
PO Box 559 86504 928-729-6705
Thomas Jackson, supt. Fax 729-5780
www.wrschool.net
Sawmill Primary Learning Center 50/K-3
PO Box 559 86504 928-729-6857
Joy Manus, prin. Fax 729-7724
Tsehootsooi Dine Bi'olta Immersion S 200/K-8
PO Box 559 86504 928-729-6842
Maggie Benally, prin. Fax 729-7563
Tse' hootsooi' ES 300/K-5
PO Box 559 86504 928-729-7802
Lorna Lewis, prin. Fax 729-7638
Tse Ho Tso MS 400/6-8
PO Box 559 86504 928-729-6802
Roberta Tayah, prin. Fax 729-7572
Other Schools – See Window Rock

Fort Huachuca, See Sierra Vista
Fort Huachuca Accommodation SD 00 1,000/PK-8
PO Box 12954 85670 520-458-5082
Dr. Ronda Frueauff, supt. Fax 515-5972
www.fthuachuca.k12.az.us
Johnston ES 400/PK-2
PO Box 12954 85670 520-459-8798
Karen Sherman, prin. Fax 452-4090
Myer ES 400/3-5
PO Box 12954 85670 520-459-8986
Connie Johnson, prin. Fax 452-4092
Smith MS 300/6-8
PO Box 12954 85670 520-459-8892
Robert Henderson, prin. Fax 459-8939

Fort Thomas, Graham
Fort Thomas USD 7 500/K-12
PO Box 28 85536 928-485-9423
Dr. Leon Ben, supt. Fax 485-3019
www.fortthomas.org/
Fort Thomas ES 200/K-6
PO Box 55 85536 928-485-2433
Lonnie Lunt, prin. Fax 485-3068

Fountain Hills, Maricopa, Pop. 23,217
Fountain Hills USD 98 2,400/PK-12
16000 E Palisades Blvd 85268 480-664-5011
Bill Myhr, supt. Fax 664-5099
fhusd.org
Fountain Hills MS 600/6-8
15414 N McDowell Mountain R 85268 480-664-5400
Tom Brennan, prin. Fax 664-5499
Four Peaks ES 500/3-5
17300 E Calaveras Ave 85268 480-664-5100
Rebecca Romans, prin. Fax 664-5199
McDowell Mountain ES 500/PK-2
14825 N Fayette Dr 85268 480-664-5200
Joanne Meehan, prin. Fax 664-5299

Fredonia, Coconino, Pop. 1,051
Fredonia-Moccasin USD 6 400/PK-12
PO Box 247 86022 928-643-7333
Nicholas Bartlett, supt. Fax 643-7044
www.fredonia.org/
Fredonia S 200/PK-8
PO Box 247 86022 928-643-7386
L. Kirt Robinson, prin. Fax 643-7324
Moccasin PS 50/K-2
PO Box 247 86022 928-643-7222
L. Kirt Robinson, prin. Fax 643-7044

Gadsden, Yuma
Gadsden ESD 32
Supt. — See San Luis
Gadsden ES 500/K-6
18745 Gadsden St 85336 928-627-6970
Carmelann Barry, prin. Fax 627-9771

Ganado, Apache, Pop. 1,257
Ganado USD 20 1,800/K-12
PO Box 1757 86505 928-755-1011
Deborah Dennison, supt. Fax 755-1012
www.ganado.k12.az.us/
Ganado IS 400/4-6
PO Box 1757 86505 928-755-1311
Keith Pertusio, prin. Fax 755-1302
Ganado MS 300/7-8
PO Box 1757 86505 928-755-1411
Fernando Madrid, prin. Fax 755-1402
Ganado PS 400/K-3
PO Box 1757 86505 928-755-1211
Helen Aseret, prin. Fax 755-1202

Gila Bend, Maricopa, Pop. 2,055
Gila Bend USD 24 500/PK-12
PO Box V 85337 928-683-2225
James Mosley, supt. Fax 683-2671
gila.az.schoolwebpages.com
Gila Bend S 300/PK-8
PO Box V 85337 928-683-2225
Jim Walker, prin. Fax 683-2671

Paloma ESD 94 100/K-8
38739 W I-8 85337 928-683-2588
Clara Vinzant, supt. Fax 683-2093
Kiser S 100/K-8
38739 W I 8 85337 928-683-2588
Clara Vinzant, prin. Fax 683-2093

Gilbert, Maricopa, Pop. 173,989
Chandler USD 80
Supt. — See Chandler
CTA Freedom Campus 800/K-6
6040 S Joslyn Ln, 480-224-2600
Wendy Nance, prin. Fax 224-2620
Patterson ES PK-6
7520 S Adora Blvd, 480-224-3600
Kristine Palbykin, prin. Fax 224-3620
Riggs ES 700/K-6
6930 S Seville Blvd W, 480-224-3400
Jan Weyenberg, prin. Fax 224-3420

Weinberg ES 1,000/K-6
5245 S Val Vista Dr, 480-812-7500
Joe Walters, prin. Fax 812-7520

Gilbert Unified SD 37,100/PK-12
140 S Gilbert Rd 85296 480-497-3300
Dave Allison Ed.D., supt. Fax 497-3398
www.gilbert.k12.az.us/
Ashland Ranch ES 1,000/PK-6
1945 S Ashland Ranch Rd, 480-917-9900
Bill Roth, prin. Fax 917-3400
Burk ES 500/PK-6
545 N Burk St 85234 480-926-3816
Brad Paes, prin. Fax 813-8789
Carol Rae Ranch ES 600/PK-6
3777 E Houston Ave 85234 480-507-1359
Geane Flournoy, prin. Fax 503-1487
Finley Farms ES 900/K-6
375 S Columbus Dr 85296 480-507-1624
John Maas, prin. Fax 507-1633
Gilbert ES 800/PK-6
175 W Elliot Rd 85233 480-892-8624
Sheila Rogers, prin. Fax 813-7284
Gilbert JHS 800/7-8
1016 N Burk St 85234 480-892-6908
Kevin Rainey, prin. Fax 813-8240
Greenfield ES 800/K-6
2550 E Elliot Rd 85234 480-892-2801
Colin Kelly, prin. Fax 926-3673
Greenfield JHS 1,000/7-8
101 S Greenfield Rd 85296 480-813-1770
Joyce Meyer, prin. Fax 813-7279
Highland Park ES PK-6
230 N Cole Ct 85234 480-832-3034
Jason Martin, prin. Fax 832-3027
Houston ES 600/PK-6
500 E Houston Ave 85234 480-497-9790
Shawn McIntosh, prin. Fax 813-6997
Islands ES 600/K-6
245 S McQueen Rd 85233 480-497-0742
Matt O'Neill, prin. Fax 813-6809
Mesquite ES 600/K-6
1000 E Mesquite St 85296 480-813-1240
Missy Udall, prin. Fax 813-7387
Mesquite JHS 1,000/7-8
130 W Mesquite St 85233 480-926-1433
Ron Izzett, prin. Fax 813-9002
Neely Traditional Academy 600/PK-6
321 W Juniper Ave 85233 480-892-2805
Dr. Caroline Chilton, prin. Fax 497-6953
Oak Tree ES 800/PK-6
505 W Houston Ave 85233 480-632-4785
Sandra Weaver, prin. Fax 632-4794
Patterson ES 600/PK-6
1211 E Guadalupe Rd 85234 480-892-2803
Nonda Chomokos, prin. Fax 926-3674
Pioneer ES 600/PK-6
1535 N Greenfield Rd 85234 480-892-2022
Mike Davis, prin. Fax 813-9010
Playa del Rey ES 700/PK-6
550 N Horne St 85233 480-892-7810
Dr. Robyn Conrad, prin. Fax 892-8842
Quartz Hill ES K-6
3680 S Quartz St 85297 480-855-5732
Michael Hallock, prin. Fax 855-5797
Settler's Point ES 800/K-6
423 E Settlers Point Dr 85296 480-507-1481
Lana Moore, prin. Fax 507-1550
Sonoma Ranch ES 700/PK-6
601 N Key Biscayne Dr 85234 480-497-9343
Terry Maurer, prin. Fax 497-9574
South Valley JHS 900/7-8
2034 S Lindsay Rd, 480-855-0015
Brian Jaeger, prin. Fax 855-3542
Spectrum ES 1,100/PK-6
2846 S Spectrum Way, 480-917-0117
Debbie Singleton, prin. Fax 917-6923
Towne Meadows ES 800/PK-6
1101 N Recker Rd 85234 480-854-1545
Jim Baker, prin. Fax 854-1641
Val Vista Lakes ES 600/PK-6
1030 N Blue Grotto Dr 85234 480-926-6301
Susie Apel, prin. Fax 813-9011
Other Schools – See Mesa

Higley USD 60 7,200/PK-12
2935 S Recker Rd, 480-279-7000
Dr. Denise Birdwell, supt. Fax 279-7005
www.husd.org
Chaparral S PK-8
3380 E Frye Rd, 480-279-7900
Jessica Edgar, prin. Fax 279-7905
Coronado S 1,100/PK-8
4333 S Deanza Blvd 85297 480-279-6900
Theodora Schiro, prin. Fax 279-6905
Higley S 900/PK-8
3391 E Vest Ave, 480-279-6800
Kathleen Hughes, prin. Fax 279-6805
Power Ranch S 1,300/PK-8
4351 S Ranch House Pkwy 85297 480-279-7600
Greg Bellemare, prin. Fax 279-7605
San Tan S 1,200/K-8
3443 E Calistoga Dr 85297 480-279-7200
Maureen Migacz, prin. Fax 279-7205
Other Schools – See Higley, Queen Creek

Bios Christian Academy 50/K-12
326 E Guadalupe Rd 85234 480-440-9203
Tim Ihms, admin. Fax 303-0578
Christ's Greenfield Lutheran S 200/K-8
425 N Greenfield Rd 85234 480-892-8314
Bob Burgess, prin. Fax 503-0437
Heritage Christian Academy 300/PK-8
919 E Guadalupe Rd 85234 480-926-1141
Cinda Thompson, prin. Fax 545-9302
Surrey Garden Christian S 400/K-12
1424 S Promenade Ln 85296 480-279-1366
Bob Bajema, admin. Fax 279-5433

Glendale, Maricopa, Pop. 239,435
Alhambra ESD 68
Supt. — See Phoenix
Barcelona MS 900/4-8
6530 N 44th Ave 85301 623-842-8616
Tyson Kelly, prin. Fax 842-1384
Peck PS 900/K-3
5810 N 49th Ave 85301 623-842-3889
Judy Gill, prin. Fax 847-7151

Deer Valley USD 97
Supt. — See Phoenix
Arrowhead ES 800/PK-6
7490 W Union Hills Dr 85308 623-376-4100
Dr. Bert Ciaramello, prin. Fax 376-4180
Bellair ES 600/PK-6
4701 W Grovers Ave 85308 602-467-5700
Sue Clark, prin. Fax 467-5780
Copper Creek ES 800/K-6
7071 W Hillcrest Blvd 85310 623-376-3900
Brian Fineberg, prin. Fax 376-3980
Desert Sage ES 800/K-6
4035 W Alameda Rd 85310 623-445-4700
Lisa Crain, prin. Fax 445-4780
Desert Sky MS 900/7-8
5130 W Grovers Ave 85308 602-467-6500
Don Morrison, prin. Fax 467-6580
Greenbrier ES 500/K-6
6150 W Greenbriar Dr 85308 602-467-5500
Jody Brammer, prin. Fax 467-5580
Highland Lakes S 1,000/K-8
19000 N 63rd Ave 85308 623-376-4300
Mark Anderson, prin. Fax 376-4380
Hillcrest MS 1,100/7-8
22833 N 71st Ave 85310 623-376-3300
Dannene Truett, prin. Fax 376-3380
Las Brisas ES 800/PK-6
5805 W Alameda Rd 85310 623-445-5500
Patricia McAlarnen, prin. Fax 445-5580
Legend Springs ES 600/K-6
21150 N Arrowhead Loop Rd 85308 623-376-4500
Carolyn Butler, prin. Fax 376-4580
Mirage ES 700/PK-6
3910 W Grovers Ave 85308 602-467-5300
Jennifer Cruz, prin. Fax 467-5380
Mountain Shadows ES 700/K-6
19602 N 45th Ave 85308 623-445-4300
Jim Pfeiffer, prin. Fax 445-4380
Park Meadows ES 600/PK-6
20012 N 35th Ave 85308 623-445-4100
Kathi Humble, prin. Fax 445-4180
Sierra Verde S 800/K-8
7241 W Rose Garden Ln 85308 623-376-4800
Cherryl Paul, prin. Fax 376-4880

Dysart USD 89
Supt. — See Surprise
Luke S 800/K-8
7300 N Dysart Rd 85307 623-876-7300
Jean Meier, prin. Fax 876-7305

Glendale ESD 40 13,600/PK-8
7301 N 58th Ave 85301 623-237-4000
Dr. Sandra Johnson, supt.
www.gesd40.org/
Bicentennial North S 700/4-8
7237 W Missouri Ave 85303 623-237-4900
Kenneth Fleming, prin. Fax 237-4915
Bicentennial South S 700/K-3
7240 W Colter St 85303 623-842-8295
Sue Pederson, prin. Fax 848-6578
Burton S 600/K-8
4801 W Maryland Ave 85301 623-842-8270
Holly Northcott, prin. Fax 842-8337
Challenger MS 1,000/4-8
6905 W Maryland Ave 85303 623-237-4011
Tiffany Molina, prin. Fax 237-5115
Coyote Ridge S 900/K-8
7677 W Bethany Home Rd 85303 623-842-8215
Susanne Hill, prin. Fax 845-0617
Desert Garden S 600/K-3
7020 W Ocotillo Rd 85303 623-237-4014
Michelle Mitchell, prin. Fax 842-8388
Desert Spirit S 800/K-8
7355 W Orangewood Ave 85303 623-237-4016
Chad Lanese, prin. Fax 237-5615
Discovery S 900/PK-8
7910 W Maryland Ave 85303 623-842-8213
Diane Pesch, prin. Fax 842-8255
Glendale American S 900/PK-8
8530 N 55th Ave 85302 623-842-8280
J.P. Ketcham, prin. Fax 842-8339
Glendale Landmark MS 800/6-8
5730 W Myrtle Ave 85301 623-237-4001
Sherry Stillman, prin. Fax 842-8330
Horizon S 900/K-8
8520 N 47th Ave 85302 623-842-8200
Diane Garner, prin. Fax 842-8338
Imes S 600/K-8
6625 N 56th Ave 85301 623-842-8220
Kathy Rudisill, prin. Fax 842-8331
Jack ES 1,000/PK-3
6600 W Missouri Ave 85301 623-237-4005
Kristen Hartsuff, prin. Fax 237-4515
Mensendick IS 800/4-8
5535 N 67th Ave 85301 623-237-4006
Angie Schultz, prin. Fax 237-4615
Sine S 900/K-8
4932 W Myrtle Ave 85301 623-842-8240
Gwen Parker, prin. Fax 842-8334
Smith ES 900/K-5
6534 N 63rd Ave 85301 623-842-8230
Dr. Rick Alvarez, prin. Fax 842-8333
Sunset Vista S 600/K-8
7775 W Orangewood Ave 85303 623-237-4017
Jacqueline Cunningham, prin. Fax 237-5708

Pendergast ESD 92
Supt. — See Phoenix
Desert Mirage S 800/PK-8
8605 W Maryland Ave 85305 623-772-2550
Susie Torrejos, prin. Fax 872-8401
Sonoran Sky S 600/K-8
10150 W Missouri Ave 85307 623-772-2640
Kristine Morris, prin. Fax 772-1005
Sunset Ridge S 500/K-8
8490 W Missouri Ave 85305 623-772-2730
Carrie Prielipp, prin. Fax 877-4935

Peoria USD 11 37,100/PK-12
6330 W Thunderbird Rd 85306 623-486-6000
Dr. Denton Santarelli, supt. Fax 486-6009
portal.peoriaud.k12.az.us/default.aspx
Canyon S 500/PK-8
5490 W Paradise Ln 85306 623-412-5050
Cheryl Neils, prin. Fax 412-5061
Copperwood S 800/K-8
11232 N 65th Ave 85304 623-412-4650
Dr. Michael Crudder, prin. Fax 412-4660
Desert Palms S 700/K-8
11441 N 55th Ave 85304 623-412-4600
Janet Swarstad, prin. Fax 412-4609
Desert Valley S 700/PK-8
12901 N 63rd Ave 85304 623-412-4750
Vivian Hunt, prin. Fax 412-4755
Foothills S 800/K-8
15808 N 63rd Ave 85306 623-412-4625
Rhea Acosta, prin. Fax 412-4635
Heritage S 800/K-8
5312 W Mountain View Rd 85302 623-412-4525
Lynn Brodie, prin. Fax 412-4535
Kachina S 500/K-8
5304 W Crocus Dr 85306 623-412-4500
Brad Henkel, prin. Fax 412-4509
Marshall Ranch S 700/K-8
12995 N Marshall Ranch Dr 85304 623-486-6450
Fritz Maynes, prin. Fax 486-6461
Pioneer S 700/K-8
6315 W Port Au Prince Ln 85306 623-412-4550
Laura Walin, prin. Fax 412-4561
Sahuaro Ranch S 700/PK-8
10401 N 63rd Ave 85302 623-412-4775
Valerie Larrison, prin. Fax 412-4786
Other Schools – See Peoria, Sun City

Washington ESD 6 24,300/PK-8
4650 W Sweetwater Ave 85304 602-347-2600
Dr. Susan Cook, supt. Fax 347-2720
www.wesdschools.org
Arroyo ES 500/K-6
4535 W Cholla St 85304 602-896-5100
Pat MacArthur, prin. Fax 896-5120
Sunburst ES 700/K-6
14218 N 47th Ave 85306 602-896-6400
Mike Christensen, prin. Fax 896-6420
Sunset ES 600/K-6
4626 W Mountain View Rd 85302 602-347-3300
Betty Paterson, prin. Fax 347-3320
Sweetwater S 500/K-8
4602 W Sweetwater Ave 85304 602-896-6500
Luanne Herman, prin. Fax 896-6520
Other Schools – See Phoenix

Atonement Lutheran S 200/PK-6
4001 W Beardsley Rd 85308 623-374-3019
Andrew Sielaff, admin. Fax 587-8512
Grace Lutheran S 100/PK-8
5600 W Palmaire Ave 85301 623-937-2010
Matthew Herbst, prin. Fax 937-4390
Joy Christian S 500/K-12
21000 N 75th Ave 85308 623-561-2000
Nate Kretzmann, dir. Fax 362-3202
Our Lady of Perpetual Help S 500/PK-8
7521 N 57th Ave 85301 623-931-7288
Mary Waldmann, prin. Fax 930-0256
St. Louis the King S 300/PK-8
4331 W Maryland Ave 85301 623-939-4260
Jane Daigle, prin. Fax 930-1129

Globe, Gila, Pop. 7,187
Globe USD 1, 455 N Willow St 85501 2,000/PK-12
Dr. Timothy Trent, supt. 928-402-6000
www.globe.k12.az.us/
Copper Rim ES 800/PK-4
455 N Willow St 85501 928-402-6000
Lorraine Cannon, prin.
High Desert MS 600/5-8
455 N Willow St 85501 928-402-5700
Steve Estatico, prin. Fax 402-5788

Holy Angels S 200/PK-8
1300 E Cedar St 85501 928-425-5703
Rebecca Grant, prin. Fax 425-3136

Gold Canyon, See Apache Junction
Apache Junction USD 43
Supt. — See Apache Junction
Peralta Trail ES 500/K-5
10965 E Peralta Rd 85218 480-982-1110
Larry LaPrise, prin. Fax 288-4490

Golden Valley, Mohave, Pop. 2,619
Kingman USD 20
Supt. — See Kingman
Black Mountain S 600/PK-8
3404 N Santa Maria Rd 86413 928-565-9111
Becky Collins, prin. Fax 565-9190

Goodyear, Maricopa, Pop. 43,941
Avondale ESD 44
Supt. — See Avondale
Centerra Mirage S 800/K-8
15151 W Centerra Dr S 85338 623-772-4800
Talmadge Tanks, prin. Fax 772-4820
Copper Trails S PK-8
16875 W Canyon Trails Blvd 85338 623-772-5088
Linda Wemple, prin. Fax 772-5001

Desert Star S 1,000/K-8
2131 S 157th Ave 85338 623-772-4600
Patricia Scarpa, prin. Fax 772-4620
Desert Thunder S 900/K-8
16750 W Garfield St 85338 623-772-4700
Wayne Deffenbaugh, prin. Fax 772-4720
Felix S 700/K-8
540 E La Pasada Blvd 85338 623-772-4300
Evangeline Diaz, prin. Fax 772-4320
Wildflower S 600/K-8
325 S Wildflower Dr 85338 623-772-5200
Ruben Lara, prin. Fax 772-5220

Liberty ESD 25
Supt. — See Buckeye
Estrella Mountain S 700/K-8
10301 S San Miguel Ave 85338 623-327-2820
Dave Bogart, prin. Fax 327-2829
Westar S 400/K-8
17777 W Westar Dr 85338 623-327-2840
Dave Richardson, prin. Fax 327-2849

Litchfield ESD 79
Supt. — See Litchfield Park
Palm Valley ES 900/PK-5
2801 N 135th Ave, 623-535-6400
Sarah Pearson, prin. Fax 935-0058
Western Sky MS 900/6-8
4905 N 144th Ave, 623-535-6300
Alan Harper, prin. Fax 935-9536

Phoenix Christian ES West Valley 200/K-7
14900 W Van Buren St 85338 623-882-2531
Donn Start, admin. Fax 234-2199
St. John Vianney S 300/PK-8
539 E La Pasada Blvd 85338 623-932-2434
Sr. Ignacia Carrillo, prin. Fax 925-0094
St. Thomas Lutheran S 50/K-8
16260 W Van Buren St 85338 623-925-1095
Craig Kiecker, prin. Fax 925-1095

Grand Canyon, Coconino
Grand Canyon USD 4 200/K-12
PO Box 519 86023 928-638-2461
Sheila Breen, supt. Fax 638-2045
www.grandcanyonschool.org
Grand Canyon S 200/K-12
PO Box 519 86023 928-638-2461
Becky Crumbo, hdmstr. Fax 638-2045

Green Valley, Pima, Pop. 13,231
Continental ESD 39 400/PK-8
PO Box 547 85622 520-625-4581
Jim Nelson, supt. Fax 648-2569
www.csd39.org/
Continental S 400/PK-8
PO Box 547 85622 520-625-4581
Jim Nelson, prin. Fax 648-2569

Guadalupe, Maricopa, Pop. 5,258
Tempe ESD 3
Supt. — See Tempe
Frank ES 700/K-5
8409 S Avenida Del Yaqui 85283 480-897-6202
Amy Uchacz, prin. Fax 777-0146

Heber, Navajo, Pop. 1,581
Heber-Overgaard USD 6 500/PK-12
PO Box 547 85928 928-535-4622
Ken VanWinkle, supt. Fax 535-5146
www.heberovergaardschools.org
Capps MS / Mogollon JHS 100/4-8
PO Box 820 85928 928-535-4622
Ron Tenney, prin. Fax 535-9044
Other Schools – See Overgaard

Hereford, Cochise
Palominas ESD 49 1,100/PK-8
PO Box 38 85615 520-366-6204
Lee Hager Ph.D., supt. Fax 366-5717
palominas.k12.az.us
Palominas S 400/PK-8
PO Box 38 85615 520-366-5441
W. Joe Holder, prin. Fax 366-5875
Valley View S 200/K-8
PO Box 38 85615 520-366-5508
Martin Ellsworth, prin. Fax 366-5592
Other Schools – See Sierra Vista

Higley, Maricopa
Higley USD 60
Supt. — See Gilbert
Gateway Pointe S 800/PK-8
2069 S De La Torre Dr 85236 480-279-7700
Paul Murray, prin. Fax 279-7705

Holbrook, Navajo, Pop. 5,126
Holbrook USD 3 2,000/K-12
PO Box 640 86025 928-524-6144
Dr. Robbie Koerperich, supt. Fax 524-3073
www.holbrook.k12.az.us
Holbrook JHS 400/6-8
PO Box 640 86025 928-524-3959
Linda Crumrine, prin. Fax 524-3766
Hulet ES 300/3-5
PO Box 640 86025 928-524-6181
Tim Newton-Pender, prin. Fax 524-2940
Indian Wells ES 300/K-5
PO Box 640 86025 928-654-3160
Dr. Jeri McKinnon, prin. Fax 654-3162
Park PS 300/K-2
PO Box 640 86025 928-524-6138
Connie McPherson, prin. Fax 524-6998

Holbrook SDA Indian S 100/1-12
PO Box 910 86025 928-524-6845
Dr. Janet Claymore-Ross, prin. Fax 524-3190
Living Word Christian S 50/PK-2
111 W Hopi Dr 86025 928-524-2388
Theodore Julien, admin.

Huachuca City, Cochise, Pop. 1,890
Tombstone USD 1
Supt. — See Tombstone
Huachuca City S 400/PK-8
100 School Dr 85616 520-456-9842
Thomas Yarborough, prin. Fax 456-9811

Humboldt, Yavapai
Humboldt USD 22
Supt. — See Prescott Valley
Humboldt ES 300/K-5
PO Box 8 86329 928-759-4400
Cole Young, prin. Fax 759-4420

Joseph City, Navajo
Joseph City USD 2 400/PK-12
PO Box 8 86032 928-288-3307
Hollis Merrell, supt. Fax 288-3309
myweb.cableone.net/joecity
Joseph City ES 300/PK-6
PO Box 8 86032 928-288-3329
Daniel Hutchens, prin. Fax 288-3317

Kayenta, Navajo, Pop. 4,372
Kayenta USD 27 2,300/PK-12
PO Box 337 86033 928-697-2008
Evangeline Wilkinson, supt. Fax 697-2160
www.kayenta.k12.az.us
Kayenta IS 400/3-5
PO Box 337 86033 928-697-2371
LaVerne Bradley, prin. Fax 697-2382
Kayenta MS 500/6-8
PO Box 337 86033 928-697-2297
Marti Gilmore, prin. Fax 697-2308
Kayenta PS 400/PK-2
PO Box 337 86033 928-697-2423
Jacqueline Benally, prin. Fax 697-2495

Keams Canyon, Navajo, Pop. 393
Cedar USD 25 400/K-12
PO Box 367 86034 928-738-2366
Damon Clarke, supt. Fax 738-5404
www.cedarusd.org
Jeddito S 300/K-8
PO Box 367 86034 928-738-2334
Kathleen Thomson, prin. Fax 738-5134

Kearny, Pinal, Pop. 2,765
Ray USD 3 700/PK-12
PO Box 427, 520-363-5515
Dr. Robert Dunn, supt. Fax 363-5642
www.ray.k12.az.us
Ray MS 200/5-8
PO Box 427, 520-363-5511
Curt Cook, prin. Fax 363-5005
Ray PS 200/PK-4
PO Box 427, 520-363-5527
Rochelle Pacheco, prin. Fax 363-5017

Kingman, Mohave, Pop. 25,547
Hackberry SD 3 100/PK-8
9501 E Nellie Dr 86401 928-692-0013
Brad Ellico, supt. Fax 692-1075
cedarhillsschool.org
Cedar Hills S 100/PK-8
9501 E Nellie Dr 86401 928-692-0013
Brad Ellico, prin. Fax 692-1075

Kingman USD 20 7,000/PK-12
3033 McDonald Ave 86401 928-753-5678
Roger Jacks, supt. Fax 753-6910
www.kusd.org
Cerbat ES 600/K-5
2689 E Jagerson Ave, 928-757-5100
Dawn McGill, prin. Fax 757-4911
Hualapai ES 800/K-5
350 Eastern Ave 86401 928-753-1919
Chris Nutt, prin. Fax 753-1418
Kingman JHS 800/6-8
1969 Detroit Ave 86401 928-753-3588
Jerry Arave, prin. Fax 753-1336
La Senita ES 700/K-5
3175 Gordon Dr, 928-757-4328
Sue Hamilton, prin. Fax 757-7537
Manzanita ES 700/PK-5
2601 Detroit Ave 86401 928-753-6197
Jeri Wolsey, prin. Fax 753-7756
Palo Christi ES 300/K-5
500 Maple St 86401 928-753-2472
Steve Hite, prin. Fax 753-7895
White Cliffs MS 6-8
400 Grandview Ave 86401 928-753-6216
John Venenga, prin. Fax 753-4042
Other Schools – See Dolan Springs, Golden Valley

Emmanuel Christian Academy 50/K-8
PO Box 4056 86402 928-681-4220
Karen Benson, admin. Fax 681-4220

Kirkland, Yavapai
Kirkland ESD 23 100/PK-6
PO Box 210 86332 928-442-3258
Pamela Hampton, supt. Fax 442-9488
www.kirklandelementaryschool.4t.com/
Kirkland ES 100/PK-6
PO Box 210 86332 928-442-3258
Pamela Hampton, prin. Fax 442-9488

Yarnell ESD 52 100/PK-8
18912 W Hays Ranch Rd 86332 928-427-3347
Andrew Smith, supt. Fax 427-3348
www.yesd52.org/
Yarnell S 100/PK-8
18912 W Hays Ranch Rd 86332 928-427-3347
Andrew Smith, prin. Fax 427-3348

Kykotsmovi Village, Navajo, Pop. 773

Hopi Mission S 50/K-6
PO Box 39 86039 928-734-2453
Betty Handrich, prin. Fax 734-5126

Lake Havasu City, Mohave, Pop. 55,338
Lake Havasu USD 1 6,100/PK-12
2200 Havasupai Blvd 86403 928-505-6900
Gail Malay, supt. Fax 505-6999
www.havasu.k12.az.us/
Daytona MS 500/6-8
98 Swanson Plz 86403 928-505-1475
Hector Fimbres, prin. Fax 505-1479
Havasupai ES 500/K-5
880 Cashmere Dr 86404 928-505-6045
Claude Sanders, prin. Fax 505-6059
Nautilus ES 400/PK-5
1425 Patrician Dr 86404 928-505-6061
Mari Jo Mulligan, prin. Fax 505-6079
Oro Grande ES 500/K-5
1250 Pawnee Dr 86406 928-505-6085
Susan Lust, prin. Fax 505-6099
Smoketree ES 600/PK-5
2395 Smoketree Ave N 86403 928-505-6025
Connie Hogard, prin. Fax 505-6039
Starline ES 600/K-5
3150 Starline Dr 86406 928-855-4088
Shaun Goodwin, prin. Fax 855-1152
Thunderbolt MS 1,100/6-8
695 Thunderbolt Ave 86406 928-855-4066
Paul Olson, prin. Fax 855-0041

Bethany Christian S 50/1-12
1200 Park Terrace Ave 86404 928-855-2661
Rev. Jerry Adams, prin. Fax 855-0807
Calvary Christian Academy 300/PK-8
1605 McCulloch Blvd S 86406 928-854-5465
Shannon Williams, admin. Fax 854-4007
Our Lady of the Lake Preschool 50/PK-PK
1975 Daytona Ave 86403 928-855-0154
Jeff Arner, dir. Fax 855-7172

Lakeside, Navajo, Pop. 3,492
Blue Ridge USD 32 2,600/PK-12
1200 W White Mountain Blvd 85929 928-368-6126
Greg Schalow, supt. Fax 368-5570
www.brusd.k12.az.us/
Blue Ridge ES 600/PK-2
1200 W White Mountain Blvd 85929 928-368-6182
Jeanne Powell, prin. Fax 368-6183
Blue Ridge IS 200/3-4
1200 W White Mountain Blvd 85929 928-368-6126
Kirstin Senske, prin. Fax 368-5570
Blue Ridge JHS 400/7-8
1200 W White Mountain Blvd 85929 928-368-2350
Loren Webb, prin. Fax 368-5570
Blue Ridge MS 400/5-6
1200 W White Mountain Blvd 85929 928-368-6126
Alicia Phillips, prin. Fax 368-5570

Laveen, Maricopa
Laveen ESD 59 3,500/PK-8
PO Box 29 85339 602-237-9100
Ron Dickson, supt. Fax 237-3376
www.laveeneld.org/
Cheatham S 900/K-8
PO Box 29 85339 602-237-7040
Michael Winters, prin. Fax 237-3376
Desert Meadows S K-8
PO Box 29 85339 602-304-2020
Steve Preis, prin. Fax 304-2025
Laveen S 1,000/PK-8
5001 W Dobbins Rd 85339 602-237-9110
Joe Roselle, prin. Fax 237-9134
Trailside Point S PK-8
7525 W Vineyard Ave 85339 602-605-8540
Bryan D'Alessio, prin. Fax 605-8545
Vista del Sur S 700/K-8
PO Box 630 85339 602-237-3046
Jim Matthies, admin. Fax 237-1976
Other Schools – See Phoenix

Maricopa Village Adventist S 50/K-8
8129 W Baseline Rd 85339 520-430-2313

Litchfield Park, Maricopa, Pop. 4,523
Litchfield ESD 79 8,800/PK-8
553 E Plaza Cir 85340 623-535-6000
Dr. Julianne Lein, supt. Fax 535-6037
www.lesd.k12.az.us/
Dreaming Summit ES 900/PK-5
553 E Plaza Cir 85340 623-547-1200
Kris Vanica, prin. Fax 547-4720
Libby ES 700/PK-5
553 E Plaza Cir 85340 623-535-6200
Lee Nelson, prin. Fax 935-7803
Litchfield ES 900/PK-5
553 E Plaza Cir 85340 623-535-6100
Ron Sterr, prin. Fax 935-3779
Robey ES 800/PK-5
553 E Plaza Cir 85340 623-547-1400
Melissa Wisner, prin. Fax 547-1947
Wigwam Creek MS 1,100/6-8
553 E Plaza Cir 85340 623-547-1100
David Mayer, prin. Fax 547-0873
Other Schools – See Avondale, Buckeye, Goodyear

St. Peter's Episcopal S 50/PK-K
400 S Litchfield Rd 85340 623-935-4215
Shiffa Mashood, dir. Fax 935-0583
Trinity Lutheran S 700/PK-8
830 E Plaza Cir 85340 623-935-4690
Dr. William Luedtke, prin. Fax 935-1203
West Valley Adventist S 50/K-8
PO Box 1257 85340 623-935-3163

Littlefield, Mohave
Littlefield USD 9 400/PK-12
PO Box 730 86432 928-347-5792
Riley Frei, supt. Fax 347-5967
www.lusd9.com/
Beaver Dam ES 300/PK-5
PO Box 730 86432 928-347-5796
Steven Peterson, prin. Fax 347-5795
Beaver Dam MS 6-8
PO Box 730 86432 928-347-5796
Riley Frei, prin. Fax 347-9795

Mc Nary, Apache, Pop. 355
Mc Nary ESD 23 200/K-8
PO Box 598, 928-334-2293
Mary Ann Wade, supt. Fax 334-2336
Mc Nary S 200/K-8
PO Box 598, 928-334-2293
Mary Ann Wade, prin. Fax 334-2336

Mc Neal, Cochise
Double Adobe ESD 45 100/K-6
7081 N Central Hwy 85617 520-364-3041
Pamela Sanders, admin. Fax 364-6796
Double Adobe ES 100/K-6
7081 N Central Hwy 85617 520-364-3041
Pamela Sanders, lead tchr. Fax 364-6796

Mc Neal ESD 55 50/K-8
PO Box 8 85617 520-642-3356
Teresa Reyna, supt. Fax 642-3356
Mc Neal S 50/K-8
PO Box 8 85617 520-642-3356
Teresa Reyna, prin. Fax 642-3356

Mammoth, Pinal, Pop. 2,167
Mammoth-San Manuel USD 8
Supt. — See San Manuel
Mammoth ES 200/PK-6
111 West Dungan Dr 85618 520-487-2242
Joe Jacobo, prin. Fax 487-9206

Many Farms, Apache, Pop. 1,294
Chinle USD 24
Supt. — See Chinle
Many Farms S 400/K-8
US Highway 191 86538 928-674-9000
Tillie Yonnie, prin. Fax 781-4227

Marana, Pima, Pop. 26,098
Marana USD 6 13,100/K-12
11279 W Grier Rd 85653 520-682-3243
Dr. Doug Wilson, supt. Fax 682-2421
www.maranausd.org
Estes ES 600/K-6
11279 W Grier Rd Ste 100 85653 520-682-4738
Nancy Paddock, prin. Fax 682-9247
Marana MS 1,000/7-8
11279 W Grier Rd Ste 105 85653 520-682-4730
Dr. Allison Murphy, prin. Fax 682-4790
Roadrunner ES 600/K-6
16651 W Calle Carmela 85653 520-616-6363
Liz Armenta, prin. Fax 616-6383
Other Schools – See Tucson

Maricopa, Pinal, Pop. 1,486
Maricopa USD 20 3,900/PK-12
45012 W Honeycutt Ave, 520-568-5100
Dr. John Flores, supt. Fax 568-5151
www.musd20.org/
Butterfield ES K-5
45012 W Honeycutt Ave, 520-568-6100
Kathy Drum, prin.
Desert Wind MS 6-8
45012 W Honeycutt Ave, 520-568-7110
Isaac Perez, prin. Fax 568-7119
Maricopa ES 900/K-5
45012 W Honeycutt Ave, 520-568-6102
Lynette Michalski, prin. Fax 568-6112
Maricopa Wells MS 900/6-8
45012 W Honeycutt Ave, 520-568-7102
Stephanie Sharp, prin. Fax 568-7104
Pima Butte ES 600/K-6
45012 W Honeycutt Ave, 520-568-7152
Matt Montoya, prin. Fax 568-7152
Saddleback ES K-5
45012 W Honeycutt Ave, 520-568-6610
Jamye Amick, prin.
Santa Cruz ES K-5
45012 W Honeycutt Ave, 520-568-5170
Lynnette Michalski, prin. Fax 568-5176
Santa Rosa ES 600/PK-5
45012 W Honeycutt Ave, 520-568-6151
Rick Abel, prin. Fax 568-6155

Mobile ESD 86 50/K-8
42798 S 99th Ave, 520-568-2280
Dr. Kit Wood, supt. Fax 568-9361
Mobile S 50/K-8
42798 S 99th Ave, 520-568-2280
Dr. Kit Wood, prin. Fax 568-9361

Mayer, Yavapai
Mayer USD 43 600/PK-12
PO Box 1059 86333 928-642-1005
Patrick Dallabetta, supt. Fax 632-4005
www.mayerschools.org
Mayer ES 300/PK-6
PO Box 1059 86333 928-642-1100
Patti Leonard, prin. Fax 632-9610

Orme S 200/K-12
HC 63 Box 3040 86333 928-632-7601
Alyce Brownridge, hdmstr. Fax 632-7605

Mesa, Maricopa, Pop. 442,780
Gilbert Unified SD
Supt. — See Gilbert
Augusta Ranch ES 1,000/K-6
9430 E Neville Ave, 480-635-2011
Susie Kreitzer, prin. Fax 635-2020
Boulder Creek ES 900/PK-6
8045 E Portobello Ave 85212 480-507-1404
Dr. Karen Coleman, prin. Fax 507-1666
Canyon Rim ES 1,100/PK-6
3045 S Canyon Rim 85212 480-984-3216
Korry Brenner, prin. Fax 380-0105
Desert Ridge JHS 1,100/7-8
10211 E Madero Ave, 480-635-2025
Jean Woods, prin. Fax 635-2044

Harris ES 600/PK-6
1820 S Harris Dr 85204 480-545-7060
Becky Henderson, prin. Fax 926-7160
Highland JHS 1,300/7-8
6915 E Guadalupe Rd 85212 480-632-4739
Brian Yee, prin. Fax 632-4729
Meridian ES 900/PK-6
3900 S Mountain Rd 85212 480-497-4032
Vicki Hester, prin. Fax 497-4039
Superstition Springs ES 900/K-6
7125 E Monterey Ave, 480-641-6413
Patty Rogers, prin. Fax 854-8871

Mesa USD 4 73,300/PK-12
63 E Main St Ste 101 85201 480-472-0000
Dr. Debra Duvall, supt. Fax 472-0204
www.mpsaz.org
Adams ES 900/PK-6
738 S Longmore 85202 480-472-4300
Terri Pearson, prin. Fax 472-4350
Alma ES 600/K-6
1313 W Medina Ave 85202 480-472-3900
Lou Perdoni, prin. Fax 472-3919
Brinton ES 800/K-6
11455 E Sunland Ave 85208 480-472-4075
Pat Estes, prin. Fax 472-4077
Bush ES 600/PK-6
4925 E Ingram St 85205 480-472-8500
Brian Corte, prin. Fax 472-8545
Crismon ES 700/PK-6
825 W Medina Ave 85210 480-472-4000
Alex MacDonald, prin. Fax 472-4058
Early Education Center 100/PK-PK
122 N Country Club Dr 85201 480-308-7320
Allen Quie, prin. Fax 308-7301
East Mesa ECC 200/PK-PK
950 N Sunvalley Blvd 85207 480-472-3975
Allen Quie, prin.
Edison ES 800/K-6
545 N Horne 85203 480-472-5300
Howard Paley, prin. Fax 472-5281
Eisenhower ES 800/PK-6
848 N Mesa Dr 85201 480-472-5200
Devon Isherwood, prin. Fax 472-5272
Emerson ES 900/K-6
415 N Westwood 85201 480-472-4700
Mark Norris, prin. Fax 472-4744
Entz ES 700/K-6
4132 E Adobe St 85205 480-472-7300
Dr. David Finley, prin. Fax 472-7373
Falcon Hill ES 700/K-6
1645 N Sterling 85207 480-472-8600
Lynn David, prin. Fax 472-8597
Field ES 800/K-6
2325 E Adobe St 85213 480-472-9800
Susan Johnston, prin. Fax 472-9819
Franklin East ES 800/K-6
1753 E 8th Ave 85204 480-472-6500
Gayle Householder, prin. Fax 472-6488
Franklin NE ES 500/K-6
7042 E Adobe St 85207 480-472-9300
Michael Heidenblut, prin. Fax 472-9339
Franklin South ES 300/K-6
5005 E Southern Ave 85206 480-472-2200
Dan Cooper, prin. Fax 472-2245
Franklin West ES 500/K-6
236 S Sirrine 85210 480-472-5400
Emily Kelly, prin. Fax 472-2245
Guerrero ES 700/K-6
463 S Alma School Rd 85210 480-472-9200
Cort Monroe, prin. Fax 472-9224
Hale ES 600/PK-6
1425 N 23rd St 85213 480-472-7400
Susan Marshall, prin. Fax 472-7377
Hawthorne ES 800/PK-6
630 N Hunt Dr 85203 480-472-7500
Scott Cumberledge, prin. Fax 472-7474
Hermosa Vista ES 700/K-6
2626 N 24th St 85213 480-472-7550
Julie Hibbard, prin. Fax 472-7549
Highland ES 600/K-6
3042 E Adobe St 85213 480-472-7600
Susan Rollins, prin. Fax 472-7606
Holmes ES 800/PK-6
948 S Horne 85204 480-472-5600
Darlene Johnson, prin. Fax 472-5555
Irving ES 600/PK-6
3220 E Pueblo Ave 85204 480-472-1700
Brenda Petties, prin. Fax 472-1699
Ishikawa ES 800/K-6
2635 N 32nd St 85213 480-472-7700
Shelley Heath, prin. Fax 472-7686
Jefferson ES 700/PK-6
120 S Jefferson Ave 85208 480-472-8700
Tim Moe, prin. Fax 472-8724
Johnson ES 700/PK-6
3807 E Pueblo Ave 85206 480-472-6800
Tracy Yslas, prin. Fax 472-6755
Keller ES 800/PK-6
1445 E Hilton Ave 85204 480-472-6200
Mario Ventura, prin. Fax 472-6150
Kerr ES 700/PK-6
125 E McLellan Rd 85201 480-472-5100
Thea Hansen, prin. Fax 472-5166
Las Sendas ES 900/PK-6
3120 N Red Mtn 85207 480-472-8750
Julia Kelly, prin. Fax 472-8735
Lehi ES 700/PK-6
2555 N Stapley Dr 85203 480-472-5500
Jason Jacobson, prin. Fax 472-5480
Lincoln ES 800/PK-6
930 S Sirrine 85210 480-472-6400
Luz Mann, prin. Fax 472-6390
Lindbergh ES 700/PK-6
930 S Lazona Dr 85204 480-472-6300
Julianne O'Shea, prin. Fax 472-6310
Longfellow ES 1,000/PK-6
345 S Hall 85204 480-472-6550
David Christensen, prin. Fax 472-6599
Lowell ES 900/PK-6
920 E Broadway Rd 85204 480-472-1400
Sandra Kuhn, prin. Fax 472-1482
MacArthur ES 600/K-6
1435 E McLellan Rd 85203 480-472-7800
Sue Paschal, prin. Fax 472-7824
Madison ES 600/K-6
849 S Sunnyvale 85206 480-472-8800
Susan Edman, prin. Fax 472-8855
Mendoza ES 800/PK-6
5831 E McLellan Rd 85205 480-472-2000
Frederica Buffmire, prin. Fax 472-1999
Mesa Academy for Advanced Studies 4-9
6919 E Brown Rd 85207 480-308-7400
Bob Crispin, prin. Fax 308-7428
O'Connor ES 700/PK-6
4840 E Adobe St 85205 480-472-7850
Bridget Braney, prin. Fax 472-7878
Patterson ES 800/K-6
615 S Cheshire 85208 480-472-9700
Maxine Sullivan, prin. Fax 472-9788
Porter ES 700/K-6
1350 S Lindsay Rd 85204 480-472-6700
Tony LaMantia, prin. Fax 472-6698
Redbird ES 700/PK-6
1020 S Extension Rd 85210 480-472-1200
Nicholas Parker, prin. Fax 472-1290
Red Mountain Ranch ES 800/K-6
6650 E Raftriver St 85215 480-472-7900
Joyce Cook, prin. Fax 472-7969
Robson ES 600/K-6
2122 E Pueblo Ave 85204 480-472-6600
Jane Carretta, prin. Fax 472-6660
Roosevelt ES 600/PK-6
828 S Valencia 85202 480-472-4200
Mary Ann Price, prin. Fax 472-4270
Salk ES 900/PK-6
7029 E Brown Rd 85207 480-472-8400
Karla Carlson, prin. Fax 472-8484
Sousa ES 700/PK-6
616 N Mountain Rd 85207 480-472-8900
Elizabeth Mullavey, prin. Fax 472-8888
Stevenson ES 800/PK-6
638 S 96th St 85208 480-472-9000
Aaron Kaczmarek, prin. Fax 472-9070
Sunridge Learning Center 200/K-6
737 W Guadalupe Rd 85210 480-472-3575
Beverly Potter, dir. Fax 472-3598
Taft ES 700/PK-6
9800 E Quarterline Rd 85207 480-472-9100
Russ Heath, prin. Fax 472-9090
Washington ES 600/K-6
2260 W Isabella Ave 85202 480-472-4100
Susan Powell, prin. Fax 472-4141
Webster ES 900/PK-6
202 N Sycamore 85201 480-472-4800
Chuck Burger, prin. Fax 472-4888
Whitman ES 800/PK-6
1829 N Grand 85201 480-472-5000
Andrea Erickson, prin. Fax 472-5058
Whittier ES 600/PK-6
733 N Longmore 85201 480-472-4900
Charles Starkey, prin. Fax 472-4905
Wilson ES 800/K-6
5619 E Glade Ave 85206 480-472-9250
John Nesbitt, prin. Fax 472-9277
Zaharis ES 900/PK-6
9410 E McKellips Rd 85207 480-308-7200
Mike Oliver, prin. Fax 308-7255
Other Schools – See Chandler

Adobe Adventist Christian S 50/K-8
9910 E Adobe Rd 85207 480-986-2310
Christ the King S 200/PK-8
1551 E Dana Ave 85204 480-844-4480
Donald Graff, prin. Fax 844-4498
Faith Christian S 100/K-12
PO Box 31300 85275 480-833-1983
Dick Buckingham, admin. Fax 503-8262
Montessori International S 100/K-8
1230 N Gilbert Rd 85203 480-890-1580
Therese Kestner, prin. Fax 292-8235
Pilgrim Lutheran S 100/PK-8
3257 E University Dr 85213 480-830-1724
Lynn Kuether, prin. Fax 807-2921
Providence Classical S 100/K-12
1720 E 8th Ave 85204 480-830-7211
David Farbishel, hdmstr. Fax 830-7211
Queen of Peace S 200/PK-8
109 N MacDonald 85201 480-969-0226
Richard Areyzaga, prin. Fax 275-2097
Redeemer Christian S 100/K-12
719 N Stapley Dr 85203 480-962-5003
Denise Monroe Ed.D., prin. Fax 833-7502
Red Rock Christian S 50/K-8
6263 E Thomas Rd 85215 480-985-3141
Mandy Coward, prin. Fax 985-3192
St. Timothy Catholic Preschool 100/PK-PK
1730 W Guadalupe Rd 85202 480-775-5237
Monica Glick, dir. Fax 820-7984
St. Timothy Catholic S 200/PK-8
2520 S Alma School Rd 85210 480-775-2650
Maureen Vick, prin. Fax 775-2651
Tempe Montessori S 50/PK-6
PO Box 40755 85274 480-966-7606
Fax 966-6805
Trinity Preschool & K 100/PK-K
2130 E University Dr 85213 480-834-9120
Cyndee Smith, dir. Fax 834-9180

Miami, Gila, Pop. 1,841
Miami USD 40 1,200/PK-12
PO Box 2070 85539 928-425-3271
Don Nelson, supt. Fax 425-7419
miami.az.schoolwebpages.com/
Bejarano ES 400/PK-PK, 3-
PO Box 2070 85539 928-425-3271
Fax 425-3051
Kornegay JHS 200/7-8
PO Box 2070 85539 928-425-3271
Susan Hocking, prin. Fax 425-5470
Las Lomas ES 300/K-2
PO Box 2070 85539 928-425-3271
Sherry Dorathy, prin. Fax 425-0111

Mohave Valley, Mohave, Pop. 6,962
Mohave Valley ESD 16 1,900/PK-8
PO Box 5070 86446 928-768-2507
Phil Sauceman, supt. Fax 768-2510
www.mvesd16.org
Mohave Valley ES 600/PK-6
1419 Willow Dr 86440 928-768-2211
Mandy Waxler, prin. Fax 768-6424
Mohave Valley JHS 400/7-8
6565 Girard Ave 86440 928-768-9196
Whitney Crow, prin. Fax 768-1129
Other Schools – See Bullhead City

Morenci, Greenlee, Pop. 1,799
Morenci USD 18 1,100/PK-12
PO Box 1060 85540 928-865-2081
Duane Howard, supt. Fax 865-3130
www.morenci.k12.az.us/
Fairbanks ES 600/PK-6
PO Box 1060 85540 928-865-3501
Philip Martinez, prin. Fax 865-5980

Morristown, Maricopa
Morristown ESD 75 100/PK-8
PO Box 98 85342 623-388-2336
Fax 388-9368
www.familyeducation.com/az/morristown
Morristown S 100/PK-8
PO Box 98 85342 623-388-2336
Lucille Thompson, lead tchr. Fax 388-9368

Naco, Cochise
Naco ESD 23 300/K-8
PO Box 397 85620 520-432-7144
Patricia Marsh, supt. Fax 432-4161
www.naco.k12.az.us/
Naco S 300/K-8
PO Box 397 85620 520-432-5060
Patricia Marsh, prin. Fax 432-4161

Nogales, Santa Cruz, Pop. 20,833
Nogales USD 1 5,900/K-12
310 W Plum St 85621 520-287-0800
Shawn McCollough, supt. Fax 287-3586
www.nusd.k12.az.us
Carpenter Middle Academy 600/6-8
595 W Kino St 85621 520-287-0820
Liza Montiel, prin. Fax 287-0817
Challenger ES 500/K-5
901 E Calle Mayer 85621 520-377-0544
Maria Vasquez, prin. Fax 377-2026
Desert Shadows MS 800/6-8
340 Boulevard Del Rey David 85621 520-377-2646
Joan Molera, prin. Fax 377-2674
Lincoln ES 400/K-5
652 N Tyler Ave 85621 520-287-0870
Lucina Romero, prin. Fax 287-0875
Mitchell ES 700/K-5
855 N Bautista St 85621 520-287-0840
Michael Young, prin. Fax 287-0847
Vasquez De Coronado ES 700/K-5
2301 N Al Harrison Rd 85621 520-377-2855
Annette Barber, prin. Fax 377-0221
Welty ES 300/K-5
1050 W Cimarron St 85621 520-287-0880
Claudia Welden, prin. Fax 287-0889

Santa Cruz ESD 28 200/K-8
HC 2 Box 50 85621 520-287-0737
James Cruice, supt. Fax 287-6791
Santa Cruz S - Little Red Schoolhouse 200/K-8
7 Duquesne Rd 85621 520-287-0737
Gail Rolinger, prin. Fax 287-6791

Lourdes S 300/PK-8
555 E Patagonia Hwy 85621 520-287-5659
Sr. Esther Hugues, prin. Fax 287-2910
Sacred Heart S 200/K-8
PO Box 968 85628 520-287-2223
Alma Teresa Salazar, prin. Fax 287-3373

Oracle, Pinal, Pop. 3,043
Oracle ESD 2 500/PK-8
725 N Carpenter Dr 85623 520-896-3071
Todd Kissick, supt. Fax 896-3088
www.osd2.org/
Mountain Vista S 400/1-8
2618 W El Paseo 85623 520-896-3000
Dennis Blauser, prin. Fax 896-3062
Oracle Ridge S 100/PK-K
725 N Carpenter Dr 85623 520-896-3071
Todd Kissick, prin. Fax 896-3088

Oro Valley, Pima, Pop. 38,438
Amphitheater USD 10
Supt. — See Tucson
Wilson S 1,400/K-8
2330 W Glover Rd, 520-696-5800
Adrian Hannah, prin. Fax 696-5900

Overgaard, Navajo
Heber-Overgaard USD 6
Supt. — See Heber
Mountain Meadows PS 200/PK-3
PO Box 40 85933 928-535-4622
Monty Williams, prin. Fax 535-6574

Page, Coconino, Pop. 6,794
Page USD 8 3,100/PK-12
PO Box 1927 86040 928-608-4100
Jim Walker, supt. Fax 608-4109
www.pageud.k12.az.us
Desert View ES 700/PK-5
PO Box 1927 86040 928-608-4137
Lorna Loy, prin. Fax 608-4169

Lake View ES 600/K-5
PO Box 1927 86040 928-608-4200
Cheryl Chuckluck, prin. Fax 645-5059
Page MS 600/6-8
PO Box 1927 86040 928-608-4306
Mark Rose, prin. Fax 645-9285

Palo Verde, Maricopa
Palo Verde ESD 49 400/K-8
PO Box 108 85343 623-327-3690
Robin Berry, supt. Fax 327-3695
Palo Verde S 400/K-8
PO Box 108 85343 623-327-3680
Robert Aldridge, prin. Fax 386-4654

Paradise Valley, Maricopa, Pop. 14,558
Scottsdale USD 48
Supt. — See Phoenix
Cherokee ES 500/PK-5
8801 N 56th St 85253 480-484-8700
Jan Howard, prin. Fax 484-8701
Kiva ES 800/K-6
6911 E McDonald Dr 85253 480-484-2200
Dr. Michael Helminski, prin. Fax 484-2201

Camelback Christian S 100/PK-K
3900 E Stanford Dr 85253 602-957-0215
Jeanne Bookhout, admin. Fax 955-7217
Camelback Desert S 100/PK-8
6050 N Invergordon Rd 85253 480-948-7520
Caroline Lynch, prin. Fax 998-5664
Phoenix Country Day S 700/PK-12
3901 E Stanford Dr 85253 602-955-8200
Geoffrey Campbell, hdmstr. Fax 955-1286
Tesseract S PK-8
4800 E Doubletree Ranch Rd 85253 480-991-1770
Nigel Taplin, hdmstr. Fax 991-1954

Parker, LaPaz, Pop. 3,222
Parker USD 27 1,900/PK-12
PO Box 1090 85344 928-669-9244
Kevin Uden, supt. Fax 669-2515
www.parkerusd.k12.az.us
Blake ES 500/PK-3
PO Box 1090 85344 928-669-8203
Lori Bachmann, prin. Fax 669-8771
Le Pera S 400/K-8
PO Box 1090 85344 928-662-4306
Dan Wolfe, prin. Fax 662-4308
Wallace ES 300/4-6
PO Box 1090 85344 928-669-2141
Brad Sale, prin. Fax 669-2515
Wallace JHS 200/7-8
PO Box 1090 85344 928-669-2141
Jay Sandusky, prin. Fax 669-2515

Parks, Coconino
Maine Consolidated SD 10 100/K-8
PO Box 50010 86018 928-635-2115
Mark Williams, supt. Fax 635-5320
Maine Consolidated S 100/K-8
PO Box 50010 86018 928-635-2115
Mark Williams, prin. Fax 635-5320

Patagonia, Santa Cruz, Pop. 825
Patagonia ESD 6 100/PK-8
PO Box 295 85624 520-394-3050
Robert Tollefson, supt. Fax 394-3051
patagonia.echalk.com
Patagonia ES 100/PK-5
PO Box 295 85624 520-394-3000
Peter Fagergren, prin. Fax 394-3001
Patagonia MS 50/6-8
PO Box 254 85624 520-394-3000
Peter Fagergren, prin. Fax 394-3001

Payson, Gila, Pop. 14,729
Payson USD 10 2,800/PK-12
PO Box 919 85547 928-474-2070
Casey O'Brien, supt. Fax 472-2013
www.pusd.k12.az.us/
Frontier ES 400/K-5
PO Box 919 85547 928-472-2052
Paula Patterson, prin. Fax 472-2047
Payson ES 400/K-5
PO Box 919 85547 928-474-5882
Will Dunman, prin. Fax 472-2045
Randall ES 500/PK-5
PO Box 919 85547 928-474-2353
Robert Varner, prin. Fax 472-2041
Rim Country MS 700/6-8
PO Box 919 85547 928-474-4511
Gary Witherspoon, prin. Fax 472-2044

Payson Community Christian S 100/PK-12
213 S Colcord Rd 85541 928-474-8050
Teresa Putree, admin. Fax 468-1176

Peach Springs, Mohave, Pop. 787
Peach Springs USD 8 100/K-8
PO Box 360 86434 928-769-2202
Steven Condict, supt. Fax 769-2676
www.psusd.k12.az.us/
Peach Springs S 100/K-8
PO Box 360 86434 928-769-2613
Steven Condict, prin. Fax 769-2892

Valentine ESD 22 100/K-8
HC 35 Box 50 86434 928-769-2310
Ron McPherson, supt. Fax 769-2389
Valentine S 100/K-8
HC 35 Box 50 86434 928-769-2310
Ron McPherson, prin. Fax 769-2389

Pearce, Cochise
Ash Creek ESD 53 50/K-8
6460 E Highway 181 85625 520-824-3340
Linda Frost, supt. Fax 824-3410
www.ashcreekschool.org
Ash Creek S 50/K-8
6460 E Highway 181 85625 520-824-3340
Linda Frost, prin. Fax 824-3410

Pearce ESD 22 100/K-8
1487 E School Rd 85625 520-826-3328
Fax 826-3531
Pearce S 100/K-8
1487 E School Rd 85625 520-826-3328
Fax 826-3531

Peoria, Maricopa, Pop. 138,200
Deer Valley USD 97
Supt. — See Phoenix
Terramar S 1,000/K-8
7000 W Happy Valley Rd 85383 623-445-7600
Jenna Moffitt, prin. Fax 445-7680
West Wing S 700/K-8
26716 N High Desert Dr 85383 623-376-5000
Sandy Luedke, prin. Fax 376-5080

Peoria USD 11
Supt. — See Glendale
Alta Loma S 1,000/K-8
9750 N 87th Ave 85345 623-412-4575
Rae Conelley, prin. Fax 412-4584
Apache S 900/K-8
8633 W John Cabot Rd 85382 623-412-4875
Larry Brodie, prin. Fax 412-4885
Cheyenne S 900/K-8
11806 N 87th Ave 85345 623-487-5100
Linda Miller, prin. Fax 487-5110
Cotton Boll S 1,100/PK-8
8540 W Butler Dr 85345 623-412-4700
David Snyder, prin. Fax 412-4705
Country Meadows S 1,400/K-8
8409 N 111th Ave 85345 623-412-5200
Ric Rodriguez, prin. Fax 412-5207
Coyote Hills S 1,400/K-8
21180 N 87th Ave 85382 623-412-5225
Terry Balliet, prin. Fax 412-5232
Desert Harbor S 900/PK-8
15585 N 91st Ave 85382 623-486-6200
Laurie Little, prin. Fax 486-6207
Frontier S 1,200/K-8
21258 N 81st Ave 85382 623-412-4900
Davita Solter, prin. Fax 412-4905
Murphy S 700/K-8
7231 W North Ln 85345 623-412-4475
Robin Dahlman, prin. Fax 412-4484
Oakwood S 700/K-8
12900 N 71st Ave 85381 623-412-4725
Paul Bower, prin. Fax 412-4734
Oasis S 700/K-8
7841 W Sweetwater Ave 85381 623-412-4800
Tom Corcoran, prin. Fax 412-4809
Parkridge S 1,000/K-8
9970 W Beardsley Rd 85382 623-412-5400
David Svorinic, prin. Fax 412-5407
Paseo Verde S 800/K-8
7880 W Greenway Rd 85381 623-412-5075
Mary Hoefner, prin. Fax 412-5084
Peoria S 800/K-8
11501 N 79th Ave 85345 623-412-4450
Phil Stanfield, prin. Fax 412-4458
Santa Fe S 800/K-8
9880 N 77th Ave 85345 623-486-6475
Robert Miller, prin. Fax 486-6487
Sky View S 600/K-8
8624 W Sweetwater Ave 85381 623-412-4850
Phil Valentine, prin. Fax 412-4861
Sundance S 800/K-8
7051 W Cholla St 85345 623-412-4675
Kathie Hornbeek, prin. Fax 412-4685
Sun Valley S 1,100/K-8
8361 N 95th Ave 85345 623-412-4825
Heidi Caine, prin. Fax 412-4837
Vistancia S K-8
30009 N Sunrise Pt 85383 623-773-6500
Steve Gillett, prin. Fax 773-6507

Cross of Glory Lutheran S 50/PK-4
10111 W Jomax Rd 85383 623-362-8668
Peter Gumm, prin. Fax 825-0096
Montessori Kingdom of Learning 200/PK-8
13111 N 94th Dr 85381 623-876-1463
Elizabeth Schneider, dir. Fax 876-1465
Northwest Christian S 100/K-6
8133 W Cactus Rd 85381 623-487-1601
Karen Nave, prin. Fax 487-3405
Southwest Indian S 50/1-12
14202 N 73rd Ave 85381 623-979-6008
Fran Pearce, prin. Fax 486-5243

Peridot, Gila, Pop. 957

Peridot Lutheran S 100/K-8
PO Box 118 85542 928-475-7537
Frederick Zimmerman, prin. Fax 475-3065

Phoenix, Maricopa, Pop. 1,461,575
Alhambra ESD 68 15,200/PK-8
4510 N 37th Ave 85019 602-336-2920
Dr. Jim Rice, supt. Fax 336-2270
www.alhambraesd.org/
Alhambra Traditional S 700/K-8
3736 W Osborn Rd 85019 602-484-8816
Tracey Lopeman, prin. Fax 484-8952
Andalucia MS 1,200/4-8
4730 W Campbell Ave 85031 623-848-8646
Scott Heusman, prin. Fax 846-6044
Andalucia PS 1,000/K-3
4530 W Campbell Ave 85031 623-848-8420
Jacqueline Doerr, prin. Fax 848-1998
Catalina Ventura S 1,100/PK-8
6331 N 39th Ave 85019 602-841-7445
Elizabeth Hargrove, prin. Fax 841-6892
Cordova MS 1,000/4-8
5631 N 35th Ave 85017 602-841-0704
Greg Gunn, prin. Fax 973-8416
Cordova PS 800/K-3
5631 N 35th Ave 85017 602-242-5828
Margaret Watral, prin. Fax 973-8416
Granada East MS 1,300/4-8
3022 W Campbell Ave 85017 602-589-0110
Sandra Kennedy, prin. Fax 589-0140
Granada PS 1,100/K-3
3232 W Campbell Ave 85017 602-841-1403
Evelyn Garcia-Rico, prin. Fax 973-8438
Montebello S 1,400/K-8
5725 N 27th Ave 85017 602-336-2000
Jeffrey Sprout, prin. Fax 249-7233
Sevilla PS 1,000/K-3
3801 W Missouri Ave 85019 602-242-0281
Mandi Caudill, prin. Fax 242-2791
Sevilla West ES 700/4-6
3851 W Missouri Ave 85019 602-347-0232
Kathy Davis, prin. Fax 347-9906
Simpson MS 1,100/4-8
5330 N 23rd Ave 85015 602-246-0699
Cynthia Nicholas, prin. Fax 246-4305
Westwood PS 1,100/K-3
4711 N 23rd Ave 85015 602-242-2442
Lori Weiss, prin. Fax 242-2514
Other Schools – See Glendale

Balsz ESD 31 2,400/PK-8
4825 E Roosevelt St 85008 602-629-6400
Dr. Jeffrey Smith, supt. Fax 629-6470
www.balsz.k12.az.us
Balsz ES 700/PK-6
4309 E Belleview St 85008 602-629-6500
Dr. Taime Bengochea, prin. Fax 629-6504
Brunson-Lee ES 500/PK-6
1350 N 48th St 85008 602-629-6900
Maria Tijerina, prin. Fax 629-6904
Crockett ES 500/PK-6
501 N 36th St 85008 602-629-6600
Tammy Tusek, prin. Fax 629-6604
Griffith ES 500/PK-6
4505 E Palm Ln 85008 602-629-6700
Alexis Wilson, prin. Fax 629-6704
Orangedale JHS Prep Academy 200/7-8
5048 E Oak St 85008 602-629-6800
Ralph Schneider, prin. Fax 629-6804

Cartwright ESD 83 19,700/K-8
3401 N 67th Ave 85033 623-691-4000
Michael Martinez, supt. Fax 691-5920
www.cartwright.k12.az.us
Atkinson MS 1,400/6-8
4315 N Maryvale Pkwy 85031 623-691-1700
Scott Winters, prin. Fax 691-1720
Borman S 1,600/K-8
3637 N 55th Ave 85031 623-691-5000
Dr. Berta Walder, prin. Fax 691-5020
Cartwright ES 1,000/K-5
2825 N 59th Ave 85035 623-691-4100
Richard Hagen, prin. Fax 691-4120
Castro MS 6-8
2730 N 79th Ave 85035 623-691-5300
Raul Pina, prin. Fax 691-5320
Davidson ES 1,000/K-5
6935 W Osborn Rd 85033 623-691-1500
Arturo Sanchez, prin. Fax 691-1520
Desert Sands MS 1,500/6-8
6308 W Campbell Ave 85033 623-691-4900
Patricia Lopez, prin. Fax 691-4920
Downs ES 700/K-5
3611 N 47th Ave 85031 623-691-4200
Sarah Hardy-Hernandez, prin. Fax 691-4220
Estrella MS 1,700/6-8
3733 N 75th Ave 85033 623-691-5400
Nick Radavich, prin. Fax 691-5420
Harris ES 900/K-5
2252 N 55th Ave 85035 623-691-4800
Dr. Rita Martinez, prin. Fax 691-4820
Heatherbrae ES 800/K-5
7070 W Heatherbrae Dr 85033 623-691-5200
Eva Stevens, prin. Fax 691-5220
Holiday Park ES 1,000/K-5
4417 N 66th Ave 85033 623-691-4500
Deby Valdez, prin. Fax 691-4520
Long ES 900/K-5
4407 N 55th Ave 85031 623-691-4300
Dr. Araceli Montoya, prin. Fax 691-4320
Palm Lane ES 900/K-5
2043 N 64th Dr 85035 623-691-5500
Enrique Gonzalez, prin. Fax 691-5520
Pena ES 900/K-5
2550 N 79th Ave 85035 623-691-3100
Dr. Cecilia Sanchez, prin. Fax 691-3120
Peralta ES 1,000/K-5
7125 W Encanto Blvd 85035 623-691-5600
Mary Kay Radavich, prin. Fax 691-5620
Spitalny ES 700/K-5
3201 N 46th Dr 85031 623-691-4400
Dr. Rachel Saunders, prin. Fax 691-4420
Starlight Park ES 1,000/K-5
7960 W Osborn Rd 85033 623-691-4700
Kristan Kurtz, prin. Fax 691-4720
Sunset ES 800/K-5
6602 W Osborn Rd 85033 623-691-4600
Kristi Langley-Wells, prin. Fax 691-4620
Tarver ES 700/K-5
4308 N 51st Ave Ste 102 85031 623-691-1900
Angela Graziano, prin. Fax 691-1920
Tomahawk ES 1,100/K-5
7820 W Turney Ave 85033 623-691-5800
Norma Jauregui, prin. Fax 691-5820

Cave Creek USD 93
Supt. — See Scottsdale
Sonoran Trails MS 700/6-8
5555 E Pinnacle Vista Dr 85085 480-272-8600
Bill Dolezal, prin. Fax 272-8699

Creighton ESD 14 7,700/K-8
2702 E Flower St 85016 602-381-6000
Dr. Charlotte Boyle, supt. Fax 381-6019
www.creightonschools.org/
Creighton S 1,000/K-8
2802 E McDowell Rd 85008 602-381-6060
Rosemary Agneessens, prin. Fax 381-6047
Excelencia S 900/K-8
2181 E McDowell Rd 85006 602-381-4670
Damon Twist, prin. Fax 381-4668
Gateway S 900/K-8
1100 N 35th St 85008 602-381-4665
Dr. Nancy Uxa, prin. Fax 381-4662
Kennedy S 800/K-8
2702 E Osborn Rd 85016 602-381-6180
Sean Hannafin, prin. Fax 381-6192
Loma Linda S 900/K-8
2002 E Clarendon Ave 85016 602-381-6080
Dr. Stephanie DeMar, prin. Fax 381-6094
Machan S 800/K-8
2140 E Virginia Ave 85006 602-381-6120
Eric Dueppen, prin. Fax 381-6125
Monte Vista S 700/K-8
3501 E Osborn Rd 85018 602-381-6140
Michael Madison, prin. Fax 381-6159
Papago S 900/K-8
2013 N 36th St 85008 602-381-6100
Jeffrey Geyer, prin. Fax 381-6118
Squaw Peak Traditional Academy 700/K-8
4601 N 34th St 85018 602-381-6160
Arnette Wessel, prin. Fax 381-6170

Deer Valley USD 97 35,100/PK-12
20402 N 15th Ave 85027 623-445-5000
Dr. Virginia McElyea, supt. Fax 445-5086
www.dvusd.org
Canyon Springs ES K-8
42901 N 45th Ave 85087 623-376-5200
Julie Ruskey, prin. Fax 376-5280
Constitution ES 800/K-6
18440 N 15th Ave 85023 602-467-6100
Stephanie Tennille, prin. Fax 467-6180
Deer Valley MS 1,000/7-8
21100 N 27th Ave 85027 623-445-3300
Dr. Lynn Miller, prin. Fax 445-3380
Desert Mountain S 1,000/K-8
35959 N 7th Ave 85086 623-445-3500
Lynda Johnson, prin. Fax 445-3580
Desert Winds ES 600/PK-6
19825 N 15th Ave 85027 623-445-3900
Kathy McNeill, prin. Fax 445-3980
Diamond Canyon S 1,200/K-8
40004 N Liberty Bell Way 85086 623-445-8000
Mark Oesterle, prin. Fax 445-8080
Esperanza ES 600/K-6
251 W Mohawk Ln 85027 623-445-3700
Denise McGloughlin, prin. Fax 445-3780
Gavilan Peak S 1,000/K-8
2701 W Memorial Dr 85086 623-445-7400
Dr. Mai-Lon Wong, prin. Fax 445-7480
New River ES 300/K-6
48827 N Black Canyon Hwy 85087 623-376-3500
Tricia Graham, prin. Fax 376-3580
Norterra Canyon S K-8
2200 W Maya Way 85085 623-445-8200
Trevor Ettenborough, prin. Fax 445-8280
Paseo Hills S 1,200/K-8
3302 W Louise Dr 85027 623-445-4500
Gayle Galligan, prin. Fax 445-4580
Stetson Hills S 1,200/K-8
25475 N Stetson Hills Loop, 623-445-5300
Krista Anderson, prin. Fax 445-5380
Sunrise ES 700/K-6
17624 N 31st Ave 85053 602-467-5900
Shelly Negron, prin. Fax 467-5980
Sunset Ridge S 1,100/K-8
35707 N 33rd Ln 85086 623-445-7800
Lynnette Byrn, prin. Fax 445-7880
Village Meadows ES 700/K-6
2020 W Morningside Dr 85023 602-467-6300
Jean Koeppen, prin. Fax 467-6380
Other Schools – See Anthem, Glendale, Peoria

Fowler ESD 45 4,400/PK-8
1617 S 67th Ave 85043 623-707-4500
Marvene Lobato, supt. Fax 707-4561
www.fesd.org
Fowler ES 600/PK-5
6707 W Van Buren St 85043 623-707-2500
Dora Barrio, prin. Fax 707-4680
Santa Maria MS 600/6-8
7250 W Lower Buckeye Rd 85043 623-707-1100
Desiree Castillo, prin. Fax 707-1110
Sun Canyon ES 700/PK-5
8150 W Durango St 85043 623-707-2000
Colleen Rodgers, prin. Fax 707-2015
Sunridge ES 600/PK-5
6244 W Roosevelt St 85043 623-707-4600
Belinda Quezada, prin. Fax 707-4630
Tuscano ES 500/PK-5
3850 S 79th Ave 85043 623-707-2300
Phillip Allen, prin. Fax 707-2304
Western Valley ES 700/PK-5
6250 W Durango St 85043 623-707-2100
Nora Ulloa, prin. Fax 707-2104
Western Valley MS 700/6-8
6250 W Durango St 85043 623-707-2200
Louis Daniels, prin. Fax 707-2204

Isaac ESD 5 8,200/PK-8
3348 W McDowell Rd 85009 602-455-6700
Carlos Bejarano, supt. Fax 455-6701
www.isaacschools.org
Alston ES 300/K-3
4006 W Osborn Rd 85019 602-442-3000
Debbie Hutson, prin. Fax 442-3099
Butler S 700/K-8
3843 W Roosevelt St 85009 602-442-2300
Jeanne Valdez, prin. Fax 442-2399
Coe ES 1,000/K-5
3801 W Roanoke Ave 85009 602-442-2400
Amanda Guerrero, prin. Fax 442-2499
Esperanza ES 400/K-5
3025 W McDowell Rd 85009 602-442-2800
Lina Munoz, prin. Fax 442-2899
Isaac MS 900/6-8
3402 W McDowell Rd 85009 602-455-6800
Armando Chavez, prin. Fax 455-6868
Mitchell ES 700/K-5
1700 N 41st Ave 85009 602-442-2600
Linda Crawford, prin. Fax 442-2699
Moya ES 600/K-4
406 N 41St Ave 85009 602-442-3100
Linda Washington, prin. Fax 442-3199
Pueblo Del Sol MS 700/6-8
3449 N 39th Ave 85019 602-455-6900
Gloria Garino Spencer, prin. Fax 484-4118
Smith MS 300/5-8
4301 W Fillmore St 85043 602-442-2850
Chad Gestson, prin. Fax 442-2897
Sutton ES 800/K-5
1001 N 31st Ave 85009 602-442-3200
Marco Ruiz, prin. Fax 442-3299
Tarver Education Complex 200/PK-PK
3101 W McDowell Rd 85009 602-442-2900
Noreen Didonna, prin. Fax 442-2999
Udall Escuela de Bellas Artes 700/K-8
3715 W Roosevelt St 85009 602-442-2700
Jose Paredes, prin. Fax 442-2799
Zito ES 900/K-5
4525 W Encanto Blvd 85035 602-442-2500
Gabriel Garcia, prin. Fax 442-2599

Kyrene ESD 28
Supt. — See Tempe
Kyrene Akimel A-al MS 1,100/6-8
2720 E Liberty Ln 85048 480-783-1600
Ernie Broderson, prin. Fax 759-7688
Kyrene Altadena MS 1,100/6-8
14620 S Desert Fthills Pkwy 85048 480-783-1300
Nancy Corner, prin. Fax 460-2094
Kyrene Centennial MS 1,200/6-8
13808 S 36th St 85044 480-783-2500
Ev Michell, prin. Fax 496-6110
Kyrene de la Colina ES 600/K-5
13612 S 36th St 85044 480-783-2600
Kelvin Inouye, prin. Fax 496-9036
Kyrene de la Esperanza ES 600/K-5
14841 S 41st Pl 85044 480-783-1700
Cheryl Greene, prin. Fax 759-6656
Kyrene de la Estrella ES 600/K-5
2620 E Liberty Ln 85048 480-783-1800
Jeff Williamson, prin. Fax 759-5776
Kyrene de la Sierra ES 700/K-5
1122 E Liberty Ln 85048 480-783-1100
Tracy Pastor, prin. Fax 460-1203
Kyrene de las Lomas ES 700/PK-5
11820 S Warner Elliot Loop 85044 480-783-2800
Brian Gibson, prin. Fax 783-5766
Kyrene del Milenio ES 500/K-5
4630 E Frye Rd 85048 480-783-3400
Jim Verrill, prin. Fax 705-4459
Kyrene de los Cerritos ES 800/PK-5
14620 S Desert Fthills Pkwy 85048 480-783-1200
Darcy Dicosmo, prin. Fax 460-0498
Kyrene de los Lagos ES 600/K-5
17001 S 34th Way 85048 480-783-1400
Tonja Yallung, prin. Fax 759-5560
Kyrene Monte Vista ES 500/K-5
15221 S Ray Rd 85048 480-783-1500
Helene Zimmerman, prin. Fax 759-4918

Laveen ESD 59
Supt. — See Laveen
Cash ES 800/PK-6
3851 W Roeser Rd 85041 602-237-9120
Lisa Sandomir, prin. Fax 237-9133

Madison ESD 38 6,200/PK-8
5601 N 16th St 85016 602-664-7900
Tim Ham Ed.D., supt. Fax 664-7999
www.msd38.org
Madison # 1 MS 800/5-8
5525 N 16th St 85016 602-664-7100
Kevin Flynn, prin. Fax 664-7199
Madison Camelview ES 700/PK-3
2002 E Campbell Ave 85016 602-664-7200
Joseph DelaHuerta, prin. Fax 664-7299
Madison Heights ES 400/PK-4
7150 N 22nd St 85020 602-664-7800
Denise Donovan, prin. Fax 664-7899
Madison Meadows MS 800/5-8
225 W Ocotillo Rd 85013 602-664-7600
Susan Doyle, prin. Fax 664-7699
Madison Park MS 700/4-8
1431 E Campbell Ave 85014 602-664-7500
Richard Ramos, prin. Fax 664-7599
Madison Rose Lane ES 900/PK-4
1155 E Rose Ln 85014 602-664-7400
Peter Morkert, prin. Fax 664-7499
Madison Simis ES 1,000/PK-4
7302 N 10th St 85020 602-664-7300
Dr. Joyce Flowers, prin. Fax 664-7399
Madison Traditional Academy 900/K-5
5525 N 16th St 85016 602-664-7119
Casey George, prin. Fax 664-7199

Murphy ESD 21 2,600/K-8
2615 W Buckeye Rd 85009 602-353-5000
Dr. Paul Mohr, supt. Fax 353-5081
www.msdaz.org
Garcia S 700/K-8
1441 S 27th Ave 85009 602-353-5110
Larry Lawrence, prin. Fax 353-5189
Hamilton S 600/K-8
2020 W Durango St 85009 602-353-5330
Mishay Tribble, prin. Fax 353-5388
Kuban S 500/K-8
3201 W Sherman St 85009 602-353-5440
Margaret Moya, prin. Fax 353-5479
Sullivan S 900/K-8
2 N 31st Ave 85009 602-353-5220
Jose Diaz, prin. Fax 353-5284

Osborn ESD 8 3,800/K-8
1226 W Osborn Rd 85013 602-707-2000
Wilma Basnett, supt. Fax 707-2040
www.osbornnet.org
Clarendon ES 500/4-6
1225 W Clarendon Ave 85013 602-707-2200
Sandra Meko, prin. Fax 707-2240
Encanto PS 700/K-3
1420 W Osborn Rd 85013 602-707-2300
Michael Robert, prin. Fax 707-2340
Longview ES 600/K-6
1209 E Indian School Rd 85014 602-707-2700
Leslie Beauchamp, prin. Fax 707-2740
Montecito Community ES 600/K-6
715 E Montecito Ave 85014 602-707-2500
Maria O'Malley, prin. Fax 707-2540
Osborn MS 700/7-8
1102 W Highland Ave 85013 602-707-2400
Marty Makar, prin. Fax 707-2440
Solano ES 800/K-6
1526 W Missouri Ave 85015 602-707-2600
Karen Epps, prin. Fax 707-2640

Paradise Valley USD 69 33,600/PK-12
15002 N 32nd St 85032 602-449-2000
John Kriekard Ed.D., supt. Fax 449-2005
www.pvschools.net
Aire Libre ES 500/K-6
16428 N 21st St 85022 602-449-5400
William Greer, prin. Fax 449-5405
Arrowhead ES 500/K-6
3820 E Nisbet Rd 85032 602-449-2700
Diana Silvestri, prin. Fax 449-2705
Boulder Creek ES 600/K-6
22801 N 22nd St 85024 602-449-4500
Robert Gibson, prin. Fax 449-4505
Cactus View ES 800/PK-6
17602 N Central Ave 85022 602-449-2500
Lara Herbein, prin. Fax 449-2505
Campo Bello ES 500/K-6
2650 E Contention Mine Rd 85032 602-449-5200
Janice Moore, prin. Fax 449-5205
Desert Cove ES 600/K-6
11020 N 28th St 85028 602-449-3400
Tom Ellinghausen, prin. Fax 449-3405
Desert Trails ES 600/K-6
4315 E Cashman Dr 85050 602-449-4100
Kristin Lee, prin. Fax 449-4105
Eagle Ridge ES 700/K-6
19801 N 13th St 85024 602-449-5700
Mary Parese, prin. Fax 449-5705
Echo Mountain IS 500/4-6
1811 E Michigan Ave Ste 6 85022 602-449-5600
Bennett MacKinney, prin. Fax 449-5605
Echo Mountain PS 600/K-3
1811 E Michigan Ave Ste 3 85022 602-449-5500
Cindy Daniels, prin. Fax 449-5505
Explorer MS 600/7-8
22401 N 40th St 85050 602-449-4200
Marianne Bursi, prin. Fax 449-4205
Foothills ES 500/K-6
17835 N 44th St 85032 602-449-7400
Dennis Reiley, prin. Fax 449-7405
Greenway MS 700/7-8
3002 E Nisbet Rd 85032 602-449-2400
Jesse Acosta, prin. Fax 449-2405
Hidden Hills ES 600/K-6
1919 E Sharon Dr 85022 602-449-3100
Lynette Geake, prin. Fax 449-3105
Indian Bend ES 600/K-6
3633 E Thunderbird Rd 85032 602-449-3200
Ibi Haghighat, prin. Fax 449-3205
Larkspur ES 600/K-6
2430 E Larkspur Dr 85032 602-449-3300
Marian Ouelette, prin. Fax 449-3305
Mercury Mine ES 700/K-6
9640 N 28th St 85028 602-449-3700
Donna Alley, prin. Fax 449-3705
Mountain Trail MS 900/7-8
2323 E Mountain Gate Pass 85024 602-449-4600
Ian Deonise, prin. Fax 449-4605
Palomino I ES 800/K-3
15833 N 29th St 85032 602-449-2800
Dr. Ana Ramos-Pell, prin. Fax 449-2805
Palomino II IS 500/4-6
15815 N 29th St 85032 602-449-2900
Jenny Robles, prin. Fax 449-2905
Quail Run ES 500/K-6
3303 E Utopia Rd 85050 602-449-4400
Gerald Michels, prin. Fax 449-4405
Shea MS 900/7-8
2728 E Shea Blvd 85028 602-449-3500
Dan Knak, prin. Fax 449-3505
Sunset Canyon ES 600/PK-6
2727 E Siesta Ln 85050 602-449-5100
Jerry Voll, prin. Fax 449-5105
Village Vista ES 400/K-6
4215 E Andora Dr 85032 602-449-3600
Jan Stevens, prin. Fax 449-3605
Vista Verde MS 800/7-8
2826 E Grovers Ave 85032 602-449-5300
Elaine Jacobs, prin. Fax 449-5305
Whispering Wind Academy 600/K-6
15844 N 43rd St 85032 602-449-7300
Brian Gilchrist, prin. Fax 449-7305
Wildfire ES K-6
3997 E Lockwood Dr 85050 602-449-4300
Dr. Troy Bales, prin. Fax 449-4305
Other Schools – See Scottsdale

Pendergast ESD 92 9,100/PK-8
3802 N 91st Ave 85037 623-772-2200
Ron Richards, supt. Fax 877-8188
www.pesd92.org/
Amberlea S K-8
8455 W Virginia Ave 85037 623-772-2900
Brenda Martin, prin. Fax 594-0207
Calderwood S 50/K-8
10730 W Campbell Ave 85037 623-772-2356
Amy Perhamus, prin. Fax 772-1022
Copper King S 1,000/K-8
10730 W Campbell Ave 85037 623-772-2580
Molly Watson, prin. Fax 872-7769
Desert Horizon S 900/PK-8
8525 W Osborn Rd 85037 623-772-2430
Suzie Jaramillo, prin. Fax 873-4691
Pendergast S 600/K-8
3802 N 91st Ave 85037 623-772-2400
Mike Woolsey, prin. Fax 877-9591
Villa De Paz S 900/PK-8
4940 N 103rd Ave 85037 623-772-2490
Kathy Welsh, prin. Fax 877-8977
Westwind IS 700/5-8
9040 W Campbell Ave 85037 623-772-2460
Brian Winefsky, prin. Fax 872-0327
Westwind PS 50/PK-4
9040 W Campbell Ave 85037 623-772-2700
Dani Williams, prin. Fax 772-8464
Other Schools – See Avondale, Glendale

Phoenix ESD 1 7,900/PK-8
1817 N 7th St 85006 602-257-3755
Myriam Roa, supt. Fax 257-3783
www.phxelem.k12.az.us
Bethune S 600/K-8
1310 S 15th Ave 85007 602-257-3831
Tracey Pastor, prin. Fax 257-2915
Capitol ES 500/K-6
330 N 16th Ave 85007 602-257-3835
Russell Sanders, prin. Fax 257-6397
Dunbar ES 200/K-6
707 W Grant St 85007 602-257-3844
Loraine Conley-Franklin, prin. Fax 257-3874
Edison ES 500/K-6
804 N 18th St 85006 602-257-3867
Fred Graef, prin. Fax 257-3704
Emerson ES 600/K-6
915 E Palm Ln 85006 602-257-3853
Garthanne Ocampo, prin. Fax 257-3937
Faith North S 300/K-8
910 E Washington St 85034 602-257-3914
Nadine Gofonia, prin. Fax 257-3926
Garfield ES 500/K-6
811 N 13th St 85006 602-257-3863
Dr. Teresa Covarrubius, prin. Fax 257-4866
Heard ES 500/K-6
2301 W Thomas Rd 85015 602-257-3879
Matthew Camacho, prin. Fax 257-3881
Herrera S 800/K-8
1350 S 11th St 85034 602-257-3885
Dr. Carolyn Davidson-Taylor, prin. Fax 257-3952
Kenilworth S 600/K-8
1210 N 5th Ave 85003 602-257-3889
Debora Moncayo, prin. Fax 257-3923
Lowell S 600/K-8
1121 S 3rd Ave 85003 602-257-3902
Rosanna Hidalgo, prin. Fax 257-6396
Magnet Traditional S 500/K-8
2602 N 23rd Ave 85009 602-257-6282
Adrian Walker, prin. Fax 257-6287
Phoenix Preparatory Academy 800/7-8
735 E Fillmore St 85006 602-257-4840
Kimberly Hertzog, dir. Fax 257-4852
Shaw ES 600/PK-6
123 N 13th St 85034 602-257-3909
Nadine Gofonia, prin. Fax 257-2954
Whittier ES 500/K-6
2000 N 16th St 85006 602-257-2890
Dr. Ronnie Pitre, prin. Fax 257-3924

Riverside ESD 2 800/K-8
1414 S 51st Ave 85043 602-477-8900
Richard Stokes, supt. Fax 272-8378
www.riverside.k12.az.us
Kings Ridge MS 400/5-8
3650 S 64th Ln 85043 602-477-8960
Tom Cox, prin. Fax 936-5531
Riverside ES 500/K-4
1414 S 51st Ave 85043 602-477-8900
Tom Cox, prin. Fax 936-5531

Roosevelt ESD 66 11,500/K-8
6000 S 7th St 85042 602-243-4800
Mary Beyda, supt. Fax 243-2637
www.rsd.k12.az.us
Barr S 400/K-8
2041 E Vineyard Rd 85042 602-232-4900
Lee Payton, prin. Fax 243-2116
Brooks Academy S 600/K-8
3146 E Wier Ave 85040 602-232-4200
Celeste Enochs, prin. Fax 243-2115
Bush S 600/K-8
602 E Siesta Dr 85042 602-232-4260
Kelly Solomon, prin. Fax 243-4932
Campbell S 600/K-8
2624 E South Mountain Ave 85042 602-304-3170
Mary Figueroa Stewart, prin. Fax 304-3182
Chavez Community S 600/K-8
4001 S 3rd St 85040 602-232-4940
Joseph Hines, prin. Fax 243-2106
Conchos S 500/K-8
1718 W Vineyard Rd 85041 602-232-4250
Ruben Gonzalez, prin. Fax 243-4969
Davis S 700/K-8
6209 S 15th Ave 85041 602-232-4930
Temako Roque, prin. Fax 232-4280
Greenfield MS 700/4-8
7009 S 10th St 85042 602-232-4240
Ernie Montoya, prin. Fax 243-4973
Jorgensen S 700/K-8
1701 W Roeser Rd 85041 602-232-4990
Patricia Welcher, prin. Fax 243-4989
Julian MS 300/5-8
2149 E Carver Dr 85040 602-232-4950
Patricia Jury, prin. Fax 243-4906
Kennedy ES 700/K-3
6825 S 10th St 85042 602-232-4220
Anita White, prin. Fax 243-4939
King ES 400/K-3
4615 S 22nd St 85040 602-232-4910
Michael Turner, prin. Fax 243-4910
Lassen S 600/K-8
909 W Vineyard Rd 85041 602-232-4210
Hamed El-Afandi, prin. Fax 232-4291
Pastor S 700/K-8
2101 W Alta Vista Rd 85041 602-304-3160
Pablo Curiel, prin. Fax 304-3169
Rose Linda S 700/K-8
4610 S 12th St 85040 602-232-4920
Irene Lopez, prin. Fax 243-4961
Sierra Vista S 500/K-8
6401 S 16th St 85042 602-232-4970
Fax 232-4979
Southwest S 700/K-8
1111 W Dobbins Rd 85041 602-232-4270
Elizabeth Minzer, prin. Fax 243-4933
Sunland S 600/K-8
5401 S 7th Ave 85041 602-232-4960
Sergio Gutierrez, prin. Fax 243-2125
Valley View S 700/K-8
8220 S 7th Ave 85041 602-232-4980
John Wann, prin. Fax 243-4926

Scottsdale USD 48 24,000/PK-12
3811 N 44th St 85018 480-484-6100
Dr. Gary Catalani, supt. Fax 484-6287
www.susd.org/
Hopi ES 800/K-5
5110 E Lafayette Blvd 85018 480-484-2000
Lori Colling, prin. Fax 484-2001
Ingleside MS 700/6-8
5402 E Osborn Rd 85018 480-484-4900
Tanya Beckwith, prin. Fax 484-4901
Tavan ES 700/PK-5
4610 E Osborn Rd 85018 480-484-3500
Margaret Serna, prin. Fax 484-3501
Other Schools – See Paradise Valley, Scottsdale

Tempe ESD 3
Supt. — See Tempe
Nevitt ES 800/K-5
4525 E Saint Anne Ave 85042 602-431-6640
Bernadette Kadel, prin. Fax 431-6887

Tolleson ESD 17
Supt. — See Tolleson
Desert Oasis S 800/K-8
8802 W McDowell Rd 85037 623-533-3901
Clint Smith, prin. Fax 533-3902
Sheely Farms S 700/K-8
9450 W Encanto Blvd 85037 623-907-5270
John Scudder, prin. Fax 907-5271

Washington ESD 6
Supt. — See Glendale
Acacia ES 700/PK-6
3021 W Evans Dr 85053 602-896-5000
Christine Hollingsworth, prin. Fax 896-5020
Alta Vista ES 700/K-6
8710 N 31st Ave 85051 602-347-2000
Carla Aronowitz, prin. Fax 347-2020
Cactus Wren ES 500/PK-6
9650 N 39th Ave 85051 602-347-2100
Kaylene Ashbridge, prin. Fax 347-2120
Chaparral ES 500/PK-6
3808 W Joan De Arc Ave 85029 602-896-5300
Ken Schofield, prin. Fax 896-5320
Cholla MS 900/7-8
3120 W Cholla St 85029 602-896-5400
Brenda Case, prin. Fax 896-5420
Desert Foothills JHS 800/7-8
3333 W Banff Ln 85053 602-896-5500
James Hall, prin. Fax 896-5520
Desert View ES 600/PK-5
8621 N 3rd St 85020 602-347-4000
Paulette Zuroff, prin. Fax 347-4020
Ironwood ES 600/PK-6
14850 N 39th Ave 85053 602-896-5600
Mike Trevillion, prin. Fax 896-5620
Jacobs ES 500/K-6
14421 N 23rd Ave 85023 602-896-5700
Candace Isherwood, prin. Fax 896-5720
Lakeview ES 600/K-6
3040 W Yucca St 85029 602-896-5800
Jaime Tejada, prin. Fax 896-5820
Lincoln Traditional S 600/K-8
10444 N 39th Ave 85051 602-896-6300
Tara Maole, prin. Fax 896-6320
Lookout Mountain ES 1,000/K-6
15 W Coral Gables Dr 85023 602-896-5900
Tricia Heller-Johnson, prin. Fax 896-5920
Manzanita ES 800/K-6
8430 N 39th Ave 85051 602-347-2200
Maria Farmer, prin. Fax 347-2220
Maryland S 800/K-8
6503 N 21st Ave 85015 602-347-2300
Adele Russell, prin. Fax 347-2320
Miller ES 600/K-5
2021 W Alice Ave 85021 602-347-3000
Jim Paczosa, prin. Fax 347-3020
Moon Mountain ES 700/PK-6
13425 N 19th Ave 85029 602-896-6000
Mary Lou Palmer, prin. Fax 896-6020
Mountain Sky JHS 900/7-8
16225 N 7th Ave 85023 602-896-6100
Linda McKeever, prin. Fax 896-6120
Mountain View S 1,000/K-8
801 W Peoria Ave 85029 602-347-4100
Joseph Negron, prin. Fax 347-4120
Ocotillo ES 900/K-6
3225 W Ocotillo Rd 85017 602-347-2400
Phil Garitson, prin. Fax 347-2420
Orangewood S 900/K-8
7337 N 19th Ave 85021 602-347-2900
Andree Charlson, prin. Fax 347-2920
Palo Verde MS 1,100/7-8
7502 N 39th Ave 85051 602-347-2500
Carmen Kemery, prin. Fax 347-2520
Roadrunner ES 800/K-6
7702 N 39th Ave 85051 602-347-3100
Karen Menaugh, prin. Fax 347-3120
Royal Palm MS 800/6-8
8520 N 19th Ave 85021 602-347-3200
Leonard Hoover, prin. Fax 347-3220
Sahuaro ES 700/PK-6
12835 N 33rd Ave 85029 602-896-6200
David Anderson, prin. Fax 896-6220
Shaw Butte ES 1,100/PK-6
12202 N 21st Ave 85029 602-347-4200
Tracy Maynard, prin. Fax 347-4220
Sunnyslope S 1,100/K-8
245 E Mountain View Rd 85020 602-347-4300
Lori Ritz, prin. Fax 347-4320
Tumbleweed ES 600/PK-6
4001 W Laurel Ln 85029 602-896-6600
Nick Gupton, prin. Fax 896-6620
Washington ES 1,100/PK-6
8033 N 27th Ave 85051 602-347-3400
David McNeil, prin. Fax 347-3420

Wilson ESD 7 1,300/PK-8
3025 E Fillmore St 85008 602-681-2200
Antonio Sanchez, supt. Fax 275-7517
www.wsd.k12.az.us
Wilson MS 700/4-8
2929 E Fillmore St 85008 602-683-2400
Cindy Campton, prin. Fax 275-8677
Wilson PS 600/PK-3
415 N 30th St 85008 602-683-2500
Araceli Cecena, prin. Fax 231-0567

All Saints' Episcopal Day S 500/PK-8
6300 N Central Ave 85012 602-274-4866
John Hyslop, hdmstr. Fax 274-0365
Christ Lutheran S 500/PK-8
3901 E Indian School Rd 85018 602-957-7010
Cheryl Ehlers, prin. Fax 955-8073
Christ the Redeemer Lutheran S 100/PK-6
8801 N 43rd Ave 85051 623-934-5896
George Leitner, prin. Fax 934-3298
Desert Springs Christian S 100/PK-PK
16215 N Tatum Blvd 85032 602-788-5060
Gwen Bailey, dir. Fax 788-7528
Emmaus S 100/PK-8
3841 W Sweetwater Ave 85029 602-843-3853
Mark Kaiser, prin. Fax 942-0223
Family of Christ Lutheran S 200/PK-K
3501 E Chandler Blvd 85048 480-759-4047
Sue Nelson, dir. Fax 759-9004
Glenview Adventist Academy 100/PK-9
6801 N 43rd Ave 85019 623-931-1846
Fax 934-3296
Good Shepherd S 50/K-8
3040 N 7th Ave 85013 602-266-3534
Richard DeFrain, prin. Fax 266-3534
Holy Trinity Academy 50/PK-3
1973 E Maryland Ave 85016 602-248-3881
James Paris, prin. Fax 230-9099
Martin Luther S 100/K-8
1806 W Glenrosa Ave 85015 602-248-0656
Fax 604-8257
Most Holy Trinity S 200/PK-8
535 E Alice Ave 85020 602-943-9058
Michael Brennan, prin. Fax 943-3188
91st Psalm Christian S 200/PK-12
2020 E Baseline Rd 85042 602-243-1900
Scott Ranney, prin. Fax 243-5919
Northwest Christian S 1,500/PK-12
16401 N 43rd Ave 85053 602-978-5134
Matthew Davidson, supt. Fax 978-5804
Paradise Valley Christian Preparatory S 400/PK-8
11875 N 24th St 85028 602-992-8140
Sheryl Temple, hdmstr. Fax 992-8152
Phoenix Christian ES Central 200/PK-6
4002 N 18th Ave 85015 602-264-4338
Dr. Kyle Brown, prin. Fax 264-6012
Phoenix Christian S 100/PK-8
2425 N 26th St 85008 602-956-9330
Sue Vander Ploeg, prin. Fax 956-4207
Phoenix Hebrew Academy 100/K-8
515 E Bethany Home Rd 85012 602-277-7479
Rabbi Isaac Entin, prin. Fax 274-0713
St. Agnes S 200/PK-8
2311 E Palm Ln 85006 602-244-1451
Denise Campbell, prin. Fax 286-0250
St. Catherine of Siena S 300/PK-8
6413 S Central Ave 85042 602-276-2241
Catherine Lucero, prin. Fax 268-7886
St. Francis Xavier S 500/K-8
4715 N Central Ave 85012 602-266-5364
Kimberly Cavnar, prin. Fax 279-0423
St. Gregory S 400/PK-8
3440 N 18th Ave 85015 602-266-9527
Maureen Fyan, prin. Fax 266-4055
St. Jerome S 300/PK-8
10815 N 35th Ave 85029 602-942-5644
Carl Hodus, prin. Fax 467-4929
St. Joan of Arc Preschool 100/PK-PK
3801 E Greenway Rd 85032 602-867-9179
Michelle Buxtrin, dir. Fax 482-7930
St. John Bosco Interparish S 600/PK-8
16035 S 48th St 85048 480-219-4848
Shelley Conner, prin. Fax 219-5767
St. Matthew S 100/K-8
2038 W Van Buren St 85009 602-254-0611
Gena McGowan, prin. Fax 393-7813

St. Paul Lutheran S 50/PK-K
6301 W Indian School Rd 85033 623-846-2235
Karen Moses, sec. ed. Fax 846-2245
St. Theresa S 600/PK-8
5001 E Thomas Rd 85018 602-840-0010
Sr. Patricia Gehling, prin. Fax 840-8323
St. Thomas the Apostle S 600/K-8
4510 N 24th St 85016 602-954-9088
Mary Coffman, prin. Fax 381-3256
St. Vincent De Paul S 400/PK-8
3130 N 51st Ave 85031 623-247-8595
Sr. Julie Kubasak, prin. Fax 245-0132
Scottsdale Christian Academy 1,200/PK-12
14400 N Tatum Blvd 85032 602-992-5100
Tim Hillen, supt. Fax 992-0575
SS. Simon & Jude S 500/K-8
6351 N 27th Ave 85017 602-242-1299
Sr. Raphael Quinn, prin. Fax 433-7608
Stone Creek Christian Learning Center 50/PK-PK
17844 N 7th Ave 85023 602-298-6630
LeAnna Sackett, dir. Fax 298-1196
Valley Classical Christian S 200/PK-8
5811 N 20th St 85016 602-955-5959
Beverly Ducey, prin.

Picacho, Pinal
Picacho ESD 33 200/K-8
PO Box 8, 520-466-7942
Allen Rogers, supt. Fax 466-7165
Picacho S 200/K-8
PO Box 8, 520-466-7942
Allen Rogers, prin. Fax 466-7165

Pima, Graham, Pop. 1,965
Pima USD 6 500/K-12
PO Box 429 85543 928-387-8000
Joseph Farnsworth, supt. Fax 485-2343
www.pima.k12.az.us/
Pima ES 400/K-6
PO Box 429 85543 928-387-8050
Lynne Jones, prin. Fax 485-8964
Pima JHS 100/7-8
PO Box 429 85543 928-387-8100
Tony Goodman, prin. Fax 485-2274

Pine, Gila
Pine Strawberry ESD 12 100/PK-8
PO Box 1150 85544 928-476-3283
Mike Clark, supt. Fax 476-2506
www.pineesd.org/
Pine Strawberry S 100/PK-8
PO Box 1150 85544 928-476-3283
Mike Clark, prin. Fax 476-2506

Pinetop, See Lakeside

St. Anthony S 50/K-3
1915 S Penrod Ln 85935 928-367-9111
Fax 367-9191

Pinon, Navajo, Pop. 468
Pinon USD 4 1,300/PK-12
PO Box 839 86510 928-725-3450
Larry Wallen, supt. Fax 725-2123
www.pusdatsa.org
Pinon ES 600/PK-5
PO Box 839 86510 928-725-2200
Rose Rooth, prin. Fax 725-2216
Pinon MS 400/6-8
PO Box 839 86510 928-725-2300
Rick Grant, prin. Fax 725-2370

Pirtleville, Cochise, Pop. 1,364
Douglas USD 27
Supt. — See Douglas
Faras ES 200/K-5
410 W 1st Ave 85626 520-364-8461
Cindy Ortega, prin. Fax 364-7470

Pomerene, Cochise
Pomerene ESD 64 100/K-8
PO Box 7 85627 520-586-2407
Dan Bailey, supt. Fax 586-7724
www.pomereneschool.org/
Pomerene S 100/K-8
PO Box 7 85627 520-586-2407
Dan Bailey, prin. Fax 586-7724

Prescott, Yavapai, Pop. 40,360
Prescott USD 1 5,400/K-12
146 S Granite St 86303 928-445-5400
Kevin Kapp, supt. Fax 713-3207
www.prescottschools.com
Granite Mountain MS 600/6-8
1800 N Williamson Valley Rd 86305 928-717-3253
Stephanie Hillig, prin. Fax 717-3284
Hicks ES 500/K-5
1845 Campbell Ave 86301 928-717-3276
Brian Moore, prin. Fax 717-3275
Judd ES 700/K-5
1749 N Williamson Valley Rd 86305 928-717-3263
Larry Peterson, prin. Fax 717-3262
Lincoln ES 300/K-5
201 Park Ave 86303 928-717-3249
Bucky Bates, prin. Fax 717-3248
Miller Valley ES 500/K-5
900 W Iron Springs Rd 86305 928-717-3268
Jeff Lane, prin. Fax 541-2281
Prescott Mile High MS 700/6-8
300 S Granite St 86303 928-717-3241
Joe Howard, prin. Fax 717-3298
Washington ES 300/K-5
300 E Gurley St 86301 928-717-3281
Harold Tenney, prin. Fax 717-3280

American Lutheran S 100/PK-PK
1085 Scott Dr 86301 928-778-7049
Lori Barbe, dir. Fax 445-8343
Christian Academy of Prescott 200/PK-8
PO Box 30 86302 928-445-2565
Cheryl Arthur, prin. Fax 778-9794
Prescott SDA S 50/K-8
2980 Willow Creek Rd 86301 928-445-3663
Sacred Heart S 200/K-8
131 N Summit Ave 86301 928-445-2621
Lynne Reuter, prin. Fax 445-0966
St. Luke's S 50/PK-K
2000 Shepherds Ln 86301 928-442-1315
Fax 778-4699
Trinity Christian S 200/PK-12
1070 Mogollon Rd 86301 928-445-6306
Kyle Maestri, admin. Fax 445-7210

Prescott Valley, Yavapai, Pop. 33,068
Humboldt USD 22 5,900/PK-12
8766 E State Route 69 86314 928-759-4000
Dr. Henry Schmitt, supt. Fax 759-4020
www.humboldtunified.com/
Coyote Springs ES 800/K-5
8101 E Highway 89 A 86314 928-759-4300
Susan Fahrni, prin. Fax 759-4320
Glassford Hill MS 700/6-8
6901 Panther Path 86314 928-759-4600
Kristen Rex, prin. Fax 759-4620
Granville ES 600/K-5
5250 N Stover Dr 86314 928-759-4800
Diana Green, prin. Fax 772-2647
Lake Valley ES 500/K-5
3900 N Starlight Dr 86314 928-759-4200
Danny Brown, prin. Fax 759-4220
Liberty Traditional S 600/PK-8
3300 N Lake Valley Rd 86314 928-759-4500
Michael DeRois, prin. Fax 759-4520
Mountain View ES 600/K-5
8601 E Loos Dr 86314 928-759-4700
JoAnne Bindell, prin. Fax 759-4720
Other Schools – See Dewey, Humboldt

Quartzsite, LaPaz, Pop. 3,397
Quartzsite ESD 4
Supt. — See Ehrenberg
Quartzsite S 100/K-8
930 Quail Trail 85359 928-927-5500
Jacque Price, prin. Fax 927-7227

Queen Creek, Maricopa, Pop. 16,628
Chandler USD 80
Supt. — See Chandler
Payne JHS 800/7-8
7655 S Higley Rd, 480-224-2400
Karen Martin, prin. Fax 224-2420

Florence USD 1
Supt. — See Florence
Circle Cross Ranch S K-8
35900 N Charbray Dr, 480-987-7600
Dr. Bob Pappalardo, prin.
Copper Basin S 900/K-8
28682 N Main St, 480-888-7500
Joanne Pike, prin. Fax 888-2134
Walker Butte S 1,200/PK-8
29697 N Desert Willow Blvd, 480-987-5360
John Allee, prin. Fax 987-5369

Higley USD 60
Supt. — See Gilbert
Cortina ES PK-8
19680 S 188th St, 480-279-7800
Bradley Jamison, prin. Fax 279-7805

Queen Creek USD 95 4,400/PK-12
20740 S Ellsworth Rd, 480-987-5935
Dr. James Murlless, supt. Fax 987-9714
www.qcusd.org/
Barnes ES 500/PK-5
20750 S 214th St, 480-987-7400
Laura Valenciano, prin. Fax 987-7415
Barney MS 6-8
24937 S Sossaman Rd, 480-474-6700
Denise Johnson, prin.
Brandon-Pickett ES 500/PK-5
22076 Village Loop, 480-987-7420
Erika Copeland, prin. Fax 987-7439
Desert Mountain ES 500/PK-5
22301 S Hawes Rd, 480-987-5912
Bill Schultz, prin. Fax 987-5914
Queen Creek ES 400/PK-5
23636 S 204th St, 480-987-5920
Sheri Horton, prin. Fax 987-0612
Queen Creek MS 900/6-8
20435 S Old Ellsworth Rd, 480-987-5940
Julie Niven, prin. Fax 987-5947

Calvary Christian S 100/PK-6
PO Box 637, 480-988-4241
Cheryl McAlister, admin. Fax 987-2717
Our Lady of Guadalupe S PK-K
PO Box 856, 480-987-0315
Anna Romley, dir. Fax 888-1159

Red Rock, Pinal
Red Rock ESD 5 100/K-8
PO Box 1010, 520-682-3331
Michael Hitchcock, supt. Fax 682-2128
redrockschools.com/
Red Rock S 100/K-8
PO Box 1010, 520-682-3331
Lillian Norris, prin. Fax 682-2128

Rimrock, Yavapai
Beaver Creek ESD 26 300/K-8
4810 E Beaver Creek Rd 86335 928-567-4631
Karin Ward, supt. Fax 567-5347
www.bcs.k12.az.us
Beaver Creek S 300/K-8
4810 E Beaver Creek Rd 86335 928-567-4631
Karin Ward, prin. Fax 567-5347

Rio Rico, Santa Cruz, Pop. 100
Santa Cruz Valley USD 35 3,700/PK-12
1374 W Frontage Rd 85648 520-375-8261
Daniel Fontes, supt. Fax 281-7093
www.santacruz.k12.az.us
Calabasas MS 900/6-8
1374 W Frontage Rd 85648 520-375-8600
David Verdugo, prin. Fax 375-8690
Coatimundi MS 6-8
1374 W Frontage Rd 85648 520-375-8800
John Fanning, prin. Fax 761-4669
Mountain View ES 600/K-5
1374 W Frontage Rd 85648 520-375-8400
Stephen Schadler, prin. Fax 281-7990
Pena Blanca ES 400/PK-5
1374 W Frontage Rd 85648 520-281-8500
Sandra Figueroa, prin. Fax 375-8590
San Cayetano ES 700/PK-5
1374 W Frontage Rd 85648 520-375-8300
Gail Rich, prin. Fax 281-7973

Rock Point, Apache, Pop. 270

Navajo Lutheran Mission S 100/K-6
PO Box 354 86545 928-659-4202
Dolores Weis, dir. Fax 659-4255

Roll, Yuma
Mohawk Valley ESD 17 200/K-8
5151 S Avenue 39 E 85347 928-785-4942
Alfredo Luna, supt. Fax 785-9496
www.mohawk.apscc.k12.az.us
Mohawk Valley S 200/K-8
5151 S Avenue 39 E 85347 928-785-4942
Alfredo Luna, admin. Fax 785-9496

Round Rock, Apache
Red Mesa USD 27
Supt. — See Teec Nos Pos
Round Rock S, PO Box CC 86547 200/K-8
Karina Roessel, prin. 928-656-4100

Sacaton, Pinal, Pop. 1,452
Sacaton ESD 18 500/PK-8
PO Box 98, 520-562-8600
Dr. James Christensen, supt. Fax 763-4410
sacatonschools.org
Sacaton ES 300/PK-5
PO Box 98, 520-562-8600
Carol Virkler, prin. Fax 763-4430
Sacaton MS 200/6-8
PO Box 98, 520-562-8600
Nicholas DePadre, prin. Fax 763-4410

Safford, Graham, Pop. 8,932
Safford USD 1 2,900/PK-12
734 W 11th St 85546 928-348-7000
Mark Tregaskes, supt. Fax 348-7001
www.saffordusd.k12.az.us
Nelson ES 500/K-6
1100 S 10th Ave 85546 928-348-7020
A.J. Taylor, prin. Fax 348-7021
Powell ES 500/K-6
1041 S 14th Ave 85546 928-348-7030
Naomi Lowery, prin. Fax 348-7031
Safford MS 400/7-8
612 W 11th St 85546 928-348-7040
Clay Emery, prin. Fax 348-7041
Stinson ES 600/PK-6
2013 S 8th Ave 85546 928-348-7010
Michael Moreno, prin. Fax 348-7011

Sahuarita, Pima, Pop. 9,007
Sahuarita USD 30 4,100/PK-12
350 W Sahuarita Rd 85629 520-625-3502
Jay St. John, supt. Fax 625-4609
sahuarita.k12.az.us
Anza Trail S K-8
350 W Sahuarita Rd 85629 520-625-3502
Kathy Shiba, prin. Fax 398-7121
Sahuarita IS 800/3-5
350 W Sahuarita Rd 85629 520-625-3502
Scott Downs, prin. Fax 648-6181
Sahuarita MS 900/6-8
350 W Sahuarita Rd 85629 520-625-3502
Terri Noe, prin. Fax 399-1870
Sahuarita PS 1,000/PK-2
350 W Sahuarita Rd 85629 520-625-3502
Tina Steward, prin. Fax 393-7036
Other Schools – See Amado

Sahuarita Christian Academy 50/PK-12
PO Box 1704 85629 520-648-0601
David Lyon, dir. Fax 871-5214

Saint David, Cochise, Pop. 1,468
Saint David USD 21 500/PK-12
PO Box 70 85630 520-720-4781
Kate Mueller, supt. Fax 720-4783
www.stdavidschools.org/
Saint David S 300/PK-8
PO Box 70 85630 520-720-4781
Mark Goodman, prin. Fax 720-4783

Saint Johns, Apache, Pop. 3,513
Saint Johns USD 1 1,100/PK-12
PO Box 3030 85936 928-337-2255
Larry Heap, supt. Fax 337-2263
www.sjusd.net
Coronado ES 300/PK-3
PO Box 609 85936 928-337-4435
Wes Brownfield, prin. Fax 337-4039
Saint Johns MS 400/4-8
PO Box 3060 85936 928-337-2132
Ed Burgoyne, prin. Fax 337-3147

Saint Michaels, Apache, Pop. 1,119

St. Michael Indian S 200/K-8
PO Box 650 86511 928-871-4636
Fax 871-3027

Salome, LaPaz
Salome Consolidated ESD 30 100/PK-8
PO Box 339 85348 928-859-3339
George Dean, supt. Fax 859-3085

Salome Consolidated S 100/PK-8
PO Box 339 85348 928-859-3339
George Dean, prin. Fax 859-3085

San Carlos, Gila, Pop. 2,918
San Carlos USD 20 1,100/PK-12
PO Box 207 85550 928-475-2315
Richard Wilde, supt. Fax 475-2301
Rice PS 300/PK-3
PO Box 207 85550 928-475-2315
Delphine Rodriguez, prin. Fax 475-2301
San Carlos IS 200/4-6
PO Box 207 85550 928-475-4836
Valerie Cervantez, prin. Fax 475-4838
San Carlos JHS 200/7-8
PO Box 207 85550 928-475-2262
Alvena Bush, prin. Fax 475-2431

St. Charles S 100/K-6
PO Box 339 85550 928-475-2449
Sr. Georgia Greene, prin. Fax 475-4860

Sanders, Apache
Sanders USD 18 1,100/K-12
PO Box 250 86512 928-688-4756
Doug McIntyre, supt. Fax 688-4723
www.susd.k12.az.us
Sanders ES 400/K-5
PO Box 250 86512 928-688-3850
Victor Caballero, prin. Fax 688-3888
Sanders MS 300/6-8
PO Box 250 86512 928-688-4772
Mindy Porter, prin. Fax 688-4773

San Luis, Yuma, Pop. 21,646
Gadsden ESD 32 4,600/PK-8
PO Box 6870 85349 928-627-6540
Raymond Aguilera, supt. Fax 627-3635
www.gesd32.org/
Arizona Desert ES 700/K-6
PO Box 6870 85349 928-627-6940
Laura Couret-Madrid, prin. Fax 627-4692
Chavez ES 700/K-6
PO Box 6870 85349 928-627-6958
Bethany Loucks, prin. Fax 627-4480
Desert View ES 700/K-6
PO Box 6870 85349 928-627-6915
Jose Urena, prin. Fax 627-1190
Pastor ES 300/K-6
PO Box 6870 85349 928-627-6980
Gretchen Gross, prin. Fax 722-0086
Rio Colorado ES 600/K-6
PO Box 6870 85349 928-627-6900
Meredith Brooks, prin. Fax 627-9717
San Luis MS 600/7-8
PO Box 6870 85349 928-627-6920
Margarito Uranga, prin. Fax 627-9339
San Luis Preschool PK-PK
PO Box 6870 85349 928-627-4774
Maria De La Fuente, dir. Fax 627-9339
Southwest JHS 600/7-8
PO Box 6870 85349 928-627-6580
Richard West, prin. Fax 627-9266
Other Schools – See Gadsden

San Manuel, Pinal, Pop. 4,009
Mammoth-San Manuel USD 8 1,000/PK-12
PO Box 406 85631 520-385-2337
Dr. Ron Rickel, supt. Fax 385-2621
www.msmusd.k12.az.us
Avenue B ES 200/4-6
PO Box 406 85631 520-385-2241
Monica Barajas, prin. Fax 385-2541
First Avenue ES 300/PK-3
PO Box 406 85631 520-385-4341
Monica Barajas, prin. Fax 385-2118
Other Schools – See Mammoth

San Simon, Cochise
San Simon USD 18 100/K-12
PO Box 38 85632 520-845-2275
Curry Donaldson, supt. Fax 845-2480
www.sansimon.k12.az.us
San Simon S 100/K-12
PO Box 38 85632 520-845-2275
Curry Donaldson, admin. Fax 845-2480

San Tan Valley, Pinal
Coolidge USD 21
Supt. — See Coolidge
Mountain Vista S K-8
33622 N Mountain Vista Blvd, 480-677-4403
Patricia Dowd, prin. Fax 677-4406
San Tan Heights S 1,400/K-8
2500 W San Tan Heights Blvd, 480-888-2930
Laurel Presnell, prin. Fax 888-2932

J.O. Combs USD 44 2,300/K-12
301 E Combs Rd, 480-987-5300
Jan Langer, supt. Fax 987-3487
www.jocombs.org/
Ellsworth ES K-6
38454 N Carolina Ave, 480-882-3520
Tammy Stimatze, prin. Fax 987-8250
Harmon ES 900/K-6
39315 N Cortona Dr, 480-882-3500
Chris Lineberry, prin. Fax 888-9143
Ranch ES K-6
43521 N Kenworthy Rd, 480-882-3530
Eric Samuels, prin. Fax 655-6412
Simonton ES 900/K-6
40300 N Simonton Blvd, 480-987-5330
Mary Griffith, prin. Fax 987-5281

Sasabe, Pima
San Fernando ESD 35 50/K-8
PO Box 80 85633 520-823-4243
Linda Arzoumanian, supt. Fax 823-4273
San Fernando S 50/K-8
PO Box 80 85633 520-823-4243
Tracy Banker-Murtadza, lead tchr. Fax 823-4273

Scottsdale, Maricopa, Pop. 226,013
Cave Creek USD 93 5,900/PK-12
33606 N 60th St 85266 480-575-2016
Dr. Debbi Burdick, supt. Fax 488-7055
www.ccusd93.org
Black Mountain ES 600/PK-5
33606 N 60th St 85266 480-575-2100
Elie Gaines, prin. Fax 488-6708
Desert Arroyo MS 800/6-8
33401 N 56th St 85262 480-575-2300
Ann Orlando, prin. Fax 488-7059
Desert Sun ES 500/PK-5
27880 N 64th Street 85262 480-575-2900
Bert Honigman, prin. Fax 502-2364
Other Schools – See Cave Creek, Phoenix

Paradise Valley USD 69
Supt. — See Phoenix
Copper Canyon ES 700/K-6
17650 N 54th St 85254 602-449-7200
Steven Bursi, prin. Fax 449-7205
Desert Shadows ES 500/PK-6
5902 E Sweetwater Ave 85254 602-449-6900
Richard McCormick, prin. Fax 449-6905
Desert Shadows MS 800/7-8
5858 E Sweetwater Ave 85254 602-449-6800
Carol Kendrick, prin. Fax 449-6805
Desert Springs ES 500/PK-6
6010 E Acoma Dr 85254 602-449-7100
Tammy Hall, prin. Fax 449-7105
Grayhawk ES 800/K-6
7525 E Grayhawk Dr 85255 602-449-6600
Don Hiemstra, prin. Fax 449-6605
Liberty ES 600/K-6
5125 E Marilyn Rd 85254 602-449-6200
Drew Davis, prin. Fax 449-6205
North Ranch ES 500/K-6
16406 N 61st Pl 85254 602-449-6400
Dr. Sarah Hartley, prin. Fax 449-6405
Pinnacle Peak ES 800/K-6
7690 E Williams Dr 85255 602-449-6700
Michael Lee, prin. Fax 449-6705
Sandpiper ES 400/K-6
6724 E Hearn Rd 85254 602-449-6300
Steve Jeras, prin. Fax 449-6305
Sonoran Sky ES 600/PK-6
12990 N 75th St 85260 602-449-6500
Patrick Sweeney, prin. Fax 449-6505
Sunrise MS 600/7-8
4960 E Acoma Dr 85254 602-449-6100
Gregory Martin, prin. Fax 449-6105

Scottsdale USD 48
Supt. — See Phoenix
Anasazi ES 600/K-5
12121 N 124th St 85259 480-484-7300
Jeff Quisberg, prin. Fax 484-7301
Arcadia Neighborhood Learning Center 600/K-8
4330 N 62nd St 85251 480-484-7500
Charles Grisier, prin. Fax 484-7501
Aztec ES 500/PK-5
9181 E Redfield Rd 85260 480-484-7700
James Selgo, prin. Fax 484-7701
Cheyenne Traditional S 900/K-8
11130 E Cholla St 85259 480-484-5600
Mike Duff, prin. Fax 484-5601
Cochise ES 500/PK-5
9451 N 84th St 85258 480-484-1100
Sarah Stammegna, prin. Fax 484-1101
Cocopah MS 1,000/6-8
6615 E Cholla St 85254 480-484-4400
Frank Rasmussen, prin. Fax 484-4401
Copper Ridge S 600/K-8
10101 E Thompson Peak Pkwy 85255 480-484-1400
Sheila Burnham, prin. Fax 484-1501
Desert Canyon ES 700/K-5
10203 E McDowell Mntn Rnch 85255 480-484-1700
Sally Norton, prin. Fax 484-4601
Desert Canyon MS 600/6-8
10203 E McDowell Mntn Ranch 85255 480-484-4600
Eileen Nilson, prin. Fax 484-4601
Hohokam ES 500/K-6
8451 E Oak St 85257 480-484-1800
Chad Caudle, prin. Fax 484-1801
Laguna ES 600/K-5
10475 E Lakeview Dr 85258 480-484-2400
Dr. Katie Root, prin. Fax 484-2401
Mohave MS 600/7-8
5520 N 86th St 85250 480-484-5200
Chris Sawyer, prin. Fax 484-5201
Mountainside MS 1,000/6-8
11256 N 128th St 85259 480-484-5500
Chris Asmussen, prin. Fax 484-5501
Navajo ES 500/PK-6
4525 N Granite Reef Rd 85251 480-484-2600
Shaun Holmes, prin. Fax 484-2601
Pima ES 600/K-6
8330 E Osborn Rd 85251 480-484-2800
Sheryl Rednor, prin. Fax 484-2801
Pueblo ES 500/K-6
6320 N 82nd St 85250 480-484-3100
Terri Kellen, prin. Fax 484-3101
Sequoya ES 600/K-5
11808 N 64th St 85254 480-484-3200
Neela Bhavnani, prin. Fax 484-3201
Supai MS 600/7-8
6720 E Continental Dr 85257 480-484-5800
Dawn Thompson, prin. Fax 484-5801
Tonalea ES 500/K-6
6801 E Oak St 85257 480-484-3600
Lesa Friend, prin. Fax 484-3601
Yavapai ES 700/PK-6
701 N Miller Rd 85257 480-484-3800
Wendy Cohen, prin. Fax 484-3801
Zuni ES 500/PK-5
9181 E Redfield Rd 85260 480-484-4000
Walter Chantler, prin. Fax 484-4001

Arizona International Academy 50/4-9
12430 N Scottsdale Rd 85254 480-948-3419
Ken Bursey, admin. Fax 948-8884
Blessed Sacrament K 100/PK-K
11300 N 64th St 85254 480-998-9466
Heather Fraher, dir. Fax 951-3844
Our Lady of Perpetual Help S 500/K-8
3801 N Miller Rd 85251 480-874-3720
Sr. Marian Brandt, prin. Fax 874-3767
Pope John XXIII S 600/K-8
16235 N 60th St 85254 480-905-0939
Christina Bernier, prin. Fax 905-0955
St. Daniel the Prophet S 100/K-8
1030 N Hayden Rd 85257 480-949-8034
Rita Standerfer, prin. Fax 949-9961
St. Maria Goretti S 100/PK-K
6261 N Granite Reef Rd 85250 480-948-3606
Kathleen Bies, dir. Fax 948-8815
Shepherd of the Desert Lutheran S 300/PK-8
9590 E Shea Blvd 85260 480-860-1677
Andy Benscoter, dir. Fax 860-4152
Thunderbird Christian S 100/1-8
7440 E Sutton Dr 85260 480-991-6705
Fax 948-1982

Sedona, Coconino, Pop. 11,220
Sedona-Oak Creek JUSD 9 1,500/PK-12
221 Brewer Rd Ste 100 86336 928-204-6800
Mike Aylstock, supt. Fax 282-0232
www.sedona.k12.az.us/
Big Park Community S 400/PK-8
25 W Saddlehorn Rd 86351 928-204-6500
Steve Gardner, prin. Fax 284-9796
West Sedona S 500/K-8
570 Posse Ground Rd 86336 928-204-6600
Lisa Hirsch, prin. Fax 282-1012

Seligman, Yavapai
Seligman USD 40 200/K-12
PO Box 650 86337 928-422-3233
Katie Fitzgerald, supt. Fax 422-3642
Seligman S 100/K-8
PO Box 650 86337 928-422-3233
Fax 422-3642

Sells, Pima, Pop. 2,750
Indian Oasis-Baboquivari USD 40 1,100/K-12
PO Box 248 85634 520-623-1031
Joe Frazier, supt. Fax 383-5441
www.iobusd40.org
Baboquivari MS 200/7-8
PO Box 248 85634 520-383-6800
Jonathan Eddy, prin. Fax 383-4852
Indian Oasis IS 300/4-6
PO Box 248 85634 520-383-2312
Lina Susee, prin. Fax 383-5930
Indian Oasis PS 400/K-3
PO Box 248 85634 520-383-6750
Lina Susee, prin. Fax 383-5970

Show Low, Navajo, Pop. 10,000
Show Low USD 10 2,300/PK-12
500 W Old Linden Rd 85901 928-537-6000
Kevin Brackney, supt. Fax 537-6009
www.show-low.k12.az.us
Homestead ES 300/K-5
500 W Old Linden Rd 85901 928-537-6150
Kevin Hall, prin. Fax 537-6199
Linden ES 200/K-5
500 W Old Linden Rd 85901 928-537-6017
Kevin Bortin, prin. Fax 537-6039
Show Low JHS 400/6-8
500 W Old Linden Rd 85901 928-537-6100
Connie Lewis, prin. Fax 537-6149
Show Low Preschool PK-PK
500 W Old Linden Rd 85901 928-537-6000
Sandy Tarbet, dir.
Whipple Ranch ES 500/K-5
500 W Old Linden Rd 85901 928-537-6050
Roy Owens, prin. Fax 537-6099

American Indian Christian S 100/K-12
924 Mission Ln Lot 1 85901 928-537-5912
Karen Slack, dir. Fax 537-5620
Mountain Christian S 50/PK-8
3171 E Show Low Lake Rd 85901 928-537-1050
Michael Granillo, admin. Fax 537-1104

Sierra Vista, Cochise, Pop. 41,908
Palominas ESD 49
Supt. — See Hereford
Coronado S 400/K-8
5148 S Coronado School Dr 85650 520-378-0616
Marylotti Copeland, prin. Fax 378-4195

Sierra Vista USD 68 6,900/PK-12
3555 E Fry Blvd 85635 520-515-2714
Brett Agenbroad, supt. Fax 515-2721
www.sierravistapublicschools.com
Apache MS 700/6-8
3555 E Fry Blvd 85635 520-515-2920
Melissa Sadorf, prin. Fax 515-2900
Bella Vista ES 400/K-5
3555 E Fry Blvd 85635 520-515-2940
Kelly Segal, prin. Fax 515-2948
Carmichael ES 400/PK-5
3555 E Fry Blvd 85635 520-515-2950
Rodney Egan, prin. Fax 515-2951
Huachuca Mountain ES 600/K-5
3555 E Fry Blvd 85635 520-515-2960
Karen Kukuchka, prin. Fax 515-2966
Pueblo Del Sol ES 500/K-5
3555 E Fry Blvd 85635 520-515-2970
John Wilson, prin. Fax 515-2973
Sierra Vista MS 600/6-8
3555 E Fry Blvd 85635 520-515-2930
Jim Sprigg, prin. Fax 515-2941
Town & Country ES 500/PK-5
3555 E Fry Blvd 85635 520-515-2980
Jennifer Rohlf, prin. Fax 515-2985

Village Meadows ES 400/K-5
3555 E Fry Blvd 85635 520-515-2990
Scot Roppe, prin. Fax 515-2994

All Saints Catholic S 200/PK-8
1425 E Yaqui St 85650 520-378-7012
Jim Gordon, prin. Fax 378-2726
First Baptist Christian Academy 300/PK-8
1447 S 7th St 85635 520-458-2983
Susan McMichael, prin. Fax 458-8399
Shiloh Christian S 50/K-12
200 North Ave 85635 520-459-2869
Angela Tumpkin, prin. Fax 459-7436
Veritas Christian Community S 100/K-12
215 Taylor Dr 85635 520-417-1113
Karen Bolton, hdmstr. Fax 417-0180

Skull Valley, Yavapai
Skull Valley ESD 15 50/K-6
PO Box 127 86338 928-442-3322
Fax 442-9198

Skull Valley ES 50/K-6
PO Box 127 86338 928-442-3322
Vicki Hilliker, lead tchr. Fax 442-9198

Snowflake, Navajo, Pop. 4,958
Snowflake USD 5 2,600/K-12
682 W School Bus Ln 85937 928-536-4156
Monte Silk, supt. Fax 536-2634
www.snowflake.k12.az.us
Highland PS 500/K-3
682 W School Bus Ln 85937 928-536-4156
Alma Yates, prin. Fax 536-3006
Snowflake IS 300/4-6
682 W School Bus Ln 85937 928-536-4156
Shon Flake, prin. Fax 536-2995
Snowflake JHS 400/7-8
682 W School Bus Ln 85937 928-536-4156
Kim Lewis, prin. Fax 536-2634
Other Schools – See Taylor

Solomon, Graham
Solomon ESD 5 200/PK-8
PO Box 167 85551 928-428-0477
Kevin England, supt. Fax 428-0398
Solomon S 200/PK-8
PO Box 167 85551 928-428-0477
Kevin England, prin. Fax 428-0398

Somerton, Yuma, Pop. 10,071
Somerton ESD 11 2,700/PK-8
PO Box 3200 85350 928-341-6005
Frank Reed, supt. Fax 341-6090
www.somerton.k12.az.us
Desert Sonora ES 400/PK-5
PO Box 3200 85350 928-341-6300
Maria Vasquez, prin. Fax 341-6390
Orange Grove ES 300/K-5
PO Box 3200 85350 928-341-6200
Connie Zepeda, prin. Fax 341-6290
Somerton MS 900/6-8
PO Box 3200 85350 928-341-6100
Cecilia Arvizo, prin. Fax 627-6190
Tierra Del Sol ES 700/PK-5
PO Box 3200 85350 928-341-6400
Veronica Lopez, prin. Fax 341-6490
Valle Del Encanto Learning Center 300/PK-5
PO Box 3200 85350 928-341-6700
Maria Delafuente, prin. Fax 341-6090

Springerville, Apache, Pop. 1,956
Round Valley USD 10 1,500/PK-12
PO Box 610 85938 928-333-6580
Travis Udall, supt. Fax 333-2823
www.elks.net
Round Valley PS 400/PK-2
PO Box 610 85938 928-333-6500
Alan Bingham, prin. Fax 333-5958
Other Schools – See Eagar

Stanfield, Pinal
Stanfield ESD 24 800/PK-8
515 S Stanfield Rd, 520-424-3353
Susan Stropko, supt. Fax 424-3798
www.stanfield.k12.az.us
Stanfield S 800/PK-8
515 S Stanfield Rd, 520-424-0235
Darrin Johnson, prin. Fax 424-0300

Sun City, Maricopa, Pop. 38,400
Peoria USD 11
Supt. — See Glendale
Zuni Hills S 1,000/K-8
10851 W Williams Rd 85373 623-412-5275
Sara Storms, prin. Fax 412-5282

Sun Valley, Navajo

Sun Valley Indian S 50/K-9
PO Box 4013 86029 928-524-6211
Mardell Shumate, admin. Fax 524-3230

Superior, Pinal, Pop. 3,158
Superior USD 15 500/PK-12
1500 W Sunset Dr Ste 101, 520-689-3000
Pete Guzman, supt. Fax 689-3009
www.superior.k12.az.us/
Kennedy ES 300/PK-6
1500 W Sunset Dr, 520-689-5841
Mary Gooday, prin. Fax 689-3170
Superior JHS 100/7-8
100 W Mary Dr, 520-689-3101
Paul Hatch, prin. Fax 689-3197

Surprise, Maricopa, Pop. 74,411
Dysart USD 89 22,900/K-12
15802 N Parkview Pl 85374 623-876-7000
Dr. Gail Pletnick, supt. Fax 876-7042
www.dysart.org
Ashton Ranch S 1,000/K-8
14898 W Acoma Dr 85379 623-523-8300
Dr. David Stoeve, prin. Fax 523-8303
Canyon Ridge S 800/K-8
17359 W Surprise Farms Loop, 623-523-8450
Kevin West, prin. Fax 523-8461
Cimarron Springs S 1,100/K-8
17032 W Surprise Farms Loop, 623-523-8600
Teresa Heatherly, prin. Fax 523-8611
Countryside S 1,100/K-8
15034 N Parkview Pl 85379 623-876-7800
Janet Korinek, prin. Fax 876-7811
Kingswood S 1,100/K-8
15150 W Mondell Rd 85374 623-876-7600
Marilee Timbrooks, prin. Fax 876-7605
Marley Park S 1,000/K-8
15042 W Sweetwater Ave 85379 623-523-8200
Cindy Mady, prin. Fax 523-8211
Parkview S 900/K-8
16066 N Parkview Pl 85374 623-523-8650
Rosalind Fisher, prin. Fax 523-8661
Public S 19 K-8
23251 N 166th Dr 85387 623-523-8900
Jayson Black, prin. Fax 523-8911
Rancho Gabriela S 900/K-8
12572 W Gabriela Dr 85374 623-523-8500
Carin Garton, prin. Fax 523-8511
Sonoran Heights S 500/K-8
11405 N Greer Ranch Pkwy 85379 623-523-8550
Emily Dean, prin. Fax 523-8561
Sunset Hills S 1,000/K-8
17825 W Sierra Montana Loop, 623-523-8700
Karen Winterstein, prin. Fax 523-8711
Western Peaks S 700/K-8
18063 W Surprise Farms Loop, 623-523-8750
Dr. Paul Tighe, prin. Fax 523-8761
West Point S 1,100/K-8
13700 W Greenway Rd 85374 623-876-7700
Christopher Kieffer, prin. Fax 876-7711
Other Schools – See El Mirage, Glendale, Waddell

Nadaburg USD 81
Supt. — See Wittmann
Desert Oasis S K-8
17161 W Bajada Dr 85387 623-556-5880
Bill Collins, prin.

Palms Christian S 50/K-3
17475 W Bell Rd 85374 623-556-2230
Betty Hall, admin. Fax 556-2240
Word of Life Christian S 100/PK-K
17525 W Bell Rd 85374 623-544-4608
Robin Taylor, dir. Fax 544-8964

Taylor, Navajo, Pop. 3,807
Snowflake USD 5
Supt. — See Snowflake
Taylor ES 400/K-3
20 S 300 E 85939 928-536-4156
Dennis Evans, prin. Fax 536-2634
Taylor IS 200/4-6
207 N 500 W 85939 928-536-4156
Jess Hughes, prin. Fax 536-7225

Teec Nos Pos, Apache, Pop. 317
Red Mesa USD 27 800/PK-12
HC 61 Box 40 86514 928-656-4100
Dr. Peter Belletto, supt. Fax 656-4106
www.rmusd.net
Red Mesa S 300/PK-8
HC 61 Box 40 86514 928-656-4141
Bob Debus, prin. Fax 656-4252
Other Schools – See Round Rock

Immanuel Mission S 100/K-12
PO Box 2000 86514 928-674-3616
John Bloom, prin. Fax 826-8120

Tempe, Maricopa, Pop. 161,143
Kyrene ESD 28 18,000/PK-8
8700 S Kyrene Rd 85284 480-783-4000
David Schauer Ed.D., supt. Fax 783-4141
www.kyrene.org
Kyrene de la Mariposa ES 500/K-5
50 E Knox Rd 85284 480-783-3200
Marianne Lescher, prin. Fax 491-1386
Kyrene de las Manitas ES 700/PK-5
1201 W Courtney Ln 85284 480-783-2000
Dan Langston, prin. Fax 592-0761
Kyrene del Norte ES 500/K-5
1331 E Redfield Rd 85283 480-783-3300
Spencer Fallgatter, prin. Fax 831-0817
Kyrene de los Ninos ES 400/PK-5
1330 E Dava Dr 85283 480-783-3100
Ana Gomez del Castillo, prin. Fax 345-2052
Kyrene MS 1,200/6-8
1050 E Carver Rd 85284 480-783-1000
Susan Poole, prin. Fax 831-0169
Waggoner ES 700/K-5
1050 E Carver Rd 85284 480-783-1900
Lisa Gibson, prin. Fax 831-0616
Other Schools – See Chandler, Phoenix

Tempe ESD 3 13,100/K-8
PO Box 27708 85285 480-730-7100
Dr. Arthur Tate, supt. Fax 730-7177
www.tempeschools.org
Aguilar ES 500/K-5
5800 S Forest Ave 85283 480-897-2544
Jolyn Gibbons, prin. Fax 838-1179
Arredondo ES 400/K-5
1330 E Carson Dr 85282 480-897-2744
Dr. Hilda Carr-Gaona, prin. Fax 839-7325
Broadmor ES 500/K-5
311 E Aepli Dr 85282 480-967-6599
Terri McCoy, prin. Fax 921-0814
Bustoz ES 300/K-5
2020 E Carson Dr 85282 480-897-2955
Tracy Harvester, prin. Fax 820-4065
Carminati ES 500/K-5
4001 S Mcallister Ave 85282 480-784-4484
Vernice Sharpe, prin. Fax 968-0626
Connolly MS 900/6-8
2002 E Concorda Dr 85282 480-967-8933
Kathryn Mullery, prin. Fax 929-9695
Curry ES 500/K-5
1974 E Meadow Dr 85282 480-967-8336
Rey Cruz, prin. Fax 894-4008
Fees MS 900/6-8
1600 E Watson Dr 85283 480-897-6063
Dr. Frank Klajda, prin. Fax 838-0853
Fuller ES 400/K-5
1975 E Cornell Dr 85283 480-897-6228
Rebeckah Winans, prin. Fax 820-7308
Gililland MS 900/6-8
1025 S Beck Ave 85281 480-966-7114
Rick Horvath, prin. Fax 829-6178
Holdeman ES 600/K-5
1326 W 18th St 85281 480-966-9934
Wendy Reeck, prin. Fax 968-3165
Hudson ES 400/K-5
1325 E Malibu Dr 85282 480-897-6608
Barry Fritch, prin. Fax 820-7335
Laird S 400/K-8
1500 N Scovel St 85281 480-941-2440
Dr. Mark Eley, prin. Fax 970-4231
McKemy MS 900/6-8
2250 S College Ave 85282 480-921-9003
Ardie Sturdivant, prin. Fax 829-6179
Meyer ES 400/K-5
2615 S Dorsey Ln 85282 480-829-8002
Howard Oechsner, prin. Fax 829-6561
Rover ES 500/K-5
1300 E Watson Dr 85283 480-897-7122
Mark Martinez, prin. Fax 820-8503
Scales Technology Academy 500/K-5
1115 W 5th St 85281 480-929-9909
David Diokno, prin. Fax 804-0384
Thew ES 600/K-5
2130 E Howe Ave 85281 480-894-5574
Julie Schroeder, prin. Fax 894-2755
Ward Traditional Academy 400/K-8
1965 E Hermosa Dr 85282 480-491-8871
Kacy Curtis, prin. Fax 491-1710
Wood ES 600/K-5
727 W Cornell Dr 85283 480-838-0711
Deborah Cotton, prin. Fax 838-0832
Other Schools – See Guadalupe, Phoenix

Abiding Savior Lutheran S 50/PK-K
515 E Continental Dr 85281 480-949-9064
Barbara McElrath, dir. Fax 947-7698
Bethany Christian S 200/1-8
6304 S Price Rd 85283 480-752-8993
Jeanine Simpkins, prin. Fax 752-7913
Emmanuel Evangelical Lutheran S 200/PK-8
715 W Southern Ave 85282 480-967-3991
Eric Brown, prin. Fax 967-2809
Gethsemane Lutheran S 200/PK-8
1035 E Guadalupe Rd 85283 480-839-0906
Wendell Robson, prin. Fax 839-8876
Grace Community Christian S 500/PK-8
1200 E Southern Ave 85282 480-966-5022
Michael Jordan, admin. Fax 968-4166
Our Lady of Mt. Carmel Preschool 100/PK-PK
2115 S Rural Rd 85282 480-966-1753
Molly Gorman, dir. Fax 967-4919
Our Lady of Mt. Carmel S 500/K-8
2117 S Rural Rd 85282 480-967-5567
Dr. Vincent Sheridan, prin. Fax 967-6038
Tempe Adventist Christian S 50/PK-8
630 W 17th Pl 85281 480-967-7152
Fax 967-2520
Tempe Christian S 100/PK-PK
3929 S Rural Rd 85282 480-838-2866
Debbie Hallman, dir. Fax 659-8000

Thatcher, Graham, Pop. 4,121
Thatcher USD 4 1,300/K-12
PO Box 610 85552 928-348-7200
Janice Given, supt. Fax 348-7220
www.thatcherud.k12.az.us
Daley PS 400/K-3
3500 W 2nd St 85552 928-348-7240
Tracy Allred, prin. Fax 348-7220
Thatcher ES 300/4-6
1386 N 4th Ave 85552 928-348-7250
James Hughes, prin. Fax 348-7220
Thatcher MS 200/7-8
1300 N 4th Ave 85552 928-348-7262
Matt Petersen, prin. Fax 348-7263

Safford SDA S 50/1-8
544 S 1st Ave 85552 928-428-3855

Tolleson, Maricopa, Pop. 5,974
Littleton ESD 65
Supt. — See Avondale
Country Place S 900/K-8
10207 W Country Place Blvd 85353 623-478-6100
Richard Stinnett, prin. Fax 478-6120
Tres Rios S K-8
5025 S 103rd Ave 85353 623-478-6300
Tracy Faulkner, prin. Fax 478-6320

Tolleson ESD 17 2,800/K-8
9261 W Van Buren St 85353 623-936-9740
Bill Christensen, supt. Fax 936-9757
www.tesd.k12.az.us
Arizona Desert S 500/K-8
8803 W Van Buren St 85353 623-907-5260
Brenda Catlett, prin. Fax 907-5261
Gonzales S 900/K-8
9401 W Garfield St 85353 623-907-5181
Juan Medrano, prin. Fax 936-0649
Other Schools – See Phoenix

Union ESD 62 1,400/PK-8
3834 S 91st Ave 85353 623-478-5005
Dr. Pat Gillespie, supt. Fax 478-5006
www.uesd.org
Dos Rios ES PK-7
2150 S 87th Ave 85353 623-474-7000
Monica Reed, prin. Fax 474-7091
Hurley Ranch ES 1,000/K-5
8950 W Illini Rd 85353 623-478-5100
Melanie Block, prin. Fax 742-9625
Union JHS 400/6-8
3834 S 91st Ave 85353 623-478-5000
Robin Gibbs, prin. Fax 478-5026

Tombstone, Cochise, Pop. 1,569
Tombstone USD 1 900/PK-12
PO Box 1000 85638 520-457-2217
Karl Uterhardt, supt. Fax 457-3270
www.tombstone.k12.az.us/
Meyer S 200/PK-8
PO Box 1000 85638 520-457-3371
Katherine Villa, prin. Fax 457-3685
Other Schools – See Huachuca City

Tonopah, Maricopa
Saddle Mountain USD 90 1,200/PK-12
38201 W Indian School Rd 85354 623-474-5115
Dr. Mark Joraanstad, supt. Fax 691-6757
www.smusd90.org
Fisher S 900/PK-8
38201 W Indian School Rd 85354 623-386-5688
Erik Haarstad, prin. Fax 386-3364
Winters Well ES K-6
35220 W Buckeye Rd 85354 623-474-5300
Jim Keith, prin. Fax 474-5341
Other Schools – See Buckeye

Tonto Basin, Gila
Tonto Basin ESD 33 100/K-8
PO Box 337 85553 928-479-2277
Johnny Ketchem, supt. Fax 479-2720
www.tontobasinschool.com/
Tonto Basin S 100/K-8
PO Box 337 85553 928-479-2490
Johnny Ketchem, prin. Fax 479-2720

Topock, Mohave
Topock ESD 12 100/PK-8
PO Box 370 86436 928-768-3344
John Warren, admin. Fax 768-9253
topockschoolk-8.net/
Topock S 100/PK-8
PO Box 370 86436 928-768-3344
John Warren, prin. Fax 768-9253

Tuba City, Coconino, Pop. 7,323
Tuba City USD 15 2,200/PK-12
PO Box 67 86045 928-283-1000
William Higgins, supt. Fax 283-5105
www.tcusd.org
Eagles Nest IS 300/4-6
PO Box 67 86045 928-283-1034
Maggie Leatherbury, prin. Fax 283-1210
Gap PS 100/K-4
PO Box 67 86045 928-283-1092
Marilyn Reed, prin. Fax 283-1244
Tuba City JHS 300/7-8
PO Box 67 86045 928-283-1042
Dr. Harold Begay, prin. Fax 283-1218
Tuba City PS 400/PK-3
PO Box 67 86045 928-283-1024
Harriet Sloan-Carter, prin. Fax 283-1222
Other Schools – See Cameron

Tucson, Pima, Pop. 515,526
Altar Valley ESD 51 700/PK-8
10105 S Sasabe Hwy 85736 520-822-1484
Douglas Roe, supt. Fax 822-1798
altarvalleyschools.org/
Altar Valley MS 300/5-8
10105 S Sasabe Hwy 85736 520-822-9343
Russ Federico, prin. Fax 822-5801
Robles ES 400/PK-4
10105 S Sasabe Hwy 85736 520-822-9418
Judi King, prin. Fax 822-9428

Amphitheater USD 10 16,500/PK-12
701 W Wetmore Rd 85705 520-696-5000
Vicki Balentine Ph.D., supt. Fax 696-5015
www.amphi.com
Amphitheater MS 800/6-8
315 E Prince Rd 85705 520-696-6230
Chuck Bermudez, prin. Fax 696-6236
Copper Creek ES 700/K-5
11620 N Copper Spring Trl 85737 520-696-6800
Diana Walker, prin. Fax 696-6806
Coronado S 1,200/K-8
3401 E Wilds Rd 85739 520-696-6610
Monica Nelson, prin. Fax 696-6701
Cross MS 900/6-8
1000 W Chapala Dr 85704 520-696-5920
Kevin Corner, prin. Fax 696-5996
Donaldson ES 400/PK-5
2040 W Omar Dr 85704 520-696-6160
Bruce Weigold, prin. Fax 696-6204
Harelson ES 500/K-6
826 W Chapala Dr 85704 520-696-6020
Andy Heinemann, prin. Fax 696-6070
Holaway ES 500/K-5
3500 N Cherry Ave 85719 520-696-6880
Ernie Galaz, prin. Fax 696-6924
Keeling ES 500/PK-5
2837 N Los Altos Ave 85705 520-696-6940
Robert Stoner, prin. Fax 696-6977
La Cima MS 700/6-8
5600 N La Canada Dr 85704 520-696-6730
Christine Sullivan, prin. Fax 696-6792
Mesa Verde ES 400/K-5
1661 W Sage St 85704 520-696-6090
Foster Hepler, prin. Fax 696-6137

Nash ES 600/K-5
515 W Kelso St 85705 520-696-6440
Alice Farley, prin. Fax 696-6490
Painted Sky ES 700/K-5
12620 N Woodburne Ave, 520-696-3800
Angela Wichers, prin. Fax 696-3888
Prince ES 700/PK-5
125 E Prince Rd 85705 520-696-6414
Tassi Call, prin. Fax 696-6413
Rio Vista ES 600/K-5
1351 E Limberlost Dr 85719 520-696-5250
Dianna Kuhn, prin. Fax 696-5260
Walker ES 500/K-5
1750 W Roller Coaster Rd 85704 520-696-6510
Jon Lansa, prin. Fax 696-6555
Other Schools – See Oro Valley

Catalina Foothills USD 16 4,900/PK-12
2101 E River Rd 85718 520-209-7500
Mary Kamerzell, supt. Fax 209-7570
www.cfsd16.org/
Canyon View ES 400/PK-5
5725 N Sabino Canyon Rd 85750 520-209-7700
Marta Gunderson, prin. Fax 209-7770
Esperero Canyon MS 600/6-8
5801 N Sabino Canyon Rd 85750 520-209-8100
Brian Lorimer, prin. Fax 209-8170
Manzanita ES 500/K-5
3000 E Manzanita Ave 85718 520-209-7800
Colleen Nichols, prin. Fax 209-7870
Orange Grove MS 600/6-8
1911 E Orange Grove Rd 85718 520-209-8200
Travis Kolter, prin. Fax 209-8275
Sunrise Drive ES 400/K-5
5301 E Sunrise Dr 85718 520-209-7900
Julie Sherrill Ph.D., prin. Fax 209-7970
Valley View Early Learning Center 100/PK-K
3435 E Sunrise Dr 85718 520-209-7650
Diane Torres, dir. Fax 209-7664
Ventana Vista ES 400/K-5
6085 N Kolb Rd 85750 520-209-8000
Kim Boling, prin. Fax 209-8070

Flowing Wells USD 8 6,000/PK-12
1556 W Prince Rd 85705 520-696-8800
Dr. Nicholas Clement, supt. Fax 690-2400
www.flowingwells.k12.az.us
Centennial ES 500/K-6
2200 W Wetmore Rd 85705 520-696-8200
Lynette Patton, prin. Fax 690-5613
Davis ES 500/K-6
4250 N Romero Rd 85705 520-696-8250
Brett Bonner, prin. Fax 690-2329
Douglas ES 600/K-6
3302 N Flowing Wells Rd 85705 520-696-8300
Sandra Thiffault, prin. Fax 690-5615
Flowing Wells ECC 100/PK-PK
1556 W Prince Rd 85705 520-696-8910
Sue Olson-Shinn, dir. Fax 690-2405
Flowing Wells JHS 1,000/7-8
4545 N La Cholla Blvd 85705 520-696-8550
Pete Wells, prin. Fax 690-2420
Hendricks ES 500/K-6
3400 W Orange Grove Rd 85741 520-696-8400
Carolyn Twohill, prin. Fax 690-5612
Laguna ES 500/K-6
5001 N Shannon Rd 85705 520-696-8450
Theresa Leal-Holmes, prin. Fax 690-5616
Richardson ES 400/K-6
6901 N Camino De La Tierra 85741 520-696-8500
Lyle Dunbar, prin. Fax 690-5617

Marana USD 6
Supt. — See Marana
Butterfield ES 700/K-6
3400 W Massingale Rd 85741 520-579-5000
Gayle Schmidt, prin. Fax 579-5029
Coyote Trail ES 900/K-6
8000 N Silverbell Rd 85743 520-579-5105
Dan Johnson, prin. Fax 579-5098
DeGrazia ES 600/K-6
5051 W Overton Rd 85742 520-579-4800
Stephen Poling, prin. Fax 579-4840
Desert Winds ES 500/K-3
12675 W Rudasill Rd 85743 520-616-4000
Denise Linsalata, prin. Fax 616-4049
Ironwood ES 900/K-6
3300 W Freer Dr 85742 520-579-5150
Eric Abrams, prin. Fax 579-5164
Picture Rocks IS 400/4-6
5875 N Sanders Rd 85743 520-616-3700
Patricia Cadigan, prin. Fax 616-3749
Quail Run ES 600/K-6
4600 W Cortaro Farms Rd 85742 520-579-4700
Pennie Harcus, prin. Fax 744-3693
Rattlesnake Ridge ES K-6
8500 N Continental Reserve 85743 520-352-7000
Jamie Meek, prin. Fax 744-3274
Thornydale ES 500/K-6
7651 N Oldfather Dr 85741 520-579-4900
Shirley Siedschlag, prin. Fax 579-4909
Tortolita MS 1,100/7-8
4101 W Hardy Rd 85742 520-579-4600
Jane D'Amore, prin. Fax 579-4646
Twin Peaks ES 800/K-6
7995 W Twin Peaks Rd 85743 520-579-4750
Dondi Luce, prin. Fax 579-4785

Sunnyside USD 12 17,000/PK-12
2238 E Ginter Rd 85706 520-545-2000
Manuel Isquierdo, supt. Fax 545-2120
www.susd12.org
Apollo MS 1,000/6-8
265 W Nebraska St 85706 520-545-4500
Ray Chavez, prin. Fax 545-4516
Challenger MS 800/6-8
100 E Elvira Rd, 520-545-4600
Wil Arias, prin. Fax 545-4616
Chaparral MS 800/6-8
3700 E Alvord Rd 85706 520-545-4700
John Benavidez, prin. Fax 545-4716

Craycroft ES 600/K-5
5455 E Littletown Rd, 520-545-2600
John Robertson, prin. Fax 545-2616
Drexel ES 700/K-5
801 E Drexel Rd 85706 520-545-2700
Debra Garcia, prin. Fax 545-2716
Elvira ES 700/K-5
250 W Elvira Rd, 520-545-2800
Tom Hubbard, prin. Fax 545-2890
Esperanza ES 900/PK-5
2353 E Bantam Rd 85706 520-545-2900
Emma Carrillo, prin. Fax 545-2916
Gallego Basic ES 600/K-5
6200 S Hemisphere Pl 85706 520-545-3000
Debra Bergman, prin. Fax 545-3016
Lauffer MS 400/6-8
5385 E Littletown Rd, 520-545-4900
Robert Miranda, prin. Fax 545-4916
Liberty ES 700/K-5
5495 S Liberty Ave 85706 520-545-3100
Bernie Cohn, prin. Fax 545-3116
Los Amigos ES 800/K-5
2200 E Drexel Rd 85706 520-545-3200
Pamela Betten, prin. Fax 545-3216
Los Ninos ES 700/K-5
5445 S Alvernon Way 85706 520-545-3300
Herb Springs, prin. Fax 545-3316
Los Ranchitos ES 700/K-5
2054 E Ginter Rd 85706 520-545-3400
Linda Swango, prin. Fax 545-3416
Mission Manor ES 700/K-5
600 W Santa Rosa St 85706 520-545-3500
Dr. Lily DeBlieux, prin. Fax 545-3516
Ocotillo ES 400/K-5
5702 S Campbell Ave 85706 520-545-3600
Steve Price, prin. Fax 545-3616
Rivera ES K-5
5102 S Cherry Ave 85706 520-545-3900
Patricia Gamez, prin. Fax 545-3916
Santa Clara ES 600/K-5
6910 S Santa Clara Ave, 520-545-3700
Eddie Islas, prin. Fax 545-3716
Sierra MS 1,000/6-8
5801 S Del Moral Blvd 85706 520-545-4800
Art Menchaca, prin. Fax 545-4816
Summit View ES 500/K-5
1900 E Summit St, 520-545-3800
Valerie Lopez-Miranda, prin. Fax 545-3816

Tanque Verde USD 13 1,300/PK-12
11150 E Tanque Verde Rd 85749 520-749-5751
Tom Rogers, supt. Fax 749-5400
www.tanq.org
Agua Caliente ES 300/PK-6
11420 E Limberlost Rd 85749 520-749-2235
Dr. Lisa Yopp, prin. Fax 749-0338
Gray JHS 300/7-8
4201 N Melpomene Way 85749 520-749-3838
Fax 749-9668
Tanque Verde ES 500/K-6
2600 N Fennimore Ave 85749 520-749-4244
Susan Centers, prin. Fax 749-4292

Tucson USD 1 58,500/PK-12
1010 E 10th St 85719 520-225-6000
Dr. Elizabeth Celania-Fagen, supt. Fax 225-6174
www.tusd.k12.az.us
Banks ES 500/K-5
3200 S Lead Flower Ave 85735 520-908-5700
Joe Herrmann, prin. Fax 908-5701
Blenman ES 600/K-5
1695 N Country Club Rd 85716 520-232-6500
Cathryn DeSalvo, prin. Fax 232-6501
Bloom ES 300/PK-5
8310 E Pima St 85715 520-731-3700
Diane Quevedo, prin. Fax 731-3701
Bonillas Magnet ES 400/K-5
4757 E Winsett Blvd 85711 520-232-6600
Richard Romero, prin. Fax 232-6601
Booth-Fickett Magnet S 900/K-8
450 S Montego Dr 85710 520-731-3800
Rosanne Neal, prin. Fax 731-3801
Borman ES 500/K-5
6630 E Lightning Dr 85708 520-584-4600
Chad Knippen, prin. Fax 584-4601
Borton Magnet PS 300/PK-2
700 E 22nd St 85713 520-225-1000
Teresa Melendez, prin. Fax 225-1001
Brichta ES 400/K-6
2110 W Brichta Dr 85745 520-225-1100
Sabrina Cruz, prin. Fax 225-1101
Carrillo Magnet IS 100/3-5
440 S Main Ave 85701 520-225-1200
Ruben Diaz, prin. Fax 225-1201
Carson MS 600/6-8
7777 E Stella Rd 85730 520-584-4700
John Howe, prin. Fax 584-4701
Cavett ES 400/K-5
2120 E Naco Vista Dr 85713 520-225-1300
Lina Armijo, prin. Fax 225-1301
Collier ES 300/K-5
3900 N Bear Canyon Rd 85749 520-584-4800
Lisa Langford, prin. Fax 584-4801
Corbett ES 600/K-5
5949 E 29th St 85711 520-584-4900
Joyce Dillon, prin. Fax 584-4901
Cragin ES 500/K-5
2945 N Tucson Blvd 85716 520-232-6700
Pearl Miller, prin. Fax 232-6701
Davidson ES 400/K-5
3950 E Paradise Falls Dr 85712 520-232-6800
Deborah Anders, prin. Fax 232-6801
Davis Bilingual Magnet ES 300/K-5
500 W Saint Marys Rd 85701 520-225-1400
Christopher Loya, prin. Fax 225-1401
Dietz ES 500/K-5
7575 E Palma St 85710 520-731-4000
Lisa McCorkle, prin. Fax 731-4001

Dodge Magnet MS 400/6-8
5831 E Pima St 85712 520-731-4100
Catherine Comstock, prin. Fax 731-4101

Doolen MS 800/6-8
2400 N Country Club Rd 85716 520-232-6900
Charlotte Patterson, prin. Fax 232-6901

Drachman Montessori Magnet ES 300/PK-6
1085 S 10th Ave 85701 520-225-1500
Jesus Celaya, prin. Fax 225-1501

Duffy ES 300/K-5
5145 E 5th St 85711 520-232-7000
David Overstreet, prin. Fax 232-7001

Dunham ES 300/K-5
9850 E 29th St 85748 520-731-4200
Helen Grijalva, prin. Fax 731-4201

Erickson ES 500/PK-5
6750 E Stella Rd 85730 520-584-5000
Helen LePage, prin. Fax 584-5001

Ford ES 300/K-5
8001 E Stella Rd 85730 520-731-4300
Julie McIntyre, prin. Fax 731-4301

Fort Lowell ES 300/K-6
5151 E Pima St 85712 520-232-7100
Andrew Kent, prin. Fax 232-7101

Fruchthendler ES 400/K-5
7470 E Cloud Rd 85750 520-731-4400
John Heidel, prin. Fax 731-4401

Gale ES 300/PK-5
678 S Gollob Rd 85710 520-731-4500
Paula Godfrey, prin. Fax 731-4501

Gridley MS 700/6-8
350 S Harrison Rd 85748 520-731-4600
Kathleen Scheppe, prin. Fax 731-4601

Grijalva ES 700/K-5
1795 W Drexel Rd 85746 520-908-3600
Anna Rivera Ph.D., prin. Fax 908-3601

Henry ES 300/PK-5
650 N Igo Way 85710 520-731-4700
Jonathan Ben-Asher, prin. Fax 731-4701

Hohokam MS 800/6-8
7400 S Settler Ave 85746 520-908-3700
John Michel, prin. Fax 908-3701

Holladay Magnet IS 200/3-5
1110 E 33rd St 85713 520-225-1600
Teri Melendez, prin. Fax 225-1601

Hollinger ES 600/K-5
150 W Ajo Way 85713 520-225-1700
Kathy Bolles, prin. Fax 225-1701

Howell ES 400/K-5
401 N Irving Ave 85711 520-232-7200
MaryAnn Jackson, prin. Fax 232-7201

Hudlow ES 400/K-5
502 N Caribe Ave 85710 520-731-4800
Cheri LaRochelle, prin. Fax 731-4801

Hughes ES 300/K-5
700 N Wilson Ave 85719 520-232-7400
Roseanne DeCesari, prin. Fax 232-7401

Jefferson Park ES 200/K-5
1701 E Seneca St 85719 520-232-7500
Jerry Gallegos Ph.D., prin. Fax 232-7501

Johnson PS 400/PK-2
6060 S Joseph Ave, 520-908-3800
Dan Weisz, prin. Fax 908-3801

Kellond ES 400/K-6
6606 E Lehigh Dr 85710 520-584-5100
Pamela Clarridge Ph.D., prin. Fax 584-5101

Lawrence IS 300/3-5
4850 W Jeffrey Rd, 520-908-3900
Ana Gallegos, prin. Fax 908-3901

Lineweaver ES 400/K-5
461 S Bryant Ave 85711 520-232-7700
Margaret Scott, prin. Fax 232-7701

Lynn/Urquides ES 900/PK-5
1573 W Ajo Way 85713 520-908-4000
Patricia Flores, prin. Fax 908-4001

Lyons ES 400/PK-5
7555 E Dogwood St 85730 520-584-6600
Sheila Govern, prin. Fax 584-6601

Magee MS 800/6-8
8300 E Speedway Blvd 85710 520-731-5000
Jerry Holmes, prin. Fax 731-5001

Maldonado ES 600/K-5
3535 W Messala Way 85746 520-908-4100
Mary Mercado, prin. Fax 908-4101

Mansfeld MS 800/6-8
1300 E 6th St 85719 520-225-1800
Elizabeth Rivera, prin. Fax 225-1801

Manzo ES 300/K-5
855 N Melrose Ave 85745 520-225-1900
Jerome Gallegos, prin. Fax 225-1901

Marshall ES 400/PK-5
9066 E 29th St 85710 520-731-4900
Paul Thompson, prin. Fax 731-4901

Maxwell MS 600/6-8
2802 W Anklam Rd 85745 520-225-2000
Yolanda Nunez, prin. Fax 225-2001

Menlo Park ES 300/PK-5
1100 W Fresno St 85745 520-225-2100
Rosanna Ortiz-Montoya, prin. Fax 225-2101

Miles Exploratory Learning Center 300/PK-8
1400 E Broadway Blvd 85719 520-225-2200
Robin Weldon, prin. Fax 225-2201

Miller ES 700/PK-6
6951 S Camino De La Tierra 85746 520-908-4200
Mary Anderson, prin. Fax 908-4201

Mission View ES 300/K-5
2600 S 8th Ave 85713 520-225-2300
Elizabeth Redondo, prin. Fax 225-2301

Myers/Ganoung ES 500/PK-5
5000 E Andrew St 85711 520-584-6700
Barbara Gonzales, prin. Fax 584-6701

Naylor MS 500/6-8
1701 S Columbus Blvd 85711 520-584-6800
Don Calhoun, prin. Fax 584-6801

Ochoa ES 300/K-5
101 W 25th St 85713 520-225-2400
Heidi Aranda, prin. Fax 225-2401

Oyama ES 500/K-5
2700 S La Cholla Blvd 85713 520-225-5700
Victoria Callison, prin. Fax 225-5701

Pistor MS 1,100/6-8
5455 S Cardinal Ave 85746 520-908-5400
Kathryn Manley-Crockett, prin. Fax 908-5411

Pueblo Gardens ES 400/PK-5
2210 E 33rd St 85713 520-225-2700
Marco Ramirez, prin. Fax 225-2701

Reynolds ES 500/K-5
7450 E Stella Rd 85730 520-584-6900
Janet Jordan, prin. Fax 584-6901

Richey S 200/K-8
2209 N 15th Ave 85705 520-225-2800
Ruben Diaz, prin. Fax 225-2801

Roberts ES 500/K-5
4355 E Calle Aurora 85711 520-584-7000
Marcos Quijada, prin. Fax 584-7001

Robins ES 500/K-5
3939 N Magnetite Ln 85745 520-908-4300
Elizabeth Minno, prin. Fax 908-4301

Robison ES 400/K-5
2745 E 18th St 85716 520-232-7800
Robert Pitts, prin. Fax 232-7801

Rogers ES 300/K-6
6000 E 14th St 85711 520-584-7100
Cricket Gallegos, prin. Fax 584-7101

Rose ES 500/K-5
710 W Michigan St 85714 520-908-4400
Stephen Trejo, prin. Fax 908-4401

Roskruge Bilingual Magnet S 200/K-8
501 E 6th St 85705 520-225-2900
Christopher Loya, prin. Fax 225-2901

Safford Magnet S 500/PK-8
200 E 13th St 85701 520-225-3000
Theresa Ross, prin. Fax 225-3001

Schumaker ES 300/K-5
501 N Maguire Ave 85710 520-731-5200
Julie Laird Ph.D., prin. Fax 731-5201

Secrist MS 600/6-8
3400 S Houghton Rd 85730 520-731-5300
Jim Christ, prin. Fax 731-5301

Sewell ES 300/K-5
425 N Sahuara Ave 85711 520-584-7200
Cricket Gallegos, prin. Fax 584-7201

Soleng Tom ES 500/K-5
10520 E Camino Quince 85748 520-731-5400
Dr. Theresa Sonnleitner, prin. Fax 731-5401

Steele ES 400/K-6
700 S Sarnoff Dr 85710 520-731-6800
Daniel Erickson, prin. Fax 731-6801

Tolson ES 500/K-5
1000 S Greasewood Rd 85745 520-225-3300
Maria Figueroa, prin. Fax 225-3301

Townsend MS 500/6-8
2120 N Beverly Ave 85712 520-232-7900
Barbara Kohl, prin. Fax 232-7901

Tully Accelerated Magnet ES 400/K-6
1701 W El Rio Dr 85745 520-225-3400
Roman Soltero, prin. Fax 225-3401

Utterback Magnet MS 900/6-8
3233 S Pinal Vis 85713 520-225-3500
Debbie Summers, prin. Fax 225-3501

Vail MS 700/6-8
5350 E 16th St 85711 520-584-5400
David Ross, prin. Fax 584-5401

Valencia MS 1,000/6-8
4400 W Irvington Rd 85746 520-908-4500
John Bellisario, prin. Fax 908-4501

Van Buskirk ES 400/PK-5
725 E Fair St 85714 520-225-3700
Ignacio Ruiz, prin. Fax 225-3701

Van Horne ES 200/K-5
7550 E Pima St 85715 520-731-6900
Diane Quevedo, prin. Fax 731-6901

Vesey ES 800/K-5
5005 S Butts Rd, 520-908-4600
David Geesey, prin. Fax 908-4601

Wakefield MS 600/6-8
101 W 44th St 85713 520-225-3800
Wade McRae, prin. Fax 225-3801

Warren ES 300/K-5
3505 W Milton Rd 85746 520-908-4700
Marianne Hernandez, prin. Fax 908-4701

Wheeler ES 300/K-5
1818 S Avenida Del Sol 85710 520-584-5500
Stacia Emert Ph.D., prin. Fax 584-5501

White ES 700/K-5
2315 W Canada St 85746 520-908-5300
David Dodge, prin. Fax 908-5301

Whitmore ES 300/K-5
5330 E Glenn St 85712 520-232-8000
Kristine Hansen, prin. Fax 232-8001

Wright ES 500/K-5
4311 E Linden St 85712 520-232-8100
Maria Marin, prin. Fax 232-8101

Wrightstown ES 200/K-5
8950 E Wrightstown Rd 85715 520-731-7000
Jonathan Ben-Asher, prin. Fax 731-7001

Vail USD 20
Supt. — See Vail

Cottonwood ES 600/K-5
9950 E Rees Loop 85747 520-879-2600
Deborah Bryson, prin. Fax 879-2601

Desert Sky MS 700/6-8
9850 E Rankin Loop 85747 520-879-2700
Micah Mortensen, prin. Fax 879-2701

Desert Willow ES 800/K-5
9400 E Esmond Loop 85747 520-879-2300
Tara Finch, prin. Fax 879-2301

Mesquite S 600/K-8
9455 E Rita Rd 85747 520-879-2100
Katie Dabney, prin. Fax 879-2101

Rincon Vista MS 6-8
10770 E Bilby 85747 520-879-3200
Kevin Carney, prin. Fax 879-3201

Senita Valley ES K-5
10750 E Bilby Rd 85747 520-879-3100
Connie Erickson, prin. Fax 879-3101

Ascension Lutheran S 100/PK-5
1220 W Magee Rd 85704 520-742-6229
Katherine Holden, admin. Fax 742-4781

Beautiful Savior Academy 100/PK-K
7570 N Thornydale Rd 85741 520-579-1453
Rhonda Karrer B.A., dir. Fax 572-2068

Calvary Chapel Christian S 100/PK-8
8725 E Speedway Blvd 85710 520-731-2100
Catherine Swearingen, admin. Fax 722-0096

Carden Christian Academy Central 100/PK-8
2727 N Swan Rd 85712 520-318-3824
Fred Lawson, admin. Fax 318-0071

Casa Ninos S of Montessori 50/PK-5
1 W Orange Grove Rd 85704 520-297-3898
Jessica Zarling, prin. Fax 575-5907

Casa Ninos S of Montessori 100/PK-5
8655 E Broadway Blvd 85710 520-751-1454
Jenny Ruth, dir. Fax 751-1479

Casas Christian S 400/PK-8
10801 N La Cholla Blvd 85742 520-297-0922
Eric Dowdle, prin. Fax 878-1212

Chapel in the Hills S 100/PK-5
5455 S Westover Ave 85746 520-883-3281
Michelle Morales, dir. Fax 883-3289

Cornerstone Christian Academy 200/K-6
6450 N Camino Miraval 85718 520-529-7080
John Saffold, prin. Fax 529-7140

Desert Christian ES 200/K-5
7525 E Speedway Blvd 85710 520-885-4800
Charlotte Beecher, prin. Fax 885-4265

Desert Christian MS 100/6-8
7525 E Speedway Blvd 85710 520-795-7161
Dennis O'Reilly, prin. Fax 795-3386

Desert Valley Christian S 50/K-7
1200 N Santa Rosa Ave 85712 520-795-0161
Fax 795-0756

Faith Community Academy 100/PK-6
2551 W Orange Grove Rd 85741 520-742-4189
Royce Nelsestuen, admin. Fax 297-2073

Faith Lutheran Parish S 100/PK-8
3925 E 5th St 85711 520-881-0670
Fax 325-5625

Family Life Academy 100/K-4
7801 E Kenyon Dr 85710 520-296-8501
Tim Boyd, admin. Fax 298-8916

Firm Foundations Christian S 100/K-8
3020 S Mission Rd 85713 520-792-4685
Bev Thompson, prin.

First Southern Christian S 100/PK-6
445 E Speedway Blvd 85705 520-624-9797
Carolyn Burger, admin. Fax 624-7770

Fountain of Life Christian S 200/PK-8
710 S Kolb Rd 85710 520-514-7688
Nadeene Jahn, prin. Fax 747-9444

Green Fields Country Day S 200/K-12
6000 N Camino De La Tierra 85741 520-297-2288
Deac Etherington M.A., hdmstr. Fax 297-2072

Imago Dei MS 50/5-8
639 N 6th Ave 85705 520-882-4008
Rev. Anne Sawyer, hdmstr. Fax 882-4011

Immaculate Heart S 400/PK-8
410 E Magee Rd 85704 520-297-6672
Lynn Cuffari, prin. Fax 297-9152

Lamad Preparatory Academy 50/1-4
4343 E 22nd St 85711 520-745-5859
Carolyn Anderson, dir. Fax 514-9501

Our Mother of Sorrows S 500/PK-8
1800 S Kolb Rd 85710 520-747-1027
Dave Keller, prin. Fax 747-0797

Redeemer Lutheran S 200/PK-8
8845 N Silverbell Rd 85743 520-572-8136
Michael Peek, prin. Fax 572-8141

River of Life Christian S 100/PK-12
6902 E Golf Links Rd 85730 520-790-7082
Denise Garcia, prin. Fax 790-3891

Saguaro Hills Adventist Christian S 50/K-8
4280 W Irvington Rd 85746 520-325-1454

St. Ambrose S 300/PK-8
300 S Tucson Blvd 85716 520-882-8678
Martha Taylor, prin. Fax 617-4860

St. Cyril S 400/K-8
4725 E Pima St 85712 520-881-4240
Ann Zeches, prin. Fax 795-0325

St. Elizabeth Ann Seton S 400/PK-8
8650 N Shannon Rd 85742 520-219-7650
Suzanne Shadonix, prin. Fax 297-1033

St. John the Evangelist S 200/K-8
600 W Ajo Way 85713 520-901-1979
Roseanne Villanueva, prin. Fax 622-3193

St. Joseph S 400/PK-8
215 S Craycroft Rd 85711 520-747-3060
Ellen Kwader-Murphy, prin. Fax 747-2024

St. Michael's Parish Day S 400/K-8
602 N Wilmot Rd 85711 520-722-8478
Barry Bedrick, hdmstr. Fax 886-0851

St. Thomas the Apostle S 100/PK-PK
5150 N Valley View Rd 85718 520-577-0503
Michelle Garmon, dir. Fax 577-0441

Santa Cruz S 200/PK-8
29 W 22nd St 85713 520-624-2093
Sr. Leonette Kochan, prin. Fax 624-2833

San Xavier Mission S 200/K-8
1980 W San Xavier Rd 85746 520-294-0628
Shirley Kalinowski, prin. Fax 294-3465

SS. Peter & Paul S 500/K-8
1436 N Campbell Ave 85719 520-325-2431
Jean McKenzie, prin. Fax 881-4690

Tucson Waldorf S 100/PK-8
3349 E Presidio Rd 85716 520-325-5514
Margery Bates, admin. Fax 325-9883

Tuller S 100/PK-8
5870 E 14th St 85711 520-747-1142
Nannette Akins, admin. Fax 747-5236

Tuscon Hebrew Academy 200/K-8
3888 E River Rd 85718 520-529-3888
Dr. Daniel Kahn, hdmstr. Fax 529-0646

Young Life Christian Learning Center 50/PK-PK
115 N Tucson Blvd 85716 520-628-1747
Sarah Wright, dir. Fax 623-3662

Vail, Pima
Vail USD 20 — 7,500/K-12
PO Box 800 85641 — 520-879-2000
Calvin Baker, supt. — Fax 879-2001
vail.k12.az.us
Acacia ES — 800/K-5
12955 E Colossal Cave Rd 85641 — 520-879-2200
Jerry Wood, prin. — Fax 879-2201
Ocotillo Ridge ES — K-5
10701 S White Lightning Ln 85641 — 520-879-3600
Justin Chesebrough, prin. — Fax 879-3601
Old Vail MS — 500/6-8
13299 E Colossal Cave Rd 85641 — 520-879-2400
Laurie Emery, prin. — Fax 879-2401
Sycamore ES — 700/K-5
16701 S Houghton Rd 85641 — 520-879-2500
Ken Graff, prin. — Fax 879-2501
Other Schools – See Corona, Tucson

Vernon, Apache
Vernon ESD 9 — 100/K-8
PO Box 89 85940 — 928-537-5463
James Devlin, supt. — Fax 537-1820
www.vernon.k12.az.us/
Vernon S — 100/K-8
PO Box 89 85940 — 928-537-5463
James Devlin, prin. — Fax 537-1820

Waddell, Maricopa
Dysart USD 89
Supt. — See Surprise
Mountain View S — 600/K-8
18302 W Burton Ave 85355 — 623-876-7450
Joel Knorr, prin. — Fax 876-7461

Wellton, Yuma, Pop. 1,862
Wellton ESD 24 — 400/K-8
PO Box 517 85356 — 928-785-3311
Laura Noel, supt. — Fax 785-4323
Wellton S — 400/K-8
PO Box 517 85356 — 928-785-3311
Laura Noel, prin. — Fax 785-4323

Wenden, LaPaz
Wenden ESD 19 — 100/PK-8
PO Box 8 85357 — 928-859-3806
Gloria Dean, supt. — Fax 859-3958
Wenden S — 100/PK-8
PO Box 8 85357 — 928-859-3806
Gloria Dean, prin. — Fax 859-3958

Whiteriver, Navajo, Pop. 3,775
Whiteriver USD 20 — 2,100/PK-12
PO Box 190 85941 — 928-338-4842
Wade McLean, supt. — Fax 338-5124
www.wusd.us
Canyon Day JHS — 300/7-8
PO Box 190 85941 — 928-338-1040
Jim Roush, prin. — Fax 338-4850
Cradleboard ES — 300/K-6
PO Box 190 85941 — 928-338-1026
Valerie Dehombreux, prin. — Fax 338-1417
Riley Seven Mile ES — 400/K-6
PO Box 190 85941 — 928-338-1353
Tyler Bangert, prin. — Fax 338-6037
Whiteriver ES — 400/PK-6
PO Box 190 85941 — 928-338-4138
Mary Good, prin. — Fax 338-6130

East Fork Lutheran S — 100/K-8
PO Box 489 85941 — 928-338-4455
Logan Block, prin. — Fax 338-1575

Wickenburg, Maricopa, Pop. 6,224
Wickenburg USD 9 — 1,500/K-12
40 W Yavapai St 85390 — 928-668-5350
Dr. Howard Carlson, supt. — Fax 668-5390
www.wickenburgschools.org/
Hassayampa ES — 500/K-5
251 S Tegner St 85390 — 928-684-6750
Michael Anderson, prin. — Fax 684-6791
Vulture Peak MS — 300/6-8
920 S Vulture Mine Rd 85390 — 928-684-6700
Ray Manker, prin. — Fax 684-6746
Other Schools – See Buckeye

Gospel Outreach Christian S — 50/PK-10
515 W Wickenburg Way 85390 — 928-684-5227
Donald Fisher, admin. — Fax 684-2878
Wickenburg Christian Academy — 100/PK-8
260 W Yavapai St 85390 — 928-684-5916
Fred West, admin. — Fax 684-6104

Wikieup, Mohave
Owens-Whitney ESD 6 — 50/K-8
PO Box 38 85360 — 928-765-2311
Susan Burdsal, supt. — Fax 765-2335
Owens S — 50/K-8
PO Box 38 85360 — 928-765-2311
Susan Burdsal, prin. — Fax 765-2335

Willcox, Cochise, Pop. 3,769
Willcox USD 13 — 1,400/PK-12
480 N Bisbee Ave 85643 — 520-384-4211
Dr. Richard Rundhaug, supt. — Fax 384-4401
www.willcox.k12.az.us
Willcox ES — 400/PK-3
501 W Delos St 85643 — 520-384-4216
Valerie Simon, prin. — Fax 384-5217
Willcox MS — 500/4-8
360 N Bisbee Ave 85643 — 520-384-4218
Doris Jones, prin. — Fax 384-6322

Williams, Coconino, Pop. 3,094
Williams USD 2 — 800/PK-12
PO Box 427 86046 — 928-635-4473
Thomas McCraley Ed.D., supt. — Fax 635-4767
www.wusd2.org
Williams S — 500/PK-8
PO Box 427 86046 — 928-635-4428
Donny Bridges, prin. — Fax 635-1213

Window Rock, Apache, Pop. 3,306
Window Rock USD 8
Supt. — See Fort Defiance
Window Rock ES — 500/K-5
PO Box 559 86515 — 928-810-7734
John McIntosh, prin. — Fax 810-7718

Winkelman, Gila, Pop. 444
Hayden-Winkelman USD 41 — 400/K-12
PO Box 409, — 520-356-7876
Jeff Gregorich, supt. — Fax 356-7303
Hambly MS — 100/6-8
PO Box 409, — 520-356-7876
Jacob Kame, prin. — Fax 356-7303
Winkelman IS — 100/4-5
PO Box 409, — 520-356-7876
Jacob Kame, prin. — Fax 356-7303
Winkelman PS — 100/K-3
PO Box 409, — 520-356-7876
Jacob Kame, prin. — Fax 356-7303

Winslow, Navajo, Pop. 9,931
Winslow USD 1 — 2,500/PK-12
PO Box 580 86047 — 928-288-8101
Robert Mansell, supt. — Fax 288-8292
www.wusd1.org
Brennan ES — 400/PK-6
PO Box 580 86047 — 928-288-8400
Daniel Hute, prin. — Fax 288-8492
Jefferson ES — 400/K-6
PO Box 580 86047 — 928-288-8500
Troy McReynolds, prin. — Fax 288-8592
Washington ES — 400/K-6
PO Box 580 86047 — 928-288-8600
John Summerville, prin. — Fax 288-8692
Winslow JHS — 400/7-8
PO Box 580 86047 — 928-288-8300
Jim MacLean, prin. — Fax 288-8393

Wittmann, Maricopa
Nadaburg USD 81 — 800/PK-8
32919 W Center St 85361 — 623-388-2321
Greg Riccio, supt. — Fax 388-2915
www.nadaburgsd.org/
Nadaburg S — 800/PK-8
21419 W Dove Valley Rd 85361 — 623-388-2321
Curtis McCandlish, prin. — Fax 388-2204
Other Schools – See Surprise

Young, Gila
Young ESD 5 — 100/PK-12
PO Box 390 85554 — 928-462-3244
Linda Cheney, supt. — Fax 462-3283
Young S — 50/PK-8
PO Box 390 85554 — 928-462-3244
Linda Cheney, prin. — Fax 462-3283

Yucca, Mohave
Yucca ESD 13 — 50/K-5
PO Box 128 86438 — 928-766-2581
Ann Marie Grant, dir. — Fax 766-2581
Yucca ES — 50/K-5
PO Box 128 86438 — 928-766-2581
Ann Marie Grant, prin. — Fax 766-2581

Yuma, Yuma, Pop. 84,688
Crane ESD 13 — 6,200/PK-8
4250 W 16th St 85364 — 928-373-3403
Cindy Didway, supt. — Fax 782-6831
craneschools.org/
Centennial MS — 700/7-8
2650 W 20th St 85364 — 928-373-3300
Paula Milner, prin. — Fax 376-7742
Crane MS — 800/7-8
4450 W 32nd St 85364 — 928-373-3200
Laurie Doering, prin. — Fax 344-6821
Knox ES — 700/K-6
2926 S 21st Dr 85364 — 928-373-5500
Laura Hurt, prin. — Fax 373-5599
Mesquite ES — K-6
4451 W 28th St 85364 — 928-373-4100
Kris Reed Ed.D., prin. — Fax 373-4199
Pueblo ES — 800/PK-6
2803 W 20th St 85364 — 928-373-3600
Lynn O'Connor, prin. — Fax 373-3699
Rancho Viejo ES — 400/4-6
1020 S Avenue C 85364 — 928-373-3800
Helen Coffeen, prin. — Fax 373-3899
Reagan Fundamental ES — 700/K-6
3200 W 16th St 85364 — 928-373-3700
Tom Fletcher, prin. — Fax 783-2635
Salida del Sol PS — 600/K-3
910 S Avenue C 85364 — 928-373-5600
Connie Jerpseth, prin. — Fax 373-5699
Suverkrup ES — 700/K-6
1590 S Avenue C 85364 — 928-373-3500
Kari Neumann, prin. — Fax 782-3132
Valley Horizon ES — 900/K-6
4501 W 20th St 85364 — 928-373-4000
Bobbie Henry, prin. — Fax 329-0504

Yuma ESD 1 — 10,200/K-8
450 W 6th St 85364 — 928-502-4300
Thomas Rushin, supt. — Fax 502-4442
www.yuma.org
Byrne ES — 300/K-5
811 W 16th St 85364 — 928-782-9585
Juli Peach, prin. — Fax 782-1942
Carver ES — 400/K-6
1341 W 5th St 85364 — 928-502-7600
Debra Drysdale Elias, prin. — Fax 782-4094
Castle Dome MS — 800/6-8
2353 S Otondo Dr 85365 — 928-341-1600
Harriet Williams, prin. — Fax 341-1700
Desert Mesa ES — 700/K-5
2350 S Avenue 7 1/2 E 85365 — 928-341-9700
Eula Baumgarner, prin. — Fax 341-9800
Fourth Avenue JHS — 500/7-8
450 S 4th Ave 85364 — 928-782-2193
Rob Monson, prin. — Fax 783-2195
Gila Vista JHS — 600/6-8
2245 S Arizona Ave 85364 — 928-782-5174
Rusty Tyndall, prin. — Fax 782-1483
Ham ES — 500/K-5
840 E 22nd St 85365 — 928-782-9241
Rebecca Kuechel, prin. — Fax 782-6737
Johnson ES — 600/K-5
1201 W 12th St 85364 — 928-502-7900
Jose Cazares, prin. — Fax 782-1535
McGraw ES — 500/K-6
2345 S Arizona Ave 85364 — 928-782-3828
Chris Clayton, prin. — Fax 782-1395
Otondo ES — 1,000/K-5
2251 S Otondo Dr 85365 — 928-344-0979
Mike Taylor, prin. — Fax 344-8168
Palmcroft ES — 500/K-5
901 W Palmcroft Dr 85364 — 928-502-8000
Patrick Koppinger, prin. — Fax 314-0685
Pecan Grove ES — 600/K-6
600 S 21st Ave 85364 — 928-502-8050
Jorge Zepeda, prin. — Fax 502-8082
Price ES — 100/K-5
1010 Barranca Rd 85365 — 928-329-4279
Tom Hurt, prin. — Fax 343-9419
Rolle ES — 800/K-6
2711 S Engler Ave 85365 — 928-726-4610
Mark Cunningham, prin. — Fax 726-6131
Roosevelt ES — 400/K-5
550 W 5th St 85364 — 928-502-8150
Karen Conde, prin. — Fax 502-8228
Sunrise ES — 600/K-5
9943 E 28th St 85365 — 928-502-8800
Edwin Richardson, prin. — Fax 502-8787
Watson MS — 500/6-8
9851 E 28th St 85365 — 928-502-7400
Donna Franklin, prin. — Fax 502-7403
Woodard JHS — 800/6-8
2250 S 8th Ave 85364 — 928-782-6546
Alan Sullivan, prin. — Fax 782-4596

Immaculate Conception S — 200/K-8
501 S Avenue B 85364 — 928-783-5225
Lydia Mendoza, prin. — Fax 343-0172
St. Francis of Assisi S — 200/K-8
700 W 18th St 85364 — 928-782-1539
Susan Armijo-Bostic, prin. — Fax 782-0403
Southwestern Christian S — 200/K-8
3261 S Avenue 6 E 85365 — 928-726-3086
Deborah Stewart, prin. — Fax 217-2172
Yuma Adventist Christian S — 50/1-8
1681 S 6th Ave 85364 — 928-783-0457
Joan Collins, prin. — Fax 376-7787
Yuma Lutheran S — 400/PK-8
2555 S Engler Ave 85365 — 928-726-8410
Karen Markin, prin. — Fax 726-5330

ARKANSAS

ARKANSAS DEPARTMENT OF EDUCATION
4 State Capitol Rm 304A, Little Rock 72201
Telephone 501-682-4475
Fax 501-682-1079
Website arkansased.org/

Commissioner of Education T. Kenneth James

ARKANSAS BOARD OF EDUCATION
4 State Capitol, Little Rock 72201

Chairperson Naccaman Williams

EDUCATION SERVICE COOPERATIVES (ESC)

Arch Ford ESC
Phillip Young, dir. 501-354-2269
101 Bulldog Dr, Plumerville 72127 Fax 354-0167
www.afsc.k12.ar.us/

Arkansas River ESC
Carolyn McCoy, dir. 870-534-6129
912 W 6th Ave, Pine Bluff 71601 Fax 534-2847
genie.arsc.k12.ar.us

Crowley's Ridge ESC
John Manning, dir. 870-578-5426
1606 Pine Grove Ln Fax 578-5896
Harrisburg 72432
crowleys.crsc.k12.ar.us/

Dawson ESC
Becky Jester, dir. 870-246-3077
711 Clinton St Ste 201 Fax 246-5892
Arkadelphia 71923
www.dawson.dsc.k12.ar.us

De Queen/Mena ESC
John Ponder, dir. 870-386-2251
PO Box 110, Gillham 71841 Fax 386-7731
nexus.dmsc.k12.ar.us/

Great Rivers ESC
Suzann McCommon, dir. 870-338-6461
PO Box 2837, West Helena 72390 Fax 338-7905
www.grsc.k12.ar.us/

Northcentral Arkansas ESC
Dr. Dennis Martin, dir. 870-368-7955
PO Box 739, Melbourne 72556 Fax 368-4920
naesc.k12.ar.us/

Northeast Arkansas ESC
Harrell Austin, dir., 211 W Hickory St 870-886-7717
Walnut Ridge 72476 Fax 886-7719
thor.nesc.k12.ar.us/

Northwest Arkansas ESC
William Auman, dir. 479-267-7450
4 N Double Springs Rd Fax 267-7456
Farmington 72730
starfish.k12.ar.us/

Ozarks Unlimited Resource Cooperative
Rick Nance, dir. 870-743-9100
525 Old Bellefonte Rd Fax 743-9099
Harrison 72601
www.oursc.k12.ar.us/

South Central Service Cooperative
Marsha Daniels, dir. 870-836-2213
400 Maul Rd, Camden 71701 Fax 836-5347
www.scsc.k12.ar.us/

Southeast Arkansas ESC
Karen Eoff, dir. 870-367-6848
1022 Scogin Dr, Monticello 71655 Fax 367-9877
se.sesc.k12.ar.us/

Southwest Arkansas ESC
Lindy Franks, dir. 870-777-3076
500 S Spruce St, Hope 71801 Fax 777-5793
etsp.k12.ar.us

Western Arkansas ESC
Guy Fenter, dir. 479-965-2191
3010 Highway 22 E Ste A Fax 965-2723
Branch 72928
www.wsc.k12.ar.us

Wilbur D. Mills ESC
Rodger Harlan, dir. 501-882-5467
PO Box 850, Beebe 72012 Fax 882-2155
wdmweb.wmsc.k12.ar.us/

PUBLIC, PRIVATE AND CATHOLIC ELEMENTARY SCHOOLS

Alexander, Saline, Pop. 622
Bryant SD
Supt. — See Bryant
Bethel MS 6-8
5415 Northlake Rd 72002 501-316-0937
Joe Fisher, prin. Fax 316-0338
Davis ES 500/K-5
12001 County Line Rd 72002 501-455-5672
Tiffany Beasley, prin. Fax 455-3290
Springhill ES 600/K-5
2716 Northlake Rd 72002 501-847-5675
Karen Metcalf, prin. Fax 847-5677

Avilla Christian Academy 100/PK-5
302 Avilla E 72002 501-316-0922
Barbara Dunn, admin. Fax 316-5053

Alma, Crawford, Pop. 4,734
Alma SD 3,300/K-12
PO Box 2359 72921 479-632-4791
Charles Dyer, supt. Fax 632-4793
almasd.net
Alma IS 800/3-5
PO Box 2259 72921 479-632-2166
Jim Warnock, prin. Fax 632-2167
Alma MS 800/6-8
PO Box 2229 72921 479-632-2168
Pat Whorton, prin. Fax 632-2160
Alma PS 800/K-2
PO Box 2299 72921 479-632-5100
Shawn Bullard, prin. Fax 632-5102

Alpena, Boone, Pop. 387
Alpena SD 600/K-12
PO Box 270 72611 870-437-2220
James Trammell, supt. Fax 437-2133
alpenaschools.k12.ar.us/
Alpena ES 300/K-6
PO Box 270 72611 870-437-2229
Geneva Bailey, prin. Fax 437-2133

Altheimer, Jefferson, Pop. 1,161
Dollarway SD
Supt. — See Pine Bluff
Martin ES 200/PK-5
PO Box 640 72004 870-766-0005
Brenda Barnes, prin. Fax 766-0007

Altus, Franklin, Pop. 835
Ozark SD
Supt. — See Ozark
Ozark MS 6-7
PO Box 339 72821 479-468-6111
Ron Hill, prin. Fax 468-2135

Amity, Clark, Pop. 741
Centerpoint SD 1,100/PK-12
755 Highway 8 E 71921 870-356-2912
Lewis Diggs, supt. Fax 356-4637
www.centerpoint.dsc.k12.ar.us/
Centerpoint IS 200/4-5
111 School St 71921 870-342-5377
Rodney Whitfield, prin. Fax 342-9559
Centerpoint JHS 300/6-8
755 Highway 8 E 71921 870-356-3612
Michael Jackson, prin. Fax 356-4519
Other Schools – See Glenwood

Arkadelphia, Clark, Pop. 10,548
Arkadelphia SD 2,100/K-12
235 N 11th St 71923 870-246-5564
Donnie Whitten, supt. Fax 246-1144
apsd.k12.ar.us/
Central PS 300/2-3
233 N 12th St 71923 870-246-4138
Mary Clay, prin. Fax 246-1157
Goza MS 500/6-8
1305 Caddo St 71923 870-246-4291
Angela Garner, prin. Fax 246-1153
Peake ES 300/4-5
1609 Pine St 71923 870-246-2361
Nikki Thomas, prin. Fax 246-1135
Perritt PS 300/K-1
1900 Walnut St 71923 870-246-2260
Wanda O'Quinn, prin. Fax 246-1158

Armorel, Mississippi
Armorel SD 400/K-12
PO Box 99 72310 870-763-6639
Mike Hunter, supt. Fax 763-0028
armorel.crsc.k12.ar.us
Armorel ES 200/K-6
PO Box 99 72310 870-763-5600
Rick Gore, prin. Fax 763-4108

Ashdown, Little River, Pop. 4,592
Ashdown SD 1,200/K-12
511 N 2nd St 71822 870-898-3208
Mike Walker, supt. Fax 898-3709
www.ashdownschools.org
Ashdown JHS 200/6-8
600 S Ellen Dr 71822 870-898-5138
James Jones, prin. Fax 898-4472
Daniel PS 200/K-1
1323 Foster Dr 71822 870-898-3711
Kay York, prin. Fax 898-4431
Franks ES 200/2-3
1321 Foster Dr 71822 870-898-2498
Teresa Wake, prin. Fax 898-4421
Henderson IS 100/4-5
410 Burke St 71822 870-898-3561
Keith Fricks, prin. Fax 898-4447

Atkins, Pope, Pop. 2,890
Atkins SD 1,100/K-12
307 N Church St 72823 479-641-7871
Boyce Watkins, supt. Fax 641-7569
ahs.afsc.k12.ar.us/
Atkins ES 400/K-4
302 NW 5th St 72823 479-641-7085
Carol Sober, prin. Fax 641-7659
Atkins MS 300/5-8
302 Avenue 2 NW 72823 479-641-1008
Allen Wilbanks, prin. Fax 641-5504

Augusta, Woodruff, Pop. 2,456
Augusta SD 500/K-12
320 Sycamore St 72006 870-347-2241
Richard Blevins, supt. Fax 347-5423
aes.wmsc.k12.ar.us
Augusta S 300/K-8
320 Sycamore St 72006 870-347-2432
Lori Lombardi, prin. Fax 347-1036
Other Schools – See Cotton Plant

Bald Knob, White, Pop. 3,316
Bald Knob SD 1,300/K-12
103 W Park Ave 72010 501-724-3273
James Staggs, supt. Fax 724-6621
bkps.wmsc.k12.ar.us
Bald Knob MS 400/5-8
103 W Park Ave 72010 501-724-5652
Brad Roberts, prin. Fax 724-2062
Lubker ES 500/K-4
103 W Park Ave 72010 501-724-3714
Wesley Roberts, prin. Fax 724-6253

Barling, Sebastian, Pop. 4,318
Fort Smith SD
Supt. — See Fort Smith
Barling ES 300/K-6
1400 D St 72923 479-452-0211
Diane Isaacs, prin. Fax 478-3152

Batesville, Independence, Pop. 9,556
Batesville SD 2,200/K-12
955 Water St 72501 870-793-6831
Ted Hall, supt. Fax 793-6760
Central Magnet ES 200/K-6
650 Vine St 72501 870-793-7498
Harvey Howard, prin. Fax 698-9829
Eagle Mountain Magnet ES 300/K-6
600 Eagle Mountain Blvd 72501 870-698-9141
Pat Rutherford, prin. Fax 793-0608
West Magnet ES 300/K-6
850 N Hill St 72501 870-793-9878
Dr. Gary Coots, prin. Fax 612-8017
Other Schools – See Sulphur Rock

Southside SD 1,500/K-12
70 Scott Dr 72501 870-251-2341
Danny Foley, supt. Fax 251-3316
southside.k12.ar.us/
Southside MS 500/5-8
70 Scott Dr 72501 870-251-2332
Joel Franks, prin. Fax 251-3316
Southside PS 600/K-4
70 Scott Dr 72501 870-251-2661
Glenda Mueller, prin. Fax 251-3316

Hope Lutheran S 50/1-8
2415 E Main St 72501 870-793-3078
Andrea Schmidt, prin. Fax 793-3078

Bauxite, Saline, Pop. 442
Bauxite SD 1,200/PK-12
800 School St 72011 501-557-5453
Mickey Billingsley, supt. Fax 557-2235
miners.k12.ar.us
Pine Haven ES 700/PK-6
500 Pine Haven Rd 72011 501-557-5361
Michael Driggers, prin. Fax 557-5874

Bay, Craighead, Pop. 1,953
Bay SD 600/K-12
PO Box 39 72411 870-781-3711
Oliver Layne, supt. Fax 781-3712
www.edline.net
Bay ES 300/K-6
PO Box 39 72411 870-781-3300
Tish Ford, prin. Fax 781-3837

Bearden, Ouachita, Pop. 1,047
Bearden SD 600/K-12
100 N Oak St 71720 870-687-2236
Denny Rozenberg, supt. Fax 687-3683
bearden.k12.ar.us/
Bearden ES 200/K-4
100 N Oak St 71720 870-687-2237
Renee McKelvin, prin. Fax 687-3683
Bearden MS 200/5-8
100 N Oak St 71720 870-687-3503
Iva Lou Stoker, prin. Fax 687-3683

Beebe, White, Pop. 5,623
Beebe SD 2,600/PK-12
1201 W Center St 72012 501-882-5463
Dr. Belinda Shook, supt. Fax 882-5465
badger.k12.ar.us/
Beebe IS 500/3-4
1201 W Center St 72012 501-882-2800
Karla Tarkington, prin. Fax 882-3117
Beebe JHS 7-8
1201 W Center St 72012 501-882-8414
Donald Sandlin, prin. Fax 882-8415
Beebe PS 800/PK-2
1201 W Center St 72012 501-882-3392
Cathy Payne, prin. Fax 882-8419
Other Schools – See Mc Rae

Bee Branch, Van Buren
South Side SD 500/K-12
334 Southside Rd 72013 501-654-2633
Billy Jackson, supt. Fax 654-2336
ssbb.k12.ar.us/
South Side ES 300/K-6
334 Southside Rd 72013 501-654-2200
Travis Love, prin. Fax 654-2326

Bella Vista, Benton, Pop. 9,083
Bentonville SD
Supt. — See Bentonville
Cooper ES K-4
2 Blowing Springs Rd 72714 479-696-3700
Ryan Oswalt, prin. Fax 855-5942

Belleville, Yell, Pop. 371
Western Yell County SD
Supt. — See Havana
Western Yell County ES 200/K-6
PO Box 250 72824 479-493-4100
Keith Jones, prin. Fax 493-4117

Benton, Saline, Pop. 25,673
Benton SD 4,600/K-12
PO Box 939 72018 501-778-4861
Dr. Tony Prothro, supt. Fax 776-5777
www.bentonschools.org
Benton MS 700/6-7
204 N Cox St 72015 501-776-5740
Sue Shults, prin. Fax 776-5749
Caldwell ES 500/K-5
1800 W Sevier St, 501-778-4444
Diane Lovell, prin. Fax 776-5711
Grant ES 500/K-5
1124 Hoover St 72015 501-778-3300
Laura Baber, prin. Fax 776-5712
Perrin ES 700/K-5
1201 Smithers 72015 501-778-7411
Gina Holstead, prin. Fax 776-5713
Ringgold ES 500/K-5
536 River St 72015 501-778-3500
Ann Kerr, prin. Fax 776-5714

Bryant SD
Supt. — See Bryant
Hurricane Creek ES K-5
6091 Alcoa Rd 72015 501-653-1012
Wanda Beggs, prin. Fax 778-7463
Salem ES 600/K-5
2701 Salem Rd, 501-316-0263
Mark Scarlett, prin. Fax 794-9043

Harmony Grove SD 900/K-12
2621 N Highway 229 72015 501-778-6271
Daniel Henley, supt. Fax 778-6271
cardinals.dsc.k12.ar.us/default.htm
Harmony Grove MS 300/5-8
2621 N Highway 229 72015 501-860-6796
Sarah Gober, prin. Fax 778-6271
Westbrook ES 400/K-4
2621 N Highway 229 72015 501-778-7331
Sheila Holicer, prin. Fax 778-6271

Our Lady of Fatima S 100/PK-8
818 W Cross St 72015 501-315-3398
Jan Cash, prin. Fax 315-1479

Bentonville, Benton, Pop. 29,538
Bentonville SD 9,400/K-12
500 Tiger Blvd 72712 479-254-5000
Dr. Gary Compton, supt. Fax 271-1159
www.bentonville.k12.ar.us
Apple Glen ES 700/K-4
1801 Brave Ln 72712 479-254-5580
Lisa St. John, prin. Fax 271-1137
Baker ES 600/K-4
301 NW 3rd St 72712 479-254-5720
Matt Young, prin. Fax 271-1116
Barker MS 5-6
500 SE 18th St 72712 479-696-3300
Dena Egger, prin. Fax 271-1161
Central Park ES K-4
1400 SW Liberty Ave 72712 479-696-3200
Galen Havner, prin. Fax 271-1148
Elm Tree ES 700/K-4
101 NW Elm Tree Rd 72712 479-254-5650
Tanya Sharp, prin. Fax 271-1175
Jefferson ES 500/K-4
810 Bella Vista Rd 72712 479-254-5860
Carol Lindman, prin. Fax 271-1186
Jones ES 600/K-4
500 SE 14th St 72712 479-254-5930
Mike Mumma, prin. Fax 271-1139
Lincoln JHS 800/7-8
1206 Leopard Ln 72712 479-254-5250
Rose Peterson, prin. Fax 271-1175
Old High MS 600/5-6
406 NW 2nd St 72712 479-254-5440
Marilyn Gilchrist, prin. Fax 254-5440
Spring Hill MS 500/5-6
3400 Highway 72 W 72712 479-254-5510
Janet McDonald, prin. Fax 271-1185
Sugar Creek ES 700/K-4
1102 Bella Vista Rd 72712 479-254-5790
Cathy Hancock, prin. Fax 271-1134
Washington JHS 800/7-8
1501 NE Wildcat Way 72712 479-254-5345
Kim Garrett, prin. Fax 271-1191
Other Schools – See Bella Vista, Centerton

Ambassadors For Christ Academy 200/PK-12
PO Box 924 72712 479-273-5635
David Welshenbaugh, admin. Fax 273-0684
Bentonville Adventist S 50/1-8
PO Box 298 72712 479-271-8887
Walnut Farm Montessori S 100/PK-6
4208 E Highway 72 72712 479-271-9424
Judy Dunn, prin. Fax 271-8766

Bergman, Boone, Pop. 438
Bergman SD 700/K-12
PO Box 1 72615 870-741-5213
Joe Couch, supt. Fax 741-6701
bergman.oursc.k12.ar.us/
Bergman ES 400/K-4
PO Box 1 72615 870-741-6404
Debbie Atkinson, prin. Fax 741-6017
Bergman MS 5-8
PO Box 1 72615 870-741-8557
Sarah Alexander, prin. Fax 741-3490

Berryville, Carroll, Pop. 4,935
Berryville SD 1,400/K-12
902 W Trimble Ave 72616 870-423-7065
Dr. Randy Byrd, supt. Fax 423-6824
bobcat.k12.ar.us
Berryville ES 500/K-2
902 W Trimble Ave 72616 870-423-3310
Teresa Wright, prin. Fax 423-4478
Berryville IS 3-5
902 W Trimble Ave 72616 870-423-3313
Shelly Osnes, prin. Fax 423-2141
Berryville MS 400/6-8
902 W Trimble Ave 72616 870-423-4512
Phillip Summers, prin. Fax 423-3195

Bigelow, Perry, Pop. 337
East End SD 700/K-12
PO Box 360 72016 501-759-2808
Myra Graham, supt. Fax 759-2667
bigelow.afsc.k12.ar.us
Watson ES 400/K-6
PO Box 360 72016 501-759-2638
Melissa Tash, prin. Fax 759-2278

Bismarck, Hot Spring
Bismarck SD 1,000/K-12
11636 Highway 84 71929 501-865-4888
David Hopkins, supt. Fax 865-3626
www.bismarcklions.net/
Bismarck ES 400/K-4
11636 Highway 84 71929 501-865-3616
Scott Henderson, prin. Fax 865-3947
Bismarck MS 300/5-8
11636 Highway 84 71929 501-865-4543
Dan Breshears, prin. Fax 865-4505

Black Rock, Lawrence, Pop. 690
Lawrence County SD
Supt. — See Walnut Ridge
Black Rock ES 200/K-6
PO Box 240 72415 870-878-6523
Lee Ann Cheadle, prin. Fax 878-6051

Blevins, Hempstead, Pop. 364
Blevins SD 500/K-12
PO Box 98 71825 870-874-2801
Randy Treat, supt. Fax 874-2889
hornet.swsc.k12.ar.us/
Blevins ES 200/K-6
PO Box 98 71825 870-874-2283
Carla Narlesky, prin. Fax 874-2300
Other Schools – See Emmet

Blytheville, Mississippi, Pop. 16,638
Blytheville SD 3,000/PK-12
PO Box 1169 72316 870-762-2053
Richard Atwill, supt. Fax 762-0141
blytheville.k12.ar.us
Blytheville IS 500/5-6
216 E Moultrie Dr 72315 870-763-5924
Geneva Harris, prin. Fax 762-0173
Blytheville Kindergarten Center 300/PK-K
1107 Byrum Rd 72315 870-763-7621
Gregg Yarbrough, prin. Fax 762-0170
Blytheville MS 500/7-8
700 Chickasawba St 72315 870-762-2983
Mike Wallace, prin. Fax 762-0174
Blytheville PS 500/1-2
1103 Byrum Rd 72315 870-763-6916
Veda Struble, prin. Fax 762-0171
Central ES 500/3-4
1124 W Moultrie Dr 72315 870-763-4485
Emma Gathen, prin. Fax 762-0169

Pathway Christian Academy 100/K-12
PO Box 466 72316 870-763-4561
Becky Brister, prin. Fax 763-7277

Bonnerdale, Hot Spring, Pop. 50

Ewing Jr Academy 50/K-10
709 Adventist Church Rd 71933 870-356-2780
Amy Clark, prin. Fax 356-2620

Booneville, Logan, Pop. 4,162
Booneville SD 1,100/K-12
381 W 7th St 72927 479-675-3504
John Parrish, supt. Fax 675-3186
www.booneville.k12.ar.us/
Booneville ES 4-6 4-6
386 W 7th St 72927 479-675-2604
Karen Garcia, prin. Fax 675-2625
Booneville ES K-3 500/K-3
386 W 7th St 72927 479-675-2604
Jeff Dyer, prin. Fax 675-2625

Bradford, White, Pop. 828
Bradford SD 500/K-12
PO Box 60 72020 501-344-2707
Arthur Dunn, supt. Fax 344-2707
bradford.wmsc.k12.ar.us/
Bradford ES 300/K-6
PO Box 60 72020 501-344-8245
Dara Burruss, prin. Fax 344-2707

Bradley, Lafayette, Pop. 553
Bradley SD 400/K-12
521 School Dr 71826 870-894-3313
Oscar Gammye Moore, supt. Fax 894-3344
bradleyweb.swsc.k12.ar.us/
Bradley ES 200/K-6
521 School Dr 71826 870-894-3477
Sherri Moore, prin. Fax 894-3474

Branch, Franklin, Pop. 366
County Line SD 500/K-12
12092 W State Highway 22 72928 479-635-2222
James Ford, supt. Fax 635-2087
indians.wsc.k12.ar.us/
County Line ES 200/K-6
12092 W State Highway 22 72928 479-635-4701
Joan Jones, prin. Fax 635-2102

Briggsville, Yell
Two Rivers SD
Supt. — See Plainview
Fourche Valley ES 100/K-6
18148 W Highway 28 72828 479-299-6215
Mary Ballard, prin. Fax 200-6212

Brinkley, Monroe, Pop. 3,520
Brinkley SD 600/K-12
200 Tigers Dr 72021 870-734-5000
Betty McGruder, supt. Fax 734-5187
www.brinkleyschools.com
Partee ES 400/K-6
400 W Lynn St 72021 870-734-5010
Linda Hamilton, prin. Fax 734-5014

Brockwell, Izard
Izard County Consolidated SD 500/K-12
PO Box 115 72517 870-258-7700
Fred Walker, supt. Fax 258-3140
icc.k12.ar.us/
Izard County Consolidated ES 200/K-4
PO Box 115 72517 870-322-7229
John Walker, prin. Fax 322-7231
Izard County Consolidated MS 200/5-8
PO Box 115 72517 870-258-7788
Monty McCurley, prin. Fax 258-3140

Brookland, Craighead, Pop. 1,442
Brookland SD 1,100/K-12
200 W School St 72417 870-932-2080
Kevin McGaughey, supt. Fax 932-2088
brookland.crsc.k12.ar.us/
Brookland ES 500/K-3
220 N Oak St 72417 870-932-2030
Nicole Covey, prin. Fax 932-9760
Brookland MS 4-6
100 W School St 72417 870-932-2080
Dr. Jeff Hernandez, prin. Fax 932-2088

Bryant, Saline, Pop. 13,185
Bryant SD 6,100/K-12
200 NW 4th St 72022 501-847-5600
Dr. Richard Abernathy, supt. Fax 847-5603
www.bryantschools.org
Bryant ES 1,100/K-5
200 NW 4th St 72022 501-847-5642
Dean Burbank, prin. Fax 847-5650
Bryant MS 900/6-8
200 NW 4th St 72022 501-847-5651
Sue Reeves, prin. Fax 847-5654
Collegeville ES 600/K-5
200 NW 4th St 72022 501-847-5670
Todd Sellers, prin. Fax 847-5672
Other Schools – See Alexander, Benton, Paron

Family Church Academy 200/PK-10
PO Box 150 72089 501-847-1559
Perry Black, admin. Fax 847-3692

Cabot, Lonoke, Pop. 21,039
Cabot SD 8,700/K-12
602 N Lincoln St 72023 501-843-3363
Dr. Tony Thurman, supt. Fax 843-0576
cabot.k12.ar.us
Cabot MS North 700/5-6
1900 N Lincoln St 72023 501-605-0192
Tanya Spillane, prin. Fax 605-8472
Cabot MS South 700/5-6
2555 Kerr Station Rd 72023 501-941-7335
Scott Jennings, prin. Fax 941-7432
Central ES 500/K-4
36 Pond St 72023 501-843-3000
Joanne Blalock, prin. Fax 843-4503
Eastside ES 600/K-4
17 Bellamy St 72023 501-743-3563
John West, prin. Fax 843-5619
Magness Creek ES 600/K-4
16150 Highway 5 72023 501-743-3565
Kelly Whiddon, prin. Fax 843-7557
Northside ES 500/K-4
814 W Locust St 72023 501-843-5920
Suzanne Proctor, prin. Fax 843-6032
Southside ES 500/K-4
2600 S Pine St 72023 501-843-6176
Lisa York, prin. Fax 843-6229
Stagecoach ES K-4
850 S Stagecoach Rd 72023 501-743-3574
Pam Waymack, prin. Fax 605-1221
Westside ES 400/K-6
1701 S 2nd St 72023 501-843-5719
Mandy Watkins, prin. Fax 843-5802
Other Schools – See Ward

Calico Rock, Izard, Pop. 1,025
Calico Rock SD 500/K-12
PO Box 220 72519 870-297-8339
Jerry Skidmore, supt. Fax 297-4233
pirates.k12.ar.us/
Calico Rock ES 200/K-6
PO Box 220 72519 870-297-8533
Debbie Moore, prin. Fax 297-4233

Camden, Ouachita, Pop. 12,204
Camden Fairview SD 2,700/K-12
625 Clifton St 71701 870-836-4193
Dr. Jerry Guess, supt. Fax 836-6039
cfsd.k12.ar.us/
Camden Fairview IS 400/4-5
255 Pope Ave 71701 870-836-6876
Artie Furlow, prin. Fax 836-8581
Camden Fairview MS 600/6-8
647 J A Dooley Womack Dr 71701 870-836-9361
Patsy Hughey, prin. Fax 836-3717
Fairview ES 400/K-1
1 Robin St 71701 870-231-5434
Vonnie Phillips, prin. Fax 231-4652
Ivory PS 400/2-3
575 J A Dooley Womack Dr 71701 870-836-7381
Melanie Churchill, prin. Fax 836-5035

Harmony Grove SD 800/K-12
401 Ouachita 88 71701 870-574-0971
Harold Davidson, supt. Fax 574-2765
harmonygrove.k12.ar.us
Harmony Grove ES 400/K-6
401 Ouachita 88 71701 870-574-0960
Jerri Courville, prin. Fax 574-2765
Other Schools – See Sparkman

Camden Christian Academy 50/K-12
1245 California Ave SW 71701 870-836-3716
Bob Taynor, admin. Fax 836-4511

Caraway, Craighead, Pop. 1,355
Riverside SD
Supt. — See Lake City
Riverside East ES 200/K-6
PO Box 699 72419 870-482-3351
Patty Hernandez, prin. Fax 482-3352

Carlisle, Lonoke, Pop. 2,419
Carlisle SD 900/PK-12
520 Center St 72024 870-552-3931
Floyd Marshall, supt. Fax 552-7967
bison.wmsc.k12.ar.us
Carlisle ES 500/PK-6
707 E 5th St 72024 870-552-3261
John Hunt, prin. Fax 552-3017

Cave City, Sharp, Pop. 1,980
Cave City SD 900/K-12
PO Box 600 72521 870-283-5391
Steven Green, supt. Fax 283-6887
www.cavecity.k12.ar.us
Cave City ES 400/K-4
PO Box 600 72521 870-283-5393
Vicki Musick, prin. Fax 283-6887
Cave City MS 200/5-8
PO Box 600 72521 870-283-5392
Mark Smith, prin. Fax 283-6887
Other Schools – See Evening Shade

Cedarville, Crawford, Pop. 1,195
Cedarville SD 1,000/K-12
PO Box 97 72932 479-474-7220
Dr. Dan Foreman, supt. Fax 410-1804
cedarville.ar.schoolwebpages.com
Cedarville ES 400/K-4
PO Box 97 72932 479-474-5073
Phillis Dickinson, prin. Fax 410-2223
Cedarville MS 300/5-8
PO Box 97 72932 479-474-5847
Curt Ledbetter, prin. Fax 471-7036

Center Ridge, Conway
Nemo Vista SD 500/PK-12
5690 Highway 9 72027 501-893-2925
Tommy Thompson, supt. Fax 893-2367
nemo.k12.ar.us/
Nemo Vista ES 300/PK-6
5690 Highway 9 72027 501-893-2435
Tresa Virden, prin. Fax 893-2367

Centerton, Benton, Pop. 5,477
Bentonville SD
Supt. — See Bentonville
Centerton-Gamble ES K-4
1550 Gamble Rd 72719 479-696-3400
Cindy Dewey, prin. Fax 795-0514

Life Way Christian S 400/PK-12
PO Box 220 72719 479-795-9322
Charles Schneider, hdmstr. Fax 795-9399

Charleston, Franklin, Pop. 3,025
Charleston SD 800/K-12
PO Box 188 72933 479-965-7160
Jeff Stubblefield, supt. Fax 965-9989
tigers.wsc.k12.ar.us/
Charleston ES 300/K-4
PO Box 188 72933 479-965-2460
Carl Underwood, prin. Fax 965-9989
Charleston MS 100/5-8
PO Box 188 72933 479-965-7170
Melissa Moore, prin. Fax 965-9989

Charlotte, Independence
Cedar Ridge SD
Supt. — See Newark
Cord-Charlotte ES 100/PK-6
225 School Rd 72522 870-799-3714
Dr. Debbie Goodwin, prin. Fax 799-3702

Cherry Valley, Cross, Pop. 702
Cross County SD 7 600/K-12
PO Box 180 72324 870-588-3338
Dr. Matt McClure, supt. Fax 588-3565
www.crosscountyschools.com
Cross County IS 100/4-6
PO Box 300 72324 870-588-3327
Melvin Bowles, prin. Fax 588-4454
Other Schools – See Vanndale

Clarendon, Monroe, Pop. 1,835
Clarendon SD 600/K-12
PO Box 248 72029 870-747-3351
George LaFargue, supt. Fax 747-5963
lions.grsc.k12.ar.us
Clarendon ES 300/K-6
PO Box 248 72029 870-747-3383
Ruby Ellis, prin. Fax 747-5963

Clarksville, Johnson, Pop. 8,311
Clarksville SD 2,400/K-12
1701 W Clark Rd 72830 479-705-3200
David Hopkins, supt. Fax 754-3748
panthernet.wsc.k12.ar.us/
Clarksville PS 500/K-1
2023 W Clark Rd 72830 479-979-6000
Steve Ziegler, prin. Fax 979-6001
Kraus MS 400/5-6
1901 W Clark Rd 72830 479-705-3240
Janice Price, prin. Fax 705-0072
Pyron ES 600/2-4
1903 W Clark Rd 72830 479-705-3256
Toby Cook, prin. Fax 754-3756

Clinton, Van Buren, Pop. 2,475
Clinton SD 1,300/K-12
683 Yellowjacket Ln 72031 501-745-6005
James McGaha, supt. Fax 745-2475
clinton.k12.ar.us/
Clinton IS 300/4-6
299 Walker St 72031 501-745-6043
Kathryn Treadaway, prin. Fax 745-4736
Cowsert ES 400/K-3
760 Yellowjacket Ln 72031 501-745-6046
Hal Ward, prin. Fax 745-8073

College Station, Pulaski, Pop. 3,000
Pulaski County Special SD
Supt. — See Little Rock
College Station ES 300/PK-5
PO Box 670 72053 501-490-5750
Blaine Alexander, prin. Fax 490-5756

Concord, Cleburne, Pop. 266
Concord SD 400/K-12
PO Box 10 72523 870-668-3844
Mike Davidson Ed.D., supt. Fax 668-3380
concord.k12.ar.us
Concord ES 200/K-6
PO Box 308 72523 870-668-3757
Sandy Brackett, prin. Fax 668-3757

Conway, Faulkner, Pop. 51,999
Conway SD 7,400/K-12
2220 Prince St 72034 501-450-4800
Dr. Greg Murry, supt. Fax 450-4898
www.conwayschools.org
Burns ES 400/K-4
1201 Donaghey Ave 72034 501-450-4825
Cynthia Thacker, prin. Fax 450-4857
Cone ES 300/K-4
1629 South Blvd 72034 501-450-4835
DeLanna Lacy, prin. Fax 450-4896
Courtway MS 700/7-8
1200 Bob Courtway Dr 72032 501-450-4832
Jerry Whitmore, prin. Fax 450-4839
Cummins ES K-4
1400 Padgett Rd 72034 501-513-4417
Charlotte Green, prin. Fax 513-0155
Doyle IS 5-6
800 Padgett Rd 72034 501-450-6675
Debi Avra, prin. Fax 450-6669
Jones ES 400/K-4
1800 Freyaldenhoven Ln 72032 501-450-6645
Tammy Woosley, prin. Fax 450-6649
Mattison ES 400/K-4
2001 Florence Mattison Dr 72032 501-450-4820
Sam Nelson, prin. Fax 450-6601
Moore ES 400/K-4
1301 Country Club Rd 72034 501-450-4830
Cathy Dunn, prin. Fax 450-6605
Simon IS 5-6
1601 E Siebenmorgan Rd 72032 501-513-6120
Larry Smith, prin. Fax 513-6127
Smith ES 500/K-4
1601 S Donaghey Ave 72034 501-450-4815
Betty Ford, prin. Fax 450-6621
Stone ES 600/K-4
4255 College Ave 72034 501-450-4808
Mark Lewis, prin. Fax 450-4807
Stuart MS 700/7-8
2745 Carl Stuart St 72034 501-329-2782
Harvey Benton, prin. Fax 450-4848
Vann ES 400/K-4
2845 Carl Stuart St 72034 501-450-4870
Cherri Wilson, prin. Fax 450-6659

Conway Christian S 400/PK-12
400 E German Ln S 72032 501-336-9067
Gloria Gwatney-Massey, admin. Fax 336-9251
St. Joseph S 500/K-12
502 Front St 72032 501-327-1204
Joe Mallett, prin. Fax 513-6805

Corning, Clay, Pop. 3,456
Corning SD 1,100/K-12
PO Box 479 72422 870-857-6818
John Edington, supt. Fax 857-5086
www.corningschools.k12.ar.us/
Central ES 300/3-6
PO Box 479 72422 870-857-6491
Terry Rapert, prin. Fax 857-1455
Park ES 300/K-2
PO Box 479 72422 870-857-3748
Mary Wiedeman, prin. Fax 857-6982

Cotter, Baxter, Pop. 1,032
Cotter SD 700/K-12
PO Box 70 72626 870-435-6171
Don Sharp, supt. Fax 435-1300
cotter.ar.schoolwebpages.com/
Gist ES 300/K-6
PO Box 70 72626 870-435-6655
Airl Cheek, prin. Fax 435-1300

Cotton Plant, Woodruff, Pop. 895
Augusta SD
Supt. — See Augusta
Cotton Plant ES K-4
457 Martin Luther King Blvd 72036 870-459-3701
Carolyn Bell, lead tchr. Fax 459-2394

Cove, Polk, Pop. 383
Van Cove SD 500/K-12
110 S 5th St 71937 870-387-6832
Andrew Curry, supt. Fax 387-2350
vancove.dmsc.k12.ar.us/
Other Schools – See Vandervoort

Crossett, Ashley, Pop. 5,802
Crossett SD 1,300/PK-12
219 Main St 71635 870-364-3112
Janice Warren, supt. Fax 364-5499
crossettschools.org
Anderson ES 500/PK-4
1100 Camp Rd 71635 870-364-6521
Joye Stephenson, prin. Fax 364-1725
Norman MS 300/5-8
100 Petersburg Rd 71635 870-364-4712
Jim Lucas, prin. Fax 364-3771

Abiding Faith Christian S 100/PK-12
1552 Highway 52 W 71635 870-364-3844
Chris Hammond, dir. Fax 364-6651

Cushman, Independence, Pop. 467
Cushman SD 300/K-12
PO Box 370 72526 870-793-0956
Gary Anderson, supt. Fax 793-7266
bulldog.k12.ar.us/
Cushman ES 200/K-6
PO Box 370 72526 870-793-6321
Mark Gipson, prin. Fax 793-5748

Danville, Yell, Pop. 2,442
Danville SD 800/K-12
PO Box 939 72833 479-495-4800
Jimmy Cunningham, supt. Fax 495-4803
www.dps-littlejohns.net/

Tucker ES 500/K-5
PO Box 939 72833 479-495-4820
Nancy Barrick, prin. Fax 495-4819

Dardanelle, Yell, Pop. 4,337
Dardanelle SD 1,800/K-12
209 Cedar St 72834 479-229-4111
John Thompson, supt. Fax 229-1387
lizardlink.afsc.k12.ar.us/
Dardanelle ES 600/3-6
2306 State Highway 7 N 72834 479-229-3707
Terry Laughinghouse, prin. Fax 229-4686
Dardanelle MS 300/7-8
2032 State Highway 7 N 72834 479-229-4550
Avis Cotton, prin. Fax 229-1697
Dardanelle PS 400/K-2
900 N 4th St 72834 479-229-4185
Sue Ann Jernigan, prin. Fax 229-5036

Decatur, Benton, Pop. 1,352
Decatur SD 600/PK-12
1498 Stadium Ave 72722 479-752-3986
LeRoy Ortman, supt. Fax 752-2490
decatur.k12.ar.us/
Decatur ES 300/PK-4
9083 Mount Olive Rd 72722 479-752-3981
Leslie Sharp, prin. Fax 752-3982
Decatur MS 100/5-7
1441 E Roller Ave 72722 479-752-3989
Tommy Baker, prin. Fax 752-3145

Deer, Newton
Deer / Mt. Judea SD 400/K-12
PO Box 56 72628 870-428-5433
Richard Denniston, supt. Fax 428-5901
deermtjudea.k12.ar.us
Deer ES 100/K-6
PO Box 56 72628 870-428-5937
Junior Edgmon, prin. Fax 428-5901
Other Schools – See Mount Judea

Delight, Pike, Pop. 303
Delight SD 400/K-12
PO Box 8 71940 870-379-2214
Lavon Flaherty, supt. Fax 379-2448
Delight ES 200/K-6
PO Box 8 71940 870-379-2214
Kathaleen Cole, prin. Fax 379-2448

De Queen, Sevier, Pop. 5,953
De Queen SD 2,200/K-12
PO Box 950 71832 870-584-4312
Bill Blackwood, supt. Fax 642-8881
leopards.k12.ar.us/
De Queen ES 500/3-5
233 S Treating Plant Rd 71832 870-584-4311
Terri Phillips, prin. Fax 642-8582
De Queen PS 600/K-2
235 S Treating Plant Rd 71832 870-642-3100
Sharon Dykes, prin. Fax 642-7360

Beacon Hill Adventist Junior Academy 50/K-10
1446 Red Bridge Rd 71832 870-642-4876
Douglas Hartzell, prin.

Dermott, Chicot, Pop. 3,463
Dermott SD 500/K-12
PO Box 380 71638 870-538-1000
Alton Newton, supt. Fax 538-1005
dermott.k12.ar.us
Dermott ES 300/K-6
PO Box 380 71638 870-538-1010
Terry Swilley, prin. Fax 538-1005

Des Arc, Prairie, Pop. 1,821
Des Arc SD 700/K-12
600 Main St 72040 870-256-4164
Rick Green, supt. Fax 256-3701
desarc.wmsc.k12.ar.us/
Des Arc ES 300/K-6
2100 Hickory St 72040 870-256-4128
Debora Carpenter, prin. Fax 256-4499

De Witt, Arkansas, Pop. 3,414
De Witt SD 1,500/K-12
422 W 1st St 72042 870-946-3576
Gary Wayman, supt. Fax 946-1491
www.dewittschooldistrict.net/
De Witt ES 600/K-5
1718 S Grandview Dr 72042 870-946-4651
Robert Franks, prin. Fax 946-4652
De Witt MS 300/6-8
301 N Jackson St 72042 870-946-3708
Jeff Rader, prin. Fax 946-1301
Other Schools – See Gillett, Humphrey

Dierks, Howard, Pop. 1,252
Dierks SD 500/K-12
PO Box 124 71833 870-286-2191
Donnie Davis, supt. Fax 286-2450
www.dmsc.k12.ar.us
Walters ES 300/K-6
PO Box 70 71833 870-286-2015
Karla Byrne, prin. Fax 286-3232

Donaldson, Hot Spring, Pop. 334
Ouachita SD 400/K-12
166 Schoolhouse Rd 71941 501-384-2318
Ronnie Kissire, supt. Fax 384-5615
www.ouachita.dsc.k12.ar.us/
Ouachita ES 200/K-6
332 Schoolhouse Rd 71941 501-384-2341
Betty Tidwell, prin. Fax 384-5616

Dover, Pope, Pop. 1,359
Dover SD 1,400/K-12
PO Box 325 72837 479-331-2916
Jerry Owens, supt. Fax 331-2205
dover.k12.ar.us/
Dover IS 300/3-5
PO Box 325 72837 479-331-2750
Roberta Shotzman, prin. Fax 331-2219
Dover MS 300/6-8
PO Box 325 72837 479-331-4814
Michael Lee, prin. Fax 331-4965
Dover PS 400/K-2
PO Box 325 72837 479-331-2702
Donald Forehand, prin. Fax 331-2106

Dumas, Desha, Pop. 4,862
Dumas SD 1,700/K-12
213 Adams St 71639 870-382-4571
Dr. Tom Cox, supt. Fax 382-4874
dumas.sesc.k12.ar.us/
Central ES 300/K-1
101 Court St 71639 870-382-4954
Mildred Miles, prin. Fax 382-6897
Reed IS 600/2-6
709 S Cherry St 71639 870-382-5363
Tammy Healey, prin. Fax 382-5356

Earle, Crittenden, Pop. 2,895
Earle SD 600/K-12
PO Box 637 72331 870-792-8486
Jack Crumbly, supt. Fax 792-8897
www.earle.crsc.k12.ar.us
Dunbar MS 5-8
PO Box 637 72331 870-792-8401
Tagwunda Smith, prin. Fax 792-8403
Earle ES 300/K-4
PO Box 637 72331 870-792-8732
Carlos Guess, prin. Fax 792-1011

Edmondson, Crittenden, Pop. 493
West Memphis SD
Supt. — See West Memphis
Wedlock ES 100/K-6
200 B J Taylor St 72332 870-735-5113
Greg Brinkley, prin. Fax 732-8653

Elaine, Phillips, Pop. 777
Marvell SD
Supt. — See Marvell
Wood ES 200/K-6
PO Box 479 72333 870-827-3471
Dana Sims, prin. Fax 827-6517

El Dorado, Union, Pop. 20,467
El Dorado SD 4,400/K-12
200 W Oak St 71730 870-864-5001
Bob Watson, supt. Fax 864-5015
www.eldoradopublicschools.com
Barton JHS 600/7-8
400 W Faulkner St 71730 870-864-5051
Sherry Hill, prin. Fax 864-5064
Brown ES 300/K-4
505 Dixie Dr 71730 870-864-5081
Connie Reed, prin. Fax 864-5080
Goodwin ES 400/K-4
201 E 5th St 71730 870-864-5071
Phillip Lansdell, prin. Fax 864-5137
Northwest ES 400/K-4
1600 N College Ave 71730 870-864-5078
Melissa Powell, prin. Fax 864-5077
Union S K-8
6049 Moro Bay Hwy 71730 870-863-8472
Beverly Overturf, prin. Fax 862-9429
Washington MS 600/5-6
601 Martin Luther King Ave 71730 870-864-5032
Jody Vines, prin. Fax 864-5041
Yocum ES 600/K-4
308 S College Ave 71730 870-864-5096
Kelly Walters, prin. Fax 864-5095

Parkers Chapel SD 700/K-12
401 Parkers Chapel Rd 71730 870-862-4641
John Gross, supt. Fax 881-5092
parkerschapel.k12.ar.us
Parkers Chapel ES 400/K-6
401 Parkers Chapel Rd 71730 870-862-9767
Jana Young, prin. Fax 881-5094

West Side Christian S 100/PK-9
2400 W Hillsboro St 71730 870-863-5636
Eldon Swenson, admin. Fax 863-3391

Elkins, Washington, Pop. 1,890
Elkins SD 900/K-12
349 N Center St 72727 479-643-2172
Mike Harris, supt. Fax 643-3605
elks.k12.ar.us/
Elkins ES 300/3-6
349 N Center St 72727 479-643-3382
Amy Evans, prin. Fax 643-4111
Elkins MS 200/7-8
349 N Center St 72727 479-643-2552
Steve Denzer, prin. Fax 643-4272
Elkins PS K-2
349 N Center St 72727 479-643-3380
Jane Vaught, prin. Fax 643-4151

Emerson, Columbia, Pop. 348
Emerson - Taylor SD 600/K-12
PO Box 129 71740 870-547-2218
James Hines, supt. Fax 547-2077
www.scsc.k12.ar.us/emerson/default2.htm
Emerson ES 200/K-6
508 W Main St 71740 870-547-2218
Regina Jean, prin. Fax 547-2077
Other Schools – See Taylor

Emmet, Nevada, Pop. 450
Blevins SD
Supt. — See Blevins
Emmet ES K-6
PO Box 330 71835 870-887-2319
Pat Loe, prin. Fax 887-2941

England, Lonoke, Pop. 3,028
England SD 700/K-12
501 Pine Bluff Hwy 72046 501-842-2996
Paula Henderson, supt. Fax 842-3698
england.k12.ar.us
England ES 400/K-6
400 E Dewitt St 72046 501-842-2041
Ray Scalf, prin. Fax 842-2986

Enola, Faulkner, Pop. 192
Mount Vernon-Enola SD
Supt. — See Mount Vernon
Mount Vernon-Enola ES 300/K-6
PO Box 99 72047 501-849-2211
Rob Rollins, prin. Fax 849-3270

Eudora, Chicot, Pop. 2,571
Lakeside SD
Supt. — See Lake Village
Eudora/Lakeside ES 200/PK-3
536 S Mabry St 71640 870-355-6040
James Maiden, prin. Fax 355-6045

Eureka Springs, Carroll, Pop. 2,350
Eureka Springs SD 700/K-12
147 Greenwood Hollow Rd 72632 479-253-5999
Wayne Carr, supt. Fax 253-5955
eurekaspringsschools.k12.ar.us
Eureka Springs ES 300/K-4
156 Greenwood Hollow Rd 72632 479-253-8704
Clare Lesieur, prin. Fax 253-7983
Eureka Springs MS 200/5-8
142 Greenwood Hollow Rd 72632 479-253-7716
Dr. Linda Trice, prin. Fax 253-7809

Clear Spring S 100/PK-12
PO Box 511 72632 479-253-7888
Phyllis Poe, hdmstr. Fax 253-0768

Evening Shade, Sharp, Pop. 480
Cave City SD
Supt. — See Cave City
Evening Shade ES K-4
200 School Dr 72532 870-266-5390
Kerry Huskey, prin. Fax 266-3657

Everton, Marion, Pop. 177
Ozark Mountain SD
Supt. — See Saint Joe
Bruno-Pyatt ES 100/K-6
4754 Highway 125 S 72633 870-427-5227
Bob Ricketts, prin. Fax 427-5255

Farmington, Washington, Pop. 4,376
Farmington SD 1,300/K-12
42 S Double Springs Rd 72730 479-266-1800
Ron Wright, supt. Fax 267-6030
www.farmcards.org/
Folsom ES K-3
230 S Grace Ln 72730 479-267-6024
Stephanie Pinkerton, prin. Fax 267-6033
Ledbetter ES 200/4-5
14 N Double Springs Rd 72730 479-266-1810
Julia Williams, prin. Fax 267-6045
Lynch MS 500/6-8
359 Rheas Mill Rd 72730 479-266-1840
Carolyn Odom, prin. Fax 267-6051
Williams ES K-3
322 Broyles St 72730 479-267-6013
Kara Gardenhire, prin. Fax 267-4506

Fayetteville, Washington, Pop. 66,655
Fayetteville SD 7,900/K-12
PO Box 849 72702 479-973-8645
Vicki Thomas, supt. Fax 973-8670
www.fayar.net
Asbell ES 500/K-5
1500 N Sang Ave 72703 479-444-3080
LaTayna Greene, prin. Fax 444-3032
Butterfield Trail ES 500/K-5
3050 N Old Missouri Rd 72703 479-444-3081
Joette Folsom, prin. Fax 444-3029
Happy Hollow ES 400/K-5
300 S Ray Ave 72701 479-444-3085
Sharon Pepple, prin. Fax 444-3031
Holcomb ES 600/K-5
2900 N Salem Rd 72704 479-527-3610
Tracy Mulvenon, prin. Fax 527-3613
Holt MS 500/6-7
2365 N Rupple Rd 72704 479-527-3670
Michael Mason, prin. Fax 527-3677
Leverett ES 300/K-5
1124 W Cleveland St 72701 479-444-3077
Cheryl Putnam, prin. Fax 444-3079
McNair MS 600/6-7
3030 E Mission Blvd 72703 479-527-3660
Michelle Owens-Hayward, prin. Fax 527-3667
Owl Creek S K-7
375 N Rupple Rd 72704 479-718-0200
Kristen Scanlon, prin. Fax 718-0201
Root ES 500/K-5
1529 E Mission Blvd 72701 479-444-3075
Rhonda Moore, prin. Fax 444-3033
Vandergriff ES 700/K-5
2975 E Township St 72703 479-527-3600
Dr. Bert Stark, prin. Fax 527-3603
Washington ES 300/K-5
425 N Highland Ave 72701 479-444-3073
Ashley Garcia, prin. Fax 527-3617

Fayetteville Christian S 300/PK-12
2006 E Mission Blvd 72703 479-442-2565
Brad Jones, supt. Fax 444-6156
New S 200/K-7
PO Box 1805 72702 479-521-7037
Bill Mandrell, dir. Fax 521-7037
St. Joseph S 300/K-7
1722 N Starr Dr 72701 479-442-4554
Ann Finch, prin. Fax 442-7887

Flippin, Marion, Pop. 1,396
Flippin SD — 900/K-12
210 Alford St 72634 — 870-453-2270
Dale Query, supt. — Fax 453-5059
flippin.ar.schoolwebpages.com
Flippin ES — 400/K-5
209 Alford St 72634 — 870-453-8860
Lewis Villines, prin. — Fax 453-8877
Flippin MS — 200/6-8
308 N 1st St 72634 — 870-453-6464
Kelvin Hudson, prin. — Fax 453-6465

Floral, Independence
Midland SD
Supt. — See Pleasant Plains
Midland ES — 300/K-6
PO Box 119 72534 — 501-345-2413
Roe Stone King, prin. — Fax 345-2273

Fordyce, Dallas, Pop. 4,409
Fordyce SD — 1,100/PK-12
PO Box 706 71742 — 870-352-3005
Pam Blake, supt. — Fax 352-7187
www.fordyceschools.org/
Fordyce ES — 500/PK-4
350 Redbug Cir 71742 — 870-352-2816
Susan Ridings, prin. — Fax 352-8693
Fordyce MS — 300/5-8
75 Redbug Blvd 71742 — 870-352-7121
Crystal Williams, prin. — Fax 352-2313

Foreman, Little River, Pop. 1,071
Foreman SD — 500/K-12
PO Box 480 71836 — 870-542-7211
Larry Lairmore, supt. — Fax 542-7225
www.foremanschooldistrict.com/
Foreman ES — 300/K-6
PO Box 480 71836 — 870-542-7214
Callie Hunley, prin. — Fax 542-6369

Forrest City, Saint Francis, Pop. 14,078
Forrest City SD — 2,800/K-12
845 N Rosser St 72335 — 870-633-1485
Dr. Jerry Woods, supt. — Fax 633-1415
mustang.grsc.k12.ar.us/
Caldwell Stewart East ES — K-5
625 Irving St 72335 — 870-663-1365
Hazel Wallace, prin. — Fax 261-1835
Central Magnet ES — 800/K-5
801 Deadrick Rd 72335 — 870-633-2141
Willie Doby, prin. — Fax 633-1415
Lincoln MS — 300/6-7
149 N Water St 72335 — 870-261-1810
Susan Berry, prin. — Fax 261-1838
Stewart ES — 700/K-5
400 Dawson Rd 72335 — 870-633-0310
Hazel Wallace, prin. — Fax 633-1415

Calvary Christian S — 300/K-12
1611 N Washington St 72335 — 870-633-5333
Suzanne Hess, prin. — Fax 633-6238

Fort Smith, Sebastian, Pop. 82,481
Fort Smith SD — 13,600/K-12
PO Box 1948 72902 — 479-785-2501
Ben Gooden Ed.D., supt. — Fax 785-1722
www.fortsmithschools.org
Ballman ES — 300/K-6
2601 S Q St 72901 — 479-783-1280
Billie Warrick, prin. — Fax 785-1513
Beard ES — 300/K-6
1600 Cavanaugh Rd 72908 — 479-646-0834
Pam Siebenmorgen, prin. — Fax 648-8262
Bonneville ES — 300/K-6
2500 S Waldron Rd 72903 — 479-478-3161
Sharla Whitson, prin. — Fax 452-7654
Carnall ES — 200/K-6
2524 Tulsa St 72901 — 479-646-3612
Michela Wiley, prin. — Fax 646-8263
Cavanaugh ES — 200/K-6
1025 School St 72908 — 479-646-1131
Hank Needham, prin. — Fax 648-8297
Cook ES — 600/K-6
3517 Brooken Hill Dr 72908 — 479-646-8880
Bill Spicer, prin. — Fax 648-8292
Euper Lane ES — 400/K-6
6601 Euper Ln 72903 — 479-452-2601
Sherri Penix, prin. — Fax 478-3118
Fairview ES — 600/K-6
2400 Dallas St 72901 — 479-783-3214
Peggy Walter, prin. — Fax 709-6099
Howard ES — 300/K-6
1301 N 8th St 72901 — 479-783-7382
Velmar Greene, prin. — Fax 784-8180
Morrison ES — 200/K-6
3415 Newlon Rd 72904 — 479-782-7045
Susan Boone, prin. — Fax 784-8192
Orr ES — 400/K-6
3609 Phoenix Ave 72903 — 479-646-3711
Kathy Haaser, prin. — Fax 648-8266
Pike ES — 400/K-6
4111 Park Ave 72903 — 479-783-4506
Bryce Dalke, prin. — Fax 784-8128
Spradling ES — 400/K-6
4949 Spradling Ave 72904 — 479-783-8048
Gary James, prin. — Fax 784-8172
Sunnymede ES — 600/K-6
4201 N O St 72904 — 479-783-6327
Krystle Smith, prin. — Fax 784-8173
Sutton ES — 500/K-6
5001 Kelley Hwy 72904 — 479-785-1778
Rebecca Plaxco, prin. — Fax 784-8174
Tilles ES — 500/K-6
815 N 16th St 72901 — 479-785-5606
Terresa Dewey, prin. — Fax 784-8152
Trusty ES — 400/K-6
3300 Harris Ave 72904 — 479-783-7720
Sarah Lavey, prin. — Fax 784-8171
Woods ES — 500/K-6
3201 Massard Rd 72903 — 479-452-5808
Stanley Wells, prin. — Fax 452-0021
Other Schools – See Barling

Christ the King S — 300/PK-6
1918 S Greenwood Ave 72901 — 479-782-0614
Marna Boltuc, prin. — Fax 782-1098
First Lutheran S — 100/PK-6
2407 Massard Rd 72903 — 479-452-5330
Eric Pralle, prin. — Fax 452-3553
Fort Smith Montessori S — 100/PK-6
3908 Jenny Lind Rd 72901 — 479-646-7225
Dr. Dustin Dooly, prin. — Fax 646-7282
Immaculate Conception S — 400/PK-6
223 S 14th St 72901 — 479-783-6798
Sharon Blentlinger, prin. — Fax 783-0510
St. Boniface S — 200/PK-6
201 N 19th St 72901 — 479-783-6601
Dr. Karen Hollenbeck, prin. — Fax 783-6605
Union Christian Academy — 700/PK-12
4201 Windsor Dr 72904 — 479-783-7327
Dr. Ralph Spencer, supt. — Fax 783-9342

Fouke, Miller, Pop. 851
Fouke SD — 1,000/K-12
PO Box 20 71837 — 870-653-4311
Paulette Smith, supt. — Fax 653-2856
fouke.swsc.k12.ar.us/home/
Fouke ES — 500/K-5
PO Box 20 71837 — 870-653-4165
Ken Endris, prin. — Fax 653-7885
Fouke MS — 200/6-8
PO Box 20 71837 — 870-653-2304
Amanda Whitehead, prin. — Fax 653-7840

Fox, Stone
Mountain View SD
Supt. — See Mountain View
Rural Special ES — K-6
13237 Highway 263 72051 — 870-363-4202
Shelia Mitchell, prin. — Fax 363-4222

Garfield, Benton, Pop. 462
Rogers SD
Supt. — See Rogers
Garfield ES — 100/K-5
PO Box 69 72732 — 479-359-3263
Anita Turner, prin. — Fax 359-2236

Gentry, Benton, Pop. 2,613
Gentry SD — 1,500/K-12
201 S Giles Ave 72734 — 479-736-2253
Dr. Randy Barrett, supt. — Fax 736-2245
www.gentrypioneers.com/
Gentry IS — 400/3-5
201 S Giles Ave 72734 — 479-736-2252
Denise Waters, prin. — Fax 736-5308
Gentry MS — 300/6-8
201 S Giles Ave 72734 — 479-736-2251
Larry Cozens, prin. — Fax 736-3414
Gentry PS — 300/K-2
201 S Giles Ave 72734 — 479-736-2300
Gayla Wilmoth, prin. — Fax 736-0316

Ozark Adventist S — 100/PK-8
21150 Dawn Hill East Rd 72734 — 479-736-8592
Steve Burton, prin. — Fax 736-3280

Gillett, Arkansas, Pop. 787
De Witt SD
Supt. — See De Witt
Gillett ES — 100/K-6
PO Box 179 72055 — 870-548-2466
Vicki Reed, prin. — Fax 548-2281

Glenwood, Pike, Pop. 2,057
Centerpoint SD
Supt. — See Amity
Centerpoint PS — 300/PK-3
1000 Lakeshore St 71943 — 870-356-3206
David Combs, prin. — Fax 356-7443

Gosnell, Mississippi, Pop. 3,661
Gosnell SD — 1,500/K-12
600 N State Highway 181 72315 — 870-532-4000
Stan Williams, supt. — Fax 532-4002
pirates.crsc.k12.ar.us
Gosnell ES — 800/K-6
600 N State Highway 181 72315 — 870-532-4003
Angie Middleton, prin. — Fax 532-4033

Gravette, Benton, Pop. 2,275
Gravette SD — 1,500/PK-12
609 Birmingham St SE 72736 — 479-787-4100
Andrea Kelly, supt. — Fax 787-4108
lions.k12.ar.us/
Duffy ES — 500/PK-2
601 El Paso St SE 72736 — 479-787-4120
Zane Vanderpool, prin. — Fax 787-4128
Gravette MS — 300/6-8
607 Dallas St SE 72736 — 479-787-4160
Mitchell Wilber, prin. — Fax 787-4178
Gravette Upper ES — 300/3-5
500 8th Ave SE 72736 — 479-787-4140
Jay Ensor, prin. — Fax 787-4148

Greenbrier, Faulkner, Pop. 3,615
Greenbrier SD — 2,800/K-12
4 School Dr 72058 — 501-679-4808
Scott Spainhour, supt. — Fax 679-1024
gps.k12.ar.us/
Greenbriar Wooster ES — K-4
9 Church Cir 72058 — 501-679-3334
Lenett Thrasher, prin.
Greenbrier Eastside ES — 500/K-4
61 Glenn Ln 72058 — 501-679-2111
Sonya Hawkins, prin. — Fax 679-1016
Greenbrier MS — 600/5-7
7 School Dr 72058 — 501-679-2113
Todd Edwards, prin. — Fax 679-1072
Greenbrier Westside ES — 600/K-5
65 Garrett Rd 72058 — 501-679-1029
Peggy Squires, prin. — Fax 679-1049

Green Forest, Carroll, Pop. 2,859
Green Forest SD — 1,300/K-12
PO Box 1950 72638 — 870-438-5201
Jeffrey Williams, supt. — Fax 438-6214
www.gf.k12.ar.us
Green Forest ES — 400/K-3
PO Box 1950 72638 — 870-438-5205
Andrea Martin, prin. — Fax 438-4380
Green Forest IS — 400/4-7
PO Box 1950 72638 — 870-438-5129
Andrea Martin, prin. — Fax 438-5017

Greenland, Washington, Pop. 1,061
Greenland SD — 900/K-12
PO Box 57 72737 — 479-521-2366
Dr. Roland Smith, supt. — Fax 521-1480
greenlandschools.k12.ar.us/
Greenland ES — 300/K-4
PO Box 57 72737 — 479-521-2366
Michael Lamb, prin. — Fax 582-8722
Greenland MS — 300/5-8
PO Box 57 72737 — 479-521-2366
Jay Gardenhire, prin. — Fax 251-1203

Greenwood, Sebastian, Pop. 7,914
Greenwood SD — 3,400/K-12
420 N Main St 72936 — 479-996-4142
Dr. Kay Johnson, supt. — Fax 996-4143
www.greenwoodarkansasschools.com
East Hills MS — 800/5-7
700 Mount Harmony Rd 72936 — 479-996-0504
Donnie Whitson, prin. — Fax 996-6614
North Main IS — 500/3-4
300 E Gary St 72936 — 479-996-6111
Susan Fox, prin. — Fax 996-6111
Westwood PS — 800/K-2
300 Westwood Ave 72936 — 479-996-7748
Dr. Sarah Turner, prin. — Fax 996-7846

Greers Ferry, Cleburne, Pop. 966
West Side SD — 500/K-12
7295 Greers Ferry Rd 72067 — 501-825-6258
Russell Hester, supt. — Fax 825-6258
westside.afsc.k12.ar.us/
West Side ES — 300/K-6
7295 Greers Ferry Rd 72067 — 501-825-7744
John Long, prin. — Fax 825-7744

Gurdon, Clark, Pop. 2,233
Gurdon SD — 800/K-12
314 Cheatman St 71743 — 870-353-4454
Bobby Smithson, supt. — Fax 353-4455
gurdon.ar.schoolwebpages.com
Cabe MS — 300/5-8
7780 Highway 67 S 71743 — 870-353-4311
Libby White, prin. — Fax 353-5149
Gurdon PS — 300/K-4
401 N 10th St 71743 — 870-353-4321
Rita Roe, prin. — Fax 353-5146

Guy, Faulkner, Pop. 551
Guy-Perkins SD — 500/K-12
492 Highway 25 N 72061 — 501-679-7224
David Westenhover, supt. — Fax 679-3508
thunderbird.k12.ar.us/
Guy-Perkins ES — 200/K-6
492 Highway 25 N 72061 — 501-679-3509
Lisa Baker, prin. — Fax 679-3508

Hackett, Sebastian, Pop. 726
Hackett SD — 600/K-12
102 N Oak St 72937 — 479-638-8822
William Pittman, supt. — Fax 638-7106
hackett.wsc.k12.ar.us/
Hackett ES — 300/K-6
102 N Oak St 72937 — 479-638-8606
George Kennedy, prin. — Fax 638-8607

Hamburg, Ashley, Pop. 2,844
Hamburg SD — 2,000/PK-12
202 E Parker St 71646 — 870-853-9851
Max Dyson, supt. — Fax 853-2842
hamburg.k12.ar.us/
Albritton Upper ES — 400/4-6
521 E Lincoln St 71646 — 870-853-2820
Lisa Atkins, prin. — Fax 853-2822
Noble Lower ES — 500/PK-3
210 S Barlett St 71646 — 870-853-2836
Tracy Streeter, prin. — Fax 853-2838
Other Schools – See Portland, Wilmot

Hampton, Calhoun, Pop. 1,512
Hampton SD — 700/K-12
PO Box 1176 71744 — 870-798-2229
Max Dyson, supt. — Fax 798-2239
hampton.k12.ar.us/
Hampton ES — 300/K-6
PO Box 1176 71744 — 870-798-2742
Lillie Randall, prin. — Fax 798-2239

Hardy, Sharp, Pop. 779
Highland SD
Supt. — See Highland
Cherokee ES — 600/K-4
PO Box 419 72542 — 870-257-3118
Tracy Webb, prin. — Fax 257-3937
Highland MS — 400/5-7
PO Box 419 72542 — 870-856-3284
Dennis Sublett, prin. — Fax 856-3288

Harrisburg, Poinsett, Pop. 2,165
Harrisburg SD 1,100/K-12
207 W Estes St 72432 870-578-2416
Danny Sample, supt. Fax 578-9366
sting.k12.ar.us
Harrisburg ES 400/K-4
1003 S Illinois St 72432 870-578-2413
Cathy Spiegel, prin. Fax 578-9630
Harrisburg MS 300/5-8
207 W Estes St 72432 870-578-2410
Karli Saracini, prin. Fax 578-2338

Trumann SD
Supt. — See Trumann
Central ES 200/5-6
15781 Highway 163 72432 870-578-5401
Bobby Benson, prin. Fax 578-5402

Harrison, Boone, Pop. 12,764
Harrison SD 2,800/K-12
110 S Cherry St 72601 870-741-7600
Dr. Jerry Moody, supt. Fax 741-4520
harrison.k12.ar.us/
Eagle Heights ES 200/K-4
500 N Chestnut St 72601 870-741-5043
Linda Pledger, prin. Fax 741-0057
Forest Heights ES 400/K-4
1124 Tamarind St 72601 870-741-5837
Paul Shrum, prin. Fax 741-8599
Harrison MS 400/5-6
1125 Goblin Dr 72601 870-741-9764
Harry Branch, prin. Fax 741-3339
Skyline Heights ES 400/K-4
1120 W Holt Ave 72601 870-741-5821
Jeffrey Winkle, prin. Fax 741-0335
Woodland Heights ES 100/K-4
520 E Womack St 72601 870-741-0581
Vicki White, prin. Fax 741-8883

Grace Christian S 100/PK-12
PO Box 7 72602 870-741-8505
Corrie Shiarla, admin. Fax 741-6605
Harrison SDA S 50/1-8
4877 Highway 392 W 72601 870-741-0169

Hartford, Sebastian, Pop. 779
Hartford SD 400/K-12
PO Box 489 72938 479-639-5002
D. Chris Rink, supt. Fax 639-2158
hartford.k12.ar.us/
Hartford ES 200/K-6
PO Box 489 72938 479-639-2831
Alan Anderson, prin. Fax 639-5031

Hartman, Johnson, Pop. 620
Westside SD 700/K-12
122 Thompson St 72840 479-497-1991
Vicki Hall, supt. Fax 497-9037
www.westsiderebels.net
Westside ES 300/K-6
PO Box 230 72840 479-497-1088
Gary Keeney, prin. Fax 497-1938

Hattieville, Conway
Wonderview SD 400/K-12
2436 Highway 95 72063 501-354-0211
Brenda Tyler, supt. Fax 354-6071
wonder.k12.ar.us
Wonderview ES 200/K-6
2436 Highway 95 72063 501-354-4736
Ted Beck, prin. Fax 354-8487

Havana, Yell, Pop. 393
Western Yell County SD 500/K-12
PO Box 214 72842 479-476-4116
Brad Spikes, supt. Fax 476-4115
wolverines.k12.ar.us
Other Schools – See Belleville

Hazen, Prairie, Pop. 1,562
Hazen SD 500/PK-12
477 N Hazen Ave 72064 870-255-4549
Matt Donaghy, supt. Fax 255-4508
hazen.wmsc.k12.ar.us/
Hazen S 300/PK-8
477 N Hazen Ave 72064 870-255-4547
Nanette Aycock, prin. Fax 255-4508

Heber Springs, Cleburne, Pop. 7,016
Heber Springs SD 1,800/K-12
800 W Moore St 72543 501-362-6712
Rick Rana, supt. Fax 362-0613
hssd.k12.ar.us/
Heber Springs ES 700/K-5
800 W Moore St 72543 501-362-8155
John Mueller, prin. Fax 362-2599
Heber Springs MS 400/6-8
800 W Moore St 72543 501-362-2488
Connie Moody, prin. Fax 362-2193

Hector, Pope, Pop. 517
Hector SD 700/K-12
11520 SR 27 72843 479-284-2021
Karen Smith, supt. Fax 284-2350
wildcats.afsc.k12.ar.us/
Hector ES 400/K-6
104 Sycamore St 72843 479-284-3586
Kathy Freeman, prin. Fax 284-4010

Helena, Phillips, Pop. 5,687
Helena/West Helena SD 2,900/K-12
PO Box 369 72342 870-338-4425
Rudolph Howard, supt. Fax 338-4434
hwh.grsc.k12.ar.us/
Wahl ES 500/1-6
125 Hickory Hills Dr 72342 870-338-4404
Becky Alexander, prin. Fax 338-4421
Other Schools – See West Helena

Hermitage, Bradley, Pop. 762
Hermitage SD 600/K-12
PO Box 38 71647 870-463-2246
Richard Rankin, supt. Fax 463-8520
se.sesc.k12.ar.us/hermitage
Hermitage ES 200/K-5
PO Box 180 71647 870-463-8500
Carla Wardlaw, prin. Fax 463-2034
Hermitage MS 200/6-8
PO Box 190 71647 870-463-2235
Carla Wardlaw, prin. Fax 463-8301

Highland, Sharp, Pop. 1,023
Highland SD 1,600/K-12
Highway 62 72542 870-856-3275
Ronnie Brogdon, supt. Fax 856-2765
highlandrebels.k12.ar.us/
Other Schools – See Hardy

Hope, Hempstead, Pop. 10,467
Hope SD 2,600/K-12
117 E 2nd St 71801 870-722-2700
Kenneth Muldrew, supt. Fax 777-4087
hope.k12.ar.us
Clinton PS 1,100/K-4
601 Lakeshore Dr 71801 870-722-2723
Jo Anne Allen, prin. Fax 722-2765
Henry ES 400/5-6
2000 S Main St 71801 870-777-6222
Roy Turner, prin. Fax 722-2751
Yerger MS 400/7-8
400 E 9th St 71801 870-722-2770
Larry Muldrew, prin. Fax 722-2707

Spring Hill SD 500/K-12
633 Highway 355 W 71801 870-777-8236
Dickie Williams, supt. Fax 777-9200
springhill.k12.ar.us
Spring Hill ES 300/K-6
633 Highway 355 W 71801 870-722-7420
Dani Elledge, prin. Fax 722-7440

Garrett Memorial Christian S 200/PK-8
1 Genesis Dr 71801 870-777-3256
Dr. Larry Silvey, prin. Fax 722-5639

Horatio, Sevier, Pop. 1,025
Horatio SD 900/PK-12
PO Box 435 71842 870-832-2340
John Ward, supt. Fax 832-2174
horatio.dmsc.k12.ar.us/
Horatio ES 400/PK-6
PO Box 435 71842 870-832-2891
Rodger Click, prin. Fax 832-2174
Other Schools – See Winthrop

Hot Springs National Park, Garland, Pop. 36,356
Cutter-Morning Star SD 700/K-12
2801 Spring St 71901 501-262-2414
Lance Robinson, supt. Fax 262-0670
eaglesnest.dsc.k12.ar.us/
Cutter-Morning Star ES 300/K-6
2801 Spring St 71901 501-262-1883
Nancy Anderson, prin. Fax 262-1884

Fountain Lake SD 1,100/K-12
4207 Park Ave 71901 501-623-5655
Dr. Darin Beckwith, supt. Fax 623-6447
flcobra.k12.ar.us/
Fountain Lake ES 600/K-6
4207 Park Ave 71901 501-624-0431
Steven Freeman, prin. Fax 318-6918

Hot Springs SD 3,000/PK-12
400 Linwood Ave 71913 501-624-3372
Joyce Craft, supt. Fax 620-7829
www.hssd.net
Gardner Math Science & Technology S 500/K-4
525 Hammond Dr 71913 501-620-7822
Brenda Seiz, prin. Fax 620-7837
Hot Springs IS 5-6
617 Main St 71913 501-620-7851
Janice McCoy, prin. Fax 620-7855
Hot Springs MS 400/7-8
700 Main St 71913 501-624-5228
George Wilson, prin. Fax 620-7833
Langston Magnet ES 400/PK-4
120 Chestnut St 71901 501-620-7821
Stephanie Nehus, prin. Fax 620-7836
Oaklawn Visual & Performing Arts S 600/K-4
301 Oaklawn St 71913 501-623-2661
Debbie Kopf, prin. Fax 620-7834
Park International Magnet S 200/K-4
617 Main St 71913 501-623-5661
Susan Beard, prin. Fax 620-7835

Lakeside SD 2,800/PK-12
2837 Malvern Ave 71901 501-262-1880
Shawn Cook, supt. Fax 262-2732
lakeside.ar.schoolwebpages.com/
Lakeside IS 600/2-4
2855 Malvern Ave 71901 501-262-2332
Cynthia McGrew, prin. Fax 262-3955
Lakeside MS 700/5-7
2923 Malvern Ave 71901 501-262-6244
Jamie Preston, prin. Fax 262-6248
Lakeside PS 400/PK-1
2841 Malvern Ave 71901 501-262-1921
Julie Burroughs, prin. Fax 262-6225

Christian Ministries Academy 100/K-12
PO Box 8500 71910 501-624-1952
Paul Kern, prin. Fax 318-2624
Hot Springs SDA S 50/PK-9
401 Weston Rd 71913 501-760-3336
Sharon Clark, prin. Fax 760-3679
Lighthouse Christian S 50/PK-12
1075 Fox Pass Cutoff 71901 501-617-4310
Dr. Harold Elder, admin.

St. Johns S 100/PK-8
583 W Grand Ave 71901 501-624-3171
Elizabeth Shackelford, prin. Fax 624-3171

Hoxie, Lawrence, Pop. 2,717
Hoxie SD 900/K-12
PO Box 240 72433 870-886-2401
Dennis Truxler, supt. Fax 886-4255
green.nesc.k12.ar.us/
Hoxie ES 500/K-6
PO Box 240 72433 870-886-4256
Tim Ryan, prin. Fax 886-4257

Hughes, Saint Francis, Pop. 1,762
Hughes SD 500/K-12
PO Box 9 72348 870-339-2570
Ray Nassar, supt. Fax 339-3317
hughes.grsc.k12.ar.us/
Hughes ES 300/K-6
PO Box 9 72348 870-339-2545
Janice Base, prin. Fax 339-3317

Humphrey, Jefferson, Pop. 787
De Witt SD
Supt. — See De Witt
Humphrey ES 100/K-5
410 S Division St 72073 870-873-1106
Iciphine Jones, prin. Fax 873-1106

Huntsville, Madison, Pop. 2,207
Huntsville SD 2,200/K-12
PO Box F 72740 479-738-2011
Shelby Sisemore, supt. Fax 738-2563
eagle.nwsc.k12.ar.us/
Huntsville IS 700/3-6
PO Box H 72740 479-738-6228
Sherry Crabtree, prin. Fax 738-2636
Huntsville MS 400/7-8
PO Box G 72740 479-738-6520
Mike Cain, prin. Fax 738-6259
Watson PS 500/K-2
PO Box H 72740 479-738-2425
Mary Holt, prin. Fax 738-6383
Other Schools – See Saint Paul

Huttig, Union, Pop. 716
Strong-Huttig SD
Supt. — See Strong
Strong-Huttig JHS 6-8
PO Box 408 71747 870-797-2944
William Neikirk, prin. Fax 943-2883

Imboden, Lawrence, Pop. 643
Sloan-Hendrix SD 400/K-12
PO Box 1080 72434 870-869-2384
Michael Holland, supt. Fax 869-2380
shsd.k12.ar.us
Sloan-Hendrix ES 200/K-4
PO Box 1080 72434 870-869-2101
Rick Tate, prin. Fax 869-2103
Sloan-Hendrix MS 5-7
PO Box 1080 72434 870-869-2101
Rick Tate, prin. Fax 869-2103

Jacksonville, Pulaski, Pop. 30,367
Pulaski County Special SD
Supt. — See Little Rock
Adkins Pre K Center 100/PK-PK
500 Cloverdale Rd 72076 501-982-3117
Lisa Peeples, prin. Fax 241-2004
Arnold Drive ES 300/PK-5
4150 Arnold Dr 72076 501-988-4145
Jackie Smith, prin. Fax 983-8204
Bayou Meto ES 400/PK-5
26405 Highway 107 72076 501-988-4131
Karen Sullards, prin. Fax 983-8218
DuPree ES 300/PK-5
700 Gregory St 72076 501-982-9541
Dr. Janice Walker, prin. Fax 985-3800
Jacksonville ES 600/PK-5
108 S Oak St 72076 501-982-6571
Gary Beck, prin. Fax 241-2034
Jacksonville MS - Boys 6-8
1320 School Dr 72076 501-982-1587
Mike Nellums, prin. Fax 241-2139
Jacksonville MS - Girls 400/6-8
201 Sharp Dr 72076 501-982-9407
Kim Forrest, prin. Fax 241-2108
Pinewood ES 400/PK-5
1919 Northeastern Ave 72076 501-982-7571
Bobby Lester, prin. Fax 241-2054
Taylor ES 400/PK-5
1401 Murrell Taylor Dr 72076 501-985-1581
Julie Davenport, prin. Fax 985-3215
Tolleson ES 300/PK-5
601 Harris Rd 72076 501-982-7456
Diane Ashenberger, prin. Fax 241-2089

Hope Lutheran S 50/PK-5
1904 McArthur Dr 72076 501-982-8678
Vickie Aukes, prin. Fax 457-5042

Jasper, Newton, Pop. 494
Jasper SD 500/K-12
PO Box 446 72641 870-446-2223
Kerry Saylors, supt. Fax 446-2305
jasper.k12.ar.us
Jasper ES 300/K-6
PO Box 446 72641 870-446-5320
Jeff Cantrell, prin. Fax 446-5549
Other Schools – See Kingston, Oark

Jessieville, Garland
Jessieville SD 600/K-12
PO Box 4 71949 501-984-5381
George Foshee, supt. Fax 984-4200
jville.k12.ar.us
Jessieville ES 400/K-5
PO Box 4 71949 501-984-5665
Terry Crumpler, prin. Fax 984-4200

Jessieville MS 6-8
PO Box 4 71949 501-984-5610
Janis Bremer, prin. Fax 984-4211

Jonesboro, Craighead, Pop. 59,358
Jonesboro SD 4,900/PK-12
2506 Southwest Sq 72401 870-933-5800
Dr. Kim Wilbanks, supt. Fax 933-5838
www.jps.k12.ar.us/
Health Wellness & Environmental Studies 500/1-6
1001 Rosemond Ave 72401 870-933-5850
Tracie Hiller, prin. Fax 933-5854
International Studies S 400/1-6
1218 Cobb St 72401 870-933-5825
Arthur Jackson, prin. Fax 933-5833
Jonesboro K 500/K-K
618 W Nettleton Ave 72401 870-933-5835
Becky Shannon, prin. Fax 933-5834
Jonesboro Preschool PK-PK
1307 Flint St 72401 870-933-5876
Sheila Stallings, prin. Fax 933-5879
Math & Science S 500/1-6
213 E Thomas Green Rd 72401 870-933-5845
Rickey Greer, prin. Fax 933-5858
MicroSociety S 400/1-6
1110 W Washington Ave 72401 870-933-5855
Dana Sims, prin. Fax 933-5819
Visual and Performing Arts S 500/1-6
1804 Hillcrest Dr 72401 870-933-5830
Ron Williams, prin. Fax 933-5809

Nettleton SD 2,700/K-12
3300 One Pl 72404 870-910-7800
James Dunivan, supt. Fax 910-7854
nettletonschools.net
Fox Meadow IS 4-6
2309 Fox Meadow Ln 72404 870-910-7812
Cathey Wilcox, prin. Fax 910-7812
Nettleton Central ES 300/K-3
2305 Promise Lane Rd 72401 870-910-7830
Debbie Bean, prin. Fax 910-7834
Nettleton Fox Meadow ES 500/K-3
2305 Fox Meadow Ln 72404 870-910-7817
Lacy Tilton, prin. Fax 910-7816
Nettleton IS 300/4-6
3801 Vera St 72401 870-910-7809
Sandy McCall, prin. Fax 910-7811
University Heights ES 300/K-3
300 Bowling Ln 72401 870-910-7823
Dale Case, prin. Fax 910-7824

Valley View SD 2,000/PK-12
2131 Valley View Dr 72404 870-935-6200
Dr. Radius Baker, supt. Fax 972-0373
blazers.k12.ar.us/
Valley View ES 600/PK-2
5603 Kersey Ln 72404 870-935-1910
Pamela Clark, prin. Fax 935-6203
Valley View IS 600/3-6
2119 Valley View Dr 72404 870-935-4602
Dr. Sharon Taylor, prin. Fax 935-6204
Valley View JHS 300/7-8
2115 Valley View Dr 72404 870-935-4602
Barry Jones, prin. Fax 935-6202

Westside Consolidated SD 1,700/K-12
1630 Highway 91 W 72404 870-935-7503
Dr. James Best, supt. Fax 935-2123
warriors.crsc.k12.ar.us/
Westside ES 600/K-4
1834 Highway 91 W 72404 870-932-8023
Katherine Glover, prin. Fax 932-9832
Westside MS 400/5-7
1800 Highway 91 W 72404 870-972-5622
Pam Dooley, prin. Fax 268-1157

Blessed Sacrament S 100/K-6
720 S Church St 72401 870-932-3684
Dee Pillow, prin. Fax 935-4444
Concordia Academy 100/PK-7
1812 Rains St 72401 870-935-2273
Cheryl Honoree, prin. Fax 935-4717
Ridgefield Christian S 400/PK-12
3824 Casey Springs Rd 72404 870-932-7540
Randy Johnson, admin. Fax 931-9711

Judsonia, White, Pop. 2,087
Riverview SD
Supt. — See Searcy
Riverview-Judsonia ES 300/K-6
1004 Boardman 72081 501-729-5196
Lance Perry, prin. Fax 729-0018

White County Central SD 700/PK-12
3259 Highway 157 72081 501-729-3992
Monty Betts, supt. Fax 729-3992
White County Central ES 400/PK-6
3259 Highway 157 72081 501-729-4292
Janice Stewart, prin. Fax 729-4292

Junction City, Union, Pop. 691
Junction City SD 700/K-12
PO Box 790 71749 870-924-4575
Danny Thomas, supt. Fax 924-4565
junctioncity.k12.ar.us/
Junction City ES 300/K-6
PO Box 790 71749 870-924-4578
Rebekah West, prin. Fax 924-4565

Keiser, Mississippi, Pop. 763
South Mississippi County SD
Supt. — See Wilson
South Mississippi ES @ Keiser 200/K-4
PO Box 18 72351 870-526-2127
Gloria Phillips, prin. Fax 655-2633

Kensett, White, Pop. 1,708
Riverview SD
Supt. — See Searcy
Riverview-Kensett ES 400/K-6
701 W Dandridge St 72082 501-742-3221
Randy Kiinhl, prin. Fax 742-1511

Kingsland, Cleveland, Pop. 454
Cleveland County SD
Supt. — See Rison
Kingsland ES 100/K-6
16650 Highway 79 71652 870-348-5335
William Durey, prin. Fax 348-5556

Kingston, Madison
Jasper SD
Supt. — See Jasper
Kingston ES K-6
PO Box 149 72742 479-665-2835
Marsha Shaver, prin. Fax 665-2577

Kirby, Pike
Kirby SD 500/K-12
PO Box 9 71950 870-398-4212
Jeff Alexander, supt. Fax 398-4442
kirby.dsc.k12.ar.us
Kirby ES 200/K-6
PO Box 9 71950 870-398-4213
Joyce Smith, prin. Fax 398-4626

Lake City, Craighead, Pop. 2,002
Riverside SD 800/K-12
PO Box 178 72437 870-237-4329
Tommy Knight, supt. Fax 237-4867
riverside.crsc.k12.ar.us
Riverside West ES 300/K-6
PO Box 178 72437 870-237-8222
Lee Ann Harrell, prin. Fax 237-4697
Other Schools – See Caraway

Lake Village, Chicot, Pop. 2,608
Lakeside SD 1,500/PK-12
1110 S Lakeshore Dr 71653 870-265-2284
Joyce Vaught, supt. Fax 265-5466
lakeside.k12.ar.us/
Lakeside Lower ES 300/PK-2
1110 S Lakeshore Dr 71653 870-265-5402
Tim Watkins, prin. Fax 265-7311
Lakeside MS 300/6-8
1110 S Lakeshore Dr 71653 870-265-2970
Arthur Gray, prin. Fax 265-7309
Lakeside Upper ES 300/3-5
1110 S Lakeshore Dr 71653 870-265-2906
Cristy Stone, prin. Fax 265-7311
Other Schools – See Eudora

St. Mary S 100/PK-6
217 Saint Mary St 71653 870-265-2921
Kelly Pieroni, prin. Fax 265-2701

Lamar, Johnson, Pop. 1,542
Lamar SD 800/K-12
301 Elberta St 72846 479-885-3907
Dennis Meins, supt. Fax 885-2380
lamarwarriors.org
Lamar ES 400/K-4
301 Elberta St 72846 479-885-3363
Pam Terry, prin. Fax 885-2380
Lamar MS 5-8
301 Elberta St 72846 479-885-6511
Johanna Kenner, prin. Fax 885-2384

Lavaca, Sebastian, Pop. 2,059
Lavaca SD 900/K-12
PO Box 8 72941 479-674-5611
Jared Cleveland, supt. Fax 674-2271
lavacapublicschools.k12.ar.us/
Lavaca ES 300/K-4
PO Box 8 72941 479-674-5613
Tara Harshaw, prin. Fax 674-2271
Lavaca MS 300/5-8
PO Box 8 72941 479-674-5618
Marcia Ford, prin. Fax 674-5518

Leachville, Mississippi, Pop. 1,847
Buffalo Island Central SD
Supt. — See Monette
Buffalo Island Central East ES 200/K-6
PO Box 110 72438 870-539-6448
Shirley Cato, prin. Fax 486-2657

Lead Hill, Boone, Pop. 295
Lead Hill SD 400/K-12
PO Box 20 72644 870-436-5249
Robert Gray, supt. Fax 436-5946
leadhill.ar.schoolwebpages.com
Lead Hill ES 200/K-6
PO Box 20 72644 870-436-2690
Regina Brown, prin. Fax 436-5946

Lepanto, Poinsett, Pop. 2,079
East Poinsett County SD 800/K-12
502 McClellan St 72354 870-475-2472
Michael Pierce, supt. Fax 475-3531
epc.k12.ar.us/
Lepanto ES 200/K-4
502 McClellan St 72354 870-475-2632
Lisa Tennyson, prin. Fax 475-2366
Other Schools – See Tyronza

Leslie, Searcy, Pop. 464
Searcy County SD
Supt. — See Marshall
Leslie ES K-6
800 Elm St 72645 870-447-2431
Patti Bohannon, prin. Fax 447-2831

Lewisville, Lafayette, Pop. 1,200
Lafayette County SD 400/K-12
PO Box 950 71845 870-921-5500
Jack Broach, supt. Fax 921-4277
lafayette.k12.ar.us/
Lafayette County ES K-6
PO Box 950 71845 870-921-4275
Betsy Griffin, prin. Fax 921-3812

Lexa, Phillips, Pop. 306
Barton-Lexa SD 800/K-12
9546 Highway 85 72355 870-572-7294
Lee Vent, supt. Fax 572-4713
blsd.grsc.k12.ar.us
Barton ES 400/K-6
9546 Highway 85 72355 870-572-3984
Kenneth Murphree, prin. Fax 572-4713

Lincoln, Washington, Pop. 1,904
Lincoln Consolidated SD 1,300/K-12
PO Box 1127 72744 479-824-3010
Dr. Frank Holman, supt. Fax 824-3045
wolfpride.k12.ar.us
Lincoln ES 600/K-5
613 County Ave 72744 479-824-3010
Marsha Hash, prin. Fax 824-3012
Lincoln MS 300/6-8
107 E School St 72744 479-824-3010
Elaine King, prin. Fax 824-3042

Little Rock, Pulaski, Pop. 184,564
Little Rock SD 25,900/PK-12
810 W Markham St 72201 501-447-1000
Dr. Linda Watson, supt. Fax 447-1001
www.lrsd.org/
Bale ES 400/PK-5
6501 W 32nd St 72204 501-447-3600
Barbara Anderson, prin. Fax 447-3601
Baseline ES 300/PK-5
3623 Baseline Rd 72209 501-447-3700
Dr. Eleanor Cox-Woodley, prin. Fax 447-3701
Booker Arts Magnet ES 600/K-5
2016 Barber St 72206 501-447-3800
Dr. Cheryl Carson, prin. Fax 447-3801
Brady ES 400/PK-5
7915 W Markham St 72205 501-447-3900
Ada Keown, prin. Fax 447-3901
Carver Magnet ES 500/PK-5
2100 E 6th St 72202 501-447-4000
Dianne Barksdale, prin. Fax 447-4001
Cloverdale Magnet MS 800/6-8
6300 Hinkson Rd 72209 501-447-2500
Willie Vinson, prin. Fax 447-2501
Dodd ES 300/PK-5
6423 Stagecoach Rd 72204 501-447-4300
Jill Brooks, prin. Fax 447-4301
Dunbar Magnet MS 800/6-8
1100 Wright Ave 72206 501-447-2600
Eunice Thrasher, prin. Fax 447-2601
Fair Park ECC 200/PK-PK
616 N Harrison St 72205 501-447-4400
Judy Milam, prin. Fax 447-4401
Forest Heights MS 700/6-8
5901 Evergreen Dr 72205 501-447-2700
Wanda Ruffins, prin. Fax 447-2701
Forest Park ES 400/PK-5
1600 N Tyler St 72207 501-447-4500
Theresa Ketcher, prin. Fax 447-4501
Franklin Communications Technology ES 400/PK-5
1701 S Harrison St 72204 501-447-4600
Cynthia Collins, prin. Fax 447-4601
Fulbright ES 700/K-5
300 Pleasant Valley Dr 72212 501-447-4700
Deborah Mitchell, prin. Fax 447-4701
Geyer Springs ES 300/PK-5
5240 Mabelvale Pike 72209 501-447-4800
Richard Mills, prin. Fax 447-4801
Gibbs Magnet ES 300/PK-5
1115 W 16th St 72202 501-447-4900
Felicia Hobbs, prin. Fax 447-4901
Henderson Magnet MS 800/6-8
401 John Barrow Rd 72205 501-447-2800
Steve Geurin, prin. Fax 447-2801
Jefferson ES 400/PK-5
2600 N McKinley St 72207 501-447-5000
Roberta Mannon, prin. Fax 447-5001
King Magnet ES 600/PK-5
905 Dr Martin Luther King 72202 501-447-5100
Tyrone Harris, prin. Fax 447-5101
Mann Magnet MS 900/6-8
1000 E Roosevelt Rd 72206 501-447-3100
Patricia Boykin, prin. Fax 447-3101
McDermott ES 400/PK-5
1200 Reservoir Rd 72227 501-447-5500
Teresa Richardson, prin. Fax 447-5501
Meadowcliff ES 400/PK-5
25 Sheraton Dr 72209 501-447-5600
Karen Carter, prin. Fax 447-5601
Otter Creek ES 500/PK-5
16000 Otter Creek Pkwy 72210 501-447-5800
Donna Hall, prin. Fax 447-5801
Pulaski Heights ES 300/PK-5
319 N Pine St 72205 501-447-5900
Lillie Carter, prin. Fax 447-5901
Pulaski Heights MS 700/6-8
401 N Pine St 72205 501-447-3200
Dr. Daniel W. Whitehorn, prin. Fax 447-3201
Rockefeller Magnet ES 500/PK-5
700 E 17th St 72206 501-447-6200
Anne Mangan, prin. Fax 447-6201
Romine Interdistrict ES 400/PK-5
3400 Romine Rd 72204 501-447-6300
Lillie Scull, prin. Fax 447-6301
Stephens ES 500/PK-5
3700 W 18th St 72204 501-447-6400
Sharon Brooks, prin. Fax 447-6401
Terry ES 700/PK-5
10800 Mara Lynn Rd 72211 501-447-6500
Becky Ramsey, prin. Fax 447-6501
Wakefield ES 500/PK-5
75 Westminister Dr 72209 501-447-6600
Leslie Taylor, prin. Fax 447-6601

Washington Magnet ES 700/PK-5
2700 Main St 72206 501-447-6700
Katherine Snyder, prin. Fax 447-6701
Watson IS 200/3-5
7000 Valley Dr 72209 501-447-6800
Betty Mosley, prin. Fax 447-6801
Western Hills ES 300/PK-5
4901 Western Hills Ave 72204 501-447-6900
Scott Morgan, prin. Fax 447-6901
Williams Magnet ES 500/K-5
7301 Evergreen Dr 72207 501-447-7100
Mary Menking, prin. Fax 447-7101
Wilson ES 300/PK-5
4015 Stannus St 72204 501-447-7200
Beverly Jones, prin. Fax 447-7201
Woodruff ES 200/PK-5
3010 W 7th St 72205 501-447-7300
Katina Ray, prin. Fax 447-7301
Other Schools – See Mabelvale

Pulaski County Special SD 17,000/PK-12
925 E Dixon Rd 72206 501-490-2000
James Sharpe, supt. Fax 490-0483
www.pcssd.org
Baker Interdistrict ES 400/PK-5
15001 Kanis Rd 72223 501-228-3250
Kyron Jones, prin. Fax 228-3257
Bates ES 500/PK-5
14300 Dineen Dr 72206 501-897-2171
Matt Mellor, prin. Fax 897-2178
Chenal ES K-5
21201 Denny Rd 72223 501-821-7450
Felicia Hamilton, prin. Fax 821-7454
Fuller MS 800/6-8
808 E Dixon Rd 72206 501-490-5730
Don Booth, prin. Fax 490-5736
Landmark ES 300/PK-5
16712 Arch St 72206 501-888-8790
Cindy Ballard, prin. Fax 888-8798
Lawson ES 300/PK-5
19901 Lawson Rd 72210 501-821-7000
Joe Scroggins, prin. Fax 821-7012
Robinson ES 400/PK-5
21600 Highway 10 72223 501-868-2420
Dr. Kim Truslow, prin. Fax 868-2442
Robinson MS 300/6-8
21001 Highway 10 72223 501-868-2410
John Pearce, prin. Fax 868-2441
Other Schools – See College Station, Jacksonville, Maumelle, North Little Rock, Scott, Sherwood

Sheridan SD
Supt. — See Sheridan
East End ES 500/K-2
21801 Arch St 72206 501-888-4264
Mark Rash, prin. Fax 888-4275
East End IS 400/3-6
5205 W Sawmill Rd 72206 501-888-1477
Margie Parker, prin. Fax 888-8937

Agape Academy 100/PK-5
701 Napa Valley Dr 72211 501-225-0068
Jo Ann Meachum, prin. Fax 687-0470
Anthony S 400/PK-8
7700 Ohio St 72227 501-225-6629
Sharon Morgan, dir. Fax 225-2149
Arkansas Baptist S 300/PK-6
62 Pleasant Valley Dr 72212 501-227-7077
Nora Yates, prin. Fax 227-0060
Arkansas River Valley Montessori S 100/PK-8
1509 N Pierce St 72207 501-603-0620
Pat Bowen, prin. Fax 603-0905
Cathedral S 200/PK-5
1616 S Spring St 72206 501-375-7997
Diane Brownlee, hdmstr. Fax 374-3481
Chenal Valley Montessori S 100/PK-8
14929 Cantrell Rd 72223 501-868-6030
Dorothy Moffett, prin. Fax 868-3894
Christ Lutheran S 300/PK-8
315 S Hughes St 72205 501-663-5212
Bruce Schrader, prin. Fax 663-9542
Christ the King S 700/PK-8
4002 N Rodney Parham Rd 72212 501-225-7883
Kathy House, prin. Fax 225-1315
Hebrew Academy 50/K-6
11905 Fairview Rd 72212 501-217-0053
Little Rock Adventist Academy 50/K-10
8708 N Rodney Parham Rd 72205 501-225-6183
Joyce Fortner, prin. Fax 225-4987
Little Rock Christian Academy 1,200/K-12
PO Box 17450 72222 501-868-9822
Gary Arnold, hdmstr. Fax 868-8766
Miss Selma's Schools 400/PK-6
7819 T St 72227 501-225-0123
Robin Smith, prin. Fax 224-4330
Our Lady the Holy Souls S 500/PK-8
1001 N Tyler St 72205 501-663-4513
Ileana Dobbins, prin. Fax 663-1014
Pulaski Academy 1,200/PK-12
12701 Hinson Rd 72212 501-604-1915
Joe Hatcher, hdmstr. Fax 225-1974
St. Edwards S 200/PK-8
805 Sherman St 72202 501-374-9166
Jason Pohlmeier, prin. Fax 907-9078
St. Theresa S 200/PK-8
6311 Baseline Rd 72209 501-565-3855
Marguerite Olberts, prin. Fax 565-9522
Second Baptist Christian Academy 100/PK-5
6111 W 83rd St 72209 501-568-3247
Darryle Hinton, prin. Fax 568-5736
Shiloh SDA S 50/PK-8
2400 S Maple St 72204 501-666-6457
Southwest Christian Academy 500/PK-12
11301 Geyer Springs Rd 72209 501-565-3276
Sharon Stewart, prin. Fax 565-3567
Word of Outreach Christian Academy 100/PK-12
3300 Asher Ave 72204 501-663-0300
Cheryl Washington, admin. Fax 558-0203

Lockesburg, Sevier, Pop. 733
Lockesburg SD 400/K-12
PO Box 88 71846 870-289-5161
Bill Blackwood, supt. Fax 289-5189
Lockesburg ES 200/K-6
PO Box 88 71846 870-289-4041
Joe Coulter, prin. Fax 289-5452

London, Pope, Pop. 955
Russellville SD
Supt. — See Russellville
London ES 200/K-4
154 School St 72847 479-293-4241
Tami Chandler, prin. Fax 293-5141

Lonoke, Lonoke, Pop. 4,552
Lonoke SD 1,800/K-12
401 W Holly St 72086 501-676-2042
Dr. John Tackett, supt. Fax 676-7074
lonokeschools.org/
Lonoke ES 400/3-5
900 W Palm St 72086 501-676-6740
Holly Dewey, prin. Fax 676-7088
Lonoke MS 400/6-8
1100 W Palm St 72086 501-676-6670
Jeannie Holt, prin. Fax 676-7013
Lonoke PS 400/K-2
800 Lincoln St 72086 501-676-3839
Ross Moore, prin. Fax 676-3726

Lowell, Benton, Pop. 7,042
Rogers SD
Supt. — See Rogers
Lowell ES 500/K-5
202 McClure Ave 72745 479-631-3610
Sharla Osbourn, prin. Fax 631-3611
Tucker ES 400/K-5
121 N School Ave 72745 479-631-3561
Cindy Viala, prin. Fax 631-3581

Grace Lutheran S 100/PK-9
415 N 6th Pl 72745 479-659-5999
Steven Gartner, prin. Fax 659-0905

Luxora, Mississippi, Pop. 1,243
South Mississippi County SD
Supt. — See Wilson
South Mississippi ES @ Luxora 100/K-4
PO Box 130 72358 870-658-2768
Gloria Phillips, prin. Fax 655-7052

Lynn, Lawrence, Pop. 305
Hillcrest SD
Supt. — See Strawberry
Hillcrest ES K-6
PO Box 70 72440 870-528-3110
Shawn Rose, prin. Fax 528-3766

Mabelvale, Pulaski
Little Rock SD
Supt. — See Little Rock
Chicot PS 400/PK-2
11100 Chicot Rd 72103 501-447-7000
Shoutell Richardson, prin. Fax 447-7001
Mabelvale ES 400/PK-5
9401 Mabelvale Cut Off Rd 72103 501-447-5400
Darian Smith, prin. Fax 447-5401
Mabelvale Magnet MS 700/6-8
10811 Mabelvale West Rd 72103 501-447-3000
Ann Blaylock, prin. Fax 447-3001

Mc Crory, Woodruff, Pop. 1,862
McCrory SD 600/K-12
PO Box 930 72101 870-731-2535
Barry Scott, supt. Fax 731-2536
Mc Crory ES 400/K-6
PO Box 930 72101 870-731-2921
Jimmy Lowery, prin. Fax 731-2160

Mc Gehee, Desha, Pop. 4,527
McGehee SD 1,200/K-12
PO Box 767 71654 870-222-3670
Dr. Barbara Wood, supt. Fax 222-6957
owls.k12.ar.us/
Mc Gehee ES 600/K-6
PO Box 767 71654 870-222-5400
Linda Tullos, prin. Fax 222-6582

Mc Rae, White, Pop. 730
Beebe SD
Supt. — See Beebe
Beebe MS 500/5-6
308 N Wilks St 72102 501-726-9705
Rhonda Smith, prin. Fax 726-4433

Magazine, Logan, Pop. 910
Magazine SD 600/PK-12
485 E Priddy St 72943 479-969-2566
Sandra Beck, supt. Fax 969-8740
magazinerattlers.k12.ar.us
Magazine ES 300/PK-5
351 E Priddy St 72943 479-969-2565
Rebekah Roberts, prin. Fax 969-8033

Magnolia, Columbia, Pop. 10,478
Magnolia SD 3,100/PK-12
PO Box 649 71754 870-234-4933
Dr. John Moore, supt. Fax 901-2508
www.magnoliaschools.net
Central ES 700/4-6
456 E North St 71753 870-234-4911
Ethel King, prin. Fax 234-8634
East Side ES 700/1-3
1310 Hollensworth 71753 870-234-5611
Lanita Talley, prin. Fax 234-8362
Walker Preschool PK-PK
655 Highway 79 S 71753 870-234-5654
Lynnetta Roberts, prin. Fax 234-3557
West Side S 200/K-K
101 Boundary St 71753 870-234-3511
Angela Waters, prin. Fax 234-0229

Columbia Christian S 300/K-12
250 Warnock Springs Rd 71753 870-234-2831
John Steelman, prin. Fax 234-1497

Malvern, Hot Spring, Pop. 9,068
Glen Rose SD 700/K-12
14334 Highway 67 72104 501-332-6764
Nathan Gills, supt. Fax 332-3031
www.glenrose.k12.ar.us/
Glen Rose ES 300/K-4
14334 Highway 67 72104 501-332-3694
Sherri Hollingsworth, prin. Fax 332-3031
Glen Rose MS 5-8
14334 Highway 67 72104 501-332-3694
Tim Holicer, prin. Fax 332-3902

Magnet Cove SD 800/K-12
472 Magnet School Rd 72104 501-332-5468
Gail McClure, supt. Fax 337-4119
magnetcove.k12.ar.us
Magnet Cove ES 400/K-6
22083 Highway 51 72104 501-337-9131
Jeff Eskola, prin. Fax 332-5747

Malvern Special SD 2,200/K-12
1517 S Main St 72104 501-332-7500
Brian Golden, supt. Fax 332-7501
malvern.dsc.k12.ar.us/
Malvern ES 800/K-4
1807 W Moline St 72104 501-467-3166
Meredith McCormack, prin. Fax 467-3161
Malvern JHS 300/7-8
1910 Roosevelt St 72104 501-332-7530
Danny Lindsey, prin. Fax 332-7532
Wilson IS 300/5-6
614 E Moline St 72104 501-332-6452
Terri Bryant, prin. Fax 332-7551

Mammoth Spring, Fulton, Pop. 1,157
Mammoth Spring SD 500/K-12
410 Goldsmith Ave 72554 870-625-3612
Ronald Taylor, supt. Fax 625-3609
mammothspringschools.k12.ar.us
Mammoth Spring ES 200/K-6
410 Goldsmith Ave 72554 870-625-7213
Wade Powell, prin. Fax 625-3609

Manila, Mississippi, Pop. 2,813
Manila SD 900/PK-12
PO Box 670 72442 870-561-4419
Pamela Castor, supt. Fax 561-4410
mps.crsc.k12.ar.us
Manila ES 400/PK-4
PO Box 670 72442 870-561-3145
Diane Baugher, prin. Fax 561-8119
Manila MS 200/5-8
PO Box 670 72442 870-561-4815
Diane Wagner, prin. Fax 561-4828

Mansfield, Scott, Pop. 1,107
Mansfield SD 1,000/K-12
402 Grove St 72944 479-928-4006
Jim Hattabaugh, supt. Fax 928-4482
www.mansfieldtigers.com
Mansfield ES 400/K-4
100 N Walnut Ave 72944 479-928-4866
Jane Ziegler, prin. Fax 928-1617
Mansfield MS 300/5-8
400 Grove St 72944 479-928-4451
Kenny Burnett, prin. Fax 928-4323

Marianna, Lee, Pop. 4,792
Lee County SD 1,400/K-12
188 W Chestnut St 72360 870-295-7100
Saul Lusk, supt. Fax 295-7125
lcsd1.grsc.k12.ar.us/
Strong ES 300/3-5
351 Moton St 72360 870-295-7185
John Jones, prin. Fax 295-7316
Strong MS 300/6-8
214 S Alabama St 72360 870-295-7140
Carolyn Love, prin. Fax 295-7134
Whitten ES 300/K-2
175 Walnut St 72360 870-295-7118
Lynn Moore Baird, prin. Fax 295-2942

Lee Academy 100/K-12
973 Highway 243 72360 870-295-3444
Billy Ferguson, hdmstr. Fax 295-2229

Marion, Crittenden, Pop. 9,792
Marion SD 3,900/K-12
200 Manor St 72364 870-739-5100
Dan Shepherd, supt. Fax 739-5156
www.msd3.org/
Marion ES 500/2-3
235 Military Rd 72364 870-739-5120
Joyce Liphford, prin. Fax 739-5123
Marion IS 600/4-5
100 L H Polk Dr 72364 870-739-5180
Margaret Buford, prin. Fax 739-5183
Marion MS 600/6-7
10 Patriot Dr 72364 870-739-5173
Dr. Robin Catt, prin. Fax 739-5156
Other Schools – See West Memphis

Marked Tree, Poinsett, Pop. 2,720
Marked Tree SD 700/K-12
406 Saint Francis St 72365 870-358-2913
Gary Masters, supt. Fax 358-3953
mtree.crsc.k12.ar.us/
Marked Tree ES 400/K-6
703 Normandy St 72365 870-358-2214
Jana Hatley, prin. Fax 358-3953

Marmaduke, Greene, Pop. 1,163
Marmaduke SD 700/K-12
1010 Greyhound Dr 72443 870-597-4693
Tim Gardner, supt. Fax 597-4336
marmaduke.nesc.k12.ar.us/

Marmaduke ES 400/K-6
2020 Greyhound Dr 72443 870-597-4324
Audrea King, prin. Fax 597-4336

Marshall, Searcy, Pop. 1,255
Searcy County SD 700/K-12
PO Box 310 72650 870-448-3011
Andrew Vining, supt. Fax 448-3012
scsd.info
Marshall ES 400/K-6
PO Box 339 72650 870-448-3333
Rose Saylors, prin. Fax 448-2510
Other Schools – See Leslie

Marvell, Phillips, Pop. 1,250
Marvell SD 900/PK-12
PO Box 1870 72366 870-829-2101
Ulicious Reed, supt. Fax 829-2044
marvell.grsc.k12.ar.us/
Marvell ES 300/PK-6
PO Box 1870 72366 870-829-2946
Elizabeth Johnson, prin. Fax 829-1349
Other Schools – See Elaine

Marvell Academy 200/K-12
PO Box 277 72366 870-829-2931
Mike Reans, hdmstr. Fax 829-2931

Maumelle, Pulaski, Pop. 14,318
Pulaski County Special SD
Supt. — See Little Rock
Maumelle MS 6-8
1000 Carnahan Dr 72113 501-851-8990
Bobby Cole, prin. Fax 851-8988
Pine Forest ES 500/PK-5
400 Pine Forest Dr 72113 501-851-5380
Rob McGill, prin. Fax 851-5386

Mayflower, Faulkner, Pop. 1,900
Mayflower SD 1,000/PK-12
15 Old Sandy Rd 72106 501-470-0506
John Gray, supt. Fax 470-1343
mayflowerschools.info
Mayflower ES 400/PK-4
4 Grove St 72106 501-470-0387
Rachel Wheeler, prin. Fax 470-2107
Mayflower MS 200/5-8
18 Eagle Dr 72106 501-470-2111
John Pipkins, prin. Fax 470-2116

Maynard, Randolph, Pop. 369
Maynard SD 500/K-12
74 Campus Dr 72444 870-647-2051
Suzanne Bailey, supt. Fax 647-2301
maynard.nesc.k12.ar.us/
Maynard ES 200/K-6
74 Campus Dr 72444 870-647-2595
Scott James, prin. Fax 647-3385

Melbourne, Izard, Pop. 1,700
Melbourne SD 500/K-12
PO Box 250 72556 870-368-4500
Gerald Cooper, supt. Fax 368-7071
bearkatz.k12.ar.us/
Melbourne ES 300/K-6
PO Box 250 72556 870-368-4500
Lori Loggains, prin. Fax 368-7071
Other Schools – See Mount Pleasant

Mena, Polk, Pop. 5,608
Mena SD 1,900/K-12
501 Hickory Ave 71953 479-394-1710
Dr. Diann Gathrig, supt. Fax 394-1713
170.211.34.2/Mena%20Public%202000/index.htm
Durham ES 400/K-2
106 Reine St N 71953 479-394-2943
Steve Davis, prin. Fax 394-2979
Harshman ES 400/3-5
1000 Geyer Dr 71953 479-394-3151
Megan Witonski, prin. Fax 394-3153
Mena MS 500/6-8
320r Mena St 71953 479-394-2572
Mike Hobson, prin. Fax 394-0258

Ouachita River SD 600/K-12
143 Polk Road 96 71953 479-394-2348
Marcus Willborg, supt. Fax 394-6687
acorn.dmsc.k12.ar.us
Acorn ES 300/K-6
143 Polk Road 96 71953 479-394-4833
Teena Bell, prin. Fax 394-5213
Maddox ES K-6
181 Polk Road 685 71953 870-326-4311
Sean Couch, prin. Fax 326-5552

Mineral Springs, Howard, Pop. 1,293
Mineral Springs SD 400/PK-12
PO Box 189 71851 870-287-4748
Max Adcock, supt. Fax 287-5301
mssd.dmsc.k12.ar.us/
Mineral Springs ES 200/PK-6
PO Box 189 71851 870-287-4746
Jeanie Gorham, prin. Fax 287-4743
Other Schools – See Saratoga

Monette, Craighead, Pop. 1,189
Buffalo Island Central SD 800/K-12
PO Box 730 72447 870-486-5411
George Holland, supt. Fax 486-2657
www.buffaloislandcentral.com/
Buffalo Island Central West ES 200/K-6
PO Box 730 72447 870-486-2212
Dr. Kima Stewart, prin. Fax 486-2657
Other Schools – See Leachville

Monticello, Drew, Pop. 9,327
Drew Central SD 800/K-12
440 Highway 83 S 71655 870-367-5369
R. Wayne Fawcett, supt. Fax 367-1932
www.drewcentral.org/
Drew Central ES 400/K-4
440 Highway 83 S 71655 870-367-6893
Mike Johnston, prin. Fax 460-5500
Drew Central MS 5-7
440 Highway 83 S 71655 870-367-5235
Joy Graham, prin. Fax 460-5502

Monticello SD 2,200/K-12
935 Scogin Dr 71655 870-367-4000
Bobby Harper, supt. Fax 367-1531
www.billies.org
Monticello ES 500/K-2
1037 Scogin Dr 71655 870-367-4010
Patricia Thomas, prin. Fax 367-2105
Monticello IS 500/3-5
280 Clyde Ross Dr 71655 870-367-4030
Mary Donaldson, prin. Fax 367-6482
Monticello MS 500/6-8
180 Clyde Ross Dr 71655 870-367-4040
Jay Hughes, prin. Fax 367-5437

Morrilton, Conway, Pop. 6,607
South Conway County SD 1,500/K-12
704 E Church St 72110 501-354-9400
Douglas Adams, supt. Fax 354-9464
www.sccsd.org
Morrilton ES 2-3
1203 N Saint Joseph St 72110 501-354-9453
Sharon Wilson, prin. Fax 354-9443
Morrilton IS 4-6
1907 Poor Farm Rd 72110 501-354-9476
Velda Thompson, prin. Fax 354-9487
Morrilton JHS 400/7-8
1400 Poor Farm Rd 72110 501-354-9437
Bruce Bryant, prin. Fax 354-9429
Morrilton PS 400/K-1
410 S Bridge St 72110 501-354-9423
Charlotte Heidenreich, prin. Fax 354-9424

Sacred Heart S 300/K-12
106 N Saint Joseph St 72110 501-354-8113
Brian Bailey, prin. Fax 354-2001

Mountainburg, Crawford, Pop. 713
Mountainburg SD 700/K-12
129 Highway 71 SW 72946 479-369-2121
Dennis Copeland, supt. Fax 369-2138
www.mountainburg.org
Mountainburg ES 300/K-4
129 Highway 71 SW 72946 479-369-2762
Marsha Crowder, prin. Fax 369-4302
Mountainburg MS 200/5-8
129 Highway 71 SW 72946 479-369-4506
Warren Bane, prin. Fax 369-4355

Mountain Home, Baxter, Pop. 11,896
Mountain Home SD 3,700/K-12
2465 Rodeo Dr 72653 870-425-1201
Dr. Charles Scriber, supt. Fax 425-1316
bombers.k12.ar.us/
Berry IS 300/4-4
1001 S Main St 72653 870-425-1261
Sondra Monger, prin. Fax 425-1290
Mountain Home K 300/K-K
1310 Post Oak Rd 72653 870-425-1256
Dr. Leigh Ann Gigliotti, prin. Fax 425-1090
Nelson-Wilks-Herron ES 1,000/1-3
618 N College St 72653 870-425-1241
Leah Cotter, prin. Fax 425-1264
Pinkston MS 900/5-7
1301 S College St 72653 870-425-1236
Michelle McWilliams, prin. Fax 425-1211

Mountain Home SDA S 50/1-8
3744 Highway 62 W 72653 870-425-1674

Mountain Pine, Garland, Pop. 827
Mountain Pine SD 600/PK-12
PO Box 1 71956 501-767-1540
Joe Cornelison, supt. Fax 767-1589
www-mpsd.dsc.k12.ar.us/
Mountain Pine ES 300/PK-6
PO Box 1 71956 501-767-2421
Pat Travis, prin. Fax 767-1549

Mountain View, Stone, Pop. 2,998
Mountain View SD 1,100/K-12
210 High School Rd 72560 870-269-3443
Greg Jackson, supt. Fax 269-3446
mvschools.k12.ar.us
Mountain View ES 600/K-5
201 Elementary St 72560 870-269-3104
Randall Lawrence, prin. Fax 269-2840
Mountain View MS 200/6-8
210 High School Rd 72560 870-269-3445
Robert Ross, prin.
Other Schools – See Fox, Timbo

Mount Ida, Montgomery, Pop. 971
Mount Ida SD 500/K-12
PO Box 1230 71957 870-867-2771
Benny Weston, supt. Fax 867-3734
www.dmsc.k12.ar.us/~mountida/cms/
Mount Ida ES 200/K-4
PO Box 1230 71957 870-867-2661
Brenda Boardman, prin. Fax 867-4552

Mount Judea, Newton
Deer / Mt. Judea SD
Supt. — See Deer
Mount Judea ES 100/K-6
PO Box 40 72655 870-434-5350
Roxanna Holt, prin. Fax 434-5700

Mount Pleasant, Izard, Pop. 407
Melbourne SD
Supt. — See Melbourne
Mount Pleasant ES K-6
PO Box 144 72561 870-346-5194
Carolyn Blevins, prin. Fax 346-5337

Mount Vernon, Faulkner, Pop. 147
Mount Vernon-Enola SD 500/K-12
PO Box 43 72111 501-849-2220
Jason Clark, supt. Fax 849-3076
mve.k12.ar.us/
Other Schools – See Enola

Mulberry, Crawford, Pop. 1,696
Mulberry/Pleasant View Bi-County SD 200/K-12
PO Box D 72947 479-997-1715
Kerry Schneider, supt. Fax 997-1897
www.mpvschools.com
Marvin PS 100/K-4
PO Box D 72947 479-997-1495
Johnny Hunter, prin. Fax 997-1367
Other Schools – See Ozark

Murfreesboro, Pike, Pop. 1,713
Murfreesboro SD 500/K-12
PO Box 339 71958 870-285-2201
Curtis Turner, supt. Fax 285-2276
mboro.k12.ar.us/
Murfreesboro ES 300/K-6
PO Box 339 71958 870-285-2193
Paul Tollett, prin. Fax 285-2276

Nashville, Howard, Pop. 4,929
Nashville SD 1,800/K-12
600 N 4th St 71852 870-845-3425
Douglas Graham, supt. Fax 845-7344
scrappers.k12.ar.us/
Nashville ES 400/4-6
200 Immanual St 71852 870-845-3262
Arlene Fugitt, prin. Fax 845-3026
Nashville PS 600/K-3
1201 N 8th St 71852 870-845-3510
Shirley Wright, prin. Fax 845-7311

Newark, Independence, Pop. 1,233
Cedar Ridge SD 500/PK-12
1502 N Hill St 72562 870-799-8691
Dr. Ann Webb, supt. Fax 799-8647
www.crsd.k12.ar.us/
Newark ES 300/PK-6
3549 Cord Rd 72562 870-799-8691
Kathy Magness, prin. Fax 799-3689
Other Schools – See Charlotte

Newport, Jackson, Pop. 7,281
Newport SD 1,600/K-12
406 Wilkerson Dr 72112 870-523-1312
Ronny Brown, supt. Fax 523-1388
greyhounds.k12.ar.us
Castleberry ES 500/K-3
400 N Pecan St 72112 870-523-1351
Judy Felts, prin. Fax 523-1374
Gibbs Albright ES 400/4-6
407 Wilkerson Dr 72112 870-523-1316
Allen Blair, prin. Fax 523-1327
Newport JHS 200/7-8
406 Wilkerson Dr 72112 870-523-1346
Lisa Tennyson, prin. Fax 523-1334

Norfork, Baxter, Pop. 521
Norfork SD 500/K-12
44 Fireball Ln 72658 870-499-5228
Mike Seay, supt. Fax 499-5109
panthers.k12.ar.us
Goforth ES 200/K-6
161 Mildred Simpson Dr 72658 870-499-7192
Vicki Hurst, prin. Fax 499-7196

Norman, Montgomery, Pop. 422
Caddo Hills SD 600/K-12
2268 Highway 8 E 71960 870-356-4495
Donald Henley, supt. Fax 356-3426
caddohills.dsc.k12.ar.us/
Caddo Hills ES 300/K-6
2268 Highway 8 E 71960 870-356-3331
Paul Shelton, prin. Fax 356-3345

Norphlet, Union, Pop. 807
Norphlet SD 500/K-12
PO Box 50 71759 870-546-2781
Eddie Miller, supt. Fax 546-2345
www.norphlet.k12.ar.us
Norphlet ES 300/K-6
PO Box 50 71759 870-546-2751
Rob Wright, prin. Fax 546-2345

North Little Rock, Pulaski, Pop. 58,803
North Little Rock SD 9,100/PK-12
2700 N Poplar St 72114 501-771-8000
Kenneth Kirspel, supt. Fax 771-8067
www.nlrsd.k12.ar.us
Amboy ES 300/K-5
2400 W 58th St 72118 501-771-8185
Michael Stone, prin. Fax 771-8187
Belwood ES 200/K-5
3902 Virginia Dr 72118 501-771-8195
Cindy Melton, prin. Fax 771-8197
Boone Park ES 400/K-5
1400 Crutcher St 72114 501-340-5160
Mavis Cherry, prin. Fax 340-5163
Crestwood ES 400/K-5
1901 Crestwood Rd 72116 501-771-8190
Lori Smith, prin. Fax 771-8192
Glenview ES 200/K-5
2101 Edmonds St 72117 501-955-3630
Carol Thornton, prin. Fax 955-3633
Indian Hills ES 500/K-5
6800 Indian Hills Dr 72116 501-835-5622
Sheryll Smith, prin. Fax 835-9580
Lakewood ES 400/K-5
1800 Fairway Ave 72116 501-771-8270
Sara Logan, prin. Fax 771-8268
Lakewood MS 700/7-8
2300 Lakeview Rd 72116 501-771-8250
Dr. Ginger Wallace, prin. Fax 771-8268

Lynch Drive ES 300/K-5
5800 Alpha St 72117 501-955-3610
Loretta Hassell, prin. Fax 955-3613
Meadow Park ES 200/K-5
400 Eureka Garden Rd 72117 501-955-3620
Rosie Coleman, prin. Fax 955-3623
North Heights ES 400/K-5
4901 Allen St 72118 501-771-8180
Dana Snowden, prin. Fax 771-8182
Park Hill ES 300/K-5
3801 John F Kennedy Blvd 72116 501-771-8175
Barbara Hartwick, prin. Fax 771-8176
Pike View ES 400/K-5
441 Mccain Blvd 72116 501-771-8170
Diane Crites, prin. Fax 771-8172
Poplar Street MS 600/6-6
2300 N Poplar St 72114 501-771-8275
Billy Bowers, prin. Fax 771-8283
Redwood ECC 200/PK-PK
401 N Redwood St 72114 501-955-3640
Jody Edrington, prin. Fax 955-3645
Rose City MS 200/7-8
5500 Lynch Dr 72117 501-955-3600
Phyllis McDonald, prin. Fax 955-3603
Seventh Street Fine Arts ES 300/K-5
1200 Bishop Lindsey Ave 72114 501-340-5170
Pam Wilcox, prin. Fax 340-5173

Pulaski County Special SD
Supt. — See Little Rock
Cato ES 400/PK-5
9906 Jacksonville Cato Rd 72120 501-833-1160
Sonja Whitfield, prin. Fax 833-1167
Crystal Hill Magnet ES 800/PK-5
5001 Northshore Dr 72118 501-791-8000
Karen Fikes, prin. Fax 791-8008
Harris ES 300/PK-5
4424 Highway 161 72117 501-955-3550
Shyrel Lee, prin. Fax 955-3555
Northwood MS 700/6-8
10200 Bamboo Ln 72120 501-833-1170
Veronica Perkins, prin. Fax 833-1178
Oak Grove ES 300/PK-5
5703 Oak Grove Rd 72118 501-851-5370
Yolanda Thomas, prin. Fax 851-5376

Central Arkansas Christian S 1,000/PK-12
1 Windsong Dr 72113 501-758-3160
Dr. Carter Lambert, pres. Fax 791-7975
Immaculate Conception S 400/PK-8
7000 John F Kennedy Blvd 72116 501-835-0771
George Robertson, prin. Fax 834-8652
Immaculate Heart of Mary S 200/PK-8
7025 Jasna Gora Dr 72118 501-851-2760
Maureen Pettei, prin. Fax 851-4769
North Little Rock Academy 200/PK-5
1518 Parker St 72114 501-374-5237
Denise Troutman, prin. Fax 374-4292

Oark, Johnson
Jasper SD
Supt. — See Jasper
Oark ES K-6
370 Highway 215 72852 479-292-3337
Anita Cooper, prin. Fax 292-3435

Ola, Yell, Pop. 1,206
Two Rivers SD
Supt. — See Plainview
Ola ES 300/K-6
PO Box 279 72853 479-489-4160
Mary Lawrence, prin. Fax 489-4159

Omaha, Boone, Pop. 172
Omaha SD 400/K-12
522 College Rd 72662 870-426-3366
Dr. David Land, supt. Fax 426-3360
omaha.k12.ar.us/
Omaha ES 300/K-8
522 College Rd 72662 870-426-3372
Matha Hicks, prin. Fax 436-4159

Osceola, Mississippi, Pop. 8,128
Osceola SD 1,200/PK-12
2750 W Semmes Ave 72370 870-563-2561
Milton Washington, supt. Fax 563-2181
www.osceola.k12.ar.us
East ES 200/3-5
315 E Union Ave 72370 870-563-6861
Clarissa Lacy, prin. Fax 622-1026
North K 200/PK-K
1230 W Semmes Ave 72370 870-563-1155
Sandra Landry, prin. Fax 622-1040
Osceola MS 200/6-8
711 W Lee Ave 72370 870-563-2918
Mary Hayden, prin. Fax 622-1030
West ES 200/PK-2
138 West Franklin St 72370 870-563-2371
Tiffany Morgan, prin. Fax 622-1035

Ozark, Franklin, Pop. 3,586
Mulberry/Pleasant View Bi-County SD
Supt. — See Mulberry
Millsap IS 5-6
5750 Hornet Ln 72949 479-997-8469
Rick Young, prin. Fax 997-1667

Ozark SD 1,300/K-12
PO Box 135 72949 479-667-4118
Donald Stone, supt. Fax 667-4092
ozark.k12.ar.us
Milton ES 600/1-5
1601 Walden Dr 72949 479-667-4745
Lori Griffin, prin. Fax 667-3936
Ozark Kindergarten K-K
700 N 12th St 72949 479-667-3021
Kelly Burns, prin. Fax 667-0171
Other Schools – See Altus

Palestine, Saint Francis, Pop. 736
Palestine-Wheatley SD 600/PK-12
PO Box 790 72372 870-581-2646
Donny Collins, supt. Fax 581-4420
www.pwsd.k12.ar.us/
Palestine-Wheatley ES 300/PK-4
PO Box 790 72372 870-581-2246
Zenna Smith, prin. Fax 581-4416
Other Schools – See Wheatley

Pangburn, White, Pop. 661
Pangburn SD 800/K-12
1100 Short St 72121 501-728-4511
Jerrod Williams, supt. Fax 728-4514
tigers.k12.ar.us/
Pangburn ES 400/K-6
1100 Short St 72121 501-728-4912
Wade Butler, prin. Fax 728-4514

Paragould, Greene, Pop. 23,775
Greene County Technical SD 3,300/PK-12
5413 W Kingshighway 72450 870-236-2762
Rita Adams, supt. Fax 236-7333
www.gctsd.k12.ar.us/
Greene County Technical ES 700/3-5
5203 W Kingshighway 72450 870-215-4430
Karen Mallard, prin. Fax 239-6975
Greene County Technical IS 500/6-7
5205 W Kingshighway 72450 870-215-4440
Marilyn Jerome, prin. Fax 239-6974
Greene County Technical PS 900/PK-2
1300 S Rockingchair Rd 72450 870-215-4420
Sherry Vance, prin. Fax 239-0680

Paragould SD 2,800/PK-12
1501 W Court St 72450 870-239-2105
Dr. Aaron Hosman, supt. Fax 239-4697
paragould.k12.ar.us/
Baldwin ES 400/K-4
612 W Mueller 72450 870-236-6369
Mike Skelton, prin. Fax 236-6389
Oak Grove ES 400/K-4
5027 Highway 135 N 72450 870-586-0439
Nicholas Jankoviak, prin. Fax 586-0485
Oak Grove MS 400/5-6
5097 Highway 135 N 72450 870-586-0483
Scott Gauntt, prin. Fax 586-0891
Paragould JHS 400/7-8
1701 W Court St 72450 870-236-7744
James Brittingham, prin. Fax 239-0185
School of the 21st Century PK-PK
427 E Poplar St 72450 870-236-8064
Vicki Shelby, dir. Fax 236-6151
Wilson ES 300/K-4
900 W Emerson St 72450 870-236-6177
Michael Allen, prin. Fax 236-7218

Crowleys Ridge Academy 300/PK-12
606 Academy Dr 72450 870-236-6909
Frank Harris, pres. Fax 236-6988
St. Marys S 100/PK-6
310 N 2nd St 72450 870-236-3681
Sharon Warren, prin. Fax 236-1073

Paris, Logan, Pop. 3,707
Paris SD 1,200/K-12
602 N 10th St 72855 479-963-3243
Jim Loyd, supt. Fax 963-3620
paris.wsc.k12.ar.us/
Paris ES 500/K-4
401 N School St 72855 479-963-3143
Sharon Donham, prin. Fax 963-1048
Paris MS 300/5-8
602 N 10th St 72855 479-963-6995
Martha Dodson, prin. Fax 963-8052

St. Joseph S 100/PK-8
25 S Spruce St 72855 479-963-2119
Brad Kent, prin. Fax 963-8039

Paron, Saline
Bryant SD
Supt. — See Bryant
Paron ES K-5
22265 Highway 9 72122 501-594-5622
Jana Starr, prin. Fax 594-5712

Pearcy, Garland
Lake Hamilton SD 4,000/K-12
205 Wolf St 71964 501-767-2306
Steve Anderson, supt. Fax 760-6549
wolves.dsc.k12.ar.us
Lake Hamilton ES 600/2-3
240 Wolf St 71964 501-767-8725
Sharon Barton, prin. Fax 767-8779
Lake Hamilton IS 600/4-5
104 Wolf St 71964 501-767-4111
Steve Davenport, prin. Fax 760-6531
Lake Hamilton MS 600/6-7
120 Wolf St 71964 501-767-3355
Dewayne Curry, prin. Fax 767-4202
Lake Hamilton PS 600/K-1
136 Oakbrook St 71964 501-767-9351
John Smalling, prin. Fax 767-7909

Pea Ridge, Benton, Pop. 3,344
Pea Ridge SD 1,200/K-12
781 W Pickens Rd 72751 479-451-8181
Michael Van Dyke, supt. Fax 451-8235
www.prs.k12.ar.us/
Pea Ridge ES 700/K-5
1536 N Davis St 72751 479-451-8183
Keith Martin, prin. Fax 451-0325
Pea Ridge MS 200/6-8
1391 Weston St 72751 479-451-0620
Sue Terry, prin. Fax 451-0624

Perryville, Perry, Pop. 1,471
Perryville SD 1,100/K-12
614 S Fourche Ave 72126 501-889-2327
Dr. Ron Wilson, supt. Fax 889-5191
mustangs.k12.ar.us/
Perryville ES 500/K-6
625 N Cedar St 72126 501-889-5146
Jeff Magie, prin. Fax 889-2153

Piggott, Clay, Pop. 3,661
Piggott SD 1,000/K-12
PO Box 387 72454 870-598-2572
Ed Winberry, supt. Fax 598-5283
piggotths.k12.ar.us/
Piggott ES 600/K-6
PO Box 387 72454 870-598-2546
Leean Mann, prin. Fax 598-3360

Pine Bluff, Jefferson, Pop. 52,693
Dollarway SD 2,100/PK-12
4900 Dollarway Rd 71602 870-534-7003
Thomas Gathen, supt. Fax 534-7859
dollarway.k12.ar.us
Dollarway MS 500/6-8
2602 W Fluker Ave 71601 870-534-5243
Herbert Harris, prin. Fax 535-1215
Matthews ES 300/PK-1
4501 Dollarway Rd 71602 870-534-0726
Vera Smith, prin. Fax 534-4515
Townsend Park North ES 300/2-3
2601 W Fluker Ave 71601 870-575-0709
Dr. Ernestine Roberts, prin. Fax 575-0712
Townsend Park South ES 200/4-5
2601 W Fluker Ave 71601 870-534-4185
Yolanda Prim, prin. Fax 541-0186
Other Schools – See Altheimer

Pine Bluff SD 4,100/PK-12
PO Box 7678 71611 870-543-4200
Frank Anthony, supt. Fax 543-4208
www.pinebluffschools.k12.ar.us/
Belair MS 200/6-7
1301 Commerce Rd 71601 870-543-4365
Robbie Williams, prin. Fax 850-2003
Broadmoor ES 300/K-5
1106 Wisconsin St 71601 870-543-4368
Clintontine Fitz, prin. Fax 543-4254
Cheney ES 300/K-5
2206 Ridgway Rd 71603 870-543-4382
Suzette Anderson, prin. Fax 535-8689
Forrest Park Preschool 50/PK-PK
1903 W 34th Ave 71603 870-543-4370
Georgia Sanders, prin. Fax 850-2021
Greenville ES 200/K-5
2501 W 10th Ave 71603 870-543-4378
Clementine Bass, prin. Fax 543-4377
Oak Park ES 300/K-5
3010 S Orange St 71603 870-543-4384
Shirley Washington, prin. Fax 543-4252
Southeast MS 400/6-7
2001 S Ohio St 71601 870-543-4350
Cheryl Hatley, prin. Fax 543-4356
Southwood ES 300/K-5
4200 S Fir St 71603 870-543-4390
Alfred Carroll, prin. Fax 850-2006
Thirty-Fourth Avenue ES 200/K-5
801 E 34th Ave 71601 870-543-4392
Verneice Lowery, prin. Fax 543-4253

Watson Chapel SD 3,300/K-12
4100 Camden Rd 71603 870-879-0220
Danny Hazelwood, supt. Fax 879-0588
watson2.arsc.k12.ar.us
Coleman IS 700/4-6
4600 W 13th Ave 71603 870-879-3697
Rose Martin, prin. Fax 870-3151
Edgewood ES 500/K-1
4100 W 32nd Ave 71603 870-879-1252
Charles Bell, prin. Fax 879-7202
Owen ES 500/2-3
3605 Oakwood Rd 71603 870-879-3741
Tim Taylor, prin. Fax 879-3570

St. Peters S 100/K-6
1515 S State St 71601 870-535-4017
Dr. Carol Beeman, prin. Fax 535-4017
Trinity Episcopal S 100/PK-6
870 W 2nd Ave 71601 870-534-7606
Terry Smith, hdmstr. Fax 534-7674

Plainview, Yell, Pop. 756
Two Rivers SD 1,000/K-12
PO Box 187 72857 479-272-3113
Sherry Holliman, supt. Fax 272-3125
tworivers.k12.ar.us
Plainview-Rover ES 200/K-6
PO Box 190 72857 479-272-3111
Mary Ballard, prin. Fax 272-3125
Other Schools – See Briggsville, Ola

Pleasant Plains, Independence, Pop. 271
Midland SD 500/K-12
PO Box 630 72568 501-345-8844
Dean Stanley, supt. Fax 345-2086
170.211.228.2
Other Schools – See Floral

Pocahontas, Randolph, Pop. 6,765
Pocahontas SD 1,900/K-12
2300 N Park St 72455 870-892-4573
Daryl Blaxton, supt. Fax 892-8857
www.nesc.k12.ar.us/
Spikes ES 500/K-2
1707 Highland Blvd 72455 870-892-4573
L. Shawn Carter, prin. Fax 892-8857
Williams IS 500/3-6
2301 N Park St 72455 870-892-4573
John Chester, prin. Fax 892-8857

St. Pauls S 100/PK-7
311 Cedar St 72455 870-892-5639
Karla Thielemier, prin. Fax 892-1869

Portland, Ashley, Pop. 528
Hamburg SD
Supt. — See Hamburg
Portland ES 200/PK-6
PO Box 8 71663 870-737-4333
Cristy West, prin. Fax 737-4334

Pottsville, Pope, Pop. 1,517
Pottsville SD 1,500/K-12
7000 SR 247 72858 479-968-8101
Larry Dugger, supt. Fax 968-6339
apache.afsc.k12.ar.us
Pottsville ES 500/K-3
87 S B St 72858 479-968-2133
Melissa Cox, prin. Fax 968-7672
Pottsville MS 400/4-6
6926 SR 247 72858 479-890-6631
Houston Townsend, prin. Fax 968-6446

Poyen, Grant, Pop. 281
Poyen SD 600/K-12
PO Box 209 72128 501-332-8884
Jerry Newton, supt. Fax 332-8886
www.poyenschool.com/
Poyen ES 300/K-6
PO Box 209 72128 501-332-2939
Tina Elliott, prin. Fax 332-7800

Prairie Grove, Washington, Pop. 2,996
Prairie Grove SD 1,700/K-12
110 School St 72753 479-846-4213
Dr. Randy Willison, supt. Fax 846-2015
tiger.nwsc.k12.ar.us
Prairie Grove IS 300/3-4
801 Viney Grove Rd 72753 479-846-4211
Jonathan Warren, prin. Fax 846-4206
Prairie Grove MS 500/5-8
807 Catlett St 72753 479-846-4221
Reba Holmes, prin. Fax 846-4275
Prairie Grove PS 400/K-2
300 Ed Staggs Dr 72753 479-846-4210
Brenda Clark, prin. Fax 846-4205

Prescott, Nevada, Pop. 4,285
Prescott SD 1,100/K-12
762 Martin St 71857 870-887-3016
Hyacinth Deon, supt. Fax 887-5021
www.prescott.k12.ar.us/
McRae MS 300/5-8
1030 E 5th St N 71857 870-887-2521
Kathie Janes, prin. Fax 887-3717
Prescott ES 400/K-4
335 School St 71857 870-887-2514
Janet Gordan, prin. Fax 887-3398

Quitman, Cleburne, Pop. 741
Quitman SD 600/K-12
PO Box 178 72131 501-589-3156
Larry Freeman, supt. Fax 589-3156
www.quitman.k12.ar.us/
Quitman ES 300/K-6
PO Box 178 72131 501-589-2807
Mary Davis, prin. Fax 589-2807

Ravenden Springs, Randolph, Pop. 137
Twin Rivers SD 400/K-12
5749 Oak Ridge Rd 72460 870-869-2479
David Gilliland, supt.
willifordschool.tripod.com/williford.html
Oak Ridge Central ES 100/K-6
5749 Oak Ridge Rd 72460 870-869-2479
Don Hamilton, prin. Fax 869-3067
Other Schools – See Williford

Rector, Clay, Pop. 1,856
Rector SD 600/K-12
PO Box 367 72461 870-595-3151
Robert Louder, supt. Fax 595-9067
www.piggott.net
Rector ES 300/K-6
PO Box 367 72461 870-595-3358
Johnny Fowler, prin. Fax 595-9067

Redfield, Jefferson, Pop. 1,173
White Hall SD
Supt. — See White Hall
Hardin ES 300/K-6
PO Box 250 72132 501-397-2450
Dan Mincy, prin. Fax 397-5037

Rison, Cleveland, Pop. 1,340
Cleveland County SD 900/K-12
PO Box 600 71665 870-325-6344
Johnnie Johnson, supt. Fax 325-7094
www.risonschools.org
Rison ES 300/K-6
PO Box 600 71665 870-325-6894
Ronald Sims, prin. Fax 325-7094
Other Schools – See Kingsland

Woodlawn SD 600/K-12
6760 Highway 63 71665 870-357-8108
Billy Williams, supt. Fax 357-8718
bears.k12.ar.us
Woodlawn ES 300/K-6
6760 Highway 63 71665 870-357-2211
Genell Davis, prin. Fax 357-2180

Rogers, Benton, Pop. 48,353
Rogers SD 10,400/K-12
500 W Walnut St 72756 479-636-3910
Dr. Janie Darr, supt. Fax 631-3504
www.rogers.k12.ar.us
Bellview ES 500/K-5
5400 Bellview Rd 72758 479-631-3605
Dr. Louise Standridge, prin. Fax 631-3584
Eastside ES 500/K-5
505 E New Hope Rd 72758 479-631-3630
Robin Wilkerson, prin. Fax 531-3632
Elmwood MS 600/6-8
1610 S 13th St 72758 479-631-3600
Bob White, prin. Fax 631-3603
Grace Hill ES 500/K-5
901 N Dixieland Rd 72756 479-631-3670
Jennie Rehl, prin. Fax 631-3672
Grimes ES 500/K-5
1801 S 13th St 72758 479-631-3660
Debra Lewis, prin. Fax 631-3661
Jones ES 500/K-5
2929 S 1st St 72758 479-631-3535
Pam Camper, prin. Fax 631-3533
Kirksey MS 900/6-8
2930 S 1st St 72758 479-631-3625
Dr. Roger Hill, prin. Fax 631-3624
Lingle MS 800/6-8
901 N 13th St 72756 479-631-3590
Mary Elmore, prin. Fax 631-3594
Mathias ES 500/K-5
1609 N 24th St 72756 479-631-3530
Tracey Montgomery, prin. Fax 631-3532
Northside ES 400/K-5
807 N 6th St 72756 479-631-3650
Dr. Yvette Williams, prin. Fax 631-3651
Oakdale MS 500/6-8
511 N Dixieland Rd 72756 479-631-3615
James Goodwin, prin. Fax 631-3617
Old Wire ES K-5
3001 S Old Wire Rd 72758 479-631-3510
Shana Maxey, prin. Fax 631-3512
Reagan ES 500/K-5
3904 W Olive St 72756 479-631-3680
Cathy Ramsey, prin. Fax 631-3682
Tillery ES 500/K-5
211 S 7th St 72756 479-631-3520
Johnnie Wilbanks, prin. Fax 631-3522
Westside ES 500/K-5
2200 W Oak St 72758 479-631-3640
Nancy Swearingen, prin. Fax 631-3642
Other Schools – See Garfield, Lowell

First Baptist Christian S 200/PK-6
626 W Olive St 72756 479-631-6390
Mitzi Bardrick, prin. Fax 621-8665
St. Vincent De Paul S 400/PK-8
1315 W Cypress St 72758 479-636-4421
Ann Morrison, prin. Fax 636-5812

Rose Bud, White, Pop. 448
Rose Bud SD 800/K-12
124 School Rd 72137 501-556-5815
Curtis Spann, supt. Fax 556-6000
rbsd.k12.ar.us
Rose Bud ES 400/K-6
124 School Rd 72137 501-556-5152
Leasha Hayes, prin. Fax 556-6001

Rosston, Nevada, Pop. 223
Nevada SD 400/K-12
PO Box 50 71858 870-871-2418
Rick McAfee, supt. Fax 871-2419
www.nevadaschooldistrict.net/
Nevada ES 200/K-6
PO Box 50 71858 870-871-2475
Mary Beth Cross, prin. Fax 871-2419

Russellville, Pope, Pop. 25,520
Russellville SD 5,000/K-12
PO Box 928 72811 479-968-1306
Randall Williams, supt. Fax 968-6381
rsdweb.k12.ar.us/
Center Valley ES 400/K-4
5401 SR 124 72802 479-968-4540
Brenda Tash, prin. Fax 968-4603
Crawford ES 400/K-4
1116 Parker Rd 72801 479-968-4677
Mark Gotcher, prin. Fax 890-4910
Dwight ES 200/K-4
1300 W 2nd Pl 72801 479-968-3967
Paula Gallagher, prin. Fax 890-4958
Oakland Heights ES 400/K-4
1501 S Detroit Ave 72801 479-968-2084
Sheri Shirley, prin. Fax 890-5956
Russellville MS 800/6-7
1203 W 4th Pl 72801 479-968-2557
Al Harpenau, prin. Fax 967-5574
Russellville Upper ES 400/5-5
1201 W 4th Pl 72801 479-968-2650
Cathy Koch, prin. Fax 967-5538
Sequoyah ES 400/K-4
1601 W 12th St 72801 479-968-2134
Don Dodson, prin. Fax 968-7973
Other Schools – See London

St. Johns S 100/K-5
1912 W Main St 72801 479-967-4644
Theresa Kolbs, prin. Fax 967-6215

Saint Joe, Searcy, Pop. 83
Ozark Mountain SD 700/K-12
250 S Highway 65 72675 870-439-2213
Dr. Delena Gammill, supt. Fax 439-2604
www.omsd.k12.ar.us
Saint Joe ES 100/K-6
250 S Highway 65 72675 870-439-2213
Cassie Gilley, prin. Fax 439-2604
Other Schools – See Everton, Western Grove

Saint Paul, Madison, Pop. 162
Huntsville SD
Supt. — See Huntsville
Saint Paul ES K-6
PO Box 125 72760 479-677-2711
David Borg, prin. Fax 677-3369

Salem, Fulton, Pop. 1,587
Salem SD 800/K-12
313 Highway 62 E Ste 1 72576 870-895-2516
Ken Rich, supt. Fax 895-4062
salem.k12.ar.us/
Salem ES 400/K-6
313 Highway 62 E Ste 4 72576 870-895-2456
David Turnbough, prin. Fax 895-4062

Saratoga, Howard, Pop. 200
Mineral Springs SD
Supt. — See Mineral Springs
Saratoga ES PK-6
PO Box 90 71859 870-388-9262
Joe Ann Harris, prin. Fax 388-9205

Scott, Pulaski
Pulaski County Special SD
Supt. — See Little Rock
Scott ES 200/PK-5
15306 Alexander Rd 72142 501-961-3300
Denise Rankin, prin. Fax 961-3307

Scranton, Logan, Pop. 263
Scranton SD 400/K-12
103 N 10th St 72863 479-938-7121
Larry Garland, supt. Fax 938-7564
www.rocketnet.k12.ar.us
Scranton ES 200/K-6
103 N 10th St 72863 479-938-7278
Gary Rhinehart, prin. Fax 938-7564

Searcy, White, Pop. 20,663
Riverview SD 1,100/K-12
800 Raider Dr 72143 501-279-0540
Howard Morris, supt. Fax 279-0737
riverview.k12.ar.us
Other Schools – See Judsonia, Kensett

Searcy SD 3,800/K-12
801 N Elm St 72143 501-268-3517
James Wood, supt. Fax 278-2220
www.searcyschools.org/
Ahlf JHS 600/7-8
308 W Vine Ave 72143 501-268-3158
Steve Garrison, prin. Fax 278-2212
Deener ES 400/K-4
163 Cloverdale Blvd 72143 501-268-3850
Richard Denney, prin. Fax 278-2232
McRae ES 500/K-4
609 W McRae Ave 72143 501-268-3936
Jim Gurchiek, prin. Fax 278-2283
Southwest MS 600/5-6
1000 W Beebe Capps Expy 72143 501-268-3125
Dr. Florence LePore, prin. Fax 278-2263
Westside ES 600/K-4
512 Country Club Rd 72143 501-268-0111
Doug Langston, prin. Fax 278-2292

Harding Academy 600/K-12
PO Box 10775 72149 501-279-7200
Mark Benton M.Ed., hdmstr. Fax 279-7213
Liberty Christian S 100/K-8
1202 Benton St 72143 501-268-4848
Hilary Polston, prin. Fax 268-1744

Sheridan, Grant, Pop. 4,349
Sheridan SD 3,900/K-12
400 N Rock St 72150 870-942-3135
Brenda Haynes, supt. Fax 942-2931
www.sheridanschools.org/
Sheridan ES 600/K-2
707 Ridge Dr 72150 870-942-3131
David Holmes, prin. Fax 942-7477
Sheridan IS 600/3-5
708 Ridge Dr 72150 870-942-7488
Joseph Judith, prin. Fax 942-3190
Sheridan MS 900/6-8
500 N Rock St 72150 870-942-3813
Peggy West, prin. Fax 942-3034
Other Schools – See Little Rock

Sherwood, Pulaski, Pop. 23,149
Pulaski County Special SD
Supt. — See Little Rock
Clinton Interdistrict Magnet ES 700/PK-5
142 Hollywood Ave 72120 501-833-1200
Jackye Parker, prin. Fax 833-1210
Oakbrooke ES 500/PK-5
2200 Thornhill Dr 72120 501-833-1190
Marilyn Conley, prin. Fax 833-1198
Sherwood ES 400/PK-5
307 Verona Ave 72120 501-833-1150
Josie Brazil, prin. Fax 833-1155
Sylvan Hills ES 400/PK-5
402 Dee Jay Hudson Dr 72120 501-833-1140
Lou Jackson, prin. Fax 833-1149
Sylvan Hills MS 700/6-8
401 Dee Jay Hudson Dr 72120 501-833-1120
Cherrie Walker, prin. Fax 833-1137

Abundant Life S 400/PK-12
9200 Highway 107 72120 501-835-3120
Dr. Russell Eudy, supt. Fax 835-4428

Shirley, Van Buren, Pop. 342
Shirley SD 500/K-12
201 Blue Devil Dr 72153 501-723-8191
Jack Robinson, supt. Fax 723-4020
shirley.k12.ar.us/
Shirley ES 300/K-6
1302 Highway 9 E 72153 501-723-8193
Cindy Coleman, prin. Fax 723-8422

Siloam Springs, Benton, Pop. 13,604
Siloam Springs SD 3,100/PK-12
PO Box 798 72761 479-524-3191
Kendall Ramey, supt. Fax 524-8002
sssd.k12.ar.us/

Allen ES 1-2
1900 N Mount Olive St 72761 479-524-0358
Cindy Covington, prin. Fax 524-0385
Northside K 300/PK-K
501 W Elgin St 72761 479-524-4126
Sheryl Braun, prin. Fax 524-4561
Siloam Springs MS 800/6-8
1500 N Mount Olive St 72761 479-524-6184
Teresa Morgan, prin. Fax 524-3228
Southside ES 900/3-5
200 W Tulsa St 72761 479-524-5146
Dan Siemens, prin. Fax 524-2328

Smackover, Union, Pop. 1,929
Smackover SD 900/K-12
112 E 8th St 71762 870-725-3132
Darrell Porter, supt. Fax 725-2385
smackover.k12.ar.us/
Smackover ES 500/K-6
701 Magnolia 71762 870-725-3601
Dan Henderson, prin. Fax 725-2580

Sparkman, Dallas, Pop. 535
Harmony Grove SD
Supt. — See Camden
Sparkman ES K-6
PO Box 37 71763 870-678-2242
Sherry Carter, prin. Fax 678-2917

Springdale, Washington, Pop. 60,096
Springdale SD 13,200/PK-12
PO Box 8 72765 479-750-8800
Dr. Jim Rollins, supt. Fax 750-8812
www.springdaleschools.org
Bayyari ES 800/K-5
2199 Scottsdale Ave 72764 479-750-8760
Martha Walker, prin. Fax 750-8762
ECC PK-PK
409 N Thompson St 72764 479-750-8889
Darlene McKinney, prin. Fax 750-8799
Elmdale ES 600/K-5
420 N West End St 72764 479-750-8859
Donald Johnson, prin. Fax 750-8861
George ES 700/K-5
2878 Powell St 72764 479-750-8710
Annette Freeman, prin. Fax 750-8810
Harp ES 600/K-5
2700 Butterfield Coach Rd 72764 479-750-8740
Linda Knapp, prin. Fax 750-8742
Hellstern MS 6-7
7771 Har Ber Ave 72762 479-750-8725
Angela Coats, prin. Fax 306-4260
Hunt ES K-5
3511 Silent Grove Rd 72762 479-750-8775
Michelle Doshier, prin. Fax 750-8774
Jones ES 500/K-5
900 Powell St 72764 479-750-8865
Melissa Fink, prin. Fax 750-8867
Kelly MS 900/6-7
1879 E Robinson Ave 72764 479-750-8730
Sara Ford, prin. Fax 750-8733
Lee ES 500/K-5
400 Quandt Ave 72764 479-750-8868
Regina Stewman, prin. Fax 750-8870
Monitor ES K-5
3955 E Monitor Rd 72764 479-750-8749
Maribel Childress, prin. Fax 750-8794
Parson Hills ES 700/K-5
2326 Cardinal Dr 72764 479-750-8877
Dr. Debbie Hardwick-Smith, prin. Fax 756-8262
Shaw ES K-5
4337 Grimsley Rd 72762 479-750-8898
Cynthia Voss, prin. Fax 333-0101
Smith ES 700/K-5
3600 Falcon Rd 72762 479-750-8846
Kim Simco, prin. Fax 750-8716
Turnbow ES K-5
3390 Habberton Rd 72764 479-750-8785
Stacey Ferguson, prin. Fax 750-8728
Tyson ES 500/K-5
1967 Chapman Ave 72762 479-750-8862
Lola Malone, prin. Fax 750-8864
Tyson MS 600/6-7
3304 S 40th St 72762 479-750-8720
Susan Buchanan, prin. Fax 750-8724
Walker ES 600/K-5
1701 S 40th St 72762 479-750-8874
Dondi Frisinger, prin. Fax 750-8717
Westwood ES 500/K-5
1850 McRay Ave 72762 479-750-8871
Dr. Jerry Rogers, prin. Fax 750-8873
Young ES 800/K-5
301 Pippin Apple Cir 72762 479-750-8770
Debbie Flora, prin. Fax 306-2002

Providence Classical Christian Academy 100/K-9
16597 Sandstone 72764 479-263-8861
Heather Russell, prin.
St. Raphael S PK-5
1721 W Sunset Ave 72762 479-756-6711
Karen LaMendola, prin. Fax 756-8818
Salem Lutheran S 200/PK-7
1800 W Emma Ave 72762 479-751-9500
Gerry Kogelman, prin. Fax 750-2028
Shiloh Christian S 700/PK-12
1707 Johnson Rd 72762 479-756-1140
Greg Jones, admin. Fax 756-7107
Springdale Adventist S 50/1-8
4001 W Oaklawn Dr 72762 479-750-4156

Star City, Lincoln, Pop. 2,321
Star City SD 1,800/K-12
206 Cleveland St 71667 870-628-4237
Rhonda Mullikin, supt. Fax 628-4228
www.starcityschools.com
Brown ES 800/K-5
206 Cleveland St 71667 870-628-5111
Hope Robinson, prin. Fax 628-5715
Star City MS 400/6-8
206 Cleveland St 71667 870-628-5125
Susan White, prin. Fax 628-1393

Stephens, Ouachita, Pop. 1,066
Stephens SD 500/K-12
315 W Chert St 71764 870-786-5443
Mark Keith, supt. Fax 786-5095
www.scsc.k12.ar.us/stephens/
Stephens ES 200/K-6
655 Arch St 71764 870-786-5402
Portia Jones, prin. Fax 786-5095

Strawberry, Lawrence, Pop. 275
Hillcrest SD 100/K-12
PO Box 50 72469 870-528-3856
Greg Crabtree, supt. Fax 528-3383
hillcrest.k12.ar.us
Other Schools – See Lynn

Strong, Union, Pop. 637
Strong-Huttig SD 400/K-12
PO Box 735 71765 870-797-7322
Dr. Terry Davis, supt. Fax 797-2257
stronghuttig.k12.ar.us/
Gardner-Strong ES 200/K-5
PO Box 736 71765 870-797-2321
Toni Barnett, prin. Fax 797-7633
Other Schools – See Huttig

Stuttgart, Arkansas, Pop. 9,376
Stuttgart SD 1,500/K-12
2501 S Main St 72160 870-674-1303
Dr. Laura Bednar, supt. Fax 673-7337
www.stuttgartschools.org/
Meekins MS 5-6
2501 S Main St 72160 870-674-1440
Kathy Hopson, prin. Fax 673-7337
Park Avenue ES 600/K-4
2501 S Main St 72160 870-674-1400
Tracy Tucker, prin. Fax 673-7337
Stuttgart JHS 300/7-8
2501 S Main St 72160 870-674-1368
Cedric Hawkins, prin. Fax 673-7337

Grand Prairie Ev. Methodist Christian S 50/K-12
1104 E 21st St 72160 870-673-2087
Thomas Bormann, prin. Fax 673-4718
Holy Rosary S 100/PK-6
920 W 19th St 72160 870-673-3211
Kathy Lorince, prin. Fax 673-3211
St. John Lutheran S 100/PK-6
2019 S Buerkle St 72160 870-673-7096
Lin Gillam, prin. Fax 673-1583

Sulphur Rock, Independence, Pop. 428
Batesville SD
Supt. — See Batesville
Sulphur Rock Magnet ES 200/K-6
480 N Main St 72579 870-799-3149
Jack Sanders, prin. Fax 799-8099

Swifton, Jackson, Pop. 811
Jackson County SD
Supt. — See Tuckerman
Swifton MS 200/5-7
PO Box 556 72471 870-485-2336
Floyd Parnell, prin. Fax 485-2711

Taylor, Columbia, Pop. 545
Emerson - Taylor SD
Supt. — See Emerson
Taylor ES 200/K-6
506 E Pine St 71861 870-694-5811
Karen McMahen, prin. Fax 694-2901

Texarkana, Miller, Pop. 30,006
Genoa Central SD 1,000/PK-12
12472 Highway 196 71854 870-653-4343
Albert Murphy, supt. Fax 653-2624
dragons1.k12.ar.us/dragons/
Cobb MS 300/5-8
11986 Highway 196 71854 870-653-2132
Deloris Coe, prin. Fax 653-6944
Genoa Central ES 400/PK-4
12018 Highway 196 71854 870-653-2248
Jane Scott, prin. Fax 653-6922

Texarkana Arkansas SD 4,400/K-12
3512 Grand Ave 71854 870-772-3371
Russell Sapaugh, supt. Fax 773-2602
texarkana.ar.schoolwebpages.com/
College Hill Magnet ES 300/K-4
3512 Grand Ave 71854 870-774-9111
Marguerite Hillier, prin. Fax 773-0643
College Hill Magnet MS 600/5-6
3512 Grand Ave 71854 870-772-0281
Carol Miller, prin. Fax 773-0068
Fairview Magnet ES 300/K-4
3512 Grand Ave 71854 870-774-9241
Theresa Cowling, prin. Fax 774-0236
Kilpatrick Magnet ES 500/K-4
3512 Grand Ave 71854 870-774-9691
David Walls, prin. Fax 772-4386
North Heights Magnet JHS 600/7-8
3512 Grand Ave 71854 870-773-1091
Gwen Adams, prin. Fax 772-2722
Trice Magnet ES 500/K-4
3512 Grand Ave 71854 870-772-8431
Jan Harris, prin. Fax 773-1492
Union Magnet ES 300/K-4
3512 Grand Ave 71854 870-772-7341
Thelma Forte, prin. Fax 772-8017

Trinity Christian S 300/PK-12
3107 Trinity Blvd 71854 870-779-1009
Ron Fellers, admin. Fax 772-1258

Tillar, Desha, Pop. 226

Cornerstone Christian Academy 200/K-12
PO Box 129 71670 870-392-2482
Monica Daniels, hdmstr. Fax 392-2328

Timbo, Stone
Mountain View SD
Supt. — See Mountain View
Timbo S K-12
PO Box 6 72680 870-746-4303
Sue Linn, prin. Fax 746-4844

Trumann, Poinsett, Pop. 6,922
Trumann SD 1,700/K-12
221 N Pine Ave 72472 870-483-6444
Ronald Waleszonia, supt. Fax 483-2602
wildcat.crsc.k12.ar.us/
Cedar Park ES 600/K-4
1200 Cedar St 72472 870-483-5314
Cynthia Wright, prin. Fax 483-6700
Other Schools – See Harrisburg

Tuckerman, Jackson, Pop. 1,721
Jackson County SD 900/K-12
PO Box 1070 72473 870-349-2232
Chester Shannon, supt. Fax 349-2355
Tuckerman ES 300/K-4
PO Box 1070 72473 870-349-2312
Pharis Smith, prin. Fax 349-2355
Other Schools – See Swifton

Turrell, Crittenden, Pop. 912
Turrell SD 400/K-12
PO Box 369 72384 870-343-2533
Alfred Hogan, supt. Fax 343-2823
turrell.k12.ar.us
Turrell ES 200/K-6
PO Box 369 72384 870-343-2688
Sylvia Moore, prin. Fax 343-2901

Tyronza, Poinsett, Pop. 890
East Poinsett County SD
Supt. — See Lepanto
Tyronza ES 200/K-6
412 S Main St 72386 870-487-2259
Lisa Tennyson, prin. Fax 487-2823

Umpire, Howard
Wickes SD
Supt. — See Wickes
Umpire S K-12
PO Box 60 71971 870-583-2141
DeWayne Taylor, prin. Fax 583-6264

Valley Springs, Boone, Pop. 173
Valley Springs SD 1,000/K-12
PO Box 640 72682 870-429-8100
Charles Trammell, supt. Fax 429-5551
valley.k12.ar.us
Valley Springs ES 400/K-4
PO Box 640 72682 870-429-8100
Beverly Frizzell, prin. Fax 429-5249
Valley Springs MS 300/5-8
PO Box 640 72682 870-429-8100
Rick Still, prin. Fax 429-8121

Van Buren, Crawford, Pop. 21,249
Van Buren SD 5,800/K-12
2221 E Pointer Trl 72956 479-474-7942
Dr. Merle Dickerson, supt. Fax 471-3146
www.vbsd.us
Central MS 400/5-6
913 N 24th St 72956 479-474-7059
Eddie Tipton, prin. Fax 471-3159
City Heights ES 300/K-4
301 Mount Vista Blvd 72956 479-474-6918
Mary McCutchen, prin. Fax 471-3139
Izard ES 400/K-4
501 N 24th St 72956 479-474-3150
Lonnie Mitchell, prin. Fax 471-3153
King ES 300/K-4
401 N 19th St 72956 479-474-2661
Martha Ragar, prin. Fax 471-3185
Northridge MS 500/5-6
120 Northridge Dr 72956 479-471-3126
Renee Risley, prin. Fax 471-3129
Parkview ES 400/K-4
605 Parkview St 72956 479-474-8730
Stacie Wood, prin. Fax 471-3149
Rena ES 500/K-4
720 Rena Rd 72956 479-471-3190
Joyce Sanders, prin. Fax 471-3193
Tate ES 400/K-4
406 Catcher Rd 72956 479-471-3130
Karen Allen, prin. Fax 471-3134

Vandervoort, Polk, Pop. 119
Van Cove SD
Supt. — See Cove
Van Cove ES 200/K-6
122 E Adair 71972 870-387-6923
Arlene Kesterson, prin. Fax 387-7468

Vanndale, Cross
Cross County SD 7
Supt. — See Cherry Valley
Cross County PS 100/K-3
PO Box 170 72387 870-238-8521
Melvin Bowles, prin. Fax 238-0188

Vilonia, Faulkner, Pop. 2,719
Vilonia SD 2,800/K-12
PO Box 160 72173 501-796-2113
Dr. Frank Mitchell, supt. Fax 796-3134
vilonia.k12.ar.us
Vilonia ES 600/K-4
PO Box 160 72173 501-796-2112
Julie Binam, prin. Fax 796-2445

Vilonia MS 700/5-7
PO Box 160 72173 501-796-2940
Cathy Riggins, prin. Fax 796-4697
Vilonia PS 400/K-4
PO Box 160 72173 501-796-2018
Brian Ratliff, prin. Fax 796-2445

Viola, Fulton, Pop. 394
Viola SD 400/K-12
PO Box 380 72583 870-458-2323
John May, supt. Fax 458-2214
violaschool.k12.ar.us
Viola ES 200/K-6
PO Box 380 72583 870-458-2511
Andy Burden, prin. Fax 458-2214

Waldron, Scott, Pop. 3,555
Waldron SD 1,800/K-12
1560 W 6th St 72958 479-637-3179
James Floyd, supt. Fax 637-3177
waldron.k12.ar.us
Waldron ES 700/K-4
1895 Rice St 72958 479-637-2454
Tammy Goodner, prin. Fax 637-3173
Waldron MS 500/5-8
2075 Rice St 72958 479-637-4549
Steve Rose, prin. Fax 637-3165

Walnut Ridge, Lawrence, Pop. 4,724
Lawrence County SD 1,000/K-12
508 E Free St 72476 870-886-6634
Terry Belcher, supt. Fax 886-6635
wrhsbobcats.nesc.k12.ar.us/
Walnut Ridge ES 400/K-6
508 E Free St 72476 870-886-3482
Kim Keen, prin. Fax 886-7622
Other Schools – See Black Rock

Ward, Lonoke, Pop. 3,271
Cabot SD
Supt. — See Cabot
Ward Central ES 500/K-4
1570 Wilson Loop 72176 501-843-9601
Michele French, prin. Fax 843-9744

Warren, Bradley, Pop. 6,263
Warren SD 1,600/K-12
PO Box 1210 71671 870-226-8500
Andrew Tolbert, supt. Fax 226-8531
se.sesc.k12.ar.us/warren/
Brunson ES 200/4-5
PO Box 1210 71671 870-226-2351
Maxwell Williams, prin. Fax 226-8541
Eastside PS 500/K-3
PO Box 1210 71671 870-226-6761
Marilyn Johnson, prin. Fax 226-8538
Warren MS 400/6-8
PO Box 1210 71671 870-226-2484
Glenetta Burks, prin. Fax 226-8511

Weiner, Poinsett, Pop. 755
Weiner SD 400/K-12
313 N Garfield St 72479 870-684-2253
Chuck Hanson, supt. Fax 684-7574
cardinal.k12.ar.us/
Weiner ES 200/K-6
313 N Garfield St 72479 870-684-2252
Cindy Armstrong, prin. Fax 684-2684

Western Grove, Newton, Pop. 404
Ozark Mountain SD
Supt. — See Saint Joe
Western Grove ES 100/K-6
300 School St 72685 870-429-5215
Steve Williams, prin. Fax 429-5276

West Fork, Washington, Pop. 2,195
West Fork SD 1,200/K-12
359 School Ave 72774 479-839-2231
Diane Barrett, supt. Fax 839-8412
www.westforktigers.k12.ar.us
West Fork ES 500/K-4
359 School Ave 72774 479-839-2236
Pat Thaler, prin. Fax 839-8412

West Fork MS 400/5-8
359 School Ave 72774 479-839-3342
David Skelton, prin. Fax 839-8412

West Helena, Phillips, Pop. 7,876
Helena/West Helena SD
Supt. — See Helena
Beech Crest ES 500/1-6
1020 Plaza 72390 870-572-4526
Joyce Stevenson, prin. Fax 572-4528
Miller JHS 500/7-8
106 Miller Loop 72390 870-572-3705
Adrian Watkins, prin. Fax 572-4525
West Side ES 400/1-6
339 S Ashlar 72390 870-572-3422
Donna Ross, prin. Fax 572-4530
Woodruff K 300/K-K
805 Cleburne Ave 72390 870-572-4500
Elnora Mitchell, prin. Fax 572-4501

De Soto S 300/K-12
PO Box 2807 72390 870-572-6717
E.G. Morris, hdmstr. Fax 572-9531

West Memphis, Crittenden, Pop. 28,181
Marion SD
Supt. — See Marion
Avondale ES 600/K-1
1402 Crestmere St 72301 870-735-4588
Glenda Bryan, prin. Fax 735-4672

West Memphis SD 6,000/K-12
PO Box 826 72303 870-735-1915
Bill Kessinger, supt. Fax 732-8643
west.grsc.k12.ar.us
Bragg ES 400/K-6
309 W Barton Ave 72301 870-735-4196
Terri McCann, prin. Fax 732-8647
Faulk ES 500/K-6
908 Vanderbilt Ave 72301 870-735-5252
Janice Donald, prin. Fax 732-8563
Jackson ES 400/K-6
2395 SL Henry St 72301 870-735-7303
Annette Frazier, prin. Fax 732-8569
Maddux ES 600/K-6
2100 E Barton Ave 72301 870-735-4242
Sheri Lowe, prin. Fax 732-8603
Richland ES 500/K-6
1011 W Barton Ave 72301 870-735-6443
Gwen Looney, prin. Fax 732-8564
Weaver ES 400/K-6
1280 E Barton Ave 72301 870-735-7670
Shelia Grissom, prin. Fax 732-8612
Wonder ES 500/K-6
801 S 16th St 72301 870-735-4219
Ora Breckinridge, prin. Fax 732-8648
Other Schools – See Edmondson

St. Michaels S 100/PK-6
405 N Missouri St 72301 870-735-1730
Michael Beauregard, prin. Fax 735-3017
West Memphis Christian S 100/K-12
1101 N Missouri St 72301 870-400-4000
Mark Lay, hdmstr. Fax 400-4001

Wheatley, Saint Francis, Pop. 348
Palestine-Wheatley SD
Supt. — See Palestine
Palestine-Wheatley MS 200/5-8
PO Box 109 72392 870-457-2121
James Williams, prin. Fax 457-4840

White Hall, Jefferson, Pop. 5,114
White Hall SD 3,100/K-12
1020 W Holland Ave 71602 870-247-2002
Dr. Larry Smith, supt. Fax 247-3707
www.whitehallsd.org/
Gandy ES 500/K-6
400 Gandy Ave 71602 870-247-4054
Peggy Swob, prin. Fax 247-4059

Moody ES 400/K-6
700 Moody Dr 71602 870-247-4363
Beth Koberlein, prin. Fax 247-4372
Taylor ES 500/K-6
805 West St 71602 870-247-1988
George Connell, prin. Fax 247-2169
Other Schools – See Redfield

Wickes, Polk, Pop. 678
Wickes SD 600/PK-12
130 School Dr 71973 870-385-7101
Allen Blackwell, supt. Fax 385-2238
www.wickes.us
Wickes ES 400/PK-6
130 School Dr 71973 870-385-2346
Netella Cureton, prin. Fax 385-2242
Other Schools – See Umpire

Williford, Sharp, Pop. 65
Twin Rivers SD
Supt. — See Ravenden Springs
Williford ES 100/K-6
423 College Ave 72482 870-966-4331
Paulette Crouthers, prin. Fax 966-4490

Wilmot, Ashley, Pop. 742
Hamburg SD
Supt. — See Hamburg
Wilmot ES 100/PK-6
PO Box 70 71676 870-473-2214
Michelle Dunbar, prin. Fax 473-2215

Wilson, Mississippi, Pop. 854
South Mississippi County SD 1,100/K-12
22 N Jefferson St 72395 870-655-8633
Gary Masters, supt. Fax 655-8841
smchs.crsc.k12.ar.us/
Rivercrest JHS 200/7-8
1702 W State Highway 14 72395 870-655-8421
Mike Smith, prin. Fax 655-9980
South Mississippi ES @ Wilson 200/K-6
1 Lee St 72395 870-655-8621
Dixie Baker, prin. Fax 655-8710
Other Schools – See Keiser, Luxora

Winthrop, Little River, Pop. 182
Horatio SD
Supt. — See Horatio
Winthrop ES 100/PK-6
PO Box 360 71866 870-381-7373
Ferrell Lisenby, prin. Fax 381-7374

Wynne, Cross, Pop. 8,569
Wynne SD 3,000/K-12
PO Box 69 72396 870-238-5000
Dr. Benjamin Perry, supt. Fax 238-5011
wynne.k12.ar.us/
Wynne IS 700/3-5
PO Box 69 72396 870-238-5060
Sandra Hollaway, prin. Fax 238-5062
Wynne JHS 700/6-8
PO Box 69 72396 870-238-5040
David Stepp, prin. Fax 238-5043
Wynne PS 700/K-2
PO Box 69 72396 870-238-5050
Debra Heath, prin. Fax 238-5052

Yellville, Marion, Pop. 1,348
Yellville-Summit SD 900/K-12
1124 N Panther Ave 72687 870-449-4061
Dr. Jack Leatherman, supt. Fax 449-5003
yspanthers.k12.ar.us/
Yellville-Summit ES 300/K-4
1124 N Panther Ave 72687 870-449-4244
Randi Connior, prin. Fax 449-2214
Yellville-Summit MS 300/5-8
1124 N Panther Ave 72687 870-449-6533
Calvin Mallett, prin. Fax 449-4330

CALIFORNIA

CALIFORNIA DEPARTMENT OF EDUCATION
1430 N St, Sacramento 95814-5901
Telephone 916-319-0800
Fax 916-319-0100
Website http://www.cde.ca.gov

Superintendent of Public Instruction Jack O'Connell

CALIFORNIA BOARD OF EDUCATION
1430 N St, Sacramento 95814-5901

President Theodore Mitchell

COUNTY SUPERINTENDENTS OF SCHOOLS

Alameda County Office of Education
Sheila Jordan, supt. 510-887-0152
313 W Winton Ave, Hayward 94544 Fax 670-4146
www.acoe.org

Alpine County Office of Education
James Parsons, supt. 530-694-2230
43 Hawkside Dr Fax 694-2379
Markleeville 96120
www.alpinecoe.k12.ca.us

Amador County Office of Education
Dick Glock, supt. 209-257-5353
217 Rex Ave, Jackson 95642 Fax 257-5360
www.amadorcoe.org/

Butte County Office of Education
Don McNelis, supt. 530-532-5650
1859 Bird St, Oroville 95965 Fax 532-5762
www.bcoe.org/

Calaveras County Office of Education
John Brophy, supt. 209-736-4662
PO Box 760, Angels Camp 95222 Fax 736-2138
www.ccoe.k12.ca.us

Colusa County Office of Education
Kay Spurgeon, supt. 530-458-0350
146 7th St, Colusa 95932 Fax 458-8054
www.ccoe.net/

Contra Costa County Office of Education
Joseph Ovick, supt. 925-942-3388
77 Santa Barbara Rd Fax 472-0875
Pleasant Hill 94523
www.cocoschools.org/

Del Norte County Office of Education
Jan Moorehouse, supt. 707-464-0200
301 W Washington Blvd Fax 464-0238
Crescent City 95531
www.delnorte.k12.ca.us

El Dorado County Office of Education
Vicki Barber, supt. 530-622-7130
6767 Green Valley Rd Fax 621-2543
Placerville 95667
www.edcoe.k12.ca.us

Fresno County Office of Education
Larry Powell, supt. 559-265-3000
1111 Van Ness Ave, Fresno 93721 Fax 265-3053
www.fcoe.k12.ca.us

Glenn County Office of Education
Arturo Barrera, supt. 530-934-6575
311 S Villa Ave, Willows 95988 Fax 934-6576
www.glenncoe.org

Humboldt County Office of Education
Garry Eagles Ph.D., supt. 707-445-7000
901 Myrtle Ave, Eureka 95501 Fax 445-7143
www.humboldt.k12.ca.us

Imperial County Office of Education
John Anderson, supt. 760-312-6464
1398 Sperber Rd, El Centro Fax 312-6565
www.icoe.k12.ca.us

Inyo County Office of Education
Dr. Terence McAteer, supt. 760-878-2426
PO Box G, Independence 93526 Fax 878-2279
www.inyo.k12.ca.us/

Kern County Office of Education
Larry Reider, supt. 661-636-4000
1300 17th St, Bakersfield 93301 Fax 636-4130
www.kern.org/

Kings County Office of Education
John Stankovich, supt. 559-584-1441
1144 W Lacey Blvd, Hanford 93230 Fax 589-7000
www.kings.k12.ca.us

Lake County Office of Education
David Geck, supt. 707-262-4100
1152 S Main St, Lakeport 95453 Fax 263-0197
www.lake-coe.k12.ca.us

Lassen County Office of Education
Jud Jensen, supt. 530-257-2196
472-013 Johnstonville Rd Fax 257-2518
Susanville 96130
www.lassencoe.org

Los Angeles County Office of Education
Darline Robles, supt. 562-922-6111
9300 Imperial Hwy, Downey 90242 Fax 922-6768
www.lacoe.edu

Madera County Office of Education
Sally Frazier Ed.D., supt. 559-673-6051
28123 Avenue 14, Madera 93638 Fax 673-5569
www.maderacoe.k12.ca.us

Marin County Office of Education
Mary Jane Burke, supt. 415-472-4110
PO Box 4925, San Rafael 94913 Fax 491-6625
www.marinschools.org/

Mariposa County Office of Education
Randy Panietz, supt. 209-742-0250
PO Box 8, Mariposa 95338 Fax 966-4549
www.mariposa.k12.ca.us/

Mendocino County Office of Education
Paul Tichinin, supt. 707-467-5000
2240 Old River Rd, Ukiah 95482 Fax 462-0379
www.mcoe.us/

Merced County Office of Education
Lee Andersen, supt. 209-381-6600
632 W 13th St, Merced 95341 Fax 381-6767
www.mcoe.org

Modoc County Office of Education
Gary Jones, supt. 530-233-7100
139 Henderson St, Alturas 96101 Fax 233-5531
www.modoccoe.k12.ca.us/

Mono County Office of Education
Catherine Hiatt, supt. 760-932-7311
PO Box 477, Bridgeport 93517 Fax 932-7278
www.monocoe.k12.ca.us

Monterey County Office of Education
Dr. Nancy Kotowski, supt. 831-755-0300
PO Box 80851, Salinas 93912 Fax 753-7888
www.monterey.k12.ca.us

Napa County Office of Education
Barbara Nemko, supt. 707-253-6800
2121 Imola Ave, Napa 94559 Fax 253-6841
www.ncoe.k12.ca.us

Nevada County Office of Education
Holly Hermansen, supt. 530-478-6400
112 Nevada City Hwy Fax 478-6410
Nevada City 95959
www.nevco.k12.ca.us/

Orange County Office of Education
William Habermehl, supt. 714-966-4000
PO Box 9050, Costa Mesa 92628 Fax 662-3570
www.ocde.us/

Placer County Office of Education
Gayle Garbolino-Mojica, supt. 530-889-8020
360 Nevada St, Auburn 95603 Fax 888-1367
www.placercoe.k12.ca.us

Plumas County Office of Education
Glenn Harris, supt. 530-283-6500
50 Church St, Quincy 95971 Fax 283-6509
www.pcoe.k12.ca.us

Riverside County Office of Education
Kenneth Young, supt. 951-826-6530
PO Box 868, Riverside 92502 Fax 826-6199
www.rcoe.us/

Sacramento County Office of Education
David Gordon, supt. 916-228-2500
PO Box 269003 Fax 228-2403
Sacramento 95826
www.scoe.net

San Benito County Office of Education
Mike Sanchez, supt. 831-637-5393
460 5th St, Hollister 95023 Fax 637-0140
sbcoe.k12.ca.us

San Bernardino Co. Office of Education
Gary Thomas, supt. 909-386-2784
601 N E St, San Bernardino 92410 Fax 386-2941
www.sbcss.k12.ca.us

San Diego County Office of Education
Randolph Ward Ed.D., supt. 858-292-3500
6401 Linda Vista Rd Fax 292-3653
San Diego 92111
www.sdcoe.net/

San Francisco County Office of Education
Carlos Garcia, supt., 555 Franklin St 415-241-6000
San Francisco 94102 Fax 241-6012
www.sfusd.edu

San Joaquin County Office of Education
Frederick Wentworth, supt. 209-468-4800
PO Box 213030, Stockton 95213 Fax 468-4819
www.sjcoe.org

San Luis Obispo Co. Office of Education
Julian Crocker, supt. 805-543-7732
3350 Education Dr Fax 541-1105
San Luis Obispo 93405
www.slocoe.org/

San Mateo County Office of Education
Dr. Jean Holbrook, supt. 650-802-5300
101 Twin Dolphin Dr Fax 802-5564
Redwood City 94065
www.smcoe.k12.ca.us

Santa Barbara County Office of Education
William Cirone, supt. 805-964-4711
PO Box 6307, Santa Barbara 93160 Fax 964-4712
www.sbceo.org

Santa Clara County Office of Education
Dr. Charles Weis, supt. 408-453-6500
1290 Ridder Park Dr Fax 453-6601
San Jose 95131
www.sccoe.org

Santa Cruz County Office of Education
Michael Watkins, supt. 831-476-7140
400 Encinal St, Santa Cruz 95060 Fax 476-5294
www.santacruz.k12.ca.us

Shasta County Office of Education
Tom Armelino, supt. 530-225-0200
1644 Magnolia Ave Fax 225-0329
Redding 96001
www.shastacoe.org/

Sierra County Office of Education
Stan Hardeman, supt. 530-994-1044
PO Box 157, Sierraville 96126 Fax 994-1045
www.sierra-coe.k12.ca.us

Siskiyou County Office of Education
Kermith Walters, dir. 530-842-8400
609 S Gold St, Yreka 96097 Fax 842-8436
www.sisnet.ssku.k12.ca.us

Solano County Office of Education
Dee Alarcon, supt. 707-399-4400
5100 Business Center Dr Fax 863-4175
Fairfield
www.solanocoe.net/

Sonoma County Office of Education
Dr. Carl Wong, supt. 707-524-2600
5340 Skylane Blvd Fax 578-0220
Santa Rosa 95403
www.sonoma.k12.ca.us

Stanislaus County Office of Education
Tom Changnon, supt. 209-525-4900
1100 H St, Modesto 95354 Fax 525-5147
www.stancoe.org/

Sutter County Office of Education
Jeff Holland, supt. 530-822-2900
970 Klamath Ln, Yuba City 95993 Fax 671-3422
www.sutter.k12.ca.us

Tehama County Office of Education
Larry Champion, supt. 530-527-5811
PO Box 689, Red Bluff 96080 Fax 529-4120
www.tcde.tehama.k12.ca.us/

Trinity County Office of Education
James French, supt. 530-623-2861
PO Box 1256, Weaverville 96093 Fax 623-4489
www.tcoek12.org/

Tulare County Office of Education
Jim Vidak, supt. 559-733-6300
PO Box 5091, Visalia 93278 Fax 737-4378
www.tcoe.net/

Tuolumne County Office of Education
Joseph Silva, supt. 209-536-2000
175 Fairview Ln, Sonora 95370 Fax 536-2003
www.tuolcoe.k12.ca.us

Ventura County Office of Education
Stan Mantooth, supt. 805-383-1900
5189 Verdugo Way Fax 383-1908
Camarillo 93012
www.vcoe.org

Yolo County Office of Education
Jorge Ayala, supt. 530-668-6700
1280 Santa Anita Ct Ste 100 Fax 668-3848
Woodland 95776
www.ycoe.org

Yuba County Office of Education
Richard Teagarden, supt. 530-749-4900
935 14th St, Marysville 95901 Fax 741-6500
www.yuba.net/

PUBLIC, PRIVATE AND CATHOLIC ELEMENTARY SCHOOLS

Acampo, San Joaquin
Lodi USD
Supt. — See Lodi
Houston S 400/K-8
4600 E Acampo Rd 95220 209-331-7475
Jann Lyall, prin. Fax 331-7405

Oak View UNESD 400/K-8
7474 E Collier Rd 95220 209-368-0636
Michael Scully, supt. Fax 368-9319
www.edserv.sjcoe.net/oakview
Oak View S 400/K-8
7474 E Collier Rd 95220 209-368-0636
Michael Scully, prin. Fax 368-9319

Lodi Christian S 100/PK-8
PO Box 268 95220 209-368-7627
Nadine Zerbe, prin. Fax 368-7600
Mokelumne River S 200/PK-12
18950 N Highway 99 95220 209-368-7271
Shannon Woodard, supt. Fax 368-7569

Acton, Los Angeles, Pop. 1,471
Acton-Agua Dulce USD 1,900/K-12
32248 Crown Valley Rd 93510 661-269-5999
Dr. Stan Halperin, supt. Fax 269-0849
aadusd.k12.ca.us/
High Desert MS 500/6-8
3620 Antelope Woods Rd 93510 661-269-0310
Gerald Watkins, prin. Fax 269-9336
Meadowlark ES 500/K-5
3015 Sacramento Ave 93510 661-269-8140
Gilbert Yoon, prin. Fax 269-9538
Other Schools – See Agua Dulce

Adelanto, San Bernardino, Pop. 24,360
Adelanto ESD 8,200/K-8
PO Box 70 92301 760-246-8691
Darin Brawley, supt. Fax 246-8259
www.aesd.net
Adelanto ES of Math & Science 600/K-5
17931 Jonathan St 92301 760-246-5892
Jesse Najera, prin. Fax 246-4880
Bradach S 700/K-8
15550 Bellflower St 92301 760-246-5016
Ann Pearson, prin. Fax 246-7896
Columbia MS 1,000/6-8
14409 Aster Rd 92301 760-530-1950
Karen Patterson, prin. Fax 530-1953
Desert Trails ES 700/K-5
14350 Bellflower St 92301 760-246-3800
Robert Foster, prin. Fax 246-6131
Magathan ES 600/K-5
11411 Holly Rd 92301 760-246-8872
Latrice Thomas, prin. Fax 246-7983
Vick ES 700/K-5
10575 Seneca Rd 92301 760-530-1750
Julie Hirst, prin. Fax 530-1761
Westside Park ES 600/K-5
18270 Casaba Rd 92301 760-246-4118
Edward Dardenne-Ankringa, prin. Fax 246-5446
Other Schools – See Victorville

Adin, Modoc
Big Valley JUSD
Supt. — See Bieber
Big Valley PS 100/K-3
PO Box 186 96006 530-299-3271
Rich Rhodes, prin. Fax 299-3493

Agoura, Los Angeles

Heschel Day S West 200/PK-6
27400 Canwood St 91301 818-707-2365
Tami Weiser, hdmstr. Fax 707-9052

Agoura Hills, Los Angeles, Pop. 22,765
Las Virgenes USD
Supt. — See Calabasas
Lindero Canyon MS 1,100/6-8
5844 Larboard Ln 91301 818-889-2134
Ronald Kaiser, prin. Fax 889-9432
Sumac ES 600/K-5
6050 Calmfield Ave 91301 818-991-4940
Carol Martino, prin. Fax 889-6729
Willow ES 500/K-5
29026 Laro Dr 91301 818-889-0677
Jessica Kiernan, prin. Fax 706-0159
Yerba Buena ES 400/K-5
6098 Reyes Adobe Rd 91301 818-889-0040
Brent Noyes, prin. Fax 889-4732

Conejo Jewish Day S 100/K-7
29900 Ladyface Ct 91301 818-879-8255
Rabbi Robbie Tombosky, hdmstr. Fax 879-8259

Agua Dulce, Los Angeles
Acton-Agua Dulce USD
Supt. — See Acton
Agua Dulce ES 300/K-5
11311 Frascati St 91390 661-268-1660
Lonnie Woodley, prin. Fax 268-0209

Aguanga, Riverside
Hemet USD
Supt. — See Hemet
Cottonwood S 300/K-8
44260 Sage Rd 92536 951-767-3870
David Farkas, prin. Fax 767-3877

Ahwahnee, Madera
Bass Lake JUNESD
Supt. — See Oakhurst
Wasuma S 300/K-8
43109 Highway 49 93601 559-642-1585
Nicole White, prin. Fax 642-1594

Alameda, Alameda, Pop. 70,576
Alameda City USD 9,900/PK-12
2200 Central Ave 94501 510-337-7000
Ardella Dailey, supt. Fax 522-6926
www.alameda.k12.ca.us
Bay Farm ES 600/K-6
200 Aughinbaugh Way 94502 510-748-4010
Jane Lee, prin. Fax 865-2194
Bridges ES 500/K-5
351 Jack London Ave 94501 510-748-4006
Jan Goodman, prin. Fax 523-8862
Chipman MS 600/6-8
401 Pacific Ave 94501 510-748-4017
Jud Kempson, prin. Fax 523-5304
Earhart ES 500/K-5
400 Packet Landing Rd 94502 510-748-4003
Joy Dean, prin. Fax 523-5837
Edison ES 400/K-5
2700 Buena Vista Ave 94501 510-748-4002
Marcheta Williams, prin. Fax 523-6131
Franklin ES 300/K-5
1433 San Antonio Ave 94501 510-748-4004
Gail Rossiter, prin. Fax 337-2439
Haight ES 400/K-5
2025 Santa Clara Ave 94501 510-748-4005
Margaret Harris, prin. Fax 523-6178
Lincoln MS 1,000/6-8
1250 Fernside Blvd 94501 510-748-4018
Judith Goodwin, prin. Fax 523-6217
Lum ES 500/K-5
1801 Sandcreek Way 94501 510-748-4009
Katie Lyons, prin. Fax 523-6717
Otis ES 400/K-5
3010 Fillmore St 94501 510-748-4013
Shirley Clem, prin. Fax 523-6880
Paden S 400/K-8
444 Central Ave 94501 510-748-4014
Tom Rust, prin. Fax 865-9427
Washington ES 300/K-5
825 Taylor Ave 94501 510-748-4007
Jesse Ramas, prin. Fax 523-8798
Wood MS 700/6-8
420 Grand St 94501 510-748-4015
Fax 523-8829

Woodstock Child Center PK-PK
190 Singleton Ave 94501 510-748-4001
Carol Barton, dir. Fax 865-9089

Alameda Christian S 100/K-8
2226 Pacific Ave 94501 510-523-1000
Jean Busby, prin. Fax 523-4022
Chinese Christian S 200/K-8
1801 N Loop Rd 94502 510-522-0200
Robin Hom, supt. Fax 522-0204
Rising Star Montessori S 200/PK-5
1421 High St 94501 510-865-4536
Katrina Ross, dir. Fax 865-4538
St. Joseph S 300/K-8
1910 San Antonio Ave 94501 510-522-4457
Monica O'Callaghan, prin. Fax 522-2890
St. Philip Neri S 300/K-8
1335 High St 94501 510-521-0787
Vikki Wojcik, prin. Fax 521-2418

Alamo, Contra Costa, Pop. 12,277
San Ramon Valley USD
Supt. — See Danville
Alamo ES 400/K-5
100 Wilson Rd 94507 925-938-0448
Amy Hink, prin. Fax 938-0454
Rancho Romero ES 600/K-5
180 Hemme Ave 94507 925-552-5675
Hope Fuss, prin. Fax 837-9030
Stone Valley MS 700/6-8
3001 Miranda Ave 94507 925-552-5640
Shaun McElroy, prin. Fax 838-5680

Albany, Alameda, Pop. 15,994
Albany City USD 3,600/K-12
904 Talbot Ave 94706 510-558-3750
Marla Stephenson, supt. Fax 559-6560
www.albany.k12.ca.us
Albany MS 900/6-8
1259 Brighton Ave 94706 510-558-3600
Robin Davis, prin. Fax 559-6547
Cornell ES 500/K-5
920 Talbot Ave 94706 510-558-3700
Wendy Holmes, prin. Fax 559-6516
Marin ES 500/K-5
1001 Santa Fe Ave 94706 510-558-4700
Laura Cardia, prin. Fax 559-6509
Ocean View ES 600/K-5
1000 Jackson St 94706 510-558-4800
Terry Georgeson, prin. Fax 528-6486

Albion, Mendocino
Mendocino USD
Supt. — See Mendocino
Albion ES 50/K-3
30400 Albion Ridge Rd 95410 707-937-2968
Suzanne Jennings, lead tchr. Fax 937-0714

Alhambra, Los Angeles, Pop. 87,410
Alhambra City SD 18,900/K-12
1515 W Mission Rd 91803 626-943-3000
Donna Perez, supt. Fax 943-8050
www.alhambra.k12.ca.us
Baldwin S 1,100/K-8
900 S Almansor St 91801 626-308-2400
Lismer Ramos-Hanacek, prin. Fax 308-2674
Emery Park S 600/K-8
2821 W Commonwealth Ave 91803 626-308-2408
Anna Kuo, prin. Fax 308-3769
Fremont S 800/K-8
2001 Elm St 91803 626-308-2411
Colleen Underwood, prin. Fax 308-2413
Garfield S 700/K-8
110 W Mclean St 91801 626-308-2415
Rachael Nicoll, prin. Fax 308-2418
Granada S 600/K-8
100 S Granada Ave 91801 626-308-2419
Dr. George Jaeger, prin. Fax 308-2421
Marguerita S 700/K-8
1603 S Marguerita Ave 91803 626-308-2423
Phyllis Evans, prin. Fax 308-2425
Northrup S 800/K-8
409 S Atlantic Blvd 91801 626-308-2431
Fax 281-4899
Park S 700/K-8
301 N Marengo Ave 91801 626-308-2435
Amy Rush, prin. Fax 308-2633
Ramona S 1,000/K-8
509 W Norwood Pl 91803 626-308-2439
Barbara Wong, prin. Fax 308-2522
Other Schools – See Monterey Park

All Souls Parish S 200/K-8
29 S Electric Ave 91801 626-282-5695
Anne Regan-Smith, prin. Fax 282-2260
Emmaus Lutheran S 200/PK-8
840 S Almansor St 91801 626-289-3664
Kit Hittinger, prin. Fax 576-0476
Oneonta Montessori S 100/K-6
2221 Poplar Blvd 91801 626-284-0840
Amie Leonida, admin.
St. Therese S 300/PK-8
1106 E Alhambra Rd 91801 626-289-3364
Christina Buckowski, prin. Fax 284-6700
St. Thomas More S 200/PK-8
2510 S Fremont Ave 91803 626-284-5778
Jennifer Schmidt, prin. Fax 284-3303

Aliso Viejo, Orange, Pop. 41,541
Capistrano USD
Supt. — See San Juan Capistrano
Aliso Viejo MS 1,100/6-8
111 Park Ave 92656 949-831-2622
Peggy Swanson, prin. Fax 643-2784
Avila ES 700/K-5
26278 Wood Canyon Dr 92656 949-349-9452
Shawn Lohman, prin. Fax 362-9108
Avila MS 1,200/6-8
26278 Wood Canyon Dr 92656 949-362-0348
Chris Carter, prin. Fax 362-9076
Canyon Vista ES 700/K-5
27800 Oak View Dr 92656 949-234-5941
Don Mahoney, prin. Fax 360-6273
Oak Grove ES 800/K-5
22705 Sanborn 92656 949-360-9001
Margie Lunder, prin. Fax 360-7372
Wood Canyon ES 400/K-5
23431 Knollwood 92656 949-448-0012
Shelley Overstreet, prin. Fax 448-0017

Aliso Viejo Christian S 400/K-8
1 Orion 92656 949-389-0300
Katherine Hutchins, prin. Fax 389-0383
St. Mary's and All Angels S 800/PK-8
7 Pursuit 92656 949-448-9027
John O'Brien, hdmstr. Fax 448-0605

Alpaugh, Tulare
Alpaugh USD 300/K-12
PO Box 9 93201 559-949-8413
Robert Hudson, supt. Fax 949-8173
www.tcoe.org/districts/alpaugh.shtm
Alpaugh ES 200/K-6
PO Box 9 93201 559-949-8413
L. Dan Barajas, prin. Fax 949-8679

Alpine, San Diego, Pop. 9,695
Alpine UNESD 2,200/PK-8
1323 Administration Way 91901 619-445-3236
Greg Ryan, supt. Fax 445-7045
alpineschooldistrict.net/
Alpine ES 500/1-5
1850 Alpine Blvd 91901 619-445-2625
Richard Miller, prin. Fax 445-0484
Boulder Oaks ES 400/1-5
2320 Tavern Rd 91901 619-445-8676
Moana Miller, prin. Fax 445-1420
Creekside Early Learning Center 200/PK-K
8818 Harbison Canyon Rd 91901 619-659-8250
Keith Malcom, prin. Fax 659-8240
MacQueen MS 800/6-8
2001 Tavern Rd 91901 619-445-3245
Katy Andersen, prin. Fax 445-6503
Shadow Hills ES 300/1-5
8770 Harbison Canyon Rd 91901 619-445-2977
Keith Malcom, prin. Fax 445-2157

Day-McKellar Preparatory S 100/K-8
2710 Alpine Blvd 91901 619-519-0317
Cara Day-McKellar, hdmstr.

Alta, Placer
Alta-Dutch Flat UNESD 100/K-8
PO Box 958 95701 530-389-8283
Jim Roberts, supt. Fax 389-2664
www.altadutchflatschool.org/
Alta-Dutch Flat S 100/K-8
PO Box 958 95701 530-389-8283
Pete Keeslar, prin. Fax 389-2664
Other Schools – See Emigrant Gap

Altadena, Los Angeles, Pop. 44,300
Pasadena USD
Supt. — See Pasadena
Altadena ES 400/K-5
743 E Calaveras St 91001 626-798-7878
Greg White, prin. Fax 296-8509

Burbank ES 400/K-5
2046 Allen Ave 91001 626-798-6769
Kelly Lawson, prin. Fax 798-7738
Eliot MS 700/6-8
2184 Lake Ave 91001 626-794-7121
Peter Pannell, prin. Fax 794-7238
Franklin ES 400/K-5
527 Ventura St 91001 626-798-9116
Caroline Bermudez, prin. Fax 791-3421
Jackson ES 400/K-5
593 W Woodbury Rd 91001 626-798-6773
Rose Ingber, prin. Fax 794-5278
Loma Alta ES 300/K-5
3544 Canon Blvd 91001 626-797-1173
Dr. Jennifer Yure, prin. Fax 797-1793

Pasadena Waldorf S 200/PK-8
209 E Mariposa St 91001 626-794-9564
Carolyn Leach, admin. Fax 794-4704
Sahag-Mesrob Christian S 400/PK-12
2501 Maiden Ln 91001 626-798-5020
Shahe Garabedian, prin. Fax 798-0036
St. Elizabeth S 300/K-8
1840 Lake Ave 91001 626-797-7727
Jeanette Cardamone, prin. Fax 797-6541
St. Mark's S 300/PK-6
1050 E Altadena Dr 91001 626-798-8858
Dr. Doreen Oleson, hdmstr. Fax 798-4180

Alta Loma, San Bernardino

Alta Loma ESD 6,900/K-8
9390 Baseline Rd 91701 909-484-5151
Rebecca Lawrence, supt. Fax 484-5155
www.alsd.k12.ca.us
Alta Loma ES 600/K-6
7085 Amethyst Ave 91701 909-484-5000
Lynda Hoppe, prin. Fax 484-5005
Alta Loma JHS 800/7-8
9000 Lemon Ave 91701 909-484-5100
Judith Neiuber, prin. Fax 484-5105
Banyan ES 700/K-6
10900 Mirador Dr 91737 909-484-5080
Ric Dahlin, prin. Fax 484-5085
Carnelian ES 600/K-6
7105 Carnelian St 91701 909-484-5010
Joan Sanders, prin. Fax 484-5015
Deer Canyon ES 700/K-6
10225 Hamilton St 91701 909-484-5030
Susanne Melton, prin. Fax 484-5035
Hermosa ES 600/K-6
10133 Wilson Ave 91737 909-484-5040
Michael Chaix, prin. Fax 484-5045
Jasper ES 600/K-6
6881 Jasper St 91701 909-484-5050
Sue Geddes, prin. Fax 484-5055
Stork ES 800/K-6
5646 Jasper St 91701 909-484-5060
Melinda Early, prin. Fax 484-5065
Victoria Groves ES 600/K-6
10950 Emerson St 91701 909-484-5070
Cindy Hall, prin. Fax 484-5075
Vineyard JHS 1,000/7-8
6440 Mayberry Ave 91737 909-484-5120
Catherine Perry, prin. Fax 484-5125

Etiwanda ESD
Supt. — See Etiwanda
Caryn ES 300/K-5
6290 Sierra Crestview Loop 91737 909-941-9551
Julie Hilberg, prin. Fax 989-3997
Lightfoot ES 700/K-5
6989 Kenyon Way 91701 909-989-6120
Rosann Marlen, prin. Fax 941-0519

Alta Loma Christian S 200/PK-8
9974 19th St 91737 909-989-2804
Lori Johnstone, prin. Fax 466-4579
St. Peter & St. Paul K 100/PK-K
9135 Banyan St 91737 909-987-7908
Patricia Ferrer, prin. Fax 987-6779

Alturas, Modoc, Pop. 2,902

Modoc JUSD 1,000/K-12
906 W 4th St 96101 530-233-7201
Lane Bates, supt. Fax 233-4362
www.modoc.k12.ca.us
Alturas ES 300/K-5
809 W 8th St 96101 530-233-7201
Diane Janssen, prin. Fax 233-7607
Modoc MS 200/6-8
906 W 4th St 96101 530-233-7201
Mike Martin, prin. Fax 233-7503
Other Schools – See Canby, Likely

Alviso, See San Jose

Santa Clara USD
Supt. — See Santa Clara
Mayne ES 500/K-5
5030 N 1st St 95002 408-423-1700
Cori Wilson, prin. Fax 423-1780

American Canyon, Napa, Pop. 15,331

Napa Valley USD
Supt. — See Napa
American Canyon MS 800/6-8
300 Benton Way 94503 707-259-8592
Dan Scudero, prin. Fax 259-8800
Canyon Oaks ES 600/K-5
475 Silver Oak Trl 94503 707-265-2363
Maren Rocca Hunt, prin. Fax 265-2365
Napa Junction ES 300/K-5
300 Napa Junction Rd 94503 707-253-3461
Dee McFarland, prin. Fax 253-6255

Calvary Baptist Christian Academy 100/K-12
117 Theresa Ave 94503 707-642-1143
Rod Burkholder, prin.

Anaheim, Orange, Pop. 331,804

Anaheim CSD 20,700/K-6
1001 S East St 92805 714-517-7500
Jose Banda, supt. Fax 517-8538
www.acsd.k12.ca.us
Barton ES 700/K-6
1926 W Clearbrook Ln 92804 714-517-8900
Nadine Skutnik, prin. Fax 517-9228
Edison ES 1,100/K-6
1526 E Romneya Dr 92805 714-517-8902
Eric Hallman, prin. Fax 517-9229
Franklin ES 900/K-6
521 W Water St 92805 714-517-8905
Maria Villegas, prin. Fax 517-9230
Gauer ES 700/K-6
810 N Gilbert St 92801 714-517-8908
Debbie Schroeder, prin. Fax 517-9232
Guinn ES 900/K-6
1051 S Sunkist St 92806 714-517-8911
Maggie Barry Ed.D., prin. Fax 517-9270
Henry ES 1,100/K-6
1123 W Romneya Dr 92801 714-517-8914
Simone Kovats Ed.D., prin. Fax 517-9233
Jefferson ES 600/1-6
504 E South St 92805 714-517-8917
Tracy Rodriguez, prin. Fax 517-9234
Juarez ES 900/K-6
841 S Sunkist St 92806 714-517-8923
Roberto Baeza, prin. Fax 517-9235
Key ES 700/K-6
2000 W Ball Rd 92804 714-517-8926
Charles Lewis Ed.D., prin. Fax 517-9236
Lincoln ES 800/K-6
1413 E Broadway 92805 714-517-8929
Alejandro Ramirez, prin. Fax 517-9237
Loara ES 700/K-6
1601 W Broadway 92802 714-517-8932
Luis Magdaleno, prin. Fax 517-9238
Madison ES 800/K-6
1510 S Nutwood St 92804 714-517-8935
Dale Hillyer Ed.D., prin. Fax 517-9239
Mann ES 1,000/K-6
600 W La Palma Ave 92801 714-517-8938
Mary Grace Ed.D., prin. Fax 517-9240
Marshall ES 1,000/K-6
2066 W Falmouth Ave 92801 714-517-8941
Aleta Peters-Schinsky Ed.D., prin. Fax 517-9241
Olive Street ES 800/K-6
890 S Olive St 92805 714-517-8920
Cheryl Moore, prin. Fax 517-8779
Orange Grove ES 800/K-6
1000 S Harbor Blvd 92805 714-517-8968
Julianne Hoefer Ph.D., prin. Fax 956-2894
Palm Lane ES 900/K-6
1010 S Harbor Blvd 92805 714-517-8944
Deanna Pelasky, prin. Fax 517-9242
Price ES 700/K-6
1516 W North St 92801 714-517-8947
Leslie Angotti, prin. Fax 517-9243
Revere ES 900/K-6
140 W Guinida Ln 92805 714-517-8950
James Gardner, prin. Fax 517-9244
Roosevelt ES 700/K-6
1600 E Vermont Ave 92805 714-517-8953
Leslie Peregrina, prin. Fax 517-9245
Ross ES 1,100/K-6
535 S Walnut St 92802 714-517-8956
Deanna Glenn Ed.D., prin. Fax 517-9246
Stoddard ES 900/K-6
1841 S Ninth St 92802 714-517-8959
Diane Eatherly, prin. Fax 517-9247
Sunkist ES 1,100/K-6
500 N Sunkist St 92806 714-517-8962
Beatrice Kirkman, prin. Fax 517-9248
Westmont ES 800/1-6
1525 W Westmont Dr 92801 714-517-8965
Dana McClanahan, prin. Fax 517-9189

Anaheim UNHSD 31,900/7-12
501 N Crescent Way 92801 714-999-3511
Joseph Farley Ed.D., supt. Fax 535-1706
www.auhsd.us
Ball JHS 1,400/7-8
1500 W Ball Rd 92802 714-999-3663
Jason Fried Ed.D., prin. Fax 563-9214
Brookhurst JHS 1,400/7-8
601 N Brookhurst St 92801 714-999-3613
Russell Earnest, prin. Fax 999-1764
Dale JHS 1,500/7-8
900 S Dale Ave 92804 714-220-4210
Kirsten Levitin, prin. Fax 220-4076
Orangeview JHS 1,200/7-8
3715 W Orange Ave 92804 714-220-4205
Kevin Astor Ed.D., prin. Fax 220-3023
South JHS 1,700/7-8
2320 E South St 92806 714-999-3667
Christian Esperanza, prin. Fax 999-3721
Sycamore JHS 1,900/7-8
1801 E Sycamore St 92805 714-999-3616
Manuel Colon, prin. Fax 776-3879
Other Schools – See Cypress, La Palma

Centralia ESD
Supt. — See Buena Park
Centralia ES 600/K-6
195 N Western Ave 92801 714-228-3210
Diana Bianco, prin. Fax 228-3213
Danbrook ES 800/K-6
320 S Danbrook Dr 92804 714-228-3230
Sara Pelly, prin. Fax 821-0328

Magnolia ESD 6,500/K-6
2705 W Orange Ave 92804 714-761-5533
Ellen Curtin Ed.D., supt. Fax 761-2771
www.msd.k12.ca.us/
Baden-Powell ES 700/K-6
2911 W Stonybrook Dr 92804 714-761-5442
Susan Smith, prin. Fax 952-3675
Disney ES 700/K-6
2323 W Orange Ave 92804 714-535-1183
Steve Pescatti, prin. Fax 635-7925
Low ES 700/K-6
215 N Ventura St 92801 714-533-2673
Debra VonSprecken, prin. Fax 533-6099
Marshall ES 600/K-6
2627 W Crescent Ave 92801 714-527-8821
Dawn Breese, prin. Fax 229-0310
Maxwell ES 800/K-6
2613 W Orange Ave 92804 714-527-2217
William Bailey, prin. Fax 229-0439
Salk ES 900/K-6
1411 S Gilbert St 92804 714-527-5143
Wendy LaDue, prin. Fax 229-5836
Schweitzer ES 700/K-6
229 S Dale Ave 92804 714-527-7761
Gregory Merwin, prin. Fax 229-5839
Walter ES 600/K-6
10802 Rustic Ln 92804 714-761-5997
Elizabeth Nordyke, prin. Fax 229-5845
Other Schools – See Stanton

Orange USD
Supt. — See Orange
Anaheim Hills ES 500/K-6
6450 E Serrano Ave 92807 714-997-6169
Sandra Miller, prin. Fax 921-0584
Canyon Rim ES 600/K-6
1090 S The Highlands 92808 714-532-7027
David Appling, prin. Fax 281-0418
Crescent IS 400/4-6
5001 E Gerda Dr 92807 714-997-6371
Randi Leach, prin. Fax 997-6260
Crescent PS 300/K-3
5125 E Gerda Dr 92807 714-997-6105
Randi Leach, prin. Fax 921-9096
Imperial ES 400/K-6
400 S Imperial Hwy 92807 714-997-6282
Tim Biland, prin. Fax 921-9098
Nohl Canyon ES 500/K-6
4100 E Nohl Ranch Rd 92807 714-997-6203
Dominique Polchow, prin. Fax 637-2946
Riverdale ES 300/K-6
4540 E Riverdale Ave 92807 714-997-6273
Sheila Thompson, prin. Fax 637-3728
Running Springs ES 800/K-6
8670 E Running Springs Dr 92808 714-281-4512
Lydia Roach, prin. Fax 281-5048

Placentia-Yorba Linda USD
Supt. — See Placentia
Glenview ES 600/K-6
1775 N Glenview Ave 92807 714-986-7150
Charles Hunter, prin. Fax 779-2633
Rio Vista ES 900/K-5
310 N Rio Vista St 92806 714-630-7680
Fax 666-0310
Woodsboro ES 600/K-6
7575 E Woodsboro Ave 92807 714-986-7040
Phil Hergenreder, prin. Fax 970-6597

Savanna ESD 2,400/K-6
1330 S Knott Ave 92804 714-236-3800
Sue Johnson, supt. Fax 827-6167
www.savsd.k12.ca.us/schools.htm
Cerritos ES 500/K-6
3731 W Cerritos Ave 92804 714-236-3830
Jerry Friedman, prin.
Hansen ES, 1300 S Knott Ave 92804 700/K-6
Greg Blanco, prin. 714-236-3835
Reid ES, 720 S Western Ave 92804 700/K-6
Bob Pipes, prin. 714-236-3845
Other Schools – See Buena Park

Acaciawood S 100/1-12
2530 W La Palma Ave 92801 714-995-1800
Michio Miyake, prin.
Calvary Baptist Church Preschool & K 50/PK-K
2780 E Wagner Ave 92806 714-630-6670
Debbie Byars, admin. Fax 630-0724
Calvary Chapel Anaheim S 200/PK-8
270 E Palais Rd 92805 714-563-9620
James Bove, prin. Fax 563-9520
Fairmont Private S 200/PK-K
121 S Citron St 92805 714-533-3930
Rae Douglas, dir.
Fairmont Private S 400/1-6
1557 W Mable St 92802 714-563-4050
Carole Calabria, dir. Fax 774-8312
Fairmont Private S 600/PK-8
5310 E La Palma Ave 92807 714-693-3812
Barry Drake, dir. Fax 693-5078
Hephatha Lutheran S 400/PK-8
5900 E Santa Ana Canyon Rd 92807 714-637-0887
Kim Voelker, prin. Fax 637-0872
Hillsborough S 100/K-8
191 S Old Springs Rd 92808 714-998-9030
Linda Adamson, dir. Fax 998-0177
Integrity Christian S 100/K-12
4905 E La Palma Ave 92807 714-693-2022
Shelly Kitada, admin.
Orange County Christian S 400/PK-12
641 S Western Ave 92804 714-821-6227
Elaine Findley, prin. Fax 952-8823
Prince of Peace Lutheran S 100/PK-8
1421 W Ball Rd 92802 714-774-0993
Rev. James Brubaker, prin. Fax 774-0183
St. Catherines Military Academy 100/K-8
215 N Harbor Blvd 92805 714-772-1363
Sr. Johnellen Turner, prin. Fax 772-3004
St. Justin Martyr S 200/K-8
2030 W Ball Rd 92804 714-772-4902
Jan Balsis, prin. Fax 772-2092
Saints of Glory S 50/K-12
1210 W Park Ave 92801 714-875-9387
Ichiro Tsuruoka, prin. Fax 817-0612

Trinity Lutheran Christian S 300/PK-8
4101 E Nohl Ranch Rd 92807 714-637-8370
Nancy Gill, admin. Fax 637-6534
Victory Christian S 100/PK-6
227 N Magnolia Ave 92801 714-220-6726
Valerie Birge, prin. Fax 220-6733
Vineyard Christian S 400/PK-12
5340 E La Palma Ave 92807 714-777-5462
Jim Wilkinson, prin. Fax 777-5422
Zion Lutheran S 200/PK-8
1244 E Cypress St 92805 714-535-3600
Julie Kangas, prin. Fax 254-7013

Anderson, Shasta, Pop. 10,528
Cascade UNESD 1,400/K-8
1645 Mill St 96007 530-378-7000
Dr. Wesley Smith, supt. Fax 378-7001
www.shastalink.k12.ca.us/cascade/
Anderson Heights ES 300/K-5
1530 Spruce St 96007 530-378-7050
Jim Evans, prin. Fax 378-7051
Anderson MS 500/6-8
1646 Ferry St 96007 530-378-7060
Carol Koppes, prin. Fax 378-7061
Meadow Lane ES 500/K-5
2770 Balls Ferry Rd 96007 530-378-7030
Brad Clagg, prin. Fax 378-7031
Verde Vale ES 200/K-5
19415 Jacqueline St 96007 530-378-7040
Genavra Williamson, prin. Fax 378-6607

Happy Valley UNESD 600/K-8
16300 Cloverdale Rd 96007 530-357-2134
Lawrence Robins, supt. Fax 357-4143
www.shastalink.k12.ca.us/happyvalley/
Happy Valley MS 300/5-8
17480 Palm Ave 96007 530-357-2111
Janet Tufts, prin. Fax 357-4193
Happy Valley PS 300/K-4
16300 Cloverdale Rd 96007 530-357-2131
Kellie Dunham, prin. Fax 357-2138

Pacheco UNESD 700/K-8
20981 Dersch Rd 96007 530-365-3335
Deidra Hoffman, supt. Fax 365-3399
www.pacheco.k12.ca.us
Prairie ES 300/K-3
20981 Dersch Rd 96007 530-365-1801
Deidra Hoffman, prin. Fax 365-7190
Other Schools – See Redding

American Christian Academy 100/K-12
PO Box 805 96007 530-365-2950
James Rose, admin. Fax 365-5689
Sacred Heart S 100/PK-8
3167 Saint Stephans Dr 96007 530-365-1429
Larry Butcher, prin. Fax 365-3039

Angels Camp, Calaveras, Pop. 2,997
Mark Twain UNESD 800/K-8
PO Box 1359 95222 209-736-1855
Kathy Northington, supt. Fax 736-6888
www.mtwain.k12.ca.us
Twain S 500/K-8
PO Box 1239 95222 209-736-6533
Karl Keller, prin. Fax 736-6537
Other Schools – See Copperopolis

Christian Family Learning Center 100/K-8
PO Box 880 95222 209-736-1175
Larry Smith, admin. Fax 736-1158

Angwin, Napa, Pop. 3,503
Howell Mountain ESD 100/K-8
525 White Cottage Rd N 94508 707-965-2423
Tom Stubbs, supt. Fax 965-0834
www.hmesd.k12.ca.us
Howell Mountain S 100/K-8
525 White Cottage Rd N 94508 707-965-2423
Tom Stubbs, prin. Fax 965-0834

Pacific Union College S 100/K-8
135 Neilsen Ct 94508 707-965-2459
James Dick Ed.D., prin. Fax 965-2480

Annapolis, Sonoma
Horicon ESD 100/K-8
35555 Annapolis Rd 95412 707-886-5322
Paul Martin Ed.D., supt. Fax 886-5422
Horicon S 100/K-8
35555 Annapolis Rd 95412 707-886-5322
Paul Martin Ed.D., prin. Fax 886-5422

Antelope, Sacramento, Pop. 70
Center JUSD 5,500/K-12
8408 Watt Ave 95843 916-338-6330
Scott Loehr, supt. Fax 338-6411
www.centerusd.k12.ca.us
Dudley ES 700/K-5
8000 Aztec Way 95843 916-338-6470
Lisa Coronado, prin. Fax 338-6472
North Country ES 500/K-5
3901 Little Rock Dr 95843 916-338-6480
Kathleen Lord, prin. Fax 338-6488
Oak Hill ES 800/K-5
3909 N Loop Blvd 95843 916-338-6460
David Grimes, prin. Fax 338-6538
Spinelli ES 400/K-5
3401 Scotland Dr 95843 916-338-6490
Kristen Schmieder, prin. Fax 338-6386
Other Schools – See Roseville

Dry Creek JESD
Supt. — See Roseville
Antelope Crossing MS 1,200/6-8
9200 Palmerson Dr 95843 916-745-2100
Greg O'Meara, prin. Fax 745-2135
Antelope Meadows ES 900/K-5
8343 Palmerson Dr 95843 916-770-8816
Amy Banks, prin. Fax 727-0373
Barrett Ranch ES 400/K-5
7720 Ocean Park Dr 95843 916-770-8839
Sara Wegner, prin. Fax 727-1336
Olive Grove ES 700/K-5
7926 Firestone Way 95843 916-727-7400
Andrew Giannini, prin. Fax 727-7410

Antelope Christian Academy 100/PK-8
4533 Antelope Rd 95843 916-727-1197
Karen Clements, admin. Fax 727-1318

Antioch, Contra Costa, Pop. 100,631
Antioch USD 21,000/K-12
510 G St 94509 925-706-4100
Dr. Deborah Sims, supt. Fax 757-2937
www.antioch.k12.ca.us
Antioch MS 1,000/6-8
1500 D St 94509 925-706-5316
Stephanie Anello, prin. Fax 706-5430
Belshaw ES 700/K-5
2801 Roosevelt Ln 94509 925-706-4140
Bill Bolio, prin. Fax 757-7725
Black Diamond MS 1,100/6-8
4730 Sterling Hill Dr 94531 925-776-5500
Tim Cooper, prin. Fax 779-2600
Dallas Ranch MS 1,300/6-8
1401 Mount Hamilton Dr 94531 925-706-4491
Bob Sanchez, prin. Fax 706-1933
Diablo Vista ES 700/K-5
4791 Prewett Ranch Dr 94531 925-706-5288
Melanie Jones, prin. Fax 754-0589
Dragon ES 700/K-5
4721 Vista Grande Dr 94531 925-776-4760
Didi Del Chiaro, prin. Fax 754-7514
Fremont ES 600/K-5
1413 F St 94509 925-706-4101
Jason Larson, prin. Fax 778-1452
Grant ES 500/K-5
4325 Spaulding St 94531 925-706-5271
Debbie Snyder-Puder, prin. Fax 756-6068
Kimball ES 600/K-5
1310 August Way 94509 925-706-4130
Sylvia Ramirez, prin. Fax 706-4137
London ES 900/K-5
4550 Country Hills Dr 94531 925-706-5400
Debra Lee, prin. Fax 778-7512
Lone Tree ES 800/K-5
1931 Mokelumne Dr 94531 925-706-8733
Wanda Apel, prin. Fax 706-9853
Marsh ES 500/K-5
2304 G St 94509 925-706-4110
Joyce Gibson, prin. Fax 754-8592
Mission ES 700/K-5
1711 Mission Dr 94509 925-706-5210
Sylvia Birdsell, prin. Fax 757-9025
Muir ES 700/K-5
615 Greystone Dr 94509 925-706-4120
David Madrigal, prin. Fax 753-0837
Park MS 1,200/6-8
1 Spartan Way 94509 925-706-5314
Essence Phillips, prin. Fax 706-2376
Sutter ES 600/K-5
3410 Longview Rd 94509 925-706-4146
Sue Tencyck, prin. Fax 754-9438
Turner ES 600/K-5
4207 Delta Fair Blvd 94509 925-706-5200
Guy Rohlfs, prin. Fax 757-2452
Other Schools – See Oakley

Cornerstone Christian S 600/PK-12
1745 E 18th St 94509 925-779-2010
Logan Heyer, admin. Fax 754-0769
Heritage Baptist Academy 100/K-12
5200 Heidorn Ranch Rd 94531 925-778-2234
John Mincy, admin.
Hilltop Christian S 100/K-10
2200 Country Hills Dr 94509 925-778-0214
Monica Greene, prin. Fax 778-7418
Holy Rosary S 600/PK-8
25 E 15th St 94509 925-757-1270
Susana Drummond, prin. Fax 757-9309
Steppingstones Academy 100/K-8
PO Box 3407 94531 925-754-2209
Trina Page, admin. Fax 548-9078

Anza, Riverside
Hemet USD
Supt. — See Hemet
Hamilton S 600/K-8
57550 Mitchell Rd 92539 951-763-1840
Paul Kankowski, prin. Fax 763-1845

Apple Valley, San Bernardino, Pop. 65,156
Apple Valley USD 14,700/K-12
22974 Bear Valley Rd 92308 760-247-8001
Robert Seevers, supt. Fax 247-4103
www.avusd.org
Apple Valley MS 1,000/6-8
12555 Navajo Rd 92308 760-247-7267
Daryl Bell, prin. Fax 247-1226
Desert Knolls ES 600/K-5
18213 Symeron Rd 92307 760-242-3441
Cynthia Breeves, prin. Fax 242-7242
Mariana ES 600/K-5
10601 Manhasset Rd 92308 760-247-7258
Viola Sims, prin. Fax 247-4406
Mojave Mesa ES 600/K-5
15552 Wichita Rd 92307 760-242-5883
Claudia Schmitt, prin. Fax 242-3888
Rancho Verde ES 700/K-5
14334 Pioneer Rd 92307 760-247-2663
Claudia Dimit, prin. Fax 247-4947
Rio Vista ES 700/K-5
13590 Havasu Rd 92308 760-240-0280
Theda Smith, prin. Fax 240-0899
Sandia ES 800/K-5
21331 Sandia Rd 92308 760-240-5125
Pat Shelby, prin. Fax 240-0515
Sitting Bull ES 500/K-5
19355 Sitting Bull Rd 92308 760-247-1481
Donna Colosky, prin. Fax 247-4562
Sitting Bull MS 1,100/6-8
19445 Sitting Bull Rd 92308 760-961-8479
Phyllis Carnahan, prin. Fax 240-8763
Sycamore Rocks ES 500/K-5
23450 South Rd 92307 760-240-3332
Jane Beckman, prin. Fax 240-3440
Vanguard Preparatory S 1,100/K-8
12951 Mesquite Rd 92308 760-961-1066
David Mobley, prin. Fax 961-1069
Vista Campana MS 900/6-8
20700 Thunderbird Rd 92307 760-242-7011
Mark Milton, prin. Fax 242-7005
Yucca Loma ES 700/K-5
21351 Yucca Loma Rd 92307 760-247-2623
Rey Rodriguez, prin. Fax 247-4300

Apple Valley Christian S 200/K-12
22434 Nisqually Rd 92308 760-247-8412
Chris Gillespie, admin. Fax 247-6988
St. Timothy's Preparatory S 100/PK-8
15757 Saint Timothy Rd 92307 760-242-4256
John Walter, admin. Fax 242-2825
Valley Christian S 50/K-12
19923 Bear Valley Rd 92308 760-247-2933
William McMinn, prin. Fax 247-4903

Aptos, Santa Cruz, Pop. 9,061
Pajaro Valley USD
Supt. — See Watsonville
Aptos JHS 700/7-8
1001 Huntington Dr 95003 831-688-3234
Brian Saxton, prin. Fax 728-8139
Mar Vista ES 300/K-5
6860 Soquel Dr 95003 831-688-5211
Chris Hertz, prin. Fax 728-6491
Rio Del Mar ES 600/K-6
819 Pinehurst Dr 95003 831-688-2053
Deborah Dorney, prin. Fax 728-6467
Valencia ES 500/K-6
250 Aptos School Rd 95003 831-728-6376
Dianna Higginbotham, prin. Fax 728-6489

Santa Cruz Montessori S 200/K-8
6230 Soquel Dr 95003 831-476-1646
Kathy Rideout, dir. Fax 476-2703
Twin Lakes Christian S 200/K-6
2701 Cabrillo College Dr 95003 831-465-3301
Meg Imel, prin. Fax 465-3389

Arbuckle, Colusa, Pop. 1,912
Pierce JUSD 1,300/K-12
PO Box 239 95912 530-476-2892
Patricia Hamilton, supt. Fax 476-2289
www.pierce.k12.ca.us
Arbuckle ES 600/K-5
PO Box 100 95912 530-476-2522
Carol Geyer, prin. Fax 476-2234
Johnson JHS 300/6-8
938 Wildwood Rd 95912 530-476-3261
Blake Kitchen, prin. Fax 476-2017
Other Schools – See Grimes

Arcadia, Los Angeles, Pop. 56,153
Arcadia USD 10,100/K-12
234 Campus Dr 91007 626-821-8300
Dr. Joel Shawn, supt. Fax 821-8647
www.ausd.k12.ca.us
Camino Grove ES 700/K-5
700 Camino Grove Ave 91006 626-821-8353
Brook Reynolds, prin. Fax 294-0911
Dana MS 800/6-8
1401 S 1st Ave 91006 626-821-8361
James Tarouilly, prin. Fax 447-1965
First Avenue MS 800/6-8
301 S 1st Ave 91006 626-821-8362
Jeffrey Wilson, prin. Fax 446-1660
Foothills MS 800/6-8
171 E Sycamore Ave 91006 626-821-8363
Patricia Hartline, prin. Fax 303-7983
Highland Oaks ES 700/K-5
10 Virginia Rd 91006 626-821-8354
Ilene Anderson, prin. Fax 821-4680
Holly Avenue ES 700/K-5
360 W Duarte Rd 91007 626-821-8355
Christine Blackstock, prin. Fax 574-3809
Longley Way ES 500/K-5
2601 Longley Way 91007 626-821-8357
Sherrie DuFresne, prin. Fax 574-3812
Reid ES 600/K-5
1000 Hugo Reid Dr 91007 626-821-8356
Thomas Bruce, prin. Fax 574-1341
Stocker ES 600/K-5
422 W Lemon Ave 91007 626-821-8351
Nadia Hillman, prin. Fax 574-3807

El Monte City ESD
Supt. — See El Monte
Rio Hondo S 1,000/K-8
11425 Wildflower Rd 91006 626-575-2308
Lance Lawson, prin. Fax 443-3508

Annunciation S 200/K-8
1307 E Longden Ave 91006 626-447-8262
Evangelina Lopez, prin. Fax 447-3841
Arcadia Christian S 500/PK-8
1900 S Santa Anita Ave 91006 626-574-8229
Fax 574-1224
Barnhart S 300/K-8
240 W Colorado Blvd 91007 626-446-5588
Joanne Testacross, hdmstr. Fax 574-3355

Holy Angels S 300/PK-8
360 Campus Dr 91007 626-447-6312
Ted Carroll, prin. Fax 447-2843

Arcata, Humboldt, Pop. 16,914

Arcata ESD 600/K-8
1435 Buttermilk Ln 95521 707-822-0351
Tim Parisi, supt. Fax 822-6589
www.humboldt.k12.ca.us/arcata_sd/index.htm

Arcata ES 300/K-5
2400 Baldwin St 95521 707-822-4858
Margaret Flenner, prin. Fax 822-6419

Sunny Brae MS 300/6-8
1430 Buttermilk Ln 95521 707-822-5988
Lynda Yeoman, prin. Fax 822-7002

Pacific UNESD 400/K-8
3001 Janes Rd 95521 707-822-4619
John McGuire, supt. Fax 822-0129
www.humboldt.k12.ca.us/pacificun_sd/

Pacific Union S 400/K-8
3001 Janes Rd 95521 707-822-4619
John McGuire, prin. Fax 822-0129

Arcata Christian S 50/PK-8
1700 Union St 95521 707-822-5986
Ronald Wunner, admin. Fax 822-2591

St. Marys S 50/K-8
1730 Janes Rd 95521 707-822-3877
James Monge, prin. Fax 822-8912

Arleta, See Los Angeles

Los Angeles USD
Supt. — See Los Angeles

Beachy Avenue ES 700/K-5
9757 Beachy Ave 91331 818-899-0241
Alan Lewis, prin. Fax 890-5532

Canterbury ES 1,100/K-5
13670 Montague St 91331 818-892-1104
Graciela Rodriguez, prin. Fax 895-2653

Sharp ES 800/K-5
13800 Pierce St 91331 818-896-9573
Kyla Hinson, prin. Fax 896-8403

Vena ES 700/K-5
9377 Vena Ave 91331 818-896-9551
Maria Nichols, prin. Fax 890-7189

Armona, Kings, Pop. 3,122

Armona UNESD 1,000/K-8
PO Box 368 93202 559-583-5000
Steve Bogan, supt. Fax 583-5004
www.kings.k12.ca.us/armona/

Armona ES 600/K-4
PO Box 368 93202 559-583-5000
Randy Howard, prin. Fax 583-5000

Parkview MS 400/5-8
PO Box 368 93202 559-583-5000
Lance Clement, prin. Fax 583-5000

Armona Union Academy 100/K-12
PO Box 397 93202 559-582-4468
Erik Borges, prin. Fax 582-6609

Arnold, Calaveras, Pop. 3,788

Vallecito UNSD
Supt. — See Avery

Fischer ES 200/K-5
1605 Blagen Rd 95223 209-795-8030
Brett Loring, prin. Fax 795-8033

Aromas, Monterey, Pop. 2,275

Aromas/San Juan USD
Supt. — See San Juan Bautista

Aromas S 400/K-8
PO Box 216 95004 831-726-5100
Stephanie Siddens, prin. Fax 726-3040

Arroyo Grande, San Luis Obispo, Pop. 16,315

Lucia Mar USD 10,900/K-12
602 Orchard Ave 93420 805-474-3000
James Hogeboom, supt. Fax 481-1398
www.lmusd.org/

Branch ES 300/K-6
970 School Rd 93420 805-474-3720
Stacey Russell, prin. Fax 473-4184

Harloe ES 700/K-6
901 Fair Oaks Ave 93420 805-474-3710
Charles Fiorentino, prin. Fax 473-5520

Mesa MS 500/7-8
2555 S Halcyon Rd 93420 805-474-3400
Jeff Martin, prin. Fax 473-4396

Ocean View ES 600/K-6
1208 Linda Dr 93420 805-474-3730
Cynthia Ravalin, prin. Fax 473-5526

Paulding MS 600/7-8
600 Crown Hill St 93420 805-474-3500
Gary Moore, prin. Fax 473-5525

Other Schools – See Grover Beach, Nipomo, Oceano, Pismo Beach

---

Coastal Christian S 200/K-12
1220 Farroll Ave 93420 805-489-1213
Lance Tullis, admin. Fax 489-5394

Royal Oaks Christian S 100/PK-6
900 Oak Park Blvd 93420 805-489-9200
Patty Clarkson, admin. Fax 489-0604

St. Patrick S 300/PK-8
900 W Branch St 93420 805-489-1210
Maureen Halderman, prin. Fax 489-7662

Valley View Adventist Academy 100/K-10
230 Vernon St 93420 805-489-2687
Philip Ermshar, prin. Fax 489-2704

Artesia, Los Angeles, Pop. 16,672

ABC USD
Supt. — See Cerritos

Burbank ES 500/K-6
17711 Roseton Ave 90701 562-865-6215
Steve Cizmar, prin. Fax 402-9856

Elliott ES 400/K-6
18415 Cortner Ave 90703 562-865-5216
Beth Bray, prin. Fax 924-8216

Kennedy ES 400/K-6
17500 Belshire Ave 90701 562-860-3378
Melissa Valentine, prin. Fax 402-9851

Niemes ES 600/K-6
16715 Jersey Ave 90701 562-865-9586
Mariaelena Jimenez, prin. Fax 402-8927

Ross MS 700/7-8
17707 Elaine Ave 90701 562-924-8331
Ricardo Brown, prin. Fax 402-6145

Our Lady of Fatima S 200/K-8
18626 Clarkdale Ave 90701 562-865-1621
Fax 403-0409

Arvin, Kern, Pop. 14,724

Arvin UNESD 3,700/K-8
737 Bear Mountain Blvd 93203 661-854-6500
Jerelle Kavanagh, supt. Fax 854-2362
www.arvinschools.com/

Bear Mountain ES 1,100/K-6
737 Bear Mountain Blvd 93203 661-854-6590
Aurora Moran, prin. Fax 854-6599

El Camino Real ES 800/K-6
737 Bear Mountain Blvd 93203 661-854-6661
Georgia Rhett, prin. Fax 854-2474

Haven Drive MS 700/7-8
737 Bear Mountain Blvd 93203 661-854-6540
David Bowling, prin. Fax 854-1440

Sierra Vista ES 1,100/K-6
737 Bear Mountain Blvd 93203 661-854-6560
Angelica Salinas, prin. Fax 854-7523

Di Giorgio ESD 200/K-8
19405 Buena Vista Blvd 93203 661-854-2604
Paul Boatman, supt. Fax 854-8746
www.digiorgio.k12.ca.us/

Di Giorgio S 200/K-8
19405 Buena Vista Blvd 93203 661-854-2604
Paul Boatman, prin. Fax 854-8746

Atascadero, San Luis Obispo, Pop. 27,130

Atascadero USD 5,000/K-12
5601 West Mall 93422 805-462-4200
John Rogers, supt. Fax 466-2941
www.atas.k12.ca.us

Atascadero Fine Arts Academy 200/4-8
6100 Olmeda Ave 93422 805-460-2500
Cheryl Hockett, prin. Fax 460-2522

Atascadero JHS 700/7-8
6501 Lewis Ave 93422 805-462-4360
Kirk Smith, prin. Fax 462-4373

Monterey Road ES 400/K-6
3355 Monterey Rd 93422 805-462-4270
Chris Allen, prin. Fax 462-4288

San Benito ES 500/K-6
4300 San Benito Rd 93422 805-462-4330
Joanne Rogoff, prin. Fax 462-4278

San Gabriel ES 500/K-6
8500 San Gabriel Rd 93422 805-462-4340
Chris Balogh, prin. Fax 462-4268

Santa Rosa Academic Academy 400/K-6
8655 Santa Rosa Rd 93422 805-462-4290
Lori Thomas-Hicks, prin. Fax 462-4358

Other Schools – See Creston, Santa Margarita

North County Christian S 200/PK-12
PO Box 6017 93423 805-466-4457
Robert McLaughlin, admin. Fax 466-7948

Atherton, San Mateo, Pop. 7,177

Las Lomitas ESD
Supt. — See Menlo Park

Las Lomitas ES 500/K-3
299 Alameda De Las Pulgas 94027 650-854-5900
Jerry Traynor, prin. Fax 854-4493

Menlo Park City ESD 2,300/K-8
181 Encinal Ave 94027 650-321-7140
Kenneth Ranella, supt. Fax 321-7184
www.mpcsd.org

Encinal ES 400/3-5
195 Encinal Ave 94027 650-326-5164
Allison Liner, prin. Fax 327-0854

Laurel ES 500/K-2
95 Edge Rd 94027 650-324-0186
Nancy Hendry, prin. Fax 325-0374

Other Schools – See Menlo Park

Redwood City ESD
Supt. — See Redwood City

Selby Lane S 600/K-8
170 Selby Ln 94027 650-368-3996
Carolyn Williams, prin. Fax 367-4366

Sacred Heart Prep S 500/PK-12
150 Valparaiso Ave 94027 650-322-1866
James Everitt, prin. Fax 322-7151

St. Joseph S 500/PK-8
50 Emilie Ave 94027 650-322-9931
Bridget Collins, prin. Fax 322-7656

Atwater, Merced, Pop. 27,107

Atwater ESD 4,600/K-8
1401 Broadway Ave 95301 209-357-6100
Melinda Hennes, supt. Fax 357-6163
www.aesd.edu

Bellevue S 800/K-8
1020 E Bellevue Rd 95301 209-357-6140
Bryan Ballenger, prin. Fax 357-6141

Colburn ES 400/K-6
2201 Heller Ave 95301 209-357-6136
Vincent Gonzalez, prin. Fax 357-6169

Heller ES 400/K-6
201 Lake View Dr 95301 209-357-6517
Nathan Hixson, prin. Fax 357-6528

Mitchell ES 600/K-6
1761 Grove Ave 95301 209-357-6112
Brian Meisenheimer, prin. Fax 357-6505

Mitchell Senior ES 800/7-8
1753 5th St 95301 209-357-6124
Andrew Kersten, prin. Fax 357-6506

Olaeta ES 500/K-6
2266 High St 95301 209-357-6148
Roger Jackson, prin. Fax 357-6167

Shaffer ES 600/K-6
1434 California St 95301 209-357-6145
Robert Ellis, prin. Fax 357-6146

Wood ES 500/K-6
1271 Bellevue Rd 95301 209-357-6143
Sylvia Nelson, prin. Fax 357-6509

King's Christian Academy 50/K-8
1683 5th St 95301 209-357-5691
Steve Shumaker, admin. Fax 356-0654

St. Anthony S 200/PK-8
1801 Winton Way 95301 209-358-3341
Dianne Silva, prin. Fax 358-3341

Auberry, Fresno, Pop. 1,866

Pine Ridge ESD 100/K-8
45828 Auberry Rd 93602 559-841-2444
Eric Bitter, supt. Fax 841-2771
www.pineridge.k12.ca.us/

Pine Ridge S 100/K-8
45828 Auberry Rd 93602 559-841-2444
Eric Bittner, prin. Fax 841-2771

Sierra USD
Supt. — See Prather

Auberry ES 400/K-5
33367 Auberry Rd 93602 559-855-2442
Ara Keledjian, prin. Fax 855-2070

Auburn, Placer, Pop. 12,912

Auburn UNESD 2,000/K-8
255 Epperle Ln 95603 530-885-7242
Michele Schuetz, supt. Fax 885-5170
www.auburn.k12.ca.us/

Auburn ES 500/K-5
11400 Lariat Ranch Rd 95603 530-887-1958
Sam Schug, prin. Fax 887-1241

Cain MS 800/6-8
150 Palm Ave 95603 530-823-6106
Randy Ittner, prin. Fax 823-0943

Rock Creek ES 300/K-5
3050 Bell Rd 95603 530-885-5189
Scott Pickett, prin. Fax 885-5196

Skyridge ES 500/K-5
800 Perkins Way 95603 530-885-7019
Doris Chandler, prin. Fax 885-4213

Calvary Chapel Christian S 200/PK-8
202 Dairy Rd 95603 530-885-9105
Paul Cross, prin. Fax 885-9194

Forest Lake Christian S 700/K-12
12515 Combie Rd 95602 530-269-1535
Jean Schoellerman, dir. Fax 269-1541

Pine Hills Adventist Academy 100/K-12
13500 Richards Ln 95603 530-885-9447
Victor Anderson, prin. Fax 885-5237

St. Joseph S 300/PK-8
11610 Atwood Rd 95603 530-885-4490
Mira Wordelman, prin. Fax 885-0182

Avalon, Los Angeles, Pop. 3,334

Long Beach USD
Supt. — See Long Beach

Avalon S 700/K-12
PO Box 557 90704 310-510-0790
Joseph Carlson, prin. Fax 510-2986

Avenal, Kings, Pop. 16,631

Reef-Sunset USD 2,500/K-12
205 N Park Ave 93204 559-386-9083
Suzanne Monroe, supt. Fax 386-5303
www.rsusd.net

Avenal ES 700/K-5
500 S 1st Ave 93204 559-386-5173
Rosemary Spencer, prin. Fax 386-5287

Reef-Sunset MS 400/6-8
608 N 1st Ave 93204 559-386-4128
Steve Bettenridge, prin. Fax 386-4918

Tamarack ES 400/K-5
1000 S Union Ave 93204 559-386-4051
Patricia Cheek, prin. Fax 386-4074

Other Schools – See Kettleman City

Avery, Calaveras, Pop. 900

Vallecito UNSD 900/K-8
PO Box 329 95224 209-795-8500
Glenn Sewell, supt. Fax 795-8505
www.vsd.k12.ca.us

Avery MS 300/6-8
PO Box 329 95224 209-795-8520
Tim Hicks, prin. Fax 795-8539

Other Schools – See Arnold, Murphys

Azusa, Los Angeles, Pop. 47,120

Azusa USD 11,000/K-12
PO Box 500 91702 626-967-6211
C. Cervantes McGuire, supt. Fax 858-6123
www.azusausd.k12.ca.us

Center MS 800/6-8
PO Box 500 91702 626-815-5184
Lynne Jorgensen, prin. Fax 815-2601

Dalton ES 400/K-5
PO Box 500 91702 626-815-5245
Roberta Monaghan, prin. Fax 815-5248

Foothill MS 900/6-8
PO Box 500 91702 626-815-6600
Jane Ostrowski, prin. Fax 815-1027

Gladstone Street ES 400/K-5
PO Box 500 91702 626-815-6700
Bettina Hunt, prin. Fax 815-6785

Hodge ES 500/K-5
PO Box 500 91702 626-815-4800
Fax 815-5531
Lee ES 500/1-5
PO Box 500 91702 626-815-5269
Hector Alegria, prin. Fax 815-5268
Longfellow S 200/K-K
PO Box 500 91702 626-815-4700
Leslie Ford, prin. Fax 815-4740
Magnolia ES 400/K-5
PO Box 500 91702 626-815-5800
Randi Carbajal-Cuccia, prin. Fax 815-2650
Mountain View ES 500/K-5
PO Box 500 91702 626-815-2900
Rita Ruminski, prin. Fax 815-7951
Murray ES 600/K-5
PO Box 500 91702 626-633-8700
Saida Valdez, prin. Fax 334-2918
Paramount ES 500/K-5
PO Box 500 91702 626-815-5104
Fax 815-5109
Powell ES 400/K-5
PO Box 500 91702 626-633-8500
Fax 633-8585
Slauson MS 900/6-8
PO Box 500 91702 626-815-5144
Ann Somers, prin. Fax 815-5147
Valleydale ES 400/K-5
PO Box 500 91702 626-633-8600
Zepure Hacopian, prin. Fax 815-5199
Other Schools – See Covina

Light & Life Christian S 100/PK-5
777 E Alosta Ave 91702 626-969-0182
Yolanda Castro, admin. Fax 969-5694
St. Frances of Rome S 200/K-8
734 N Pasadena Ave 91702 626-334-2018
Christina Arellano, prin. Fax 815-2760

Badger, Tulare
Cutler-Orosi JUSD
Supt. — See Orosi
Sierra S 50/K-8
PO Box 170 93603 559-337-2514
Ramon Oyervidez, prin. Fax 337-2895

Baker, San Bernardino
Baker Valley USD 200/K-12
PO Box 460 92309 760-733-4567
Keith Tomes, supt. Fax 733-4605
www.baker.k12.ca.us/
Baker ES 100/K-6
PO Box 460 92309 760-733-4567
Ronda Tremblay, prin. Fax 733-4605
Baker JHS 50/7-8
PO Box 460 92309 760-733-4567
Ronda Tremblay, prin. Fax 733-4605

Bakersfield, Kern, Pop. 295,536
Bakersfield CSD 27,300/K-8
1300 Baker St 93305 661-631-4600
Michael Lingo, supt. Fax 326-1485
www.bcsd.com
Casa Loma ES 700/K-5
525 E Casa Loma Dr 93307 661-631-5200
Gwen Johnson, prin. Fax 631-3181
Chavez ES 500/K-6
4201 Mesa Marin Dr 93306 661-631-5870
Ruscel Reader, prin. Fax 631-3264
Chipman JHS 900/7-8
2905 Eissler St 93306 661-631-5210
Russell Taylor, prin. Fax 631-3229
College Heights ES 800/K-6
2551 Sunny Ln 93305 661-631-5220
Ricardo Zavala, prin. Fax 631-4510
Compton JHS 700/7-8
3211 Pico Ave 93306 661-631-5230
Alex Soriano, prin. Fax 631-3166
Curran MS 1,000/6-8
1116 Lymric Way 93309 661-631-5240
Jason Brannen, prin. Fax 631-4538
Downtown S 300/K-8
2021 M St 93301 661-631-5920
Jennifer Painter, prin. Fax 631-3276
Eissler ES 600/K-6
2901 Eissler St 93306 661-631-5250
Diane Adame, prin. Fax 631-4504
Emerson MS 900/6-8
801 4th St 93304 661-631-5260
Kempton Coman, prin. Fax 631-3157
Evergreen ES 600/K-5
2600 Rose Marie Dr 93304 661-631-5930
Brandon Johnson, prin. Fax 631-3190
Franklin ES 400/K-6
2400 Truxtun Ave 93301 661-631-5270
Carla Tafoya, prin. Fax 631-3210
Fremont ES 900/K-6
607 Texas St 93307 661-631-5280
Jesse Beed, prin. Fax 631-4527
Garza ES 800/K-5
2901 Center St 93306 661-631-5290
Teresa Arambula, prin. Fax 631-3110
Harding ES 500/K-6
3201 Pico Ave 93306 661-631-5300
Bridget Fitch, prin. Fax 631-4587
Harris ES 400/K-5
4110 Garnsey Ln 93309 661-631-5310
Sarita Arredondo, prin. Fax 631-3178
Hills ES 600/K-5
3800 Jewett Ave 93301 661-631-5320
Jon Hughes, prin. Fax 631-3119
Hort ES 700/K-5
2301 Park Dr 93306 661-631-5330
Steve Robinson, prin. Fax 631-3208
Jefferson ES 500/K-5
816 Lincoln St 93305 661-631-5340
Eugenia Delouth, prin. Fax 631-3104

Longfellow ES 700/K-6
1900 Stockton St 93305 661-631-5350
Mario Castro, prin. Fax 631-3151
Mann ES 800/K-5
2710 Niles St 93306 661-631-5360
Dayna Gardner, prin. Fax 631-3256
McKinley ES 700/K-5
601 4th St 93304 661-631-5370
Rene Beed, prin. Fax 631-4553
Mt. Vernon ES 700/K-6
2161 Potomac Ave 93307 661-631-5380
Eva Zavala, prin. Fax 631-3126
Munsey ES 700/K-5
3801 Brave Ave 93309 661-631-5390
Fax 631-3222
Nichols ES 600/K-6
3401 Renegade Ave 93306 661-631-5400
Debra Craig, prin. Fax 631-4902
Noble ES 800/K-5
1015 Noble Ave 93305 661-631-5410
Juanita Sanchez, prin. Fax 631-3248
Owens IS 500/4-6
815 Eureka St 93305 661-631-5950
Carol Sherrill, prin. Fax 631-3269
Owens PS 600/K-3
815 Potomac Ave 93307 661-631-5420
Anne Lopez, prin. Fax 631-3134
Pauly ES 700/K-5
313 Planz Rd 93304 661-631-5430
Rachelle Montoya, prin. Fax 631-3215
Penn ES 300/K-5
2201 San Emidio St 93304 661-631-5440
Gabriela Ulloa-Espinosa, prin. Fax 631-3279
Pioneer Drive ES 700/K-6
4404 Pioneer Dr 93306 661-631-5450
Traci Hicks, prin. Fax 631-3196
Roosevelt ES 400/K-5
2324 Verde St 93304 661-631-5460
Warren Ramay, prin. Fax 631-4912
Sequoia MS 1,000/6-8
900 Belle Ter 93304 661-631-5940
Gary McCloskey, prin. Fax 631-3236
Sierra MS 800/6-8
3017 Center St 93306 661-631-5470
Tomas Prieto, prin. Fax 631-4541
Stiern MS 1,400/6-8
2551 Morning Dr 93306 661-631-5480
Julie Short, prin. Fax 631-3241
Thorner ES 800/K-6
5501 Thorner St 93306 661-631-5490
Wanda Bradford, prin. Fax 631-4567
Voorhies ES 800/K-6
6001 Pioneer Dr 93306 661-631-5800
Dr. Vivian Gayles, prin. Fax 631-4579
Washington MS 600/6-8
1101 Noble Ave 93305 661-631-5810
Jeff Fenske, prin. Fax 631-3172
Wayside ES 700/K-5
1000 Ming Ave 93307 661-631-5820
Dr. Michelle McLean, prin. Fax 631-4593
West ES 600/K-5
2400 Benton St 93304 661-631-5830
Dawn Slaybaugh, prin. Fax 631-4519
Williams ES 500/K-5
1201 Williams St 93305 661-631-5840
Jennifer Payne, prin. Fax 631-4560

Beardsley ESD 1,800/K-8
1001 Roberts Ln 93308 661-393-8550
Dick Stotler, supt. Fax 393-5965
www.beardsleyschool.org/
Beardsley IS 400/4-6
1001 Roberts Ln 93308 661-392-1417
Kevin Williams, prin. Fax 393-5965
Beardsley JHS 400/7-8
1001 Roberts Ln 93308 661-392-9254
David Hilton, prin. Fax 399-3925
North Beardsley PS 600/K-3
900 Sanford Dr 93308 661-392-0878
Aimee Williamson, prin. Fax 392-1399
San Lauren ES 400/K-6
5210 Victor St 93308 661-393-5511
Terri Chamberlin, prin. Fax 393-9064

Edison ESD 1,100/K-8
11518 School St 93307 661-363-5394
Stephen Ventura, supt. Fax 363-4631
www.edisonschooldistrict.org
Edison MS 500/5-8
721 S Edison Rd 93307 661-366-8216
Loreda Clevenger, prin. Fax 366-0922
Orangewood ES 600/K-4
9600 Eucalyptus Dr 93306 661-366-8440
Jennifer Delmarter, prin. Fax 366-0159

Fairfax ESD 2,000/K-8
1500 S Fairfax Rd 93307 661-366-7221
Desiree Von Flue, supt. Fax 366-1901
www.fairfax.k12.ca.us/
Fairfax MS 700/6-8
1500 S Fairfax Rd 93307 661-366-4461
Alice Pacheco, prin. Fax 366-5831
Shirley Lane ES 600/3-5
6714 Shirley Ln 93307 661-363-7684
Cindy Castro, prin. Fax 363-7552
Virginia Avenue ES 700/K-2
3301 Virginia Ave 93307 661-366-3223
Lora Brown, prin. Fax 366-2043

Fruitvale ESD 3,200/K-8
7311 Rosedale Hwy 93308 661-589-3830
Dr. Carl Olsen, supt. Fax 589-3674
www.fruitvale.k12.ca.us/
Columbia ES 500/K-6
703 Mondavi Way 93312 661-588-3540
Bill Jager, prin. Fax 589-5264
Discovery ES 700/K-6
7500 Vaquero Ave 93308 661-589-7336
Danyel Kelly, prin. Fax 587-9413

Endeavour ES 900/K-6
9300 Meacham Rd 93312 661-588-3550
Deanna Clarke, prin. Fax 587-9318
Fruitvale JHS 800/7-8
2114 Calloway Dr 93312 661-589-3933
Susan Richardson, prin. Fax 588-3259
Quailwood ES 300/K-6
7301 Remington Ave 93309 661-832-6415
Steve Duke, prin. Fax 831-7391

General Shafter ESD 200/K-8
1825 Shafter Rd 93313 661-837-1931
Deborah Rodrigues, supt. Fax 837-8261
Shafter S 200/K-8
1825 Shafter Rd 93313 661-837-1931
Deborah Rodrigues, prin. Fax 837-8261

Greenfield UNESD 7,800/K-8
1624 Fairview Rd 93307 661-837-6000
Chris Crawford, supt. Fax 832-2873
www.gfusd.k12.ca.us/
Fairview ES 500/K-5
425 E Fairview Rd 93307 661-837-6050
Michael Barella, prin. Fax 837-6056
Granite Pointe ES K-5
2900 Berkshire Rd 93313 661-837-6040
Anne Fisk, prin. Fax 837-3491
Greenfield MS 1,000/6-8
1109 Pacheco Rd 93307 661-837-6110
Scott McArthur, prin. Fax 832-7431
Horizon ES 700/K-5
7901 Monitor St 93307 661-837-3730
Brenda Cassell, prin. Fax 837-3734
Kendrick ES 700/K-5
2200 Faith Ave 93304 661-837-6190
Lucas Hogue, prin. Fax 397-0226
McKee MS 700/6-8
205 McKee Rd 93307 661-837-6060
Carol Schaefer, prin. Fax 834-7566
Ollivier MS 1,000/6-8
7310 Monitor St 93307 661-837-6120
Sheila Johnson, prin. Fax 396-0963
Palla ES 1,000/K-5
800 Fairview Rd 93307 661-837-6100
Margie Berumen, prin. Fax 837-6106
Plantation ES 700/K-5
901 Plantation Ave 93304 661-837-6070
Deloris Sill, prin. Fax 837-6077
Planz ES 700/K-5
2400 E Planz Rd 93307 661-837-6080
Valerie Park, prin. Fax 831-5467
Valle Verde ES 700/K-5
400 Berkshire Rd 93307 661-837-6150
Shayleen Harte, prin. Fax 837-6159

Lakeside UNSD 1,400/K-8
14535 Old River Rd 93311 661-836-6658
Nick Kouklis, supt. Fax 836-8059
www.lakesideusd.org/
Lakeside S 600/K-8
14535 Old River Rd 93311 661-831-3503
Mike McGrath, prin. Fax 831-7709
Suburu ES 800/K-5
7315 Harris Rd 93313 661-665-8190
Gary Mullen, prin. Fax 665-8282

Norris SD 4,100/K-8
6940 Calloway Dr 93312 661-387-7000
Wallace McCormick Ph.D., supt. Fax 399-9750
www.norris.k12.ca.us/
Bimat ES 600/K-5
8600 Northshore Dr 93312 661-387-7080
Dan Weirather, prin. Fax 589-7849
Norris ES 1,300/K-5
7110 Old Farm Rd 93312 661-387-7020
Corey Osvog, prin. Fax 399-0435
Norris MS 1,100/6-8
6940 Calloway Dr 93312 661-387-7060
Jon Boles, prin. Fax 399-9356
Olive Drive ES 600/K-5
7800 Darrin Ave 93308 661-387-7040
Darren Grisham, prin. Fax 399-3149
Veterans ES 500/K-5
6301 Old Farm Rd 93312 661-387-7050
Kelly Miller, prin. Fax 589-5758

Panama-Buena Vista UNSD 16,400/K-8
4200 Ashe Rd 93313 661-831-8331
Kip Hearron, supt. Fax 398-2141
www.pbvusd.k12.ca.us
Actis JHS 800/7-8
2400 Westholme Blvd 93309 661-833-1250
Patrick Spears, prin. Fax 833-9656
Berkshire ES 1,000/K-6
3900 Berkshire Rd 93313 661-834-9472
Marsha Ketchell, prin. Fax 834-7876
Buena Vista ES 1,100/K-6
6547 Buena Vista Rd 93311 661-831-0818
Brandie Haining, prin. Fax 831-4842
Castle ES 800/K-6
6001 Edgemont Dr 93309 661-834-5311
Lisa Beasley, prin. Fax 834-9422
Hart ES 600/K-6
9501 Ridge Oak Dr 93311 661-664-1296
Daryl Newton, prin. Fax 664-0176
Laurelglen ES 600/K-6
2601 El Portal Dr 93309 661-831-4444
Brian Mark, prin. Fax 831-6689
Loudon ES 800/K-6
4000 Loudon St 93313 661-398-3210
Sharon Dunn, prin. Fax 398-6233
Lum ES 700/K-6
4600 Chaney Ln 93311 661-664-1611
Shawna Manning, prin. Fax 664-1852
McAuliffe ES 600/K-6
8900 Westwold Dr 93311 661-665-9471
Dan Pokett, prin. Fax 665-9821

Miller ES K-6
7345 Mountain Ridge Dr 93313 661-836-6689
Judy Nightengale, prin. Fax 836-8452
Old River ES 600/K-6
9815 Campus Park Dr 93311 661-664-7009
Mike Boles, prin. Fax 664-8247
Panama ES 1,000/K-6
9400 Stine Rd 93313 661-831-1741
Brian Malavar, prin. Fax 831-6662
Reagan ES 900/K-6
10800 Rosslyn Ln 93311 661-665-8099
Tom Irvin, prin. Fax 665-8311
Sandrini ES 700/K-6
4100 Alum Ave 93309 661-397-1515
Marshall Dillard, prin. Fax 397-3817
Seibert ES 700/K-6
2800 Agate St 93304 661-832-4141
Matthew Merickel, prin. Fax 832-3734
Stine ES 800/K-6
4300 Wilson Rd 93309 661-831-1022
Matthew Kennedy, prin. Fax 831-6610
Stockdale ES 600/K-6
7801 Kroll Way 93309 661-831-7835
Ron Madding, prin. Fax 831-7701
Stonecreek JHS 600/7-8
8000 Akers Rd 93313 661-834-4521
Darryl Johnson, prin. Fax 834-6908
Tevis JHS 800/7-8
3901 Pin Oak Park Blvd 93311 661-664-7211
Robert Machado, prin. Fax 664-9659
Thompson JHS 900/7-8
4200 Planz Rd 93309 661-832-8011
Darryl Pope, prin. Fax 832-5165
Van Horn ES 600/K-6
5501 Kleinpell Ave 93309 661-324-6538
James Lopez, prin. Fax 324-2007
Warren JHS 700/7-8
4615 Mountain Vista Dr 93311 661-665-9210
George Thornburgh, prin. Fax 665-9507
Williams ES 700/K-6
5601 Harris Rd 93313 661-837-8070
Dion Lovio, prin. Fax 837-4459

Rio Bravo-Greeley UNESD 900/K-8
6521 Enos Ln, 661-589-2696
Ernie Unruh, supt. Fax 589-2218
www.rbgusd.k12.ca.us
Rio Bravo ES 300/K-3
22725 Elementary Ln, 661-588-6313
Stacy Monroe, prin. Fax 588-6318
Rio Bravo-Greeley MS 500/4-8
6601 Enos Ln, 661-589-2505
Joost Demoes, prin. Fax 588-7204

Rosedale UNESD 5,200/K-8
2553 Old Farm Rd 93312 661-588-6000
Jamie Henderson, supt. Fax 588-6009
www.ruesd.net/
Almondale ES 600/K-6
10510 Chippewa St 93312 661-588-6060
Crysta Silver-Hill, prin. Fax 588-6063
American ES 600/K-6
800 Verdugo Ln 93312 661-587-2277
Rob Bray, prin. Fax 829-2591
Centennial ES 500/K-6
15200 Westdale Dr, 661-588-6020
Susan Denton, prin. Fax 588-6023
Del Rio ES 500/K-6
600 Hidalgo Dr, 661-588-6050
Bruce Carlile, prin. Fax 588-6053
Freedom MS 700/7-8
11445 Noriega Rd 93312 661-588-6044
Trica Lazenby, prin. Fax 588-6048
Independence ES 400/K-6
2345 Old Farm Rd 93312 661-588-6011
Judith Silver, prin. Fax 588-6018
Patriot ES 800/K-6
4410 Old Farm Rd 93312 661-588-6065
Diane Dalton-Rivard, prin. Fax 587-2272
Rosedale MS 600/7-8
12463 Rosedale Hwy 93312 661-588-6030
Jennifer Keyes, prin. Fax 588-6039
Rosedale-North ES 600/K-6
11500 Meacham Rd 93312 661-588-6040
Erin Hawkins, prin. Fax 588-6043

Standard ESD 2,900/K-8
1200 N Chester Ave 93308 661-392-2110
Kevin Silberberg Ed.D., supt. Fax 392-0681
www.standard.k12.ca.us
Highland ES 800/K-5
2900 Barnett St 93308 661-392-2115
Stuart Packard, prin. Fax 392-2142
Standard ES 500/K-5
115 E Minner Ave 93308 661-392-2120
Richard Morosa, prin. Fax 392-2137
Standard MS 1,000/6-8
1222 N Chester Ave 93308 661-392-2130
Tonny Gisbertz, prin. Fax 392-2134
Wingland ES 700/K-5
701 Douglas St 93308 661-392-2125
Robert Sheldon, prin. Fax 392-2139

Vineland ESD 900/K-8
14713 Weedpatch Hwy 93307 661-845-3713
Adolph Wirth, supt. Fax 845-8449
www.vinelandschooldistrict.com
Sunset MS 400/5-8
8301 Sunset Blvd 93307 661-845-1320
Mike Gonzalez, prin. Fax 845-3952
Vineland ES 500/K-4
14327 S Vineland Rd 93307 661-845-3917
Maureen Angelini, prin. Fax 845-1599

Agapeland Christian Academy 100/PK-6
1030 4th St 93304 661-325-4321
Marisa Banks, admin. Fax 325-5213
Bakersfield Adventist Academy 200/K-12
3333 Bernard St 93306 661-871-1591
Mike Schwartz, prin. Fax 871-1594
Cornerstone Christian Academy 100/PK-5
PO Box 80743 93380 661-399-4233
Donna Coe, prin.
Country Christian S 100/PK-6
2416 Dean Ave 93312 661-589-4703
Rose Merriman, admin. Fax 588-5944
Eternity Preparatory Academy 50/K-12
PO Box 13158 93389 661-324-2759
Mike Kirkland, hdmstr.
Heritage Christian S 100/PK-8
2401 Bernard St 93306 661-871-4545
Dr. Kent McClain, supt. Fax 871-5627
New Life Christian S 100/PK-8
4201 Stine Rd 93313 661-831-6252
Ginger Martinez, admin. Fax 831-5607
Olive Knolls Christian S 400/PK-8
6201 Fruitvale Ave 93308 661-393-3566
Suzanne Hunter, prin. Fax 393-3467
Our Lady of Guadalupe S 200/PK-8
609 E California Ave 93307 661-323-6059
Sr. Eva Lujano, prin. Fax 323-1860
Our Lady of Perpetual Help S 300/K-8
124 Columbus St 93305 661-327-7741
Donna Smith, prin. Fax 325-7067
St. Francis S 600/PK-8
2516 Palm St 93304 661-326-7955
Cindy Meek, prin. Fax 327-0395
St. John Lutheran S 300/K-8
4500 Buena Vista Rd 93311 661-664-8090
Stephen Dinger M.Ed., admin. Fax 661-1327
Stockdale Christian S 800/PK-8
4901 California Ave 93309 661-327-3927
Doug Pike, supt. Fax 327-9802
Turner Christian Academy 100/1-12
48 Manor St 93308 661-366-4520
Peggy Turner, prin.
Valley S 200/PK-7
PO Box 60607 93386 661-325-5084
Tiffany Touchstone, prin. Fax 325-5087

Baldwin Park, Los Angeles, Pop. 78,861
Baldwin Park USD 16,800/PK-12
3699 Holly Ave 91706 626-962-3311
Mark Skvarna, supt. Fax 856-4901
www.bpusd.net
Bursch ES 700/K-6
4245 Merced Ave 91706 626-338-4319
Michael Garcia, prin. Fax 856-4086
Central ES 800/K-6
14741 Central Ave 91706 626-962-7915
Christine Medina, prin. Fax 962-0676
DeAnza ES 800/K-6
12820 Bess Ave 91706 626-338-4019
Christine Simmons, prin. Fax 856-4495
Elwin ES 600/K-6
13010 Waco St 91706 626-962-8015
Arthur Cunha, prin. Fax 856-4444
Foster ES 800/K-6
13900 Foster Ave 91706 626-962-8111
Christine Simmons, prin. Fax 856-4286
Geddes ES 900/K-5
14600 Cavette Pl 91706 626-962-8114
M. Virginia Castro, prin. Fax 856-4966
Heath ES 500/K-6
14321 School St 91706 626-338-4013
Maria Rios, prin. Fax 856-4967
Holland MS 800/6-8
4733 Landis Ave 91706 626-962-8412
James Rust, prin. Fax 813-6148
Holliday Childrens Center PK-PK
13529 Francisquito Ave 91706 626-337-2711
Jenice Broomfield, prin. Fax 814-4635
Jones JHS 600/7-8
14250 Merced Ave 91706 626-962-8312
Elizabeth Cox, prin. Fax 856-4291
Kenmore ES 700/K-6
3823 Kenmore Ave 91706 626-962-8316
Lawrence King, prin. Fax 856-4968
Olive MS 600/6-8
13701 Olive St 91706 626-962-8416
Richard Novlett, prin. Fax 856-4568
Pleasant View ES 600/K-6
14900 Nubia St 91706 626-962-8512
Russhell Ortega, prin. Fax 856-4369
Santa Fe S 400/3-8
4650 Baldwin Park Blvd 91706 626-856-1525
Kathy Warden, prin. Fax 813-0614
Sierra Vista JHS 800/7-8
13400 Foster Ave 91706 626-962-1300
Angela Salazar, prin. Fax 856-4577
Tracy ES 800/K-6
13350 Tracy St 91706 626-962-9718
Christine Heinrichs, prin. Fax 856-4213
Vineland ES 800/K-6
3609 Vineland Ave 91706 626-962-9719
Laura Rodriguez, prin. Fax 856-4929
Walnut ES 700/K-5
4701 Walnut St 91706 626-939-4368
Marie Porcell, prin. Fax 856-4373

Creative Planet S of the Arts 100/K-8
4428 Stewart Ave 91706 626-856-1710
Billy Rugh, admin.
East Valley Adventist S 50/K-8
3554 Maine Ave 91706 626-960-4751
Paul Negrete, prin. Fax 960-4752
St. John the Baptist S 400/PK-8
3870 Stewart Ave 91706 626-337-1421
Sr. Rosario Mediavilla, prin. Fax 337-3733

Ballard, Santa Barbara
Ballard ESD 100/K-6
2425 School St 93463 805-688-4812
Allen Pelletier, supt. Fax 688-7325
www.ballardschool.org/
Ballard ES 100/K-6
2425 School St 93463 805-688-4812
Allen Pelletier, prin. Fax 688-7325

Ballico, Merced
Ballico-Cressey ESD 300/K-8
11818 Gregg Ave 95303 209-632-5371
Jose Gonzalez, supt. Fax 632-8929
www.ballicocressey.com
Ballico S 200/4-8
11818 Gregg Ave 95303 209-632-5371
Jose Gonzalez, prin. Fax 632-8929
Other Schools – See Cressey

Bangor, Butte
Bangor UNESD 100/K-8
PO Box 340 95914 530-679-2434
Paul Arnold, supt. Fax 679-1018
www.bcoe.org/home/districts/Bangor/index.htm
Bangor S 100/K-8
PO Box 340 95914 530-679-2434
Paul Arnold, prin. Fax 679-1018

Banning, Riverside, Pop. 29,308
Banning USD 5,000/K-12
161 W Williams St 92220 951-922-0200
Lynne Kennedy Ph.D., supt. Fax 922-0227
www.banning.k12.ca.us
Cabazon ES 200/K-4
50575 Carmen 92220 951-922-0252
John Curtis, prin. Fax 922-2763
Central ES 600/K-4
295 N San Gorgonio Ave 92220 951-922-0264
Spencer Holtom, prin. Fax 922-2718
Coombs IS 800/5-6
1151 W Wilson St 92220 951-922-0268
Mark Baldwin, prin. Fax 922-2723
Hemmerling ES 500/K-4
1928 W Nicolet St 92220 951-922-0254
Ed Young, prin. Fax 922-0294
Hoffer ES 700/K-4
1115 E Hoffer St 92220 951-922-0257
Sonya Balingit, prin. Fax 922-0260
Nicolet MS 800/7-8
101 E Nicolet St 92220 951-922-0280
Robert Meteau, prin. Fax 922-2748

Precious Blood S 50/PK-PK
117 W Nicolet St 92220 951-849-2433
Cindy Gomez, dir. Fax 849-0843

Barstow, San Bernardino, Pop. 23,737
Barstow USD 7,000/K-12
551 S Avenue H 92311 760-255-6006
Fax 255-6007
www.barstow.k12.ca.us/
Barstow IS 1,100/5-6
500 G St 92311 760-255-6304
Larry Notario, prin. Fax 255-6302
Barstow JHS 1,000/7-8
1000 Armory Rd 92311 760-255-6200
Carolyn Norman, prin. Fax 255-6205
Cameron ES 600/K-4
801 S Muriel Dr 92311 760-255-6260
Derrick Delton, prin. Fax 255-6261
Crestline ES 400/K-4
2020 Monterey Ave 92311 760-252-5121
Dave Finch, prin. Fax 252-5152
Henderson ES 400/K-4
400 Avenue E 92311 760-255-6250
Jan Rhoads, prin. Fax 255-6253
Lenwood ES 300/K-4
34374 Ash Rd 92311 760-253-7715
Laura May, prin. Fax 253-7708
Montara ES 400/K-4
700 Montara Rd 92311 760-252-5150
Keith Acedo, prin. Fax 252-5185
Skyline North ES 200/K-4
36968 Camarillo Ave 92311 760-255-6090
Kim Barilone, prin. Fax 255-6095
Thomson ES 300/K-4
310 W Mountain View St 92311 760-255-6150
Theresa Gonzales, prin. Fax 255-6104
Other Schools – See Hinkley

Barstow Christian S 200/PK-8
800 Yucca Ave 92311 760-256-3556
Heather Bradford, prin. Fax 256-1326

Bass Lake, Madera
Bass Lake JUNESD
Supt. — See Oakhurst
Bass Lake ES 100/K-5
40356 Road 331 93604 559-642-1560
Glenn Reid, prin. Fax 642-1564

Bayside, Humboldt

Humboldt Bay Christian S 50/K-8
70 Stephens Ln 95524 707-822-1738
Laurel Baker, prin. Fax 822-1739

Beale AFB, Yuba, Pop. 6,912
Wheatland ESD
Supt. — See Wheatland
Lone Tree ES 400/K-5
123 Beale Hwy 95903 530-788-0248
Angela Gouker, prin. Fax 788-0518

Bear Valley, Calaveras, Pop. 550
Alpine County USD
Supt. — See Markleeville
Bear Valley S 50/K-8
PO Box 5070 95223 209-753-2880
Sally Clark, prin. Fax 753-6303

Beaumont, Riverside, Pop. 20,530
Beaumont USD 6,700/K-12
PO Box 187 92223 951-845-1631
Dr. Barry Kayrell, supt. Fax 845-2319
www.beaumontusd.k12.ca.us/
Brookside ES 700/K-5
PO Box 187 92223 951-845-3473
Fax 845-3714
Hause ES K-5
PO Box 187 92223 951-769-1674
Wilson Cuellar, prin. Fax 845-8538
Mountain View MS 700/6-8
PO Box 187 92223 951-845-1627
Victor Kezer, prin. Fax 845-8679
Palm ES 700/K-5
PO Box 187 92223 951-845-9579
Beatrice Gray, prin. Fax 845-5604
San Gorgonio MS 900/6-8
PO Box 187 92223 951-769-4391
Brian Wood, prin. Fax 769-8750
Sundance ES 700/K-5
PO Box 187 92223 951-845-2621
Lauren Kinney, prin. Fax 769-8752
Three Rings Ranch ES 700/K-5
PO Box 187 92223 951-845-5052
Aurora Perry, prin. Fax 769-3528
Tournament Hills ES 300/K-5
PO Box 187 92223 951-769-0711
Shawn Mitchell, prin. Fax 769-0592

Bell, Los Angeles, Pop. 37,521
Los Angeles USD
Supt. — See Los Angeles
Corona ES 1,300/K-5
3825 Bell Ave 90201 323-560-1323
Jack Baumann, prin. Fax 560-8166
Escutia ES K-6
6401 Bear Ave 90201 323-585-8237
Marcus Billson, prin. Fax 585-3797
Nueva Vista ES 1,000/K-5
4412 Randolph St 90201 323-562-3015
Barbara Howington, prin. Fax 560-3507
Ochoa Learning Center 2,000/K-8
5027 Live Oak St 90201 323-869-1300
Mara Bommarito, prin. Fax 562-8015
Woodlawn Avenue ES 1,000/K-5
6314 Woodlawn Ave 90201 323-560-1445
Natividad Rozsa, prin. Fax 560-7049

Bella Vista, Shasta
Bella Vista ESD 400/K-8
22661 Old Alturas Rd 96008 530-549-4415
George DeFillipo, supt. Fax 549-4506
www.shastalink.k12.ca.us/bellavista/
Bella Vista S 400/K-8
22661 Old Alturas Rd 96008 530-549-4415
George DeFillipo, prin. Fax 549-4506

Bellflower, Los Angeles, Pop. 74,570
Bellflower USD 14,900/K-12
16703 Clark Ave 90706 562-866-9011
Rick Kemppainen, supt. Fax 866-7713
www.busd.k12.ca.us/
Baxter ES 500/K-6
14929 Cerritos Ave 90706 562-531-1602
Debbie Apple, prin. Fax 531-4073
Jefferson ES 700/K-6
10027 Rose St 90706 562-804-6521
Dina Hernandez, prin. Fax 804-6577
Las Flores ES 200/K-6
10039 Palm St 90706 562-804-6565
Ruben Presiado, prin. Fax 804-6566
Pyle ES 600/K-6
14500 Woodruff Ave 90706 562-804-6528
Sulema Holguin, prin. Fax 804-6530
Ramona ES 800/K-6
9351 Laurel St 90706 562-804-6532
Bonnie Carter, prin. Fax 804-6562
Washington ES 900/K-6
9725 Jefferson St 90706 562-804-6535
Isel Taylor, prin. Fax 804-6539
Woodruff ES 800/K-6
15332 Eucalyptus Ave 90706 562-804-6545
Susan Curtiss, prin. Fax 804-6583
Other Schools – See Lakewood

Adventist Union S 100/K-8
15548 Santa Ana Ave 90706 562-867-0718
Terry Tryon, prin. Fax 866-9968
St. Bernard S 200/PK-8
9626 Park St 90706 562-867-9410
Melissa Oswald, prin. Fax 866-3210
St. Dominic Savio S 400/PK-8
9750 Foster Rd 90706 562-866-3617
Sr. Josephine Ochoa, prin. Fax 804-6638
Southland Christian Academy 200/K-6
16400 Woodruff Ave 90706 562-867-8594
Arthur Fagan, prin. Fax 867-8594
Valley Christian ES 400/PK-6
17408 Grand Ave 90706 562-920-9902
Ann Samuelson, prin. Fax 920-9778

Bell Gardens, Los Angeles, Pop. 45,135
Montebello USD
Supt. — See Montebello
Bell Gardens ES 1,000/K-4
5620 Quinn St 90201 562-927-1223
Gudiel Crosthwaite, prin. Fax 806-5134
Bell Gardens IS 1,900/5-8
5841 Live Oak St 90201 562-927-1319
Rick Mendez, prin. Fax 806-5131
Chavez ES 800/K-5
6139 Loveland St 90201 323-773-1804
Teresa Alonzo, prin. Fax 826-5164
Garfield ES 800/K-4
7425 Garfield Ave 90201 562-927-1915
Melodie Santana, prin. Fax 806-5135
Suva ES 800/K-5
6740 Suva St 90201 562-927-1827
Janice Riddle, prin. Fax 806-5137
Suva IS 1,000/6-8
6660 Suva St 90201 562-927-2679
Raymond Rivera, prin. Fax 806-5132

Bell Gardens Christian S 100/PK-8
6262 Gage Ave 90201 323-773-3968
Verdell Winslow, admin. Fax 773-2422
St. Gertrude S 300/PK-8
6824 Toler Ave 90201 562-927-1216
Joanne Dalton, prin. Fax 928-9099

Belmont, San Mateo, Pop. 24,522
Belmont-Redwood Shores ESD 2,500/K-8
2960 Hallmark Dr 94002 650-637-4800
Dr. Emerita Orta-Camilleri, supt. Fax 637-4811
www.belmont.k12.ca.us
Central ES 300/K-5
525 Middle Rd 94002 650-637-4820
Cori McKenzie, prin. Fax 637-4827
Cipriani ES 200/K-5
2525 Buena Vista Ave 94002 650-637-4840
Maria Lang-Gavidia, prin. Fax 637-4839
Fox ES 300/K-5
3100 Saint James Rd 94002 650-637-4850
Chris Marchetti, prin. Fax 637-4858
Nesbit ES 400/K-5
500 Biddulph Way 94002 650-637-4860
Kathy Kelley, prin. Fax 637-4867
Ralston MS 800/6-8
2675 Ralston Ave 94002 650-637-4880
Jennifer Kollmann, prin. Fax 637-4888
Other Schools – See Redwood City

Armstrong S 300/1-8
1405 Solana Dr 94002 650-592-7570
Rosalie Whitlock Ph.D., hdmstr. Fax 591-3114
Belmont Oaks Academy 200/K-5
2200 Carlmont Dr 94002 650-593-6175
Christine Shales, hdmstr. Fax 593-7937
Gloria Dei Lutheran S 50/K-5
2600 Ralston Ave 94002 650-593-3361
Johnold Strey, prin. Fax 593-3361
Immaculate Heart of Mary S 300/K-8
1000 Alameda De Las Pulgas 94002 650-593-4265
Sandra Larragoiti, prin. Fax 593-4342
Notre Dame S 200/PK-8
1200 Notre Dame Ave 94002 650-591-2209
Noreen Browning, prin. Fax 591-4798

Benicia, Solano, Pop. 26,489
Benicia USD 5,000/PK-12
350 E K St 94510 707-747-8300
Janice Adams Ph.D., supt. Fax 748-0146
www.beniciaunified.org
Benicia MS 1,200/6-8
1100 Southampton Rd 94510 707-747-8340
Susan Hutchinson, prin. Fax 747-8349
Farmar ES 500/K-5
901 Military W 94510 707-747-8350
Susan Sullivan, prin. Fax 747-8359
Henderson ES 600/K-5
650 Hastings Dr 94510 707-747-8370
Bobbi Horack, prin. Fax 747-8379
Semple ES 400/PK-5
2015 E 3rd St 94510 707-747-8360
Gary Dias, prin. Fax 747-8369
Turner ES 500/K-5
540 Rose Dr 94510 707-747-8390
Barbara Sanders, prin. Fax 747-8399

St. Dominic S 300/PK-8
935 E 5th St 94510 707-745-1266
Theresa Cullen, prin. Fax 745-1841

Ben Lomond, Santa Cruz, Pop. 7,884
San Lorenzo Valley USD 2,600/K-12
325 Marion Ave 95005 831-336-5194
Julie Haff, supt. Fax 336-9531
www.slv.k12.ca.us
Other Schools – See Boulder Creek, Felton

Benton, Mono
Eastern Sierra USD
Supt. — See Bridgeport
Beaman S 100/K-8
PO Box 947 93512 760-933-2397
Steven Childs, prin. Fax 933-2355

Berkeley, Alameda, Pop. 100,744
Berkeley USD 9,100/K-12
2134 Mrtn Lther King Jr Way 94704 510-644-6206
William Huyett, supt. Fax 540-5358
www.berkeley.k12.ca.us
Berkeley Arts Magnet S at Whittier 400/K-5
2015 Virginia St 94704 510-644-6225
Kristin Collins, prin. Fax 644-6265
Cragmont ES 400/K-5
830 Regal Rd 94708 510-644-8810
Evelyn Bradley, prin. Fax 644-7717
Emerson ES 300/K-5
2800 Forest Ave 94705 510-644-6891
Susan Hodge, prin. Fax 644-7758
Jefferson ES 300/K-5
1400 Ada St 94702 510-644-6298
Maggie Riddle, prin. Fax 644-6984
King MS 1,000/6-8
1781 Rose St 94703 510-644-6280
Jason Lustig, prin. Fax 644-8783
LeConte ES 300/K-5
2241 Russell St 94705 510-644-6290
Cheryl Wilson, prin. Fax 644-7767
Longfellow Arts & Technology MS 400/6-8
1500 Derby St 94703 510-644-6360
Patricia Saddler, prin. Fax 644-8707
Malcolm X ES 400/K-5
1731 Prince St 94703 510-644-6313
Cheryl Chinn, prin. Fax 644-6297
Muir ES 200/K-5
2955 Claremont Ave 94705 510-644-6410
Javier Mendieta, prin. Fax 644-8643
Oxford ES 300/K-5
1130 Oxford St 94707 510-644-6300
Janet Levenson, prin. Fax 644-4869
Parks Magnet ES 400/K-5
920 Allston Way 94710 510-644-8812
Kathy Hatzke, prin. Fax 883-6986
Thousand Oaks ES 400/K-5
840 Colusa Ave 94707 510-644-6368
Julianna Sikes, prin. Fax 644-4825
Washington ES 300/K-5
2300 Mrtn Lther King Jr Way 94704 510-644-6310
Rita Kimball, prin. Fax 644-7718
Willard MS 500/6-8
2425 Stuart St 94705 510-644-6330
Robert Ithurburn, prin. Fax 548-4219

Academy S 100/K-8
2722 Benvenue Ave 94705 510-549-0605
Gina Claudeanos, admin. Fax 549-9119
Berkeley Montessori S 100/PK-K
2030 Francisco St 94709 510-849-8340
Janet Stork, hdmstr. Fax 841-4460
Berkeley Montessori S 200/K-8
1310 University Ave 94702 510-665-8800
Janet Stork, hdmstr. Fax 665-8700
Black Pine Circle S 200/K-8
2027 7th St 94710 510-845-0876
John Carlstroem, dir. Fax 845-0336
Ecole Bilingue De Berkeley 500/PK-8
1009 Heinz Ave 94710 510-549-3867
Frederic Canadas, prin. Fax 845-3209
School of the Madeleine 300/K-8
1225 Milvia St 94709 510-526-4744
Catherine Deehan, prin. Fax 526-5152

Bermuda Dunes, Riverside, Pop. 4,571
Desert Sands USD
Supt. — See La Quinta
Monroe ES 500/K-5
42100 Yucca Ln, 760-772-4130
Mike Kint, prin. Fax 772-4135

Christian School of the Desert 500/PK-12
40700 Yucca Ln, 760-345-2848
David Fulton, prin. Fax 345-9948

Berry Creek, Butte
Pioneer UNESD 100/K-8
286 Rockerfeller Rd 95916 530-589-1633
Ted Fredenburg, supt. Fax 589-5021
pioneer.bcoe.butte.k12.ca.us/
Berry Creek S 100/K-8
286 Rockerfeller Rd 95916 530-589-1633
Ted Fredenburg, prin. Fax 589-5021

Beverly Hills, Los Angeles, Pop. 35,078
Beverly Hills USD 5,200/K-12
255 S Lasky Dr 90212 310-551-5100
Jerry Gross Ph.D., supt. Fax 286-2138
www.bhusd.org/
Beverly Vista S 700/K-8
200 S Elm Dr 90212 310-229-3669
Erik Warren, prin. Fax 275-3532
El Rodeo S 700/K-8
605 N Whittier Dr 90210 310-229-3670
Pat Escalante, prin. Fax 275-3185
Hawthorne S 700/K-8
624 N Rexford Dr 90210 310-229-3675
Toni Staser, prin. Fax 276-5023
Mann S 700/K-8
8701 Charleville Blvd 90211 310-229-3680
D. Murakawa-Leopard Ed.D., prin. Fax 652-8841

Good Shepherd S 200/PK-8
148 S Linden Dr 90212 310-275-8601
Terry Miller, prin. Fax 275-0366
Harkham Hillel Hebrew Academy 600/K-8
9120 W Olympic Blvd 90212 310-276-6135
Rabbi Yisroel Sufrin, hdmstr. Fax 276-6134
Page Private S of Beverly Hills 100/PK-6
419 S Robertson Blvd 90211 323-272-3429
Arlene Martus, dir. Fax 273-0497

Bieber, Lassen
Big Valley JUSD 300/K-12
PO Box 157 96009 530-294-5266
Rich Rhodes, supt. Fax 294-5396
www.bigvalleyschool.org/
Big Valley IS 100/4-8
PO Box 157 96009 530-294-5214
Rich Rhodes, prin. Fax 294-5109
Other Schools – See Adin

Big Bar, Trinity
Cox Bar ESD 50/K-8
PO Box 529 96010 530-623-6316
Cherie Donahue, supt. Fax 623-6316
Cox Bar S 50/K-8
PO Box 529 96010 530-623-6316
Cherie Donahue, prin. Fax 623-6316

Big Bear Lake, San Bernardino, Pop. 6,158
Bear Valley USD 3,100/K-12
PO Box 1529 92315 909-866-4631
Dr. Rudy Macioge, supt. Fax 866-2040
www.bigbear.k12.ca.us
Big Bear ES 400/K-6
PO Box 1627 92315 909-866-4638
Jeanette Haston, prin. Fax 866-1113
Big Bear MS 500/7-8
PO Box 1607 92315 909-866-4634
Julie Chamberlin, prin. Fax 866-5679

North Shore ES 500/K-6
PO Box 1887 92315 909-866-7501
Kevin Amburgey, prin. Fax 866-7510
Other Schools – See Forest Falls, Sugarloaf

Big Bend, Shasta
Indian Springs ESD 50/K-8
PO Box 70 96011 530-337-6219
Merle Stolz, supt. Fax 337-6456
www.shastalink.k12.ca.us/indiansprings/
Indian Springs S 50/K-8
PO Box 70 96011 530-337-6219
Merle Stolz, prin. Fax 337-6456

Big Creek, Fresno
Big Creek ESD 50/K-8
PO Box 98 93605 559-893-3314
Judy Statler, supt. Fax 893-3315
Big Creek S 50/K-8
PO Box 98 93605 559-893-3314
Judy Statler, prin. Fax 893-3315

Biggs, Butte, Pop. 1,803
Biggs USD 500/K-12
300 B St 95917 530-868-1281
Bill Cornelius, supt. Fax 868-1615
www.biggs.org/
Biggs S, 300 B St 95917 200/K-8
Jerry Walker, prin. 530-868-5870
Richvale ES, 300 B St 95917 50/K-6
Jerry Walker, prin. 530-882-4273

Big Pine, Inyo, Pop. 1,158
Big Pine USD 200/K-12
PO Box 908 93513 760-938-2005
Pamela Jones, supt. Fax 938-2310
www.bp.k12.ca.us
Big Pine S 100/K-8
PO Box 908 93513 760-938-2222
Pamela Jones, prin. Fax 938-2310

Big Sur, Monterey
Carmel USD
Supt. — See Carmel
Cooper ES 100/K-5
PO Box 250 93920 831-667-2452
Paula Terui, prin. Fax 667-2760

Pacific USD 50/K-12
69325 Highway 1 93920 805-927-4507
Raeanna Thomasson, supt. Fax 927-8123
www.pacificvalleyschool.com
Pacific Valley S 50/K-12
69325 Highway 1 93920 805-927-4507
Raeanna Thomasson, prin. Fax 927-8123

Bishop, Inyo, Pop. 3,606
Bishop UNESD 1,300/K-8
800 W Elm St 93514 760-872-4352
Barry Simpson, supt. Fax 872-1063
www.buesd.k12.ca.us
Elm Street S 400/K-2
800 W Elm St 93514 760-872-1278
Betsy McDonald, prin. Fax 872-5113
Home Street MS 500/6-8
201 Home St 93514 760-872-1381
Randy Cook, prin. Fax 872-1877
Pine Street S 500/3-5
800 W Pine St 93514 760-872-1658
Betsy McDonald, prin. Fax 872-5113

Round Valley JESD 100/K-8
300 N Round Valley Rd 93514 760-387-2525
Robert Barker, supt. Fax 387-2330
www.rv.k12.ca.us
Round Valley S 100/K-8
300 N Round Valley Rd 93514 760-387-2525
Robert Barker, prin. Fax 387-2330

Blocksburg, Humboldt
Southern Humbolt JUSD
Supt. — See Miranda
Casterlin S 100/K-8
24790 Alderpoint Rd 95514 707-926-5402
Marc Wilson, prin. Fax 926-5150

Bloomington, San Bernardino, Pop. 15,116
Colton JUSD
Supt. — See Colton
Bloomington MS 900/7-8
18829 Orange St 92316 909-876-4101
Nuh Kimbwala, prin. Fax 876-4195
Crestmore ES 900/K-6
18870 Jurupa Ave 92316 909-876-4151
Patricia Frost, prin. Fax 872-6408
Grimes ES 700/K-6
1609 S Spruce Ave 92316 909-876-4156
Laurie Carlton, prin. Fax 876-4213
Harris MS 1,000/7-8
11150 Alder Ave 92316 909-876-6300
Sandy Torres, prin. Fax 820-2238
Lewis ES 800/K-6
18040 San Bernardino Ave 92316 909-876-4236
Judy Scates, prin. Fax 876-4236
Smith ES 800/K-6
9551 Linden Ave 92316 909-876-4250
Brian Butler, prin. Fax 430-2835
Zimmerman ES 800/K-6
11050 Linden Ave 92316 909-876-4246
Raquel Posadas-Gonzalez, prin. Fax 872-6481

Blue Lake, Humboldt, Pop. 1,128
Blue Lake UNESD 200/K-8
PO Box 268 95525 707-668-5674
Paula Wyant-Kelso, supt. Fax 668-5619
www.humboldt.k12.ca.us/bluelake/
Blue Lake S 200/K-8
PO Box 268 95525 707-668-5674
Paula Wyant-Kelso, prin. Fax 668-5619

Green Point ESD 50/K-8
180 Valkensar Ln 95525 707-668-5921
Carole Boshears, supt. Fax 668-1986
www.humboldt.k12.ca.us/greenpoint_sd/
Green Point S 50/K-8
180 Valkensar Ln 95525 707-668-5921
Kathleen Wolfberg, prin. Fax 668-1986

Blythe, Riverside, Pop. 22,130
Palo Verde USD 3,700/K-12
295 N 1st St 92225 760-922-4164
Dr. Alan Jensen, supt. Fax 922-5942
www.pvusd-bly.k12.ca.us
Appleby ES 500/K-5
811 W Chanslor Way 92225 760-922-7174
Jeremy James, prin. Fax 922-0504
Blythe MS 800/6-8
825 N Lovekin Blvd 92225 760-922-1300
Lois Shaffer, prin. Fax 922-3748
Brown ES 700/K-5
241 N 7th St 92225 760-922-7164
Jeff Blansett, prin. Fax 922-0636
White ES 700/K-5
610 N Broadway 92225 760-922-5159
Josie Koivisto, prin. Fax 922-1367

Bodega Bay, Sonoma, Pop. 1,127
Shoreline USD
Supt. — See Tomales
Bodega Bay ES 50/K-5
PO Box 155 94923 707-875-2724
Jane Realon, prin. Fax 875-2182

Bolinas, Marin, Pop. 1,098
Bolinas-Stinson UNESD 100/K-8
125 Olema Bolinas Rd 94924 415-868-1603
Lawrence Enos, supt. Fax 868-9406
www.bolinas-stinson.org/
Bolinas-Stinson S 100/K-8
125 Olema Bolinas Rd 94924 415-868-1603
Leo Kostelnik, prin. Fax 868-9406

Bonita, San Diego, Pop. 12,542
Chula Vista ESD
Supt. — See Chula Vista
Allen ES 400/K-6
4300 Allen School Ln 91902 619-479-3662
Toni Jones, prin. Fax 267-6237
Sunnyside ES 400/K-6
5430 San Miguel Rd 91902 619-479-0571
David Schlottman, prin. Fax 479-7297
Valley Vista ES 500/K-6
3724 Valley Vista Way 91902 619-479-7171
Carmen Emery, prin. Fax 479-7024

Bonsall, San Diego, Pop. 1,881
Bonsall UNESD 1,700/K-8
31505 Old River Rd 92003 760-631-5200
Justin Cunningham, supt. Fax 941-4409
www.bonsallusd.com/
Bonsall ES 800/K-5
31555 Old River Rd 92003 760-631-5205
Lori Cummins, prin. Fax 758-3193
Sullivan MS 600/6-8
7350 W Lilac Rd 92003 760-631-5210
Janet Whiddon, prin. Fax 631-5230
Other Schools – See Oceanside

Boonville, Mendocino
Anderson Valley USD 600/PK-12
PO Box 457 95415 707-895-3774
James Collins, supt. Fax 895-2665
www.avusd.k12.ca.us/
Anderson Valley ES 300/K-6
PO Box 830 95415 707-895-3010
Donna Pierson-Pugh, prin. Fax 895-2197
Peachland Preschool PK-PK
PO Box 457 95415 707-895-2761
Donna Pearson-Pugh, prin. Fax 895-2665

Boron, Kern, Pop. 2,101
Muroc JUSD
Supt. — See North Edwards
West Boron ES 400/K-6
12300 Del Oro St 93516 760-762-5430
Janie White, prin. Fax 762-5019

Borrego Springs, San Diego, Pop. 2,244
Borrego Springs USD 500/K-12
1315 Palm Canyon Dr 92004 760-767-5357
Consuela Smith, supt. Fax 767-0494
www.sdcoe.k12.ca.us/districts/borrego/
Borrego Springs ES 200/K-5
1315 Palm Canyon Dr 92004 760-767-5333
Martha Deichler, prin. Fax 767-7438
Borrego Springs MS 100/6-8
1315 Palm Canyon Dr 92004 760-767-5335
Anne Bogardt, prin. Fax 767-5999

Boulder Creek, Santa Cruz, Pop. 6,725
San Lorenzo Valley USD
Supt. — See Ben Lomond
Boulder Creek ES 500/K-5
400 W Lomond St 95006 831-338-6413
Lynn Chappell, prin. Fax 338-6118

Boulevard, San Diego
Mountain Empire USD
Supt. — See Pine Valley
Clover Flat ES 100/3-7
39639 Old Highway 80 91905 619-766-4655
Mr. Brennan McLaughlin, prin. Fax 766-4537

Bradley, Monterey
Bradley UNESD 50/K-8
PO Box 60 93426 805-472-2310
Catherine Reimer, supt. Fax 472-2339
schools.monterey.k12.ca.us/~bradley/
Bradley S 50/K-8
PO Box 60 93426 805-472-2310
Catherine Reimer, prin. Fax 472-2339

Brawley, Imperial, Pop. 22,433
Brawley ESD 3,700/K-8
261 D St 92227 760-344-2330
Terri Decker, supt. Fax 344-8928
www.besd.org/
Hildalgo ES 600/K-K, 4-6
615 S Cesar Chavez St 92227 760-344-0431
Celia Santana, prin. Fax 344-2423
Oakley ES 800/K-3
1401 B St 92227 760-344-4620
Craig Casey, prin. Fax 344-2019
Swing ES 800/K-K, 4-6
245 W A St 92227 760-344-3350
Brian Taylor, prin. Fax 344-2613
Witter ES 700/K-3
150 K St 92227 760-344-0750
Gail Watkins, prin. Fax 351-3097
Worth JHS 900/7-8
385 W D St 92227 760-344-2153
Luis Panduro, prin. Fax 351-5043

Magnolia UNESD 100/K-8
4502 Casey Rd 92227 760-344-2494
Blaine Smith, supt. Fax 344-8584
www.magnoliatigers.com
Magnolia Union S 100/K-8
4502 Casey Rd 92227 760-344-2494
Blaine Smith, prin. Fax 344-8584

Mulberry ESD 100/K-8
1391 Rutherford Rd 92227 760-344-8600
Danny Eddins, supt. Fax 351-1769
www.mulberrymustangs.com/
Mulberry S 100/K-8
1391 Rutherford Rd 92227 760-344-8600
Danny Eddins, prin. Fax 351-1769

Brawley Christian Academy 100/PK-12
430 N 2nd St 92227 760-344-3911
Robert Feist, prin. Fax 344-5864
Sacred Heart S 100/PK-8
428 S Imperial Ave 92227 760-344-2662
Yvonne Burns, prin. Fax 344-1910

Brea, Orange, Pop. 38,465
Brea-Olinda USD 6,100/K-12
PO Box 300 92822 714-990-7800
A.J Roland, supt. Fax 529-2137
www.bousd.k12.ca.us
Arovista ES 600/K-6
900 Eadington Dr 92821 714-529-2185
Bob Phelps, prin. Fax 990-7899
Brea Country Hills ES 600/K-6
150 N Associated Rd 92821 714-990-3221
Bob Rendon, prin. Fax 990-3222
Brea JHS 1,000/7-8
400 N Brea Blvd 92821 714-990-7500
Pam Gallarda, prin. Fax 990-7585
Fanning ES 500/K-6
650 Apricot Ave 92821 714-529-3908
Brenda Clark, prin. Fax 529-3909
Laurel ES 500/K-6
200 S Flower Ave 92821 714-529-2520
Daryn Coburn, prin. Fax 990-7542
Mariposa ES 500/K-6
1111 Mariposa Dr 92821 714-529-4916
Helene Cunningham, prin. Fax 990-7552
Olinda ES 300/K-6
109 Lilac Ln 92823 714-528-7475
Kelly Anderson, prin. Fax 528-7481

Brea-Olinda Friends Christian S 200/PK-6
200 S Associated Rd 92821 714-990-8780
Jodie Whittemore, prin. Fax 990-4879
Christ Lutheran S 300/PK-8
820 W Imperial Hwy 92821 714-529-0892
Fax 529-2157
St. Angela Merici S 300/K-8
575 S Walnut Ave 92821 714-529-6372
Nancy Windisch, admin. Fax 529-7755

Brentwood, Contra Costa, Pop. 43,794
Brentwood UNESD 7,700/K-8
255 Guthrie Ln 94513 925-513-6300
Merrill Grant Ed.D., supt. Fax 634-8583
www.brentwood.k12.ca.us
Adams MS 800/6-8
401 American Ave 94513 925-513-6450
Scott Vernoy, prin. Fax 513-3470
Brentwood ES 800/K-5
200 Griffith Ln 94513 925-513-6360
Guy Rohlfs, prin. Fax 513-0697
Bristow MS 900/6-8
855 Minnesota Ave 94513 925-513-6460
Russ Cornell, prin. Fax 516-8725
Garin ES 800/K-5
250 1st St 94513 925-513-6370
Stacy Joslin, prin. Fax 513-0698
Hill MS 800/6-8
140 Birch St 94513 925-513-6440
Kirsten Jobb, prin. Fax 513-0696
Krey ES 900/K-5
190 Crawford Dr 94513 925-513-6400
Brian Jones, prin. Fax 240-1628
Loma Vista ES 700/K-5
2110 San Jose Ave 94513 925-513-6390
Lauri James, prin. Fax 240-5456
Marsh Creek ES 500/K-5
601 Grant St 94513 925-513-6420
Michael Bowen, prin. Fax 240-5382
Nunn ES 600/K-5
1755 Central Blvd 94513 925-513-6380
Charla Hernandez, prin. Fax 513-0995
Pioneer ES 700/K-5
2010 Shady Willow Ln 94513 925-513-6410
Rusty Ehrlich, prin. Fax 513-6419

Knightsen ESD
Supt. — See Knightsen
Old River S K-8
30 Learning Ln 94513 925-625-3330
Ray Witte, prin. Fax 516-1011

Dainty Center/Willow Wood S 200/K-6
1265 Dainty Ave 94513 925-634-4539
Adrienne Guinn, dir.
Gateway Christian S 200/K-12
2401 Shady Willow Ln 94513 925-634-0493
Kathy Zamora, prin. Fax 634-0402

Bridgeport, Mono
Eastern Sierra USD 500/K-12
PO Box 575 93517 760-932-7443
Don Clark, supt. Fax 932-7140
www.esusd.org
Bridgeport S 100/K-8
PO Box 577 93517 760-932-7441
Roger Yost, prin. Fax 932-1188
Other Schools – See Benton, Coleville, Lee Vining

Bridgeville, Humboldt
Bridgeville ESD 50/K-8
PO Box 98 95526 707-777-3311
Mike Mullan, supt. Fax 777-3023
www.humboldt.k12.ca.us/bridgeville_sd/
Bridgeville S 50/K-8
PO Box 98 95526 707-777-3311
Mike Mullan, prin. Fax 777-3023

Southern Trinity JUSD 100/K-12
680 Van Duzen Rd 95526 707-574-6237
Peggy Canale, supt. Fax 574-6538
www.tcoe.trinity.k12.ca.us/~sotrin/
Van Duzen S 100/K-8
680 Van Duzen Rd 95526 707-574-6237
Peggy Canale, prin. Fax 574-6538
Other Schools – See Zenia

Brisbane, San Mateo, Pop. 3,556
Brisbane ESD 600/K-8
1 Solano St 94005 415-467-0550
Toni Presta, supt. Fax 467-2914
brisbane.ca.campusgrid.net/home
Brisbane ES 200/K-5
500 San Bruno Ave 94005 415-467-0120
Bob Abaya, prin. Fax 468-8257
Lipman MS 200/6-8
1 Solano St 94005 415-467-9541
Pennie Pine, prin. Fax 467-5073
Other Schools – See Daly City

Browns Valley, Yuba
Marysville JUSD
Supt. — See Marysville
Browns Valley ES 200/K-5
PO Box 190 95918 530-741-6107
Gina Lanphier, prin. Fax 741-7831

Buellton, Santa Barbara, Pop. 4,293
Buellton UNSD 700/K-8
595 2nd St 93427 805-686-2767
Tom Cooper, supt. Fax 686-2719
buellton.ca.schoolwebpages.com/
Jonata MS 200/6-8
301 2nd St 93427 805-688-4222
Fax 688-6611
Oak Valley ES 400/K-5
595 2nd St 93427 805-688-6992
Joel Williamson, prin. Fax 688-1364

Buena Park, Orange, Pop. 79,174
Buena Park ESD 6,000/K-8
6885 Orangethorpe Ave 90620 714-522-8412
Greg Magnuson, supt. Fax 994-1506
www.ocde.k12.ca.us/bpsd
Beatty ES 1,100/K-6
8201 Country Club Dr 90621 714-523-1160
Nancy Rios, prin. Fax 670-7628
Buena Park JHS 1,200/7-8
6931 Orangethorpe Ave 90620 714-522-8491
Jody Black, prin. Fax 523-1602
Corey ES 700/K-6
7351 Holder St 90620 714-522-8389
Annie Oei, prin. Fax 739-4058
Emery ES 800/K-6
8600 Somerset St 90621 714-521-5134
Debbie Diaz, prin. Fax 562-0541
Gilbert ES 800/K-6
7255 8th St 90621 714-522-7281
Jason Kuncewicki, prin. Fax 670-7748
Pendleton ES 600/K-6
7101 Stanton Ave 90621 714-521-8568
Renee Jeffrey, prin. Fax 670-9391
Whitaker ES 800/K-6
8401 Montana Ave 90621 714-521-9770
Valerie Connolly, prin. Fax 521-3487

Centralia ESD 4,800/K-6
6625 La Palma Ave 90620 714-228-3100
Diane Scheerhorn, supt. Fax 228-3111
www.cesd.us
Buena Terra ES 400/K-6
8299 Holder St 90620 714-228-3220
Peter Cole, prin. Fax 821-3716
Dysinger ES 500/K-6
7770 Camellia Dr 90620 714-228-3240
Pam Carlson, prin. Fax 228-3246
Knott ES 500/K-6
7300 La Palma Ave 90620 714-228-3250
Michelle Newman, prin. Fax 826-4047
San Marino ES 600/K-6
6215 San Rolando Cir 90620 714-228-3280
Randy Helms, prin. Fax 220-0521
Temple ES 400/K-6
7800 Holder St 90620 714-228-3290
Linda Rader, prin. Fax 736-0250
Other Schools – See Anaheim, La Palma

Cypress ESD
Supt. — See Cypress
Vessels ES 400/K-6
10051 Bernadette Ave 90620 714-220-6990
Jane Snyder, prin. Fax 220-6993

Savanna ESD
Supt. — See Anaheim
Holder ES, 9550 Holder St 90620 500/K-6
Ona Sandi, prin. 714-236-3840

Bethel Baptist Academy 200/K-12
8433 Philodendron Way 90620 714-521-5586
Sharon Wallace, admin.
Crescent Avenue Christian S 100/K-6
5600 Crescent Ave 90620 714-527-6673
Loretta Scott, admin. Fax 527-2820
St. Pius V S 600/K-8
7681 Orangethorpe Ave 90621 714-522-5313
Sandy Lewis, prin. Fax 522-1767
Speech and Language Development Ctr 200/K-12
8699 Holder St 90620 714-821-3620
Dawn O'Connor, dir.

Burbank, Los Angeles, Pop. 104,108
Burbank USD 15,200/K-12
1900 W Olive Ave 91506 818-729-4400
Dr. Kevin Jolly, supt. Fax 729-4483
www.burbankusd.org/
Burbank MS 1,000/6-8
3700 W Jeffries Ave 91505 818-558-4646
Anita Schackmann, prin. Fax 842-3727
Disney ES 400/K-5
1220 W Orange Grove Ave 91506 818-558-5385
Sandra Cavalheiro, prin. Fax 558-4664
Edison ES 600/K-5
2110 Chestnut St 91506 818-558-4644
Laura Flosi, prin. Fax 558-5566
Emerson ES 500/K-5
720 E Cypress Ave 91501 818-558-5419
Linda Acuff, prin. Fax 843-2359
Harte ES 600/K-5
3200 W Jeffries Ave 91505 818-558-5533
Sheari Taylor, prin. Fax 955-7630
Jefferson ES 700/K-5
1900 N 6th St 91504 818-558-4635
Melissa Kistler, prin. Fax 558-4666
Jordan MS 1,200/6-8
420 S Mariposa St 91506 818-558-4622
Sharon Cuseo, prin. Fax 843-3509
McKinley ES 500/K-5
349 W Valencia Ave 91506 818-558-5477
Roberta Kavanaugh, prin. Fax 558-5485
Miller ES 700/K-5
720 E Providencia Ave 91501 818-558-5460
Judy Hession, prin. Fax 843-6077
Muir MS 1,500/6-8
1111 N Kenneth Rd 91504 818-558-5320
Dr. Daniel Hacking, prin. Fax 841-4637
Providencia ES 400/K-5
1919 N Ontario St 91505 818-558-5470
Tom Kissinger, prin. Fax 558-5475
Roosevelt ES 500/K-5
850 N Cordova St 91505 818-558-4668
Betsy Quinn, prin. Fax 955-7648
Stevenson ES 400/K-5
3333 W Oak St 91505 818-558-5522
Debbie Ginnetti, prin. Fax 841-3435
Washington ES 500/K-5
2322 N Lincoln St 91504 818-558-5550
Arlene Zenian, prin. Fax 558-5556

First Lutheran S 50/K-6
1001 S Glenoaks Blvd 91502 818-848-3076
Carol McDowell, prin. Fax 848-3801
St. Finbar S 200/K-8
2120 W Olive Ave 91506 818-848-0191
Michael Marasco, prin. Fax 848-4315
St. Francis Xavier S 300/K-8
3601 Scott Rd 91504 818-504-4422
Dr. Paul Sullivan, prin. Fax 504-4424
St. Robert Bellarmine S 300/PK-8
154 N 5th St 91501 818-842-5033
Dr. June Rosena, prin. Fax 842-3246

Burlingame, San Mateo, Pop. 27,380
Burlingame ESD 2,300/K-8
1825 Trousdale Dr 94010 650-259-3800
Dianne Talarico, supt. Fax 259-3820
www.bsd.k12.ca.us/
Burlingame IS 800/6-8
1715 Quesada Way 94010 650-259-3830
Pamela Scott, prin. Fax 259-3843
Franklin ES 500/K-5
2385 Trousdale Dr 94010 650-259-3850
Lisa Booth, prin. Fax 259-3854
Lincoln ES 400/K-5
1801 Devereaux Dr 94010 650-259-3860
Diane Garber, prin. Fax 259-3868
McKinley ES 200/K-5
701 Paloma Ave 94010 650-259-3870
Paula Valerio, prin. Fax 259-3879
Roosevelt ES 300/K-5
1151 Vancouver Ave 94010 650-259-3890
Dennis Hills, prin. Fax 259-0111
Washington ES 200/K-5
801 Howard Ave 94010 650-259-3880
Julie Eastman, prin. Fax 259-3884

Our Lady of Angels S 300/PK-8
1328 Cabrillo Ave 94010 650-343-9200
Pat Bordin, prin. Fax 343-5620
St. Catherine of Siena S 300/K-8
1300 Bayswater Ave 94010 650-344-7176
Sr. Antonella Manca, prin. Fax 344-7426

Burney, Shasta, Pop. 3,423
Fall River JUSD 1,300/K-12
20375 Tamarack Ave 96013 530-335-4538
Larry Snelling, supt. Fax 335-3115
www.shastalink.k12.ca.us/frjusd/
Burney ES 400/K-6
37403 Toronto Ave 96013 530-335-2279
Dianna Fischer, prin. Fax 335-2360
Other Schools – See Fall River Mills

Burnt Ranch, Trinity
Burnt Ranch ESD 100/K-8
PO Box 39 95527 530-629-2543
Sarah Supahan, supt. Fax 629-2479
www.tcoek12.org/~br/
Burnt Ranch S 100/K-8
PO Box 39 95527 530-629-2543
Terry NaDeau, prin. Fax 629-2479

Buttonwillow, Kern, Pop. 1,301
Buttonwillow UNESD 400/K-8
42600 Highway 58 93206 661-764-5166
James Murphy, supt. Fax 764-5165
Buttonwillow S 400/K-8
42600 Highway 58 93206 661-764-5248
Fax 764-5165

Byron, Contra Costa
Byron UNESD 1,700/K-8
14301 Byron Hwy 94514 925-634-6644
Eric Prater, supt. Fax 634-9421
www.byronusd.com
Excelsior MS 500/6-8
14301 Byron Hwy 94514 925-634-2128
Ben Scinto, prin. Fax 634-5120
Other Schools – See Discovery Bay

Mountain House ESD 50/K-8
3950 Mountain House Rd 94514 209-835-2283
Fax 832-0284
www.mountainhouseschool.com/
Mountain House S 50/K-8
3950 Mountain House Rd 94514 209-835-2283
Fax 832-0284

Calabasas, Los Angeles, Pop. 21,908
Las Virgenes USD 11,900/K-12
4111 Las Virgenes Rd 91302 818-880-4000
Dr. Donald Zimring, supt. Fax 880-4200
corp.lvusd.org
Bay Laurel ES 700/K-5
24740 Paseo Primario 91302 818-222-9022
Susan Wachtel, prin. Fax 222-0231
Chaparral ES 600/K-5
22601 Liberty Bell Rd 91302 818-591-2428
Somer Harding, prin. Fax 591-7056
Lupin Hill ES 700/K-5
26210 Adamor Rd 91302 818-880-4434
Sheila Grady, prin. Fax 880-2201
Round Meadow ES 600/K-5
5151 Round Meadow Rd 91302 818-883-6750
Tom Spence, prin. Fax 883-7121
Stelle MS 1,000/6-8
22450 Mulholland Hwy 91302 818-224-4107
Mary Sistrunk, prin. Fax 224-4989
Wright MS 900/6-8
4029 Las Virgenes Rd 91302 818-880-4614
Kimmarie Taylor, prin. Fax 878-0453
Other Schools – See Agoura Hills, Westlake Village

Arbor Academy 200/1-12
26245 Hatmor Dr 91302 805-624-6666
Stephanie Mitchell, admin.
Calmont S 100/PK-9
1666 Las Virgenes Canyon Rd 91302 818-880-8820
Judith Chamberlain, dir. Fax 880-8860
Viewpoint S 1,200/K-12
23620 Mulholland Hwy 91302 818-340-2901
Dr. Robert Dworkoski, hdmstr. Fax 591-0834

Calexico, Imperial, Pop. 36,005
Calexico USD 9,400/K-12
PO Box 792 92232 760-768-3888
David Groesbeck, supt. Fax 768-3856
www.calexico.k12.ca.us/
Charles ES 900/K-6
PO Box 792 92232 760-768-3910
Alejandra Sandoval, prin. Fax 768-9640
Dool ES 700/K-6
PO Box 792 92232 760-768-3820
Liliana Dimian, prin. Fax 357-8909
Jefferson ES 1,000/K-6
PO Box 792 92232 760-768-3812
Lucio Padilla, prin. Fax 768-1827
Kennedy Gardens ES 900/K-6
PO Box 792 92232 760-768-7416
Alba Zazueta, prin. Fax 768-1670
Mains ES 500/K-6
PO Box 792 92232 760-768-3900
Carlos Gonzales, prin. Fax 768-1446
Rockwood ES 800/K-6
PO Box 792 92232 760-768-3832
Gloria Martinez, prin. Fax 768-1893

Calexico Mission S 400/K-12
601 E 1st St 92231 760-357-3711
Susan Smith, prin. Fax 357-3713
Our Lady of Guadalupe Academy 600/PK-8
535 Rockwood Ave 92231 760-357-1986
Sr. Maria Elvia Gonzalez, prin. Fax 357-3282

Caliente, Kern
Caliente UNESD 100/K-8
12400 Caliente Creek Rd 93518 661-867-2301
Marv Baker, supt. Fax 867-6902
www.calienteschooldistrict.org/
Caliente S 50/K-8
12400 Caliente Creek Rd 93518 661-867-2302
Marv Baker, prin.

Piute Mountain S 100/K-8
12400 Caliente Creek Rd 93518 661-867-2301
Marv Baker, prin. Fax 867-6902

California City, Kern, Pop. 11,790
Mojave USD
Supt. — See Mojave
California City MS 500/6-8
9736 Redwood Blvd 93505 760-373-3241
Starletta Darbeau, prin. Fax 373-1355
Hacienda ES 500/K-3
19950 Hacienda Blvd 93505 760-373-5824
Shawnee Moore, prin. Fax 373-5787
Ulrich ES 1,000/K-5
9124 Catalpa Ave 93505 760-373-4824
Bonnie Ulrich, prin. Fax 373-3309

California Hot Springs, Tulare
Hot Springs ESD 50/K-8
PO Box 38 93207 661-548-6544
I.J. Blevens, supt. Fax 548-6254
www.hot-springs.k12.ca.us
Hot Springs S 50/K-8
PO Box 38 93207 661-548-6544
I.J. Blevens, prin. Fax 548-6254
Other Schools – See Kernville

Calimesa, Riverside, Pop. 7,491

Mesa Grande Academy 300/K-12
975 Fremont St 92320 909-795-1112
Alfred Riddle, prin. Fax 795-1653

Calipatria, Imperial, Pop. 7,725
Calipatria USD 1,100/K-12
501 W Main St 92233 760-348-2892
Douglas Kline, supt. Fax 344-8926
calipatria.k12.ca.us/
Fremont PS 300/K-4
401 W Main St 92233 760-348-5025
Susan Casey, prin. Fax 348-5525
Young MS 300/5-8
220 S International Blvd 92233 760-348-2842
Joe Derma, prin. Fax 348-2848
Other Schools – See Niland

Calistoga, Napa, Pop. 5,190
Calistoga JUSD 1,000/K-12
1520 Lake St 94515 707-942-4703
Jeff Johnson, supt. Fax 942-6589
www.calistoga.k12.ca.us
Calistoga ES 500/K-6
1327 Berry St 94515 707-942-4398
Michele Treuscorff, prin. Fax 942-0970

Calpella, Mendocino

Waldorf S of Mendocino County 200/PK-8
PO Box 349 95418 707-485-8719
Fax 485-7335

Camarillo, Ventura, Pop. 61,576
Pleasant Valley SD 6,700/PK-8
600 Temple Ave 93010 805-482-2763
Dr. Luis Villegas, supt. Fax 987-5511
www.pvsd.k12.ca.us
Camarillo Heights ES 500/K-5
35 Catalina Dr 93010 805-482-9838
Elizabeth Silverman, prin. Fax 987-7189
Dos Caminos ES 500/PK-5
3635 Appian Way 93010 805-482-9894
Erica Williams, prin. Fax 482-7478
El Descanso ES 500/PK-5
1099 Bedford Dr 93010 805-482-1954
Beverly Eidmann, prin. Fax 388-8593
La Mariposa ES 600/K-5
4800 Corte Olivas 93012 805-987-8333
Jay Greenlinger, prin. Fax 383-8977
Las Colinas MS 1,000/6-8
5750 Fieldcrest Dr 93012 805-484-0461
Pam Gonzalez, prin. Fax 482-2443
Las Posas ES 500/PK-5
75 E Calle La Guerra 93010 805-482-4606
James Martinez, prin. Fax 388-5431
Monte Vista MS 800/6-8
888 Lantana St 93010 805-482-8891
Joe Herzog, prin. Fax 987-8951
PVIC PEEP Preschool PK-PK
2222 Ventura Blvd 93010 805-482-8861
Laurie Matson, contact Fax 388-2532
Rancho Rosal ES 600/K-5
3535 Village at the Park Dr 93012 805-445-1147
Sue Sigler, prin. Fax 445-1244
Tierra Linda ES 700/K-5
1201 Woodcreek Rd 93012 805-445-8800
June Pack, prin. Fax 445-8804
Other Schools – See Santa Rosa Vlly

Cornerstone Christian S 600/PK-12
1777 Arneill Rd 93010 805-987-8621
Lory Selby, supt. Fax 987-8208
Mt. Cross Child Development Center 50/PK-K
102 Camino Esplendido 93010 805-482-9706
Catherine Channels, dir.
Pleasant Valley Christian S 300/PK-8
1101 E Ponderosa Dr 93010 805-383-2672
Susan Wilson, prin. Fax 384-9328
St. Mary Magdalen S 300/PK-8
2534 Ventura Blvd 93010 805-482-2611
Dr. Marquita Yriarte, prin. Fax 987-8211

Cambria, San Luis Obispo, Pop. 5,382
Coast USD 900/K-12
1350 Main St 93428 805-927-3880
Chris Adams, supt. Fax 927-0312
www.cambria.k12.ca.us
Cambria ES 300/K-5
3223 Main St 93428 805-927-4400
Carol Stoner, prin. Fax 927-6753

Santa Lucia MS 200/6-8
2850 Schoolhouse Ln 93428 805-927-3693
Denis deClercq, prin. Fax 927-4615

Cameron Park, El Dorado, Pop. 11,897
Buckeye UNSD
Supt. — See Shingle Springs
Blue Oak ES 700/K-5
2391 Merrychase Dr 95682 530-676-0164
Sally Traub, prin. Fax 676-0758
Camerado Springs MS 700/6-8
2480 Merrychase Dr 95682 530-677-1658
Meg Enns, prin. Fax 677-9537

Camino, El Dorado
Camino UNESD 400/K-8
3060 Snows Rd 95709 530-644-4552
Suzanne Egger, supt. Fax 644-5412
www.caminoschool.org
Camino S 400/K-8
3060 Snows Rd 95709 530-644-2204
Eric Bonniksen, prin. Fax 644-5412

Campbell, Santa Clara, Pop. 37,042
Campbell UNESD 2,900/K-8
155 N 3rd St 95008 408-364-4200
Dr. Johanna VanderMolen, supt. Fax 341-7280
www.campbellusd.k12.ca.us
Campbell MS 700/5-8
295 Cherry Ln 95008 408-364-4222
Cynthia Dodd, prin. Fax 341-7150
Rosemary ES 400/K-5
401 W Hamilton Ave 95008 408-364-4254
Edna Laskin, prin. Fax 341-7010
Other Schools – See San Jose, Saratoga

Campbell Christian S 400/PK-5
1075 W Campbell Ave 95008 408-370-4900
Dr. Shawn Stuart, prin. Fax 370-4907
Canyon Heights Academy 200/PK-8
775 Waldo Rd 95008 408-370-6727
Paul Parker, prin. Fax 370-7147
Casa Di Mir Montessori S 100/PK-6
90 E Latimer Ave 95008 408-370-3073
Wanda Whitehead, prin. Fax 370-3153
Old Orchard S 200/PK-8
400 W Campbell Ave 95008 408-378-5935
Bonnie Weston, dir. Fax 341-0782
St. Lucy S 300/K-8
76 Kennedy Ave 95008 408-871-8023
Jennifer Martin, prin. Fax 378-4945
San Jose Christian S 300/PK-8
1300 Sheffield Ave 95008 408-371-7741
Dan Meester, supt. Fax 371-5596
Veritas Christian Academy 50/K-12
400 Llewellyn Ave Unit 2 95008 408-984-1255
David Wallace, admin. Fax 871-7929
West Valley Christian S 50/K-8
95 Dot Ave 95008 408-378-4327
Yuritzy Villasenor, prin. Fax 378-4371

Campo, San Diego
Mountain Empire USD
Supt. — See Pine Valley
Campo ES 300/K-7
1654 Buckman Springs Rd 91906 619-478-5583
Diane Yops, prin. Fax 478-5982

Camptonville, Yuba
Camptonville ESD 100/K-8
PO Box 278 95922 530-288-3277
Steve Kelly, supt. Fax 288-0805
www.cville.k12.ca.us/
Camptonville S 100/K-8
PO Box 278 95922 530-288-3277
Steve Kelly, prin. Fax 288-0805

Canby, Modoc
Modoc JUSD
Supt. — See Alturas
Arlington S 50/K-8
PO Box 7 96015 530-233-7201
Mike Martin, prin. Fax 233-3253

Canoga Park, See Los Angeles
Los Angeles USD
Supt. — See Los Angeles
Canoga Park ES 800/K-5
7438 Topanga Canyon Blvd 91303 818-340-3591
Lorraine Mariglia, prin. Fax 592-0845
Capistrano Avenue ES 400/K-5
8118 Capistrano Ave 91304 818-883-8981
Alice Gibbs, prin. Fax 340-2187
Columbus MS 1,200/6-8
22250 Elkwood St 91304 818-702-1200
Ann Allocca, prin. Fax 348-2894
Fullbright Avenue ES 600/K-5
6940 Fullbright Ave 91306 818-340-6677
Claudia Ruiz, prin. Fax 340-1052
Hamlin Street ES 300/K-5
22627 Hamlin St 91307 818-348-4741
Victoria Christie, prin. Fax 348-3506
Hart Street ES 800/K-5
21040 Hart St 91303 818-340-6222
Susan Klein, prin. Fax 340-8149
Justice Street ES 400/K-5
23350 Justice St 91304 818-346-4388
Jill Frieze, prin. Fax 346-4649
Limerick Avenue ES 1,000/K-5
8530 Limerick Ave 91306 818-341-1730
Betsy Garvin, prin. Fax 998-4912
Nevada ES 600/K-5
22120 Chase St 91304 818-348-2169
Murray MacPherson, prin. Fax 592-0894
Pomelo ES 700/K-5
7633 March Ave 91304 818-887-9700
Masha Gardner, prin. Fax 887-1744
Sunny Brae ES 800/K-5
20620 Arminta St 91306 818-341-0931
Susan Lasken, prin. Fax 709-1232

Sutter MS 1,700/6-8
7330 Winnetka Ave 91306 818-773-5800
Michael Smith, prin. Fax 341-3039
Welby Way ES 700/K-5
23456 Welby Way 91307 818-348-1975
Dustin Merritt, prin. Fax 704-8726
Winnetka ES 600/K-5
8240 Winnetka Ave 91306 818-341-5422
Jackie Adelman, prin. Fax 998-1871

AGBU Manoogian-Demirdjian S 900/PK-12
6844 Oakdale Ave 91306 818-883-2428
Hagop Hagopian, prin. Fax 883-8353
Canoga Park Lutheran S 100/K-8
7357 Jordan Ave 91303 818-348-5714
Karen Jonas, prin. Fax 348-1516
Faith Baptist S 1,300/PK-12
7644 Farralone Ave 91304 818-340-6131
Dr. Roland Rasmussen, dir. Fax 592-0279
Our Lady of the Valley S 200/PK-8
22041 Gault St 91303 818-592-2894
Kathleen Delgado, prin. Fax 592-2896

Cantua Creek, Fresno
Golden Plains USD
Supt. — See San Joaquin
Cantua S 200/K-8
PO Box 369 93608 559-829-3331
Mario Cobarruvias, prin. Fax 829-6783

Canyon, Contra Costa
Canyon ESD 100/K-8
PO Box 187 94516 925-376-4671
Gloria Faircloth, supt. Fax 376-2343
www.canyon.k12.ca.us
Canyon S 100/K-8
PO Box 187 94516 925-376-4671
Chris Kerrigan, prin. Fax 376-2343

Canyon Country, See Santa Clarita
Saugus UNESD
Supt. — See Santa Clarita
Cedarcreek ES 600/K-6
27792 Camp Plenty Rd 91351 661-298-3251
Rudy Ramirez, prin. Fax 298-3255
Rio Vista ES 900/K-6
20417 Cedarcreek St 91351 661-298-3242
Isa DeArmas, prin. Fax 251-7466
Skyblue Mesa ES 500/K-6
28040 Hardesty Ave 91351 661-298-3260
Deborah Bohn, prin. Fax 298-3256

Sulphur Springs UNESD 5,700/K-6
27000 Weyerhauser Way 91351 661-252-5131
Dr. Robert Nolet, supt. Fax 252-3589
www.sssd.k12.ca.us
Canyon Springs Community ES 800/K-6
19059 Vicci St 91351 661-252-4322
Lynn David, prin. Fax 252-0974
Cox Community ES 500/K-6
18643 Oakmoor St 91351 661-252-2100
Sandra Smith, prin. Fax 299-4916
Mint Canyon Community ES 400/K-6
16400 Sierra Hwy 91351 661-252-2570
Betsy Letzo, prin. Fax 298-3383
Mitchell Community ES 800/K-6
16821 Goodvale Rd 91387 661-252-9110
Roni Andrus, prin. Fax 252-6537
Pinetree Community ES 800/K-6
29156 Lotusgarden Dr 91387 661-298-2280
Jane D'Anna, prin. Fax 298-0331
Sulphur Springs Community ES 700/K-6
16628 Lost Canyon Rd 91387 661-252-2725
Josh Randall, prin. Fax 252-5403
Other Schools – See Newhall, Santa Clarita

William S. Hart UNHSD
Supt. — See Santa Clarita
Sierra Vista JHS 1,300/7-8
19425 Stillmore St 91351 661-252-3113
Mark Crawford, prin. Fax 252-2790

Pinecrest S 200/K-8
16530 Lost Canyon Rd 91387 661-298-2127
Iliana Faraldo, admin.
Santa Clarita Christian S 600/K-12
27249 Luther Dr 91351 661-252-7371
Derek Swales, prin. Fax 252-4354

Capistrano Beach, See Dana Point
Capistrano USD
Supt. — See San Juan Capistrano
Palisades ES 500/K-5
26462 Via Sacramento 92624 949-496-5942
Melissa Murray, prin. Fax 496-7290

Capo Beach Calvary S 100/PK-8
25975 Domingo Ave 92624 949-496-3513
Maggie McMillion, prin. Fax 496-2138

Capitola, Santa Cruz, Pop. 9,553
Soquel UNESD 1,700/K-8
620 Monterey Ave 95010 831-464-5630
Kathleen Howard, supt. Fax 475-5196
www.soqueldo.santacruz.k12.ca.us/
New Brighton MS 600/6-8
250 Washburn Ave 95010 831-464-5660
Robert Martin, prin. Fax 475-8236
Other Schools – See Santa Cruz, Soquel

Cardiff by the Sea, See Encinitas
Cardiff ESD 700/K-6
1888 Montgomery Ave 92007 760-632-5890
Tom Pellegrino, supt. Fax 942-5831
www.cardiffschools.com
Cardiff ES 300/K-3
1888 Montgomery Ave 92007 760-632-5892
Julie Parker, prin. Fax 632-5375

Harris S 400/3-6
1888 Montgomery Ave 92007 760-632-5894
Jill Heichel, prin. Fax 632-0585

Carlotta, Humboldt
Cuddeback UNESD 100/K-8
PO Box 7 95528 707-768-3372
Ronan Collver, supt. Fax 768-3211
www.humboldt.k12.ca.us/cuddeback_sd/
Cuddeback S 100/K-8
PO Box 7 95528 707-768-3372
Ronan Collver, prin. Fax 768-3211

Carlsbad, San Diego, Pop. 90,773
Carlsbad USD 10,900/K-12
6225 El Camino Real 92009 760-331-5000
John Roach Ed.D., supt. Fax 431-6707
www.carlsbadusd.k12.ca.us
Aviara Oaks ES 900/K-5
6900 Ambrosia Ln, 760-331-6000
Kimberly Huesing, prin. Fax 438-4576
Aviara Oaks MS 900/6-8
6880 Ambrosia Ln, 760-331-6100
Carolyn Millikin, prin. Fax 438-7894
Buena Vista ES 300/K-5
1330 Buena Vista Way 92008 760-331-5400
Tina Howard, prin. Fax 720-0741
Calavera Hills ES 600/K-5
4104 Tamarack Ave, 760-331-6400
Leslie Harden, prin. Fax 729-3040
Calavera Hills MS 500/6-8
4104 Tamarack Ave, 760-331-6400
Catina Hancock, prin. Fax 729-4758
Hope ES 500/K-5
3010 Tamarack Ave, 760-331-5900
Richard Tubbs, prin. Fax 729-4758
Jefferson ES 600/K-5
3743 Jefferson St 92008 760-331-5500
Jane Hartman, prin. Fax 720-3809
Kelly ES 700/K-5
4885 Kelly Dr 92008 760-331-5800
Tressie Armstrong, prin. Fax 720-0635
Magnolia ES 400/K-5
1905 Magnolia Ave 92008 760-331-5600
Jimmy Hines, prin. Fax 720-3879
Pacific Rim ES 800/K-5
1100 Camino de las Ondas 92009 760-331-6200
Robert Devich, prin. Fax 929-1778
Poinsettia ES 400/K-5
2445 Mica Rd 92009 760-331-6500
Steve Ahle, prin. Fax 930-6005
Valley MS 1,100/6-8
1645 Magnolia Ave 92008 760-331-5300
Cesar Morales, prin. Fax 720-2326

Encinitas UNESD
Supt. — See Encinitas
El Camino Creek ES 900/K-6
7885 Paseo Aliso 92009 760-943-2051
Carrie Brown, prin. Fax 943-2052
La Costa Heights ES 600/K-6
3035 Levante St 92009 760-944-4375
Leighangela Brady, prin. Fax 632-7627
Mission Estancia ES 600/K-6
3330 Calle Barcelona 92009 760-943-2004
Gregg Sonken, prin. Fax 943-2008
Olivenhain Pioneer ES 700/K-6
8000 Calle Acervo 92009 760-943-2000
Erin English, prin. Fax 943-2028

San Marcos USD
Supt. — See San Marcos
Carrillo ES 800/K-5
2875 Poinsettia Ln 92009 760-290-2900
Fran Pistone, prin. Fax 736-2203
La Costa Meadows ES 700/K-5
6889 El Fuerte St 92009 760-290-2121
Jennifer Carter, prin. Fax 290-2120

Beautiful Saviour Lutheran S 100/K-8
3030 Valley St 92008 760-729-6272
Daniel Unke, prin. Fax 729-6573
St. Patrick's S 400/K-8
3820 Pio Pico Dr 92008 760-729-1333
Denise Coates, prin. Fax 729-5174

Carmel, Monterey, Pop. 4,084
Carmel USD 2,100/K-12
PO Box 222700 93922 831-624-1546
Marvin Biasotti, supt. Fax 626-4052
www.carmelunified.org
Carmel MS 500/6-8
PO Box 222740 93922 831-624-2785
Ken Griest, prin. Fax 624-0839
Carmel River ES 400/K-5
PO Box 222700 93922 831-624-4609
Jay Marden, prin. Fax 624-6633
Other Schools – See Big Sur, Carmel Valley

All Saints' Episcopal Day S 200/PK-8
8060 Carmel Valley Rd 93923 831-624-9171
Michele Rench, hdmstr. Fax 624-3960
Junipero Serra S 200/K-8
2992 Lasuen Dr 93923 831-624-8322
Peggy Burger, prin. Fax 624-8311
St. Dunstan's S 50/PK-K
28003 Robinson Canyon Rd 93923 831-624-9250
Elizabeth Buche, dir. Fax 624-9153
Stevenson S 200/K-8
PO Box AP 93921 831-626-5200
Ronald Provost, hdmstr. Fax 624-9044

Carmel Valley, Monterey, Pop. 980
Carmel USD
Supt. — See Carmel
Tularcitos ES 400/K-5
35 Ford Rd 93924 831-659-2276
Karen Camilli, prin. Fax 659-1049

Carmichael, Sacramento, Pop. 49,900
San Juan USD 42,000/K-12
PO Box 477 95609 916-971-7700
Pat Jaurequi, supt. Fax 971-7758
www.sanjuan.edu
Barrett MS 800/6-8
4243 Barrett Rd 95608 916-971-7842
Lisa Herstrom-Smith, prin. Fax 971-7839
Cameron Ranch ES 300/K-6
4333 Hackberry Ln 95608 916-575-2302
Theresa Altieri, prin. Fax 575-2305
Carmichael ES 500/K-6
6141 Sutter Ave 95608 916-971-5727
Fax 971-5728
Churchill MS 800/6-8
4900 Whitney Ave 95608 916-971-7324
Jim Shoemake, prin. Fax 971-7856
Coyle Avenue ES 500/K-6
6330 Coyle Ave 95608 916-867-2012
Dianna Batt, prin. Fax 867-2019
Del Dayo ES 400/K-6
1301 Mcclaren Dr 95608 916-575-2323
Thomas Harp, prin. Fax 575-2328
Deterding ES 500/K-6
6000 Stanley Ave 95608 916-575-2338
Sandra Rangel, prin. Fax 575-2341
Garfield ES 500/K-6
3700 Garfield Ave 95608 916-575-2349
Anne Birchfield, prin. Fax 575-2352
Kelly ES 400/K-6
6301 Moraga Dr 95608 916-867-2041
Deanna Terry, prin. Fax 867-2045
Mission Avenue Open ES 400/K-6
2925 Mission Ave 95608 916-575-2362
Janis Stonebreaker, prin. Fax 575-2413
Peck ES 500/K-6
6230 Rutland Dr 95608 916-867-2071
Jane Schabinger, prin. Fax 867-2075
Schweitzer ES 400/K-6
4350 Glenridge Dr 95608 916-867-2094
Janice Bowdler, prin. Fax 867-2092
Starr King S 300/K-8
4848 Cottage Way 95608 916-971-7318
John Garrard, prin. Fax 971-7316
Other Schools – See Citrus Heights, Fair Oaks, Gold River, Orangevale, Sacramento

---

Our Lady of Assumption S 300/K-8
2141 Walnut Ave 95608 916-489-8958
Robert Love, prin. Fax 489-3237
Sacramento Adventist Academy 300/K-12
5601 Winding Way 95608 916-481-2300
Bettesue Constanzo, prin. Fax 481-7426
St. John the Evangelist S 300/PK-8
5701 Locust Ave 95608 916-481-8845
Nancy Conroy, prin. Fax 481-1319
St. Michael's Episcopal Day S 200/PK-8
2140 Mission Ave 95608 916-485-3418
Fr. Jesse Vaughan, hdmstr. Fax 485-9084
Victory Christian S Carmichael Campus 300/K-6
3045 Garfield Ave 95608 916-488-6740
Dora Marques, prin. Fax 488-2589

Carpinteria, Santa Barbara, Pop. 13,549
Carpinteria USD 2,300/K-12
1400 Linden Ave 93013 805-684-4511
Paul Cordeiro, supt. Fax 684-0218
www.cusd.net
Aliso ES 300/K-5
4545 Carpinteria Ave 93013 805-684-4539
Tricia Price, prin. Fax 566-4759
Canalino ES 500/K-5
1480 Linden Ave 93013 805-684-4141
Sally Green, prin. Fax 684-3384
Carpinteria MS 400/6-8
5351 Carpinteria Ave 93013 805-684-4544
Felicia Sexsmith, prin. Fax 566-3839
Other Schools – See Summerland

Carson, Los Angeles, Pop. 93,955
Compton USD
Supt. — See Compton
Bunche ES 400/K-5
16223 Haskins Ln 90746 310-898-6120
Synee Pearson, prin. Fax 329-6056

Los Angeles USD
Supt. — See Los Angeles
Ambler ES 600/K-5
319 E Sherman Dr 90746 310-532-4090
Gina Ellis, prin. Fax 719-9881
Annalee Avenue ES 400/K-5
19410 Annalee Ave 90746 310-537-4740
Robin Willis, prin. Fax 764-4729
Bonita Street ES 600/K-5
21929 Bonita St 90745 310-834-8588
Eva Ybarra, prin. Fax 834-8033
Broadacres Avenue ES 400/K-5
19424 Broadacres Ave 90746 310-537-1980
Barbara Sparks, prin. Fax 639-4240
Carnegie MS 1,700/6-8
21820 Bonita St 90745 310-952-5700
Verna Stroud, prin. Fax 830-9015
Caroldale Avenue S 1,100/K-8
22424 Caroldale Ave 90745 310-320-8570
Suzanne Zopatti, prin. Fax 320-6803
Carson Street ES 700/K-5
161 E Carson St 90745 310-834-4508
Martin Leon, prin. Fax 549-9660
Catskill Avenue ES 800/K-5
23536 Catskill Ave 90745 310-834-7241
Hoff Brooks, prin. Fax 549-3742
Curtiss MS 1,400/6-8
1254 E Helmick St 90746 310-661-4500
Edna Burems, prin. Fax 537-2115
Del Amo ES 500/K-5
21228 Water St 90745 310-830-5351
Cheryl Nakada Becerra, prin. Fax 830-6466

Dolores Street ES 700/K-5
22526 Dolores St 90745 310-834-2565
Anna Barraza, prin. Fax 830-6730
Leapwood Avenue ES 400/K-5
19302 Leapwood Ave 90746 310-327-8245
Camellia Hudley, prin. Fax 527-7240
Towne Avenue ES 400/K-5
18924 Towne Ave 90746 310-329-3505
Mark Hirata, prin. Fax 329-3467
232nd Place ES 500/K-5
23240 Archibald Ave 90745 310-830-8710
Rosalyn Leach, prin. Fax 835-1946
White MS 2,000/6-8
22102 Figueroa St 90745 310-783-4900
James Noble, prin. Fax 782-8954

St. Philomena S 200/PK-8
21832 Main St 90745 310-835-4827
Sr. Maureen Cochrane, prin. Fax 835-1655

Caruthers, Fresno, Pop. 1,603
Caruthers USD 1,500/K-12
PO Box 127 93609 559-864-6500
James Sargent, supt. Fax 864-8857
www.caruthers.k12.ca.us
Caruthers S 800/K-8
PO Box 7 93609 559-864-6500
Roxie Martin, prin. Fax 864-0610

Castaic, Los Angeles
Castaic UNESD
Supt. — See Valencia
Castaic ES 800/K-5
30455 Park Vista Dr 91384 661-257-4530
Mark Evans, prin. Fax 294-7854
Castaic MS 1,200/6-8
28900 Hillcrest Pkwy 91384 661-257-4550
Ellen Edeburn, prin. Fax 294-9714
Live Oak ES 800/K-5
27715 Saddleridge Way 91384 661-257-4540
Cynthia Seamands, prin. Fax 257-6384
Northlake Hills ES 700/K-5
32545 Ridge Route Rd 91384 661-257-4560
Bob Brauneisen, prin. Fax 295-3924

Castella, Shasta
Castle Rock UNESD 100/K-8
PO Box 180 96017 530-235-0101
Mark Telles, supt. Fax 235-0257
www.shastalink.k12.ca.us/castlerock
Castle Rock S 100/K-8
PO Box 180 96017 530-235-0101
Mark Telles, prin. Fax 235-0257

Castro Valley, Alameda, Pop. 59,300
Castro Valley USD 8,600/K-12
PO Box 2146 94546 510-537-3000
James Fitzpatrick, supt. Fax 886-8962
www.cv.k12.ca.us
Canyon MS 1,300/6-8
PO Box 2146 94546 510-538-8833
Mark Croghan, prin. Fax 247-9439
Castro Valley ES 400/K-5
PO Box 2146 94546 510-537-1919
Denise Hohn, prin. Fax 537-9892
Chabot ES 400/K-5
PO Box 2146 94546 510-537-2342
Terry Hoops, prin. Fax 537-9418
Creekside MS 800/6-8
PO Box 2146 94546 510-247-0665
Mary Ann DeGrazia, prin. Fax 581-6617
Independent ES 500/K-5
PO Box 2146 94546 510-537-9558
Jim Kentris, prin. Fax 537-9591
Jensen Ranch ES 400/K-5
PO Box 2146 94546 510-537-6365
Joe Nguyen, prin. Fax 728-9853
Marshall ES 400/K-5
PO Box 2146 94546 510-537-2431
Walt Lewis, prin. Fax 247-9826
Palomares ES 100/K-5
PO Box 2146 94546 510-582-4207
Melodie Stibich, prin. Fax 582-3948
Proctor ES 500/K-5
PO Box 2146 94546 510-537-0630
Lisa Garcia, prin. Fax 537-6752
Stanton ES 400/K-5
PO Box 2146 94546 510-727-9192
Jennifer Yamashita, prin. Fax 247-9610
Vannoy ES 400/K-5
PO Box 2146 94546 510-537-1832
Greg Ko, prin. Fax 582-8599

Hayward USD
Supt. — See Hayward
Strobridge ES 500/K-6
21400 Bedford Dr 94546 510-293-8576
Donald Oliver, prin. Fax 582-8566

Bright World Preschool 50/PK-PK
20613 Stanton Ave 94546 510-581-1580
Diana Wood, admin. Fax 582-8655
Our Lady of Grace S 200/K-8
3433 Somerset Ave 94546 510-581-3155
Colleen Wahl, prin. Fax 581-1059
Redwood Christian S - Crossroads Campus 200/K-6
20600 John Dr 94546 510-537-4277
Mike Kady, prin. Fax 537-0148
Redwood Christian S - Redwood Campus 200/K-6
19300 Redwood Rd 94546 510-537-4288
Timothy Ball, prin. Fax 728-4383

Castroville, Monterey, Pop. 5,272
North Monterey County USD
Supt. — See Moss Landing
Castroville ES 600/PK-6
11161 Merritt St 95012 831-633-2570
Aida Ramirez, prin. Fax 633-0642

Elkhorn ES 600/PK-6
2235 Elkhorn Rd 95012 831-633-2405
Sandra Cuevas, prin. Fax 633-0863
North Monterey County MS 700/7-8
10301 Seymour St 95012 831-633-3391
David Burke, prin. Fax 633-3680

Cathedral City, Riverside, Pop. 51,713
Palm Springs USD
Supt. — See Palm Springs
Agua Caliente ES 800/K-5
30800 San Luis Rey Dr 92234 760-416-8235
Lucy Medina, prin. Fax 416-8245
Cathedral City ES 900/K-5
69300 Converse Rd 92234 760-770-8583
Jessica Arduini, prin. Fax 770-4703
Coffman MS 1,200/6-8
34603 Plumley Rd 92234 760-770-8617
Lucinda Killebrew, prin. Fax 770-8623
Landau ES 900/K-5
30310 Landau Blvd 92234 760-770-8600
Lynne Keating, prin. Fax 770-8607
Rio Vista ES 600/K-5
67700 Verona Rd 92234 760-416-0032
Mike Long, prin. Fax 416-0087
Sunny Sands ES 1,000/K-5
69310 McCallum Way 92234 760-770-8635
Karen Cornett, prin. Fax 770-8641
Workman MS 1,600/6-8
69300 30th Ave 92234 760-770-8540
Brad Sauer, prin. Fax 770-8545

Catheys Valley, Mariposa
Mariposa County USD
Supt. — See Mariposa
Catheys Valley ES 100/K-6
4952 School House Rd 95306 209-742-0300
Carol Fincham, prin. Fax 742-0301

Cayucos, San Luis Obispo, Pop. 2,960
Cayucos ESD 200/K-8
301 Cayucos Dr 93430 805-995-3694
George Erdelyi, supt. Fax 995-2876
www.cesdschool.net/
Cayucos S 200/K-8
301 Cayucos Dr 93430 805-995-3694
George Erdelyi, prin. Fax 995-2876

Cazadero, Sonoma
Fort Ross ESD 50/K-8
30600 Seaview Rd 95421 707-847-3390
James Johnson, supt. Fax 847-3312
www.ftrosssd.k12.ca.us
Fort Ross S 50/K-8
30600 Seaview Rd 95421 707-847-3390
James Johnson, prin. Fax 847-3312

Montgomery ESD 50/K-8
PO Box 286 95421 707-632-5221
John Quinn, supt. Fax 632-5749
Montgomery S 50/K-8
PO Box 286 95421 707-632-5221
Judy Mercieca, prin. Fax 632-5749

Cedarville, Modoc
Surprise Valley JUSD 200/K-12
PO Box 100 96104 530-279-6141
Don Demsher, supt. Fax 279-2210
Surprise Valley ES 100/K-6
PO Box 100 96104 530-279-6161
Janelle Anderson, prin. Fax 279-6154

Ceres, Stanislaus, Pop. 40,571
Ceres USD 10,600/K-12
PO Box 307 95307 209-556-1500
Walt Hanline Ed.D., supt. Fax 556-1090
www.ceres.k12.ca.us
Blaker-Kinser JHS 800/7-8
PO Box 307 95307 209-556-1810
Kristi Britton, prin. Fax 541-0174
Caswell ES 500/K-6
PO Box 307 95307 209-556-1620
Carol Lubinsky, prin. Fax 538-1536
Don Pedro ES 500/K-6
PO Box 307 95307 209-556-1630
Rick Hall, prin. Fax 538-2856
Fowler ES 600/K-6
PO Box 307 95307 209-556-1640
Bruce Clifton, prin. Fax 538-7822
Hensley JHS 800/7-8
PO Box 307 95307 209-556-1820
Lynda Maben, prin. Fax 538-9428
Hidahl ES 500/K-6
PO Box 307 95307 209-556-1650
Vaughn Williams, prin. Fax 581-9761
La Rosa ES 400/K-6
PO Box 307 95307 209-556-1660
Lori Mariani, prin. Fax 538-7346
Parks ES 600/K-6
PO Box 307 95307 209-556-1670
Jennifer Backman, prin. Fax 531-0619
Sinclear ES 600/K-6
PO Box 307 95307 209-556-1680
Connie Stark, prin. Fax 538-3910
Vaughn ES 600/K-6
PO Box 307 95307 209-556-1690
Amy Peterman, prin. Fax 541-1363
White ES 700/K-6
PO Box 307 95307 209-556-1710
Jose Beltran, prin. Fax 538-0276
Other Schools – See Modesto

Central Valley Christian Academy 300/PK-12
2020 Academy Pl 95307 209-537-4521
Wayne Dunbar, prin. Fax 538-0706

Cerritos, Los Angeles, Pop. 52,561
ABC USD 21,000/K-12
16700 Norwalk Blvd 90703 562-926-5566
Dr. Gary Smuts, supt. Fax 404-1092
www.abcusd.k12.ca.us
Bragg ES 600/K-6
11501 Bos St 90703 562-860-5580
Annette Janeway, prin. Fax 402-2580
Carmenita MS 700/7-8
13435 166th St 90703 562-926-4405
Rhonda Buss, prin. Fax 404-7807
Carver ES 500/K-6
19200 Ely Ave 90703 562-865-1257
Deborah Berlyn, prin. Fax 402-8678
Cerritos ES 600/K-6
13600 183rd St 90703 562-926-1315
Dennis Wilson, prin. Fax 404-4635
Gonsalves ES 600/K-6
13650 Park St 90703 562-926-1347
Claudia Ross, prin. Fax 802-0483
Haskell MS 600/7-8
11525 Del Amo Blvd 90703 562-860-6529
Fax 809-7250
Juarez ES 400/K-6
11939 Aclare St 90703 562-865-6278
LuAnn Adler, prin. Fax 809-3093
Leal ES 700/K-6
12920 Droxford St 90703 562-865-0209
Laura Makely, prin. Fax 402-5950
Nixon ES 700/K-6
19600 Jacob Ave 90703 562-860-6549
Melinda Baek, prin. Fax 865-1249
Stowers ES 500/K-6
13350 Beach St 90703 562-926-2326
Eileen Blagden, prin. Fax 404-9017
Tetzlaff MS 600/7-8
12351 Del Amo Blvd 90703 562-865-9539
Crechena Wise, prin. Fax 402-6412
Wittmann ES 500/K-6
16801 Yvette Ave 90703 562-926-1321
Patrick Walker, prin. Fax 921-3940
Other Schools – See Artesia, Hawaiian Gardens, Lakewood

Concordia Lutheran S 100/PK-6
13633 183rd St 90703 562-926-2491
Mary Anne McCombs, prin. Fax 407-0610
Valley Christian MS 300/7-8
18100 Dumont Ave 90703 562-865-6519
Paul Theule, prin. Fax 403-3159

Challenge, Yuba, Pop. 1,096
Marysville JUSD
Supt. — See Marysville
Yuba Feather S 200/K-8
PO Box 398 95925 530-675-2382
Lynne Cardoza, prin. Fax 675-2618

Chatsworth, See Los Angeles
Los Angeles USD
Supt. — See Los Angeles
Chatsworth Park ES 400/K-5
22005 Devonshire St 91311 818-341-1371
Patricia Chavez Del Pino, prin. Fax 882-3540
Germain Street ES 700/K-5
20730 Germain St 91311 818-341-5821
Sonia Ugarte, prin. Fax 882-3599
Lawrence MS 1,900/6-8
10100 Variel Ave 91311 818-678-7900
Christopher Rosas, prin. Fax 349-4539
Superior ES 500/K-5
9756 Oso Ave 91311 818-349-1410
Jerilyn Schubert, prin. Fax 886-8748

Chaminade MS 700/6-8
19800 Devonshire St 91311 818-363-8127
Mike Valentine, prin. Fax 363-1219
Chatsworth Hills Academy 200/PK-8
PO Box 5077 91313 818-998-4037
Graham Brown, hdmstr. Fax 998-4062
Egremont S 200/K-8
19850 Devonshire St 91311 818-363-7803
Coleen Callahan, dir. Fax 831-5670
St. John Eudes S 300/K-8
9925 Mason Ave 91311 818-341-1454
Barbara Danowitz, prin. Fax 341-3093
Sierra Canyon S 500/PK-6
11052 Independence Ave 91311 818-882-8121
James Skrumbis, hdmstr. Fax 882-8218

Cherry Valley, Riverside, Pop. 5,945

Cherry Valley Brethren S 100/PK-12
39205 Vineland St 92223 951-845-2653
Judy Polman, prin. Fax 845-2026

Chester, Plumas, Pop. 2,082
Plumas USD
Supt. — See Quincy
Chester ES 300/K-6
PO Box 826 96020 530-258-3194
Sally McGowan, prin. Fax 258-3195

Chico, Butte, Pop. 71,427
Chico USD 12,700/K-12
1163 E 7th St 95928 530-891-3000
Kelly Staley, supt. Fax 891-3220
www.chicousd.org
Bidwell JHS 700/7-8
2376 North Ave 95926 530-891-3080
Brian Boyer, prin. Fax 891-3082
Chapman ES 300/K-6
1071 E 16th St 95928 530-891-3100
Ted Sullivan, prin. Fax 891-3294
Chico JHS 700/7-8
280 Memorial Way 95926 530-891-3066
John Bohannon, prin. Fax 891-3264
Citrus Avenue ES 500/K-6
1350 Citrus Ave 95926 530-891-3107
Michelle Sanchez, prin. Fax 891-3180
Dow ES 500/K-6
1420 Neal Dow Ave 95926 530-891-3110
Marilyn Rees, prin. Fax 891-3184
Hooker Oak Open S 400/K-8
1238 Arbutus Ave 95926 530-891-3119
Sue Hegedus, prin. Fax 891-3120
Little Chico Creek ES 600/K-6
2090 Amanda Way 95928 530-891-3285
Suzanne Michelony, prin. Fax 891-3288
Marigold ES 500/K-6
2446 Marigold Ave 95926 530-891-3121
Rhys Severe, prin. Fax 891-3242
Marsh JHS, 2253 Humboldt Rd 95928 600/7-8
Jay Marchant, prin. 530-895-4110
McManus ES 600/K-6
988 East Ave 95926 530-891-3128
Diane Bird, prin. Fax 891-3130
Parkview ES 500/K-6
1770 E 8th St 95928 530-891-3114
Liz Capen, prin. Fax 891-3230
Rosedale ES 500/K-6
100 Oak St 95928 530-891-3104
Claudia de la Torre, prin. Fax 891-3169
Shasta ES 600/K-6
169 Leora Ct 95973 530-891-3141
Larry Spini, prin. Fax 891-3239
Sierra View ES 600/K-6
1598 Hooker Oak Ave 95926 530-891-3117
Debbie Aldred, prin. Fax 891-3186
Wilson ES 700/K-6
1530 W 8th Ave 95926 530-891-3297
Kim Rodgers, prin. Fax 891-4097

Chico Christian S 300/PK-8
2801 Notre Dame Blvd 95928 530-879-8989
Beverly Landers, prin. Fax 879-8987
Chico Oaks Adventist S 100/K-8
1859 Hooker Oak Ave 95926 530-342-5043
Rick Nelson, prin. Fax 342-8402
King's Christian S 100/PK-6
1137 Arbutus Ave 95926 530-345-1377
Sandra Husband, prin. Fax 345-1727
Notre Dame S 200/K-8
435 Hazel St 95928 530-342-2502
Michael Garcia, prin. Fax 342-6292

Chinese Camp, Tuolumne
Chinese Camp ESD 50/K-6
PO Box 100 95309 209-984-5421
Bill Scheiderman, supt. Fax 984-4362
Chinese Camp ES 50/K-6
PO Box 100 95309 209-984-5421
Bill Scheiderman, prin. Fax 984-4362

Chino, San Bernardino, Pop. 77,578
Chino Valley USD 31,800/K-12
5130 Riverside Dr 91710 909-628-1201
Edmond Heatley Ed.D., supt. Fax 590-4911
www.chino.k12.ca.us
Borba Fundamental ES 600/K-6
12970 3rd St 91710 909-627-9613
Kathy Hemlock, prin. Fax 548-6086
Briggs Fundamental S 900/K-8
11880 Roswell Ave 91710 909-628-6497
Mike Harrell, prin. Fax 548-6085
Cattle ES 800/K-6
13590 Cypress Ave 91710 909-591-2755
Fax 465-9414
Cortez ES 700/K-6
12750 Carissa Ave 91710 909-627-9438
Rod Federwisch, prin. Fax 548-6069
Dickson ES 600/K-6
3930 Pamela Dr 91710 909-591-2653
Sue Pederson, prin. Fax 548-6070
El Rancho ES 600/K-6
5862 C St 91710 909-627-9496
Grace Park, prin. Fax 465-9401
Gird ES 700/K-6
4980 Riverside Dr 91710 909-627-9638
Jesus Luna, prin. Fax 902-9126
Magnolia JHS 1,000/7-8
13150 Mountain Ave 91710 909-627-9263
Kimberly Watson, prin. Fax 627-2165
Marshall ES 700/K-6
12045 Telephone Ave 91710 909-627-9741
Rick Edwards, prin. Fax 364-1283
Newman ES 900/K-6
4150 Walnut Ave 91710 909-627-9758
Iraida Pisano, prin. Fax 548-6064
Ramona JHS 900/7-8
4575 Walnut Ave 91710 909-627-9144
Mike Finkbiner, prin. Fax 548-6055
Rhodes ES 600/K-6
6655 Schaefer Ave 91710 909-364-0683
Sue Roche, prin. Fax 548-4399
Walnut Avenue ES 700/K-6
5550 Walnut Ave 91710 909-627-9817
Dan Galindo, prin. Fax 548-0205
Other Schools – See Chino Hills, Ontario

Chino Valley Christian Academy 100/K-12
12205 Pipeline Ave 91710 909-464-8255
Dennis Leonard, dir.
Chino Valley Christian S 300/PK-8
4136 Riverside Dr 91710 909-613-1381
Eugene Huang, admin. Fax 613-1383
Cornerstone Christian S 200/PK-6
13000 Pipeline Ave 91710 909-628-6812
Cynthia Bayer, prin. Fax 590-1482
Kiddie Korner 100/PK-K
5559 Park Pl 91710 909-627-1621
Nickie Lee Bennett, admin. Fax 613-1265

New Hope Christian S 200/PK-6
13333 Ramona Ave 91710 909-591-2717
Dave Scott, prin. Fax 591-9305
St. Margaret Mary S 300/PK-8
12664 Central Ave 91710 909-591-8419
Joan Blank, prin. Fax 591-6960

Chino Hills, San Bernardino, Pop. 75,722
Chino Valley USD
Supt. — See Chino
Butterfield Ranch ES 900/K-6
6350 Mystic Canyon Dr 91709 909-591-0766
Ken Hawkins, prin. Fax 548-6078
Canyon Hills JHS 1,200/7-8
2500 Madrugada Dr 91709 909-464-9938
Jaime Camacho, prin. Fax 548-6058
Country Springs ES 700/K-6
14145 Village Center Dr 91709 909-590-8212
Tracy MacArthur, prin. Fax 548-6079
Eagle Canyon ES 600/K-6
13435 Eagle Canyon Dr 91709 909-590-2707
Sarah Barraza, prin. Fax 548-6073
Glenmeade ES 500/K-6
15000 Whirlaway Ln 91709 909-393-4087
Connie Daigle, prin. Fax 393-3285
Hidden Trails ES 700/K-6
2250 Ridgeview Dr 91709 909-597-0288
Kristen Robinson, prin. Fax 548-6081
Litel ES 700/K-6
3425 Eucalyptus Ave 91709 909-591-1336
Brian Martinez, prin. Fax 548-6072
Los Serranos ES 400/K-6
15650 Pipeline Ave 91709 909-591-3682
Lisa Hall, prin. Fax 548-6065
Oak Ridge ES 800/K-6
15452 Valle Vista Dr 91709 909-591-1239
Don Wilson, prin. Fax 393-0792
Rolling Ridge ES 600/K-6
13677 Calle San Marcos 91709 909-628-9375
Amy Nguyen-Hernandez, prin. Fax 591-1435
Townsend JHS 1,200/7-8
15359 Ilex Dr 91709 909-591-2161
Melody Kohn, prin. Fax 548-6057
Wickman ES 900/K-6
16250 Pinehurst Dr 91709 909-393-3774
Robert Clements, prin. Fax 597-2726

Chino Hills Christian S 200/K-6
2549 Madrugada Dr 91709 909-465-9905
Randy Long, prin. Fax 902-0556
Loving Savior Lutheran S 400/PK-8
14816 Peyton Dr 91709 909-597-2948
Liz Page, prin. Fax 393-4659
St. Paul the Apostle Preschool 50/PK-PK
14085 Peyton Dr 91709 909-465-5503
Christina Stutzman, dir. Fax 465-1683

Chowchilla, Madera, Pop. 16,525
Alview-Dairyland UNESD 300/K-8
12861 Avenue 18 1/2 93610 559-665-2394
Lori Flanagan, supt. Fax 665-7347
www.adusd.k12.ca.us
Alview S 200/K-3
20513 Road 4 93610 559-665-2275
Lori Flanagan, prin. Fax 665-8510
Dairyland S 200/4-8
12861 Avenue 18 1/2 93610 559-665-2394
Lori Flanagan, prin. Fax 665-7347

Chowchilla ESD 1,700/K-8
PO Box 910 93610 559-665-8000
Dr. Charles Martin, supt. Fax 665-3036
www.chowchillaelem.k12.ca.us
Fairmead ES 200/5-6
PO Box 910 93610 559-665-8040
Terry Barnes, prin. Fax 665-8003
Fuller ES 400/1-2
PO Box 910 93610 559-665-8050
Jan Crader, prin. Fax 665-8026
Reagan ES 400/3-4
PO Box 910 93610 559-665-8080
Kari Anderson, prin. Fax 665-8083
Stephens K 200/K-K
PO Box 910 93610 559-665-8060
Sandy Frisby, prin. Fax 665-0219
Wilson MS 500/7-8
PO Box 910 93610 559-665-8070
Jennifer Euker Ed.D., prin. Fax 665-8004

Chowchilla SDA S 50/K-12
22310 Rd 13 93610 559-665-1853
Jeanie de la Torre, prin. Fax 665-0612

Chualar, Monterey
Chualar UNESD 300/K-8
PO Box 188 93925 831-679-2504
Sergio Montenegro, supt. Fax 679-0345
Chualar S 300/K-8
PO Box 188 93925 831-679-2313

Chula Vista, San Diego, Pop. 210,497
Chula Vista ESD 22,400/K-6
84 E J St 91910 619-425-9600
Lowell Billings Ed.D., supt. Fax 427-0463
www.cvesd.org
Casillas ES 700/K-6
1130 E J St 91910 619-421-7555
Del Merlan, prin. Fax 421-3008
Castle Park ES 500/K-6
25 Emerson St 91911 619-422-5301
Alicia Moreno, prin. Fax 422-4452
Chula Vista Hills ES 600/K-6
980 Buena Vista Way 91910 619-482-7066
Monica Sorenson, prin. Fax 482-6823
Cook ES 500/K-6
875 Cuyamaca Ave 91911 619-422-8381
Pamela Page, prin. Fax 427-3407
Eastlake ES 700/K-6
1955 Hillside Dr 91913 619-421-4798
Douglas Ricketts, prin. Fax 421-4516
Halecrest ES 500/K-6
475 E J St 91910 619-421-0771
Fax 421-8746
Harborside ES 700/K-6
681 Naples St 91911 619-422-8369
Matthew Tessier, prin. Fax 422-7361
Hedenkamp ES 1,000/K-6
930 E Palomar St 91913 619-397-5828
Richard Hanks, prin. Fax 397-7174
Heritage ES 900/K-6
1450 Santa Lucia Rd 91913 619-421-7080
Gloria Ciriza, prin. Fax 421-8525
Hilltop Drive ES 600/K-6
30 Murray St 91910 619-422-8323
Lisa Parker, prin. Fax 691-1375
Kellogg ES 400/K-6
229 E Naples St 91911 619-420-4151
Emily Acosta-Thompson, prin. Fax 498-1433
Lauderbach ES 800/K-6
390 Palomar St 91911 619-422-1127
Charlene Sapien, prin. Fax 426-5875
Liberty ES 700/K-6
2175 Proctor Valley Rd 91914 619-397-5225
Santos Gonzalez, prin. Fax 397-2833
Loma Verde ES 500/K-6
1450 Loma Ln 91911 619-420-3940
Jane Clark, prin. Fax 422-2667
Marshall ES 700/K-6
2295 MacKenzie Creek Rd 91914 619-656-6252
Fax 656-4248
McMillin ES 900/K-6
1201 Santa Cora Ave 91913 619-397-0103
Jorge Mora, prin. Fax 397-0122
Montgomery ES 400/K-6
1601 4th Ave 91911 619-422-6131
Francisco Velasco, prin. Fax 426-6836
Olympic View ES 800/K-6
1220 S Greensview Dr 91915 619-656-2030
Gloria McKearney, prin. Fax 656-8752
Otay ES 600/K-6
1651 Albany Ave 91911 619-425-4311
Rosario Villareal, prin. Fax 425-2018
Palomar ES 400/K-6
300 E Palomar St 91911 619-420-0134
Erin Dare, prin. Fax 420-8416
Parkview ES 500/K-6
575 Juniper St 91911 619-421-5483
Bonnie Nelson, prin. Fax 421-2119
Rice ES 700/K-6
915 4th Ave 91911 619-420-7071
Emiko Nakamura, prin. Fax 420-6124
Rogers ES 500/K-6
510 E Naples St 91911 619-656-2082
Sherrol Stogsdill-Posey, prin. Fax 421-1423
Rohr ES 400/K-6
1540 Malta Ave 91911 619-420-5533
Rosalba Ponce, prin. Fax 476-0850
Rosebank ES 700/K-6
80 Flower St 91910 619-422-8329
Scott Woodward, prin. Fax 422-5014
Salt Creek ES 900/K-6
1055 Hunte Pkwy 91914 619-397-5494
Dan Winters, prin. Fax 397-4669
Tiffany ES 600/K-6
1691 Elmhurst St 91913 619-421-6300
Charles Padilla, prin. Fax 482-3115
Valle Lindo ES 600/K-6
1515 Oleander Ave 91911 619-421-5151
Theresa Corona, prin. Fax 421-1802
Veterans ES 500/K-6
1550 Magdalena Ave 91913 619-216-1226
Olga West, prin. Fax 216-9226
Vista Square ES 700/K-6
540 G St 91910 619-422-8374
Anateresa Herrera-Wood, prin. Fax 691-1086
Wolf Canyon ES 200/K-6
1950 Wolf Canyon Loop 91913 619-482-8877
Debra McLaren, prin. Fax 482-7766
Other Schools – See Bonita, San Diego

Sweetwater UNHSD 41,600/7-12
1130 5th Ave 91911 619-691-5500
Jesus Gandara Ed.D., supt. Fax 498-1997
www.suhsd.k12.ca.us
Bonita Vista MS 1,200/7-8
650 Otay Lakes Rd 91910 619-397-2200
Bernard Balanay, prin. Fax 482-9356
Castle Park MS 1,200/7-8
160 Quintard St 91911 619-691-5490
V. Sandoval-Johnson, prin. Fax 427-8045
Chula Vista MS 1,200/7-8
415 5th Ave 91910 619-498-6800
Jan Godfrey, prin. Fax 427-5723
Eastlake MS 1,400/7-8
900 Duncan Ranch Rd 91914 619-591-4000
Doug Jenkins, prin. Fax 482-0553
Hilltop MS 1,400/7-8
44 E J St 91910 619-498-2700
Linda Stanley, prin. Fax 585-3576
Rancho del Rey MS 1,500/7-8
1174 E J St 91910 619-397-2500
Tom Rodrigo, prin. Fax 656-3810
Other Schools – See National City, San Diego

Bonita Road Christian S 200/K-6
73 E Bonita Rd 91910 619-422-5850
Brenda Sniff, prin. Fax 422-5012
Calvary Christian Academy 500/PK-12
1771 E Palomar St 91913 619-591-2260
Dr. Chapin Marsh, hdmstr. Fax 591-2261
Christian Academy of Chula Vista 100/PK-6
494 E St 91910 619-422-7167
Carla Foster, dir. Fax 422-7196
Chula Vista Christian S 100/K-8
960 5th Ave 91911 619-425-0132
Von Thomas, prin. Fax 425-0135
Covenant Christian S 100/K-12
505 E Naples St 91911 619-421-8822
Thomas McManus, prin. Fax 216-9846
Highland Prince Academy 50/1-12
880 Kuhn Dr 91914 619-482-8485
Leon Hernandez, admin.
Pilgrim Lutheran S 200/PK-8
497 E St 91910 619-420-6233
Peter Halvorson, prin. Fax 422-2740
St. John's Episcopal S 500/PK-8
760 1st Ave 91910 619-422-6414
Frances Shorkey, prin. Fax 422-6946
St. Pius X S 300/K-8
37 E Emerson St 91911 619-422-2015
Eileen Hanson, prin. Fax 422-0048
St. Rose of Lima S 300/K-8
473 3rd Ave 91910 619-422-1121
Maria Tollefson, prin. Fax 422-8007
Southwestern Christian S 200/K-6
482 L St 91911 619-425-8940
Chelsey Watkins, prin. Fax 425-1014

Citrus Heights, Sacramento, Pop. 86,272
San Juan USD
Supt. — See Carmichael
Arlington Heights ES 500/K-6
6401 Trenton Way 95621 916-971-5234
Tambria Swift, prin. Fax 725-4599
Cambridge Heights ES 400/K-6
5555 Fleetwood Dr 95621 916-867-2000
Meredith Ryan, prin. Fax 867-2004
Carriage Drive ES 600/K-6
7519 Carriage Dr 95621 916-971-5241
Michelle Ramirez, prin. Fax 971-5326
Citrus Heights ES 500/K-6
7085 Auburn Blvd 95621 916-971-5230
Alicia Legarda, prin. Fax 722-6209
Grand Oaks ES 500/K-6
7901 Rosswood Dr 95621 916-971-5208
Greg Peterson, prin. Fax 722-3897
Kingswood ES 600/K-6
5700 Primrose Dr 95610 916-867-2046
Kathy Brann, prin. Fax 867-2053
Lichen S 600/K-8
8319 Lichen Dr 95621 916-971-5237
Sandy Butorac, prin. Fax 729-4578
Mariposa Avenue ES 600/K-6
7940 Mariposa Ave 95610 916-971-5212
Debbie MacDonald, prin. Fax 725-8793
Skycrest ES 700/K-6
5641 Mariposa Ave 95610 916-867-2098
Mary Ann Pivetti, prin. Fax 867-2083
Sylvan MS 700/7-8
7137 Auburn Blvd 95610 916-971-7873
Jeff Banks, prin. Fax 971-7896
Woodside S 500/K-8
8248 Villa Oak Dr 95610 916-971-5216
Greg Barge, prin. Fax 726-7169

American Christian Academy 500/K-12
7412 Hollyhock Ct 95621 916-725-8316
Karen Davis, admin.
Carden Christian Academy 100/PK-8
7723 Old Auburn Rd 95610 916-722-8668
Diana Owen, dir. Fax 722-7698
Creative Frontiers S 100/K-6
6446 Sylvan Rd 95610 916-723-2500
Robert Adams, prin.
Faith Christian Academy 100/PK-8
7737 Highland Ave 95610 916-725-5707
Beverly Wrinkle, admin.
Holy Family S 500/PK-8
7817 Old Auburn Rd 95610 916-722-7788
Charles Suarez, prin. Fax 722-5297
St. Mark's Lutheran S 100/K-8
7869 Kingswood Dr 95610 916-961-6894
Matthew Bauer, prin. Fax 961-5034

City of Industry, Los Angeles, Pop. 616
Bassett USD
Supt. — See La Puente
Torch Magnet MS 800/6-8
751 Vineland Ave 91746 626-931-2700
Joe Medina, prin. Fax 931-2702

Hacienda La Puente USD 22,000/K-12
PO Box 60002 91716 626-933-1000
Dr. Barbara Nakaoka, supt. Fax 855-3505
www.hlpusd.k12.ca.us/
Other Schools – See Hacienda Heights, La Puente, Valinda

Claremont, Los Angeles, Pop. 35,182
Claremont USD 6,800/K-12
170 W San Jose Ave 91711 909-398-0609
Terry Nichols, supt. Fax 398-0690
www.cusd.claremont.edu
Chaparral ES 600/K-6
451 Chaparral Dr 91711 909-398-0305
Laura Kerns, prin. Fax 398-0306
Condit ES 600/K-6
1750 N Mountain Ave 91711 909-398-0300
Christine Malally, prin. Fax 398-0479
El Roble IS 1,100/7-8
665 N Mountain Ave 91711 909-398-0343
Kevin Grier, prin. Fax 398-0399
Mountain View ES 400/K-6
851 Santa Clara Ave 91711 909-398-0308
Clara Arocha, prin. Fax 624-0289
Oakmont ES 300/K-6
120 W Green St 91711 909-398-0313
Kevin Ward, prin. Fax 625-8463
Sumner ES 600/K-6
1770 Sumner Ave 91711 909-398-0320
Frank D'Emilio, prin. Fax 398-0380

Sycamore ES 400/K-6
225 W 8th St 91711 909-398-0324
Amy Stanger, prin. Fax 625-6004
Vista Del Valle ES 300/K-6
550 Vista Dr 91711 909-398-0331
Ley Yeager, prin. Fax 398-0017

Foothill Country Day S 200/K-8
1035 Harrison Ave 91711 909-626-5681
Dr. Mark Lauria, hdmstr. Fax 625-4251
Our Lady of the Assumption S 500/PK-8
611 W Bonita Ave 91711 909-626-7135
Bernadette Boyle, prin. Fax 398-1395
Western Christian S 400/PK-8
3105 Padua Ave 91711 909-624-8291
Michelle Browning, prin. Fax 624-0651

Clayton, Contra Costa, Pop. 11,142
Mount Diablo USD
Supt. — See Concord
Diablo View MS 700/6-8
300 Diablo View Ln 94517 925-672-0898
Patti Bannister, prin. Fax 672-4327
Mount Diablo ES 900/K-5
5880 Mt Zion Dr 94517 925-672-4840
Bob Dodson, prin. Fax 673-9723

Clearlake, Lake, Pop. 14,728
Konocti USD
Supt. — See Lower Lake
Burns Valley ES 400/K-6
3620 Pine St 95422 707-994-2272
Troy Sherman, prin. Fax 994-7349
Oak Hill MS 600/6-8
15850A Dam Road Ext 95422 707-994-6447
Marie Munguia, prin. Fax 994-5047
Pomo ES 500/K-6
3350 Acacia St 95422 707-994-6744
April Leiferman, prin. Fax 994-4558

Clearlake SDA Christian S 50/K-8
PO Box 5686 95422 707-994-6356
Suzanne Aikin, prin. Fax 994-6356

Clearlake Oaks, Lake, Pop. 2,419
Konocti USD
Supt. — See Lower Lake
East Lake ES 200/K-7
PO Box 577 95423 707-998-3387
Debra Sorensen-Malley, prin. Fax 998-4936

Clements, San Joaquin
Lodi USD
Supt. — See Lodi
Clements ES 100/K-1
PO Box 743 95227 209-331-7300
Virginia Anderson, prin. Fax 759-9105

Cloverdale, Sonoma, Pop. 8,016
Cloverdale USD 1,500/K-12
97 School St 95425 707-894-1920
Claudia Rosatti, supt. Fax 894-1922
www.cusd.org/
Jefferson ES 500/K-3
315 North St 95425 707-894-1930
Aracely Romo-Flores, prin. Fax 894-1906
Washington MS 600/4-8
129 S Washington St 95425 707-894-1940
Julie Brandt, prin. Fax 894-1946

Cloverdale SDA S 50/K-8
1081 S Cloverdale Blvd 95425 707-894-5703
Janelle Griswold, prin. Fax 894-5703

Clovis, Fresno, Pop. 86,527
Clovis USD 38,600/K-12
1450 Herndon Ave 93611 559-327-9000
David Cash Ed.D., supt. Fax 327-9109
www.cusd.com/
Alta Sierra IS 1,800/7-8
380 W Teague Ave, 559-327-3500
Devin Blizzard, prin. Fax 327-3590
Cedarwood ES 700/K-6
2851 Palo Alto Ave 93611 559-327-6000
Colin Hintergardt, prin. Fax 327-6090
Century ES 800/K-6
965 N Sunnyside Ave 93611 559-327-8400
Gary Comstock, prin. Fax 327-8490
Clark IS 1,300/7-8
902 5th St 93612 559-327-1500
Scott Steele, prin. Fax 327-1556
Clovis ES 600/K-6
1100 Armstrong Ave 93611 559-327-6100
Isabel Facio, prin. Fax 327-6190
Cole ES 700/K-6
615 W Stuart Ave 93612 559-327-6200
Annette Bitter, prin. Fax 327-6290
Cox ES 600/K-6
2191 Sierra Ave 93611 559-327-6400
Cheryl Floth, prin. Fax 327-6490
Dry Creek ES 1,000/K-6
1273 N Armstrong Ave, 559-327-6500
Bob Hansen, prin. Fax 327-6590
Freedom ES 800/K-6
2955 Gettysburg Ave 93611 559-327-4800
Suzi Erickson, prin. Fax 327-4890
Garfield ES 700/K-6
1315 N Peach Ave, 559-327-6800
Jessica Mele, prin. Fax 327-6890
Gettysburg ES 700/K-6
2100 Gettysburg Ave 93611 559-327-6900
Scott Dille, prin. Fax 327-6990
Jefferson ES 700/K-6
1880 Fowler Ave 93611 559-327-7000
Geoffrey Tiftick, prin. Fax 327-7090
Miramonte ES 700/K-6
1590 Bellaire Ave 93611 559-327-7400
Dave Bower, prin. Fax 327-7490
Reagan ES 300/K-6
3701 Ashlan Ave, 559-327-8900
Robb Christopherson Ed.D., prin. Fax 327-8901
Red Bank ES 700/K-6
1454 Locan Ave, 559-327-7800
Kevin Peterson, prin. Fax 327-7890
Reyburn IS 1,500/7-8
2901 De Wolf Ave, 559-327-4500
Barry Jager, prin. Fax 327-4791
Sierra Vista ES 500/K-6
510 Barstow Ave 93612 559-327-7900
Cathy Dodd, prin. Fax 327-7990
Tarpey ES 800/K-6
2700 Minnewawa Ave 93612 559-327-8000
Darrin Holtermann, prin. Fax 327-8090
Weldon ES 700/K-6
150 Dewitt Ave 93612 559-327-8300
Ray Lozano, prin. Fax 327-8390
Woods ES 600/K-6
700 Teague Ave, 559-327-8800
Tracy Smith, prin. Fax 327-8801
Other Schools – See Fresno, Pinedale

Bright Beginnings Learning Center 100/PK-PK
2080 Tollhouse Rd 93611 559-299-5247
Kelli Austin, dir. Fax 299-0748
Clovis Christian S 400/PK-12
3105 Locan Ave, 559-291-6302
Kim Bonjorni, supt. Fax 291-6278
Our Lady of Perpetual Help S 200/K-8
836 Dewitt Ave 93612 559-299-7504
Kim Cochran, prin. Fax 299-4627
Tower Christian S 300/K-12
8753 Chickadee Ln, 559-298-2772
Ann Raber, admin.

Coachella, Riverside, Pop. 32,432
Coachella Valley USD
Supt. — See Thermal
Cahuilla Desert Academy 1,500/7-8
82489 Avenue 52 92236 760-398-0097
Estella Palacio, prin. Fax 398-0088
Chavez ES 1,000/K-6
49601 Avenida De Oro 92236 760-398-2004
Maria Ponce, prin. Fax 398-6713
Coral Mountain Academy 600/K-6
51375 Van Buren St 92236 760-398-3525
Jesse Alvarez, prin. Fax 393-0591
Duke MS 400/7-8
85358 Bagdad Ave 92236 760-398-0139
Erasmo Garcia, prin. Fax 398-5399
Palm View ES 600/K-6
1390 7th St 92236 760-398-2861
Leiala Montoya, prin. Fax 398-2592
Pendleton ES 700/K-6
84750 Calle Rojo 92236 760-398-0178
Armando Rivera, prin. Fax 398-0628
Valle Del Sol ES 600/K-6
51433 Education Way 92236 760-398-1025
Catherine Loy, prin. Fax 398-1746
Valley View ES 900/K-6
85270 Valley Rd 92236 760-398-4651
Maria Inzunza, prin. Fax 398-5931

Jordan Christian Academy 50/PK-7
50930 Calhoun St 92236 760-398-1614
Joe Jordan, admin. Fax 398-6352

Coalinga, Fresno, Pop. 17,350
Coalinga - Huron JUSD 4,300/K-12
657 Sunset St 93210 559-935-7500
Dr. C. Greenberg-English, supt. Fax 935-5329
www.coalinga-huron.org/chusd/
Bishop ES 300/K-1
1501 Sunset St 93210 559-935-7570
Judy Horn, prin. Fax 935-7573
Cheney K 100/K-K
149 Adams St 93210 559-935-7515
Judy Horn, prin. Fax 935-2950
Coalinga MS 600/6-8
265 Cambridge Ave 93210 559-935-7550
Jim Allen, prin. Fax 934-1311
Dawson ES 400/2-3
1303 Sunset St 93210 559-935-7580
Michael Motter, prin. Fax 935-7588
Sunset ES 400/4-5
985 Sunset Ave 93210 559-935-7590
Shirley Marsh, prin. Fax 935-7509
Other Schools – See Huron

Faith Christian Academy 100/PK-12
450 W Elm Ave 93210 559-935-9209
Tara Davis, prin. Fax 935-0745

Coarsegold, Madera
Yosemite USD
Supt. — See Oakhurst
Coarsegold S 500/K-8
45426 Road 415 93614 559-683-4842
Bob Rose, prin. Fax 683-2625
Rivergold S 600/K-8
31800 Road 400 93614 559-658-7566
Al Nocciolo, prin. Fax 658-7244

Coleville, Mono
Eastern Sierra USD
Supt. — See Bridgeport
Antelope S 100/K-8
111527 US Highway 395 96107 530-495-2231
Jason Reid, prin. Fax 495-1831

Colfax, Placer, Pop. 1,720
Colfax ESD 400/K-8
24825 Ben Taylor Rd 95713 530-346-2202
Jon Ray, supt. Fax 346-2205
www.colfax.k12.ca.us
Colfax S 400/K-8
24825 Ben Taylor Rd 95713 530-346-2202
Jon Ray, prin. Fax 346-2205
Iowa Hill S 50/K-8
24825 Ben Taylor RD 95713 530-913-9680
Jon Ray, prin. Fax 346-2205

Colma, San Mateo, Pop. 1,394

Holy Angels S 300/K-8
20 Reiner St 94014 650-755-0220
Sr. Leonarda Montealto, prin. Fax 755-0258

Colton, San Bernardino, Pop. 51,350
Colton JUSD 24,400/PK-12
1212 Valencia Dr 92324 909-580-5000
James Downs, supt. Fax 433-9471
www.colton.k12.ca.us
Birney ES 800/K-6
1050 E Olive St 92324 909-876-4206
Jessica Gomez, prin. Fax 433-9474
Colton MS 1,200/7-8
670 W Laurel St 92324 909-580-5009
Chris Marin, prin. Fax 876-4095
Cooley Ranch ES 700/K-6
1000 S Cooley Dr 92324 909-876-4272
Valerie Villareal, prin. Fax 430-2834
Grant ES 800/K-6
550 W Olive St 92324 909-876-4126
Kathy Houle-Jackson, prin. Fax 876-6325
Lincoln ES 800/K-6
444 E Olive St 92324 909-876-4176
Jessica Gomez, prin. Fax 876-6348
McKinley ES 600/K-6
600 Johnston St 92324 909-876-4201
Dr. Frank Miranda, prin. Fax 876-6305
Reche Canyon ES 800/K-6
3101 Canyon Vista Dr 92324 909-876-4155
Diane Mumper, prin. Fax 876-6336
Rogers ES 700/K-6
955 W Laurel St 92324 909-876-4211
Lisa Mannes, prin. Fax 876-4252
San Salvador Preschool PK-PK
471 Agua Mansa Rd 92324 909-876-4240
Kathleen McGinn, admin. Fax 824-7406
Wilson ES 700/K-6
750 S 8th St 92324 909-876-4242
Diana Carreon, prin. Fax 872-6480
Other Schools – See Bloomington, Fontana, Grand Terrace

Rialto USD
Supt. — See Rialto
Garcia ES 800/K-5
1390 W Randall Ave 92324 909-421-7620
Jasmin Valenzuela, prin. Fax 421-7624
Jehue MS 1,500/6-8
1500 N Eucalyptus Ave 92324 909-421-7377
Leonard Buckner, prin. Fax 421-7376
Morris ES 800/K-5
1900 W Randall Ave 92324 909-820-6864
Nils Karlsson, prin. Fax 820-7944

Columbia, Tuolumne, Pop. 1,799
Columbia UNSD 600/K-8
22540 Parrotts Ferry Rd 95310 209-532-0202
Dr. John Pendley, supt. Fax 533-7709
www.columbia49er.k12.ca.us
Columbia S 600/K-8
22540 Parrotts Ferry Rd 95310 209-533-7700
Don Foster, prin. Fax 533-4998

Colusa, Colusa, Pop. 5,826
Colusa USD 1,300/K-12
745 10th St 95932 530-458-7791
Larry Yeghoian, supt. Fax 458-4030
www.colusa.k12.ca.us
Burchfield PS 400/K-3
400 Fremont St 95932 530-458-5853
Dave Tarr, prin. Fax 458-8874
Egling MS 500/4-8
813 Webster St 95932 530-458-7631
Ed Conrado, prin. Fax 458-8107

Our Lady of Lourdes S 100/PK-8
741 Ware Ave 95932 530-458-8208
Barbara Genera, prin. Fax 458-8657

Commerce, Los Angeles, Pop. 13,455
Montebello USD
Supt. — See Montebello
Bandini ES 400/K-5
2318 Couts Ave 90040 323-261-8782
Karen Pugh, prin. Fax 887-5856
Laguna Nueva S 800/K-8
6360 Garfield Ave 90040 562-806-7812
Juan Herrera, prin. Fax 806-5138
Rosewood Park S 900/K-8
2353 Commerce Way 90040 323-887-7862
Robert Cornejo, prin. Fax 887-7863

Comptche, Mendocino
Mendocino USD
Supt. — See Mendocino
Comptche ES 50/K-3
PO Box 144 95427 707-937-5945
Judy Stavely, lead tchr. Fax 937-0714

Compton, Los Angeles, Pop. 95,659
Compton USD 28,300/PK-12
501 S Santa Fe Ave 90221 310-639-4321
Dr. Kaye Burnside, supt. Fax 632-3014
www.compton.k12.ca.us
Anderson ES 600/PK-5
2210 E 130th St 90222 310-898-6110
Martha Funes, prin. Fax 604-4314
Bunche MS 800/6-8
12338 S Mona Blvd 90222 310-898-6010
Paul Hernandez, prin. Fax 638-4935

Bursch ES 400/PK-5
2505 W 156th St 90220 310-898-6130
Rochelle Johnson-Evans, prin. Fax 638-6716
Caldwell Street ES 300/PK-5
2300 W Caldwell St 90220 310-898-6140
Laura Brown-Henry, prin. Fax 764-2573
Clinton ES 800/PK-5
6500 E Compton Blvd 90221 562-630-7912
Virginia Ward-Roberts, prin. Fax 630-7914
Davis MS 1,400/6-8
621 W Poplar St 90220 310-898-6020
Betty Jones, prin. Fax 631-5725
Dickison ES 900/K-5
905 N Aranbe Ave 90220 310-898-6160
Pamela Neal-Robinson, prin. Fax 631-5675
Emerson ES 700/PK-5
1011 E Caldwell St 90221 310-898-6170
Lisa Davis, prin. Fax 632-8316
Enterprise MS 600/6-8
2600 W Compton Blvd 90220 310-898-6030
Dr. Teodor Brancov, prin. Fax 632-4183
Foster ES 700/PK-5
1620 N Pannes Ave 90221 310-898-6180
Jacqueline Sanderlin Ed.D., prin. Fax 638-4553
Jefferson ES 500/K-5
2508 E 133rd St 90222 310-898-6190
Irella Martinez Ed.D., prin. Fax 537-3421
Kelly ES 1,000/K-5
2320 E Alondra Blvd 90221 310-898-6410
Valerie Quarles, prin. Fax 632-0583
Kennedy ES 700/K-5
1305 S Oleander Ave 90220 310-898-6420
Sidney Ritchey-Burnett, prin. Fax 762-9847
King ES 600/PK-5
2270 E 122nd St 90222 310-898-6430
Stephanie Richardson, prin. Fax 631-9208
Laurel Street ES 500/PK-5
1321 W Laurel St 90220 310-898-6440
Francisca Owoaje, prin. Fax 639-8409
Longfellow ES 700/PK-5
1101 S Dwight Ave 90220 310-898-6460
Cowana Emile, prin. Fax 632-5406
Mayo ES 600/K-2
915 N Mayo Ave 90221 310-898-6310
Diana Stephens, prin. Fax 638-5660
McKinley ES 300/PK-5
14431 S Stanford Ave 90220 310-898-6320
Fleming Robinson, prin. Fax 516-1322
McNair ES 500/K-5
1450 W El Segundo Blvd 90222 310-898-6330
Jacquelyn Arion Ed.D., prin. Fax 898-6098
Roosevelt ES 1,100/PK-5
700 N Bradfield Ave 90221 310-898-6350
Ronald Keaton, prin. Fax 632-0338
Roosevelt MS 1,300/6-8
1200 E Alondra Blvd 90221 310-898-6040
Edd Bond, prin. Fax 631-3298
Rosecrans ES 500/PK-5
1301 N Acacia Ave 90222 310-898-6360
Umar Baba, prin. Fax 639-2224
Tibby ES 500/PK-5
1400 W Poplar St 90220 310-898-6370
Fredricka Brown, prin. Fax 638-7015
Walton MS 600/6-8
900 W Greenleaf Dr 90220 310-898-6060
Gipson Lyles, prin. Fax 631-3409
Washington ES 600/K-5
1421 N Wilmington Ave 90222 310-898-6390
Ontrece Ellerbe, prin. Fax 898-6038
Whaley MS 1,100/6-8
14401 S Gibson Ave 90221 310-898-6070
Renee Cobb, prin. Fax 638-7079
Willard ES 500/3-5
310 E El Segundo Blvd 90222 310-898-6434
Freda Rossi, prin. Fax 639-8715
Willowbrook MS 700/6-8
2601 N Wilmington Ave 90222 310-898-6080
Janet Robinson, prin. Fax 537-2932
Other Schools – See Carson, Los Angeles

Optimal Christian Academy 300/K-8
1300 E Palmer St 90221 310-603-0378
Carolyn Dowell, admin. Fax 603-0604
Our Lady of Victory S 200/PK-8
601 E Palmer St 90221 310-631-1320
Manuel Gonzalez, prin. Fax 631-4280
St. Albert the Great S 200/PK-8
804 E Compton Blvd 90220 310-323-4559
Tina Johnson, prin. Fax 323-4825

Concord, Contra Costa, Pop. 123,252

Mount Diablo USD 35,300/PK-12
1936 Carlotta Dr 94519 925-682-8000
Gary McHenry, supt. Fax 689-1649
www.mdusd.k12.ca.us
Ayers ES 400/K-5
5120 Myrtle Dr 94521 925-682-7686
Nancy Baum, prin. Fax 827-2521
Cambridge ES 700/K-5
1135 Lacey Ln 94520 925-686-4749
Marie Schirmer, prin. Fax 798-5068
El Dorado MS 1,000/6-8
1750 West St 94521 925-682-5700
Robert Humphrey, prin. Fax 685-1460
El Monte ES 500/K-5
1400 Dina Dr 94518 925-685-3113
Christina Boman, prin. Fax 827-5471
Glenbrook MS 700/6-8
2351 Olivera Rd 94520 925-685-6835
Gary McAdam, prin. Fax 671-9532
Highlands ES 700/K-5
1326 Pennsylvania Blvd 94521 925-672-5252
Mary Ann Tucker, prin. Fax 672-6910
Holbrook ES 500/K-5
3333 Ronald Way 94519 925-685-6446
Nancy Edwards-Dasho, prin. Fax 827-1138
Meadow Homes ES 900/K-5
1371 Detroit Ave 94520 925-685-8760
Toby Montez, prin. Fax 689-7217
Monte Gardens ES 600/K-5
3841 Larkspur Dr 94519 925-685-3834
Patt Hoellwarth, prin. Fax 689-8291
Mountain View ES 400/K-5
1705 Thornwood Dr 94521 925-689-6450
Diana DeMott-Rigoli, prin. Fax 687-8622
Oak Grove MS 600/6-8
2050 Minert Rd 94518 925-682-1843
Teresa McCormick, prin. Fax 682-2083
Pine Hollow MS 700/6-8
5522 Pine Hollow Rd 94521 925-672-5444
Shelley Bain, prin. Fax 672-9751
Silverwood ES 400/K-5
1679 Claycord Ave 94521 925-687-1150
Dr. Sandra Rogers-Hare, prin. Fax 689-8199
Sun Terrace ES 600/K-5
2448 Floyd Ln 94520 925-682-4861
Felicia Stuckey-Smith, prin. Fax 798-7476
Westwood ES 400/K-5
1748 West St 94521 925-685-4202
Jennifer Vargas, prin. Fax 680-0431
Woodside ES 500/K-5
761 San Simeon Dr 94518 925-689-7671
Michele Batesole, prin. Fax 689-4974
Wren Avenue ES 400/K-5
3339 Wren Ave 94519 925-685-7002
Sandra Seskin, prin. Fax 609-9506
Ygnacio Valley ES 500/K-5
2217 Chalomar Rd 94518 925-682-9336
Christine Richardson, prin. Fax 609-7759
Other Schools – See Clayton, Martinez, Pittsburg, Pleasant Hill, Walnut Creek

---

Calvary Temple Christian S 200/PK-8
4725 Evora Rd 94520 925-458-9870
John Jackson, prin. Fax 458-9001
Concordia S 100/PK-6
2353 5th Ave 94518 925-689-6910
Kathryn Linzey, prin. Fax 680-8040
King's Valley Christian S 300/PK-8
4255 Clayton Rd 94521 925-687-2020
Dan Prescott, prin. Fax 687-7829
Queen of all Saints S 200/K-8
2391 Grant St 94520 925-685-8700
Maryalice Clare, prin. Fax 685-2034
St. Agnes S 300/K-8
3886 Chestnut Ave 94519 925-689-3990
Karen Mangini, prin. Fax 689-3455
St. Francis of Assisi S 300/K-8
866 Oak Grove Rd 94518 925-682-5414
Sr. James Dyer, prin. Fax 682-5480
Tabernacle Christian S 500/PK-8
4380 Concord Blvd 94521 925-685-9169
Margaret Bridges, dir. Fax 685-9176
Ygnacio Valley Christian S 200/PK-8
4977 Concord Blvd 94521 925-798-3131
Gary Falk, hdmstr. Fax 798-6150

Cool, El Dorado

Black Oak Mine USD
Supt. — See Georgetown
Northside S 600/K-8
860 Cave Valley Rd 95614 530-333-8355
Bill Jensen, prin. Fax 333-8355

Copperopolis, Calaveras

Mark Twain UNESD
Supt. — See Angels Camp
Copperopolis ES 300/K-6
217 School St 95228 209-785-2236
Julia Tidball, prin. Fax 785-4309

Corcoran, Kings, Pop. 22,456

Corcoran JUSD 3,200/PK-12
1520 Patterson Ave 93212 559-992-8888
Rich Merlo, supt. Fax 992-3957
www.corcoran.k12.ca.us
Fremont ES 400/2-3
1520 Patterson Ave 93212 559-992-8888
Lora Cartwright, prin. Fax 992-5105
Harte ES 500/PK-1
1520 Patterson Ave 93212 559-992-8888
Elizabeth Mendoza, prin. Fax 992-3299
Muir MS 800/6-8
1520 Patterson Ave 93212 559-992-8888
Mike Graville, prin. Fax 992-4423
Twain MS 500/4-5
1520 Patterson Ave 93212 559-992-8888
Mike Anderson, prin. Fax 992-1018

Corning, Tehama, Pop. 7,140

Corning UNESD 2,000/K-8
1590 South St 96021 530-824-7700
Stephen Kelish, supt. Fax 824-2493
www.cuesd.tehama.k12.ca.us
Maywood MS 700/6-8
1666 Marguerite Ave 96021 530-824-7730
Jeff Harris, prin. Fax 824-7742
Olive View ES 600/K-5
1402 Fig St 96021 530-824-7715
Beckie Bouchard Ed.D., prin. Fax 824-7740
Rancho Tehama ES 100/K-6
PO Box 5775 96021 530-585-2800
Mona Miller, prin. Fax 585-2802
West Street ES 200/K-5
900 West St 96021 530-824-7705
Beckie Bouchard Ed.D., prin. Fax 824-7741
Woodson ES 400/K-5
150 N Toomes Ave 96021 530-824-7720
Mona Miller, prin. Fax 824-7745
Kirkwood ESD 50/K-8
2049 Kirkwood Rd 96021 530-824-7773
John Lalaguna, supt. Fax 824-6995
www.ksd.tehama.k12.ca.us/
Kirkwood S 50/K-8
2049 Kirkwood Rd 96021 530-824-7773
Fax 824-6995

Richfield ESD 200/K-8
23875 River Rd 96021 530-824-3354
Todd Brose, supt. Fax 824-0569
www.resd.tehama.k12.ca.us/
Richfield S 200/K-8
23875 River Rd 96021 530-824-3354
Todd Brose, prin. Fax 824-0569

Corona, Riverside, Pop. 149,387

Alvord USD
Supt. — See Riverside
Promenade ES 1,000/K-5
550 Hamilton Dr 92879 951-358-1650
Lori Copeland, prin. Fax 358-1651

Corona-Norco USD
Supt. — See Norco
Adams ES 800/K-6
2350 Border Ave 92882 951-736-3313
Trevor Dietrich, prin. Fax 736-7130
Anthony ES 1,000/K-6
2665 Gilbert Ave 92881 951-739-5655
Dr. Jo Melillo Long, prin. Fax 739-5662
Auburndale IS 1,100/7-8
1255 River Rd 92880 951-736-3231
Linda Lanyi, prin. Fax 736-3360
Barton ES 1,200/K-6
7437 Corona Valley Ave 92880 951-736-4545
Susan Helms, prin. Fax 736-4538
Chavez ES 600/K-6
1150 Paseo Grande 92882 951-736-4640
Dr. Felicia Cruz-Delgado, prin. Fax 736-4648
Citrus Hills IS 1,700/7-8
3211 S Main St 92882 951-736-4600
Lisa Simon, prin. Fax 736-4623
Corona Fundamental IS 1,100/7-8
1230 S Main St 92882 951-736-3321
Bonnie Paskey, prin. Fax 736-3417
Corona Ranch ES 1,000/K-6
785 Village Loop Dr 92879 951-736-4626
Adriana Burkhart, prin. Fax 736-4633
Coronita ES 800/K-6
1757 Via Del Rio 92882 951-736-3389
Beth Feaster, prin. Fax 736-3485
Eastvale ES 1,000/K-6
13031 Orange St 92880 951-738-2180
Steve Rachunok, prin. Fax 738-2186
Eisenhower ES 1,000/K-6
3355 Mountain Gate Dr 92882 951-739-5960
Jeanne Trevino, prin. Fax 739-5968
El Cerrito MS 800/6-8
7610 El Cerrito Rd 92881 951-736-3216
Shelly Yarbrough, prin. Fax 736-3286
Foothill ES 1,200/K-6
2601 S Buena Vista Ave 92882 951-736-3441
Ryan Reider, prin. Fax 736-3251
Franklin ES 800/K-6
2650 Oak Ave 92882 951-739-5645
Jason Scott, prin. Fax 739-5650
Garretson ES 1,100/K-6
1650 Garretson Ave 92879 951-736-3345
John Reynoso, prin. Fax 736-3347
Harada ES 1,100/K-6
12884 Oakdale St 92880 951-739-6820
Melanie Murphy-Corwin, prin. Fax 739-6825
Home Gardens ES 800/K-6
13550 Tolton Ave 92879 951-736-3219
Cassandra Willis, prin. Fax 736-7151
Jefferson ES 800/K-6
1040 S Vicentia Ave 92882 951-736-3226
Patricio Vargas, prin. Fax 736-3270
McKinley ES 900/K-6
2050 Aztec Ln 92879 951-736-7190
Janette Neumann, prin. Fax 736-7192
Orange ES 1,100/K-6
1350 Valencia Rd 92881 951-736-3455
Shanda Morgan, prin. Fax 736-3490
Parkridge S for the Arts 1,000/K-6
750 Corona Ave 92879 951-736-3236
Judy Now, prin. Fax 736-3478
Parks ES 900/K-6
13830 Whispering Hills Dr 92880 951-736-7305
Philip Saxena, prin. Fax 736-3478
Prado View ES 1,000/K-6
2800 Ridgeline Dr 92882 951-736-3474
Carol Ackermann, prin. Fax 739-5810
Raney IS 1,400/6-8
1010 W Citron St 92882 951-736-3221
Allen Pietrok, prin. Fax 736-3439
River Heights IS 1,200/7-8
7227 Cleveland Ave 92880 951-738-2155
Karen Fisher, prin. Fax 738-2175
Stallings ES 800/K-6
1980 Fullerton Ave 92881 951-736-3249
Carol Cornell, prin. Fax 739-5811
Temescal Valley ES 1,100/K-6
22950 Claystone Ave 92883 951-736-7110
Nancy Moler, prin. Fax 736-7178
Todd ES 600/K-6
25105 Mayhew Canyon Rd 92883 951-736-8285
Grace Eden, prin. Fax 736-8286
Vicentia ES 900/K-6
2005 S Vicentia Ave 92882 951-736-3228
Ryan Lewis, prin. Fax 736-7140
Wilson ES 1,100/K-6
1750 Spyglass Dr 92883 951-739-5820
Karen Hall, prin. Fax 739-5827

Lake Elsinore USD
Supt. — See Lake Elsinore
Luiseno ES 800/K-5
13500 Mountain Rd 92883 951-674-0750
Susan Jones, prin. Fax 245-6847

Amor Christian Academy 50/1-12
PO Box 2650 92878 951-735-6609
Jesse Reyes, admin. Fax 735-5185
Calvary Chapel Christian Academy 100/K-6
130 W Chase Dr 92882 951-278-0600
Roger Kerwin, prin. Fax 284-1686
Christian Heritage S 400/K-12
PO Box 1780 92878 951-736-3033
Arleen Morris, admin.
Corona Christian S 50/PK-K
1901 W Ontario Ave 92882 951-734-5683
Dr. David Howard, supt. Fax 734-3809
Crossroads Christian S 1,000/PK-8
2380 Fullerton Ave 92881 951-278-3199
Beth Frobisher, admin. Fax 493-2169
Grace Lutheran S 100/K-8
1811 S Lincoln Ave 92882 951-737-2187
Teresa Bustos, prin. Fax 737-1750
Montessori S of Corona 100/K-6
260 W Ontario Ave 92882 951-371-6731
Sandra Perez, admin.
Olive Branch Christian Academy 200/PK-8
7702 El Cerrito Rd 92881 951-279-9977
Mandy Logan, admin. Fax 520-9797
St. Edward S 500/PK-8
500 S Merrill St 92882 951-737-2530
Leilani Lister, prin. Fax 737-1074

Corona del Mar, Orange
Newport - Mesa USD
Supt. — See Costa Mesa
Harbor View ES 400/PK-6
900 Goldenrod Ave 92625 949-515-6940
Charlene Metoyer, prin. Fax 515-6811
Lincoln ES 600/K-6
3101 Pacific View Dr 92625 949-515-6955
Jane Holm, prin. Fax 515-6806

Harbor Day S 400/K-8
3443 Pacific View Dr 92625 949-640-1410
Douglas Phelps, hdmstr. Fax 640-0908

Coronado, San Diego, Pop. 26,424
Coronado USD 3,000/K-12
201 6th St 92118 619-522-8900
Jeffrey Felix, supt. Fax 437-6570
www.coronado.k12.ca.us
Coronado MS 700/6-8
550 F Ave 92118 619-522-8921
Jay Marquard, prin. Fax 522-6948
Coronado Village ES 800/K-5
600 6th St 92118 619-522-8919
Deeba Zaher, prin. Fax 522-8988
Silver Strand ES 300/K-5
1350 Leyte Rd 92118 619-522-8934
Bill Cass, prin. Fax 437-8041

Christ Church Day S 100/K-6
1114 9th St 92118 619-435-6393
Nancy Roberts, hdmstr. Fax 435-4574
Sacred Heart S 200/K-8
706 C Ave 92118 619-437-4431
Peter Harris, prin. Fax 437-1559

Corralitos, Santa Cruz, Pop. 2,513

Salesian S 200/K-8
605 Enos Ln 95076 831-728-5518
Sr. Carmen Botello, prin. Fax 728-0273

Corte Madera, Marin, Pop. 9,120
Larkspur ESD
Supt. — See Larkspur
Cummins ES 700/K-4
58 Mohawk Ave 94925 415-927-6965
Marilyn Clark, prin. Fax 927-6967

Lycee Francais International Laperouse S 200/K-5
330 Golden Hind Psge 94925 415-661-5232
Frederick Arzelier, hdmstr. Fax 924-2849
Marin Country Day S 500/K-8
5221 Paradise Dr 94925 415-927-5900
Lucinda Kutz, hdmstr.
Marin Montessori S 200/PK-8
5200 Paradise Dr 94925 415-924-5388
Jim Fitzpatrick, hdmstr. Fax 924-5305

Costa Mesa, Orange, Pop. 109,830
Newport - Mesa USD 20,400/PK-12
2985 Bear St 92626 714-424-5000
Dr. Jeffrey Hubbard, supt. Fax 424-5018
www.nmusd.us
Adams ES 500/PK-6
2850 Clubhouse Rd 92626 714-424-7935
Candy Cloud, prin. Fax 424-4701
California ES 400/K-6
3232 California St 92626 714-424-7940
Kelli Smith, prin. Fax 424-4711
College Park ES 400/PK-5
2380 Notre Dame Rd 92626 714-424-7960
John Sanders, prin. Fax 424-4721
Davis ES 700/4-6
1050 Arlington Dr 92626 714-424-7930
Patricia Mulhaupt, prin. Fax 424-4711
Kaiser ES 700/3-6
2130 Santa Ana Ave 92627 949-515-6950
Barbara Harrington, prin. Fax 515-6851
Killybrooke ES 400/K-6
3155 Killybrooke Ln 92626 714-424-7945
Kathy Sanchez, prin. Fax 424-4731
Paularino ES 300/PK-5
1060 Paularino Ave 92626 714-424-7950
Stacy DeBoom, prin. Fax 424-4741
Pomona ES 500/PK-4
2051 Pomona Ave 92627 949-515-6980
Stacy Holmes, prin. Fax 515-6891
Rea ES 700/PK-6
661 Hamilton St 92627 949-515-6905
Anna Corral, prin. Fax 515-6835
Sonora ES 300/PK-5
966 Sonora Rd 92626 949-424-7955
Christine Anderson, prin. Fax 424-4751
TeWinkle MS 700/7-8
3224 California St 92626 714-424-7965
Kirk Bauermeister, prin. Fax 424-5680
Victoria ES 300/K-6
1025 Victoria St 92627 949-515-6985
Judy Laakso, prin. Fax 515-6841
Whittier ES 600/PK-4
1800 Whittier Ave 92627 949-515-6990
Tracey Carter, prin. Fax 515-6815
Wilson ES 500/PK-6
801 W Wilson St 92627 949-515-6995
Candy Sperling, prin. Fax 515-6825
Woodland ES 500/K-2
2025 Garden Ln 92627 949-515-6945
Lauren Medve, prin. Fax 515-6861
Other Schools – See Corona del Mar, Newport Beach, Newport Coast

---

Christ Lutheran S 300/PK-8
760 Victoria St 92627 949-548-6866
Richard Nordmeyer, prin. Fax 631-6224
Kline S of Technology 100/K-8
1620 Adams Ave 92626 714-421-4700
Susan Kline, dir.
Mariners Christian S 600/K-8
300 Fischer Ave 92626 714-437-1700
Don Cole, hdmstr. Fax 437-7976
Page Private S of Costa Mesa 100/K-8
PO Box 10909 92627 949-642-0411
Jill Sebasto, dir.
Prince of Peace Christian S 100/PK-6
2987 Mesa Verde Dr E 92626 714-549-0562
Sherry Williams, prin. Fax 434-3845
St. Joachim S 300/PK-8
1964 Orange Ave 92627 949-574-7411
Sr. Kathleen Pughe, prin. Fax 646-8948
St. John the Baptist S 600/K-8
1021 Baker St 92626 714-557-5060
Sr. Mary Vianney Ennis, prin. Fax 557-9263
Waldorf S of Orange County 300/PK-12
2350 Canyon Dr 92627 949-574-7775
Gina Illes, admin. Fax 574-7740

Cotati, Sonoma, Pop. 7,138
Cotati-Rohnert Park USD
Supt. — See Rohnert Park
Page ES 200/K-5
1075 Madrone Ave 94931 707-792-4860
Mary Campbell, prin. Fax 792-4514

Coto de Caza, Orange, Pop. 2,853
Capistrano USD
Supt. — See San Juan Capistrano
Wagon Wheel ES 900/K-5
30912 Bridle Path 92679 949-589-1953
Kathy Parker, prin. Fax 589-2813

Cottonwood, Shasta, Pop. 1,747
Cottonwood UNESD 1,200/K-8
20512 1st St 96022 530-347-3165
Robert Lowden, supt. Fax 347-0247
www.shastalink.k12.ca.us/cottonwood/
East Cottonwood ES 400/K-2
20512 1st St 96022 530-347-3071
Rose Scott, prin. Fax 347-1941
North Cottonwood ES 400/3-5
20512 1st St 96022 530-347-1698
Mark Boyle, prin. Fax 347-7233
West Cottonwood JHS 400/6-8
20512 1st St 96022 530-347-3123
Douglas Geren, prin. Fax 347-0247

Evergreen UNSD 900/K-8
19500 Learning Way 96022 530-347-3411
Harley North, supt. Fax 347-7954
www.eusd.tehama.k12.ca.us
Evergreen ES 500/K-4
19500 Learning Way 96022 530-347-3411
Debbie Oppezzo, prin. Fax 347-4639
Evergreen MS 500/5-8
19500 Learning Way 96022 530-347-3411
Brad Mendenhall, prin. Fax 347-7953

Coulterville, Mariposa
Mariposa County USD
Supt. — See Mariposa
Coulterville-Greeley S 100/K-8
10326 Fiske Rd 95311 209-878-3481
Daniel Hoffman, prin. Fax 878-3096

Courtland, Sacramento
River Delta USD
Supt. — See Rio Vista
Bates ES 300/K-6
PO Box 308 95615 916-775-1771
Vicky Turk, prin. Fax 775-1702

Covelo, Mendocino, Pop. 1,057
Round Valley USD 400/K-12
PO Box 276 95428 707-983-6171
Dennis Ivey, supt. Fax 983-6655
Round Valley S 200/K-8
PO Box 276 95428 707-983-6175
Cheryl Tuttle, prin. Fax 983-6377

Covelo's SDA S 50/1-8
77650 Crawford Rd 95428 707-983-6822
Arla Nummelin, prin. Fax 983-8297

Covina, Los Angeles, Pop. 47,850
Azusa USD
Supt. — See Azusa
Ellington ES 300/K-5
5034 N Clydebank Ave 91722 626-858-6800
Paula Rode, prin. Fax 974-8232

Charter Oak USD 6,300/K-12
20240 E Cienega Ave 91724 626-966-8331
Clint Harwick Ed.D., supt. Fax 967-9580
www.cousd.k12.ca.us
Badillo ES 600/K-6
1771 E Old Badillo St 91724 626-966-1753
Carren Acevedo, prin. Fax 859-5765
Cedargrove ES 1,000/K-6
1209 N Glendora Ave 91724 626-966-8675
Debra Tarbox, prin. Fax 966-6773
Glen Oak ES 500/K-6
1000 N Sunflower Ave 91724 626-331-5341
Margaret Grosjean, prin. Fax 331-5312
Royal Oak MS 1,000/7-8
303 S Glendora Ave 91724 626-967-6354
Dr. Mary Martinez, prin. Fax 331-2074
Other Schools – See Glendora

Covina-Valley USD 13,900/K-12
PO Box 269 91723 626-974-7000
Louis Pappas, supt. Fax 974-7032
www.cvusd.k12.ca.us
Barranca ES 600/K-5
PO Box 269 91723 626-974-4000
Zoe Vanek, prin. Fax 974-4015
Ben Lomond ES 400/K-5
PO Box 269 91723 626-974-4100
Cheri Howell, prin. Fax 974-4115
Cypress ES 600/K-5
PO Box 269 91723 626-974-4300
Adin Rudd, prin. Fax 974-4315
Lark Ellen ES 500/K-5
PO Box 269 91723 626-974-4500
Susan Perez-May, prin. Fax 974-4515
Las Palmas MS 1,200/6-8
PO Box 269 91723 626-974-7200
Josie Paredes, prin. Fax 974-7215
Manzanita ES 500/K-5
PO Box 269 91723 626-472-7640
Sue Cytryn, prin. Fax 472-7655
Sierra Vista MS 1,300/6-8
PO Box 269 91723 626-974-7300
Robert Shivers, prin. Fax 974-7315
Other Schools – See Irwindale, West Covina

Sacred Heart S 300/PK-8
360 W Workman St 91723 626-332-7222
April Luchonok, prin. Fax 967-8836
St. Louise De Marillac S 300/K-8
1728 E Covina Blvd 91724 626-966-2317
Elizabeth LaDou, prin. Fax 332-4431
Sonrise Christian S 600/PK-8
1220 E Ruddock St 91724 626-331-0559
Dr. Timothy Burlingame, supt. Fax 339-8029

Crescent City, Del Norte, Pop. 7,825
Del Norte County USD 4,100/K-12
301 W Washington Blvd 95531 707-464-6141
Jan Moorehouse, supt. Fax 464-0238
www.delnorte.k12.ca.us
Crescent Elk MS 600/6-8
994 G St 95531 707-464-0320
Billy Hartwick, prin. Fax 464-0326
Hamilton ES 400/K-5
1050 E St 95531 707-464-0330
Tony Fabricius, prin. Fax 465-4844
Maxwell ES 300/K-5
1124 El Dorado St 95531 707-464-0310
Katy Cunningham, prin. Fax 464-0316
Peacock ES 400/K-6
1720 Arlington Dr 95531 707-464-0301
Brooke Davis, prin. Fax 464-3399
Pine Grove ES 200/K-6
900 Pine Grove Rd 95531 707-464-0350
Connie Gilman, prin. Fax 465-4775
Redwood S 400/K-8
6900 Lake Earl Dr 95531 707-464-0360
Alisa Vervilos, prin. Fax 487-9051
Other Schools – See Gasquet, Klamath, Smith River

Crescent City Jr. Academy 50/K-8
1770 Northcrest Dr 95531 707-464-5229
Georgine Hultz, prin. Fax 464-4671
Foursquare Christian S 100/PK-12
144 Butte St 95531 707-464-9501
Roger Bodenstab, admin. Fax 465-3254
St. Joseph S 50/K-8
330 E St 95531 707-464-3477
Patricia Foht, prin. Fax 465-1763

Cressey, Merced, Pop. 350
Ballico-Cressey ESD
Supt. — See Ballico
Cressey ES 100/K-3
9921 W Crocker Ave 95312 209-394-3031
Jose Gonzalez, prin. Fax 394-3031

Crestline, San Bernardino, Pop. 8,594
Rim of the World USD
Supt. — See Lake Arrowhead
Valley of Enchantment ES 500/K-3
22836 Fir Ln 92325 909-336-0375
Susan Brown, prin. Fax 336-0380

Creston, San Luis Obispo
Atascadero USD
Supt. — See Atascadero

Creston ES 100/K-6
PO Box 238 93432 805-238-4771
Wendy Smith, prin. Fax 238-4185

Crockett, Contra Costa, Pop. 3,228
John Swett USD
Supt. — See Rodeo
Carquinez MS 400/6-8
1099 Pomona St 94525 510-787-1081
Linda Steensrud, prin. Fax 787-2359

Crowley Lake, Mono

Crowley Christian S 50/K-8
80 S Landing Rd 93546 760-935-4722
Kevin Sapp, prin. Fax 935-4273

Crows Landing, Stanislaus
Chatom UNESD
Supt. — See Turlock
Mountain View MS 200/6-8
10001 Crows Landing Rd 95313 209-664-8515
Cherise Olvera, prin. Fax 669-1733

Newman-Crows Landing USD
Supt. — See Newman
Bonita ES 100/K-5
425 Fink Rd 95313 209-837-4401
Richard Jukes, prin. Fax 837-0431

Cudahy, Los Angeles, Pop. 25,004
Los Angeles USD
Supt. — See Los Angeles
Elizabeth Learning Center 2,700/K-12
4811 Elizabeth St 90201 323-271-3600
Michael Perez, prin. Fax 560-8412
Hughes ES 1,200/K-6
4242 Clara St 90201 323-560-4422
Grace Fuller, prin. Fax 773-7568
Park Avenue ES 700/K-6
8020 Park Ave 90201 323-832-1860
Ofelia Valdez, prin. Fax 560-9912

Culver City, Los Angeles, Pop. 39,603
Culver City USD 6,500/K-12
4034 Irving Pl 90232 310-842-4220
Dr. Myrna Rivera-Cote, supt. Fax 842-4205
www.ccusd.k12.ca.us
Culver City MS 1,600/6-8
4601 Elenda St 90230 310-842-4200
Jon Pearson, prin. Fax 842-4304
El Marino ES 700/K-5
11450 Port Rd 90230 310-842-4241
Tracy Pumilia, prin. Fax 572-9420
El Rincon ES 500/K-5
11177 Overland Ave 90230 310-842-4340
Dr. Tom Tracy, prin. Fax 842-4317
Farragut ES 500/K-5
10820 Farragut Dr 90230 310-842-4323
Eileen Carroll, prin. Fax 842-4320
Howe ES 500/K-5
4100 Irving Pl 90232 310-842-4338
Amy Anderson, prin. Fax 842-4330
La Ballona ES 500/K-5
10915 Washington Blvd 90232 310-842-4334
Christine Collins, prin. Fax 842-4298

Los Angeles USD
Supt. — See Los Angeles
Braddock Drive ES 500/K-5
4711 Inglewood Blvd 90230 310-391-6707
Deborah Brandy, prin. Fax 390-5134
Playa Del Rey ES 200/K-5
12221 Juniette St 90230 310-827-3560
Mary Pierce, prin. Fax 301-9541
Stoner ES 500/K-5
11735 Braddock Dr 90230 310-390-3396
Pamela Williams, prin. Fax 397-6946

Echo Horizon S 300/PK-6
3430 McManus Ave 90232 310-838-2442
Paula Dashiell, prin. Fax 838-0479
St. Augustine S 300/K-8
3819 Clarington Ave 90232 310-838-3144
Norman Mezey, prin. Fax 838-7479
Turning Point S 400/PK-8
8780 National Blvd 90232 310-841-2505
Deborah Richman, hdmstr. Fax 841-5420
Willows Community S 400/K-8
8509 Higuera St 90232 310-815-0411
Lisa Rosenstein, hdmstr. Fax 815-0425
Yeshiva Aharon Yaakov Ohr Eliyahu 300/PK-8
5950 Stoneview Dr 90232 310-559-3330
Rabbi Shlomo Goldberg, prin. Fax 559-2211

Cupertino, Santa Clara, Pop. 52,171
Cupertino UNSD 17,000/K-8
10301 Vista Dr 95014 408-252-3000
Phil Quon Ph.D., supt. Fax 255-4450
cupertino.ca.campusgrid.net
Collins ES 600/K-5
10300 N Blaney Ave 95014 408-252-6002
Jones Wong, prin. Fax 253-3142
Eaton ES 500/K-5
20220 Suisun Dr 95014 408-255-2848
Connie Rowe, prin. Fax 255-0610
Faria ES 600/K-5
10155 Barbara Ln 95014 408-252-0706
Steven Woo, prin. Fax 253-0271
Garden Gate ES 700/K-5
10500 Ann Arbor Ave 95014 408-252-5414
Nancy Wood, prin. Fax 996-9725
Hyde MS 1,000/6-8
19325 Bollinger Rd 95014 408-252-6290
Todd Shimada, prin. Fax 255-3288
Kennedy MS 1,400/6-8
821 Bubb Rd 95014 408-253-1525
Russ Ottey, prin. Fax 257-5777
Lawson MS 900/6-8
10401 Vista Dr 95014 408-255-7500
Karl Sonntag, prin. Fax 446-4987
Lincoln ES 600/K-5
21710 McClellan Rd 95014 408-252-4798
Lynn Shimada, prin. Fax 865-0813
Regnart ES 600/K-5
1170 Yorkshire Dr 95014 408-253-5250
Lorrie Wernick, prin. Fax 253-2604
Sedgwick ES 400/K-5
19200 Phil Ln 95014 408-252-3103
Lisa Hickey, prin. Fax 253-2213
Stevens Creek ES 600/K-5
10300 Ainsworth Dr 95014 408-245-3312
Vivian Franklin, prin. Fax 245-7484
Other Schools – See Los Altos, San Jose, Santa Clara, Saratoga, Sunnyvale

Montebello ESD 50/K-6
15101 Montebello Rd 95014 408-867-3618
Alicia Mommer, supt. Fax 867-8627
www.montebelloschool.org/
Montebello ES 50/K-6
15101 Montebello Rd 95014 408-867-3618
Alicia Mommer, prin. Fax 867-8627

Bethel Lutheran S 200/PK-5
10181 Finch Ave 95014 408-252-8512
Christine Stroud, prin. Fax 252-8465
St. Joseph of Cupertino S 300/K-8
10120 N De Anza Blvd 95014 408-252-6441
Mary Lyons, prin. Fax 252-9771

Cutler, Tulare, Pop. 4,450
Cutler-Orosi JUSD
Supt. — See Orosi
Cutler ES 700/K-5
40532 Road 128 93615 559-528-6931
Miguel Flores, prin. Fax 528-0932

Cypress, Orange, Pop. 47,383
Anaheim UNHSD
Supt. — See Anaheim
Lexington JHS 1,200/7-8
4351 Orange Ave 90630 714-220-4201
Jodie Wales Ed.D., prin. Fax 761-4989

Cypress ESD 3,900/K-6
9470 Moody St 90630 714-220-6900
Sheri Loewenstein, supt. Fax 828-6652
www.cypsd.k12.ca.us
Arnold ES 600/K-6
9281 Denni St 90630 714-220-6965
Mark Brown, prin. Fax 220-6968
Cawthon ES 500/K-6
4545 Myra Ave 90630 714-220-6970
Jacki Teschke, prin. Fax 220-6973
King ES 500/K-6
8710 Moody St 90630 714-220-6980
Carol Erbe, prin. Fax 220-6983
Landell ES 600/K-6
9739 Denni St 90630 714-220-6960
Tracy Mouren-Laurens, prin. Fax 229-7720
Morris ES 500/K-6
9952 Graham St 90630 714-220-6995
Jeannette Lohrman, prin. Fax 821-9412
Swain ES 400/K-6
5851 Newman St 90630 714-220-6985
Denine Kelly, prin. Fax 220-6988
Other Schools – See Buena Park, La Palma

Calvary Chapel Christian S 200/PK-6
PO Box 769 90630 714-236-1293
Rene Hill, prin. Fax 821-0929
Grace Christian S 400/K-6
5100 Cerritos Ave 90630 714-761-5200
Don Pettinger, supt. Fax 761-1200
Holy Cross Lutheran S 100/PK-8
4321 Cerritos Ave 90630 714-527-7928
Marty Miller, prin. Fax 527-8472
St. Irenaeus Catholic S 400/K-8
9201 Grindlay St 90630 714-827-4500
Darlene Hembreiker, prin. Fax 827-2930

Daly City, San Mateo, Pop. 100,339
Bayshore ESD 400/K-8
1 Martin St 94014 415-467-5444
Norman Forbert, supt. Fax 467-1542
www.bayshore.k12.ca.us
Bayshore ES 200/K-4
155 Oriente St 94014 415-467-0442
Fax 657-3449
Robertson IS 200/4-8
1 Martin St 94014 415-467-5443
Norman Fobert, prin. Fax 467-1542

Brisbane ESD
Supt. — See Brisbane
Panorama ES 200/K-5
25 Bellevue Ave 94014 415-586-6595
Robin Pang-Maganaris, prin. Fax 586-0782

Jefferson ESD 6,000/K-8
101 Lincoln Ave 94015 650-991-1000
Matteo Rizzo, supt. Fax 992-2265
www.jsd.k12.ca.us/
Anthony ES 500/K-5
575 Abbot Ave 94014 650-997-7880
Gay Gardner-Berk, prin. Fax 755-8303
Brown ES 400/K-6
305 Eastmoor Ave 94015 650-991-1243
Dianne Lakatta, prin. Fax 997-0351
Edison ES 500/K-6
1267 Southgate Ave 94015 650-991-1250
Jennifer Larocque, prin. Fax 755-3040
Franklin IS 500/7-8
700 Stewart Ave 94015 650-991-1200
James Parrish, prin. Fax 756-5475
Garden Village ES 300/K-6
208 Garden Ln 94015 650-991-1233
Joseph McCreary, prin. Fax 755-1916
Kennedy ES 500/K-5
785 Price St 94014 650-991-1239
Carolyn Casey, prin. Fax 755-1937
Pollicita MS 700/6-8
550 E Market St 94014 650-991-1216
Catalina Rico, prin. Fax 755-2170
Rivera IS 500/7-8
1255 Southgate Ave 94015 650-991-1225
Brent Marquez-Valenti, prin. Fax 755-6273
Roosevelt ES 300/K-6
1200 Skyline Dr 94015 650-991-1230
Sharon Yniguez, prin. Fax 755-5046
Tobias ES 300/K-6
725 Southgate Ave 94015 650-991-1246
Will Anderson, prin. Fax 755-1599
Washington ES 400/K-5
251 Whittier St 94014 650-991-1236
Rochelle Pimentel-Yuen, prin. Fax 991-1326
Webster ES 500/K-6
425 El Dorado Dr 94015 650-991-1222
Rochelle Yatomi, prin. Fax 755-8214
Westlake ES 400/K-6
80 Fieldcrest Dr 94015 650-991-1252
Jessica Pace, prin. Fax 994-6137
Wilson ES 400/K-6
43 Miriam St 94014 650-991-1255
Aurora Sweet, prin. Fax 994-5946

South San Francisco USD
Supt. — See South San Francisco
Junipero Serra ES 400/K-5
151 Victoria St 94015 650-877-8853
John Schmella, prin. Fax 878-4743
Skyline ES 400/K-5
55 Christen Ave 94015 650-877-8941
Tim Sullivan, prin. Fax 754-1746

Hope Lutheran S 100/PK-K
55 San Fernando Way 94015 650-991-4673
Cynthia Huang, admin. Fax 991-9723
Our Lady of Mercy S 500/K-8
7 Elmwood Dr 94015 650-756-3395
Alex Endo, prin. Fax 756-5872
Our Lady of Perpetual Help S 300/K-8
80 Wellington Ave 94014 650-755-4438
William Kovacich, prin. Fax 755-7366

Dana Point, Orange, Pop. 35,867
Capistrano USD
Supt. — See San Juan Capistrano
Dana ES 300/K-5
24242 La Cresta Dr 92629 949-496-5784
Christina Portillo, prin. Fax 488-3867

St. Edward the Confessor S 600/K-8
33866 Calle La Primavera 92629 949-496-1241
Sharon Rands, prin. Fax 496-1819

Danville, Contra Costa, Pop. 41,852
San Ramon Valley USD 26,400/K-12
699 Old Orchard Dr 94526 925-552-5500
Steven Enoch, supt. Fax 838-3147
www.srvusd.net/
Baldwin ES 600/K-5
741 Brookside Dr 94526 925-855-5200
Darlene Hale, prin. Fax 820-8307
Diablo Vista MS 700/6-8
4100 Camino Tassajara 94506 925-648-8560
Becky Ingram, prin. Fax 648-7167
Greenbrook ES 700/K-5
1475 Harlan Dr 94526 925-855-5300
Tom Ladouceur, prin. Fax 837-8727
Green Valley ES 700/K-5
1001 Diablo Rd 94526 925-855-5400
Tasha Anestos, prin. Fax 837-3807
Los Cerros MS 600/6-8
968 Blemer Rd 94526 925-552-5620
Phyllis Roach, prin. Fax 837-3512
Montair ES 500/K-5
300 Quinterra Ln 94526 925-855-5100
Matt Hermann, prin. Fax 820-6713
Sycamore Valley ES 700/K-5
2200 Holbrook Dr 94506 925-736-0102
Robert Scott, prin. Fax 736-0224
Tassajara Hills ES 700/K-5
4675 Camino Tassajara 94506 925-648-7150
Luann Duggan, prin. Fax 648-3190
Vista Grande ES 600/K-5
667 Diablo Rd 94526 925-314-1000
Patricia Hansen, prin. Fax 837-5918
Wood MS 1,100/6-8
600 El Capitan Dr 94526 925-552-5600
Sandy Budde, prin. Fax 820-1857
Other Schools – See Alamo, San Ramon

Rainbow Montessori & Child Development 100/PK-K
101 Sonora Ave 94526 925-831-6199
Giti Jomehri, prin. Fax 831-1523
St. Isidore S 600/K-8
435 La Gonda Way 94526 925-837-2977
Jean Schroeder, prin. Fax 837-2407
San Ramon Valley Christian Academy 300/K-8
220 W El Pintado 94526 925-838-9622
Janis Brunkal, prin. Fax 838-8934

Davenport, Santa Cruz
Pacific ESD, PO Box H 95017 100/K-6
Sharon Smith, supt. 831-425-7002
www.pacific.santacruz.k12.ca.us/
Pacific ES, PO Box H 95017 100/K-6
Sharon Smith, prin. 831-425-7002

Davis, Yolo, Pop. 60,709
Davis JUSD 8,100/K-12
526 B St 95616 530-757-5300
James Hammond, supt. Fax 757-5423
www.djusd.k12.ca.us
Birch Lane ES 600/K-6
1600 Birch Ln 95618 530-757-5395
Kathy Tyzzer, prin. Fax 757-5413
Chavez ES 600/K-6
1221 Anderson Rd 95616 530-757-5490
Denise Beck, prin. Fax 757-5427
Fairfield ES 100/K-3
26960 County Road 96 95616 530-757-5370
Pam Mari, prin. Fax 757-5412
Korematsu ES, 3100 Loyola Dr 95618 K-6
Mary Ponce, prin. 530-757-5425
Montgomery ES 500/K-6
1441 Danbury St 95618 530-759-2100
Shelly Wickwire, prin. Fax 759-2103
North Davis ES 500/K-6
555 E 14th St 95616 530-757-5475
Ramon Cusi, prin. Fax 757-5477
Patwin ES 500/K-6
2222 Shasta Dr 95616 530-757-5383
Michelle Azevedo, prin. Fax 757-5417
Pioneer ES 600/K-6
5215 Hamel St 95618 530-757-5480
Fax 757-5482
Willet ES 500/K-6
1207 Sycamore Ln 95616 530-757-5460
Heidi Perry, prin. Fax 757-5428

Davis Waldorf S 200/PK-8
3100 Sycamore Ln 95616 530-753-1651
Kelly Brewer, admin. Fax 753-0944
Grace Valley Christian Academy 100/K-9
27173 County Road 98 95616 530-758-6590
Jack Armstrong, prin. Fax 758-2406
St. James S 300/K-8
1215 B St 95616 530-756-3946
David Perry, prin. Fax 753-9765

Delano, Kern, Pop. 45,531
Columbine ESD 200/K-8
2240 Road 160 93215 661-725-8501
Timothy Jones, supt. Fax 725-6006
Columbine S 200/K-8
2240 Road 160 93215 661-725-8501
Timothy Jones, prin. Fax 725-6006

Delano UNESD 7,600/K-8
1405 12th Ave 93215 661-721-5000
Robert Aguilar, supt. Fax 725-2446
www.duesd.org
Albany Park ES 500/K-5
235 W 20th Ave 93215 661-721-5020
Mark Luque, prin. Fax 720-2833
Almond Tree MS 900/6-8
200 W 15th Ave 93215 661-721-3641
Mike Havens, prin. Fax 721-3649
Cecil Avenue MS 900/6-8
1430 Cecil Ave 93215 661-721-5030
Martin Bans, prin. Fax 721-5097
Del Vista ES 600/K-5
710 Quincy St 93215 661-721-5040
Shirley Gibbs, prin. Fax 721-5087
Fremont ES 800/K-5
1318 Clinton St 93215 661-721-5050
Rosa Montes, prin. Fax 721-5058
Harvest ES 500/K-5
1320 Vassar Dr 93215 661-720-2725
Dannette Mehling, prin. Fax 720-2715
La Vina MS 700/6-8
1331 Browning Rd 93215 661-721-3601
Jennifer Townson, prin. Fax 721-3662
Morningside ES 700/K-5
2100 Summer Dr 93215 661-720-2700
Christine Chapman, prin. Fax 720-2838
Princeton Street ES 700/K-5
1959 Princeton St 93215 661-721-5080
Ricardo Chavez, prin. Fax 721-5084
Terrace ES 600/K-5
1999 Norwalk St 93215 661-721-5060
Linda Enriquez, prin. Fax 721-5074
Valle Vista ES 600/K-5
120 Garces Hwy 93215 661-721-5070
Nora Tapia, prin. Fax 721-3638

Sequoia Christian Academy 50/K-12
1009 7th Ave 93215 661-721-2721
Roberta Hunter, prin. Fax 721-2722

Delhi, Merced, Pop. 3,280
Delhi USD 2,300/K-12
9716 Hinton Ave 95315 209-656-2000
Bill Baltazar, supt. Fax 668-6133
www.delhi.k12.ca.us
El Capitan S 400/K-8
9716 Hinton Ave 95315 209-656-2030
Anthony Arista, prin. Fax 668-6146
Harmony S 600/K-8
9716 Hinton Ave 95315 209-656-2010
Richrd Perez, prin. Fax 669-3164
Schendel S 600/K-8
9716 Hinton Ave 95315 209-656-2040
Alicia Valenzuela, prin. Fax 668-6124

Del Mar, San Diego, Pop. 4,378
Del Mar UNESD 4,300/K-6
225 9th St 92014 858-755-9301
Sharon McClain, supt. Fax 755-4361
www.dmusd.org/
Del Mar Heights ES 500/K-6
13555 Boquita Dr 92014 858-755-9367
Wendy Wardlow, prin. Fax 509-1412
Del Mar Hills Academy of Arts & Sciences 400/K-6
14085 Mango Dr 92014 858-755-9763
Susan Fitzpatrick, prin. Fax 755-6107
Other Schools – See San Diego

Del Rey, Fresno, Pop. 1,150
Sanger USD
Supt. — See Sanger
Del Rey ES 300/K-6
PO Box 70 93616 559-888-2056
Susan Fitzgerald, prin. Fax 888-0901

Denair, Stanislaus, Pop. 3,693
Denair USD 1,200/K-12
3460 Lester Rd 95316 209-632-7514
Edward Parraz, supt. Fax 632-9194
dusd.k12.ca.us
Denair ES 500/K-4
3460 Lester Rd 95316 209-632-8887
Fawn Oliver, prin. Fax 632-8442
Denair MS 300/5-8
3460 Lester Rd 95316 209-632-2510
Darrin Allen, prin. Fax 632-0269

Gratton ESD 100/K-8
4500 S Gratton Rd 95316 209-632-0505
Shannon Sanford-Rice, supt. Fax 632-7810
Gratton S 100/K-8
4500 S Gratton Rd 95316 209-632-0505
Shannon Sanford-Rice, prin. Fax 632-7810

Descanso, San Diego
Mountain Empire USD
Supt. — See Pine Valley
Descanso ES 100/4-7
24842 Viejas Blvd 91916 619-445-2126
Joan Baumann, prin. Fax 445-2292

Desert Center, Riverside
Desert Center USD 50/K-8
PO Box 6 92239 760-392-4217
Dr. Norman Guith, supt. Fax 392-4218
Eagle Mountain S 50/K-8
PO Box 6 92239 760-392-4227
Dr. Norman Guith, prin. Fax 392-4218

Desert Hot Springs, Riverside, Pop. 20,492
Palm Springs USD
Supt. — See Palm Springs
Bubbling Wells ES 800/K-5
67501 Camino Campanero 92240 760-251-7230
Steven Marlatt, prin. Fax 251-7237
Cabot Yerxa ES K-5
67067 Desert View Ave 92240 760-416-6000
Mike Grein, prin.
Corsini ES 900/K-5
68750 Hacienda Ave 92240 760-251-7260
Kiela Bonelli, prin. Fax 251-7263
Desert Springs MS 1,700/6-8
66755 Two Bunch Palms Trl 92240 760-251-7200
Ryan Saunders, prin. Fax 251-7206
Two Bunch Palms ES 900/K-5
14250 West Dr 92240 760-251-7220
Arlan Anderson, prin. Fax 251-7272
Wenzlaff ES 800/K-5
11625 West Dr 92240 760-251-7244
Karen Renfield, prin. Fax 251-7255

Diamond Bar, Los Angeles, Pop. 57,975
Pomona USD
Supt. — See Pomona
Armstrong ES 400/K-6
22750 Beaverhead Dr 91765 909-397-4563
Patricia Savage, prin. Fax 397-4565
Diamond Point ES 400/K-6
24150 Sunset Crossing Rd 91765 909-397-4587
Krystana Walks-Harper, prin. Fax 396-4017
Golden Springs ES 500/K-6
245 Ballena Dr 91765 909-397-4596
Alan Pantanini, prin. Fax 860-0780
Lorbeer MS 900/7-8
501 S Diamond Bar Blvd 91765 909-397-4527
Kathrine Morillo-Shone, prin. Fax 396-9022
Pantera ES 400/K-6
801 Pantera Dr 91765 909-397-4475
Todd Riffell, prin. Fax 396-8568

Walnut Valley USD
Supt. — See Walnut
Castle Rock ES 600/K-5
2975 Castle Rock Rd 91765 909-598-5006
Jackie Brown, prin. Fax 598-5960
Chaparral MS 1,300/6-8
1405 Spruce Tree Dr 91765 909-861-6227
Dr. Michael Chavez, prin. Fax 396-0749
Evergreen ES 700/K-5
2450 Evergreen Springs Dr 91765 909-594-1041
Dr. Don Trimmer, prin. Fax 468-5217
Maple Hill ES 500/K-5
1350 Maple Hill Rd 91765 909-861-6224
Linda Carefoot, prin. Fax 861-9825
Quail Summit ES 600/K-5
23330 Quail Summit Dr 91765 909-861-3004
Alysia Hobbs, prin. Fax 444-4476

Mt. Calvary Lutheran S 300/PK-8
23300 Golden Springs Dr 91765 909-861-2740
Claudia Randall, prin. Fax 861-5481

Dinuba, Tulare, Pop. 19,308
Dinuba USD 5,800/K-12
1327 E El Monte Way 93618 559-595-7200
Joe Hernandez Ed.D., supt. Fax 591-3334
www.dinubausd.org/
Grand View ES 400/K-5
1327 E El Monte Way 93618 559-595-7275
Cynthia James, prin. Fax 595-8189
Jefferson ES 600/K-5
1327 E El Monte Way 93618 559-595-7266
Chris Meyer, prin. Fax 595-7269
Kennedy Sixth Grade Academy 400/6-6
1327 E El Monte Way 93618 559-595-7300
Sandy Chavez, prin. Fax 596-2050
Lincoln ES 500/K-5
1327 E El Monte Way 93618 559-595-7260
Gina Ramshaw, prin. Fax 595-7287
Roosevelt ES 500/K-5
1327 E El Monte Way 93618 559-595-7290
Fax 595-9628
Washington IS 900/7-8
1327 E El Monte Way 93618 559-595-7252
Nancy Ruble, prin. Fax 595-8158
Wilson ES 500/K-5
1327 E El Monte Way 93618 559-595-7270
Fax 595-7279

Dinuba Jr. Academy 50/K-10
218 S Crawford Ave 93618 559-591-0194
Allen Lipps, prin. Fax 591-4835

Discovery Bay, Contra Costa, Pop. 5,351
Byron UNESD
Supt. — See Byron
Discovery Bay ES 600/K-5
1700 Willow Lake Rd, 925-634-2150
Allen Petersdorf, prin. Fax 634-2106
Timber Point ES 600/K-5
40 Newberry Ln, 925-634-4369
Brian Burnight, prin. Fax 516-9318

Dixon, Solano, Pop. 17,330
Dixon USD 3,600/K-12
180 S 1st St Ste 6 95620 707-678-5582
Roger Halberg, supt. Fax 678-0726
www.dixonusd.org
Anderson ES 400/K-6
415 E C St 95620 707-678-5508
Fax 678-2073
Higgins ES 600/K-6
1525 Pembroke Way 95620 707-678-6271
Tracy Linyard, prin. Fax 693-1960
Jacobs IS 600/7-8
200 N Lincoln St 95620 707-678-9222
Jason Hofhenke, prin. Fax 678-1245
Tremont ES 700/K-6
355 Pheasant Run Dr 95620 707-678-9533
Matt Banuelos, prin. Fax 678-0298

Neighborhood Christian S 200/PK-8
655 S 1st St Ste C 95620 707-678-9336
Rick Vidmar, admin. Fax 678-6640

Dobbins, Yuba
Marysville JUSD
Supt. — See Marysville
Dobbins ES 100/K-5
PO Box 129 95935 530-692-1665
Judy Hart, prin. Fax 692-2410

Dorris, Siskiyou, Pop. 875
Butte Valley USD 300/K-12
PO Box 709 96023 530-397-4000
H. Wayne Campbell, supt. Fax 397-3999
www.bvalusd.org/
Butte Valley ES 200/K-6
PO Box 709 96023 530-397-3900
H. Wayne Campbell, prin. Fax 397-3899

Dos Palos, Merced, Pop. 5,036
Dos Palos Oro Loma JUSD 2,100/K-12
2041 Almond St 93620 209-392-0200
Brian Walker, supt. Fax 392-3347
www.dpol.net
Bryant MS 600/6-8
16695 Bryant Ave 93620 209-392-0240
David McIntyre, prin. Fax 392-2636
Dos Palos ES 300/K-2
2149 Almond St 93620 209-392-0260
Dwight Thompson, prin. Fax 392-1006
Marks ES 200/3-5
1717 Valeria St 93620 209-392-0250
Norma Delgado, prin. Fax 392-4115
Other Schools – See Firebaugh

Douglas City, Trinity
Douglas City ESD 100/K-8
PO Box 280 96024 530-623-6350
Marilyn Myrick, supt. Fax 623-3412
www.tcoek12.org/~dc/
Douglas City S 100/K-8
PO Box 280 96024 530-623-6350
Marilyn Myrick, prin. Fax 623-3412

Downey, Los Angeles, Pop. 109,718
Downey USD 22,500/K-12
PO Box 7017 90241 562-469-6500
Dr. Wendy Doty, supt. Fax 469-6515
www.dusd.net/
Alameda ES 600/K-3
8613 Alameda St 90242 562-904-3589
Lisa Rawlings, prin. Fax 469-7100
Carpenter ES 800/4-5
9439 Foster Rd 90242 562-904-3588
Vicki Rusick, prin. Fax 469-7110
East MS 1,300/6-8
10301 Woodruff Ave 90241 562-904-3586
Brent Shubin, prin. Fax 469-7240
Gallatin ES 700/K-5
9513 Brookshire Ave 90240 562-904-3583
Rani Bertsch Ed.D., prin. Fax 469-7120
Gauldin ES 800/K-5
9724 Spry St 90242 562-904-3582
Dolores Goble, prin. Fax 469-7130
Griffiths MS 1,300/6-8
9633 Tweedy Ln 90240 562-904-3580
Gregg Stapp, prin. Fax 469-7260
Imperial ES 600/K-3
8133 Imperial Hwy 90242 562-904-3578
Karen Trejo, prin. Fax 469-7140
Lewis ES 800/K-5
13220 Bellflower Blvd 90242 562-904-3590
Robin Martin, prin. Fax 469-7150

Old River ES 800/4-5
11995 Old River School Rd 90242 562-904-3561
T. Medina, prin. Fax 469-7160
Price ES 700/K-5
9525 Tweedy Ln 90240 562-904-3575
J. Hobson, prin. Fax 469-7180
Rio Hondo ES 900/K-5
7731 Muller St 90241 562-904-3568
Theresa Ford, prin. Fax 469-7190
Rio San Gabriel ES 800/K-5
9338 Gotham St 90241 562-904-3567
Paula Barnes, prin. Fax 469-7200
Sussman MS 1,500/6-8
12500 Birchdale Ave 90242 562-904-3572
Gloria Widmann, prin. Fax 469-7280
Unsworth ES 600/K-5
9001 Lindsey Ave 90240 562-904-3576
Yolanda Cornair, prin. Fax 469-7210
Ward ES 500/K-3
8851 Adoree St 90242 562-904-3591
Jennifer Robbins, prin. Fax 469-7220
West MS 1,400/6-8
11985 Old River School Rd 90242 562-904-3565
Craig Bertsch, prin. Fax 469-7300
Williams ES 700/K-3
7530 Arnett St 90241 562-904-3564
M. Weyers, prin. Fax 469-7230

Calvary Chapel Christian S 1,100/K-12
12808 Woodruff Ave 90242 562-803-4076
Yuri Escandon, admin. Fax 803-9916
Creative Beginnings S 200/K-5
8033 3rd St 90241 562-861-1499
Kathleen LeCompte, prin. Fax 861-1151
Keystone Academy 200/K-12
8615 Florence Ave Ste 207 90240 562-862-7134
Philip Troutt, hdmstr.
Kirkwood Christian S 100/PK-3
10822 Brookshire Ave 90241 562-862-4252
Jennifer Hartl, prin. Fax 904-6912
Our Lady of Perpetual Help S 300/K-8
10441 Downey Ave 90241 562-869-9969
Steffani McMains, prin. Fax 923-0659
St. Mark's Episcopal S 100/PK-8
10354 Downey Ave 90241 562-869-7213
Glenda Roberts, hdmstr. Fax 861-9523
St. Raymond S 300/K-8
12320 Paramount Blvd 90242 562-862-3210
Sr. Kathleen O'Connor, prin. Fax 862-6328

Downieville, Sierra
Sierra-Plumas JUSD
Supt. — See Sierraville
Downieville ES 50/K-6
PO Box B 95936 530-289-3473
James Berardi, prin. Fax 289-3693

Duarte, Los Angeles, Pop. 22,194
Duarte USD 4,400/K-12
1620 Huntington Dr 91010 626-599-5000
Dr. Dean Conklin, supt. Fax 599-5078
www.duarte.k12.ca.us
Beardslee ES 400/K-6
1620 Huntington Dr 91010 626-599-5200
Jennifer Janetzke, prin. Fax 599-5284
Duarte ES 500/K-6
1620 Huntington Dr 91010 626-599-5100
Joilyn Campitiello, prin. Fax 599-5184
Maxwell ES 500/K-6
1620 Huntington Dr 91010 626-599-5300
Mary Gonzales, prin. Fax 599-5384
Northview IS 700/7-8
1620 Huntington Dr 91010 626-599-5600
Miriam Fox, prin. Fax 599-5684
Royal Oaks ES 600/K-6
1620 Huntington Dr 91010 626-599-5400
Janice Kolodinski, prin. Fax 599-5484
Valley View ES 400/K-6
1620 Huntington Dr 91010 626-599-5500
Robin Nelson, prin. Fax 599-5584

Anita Oaks S 100/PK-8
822 Bradbourne Ave 91010 626-301-1354
Nancy Lopez, hdmstr. Fax 301-1342

Dublin, Alameda, Pop. 39,328
Dublin USD 5,500/K-12
7471 Larkdale Ave 94568 925-828-2551
Dr. Stephen Hanke, supt. Fax 829-6532
www.dublin.k12.ca.us
Dougherty ES 600/K-5
5301 Hibernia Dr 94568 925-803-4444
Lynn Medici, prin. Fax 556-3488
Dublin ES 300/K-5
7997 Vomac Rd 94568 925-833-1204
Kara Holthe, prin. Fax 833-3362
Fallon S 1,000/K-8
3601 Kohnen Way 94568 925-875-9376
Tess Thomas, prin. Fax 829-6532
Fredericksen ES 500/K-5
7243 Tamarack Dr 94568 925-828-1037
Holly Scroggins, prin. Fax 829-2562
Green ES 700/K-5
3300 Antone Way 94568 925-833-4200
Keith Nomura, prin. Fax 829-1076
Murray ES 300/K-5
8435 Davona Dr 94568 925-828-2568
Rick Boster, prin. Fax 803-1367
Wells MS 700/6-8
6800 Penn Dr 94568 925-828-6227
Kathy Rosselle, prin. Fax 829-8851

St. Philip Lutheran S 100/PK-8
8850 Davona Dr 94568 925-829-3857
Char Nale, prin. Fax 829-6672
St. Raymond S 300/K-8
11557 Shannon Ave 94568 925-574-7425
Madeline de la Fontaine, prin. Fax 828-2454
Valley Christian S 600/PK-6
7500 Inspiration Dr 94568 925-560-6270
Jeri Schall, prin. Fax 828-6725

Ducor, Tulare
Ducor UNESD 200/K-8
PO Box 249 93218 559-534-2261
Franklin Samples, supt. Fax 534-2271
Ducor Union S 200/K-8
PO Box 249 93218 559-534-2261
Franklin Samples, prin. Fax 534-2271

Dunlap, Fresno
Kings Canyon JUSD
Supt. — See Reedley
Dunlap S 400/K-8
PO Box 100 93621 559-305-7310
Karen Snell, prin. Fax 338-2026

Dunsmuir, Siskiyou, Pop. 1,870
Dunsmuir ESD 200/K-8
4760 Siskiyou Ave 96025 530-235-4828
Michael Michelon, supt. Fax 235-0145
www.sisnet.ssku.k12.ca.us/~desftp/
Dunsmuir S 200/K-8
4760 Siskiyou Ave 96025 530-235-4828
Kale Riccomini, prin. Fax 235-0145

Durham, Butte, Pop. 4,784
Durham USD 1,100/K-12
PO Box 300 95938 530-895-4675
Mike Stuart, supt. Fax 895-4692
www.durhamunified.org/
Durham ES 500/K-5
PO Box 700 95938 530-895-4695
Bobbi Abold, prin. Fax 895-4665
Durham IS 300/6-8
PO Box 310 95938 530-895-4690
Greg Blake, prin. Fax 895-4305

Earlimart, Tulare, Pop. 5,881
Allensworth ESD 100/K-8
HC 1 Box 136 93219 661-849-2401
Roberto Cardenas, supt. Fax 849-6634
Allensworth S 100/K-8
HC 1 Box 136 93219 661-849-2401
Roberto Cardenas, prin. Fax 849-6634

Earlimart ESD 2,000/K-8
PO Box 11970 93219 661-849-3386
Dr. Marcella Smith, supt. Fax 849-2352
www.earlimart.org
Alila IS 700/3-5
PO Box 11970 93219 661-849-4202
Andres Gomez, prin. Fax 849-4206
Earlimart ES 700/K-2
PO Box 11970 93219 661-849-2651
Jane Mitchell, prin. Fax 849-1533
Earlimart MS 600/6-8
PO Box 11970 93219 661-849-2611
Phillip Nystrom, prin. Fax 849-4214

East Nicolaus, Sutter
Marcum-Illinois UNESD 100/PK-8
2452 El Centro Blvd 95659 530-656-2407
Sharon McIntosh, supt. Fax 755-4302
www.marcum-illinois.org/
Marcum-Illinois Union S 100/PK-8
2452 El Centro Blvd 95659 530-656-2407
Sharon McIntosh, prin. Fax 755-4302

East Palo Alto, San Mateo, Pop. 32,242
Ravenswood City ESD 3,100/PK-8
2160 Euclid Ave 94303 650-329-2800
Maria De La Vega, supt. Fax 323-1072
www.ravenswood.k12.ca.us
Chavez Academy 400/4-8
2450 Ralmar Ave 94303 650-329-6700
David Herrera, prin. Fax 326-8902
Costano S 400/K-8
2695 Fordham St 94303 650-329-2830
Gina Sudaria, prin. Fax 328-3214
Green Oaks Academy 400/K-3
2450 Ralmar Ave 94303 650-329-6536
Fax 325-8312
McNair Academy 400/5-8
2033 Pulgas Ave 94303 650-329-2800
Michael Lyons, prin. Fax 473-9247
Ravenswood Child Development Center PK-PK
2450 Ralmar Ave 94303 650-838-3460
Vera Clark, dir. Fax 329-6798
San Francisco 49er Academy 100/6-8
2086 Clarke Ave 94303 650-614-4300
Michele Sharky, dir. Fax 614-4310
Other Schools – See Menlo Park

Edwards, Kern
Muroc JUSD
Supt. — See North Edwards
Branch ES 500/K-6
1595 Bailey Ave 93523 661-258-4411
Kevin Cordes, prin. Fax 258-4411

El Cajon, San Diego, Pop. 92,487
Cajon Valley UNESD 15,100/K-8
PO Box 1007 92022 619-588-3000
Janice Cook Ed.D., supt. Fax 588-7653
www.cajonvalley.net/
Anza ES 500/K-5
1005 S Anza St 92020 619-588-3116
Christina Willis, prin. Fax 579-4815
Blossom Valley ES 500/K-5
9863 Oakmont Ter 92021 619-588-3678
Colleen Newman, prin. Fax 588-3022
Bostonia ES 600/K-5
1390 Broadway 92021 619-588-3121
Cindy Knight, prin. Fax 579-4849
Cajon Valley MS 800/6-8
505 E Park Ave 92020 619-588-3092
Ernesto Villanueva, prin. Fax 579-4817
Chase Ave ES 500/K-5
195 E Chase Ave 92020 619-588-3123
Sue Geller, prin. Fax 588-3184
Crest ES 200/K-5
2000 Suncrest Blvd 92021 619-588-3128
Martin Jaquez, prin. Fax 579-4855
Emerald MS 900/6-8
1221 Emerald Ave 92020 619-588-3097
Rod Girvin, prin. Fax 588-3225
Flying Hills ES 500/K-6
1251 Finch St 92020 619-588-3132
Susan Cunningham, prin. Fax 579-4877
Fuerte ES 600/K-5
11625 Fuerte Dr 92020 619-588-3134
Karen Sapper, prin. Fax 579-4825
Greenfield MS 900/6-8
1495 Greenfield Dr 92021 619-588-3103
Froylan Villanueva, prin. Fax 588-3648
Hall ES 500/K-5
1376 Pepper Dr 92021 619-588-3136
Steve Boyle, prin. Fax 579-4887
Hillsdale MS 1,600/6-8
1301 Brabham St 92019 619-441-6156
Don Hohimer, prin. Fax 441-6185
Jamacha ES 500/K-5
2962 Jamul Dr 92019 619-441-6150
Dana Stevenson, prin. Fax 588-3682
Johnson ES 600/K-5
500 W Madison Ave 92020 619-588-3139
Regula Schmid, prin. Fax 579-4852
Lexington ES 700/K-5
533 S 1st St 92019 619-588-3075
Sylvia Casas-Werkman, prin. Fax 588-3675
Madison Avenue ES 500/K-5
1615 E Madison Ave 92019 619-588-3077
Michelle Hayes, prin. Fax 441-6183
Magnolia ES 500/K-5
650 Greenfield Dr 92021 619-588-3080
Valerie Simpson, prin. Fax 579-4854
Meridian ES 600/K-5
651 S 3rd St 92019 619-588-3083
Gail Boone, prin. Fax 579-4824
Montgomery MS 1,000/6-8
1570 Melody Ln 92019 619-588-3107
Kelly Madden, prin. Fax 441-6122
Naranca ES 700/K-5
1030 Naranca Ave 92021 619-588-3087
Amanda Lang, prin. Fax 441-6176
Rancho San Diego ES 500/K-5
12151 Calle Albara 92019 619-588-3211
Maria Kehoe, prin. Fax 579-4858
Rios ES 300/K-5
14314 Rios Canyon Rd 92021 619-588-3090
Martin Jaquez, prin. Fax 579-4842
Vista Grande ES 600/K-5
1908 Vista Grande Rd 92019 619-588-3170
Brian Handley, prin. Fax 579-4822
Other Schools – See La Mesa

Dehesa ESD 200/K-6
4612 Dehesa Rd 92019 619-444-2161
Janet Wilson, supt. Fax 444-2105
www.sdcoe.k12.ca.us/districts/dehesa
Dehesa ES 200/K-6
4612 Dehesa Rd 92019 619-444-2161
Janet Wilson, prin. Fax 444-2105

La Mesa-Spring Valley SD
Supt. — See La Mesa
Fletcher Hills ES 500/K-5
2330 Center Pl 92020 619-668-5820
Lisa Conry, prin. Fax 668-8353

Santee ESD
Supt. — See Santee
Pepper Drive S 700/K-8
1935 Marlinda Way 92021 619-956-5100
Debbie Brenner, prin. Fax 956-5114

Christian S East Campus 100/K-6
2100 Greenfield Dr 92019 619-590-1794
Karyn Sterkowitz, prin. Fax 579-1697
Christian S West Campus 100/K-6
211 S 3rd St 92019 619-442-9843
Karyn Sterkowitz, prin. Fax 442-9009
El Cajon SDA Christian S 50/K-8
1640 E Madison Ave 92019 619-442-6544
Tamara Luppens, prin. Fax 442-0490
First Lutheran S 100/PK-K
867 S Lincoln Ave 92020 619-444-0559
Kathleen Perez, dir. Fax 444-9892
Holy Trinity S 300/PK-8
509 Ballard St 92019 619-444-7529
Frances Wright, prin. Fax 444-3721
Our Lady of Grace S 300/K-8
2766 Navajo Rd 92020 619-466-0055
Susan Hause, prin. Fax 466-8994
St. Kierans S 200/PK-8
1347 Camillo Way 92021 619-588-6398
Patricia Provo, prin. Fax 588-6382

El Centro, Imperial, Pop. 39,636
El Centro ESD 5,800/K-8
1256 Broadway St, 760-352-5712
Robert Pletka, supt. Fax 312-9522
www.ecsd.k12.ca.us/
De Anza S 300/K-7
1530 S Waterman Ave, 760-352-9811
Terri Mason, prin. Fax 352-0920
Desert Garden ES 500/K-6
1900 S 6th St, 760-352-2051
Kathy Brandenberg, prin. Fax 352-3802
Harding ES 500/K-6
950 S 7th St, 760-352-4791
Juan Cruz, prin. Fax 353-7204

Hedrick ES 600/K-6
550 S Waterman Ave, 760-352-4750
Rauna Fox, prin. Fax 353-6832
Kennedy MS 700/6-8
900 N 6th St, 760-352-0444
Renato Montano, prin. Fax 353-0325
King ES 400/K-5
1950 Villa Ave, 760-337-6555
Nancy Johnson, prin. Fax 353-6714
Lincoln ES 400/K-5
200 N 12th St, 760-352-3060
Michael Minnix, prin. Fax 352-4477
McKinley ES 500/K-5
1177 N 8th St, 760-352-3225
Karla Sigmond, prin. Fax 353-2858
Sunflower ES 500/K-6
2450 W Main St, 760-337-4890
Spencer Wavra, prin. Fax 337-4894
Washington ES 600/K-6
223 S 1st St, 760-352-6611
Eddie Hernandez, prin. Fax 370-3089
Wilson JHS 900/7-8
600 S Wilson St, 760-352-5341
Matt Phillips, prin. Fax 337-3800

Imperial USD
Supt. — See Imperial
Westside ES 100/K-5
2294 W Vaughn Rd, 760-355-3208
Nancy Rood, prin. Fax 353-6917

McCabe UNESD 1,000/K-8
701 W McCabe Rd, 760-335-5200
Amanda Brooke, supt. Fax 352-4398
www.mccabeschool.net
McCabe S 1,000/K-8
701 W McCabe Rd, 760-352-5443
Laura Dubbe, prin. Fax 352-6812

Meadows UNESD 500/K-8
2059 Bowker Rd, 760-352-7512
Sue Hess, supt. Fax 337-1275
Meadows S 500/K-8
2059 Bowker Rd, 760-352-7512
Sue Hess, prin. Fax 337-1275

Christ Community S 100/K-6
585 W Orange Ave, 760-337-9444
Patricia Rudolph, prin. Fax 337-1330
St. Mary S 300/PK-8
700 S Waterman Ave, 760-352-7285
Juanita Pereyra, prin. Fax 352-9727

El Cerrito, Contra Costa, Pop. 22,868

West Contra Costa USD
Supt. — See Richmond
Castro ES 300/K-6
7125 Donal Ave 94530 510-234-6200
Galen Murphy, prin. Fax 235-7213
Fairmont ES 300/K-6
724 Kearney St 94530 510-525-5235
Brenda Surgers, prin. Fax 528-9206
Harding ES 300/K-6
7230 Fairmount Ave 94530 510-231-1413
Valerie Garrett, prin. Fax 559-1365
Madera ES 400/K-5
8500 Madera Dr 94530 510-231-1412
Doris Holland, prin. Fax 235-8003
Portola MS 600/6-8
1021 Navellier St 94530 510-524-0405
Denise VanHook, prin. Fax 559-8784

Montessori Family S 100/K-6
7075 Cutting Blvd 94530 510-236-8802
Jane Wechsler, hdmstr. Fax 236-8805
Prospect Sierra ES K-4
2060 Tapscott Ave 94530 510-232-4123
.prospectsierra.org, hdmstr. Fax 232-7615
Prospect Sierra MS 100/5-6
960 Avis Dr 94530 510-528-5800
Katherine Dinh, prin. Fax 527-3728
St. Jerome S 200/K-8
320 San Carlos Ave 94530 510-525-9484
Marla Korte, prin. Fax 525-5227
St. John the Baptist S 300/K-8
11156 San Pablo Ave 94530 510-234-2244
Teresa Barber, prin. Fax 234-3726
Tehiyah Day S 300/K-8
2603 Tassajara Ave 94530 510-233-3013
Bathea James, hdmstr. Fax 233-0171
Windrush S 300/K-8
1800 Elm St 94530 510-970-7580
Ilana Kaufman, hdmstr. Fax 215-2326

El Dorado, El Dorado

Mother Lode UNESD
Supt. — See Placerville
Brown ES 400/K-5
6520 Oakdell Dr 95623 530-622-5775
Ed Watkins, prin. Fax 622-4081

El Dorado Hills, El Dorado, Pop. 6,395

Buckeye UNSD
Supt. — See Shingle Springs
Brooks ES 500/K-5
3610 Park Dr 95762 916-933-6618
Kathi Jensen, prin. Fax 933-3910
Oak Meadow ES 700/K-5
7701 Silva Valley Pkwy 95762 916-933-9746
Barbara Narez, prin. Fax 933-9784
Rolling Hills MS 1,000/6-8
7141 Silva Valley Pkwy 95762 916-933-9290
Debra Bowers, prin. Fax 939-7454
Silva Valley ES 700/K-5
3001 Golden Eagle Ln 95762 916-933-3767
Kathy Holliman, prin. Fax 933-6389

Rescue UNESD
Supt. — See Rescue
Jackson ES 400/K-5
2561 Francisco Dr 95762 916-933-1828
Michele Miller, prin. Fax 933-5569
Lake Forest ES 600/K-5
2240 Sailsbury Dr 95762 916-933-0652
Bruce Peters, prin. Fax 933-0654
Lakeview ES 400/K-5
3371 Brittany Way 95762 916-941-2600
Judy Chance, prin. Fax 941-3826
Marina Village MS 700/6-8
1901 Francisco Dr 95762 916-933-3993
Jeff Warshaw, prin. Fax 933-3995

Golden Hills School 200/K-8
1060 Suncast Ln 95762 916-933-0100
Joe Krutulis, hdmstr.
Holy Trinity S 300/K-8
3115 Tierra de Dios Dr 95762 530-677-3591
Trisha Uhrhammer, prin. Fax 350-3202
Marble Valley S 100/K-8
5001 Windplay Dr 95762 916-933-5122
Gwendolyn Andrus, prin. Fax 933-5171

Elk, Mendocino

Mendocino USD
Supt. — See Mendocino
Greenwood ES 50/K-3
PO Box 39 95432 707-877-3361
Kathy White, lead tchr. Fax 937-0714

Elk Creek, Glenn

Stony Creek JUSD 100/K-12
PO Box 68 95939 530-968-5361
John McIntosh, supt. Fax 968-5102
www.scjusd.org/index.cfm
Elk Creek ES 50/K-6
PO Box 68 95939 530-968-5288
Holly McLaughlin, prin. Fax 968-5535
Other Schools – See Stonyford

Elk Grove, Sacramento, Pop. 112,338

Elk Grove USD 61,100/PK-12
9510 Elk Grove Florin Rd 95624 916-686-5085
Steven Ladd Ed.D., supt. Fax 686-7787
www.egusd.net/
Albiani MS 1,200/7-8
9140 Bradshaw Rd 95624 916-686-5210
Ramona Nelson, prin. Fax 686-5538
Batey ES 1,100/K-6
9421 Stonebrook Dr 95624 916-714-5520
Michael Sompayrac, prin. Fax 714-5588
Butler ES 1,000/K-6
9180 Brown Rd 95624 916-681-7595
Carla Victor, prin. Fax 681-7599
Carroll ES 800/K-6
10325 Stathos Dr, 916-714-0106
Paul Hauder, prin. Fax 714-0828
Case ES 900/K-6
8565 Shasta Lily Dr 95624 916-681-8820
Abelardo Cordova, prin. Fax 681-8807
Case Partners Preschool PK-PK
8565 Shasta Lily Dr 95624 916-686-2013
Darla Webb, lead tchr.
Castello ES 700/K-6
9850 Fire Poppy Dr, 916-686-1725
Ilesha Graham, prin. Fax 686-3082
Donner ES 1,100/K-6
9461 Soaring Oaks Dr 95758 916-683-3073
Michelle Jenkins, prin. Fax 683-3136
Eddy MS 1,300/7-8
9329 Soaring Oaks Dr 95758 916-683-1302
Peter Lambert, prin. Fax 684-6142
Ehrhardt ES 1,000/K-6
8900 Old Creek Dr 95758 916-684-7259
Steve Brenizer, prin. Fax 684-0351
Ehrhardt Preschool PK-PK
8900 Old Creek Dr 95758 916-683-6751
Mary Beth Frutchey, lead tchr.
Elk Grove ES 800/K-6
9373 Crowell Dr 95624 916-686-3766
Dave Neves, prin. Fax 686-1299
Elliott Ranch ES 1,000/K-6
10000 E Taron Dr, 916-683-3877
Mary Rountree, prin. Fax 683-3862
Feickert ES 700/K-6
9351 Feickert Dr 95624 916-686-7716
Patrick Dolinar, prin. Fax 686-8921
Foulks Ranch ES 1,100/K-6
6211 Laguna Park Dr 95758 916-684-8177
Mary Beth Kropp, prin. Fax 684-0533
Franklin ES 600/K-6
4011 Hood Franklin Rd, 916-684-6518
John Santin, prin. Fax 684-6039
Harris MS 1,300/7-8
8691 Power Inn Rd 95624 916-688-0075
Felicia Bessent, prin. Fax 688-0084
Hein ES 900/K-6
6820 Bellaterra Dr, 916-714-0654
Toni Westermann, prin. Fax 714-0216
Herburger ES 700/K-6
8670 Maranello Way 95624 916-681-1390
Rebecca Davis, prin. Fax 682-5477
Johnson MS 1,500/7-8
10099 Franklin High Rd, 916-714-8181
Dawnelle Maffei, prin. Fax 714-8177
Kerr MS 1,000/7-8
8865 Elk Grove Blvd 95624 916-686-7728
Cecil Duke, prin. Fax 685-2952
Markofer ES 600/K-6
9759 Tralee Way 95624 916-686-7714
Eric Murchison, prin. Fax 685-7653
McKee ES 600/K-6
8701 Halverson Dr 95624 916-686-3715
Steve Looper, prin. Fax 685-9614
McKee Preschool PK-PK
8701 Halverson Dr 95624 916-686-8933
Gail Womack, lead tchr.
Pinkerton MS 7-8
8365 Whitelock Pkwy, 916-683-7670
Patrick McDougall, prin. Fax 683-4522
Pleasant Grove ES 500/K-6
10160 Pleasant Grove Sch Rd 95624 916-685-9630
Joe Donovan, prin. Fax 685-7910
Sims ES 1,200/K-6
3033 Buckminster Dr 95758 916-683-7445
Shelly Hughes, prin. Fax 683-6313
Stone Lake ES 1,100/K-6
9673 Lakepoint Dr 95758 916-683-4096
Michael Anderson, prin. Fax 683-4098
West ES 1,000/K-6
8625 Serio Way 95758 916-683-4362
Marty Powers, prin. Fax 683-4363
Other Schools – See Rancho Cordova, Sacramento, Sloughhouse, Wilton

---

St. Elizabeth Ann Seton S 300/K-8
9539 Racquet Ct 95758 916-684-7903
Trina Koontz, prin. Fax 691-4064
St. Peter's Lutheran S 200/PK-8
8701 Elk Grove Florin Rd 95624 916-689-3050
Ann Cunningham, prin. Fax 689-3462

El Monte, Los Angeles, Pop. 122,513

El Monte City ESD 9,100/K-8
3540 Lexington Ave 91731 626-453-3700
Jeffrey Seymour, supt. Fax 442-1063
www.emcsd.org/
Cherrylee ES 600/K-6
5025 Buffington Rd 91732 626-575-2326
Dr. Darice Wallace, prin. Fax 279-7059
Columbia S 1,000/K-8
3400 California Ave 91731 626-575-2306
Maribel Garcia, prin. Fax 279-1603
Cortada ES 600/K-6
3111 Potrero Ave 91733 626-575-2391
Cynthia Flores, prin. Fax 442-2038
Durfee/Thompson S 600/K-8
12233 Star St 91732 626-443-3900
Dianna Mercado, prin. Fax 579-0451
Gidley S 600/K-8
10226 Lower Azusa Rd 91731 626-575-2323
Lorraine Torres, prin. Fax 455-0538
Legore ES 500/K-6
11121 Bryant Rd 91731 626-575-2329
Adriana Garcia, prin. Fax 448-6921
New Lexington ES 500/K-6
10410 Bodger St 91733 626-575-2320
Karin Smith, prin. Fax 575-2228
Potrero S 800/K-8
2611 Potrero Ave 91733 626-350-9386
Liz Raymond, prin. Fax 443-8707
Rio Vista ES 400/K-6
4300 Esto Ave 91731 626-575-2310
Loan Mascorro, prin. Fax 579-3729
Shirpser ES 600/K-6
4020 Gibson Rd 91731 626-575-2393
Brenda Ruiz, prin. Fax 443-2140
Wilkerson ES 600/K-6
2700 Doreen Ave 91733 626-575-2331
Larry Herrera, prin. Fax 443-8659
Wright S 900/K-8
11317 McGirk Ave 91732 626-575-2333
Jose Marquez, prin. Fax 443-8711
Other Schools – See Arcadia, Temple City

Mountain View ESD 9,300/K-8
3320 Gilman Rd 91732 626-652-4000
John Stoddard, supt. Fax 652-4052
www.mtviewschools.com/
Baker ES 900/K-5
12043 Exline St 91732 626-652-4700
Roberto Lopez, prin. Fax 652-4715
Cogswell ES 600/K-6
11050 Fineview St 91733 626-652-4100
Mario Ganzales, prin. Fax 652-4115
Kranz IS 1,200/7-8
12460 Fineview St 91732 626-652-4200
Dr. Kristen McGregor, prin. Fax 652-4215
La Primaria ES 300/K-3
4220 Gilman Rd 91732 626-652-4150
Aileen LaCorte, prin. Fax 652-4165
Madrid MS 1,200/6-8
3300 Gilman Rd 91732 626-652-4300
Bonnie Tanaka, prin. Fax 652-4315
Maxson ES 900/K-6
12380 Felipe St 91732 626-652-4540
Helen Vega-Heller, prin. Fax 652-4515
Miramonte ES 600/K-6
10620 Schmidt Rd 91733 626-652-4600
Jeff Lagozzino, prin. Fax 652-4615
Monte Vista ES 700/K-6
11111 Thienes Ave 91733 626-652-4650
Donelle Soto-Magat, prin. Fax 652-4665
Parkview ES 1,000/K-6
12044 Elliott Ave 91732 626-652-4800
Anamarie Sanchez, prin. Fax 652-4815
Payne ES 700/K-6
2850 Mountain View Rd 91732 626-652-4900
Sylvia Puente, prin. Fax 652-4915
Twin Lakes ES 600/K-5
3900 Gilman Rd 91732 626-652-4400
Sylvia Rivera, prin. Fax 652-4415
Voorhis ES 600/K-5
3501 Durfee Ave 91732 626-652-4450
Roberta Vincent, prin. Fax 652-4465

Nativity S 200/K-8
10907 Saint Louis Dr 91731 626-448-2414
Sr. Stacy Reineman, prin. Fax 448-2763

El Nido, Merced
El Nido ESD 200/K-8
161 E El Nido Rd 95317 209-385-8420
Marilyn Blake, supt. Fax 723-9169
www.elnido.k12.ca.us/
El Nido S 200/K-8
161 E El Nido Rd 95317 209-385-8420
Marilyn Blake, prin. Fax 723-9169

El Portal, Mariposa
Mariposa County USD
Supt. — See Mariposa
El Portal ES 100/K-6
PO Box 190 95318 209-379-2382
Phyllis Weber, prin. Fax 379-9138

El Segundo, Los Angeles, Pop. 16,517
El Segundo USD 3,300/K-12
641 Sheldon St 90245 310-615-2650
Geoff Yantz, supt. Fax 640-8272
elsegundousd.org/
Center Street ES 700/K-5
641 Sheldon St 90245 310-615-2676
Marisa Janicek, prin. Fax 640-9105
El Segundo MS 800/6-8
641 Sheldon St 90245 310-615-2690
Dave Lubs, prin. Fax 640-9634
Richmond Street ES 600/K-5
641 Sheldon St 90245 310-606-6831
Dickie Van Breene, prin. Fax 322-8512

St. Anthony S 100/K-8
233 Lomita St 90245 310-322-4218
Georgina Curcio, prin. Fax 322-2659

El Sobrante, Contra Costa, Pop. 9,852
West Contra Costa USD
Supt. — See Richmond
Crespi JHS 700/7-8
1121 Allview Ave 94803 510-223-8611
Sherry Bell, prin. Fax 243-2090
El Sobrante ES 200/K-6
1060 Manor Rd 94803 510-223-4500
Stephen Riave, prin. Fax 243-1540
Murphy ES 300/K-6
4350 Valley View Rd 94803 510-231-1427
Carlena Moss, prin. Fax 223-4111
Olinda ES 300/K-6
5855 Olinda Rd 94803 510-223-2800
Dennis Lods, prin. Fax 223-4514
Sheldon ES 400/K-6
2601 May Rd 94803 510-231-1414
Cynthia Swainbank, prin. Fax 243-2093

Calvary Christian Academy 200/PK-12
4892 San Pablo Dam Rd 94803 510-222-3828
Susan Blankenchip, admin. Fax 222-3702
Contra Costa Christian Academy 50/1-5
5435 San Pablo Dam Rd 94803 510-325-4459
Shirley Reed, admin. Fax 223-4404
East Bay Waldorf S 200/PK-8
3800 Clark Rd 94803 510-223-3570
Audrey Lee, admin. Fax 222-3141
El Sobrante Christian S 200/K-6
5100 Argyle Rd 94803 510-223-2242
C. Scott Wells, prin. Fax 223-8453

Elverta, Sacramento
Elverta JESD 300/K-8
8920 Elwyn Ave 95626 916-991-4726
Elizabeth Golchert, supt. Fax 991-5888
www.elverta.k12.ca.us/
Alpha Technology MS 100/6-8
8920 Elwyn Ave 95626 916-991-4726
Elizabeth Golchert, prin. Fax 991-5888
Elverta ES 200/K-5
7900 Eloise Ave 95626 916-991-2244
Elizabeth Golchert, prin. Fax 991-0271

Emeryville, Alameda, Pop. 8,528
Emery USD 800/K-12
4727 San Pablo Ave 94608 510-601-4000
John Sugiyama, supt. Fax 601-4913
www.emeryusd.org/
Yates ES 400/K-6
1070 41st St 94608 510-601-4917
Jaguanana Lathan, prin. Fax 601-4948

Emigrant Gap, Placer
Alta-Dutch Flat UNESD
Supt. — See Alta
Emigrant Gap S 50/K-8
42420 Emigrant Gap Rd 95715 530-389-8225
Fax 389-2204

Empire, Stanislaus
Empire UNESD
Supt. — See Modesto
Empire S 500/K-8
PO Box 1269 95319 209-521-2970
Chris Schoeneman, prin. Fax 527-5620

Encinitas, San Diego, Pop. 59,525
Encinitas UNESD 5,600/K-6
101 S Rancho Santa Fe Rd 92024 760-944-4300
Timothy Baird, supt. Fax 942-7094
www.eusd.k12.ca.us
Capri ES 600/K-6
941 Capri Rd 92024 760-944-4360
Dr. Belinda Minor, prin. Fax 944-4364
Ecke-Central ES 500/K-6
185 Union St 92024 760-944-4323
Adriana Chavarin, prin. Fax 944-4370
Flora Vista ES 500/K-6
1690 Wandering Rd 92024 760-944-4329
Stephanie Casperson, prin. Fax 944-4385
Ocean Knoll ES 500/K-6
910 Melba Rd 92024 760-944-4351
Angelica Lopez, prin. Fax 944-4353
Park Dale Lane ES 700/K-6
2050 Park Dale Ln 92024 760-944-4344
Dr. Tim Reeve, prin. Fax 632-1692
Other Schools – See Carlsbad

San Dieguito UNHSD 12,400/7-12
710 Encinitas Blvd 92024 760-753-6491
Ken Noah, supt. Fax 943-3501
www.sduhsd.net
Diegueno MS 900/7-8
710 Encinitas Blvd 92024 760-944-1892
MaryAnne Nuskin, prin. Fax 944-3717
Oak Crest MS 900/7-8
710 Encinitas Blvd 92024 760-753-6241
Terry Calen, prin. Fax 942-0520
Other Schools – See San Diego, Solana Beach

Encinitas Country Day 200/K-8
3616 Manchester Ave 92024 760-942-1111
Kathleen Porterfield, dir.
Lighthouse Christian Preschool 50/PK-PK
510 S El Camino Real 92024 760-942-8500
Maxine Tellchea, admin. Fax 942-9383
Rhoades S 300/K-8
141 S Rancho Santa Fe Rd 92024 760-436-1102
Luanne Kittle, hdmstr. Fax 436-8128
St. John S 500/K-8
1003 Encinitas Blvd 92024 760-944-8227
Barbara Picco, prin. Fax 944-8939
Sanderling Waldorf S 100/PK-6
1578 S El Camino Real 92024 760-635-3747
Fax 635-1037

Encino, See Los Angeles
Los Angeles USD
Supt. — See Los Angeles
Emelita ES 500/K-5
17931 Hatteras St 91316 818-342-6353
Marta Norton, prin. Fax 774-9352
Encino ES 500/K-5
16941 Addison St 91316 818-784-1762
Bette Kaplan, prin. Fax 995-7110
Hesby Oaks S 300/K-8
15530 Hesby St 91436 818-528-7000
Judith Mintz, prin. Fax 907-0788
Lanai Road ES 500/K-5
4241 Lanai Rd 91436 818-788-1590
Mary Melvin, prin. Fax 788-4263

Los Encinos S 100/K-6
17114 Ventura Blvd 91316 818-990-1006
Irene Reinfeld, prin.
Our Lady of Grace S 300/PK-8
17720 Ventura Blvd 91316 818-344-4126
Patricia Chaimowitz, prin. Fax 344-1736
St. Cyril of Jerusalem S 300/PK-8
4548 Haskell Ave 91436 818-501-4155
Michael Muir, prin. Fax 501-8480
Valley Beth Shalom Day S 300/K-6
15739 Ventura Blvd 91436 818-788-2199
Sheva Locke, hdmstr. Fax 788-7932
Westmark S 200/3-12
5461 Louise Ave 91316 818-986-5045
Donald Cook, hdmstr. Fax 986-2605

Escalon, San Joaquin, Pop. 7,171
Escalon USD 3,100/K-12
1520 Yosemite Ave 95320 209-838-3591
Dave Mantooth, supt. Fax 838-6703
www.escalonusd.org/
Dent ES 800/K-5
1998 Yosemite Ave 95320 209-838-7031
Kendra Helsley, prin. Fax 838-8916
El Portal MS 700/6-8
805 1st St 95320 209-838-7095
Mark Vos, prin. Fax 838-3017
Van Allen ES 200/K-5
21051 State Highway 120 95320 209-838-2931
Scott Ferreira, prin. Fax 838-1832
Other Schools – See Farmington, Stockton

Escondido, San Diego, Pop. 134,085
Escondido Union SD 18,500/PK-8
2310 Aldergrove Ave 92029 760-432-2400
Jennifer Walters, supt. Fax 735-2874
www.eusd4kids.org/
Bear Valley MS 1,200/6-8
3003 Bear Valley Pkwy S 92025 760-432-4060
Mark Garner, prin. Fax 504-0158
Bernardo ES 600/K-5
1122 Mountain Heights Dr 92029 760-432-2700
Lisa Clark, prin. Fax 432-2720
Central ES 800/K-5
122 W 4th Ave 92025 760-432-2431
Fabiola Elias, prin. Fax 735-2862
Conway ES 800/K-5
1325 Conway Dr 92027 760-432-2435
Steve White, prin. Fax 480-4312
Del Dios MS 1,100/6-8
1400 W 9th Ave 92029 760-432-2439
Darren McDuffie, prin. Fax 432-0728
Farr Avenue ES 800/K-5
933 Farr Ave 92026 760-735-3049
Angel Gotay, prin. Fax 504-0170
Felicita ES 700/K-5
737 W 13th Ave 92025 760-432-2444
Henry Leso, prin. Fax 745-1462
Glen View ES 700/K-5
2201 E Mission Ave 92027 760-432-2448
Leticia Ortegon, prin. Fax 480-8302
Green ES 800/K-5
3115 Las Palmas Ave 92025 760-432-2260
Susan Freeman, prin. Fax 745-9173
Hidden Valley MS 1,200/6-8
2700 Reed Rd 92027 760-432-2457
Trent Smith, prin. Fax 480-0845
Juniper ES 700/K-5
1809 S Juniper St 92025 760-432-2462
Kelly Mussatti, prin. Fax 746-2041
Lincoln ES 600/K-5
1029 N Broadway 92026 760-432-2466
Elisa Fregoso, prin. Fax 745-3402
Miller ES 500/K-5
1975 Miller Ave 92025 760-432-2470
Jim Scott, prin. Fax 745-2766
Mission MS 1,100/6-8
939 E Mission Ave 92025 760-432-2452
Leticia Aroyo, prin. Fax 737-9085
North Broadway ES 600/K-5
2301 N Broadway 92026 760-432-2479
Libby Campbell, prin. Fax 745-5230
Oak Hill ES 1,000/K-5
1820 Oak Hill Dr 92027 760-432-2483
Cliff Smith, prin. Fax 745-5067
Orange Glen ES 800/K-5
2861 E Valley Pkwy 92027 760-432-2487
Rick Ausby, prin. Fax 735-2840
Pioneer ES 800/K-5
980 N Ash St 92027 760-432-2412
Marcia Karadashian, prin. Fax 745-7536
Preschool PK-PK
835 W 15th Ave 92025 760-489-4131
Jan Zelasko, prin. Fax 489-6431
Reidy Creek ES 700/K-5
2869 N Broadway 92026 760-739-5800
Beth Crooks, prin. Fax 739-5813
Rincon MS 1,500/6-8
925 Lehner Ave 92026 760-432-2491
Jon Centofranchi, prin. Fax 743-6713
Rock Springs ES 700/K-5
1155 Deodar Rd 92026 760-432-2284
Kathy Morris, prin. Fax 745-3549
Rose ES 800/K-5
906 N Rose St 92027 760-432-2495
Cesar Carrasco, prin. Fax 745-3251

San Pasqual UNESD 600/PK-8
15305 Rockwood Rd 92027 760-745-4931
Frank Gomez, supt. Fax 745-2473
www.sanpasqualunion.com
San Pasqual Union S 600/PK-8
15305 Rockwood Rd 92027 760-745-4931
Frank Gomez, prin. Fax 745-2473

Ascension Lutheran S 50/K-8
1140 N Midway Dr 92027 760-747-4276
Andrew Plocher, prin. Fax 747-4156
Calvin Christian S 200/PK-5
1868 N Broadway 92026 760-489-1159
Terry Kok, prin. Fax 489-0335
Christian LIFE Academy 200/K-12
PO Box 300038 92030 760-741-7651
Emilie Mahoney, admin.
Escondido Adventist Academy 200/K-12
1301 Deodar Rd 92026 760-746-1800
Kristine Fuentes, prin. Fax 743-3499
Escondido Christian S 400/PK-8
PO Box 300157 92030 760-745-2071
Dr. Pat Klose, prin. Fax 745-1905
Grace Lutheran S 400/PK-8
643 W 13th Ave 92025 760-747-3029
Sandy Zielinski, prin. Fax 745-1612
Light & Life Christian S 400/PK-8
120 N Ash St 92027 760-745-2832
Al Fikse, admin. Fax 745-4318
St. Mary S 300/K-8
130 E 13th Ave 92025 760-743-3431
Cynthia Asbury, prin. Fax 743-6808

Esparto, Yolo, Pop. 1,487
Esparto USD 1,000/K-12
26675 Plainfield St 95627 530-787-3446
Aida Buelna, supt. Fax 787-3033
www.espartok12.org
Esparto ES 500/K-5
26675 Plainfield St 95627 530-787-3417
Veronica Michael, prin. Fax 787-4844
Esparto MS 300/6-8
26675 Plainfield St 95627 530-787-4151
Robert Verdugo, prin. Fax 787-3890

Etiwanda, See Rancho Cucamonga
Etiwanda ESD 12,900/K-8
6061 East Ave 91739 909-899-2451
Shawn Judson, supt. Fax 899-1656
www.etiwanda.k12.ca.us
Day Creek IS 1,000/6-8
12345 Coyote Dr 91739 909-803-3300
Charlayne Sprague, prin. Fax 803-3309
Etiwanda Colony ES 800/K-5
13144 Banyan St 91739 909-803-3911
Darlene Carlmark, prin. Fax 803-3917
Etiwanda IS 1,200/6-8
6925 Etiwanda Ave 91739 909-899-1701
Janella Cantu-Myricks, prin. Fax 899-5676
Golden ES 700/K-5
12400 Banyan St 91739 909-463-9105
Sherri Carmean, prin. Fax 463-9124
Grapeland ES 900/K-5
7171 Etiwanda Ave 91739 909-463-7026
Jeff Sipos, prin. Fax 463-4838
Summit IS 800/6-8
5959 East Ave 91739 909-899-1704
Lori Arita, prin. Fax 899-7596
Windrows ES 600/K-5
6855 Victoria Park Ln 91739 909-899-2641
Josh Lautenslager, prin. Fax 899-3197
Other Schools – See Alta Loma, Fontana, Rancho Cucamonga

Etna, Siskiyou, Pop. 796
Scott Valley USD
Supt. — See Fort Jones

Etna ES 200/K-6
PO Box 490 96027 530-467-3320
Jim Pindell, prin. Fax 467-3465

Eureka, Humboldt, Pop. 25,579
Cutten ESD 600/K-6
4182 Walnut Dr 95503 707-441-3900
Ron Pontoni, supt. Fax 441-3906
www.humboldt.k12.ca.us/cutten_sd
Cutten ES 300/3-6
4182 Walnut Dr 95503 707-441-3900
Ron Pontoni, prin. Fax 441-3906
Ridgewood ES 200/K-2
4182 Walnut Dr 95503 707-441-3930
Julie Osborne, prin. Fax 441-3933

Eureka City SD 3,500/K-12
3200 Walford Ave 95503 707-441-2400
Gregg Haulk, supt. Fax 441-3326
www.eurekacityschools.org
Birney ES 300/K-6
717 South Ave 95503 707-441-2495
Georgeanne Pucillo, prin. Fax 444-3524
Grant ES 200/K-6
3901 G St 95503 707-441-2552
Laurie Alexander, prin. Fax 441-3321
LaFayette ES 300/K-6
3100 Park St 95501 707-441-2482
Kathleen Honsal, prin. Fax 441-3320
Washington ES 400/K-6
3322 Dolbeer St 95503 707-441-2547
Jan Schmidt, prin. Fax 441-3323
Zane MS 400/7-8
2155 S St 95501 707-441-2470
Heidi Moore, prin. Fax 441-0286

Garfield ESD 100/K-6
2200 Freshwater Rd 95503 707-442-5471
Barbara McMahon, supt. Fax 442-1932
www.humboldt.k12.ca.us/garfield_sd/
Garfield ES 100/K-6
2200 Freshwater Rd 95503 707-442-5471
Barbara McMahon, prin. Fax 442-1932

South Bay UNESD 400/K-6
6077 Loma Ave 95503 707-476-8549
Marie Twibell, supt. Fax 476-8968
www.humboldt.k12.ca.us/sobay_sd/district/index.htm
Pine Hill ES 200/K-6
5230 Vance St 95503 707-443-4596
Pam Olson, prin. Fax 443-1312
South Bay ES 200/K-6
6077 Loma Ave 95503 707-443-4828
Marie Twibell, prin. Fax 444-3690

Gospel Outreach S 50/K-12
PO Box 1022 95502 707-445-1167
Jerry Kent, prin. Fax 445-1562
Rebecca's Sunnybrook Farm 50/PK-PK
1405 L St 95501 707-443-1954
Raymond Sanders, admin.
Redwood Christian S 100/K-8
2039 E St 95501 707-442-4625
Bob Giacomini, prin. Fax 442-4685
St. Bernard S 200/PK-12
222 Dollison St 95501 707-443-2735
Patrick Daly, pres. Fax 443-4723

Exeter, Tulare, Pop. 9,974
Exeter UNSD 3,100/K-12
134 S E St 93221 559-592-9421
Renee Whitson, supt. Fax 592-9445
www.exeterpublicschools.org/
Lincoln ES 600/K-2
333 S D St 93221 559-592-2141
Donna Jackson, prin. Fax 592-5249
Rocky Hill ES 700/3-5
313 Sequoia Dr 93221 559-592-5490
Jessica Bradshaw, prin. Fax 592-3715
Wilson MS 600/6-8
265 Albert Ave 93221 559-592-2144
Heather Keran, prin. Fax 592-5536

Sierra View Junior Academy 100/K-10
19933 Avenue 256 93221 559-592-3689
Robert Bramhall, prin. Fax 592-5615

Fairfax, Marin, Pop. 7,106
Ross Valley ESD
Supt. — See San Anselmo
Manor ES 300/K-5
150 Oak Manor Dr 94930 415-453-1544
Catalina Nocon, prin. Fax 453-0680
White Hill MS 600/6-8
101 Glen Dr 94930 415-454-8390
Michele Patterson, prin. Fax 454-3980

St. Rita S 100/PK-8
102 Marinda Dr 94930 415-456-1003
Marilyn Porto, prin. Fax 456-7946

Fairfield, Solano, Pop. 104,476
Fairfield-Suisun USD 21,600/K-12
2490 Hilborn Rd, 707-399-5000
Jacki Cottingim Ph.D., supt. Fax 399-5154
www.fsusd.k12.ca.us
Cordelia Hills ES 800/K-6
4770 Canyon Hills Dr, 707-864-1905
Nancy Allen, prin. Fax 864-1778
Fairview ES 500/K-5
830 1st St 94533 707-421-4165
Gloria Bandy, prin. Fax 427-3348
Gordon ES 400/K-5
1950 Dover Ave 94533 707-421-4125
Victor Romualdi Ph.D., prin. Fax 421-4262
Grange MS 600/6-8
1975 Blossom Ave 94533 707-421-4175
Christine Harrison, prin. Fax 422-4004
Green Valley MS 800/6-8
1350 Gold Hill Rd, 707-646-7000
Greg Hubbs, prin. Fax 864-1503
Jones ES 900/K-6
2001 Winston Dr, 707-421-4195
Cheryl Jones, prin. Fax 421-3909
Kyle ES 600/K-5
1600 Kidder Ave 94533 707-421-4105
Sandy Holland, prin. Fax 421-3932
Laurel Creek ES 800/K-5
2900 Gulf Dr 94533 707-421-4291
Bill Stockman, prin. Fax 421-4305
Mundy ES 800/K-6
570 Vintage Valley Dr, 707-863-7920
Kristen Cherry, prin. Fax 863-7927
Oakbrook ES 900/K-6
700 Oakbrook Dr, 707-863-7930
Justine Turner, prin. Fax 863-7931
Rolling Hills ES 800/K-6
2025 Fieldcrest Ave, 707-399-9566
Rona Portalupi, prin. Fax 399-8452
Sheldon ES 500/K-6
1901 Woolner Ave 94533 707-421-4150
Lauran Hawker, prin. Fax 421-3203
Sullivan MS 800/6-8
2195 Union Ave 94533 707-421-4115
Catherine Pickett, prin. Fax 421-3964
Tolenas ES 600/K-5
4500 Tolenas Rd 94533 707-421-4350
Pamela Moore, prin. Fax 421-3220
Weir ES 500/K-5
1975 Pennsylvania Ave 94533 707-399-3300
Martha Lacy-Meeks, prin. Fax 399-3370
Wilson S 900/K-8
3301 Cherry Hills Ct, 707-421-4225
Jeff Crane, prin. Fax 421-3937
Other Schools – See Suisun City

Travis USD 5,300/K-12
2751 De Ronde Dr 94533 707-437-4604
Kate Wren Gavlak, supt. Fax 437-3378
www.travisusd.k12.ca.us
Golden West MS 800/7-8
2651 De Ronde Dr 94533 707-437-8240
Jackie Tretten, prin. Fax 437-3416
Other Schools – See Travis AFB, Vacaville

Holy Spirit S 300/K-8
1050 N Texas St 94533 707-422-5016
Sr. Elizabeth Curtis, prin. Fax 422-0874
Solano Christian Academy 200/PK-8
2200 Fairfield Ave 94533 707-425-7715
Michelle Bounds, admin. Fax 429-2999
Trinity Lutheran S 100/PK-K
2075 Dover Ave 94533 707-435-1123
Gloria Cantrell, lead tchr. Fax 435-1122

Fair Oaks, Sacramento, Pop. 28,300
San Juan USD
Supt. — See Carmichael
Dewey Fundamental ES 400/K-6
7025 Falcon Rd 95628 916-867-2020
Jeanne Lazar, prin. Fax 867-2023
LeGette ES 500/K-6
4623 Kenneth Ave 95628 916-867-2054
Dennis Pedersen, prin. Fax 867-2058
Northridge ES 500/K-6
5150 Cocoa Palm Way 95628 916-867-2066
Michele Flagler, prin. Fax 867-2070
Orangevale Open S 600/K-8
5630 Illinois Ave 95628 916-867-2067
Judi McGuire, prin.
Rogers MS 800/7-8
4924 Dewey Dr 95628 916-971-7889
Kamaljit Pannu, prin. Fax 971-7903

Faith Lutheran S 100/PK-4
4000 San Juan Ave 95628 916-961-4253
Cynthia Finn, dir. Fax 961-2604
Freedom Christian S 100/K-12
7736 Sunset Ave 95628 916-962-3247
Annette Coller, admin. Fax 962-0783
Sacramento Waldorf S 400/K-12
3750 Bannister Rd 95628 916-961-3900
Elizabeth Beaven, admin. Fax 961-3970
St. Mel S 300/K-8
4745 Pennsylvania Ave 95628 916-967-2814
Janet Nagel, prin. Fax 967-0705
Victory Christian S - Fair Oaks 100/K-8
5010 Hazel Ave 95628 916-967-6565
Paul Eggenberger, prin. Fax 967-6576

Fallbrook, San Diego, Pop. 22,095
Fallbrook UNESD 5,700/K-8
321 Iowa St 92028 760-731-5420
Brian Jacobs Ed.D., supt. Fax 723-3895
www.fuesd.k12.ca.us
Ellis ES 400/K-3
400 W Elder St 92028 760-731-4300
Andy Santamaria, prin. Fax 723-2763
Fallbrook Street ES 500/K-2
405 W Fallbrook St 92028 760-731-4000
Diane McClelland, prin. Fax 723-4871
Frazier ES 600/K-3
1835 Gum Tree Ln 92028 760-723-6770
Leonard Rodriguez, prin. Fax 731-2707
Iowa Street S 200/K-8
321 Iowa St 92028 760-731-5440
Tom Rhine, prin. Fax 723-5294
La Paloma ES 700/4-6
300 Heald Ln 92028 760-731-4220
Lea Curcio, prin. Fax 731-3202
Live Oak ES 800/3-6
1978 Reche Rd 92028 760-731-4430
Lilly Perez, prin. Fax 731-0446
Potter IS 1,100/7-8
1743 Reche Rd 92028 760-731-4150
Tere Peterson, prin. Fax 723-5740
Other Schools – See Oceanside, San Clemente

Vallecitos ESD 200/K-8
5253 5th St 92028 760-728-7092
Dr. Paul Cartas, supt. Fax 728-7712
www.sdcoe.k12.ca.us/districts/vallecitos
Vallecitos S 200/K-8
5253 5th St 92028 760-728-7092
Leslie Lyle, prin. Fax 728-7712

St. Peters S 200/K-8
450 S Stage Coach Ln 92028 760-728-6961
Anne Lewis, prin. Fax 723-8973
St. Stephen Lutheran S 100/PK-8
1636 E Mission Rd 92028 760-728-6814
James Hussman, prin. Fax 728-2958
Zion Lutheran S 300/PK-8
1405 E Fallbrook St 92028 760-723-3500
Nancy Swanlund, prin. Fax 723-3951

Fall River Mills, Shasta
Fall River JUSD
Supt. — See Burney
Fall River ES 300/K-6
24977 Curve St 96028 530-336-5551
Christine Knoch, prin. Fax 336-6892

Farmersville, Tulare, Pop. 9,918
Farmersville USD 2,400/K-12
571 E Citrus Dr 93223 559-592-2010
Janet Jones, supt. Fax 592-2203
www.farmersville.k12.ca.us
Farmersville JHS 600/6-8
650 N Virginia Ave 93223 559-747-0764
Richard Albay, prin. Fax 747-2704
Freedom ES 400/4-5
575 E Citrus Dr 93223 559-592-2662
Judy Lucas, prin. Fax 592-4841
Hester ES 400/K-1
477 E Ash St 93223 559-594-5801
Terrence Keller, prin. Fax 594-4022
Snowden ES 400/2-3
301 S Farmersville Blvd 93223 559-747-0781
Randy DeGraw, prin. Fax 747-2709

Farmington, San Joaquin
Escalon USD
Supt. — See Escalon
Farmington ES 200/K-5
PO Box 68 95230 209-886-5344
Bob Amato, prin. Fax 886-5014

Fellows, Kern
Midway ESD 100/K-8
PO Box 39 93224 661-768-4344
Greg Coker, supt. Fax 768-4746
Midway S 100/K-8
PO Box 39 93224 661-768-4344
Greg Coker, prin. Fax 768-4746

Felton, Santa Cruz, Pop. 5,350
San Lorenzo Valley USD
Supt. — See Ben Lomond
San Lorenzo Valley ES 600/K-5
7155 Highway 9 95018 831-335-4475
Michelle McKinny, prin. Fax 335-4768
San Lorenzo Valley MS 500/6-8
7179 Hacienda Way 95018 831-335-4452
Christopher Schiermeyer, prin. Fax 335-3812

St. Lawrence Academy 50/K-8
6184 Highway 9 95018 831-335-0328
Marcel Herle, prin. Fax 335-0353

Ferndale, Humboldt, Pop. 1,394
Ferndale USD 500/K-12
1231 Main St 95536 707-786-5900
Sam Garamendi, supt. Fax 786-4865
www.ferndalek12.org/
Ferndale S 300/K-8
164 Shaw Ave 95536 707-786-5300
Paul Meyers, prin. Fax 786-4284

Fieldbrook, Humboldt
Fieldbrook ESD 100/K-8
4070 Fieldbrook Rd, 707-839-3201
Daria Lowery, supt. Fax 839-8832
www.nohum.k12.ca.us
Fieldbrook S 100/K-8
4070 Fieldbrook Rd, 707-839-3201
Daria Lowery, prin. Fax 839-8832

Fillmore, Ventura, Pop. 14,895
Fillmore USD 3,800/K-12
PO Box 697 93016 805-524-6000
Jeff Sweeney, supt. Fax 524-6060
www.fillmore.k12.ca.us
Fillmore MS 900/6-8
PO Box 697 93016 805-524-6070
Todd Schieferle, prin. Fax 524-6063
Mountain Vista ES 400/K-5
PO Box 697 93016 805-524-6781
Christine Schieferle, prin. Fax 524-6785
San Cayetano ES 400/K-5
PO Box 697 93016 805-524-6040
Jan Marholin, prin. Fax 524-6185
Sespe ES 500/K-5
PO Box 697 93016 805-524-6161
Rosemarie Hibler, prin. Fax 524-6178
Other Schools – See Piru

Fillmore Christian Academy 100/K-8
461 Central Ave 93015 805-524-1572
Gene Signor, admin. Fax 524-1139

Firebaugh, Fresno, Pop. 7,001
Dos Palos Oro Loma JUSD
Supt. — See Dos Palos

Oro Loma ES 100/K-5
5609 N Russell Ave 93622 209-392-0270
Norma Delgado, prin. Fax 364-6322

Firebaugh-Las Deltas JUSD 2,200/K-12
1976 Morris Kyle Dr 93622 559-659-1476
Violet Chuck, supt. Fax 659-2355
www.fldusd.k12.ca.us/
Bailey PS 600/K-3
1976 Morris Kyle Dr 93622 559-659-1421
Ana Fuentes, prin. Fax 659-3929
Firebaugh MS 500/6-8
1976 Morris Kyle Dr 93622 559-659-1481
Marvin Baker, prin. Fax 659-7106
Mills IS 300/4-5
1976 Morris Kyle Dr 93622 559-659-2317
Karyn Albert, prin. Fax 659-3927

Five Points, See San Diego
Westside ESD 300/K-8
PO Box 398 93624 559-884-2492
Baldomero Hernandez, supt. Fax 884-2206
Westside S 300/K-8
PO Box 398 93624 559-884-2492
Baldomero Hernandez, prin. Fax 884-2206

Flournoy, Tehama
Flournoy UNESD 50/K-8
PO Box 2260 96029 530-833-5331
Ken Burkhart, supt. Fax 833-5332
www.flournoyschool.org/
Flournoy S 50/K-8
PO Box 2260 96029 530-833-5331
Ken Burkhart, prin. Fax 833-5332

Folsom, Sacramento, Pop. 65,611
Folsom-Cordova USD 19,600/PK-12
125 E Bidwell St 95630 916-355-1100
Patrick Godwin, supt. Fax 985-0722
www.fcusd.k12.ca.us
Empire Oaks ES 700/K-5
1830 Bonhill Dr 95630 916-983-0120
Monika Himmrich, prin. Fax 983-0399
Folsom Hills ES 600/K-6
106 Manseau Dr 95630 916-985-0771
Shawn Lundberg, prin. Fax 985-4673
Folsom MS 1,100/6-8
500 Blue Ravine Rd 95630 916-983-4466
Karen Knight, prin. Fax 983-3462
Gallardo ES 700/K-5
775 Russi Rd 95630 916-294-0334
Joanie Cunningham, prin. Fax 294-0713
Gold Ridge ES 600/K-5
735 Halidon Way 95630 916-984-5151
Curtis Wilson, prin. Fax 984-5353
Judah ES 400/K-6
101 Dean Way 95630 916-983-4469
Joan Jarman, prin. Fax 983-0381
Natoma Station ES 600/K-6
500 Turn Pike Dr 95630 916-351-0565
Canen Peterson, prin. Fax 351-9209
Oak Chan ES 600/K-5
101 Prewett Dr 95630 916-983-0190
James Cagney, prin. Fax 983-0225
Russell Ranch ES 300/K-5
375 Dry Creek Rd 95630 916-294-2430
Tony Peterson, prin. Fax 294-2431
Sprentz ES 300/K-5
249 Flower Dr 95630 916-985-3626
Trisha Ruckle, prin. Fax 985-7748
Sundahl ES 400/K-6
9932 Inwood Rd 95630 916-989-9182
Donna Hays, prin. Fax 989-2510
Sutter MS 1,100/6-8
715 Riley St 95630 916-985-3644
Keri Phillips, prin. Fax 985-7044
Other Schools – See Mather, Rancho Cordova

Folsom S 400/K-8
650 Willard Dr 95630 916-353-0185
Sandy Hanavan, prin. Fax 353-0637
St. John's Notre Dame S 300/K-8
309 Montrose Dr 95630 916-985-4129
Susan Halfman, prin. Fax 985-7958

Fontana, San Bernardino, Pop. 163,860
Colton JUSD
Supt. — See Colton
D'Arcy ES 600/K-6
11645 Elm Ave 92337 909-430-2800
Neera Kohli, prin. Fax 350-9637
Jurupa Vista ES 700/K-6
15920 Village Dr 92337 909-580-5021
Syed Hyder, prin. Fax 554-1875
Sycamore Hills ES 800/K-6
11036 Mahogany Dr 92337 909-580-5029
Cecilia Smith, prin. Fax 349-2393

Etiwanda ESD
Supt. — See Etiwanda
East Heritage ES 700/K-5
14250 E Constitution Way 92336 909-823-5696
Betty Rose, prin. Fax 823-2517
Heritage IS 1,300/6-8
13766 S Heritage Cir 92336 909-357-1345
Laura Rowland, prin. Fax 357-8945
Long ES 700/K-5
5383 N Bridlepath Dr 92336 909-463-1626
Carol Alexander, prin. Fax 463-0810
Solorio ES 800/K-5
15172 Walnut St 92336 909-357-8691
Carol Bidwell-Pilgren, prin. Fax 357-7329
West Heritage ES 600/K-5
13690 W Constitution Way 92336 909-899-1199
Ben Lautenslager, prin. Fax 899-2297

Fontana USD 42,400/PK-12
9680 Citrus Ave 92335 909-357-5000
Cali Olsen-Binks, supt. Fax 357-5012
www.fusd.net/
Alder MS 1,400/6-8
7555 Alder Ave 92336 909-357-5330
Mark McLaughlin, prin. Fax 357-5348
Almeria MS 1,100/6-8
7723 Almeria Ave 92336 909-357-5350
Gregory Fromm, prin. Fax 357-5360
Almond ES 700/K-6
8172 Almond Ave 92335 909-357-5130
Karolee Rosen Ph.D., prin. Fax 357-5139
Beech Avenue ES 600/K-6
9206 Beech Ave 92335 909-357-5060
Michele Mower, prin. Fax 357-7675
Binks ES 600/K-5
7358 Cypress Ave 92336 909-357-5030
Joanne Thoring, prin. Fax 357-7678
Canyon Crest ES 800/PK-5
11851 Cherry Ave 92337 909-357-5440
Susan Ruoff Ed.D., prin. Fax 357-5449
Chaparrel ES 500/PK-5
14000 Shadow Dr 92337 909-357-5450
Craig Baker, prin. Fax 357-5459
Citrus ES 800/K-6
16041 Randall Ave 92335 909-357-5140
Kevin Tierney, prin. Fax 357-5149
Cypress ES 800/PK-5
9751 Cypress Ave 92335 909-357-5460
Ron Dillender, prin. Fax 357-5469
Date ES 700/PK-5
9011 Oleander Ave 92335 909-357-5240
Larry Elwell, prin. Fax 357-5249
Fontana MS 1,300/6-8
8425 Mango Ave 92335 909-357-5370
Giovanni Annous, prin. Fax 357-5391
Grant ES 600/PK-5
7069 Isabel Ln 92336 909-357-5540
Chris Ridge, prin. Fax 357-5549
Hemlock ES 600/PK-5
PO Box 5090 92334 909-357-5470
Gerald Mullins, prin. Fax 357-5479
Juniper ES 900/PK-5
7655 Juniper Ave 92336 909-357-5480
Adele Thomas, prin. Fax 357-5483
Live Oak ES 800/PK-5
9522 Live Oak Ave 92335 909-357-5640
Ricardo Chaparro, prin. Fax 357-5648
Locust ES 600/PK-6
7420 Locust Ave 92336 909-357-5650
Sandra Gray, prin. Fax 357-5659
Mango ES 700/PK-5
7450 Mango Ave 92336 909-357-5660
Sara Najaro, prin. Fax 357-5669
Maple ES 800/PK-5
751 S Maple Ave 92335 909-357-5670
Michael Garcia, prin. Fax 357-5679
North Tamarind ES 500/PK-6
7961 Tamarind Ave 92336 909-357-5680
Dan Fitzgerald, prin. Fax 357-5683
Oak Park ES 600/PK-5
14200 Live Oak Ave 92337 909-357-5690
Antonio Viramontes, prin. Fax 357-5699
Oleander ES 700/PK-5
8650 Oleander Ave 92335 909-357-5700
Gorge Santiago, prin. Fax 357-5707
Palmetto ES 1,000/PK-5
9325 Palmetto Ave 92335 909-357-5710
Mercedes Walker, prin. Fax 357-5718
Poplar ES 700/K-6
9937 Poplar Ave 92335 909-357-5720
Michelle Hiser, prin. Fax 357-5729
Porter ES 700/PK-5
8330 Locust Ave 92335 909-357-5320
J.J. Francoisse, prin. Fax 357-5329
Primrose ES 800/PK-5
751 N Maple Ave 92336 909-357-5790
Darlene Duquette, prin. Fax 357-5799
Randall-Pepper ES 800/PK-5
16613 Randall Ave 92335 909-357-5730
Sylvia Rivera, prin. Fax 357-5736
Redwood ES 800/K-6
8570 Redwood Ave 92335 909-357-5740
Sergio Chavez, prin. Fax 357-5749
Ruble MS 1,400/6-8
6762 Juniper Ave 92336 909-357-5530
Crystal Whitley, prin. Fax 357-5539
Sequoia MS 1,400/7-8
9452 Hemlock Ave 92335 909-357-5400
Rita Bucheli, prin. Fax 357-5419
Shadow Hills ES 600/PK-5
14300 Shadow Dr 92337 909-357-5750
Frank Donahue, prin. Fax 357-5759
Sierra Lakes ES 700/K-5
5740 Avenal Pl 92336 909-357-5270
Andrea Credille, prin. Fax 357-5279
Southridge MS 1,200/6-8
14500 Live Oak Ave 92337 909-357-5420
Linda Buck, prin. Fax 822-4609
South Tamarind ES 800/PK-5
8561 Tamarind Ave 92335 909-357-5760
Joel Avina Sanchez, prin. Fax 357-5769
Tokay ES 800/PK-5
7846 Tokay Ave 92336 909-357-5770
Terry Abernathy, prin. Fax 357-5779
Truman MS 1,200/6-8
PO Box 5090 92334 909-357-5190
Paul Pagano, prin. Fax 357-5199
West Randall ES 1,000/K-6
15620 Randall Ave 92335 909-357-5780
Albert Martin, prin. Fax 357-5789

Life Covenant Christian Academy 100/K-8
9315 Citrus Ave 92335 909-429-7707
Barbara Carroll, prin. Fax 823-3499
Peace in the Valley Christian Academy 50/K-8
17487 Arrow Blvd 92335 909-355-2008
Carlos Cabello, admin. Fax 355-5228
Resurrection Academy 200/PK-8
PO Box 816 92334 909-822-4431
Madeleine Thomas, prin. Fax 822-0617
Water of Life Christian S 300/PK-5
7623 East Ave 92336 909-463-3915
Arden Schlecht, admin. Fax 463-1436

Foothill Ranch, Orange
Saddleback Valley USD
Supt. — See Mission Viejo
Foothill Ranch ES 1,400/K-6
1 Torino 92610 949-470-4885
Ed MacNevin, prin. Fax 586-9982

Forest Falls, San Bernardino
Bear Valley USD
Supt. — See Big Bear Lake
Fallsvale ES 50/K-6
PO Box 100 92339 909-794-8630
Jacque Williams, prin. Fax 794-2975

Foresthill, Placer, Pop. 1,409
Foresthill UNESD 600/K-8
24750 Main St 95631 530-367-2966
Jim Roberts, supt. Fax 367-2470
www.fusd.org
Foresthill Divide MS 300/5-8
22888 Foresthill Rd 95631 530-367-3782
Shannon Jacinto, prin. Fax 367-4526
Foresthill ES 300/K-4
24750 Main St 95631 530-367-2211
Jim Roberts, prin. Fax 367-4568

Forks of Salmon, Siskiyou
Forks of Salmon ESD 50/K-8
15616 Salmon River Rd 96031 530-462-4762
Joel Kurtzman, supt. Fax 462-4735
www.sisnet.ssku.k12.ca.us/~forksftp/
Forks of Salmon S 50/K-8
15616 Salmon River Rd 96031 530-462-4762
Cathy Leavens, admin. Fax 462-4735

Fort Bragg, Mendocino, Pop. 6,814
Fort Bragg USD 1,900/K-12
312 S Lincoln St 95437 707-961-2850
Dr. Donald Armstrong, supt. Fax 964-5002
www.fbusd.us/
Fort Bragg MS 400/6-8
500 N Harold St 95437 707-961-2870
Donna Miller, prin. Fax 964-9416
Gray ES 400/3-5
1197 E Chestnut St 95437 707-961-2865
Nancy Doll, prin. Fax 961-2887
Redwood ES 400/K-2
324 S Lincoln St 95437 707-961-2860
Mary Kaye Champagne, prin. Fax 961-4231
Westport Village ES 50/K-5
324 S Lincoln St 95437 707-961-6336
Mary Kaye Champagne, prin. Fax 961-2887

Fort Irwin, San Bernardino
Silver Valley USD
Supt. — See Yermo
Fort Irwin MS 300/6-8
1700 Pork Chop Hill St 92310 760-386-1133
Charles Thatch, prin. Fax 386-2448
Lewis ES 700/K-2
1800 Blackhawk Dr 92310 760-386-1900
Patti Baer, prin. Fax 386-1956
Tiefort View ES 400/3-5
8700 Anzio St 92310 760-386-3123
Ruth Williams, prin. Fax 386-4353

Fort Jones, Siskiyou, Pop. 669
Scott Valley USD 700/K-12
PO Box 687 96032 530-468-2727
Dr. Emily Houck, supt. Fax 468-2729
users.sisqtel.net/svcoc/schools.html
Fort Jones ES 100/K-6
PO Box 249 96032 530-468-2412
Bruce Bishop, prin. Fax 468-2742
Quartz Valley S 50/K-8
11033 Quartz Valley Rd 96032 530-468-2448
James Pindell, prin. Fax 468-5284
Other Schools – See Etna

Fortuna, Humboldt, Pop. 11,155
Fortuna UNESD 800/K-8
843 L St 95540 707-725-2293
Dr. Patti Hafner, supt. Fax 725-2228
www.humboldt.k12.ca.us/fortuna_un/
Fortuna MS 300/5-8
843 L St 95540 707-725-3415
Dr. Shannon Lynch, prin. Fax 725-2228
South Fortuna ES 400/K-4
2089 Newburg Rd 95540 707-725-2519
Jeff Northern, prin. Fax 725-2085

Rohnerville ESD 600/K-8
2800 Thomas St 95540 707-725-7823
Robert Williams Ed.D., supt. Fax 725-5776
www.humboldt.k12.ca.us/rohnerville_sd/index.html
Ambrosini ES 300/K-3
3850 Rohnerville Rd 95540 707-725-4688
Robert Williams Ed.D., prin. Fax 725-4941
Thomas MS 300/4-8
2800 Thomas St 95540 707-725-5197
Linda Meitner, prin. Fax 725-8637

Fortuna Junior Academy 50/K-8
1200 Ross Hill Rd 95540 707-725-2988
Raemel Oliveira, prin. Fax 725-3986
New Life Christian S 100/PK-12
1736 Newburg Rd 95540 707-725-9136
Anita Horner, supt. Fax 725-1638

Foster City, San Mateo, Pop. 28,756
San Mateo-Foster City ESD 10,000/K-8
1170 Chess Dr 94404 650-312-7700
Pendery Clark Ed.D., supt. Fax 312-7348
www.smfc.k12.ca.us
Audubon ES 500/K-5
841 Gull Ave 94404 650-312-7500
Rick Giannotti, prin. Fax 312-7506
Bowditch MS 1,000/6-8
1450 Tarpon St 94404 650-312-7680
Judy Ross, prin. Fax 312-7639
Brewer Island ES 600/K-5
1151 Polynesia Dr 94404 650-312-7532
Alice Wycke, prin. Fax 638-7044
Foster City ES 800/K-5
461 Beach Park Blvd 94404 650-312-7522
David Holcombe, prin. Fax 312-7640
Other Schools – See San Mateo

Kids Connection S 200/K-5
1998 Beach Park Blvd 94404 650-578-6691
Diane Marcum, admin. Fax 372-0583
St. Ambrose/Sea Breeze S 200/PK-K
900 Edgewater Blvd 94404 650-574-5437
Maryanne Lewis, hdmstr. Fax 574-5833
Wornick Jewish Day S 300/K-8
800 Foster City Blvd 94404 650-378-2600
Susan Weintrob, hdmstr. Fax 378-2669

Fountain Valley, Orange, Pop. 55,942
Fountain Valley ESD 6,100/K-8
10055 Slater Ave 92708 714-843-3200
Marc Ecker, supt. Fax 841-0356
www.fvsd.k12.ca.us
Courreges ES 600/K-5
18313 Santa Carlotta St 92708 714-378-4280
Joyce Buehler, prin. Fax 378-4289
Cox ES 700/K-5
17615 Los Jardines E 92708 714-378-4241
Julianne Hoefer, prin. Fax 378-4249
Fulton MS 700/6-8
8778 El Lago Cir 92708 714-375-2816
Chris Christensen, prin. Fax 375-2825
Gisler ES 500/K-5
18720 Las Flores St 92708 714-378-4210
Jennifer Perkins, prin. Fax 378-4219
Masuda MS 800/6-8
17415 Los Jardines W 92708 714-378-4250
Chris Mullin, prin. Fax 378-4259
Moiola S 600/K-8
9790 Finch Ave 92708 714-378-4270
Erin Bains, prin. Fax 378-4279
Plavan ES 400/K-5
9675 Warner Ave 92708 714-378-4230
Julie Hunter, prin. Fax 378-4239
Tamura ES 400/K-5
17340 Santa Suzanne St 92708 714-375-6226
Jay Adams, prin. Fax 375-6235
Other Schools – See Huntington Beach

Garden Grove USD
Supt. — See Garden Grove
Allen ES 600/K-6
16200 Bushard St 92708 714-663-6228
Lynn Hardin, prin. Fax 531-6348
Monroe ES 400/K-6
16225 Newhope St 92708 714-663-6264
Michelle Rushall, prin. Fax 663-6213
Northcutt ES 500/K-6
11303 Sandstone Ave 92708 714-663-6537
Kai Chang, prin.

Ocean View SD
Supt. — See Huntington Beach
Vista View MS 800/6-8
16250 Hickory St 92708 714-842-0626
Robert Miller, prin. Fax 843-9156

Shoreline Christian S 400/PK-8
10350 Ellis Ave 92708 714-962-6886
Rev. Larrey Noia, admin. Fax 968-6195
Sycamore Academy 300/K-12
17150 Newhope St Ste 701 92708 888-334-6711
Sandra Gogel, dir. Fax 668-1344

Fowler, Fresno, Pop. 4,713
Fowler USD 2,300/K-12
658 E Adams Ave 93625 559-834-6080
John Cruz, supt. Fax 834-3390
www.fowlerusd.org
Fremont ES 400/3-5
306 E Tuolumne St 93625 559-834-6130
Glen Billington, prin. Fax 834-3241
Marshall ES 400/K-2
142 N Armstrong Ave 93625 559-834-6120
Gloria Regier, prin. Fax 834-9125
Sutter MS 500/6-8
701 E Walter Ave 93625 559-834-6180
Lori Gonzalez, prin. Fax 834-4739
Other Schools – See Fresno

Freedom, Santa Cruz, Pop. 8,361
Pajaro Valley USD
Supt. — See Watsonville
Freedom ES 600/K-6
25 Holly Dr 95019 831-728-6260
Jean Gottlob, prin. Fax 761-6196

Fremont, Alameda, Pop. 200,468
Fremont USD 31,800/K-12
PO Box 5008 94537 510-657-2350
Milton Werner Ed.D., supt. Fax 659-2597
www.fremont.k12.ca.us
Ardenwood ES 800/K-6
33955 Emilia Ln 94555 510-794-0392
Paula Rugg, prin. Fax 794-8261
Azevada ES 400/K-6
39450 Royal Palm Dr 94538 510-657-3900
Carole Diamond, prin. Fax 657-2749
Blacow ES 600/K-6
40404 Sundale Dr 94538 510-656-5121
Brad Hermann, prin. Fax 651-6933
Brier ES 600/K-6
39201 Sundale Dr 94538 510-657-5020
Jan March, prin. Fax 651-4367
Brookvale ES 500/K-6
3400 Nicolet Ave 94536 510-797-5940
Cindy Hicks, prin. Fax 797-0151
Cabrillo ES 400/K-6
36700 San Pedro Dr 94536 510-792-3232
Giselle Hudson, prin. Fax 792-0245
Centerville JHS 1,000/7-8
37720 Fremont Blvd 94536 510-797-2072
Sherry Strausbaugh, prin. Fax 794-7588
Chadbourne ES 700/K-6
801 Plymouth Ave 94539 510-656-5242
Tess Melendez, prin. Fax 656-6026
Durham ES 500/K-6
40292 Leslie St 94538 510-657-7080
Annette LeTourneau, prin. Fax 656-3092
Forest Park ES 900/K-6
34400 Maybird Cir 94555 510-713-0141
Chuck Graves, prin. Fax 713-7866
Glenmoor ES 600/K-6
4620 Mattos Dr 94536 510-797-0740
Vivian Martin, prin. Fax 797-0203
Gomes ES 900/K-6
555 Lemos Ln 94539 510-656-3414
Doug Whipple, prin. Fax 656-6817
Green ES 400/K-6
42875 Gatewood St 94538 510-656-6438
Nanci Pass, prin. Fax 656-2833
Grimmer ES 400/K-6
43030 Newport Dr 94538 510-656-1250
Donna Tonry, prin. Fax 656-2804
Hirsch ES 400/K-6
41399 Chapel Way 94538 510-657-3537
Jennifer Casey, prin. Fax 657-9574
Hopkins JHS 1,100/7-8
600 Driscoll Rd 94539 510-656-3500
Mary Miller, prin. Fax 656-3731
Horner JHS 900/7-8
41365 Chapel Way 94538 510-656-4000
Greg Bailey, prin. Fax 656-2793
Leitch ES 600/K-2
47100 Fernald St 94539 510-657-6100
Debbie Amundson, prin. Fax 659-9298
Maloney ES 500/K-6
38700 Logan Dr 94536 510-797-4422
Barbara Okuda, prin. Fax 797-1972
Mattos ES 500/K-6
37944 Farwell Dr 94536 510-793-1359
Marsha Parker, prin. Fax 793-8642
Millard ES 600/K-6
5200 Valpey Park Ave 94538 510-657-0344
Mary Anne Kolda, prin. Fax 657-8720
Mission San Jose ES 600/K-6
43545 Bryant St 94539 510-656-1200
Bonnie Curtis, prin. Fax 651-4211
Mission Valley ES 800/K-6
41700 Denise St 94539 510-656-2000
Carry Bossi, prin. Fax 226-7056
Niles ES 500/K-6
37141 2nd St 94536 510-793-1141
Jim Hough, prin. Fax 793-3742
Oliveira ES 600/K-6
4180 Alder Ave 94536 510-797-1132
Linda Anderson, prin. Fax 797-0861
Parkmont ES 800/K-6
2601 Parkside Dr 94536 510-793-7492
Marianne Schmidt, prin. Fax 793-1476
Patterson ES 600/K-6
35521 Cabrillo Dr 94536 510-793-0420
Marlene Davis, prin. Fax 793-6581
Thornton JHS 1,000/7-8
4357 Thornton Ave 94536 510-793-9090
Phyllis Hamilton, prin. Fax 793-9756
Vallejo Mill ES 500/K-6
38569 Canyon Heights Dr 94536 510-793-1441
Mary Lou Ulloa, prin. Fax 793-0564
Walters JHS 800/7-8
39600 Logan Dr 94538 510-656-7211
Vinh Lam, prin. Fax 656-4056
Warm Springs ES 700/3-6
47370 Warm Springs Blvd 94539 510-656-1611
Brett Nelson, prin. Fax 656-7682
Warwick ES 800/K-6
3375 Warwick Rd 94555 510-793-8660
Vivienne Paratore, prin. Fax 793-6041
Weibel ES 800/K-6
45135 S Grimmer Blvd 94539 510-651-6958
Genevieve Johnson, prin. Fax 651-6653

Bethel Christian Academy 50/K-8
36060 Fremont Blvd 94536 510-795-1234
William Kintner, hdmstr. Fax 742-8334
Centerville Montessori S 100/PK-3
4209 Baine Ave 94536 510-797-3634
Elizabeth Thurairatnam, prin. Fax 797-3634
Christian Community S 500/PK-8
39700 Mission Blvd 94539 510-651-5437
Tina Sevilla, admin. Fax 656-8793
Dominican K 50/K-K
PO Box 3908 94539 510-651-7978
Sr. Jane Estoesta, dir. Fax 657-1734
Fremont Christian S 1,400/PK-12
4760 Thornton Ave 94536 510-744-2249
Rev. C.K. Rankin, supt. Fax 744-2255
Holy Spirit S 400/PK-8
3930 Parish Ave 94536 510-793-3553
Susan Buchanan, prin. Fax 793-2694
Mission Hills SDA S 50/K-8
225 Driscoll Rd 94539 510-490-7709
Jim Beierle, prin.
Montessori S of Fremont 100/K-6
155 Washington Blvd 94539 510-490-0919
Cynthia Leahy, admin.
New Horizons S 200/K-8
2550 Peralta Blvd 94536 510-791-5683
Kaye Liu, pres.
Our Lady of Guadalupe S 200/K-8
40374 Fremont Blvd 94538 510-657-1674
Linda Parini, prin. Fax 657-3659
Peace Terrace Academy 100/K-8
33330 Peace Ter 94555 510-477-9946
Niloufer Wahid, prin. Fax 477-9963
Prince of Peace Lutheran S 200/PK-8
38451 Fremont Blvd 94536 510-797-8186
Marcia Houseworth, prin. Fax 793-6993
St. Joseph S 300/K-8
PO Box 3246 94539 510-656-6525
Jan Cooper, prin. Fax 656-3608
Scribbles Montessori S 100/PK-3
38660 Lexington St 94536 510-797-9944
Elizabeth Thurairatnam, prin. Fax 797-9945
Stratford S 200/K-5
5301 Curtis St 94538 510-438-9745
Ellie Tariverdi, prin. Fax 438-9749

French Camp, San Joaquin, Pop. 3,018
Manteca USD
Supt. — See Lathrop
French Camp S 700/K-8
241 E 4th St 95231 209-938-6370
Joanne Balestreri, prin. Fax 858-3004

French Gulch, Shasta
French Gulch-Whiskeytown ESD 50/K-8
PO Box 368 96033 530-359-2151
Kirk Heims, supt. Fax 359-2010
www.shastalink.k12.ca.us/frenchgulch/
French Gulch-Whiskeytown S 50/K-8
PO Box 368 96033 530-359-2151
Kirk Heims, prin. Fax 359-2010

Fresno, Fresno, Pop. 461,116
American UNESD 300/K-8
2801 W Adams Ave 93706 559-268-1213
Ed Gonzalez, supt. Fax 268-5708
www.americanunion.k12.ca.us
American S 300/K-8
2801 W Adams Ave 93706 559-268-1213
Ed Gonzalez, prin. Fax 268-5708

Central USD 12,500/K-12
4605 N Polk Ave 93722 559-274-4700
Marilou Ryder Ed.D., supt. Fax 271-8200
www.centralusd.k12.ca.us
Biola-Pershing ES 100/K-6
4885 N Biola Ave, 559-276-5235
Irene Bruno, prin. Fax 276-2151
El Capitan MS 800/7-8
4443 W Weldon Ave 93722 559-276-5270
Cheryl Coddington, prin. Fax 276-3121
Harvest ES K-6
6514 W Gettysburg Ave, 559-271-0420
Andrew Manouelian, prin. Fax 271-0767
Herndon-Barstow ES 500/K-6
6265 N Grantland Ave, 559-276-5250
Melody Burriss, prin. Fax 276-3111
Houghton-Kearney S 200/K-8
8905 W Kearney Blvd 93706 559-276-5285
Dave Holtermann, prin. Fax 264-9557
Liddell ES 700/K-6
5455 W Alluvial Ave 93722 559-276-3176
Susan Roque, prin. Fax 276-3181
Madison ES 700/K-6
330 S Brawley Ave 93706 559-276-5280
Chuck Howell, prin. Fax 276-3103
McKinley ES 800/K-6
4444 W Mckinley Ave 93722 559-276-5232
Eliseo Cuellar, prin. Fax 276-8383
Polk ES 600/K-6
2195 N Polk Ave 93722 559-274-9780
Karen Garlick, prin. Fax 274-9487
Rio Vista MS 1,300/7-8
6240 W Palo Alto Ave 93722 559-276-3185
Tim Swain, prin. Fax 276-3199
River Bluff ES 800/K-6
6150 W Palo Alto Ave 93722 559-276-6001
Leah Spate, prin. Fax 276-6006
Roosevelt ES 600/K-6
2600 N Garfield Ave, 559-276-5257
Danny Teevens, prin. Fax 277-1847
Saroyan ES 800/K-6
5650 W Escalon Ave 93722 559-276-3131
Sumer Avila, prin. Fax 276-3135
Steinbeck ES 700/K-6
3550 N Milburn Ave 93722 559-276-3141
Christine Pennington, prin. Fax 276-3145
Teague ES 700/K-6
4725 N Polk Ave 93722 559-276-5260
Gina Amaro, prin. Fax 275-9116

Clovis USD
Supt. — See Clovis
Copper Hills ES 600/K-6
1881 E Plymouth Way 93720 559-327-6300
Christine Archer, prin. Fax 327-6390
Fancher Creek ES 800/K-6
5948 E Tulare Ave 93727 559-327-6700
Kevin Kerney, prin. Fax 327-6790
Fort Washington ES 500/K-6
960 E Teague Ave 93720 559-327-6600
Ann Kalashian, prin. Fax 327-6690
Fugman ES 500/K-6
10825 N Cedar Ave, 559-327-8700
Sharon Uyeno, prin. Fax 327-8750
Granite Ridge IS 700/7-8
2770 E International Ave, 559-327-5000
Norm Anderson, prin. Fax 327-5090

Kastner IS 1,300/7-8
7676 N 1st St 93720 559-327-2500
Johnny Alvarado, prin. Fax 327-2790
Liberty ES 500/K-6
1250 E Liberty Hill Rd 93720 559-327-7100
George Petersen, prin. Fax 327-7190
Lincoln ES 600/K-6
774 E Alluvial Ave 93720 559-327-7200
Roann Carpenter, prin. Fax 327-7290
Maple Creek ES 800/K-6
2025 E Teague Ave 93720 559-327-7300
Gina Kismet, prin. Fax 327-7390
Mountain View ES 800/K-6
2002 E Alluvial Ave 93720 559-327-7500
Monica Everson, prin. Fax 327-7590
Riverview ES 700/K-6
2491 E Behymer Ave, 559-327-8600
Kristie Wiens, prin. Fax 327-8660
Temperance-Kutner ES 600/K-6
1448 N Armstrong Ave 93727 559-327-8100
Randy Hein, prin. Fax 327-8190
Valley Oak ES 500/K-6
465 E Champlain Dr, 559-327-8200
Jennifer Watson, prin. Fax 327-8290

Fowler USD
Supt. — See Fowler
Malaga ES 200/K-5
3910 S Ward Ave 93725 559-834-6140
Danell Stepp, prin. Fax 264-1904

Fresno USD 75,700/PK-12
2309 Tulare St 93721 559-457-3000
Michael Hanson, supt. Fax 457-3786
www.fresno.k12.ca.us/
Addams ES 900/K-6
2117 W McKinley Ave 93728 559-457-2510
Juanita Varela, prin. Fax 495-0311
Ahwahnee MS 600/7-8
1127 E Escalon Ave 93710 559-451-4300
Lisa DeLeon, prin. Fax 439-1808
Anthony ES 500/K-6
1542 E Webster Ave 93728 559-457-2520
Kim Collins, prin. Fax 485-1177
Ayer ES 700/K-6
5272 E Lowe Ave 93727 559-253-6400
Lynn Rocha-Salazar, prin. Fax 452-0553
Aynesworth ES 1,000/K-6
4765 E Burns Ave 93725 559-253-6410
Ermelinda Sanchez, prin. Fax 253-6413
Baird MS 600/5-8
5500 N Maroa Ave 93704 559-451-4310
Janetta McGensy, prin. Fax 432-4075
Bakman ES, 580 N Helm Ave 93727 500/K-6
Mike Jones, prin. 559-253-6610
Balderas ES 700/K-6
4625 E Florence Ave 93725 559-253-6420
Robert Stiffler, prin. Fax 253-6424
Birney ES 800/K-6
3034 E Cornell Ave 93703 559-248-7000
Margaret Navarrette, prin. Fax 244-0433
Bullard Project Talent S 700/K-8
4950 N Harrison Ave 93704 559-248-7030
Sue Fuentes, prin. Fax 248-7032
Burroughs ES 1,000/K-6
166 N Sierra Vista Ave 93702 559-253-6430
Misty Her, prin. Fax 253-6431
Calwa ES 700/K-6
4303 E Jensen Ave 93725 559-457-2610
Rosalinda Gutierrez, prin. Fax 266-2021
Carver Academy 400/5-8
2463 Martin L King Jr Blvd 93706 559-457-2620
Stephen Morris, prin. Fax 497-5336
Centennial ES 800/K-6
3830 E Saginaw Way 93726 559-248-7040
David Gonzalez, prin. Fax 248-7043
Columbia ES 500/K-6
1025 S Trinity St 93706 559-457-2630
Terri Edwards, prin. Fax 495-1210
Computech MS 800/7-8
555 E Belgravia Ave 93706 559-457-2640
Fax 457-2643
Cooper MS 700/7-8
2277 W Bellaire Way 93705 559-248-7050
Scott Lamm, prin. Fax 224-7255
Del Mar ES 600/K-6
4122 N Del Mar Ave 93704 559-248-7070
Reynaldo Villalobos, prin. Fax 225-3850
Easterby ES 900/K-6
5211 E Tulare Ave 93727 559-253-6440
Greg Brock Jones, prin. Fax 253-6442
Eaton ES 500/K-6
1451 E Sierra Ave 93710 559-451-4470
Lisa Harrington, prin. Fax 261-2170
Ericson ES 700/K-6
4774 E Yale Ave 93703 559-253-6450
Karen Walker, prin. Fax 452-8834
Ewing ES 800/K-6
4873 E Olive Ave 93727 559-451-4480
Stephanie Collom, prin. Fax 252-7533
Figarden ES 700/K-6
6235 N Brawley Ave 93722 559-451-4480
Larry Petersen, prin. Fax 437-9411
Forkner ES 500/K-6
7120 N Valentine Ave 93711 559-451-4490
Kay Davies, prin. Fax 457-4492
Ft. Miller MS 900/7-8
1302 E Dakota Ave 93704 559-248-7100
Debbie Buckman, prin. Fax 221-7548
Fremont ES 500/K-6
1005 W Weldon Ave 93705 559-457-2910
Deborah Schlueter, prin. Fax 266-1264
Gibson ES 400/K-6
1266 W Barstow Ave 93711 559-451-4500
Helen Cabe, prin. Fax 451-4503
Greenberg ES 900/K-6
5081 E Lane Ave 93727 559-253-6550
Katie Russell, prin. Fax 253-6555

Hamilton S, 102 E Clinton Ave 93704 600/K-6
Bobbi Hanada, prin. 559-248-7370
Heaton ES 700/K-6
1533 N San Pablo Ave 93728 559-457-2920
Carla Hartunian, prin. Fax 495-0422
Hidalgo ES 600/K-6
3550 E Thomas Ave 93702 559-457-2930
Jack Jarvis, prin. Fax 457-2931
Holland ES 500/K-6
4676 N Fresno St 93726 559-248-7140
Phyllis Grossman, prin. Fax 224-2594
Homan ES 800/K-6
1602 W Harvard Ave 93705 559-457-2940
Suzanne Webster-Jones, prin. Fax 266-1079
Jackson ES 500/K-6
3733 E Kerckhoff Ave 93702 559-457-2950
Tom Fuentes, prin. Fax 498-0335
Jefferson ES 500/K-6
202 N Mariposa St 93701 559-457-2960
Edward Gomes, prin. Fax 457-2963
King ES 500/K-6
1001 E Florence Ave 93706 559-457-2970
Faith Medina, prin. Fax 497-6442
Kings Canyon MS 1,000/7-8
5117 E Tulare Ave 93727 559-253-6470
Clark Mello, prin. Fax 253-1005
Kirk ES 400/K-6
2000 E Belgravia Ave 93706 559-457-2980
Carla Manning, prin. Fax 497-8511
Kratt ES 600/K-6
650 W Sierra Ave 93704 559-451-4510
Terri Bricker, prin. Fax 436-8577
Lane ES 800/K-6
4730 E Lowe Ave 93702 559-253-6480
Rosemary Baiz, prin. Fax 456-2916
Lawless S 700/K-8
5255 N Reese Ave 93722 559-451-4520
John Maurer, prin. Fax 271-1885
Leavenworth ES 900/K-6
4420 E Thomas Ave 93702 559-253-6490
Jan Zoller, prin. Fax 253-6491
Lincoln ES 500/K-6
1100 Mono St 93706 559-457-3010
Rosario Sanchez, prin. Fax 495-1134
Lowell ES 500/K-6
171 N Poplar Ave 93701 559-457-3020
Miguel Narajo, prin. Fax 498-8614
Malloch ES 500/K-6
2251 W Morris Ave 93711 559-451-4530
Robert Avedesian, prin. Fax 451-4533
Manchester GATE ES 700/2-6
2307 E Dakota Ave 93726 559-248-7220
Russ Painter, prin. Fax 222-8854
Mayfair ES 800/K-6
3305 E Home Ave 93703 559-457-3140
Bill Serns, prin. Fax 268-0134
McCardle ES 500/K-6
577 E Sierra Ave 93710 559-451-4540
Kathy Dennen, prin. Fax 447-1125
Muir ES 600/K-6
410 E Dennett Ave 93728 559-457-3150
Virginia Mendez-Buelna, prin. Fax 443-5172
Norseman ES 900/K-6
4636 E Weldon Ave 93703 559-253-6500
Joy Nunes, prin. Fax 253-1778
Olmos ES 800/K-6
550 S Garden Ave 93727 559-253-6620
Teresa Calderon, prin. Fax 253-6622
Powers/Ginsberg ES 500/PK-6
110 E Swift Ave 93704 559-248-7230
Janet Melton, prin. Fax 225-7316
Pyle ES 700/K-6
4140 N Augusta St 93726 559-248-7240
Cindy Ferdinandi, prin. Fax 248-7246
Robinson ES 400/K-6
555 E Browning Ave 93710 559-451-4550
Denver Stairs, prin. Fax 435-2711
Roeding ES 800/K-6
1225 W Dakota Ave 93705 559-248-7250
Rob Gaertig, prin. Fax 225-3234
Rowell ES 900/K-6
3460 E McKenzie Ave 93702 559-457-3200
John Martinez, prin. Fax 498-6315
Scandinavian MS 800/7-8
3232 N Sierra Vista Ave 93726 559-253-6510
Julie Goorabian-Raley, prin. Fax 252-7608
Sequoia MS 800/7-8
4050 E Hamilton Ave 93702 559-457-3210
Mike Ribera, prin. Fax 497-1745
Slater ES 900/K-6
4472 N Emerson Ave 93705 559-248-7260
Joan Steinhauer, prin. Fax 244-0432
Starr ES 400/K-6
1780 W Sierra Ave 93711 559-451-4560
Kathleen Scott, prin. Fax 446-0421
Storey ES 800/K-6
5250 E Church Ave 93725 559-253-6530
Bruce Thele, prin. Fax 253-6535
Tehipite MS 700/7-8
630 N Augusta St 93701 559-457-3420
Richard Pascual, prin. Fax 457-3423
Tenaya MS 1,000/7-8
1239 W Mesa Ave 93711 559-451-4570
Elizabeth Hayden, prin. Fax 431-0771
Terronez MS 900/7-8
2300 S Willow Ave 93725 559-253-6570
Fax 253-6572
Thomas ES 700/K-6
4444 N Millbrook Ave 93726 559-248-7270
Bob Nelson, prin. Fax 228-1933
Tioga MS 800/7-8
3232 E Fairmont Ave 93726 559-248-7280
Ray Avila, prin. Fax 226-1296
Turner ES 800/K-6
5218 E Clay Ave 93727 559-253-6540
Steve Gettman, prin. Fax 253-1303

Viking ES 700/K-6
4251 N Winery Ave 93726 559-248-7290
Ron Bohigian, prin. Fax 291-1960
Vinland ES 500/K-6
4666 N Maple Ave 93726 559-248-7300
Mary Bailey-Dougherty, prin. Fax 294-7331
Wawona MS 800/7-8
4524 N Thorne Ave 93704 559-248-7310
Mike Darling, prin. Fax 227-5206
Webster ES 400/K-6
930 N Augusta St 93701 559-457-3430
Noe Cruz, prin. Fax 266-2277
Williams ES K-6
525 W Saginaw Way 93705 559-248-7540
Karen Osbourne, prin.
Wilson ES 900/K-6
2131 W Ashlan Ave 93705 559-248-7320
Melissa Dutra, prin. Fax 221-8373
Winchell ES 900/K-6
3722 E Lowe Ave 93702 559-457-3440
Mike Perez, prin. Fax 266-5755
Wishon ES 700/K-6
3857 E Harvard Ave 93703 559-248-7330
Dr. Davinder Sidhu, prin. Fax 248-7331
Wolters ES 600/K-6
5174 N 1st St 93710 559-248-7340
Debbie Hawkins, prin. Fax 225-2235
Yokomi ES 700/K-6
2323 E McKenzie Ave 93701 559-457-6140
Steven Gonzalez, prin. Fax 457-6142
Yosemite MS 800/7-8
1292 N 9th St 93703 559-457-3450
Kathy Chambas, prin. Fax 264-0933

Monroe ESD 200/K-8
11842 S Chestnut Ave 93725 559-834-2895
Shelley Manser, supt. Fax 834-1085
www.monroe.k12.ca.us/
Monroe S 200/K-8
11842 S Chestnut Ave 93725 559-834-2895
Shelley Manser, prin. Fax 834-1085

Orange Center ESD 300/K-8
3530 S Cherry Ave 93706 559-237-0437
John Stahl, supt. Fax 237-9380
www.orangecenter.org/
Orange Center S 300/K-8
3530 S Cherry Ave 93706 559-237-0437
John Stahl, prin. Fax 237-9380

Pacific UNESD 400/K-8
2065 E Bowles Ave 93725 559-834-2533
Warren Jennings, supt. Fax 834-6433
www.pacificunion.k12.ca.us/
Pacific Union S 400/K-8
2065 E Bowles Ave 93725 559-834-2533
Warren Jennings, prin. Fax 834-6433

Sanger USD
Supt. — See Sanger
Lone Star ES 500/K-6
2617 S Fowler Ave 93725 559-268-8064
Dick Larimer, prin. Fax 268-8452
Wash ES 300/K-6
6350 E Lane Ave 93727 559-251-7543
Wesley Sever, prin. Fax 251-2643

Washington Colony ESD 400/K-8
130 E Lincoln Ave 93706 559-233-0706
Dale Drew, supt. Fax 233-9583
www.wcesd.org/
Washington Colony S 400/K-8
130 E Lincoln Ave 93706 559-233-0706
Dale Drew, prin. Fax 233-9583

West Fresno ESD 900/PK-8
2888 S Ivy Ave 93706 559-495-5600
Dolphas Trotter, supt. Fax 495-5608
www.westfresno.net/
West Fresno ES 600/K-5
2910 S Ivy Ave 93706 559-495-5615
Armando Ayala, dir. Fax 233-6446
West Fresno MS 300/6-8
2888 S Ivy Ave 93706 559-495-5607
Joey Adame, prin. Fax 485-3006
West Fresno Preschool PK-PK
2888 S Ivy Ave 93706 559-495-5606
Jan Breazell, dir.

West Park ESD 300/K-8
2695 S Valentine Ave 93706 559-233-6501
Ralph Vigil, supt. Fax 233-8626
www.westpark.k12.ca.us
West Park S 300/K-8
2695 S Valentine Ave 93706 559-233-6501
Steven Irby, prin. Fax 233-8626

Carden S of Fresno 200/PK-8
6901 N Maple Ave Ste 101 93710 559-323-0126
Fax 323-0980
Central Valley Christian Academy 100/K-12
4147 E Dakota Ave 93726 559-226-4644
Timothe Addelsee, prin. Fax 248-2775
First Church Christian Academy 200/PK-8
3920 N 1st St 93726 559-227-3222
Lisa Pielstick, admin. Fax 227-0723
Fresno Adventist Academy 200/K-12
5397 E Olive Ave 93727 559-251-5548
Daniel Kittle, prin. Fax 456-1735
Fresno Christian S - Northeast Campus 100/K-2
7280 N Cedar Ave 93720 559-292-7704
Pat Unruh, prin. Fax 299-1051
Fresno Christian S - Peoples Campus 600/3-12
7280 N Cedar Ave 93720 559-299-1695
Jon Endicott, prin. Fax 299-1051
Mountain View Christian S 100/PK-6
1284 E Bullard Ave 93710 559-435-2923
Bev Drury, prin. Fax 435-6140

Next Level Christian Academy 50/PK-1
735 E Church Ave 93706 559-824-9677
Mikol Brown, dir. Fax 266-1764
Our Lady of Victory S 200/PK-8
1626 W Princeton Ave 93705 559-229-0205
Joan Bouchard, prin. Fax 229-3230
Sacred Heart S 100/PK-8
4460 E Yale Ave 93703 559-251-3171
Sr. Kathleen Drilling, prin. Fax 251-7778
St. Anthony S 600/K-8
5680 N Maroa Ave 93704 559-435-0700
Tim McConnico, prin. Fax 435-6749
St. Helen S 300/PK-8
4888 E Belmont Ave 93727 559-251-5855
Dr. Toni Amodio, prin. Fax 251-5948
Truth Tabernacle Christian S 100/K-12
PO Box 5393 93755 559-225-1027
Diane Estes, prin. Fax 225-0465

Fullerton, Orange, Pop. 132,787

Fullerton SD 13,600/K-8
1401 W Valencia Dr 92833 714-447-7400
Mitch Hovey Ed.D., supt. Fax 447-7414
www.fsd.k12.ca.us
Acacia ES 500/K-6
1200 N Acacia Ave 92831 714-447-7700
Sue Faassen, prin. Fax 447-7595
Beechwood S 600/K-8
780 Beechwood Ave 92835 714-447-2850
Ramon Miramontes, prin. Fax 447-2853
Commonwealth ES 400/K-6
2200 E Commonwealth Ave 92831 714-447-7705
Sherry Hoyt, prin. Fax 447-7777
Fern Drive ES 500/K-6
1400 W Fern Dr 92833 714-447-7710
Gaye Besler, prin. Fax 447-7452
Fisler S 800/K-8
1350 Starbuck St 92833 714-447-2890
Jackie Pearce, prin. Fax 447-2893
Golden Hill ES 700/K-6
732 Barris Dr 92832 714-447-7715
Robert Johnson, prin. Fax 447-2881
Hermosa Drive ES 400/K-6
400 E Hermosa Dr 92835 714-447-7720
Robin Gilligan, prin. Fax 447-7723
Ladera Vista JHS 900/7-8
1700 E Wilshire Ave 92831 714-447-7765
Margy Price, prin. Fax 447-7554
Laguna Road ES 600/K-6
300 Laguna Rd 92835 714-447-7725
Harold Sullivan, prin. Fax 447-7432
Maple ES 400/K-6
244 E Valencia Dr 92832 714-447-7590
Susan Mercado, prin. Fax 447-7546
Nicolas JHS 1,000/7-8
1100 W Olive Ave 92833 714-447-7775
Mathew Barnett, prin. Fax 447-7586
Orangethorpe ES 900/K-6
1400 S Brookhurst Rd 92833 714-447-7730
Ken Valburg, prin. Fax 447-7527
Pacific Drive ES 700/K-6
1501 W Valencia Dr 92833 714-447-7735
Gretchen Francisco, prin. Fax 447-7585
Parks JHS 1,000/7-8
1710 Rosecrans Ave 92833 714-447-7785
Sherry Dustin, prin. Fax 447-7753
Raymond ES 500/K-6
517 N Raymond Ave 92831 714-447-7740
Yolanda McComb, prin. Fax 447-2802
Richman ES 800/K-6
700 S Richman Ave 92832 714-447-7745
Estella Grimm, prin. Fax 447-7769
Rolling Hills ES 500/K-6
1460 Rolling Hills Dr 92835 714-447-7795
Randa Schmalfeld, prin. Fax 447-7704
Sunset Lane ES 800/K-6
2030 Sunset Ln 92833 714-447-7750
Paula Pitluk, prin. Fax 447-7768
Valencia Park ES 800/K-6
3441 W Valencia Dr 92833 714-447-7755
Linda Moser, prin. Fax 447-2868
Woodcrest ES 500/K-6
455 W Baker Ave 92832 714-447-7760
Alfonso Jimenez, prin. Fax 447-7724

Placentia-Yorba Linda USD
Supt. — See Placentia
Topaz ES 500/K-6
3232 Topaz Ln 92831 714-993-9977
Rafael Plascencia, prin. Fax 993-1284

Annunciation S 100/PK-5
215 S Pine Dr 92833 714-871-6121
Clara Ann Habich, admin. Fax 992-4167
Eastside Christian S 500/PK-12
2505 Yorba Linda Blvd 92831 714-879-2187
David Schoen, supt. Fax 526-5074
Ivycrest Montessori Private S 100/K-6
2025 E Chapman Ave 92831 714-879-6091
Aida King, dir. Fax 879-1921
St. Juliana Falconieri S 300/K-8
1320 N Acacia Ave 92831 714-871-2829
Mary Santoni, prin. Fax 526-6673
West Fullerton Christian S 100/1-8
2353 W Valencia Dr 92833 714-526-5039
Jacinda Gonzales, prin. Fax 526-7761

Galt, Sacramento, Pop. 23,173

Galt JUNESD 3,100/K-8
1018 C St Ste 210 95632 209-744-4545
Karen Schauer, supt. Fax 744-4553
www.galt.k12.ca.us/
Greer ES 200/K-6
248 W A St 95632 209-745-2641
Emily Peckham, prin. Fax 745-9202
Lake Canyon ES 400/K-6
800 Lake Canyon Ave 95632 209-744-5200
Suzanne Souligny, prin. Fax 745-5014
Marengo Ranch ES 600/K-6
1000 Elk Hills Dr 95632 209-745-5470
Terry Metzger, prin. Fax 745-5474
McCaffrey MS 500/7-8
997 Park Terrace Dr 95632 209-745-5462
Ron Rammer, prin. Fax 745-5465
River Oaks ES 600/K-6
905 Vintage Oak Ave 95632 209-745-4614
Lois Yount, prin. Fax 745-7817
Valley Oaks ES 800/K-6
21 C St 95632 209-745-1564
Annette Lane, prin. Fax 744-4565

Galt Adventist Christian S 50/K-8
619 Myrtle Ave 95632 209-745-3577
Janice Deibel, prin. Fax 745-1971
Galt Christian S 100/K-8
801 Church St 95632 209-745-3316
Orlando Morazan, admin. Fax 745-0705
Valley Christian S 50/K-10
501 B St 95632 209-745-2049
Denise Much, admin. Fax 745-9009

Garberville, Humboldt

Southern Humbolt JUSD
Supt. — See Miranda
Ettersburg ES 50/K-3
4500 Ettersburg Rd 95542 707-986-7677
Susie Jennings, prin. Fax 986-7677

Gardena, Los Angeles, Pop. 59,891

Los Angeles USD
Supt. — See Los Angeles
Amestoy ES 900/K-5
1048 W 149th St 90247 310-327-5592
Hugh Ryan, prin. Fax 719-8710
Chapman ES 400/K-5
1947 Marine Ave 90249 310-324-2275
Cindy Miller, prin. Fax 327-3898
Denker ES 800/K-5
1620 W 162nd St 90247 310-327-9420
Cindy Ahn, prin. Fax 324-6949
Gardena ES 800/K-5
647 W Gardena Blvd 90247 310-324-6967
Christy McCartney, prin. Fax 217-1876
186th Street ES 800/K-5
1581 W 186th St 90248 310-324-1153
Marcia Reed, prin. Fax 323-0388
156th Street ES 300/K-5
2100 W 156th St 90249 310-324-6639
Esther Kim, prin. Fax 532-2306
153rd Street ES 600/K-5
1605 W 153rd St 90247 310-323-1029
Albert Lozano, prin. Fax 769-5742
135th Street ES 800/K-5
801 W 135th St 90247 310-324-4454
Antonio Camacho, prin. Fax 538-4976
Peary MS 2,500/6-8
1415 W Gardena Blvd 90247 310-225-4200
L. Gail Garrett, prin. Fax 329-3957
Purche Avenue ES 600/K-5
13210 Purche Ave 90249 310-323-3184
Thaddus Jackson, prin. Fax 532-0967

CrossRoad Christian Academy 300/PK-8
2818 Manhattan Beach Blvd 90249 310-327-3094
Dr. Robert Bowman, hdmstr. Fax 327-8543
Gardena Valley Christian S 300/K-8
1473 W 182nd St 90248 310-327-4987
Judy Pickens, prin. Fax 327-2110
Maria Regina S 300/K-8
13510 Van Ness Ave 90249 310-327-9133
Lynette Lino, prin. Fax 327-2636
St. Anthony of Padua S 200/PK-8
1003 W 163rd St 90247 310-329-7170
Maria Cunanan, prin. Fax 329-9843

Garden Grove, Orange, Pop. 166,075

Garden Grove USD 48,000/K-12
10331 Stanford Ave 92840 714-663-6000
Laura Schwalm Ph.D., supt. Fax 663-6100
www.ggusd.k12.ca.us
Alamitos IS 900/7-8
12381 Dale St 92841 714-663-6101
Bill Gates, prin. Fax 663-6277
Barker ES 300/K-6
12565 Springdale St 92845 714-663-6164
Susie Dollbaum, prin. Fax 663-6016
Bell IS 800/7-8
12345 Springdale St 92845 714-663-6466
Lorraine Rae, prin. Fax 663-6238
Brookhurst ES 500/K-6
9821 Catherine Ave 92841 714-663-6556
Lynn Cudd, prin. Fax 663-6019
Bryant ES 600/K-6
8371 Orangewood Ave 92841 714-663-6451
Monica Acosta, prin. Fax 663-6014
Clinton-Mendenhall ES 700/K-6
13641 Clinton St 92843 714-663-6146
Carrie Mitchell Ed.D., prin. Fax 663-6481
Cook ES 400/K-6
9802 Woodbury Ave 92844 714-663-6251
Melissa Sais, prin. Fax 663-6087
Crosby ES 500/K-6
12181 West St 92840 714-663-6346
Don Terreri, prin. Fax 663-6553
Doig IS, 12752 Trask Ave 92843 900/7-8
Jason Bevacqua, prin. 714-663-6241
Eisenhower ES, 13221 Lilly St 92843 600/K-6
Jay Camerino, prin. 714-663-6401
Enders ES 600/K-6
12302 Springdale St 92845 714-663-6205
Gloria Spelber, prin. Fax 663-6220
Evans ES 600/K-6
12281 Nelson St 92840 714-663-6558
Wayne Kelley, prin. Fax 663-6496
Excelsior ES 600/K-6
10421 Woodbury Rd 92843 714-663-6106
Kim Kroyer, prin.
Faylane ES, 11731 Morrie Ln 92840 600/K-6
Thorsten Hegberg, prin. 714-663-6253
Garden Park ES 300/K-6
6562 Stanford Ave 92845 714-663-6074
Gary Gerstner, prin. Fax 663-6076
Gilbert ES 700/K-6
9551 Orangewood Ave 92841 714-663-6318
Beth Cusimano, prin. Fax 663-6067
Hill ES 400/K-6
9681 11th St 92844 714-663-6561
Marie Kennedy, prin. Fax 663-6499
Irvine IS 900/7-8
10552 Hazard Ave 92843 714-663-6551
Betsy Arns, prin. Fax 663-6013
Jordan IS 700/7-8
9821 Woodbury Ave 92844 714-663-6124
Steve Osborne, prin. Fax 663-6123
Lake IS 600/7-8
10801 Orangewood Ave 92840 714-663-6506
Dave Biniasz, prin. Fax 663-6065
Lawrence ES, 12521 Monroe St 92841 600/K-6
Valerie Shedd, prin. 714-663-6255
Mitchell ES 600/K-6
13451 Taft St 92843 714-663-6131
Kathy Roe, prin. Fax 663-6025
Morningside ES 600/K-6
10521 Morningside Dr 92843 714-663-6328
Gail Sugamura, prin. Fax 663-6033
Murdy ES, 14851 Donegal Dr 92844 500/K-6
Marc Patterson, prin. 714-663-6405
Paine ES 500/K-6
15792 Ward St 92843 714-663-6118
Lisa Chavez, prin. Fax 663-6035
Parkview ES 600/K-6
12272 Wilken Way 92840 714-663-6266
Joy Ellsworth, prin. Fax 663-6066
Patton ES 900/K-6
6861 Santa Rita Ave 92845 714-663-6584
Linda Chrystal, prin. Fax 663-6034
Peters 4-6 ES 4-6
13200 Newhope St 92843 714-663-6070
Adam Bernstein, prin. Fax 663-6072
Peters ES 600/K-3
13162 Newhope St 92843 714-663-6085
Barbara Batson, prin. Fax 663-6570
Ralston IS 600/7-8
10851 Lampson Ave 92840 714-663-6366
Jan Cody, prin. Fax 638-7155
Riverdale ES, 13222 Lewis St 92843 600/K-6
Bonnie Strand, prin. 714-663-6563
Simmons ES, 11602 Steele Dr 92840 500/K-6
Omaire Lee, prin. 714-663-6096
Skylark ES 600/K-6
11250 MacMurray St 92841 714-663-6336
Jesus Vasquez, prin. Fax 663-6135
Stanford ES, 12721 Magnolia St 92841 600/K-6
Trena Gonzalez, prin. 714-663-6458
Stanley ES 400/K-6
12201 Elmwood St 92840 714-663-6484
Jorge Velastegui, prin. Fax 663-6073
Sunnyside ES 600/K-6
9972 Russell Ave 92844 714-663-6158
Eileen Young, prin.
Violette ES 600/K-6
12091 Lampson Ave 92840 714-663-6203
Janet Luya, prin. Fax 663-6023
Wakeham ES 400/K-6
7772 Chapman Ave 92841 714-663-6407
Alicia Corulla, prin. Fax 897-7214
Walton IS 800/7-8
12181 Buaro St 92840 714-663-6040
Kelly McAmis, prin. Fax 534-4814
Warren ES 600/K-6
12871 Estock Dr 92840 714-663-6331
Terey Kroy, prin. Fax 663-6012
Woodbury ES 600/K-6
11362 Woodbury Rd 92843 714-663-6461
Edie Smith, prin. Fax 663-6463
Zeyen ES 500/K-6
12081 Magnolia St 92841 714-663-6535
Emma Druitt, prin. Fax 663-6039
Other Schools – See Fountain Valley, Santa Ana, Stanton, Westminster

Orange USD
Supt. — See Orange
Lampson ES 800/K-5
13321 Lampson Ave 92840 714-997-6153
Laurie Dieppa, prin. Fax 971-8516

Westminster ESD
Supt. — See Westminster
Anderson ES 700/PK-6
8902 Hewitt Pl 92844 714-894-7201
Lori Rogers, prin. Fax 895-7804
Meairs ES 600/PK-5
8441 Trask Ave 92844 714-638-0450
Trish Urbaniec, prin. Fax 638-0127

Crystal Cathedral Academy 400/PK-12
13280 Chapman Ave 92840 714-971-4158
Dr. Sheila Coleman, supt. Fax 971-4028
Hope Christian Academy 200/K-12
12211 Magnolia St 92841 714-534-6733
Deborah Haller, dir. Fax 534-6707
King of Kings Lutheran S 100/K-8
13431 Newhope St 92843 714-530-2152
Karl Grebe, prin. Fax 530-6553
Montessori Greenhouse S 300/PK-6
5856 Belgrave Ave 92845 714-897-3833
Catherine Smythe, prin. Fax 892-8595
Orange Crescent S 400/K-8
1 Al Rahman Plz 92844 714-531-1451
Nehad Ahmed, prin.

Orangewood Adventist Academy 300/PK-12
13732 Clinton St 92843 714-534-4694
Ruben Escalante, prin. Fax 534-5931

St. Callistus S 300/PK-8
12901 Lewis St 92840 714-971-2023
Margaret Meland, prin. Fax 971-2031

St. Columban S 200/K-8
10855 Stanford Ave 92840 714-534-3947
Fax 590-9153

St. Paul Lutheran S 200/PK-8
13082 Bowen St 92843 714-534-6320
Carol Smallwood, prin. Fax 741-8353

Gasquet, Del Norte

Del Norte County USD
Supt. — See Crescent City

Mountain ES 50/K-5
PO Box 25 95543 707-457-3211
Jeff Slayton, prin. Fax 457-3902

Gaviota, Santa Barbara, Pop. 70

Vista del Mar UNESD 100/K-8
9467 San Julian Rd 93117 805-686-1880
Gregory Pruitt, supt. Fax 686-8536

Vista de Las Cruces S 100/K-8
9467 San Julian Rd 93117 805-686-1880
Gregory Pruitt, prin. Fax 686-8536

Gazelle, Siskiyou

Gazelle UNESD 100/K-8
PO Box 6 96034 530-435-2321
Jeannette Eiler, supt. Fax 435-2298
www.sisnet.ssku.k12.ca.us/~gazelftp/

Gazelle S 100/K-8
PO Box 6 96034 530-435-2321
Jeannette Eiler, prin. Fax 435-2298

Georgetown, El Dorado

Black Oak Mine USD 1,800/K-12
PO Box 4510 95634 530-333-8300
Roger Yohe, supt. Fax 333-8303
www.bomusd.org/

Georgetown S 400/K-8
PO Box 4630 95634 530-333-8320
Karen Shadle, prin. Fax 333-8324

Otter Creek ES 50/K-5
PO Box 4316 95634 530-333-8347
Karen Shadle, prin. Fax 333-8347

Other Schools – See Cool

Gerber, Tehama, Pop. 1,143

Gerber UNESD 400/K-8
23014 Chard Ave 96035 530-385-1041
Rod Stone, supt. Fax 385-1451
www.tcde.tehama.k12.ca.us/gerberusd.html

Gerber S 400/K-8
23014 Chard Ave 96035 530-385-1041
Rod Stone, prin. Fax 385-1451

Geyserville, Sonoma

Geyserville USD 300/K-12
1300 Moody Ln 95441 707-857-3592
Joseph Carnation, supt. Fax 857-3071
www.gusd.com

Geyserville ES 100/K-5
21485 Geyserville Ave 95441 707-857-3410
Tonya Giusso, prin. Fax 857-3072

Geyserville MS 100/6-8
1300 Moody Ln 95441 707-857-3592
Katherine Hadden, prin. Fax 857-3071

Gilroy, Santa Clara, Pop. 45,718

Gilroy USD 9,900/K-12
7810 Arroyo Cir 95020 408-847-2700
Deborah Flores, supt. Fax 847-4717
www.gusd.k12.ca.us

Aprea Fundamental ES 800/K-5
9225 Calle del Rey 95020 408-842-3135
Richard Rodriguez, prin. Fax 846-7541

Brownell MS 700/6-8
7800 Carmel St 95020 408-847-3377
Greg Camacho Light, prin. Fax 846-7521

Del Buono ES 700/K-5
9300 Wren Ave 95020 408-848-5161
Velia Codiga, prin. Fax 846-6833

Eliot ES 500/K-5
475 Old Gilroy St 95020 408-842-5618
James Dent, prin. Fax 846-7531

El Roble ES 600/K-5
930 3rd St 95020 408-842-8234
Leigh Schwartz, prin. Fax 842-3874

Glen View ES 600/K-5
600 W 8th St 95020 408-842-8292
Scott Otteson, prin. Fax 842-1237

Kelley ES 700/K-5
8755 Kern Ave 95020 408-847-1932
Luis Carrillo, prin. Fax 847-5562

Las Animas ES 500/K-5
6550 Cimino St 95020 408-842-6414
Silvia Reyes, prin. Fax 842-3374

Rucker ES 500/K-5
325 Santa Clara Ave 95020 408-842-6471
Barbara Keesaw, prin. Fax 842-3563

Solorsano MS 800/6-8
7121 Grenache Way 95020 408-848-4121
Sal Tomasello, prin. Fax 848-7121

South Valley MS 800/6-8
385 I O O F Ave 95020 408-847-2828
Greg Kapaku, prin. Fax 847-5708

Pacific West Christian Academy 300/K-8
1575A Mantelli Dr 95020 408-847-7922
Donna Garcia, prin. Fax 847-3003

St. Mary S 300/K-8
7900 Church St 95020 408-842-2827
Christa Hanson, prin. Fax 847-7679

Glendale, Los Angeles, Pop. 200,065

Glendale USD 27,000/K-12
223 N Jackson St 91206 818-241-3111
Michael Escalante Ed.D., supt. Fax 548-9041
www.gusd.net/

Balboa ES 600/K-6
1844 Bel Aire Dr 91201 818-241-1801
Linda Russo Milano, prin. Fax 241-5557

Cerritos ES 500/K-6
120 E Cerritos Ave 91205 818-244-7207
Janice Hanada, prin. Fax 247-2532

Columbus ES 700/K-6
425 Milford St 91203 818-242-7722
Beatriz Bautista, prin. Fax 247-2542

Edison ES 700/K-6
435 S Pacific Ave 91204 818-241-1807
Kelly King Ed.D., prin. Fax 241-8028

Franklin ES 400/K-6
1610 Lake St 91201 818-243-1809
Stephen Williams, prin. Fax 552-5097

Fremont ES 600/K-6
3320 Las Palmas Ave 91208 818-249-3241
Cynthia Livingston Ed.D., prin. Fax 249-7921

Glenoaks ES 600/K-6
2015 E Glenoaks Blvd 91206 818-242-3747
Cynthia McCarty Ed.D., prin. Fax 247-4423

Jefferson ES 500/K-6
1540 5th St 91201 818-243-4279
Greg Mooshagian, prin. Fax 551-1069

Keppel ES 900/K-6
730 Glenwood Rd 91202 818-244-2113
Mary Mason Ed.D., prin. Fax 507-6542

Mann ES 800/K-5
501 E Acacia Ave 91205 818-246-2421
Rosa Alonso, prin. Fax 507-6238

Marshall ES 700/K-6
1201 E Broadway 91205 818-242-6834
Jacqueline Mora, prin. Fax 242-1761

Muir ES 900/K-6
912 S Chevy Chase Dr 91205 818-241-4848
Linda Junge Ed.D., prin. Fax 241-1058

Roosevelt MS 900/7-8
1017 S Glendale Ave 91205 818-242-6845
Lynn Marso, prin. Fax 552-5188

Toll MS 1,100/7-8
700 Glenwood Rd 91202 818-244-8414
Paula Nelson Ed.D., prin. Fax 500-1487

Verdugo Woodlands ES 600/K-6
1751 N Verdugo Rd 91208 818-241-2433
Janet Buhl, prin. Fax 548-4173

White ES 800/K-6
744 E Doran St 91206 818-241-2164
Suzanne Risse, prin. Fax 409-8974

Wilson MS 1,000/7-8
1221 Monterey Rd 91206 818-244-8145
Richard Lucas, prin. Fax 244-2050

Other Schools – See La Crescenta

A Plus Adventist S 50/K-1
234 N Isabel St 91206 818-241-9353
Jeanie Drake, prin. Fax 547-4824

Chamlian Armenian S 500/1-8
4444 Lowell Ave 91214 818-957-3399
Vazken Madenlian, prin. Fax 957-1827

First Lutheran S 100/PK-8
1300 E Colorado St 91205 818-244-7319
Julie Sanchez, prin. Fax 550-7563

Glendale Adventist Academy 700/K-12
700 Kimlin Dr 91206 818-244-8671
Dr. Glen Baker, prin. Fax 546-1180

Holy Family S 300/K-8
400 S Louise St 91205 818-243-9239
Marian Heintz, prin. Fax 243-0976

Incarnation S 300/K-8
123 W Glenoaks Blvd 91202 818-241-2269
Olivia Carrillo, prin. Fax 241-4734

Salem Lutheran S 200/K-6
1211 N Brand Blvd 91202 818-243-8264
Ghada Huleis, prin. Fax 243-4491

Zion Lutheran S 100/PK-7
301 N Isabel St 91206 818-243-3119
Donna Lucas, prin. Fax 243-9640

Glendora, Los Angeles, Pop. 50,540

Charter Oak USD
Supt. — See Covina

Washington ES 400/K-6
325 W Gladstone St 91740 626-914-2704
Jeanine Robertson, prin. Fax 852-7690

Willow ES 300/K-6
1427 Willow Ave 91740 626-914-5839
Mary Ireland, prin. Fax 852-7689

Glendora USD 7,600/K-12
500 N Loraine Ave 91741 626-963-1611
Catherine Nichols, supt. Fax 335-2196
www.glendora.k12.ca.us

Cullen ES 600/K-5
440 N Live Oak Ave 91741 626-852-4593
Cheryl Bonner, prin. Fax 852-4570

Goddard MS 900/6-8
859 E Sierra Madre Ave 91741 626-852-4500
Dominic DiGrazia, prin. Fax 852-4520

La Fetra ES 600/K-5
547 W Bennett Ave 91741 626-852-4566
Elizabeth Eminhizer, prin. Fax 852-4571

Sandburg MS 900/6-8
819 W Bennett Ave 91741 626-852-4530
Scott Bell, prin. Fax 852-4521

Sellers ES 500/K-5
500 N Loraine Ave 91741 626-852-4574
Steve Bishop, prin. Fax 852-4572

Stanton ES 500/K-5
725 S Vecino Dr 91740 626-852-4604
Kristina McCauley, prin. Fax 852-4573

Sutherland ES 500/K-5
1330 Amelia Ave 91740 626-852-4614
Jennifer Root, prin. Fax 852-4660

Williams ES 400/K-5
301 S Loraine Ave 91741 626-852-4586
Mary Suzuki, prin. Fax 852-4585

Foothill Christian S 600/K-8
242 W Baseline Rd 91740 626-914-1849
Robert Gutzwiller, supt. Fax 914-5940

Foothill Christian S 200/3-5
901 S Grand Ave 91740 626-335-4035
Robert Gutzwiller, supt. Fax 963-4599

Grace Preschool 100/PK-PK
1515 S Glendora Ave 91740 626-335-4067
Lynn Elliott, dir. Fax 335-1968

Hope Lutheran S 200/PK-8
1041 E Foothill Blvd 91741 626-335-5315
Jerry White, prin. Fax 852-0836

St. Dorothy S 300/PK-8
215 S Valley Center Ave 91741 626-335-0772
Carol Burke, prin. Fax 335-0059

Glen Ellen, Sonoma, Pop. 1,191

Sonoma Valley USD
Supt. — See Sonoma

Dunbar ES 200/K-5
11700 Dunbar Rd 95442 707-935-6070
Melanie Blake, prin. Fax 935-4268

Glennville, Kern

Linns Valley-Poso Flat SD 50/K-8
PO Box 399 93226 661-536-8811
Curtis Guaglianone, supt. Fax 536-8878
kcsos.kern.org/LinnsValley/

Linns Valley-Poso Flat Union S 50/K-8
PO Box 399 93226 661-536-8811
Kay Yarger, prin. Fax 536-8878

Gold River, Sacramento

San Juan USD
Supt. — See Carmichael

Gold River Discovery Center 700/K-8
2200 Roaring Camp Dr 95670 916-867-2109
Vincent Arias, prin. Fax 867-2040

Goleta, Santa Barbara, Pop. 29,367

Goleta UNESD 3,500/K-6
401 N Fairview Ave 93117 805-681-1200
Dr. Kathleen Boomer, supt. Fax 681-1258
www.goleta.k12.ca.us

Brandon ES 400/K-6
195 Brandon Dr 93117 805-571-3770
Lynette Meyer, prin. Fax 571-3771

Ellwood ES 400/K-6
7686 Hollister Ave 93117 805-571-3774
Liz Rocha, prin. Fax 571-3775

Isla Vista ES 400/K-6
6875 El Colegio Rd 93117 805-685-4418
Lisa Maglione, prin. Fax 968-1338

Kellogg ES 400/K-6
475 Cambridge Dr 93117 805-681-1277
Nancy Knight, prin. Fax 681-4823

La Patera ES 400/K-6
555 N La Patera Ln 93117 805-681-1280
Patty Santiago, prin. Fax 964-7402

Other Schools – See Santa Barbara

Santa Barbara SD
Supt. — See Santa Barbara

Goleta Valley JHS 800/7-8
6100 Stow Canyon Rd 93117 805-967-3486
Veronica Rogers, prin. Fax 967-8176

Coastline Christian Academy 100/K-8
5950 Cathedral Oaks Rd 93117 805-967-5834
Mary Osgood, prin. Fax 967-5834

Montessori Center S 300/PK-6
401 N Fairview Ave Ste 1 93117 805-683-9383
Nelda Nutter, hdmstr. Fax 683-9384

Santa Barbara Montessori S 100/PK-8
7421 Mirano Dr 93117 805-685-7600
James Fitzpatrick, admin. Fax 685-7660

Waldorf S of Santa Barbara 100/PK-8
PO Box 788 93116 805-967-6656
Fax 696-6228

Gonzales, Monterey, Pop. 8,498

Gonzales USD 2,300/K-12
PO Box G 93926 831-675-0100
Elizabeth Modena, supt. Fax 675-2763
www.gusd-district.com/GUSD

Fairview MS 700/5-8
PO Box G 93926 831-675-3704
Al Velasquez, prin. Fax 675-3274

La Gloria ES 900/K-4
PO Box G 93926 831-675-3663
Matthew Fleming, prin. Fax 675-3260

Gorman, Los Angeles

Gorman ESD 50/K-8
PO Box 104 93243 661-248-6441
Sue Page, supt. Fax 248-6849

Gorman S 50/K-8
PO Box 104 93243 661-248-6441
Sue Page, prin. Fax 248-6849

Granada Hills, See Los Angeles

Los Angeles USD
Supt. — See Los Angeles

Danube Avenue ES 400/K-5
11220 Danube Ave 91344 818-366-6463
Sharon Geier, prin. Fax 363-4047

El Oro Way ES 500/K-5
12230 El Oro Way 91344 818-360-2288
Royce Goldman, prin. Fax 360-3264

Frost MS 1,800/6-8
12314 Bradford Pl 91344 818-362-6900
Elias De La Torre, prin. Fax 360-9584

Granada ES 500/K-5
17170 Tribune St 91344 818-363-3188
Cynthia Van Houten, prin. Fax 368-0821

Haskell ES 600/K-5
15850 Tulsa St 91344 818-366-6431
Lorie Thompson, prin. Fax 360-4627
Henry MS 1,300/6-8
17340 San Jose St 91344 818-832-3870
Michael Bennett, prin. Fax 368-7333
Knollwood ES 500/K-5
11822 Gerald Ave 91344 818-363-9558
Barbara Cohen, prin. Fax 832-9276
Porter MS 1,800/6-8
15960 Kingsbury St 91344 818-920-2050
Joyce Edelson, prin. Fax 891-7826
Tulsa ES 500/K-5
10900 Hayvenhurst Ave 91344 818-363-5061
Shari Moelter, prin. Fax 831-6935
Van Gogh ES 400/K-5
17160 Van Gogh St 91344 818-360-2141
Susan Gundersen, prin. Fax 831-9081

Bethlehem Lutheran K 100/PK-K
12227 Balboa Blvd 91344 818-368-6947
Fax 360-5559
De La Salle S 600/K-8
16535 Chatsworth St 91344 818-363-2270
Patricia Melch, prin. Fax 832-8950
Granada Hills Baptist S 200/K-6
10949 Zelzah Ave 91344 818-360-2104
Elayne Vanasse, prin. Fax 360-0175
Hillcrest Christian S 700/K-12
17531 Rinaldi St 91344 818-368-7071
David Kendrick, supt. Fax 363-4455
Our Savior's First Lutheran S 100/PK-6
16603 San Fernando Mission 91344 818-368-0892
Katherine Moore, prin. Fax 831-9222
St. Euphrasia S 300/K-8
17637 Mayerling St 91344 818-363-5515
Mary Blair, prin. Fax 832-6678
St. Stephen Lutheran K 50/PK-K
15950 Chatsworth St 91344 818-891-0801
Anjie Emeka, dir. Fax 891-5970

Grand Terrace, San Bernardino, Pop. 12,342
Colton JUSD
Supt. — See Colton
Grand Terrace ES 700/K-6
12066 Vivienda Ave 92313 909-876-4146
Cynthia Coello, prin. Fax 876-4059
Terrace Hills MS 1,000/7-8
22579 De Berry St 92313 909-876-4256
Joda Murphy, prin. Fax 783-3836
Terrace View ES 700/K-6
22731 Grand Terrace Rd 92313 909-876-4266
Dr. Joseph Adeyemo, prin. Fax 876-6366

Granite Bay, Placer
Eureka UNSD 3,500/K-8
5455 Eureka Rd 95746 916-791-4939
Tim McCarty, supt. Fax 791-5527
www.eureka-usd.k12.ca.us
Cavitt JHS 500/7-8
7200 Fuller Dr 95746 916-791-4152
Jennifer Platt, prin. Fax 791-7414
Greenhills ES 500/K-3
8200 Greenhills Way 95746 916-791-4230
Peter Towne, prin. Fax 791-4212
Oakhills ES 500/K-3
9233 Twin School Rd 95746 916-791-5391
Kristi Ellison, prin. Fax 791-6484
Ridgeview ES 500/4-6
9177 Twin School Rd 95746 916-791-3477
Patrice McCallum, prin. Fax 774-2707
Other Schools – See Roseville

Grass Valley, Nevada, Pop. 12,449
Chicago Park ESD 200/K-8
15725 Mount Olive Rd 95945 530-346-2153
Dan Zeisler, supt. Fax 346-8559
www.nevco.k12.ca.us/cpark/
Chicago Park S 200/K-8
15725 Mount Olive Rd 95945 530-346-2153
Dan Zeisler, prin. Fax 346-8559

Clear Creek ESD 100/K-8
17700 McCourtney Rd 95949 530-273-3664
Scott Lay, supt. Fax 273-4168
clearcreekschool.com
Clear Creek S 100/K-8
17700 McCourtney Rd 95949 530-273-3664
Scott Lay, prin. Fax 273-4168

Grass Valley ESD 1,500/K-8
10840 Gilmore Way 95945 530-273-4483
Jon Byerrum, supt. Fax 273-0248
www.gvsd.k12.ca.us
Gilmore MS 500/6-8
10837 Rough and Ready Hwy 95945 530-273-8479
Brian Buckley, prin. Fax 273-1675
Hennessy ES 500/K-5
225 S Auburn St 95945 530-273-2281
Deborah Plate, prin. Fax 273-3219
Scotten ES 400/K-5
10821 Squirrel Creek Rd 95945 530-273-6472
John Baggett, prin. Fax 273-6233

Pleasant Ridge UNESD 1,800/K-8
22580 Kingston Ln 95949 530-268-2800
James Meshwert, supt. Fax 268-2804
www.prsd.k12.ca.us/
Alta Sierra ES 400/K-5
16607 Annie Dr 95949 530-272-2319
Pat Rath, prin. Fax 274-8761
Cottage Hill ES 500/K-5
22600 Kingston Ln 95949 530-268-2808
Scotia Sanchez, prin. Fax 268-2810
Magnolia IS 700/6-8
22431 Kingston Ln 95949 530-268-2815
Mark Rodriguez, prin. Fax 268-2819
Pleasant Ridge ES 300/K-5
16229 Duggans Rd 95949 530-268-2820
Derek Cooper, prin. Fax 268-2823

Union Hill ESD 800/K-8
10879 Bartlett Dr 95945 530-273-0647
Eric Fredrickson, supt. Fax 273-5626
www.uhsd.k12.ca.us
Union Hill S 700/K-8
11638 Colfax Hwy 95945 530-273-8456
Eileen Barker, prin. Fax 273-0152

Crossroads Christian S 100/K-8
10062 Wolf Rd 95949 530-268-2597
Duane Triplett, supt. Fax 268-6762
Mt. St. Mary S 100/K-8
400 S Church St 95945 530-273-4694
Edee Wood, prin. Fax 273-1724

Greenfield, Monterey, Pop. 13,330
Greenfield UNSD 2,500/K-8
493 El Camino Real 93927 831-674-2840
Elida Garza Ed.D., supt. Fax 674-3712
www.greenfield.k12.ca.us/
Cesar Chavez ES 500/K-5
490 El Camino Real 93927 831-674-2412
Michelle Archuleta, prin. Fax 674-2469
Greenfield ES 600/K-5
490 El Camino Real 93927 831-674-5586
Alicia Estigoy, prin. Fax 674-3510
Oak Avenue S 600/K-5
1239 Oak Ave 93927 831-674-5916
Tina Martinez, prin. Fax 674-3682
Vista Verde MS 800/6-8
1199 Elm Ave 93927 831-674-1420
Stella Laurel, prin. Fax 674-1425

Greenville, Plumas, Pop. 1,396
Plumas USD
Supt. — See Quincy
Greenville ES 100/K-6
225 Grand St 95947 530-284-7195
Laura Blesse, prin. Fax 284-6720

Grenada, Siskiyou
Grenada ESD 100/K-8
PO Box 10 96038 530-436-2233
Mike Michelon, supt. Fax 436-2235
www.sisnet.ssku.k12.ca.us/~grenftp/
Grenada S 100/K-8
PO Box 10 96038 530-436-0345
GingerLee Charles, prin. Fax 436-2235

Gridley, Butte, Pop. 5,588
Gridley USD 2,100/K-12
429 Magnolia St 95948 530-846-4721
Clark Redfield, supt. Fax 846-4595
www.gridley.k12.ca.us/
McKinley ES 300/K-1
1045 Sycamore St 95948 530-846-5686
Chris McIntire, prin. Fax 846-3283
Sycamore MS 400/6-8
1125 Sycamore St 95948 530-846-3636
Christine McCormick, prin. Fax 846-6796
Wilson ES 600/2-5
409 Magnolia St 95948 530-846-3675
Chris McIntire, prin. Fax 846-4595

Manzanita ESD 300/K-8
627 E Evans Reimer Rd 95948 530-846-5594
Brad Roberts, supt. Fax 846-4084
www.manzanitaelementaryschool.com
Manzanita S 300/K-8
627 E Evans Reimer Rd 95948 530-846-5594
Brad Roberts, prin. Fax 846-4084

Grimes, Colusa
Pierce JUSD
Supt. — See Arbuckle
Grand Island ES 100/K-5
PO Box 30 95950 530-437-2416
Carol Geyer, prin. Fax 437-2296

Grizzly Flats, El Dorado
Pioneer UNESD
Supt. — See Somerset
Grizzly Pines ES 50/K-5
PO Box 26 95636 530-622-2995
Robin Kelley, lead tchr. Fax 622-2896

Groveland, Tuolumne, Pop. 2,753
Big Oak Flat-Groveland USD 600/K-12
19177 State Highway 120 95321 209-962-7846
Fax 962-5076
www.bofg.k12.ca.us
Tenaya S 300/K-8
19177 State Highway 120 95321 209-962-7846
Marianne Quinn, prin. Fax 962-5076

Grover Beach, San Luis Obispo, Pop. 12,887
Lucia Mar USD
Supt. — See Arroyo Grande
Grover Beach ES 500/K-6
365 S 10th St 93433 805-474-3770
Juan Olivarria, prin. Fax 473-5502
Grover Heights ES 500/K-6
770 N 8th St 93433 805-474-3700
Jennifer Bowen, prin. Fax 473-4323
North Oceano ES 500/K-6
2101 The Pike 93433 805-474-3740
Andy Stenson, prin. Fax 473-4109

Guadalupe, Santa Barbara, Pop. 6,346
Guadalupe UNESD 1,100/K-8
PO Box 788 93434 805-343-2114
Hugo Lara, supt. Fax 343-6155
www.sbceo.org/districts/guadalupeusd/
Buren ES 700/K-5
PO Box 788 93434 805-343-2411
Sandra Bravo Ph.D., prin. Fax 343-2512
McKenzie JHS 400/6-8
PO Box 788 93434 805-343-1951
Celia Ramos, prin. Fax 343-6931

Guerneville, Sonoma, Pop. 1,966
Guerneville ESD 300/K-8
14630 Armstrong Woods Rd 95446 707-869-2864
Diane Ogden Ed.D., supt. Fax 869-3149
www.guernevilleschool.org
Guerneville S 300/K-8
14630 Armstrong Woods Rd 95446 707-869-2864
Elaine Carlson, prin. Fax 869-3149

Gustine, Merced, Pop. 5,324
Gustine USD 2,000/K-12
1500 Meredith Ave 95322 209-854-3784
Gail McWilliams, supt. Fax 854-9164
www.gustine.k12.ca.us
Gustine ES 600/K-5
2806 Grove Ave 95322 209-854-6496
Donna Ross, prin. Fax 854-9165
Gustine MS 400/6-8
28075 Sullivan Rd 95322 209-854-5030
Rita Azevedo, prin. Fax 854-9592
Romero ES 300/K-5
13500 Luis Ave 95322 209-854-6177
Karen Azevedo, prin. Fax 826-6858

Our Lady of Miracles S 200/PK-8
370 Linden Ave 95322 209-854-3180
Mary Salvador, prin. Fax 854-3961

Hacienda Heights, Los Angeles, Pop. 53,300
Hacienda La Puente USD
Supt. — See City of Industry
Bixby ES 400/K-5
16446 Wedgeworth Dr 91745 626-933-8200
Rosalie Sinapi, prin. Fax 855-3506
Cedarlane MS 500/6-8
16333 Cedarlane Dr 91745 626-933-8000
Janine Ezaki, prin. Fax 855-3819
Glenelder ES 200/K-5
16234 Folger St 91745 626-933-6200
Ken Quon, prin. Fax 855-3836
Grazide ES 600/K-5
2850 Leopold Ave 91745 626-933-6100
Gloria Alderete, prin. Fax 369-0653
Kwis ES 300/K-5
1925 Kwis Ave 91745 626-933-2100
Dr. Leslie Rapkine-Miller, prin. Fax 855-3198
Los Altos ES 400/K-5
15565 Los Altos Dr 91745 626-933-2300
Dr. Margaret Hesselgrave, prin. Fax 855-3735
Los Molinos ES 300/K-5
3112 Las Marias Ave 91745 626-933-2200
Dr. Angela Lin, prin. Fax 855-3746
Los Robles Academy 500/K-5
1530 Ridley Ave 91745 626-933-7200
Charles Coulter, prin. Fax 855-3157
Mesa Robles S 1,000/K-8
16060 Mesa Robles Dr 91745 626-933-6000
Dr. Amy Baumann, prin. Fax 855-3827
Newton MS 700/6-8
15616 Newton St 91745 626-933-2400
Dr. Stephen Lee, prin. Fax 855-3832
Orange Grove MS 600/6-8
14505 Orange Grove Ave 91745 626-933-7000
Dr. Alejandro Rojas, prin. Fax 855-3837
Palm ES 400/K-5
14740 Palm Ave 91745 626-933-7400
Edna Moore, prin. Fax 855-3761
Wedgeworth ES 200/K-5
16949 Wedgeworth Dr 91745 626-933-8100
Ellen Park, prin. Fax 855-3790

Molokan Christian S 100/PK-6
16222 Soriano Dr 91745 626-336-5958
Tanya Nevarov, prin. Fax 336-6999
Morning Star Christian S 100/K-12
15716 Tetley St 91745 626-333-7784
Marlene Guerrero, admin. Fax 330-8636
St. Mark's Lutheran S 700/K-8
2323 Las Lomitas Dr 91745 626-968-0428
Barbara Clark, prin. Fax 333-4998

Half Moon Bay, San Mateo, Pop. 12,203
Cabrillo USD 3,400/K-12
498 Kelly Ave 94019 650-712-7100
Robert Gaskill, supt. Fax 726-0279
www.cabrillo.k12.ca.us/
Cunha IS 700/6-8
498 Kelly Ave 94019 650-712-7190
Michael Andrews, prin. Fax 712-7195
El Granada ES 500/K-5
498 Kelly Ave 94019 650-712-7150
Carrie Betti, prin. Fax 712-0126
Hatch ES 500/K-5
498 Kelly Ave 94019 650-712-7160
Mark Loos Ed.D., prin. Fax 712-1623
Other Schools – See Montara, Woodside

Sea Crest S 200/K-8
901 Arnold Way 94019 650-712-9892
Bruce Pollock, hdmstr. Fax 712-9171

Hamilton City, Glenn, Pop. 1,811
Hamilton UNESD 500/K-8
PO Box 277 95951 530-826-3474
David Moss, supt. Fax 826-0419
www.huesd.org/
Hamilton S 500/K-8
PO Box 277 95951 530-826-3474
David Moss, prin. Fax 826-0419

Hanford, Kings, Pop. 47,485
Delta View JUNESD 100/K-8
1201 Lacey Blvd 93230 559-582-3122
Carmen Barnhart, supt. Fax 582-3139

Delta View ES 100/K-8
1201 Lacey Blvd 93230 559-582-3122
Fax 582-3139

Hanford ESD 5,500/K-8
PO Box 1067 93232 559-585-3601
Paul Terry, supt. Fax 584-7833
www.hesd.k12.ca.us/
Hamilton ES 400/K-6
PO Box 1067 93232 559-585-3820
Javier Espindola, prin. Fax 583-7295
Jefferson ES 400/K-6
PO Box 1067 93232 559-585-3700
Javier Espindola, prin. Fax 585-2272
Kennedy JHS 600/7-8
PO Box 1067 93232 559-585-3850
Jason Strickland, prin. Fax 585-2374
King ES 600/K-6
PO Box 1067 93232 559-585-3715
Debra Colvard, prin. Fax 585-2363
Lincoln ES 500/K-6
PO Box 1067 93232 559-585-3730
Jen Pitkin, prin. Fax 585-2282
Monroe ES 400/K-6
PO Box 1067 93232 559-585-3745
Jaime Martinez, prin. Fax 585-2288
Richmond ES 500/K-6
PO Box 1067 93232 559-585-3760
Lucy Gomez, prin. Fax 585-2302
Roosevelt ES 500/K-6
PO Box 1067 93232 559-585-3775
Jill Rubalcava, prin. Fax 585-2317
Simas ES 500/K-6
PO Box 1067 93232 559-585-3790
Silvia Duvall, prin. Fax 585-2386
Washington ES 500/K-6
PO Box 1067 93232 559-585-3805
Charlotte Hines, prin. Fax 585-2325
Wilson JHS 600/7-8
PO Box 1067 93232 559-585-3870
Kenneth Eggert, prin. Fax 585-2336

Kit Carson UNESD 400/K-8
9895 7th Ave 93230 559-582-2843
John Sousa, supt. Fax 582-7565
www.kings.k12.ca.us/kcusd/index.htm
Kit Carson Union S 400/K-8
9895 7th Ave 93230 559-582-2843
John Sousa, prin. Fax 582-7565

Lakeside UNESD 300/K-8
9100 Jersey Ave 93230 559-582-2868
Dale Ellis, supt. Fax 582-7638
www.lakeside.k12.ca.us/
Gardenside ES 100/K-1
9100 Jersey Ave 93230 559-584-3792
Dale Ellis, prin. Fax 582-7638
Lakeside ES 200/2-8
9100 Jersey Ave 93230 559-582-2868
Dale Ellis, prin. Fax 582-7638

Hanford Christian S 200/PK-8
11948 Flint Ave 93230 559-584-9207
Gary Cookson, admin. Fax 584-2602
St. Rose/McCarthy S 200/K-8
1000 N Harris St 93230 559-584-5218
Jim Carpenter, prin. Fax 584-0899
Western Christian S 100/K-8
1594 W Grangeville Blvd 93230 559-584-1571
Kelly Virden, prin. Fax 584-1557

Happy Camp, Siskiyou
Happy Camp UNESD 100/K-8
PO Box 467 96039 530-493-2267
Casey Chambers, supt. Fax 493-2734
www.sisnet.ssku.k12.ca.us/~happyftp/
Happy Camp Union S 100/K-8
PO Box 467 96039 530-493-2267
Casey Chambers, prin. Fax 493-2734

Harbor City, See Los Angeles
Los Angeles USD
Supt. — See Los Angeles
Harbor City ES 600/K-5
1508 254th St 90710 310-326-5075
Akida Long, prin. Fax 326-8914
Normont ES 500/K-5
1001 253rd St 90710 310-326-5261
Tracy Joseph, prin. Fax 326-8034
President ES 500/K-5
1465 243rd St 90710 310-326-7400
Emmanuel Annor, prin. Fax 326-4936

Pines Christian S 100/PK-5
25200 Western Ave 90710 310-325-1213
Linda Ingersoll, prin. Fax 325-8292

Hawaiian Gardens, Los Angeles, Pop. 15,398
ABC USD
Supt. — See Cerritos
Fedde MS 500/7-8
21409 Elaine Ave 90716 562-924-2309
Rochelle Wollman, prin. Fax 809-6895
Furgeson ES 600/K-6
22215 Elaine Ave 90716 562-421-8285
Mayra Lozano, prin. Fax 421-5345
Hawaiian ES 600/K-6
12350 226th St 90716 562-594-9525
Laurie Cordova, prin. Fax 431-9547

Hawthorne, Los Angeles, Pop. 85,697
Hawthorne SD 8,900/K-8
14120 Hawthorne Blvd 90250 310-676-2276
Donald Carrington, supt. Fax 675-2308
www.hawthorne.k12.ca.us
Carson MS 900/6-8
13838 Yukon Ave 90250 310-676-1908
Patricia Jordan, prin. Fax 676-0634
Davis ES 1,300/K-5
13435 Yukon Ave 90250 310-679-1771
Mara Pagniano, prin. Fax 675-4962
Eucalyptus ES 1,100/K-5
12044 Eucalyptus Ave 90250 310-675-3369
Kathy Carbajal, prin. Fax 675-5628
Hawthorne MS 1,000/6-8
4366 W 129th St 90250 310-676-0167
Wendy Ostenson, prin. Fax 675-0924
Jefferson ES 600/K-5
4091 W 139th St 90250 310-676-9423
Brian Markarian, prin. Fax 676-4234
Kornblum ES 900/K-5
3620 W El Segundo Blvd 90250 310-970-4294
Jeff VanHulzen, prin. Fax 970-4298
Prairie Vista MS 1,000/6-8
13600 Prairie Ave 90250 310-679-1003
Christine Fagnano, prin. Fax 679-1142
Ramona ES 700/K-5
4617 W 136th St 90250 310-675-7189
Michael Collins, prin. Fax 675-6593
Washington ES 700/K-5
4339 W 129th St 90250 310-676-3422
Jennifer Gutierrez, prin. Fax 644-4824
York ES 700/K-5
11838 York Ave 90250 310-675-1189
Jennifer Beekman, prin. Fax 675-4892

Lawndale ESD
Supt. — See Lawndale
Carson ES 400/K-2
3530 W 147th St 90250 310-263-6830
Venecia Lizarzaburu, prin. Fax 676-0816

Los Angeles USD
Supt. — See Los Angeles
Cimarron Avenue ES 400/K-5
11559 Cimarron Ave 90250 323-757-1226
Cynthia Williams, prin. Fax 756-1686

Wiseburn ESD 2,100/K-8
13530 Aviation Blvd 90250 310-643-3025
Dr. Tom Johnstone, supt. Fax 643-7659
www.wiseburn.k12.ca.us/
Anza ES 600/K-5
12110 Hindry Ave 90250 310-725-2100
Dr. Christopher Jones, prin. Fax 643-0383
Burnett ES 400/3-5
5403 W 138th St 90250 310-725-2151
Fax 643-4306
Cabrillo ES 400/K-2
5309 W 135th St 90250 310-643-6165
Jane Comitz, prin. Fax 643-0208
Dana MS 800/6-8
5504 W 135th St 90250 310-725-4700
Aileen Harbeck, prin. Fax 536-9091

Al Huda Islamic S 100/K-8
12227 Hawthorne Way 90250 310-973-0500
Entesar Hamdan, prin. Fax 355-0554
Hawthorne Academy 100/K-12
12500 Ramona Ave 90250 310-644-8841
Ray Richard, dir.
New Journey Christian S 100/PK-12
14204 Prairie Ave 90250 310-676-9042
Colette Arce, prin. Fax 676-9043
St. Joseph S 500/PK-8
11886 Acacia Ave 90250 310-679-1014
Christina Whelan, prin. Fax 679-1310
Trinity Lutheran S 100/K-6
4783 W 130th St 90250 310-675-3379
Alex Cardenas, prin. Fax 675-9523

Hayfork, Trinity, Pop. 2,605
Mountain Valley USD 400/K-12
PO Box 339 96041 530-628-5265
Tom Barnett, supt. Fax 628-5267
www.mvusd.us
Hayfork S 200/K-8
PO Box 70 96041 530-628-5294
Deborah Hansen, prin. Fax 628-5344
Other Schools – See Hyampom

Hayfork SDA S 50/1-12
PO Box 580 96041 530-628-1601

Hayward, Alameda, Pop. 140,293
Hayward USD 20,500/PK-12
PO Box 5000 94540 510-784-2600
Dr. Dale Vigil, supt. Fax 784-2641
www.husd.k12.ca.us
Bowman ES 500/K-6
PO Box 5000 94540 510-723-3800
Maria Rivera, prin. Fax 582-7178
Burbank ES 600/K-6
PO Box 5000 94540 510-293-8568
Sandra Escobedo, prin. Fax 582-7142
Chavez MS 800/7-8
PO Box 5000 94540 510-723-3110
Vanessa Smith, prin. Fax 538-8478
Cherryland ES 900/K-6
PO Box 5000 94540 510-723-3810
Curtis Brock, prin. Fax 582-7133
East Avenue ES 400/K-6
PO Box 5000 94540 510-723-3820
Christine Jones-Crubaugh, prin. Fax 582-7016
Eden ES 500/K-6
PO Box 5000 94540 510-293-8509
Kim Watts, prin. Fax 783-2839
Eden Gardens ES 600/K-6
PO Box 5000 94540 510-723-3820
Gary Dobbs, prin. Fax 783-4069
Eldridge ES 500/K-6
PO Box 5000 94540 510-723-3825
Nancy Eaton, prin. Fax 783-3922
Fairview ES 400/K-6
PO Box 5000 94540 510-293-8571
Kris Martin-Meyer, prin. Fax 733-0342
Glassbrook ES 400/K-4
PO Box 5000 94540 510-293-8505
Jeanne Duarte-Armas, prin. Fax 782-8796
Harder ES 600/K-6
PO Box 5000 94540 510-293-8572
Enikia Ford Morthel, prin. Fax 733-0951
Harte MS 500/7-8
PO Box 5000 94540 510-723-3100
Lisa Davies, prin. Fax 886-5926
King MS 700/7-8
PO Box 5000 94540 510-723-3120
Estella Santos, prin. Fax 786-4139
Longwood ES 800/K-6
PO Box 5000 94540 510-293-8507
Gloria Prada, prin. Fax 783-2165
Markham ES 300/2-6
PO Box 5000 94540 510-293-8574
Diana Levy, prin. Fax 582-5814
Ochoa MS 600/7-8
PO Box 5000 94540 510-723-3130
Brent Stephens, prin. Fax 786-0559
Palma Ceia ES 600/K-6
PO Box 5000 94540 510-293-8512
Irma Fitzsimons, prin. Fax 783-2836
Park ES 600/K-6
PO Box 5000 94540 510-293-8515
Michele Perez, prin. Fax 781-6106
Ruus ES 700/K-6
PO Box 5000 94540 510-293-8517
John Hazatone, prin. Fax 783-2536
Schafer Park ES 500/K-6
PO Box 5000 94540 510-293-8520
Zarina Zanipatin, prin. Fax 783-2532
Southgate ES 600/K-6
PO Box 5000 94540 510-293-8524
Richard Aguirre, prin. Fax 781-0840
Stonebrae ES 500/K-6
PO Box 5000 94540 510-723-3910
Lisa Nolting, prin. Fax 733-1437
Treeview ES 300/2-6
PO Box 5000 94540 510-293-8577
William Grasty, prin. Fax 489-1211
Treeview ES Annex PK-1
PO Box 5000 94540 510-675-9091
William Grasty, prin. Fax 471-5783
Turner Childrens Center PK-PK
PO Box 5000 94540 510-293-8547
Bonnie Gutierrez, prin. Fax 783-9018
Tyrrell ES 400/K-6
PO Box 5000 94540 510-293-8526
Rosanna Mucetti, prin. Fax 783-2352
Winton MS 700/7-8
PO Box 5000 94540 510-723-3140
Donald West, prin. Fax 733-9043
Other Schools – See Castro Valley

New Haven USD
Supt. — See Union City
Hillview Crest ES 700/K-5
31410 Wheelon Ave 94544 510-471-5720
Beth Davies, prin. Fax 471-1436

San Lorenzo USD
Supt. — See San Lorenzo
Colonial Acres ES 600/K-5
17115 Meekland Ave 94541 510-317-4500
Linda Santillan, prin. Fax 481-1423
Lorenzo Manor ES 600/K-5
18250 Bengal Ave 94541 510-317-5400
Eileen Blood-Golden, prin. Fax 481-1312
Royal Sunset State Preschool PK-PK
20450 Royal Ave 94541 510-317-4412
Fax 317-4495

All Saints S 100/K-8
22870 2nd St 94541 510-582-1910
Gerry Marchi, prin. Fax 582-0866
Bayside SDA Christian S 50/K-8
26400 Gading Rd 94544 510-785-1313
Deborah Joplin, prin. Fax 785-3302
Elmhurst Learning Center/Grace Academy 100/PK-3
380 Elmhurst St 94544 510-786-1289
Marilyn Escoto, prin. Fax 786-1321
St. Bede S 200/K-8
26910 Patrick Ave 94544 510-782-3444
Toni Cosentino, prin. Fax 782-2243
St. Clement S 300/K-8
790 Calhoun St 94544 510-538-5885
Lana Jang, prin. Fax 538-1643
St. Joachim S 300/PK-8
21250 Hesperian Blvd 94541 510-783-3177
Armond Seishas, prin. Fax 783-2161

Healdsburg, Sonoma, Pop. 11,051
Alexander Valley Union ESD 100/K-6
8511 Highway 128 95448 707-433-1375
Bob Raines, supt. Fax 431-0102
www.alexandervalleyusd.org/
Alexander Valley ES 100/K-6
8511 Highway 128 95448 707-433-1375
Bob Raines, prin. Fax 431-0102

Healdsburg USD 2,800/K-12
1028 Prince Ave 95448 707-431-3488
Jeff Harding Ed.D., supt. Fax 433-8403
www.husd.com
Healdsburg ES - Fitch Mountain Campus 800/3-5
520 Monte Vista Ave 95448 707-473-4449
Amber Stringfellow, prin. Fax 473-4483
Healdsburg ES - HES Campus 400/K-2
400 1st St 95448 707-431-3440
Peter Fong, prin. Fax 431-3592
Healdsburg JHS 600/6-8
315 Grant St 95448 707-431-3410
Deborah Hall, prin. Fax 431-3593

West Side UNESD 200/K-6
1201 Felta Rd 95448 707-433-3923
Rhonda Bellmer, supt. Fax 431-7341
www.westsideusd.org/
West Side ES 200/K-6
1201 Felta Rd 95448 707-433-3923
Rhonda Bellmer, prin. Fax 431-8077

St. John the Baptist S 300/PK-8
217 Fitch St 95448 707-433-2758
Donna Garcia, prin. Fax 433-0353

Heber, Imperial, Pop. 2,566
Heber ESD 900/K-8
1052 Heber Ave 92249 760-337-6530
Jaime Silva, supt. Fax 353-3421
www.heber.k12.ca.us/
Heber S 900/K-8
1052 Heber Ave 92249 760-337-6534
Arturo Camacho, prin. Fax 352-3534

Helendale, San Bernardino
Helendale ESD 600/K-8
PO Box 249 92342 760-952-1180
Brian Dietz, supt. Fax 952-1178
www.helendalesd.org/
Helendale ES 400/K-5
PO Box 249 92342 760-952-1204
Jeff Fleury, prin. Fax 952-1762
Riverview MS 200/6-8
PO Box 249 92342 760-952-1266
Donna Cannon, prin. Fax 952-1178

Helm, Fresno
Golden Plains USD
Supt. — See San Joaquin
Helm S 100/K-8
PO Box 38 93627 559-866-5683
Aurora Ramirez, prin. Fax 866-5209

Hemet, Riverside, Pop. 68,063
Hemet USD 24,500/K-12
1791 W Acacia Ave 92545 951-765-5100
Dr. Philip Pendley, supt. Fax 765-5115
www.hemetusd.k12.ca.us
Acacia MS 1,000/6-8
1200 E Acacia Ave 92543 951-765-1620
Derek Jindra, prin. Fax 765-5149
Bautista Creek ES 1,000/K-5
441 N Lake St 92544 951-927-0822
David Howland, prin. Fax 927-0821
Cawston ES 800/K-5
4000 W Menlo Ave 92545 951-765-0277
Tracy Chambers, prin. Fax 929-2496
Dartmouth MS 1,200/6-8
41535 Mayberry Ave 92544 951-765-2550
Sharleen Rainville, prin. Fax 765-2559
Diamond Valley MS 1,500/6-8
291 W Chambers Ave 92543 951-925-2899
Patrice Ballinger, prin. Fax 925-6297
Fruitvale ES 900/K-6
2800 W Fruitvale Ave 92545 951-765-1680
Fax 765-1685
Harmony ES 800/K-5
1500 S Cawston Ave 92545 951-791-1830
Carol Robilotta, prin. Fax 791-1876
Hemet ES 800/K-5
26400 Dartmouth St 92544 951-765-1630
Marco Baeza, prin. Fax 765-1636
Little Lake ES 800/K-5
26091 Meridian St 92544 951-765-1660
Jinane Annous, prin. Fax 765-1696
McSweeny ES 700/K-5
451 W Chambers Ave 92543 951-925-4366
Daryl Wallace, prin. Fax 925-8321
Ramona ES 800/K-5
41051 Whittier Ave 92544 951-765-1670
John Wilder, prin. Fax 765-1677
Rancho Viejo MS 6-8
985 N Cawston Ave 92545 951-765-6287
John Huber, prin. Fax 925-5244
Valle Vista ES 700/K-5
43900 Mayberry Ave 92544 951-927-0800
Emily Shaw, prin. Fax 927-0808
Whittier ES 1,000/K-5
400 W Whittier Ave 92543 951-765-1650
Marc Horton, prin. Fax 765-1654
Wiens ES 700/K-5
935 E Campus Way 92543 951-929-3734
Sharon Bowman, prin. Fax 929-4425
Other Schools – See Aguanga, Anza, Idyllwild, Winchester

Baptist Christian S 400/PK-12
26089 Girard St 92544 951-658-3203
Ed Cardwell, prin. Fax 658-0723
Community Christian S 200/PK-8
41762 Stetson Ave 92544 951-929-2135
Cynthia Henninger, prin. Fax 765-6696
Crosspoint Academy 100/PK-8
825 S Gilbert St 92543 951-925-8967
Jack Stamback, admin. Fax 765-0716
Hemet Adventist Christian S 100/K-8
26312 Hemet St 92544 951-927-3972
Gary Brown, prin.
St. John's Lutheran S 200/PK-6
26410 Columbia St 92544 951-652-5909
Vickie Leitz, prin. Fax 925-6136

Herald, Sacramento
Arcohe UNESD 500/K-8
PO Box 93 95638 209-748-2313
Mark Cornfield, supt. Fax 748-5798
www.arcohe.net
Arcohe S 500/K-8
PO Box 93 95638 209-748-2313
Lori Salfen, prin. Fax 748-5798

Hercules, Contra Costa, Pop. 24,109
West Contra Costa USD
Supt. — See Richmond
Hanna Ranch ES 500/K-5
2480 Refugio Valley Rd 94547 510-245-9902
Anita Hayward, prin. Fax 799-5795
Lupine Hills ES 400/K-5
1919 Lupine Rd 94547 510-231-1411
Kathleen Brady, prin. Fax 799-1587
Ohlone ES 500/K-5
1616 Pheasant Dr 94547 510-799-0889
Elizabeth Lonsdale, prin. Fax 799-1556

Herlong, Lassen
Fort Sage USD 200/K-12
PO Box 6 96113 530-827-2129
Bryan Young, supt. Fax 827-2019
www.fortsage.org
Sierra ES 100/K-6
PO Box 6 96113 530-827-2126
Bryan Young, prin. Fax 827-3239

Hermosa Beach, Los Angeles, Pop. 19,500
Hermosa Beach City ESD 1,100/K-8
1645 Valley Dr 90254 310-937-5877
Sharon McClain Ed.D., supt. Fax 376-4974
www.hbcsd.org
Hermosa Valley MS 700/3-8
1645 Valley Dr 90254 310-937-5888
Sylvia Gluck, prin. Fax 798-4365
Hermosa View ES 400/K-2
1800 Prospect Ave 90254 310-798-1680
Carol Caballero, prin. Fax 798-4681

Hope Chapel Academy 200/K-12
2420 Pacific Coast Hwy 90254 310-374-4673
Kevin Bryan, prin.
Our Lady of Guadalupe S 200/PK-8
340 Massey St 90254 310-372-7486
Cheryl Hunt, prin. Fax 798-4051

Hesperia, San Bernardino, Pop. 77,984
Hesperia USD 22,100/K-12
15576 Main St 92345 760-244-4411
Mark McKinney, supt. Fax 244-2806
www.hesperia.org
Carmel ES 900/K-6
9321 Glendale Ave 92345 760-947-3188
Chris Mauger, prin. Fax 947-6545
Cedar MS 600/7-8
13565 Cedar St, 760-244-6093
David Olney, prin. Fax 244-5439
Cottonwood ES 900/K-5
8850 Cottonwood Ave 92345 760-949-1390
Sue Knuth, prin. Fax 949-6172
Cypress Academy 500/6-6
10365 Cypress Ave 92345 760-949-2596
Scott Sheffield, prin. Fax 949-3179
Eucalyptus ES 800/K-6
11224 10th Ave 92345 760-949-0815
Craig Gunter, prin. Fax 949-2886
Hesperia JHS 2,100/7-8
10275 Cypress Ave 92345 760-244-9386
Robert McCollum, prin. Fax 244-0595
Joshua Circle ES 900/K-6
10140 8th Ave 92345 760-244-6133
Lois Reaber, prin. Fax 244-3564
Juniper ES 800/K-6
9400 I Ave 92345 760-244-6161
Stephanie Poindexter, prin. Fax 244-1931
Kingston ES 900/K-5
7473 Kingston Ave 92345 760-244-8869
Teri Green, prin. Fax 947-2719
Lime Street ES 800/K-5
16852 Lime St 92345 760-244-0512
Sue Yarbrough, prin. Fax 244-2326
Maple ES 800/K-6
10616 Maple Ave 92345 760-244-3096
Karen Elgan, prin. Fax 244-0337
Mesa Grande ES 800/K-6
9172 3rd Ave 92345 760-244-3709
Pam Seeger, prin. Fax 244-5259
Mesquite Trails ES 700/K-5
13884 Mesquite St, 760-949-3149
David Stewart, prin. Fax 949-3602
Mission Crest ES 700/K-5
12850 Muscatel St, 760-949-8265
Michelle Murphy, prin. Fax 949-8202
Oxford Academy 300/6-6
7280 Oxford Ave 92345 760-949-8364
Patricia Baer, prin. Fax 949-6684
Ranchero MS 1,400/7-8
17607 Ranchero Rd 92345 760-948-0175
Cindy Costa, prin. Fax 948-0381
Topaz ES 600/K-5
14110 Beech St 92345 760-244-4622
Alan Giles, prin. Fax 244-2511
Other Schools – See Victorville

Hesperia Christian S 600/PK-12
16775 Olive St 92345 760-244-6164
Cindy Harmon, admin. Fax 244-9756
New Life Christian Academy 100/PK-6
15975 Hercules St 92345 760-244-1283
Debbie Lund, prin. Fax 244-3403
Tri-City Christian Academy 100/PK-8
11616 Hesperia Rd 92345 760-948-8877
Tammy Osborne, prin. Fax 948-5056

Highland, San Bernardino, Pop. 50,892
Redlands USD
Supt. — See Redlands
Arroyo Verde ES 500/K-5
7701 Church St 92346 909-307-5590
Jennifer Sherman, prin. Fax 307-5594
Beattie MS 1,300/6-8
7800 Orange St 92346 909-307-2400
Angela Neuhaus, prin. Fax 307-2416
Cram ES 700/K-5
29700 Water St 92346 909-425-9300
Julie Cinq-Mars, prin. Fax 425-9393
Highland Grove ES 500/K-5
7700 Orange St 92346 909-307-2420
David Cisneros, prin. Fax 307-2429

San Bernardino City USD
Supt. — See San Bernardino
Belvedere ES 800/K-6
2501 Marshall Blvd 92346 909-862-7111
Maribel Lopez-Tyus, prin. Fax 862-6575
Cole ES 500/K-6
1331 Cole Ave 92346 909-388-6510
Diana Silva, prin. Fax 862-8453
Cypress ES 700/K-6
26825 Cypress St 92346 909-388-6514
David Delgado, prin. Fax 862-5783
Highland-Pacific ES 400/K-6
3340 Pacific St 92346 909-388-6518
Brad McDuffee, prin. Fax 864-9853
Lankershim ES 1,000/K-6
7499 Lankershim Ave 92346 909-862-4213
Guadalupe Manee, prin. Fax 862-1899
Oehl ES 700/K-6
2525 Palm Ave 92346 909-388-6532
Heidi Vazquez, prin. Fax 862-3306
Serrano MS 1,000/7-8
3131 Piedmont Dr 92346 909-388-6530
Susan Keidel, prin. Fax 864-6232
Thompson ES 700/K-6
7401 Church Ave 92346 909-388-6512
Lynn Kvalheim, prin. Fax 862-4729

Banner S 300/K-6
2626 Pacific St 92346 909-864-1794
Gayle Linn, prin. Fax 425-5267
St. Adelaide S 200/PK-8
27487 Baseline St 92346 909-862-5851
Greg Blanco, prin. Fax 862-2877

Hillsborough, San Mateo, Pop. 10,615
Hillsborough CSD 1,400/K-8
300 El Cerrito Ave 94010 650-342-5193
Marilyn Loushin-Miller, supt. Fax 342-6964
www.hcsd.k12.ca.us/
Crocker MS 500/6-8
2600 Ralston Ave 94010 650-342-6331
Janet Chun, prin. Fax 579-5943
North Hillsborough ES 300/K-5
545 Eucalyptus Ave 94010 650-347-4175
Linda Miles, prin. Fax 347-2832
South Hillsborough ES 300/K-5
303 El Cerrito Ave 94010 650-344-0303
Jane Fletcher, prin. Fax 548-9443
West Hillsborough ES 400/K-5
376 Barbara Way 94010 650-344-9870
Anthony Ranii, prin. Fax 340-1630

Nueva S 400/PK-8
6565 Skyline Blvd 94010 650-348-2272
Diane Rosenberg, hdmstr. Fax 344-9302

Hilmar, Merced, Pop. 3,392
Hilmar USD 2,400/K-12
7807 Lander Ave 95324 209-667-5701
Isabel Cabral-Johnson, supt. Fax 667-1721
www.hilmar.k12.ca.us
Elim ES 800/K-5
7807 Lander Ave 95324 209-667-1082
Stephen Harrison, prin. Fax 667-9066
Hilmar MS 600/6-8
7807 Lander Ave 95324 209-632-8847
Eric Hixson, prin. Fax 667-7018
Other Schools – See Stevinson

Hinkley, San Bernardino
Barstow USD
Supt. — See Barstow
Hinkley S 300/K-8
37600 Hinkley Rd 92347 760-253-5512
Dennis Hirsch, prin. Fax 253-5518

Hollister, San Benito, Pop. 35,941
Cienega UNESD 50/K-8
11936 Cienega Rd 95023 831-637-3821
Nancy MacLean, supt. Fax 637-3961
www.sbcoe.k12.ca.us/cienega.html
Cienega S 50/K-8
11936 Cienega Rd 95023 831-637-3821
Nancy MacLean, prin. Fax 637-3961

Hollister SD 6,000/K-8
2690 Cienega Rd 95023 831-630-6300
Ronald Crates Ed.D., supt. Fax 634-2080
www.hesd.org/
Calaveras S 500/K-7
1151 Buena Vista Rd 95023 831-636-4460
Christine White, prin. Fax 634-4960
Cerra Vista ES 700/K-5
2151 Cerra Vista Dr 95023 831-636-4470
Pam Little, prin. Fax 634-4970
Gabilan Hills S 600/K-8
921 Santa Ana Rd Ste 100 95023 831-636-4430
Cindy Cordova, prin. Fax 636-3908
Hardin ES 700/K-5
881 Line St 95023 831-636-4440
Aggie Obeso-Bradley, prin. Fax 636-7537
Hollister Dual Language Academy K-3
873 Santa Ana Rd Ste 200 95023 831-634-4930
Delia Gomez, prin. Fax 634-4934
Ladd Lane ES 700/K-5
161 Ladd Ln 95023 831-636-4490
Maxine Stewart-Carlson, prin. Fax 634-4992
Maze MS 900/6-8
900 Meridian St 95023 831-636-4480
Bernice Smith, prin. Fax 636-4488

Rancho San Justo MS 1,000/6-8
1201 Rancho Dr 95023 831-636-4450
Don Knapp, prin. Fax 634-4952
Sunnyslope ES 700/K-5
1475 Memorial Dr 95023 831-636-4420
Melinda Scott, prin. Fax 634-4920

North County JUNESD 600/K-8
500 Spring Grove Rd 95023 831-637-5574
Evelyn Muro, supt. Fax 637-0682
www.ncjusd.k12.ca.us/
Spring Grove S 600/K-8
500 Spring Grove Rd 95023 831-637-3745
Jenny Bernosky, prin. Fax 637-0682

Southside ESD 200/K-8
4991 Southside Rd 95023 831-637-4439
Eric Johnson, supt. Fax 634-0156
www.southsideschool.net
Southside S 200/K-8
4991 Southside Rd 95023 831-637-4439
Eric Johnson, prin. Fax 634-0156

Calvary Christian S 100/K-12
1900 Highland Dr 95023 831-637-2909
Dave Cannon, admin. Fax 637-7268
Hollister SDA Christian S 50/K-8
2020 Santa Ana Rd 95023 831-637-5570
Roymond Koubong, prin. Fax 637-4560
Sacred Heart Parish S 400/PK-8
670 College St 95023 831-637-4157
Gayla Jurevich, admin. Fax 637-4164

Hollywood, See Los Angeles
Los Angeles USD
Supt. — See Los Angeles
Le Conte MS 2,000/6-8
1316 N Bronson Ave 90028 323-308-1700
Donald Foote, prin. Fax 856-3053

Pacific Southwest Lutheran Learning Ctr 50/K-8
1518 N Alexandria Ave 90027 323-667-3044
Aleta Williams, prin. Fax 667-3044

Holtville, Imperial, Pop. 5,470
Holtville USD 1,800/K-12
621 E 6th St 92250 760-356-2974
Jon LeDoux, supt. Fax 356-4936
www.holtville.k12.ca.us/
Finley ES 600/K-5
627 E 6th St 92250 760-356-2929
David Martinez, prin. Fax 356-2052
Holtville JHS 400/6-8
800 Beale Ave 92250 760-356-2811
Mitchell Drye, prin. Fax 356-5741
Pine S 200/K-8
3295 Holt Rd 92250 760-356-2615
Margie Stacey, prin. Fax 356-1354

Homeland, Riverside, Pop. 3,312
Romoland ESD 2,800/K-8
25900 Leon Rd 92548 951-926-9244
Bobbie Plough, supt. Fax 926-2170
www.romoland.k12.ca.us
Other Schools – See Romoland

Honeydew, Humboldt
Mattole USD 50/K-12
29289 Chambers Rd 95545 707-629-3311
Richard Graey, supt. Fax 629-3575
www.humboldt.k12.ca.us/mattole_usd
Honeydew ES 50/K-4
Wilder Ridge Rd 95545 707-629-3230
Richard Graey, prin. Fax 629-3239
Other Schools – See Petrolia

Hoopa, Humboldt
Klamath-Trinity JUSD 1,100/K-12
PO Box 1308 95546 530-625-5600
Douglas Oliveira, supt. Fax 625-5611
www.ktjusd.k12.ca.us/
Hoopa Valley S 500/K-8
PO Box 1308 95546 530-625-5600
Rosie Leazer, prin. Fax 625-4697
Norton S 50/K-8
PO Box 1308 95546 707-444-0262
Sandra Moon, prin. Fax 222-4109
Weitchpec ES 50/K-3
PO Box 1308 95546 530-625-5600
Sandra Moon, prin. Fax 625-4133
Other Schools – See Orleans, Willow Creek

Hopland, Mendocino
Ukiah USD
Supt. — See Ukiah
Hopland ES 100/K-6
PO Box 368 95449 707-744-1333
Jeanne Yttreness, prin. Fax 744-1463

Hornbrook, Siskiyou
Hornbrook ESD 50/K-8
PO Box 169 96044 530-475-3598
Pedro Abeyta, admin. Fax 475-0929
www.sisnet.ssku.k12.ca.us/~hornftp/
Hornbrook S 50/K-8
PO Box 169 96044 530-475-3598
Pedro Abeyta, prin. Fax 475-0929

Horse Creek, Siskiyou
Klamath River UNESD 50/K-8
30438 Walker Rd 96050 530-496-3406
Fax 496-3426
Klamath River S 50/K-8
30438 Walker Rd 96050 530-496-3406
Nadine Bideler, lead tchr. Fax 496-3426

Hughson, Stanislaus, Pop. 5,705
Hughson USD 2,200/K-12
PO Box 189 95326 209-883-4428
Brian Beck, supt. Fax 883-4639
www.hughson.k12.ca.us/
Fox Road ES 300/4-5
PO Box 189 95326 209-883-2256
Mark Taylor, prin. Fax 883-2279
Hughson ES 600/K-3
PO Box 189 95326 209-883-4412
Brenda Vaca, prin. Fax 883-4784
Ross MS 500/6-8
PO Box 189 95326 209-883-4425
Mark Taylor, prin. Fax 883-2017

Keyes UNESD
Supt. — See Keyes
Spratling MS 300/6-8
5277 Washington Rd 95326 209-664-3833
Mike Richter, prin. Fax 656-2384

Huntington Beach, Orange, Pop. 194,457
Fountain Valley ESD
Supt. — See Fountain Valley
Newland ES 400/K-5
8787 Dolphin Dr 92646 714-378-4200
Kathy Davis, prin. Fax 378-4209
Oka ES 400/K-5
9800 Yorktown Ave 92646 714-378-4260
Brandi Loyd, prin. Fax 378-4269
Talbert MS 600/6-8
9101 Brabham Dr 92646 714-378-4220
Cara Robinson, prin. Fax 378-4229

Huntington Beach City ESD 6,600/K-8
20451 Craimer Ln 92646 714-964-8888
Kathy Kessler, supt. Fax 963-9565
www.hbcsd.k12.ca.us
Dwyer MS 1,200/6-8
1502 Palm Ave 92648 714-536-7507
Donald Ruisinger, prin. Fax 960-0955
Eader ES 500/K-5
9291 Banning Ave 92646 714-962-2451
Cynthia Guerrero, prin. Fax 378-3601
Hawes ES 500/K-5
9682 Yellowstone Dr 92646 714-963-8302
Heidi Harvey, prin. Fax 378-3603
Huntington Seacliff ES 600/K-5
6701 Garfield Ave 92648 714-841-7081
Ann Sullivan, prin. Fax 841-4593
Moffett ES 500/K-5
8800 Burlcrest Dr 92646 714-963-8985
Billie Baker, prin. Fax 378-3602
Perry ES 500/K-5
19231 Harding Ln 92646 714-962-3348
Monique Van Zeebroeck, prin. Fax 962-3347
Peterson ES 700/K-5
20661 Farnsworth Ln 92646 714-378-1515
Barbara Crissman, prin. Fax 378-1520
Smith ES 800/K-5
770 17th St 92648 714-536-1469
Michael Andrzejewski, prin. Fax 536-7484
Sowers MS 1,200/6-8
9300 Indianapolis Ave 92646 714-962-7738
Deborah Randall, prin. Fax 968-5580

Ocean View SD 9,500/PK-8
17200 Pinehurst Ln 92647 714-847-2551
Alan Rasmussen, supt. Fax 847-1430
www.ovsd.org
Circle View ES 700/K-5
6261 Hooker Dr 92647 714-893-5035
Kathleen Jaquin Ed.D., prin. Fax 898-6495
College View ES 500/K-5
6582 Lennox Dr 92647 714-847-3505
Kristine White Ed.D., prin. Fax 847-8615
Golden View ES 500/K-5
17251 Golden View Ln 92647 714-847-2516
Anna Dreifus, prin. Fax 375-0736
Harbour View ES 800/K-5
4343 Pickwick Cir 92649 714-846-6602
Cindy Osterhout, prin. Fax 377-0952
Hope View ES 700/K-5
17622 Flintstone Ln 92647 714-847-8571
Kathy Smith, prin. Fax 841-1591
Lake View ES 400/K-5
17451 Zeider Ln 92647 714-842-2589
Colette Wright, prin. Fax 375-9269
Marine View MS 900/6-8
5682 Tilburg Dr 92649 714-846-0624
Roni Ellis, prin. Fax 846-2074
Mesa View MS 700/6-8
17601 Avilla Ln 92647 714-842-6608
Leona Olson, prin. Fax 842-8798
Oak View ES 800/K-5
17241 Oak Ln 92647 714-842-4459
Joyce Horowitz, prin. Fax 842-4769
Oak View Preschool PK-PK
17131 Emerald Ln 92647 714-843-6938
Claudine Dumais Ed.D., coord. Fax 375-6354
Pleasant View Preschool/OVPP PK-PK
16692 Landau Ln 92647 714-845-5000
Paul James, prin.
Spring View MS 900/6-8
16662 Trudy Ln 92647 714-846-2891
John Drake, prin. Fax 377-9821
Sun View ES 400/K-5
7721 Juliette Low Dr 92647 714-847-9643
Kristi Hickman, prin. Fax 847-4173
Village View ES 600/K-5
5361 Sisson Dr 92649 714-846-2801
Aaron Jetzer, prin. Fax 846-1631
Other Schools – See Fountain Valley, Midway City, Westminster

Westminster ESD
Supt. — See Westminster
Clegg ES 500/K-5
6311 Larchwood Dr 92647 714-894-7218
John Staggs, prin. Fax 898-6176
Schroeder ES 600/PK-6
15151 Columbia Ln 92647 714-894-7268
Kim Breckenridge, prin. Fax 379-5861
Stacey MS 1,000/6-8
6311 Larchwood Dr 92647 714-894-7212
Kathy Kane, prin. Fax 373-0478

Carden Academy 200/K-8
721 E Utica Ave 92648 714-563-1441
Fax 536-3448
Carden Conservatory 100/K-10
5702 Clark Dr 92649 714-840-5127
Paul Hunt, dir.
Coastline Christian S 100/PK-PK
2721 Delaware St 92648 714-536-1740
Olivia Woerz, dir. Fax 960-6691
Grace Lutheran S 400/PK-8
5172 McFadden Ave 92649 714-899-1600
Dr. Janie Andrich, admin. Fax 899-1615
Hebrew Academy 200/PK-12
14401 Willow Ln 92647 714-898-0051
Rabbi Yitzchok Newman, dir. Fax 898-0633
Huntington Christian S 500/K-8
9700 Levee Dr 92646 714-378-9932
Art Blietz, admin. Fax 378-9973
Liberty Christian S 400/PK-12
7661 Warner Ave 92647 714-842-5992
Thomas Doney, prin. Fax 848-7484
Pegasus S 600/PK-8
19692 Lexington Ln 92646 714-964-1224
Laura Hathaway, hdmstr. Fax 962-6047
St. Bonaventure S 600/K-8
16390 Springdale St 92647 714-846-2472
Judy Luttrell, prin. Fax 840-0498
SS. Simon & Jude S 600/PK-8
20400 Magnolia St 92646 714-962-4451
Crystal Smith, prin. Fax 968-1329

Huntington Park, Los Angeles, Pop. 62,491
Los Angeles USD
Supt. — See Los Angeles
Gage MS 3,500/6-8
2880 E Gage Ave 90255 323-826-1500
Walter Flores, prin. Fax 589-6925
Hope ES 500/K-4
7560 State St 90255 323-586-5700
Dee Nishimoto, prin. Fax 585-6885
Huntington Park ES 500/K-5
6055 Corona Ave 90255 323-869-5920
April Ramos, prin. Fax 560-1615
Middleton ES 1,300/K-5
6537 Malabar St 90255 323-582-6387
Javier Miranda, prin. Fax 587-7006
Middleton Primary Center 200/K-K
2410 Zoe Ave 90255 323-826-9533
Laura Rosales, prin. Fax 826-9556
Miles Avenue ES 1,900/K-5
6720 Miles Ave 90255 323-588-8296
Pamela Robertson, prin. Fax 581-4567
Nimitz MS 3,300/6-8
6021 Carmelita Ave 90255 323-887-5400
Francisco Vasquez, prin. Fax 773-5201
Pacific Boulevard ES 600/K-5
2660 E 57th St 90255 323-586-8640
Gabriel Duran, prin. Fax 586-8677
San Antonio ES 700/K-5
6222 State St 90255 323-582-1250
Mark Browning, prin. Fax 582-1710
Walnut Park ES 1,100/K-5
2642 Olive St 90255 323-588-3145
Lewin Dover, prin. Fax 588-5965

St. Matthias S 200/PK-8
7130 Cedar St 90255 323-588-7253
Vannessa Rivas, prin. Fax 588-1136

Huron, Fresno, Pop. 7,187
Coalinga - Huron JUSD
Supt. — See Coalinga
Huron ES 800/K-5
PO Box 370 93234 559-945-2236
Arturo Duran, prin. Fax 945-1215
Huron MS 400/6-8
PO Box 99 93234 559-945-2926
Irene Fernandez, prin. Fax 945-8482

Hyampom, Trinity
Mountain Valley USD
Supt. — See Hayfork
Hyampom Arts Magnet S 50/K-8
PO Box 140 96046 530-628-5912
Deborah Hansen, prin. Fax 628-5902

Hydesville, Humboldt, Pop. 1,131
Hydesville ESD 100/K-8
PO Box 551 95547 707-768-3610
John Blakely, supt. Fax 768-3612
www.humboldt.k12.ca.us/hydesville_sd/
Hydesville S 100/K-8
PO Box 551 95547 707-768-3610
John Blakely, prin. Fax 768-3612

Idyllwild, Riverside, Pop. 2,853
Hemet USD
Supt. — See Hemet
Idyllwild S 300/K-8
PO Box 97 92549 951-659-0750
Matt Kraemer, prin. Fax 659-0757

Igo, Shasta
Igo-Ono-Platina UNESD
Supt. — See Redding

Igo-Ono S 100/K-8
PO Box 250 96047 530-396-2841
Heidi Gerig, prin. Fax 396-2848
Platina S 50/K-8
PO Box 250 96047 530-352-4341
Heidi Gerig, prin. Fax 352-4396

Imperial, Imperial, Pop. 9,707
Imperial USD 3,300/K-12
219 N E St 92251 760-355-3200
Madeline Willis, supt. Fax 355-4511
iusd.imperial.k12.ca.us/
Hulse ES 900/K-5
303 S D St 92251 760-355-3210
Jerry Johnson, prin. Fax 355-3248
Waggoner ES 600/K-5
627 Joshua Tree St 92251 760-355-3266
Roger Ruvalcaba, prin. Fax 355-3180
Wright MS 800/6-8
885 N Imperial Ave 92251 760-355-3240
Diego Lopez, prin. Fax 355-3256
Other Schools – See El Centro

Imperial Beach, San Diego, Pop. 26,374
South Bay UNSD 8,300/K-6
601 Elm Ave 91932 619-628-1600
Carol Parish Ed.D., supt. Fax 628-1608
www.sbusd.org
Bayside ES 400/K-6
490 Emory St 91932 619-628-2500
Patty Valdivia, prin. Fax 628-2580
Central ES 600/K-6
1290 Ebony Ave 91932 619-628-5000
Linda Sullivan, prin. Fax 628-5080
Imperial Beach ES 600/K-6
650 Imperial Beach Blvd 91932 619-628-5600
Matt Carlton, prin. Fax 628-5680
Oneonta ES 600/K-6
1311 10th St 91932 619-628-8600
Marla Fernandez, prin. Fax 628-8680
West View ES 400/K-6
525 3rd St 91932 619-628-8900
Matt Carlton, prin. Fax 628-8980
Other Schools – See San Diego, San Ysidro

Independence, Inyo
Owens Valley USD 100/K-12
PO Box E 93526 760-878-2405
Joel Hampton, supt. Fax 878-2626
www.ovusd.org
Owens Valley S 50/K-8
PO Box E 93526 760-878-2405
Joel Hampton, prin. Fax 878-2626

Indian Wells, Riverside, Pop. 4,933
Desert Sands USD
Supt. — See La Quinta
Ford ES 700/K-5
44210 Warner Trl 92210 760-772-4120
Theresa Kachiroubas, prin. Fax 772-4125

Indio, Riverside, Pop. 70,542
Coachella Valley USD
Supt. — See Thermal
Mountain Vista ES 1,000/K-6
49750 Hjorth St 92201 760-775-6888
Valerie Perez, prin. Fax 775-6568

Desert Sands USD
Supt. — See La Quinta
Carreon Academy 800/K-5
47368 Monroe ST 92201 760-863-1544
Regina Heredia, prin. Fax 863-1540
Carrillo Ranch ES 500/K-5
43775 Madison St 92201 760-238-9700
John Waybrant, prin. Fax 347-0489
Desert Ridge Academy 6-8
79767 Avenue 39 92203 760-393-5500
Dan Borgen, prin. Fax 393-5502
Earhart ES of Intl Studies 900/K-5
45250 Dune Palms Rd 92201 760-200-3720
Bradley Fisher, prin. Fax 200-3729
Eisenhower ES 600/K-5
83391 Dillon Ave 92201 760-775-3810
Theresa Kramer, prin. Fax 775-3598
Glenn MS of International Studies 1,100/6-8
79655 Miles Ave 92201 760-200-3700
Marcus Wood, prin. Fax 200-3709
Hoover ES 600/K-5
44300 Monroe St 92201 760-775-3820
Maria Fernandez, prin. Fax 775-3863
Indio MS 1,100/6-8
81195 Miles Ave 92201 760-775-3800
Jesus Jimenez, prin. Fax 775-3807
Jackson ES 600/K-5
82850 Kenner Ave 92201 760-775-3830
Michael Wilhite, prin. Fax 775-3836
Jefferson MS 800/6-8
83089 US Highway 111 92201 760-863-3660
Esther Lopez, prin. Fax 775-3597
Johnson ES 700/K-5
44640 Clinton St 92201 760-863-3680
Maryalice Alberg, prin. Fax 863-3684
Kennedy ES 600/K-5
45100 Clinton St 92201 760-775-3840
Fax 347-5187
Madison ES 800/K-5
80845 Avenue 46 92201 760-775-3850
David Karlquist, prin. Fax 775-3855
Roosevelt ES 700/K-5
83200 Doctor Carreon Blvd 92201 760-775-3860
Clayton Hill, prin. Fax 775-3856
Van Buren ES 500/K-5
47733 Van Buren St 92201 760-775-3870
Melinda Wallace, prin. Fax 775-3846

Destiny Academy 50/K-6
82545 Showcase Pkwy Ste 112 92203 760-863-0700
Cheri Steinker, prin. Fax 863-4707

Grace Academy 100/K-8
48395 Madison St 92201 760-775-3440
Richard Matley, prin. Fax 775-2866
Our Lady of Perpetual Help S 200/PK-8
82470 Bliss Ave 92201 760-347-3786
Diane Arias, prin. Fax 347-7207

Inglewood, Los Angeles, Pop. 114,467
Inglewood USD 15,400/K-12
401 S Inglewood Ave 90301 310-419-2700
Dr. Pamela Short-Powell, supt. Fax 680-5128
inglewood.k12.ca.us
Bennett/Kew ES 800/K-5
11710 Cherry Ave 90303 310-680-5400
Kelly McGowens, prin. Fax 680-5409
Centinela ES 1,000/K-6
1123 Marlborough Ave 90302 310-680-5440
Lorna Martin, prin. Fax 680-5347
Crozier MS 1,100/6-8
120 W Regent St 90301 310-680-5280
Steve Donahue, prin. Fax 680-5299
Freeman ES 400/K-6
2602 W 79th St 90305 310-680-5380
Geraldine Gamby-Turner, prin. Fax 680-5389
Highland ES 600/K-5
430 Venice Way 90302 310-680-5460
Susan Ippongi, prin. Fax 680-5478
Hudnall ES 500/K-5
331 W Olive St 90301 310-680-5420
Thomas Washington, prin. Fax 680-5428
Kelso ES 800/K-5
809 E Kelso St 90301 310-680-5480
Ugema Hosea-James, prin. Fax 680-5489
Lane S 800/K-8
9330 S 8th Ave 90305 310-680-5330
Douglas Howard, prin. Fax 680-5336
La Tijera S 700/K-8
1415 S La Tijera Blvd 90302 310-680-5260
Judith Washington, prin. Fax 680-5277
Monroe MS 1,100/6-8
10711 S 10th Ave 90303 310-680-5310
Barbara Searcy, prin. Fax 680-5317
Oak Street ES 800/K-5
633 S Oak St 90301 310-680-5340
Richard Barter, prin. Fax 680-5347
Parent S 800/K-8
5354 W 64th St 90302 310-680-5430
Garry Gregory, prin. Fax 680-5436
Payne ES 800/K-5
215 W 94th St 90301 310-680-5410
Marie Blanco, prin. Fax 680-5418
Woodworth ES 600/K-5
3200 W 104th St 90303 310-680-5361
Josephine Taylor, prin. Fax 680-5377
Worthington ES 800/K-5
11101 Yukon Ave 90303 310-680-5350
Angelina Marquez, prin. Fax 680-5359

Los Angeles USD
Supt. — See Los Angeles
Century Park ES 600/K-5
10935 Spinning Ave 90303 323-757-8231
Kim Polk, prin. Fax 757-7449

Anthony's S 100/2-6
8420 Crenshaw Blvd 90305 323-758-1187
Brady Johnson, prin.
First Lutheran K 50/PK-K
600 W Queen St 90301 310-674-0310
Michele Graveline, dir.
Inglewood Christian S 100/K-8
215 E Hillcrest Blvd 90301 310-671-7666
Mary Waymon, admin. Fax 671-1288
St. John Chrysostom S 300/K-8
530 E Florence Ave 90301 310-677-5868
Sr. Antoinette Czuleger, prin. Fax 677-3429
YDP of Greater Los Angeles 100/K-9
3320 W 85th St 90305 310-680-9400

Inyokern, Kern
Sierra Sands USD
Supt. — See Ridgecrest
Inyokern ES 200/K-5
PO Box 1597 93527 760-377-4336
Virginia Cornell, prin. Fax 377-5995

Ione, Amador, Pop. 7,607
Amador County USD
Supt. — See Jackson
Ione ES 600/K-6
415 S Ione St 95640 209-257-7000
Laurie Amick, prin. Fax 274-2167
Ione JHS 400/6-8
450 S Mill St 95640 209-257-5500
Bill Murray, prin. Fax 274-0671

Irvine, Orange, Pop. 186,852
Irvine USD 25,400/PK-12
5050 Barranca Pkwy 92604 949-936-5000
Dr. Gwen Gross, supt. Fax 936-5259
www.iusd.org
Alderwood Basics ES 700/K-6
2005 Knollcrest 92603 949-936-5400
Ken Horner, prin. Fax 936-5409
Bonita Canyon ES 500/K-6
1 Sundance 92603 949-936-5450
Robin Beacham, prin. Fax 936-5459
Brywood ES 600/K-6
1 Westwood 92620 949-936-5500
Christine Amoroso, prin. Fax 936-5509
Canyon View ES 800/K-6
12025 Yale Ct 92620 949-936-6900
Susan Kemp, prin. Fax 936-6909
College Park ES 700/K-6
3700 Chaparral Ave 92606 949-936-5550
Alan Battenfield, prin. Fax 936-5559
Culverdale ES 600/K-6
2 Paseo Westpark 92614 949-936-5600
Allie Nixon, prin. Fax 936-5609

Deerfield ES 500/K-6
2 Deerfield Ave 92604 949-936-5650
Kathy McKeown, prin. Fax 936-5659
Early Childhood Education Center PK-PK
1 Smoketree 92604 949-936-5860
Pat Desimone, prin. Fax 936-5809
Eastshore ES 500/K-6
155 Eastshore 92604 949-936-5700
Lisa Kadam, prin. Fax 936-5709
Greentree ES 500/K-6
4200 Manzanita 92604 949-936-5800
Tamara Brown, prin. Fax 936-5809
Lakeside MS 700/7-8
3 Lemongrass 92604 949-936-6100
Craig Ritter, prin. Fax 936-6109
Meadow Park ES 600/K-6
50 Blue Lk S 92614 949-936-5900
Lisa Livernois, prin. Fax 936-5909
Northwood ES 500/K-6
28 Carson 92620 949-936-5950
Stuart Payne, prin. Fax 936-5959
Oak Creek ES 700/K-6
1 Dove Creek 92618 949-936-8550
Jenna Berumen, prin. Fax 936-8559
Plaza Vista S 900/K-8
670 Paseo Westpark 92606 949-936-6950
Heather Phillips, prin. Fax 936-6959
Rancho San Joaquin MS 800/7-8
4861 Michelson Dr 92612 949-936-6500
Scott Bowman, prin. Fax 936-6509
Santiago Hills ES 500/K-6
29 Christamon W 92620 949-936-6000
Alan Schlichting, prin. Fax 936-6009
Sierra Vista MS 1,000/7-8
2 Liberty 92620 949-936-6600
Lynn Matassrin, prin. Fax 936-6609
South Lake MS 600/7-8
655 W Yale Loop 92614 949-936-6700
Bruce Baron, prin. Fax 936-6709
Springbrook ES 600/K-6
655 Springbrook N 92614 949-936-6050
Robert Curley, prin. Fax 936-6059
Stone Creek ES 400/K-6
2 Stone Crk S 92604 949-936-6200
Michael Shackelford, prin. Fax 936-6209
Turtle Rock ES 800/K-6
5151 Amalfi Dr 92603 949-936-6250
Karen Catabijan, prin. Fax 936-6259
University Park ES 500/K-6
4572 Sandburg Way 92612 949-936-6300
Kara Rydman, prin. Fax 936-6309
Venado MS 700/7-8
4 Deerfield Ave 92604 949-936-6800
Keith Tuominen, prin. Fax 936-6809
Vista Verde S 700/K-8
6 Federation Way 92603 949-936-6350
Jean Mylen, prin. Fax 936-6359
Westpark ES 600/K-6
25 San Carlo 92614 949-936-6400
Erica Hoegh, prin. Fax 936-6409
Westwood Basics ES 400/K-6
1 Liberty 92620 949-936-6450
Stan Machesky, prin. Fax 936-6459
Woodbury ES K-6
125 Great Lawn 92620 949-936-5750
Chriss Shane, prin. Fax 936-5759

Tustin USD
Supt. — See Tustin
Hicks Canyon ES 700/K-5
3817 View Park 92602 714-734-1878
Rich Montgomery, prin. Fax 669-0564
Myford ES 700/K-5
3181 Trevino Dr 92602 714-734-1875
Amy Fedderly, prin. Fax 731-7614

Mariners Church Preschool 200/PK-PK
5001 Newport Coast Dr 92603 949-854-7030
Linda Jahneke, dir. Fax 854-4396
New Horizon S - Irvine 100/K-6
1 Truman St 92620 949-552-5411
Dina Eletreby, hdmstr.
Northwood Montessori S 200/PK-1
12100 Yale Ct 92620 714-508-0400
Amy Martin, dir. Fax 508-0444
Tarbut V'Torah Day ES 300/K-5
5200 Bonita Canyon Dr 92603 949-509-9500
Dr. Jean Oleson, prin. Fax 856-2400

Irwindale, Los Angeles, Pop. 1,480
Covina-Valley USD
Supt. — See Covina
Merwin ES 400/K-5
16125 Cypress Ave 91706 626-472-7660
Joan Moorman, prin. Fax 472-7675

Isleton, Sacramento, Pop. 820
River Delta USD
Supt. — See Rio Vista
Isleton ES 100/K-6
PO Box 728 95641 916-777-6515
Kathy Wright, prin. Fax 777-6525

Ivanhoe, Tulare, Pop. 3,293
Visalia USD
Supt. — See Visalia
Ivanhoe ES 700/K-6
16030 Avenue 332 93235 559-730-7849
Deborah Cardoza, prin. Fax 730-7848

Jackson, Amador, Pop. 4,303
Amador County USD 4,200/K-12
217 Rex Ave 95642 209-223-1750
Richard Glock, supt. Fax 296-3133
www.amadorcoe.org/
Jackson ES 400/K-6
217 Rex Ave 95642 209-257-5600
Barbara Magpusao, prin. Fax 223-2366

Jackson JHS 400/6-8
217 Rex Ave 95642 209-257-5700
Janet Pabst, prin. Fax 257-5311
Other Schools – See Ione, Pine Grove, Pioneer, Plymouth, Sutter Creek

Jacumba, San Diego
Mountain Empire USD
Supt. — See Pine Valley
Jacumba ES 100/K-2
44343 Old Highway 80 91934 619-766-4464
Brennan McLaughlin, prin. Fax 766-4532

Jamestown, Tuolumne, Pop. 2,178
Jamestown ESD 500/K-8
18299 5th Ave 95327 209-984-4058
Diane Dotson, supt. Fax 984-0434
www.jamestown.k12.ca.us
Jamestown S 500/K-8
18299 5th Ave 95327 209-984-5217
Lucinda Jaconette, prin. Fax 984-2069

Sierra Waldorf S 100/PK-8
19234 Rawhide Rd 95327 209-984-0454
Wendy Burkhard, admin. Fax 984-4125

Jamul, San Diego, Pop. 2,258
Jamul-Dulzura UNSD 1,000/K-8
14581 Lyons Valley Rd 91935 619-669-7700
Nadine Bennett, supt. Fax 669-0254
www.jdusd.net/
Jamul IS 200/4-5
14545 Lyons Valley Rd 91935 619-669-7900
Liz Bystedt, prin. Fax 669-5324
Jamul PS 400/K-3
14567 Lyons Valley Rd 91935 619-669-7800
Liz Bystedt, prin. Fax 669-0438
Oak Grove MS 400/6-8
14344 Olive Vista Dr 91935 619-669-2700
Chris Callaway, prin. Fax 669-7632

Janesville, Lassen
Janesville UNESD 400/K-8
PO Box 280 96114 530-253-3660
Zach Thurman, supt. Fax 253-3891
www.janesvilleschool.org
Janesville S 400/K-8
PO Box 280 96114 530-253-3551
Zach Thurman, prin. Fax 253-2127

Johannesburg, Kern
Sierra Sands USD
Supt. — See Ridgecrest
Rand ES 50/K-3
PO Box 157 93528 760-374-2326
Virginia Cornell, prin. Fax 374-2167

Joshua Tree, San Bernardino, Pop. 3,898
Morongo USD
Supt. — See Twentynine Palms
Friendly Hills S 500/K-8
7252 Sunny Vista Rd 92252 760-366-3812
Garrett Gruwell, prin. Fax 366-1061
Joshua Tree ES 400/K-6
6051 Sunburst St 92252 760-366-8459
Daniele Hunter, prin. Fax 366-5364

Julian, San Diego, Pop. 1,284
Julian UNESD 400/K-8
PO Box 337 92036 760-765-0661
Kevin Ogden, supt. Fax 765-0220
www.sdcoe.k12.ca.us/districts/julianel/
Julian ES 300/K-6
PO Box 337 92036 760-765-0661
Brian Duffy, prin. Fax 765-0220
Julian JHS 100/7-8
PO Box 337 92036 760-765-0575
Brian Duffy, prin. Fax 765-3340

Junction City, Trinity
Junction City ESD 100/K-8
430 Red Hill Rd 96048 530-623-6381
Christine Camara, supt. Fax 623-5652
www.junctioncityschool.org/
Junction City S 100/K-8
430 Red Hill Rd 96048 530-623-6381
Christine Camara, prin. Fax 623-5652

Kelseyville, Lake, Pop. 2,861
Kelseyville USD 1,900/K-12
4410 Konocti Rd 95451 707-279-1511
Boyce McClain, supt. Fax 279-9221
www.kusd.lake.k12.ca.us
Kelseyville ES 500/K-5
5065 Konocti Rd 95451 707-279-4232
Dave McQueen, prin. Fax 279-8748
Mountain Vista MS 400/6-8
5081 Konocti Rd 95451 707-279-4060
John Berry, prin. Fax 279-8835
Riviera ES 300/K-5
10505 Fairway Dr 95451 707-277-6050
Enrico Frediani, prin. Fax 277-6060

Kensington, Contra Costa, Pop. 4,974
West Contra Costa USD
Supt. — See Richmond
Kensington ES 500/K-6
90 Highland Blvd 94708 510-231-1415
Judith Sanders, prin. Fax 526-3189

Kentfield, Marin, Pop. 6,030
Kentfield ESD 1,000/K-8
750 College Ave 94904 415-458-5130
Mary Jo Pettegrew, supt. Fax 458-5137
www.kentfieldschools.org/
Bacich ES 500/K-4
25 McAllister Ave 94904 415-925-2220
Sally Peck, prin. Fax 925-2226
Kent MS 400/5-8
800 College Ave 94904 415-458-5970
Skip Kniesche, prin. Fax 458-5973

Kenwood, Sonoma
Kenwood ESD 200/K-6
PO Box 220 95452 707-833-2500
Robert Bales, supt. Fax 833-2181
www.kenwoodschool.org/
Kenwood ES 200/K-6
PO Box 220 95452 707-833-2500
Robert Bales, prin. Fax 833-2181

Kerman, Fresno, Pop. 11,223
Kerman USD 4,100/K-12
151 S 1st St 93630 559-846-5383
Robert Frausto, supt. Fax 846-5941
www.kermanusd.com
Kerman-Floyd ES 1,000/K-4
14655 W F St 93630 559-842-4500
Kathy Goodlad, prin. Fax 846-3366
Kerman MS 700/7-8
601 S 1st St 93630 559-842-3000
Amanda Guizar, prin. Fax 846-5217
Liberty IS 600/5-6
16001 W E St 93630 559-842-6000
Melissa Andresen, prin. Fax 846-4068
Sun Empire ES 700/K-4
2649 N Modoc Ave 93630 559-842-4000
Albert DeLeon, prin. Fax 846-5397

Central Valley Christian Molokan S 50/PK-6
PO Box 663 93630 559-846-6042
Sarah Morozov, prin. Fax 846-3771
Kerman Christian S 100/PK-6
15495 W Whitesbridge Ave 93630 559-846-7200
Madeline Rahal, prin. Fax 842-7491

Kernville, Kern, Pop. 1,656
Hot Springs ESD
Supt. — See California Hot Springs
Johnsondale S 50/K-8
HC 1 Box 104 93238 760-376-2427
I.J. Blevens, prin. Fax 376-2427

Kernville UNESD
Supt. — See Lake Isabella
Kernville ES 200/K-5
PO Box 2007 93238 760-376-2249
Aileen Delapp, prin. Fax 376-1935

Kettleman City, Kings, Pop. 1,411
Reef-Sunset USD
Supt. — See Avenal
Kettleman City S 300/K-8
PO Box 599 93239 559-386-5702
Carmel Draper, prin. Fax 386-0207

Keyes, Stanislaus, Pop. 2,878
Keyes UNESD 800/K-8
PO Box 310 95328 209-669-2921
Karen Poppen, supt. Fax 669-2923
www.keyes.k12.ca.us/
Keyes ES 500/K-5
PO Box 549 95328 209-667-1660
Cynthia Schaefer, prin. Fax 668-8714
Other Schools – See Hughson

King City, Monterey, Pop. 11,004
Bitterwater-Tully UNESD 50/K-8
Lonoak Route Box 10 93930 831-385-5339
Kevin Kirschman, supt. Fax 385-9105
Bitterwater-Tully S 50/K-8
Lonoak Route Box 10 93930 831-385-5339
Kevin Kirschman, prin. Fax 385-9105

King City UNSD 2,300/K-8
800 Broadway St 93930 831-385-1144
Tom Michaelson Ed.D., supt. Fax 385-0695
www.kingcity.k12.ca.us/
Chalone Peaks MS 800/6-8
667 Meyer St 93930 831-385-4400
Mike Barbree, prin. Fax 385-4422
Del Rey ES 800/K-5
502 King St 93930 831-385-4884
Dee Shires, prin. Fax 385-1045
Santa Lucia ES 700/K-5
502 Collins St 93930 831-385-3246
Patrick Gross, prin. Fax 385-6310

Kings Beach, Placer, Pop. 2,796
Tahoe-Truckee JUSD
Supt. — See Truckee
Kings Beach ES 400/K-5
PO Box 1177 96143 530-546-2605
Eileen Fahrner, prin. Fax 546-5066

Kingsburg, Fresno, Pop. 11,148
Clay JESD 200/K-8
12449 S Smith Ave 93631 559-897-4185
Bill Mannlein, supt. Fax 897-2280
www.clayschool.k12.ca.us/
Clay S 200/K-8
12449 S Smith Ave 93631 559-897-4185
Bill Mannlein, prin. Fax 897-2280

Kings River UNESD 500/K-8
3961 Avenue 400 93631 559-897-2878
Ed Snell, supt. Fax 897-0320
kingsriverelementary.org/
Kings River S 500/K-8
3961 Avenue 400 93631 559-897-2878
Ed Snell, prin. Fax 897-0320

Kingvale, Nevada
Tahoe-Truckee JUSD
Supt. — See Truckee
Donner Trail ES 100/K-5
11661 Donner Pass Rd 95728 530-426-3639
Susan Phebus, prin. Fax 426-0530

Klamath, Del Norte, Pop. 827
Del Norte County USD
Supt. — See Crescent City
Keating ES 100/K-5
PO Box 65 95548 707-464-0340
William Einman, prin. Fax 464-0348

Kneeland, Humboldt
Kneeland ESD 50/K-8
9313 Kneeland Rd 95549 707-442-5472
Carole Boshears, supt. Fax 442-7784
www.humboldt.k12.ca.us/kneeland_sd/
Kneeland S 50/K-8
9313 Kneeland Rd 95549 707-442-5472
Carole Boshears, prin. Fax 442-7784

Knightsen, Contra Costa
Knightsen ESD 500/K-8
PO Box 265 94548 925-625-0073
Vickey Rinehart, supt. Fax 625-8766
www.knightsen.k12.ca.us
Knightsen S 500/K-8
PO Box 265 94548 925-625-0073
Theresa Estrada, prin. Fax 625-8766
Other Schools – See Brentwood

Knights Ferry, Stanislaus
Knights Ferry ESD 100/K-8
PO Box 840 95361 209-881-3382
Cheryl Griffiths, supt. Fax 881-3525
www.knightsferry.k12.ca.us
Knights Ferry S 100/K-8
PO Box 840 95361 209-881-3382
Cheryl Griffiths, prin. Fax 881-3525

Knights Landing, Yolo
Woodland JUSD
Supt. — See Woodland
Grafton ES 100/K-6
PO Box 458 95645 530-735-6435
Roberto Barajas, prin. Fax 735-6156

Korbel, Humboldt
Maple Creek ESD 50/K-8
15933 Maple Creek Rd 95550 707-668-5596
Karen Schatz, supt. Fax 668-5596
www.humboldt.k12.ca.us/mapleck_sd/
Maple Creek S 50/K-8
15933 Maple Creek Rd 95550 707-668-5596
John Cromwell, prin. Fax 668-5596

Kyburz, El Dorado
Silver Fork ESD
Supt. — See Pollock Pines
Silver Fork S 50/K-8
PO Box 45 95720 530-293-3163
Fax 293-3193

La Canada Flintridge, Los Angeles, Pop. 20,998
La Canada USD 4,100/K-12
4490 Cornishon Ave 91011 818-952-8300
Jim Stratton, supt. Fax 952-8309
www.lcusd.net
La Canada ES 700/K-6
4540 Encinas Dr 91011 818-952-8350
Elissa DeAngelo, prin. Fax 952-8355
Palm Crest ES 600/K-6
5025 Palm Dr 91011 818-952-8360
Anais Wenn, prin. Fax 952-8365
Paradise Canyon ES 700/K-6
471 Knight Way 91011 818-952-8340
Donna Robinson, prin. Fax 952-8337

Crestview Preparatory S 200/K-6
140 Foothill Blvd 91011 818-952-0925
Marie Kidd, hdmstr. Fax 952-8470
Learning Castle S & La Canada Prep 400/K-8
4490 Cornishon Ave 91011 818-952-8008
Terry Villanueva, dir. Fax 952-5101
Renaissance Academy 100/K-12
4490 Cornishon Ave 91011 818-952-3055
Sandra Staffer, prin. Fax 952-3069
St. Bede the Venerable S 300/PK-8
4524 Crown Ave 91011 818-790-7884
Ralph Valente, prin. Fax 790-7887

La Crescenta, Los Angeles, Pop. 16,968
Glendale USD
Supt. — See Glendale
Dunsmore ES 500/K-6
4717 Dunsmore Ave 91214 818-248-1758
Karen Stegman, prin. Fax 249-7918
La Crescenta ES 500/K-6
4343 La Crescenta Ave 91214 818-249-3187
Kim Bishop, prin. Fax 248-3168
Lincoln ES 500/K-6
4310 New York Ave 91214 818-249-1863
Bill Card, prin. Fax 249-7876
Monte Vista ES 600/K-6
2620 Orange Ave 91214 818-248-2617
Susan Hoge Ed.D., prin. Fax 248-5263
Mountain Avenue ES 600/K-6
2307 Mountain Ave 91214 818-248-7766
Rebecca Witt, prin. Fax 248-6352
Rosemont MS 1,300/7-8
4725 Rosemont Ave 91214 818-248-4224
Michele Doll Ed.D., prin. Fax 248-3790
Valley View ES 400/K-6
4900 Maryland Ave 91214 818-236-3771
Carla Walker, prin. Fax 542-6480

Crescenta Valley Adventist S 100/K-8
6245 Honolulu Ave 91214 818-249-1504
Elaine Pugh, prin. Fax 249-1595
St. James the Less S 200/K-8
4635 Dunsmore Ave 91214 818-248-7778
Susan Romero, prin. Fax 248-5242

Ladera Ranch, Orange
Capistrano USD
Supt. — See San Juan Capistrano

Chaparral ES 900/K-5
29001 Sienna Pkwy 92694 949-234-5349
Dr. Kevin Rafferty, prin. Fax 364-3952
Ladera Ranch ES 800/K-5
29551 Sienna Pkwy 92694 949-234-5915
Meg Gwyn, prin. Fax 364-1149
Ladera Ranch MS 900/6-8
29551 Sienna Pkwy 92694 949-234-5922
Karen Gerhard, prin. Fax 364-1149
Oso Grande ES 500/K-5
30251 Sienna Pkwy 92694 949-234-5966
Jayne Martin, prin. Fax 365-1716

Ladera Ranch ES 200/PK-6
26122 ONeill Dr 92694 949-429-3811
Jim Berkompas, prin. Fax 429-3818
Ladera Ranch JHS 100/7-8
26122 ONeill Dr 92694 949-429-3812
Lloyd Grim, prin. Fax 429-3820

Lafayette, Contra Costa, Pop. 24,767
Lafayette ESD 3,200/K-8
PO Box 1029 94549 925-927-3500
Fred Brill, supt. Fax 284-1525
www.lafsd.k12.ca.us
Burton Valley ES 700/K-5
561 Merriewood Dr 94549 925-927-3550
Sue Rusk, prin. Fax 284-5891
Happy Valley ES 400/K-5
3855 Happy Valley Rd 94549 925-927-3560
Wendy Patterson, prin. Fax 284-5973
Lafayette ES 400/K-5
950 Moraga Rd 94549 925-927-3570
Mary Maddux, prin. Fax 283-4091
Springhill ES 500/K-5
3301 Springhill Rd 94549 925-927-3580
Bruce Wodhams, prin. Fax 283-3675
Stanley MS 1,200/6-8
3455 School St 94549 925-927-3530
David Schrag, prin. Fax 283-1797

Contra Costa Jewish Day S 100/K-8
3800 Mt Diablo Blvd 94549 925-284-8288
Dean Goldfein, hdmstr.
Meher S 200/K-5
999 Leland Dr 94549 925-938-9958
Ellen Evans, prin. Fax 938-9183
St. Perpetua S 300/K-8
3445 Hamlin Rd 94549 925-284-1640
Karen Goodshaw, prin. Fax 284-5676

La Grange, Stanislaus
La Grange ESD 50/K-8
PO Box 66 95329 209-853-2132
Joseph Magnu, supt. Fax 853-2007
La Grange S 50/K-8
PO Box 66 95329 209-853-2132
Joseph Magnu, prin. Fax 853-2007

Mariposa County USD
Supt. — See Mariposa
Lake Don Pedro S 200/K-8
2411 Hidalgo St 95329 209-852-2144
Ron Henderson, prin. Fax 852-2184

Laguna Beach, Orange, Pop. 24,127
Laguna Beach USD 2,900/K-12
550 Blumont St 92651 949-497-7700
Robert Fraisse, supt. Fax 497-6021
www.lagunabeachschools.org
El Morro ES 500/K-5
8681 N Coast Hwy 92651 949-497-7780
Christopher Duddy, prin. Fax 497-7784
Thurston MS 700/6-8
2100 Park Ave 92651 949-497-7785
Dr. Joanne Culverhouse, prin. Fax 497-7798
Top of the World ES 600/K-5
21601 Treetop Ln 92651 949-497-7790
Ron LaMotte, prin. Fax 497-5397

Anneliese's S 300/K-8
20062 Laguna Canyon Rd 92651 949-497-8310
Kimberly Hanson, dir.
St. Catherine of Siena S 200/K-8
3090 S Coast Hwy 92651 949-494-7339
Jan Callender, prin. Fax 376-5752

Laguna Hills, Orange, Pop. 32,198
Saddleback Valley USD
Supt. — See Mission Viejo
Lomarena ES 600/K-6
25100 Earhart Rd 92653 949-581-1370
Laura Canzone, prin. Fax 581-8520
San Joaquin ES 600/K-6
22182 Barbera 92653 949-581-3450
Jonathan Kaplan, prin. Fax 581-1031
Valencia ES 600/K-6
25661 Paseo De Valencia 92653 949-830-3650
Jeremy Stonebarger, prin. Fax 830-1868

Cornerstone Community S 100/K-8
23331 Moulton Pkwy 92653 949-595-0070
Sharon Cannavo, admin. Fax 472-0747
Pathway S 50/3-8
23802 Avenida De La Carlota 92653 949-837-1203
Ellie Watkins, hdmstr. Fax 837-1205
St. Augustine Classical Academy 50/K-8
25382 MacKenzie St 92653 949-395-2734
Shaun Howington, dir.
St. George's Academy 50/PK-K
23802 Avenida De La Carlota 92653 949-837-4530
Lori Burwell, dir. Fax 581-5810

Laguna Niguel, Orange, Pop. 64,664
Capistrano USD
Supt. — See San Juan Capistrano
Bergeson ES 500/K-5
25302 Rancho Niguel Rd 92677 949-643-1540
Barbara Scholl, prin. Fax 643-7931
Crown Valley ES 500/K-5
29292 Crown Valley Pkwy 92677 949-495-5115
Tony Bogle, prin. Fax 495-6103
Hidden Hills ES 500/K-5
25142 Hidden Hills Rd 92677 949-495-0050
Aida Nunez, prin. Fax 495-6920
Laguna Niguel ES 600/K-5
27922 Niguel Heights Blvd 92677 949-234-5308
Ellen Fine, prin. Fax 360-4407
Malcom ES 700/K-5
32261 Charles Rd 92677 949-248-0542
Dr. Faith Morris, prin. Fax 248-7697
Moulton ES 700/K-5
29851 Highlands Ave 92677 949-234-5980
Jerry Vlasic, prin. Fax 495-5233
Niguel Hills MS 1,400/6-8
29070 Paseo De La Escuela 92677 949-234-5360
Tim Reece, prin. Fax 249-2069
White ES 800/K-5
25422 Chapparosa Park Rd 92677 949-249-3875
Mike Spelber, prin. Fax 249-5316

Childrens Choice/McDowell S 100/K-6
29028 Aloma Ave 92677 949-495-5162
Cari Caris, admin.
Laguna Niguel Jr. Academy 100/K-10
29702 Kensington Dr 92677 949-495-3428
David Tripp, prin. Fax 495-3438
Laguna Niguel Montessori Center 200/PK-1
28083 Moulton Pkwy 92677 949-643-1200
Debbie McLane, hdmstr. Fax 643-1588
St. Anne S 800/PK-8
32451 Bear Brand Rd 92677 949-487-2663
Randy Adams, admin. Fax 487-2137
Vine Preparatory Academy 100/K-8
27632 El Lazo 92677 949-280-8641
Jodie Atkinson, admin. Fax 389-0270

La Habra, Orange, Pop. 59,326
La Habra City ESD 5,900/K-8
PO Box 307 90633 562-690-2300
Susan Belenardo Ed.D., supt. Fax 690-4154
www.lhcsd.k12.ca.us
Arbolita ES 400/K-2
PO Box 307 90633 562-690-2352
Teresa Egan, prin. Fax 697-8862
El Cerrito ES 500/K-2
PO Box 307 90633 562-690-2340
Pam Cunningham, prin. Fax 690-2342
Imperial MS 1,000/6-8
PO Box 307 90633 562-690-2344
Cathy Seighman, prin. Fax 526-3678
Ladera Palma ES 500/K-2
PO Box 307 90633 562-690-2348
Cathy Kalcevich, prin. Fax 697-9734
Las Lomas ES 500/K-2
PO Box 307 90633 562-690-2353
Sheryl Tecker, prin. Fax 870-9049
Las Positas ES 600/3-5
PO Box 307 90633 562-690-2356
Sandi Baltes, prin. Fax 871-2073
Sierra Vista ES 700/3-5
PO Box 307 90633 562-690-2359
Rick Snyder, prin. Fax 690-2093
Walnut ES 600/3-5
PO Box 307 90633 562-690-2369
Mike Klewer, prin. Fax 697-3621
Washington MS 1,000/6-8
PO Box 307 90633 562-690-2374
Gary Mantey, prin. Fax 690-7834

Lowell JSD
Supt. — See Whittier
El Portal ES 500/K-6
200 Nada St 90631 562-902-4211
Kim Likert, prin. Fax 694-0022
Macy ES 400/K-6
2301 Russell St 90631 562-902-4231
Tara Ryan, prin. Fax 690-8989
Olita ES 400/K-6
950 Briercliff Dr 90631 562-902-4251
Krista Van Hoogmoed, prin. Fax 690-0273

Our Lady of Guadalupe S 400/K-8
920 W La Habra Blvd 90631 562-697-9726
Francine Kubasek, prin. Fax 905-0095

La Honda, San Mateo
La Honda-Pescadero USD
Supt. — See Pescadero
La Honda ES 100/K-5
PO Box 87 94020 650-747-0051
Kristen Lindstrom, prin. Fax 747-0617

La Jolla, See San Diego
San Diego USD
Supt. — See San Diego
Bird Rock ES 500/K-5
5371 La Jolla Hermosa Ave 92037 858-488-0537
Beverly Candage, prin. Fax 539-0541
La Jolla ES 500/K-5
1111 Marine St 92037 858-454-7196
Donna Tripi, prin. Fax 459-6918
Muirlands MS 1,100/6-8
1056 Nautilus St 92037 858-459-4211
Christine Hargrave, prin. Fax 459-8075
Torrey Pines ES 400/K-5
8350 Cliffridge Ave 92037 858-453-2323
James Solo, prin. Fax 452-6923

All Hallows Academy 300/K-8
2390 Nautilus St 92037 858-459-6074
Michaele Durant, prin. Fax 459-4602
Childrens S 200/PK-8
2225 Torrey Pines Ln 92037 858-454-0184
Molly Huffman, hdmstr. Fax 454-0186
Evans S 100/K-6
6510 La Jolla Scenic Dr S 92037 858-459-2066
Gillispie S 200/K-6
7380 Girard Ave 92037 858-459-3773
Alison Fleming, hdmstr. Fax 459-3834
La Jolla Country Day S 1,000/PK-12
9490 Genesee Ave 92037 858-453-3440
Christopher Schuck, hdmstr. Fax 453-8210
San Diego French American S 200/PK-8
6550 Soledad Mountain Rd 92037 858-456-2807
Andre Bordes, prin. Fax 459-2670
Stella Maris Academy 200/K-8
7654 Herschel Ave 92037 858-454-2461
Patricia Lowell, prin. Fax 454-4913

Lake Almanor, Plumas

Lake Almanor Christian S 50/K-12
2610 State Route A13 96137 530-596-4100
Gwen Meinhardt, prin. Fax 596-4682

Lake Arrowhead, San Bernardino, Pop. 6,539
Rim of the World USD 5,300/K-12
PO Box 430 92352 909-336-2031
Ronald Peavy Ed.D., supt. Fax 337-4527
www.rimsd.k12.ca.us
Henck IS 800/7-8
PO Box 430 92352 909-336-0360
Robert Turner, prin. Fax 336-3449
Lake Arrowhead ES 700/K-6
PO Box 430 92352 909-336-0387
Debbie Wogen, prin. Fax 336-3440
Lake Gregory ES 400/4-6
PO Box 430 92352 909-336-3474
David Bealer, prin. Fax 336-3450
Other Schools – See Crestline, Running Springs, Twin Peaks

Lake Arrowhead Christian S 100/K-12
PO Box 179 92352 909-337-3739
Randall Leonard, prin. Fax 337-4550

Lake Elsinore, Riverside, Pop. 39,258
Lake Elsinore USD 20,600/K-12
545 Chaney St 92530 951-253-7000
Dr. Frank Passarella, supt. Fax 253-7084
www.leusd.k12.ca.us
Butterfield ES 900/K-5
16275 Grand Ave 92530 951-253-7470
Dorri Neal, prin. Fax 253-7471
Canyon Lake MS 1,300/6-8
33005 Canyon Hills Rd 92532 951-244-2123
Dr. Tamerin Capellino, prin. Fax 244-2103
Cottonwood Canyon ES 900/K-5
32100 Lost Rd 92532 951-244-2585
Preston Perez, prin. Fax 244-2549
Elsinore ES 500/K-5
512 W Sumner Ave 92530 951-253-7615
Rita Post, prin. Fax 674-8289
Elsinore MS 800/6-8
1203 W Graham Ave 92530 951-674-2118
Narciso Iglesias, prin. Fax 674-6302
Lakeland Village MS 900/6-8
18730 Grand Ave 92530 951-253-7400
Billie DaVolt, prin. Fax 253-7424
Machado ES 800/K-5
15150 Joy St 92530 951-253-7500
Gail Forseth, prin. Fax 253-7501
Railroad Canyon ES 600/K-5
1300 Mill St 92530 951-674-8671
Jeri Peterson, prin. Fax 674-0871
Rice Canyon ES 800/K-5
29535 Westwind Dr 92530 951-471-2184
Dr. Corene Barr, prin. Fax 471-2186
Terra Cotta MS 1,500/6-8
29291 Lake St 92530 951-253-7380
Sarah Arredondo, prin. Fax 674-5191
Tuscany Hills ES 600/K-5
23 Ponte Russo 92532 951-245-6850
Jeff Marks, prin. Fax 245-6857
Warren ES K-5
41221 Rosetta Canyon Dr 92532 951-253-7810
Whitney Naughton, prin. Fax 253-7817
Withrow ES 700/K-5
30100 Audelo St 92530 951-678-0132
Carolyn Berry, prin. Fax 678-9796
Other Schools – See Corona, Wildomar

Lake Forest, Orange, Pop. 76,412
Saddleback Valley USD
Supt. — See Mission Viejo
Aliso ES 400/K-6
22882 Loumont Dr 92630 949-830-4670
Crystal Turner, prin. Fax 859-2071
Lake Forest ES 800/K-6
21801 Pittsford 92630 949-830-9945
Michelle Vaught, prin. Fax 830-6478
La Madera ES 600/K-6
25350 Serrano Rd 92630 949-770-1415
Roger Mayer, prin. Fax 770-0257
Olivewood ES 500/K-6
23391 Dune Mear Rd 92630 949-837-6682
Patty Murphey, prin. Fax 586-8014
Rancho Canada ES 700/K-6
21801 Winding Way 92630 949-768-5252
Tom Potwara, prin. Fax 768-5741
Santiago ES 400/K-6
24982 Rivendell Dr 92630 949-586-2820
Andrea Norman, prin. Fax 586-4232
Serrano IS 1,500/7-8
24642 Jeronimo Rd 92630 949-586-3221
Robert Presby, prin. Fax 586-3773

Abiding Savior Lutheran S 300/K-8
23262 El Toro Rd 92630 949-830-1461
Dr. Carolyn Sims, prin. Fax 830-7921
El Toro Baptist S 100/PK-6
23302 El Toro Rd 92630 949-855-4599
Faye Martnick, dir. Fax 855-3891
Grace Christian S 400/PK-3
26052 Trabuco Rd 92630 949-951-8683
Sandi Brakebush, prin.
Montessori on the Lake S 100/K-8
23311 Muirlands Blvd 92630 949-855-5630
Sarah Smith, prin. Fax 855-5633

Lake Hughes, Los Angeles
Hughes-Elizabeth Lakes UNESD 400/K-8
PO Box 530 93532 661-724-1231
Sandra Lyon, supt. Fax 724-0967
www.heluesd.org
Hughes-Elizabeth Lakes S 400/K-8
PO Box 530 93532 661-724-1231
Sandra Lyon, prin. Fax 724-1485

Lake Isabella, Kern, Pop. 3,323
Kernville UNESD 900/K-8
PO Box 3077 93240 760-379-3651
Mary Barlow, supt. Fax 379-3812
Wallace ES 400/K-5
PO Box 3077 93240 760-379-2621
Stephanie Pope, prin. Fax 379-1324
Wallace MS 300/6-8
PO Box 3077 93240 760-379-4646
Stephanie Pope, prin. Fax 379-1322
Other Schools – See Kernville

Lakeport, Lake, Pop. 5,241
Lakeport USD 1,700/K-12
2508 Howard Ave 95453 707-262-3000
Erin Smith-Hagberg, supt. Fax 263-7332
www.lakeport.k12.ca.us
Lakeport ES 400/K-3
2508 Howard Ave 95453 707-262-3005
Nancy Kirby, prin. Fax 262-5531
Terrace MS 700/4-8
2508 Howard Ave 95453 707-262-3007
Jill Falconer, prin. Fax 262-5532

Konocti Christian Academy 50/K-8
PO Box 1515 95453 707-262-1522
Jeff Rein, dir. Fax 263-4466
Westlake SDA S 50/K-8
6585 Westlake Rd 95453 707-263-4607
Margaret Utt, prin. Fax 263-7160

Lakeside, San Diego, Pop. 56,225
Lakeside UNSD 4,000/K-8
12335 Woodside Ave 92040 619-390-2600
Stephen Halfaker, supt. Fax 561-7929
www.lsschools.k12.ca.us/lakeside/default.htm
Lakeside Farms ES 500/K-5
11915 Lakeside Ave 92040 619-390-2646
Scott Goergens, prin. Fax 390-2648
Lakeside MS 600/6-8
11833 Woodside Ave 92040 619-390-2636
Steve Mull, prin. Fax 390-2643
Lakeview ES 500/K-5
9205 Lakeview Rd 92040 619-390-2652
Rhonda Taylor, prin. Fax 390-2693
Lemon Crest ES 500/K-5
12463 Lemon Crest Dr 92040 619-390-2527
Larry Skeels, prin. Fax 390-2563
Lindo Park ES 500/K-5
12824 Lakeshore Dr 92040 619-390-2656
Virginia Van Zant, prin. Fax 390-2551
Riverview ES 400/K-5
9308 Winter Gardens Blvd 92040 619-390-2662
Olympia Kyriakidis, prin. Fax 390-2668
Tierra Del Sol MS 800/6-8
9611 Petite Ln 92040 619-390-2670
Chris McDuffie, prin. Fax 390-2518
Winter Gardens ES 100/K-5
8501 Pueblo Rd 92040 619-390-2687
Suzie Smith, prin. Fax 390-2695

Foothills Christian S 200/K-8
PO Box 2029 92040 619-561-2295
Regina Hoffman, prin. Fax 561-0238
Our Lady of Perpetual Help S 200/K-8
9825 Pino Dr 92040 619-443-1440
Jeanne Pate, prin. Fax 443-1733

Lakewood, Los Angeles, Pop. 80,467
ABC USD
Supt. — See Cerritos
Aloha ES 500/K-6
11737 214th St 90715 562-924-8329
Julie Yabumoto, prin. Fax 809-3297
Melbourne ES 600/K-6
21314 Claretta Ave 90715 562-924-1658
Kathy Neder-Olivos, prin. Fax 402-2764
Palms ES 600/K-6
12445 207th St 90715 562-924-5549
Beverly Spicer, prin. Fax 924-9439
Willow ES 600/K-6
11733 205th St 90715 562-865-6209
Linda Dohm, prin. Fax 402-9837

Bellflower USD
Supt. — See Bellflower
Foster ES 700/K-6
5223 Bigelow St 90712 562-804-6518
Deirdre Reyes, prin. Fax 804-6520
Intensive Learning Center 800/K-6
4718 Michelson St 90712 562-804-6513
Lisa Paioni, prin. Fax 633-3957
Lindstrom ES 900/K-6
5900 Canehill Ave 90713 562-804-6525
Beverly Swanson, prin. Fax 804-6579
Williams ES 800/K-6
6144 Clark Ave 90712 562-804-6540
Keisha Sawyer, prin. Fax 804-6543

Long Beach USD
Supt. — See Long Beach
Cleveland ES 600/K-5
4760 Hackett Ave 90713 562-420-7552
Julie Drysdale, prin. Fax 420-7820
Gompers S 700/K-8
5206 Briercrest Ave 90713 562-925-2285
Gray Lange, prin. Fax 920-0053
Holmes ES 600/K-5
5020 Barlin Ave 90712 562-633-4427
Kelly Koga, prin. Fax 633-3083
Hoover MS 1,100/6-8
3501 Country Club Dr 90712 562-421-1213
Michael Troyer, prin. Fax 421-8063
MacArthur ES 400/K-5
6011 Centralia St 90713 562-420-3588
Wayne Wong, prin. Fax 420-7883
Madison ES 600/K-5
2801 Bomberry St 90712 562-420-7731
Geraldine Rescinito, prin. Fax 420-7819
Monroe S 900/K-8
4400 Ladoga Ave 90713 562-429-8911
Cathleen Imbroane, prin. Fax 420-7667
Riley ES 600/K-5
3319 Sandwood St 90712 562-420-9595
Stacy Sanchez, prin. Fax 420-7708

Paramount USD
Supt. — See Paramount
Lakewood S 400/K-8
3701 Michelson St 90712 562-602-8032
Alvaretta Baxter, prin. Fax 602-8033

St. Pancratius S 300/K-8
3601 Saint Pancratius Pl 90712 562-634-6310
Carol Kulesza, prin. Fax 633-0731

La Mesa, San Diego, Pop. 53,081
Cajon Valley UNESD
Supt. — See El Cajon
Avocado ES 500/K-5
3845 Avocado School Rd 91941 619-588-3100
Ryan Burke, prin. Fax 579-4872

La Mesa-Spring Valley SD 13,000/K-8
4750 Date Ave 91942 619-668-5700
Brian Marshall, supt. Fax 668-5809
www.lmsvsd.k12.ca.us
La Mesa Dale ES 400/K-5
4370 Parks Ave 91941 619-668-5740
Diane Avery, prin. Fax 668-8352
La Mesa MS 1,200/6-8
4200 Parks Ave 91941 619-668-5730
Beth Thomas, prin. Fax 668-8303
Lemon Avenue ES 600/K-5
8787 Lemon Ave 91941 619-668-5835
Jennifer Luibel, prin. Fax 668-8354
Maryland Avenue ES 300/K-5
5400 Maryland Ave 91942 619-668-5744
Laura Hollis, prin. Fax 668-5746
Murdock ES 600/K-5
4354 Conrad Dr 91941 619-668-5775
John Ashley, prin. Fax 668-8343
Murray Manor ES 600/K-5
8305 El Paso St 91942 619-668-5865
James Parker, prin. Fax 668-8343
Northmont ES 400/K-5
9405 Gregory St 91942 619-668-5830
Melody Belcher, prin. Fax 668-8340
Parkway MS 1,200/6-8
9009 Park Plaza Dr 91942 619-668-5810
Cyndi Sutton, prin. Fax 668-5779
Rolando ES 400/K-5
6925 Tower St 91942 619-688-5800
Guido MagLiato, prin. Fax 668-5805
Other Schools – See El Cajon, Spring Valley

Lemon Grove ESD
Supt. — See Lemon Grove
Vista La Mesa ES 500/K-5
3900 Violet St 91941 619-825-5645
Glenn Heath, prin. Fax 825-5783

Calvary Chapel of La Mesa Christian S 100/K-8
7525 El Cajon Blvd 91942 619-697-0165
Dr. Kathy Kotowski, prin. Fax 697-7258
Christ Lutheran S 300/PK-8
7929 La Mesa Blvd 91942 619-462-5211
Xavria Schwarz, prin. Fax 462-5275
Mount Helix Academy 200/K-8
5955 Severin Dr 91942 619-466-1434
Barbara Moulaison, dir. Fax 466-1448
St. Martin of Tours Academy 300/PK-8
7708 El Cajon Blvd 91942 619-466-3241
Antoinette Dimuzio, prin. Fax 466-0285
Shepherd of the Hills S 50/K-8
9191 Fletcher Pkwy 91942 619-469-9443
Andrew Mildebrandt, prin. Fax 469-9443

La Mirada, Los Angeles, Pop. 49,640
Norwalk-La Mirada USD
Supt. — See Norwalk
Benton MS 600/6-8
15709 Olive Branch Dr 90638 562-943-1553
Craig Hauke, prin. Fax 947-3861
Dulles ES 400/K-5
12726 Meadow Green Rd 90638 562-943-6734
Susan Shanks, prin. Fax 902-0438
Eastwood ES 600/K-5
15730 Pescados Dr 90638 714-521-6480
Yvette Cantu, prin. Fax 521-6485
Escalona ES 500/K-5
15135 Escalona Rd 90638 714-521-0970
Bonnie Lytle, prin. Fax 521-1173
Foster Road ES 500/K-5
13930 Foster Rd 90638 562-921-9908
Dr. Jean Maddox, prin. Fax 404-3952
Gardenhill ES 600/K-5
14607 Gardenhill Dr 90638 562-944-6128
Eileen Burkholder, prin. Fax 944-8188
Hutchinson MS 600/6-8
13900 Estero Rd 90638 562-944-3268
Sara Siemens, prin. Fax 944-3269
La Pluma ES 500/K-5
14420 La Pluma Dr 90638 562-943-7104
Michelle Green, prin. Fax 943-6884
Los Coyotes MS 600/6-8
14640 Mercado Ave 90638 714-523-2051
Dr. Sylvia Begtrup, prin. Fax 739-2368

Beatitudes of Our Lord S 300/PK-8
13021 Santa Gertrudes Ave 90638 562-943-3218
Leonard Payette, prin. Fax 902-7627
Heights Christian JHS 300/7-8
12900 Bluefield Ave 90638 562-947-3309
Rolland Esslinger, prin. Fax 947-1001
La Mirada Heights Christian S 400/PK-6
12200 Oxford Dr 90638 562-902-1779
Luann Macdonald, prin. Fax 902-1769
St. Paul of the Cross S 200/K-8
14030 Foster Rd 90638 562-921-2118
Lorraine Mendiaz, prin. Fax 802-2048

Lamont, Kern, Pop. 11,517
Lamont ESD 2,700/K-8
7915 Burgundy Ave 93241 661-845-0751
Cheryl McConaughey, supt. Fax 845-0689
www.lamontschooldistrict.org/
Alicante Avenue ES 1,100/K-6
7915 Burgundy Ave 93241 661-845-1452
Jonathan Martinez, prin. Fax 845-5114
Lamont ES 600/K-3
7915 Burgundy Ave 93241 661-845-4404
Richard Martinez, prin. Fax 845-5837
Mountain View MS 600/7-8
7915 Burgundy Ave 93241 661-845-2291
Fred Molina, prin. Fax 845-1839
Myrtle Avenue ES 400/4-6
7915 Burgundy Ave 93241 661-845-2217
Dolores Lopez, prin. Fax 845-4816

Lancaster, Los Angeles, Pop. 134,032
Eastside UNSD 3,300/K-8
45006 30th St E 93535 661-952-1200
Dr. Roberto Villa, supt. Fax 952-1220
www.eastside.k12.ca.us
Cole MS 1,000/6-8
3126 E Avenue I 93535 661-946-1041
Matt Ross, prin. Fax 946-0166
Columbia ES 800/K-5
2640 E Avenue J4 93535 661-946-1927
Francisco Pinto, prin. Fax 946-1628
Eastside ES 800/K-6
6742 E Avenue H 93535 661-946-3907
Troy Cox, prin. Fax 946-5431
Tierra Bonita South ES 700/K-6
44820 27th St E 93535 661-946-3038
George Guerrero, prin. Fax 946-3198

Lancaster ESD 16,200/K-8
44711 Cedar Ave 93534 661-948-4661
Dr. Howard Sunberg, supt. Fax 948-9398
www.lancaster.k12.ca.us
Amargosa Creek MS 1,200/6-8
44333 27th St W 93536 661-729-6064
Julie Vela, prin. Fax 729-6858
Cory ES 800/K-5
3540 W Avenue K4 93536 661-722-1010
Michael Choate, prin. Fax 722-0625
Desert View ES 1,000/K-5
1555 W Avenue H10 93534 661-942-9521
Staci Jordan, prin. Fax 942-4321
El Dorado ES 800/K-5
361 E Pondera St 93535 661-942-8487
Doug Duncan, prin. Fax 942-2267
Endeavour MS 700/6-8
43755 45th St W 93536 661-723-0351
Robert Porter, prin. Fax 723-1362
Joshua ES 1,000/K-5
43926 2nd St E 93535 661-948-0743
Denise Trentham, prin. Fax 940-6671
Lincoln ES 1,000/K-5
44021 15th St E 93535 661-726-9913
Donna Shoffner, prin. Fax 726-4353
Linda Verde ES 800/K-5
44924 5th St E 93535 661-942-0431
Lorraine Zapata, prin. Fax 942-7621
Mariposa ES 700/K-5
737 W Avenue H6 93534 661-942-0437
Mark Gross, prin. Fax 949-1324
Monte Vista ES 900/K-5
1235 W Kettering St 93534 661-942-1477
Elaine Darby, prin. Fax 949-1328
New Vista MS 1,300/6-8
753 E Avenue K2 93535 661-726-4271
Deborah Lewis, prin. Fax 726-4278
Northrop ES 900/K-5
835 E Avenue K4 93535 661-949-0435
Karen Stults, prin. Fax 945-3463
Park View MS 1,200/6-8
808 W Avenue J 93534 661-942-0496
Eric George, prin. Fax 940-5732
Piute MS 1,300/6-8
425 E Avenue H11 93535 661-942-9508
Kathy Lee, prin. Fax 940-6676
Sierra ES 1,000/K-5
747 W Avenue J12 93534 661-942-9536
Ed Drenner, prin. Fax 942-0682
Sunnydale ES 700/K-5
1233 W Avenue J8 93534 661-948-2636
Rick Filloon, prin. Fax 940-6670

West Wind ES 1,000/K-5
44044 36th St W 93536 661-948-0192
Linda Edmond, prin. Fax 940-8388

Westside UNESD 9,000/K-8
41914 50th St W 93536 661-722-0716
Regina Rossalli, supt. Fax 772-5223
www.westside.k12.ca.us
Del Sur S 900/K-8
9023 W Avenue H 93536 661-942-0488
Timothy Barker, prin. Fax 722-0747
Sundown ES 1,000/K-6
6151 W Avenue J8 93536 661-722-3026
Shelly Dearinger, prin. Fax 722-0196
Valley View ES 900/K-6
3310 W Avenue L8 93536 661-943-2451
Scott Brewer, prin. Fax 943-9103
Other Schools – See Leona Valley, Palmdale, Quartz Hill

Wilsona SD
Supt. — See Palmdale
Challenger MS 600/6-8
41725 170th St E 93535 661-264-1790
Bill Perry, prin. Fax 264-1793
Wilsona ES 600/K-5
41625 170th St E 93535 661-264-2118
Janice Stowers, prin. Fax 264-3625

Antelope Valley Adventist S 100/PK-8
45002 Fern Ave 93534 661-942-6552
James Smith, prin. Fax 942-5699
Antelope Valley Christian S 400/PK-12
3700 W Avenue L 93536 661-943-0044
Karen Hester, prin. Fax 943-6774
Bethel Christian S 500/PK-12
3100 W Avenue K 93536 661-943-2224
Mathias Konnerth, prin. Fax 943-6574
Calvary Chapel Christian S 100/1-12
1833 W Avenue J 93534 661-942-0404
Terese Wilson, prin. Fax 942-6040
Desert Christian ES 500/K-5
44662 15th St W 93534 661-948-5071
Lisa Horner, prin. Fax 948-0858
Desert Christian MS 300/6-8
44662 15th St W 93534 661-723-0665
Brian Roseborough, prin. Fax 723-6774
Grace Lutheran S 200/PK-8
856 W Newgrove St 93534 661-948-1018
Wanda Vandrey, prin. Fax 948-2731
Lancaster Baptist S 400/K-12
4020 E Lancaster Blvd 93535 661-946-4663
Dr. Manuel Salazar, admin. Fax 946-7374
Pinecrest S 200/K-8
2110 W Avenue K 93536 661-723-0366
Lisa Latimer, admin. Fax 723-0713
Sacred Heart S 300/PK-8
45002 Date Ave 93534 661-948-3613
David Schatz, prin. Fax 948-4486
Sonshine Factory Preschool 200/PK-K
44514 20th St W 93534 661-949-3550
Gara Doll, dir. Fax 945-9985
Vineyard Christian S 200/PK-6
1011 E Avenue I 93535 661-948-3766
Denise Baldridge, admin. Fax 942-2908

Landers, San Bernardino
Morongo USD
Supt. — See Twentynine Palms
Landers ES 200/K-6
56450 Reche Rd 92285 760-364-2382
Melinda Peterson, prin. Fax 364-1397

La Palma, Orange, Pop. 15,805
Anaheim UNHSD
Supt. — See Anaheim
Walker JHS 1,300/7-8
8132 Walker St 90623 714-220-4051
Daphne Hammer, prin. Fax 220-2237

Centralia ESD
Supt. — See Buena Park
Los Coyotes ES 500/K-6
8122 Moody St 90623 714-228-3260
Lorraine Test, prin. Fax 826-5641
Miller ES 500/K-6
7751 Furman Rd 90623 714-228-3270
Cindy Chaffee, prin. Fax 522-7978

Cypress ESD
Supt. — See Cypress
Luther ES 500/K-6
4631 La Palma Ave 90623 714-220-6918
M.J. Beatty, prin. Fax 229-7738

La Palma Christian S 100/PK-6
8082 Walker St 90623 714-527-3231
Zsalene Lovetere, dir. Fax 995-8046

La Puente, Los Angeles, Pop. 41,762
Bassett USD 4,900/K-12
904 Willow Ave 91746 626-931-3000
Jim Ballard, supt. Fax 918-9579
www.bassett.k12.ca.us
Edgewood Academy 600/K-8
14135 Fairgrove Ave 91746 626-931-7800
Albert Cahueque, prin. Fax 931-7810
Julian S 700/K-8
13855 Don Julian Rd 91746 626-931-2900
Salvador Flores, prin. Fax 931-2951
Sunkist S 600/K-8
935 Mayland Ave 91746 626-931-7700
Cynthia Medeiros, prin. Fax 931-7710
Vanwig S 600/K-8
1151 Van Wig Ave 91746 626-931-8000
Albert Michel, prin. Fax 931-8010
Other Schools – See City of Industry

Hacienda La Puente USD
Supt. — See City of Industry
Baldwin Academy 800/K-6
1616 Griffith Ave 91744 626-933-3700
Jan Castle, prin. Fax 855-3700
California ES 500/K-6
1111 N California Ave 91744 626-933-5200
Kathryne Meade, prin. Fax 855-3712
Del Valle ES 600/K-6
801 Del Valle Ave 91744 626-933-4100
Mona Diaz, prin. Fax 855-3158
Fairgrove Academy 900/K-8
15540 Fairgrove Ave 91744 626-933-8500
Penny Fraumeni, prin. Fax 333-5794
Lassalette S 600/K-8
14333 Lassalette St 91744 626-933-3000
Cristina Sanchez, prin. Fax 855-3536
Nelson ES 500/K-6
330 N California Ave 91744 626-933-8400
Patricia Graham, prin. Fax 855-3537
Sierra Vista MS 400/7-8
15801 Sierra Vista Ct 91744 626-933-4000
Sue Kaiser, prin. Fax 855-3817
Sparks ES 400/K-6
15151 Temple Ave 91744 626-933-5100
Greg O'Brien, prin. Fax 855-3770
Sparks MS 600/7-8
15100 Giordano St 91744 626-933-5000
Sherri Franson, prin. Fax 855-3848
Sunset ES 300/K-6
800 Tonopah Ave 91744 626-933-3200
Donna Esperon, prin. Fax 918-9531
Temple Academy 400/K-6
635 N California Ave 91744 626-933-3100
Mary Castner, prin. Fax 855-3782
Valinda S 700/K-8
1030 Indian Summer Ave 91744 626-933-4700
Cynthia Gomez, prin. Fax 855-3787
Workman ES 500/K-6
16000 Workman St 91744 626-933-4200
Arlene Gallego, prin. Fax 855-3799

Rowland USD
Supt. — See Rowland Heights
Hurley ES 800/K-6
535 Dora Guzman Ave 91744 626-965-2429
Van Windham, prin. Fax 965-1499
La Seda ES 600/K-6
341 La Seda Rd 91744 626-965-3496
Liz Leon, prin. Fax 965-0447
Northam ES 700/K-6
17800 Renault St 91744 626-965-2404
Fax 965-3014
Rorimer ES 600/K-6
18750 Rorimer St 91744 626-965-3333
Audrey Hicks, prin. Fax 965-8983
Villacorta ES 700/K-6
17840 Villa Corta St 91744 626-964-2385
John Martinez, prin. Fax 964-8701
Yorbita ES 800/K-6
520 Vidalia Ave 91744 626-964-3486
Erika Krohn, prin. Fax 964-3736

St. Joseph S 200/PK-8
15650 Temple Ave 91744 626-336-2821
Sr. Anne Valencia, prin. Fax 369-8921
St. Louis of France S 300/K-8
13901 Temple Ave 91746 626-918-6210
Christopher Martinez, prin. Fax 918-9549
St. Martha S 200/PK-8
440 N Azusa Ave 91744 626-964-1093
Sr. Azucena Del Rio, prin. Fax 912-2014
Sunset Christian S 200/PK-8
400 N Sunset Ave 91744 626-336-1206
Maxine Kyker, admin. Fax 336-1207

La Quinta, Riverside, Pop. 38,232
Desert Sands USD 25,900/K-12
47950 Dune Palms Rd 92253 760-777-4200
Sharon McGehee Ph.D., supt. Fax 771-8505
www.dsusd.us
Adams ES 500/K-5
50800 Desert Club Dr 92253 760-777-4260
Pattie Rice, prin. Fax 777-4265
Franklin ES 700/K-5
77800 Calle Tampico 92253 760-238-9424
Matt Bugg, prin. Fax 238-9433
La Quinta MS 900/6-8
78900 Avenue 50 92253 760-777-4220
Janet Seto, prin. Fax 777-4216
Paige MS 1,000/6-8
43495 Palm Royale Dr 92253 760-238-9710
Derrick Lawson, prin. Fax 345-1202
Truman ES 800/K-5
78870 Avenue 50 92253 760-777-4240
Carol Bishop, prin. Fax 777-4237
Other Schools – See Bermuda Dunes, Indian Wells, Indio, Palm Desert

Larkspur, Marin, Pop. 11,724
Larkspur ESD 1,200/K-8
230 Doherty Dr 94939 415-927-6960
Valerie Pitts, supt. Fax 927-6964
www.larkspurschools.org
Hall MS 500/5-8
200 Doherty Dr 94939 415-927-6978
Daniel A. Norbutas, prin. Fax 927-6985
Other Schools – See Corte Madera

Marin S 300/PK-8
20 Magnolia Ave 94939 415-924-2608
Julie Elam, hdmstr. Fax 924-9351
St. Patrick S 300/K-8
120 King St 94939 415-924-0501
Linda Kinkade, prin. Fax 924-3544

Las Flores, Orange
Capistrano USD
Supt. — See San Juan Capistrano
Las Flores ES 700/K-5
25862 Antonio Pkwy, Rcho Sta Marg CA 92688
949-589-6935
Shele Tamaki, prin. Fax 589-9286
Las Flores MS 1,400/6-8
25862 Antonio Pkwy, Rcho Sta Marg CA 92688
949-589-6543
Shannon Soto, prin. Fax 589-9286

Lathrop, San Joaquin, Pop. 13,116
Manteca USD 24,600/K-12
2901 E Louise Ave 95330 209-825-3200
Jason Messer, supt. Fax 825-3295
www.mantecausd.net/
Lathrop S 1,100/K-8
15851 5th St 95330 209-858-7250
David Silveira, prin. Fax 858-3056
Mossdale S 1,200/K-8
455 Brookhurst Blvd 95330 209-938-6285
Susan Sanders, prin. Fax 234-7494
Widmer S 1,000/K-8
751 Stonebridge Ave 95330 209-858-0650
Suzan Turner-Kelley, prin. Fax 858-4414
Other Schools – See French Camp, Manteca, Stockton

Laton, Fresno, Pop. 1,415
Laton JUSD 600/PK-12
PO Box 248 93242 559-922-4015
Ralph Vandro, supt. Fax 923-4791
www.laton.k12.ca.us
Laton/Conejo S 400/K-8
PO Box 7 93242 559-922-4030
Terry Hirschfield, prin. Fax 923-9651
Laton Preschool PK-PK
6045 E Mount Whitney Ave 93242 559-922-4075
Ann Larson, lead tchr.

La Verne, Los Angeles, Pop. 33,185
Bonita USD
Supt. — See San Dimas
Laverne Heights ES 500/K-5
1550 Base Line Rd 91750 909-971-8205
Gary Tempkin, prin. Fax 971-8255
Miller ES 400/K-5
1629 Holly Oak St 91750 909-971-8206
Deanne Spencer, prin. Fax 971-8256
Oak Mesa ES 500/K-5
5200 Wheeler Ave 91750 909-971-8209
Karen Eberhart, prin. Fax 971-8259
Ramona MS 1,500/6-8
3490 Ramona Ave 91750 909-971-8260
Anne Neal, prin. Fax 971-8269
Roynon ES 700/K-5
2715 E St 91750 909-971-8207
Sean Grycel, prin. Fax 971-8257

Calvary Baptist S 100/PK-12
2990 Damien Ave 91750 909-593-4672
Taylora Dial, prin. Fax 392-9533

Lawndale, Los Angeles, Pop. 32,193
Lawndale ESD 5,200/K-8
4161 W 147th St 90260 310-973-1300
Ellen Dougherty Ed.D., supt. Fax 675-6462
www.lawndale.k12.ca.us
Addams MS 100/6-8
4161 W 147th St 90260 310-676-4806
Frank Noyes, prin. Fax 676-8621
Anderson ES 800/K-5
4161 W 147th St 90260 310-676-0197
Dayla Sims, prin. Fax 676-8053
Green ES 800/K-5
4161 W 147th St 90260 310-370-3585
Stephen McCray, prin. Fax 370-0522
Mitchell ES 600/K-5
4161 W 147th St 90260 310-676-6140
Lucia Karaptian, prin. Fax 676-7616
Rogers MS 1,100/6-8
4161 W 147th St 90260 310-676-1197
Tina Nielsen, prin. Fax 675-0489
Roosevelt ES 400/3-5
4161 W 147th St 90260 310-675-1121
Denise Appell Ed.D., prin. Fax 219-3180
Smith ES 500/K-5
4161 W 147th St 90260 310-970-2915
Jennifer Harris, prin. Fax 675-7584
Twain ES 400/K-5
4161 W 147th St 90260 310-675-9134
Beth Mossman, prin. Fax 675-6367
Other Schools – See Hawthorne

Laytonville, Mendocino, Pop. 1,133
Laytonville USD 400/K-12
PO Box 868 95454 707-984-6414
Joan Potter, supt. Fax 984-8223
layt.k12.ca.us/
Branscomb ES 50/K-3
PO Box 325 95454 707-984-8718
Lorre Stange, prin. Fax 984-8761
Laytonville S 200/K-8
PO Box 325 95454 707-984-6123
Lorre Stange, prin. Fax 984-8761
Spy Rock ES 50/K-6
PO Box 325 95454 707-984-6172
Lorre Stange, prin. Fax 984-8761

Lebec, Kern
El Tejon USD 1,300/K-12
PO Box 876 93243 661-248-6247
Shelly Mason, supt. Fax 248-6714
www.el-tejon.k12.ca.us
El Tejon MS 500/4-8
PO Box 876 93243 661-248-6680
Dena Kiouses, prin. Fax 248-5203

Frazier Park ES 300/K-3
PO Box 876 93243 661-245-3312
Dena Kiouses, prin. Fax 245-3424

Lee Vining, Mono
Eastern Sierra USD
Supt. — See Bridgeport
Lee Vining ES 100/K-6
PO Box 270 93541 760-647-6460
Sally Hadden, prin. Fax 647-6489

Leggett, Mendocino
Leggett Valley USD 200/K-12
PO Box 186 95585 707-925-6285
Gordon Piffero, supt. Fax 925-6396
leggett.k12.ca.us
Leggett Valley S 100/K-8
PO Box 186 95585 707-925-6230
Gordon Piffero, prin. Fax 925-6396
Other Schools – See Whitethorn

Le Grand, Merced, Pop. 1,205
Le Grand UNESD 400/K-8
PO Box 27 95333 209-389-4515
J. Scott Lucas, supt. Fax 389-4041
www.legrand.k12.ca.us/
Le Grand S 400/K-8
PO Box 27 95333 209-389-4515
J. Scott Lucas, prin. Fax 389-4041

Lemon Cove, Tulare
Sequoia UNESD 400/K-8
PO Box 44260 93244 559-564-2106
Larry Lakey, supt. Fax 564-2126
www.sequoiaunion.org
Sequoia S 400/K-8
PO Box 44260 93244 559-564-2106
Larry Lakey, prin. Fax 564-2126

Lemon Grove, San Diego, Pop. 24,124
Lemon Grove ESD 4,100/K-8
8025 Lincoln St 91945 619-825-5600
Ernie Anastos, supt. Fax 462-7959
www.lgsd.k12.ca.us
Golden Avenue ES 400/K-5
7885 Golden Ave 91945 619-825-5637
Rick Oser, prin. Fax 825-5782
Lemon Grove MS 800/6-8
7866 Lincoln St 91945 619-825-5628
Ambler Moss, prin. Fax 825-5781
Monterey Heights ES 400/K-5
7550 Canton Dr 91945 619-825-5633
Yolanda Cole, prin. Fax 825-5784
Mt. Vernon ES 400/K-5
8350 Mount Vernon St 91945 619-825-5613
Gustavo Vazquez, prin. Fax 825-5788
Palm MS 700/6-8
8425 Palm St 91945 619-825-5641
Russell Little, prin. Fax 628-5786
San Altos ES 400/K-5
1750 Madera St 91945 619-825-5621
Larry Buchanan, prin. Fax 825-5787
San Miguel ES 500/K-5
7059 San Miguel Ave 91945 619-825-5619
Marcia Mattson, prin. Fax 825-5785
Other Schools – See La Mesa

Christian Creative Learning Academy 100/PK-K
2920 Main St 91945 619-698-4306
Terrie Bearden, admin. Fax 698-4340
St. John of the Cross S 600/PK-8
8175 Lemon Grove Way 91945 619-466-8624
Sr. Marilupe Teran, prin. Fax 466-0034

Lemoore, Kings, Pop. 22,699
Central UNESD 1,900/K-8
PO Box 1339 93245 559-924-3405
Ron Seaver, supt. Fax 924-1153
www.central.k12.ca.us/district/
Akers S 700/K-8
PO Box 1339 93245 559-998-5707
Heiko Sweeney, prin. Fax 998-7517
Central S 400/K-8
PO Box 1339 93245 559-924-7797
Nancy Davis, prin. Fax 924-0919
Neutra ES 500/K-5
PO Box 1339 93245 559-998-6823
John Partin, prin. Fax 998-7521
Other Schools – See Stratford

Lemoore UNESD 3,200/K-8
100 Vine St 93245 559-924-6800
Richard Rayburn, supt. Fax 924-6809
www.luesd.k12.ca.us/
Cinnamon ES 600/K-6
100 Vine St 93245 559-924-6870
Rosemary Montoya, prin. Fax 924-6879
Engvall ES 700/K-6
100 Vine St 93245 559-924-6850
Eric Wyand, prin. Fax 924-6859
Lemoore ES 700/K-6
100 Vine St 93245 559-924-6820
Cathlene Bullard, prin. Fax 924-6829
Liberty MS 600/7-8
100 Vine St 93245 559-924-6860
Eric Smyers, prin. Fax 924-6869
Meadow Lane ES 600/K-6
100 Vine St 93245 559-924-6840
Patty Stratton, prin. Fax 924-6849

Kings Christian S 300/PK-12
900 E D St 93245 559-924-8301
Duane Daniel, admin. Fax 924-0607
Mary Immaculate Queen S 200/PK-8
884 N Lemoore Ave 93245 559-924-3424
Sr. Tessy Acharuparambil, prin. Fax 924-7848

Lennox, Los Angeles, Pop. 22,757
Lennox ESD 6,000/K-8
10319 Firmona Ave 90304 310-695-4000
Dr. Bruce McDaniel, supt. Fax 695-4000
www.lennox.k12.ca.us
Buford ES 800/K-5
10319 Firmona Ave 90304 310-330-4920
Martha Pardo, prin. Fax 672-5829
Felton ES 700/K-5
10319 Firmona Ave 90304 310-680-8950
Lissett Pichardo, prin. Fax 673-6101
Huerta ES 600/K-5
10319 Firmona Ave 90304 310-677-7050
Susan Ramos, prin. Fax 330-4574
Jefferson ES 900/K-5
10319 Firmona Ave 90304 310-680-5650
Jason Holmes, prin. Fax 672-5031
Lennox MS - 6 700/6-6
10319 Firmona Ave 90304 310-419-1800
Dr. Cesar Morales, dir. Fax 677-4635
Lennox MS 1,400/7-8
10319 Firmona Ave 90304 310-419-1800
Brian Johnson, prin. Fax 677-4635
Moffett ES 1,000/K-5
10319 Firmona Ave 90304 310-680-6200
JoAnn Isken, prin. Fax 412-3275

Leona Valley, Los Angeles
Westside UNESD
Supt. — See Lancaster
Leona Valley S 200/K-8
9063 Leona Ave 93551 661-948-9010
Scott Brewer, prin. Fax 270-9758

Lewiston, Trinity, Pop. 1,187
Lewiston ESD 100/K-8
685 Lewiston Rd 96052 530-778-3984
Duncan Hobbs, supt. Fax 778-3103
www.tcoek12.org/~les/
Lewiston S 100/K-8
685 Lewiston Rd 96052 530-778-3984
Duncan Hobbs, prin. Fax 778-3103

Likely, Modoc
Modoc JUSD
Supt. — See Alturas
South Fork S 50/K-8
PO Box 115 96116 530-233-7210
Diane Janssen, prin. Fax 233-4362

Lincoln, Placer, Pop. 32,804
Western Placer USD 6,100/K-12
600 6th St Fl 4 95648 916-645-6350
Scott Leaman, supt. Fax 645-6356
www.wpusd.k12.ca.us
Coppin ES 500/K-5
150 E 12th St 95648 916-645-6390
Terri Dorow, prin. Fax 645-6363
Creekside Oaks ES 700/K-5
2030 1st St 95648 916-645-6380
Linda Pezanoski, prin. Fax 645-6383
Edwards MS 700/6-8
204 L St 95648 916-645-6370
Michael Doherty, prin. Fax 645-6379
First Street ES 500/K-5
1400 1st St 95648 916-645-6330
Ruben Ayala, prin. Fax 645-6284
Foskett Ranch ES 500/K-5
1561 Joiner Pkwy 95648 916-434-5220
Kelly Castillo, prin. Fax 434-5240
Lincoln Crossing ES 600/K-5
635 Groveland Ln 95648 916-434-5292
Kevin Kurtz, prin. Fax 434-5261
Twelve Bridges ES 700/K-5
2450 Eastridge Dr 95648 916-434-5220
Jeremy Lyche, prin. Fax 434-5201
Twelve Bridges MS 600/6-8
770 Westview Dr 95648 916-434-5270
Stacey Brown, prin. Fax 434-5240
Other Schools – See Sheridan

Community Christian S 100/PK-8
PO Box 870 95648 916-645-6280
Becky Romness, admin. Fax 645-1345

Linden, San Joaquin, Pop. 1,339
Linden USD 2,800/K-12
18527 E Main St 95236 209-887-3894
Ronald Estes, supt. Fax 887-2250
www.sjcoe.net/LUSD/DO.html
Linden ES 500/K-4
18100 E Front St 95236 209-887-3600
Anthony Pimentel, prin. Fax 887-2252
Other Schools – See Stockton

Lindsay, Tulare, Pop. 10,767
Lindsay USD 4,000/K-12
371 E Hermosa St 93247 559-562-5111
Janet Kliegl, supt. Fax 562-4637
www.lindsay.k12.ca.us
Garvey JHS 600/7-8
340 N Harvard Ave 93247 559-562-1311
Rebecca Mestaz, prin. Fax 562-1411
Jefferson ES 700/K-6
333 N Westwood Ave 93247 559-562-6303
Chris Saenz, prin. Fax 562-8529
Lincoln ES 800/K-6
851 N Stanford Ave 93247 559-562-2571
Pam Canby, prin. Fax 562-8555
Washington ES 700/K-6
451 E Samoa St 93247 559-562-5916
Cinnamon Scheufele, prin. Fax 562-8518

Litchfield, Lassen
Shaffer UNESD 300/K-8
PO Box 320 96117 530-254-6577
Jason Waddell, supt. Fax 254-6126
www.shafferschool.com/
Shaffer S 300/K-8
PO Box 320 96117 530-254-6577
Jason Waddell, prin. Fax 254-6126

Littlerock, Los Angeles, Pop. 1,320
Keppel UNESD
Supt. — See Pearblossom
Almondale MS 600/7-8
9330 E Avenue U 93543 661-944-2152
Melanie Pumphrey, prin. Fax 944-0694
Alpine ES 600/K-6
8244 Pearblossom Hwy 93543 661-944-3221
Larry Lueck, prin. Fax 944-0597
Antelope ES 300/K-6
37237 100th St E 93543 661-944-2148
Gerilyn Cherland, prin. Fax 944-0683

Live Oak, Sutter, Pop. 7,128
Live Oak USD 1,900/K-12
2201 Pennington Rd 95953 530-695-5400
Tom Pritchard, supt. Fax 695-5460
www.lousd.k12.ca.us/
Encinal S 100/K-8
6484 Larkin Rd 95953 530-695-5458
Mary Page, prin. Fax 695-5459
Live Oak MS 600/5-8
2082 Pennington Rd 95953 530-695-5435
Parm Virk, prin. Fax 695-5443
Luther ES 600/K-4
10123 Connecticut Ave 95953 530-695-5450
Marjorie Jones, prin. Fax 695-5429

Nuestro ESD 100/K-8
3934 Broadway 95953 530-822-5100
Irwin Karp, supt. Fax 822-5178
Nuestro S 100/K-8
3934 Broadway 95953 530-822-5100
Irwin Karp, prin. Fax 822-5178

Livermore, Alameda, Pop. 78,409
Livermore Valley JUSD 13,400/K-12
685 E Jack London Blvd 94551 925-606-3200
Brenda Miller, supt. Fax 606-3329
www.livermoreschools.com
Altamont Creek ES 600/K-5
6500 Garaventa Ranch Rd 94551 925-454-5575
Beverly Tom, prin. Fax 454-5591
Arroyo Seco ES 700/K-5
5280 Irene Way 94550 925-606-4700
Steve Bering, prin. Fax 606-3427
Christenson MS 700/6-8
5757 Haggin Oaks Ave 94551 925-606-4702
Amy Robbins, prin. Fax 606-4705
Croce ES 700/K-5
5650 Scenic Ave 94551 925-606-4706
Shari Johnston, prin. Fax 606-4708
East Avenue MS 700/6-8
3951 East Ave 94550 925-606-4711
Vicki Scudder, prin. Fax 606-4763
Jackson Avenue ES 500/K-5
554 Jackson Ave 94550 925-606-4717
Tammy Rankin-Conover, prin. Fax 606-4766
Junction Avenue MS 700/6-8
298 Junction Ave 94551 925-606-4720
Susan Sambuceti, prin. Fax 606-3318
Marylin Avenue ES 500/K-5
800 Marylin Ave 94551 925-606-4724
Jeff Keller, prin. Fax 606-4730
Mendenhall MS 900/6-8
1701 El Padro Dr 94550 925-606-4731
Helen Foster, prin. Fax 606-4737
Michell ES 400/K-5
1001 Elaine Ave 94550 925-606-4738
Angela Ehrlich, prin. Fax 455-5504
Portola ES 400/K-5
2451 Portola Ave 94551 925-606-4743
Jamal Fields, prin. Fax 606-4747
Rancho Las Positas ES 500/K-5
401 E Jack London Blvd 94551 925-606-4748
Chris Calabrese, prin. Fax 606-3346
Smith ES 700/K-5
391 Ontario Dr 94550 925-606-4750
Denise Nathanson, prin. Fax 606-3330
Sunset ES 600/K-5
1671 Frankfurt Way 94550 925-606-5230
Candice Flint, prin. Fax 606-4753

Our Savior Lutheran S 600/PK-8
1385 S Livermore Ave 94550 925-447-2082
Dennis Dirks, prin. Fax 447-0201
St. Michael S 300/K-8
345 Church St 94550 925-447-1888
Sr. Emmanuel Cardinale, prin. Fax 447-6720
Sunset Christian S 100/PK-5
2200 Arroyo Rd 94550 925-243-0972
Andrea Anderson, dir. Fax 447-0310
Valley Montessori S 500/PK-8
1273 N Livermore Ave 94551 925-455-8021
Mary Ellen Kordas, dir. Fax 455-8002

Livingston, Merced, Pop. 12,585
Livingston UNESD 2,500/K-8
922 B St 95334 209-394-5400
Henry Escobar, supt. Fax 394-5401
www.lusd.k12.ca.us
Campus Park ES 500/K-5
1845 H St 95334 209-394-5460
George Solis, prin. Fax 394-5461
Herndon ES 600/K-5
714 Prusso St 95334 209-394-5480
Stella Montanez, prin. Fax 394-5481
Livingston MS 800/6-8
101 F St 95334 209-394-5450
Filomena Sousa, prin. Fax 394-5451
Yamato Colony ES 500/K-5
800 Livingston Cressey Rd 95334 209-394-5470
Robin Hopper, prin. Fax 394-5471

Lockeford, San Joaquin, Pop. 2,722
Lodi USD
Supt. — See Lodi
Lockeford ES 300/K-6
19456 N Tully Rd 95237 209-331-7214
Virginia Anderson, prin. Fax 727-5802

Lockwood, Monterey
San Antonio UNESD 200/K-8
PO Box 5000 93932 831-385-3051
Linda Irving, supt. Fax 385-4240
schools.monterey.k12.ca.us/~santonio/
San Antonio S 200/K-8
PO Box 5000 93932 831-385-3051
Linda Irving, prin. Fax 385-4240

Lodi, San Joaquin, Pop. 62,133
Lodi USD 29,700/PK-12
1305 E Vine St 95240 209-331-7000
Cathy Nichols-Washer, supt. Fax 331-7256
www.lodiusd.k12.ca.us
Beckman ES 600/K-6
2201 Scarborough Dr 95240 209-331-7410
Maria Martinez, prin. Fax 331-8301
Borchardt ES 700/K-6
375 Culbertson Dr 95240 209-331-8212
Janis Morehead, prin. Fax 331-8241
Heritage ES 500/K-3
509 Eden St 95240 209-331-7334
Maria Cervantes, prin. Fax 331-7341
Lakewood ES 400/K-6
1100 N Ham Ln 95242 209-331-7348
Bruce Spaulding, prin. Fax 331-7353
Larson ES 700/K-6
2375 Giannoni Way 95242 209-331-8391
Cheryl Nilmeyer, prin. Fax 331-8375
Lawrence ES 500/PK-6
721 Calaveras St 95240 209-331-7356
Graciela Uribes, prin. Fax 331-7357
Live Oak ES 300/K-6
5099 Bear Creek Rd 95240 209-331-7370
Marianne Varni, prin. Fax 331-7302
Lodi MS 900/7-8
945 S Ham Ln 95242 209-331-7540
Marco Sanchez, prin. Fax 331-7550
Millswood MS 800/7-8
233 N Mills Ave 95242 209-331-8332
Sheree Perez, prin. Fax 331-8347
Needham IS 300/4-6
420 S Pleasant Ave 95240 209-331-7375
Carol Rivas, prin. Fax 331-7483
Nichols ES 400/K-6
1301 S Crescent Ave 95240 209-331-7378
Elaine Douglas, prin. Fax 331-7380
Reese ES 600/K-6
1800 W Elm St 95242 209-331-7424
Celeste Bordner, prin. Fax 331-7431
Tokay Colony ES 100/K-6
13520 E Live Oak Rd 95240 209-331-7438
Carlos Villafana, prin. Fax 953-3200
Turner ES 100/K-6
18051 N Ray Rd 95242 209-331-7440
Jann Lyall, prin. Fax 331-7533
Vinewood ES 600/K-6
1600 W Tokay St 95242 209-331-7445
Kitsy Smith, prin. Fax 331-7447
Washington ES 500/K-6
831 W Lockeford St 95240 209-331-7451
Linda Denman, prin. Fax 331-7320
Woodbridge ES, 1290 Lilac St 95242 400/K-6
John Kirilov, prin. 209-331-8160
Other Schools – See Acampo, Clements, Lockeford, Stockton, Victor

---

Century Christian S 400/PK-8
550 W Century Blvd 95240 209-334-3230
Chris Finch, admin. Fax 334-6656
Lodi SDA S 200/K-8
1240 S Central Ave 95240 209-368-5341
Dann Dodd, prin. Fax 368-5370
St. Anne S 200/K-8
200 S Pleasant Ave 95240 209-333-7580
Dennis Taricco, prin. Fax 369-1971
St. Peter Lutheran S 200/PK-8
2400 Oxford Way 95242 209-333-2225
Caleb Hardy, prin. Fax 334-4633
Vineyard Christian MS 100/6-8
2301 W Lodi Ave 95242 209-333-8300
Karen Hale, prin. Fax 339-4327

Loleta, Humboldt
Loleta UNESD 100/K-8
PO Box 547 95551 707-733-5705
Louis Hoiland, supt. Fax 733-5367
www.humboldt.k12.ca.us/loleta_sd/
Loleta S 100/K-8
PO Box 547 95551 707-733-5705
Louis Hoiland, prin. Fax 733-5367

Loma Linda, San Bernardino, Pop. 20,901
Redlands USD
Supt. — See Redlands
Bryn Mawr ES 900/K-5
11680 Whittier Ave 92354 909-478-5650
Jim O'Neill, prin. Fax 478-5654

Loma Linda Academy 1,600/K-12
10656 Anderson St 92354 909-796-0161
Dr. L. Roo McKenzie, prin. Fax 478-6829

Lomita, Los Angeles, Pop. 20,515
Los Angeles USD
Supt. — See Los Angeles
Eshelman Avenue ES 600/K-5
25902 Eshelman Ave 90717 310-326-1576
Milica Mladinich, prin. Fax 326-2749
Fleming MS 2,000/6-8
25425 Walnut St 90717 310-257-4500
Janice Hackett, prin. Fax 326-9071
Lomita Math & Science Magnet S 1,000/K-5
2211 247th St 90717 310-326-1655
Sandy Du, prin. Fax 326-0632

Coastal Academy 200/K-12
25501 Oak St 90717 310-644-0433
Grace DiPasquale, dir.
Harbor Church S 200/PK-8
1716 254th St 90717 310-534-8278
Lee Ann Bowman, prin. Fax 325-1890
Maimonides Torah Academy 50/K-8
24412 Narbonne Ave 90717 310-326-8234
Rabbi Eli Hecht, dir. Fax 326-1555
Nishiyamato Academy 100/K-9
2458 Lomita Blvd 90717 310-325-7040
Katsuyuki Nishikawa, prin.
St. Margaret Mary Alacoque S 300/PK-8
25515 Eshelman Ave 90717 310-326-9494
Douglas Erhard, prin. Fax 539-1570

Lompoc, Santa Barbara, Pop. 39,985
Lompoc USD 9,700/K-12
PO Box 8000 93438 805-742-3300
Dr. Frank Lynch, supt. Fax 735-8452
www.lusd.org
Buena Vista ES 400/K-6
PO Box 8000 93438 805-742-2020
Dr. Diane Burton, prin. Fax 742-2021
Crestview ES 500/K-5
PO Box 8000 93438 805-742-2050
Ken Faulk, prin. Fax 742-2083
Fillmore ES 600/K-6
PO Box 8000 93438 805-742-2100
Janet Boehme, prin. Fax 742-2135
Hapgood ES 500/K-6
PO Box 8000 93438 805-742-2200
Carol Pace, prin. Fax 742-3309
La Canada ES 700/K-6
PO Box 8000 93438 805-742-2250
Carmen Chavez, prin. Fax 742-2217
La Honda ES 400/K-6
PO Box 8000 93438 805-742-2300
Nancy Hardy, prin. Fax 742-2307
Lompoc Valley MS 600/7-8
PO Box 8000 93438 805-742-2600
Jeff Wagonseller, prin. Fax 737-9480
Los Berros ES 400/K-6
PO Box 8000 93438 805-742-2350
Leslie Wagonseller, prin. Fax 742-2352
Miguelito ES 600/K-6
PO Box 8000 93438 805-742-2440
Paula Davis, prin. Fax 742-2450
Ruth ES 600/K-6
PO Box 8000 93438 805-742-2500
Carl Krugmeier, prin. Fax 742-2504
Vandenberg MS 1,000/6-8
PO Box 8000 93438 805-742-2700
Kathu Froemming, prin. Fax 742-2759

Childrens Montessori S 50/PK-8
PO Box 3510 93438 805-733-2290
Jim Murphy, dir. Fax 733-2290
La Purisima Concepcion S 200/K-8
219 W Olive Ave 93436 805-736-6210
Tina Steele, prin. Fax 735-7649

Lone Pine, Inyo, Pop. 1,818
Lone Pine USD 400/K-12
PO Box 159 93545 760-876-5579
Larry Todd, supt. Fax 876-5438
www.lpusd.k12.ca.us/
Lo-Inyo S 300/K-8
PO Box 159 93545 760-876-5581
Diane Gross, prin. Fax 876-5584

Long Beach, Los Angeles, Pop. 474,014
Long Beach USD 88,800/PK-12
1515 Hughes Way 90810 562-997-8000
Christopher Steinhauser, supt. Fax 997-8280
www.lbschools.net/
Addams ES 1,100/K-5
5320 Pine Ave 90805 562-428-0202
Yvette Streeter, prin. Fax 428-4322
Bancroft MS 1,300/6-8
5301 E Centralia St 90808 562-425-7461
Pamela Sawyer, prin. Fax 425-9741
Barton ES 1,000/K-5
1100 E Del Amo Blvd 90807 562-428-0555
Luana Wesley, prin. Fax 984-8509
Birney ES 700/K-5
710 W Spring St 90806 562-427-8512
Jeffrey Wood, prin. Fax 424-9417
Bixby ES 400/K-5
5251 E Stearns St 90815 562-498-3794
Juan Gutierrez, prin. Fax 498-1711
Bryant ES 400/K-5
4101 E Fountain St 90804 562-498-3802
Doris Robinson, prin. Fax 494-6952
Buffum ES 300/K-5
2350 Ximeno Ave 90815 562-498-2431
Deborah Anderson, prin. Fax 494-4898
Burbank ES 800/K-5
501 Junipero Ave 90814 562-439-0997
Lorraine Griego, prin. Fax 434-8285
Burcham ES 500/K-7
5610 E Monlaco Rd 90808 562-420-2685
LaShell Diggs, prin. Fax 420-7865
Burnett ES 1,000/K-5
565 E Hill St 90806 562-595-9466
Lucy Salazar, prin. Fax 424-8796
Butler S 900/K-8
1400 E 20th St 90806 562-591-7477
Terri Rennard, prin. Fax 218-3667
Carver ES 400/K-5
5335 E Pavo St 90808 562-420-2697
Lisa Stephenson, prin. Fax 420-7868
Chavez ES 500/K-5
730 W 3rd St 90802 562-590-0904
Kimberly Weber, prin. Fax 590-6538
Cubberley S 1,000/K-8
3200 Monogram Ave 90808 562-420-8810
Michael Navia, prin. Fax 420-7821
DeMille MS 1,100/6-8
7025 E Parkcrest St 90808 562-421-8424
Timothy Spivey, prin. Fax 429-1054
Dooley ES 1,000/K-5
5075 Long Beach Blvd 90805 562-428-7274
Julie Nyssen, prin. Fax 428-6010
Edison ES 900/K-5
625 Maine Ave 90802 562-590-8481
Richard Littlejohn, prin. Fax 435-2605
Franklin MS 1,100/6-8
540 Cerritos Ave 90802 562-435-4952
David Taylor, prin. Fax 432-6308
Fremont ES 400/K-5
4000 E 4th St 90814 562-439-6873
Matthew Hammond, prin. Fax 433-1826
Gant ES 700/K-5
1854 N Britton Dr 90815 562-430-3384
Patricia Lambert, prin. Fax 431-6091
Garfield ES 900/K-5
2240 Baltic Ave 90810 562-424-8167
Donna McKeehan, prin. Fax 595-8823
Grant ES 1,300/K-5
1225 E 64th St 90805 562-428-4616
Mona Cook, prin. Fax 428-0926
Hamilton MS 1,400/6-8
1060 E 70th St 90805 562-602-0302
David Downing, prin. Fax 602-1354
Harte ES 1,100/K-5
1671 E Phillips St 90805 562-428-0333
Scott Tardibuono, prin. Fax 428-7985
Henry ES 400/K-5
3720 Canehill Ave 90808 562-421-3754
Claire Alvarez, prin. Fax 420-7849
Hill MS 1,100/6-8
1100 Iroquois Ave 90815 562-598-7611
Peter Davis, prin. Fax 598-6329
Hudson S 1,100/K-8
2335 Webster Ave 90810 562-426-0470
Wendy Claflin, prin. Fax 424-1569
Hughes MS 1,600/6-8
3846 California Ave 90807 562-595-0831
Monica Daley, prin. Fax 595-9221
International ES 700/PK-5
700 Locust Ave 90813 562-436-4420
Kimberley Baril, prin. Fax 437-0690
Jefferson Leadership Academies 1,100/6-8
750 Euclid Ave 90804 562-438-9904
Lori Clark, prin. Fax 439-3718
Keller ES 500/K-5
7020 E Brittain St 90808 562-421-8851
Marjean Hughes, prin. Fax 420-2759
Kettering ES 400/K-5
550 Silvera Ave 90803 562-598-9486
Kelly Ludden, prin. Fax 594-9359
King ES 1,000/K-5
145 E Artesia Blvd 90805 562-428-1232
Rosana Madrid-Arroyo, prin. Fax 422-1481
LaFayette ES 900/K-5
2445 Chestnut Ave 90806 562-426-7075
Damita Myers-Miller, prin. Fax 490-7318
Lee ES 1,000/K-5
1620 Temple Ave 90804 562-494-5101
Thomas Malkus, prin. Fax 494-5198
Lincoln ES 1,200/K-5
1175 E 11th St 90813 562-599-5005
Christi Granado, prin. Fax 591-5375
Lindbergh MS 1,100/6-8
1022 E Market St 90805 562-422-2845
Dr. Avery Hall, prin. Fax 423-8176
Lindsey Academy 500/6-8
5075 Daisy Ave 90805 562-423-6451
Stephanie Dunn, prin. Fax 422-3800
Longfellow ES 800/K-5
3800 Olive Ave 90807 562-595-0308
Brian Moskovitz, prin. Fax 424-3991
Los Cerritos ES 500/K-5
515 W San Antonio Dr 90807 562-595-6337
Lauren Price, prin. Fax 595-7994
Lowell ES 700/K-5
5201 E Broadway 90803 562-433-6757
Laurie Murrin, prin. Fax 438-3264
Mann ES 400/K-5
257 Coronado Ave 90803 562-439-6897
Wanda Oliver, prin. Fax 439-8046
Marshall MS 1,100/6-8
5870 E Wardlow Rd 90808 562-429-7013
Sherryl Johnson, prin. Fax 429-6973
McKinley ES 900/K-5
6822 N Paramount Blvd 90805 562-630-6200
Thomas Espinosa, prin. Fax 633-2891
Muir ES 900/K-6
3038 Delta Ave 90810 562-426-5571
Gerardo Gloria, prin. Fax 426-0828
Naples Bayside Academy 200/K-5
5537 E The Toledo 90803 562-433-0489
Diane Prince, prin. Fax 434-9016
Newcomb Academy 1,000/K-8
3351 Val Verde Ave 90808 562-493-3596
Elizabeth Flynn, prin. Fax 430-2359
Powell Academy for Success 1,400/K-8
150 W Victoria St 90805 310-631-8794
Denise Peterson, prin. Fax 631-8983
Prisk ES 500/K-5
2375 Fanwood Ave 90815 562-598-9601
Cynthia Young, prin. Fax 431-8718
Robinson Academy 1,000/K-8
2750 Pine Ave 90806 562-492-6003
Stephanie Jones, prin. Fax 492-6013

Rogers MS 900/6-8
365 Monrovia Ave 90803 562-434-7411
Thomas Huff, prin. Fax 434-0581
Roosevelt ES 1,100/K-5
1574 Linden Ave 90813 562-599-1888
Christopher Lund, prin. Fax 591-4883
Stanford MS 1,400/6-8
5871 E Los Arcos St 90815 562-594-9793
Kathleen Cruz, prin. Fax 594-8591
Stephens MS 1,400/6-8
1830 W Columbia St 90810 562-595-0841
Shivaun Williams, prin. Fax 426-5631
Stevenson ES 800/K-5
515 Lime Ave 90802 562-437-0407
Gonzalo Moraga, prin. Fax 435-2862
Tincher Prep S 1,100/K-8
1701 Petaluma Ave 90815 562-493-2636
William Vogel, prin. Fax 594-0818
Twain ES 700/K-5
5021 E Centralia St 90808 562-421-8421
Ellen Ryan, prin. Fax 420-7654
Washington MS 1,000/4-8
1450 Cedar Ave 90813 562-591-2434
Constance McKivett, prin. Fax 591-6888
Webster ES 700/K-5
1755 W 32nd Way 90810 562-595-6568
Kevin Maddox, prin. Fax 595-5710
Whittier ES 900/K-5
1761 Walnut Ave 90813 562-599-6263
Edward Garcia, prin. Fax 591-4046
Willard ES 900/K-5
1055 Freeman Ave 90804 562-438-9934
Linda Fletcher, prin. Fax 439-8156
Other Schools – See Avalon, Lakewood, Signal Hill

Los Angeles USD
Supt. — See Los Angeles
Dominguez ES 700/K-5
21250 S Santa Fe Ave 90810 310-835-7137
Michelle Heron-Archie, prin. Fax 835-6071

Paramount USD
Supt. — See Paramount
Collins S 700/K-8
6125 Coke Ave 90805 562-602-8008
Pamela Houston, prin. Fax 633-8009

Bethany Lutheran S 400/PK-8
5100 E Arbor Rd 90808 562-420-7783
Mary Fink, prin. Fax 429-1693
Bethany S 400/PK-8
2244 Clark Ave 90815 562-597-2814
Bill Cook, prin. Fax 597-1396
First Baptist Church S 200/K-12
1000 Pine Ave 90813 562-432-8447
James Allen, admin. Fax 499-6847
Grace Christian S 200/PK-12
3601 Linden Ave 90807 562-595-1674
Pearlie Davis, prin. Fax 595-5566
Holy Innocents S 200/PK-8
2500 Pacific Ave 90806 562-424-1018
Fax 424-4126
Lakewood Christian S 400/PK-8
5336 E Arbor Rd 90808 562-425-3358
Patrick Major, admin. Fax 420-9140
Los Altos Brethren S 100/PK-6
6565 E Stearns St 90815 562-430-6983
Kathy Shaw, prin. Fax 431-7013
Nazarene Christian S 50/PK-PK
5253 E Los Coyotes Diagonal 90815 562-597-3900
Jerry Cordell, admin. Fax 494-4079
Oakwood Academy 100/K-8
2951 Long Beach Blvd 90806 562-424-4816
Jennifer Davis, prin.
Our Lady of Refuge S 200/PK-8
5210 E Los Coyotes Diagonal 90815 562-597-0819
Dr. Joan Bravo de Murillo, prin. Fax 597-1419
Pacific Baptist S 100/K-12
3332 Magnolia Ave 90806 562-426-5214
Joseph Esposito, prin.
Parkridge Private S 100/K-12
3605 Long Beach Blvd 90807 562-424-5528
Joan Horton, dir.
St. Anthony S 200/PK-8
855 E 5th St 90802 562-432-5946
Bradford Detanna, prin. Fax 435-8606
St. Athanasius S 200/K-8
5369 Linden Ave 90805 562-428-7422
Sr. Rita Campos, prin. Fax 422-0306
St. Barnabas S 300/PK-8
3980 Marron Ave 90807 562-424-7476
Carol Schmitz, prin. Fax 981-3351
St. Cornelius S 300/K-8
3330 N Bellflower Blvd 90808 562-425-7813
Nancy Hayes, prin. Fax 425-2743
St. Cyprian S 200/K-8
5133 E Arbor Rd 90808 562-425-7341
Dawn Still, prin. Fax 421-1642
St. Joseph S 300/K-8
6200 E Willow St 90815 562-596-6115
Brigid Considine, prin. Fax 596-6725
St. Lucy S 200/K-8
2320 Cota Ave 90810 562-424-9062
Diane Pedroni, prin. Fax 424-8572
St. Maria Goretti S 100/PK-8
3950 Palo Verde Ave 90808 562-425-5112
Mary Ann Fitzpatrick, prin. Fax 425-5672
Westerly S 100/K-8
2950 E 29th St 90806 562-981-3151
Timothy Johnson, hdmstr. Fax 981-3153

Loomis, Placer, Pop. 6,577
Loomis UNESD 2,300/K-8
3290 Humphrey Rd 95650 916-652-1800
Paul Johnson, supt. Fax 652-1809
www.loomis-usd.k12.ca.us/
Franklin S 600/K-8
7050 Franklin School Rd 95650 916-652-1818
Shawn Shaw, prin. Fax 652-1821
Loomis S 400/K-8
3505 Taylor Rd 95650 916-652-1824
Rick Judd, prin. Fax 652-1826
Placer S 500/K-8
8650 Horseshoe Bar Rd 95650 916-652-1830
Carolyn Cowles, prin. Fax 652-1832
Powers S 400/K-8
3296 Humphrey Rd 95650 916-652-2635
Glenn Lockwood, prin. Fax 652-2679
Other Schools – See Newcastle, Penryn

Los Alamitos, Orange, Pop. 11,657
Los Alamitos USD 9,200/PK-12
10293 Bloomfield St 90720 562-799-4700
Gregory Franklin Ed.D., supt. Fax 799-4711
www.losal.org
Hopkinson ES 600/K-5
12582 Kensington Rd 90720 562-799-4500
Linda Stewart, prin. Fax 799-4510
Lee ES 600/K-5
11481 Foster Rd 90720 562-799-4540
Andrew Pulver, prin. Fax 799-4550
Los Alamitos ES 600/K-5
10862 Bloomfield St 90720 714-816-3300
Sunghie Okino, prin. Fax 816-3315
McAuliffe MS 1,200/6-8
4112 Cerritos Ave 90720 714-816-3320
Dennis Sackett, prin. Fax 816-3362
Oak MS 1,100/6-8
10821 Oak St 90720 562-799-4740
Sally Neiser, prin. Fax 799-4773
Rossmoor ES 600/K-5
3272 Shakespeare Dr 90720 562-799-4520
Kiva Adele, prin. Fax 799-4530
Weaver ES 600/PK-5
11872 Wembley Rd 90720 562-799-4580
Erin Kominsky, prin. Fax 799-4589
Other Schools – See Seal Beach

Montessori Greenhouse S 50/PK-6
4001 Howard Ave 90720 562-430-4409
Cathy Smythe, dir.
St. Hedwig S 500/K-8
3591 Orangewood Ave 90720 562-296-9060
Suzanne DeVaeney, prin. Fax 296-9089

Los Alamos, Santa Barbara
Los Alamos ESD 200/K-8
PO Box 318 93440 805-344-2401
Fax 344-2321
www.losalamosschool.org/
Reed S 200/K-8
PO Box 318 93440 805-344-2401
Fax 344-2321

Los Altos, Santa Clara, Pop. 27,096
Cupertino UNSD
Supt. — See Cupertino
Montclaire ES 500/K-5
1160 Saint Joseph Ave 94024 650-967-9388
Gail Moberg, prin. Fax 938-0342

Los Altos ESD 4,200/K-8
201 Covington Rd 94024 650-947-1150
Tim Justus, supt. Fax 947-0118
www.losaltos.k12.ca.us
Almond ES 600/K-6
550 Almond Ave 94022 650-917-5400
Terri Stromfeld, prin. Fax 948-7338
Blach IS 500/7-8
1120 Covington Rd 94024 650-934-3800
Leslie Crane, prin. Fax 968-3918
Covington ES 500/K-6
205 Covington Rd 94024 650-947-1100
Erin Green, prin. Fax 941-8175
Egan IS 500/7-8
100 W Portola Ave 94022 650-917-2200
Brenda Dyckman, prin. Fax 949-3748
Loyola ES 500/K-6
770 Berry Ave 94024 650-254-2400
Kimberly Attell, prin. Fax 967-7531
Oak Avenue ES 400/K-6
1501 Oak Ave 94024 650-237-3900
Amy Rettberg, prin. Fax 964-9634
Santa Rita ES 600/K-6
700 Los Altos Ave 94022 650-559-1600
Alyssa Gallagher, prin. Fax 941-5316
Other Schools – See Los Altos Hills, Mountain View

Canterbury Christian S 100/K-6
101 N El Monte Ave 94022 650-949-0909
Rev. Norman Milbank, admin. Fax 949-0909
Los Altos Christian S 200/PK-8
625 Magdalena Ave 94024 650-948-3738
Susan Torode, prin. Fax 949-6092
Miramonte SDA S 200/K-8
1175 Altamead Dr 94024 650-967-2783
Gerald Corson, prin. Fax 967-0833
Pinewood Private S 200/3-6
327 Fremont Ave 94024 650-209-3030
Scott Riches, pres. Fax 941-2459
Pinewood Private S Lower Campus 100/K-2
477 Fremont Ave 94024 650-209-3050
Scott Riches, pres. Fax 948-0916
St. Simon S 500/K-8
1840 Grant Rd 94024 650-968-9952
Steven Clossick, prin. Fax 988-9308
Waldorf S of the Peninsula 300/PK-12
11311 Mora Dr 94024 650-948-8433
Stephanie Rynas, admin. Fax 949-2494

Los Altos Hills, Santa Clara, Pop. 8,164
Los Altos ESD
Supt. — See Los Altos
Gardner Bullis ES 100/K-6
25890 W Fremont Rd 94022 650-559-3200
Erica Gilbert, prin. Fax 949-1312

St. Nicholas S 200/K-8
12816 El Monte Rd 94022 650-941-4056
Matt Komar, prin. Fax 917-9872

Los Angeles, Los Angeles, Pop. 3,844,829
Compton USD
Supt. — See Compton
Carver ES 400/PK-5
1425 E 120th St 90059 310-898-6150
Theophanie Korie, prin. Fax 569-7133
Lincoln Drew ES 400/PK-5
1667 E 118th St 90059 310-898-6450
Kanika White, prin. Fax 563-1268
Vanguard Learning Center 500/6-8
13305 S San Pedro St 90061 310-898-6050
Lori Body, prin. Fax 327-7180

Los Angeles USD 652,100/PK-12
333 S Beaudry Ave 90017 213-241-7000
Ramon Cortinas, supt. Fax 241-8442
www.lausd.k12.ca.us
Adams MS 1,700/6-8
151 W 30th St 90007 213-745-3700
Joseph Santana, prin. Fax 749-8542
Albion Street ES 400/K-5
322 S Avenue 18 90031 323-221-3108
Cheryl Morelan, prin. Fax 223-4077
Aldama ES 700/K-5
632 N Avenue 50 90042 323-255-1434
Joy Naval, prin. Fax 254-2159
Alexander Science Center S 600/K-5
3737 S Figueroa St 90007 213-746-1995
Paula Denen, prin. Fax 746-7443
Alexandria ES 1,100/K-5
4211 Oakwood Ave 90004 323-660-1936
Manuel Ponce, prin. Fax 666-3977
Allesandro ES 500/K-5
2210 Riverside Dr 90039 323-666-7162
Lynn Andrews, prin. Fax 669-8096
Alta Loma ES 800/K-5
1745 Vineyard Ave 90019 323-939-2113
Ellen Deleston, prin. Fax 965-9233
Amanecer Primary Center 200/K-1
832 S Eastman Ave 90023 323-264-6494
Marianne Roberts, prin. Fax 264-6505
Angeles Mesa ES 500/K-5
2611 W 52nd St 90043 323-294-5103
Elizabeth Pratt, prin. Fax 294-0930
Annandale ES 300/K-5
6125 Poppy Peak Dr 90042 323-254-9168
Barbara Wilson, prin. Fax 254-3023
Ann ES 200/K-5
126 Bloom St 90012 323-221-3194
Jane Urbina, prin. Fax 225-6079
Aragon Avenue ES 600/K-5
1118 Aragon Ave 90065 323-221-5173
Louie Carrillo, prin. Fax 221-6708
Arco Iris PS 200/K-K
4504 Ascot Ave 90011 323-233-2403
Thomas Kaminski, prin. Fax 233-3306
Arlington Heights ES 800/K-5
1717 7th Ave 90019 323-735-1021
Zolieta Jefferson, prin. Fax 732-6061
Ascot ES 1,000/K-5
1447 E 45th St 90011 323-235-3178
Donna Gilliland, prin. Fax 231-1486
Atwater ES 400/K-5
3271 Silver Lake Blvd 90039 323-665-5941
Karen Sulahian, prin. Fax 665-5708
Audubon MS 1,500/6-8
4120 11th Ave 90008 323-290-6300
James Downing, prin. Fax 296-2433
Aurora ES 700/K-5
1050 E 52nd Pl 90011 323-238-1500
Heather Lowe, prin. Fax 233-5228
Avalon Gardens ES 200/K-5
13940 S San Pedro St 90061 310-532-8540
Marianne J. Teola, prin. Fax 217-1586
Bakewell Primary Center K-K
8621 Baring Cross St 90044 323-751-3887
Robbie Mae Belcher, prin. Fax 751-5990
Baldwin Hills ES 500/K-5
5421 Rodeo Rd 90016 323-937-7223
Joanne Polite, prin. Fax 937-6529
Bancroft MS 1,300/6-8
929 N Las Palmas Ave 90038 323-993-3400
Cheryl Hildreth, prin. Fax 461-8246
Barrett ES 1,200/K-5
419 W 98th St 90003 323-756-1419
Prescious Robinson, prin. Fax 418-0227
Beethoven Street ES 400/K-5
3711 Beethoven St 90066 310-398-6286
Althea C. Ford, prin. Fax 390-7587
Bellevue PS 100/K-1
610 Micheltorena St 90026 323-664-6899
Marie Leyva, prin. Fax 664-2868
Belvedere ES 1,000/K-5
3724 E 1st St 90063 323-269-0345
Jose J. Hernandez, prin. Fax 269-5581
Belvedere MS 2,400/6-8
312 N Record Ave 90063 323-266-5400
Leo Salazar, prin. Fax 269-6769
Berendo MS 3,000/6-8
1157 S Berendo St 90006 213-739-5600
Robert Bilovsky, prin. Fax 382-8599
Bethune MS 2,500/6-8
155 W 69th St 90003 323-541-1800
Daryl Narimatsu, prin. Fax 759-1271
Bradley ES 600/K-5
3875 Dublin Ave 90008 323-292-8195
Genevieve Shepherd, prin. Fax 292-2413
Breed ES 700/K-5
2226 E 3rd St 90033 323-269-4343
Carmel Madady, prin. Fax 269-0733

Brentwood Science ES 1,200/K-5
740 S Gretna Green Way 90049 310-826-5631
Jeanne Malia, prin. Fax 826-1021
Bridge ES 400/K-5
605 N Boyle Ave 90033 323-222-0165
Theresa Arreguin, prin. Fax 226-0494
Bright ES 800/K-5
1771 W 36th St 90018 323-733-1178
Rene Robinson, prin. Fax 735-5103
Brockton ES 300/K-5
1309 Armacost Ave 90025 310-479-6090
Kim Lattimore, prin. Fax 996-1168
Brooklyn Avenue ES 500/K-5
4620 E Cesar E Chavez Ave 90022 323-269-8161
Nora Gonzalez, prin. Fax 264-6144
Buchanan Street ES 600/K-5
5024 Buchanan St 90042 323-255-7118
Patrice Velasquez, prin. Fax 254-9363
Budlong Avenue ES 1,200/K-5
5940 S Budlong Ave 90044 323-750-6955
Cheri McDonald, prin. Fax 778-3811
Burbank MS 1,800/6-8
6460 N Figueroa St 90042 323-340-4400
John Samaniego, prin. Fax 257-7420
Burroughs MS 2,200/6-8
600 S Mccadden Pl 90005 323-549-5000
Mirta McKay, prin. Fax 934-9051
Bushnell Way ES 500/K-5
5507 Bushnell Way 90042 323-255-6511
Nery Paiz, prin. Fax 255-6343
Cahuenga ES 900/K-5
220 S Hobart Blvd 90004 213-386-6303
Lloyd Houske, prin. Fax 387-7010
Canfield ES 400/K-5
9233 Airdrome St 90035 310-552-2525
Tamara Gullatt, prin. Fax 551-3012
Carthay Center ES 400/K-5
6351 W Olympic Blvd 90048 323-935-8173
Gwen McGee, prin. Fax 933-2698
Carver MS 2,400/6-8
4410 McKinley Ave 90011 323-846-2900
Evelyn Wesley, prin. Fax 232-5344
Castelar ES 800/K-5
840 Yale St 90012 213-626-3674
Cheuk Choi, prin. Fax 680-1894
Castle Heights ES 600/K-5
9755 Cattaraugus Ave 90034 310-839-4528
Patricia Godon Tann, prin. Fax 839-3097
Charnock Road ES 400/K-5
11133 Charnock Rd 90034 310-838-6110
Germaine England, prin. Fax 838-2950
Chavez ES 500/K-6
5243 Oakland St 90032 323-276-1440
Maryhelen Torres, prin. Fax 276-1232
Cheremoya ES 300/K-6
6017 Franklin Ave 90028 323-464-1722
Armineh Papazian, prin. Fax 463-2928
Cienega ES 800/K-5
2611 S Orange Dr 90016 323-939-1138
Kandice Hasani, prin. Fax 933-5316
City Terrace ES 400/K-5
4350 City Terrace Dr 90063 323-269-0581
Christopher Ortiz, prin. Fax 267-9959
Clay MS 1,800/6-8
12226 S Western Ave 90047 323-600-6000
Keri Lew, prin. Fax 777-6056
Clifford ES 200/K-5
2150 Duane St 90039 323-663-0474
Kerry Kehrley, prin. Fax 663-6822
Clinton MS 6-8
3500 S Hill St 90007 323-235-7200
Beverley Clarkson, prin. Fax 846-0054
Clover Avenue ES 500/K-5
11020 Clover Ave 90034 310-479-7739
Sharon Fabian, prin. Fax 444-9744
Cochran MS 1,900/6-8
4066 W 17th St 90019 323-730-4300
Scott Schmerelson, prin. Fax 733-9106
Coliseum Street ES 300/K-5
4400 Coliseum St 90016 323-294-5244
Lisa Le Sassier, prin. Fax 292-9490
Commonwealth Avenue ES 800/1-5
215 S Commonwealth Ave 90004 213-384-2546
Young Park, prin. Fax 386-3652
Compton ES 400/K-5
1515 E 104th St 90002 323-564-5767
TaJuana Starks, prin. Fax 563-6311
Cowan Avenue ES 500/K-5
7615 Cowan Ave 90045 310-645-1973
Richard DaSylveira, prin. Fax 645-6273
Crescent Heights Boulevard ES 400/K-5
1661 S Crescent Hts Blvd 90035 323-931-2761
Cherise Caver, prin. Fax 939-7560
Dahlia Heights ES 400/K-6
5063 Floristan Ave 90041 323-255-1419
Rona Greenstadt, prin. Fax 344-9129
Dayton Heights ES 600/K-5
607 N Westmoreland Ave 90004 323-661-3308
Dona Lawrie, prin. Fax 662-5278
Delevan Drive ES 600/K-6
4168 W Avenue 42 90065 323-255-0571
Yolanda Hamilton, prin. Fax 254-8368
Del Olmo ES 900/K-5
100 N New Hampshire Ave 90004 213-427-7200
Eugene Hernandez, prin. Fax 487-0788
Dena ES 600/K-5
1314 S Dacotah St 90023 323-269-9222
Liliana Narvaez, prin. Fax 263-2371
Dorris Place ES 400/K-5
2225 Dorris Pl 90031 323-222-9185
Susan Grant, prin. Fax 222-3686
Drew MS 2,600/6-8
8511 Compton Ave 90001 323-826-1700
David Garcia, prin. Fax 583-6030
Eagle Rock ES 1,000/K-6
2057 Fair Park Ave 90041 323-254-6851
Mary Jane Collier, prin. Fax 344-9720

Eastman ES 1,300/K-5
4112 E Olympic Blvd 90023 323-269-0456
Ileana Davalos, prin. Fax 269-3625
Edison MS 2,200/6-8
6500 Hooper Ave 90001 323-826-2500
Coleen Kaiwi, prin. Fax 581-8389
El Sereno ES 600/K-5
3838 Rosemead Ave 90032 323-222-3389
Alice M. Treptow, prin. Fax 226-0200
El Sereno MS 2,200/6-8
2839 N Eastern Ave 90032 323-224-4700
Arthur Duardo, prin. Fax 223-9024
Elysian Heights ES 300/K-5
1562 Baxter St 90026 323-665-6315
Sally Olguin, prin. Fax 661-5961
Emerson MS 1,400/6-8
1650 Selby Ave 90024 310-234-3100
Katherine Gonnella, prin. Fax 474-6517
Esperanza ES 1,000/K-5
680 Little St 90017 213-484-0326
Felicia Mitchell, prin. Fax 484-1137
Euclid Avenue ES 1,000/K-5
806 Euclid Ave 90023 323-263-6792
Olga Garcia, prin. Fax 780-7992
Evergreen ES 900/K-5
2730 Ganahl St 90033 323-269-0415
Raul Navar, prin. Fax 261-1128
Fairburn Avenue ES 400/K-5
1403 Fairburn Ave 90024 310-470-1344
Elizabeth Abramowitz, prin. Fax 470-3981
Farmdale ES 600/K-5
2660 Ruth Swiggett Dr 90032 323-222-6659
Teresita DePalma, prin. Fax 222-9693
Fifty-Fourth Street ES 500/K-5
5501 Eileen Ave 90043 323-294-5275
Dewayne Davis, prin. Fax 298-0820
Fifty-Ninth Street ES 500/K-5
5939 2nd Ave 90043 323-294-5118
Patricia Williams, prin. Fax 291-9424
Fifty-Second Street ES 900/K-5
816 W 51st St 90037 323-753-3175
Beverly Crosby, prin. Fax 750-9542
Figueroa ES 700/K-5
510 W 111th St 90044 323-756-9268
Tanya Stokes-Mack, prin. Fax 754-1905
First Street ES 700/K-5
2820 E 1st St 90033 323-269-0138
Hobart F. Cress, prin. Fax 269-8776
Fletcher Drive ES 800/K-5
3350 Fletcher Dr 90065 323-254-5246
Maria Manzur, prin. Fax 258-8014
Florence ES 900/K-5
7211 Bell Ave 90001 323-582-0758
Luis Montoya, prin. Fax 582-7804
Flournoy ES 700/K-5
1630 E 111th St 90059 323-564-2545
Catherine Andrews, prin. Fax 567-0816
Ford Boulevard ES 1,200/K-5
1112 S Ford Blvd 90022 323-268-8508
Jeanette Rodriguez Chien, prin. Fax 264-6953
Forty-Ninth Street ES 1,200/K-5
750 E 49th St 90011 323-234-9045
Daniel A. Balderrama, prin. Fax 234-3824
Forty-Second Street ES 500/K-5
4231 4th Ave 90008 323-296-7550
Darneika Watson, prin. Fax 292-7680
Fourth Street ES 700/K-5
420 Amalia Ave 90022 323-266-0182
Marguerite Murphy, prin. Fax 264-4071
Fourth Street Primary Center PK-1
469 Amalia Ave 90022 323-268-8775
Vermel Taylor, prin. Fax 268-8755
Franklin ES 400/K-6
1910 N Commonwealth Ave 90027 323-663-0320
Veronica Sasso, prin. Fax 663-1684
Gardner ES 400/K-6
7450 Hawthorn Ave 90046 323-876-4710
Kenneth L. Urbina, prin. Fax 878-0954
Garvanza ES 500/K-5
317 N Avenue 62 90042 323-254-7328
Shannon Corbett, prin. Fax 256-6351
Garza Primary Center 100/K-1
2750 Hostetter St 90023 323-981-0270
Patricia Romero, prin. Fax 981-0951
Gates ES 800/K-5
3333 Manitou Ave 90031 323-225-9574
Margaret DeLaMora, prin. Fax 225-8562
Glassell Park ES 700/K-5
2211 W Avenue 30 90065 323-223-2277
Eileen Hatrick, prin. Fax 227-6391
Glen Alta ES 300/K-5
3410 Sierra St 90031 323-223-1195
Cecile Rico, prin. Fax 223-3573
Glenfeliz Boulevard ES 500/K-5
3955 Glenfeliz Blvd 90039 323-666-1431
Carole Rosenblum, prin. Fax 666-5735
Gompers MS 1,900/6-8
234 E 112th St 90061 323-241-4000
Sonia Miller, prin. Fax 418-0778
Graham ES 900/K-5
8407 S Fir Ave 90001 323-583-1263
Ruben Valles, prin. Fax 583-5367
Grand View Boulevard ES 700/K-5
3951 Grand View Blvd 90066 310-390-3618
Alfredo Ortiz, prin. Fax 390-5836
Grant ES 1,000/K-5
1530 N Wilton Pl 90028 323-469-4046
Christopher Ikeanyi, prin. Fax 469-4861
Grape ES 700/K-5
1940 E 111th St 90059 323-564-5941
Jera Turner, prin. Fax 564-7168
Gratts ES 900/K-5
309 Lucas Ave 90017 213-250-2932
Titus Campos, prin. Fax 250-3648
Griffin Avenue ES 600/K-5
2025 Griffin Ave 90031 323-222-8131
Susan Saenz, prin. Fax 222-0837

Griffith Joyner ES 1,000/K-5
1963 E 103rd St 90002 323-569-8141
John P. Sayers, prin. Fax 249-0939
Griffith MS 2,000/6-8
4765 E 4th St 90022 323-266-7400
Teresa Hurtado, prin. Fax 268-6375
Hamasaki ES 400/K-5
4865 E 1st St 90022 323-263-3869
Ana Maria Perez, prin. Fax 268-8830
Hammel Street ES 900/K-5
438 N Brannick Ave 90063 323-263-9461
Jose Cantu, prin. Fax 263-6872
Hancock Park ES 700/K-5
408 S Fairfax Ave 90036 323-935-5272
Judith Perez, prin. Fax 857-1795
Harmony ES 900/K-5
899 E 42nd Pl 90011 323-238-0791
Robert Cordova, prin. Fax 238-0793
Harrison S 900/K-8
3529 City Terrace Dr 90063 323-263-9191
Isaias Martinez, prin. Fax 263-7708
Harte Prep MS 1,600/6-8
9301 S Hoover St 90044 323-242-5400
Lester Davidson, prin. Fax 757-0408
Harvard ES 500/K-5
330 N Harvard Blvd 90004 323-953-4540
Marilyn Estrada, prin. Fax 669-2833
Hillcrest Drive ES 1,000/K-5
4041 Hillcrest Dr 90008 323-296-6867
Doreen Evans, prin. Fax 292-9180
Hillside ES 400/K-5
120 E Avenue 35 90031 323-222-2665
Hilda Maldonado, prin. Fax 222-6033
Hobart Boulevard ES 1,300/K-5
980 S Hobart Blvd 90006 213-386-8661
Mercedes Villalvazo, prin. Fax 382-2859
Hollenbeck MS 2,600/6-8
2510 E 6th St 90023 323-780-3000
Jose Torres, prin. Fax 265-0865
Hollywood Primary Center 100/PK-1
1115 Tamarind Ave 90038 323-464-0331
Marco Nava, prin. Fax 464-4206
Hooper ES 1,400/K-5
1225 E 52nd St 90011 323-232-3571
Eufrosino Espinoza, prin. Fax 235-0847
Hooper Primary Center 300/K-K
1280 E 52nd St 90011 323-233-5866
Michael Shaw, prin. Fax 233-3188
Hoover ES 1,600/K-5
2726 Francis Ave 90005 213-387-3296
May Arakaki, prin. Fax 387-9054
Humphreys Avenue ES 900/K-5
500 S Humphreys Ave 90022 323-263-6958
Maricela Sanchez Robles, prin. Fax 780-2978
Huntington Drive ES 600/K-5
4435 Huntington Dr N 90032 323-223-1336
Roberto Salazar, prin. Fax 223-7931
Hyde Park ES 800/K-5
3140 Hyde Park Blvd 90043 323-778-4992
Carolyn S. Mayes, prin. Fax 753-2280
Irving MS 1,600/6-8
3010 Estara Ave 90065 323-259-3700
Kimberly Noble, prin. Fax 254-6447
Ivanhoe ES 300/K-5
2828 Herkimer St 90039 323-664-0051
Lillian Sugahara, prin. Fax 666-7417
Jones Primary Center PK-2
1017 W 47th St 90037 323-235-8911
Arnold Hernandez, prin. Fax 235-1887
Kennedy ES 600/K-5
4010 Ramboz Dr 90063 323-263-9627
Rafael Escobar, prin. Fax 263-6871
Kentwood ES 300/K-5
8401 Emerson Ave 90045 310-670-8977
Jean Pennicooke, prin. Fax 670-6957
Kim ES 600/K-5
225 S Oxford Ave 90004 213-368-5600
Jim Canelas, prin. Fax 739-2550
King ES 900/K-5
3989 S Hobart Blvd 90062 323-294-0031
David Bell, prin. Fax 294-0277
King MS 2,800/6-8
4201 Fountain Ave 90029 323-664-6700
Kristen Murphy, prin. Fax 913-3594
Kingsley ES 500/K-5
5200 Virginia Ave 90029 323-644-7700
Renee Fuentes Campa, prin. Fax 913-3360
Lafayette Park Primary Center 200/K-K
310 S La Fayette Park Pl 90057 213-380-5039
Dean Tagawa, prin. Fax 380-5196
Lake Street PS 200/K-K
135 N Lake St 90026 213-413-3305
Julie Gonzalez, prin. Fax 413-3827
La Salle Avenue ES 900/K-5
8715 La Salle Ave 90047 323-759-1161
Debora Weathersby, prin. Fax 751-5591
Latona ES 400/K-5
4312 Berenice Ave 90031 323-221-5148
Brian Lucas, prin. Fax 225-6417
Laurel ES 300/K-5
925 N Hayworth Ave 90046 323-654-1930
Patricia Dachenhausen, prin. Fax 656-5801
Lexington Ave Primary Center 200/PK-1
4564 Lexington Ave 90029 323-644-2884
Traci Calhoun, prin. Fax 644-8115
Liechty MS 1,700/6-8
650 S Union Ave 90017 213-989-1200
Jeanette Stevens, prin. Fax 484-2700
Lillian Street ES 700/K-5
5909 Lillian St 90001 323-582-0705
Susan Ahern, prin. Fax 582-8873
Lizarraga ES K-4
401 E 40th Pl 90011 323-235-6960
Veronica Moscosco, prin. Fax 846-9824
Lockwood Avenue ES 600/K-5
4345 Lockwood Ave 90029 323-662-2101
Andrea Donahoo, prin. Fax 663-3136

Logan ES 700/K-5
1711 Montana St 90026 213-413-6353
Diane R. Ramirez, prin. Fax 413-1261
Lorena Street ES 800/K-5
1015 S Lorena St 90023 323-268-1128
Luis Cuevas, prin. Fax 264-9437
Loreto ES 600/K-5
3408 Arroyo Seco Ave 90065 323-222-5176
Delores Manrique, prin. Fax 222-6370
Los Angeles Academy 2,400/6-8
644 E 56th St 90011 323-238-1800
Maria Borges, prin. Fax 231-0136
Los Angeles ES 900/K-5
1211 S Hobart Blvd 90006 323-734-8233
Bruce Clark, prin. Fax 734-8639
Los Feliz ES 500/K-5
1740 N New Hampshire Ave 90027 323-663-0674
Katherine Pilkinton, prin. Fax 664-6045
Loyola Village ES 600/K-5
8821 Villanova Ave 90045 310-670-0480
Melinda L. Goodall, prin. Fax 216-9529
MacArthur Park Primary Center 300/K-2
2300 W 7th St 90057 213-381-7217
Deborah Siegel, prin. Fax 381-1872
Mack ES 500/K-5
3020 S Catalina St 90007 323-730-7620
Brenda Grady, prin. Fax 373-9655
Magnolia ES 1,400/K-5
1626 Orchard Ave 90006 213-748-6281
Luis Velasco, prin. Fax 748-3722
Main Street ES 1,200/K-5
129 E 53rd St 90011 323-232-4856
Eva Garcia, prin. Fax 231-1260
Malabar Street ES 900/K-5
3200 Malabar St 90063 323-261-1103
Jorge Rios, prin. Fax 261-3252
Manchester ES 1,100/K-5
661 W 87th St 90044 323-778-3472
Gregory Hooker, prin. Fax 751-5321
Manhattan Place ES 600/K-5
1850 W 96th St 90047 323-756-1308
Shirley Gideon, prin. Fax 756-9685
Mann MS 1,400/6-8
7001 S St Andrews Pl 90047 323-541-1900
Cynthia Arceneaux, prin. Fax 758-8203
Maple Primary Center 100/K-K
3601 Maple Ave 90011 323-232-0984
Elaine Fujiu, prin. Fax 238-0780
Marianna ES 500/K-6
4215 Gleason St 90063 323-262-6382
Robert Martinez, prin. Fax 780-0971
Marina Del Rey MS 1,300/6-8
12500 Braddock Dr 90066 310-578-2700
Erick Mata, prin. Fax 821-3248
Mariposa-Nabi PS 200/PK-5
987 S Mariposa Ave 90006 213-385-0241
Salvador Rodriguez, prin. Fax 385-0257
Marvin ES 800/K-5
2411 S Marvin Ave 90016 323-938-3608
Ivalene Cass, prin. Fax 938-0411
Mar Vista ES 600/K-5
3330 Granville Ave 90066 310-391-1175
Brenda Weinstock, prin. Fax 398-0924
Mayberry Street ES 400/K-5
2414 Mayberry St 90026 213-413-3420
Paula Bennett, prin. Fax 413-5975
McKinley Avenue ES 1,000/K-5
7812 McKinley Ave 90001 323-582-7481
Gabriela Rodriguez, prin. Fax 588-1858
Melrose ES 200/K-5
731 N Detroit St 90046 323-938-6275
Bernadette Lucas, prin. Fax 938-4981
Menlo Avenue ES 1,100/K-5
4156 Menlo Ave 90037 323-232-4291
Vive Berry, prin. Fax 232-0696
Micheltorena Street ES 400/K-6
1511 Micheltorena St 90026 323-661-2125
Susanna Furfari, prin. Fax 661-2086
Mid-City Magnet S 400/K-8
3150 W Adams Blvd 90018 323-731-9346
Herbert Jones, prin. Fax 730-1976
Miller ES 1,100/K-5
830 W 77th St 90044 323-753-4445
Jean Mitchell, prin. Fax 758-5081
Miramonte ES 1,800/K-5
1400 E 68th St 90001 323-583-1257
Richard Lopez, prin. Fax 582-6736
Monte Vista Street ES 500/2-5
5423 Monte Vista St 90042 323-254-7261
Jose Posada, prin. Fax 259-9757
Mt. Washington ES 300/K-6
3981 San Rafael Ave 90065 323-225-8320
Sosie Kralian, prin. Fax 223-2514
Muir MS 2,400/6-8
5929 S Vermont Ave 90044 323-565-2200
Michael Olivo, prin. Fax 778-9824
Multnomah ES 600/K-5
2101 N Indiana Ave 90032 323-225-6005
Beth Eythrow, prin. Fax 226-0220
Murchison Street ES 600/K-5
1501 Murchison St 90033 323-222-0148
Margarita Gutierrez, prin. Fax 225-2418
Nevin ES 900/K-5
1569 E 32nd St 90011 323-232-2236
Kevin Baker, prin. Fax 232-5648
Nightingale MS 1,900/6-8
3311 N Figueroa St 90065 323-224-4800
Manuel Diaz, prin. Fax 222-4506
Ninety-Fifth Street ES 1,100/K-5
1109 W 96th St 90044 323-756-1466
Carlen Powell, prin. Fax 754-8339
Ninety-Ninth Street ES 600/K-5
9900 Wadsworth Ave 90002 323-564-2677
Sherri Williams, prin. Fax 249-9354
Ninety-Second Street ES 900/K-5
9211 Grape St 90002 323-564-7946
Nanetta Arceneaux, prin. Fax 249-9417

Ninety-Sixth Street ES 900/K-5
1471 E 96th St 90002 323-567-8871
Luis Heckmuller, prin. Fax 567-3491
Ninety-Third Street ES 1,200/K-5
330 E 93rd St 90003 323-754-2869
Arne Rubenstein, prin. Fax 756-8345
Ninth Street ES 400/K-5
820 Towne Ave 90021 213-622-0669
Anne Barry, prin. Fax 622-6557
Normandie ES 1,000/K-5
4505 S Raymond Ave 90037 323-294-5171
Gustgavo Ortiz, prin. Fax 294-7061
Norwood Street ES 900/K-5
2020 Oak St 90007 213-748-3733
Bruce Onodera, prin. Fax 747-3380
Olympic Primary Center 200/PK-1
950 Albany St 90015 213-739-2753
Helen Yu, prin. Fax 739-0048
118th Street ES 700/K-5
144 E 118th St 90061 323-757-1717
Tina Choyce, prin. Fax 757-9916
109th Street ES 500/K-5
10915 McKinley Ave 90059 323-756-9206
Priscilla Currie, prin. Fax 755-2307
107th Street ES 1,100/K-5
147 E 107th St 90003 323-756-8137
Reuben Rios, prin. Fax 779-6942
116th Street ES 500/K-5
11610 Stanford Ave 90059 323-754-3121
Carolin McKie, prin. Fax 777-5977
112th Street ES 600/K-5
1265 E 112th St 90059 323-567-2108
Brenda A. Manuel, prin. Fax 567-2611
122nd Street ES 800/K-5
405 E 122nd St 90061 323-757-8117
Robin Benton, prin. Fax 757-0689
Overland ES 500/K-5
10650 Ashby Ave 90064 310-838-7308
Anna Born, prin. Fax 842-9392
Palms ES 400/K-5
3520 Motor Ave 90034 310-838-7337
Keith Abrahams, prin. Fax 841-0814
Palms MS 1,900/6-8
10860 Woodbine St 90034 310-253-7600
Bonnie Murrow, prin. Fax 559-0397
Parks/Huerta Primary Center 100/K-K
1020 W 58th Pl 90044 323-759-0667
Dianne Island, prin. Fax 759-1369
Parmelee ES 1,200/K-5
1338 E 76th Pl 90001 323-587-4235
Arthur Chandler, prin. Fax 587-0257
Pio Pico S 1,900/K-8
1512 Arlington Ave 90019 323-733-8801
Dina Sim, prin. Fax 735-2665
Plasencia ES 1,100/K-5
1321 Cortez St 90026 213-250-7450
Eleanor Page, prin. Fax 482-1815
Politi ES 900/K-5
2481 W 11th St 90006 213-480-1244
Bradley Rumble, prin. Fax 736-0486
Queen Anne Place ES 500/K-5
1212 Queen Anne Pl 90019 323-939-7322
Mary Hall, prin. Fax 939-6605
Ramona ES 800/K-5
1133 N Mariposa Ave 90029 323-663-2158
Susan Arcaris, prin. Fax 665-4934
Raymond Avenue ES 700/K-5
7511 Raymond Ave 90044 323-759-1183
Linda McClellan, prin. Fax 778-2569
Richland Avenue ES 300/K-5
11562 Richland Ave 90064 310-473-0467
Karina Salazar, prin. Fax 268-7948
Riordan PS 300/K-1
5531 Monte Vista St 90042 323-551-6822
Marilee Wood, prin. Fax 551-6944
Rockdale ES 300/K-6
1303 Yosemite Dr 90041 323-255-6793
Desiree DeBond, prin. Fax 255-2906
Roscomare Road ES 500/K-5
2425 Roscomare Rd 90077 310-472-9829
Giuseppa Dimarco, prin. Fax 476-7970
Rosemont Avenue ES 1,100/K-5
421 Rosemont Ave 90026 213-413-5310
Evaristo Barrett, prin. Fax 483-4341
Rosewood ES 500/K-5
503 N Croft Ave 90048 323-651-0166
Janet Chapman, prin. Fax 852-9653
Rowan Avenue ES 1,000/K-5
600 S Rowan Ave 90023 323-261-7191
Thomas Delgado, prin. Fax 261-0610
Russell ES 1,200/K-5
1263 Firestone Blvd 90001 323-582-7247
Adalberto Vega, prin. Fax 582-3751
San Pascual Avenue ES 300/K-5
815 San Pascual Ave 90042 323-255-8354
James Allen, prin. Fax 255-5663
San Pedro Street ES 800/K-5
1635 S San Pedro St 90015 213-747-9538
Armando Ramirez, prin. Fax 747-6332
Saturn Street ES 600/K-5
5360 Saturn St 90019 323-931-1688
Tracie Bryant, prin. Fax 933-6370
Second Street ES 600/K-5
1942 E 2nd St 90033 323-269-9401
Edgardo Soberanes, prin. Fax 780-2912
Selma Avenue ES 400/K-5
6611 Selma Ave 90028 323-461-9418
Julie Kane, prin. Fax 962-9258
Seventy-Fifth Street ES 1,500/K-5
142 W 75th St 90003 323-971-8885
Miguel Campa, prin. Fax 778-0783
Seventy-Fourth Street ES 700/K-5
2112 W 74th St 90047 323-753-2338
Andre Cunningham, prin. Fax 778-2347
Shenandoah ES 800/K-5
2450 S Shenandoah St 90034 310-838-3142
Carmen Dominguez, prin. Fax 842-9892

Sheridan Street ES 1,200/K-5
416 Cornwell St 90033 323-263-9818
Genaro Carapia, prin. Fax 261-4710
Short ES 300/K-5
12814 Maxella Ave 90066 310-397-4234
Stephanie Harris, prin. Fax 390-8940
Sierra Park ES 600/K-5
3170 Budau Ave 90032 323-223-1081
Letecia De Carreon, prin. Fax 222-1661
Sierra Vista ES 200/K-5
4342 Alpha St 90032 323-222-2530
Heidi Morteo, prin. Fax 222-4347
Sixth Avenue ES 800/K-5
3109 6th Ave 90018 323-733-9107
Jaime Miranda, prin. Fax 732-4001
Sixty-Eighth Street ES 1,100/K-5
612 W 68th St 90044 323-753-2133
Rosalinda Lugo, prin. Fax 752-9909
Sixty-First Street ES 900/K-5
6020 S Figueroa St 90003 323-759-1138
Jose Macias, prin. Fax 750-9685
Sixty-Sixth Street ES 1,300/K-5
6600 S San Pedro St 90003 323-753-1589
Lisa Jeffery, prin. Fax 758-6505
Solano Avenue ES 300/K-6
615 Solano Ave 90012 323-223-4291
Richard Hickcox, prin. Fax 343-1975
Soto Street ES 300/K-5
1020 S Soto St 90023 323-262-6513
Elva Reyes, prin. Fax 268-7453
South Park ES 1,000/K-5
8510 Towne Ave 90003 323-753-4591
Karen Rose, prin. Fax 753-7256
Sterry ES 400/K-5
1730 Corinth Ave 90025 310-473-2172
Freida Smith, prin. Fax 444-1988
Stevenson MS 2,600/6-8
725 S Indiana St 90023 323-780-6400
L. Gonzalez, prin. Fax 265-3952
Tenth Street ES 1,200/K-5
1000 Grattan St 90015 213-380-8990
Linda Ariyasu, prin. Fax 480-6732
Third Street ES 700/K-5
201 S June St 90004 323-939-8337
Suzie Oh, prin. Fax 939-3098
Thirty Second Street USC Magnet S 1,000/K-12
822 W 32nd St 90007 213-748-0126
Larverne Brunt, prin. Fax 744-1608
Toland Way ES 500/K-6
4545 Toland Way 90041 323-255-3142
Juan Gonzalez, prin. Fax 255-0555
Trinity Street ES 800/K-5
3736 Trinity St 90011 323-232-2358
Robin Shuffer, prin. Fax 231-2441
Twain MS 1,100/6-8
2224 Walgrove Ave 90066 310-305-3100
Raul Fernandez, prin. Fax 398-1627
Twentieth Street ES 700/K-5
1353 E 20th St 90011 213-747-7151
Bethsaida Castillo, prin. Fax 745-7606
Twenty-Eighth Street ES 1,500/K-5
2807 Stanford Ave 90011 323-232-3496
Rigoberto Rodriguez, prin. Fax 232-3029
Twenty-Fourth Street ES 1,000/K-5
2055 W 24th St 90018 323-735-0278
Renee Dolberry, prin. Fax 730-1865
Union ES 1,200/K-5
150 S Burlington Ave 90057 213-483-1345
Giuseppe Nardulli, prin. Fax 483-8109
Utah ES 300/K-5
255 Gabriel Garcia Marquez 90033 323-261-1171
Patricia Castro, prin. Fax 265-2090
Valley View ES 200/K-6
6921 Woodrow Wilson Dr 90068 323-851-0020
Harold Klein, prin. Fax 851-6185
Van Ness Avenue ES 300/K-5
501 N Van Ness Ave 90004 323-469-0992
Katty Iriarte, prin. Fax 469-8376
Vermont ES 900/K-5
1435 W 27th St 90007 323-733-2195
Major DeBerry, prin. Fax 766-0577
Vine Street ES 700/K-5
955 Vine St 90038 323-469-0877
Christopher Stehr, prin. Fax 461-7536
Virgil MS 2,800/6-8
152 N Vermont Ave 90004 213-368-2800
Ada Stevens, prin. Fax 383-8774
Virginia Road ES 600/K-5
2925 Virginia Rd 90016 323-735-0570
Odessa Taylor, prin. Fax 735-8224
Wadsworth ES 1,100/K-5
981 E 41st St 90011 323-232-5234
Lorraine Abner, prin. Fax 233-9612
Walgrove Avenue ES 300/K-5
1630 Walgrove Ave 90066 310-391-7104
Arlene Fortier, prin. Fax 391-9809
Warner ES 600/K-5
615 Holmby Ave 90024 310-475-5893
Jeffrey Kaufman, prin. Fax 470-5840
Washington Primary Center 200/K-1
860 W 112th St 90044 323-779-7550
Allison Speight, prin. Fax 779-7473
Webster MS 1,200/6-8
11330 Graham Pl 90064 310-235-4600
Kendra Wallace, prin. Fax 477-0146
Weemes ES 1,200/K-5
1260 W 36th Pl 90007 323-733-9186
Lynn Brown, prin. Fax 732-3973
Weigand ES 500/K-5
10401 Weigand Ave 90002 323-567-9606
Frances Pasillas, prin. Fax 564-2916
West Athens ES 1,000/K-5
1110 W 119th St 90044 323-756-9114
Maxine Hawk, prin. Fax 418-8467
Western ES 800/K-5
1724 W 53rd St 90062 323-295-3261
Bettye Johnson, prin. Fax 295-4809

Westport Heights ES 500/K-5
6011 W 79th St 90045 310-645-5611
Karen Long, prin. Fax 645-4258
West Vernon ES 1,200/K-5
4312 S Grand Ave 90037 323-232-4218
Margaret Just, prin. Fax 232-7801
White ES 500/2-5
2401 Wilshire Blvd 90057 213-487-9172
Carol Greene, prin. Fax 487-9177
Whitehouse Place PS 200/K-2
108 Bimini Pl 90004 213-383-6024
Rosa Maria Ashaq, prin. Fax 739-8516
Wilshire Crest ES 400/K-5
5241 W Olympic Blvd 90036 323-938-5291
Joan McConico, prin. Fax 933-1481
Wilshire Park ES 500/K-5
4063 Ingraham St 90005 213-739-4760
Enrique Franco, prin. Fax 381-6178
Wilton Place ES 1,000/K-5
745 S Wilton Pl 90005 213-389-1181
Jung Kim, prin. Fax 387-5192
Windsor Hills Math/Science/Aerospace ES 700/K-5
5215 Overdale Dr 90043 323-293-6251
Kathy Crowe, prin. Fax 293-2021
Wonderland Avenue ES 400/K-5
8510 Wonderland Ave 90046 323-654-4401
Donald Wilson, prin. Fax 656-3228
Woodcrest ES 1,000/K-5
1151 W 109th St 90044 323-756-1371
Zelendria Robinson, prin. Fax 756-1432
Wright MS 1,100/6-8
6550 W 80th St 90045 310-258-6600
Fax 568-8942
Yorkdale ES 500/K-5
5657 Meridian St 90042 323-255-0587
Clayton Forrest Baird, prin. Fax 255-1348
Other Schools – See Arleta, Bell, Canoga Park, Carson, Chatsworth, Cudahy, Culver City, Encino, Gardena, Granada Hills, Harbor City, Hawthorne, Hollywood, Huntington Park, Inglewood, Lomita, Long Beach, Maywood, Mission Hills, Monterey Park, North Hills, North Hollywood, Northridge, Pacoima, Panorama City, Playa Del Rey, Rancho Palos Verdes, Reseda, San Fernando, San Pedro, Sepulveda, Sherman Oaks, South Gate, Studio City, Sunland, Sun Valley, Sylmar, Tarzana, Torrance, Tujunga, Van Nuys, Venice, Vernon, West Hills, West Hollywood, Wilmington, Woodland Hills

Montebello USD
Supt. — See Montebello
Gascon ES 1,100/K-4
630 Leonard Ave 90022 323-721-2025
Stephanie Hardaway, prin. Fax 887-3034
Montebello Park ES 600/K-4
6300 Northside Dr 90022 323-721-3305
Margie Rodriguez, prin. Fax 887-3073
Winter Gardens ES 600/K-5
1277 Clela Ave 90022 323-268-0477
Olga Moreno, prin. Fax 887-7894

All Saints S 100/PK-8
3420 Portola Ave 90032 323-225-7264
Maria Palermo, prin. Fax 225-1240
Ascension S 200/PK-8
500 W 111th Pl 90044 323-756-4064
Dr. Karen Kallay, prin. Fax 756-1060
Assumption S 200/PK-8
3016 Winter St 90063 323-269-4319
Carolina Gomez, prin. Fax 269-2434
Bais Chaya Mushka S 200/PK-8
9051 W Pico Blvd 90035 310-859-8840
Rabbi Danny Yiftach, admin. Fax 859-9824
Bais Tzivia Girls' S 300/PK-8
7269 Beverly Blvd 90036 323-935-9274
Berkeley Hall S 300/PK-8
16000 Mulholland Dr 90049 310-476-6421
Craig Barrows, hdmstr. Fax 476-5748
Blessed Sacrament S 100/K-8
6641 W Sunset Blvd 90028 323-467-4177
Ava Haylock, prin. Fax 467-6099
Brawerman S 200/K-6
11661 W Olympic Blvd 90064 310-445-1280
Nadine Breuer, hdmstr.
Brentwood S 300/K-6
12001 W Sunset Blvd 90049 310-471-1041
Dr. Michael Pratt, hdmstr. Fax 440-1989
Cathedral Chapel S 300/K-8
755 S Cochran Ave 90036 323-938-9976
Tina Kipp, prin. Fax 938-9930
Cheder Menachem 300/K-8
5120 Melrose Ave 90038 323-769-8200
Rabbi Menachem Greenbaum, prin. Fax 769-8204
Christ the King S 200/K-8
617 N Arden Blvd 90004 323-462-4753
Mary Kurban, prin. Fax 462-8475
Communion Christian Academy 100/PK-6
6201 S La Brea Ave 90056 323-296-8761
Dr. Noble Henson, admin. Fax 296-1857
Culver City Adventist S 100/K-8
11828 W Washington Blvd 90066 310-398-3305
Culver City Christian S 100/PK-K
11312 W Washington Blvd 90066 310-391-6963
Deanna Zamora, dir. Fax 397-8031
Curtis S 500/PK-6
15871 Mulholland Dr 90049 310-476-1251
Stephen Switzer, prin. Fax 476-1542
Divine Savior S 200/K-8
624 Cypress Ave 90065 323-222-6077
Maria Jimenez, prin. Fax 222-6994
Dolores Mission S 200/PK-8
170 S Gless St 90033 323-881-0001
Karina Moreno, prin. Fax 881-0034
Dye S 300/K-6
11414 Chalon Rd 90049 310-476-2811
Raymond Michaud, prin. Fax 476-9176

E Los Angeles Light & Life Christian S 100/K-8
207 S Dacotah St 90063 323-269-5236
Veronica Guerrero, prin. Fax 269-3370
Golden Day S 400/K-6
4508 Crenshaw Blvd 90043 323-296-6280
Dr. Clark Parker, prin. Fax 290-0190
Good Shepherd Lutheran S 50/PK-6
6338 N Figueroa St 90042 323-255-2786
Patricia Rafacz, prin. Fax 255-8452
Hollywood Schoolhouse 200/K-8
1233 N McCadden Pl 90038 323-465-1320
Stephen Bloodworth, hdmstr. Fax 465-1720
Holy Name of Jesus S 200/K-8
1955 W Jefferson Blvd 90018 323-731-2255
Marva Belisle, prin. Fax 730-0321
Holy Spirit S 100/K-8
1418 S Burnside Ave 90019 323-933-7775
Sr. Loretto O'Leary, prin. Fax 933-7453
Holy Trinity S 200/K-8
3716 Boyce Ave 90039 323-663-2064
Alice Martinez, prin. Fax 663-0732
Immaculate Conception S 200/K-8
830 Green Ave 90017 213-382-5931
Mary Murphy, prin. Fax 382-4563
Immaculate Heart MS 200/6-8
5515 Franklin Ave 90028 323-461-3651
Ann Phelps, prin. Fax 462-0610
Immaculate Heart of Mary S 200/K-8
1055 N Alexandria Ave 90029 323-663-4611
Paula Simpson, prin. Fax 663-6216
La Senda Antigua Christian S 50/K-12
631 E Adams Blvd 90011 213-746-5274
Jose Galan, prin. Fax 746-5274
Le Lycee Francais de Los Angeles 800/PK-12
3261 Overland Ave 90034 310-836-3464
Alain Anselme, dir. Fax 558-8069
Le Lycee Francais de Los Angeles 100/K-1
10361 W Pico Blvd 90064 310-553-7444
Michel Zala, hdmstr.
Little Citizens Westside Academy 100/1-12
4256 S Western Ave 90062 323-293-9775
Angela Moore, admin.
Los Angeles Adventist Academy 300/PK-12
846 E El Segundo Blvd 90059 323-321-2585
Lorenzo Paytee, prin. Fax 324-3207
Los Angeles Cheder 300/PK-8
801 N La Brea Ave 90038 323-932-6347
Rabbi Simcha Ullman, prin. Fax 932-6335
Los Angeles Christian S 100/K-8
1620 W 20th St 90007 323-735-2867
Michelle Milburn, prin. Fax 735-2576
Lycee International De Los Angeles 500/PK-12
4155 Russell Ave 90027 323-665-4526
Deborah Thornburg, dir. Fax 665-2607
Maimonides Academy 400/PK-8
310 Huntley Dr 90048 310-659-2456
Rabbi Aharon Wilk, prin. Fax 659-2865
Miracle Baptist Christian S 100/K-8
8300 S Central Ave 90001 323-582-3898
Andrea Thompson, prin. Fax 582-8363
Mirman S 300/1-9
16180 Mulholland Dr 90049 310-476-2868
John West, hdmstr. Fax 471-1532
Mother of Sorrows S 200/PK-8
100 W 87th Pl 90003 323-758-6204
Jennifer Beltram, prin. Fax 758-7853
Nativity S 300/K-8
943 W 57th St 90037 323-752-0720
Sr. Judy Flahavan, prin. Fax 752-1945
Netan Eli Hebrew Academy 100/PK-K
1518 S Robertson Blvd 90035 310-274-2526
Benjamin Jadidi, dir. Fax 860-9086
New Covenant Academy 100/1-12
1111 W Sunset Blvd 90012 213-250-1600
Jason Song, hdmstr. Fax 250-1601
New Roads ES 100/K-5
2000 Stoner Ave 90025 310-479-8500
David Bryan Ph.D., hdmstr. Fax 479-8556
New Wave Christian Academy 100/PK-6
10525 S Western Ave 90047 323-757-1200
Patricia Fargas, prin. Fax 418-7605
Normandie Christian S 100/K-6
6306 S Normandie Ave 90044 323-752-3122
Teresa Wilson, prin. Fax 750-5180
Notre Dame Academy 300/PK-8
2911 Overland Ave 90064 310-287-3895
Kathleen Nocella, prin. Fax 838-8983
Oaks S 200/K-6
6817 Franklin Ave 90028 323-850-3755
Mary Fauvre, hdmstr. Fax 850-3758
Our Lady Help of Christians S 200/K-8
2024 Darwin Ave 90031 323-222-3913
Sr. Maria Gonzalez, prin. Fax 222-2561
Our Lady of Guadalupe S 100/K-8
4522 Browne Ave 90032 323-221-8187
Juan Garcia, prin. Fax 221-8197
Our Lady of Guadalupe S 200/K-8
436 N Hazard Ave 90063 323-269-4998
Fax 780-7001
Our Lady of Loretto S 200/PK-8
258 N Union Ave 90026 213-483-5251
Fidela Suelto, prin. Fax 483-6709
Our Lady of Lourdes S 200/PK-8
315 S Eastman Ave 90063 323-526-3813
Annette Olivas, prin. Fax 526-3814
Our Lady of Talpa S 200/PK-8
411 S Evergreen Ave 90033 323-261-0583
Annie Delgado, prin. Fax 261-0352
Our Mother of Good Counsel S 200/K-8
4622 Ambrose Ave 90027 323-664-2131
Andrea Deebs, prin. Fax 664-1906
Page Private S of Hancock Park 100/K-8
565 N Larchmont Blvd 90004 323-463-5118
Connie Rivera, dir.
Perutz Etz Jacob Hebrew Academy 100/K-8
7951 Beverly Blvd 90048 323-655-5766
Rabbi Shlomo Harrosh, prin. Fax 655-0602

Pilgrim S 300/PK-12
540 S Commonwealth Ave 90020 213-385-7351
Mark Brooks, prin. Fax 386-7264
Pilibos Armenian S 600/K-12
1615 N Alexandria Ave 90027 323-668-2661
Viken Yacoubian, prin. Fax 662-0332
Precious Blood S 200/PK-8
307 S Occidental Blvd 90057 213-382-3345
Dottie Bessares, prin. Fax 382-2078
Pressman Academy 400/K-8
1055 S La Cienega Blvd 90035 310-652-2002
Rabbi Mitchel Malkus, hdmstr. Fax 360-0850
Price S 200/PK-12
7901 S Vermont Ave 90044 323-565-4199
Angela Evans, supt. Fax 753-6770
Redeemer Baptist S 200/K-6
10792 National Blvd 90064 310-475-4598
Meredith Rapinchuk, admin. Fax 475-2123
ReJOYce in Jesus Christian S 50/K-8
PO Box 47775 90047 323-934-5962
Rachel Daniel, prin. Fax 954-9936
Resurrection S 200/PK-8
3360 Opal St 90023 323-261-5750
Angelica Figuero, prin. Fax 268-1141
Ribet Academy 400/PK-12
2911 N San Fernando Rd 90065 323-344-4330
Ronald Dauzat, hdmstr. Fax 344-4339
Sacred Heart S 300/PK-8
2109 Sichel St 90031 323-225-4177
Sr. Maria Gutierrez, prin. Fax 225-2615
St. Agnes S 300/K-8
1428 W Adams Blvd 90007 323-734-6441
Kevin Dempsey, prin. Fax 731-6186
St. Aloysius Gonzaga S 200/PK-8
2023 Nadeau St 90001 323-582-4965
Erica Flores, prin. Fax 589-8485
St. Alphonsus S 300/PK-8
552 Amalia Ave 90022 323-268-5165
Kathleen Hughes, prin. Fax 264-4858
St. Anastasia S 300/PK-8
8631 Stanmoor Dr 90045 310-645-8816
Rosemary Connolly, prin. Fax 645-6923
St. Bernadette S 200/PK-8
4196 Marlton Ave 90008 323-291-4284
Barbara Davis, prin. Fax 291-0839
St. Bernard S 200/K-8
3254 Verdugo Rd 90065 323-256-4989
Laurin Boadt, prin. Fax 256-4963
St. Brendan S 300/PK-8
238 S Manhattan Pl 90004 213-382-7401
Sr. Maureen O'Connor, prin. Fax 382-8918
St. Cecilia S 300/K-8
4224 S Normandie Ave 90037 323-293-4266
Michelle Flippen, prin. Fax 293-5556
St. Columbkille S 300/PK-8
131 W 64th St 90003 323-758-2284
Karla Biceno, prin. Fax 750-7141
St. Dominic S 300/K-8
2005 Merton Ave 90041 323-255-5803
Elida Lujan, prin. Fax 255-3076
St. Eugene S 200/K-8
9521 Haas Ave 90047 323-754-9536
Leona Sorrell, prin. Fax 754-0913
St. Frances X Cabrini S 200/K-8
1428 W Imperial Hwy 90047 323-756-1354
Michelle Sarmien, prin. Fax 756-1157
St. Francis of Assisi S 200/K-8
1550 Maltman Ave 90026 323-665-3601
Frank Cavallo, prin. Fax 665-4143
St. Gregory Nazianzen S 200/1-8
911 S Norton Ave 90019 323-936-2542
Zulay Chavez, prin. Fax 936-1690
St. Ignatius of Loyola S 300/PK-8
6025 Monte Vista St 90042 323-255-6456
Sr. Georgette Coulombe, prin. Fax 255-0959
St. James S 300/PK-6
625 S St Andrews Pl 90005 213-382-2315
Stephen Bowers, hdmstr. Fax 382-2436
St. Jerome S 300/K-8
5580 Thornburn St 90045 310-670-1678
Sr. Donna Bachman, prin. Fax 670-1678
St. Joan of Arc S 200/PK-8
11561 Gateway Blvd 90064 310-479-3607
Norma Moreno, prin. Fax 478-1398
St. John the Evangelist S 200/PK-8
6028 S Victoria Ave 90043 323-751-8545
Karen Velasquez, prin. Fax 751-1651
St. Lawrence Brindisi S 300/K-8
10044 Compton Ave 90002 323-564-3051
Lilliam Paetzold, prin. Fax 564-4050
St. Malachy S 200/K-8
1200 E 81st St 90001 323-582-3112
Daniel Garcia, prin. Fax 582-9340
St. Martin of Tours S 300/PK-8
11955 W Sunset Blvd 90049 310-472-7419
Cecile Oswald, prin. Fax 440-2298
St. Mary Magdalen S 100/1-8
1241 S Corning St 90035 310-652-4723
Sr. Loretto O'Leary, prin. Fax 933-7453
St. Mary S 300/K-8
416 S St Louis St 90033 323-262-3395
Sr. Anna Bui, prin. Fax 262-4738
St. Michael S 200/PK-8
1027 W 87th St 90044 323-752-6101
James McMains, prin. Fax 752-6785
St. Odilia S 200/PK-8
5300 Hooper Ave 90011 323-232-5449
Sharon Oliver, prin. Fax 231-9714
St. Paul S 200/1-8
1908 S Bronson Ave 90018 323-734-4022
Mario Pandy, prin. Fax 734-5266
St. Paul the Apostle S 500/K-8
1536 Selby Ave 90024 310-474-1588
Sr. Stella Enright, prin. Fax 475-4272
St. Raphael S 300/K-8
924 W 70th St 90044 323-751-2774
Barbara Curtis, prin. Fax 751-1244

St. Sebastian S 200/PK-8
1430 Federal Ave 90025 310-473-3337
Edward Hermeno, prin. Fax 473-3178
St. Teresa of Avila S 200/K-8
2215 Fargo St 90039 323-662-3777
Christina Fernandez-Caso, prin. Fax 662-3420
St. Thomas the Apostle S 300/PK-8
2632 W 15th St 90006 323-737-4730
Raymond Saborio, prin. Fax 737-6348
St. Timothy S 100/K-8
10479 W Pico Blvd 90064 310-474-1811
Iselda Richmond, prin. Fax 470-1391
St. Turibius S 200/PK-8
1524 Essex St 90021 213-749-8894
Claudia Moreno, prin. Fax 749-0424
St. Vincent S 300/K-8
2333 S Figueroa St 90007 213-748-5367
Sr. Cabrini Thomas, prin. Fax 748-5347
San Miguel S 200/K-8
2270 E 108th St 90059 323-567-6892
Maryann Reynos, prin. Fax 567-1850
Santa Isabel S 200/K-8
2424 Whittier Blvd 90023 323-263-3716
Fax 263-3763
Santa Teresita S 200/K-8
2646 Zonal Ave 90033 323-221-1129
Sr. Mary Antczak, prin. Fax 221-6339
Shalhevet S 200/K-12
910 S Fairfax Ave 90036 323-930-9333
Jay Weinbach, hdmstr. Fax 930-9444
Sinai Akiba Academy 600/PK-8
10400 Wilshire Blvd 90024 310-475-6401
Rabbi Larry Scheindlin, hdmstr. Fax 234-9184
Star Christian S 200/PK-6
2120 Estrella Ave 90007 213-746-6900
Margarita Robaina, admin. Fax 748-5301
Summit View S - Westside 200/1-12
12101 W Washington Blvd 90066 310-751-1100
Nancy Rosenfelt, dir.
Sycamore Grove S 100/K-8
4900 N Figueroa St 90042 323-255-6550
Elizabeth Cruver, prin. Fax 255-2330
T.C.A. Arshag Dickranian Armenian S 300/PK-12
1200 N Cahuenga Blvd 90038 323-461-4377
Vartkes Kourouyan, prin. Fax 461-4247
Temple Israel of Hollywood S 200/K-6
7300 Hollywood Blvd 90046 323-876-8330
Rosalyn Siegel, hdmstr. Fax 876-8193
Torat-Hayim Hebrew Academy 200/K-8
1210 S La Cienega Blvd 90035 310-652-8349
Daniel Taban, prin. Fax 652-6979
Transfiguration S 200/PK-8
4020 Roxton Ave 90008 323-292-3011
Mechele Yerima, prin. Fax 292-1527
Village Glen S - Westside 200/K-12
4160 Grand View Blvd 90066 310-751-1101
Nata Preis, hdmstr.
Visitation S 200/K-8
8740 Emerson Ave 90045 310-645-6620
Dr. Carol Crede, prin. Fax 645-4407
Vista S 200/K-12
3200 Motor Ave 90034 310-836-1223
Donna Baker, dir. Fax 836-3506
Westchester Lutheran S 500/PK-8
7831 S Sepulveda Blvd 90045 310-670-5422
Sandra Masted, admin. Fax 670-1476
Westland S 100/K-6
16200 Mulholland Dr 90049 310-472-5544
Janie Hirsch, prin.
Westside Neighborhood S 300/K-8
5401 Beethoven St 90066 310-574-8650
Bradley Zacuto, hdmstr. Fax 574-8657
White Memorial Adventist S 100/K-8
1605 New Jersey St 90033 323-268-7159
Devon Ludwig, prin. Fax 268-7033
Wildwood S 300/K-5
12201 Washington Pl 90066 310-397-3134
Landis Green, hdmstr. Fax 397-5134
Wilshire S 100/K-6
4900 Wilshire Blvd 90010 323-939-3800
Marlin Miller M.Ed., hdmstr. Fax 937-0093
Wise Temple S 400/K-12
15500 Stephen S Wise Dr 90077 310-889-2300
Metuka Benjamin, dir. Fax 476-2353
Woodcrest Nazarene Christian S 100/PK-6
10936 S Normandie Ave 90044 323-754-4933
Vanessa Beverly, prin. Fax 754-1642
Yavneh Hebrew Academy 500/PK-8
5353 W 3rd St 90020 323-931-5808
Rabbi Moshe Dear, hdmstr. Fax 931-5818
Yeshiva Rav Isacsohn Girls' S 1,000/PK-8
555 N La Brea Ave 90036 323-549-3188
Faigy Back, prin. Fax 935-5060
Yeshiva Rav Isacsohn/Torah Emeth Academy
1,000/PK-8
540 N La Brea Ave 90036 323-549-3170
Rabbi Yakov Krause, dir. Fax 938-5232

Los Banos, Merced, Pop. 33,506
Los Banos USD 9,000/K-12
1717 S 11th St 93635 209-826-3801
Steve Tietjen, supt. Fax 826-6810
www.losbanosusd.k12.ca.us
Charleston ES 400/K-6
18463 Charleston Rd 93635 209-826-5270
Lou Ruiz, prin. Fax 826-5288
Falasco ES 800/K-6
310 Overland Rd 93635 209-827-5834
Jane Brittell, prin. Fax 827-6009
Los Banos ES 1,000/K-6
1260 7th St 93635 209-826-4981
Pat Patterson, prin. Fax 826-5551
Los Banos JHS 1,500/7-8
1750 San Luis St 93635 209-826-0867
Paul Enos, prin. Fax 826-8532
Miano ES 900/K-6
1129 E B St 93635 209-826-3877
Paula Mastrangelo, prin. Fax 826-9201
Miller ES 900/K-6
545 W L St 93635 209-826-3816
Patrick Atkins, prin. Fax 826-9772
Volta ES 300/K-6
24307 Ingomar Grade 93635 209-826-2912
Jan Whitehurst, prin. Fax 826-0855
Westside Union ES 800/K-6
659 K St 93635 209-827-9390
Bill Garcia, prin. Fax 827-6003

Our Lady of Fatima S 200/K-8
1625 Center Ave 93635 209-826-2709
Connie McGhee, prin. Fax 826-7320

Los Gatos, Santa Clara, Pop. 28,029
Lakeside JESD 100/K-6
19621 Black Rd 95033 408-354-2372
Bob Chrisman, supt. Fax 354-8819
www.lakesidelosgatos.org/
Lakeside ES 100/K-6
19621 Black Rd 95033 408-354-2372
Bob Chrisman, prin. Fax 354-8819

Loma Prieta JUNESD 500/K-8
23800 Summit Rd 95033 408-353-1101
Henry Castaniada, supt. Fax 353-8051
www.loma.k12.ca.us
English MS 200/6-8
23800 Summit Rd 95033 408-353-1123
Corey Kidwell, prin. Fax 353-5024
Loma Prieta ES 300/K-5
23800 Summit Rd 95033 408-353-1106
Corey Kidwell, prin. Fax 353-3274

Los Gatos UNESD 2,600/K-8
17010 Roberts Rd 95032 408-335-2000
J. Richard Whitmore, supt. Fax 395-6481
www.lgusd.k12.ca.us
Blossom Hill ES 600/K-5
16400 Blossom Hill Rd 95032 408-335-2100
Lisa Reynolds, prin. Fax 358-6438
Daves Avenue ES 500/K-5
17770 Daves Ave 95030 408-335-2200
Susan von Felten, prin. Fax 395-6314
Fisher MS 900/6-8
19195 Fisher Ave 95032 408-335-2300
Lisa Fraser, prin. Fax 356-7616
Lexington ES 100/K-5
19700 Santa Cruz Hwy 95033 408-335-2150
David Freed, prin. Fax 354-2014
Van Meter ES 500/K-5
16445 Los Gatos Blvd 95032 408-335-2250
Rosanne Adona, prin. Fax 356-9487

Union ESD
Supt. — See San Jose
Alta Vista ES 500/K-5
200 Blossom Valley Dr 95032 408-356-6146
Karen Miller, prin. Fax 356-6706

Hillbrook S 400/PK-8
300 Marchmont Dr 95032 408-356-6116
Mark Silver, hdmstr. Fax 358-1286
Los Gatos Christian S 500/PK-8
16845 Hicks Rd 95032 408-997-4682
Treva Black, admin. Fax 268-4107
Mulberry S 100/K-5
220 Belgatos Rd 95032 408-358-9080
Patti Wilczek, prin. Fax 358-9082
St. Mary S 300/K-8
30 Lyndon Ave 95030 408-354-3944
Sr. Nicki Thomas, prin. Fax 395-9151
Stratford S 300/PK-5
220 Kensington Way 95032 408-371-3020
Tekla Petrinovich, prin.
Yavneh Day S 100/K-8
14855 Oka Rd Ste 100 95032 408-984-6700
Steven Bogad, hdmstr. Fax 984-3696

Los Molinos, Tehama, Pop. 1,709
Lassen View UNESD 300/K-8
10818 State Highway 99E 96055 530-527-5162
Mancill Tiss, supt. Fax 527-2331
www.lvuesd.tehama.k12.ca.us
Lassen View Community Day S 50/K-8
10818 State Highway 99E 96055 530-527-5162
Mancill Tiss, prin. Fax 527-2331
Lassen View S 300/K-8
10818 State Highway 99E 96055 530-527-5162
Mancill Tiss, prin. Fax 527-2331

Los Molinos USD 600/K-12
7851 State Highway 99 E 96055 530-384-7826
Charles Ward, supt. Fax 384-7832
www.lmusd.tehama.k12.ca.us
Los Molinos S 300/K-8
PO Box 7 96055 530-384-7903
Dane Hansen, prin. Fax 384-7918
Other Schools – See Vina

Los Nietos, Los Angeles, Pop. 24,164
Los Nietos ESD 2,100/K-8
8324 Westman Ave 90606 562-692-0271
Lillian Maldonado-French, supt. Fax 699-3395
www.losnietos.k12.ca.us
Los Nietos MS 600/6-8
11425 Rivera Rd 90606 562-695-0637
Olga Hofreiter, prin. Fax 695-3805
Other Schools – See Santa Fe Springs, Whittier

Los Olivos, Santa Barbara
Los Olivos ESD 300/K-8
PO Box 208 93441 805-688-4025
Marsha Filbin, supt. Fax 688-4885
www.losolivosschool.com
Los Olivos S 300/K-8
PO Box 208 93441 805-688-4025
Gary Crispin, prin. Fax 688-4885

Los Osos, San Luis Obispo, Pop. 14,377
San Luis Coastal USD
Supt. — See San Luis Obispo
Baywood ES 400/K-6
1330 9th St 93402 805-534-2856
Douglas Jenison, prin. Fax 528-8065
Los Osos MS 400/7-8
1555 El Morro Ave 93402 805-534-2835
Terry Elfrink, prin. Fax 528-5133
Monarch Grove ES 400/K-6
348 Los Osos Valley Rd 93402 805-534-2844
James Scoolis, prin. Fax 528-5374

Lost Hills, Kern, Pop. 1,212
Lost Hills Union ESD 500/K-8
PO Box 158 93249 661-797-2626
Jerry Scott, supt. Fax 797-2580
Lost Hills ES 400/K-5
PO Box 158 93249 661-797-2626
David Day, prin. Fax 797-3015
Thomas MS 200/6-8
PO Box 158 93249 661-797-2626
Jerry Scott, prin. Fax 797-3015

Lower Lake, Lake, Pop. 1,217
Konocti USD 3,100/K-12
PO Box 759 95457 707-994-6475
William McDougall Ed.D., supt. Fax 994-0210
www.konoctiusd.lake.k12.ca.us/
Lower Lake ES 500/K-6
9240 Lake St 95457 707-994-5787
Greg Mucks, prin. Fax 994-7707
Other Schools – See Clearlake, Clearlake Oaks

Loyalton, Sierra, Pop. 817
Sierra-Plumas JUSD
Supt. — See Sierraville
Loyalton ES 200/K-5
PO Box 127 96118 530-993-4482
Penny Berry, prin. Fax 993-1007
Loyalton MS 100/6-8
PO Box 5 96118 530-993-4186
Penny Berry, prin. Fax 993-0828

Lucerne, Lake, Pop. 2,011
Lucerne ESD 300/K-8
PO Box 1083 95458 707-274-5578
Mike Brown, supt. Fax 274-9865
www.lucerne.k12.ca.us
Lucerne S 300/K-8
PO Box 1083 95458 707-274-5578
Mike Brown, prin. Fax 274-9865

Lucerne Valley, San Bernardino
Lucerne Valley USD 900/K-12
8560 Aliento Rd 92356 760-248-6108
Michael Noga, supt. Fax 248-6677
www.lvsd.k12.ca.us/
Lucerne Valley ES 500/K-6
10788 Barstow Rd 92356 760-248-7659
Suzette Davis, prin. Fax 248-2806

Lynwood, Los Angeles, Pop. 71,208
Lynwood USD 16,700/K-12
11321 Bullis Rd 90262 310-886-1600
Dr. Dhyan Lal, supt. Fax 608-7483
www.lynwoodusd.org/
Abbott ES 700/K-5
5260 Clark St 90262 310-603-1498
Darlene Spoeri, prin. Fax 632-5897
Chavez MS 700/7-8
3898 Abbott Rd 90262 310-886-7300
Dr. Nick Velasquez, prin. Fax 603-2048
Hosler MS 900/7-8
11300 Spruce St 90262 310-603-1447
Yvette MayhornHarps, prin. Fax 764-4124
Keller ES 700/K-5
3521 Palm Ave 90262 310-886-5700
Dixie Scott, prin. Fax 637-8033
Lincoln ES 700/K-5
11031 State St 90262 310-603-1518
Fax 632-5673
Lindbergh ES 800/K-5
3309 Cedar Ave 90262 310-603-1521
Gary Furuno, prin. Fax 632-8242
Lugo ES 500/K-6
4345 Pendleton Ave 90262 310-603-1493
Susan Skornia, prin. Fax 639-3682
Lynwood MS 1,900/6-8
12124 Bullis Rd 90262 310-603-1466
Dr. Anim Mener, prin. Fax 638-2156
Marshall ES 800/K-5
3593 Martin Luther King Blv 90262 310-886-5900
Carlos Hernandez, prin. Fax 604-3000
Parks ES 500/K-6
3900 Agnes Ave 90262 310-603-1401
Simmie Coffey, prin. Fax 603-2013
Rogers ES 900/K-5
11220 Duncan Ave 90262 310-603-1542
Victor Ebanks, prin. Fax 631-3923
Roosevelt ES 500/K-6
10835 Mallison Ave 90262 310-603-1511
Fax 669-8631
Twain ES 600/K-5
12315 Thorson Ave 90262 310-603-1509
Dr. Helen Martinez, prin. Fax 632-8269
Washington ES 800/K-5
4225 Sanborn Ave 90262 310-603-1513
Patricia Gould, prin. Fax 608-2694
Wilson ES 700/K-5
11700 School St 90262 310-603-1525
Nancy Nichols, prin. Fax 635-5237

St. Emydius S 400/K-8
10990 California Ave 90262 310-635-7184
Jesus Vasquez, prin. Fax 605-3041
St. Philip Neri S 200/PK-8
12522 Stoneacre Ave 90262 310-638-0341
Elvia Villasenor, prin. Fax 638-9805

Mc Clellan, Sacramento
Twin Rivers USD 25,900/PK-12
5115 Dudley Blvd Bldg 250B, 916-566-1600
Frank Porter, supt. Fax 566-1784
www.twinriversusd.org/
Other Schools – See North Highlands, Rio Linda, Sacramento

Mc Cloud, Siskiyou, Pop. 1,555
McCloud UNESD 100/K-8
PO Box 700, 530-964-2133
Mike Michelon, supt. Fax 964-2153
www.sisnet.ssku.k12.ca.us/~cloudftp/mccloud_home_page
McCloud S 100/K-8
PO Box 700, 530-964-2133
Gil Steele, prin. Fax 964-2153

Mc Farland, Kern, Pop. 7,133
McFarland USD 3,200/K-12
601 2nd St 93250 661-792-3081
Gabriel McCurtis, supt. Fax 792-2447
www.mcfarlandusd.com
Browning Road ES 600/K-5
410 E Perkins Ave 93250 661-792-2113
Maria Gonzalez-Salgado, prin. Fax 792-5423
Kern Avenue ES 900/K-5
356 W Kern Ave 93250 661-792-3033
Ty Bryson, prin. Fax 792-6036
Mc Farland MS 800/6-8
405 Mast Ave 93250 661-792-3340
Roberta Burgh, prin. Fax 792-5681

Mc Kinleyville, Humboldt, Pop. 10,749
Mc Kinleyville UNESD 1,200/K-8
2275 Central Ave, 707-839-1549
Dena McCullough, supt. Fax 839-1540
www.nohum.k12.ca.us/msd/
Dows Prairie ES 400/K-5
3940 Dows Prairie Rd, 707-839-1558
Jane Rowland, prin. Fax 839-5652
Mc Kinleyville MS 400/6-8
2285 Central Ave, 707-839-1508
Anne Hartline, prin. Fax 839-2548
Morris ES 400/K-5
2395 McKinleyville Ave, 707-839-1520
Michael Davies-Hughes, prin. Fax 839-4754

Mc Kittrick, Kern
Belridge ESD 50/K-8
19447 Wagon Wheel Rd 93251 661-762-7381
Tammy Reynolds, supt. Fax 762-9751
Belridge S 50/K-8
19447 Wagon Wheel Rd 93251 661-762-7381
Tammy Reynolds, prin. Fax 762-9751

Mc Kittrick ESD 100/K-8
PO Box 277 93251 661-762-7303
Barry Koerner, supt. Fax 762-7283
Mc Kittrick S 100/K-8
PO Box 277 93251 661-762-7303
Barry Koerner, prin. Fax 762-7283

Madera, Madera, Pop. 52,147
Golden Valley USD 2,000/K-12
37479 Avenue 12, 559-645-7500
Sarah Koligian, supt. Fax 645-7144
www.gvusd.k12.ca.us
Ranchos MS 300/7-8
12220 Road 36, 559-645-3550
Shane Pinkard, prin. Fax 645-3565
Sierra View ES 400/K-6
16436 Paula Rd, 559-645-1122
Scott Tefft, prin. Fax 645-5161
Webster ES 700/K-6
36477 Ruth Ave, 559-645-1322
Kevin Hatch, prin. Fax 276-1921

Madera USD 16,100/K-12
1902 Howard Rd 93637 559-675-4500
John Stafford, supt. Fax 661-7764
www.madera.k12.ca.us
Adams ES 800/K-6
1822 National Ave 93637 559-674-4631
Kendall Jones, prin. Fax 674-3867
Alpha ES 800/K-6
900 Stadium Rd 93637 559-661-4101
Carsten Christiansen, prin. Fax 673-0931
Berenda ES 900/K-6
26820 Club Dr 93638 559-674-3325
Lisa Fernandez, prin. Fax 674-5617
Chavez ES 700/K-6
2600 E Pecan 93638 559-664-9701
Elizabeth Runyon, prin. Fax 664-9716
Desmond MS 900/7-8
26490 Martin St 93638 559-664-1775
Michael Lennemann, prin. Fax 664-1308
Dixieland S 300/K-8
18440 Road 19 93637 559-673-9119
Kliff Justesen, prin. Fax 673-8232
Howard S 500/K-8
13878 Road 21 1/2 93637 559-674-8568
Mark Beveridge, prin. Fax 673-5882
Jefferson MS 800/7-8
1407 Sunset Ave 93637 559-673-9286
Jesse Carrasco, prin. Fax 673-6930
King MS 800/7-8
601 Lilly St 93638 559-674-4681
Daren Miller, prin. Fax 674-4261
La Vina S 300/K-8
8594 Road 23 93637 559-673-5194
Alma Juarequi, prin. Fax 673-9091
Lincoln ES 900/K-6
650 Liberty Ln 93637 559-675-4600
Kim Bondietti, prin. Fax 674-3061
Madison ES 700/K-6
109 Stadium Rd 93637 559-675-4630
Armando Gomez, prin. Fax 661-8397
Millview ES 900/K-6
1609 Clinton St 93638 559-674-8509
Rachel Church, prin. Fax 674-9683
Monroe ES 1,000/K-6
1819 N Lake St 93638 559-674-5679
Tom Chagoya, prin. Fax 674-3008
Nishimoto ES 800/K-6
26460 Martin St 93638 559-664-8110
Raul Lozano, prin. Fax 664-8343
Sierra Vista ES 800/K-6
917 E Olive Ave 93638 559-674-8579
Sherri DeFina, prin. Fax 674-1503
Washington ES 700/K-6
509 E South St 93638 559-674-6705
Bill Holden, prin. Fax 674-7386

Crossroads Christian S 100/K-8
17755 Rd 26 93638 559-662-1624
Patty Dougherty, prin. Fax 662-1625
St. Joachim S 300/PK-8
310 N I St 93637 559-674-7628
Thomas Spencer, prin. Fax 674-8770

Magalia, Butte, Pop. 8,987
Paradise USD
Supt. — See Paradise
Cedarwood ES 300/K-5
6400 Columbine Rd 95954 530-873-3785
Fax 873-1017
Pine Ridge S 300/K-8
13878 Compton Dr 95954 530-873-3800
Fax 873-2828

Pines Christian Academy 50/PK-12
PO Box 1821 95954 530-873-1412
Martin Glasenapp, admin. Fax 873-3455

Malibu, Los Angeles, Pop. 13,208
Santa Monica-Malibu USD
Supt. — See Santa Monica
Cabrillo ES 300/K-5
30237 Morning View Dr 90265 310-457-0360
Barry Yates, prin. Fax 457-0367
Point Dume ES 300/K-5
6955 Fernhill Dr 90265 310-457-9370
Chi Kim, prin. Fax 457-8064
Webster ES 400/K-5
3602 Winter Canyon Rd 90265 310-456-6494
Phillip Cott, prin. Fax 456-9304

Our Lady of Malibu S 100/K-8
3625 Winter Canyon Rd Ste 1 90265 310-456-8071
Suzanne Ricci, prin. Fax 456-7767

Mammoth Lakes, Mono, Pop. 7,156
Mammoth USD 1,200/K-12
PO Box 3509 93546 760-934-6802
Michael Derisi, supt. Fax 934-6803
www.mammothusd.org/
Mammoth ES 500/K-5
PO Box 3209 93546 760-934-7545
Frank Romero, prin. Fax 934-7341
Mammoth MS 300/6-8
PO Box 2429 93546 760-934-7072
Gabriel Solorio, prin. Fax 934-7073

Manchester, Mendocino
Manchester UNESD 100/K-8
PO Box 98 95459 707-882-2374
Cynthia Biaggi-Gonzalez, supt. Fax 882-3106
Manchester S 100/K-8
PO Box 98 95459 707-882-2374
Cynthia Biaggi-Gonzalez, prin. Fax 882-3106

Manhattan Beach, Los Angeles, Pop. 36,481
Manhattan Beach USD 6,700/PK-12
325 S Peck Ave 90266 310-318-7345
Dr. Beverly Rohrer, supt. Fax 303-3822
www.mbusd.org/
Grand View ES 700/K-5
325 S Peck Ave 90266 310-546-8022
Rhonda Steinberg, prin. Fax 303-3817
Manhattan Beach MS 1,300/6-8
325 S Peck Ave 90266 310-545-4878
John Jackson, prin. Fax 303-3829
Manhattan Beach Preschool 500/PK-PK
325 S Peck Ave 90266 310-546-7655
Kim Johnson, prin.
Meadows Avenue ES 500/K-5
325 S Peck Ave 90266 310-546-8033
Connie Harrington, prin. Fax 303-3819
Pacific ES 600/K-5
325 S Peck Ave 90266 310-546-8044
Debborah Mabry, prin. Fax 303-3806
Pennekamp ES 500/K-5
325 S Peck Ave 90266 310-546-8073
Dale Keldrauk, prin. Fax 303-3839
Robinson ES 400/K-5
325 S Peck Ave 90266 310-318-5120
Nancy Doyle, prin. Fax 303-3812

American Martyrs S 600/K-8
1701 Laurel Ave 90266 310-545-8559
Dr. Kevin Baxter, prin. Fax 546-7219
Journey of Faith Christian S 100/PK-K
1243 Artesia Blvd 90266 310-374-0583
Shirley Hippler, admin. Fax 374-0402

Manteca, San Joaquin, Pop. 62,651
Manteca USD
Supt. — See Lathrop
Brockman S 800/K-8
763 Silverado Dr 95337 209-858-7200
Diane Medeiros, prin. Fax 858-7202
Cowell S 600/K-8
740 Pestana Ave 95336 209-825-3310
Harriet Myrick, prin. Fax 825-3314
Elliott S 800/K-8
1110 Stonum Ln 95337 209-858-7260
Debbie Ruger, prin. Fax 825-3332
Golden West S 700/K-8
1031 N Main St 95336 209-858-7300
Sherie Gates, prin. Fax 825-3343
Hafley S 900/K-8
849 Northgate Dr 95336 209-825-3350
Steve Anderson, prin. Fax 825-3354
Lincoln S 700/K-8
750 E Yosemite Ave 95336 209-825-3380
Cheryl Spiegel, prin. Fax 825-3387
McParland S 1,300/K-8
1601 Northgate Dr 95336 209-858-7290
Dale Borgeson, prin. Fax 825-3394
New Haven S 600/K-8
14600 S Austin Rd 95336 209-825-3400
David O'Leary, prin. Fax 825-3403
Nile Garden S 600/K-8
5700 Nile Rd 95337 209-825-3410
Joe Cook, prin. Fax 825-3412
Sequoia S 800/K-8
710 Martha St 95337 209-858-7440
Jacqui Breitenbucher, prin. Fax 825-3445
Shasta S 800/K-8
751 E Edison St 95336 209-825-3450
Richard Mello, prin. Fax 825-3453
Woodward S 800/K-8
575 Tannehill Dr 95337 209-824-0633
Roger Goatcher, prin. Fax 824-8783

Alta Vista Christian S 50/PK-12
1050 S Union Rd 95337 209-629-8842
Rita Torres, admin. Fax 629-8843
Manteca Christian S 200/PK-8
486 Button Ave 95336 209-239-3436
Christian Grigson, prin. Fax 239-5072
Manteca SDA S, PO Box 2548 95336 50/1-8
Cheryl Griffith, prin. 209-239-3140
St. Anthony S 300/PK-8
323 N Fremont St 95336 209-823-4513
MaryLou Hoffman, prin. Fax 825-7447

Manton, Tehama
Manton JUNESD 50/K-8
PO Box 410 96059 530-474-3167
Joanne Barrow, supt. Fax 474-5550
www.tcde.tehama.k12.ca.us/mantonusd.html
Manton S 50/K-8
PO Box 410 96059 530-474-3167
Jake Hosler, prin. Fax 474-5550

Maricopa, Kern, Pop. 1,160
Maricopa USD 400/K-12
955 Stanislaus St 93252 661-769-8231
Terry Wolfe, supt. Fax 769-8168
www.maricopaschools.org/
Maricopa S 200/K-8
955 Stanislaus St 93252 661-769-8231
Terry Wolfe, prin. Fax 769-8168

Marina, Monterey, Pop. 19,006
Monterey Peninsula USD
Supt. — See Monterey
Crumpton ES 400/K-5
460 Carmel Ave 93933 831-392-3520
Katie Loftus, prin. Fax 392-3520
Los Arboles MS 600/6-8
294 Hillcrest Ave 93933 831-384-3550
Xavier Rodriguez, prin. Fax 384-6353
Marina Children's Center PK-PK
261 Beach Rd 93933 831-384-7952
Christopher Oliver, lead tchr. Fax 384-8526
Marina Del Mar ES 300/K-6
3066 Lake Dr 93933 831-384-0255
Joanne Vanderhorst, prin. Fax 384-7451
Marina Vista ES 400/K-5
390 Carmel Ave 93933 831-384-2384
Lupe Gutierrez, prin. Fax 384-0916
Olson ES 400/K-5
261 Beach Rd 93933 831-384-6688
Daniel Lee, prin. Fax 384-2369

Mariposa, Mariposa, Pop. 1,152
Mariposa County USD 2,200/K-12
PO Box 8 95338 209-742-0250
Randy Panietz, supt. Fax 966-4549
www.mariposa.k12.ca.us/
Mariposa ES 300/K-6
PO Box 5002 95338 209-742-0340
Brian Goodbar, prin. Fax 742-0383
Mariposa MS 300/7-8
5171 Silva Rd 95338 209-742-0320
Dr. Bill Atwood, prin. Fax 742-0382
Woodland ES 400/K-6
3394 Woodland Dr 95338 209-742-0310
Mary Brownell, prin. Fax 742-0313
Other Schools – See Catheys Valley, Coulterville, El Portal, La Grange, Yosemite National Park

Mariposa SDA S, PO Box 865 95338 50/1-8
Judith Wagner, admin. 209-966-4994

Markleeville, Alpine
Alpine County USD 100/K-8
43 Hawkside Dr 96120 530-694-2230
James Parsons Ed.D., supt. Fax 694-2379
alpinecoe.k12.ca.us
Diamond Valley S 100/K-8
35 Hawkside Dr 96120 530-694-2238
Sally Clark, prin. Fax 694-2386
Other Schools – See Bear Valley

Martinez, Contra Costa, Pop. 35,916
Martinez USD 4,100/K-12
921 Susana St 94553 925-335-5800
Rami Muth, supt. Fax 335-5960
www.martinez.k12.ca.us/

Briones S 100/K-12
614 F St 94553 925-228-9232
Carol Adams, prin. Fax 313-9890
Las Juntas ES 300/K-5
4105 Pacheco Blvd 94553 925-335-5831
Fax 335-5980
Martinez JHS 1,000/6-8
1600 Court St 94553 925-313-0414
Helen Rossi, prin. Fax 370-0143
Morello Park ES 500/K-5
244 Morello Ave 94553 925-335-5841
Christopher Cammack, prin. Fax 228-2573
Muir ES 300/K-5
205 Vista Way 94553 925-313-0470
Kathlean Kizziee, prin. Fax 372-0153
Swett ES 500/K-5
4955 Alhambra Valley Rd 94553 925-335-5860
Marjorie Pampe, prin. Fax 229-1220

Mount Diablo USD
Supt. — See Concord
Hidden Valley ES 700/K-5
500 Glacier Dr 94553 925-228-9530
Lorie O'Brien, prin. Fax 313-8938

St. Catherine of Siena S 200/PK-8
604 Mellus St 94553 925-228-4140
Andrew VonHaunalter, prin. Fax 228-0697

Marysville, Yuba, Pop. 12,131
Marysville JUSD 8,800/PK-12
1919 B St 95901 530-741-6000
Gay Todd Ed.D., supt. Fax 742-0573
www.mjusd.k12.ca.us
Arboga ES 300/K-5
1686 Broadway St, 530-741-6101
Eric Preston, prin. Fax 741-7836
Cedar Lane ES 600/K-5
841 Cedar Ln, 530-741-6112
Rob Gregor, prin. Fax 741-7860
Cordua ES 100/K-5
2830 State Highway 20 95901 530-741-6115
Gina Lanphier, prin. Fax 741-6013
Covillaud ES 500/K-5
628 F St 95901 530-741-6121
Doug Escheman, prin. Fax 741-7868
Foothill IS 300/6-8
5351 Fruitland Rd 95901 530-741-6130
Chris Meyer, prin. Fax 741-6017
Johnson Park ES 400/K-5
4364 Lever Ave, 530-741-6133
Lori Guy, prin. Fax 741-7864
Kynoch ES 600/K-5
1905 Ahern St 95901 530-741-6141
Monica Oakes, prin. Fax 741-6020
Linda ES 700/K-5
6180 Dunning Ave 95901 530-741-6196
Terry Heenan, prin. Fax 741-7849
Loma Rica ES 200/K-5
5150 Fruitland Rd 95901 530-741-6144
Judy Hart, prin. Fax 741-6098
Marysville Preschool PK-PK
1919 B St 95901 530-741-6165
Kathy Woods, prin. Fax 742-0573
McKenney IS 500/6-8
1904 Huston St 95901 530-741-6187
Rocco Greco, prin. Fax 742-0573
Other Schools – See Browns Valley, Challenge, Dobbins, Olivehurst

Mather, Sacramento, Pop. 4,885
Folsom-Cordova USD
Supt. — See Folsom
Mather Heights ES 400/K-6
4370 Mather School Rd 95655 916-362-4153
Angi Hamlin, prin. Fax 362-1570

Maxwell, Colusa
Maxwell USD 500/K-12
PO Box 788 95955 530-438-2291
Ron Turner, supt. Fax 438-2693
www.maxwell.k12.ca.us
Maxwell S 300/K-8
PO Box 788 95955 530-438-2401
Brett Denhalter, prin. Fax 438-2460

Maywood, Los Angeles, Pop. 28,600
Los Angeles USD
Supt. — See Los Angeles
Fishburn Avenue ES 700/K-5
5701 Fishburn Ave 90270 323-560-0878
Susan Espinoza, prin. Fax 560-6391
Heliotrope ES 900/K-5
5911 Woodlawn Ave 90270 323-560-1230
Luis Camarena, prin. Fax 562-4415
Loma Vista ES 900/K-5
3629 E 58th St 90270 323-582-6153
Carmen Hernandez, prin. Fax 585-2139
Maywood ES 500/K-5
5200 Cudahy Ave 90270 323-890-2440
Lupe Hernandez, prin. Fax 560-2889

St. Rose of Lima S 200/K-8
4422 E 60th St 90270 323-560-3376
Carin Buckel, prin. Fax 560-8539

Meadow Vista, Placer, Pop. 3,067
Placer Hills UNESD 1,100/K-8
16801 Placer Hills Rd 95722 530-878-2606
Fred Adam, supt. Fax 878-2663
www.phusd.k12.ca.us/
Sierra Hills ES 400/K-3
16505 Placer Hills Rd 95722 530-878-9473
Ella Dobrec, prin. Fax 878-9475
Other Schools – See Weimar

Live Oak Waldorf S 200/PK-8
410 Crother Rd 95722 530-878-8720
Fax 878-0624

Mecca, Riverside, Pop. 1,966
Coachella Valley USD
Supt. — See Thermal
Martinez ES 1,000/K-6
65705 Johnson St 92254 760-396-1935
Delia Alvarez, prin. Fax 396-2103
Mecca ES 700/K-6
65250 Coahuilla St 92254 760-396-2143
Manuela Silvestre, prin. Fax 396-0463

Mendocino, Mendocino
Mendocino USD 500/K-12
PO Box 1154 95460 707-937-5868
Catherine Stone, supt. Fax 937-0714
musd.mcn.org/
Mendocino S 200/K-8
PO Box 226 95460 707-937-0515
Bronwyn Rhoades, prin. Fax 937-1538
Other Schools – See Albion, Comptche, Elk

Mendota, Fresno, Pop. 8,942
Mendota USD 2,500/K-12
115 McCabe Ave 93640 559-655-4942
Gilbert Rossette, supt. Fax 655-4944
www.mendotausd.k12.ca.us/
McCabe ES 800/3-6
115 McCabe Ave 93640 559-655-4262
Paul Lopez, prin. Fax 655-1220
McCabe JHS 400/7-8
115 McCabe Ave 93640 559-655-4301
Manuel Bautista, prin. Fax 655-1229
Washington ES 700/K-2
115 McCabe Ave 93640 559-655-4365
Rebecca Gamez, prin. Fax 655-7007

Menifee, Riverside, Pop. 100
Menifee UNESD 7,700/K-9
30205 Menifee Rd 92584 951-672-1851
Linda Callaway Ed.D., supt. Fax 672-6447
www.menifeeusd.org
Bell Mountain MS 1,700/6-8
28525 La Piedra Rd 92584 951-301-8496
Cynthia Deavers, prin. Fax 301-5286
Evans Ranch ES 500/K-5
30465 Evans Rd 92584 951-246-7690
Ken Murdock, prin. Fax 246-7805
Freedom Crest ES 1,000/K-5
29282 Menifee Rd 92584 951-679-5285
Jennifer Adcock, prin. Fax 672-2651
Kirkpatrick ES 800/K-5
28800 Reviere Dr 92584 951-672-6420
Daphne Donoho, prin. Fax 672-6423
Menifee Valley MS 1,200/6-8
26255 Garbani Rd 92584 951-672-6400
Robert Voelkel, prin. Fax 672-6415
Morrison ES 500/K-5
30250 Bradley Rd 92584 951-679-7076
Caroline Luke, prin. Fax 672-6436
Southshore ES K-5
30975 Southshore Dr 92584 951-672-0013
Ellen Kane, prin. Fax 723-1230
Other Schools – See Murrieta, Quail Valley, Sun City

Good Shepherd Lutheran S 300/PK-7
26800 Newport Rd 92584 951-672-6675
Robert McDowell, prin. Fax 672-6680
Revival Christian Academy 200/K-12
29220 Scott Rd 92584 951-672-3157
Diana Miller, dir. Fax 672-9187

Menlo Park, San Mateo, Pop. 29,661
Las Lomitas ESD 1,100/K-8
1011 Altschul Ave 94025 650-854-2880
Eric Hartwig, supt. Fax 854-0882
www.llesd.k12.ca.us
La Entrada MS 600/4-8
2200 Sharon Rd 94025 650-854-3962
Larry Thomas, prin. Fax 854-5947
Other Schools – See Atherton

Menlo Park City ESD
Supt. — See Atherton
Hillview MS 700/6-8
1100 Elder Ave 94025 650-326-4341
Michael Moore, prin. Fax 325-3861
Oak Knoll ES 700/K-5
1895 Oak Knoll Ln 94025 650-854-4433
David Ackerman, prin. Fax 854-0179

Ravenswood City ESD
Supt. — See East Palo Alto
Belle Haven S 600/K-8
415 Ivy Dr 94025 650-329-2898
Maria Ibarra, prin. Fax 566-9386
Flood Magnet S 300/K-8
320 Sheridan Dr 94025 650-329-2891
Cammie Harris, prin. Fax 327-9163
Willow Oaks S 600/K-8
620 Willow Rd 94025 650-329-2850
Fax 326-1419

Beechwood S 200/K-8
50 Terminal Ave 94025 650-327-5052
David Laurance, prin. Fax 327-5066
German-American International S 200/K-8
275 Elliott Dr 94025 650-324-8617
Ursula Waite, prin. Fax 324-9548
Nativity S 300/K-8
1250 Laurel St 94025 650-325-7304
Carol Trelut, prin. Fax 325-3841
Peninsula S 200/PK-8
920 Peninsula Way 94025 650-325-1584
Katy Dalgleish, dir. Fax 325-1313

Phillips Brooks S 200/PK-5
2245 Avy Ave 94025 650-854-4545
Kristi Kerins, hdmstr. Fax 854-6532
St. Raymond S 200/K-8
1211 Arbor Rd 94025 650-322-2312
Sr. Ann Bernard O'Shea, prin. Fax 322-2910
Trinity S 200/PK-5
2650 Sand Hill Rd 94025 650-854-0288
Mary Menacho, hdmstr. Fax 854-1374

Mentone, San Bernardino, Pop. 5,675
Redlands USD
Supt. — See Redlands
Mentone ES 500/K-5
1320 Crafton Ave 92359 909-794-8610
Kimberly Cavanagh, prin. Fax 794-8614

Mentone Adventist Team S K-8
1230 Olivine Ave 92359 909-794-1610
Ingrid Wahjudi, prin.

Merced, Merced, Pop. 73,767
McSwain UNESD 800/K-8
926 Scott Rd 95341 209-723-7877
Stan Mollart, supt. Fax 723-2267
www.mcswain.k12.ca.us
McSwain S 800/K-8
922 Scott Rd 95341 209-723-3266
Terrie Rohrer, prin. Fax 723-2630

Merced City ESD 10,400/K-8
444 W 23rd St 95340 209-385-6600
Rosemary Duran Ed.D., supt. Fax 385-6316
www.mcsd.k12.ca.us/
Burbank ES 600/K-5
609 E Alexander Ave 95340 209-385-6674
Rogelio Gutierrez, prin. Fax 385-6377
Chenoweth ES 700/K-5
3200 N Parsons Ave 95340 209-385-6620
Paula Heupel, prin. Fax 385-6386
Cruickshank MS 1,000/6-8
601 Mercy Ave 95340 209-385-6330
Elena Bubenchik, prin. Fax 385-6338
Franklin ES 400/K-2
2736 Franklin Rd 95348 209-385-6623
Lori Slaven, prin. Fax 385-6303
Givens ES 500/K-5
2900 Green St 95340 209-385-6610
Dalinda Saich, prin. Fax 385-6388
Gracey ES 600/K-5
945 N West Ave 95341 209-385-6710
Irma Ayala-Olson, prin. Fax 385-6748
Hoover MS 800/6-8
800 E 26th St 95340 209-385-6631
Doug Collins, prin. Fax 385-6799
Muir ES 500/K-5
300 W 26th St 95340 209-385-6667
Sandi Hamilton, prin. Fax 385-6320
Peterson ES 700/K-5
848 E Donna Dr 95340 209-385-6700
Nolan Harris, prin. Fax 385-6379
Reyes ES 600/K-5
123 S N St 95341 209-385-6761
Teresa Saldivar-Morse, prin. Fax 385-6775
Rivera MS 1,100/6-8
945 Buena Vista Dr 95348 209-385-6680
Brian Ferguson, prin. Fax 385-6702
Sheehy ES 600/K-5
1240 W 6th St 95341 209-385-6676
Lucrecia Sicairos, prin. Fax 385-6389
Stefani ES 400/3-5
2768 Ranchero Ln 95348 209-385-6600
Connie Hadley, prin. Fax 724-2500
Stowell ES 400/K-5
251 E 11th St 95341 209-381-2803
Cesar Hernandez, prin. Fax 381-2807
Tenaya MS 900/6-8
760 W 8th St 95341 209-385-6687
Tara Bright, prin. Fax 385-6365
Wright ES 500/K-5
900 E 20th St 95340 209-385-6615
Jose Munoz, prin. Fax 385-6302

Plainsburg UNESD 100/K-8
3708 Plainsburg Rd 95341 209-389-4707
Vernon Snodderly, supt. Fax 389-4817
www.plainsburg.k12.ca.us/
Plainsburg Union S 100/K-8
3708 Plainsburg Rd 95341 209-389-4707
Vernon Snodderly, prin. Fax 389-4817

Weaver UNESD 2,600/K-8
3076 E Childs Ave 95341 209-723-7606
Steve Becker, supt. Fax 725-7128
www.weaverusd.k12.ca.us
Farmdale ES 800/K-5
100 Winder Ave 95341 209-725-7170
Karen Snell, prin. Fax 725-7175
Pioneer ES 1,100/K-5
2950 E Gerard Ave 95341 209-725-7111
Brenda Jones, prin. Fax 725-7117
Weaver MS 800/6-8
3076 E Childs Ave 95341 209-723-2174
Teresa Langford, prin. Fax 725-7116

Merced Adventist S 50/1-8
2300 E Olive Ave 95340 209-384-2433
Joan Hacko, prin. Fax 384-2485
Merced Christian S 200/PK-8
3312 G St 95340 209-384-1940
William Martin, prin. Fax 384-1546
Our Lady of Mercy S 400/PK-8
1400 E 27th St 95340 209-722-7496
Judy Blackburn, prin. Fax 722-7532
St. Paul Lutheran S 100/PK-5
2916 McKee Rd 95340 209-383-3302
Sanna Klipfel, prin. Fax 383-3642

Meridian, Sutter
Meridian ESD 100/K-8
15898 Central St 95957 530-696-2604
Benjamin Moss, supt. Fax 696-0406
meridian.sutter.k12.ca.us/
Meridian S 100/K-8
15898 Central St 95957 530-696-2604
Benjamin Moss, prin. Fax 696-0406

Winship-Robbins ESD 100/K-8
4305 S Meridian Rd 95957 530-696-2451
Katherine Anderson, supt. Fax 696-2262
winship.sutter.k12.ca.us/
Winship S 50/K-8
4305 S Meridian Rd 95957 530-696-2451
Katherine Anderson, prin. Fax 696-2262
Other Schools – See Robbins

Middletown, Lake
Middletown USD 1,800/K-12
20932 Big Canyon Rd 95461 707-987-4100
Korby Olson Ed.D., supt. Fax 987-4105
www.middletownusd.org
Cannon ES 200/K-6
20932 Big Canyon Rd 95461 707-987-4130
Dan Morgan, prin. Fax 987-4136
Cobb Mountain ES 200/K-6
20932 Big Canyon Rd 95461 707-928-5229
Tracy Skeen, prin. Fax 928-5414
Coyote Valley ES 500/K-6
20932 Big Canyon Rd 95461 707-987-3357
Tom Hoskins, prin. Fax 987-4111
Middletown MS 300/7-8
20932 Big Canyon Rd 95461 707-987-4160
Daniel Morgan, prin. Fax 987-4162

Middletown Christian S 100/K-12
PO Box 989 95461 707-987-2556
Melanie Brown, admin. Fax 987-2126
Middletown SDA S 50/1-8
PO Box 1664 95461 707-987-9147
Paul Lockwood, prin. Fax 987-3546

Midway City, Orange, Pop. 4,400
Ocean View SD
Supt. — See Huntington Beach
Star View ES 500/K-5
8411 Worthy Dr 92655 714-897-1009
Pauline Tressler Ed.D., prin. Fax 373-0769

Westminster ESD
Supt. — See Westminster
DeMille ES 600/PK-6
15400 Van Buren St 92655 714-894-7224
Shannon Villanueva, prin. Fax 892-0527
Hayden ES 700/PK-5
14782 Eden St 92655 714-894-7261
Dr. Paula Mills, prin. Fax 379-1774

Millbrae, San Mateo, Pop. 20,342
Millbrae ESD 2,100/K-8
555 Richmond Dr 94030 650-697-5693
Dr. Shirley Martin, supt. Fax 697-6865
millbraeschooldistrict.org/
Green Hills ES 300/K-5
401 Ludeman Ln 94030 650-588-6485
Kristen Ugrin, prin. Fax 583-8052
Meadows ES 400/K-5
1101 Helen Dr 94030 650-583-7590
Molly Whiteley, prin. Fax 588-5461
Spring Valley ES 400/K-5
817 Murchison Dr 94030 650-697-5681
Phil White, prin. Fax 697-2931
Taylor MS 900/6-8
850 Taylor Blvd 94030 650-697-4096
David Erwin, prin. Fax 697-8435
Other Schools – See San Bruno

St. Dunstan S 300/K-8
1150 Magnolia Ave 94030 650-697-8119
Dr. Bruce Colville, prin. Fax 697-9295

Mill Valley, Marin, Pop. 13,286
Mill Valley ESD 2,300/K-8
411 Sycamore Ave 94941 415-389-7700
Ken Benny, supt. Fax 389-7773
www.mvschools.org
Maguire ES 400/K-5
80 Lomita Dr 94941 415-389-7733
Lisa Zimmer, prin. Fax 389-7776
Mill Valley MS 700/6-8
425 Sycamore Ave 94941 415-389-7711
Matt Huxley, prin. Fax 389-7780
Old Mill ES 300/K-5
352 Throckmorton Ave 94941 415-389-7727
Jane McDonough, prin. Fax 389-7778
Park ES 300/K-5
360 E Blithedale Ave 94941 415-389-7735
Peg Katz, prin. Fax 389-7779
Strawberry Point ES 300/K-5
117 E Strawberry Dr 94941 415-389-7660
Leslie Thornton, prin. Fax 380-2499
Tamalpais Valley ES 400/K-5
350 Bell Ln 94941 415-389-7731
Gail van Adelsberg, prin. Fax 389-7781

Marin Horizon S 300/PK-8
305 Montford Ave 94941 415-388-8408
Rosalind Hamar, prin. Fax 388-7831
Mt. Tamalpais S 200/K-8
100 Harvard Ave 94941 415-383-9434
Dr. Kathleen Mecca, dir. Fax 383-7519

Millville, Shasta
Millville ESD 200/K-8
8570 Brookdale Rd 96062 530-547-4471
Mindy DeSantis, supt. Fax 547-3760
www.shastalink.k12.ca.us/millville/
Millville S 200/K-8
8570 Brookdale Rd 96062 530-547-4471
Mindy DeSantis, prin. Fax 547-3760

Milpitas, Santa Clara, Pop. 63,383
Milpitas USD 9,800/PK-12
1331 E Calaveras Blvd 95035 408-635-2600
Karl Black Ed.D., supt. Fax 635-2616
www.musd.org
Burnett ES 600/K-6
400 Fanyon St 95035 408-635-2650
Catherine Waslif, prin. Fax 635-2655
Curtner ES 700/K-6
275 Redwood Ave 95035 408-635-2852
Todd Gaviglio, prin. Fax 635-2857
Pomeroy ES 700/K-6
1505 Escuela Pkwy 95035 408-635-2858
Barbara Berman, prin. Fax 635-2863
Rancho Milpitas MS 700/7-8
1915 Yellowstone Ave 95035 408-635-2656
Leticia Villa-Gascon, prin. Fax 635-2661
Randall ES 500/K-6
1300 Edsel Dr 95035 408-635-2662
Kristian Lecours, prin. Fax 635-2667
Rose Child Development Center 100/PK-PK
250A Roswell Dr 95035 408-635-2686
Kathleen Lincoln, prin. Fax 635-9503
Rose ES 400/K-6
250 Roswell Dr 95035 408-635-2668
Mindy Bolar, prin. Fax 635-2673
Russell MS 800/7-8
1500 Escuela Pkwy 95035 408-635-2864
Laura Foegal, prin. Fax 635-2869
Sinnott ES 700/K-6
2025 Yellowstone Ave 95035 408-635-2674
Stacey Espino, prin. Fax 635-2679
Spangler ES 500/K-6
140 N Abbott Ave 95035 408-635-2870
Normajean McClellan, prin. Fax 635-2875
Sunnyhills Child Development Center 100/PK-PK
356 Dixon Rd 95035 408-945-5577
Kathleen Lincoln, prin. Fax 945-2779
Weller ES 500/K-6
345 Boulder St 95035 408-635-2876
Damon James, prin. Fax 635-2880
Zanker ES 500/K-6
1585 Fallen Leaf Dr 95035 408-635-2882
Kathy Doi, prin. Fax 635-2887

Foothill SDA S 100/K-8
1991 Landess Ave 95035 408-263-2568
Justine Leonie, prin. Fax 263-1994
Plantation Christian S 100/1-12
PO Box 360743 95036 408-956-1557
St. John the Baptist S 300/PK-8
360 S Abel St 95035 408-262-8110
Judith Perkowski, prin. Fax 262-8134

Mineral, Tehama
Mineral ESD 50/K-8
PO Box 130 96063 530-595-3322
Brenda Wolfe, admin. Fax 595-3298
www.mineralschool.net
Mineral S 50/K-8
PO Box 130 96063 530-595-3322
Brenda Wolfe, admin. Fax 595-3298

Mira Loma, Riverside, Pop. 15,786
Corona-Norco USD
Supt. — See Norco
VanderMolen Fundamental ES K-6
6744 Carnelian 91752 951-739-7120
Russ Schriver, prin. Fax 739-7128

Jurupa USD
Supt. — See Riverside
Sky Country ES 700/K-6
5520 Lucretia Ave 91752 951-360-2816
Joan Lauritzen, prin. Fax 681-5197
Troth Street ES 900/K-6
5565 Troth St 91752 951-360-2866
Laz Barreiro, prin. Fax 360-5342

Olive Tree Christian S 200/K-12
5430 Galaxy Ln 91752 951-360-1160
Rebecca Kocsis, admin. Fax 360-1160

Miranda, Humboldt
Southern Humbolt JUSD 800/K-12
PO Box 650 95553 707-943-1789
Clifton Anderson, supt. Fax 943-1921
internet.humboldt.k12.ca.us/sohumb_usd/school/
Other Schools – See Blocksburg, Garberville, Redway, Weott, Whitethorn

Mission Hills, Los Angeles, Pop. 3,112
Los Angeles USD
Supt. — See Los Angeles
San Jose ES 700/K-5
14928 Clymer St 91345 818-365-3218
Janet Johnson, prin. Fax 365-5067

Mission Viejo, Orange, Pop. 94,982
Capistrano USD
Supt. — See San Juan Capistrano
Barcelona Hills ES 500/K-5
23000 Via Santa Maria 92691 949-581-5240
Kathy Kirtz, prin. Fax 581-6897
Bathgate ES 700/K-5
27642 Napoli Way 92692 949-348-0451
Kimberly Hall, prin. Fax 348-0426
Castille ES 700/K-5
24042 Via La Coruna 92691 949-234-5976
Laura Lyon, prin. Fax 586-6739
Hankey ES 500/K-7
27252 Nubles 92692 949-234-5315
Scott Wilbur, prin. Fax 347-0536
Newhart MS 1,800/6-8
25001 Veterans Way 92692 949-855-0162
George Knights, prin. Fax 770-1262
Reilly ES 600/K-5
24171 Pavion 92692 949-454-1590
Judy Shades, prin. Fax 588-6315
Viejo ES 500/K-5
26782 Via Grande 92691 949-582-2424
Doug Kramer, prin. Fax 348-2499

Saddleback Valley USD 32,400/K-12
25631 Peter A Hartman Way 92691 949-586-1234
Steven Fish Ed.D., supt. Fax 951-0994
www.svusd.k12.ca.us
Cordillera ES 600/K-6
25952 Cordillera Dr 92691 949-830-3400
Liza Zielasko, prin. Fax 830-7673
Del Cerro ES 500/K-6
24382 Regina St 92691 949-830-5430
Larry Callison, prin. Fax 830-5151
Del Lago ES 500/K-6
27181 Entidad 92691 949-855-1125
Doug Dick, prin. Fax 829-6733
De Portola ES 600/K-6
27031 Preciados Dr 92691 949-586-5830
Bob Gaebel, prin. Fax 586-5876
Glen Yermo ES 600/K-6
26400 Trabuco Rd 92691 949-586-6766
Lisa Graham, prin. Fax 837-3528
La Paz IS 1,200/7-8
25151 Pradera Dr 92691 949-830-1720
Jean Carroll, prin. Fax 830-3320
Linda Vista ES 600/K-6
25222 Pericia Dr 92691 949-830-0970
Terry Petersen, prin. Fax 830-9237
Los Alisos IS 1,300/7-8
25171 Moor Ave 92691 949-830-9700
Dr. Jerry Ray, prin. Fax 472-3968
Montevideo ES 600/K-6
24071 Carrillo Dr 92691 949-586-8050
Jim Schmalbach, prin. Fax 586-0518
Other Schools – See Foothill Ranch, Laguna Hills, Lake Forest, Rancho Santa Margarita, Trabuco Canyon

---

Agape Academy 100/K-12
23632 Via Calzada 92691 949-701-9086
Denise Justiniano, admin.
Carden Academy 200/K-8
24741 Chrisanta Dr 92691 949-458-1776
Fax 458-5071
Heritage Christian S 100/PK-12
24162 Alicia Pkwy 92691 949-598-9166
George Gay, prin. Fax 598-1892
Living Word Christian Academy 50/K-8
23561 Alicia Pkwy 92691 949-830-3763
Brad Gurgel, prin. Fax 830-3763
Master's Academy 50/K-12
23052 Alicia Pkwy Ste H107 92692 949-459-5293
Helen Martinez, admin. Fax 459-5293
Mission Viejo Christian S 200/PK-8
27192 Jeronimo Rd 92692 949-465-1950
James Downey, prin. Fax 465-1949
Saddleback Christian Academy 300/K-12
26861 Trabuco Rd Ste E 92691 949-587-9650
Tracey Hodge, hdmstr.

Modesto, Stanislaus, Pop. 207,011
Ceres USD
Supt. — See Ceres
Adkison ES 400/K-6
1824 Nadine Ave 95351 209-556-1600
Lynnette Chirrick, prin. Fax 531-0216
Westport ES 400/K-6
5218 S Carpenter Rd 95358 209-556-1700
Marla Mack, prin. Fax 537-9589

Empire UNESD 2,800/K-8
116 N McClure Rd 95357 209-521-2800
Dr. Robert Price, supt. Fax 526-6421
www.empire.k12.ca.us
Capistrano ES 500/K-6
400 Capistrano Dr 95354 209-521-8664
Dante Alvarez, prin. Fax 575-0734
Glick MS 400/7-8
400 Frazine Rd 95357 209-577-3945
Janet Mikkelsen, prin. Fax 577-3975
Hughes ES 500/K-6
512 N McClure Rd 95357 209-527-1330
Rosalie Reberg, prin. Fax 550-0537
Sipherd ES 500/K-6
3420 E Orangeburg Ave 95355 209-524-4844
Nancy Fox, prin. Fax 569-0913
Stroud ES 400/K-6
815 Frazine Rd 95357 209-491-0754
Lorinda Ferguson, prin. Fax 529-3738
Other Schools – See Empire

Hart-Ransom UNESD 700/K-8
3920 Shoemake Ave 95358 209-523-9996
Dr. Ream Lochry, supt. Fax 523-9997
www.hartransom.org
Hart-Ransom S 700/K-8
3930 Shoemake Ave 95358 209-523-9979
Jerrianna Boer, prin. Fax 523-0588

Modesto CSD 31,500/K-12
426 Locust St 95351 209-576-4011
Arturo Flores, supt. Fax 576-4184
www.monet.k12.ca.us
Beard ES 500/K-6
915 Bowen Ave 95350 209-576-4689
Gregory Elliott, prin. Fax 569-2757
Bret Harte ES 900/K-6
909 Glenn Ave 95358 209-576-4673
Ruth Flores, prin. Fax 576-4288
Burbank ES 700/K-6
1135 Paradise Rd 95351 209-576-4709
Pamela Corbett, prin. Fax 576-4859

El Vista ES 400/K-6
450 El Vista Ave 95354 209-576-4665
Marilyn Rockey, prin. Fax 576-4567
Enslen ES 400/K-6
515 Coldwell Ave 95354 209-576-4701
Deborah Grochau, prin. Fax 569-2731
Everett ES 400/K-6
1530 Mount Vernon Dr 95350 209-576-4009
Michael Brady, prin. Fax 576-4069
Fairview ES 1,000/K-6
1937 W Whitmore Ave 95358 209-576-4693
Heather Sharp, prin. Fax 576-4696
Franklin ES 800/2-6
120 S Emerald Ave 95351 209-576-4850
Fax 576-4853
Fremont ES 600/K-6
1220 W Orangeburg Ave 95350 209-576-4679
Jane Manley, prin. Fax 569-2754
Garrison ES 300/K-6
1811 Teresa St 95350 209-576-4648
LaVerne Shireman, prin. Fax 576-4640
Hanshaw MS 1,000/7-8
1725 Las Vegas St 95358 209-576-4847
Brooke Thomas, prin. Fax 576-4723
Kirschen ES 700/K-6
1900 Kirschen Dr 95351 209-576-4611
Rob Williams, prin. Fax 576-4270
Lakewood ES 400/K-6
2920 Middleboro Pl 95355 209-576-4841
Jennifer Ortiz, prin. Fax 576-4980
La Loma JHS 900/7-8
1800 Encina Ave 95354 209-576-4627
Ed Miller, prin. Fax 576-4631
Marshall ES 800/K-6
515 Sutter Ave 95351 209-576-4697
Theresa Finley, prin. Fax 576-4699
Martone ES 800/K-6
1413 Poust Rd 95358 209-576-4613
Carol Brooks, prin. Fax 569-2753
Muir ES 500/K-6
1215 Lucern Ave 95350 209-576-4835
Kuljinder Sekhon, prin. Fax 569-2755
Pearson ES 300/K-1
500 Locust St 95351 209-576-4110
Fax 576-4146
Robertson Road ES 500/K-6
1821 Robertson Rd 95351 209-576-4646
Michele Gutierrez, prin. Fax 576-4642
Roosevelt JHS 800/7-8
1330 College Ave 95350 209-576-4871
Dave Kline, prin. Fax 569-2713
Rose Avenue ES 500/K-6
1120 Rose Ave 95355 209-576-4712
Diane Scott, prin. Fax 569-2752
Shackelford ES 500/K-6
100 School Ave 95351 209-576-4831
Cecilia Cobb, prin. Fax 576-4860
Sonoma ES 500/K-6
1325 Sonoma Ave 95355 209-576-4683
Jane Moffett, prin. Fax 576-2725
Tuolumne ES 800/K-6
707 Herndon Rd 95351 209-576-4661
Mark Lewis, prin. Fax 576-4663
Twain JHS 900/7-8
707 S Emerald Ave 95351 209-576-4814
Julie Beebe, prin. Fax 576-4843
Wilson ES 300/K-6
201 Wilson Ave 95354 209-576-4827
Ignacio Cantu, prin. Fax 569-2756
Wright ES 500/K-6
1602 Monterey Ave 95354 209-576-4821
Heather Sherburn, prin. Fax 576-4824

Paradise ESD 100/K-8
3361 California Ave 95358 209-524-0184
Bill Stires, supt. Fax 524-0363
www.paradiseesd.org/
Paradise S 100/K-8
3361 California Ave 95358 209-524-0184
Bill Stires, prin. Fax 524-0363

Salida UNESD
Supt. — See Salida
Perkins ES 400/K-5
3920 Blue Bird Dr 95356 209-545-4415
Philip Menchaca, prin. Fax 545-4248

Shiloh ESD 100/K-8
6633 Paradise Rd 95358 209-522-2261
Seth Ehrler, supt. Fax 522-0188
www.shiloh.k12.ca.us/
Shiloh S 100/K-8
6633 Paradise Rd 95358 209-522-2261
Seth Ehrler, prin. Fax 522-0188

Stanislaus UNESD 3,000/K-8
3601 Carver Rd 95356 209-529-9546
Wayne Brown, supt. Fax 529-0243
www.stanunion.k12.ca.us
Baptist ES 600/K-6
1825 Cheyenne Way 95356 209-527-0450
Tom Price, prin. Fax 527-6351
Chrysler ES 600/K-6
2818 Conant Ave 95350 209-529-5430
Scott Borba, prin. Fax 529-4401
Dieterich ES 600/K-6
2412 Warm Springs Dr 95356 209-550-8400
Loren York, prin. Fax 578-1520
Eisenhut ES 300/K-6
1809 Sheldon Dr 95350 209-527-7867
Dru Howenstine, prin. Fax 527-3438
Prescott Senior ES 700/7-8
2243 W Rumble Rd 95350 209-529-9892
Tom Freeman Ed.D., prin. Fax 529-4406
Stanislaus ES 200/K-6
1931 Kiernan Ave 95356 209-545-0718
Pamela Collinsworth, prin. Fax 543-7909

Sylvan Union ESD 9,300/K-8
605 Sylvan Ave 95350 209-574-5000
Dr. John Halverson, supt. Fax 524-2672
www.sylvan.k12.ca.us
Brown ES 600/K-5
2024 Vera Cruz Dr 95355 209-574-5100
Mitch Wood, prin. Fax 524-6278
Coffee ES 800/K-5
3900 Northview Dr 95355 209-574-5500
Joe Berry, prin. Fax 521-5601
Freedom ES 900/K-5
2101 Fine Ave 95355 209-552-3400
Jonette DeCamp, prin. Fax 552-3405
Orchard ES 700/K-5
1800 Wisdom Way 95355 209-552-3100
Vickie Briscoe, prin. Fax 552-3105
Sanders ES 600/K-5
3101 Fine Ave 95355 209-574-5000
Russell Antracoli, prin. Fax 552-3205
Savage MS 700/6-8
1900 Maid Mariane Ln 95355 209-552-3300
Dave Garcia, prin. Fax 552-3305
Sherwood ES 600/K-5
819 E Rumble Rd 95350 209-574-5200
Tedde Vaupel, prin. Fax 574-5202
Somerset MS 1,100/6-8
1037 Floyd Ave 95350 209-574-5300
Janice Latham, prin. Fax 529-1110
Standiford ES 500/K-5
605 Tokay Ave 95350 209-574-5400
Matthew Shipley, prin. Fax 524-7405
Sylvan ES 600/K-5
2908 Coffee Rd 95355 209-574-5600
Carrie Albert, prin. Fax 527-6259
Ustach MS 1,100/6-8
2701 Kodiak Dr 95355 209-552-3000
Laura Wharff, prin. Fax 552-3010
Woodrow ES 500/K-5
800 Woodrow Ave 95350 209-574-5700
Sherryl Price, prin. Fax 574-5010
Other Schools – See Riverbank

Big Valley Christian S 900/PK-12
4040 Tully Rd Ste D 95356 209-527-3481
Scott Edwards, supt. Fax 569-0138
Brethren Heritage S 100/K-12
3549 Dakota Ave 95358 209-543-7860
James Shuman, prin. Fax 543-7862
Calvary Temple Preschool 100/PK-PK
1601 Coffee Rd 95355 209-529-7154
Loren Mauch, admin. Fax 529-1129
Grace Lutheran S 200/PK-8
617 W Orangeburg Ave 95350 209-529-1800
Jim Scriven, prin. Fax 529-7721
Heritage Christian S 50/K-12
812 Thieman Rd 95356 209-545-9009
Kimberly Meyer, prin. Fax 545-9009
Modesto Christian ES 200/K-5
5901 Sisk Rd 95356 209-529-5510
Nancee Davis, prin. Fax 545-1369
Modesto Christian MS 100/6-8
5901 Sisk Rd 95356 209-529-5510
Nancee Davis, prin. Fax 545-1369
Orangeburg Christian S 100/PK-8
313 E Orangeburg Ave 95350 209-577-2576
Elaine Bartels, prin. Fax 577-3190
Our Lady of Fatima S 300/K-8
501 W Granger Ave 95350 209-524-4170
Linda Partlow, prin. Fax 524-3960
St. Peter Lutheran S 50/K-8
3461 Merle Ave 95355 209-551-4963
Matthew Linton, prin. Fax 551-8827
St. Stanislaus S 300/PK-8
1416 Maze Blvd 95351 209-524-9036
Donna O'Connor, prin. Fax 524-4344
Wood Colony Brethren S 100/K-12
2524 Finney Rd 95358 209-544-9227
Nancy Walton, admin. Fax 544-9229

Mojave, Kern, Pop. 3,763
Mojave USD 3,700/K-12
3500 Douglas Ave 93501 661-824-4001
Larry Phelps, supt. Fax 824-2686
www.mojave.k12.ca.us/
Joshua MS 200/4-6
3200 Pat Ave 93501 661-824-2411
Marv Baker, prin. Fax 824-5251
Mojave ES 300/K-3
15800 O St 93501 661-824-2456
Marv Baker, prin. Fax 824-2461
Other Schools – See California City

Mokelumne Hill, Calaveras
Calaveras USD
Supt. — See San Andreas
Mokelumne Hill ES 100/K-6
8350 Highway 26 95245 209-754-2140
Michelle Besmer, prin. Fax 286-1038

Monrovia, Los Angeles, Pop. 37,954
Monrovia USD 6,300/PK-12
325 E Huntington Dr 91016 626-471-2000
Linda Wagner, supt. Fax 471-2077
www.monroviaschools.net
Bradoaks ES 600/K-5
930 E Lemon Ave 91016 626-471-2100
Valerie Bires, prin. Fax 471-2110
Canyon Early Learning Center PK-PK
1000 S Canyon Blvd 91016 626-471-2001
Suzanne Heck, prin. Fax 471-2086
Clifton MS 700/6-8
226 S Ivy Ave 91016 626-471-2600
Traci Gholar, prin. Fax 471-2610
Mayflower ES 600/K-5
210 N Mayflower Ave 91016 626-471-2200
Kirk McGinnis, prin. Fax 471-2210
Monroe ES 500/K-5
402 W Colorado Blvd 91016 626-471-2300
Cindy Lathrop, prin. Fax 471-2310
Plymouth ES 500/K-5
1300 Boley St 91016 626-471-2400
Michael Hoon, prin. Fax 471-2410
Santa Fe MS 700/6-8
148 W Duarte Rd 91016 626-471-2700
Ron Letourneau, prin. Fax 471-2710
Wild Rose ES 500/K-5
232 Jasmine Ave 91016 626-471-2500
Stacy Ayers, prin. Fax 471-2510

Excellence in Education Academy 500/K-12
2640 S Myrtle Ave 91016 626-821-0025
Carolyn Forte, prin. Fax 821-0216
First Lutheran S 100/PK-8
1323 S Magnolia Ave 91016 626-357-3543
Deborah Martinez, dir. Fax 357-8296
Immaculate Conception S 200/K-8
726 S Shamrock Ave 91016 626-358-5129
Dr. Patricia Taepke, prin. Fax 358-3933

Montague, Siskiyou, Pop. 1,504
Big Springs UNESD 100/K-8
7405 County Highway A12 96064 530-459-3189
Terry Weatherby, supt. Fax 459-3201
Big Springs S 100/K-8
7405 County Highway A12 96064 530-459-3189
Terry Weatherby, prin. Fax 459-3201

Bogus ESD 50/K-8
13735 Ager Beswick Rd 96064 530-459-3163
Fred Ehmke, supt. Fax 459-0706
www.sisnet.ssku.k12.ca.us/bogusdirectory.html
Bogus S 50/K-8
13735 Ager Beswick Rd 96064 530-459-3163
Fred Ehmke, prin. Fax 459-0706

Delphic ESD 50/K-8
1420 Delphic Rd 96064 530-842-3653
Debbie Faulkner, supt. Fax 842-0249
www.sisnet.ssku.k12.ca.us/delphicdir.html
Delphic S 50/K-8
1420 Delphic Rd 96064 530-842-3653
Debbie Faulkner, prin. Fax 842-0249

Little Shasta ESD 50/K-6
8409 Lower Little Shasta Rd 96064 530-459-3269
Kathleen Koon, supt. Fax 459-1619
Little Shasta ES 50/K-6
8409 Lower Little Shasta Rd 96064 530-459-3269
Kathleen Koon, prin. Fax 459-1619

Montague ESD 100/K-8
PO Box 308 96064 530-459-3001
Mike Michelon, supt. Fax 459-3788
www.sisnet.ssku.k12.ca.us/~montagftp/
Montague S 100/K-8
PO Box 308 96064 530-459-3001
Renee McKay, prin. Fax 459-3788

Willow Creek ESD 50/K-8
5321 York Rd 96064 530-459-3313
Ron Ferrando, supt. Fax 459-1537
www.sisnet.ssku.k12.ca.us/~willoweb
Willow Creek S 50/K-8
5321 York Rd 96064 530-459-3313
Ron Ferrando, prin. Fax 459-1537

Montara, San Mateo, Pop. 2,552
Cabrillo USD
Supt. — See Half Moon Bay
Farallone View ES 500/K-5
250 Laconte and Kanoff 94037 650-712-7170
Catherine Werdel, prin. Fax 728-3352

Montclair, San Bernardino, Pop. 35,474
Ontario-Montclair ESD
Supt. — See Ontario
Buena Vista Arts ES 400/K-6
5685 San Bernardino St 91763 909-984-9556
Stu Bernhard, prin. Fax 459-2602
Howard ES 700/K-6
4650 Howard St 91763 909-591-2339
Tammy Lipschultz, prin. Fax 517-3943
Kingsley ES 800/K-6
5625 Kingsley St 91763 909-984-3634
Lynn Gage, prin. Fax 459-2848
Lehigh ES 700/PK-6
10200 Lehigh Ave 91763 909-624-5697
Anthony Ortiz, prin. Fax 445-1613
Montera ES 600/PK-6
4825 Bandera St 91763 909-445-1062
Vickie Lamborn, prin. Fax 445-1493
Monte Vista ES 800/PK-6
4900 Orchard St 91763 909-626-5046
Sultana Dixon, prin. Fax 445-1650
Moreno ES 700/PK-6
4825 Moreno St 91763 909-445-1661
Amy D'Andrea, prin. Fax 445-1662
Ramona ES 700/PK-6
4225 Howard St 91763 909-627-3411
Jennifer Clark, prin. Fax 517-3987
Serrano MS 900/7-8
4725 San Jose St 91763 909-624-0029
Leticia Zaragoza, prin. Fax 445-1687
Vernon MS 900/6-8
9775 Vernon Ave 91763 909-624-5036
Brian Bettger, prin. Fax 445-1720

Montclair Christian S 50/PK-6
PO Box 2507 91763 909-626-4702
Barbara Rhodes, admin. Fax 398-4162
Our Lady of Lourdes S 200/K-8
5303 Orchard St 91763 909-621-4418
Sr. Fidelma Lyne, prin. Fax 625-5034

Montebello, Los Angeles, Pop. 63,290
Montebello USD 32,900/K-12
123 S Montebello Blvd 90640 323-887-7900
Edward Velasquez, supt. Fax 887-5890
www.montebello.k12.ca.us
Eastmont IS 1,700/5-8
400 Bradshawe St 90640 323-721-5133
Lorraine Verduzco, prin. Fax 887-3058
Fremont ES 600/K-4
200 W Madison Ave 90640 323-721-2435
Chuck Cota, prin. Fax 887-3139
Greenwood ES 800/K-4
900 S Greenwood Ave 90640 323-721-4605
Lourdes Hale, prin. Fax 887-5882
La Merced ES 800/K-4
724 N Poplar Ave 90640 323-721-5043
John Olague, prin. Fax 887-5806
La Merced IS 1,900/5-8
215 E Avenida De La Merced 90640 323-722-7262
Eugene Kerr, prin. Fax 887-5816
Montebello IS 2,000/5-8
1600 W Whittier Blvd 90640 323-721-5111
Susan Donnelly, prin. Fax 887-3192
Washington ES 900/K-4
1400 W Madison Ave 90640 323-721-3621
Cynthia Herrera, prin. Fax 887-5891
Wilcox ES 700/K-4
816 Donna Way 90640 323-728-1833
Leo Gallegos, prin. Fax 887-3096
Other Schools – See Bell Gardens, Commerce, Los Angeles, Monterey Park, Pico Rivera, South San Gabriel

---

Cross & Crown Lutheran S 50/PK-K
809 W Beverly Blvd 90640 323-725-7050
Silvia Losoya, dir.
Montebello Christian S 200/K-8
136 S 7th St 90640 323-728-4119
Ernest Castro, prin. Fax 728-8396
Our Lady of Miraculous Medal S 500/PK-8
840 N Garfield Ave 90640 323-728-5435
Analisa Hernandez, prin. Fax 728-8038
St. Benedict S 600/K-8
217 N 10th St 90640 323-721-3348
Frank Loya, prin. Fax 721-8698
St. John Lutheran S 50/PK-6
417 N 18th St 90640 323-721-3910
Marie Garcia, prin. Fax 721-3910

Monterey, Monterey, Pop. 29,217
Monterey Peninsula USD 10,900/PK-12
PO Box 1031 93942 831-645-1200
Dr. Marilyn Shepherd, supt. Fax 649-4175
www.mpusd.k12.ca.us
Bay View ES 300/K-5
680 Belden St 93940 831-649-1264
Jone Amador, prin. Fax 647-9448
Colton S 800/K-8
100 Toda Vis 93940 831-649-1951
Kim Cooper, prin. Fax 649-4692
Foothill ES 400/K-6
1700 Via Casoli 93940 831-649-1744
Tom VanHeukeleum, prin. Fax 649-3428
La Mesa ES 500/K-6
1 La Mesa Way 93940 831-649-1872
Bob Miller, prin. Fax 649-3942
Other Schools – See Marina, Seaside

San Carlos S 300/K-8
450 Church St 93940 831-375-1324
Teresa Bennett, prin. Fax 375-9736
Santa Catalina S 600/PK-12
1500 Mark Thomas Dr 93940 831-655-9300
Sr. Claire Barone, hdmstr. Fax 649-3056

Monterey Park, Los Angeles, Pop. 62,065
Alhambra City SD
Supt. — See Alhambra
Brightwood S 900/K-8
1701 Brightwood St 91754 626-308-2404
Amy Tambara, prin. Fax 308-2407
Monterey Highlands S 800/K-8
400 Casuda Canyon Dr 91754 626-308-2427
Joe Cash, prin. Fax 308-2429
Repetto S 700/K-8
650 S Grandridge Ave 91754 626-572-2231
Natalie Tee-Gaither, prin. Fax 572-2233
Ynez S 900/K-8
120 S Ynez Ave 91754 626-572-2236
Carla Danner Powell, prin. Fax 571-8265

Garvey ESD
Supt. — See Rosemead
Hillcrest ES 500/K-6
795 Pepper St 91755 626-307-3371
Robin Libby, prin. Fax 572-4225
Monterey Vista ES 400/K-6
901 E Graves Ave 91755 626-307-3300
Hing Chow, prin. Fax 307-3490

Los Angeles USD
Supt. — See Los Angeles
Lane ES 400/K-5
1500 Avenida Cesar Chavez 91754 323-263-3877
Lupe Buenrostro, prin. Fax 263-7600

Montebello USD
Supt. — See Montebello
Bella Vista ES 700/K-5
2410 Findlay Ave 91754 323-721-4335
Sandra Vega, prin. Fax 887-3077
Macy IS 1,000/6-8
2101 Lupine Ave 91755 323-722-0260
Stacey Honda, prin. Fax 887-3068

Meher Montessori S 100/K-6
2009 S Garfield Ave 91754 323-724-0683
Adela Munoz, dir. Fax 724-0028
New Avenue S, 126 N New Ave 91755 300/K-8
Nancy Huang, admin. 626-280-5536
St. Stephen S 200/PK-8
119 S Ramona Ave 91754 626-573-1716
Josefina Solomonson, prin. Fax 573-3251
St. Thomas Aquinas S 200/K-8
1501 S Atlantic Blvd 91754 323-261-6583
Marinia De la Rosa, prin. Fax 261-5972

Monte Rio, Sonoma, Pop. 1,058
Monte Rio UNESD 100/K-8
20700 Foothill Dr 95462 707-865-2266
Diane Ogden Ed.D., supt. Fax 865-9356
Monte Rio S 100/K-8
20700 Foothill Dr 95462 707-865-2266
Jennifer Schwinn, prin. Fax 865-9356

Montgomery Creek, Shasta
Mountain UNESD 50/K-8
PO Box 368 96065 530-337-6214
Matthew Carroll, supt. Fax 337-6215
www.shastalink.k12.ca.us/muesd/
Montgomery Creek MS 50/K-8
PO Box 368 96065 530-337-6214
Matthew Carroll, prin. Fax 337-6215

Montrose, See La Crescenta

Armenian Sisters Academy 200/1-8
2361 Florencita Ave 91020 818-249-8783
Sr. Lucia Al-Haik, prin. Fax 249-7288
Holy Redeemer S 200/PK-8
2361 Del Mar Rd 91020 818-541-9005
Susan Fite, prin. Fax 541-9006
Montrose Christian Montessori S 200/K-6
2545 Honolulu Ave 91020 818-249-2319
Stephanie McReynolds, dir. Fax 249-6290

Moorpark, Ventura, Pop. 35,844
Moorpark USD 7,600/PK-12
5297 Maureen Ln 93021 805-378-6300
Ellen Smith, supt. Fax 529-8592
www.mrpk.org/
Arroyo West ES 500/2-5
4117 Country Hill Rd 93021 805-378-6308
Susanne Smith-Stein, prin. Fax 531-6611
Campus Canyon ES 400/K-5
15300 Monroe Ave 93021 805-378-6301
Stephanie Brazell, prin. Fax 531-6612
Chaparral MS 900/6-8
280 Poindexter Ave 93021 805-378-6302
Creighton Nicks, prin. Fax 378-6324
ECC PK-PK
240 Flory Ave 93021 805-531-6466
Fax 378-6362
Flory Academy of Sciences and Technology 500/K-5
240 Flory Ave 93021 805-378-6303
Michael Winters, prin. Fax 531-6609
Mesa Verde MS 900/6-8
14000 Peach Hill Rd 93021 805-378-6309
Kelli Hays, prin. Fax 531-6622
Mountain Meadows ES 400/K-2
4200 Mountain Meadow Dr 93021 805-378-6306
Christine Kelley, prin. Fax 531-6624
Peach Hill Academy 600/K-5
13400 Christian Barrett Dr 93021 805-378-6300
Donna Welch, prin. Fax 531-6450
Walnut Canyon ES 600/K-5
280 Casey Rd 93021 805-517-1722
Linda Bowe, prin. Fax 517-1726

Pinecrest S 300/PK-5
14100 Peach Hill Rd 93021 805-529-3255
April Cauthron, prin.

Moraga, Contra Costa, Pop. 16,869
Moraga ESD 1,700/K-8
PO Box 158 94556 925-376-5943
Richard Schafer, supt. Fax 376-8132
www.moraga.k12.ca.us
Camino Pablo ES 400/K-5
1111 Camino Pablo 94556 925-376-4435
Neil Jennings, prin. Fax 376-6749
Los Perales ES 300/K-5
22 Wakefield Dr 94556 925-631-0105
William Walters, prin. Fax 376-7452
Moraga IS 700/6-8
1010 Camino Pablo 94556 925-376-7206
Bruce Burns, prin. Fax 376-6836
Rheem ES 300/K-5
90 Laird Dr 94556 925-376-4441
Elaine Frank, prin. Fax 376-3248

Saklan Valley S 100/PK-8
1678 School St 94556 925-376-7900
David Hague, hdmstr. Fax 376-1156

Moreno Valley, Riverside, Pop. 178,367
Moreno Valley USD 36,900/K-12
25634 Alessandro Blvd 92553 951-571-7500
Rowena Lagrosa, supt. Fax 571-7550
www.mvusd.net
Armada ES 700/K-5
25201 John F Kennedy Dr 92551 951-571-4500
Dr. John Lawson, prin. Fax 571-4505
Badger Springs MS 1,500/6-8
24750 Delphinium Ave 92553 951-571-4200
Rose Gasser, prin. Fax 571-4205
Bear Valley ES 800/K-5
26125 Fir Ave 92555 951-571-4520
Lillian Saldana, prin. Fax 571-4525
Box Springs ES 500/K-5
11900 Athens Dr 92557 951-571-4530
Samuel Stager, prin. Fax 571-4535
Butterfield ES 800/K-5
13400 Kitching St 92553 951-571-4540
Tia May, prin. Fax 571-4545
Chaparral Hills ES 800/K-5
24850 Delphinium Ave 92553 951-571-4730
Kirk Skorpanich, prin. Fax 571-4735
Cloverdale ES 900/K-5
12050 Kitching St 92557 951-571-4550
Ken Sims, prin. Fax 571-4555
Creekside ES 800/K-5
13563 Heacock St 92553 951-571-4560
Andrea Aragon, prin. Fax 571-4565
Edgemont ES 700/K-5
21790 Eucalyptus Ave 92553 951-571-4570
Melissa Bazanos, prin. Fax 571-4575
Hendrick Ranch ES 800/K-5
25570 Brodiaea Ave 92553 951-571-4580
Robert Gordon, prin. Fax 571-4585
Hidden Springs ES 500/K-5
9801 Hidden Springs Dr 92557 951-571-4590
Misty Kelley, prin. Fax 571-4595
Honey Hollow ES 800/K-5
11765 Honey Holw 92557 951-571-4600
Dolores Vasquez, prin. Fax 571-4605
La Jolla ES 900/K-5
14745 Willow Grove Pl 92555 951-571-4740
Wade Hamilton, prin. Fax 571-4745
Landmark MS 1,400/6-8
15261 Legendary Dr 92555 951-571-4220
Chris Schiermeyer, prin. Fax 571-4225
Midland ES 800/K-5
11440 Davis St 92557 951-571-4610
Todd Flowers, prin. Fax 571-4615
Moreno ES 600/K-5
26700 Cottonwood Ave 92555 951-571-4620
Jeffrey Jones, prin. Fax 571-4625
Mountain View MS 1,500/6-8
13130 Morrison St 92555 951-571-4240
Deborah Fay, prin. Fax 571-4245
North Ridge ES 700/K-5
25101 Kalmia Ave 92557 951-571-4630
Tony Knapp, prin. Fax 571-4635
Palm MS 1,600/6-8
11900 Slawson Ave 92557 951-571-4260
Nancy Ross, prin. Fax 571-4265
Ramona ES 800/K-5
24801 Bay Ave 92553 951-571-4720
Sandra Bunting, prin. Fax 571-4725
Ridge Crest ES 500/K-5
28500 John F Kennedy Dr 92555 951-571-4640
Diana Emanuel, prin. Fax 571-4645
Seneca ES 600/K-5
11615 Wordsworth Rd 92557 951-571-4650
Emilio Gallegos, prin. Fax 571-4655
Serrano ES 800/K-5
24100 Delphinium Ave 92553 951-571-4660
Martha Palomino, prin. Fax 571-4665
Sugar Hill ES 800/K-5
24455 Old Country Rd 92557 951-571-4670
Penny Macon, prin. Fax 571-4675
Sunnymead ES 800/K-5
24050 Dracaea Ave 92553 951-571-4680
Maria Torrez, prin. Fax 571-4685
Sunnymead MS 1,300/6-8
23996 Eucalyptus Ave 92553 951-571-4280
Lilia Villa, prin. Fax 571-4285
Sunnymeadows ES 800/K-5
23200 Eucalyptus Ave 92553 951-571-4690
Cheryl Smith, prin. Fax 571-4695
Towngate ES 800/K-5
22480 Dracaea Ave 92553 951-571-4700
Paula Rynders, prin. Fax 571-4705
Vista Heights MS 1,500/6-8
23049 Old Lake Dr 92557 951-571-4300
Mark Hasson, prin. Fax 571-4305

Val Verde USD
Supt. — See Perris
Bethune ES 600/K-5
25390 Krameria St 92551 951-490-0380
Kimberly Hendricks, prin. Fax 490-0385
Lasselle ES 600/K-5
26446 Krameria Ave 92555 951-490-0350
Thelma Almuena, prin. Fax 490-0355
March MS 900/6-8
15800 Indian St 92551 951-490-0430
Wendy Pospichal, prin. Fax 490-0435
Rainbow Ridge ES 600/K-5
15950 Indian St 92551 951-490-0420
Tim Tanner, prin. Fax 490-0425
Red Maple ES 600/K-5
25100 Red Maple Ln 92551 951-443-2450
Tom Gronotte, prin. Fax 443-2455
Victoriano ES 500/K-5
25650 Los Cabos Dr 92551 951-490-0390
Rick Aleksak, prin. Fax 490-0395
Vista Verde MS 1,100/6-8
25777 Krameria St 92551 951-485-6270
Gary Roughton, prin. Fax 485-6278

Calvary Chapel Christian S 600/K-12
11960 Pettit St 92555 951-485-6088
Tim Hamilton, prin. Fax 485-6718
Moreno Valley Christian S 100/PK-8
25560 Alessandro Blvd 92553 951-924-6282
Jack Clark, admin. Fax 924-6282
St. Christopher Preschool 50/PK-PK
25075 Cottonwood Ave 92553 951-924-1968
Rebecca Reynoso, dir. Fax 247-6477
Valley Adventist Christian S 50/K-8
12649 Indian St 92553 951-242-3012
Toni Hollier, prin.
Valley Christian Academy 200/PK-8
26755 Alessandro Blvd 92555 951-242-5683
Cathleen Peacock, prin. Fax 242-6185

Morgan Hill, Santa Clara, Pop. 34,852
Morgan Hill USD 8,600/K-12
15600 Concord Cir 95037 408-201-6000
Dr. Alan Nishino, supt. Fax 778-0486
www.mhu.k12.ca.us

Barrett ES 500/K-6
895 Barrett Ave 95037 408-201-6340
Lisa Atlas, prin. Fax 776-8693
Britton MS 700/7-8
80 W Central Ave 95037 408-201-6160
Carol Coursey, prin. Fax 778-2550
El Toro ES 600/K-6
455 E Main Ave 95037 408-201-6380
Patrick Buchser, prin. Fax 779-1690
Jackson ES 500/K-6
2700 Fountain Oaks Dr 95037 408-201-6400
Garry Dudley, prin. Fax 776-8065
Nordstrom ES 700/K-6
1425 E Dunne Ave 95037 408-201-6440
Kathy Yeager, prin. Fax 776-9714
Paradise Valley/Machado ES 500/K-6
1400 La Crosse Dr 95037 408-201-6460
Fax 779-8307
Walsh ES 300/K-6
353 W Main Ave 95037 408-201-6500
Natalie Gioco, prin. Fax 776-0392
Other Schools – See San Jose, San Martin

Crossroads Christian S 200/PK-8
145 Wright Ave 95037 408-779-8850
Jim Wallace, supt. Fax 779-0444
Oakwood S 400/PK-12
105 John Wilson Way 95037 408-782-7177
Fax 782-7138
St. Catherine S 300/K-8
17500 Peak Ave 95037 408-779-9950
Fabienne Esparza, prin. Fax 779-9928
Shadow Mountain Baptist S 100/K-12
17810 Monterey St 95037 408-782-7806

Morongo Valley, San Bernardino, Pop. 1,544
Morongo USD
Supt. — See Twentynine Palms
Morongo Valley ES 200/K-6
10951 Hess Blvd 92256 760-363-6216
Melinda Peterson, prin. Fax 363-8185

Morro Bay, San Luis Obispo, Pop. 10,208
San Luis Coastal USD
Supt. — See San Luis Obispo
Del Mar ES 400/K-6
501 Sequoia St 93442 805-771-1858
Janet Gould, prin. Fax 772-0859

Moss Landing, Monterey
North Monterey County USD 4,700/PK-12
8142 Moss Landing Rd 95039 831-633-3343
Sergio Montenegro, supt. Fax 633-2937
www.nmcusd.org
Other Schools – See Castroville, Salinas

Mountain House, San Joaquin
Lammersville ESD 1,500/K-8
300 E Legacy Dr 95391 209-836-7400
Dale Hansen, supt. Fax 835-1113
www.lammersvilleschooldistrict.net
Bethany S 400/K-8
570 S Escuela Dr 95391 209-836-7250
Keri Buckley, prin. Fax 839-0446
Wicklund S 800/K-8
300 E Legacy Dr 95391 209-836-7200
Lem Vergara, prin. Fax 830-6746
Other Schools – See Tracy

Mountain View, Santa Clara, Pop. 69,276
Los Altos ESD
Supt. — See Los Altos
Springer ES 500/K-6
1120 Rose Ave 94040 650-943-4200
Wade Spenader, prin. Fax 965-9683

Mountain View Whisman SD 4,300/K-8
750A San Pierre Way 94043 650-526-3500
Maurice Ghysels, supt. Fax 964-8907
www.mvwsd.org/
Bubb ES 500/K-5
525 Hans Ave 94040 650-526-3480
Mary Dietrich, prin. Fax 428-1556
Castro ES 500/K-5
505 Escuela Ave 94040 650-526-3590
Judy Crates, prin. Fax 964-9013
Crittenden MS 600/6-8
1701 Rock St 94043 650-903-6945
Karen Robinson, prin. Fax 967-1707
Graham MS 600/6-8
1175 Castro St 94040 650-526-3570
Gretchen Jacobs, prin. Fax 965-9278
Huff ES 500/K-5
253 Martens Ave 94040 650-526-3490
Sharon Burns, prin. Fax 564-9046
Landels ES 500/K-5
115 W Dana St 94041 650-526-3520
Carmen Mizell, prin. Fax 969-7036
Monta Loma ES 500/K-5
460 Thompson Ave 94043 650-903-6915
Cathy Baur, prin. Fax 903-6921
Stevenson PACT ES K-5
750 San Pierre Way 94043 650-526-3500
Steve Gilbert, prin.
Theurkauf ES 500/K-5
1625 San Luis Ave 94043 650-903-6925
Connie Sawdey, prin. Fax 903-6931

German International S of Silicon Valley 200/K-12
310 Easy St 94043 650-254-0748
Maja Oelschlagel, prin. Fax 254-0749
Girls' MS 100/6-8
180 N Rengstorff Ave 94043 650-968-8338
Deborah Hof, hdmstr. Fax 968-4775
St. Joseph S 300/K-8
1120 Miramonte Ave 94040 650-967-1839
Stephanie Mirenda-Knight, prin. Fax 691-1530

Mount Baldy, Los Angeles
Mount Baldy JESD 100/K-8
PO Box 489 91759 909-985-0991
Kevin Vaughn Ph.D., supt. Fax 982-8009
www.mtbaldy.k12.ca.us
Mount Baldy S 100/K-8
PO Box 489 91759 909-985-0991
Kevin Vaughn, prin. Fax 982-8009

Mount Shasta, Siskiyou, Pop. 3,623
Mount Shasta UNSD 700/K-8
595 E Alma St 96067 530-926-6007
Gary Lampella, supt. Fax 926-6103
www.mtshasta.k12.ca.us/
Mount Shasta ES 300/K-3
501 Cedar St 96067 530-926-3434
Sally Gasaway, prin. Fax 926-2827
Sisson S 400/4-8
601 E Alma St 96067 530-926-3846
Kathi Emerson, prin. Fax 926-2152

Weed UNESD 400/K-8
595 E Alma St 96067 530-926-6007
Gary Lampella, supt. Fax 926-6103
Other Schools – See Weed

Siskiyou Christian S 50/K-8
1030 W A Barr Rd 96067 530-926-1784
Regina Wagner, admin. Fax 926-2700

Murphys, Calaveras, Pop. 1,517
Vallecito UNSD
Supt. — See Avery
Michelson ES 300/K-5
196 Pennsylvania Gulch Rd 95247 209-728-3441
Phyllis Parisi, prin. Fax 795-2510

Murrieta, Riverside, Pop. 82,778
Menifee UNESD
Supt. — See Menifee
Oak Meadows ES 1,000/K-5
28600 Poinsettia St 92563 951-246-4210
Linda Carpenter, prin. Fax 679-4637

Murrieta Valley USD 22,100/K-12
41870 McAlby Ct 92562 951-696-1600
Dr. Stan Scheer, supt. Fax 696-1641
www.murrieta.k12.ca.us
Alta Murrieta ES 700/K-5
39475 Whitewood Rd 92563 951-696-1403
Terry Picchiottino, prin. Fax 304-1766
Antelope Hills ES 700/K-5
36105 Murrieta Oaks Ave 92562 951-445-4110
Karen Briski, prin. Fax 304-1871
Avaxat ES 700/K-5
24300 Las Brisas Rd 92562 951-696-1402
David Ciabattini, prin. Fax 304-1629
Buchanan ES 1,100/K-5
40121 Torrey Pines Rd 92563 951-696-1428
Mike Lorimer, prin. Fax 304-1851
Cole Canyon ES 1,100/K-5
23750 Via Alisol 92562 951-696-1421
Karen Michaud, prin. Fax 304-1861
Curran ES 900/K-5
40855 Chaco Canyon Rd 92562 951-696-1405
David Koltovich, prin. Fax 304-1726
Mails ES, 35185 Briggs Rd 92563 900/K-6
Faythe Mutchnick-Jayx, prin. 951-696-1600
Monte Vista ES 1,200/K-5
37420 Via Mira Mosa 92563 951-894-5085
Randy Rogers, prin. Fax 304-1842
Murrieta ES 1,000/K-5
24725 Adams Ave 92562 951-696-1401
Estelle Jaurequi, prin. Fax 304-1705
Rail Ranch ES 800/K-5
25030 Via Santee 92563 951-696-1404
Kerry Wise, prin. Fax 304-1745
Shivela MS 1,800/6-8
24515 Lincoln Ave 92562 951-696-1406
Gary Farmer, prin. Fax 304-1643
Thompson MS 1,800/6-8
24040 Hayes Ave 92562 951-696-1410
Dale Velk, prin. Fax 304-1691
Tovashal ES 800/K-5
23801 Saint Raphael Dr 92562 951-696-1411
Andy Banks, prin. Fax 304-1783
Warm Springs MS 1,600/6-8
39245 Calle de Fortuna 92563 951-696-3503
Timothy Custer, prin. Fax 304-1611

Temecula Valley USD
Supt. — See Temecula
Alamos ES 900/K-5
38200 Pacific Park Dr 92563 951-294-6760
Penny Kubly, prin. Fax 294-6770
Bella Vista MS 1,200/6-8
31650 Browning St 92563 951-294-6600
Pam Blasich, prin. Fax 294-6624

Calvary Murrieta Christian S 1,100/PK-12
24225 Monroe Ave 92562 951-834-9190
Desmond Starr, supt. Fax 698-4896
Las Brisas Christian Academy 100/PK-4
24270 Adams Ave 92562 951-677-8468
Blake Withers, prin. Fax 696-7597
Murrieta Springs Adventist Christian S 100/K-8
32477 Starbuck Cir 92562 951-461-2243
Darena Shetler, prin. Fax 461-9565
Oak Grove Institute - Jack Weaver 100/K-12
24275 Jefferson Ave 92562 951-677-5599
Michael Brown, dir.
Sierra Springs Christian S 100/1-12
40960 California Oaks Rd 92562 951-304-3304
Pamela Healey, admin.

Napa, Napa, Pop. 74,782
Napa Valley USD 14,500/K-12
2425 Jefferson St 94558 707-253-3511
John Glaser, supt. Fax 253-3855
www.nvusd.k12.ca.us
Alta Heights ES 400/K-5
15 Montecito Blvd 94559 707-253-3671
Fax 253-6291
Browns Valley ES 400/K-5
1001 Buhman Ave 94558 707-253-3761
Frank Silva, prin. Fax 259-8421
Capell Valley ES 50/K-5
1192 Capell Valley Rd 94558 707-255-4913
Donna Drago, prin. Fax 253-3879
Carneros ES 200/K-5
1680 Los Carneros Ave 94559 707-253-3466
Donna Drago, prin. Fax 253-3870
El Centro ES 300/K-5
1480 El Centro Ave 94558 707-253-3771
Molly McClurg-Wong, prin. Fax 259-8422
Harvest MS 900/6-8
2449 Old Sonoma Rd 94558 707-259-8866
Linda Beckstrom, prin. Fax 253-4013
McPherson ES 600/K-5
2670 Yajome St 94558 707-253-3488
Tamara Sanguinetti, prin. Fax 259-8423
Mt. George ES 200/K-5
1019 2nd Ave 94558 707-253-3766
Janine Burt, prin. Fax 253-3624
Northwood ES 400/K-5
2214 Berks St 94558 707-253-3471
Chuck Niedhoefer, prin. Fax 259-8424
Pueblo Vista ES 200/K-5
1600 Barbara Rd 94558 707-253-3491
Patrick Warfield, prin. Fax 253-6239
Redwood MS 1,100/6-8
3600 Oxford St 94558 707-253-3415
Michael Pearson, prin. Fax 259-0718
Salvador ES 200/K-5
1850 Salvador Ave 94558 707-253-3476
Sarah Williams, prin. Fax 253-6293
Silverado MS 800/6-8
1133 Coombsville Rd 94558 707-253-3688
Mike Mansuy, prin. Fax 253-3830
Snow ES 300/K-5
1130 Foster Rd 94558 707-253-3666
MaryAnn Salinger, prin. Fax 253-6241
West Park ES 300/K-5
2315 W Park Ave 94558 707-253-3516
Julie Herdell, prin. Fax 253-6244
Wooden Valley ES 50/K-5
1340 Wooden Valley Rd 94558 707-255-4956
Donna Drago, prin. Fax 259-8428
Other Schools – See American Canyon, Vallejo, Yountville

Blue Oak S 200/K-8
1436 Polk St 94559 707-261-4500
Scott Duyan, hdmstr. Fax 261-4509
First Christian S 100/PK-8
2659 1st St 94558 707-253-7226
Dawnelle Ellis, admin. Fax 253-1261
Napa Christian S 200/K-12
2201 Pine St 94559 707-255-5233
Greg Coryell, prin. Fax 255-8530
St. Apollinaris S 300/K-8
3700 Lassen St 94558 707-224-6525
Jack Kersting, prin. Fax 224-5400
St. John's Lutheran S 300/PK-8
3521 Linda Vista Ave 94558 707-226-7970
Joel Wahlers, prin. Fax 226-7974
St. John the Baptist S 200/K-8
983 Napa St 94559 707-224-8388
Nancy Jordan, prin. Fax 224-0236
Sunrise Montessori of Napa Valley 100/PK-8
1226 Salvador Ave 94558 707-253-1105
Janice Tres, prin. Fax 253-8230

National City, San Diego, Pop. 61,419
National ESD 5,900/K-6
1500 N Ave 91950 619-336-7500
Fax 336-7505
nsd.us/
Central ES 800/K-6
933 E Ave 91950 619-336-7400
Alfonso Denegri, prin. Fax 336-7455
El Toyon ES 400/K-6
2000 E Division St 91950 619-336-8000
Manuel Machado, prin. Fax 336-8055
Harbison ES 600/K-6
3235 E 8th St 91950 619-336-8200
Beverly Hayes, prin. Fax 336-8255
Kimball ES 400/K-6
302 W 18th St 91950 619-336-8300
Sonia Ruan, prin. Fax 336-8355
Las Palmas ES 700/K-6
1900 E 18th St 91950 619-336-8500
Gina Mazeau, prin. Fax 336-8555
Lincoln Acres ES 700/K-6
2200 S Lanoitan Ave 91950 619-336-8600
Angela Franco, prin. Fax 336-8655
Olivewood ES 800/K-6
2505 F Ave 91950 619-336-8700
Luz Vicario, prin. Fax 336-8755
Otis ES 400/K-6
621 E 18th St 91950 619-336-8800
Steve Sanchez, prin. Fax 336-8855
Palmer Way ES 600/K-6
2900 Palmer St 91950 619-336-8900
Deborah Hernandez, prin. Fax 336-8955
Rancho de la Nacion S 400/K-6
1830 E Division St 91950 619-336-8100
Cindy Vasquez, prin. Fax 336-8155

Sweetwater UNHSD
Supt. — See Chula Vista
National City MS 800/7-8
1701 D Ave 91950 619-336-2600
Arturo Montano, prin. Fax 474-1756

Faithful Ambassadors Bible Baptist Acdmy 100/K-12
2432 E 18th St 91950 619-434-2265
Ireneo Austria, admin.
San Diego Academy 300/K-12
2800 E 4th St 91950 619-267-9550
Mervin Kesler, prin. Fax 267-8662

Needles, San Bernardino, Pop. 5,348
Needles USD 1,200/K-12
1900 Erin Dr 92363 760-326-3891
Dave Renquest, supt. Fax 326-4218
www.needles.k12.ca.us/
Chemehuevi Valley S 50/K-8
1900 Erin Dr 92363 760-858-4607
Dave Renquest, prin. Fax 858-1107
Hohstadt ES 100/K-2
1900 Erin Dr 92363 760-326-2177
Don Hoyle, prin. Fax 326-1127
Needles MS 300/6-8
1900 Erin Dr 92363 760-326-3894
Jim Rolls, prin. Fax 326-4052
Vista Colorado ES 300/K-5
1900 Erin Dr 92363 760-326-2167
Don Hoyle, prin. Fax 326-6565
Other Schools – See Parker Dam

Needles AG Christian S 100/1-12
PO Box 457 92363 760-326-2751
Debra Lamb, prin. Fax 326-2751
Needles SDA S 50/1-8
PO Box 306 92363 760-326-4406
Norma Howard, prin. Fax 326-4300

Nevada City, Nevada, Pop. 3,032
Nevada City ESD 1,200/K-8
800 Hoover Ln 95959 530-265-1820
Roger Steel, supt. Fax 265-1822
www.ncsd.k12.ca.us
Deer Creek ES 400/3-5
805 Lindley Ave 95959 530-265-1870
Susan Barry, prin. Fax 265-1876
Gold Run ES 200/K-2
470 Searls Ave 95959 530-265-1860
Kate Wiley, prin. Fax 265-1866
Nevada City ES 200/K-2
505 Main St 95959 530-265-1830
Teena Corker, prin. Fax 265-1832
Seven Hills IS 500/6-8
700 Hoover Ln 95959 530-265-1840
Joe Limov, prin. Fax 265-1846

Twin Ridges ESD 100/K-8
16661 Old Mill Rd 95959 530-265-9052
Joan Little, supt. Fax 265-3049
www.tresd.k12.ca.us
Grizzly Hill S 100/K-8
16661 Old Mill Rd 95959 530-265-9052
Joan Little, prin. Fax 265-3049
Other Schools – See Washington

Echo Ridge Christian S 50/K-8
15504 Liberty Cir 95959 530-265-2057
Sara Griesert, prin. Fax 265-2045
Sierra Christian S 100/PK-7
PO Box 268 95959 530-265-5890
Jeff Patton, admin. Fax 265-3384

Newark, Alameda, Pop. 41,956
Newark USD 7,100/PK-12
5715 Musick Ave 94560 510-818-4100
Kevin Harrigan, supt. Fax 794-2199
www.nusd.k12.ca.us
Bunker ES 600/K-6
6071 Smith Ave 94560 510-818-3100
Robert Chamberlin, prin. Fax 792-5624
Graham ES 500/K-6
36270 Cherry St 94560 510-818-3300
Peter Parenti, prin. Fax 494-0582
Kennedy ES 500/K-6
35430 Blackburn Dr 94560 510-818-3400
Kathleen Waffle, prin. Fax 793-1579
Lincoln ES 300/K-6
36111 Bettencourt St 94560 510-818-3500
Pamela Hughes, prin. Fax 793-3446
Milani ES 400/K-6
37490 Birch St 94560 510-818-3600
LaKimbre Brown, prin. Fax 793-2437
Musick ES 500/K-6
5735 Musick Ave 94560 510-818-4000
Debbie Ashmore, prin. Fax 791-5792
Newark JHS 1,100/7-8
6201 Lafayette Ave 94560 510-818-3000
Catherine Ward-Mikes, prin. Fax 794-2079
Schilling ES 500/K-6
36901 Spruce St 94560 510-818-3800
Nicole Paredes, prin. Fax 791-9203
Snow ES 400/K-6
6580 Mirabeau Dr 94560 510-818-3900
Jan Schmitt, prin. Fax 791-8942
Whiteford S PK-PK
35725 Cedar Blvd 94560 510-818-3232
Anjanette Pelletier, dir. Fax 818-3242

Challenger S - Ardenwood 1,000/PK-8
35487 Dumbarton Ct 94560 510-739-0300
Joey Morrison, hdmstr. Fax 739-1796
Challenger S - Newark 400/PK-K
39600 Cedar Blvd 94560 510-770-1771
Maria Jayne, dir.

St. Edward S 300/K-8
5788 Thornton Ave 94560 510-793-7242
Sr. Diane Aruda, prin. Fax 793-3189

Newbury Park, See Thousand Oaks
Conejo Valley USD
Supt. — See Thousand Oaks
Banyan ES 500/K-5
1120 Knollwood Dr 91320 805-498-6641
Sally Wennes, prin. Fax 375-6626
Cypress ES 500/K-5
4200 Kimber Dr 91320 805-498-6683
Judie Tetzlaff, prin. Fax 375-5600
Environmental Academy of Research Tech K-5
2626 Michael Dr 91320 805-408-3686
Jennifer Boone, prin.
Maple ES 400/K-5
3501 Kimber Dr 91320 805-498-6748
Christina Palmer, prin. Fax 375-5603
Sequoia MS 1,200/6-8
2855 Borchard Rd 91320 805-498-3617
Vivian Vina-Hunt, prin. Fax 375-5605
Sycamore Canyon S 1,300/K-8
4601 Via Rio 91320 805-498-1573
Jon Sand, prin. Fax 498-0385
Walnut ES 400/K-5
581 Dena Dr 91320 805-498-3608
Linda Hensley, prin. Fax 375-5604

Conejo Adventist S 100/K-8
1250 Academy Dr 91320 805-498-2391
Phil Hudema, prin. Fax 498-1816

Newcastle, Placer
Loomis UNESD
Supt. — See Loomis
Ophir S 200/K-8
1373 Lozanos Rd 95658 530-885-3495
Mary Zaun, prin. Fax 823-9101

Newcastle ESD 200/K-8
8951 Valley View Dr 95658 916-663-3307
Kathleen Daugherty, supt. Fax 663-3524
www.newcastle.k12.ca.us
Newcastle S 200/K-8
8951 Valley View Dr 95658 916-663-3307
Kathleen Daugherty, prin. Fax 663-3524

New Cuyama, Santa Barbara
Cuyama JUSD 300/K-12
PO Box 271 93254 661-766-2482
Jan Hensley, supt. Fax 766-2255
Cuyama S 200/K-8
PO Box 271 93254 661-766-2642
Jan Hensley, prin. Fax 766-2244

Newhall, See Santa Clarita
Newhall ESD
Supt. — See Valencia
McGrath ES 600/K-6
21501 Deputy Jake Dr 91321 661-291-4090
Larry Heath, prin. Fax 291-4091
Newhall ES 700/K-6
24607 Walnut St 91321 661-291-4010
Tim Lankford, prin. Fax 291-4011
Peachland Avenue ES 600/K-6
24800 Peachland Ave 91321 661-291-4020
Sarah Johnson, prin. Fax 291-4021
Wiley Canyon ES 700/K-6
24240 La Glorita Cir 91321 661-291-4030
Alexis Yannich, prin. Fax 291-4031

Sulphur Springs UNESD
Supt. — See Canyon Country
Valley View Community ES 800/K-6
19414 Sierra Estates Dr 91321 661-251-2000
Rick Drew, prin. Fax 298-5428

William S. Hart UNHSD
Supt. — See Santa Clarita
Placerita JHS 1,000/7-8
25015 Newhall Ave 91321 661-259-1551
Mike Kuhlman, prin. Fax 287-9748

Little Light Preschool 100/PK-PK
24551 Valley St 91321 661-259-1515
Cori Hanes, admin. Fax 259-9525

Newman, Stanislaus, Pop. 9,623
Newman-Crows Landing USD 2,900/K-12
890 Main St 95360 209-862-2933
Rick Fauss, supt. Fax 862-0113
www.nclusd.k12.ca.us/
Hunt ES 500/K-5
907 R St 95360 209-862-1020
Justin Pruett, prin. Fax 862-0579
Von Renner ES 700/K-5
1388 Patchett Dr 95360 209-862-2868
Audry Garza, prin. Fax 862-3639
Yolo MS 500/6-8
901 Hoyer Rd 95360 209-862-2984
Dan Cope, prin. Fax 862-3734
Other Schools – See Crows Landing

Newport Beach, Orange, Pop. 79,834
Newport - Mesa USD
Supt. — See Costa Mesa
Andersen ES 500/K-6
1900 Port Seabourne Way 92660 949-515-6935
Mary Manos, prin. Fax 515-6821
Eastbluff ES 400/K-6
2627 Vista Del Oro 92660 949-515-5920
Cheryl Beck, prin. Fax 515-6848
Ensign IS 1,200/7-8
2000 Cliff Dr 92663 949-515-6910
Steve McLaughlin, prin. Fax 515-3370
Mariners ES 600/K-6
2100 Mariners Dr 92660 949-515-6960
Pam Coughlin, prin. Fax 515-6801
Newport ES 400/K-6
1327 W Balboa Blvd 92661 949-515-6965
Amy Nagy, prin. Fax 515-6831
Newport Heights ES 600/K-6
300 E 15th St 92663 949-515-6970
Kurt Suhr, prin. Fax 515-6871

Carden Hall 500/K-8
1541 Monrovia Ave 92663 949-645-1773
Cicek Chek, prin. Fax 645-3782
Our Lady Queen of Angels S 400/PK-8
750 Domingo Dr 92660 949-644-1166
Eileen Ryan, prin. Fax 644-6213

Newport Coast, Orange
Newport - Mesa USD
Supt. — See Costa Mesa
Newport Coast ES 700/K-6
6655 Ridge Park Rd 92657 949-515-6975
Rich Rodriguez, prin. Fax 515-6881

Nicasio, Marin
Nicasio ESD 100/K-8
PO Box 711 94946 415-662-2184
Stephen Rosenthal, supt. Fax 662-2250
www.nicasioschool.org/
Nicasio S 100/K-8
PO Box 711 94946 415-662-2184
Christy Stocker, prin. Fax 662-2250

Niland, Imperial, Pop. 1,183
Calipatria USD
Supt. — See Calipatria
Smith ES 100/K-5
PO Box 1005 92257 760-348-0636
Linda Aleksick, prin. Fax 359-3612

Nipomo, San Luis Obispo, Pop. 7,109
Lucia Mar USD
Supt. — See Arroyo Grande
Dana ES 600/K-6
920 W Tefft St 93444 805-474-3790
Paul Jarvis, prin. Fax 473-5521
Lange ES 600/K-6
1661 Via Alta Mesa 93444 805-474-3670
Jeff Madrigal, prin. Fax 473-4303
Nipomo ES 400/K-6
190 E Price St 93444 805-474-3780
Ron Walton, prin. Fax 473-4229

Highland Preparatory S 100/K-12
747 Live Oak Ridge Rd 93444 805-929-4059
Kristin Holder, admin. Fax 929-1837

Norco, Riverside, Pop. 26,960
Corona-Norco USD 50,900/K-12
2820 Clark Ave 92860 951-736-5000
Kent Bechler Ph.D., supt. Fax 736-5016
www.cnusd.k12.ca.us
Highland ES 1,000/K-6
2301 Alhambra St 92860 951-736-3308
Keith Adams, prin. Fax 736-3488
Norco ES 700/K-6
1700 Temescal Ave 92860 951-736-3348
Amy Shainman, prin. Fax 736-7145
Norco IS 700/7-8
2711 Temescal Ave 92860 951-736-3206
Teri Dudley, prin. Fax 736-3208
Riverview ES 600/K-6
4600 Pedley Ave 92860 951-736-3245
Russ Marsh, prin. Fax 736-3341
Sierra Vista ES 600/K-6
3560 Corona Ave 92860 951-736-3311
Doris Hust, prin. Fax 736-7154
Washington ES 1,100/K-6
1220 Parkridge Ave 92860 951-736-3326
Bonita Barnett, prin. Fax 736-3479
Other Schools – See Corona, Mira Loma

New Life Christian S 100/K-8
PO Box 6166 92860 951-734-7032
Debra Panetta, admin.

North Edwards, Kern, Pop. 1,259
Muroc JUSD 1,500/K-12
17100 Foothill Ave 93523 760-769-4821
Robert Challinor, supt. Fax 769-4241
www.muroc.k12.ca.us
Other Schools – See Boron, Edwards

North Fork, Madera
Chawanakee USD 600/K-12
PO Box 400 93643 559-877-6209
Dr. Stephen Foster, supt. Fax 877-2065
www.chawanakee.k12.ca.us
North Fork Digital MS 6-8
33087 Road 228 93643 559-877-2215
Stuart Pincus, prin. Fax 877-2377
North Fork ES 50/K-5
33087 Road 228 93643 559-877-2215
Stuart Pincus, prin. Fax 877-2377
Other Schools – See O Neals

North Highlands, Sacramento, Pop. 44,600
Twin Rivers USD
Supt. — See Mc Clellan
Aero Haven ES 400/K-6
5450 Georgia Dr 95660 916-566-1800
Karen Snyder, prin. Fax 331-2316
Allison ES 400/K-6
4315 Don Julio Blvd 95660 916-566-1810
Vivian Riley, prin. Fax 332-3597
Highlands Academy of Arts & Design West 7-8
6444 Walerga Rd 95660 916-286-1800
Heather Westerman, prin. Fax 286-1871
Hillsdale ES 400/K-6
6469 Guthrie St 95660 916-566-1860
Ken Gammelgard, prin. Fax 339-2033

Joyce ES 400/K-6
6050 Watt Ave 95660 916-556-1880
Kelli Hanson, prin. Fax 344-5835
Kohler ES 400/K-6
4004 Bruce Way 95660 916-566-1850
Kelly Grashoff, prin. Fax 334-6320
Larchmont ES 300/K-6
6560 Melrose Dr 95660 916-566-1890
Doretha Hayes, prin. Fax 332-6188
Madison ES 500/K-6
5241 Harrison St 95660 916-566-1900
Jana Fields, prin. Fax 331-1071
Oakdale ES 400/K-6
3708 Myrtle Ave 95660 916-566-1910
Linda Kyle, prin. Fax 339-2031
Sierra View ES 400/K-6
3638 Bainbridge Dr 95660 916-566-1960
John Baggett, prin. Fax 331-0643
Village ES 400/K-6
6845 Larchmont Dr 95660 916-566-1970
Fax 332-0823

New Testament Christian S 50/PK-1
6746 34th St 95660 916-344-6463
Karin Green, dir. Fax 344-3246

North Hills, Los Angeles
Los Angeles USD
Supt. — See Los Angeles
Parthenia ES 700/K-5
16825 Napa St 91343 818-891-6955
Marcia Jackman, prin. Fax 892-7467

Centers of Learning 100/PK-12
PO Box 2037 91393 818-894-3213
Debra Grill, prin. Fax 893-8074
Holy Martyrs Armenian S 200/PK-5
16617 Parthenia St 91343 818-892-7991
John Kossakian, dir. Fax 892-5044
Valley Presbyterian S 300/PK-6
9240 Haskell Ave 91343 818-894-3674
Claudia Moreland, prin. Fax 893-3754

North Hollywood, See Los Angeles
Los Angeles USD
Supt. — See Los Angeles
Arminta ES 800/K-5
11530 Strathern St 91605 818-765-5911
Yolanda Guerra, prin. Fax 764-9648
Bellingham Primary Center 200/K-K
6728 Bellingham Ave 91606 818-759-0119
Jesus Limon, prin. Fax 759-0181
Burbank ES 400/K-5
12215 Albers St 91607 818-763-6497
Andrea R. Gordon, prin. Fax 763-1431
Camellia Avenue ES 1,100/K-5
7451 Camellia Ave 91605 818-765-5255
Dora M. Baxter, prin. Fax 765-4909
Coldwater Canyon Avenue ES 1,100/K-5
6850 Coldwater Canyon Ave 91605 818-765-6634
Lydia Stephens, prin. Fax 982-1387
Fair Avenue ES 1,400/K-5
6501 Fair Ave 91606 818-761-5444
Rosalba Manrique, prin. Fax 762-5316
Lankershim ES 600/K-5
5250 Bakman Ave 91601 818-769-3130
Sophia Mendoza, prin. Fax 769-2802
Madison MS 2,300/6-8
13000 Hart St 91605 818-255-5200
Estelle Baptiste, prin. Fax 765-4692
Monlux ES 700/K-5
6051 Bellaire Ave 91606 818-763-4693
Alma Flores, prin. Fax 762-7509
Oxnard Street ES 600/K-5
10912 Oxnard St 91606 818-762-3397
Kay Jeffries, prin. Fax 753-4935
Reed MS 2,000/6-8
4525 Irvine Ave 91602 818-487-7600
Donna Tobin, prin. Fax 766-9069
Rio Vista ES 400/K-5
4243 Satsuma Ave 91602 818-761-6147
Marlene Breitenbach, prin. Fax 508-8158
Romer MS 6-8
6501 Laurel Canyon Blvd 91606 818-505-2200
John McLaughlin, prin. Fax 761-9343
Saticoy ES 700/K-5
7850 Ethel Ave 91605 818-765-0783
Roger Avila, prin. Fax 503-4781
Sendak ES 700/K-5
11414 Tiara St 91601 818-509-3400
Nancy Oda, prin. Fax 487-3727
Strathern ES 1,000/K-5
7939 Saint Clair Ave 91605 818-765-4234
Linda Mae Williams, prin. Fax 764-5912
Toluca Lake ES 500/K-5
4840 Cahuenga Blvd 91601 818-761-3339
Carol Bove, prin. Fax 761-7197
Victory ES 900/K-5
6315 Radford Ave 91606 818-761-4676
Michelle Diamond, prin. Fax 769-2729

Campbell Hall S 1,100/K-12
4533 Laurel Canyon Blvd 91607 818-980-7280
Rev. Julian Bull, hdmstr. Fax 505-5362
Country S 200/PK-8
5243 Laurel Canyon Blvd 91607 818-769-2473
Joseph Perez, hdmstr. Fax 752-3097
Laurel Hall S 600/PK-8
11919 Oxnard St 91606 818-763-5434
Kathleen Haworth, prin. Fax 509-6979
Messiah Lutheran S 100/K-8
12020 Cantara St 91605 818-768-8375
Chris Treder, prin. Fax 768-8375
Oakwood S 300/K-6
11230 Moorpark St 91602 818-752-4444
Dr. James Astman, hdmstr. Fax 752-4466
Or Hachaim Academy 100/K-6
6021 Laurel Canyon Blvd 91606 818-505-1614
Amram Gabay, admin.
St. Charles Borromeo S 200/K-8
10850 Moorpark St 91602 818-508-5359
Jayne Quinn, prin. Fax 508-4511
St. Jane Frances De Chantal S 300/PK-8
12950 Hamlin St 91606 818-766-1714
Edgar Sedano, prin. Fax 766-5372
St. Patrick S 200/PK-8
10626 Erwin St 91606 818-761-7363
Rosselle Azar, prin. Fax 761-6349
St. Paul's First Lutheran S 100/K-8
11330 McCormick St 91601 818-763-2892
Rendell Koeppel, prin. Fax 487-1378
Summit View S 200/1-12
6455 Coldwater Canyon Ave 91606 818-623-6300
Nancy Rosenfelt, dir.
Wesley S 200/K-8
4832 Tujunga Ave 91601 818-508-4542
Ruth Glass, hdmstr. Fax 508-4570

Northridge, See Los Angeles
Los Angeles USD
Supt. — See Los Angeles
Andasol ES 500/K-5
10126 Encino Ave 91325 818-349-8631
Charleen Curry, prin. Fax 886-7156
Balboa Gifted High Ability Magnet ES 700/1-5
17020 Labrador St 91325 818-349-4801
Rajinder Schindl, prin. Fax 993-3470
Beckford ES 600/K-5
19130 Tulsa St 91326 818-360-1924
Barbara Friedrich, prin. Fax 832-9831
Calahan ES 500/K-5
18722 Knapp St 91324 818-886-4612
Liane Jacob, prin. Fax 886-0760
Castlebay Lane ES 800/K-5
19010 Castlebay Ln 91326 818-360-1908
Vivian K. Ihori, prin. Fax 831-5492
Darby Avenue ES 500/K-5
10818 Darby Ave 91326 818-360-1824
Virginia Ghoniem, prin. Fax 832-9761
Dearborn ES 500/K-5
9240 Wish Ave 91325 818-349-4381
Debra Hirsch, prin. Fax 886-2149
Holmes MS 1,500/6-8
9351 Paso Robles Ave 91325 818-678-4100
Gregory Vallone, prin. Fax 886-3358
Lorne Street ES 600/K-5
17440 Lorne St 91325 818-342-3123
Sharon Kaiser, prin. Fax 705-0860
Napa Street ES 700/K-5
19010 Napa St 91324 818-885-1441
Susan Babit, prin. Fax 993-4824
Nobel MS 2,400/6-8
9950 Tampa Ave 91324 818-773-4700
Bob Coburn, prin. Fax 701-9480
Northridge MS 1,200/6-8
17960 Chase St 91325 818-678-5100
Deborah Wiltz, prin. Fax 885-1461
Topeka Drive ES 500/K-5
9815 Topeka Dr 91324 818-886-2266
Chiae Byun-Kitayama, prin. Fax 885-7682

Casa Montessori 100/PK-6
17633 Lassen St 91325 818-886-7922
Sakura Long, prin. Fax 886-7923
First Lutheran Christian S 100/K-8
18355 Roscoe Blvd 91325 818-885-1655
Sheree Spraglin, dir. Fax 885-6483
First Presbyterian Weekday S 200/PK-5
10400 Zelzah Ave 91326 818-368-7254
Marylou Pennington, dir. Fax 832-0295
Heschel Day S 400/PK-8
17701 Devonshire St 91325 818-368-5781
Betty Winn, hdmstr. Fax 363-3860
Highland Hall Waldorf S 400/PK-12
17100 Superior St 91325 818-349-1394
Ed Eadon, hdmstr. Fax 349-2390
New Heights Preparatory School 100/3-12
8756 Canby Ave 91325 818-993-3800
Igaal Barak, dir.
Northridge Community S 100/K-12
8212 Louise Ave 91325 818-776-2440
Karen Richardson, admin.
Our Lady of Lourdes S 300/K-8
18437 Superior St 91325 818-349-0245
Patricia Hager, prin. Fax 349-4156
Pinecrest S 600/PK-8
17081 Devonshire St 91325 818-368-7241
Janice Rudd, dir. Fax 363-9768
St. Nicholas S 300/PK-8
9501 Balboa Blvd 91325 818-886-6751
Helen Kamenos, prin. Fax 886-3933
San Fernando Valley Academy 200/PK-12
17601 Lassen St 91325 818-349-1373
Fax 773-6353

Norwalk, Los Angeles, Pop. 105,834
Little Lake City SD
Supt. — See Santa Fe Springs
Cresson ES 400/K-5
11650 Cresson St 90650 562-868-6620
Tannie Wise, prin. Fax 868-2454
Lakeland ES 400/K-5
11224 Bombardier Ave 90650 562-868-8887
Yolanda McIntosh, prin. Fax 868-0247
Lakeside MS 800/6-8
11000 Kenney St 90650 562-868-9422
David Grant, prin. Fax 863-9252
Orr ES 500/K-5
12130 Jersey Ave 90650 562-868-7988
Sonya Cuellar, prin. Fax 863-2518
Paddison ES 500/K-5
12100 Crewe St 90650 562-868-7741
Ana Gutirrez, prin. Fax 864-1591
Studebaker ES 500/K-5
11800 Halcourt Ave 90650 562-868-7882
Yvette Sugino, prin. Fax 929-0092

Norwalk-La Mirada USD 21,400/PK-12
12820 Pioneer Blvd 90650 562-868-0431
Ruth Perez Ed.D., supt. Fax 864-9857
www.nlmusd.k12.ca.us
Chavez ES 500/K-5
12110 Walnut St 90650 562-868-3565
Bob Rayburn, prin. Fax 863-8193
Corvallis MS 1,000/6-8
11032 Leffingwell Rd 90650 562-868-2678
Bob Easton, prin. Fax 863-4755
Dolland ES 800/K-5
15021 Bloomfield Ave 90650 562-921-9934
Bart McNeil, prin. Fax 404-4302
Edmondson ES 400/K-5
15121 Grayland Ave 90650 562-864-9501
Jacob Muniz, prin. Fax 929-4861
Glazier ES 600/K-5
10932 Excelsior Dr 90650 562-863-8796
Kristine Cvar, prin. Fax 863-8797
Johnston ES 600/K-5
13421 Fairford Ave 90650 562-864-2508
Veronica Lizardi, prin. Fax 868-5799
Lampton ES 600/K-5
14716 Elmcroft Ave 90650 562-462-9273
Cindy Rayburn, prin. Fax 484-0223
Los Alisos MS 1,000/6-8
14800 Jersey Ave 90650 562-868-0865
Ligia Hallstrom, prin. Fax 864-2967
Moffitt ES 800/K-5
13323 Goller Ave 90650 562-864-3071
Maureen Raul, prin. Fax 864-0471
Morrison ES 600/K-5
13510 Maidstone Ave 90650 562-868-9878
Marsha Guerrero, prin. Fax 868-9879
New River ES 700/K-5
13432 Halcourt Ave 90650 562-868-9848
Michelle Centeno, prin. Fax 868-0726
Nuffer ES 600/K-5
14821 Jersey Ave 90650 562-868-3788
Sherry Herrera, prin. Fax 868-5167
Ramona Preschool PK-PK
14616 Dinard Ave 90650 562-921-7610
Laurel Parker, dir. Fax 921-1605
Sanchez ES 500/K-5
11960 162nd St 90650 562-926-2365
Irene Mora, prin. Fax 926-2366
Waite MS 900/6-8
14320 Norwalk Blvd 90650 562-921-7981
Willie Norman, prin. Fax 921-8114
Other Schools – See La Mirada

New Harvest Christian S 200/PK-12
11364 Imperial Hwy 90650 562-929-6034
Sergio Romo, admin. Fax 484-3260
Norwalk Christian Academy 200/PK-8
11005 Foster Rd 90650 562-863-6282
Don Pettinger, supt. Fax 863-2394
Norwalk Christian S 100/PK-8
11129 Pioneer Blvd 90650 562-863-5751
Anna Hernandez, prin. Fax 862-5245
St. John of God S 300/PK-8
13817 Pioneer Blvd 90650 562-863-5721
Mary Pekarcik, prin. Fax 406-3927
St. Linus S 300/K-8
13913 Shoemaker Ave 90650 562-921-0336
Sr. Catherine Casey, prin. Fax 926-9077
Trinity Christian S 200/PK-8
11507 Studebaker Rd 90650 562-864-3712
Jeff Jepson, prin. Fax 864-1877

Novato, Marin, Pop. 50,335
Novato USD 7,500/K-12
1015 7th St 94945 415-897-4201
Jan La Torre-Derby, supt. Fax 898-5790
do.nusd.org
Hamilton S 500/K-8
1 Main Gate Rd 94949 415-883-4691
Ruthanne Bexton, prin. Fax 883-2249
Hill MS 600/6-8
720 Diablo Ave 94947 415-893-1557
Chona Killeen, prin. Fax 898-3910
Loma Verde ES 400/K-5
399 Alameda De La Loma 94949 415-883-4681
Eileen Smith, prin. Fax 883-0834
Lu Sutton ES 400/K-5
1800 Center Rd 94947 415-897-3196
Suzanne Thompson, prin. Fax 897-7016
Lynwood ES 400/K-5
1320 Lynwood Dr 94947 415-897-4161
Ivy Morritt, prin. Fax 897-3322
Olive ES 400/K-5
629 Plum St 94945 415-897-2131
Lenard Banaag, prin. Fax 897-0931
Pleasant Valley ES 400/K-5
755 Sutro Ave 94947 415-897-5104
Terry Gavin-Brown, prin. Fax 897-5704
Rancho ES 500/K-5
1430 Johnson St 94947 415-897-3101
Fax 897-7492
San Jose MS 500/6-8
1000 Sunset Pkwy 94949 415-883-7831
Jeff King, prin. Fax 883-0624
San Ramon ES 500/K-5
45 San Ramon Way 94945 415-897-1196
Mary Pritchard, prin. Fax 897-2326
Sinaloa MS 600/6-8
2045 Vineyard Rd 94947 415-897-2111
Kit Gabbard, prin. Fax 892-1201

Good Shepherd Lutheran S 100/K-6
1180 Lynwood Dr 94947 415-897-2510
Carol Wise, admin. Fax 892-0663

Marin Christian Academy 200/PK-8
1370 S Novato Blvd 94947 415-892-5713
Christopher Mychajluk, prin. Fax 892-1818
North Bay Christian Academy 100/K-12
6965 Redwood Blvd 94945 415-892-8921
Pam Carraher, prin. Fax 893-1750
Our Lady of Loretto S 200/K-8
1811 Virginia Ave 94945 415-892-8621
Sue Maino, prin. Fax 892-9631

Nuevo, Riverside, Pop. 3,010
Nuview UNESD 1,600/K-8
29780 Lakeview Ave 92567 951-928-0066
Jay Hoffman, supt. Fax 928-0324
www.nuview.k12.ca.us
Mountain Shadows MS 600/6-8
30401 Reservoir Ave 92567 951-928-3836
Jeff Simmons, prin. Fax 928-3015
Nuview ES 500/K-5
29680 Lakeview Ave 92567 951-928-0201
Thomas Seigel, prin. Fax 928-9171
Valley View ES 500/K-5
21220 Maurice St 92567 951-928-1841
David Pyle, prin. Fax 928-9581

Oakdale, Stanislaus, Pop. 18,561
Oakdale JUSD 5,200/K-12
168 S 3rd Ave 95361 209-848-4884
Fred Rich, supt. Fax 847-0155
www.oakdale.k12.ca.us
Cloverland ES 500/K-6
201 Johnson Ave 95361 209-847-4276
Stacey Aprile, prin. Fax 847-9059
Fair Oaks ES 800/K-6
151 N Lee Ave 95361 209-847-0391
David Kindred, prin. Fax 847-9067
Magnolia ES 600/K-6
739 Magnolia St 95361 209-847-3056
Julie Minabe, prin. Fax 848-0815
Oakdale JHS 800/7-8
400 S Maag Ave 95361 209-847-2294
John Simons, prin. Fax 847-8521
Sierra View ES 700/K-6
1323 E J St 95361 209-848-4200
Terri Taylor, prin. Fax 848-4203

Oakhurst, Madera, Pop. 2,602
Bass Lake JUNESD 1,000/K-8
40096 Indian Springs Rd 93644 559-642-1555
Glenn Reid, supt. Fax 642-1556
www.basslakeschooldistrict.com/
Oak Creek IS 200/6-8
40094 Indian Springs Rd 93644 559-642-1570
Kirk Huckabone, prin. Fax 683-7279
Oakhurst ES 300/K-5
49495 Road 427 93644 559-642-1580
Kathy Murphy, prin. Fax 642-1584
Other Schools – See Ahwahnee, Bass Lake, Yosemite National Park

Yosemite USD 2,400/K-12
50200 Road 427 93644 559-683-8801
Steve Raupp, supt. Fax 683-4160
www.yosemiteusd.com/
Other Schools – See Coarsegold

Oakhurst Adventist S 50/1-8
50690 Rd 426 93644 559-683-7020
Gayla Rumble, prin. Fax 683-7020

Oakland, Alameda, Pop. 395,274
Oakland USD 40,000/PK-12
1025 2nd Ave 94606 510-879-8200
Dr. Roberta Mayor, supt. Fax 879-8800
www.ousd.k12.ca.us/
Acorn Woodland ES 300/K-5
1025 81st Ave 94621 510-879-0190
Kimi Kean, prin. Fax 879-0199
Allendale ES 400/K-5
3670 Penniman Ave 94619 510-879-1010
Steven Thomasberger, prin. Fax 879-1019
Alliance Academy 200/6-7
1800 98th Ave 94603 510-879-2733
Yvette Renteria, prin. Fax 879-2025
Ascend S 300/K-8
3709 E 12th St 94601 510-879-3140
Larissa Adam, prin. Fax 879-3149
Bella Vista ES 500/K-5
1025 E 28th St 94610 510-879-1020
Shannon Yip, prin. Fax 879-1027
Brewer MS 700/6-8
3748 13th Ave 94610 510-879-2100
Jamie Marantz, prin. Fax 879-2109
Bridges Academy 400/K-5
1325 53rd Ave 94601 510-879-1410
Clara Tarango, prin. Fax 879-1419
Brookfield Village ES 500/K-5
401 Jones Ave 94603 510-879-1030
Adam Taylor, prin. Fax 879-1039
Burckhalter ES 200/K-5
3994 Burckhalter Ave 94605 510-879-1050
Carin Geathers, prin. Fax 879-1059
Chabot ES 500/K-5
6686 Chabot Rd 94618 510-879-1060
Jonathan Mayer, prin. Fax 879-1069
Claremont MS 400/6-8
5750 College Ave 94618 510-879-2010
David Chambliss, prin. Fax 879-2019
Cleveland ES 300/K-5
745 Cleveland St 94606 510-879-1080
Mia Settles, prin. Fax 879-1089
Cole MS 200/7-8
1011 Union St 94607 510-879-1090
Ivory Brooks, prin. Fax 879-1099
Coliseum College Prep Academy 200/6-8
1390 66th Ave 94621 510-879-2456
Aaron Townsend, prin. Fax 879-2453
Community United ES 400/K-4
6701 International Blvd 94621 510-879-1340
Patricia Ceja, prin. Fax 879-1349
Crocker Highlands ES 300/K-5
525 Midcrest Rd 94610 510-879-1110
Fax 879-1119
East Oakland Pride ES 400/K-4
8000 Birch St 94621 510-879-1620
Viet Nguyen, prin. Fax 879-1629
Elmhurst Community Prep MS 200/6-8
1800 98th Ave 94603 510-879-2021
Matthew Duffy, prin. Fax 879-2029
Emerson ES 200/K-5
4803 Lawton Ave 94609 510-879-1150
Wendy Caporicci, prin. Fax 879-1159
Encompass Academy 200/K-4
1025 81st Ave 94621 510-879-0207
Minh-Tram Nguyen, prin. Fax 879-0209
Esperanza Academy 300/K-5
10315 E St 94603 510-879-1551
Sondra Aguilera, prin. Fax 879-1559
Explore College Prep MS 300/6-8
3550 64th Ave 94605 510-879-1040
Michael Scott, prin. Fax 879-1049
Franklin ES 700/K-5
915 Foothill Blvd 94606 510-879-1160
Jeanette MacDonald, prin. Fax 879-1164
Frick MS 600/6-8
2845 64th Ave 94605 510-879-2030
Jerome Gourdine, prin. Fax 879-2039
Fruitvale ES 600/K-5
3200 Boston Ave 94602 510-879-1170
Terry Edwards, prin. Fax 879-1179
Futures ES 400/K-4
6701 International Blvd 94621 510-636-0520
Steven Daubenspeck, prin. Fax 879-1349
Garfield ES 700/K-5
1640 22nd Ave 94606 510-879-1180
Michael Rothhammer, prin. Fax 879-1189
Glenview ES 400/K-5
4215 La Cresta Ave 94602 510-879-1190
Deitra Atkins, prin. Fax 879-1199
Global Family ES 400/K-4
2035 40th Ave 94601 510-879-1280
Reyna Diaz, prin. Fax 879-1289
Grass Valley ES 200/K-5
4720 Dunkirk Ave 94605 510-879-1220
Rosella Jackson, prin. Fax 879-1229
Greenleaf ES 400/K-4
6328 E 17th St 94621 510-879-1630
Monica Thomas, prin. Fax 879-1639
Harte MS 900/6-8
3700 Coolidge Ave 94602 510-879-2060
Teresa Williams, prin. Fax 879-2069
Hillcrest S 300/K-8
30 Marguerite Dr 94618 510-879-1270
Beverly Rothenberg, prin. Fax 879-1279
Hoover ES 300/K-5
890 Brockhurst St 94608 510-879-1700
LaResha Martin-Smith, prin. Fax 879-1709
Howard ES 300/K-5
8755 Fontaine St 94605 510-879-1660
Carolyn Howard, prin. Fax 879-1669
International Community S 200/PK-5
2825 International Blvd 94601 510-879-4286
Karen Monroe, prin. Fax 879-4287
Jefferson ES 100/5-5
2035 40th Ave 94601 510-879-1280
Reyna Diaz, prin. Fax 879-1289
Kaiser ES 200/K-5
25 S Hill Ct 94618 510-879-1710
Mel Stenger, prin. Fax 879-1719
King ES 300/K-4
960 10th St 94607 510-879-1820
Patricia Washington, prin. Fax 879-1829
Korematsu Discovery Academy 300/K-5
10315 E St 94603 510-879-2795
Charles Wilson, prin. Fax 879-2798
La Escuelita ES 300/K-5
1100 3rd Ave 94606 510-879-1210
Tammy Rose, prin. Fax 879-1216
Lafayette ES 300/K-5
1700 Market St 94607 510-879-1290
Karen Haynes, prin. Fax 879-1299
Lakeview ES 300/K-5
746 Grand Ave 94610 510-879-1300
Clara Roberts, prin. Fax 879-1309
Laurel ES 500/K-5
3750 Brown Ave 94619 510-879-1310
Ron Smith, prin. Fax 879-1319
Lazear ES 300/K-5
824 29th Ave 94601 510-879-1320
Pia Jara, prin. Fax 879-1329
Learning Without Limits ES 400/K-4
2035 40th Ave 94601 510-879-1282
Leo Fuchs, prin. Fax 879-1289
Lincoln ES 600/K-5
225 11th St 94607 510-879-1330
John Melvin, prin. Fax 879-1339
Lockwood ES 500/5-5
6701 International Blvd 94621 510-879-1340
Pati Ceja, prin. Fax 879-1349
Madison MS 300/6-8
400 Capistrano Dr 94603 510-879-2150
Lucinda Taylor, prin. Fax 879-2159
Mann ES 300/K-5
5222 Ygnacio Ave 94601 510-879-1360
Alanna Lim, prin. Fax 879-1369
Manzanita Community S 300/K-5
2409 E 27th St 94601 510-879-1370
Eyana Spencer, prin. Fax 879-1379
Manzanita SEED ES 200/K-5
2409 E 27th St 94601 510-879-1373
Katherine Carter, prin. Fax 879-0139
Markham ES 400/K-5
7220 Krause Ave 94605 510-879-1380
Pam Booker, prin. Fax 879-1389
Marshall ES 200/K-5
3400 Malcolm Ave 94605 510-879-1740
Maya Woods-Cadiz, prin. Fax 879-1749
Maxwell Park International Academy 300/K-5
4730 Fleming Ave 94619 510-879-1390
Mary Louise-Newling, prin. Fax 879-1399
Melrose Leadership Academy 200/6-8
5328 Brann St 94619 510-879-1530
Moyra Contreras, prin. Fax 879-1539
Miller ES 300/K-5
5525 Ascot Dr 94611 510-879-1420
Ifeoma Obodozie, prin. Fax 879-1429
Montclair ES 300/K-5
1757 Mountain Blvd 94611 510-879-1430
Nancy Bloom, prin. Fax 879-1439
Montera JHS 900/6-8
5555 Ascot Dr 94611 510-879-2110
Russom Mesfun, prin. Fax 879-2119
Munck ES 300/K-5
11900 Campus Dr 94619 510-879-1680
Denise Burroughs, prin. Fax 879-1689
New Highland Academy 300/K-5
8521 A St 94621 510-879-1260
Liz Ozol, prin. Fax 879-1269
Parker ES 300/K-5
7929 Ney Ave 94605 510-879-1440
Deborah Davis, prin. Fax 879-1449
Peralta Creek MS 200/8-8
2101 35th Ave 94601 510-879-2051
Greg McNamara, prin. Fax 879-2059
Peralta ES 200/K-5
460 63rd St 94609 510-879-1450
Rosette Costello, prin. Fax 879-1459
Piedmont Avenue ES 300/K-5
4314 Piedmont Ave 94611 510-879-1460
Zarina Ahmad, prin. Fax 879-1469
Prep Literary Acad Cultural Excellence 300/K-5
920 Campbell St 94607 510-879-1470
Enomwoyi Booker, prin. Fax 879-1479
Reach Academy 200/K-5
9860 Sunnyside St 94603 510-879-1100
Mishaa Degraw, prin. Fax 879-1109
Redwood Heights ES 300/K-5
4401 39th Ave 94619 510-879-1480
Fax 879-1489
Rise Academy 300/K-5
8521 A St 94621 510-879-2487
Connie Tillman, prin. Fax 879-1263
Roosevelt MS 800/6-8
1926 E 19th St 94606 510-879-2120
Theresa Clincy, prin. Fax 879-2129
ROOTS International Academy 200/6-7
1390 66th Ave 94621 510-879-2625
Brandee Stewart, prin. Fax 879-2078
Sankofa Academy 100/K-5
581 61st St 94609 510-879-1610
Danielle Neves, prin. Fax 879-1619
Santa Fe ES 300/K-5
915 54th St 94608 510-879-1500
Carol Johnson, prin. Fax 879-1507
Sequoia ES 300/K-5
3730 Lincoln Ave 94602 510-879-1510
Kyla Johnson-Trammel, prin. Fax 879-1519
Sobrante Park ES 300/K-5
470 El Paseo Dr 94603 510-879-1540
Marco Franco, prin. Fax 879-1549
Think College Now 300/K-5
2825 International Blvd 94601 510-879-1490
David Silver, prin. Fax 879-5430
Thornhill ES 400/K-5
5880 Thornhill Dr 94611 510-879-1570
Sallyann Tomlin, prin. Fax 879-1579
United for Success Academy 200/6-7
2101 35th Ave 94601 510-879-1494
Phil Cotty, prin. Fax 879-1493
Urban Promise Academy 300/6-8
3031 E 18th St 94601 510-879-1640
Mark Triplett, prin. Fax 879-4297
Webster Academy 500/5-5
8000 Birch St 94621 510-394-9077
Fax 639-5532
Westlake MS 700/6-8
2629 Harrison St 94612 510-879-2130
Misha Karigaca, prin. Fax 879-2139
West Oakland MS 400/6-7
991 14th St 94607 510-879-2093
Seyana Mawusi, prin. Fax 879-8012
Whittier ES 500/5-5
6328 E 17th St 94621 510-879-1630
Fax 879-1639

ACTS Christian Academy 200/K-8
1034 66th Ave 94621 510-568-3333
Dr. Doris Limbrick, prin. Fax 568-4125
Archway S, 250 41st St 94611 100/K-8
Sarah Flowers, prin. 510-547-4747
Aurora S 100/K-5
40 Dulwich Rd 94618 510-428-2606
Reynaldo Almeida, hdmstr. Fax 428-9183
Beacon Day S 300/PK-8
2101 Livingston St 94606 510-436-4466
Richard Hof, hdmstr. Fax 437-2314
Bentley S 400/K-8
1 Hiller Dr 94618 510-843-2512
Arlene Hogan, hdmstr. Fax 843-5162
Head-Royce S 800/K-12
4315 Lincoln Ave 94602 510-531-1300
Paul Chapman Ph.D., hdmstr. Fax 531-2649
Morgan S for Girls 200/6-8
PO Box 9966 94613 510-632-6000
Sandra Luna, hdmstr. Fax 632-6301
Muhammad University of Islam 100/K-12
5277 Foothill Blvd 94601 510-436-0206
Salamah Muhammad, admin.
Northern Light S 100/K-8
3710 Dorisa Ave 94605 510-957-0570
Jennifer Diaz, admin.

Oakland Hebrew Day S 200/K-8
5500 Redwood Rd 94619 510-531-8600
Mark Shinar, dir. Fax 531-8686
Park Day S 300/K-8
370 43rd St 94609 510-653-0317
Tom Little, dir. Fax 653-0637
Patten Academy of Christian Education 200/K-12
2433 Coolidge Ave 94601 510-533-3121
Sharon Anderson, prin. Fax 535-9381
Redwood Day S 400/K-8
3245 Sheffield Ave 94602 510-534-0800
Michael Riera, hdmstr. Fax 534-0806
St. Anthony S 100/K-8
1500 E 15th St 94606 510-534-3334
Sr. Barbara Flannery, prin. Fax 534-3378
St. Bernard S 100/K-8
1630 62nd Ave 94621 510-632-6323
Ellen Spencer, prin. Fax 632-6110
St. Elizabeth S 400/K-8
1516 33rd Ave 94601 510-532-7392
Sr. Rose Hennessy, prin. Fax 532-0321
St. Jarlath S 200/K-8
2634 Pleasant St 94602 510-532-4387
Kathy Capra, prin. Fax 532-1001
St. Lawrence O'Toole S 200/K-8
3695 High St 94619 510-530-0266
Barbara McCullough, prin. Fax 530-7568
St. Leo S 200/PK-8
4238 Howe St 94611 510-654-7828
Sonya Simril, prin. Fax 654-4057
St. Martin de Porres S 100/K-5
675 41st St 94609 510-652-2220
Sr. Barbara Dawson, pres. Fax 652-2294
St. Martin de Porres S 100/6-8
1630 10th St 94607 510-832-1757
Sr. Barbara Dawson, pres. Fax 832-6481
St. Paul's Episcopal S 400/K-8
116 Montecito Ave 94610 510-285-9600
Karan Merry, hdmstr. Fax 899-7297
St. Theresa S 300/K-8
4850 Clarewood Dr 94618 510-547-3146
Judy KoneffKlatt, prin. Fax 547-3253

Oakley, Contra Costa, Pop. 27,177
Antioch USD
Supt. — See Antioch
Orchard Park ES 800/K-5
5150 Live Oak Ave 94561 925-779-7445
Ed Dacus, prin. Fax 679-2639

Oakley UNESD 4,500/K-8
91 Mercedes Ln 94561 925-625-0700
Richard Rogers Ed.D., supt. Fax 625-1863
www.ouesd.k12.ca.us
Delta Vista MS 900/6-8
4901 Frank Hengel Way 94561 925-625-6840
Greg Hetrick, prin. Fax 625-6850
Gehringer ES 600/K-5
100 Simoni Ranch Rd 94561 925-625-7070
Maria Bordanaro, prin. Fax 625-6356
Iron House ES 400/K-5
4801 Frank Hengel Way 94561 925-625-6825
Michele Gaudinier, prin. Fax 625-6866
Laurel ES 700/K-5
1141 Laurel Rd 94561 925-625-7090
Mimi Curran, prin. Fax 625-8300
Oakley ES 500/K-5
501 Norcross Ln 94561 925-625-7050
Kathy Kruse, prin. Fax 625-7068
O'Hara Park MS 700/6-8
1100 OHara Ave 94561 925-625-5060
Roger Macdonald, prin. Fax 625-5096
Vintage Parkway ES 600/K-5
1000 Vintage Pkwy 94561 925-625-6800
Christina Karg, prin. Fax 625-6813

Faith Christian Learning Center 50/K-12
PO Box 1399 94561 925-625-2161
Karen Lyles, admin. Fax 625-2161
Trinity Christian S 100/PK-9
5000 Amaryllis Dr 94561 925-625-9014
Geannine Mijares, prin. Fax 625-9003

Oak Park, Ventura, Pop. 2,412
Oak Park USD 3,700/PK-12
5801 Conifer St 91377 818-735-3200
Anthony Knight, supt. Fax 879-0372
www.oakparkusd.org/
Brookside ES 500/K-5
165 Satinwood Ave 91377 818-597-4200
Debra Burgher, prin. Fax 889-0725
Medea Creek MS 900/6-8
1002 Doubletree Rd 91377 818-707-7922
Brad Benioff, prin. Fax 865-8641
Oak Hills ES 400/K-5
1010 Kanan Rd 91377 818-707-4224
Leslie Heilbron, prin. Fax 707-4232
Oak Park Neighborhood S PK-PK
1010 Kanan Rd 91377 818-707-7742
Kim Gregorchuk, prin.
Red Oak ES 500/K-5
4857 Rockfield St 91377 818-707-7972
Jon Duim, prin. Fax 597-4244

Oak Run, Shasta
Oak Run ESD 100/K-8
PO Box 48 96069 530-472-3241
Bruce Katz, supt. Fax 472-1087
www.shastalink.k12.ca.us/oakrun/
Oak Run S 100/K-8
PO Box 48 96069 530-472-3241
Bruce Katz, prin. Fax 472-1087

Oak View, Ventura, Pop. 3,606
Ventura USD
Supt. — See Ventura
Sunset ES 300/K-5
400 Sunset Ave 93022 805-649-6600
Peter Aguirre, prin. Fax 649-8745

Occidental, Sonoma, Pop. 1,300
Harmony UNESD 100/K-3
1935 Bohemian Hwy 95465 707-874-3280
Dave Miller, supt. Fax 874-1226
www.harmony.k12.ca.us
Harmony ES 100/K-3
1935 Bohemian Hwy 95465 707-874-3280
Dave Miller, prin. Fax 874-1226

Oceano, San Luis Obispo, Pop. 6,169
Lucia Mar USD
Supt. — See Arroyo Grande
Oceano ES 400/K-6
1551 17th St 93445 805-474-3800
Tom Butler, prin. Fax 473-5519

Oceanside, San Diego, Pop. 166,108
Bonsall UNESD
Supt. — See Bonsall
Bonsall West ES 300/K-6
5050 El Mirlo Dr 92057 760-721-8001
Eric Kosch, prin. Fax 721-8117

Fallbrook UNESD
Supt. — See Fallbrook
Pendleton ES 800/K-6
110 Marine Dr 92058 760-731-4050
Wendy Hill, prin. Fax 385-4254

Oceanside USD 20,600/K-12
2111 Mission Ave 92058 760-966-4000
Larry Perondi, supt. Fax 433-8620
www.oside.k12.ca.us
Chavez MS 900/6-8
202 Oleander Dr 92057 760-966-4900
Cheri Sanders, prin. Fax 945-4665
Del Rio ES 500/K-5
4991 Macario Dr 92057 760-901-7300
Marie Higareda de Ochoa, prin. Fax 433-3240
Foussat ES 600/K-5
3800 Pala Rd 92058 760-721-2200
Frank Balanon, prin. Fax 754-1567
Garrison ES 400/K-5
333 Garrison St 92054 760-757-8270
Margie Yeomans-Oliver, prin. Fax 757-5008
Ivey Ranch ES 800/K-5
4275 Via Rancho Rd 92057 760-967-9720
Charlotte Turner, prin. Fax 967-4077
Jefferson MS 1,200/6-8
823 Acacia Ave 92058 760-757-6060
Eileen Frazier, prin. Fax 757-5791
King MS 1,800/6-8
1290 Ivey Ranch Rd 92057 760-901-8800
Bob Rowe, prin. Fax 967-4154
Laurel ES 500/K-5
1410 Laurel St 92058 760-966-4200
Linda Sanchez-Guerrero, prin. Fax 966-4202
Libby ES 600/K-5
423 W Redondo Dr 92057 760-901-7000
Laura Philyaw, prin. Fax 967-0623
Lincoln MS 1,300/6-8
2000 California St 92054 760-757-0153
Steve Bessant, prin. Fax 433-2035
McAuliffe ES 700/K-5
3701 Kelton Dr 92056 760-722-8357
Mary Gleisberg, prin. Fax 722-1576
Mission ES 600/K-5
2100 Mission Ave 92058 760-966-8700
Todd McAteer, prin. Fax 757-6492
Nichols ES 800/K-5
4250 Old Grove Rd 92057 760-435-7400
Kasia Obrzut, prin. Fax 435-7402
North Terrace ES 500/K-5
940 Capistrano Dr 92058 760-757-4343
Betsy Wilcox, prin. Fax 757-5872
Palmquist ES 600/K-5
1999 California St 92054 760-757-0337
Phyllis Morgan, prin. Fax 433-6795
Reynolds ES 800/K-5
4575 Douglas Dr 92057 760-433-8949
Paulette Thompson, prin. Fax 433-5329
San Luis Rey ES 800/K-5
3535 Hacienda Dr 92054 760-757-2360
Michael Hargrove, prin. Fax 757-3945
Santa Margarita ES 500/K-5
1 Carnes Rd 92058 760-430-7110
Pat Kurtz, prin. Fax 430-1415
South Oceanside ES 500/K-5
1806 S Horne St 92054 760-435-2100
Rand Johnston, prin. Fax 439-9954
Stuart Mesa ES 600/K-5
100 Yamanaka Way 92058 760-430-3331
Lois Grazioli, prin. Fax 430-8288

Vista USD
Supt. — See Vista
Alamosa Park ES 600/K-5
5130 Alamosa Park Dr 92057 760-940-0700
Vivian Firestone, prin. Fax 940-0522
Empresa ES 800/K-5
4850 Avenida Empresa 92056 760-940-8454
Debbie Gosselin, prin. Fax 940-1578
Lake ES 800/K-5
4950 Lake Blvd 92056 760-945-5300
Diane Lambert, prin. Fax 945-7102
Madison MS 1,500/6-8
4930 Lake Blvd 92056 760-940-0176
Dr. Robert Pack, prin. Fax 940-2081
Mission Meadows ES 600/K-5
5657 Spur Ave 92057 760-630-7884
Denise Shaver, prin. Fax 630-8598
Roosevelt MS 1,300/6-8
850 Sagewood Dr 92057 760-726-8003
Raif Henry, prin. Fax 726-8596
Temple Heights ES 600/K-5
1550 Temple Heights Dr 92056 760-631-6242
Shari Fernandez, prin. Fax 631-6240

Lighthouse Christian S 100/PK-3
4700 Mesa Dr 92056 760-726-0590
Teri Pickard, dir. Fax 560-0653
New Venture Christian S 200/PK-9
4000 Mystra Way 92056 760-630-0712
Rachel Torres, prin. Fax 630-0388
Oceanside Adventist S 100/K-8
1943 California St 92054 760-722-6894
Julia Payaban, prin. Fax 757-5772
Old Mission Montessori S 300/PK-8
4070 Mission Ave 92057 760-757-3232
Wanda King, prin. Fax 721-0305
St. Mary Star of the Sea S 300/PK-8
515 Wisconsin Ave 92054 760-722-7259
Alan Hicks, prin. Fax 722-0862

Ojai, Ventura, Pop. 7,945
Ojai USD 3,200/K-12
PO Box 878 93024 805-640-4300
Fax 640-4321
www.ojai.k12.ca.us
Matilija JHS 600/7-8
703 El Paseo Rd 93023 805-640-4355
Emily Mostovoy, prin. Fax 640-4398
Meiners Oaks ES 400/K-6
400 S Lomita Ave 93023 805-640-4378
Martin Babayco, prin. Fax 640-4380
Mira Monte ES 400/K-6
1216 Loma Dr 93023 805-640-4300
Kathy White, prin. Fax 640-4419
San Antonio ES 200/K-6
650 Carne Rd 93023 805-640-4373
Theresa Dutter, prin. Fax 640-4376
Summit ES 50/K-6
12525 Ojai Santa Paula Rd 93023 805-640-4391
Marilyn Smith, prin. Fax 525-0698
Topa Topa ES 400/K-6
916 Mountain View Ave 93023 805-640-4366
John LeSuer, prin. Fax 640-4369

Laurel Springs S 2,000/K-12
PO Box 1440 93024 805-646-2473
Thomas Edwards, dir. Fax 646-0186
Montessori S of Ojai 100/PK-8
806 Baldwin Rd 93023 805-649-2525
Janet Lindquist-Lang, prin. Fax 649-3718
Oak Grove S 200/PK-12
220 W Lomita Ave 93023 805-646-8236
Meredy Rice, hdmstr. Fax 646-6509
Ojai Christian Academy 50/K-8
190 E El Roblar Dr 93023 805-646-7386
Michelle Gross, admin. Fax 646-5842
Ojai Valley S 300/PK-12
723 El Paseo Rd 93023 805-646-1423
Michael Hermes, pres. Fax 646-0362

Olivehurst, Yuba, Pop. 9,738
Marysville JUSD
Supt. — See Marysville
Ella ES 500/K-5
4850 Olivehurst Ave 95961 530-741-6124
John Green, prin. Fax 741-7806
Olivehurst ES 500/K-5
1778 Mcgowan Pkwy 95961 530-741-6191
Jimmie Eggers, prin. Fax 741-7827
Yuba Gardens IS 600/6-8
1964 11th Ave 95961 530-741-6194
Cindy Thomas, prin. Fax 741-7847

New Life Christian S 200/PK-12
5736 Arboga Rd 95961 530-742-3033
John Lewallen, admin. Fax 741-8221

O Neals, Madera
Chawanakee USD
Supt. — See North Fork
O'Neals Digital MS 6-8
PO Box 9 93645 559-868-3343
Diane Jackson, prin. Fax 868-3407
Spring Valley ES 100/K-5
PO Box 9 93645 559-868-3343
Diane Jackson, prin. Fax 868-3407

Ontario, San Bernardino, Pop. 172,679
Chino Valley USD
Supt. — See Chino
Dickey ES 700/K-6
2840 S Parco Ave 91761 909-947-6693
Pat Miller, prin. Fax 548-6071
Liberty ES 800/K-6
2730 S Bon View Ave 91761 909-947-9749
Bob Whale, prin. Fax 673-1348
Woodcrest JHS 500/7-8
2725 S Campus Ave 91761 909-923-3455
Diana Yarboi, prin. Fax 548-6059

Cucamonga ESD
Supt. — See Rancho Cucamonga
Ontario Center S 700/K-5
835 N Center Ave 91764 909-948-3044
Steven Markley, prin. Fax 948-1712

Mountain View ESD 3,100/K-8
2585 S Archibald Ave 91761 909-947-2205
Dr. Rick Carr, supt. Fax 947-2291
www.mtnview.k12.ca.us
Creek View ES 700/K-5
3742 Lytle Creek Loop 91761 909-947-8385
Curtis Schibye, prin.
Mountain View ES 500/K-5
2825 E Walnut St 91761 909-947-3516
Jeremy Currier, prin.
Ranch View ES 700/K-5
3300 Old Archibald Ranch Rd 91761
Peggy Van Dyk, prin. 909-947-5545
Yokley JHS, 2947 S Turner Ave 91761 1,200/6-8
Eric Mills, prin. 909-947-6774

Ontario-Montclair ESD 23,400/PK-8
950 W D St 91762 909-459-2500
Dr. Virgil Barnes, supt. Fax 459-2542
www.omsd.k12.ca.us
Arroyo ES 600/K-6
1700 E 7th St 91764 909-985-1012
Janet Catchings, prin. Fax 608-7385
Berlyn ES 800/K-6
1320 N Berlyn Ave 91764 909-986-8995
Kristy Tibbetts, prin. Fax 459-2586
Bon View ES 800/K-6
2121 S Bon View Ave 91761 909-947-3932
Kristie Marino, prin. Fax 930-6751
Central ES 600/K-6
415 E G St 91764 909-983-8522
Gorman Bentley, prin. Fax 459-2611
Corona ES 700/PK-6
1140 N Corona Ave 91764 909-984-6411
Marco Villegas, prin. Fax 459-2632
Danks MS 1,100/6-8
1020 N Vine Ave 91762 909-983-2691
Ellen Ransons, prin. Fax 459-2959
De Anza MS 1,000/6-8
1450 S Sultana Ave 91761 909-986-8577
Jack Young, prin. Fax 459-2673
Del Norte ES 700/K-6
850 N Del Norte Ave 91764 909-986-9515
Bob Gallagher, prin. Fax 459-2662
Edison ES 500/K-5
515 E 6th St 91764 909-984-5618
Joy Parker, prin. Fax 459-2698
El Camino ES 800/K-6
1525 W 5th St 91762 909-986-6402
Lisa Gettler, prin. Fax 459-2716
Elderberry ES 700/K-5
950 N Elderberry Ave 91762 909-986-0108
Veronica Castenada, prin. Fax 459-2741
Euclid ES 600/K-6
1120 S Euclid Ave 91762 909-984-5119
Rhonda Cleeland, prin. Fax 459-2769
Hawthorne ES 800/K-6
705 W Hawthorne St 91762 909-986-6582
Michelle Harold, prin. Fax 459-2808
Haynes ES 900/K-6
715 W Francis St 91762 909-984-1759
Ann Masters, prin. Fax 459-2775
Lincoln ES 300/PK-3
440 N Allyn Ave 91764 909-983-9803
Mario Vanheuckelom, prin. Fax 459-2865
Mariposa ES 800/K-6
1605 E D St 91764 909-983-4116
Miriam Locklair, prin. Fax 459-2906
Mission ES 800/K-6
5555 Howard St 91762 909-627-3010
Karen Reiter, prin. Fax 517-3971
Oaks MS 1,000/7-8
1221 S Oaks Ave 91762 909-988-2050
Dave Foley, prin. Fax 988-2081
Sultana ES 700/K-5
1845 S Sultana Ave 91761 909-986-1215
Anne Michaelson, prin. Fax 459-2916
Vineyard ES 600/K-6
1500 E 6th St 91764 909-984-2306
Keri Applegate, prin. Fax 459-2965
Vista Grande ES 600/K-6
1390 W Francis St 91762 909-988-2234
Bruce Lauria, prin. Fax 986-6609
Wiltsey MS 1,000/7-8
1450 E G St 91764 909-986-5838
Lisa Somerville, prin. Fax 459-2834
Other Schools – See Montclair

Ontario Christian S 1,000/PK-8
1907 S Euclid Ave 91762 909-983-1010
Keith Lucas, prin. Fax 984-3270
Redeemer Lutheran S 100/PK-8
920 W 6th St 91762 909-986-6510
David Oleson, prin. Fax 986-0757
St. George S 200/K-8
322 W D St 91762 909-984-9123
Peter Horton, prin. Fax 984-0921
San Antonio Christian S 100/K-10
1722 E 8th St 91764 909-982-2301
Shelley Hulin, prin. Fax 982-0921

Orange, Orange, Pop. 134,950
Orange USD 27,700/PK-12
PO Box 11022 92856 714-628-4040
Renae Dreier Ed.D., supt. Fax 628-4041
www.orangeusd.org/
California ES 600/K-6
1080 N California St 92867 714-997-6104
Cyndi Paik Ed.D., prin. Fax 532-4753
Cambridge ES 500/K-6
425 N Cambridge St 92866 714-997-6103
Karen Merkow, prin. Fax 532-4754
Chapman Hills ES 400/K-6
170 Aspen 92869 714-532-8043
Julie Lucas, prin. Fax 289-0302
Esplanade ES 500/K-6
381 N Esplanade St 92869 714-997-6157
Amy Hitt, prin. Fax 532-6369
Fletcher ES 400/K-6
515 W Fletcher Ave 92865 714-997-6181
Christina Varela, prin. Fax 921-9155
Handy ES 600/K-6
860 N Handy St 92867 714-997-6183
Sandra Schaffer, prin. Fax 532-6368
Jordan ES 400/K-6
4319 E Jordan Ave 92869 714-997-6187
Elizabeth Cosnell, prin. Fax 532-6360
LaVeta ES 700/K-6
2800 E La Veta Ave 92869 714-997-6155
Jaymi Abusham, prin. Fax 639-5990
Linda Vista ES 400/K-6
1200 N Cannon St 92869 714-997-6201
Sally Hughson, prin. Fax 532-5705
McPherson Magnet S 800/K-8
333 S Prospect St 92869 714-997-6384
Jeanne Bentley, prin. Fax 628-4321
Olive ES 500/K-6
3038 N Magnolia Ave 92865 714-637-8218
Kathryn Martin, prin. Fax 637-8237
Palmyra ES 600/K-6
1325 E Palmyra Ave 92866 714-997-6207
Connie Smith, prin. Fax 532-5704
Parkside Pre-Kindergarten 50/PK-K
2345 E Palmyra Ave 92869 714-997-6202
Kristi Franco, coord. Fax 997-6270
Portola MS 900/6-8
270 N Palm Dr 92868 714-997-6361
Debra Backstrom, prin. Fax 978-0274
Prospect ES 500/K-6
379 N Virage St 92869 714-997-6271
Elera Stoces, prin. Fax 532-4092
Sycamore ES 600/K-6
340 N Main St 92868 714-997-6277
Kathy Bruce, prin. Fax 532-5896
Taft ES 600/K-6
1829 N Cambridge St 92865 714-997-6254
Antoinette Coe, prin. Fax 997-6259
West Orange ES 500/K-5
243 S Bush St 92868 714-997-6283
Michael Olander, prin. Fax 532-5894
Yorba MS 700/7-8
935 N Cambridge St 92867 714-997-6161
Tara Saraye, prin. Fax 532-4759
Other Schools – See Anaheim, Garden Grove, Santa Ana, Villa Park

---

Covenant Christian S 200/PK-8
1855 N Orange Olive Rd 92865 714-998-4852
Larry Ahl, prin. Fax 998-5425
Eldorado S for the Gifted Child 200/PK-12
4100 E Walnut Ave 92869 714-633-4774
Cathie Peterson, admin. Fax 744-3304
Holy Family S 500/PK-8
530 S Glassell St 92866 714-538-6012
Margaret Harlow, prin. Fax 633-5892
Immanuel Lutheran S 100/PK-8
147 S Pine St 92866 714-538-2374
Mark Grewe, prin. Fax 538-5275
Independence Christian S 200/PK-8
1820 E Meats Ave 92865 714-974-3995
Ron Cushing, prin. Fax 921-3273
La Purisima S 300/PK-8
11712 Hewes St 92869 714-633-5411
Debbie Vallas, prin. Fax 633-1588
Oakridge Private S 300/K-10
19111 Villa Park Rd 92869 714-288-1432
Patricia Burry, dir.
St. John Lutheran S 700/K-8
154 S Shaffer St 92866 714-288-4406
Randy Einem, prin. Fax 997-4521
St. Norbert S 300/K-8
300 E Taft Ave 92865 714-637-6822
John Loffer, prin. Fax 637-1604
St. Paul's Lutheran S 600/K-8
901 E Heim Ave 92865 714-921-3188
James Beaudoin, prin. Fax 921-0131
Salem Lutheran S 600/PK-8
6411 E Frank Ln 92869 714-639-1946
Philip Duerr, prin. Fax 639-6484

Orange Cove, Fresno, Pop. 9,578
Kings Canyon JUSD
Supt. — See Reedley
Citrus MS 600/6-8
1400 Anchor Ave 93646 559-305-7370
Roberto Gutierrez, prin. Fax 626-7255
Connor ES 400/K-5
222 4th St 93646 559-305-7200
Gabriela Cazares, prin. Fax 626-3008
McCord ES 400/K-5
333 Center St 93646 559-305-7250
Sheila Wiebe, prin. Fax 626-3332
Sheridan ES 400/K-5
1001 9th St 93646 559-305-7260
Linda Klein, prin. Fax 626-3137

Orangevale, Sacramento, Pop. 26,800
San Juan USD
Supt. — See Carmichael
Carnegie MS 900/7-8
5820 Illinois Ave 95662 916-971-7853
Patricia Baldwin, prin. Fax 971-7849
Green Oaks Fundamental ES 400/K-6
7145 Filbert Ave 95662 916-986-2209
Robert Reynolds, prin. Fax 986-2214
Oakview Community ES 500/K-6
7229 Beech Ave 95662 916-986-2215
Bonnie Hutson, prin. Fax 986-2219
Ottomon Way ES 400/K-6
9460 Ottomon Way 95662 916-986-2228
Dave Cowles, prin. Fax 986-2235
Pasteur MS 800/7-8
8935 Elm Ave 95662 916-971-7891
Janet Deal, prin. Fax 971-7893
Pershing ES 600/K-6
9010 Pershing Ave 95662 916-867-2076
Loni Mellerup, prin. Fax 867-2081
Trajan ES 600/K-6
6601 Trajan Dr 95662 916-971-5200
Cristina Petroni, prin. Fax 726-4137
Twin Lakes ES 700/K-6
5515 Main Ave 95662 916-986-2243
Christine Ohlinger, prin. Fax 986-2249

Orangevale SDA S 100/K-8
5810 Pecan Ave 95662 916-988-4310
Brad Davis, prin. Fax 988-8026

Orcutt, Santa Barbara
Orcutt UNESD 4,800/K-8
500 Dyer St 93455 805-938-8900
Dr. Sharon McHolland, supt. Fax 938-8919
www.orcutt-schools.net
Grisham ES 600/K-6
610 Pinal Ave 93455 805-938-8550
Don Nicholson, prin. Fax 938-8599
Orcutt JHS 500/7-8
608 Pinal Ave 93455 805-938-8700
Alan Majewski, prin. Fax 938-8749
Other Schools – See Santa Maria

Orick, Humboldt
Orick ESD 50/K-8
PO Box 128 95555 707-488-2821
John Sutter, supt. Fax 488-2831
www.humboldt.k12.ca.us/orick_sd/
Orick S 50/K-8
PO Box 128 95555 707-488-2821
John Sutter, prin. Fax 488-2831

Orinda, Contra Costa, Pop. 18,259
Orinda UNESD 2,500/K-8
8 Altarinda Rd 94563 925-254-4901
Joe Jaconette Ed.D., supt. Fax 254-5261
www.orindaschools.org/
Del Rey ES 400/K-5
25 El Camino Moraga 94563 925-258-3099
Kirsten Theurer, prin. Fax 376-1832
Glorietta ES 400/K-5
15 Martha Rd 94563 925-254-8770
Wendy Sparks, prin. Fax 254-4856
Orinda IS 900/6-8
80 Ivy Dr 94563 925-258-3090
Michael Randall, prin. Fax 631-7985
Sleepy Hollow ES 400/K-5
20 Washington Ln 94563 925-254-8711
Diane Kanegae, prin. Fax 253-8320
Wagner Ranch ES 400/K-5
350 Camino Pablo 94563 925-258-0016
Janis Arnerich, prin. Fax 258-0351

Orland, Glenn, Pop. 6,757
Capay JUNESD 100/K-8
7504 Cutting Ave 95963 530-865-1222
Jim Scribner, supt. Fax 865-1214
Capay Joint Union S 100/K-8
7504 Cutting Ave 95963 530-865-1222
Jim Scribner, prin. Fax 865-1214

Lake ESD 100/K-8
4672 County Rd N 95963 530-865-1255
Grant Sandro, supt. Fax 865-1203
www.lakeschool.org/
Lake S 100/K-8
4672 County Rd N 95963 530-865-1255
Beverlee Seale, prin. Fax 865-1203

Orland JUSD 2,300/K-12
1320 6th St 95963 530-865-1200
Chris von Kleist, supt. Fax 865-1202
www.orlandusd.net
Fairview ES 500/3-5
1320 6th St 95963 530-865-1235
Steven Hiscock, prin. Fax 865-1238
Mill Street ES 500/K-2
1320 6th St 95963 530-865-1240
Annette Thole, prin. Fax 865-1129
Price IS 500/6-8
1320 6th St 95963 530-865-1225
Theresa Johansen, prin. Fax 865-1227

Plaza ESD 100/K-8
7322 County Road 24 95963 530-865-1250
Grant Sandro, supt. Fax 865-1252
www.plazaschool.org/
Plaza S 100/K-8
7322 County Road 24 95963 530-865-1250
Martha Bradshaw, prin. Fax 865-1252

North Valley Christian S 100/K-12
1148 E Walker St 95963 530-865-4924
Gordon Wiens, supt. Fax 865-4926

Orleans, Humboldt
Klamath-Trinity JUSD
Supt. — See Hoopa
Orleans S 50/K-8
PO Box 130 95556 530-625-5600
Sandra Moon, prin. Fax 627-3332

Oro Grande, San Bernardino
Oro Grande ESD 100/K-6
PO Box 386 92368 760-245-9260
Dr. Kim Moore, supt. Fax 245-1339
www.orogrande.net
Oro Grande ES 100/K-6
PO Box 386 92368 760-245-9260
Dr. Kim Moore, prin. Fax 245-1339

Orosi, Tulare, Pop. 5,486
Cutler-Orosi JUSD 3,900/K-12
12623 Avenue 416 93647 559-528-4763
Carolyn Kehrli Ed.D., supt. Fax 528-3132
www.cojusd.org
El Monte JHS 600/7-8
42111 Road 128 93647 559-528-3017
Roel Alvarado, prin. Fax 528-2822
Golden Valley ES 800/K-6
41465 Road 127 93647 559-528-9004
Pablo Gonzalez, prin. Fax 528-9137
Palm ES 700/K-6
12915 Avenue 419 93647 559-528-4751
Roy Woods, prin. Fax 528-9260
Other Schools – See Badger, Cutler

Oroville, Butte, Pop. 13,468
Feather Falls UNESD 50/K-8
2651 Lumpkin Rd 95966 530-589-1810
Deborah Nelson, supt. Fax 589-1446

Feather Falls S 50/K-8
2651 Lumpkin Rd 95966 530-589-1810
Deborah Nelson, prin. Fax 589-1446

Golden Feather UNESD 200/K-8
11679 Nelson Bar Rd 95965 530-533-3833
Lora Haston, supt. Fax 533-3887
www.bcoe.org/home/districts/golden.htm
Concow MS 100/4-8
11679 Nelson Bar Rd 95965 530-533-6033
Lora Haston, prin. Fax 533-3887
Spring Valley ES 100/K-3
2771 Pentz Rd 95965 530-533-3258
Lora Haston, prin. Fax 533-3879

Oroville City ESD 2,800/K-8
2795 Yard St 95966 530-532-3000
Penny Chennell-Carter, supt. Fax 532-3050
www.ocesd.org/
Bird Street ES 100/K-4
1421 Bird St 95965 530-532-3001
Lori Strieby, prin. Fax 532-3041
Central MS 500/7-8
2565 Mesa Ave 95966 530-532-3002
Donald Phillips, prin. Fax 532-3042
Ishi Hills MS 400/6-8
1 Ishi Hills Way 95966 530-532-3078
Kathy Myszka, prin. Fax 532-3040
Oakdale Heights ES 400/K-6
2255 Las Plumas Ave 95966 530-532-3004
Rick Desimone, prin. Fax 532-3044
Ophir ES 600/K-6
210 Oakvale Ave 95966 530-532-3005
Rex Moseley, prin. Fax 532-3045
Stanford Avenue ES 400/K-5
1801 Stanford Ave 95966 530-532-3006
Charles Gallivan, prin. Fax 532-3046
Wyandotte Avenue ES 400/K-6
2800 Wyandotte Ave 95966 530-532-3007
Rita Costa, prin. Fax 532-3047

Palermo UNESD
Supt. — See Palermo
Golden Hills ES 300/4-5
2400 Via Canela 95966 530-532-6000
Carol Brown, prin. Fax 534-7982
Honcut ES 50/K-2
68 School St 95966 530-742-5284
Heather Scott, prin. Fax 742-2955
Wilcox ES 600/K-3
5737 Autrey Ln 95966 530-533-7627
Heather Scott, prin. Fax 533-6949

Thermalito UNESD 1,500/K-8
400 Grand Ave 95965 530-538-2900
Gregory Kampf, supt. Fax 538-2909
www.thermalito.org/
Nelson Avenue MS 500/6-8
2255 6th St 95965 530-538-2940
Julian Diaz, prin. Fax 538-2949
Plumas Avenue ES 300/K-5
440 Plumas Ave 95965 530-538-2930
Anthony Catalano, prin. Fax 538-2939
Poplar Avenue ES 300/K-5
2075 20th St 95965 530-538-2910
Jeanette Spencer, prin. Fax 538-2919
Sierra Avenue ES 300/K-5
1050 Sierra Ave 95965 530-538-2920
Ed Gregorio, prin. Fax 538-2929

Feather River Adventist S 50/1-8
27 Cox Ln 95965 530-533-8848
J. Marvin Whitney, prin. Fax 533-6496
Oroville Christian S 100/PK-8
3785 Olive Hwy 95966 530-533-2888
Thomas Hammonds, prin. Fax 533-4155
St. Thomas the Apostle S 100/PK-8
1380 Bird St 95965 530-534-6969
Joani Briggs, prin. Fax 534-9374

Oxnard, Ventura, Pop. 183,628
Hueneme ESD
Supt. — See Port Hueneme
Blackstock JHS 1,200/6-8
701 E Bard Rd 93033 805-488-3644
Elena Coronado, prin. Fax 488-1250
Green JHS 1,100/6-8
3739 S C St 93033 805-986-8750
Carlos Dominguez, prin. Fax 986-8756
Hathaway ES 600/K-6
405 E Dollie St 93033 805-488-2217
Helen Cosgrove, prin. Fax 488-1304
Haycox ES 700/K-5
5400 Perkins Rd 93033 805-488-3578
Janet Lee, prin. Fax 488-2459
Hollywood Beach ES 300/K-6
4000 Sunset Ln 93035 805-986-8720
Cheryl Davidson, prin. Fax 986-8719
Larsen ES 700/K-5
550 Thomas Ave 93033 805-986-8740
Irma Villanueva, prin. Fax 986-8781
Williams ES 700/K-5
4300 Anchorage St 93033 805-488-3541
Sandy Schiffner, prin. Fax 986-1184

Ocean View ESD 2,500/PK-8
4200 Olds Rd 93033 805-488-4441
Dr. Nancy Carroll, supt. Fax 986-6797
www.oceanviewsd.org
Laguna Vista ES 500/PK-5
5084 Etting Rd 93033 805-488-3638
Suzanne Lange, prin. Fax 986-6759
Mar Vista ES 700/K-5
2382 Etting Rd 93033 805-488-3659
Jaime Verdugo, prin. Fax 986-6754
Ocean View Early Education Center PK-PK
4600 Olds Rd 93033 805-488-5277
Antoinette Dodge, dir. Fax 488-5669
Ocean View JHS 800/6-8
4300 Olds Rd 93033 805-488-6421
Sharon Anderson, prin. Fax 488-4132
Ocean Vista Early Education S PK-PK
5191 Squires Dr 93033 805-986-3186
Shahida Chaudry, dir. Fax 986-6857
Tierra Vista ES 600/PK-5
2001 Sanford St 93033 805-488-4454
Marlene Carabello-Dalton, prin. Fax 986-6792

Oxnard SD 15,500/K-8
1051 S A St 93030 805-487-3918
Anthony Monreal, supt. Fax 483-7426
www.oxnardsd.org
Brekke ES 900/K-6
1400 Martin Luther King Jr 93030 805-485-1224
Kelly Castillo, prin. Fax 485-4467
Chavez ES 600/K-6
301 N Marquita St 93030 805-483-2389
Julia Villalpando, prin. Fax 483-4799
Curren ES 700/K-6
1101 N F St 93030 805-485-3323
Marikaye Phipps, prin. Fax 485-7593
Driffill ES 900/K-6
910 S E St 93030 805-486-3563
Maria Elena Plaza, prin. Fax 487-8223
Elm Street ES 500/K-6
450 E Elm St 93033 805-487-7581
Arthur Barragan, prin. Fax 487-9961
Frank IS 1,200/7-8
701 N Juanita Ave 93030 805-981-1733
Robin Poe, prin. Fax 981-1754
Fremont IS 1,300/7-8
1130 N M St 93030 805-485-5900
Anne Gibson, prin. Fax 485-2486
Harrington ES 600/K-6
2501 Gisler Ave 93033 805-487-7574
Debra Cordes, prin. Fax 486-8364
Haydock IS 900/7-8
647 Hill St 93033 805-487-6797
Amelia Sugden, prin. Fax 487-7159
Kamala ES 800/K-6
634 W Kamala St 93033 805-483-1153
Christine McDaniels, prin. Fax 486-2893
Lemonwood ES 700/K-6
2200 Carnegie Ct 93033 805-487-7583
Louise Platt, prin. Fax 487-7293
Marina West ES 900/K-6
2501 Carob St 93035 805-985-2844
Anna Thomas, prin. Fax 984-5494
Marshall ES 600/K-6
2900 Thurgood Marshall Dr, 805-983-7155
Pamela Morrison, prin. Fax 983-7215
McAuliffe ES 900/K-6
3300 Via Marina Ave 93035 805-984-0010
Christine Anderson, prin. Fax 985-4690
McKinna ES 700/K-6
1611 S J St 93033 805-483-1171
Anne Jenks, prin. Fax 487-2231
Ramona ES 600/K-6
804 Cooper Rd 93030 805-483-5450
Jairo Arellano, prin. Fax 486-7049
Ritchen ES 800/K-6
2200 Cabrillo Way 93030 805-981-9428
Cheryl Vice, prin. Fax 981-4685
Rose Avenue ES 1,000/K-6
220 S Driskill St 93030 805-485-1991
Shannon Coletti, prin. Fax 485-8061
Sierra Linda ES 700/K-6
2201 Jasmine Ave, 805-983-2280
Ronit Driver, prin. Fax 485-5796
Soria ES, 3101 Dunkirk Dr 93035 100/K-6
Ana DeGenna, prin. 805-385-1584

Rio SD 4,600/PK-8
2500 E Vineyard Ave, 805-485-3111
Sherianne Cotterell, supt. Fax 983-0221
www.rio.k12.ca.us
Rio del Mar ES 600/K-5
2500 E Vineyard Ave, 805-485-0560
Refugio Villalpando, prin. Fax 485-6634
Rio del Norte ES 700/K-5
2500 E Vineyard Ave, 805-604-1412
Delfin Merlan, prin. Fax 604-1792
Rio Del Valle MS 900/6-8
2500 E Vineyard Ave, 805-485-3119
Maria Hernandez, prin. Fax 981-7737
Rio Lindo ES 500/K-5
2500 E Vineyard Ave, 805-485-3113
Jeff Turner, prin. Fax 981-7738
Rio Plaza ES 400/K-5
2500 E Vineyard Ave, 805-485-3121
Cassandra Bautista, prin. Fax 981-7740
Rio Real ES 400/K-5
2500 E Vineyard Ave, 805-485-3117
Carolyn Bernal, prin. Fax 981-7739
Rio Rosales ES 400/PK-5
2500 E Vineyard Ave, 805-983-0277
Nicholas Bruski, prin. Fax 983-0617
Rio Vista MS 700/6-8
2500 E Vineyard Ave, 805-981-1507
Shirley Shaw, prin. Fax 981-6791

Linda Vista Adventist S 100/K-8
5050 Perry Way, 805-647-2220
Sharron Crooms, prin. Fax 647-3971
New Harvest Christian S 100/K-8
723 S D St 93030 805-486-4656
Carol Ford, admin. Fax 201-6687
Our Lady of Guadalupe S 300/PK-8
530 N Juanita Ave 93030 805-483-5116
Siobhain Hill, prin. Fax 385-7242
Our Redeemer Preschool & Kindergarten 200/PK-K
721 Doris Ave 93030 805-983-0619
Fax 983-0443
St. Anthony S 200/K-8
2421 S C St 93033 805-487-5317
Mike Livingston, prin. Fax 486-1537
St. John's Lutheran S 200/K-8
1500 N C St 93030 805-983-0330
Gary Krumdieck, admin. Fax 983-2171
Santa Clara S 200/PK-8
324 S E St 93030 805-483-6935
Dotty Massa, prin. Fax 487-6686

Pacifica, San Mateo, Pop. 37,092
Pacifica SD 3,100/K-8
375 Reina Del Mar Ave 94044 650-738-6600
Susan Vickrey, supt. Fax 557-9672
www.pacificasd.org/
Cabrillo S 600/K-8
601 Crespi Dr 94044 650-738-6660
Scott Carson, prin. Fax 738-2870
Lacy MS 600/6-8
1427 Palmetto Ave 94044 650-738-6665
Tina Van Raaphorst, prin. Fax 738-6669
Ocean Shore S 300/K-8
411 Oceana Blvd 94044 650-738-6650
Laura Shain, prin. Fax 355-0660
Ortega ES 400/K-5
1283 Terra Nova Blvd 94044 650-738-6670
Marc Lorenzen, prin. Fax 738-6672
Sunset Ridge ES 600/K-5
340 Inverness Dr 94044 650-738-6687
Ellie Cundiff, prin. Fax 355-4042
Vallemar S 600/K-8
377 Reina Del Mar Ave 94044 650-738-6655
Barbara Ng, prin. Fax 359-2476

Alma Heights Christian Academy 300/K-12
1295 Seville Dr 94044 650-359-0555
David Welling, dir. Fax 359-5020
Good Shepherd S 300/K-8
909 Oceana Blvd 94044 650-359-4544
Patricia Volan, prin. Fax 359-4558

Pacific Grove, Monterey, Pop. 15,091
Pacific Grove USD 1,700/K-12
555 Sinex Ave 93950 831-646-6520
Ralph Porras, supt. Fax 646-6500
pgusd.org
Down ES 400/K-5
485 Pine Ave 93950 831-646-6540
Linda Williams, prin. Fax 648-8414
Forest Grove ES 300/K-5
1065 Congress Ave 93950 831-646-6560
Mariphil Romanow-Cole, prin. Fax 648-8415
Pacific Grove MS 400/6-8
835 Forest Ave 93950 831-646-6568
Mary Riedel, prin. Fax 646-6652

St. Angela's Children's Center 100/PK-PK
136 8th St 93950 831-372-3555
Virginia Ziomek, prin. Fax 372-1965

Pacific Palisades, See Los Angeles

Calvary Christian S 400/PK-8
701 Palisades Dr 90272 310-573-0082
Teresa Roberson, hdmstr. Fax 230-9268
Corpus Christi S 300/K-8
890 Toyopa Dr 90272 310-454-9411
Catherine Carvalho, prin. Fax 454-3776
St. Matthew's Parish S 300/PK-8
PO Box 1710 90272 310-454-1350
Les Frost, hdmstr. Fax 573-7423
Seven Arrows ES 100/K-6
15240 La Cruz Dr 90272 310-230-0257
Margarita Pagliai, dir. Fax 230-7725
Village S 300/PK-6
780 Swarthmore Ave 90272 310-459-8411
Nora Malone, hdmstr. Fax 459-3285
Westside Waldorf S 200/PK-8
17310 W Sunset Blvd 90272 310-454-7064
Fax 454-7084

Pacoima, See Los Angeles
Los Angeles USD
Supt. — See Los Angeles
Broadous ES 900/K-5
12561 Filmore St 91331 818-896-5236
Aurora Arreola, prin. Fax 834-4961
Coughlin ES 300/K-2
11035 Borden Ave 91331 818-686-6428
Giovanni Foschetti, prin. Fax 686-6509
Haddon Avenue ES 1,000/K-5
10115 Haddon Ave 91331 818-899-0244
Loraine Mason, prin. Fax 834-6024
MacLay MS 1,100/6-8
12540 Pierce St 91331 818-686-3800
Veronica Arreguin, prin. Fax 834-1012
Pacoima MS 2,200/6-8
9919 Laurel Canyon Blvd 91331 818-686-4200
Marsha Hamm, prin. Fax 834-2021
Telfair ES 1,100/K-5
10975 Telfair Ave 91331 818-896-7411
Alfonso Jimenez, prin. Fax 834-9582

Guardian Angel S 200/K-8
10919 Norris Ave 91331 818-896-1113
Mario Landeros, prin. Fax 834-4014
Mary Immaculate S 300/PK-8
10390 Remick Ave 91331 818-834-8551
Federina Gullano, prin. Fax 896-7996

Paicines, San Benito
Jefferson ESD 50/K-8
221 Old Hernandez Rd 95043 831-389-4593
Tina Plunkett, supt. Fax 389-4593
Jefferson S 50/K-8
221 Old Hernandez Rd 95043 831-389-4593
Tina Plunkett, prin. Fax 389-4593

Panoche ESD 50/K-8
31441 Panoche Rd 95043 831-628-3438
Ottalie Davis, supt. Fax 628-3438
Panoche S 50/K-8
31441 Panoche Rd 95043 831-628-3438
Ottalie Davis, prin. Fax 628-3438

Willow Grove UNESD 50/K-8
PO Box 46 95043 831-628-3256
Carole Brummet, supt. Fax 628-3458
Willow Grove S 50/K-8
PO Box 46 95043 831-628-3256
Carole Brummet, prin. Fax 628-3458

Pala, San Diego

Aswe-t Pati'a Christian Academy 50/K-12
35008 Pala Temecula Rd 92059 760-742-3071
Diana Dreibelbis, prin. Fax 742-3851

Palermo, Butte, Pop. 5,260
Palermo UNESD 1,300/K-8
7390 Bulldog Way 95968 530-533-4842
Sam Chimento, supt. Fax 532-1047
www.palermoschools.org
Palermo MS 500/6-8
7350 Bulldog Way 95968 530-533-4708
Kathleen Coleman, prin. Fax 532-7801
Other Schools – See Oroville

Palmdale, Los Angeles, Pop. 134,570
Keppel UNESD
Supt. — See Pearblossom
Gibson ES 600/K-6
9650 E Palmdale Blvd 93591 661-944-6590
Michael Perkins, prin. Fax 944-0656
Lake Los Angeles S 500/K-8
16310 E Avenue Q 93591 661-264-3700
Michele Bowes, prin. Fax 264-4570

Palmdale ESD 22,000/K-8
39139 10th St E 93550 661-947-7191
Roger Gallizzi, supt. Fax 273-5137
www.psd.k12.ca.us
Barrel Springs ES 800/K-6
3636 Ponderosa Way 93550 661-285-9270
Kim Wright, prin. Fax 456-1159
Buena Vista S 900/K-8
37005 Hillcrest Dr 93552 661-285-4158
Chad Gray, prin. Fax 285-0240
Cactus MS 1,100/6-8
38060 20th St E 93550 661-273-0847
Kate Laferriere, prin. Fax 273-5514
Chaparral ES 1,000/K-6
37500 50th St E 93552 661-285-9777
Pam Williams, prin. Fax 285-3702
Cimarron ES 900/K-6
36940 45th St E 93552 661-285-9780
David Armstrong, prin. Fax 285-9185
Desert Rose ES 1,100/K-6
37730 27th St E 93550 661-272-0584
Sergei Orloff, prin. Fax 224-1329
Desert Willow IS 800/7-8
37230 37th St E 93550 661-285-5866
Thomas Pitts, prin. Fax 456-1145
Golden Poppy S 900/K-8
37802 Rockie Ln 93552 661-285-3683
Melanie Pagliaro, prin. Fax 456-1540
Joshua Hills ES 800/K-6
3030 Fairfield Ave 93550 661-265-9992
Arland Atwood, prin. Fax 265-7211
Juniper IS 1,000/7-8
39066 Palm Tree Way 93551 661-947-0181
David Ellms, prin. Fax 456-1576
Los Amigos S 900/K-8
6640 E Avenue R8 93552 661-285-1546
Matthew Heinrich, prin. Fax 456-2959
Manzanita ES 700/K-6
38620 33rd St E 93550 661-947-3128
Dr. Thomas Leveque, prin. Fax 947-2980
Mesa IS 900/7-8
3243 E Avenue R8 93550 661-947-0188
Ruth James, prin. Fax 456-1338
Mesquite ES 1,000/K-6
37622 43rd St E 93552 661-285-8376
Barbara Gaines, prin. Fax 285-2530
Ocotillo ES 1,200/K-6
38737 Ocotillo Dr 93551 661-947-9987
Kathy Wehunt, prin. Fax 267-2186
Palm Tree ES 900/K-6
326 E Avenue R 93550 661-265-9357
Pam Egbert, prin. Fax 266-3790
Quail Valley ES 800/K-6
37236 58th St E 93552 661-533-7100
Donna Lebetsames, prin. Fax 533-7155
Shadow Hills IS 800/7-8
37315 60th St E 93552 661-533-7400
Suresh Bajnath, prin. Fax 533-7445
Summerwind ES 800/K-6
39360 Summerwind Dr 93551 661-947-3863
Bob Rodrigo, prin. Fax 947-4692
Tamarisk ES 800/K-6
1843 E Avenue Q5 93550 661-273-5770
Jezelle Fullwood, prin. Fax 273-7245
Tumbleweed ES 1,100/K-6
1100 E Avenue R4 93550 661-273-4166
Debra Hollis, prin. Fax 273-9384
Wildflower S 900/K-6
38136 35th St E 93550 661-272-1571
Chris O'Neill, prin. Fax 272-0637
Yucca ES 800/K-6
38440 2nd St E 93550 661-273-5052
Kim Shaw, prin. Fax 273-1995

Westside UNESD
Supt. — See Lancaster
Ana Verde Hills S 300/K-6
2740 W Avenue P8 93551 661-575-9923
Paula Sour, prin. Fax 575-0946
Cottonwood ES 800/K-6
2740 W Avenue P8 93551 661-267-2825
Paula Sour, prin. Fax 267-1847
Esperanza ES 1,100/K-6
40521 35th St W 93551 661-575-0420
Joe Andrews, prin. Fax 942-2576
Hillview MS 1,000/7-8
40525 Peonza Ln 93551 661-722-9993
Robert Garza, prin. Fax 722-9483
Rancho Vista ES 900/K-6
40641 Peonza Ln 93551 661-722-0148
Rodney Lots, prin. Fax 722-9962

Wilsona SD 2,000/K-8
18050 E Avenue O 93591 661-264-1111
David Andreasen, supt. Fax 261-3259
Vista San Gabriel ES 700/K-5
18020 E Avenue O 93591 661-264-1155
Teresa Grey, prin. Fax 261-9348
Other Schools – See Lancaster

Covenant Christian S 100/1-12
2013 Clearwater Ave 93551 661-274-8285
Susan Mitchell, admin.
St. Mary S 300/PK-8
1600 E Avenue R4 93550 661-273-5555
Carolyn Gries, prin. Fax 273-3845
Westside Christian S 300/K-8
40027 11th St W 93551 661-947-7000
Charles Miller, admin. Fax 947-2366

Palm Desert, Riverside, Pop. 47,058
Desert Sands USD
Supt. — See La Quinta
Carter ES 600/K-5
74251 Hovley Ln E 92260 760-862-4370
Jeff Hisgen, prin. Fax 862-4375
Lincoln ES 800/K-5
74100 Rutledge Way 92260 760-862-4340
Jill Garner, prin. Fax 862-4344
Reagan ES 500/K-5
39800 Liberty Dr 92211 760-772-0456
Kim McLaughlin, prin. Fax 360-4304

Desert Adventist Academy 100/K-8
74200 Country Club Dr 92260 760-779-1799
C. William Rouse, prin. Fax 779-0179
Oasis Preparatory S 50/1-12
39605 Entrepreneur Ln 92211 760-772-8255
Susan Roberts, prin. Fax 772-7446
Palm Desert Learning Tree Center 100/PK-5
42675 Washington St 92211 760-345-8100
Robert Craven, prin. Fax 360-1909
Sacred Heart S 500/PK-8
43775 Deep Canyon Rd 92260 760-346-3513
Alan Bruzzio, prin. Fax 773-0673
St. Margaret's Episcopal S 200/PK-8
47535 State Highway 74 92260 760-346-6268
Dr. Kim Marshall, hdmstr. Fax 836-3267

Palm Springs, Riverside, Pop. 47,082
Palm Springs USD 24,200/PK-12
980 E Tahquitz Canyon Way 92262 760-416-6000
Lorri McCune Ed.D., supt. Fax 416-6015
www.psusd.k12.ca.us
Cahuilla ES 600/K-5
833 E Mesquite Ave 92264 760-416-8161
Denise Ellis, prin. Fax 416-8164
Cielo Vista ES 600/K-5
650 S Paseo Dorotea 92264 760-416-8250
Lynda Lake, prin. Fax 416-8253
Cree MS 1,100/6-8
1011 E Vista Chino 92262 760-416-8283
Tony Signoret, prin. Fax 416-8287
Early Childhood Education PK-PK
1000 E Tahquitz Canyon Way 92262 760-416-8090
Joan Prehoda, prin. Fax 416-8413
Finchy ES 700/K-5
777 E Tachevah Dr 92262 760-416-8190
Mark Arnold, prin. Fax 416-8201
Vista Del Monte ES 600/K-5
2744 N Via Miraleste 92262 760-416-8176
Joseph Scudder, prin. Fax 416-8178
Other Schools – See Cathedral City, Desert Hot Springs, Rancho Mirage, Thousand Palms

Desert Chapel Christian S 300/K-12
630 S Sunrise Way 92264 760-327-2772
Frank Marshall, admin. Fax 325-7048
King's S 400/PK-8
67675 Bolero Rd 92264 760-324-5464
Don De Lair, hdmstr. Fax 321-0266
St. Theresa S 400/PK-8
455 S Compadre Rd 92262 760-327-4919
Cheryl Corey, prin. Fax 327-4429

Palo Alto, Santa Clara, Pop. 56,982
Palo Alto USD 10,900/K-12
25 Churchill Ave 94306 650-329-3700
Kevin Skelly Ph.D., supt. Fax 329-3803
www.pausd.org
Addison ES 400/K-5
650 Addison Ave 94301 650-322-5935
John Lents, prin. Fax 322-3306
Barron Park ES 300/K-5
800 Barron Ave 94306 650-858-0508
Catherine Howard, prin. Fax 813-1031
Briones ES 300/K-5
4100 Orme St 94306 650-856-0877
Michael O'Neill, prin. Fax 856-3750
Duveneck ES 500/K-5
705 Alester Ave 94303 650-322-5946
Kathleen Meagher, prin. Fax 322-4387
El Carmelo ES 400/K-5
3024 Bryant St 94306 650-856-0960
Chuck Merritt, prin. Fax 856-4817
Fairmeadow ES 400/K-5
500 E Meadow Dr 94306 650-856-0845
Eric Goddard, prin. Fax 852-9436
Hays ES 500/K-5
1525 Middlefield Rd 94301 650-322-5956
Fax 329-8713
Hoover ES 400/K-5
445 E Charleston Rd 94306 650-320-8106
Susanne Scott, prin. Fax 493-8130
Jordan MS 900/6-8
750 N California Ave 94303 650-494-8120
Michael Milliken, prin. Fax 858-1310
Nixon ES 400/K-5
1711 Stanford Ave 94305 650-856-1622
Mary O'Connell, prin. Fax 813-1417
Ohlone ES 400/K-5
950 Amarillo Ave 94303 650-856-1726
Susan Charles, prin. Fax 852-9447
Palo Verde ES 400/K-5
3450 Louis Rd 94303 650-856-1672
Lupe Garcia, prin. Fax 856-6316
Stanford MS 900/6-8
480 E Meadow Dr 94306 650-856-5188
Don Cox, prin. Fax 856-3248
Terman MS 700/6-8
655 Arastradero Rd 94306 650-856-9810
Carmen Giedt, prin. Fax 856-9878
Other Schools – See Stanford

Bowman International S 200/K-8
4000 Terman Dr 94306 650-813-9131
Mary Ricks, prin. Fax 813-9132
Challenger S - Middlefield 500/PK-8
3880 Middlefield Rd 94303 650-213-8245
Sanny Figueroa, hdmstr.
Emerson S 50/PK-8
2800 W Bayshore Rd 94303 650-424-1267
Tracy Bootz, dir. Fax 856-2778
Hausner Jewish Day S 400/K-8
450 San Antonio Rd 94306 650-494-8200
Julie Smith, hdmstr. Fax 424-0714
International S of the Peninsula 500/K-8
151 Laura Ln 94303 650-251-8500
Philippe Dietz, hdmstr.
Keys S 200/K-8
2890 Middlefield Rd 94306 650-328-1711
Jonathon Ninnemann, hdmstr. Fax 328-4506
St. Elizabeth Seton S 200/K-8
1095 Channing Ave 94301 650-326-9004
Sr. Adella Armentrout, prin. Fax 326-2949
Stratford S 300/PK-5
870 N California Ave 94303 650-493-1151
Sherrie Paregian, prin.
Torah Academy 50/PK-K
3070 Louis Rd 94303 650-424-9800

Palo Cedro, Shasta
Junction ESD 400/K-8
9087 Deschutes Rd 96073 530-547-5494
Mary Sakuma, supt. Fax 547-4829
www.junctionesd.net
Junction ES 200/K-5
9087 Deschutes Rd 96073 530-547-3274
Mary Sakuma, prin. Fax 547-4080
Junction IS 200/6-8
9019 Deschutes Rd 96073 530-547-5494
Mary Sakuma, prin. Fax 547-4829

North Cow Creek ESD 300/K-8
10619 Swede Creek Rd 96073 530-549-4488
Tom Mancuso, supt. Fax 549-4490
www.shastalink.k12.ca.us/nccs
North Cow Creek S 300/K-8
10619 Swede Creek Rd 96073 530-549-4488
Tom Mancuso, prin. Fax 549-4490

Palos Verdes Estates, Los Angeles, Pop. 13,812
Palos Verdes Peninsula USD 12,000/K-12
3801 Via La Selva 90274 310-378-9966
Walker Williams, supt. Fax 378-0732
www.pvpusd.k12.ca.us
Lunada Bay ES 400/K-5
520 Paseo Lunado 90274 310-377-3005
Joan Romano, prin. Fax 544-1265
Montemalaga ES 500/K-5
1121 Via Nogales 90274 310-378-5228
Patricia Stewart, prin. Fax 375-7484
Palos Verdes IS 1,000/6-8
2161 Via Olivera 90274 310-544-4816
Frank Califano, prin. Fax 265-5944
Other Schools – See Rancho Palos Verdes, Rolling Hills

Palos Verdes Peninsula, See Rolling Hills Estates

Chadwick S 800/K-12
26800 Academy Dr 90274 310-377-1543
Frederick Hill, hdmstr. Fax 377-0380

Panorama City, See Los Angeles
Los Angeles USD
Supt. — See Los Angeles
Burton ES 700/K-5
8111 Calhoun Ave 91402 818-908-1287
Roger W. Wilcox, prin. Fax 785-6680
Chase Street ES 900/K-5
14041 Chase St 91402 818-892-4329
Andres Chait, prin. Fax 892-8136
Liggett ES 1,100/K-5
9373 Moonbeam Ave 91402 818-892-4388
Lynda Diamond, prin. Fax 830-0880
Panorama City ES 700/K-5
8600 Kester Ave 91402 818-895-4230
Sylvia Guzman, prin. Fax 895-2884
Primary Academy for Success 300/K-1
9075 Willis Ave 91402 818-920-2932
Irene Belden, prin. Fax 893-5718

Ranchito Avenue ES 700/K-5
7940 Ranchito Ave 91402 818-988-1710
Alan O'Hara, prin. Fax 988-4238

St. Genevieve S 600/PK-8
14024 Community St 91402 818-892-3802
Sr. Teresa Lynch, prin. Fax 893-8143

Paradise, Butte, Pop. 26,517
Paradise USD 4,100/K-12
6696 Clark Rd 95969 530-872-6400
Roger Bylund, supt. Fax 872-6409
www.pusdk12.org
Paradise ES 600/K-5
588 Pearson Rd 95969 530-872-6415
Michelle John, prin. Fax 872-6419
Paradise IS 500/6-8
5657 Recreation Dr 95969 530-872-6465
Michael Ervin, prin. Fax 876-1852
Ponderosa ES 500/K-5
6593 Pentz Rd 95969 530-872-6470
Tom Taylor, prin. Fax 872-6474
Other Schools – See Magalia

Cornerstone Christian S 50/K-5
6500 Clark Rd 95969 530-877-3240
Brad Wells, admin. Fax 877-3557
Lighthouse Christian S 50/K-12
PO Box 399 95967 530-872-9029
Wendy Lightbody, prin. Fax 877-2246
Paradise Adventist Academy 200/K-12
PO Box 2169 95967 530-877-6540
Ken Preston, prin. Fax 877-0870

Paramount, Los Angeles, Pop. 56,540
Paramount USD 15,700/K-12
15110 California Ave 90723 562-602-6000
David Verdugo Ed.D., supt. Fax 602-8111
www.paramount.k12.ca.us
Alondra S 900/K-8
16200 Downey Ave 90723 562-602-8004
Carolynn Butler, prin. Fax 602-8005
Gaines S 400/K-3
7340 Jackson St 90723 562-602-8012
Linda Harju-Stevens, prin. Fax 602-8013
Jackson MS 500/4-8
7220 Jackson St 90723 562-602-8020
Lupe Hernandez, prin. Fax 602-8021
Jefferson S 600/K-8
8600 Jefferson St 90723 562-602-8024
Yuki Mio, prin. Fax 602-8025
Keppel S 600/K-8
6630 Mark Keppel St 90723 562-602-8028
Concepcion Toscano, prin. Fax 602-8029
Lincoln S 700/K-8
15324 California Ave 90723 562-602-8036
Linda Go, prin. Fax 602-8037
Los Cerritos S 900/K-8
14626 Gundry Ave 90723 562-602-8040
Elizabeth Salcido, prin. Fax 602-8041
Mokler S 700/K-8
8571 Flower Ave 90723 562-602-8044
Beatriz Spelker, prin. Fax 602-8045
Paramount Park S 700/K-8
14608 Paramount Blvd 90723 562-602-8052
Topekia Jones, prin. Fax 602-8053
Roosevelt S 800/K-8
13451 Merkel Ave 90723 562-602-8056
Michele Dutton, prin. Fax 602-8057
Tanner S 700/K-8
7210 Rosecrans Ave 90723 562-602-8060
Patricia Brent, prin. Fax 602-8061
Wirtz S 900/K-8
8535 Contreras St 90723 562-602-8068
Kelly Williams, prin. Fax 602-8069
Zamboni S 700/K-8
15733 Orange Ave 90723 562-602-8048
Valanitta Richard, prin. Fax 602-8049
Other Schools – See Lakewood, Long Beach, South Gate

Our Lady of the Rosary S 200/PK-8
14813 Paramount Blvd 90723 562-633-6360
Sr. Anna O'Reilly, prin. Fax 633-2641

Parker Dam, San Bernardino
Needles USD
Supt. — See Needles
Parker Dam S 100/K-8
California and Utah Sts 92267 760-663-4926
Lisa Cain, prin. Fax 663-3184

Parlier, Fresno, Pop. 13,025
Kings Canyon JUSD
Supt. — See Reedley
Riverview S 400/K-8
8662 S Lac Jac Ave 93648 559-305-7290
Bendta Friesen, prin. Fax 637-1279

Parlier USD 3,800/K-12
900 S Newmark Ave 93648 559-646-2731
Rick Rodriguez, supt. Fax 646-0626
www.parlierunified.org/
Benavidez ES 600/K-6
13900 Tuolumne St 93648 559-646-2963
Julissa Alvarado, prin. Fax 646-2975
Brletic ES 600/K-6
601 3rd St 93648 559-646-3551
Angelina Rodriguez, prin. Fax 646-2850
Chavez ES 500/K-6
500 Tuolumne St 93648 559-646-3595
Theressa Manzanedo, prin. Fax 646-0782
Martinez ES 600/K-6
13174 E Parlier Ave 93648 559-646-3527
Gudelia Sandoval, prin. Fax 646-2025
Parlier JHS 600/7-8
1200 E Parlier Ave 93648 559-646-1660
Juan Lopez, prin. Fax 646-1633

Pasadena, Los Angeles, Pop. 143,731
Pasadena USD 19,800/K-12
351 S Hudson Ave 91101 626-795-6981
Edwin Diaz, supt. Fax 795-5309
www.pusd.us/
Cleveland ES 300/K-5
524 Palisade St 91103 626-794-7169
Dr. Francine Williams, prin. Fax 794-2556
Don Benito Fundamental ES 700/K-5
3700 Denair St 91107 626-351-8895
Victoria Rueda, prin. Fax 351-8892
Field ES 300/K-5
3600 E Sierra Madre Blvd 91107 626-351-8812
Ana Apodaca, prin. Fax 351-4202
Hamilton ES 400/K-5
2089 Rose Villa St 91107 626-793-0678
Sarah Rudchenko, prin. Fax 793-7581
Jefferson ES 700/K-5
1500 E Villa St 91106 626-793-0656
Jill Girod, prin. Fax 793-6994
Longfellow ES 500/K-5
1065 E Washington Blvd 91104 626-794-1134
Erica Ingber, prin. Fax 398-6340
Madison ES 600/K-5
515 E Ashtabula St 91104 626-793-1181
Sandra Macis, prin. Fax 793-6868
McKinley S 1,100/K-8
325 S Oak Knoll Ave 91101 626-844-7880
Marisa Sarian, prin. Fax 844-7838
Roosevelt S 300/K-12
315 N Pasadena Ave 91103 626-795-9501
Dr. Kathleen Bautista, prin. Fax 795-5180
San Rafael ES 400/K-5
1090 Nithsdale Rd 91105 626-793-4189
Alyson Beecher, prin. Fax 683-7429
Washington Accelerated ES 800/K-5
1520 N Raymond Ave 91103 626-791-4573
Karrone Meeks-Clark, prin. Fax 296-2693
Washington MS 500/6-8
1505 N Marengo Ave 91103 626-798-6708
Alejandro Ruvalcaba, prin. Fax 798-2844
Webster ES 400/K-5
2101 E Washington Blvd 91104 626-798-7866
Sharon Lefler, prin. Fax 798-8216
Willard ES 600/K-5
301 Madre St 91107 626-793-6163
Kathy Onoye, prin. Fax 744-3375
Wilson MS 900/6-8
300 Madre St 91107 626-449-7390
Ruth Esseln, prin. Fax 584-9895
Other Schools – See Altadena, Sierra Madre

Assumption of the Blessed Virgin Mary S 300/PK-8
2660 E Orange Grove Blvd 91107 626-793-2089
Christine Hunter, prin. Fax 793-4070
Chandler S 400/K-8
1005 Armada Dr 91103 626-795-9314
John Finch, hdmstr. Fax 795-6508
Friends Western S 50/K-6
524 E Orange Grove Blvd 91104 626-793-2727
Peter Day, hdmstr. Fax 243-4719
Grace Christian Academy 100/K-8
73 N Hill Ave 91106 626-792-7725
Vsev Krawczeniuk, dir. Fax 792-6830
Harambee Preparatory S 50/PK-6
1609 Navarro Ave 91103 626-798-7431
Kafi Carrasco, prin. Fax 798-1865
High Point Academy 400/K-8
1720 Kinneloa Canyon Rd 91107 626-798-8989
John Higgins, prin. Fax 798-8751
Judson International S 100/K-8
1610 E Elizabeth St 91104 626-398-2476
Diana Bjoraker, prin. Fax 398-2222
Mayfield Junior S 500/PK-8
405 S Euclid Ave 91101 626-796-2774
Stephanie Griffin, prin. Fax 796-5753
New Horizon S 200/PK-8
651 N Orange Grove Blvd 91103 626-795-5186
Amira Al-Sarraf, hdmstr. Fax 395-9519
Pasadena Christian S 500/PK-8
1515 N Los Robles Ave 91104 626-791-1214
Steven Gray Ph.D., supt. Fax 791-1256
Polytechnic S 900/K-12
1030 E California Blvd 91106 626-792-2147
Deborah Reed, hdmstr. Fax 796-2249
St. Andrew S 200/K-8
42 Chestnut St 91103 626-796-7697
Sr. Daleen Larkin, prin. Fax 796-1931
St. Gregory's A & M Hovsepian S 100/K-8
2215 E Colorado Blvd 91107 626-578-1343
Fax 578-7378
St. Monica Academy 100/1-12
301 N Orange Grove Blvd 91103 626-229-0351
Marguerite Grimm, hdmstr.
St. Philip the Apostle S 400/K-8
1363 Cordova St 91106 626-795-9691
Jennifer Ramirez, prin. Fax 795-9946
San Marino Montessori S 100/K-8
444 S Sierra Madre Blvd 91107 626-577-8007
Linda Hughes, dir. Fax 577-4566
Sequoyah S 200/K-8
535 S Pasadena Ave 91105 626-795-4351
Josh Brody, dir. Fax 795-8773
Walden S of California 300/PK-6
74 S San Gabriel Blvd 91107 626-792-6166
Matt Allio, dir. Fax 792-1335
Waverly ES 100/K-6
67 W Bellevue Dr 91105 626-792-5940
Heidi Johnson, hdmstr. Fax 683-5460
Westminster Academy 200/K-8
1206 Lincoln Ave 91103 626-398-7576
David Thibault, prin. Fax 398-7577

Paskenta, Tehama
Elkins ESD 50/K-8
PO Box 407 96074 530-833-5582
Marla Katzler, supt. Fax 833-9859
www.tcde.tehama.k12.ca.us/elkinssd.html
Elkins S 50/K-8
PO Box 407 96074 530-833-5582
Marla Katzler, prin. Fax 833-9859

Paso Robles, San Luis Obispo, Pop. 20,187
Paso Robles JUSD 6,800/K-12
PO Box 7010 93447 805-238-2222
Kathleen McNamara Ed.D., supt. Fax 237-3339
www.pasoschools.org/
Bauer/Speck ES 500/K-5
PO Box 7010 93447 805-237-3413
Tracey Hockett, prin. Fax 237-3498
Brown ES 500/K-5
PO Box 7010 93447 805-237-3387
Rigoberto Elenes, prin. Fax 237-3426
Butler ES 500/K-5
PO Box 7010 93447 805-237-3407
Dorothy Halic, prin. Fax 237-3496
Flamson MS 700/6-8
PO Box 7010 93447 805-237-3350
Gene Miller, prin. Fax 237-3427
Kermit King ES 400/K-5
PO Box 7010 93447 805-237-6170
Carol Kenyon, prin. Fax 237-6169
Lewis MS 700/6-8
PO Box 7010 93447 805-237-3450
Rick Oyler, prin. Fax 237-3458
Peterson ES 500/K-5
PO Box 7010 93447 805-237-3401
Wayne Peterson, prin. Fax 237-3497
Pifer ES 500/K-5
PO Box 7010 93447 805-237-3393
Ruben Canales, prin. Fax 237-3398

San Miguel JUNESD
Supt. — See San Miguel
Culver S 100/K-6
11011 Heritage Loop Ranch, 805-227-1040
Marshall Dennis, prin. Fax 227-1045

Advanced Christian Training S 100/K-12
PO Box 97 93447 805-239-0707
William Thompson, supt. Fax 238-1133
St. Rose of Lima S 200/PK-8
900 Tucker Ave 93446 805-238-0304
Sr. Rebecca Munoz, prin. Fax 238-7393
Solid Rock Christian Academy 50/1-12
4675 Whispering Oak Way 93446 805-610-5318
Yasmin Nason, dir. Fax 238-4471
Trinity Lutheran S 200/PK-8
940 Creston Rd 93446 805-238-0335
Jane Fairbank, prin. Fax 238-0892

Patterson, Stanislaus, Pop. 15,500
Patterson JUSD 5,100/K-12
510 Keystone Blvd 95363 209-895-7700
Patrick Sweeney Ed.D., supt.
www.patterson.k12.ca.us/
Apricot Valley ES 600/K-5
1320 Henley Pkwy 95363 209-895-4301
Jose Sanchez, prin. Fax 892-4310
Creekside MS 1,300/6-8
535 Peregrine Dr 95363 209-892-3600
Shawn Posey, prin. Fax 892-7101
Las Palmas ES 600/K-5
624 W Las Palmas Ave 95363 209-892-7457
Jennifer Yacoub, prin. Fax 892-7769
Northmead ES 900/K-5
625 L St 95363 209-892-7460
Veronica Miranda, prin. Fax 892-7770
Other Schools – See Vernalis

Sacred Heart S 300/PK-8
505 M St 95363 209-892-3544
Jason Oliveira, prin. Fax 892-3214

Pauma Valley, San Diego
Valley Center-Pauma USD
Supt. — See Valley Center
Pauma S 300/K-8
33158 Cole Grade 92061 760-742-3741
Bryan Farmer, prin. Fax 742-1214

Paynes Creek, Tehama
Plum Valley ESD 50/K-8
29950 Plum Creek Rd 96075 530-597-2248
Pat Sinclair, supt. Fax 597-2890
www.pvsd.tehama.k12.ca.us/
Plum Valley S 50/K-8
29950 Plum Creek Rd 96075 530-597-2248
Pat Sinclair, prin. Fax 597-2890

Pearblossom, Los Angeles
Keppel UNESD 3,100/K-8
PO Box 186 93553 661-944-2155
Steve Doyle, supt. Fax 944-2933
www.keppel.k12.ca.us
Pearblossom ES 400/K-6
PO Box 205 93553 661-944-6019
Lynn Boop, prin. Fax 944-0733
Other Schools – See Littlerock, Palmdale

Penngrove, Sonoma, Pop. 1,100
Petaluma SD
Supt. — See Petaluma
Penngrove ES 300/K-6
365 Adobe Rd 94951 707-778-4755
Kathleen Larsen, prin. Fax 778-4831

Penn Valley, Nevada, Pop. 1,242
Pleasant Valley ESD 600/K-8
14806 Pleasant Valley Rd 95946 530-432-7311
Debra Sandoval, supt. Fax 432-7314
www.pennvalleyschools.k12.ca.us

Pleasant Valley S 400/4-8
14685 Pleasant Valley Rd 95946 530-432-7333
Clint Johnson, prin. Fax 432-7338
Williams Ranch ES 300/K-3
14804 Pleasant Valley Rd 95946 530-432-7300
Anne Stone, prin. Fax 432-7305

Ready Springs UNESD 200/K-8
14806 Pleasant Valley Rd 95946 530-432-7311
Debra Sandoval, supt. Fax 432-7314
www.pennvalleyschools.k12.ca.us
Ready Springs S 200/K-8
10862 Spenceville Rd 95946 530-432-1118
Thomas Bivens, prin. Fax 432-9473

Penryn, Placer
Loomis UNESD
Supt. — See Loomis
Penryn S 300/K-8
6885 English Colony Way 95663 916-663-3993
Andy Withers, prin. Fax 663-2127

Hope Lutheran S 50/K-8
7117 Hope Way 95663 916-652-0459
Paul Leifer, prin. Fax 652-0459

Perris, Riverside, Pop. 45,671
Perris ESD 5,600/K-6
143 E 1st St 92570 951-657-3118
Edward Aqundez, supt. Fax 940-5115
www.perris.k12.ca.us
Enchanted Hills ES 600/K-6
1357 Mount Baldy St 92570 951-443-4790
Robin Jones, prin. Fax 443-1692
Good Hope ES 900/K-6
24050 Theda St 92570 951-657-5181
Margaret Briggs, prin. Fax 657-9961
Palms ES 800/K-6
255 E Jarvis St 92571 951-940-5112
Juan Hernandez, prin. Fax 940-5179
Park Avenue ES 500/K-6
445 Park Ave 92570 951-940-5140
Gloria Johnson, prin. Fax 657-5743
Perris ES 600/K-6
500 S A St 92570 951-657-2124
Tiffany Martinez, prin. Fax 657-0854
Railway ES 500/K-6
555 Alpine Dr 92570 951-943-3259
Dennis Stevens, prin. Fax 943-8517
Sanders ES 800/K-6
1461 N A St 92570 951-657-0728
Sandra Dial, prin. Fax 940-5103
Sky View ES 800/K-6
625 Mildred St 92571 951-657-4214
Robert French, prin. Fax 940-5816

Perris UNHSD 10,300/7-12
155 E 4th St 92570 951-943-6369
Dr. Jonathan Greenberg, supt. Fax 940-5378
www.puhsd.org/
Pinacate MS 1,300/7-8
1990 S A St 92570 951-943-6441
Charles Newman, prin. Fax 940-5344

Val Verde USD 17,200/PK-12
975 Morgan St 92571 951-940-6100
Alan Jensen Ed.D., supt. Fax 940-6121
www.valverde.edu
Avalon ES 800/K-5
1815 E Rider St 92571 951-490-0360
Marilyn Lezine, prin. Fax 490-0365
Columbia ES 700/K-5
21350 Rider St 92570 951-443-2460
Deborah Bryant, prin. Fax 443-2465
Glen View Headstart / Preschool PK-PK
21200 Oleander Ave 92570 951-940-8530
Julie Singletary, prin. Fax 940-8535
Lakeside MS 1,400/6-8
27720 Walnut St 92571 951-443-2440
Robert Block, prin. Fax 443-2445
May Ranch ES K-5
900 E Morgan St 92571 951-490-4670
Jim Owen, prin. Fax 490-4675
Mead Valley ES 700/K-5
21100 Oleander Ave 92570 951-940-8540
Ruth Salazar, prin. Fax 940-8545
Real ES 700/K-5
19150 Clark St 92570 951-940-8520
Paz Enciso, prin. Fax 940-8525
Rivera MS 1,200/6-8
21675 Martin St 92570 951-940-8570
Ernesto Lizarraga, prin. Fax 940-6133
Sierra Vista ES 800/K-5
20300 Sherman Rd 92571 951-443-2430
Corby Warren, prin. Fax 443-2435
Triple Crown ES K-5
530 Orange Ave 92571 951-490-0440
Laura Muehlebach, prin. Fax 490-0445
Val Verde ES 800/K-5
2656 Indian Ave 92571 951-940-8550
Anu Menon, prin. Fax 940-8555
Other Schools – See Moreno Valley

St. James S 200/K-8
250 W 3rd St 92570 951-657-5226
Sr. Sylvia Parkes, prin. Fax 657-1793
Temple Christian S 200/PK-8
745 N Perris Blvd 92571 951-657-7326
Craig Brooks, prin.

Pescadero, San Mateo
La Honda-Pescadero USD 400/K-12
PO Box 189 94060 650-879-0286
Timothy Beard, supt. Fax 879-0816
www.lhpusd.net/
Pescadero S 200/K-8
PO Box 207 94060 650-879-0332
Patty Able, prin. Fax 879-0816
Other Schools – See La Honda

Petaluma, Sonoma, Pop. 54,846
Cinnabar ESD 200/K-6
PO Box 750399 94975 707-765-4345
Robert Ecker, supt. Fax 765-4349
www.cinnabar.k12.ca.us
Cinnabar ES 200/K-6
PO Box 750399 94975 707-765-4345
Robert Ecker, prin. Fax 765-4349

Dunham ESD 200/K-6
4111 Roblar Rd 94952 707-795-5050
Kimberlee Wilding, supt. Fax 795-5166
www.dunhamsd.k12.ca.us
Dunham ES 200/K-6
4111 Roblar Rd 94952 707-795-5050
Kimberlee Wilding, prin. Fax 795-5166

Laguna JESD 50/K-6
2657 Chileno Valley Rd 94952 707-762-6051
Luke McCann, supt. Fax 762-6051
Laguna ES 50/K-6
2657 Chileno Valley Rd 94952 707-762-6051
Pamela Brambila, prin. Fax 762-6051

Liberty ESD 200/K-6
170 Liberty School Rd 94952 707-795-4380
Chris Rafanelli, supt. Fax 795-6468
www.libertysd.org
Liberty ES 200/K-6
170 Liberty School Rd 94952 707-795-4380
Chris Rafanelli, prin. Fax 795-6468

Lincoln ESD 50/K-6
1300 Hicks Valley Rd 94952 707-763-0045
Luke McCann, supt. Fax 763-1255
Lincoln ES 50/K-6
1300 Hicks Valley Rd 94952 707-763-0045
Sandy Doyle, prin. Fax 763-1255

Old Adobe UNESD 1,900/K-6
845 Crinella Dr 94954 707-765-4322
Dr. Diane Zimmerman, supt. Fax 765-4343
www.oldadobe.org
Eldredge ES 300/K-6
207 Maria Dr 94954 707-765-4302
Lisa Jimenez, prin. Fax 765-4317
La Tercera ES 400/K-6
1600 Albin Way 94954 707-765-4303
Ken Schwinn, prin. Fax 765-4333
Miwok Valley ES 500/K-6
1010 Saint Francis Dr 94954 707-765-4304
Kim Harper, prin. Fax 765-4380
Old Adobe ES 300/K-6
2856 Old Adobe Rd 94954 707-765-4301
Jeff Williamson, prin. Fax 765-4334
Sonoma Mountain ES 400/K-6
1900 Rainier Cir 94954 707-765-4305
Suzanne Martin, prin. Fax 765-4385

Petaluma SD 7,500/K-12
200 Douglas St 94952 707-778-4604
Greta Viguie, supt. Fax 778-4736
www.petalumacityschools.org
Grant ES 300/K-6
200 Grant Ave 94952 707-778-4742
Judith Martin, prin. Fax 778-4852
Kenilworth JHS 900/7-8
800 Riesling Rd 94954 707-778-4710
Toni Beal, prin. Fax 766-8231
McDowell ES 300/K-6
421 S McDowell Blvd 94954 707-778-4745
Maureen Rudder, prin. Fax 778-4789
McKinley ES 300/K-6
110 Ellis St 94952 707-778-4750
Sherry Devine, prin. Fax 766-8337
McNear ES 400/K-6
605 Sunnyslope Ave 94952 707-778-4752
Jason Sutter, prin. Fax 778-4859
Petaluma JHS 700/7-8
700 Bantam Way 94952 707-778-4724
John Lehmann, prin. Fax 778-4600
Valley Vista ES 400/K-6
730 N Webster St 94952 707-778-4762
Emily Blecher, prin. Fax 778-4840
Other Schools – See Penngrove

Two Rock UNESD 200/K-6
5001 Spring Hill Rd 94952 707-762-6617
Michael Simpson, supt. Fax 762-1923
www.trusd.org/
Two Rock ES 200/K-6
5001 Spring Hill Rd 94952 707-762-6617
Michael Simpson, prin. Fax 762-1923

Union JESD 50/K-6
5300 Red Hill Rd 94952 707-762-2047
Luke McCann, supt. Fax 781-9258
mcoeweb.marin.k12.ca.us/rurals/union/
Union ES 50/K-6
5300 Red Hill Rd 94952 707-762-2047
Cynthia Haydon, prin. Fax 781-9258

Waugh ESD 900/K-6
1851 Hartman Ln 94954 707-765-3331
Scott Mahoney Ed.D., supt. Fax 782-9666
www.waughsd.org/
Corona Creek ES 500/K-6
1851 Hartman Ln 94954 707-765-3331
Scott Mahoney, prin. Fax 782-9666
Meadow ES 500/K-6
880 Maria Dr 94954 707-762-4905
Melissa Becker, prin. Fax 762-5751

Wilmar UNESD 200/PK-6
3775 Bodega Ave 94952 707-765-4340
Eric Hoppes, supt. Fax 765-4342
www.wilsonschoolpetaluma.org/
Wilson ES 200/PK-6
3775 Bodega Ave 94952 707-765-4340
Eric Hoppes, prin. Fax 765-4342

Harvest Christian S 100/K-9
3700 Lakeville Hwy Ste 210 94954 707-763-2954
Jonathan Wraith, prin. Fax 763-0159
St. Vincent de Paul S 300/K-8
100 Union St 94952 707-762-6426
Susan Roffmann, prin. Fax 762-6791

Petrolia, Humboldt
Mattole USD
Supt. — See Honeydew
Mattole S 50/K-8
PO Box 211 95558 707-629-3240
Glenda Short, prin. Fax 629-3611

Phelan, San Bernardino
Snowline JUSD 8,700/K-12
PO Box 296000 92329 760-868-5817
Eric Johnston, supt. Fax 868-5309
www.snowlineschools.com/
Baldy Mesa ES 1,000/K-5
PO Box 296000 92329 760-949-1232
Dan MacDonald, prin. Fax 949-2770
Heritage S 500/K-8
PO Box 296000 92329 760-868-2422
John Garner, prin. Fax 868-0589
Phelan ES 700/K-5
PO Box 296000 92329 760-868-3252
Stacey Stewart, prin. Fax 868-1044
Pinon Mesa MS 1,000/6-8
PO Box 296000 92329 760-868-3126
Burt Umstead, prin. Fax 868-3033
Quail Valley MS 1,000/6-8
PO Box 296000 92329 760-949-4888
Dennis Zimmerman, prin. Fax 949-3663
Other Schools – See Pinon Hills, Victorville, Wrightwood

Pico Rivera, Los Angeles, Pop. 64,679
El Rancho USD 10,200/PK-12
9333 Loch Lomond Dr 90660 562-942-1500
Norbert Genis, supt. Fax 949-2821
www.erusd.k12.ca.us
Birney ES 500/K-5
8501 Orange Ave 90660 562-801-5153
Gisela Castanon, prin. Fax 801-9354
Burke MS 800/6-8
8101 Orange Ave 90660 562-801-5059
Mark Matthews, prin. Fax 801-5067
Child Development Center PK-PK
7601 Cord Ave 90660 562-801-5117
Roberta Gonzalez, prin. Fax 801-0164
Durfee ES 500/K-5
4220 Durfee Ave 90660 562-801-5070
Gloria Lopez, prin. Fax 692-8922
Magee ES 500/K-5
8200 Serapis Ave 90660 562-801-5000
Yolanda Aguerrebere, prin. Fax 801-5004
North Park MS 1,000/6-8
4450 Durfee Ave 90660 562-801-5137
John Lopez, prin. Fax 801-5143
North Ranchito ES 500/K-5
8837 Olympic Blvd 90660 562-801-5031
Cynthia Alvarez, prin. Fax 699-0216
Rio Vista ES 500/K-5
8809 Coffman Pico Rd 90660 562-801-5049
Dean Cochran, prin. Fax 942-7989
Rivera ES 500/K-5
7250 Citronell Ave 90660 562-801-5095
Barbara Keenoy, prin. Fax 801-0383
Rivera MS 1,000/6-8
7200 Citronell Ave 90660 562-801-5088
Andrew Alvidrez, prin. Fax 801-9158
South Ranchito ES 600/K-5
5241 Passons Blvd 90660 562-801-5177
Margaret Norman, prin. Fax 942-8927
Valencia ES 300/K-5
9241 Cosgrove St 90660 562-801-5079
Roxane Cicciarelli, prin. Fax 801-0146

Montebello USD
Supt. — See Montebello
Montebello Gardens ES 300/K-4
4700 Pine St 90660 562-463-5191
Norma Perez, prin. Fax 463-5196

Armenian Mesrobian S 200/PK-12
8420 Beverly Rd 90660 323-723-3181
Hilda Saliba, prin. Fax 699-0757
St. Hilary S 300/K-8
5401 Citronell Ave 90660 562-942-7361
Sr. Richardine Rempe, prin. Fax 801-9131
St. Marianne De Paredes S 200/PK-8
7911 Buhman Ave 90660 562-949-1234
Karen Lloyd, prin. Fax 948-3855

Piedmont, Alameda, Pop. 10,559
Piedmont City USD 2,600/K-12
760 Magnolia Ave 94611 510-594-2600
Constance Hubbard, supt. Fax 654-7374
www.piedmont.k12.ca.us
Beach ES 300/K-5
100 Lake Ave 94611 510-594-2666
Julie Valdez, prin. Fax 655-6751
Havens ES 500/K-5
1800 Oakland Ave 94611 510-594-2680
Tery Susman, prin. Fax 654-9266
Piedmont MS 600/6-8
740 Magnolia Ave 94611 510-594-2660
Jeanne Donovan, prin. Fax 595-3523
Wildwood ES 300/K-5
301 Wildwood Ave 94611 510-594-2710
Carol Cramer, prin. Fax 451-8134

Corpus Christi S 300/K-8
1 Estates Dr 94611 510-530-4056
Kathleen Murphy, prin. Fax 530-5926
Zion Lutheran S 100/K-8
5201 Park Blvd 94611 510-530-7909
John Heinitz, prin. Fax 530-2635

Pinecrest, Tuolumne
Twain Harte-Long Barn UESD
Supt. — See Twain Harte
Pinecrest S 50/K-8
30433 Old Strawberry Rd 95364 209-965-3521
John Keiter Ed.D., prin. Fax 965-0226

Pinedale, Fresno
Clovis USD
Supt. — See Clovis
Nelson ES 600/K-6
1336 W Spruce Ave 93650 559-327-7600
Chuck Sandoval, prin. Fax 327-7690
Pinedale ES 500/K-6
7171 N Sugar Pine Ave 93650 559-327-7700
Allison Hernandez, prin. Fax 327-7790

Pine Grove, Amador
Amador County USD
Supt. — See Jackson
Pine Grove ES 300/K-6
20101 Highway 88 95665 209-296-2800
Tom Reed, prin. Fax 296-3133

Community Christian S 100/PK-8
14045 Ponderosa Way 95665 209-296-7773
Les Darrow, admin. Fax 296-7744

Pine Valley, San Diego, Pop. 1,297
Mountain Empire USD 1,300/K-12
3291 Buckman Springs Rd 91962 619-473-9022
Steve VanZant, supt. Fax 473-9728
www.meusd.net
Mountain Empire MS 100/8-8
3305 Buckman Springs Rd 91962 619-473-8601
Ernie Sopp, prin. Fax 473-8038
Pine Valley ES 50/K-3
PO Box 571 91962 619-473-8693
Joan Baumann, prin. Fax 473-8026
Other Schools – See Boulevard, Campo, Descanso, Jacumba, Potrero

Pinole, Contra Costa, Pop. 19,061
West Contra Costa USD
Supt. — See Richmond
Collins ES 400/K-6
1224 Pinole Valley Rd 94564 510-724-3086
Anne Shin, prin. Fax 741-1268
Ellerhorst ES 400/K-6
3501 Pinole Valley Rd 94564 510-231-1426
Grethe Holtan, prin. Fax 243-6754
Pinole MS 700/7-8
1575 Mann Dr 94564 510-724-4042
Katie von Husen, prin. Fax 724-9583
Shannon ES 400/K-6
685 Marlesta Rd 94564 510-724-0943
Frank Bianchi, prin. Fax 741-8690
Stewart S 500/K-8
2040 Hoke Dr 94564 510-231-1410
Carol Butcher, prin. Fax 758-1639

St. Joseph S 300/K-8
1961 Plum St 94564 510-724-0242
Arlene Marseille, prin. Fax 724-9886

Pinon Hills, San Bernardino
Snowline JUSD
Supt. — See Phelan
Pinon Hills ES 500/K-5
878 Mono Rd 92372 760-868-4424
Shawn Premo, prin. Fax 868-1028

Pioneer, Amador
Amador County USD
Supt. — See Jackson
Pioneer ES 200/K-6
24625 Highway 88 95666 209-295-6500
Donna Custodio, prin. Fax 295-1660

Piru, Ventura, Pop. 1,157
Fillmore USD
Supt. — See Fillmore
Piru ES 300/K-6
3811 E Center St 93040 805-524-8251
Leticia Ramos, prin. Fax 521-1044

Pismo Beach, San Luis Obispo, Pop. 8,419
Lucia Mar USD
Supt. — See Arroyo Grande
Judkins MS 500/7-8
680 Wadsworth Ave 93449 805-474-3600
Bryant Smith, prin. Fax 473-4376
Shell Beach ES 400/K-6
2100 Shell Beach Rd 93449 805-474-3760
Rob Bergan, prin. Fax 473-5517

Pittsburg, Contra Costa, Pop. 62,547
Mount Diablo USD
Supt. — See Concord
Bel Air ES 500/K-5
663 Canal Rd 94565 925-458-2606
Tom Carmen, prin. Fax 458-2065
Delta View ES 600/K-5
2916 Rio Verde 94565 925-261-0240
Susan Petersen, prin. Fax 261-0246
Rio Vista ES 400/K-5
611 Pacifica Ave 94565 925-458-6101
Barbara Blankenship, prin. Fax 458-8765
Riverview MS 900/6-8
205 Pacifica Ave 94565 925-458-3216
Denise Rugani, prin. Fax 458-0875
Shore Acres ES 600/K-5
351 Marina Rd 94565 925-458-3261
Kari Rees, prin. Fax 458-6465

Pittsburg USD 8,300/PK-12
2000 Railroad Ave 94565 925-473-2300
Dr. Barbara Wilson, supt. Fax 473-4274
www.pittsburg.k12.ca.us
Foothill ES 700/K-5
1200 Jensen Dr 94565 925-473-2450
Ricardo Araiza, prin. Fax 473-4305
Heights ES 600/K-5
163 West Blvd 94565 925-473-2410
Karen Clark, prin. Fax 473-4315
Highlands ES 700/K-5
4141 Harbor St 94565 925-473-2440
Steve Ahonen, prin. Fax 473-4311
Hillview JHS 1,000/6-8
333 Yosemite Dr 94565 925-473-2380
Shelley Velasco, prin. Fax 473-4406
King Preschool PK-PK
950 El Pueblo Ave 94565 925-473-4370
Karan Latimer, coord. Fax 473-4371
Los Medanos ES 600/K-5
610 Crowley Ave 94565 925-473-2460
Angela Stevenson, prin. Fax 473-4335
Marina Vista ES K-5
50 E 8th St 94565 925-473-2490
Lynne Plunkett, prin. Fax 473-9039
Parkside ES 600/K-5
985 W 17th St 94565 925-473-2420
Jeff Varner, prin. Fax 473-4343
Rancho Medanos JHS 6-8
2301 Range Rd 94565 925-473-2490
Eric Peyko, prin. Fax 473-1060
Stoneman ES 600/K-5
2929 Loveridge Rd 94565 925-473-2430
Donna Marshall, prin. Fax 473-4355
Willow Cove ES 700/K-5
1880 Hanlon Way 94565 925-473-2470
Jan Kuhl, prin. Fax 709-2005

Christian Center S 200/PK-12
1210 Stoneman Ave 94565 925-439-2552
Edward Marquardt, admin. Fax 439-2555
St. Peter Martyr S 300/PK-8
425 W 4th St 94565 925-439-1014
Joseph Siino, prin. Fax 439-1506

Pixley, Tulare, Pop. 2,457
Pixley UNESD 900/K-8
300 N School St 93256 559-757-3131
Dr. Saddie Nishitani, supt. Fax 757-1701
www.pixley.k12.ca.us/
Pixley S 900/K-8
300 N School St 93256 559-757-3131
Fax 757-0705

Placentia, Orange, Pop. 49,795
Placentia-Yorba Linda USD 26,300/K-12
1301 E Orangethorpe Ave 92870 714-996-2550
Dennis Smith Ed.D., supt. Fax 524-3034
www.pylusd.org/
Brookhaven ES 500/K-6
1851 Brookhaven Ave 92870 714-996-7110
Shirley Fargo, prin. Fax 996-4308
Golden Ave ES 800/K-6
740 Golden Ave 92870 714-986-7160
Kathy Chakan, prin. Fax 996-7690
Kraemer MS 1,600/6-8
645 N Angelina Dr 92870 714-996-1551
Richard McAlindin, prin. Fax 996-8407
Melrose ES 600/K-5
974 S Melrose St 92870 714-630-4992
Vivian Cuesta, prin. Fax 630-6742
Morse Ave ES 500/K-6
431 Morse Ave 92870 714-524-6300
Kathi DiRocco, prin. Fax 524-3260
Ruby Drive ES 500/K-6
601 Ruby Dr 92870 714-996-1921
Monica Barrera, prin. Fax 996-2143
Sierra Vista ES 500/K-6
1811 N Placentia Ave 92870 714-986-7270
Joan Bonn, prin. Fax 572-9506
Tuffree MS 800/7-8
2151 N Kraemer Blvd 92870 714-986-7480
Rosie Baldwin-Shirey, prin. Fax 993-6359
Tynes ES 800/K-6
735 Stanford Dr 92870 714-986-7290
Cristina McCall, prin. Fax 996-7931
Valadez MS Academy 6-8
161 E La Jolla St 92870 714-986-7440
Minerva Gandara, prin. Fax 238-9159
Van Buren ES 700/K-6
1245 N Van Buren St 92870 714-986-7290
Caryn Lewis, prin. Fax 996-5133
Wagner ES 400/K-6
717 E Yorba Linda Blvd 92870 714-986-7180
Katherine Dailey, prin. Fax 792-0852
Other Schools – See Anaheim, Fullerton, Yorba Linda

St. Joseph S 300/PK-8
801 N Bradford Ave 92870 714-528-1794
Dr. Judith Johnston, prin. Fax 528-0668

Placerville, El Dorado, Pop. 10,184
Gold Oak UNESD 600/K-8
3171 Pleasant Valley Rd 95667 530-626-3150
Richard Williams, supt. Fax 626-3145
www.gousd.k12.ca.us
Gold Oak ES 400/K-5
3171 Pleasant Valley Rd 95667 530-626-3160
Sylvia Shannon, prin. Fax 626-3144
Pleasant Valley MS 200/6-8
4120 Pleasant Valley Rd 95667 530-644-9620
Dr. Jerry Kosch, prin. Fax 644-9622

Gold Trail UNESD 500/K-8
1575 Old Ranch Rd 95667 530-626-3194
Joe Murchison, supt. Fax 626-3199
www.gtusd.org/
Gold Trail S 300/4-8
889 Cold Springs Rd 95667 530-626-2595
Stephany Rewick, prin. Fax 626-3289
Sutter's Mill PS 200/K-3
4801 Luneman Rd 95667 530-626-2591
Joe Murchison, prin. Fax 626-2593

Mother Lode UNESD 1,500/K-8
3783 Forni Rd 95667 530-622-6464
Shanda Hahn, supt. Fax 622-6163
www.mlusd.net
Green MS 500/6-8
3781 Forni Rd 95667 530-622-4668
Tim Smith, prin. Fax 622-4680
Indian Creek ES 500/K-5
6701 Green Valley Rd 95667 530-626-0765
Bob Bassett, prin. Fax 626-9695
Other Schools – See El Dorado

Placerville UNSD 1,200/K-8
1032 Thompson Way 95667 530-622-7216
Nancy Lynch Ed.D., supt. Fax 622-0336
www.pusdk8.us/
Louisiana Schnell S 400/K-5
2871 Schnell School Rd 95667 530-622-6244
Sam LaCara, prin. Fax 622-2309
Markham MS 400/6-8
2800 Moulton Dr 95667 530-622-0403
Steve Mizera, prin. Fax 622-5584
Sierra S 400/K-5
1100 Thompson Way 95667 530-622-0814
Natalie Miller, prin. Fax 622-0532

Cedar Springs Waldorf S 200/PK-8
6029 Gold Meadows Rd 95667 530-642-9903
Scott Krieger, admin. Fax 642-1904
El Dorado Adventist S 200/K-12
1900 Broadway 95667 530-622-3560
Larry Ballew, prin. Fax 622-2604

Planada, Merced, Pop. 3,531
Planada ESD 800/K-8
PO Box 236 95365 209-382-0756
Steve Gomes, supt. Fax 382-1750
www.planada.k12.ca.us/
Chavez MS 300/6-8
PO Box 236 95365 209-382-0768
Ildefonso Nava, prin. Fax 382-0775
Planada ES 500/K-5
PO Box 236 95365 209-382-0272
Richard Lopez, prin. Fax 382-0113

Playa Del Rey, See Los Angeles
Los Angeles USD
Supt. — See Los Angeles
Paseo Del Rey Fundamental ES 500/K-5
7751 Paseo Del Rey 90293 310-823-2356
Jennifer Sullivan, prin. Fax 305-0251

Pleasant Grove, Sutter
Pleasant Grove Joint Union SD 200/K-8
3075 Howsley Rd 95668 916-655-3235
Rebecca Gillespie, supt. Fax 655-3501
Pleasant Grove S 200/K-8
3075 Howsley Rd 95668 916-655-3235
Rebecca Gillespie, prin. Fax 655-3501

Pleasant Hill, Contra Costa, Pop. 33,153
Mount Diablo USD
Supt. — See Concord
Fair Oaks ES 400/K-5
2400 Lisa Ln 94523 925-685-4494
Cheryl Champion, prin. Fax 687-3170
Gregory Gardens ES 400/K-5
1 Corritone Ct 94523 925-827-3770
Candace Raitano, prin. Fax 687-8677
Pleasant Hill ES 600/K-5
2097 Oak Park Blvd 94523 925-934-3341
Jennifer Voris, prin. Fax 935-3748
Pleasant Hill MS 800/6-8
1 Santa Barbara Rd 94523 925-256-0791
Jonathan Roslin, prin. Fax 937-6271
Sequoia ES 600/K-5
277 Boyd Rd 94523 925-935-5721
Cindy Matteoni, prin. Fax 988-8049
Sequoia MS 900/6-8
265 Boyd Rd 94523 925-934-8174
Hellena Postrik, prin. Fax 946-9063
Shearer Preschool PK-PK
1 Corritone Ct 94523 925-685-1960
Candace Raitano, prin. Fax 685-1961
Strandwood ES 600/K-5
416 Gladys Dr 94523 925-685-3212
Liz Kim, prin. Fax 798-4582
Valhalla S 500/K-8
530 Kiki Dr 94523 925-687-1700
Marji Calbeck, prin. Fax 687-3083
Valley View MS 800/6-8
181 Viking Dr 94523 925-686-6136
Nadine Rosenzweig, prin. Fax 687-5381

Christ the King S 300/K-8
195 Brandon Rd 94523 925-685-1109
Linda Basman, prin. Fax 685-1289
Pleasant Hill Adventist Academy 300/K-12
796 Grayson Rd 94523 925-934-9261
Alexis Emmerson, prin. Fax 934-5871

Pleasanton, Alameda, Pop. 65,950
Pleasanton USD 14,600/K-12
4665 Bernal Ave 94566 925-462-5500
John Casey, supt.
www.pleasanton.k12.ca.us

Alisal ES 700/K-5
1454 Santa Rita Rd 94566 925-426-4201
Amy Simione, prin. Fax 426-9852
Apperson Hearst ES 700/K-5
5301 Case Ave 94566 925-426-3772
Mike Kuhfal, prin. Fax 846-2841
Donlon ES 700/K-5
4150 Dorman Rd 94588 925-426-4221
Marc Schweitzer, prin. Fax 484-5423
Fairlands ES 700/K-5
4141 W Las Positas Blvd 94588 925-426-4211
Kim Michels, prin. Fax 417-1245
Hart MS 1,200/6-8
4433 Willow Rd 94588 925-426-3102
Steve Maher, prin. Fax 460-0799
Harvest Park MS 1,100/6-8
4900 Valley Ave 94566 925-426-4444
Jim Hansen, prin. Fax 426-9613
Lydiksen ES 700/K-5
7700 Highland Oaks Dr 94588 925-426-4421
Colleen Henry, prin. Fax 417-8987
Mohr ES 700/K-5
3300 Dennis Dr 94588 925-426-4256
Robin Sehrt, prin. Fax 484-9430
Pleasanton MS 1,200/6-8
5001 Case Ave 94566 925-426-4390
John Whitney, prin. Fax 426-1382
Valley View ES 700/K-5
480 Adams Way 94566 925-426-4230
Rafael Cruz, prin. Fax 426-0731
Vintage Hills ES 600/K-5
1125 Concord St 94566 925-426-4240
Carolyn Parker, prin. Fax 417-7388
Walnut Grove ES 700/K-5
1999 Harvest Rd 94566 925-426-4250
Bill Radulovich, prin. Fax 462-6382

Hacienda S 100/PK-8
3800 Stoneridge Dr 94588 925-485-5750
JoAnne Camara M.Ed., dir. Fax 485-5757
Quarry Lane 200/PK-12
6363 Tassajara Rd 94588 925-829-8000
Gabrielle Denton, dir. Fax 829-4928

Plumas Lake, Yuba

Plumas Lake ESD 1,000/K-8
2743 Plumas School Rd, 530-743-4428
Jeffrey Roberts, supt. Fax 743-1408
www.plusd.org
Cobblestone ES 300/K-5
1718 Churchill Way, 530-634-9723
Kirsten Spallino, prin. Fax 749-9765
Rio Del Oro ES 400/K-5
1220 Zanes Dr, 530-749-0690
Baljinder Dhillon, prin. Fax 749-0689
Riverside Meadows IS 400/5-8
1751 Cimarron Dr, 530-743-1271
Christopher Morris, prin. Fax 743-8970

Plymouth, Amador, Pop. 1,072

Amador County USD
Supt. — See Jackson
Plymouth ES 200/K-6
10601 Sherwood St 95669 209-257-7800
Rosalie McProuty, prin. Fax 245-6376

Point Arena, Mendocino, Pop. 475

Arena UNESD 200/K-8
PO Box 87 95468 707-882-2803
Mark Iacuaniello, supt. Fax 882-2848
www.pointarenaschools.org/
Arena S 200/K-8
PO Box 45 95468 707-882-2131
Paula Patterson, prin. Fax 882-3076

Point Reyes Station, Marin

Shoreline USD
Supt. — See Tomales
Inverness ES 50/K-1
PO Box 300 94956 415-669-1018
Anne Harris, prin. Fax 669-1581
West Marin S 100/2-8
PO Box 300 94956 415-663-1014
Anne Harris, prin. Fax 663-8558

Pollock Pines, El Dorado, Pop. 4,291

Pollock Pines ESD 800/K-8
2701 Amber Trl 95726 530-644-5416
Susan Spencer, supt. Fax 644-5483
www.ppesd.org
Pinewood ES 400/K-4
6181 Pine St 95726 530-644-2384
Ralph Haslam, prin. Fax 644-6215
Sierra Ridge MS 400/5-8
2700 Amber Trl 95726 530-644-2031
Rich Callaghan, prin. Fax 644-0198

Silver Fork ESD 50/K-8
2701 Amber Trl 95726 530-644-5416
Susan Spencer, supt. Fax 644-5483
www.ppsd.k12.ca.us/silverfork
Other Schools – See Kyburz

Pomona, Los Angeles, Pop. 153,787

Pomona USD 31,300/K-12
PO Box 2900 91769 909-397-4800
Dr. Thelma Melendez, supt. Fax 397-4881
www.pusd.org
Alcott ES 1,000/K-6
1600 S Towne Ave 91766 909-397-4552
Maria Slater, prin. Fax 623-4601
Allison ES 500/K-6
1011 Russell Pl 91767 909-397-4556
Petra Franco, prin. Fax 622-3760
Arroyo ES 900/K-5
1605 Arroyo Ave 91768 909-397-4568
Celia Asebedo, prin. Fax 865-9440
Barfield ES 600/K-6
2181 N San Antonio Ave 91767 909-397-4575
Rosa Mendieta, prin. Fax 623-5479
Cortez ES 800/K-6
1300 N Dudley St 91768 909-397-4750
Janet Alvarez, prin. Fax 623-8473
Decker ES 600/K-6
20 Village Loop Rd 91766 909-397-4581
Lisa Minami-Lin, prin. Fax 397-4585
Emerson MS 900/6-8
635 Lincoln Ave 91767 909-397-4516
Jorge Amancio, prin. Fax 397-5280
Fremont MS 800/7-8
725 W Franklin Ave 91766 909-397-4521
Susan Williams, prin. Fax 620-6229
Harrison ES 500/K-6
425 E Harrison Ave 91767 909-397-4601
Diane Betance, prin. Fax 626-2135
Kellogg Polytechnic ES 500/K-6
610 Medina St 91768 909-397-4604
Olga McCullough, prin. Fax 444-9782
Kingsley ES 800/K-5
1170 Washington Ave 91767 909-397-4609
Gloria Moreno, prin. Fax 620-3910
Lexington ES 700/K-6
550 W Lexington Ave 91766 909-397-4616
Louise Champan, prin. Fax 865-3138
Lincoln ES 600/K-5
1200 N Gordon St 91768 909-397-4624
Michele Bauer, prin. Fax 397-4627
Lopez ES 300/4-6
701 S White Ave 91766 909-397-4438
Marlo Yep-Vaughan, prin. Fax 397-7751
Madison ES 700/K-6
351 W Phillips Blvd 91766 909-397-4643
Jesus Peralta Cervantes, prin. Fax 629-4351
Marshall MS 1,000/6-8
1921 Arroyo Ave 91768 909-397-4532
Teresa Mora, prin. Fax 629-8275
Mendoza ES 500/K-3
851 S Hamilton Blvd 91766 909-397-4648
Alicia McMullin, prin. Fax 397-5281
Montvue ES 400/K-6
1440 San Bernardino Ave 91767 909-397-4655
Rachel Heller, prin. Fax 397-4658
Palomares MS 600/6-8
2211 N Orange Grove Ave 91767 909-397-4539
Neville Brown, prin. Fax 625-0337
Philadelphia ES 900/K-6
600 Philadelphia St 91766 909-397-4660
Miguel Hurtado, prin. Fax 397-4607
Pueblo S 1,000/K-8
1460 E Holt Ave Ste 100 91767 909-397-4900
Maria Bolado, prin. Fax 622-4301
Ranch Hills ES 400/K-6
2 Trabuco Rd 91766 909-397-4978
Cynthia Quan, prin. Fax 623-3628
Roosevelt ES 1,000/K-5
701 N Huntington Blvd 91768 909-397-4666
Fernando Esparza, prin. Fax 623-2720
San Antonio ES 500/K-5
855 E Kingsley Ave 91767 909-397-4981
Dolores Villasenor, prin. Fax 623-9789
San Jose ES 500/K-6
2015 Cadillac Dr 91767 909-397-4670
Lilia Fuentes, prin. Fax 469-9890
Simons MS 1,000/6-8
900 E Franklin Ave 91766 909-397-4544
Juaniqua Brimm, prin. Fax 623-4691
Vejar ES 700/K-6
950 W Grand Ave 91766 909-397-4985
Terry Whittington, prin. Fax 865-3627
Washington ES 700/K-5
975 E 9th St 91766 909-397-4675
Carmen Mejico, prin. Fax 397-4677
Westmont ES 700/K-6
1780 W 9th St 91766 909-397-4680
Cynthia Badillo, prin. Fax 620-1686
Yorba ES 400/K-6
250 W La Verne Ave 91767 909-397-4684
Janet Chung-MacCormick, prin. Fax 392-0191
Other Schools – See Diamond Bar

Charisma Christian Academy 100/PK-6
305 E Arrow Hwy 91767 909-624-1455
Florence Amecillo, prin. Fax 626-0818
City of Knowledge S 200/K-12
3285 N Garey Ave 91767 909-392-0251
Haleema Shaikley, prin. Fax 392-0295
St. Joseph S 200/PK-8
1200 W Holt Ave 91768 909-622-3365
Amelita Martinez, prin. Fax 469-5146
St. Madeleine S 200/K-8
935 E Kingsley Ave 91767 909-623-9602
Adela Solis, prin. Fax 620-5766
Young People Corporation Academy 100/K-8
1750 W Holt Ave 91768 909-949-3851
Jennifer Johnson, admin.

Pond, Kern

Pond UNESD 200/K-8
29585 Pond Rd 93280 661-792-2545
Robert Parsons, supt. Fax 792-2303
www.pond.k12.ca.us/
Pond S 200/K-8
29585 Pond Rd 93280 661-792-2545
Robert Parsons, prin. Fax 792-2303

Pope Valley, Napa

Pope Valley UNESD 100/K-8
PO Box 167 94567 707-965-2402
Florence Eaton, supt. Fax 965-0946
Pope Valley S 100/K-8
PO Box 167 94567 707-965-2402
Florence Eaton, prin. Fax 965-0946

Porterville, Tulare, Pop. 44,959

Alta Vista ESD 500/K-8
2293 E Crabtree Ave 93257 559-782-5700
Jasper Land, supt. Fax 782-5715
www.alta-vista.k12.ca.us/
Alta Vista S 500/K-8
2293 E Crabtree Ave 93257 559-782-5700
Ruthie Gale, prin. Fax 788-2320

Burton ESD 2,900/K-8
264 N Westwood St 93257 559-781-8020
Gary McKeel, supt. Fax 781-1403
www.burtonschools.org
Buckley ES 500/K-4
2573 W Westfield Ave 93257 559-788-6412
Skip Sonksen, prin. Fax 788-6417
Burton ES 600/K-4
2375 W Morton Ave 93257 559-784-2401
Phil Nava, prin. Fax 793-1686
Burton MS 600/7-8
1155 N Elderwood St 93257 559-781-2671
Michelle Pengilly, prin. Fax 788-6424
Maples Academy 600/5-6
252 N Westwood St 93257 559-781-1658
Chastity Lollis, prin. Fax 781-8574
Oak Grove ES 500/K-4
1873 W Mulberry Ave 93257 559-784-0310
Treasure Weisenberger, prin. Fax 788-6411

Citrus South Tule ESD 100/K-6
31374 Success Valley Dr 93257 559-784-6333
J. Norman Brown, supt. Fax 784-0413
Citrus South Tule ES 100/K-6
31374 Success Valley Dr 93257 559-784-6333
J. Norman Brown, prin. Fax 784-0413

Hope ESD 100/K-8
613 W Teapot Dome Ave 93257 559-784-1064
Deborah McCaskill, supt. Fax 784-1905
www.vip.ocsnet.net/~hopeschool
Hope S 100/K-8
613 W Teapot Dome Ave 93257 559-784-1064
Deborah McCaskill, prin. Fax 784-1905

Pleasant View ESD 600/K-8
14004 Road 184 93257 559-784-6769
Collin Bromley, supt. Fax 784-6819
www.pleasant-view.k12.ca.us
Pleasant View ES 200/K-1
18900 Avenue 145 93258 559-788-2002
Mark Odsather, prin. Fax 788-2030
Pleasant View West S 400/2-8
14004 Road 184 93257 559-784-6769
Mark Odsather, prin. Fax 784-6819

Porterville USD 13,400/K-12
600 W Grand Ave 93257 559-793-2455
John Snavely Ed.D., supt. Fax 793-1088
www.portervilleschools.org
Bartlett MS 500/7-8
600 W Grand Ave 93257 559-782-7100
Jeremy Powell, prin. Fax 784-3432
Belleview ES 400/K-6
600 W Grand Ave 93257 559-782-7110
Chris Barrera, prin. Fax 788-0216
Doyle ES 700/K-6
600 W Grand Ave 93257 559-782-7140
Lorenzo Cruz, prin. Fax 788-0214
Los Robles ES 500/K-6
600 W Grand Ave 93257 559-782-7011
Lissa Lambie, prin. Fax 788-0139
Monte Vista ES 600/K-6
600 W Grand Ave 93257 559-782-7350
Carol Woodley, prin. Fax 793-0150
Olive Street ES 700/K-6
600 W Grand Ave 93257 559-782-7190
Tony Navarro, prin. Fax 783-9233
Pioneer MS 500/7-8
600 W Grand Ave 93257 559-782-7200
Isaac Nunez, prin. Fax 784-3507
Roche Avenue ES 400/K-6
600 W Grand Ave 93257 559-782-7250
Julissa Leyva, prin. Fax 783-8356
Santa Fe ES 600/K-6
600 W Grand Ave 93257 559-782-6614
Angel Valdez, prin. Fax 782-6613
Sequoia MS 400/7-8
600 W Grand Ave 93257 559-788-0925
Joe Santos, prin. Fax 788-0927
Vandalia ES 800/K-6
600 W Grand Ave 93257 559-782-7260
Israel Longoria, prin. Fax 782-7268
Westfield ES 700/K-6
600 W Grand Ave 93257 559-782-7270
John Buckley, prin. Fax 783-8219
West Putnam ES 500/K-6
600 W Grand Ave 93257 559-782-7280
Laura Geren, prin. Fax 783-2969

Rockford ESD 400/K-8
14983 Road 208 93257 559-784-5406
Andrew Schultz, supt. Fax 784-8608
Rockford S 400/K-8
14983 Road 208 93257 559-784-5406
Andrew Schultz, prin. Fax 784-8608

Woodville Union ESD 600/K-8
16563 Road 168 93257 559-686-9713
Dr. Clifford Turk, supt. Fax 685-0875
www.tcoe.org/districts/woodville.shtm
Woodville Union S 600/K-8
16541 Road 168 93257 559-686-9713
Dondreia Bradley, prin. Fax 685-0875

Landmark Christian Academy 50/K-6
2380 W Olive Ave 93257 559-781-9500
Anthony Hendley, prin. Fax 784-2861
St. Anne S 200/PK-8
385 N F St 93257 559-784-4096
Sr. Carmen Fernandez, prin. Fax 784-4338

Port Hueneme, Ventura, Pop. 22,032
Hueneme ESD 7,900/K-8
205 N Ventura Rd 93041 805-488-3588
Dr. Jerry Dannenberg, supt. Fax 986-8755
www.huensd.k12.ca.us
Bard ES 700/K-6
622 E Pleasant Valley Rd 93041 805-488-3583
Christine McCloskey, prin. Fax 488-1303
Hueneme ES 500/K-6
354 N 3rd St 93041 805-488-3569
Colleen Robertson, prin. Fax 986-8765
Parkview ES 700/K-5
1416 N 6th Pl 93041 805-986-8730
Heidi Haines, prin. Fax 986-8734
Sunkist ES 700/K-5
1400 Teakwood St 93041 805-986-8722
Joy Epstein, prin. Fax 486-8753
Other Schools – See Oxnard

Hueneme Christian S 300/K-8
312 N Ventura Rd 93041 805-488-8781
Luzviminda Cajiuat, prin. Fax 488-2891

Portola, Plumas, Pop. 2,242
Plumas USD
Supt. — See Quincy
Carmichael ES 400/K-6
895 West St 96122 530-832-0211
Edeltra Marquette, prin. Fax 832-0667

Portola Valley, San Mateo, Pop. 4,417
Portola Valley ESD 700/K-8
4575 Alpine Rd 94028 650-851-1777
Anne Campbell, supt. Fax 851-3700
www.pvsd.net
Corte Madera MS 400/4-8
4575 Alpine Rd 94028 650-851-1777
Carol Piraino, prin. Fax 529-8553
Ormondale ES 300/K-3
200 Shawnee Pass 94028 650-851-1777
Jennifer Warren, prin. Fax 529-2086

Woodland S 200/PK-8
360 La Cuesta Dr 94028 650-854-9065
John Ora, hdmstr. Fax 854-6006
Woodside Priory MS 100/6-8
302 Portola Rd 94028 650-851-8221
Kathy Hume, prin. Fax 851-2839

Potrero, San Diego
Mountain Empire USD
Supt. — See Pine Valley
Potrero ES 200/K-7
24875 Potrero Valley Rd 91963 619-478-5930
Barbara Cowling, prin. Fax 478-5821

Potter Valley, Mendocino
Potter Valley Community USD 200/K-12
PO Box 219 95469 707-743-2101
Gary Barr, supt. Fax 743-1930
www.pottervalleyschools.us/
Potter Valley ES 100/K-5
PO Box 219 95469 707-743-1115
Gary Barr, prin. Fax 743-1483

Poway, San Diego, Pop. 48,476
Poway USD 33,500/K-12
13626 Twin Peaks Rd 92064 858-748-0010
Dr. Donald Phillips, supt. Fax 679-2642
www.powayusd.com
Chaparral ES 800/K-5
17250 Tannin Dr 92064 858-485-0042
Dawn Zwibel, prin. Fax 673-8579
Garden Road ES 500/K-5
14614 Garden Rd 92064 858-748-0230
Jeannie Miller, prin. Fax 748-2961
Meadowbrook MS 1,400/6-8
12320 Meadowbrook Ln 92064 858-748-0802
Cathy Brose, prin. Fax 679-0149
Midland ES 600/K-5
13910 Midland Rd 92064 858-748-0047
Julie Lerner, prin. Fax 748-8934
Painted Rock ES 600/K-5
16711 Martincoit Rd 92064 858-487-1180
Sal Embry, prin. Fax 673-8254
Pomerado ES 500/K-5
12321 9th St 92064 858-748-1320
Lisa Danzer, prin. Fax 748-8695
Tierra Bonita ES 500/K-5
14678 Tierra Bonita Rd 92064 858-748-8540
Joe Erpelding, prin. Fax 748-8864
Twin Peaks MS 1,400/6-8
14640 Tierra Bonita Rd 92064 858-748-5131
Lyn Antrim, prin. Fax 679-6823
Valley ES 700/K-5
13000 Bowron Rd 92064 858-748-2007
Andy Johnsen, prin. Fax 748-6587
Other Schools – See San Diego

Country Montessori S of Poway 200/PK-5
12642 Monte Vista Rd 92064 858-673-1756
Holly Williamson, prin. Fax 673-8379
St. Michael's S 500/K-8
15542 Pomerado Rd 92064 858-485-1303
Kathleen Mock, prin. Fax 485-5059

Prather, Fresno, Pop. 30
Sierra USD 1,900/K-12
29143 Auberry Rd 93651 559-855-3662
Michael Gardner Ph.D., supt. Fax 855-3585
www.sierra.k12.ca.us
Foothill MS 400/6-8
29147 Auberry Rd 93651 559-855-3551
Brad Barcus, prin. Fax 855-5350
Other Schools – See Auberry, Shaver Lake, Tollhouse

Princeton, Colusa
Princeton JUSD 200/K-12
PO Box 8 95970 530-439-2261
John Greene, supt. Fax 439-2113
www.pjusd.org/
Princeton ES 100/K-6
PO Box 8 95970 530-439-2501
John Greene, prin. Fax 439-2512

Prunedale, Monterey, Pop. 7,393

Prunedale Christian Academy 100/PK-12
8145 Prunedale North Rd 93907 831-663-2211
Dr. E.L. Moon, admin. Fax 663-1663

Quail Valley, Riverside, Pop. 1,937
Menifee UNESD
Supt. — See Menifee
Quail Valley ES K-5
23757 Canyon Heights Dr 92587 951-244-1937
Linda Hickey, prin. Fax 244-6842

Quartz Hill, Los Angeles, Pop. 9,626
Westside UNESD
Supt. — See Lancaster
Quartz Hill ES 1,000/K-6
41820 50th St W 93536 661-943-3236
Cathy Bennett, prin. Fax 943-1496
Walker MS 900/7-8
5632 W Avenue L8 93536 661-943-3258
Christine Fitzgerald, prin. Fax 943-2969

Quincy, Plumas, Pop. 4,271
Plumas USD 2,400/K-12
50 Church St 95971 530-283-6500
Glenn Harris, supt. Fax 283-6509
www.pcoe.k12.ca.us
Pioneer-Quincy ES 200/K-2
175 N Mill Creek Rd 95971 530-283-6520
Kest Porter, prin. Fax 283-6517
Pioneer-Quincy ES 200/3-6
246 Alder St 95971 530-283-6550
Bruce Williams, prin. Fax 283-6508
Other Schools – See Chester, Greenville, Portola, Taylorsville

Plumas Christian S 100/K-12
49 S Lindan Ave 95971 530-283-0415
John Sturley, admin. Fax 283-2933

Rail Road Flat, Calaveras
Calaveras USD
Supt. — See San Andreas
Rail Road Flat ES 100/K-6
PO Box 217 95248 209-754-2275
Randall Youngblood, lead tchr. Fax 293-7709

Raisin City, Fresno
Raisin City ESD 300/PK-8
PO Box 69 93652 559-233-0128
Beatriz Ramirez, supt. Fax 486-0891
www.raisincity.k12.ca.us/
Raisin City S 300/PK-8
PO Box 69 93652 559-233-0128
Beatriz Ramirez, prin. Fax 486-0891

Ramona, San Diego, Pop. 13,040
Ramona USD 6,700/K-12
720 9th St 92065 760-787-2000
Bob Graeff, supt. Fax 789-9168
www.ramonausd.net/
Barnett ES 600/K-6
23925 Couna Way 92065 760-787-3500
Kim Reed, prin. Fax 788-5358
Dukes ES 600/K-6
24908 Abalar Way 92065 760-788-5060
Paige Schwartz, prin. Fax 788-6170
Hanson ES 700/K-6
2520 Boundary Ave 92065 760-787-2100
Shelagh Appleman, prin. Fax 788-5363
Mt. Woodson ES 600/K-6
17427 Archie Moore Rd 92065 760-788-5120
Theresa Grace, prin. Fax 788-5353
Peirce MS 1,000/7-8
1521 Hanson Ln 92065 760-787-2400
Linda Solis, prin. Fax 788-5014
Ramona ES 600/K-6
415 8th St 92065 760-787-4400
Phyllis Munoz, prin. Fax 788-5110

Montessori Children's House 100/PK-8
719 9th St 92065 760-789-5363
Linda Jordan, prin. Fax 788-8130
Ramona Lutheran S 100/PK-8
520 16th St 92065 760-789-4804
Nancy Knight, prin. Fax 789-8110

Rancho Cordova, Sacramento, Pop. 57,164
Elk Grove USD
Supt. — See Elk Grove
Sunrise ES 500/K-6
11821 Cobble Brook Dr 95742 916-985-4350
Judy Brown, prin. Fax 985-8927

Folsom-Cordova USD
Supt. — See Folsom
Cordova Gardens ES 400/K-6
2400 Dawes St 95670 916-363-2601
Patricia Carbone, prin. Fax 363-5359
Cordova Lane ES 400/K-5
2460 Cordova Ln 95670 916-635-4301
Richard Tapia, prin. Fax 635-1806
Cordova Meadows ES 400/K-5
2550 La Loma Dr 95670 916-363-9406
Carol LaPierre, prin. Fax 362-5395
Cordova Villa ES 400/K-5
10359 S White Rock Rd 95670 916-366-6181
Jon Wallace, prin. Fax 362-8104
Mills MS 1,000/6-8
10439 Coloma Rd 95670 916-363-6544
Peter Maroon, prin. Fax 361-3744
Mitchell MS 800/6-8
2100 Zinfandel Dr 95670 916-635-8460
Jay Berns, prin. Fax 635-8979
Navigator ES 300/K-5
10679 Bear Hollow Dr 95670 916-294-2420
Denise Burns, prin. Fax 859-0740
Rancho Cordova ES 400/K-6
2562 Chassella Way 95670 916-363-4874
David Frankel, prin. Fax 362-2949
Reymouth Preschool 100/PK-PK
10460 Reymouth Ave 95670 916-363-4377
Joan Lopez-Jarman, prin. Fax 362-8104
Riverview ES 300/K-6
10700 Ambassador Dr 95670 916-635-8402
Andrew Smith, prin. Fax 635-3801
Shields ES 300/K-5
10434 Georgetown Dr 95670 916-635-5152
Judy Delise, prin. Fax 635-6448
White Rock ES 500/K-6
10487 White Rock Rd 95670 916-363-9441
Elana Cabrera, prin. Fax 363-5283
Williamson ES 400/K-5
2275 Benita Dr 95670 916-635-5225
Linda Liebert, prin. Fax 635-5864

IHS Christian S 100/K-12
PO Box 2191 95741 916-638-7755
St. John Vianney S 300/K-8
10499 Coloma Rd 95670 916-363-4610
Julia Boen, prin. Fax 363-3243

Rancho Cucamonga, San Bernardino, Pop. 169,353
Central ESD 4,900/K-8
10601 Church St Ste 112 91730 909-989-8541
Sharon Nagel, supt. Fax 941-1732
www.csd.k12.ca.us/
Bear Gulch ES 600/K-5
8355 Bear Gulch Pl 91730 909-989-9396
Susan Kohn, prin. Fax 484-2730
Central ES 600/K-5
7955 Archibald Ave 91730 909-987-2541
Mary Perez, prin. Fax 484-2740
Coyote Canyon ES 700/K-4
7889 Elm Ave 91730 909-980-4743
Lilia Gonzalez-Gomez, prin. Fax 980-1596
Cucamonga MS 900/6-8
7611 Hellman Ave 91730 909-987-1788
Jeffrey Koenig, prin. Fax 483-3201
Dona Merced ES 600/K-5
10333 Palo Alto St 91730 909-980-1600
Eileen Galarze, prin. Fax 980-0066
Musser MS 1,100/5-8
10789 Terra Vista Pkwy 91730 909-980-1230
David Soden, prin. Fax 980-3042
Valle Vista ES 500/K-5
7727 Valle Vista Dr 91730 909-981-8697
Luanne Weaver, prin. Fax 981-9718

Cucamonga ESD 2,700/K-8
8776 Archibald Ave 91730 909-987-8942
Claudia Maidenberg, supt. Fax 980-3628
www.cuca.k12.ca.us
Cucamonga ES 600/K-5
8677 Archibald Ave 91730 909-980-1318
Joyce Kozyra, prin. Fax 980-4040
Los Amigos ES 500/K-5
8498 9th St 91730 909-982-8387
Mariza Naylor, prin. Fax 982-8679
Rancho Cucamonga MS 900/6-8
10022 Feron Blvd 91730 909-980-0969
Bruce LaVallee, prin. Fax 481-5381
Other Schools – See Ontario

Etiwanda ESD
Supt. — See Etiwanda
Perdew ES 900/K-5
13051 Miller Ave 91739 909-803-3316
Kelly Bray, prin. Fax 803-3941
Terra Vista ES 800/K-5
7497 Mountain View Dr 91730 909-945-5715
Cecille Peace, prin. Fax 945-3373

Highland Avenue Christian S 50/PK-PK
9944 Highland Ave 91737 909-989-3009
John Watkin, admin. Fax 980-5405
Sacred Heart S 300/K-8
12676 Foothill Blvd 91739 909-899-1049
Trenna Meins, prin. Fax 899-0413

Rancho Mirage, Riverside, Pop. 16,514
Palm Springs USD
Supt. — See Palm Springs
Rancho Mirage ES 500/K-5
42985 Indian Trl 92270 760-836-3680
Marsha Boring, prin. Fax 836-3684

Marywood Palm Valley S 500/PK-12
35525 Da Vall Dr 92270 760-328-0861
Vincent Downey, admin. Fax 770-4541

Rancho Palos Verdes, Los Angeles, Pop. 41,949
Los Angeles USD
Supt. — See Los Angeles
Crestwood Street ES 500/K-5
1946 W Crestwood St 90275 310-832-8130
David Gonzales, prin. Fax 832-7458
Dodson MS 1,900/6-8
28014 S Montereina Dr 90275 310-241-1900
Elmore Collier, prin. Fax 832-4709

Palos Verdes Peninsula USD
Supt. — See Palos Verdes Estates
Cornerstone at Pedregal ES 400/K-5
6069 Groveoak Pl 90275 310-378-0324
Jody Pastell, prin. Fax 378-1484

Mira Catalina ES 400/K-5
30511 Lucania Dr 90275 310-377-6731
Jeffrey Keeney, prin. Fax 541-4220
Miraleste ES 100/K-1
6245 Via Canada 90275 310-377-6731
Jeffrey Keeney, prin. Fax 541-4220
Miraleste IS 1,000/6-8
29323 Palos Verdes Dr E 90275 310-732-0900
Beth Hadley, prin. Fax 521-8915
Point Vicente ES 400/K-5
30540 Rue De La Pierre 90275 310-377-6972
Becky Cash, prin. Fax 377-7692
Ridgecrest IS 900/6-8
28915 Northbay Rd 90275 310-547-2747
Pat Corwin, prin. Fax 265-1716
Silver Spur ES 600/K-5
5500 Ironwood St 90275 310-378-5011
Meriam Wilhelm, prin. Fax 378-7674
Soleado ES 500/K-5
27800 Longhill Dr 90275 310-377-6854
Kevin Allen, prin. Fax 544-0916
Vista Grande ES 600/K-5
7032 Purple Ridge Dr 90275 310-377-6066
Patricia Vincent, prin. Fax 541-4692

Christ Lutheran S 300/PK-8
28850 S Western Ave 90275 310-831-0848
Patricia Mayer, prin. Fax 831-0090
Peninsula Montessori S 100/PK-6
31100 Hawthorne Blvd 90275 310-544-3099
Claudia Krikorian, prin. Fax 544-2629
St. John Fisher S 200/PK-8
5446 Crest Rd 90275 310-377-2800
Anne Marie Hudami, prin. Fax 377-3863

Rancho Santa Fe, San Diego, Pop. 7,000
Rancho Santa Fe ESD 600/K-8
PO Box 809 92067 858-756-1141
Lindy Delaney, supt. Fax 756-0712
www.rsf.k12.ca.us
Rowe ES 400/K-4
PO Box 809 92067 858-756-1141
Kim Pinkerton, prin. Fax 756-0712
Rowe MS 200/5-8
PO Box 809 92067 858-756-1141
Suzanne Roy, prin. Fax 759-0712

Solana Beach ESD
Supt. — See Solana Beach
Solana Santa Fe ES 400/K-6
PO Box 8940 92067 858-794-4700
Julie Norby, prin. Fax 794-4750

Diegueno Country S 100/K-6
PO Box 8126 92067 858-756-3603
Michael Cole, hdmstr.
Horizon Prep S 400/PK-8
PO Box 9070 92067 858-756-5599
Ken Kush, hdmstr. Fax 759-5827
Nativity S 200/K-8
PO Box 9180 92067 858-756-6763
Margaret Heveron, prin. Fax 756-9128

Rancho Santa Margarita, Orange, Pop. 50,682
Capistrano USD
Supt. — See San Juan Capistrano
Arroyo Vista S 700/K-8
23371 Arroyo Vis 92688 949-234-5951
Tim Brooks, prin. Fax 589-6924
Tijeras Creek ES 700/K-5
23072 Avenida Empresa 92688 949-234-5300
Diann Buckingham, prin. Fax 858-3862

Saddleback Valley USD
Supt. — See Mission Viejo
Cielo Vista ES 1,000/K-6
21811 Avnida De Los Fundado 92688 949-589-7456
Karen Schibler, prin. Fax 589-8671
Melinda Heights ES 1,300/K-6
21001 Rancho Trabuco 92688 949-888-7311
Joel Rawlins, prin. Fax 888-7429
Rancho Santa Margarita IS 1,700/7-8
21931 Alma Aldea 92688 949-459-8253
Rick Jameson, prin. Fax 459-8258
Trabuco Mesa ES 700/K-6
21301 Avenida De Las Flores 92688 949-858-3339
Suzanne Westmoreland, prin. Fax 858-5476

Mission Hills Christian S 500/PK-8
29582 Aventura 92688 949-589-4504
Robert Sladek, prin. Fax 589-7566
St. John's Episcopal S 800/PK-8
30382 Via Con Dios 92688 949-858-5144
James Lusby, hdmstr. Fax 858-1403
Serra Catholic S 1,000/PK-8
23652 Antonio Pkwy 92688 949-888-1990
Angeline Trudell, prin. Fax 888-1994

Raymond, Madera
Raymond-Knowles UNESD 100/K-8
PO Box 47 93653 559-689-3336
Ron Johnson, supt. Fax 689-3203
www.rkusd.k12.ca.us/
Raymond-Knowles S 100/K-8
PO Box 47 93653 559-689-3336
Ron Johnson, prin. Fax 689-3203

Red Bluff, Tehama, Pop. 14,059
Antelope ESD 700/K-8
22630 Antelope Blvd 96080 530-527-1272
Earnie Graham, supt. Fax 527-2931
www.asd.tehama.k12.ca.us/
Antelope ES 400/K-5
22630 Antelope Blvd 96080 530-527-1272
Earnie Graham, prin. Fax 527-2931
Berrendos MS 300/6-8
401 Chestnut Ave 96080 530-527-6700
Teresa Cottier, prin. Fax 527-2506

Bend ESD 100/K-8
22270 Bend Ferry Rd 96080 530-527-4648
Roxy Williams, supt. Fax 527-4670
Bend S 100/K-8
22270 Bend Ferry Rd 96080 530-527-4648
Fax 527-4670

Red Bluff UNESD 2,200/K-8
1755 Airport Blvd 96080 530-527-7200
Charles Allen, supt. Fax 527-9308
www.rbuesd.tehama.k12.ca.us
Bidwell ES 600/K-6
1256 Walnut St 96080 530-527-7171
Isaac Scharaga, prin. Fax 527-8439
Jackson Heights ES 500/K-6
225 S Jackson St 96080 530-527-7150
Dottie Renstrom, prin. Fax 527-1172
Metteer S 600/K-8
695 Kimball Rd 96080 530-527-9015
William McCoy, prin. Fax 527-7240
Vista MS 500/7-8
1770 S Jackson St 96080 530-527-7840
Gordon Yates, prin. Fax 527-9374

Reeds Creek ESD 100/K-8
18335 Johnson Rd 96080 530-527-6006
Jake Hosler, supt. Fax 527-6849
www.rcesd.tehama.k12.ca.us
Reeds Creek S 100/K-8
18335 Johnson Rd 96080 530-527-6006
Jake Hosler, prin. Fax 527-6849

Community Christian S 100/PK-7
598 Roundup Ave 96080 530-527-7040
Mark Franklin, admin. Fax 527-4302
Sacred Heart S 100/PK-8
2255 Monroe Ave 96080 530-527-6727
Terri Sobieralski, prin. Fax 527-5026

Redding, Shasta, Pop. 89,641
Columbia ESD 1,000/K-8
10140 Old Oregon Trl 96003 530-223-1915
Frank Adelman, supt. Fax 223-4168
www.columbiasd.com
Columbia ES 600/K-5
10142 Old Oregon Trl 96003 530-223-4070
Clay Ross, prin. Fax 223-5245
Mountain View MS 400/6-8
675 Shasta View Dr 96003 530-221-6224
Mike Freeman, prin. Fax 221-5620

Enterprise ESD 3,500/K-8
1155 Mistletoe Ln 96002 530-224-4100
Brian Winstead Ed.D., supt. Fax 224-4101
www.eesd.net/
Alta Mesa ES 300/K-5
2301 Saturn Skwy 96002 530-224-4130
Shari Biscotti, prin. Fax 224-4131
Boulder Creek ES 600/K-5
505 Springer Dr 96003 530-224-4140
Dale Porter, prin. Fax 224-4141
Lassen View ES 400/K-5
705 Loma Vista Dr 96002 530-224-4150
Debbie Lungi, prin. Fax 224-4151
Mistletoe S 600/K-8
1225 Mistletoe Ln 96002 530-224-4160
Denny Mills, prin. Fax 224-4161
Parsons MS 800/6-8
750 Hartnell Ave 96002 530-224-4190
Tony Moebes, prin. Fax 224-4191
Rother ES 400/K-5
795 Hartnell Ave 96002 530-224-4170
Kelly Rizzi, prin. Fax 224-4171
Shasta Meadows ES 400/K-5
2825 Yana Ave 96002 530-224-4180
Rick Fitzpatrick, prin. Fax 224-4181

Gateway USD 2,800/K-12
4411 Mountain Lakes Blvd 96003 530-245-7900
Robert Hubbell, supt. Fax 245-7920
www.gateway-schools.org/home.aspx
Buckeye S of the Arts 500/K-6
3407 Hiatt Dr 96003 530-225-0420
Todd Clark, prin. Fax 225-0402
Other Schools – See Shasta Lake

Grant ESD 600/K-8
8835 Swasey Dr 96001 530-243-4952
John Krinkel, supt. Fax 243-7014
www.grantesd.k12.ca.us/
Grant S 600/K-8
8835 Swasey Dr 96001 530-243-4952
Robert Effa, prin. Fax 243-7014

Igo-Ono-Platina UNESD 100/K-8
6429 Placer Rd 96001 530-396-2841
Diane Kempley, supt. Fax 396-2848
igoono.echalk.com/
Other Schools – See Igo

Pacheco UNESD
Supt. — See Anderson
Pacheco S 400/4-8
7430 Pacheco School Rd 96002 530-224-4585
Joy Tucker, prin. Fax 224-4588

Redding ESD 3,400/K-8
PO Box 992418 96099 530-225-0011
Diane Kempley, supt. Fax 225-0015
redding.echalk.com
Bonny View ES 300/K-5
PO Box 992418 96099 530-225-0030
David Alexander, prin. Fax 225-0034
Cypress ES 300/K-5
PO Box 992418 96099 530-225-0040
Cindy Bishop, prin. Fax 225-0044
Juniper Academy 200/K-8
PO Box 992418 96099 530-225-0045
Margaret Arthofer, prin. Fax 225-0049

Manzanita ES 600/K-5
PO Box 992418 96099 530-225-0050
Kim McKenzie, prin. Fax 225-0054
Sequoia MS 800/6-8
PO Box 992418 96099 530-225-0020
Cass Ditzler, prin. Fax 225-0029
Sycamore ES 300/K-5
PO Box 992418 96099 530-225-0055
Lana Rylee, prin. Fax 225-0059
Turtle Bay S 800/K-8
PO Box 992418 96099 530-225-0035
Linda Lawhon, prin. Fax 225-0039

Bethel Christian S 300/PK-8
933 College View Dr 96003 530-246-6010
H. Don Mayer, prin. Fax 246-6020
Country Christian S 200/PK-8
873 Canby Rd 96003 530-222-0675
Dennis McGowan, admin. Fax 222-2631
Hope S International 100/K-12
4824 Aloe Vera Dr 96001 530-222-2095
Dee Haselhuhn, prin. Fax 242-0543
Liberty Christian S 300/PK-12
3782 Churn Creek Rd 96002 530-222-2232
Stephen Roberts, supt. Fax 222-1784
Mt. Calvary Lutheran S 50/K-8
3961 Alta Mesa Dr 96002 530-221-2451
Daniel Douglas, prin. Fax 222-1403
Redding Adventist Academy 200/K-12
1356 E Cypress Ave 96002 530-222-1018
Timothy Erich, prin. Fax 222-4260
Redding Christian S 500/K-12
777 Loma Vista Dr 96002 530-223-1226
Michael Wenger, prin. Fax 223-4755
St. Joseph S 200/K-8
2460 Gold St 96001 530-243-2302
Patricia Cole, prin. Fax 243-2747
Trinity Lutheran S 100/PK-1
2440 Hilltop Dr 96002 530-221-6686
Denise Killgore, prin. Fax 221-6695

Redlands, San Bernardino, Pop. 69,995
Redlands USD 21,300/K-12
PO Box 3008 92373 909-307-5300
Lori Rhodes, supt. Fax 307-5320
www.redlands.k12.ca.us
Clement MS 1,100/6-8
501 E Pennsylvania Ave 92374 909-307-5400
Robert Clarey, prin. Fax 307-5414
Cope MS 1,300/6-8
1000 W Cypress Ave 92373 909-307-5420
Kate Pearne, prin. Fax 307-5436
Crafton ES 700/K-5
311 N Wabash Ave 92374 909-794-8600
Luanna Kloepfer, prin. Fax 794-8605
Franklin ES 800/K-5
850 E Colton Ave 92374 909-307-5530
Rhonda Bruce, prin. Fax 307-5539
Judson & Brown ES 400/K-5
1401 E Pennsylvania Ave 92374 909-307-2430
Robert Cmelak, prin. Fax 307-2438
Kimberly ES 600/K-5
301 W South Ave 92373 909-307-5540
Marcia Fagan, prin. Fax 307-5545
Kingsbury ES 500/K-5
600 Cajon St 92373 909-307-5550
Toni Marshburn, prin. Fax 307-5555
Lugonia ES 600/K-5
202 E Pennsylvania Ave 92374 909-307-5560
Kathy Jeide, prin. Fax 307-5566
Mariposa ES 600/K-5
30800 Palo Alto Dr 92373 909-794-8620
Scott Bohlender, prin. Fax 794-8624
McKinley ES 400/K-5
645 W Olive Ave 92373 909-307-5570
Tim Hoch, prin. Fax 307-5579
Moore MS 1,200/6-8
1550 E Highland Ave 92374 909-307-5440
Julie Swan, prin. Fax 307-5453
Smiley ES 700/K-5
1210 W Cypress Ave 92373 909-307-5580
Caroleen Cosand, prin. Fax 307-5339
Other Schools – See Highland, Loma Linda, Mentone, San Bernardino

---

Citrus Valley Christian Academy 100/K-12
PO Box 8037 92375 909-556-7201
Cheryl VanGelder, admin.
Montessori S in Redlands 300/PK-9
1890 Orange Ave 92373 909-793-6989
Maura Joyce, hdmstr. Fax 335-2749
Packinghouse Christian Academy 300/K-12
27165 San Bernardino Ave 92374 909-793-4984
Paul Verhoeven, prin. Fax 307-1852
Redlands Adventist Academy 500/K-12
130 Tennessee St 92373 909-793-1000
Geoff Hayton, prin. Fax 793-9862
Redlands Christian S 500/PK-8
1145 Church St 92374 909-793-5172
Ray Leenstra, admin. Fax 335-9593
Sacred Heart S 300/K-8
215 S Eureka St 92373 909-792-3958
Sr. Linda Nicholson, prin. Fax 792-7292
Valley Preparatory S 200/PK-8
1605 Ford St 92373 909-793-3063
Michael Hughes Ph.D., hdmstr. Fax 798-5963
Westside Christian S 200/PK-6
1495 W Olive Ave 92373 909-793-5811
Willie Guida, prin. Fax 793-3253

Redondo Beach, Los Angeles, Pop. 66,824
Redondo Beach Unified SD 8,200/PK-12
1401 Inglewood Ave 90278 310-379-5449
Steven Keller Ed.D., supt. Fax 798-8610
www.rbusd.org

Adams MS 800/6-8
2600 Ripley Ave 90278 310-798-8636
Dr. Nicole Wesley, prin. Fax 318-3064
Alta Vista ES 500/PK-5
815 Knob Hill Ave 90277 310-798-8650
Anthony Taranto, prin. Fax 798-8662
Beryl Heights ES 300/K-5
920 Beryl St 90277 310-798-8611
Karen Mohr, prin. Fax 937-6513
Birney ES 300/K-6
1600 Green Ln 90278 310-798-8626
Jacquelin O'Sullivan, prin. Fax 937-6511
Jefferson ES 600/K-6
600 Harkness Ln 90278 310-798-8631
Stephen Edmunds, prin. Fax 937-6506
Lincoln ES 600/K-6
2223 Plant Ave 90278 310-798-8646
Samantha Leddel, prin. Fax 793-6786
Madison ES 400/K-5
2200 MacKay Ln 90278 310-798-8623
David Hoffman, prin. Fax 798-3923
Parras MS 900/6-8
200 N Lucia Ave 90277 310-798-8616
Lars Nygren, prin. Fax 798-8660
Tulita ES 400/K-6
1520 S Prospect Ave 90277 310-798-8628
Danielle Allphin, prin. Fax 798-8698
Washington ES 600/K-5
1100 Lilienthal Ln 90278 310-798-8641
Nino Torres, prin. Fax 798-8302

Carden Dominion S 100/K-6
320 Knob Hill Ave 90277 310-316-9733
Carol Hermanns, prin. Fax 316-9733
Coast Christian S 300/PK-8
525 Earle Ln 90278 310-798-5181
Cyndy Keenan, prin. Fax 798-1575
Riviera Hall S 200/K-8
330 Palos Verdes Blvd 90277 310-375-5528
Phyllis Nollan, admin. Fax 791-8939
St. Lawrence Martyr S 300/PK-8
1950 S Prospect Ave 90277 310-316-3049
Shannon Gomez, prin. Fax 316-0888
South Bay Faith Academy 400/K-12
PO Box 7000 90277 310-379-8242
Roslyn Ballard, prin.

Redway, Humboldt, Pop. 1,212
Southern Humbolt JUSD
Supt. — See Miranda
Redway ES 300/K-7
PO Box 369 95560 707-923-2526
Patrick Mayer, prin. Fax 923-3289

Redwood City, San Mateo, Pop. 73,114
Belmont-Redwood Shores ESD
Supt. — See Belmont
Sandpiper ES 500/K-5
801 Redwood Shores Pkwy 94065 650-631-5510
Linda McDaniel, prin. Fax 631-5515

Redwood City ESD 7,700/PK-8
750 Bradford St 94063 650-423-2200
Jan Christensen, supt. Fax 423-2204
www.rcsd.k12.ca.us
Child Development Center PK-PK
903 10th Ave 94063 650-366-6819
Merrily Frisz, coord. Fax 482-5998
Clifford S 700/K-8
225 Clifford Ave 94062 650-366-8011
Phil Lind, prin. Fax 367-4354
Cloud S 700/K-8
3790 Red Oak Way 94061 650-369-2264
Fax 367-4355
Fair Oaks ES 500/K-5
2950 Fair Oaks Ave 94063 650-368-3953
Larry Johnson, prin. Fax 367-4356
Ford ES 500/K-5
2498 Massachusetts Ave 94061 650-368-2981
Lynne Griffiths, prin. Fax 367-4357
Gill ES 400/K-5
555 Avenue Del Ora 94062 650-365-8320
Wendy Kelly, prin. Fax 367-4359
Hawes ES 400/K-5
909 Roosevelt Ave 94061 650-366-3122
Josh Griffith, prin. Fax 367-4360
Hoover S 800/K-8
701 Charter St 94063 650-366-8415
Greg Land, prin. Fax 367-4361
Kennedy MS 900/6-8
2521 Goodwin Ave 94061 650-365-4611
Warren Sedar, prin. Fax 367-4362
McKinley Institute of Technology 300/6-8
400 Duane St 94062 650-366-3827
Cheryl Bracco, prin. Fax 367-4363
Newcomer Academy 3-8
400 Duane St 94062 650-366-3827
North Star Academy 500/3-8
400 Duane St 94062 650-482-5973
Ray Dawley, prin. Fax 482-5980
Roosevelt ES 400/K-5
2223 Vera Ave 94061 650-369-5597
Sonya Dineen, prin. Fax 367-4365
Taft ES 500/K-5
903 10th Ave 94063 650-369-2589
Michelle Griffith, prin. Fax 367-4367
Other Schools – See Atherton

Our Lady of Mt. Carmel S 300/PK-8
301 Grand St 94062 650-366-6127
Teresa Anthony, prin. Fax 366-0902
Peninsula Christian S 100/PK-8
1305 Middlefield Rd 94063 650-366-3842
Ed Swift, prin. Fax 368-0790
Redeemer Lutheran S 200/K-8
468 Grand St 94062 650-366-3466
Michael Mancini, prin. Fax 366-5897

St. Pius S 300/K-8
1100 Woodside Rd 94061 650-368-8327
Rita Carroll, prin. Fax 368-7031

Redwood Valley, Mendocino
Ukiah USD
Supt. — See Ukiah
Eagle Peak MS 400/6-8
8601 West Rd 95470 707-485-8154
Dan Stearns, prin. Fax 485-9542
Redwood Valley ES 300/3-5
700 E School Way 95470 707-485-8741
Tina Burrell, prin. Fax 485-5723

Deep Valley Christian S 100/PK-12
PO Box 9 95470 707-485-8778
Joseph Fry, admin. Fax 485-9362

Reedley, Fresno, Pop. 22,368
Kings Canyon JUSD 9,300/K-12
675 W Manning Ave 93654 559-305-7010
Juan Garza, supt. Fax 637-1292
www.kc-usd.k12.ca.us
Alta ES 400/K-5
21771 E Parlier Ave 93654 559-305-7210
Vickie Nishida, prin. Fax 637-1277
Bartsch S K-8
2225 E North Ave 93654 559-305-7360
Jeremy Brown, prin. Fax 638-5308
Grant MS 600/6-8
360 N East Ave 93654 559-305-7330
Monica Benner, prin. Fax 638-6772
Great Western ES 300/K-5
5051 S Frankwood Ave 93654 559-305-7220
Sharon Matsuzaki, prin. Fax 637-1348
Jefferson ES 600/K-5
1037 E Duff Ave 93654 559-305-7230
Ruth White, prin. Fax 638-2486
Lincoln ES 400/K-5
374 E North Ave 93654 559-305-7240
Kelli Duckworth, prin. Fax 638-3064
Navelencia MS 400/6-8
22620 Wahtoke Ave 93654 559-305-7350
Pablo Saenz, prin. Fax 637-1316
Reed S 600/K-8
1400 N Frankwood Ave 93654 559-305-7300
Virginia Zalky, prin. Fax 637-9486
Washington ES 400/K-5
1250 K St 93654 559-305-7270
Mary Stanley, prin. Fax 637-1223
Other Schools – See Dunlap, Orange Cove, Parlier

Immanuel ES 200/K-6
5018 Avenue 416 93654 559-638-0024
Jerry Meadows, supt. Fax 638-7030
St. La Salle S 300/PK-8
404 E Manning Ave 93654 559-638-2621
Sr. Lucy Cassarino, prin. Fax 638-5542

Rescue, El Dorado
Rescue UNESD 3,900/K-8
2390 Bass Lake Rd 95672 530-677-4461
Carol Bly Ed.D., supt. Fax 677-0719
www.rescue.k12.ca.us/
Green Valley ES 700/K-5
2380 Bass Lake Rd 95672 530-677-3686
Darrien Johnson, prin. Fax 677-6532
Pleasant Grove MS 700/6-8
2540 Green Valley Rd 95672 530-672-4400
Reid Briggs, prin. Fax 677-5829
Rescue ES 500/K-5
3880 Green Valley Rd 95672 530-677-2720
Sandee Barrett, prin. Fax 677-9705
Other Schools – See El Dorado Hills

Reseda, See Los Angeles
Los Angeles USD
Supt. — See Los Angeles
Bertrand Avenue ES 400/K-5
7021 Bertrand Ave 91335 818-342-1103
Esta Herman, prin. Fax 609-8761
Blythe Street ES 500/K-5
18730 Blythe St 91335 818-345-4066
Randy Haege, prin. Fax 344-1637
Cantara Street ES 700/K-5
17950 Cantara St 91335 818-342-5191
Meline Karabedian, prin. Fax 344-1214
Garden Grove ES 500/K-5
18141 Valerio St 91335 818-343-4762
Connie Hershelman, prin. Fax 343-4793
Melvin Avenue ES 700/K-5
7700 Melvin Ave 91335 818-886-7171
Danny Dixon, prin. Fax 886-3658
Newcastle ES 400/K-5
6520 Newcastle Ave 91335 818-343-8795
Luis Rojas, prin. Fax 343-8864
Reseda ES 500/K-5
7265 Amigo Ave 91335 818-343-1312
Rosemarie Kubena, prin. Fax 705-7346
Shirley ES 700/K-5
19452 Hart St 91335 818-342-6183
Donna Zero, prin. Fax 774-9051
Vanalden ES 500/K-5
19019 Delano St 91335 818-342-5131
Lance Moore, prin. Fax 996-5109

Heart of the Valley Christian S 200/PK-6
18644 Sherman Way 91335 818-881-9828
Stephanie Jones, prin. Fax 776-9925
Kirk O' the Valley S 200/PK-5
19620 Vanowen St 91335 818-344-1242
Carol Piekaar, dir. Fax 881-4217
Netan Eli Hebrew Academy 50/K-8
PO Box 370037 91337 818-345-6090
Benjamin Yadidi, dir. Fax 345-6857
St. Catherine of Siena S 200/K-8
18125 Sherman Way 91335 818-343-9880
Roberta Fox, prin. Fax 343-6851

Rialto, San Bernardino, Pop. 99,513
Rialto USD 27,700/K-12
182 E Walnut Ave 92376 909-820-7700
Edna Davis-Herring, supt. Fax 873-0448
www.rialto.k12.ca.us
Bemis ES 800/K-5
774 E Etiwanda Ave 92376 909-820-7917
Chantal Anderson, prin. Fax 873-8557
Boyd ES 700/K-5
310 E Merrill Ave 92376 909-820-7929
Aaron Rogers, prin. Fax 820-6889
Casey ES 900/K-5
219 N Eucalyptus Ave 92376 909-820-7904
James Nava, prin. Fax 820-7957
Curtis ES 900/K-5
451 S Lilac Ave 92376 909-421-7366
Karen Elias, prin. Fax 421-7369
Dollahan ES 800/K-5
1060 W Etiwanda Ave 92376 909-820-7943
Mariyon Thompson, prin. Fax 421-7644
Dunn ES 800/K-5
830 N Lilac Ave 92376 909-820-7872
Elizabeth Curtiss, prin. Fax 421-3462
Fitzgerald ES 800/K-5
2568 W Terra Vista Dr 92377 909-421-7625
David Culberhouse, prin. Fax 421-7633
Frisbie MS 1,500/6-8
1442 N Eucalyptus Ave 92376 909-820-7887
Teresa Brown, prin. Fax 820-7885
Henry ES 600/K-5
470 E Etiwanda Ave 92376 909-820-7910
Debra Steinmiller, prin. Fax 820-7947
Hughbanks ES 800/K-5
2241 N Apple Ave 92377 909-820-7970
Gonzalo Avila, prin. Fax 421-7607
Kelley ES 900/K-5
380 S Meridian Ave 92376 909-820-7924
Linda Miner, prin. Fax 820-6880
Kolb MS 1,300/6-8
2351 N Spruce Ave 92377 909-820-7849
John Roach, prin. Fax 875-0374
Kucera MS 1,400/6-8
2140 W Buena Vista Dr 92377 909-421-7662
Monique Conway, prin. Fax 421-7681
Morgan ES 800/K-5
1571 N Sycamore Ave 92376 909-820-7883
Robbin Santiago, prin. Fax 421-3472
Myers ES 800/K-5
975 N Meridian Ave 92376 909-820-7921
Angela Brantley, prin. Fax 421-7532
Preston ES 900/K-5
1750 N Willow Ave 92376 909-820-7932
Erick Witherspoon, prin. Fax 421-7697
Rialto MS 1,300/6-8
324 N Palm Ave 92376 909-820-7838
Mark Bline, prin. Fax 820-7940
Simpson ES 800/K-5
1050 S Lilac Ave 92376 909-820-7954
Deidre Marshall, prin. Fax 421-3456
Trapp ES 800/K-5
2750 N Riverside Ave 92377 909-820-7914
Daniel Sosa, prin. Fax 421-7643
Werner ES, 1050 W Rialto Ave 92376 K-5
Rhea McIver, prin. 909-820-6830
Other Schools – See Colton

Bloomington Christian S 1,000/PK-12
955 Bloomington Ave 92376 909-877-1239
Yvonna Williams, admin. Fax 873-3160
Calvary Chapel Rialto Christian S 50/K-6
1391 W Merrill Ave 92376 909-820-9072
Roland Dooley, prin. Fax 820-7399
St. Catherine of Siena S 200/PK-8
335 N Sycamore Ave 92376 909-875-7821
Enrique Landin, prin. Fax 875-7948
Valley Fellowship Resource Center 50/K-8
275 E Grove St 92376 909-874-5579
Michelle Washington, prin. Fax 874-5152

Richgrove, Tulare, Pop. 1,899
Richgrove ESD 700/K-8
PO Box 540 93261 661-725-2427
Frank Chavez, supt. Fax 725-5772
www.richgrove.org
Richgrove S 700/K-8
PO Box 540 93261 661-725-2427
Mario Millan, prin. Fax 725-5772

Richmond, Contra Costa, Pop. 102,186
West Contra Costa USD 30,200/K-12
1108 Bissell Ave 94801 510-231-1100
Bruce Harter, supt. Fax 236-6784
www.wccusd.k12.ca.us
Adams MS 800/6-8
5000 Patterson Cir 94805 510-235-5464
Julian Szot, prin. Fax 233-9450
Chavez ES 600/K-5
960 17th St 94801 510-412-5081
Sara Dieli, prin. Fax 412-3353
Coronado ES 400/K-5
2001 Virginia Ave 94804 510-231-1419
Linda Cohen, prin. Fax 215-4181
DeJean MS 800/6-8
3400 MacDonald Ave 94805 510-231-1430
Antoinette Henry-Evans, prin. Fax 236-6680
Ford ES 500/K-5
2711 Maricopa Ave 94804 510-231-1421
Barbara Penny-James, prin. Fax 234-3243
Grant ES 600/K-6
2400 Downer Ave 94804 510-231-1422
Susan Berrington, prin. Fax 412-5005
Highland ES 600/K-6
2829 Moyers Rd 94806 510-231-1424
Sara Danielson, prin. Fax 758-4445
King ES 300/K-5
234 S 39th St 94804 510-231-1403
Ronald Richardson, prin. Fax 235-7206

Lincoln ES 400/K-5
29 6th St 94801 510-231-1404
Mimi Melodia, prin. Fax 235-7205
Mira Vista ES 400/K-6
6397 Hazel Ave 94805 510-231-1416
Katherine Hendon, prin. Fax 234-8739
Nystrom ES 400/K-5
230 Harbour Way S 94804 510-231-1406
Reginald Richardson, prin. Fax 215-8165
Peres ES 500/K-6
719 5th St 94801 510-231-1407
Janet Amani-Scott, prin. Fax 215-8103
Riverside ES 300/K-6
1300 Amador St 94806 510-231-1409
Greg Santiago, prin. Fax 237-6991
Stege ES 300/K-5
4949 Cypress Ave 94804 510-231-1425
Linda Adams, prin. Fax 235-7239
Valley View ES 400/K-6
3416 Maywood Dr 94803 510-223-6363
Cheryl Cotton, prin. Fax 222-8896
Verde ES 300/K-6
2000 Giaramita St 94801 510-231-1408
Rosemary Mauldin, prin. Fax 215-9485
Washington ES 500/K-6
565 Wine St 94801 510-231-1417
Lisa Levi, prin. Fax 236-1642
Wilson ES 500/K-5
629 42nd St 94805 510-232-6852
Sonja Neely-Johnson, prin. Fax 412-5011
Other Schools – See El Cerrito, El Sobrante, Hercules, Kensington, Pinole, San Pablo

---

St. Cornelius S 200/K-8
201 28th St 94804 510-232-3326
Sherri Moradi, prin. Fax 232-4071
St. David S 200/PK-8
871 Sonoma St 94805 510-232-2283
Ann Pires, prin. Fax 231-0484
Vista Christian S 100/K-8
2354 Andrade Ave 94804 510-237-4981
Adrienne Reynolds, prin. Fax 237-4981

Ridgecrest, Kern, Pop. 25,974

Sierra Sands USD 5,700/K-12
113 W Felspar Ave 93555 760-375-3363
Joanna Rummer, supt. Fax 375-3338
www.ssusd.org
Faller ES 500/K-5
1500 W Upjohn Ave 93555 760-375-5081
Melissa Christman, prin. Fax 375-7328
Gateway ES 500/K-5
501 S Gateway Blvd 93555 760-384-3228
Lisa Decker, prin. Fax 384-2608
Las Flores ES 500/K-5
720 W Las Flores Ave 93555 760-375-8431
Ron Carter, prin. Fax 375-1797
Monroe MS 600/6-8
340 W Church Ave 93555 760-375-1301
Clara Finneran, prin. Fax 375-8781
Murray MS 700/6-8
921 E Inyokern Rd 93555 760-446-5525
Kirsti Smith, prin. Fax 446-3838
Pierce ES 400/K-5
674 N Gold Canyon St 93555 760-375-5016
Pam Barnes, prin. Fax 375-6413
Richmond ES 400/K-5
1206 Kearsarge Ave 93555 760-446-2531
Beverly Estis, prin. Fax 446-3302
Other Schools – See Inyokern, Johannesburg

Adventist Christian S 50/1-8
555 W Las Flores Ave 93555 760-375-8673
Mary Adams, prin. Fax 375-8402
Calvary Christian S 100/K-12
PO Box 2138 93556 760-375-3133
David Shipley, admin. Fax 375-2694
Immanuel Christian S 200/PK-12
201 W Graaf Ave 93555 760-446-6114
Dr. Wes Johnston, prin. Fax 446-7035
St. Ann S 100/K-8
446 W Church Ave 93555 760-375-4713
Mary Little, prin. Fax 375-6345

Rio Dell, Humboldt, Pop. 3,158

Rio Dell ESD 300/K-8
95 Center St 95562 707-764-5694
Mary Varner, supt. Fax 764-2656
internet.humboldt.k12.ca.us/riodell_sd/
Eagle Prairie ES 200/K-5
95 Center St 95562 707-764-5694
Chris Byrne, prin. Fax 764-2656
Monument MS 100/6-8
95 Center St 95562 707-764-3783
Chris Byrne, prin. Fax 764-2656

Rio Linda, Sacramento, Pop. 9,481

Twin Rivers USD
Supt. — See Mc Clellan
Dry Creek ES 400/K-6
1230 G St 95673 916-566-1820
Sal Garcia, prin. Fax 991-3571
Orchard ES 400/K-6
1040 Q St 95673 916-566-1930
Ed Delgado, prin. Fax 991-6301
Rio Linda ES 300/K-6
631 L St 95673 916-566-1920
Paula Roach, prin. Fax 991-0240
Rio Linda JHS 600/7-8
1101 G St 95673 916-286-1601
Harjinder Mattu, prin. Fax 263-4674
Westside ES 400/K-6
6537 W 2nd St 95673 916-566-1990
Janelle Scheftner, prin. Fax 991-5842

Rio Oso, Sutter

Browns ESD 100/K-8
1248 Pacific Ave 95674 530-633-2523
Karin Jelavich, supt. Fax 633-0345
www.brownsschool.org
Browns S 100/K-8
1248 Pacific Ave 95674 530-633-2523
Karin Jelavich, prin. Fax 633-0345

Rio Vista, Solano, Pop. 7,077

River Delta USD 1,900/K-12
445 Montezuma St 94571 707-374-6381
Richard Hennes, supt. Fax 374-2995
www.riverdelta.k12.ca.us/
Riverview MS 300/5-8
525 S 2nd St 94571 707-374-2345
Pierre Laleau, prin. Fax 374-5623
White ES 400/K-4
500 Elm Way 94571 707-374-5335
Linda Costlow, prin. Fax 374-4364
Other Schools – See Courtland, Isleton, Walnut Grove

Ripon, San Joaquin, Pop. 13,658

Ripon USD 3,000/K-12
304 N Acacia Ave 95366 209-599-2131
Louise Nan, supt. Fax 599-6271
www.riponusd.net/
Colony Oak S 500/K-8
22241 S Murphy Rd 95366 209-599-7145
Sylvia Eheler, prin. Fax 599-2772
Park View ES 200/K-4
751 Cindy Dr 95366 209-599-1882
Kathryn Coleman, prin. Fax 599-1886
Ripona S 500/K-8
415 Oregon St 95366 209-599-4104
Warren Council, prin. Fax 599-1886
Ripon S 400/K-8
509 W Main St 95366 209-599-4225
Mike Larson, prin. Fax 599-8725
Weston S 500/K-8
1660 Stanley Dr 95366 209-599-7113
Lisa Fereria, prin. Fax 599-4063

Ripon Christian S 400/K-8
217 Maple Ave 95366 209-599-2155
Dale De Weerd, prin. Fax 599-9487

Riverbank, Stanislaus, Pop. 19,727

Riverbank USD 3,000/K-12
6715 7th St 95367 209-869-2538
Ken Geisick, supt. Fax 869-1487
www.riverbank.k12.ca.us
California Avenue ES 600/K-5
3800 California Ave 95367 209-869-2597
Laurie Sacknitz, prin. Fax 869-7375
Cardozo MS 700/6-8
3525 Santa Fe St 95367 209-869-2591
Alice Solis, prin. Fax 869-2714
Mesa Verde ES, 4850 Mesa Dr 95367 100/K-5
Kim Newton, prin.
Rio Altura ES 800/K-5
2400 Stanislaus St 95367 209-869-3633
Kevin Bizzini, prin. Fax 869-0430

Sylvan Union ESD
Supt. — See Modesto
Crossroads ES 700/K-5
5800 Saxon Way 95367 209-574-5000
Marti Reed, prin. Fax 869-7425

Riverdale, Fresno, Pop. 1,980

Burrel UNESD 200/K-8
16704 S Jameson Ave 93656 559-866-5634
Timothy Bybee, supt. Fax 866-5280
burrel.ca.schoolwebpages.com
Burrel Union S 200/K-8
16704 S Jameson Ave 93656 559-866-5634
Timothy Bybee, prin. Fax 866-5280

Riverdale JUSD 1,600/K-12
PO Box 1058 93656 559-867-8200
Elaine Cash, supt. Fax 867-6722
www.riverdale.k12.ca.us
Fipps PS 500/K-3
PO Box 338 93656 559-867-3353
Sherry Martin, prin. Fax 867-4949
Riverdale ES 600/4-8
PO Box 338 93656 559-867-3589
Mark Allein, prin. Fax 867-3393

Riverside, Riverside, Pop. 290,086

Alvord USD 21,400/K-12
10365 Keller Ave 92505 951-509-5070
Wendel Tucker, supt. Fax 509-6070
www.alvord.k12.ca.us
Arizona MS 1,200/6-8
10365 Keller Ave 92505 951-358-1675
Angela Hopkins, prin. Fax 358-1676
Arlanza ES 600/K-5
10365 Keller Ave 92505 951-358-1600
Gerardo Aguilar, prin. Fax 358-1601
Collett ES 800/K-5
10365 Keller Ave 92505 951-358-1605
Brad Shearer, prin. Fax 358-1606
Foothill ES 800/K-5
10365 Keller Ave 92505 951-358-1610
Hector Zaldivar, prin. Fax 358-1611
Kennedy ES 800/K-5
10365 Keller Ave 92505 951-358-1655
Jackie Casillas, prin. Fax 358-1656
La Granada ES 600/K-5
10365 Keller Ave 92505 951-358-1615
Martha Martinez, prin. Fax 358-1616
Lake Hills ES 800/K-5
10365 Keller Ave 92505 951-358-1620
Charla Capps, prin. Fax 358-1621
Linn ES 700/K-5
10365 Keller Ave 92505 951-358-1630
Mary Parsons, prin. Fax 358-1631
Loma Vista MS 1,200/6-8
10365 Keller Ave 92505 951-358-1685
Susan Boyd, prin. Fax 358-1686
McAuliffe ES 1,100/K-5
10365 Keller Ave 92505 951-358-1625
Denise Edwards, prin. Fax 358-1626
Orrenmaa ES 900/K-5
10365 Keller Ave 92505 951-358-1635
Debra Johnson, prin. Fax 358-1636
Stokoe ES 800/K-5
10365 Keller Ave 92505 951-358-1640
Katherine Delgado, prin. Fax 358-1641
Terrace ES 800/K-5
10365 Keller Ave 92505 951-358-1660
Kathleen Kennedy, prin. Fax 358-1661
Twinhill ES 600/K-5
10365 Keller Ave 92505 951-358-1665
Emily Devor, prin. Fax 358-1666
Valley View ES 500/K-5
10365 Keller Ave 92505 951-358-1670
Peggy Nelson, prin. Fax 358-1671
Villegas MS 1,400/6-8
10365 Keller Ave 92505 951-358-1695
Julie Koehler-Mount, prin. Fax 358-1696
Wells MS 1,000/6-8
10365 Keller Ave 92505 951-358-1705
Chuck Fischer, prin. Fax 358-1706
Other Schools – See Corona

Jurupa USD 22,800/K-12
4850 Pedley Rd 92509 951-360-4100
Elliott Duchon, supt. Fax 360-4194
www.jusd.k12.ca.us
Arbuckle ES 700/K-6
3600 Packard St 92509 951-222-7788
Karina Becerra-Murillo, prin. Fax 369-3913
Camino Real ES 700/K-6
4655 Camino Real 92509 951-360-2714
Jose Campos, prin. Fax 360-2819
Glen Avon ES 700/K-6
4352 Pyrite St 92509 951-360-2764
Dave Doubravsky, prin. Fax 685-6938
Granite Hill ES 700/K-6
9371 Granite Hill Dr 92509 951-360-2725
Sylvia Bottom, prin. Fax 685-6568
Indian Hills ES 700/K-6
7750 Linares Ave 92509 951-360-2724
Cynthia Johnson, prin. Fax 681-4742
Jurupa MS 1,100/7-8
8700 Galena St 92509 951-360-2846
Walter Lancaster, prin. Fax 360-8928
Mira Loma MS 1,100/7-8
5051 Steve Ave 92509 951-360-2883
Cindy Freeman, prin. Fax 685-7405
Mission Bell ES 600/K-6
4020 Conning St 92509 951-360-2748
Andrew Huben, prin. Fax 681-7714
Mission MS 1,100/7-8
5961 Mustang Ln 92509 951-222-7842
Luz Mendez, prin. Fax 369-1407
Pacific Avenue ES 500/K-6
6110 45th St 92509 951-222-7877
Maureen Dalimot, prin. Fax 684-4540
Pedley ES 700/K-6
5871 Hudson St 92509 951-360-2793
Victoria Jobe, prin. Fax 360-2791
Peralta ES 700/K-6
6450 Peralta Pl 92509 951-222-7701
Marcy Hale, prin. Fax 779-9143
Rustic Lane ES 800/K-6
6420 Rustic Ln 92509 951-222-7837
Sandra Amatriain, prin. Fax 788-6401
Stone Avenue ES 700/K-6
5111 Stone Ave 92509 951-360-2859
Caron Winston, prin. Fax 681-5933
Sunnyslope ES 600/K-6
7050 38th St 92509 951-360-2781
Gary Dixon, prin. Fax 360-5462
Van Buren ES 700/K-6
9501 Jurupa Rd 92509 951-360-2865
Raul Espinoza, prin. Fax 685-3314
West Riverside ES 800/K-6
3972 Riverview Dr 92509 951-222-7759
Terri Stevens, prin. Fax 781-6873
Other Schools – See Mira Loma

Riverside USD 43,500/K-12
PO Box 2800 92516 951-788-7131
Gladys Walker, supt. Fax 778-5668
www.rusd.k12.ca.us
Adams ES 600/K-6
8362 Colorado Ave 92504 951-352-6709
Paul DeFoe, prin. Fax 328-2547
Alcott ES 900/K-6
2433 Central Ave 92506 951-788-7451
Joseph Nieto, prin. Fax 328-5480
Beatty ES 700/K-6
4261 Latham St 92501 951-276-2070
Debbie Ausman-Haskins, prin. Fax 274-4231
Bryant ES 300/K-6
4324 3rd St 92501 951-788-7453
Jamelia Oliver, prin. Fax 328-4080
Castle View ES 600/K-6
6201 Shaker Dr 92506 951-788-7460
Hayley Calhoun, prin. Fax 778-5780
Central MS 700/7-8
4795 Magnolia Ave 92506 951-788-7282
Fax 328-2580
Chemawa MS 1,300/7-8
8830 Magnolia Ave 92503 951-352-8244
Sean Curtin, prin. Fax 328-2980
Earhart MS 1,600/7-8
20202 Aptos St 92508 951-697-5700
Coleman Kells, prin. Fax 328-7580
Emerson ES 500/K-6
4660 Ottawa Ave 92507 951-788-7462
John McCombs, prin. Fax 274-4221

Franklin ES 800/K-6
19661 Orange Terrace Pkwy 92508 951-571-6502
Vivian Lee, prin. Fax 328-7280
Fremont ES 1,100/K-6
1925 N Orange St 92501 951-788-7466
Patti Popovich, prin. Fax 778-5380
Gage MS 1,200/7-8
6400 Lincoln Ave 92506 951-788-7350
Chuck Hiroto, prin. Fax 328-5680
Harrison ES 800/K-6
2901 Harrison St 92503 951-352-6712
Jean Aklufi, prin. Fax 274-4227
Hawthorne ES 600/K-6
2700 Irving St 92504 951-352-6716
Linda Daltrey, prin. Fax 778-5180
Highgrove ES 700/K-6
690 Center St 92507 951-788-7296
Esther Garcia, prin. Fax 342-4080
Highland ES 800/K-6
700 Highlander Dr 92507 951-788-7292
Lia Boucher, prin. Fax 778-5280
Hyatt ES 400/K-6
4466 Mount Vernon Ave 92507 951-788-7308
Raul Ayala, prin. Fax 788-7535
Jackson ES 900/K-6
4585 Jackson St 92503 951-352-8211
David Marshall, prin. Fax 687-8932
Jefferson ES 1,000/K-6
4285 Jefferson St 92504 951-352-8218
Maria Ortega, prin. Fax 342-2780
Kennedy ES 1,000/K-6
19125 School House Ln 92508 951-789-7570
Russ Bouton, prin. Fax 328-7380
Lake Mathews ES 600/K-6
12252 Blackburn Rd 92503 951-352-5520
Pamela Williams, prin. Fax 328-7180
Liberty ES 800/K-6
9631 Hayes St 92503 951-352-8225
Joshua Lightle, prin. Fax 328-5580
Longfellow ES 700/K-6
3610 Eucalyptus Ave 92507 951-788-7335
Melanie Maxwell, prin. Fax 328-5080
Madison ES 900/K-6
3635 Madison St 92504 951-352-8236
Loretta Houston, prin. Fax 689-6420
Magnolia ES 700/K-6
3975 Maplewood Pl 92506 951-788-7274
Joyce Harshman, prin. Fax 369-1608
Monroe ES 700/K-6
8535 Garfield St 92504 951-352-8241
Rob Murphy, prin. Fax 359-1757
Mountain View ES 1,000/K-6
6180 Streeter Ave 92504 951-788-7433
Paula Allbeck, prin. Fax 778-5580
Pachappa ES 700/K-6
6200 Riverside Ave 92506 951-788-7355
Kiersten Reno-Frausto, prin. Fax 276-7643
Rivera ES 800/K-6
20440 Red Poppy Ln 92508 951-697-5757
Char Gebeau, prin. Fax 328-7480
Sierra MS 1,000/7-8
4950 Central Ave 92504 951-788-7500
Lou Mason, prin. Fax 788-7561
Taft ES 800/K-6
959 Mission Grove Pkwy N 92506 951-776-3018
Janelle Woodward, prin. Fax 328-2921
Twain ES 800/K-6
19411 Krameria Ave 92508 951-789-8170
Jacqueline Hall, prin. Fax 274-4280
University Heights MS 900/7-8
1155 Massachusetts Ave 92507 951-788-7382
Patricia Grice, prin. Fax 276-7649
Victoria ES 600/K-6
2910 Arlington Ave 92506 951-788-7441
Lari Nelson, prin. Fax 274-4223
Washington ES 700/K-6
2760 Jane St 92506 951-788-7305
Kyley Ybarra, prin. Fax 328-4011
Woodcrest ES 600/K-6
16940 Krameria Ave 92504 951-776-4122
Randy Caudill, prin. Fax 328-7080

Bethel Christian S 400/PK-12
2425 Van Buren Blvd 92503 951-359-1123
Pattie Valenzuela, supt. Fax 359-1719
Harvest Christian S 400/K-6
6115 Arlington Ave 92504 951-359-3932
Dell Campbell, prin. Fax 637-1217
Hawarden Hills Academy 400/K-8
6696 Via Vista Dr 92506 951-780-1616
Lennett Logan, prin. Fax 780-0699
Immanuel Lutheran S 200/PK-6
5545 Alessandro Blvd 92506 951-682-4211
Susan Winscher, prin. Fax 682-9403
La Sierra Academy 800/K-12
4900 Golden Ave 92505 951-351-1445
Dr. Cyril Connelly, prin. Fax 689-3708
Life Christian Academy 100/PK-6
3349 Rubidoux Blvd 92509 951-681-3639
Demetria King, prin. Fax 684-7093
Our Lady of Perpetual Help S 300/PK-8
6686 Streeter Ave 92504 951-689-2125
Laurie Moore, prin. Fax 689-9354
Riverside Christian Day S 400/K-6
3612 Arlington Ave 92506 951-686-1818
Laurie Leach, prin. Fax 686-4041
Riverside Christian MS 200/6-8
8223 California Ave 92504 951-687-4610
Pat VanDyke, prin. Fax 687-4601
Riverside Christian S 400/K-5
3532 Monroe St 92504 951-687-0077
James Carter, prin. Fax 687-3340
Riverside Garden S 100/K-6
1085 W Linden St 92507 951-683-6602
Meg Shannon, prin. Fax 683-6602
St. Catherine of Alexandria S 300/K-8
7025 Brockton Ave 92506 951-684-1091
Rick Howick, prin. Fax 684-4936
St. Francis De Sales S 300/PK-8
4205 Mulberry St 92501 951-683-5083
Kathy Kothlow, prin. Fax 683-0249
St. Thomas the Apostle S 300/K-8
9136 Magnolia Ave 92503 951-689-1981
Cathy Thompson, prin. Fax 689-1985

Robbins, Sutter
Winship-Robbins ESD
Supt. — See Meridian
Robbins S 100/K-8
PO Box 237 95676 530-738-4386
Kim Richter, prin. Fax 738-4291

Rocklin, Placer, Pop. 49,626
Rocklin USD 9,700/K-12
2615 Sierra Meadows Dr 95677 916-624-2428
Kevin Brown, supt. Fax 630-2229
www.rocklin.k12.ca.us
Antelope Creek ES 500/K-6
6185 Springview Dr 95677 916-632-1095
Matt Murphy, prin. Fax 632-2381
Breen ES 600/K-6
2751 Breen Dr 95765 916-632-1155
Charles Thibideau, prin. Fax 632-9471
Cobblestone ES 500/K-6
5740 Cobblestone Dr 95765 916-632-0140
Kathleen Goddard, prin. Fax 632-9732
Granite Oaks MS 800/7-8
2600 Wyckford Blvd 95765 916-315-9009
Mike Melton, prin. Fax 315-9885
Parker Whitney ES 500/K-6
5145 Topaz Ave 95677 916-624-2491
Denny Rush, prin. Fax 624-0335
Rock Creek ES 600/K-6
2140 Collet Quarry Dr 95765 916-788-4282
Dorothy Sutter, prin. Fax 788-8161
Rocklin ES 500/K-6
5025 Meyers St 95677 916-624-3311
James Trimble, prin. Fax 624-5908
Ruhkala ES 400/K-6
6530 Turnstone Way 95765 916-632-6560
Gary Yee, prin. Fax 797-2062
Sierra ES 500/K-6
6811 Camborne Way 95677 916-788-7141
Fax 788-7161
Spring View MS 800/7-8
5040 5th St 95677 916-624-3381
Marjorie Crawford, prin. Fax 624-5737
Twin Oaks ES 500/K-6
2835 Club Dr 95765 916-315-1400
Sarah James, prin. Fax 315-1872
Valley View ES 500/K-6
3000 Crest Dr 95765 916-435-4844
Charles Kilbourne, prin. Fax 435-4944

Sierra Christian Academy 500/PK-12
6900 Destiny Dr 95677 916-772-1440
Cynthia White, prin. Fax 773-0304

Rodeo, Contra Costa, Pop. 7,589
John Swett USD 1,800/K-12
400 Parker Ave 94572 510-245-4300
Fax 245-4312
www.jsusd.k12.ca.us
Rodeo Hills ES 700/K-5
545 Garretson Ave 94572 510-799-4431
Linda Larson, prin. Fax 799-5230
Other Schools – See Crockett

St. Patrick S 300/PK-8
907 7th St 94572 510-799-2506
Kelly Stevens, prin. Fax 799-6781

Rohnert Park, Sonoma, Pop. 41,101
Cotati-Rohnert Park USD 6,100/K-12
5860 Labath Ave 94928 707-792-4722
Dr. Barbara Vrankovich, supt. Fax 792-4537
www.crpusd.org/
Creekside MS 700/6-8
5154 Snyder Ln 94928 707-588-5600
Sandy Kuzma, prin. Fax 588-5607
Evergreen ES 400/K-5
1125 Emily Ave 94928 707-588-5715
Gaylene Rosaschi, prin. Fax 588-5720
Hahn ES 400/K-5
825 Hudis St 94928 707-588-5675
Bonnie Barron, prin. Fax 588-5680
Monte Vista ES 500/K-5
1400 Magnolia Ave 94928 707-792-4531
Jane Wheeler, prin. Fax 792-4513
Mountain Shadows MS 900/6-8
7165 Burton Ave 94928 707-792-4800
Laura Mason, prin. Fax 792-4516
Reed ES 400/K-5
390 Arlen Dr 94928 707-792-4845
Amy Goodwin, prin. Fax 792-4517
Rohnert ES 400/K-5
550 Bonnie Ave 94928 707-792-4830
Barbara Bickford, prin. Fax 792-4519
Other Schools – See Cotati

Cross & Crown Lutheran S 200/PK-8
5475 Snyder Ln 94928 707-795-7863
Jean Bashi, admin. Fax 795-0509

Rolling Hills, Los Angeles, Pop. 1,933
Palos Verdes Peninsula USD
Supt. — See Palos Verdes Estates
Dapplegray ES 700/K-5
3011 Palos Verdes Dr N 90274 310-541-3706
Fred London, prin. Fax 541-8265
Rancho Vista ES 500/K-5
4323 Palos Verdes Dr N 90274 310-378-8388
Debra Loob, prin. Fax 378-4980

Peninsula Heritage S 100/K-5
26944 Rolling Hills Rd 90274 310-541-4795
Patricia Cailler, hdmstr. Fax 541-8264
Rolling Hills Country S 400/K-8
26444 Crenshaw Blvd 90274 310-377-4848
Karen Mayfield, dir. Fax 377-9651

Romoland, Riverside, Pop. 2,319
Romoland ESD
Supt. — See Homeland
Boulder Ridge MS 800/6-8
27327 Junipero Rd 92585 951-723-8931
Susan Scott, prin. Fax 723-8929
Harvest Valley ES 600/K-5
29955 Watson Rd 92585 951-928-2915
Michelle Rodriquez, prin. Fax 928-2920
Mesa View ES 600/K-5
27227 Heritage Lake Dr 92585 951-723-1284
Manuel Valdes, prin. Fax 723-1325
Romoland S 800/K-8
25890 Antelope Rd 92585 951-928-2910
Barbara Sanchez, prin. Fax 928-2918

Rosamond, Kern, Pop. 7,430
Southern Kern USD 2,400/K-12
PO Box CC 93560 661-256-5000
Rodney Van Norman, supt. Fax 256-1247
www.skusd.k12.ca.us
Rosamond ES 500/K-5
PO Box CC 93560 661-256-5050
Ann Buxton, prin. Fax 256-6248
Tropico MS 800/6-8
PO Box CC 93560 661-256-5040
Steve Smith, prin. Fax 256-0630

Rosemead, Los Angeles, Pop. 55,119
Garvey ESD 5,700/K-8
2730 Del Mar Ave 91770 626-307-3400
Virginia Peterson, supt. Fax 307-1964
www.garvey.k12.ca.us
Bitely ES 600/K-6
7501 Fern Ave 91770 626-307-3318
Laurie Narro, prin. Fax 307-8156
Emerson ES 500/K-6
7544 Emerson Pl 91770 626-307-3333
Annamarie Knight, prin. Fax 312-3566
Garvey IS 900/7-8
2720 Jackson Ave 91770 626-307-3385
Gema Macias, prin. Fax 307-3443
Rice ES 700/K-6
2150 Angelus Ave 91770 626-307-3348
John Turmes, prin. Fax 307-8163
Sanchez ES 400/K-6
8470 Fern Ave 91770 626-307-3368
Rene Hernandez, prin. Fax 312-2035
Temple IS 500/7-8
8470 Fern Ave 91770 626-307-3360
C.P. Cheung, prin. Fax 307-8162
Willard ES 600/K-6
3152 Willard Ave 91770 626-307-3375
Michelle Collaso, prin. Fax 312-3571
Other Schools – See Monterey Park, San Gabriel

Rosemead ESD 3,200/K-8
3907 Rosemead Blvd 91770 626-312-2900
Amy Enomoto-Perez Ed.D., supt. Fax 312-2906
www.rosemead.k12.ca.us
Encinita ES 400/K-6
4515 Encinita Ave 91770 626-286-3155
Dawn Rock, prin. Fax 285-8584
Janson ES 700/K-6
8628 Marshall St 91770 626-288-3150
Janieta Villagrana, prin. Fax 307-6184
Muscatel MS 700/7-8
4201 Ivar Ave 91770 626-287-1139
Dean Wharton, prin. Fax 307-6185
Savannah ES 700/K-6
3720 Rio Hondo Ave 91770 626-443-4015
Ruth Soto, prin. Fax 442-5478
Shuey ES 600/K-6
8472 Wells St 91770 626-287-5221
Carlos Moran, prin. Fax 307-6187

Roseville, Placer, Pop. 105,940
Center JUSD
Supt. — See Antelope
Riles MS 1,300/6-8
4747 PFE Rd 95747 916-787-8100
Joyce Duplissea, prin. Fax 773-4131

Dry Creek JESD 7,400/K-8
9707 Cook Riolo Rd 95747 916-770-8850
Mark Geyer, supt. Fax 771-0650
www.drycreek.k12.ca.us
Coyote Ridge ES 900/K-5
1751 Morningstar Dr 95747 916-774-8282
Michelle Harmeier, prin. Fax 774-8292
Creekview Ranch MS 6-8
8779 Cook Riolo Rd 95747 916-770-8845
George Tsai, prin. Fax 772-4145
Dry Creek ES 400/K-5
2955 PFE Rd 95747 916-770-8809
Tracy Robinson, prin. Fax 771-2072
Heritage Oak ES 700/K-5
2271 Americana Dr 95747 916-773-3960
Gabe Simon, prin. Fax 773-3955
Quail Glen ES 800/K-5
1250 Canevari Dr 95747 916-789-7100
James Ferguson, prin. Fax 789-7113
Silverado MS 1,400/6-8
2525 Country Club Dr 95747 916-780-2620
Priscilla Rasanen, prin. Fax 780-2635
Other Schools – See Antelope

Eureka UNSD
Supt. — See Granite Bay
Excelsior ES 500/4-6
2701 Eureka Rd 95661 916-780-2701
Diane Duncan, prin. Fax 780-4314

Maidu ES 500/K-3
1950 Johnson Ranch Dr 95661 916-789-7910
Stephanie Groat, prin. Fax 789-7914
Olympus JHS 500/7-8
2625 La Croix Dr 95661 916-782-1667
Kelly Graham, prin. Fax 782-1339

Roseville City ESD 8,400/K-8
1050 Main St 95678 916-771-1600
Richard Pierrucci, supt. Fax 786-5098
www.rcsdk8.org
Blue Oaks ES 600/K-5
8150 Horncastle Ave 95747 916-771-1700
Jeff Ancker, prin. Fax 772-7839
Brown ES 500/K-5
250 Trestle Rd 95678 916-771-1710
Marc Buljan, prin. Fax 773-1808
Buljan MS 1,000/6-8
100 Hallissey Dr 95678 916-771-1720
Greg Gunn, prin. Fax 773-2696
Cirby ES 400/K-5
814 Darling Way 95678 916-771-1730
David Dominguez, prin. Fax 783-1020
Cooley MS 900/6-8
9300 Prairie Woods Way 95747 916-771-1740
Karen Calkins, prin. Fax 786-3003
Crestmont ES 500/K-6
1501 Sheridan Ave 95661 916-771-1750
Richard Sorenson, prin. Fax 781-2042
Diamond Creek ES 600/K-5
3151 Hopscotch Way 95747 916-771-1760
Marty Brown, prin. Fax 626-2014
Eich IS 600/7-8
1509 Sierra Gardens Dr 95661 916-771-1770
Christine Hudson, prin. Fax 783-7292
Gates ES 600/K-5
1051 Trehowell Dr 95678 916-771-1780
Meghan Baichtal, prin. Fax 786-2060
Jefferson ES 400/K-5
750 Central Park Dr 95678 916-771-1840
Barbara Jelicich, prin. Fax 772-7195
Junction ES K-5
2150 Ellison Dr 95747 916-771-1860
Dave Phillips, prin. Fax 771-1861
Kaseberg ES 400/K-5
1040 Main St 95678 916-771-1790
Karen Quinlan, prin. Fax 782-4090
Sargeant ES 500/K-6
1200 Ridgecrest Way 95661 916-771-1800
Teri Seaman, prin. Fax 782-1090
Sierra Gardens ES 500/K-6
711 Oak Ridge Dr 95661 916-771-1810
Vickie Raymond, prin. Fax 782-4373
Spanger ES 400/K-5
699 Shasta St 95678 916-771-1820
Jodi Westphal, prin. Fax 773-2404
Stoneridge ES 500/K-6
2501 Alexandra Dr 95661 916-771-1830
Rebecca Toto, prin. Fax 786-5898
Woodbridge ES 300/K-3
515 Niles Ave 95678 916-771-1850
Dave Phillips, prin. Fax 782-4363

Adventure Christian S 500/PK-8
6401 Stanford Ranch Rd # B 95678 916-781-2986
Renee Flores, prin. Fax 773-5683
Christian Life Academy 100/K-12
1301 Coloma Way 95661 916-956-4662
Gary Gubitz, prin. Fax 786-7916
Cornerstone Christian S 100/K-12
143 Clinton Ave 95678 916-783-7779
H.D. Lowery, hdmstr. Fax 783-1856
Merryhill Sierra Gardens S 100/K-5
1622 Sierra Gardens Dr 95661 916-783-3010
Connie Curiel, prin. Fax 783-3017
St. Albans Country Day S 200/PK-8
2312 Vernon St 95678 916-782-3557
Laura Bernauer, hdmstr. Fax 782-3505
St. John's School 200/PK-8
4501 Bob Doyle Dr 95747 916-786-5400
Rev. Paul Hancock, hdmstr. Fax 789-2064
St. Rose S 300/K-8
633 Vine Ave 95678 916-782-1161
Suzanne Smoley, prin. Fax 782-7862
Valley Christian Academy 300/PK-12
301 W Whyte Ave 95678 916-728-5500
Brad Gunter, admin. Fax 721-3305

Ross, Marin, Pop. 2,283
Ross ESD 400/K-8
PO Box 1058 94957 415-457-2705
Tammy Murphy, supt. Fax 457-6724
www.rossschool.net/
Ross S 400/K-8
PO Box 1058 94957 415-457-2705
Carole Ramsey, prin. Fax 457-8923

Rowland Heights, Los Angeles, Pop. 49,900
Rowland USD 17,200/K-12
1830 Nogales St 91748 626-965-2541
Dr. Maria Ott, supt. Fax 854-8302
www.rowlandschools.org
Alvarado IS 1,000/7-8
1901 Desire Ave 91748 626-964-2358
Ying Tsao, prin. Fax 810-5579
Blandford ES 700/K-6
2601 Blandford Dr 91748 626-965-3410
Mercedes Lovie, prin. Fax 965-2360
Farjardo ES 500/K-6
18550 Farjardo St 91748 626-965-1537
Elaine McCauley, prin. Fax 965-7557
Jellick ES 400/K-6
1400 Jellick Ave 91748 626-964-1275
John Staumont, prin. Fax 964-8345
Killian ES 600/K-6
19100 Killian Ave 91748 626-964-6409
Jason Gass, prin. Fax 965-7729

Rowland ES 500/K-6
2036 Fullerton Rd 91748 626-964-3441
Sandy Johnson, prin. Fax 964-0931
Shelyn ES 600/K-6
19500 Nacora St 91748 909-444-0584
Sarah Opatkiewicz, prin. Fax 444-0582
Other Schools – See La Puente, Walnut, West Covina

American Chinese S 100/K-12
19100 Killian Ave 91748 909-762-1688
Ted Yeh, prin.
Fullerton Christian S 50/PK-K
2628 Fullerton Rd 91748 626-709-4557
Gloria Chang, admin. Fax 810-6686

Running Springs, San Bernardino, Pop. 4,195
Rim of the World USD
Supt. — See Lake Arrowhead
Hoffmann ES 500/K-6
2851 Running Springs School 92382 909-336-0370
Cherie Singer, prin. Fax 867-5244

Sacramento, Sacramento, Pop. 456,441
Elk Grove USD
Supt. — See Elk Grove
Adreani ES 600/K-6
9927 Wildhawk Dr W 95829 916-525-0630
Leanne Teuber, prin. Fax 525-0725
Beitzel ES 900/K-6
8140 Caymus Dr 95829 916-688-8484
Martin Martinez, prin. Fax 688-5371
Fite ES 800/K-6
9561 Fite School Rd 95829 916-689-2854
Bindy Grewal, prin. Fax 689-2917
Florin ES 700/K-6
7300 Kara Dr 95828 916-383-0530
Bob Pasley, prin. Fax 383-6404
Jackman MS 1,100/7-8
7925 Kentwall Dr 95823 916-393-2352
William Del Bonta, prin. Fax 393-4053
Jackson ES 900/K-6
8351 Cutler Way 95828 916-689-2115
Martin Fine, prin. Fax 689-2091
Kennedy ES 1,000/K-6
7037 Briggs Dr 95828 916-383-3311
Clarice Hespeler, prin. Fax 383-0242
Kirchgater ES 900/K-6
8141 Stevenson Ave 95828 916-689-9150
Larry Quismondo, prin. Fax 689-7938
Leimbach ES 800/K-6
8101 Grandstaff Dr 95823 916-689-2120
Jeanette Seamans, prin. Fax 689-8400
Mack ES 1,000/K-6
4701 Brookfield Dr 95823 916-422-5524
Roberta Collier, prin. Fax 422-2673
Morse ES 900/K-6
7000 Cranleigh Ave 95823 916-688-8586
Kilolo Umi, prin. Fax 682-5098
Prairie ES 1,000/K-6
5251 Valley Hi Dr 95823 916-422-1843
Fawzia Keval, prin. Fax 422-4722
Reese ES 1,000/K-6
7600 Lindale Dr 95828 916-422-2450
Margaret Campos, prin. Fax 422-4790
Reith ES 900/K-6
8401 Valley Lark Dr 95823 916-399-0110
Gordon Blackwood, prin. Fax 391-6763
Rutter MS 1,100/7-8
7350 Palmer House Dr 95828 916-422-7590
Yuri Penermon, prin. Fax 422-8354
Sierra-Enterprise ES 500/K-6
9115 Fruitridge Rd 95826 916-381-2767
Jason Campbell, prin. Fax 381-0572
Smedberg MS 1,200/7-8
8239 Kingsbridge Dr 95829 916-681-7525
Sharon Barnes, prin. Fax 681-7530
Tsukamoto ES 1,100/K-6
8737 Brittany Park Dr 95828 916-689-7580
Mark Leal, prin. Fax 682-7955
Union House ES 900/K-6
7850 Deer Creek Dr 95823 916-424-9201
Dan Owens, prin. Fax 424-3510
Valley Partners Preschool PK-PK
6300 Ehrhardt Ave 95823 916-689-3562
Debbie Benton, lead tchr.

Natomas USD 9,300/K-12
1901 Arena Blvd 95834 916-567-5400
Dr. Steve Farrar, supt. Fax 567-5405
www.natomas.k12.ca.us
American Lakes ES 500/K-5
2800 Stonecreek Dr 95833 916-567-5500
Rafael Soler, prin. Fax 567-5509
Bannon Creek ES 600/K-5
2775 Millcreek Dr 95833 916-567-5600
Linda Wilkinson, prin. Fax 567-5609
Greene MS 900/6-8
2950 W River Dr 95833 916-567-5560
Bob Evans, prin. Fax 567-5569
Heron S 900/K-8
5151 Banfield Dr 95835 916-567-5680
Mary Patrick, prin. Fax 567-5689
Hight ES K-5
3200 N Park Dr 95835 916-567-5700
Hervey Taylor, prin. Fax 567-5709
Jefferson ES 700/K-5
2001 Pebblewood Dr 95833 916-567-5580
Carrie Lopes, prin. Fax 567-5589
Natomas MS 800/6-8
3200 N Park Dr 95835 916-567-5540
Carla Najera-Kunsemiller, prin. Fax 567-5549
Natomas Park ES 800/K-5
4700 Crest Dr 95835 916-925-5234
Brent Johnson, prin. Fax 928-5219
Two Rivers ES 600/K-5
3201 W River Dr 95833 916-567-5520
Amanda Segovia Hale, prin. Fax 567-5529

Witter Ranch ES 800/K-5
3790 Poppy Hill Way 95834 916-567-5620
Julia True, prin. Fax 567-5629

Robla ESD 1,800/PK-6
5248 Rose St 95838 916-991-1728
Ralph Friend, supt. Fax 992-0308
www.robla.k12.ca.us
Bell Avenue ES 400/K-6
1900 Bell Ave 95838 916-922-0202
Lisa Hall, prin. Fax 568-7774
Glenwood ES 400/K-6
201 Jessie Ave 95838 916-922-2767
Marie Booth, prin. Fax 922-5035
Main Avenue ES 100/K-2
1400 Main Ave 95838 916-929-9559
Ruben Reyes, prin. Fax 929-4253
Robla ES 400/K-6
5200 Marysville Blvd 95838 916-991-1006
Mario Penman, prin. Fax 991-8643
Robla Preschool PK-PK
4351 Pinell St 95838 916-927-0136
Laura Lystrup, prin. Fax 568-7808
Taylor Street ES 500/K-6
4350 Taylor St 95838 916-927-5340
Arthur Estrada, prin. Fax 927-6396

Sacramento City USD 44,800/K-12
PO Box 269003 95826 916-643-7400
Susan Miller, supt. Fax 643-9480
www.scusd.edu
Anthony ES 300/K-6
7864 Detroit Blvd 95832 916-433-5353
Candas Colen, prin. Fax 433-5578
Bacon Basic MS 1,000/6-8
4140 Cuny Ave 95823 916-433-5000
David Sachs, prin. Fax 433-5166
Baker ES 600/K-6
5717 Laurine Way 95824 916-433-5444
Olga Arellano, prin. Fax 433-5533
Bancroft ES 400/K-6
2929 Belmar St 95826 916-382-5940
Enrique Flores, prin. Fax 382-5943
Bidwell ES 400/K-6
1730 65th Ave 95822 916-433-5047
Charlotte Chadwick, prin. Fax 433-5557
Birney ES 300/K-6
6251 13th St 95831 916-433-5420
Manuel Huezo, prin. Fax 433-5509
Bonnheim ES 400/K-6
7300 Marin Ave 95820 916-277-6294
Susan Dresser, prin. Fax 277-6697
Brannan MS 900/7-8
5301 Elmer Way 95822 916-264-4350
Peter Callas, prin. Fax 264-4481
Burnett ES 600/K-6
6032 36th Ave 95824 916-277-6685
Irma Marquez, prin. Fax 277-6442
Cabrillo ES 400/K-6
1141 Seamas Ave 95822 916-264-4171
Lynette Dilley, prin. Fax 264-4005
California MS 600/7-8
1600 Vallejo Way 95818 916-264-4550
Elizabeth Vigil, prin. Fax 264-4477
Camellia Basic ES 400/K-6
6600 Cougar Dr 95828 916-382-5980
Dr. Patricia Boyd, prin. Fax 382-5918
Carson MS 500/6-8
5301 N St 95819 916-277-6750
Catherine Beckworth, prin. Fax 277-6550
Chavez IS 400/4-6
7500 32nd St 95822 916-433-7397
Antonio Medrano, prin. Fax 433-7396
Cohen ES 300/K-6
9025 Salmon Falls Dr 95826 916-228-5840
Virginia Grabbe, prin. Fax 228-5818
Crocker/Riverside ES 500/K-6
2970 Riverside Blvd 95818 916-264-4183
Alvin Lee, prin. Fax 264-3223
DaVinci S 600/K-8
4701 Joaquin Way 95822 916-277-6496
Devon Davis, prin. Fax 277-6806
Didion S 600/K-8
6490 Harmon Dr 95831 916-433-5039
Norman Policar, prin. Fax 433-5189
Einstein MS 900/7-8
9325 Mirandy Dr 95826 916-228-5800
Leise Martinez, prin. Fax 228-5813
Elder Creek ES 700/K-6
7934 Lemon Hill Ave 95824 916-382-5970
Mary DeSplinter, prin. Fax 382-5959
Erlewine ES 400/K-6
2441 Stansberry Way 95826 916-228-5870
Terry Nicholson-Smith, prin. Fax 228-5872
Freeport ES 400/K-6
2118 Meadowview Rd 95832 916-433-5032
Amy Whitten, prin. Fax 433-5165
Fruit Ridge ES 500/K-6
4625 44th St 95820 916-277-6283
Fax 277-7179
Golden Empire ES 600/K-6
9045 Canberra Dr 95826 916-228-5890
Dr. Irene Eister, prin. Fax 228-5838
Greenwood S 600/K-8
5457 Carlson Dr 95819 916-277-6266
Christine Plumb, prin. Fax 277-6591
Harkness ES 300/K-6
2147 54th Ave 95822 916-433-5042
Eric Chapman, prin. Fax 433-5346
Harte ES 500/K-6
2751 9th Ave 95818 916-277-6261
Santiago Chapa, prin. Fax 277-6456
Hearst ES 500/1-6
1410 60th St 95819 916-277-6690
Charlie Watters, prin. Fax 277-6739
Hollywood Park ES 400/K-6
4915 Harte Way 95822 916-277-6290
Hamed Razawi, prin. Fax 277-6292

Hopkins ES 400/K-6
2221 Matson Dr 95822 916-433-5072
Laura Reed, prin. Fax 433-5274

Huntington ES 300/K-6
5921 26th St 95822 916-433-5435
Jacqualynn Bonini, prin. Fax 433-5532

Jefferson ES 300/K-6
2635 Chestnut Hill Dr 95826 916-382-5960
Angelia Brye-Jones, prin. Fax 382-5965

Judah ES 300/K-6
3919 McKinley Blvd 95819 916-277-6364
Robin Riley, prin. Fax 277-6388

Kemble ES 500/K-3
7495 29th St 95822 916-433-5025
Shana Henry, prin. Fax 433-5579

King S 500/K-8
480 Little River Way 95831 916-433-5062
Reginald Brown, prin. Fax 433-5179

Land ES 300/K-6
2120 12th St 95818 916-264-4166
Ellen Lee Carlson, prin. Fax 264-4357

Lincoln ES 500/K-6
3324 Glenmoor Dr 95827 916-228-5830
Laura Butler, prin. Fax 228-5834

Lisbon ES 400/K-6
7555 S Land Park Dr 95831 916-433-5057
Frank Lawler, prin. Fax 433-5289

Lubin ES 500/K-6
3535 M St 95816 916-277-6271
Lynn Soto, prin. Fax 277-6526

Maple ES 300/K-6
3301 37th Ave 95824 916-433-5067
Lorena Carrillo, prin. Fax 433-5069

Marshall ES 500/K-6
9525 Goethe Rd 95827 916-228-5860
Marla VanLaningham, prin. Fax 228-5819

Matsuyama ES 600/K-6
7680 Windbridge Dr 95831 916-433-5535
Doug Huscher, prin. Fax 433-5556

Morse Waldorf S 300/K-8
1901 60th Ave 95822 916-433-5544
Cheryl Eining, prin. Fax 433-5589

Nicholas ES 600/K-6
6601 Steiner Dr 95823 916-433-5076
Olga Bautista, prin. Fax 433-5560

Oak Ridge ES 500/K-6
4501 M L King Blvd 95820 916-277-6679
Stephen Lewis, prin. Fax 277-6849

Pacific ES 500/K-5
6201 41st St 95824 916-433-5089
Kathy Kingsbury, prin. Fax 433-5439

Parks MS 700/7-8
2250 68th Ave 95822 916-433-5400
Renee Balestrieri, prin. Fax 433-5518

Parkway ES 500/K-6
4720 Forest Pkwy 95823 916-433-5082
Deborah Nelson, prin. Fax 433-5572

Phillips ES 500/K-6
2930 21st Ave 95820 916-277-6277
Danny Hernandez, prin. Fax 277-6762

Pony Express ES 400/K-6
1250 56th Ave 95831 916-433-5350
Amelia Williams, prin. Fax 433-5267

Sequoia ES 500/K-6
3333 Rosemont Dr 95826 916-228-5850
William Aydlett, prin. Fax 228-5853

Sloat Basic ES 300/K-6
7525 Candlewood Way 95822 916-433-5051
Robert Sullivan, prin. Fax 433-5272

Smith ES 300/K-6
401 McClatchy Way 95818 916-264-4175
Faye Sharpe, prin. Fax 264-4182

Still ES 400/K-6
2200 John Still Dr 95832 916-433-5191
Jeff Kilty, prin. Fax 433-2716

Still MS, 2250 John Still Dr 95832 700/7-8
Andy O'Neill, prin. 916-433-5375

Sutter MS 1,300/7-8
3150 I St 95816 916-264-4150
Chad Sweitzer, prin. Fax 264-3436

Sutterville ES 500/K-6
4967 Monterey Way 95822 916-277-6693
Lori Aoun, prin. Fax 277-6590

Tahoe ES 400/K-6
3110 60th St 95820 916-277-6360
Katie Curry, prin. Fax 277-6419

Twain ES 400/K-6
4914 58th St 95820 916-277-6670
Rosario Guillen, prin. Fax 277-6486

Warren ES 500/K-6
5420 Lowell St 95820 916-382-5930
Tu Moua, prin. Fax 382-5977

Washington ES 200/K-4
520 18th St, 916-264-4160
Marilyn Collins, prin. Fax 264-4360

Wenzel ES 400/K-6
6870 Greenhaven Dr 95831 916-433-5432
Judy Montgomery, prin. Fax 433-5285

Winn ES 500/K-6
3351 Explorer Dr 95827 916-228-5880
Jill Tabachnick, prin. Fax 228-5820

Wire ES 600/K-6
5100 El Paraiso Ave 95824 916-433-5440
Susan Gibson, prin. Fax 433-5443

Woodbine ES 400/K-6
2500 52nd Ave 95822 916-433-5358
Scott Oltmanns, prin. Fax 433-5094

Wood MS 800/7-8
6201 Lemon Hill Ave 95824 916-382-5900
George Porter, prin. Fax 382-5914

San Juan USD
Supt. — See Carmichael

Arcade Fundamental MS 600/6-8
3500 Edison Ave 95821 916-971-7300
Tony Oddo, prin. Fax 971-7821

Arden MS 700/6-8
1640 Watt Ave 95864 916-971-7306
Peggy Picardo, prin. Fax 971-7830

Cottage ES 400/K-6
2221 Morse Ave 95825 916-575-2306
Rich Carlson, prin. Fax 575-2311

Cowan Fundamental ES 400/K-6
3350 Becerra Way 95821 916-575-2312
Karen Adicoff, prin. Fax 575-2316

Del Paso Manor ES 500/K-6
2700 Maryal Dr 95821 916-575-2330
Phyllis Westrup, prin. Fax 575-2335

Dyer-Kelly ES 500/K-5
2236 Edison Ave 95821 916-566-2150
Debi Wegsteen, prin. Fax 566-2156

Edison ES 400/K-6
1500 Dom Way 95864 916-575-2342
Todd Lindeman, prin. Fax 575-2348

Greer ES 400/K-6
2301 Hurley Way 95825 916-566-2157
Debbie Kraus, prin. Fax 566-2161

Howe Avenue ES 600/K-5
2404 Howe Ave 95825 916-566-2165
Carl Fahle, prin. Fax 566-2180

Mariemont ES 500/K-6
1401 Corta Way 95864 916-575-2360
Linda Dismukes, prin. Fax 575-2353

Pasadena Avenue ES 400/K-6
4330 Pasadena Ave 95821 916-575-2373
Phyllis Caesar, prin. Fax 575-2376

Salk High Tech Academy 600/6-8
2950 Hurley Way 95864 916-971-7312
Valerie Turner, prin. Fax 971-7694

Sierra Oaks S 500/K-8
171 Mills Rd 95864 916-575-2390
Donna Kenfield, prin. Fax 575-2395

Whitney Avenue ES 400/K-6
4248 Whitney Ave 95821 916-575-2407
Barbara Githens, prin. Fax 575-2412

Twin Rivers USD
Supt. — See Mc Clellan

Babcock ES 500/K-6
2400 Cormorant Way 95815 916-263-8324
Betty von Werlhof, prin. Fax 263-8332

Castori ES 500/K-6
1801 South Ave 95838 916-263-8352
Patrick Birdsong, prin. Fax 263-8358

Del Paso Heights ES 400/K-6
590 Morey Ave 95838 916-643-8700
Leo Alvarez, prin. Fax 643-8716

Fairbanks ES 300/K-6
227 Fairbanks Ave 95838 916-643-8640
Kenneth Kolster, prin. Fax 643-8666

Foothill Farms JHS 800/7-8
5001 Diablo Dr 95842 916-286-1400
Jeff James, prin. Fax 263-3756

Foothill Oaks ES 600/K-6
5520 Lancelot Dr 95842 916-566-1830
Linda Reuter, prin. Fax 339-2027

Frontier ES 500/K-6
6691 Silverthorne Cir 95842 916-566-1840
Ellen Giffin, prin. Fax 344-8932

Garden Valley ES 400/K-6
3601 Larchwood Dr 95834 916-643-8750
Michele Williams, prin. Fax 643-8766

Hagginwood ES 400/K-6
1418 Palo Verde Ave 95815 916-263-8365
Alberto Beccora, prin. Fax 263-8377

Johnson ES 400/K-6
2591 Edgewater Rd 95815 916-263-8388
David Nevarez, prin. Fax 263-8392

King Technology Academy 800/7-8
3051 Fairfield St 95815 916-286-4700
Samuel Harris, prin. Fax 263-6701

Morey Ave ECC 50/PK-K
155 Morey Ave 95838 916-643-8680
Dr. Lois Graham, prin. Fax 643-8681

Noralto ES 700/K-6
477 Las Palmas Ave 95815 916-263-8411
Brad Allen, prin. Fax 263-8404

North Avenue ES 200/K-6
1281 North Ave 95838 916-643-8775
Janis Wade, prin. Fax 643-8791

Northwood ES 400/K-6
2630 Taft St 95815 916-263-8426
Renee Scott-Femenella, prin. Fax 263-8424

Norwood JHS 600/7-8
4601 Norwood Ave 95838 916-649-6600
Roxanne Mitchell, prin. Fax 649-6696

Pioneer ES 500/K-6
5816 Pioneer Way 95841 916-566-1940
Michelle Nunn, prin. Fax 332-6374

Regency Park ES 700/K-6
5901 Bridgecross Dr 95835 916-566-1660
Mike Reed, prin. Fax 419-4958

Ridgepoint ES 600/K-6
4680 Monument Dr 95842 916-566-1950
Jim McLaughlin, prin. Fax 344-3951

Rio Tierra JHS 600/7-8
3201 Northstead Dr 95833 916-286-1500
Paul Orlando, prin. Fax 263-6971

Strauch ES 600/K-6
3141 Northstead Dr 95833 916-263-8477
Axel Hannemann, prin. Fax 263-8487

Woodlake ES 400/K-6
700 Southgate Rd 95815 916-263-8491
Maria Oropeza, prin. Fax 263-8494

Woodridge ES 600/K-6
5761 Brett Dr 95842 916-566-1650
Roberta Raymond, prin. Fax 331-7183

Al-Arqam Islamic S 300/K-12
6990 65th St 95823 916-391-3333
Dalia Wardany, prin.

Bergamo Montessori S 100/K-8
8200 Pocket Rd 95831 916-399-1900
Pamela Barrow-Lynn, prin. Fax 394-0551

Bradshaw Christian S 1,000/PK-12
8324 Bradshaw Rd 95829 916-688-0521
Carl Eastvold, supt. Fax 688-0502

Calvary Christian S 100/K-12
5051 47th Ave 95824 916-393-3633
Rodney Barlow, prin. Fax 393-5000

Camellia Waldorf S 200/PK-8
5701 Freeport Blvd 95822 916-427-5022
Meredith Johanson, admin. Fax 427-8287

Capital Christian S 500/K-5
9470 Micron Ave 95827 916-856-5633
Todd Jacobs, prin. Fax 856-5609

Courtyard Private S 100/K-6
205 24th St 95816 916-442-5395
Jonathan Molnar, prin. Fax 442-5398

Gloria Dei Lutheran S 200/PK-8
4910 Lemon Hill Ave 95824 916-428-1127
Randall Smith, admin. Fax 428-2766

Holy Spirit S 300/K-8
3920 W Land Park Dr 95822 916-448-5663
Marilee Bellotti, prin. Fax 448-1465

John Paul II S 200/PK-8
5700 13th Ave 95820 916-457-5621
Frances Wise, prin. Fax 736-0204

Liberty Towers Christian S 200/PK-8
5132 Elkhorn Blvd 95842 916-332-4070
Mary Mast, prin. Fax 339-3515

Merryhill Eastern ES 100/K-5
2730 Eastern Ave 95821 916-485-2177
Sue Stewart, prin.

Merryhill ES 200/PK-5
9036 Calvine Rd 95829 916-689-7236
Nieva Gatbonton, prin. Fax 689-7289

Merryhill Millcreek S 200/K-5
2565 Millcreek Dr 95833 916-564-7343
Lezli Warburton, prin.

Merryhill Pocket S 100/K-5
7450 Pocket Rd 95831 916-429-6044
Claudia Sherry, prin.

Nehemiah Christian Academy 100/PK-6
PO Box 15010 95851 916-922-2033
Brenda Goudeaux, admin. Fax 922-6542

Peace Lutheran S 100/PK-PK
924 San Juan Rd 95834 916-927-4060
Penny Nixon, prin. Fax 920-3412

Presentation S 200/PK-8
3100 Norris Ave 95821 916-482-0351
Kathryn Lucchesi, prin. Fax 482-0377

Sacramento Country Day S 500/PK-12
2636 Latham Dr 95864 916-481-8811
Stephen Repsher, hdmstr. Fax 481-6016

Sacred Heart S 300/K-8
3933 I St 95816 916-456-1576
Theresa Sparks, prin. Fax 456-4773

St. Charles Borromeo S 300/K-8
7580 Center Pkwy 95823 916-421-6189
Susan Jaftok, prin. Fax 421-3954

St. Francis S 300/K-8
2500 K St 95816 916-442-5494
Laurie Power, prin. Fax 442-1390

St. Ignatius S 400/PK-8
3245 Arden Way 95825 916-488-3907
Patricia Lane, prin. Fax 488-0569

St. Joseph S 200/PK-8
1718 El Monte Ave 95815 916-925-1465
Patricia Peterson, prin. Fax 925-0963

St. Mary S 300/K-8
1351 58th St 95819 916-452-1100
Laura Allen, prin. Fax 453-2750

St. Patrick S 200/K-8
5945 Franklin Blvd 95824 916-421-4963
John Rieschick, prin. Fax 421-3849

St. Philomene S 300/PK-8
2320 El Camino Ave 95821 916-489-1506
Debra Mosbrucker, prin. Fax 489-2642

St. Robert S 300/K-8
2251 Irvin Way 95822 916-452-2111
Brian James, prin. Fax 452-5765

Shalom Day S 200/PK-6
2320 Sierra Blvd 95825 916-485-4151
Dr. Joan Gusinow, dir. Fax 485-3970

Southpointe Christian S 100/PK-12
7520 Stockton Blvd 95823 916-423-2060
Dr. Rick Hackney, supt. Fax 681-4538

Town & Country Lutheran S 100/K-8
4049 Marconi Ave 95821 916-481-2542
Myia Stewart, prin. Fax 481-0648

Trinity Christian S 200/PK-8
5225 Hillsdale Blvd 95842 916-331-7377
Dr. Charles Seielstad, dir. Fax 331-3152

Saint Helena, Napa, Pop. 6,028

St. Helena USD 1,400/K-12
465 Main St 94574 707-967-2708
Dr. Robert Haley, supt. Fax 963-1335
www.sthelena.k12.ca.us

St. Helena ES 300/3-5
1325 Adams St 94574 707-967-2712
Stan Augustine, prin. Fax 967-2756

St. Helena PS 300/K-2
1701 Grayson Ave 94574 707-967-2772
Rob Grace, prin. Fax 963-2959

Stevenson MS 400/6-8
1316 Hillview Pl 94574 707-967-2725
Mary Allen, prin. Fax 967-2734

Foothills Adventist S 100/PK-8
711 Sunnyside Rd 94574 707-963-3546
Josue Rosado, prin. Fax 963-7651

St. Helena S 100/K-8
1255 Oak Ave 94574 707-963-4677
Jim Ritchie, prin. Fax 963-4659

Salida, Stanislaus, Pop. 4,499
Salida UNESD 3,300/K-8
4801 Sisk Rd 95368 209-545-0339
Douglas Baughn, supt. Fax 545-2682
www.salida.k12.ca.us/
Boer ES 600/K-5
4801 Gold Valley Rd 95368 209-543-8163
Rex Tschetter, prin. Fax 543-0669
Salida ES 500/K-5
4519 Finney Rd 95368 209-545-9394
Jeri Passalaqua, prin. Fax 545-3711
Salida MS - Vella Campus 1,100/6-8
5041 Toomes Rd 95368 209-545-1633
Shannon Kettering, prin. Fax 545-0831
Sisk ES 700/K-5
5337 Sugar Creek Ln 95368 209-545-1671
Ana Garcia, prin. Fax 545-1624
Other Schools – See Modesto

Salinas, Monterey, Pop. 146,431
Alisal UNSD 7,300/K-6
1205 E Market St 93905 831-753-5700
Dr. Esperanza Zendejas, supt. Fax 753-5709
www.alisal.org
Alisal Community ES 600/K-6
1437 Del Monte Ave 93905 831-753-5720
Elizabeth Armenta, prin. Fax 753-5725
Bardin ES 700/K-6
425 Bardin Rd 93905 831-753-5730
Esteban Hernandez, prin. Fax 753-5758
Chavez ES 700/K-6
1225 Towt St 93905 831-753-5224
Sonia Jaramillo, prin. Fax 753-5230
Creekside ES 700/K-6
1770 Kittery St 93906 831-753-5252
Hecate Rosewood, prin. Fax 753-5256
Fremont ES 700/K-6
1255 E Market St 93905 831-753-5750
Trine Rodriguez, prin. Fax 753-5754
King Academy 500/4-6
925 N Sanborn Rd 93905 831-796-3916
Luisa Resendiz, prin. Fax 796-3921
Loya ES 800/K-6
1505 Cougar Dr 93905 831-751-1945
Mary Magana, prin. Fax 751-1953
Paul ES 700/K-6
1300 Rider Ave 93905 831-753-5740
Ricardo Cabrera, prin. Fax 753-5268
Rocca Barton ES 600/K-6
680 Las Casitas Dr 93905 831-753-5770
Anastacio Cabral, prin. Fax 753-5797
Sanchez ES 500/K-3
901 N Sanborn Rd 93905 831-753-5760
Alicia Fletcher, prin. Fax 753-5764
Steinbeck ES 600/K-6
1714 Burlington Dr 93906 831-753-5780
Dora Salazar, prin. Fax 443-0977

Graves ESD 50/K-8
15 McFadden Rd 93908 831-422-6392
Rosemarie Grounds, supt. Fax 422-3211
schools.monterey.k12.ca.us/~graves/
Graves S 50/K-8
15 McFadden Rd 93908 831-422-6392
Rosemarie Grounds, prin. Fax 422-3211

Lagunita ESD 100/K-8
975 San Juan Grade Rd 93907 831-449-2800
Sharon Theis, supt. Fax 449-9671
Lagunita S 100/K-8
975 San Juan Grade Rd 93907 831-449-2800
Sharon Theis, prin. Fax 449-9671

North Monterey County USD
Supt. — See Moss Landing
Echo Valley ES 500/PK-6
147 Echo Valley Rd 93907 831-663-2308
Rachelle Morgan-Lewis, prin. Fax 663-1006
N Monterey Co. Ctr for Independent Study 200/K-12
17500 Pesante Rd 93907 831-663-6154
Ken Jordan, prin. Fax 663-6184
Prunedale ES 700/PK-6
17719 Pesante Rd 93907 831-663-3963
Margarita Palacios, prin. Fax 663-5295

Salinas City ESD 8,400/PK-6
840 S Main St 93901 831-753-5600
Donna Alonzo Vaughan, supt. Fax 753-5610
schools.monterey.k12.ca.us/~salcity/
Boronda Meadows ES 600/K-6
915 Larkin St 93907 831-784-5400
Rosie Alvarez, prin. Fax 770-1987
El Gabilan ES 700/K-6
1256 Linwood Dr 93906 831-753-5660
Michael Trujillo, prin. Fax 442-9860
Kammann ES 800/K-6
521 Rochex Ave 93906 831-753-5665
Jennifer Zanzot, prin. Fax 753-5223
Laurel Wood ES 500/K-6
645 Larkin St 93907 831-753-5620
Marsha Nichols, prin. Fax 783-3050
Lincoln ES 600/PK-2
705 California St 93901 831-753-5625
Chris Banks, prin. Fax 753-5699
Loma Vista ES 600/K-6
757 Sausal Dr 93906 831-753-5670
Ernesto Gonzalez, prin. Fax 443-2181
Los Padres ES 700/K-6
1130 John St 93905 831-753-5630
Hilda Huerta, prin. Fax 751-3564
Mission Park ES 700/K-6
403 W Acacia St 93901 831-753-5635
Melissa Lewington, prin. Fax 753-4191
Monterey Park ES 600/K-6
410 San Miguel Ave 93901 831-753-5640
Diane Middaugh, prin. Fax 751-3626
Natividad ES 700/K-6
1465 Modoc Ave 93906 831-753-5675
Lori Sanders, prin. Fax 753-5218
Roosevelt ES 600/K-6
120 Capitol St 93901 831-753-5645
Brinet Greenlee, prin. Fax 769-0956
Sherwood ES 800/K-6
110 S Wood St 93905 831-753-5650
Terri Dye, prin. Fax 751-3616
University Park ES 600/K-6
833 W Acacia St 93901 831-753-5655
Anne Crawford, prin. Fax 751-3622

Salinas UNHSD 13,500/7-12
431 W Alisal St 93901 831-796-7000
Roger Anton, supt. Fax 796-7005
www.salinas.k12.ca.us
El Sausal MS 900/7-8
1155 E Alisal St 93905 831-796-7200
Francisco Huerta, prin. Fax 796-7205
Harden MS 1,200/7-8
1561 McKinnon St 93906 831-796-7310
Jacqui Axtell, prin. Fax 796-7305
La Paz MS 1,000/7-8
1300 N Sanborn Rd 93905 831-796-7900
Steve Oliver, prin. Fax 796-7905
Washington MS 1,000/7-8
560 Iverson St 93901 831-796-7100
Judith Roney, prin. Fax 796-7105

Santa Rita UNESD 2,900/K-8
57 Russell Rd 93906 831-443-7200
James Fontana, supt. Fax 442-1729
www.santaritaschools.org
Gavilan View MS 1,000/6-8
18250 Van Buren Ave 93906 831-443-7212
John Gutierrez, prin. Fax 443-0908
La Joya ES 400/K-5
55 Rogge Rd 93906 831-443-7216
Mary Stefan, prin. Fax 443-9539
McKinnon ES 500/K-5
2100 McKinnon St 93906 831-443-7224
Susan Fisher, prin. Fax 443-7240
New Republic ES 400/K-5
636 Arcadia Way 93906 831-443-7246
Ana Butler, prin. Fax 443-7256
Santa Rita ES 500/K-5
2014 Santa Rita St 93906 831-443-7221
Jose Garcia, prin. Fax 443-7228

Spreckels UNESD
Supt. — See Spreckels
Buena Vista MS 300/6-8
18250 Tara Dr 93908 831-455-8936
Eric Tarallo, prin. Fax 455-8832

Washington UNESD 1,000/K-8
43 San Benancio Rd 93908 831-484-2166
Dee Baker, supt. Fax 484-2828
schools.monterey.k12.ca.us/~sbenanci/
San Benancio MS 300/6-8
43 San Benancio Rd 93908 831-484-1172
Gina Uccelli, prin. Fax 484-6509
Toro Park ES 400/K-3
43 San Benancio Rd 93908 831-484-9691
Barbara Brown, prin. Fax 484-5666
Washington Union S 200/4-5
43 San Benancio Rd 93908 831-484-1331
Sandi Young, prin. Fax 484-5736

Church of the Good Shepherd Preschool 100/PK-K
301 Corral de Tierra Rd 93908 831-484-2363
Fax 484-2647
Madonna Del Sasso S 300/PK-8
20 Santa Teresa Way 93906 831-424-7813
Dr. Charles White, prin. Fax 424-3359
Montessori Learning Center 100/PK-8
PO Box 2387 93902 831-455-1546
Adrii Helgren, admin. Fax 455-9628
Pacific Coast Christian Academy 100/PK-8
381 San Juan Grade Rd 93906 831-449-0140
Robin Young, prin. Fax 449-7161
Sacred Heart S 300/K-8
123 W Market St 93901 831-771-1310
Jennifer Dean, prin. Fax 771-1314
Salinas Christian S 200/PK-8
345 E Alvin Dr 93906 831-449-5421
Debbie Cabitac, prin. Fax 449-5354
Soaring Eagles Christian Academy 100/K-12
PO Box 875 93902 831-758-5849
Maria Musumeci, dir. Fax 758-5279

Salton City, Imperial
Coachella Valley USD
Supt. — See Thermal
Sea View ES 400/K-6
2467 Sea Shore Ave 92275 760-394-4124
Carrie Macy, prin. Fax 394-0971

Samoa, Humboldt
Peninsula UNESD 50/K-8
PO Box 175 95564 707-443-2731
Dr. Mary Wolford, supt. Fax 443-3685
www.humboldt.k12.ca.us/peninsula_sd/
Peninsula Union S 50/K-8
PO Box 175 95564 707-443-2731
Dr. Mary Wolford, prin. Fax 443-3685

San Andreas, Calaveras, Pop. 2,115
Calaveras USD 3,600/K-12
PO Box 788 95249 209-754-3504
Mark Campbell, supt. Fax 754-5361
www.calaveras.k12.ca.us
San Andreas ES 300/K-6
PO Box 67 95249 209-754-2136
Maria Ortner, prin. Fax 754-2162
Other Schools – See Mokelumne Hill, Rail Road Flat, Valley Springs, West Point

San Anselmo, Marin, Pop. 12,018
Ross Valley ESD 1,900/K-8
110 Shaw Dr 94960 415-454-2160
Bryce Sumnick, supt. Fax 454-6840
rossvalleyschools.org/
Brookside ES 300/K-2
116 Butterfield Rd 94960 415-453-2948
David Finnane, prin. Fax 453-0243
Brookside ES 300/2-5
46 Green Valley Ct 94960 415-454-7409
Tracy Smith, prin. Fax 454-3782
Thomas ES 300/K-5
150 Ross Ave 94960 415-454-4603
Chad Carvey, prin. Fax 485-5506
Other Schools – See Fairfax

St. Anselm S 300/K-8
40 Belle Ave 94960 415-454-8667
Odile Steel, prin. Fax 454-4730
San Domenico MS 200/6-8
1500 Butterfield Rd 94960 415-258-1908
Jay Buckley, prin. Fax 258-1901
San Domenico S 200/PK-5
1500 Butterfield Rd 94960 415-258-1910
Carole Chase, prin. Fax 258-1901

San Ardo, Monterey
San Ardo UNESD 100/K-8
PO Box 170 93450 831-627-2520
Carlos Vega, supt. Fax 627-2078
schools.monterey.k12.ca.us/~sanardo/
San Ardo S 100/K-8
PO Box 170 93450 831-627-2520
Carlos Vega, prin. Fax 627-2078

San Bernardino, San Bernardino, Pop. 198,550
Redlands USD
Supt. — See Redlands
Victoria ES 600/K-5
1505 Richardson St 92408 909-478-5670
Larry Elwell, prin. Fax 478-5676

San Bernardino City USD 55,600/K-12
777 N F St 92410 909-381-1100
Dr. Arturo Delgado, supt. Fax 885-6392
www.sbcusd.com/
Anton ES 500/K-5
1501 Anton Ct 92404 909-386-2000
Debra Fields, prin. Fax 891-1922
Arrowhead ES 400/K-5
3825 N Mountain View Ave 92405 909-881-8100
Tasha Lindsay-Doizan, prin. Fax 881-8104
Arrowview MS 900/7-8
2299 N G St 92405 909-881-8109
Arwyn Wild, prin. Fax 881-8119
Barton ES 500/K-5
2214 Pumalo St 92404 909-388-6534
Charles Van Frank, prin. Fax 862-3583
Bradley ES 800/K-6
1300 Valencia Ave 92404 909-388-6317
Art Gallardo, prin. Fax 888-9716
Burbank ES 400/K-6
198 W Mill St 92408 909-388-6324
Dorothy Fenster, prin. Fax 384-0625
Chavez MS 1,400/6-8
6650 Magnolia Ave 92407 909-386-2050
Karen Strong, prin. Fax 473-8443
Curtis MS 1,400/6-8
1050 Del Rosa Ave 92410 909-388-6332
Steven Perlut, prin. Fax 388-6339
Davidson ES 600/K-6
2844 Davidson Ave 92405 909-881-8153
Joyce Payne, prin. Fax 881-5633
Del Rosa ES 1,000/K-6
3395 Mountain Ave 92404 909-881-8160
Elizabeth Atkinson, prin. Fax 881-2926
Del Vallejo MS 1,700/6-8
1885 E Lynwood Dr 92404 909-881-8280
Charles McWilliams, prin. Fax 881-8285
Emmerton ES 800/K-6
1888 Arden Ave 92404 909-388-6522
Dottie Podolak, prin. Fax 862-4353
Fairfax ES 400/K-6
1362 Pacific St 92404 909-381-1283
Ruth Curry, prin. Fax 384-0582
Golden Valley MS 1,300/6-8
3800 N Waterman Ave 92404 909-881-8168
Marguerite Williams, prin. Fax 881-5196
Hillside ES 700/K-6
4975 N Mayfield Ave 92407 909-881-8264
Linda Brown, prin. Fax 881-4270
Hunt ES 800/K-5
1342 Pumalo St 92404 909-881-8178
E. Cochrane-Benoit, prin. Fax 881-8175
Ingham ES 500/K-5
1695 W 19th St 92411 909-880-6633
Joan West, prin. Fax 880-6638
Jones ES 600/K-6
700 N F St 92410 909-386-2020
Alvina Pawlik, prin. Fax 885-8181
Kimbark ES 500/K-6
18021 W Kenwood Ave 92407 909-880-6641
Karen Hoag, prin. Fax 880-9341
King MS 1,100/6-8
1250 Medical Center Dr 92411 909-388-6350
James Espinoza, prin. Fax 388-6361
Lincoln ES 1,000/K-6
255 W 13th St 92405 909-388-6370
Kristin Kolling, prin. Fax 388-6379
Lytle Creek ES 800/K-6
275 S K St 92410 909-388-6382
Edwin Gomez, prin. Fax 381-0483
Marshall ES 700/K-6
3288 N G St 92405 909-881-8185
Yodit Terrefe, prin. Fax 882-6705
Monterey ES 800/K-5
794 E Monterey Ave 92410 909-388-6391
Ernestine Landeros, prin. Fax 381-5031

Mt. Vernon ES 800/K-5
1271 W 10th St 92411 909-388-6400
Luis Chavez-Andere, prin. Fax 889-9797
Muscoy ES 800/K-6
2119 Blake St 92407 909-880-6649
Alejandro Hernandez, prin. Fax 880-6654
Newmark ES 500/K-5
4121 N 3rd Ave 92407 909-881-8192
Santosh Trikha, prin. Fax 881-9563
North Park ES 900/K-6
5378 N H St 92407 909-881-8202
Janie Morales, prin. Fax 882-7142
North Verdemont ES 500/K-6
3555 W Meyers Rd 92407 909-880-6730
Denise Martinez, prin. Fax 880-6734
Palm Avenue ES 800/K-6
6565 Palm Ave 92407 909-880-6753
Christopher Tickell, prin. Fax 880-6759
Parkside ES 700/K-6
3775 N Waterman Ave 92404 909-881-8209
Kevin Goodly, prin. Fax 881-1359
Ramona-Alessandro ES 700/K-5
670 Ramona Ave 92411 909-388-6300
Jack Oakes, prin. Fax 381-1993
Richardson Prep MS 600/6-8
455 S K St 92410 909-388-6438
Natalie Raymundo, prin. Fax 383-0368
Riley ES 900/K-6
1266 N G St 92405 909-388-6460
Sane Mataitusi, prin. Fax 388-6467
Rio Vista ES 700/K-5
1451 N California St 92411 909-388-6450
Charles Brown, prin. Fax 884-9518
Roberts ES 900/K-6
494 E 9th St 92410 909-388-6409
Velia Martinez, prin. Fax 885-0536
Rodriguez Prep MS 6-8
1985 Guthrie St 92404 909-884-6030
Perry Wiseman, prin. Fax 863-7869
Roosevelt ES 700/K-6
1554 Garner Ave 92411 909-388-6470
Michele Tesauro, prin. Fax 889-1378
Salinas ES 600/K-5
2699 N California St 92407 909-880-6600
Daniel Marin, prin. Fax 880-9607
Shandin Hills MS 1,600/6-8
4301 Little Mountain Dr 92407 909-880-6666
Carmen Beck, prin. Fax 880-6672
Urbita ES 500/K-6
771 S J St 92410 909-388-6488
Pat King, prin. Fax 388-7488
Vermont ES 700/K-6
3695 Vermont St 92407 909-880-6658
Aldo Ramirez, prin. Fax 880-1348
Warm Springs ES 800/K-6
7497 Sterling Ave 92410 909-388-6500
Ana Applegate, prin. Fax 888-6045
Wilson ES 800/K-6
2894 Belle St 92404 909-881-8253
Nelson Togerson, prin. Fax 886-6943
Wong ES K-6
1250 E 9th St 92410 909-888-1500
Irma Gastelum, prin. Fax 889-8929
Other Schools – See Highland

Congregation Emanu El Clare Cherry S 100/PK-6
3512 N E St 92405 909-883-9168
Gina Howard, dir. Fax 886-4048
Del Rosa Christian S 100/PK-6
1333 E 39th St 92404 909-882-3004
Steve Spray, prin. Fax 886-8630
Dikaios Christian Academy 300/K-12
PO Box 9067 92427 909-473-0118
Von Sommerville, admin.
Holy Rosary Academy 200/K-8
2620 N Arrowhead Ave 92405 909-886-1088
Cheryll Austin, prin. Fax 475-5263
Northpark Christian Academy 50/PK-2
5395 N F St 92407 909-882-3277
Lee Leslie, admin. Fax 882-2898
Our Lady of the Assumption S 200/K-8
796 W 48th St 92407 909-881-2416
Sue Long, prin. Fax 886-7892
St. Anthony S 200/K-8
1510 W 16th St 92411 909-887-5413
Lori Campbell, prin. Fax 887-9908
San Bernardino Christian S 100/K-6
2898 N G St 92405 909-883-1622
Diana Fuentes, prin. Fax 886-3593
Temple Learning Center 50/PK-12
1777 W Base Line St 92411 909-885-4695
Rev. Raymond Turner, admin. Fax 383-0438

San Bruno, San Mateo, Pop. 39,752

Millbrae ESD
Supt. — See Millbrae
Lomita Park ES 200/K-5
200 Santa Helena Ave 94066 650-588-5852
Lynne Ferrario, prin. Fax 873-8014

San Bruno Park ESD 2,600/K-8
500 Acacia Ave 94066 650-624-3100
David Hutt, supt. Fax 266-9626
sbpsd.k12.ca.us
Allen ES 400/K-6
875 Angus Ave W 94066 650-624-3140
Kathleen Obar-Cosgriff, prin. Fax 875-7490
Belle Air ES 400/K-6
450 3rd Ave 94066 650-624-3155
Claire Beltrami, prin. Fax 875-7596
Crestmoor ES 200/K-6
2322 Crestmoor Dr 94066 650-624-3145
Natalie Sheridon, prin. Fax 875-7781
El Crystal ES 200/K-6
201 Balboa Way 94066 650-624-3150
Karl Johnson, prin. Fax 875-9308

Muir ES 300/K-6
130 Cambridge Ln 94066 650-624-3160
Francis Dunleavy, prin. Fax 875-9462
Parkside IS 600/7-8
1801 Niles Ave 94066 650-624-3180
Angela Addiego, prin. Fax 877-8195
Portola ES 200/K-6
300 Amador Ave 94066 650-624-3175
Charles Rohrbach, prin. Fax 738-6697
Rollingwood ES 300/K-6
2500 Cottonwood Dr 94066 650-624-3165
Sande Mikulik, prin. Fax 877-8298

South San Francisco USD
Supt. — See South San Francisco
Monte Verde ES 500/K-5
2551 Saint Cloud Dr 94066 650-877-8838
Deborah Mirt, prin. Fax 952-0904

Highlands Christian S 900/PK-12
1900 Monterey Dr 94066 650-873-4090
Vernita Sheley, supt. Fax 742-6228
St. Robert S 300/K-8
345 Oak Ave 94066 650-583-5065
Yvonne Olcomendy, prin. Fax 583-1418

San Carlos, San Mateo, Pop. 26,821

San Carlos ESD 600/5-8
826 Chestnut St 94070 650-508-7333
Steven Mitrovich, supt. Fax 508-7340
www.sancarlos.k12.ca.us
Central MS 600/5-8
828 Chestnut St 94070 650-508-7321
Lynette Hovland, prin. Fax 508-7342

St. Charles S 300/K-8
850 Tamarack Ave 94070 650-593-1629
Maureen Grazioli, prin. Fax 593-9723

San Clemente, Orange, Pop. 60,235

Capistrano USD
Supt. — See San Juan Capistrano
Ayer MS 800/6-8
1271 Calle Sarmentoso 92673 949-366-9607
Dr. Cheryl Baughn, prin. Fax 366-1519
Benedict ES 700/K-5
1251 Calle Sarmentoso 92673 949-498-6617
Dr. Charlotte Hibsch, prin. Fax 361-8462
Concordia ES 700/K-5
3120 Avenida Del Presidente 92672 949-492-3060
Dave Gerhard, prin. Fax 361-8652
Las Palmas ES 600/K-5
1101 Calle Puente 92672 949-234-5333
Kristen Nelson, prin. Fax 369-1427
Lobo ES 500/K-5
200 Avenida Vista Montana 92672 949-366-6740
Sandra McKinney, prin. Fax 366-0764
Marblehead ES 500/K-5
2410 Via Turqueza 92673 949-234-5339
Jackie Campbell, prin. Fax 361-0712
Shorecliffs MS 1,000/6-8
240 Via Socorro 92672 949-498-1660
Kenny Moe, prin. Fax 498-0826
Vista Del Mar ES 900/K-5
1130 Avenida Talega 92673 949-234-5950
Scott Young, prin. Fax 940-0262
Vista del Mar MS 600/6-8
1130 Avenida Talega 92673 949-234-5955
Adam Ochwat, prin. Fax 940-0262

Fallbrook UNESD
Supt. — See Fallbrook
San Onofre S 700/K-8
200 Pate Dr 92672 949-492-3372
Bill Billingsley, prin. Fax 492-1368

Our Lady of Fatima S 300/PK-8
105 N La Esperanza 92672 949-492-7320
Julie Tipton, prin. Fax 492-3793
Our Savior's Lutheran S 200/PK-5
200 Avenida San Pablo 92672 949-492-6165
Dunya Shaw, prin. Fax 492-6132
St. Michael's Academy 100/K-12
107 W Marquita 92672 949-366-9468
Phillip Johnson, prin. Fax 492-7238

San Diego, San Diego, Pop. 1,255,540

Chula Vista ESD
Supt. — See Chula Vista
Finney ES 500/K-6
3950 Byrd St 92154 619-690-1334
Olivia Amador-Valerio, prin. Fax 428-4138
Juarez-Lincoln ES 600/K-6
849 Twining Ave 92154 619-690-9222
Cristina Flores-Speer, prin. Fax 662-9679
Los Altos ES 400/K-6
1332 Kenalan Dr 92154 619-690-5880
Dei Romero, prin. Fax 428-4712
Silver Wing ES 500/K-6
3730 Arey Dr 92154 619-423-3950
Alex Cortes, prin. Fax 423-7438

Del Mar UNESD
Supt. — See Del Mar
Ashley Falls ES 600/K-6
13030 Ashley Falls Dr 92130 858-259-7812
Shelley Petersen, prin. Fax 259-1828
Carmel Del Mar ES 500/K-6
12345 Carmel Park Dr 92130 858-481-6789
David Jones, prin. Fax 481-7418
Ocean Air ES 500/K-6
11444 Canter Heights Dr 92130 858-481-4040
Gary Wilson, prin. Fax 481-6657
Sage Canyon ES 800/K-6
5290 Harvest Run Dr 92130 858-481-7844
Peg LaRose, prin. Fax 481-7949

Sycamore Ridge ES 400/K-6
5333 Old Carmel Valley Rd 92130 858-755-1060
Emily Disney, prin. Fax 755-1258
Torrey Hills ES 800/K-6
10830 Calle Mar De Mariposa 92130 858-481-4266
Susan Paul, prin. Fax 481-0344

Poway USD
Supt. — See Poway
Adobe Bluffs ES 700/K-5
8707 Adobe Bluffs Dr 92129 858-538-8403
Mark Atkins, prin. Fax 538-2749
Bernardo Heights MS 1,300/6-8
12990 Paseo Lucido 92128 858-485-4850
Elaine Johnson, prin. Fax 485-4865
Black Mountain MS 1,300/6-8
9353 Oviedo St 92129 858-484-1300
David Hall, prin. Fax 538-9440
Canyon View ES 600/K-5
9225 Adolphia St 92129 858-484-0981
Jack Troxell, prin. Fax 538-9441
Creekside ES 800/K-5
12362 Springhurst Dr 92128 858-391-1514
Robin Robinson, prin. Fax 391-1511
Deer Canyon ES 600/K-5
13455 Russet Leaf Ln 92129 858-484-6064
Terry Worthington, prin. Fax 538-9453
Del Sur ES 200/K-5
15665 Paseo Del Sur 92127 858-674-6200
Doug Johnson, prin.
Highland Ranch ES 600/K-5
14840 Waverly Downs Way 92128 858-674-4707
Anita Watson, prin. Fax 485-7642
Los Penasquitos ES 600/K-5
14125 Cuca St 92129 858-672-3600
Deanne McLaughlin, prin. Fax 672-4390
Mesa Verde MS 1,400/6-8
8375 Entreken Way 92129 858-538-5478
Cliff Mitchell, prin. Fax 538-8636
Monterey Ridge ES 500/K-5
17117 4S Ranch Pkwy 92127 858-487-6887
Rich Newman, prin. Fax 487-2050
Morning Creek ES 600/K-5
10925 Morning Creek Dr S 92128 858-748-4334
Carol Osborne, prin. Fax 748-8672
Oak Valley MS 800/6-8
16055 Wine Creek Rd 92127 858-487-2939
Sonya Wrisley, prin. Fax 457-0991
Park Village ES 800/K-5
7930 Park Village Rd 92129 858-484-5621
Ricardo Cecena, prin. Fax 484-5138
Rolling Hills ES 400/K-5
15255 Penasquitos Dr 92129 858-672-3400
Kathleen Marshack, prin. Fax 672-4324
Shoal Creek ES 700/K-5
11775 Shoal Creek Dr 92128 858-613-9080
Libby Keller, prin. Fax 613-0375
Stone Ranch ES 900/K-5
16150 4S Ranch Pkwy 92127 858-487-8474
Cindy Venolia, prin. Fax 487-6225
Sundance ES 500/K-5
8944 Twin Trails Dr 92129 858-484-2950
Earl Scull, prin. Fax 538-9452
Sunset Hills ES 600/K-5
9291 Oviedo St 92129 858-484-1600
Kathy Brown, prin. Fax 538-9451
Turtleback ES 500/K-5
15855 Turtleback Rd 92127 858-673-5514
Celeste Campbell, prin. Fax 673-8884
Westwood ES 800/K-5
17449 Matinal Rd 92127 858-487-2026
Mike Mosgrove, prin. Fax 673-9103
Willow Grove ES 200/K-5
14727 Via Azul 92127 858-674-6300
Cindy DeClercq, prin. Fax 759-8511

San Diego USD 119,400/K-12
4100 Normal St 92103 619-725-8000
Dr. Terry Grier, supt. Fax 291-7182
www.sandi.net/
Adams ES 400/K-5
4672 35th St 92116 619-284-1158
Judith Brings, prin. Fax 563-7532
Alcott ES 300/K-5
4680 Hidalgo Ave 92117 858-273-3415
Michelle Riley, prin. Fax 581-6429
Angier ES 400/K-5
8450 Hurlbut St 92123 858-496-8295
Kimberlee Kidd, prin. Fax 277-9279
Audubon S 500/K-8
8111 San Vicente St 92114 619-469-6139
Sharon Carr, prin. Fax 469-7859
Baker ES 500/K-6
4041 T St 92113 619-264-3139
Linette DaRosa, prin. Fax 264-2318
Balboa ES 700/K-6
1844 S 40th St 92113 619-263-8151
Fabiola Bagula, prin. Fax 263-5742
Barnard ES 200/K-4
2930 Barnard St 92110 619-224-3306
Edward Park, prin. Fax 224-8721
Bay Park ES 500/K-5
2433 Denver St 92110 619-276-1471
Eric Takeshita, prin. Fax 276-3243
Bayview Terrace ES 300/K-5
2445 Fogg St 92109 858-273-5244
Magdalena Tavasci, prin. Fax 272-0191
Bell MS 1,000/6-8
620 Briarwood Rd 92139 619-479-7111
Michael Dodson, prin. Fax 470-6054
Benchley/Weinberger ES 600/K-5
6269 Twin Lake Dr 92119 619-463-9271
Marian Jacobs, prin. Fax 697-8617
Bethune S 500/K-8
6835 Benjamin Holt Rd 92114 619-267-2271
Robert Morgenstein, prin. Fax 475-5068

Birney ES 300/K-6
4345 Campus Ave 92103 619-497-3500
Amanda Hammond-Williams, prin. Fax 688-3017
Boone ES 600/K-6
7330 Brookhaven Rd 92114 619-479-3111
Joel Sachs, prin. Fax 470-6529
Burbank ES 300/K-5
2146 Julian Ave 92113 619-652-4500
Diana Grijalva, prin. Fax 231-4106
Cabrillo ES 200/K-4
3120 Talbot St 92106 619-223-7154
Nestor Suarez, prin. Fax 221-9051
Cadman ES 200/K-5
4370 Kamloop Ave 92117 858-273-3003
Jacquelyn McCabe, prin. Fax 273-3907
Carson ES 500/K-5
6905 Kramer St 92111 858-496-8060
Anne Worrall, prin. Fax 496-8358
Carver S 400/K-8
3251 Juanita St 92105 619-583-7021
Stephanie Mahan, prin. Fax 286-4817
Central ES 900/K-5
4063 Polk Ave 92105 619-281-6644
Cynthia Marten, prin. Fax 281-1732
Challenger MS 1,200/6-8
10810 Parkdale Ave 92126 858-586-7001
Sheelagh Moran, prin. Fax 271-5203
Chavez ES 500/K-6
1404 S 40th St 92113 619-527-4098
Julia Carrillo, prin. Fax 527-8944
Cherokee Point ES 500/K-5
3735 38th St 92105 619-641-3400
Godwin Higa, prin. Fax 282-2665
Chesterton ES 600/K-5
7335 Wheatley St 92111 858-496-8070
Jean Richmond, prin. Fax 571-5766
Chollas-Mead ES 800/K-6
4525 Market St 92102 619-264-3113
Carolanne Buguey, prin. Fax 266-2217
Clark MS 1,400/6-8
4388 Thorn St 92105 619-563-6801
Thomas Liberto, prin. Fax 563-9653
Clay ES 300/K-5
6506 Solita Ave 92115 619-583-0690
Valerie Voss, prin. Fax 583-9643
Correia JHS 1,000/7-8
4302 Valeta St 92107 619-222-0476
Patricia Ladd, prin. Fax 221-0147
Creative Performing & Media Arts S 600/6-8
5050 Conrad Ave 92117 858-278-5917
Fred Hilgers, prin. Fax 293-7235
Crown Point ES 100/K-5
4033 Ingraham St 92109 858-273-9830
Barbara Boone, prin. Fax 274-5165
Cubberley ES 300/K-5
3201 Marathon Dr 92123 858-496-8075
Rosemary Cruz, prin. Fax 496-8325
Curie ES 600/K-5
4080 Governor Dr 92122 858-453-4184
Chris Juarez, prin. Fax 546-3972
Dailard ES 500/K-5
6425 Cibola Rd 92120 619-286-1550
Jonathan McDade, prin. Fax 286-8395
Dana MS 900/5-6
1775 Chatsworth Blvd 92107 619-225-3897
Diane Ryan, prin. Fax 225-3878
De Portola MS 1,000/6-8
11010 Clairemont Mesa Blvd 92124 858-496-8080
Listy Gillingham, prin. Fax 576-4419
Dewey ES 400/K-4
3251 Rosecrans St 92110 619-223-8131
Vera Valdivia, prin. Fax 523-9338
Dingeman ES 800/K-6
11840 Scripps Creek Dr 92131 858-549-4437
Kimie Lochtfeld, prin. Fax 635-8948
Doyle ES 800/K-5
3950 Berino Ct 92122 858-455-6230
Kimberly Moore, prin. Fax 455-9486
Edison ES 600/K-5
4077 35th St 92104 619-283-5961
Tavga Bustani, prin. Fax 282-3179
Emerson/Bandini ES 800/K-6
3510 Newton Ave 92113 619-525-7418
Mirna Estrada, prin. Fax 525-7352
Encanto ES 700/K-5
822 65th St 92114 619-264-3191
Kristi Dean, prin. Fax 264-5484
Ericson ES 800/K-5
11174 Westonhill Dr 92126 858-271-0505
Maria Gomez, prin. Fax 566-6614
Euclid ES 600/K-5
4166 Euclid Ave 92105 619-282-2192
Vickie Jacobson, prin. Fax 283-7351
Farb MS 800/6-8
4880 La Cuenta Dr 92124 858-496-8090
Susan Levy, prin. Fax 576-0931
Fay ES, 4080 52nd St 92105 K-5
Eileen Moreno, prin. 619-624-2600
Field ES 300/K-6
4375 Bannock Ave 92117 858-273-3323
Robin Stern, prin. Fax 581-0873
Fletcher ES 300/K-5
7666 Bobolink Way 92123 858-496-8100
Kathleen Phillips, prin. Fax 496-8045
Florence ES 300/K-6
3914 1st Ave 92103 619-293-4440
Mary Estill, prin. Fax 725-4028
Foster ES 400/K-5
6550 51st St 92120 619-582-2728
David Downey, prin. Fax 583-6812
Franklin ES 300/K-5
4481 Copeland Ave 92116 619-284-9279
Jean Small, prin. Fax 282-6112
Freese ES 600/K-6
8140 Greenlawn Dr 92114 619-479-2727
Alma Hills, prin. Fax 475-7305

Fulton S 400/K-8
7055 Skyline Dr 92114 619-262-0777
Carol King, prin. Fax 527-4172
Gage ES 500/K-5
6811 Bisby Lake Ave 92119 619-463-0202
Cheryl Zitsman, prin. Fax 463-0534
Garfield ES 400/K-5
4487 Oregon St 92116 619-284-2076
Charles Moriarty, prin. Fax 284-2096
Golden Hill S 500/K-8
1240 33rd St 92102 619-236-5600
Juan Romo, prin. Fax 236-5690
Grant S 400/K-8
1425 Washington Pl 92103 619-293-4420
Bruce McGirr, prin. Fax 297-8404
Green ES 400/K-5
7030 Wandermere Dr 92119 619-460-5755
Timothy Dale, prin. Fax 465-8814
Hage ES 700/K-5
9750 Galvin Ave 92126 858-566-0273
Ethel Daniels, prin. Fax 693-7942
Hamilton ES 800/K-5
2807 Fairmount Ave 92105 619-262-2483
Lillie McMillan, prin. Fax 262-8251
Hancock ES 800/K-5
3303 Taussig St 92124 858-496-8310
Bonnie Remington, prin. Fax 278-6549
Hardy ES 400/K-5
5420 Montezuma Rd 92115 619-582-0136
Bruce Ferguson, prin. Fax 286-2016
Hawthorne ES 300/K-6
4750 Lehrer Dr 92117 858-273-3341
Momiji Seligman, prin. Fax 274-6379
Hearst ES 400/K-5
6230 Del Cerro Blvd 92120 619-583-5704
Jamie Jorgensen, prin. Fax 287-9921
Hickman ES 700/K-5
10850 Montongo St 92126 858-271-5210
Dr. Dianette Mitchell-Ricks, prin. Fax 566-9010
Holmes ES 500/K-6
4902 Mount Ararat Dr 92111 858-496-8110
Jean Brown, prin. Fax 496-8734
Horton ES 600/K-6
5050 Guymon St 92102 619-264-0171
Robin McCulloch, prin. Fax 262-8023
Ibarra ES, 4877 Orange Ave 92115 600/K-5
Susie Sovereign, prin. 619-641-5400
Innovation MS 200/7-8
5095 Arvinels Ave 92117 858-278-5948
Harlan Klein, prin.
Jefferson ES 300/K-5
3770 Utah St 92104 619-293-4406
Mary Jo Longo, prin. Fax 297-7053
Jerabek ES 800/K-5
10050 Avenida Magnifica 92131 858-578-5330
Paul Gilroy, prin. Fax 578-7367
Johnson ES 400/K-6
1355 Kelton Rd 92114 619-264-0103
Charlie Smith, prin. Fax 266-0424
Jones ES 300/K-5
2751 Greyling Dr 92123 858-496-8140
Annette Brady, prin. Fax 571-2877
Joyner ES 700/K-5
4271 Myrtle Ave 92105 619-640-4000
Gilbert Gutierrez, prin. Fax 640-4090
Juarez ES 300/K-5
2633 Melbourne Dr 92123 858-496-8145
Marceline Clausen, prin. Fax 627-7410
Kimbrough ES 900/K-5
321 Hoitt St 92102 619-525-2010
Leah Tussey, prin. Fax 525-2018
Knox S 500/K-8
1098 S 49th St 92113 619-262-2473
Ana Biffle, prin. Fax 263-6476
Kumeyaay ES 500/K-5
6475 Antigua Blvd 92124 858-279-1022
Steven Mosher, prin. Fax 569-7418
Lafayette ES 400/K-6
6125 Printwood Way 92117 858-496-8160
Jerrilee Fischer-Garza, prin. Fax 576-9739
Language Academy 800/K-8
4961 64th St 92115 619-287-1182
Veronika Mendez, prin. Fax 582-1769
Lee ES 600/K-6
6196 Childs Ave 92139 619-475-2020
James Jimenez, prin. Fax 475-2091
Lewis MS 1,100/6-8
5170 Greenbrier Ave 92120 619-583-3233
Brad Callahan, prin. Fax 229-1338
Linda Vista Annex ES 500/K-5
7260 Linda Vista Rd 92111 858-496-8190
Dana Robinson, prin.
Linda Vista ES 500/K-5
2772 Ulric St 92111 858-496-8196
Deborah Hatchell-Carter, prin. Fax 292-0326
Lindbergh/Schweitzer ES 600/K-6
4133 Mount Albertine Ave 92111 858-496-8400
Deanne Rohde, prin. Fax 292-0746
Logan S 800/K-8
2875 Ocean View Blvd 92113 619-525-7440
Antonio Villar, prin. Fax 237-1004
Loma Portal ES 400/K-4
3341 Browning St 92106 619-223-1683
Glenda Gerde, prin. Fax 224-1352
Longfellow S 700/K-8
5055 July St 92110 619-276-4206
Flavia Soria, prin. Fax 276-7008
Mann MS 300/6-8
4345 54th St 92115 619-582-8990
Esther Omogbehin, prin. Fax 583-2637
Marshall ES 600/K-5
3550 Altadena Ave 92105 619-283-5924
Yesenia Robinson, prin. Fax 563-4762
Marshall MS 1,100/6-8
9700 Avenue of Nations 92131 858-549-5400
Michelle Irwin, prin. Fax 549-5490

Marston MS 1,100/6-8
3799 Clairemont Dr 92117 858-273-2030
Dr. Elizabeth Cook, prin. Fax 272-3460
Marvin ES 400/K-5
5720 Brunswick Ave 92120 619-583-1355
E. Jay Derwae, prin. Fax 582-7853
Mason ES 800/K-5
10340 San Ramon Dr 92126 858-271-0410
Deidre Hardson, prin. Fax 578-6822
McKinley ES 400/K-6
3045 Felton St 92104 619-282-7694
Julie Ashton-Gray, prin. Fax 281-3478
Memorial Prep for Scholars & Athletes 300/6-8
2850 Logan Ave 92113 619-231-8581
Joe Lara, prin.
Millennial Tech S 200/6-7
1110 Carolina Ln 92102 619-527-6933
Helen Griffith, prin.
Miller ES 800/K-5
4343 Shields St 92124 858-496-8319
Stacy Jones, prin. Fax 278-1649
Miramar Ranch ES 800/K-6
10770 Red Cedar Dr 92131 858-271-0470
Jennifer Wroblewski, prin. Fax 549-6817
Montgomery MS 600/6-8
2470 Ulric St 92111 858-496-8330
Jonathan Ton, prin. Fax 292-0125
Normal Heights ES 400/K-5
3750 Ward Rd 92116 619-584-6000
John Aguilar, prin.
North Park ES 200/K-5
4041 Oregon St 92104 619-293-4468
Leslie Barnes, prin. Fax 293-8118
Nye ES 600/K-5
981 Valencia Pkwy 92114 619-527-4901
Karen Mooney, prin. Fax 527-0472
Oak Park ES 800/K-5
2606 54th St 92105 619-264-3179
Tanya Belsan, prin. Fax 527-7152
Ocean Beach ES 300/K-4
4741 Santa Monica Ave 92107 619-223-1631
Margaret Johnson, prin. Fax 224-0141
Pacific Beach ES 300/K-5
1234 Tourmaline St 92109 858-488-8316
Sherry Turner, prin. Fax 488-7852
Pacific Beach MS 800/6-8
4676 Ingraham St 92109 858-273-9070
Dr. Julie Martel, prin. Fax 270-8063
Paradise Hills ES 400/K-6
5816 Alleghany St 92139 619-479-3145
Donald Craig, prin. Fax 472-8889
Parks ES 1,300/K-5
4510 Landis St 92105 619-282-6803
Peggy Crane, prin. Fax 282-5895
Penn ES 700/K-6
2797 Utica Dr 92139 619-479-5638
Joan Nelson, prin. Fax 479-2225
Perkins S 400/K-8
1770 Main St 92113 619-525-7482
Fernando Hernandez, prin. Fax 234-7418
Perry ES 400/K-6
6290 Oriskany Rd 92139 619-479-4040
Elizabeth Austin, prin. Fax 267-6172
Pershing MS 1,000/6-8
8204 San Carlos Dr 92119 619-465-3234
Sarah Sullivan, prin. Fax 461-5447
Porter North ES, 445 S 47th St 92113 K-K, 4-6
Evva Cross, prin. 619-266-7700
Porter South ES 600/K-5
4800 T St 92113 619-266-4500
Evva Cross, prin. Fax 266-4590
Rodriguez ES 700/K-5
825 S 31st St 92113 619-699-4500
Claudia Jordan, prin. Fax 699-4590
Rolando Park ES 200/K-5
6620 Marlowe Dr 92115 619-582-5414
Yolanda Lewis, prin. Fax 582-3872
Roosevelt MS 1,000/6-8
3366 Park Blvd 92103 619-293-4450
Dr. Carmen Garcia, prin. Fax 497-0918
Ross ES 400/K-5
7470 Bagdad St 92111 858-496-8300
Timothy Suanico, prin. Fax 467-9313
Rowan ES 300/K-5
1755 Rowan St 92105 619-262-7541
Kimberlee Kossyta, prin. Fax 262-0971
Sandburg ES 700/K-5
11230 Avenida Del Gato 92126 858-566-0510
Laurie Hinzman, prin. Fax 693-3896
Scripps ES 500/K-5
11778 Cypress Canyon Rd 92131 858-693-8593
Gregory Collamer, prin. Fax 536-2364
Sequoia ES 300/K-6
4690 Limerick Ave 92117 858-496-8240
Susan Izu, prin. Fax 496-8329
Sessions ES 400/K-5
2150 Beryl St 92109 858-273-3111
Susan DeVicariis, prin. Fax 272-0260
Sherman ES, 301 22nd St 92102 700/K-5
Eddie Caballero, prin. 619-615-7000
Silver Gate ES 400/K-4
1499 Venice St 92107 619-222-1139
Sandra McClure, prin. Fax 226-3058
Spreckels ES 700/K-5
6033 Stadium St 92122 858-453-5377
Dr. Cecilia Fernandez, prin. Fax 546-1269
Standley MS 1,400/6-8
6298 Radcliffe Dr 92122 858-455-0550
Heidi Eastcott, prin. Fax 546-7627
Sunset View ES 400/K-4
4365 Hill St 92107 619-223-7156
Linda Parker, prin. Fax 224-6920
Taft MS 800/6-8
9191 Gramercy Dr 92123 858-496-8245
Michael George, prin. Fax 496-8138
Tierrasanta ES 500/K-5
5450 La Cuenta Dr 92124 858-496-8255
Mary Olsen, prin. Fax 627-9753

Toler ES 300/K-5
3350 Baker St 92117 858-273-0294
Peggy Lewis, prin. Fax 483-3832
Valencia Park ES 600/K-5
5880 Skyline Dr 92114 619-264-0125
Penny Simmons, prin. Fax 266-8801
Vista Grande ES 500/K-5
5606 Antigua Blvd 92124 858-496-8290
Alan Richmond, prin. Fax 569-7647
Walker ES 600/K-5
9225 Hillery Dr 92126 858-271-8050
Rochelle Dawes, prin. Fax 578-8364
Wangenheim MS 1,300/6-8
9230 Gold Coast Dr 92126 858-578-1400
Robert Grano, prin. Fax 578-9481
Washington ES 300/K-6
1789 State St 92101 619-525-7475
Janie Wardlow, prin. Fax 231-3562
Webster ES 500/K-6
4801 Elm St 92102 619-263-6628
Minerva Salas, prin. Fax 262-3160
Wegeforth ES 300/K-5
3443 Ediwhar Ave 92123 858-496-8274
Bob Frain, prin. Fax 496-8109
Whitman ES 400/K-6
4050 Appleton St 92117 858-273-2700
Pam Thompson, prin. Fax 483-8946
Wilson MS 900/6-8
3838 Orange Ave 92105 619-280-1661
Bernadette Nguyen, prin. Fax 280-6437
Zamorano ES 1,400/K-6
2655 Casey St 92139 619-267-8007
Marian Phelps, prin. Fax 475-9748
Other Schools – See La Jolla

San Dieguito UNHSD
Supt. — See Encinitas
Carmel Valley MS 1,400/7-8
3800 Mykonos Ln 92130 858-481-8221
Laurie Francis, prin. Fax 481-8256

San Ysidro ESD
Supt. — See San Ysidro
Ocean View Hills S 1,100/K-8
4919 Del Sol Blvd 92154 619-661-0457
Jose Luis Valdivia, prin. Fax 710-0280

Solana Beach ESD
Supt. — See Solana Beach
Carmel Creek ES 500/K-4
4210 Carmel Center Rd 92130 858-794-4400
Terri Davis, prin. Fax 794-4450
Solana Highlands ES 500/K-4
3520 Long Run Dr 92130 858-794-4300
Jerry Jones, prin. Fax 794-4350
Solana Pacific ES 500/5-6
3901 Townsgate Dr 92130 858-794-4500
Brian McBride, prin. Fax 794-4550

South Bay UNSD
Supt. — See Imperial Beach
Berry ES 700/K-6
2001 Rimbey Ave 92154 619-628-3500
Paul Bloomberg, prin. Fax 628-3580
Emory ES 700/K-6
1915 Coronado Ave 92154 619-628-5300
Jil Palmer, prin. Fax 628-5380
Mendoza ES 1,000/K-6
2050 Coronado Ave 92154 619-424-0100
Don Visnick, prin. Fax 424-0180
Nestor ES 900/K-6
1455 Hollister St 92154 619-628-0900
Guadalupe Avilez-Herrera, prin. Fax 628-0980
Pence ES 700/K-6
877 Via Tonga Ct 92154 619-662-8100
Bob Daily, prin. Fax 662-8180
Sunnyslope ES 700/K-6
2500 Elm Ave 92154 619-628-8800
Marisol Rerucha, prin. Fax 628-8880

Sweetwater UNHSD
Supt. — See Chula Vista
Mar Vista MS 1,100/7-8
1267 Thermal Ave 92154 619-628-5100
Scott Tanner, prin. Fax 423-8431
Montgomery MS 1,000/7-8
1051 Picador Blvd 92154 619-662-9200
Maria Lizarraga, prin. Fax 428-6517
Southwest MS 800/7-8
2710 Iris Ave 92154 619-628-4000
Steve Lizarraga, prin. Fax 423-1151

All Saints Episcopal S 100/PK-8
3674 7th Ave 92103 619-298-1671
Fax 298-4335
Blessed Sacrament S 300/PK-8
4551 56th St 92115 619-582-3862
Theodora Furtado, prin. Fax 265-9310
Cambridge S 50/PK-5
10075 Azuaga St 92129 858-484-3488
Jean Kim, hdmstr. Fax 484-3458
Chabad Hebrew Academy 300/PK-8
10785 Pomerado Rd 92131 858-566-1996
Yosef Fradkin, hdmstr. Fax 547-8078
Childrens Creative/Performing Arts Acad. 300/K-12
3051 El Cajon Blvd 92104 619-584-2454
Janet Cherif, prin. Fax 584-2422
Christ the Cornerstone Academy 200/PK-6
9028 Westmore Rd 92126 858-566-1741
Lark Mayeski, admin. Fax 566-1965
City Tree Christian S 300/PK-8
320 Date St 92101 619-232-3794
Sue Kennedy, prin. Fax 232-2447
Del Mar Pines S 200/K-6
3975 Torrington St 92130 858-481-5615
Marci McCord, dir.
Faith Community S 100/K-6
2285 Murray Ridge Rd 92123 858-565-4812
Dotty Carter, admin. Fax 565-6726

Good Shepherd S 300/K-8
8180 Gold Coast Dr 92126 858-693-1522
Christine Corpora, prin. Fax 693-3439
Grace Lutheran S 50/PK-PK
3967 Park Blvd 92103 619-299-2890
Fax 295-4472
Holy Family S 200/PK-8
1945 Coolidge St 92111 858-277-0222
Dan O'Neal, prin. Fax 277-0224
Horizon Christian S 400/PK-6
4520 Pocahontas Ave 92117 858-490-5000
Carrie DeMoll, prin. Fax 490-5005
Islamic S of San Diego 200/K-8
7050 Eckstrom Ave 92111 858-278-7970
Sharifa Abukar, prin. Fax 278-7995
Maranatha Christian S 600/PK-12
9050 Maranatha Dr 92127 858-759-9737
Dennis Frey, supt. Fax 759-4001
Maria Montessori S 100/PK-5
4544 Pocahontas Ave 92117 858-270-9350
Lo Ann Jundt, dir. Fax 273-4254
Midway Baptist S 300/K-12
2460 Palm Ave 92154 619-424-7875
Stephen Johnson, prin. Fax 424-9204
Mira Mesa Christian S 100/PK-6
9696 Candida St 92126 858-578-0262
Terri Clark, prin. Fax 578-0319
Mission Bay Montessori Academy 400/PK-6
2640 Soderblom Ave 92122 858-457-5895
Nan Madden, dir.
Mt. Erie Christian Academy 50/K-6
504 S 47th St 92113 619-263-1914
Walter Wells, prin. Fax 263-5002
Nazareth S 300/PK-8
10728 San Diego Mission Rd 92108 619-280-3140
Dr. Colleen Mauricio, prin. Fax 280-4652
Notre Dame Academy 400/PK-8
4345 Del Mar Trails Rd 92130 858-509-2300
Sr. Marie Pascale, prin. Fax 509-5915
Our Lady of the Sacred Heart S 200/PK-8
4106 42nd St 92105 619-284-1715
Christine Haddad, prin. Fax 284-8332
Our Lady's S 200/PK-8
650 24th St 92102 619-233-8888
Noel Bishop, prin. Fax 501-2951
Parker S 400/PK-5
4201 Randolph St 92103 619-298-9110
Dr. Robert Gillingham, prin. Fax 298-5128
Reformation Lutheran S 100/PK-8
4670 Mount Abernathy Ave 92117 858-279-3311
Joel Walker, prin. Fax 627-9898
Rock Academy 300/PK-12
2277 Rosecrans St 92106 619-764-5200
Dr. Richard Andujo, hdmstr. Fax 764-5201
Sacred Heart Academy 200/K-8
4895 Saratoga Ave 92107 619-222-7252
Jeff Saavedra, prin. Fax 222-2836
St. Charles Borromeo S 200/K-8
2808 Cadiz St 92110 619-223-8271
Thomas Mamara, prin. Fax 223-2695
St. Charles S 300/K-8
929 18th St 92154 619-423-3701
Steve Stutz, prin. Fax 423-5331
St. Columba S 200/PK-8
3327 Glencolum Dr 92123 858-279-1882
Geraldine Nau, prin. Fax 279-1653
St. Didacus S 300/PK-8
4630 34th St 92116 619-284-8730
Elizabeth LaCosta, prin. Fax 284-1764
St. Gregory the Great S K-4
15315 Stonebridge Pkwy 92131 858-397-1290
Maeve O'Connell, prin. Fax 397-1294
St. Jude Academy 200/PK-8
1228 S 38th St 92113 619-264-3154
Yolanda Minton, prin. Fax 264-8050
St. Michaels Academy 200/PK-8
2637 Homedale St 92139 619-470-4880
Evelyn Urbitztondo, prin. Fax 470-1050
St. Patricks S 200/K-8
3583 30th St 92104 619-297-1314
Daniel O'Neal, prin. Fax 297-3346
St. Paul's Lutheran S 100/PK-8
1376 Felspar St 92109 858-272-6282
Fred Friedrichs, prin. Fax 272-4397
St. Rita's S 200/PK-8
5165 Imperial Ave 92114 619-264-0109
Amber Johnson, prin. Fax 269-4316
St. Therese Academy 300/PK-8
6046 Camino Rico 92120 619-583-6270
Mark Sperrazzo, prin. Fax 583-5721
St. Vincent de Paul S 200/K-8
4061 Ibis St 92103 619-296-2222
Kathleen Walsh, prin. Fax 296-2763
San Diego Jewish Academy 600/K-12
11860 Carmel Creek Rd 92130 858-704-3700
Larry Acheatel, dir. Fax 704-3850
School of the Madeleine 600/PK-8
1875 Illion St 92110 619-276-6545
Donna Wittouck, prin. Fax 276-5359
Scripps Montessori S 100/PK-6
9939 Old Grove Rd 92131 858-566-3632
M.K. Newton, admin. Fax 653-3085
Soille San Diego Hebrew Day S 300/PK-8
3630 Afton Rd 92123 858-279-3300
Rabbi Simcha Weiser, hdmstr. Fax 279-3389
Waldorf S of San Diego 300/PK-9
3547 Altadena Ave 92105 619-280-8016
Kris Iselin-Bradley, admin. Fax 280-8071
Warren-Walker S 400/PK-8
4605 Point Loma Ave 92107 619-223-3663
Pamela Volker, hdmstr. Fax 223-5567

San Dimas, Los Angeles, Pop. 35,850
Bonita USD 10,100/K-12
115 W Allen Ave 91773 909-971-8200
Dr. Gary Rapkin, supt. Fax 971-8329
www.bonita.k12.ca.us

Allen Avenue ES 500/K-5
115 W Allen Ave 91773 909-971-8202
Debra McCaleb, prin. Fax 971-8252
Ekstrand ES 500/K-5
115 W Allen Ave 91773 909-971-8203
Albert Cahueque, prin. Fax 971-8253
Gladstone ES 500/K-5
115 W Allen Ave 91773 909-971-8204
Nanette Shapiro, prin. Fax 971-8254
Lone Hill MS 1,000/6-8
115 W Allen Ave 91773 909-971-8270
Ray Arredondo, prin. Fax 971-8279
Shull ES 500/K-5
115 W Allen Ave 91773 909-394-3171
Chris Ann Horsley, prin. Fax 971-8258
Other Schools – See La Verne

Canyon View S, 762 Cypress St 91773 100/K-12
John Mann, prin. 909-599-1227
Holy Name of Mary S 300/PK-8
124 S San Dimas Canyon Rd 91773 909-542-0449
Candice Kuzmickas, prin. Fax 592-3884
Sonrise Christian S 200/PK-5
1400 W Covina Blvd 91773 909-599-5958
Dr. Timothy Burlingame, supt. Fax 599-3780

San Fernando, Los Angeles, Pop. 24,207
Los Angeles USD
Supt. — See Los Angeles
Gridley ES 1,000/K-5
1907 8th St 91340 818-361-1243
Victoria Verches, prin. Fax 361-5959
Morningside ES 1,000/K-5
576 N Maclay Ave 91340 818-365-7181
Oliver Ramirez, prin. Fax 365-8359
O'Melveny ES 600/K-5
728 Woodworth St 91340 818-365-5621
Henry Vidrio, prin. Fax 837-7974
San Fernando ES 700/K-5
1130 Mott St 91340 818-365-3201
Mary Ellen Mendoza, prin. Fax 365-3632
San Fernando MS 2,000/6-8
130 N Brand Blvd 91340 818-837-5400
Rafael Balderas, prin. Fax 365-8911

First Lutheran S 100/K-6
777 N Maclay Ave 91340 818-361-4800
Peggy Courtney, admin. Fax 361-9725
St. Ferdinand S 200/PK-8
1012 Coronel St 91340 818-361-3264
Sr. Eleanor Ortega, prin. Fax 361-5894
Santa Rosa De Lima S 200/PK-8
1309 Mott St 91340 818-361-5096
Sr. Antionette Clay, prin. Fax 361-2259

San Francisco, San Francisco, Pop. 739,426
San Francisco USD 52,100/PK-12
555 Franklin St 94102 415-241-6000
Carlos Garcia, supt. Fax 555-5555
www.sfusd.edu
Alamo ES 600/K-5
250 23rd Ave 94121 415-750-8456
Pamela Gire, prin. Fax 750-8434
Alvarado ES 500/K-5
625 Douglass St 94114 415-695-5695
Robert Broeker, prin. Fax 695-5447
Aptos MS 900/6-8
105 Aptos Ave 94127 415-469-4520
Paul Marcoux, prin. Fax 333-9038
Brown ES 100/K-5
2055 Silver Ave 94124 415-695-5400
Tareyton Russ, prin. Fax 695-5335
Bryant ES 200/K-5
1050 York St 94110 415-695-5780
Veronica Chavez, prin. Fax 206-0538
Carmichael ES 400/K-5
375 7th St 94103 415-355-6916
Jeffrey T. Burgos, prin. Fax 355-7683
Carmichael MS 6-7
824 Harrison St 94107 415-291-7984
Kristin Tavernetti, prin. Fax 291-7985
Carver ES 300/K-5
1360 Oakdale Ave 94124 415-330-1540
Emily Wade-Thompson, prin. Fax 467-7217
Chavez ES 400/PK-5
825 Shotwell St 94110 415-695-5765
Adelina Aramburo, prin. Fax 695-5843
Chin ES 200/K-5
350 Broadway 94133 415-291-7946
Allen Lee, prin. Fax 291-7943
Cleveland ES 300/K-5
455 Athens St 94112 415-469-4709
Katerina Palomares, prin. Fax 469-4051
Cobb ES 200/K-5
2725 California St 94115 415-749-3505
Pat Forte, prin. Fax 749-3436
Denman MS 600/6-8
241 Oneida Ave 94112 415-469-4535
Han Phung, prin. Fax 585-8402
Drew ES 300/K-5
50 Pomona St 94124 415-330-1526
Tamitrice Rice, prin. Fax 822-9210
El Dorado ES 300/K-5
70 Delta St 94134 415-330-1537
Tai-Sun Schoeman, prin. Fax 467-2435
Everett MS 500/6-8
450 Church St 94114 415-241-6344
Richard Curci, prin. Fax 241-6361
Fairmount ES 400/K-5
65 Chenery St 94131 415-695-5669
Ana Lunardi, prin. Fax 695-5343
Feinstein ES 200/K-5
2550 25th Ave 94116 415-615-8460
Michelle Chang, prin. Fax 242-2532
Flynn ES 400/K-5
3125 Cesar Chavez 94110 415-695-5770
Charles Addcox, prin. Fax 695-5837

Francisco MS 600/6-8
2190 Powell St 94133 415-291-7900
Judith Giampaoli, prin. Fax 291-7910
Garfield ES 200/K-5
420 Filbert St 94133 415-291-7924
Karen Law, prin. Fax 291-7916
Giannini MS 1,300/6-8
3151 Ortega St 94122 415-759-2770
Leslie Trook, prin. Fax 664-8541
Glen Park ES 300/K-5
151 Lippard Ave 94131 415-469-4713
Marion Grady, prin. Fax 337-6942
Grattan ES 300/K-5
165 Grattan St 94117 415-759-2815
Jean Robertson, prin. Fax 759-2803
Guadalupe ES 400/K-5
859 Prague St 94112 415-469-4718
Gene Barresi, prin. Fax 469-4066
Harte ES 300/K-5
1035 Gilman Ave 94124 415-330-1520
Vidrale Franklin, prin. Fax 330-1555
Hillcrest ES 500/K-5
810 Silver Ave 94134 415-469-4722
Richard Zapien, prin. Fax 469-4067
Hoover MS 1,200/6-8
2290 14th Ave 94116 415-759-2783
Judy Dong, prin. Fax 759-2881
Jefferson ES 500/K-5
1725 Irving St 94122 415-759-2821
Victor Tam, prin. Fax 759-2806
Key ES 500/K-5
1530 43rd Ave 94122 415-759-2811
David Wong, prin. Fax 759-2810
King Academic MS 500/6-8
350 Girard St 94134 415-330-1500
Cami Okubo, prin. Fax 468-7295
King ES 200/K-5
1215 Carolina St 94107 415-695-5797
Christopher Rosenberg, prin. Fax 695-5338
Lafayette ES 400/K-5
4545 Anza St 94121 415-750-8483
Ruby Brown, prin. Fax 750-8472
Lau ES 700/K-5
950 Clay St 94108 415-291-7921
Marlene Callejas, prin. Fax 291-7952
Lick MS 600/6-8
1220 Noe St 94114 415-695-5675
Bita Nazarian, prin. Fax 695-5360
Longfellow ES 600/K-5
755 Morse St 94112 415-469-4730
Phyllis Matsuno, prin. Fax 469-4068
Malcom X Academy 200/K-5
350 Harbor Rd 94124 415-695-5950
Cheryl Foster, prin. Fax 647-1647
Mann MS 500/6-8
3351 23rd St 94110 415-695-5881
Paul Jacobsen, prin. Fax 282-7868
Marina MS 1,000/6-8
3500 Fillmore St 94123 415-749-3495
Dennis Chew, prin. Fax 921-7539
Marshall ES 200/K-5
1575 15th St 94103 415-241-6280
Peter Avila, prin. Fax 241-6547
McCoppin ES 200/K-5
651 6th Ave 94118 415-750-8475
Bennett Lee, prin. Fax 750-8474
McKinley ES 200/K-5
1025 14th St 94114 415-241-6300
Rosa Fong, prin. Fax 241-6548
Milk Civil Rights Academy 200/K-5
4235 19th St 94114 415-241-6276
Sandra Leigh, prin. Fax 241-6545
Miraloma ES 300/K-5
175 Omar Way 94127 415-469-4734
Ronnie Machado, prin. Fax 469-4069
Monroe ES 500/K-5
260 Madrid St 94112 415-469-4736
Jennifer Steiner, prin. Fax 469-4070
Moscone ES 300/K-5
2576 Harrison St 94110 415-695-5736
Susan Zielenski, prin. Fax 695-5341
Muir ES 300/K-5
380 Webster St 94117 415-241-6335
Alene Wheaton, prin. Fax 431-9938
New Traditions ES 200/K-5
2049 Grove St 94117 415-750-8490
Maria Luz Agudelo, prin. Fax 750-8479
Ortega ES 200/K-5
400 Sargent St 94132 415-469-4726
Jolynn Washington, prin. Fax 584-7972
Parker ES 300/K-5
840 Broadway 94133 415-291-7990
Janet Dong, prin. Fax 291-7996
Parks ES 400/K-5
1501 Ofarrell St 94115 415-749-3519
Monica Nagy, prin. Fax 749-3610
Peabody ES 200/K-5
251 6th Ave 94118 415-750-8480
Willem Vroegh, prin. Fax 750-8487
Presidio MS 1,200/6-8
450 30th Ave 94121 415-750-8435
Alvin Dea, prin. Fax 750-8445
Redding ES 300/K-5
1421 Pine St 94109 415-749-3525
Darlene Lau, prin. Fax 749-3527
Revere ES 300/K-5
555 Tompkins Ave 94110 415-695-5656
Lance Tagomori, prin. Fax 647-0878
Roosevelt MS 700/6-8
460 Arguello Blvd 94118 415-750-8446
Diane Panagotacos, prin. Fax 750-8455
Sanchez ES 300/K-5
325 Sanchez St 94114 415-241-6380
Raymond Isola, prin. Fax 522-6729
Serra ES 300/K-5
625 Holly Park Cir 94110 415-695-5685
Eve Cheung, prin. Fax 920-5194

Sheridan ES 200/K-5
431 Capitol Ave 94112 415-469-4743
NurJehan Khalique, prin. Fax 469-4089
Sherman ES 400/K-5
1651 Union St 94123 415-749-3530
Sara Shenkan-Rich, prin. Fax 749-3433
Sloat ES 400/K-5
50 Darien Way 94127 415-759-2807
Deborah Faigenbaum, prin. Fax 759-2843
Spring Valley ES 300/K-5
1451 Jackson St 94109 415-749-3535
Lonnie Chin, prin. Fax 749-3555
Stevenson ES 400/K-5
2051 34th Ave 94116 415-759-2837
V. Kanani Choy, prin. Fax 759-2844
Sunnyside ES 300/K-5
250 Foerster St 94112 415-469-4746
Nancy Schlenke, prin. Fax 334-3569
Sunset ES 300/K-5
1920 41st Ave 94116 415-759-2760
Sophie Lee, prin. Fax 759-2729
Sutro ES 300/K-5
235 12th Ave 94118 415-750-8525
Andrew Poon, prin. Fax 750-8498
Taylor ES 600/K-5
423 Burrows St 94134 415-330-1530
Virginia Dold, prin. Fax 468-1742
Ulloa ES 500/K-5
2650 42nd Ave 94116 415-759-2841
Carol Fong, prin. Fax 759-2845
Visitacion Valley ES 400/K-5
55 Schwerin St 94134 415-469-4796
Vincent Chao, prin. Fax 469-4099
Visitacion Valley MS 400/6-8
450 Raymond Ave 94134 415-469-4590
James Dierke, prin. Fax 469-4703
Webster ES 200/K-5
465 Missouri St 94107 415-695-5787
Moraima Machado, prin. Fax 826-6813
West Portal ES 600/K-5
5 Lenox Way 94127 415-759-2846
William Lucey, prin. Fax 242-2526
Yick Wo ES 300/K-5
2245 Jones St 94133 415-749-3540
Yvonne Chong, prin. Fax 749-3543
Other Schools – See Treasure Island

Brandeis Hillel Day S 500/K-8
655 Brotherhood Way 94132 415-406-1035
Chaim Heller, hdmstr. Fax 584-1099
Burke S 400/K-8
7070 California St 94121 415-751-0177
Kim Wargo, hdmstr. Fax 666-0535
Cathedral S for Boys 200/K-8
1275 Sacramento St 94108 415-771-6600
Michael Ferreboeuf, hdmstr. Fax 771-2547
Children's Day S 300/PK-8
333 Dolores St 94110 415-861-5432
Rick Ackerly, hdmstr. Fax 861-5419
Chinese American International S 400/PK-8
150 Oak St 94102 415-865-6000
Andrew Corcoran, hdmstr. Fax 865-6089
Clevenger Jr Preparatory S 100/K-8
180 Fair Oaks St 94110 415-824-2240
Carol Harrison, dir.
Convent of the Sacred Heart S 300/K-8
2222 Broadway St 94115 415-563-2900
Sr. Anne Wachter, hdmstr. Fax 563-0438
Cornerstone Academy 900/PK-4
801 Silver Ave 94134 415-587-7256
Derrick Wong, prin. Fax 333-6923
Corpus Christi S 200/K-8
75 Francis St 94112 415-587-7014
Sr. Martina Ponce, prin. Fax 587-1575
De Marillac Academy 100/4-8
175 Golden Gate Ave 94102 415-552-5220
Eileen Emerson, prin. Fax 621-5632
Ecole Notre Dame des Victoires S 300/K-8
659 Pine St 94108 415-421-0069
Mary Ghisolfo, prin. Fax 421-1440
French-American International S 900/PK-12
150 Oak St 94102 415-558-2000
Jane Camblin, hdmstr. Fax 558-2024
Furth Academy 100/K-8
2445 Pine St 94115 415-346-9500
Nicole McAuliffe, prin. Fax 346-8001
Hamlin S 400/K-8
2120 Broadway St 94115 415-922-0300
Wanda Holland-Green, hdmstr. Fax 674-5409
Hebrew Academy of San Francisco 100/PK-12
645 14th Ave 94118 415-752-7333
Rabbi Pinchas Lipner, dean Fax 752-5851
Holy Name S 300/K-8
1560 40th Ave 94122 415-731-4077
Judy Cosmos, prin. Fax 731-3328
KZV Armenian S 100/PK-8
825 Brotherhood Way 94132 415-586-8686
Yeprem Mehranian, prin. Fax 586-8689
Live Oak S 300/K-8
1555 Mariposa St 94107 415-861-8840
Holly Horton, hdmstr. Fax 861-7153
Lycee Francais-Laperouse S 600/K-5
755 Ashbury St 94117 415-661-5232
Frederick Arzelier, hdmstr. Fax 661-0245
Mission Dolores S 200/K-8
3371 16th St 94114 415-861-7673
Andreina Gualco, prin. Fax 861-7620
Our Lady of the Visitacion S 200/K-8
785 Sunnydale Ave 94134 415-239-7840
Sr. Louise Camous, prin. Fax 239-2559
Presidio Hill S 200/K-8
3839 Washington St 94118 415-751-9318
Brian Thomas, hdmstr. Fax 751-9334
St. Anne S 500/K-8
1320 14th Ave 94122 415-664-7977
Thomas White, prin. Fax 661-6904

St. Anthony-Immaculate Conception S 200/K-8
299 Precita Ave 94110 415-648-2008
Dennis Ruggiero, prin. Fax 648-1825
St. Brendan S 300/K-8
940 Laguna Honda Blvd 94127 415-731-2665
Carol Grewal, prin. Fax 731-7207
St. Brigid S 300/K-8
2250 Franklin St 94109 415-673-4523
Sr. Carmen Santiuste, prin. Fax 674-4187
St. Cecilia S 600/K-8
660 Vicente St 94116 415-731-8400
Sr. Marilyn Miller, prin. Fax 731-5686
St. Charles Borromeo S 300/K-8
3250 18th St 94110 415-861-7652
Daniel Dean, prin. Fax 861-0221
St. Elizabeth S 200/K-8
450 Somerset St 94134 415-468-3247
Gene Dabdoub, prin. Fax 468-1804
St. Finn Barr S 200/K-8
419 Hearst Ave 94112 415-333-1800
Tom Dooher, prin. Fax 452-0177
St. Gabriel S 500/K-8
2550 41st Ave 94116 415-566-0314
Sr. Pauline Borghello, prin. Fax 566-3223
St. James S 200/K-8
321 Fair Oaks St 94110 415-647-8972
Sr. Mary Susanna Vasquez, prin. Fax 647-0166
St. John Orthodox Academy 100/K-12
6210 Geary Blvd 94121 415-221-3484
Maria Kotar, admin.
St. John S 200/K-8
925 Chenery St 94131 415-584-8383
Kenneth Willers, prin. Fax 584-8359
St. Mary Chinese Day S 100/K-8
910 Broadway 94133 415-929-4690
Evelyn Hall Ph.D., prin. Fax 929-4699
St. Monica S 200/K-8
5950 Geary Blvd 94121 415-751-9564
Vincent Sweeters, prin. Fax 751-0781
St. Paul S 200/PK-8
1690 Church St 94131 415-648-2055
Arleen Guaraglia, prin. Fax 648-1920
St. Peter S 400/K-8
1266 Florida St 94110 415-647-8662
Victoria Butler, prin. Fax 647-4618
St. Philip S 200/PK-8
665 Elizabeth St 94114 415-824-8467
Remy Everett, prin. Fax 282-0121
St. Stephen S 300/K-8
401 Eucalyptus Dr 94132 415-664-8331
Sharon McCarthy Allen, prin. Fax 242-5608
St. Thomas More S 300/K-8
50 Thomas More Way 94132 415-337-0100
Joseph Elsbernd, prin. Fax 333-2564
St. Thomas the Apostle S 300/K-8
3801 Balboa St 94121 415-221-2711
Judy Borelli, prin. Fax 221-8611
St. Vincent de Paul S 300/K-8
2350 Green St 94123 415-346-5505
Barbara Harvey, prin. Fax 346-0970
San Francisco Adventist S 50/K-8
66 Geneva Ave 94112 415-585-5550
Rob Robinson, prin. Fax 585-4155
San Francisco Christian S 200/K-12
25 Whittier St 94112 415-586-1117
Mark Asire, admin. Fax 841-0833
San Francisco City Academy 50/K-8
PO Box 16217 94116 415-345-0924
Marie-France Ladine, prin. Fax 345-0925
San Francisco Day S 400/K-8
350 Masonic Ave 94118 415-931-2422
Dr. David Jackson, hdmstr. Fax 931-1753
San Francisco Friends S 300/K-8
250 Valencia St 94103 415-565-0400
Catherine Hunter, prin. Fax 565-0403
San Francisco S 300/PK-8
300 Gaven St 94134 415-239-5065
Steven Morris, hdmstr. Fax 239-4833
San Francisco Waldorf S 400/PK-12
2938 Washington St 94115 415-931-2750
Corinne Fendell, admin. Fax 931-0590
School of the Epiphany 600/K-8
600 Italy Ave 94112 415-337-4030
Diane Elkins, prin. Fax 337-8583
SS. Peter & Paul S 200/PK-8
660 Filbert St 94133 415-421-5219
Dr. Lisa Harris, prin. Fax 421-1831
Star of the Sea S 200/K-8
360 9th Ave 94118 415-221-8558
Terry Hanley, prin. Fax 221-7118
Stuart Hall for Boys S 300/K-8
2222 Broadway St 94115 415-563-2900
Jamie Dominguez, prin. Fax 292-3165
Synergy S 200/K-8
1387 Valencia St 94110 415-567-6177
Harriet Damon, prin. Fax 567-0607
Town S for Boys 400/K-8
2750 Jackson St 94115 415-921-3747
Brewster Ely, hdmstr. Fax 921-2968
West Portal Lutheran S 500/K-8
200 Sloat Blvd 94132 415-665-6330
Gary Beyer, prin. Fax 242-8876
Zion Lutheran S 200/K-8
495 9th Ave 94118 415-221-7500
Donna Laughlin, prin. Fax 221-7141

San Gabriel, Los Angeles, Pop. 41,056

Garvey ESD
Supt. — See Rosemead
Dewey Avenue ES 300/K-6
525 Dewey Ave 91776 626-307-3341
Elizabeth Silva, prin. Fax 307-3473
Marshall ES 300/K-6
1817 Jackson Ave 91776 626-307-3381
Carol Brotsky, prin. Fax 307-8151

San Gabriel USD — 5,500/K-12
408 Junipero Serra Dr 91776 — 626-451-5400
Susan Parks Ed.D., supt. — Fax 451-5494
www.sgusd.k12.ca.us
Coolidge ES — 400/K-5
421 N Mission Dr 91775 — 626-282-6952
Martin Hranek, prin. — Fax 308-0354
Jefferson MS — 1,200/6-8
1372 E Las Tunas Dr 91776 — 626-287-5260
Janice Canfield, prin. — Fax 285-5387
McKinley ES — 700/K-5
1425 Manley Dr 91776 — 626-288-6681
Anna Molinar, prin. — Fax 288-3021
Roosevelt ES — 400/K-5
401 S Walnut Grove Ave 91776 — 626-287-0512
Mayra Perez, prin. — Fax 287-4604
Washington ES — 500/K-5
300 N San Marino Ave 91775 — 626-282-3926
Thomas Chen, prin. — Fax 282-9970
Wilson ES — 400/K-5
8317 Sheffield Rd 91775 — 626-287-0497
Jeannine McGuigan, prin. — Fax 285-4247

Temple City USD
Supt. — See Temple City
Emperor ES — 600/K-6
6415 N Muscatel Ave 91775 — 626-548-5084
Kathy Perini, prin. — Fax 548-5090

Clairbourn S — 400/PK-8
8400 Huntington Dr 91775 — 626-286-3108
Robert Nafie, prin. — Fax 286-1528
St. Anthony S — 300/PK-8
1905 S San Gabriel Blvd 91776 — 626-280-7255
Pauline Ortega, prin. — Fax 280-3870
San Gabriel Christian S — 600/K-8
117 N Pine St 91775 — 626-287-0486
Jan VanSpronsen, prin. — Fax 287-0628
San Gabriel Mission S — 200/K-8
416 S Mission Dr 91776 — 626-281-2454
Sr. Sharon Dempsey, prin. — Fax 281-4817
San Gabriel SDA Academy — 400/PK-12
8827 E Broadway 91776 — 626-292-1156
David Gillham, prin. — Fax 285-4949

Sanger, Fresno, Pop. 22,041
Sanger USD — 8,500/K-12
1905 7th St 93657 — 559-875-6521
Marcus Johnson, supt. — Fax 875-0311
www.sangerusd.com/
Centerville ES — 300/K-6
48 S Smith Ave 93657 — 559-787-2511
Lisa Houston, prin. — Fax 787-3101
Fairmont S — 500/K-8
3095 N Greenwood Ave 93657 — 559-875-7581
Tim Lopez, prin. — Fax 875-1365
Jackson ES — 500/K-5
1810 3rd St 93657 — 559-875-5549
Adela Jones, prin. — Fax 875-1363
Jefferson ES — 400/K-5
1110 Tucker Ave 93657 — 559-875-4591
Cathy Padilla, prin. — Fax 875-1352
Lincoln ES — 400/K-5
1700 14th St 93657 — 559-875-5541
Ketti Davis, prin. — Fax 875-1332
Madison ES — 500/K-5
2324 Cherry Ave 93657 — 559-875-4530
Karl Kesterke, prin. — Fax 875-1219
Reagan ES — 200/K-5
1586 S Indianola Ave 93657 — 559-875-5098
John Hannigan, prin. — Fax 876-0170
Washington Academic MS — 1,500/6-8
1705 10th St 93657 — 559-875-5561
Jon Yost, prin. — Fax 875-6365
Wilson ES — 500/K-5
610 Faller Ave 93657 — 559-875-4501
David Paliughi, prin. — Fax 875-1328
Other Schools – See Del Rey, Fresno

San Geronimo, Marin
Lagunitas ESD — 300/K-8
PO Box 308 94963 — 415-488-4118
Lawrence Enos, supt. — Fax 488-9617
lagunitas.marin.k12.ca.us
Lagunitas S — 100/K-8
PO Box 308 94963 — 415-488-9437
Goldie Curry, prin. — Fax 488-9617
San Geronimo Valley ES — 100/K-6
PO Box 308 94963 — 415-488-9421
Goldie Curry, prin. — Fax 488-1011

San Jacinto, Riverside, Pop. 30,253
San Jacinto USD — 8,800/K-12
2045 S San Jacinto Ave 92583 — 951-929-7700
Shari Fox Ed.D., supt. — Fax 658-3574
www.sanjacinto.k12.ca.us/
De Anza ES — 900/K-5
1089 De Anza Dr 92582 — 951-654-4777
Karen Kirschinger, prin. — Fax 654-7720
Estudillo ES — 700/K-5
900 Las Rosas Dr 92583 — 951-654-1003
Joe Dominguez, prin. — Fax 654-1101
Hyatt ES — 500/K-5
400 E Shaver St 92583 — 951-654-9391
Vincent Record, prin. — Fax 654-8034
Monte Vista MS — 1,000/6-8
181 N Ramona Blvd 92583 — 951-654-9361
Sharon Raffiee, prin. — Fax 654-0173
North Mountain MS — 1,100/6-8
1202 E 7th St 92583 — 951-487-7797
Jordan Reeves, prin. — Fax 487-7799
Park Hill ES — 800/K-5
1157 E Commonwealth Ave 92583 — 951-654-6651
Matt Hixson, prin. — Fax 487-7756
Record ES — 600/K-5
1600 Malaga Dr 92583 — 951-487-6644
Fax 487-6557

San Jacinto ES — 600/K-5
136 N Ramona Blvd 92583 — 951-654-7349
Juan Penaloza, prin. — Fax 487-7721

St. Hyacinth Academy — 300/PK-8
275 S Victoria Ave 92583 — 951-654-2013
Ladonna Lambert, prin. — Fax 654-5644

San Joaquin, Fresno, Pop. 3,579
Golden Plains USD — 2,000/K-12
PO Box 937 93660 — 559-693-1115
Susana Ramirez, supt. — Fax 693-4366
www.gpusd.org
San Joaquin S — 900/K-8
PO Box 408 93660 — 559-693-4321
Diane Steele, prin. — Fax 693-2369
Other Schools – See Cantua Creek, Helm, Tranquillity

San Jose, Santa Clara, Pop. 912,332
Alum Rock UNESD — 12,200/PK-8
2930 Gay Ave 95127 — 408-928-6800
Norma Martinez, supt. — Fax 928-6416
www.arusd.org/
Adelante Dual Language Academy — K-4
2999 Ridgemont Dr 95127 — 408-928-1900
Sandra Garcia, prin. — Fax 928-1901
Arbuckle ES — 400/PK-5
1970 Cinderella Ln 95116 — 408-928-7100
Zarpana Reitman, prin. — Fax 928-7101
Cassell ES — 600/PK-6
1300 Tallahassee Dr 95122 — 408-928-7200
Carolyn Barnaba, prin. — Fax 928-7201
Chavez ES — 600/PK-5
2000 Kammerer Ave 95116 — 408-928-7300
Rene Sanchez, prin. — Fax 928-7301
Cureton ES — 600/PK-5
3720 E Hills Dr 95127 — 408-928-7350
Jason Sorich, prin. — Fax 928-7351
Dorsa ES — 600/PK-5
1290 Bal Harbor Way 95122 — 408-928-7400
Norma Rodriguez, prin. — Fax 928-7401
Fischer MS — 600/6-8
1720 Hopkins Dr 95122 — 408-928-7500
Nancy Gutierrez, prin. — Fax 928-7501
George MS — 500/6-8
277 Mahoney Dr 95127 — 408-928-7600
David Franklin, prin. — Fax 928-7601
Goss ES — 400/K-5
2475 Van Winkle Ln 95116 — 408-928-7650
Brian Schmaedick, prin. — Fax 928-7651
Hubbard ES — 500/K-6
1745 June Ave 95122 — 408-928-7700
Pat Perez, prin. — Fax 928-7701
Linda Vista ES — 700/PK-5
100 Kirk Ave 95127 — 408-928-7800
Paddy Douglas, prin. — Fax 928-7801
L.U.C.H.A. S — K-5
1250 S King Rd 95122 — 408-928-8300
Kristen Henney, prin. — Fax 928-8301
Lyndale ES — 600/PK-5
13901 Nordyke Dr 95127 — 408-928-7900
Lita Fox, prin. — Fax 928-7901
Mathson MS — 700/6-8
2050 Kammerer Ave 95116 — 408-928-7950
Helen Rodriguez, prin. — Fax 928-7951
McCollam ES — 500/PK-5
3311 Lucian Ave 95127 — 408-928-8000
Pablo Fiene, prin. — Fax 928-8001
McEntee Academy — 3-6
2851 Gay Ave 95127 — 408-928-8850
Trevor McDonald, prin. — Fax 928-8851
Meyer ES — 600/PK-5
1824 Daytona Dr 95122 — 408-928-8200
Markeeta Fields, prin. — Fax 928-8201
Ocala MS — 700/6-8
2800 Ocala Ave 95148 — 408-928-8350
Oscar Leon, prin. — Fax 928-8351
Painter ES — 500/PK-5
500 Rough and Ready Rd 95133 — 408-928-8400
Tereasa Smith, prin. — Fax 928-8401
Pala MS — 400/7-8
149 N White Rd 95127 — 408-928-8500
Imee Almazan, prin. — Fax 928-8501
Renaissance Academy — 200/6-8
1720 Hopkins Dr 95122 — 408-928-1950
Fax 928-1951
Rogers ES — 300/PK-5
2999 Ridgemont Dr 95127 — 408-928-8600
Loc Nguyen, prin. — Fax 928-8601
Russo Academy — K-2
2851 Gay Ave 95127 — 408-928-8900
Silvia Villarreal, prin. — Fax 928-8901
Ryan ES — 500/K-6
1241 McGinness Ave 95127 — 408-928-8650
Doug Paganelli, prin. — Fax 928-8651
San Antonio ES — 600/K-5
1855 E San Antonio St 95116 — 408-928-8700
Gail Smith, prin. — Fax 928-8701
Sheppard MS — 600/6-8
480 Rough and Ready Rd 95133 — 408-928-8800
John Rastatter, prin. — Fax 928-8801
Slonaker Academy — 500/PK-6
1601 Cunningham Ave 95122 — 408-928-8950
Ricardo Balderas, prin. — Fax 928-8951

Berryessa UNESD — 8,300/K-8
1376 Piedmont Rd 95132 — 408-923-1800
Marc Liebman Ph.D., supt. — Fax 923-0623
www.berryessa.k12.ca.us
Brooktree ES — 500/K-5
1781 Olivetree Dr 95131 — 408-923-1910
Parisa Goshtasb, prin. — Fax 923-1635
Cherrywood ES — 500/K-5
2550 Greengate Dr 95132 — 408-923-1915
Virgie Catbagan, prin. — Fax 258-8356
Laneview ES — 500/K-5
2095 Warmwood Ln 95132 — 408-923-1920
Sheila Nunez, prin. — Fax 262-5804

Majestic Way ES — 500/K-5
1855 Majestic Way 95132 — 408-923-1925
Carol Mar, prin. — Fax 254-1315
Morrill MS — 900/6-8
1970 Morrill Ave 95132 — 408-923-1930
Christopher Mosley, prin. — Fax 946-0776
Noble ES — 500/K-5
3466 Grossmont Dr 95132 — 408-923-1935
A.J. Winckler, prin. — Fax 937-5006
Northwood ES — 400/K-5
2760 E Trimble Rd 95132 — 408-923-1940
Patty McDonald, prin. — Fax 942-9032
Piedmont MS — 1,100/6-8
955 Piedmont Rd 95132 — 408-923-1945
Steve Lopez, prin. — Fax 251-2392
Ruskin ES — 700/K-5
1401 Turlock Ln 95132 — 408-923-1950
Nora Ho, prin. — Fax 937-4846
Sierramont MS — 900/6-8
3155 Kimlee Dr 95132 — 408-923-1955
James Hamilton, prin. — Fax 729-5840
Summerdale ES — 600/K-5
1100 Summerdale Dr 95132 — 408-923-1960
Bobbie Infelise, prin. — Fax 937-4923
Toyon ES — 500/K-5
995 Bard St 95127 — 408-923-1965
Gayle Calhoun, prin. — Fax 937-4908
Vinci Park ES — 700/K-5
1311 Vinci Park Way 95131 — 408-923-1970
Lihn Nguyen, prin. — Fax 254-3790

Cambrian ESD — 700/K-5
4115 Jacksol Dr 95124 — 408-377-2103
Thomas Dase, supt. — Fax 559-3122
www.cambrian.k12.ca.us
Bagby ES — 700/K-5
1840 Harris Ave 95124 — 408-377-3882
Kathy Kimpel, prin. — Fax 377-8648

Campbell UNESD
Supt. — See Campbell
Blackford ES — 600/K-5
1970 Willow St 95125 — 408-978-4675
Matthew Nagle, prin. — Fax 341-7110
Forest Hill ES — 600/K-5
4450 Mccoy Ave 95130 — 408-364-4279
Lani Potts, prin. — Fax 341-7140

Cupertino UNSD
Supt. — See Cupertino
de Vargas ES — 400/K-5
5050 Moorpark Ave 95129 — 408-252-0303
Karen Wright, prin. — Fax 253-4962
Dilworth ES — 500/K-5
1101 Strayer Dr 95129 — 408-253-2850
Joanne Matala, prin. — Fax 366-0743
Meyerholtz ES — 700/K-5
6990 Melvin Dr 95129 — 408-252-7450
Marge Zellner, prin. — Fax 446-2597
Miller MS — 1,200/6-8
6151 Rainbow Dr 95129 — 408-252-3755
Richard Taylor, prin. — Fax 255-5269
Muir ES — 500/K-5
6560 Hanover Dr 95129 — 408-252-5265
Jones Wong, prin. — Fax 253-3116
Murdock - Portal ES — 500/K-5
1188 Wunderlich Dr 95129 — 408-973-8191
Julie Ales, prin. — Fax 973-8259

Evergreen ESD — 13,100/K-8
3188 Quimby Rd 95148 — 408-270-6800
Clif Black, supt. — Fax 274-3894
www.eesd.org/
Cadwallader ES — 400/K-6
3799 Cadwallader Ave 95121 — 408-270-4950
Roberta Ortega, prin. — Fax 223-4839
Cedar Grove ES — 700/K-6
2702 Sugarplum Dr 95148 — 408-270-4958
Bob Pruitt, prin. — Fax 223-4852
Chaboya MS — 1,100/6-8
3276 Fowler Rd 95135 — 408-270-6900
Mary Helmer, prin. — Fax 270-6916
Clark ES — 800/K-6
3701 Rue Mirassou 95148 — 408-223-4560
Brian Martes, prin. — Fax 223-4567
Dove Hill ES — 700/K-6
1460 Colt Way 95121 — 408-270-4964
Tina Tong Choy, prin. — Fax 223-4536
Evergreen ES — 700/K-6
3010 Fowler Rd 95135 — 408-270-4966
Jeff Smith, prin. — Fax 270-4968
Holly Oak ES — 800/K-6
2995 Rossmore Way 95148 — 408-270-4975
Chris Corpus, prin. — Fax 223-4513
Laurelwood ES — 400/K-6
4280 Partridge Dr 95121 — 408-270-4983
Linda Mora, prin. — Fax 270-6922
LeyVa MS — 800/7-8
1865 Monrovia Dr 95122 — 408-270-4992
Dolores Garcia, prin. — Fax 270-5462
Matsumoto ES — 800/K-5
4121 Mackin Woods Ln 95135 — 408-223-4873
Jim Sherman, prin. — Fax 223-4883
Millbrook ES — 700/K-6
3200 Millbrook Dr 95148 — 408-270-6767
Leila Welch, prin. — Fax 223-4887
Montgomery ES — 600/K-6
2010 Daniel Maloney Dr 95121 — 408-270-6718
Hedwig Rucker, prin. — Fax 223-4848
Norwood Creek ES — 600/K-6
3241 Remington Way 95148 — 408-270-6726
Dan Deguara, prin. — Fax 223-9266
Quimby Oak MS — 1,000/7-8
3190 Quimby Rd 95148 — 408-270-6735
Phil Bond, prin. — Fax 223-4533
Silver Oak ES — 800/K-6
5000 Farnsworth Dr 95138 — 408-223-4515
Carole Schmitt, prin. — Fax 223-4540

Smith ES 700/K-6
2220 Woodbury Ln 95121 408-532-2150
Keith Hodgin, prin. Fax 223-2165
Smith ES 800/K-6
2025 Clarice Dr 95122 408-270-6751
Nick Radley, prin. Fax 270-6877
Whaley ES 700/K-6
2655 Alvin Ave 95121 408-270-6759
Lyn Vijayendran, prin. Fax 223-4537

Franklin-McKinley ESD 9,700/K-8
645 Wool Creek Dr 95112 408-283-6000
Dr. John Porter, supt. Fax 283-6022
www.fmsd.k12.ca.us
Dahl ES 700/K-6
3200 Water St 95111 408-363-5650
Joyce Bacoccina, prin. Fax 363-5669
Fair MS 800/7-8
1702 Mclaughlin Ave 95122 408-283-6400
Beverly Hill, prin. Fax 283-6419
Franklin ES 700/K-6
420 Tully Rd 95111 408-283-6375
Cesar Torrico, prin. Fax 283-6060
Hellyer ES 500/K-6
725 Hellyer Ave 95111 408-363-5750
Sheilah Lane, prin. Fax 363-5761
Kennedy ES 700/K-6
1602 Lucretia Ave 95122 408-283-6325
Linda Barker, prin. Fax 283-6337
Los Arboles ES 600/K-6
455 Los Arboles St 95111 408-363-5675
Carla Haakma, prin. Fax 363-5641
McKinley ES 500/K-6
651 Macredes Ave 95116 408-283-6350
Aurora Garcia, prin. Fax 283-6355
Meadows ES 700/K-6
1250 Taper Ln 95122 408-283-6300
Wayne Leach, prin. Fax 283-6061
Ramblewood ES 300/K-6
1351 Lightland Rd 95121 408-283-6272
Jeanie Sharrock, prin. Fax 283-6217
Santee ES 500/K-6
1313 Audubon Dr 95122 408-283-6450
Guillermina Gutierrez, prin. Fax 283-6062
Seven Trees ES 600/K-6
3975 Mira Loma Way 95111 408-363-5775
Dan Lairon, prin. Fax 363-5642
Shirakawa S 800/K-8
665 Wool Creek Dr 95112 408-938-3200
Manuel Porras, prin. Fax 938-3260
Stonegate ES 600/K-6
2605 Gassmann Dr 95121 408-363-5626
Mary Akin, prin. Fax 363-5631
Sylvandale JHS 1,000/7-8
653 Sylvandale Ave 95111 408-363-5700
David Kennedy, prin. Fax 363-5649
Windmill Springs S 600/K-8
2880 Aetna Way 95121 408-363-5600
Dan Fowler, prin. Fax 363-5606

Luther Burbank ESD 500/PK-8
4 Wabash Ave 95128 408-295-2450
Dr. Fernando Elizondo, supt. Fax 295-3168
www.lbsd.k12.ca.us
Burbank Child Development Center PK-PK
4 Wabash Ave 95128 408-295-1731
Dana Arebalo, prin. Fax 295-3168
Burbank S 500/K-8
4 Wabash Ave 95128 408-295-1814
Marvelyn Maldonado, prin. Fax 295-3168

Moreland ESD 3,800/K-8
4711 Campbell Ave 95130 408-874-2900
Glen Ishiwata, supt. Fax 374-8863
www.moreland.org
Anderson ES 400/K-5
4000 Rhoda Dr 95117 408-874-3100
Destiny Ortega, prin. Fax 243-4312
Baker ES 600/K-5
4845 Bucknall Rd 95130 408-874-3200
Ann Doumain, prin. Fax 379-3726
Country Lane ES 600/K-5
5140 Country Ln 95129 408-874-3400
Nancy Cisler, prin. Fax 252-4576
Easterbrook Discovery S 400/K-5
4835 Doyle Rd 95129 408-874-3500
Sherri Vasquez, prin. Fax 253-7321
Moreland MS 1,200/6-8
4600 Student Ln 95130 408-874-3300
Norma Jeanne Ready, prin. Fax 379-3622
Payne ES 500/K-5
3750 Gleason Ave 95130 408-874-3700
Theresa Molinelli, prin. Fax 241-4932

Morgan Hill USD
Supt. — See Morgan Hill
Los Paseos ES 600/K-6
121 Avenida Grande 95139 408-201-6420
Rex Coffman, prin. Fax 281-4021
Murphy MS 600/7-8
141 Avenida Espana 95139 408-201-6260
Barbara Nakasone, prin. Fax 281-0312

Mount Pleasant ESD 2,600/K-8
3434 Marten Ave 95148 408-223-3700
George Perez, supt. Fax 223-3715
www.mountpleasant.k12.ca.us
Boeger MS 600/6-8
1944 Flint Ave 95148 408-223-3770
Diane Haywood, prin. Fax 223-6959
Jew ES 600/K-5
1966 Flint Ave 95148 408-223-3750
Mariann Engle, prin. Fax 223-7346
Mount Pleasant ES 400/K-5
14275 Candler Ave 95127 408-258-6451
Jose Gonzales, prin. Fax 272-9705
Sanders ES 500/K-5
3411 Rocky Mountain Dr 95127 408-258-7288
Laurie Aknin, prin. Fax 272-9646

Valle Vista ES 500/K-5
2400 Flint Ave 95148 408-238-3525
Patty Pizziol, prin. Fax 223-7465

Oak Grove ESD 11,700/K-8
6578 Santa Teresa Blvd 95119 408-227-8300
Tony Garcia, supt. Fax 227-2719
www.ogsd.k12.ca.us
Anderson ES 600/K-6
5800 Calpine Dr 95123 408-225-6556
Tammy Unck, prin. Fax 224-6964
Baldwin ES 500/K-6
280 Martinvale Ln 95119 408-226-3370
Susan Wright, prin. Fax 224-8506
Bernal IS 900/7-8
6610 San Ignacio Ave 95119 408-578-5731
Katherine Baker, prin. Fax 578-7367
Christopher ES 500/K-6
565 Coyote Rd 95111 408-227-8550
Bill Abraham, prin. Fax 224-8265
Davis IS 900/7-8
5035 Edenview Dr 95111 408-227-0616
Oscar Ortiz, prin. Fax 224-8957
Del Roble ES 600/K-6
5345 Avenida Almendros 95123 408-225-5675
Yolanda Ross, prin. Fax 224-8748
Edenvale ES 600/K-6
285 Azucar Ave 95111 408-227-7060
Alma Maldonado-Castro, prin. Fax 224-8732
Frost ES 500/K-6
530 Gettysburg Dr 95123 408-225-1881
Robert Topf, prin. Fax 224-8932
Glider ES 600/K-6
511 Cozy Dr 95123 408-227-1505
Larry Harris, prin. Fax 224-8386
Hayes ES 500/K-6
5035 Poston Dr 95136 408-227-0424
Tracy Cochran, prin. Fax 224-7191
Herman IS 800/7-8
5955 Blossom Ave 95123 408-226-1886
Julie Hing-Pacheco, prin. Fax 226-1897
Ledesma ES 500/K-6
1001 Schoolhouse Rd 95138 408-224-2191
Barbara Harris, prin. Fax 224-1566
Miner ES 600/K-6
5629 Lean Ave 95123 408-225-2144
Lisa Barlesi, prin. Fax 224-5891
Oak Ridge ES 500/K-6
5920 Bufkin Dr 95123 408-578-5900
Lory Hapeman, prin. Fax 224-3960
Parkview ES 700/K-6
330 Bluefield Dr 95136 408-226-4655
Debbie Roach, prin. Fax 224-9105
Sakamoto ES 600/K-6
6280 Shadelands Dr 95123 408-227-3411
Ziem Nuebert, prin. Fax 224-8784
Santa Teresa ES 600/K-6
6200 Encinal Dr 95119 408-227-3303
Diana Elia, prin. Fax 226-3379
Stipe ES 500/K-6
5000 Lyng Dr 95111 408-227-7332
Paula Cornia, prin. Fax 224-2231
Taylor ES 600/K-6
410 Sautner Dr 95123 408-226-0462
Donna Loose, prin. Fax 224-3279

Orchard ESD 800/K-8
921 Fox Ln 95131 408-944-0397
Joseph Amelio, supt. Fax 944-0394
www.orchardsd.org/
Orchard S 800/K-8
921 Fox Ln 95131 408-994-0388
Bradley Yee, prin. Fax 994-0394

San Jose USD 30,800/K-12
855 Lenzen Ave 95126 408-535-6000
Don Iglesias, supt. Fax 535-2362
www.sjusd.org
Allen ES 800/K-5
820 Steinbeck Dr 95123 408-535-6205
Nico Flores, prin. Fax 578-6059
Almaden ES 400/K-5
1295 Dentwood Dr 95118 408-535-6207
Enrique Pin, prin. Fax 535-2328
Bachrodt ES 500/K-5
102 Sonora Ave 95110 408-535-6211
Lupe Mendoza-Ramirez, prin. Fax 535-6588
Booksin ES 700/K-5
1590 Dry Creek Rd 95125 408-535-6213
Cyndi Maijala, prin. Fax 448-2507
Burnett MS 1,000/6-8
850 N 2nd St 95112 408-535-6267
Lisa Aguerria-Lewis, prin. Fax 298-1675
Canoas ES 400/K-5
880 Wren Dr 95125 408-535-6391
Vinh An Nguyen, prin. Fax 265-4126
Carson ES 400/K-5
4245 Meg Dr 95136 408-535-6287
Betsy Doss, prin. Fax 264-6743
Castillero MS 1,300/6-8
6384 Leyland Park Dr 95120 408-535-6385
Katrina Johnson, prin. Fax 268-4489
Darling ES 600/K-5
333 N 33rd St 95133 408-535-6209
Patsy Storie, prin. Fax 535-6334
Empire Gardens ES 400/K-5
1060 E Empire St 95112 408-535-6221
Carlos Acosta, prin. Fax 297-6914
Galarza ES 500/K-5
1610 Bird Ave 95125 408-535-6671
Susana Parades, prin. Fax 265-3495
Gardner ES 500/K-5
502 Illinois Ave 95125 408-535-6225
Janis Hubbs, prin. Fax 535-2358
Grant ES 500/K-5
470 Jackson St 95112 408-535-6227
Cecilia Barrie, prin. Fax 535-6061

Graystone ES 800/K-5
6982 Shearwater Dr 95120 408-535-6317
Dave Beymer, prin. Fax 323-1034
Hacienda Science/Environmental Magnet ES 600/K-5
1290 Kimberly Dr 95118 408-535-6259
Melissa Mohamed, prin. Fax 723-8225
Harte MS 1,300/6-8
7050 Bret Harte Dr 95120 408-535-6270
Dominic Bejarano, prin. Fax 927-0698
Hoover MS 1,300/6-8
1635 Park Ave 95126 408-535-6274
Suzanne Barbarasch, prin. Fax 286-4864
Los Alamitos ES 700/K-5
6130 Silberman Dr 95120 408-535-6297
Shyril McGuiness, prin. Fax 268-8929
Lowell ES 400/K-5
625 S 7th St 95112 408-535-6243
Jodi Lax, prin. Fax 298-3708
Mann ES 500/K-5
55 N 7th St 95112 408-535-6237
Juan Correa, prin. Fax 535-2315
Muir MS 1,200/6-8
1260 Branham Ln 95118 408-535-6281
Gloria Marchant, prin. Fax 535-2319
Olinder ES 500/K-5
890 E William St 95116 408-535-6245
Al Rosell, prin. Fax 535-2313
Reed ES 400/K-5
1524 Jacob Ave 95118 408-535-6247
Bonnie Thurston, prin. Fax 978-0842
River Glen S 500/K-8
1088 Broadway Ave 95125 408-535-6240
Milly Colon-Arellano, prin. Fax 298-8377
Schallenberger ES 500/K-5
1280 Koch Ln 95125 408-535-6253
Angelic Ruiz, prin. Fax 445-9638
Simonds ES 600/K-5
6515 Grapevine Way 95120 408-535-6251
Janice Samuels, prin. Fax 268-6868
Terrell ES 500/K-5
3925 Pearl Ave 95136 408-535-6255
Anita Sunseri, prin. Fax 265-2917
Trace IS 400/3-5
651 Dana Ave 95126 408-535-6257
Mary Martinez, prin. Fax 535-2304
Washington ES 600/K-5
100 Oak St 95110 408-535-6261
Maria Evans, prin. Fax 535-2369
Williams ES 700/K-5
1150 Rajkovich Way 95120 408-535-6196
Karen Heverling, prin. Fax 535-6525
Willow Glen ES 600/K-5
1425 Lincoln Ave 95125 408-535-6265
Dayle D'anna, prin. Fax 535-6535
Willow Glen MS 1,200/6-8
2105 Cottle Ave 95125 408-535-6277
Erin Green, prin. Fax 535-2353

Union ESD 4,400/K-8
5175 Union Ave 95124 408-377-8010
Jacki Horejs Ed.D., supt. Fax 377-7182
www.unionsd.org
Carlton ES 400/K-5
2421 Carlton Ave 95124 408-356-1141
Cathy Stewart, prin. Fax 356-5993
Dartmouth MS 800/6-8
5575 Dartmouth Dr 95118 408-264-1122
Carole Carlson, prin. Fax 264-9332
Guadalupe ES 500/K-5
6044 Vera Cruz Dr 95120 408-268-1030
Martha Lux, prin. Fax 268-6914
Lietz ES 400/K-5
5300 Carter Ave 95118 408-264-8314
Chris Izor, prin. Fax 264-9615
Noddin ES 600/K-5
1755 Gilda Way 95124 408-356-2126
Robin Jones, prin. Fax 358-9807
Oster ES 400/K-5
1855 Lencar Way 95124 408-266-8121
Randy Martino, prin. Fax 266-3751
Union MS 800/6-8
2130 Los Gatos Almaden Rd 95124 408-371-0366
Erik Burmeister, prin. Fax 371-1217
Other Schools – See Los Gatos

Achiever Christian S 300/PK-8
540 Sands Dr 95125 408-264-6789
Denise Chester, prin. Fax 264-2001
Almaden Country S 300/PK-8
6835 Trinidad Dr 95120 408-997-0424
Dr. Olaf Jorgenson, hdmstr. Fax 997-6823
Apostles Lutheran S 200/K-8
5828 Santa Teresa Blvd 95123 408-578-4800
Shaun Luehring, prin. Fax 225-0720
Calvary Chapel Christian S 100/PK-K
1175 Hillsdale Ave 95118 408-269-2222
Denise Higuera, dir. Fax 269-8341
Challenger S 900/PK-8
711 E Gish Rd 95112 408-998-2860
Dave Mounteer, hdmstr. Fax 998-1852
Challenger S - Almaden 500/PK-8
19950 McKean Rd 95120 408-927-5771
Judy Burbank, prin.
Challenger S - Harwood 300/PK-8
4949 Harwood Rd 95124 408-723-0111
Aaron Schiffner, prin.
Challenger S - Shawnee 500/PK-8
500 Shawnee Ln 95123 408-365-9298
Deepali Deshmukh, prin.
Challenger S - Strawberry Park 600/PK-8
730 Camina Escuela 95129 408-213-0083
Tiffanie Moyano, prin.
Grace Christian S 50/K-8
2350 Leigh Ave 95124 408-377-2387
Connie Cossell, prin.

Harker ES K-5
4300 Bucknall Rd 95130 408-871-4600
Christopher Nikoloff, hdmstr. Fax 871-4320
Harker MS 6-8
3800 Blackford Ave 95117 408-248-2510
Christopher Nikoloff, hdmstr. Fax 248-2502
Holy Family S 500/K-8
4850 Pearl Ave 95136 408-978-1355
Gail Harrell, prin. Fax 978-0290
Holy Spirit S 600/PK-8
1198 Redmond Ave 95120 408-268-0794
Mark Bistricky, prin. Fax 268-5281
Legacy Christian S 50/PK-6
479 Blossom Hill Rd 95123 408-483-4866
Debbie Hudson, prin.
Liberty Baptist S 300/PK-12
2790 S King Rd 95122 408-274-5613
Russel Barnes, prin. Fax 274-1363
Milpitas Christian S 500/PK-8
3435 Birchwood Ln 95132 408-945-6530
Ken VanMeter, supt. Fax 945-9746
Most Holy Trinity S 300/K-8
1940 Cunningham Ave 95122 408-729-3431
Dorothy Suarez, prin. Fax 272-4945
Nativity S of San Jose 100/6-8
310 Edwards Ave 95110 408-993-1293
Kevin Eagleson, prin. Fax 292-0675
Primary Plus S 300/K-4
3500 Amber Dr 95117 408-248-2464
Mary Lou Rodriguez, prin. Fax 248-9447
Queen of Apostles S 300/K-8
4950 Mitty Way 95129 408-252-3659
Martin Chargin, prin. Fax 873-2645
St. Christopher S 600/K-8
2278 Booksin Ave 95125 408-723-7223
Anne Ivie, prin. Fax 978-5458
St. Frances Cabrini S 600/PK-8
15325 Woodard Rd 95124 408-377-6545
Gail Cirrone, prin. Fax 377-8491
St. John Vianney S 600/K-8
4601 Hyland Ave 95127 408-258-7677
Sr. Michele Anne Murphy, prin. Fax 258-5997
St. Leo the Great S 300/K-8
1051 W San Fernando St 95126 408-293-4846
Marie Bordeleau, prin. Fax 293-3516
St. Martin of Tours S 300/K-8
300 OConnor Dr 95128 408-287-3630
Karen DeMonner, prin. Fax 287-4313
St. Patrick S 200/K-8
51 N 9th St 95112 408-283-5858
Sr. Rosemarie Carroll, prin. Fax 283-5852
St. Timothy Lutheran S 100/PK-5
5100 Camden Ave 95124 408-265-0244
Gayle Renken, admin. Fax 265-0275
St. Victor S 300/K-8
3150 Sierra Rd 95132 408-251-1740
Patricia Wolf, prin. Fax 251-1492
Stratford S 200/PK-5
6670 San Anselmo Way 95119 408-363-2130
Beth Ann Zuvella, prin. Fax 363-2131
Valley Christian ES 400/K-5
1450 Leigh Ave 95125 408-559-4400
Gabriel Guven, prin. Fax 559-4022
Valley Christian JHS 600/6-8
100 Skyway Dr Ste 140 95111 408-513-2460
Robert Bridges, prin. Fax 513-2466
White Road Baptist Academy 50/1-12
480 S White Rd 95127 408-272-7713
Anthony Aheav, admin. Fax 272-7666
Willow Vale Christian Children's Center 100/PK-12
1730 Curtner Ave 95125 408-448-0656
Carollyn Ellis, admin. Fax 264-2817

San Juan Bautista, San Benito, Pop. 1,652
Aromas/San Juan USD 1,300/K-12
2300 San Juan Hwy 95045 831-623-4500
Jacquelyn Munoz, supt. Fax 623-4907
www.asjusd.k12.ca.us
San Juan S 500/K-8
100 Nyland Dr 95045 831-623-4538
Alicia Saballa-Santana, prin. Fax 623-0614
Other Schools – See Aromas

San Juan Capistrano, Orange, Pop. 34,673
Capistrano USD 50,700/K-12
33122 Valle Rd 92675 949-234-9200
A. Woodrow Carter, supt. Fax 489-8646
www.capousd.org/
Ambuehl ES 600/K-5
28001 San Juan Creek Rd 92675 949-661-0400
Curt Visca, prin. Fax 488-3158
Del Obispo ES 500/K-5
25591 Camino Del Avion 92675 949-234-5905
Eric Gruenewald, prin. Fax 488-3062
Forster MS 1,400/6-8
25601 Camino Del Avion 92675 949-234-5907
Carrie Bertini, prin. Fax 488-3567
Kinoshita ES 600/K-5
2 Via Positiva 92675 949-489-2131
Erick Fineberg, prin. Fax 234-0405
San Juan ES 600/K-5
31642 El Camino Real 92675 949-493-4533
Silvia Pule, prin. Fax 240-9174
Other Schools – See Aliso Viejo, Capistrano Beach, Coto de Caza, Dana Point, Ladera Ranch, Laguna Niguel, Las Flores, Mission Viejo, Rancho Santa Margarita, San Clemente

---

Capistrano Valley Christian S 500/PK-12
32032 Del Obispo St 92675 949-493-5683
Dr. Dave Baker, hdmstr. Fax 493-6057
Mission S 300/K-8
31641 El Camino Real 92675 949-234-1385
Tina Rolewicz, prin. Fax 234-1397
Rancho Capistrano Christian S 100/PK-8
29251 Camino Capistrano 92675 949-347-7860
Jenda Turner, prin. Fax 364-0849
Saddleback Valley Christian S 600/PK-12
26333 Oso Rd 92675 949-443-4050
Mike Henjum, prin. Fax 443-3941
St. Margaret Episcopal S 1,200/PK-12
31641 La Novia Ave 92675 949-661-0108
Marcus Hurlbut, hdmstr. Fax 489-8042
Stoneybrooke Christian S 400/PK-8
26300 Via Escolar 92692 949-364-4407
Sherry Worel, supt. Fax 364-6303

San Leandro, Alameda, Pop. 78,178
San Leandro USD 8,700/K-12
14735 Juniper St 94579 510-667-3500
Christine Lim, supt. Fax 667-3569
www.sanleandro.k12.ca.us
Bancroft MS 1,000/6-8
1150 Bancroft Ave 94577 510-618-4380
Mary Ann Valles, prin. Fax 895-4113
Garfield ES 400/K-5
13050 Aurora Dr 94577 510-618-4300
Jan Nuno, prin. Fax 352-5399
Jefferson ES 500/K-5
14300 Bancroft Ave 94578 510-618-4310
Ruben Aurelio, prin. Fax 895-4161
Madison ES 400/K-5
14751 Juniper St 94579 510-895-7944
Garry Grotke, prin. Fax 895-7959
McKinley ES 500/K-5
2150 E 14th St 94577 510-618-4320
Cher Mott, prin. Fax 895-7457
Monroe ES 400/K-5
3750 Monterey Blvd 94578 510-618-4340
Queta Beltran-Bannon, prin. Fax 614-0298
Muir MS 1,100/6-8
1444 Williams St 94577 510-618-4400
Belen Magers, prin. Fax 667-3545
Roosevelt ES 500/K-5
951 Dowling Blvd 94577 510-618-4350
Victoria Forrester, prin. Fax 639-0832
Washington ES 400/K-5
250 Dutton Ave 94577 510-618-4360
Tracey Lantz, prin. Fax 895-4112
Wilson ES 800/K-5
1300 Williams St 94577 510-618-4370
Fax 895-4179

San Lorenzo USD
Supt. — See San Lorenzo
Corvallis ES 600/K-5
14790 Corvallis St 94579 510-317-4900
Gail Drake, prin. Fax 317-4925
Dayton ES 500/K-5
1500 Dayton Ave 94579 510-317-3600
Neal Bloch, prin. Fax 317-3690
Hillside ES 500/K-5
15980 Marcella St 94578 510-317-5300
Pam VandeCamp, prin. Fax 317-5322
Washington Manor MS 900/6-8
1170 Fargo Ave 94579 510-317-5500
Wendilynn Warda, prin. Fax 317-5597

Assumption S 300/K-8
1851 136th Ave 94578 510-357-8772
Pamela Lyons, prin. Fax 357-7018
Chinese Christian S 900/K-12
750 Fargo Ave 94579 510-351-4957
Robin Hom, supt. Fax 351-1789
Montessori S of San Leandro 100/PK-1
16492 Foothill Blvd 94578 510-278-0288
Angie Sebastian, admin. Fax 278-1181
St. Felicitas S 300/K-8
1650 Manor Blvd 94579 510-357-2530
Rodney Pierre-Antoine, prin. Fax 357-5358
St. Leander S 300/PK-8
451 Davis St 94577 510-351-4144
Lynne Mullen, prin. Fax 483-6060

San Lorenzo, Alameda, Pop. 19,987
San Lorenzo USD 11,500/PK-12
15510 Usher St 94580 510-317-4600
Dennis Byas, supt. Fax 278-4344
www.sanlorenzousd.k12.ca.us
Bay ES 500/K-5
2001 Bockman Rd 94580 510-317-4300
Diana Tavares, prin. Fax 317-4350
Bohannon MS 900/6-8
800 Bockman Rd 94580 510-317-3800
Gail Yothers, prin. Fax 278-7794
Del Rey ES 600/K-5
1510 Via Sonya 94580 510-317-5000
Robert Patrick, prin. Fax 481-1422
Edendale MS 900/6-8
16160 Ashland Ave 94580 510-317-5100
Thomas Merritt, prin. Fax 317-5190
Grant ES 400/K-5
879 Grant Ave 94580 510-317-3700
Robert Kaminski, prin. Fax 317-3720
Hesperian ES 700/K-5
620 Drew St 94580 510-317-5200
Babette Jackson, prin. Fax 317-5230
Other Schools – See Hayward, San Leandro

Calvary Lutheran S 200/PK-8
17200 Via Magdalena 94580 510-278-2598
Trudy Packard, prin. Fax 278-2557
St. John S 300/PK-8
270 E Lewelling Blvd 94580 510-276-6632
Eliizabeth Guneratne, prin. Fax 276-5645

San Lucas, Monterey
San Lucas UNESD 100/K-8
PO Box 310 93954 831-382-4426
Catherine Reimer, supt. Fax 382-4088
schools.monterey.k12.ca.us/~sanlucas/
San Lucas S 100/K-8
PO Box 310 93954 831-382-4426
Ian Trejo, prin. Fax 382-4088

San Luis Obispo, San Luis Obispo, Pop. 43,509
San Luis Coastal USD 7,000/K-12
1500 Lizzie St 93401 805-549-1200
Edward Valentine, supt. Fax 549-9074
www.slcusd.org
Bishop's Peak/Teach ES 300/K-6
451 Jaycee Dr 93405 805-596-4030
Dan Block, prin. Fax 544-9308
Hawthorne ES 300/K-6
2125 Story St 93401 805-596-4070
Kirt Collins, prin. Fax 544-5759
Laguna MS 700/7-8
11050 Los Osos Valley Rd 93405 805-596-4055
Diane Frost, prin. Fax 544-2449
Los Ranchos ES 400/K-6
5785 Los Ranchos Rd 93401 805-596-4075
Marylou Gooden, prin. Fax 543-2366
Pacheco ES 400/K-6
261 Cuesta Dr 93405 805-596-4081
Rick Mayfield, prin. Fax 782-0597
Sinsheimer ES 400/K-6
2755 Augusta St 93401 805-596-4088
Joyce Hunter, prin. Fax 544-9634
Smith ES 300/K-6
1375 Balboa St 93405 805-596-4094
Amy Shields, prin. Fax 544-0703
Other Schools – See Los Osos, Morro Bay

Laureate Private S 100/K-8
880 Laureate Ln 93405 805-544-2141
Roz Reymers, prin.
Old Mission S 300/PK-8
761 Broad St 93401 805-543-6019
Tina Ballantyne, prin. Fax 543-6246
San Luis Obispo Christian S 50/K-9
PO Box 385 93406 805-543-1146
Jonell Griffith, prin. Fax 548-0546

San Marcos, San Diego, Pop. 73,487
San Marcos USD 16,400/K-12
255 Pico Ave Ste 250 92069 760-752-1299
Kevin Holt Ed.D., supt. Fax 471-4928
www.smusd.org/
Discovery ES 900/K-5
730 Applewilde Dr 92078 760-290-2077
Dan Trujillo, prin. Fax 744-8847
Dunn ES 900/K-5
3697 La Mirada Dr 92078 760-290-2000
Whitney DeSantis, prin. Fax 598-5727
Knob Hill ES 800/K-5
1825 Knob Hill Rd 92069 760-290-2080
Carrie Geldard, prin. Fax 741-7843
Paloma ES 1,100/K-5
660 Camino Magnifico 92069 760-290-2199
Tracy Garcia, prin. Fax 736-2212
Richland ES 1,000/K-5
910 Borden Rd 92069 760-290-2400
Monika Hazel, prin. Fax 290-2412
San Elijo ES 500/K-5
1615 Schoolhouse Way 92078 760-290-2600
Lynda McDonell, prin. Fax 290-2807
San Elijo MS 1,100/6-8
1600 Schoolhouse Way 92078 760-290-2800
Doug Hall, prin. Fax 290-2828
San Marcos ES 500/K-5
300 W San Marcos Blvd 92069 760-290-2430
Stephanie Wallace, prin. Fax 736-2213
San Marcos MS 1,300/6-8
650 W Mission Rd 92069 760-290-2500
Brian Randall, prin. Fax 744-0893
Twin Oaks ES 900/K-5
1 Cassou Rd 92069 760-290-2588
Steve Baum, prin. Fax 752-3155
Woodland Park MS 1,400/6-8
1270 Rock Springs Rd 92069 760-290-2455
David Cochrane, prin. Fax 741-6178
Other Schools – See Carlsbad, Vista

Community Christian S 100/PK-8
1645 S Rancho Santa Fe Rd 92078 760-744-9237
Suzanne Law, admin. Fax 744-0318
Valley Christian S 200/K-8
1350 Discovery St 92078 760-744-0207
Susie Koons, prin. Fax 744-6231

San Marino, Los Angeles, Pop. 13,165
San Marino USD 3,200/K-12
1665 West Dr 91108 626-299-7000
Dr. Gary Woods, supt. Fax 299-7010
www.san-marino.k12.ca.us
Carver ES 600/K-5
3100 Huntington Dr 91108 626-299-7080
Elizabeth Hollingsworth, prin. Fax 299-7086
Huntington MS 800/6-8
1700 Huntington Dr 91108 626-299-7060
Gary McGuigan, prin. Fax 299-7064
Valentine ES 700/K-5
1650 Huntington Dr 91108 626-299-7090
Traynor Schreiber, prin. Fax 299-7094

SS. Felicitas & Perpetua S 300/PK-8
2955 Huntington Dr 91108 626-796-8223
Patricia Aparicio, prin. Fax 683-8129

San Martin, Santa Clara, Pop. 1,713
Morgan Hill USD
Supt. — See Morgan Hill
San Martin/Gwinn ES 500/K-6
100 North St 95046 408-201-6480
Barbara Neal, prin. Fax 683-0851

San Mateo, San Mateo, Pop. 91,081
San Mateo-Foster City ESD
Supt. — See Foster City
Abbott MS 800/6-8
600 36th Ave 94403 650-312-7600
Cathy Ennon, prin. Fax 312-7605

Bayside S.T.E.M. Academy 700/6-8
2025 Kehoe Ave 94403 650-312-7660
Jeanne Elliot, prin. Fax 312-7634
Baywood ES 500/K-5
600 Alameda De Las Pulgas 94402 650-312-7511
Joanne Day, prin. Fax 312-7508
Beresford ES 200/K-5
300 28th Ave 94403 650-312-7551
Alicia Heneghan, prin. Fax 312-1970
Borel MS 900/6-8
425 Barneson Ave 94402 650-312-7670
John Cosmos, prin. Fax 312-7644
College Park ES 300/K-5
715 Indian Ave 94401 650-312-7766
Diana Hallock, prin. Fax 312-7729
Fiesta Gardens International ES 400/K-5
1001 Bermuda Dr 94403 650-312-7737
Shiela Spieller, prin. Fax 312-7697
Hall ES 400/K-5
130 San Miguel Way 94403 650-312-7533
Pam Weinstein, prin. Fax 312-7637
Highlands ES 400/K-5
2320 Newport St 94402 650-312-7544
Maria Majka, prin. Fax 312-7635
Horrall ES 400/K-5
949 Ocean View Ave 94401 650-312-7550
John Dean, prin. Fax 312-7641
Laurel ES 400/K-5
316 36th Ave 94403 650-312-7555
Susan Glines, prin. Fax 312-7636
Meadow Heights ES 300/K-5
2619 Dolores St 94403 650-312-7566
Heather Olsen, prin. Fax 312-7560
North Shoreview ES 300/K-5
1301 Cypress Ave 94401 650-312-7588
Phyllis Harrison, prin. Fax 312-7642
Park ES 400/K-5
161 Clark Dr 94402 650-312-7577
Bob Abaya, prin. Fax 312-7643
Parkside ES 400/K-5
1685 Eisenhower St 94403 650-312-7575
Lynn Gurnee, prin. Fax 312-7638
Sunnybrae ES 400/K-5
1031 S Delaware St 94402 650-312-7599
Shelley Ferguson, prin. Fax 312-7596

Alpha Beacon Christian S 200/PK-12
525 42nd Ave 94403 650-212-4222
Dr. Lillian Mark, supt. Fax 212-1026
Carey S 200/K-5
1 Carey School Ln 94403 650-345-8205
Eric Temple, hdmstr. Fax 345-2528
Grace Lutheran S 100/K-8
2825 Alameda De Las Pulgas 94403 650-345-9082
Robert Meier, prin. Fax 377-4831
Pacific Rim International S 100/PK-12
454 Peninsula Ave 94401 650-685-1881
Christinia Cheung, prin. Fax 685-1820
St. Gregory S 300/K-8
2701 Hacienda St 94403 650-573-0111
Lorraine Paul, prin. Fax 573-6548
St. Matthew Catholic S 600/K-8
910 S El Camino Real 94402 650-343-1373
Kenneth Boegel, prin. Fax 343-2046
St. Matthew's Episcopal S 200/PK-8
16 Baldwin Ave 94401 650-342-5436
Mark McKee, hdmstr. Fax 342-4019
St. Timothy S 300/K-8
1515 Dolan Ave 94401 650-342-6567
Evelyn Nordberg, prin. Fax 342-5913

San Miguel, San Luis Obispo, Pop. 1,123
Pleasant Valley JUNESD 100/K-8
7000 Ranchita Canyon Rd 93451 805-467-3453
Thomas Apkarian, supt. Fax 467-2306
Pleasant Valley S 100/K-8
7000 Ranchita Canyon Rd 93451 805-467-3453
Thomas Apkarian, prin. Fax 467-2306

San Miguel JUNESD 500/K-8
1601 L St 93451 805-467-3216
Dean Smith, supt. Fax 467-3410
Larsen S 400/K-8
1601 L St 93451 805-467-3216
Dean Smith, prin. Fax 467-3410
Other Schools – See Paso Robles

Shandon JUSD
Supt. — See Shandon
Parkfield ES 50/K-6
70585 Parkfield Coalinga Rd 93451 805-463-2331
Dan Peverini, lead tchr.

San Pablo, Contra Costa, Pop. 31,004
West Contra Costa USD
Supt. — See Richmond
Bayview ES 500/K-6
3001 16th St 94806 510-231-1401
Merrilee Cavenecia, prin. Fax 215-6681
Dover ES 600/K-5
1871 21st St 94806 510-231-1420
Matthew Wayne, prin. Fax 236-5483
Downer ES 700/K-6
1777 Sanford Ave 94806 510-234-3851
Marco Gonzales, prin. Fax 233-8961
Helms MS 800/6-8
2500 Road 20 94806 510-233-3988
Rachel Bartlett-Preston, prin. Fax 234-5977
Lake ES 500/K-6
2700 11th St 94806 510-234-7395
Grace Morizawa, prin. Fax 215-8948
Montalvin Manor ES 400/K-6
300 Christine Dr 94806 510-231-1405
Wendy Forrest-Scott, prin. Fax 758-8742
Tara Hills ES 500/K-6
2300 Dolan Way 94806 510-231-1428
Denise Weis, prin. Fax 724-3224

St. Paul S 300/K-8
1825 Church Ln 94806 510-233-3080
Connie Howard, prin. Fax 231-8776

San Pedro, See Los Angeles
Los Angeles USD
Supt. — See Los Angeles
Bandini Street ES 400/K-5
425 N Bandini St 90731 310-832-4593
Robert Fenton, prin. Fax 547-3300
Barton Hill ES 800/K-5
423 N Pacific Ave 90731 310-547-2471
Louie J. Mardesich, prin. Fax 832-4531
Cabrillo Avenue ES 500/K-5
732 S Cabrillo Ave 90731 310-832-6446
Suzanne Russo, prin. Fax 833-2699
Dana MS 1,900/6-8
1501 S Cabrillo Ave 90731 310-241-1100
Terry Ball, prin. Fax 514-9925
Fifteenth Street ES 700/K-5
1527 S Mesa St 90731 310-547-3323
Jennifer Mak, prin. Fax 547-1156
Leland Street ES 500/K-5
2120 S Leland St 90731 310-832-0505
Susan Masero, prin. Fax 831-0837
Park Western Place ES 600/K-5
1214 Park Western Pl 90732 310-833-3591
Christine Cassidy, prin. Fax 833-6413
Point Fermin ES 300/K-5
3333 S Kerckhoff Ave 90731 310-832-2649
Bonnie Taft, prin. Fax 833-4307
Seventh Street ES 500/K-5
1570 W 7th St 90732 310-832-1538
Constantine Colazas, prin. Fax 548-7004
South Shores Performing Arts Magnet S 500/K-5
2060 W 35th St 90732 310-832-6596
Paul Suzuki, prin. Fax 832-4994
Taper Avenue ES 700/K-5
1824 N Taper Ave 90731 310-832-3056
Doreen Steinbach, prin. Fax 548-4485
White Point ES 400/K-5
1410 Silvius Ave 90731 310-833-5232
Lisa O'Brien, prin. Fax 514-8726

Holy Trinity S 600/PK-8
1226 W Santa Cruz St 90732 310-833-0703
Linda Wiley, prin. Fax 833-5219
Mary Star of the Sea S 300/PK-8
717 S Cabrillo Ave 90731 310-831-0875
Noreen Maricich, prin. Fax 831-0877

San Rafael, Marin, Pop. 55,716
Dixie ESD 1,700/K-8
380 Nova Albion Way 94903 415-492-3700
Thomas Lohwasser, supt. Fax 492-3707
dixiesd.marin.k12.ca.us/
Dixie ES 400/K-5
1175 Idylberry Rd 94903 415-492-3730
Patty Flynn, prin. Fax 492-3736
Miller Creek MS 600/6-8
2255 Las Gallinas Ave 94903 415-492-3760
Greg Johnson, prin. Fax 492-3765
Silveira ES 400/K-5
375 Blackstone Dr 94903 415-492-3741
Jeanne Casella, prin. Fax 507-9783
Vallecito ES 400/K-5
50 Nova Albion Way 94903 415-492-3750
Betty Jordan, prin. Fax 492-3757

San Rafael CSD 5,700/K-12
310 Nova Albion Way 94903 415-492-3233
Dr. Michael Watenpaugh, supt. Fax 492-3245
www.srcs.org
Bahia Vista ES 400/K-5
125 Bahia Way 94901 415-485-2415
Juan Rodriguez, prin. Fax 485-2474
Coleman ES 300/K-5
800 Belle Ave 94901 415-485-2420
Ruth Reynolds, prin. Fax 485-2494
Davidson MS 900/6-8
280 Woodland Ave 94901 415-485-2400
Harriet MacLean, prin. Fax 485-2476
Glenwood ES 400/K-5
25 W Castlewood Dr 94901 415-485-2430
Robert Marcucci, prin. Fax 485-2434
Laurel Dell ES 200/K-5
225 Woodland Ave 94901 415-485-2317
Elizabeth Block, prin. Fax 485-2361
San Pedro ES 400/K-5
498 Point San Pedro Rd 94901 415-485-2450
Kathryn Gibney, prin. Fax 485-2454
Sun Valley ES 400/K-5
75 Happy Ln 94901 415-485-2440
Julie Harris, prin. Fax 485-2443
Venetia Valley S 600/K-8
177 N San Pedro Rd 94903 415-492-3150
Pepe Gonzalez, prin. Fax 492-3160

Marin Waldorf S 200/PK-8
755 Idylberry Rd 94903 415-479-8190
Jean Bowler, admin. Fax 479-9921
Montessori De Terra Linda 100/PK-6
PO Box 6093 94903 415-479-7373
Mary Yahnke, hdmstr. Fax 479-5394
St. Isabella S 300/K-8
PO Box 6188 94903 415-479-3727
Ann Kalayjian, prin. Fax 479-9961
St. Mark's S 400/K-8
39 Trellis Dr 94903 415-472-8000
Damon Kerby, hdmstr. Fax 472-0722
St. Raphael S 200/K-8
1100 5th Ave 94901 415-454-4455
Maureen Albritton, prin. Fax 454-5927

San Ramon, Contra Costa, Pop. 49,999
San Ramon Valley USD
Supt. — See Danville
Armstrong ES 500/K-5
2849 Calais Dr 94583 925-479-1600
Paul Foucart, prin. Fax 828-8473
Bollinger Canyon ES 500/K-5
2300 Talavera Dr 94583 925-242-3200
Shawn Wells, prin. Fax 830-9595
Country Club ES 600/K-5
7534 Blue Fox Way 94583 925-803-7430
Michael Biondi, prin. Fax 803-9827
Coyote Creek ES 800/K-5
8700 Northgale Ridge Rd, 925-735-1183
Marsha Tokuyoshi, prin. Fax 735-1197
Disney ES 500/K-5
3250 Pine Valley Rd 94583 925-479-3900
Sandra King, prin. Fax 829-8957
Gale Ranch MS 400/6-8
6400 Main Branch Rd, 925-479-1500
Lisa Ward, prin. Fax 479-1595
Golden View ES 600/K-5
5025 Canyon Crest Dr, 925-735-0555
Nancy White, prin. Fax 735-2104
Hidden Hills ES 800/K-5
12995 Harcourt Way, 925-479-3800
Desiree Braganza, prin. Fax 803-9792
Iron Horse MS 900/6-8
12601 Alcosta Blvd 94583 925-824-2820
Michelle Cooper, prin. Fax 824-2830
Live Oak ES 900/K-5
5151 Sherwood Way, 925-803-3100
Don Loflin, prin. Fax 803-3197
Montevideo ES 500/K-5
13000 Broadmoor Dr 94583 925-803-7450
Sharon Keeton, prin. Fax 828-1727
Pine Valley MS 900/6-8
3000 Pine Valley Rd 94583 925-479-7700
Jason Law, prin. Fax 828-1972
Quail Run ES 600/K-5
4000 Goldenbay Ave, 925-560-4000
Carol Loflin, prin. Fax 560-4059
Twin Creeks ES 500/K-5
2785 Marsh Dr 94583 925-552-5650
Kathleen Crosthwait, prin. Fax 838-8431
Windemere Ranch MS 800/6-8
11611 E Branch Pkwy, 925-479-7400
David Bolin, prin. Fax 479-7469

Santa Ana, Orange, Pop. 340,368
Garden Grove USD
Supt. — See Garden Grove
Fitz IS, 4600 W McFadden Ave 92704 1,000/7-8
Vicki Braddock, prin. 714-663-6351
Hazard ES 700/K-6
4218 W Hazard Ave 92703 714-663-6403
Nanci Cole, prin.
Heritage ES 700/K-6
426 S Andres Pl 92704 714-663-6108
Rebekah Schneider, prin. Fax 663-6032
Newhope ES 700/K-6
4419 W Regent Dr 92704 714-663-6581
Mike Ingalls, prin.
Rosita ES 700/K-6
4726 W Hazard Ave 92703 714-663-6418
Melanie Salazar, prin. Fax 663-6015
Russell ES 700/K-6
600 S Jackson St 92704 714-663-6151
Maurita De La Torre, prin. Fax 663-6026

Orange USD
Supt. — See Orange
Fairhaven ES 600/K-6
1415 Fairhaven Ave 92705 714-997-6178
Andrew Fisher, prin. Fax 532-8073
Panorama ES 300/K-6
10512 Crawford Canyon Rd 92705 714-997-6265
Michelle Moore, prin. Fax 771-3402

Santa Ana USD 56,500/PK-12
1601 E Chestnut Ave 92701 714-558-5501
Jane Russo Ph.D., supt. Fax 558-5610
www.sausd.us/
Adams ES 600/K-5
2130 S Raitt St 92704 714-430-5900
Melanie Champion, prin. Fax 430-5999
Carr IS 1,700/6-8
2120 W Edinger Ave 92704 714-431-7600
P. Yrarrazaval-Correa, prin. Fax 431-7699
Carver ES 600/K-3
1401 W Santa Ana Blvd 92703 714-564-2000
Edna Velado, prin. Fax 564-2099
Davis ES 600/K-5
1405 French St 92701 714-564-2200
Damaris Molina, prin. Fax 564-2299
Diamond ES 600/K-5
1450 S Center St 92704 714-430-6100
Denise Bertrand, prin. Fax 430-6199
Edison ES 800/K-5
2063 Orange Ave 92707 714-433-6900
Jane Mitchell, prin. Fax 433-6999
Esqueda ES 700/K-5
2240 S Main St 92707 714-431-1500
Art Jimenez, prin. Fax 431-1599
Franklin ES 400/K-5
210 W Cubbon St 92701 714-564-2900
Rita Pereira, prin. Fax 564-2999
Fremont ES 800/K-5
1930 W 10th St 92703 714-972-4300
Marisela Roque, prin. Fax 972-4399
Garfield ES 700/K-5
850 Brown St 92701 714-972-5300
Linda DeLeon, prin. Fax 972-5399
Greenville Fundamental ES 1,000/K-5
3600 S Raitt St 92704 714-431-3200
Felicia Gear, prin. Fax 431-3299
Griset Academy 300/K-5
1915 W McFadden Ave 92704 714-648-2900
Virginia Eshtehardi, prin. Fax 648-2996
Harvey ES 500/K-5
1635 S Center St 92704 714-430-6200
Teresa Stetler, prin. Fax 430-6299

Heninger ES 800/K-5
417 W Walnut St 92701 714-953-3800
William Skelly, prin. Fax 953-3899
Heroes ES K-5
1111 W Civic Center Dr 92703 714-568-9600
Maria Duran-Smith, prin. Fax 568-9699
Hoover Academy 800/K-5
408 E Santa Clara Ave 92706 714-564-2100
Richard Valle, prin. Fax 564-2199
Jackson ES 1,100/K-5
1143 S Nakoma Dr 92704 714-431-3700
Marisela Longacre, prin. Fax 431-3799
Jefferson ES 900/K-5
1522 W Adams St 92704 714-431-3800
Anita Ford, prin. Fax 431-3899
Kennedy ES 800/K-5
1300 E McFadden Ave 92705 714-972-5700
Carol Muse, prin. Fax 972-5799
King ES 900/K-5
1001 Graham Ln 92703 714-972-6000
Eleanor Rodriguez, prin. Fax 972-6099
Lathrop IS 1,400/6-8
1111 S Broadway 92707 714-567-3300
Martha Brambila, prin. Fax 567-3399
Lincoln ES 1,100/K-5
425 S Sullivan St 92704 714-972-6200
Manuel Fuentes Ed.D., prin. Fax 972-6299
Lowell ES 900/K-5
700 S Flower St 92703 714-972-6300
Paulita Martinez, prin. Fax 972-6399
MacArthur Fundamental IS 1,300/6-8
600 W Alton Ave 92707 714-513-9800
Marvin Smulowitz, prin. Fax 513-9899
Madison ES 900/K-5
1124 Hobart St 92707 714-972-6400
Martha Baker, prin. Fax 972-6499
Martin ES 700/K-5
939 W Wilshire Ave 92707 714-431-7200
Lisa Gonzales-Solomon, prin. Fax 431-7299
McFadden IS 1,500/6-8
2701 S Raitt St 92704 714-435-3700
Lisa Hinshaw, prin. Fax 435-3799
Mendez Fundamental IS 1,500/6-8
2000 N Bristol St 92706 714-972-7800
Cynthia Landsiedel, prin. Fax 972-7899
Mitchell Child Development Center PK-PK
3001 W Harvard St 92704 714-430-5600
Mark Bello, prin. Fax 430-5699
Monroe ES 500/K-5
417 E Central Ave 92707 714-431-3900
Betty Tamara-Rios, prin. Fax 431-3999
Monte Vista ES 700/K-5
2116 W Monta Vista Ave 92704 714-564-8500
Paulina Jacobs, prin. Fax 564-8599
Muir Fundamental ES 900/K-5
1951 Mabury St 92705 714-972-6700
Donna Kertman, prin. Fax 972-6799
Pio Pico ES 800/PK-5
931 Highland St 92703 714-972-7500
Robert Anguiano, prin. Fax 972-7599
Remington ES 400/K-5
1325 E 4th St 92701 714-972-7600
Robert McDonald, prin. Fax 972-7699
Romero-Cruz ES 400/3-5
1512 W Santa Ana Blvd 92703 714-564-8000
Edna Velado, prin. Fax 564-8099
Roosevelt ES 700/K-5
501 S Halladay St 92701 714-564-1200
Dennis McGeeney, prin. Fax 564-1299
Santiago ES 900/K-5
2212 N Baker St 92706 714-564-8400
Debra Prieto, prin. Fax 564-8799
Sepulveda ES 600/K-5
1801 S Poplar St 92704 714-433-6500
Pamela Mayle, prin. Fax 433-6599
Sierra IS 1,100/5-8
2021 N Grand Ave 92705 714-567-3500
Brenda McGaffigan, prin. Fax 567-3591
Spurgeon IS 1,600/6-8
2701 W 5th St 92703 714-480-2200
Robert Laxton Ed.D., prin. Fax 480-2215
Taft S 1,200/PK-8
500 Keller Ave 92707 714-431-7700
Steven Longacre, prin. Fax 431-7799
Thorpe Fundamental ES 800/K-5
2450 W Alton Ave 92704 714-430-5800
Linda Bell, prin. Fax 430-5899
Villa Fundamental IS 1,400/6-8
1441 E Chestnut Ave 92701 714-558-5100
Cheryl Weaver, prin. Fax 558-5103
Walker ES 600/K-5
811 E Bishop St 92701 714-647-2800
Roxanna Owings, prin. Fax 647-2899
Washington ES 1,200/K-5
910 W Anahurst Pl 92707 714-445-5100
Fernando Duran Ph.D., prin. Fax 445-5199
Willard IS 1,600/5-8
1342 N Ross St 92706 714-480-4800
Jeff Bishop, prin. Fax 480-4899
Wilson ES 700/K-4
1317 N Baker St 92706 714-564-8100
Norris Perez, prin. Fax 564-8199

Tustin USD
Supt. — See Tustin
Arroyo ES 600/K-5
11112 Coronel Rd 92705 714-730-7381
Maggie Villegas, prin. Fax 734-9462
Foss ES 400/K-5
18492 Vanderlip Ave 92705 714-730-7552
Nancy Jenkins, prin. Fax 838-5287
Hewes MS 900/6-8
13232 Hewes Ave 92705 714-730-7348
Tracey VanderHayden, prin. Fax 730-7315
Loma Vista ES 600/K-5
13822 Prospect Ave 92705 714-730-7528
Molly Murphy, prin. Fax 730-7550
Red Hill ES 500/K-5
11911 Red Hill Ave 92705 714-730-7543
Wendy Hudson, prin. Fax 730-1306
Tustin Memorial Academy 600/K-5
12712 Browning Ave 92705 714-730-7546
Cindy Agopian, prin. Fax 730-7524

Bethel Baptist S 300/PK-12
901 S Euclid St 92704 714-839-3600
Dr. Terry Cantrell, admin. Fax 839-4953
Calvary Chapel S 1,700/K-12
3800 S Fairview St 92704 714-556-0965
Jay Henry, supt. Fax 751-3718
Calvary Christian S 500/PK-8
1010 N Tustin Ave 92705 714-973-2056
Mary Malyon, admin. Fax 558-8043
Fairmont Private S - Edgewood Campus 300/PK-8
12421 Newport Ave 92705 714-832-4867
Darcy Krulisky, dir. Fax 832-8336
Grand Avenue Christian S 50/PK-6
2121 N Grand Ave 92705 714-547-5039
John Hernandez, admin. Fax 547-0484
Lycée International de Los Angeles 100/K-6
2625 N Tustin Ave 92705 714-771-4710
Pascal Stricher, prin.
Prentice S, 18341 Lassen Dr 92705 200/PK-8
Carol Clark, dir. 714-538-4511
St. Anne S 200/PK-8
1324 S Main St 92707 714-542-9328
Sr. Cecilia Duran, prin. Fax 542-3431
St. Barbara S 500/K-8
5306 W McFadden Ave 92704 714-775-9477
Judy Bloom, prin. Fax 775-9468
St. Joseph S 200/K-8
608 E Civic Center Dr 92701 714-542-2704
Brad Snyder, prin. Fax 542-2132
School of our Lady 200/K-8
2204 W McFadden Ave 92704 714-545-8185
Priscilla Doorbar, prin. Fax 545-2362

Santa Barbara, Santa Barbara, Pop. 85,899

Cold Spring ESD 200/K-6
2243 Sycamore Canyon Rd 93108 805-969-2678
Dr. Bryan McCabe, supt. Fax 969-0787
www.coldspringschool.net
Cold Spring ES 200/K-6
2243 Sycamore Canyon Rd 93108 805-969-2678
Dr. Bryan McCabe, prin. Fax 969-0787

Goleta UNESD
Supt. — See Goleta
El Camino ES 300/K-6
5020 San Simeon Dr 93111 805-692-5574
Kim Bruzzese, prin. Fax 692-5578
Foothill ES 300/K-6
711 Ribera Dr 93111 805-681-1268
Craig Richter, prin. Fax 681-0700
Hollister ES 400/K-6
4950 Anita Ln 93111 805-681-1271
Ryan Sparre, prin. Fax 681-0331
Mountain View ES 400/K-6
5465 Queen Ann Ln 93111 805-681-1284
Ned Schoenwetter, prin. Fax 681-4814

Hope ESD 1,300/K-6
3970 La Colina Rd Ste 14 93110 805-682-2564
Gerrie Fausett, supt. Fax 687-7954
www.hopeschooldistrict.org
Hope ES 400/K-6
3970-A La Colina Rd 93110 805-563-2974
Barbara LaCorte, prin. Fax 563-4906
Monte Vista ES 500/K-6
730 N Hope Ave 93110 805-687-5333
Nancy Lorenzen, prin. Fax 687-0457
Vieja Valley ES 400/K-6
434 Nogal Dr 93110 805-967-1239
Judy Stettler, prin. Fax 967-5947

Montecito UNESD 400/K-6
385 San Ysidro Rd 93108 805-969-3249
Dick Douglas, supt. Fax 969-9714
www.montecitou.org
Montecito Union S 400/K-6
385 San Ysidro Rd 93108 805-969-3249
Kris Bergstrom, prin. Fax 969-9714

Santa Barbara SD 14,900/K-12
720 Santa Barbara St 93101 805-963-4331
J. Brian Sarvis, supt. Fax 962-3146
www.sbsdk12.org/
Adams ES 600/K-6
2701 Las Positas Rd 93105 805-563-2515
Amy Alzina, prin. Fax 563-4365
Cleveland ES 400/K-6
123 Alameda Padre Serra 93103 805-963-8873
Michael Vail, prin. Fax 965-3523
Franklin ES 600/K-6
1111 E Mason St 93103 805-963-4283
Casie Killgore, prin. Fax 962-6846
Harding ES 500/K-6
1625 Robbins St 93101 805-965-8994
Sally Kingston Ph.D., prin. Fax 962-1846
La Colina JHS 1,000/7-8
4025 Foothill Rd 93110 805-967-4506
David Ortiz, prin. Fax 967-3056
La Cumbre JHS 500/7-8
2255 Modoc Rd 93101 805-687-0761
Jo Ann Caines, prin. Fax 563-4636
McKinley ES 400/K-6
350 Loma Alta Dr 93109 805-966-9926
Emilio Handall, prin. Fax 899-3286
Monroe ES 500/K-6
431 Flora Vista Dr 93109 805-966-7023
Brent Millhollen, prin. Fax 963-4198
Roosevelt ES 500/K-6
1990 Laguna St 93101 805-563-2062
Donna Ronzone, prin. Fax 563-6092
Santa Barbara Community Academy 300/K-6
850 Portesuello Ave 93101 805-687-2081
Eric Nichols, prin.
Santa Barbara JHS 800/7-8
721 E Cota St 93103 805-963-7751
John Becchio, prin. Fax 962-7196
Washington ES 600/K-6
290 Lighthouse Rd 93109 805-965-6653
Demian Barnett, prin. Fax 962-5328
Other Schools – See Goleta

Crane Country Day S 300/K-8
1795 San Leandro Ln 93108 805-969-7732
Joel Weiss, hdmstr. Fax 969-3635
El Montecito S 100/PK-6
630 E Canon Perdido St 93103 805-962-3091
R. Jeannine Morgan, dir. Fax 962-3092
Laguna Blanca S 400/K-12
4125 Paloma Dr 93110 805-687-2461
Douglas Jessup, hdmstr. Fax 682-2553
Marymount S 200/PK-8
2130 Mission Ridge Rd 93103 805-569-1811
Deborah David, hdmstr. Fax 682-6892
Notre Dame S 200/PK-8
33 E Micheltorena St 93101 805-965-1033
Henry Barajas, prin. Fax 965-1034
Our Lady of Mt. Carmel S 200/K-8
530 Hot Springs Rd 93108 805-969-5965
Karen Regan, prin. Fax 565-9841
St. Raphael S 300/PK-8
160 Saint Josephs St 93111 805-967-2115
Ellen Manning, prin. Fax 683-9765
San Roque S 300/PK-6
3214 Calle Cedro 93105 805-687-3717
Fax 569-3767
Santa Barbara Adventist S 50/K-8
425 Arroyo Rd 93110 805-967-9914
Gladys Cerha, prin. Fax 967-9882
Santa Barbara Christian S 100/K-8
3723 Modoc Rd 93105 805-563-4770
Sandra Calkins, prin. Fax 563-4780

Santa Clara, Santa Clara, Pop. 105,402

Cupertino UNSD
Supt. — See Cupertino
Eisenhower ES 600/K-5
277 Rodonovan Dr 95051 408-248-4313
Nicole Johnston, prin. Fax 248-2063

Santa Clara USD 14,100/K-12
1889 Lawrence Rd 95051 408-423-2000
Steve Stavis, supt. Fax 423-2285
www.scu.k12.ca.us
Bowers ES 400/K-5
2755 Barkley Ave 95051 408-423-1100
Robert Moss, prin. Fax 423-1180
Bracher ES 400/K-5
2700 Chromite Dr 95051 408-423-1200
Dr. Jerry Krumbein, prin. Fax 423-1280
Briarwood ES 400/K-5
1930 Townsend Ave 95051 408-423-1300
Julie Topliff, prin. Fax 423-1380
Buchser MS 1,100/6-8
1111 Bellomy St 95050 408-423-3000
Kyle Eaton, prin. Fax 423-3080
Cabrillo MS 900/6-8
2550 Cabrillo Ave 95051 408-423-3700
Stan Garber, prin. Fax 423-3780
Callejon S 500/K-8
4176 Lick Mill Blvd 95054 408-423-3300
Hans Barber, prin. Fax 423-3380
Haman ES 400/K-5
865 Los Padres Blvd 95050 408-423-1400
Pam Fox, prin. Fax 423-1480
Hughes ES 400/K-5
4949 Calle De Escuela 95054 408-423-1500
Kevin Keegan, prin. Fax 423-1580
Laurelwood ES 500/K-5
955 Teal Dr 95051 408-423-1600
Lori Paolinetti, prin. Fax 423-1680
Millikin ES 400/K-5
2720 Sonoma Pl 95051 408-423-1800
Melba Rhodes-Stanford, prin. Fax 423-1880
Montague ES 300/K-5
750 Laurie Ave 95054 408-423-1900
Eric Lewis, prin. Fax 423-1980
Pomeroy ES 500/K-5
1250 Pomeroy Ave 95051 408-423-3800
Tricia Fryer, prin. Fax 423-3880
Scott Lane ES 500/K-5
1925 Scott Blvd 95050 408-985-4100
Melissa Alatorre, prin. Fax 423-4180
Sutter ES 400/K-5
3200 Forbes Ave 95051 408-423-4200
Tom Funcheon, prin. Fax 423-4280
Washington Open S 400/K-5
270 Washington St 95050 408-423-3900
Lori King, prin. Fax 423-3980
Westwood ES 400/K-5
435 Saratoga Ave 95050 408-423-4300
Tommye Wintle, prin. Fax 423-4380
Other Schools – See Alviso, Sunnyvale

Carden Academy of Santa Clara 300/PK-8
615 Hobart Ter 95051 408-244-5041
William Ries, prin. Fax 244-0684
Challenger S - Pomeroy 300/PK-K
890 Pomeroy Ave 95051 408-243-6190
Christel Soriano, dir.
Delphi Academy of the San Francisco Bay 100/K-8
890 Pomeroy Ave Ste 201 95051 408-260-2300
Marcy Green, hdmstr.
Granada Islamic S 400/PK-8
3003 Scott Blvd 95054 408-980-1161
Nihad Mourad, prin. Fax 980-1120

Monticello Academy 100/K-8
3345 Lochinvar Ave 95051 408-615-9416
Trinh Trinh, prin.
North Valley Baptist S 200/K-12
941 Clyde Ave 95054 408-988-8883
Dan Azzarello, prin.
St. Clare S 300/K-8
725 Washington St 95050 408-246-6797
Madeline Rader, prin. Fax 246-6726
St. Justin S 300/K-8
2655 Homestead Rd 95051 408-248-1094
Kim Shields, prin. Fax 246-0691
St. Lawrence the Martyr S 300/PK-8
1977 Saint Lawrence Dr 95051 408-296-2260
Priscilla Murphy, prin. Fax 296-1068
Santa Clara Christian S 100/PK-5
3421 Monroe St 95051 408-246-5423
Stuart Nice, prin. Fax 246-4883

Santa Clarita, Los Angeles, Pop. 168,253
Newhall ESD
Supt. — See Valencia
Old Orchard ES 500/K-6
25141 Avenida Rondel 91355 661-291-4040
Sandra Reveles, prin. Fax 291-4041

Saugus UNESD 10,500/K-6
24930 Avenue Stanford 91355 661-294-5300
Dr. Judy Fish, supt. Fax 294-3111
www.saugus.k12.ca.us
Bridgeport ES 900/K-6
23670 Newhall Ranch Rd 91355 661-286-1590
Susan Bender, prin. Fax 286-1598
Other Schools – See Canyon Country, Saugus, Valencia

Sulphur Springs UNESD
Supt. — See Canyon Country
Fair Oaks Ranch Community ES 1,000/K-6
26933 Silverbell Ln 91387 661-299-1790
Marie Stump, prin. Fax 299-1879
Golden Oak Community ES K-6
25201 Via Princessa 91387 661-251-8929
Gayle Abril, prin. Fax 251-8727

William S. Hart UNHSD 22,400/7-12
21515 Centre Pointe Pkwy 91350 661-259-0033
Jaime Castellanos, supt. Fax 254-8653
www.hartdistrict.org
La Mesa JHS 1,300/7-8
26623 May Way 91351 661-250-0022
Pete Fries, prin. Fax 252-3326
Other Schools – See Canyon Country, Newhall, Stevenson Ranch, Valencia

---

Advantage Preparatory S 200/K-12
PO Box 802274 91380 661-296-5466
Cynthia Grant, admin.
Our Lady of Perpetual Help S 300/PK-8
23225 Lyons Ave 91321 661-259-1141
Sharon Krahl, prin. Fax 259-8254

Santa Cruz, Santa Cruz, Pop. 54,760
Bonny Doon UNESD 100/K-6
1492 Pine Flat Rd 95060 831-427-2300
Gail Levine, supt. Fax 427-2800
www.bonnydoon.santacruz.k12.ca.us/
Bonny Doon ES 100/K-6
1492 Pine Flat Rd 95060 831-427-2300
Gail Levine, prin. Fax 427-2800

Happy Valley ESD 100/K-6
3125 Branciforte Dr 95065 831-429-1456
Chris McGriff, supt. Fax 429-6205
www.happyvalley.santacruz.k12.ca.us
Happy Valley ES 100/K-6
3125 Branciforte Dr 95065 831-429-1456
Chris McGriff, prin. Fax 429-6205

Live Oak SD 1,900/K-8
984 Bostwick Ln Ste 1 95062 831-475-6333
Tamra Taylor, supt. Fax 475-2638
www.lodo.santacruz.k12.ca.us
Del Mar ES 500/K-5
1959 Merrill St 95062 831-477-2063
Pamela Randall, prin. Fax 477-9555
Green Acres ES 400/K-5
966 Bostwick Ln 95062 831-475-0111
Doug Fritsch, prin. Fax 475-4813
Live Oak ES 400/K-5
1916 Capitola Rd 95062 831-475-2000
Deborah Wilson, prin. Fax 475-0458
Shoreline MS 700/6-8
855 17th Ave 95062 831-475-6565
Robert Greenlee, prin. Fax 462-1653

Santa Cruz CSD
Supt. — See Soquel
Bay View ES 500/K-5
1231 Bay St 95060 831-429-3991
Mary Ann Robb, prin. Fax 429-3513
Branciforte MS 400/6-8
315 Poplar Ave 95062 831-429-3883
Kris Munro, prin. Fax 429-3962
De Laveaga ES 600/K-5
1145 Morrissey Blvd 95065 831-429-3807
Ruth Smith, prin. Fax 429-3999
Gault ES 400/K-5
1320 Seabright Ave 95062 831-429-3856
Molly Parks, prin. Fax 427-4812
Mission Hill MS 600/6-8
425 King St 95060 831-429-3860
Valerie Quandt, prin. Fax 427-4846
Westlake ES 500/K-5
1000 High St 95060 831-429-3878
Clyde Curley, prin. Fax 429-3835

Scotts Valley USD
Supt. — See Scotts Valley
Brook Knoll ES 600/K-5
151 Brook Knoll Dr 95060 831-423-2454
Kathy Frandle, prin. Fax 429-8508

Soquel UNESD
Supt. — See Capitola
Santa Cruz Gardens ES 300/K-5
8005 Winkle Ave 95065 831-464-5670
Alicia Escobar, prin. Fax 476-5827

Gateway S 300/K-8
126 Eucalyptus Ave 95060 831-423-0341
Percy Abram, hdmstr. Fax 454-0843
Good Shepherd S 200/PK-8
2727 Mattison Ln 95065 831-476-4000
Daniel Anderson, prin. Fax 476-0948
Holy Cross S 300/PK-8
150 Emmett St 95060 831-423-4447
Kathleen Ryan, prin. Fax 423-0752
Santa Cruz Waldorf S 200/PK-12
2190 Empire Grade 95060 831-425-0519
Sally Donnelly, admin. Fax 425-1326
Spring Hill Advanced S 100/K-6
250 California St 95060 831-427-2641
Sylvie Hill, prin. Fax 427-2958
VHM Christian S 100/K-8
427 Capitola Road Ext 95062 831-475-4762
Donald Ramey, prin. Fax 475-4845

Santa Fe Springs, Los Angeles, Pop. 17,058
Little Lake City SD 5,100/K-8
10515 Pioneer Blvd 90670 562-868-8241
Phillip Perez Ph.D., supt. Fax 868-1192
www.littlelake.k12.ca.us
Jersey Avenue ES 400/K-5
9400 Jersey Ave 90670 562-948-3772
Monica Johnson, prin. Fax 942-7902
Lake Center MS 1,000/6-8
10503 Pioneer Blvd 90670 562-868-4977
David Weiss, prin. Fax 929-4527
Lakeview ES 600/K-5
11500 Joslin St 90670 562-868-8655
William Crean Ph.D., prin. Fax 868-1647
Other Schools – See Norwalk

Los Nietos ESD
Supt. — See Los Nietos
Rancho Santa Gertrudes ES 500/K-5
11233 Charlesworth Rd 90670 562-692-0841
Jeanette Salinas, prin. Fax 699-6955

St. Pius X S 300/PK-8
10855 Pioneer Blvd 90670 562-864-4818
Cynthia Valencia, prin. Fax 864-7120
Santa Fe Springs Christian S 200/K-8
11457 Florence Ave 90670 562-868-2263
Richard Brown, prin. Fax 868-8398

Santa Margarita, San Luis Obispo
Atascadero USD
Supt. — See Atascadero
Carrisa Plains ES 50/K-6
9640 Carrisa Hwy 93453 805-475-2244
Kathy Hannemann, prin. Fax 475-2046
Santa Margarita ES 300/K-6
PO Box 380 93453 805-438-5633
Melanie Karp, prin. Fax 438-3323

Santa Maria, Santa Barbara, Pop. 84,346
Blochman UNESD 100/K-8
4949 Foxen Canyon Rd 93454 805-937-1148
Kristin Garrison-Lima, supt. Fax 937-2291
Foxen S 100/K-8
4949 Foxen Canyon Rd 93454 805-937-1148
Doug Brown, prin. Fax 937-2291

Orcutt UNESD
Supt. — See Orcutt
Dunlap ES 600/K-6
1220 Oak Knoll Rd 93455 805-938-8500
Joe Dana, prin. Fax 938-8549
Lakeview JHS 700/7-8
3700 Orcutt Rd 93455 805-938-8600
Jeff Carlovsky, prin. Fax 938-8649
Nightingale ES 800/K-6
255 Winter Rd 93455 805-938-8650
Holly Edds, prin. Fax 938-8699
Patterson Road ES 500/K-6
400 Patterson Rd 93455 805-938-8750
Don Hart, prin. Fax 938-8799
Pine Grove ES 400/K-6
1050 E Rice Ranch Rd 93455 805-938-8800
Elizabeth Herbstreith, prin. Fax 938-8849
Shaw ES 600/K-6
759 Dahlia Pl 93455 805-938-8850
Janet Bertoldi, prin. Fax 938-8899

Santa Maria-Bonita ESD 12,900/K-8
708 S Miller St 93454 805-928-1783
Phillip Alvarado, supt. Fax 928-7874
www.smbsd.org/
Adam ES 600/K-6
500 Windsor St 93458 805-361-6700
Laurie Graack, prin. Fax 352-9104
Alvin ES 600/K-6
301 E Alvin Ave 93454 805-361-6760
Ann Wicklund, prin. Fax 349-2737
Arellanes ES 300/K-6
1890 Sandalwood Dr 93455 805-361-6860
Leslie Brown, prin. Fax 346-8540
Arellanes JHS 500/7-8
1890 Sandalwood Dr 93455 805-361-6820
Patty Grady, prin. Fax 346-8535
Battles ES 800/K-6
605 E Battles Rd 93454 805-361-6880
Jim Bissin, prin. Fax 346-1836

Bonita ES 300/K-6
2715 W Main St 93458 805-361-8280
Aaron Shrogin, prin. Fax 925-1179
Bruce ES 800/K-6
601 W Alvin Ave 93458 805-361-6940
Ann Sawyer, prin. Fax 346-1838
El Camino JHS 700/7-8
219 W El Camino St 93458 805-361-7800
Ann Orton, prin. Fax 346-1851
Fairlawn ES 600/K-6
120 Mary Dr 93458 805-361-7500
Polly Nelson, prin. Fax 346-1839
Fesler JHS 800/7-8
1100 E Fesler St 93454 805-361-7880
Barbara Walker, prin. Fax 346-1849
Kunst JHS 800/7-8
930 Hidden Pines Way 93458 805-361-5800
Ed Cora, prin. Fax 925-8239
Liberty ES 700/K-6
1300 Sonya Ln 93458 805-361-4530
Jamie LeBlanc, prin. Fax 925-2165
Miller ES 700/K-6
410 E Camino Colegio 93454 805-361-7560
Karen Porter, prin. Fax 346-1840
Oakley ES 800/K-6
1120 W Harding Ave 93458 805-361-7620
Bronwyn Rafferty, prin. Fax 346-1841
Ontiveros ES 800/K-6
930 Rancho Verde 93458 805-361-7680
Margaret Ontiveros, prin. Fax 346-1846
Rice ES 800/K-6
700 Vickie Ave 93454 805-361-7740
Rebecca Herrick, prin. Fax 346-1842
Sanchez ES 700/K-6
804 Liberty St 93458 805-361-4625
Virginia Bauer, prin. Fax 925-8410
Taylor ES 1,000/K-6
1921 Carlotti Dr 93454 805-361-6250
Sherry Peterson, prin. Fax 346-2683
Tunnell S 800/K-6
1248 Dena Way 93454 805-361-7940
Niccole Wiseman, prin. Fax 349-2017

Crossroads Christian JHS 100/7-8
1550 S College Dr 93454 805-922-0237
Susan Pruett, admin. Fax 925-9690
Pacific Christian S 300/PK-8
3435 Santa Maria Way 93455 805-934-1253
Joseph Hunt, admin. Fax 934-3445
St. Louis De Montfort S 300/K-8
5095 Harp Rd 93455 805-937-5571
Kathy Crow, prin. Fax 937-3181
St. Mary of the Assumption S 200/K-8
424 E Cypress St 93454 805-925-6713
Carmen Vadillo, prin. Fax 925-3815
Valley Christian Academy 300/K-12
2970 Santa Maria Way 93455 805-937-6317
Charles Mason, prin. Fax 934-2563

Santa Monica, Los Angeles, Pop. 87,800
Santa Monica-Malibu USD 11,900/PK-12
1651 16th St 90404 310-450-8338
Tim Cuneo, supt. Fax 450-1667
www.smmusd.org
Adams MS 1,100/6-8
2425 16th St 90405 310-452-2326
Martha Shaw, prin. Fax 452-5352
Child Development Services PK-PK
2802 4th St 90405 310-399-5865
Judy Abdo, dir. Fax 396-1618
Edison Language Academy 400/K-5
2425 Kansas Ave 90404 310-828-0335
Lori Orum, prin. Fax 449-1250
Franklin ES 800/K-5
2400 Montana Ave 90403 310-828-2814
Tara Brown, prin. Fax 449-1252
Grant ES 700/K-5
2368 Pearl St 90405 310-450-7651
Alan Friedenberg, prin. Fax 452-4350
Lincoln MS 1,200/6-8
1501 California Ave 90403 310-393-9227
Suzanne Webb, prin. Fax 393-4297
McKinley ES 400/K-5
2401 Santa Monica Blvd 90404 310-828-5011
Irene Gonzalez, prin. Fax 449-1251
Muir ES 300/K-5
2526 6th St 90405 310-399-7721
Tristan Komlos, prin. Fax 452-4351
Pine Street Preschool PK-PK
731 Pine St 90405 310-450-5022
Judy Abdo, dir. Fax 396-1618
Rogers ES 600/K-5
2401 14th St 90405 310-452-2364
Irma Lyons, prin. Fax 452-9035
Roosevelt ES 800/K-5
801 Montana Ave 90403 310-395-0941
Natalie Burton, prin. Fax 587-1169
Other Schools – See Malibu

Carlthorp S 300/K-6
438 San Vicente Blvd 90402 310-451-1332
Dorothy Menzies, hdmstr. Fax 451-8559
Crossroads S for Arts & Sciences 1,100/K-12
1714 21st St 90404 310-829-7391
Roger Weaver, hdmstr. Fax 828-5636
Lighthouse S 100/PK-12
1220 20th St 90404 310-829-1741
Willette Lever, prin. Fax 829-1743
New Roads MS 200/6-8
1238 Lincoln Blvd 90401 310-587-2255
David Bryan, hdmstr. Fax 587-2258
Pilgrim Lutheran Preschool 50/PK-PK
1730 Wilshire Blvd 90403 310-829-2239
Shelley McDermott, dir. Fax 453-5345
Pluralistic S #1 200/K-6
1454 Euclid St 90404 310-394-1313
Joel Pelcyger, hdmstr. Fax 395-1093

St. Anne Mission S — 200/PK-8
2015 Colorado Ave 90404 — 310-829-2775
Michael Browning, prin. — Fax 829-3945
St. Monica S — 300/K-8
1039 7th St 90403 — 310-451-9801
Sharon Dandorf, prin. — Fax 394-6001

Santa Paula, Ventura, Pop. 28,478
Briggs ESD — 400/PK-8
12465 Foothill Rd 93060 — 805-525-7540
Ken Moffett, supt. — Fax 933-1111
www.briggsesd.org/
Briggs MS — 200/4-8
14438 W Telegraph Rd 93060 — 805-525-7151
Brandon Gallagher, prin. — Fax 933-3565
Olivelands ES — 200/PK-3
12465 Foothill Rd 93060 — 805-933-2254
Deborah Cuevas, prin. — Fax 933-1111

Mupu ESD — 100/K-8
4410 Ojai Rd 93060 — 805-525-6111
Jeanine Gore, supt. — Fax 525-2871
www.mupu.k12.ca.us
Mupu S — 100/K-8
4410 Ojai Rd 93060 — 805-525-6111
Jeanine Gore, prin. — Fax 525-2871

Santa Clara ESD — 100/K-6
20030 E Telegraph Rd 93060 — 805-525-4573
Kari Skidmore, supt. — Fax 525-4985
www.scesd.k12.ca.us
Santa Clara ES — 100/K-6
20030 E Telegraph Rd 93060 — 805-525-4573
Kari Skidmore, prin. — Fax 525-4985

Santa Paula ESD — 3,700/K-8
201 S Steckel Dr 93060 — 805-933-8800
Winston Braham Ed.D., supt. — Fax 933-3023
www.spesd.org/
Bedell ES — 300/K-5
1305 Laurel Rd 93060 — 805-933-8950
Lori Sanchez, prin. — Fax 933-9735
Blanchard ES — 500/K-5
115 N Peck Rd 93060 — 805-933-8866
Mary Fennell, prin. — Fax 933-4409
Glen City ES — 600/K-5
141 S Steckel Dr 93060 — 805-933-8850
Raul Betancourt, prin. — Fax 525-2821
Isbell MS — 1,200/6-8
221 S 4th St 93060 — 805-933-8880
Laura Rynott, prin. — Fax 933-5582
McKevett ES — 300/K-5
955 E Pleasant St 93060 — 805-933-8910
Sheryl Misenhimer, prin. — Fax 933-0542
Thille ES — 300/K-5
1144 E Ventura St 93060 — 805-933-8920
Frances Contreras, prin. — Fax 933-0192
Webster ES — 400/K-5
1150 Saticoy St 93060 — 805-933-8930
Patti Fulbright, prin. — Fax 933-5588

St. Sebastian S — 200/PK-8
325 E Santa Barbara St 93060 — 805-525-1575
Kathleen Garcia, prin. — Fax 525-1576

Santa Rosa, Sonoma, Pop. 153,158
Bellevue UNESD — 2,000/K-6
3223 Primrose Ave 95407 — 707-542-5197
Dr. Tony Roehrick, supt. — Fax 542-6127
www.bellevueusd.org/
Bellevue ES — 600/K-6
3223 Primrose Ave 95407 — 707-542-5196
John Eberly, prin. — Fax 542-6083
Kawana ES — 600/K-6
2121 Moraga Dr 95404 — 707-545-4283
Jesse Escobedo, prin. — Fax 573-9065
Meadow View ES — 500/K-6
2665 Dutton Mdw 95407 — 707-541-3715
Terri Palladino, prin. — Fax 541-3717
Taylor Mountain ES — 400/K-6
1210 E Bellevue Ave 95407 — 707-542-3671
Elizabeth Sesma-Olinyk, prin. — Fax 542-3904

Bennett Valley UNESD — 900/K-6
2250 Mesquite Dr 95405 — 707-542-2201
Susan Field, supt. — Fax 544-6629
www.bvusd.org
Strawberry ES — 400/4-6
2311 Horseshoe Dr 95405 — 707-526-4433
Scott Humble, prin. — Fax 526-0906
Yulupa ES — 500/K-3
2250 Mesquite Dr 95405 — 707-542-6272
Sue Simon, prin. — Fax 544-0360

Mark West UNESD — 1,300/K-6
305 Mark West Springs Rd 95404 — 707-524-2970
Kay Schultz, supt. — Fax 524-2976
www.mwusd.k12.ca.us/
Riebli ES — 500/K-6
315 Mark West Springs Rd 95404 — 707-524-2980
Bethany Wilson, prin. — Fax 524-2986
San Miguel ES — 400/K-6
5350 Faught Rd 95403 — 707-524-2960
Ron Calloway, prin. — Fax 524-2968
West ES — 400/K-6
4600 Lavell Rd 95403 — 707-524-2990
Tracy Lavin-Kendall, prin. — Fax 524-2999

Oak Grove UNESD — 700/K-8
5285 Hall Rd 95401 — 707-545-0171
Noel Buehler, supt. — Fax 545-0176
www.ogusd.org/
Willowside MS — 400/6-8
5285 Hall Rd 95401 — 707-542-3322
Adam Schaible, prin. — Fax 525-4439
Other Schools – See Sebastopol

Piner-Olivet UNESD — 1,400/K-6
3450 Coffey Ln 95403 — 707-522-3000
Marion Guillen, supt. — Fax 522-3007
www.pousd.org
London ES — 300/K-6
2707 Francisco Ave 95403 — 707-522-3310
Jack Potter, prin. — Fax 522-3317
Olivet ES — 300/K-6
1825 Willowside Rd 95401 — 707-522-3045
Emily Davis, prin. — Fax 522-3047
Piner ES — 400/K-6
2590 Piner Rd 95401 — 707-522-3030
Joe Hamp, prin. — Fax 522-3032
Schaefer ES — 400/K-6
1370 San Miguel Rd 95403 — 707-522-3015
Jennie Snyder, prin. — Fax 522-3017

Rincon Valley UNESD — 2,800/K-6
1000 Yulupa Ave 95405 — 707-542-7375
Diane Moresi, supt. — Fax 542-9802
www.rvusd.org
Austin Creek ES — 400/K-6
1480 Snowy Egret Dr 95409 — 707-538-2122
Dr. Devon Leaf, prin. — Fax 538-1774
Binkley ES — 300/K-6
4965 Canyon Dr 95409 — 707-539-6060
Mike Herfurth, prin. — Fax 539-4862
Madrone ES — 400/K-6
4550 Rinconada Dr 95409 — 707-539-9665
Michael Kellison, prin. — Fax 539-1362
Matanzas ES — 300/K-6
1687 Yulupa Ave 95405 — 707-546-6183
Jim Currie, prin. — Fax 528-8027
Sequoia ES — 400/K-6
5305 Dupont Dr 95409 — 707-539-3410
Matt Reno, prin. — Fax 537-1791
Spring Creek ES — 300/K-6
4675 Mayette Ave 95405 — 707-545-1771
Randy Coleman, prin. — Fax 545-6926
Village ES — 400/K-6
900 Yulupa Ave 95405 — 707-545-5754
Maria McCormick, prin. — Fax 573-0951
Whited ES — 400/K-6
4995 Sonoma Hwy 95409 — 707-539-2400
Tom Castagnola, prin. — Fax 539-9253

Roseland ESD — 1,400/K-6
1934 Biwana Dr 95407 — 707-545-0102
Gail Ahlas, supt. — Fax 545-5096
www.roselandsd.org/
Roseland ES — 800/K-6
950 Sebastopol Rd 95407 — 707-545-0100
Dana Pedersen, prin. — Fax 542-2111
Sheppard Accelerated ES — 700/K-6
1777 West Ave 95407 — 707-546-7050
Jenny Young, prin. — Fax 546-0434

Santa Rosa CSD — 16,700/K-12
211 Ridgway Ave 95401 — 707-528-5388
Sharon Liddell Ed.D., supt. — Fax 528-5440
www.srcs.k12.ca.us
Biella ES — 500/K-6
2140 Jennings Ave 95401 — 707-522-3110
Winnie Hogoboom, prin. — Fax 522-3109
Brook Hill ES — 400/K-6
1850 Vallejo St 95404 — 707-522-3120
Guadalupe Perez-Cook, prin. — Fax 522-3127
Burbank ES — 300/K-6
203 S A St 95401 — 707-522-3140
Patricia Turner, prin. — Fax 522-3149
Comstock MS — 400/7-8
2750 W Steele Ln 95403 — 707-528-5266
Robert Dahlstet, prin. — Fax 528-5480
Cook MS — 600/7-8
2480 Sebastopol Rd 95407 — 707-528-5156
Harriet Gray, prin. — Fax 528-5163
Doyle Park ES — 300/K-6
1350 Sonoma Ave 95405 — 707-522-3150
Kaesa Enemark, prin. — Fax 522-3159
Hidden Valley ES — 700/K-6
3435 Bonita Vista Ln 95404 — 707-522-3180
Patricia McCaffrey, prin. — Fax 522-3181
Hidden Valley ES Satellite — 700/K-6
3555 Parker Hill Rd 95404 — 707-522-3190
Patricia McCaffrey, prin. — Fax 522-3193
Lehman ES — 400/K-6
1700 Jennings Ave 95401 — 707-522-3200
Beverley Jones, prin. — Fax 522-3195
Lincoln ES — 400/K-6
850 W 9th St 95401 — 707-522-3210
Barbara Babin, prin. — Fax 522-3213
Monroe ES — 400/K-6
2567 Marlow Rd 95403 — 707-522-3230
Rachel Valenzuela, prin. — Fax 522-3229
Proctor Terrace ES — 400/K-6
1711 Bryden Ln 95404 — 707-522-3240
Stephen Mayer, prin. — Fax 522-3249
Rincon Valley MS — 800/7-8
4650 Badger Rd 95409 — 707-528-5255
Matt Marshall, prin. — Fax 528-5644
Santa Rosa MS — 700/7-8
500 E St 95404 — 707-528-5281
Kathy Coker, prin. — Fax 528-5283
Slater MS — 800/7-8
3500 Sonoma Ave 95405 — 707-528-5241
Jason Lea, prin. — Fax 528-5733
Steele Lane ES — 400/K-6
301 Steele Ln 95403 — 707-522-3260
Barry Kelly, prin. — Fax 522-3256

Windsor USD
Supt. — See Windsor
Washburn ES — 500/K-1
75 Pleasant Ave 95403 — 707-837-7727
Benita Jones, prin. — Fax 837-7732

Wright ESD — 1,400/K-6
4385 Price Ave 95407 — 707-542-0550
Casey D'Angelo Ed.D., supt. — Fax 577-7962
www.wrightesd.org/
Stevens ES — 500/K-6
2345 Giffen Ave 95407 — 707-575-8883
Maxine Reagh, prin. — Fax 573-0317
Wilson ES — 500/K-6
246 Brittain Ln 95401 — 707-525-8350
Jane Futrell, prin. — Fax 525-0116
Wright ES — 400/K-6
4389 Price Ave 95407 — 707-542-0556
Terrena Rodebaugh, prin. — Fax 542-0418

Brush Creek Montessori S — 100/PK-8
1569 Brush Creek Rd 95404 — 707-539-7980
Susan Cohn, prin. — Fax 539-7549
Hall's New Song S — 100/K-12
233 Fairway Dr 95409 — 707-539-1725
Heidi Dafler-Hall, admin.
Merryhill Bennett Valley S — 200/K-8
4580 Bennett View Dr 95404 — 707-575-0910
Sherry Banks, prin.
Redwood Adventist Academy — 100/PK-12
385 Mark West Springs Rd 95404 — 707-545-1697
Rob Fenderson, prin. — Fax 545-8020
Rincon Valley Christian S — 300/PK-12
4585 Badger Rd 95409 — 707-539-1486
Brent Mitten, admin. — Fax 539-1493
St. Eugene Cathedral S — 400/PK-8
300 Farmers Ln 95405 — 707-545-7252
Barbara Gasparini, prin. — Fax 545-2594
St. Luke Lutheran S — 100/PK-8
905 Mendocino Ave 95401 — 707-545-0526
Marla Kuefner, prin. — Fax 544-2112
St. Rose S — 300/PK-8
4300 Old Redwood Hwy 95403 — 707-545-0379
Kathy Ryan, prin. — Fax 545-7150
Santa Rosa Christian S — 200/K-12
50 Mark West Springs Rd 95403 — 707-542-6414
Dr. Lois Sowers, hdmstr. — Fax 542-0421
Sonoma Country Day S — 300/K-8
4400 Day School Pl 95403 — 707-284-3200
Philip Nix, hdmstr. — Fax 284-3254
Summerfield Waldorf S — 400/PK-12
655 Willowside Rd 95401 — 707-575-7194
Fax 575-3217

Santa Rosa Vlly, Ventura
Pleasant Valley SD
Supt. — See Camarillo
Santa Rosa Technology Magnet S — 500/K-8
13282 Santa Rosa Rd, — 805-491-3822
Thomas Holtke, prin. — Fax 491-2702

Santa Ynez, Santa Barbara, Pop. 4,200
College ESD — 200/K-8
3525 Pine St 93460 — 805-686-7300
James Brown, supt. — Fax 686-7305
www.collegeschooldistrict.org
College ES — 100/K-1
3525 Pine St 93460 — 805-686-7300
Lorna Glenn, prin. — Fax 686-7305
Santa Ynez S — 200/2-8
3325 Pine St 93460 — 805-686-7310
Lorna Glenn, prin. — Fax 686-7340

Santa Ynez Valley Chrstian Academy — 100/K-8
891 N Refugio Rd 93460 — 805-688-3830
Susan Kindschy, admin. — Fax 686-9380

Santa Ysabel, San Diego
Spencer Valley ESD — 50/K-8
PO Box 159 92070 — 760-765-0336
Julie Weaver, supt. — Fax 765-3135
www.sdcoe.k12.ca.us/districts/spencer/welcome.html
Spencer Valley S — 50/K-8
PO Box 159 92070 — 760-765-0336
Julie Weaver, prin. — Fax 765-3135

Santee, San Diego, Pop. 52,306
Santee ESD — 6,300/K-8
9625 Cuyamaca St 92071 — 619-258-2300
Patrick Shaw, supt. — Fax 258-2305
www.santeesd.net/
Cajon Park S — 1,000/K-8
10300 N Magnolia Ave 92071 — 619-956-2400
Marcia Ginn-May, prin. — Fax 956-2408
Carlton Hills S — 600/K-8
9353 Pike Rd 92071 — 619-258-3400
Terry Heck, prin. — Fax 258-3414
Carlton Oaks S — 800/K-8
9353 Wethersfield Rd 92071 — 619-956-4500
Ann Bray, prin. — Fax 956-4509
Harritt S — 700/K-8
8120 Arlette St 92071 — 619-258-4800
Andrew Johnston, prin. — Fax 258-4816
Hill Creek S — 800/K-8
9665 Jeremy St 92071 — 619-956-5000
Jerelyn Lindsay, prin. — Fax 956-5014
Prospect Avenue S — 500/K-8
9303 Prospect Ave 92071 — 619-956-5200
Stephanie Southcott, prin. — Fax 956-5212
Rio Seco S — 800/K-8
9545 Cuyamaca St 92071 — 619-956-5500
Lisa McColl, prin. — Fax 956-5514
Sycamore Canyon ES — 300/K-6
10201 Settle Rd 92071 — 619-956-5400
Debra Simpson, prin. — Fax 956-5412
Other Schools – See El Cajon

San Ysidro, See San Diego
San Ysidro ESD — 4,000/K-8
4350 Otay Mesa Rd 92173 — 619-428-4476
Manuel Paul, supt. — Fax 428-1505
www.sysd.k12.ca.us

Beyer ES 300/K-3
2312 E Beyer Blvd 92173 619-428-1154
Ana Gonzalez, prin. Fax 428-6564
La Mirada ES 300/4-6
222 Avenida De La Madrid 92173 619-428-4424
Manuel Bojorquez, prin. Fax 428-0858
San Ysidro MS 1,000/7-8
4345 Otay Mesa Rd 92173 619-428-5551
David Torres, prin. Fax 690-2837
Smythe ES 500/K-3
1880 Smythe Ave 92173 619-428-4447
Manuela Colom, prin. Fax 428-0041
Sunset ES 800/K-6
3825 Sunset Ln 92173 619-428-1148
Jason Romero, prin. Fax 428-0065
Other Schools – See San Diego

South Bay UNSD
Supt. — See Imperial Beach
Nicoloff ES 1,000/K-6
1777 Howard Ave 92173 619-428-7000
Ruth Frazier, prin. Fax 428-7080

Our Lady of Mt. Carmel S 300/K-8
4141 Beyer Blvd 92173 619-428-2091
Sr. Ana Aceves, prin. Fax 428-8324

Saratoga, Santa Clara, Pop. 29,663
Campbell UNESD
Supt. — See Campbell
Marshall Lane ES 600/K-5
14114 Marilyn Ln 95070 408-364-4259
Claudia Gallaher, prin. Fax 341-7080

Cupertino UNSD
Supt. — See Cupertino
Blue Hills ES 500/K-5
12300 De Sanka Ave 95070 408-257-9282
Susan Tsolinas, prin. Fax 366-0611
McAuliffe S 500/K-8
12211 Titus Ave 95070 408-253-4696
Louise Ostrov, prin. Fax 865-0684

Saratoga UNESD 2,300/K-8
20460 Forrest Hills Dr 95070 408-867-3424
Lane Weiss, supt. Fax 867-2312
www.saratogausd.org
Argonaut ES 500/K-5
13200 Shadow Mountain Dr 95070 408-867-4773
Alex Chapman, prin. Fax 867-5737
Foothill ES 500/K-5
13919 Lynde Ave 95070 408-867-4036
Nancy Ondrejka, prin. Fax 867-7959
Redwood MS 900/6-8
13925 Fruitvale Ave 95070 408-867-3042
Kelly Green, prin. Fax 867-3195
Saratoga ES 400/K-5
14592 Oak St 95070 408-867-3476
Diane Smalley, prin. Fax 867-0538

Sacred Heart S 300/PK-8
13718 Saratoga Ave 95070 408-867-9241
Tom Pulchny, prin. Fax 867-9242
St. Andrew's S 300/PK-8
13601 Saratoga Ave 95070 408-867-3785
Harry McKay, admin. Fax 741-1852

Saugus, See Santa Clarita
Saugus UNESD
Supt. — See Santa Clarita
Bouquet Canyon ES 600/K-6
28110 Wellston Dr 91350 661-297-8865
Jeff Pettipas, prin. Fax 297-8633
Emblem ES 200/K-6
22635 Espuella Dr 91350 661-297-8870
Julie Bogosian, prin. Fax 296-3265
Foster ES 700/K-6
22500 Pamplico Dr 91350 661-297-8840
Gina Nolte, prin. Fax 297-8844
Highlands ES 700/K-6
27332 Catala Ave 91350 661-297-8875
Paul Martinsen, prin. Fax 297-8632
Mountainview ES 1,000/K-6
22201 Cypress Pl 91390 661-297-8835
Christine Hamlin, prin. Fax 297-8637
Plum Canyon ES 700/K-6
28360 Alfreds Way 91350 661-297-8621
Mary Jane Kelly, prin. Fax 297-8625
Rosedell ES 700/K-6
27853 Urbandale Ave 91350 661-297-8860
Cory Pak, prin. Fax 297-8619
Santa Clarita ES 600/K-6
27177 Seco Canyon Rd 91350 661-297-8845
Dianne Saunders, prin. Fax 297-8631

Sausalito, Marin, Pop. 7,184
Sausalito Marin CSD 100/K-8
630 Nevada St 94965 415-332-3190
Debra Bradley Ed.D., supt. Fax 332-9643
www.sausalitomarincityschools.org/
Bayside ES 100/K-6
630 Nevada St 94965 415-332-1024
Cherisse Baatin, prin. Fax 332-7816
King Jr Academy 50/7-8
630 Nevada St 94965 415-332-3573
Cherisse Baatin, prin. Fax 332-2492

Scotia, Humboldt
Scotia UNESD 200/K-8
PO Box 217 95565 707-764-2212
Jaenelle Lampp, supt. Fax 764-5111
www.humboldt.k12.ca.us/scotia_sd
Murphy S 200/K-8
PO Box 217 95565 707-764-2212
Jaenelle Lampp, prin. Fax 764-5111

Scotts Valley, Santa Cruz, Pop. 11,154
Scotts Valley USD 2,700/K-12
4444 Scotts Valley Dr Ste 5 95066 831-438-1820
Dr. Susan Silver, supt. Fax 438-1518
www.svusd.santacruz.k12.ca.us
Scotts Valley MS 600/6-8
8 Bean Creek Rd 95066 831-438-0610
Mary Lonhart, prin. Fax 439-8935
Vine Hill ES 600/K-5
151 Vine Hill School Rd 95066 831-438-1090
Kathy Dunton, prin. Fax 438-4087
Other Schools – See Santa Cruz

Baymonte Christian S 500/PK-8
5000B Granite Creek Rd 95066 831-438-0100
Steve Patterson, prin. Fax 438-0715

Seal Beach, Orange, Pop. 24,295
Los Alamitos USD
Supt. — See Los Alamitos
McGaugh ES 700/K-5
1698 Bolsa Ave 90740 562-799-4560
Daryle Palmer, prin. Fax 799-4570

Seaside, Monterey, Pop. 34,214
Monterey Peninsula USD
Supt. — See Monterey
Del Rey Woods ES 500/K-5
1281 Plumas Ave 93955 831-392-3907
Antonio Panganiban, prin. Fax 394-8207
Fitch MS 800/6-8
999 Coe Ave 93955 831-899-7080
Joan Nugent, prin. Fax 899-0663
Highland ES 500/K-5
1650 Sonoma Ave 93955 831-583-2024
Taffra Purnsley, prin. Fax 899-3857
King S 800/K-8
1713 Broadway Ave 93955 831-392-3970
Denise Estrella, prin. Fax 394-0859
Marshall ES 600/K-5
300 Normandy Rd 93955 831-899-7052
Bob Morgan, prin. Fax 899-4773
Ord Terrace ES 600/K-5
1755 La Salle Ave 93955 831-392-3922
Laura Thorpe, prin.
Seaside Childen's Center PK-PK
1450 Elm Ave 93955 831-899-7005
Sandra Wade, lead tchr. Fax 899-9238

Chartwell S 100/1-8
2511 Numa Watson Rd 93955 831-394-3468
Douglas Atkins, dir.
Monterey Bay Christian S 200/PK-8
1184 Hilby Ave 93955 831-899-2060
Albert Vredenburg, prin. Fax 899-1250
Peninsula Adventist S 50/K-8
1025 Mescal St 93955 831-394-5578
Sarah Seaman, prin. Fax 393-8530

Sebastopol, Sonoma, Pop. 7,598
Gravenstein UNESD 500/PK-8
3840 Twig Ave 95472 707-823-7008
Linda LaMarre, supt. Fax 823-2108
www.grav.k12.ca.us/
Gravenstein ES 300/PK-5
3840 Twig Ave 95472 707-823-5361
Linda LaMarre, prin. Fax 823-0478
Hillcrest MS 300/6-8
725 Bloomfield Rd 95472 707-823-7653
Keri Pugno, prin. Fax 823-4630

Oak Grove UNESD
Supt. — See Santa Rosa
Oak Grove ES 300/K-5
8760 Bower St 95472 707-823-5225
Beth Acosta, prin. Fax 829-2614

Sebastopol UNESD 900/K-8
7611 Huntley St 95472 707-829-4570
David Wheeler, supt. Fax 829-7427
www.sebusd.org/
Brook Haven MS 400/6-8
7905 Valentine Ave 95472 707-829-4590
Kent Cromwell, prin. Fax 829-6285
Park Side ES 300/K-3
7450 Bodega Ave 95472 707-829-7400
Laurie Whiteside, prin. Fax 829-7409
Pine Crest S 200/3-5
7285 Hayden Ave 95472 707-829-7411
Liz Schott, prin. Fax 829-7403

Twin Hills UNESD 300/K-5
700 Watertrough Rd 95472 707-823-0871
Les Crawford, supt. Fax 823-5832
www.thusd.k12.ca.us/
Apple Blossom ES 300/K-5
700 Watertrough Rd 95472 707-823-1041
Jill Rosenquist, prin. Fax 823-8946

Pleasant Hill Christian S 100/K-6
1782 Pleasant Hill Rd 95472 707-823-5868
Sandi King, admin. Fax 823-7092
Sebastopol Christian S 100/K-8
7789 Healdsburg Ave 95472 707-823-2754
Christine Siville, prin. Fax 823-5711

Seeley, Imperial, Pop. 1,228
Seeley UNESD 500/K-8
PO Box 868 92273 760-352-3571
Cathy Denton, supt. Fax 352-1629
www.seeley.k12.ca.us
Seeley S 500/K-8
PO Box 868 92273 760-352-3571
Ruben Castro, prin. Fax 352-1629

Seiad Valley, Siskiyou
Seiad ESD 50/K-8
PO Box 647 96086 530-496-3308
Carol Lawrence, supt. Fax 496-3310
Seiad S 50/K-8
PO Box 647 96086 530-496-3308
Carol Lawrence, prin. Fax 496-3310

Selma, Fresno, Pop. 22,261
Selma USD 6,400/K-12
3036 Thompson Ave 93662 559-898-6500
Mark Sutton, supt. Fax 896-7147
www.selma.k12.ca.us
Garfield ES 200/K-6
2535 B St 93662 559-898-6740
Gay Mukai, prin. Fax 896-6084
Indianola ES 500/K-6
11524 E Dinuba Ave 93662 559-898-6680
Victoria Armstrong, prin. Fax 896-0120
Jackson ES 700/K-6
2220 Huntsman Ave 93662 559-898-6690
Diane Clements, prin. Fax 891-8618
Lincoln MS 1,000/7-8
1239 Nelson Blvd 93662 559-898-6600
Drew Sylvia, prin. Fax 896-0733
Roosevelt ES 800/K-6
1802 Floral Ave 93662 559-898-6700
Tim Smith, prin. Fax 896-4655
Terry ES 200/K-6
12906 S Fowler Ave 93662 559-898-6710
Rosa Baly, prin. Fax 891-7889
Washington ES 200/K-1
1420 2nd St 93662 559-898-6720
Alicia Gonzalez, prin. Fax 891-8626
White ES 500/2-6
2001 Mitchell Ave 93662 559-898-6650
Sandra Aguilera, prin. Fax 891-0633
Wilson ES 400/K-6
1325 Stillman St 93662 559-898-6730
Brenda Sylvia, prin. Fax 898-0711

Valley Christian Academy 50/K-6
3200 McCall Ave 93662 559-896-2790
Jackie Gammon, prin. Fax 896-8742

Sepulveda, See Los Angeles
Los Angeles USD
Supt. — See Los Angeles
Gledhill Street ES 800/K-5
16030 Gledhill St 91343 818-894-1151
Marc Dyen, prin. Fax 894-2462
Langdon Avenue ES 1,200/K-5
8817 Langdon Ave 91343 818-892-0779
Leah Perrotti, prin. Fax 830-7532
Lassen ES 700/K-5
15017 Superior St 91343 818-892-8618
Dana Carter, prin. Fax 892-5731
Mayall Street ES 500/K-5
16701 Mayall St 91343 818-363-5058
Nancy Vallens, prin. Fax 831-3379
Noble Avenue ES 1,300/K-5
8329 Noble Ave 91343 818-892-1151
Cara Schneider, prin. Fax 830-1898
Parks Learning Center 1,000/K-5
8855 Noble Ave 91343 818-895-9620
Judith Schear, prin. Fax 894-4711
Plummer ES 1,000/K-5
9340 Noble Ave 91343 818-895-2481
Angel Barrett, prin. Fax 891-1594
Sepulveda MS 2,200/6-8
15330 Plummer St 91343 818-920-2130
Patricia Pelletier, prin. Fax 891-5754
Vintage Street Fundamental Magnet ES 700/K-5
15848 Stare St 91343 818-892-8661
John Rome, prin. Fax 830-9456

Our Lady of Peace S 300/PK-8
9022 Langdon Ave 91343 818-894-4059
Christopher Watson, prin. Fax 894-6759

Shafter, Kern, Pop. 14,569
Maple ESD 300/K-8
29161 Fresno Ave 93263 661-746-4439
Rebecca Devahl, supt. Fax 746-4765
www.maple.k12.ca.us/
Maple S 300/K-8
29161 Fresno Ave 93263 661-746-4439
Rebecca Devahl, prin. Fax 746-4765

Richland UNESD 2,700/K-8
331 N Shafter Ave 93263 661-746-8600
Kenneth Bergevin, supt. Fax 746-8614
www.richland.k12.ca.us
Golden Oak ES 700/K-6
331 N Shafter Ave 93263 661-746-8670
Rose Shannon, prin. Fax 746-8614
Redwood ES 700/K-6
331 N Shafter Ave 93263 661-746-8650
Heidi Witcher, prin. Fax 746-8614
Richland JHS 700/7-8
331 N Shafter Ave 93263 661-746-8630
Kathy Mayes, prin. Fax 746-8614
Sequoia ES 600/K-6
331 N Shafter Ave 93263 661-746-8740
Jason Hutchison, prin. Fax 746-8614

Kern SDA S 50/1-8
30105 Riverside St 93263 661-746-4467
Elaine Garcia, prin.

Shandon, San Luis Obispo
Shandon JUSD 400/K-12
PO Box 79 93461 805-238-0286
Chris Crawford, supt. Fax 238-0777
shandon.echalk.com
Shandon ES 200/K-6
PO Box 49 93461 805-238-1782
Dan Peverini, prin. Fax 238-6314
Other Schools – See San Miguel

Shasta, Shasta
Shasta UNESD 100/K-8
PO Box 1125 96087 530-225-0011
Dr. Diane Kempley, supt. Fax 241-5193
www.shastalink.k12.ca.us/sue/
Shasta S 100/K-8
PO Box 1125 96087 530-243-1110
Jim Lightner, prin. Fax 241-5193

Shasta Lake, Shasta, Pop. 10,233
Gateway USD
Supt. — See Redding
Grand Oaks ES 400/K-6
5309 Grand Ave 96019 530-275-7040
Steve Henson, prin. Fax 275-7045
Shasta Lake S 800/K-8
4620 Vallecito St 96019 530-275-7020
Helen Herd, prin. Fax 275-7025

Shaver Lake, Fresno
Sierra USD
Supt. — See Prather
Pole Corral S 50/K-8
65265 Hall Meadow Ln 93664 559-865-3639

Sheridan, Placer
Western Placer USD
Supt. — See Lincoln
Sheridan S 100/K-8
4730 H St 95681 530-633-2591
Kris Knutson, prin. Fax 633-9565

Sherman Oaks, See Los Angeles
Los Angeles USD
Supt. — See Los Angeles
Dixie Canyon Avenue ES 500/K-5
4220 Dixie Canyon Ave 91423 818-784-6283
Judith Dichter, prin. Fax 788-3340
Millikan MS 2,000/6-8
5041 Sunnyslope Ave 91423 818-528-1600
Derek Horowitz, prin. Fax 990-7651
Riverside Drive ES 700/K-5
13061 Riverside Dr 91423 818-990-4525
Jennifer Kessler, prin. Fax 789-4835
Sherman Oaks ES 800/K-5
14755 Greenleaf St 91403 818-784-8283
Kerry Harr, prin. Fax 981-8258

Bridgeport S 200/K-12
13130 Burbank Blvd 91401 818-781-0360
Pamela Clark, prin.
Buckley S 800/K-12
3900 Stansbury Ave 91423 818-783-1610
Dr. Larry Dougherty, hdmstr. Fax 461-6715
C & E Merdinian Armenian Evangelical S 200/PK-8
13330 Riverside Dr 91423 818-907-8149
Hovsep Injejikian, prin. Fax 907-6147
Emek Hebrew Academy 600/K-8
15365 Magnolia Blvd 91403 818-783-3663
Gabriela Shapiro, prin. Fax 783-3739
St. Francis De Sales S 300/PK-8
13368 Valleyheart Dr 91423 818-784-9573
Anthony Galla, prin. Fax 784-9649
Village Glen S 200/K-12
13130 Burbank Blvd 91401 818-781-0360
Pamela Clark, prin.

Shingle Springs, El Dorado, Pop. 2,049
Buckeye UNSD 4,700/K-8
PO Box 547 95682 530-677-2261
Teresa Wenig, supt. Fax 677-1015
www.buckeyeusd.org/
Buckeye ES 500/K-5
4561 Buckeye Rd 95682 530-677-2277
Deedra Devine, prin. Fax 672-1483
Other Schools – See Cameron Park, El Dorado Hills

Latrobe SD 200/K-8
7900 S Shingle Rd 95682 916-677-0260
Jean Pinotti, supt. Fax 672-0463
www.latrobeschool.com/
Latrobe ES 100/K-3
7900 S Shingle Rd 95682 530-677-0260
Jean Pinotti, prin. Fax 672-0463
Millers Hill S 100/4-8
7900 S Shingle Rd 95682 530-677-0260
Jean Pinotti, prin. Fax 672-0463

Providence Christian S 100/PK-8
3800 N Shingle Rd 95682 530-672-6657
Gail Gilbertson, admin. Fax 672-6189

Shingletown, Shasta
Black Butte UNESD 300/K-8
7752 Ponderosa Way 96088 530-474-3125
Don Aust, supt. Fax 474-3118
www.shastalink.k12.ca.us/bbutte/
Black Butte ES 200/K-6
7752 Ponderosa Way 96088 530-474-3125
Don Aust, prin. Fax 474-3118
Black Butte JHS 100/7-8
7946 Ponderosa Way 96088 530-474-3441
Don Aust, prin. Fax 474-1361

Shoshone, Inyo
Death Valley USD 100/K-12
PO Box 217 92384 760-852-4303
James Copeland, supt. Fax 852-4395
Death Valley ES 50/K-6
PO Box 217 92384 760-786-2318
James Copeland, prin. Fax 786-2193
Shoshone ES 50/K-6
PO Box 217 92384 760-852-4303
James Copeland, prin. Fax 852-4395
Tecopa-Francis ES 50/K-6
PO Box 217 92384 760-852-4530
James Copeland, prin. Fax 852-4395

Sierra Madre, Los Angeles, Pop. 10,988
Pasadena USD
Supt. — See Pasadena
Sierra Madre S 900/K-8
160 N Canon Ave 91024 626-355-1428
Gayle Bluemel, prin. Fax 355-0388

Bethany Christian S 300/PK-8
93 N Baldwin Ave 91024 626-355-3527
James Lugenbuehl, admin. Fax 355-0438
Gooden S 200/K-8
192 N Baldwin Ave 91024 626-355-2410
Patricia Patano, hdmstr. Fax 355-4212
St. Rita S 300/K-8
322 N Baldwin Ave 91024 626-355-6114
Joanne Harabedian, prin. Fax 355-0713

Sierraville, Sierra
Sierra-Plumas JUSD 500/K-12
PO Box 157 96126 530-994-1044
Stan Hardeman, supt. Fax 994-1045
www.sierra-coe.k12.ca.us
Other Schools – See Downieville, Loyalton

Signal Hill, Los Angeles, Pop. 10,851
Long Beach USD
Supt. — See Long Beach
Alvarado ES 400/K-5
1900 E 21st St, 562-985-0019
Brett Geithman, prin. Fax 494-8139
Burroughs ES 300/K-5
1260 E 33rd St, 562-426-8144
Teresa Montoya, prin. Fax 427-8495
Signal Hill ES 800/K-5
2285 Walnut Ave, 562-426-8170
Karen Williams, prin. Fax 426-6072

Simi Valley, Ventura, Pop. 118,687
Simi Valley USD 21,300/K-12
875 Cochran St 93065 805-520-6500
Kathryn Scroggin Ed.D., supt. Fax 520-6504
www.simi.k12.ca.us
Arroyo ES 400/K-6
225 Ulysses St 93065 805-306-4420
Nancy Mason, prin. Fax 520-6763
Atherwood ES 500/K-6
2350 Greensward St 93065 805-520-6730
Kathy Roth, prin. Fax 520-6738
Berylwood ES 800/K-6
2300 Heywood St 93065 805-520-6705
Nidia Grijalva-Imbler, prin. Fax 520-6102
Big Springs ES 600/K-6
3401 Big Springs Ave 93063 805-520-6710
Beverley Radloff, prin. Fax 520-6103
Crestview ES 500/K-6
900 Crosby Ave 93065 805-520-6715
Phil Ross, prin. Fax 520-6104
Garden Grove ES 500/K-6
2250 Tracy Ave 93063 805-520-6700
Mary Curtis, prin. Fax 520-6105
Hillside JHS 1,100/6-8
2222 Fitzgerald Rd 93065 805-520-6810
Sara Davis, prin. Fax 520-6156
Hollow Hills ES 700/K-6
828 Gibson Ave 93065 805-520-6720
Aldo Calcagno, prin. Fax 520-6106
Justin ES 400/K-6
2245 N Justin Ave 93065 805-520-6619
Marian Weaver, prin. Fax 520-6107
Katherine ES 500/K-6
5455 Katherine St 93063 805-520-6780
Sean Platt, prin. Fax 520-6108
Knolls ES 500/K-6
6334 Katherine Rd 93063 805-520-6735
Bonny Porter, prin. Fax 520-6109
Lincoln ES 400/K-6
1220 4th St 93065 805-520-6725
Brenda Montaine, prin. Fax 520-6727
Madera ES 400/K-6
250 Royal Ave 93065 805-520-6740
Suzanne Wolf, prin. Fax 520-6742
Mountain View ES 300/K-6
2925 Fletcher St 93065 805-520-6775
Irene Stambolos, prin. Fax 520-6110
Park View ES 400/K-6
1500 Alexander St 93065 805-520-6755
Tony Karch, prin. Fax 520-6120
Santa Susana ES 500/K-6
4300 Apricot Rd 93063 805-520-6765
Dr. Robin Hunter, prin. Fax 520-6121
Simi ES 300/K-6
2956 School St 93065 805-520-6760
Susan Koch, prin. Fax 520-6649
Sinaloa JHS 1,100/6-8
601 Royal Ave 93065 805-520-6830
Leslie Frank, prin. Fax 520-6835
Sycamore ES 400/K-6
2100 Ravenna St 93063 805-520-6745
Donna Stapleton, prin. Fax 520-6123
Township ES 500/K-6
4101 Township Ave 93063 805-520-6770
Laura Tyre, prin. Fax 520-6124
Valley View JHS 1,400/6-8
3347 Tapo St 93063 805-520-6820
Terry Webb, prin. Fax 520-6157
Vista ES 700/K-6
2175 Wisteria St 93065 805-520-6750
Denise Ferguson, prin. Fax 520-6752
White Oak ES 600/K-6
2201 Alscot Ave 93063 805-520-6617
Dolores Pekrul, prin. Fax 520-6126
Wood Ranch ES 700/K-6
455 Circle Knoll Dr 93065 805-579-6370
Ron Todo, prin. Fax 579-6373

Good Shepherd Lutheran S 100/K-8
2949 Alamo St 93063 805-526-2482
Nancy Hawthorne, prin. Fax 526-4857
Grace Brethren Preschool East 100/PK-PK
2762 Avenida Simi 93065 805-582-4270
Julia Chandler, dir. Fax 522-0702
Grace Brethren S 500/K-6
1717 Arcane St 93065 805-527-0101
Howard Lee, prin. Fax 527-4011
Heritage Christian Academy 100/K-12
1559 Rosita Dr 93065 805-428-2511
Cheryl Neher, admin.
Phoenix Ranch S, 1845 Oak Rd 93063 200/K-8
Frances Alascano, admin. 805-526-0136
Pinecrest S 300/PK-8
4974 Cochran St 93063 805-527-7764
Debra Adams, dir. Fax 527-8681
St. Rose of Lima S 300/1-8
1325 Royal Ave 93065 805-526-5304
Kathleen Barrantes, prin. Fax 526-0939
Simi Valley SDA S 50/K-8
1636 Sinaloa Rd 93065 805-583-1866
Timothy Kripps, prin. Fax 526-7657

Sloughhouse, Sacramento
Elk Grove USD
Supt. — See Elk Grove
Cosumnes River ES 500/K-6
13580 Jackson Rd 95683 916-682-2653
Michael Gulden, prin. Fax 682-5320

Smith River, Del Norte
Del Norte County USD
Supt. — See Crescent City
Smith River S 300/K-8
564 W First St 95567 707-464-0370
Paige Swan, prin. Fax 487-8932

Snelling, Merced
Merced River UNESD
Supt. — See Winton
Hopeton ES 100/K-3
2241 Turlock Rd 95369 209-722-4581
Dr. Helio Brasil, prin. Fax 563-1045

Snelling-Merced Falls UNESD 100/K-8
PO Box 189 95369 209-563-6414
Bette Woolstenhulme, supt. Fax 563-6672
Snelling-Merced Falls S 100/K-8
PO Box 189 95369 209-563-6414
Bette Woolstenhulme, prin. Fax 563-6672

Solana Beach, San Diego, Pop. 12,716
San Dieguito UNHSD
Supt. — See Encinitas
Warren MS 600/7-8
155 Stevens Ave 92075 858-755-1558
Anna Pedroza, prin. Fax 755-0891

Solana Beach ESD 2,700/K-6
309 N Rios Ave 92075 858-794-7100
Leslie Fausset, supt. Fax 794-7105
www.sbsd.k12.ca.us
Skyline ES 500/K-6
606 Lomas Santa Fe Dr 92075 858-794-3600
Lisa Denham, prin. Fax 755-3650
Solana Vista ES 400/K-3
780 Santa Victoria 92075 858-794-3700
Lisa Platt, prin. Fax 794-3750
Other Schools – See Rancho Santa Fe, San Diego

St. James Academy 300/K-8
623 S Nardo Ave 92075 858-755-1777
Kathryn Dunn, prin. Fax 755-3124
Santa Fe Christian S 1,000/PK-12
838 Academy Dr 92075 858-755-8900
Tom Bennett, hdmstr. Fax 755-2480
Santa Fe Montessori S 200/PK-6
PO Box 745 92075 858-755-3232
Walter Huebscher, prin. Fax 755-1460

Soledad, Monterey, Pop. 27,210
Mission UNESD 100/K-8
36825 Foothill Rd 93960 831-678-3524
Jerry Tollefson, supt. Fax 678-0491
Mission S 100/K-8
36825 Foothill Rd 93960 831-678-3524
Elizabeth Bozzo, prin. Fax 678-0491

Soledad USD 4,200/K-12
PO Box 186 93960 831-678-3987
Jorge Guzman, supt. Fax 678-2866
www.soledad.monterey.k12.ca.us/
Ferrero ES 400/K-6
400 Entrada Dr 93960 831-678-6480
Julie Brush, prin. Fax 678-4241
Franscion ES 400/K-6
779 Orchard Ln 93960 831-678-6340
Jeanne Hernandez-Tutop, prin. Fax 678-3442
Gabilan ES 400/K-6
330 N Walker Dr 93960 831-678-6440
Terri Lambert, prin. Fax 678-3467
Ledesma ES 600/K-6
973 Vista de Soledad 93960 831-678-6320
Jamie Mumau, prin. Fax 678-8029
Main Street MS 600/7-8
441 Main St 93960 831-678-6460
Lori Villanueva, prin. Fax 678-0797
San Vincente ES 600/K-6
1300 Metz Rd 93960 831-678-6420
Ellen Brusa, prin. Fax 678-2786

Liberty Christian S 50/K-12
274 Kidder St 93960 831-678-2885
Barbara Stewart, admin. Fax 678-2804

Solvang, Santa Barbara, Pop. 5,141
Solvang ESD 600/K-8
565 Atterdag Rd 93463 805-688-4810
Thomas Allcock, supt. Fax 688-7012
www.solvangschool.org

Solvang S 600/K-8
565 Atterdag Rd 93463 805-688-4810
Lisa O'Neill, prin. Fax 688-7012

Somerset, El Dorado
Indian Diggings ESD 50/K-8
6020 Omo Ranch Rd 95684 530-620-6546
James Vardy, supt. Fax 620-8690
www.edcoe.k12.ca.us/districts/idsd.html
Indian Diggings S 50/K-8
6020 Omo Ranch Rd 95684 530-620-6546
James Vardy, prin. Fax 620-8690

Pioneer UNESD 400/K-8
6862 Mount Aukum Rd 95684 530-620-3556
Richard Williams, supt. Fax 620-4932
pioneer.k12.ca.us/
Mountain Creek MS 200/6-8
6862 Mount Aukum Rd 95684 530-620-4393
Jeannine Wheeler, prin. Fax 620-6509
Pioneer ES 300/K-5
6862 Mount Aukum Rd 95684 530-620-7210
Jeannine Wheeler, prin. Fax 620-9509
Other Schools – See Grizzly Flats

Somesbar, Siskiyou
Junction ESD 50/K-8
98821 Highway 96 95568 530-469-3373
Michael Stearns, supt. Fax 469-3390
www.sisnet.ssku.k12.ca.us/~junctftp/
Junction S 50/K-8
98821 Highway 96 95568 530-469-3373
Michael Stearns, prin. Fax 469-3390

Somis, Ventura
Mesa UNESD 600/K-8
3901 Mesa School Rd 93066 805-485-1411
Dr. John Puglisi, supt. Fax 485-4387
www.mesaschool.org/
Mesa S 600/K-8
3901 Mesa School Rd 93066 805-485-1411
Marilyn Renger, prin. Fax 485-4387

Somis UNESD 400/K-8
PO Box 900 93066 805-386-8258
Mary McKee, supt. Fax 386-2324
www.somis.k12.ca.us
Somis S 400/K-8
PO Box 900 93066 805-386-5711
Mary McKee, prin. Fax 386-4596

Sonoma, Sonoma, Pop. 9,885
Sonoma Valley USD 4,400/K-12
17850 Railroad Ave 95476 707-935-6000
Pamela Martens Ph.D., supt. Fax 939-2235
www.sonomavly.k12.ca.us
Altimira MS 500/6-8
17805 Arnold Dr 95476 707-935-6020
Sydney Smith, prin. Fax 935-6027
El Verano ES 400/K-5
18606 Riverside Dr 95476 707-935-6050
Maite Iturri, prin. Fax 935-4256
Flowery ES 400/K-5
17600 Sonoma Hwy 95476 707-935-6060
Esmerelda Moseley, prin. Fax 935-4256
Harrison MS 500/6-8
1150 Broadway 95476 707-935-6080
Karla Conroy, prin. Fax 935-6083
Prestwood ES 500/K-5
343 E MacArthur St 95476 707-935-6030
Beth Wolk, prin. Fax 935-4262
Sassarini ES 400/K-5
652 5th St W 95476 707-935-6040
Leticia Cruz Ed.D., prin. Fax 935-6049
Other Schools – See Glen Ellen

St. Francis Solano S 300/K-8
342 W Napa St 95476 707-996-4994
Lydia Blecksmith Ed.D., prin. Fax 996-2662

Sonora, Tuolumne, Pop. 4,668
Belleview ESD 200/K-8
22736 Kuien Mill Rd 95370 209-586-5510
T. Kevin Hart, supt. Fax 586-5516
www.belleview.k12.ca.us/
Belleview S 200/K-8
22736 Kuien Mill Rd 95370 209-586-5510
T. Kevin Hart, prin. Fax 586-5516

Curtis Creek ESD 600/K-8
18755 Standard Rd 95370 209-533-1083
Britta Skavdahl, supt. Fax 532-6080
www.ccreek.k12.ca.us/
Curtis Creek S 500/K-8
18755 Standard Rd 95370 209-532-1428
Terri Bell, prin. Fax 588-9593
Sullivan Creek ES 200/K-5
16331 Hidden Valley Rd 95370 209-532-9756
Elizabeth Burr, prin. Fax 532-8557

Sonora ESD 900/K-8
830 Greenley Rd 95370 209-532-5491
Marguerite Bulkin, supt. Fax 532-4828
www.ses.k12.ca.us/
Sonora S 900/K-8
830 Greenley Rd 95370 209-532-3159
Pam Vlach, prin. Fax 532-7244

Mother Lode Adventist Junior Academy 100/K-10
80 N Forest Rd 95370 209-532-2855
Emily Villeda, prin. Fax 532-7757

Soquel, Santa Cruz, Pop. 9,188
Mountain ESD 200/K-6
3042 Old San Jose Rd 95073 831-475-6812
Ken Miller, supt. Fax 464-7200
www.mountain.santacruz.k12.ca.us
Mountain ES 200/K-6
3042 Old San Jose Rd 95073 831-475-6812
Ken Miller, prin. Fax 464-7200

Santa Cruz CSD 7,000/K-12
405 Old San Jose Rd 95073 831-429-3410
Gary Bloom, supt. Fax 429-3439
www.sccs.santacruz.k12.ca.us
Other Schools – See Santa Cruz

Soquel UNESD
Supt. — See Capitola
Main Street ES 500/K-5
3430 N Main St 95073 831-464-5650
Brenda Payne, prin. Fax 462-6295
Soquel ES 400/K-5
2700 Porter St 95073 831-464-5655
Eric Gross, prin. Fax 475-4678

Soulsbyville, Tuolumne, Pop. 1,732
Soulsbyville ESD 600/K-8
20300 Soulsbyville Rd 95372 209-532-1419
Jeff Winfield, supt. Fax 532-4371
www.soulsbyville.k12.ca.us
Soulsbyville S 600/K-8
20300 Soulsbyville Rd 95372 209-532-1419
Bart Taylor, prin. Fax 533-2922

South El Monte, Los Angeles, Pop. 21,666
Valle Lindo ESD 1,300/K-8
1431 Central Ave 91733 626-580-0610
Mary Labrucherie, supt. Fax 575-1534
www.vallelindo.k12.ca.us/
New Temple ES 500/K-3
11033 Central Ave 91733 626-580-0692
John Gannon, prin. Fax 580-0691
Shively MS 700/4-8
1431 Central Ave 91733 626-580-0610
Lynn Bulgin, prin. Fax 575-1534

Epiphany S 200/PK-8
10915 Michael Hunt Dr 91733 626-442-6264
Gina Garcia, prin. Fax 442-6074

South Gate, Los Angeles, Pop. 98,897
Los Angeles USD
Supt. — See Los Angeles
Bryson ES 1,200/K-5
4470 Missouri Ave 90280 323-569-7141
Lisa Trujillo, prin. Fax 567-5386
Independence ES 900/K-5
8435 Victoria Ave 90280 323-249-9559
Kathleen Hannum, prin. Fax 564-9165
Liberty Boulevard ES 800/K-5
2728 Liberty Blvd 90280 323-583-4196
Leo Garcia, prin. Fax 589-5680
Madison ES 600/K-5
9820 Madison Ave 90280 323-568-3900
Gretchen Young, prin. Fax 357-0301
Montara Avenue ES 900/K-5
10018 Montara Ave 90280 323-567-1451
Juana Cortez, prin. Fax 249-7394
San Gabriel Avenue ES 900/K-5
8628 San Gabriel Ave 90280 323-567-1488
Beatriz Gonzalez, prin. Fax 563-3762
San Miguel Avenue ES 1,200/K-5
9801 San Miguel Ave 90280 323-567-0511
Andrea Johnson, prin. Fax 249-0997
Southeast Area MS 1,400/6-8
2560 Tweedy Blvd 90280 323-568-3100
Wanda Sequeira, prin. Fax 564-9398
South Gate MS 3,000/6-8
4100 Firestone Blvd 90280 323-568-4000
German Cerda, prin. Fax 564-7434
Stanford ES 1,000/K-5
2833 Illinois Ave 90280 323-569-8117
Mark Reiland, prin. Fax 569-1786
Stanford Primary Center 200/K-K
3020 Kansas Ave 90280 323-563-9208
Romero Gogue, prin. Fax 563-9225
State ES 1,100/K-5
3211 Santa Ana St 90280 323-582-7358
Cora Watkins, prin. Fax 582-5981
Tweedy ES 700/K-5
9724 Pinehurst Ave 90280 323-568-2828
Paula Morrell, prin. Fax 249-1788
Victoria ES 900/K-5
3320 Missouri Ave 90280 323-567-1261
Lynne Uyehara, prin. Fax 563-2056

Paramount USD
Supt. — See Paramount
Hollydale S 1,100/K-8
5511 Century Blvd 90280 562-602-8016
Susan Marilley, prin. Fax 602-8017

Redeemer Lutheran S 100/K-8
2626 Liberty Blvd 90280 323-588-0934
Bridget Valadez, prin. Fax 588-0701
St. Helen S 300/PK-8
9329 Madison Ave 90280 323-566-5491
Sr. Mary Wahl, prin. Fax 566-2810

South Lake Tahoe, El Dorado, Pop. 24,016
Lake Tahoe USD 4,300/K-12
1021 Al Tahoe Blvd 96150 530-541-2850
Dr. James Tarwater, supt. Fax 541-5930
www.ltusd.org/
Bijou Community S 500/K-5
3501 Spruce Ave 96150 530-543-2337
Karen Tinlin, prin. Fax 543-2342
Lake Tahoe Environmental Sci Magnet S 300/K-5
1095 E San Bernardino Ave 96150 530-543-2371
James Tarwater, prin. Fax 543-2375
Sierra House ES 500/K-5
1709 Remington Trl 96150 530-543-2327
Ryan Galles, prin. Fax 543-2330
South Tahoe MS 1,000/6-8
2940 Lake Tahoe Blvd 96150 530-541-6404
Beth Delacour, prin. Fax 541-4624
Tahoe Valley ES 500/K-5
943 Tahoe Island Dr 96150 530-543-2350
Mark Romagnolo, prin. Fax 543-2362

St. Theresa S 200/PK-8
1081 Lyons Ave 96150 530-544-8944
Dannette Winslow, prin. Fax 544-8909

South Pasadena, Los Angeles, Pop. 24,889
South Pasadena USD 4,300/K-12
1020 El Centro St 91030 626-441-5800
Brian Bristol Ed.D., supt. Fax 441-5815
www.spusd.net
Arroyo Vista ES 600/K-5
335 El Centro St 91030 626-441-5840
Rebecca Speh, prin. Fax 441-5845
Marengo ES 600/K-5
1400 Marengo Ave 91030 626-441-5850
Betsy Hamilton, prin. Fax 441-5855
Monterey Hills ES 500/K-5
1624 Via Del Rey 91030 626-441-5860
Joe Johnson, prin. Fax 441-5865
South Pasadena MS 1,100/6-8
1600 Oak St 91030 626-441-5830
Fax 441-5835

Almansor Center 100/K-12
1955 Fremont Ave 91030 323-257-3006
Jason Rubin, prin.
Holy Family S 300/K-8
1301 Rollin St 91030 626-799-4354
Carolyn Strong, prin. Fax 403-6180
St. James Parish Day S 200/PK-K
1325 Monterey Rd 91030 626-799-6906
Fax 799-4272

South San Francisco, San Mateo, Pop. 60,735
South San Francisco USD 9,300/PK-12
398 B St 94080 650-877-8700
Howard Cohen, supt. Fax 583-4717
www.ssfusd.org
Alta Loma MS 800/6-8
116 Romney Ave 94080 650-877-8797
Lou Delorio, prin. Fax 877-8824
Buri Buri ES 600/K-5
120 El Campo Dr 94080 650-877-8776
Joseph Spaulding, prin. Fax 583-5742
Childrens Center PK-PK
530 Tamarack Ln 94080 650-877-8836
Sheryl Chan, prin. Fax 877-5232
Los Cerritos ES 400/K-5
210 W Orange Ave 94080 650-877-8841
Jammie Behrendt, prin. Fax 589-8093
Martin ES 400/K-5
35 School St 94080 650-877-3955
Rona Jawetz, prin. Fax 877-3957
Parkway Heights MS 600/6-8
650 Sunset Ave 94080 650-877-8788
Jay Rowley, prin. Fax 225-9427
Ponderosa ES 400/K-5
295 Ponderosa Rd 94080 650-877-8825
Janet Ingersoll, prin. Fax 583-8275
Spruce ES 500/K-5
501 Spruce Ave 94080 650-877-8780
Riza Gutierrez, prin. Fax 589-9376
Sunshine Gardens ES 400/K-5
1200 Miller Ave 94080 650-877-8784
Sheila Milosky, prin. Fax 877-5285
Westborough MS 700/6-8
2570 Westborough Blvd 94080 650-877-8848
Beth Orofino, prin. Fax 871-5356
Other Schools – See Daly City, San Bruno

All Souls S 300/K-8
479 Miller Ave 94080 650-583-3562
Vincent Riener, prin. Fax 952-1167
Hillside Christian Academy 100/PK-4
1415 Hillside Blvd 94080 650-588-6866
Michael Coutts, admin. Fax 588-6827
St. Veronica S 300/K-8
434 Alida Way 94080 650-589-3909
Teresa Pallitto, prin. Fax 589-2826

South San Gabriel, Los Angeles, Pop. 7,700
Montebello USD
Supt. — See Montebello
Potrero Heights ES 500/K-5
8026 Hill Dr, Rosemead CA 91770 626-307-7010
Jill Rojas, prin. Fax 307-7013

Spreckels, Monterey
Spreckels UNESD 900/K-8
PO Box 7362 93962 831-455-2550
Harold Kahn Ed.D., supt. Fax 455-1871
schools.monterey.k12.ca.us/~sprckldo/
Spreckels ES 500/K-5
PO Box 7308 93962 831-455-1831
Harold Kahn Ed.D., prin. Fax 455-0786
Other Schools – See Salinas

Spring Valley, San Diego, Pop. 27,100
La Mesa-Spring Valley SD
Supt. — See La Mesa
Avondale ES 500/K-5
8401 Stansbury St 91977 619-668-5880
Claudia Burris, prin. Fax 668-8330
Bancroft ES 400/K-5
8805 Tyler St 91977 619-668-5890
Dr. Lois DeKock, prin. Fax 668-8335
Casa De Oro ES 400/K-5
10227 Ramona Dr 91977 619-668-5715
Dr. John Parsons, prin. Fax 668-8337
Highlands ES 400/K-5
3131 S Barcelona St 91977 619-668-5780
Eileen Cotter, prin. Fax 668-8320
Kempton Street ES 800/K-5
740 Kempton St 91977 619-668-5870
Elisa Holston, prin. Fax 668-8317
La Presa ES 500/K-5
519 La Presa Ave 91977 619-668-5790
Peter Dean, prin. Fax 668-5795

La Presa MS 1,000/6-8
1001 Leland St 91977 619-668-5720
Mike Allmann, prin. Fax 668-8305
Loma ES 500/K-5
10355 Loma Ln 91978 619-668-5862
Mary Beason, prin. Fax 670-6839
Rancho ES 400/K-5
8845 Noeline Ave 91977 619-668-5885
Andrew Smith, prin. Fax 668-8339
Spring Valley MS 1,300/6-8
3900 Conrad Dr 91977 619-668-5750
Dana Wright, prin. Fax 668-8302
Sweetwater Springs Community ES 500/K-5
10129 Austin Dr 91977 619-668-5895
Monica Robinson, prin. Fax 668-8324

Santa Sophia Academy 200/PK-8
9806 San Juan St 91977 619-463-0488
Karen Laaperi, prin. Fax 668-5469
Trinity Christian S 200/PK-8
3902 Kenwood Dr 91977 619-462-6440
Sharlene Park, prin. Fax 462-4011

Springville, Tulare
Springville UNESD 400/K-8
PO Box 349 93265 559-539-2605
Connie Owens, supt. Fax 539-5616
www.springvilleschool.org/
Springville S 400/K-8
PO Box 349 93265 559-539-2605
Connie Owens, prin. Fax 539-5616

Stanford, Santa Clara, Pop. 18,097
Palo Alto USD
Supt. — See Palo Alto
Escondido ES 500/K-5
890 Escondido Rd 94305 650-856-1337
Gary Prehn, prin. Fax 424-1079

Stanton, Orange, Pop. 37,661
Garden Grove USD
Supt. — See Garden Grove
Carver ES 300/K-6
11150 Santa Rosalia St 90680 714-663-6437
Jan Schmidt, prin. Fax 663-6428

Magnolia ESD
Supt. — See Anaheim
Pyles ES 900/K-6
10411 Dale Ave 90680 714-761-6324
Dianna Rangel, prin. Fax 229-5832

St. Polycarp S 100/K-8
8182 Chapman Ave 90680 714-893-8882
Theresa Wyles, prin. Fax 897-3357

Stevenson Ranch, Los Angeles
Newhall ESD
Supt. — See Valencia
Pico Canyon ES 900/K-6
25255 Pico Canyon Rd 91381 661-291-4080
Laura Banda, prin. Fax 291-4081
Stevenson Ranch ES 1,000/K-6
25820 Carroll Ln 91381 661-291-4070
Candace Fleece, prin. Fax 291-4071

William S. Hart UNHSD
Supt. — See Santa Clarita
Rancho Pico JHS 900/7-8
26250 Valencia Blvd 91381 661-284-3260
Michele Krantz, prin. Fax 255-7523

Stevinson, Merced
Hilmar USD
Supt. — See Hilmar
Merquin ES 200/K-5
20316 3rd Ave 95374 209-634-4938
Geraldine Eastman, lead tchr. Fax 634-1542

Stewarts Point, Sonoma
Kashia ESD 50/K-8
PO Box 129 95480 707-322-5484
Les Crawford, supt. Fax 785-2802
Kashia S 50/K-8
PO Box 129 95480 707-785-9682
Mary Caponio, lead tchr. Fax 785-2802

Stockton, San Joaquin, Pop. 286,926
Escalon USD
Supt. — See Escalon
Collegeville ES 200/K-5
6701 S Jack Tone Rd 95215 209-941-2007
Bob Amato, prin. Fax 462-7126

Lincoln USD 8,300/PK-12
2010 W Swain Rd 95207 209-953-8700
Steve Lowder Ed.D., supt. Fax 474-7817
www.lusd.net
Barron S 700/K-8
6835 Cumberland Pl 95219 209-953-8796
Ellen Wehrs, prin. Fax 478-2736
Brookside S 800/K-8
2962 Brookside Rd 95219 209-953-8642
Fax 953-8640
Colonial Heights S 500/K-8
8135 Balboa Ave 95209 209-953-8783
Maureen Oechel, prin. Fax 953-8785
Knoles S 500/PK-8
6511 Clarksburg Pl 95207 209-953-8775
Kelly Sandstrom, prin. Fax 474-2107
Landeen S 700/K-8
4128 Feather River Dr 95219 209-953-8660
Pam Warman, prin. Fax 953-8821
Lincoln ES 500/K-6
818 W Lincoln Rd 95207 209-953-8652
Scott Tatum, prin. Fax 953-8651
Riggio S 600/K-8
3110 Brookside Rd 95219 209-953-8753
Joan Calonico, prin. Fax 953-8823

Sierra MS 500/7-8
6768 Alexandria Pl 95207 209-953-8749
Terry Asplund, prin. Fax 953-8747
Williams S 500/K-8
2450 Meadow Ave 95207 209-953-8768
Nancy Martin, prin. Fax 952-4642

Linden USD
Supt. — See Linden
Glenwood S 500/K-8
2005 N Alpine Rd 95215 209-931-3229
Gary Phillips, prin. Fax 931-2612
Waterloo MS 400/5-8
7007 Pezzi Rd 95215 209-931-0818
Mike McCandless, prin. Fax 931-2915
Waverly S 300/K-8
3507 Wilmarth Rd 95215 209-931-0735
Lisa Pettis, prin. Fax 931-3509

Lodi USD
Supt. — See Lodi
Adams ES 900/K-6
9275 Glacier Point Dr 95212 209-953-9506
Patti Morone, prin. Fax 953-9603
Clairmont ES 500/K-6
8282 Le Mans Ave 95210 209-953-8267
Susan Hitchcock, prin. Fax 953-8276
Creekside ES 800/K-6
2515 Estate Dr 95209 209-953-8285
Brandon Krueger, prin. Fax 953-8296
Davis ES 400/K-6
5224 E Morada Ln 95212 209-953-8301
Tim Shepherd, prin. Fax 953-8304
Delta Sierra MS 600/7-8
2255 Wagner Heights Rd 95209 209-953-8510
Steven Takemoto, prin. Fax 953-8139
Elkhorn MS 300/4-8
10505 Davis Rd 95209 209-953-8312
Scott McGregor, prin. Fax 953-8319
McAuliffe MS 900/7-8
3880 Iron Canyon Cir 95209 209-953-9431
Randy Malandro, prin. Fax 953-9430
Morada MS 900/7-8
5001 Eastview Dr 95212 209-953-8490
Janet Perez, prin. Fax 953-8502
Morgan ES 700/K-6
3777 A G Spanos Blvd 95209 209-953-8453
Jan Glassco, prin. Fax 953-8090
Mosher ES 400/K-6
3220 Buddy Holly Dr 95212 209-953-9298
Harold Brown, prin. Fax 953-3218
Muir ES 700/K-6
2303 Whistler Way 95209 209-953-8106
Virginia Medford, prin. Fax 953-8110
Oakwood ES 700/K-6
1315 Woodcreek Way 95209 209-953-8392
Denice Shigematsu, prin. Fax 953-8004
Parklane ES 600/K-3
8405 Tam O Shanter Dr 95210 209-953-8410
Princetta Purkins, prin. Fax 953-8084
Silva ES 700/K-6
6250 Scotts Creek Dr 95219 209-953-9302
Dan Faith, prin. Fax 953-9309
Sutherland ES 400/4-6
550 Spring River Cir 95210 209-953-8999
Allison Gerrity, prin. Fax 953-8031
Wagner-Holt ES 600/PK-6
8778 Brattle Pl 95209 209-953-8407
Janet Rogers, prin. Fax 953-8403
Westwood ES 600/K-6
9444 Caywood Dr 95210 209-953-8333
Mary Miller, prin. Fax 953-8337

Manteca USD
Supt. — See Lathrop
Great Valley S 1,400/K-8
4223 McDougald Blvd 95206 209-234-1130
Sonya Arellano, prin. Fax 858-3094
Knodt S 1,000/K-8
3939 Ews Woods Blvd 95206 209-938-6200
Frank Souza, prin. Fax 938-6219
Komure S 1,300/K-8
2121 Henry Long Blvd 95206 209-234-4812
JoElla Allen, prin. Fax 234-8763

Stockton USD 34,700/K-12
701 N Madison St 95202 209-933-7000
Anthony Amato, supt. Fax 933-7071
www.stockton.k12.ca.us
Adams S 700/K-8
6402 Inglewood Ave 95207 209-933-7155
Pam Whitted, prin. Fax 952-9208
August S 600/K-8
2101 Sutro Ave 95205 209-933-7160
Diane Hernandez-Dutra, prin. Fax 463-1179
Bush S 800/K-8
5420 Fred Russo Dr 95212 209-933-7350
Sylvia Ulmer, prin. Fax 473-9792
Cleveland S 800/K-8
20 E Fulton St 95204 209-933-7165
Heidi Mohammadkhan, prin. Fax 943-6592
El Dorado S 700/K-8
1540 N Lincoln St 95204 209-933-7175
Teresa Oden, prin. Fax 465-4358
Elmwood S 800/K-8
840 S Cardinal Ave 95215 209-933-7180
John Semillo, prin. Fax 465-1042
Fillmore S 800/K-8
2644 E Poplar St 95205 209-933-7185
Gina Hall, prin. Fax 467-3672
Fremont S 700/K-8
2021 E Flora St 95205 209-933-7385
Marlesse Cavazos, prin. Fax 466-7342
Grant S 300/K-8
1800 S Sutter St 95206 209-933-7195
Suzanne Loera, prin. Fax 943-7716
Grunsky S 600/K-8
1550 School Ave 95205 209-933-7200
Michael Sousa, prin. Fax 467-3190

Hamilton S 700/K-8
2245 E 11th St 95206 209-933-7395
Dr. Gurmel Singh, prin. Fax 464-4851
Harrison S 600/K-8
3203 Sanguinetti Ln 95205 209-933-7205
Henry Phillips, prin. Fax 948-3345
Hazelton S 500/K-6
535 W Jefferson St 95206 209-933-7210
Olivia Castillo, prin. Fax 465-5925
Henry S, 1107 S Wagner Ave 95215 800/K-8
Yanik Ruley, prin. 209-933-7490
Hoover S 700/K-8
2900 Kirk St 95204 209-933-7215
Janna Schumacher, prin. Fax 943-6207
Huerta S 400/K-8
1644 S Lincoln St 95206 209-933-7220
Sandra Lepe, prin. Fax 933-7221
Kennedy S 700/K-8
630 Ponce De Leon Ave 95210 209-933-7225
Suzanne Anderson, prin. Fax 474-6449
King S 900/K-8
2640 E Lafayette St 95205 209-933-7230
Connie Fabian, prin. Fax 466-4528
Kingston S 800/K-8
6324 N Alturas Ave 95207 209-933-7493
Ruben Garza, prin. Fax 478-3256
Kohl Open S 200/K-8
4115 Crown Ave 95207 209-933-7235
Bud West, prin. Fax 472-7425
Madison S 800/K-8
2939 Mission Rd 95204 209-933-7240
Carol Becker, prin. Fax 942-0438
Marshall S 600/K-8
1141 Lever Blvd 95206 209-933-7405
Dr. Ron Small, prin. Fax 466-4962
McKinley S 700/K-8
30 W 9th St 95206 209-933-7245
Danielle Valtierra, prin. Fax 948-2260
Monroe S 600/K-8
2236 E 11th St 95206 209-933-7250
Girlie Hale, prin. Fax 948-2648
Montezuma S 700/K-8
2843 Farmington Rd 95205 209-933-7255
James Cowan, prin. Fax 465-4036
Nightingale S 500/K-8
1721 Carpenter Rd 95206 209-933-7260
Kathryn Byers, prin. Fax 234-1850
Pittman S 700/K-7
701 E Park St 95202 209-933-7040
Adrienne Machado, prin. Fax 942-2769
Pulliam S 700/K-8
230 Presidio Way 95207 209-933-7265
Vendetta Brown, prin. Fax 473-3540
Rio Calaveras S 900/K-8
1819 E Bianchi Rd 95210 209-933-7270
Barbara Miller, prin. Fax 957-5182
Roosevelt S 600/K-8
776 S Broadway Ave 95205 209-933-7275
Reyes Gauna, prin. Fax 946-0657
San Joaquin S 700/K-8
2020 S Fresno Ave 95206 209-933-7280
Nicholle Medina, prin. Fax 467-7057
Taft S 500/K-8
419 Downing Ave 95206 209-933-7285
Dee Johnson, prin. Fax 982-4257
Taylor S 600/K-8
1101 Lever Blvd 95206 209-933-7290
Jacquelyne Green, prin. Fax 462-7143
Tyler S 700/K-8
3830 Webster Ave 95204 209-933-7295
Louie Campos, prin. Fax 943-7631
Van Buren S 600/K-7
1628 E 10th St 95206 209-933-7305
Lynn Johnson, prin. Fax 466-3705
Victory S 600/K-8
1838 W Rose St 95203 209-933-7310
Mitchell Kanter, prin. Fax 948-2259
Washington S 200/K-8
1735 W Sonora St 95203 209-933-7320
Laurie Leffler, prin. Fax 943-6209
Wilson S 300/K-8
150 E Mendocino Ave 95204 209-933-7325
Mingo Greco, prin. Fax 948-3480

Tracy JUSD
Supt. — See Tracy
Delta Island S 200/K-8
11022 Howard Rd 95206 209-830-3306
Carla Washington, prin. Fax 830-3307

Annunciation S 300/PK-8
1110 N Lincoln St 95203 209-444-4000
Carla Donaldson, prin. Fax 444-4013
Children's Home of Stockton 100/K-12
PO Box 201068 95201 209-466-0853
Michael Dutra, dir.
First Baptist Christian S 200/K-8
3535 N El Dorado St 95204 209-466-1577
Nan Beattie, prin. Fax 466-4337
Lakside Christian S 500/K-8
2111 Quail Lakes Dr 95207 209-954-7653
Jessica Carter, prin. Fax 954-7670
Merryhill S 300/K-8
4811 Riverbrook Dr 95219 209-477-9005
Presentation S 300/K-8
1635 W Benjamin Holt Dr 95207 209-472-2140
Diane Rothschild, prin. Fax 320-1515
St. George S 200/K-8
144 W 5th St 95206 209-463-1540
Frank Remkiewicz, prin. Fax 463-2707
St. Luke S 300/PK-8
4005 N Sutter St 95204 209-464-0801
Patricia Simon, prin. Fax 466-1150
Sierra Christian S 100/K-8
4368 N Sutter St 95204 209-941-2877
Alan Perkins, prin. Fax 288-1858

Stockton Christian S — 300/K-12
9021 West Ln 95210 — 209-957-3043
Harry Meeks, admin. — Fax 957-4120
Stockton SDA S — 50/K-8
PO Box 5066 95205 — 209-944-9818
Sherry Riley, prin. — Fax 944-9829

Stonyford, Colusa
Stony Creek JUSD
Supt. — See Elk Creek
Indian Valley ES — 50/K-6
PO Box 279 95979 — 530-963-3210
Holly McLaughlin, prin. — Fax 963-3047

Stratford, Kings
Central UNESD
Supt. — See Lemoore
Stratford S — 300/K-8
19348 Empire Ave 93266 — 559-947-3391
Bill Bilbo, prin. — Fax 947-3840

Strathmore, Tulare, Pop. 2,353
Strathmore UNESD — 700/K-8
PO Box 247 93267 — 559-568-1283
David DePaoli, supt. — Fax 568-1262
www.suesd.k12.ca.us
Strathmore ES — 400/K-4
PO Box 247 93267 — 559-568-2118
Richard Radtke, prin. — Fax 568-1280
Strathmore MS — 200/5-8
PO Box 247 93267 — 559-568-9293
Evelyn Erquhart, prin. — Fax 568-2944

Sunnyside UNESD — 400/K-8
21644 Avenue 196 93267 — 559-568-1741
Steve Tsuboi, supt. — Fax 568-0291
www.sunnysideunion.com/
Sunnyside S — 400/K-8
21644 Avenue 196 93267 — 559-568-1741
Steve Tsuboi, prin. — Fax 568-0291

Studio City, See Los Angeles
Los Angeles USD
Supt. — See Los Angeles
Carpenter Avenue ES — 800/K-5
3909 Carpenter Ave 91604 — 818-761-4363
Linda Parth, prin. — Fax 508-6724

Sugarloaf, San Bernardino
Bear Valley USD
Supt. — See Big Bear Lake
Baldwin Lane ES — 500/K-6
44500 Baldwin Ln 92386 — 909-585-7766
Rosa Murillo, prin. — Fax 585-8135

Suisun City, Solano, Pop. 26,762
Fairfield-Suisun USD
Supt. — See Fairfield
Crescent ES — 700/K-5
1001 Anderson Dr 94585 — 707-435-2771
Stephanie Wheeler, prin. — Fax 428-1536
Crystal MS — 800/6-8
400 Whispering Bay Ln 94585 — 707-435-5800
David Marshall, prin. — Fax 435-5806
Root ES — 700/K-5
820 Harrier Dr 94585 — 707-421-4240
Jodie Phan, prin. — Fax 421-4298
Suisun City ES — 600/K-5
725 Golden Eye Way 94585 — 707-421-4210
Richard Yee, prin. — Fax 421-3981
Suisun Valley S — 300/K-8
4985 Lambert Rd, — 707-421-4338
Janice Napier, prin. — Fax 422-5710

Sultana, Tulare
Monson-Sultana JUESD — 400/K-8
PO Box 25 93666 — 559-591-1634
Thomas Giampietro, supt. — Fax 591-0717
www.msschool.org/
Monson-Sultana S — 400/K-8
PO Box 25 93666 — 559-591-1634
Thomas Giampietro, prin. — Fax 591-0717

Summerland, Santa Barbara
Carpinteria USD
Supt. — See Carpinteria
Summerland ES — 100/K-6
PO Box 460 93067 — 805-969-1011
Tricia Price, prin. — Fax 969-1524

Sun City, Riverside, Pop. 14,930
Menifee UNESD
Supt. — See Menifee
Ridgemoor ES — 900/K-5
25455 Ridgemoor Rd 92586 — 951-672-6450
Midge James, prin. — Fax 672-6456

Sunland, See Los Angeles
Los Angeles USD
Supt. — See Los Angeles
Apperson ES — 500/K-5
10233 Woodward Ave 91040 — 818-353-5544
Eleanor Purcell, prin. — Fax 951-6682
Mt. Gleason MS — 1,500/6-8
10965 Mount Gleason Ave 91040 — 818-951-2580
Deborah Acosta, prin. — Fax 352-6209
Sunland ES — 500/K-5
8350 Hillrose St 91040 — 818-353-1631
Lisa Ornelas, prin. — Fax 951-3814

Trinity Christian S — 100/K-6
10614 Oro Vista Ave 91040 — 818-352-7980
Debbie Gustaveson, admin. — Fax 352-2721

Sunnyvale, Santa Clara, Pop. 128,902
Cupertino UNSD
Supt. — See Cupertino
Cupertino MS — 1,200/6-8
1650 S Bernardo Ave 94087 — 408-245-0303
Kara Butler, prin. — Fax 732-4152
Nimitz ES — 600/K-5
545 Cheyenne Dr 94087 — 408-736-2180
Dale Jones, prin. — Fax 737-7182
Stocklmeir ES — 800/K-5
592 Dunholme Way 94087 — 408-732-3363
Leslie Mains, prin. — Fax 738-5904
West Valley ES — 600/K-5
1635 Belleville Way 94087 — 408-245-0148
Anne Brown, prin. — Fax 736-7543

Santa Clara USD
Supt. — See Santa Clara
Braly ES — 300/K-5
675 Gail Ave 94086 — 408-423-1000
Miakje Kamstra, prin. — Fax 423-1080
Peterson MS — 800/6-8
1380 Rosalia Ave 94087 — 408-423-2800
Sue Harris, prin. — Fax 423-2880
Ponderosa ES — 500/K-5
804 Ponderosa Ave 94086 — 408-423-4000
Meg Jackson, prin. — Fax 423-4080

Sunnyvale ESD — 6,000/K-8
PO Box 3217 94088 — 408-522-8200
Benjamin Picard Ed.D., supt. — Fax 522-8338
www.sesd.org
Bishop ES — 600/K-5
450 N Sunnyvale Ave 94085 — 408-522-8229
Eric Panosian, prin. — Fax 522-8238
Cherry Chase ES — 600/K-5
1138 Heatherstone Way 94087 — 408-522-8241
Diane Hemmes, prin. — Fax 522-4679
Columbia MS — 900/6-8
739 Morse Ave 94085 — 408-522-8247
Jocelyn Lee, prin. — Fax 522-8254
Cumberland ES — 500/K-5
824 Cumberland Dr 94087 — 408-522-8255
Mala Ahuja, prin. — Fax 522-8314
Ellis ES — 600/K-5
550 E Olive Ave 94086 — 408-522-8260
Christine Muzik, prin. — Fax 522-8232
Fairwood ES — 300/K-5
1110 Fairwood Ave 94089 — 408-523-4870
James Medina, prin. — Fax 523-4873
Lakewood ES — 500/K-5
750 Lakechime Dr 94089 — 408-522-8272
Annette Grasty, prin. — Fax 522-8276
San Miguel ES — 500/K-5
777 San Miguel Ave 94085 — 408-522-8278
Brenda Guy, prin. — Fax 522-8328
Sunnyvale MS — 900/6-8
1080 Mango Ave 94087 — 408-522-8288
Frances Dampier, prin. — Fax 522-8296
Vargas ES — 500/K-5
1054 Carson Dr 94086 — 408-522-8267
Ana Bonilla, prin. — Fax 522-8308

Challenger S - Sunnyvale — 800/PK-8
1185 Hollenbeck Ave 94087 — 408-245-7170
Jesse Grapes, prin.
French American S of Silicon Valley — 100/K-5
1522 Lewiston Dr 94087 — 408-746-0460
Bernard Moreau, hdmstr.
King's Academy — 800/K-12
562 N Britton Ave 94085 — 408-481-9900
Bob Kellogg, prin. — Fax 481-9932
Rainbow Montessori S — 400/K-6
790 E Duane Ave 94085 — 408-738-3261
Spyroula Rodenborn, dir. — Fax 727-4741
Resurrection S — 300/PK-8
1395 Hollenbeck Ave 94087 — 408-245-4571
Sr. Georgianna Coonis, prin. — Fax 733-7301
St. Cyprian S — 200/K-8
195 Leota Ave 94086 — 408-738-3444
Paul Wilson, prin. — Fax 733-3730
St. Martin S — 200/PK-8
597 Central Ave 94086 — 408-736-5534
Genie Florczyk, prin. — Fax 736-1034
South Penninsula Hebrew S — 300/PK-8
1030 Astoria Dr 94087 — 408-738-3060
Rabbi Avi Schochet, hdmstr. — Fax 738-0237
Stratford S - De Anza Park — 500/PK-5
1196 Lime Dr 94087 — 408-732-4424
Gigi Tate, prin.
Stratford S - Washington Park — 200/K-5
820 W McKinley Ave 94086 — 408-737-1500
Nicole Carpenter, prin.
Sunnyvale Christian S — 200/PK-5
445 S Mary Ave 94086 — 408-736-3286
Leanna Christie, prin. — Fax 736-3549

Sunol, Alameda
Sunol Glen USD — 200/K-8
11601 Main St 94586 — 925-862-2026
Molleen Barnes, supt. — Fax 862-2026
www.sunol.k12.ca.us
Sunol Glen S — 200/K-8
11601 Main St 94586 — 925-862-2026
Molleen Barnes, prin. — Fax 862-2026

Sun Valley, See Los Angeles
Los Angeles USD
Supt. — See Los Angeles
Byrd MS — 1,800/6-8
8501 Arleta Ave 91352 — 818-394-4300
Sondra Reynolds, prin. — Fax 768-1837
Fernangeles ES — 1,100/K-5
12001 Art St 91352 — 818-767-0380
Karen Jaye, prin. — Fax 504-9905
Glenwood ES — 600/K-5
8001 Ledge Ave 91352 — 818-767-6406
Christina Garcia, prin. — Fax 504-8081
Roscoe ES — 1,000/K-5
10765 Strathern St 91352 — 818-767-3018
Richard Lioy, prin. — Fax 504-1597
Stonehurst Avenue ES — 300/K-5
9851 Stonehurst Ave 91352 — 818-767-8014
Jill Imperiale, prin. — Fax 768-7564
Sun Valley MS — 2,700/6-8
7330 Bakman Ave 91352 — 818-255-5100
Antonio Delgado, prin. — Fax 503-9846
Vinedale ES — 300/K-5
10150 La Tuna Canyon Rd 91352 — 818-767-0106
Linda Rolls, prin. — Fax 768-2452

Grace Community S — 300/K-9
13248 Roscoe Blvd 91352 — 818-909-5611
Tom Chaffin, admin. — Fax 909-5546
Our Lady of the Holy Rosary S — 300/PK-8
7802 Vineland Ave 91352 — 818-765-4897
Sr. Remedios Aguilar, prin. — Fax 765-5791
Sol del Valle Christian S — 50/K-8
10803 Penrose St 91352 — 818-252-7305
James Hooyenya, prin. — Fax 767-5176
Village Christian ES — 600/K-5
8930 Village Ave 91352 — 818-768-1900
David Vegas, prin. — Fax 767-7553
Village Christian MS — 500/6-8
8930 Village Ave 91352 — 818-768-1588
Thomas Nare, prin. — Fax 504-0982

Susanville, Lassen, Pop. 18,101
Johnstonville ESD — 200/K-8
704-795 Bangham Ln 96130 — 530-257-2471
Lou Istrice, supt. — Fax 251-5557
www.johnstonvilleusd.org/
Johnstonville S — 200/K-8
704-795 Bangham Ln 96130 — 530-257-2471
Lou Istrice, prin. — Fax 251-5557

Ravendale-Termo ESD — 50/K-8
472-013 Johnstonville Rd 96130 — 530-234-2010
Robert Pace, supt. — Fax 234-2132
Juniper Ridge S — 50/K-8
472-013 Johnstonville Rd 96130 — 530-234-2010
Robert Pace, prin. — Fax 234-2132

Richmond ESD — 200/K-8
700-585 Richmond Rd E 96130 — 530-257-2338
Cynthia Nellums, supt. — Fax 257-6398
www.richmondelementary.com/
Richmond S — 200/K-8
700-585 Richmond Rd E 96130 — 530-257-2338
Cynthia Nellums, prin. — Fax 257-6398

Susanville ESD — 800/K-8
109 S Gilman St 96130 — 530-257-8200
Gary McIntire, supt. — Fax 257-8246
www.susanvillesd.org
Diamond View MS — 300/7-8
1200 Paiute Ln 96130 — 530-257-5144
Patricia Gunderson, prin. — Fax 257-7232
McKinley ES — 300/K-3
2005 4th St 96130 — 530-257-5161
Donna Wix, prin. — Fax 257-4967
Meadow View ES — 200/4-6
1200 Paiute Ln 96130 — 530-257-3000
Vicky Leitaker, prin. — Fax 257-2631

Lassen Christian Academy — 50/K-9
2545 Riverside Dr 96130 — 530-257-4643
Mark Snyder, admin. — Fax 257-4295
Susanville SDA S — 50/1-8
455 Cedar St 96130 — 530-257-5045

Sutter, Sutter, Pop. 2,606
Brittan ESD — 600/K-8
2340 Pepper St 95982 — 530-822-5155
Staci Kaelin, supt. — Fax 822-5143
www.brittan.k12.ca.us/
Brittan S — 600/K-8
2340 Pepper St 95982 — 530-822-5155
Staci Kaelin, prin. — Fax 822-5143

Sutter Creek, Amador, Pop. 2,748
Amador County USD
Supt. — See Jackson
Sutter Creek ES — 200/4-6
340 Spanish St 95685 — 209-257-7200
Sean Snider, prin. — Fax 267-1231
Sutter Creek PS — K-3
110 Broad St 95685 — 209-257-7100
Sean Snider, prin. — Fax 267-9210

Sutter Hill SDA S — 50/K-8
12900 Ridge Rd 95685 — 209-267-5849
Lynnae Webster, prin. — Fax 267-2234

Sylmar, See Los Angeles
Los Angeles USD
Supt. — See Los Angeles
Brainard Avenue ES — 300/K-5
11407 Brainard Ave 91342 — 818-899-5241
Anthony Aguilar, prin. — Fax 890-9991
Dyer Street ES — 1,000/K-5
14500 Dyer St 91342 — 818-367-1932
Ernestina Gandera, prin. — Fax 364-1913
El Dorado Avenue ES — 600/K-5
12749 El Dorado Ave 91342 — 818-367-5816
Eric Maxey, prin. — Fax 362-6576
Harding Street ES — 600/K-5
13060 Harding St 91342 — 818-365-9237
Christopher Clarke, prin. — Fax 365-0759
Herrick Avenue ES — 800/K-5
13350 Herrick Ave 91342 — 818-367-1864
Louis Owens, prin. — Fax 364-9304
Hubbard Street ES — 1,000/K-5
13325 Hubbard St 91342 — 818-367-1944
Suellen Torres, prin. — Fax 362-7495
Olive Vista MS — 1,900/6-8
14600 Tyler St 91342 — 818-833-3900
Danford Schar, prin. — Fax 367-8273
Osceola Street ES — 400/K-5
14940 Osceola St 91342 — 818-362-1556
Julie Maravilla, prin. — Fax 362-8456

Sylmar ES 900/K-5
13291 Phillippi Ave 91342 818-367-1078
Susana Rubinstein, prin. Fax 362-4844

Delphi Academy of Los Angeles 200/K-12
11341 Brainard Ave 91342 818-583-1070
Karen Dale, hdmstr.

St. Didacus S 300/PK-8
14325 Astoria St 91342 818-367-5886
Kathryn Sweeney, prin. Fax 364-5486

Sylmar Light & Life Christian S 100/PK-6
14019 Sayre St 91342 818-362-9497
Bob Managbanag, admin. Fax 833-1235

Taft, Kern, Pop. 9,106

Taft CSD 2,100/K-8
820 6th St 93268 661-763-1521
Fax 763-1495
www.taftcity.k12.ca.us

Conley ES 300/K-3
623 Rose Ave 93268 661-765-4117
Lisa Kindred, prin. Fax 765-2065

Jefferson ES 200/K-3
318 Taylor St 93268 661-763-4236
Sylvia Hazel, prin. Fax 763-3054

Lincoln JHS 700/6-8
810 6th St 93268 661-765-2127
Dr. Kathy Orrin, prin. Fax 763-3970

Parkview ES 300/K-3
520 A St 93268 661-763-4164
Gay Anderson, prin. Fax 763-3020

Roosevelt S 500/4-5
811 6th St 93268 661-763-3113
Nancy Hickernell, prin. Fax 763-3732

Taft PS 200/K-3
212 Lucard St 93268 661-765-4151
Sylvia Hazel, prin. Fax 763-3783

Tahoe City, Placer, Pop. 1,643

Tahoe-Truckee JUSD
Supt. — See Truckee

North Tahoe MS 300/6-8
PO Box 5099 96145 530-581-7050
Teresa Rensch, prin. Fax 581-1237

Tahoe Lake ES 200/K-5
PO Box 856 96145 530-583-3010
Dan Hyde, prin. Fax 583-7623

Tarzana, See Los Angeles

Los Angeles USD
Supt. — See Los Angeles

Nestle Avenue ES 500/K-5
5060 Nestle Ave 91356 818-342-6148
Ibia Gomez, prin. Fax 609-9864

Portola MS 2,000/6-8
18720 Linnet St 91356 818-654-3300
Adrienne Shaha, prin. Fax 996-0292

Tarzana ES 500/K-5
5726 Topeka Dr 91356 818-881-1424
Vicki Lee, prin. Fax 343-4418

Wilbur ES 700/K-5
5213 Crebs Ave 91356 818-345-1090
David Hirsch, prin. Fax 881-8128

Assyrian American Christian S 50/2-12
5955 Lindley Ave 91356 818-996-1226
Robin Alkhas, prin. Fax 996-6467

Woodcrest S 200/K-5
6043 Tampa Ave Ste 101A 91356 818-345-3002
Andrea Miller, admin. Fax 345-7880

Taylorsville, Plumas

Plumas USD
Supt. — See Quincy

Taylorsville ES 100/1-6
PO Box 202 95983 530-284-7421
Tori Willits, prin. Fax 284-6730

Tecate, San Diego

Tecate Christian S 100/1-12
PO Box 1000 91980 619-468-3355
Rick Rowe, admin. Fax 478-5910

Tehachapi, Kern, Pop. 11,752

Tehachapi USD 4,900/K-12
400 S Snyder Ave 93561 661-822-2100
Dr. Richard Swanson, supt. Fax 822-2159
www.teh.k12.ca.us

Cummings Valley ES 700/K-5
24220 Bear Valley Rd 93561 661-822-2190
David Spencer, prin. Fax 822-2128

Golden Hills ES 700/K-5
20215 Park Rd 93561 661-822-2180
Pat Thomas, prin. Fax 822-2185

Jacobsen MS 1,100/6-8
711 Anita Dr 93561 661-822-2150
Susan Ortega, prin. Fax 822-2156

Tompkins ES 700/K-5
1120 S Curry St 93561 661-822-2170
Traci Minjares, prin. Fax 822-2198

Heritage Oak S 100/K-12
20915 Schout Rd 93561 661-823-0885
Vanessa Cross, admin. Fax 823-0863

Temecula, Riverside, Pop. 85,799

Temecula Valley USD 28,400/K-12
31350 Rancho Vista Rd 92592 951-676-2661
Carol Leighty, supt. Fax 695-7121
www.tvusd.k12.ca.us

Barnett ES 600/K-5
39925 Harveston Dr 92591 951-296-5579
Chris Dixon, prin. Fax 296-9029

Crowne Hill ES 700/K-5
33535 Old Kent Rd 92592 951-294-6370
Karen Johnson, prin. Fax 294-6373

Day MS 1,000/6-8
40775 Camino Campos Verde 92591 951-699-8138
Greg Cooke, prin. Fax 699-4198

Gardner MS 900/6-8
45125 Via Del Coronado 92592 951-699-0080
Jim Flesuras, prin. Fax 699-0081

Jackson ES 700/K-5
32400 Camino San Dimas 92592 951-302-5199
Shery Stewart, prin. Fax 302-6643

Margarita MS 1,000/6-8
30600 Margarita Rd 92591 951-695-7370
Karen Hayes, prin. Fax 695-7378

Nicolas Valley ES 900/K-5
39600 N General Kearny Rd 92591 951-695-7180
Shelley Maxwell, prin. Fax 695-7186

Paloma ES 700/K-5
42940 Via Rami 92592 951-302-5165
Sandra McKay, prin. Fax 302-5176

Pauba Valley ES 800/K-5
33125 Regina Dr 92592 951-302-5140
Kimberley Velez, prin. Fax 302-5146

Rancho ES 700/K-5
31530 La Serena Way 92591 951-695-7150
Pam May, prin. Fax 695-7154

Red Hawk ES 700/K-5
32045 Camino San Jose 92592 951-302-5125
Melanie Aamodt, prin. Fax 302-5133

Reinke ES 900/K-5
43799 Sunny Meadows Dr 92592 951-302-6610
Katie Johnson, prin. Fax 302-6616

Sparkman ES 400/K-5
32225 Pio Pico Rd 92592 951-302-5100
Pilar Byham, prin. Fax 302-5104

Temecula ES 800/K-5
41951 Moraga Rd 92591 951-695-7130
Susan Yakich, prin. Fax 695-7137

Temecula Luiseno ES 500/K-5
45754 Wolf Creek Dr 92592 951-294-6340
Andree Grey, prin. Fax 294-6343

Temecula MS 1,400/6-8
42075 Meadows Pkwy 92592 951-302-5151
Rob Sousa, prin. Fax 302-5160

Tobin ES 700/K-5
45200 Morgan Hl 92592 951-294-6355
Michael McTasney, prin. Fax 294-6358

Vail ES 600/K-5
29915 Mira Loma Dr 92592 951-695-7140
Barbara Oglesby, prin. Fax 695-7148

Vail Ranch MS 1,200/6-8
33340 Camino Piedra Rojo 92592 951-302-5188
Kevin Groepper, prin. Fax 302-5195

Vintage Hills ES 900/K-5
42240 Camino Romo 92592 951-695-4260
Jennifer Carpenter, prin. Fax 695-4268

Other Schools – See Murrieta, Winchester

Hillcrest Academy 200/K-8
29275 Santiago Rd 92592 951-676-4754
Maureen Manion, hdmstr. Fax 676-5316

Linfield Christian S 900/K-12
31950 Pauba Rd 92592 951-676-8111
Karen Raftery, supt. Fax 695-1291

Rancho Community Christian S 600/PK-9
31300 Rancho Community Way 92592
951-303-1408
Michael Rea, supt. Fax 302-1580

St. Jeanne De Lestonnac S 500/PK-8
32650 Avenida Lestonnac 92592 951-587-2505
Sr. Esperanza Flores, prin. Fax 587-2515

Temecula Christian S 100/K-8
29825 Santiago Rd 92592 951-695-0025
Brent Yim, admin. Fax 676-3689

Van Avery Preparatory S 500/K-8
29851 Santiago Rd 92592 951-506-3123
Christine McCusker, admin.

Temple City, Los Angeles, Pop. 37,363

El Monte City ESD
Supt. — See El Monte

Cleminson ES 400/K-6
5213 Daleview Ave 91780 626-575-2327
Dr. Lillian Prince, prin. Fax 443-8661

Temple City USD 5,700/K-12
9700 Las Tunas Dr 91780 626-548-5000
Dr. Chelsea Kang-Smith, supt. Fax 548-5022
www.tcusd.net

Cloverly ES 500/4-6
5476 Cloverly Ave 91780 626-548-5092
Trang Lai, prin. Fax 548-5095

La Rosa ES 500/K-3
9301 La Rosa Dr 91780 626-548-5076
Tiffany Haeberlein, prin. Fax 548-5081

Longden ES 1,000/K-6
9501 Wendon St 91780 626-548-5068
Cheryl Busick, prin. Fax 548-5175

Oak Avenue IS 900/7-8
6623 Oak Ave 91780 626-548-5060
Lawton Gray, prin. Fax 548-5170

Other Schools – See San Gabriel

First Lutheran S 100/PK-8
9123 Broadway 91780 626-287-0968
Richard Swanson, prin. Fax 285-8648

Pacific Friends S 100/PK-PK
6210 Temple City Blvd 91780 626-287-6880
Kellie McKinley, dir. Fax 292-3896

St. Luke S 200/K-8
5521 Cloverly Ave 91780 626-291-5959
Erin Barisano, prin. Fax 285-5367

Templeton, San Luis Obispo, Pop. 2,887

Templeton USD 2,400/K-12
960 Old County Rd 93465 805-434-5800
Deborah Bowers Ed.D., supt. Fax 434-5879
www.tusdnet.net/

Templeton ES 400/K-2
215 8th St 93465 805-434-5820
Katie Mammen, prin. Fax 434-5811

Templeton MS 500/6-8
925 Old County Rd 93465 805-434-5813
Tom Harrington, prin. Fax 434-5812

Vineyard ES 500/3-5
2121 Vineyard Dr 93465 805-434-5840
Kyle Pruitt, prin. Fax 434-3105

Terra Bella, Tulare, Pop. 2,740

Saucelito ESD 100/K-8
17615 Avenue 104 93270 559-784-2164
Cynthia Lamb, supt. Fax 784-7109

Saucelito S 100/K-8
17615 Avenue 104 93270 559-784-2164
Cynthia Lamb, prin. Fax 784-7109

Terra Bella UNESD 900/K-8
9121 Road 240 93270 559-535-4451
Frank Betry, supt. Fax 535-0314
www.tbuesd.org/

Smith MS 200/6-8
23825 Avenue 92 93270 559-535-4451
Guadalupe Roman, prin. Fax 535-0829

Terra Bella ES 700/K-5
9364 Road 238 93270 559-535-4451
Debby Tupper, prin. Fax 535-4457

Zion Lutheran S 50/K-8
10368 Road 256 93270 559-535-4346
Eloise Anderson, prin. Fax 535-2719

Thermal, Riverside

Coachella Valley USD 17,900/K-12
PO Box 847 92274 760-399-5137
Ricardo Medina, supt. Fax 399-1008
www.cvusd.us/

Kelley ES 600/K-6
87163 Center St 92274 760-399-5101
Luis Rodriguez, prin. Fax 399-1427

Las Palmitas ES 800/K-6
86150 Avenue 66 92274 760-397-2200
Michael Williams, prin. Fax 397-8790

Oasis ES 700/K-6
88175 74th Ave 92274 760-397-4112
Elizabeth Ramirez, prin. Fax 397-0192

Toro Canyon MS 1,000/7-8
86150 Avenue 66 92274 760-397-2244
Raul Hernandez, prin. Fax 397-8760

Westside ES 600/K-6
82225 Airport Blvd 92274 760-399-5171
Bernice Rummonds, prin. Fax 399-1284

Other Schools – See Coachella, Indio, Mecca, Salton City

Thornton, San Joaquin

New Hope ESD 200/K-8
PO Box 238 95686 209-794-2376
Joanne Oien, supt. Fax 794-2230

New Hope S 200/K-8
PO Box 238 95686 209-794-2376
Joanne Oien, prin. Fax 794-2230

Thousand Oaks, Ventura, Pop. 124,359

Conejo Valley USD 20,900/K-12
1400 E Janss Rd 91362 805-497-9511
Mario Contini, supt. Fax 371-9170
www.conejo.k12.ca.us

Acacia ES 500/K-5
55 W Norman Ave 91360 805-495-5550
Kirsten Walker, prin. Fax 374-1156

Aspen ES 500/K-5
1870 Oberlin Ave 91360 805-495-2810
Amie Mills, prin. Fax 374-1157

Colina MS 1,200/6-8
1500 E Hillcrest Dr 91362 805-495-7429
Shane Frank, prin. Fax 374-1163

Conejo ES 500/K-5
280 N Conejo School Rd 91362 805-495-7058
Dena Sellers, prin. Fax 374-1158

Glenwood ES 400/K-5
1135 Windsor Dr 91360 805-495-2118
Martha Tureen, prin. Fax 374-1159

Ladera ES 400/K-5
1211 Calle Almendro 91360 805-492-3565
Pamela Chasse, prin. Fax 493-8851

Lang Ranch ES 800/K-5
2450 Whitechapel Pl 91362 805-241-4417
Brad Baker, prin. Fax 241-4617

Los Cerritos MS 1,200/6-8
2100 E Ave De Las Flores 91362 805-492-3538
Eleanor Love, prin. Fax 493-8854

Madrona ES 600/K-5
612 Camino Manzanas 91360 805-498-6102
Jean Gordon, prin. Fax 375-5601

Park Oaks ES 300/K-5
1335 Calle Bouganvilla 91360 805-492-3569
Paula Willebrands, prin. Fax 493-8852

Redwood MS 1,100/6-8
233 W Gainsborough Rd 91360 805-497-7264
Steve Lepire, prin. Fax 497-3734

Weathersfield ES 300/K-5
3151 Darlington Dr 91360 805-492-3563
Jeanne Valentine, prin. Fax 492-4452

Wildwood ES 300/K-5
620 Velarde Dr 91360 805-492-3531
Doug Hedin, prin. Fax 493-8855

Other Schools – See Newbury Park, Westlake Village

Ascension Lutheran S 200/K-8
1600 E Hillcrest Dr 91362 805-496-2419
Diann Lavik, prin.

Bethany Christian S 300/PK-6
200 Bethany Ct 91360 805-497-7072
Shirley Hackleman, prin. Fax 494-4879

First Baptist Academy 100/PK-6
1250 Erbes Rd 91362 805-495-2531
Dean Johnson, admin. Fax 495-6167
Hillcrest Christian S 400/PK-12
384 Erbes Rd 91362 805-497-7501
Stephen Allen, hdmstr. Fax 494-9355
Honey Tree ECC 200/PK-K
1 W Avenida De Los Arboles 91360 805-492-1232
Calla Chevalier, dir. Fax 493-5390
Little Oaks S 100/PK-6
101 N Skyline Dr 91362 805-495-5513
Miriam Lockin, admin. Fax 496-7356
Pinecrest S 300/K-6
449 E Wilbur Rd 91360 805-497-8533
Richele Petersen, dir. Fax 494-7104
St. Paschal Baylon S 400/K-8
154 E Janss Rd 91360 805-495-9340
Suzanne Duffy, prin. Fax 778-1509
St. Patrick's Day S 100/K-6
1 Church Rd 91362 805-497-1416
Eileen Doyle, hdmstr. Fax 496-8331
Trinity Pacific Christian S 400/K-12
3389 Camino Calandria 91360 805-492-0863
Barbara Richert, prin.

Thousand Palms, Riverside, Pop. 4,122
Palm Springs USD
Supt. — See Palm Springs
Lindley ES 700/K-5
31495 Robert Rd 92276 760-343-7570
Simone Kovats, prin. Fax 343-7576

Three Rivers, Tulare
Three Rivers UNESD 200/K-8
PO Box 99 93271 559-561-4466
Susan Sherwood, supt. Fax 561-4468
www.three-rivers.k12.ca.us/
Three Rivers S 200/K-8
PO Box 99 93271 559-561-4466
Susan Sherwood, prin. Fax 561-4468

Tiburon, Marin, Pop. 8,671
Reed UNESD 1,100/K-8
277 Karen Way Ste A 94920 415-381-1112
Christine Carter, supt. Fax 384-0890
www.reedschools.org
Bel Aire ES 400/3-5
277 Karen Way 94920 415-388-7100
Patti Purcell, prin. Fax 388-7176
Del Mar MS 300/6-8
105 Avenida Miraflores 94920 415-435-1468
Kit Pappenheimer, prin. Fax 435-6190
Reed ES 400/K-2
1199 Tiburon Blvd 94920 415-435-7840
Lexie Sifford, prin. Fax 435-7853

St. Hilary S 300/PK-8
765 Hilary Dr 94920 415-435-2224
Bryan Clement, prin. Fax 435-5895

Tipton, Tulare, Pop. 1,383
Tipton ESD 600/K-8
PO Box 787 93272 559-752-4213
Mike Salcido, supt. Fax 687-2221
www.tiptonschool.org/
Tipton S 600/K-8
PO Box 787 93272 559-752-4213
Christine Griesbach, prin. Fax 687-2221

Tollhouse, Fresno
Sierra USD
Supt. — See Prather
Lodge Pole S 50/K-8
33467 Lodge Rd 93667 559-855-4347
Larry Silva, prin. Fax 855-4348
Sierra ES 300/K-5
27444 Tollhouse Rd 93667 559-855-2332
Donna Wright, prin. Fax 855-2016

Tomales, Marin
Shoreline USD 600/K-12
PO Box 198 94971 707-878-2266
Dr. Stephen Rosenthal, supt. Fax 878-2554
shoreline.marin.k12.ca.us/
Tomales S 200/K-8
PO Box 198 94971 707-878-2214
Jane Realon, prin. Fax 878-2467
Other Schools – See Bodega Bay, Point Reyes Station

Torrance, Los Angeles, Pop. 142,384
Los Angeles USD
Supt. — See Los Angeles
Halldale ES 600/K-5
21514 Halldale Ave 90501 310-328-3100
Linda Sakurai, prin. Fax 328-7928
Meyler ES 1,000/K-5
1123 W 223rd St 90502 310-328-3910
Nancy Wloch, prin. Fax 787-9116
Van Deene ES 400/K-5
826 Javelin St 90502 310-320-8680
Ellen Hodnett, prin. Fax 782-6537

Torrance USD 25,100/K-12
2335 Plaza Del Amo 90501 310-972-6500
George Mannon Ed.D., supt. Fax 972-6012
www.tusd.org
Adams ES 400/K-5
2121 W 238th St 90501 310-533-4480
Sandy Skora, prin. Fax 972-6385
Anza ES 500/K-5
21400 Ellinwood Dr 90503 310-533-4559
Barbara Marks, prin. Fax 972-6386
Arlington ES 600/K-5
17800 Van Ness Ave 90504 310-533-4510
Vicki Roloff, prin. Fax 972-6387
Arnold ES 700/K-5
4100 W 227th St 90505 310-533-4524
Jane Sifford Tasker, prin. Fax 972-6388

Calle Mayor MS 800/6-8
4800 Calle Mayor 90505 310-533-4548
Chris Sheck, prin. Fax 972-6389
Carr ES 500/K-5
3404 W 168th St 90504 310-533-4467
Richard Peterson, prin. Fax 972-6390
Casimir MS 700/6-8
17220 Casimir Ave 90504 310-533-4498
Susan Holmes, prin. Fax 972-6391
Edison ES 600/K-5
3800 W 182nd St 90504 310-533-4513
Erin Lahr, prin. Fax 972-6392
Fern ES 600/K-5
1314 Fern Ave 90503 310-533-4506
Valerie Williams, prin. Fax 972-6393
Hickory ES 800/K-5
2800 W 227th St 90505 310-533-4672
Edna Schumacher, prin. Fax 972-6396
Hull MS at Levy 700/6-8
3420 W 229th Pl 90505 310-533-4516
Barry Lafferty, prin. Fax 972-6397
Jefferson MS 700/6-8
21717 Talisman St 90503 310-533-4794
Lee Chou, prin. Fax 972-6398
Lincoln ES 500/K-5
2418 W 166th St 90504 310-533-4464
Katherine Castleberry, prin. Fax 972-6400
Lynn MS 800/6-8
5038 Halison St 90503 310-533-4495
Leroy Jackson, prin. Fax 972-6401
Madrona MS 800/6-8
21364 Madrona Ave 90503 310-533-4562
Ron Richardson, prin. Fax 972-6402
Magruder MS 900/6-8
4100 W 185th St 90504 310-533-4527
Michael Voight, prin. Fax 972-6403
Richardson MS 700/6-8
23751 Nancylee Ln 90505 310-533-4790
Michelle Stupnik, prin. Fax 972-6405
Riviera ES 700/K-5
365 Paseo De Arena 90505 310-533-4460
Christie Forshey, prin. Fax 972-6406
Seaside ES 700/K-5
4651 Sharynne Ln 90505 310-533-4532
Tom Dimercurio, prin. Fax 972-6407
Torrance ES 500/K-5
2125 Lincoln Ave 90501 310-533-4500
Gerardo Yepez, prin. Fax 972-6453
Towers ES 600/K-5
5600 Towers St 90503 310-533-4535
Dr. Kaivan Yuen, prin. Fax 972-6456
Victor ES 1,100/K-5
4820 Spencer St 90503 310-533-4542
William Baker, prin. Fax 972-6457
Walteria ES 600/K-5
24456 Madison St 90505 310-533-4487
Pamela Williams, prin. Fax 972-6458
Wood ES 400/K-5
2250 W 235th St 90501 310-533-4484
Teresa Lanphere, prin. Fax 972-6484
Yukon ES 400/K-5
17815 Yukon Ave 90504 310-533-4477
Elaine Wassil, prin. Fax 972-6485

Ascension Lutheran S 200/PK-8
17910 Prairie Ave 90504 310-371-3531
Carol Woods, prin. Fax 214-4657
First Lutheran S 600/PK-8
2900 W Carson St 90503 310-320-9920
Sandy Ammentorp, prin. Fax 320-1963
Nativity S 300/K-8
2371 W Carson St 90501 310-328-5387
Michael Falco, prin. Fax 328-5365
St. Catherine Laboure S 500/K-8
3846 Redondo Beach Blvd 90504 310-324-8732
Kathleen Gorze, prin. Fax 324-2471
St. James S 300/PK-8
4625 Garnet St 90503 310-371-0416
Sr. Mary Margaret Krueper, prin. Fax 371-8377
South Bay Junior Academy 200/PK-10
4400 Del Amo Blvd 90503 310-370-6215
Susan Vlach, prin. Fax 793-8665
Zion Lutheran S 50/K-8
1001 W 223rd St 90502 310-320-1771
Nicholas Bush, prin. Fax 320-1771

Trabuco Canyon, Orange
Saddleback Valley USD
Supt. — See Mission Viejo
Portola Hills ES 900/K-6
19422 Saddleback Ranch Rd 92679 949-459-9370
Susan Navarro-Sims, prin. Fax 459-9376
Robinson ES 900/K-6
21400 Lindsay Dr 92679 949-589-2446
Don Snyder, prin. Fax 589-1374
Trabuco ES 100/K-6
PO Box 277 92678 949-858-0343
Suzanne Westmoreland, prin. Fax 858-9188

Tracy, San Joaquin, Pop. 79,964
Banta ESD 300/K-8
22375 El Rancho Rd 95304 209-835-0843
William Draa, supt. Fax 835-9851
www.bantaesd.org
Banta S 300/K-8
22345 El Rancho Rd 95304 209-835-0171
Albert Garibaldi, prin. Fax 835-0319

Jefferson ESD 2,400/K-8
1219 Whispering Wind Dr 95377 209-836-3388
Ed Quinn, supt. Fax 836-2930
www.jeffersonschooldistrict.com/
Hawkins S 800/K-8
475 Darlene Ln 95377 209-839-2380
Paula Finton, prin. Fax 839-2384
Jefferson S 400/5-8
7500 W Linne Rd 95304 209-835-3053
Jim Bridges, prin. Fax 835-4419

Monticello ES 500/K-4
1001 Cambridge Ln 95377 209-833-9300
Leslie Adair, prin. Fax 833-9317
Traina S 700/K-8
4256 Windsong Dr 95377 209-839-2379
Susan Moffitt, prin. Fax 839-2314

Lammersville ESD
Supt. — See Mountain House
Lammersville S 300/K-8
16555 Von Sosten Rd 95304 209-835-0138
Samy D'Amico, prin. Fax 835-3861

New Jerusalem ESD 200/K-8
31400 S Koster Rd 95304 209-835-2597
David Thoming, supt. Fax 835-1613
www.newjfalcons.com/
New Jerusalem S 200/K-8
31400 S Koster Rd 95304 209-835-2597
Steve Payne, prin. Fax 835-2613

Tracy JUSD 16,600/K-12
1875 W Lowell Ave 95376 209-830-3200
James Franco, supt. Fax 830-3259
www.tracy.k12.ca.us
Bohn ES 500/K-5
350 E Mount Diablo Ave 95376 209-830-3300
Charles Hill, prin. Fax 830-3301
Central ES 500/K-5
1370 Parker Ave 95376 209-831-5300
Nancy Link, prin. Fax 831-5309
Freiler S 1,100/K-8
2421 W Lowell Ave 95377 209-831-5170
Laurie Fracolli, prin. Fax 831-5177
Hirsch ES 700/K-5
1280 Dove Dr 95376 209-830-3312
Jon Fine, prin. Fax 830-3313
Jacobson ES 700/K-5
1750 W Kavanagh Ave 95376 209-830-3315
Cindy Sasser, prin. Fax 830-3316
Kelly S 1,100/K-8
535 Mabel Josephine Dr 95377 209-831-5000
Fax 831-5031
McKinley ES 500/K-5
800 W Carlton Way 95376 209-830-3319
Fax 830-3320
Monte Vista MS 900/6-8
751 W Lowell Ave 95376 209-830-3340
Stephanie Prioste, prin. Fax 830-3341
North S 800/K-8
2875 Holly Dr 95376 209-830-3350
Fred Medina, prin. Fax 830-3351
Poet-Christian S 700/K-8
1701 S Central Ave 95376 209-831-5252
William Masylar, prin. Fax 831-5344
South/West Park ES 400/K-2
501 Mount Oso Ave 95376 209-830-3335
Ramona Soto, prin. Fax 830-3336
South/West Park ES 500/3-5
500 W Mount Diablo Ave 95376 209-830-3328
Ramona Soto, prin. Fax 830-3329
Villalovoz ES 600/K-5
1550 Cypress Dr 95376 209-830-3331
Lisa Beeso, prin. Fax 830-3332
Williams MS 1,300/6-8
1600 Tennis Ln 95376 209-831-5289
Barbara Montgomery, prin. Fax 831-5294
Other Schools – See Stockton

Bella Vista Christian Academy 300/PK-8
1635 Chester Dr 95376 209-835-7438
Larry Tietmeyer, prin. Fax 835-7951
Montessori S of Tracy 200/PK-6
100 S Tracy Blvd 95376 209-833-3458
Ana Rodrigues, prin. Fax 833-0194
St. Bernard S 200/K-8
165 W Eaton Ave 95376 209-835-8018
Gary Abate, prin. Fax 835-2496
Tracy SDA S 50/K-8
126 W 21st St 95376 209-835-6607
Patsy Iverson, prin. Fax 835-3036
West Valley Christian Academy 300/PK-8
1790 Sequoia Blvd 95376 209-832-4072
Teresa Smith, prin. Fax 832-4073

Tranquillity, Fresno
Golden Plains USD
Supt. — See San Joaquin
Tranquillity S 300/K-8
PO Box 337 93668 559-698-5517
Debbie Gleason, prin. Fax 698-5546

Traver, Tulare
Traver JESD 200/K-8
PO Box 69 93673 559-897-2755
Steve Ramirez, supt. Fax 897-0239
Traver S 200/K-8
PO Box 69 93673 559-897-2755
Steve Ramirez, prin. Fax 897-0239

Travis AFB, See Fairfield
Travis USD
Supt. — See Fairfield
Center ES 500/K-6
2900 Armstrong St 94535 707-437-4621
Pat Zetah, prin. Fax 437-1226
Scandia ES 400/K-6
100 Broadway St 94535 707-437-4691
Lucy Salerno, prin. Fax 437-9234
Travis ES 600/K-6
100 Hickam Ave 94535 707-437-2070
Nancy Kawata, prin. Fax 437-2687

Treasure Island, San Francisco
San Francisco USD
Supt. — See San Francisco
Tenderloin Community S 400/K-5
627 Turk St, San Francisco CA 94102 415-749-3567
Herb Packer, prin. Fax 749-3643

Tres Pinos, San Benito
Tres Pinos UNESD 100/K-8
PO Box 188 95075 831-637-0503
Luciano Medeiros, supt. Fax 637-9423
Tres Pinos S 100/K-8
PO Box 188 95075 831-637-0503
Luciano Medeiros, prin. Fax 637-9423

Trinidad, Humboldt, Pop. 309
Big Lagoon UNESD 50/K-8
269 Big Lagoon Park Rd 95570 707-677-3688
Kim Blanc, supt. Fax 677-3642
www.humboldt.k12.ca.us/blagoon_sd/index.html
Big Lagoon S 50/K-8
269 Big Lagoon Park Rd 95570 707-677-3688
Kim Blanc, prin. Fax 677-3642

Trinidad UNESD 100/K-8
PO Box 3030 95570 707-677-3631
Geoff Proust, supt. Fax 677-0954
www.humboldt.k12.ca.us/trinidad_sd/index.html
Trinidad S 100/K-8
PO Box 3030 95570 707-677-3631
Geoff Proust, prin. Fax 677-0954

Trinity Center, Trinity
Coffee Creek ESD 50/K-8
HC 2 Box 4740 96091 530-266-3344
Fax 266-3344
www.tcoe.trinity.k12.ca.us/~ccschool/
Coffee Creek S 50/K-8
HC 2 Box 4740 96091 530-266-3344
Fax 266-3344

Trinity Center ESD 50/K-8
PO Box 127 96091 530-266-3342
Marilyn Myrick, supt. Fax 266-3342
www.tcoek12.org/~tces/index.html
Trinity Center S 50/K-8
PO Box 127 96091 530-266-3342
Stephanie Petrick, prin. Fax 266-3342

Trona, San Bernardino
Trona JUSD 300/K-12
83600 Trona Rd 93562 760-372-2861
Charles Raff, supt. Fax 372-4534
www.trona.k12.ca.us/
Trona ES 200/K-6
83600 Trona Rd 93562 760-372-2868
Alan Tsubota, prin. Fax 372-5519

Truckee, Nevada, Pop. 15,737
Tahoe-Truckee JUSD 4,100/K-12
11839 Donner Pass Rd 96161 530-582-2500
Stephen Jennings, supt. Fax 582-7606
www.ttusd.org
Alder Creek MS 600/6-8
10931 Alder Dr 96161 530-582-2750
Susan Phebus, prin. Fax 582-7640
Glenshire ES 500/K-5
10990 Dorchester Dr 96161 530-582-7675
Kathleen Gauthier, prin. Fax 582-7676
Truckee ES 700/K-5
11911 Donner Pass Rd 96161 530-582-2650
Cathy Valle, prin. Fax 582-7696
Other Schools – See Kings Beach, Kingvale, Tahoe City

Tujunga, See Los Angeles
Los Angeles USD
Supt. — See Los Angeles
Mountain View ES 400/K-5
6410 Olcott St 91042 818-352-1616
Elizabeth Harker, prin. Fax 951-9286
Pinewood ES 500/K-5
10111 Silverton Ave 91042 818-353-2515
Steven Gediman, prin. Fax 353-3179
Plainview ES 400/K-5
10819 Plainview Ave 91042 818-353-1730
Wing Kwan Leung, prin. Fax 353-6658

Mekhitarist Armenian S 100/PK-8
6470 Foothill Blvd 91042 818-353-3003
Rev. Augustin Szekul, prin. Fax 353-0815
Our Lady of Lourdes S 200/K-8
7324 Apperson St 91042 818-353-1106
Kathleen Jones, prin. Fax 951-4276
Smart Academy 50/K-12
7754 McGroarty St 91042 818-951-7182
Brandon Moore, prin. Fax 951-7183

Tulare, Tulare, Pop. 50,127
Buena Vista ESD 200/K-8
21660 Road 60 93274 559-686-2015
Carole Mederos, supt. Fax 684-0932
Buena Vista S 200/K-8
21660 Road 60 93274 559-686-2015
Carole Mederos, prin. Fax 684-0932

Oak Valley UNESD 400/K-8
24500 Road 68 93274 559-688-2908
Kerry Beauchaine, supt. Fax 688-8023
Oak Valley S 400/K-8
24500 Road 68 93274 559-688-2908
Kerry Beauchaine, prin. Fax 688-8023

Palo Verde UNESD 500/PK-8
9637 Avenue 196 93274 559-688-0648
John Manning, supt. Fax 688-0640
Palo Verde Union S 500/PK-8
9637 Avenue 196 93274 559-688-0648
John Manning, prin. Fax 688-0640

Sundale UNESD 700/K-8
13990 Avenue 240 93274 559-688-7451
Terri Rufert, supt. Fax 688-5905
www.sundaleschool.com
Sundale S 700/K-8
13990 Avenue 240 93274 559-688-7451
Cindy Gist, prin. Fax 688-5905

Tulare CSD 9,000/K-8
600 N Cherry St 93274 559-685-7200
Luis Castellanoz, supt. Fax 685-7287
www.tcsdk8.org/
Cherry Avenue MS 700/6-8
540 N Cherry St 93274 559-685-7320
Joe Terri, prin. Fax 685-5621
Cypress ES 600/K-5
1870 S Laspina St 93274 559-685-7290
Valerie Brown, prin. Fax 685-7299
Garden ES 800/K-5
640 E Pleasant Ave 93274 559-685-7330
Barbara Xavier, prin. Fax 685-7336
Heritage ES 700/K-5
895 W Gail Ave 93274 559-685-7360
Loren Johnson, prin. Fax 685-7369
Kohn ES 700/K-5
500 S Laspina St 93274 559-685-7340
Paula Adair, prin. Fax 685-7344
Lincoln ES 400/K-6
909 E Cedar Ave 93274 559-685-7350
Tim Williams, prin. Fax 685-7355
Live Oak MS 700/6-8
980 N Laspina St 93274 559-685-7310
Tracey Jenkins, prin. Fax 685-7313
Los Tules MS 700/6-8
801 W Gail Ave 93274 559-687-3156
Gary Yentes, prin. Fax 685-7374
Maple ES 700/K-5
640 W Cross Ave 93274 559-685-7270
Terri Slover, prin. Fax 685-7337
Mission Valley ES 500/K-6
1695 Bella Oaks Dr 93274 559-685-7396
Brian Hollingshead, prin. Fax 685-7392
Mulcahy MS 600/5-8
1001 W Sonora Ave 93274 559-685-7250
John Pendleton, prin. Fax 687-6412
Pleasant ES 700/K-5
1855 W Pleasant Ave 93274 559-685-7300
Elaine Sewell, prin. Fax 687-6413
Roosevelt ES 600/K-4
1046 W Sonora Ave 93274 559-685-7280
Ira Porchia, prin. Fax 685-7386
Wilson ES 500/K-5
955 E Tulare Ave 93274 559-685-7260
Greg Anderson, prin. Fax 687-6414

Waukena JUNESD 200/K-8
19113 Road 28 93274 559-686-3328
Terri Lancaster, supt. Fax 686-8136
www.tcoe.org/districts/waukena.shtm
Waukena Joint Union S 200/K-8
19113 Road 28 93274 559-686-3328
Terri Lancaster, prin. Fax 686-8136

St. Aloysius S 200/K-8
627 N Beatrice Dr 93274 559-686-6250
Sr. Kay O'Brien, prin. Fax 686-0479
Tulare Christian S 100/K-8
PO Box 1477 93275 559-688-2010
Michael Young, admin. Fax 688-2009

Tulelake, Siskiyou, Pop. 1,010
Tulelake Basin JUSD 500/K-12
PO Box 640 96134 530-667-2295
Patricia Reeder, supt. Fax 667-4298
www.tulelake.k12.ca.us
Newell ES 100/K-2
407 County Road 160 96134 530-664-2131
Vanessa Jones, prin. Fax 664-2144
Tulelake Basin ES 200/3-6
PO Box 610 96134 530-667-2294
Vanessa Jones, prin. Fax 667-3448

Tuolumne, Tuolumne
Summerville ESD 400/K-8
18451 Carter St 95379 209-928-4291
Leigh Shampain, supt. Fax 928-1602
www.sumel.k12.ca.us/
Summerville S 400/K-8
18451 Carter St 95379 209-928-4291
T.Y. Atkins, prin. Fax 928-1602

Mother Lode Christian S 100/PK-12
18393 Gardner Ave 95379 209-928-4126
Linda Larson, admin. Fax 928-4613

Tupman, Kern
Elk Hills ESD 100/K-8
PO Box 129 93276 661-765-7431
Leslie Roberts, supt. Fax 765-4583
www.elkhills.k12.ca.us
Elk Hills S 100/K-8
PO Box 129 93276 661-765-7431
Leslie Roberts, prin. Fax 765-4583

Turlock, Stanislaus, Pop. 67,669
Chatom UNESD 700/K-8
7201 Clayton Rd 95380 209-664-8505
Barbara Patman, supt. Fax 664-8508
www.chatom.k12.ca.us
Chatom ES 500/K-5
7221 Clayton Rd 95380 209-664-8500
Chanda Rowley, prin. Fax 664-8520
Other Schools – See Crows Landing

Turlock USD 13,800/PK-12
PO Box 819013 95381 209-667-0632
Sonny DaMarto Ed.D., supt. Fax 667-6520
www.turlock.k12.ca.us
Brown ES 700/K-6
1400 Georgetown Ave 95382 209-634-7231
Jeff Persons, prin. Fax 668-3584
Crane Early Learning Center 100/PK-K
1100 Cahill Ave 95380 209-632-1043
Wendy Lankford, prin. Fax 668-3591
Crowell ES 800/K-6
118 North Ave 95382 209-667-0885
Linda Alaniz, prin. Fax 668-3631
Cunningham ES 800/K-6
324 W Linwood Ave 95380 209-667-0794
Tim Norton, prin. Fax 668-3730
Dutcher MS 500/7-8
1441 Colorado Ave 95380 209-667-8817
Jessie Ceja, prin. Fax 667-1332
Earl ES 800/K-6
4091 N Olive Ave 95382 209-634-1090
Tami Truax, prin. Fax 634-6750
Julien ES 900/K-6
1924 E Canal Dr 95380 209-667-0891
Linda Murphy-Lopes, prin. Fax 668-3782
Medeiros ES 700/K-6
651 W Springer Dr 95382 209-668-9600
Al Silveira, prin. Fax 668-4669
Osborn ES 900/K-6
201 N Soderquist Rd 95380 209-667-0893
Ed Ewing, prin. Fax 668-3910
Turlock JHS 1,500/7-8
3951 N Walnut Rd 95382 209-667-0881
Heidi Lawler, prin. Fax 668-3985
Wakefield ES 700/K-6
400 South Ave 95380 209-667-0895
Aaron Mello, prin. Fax 668-3945
Walnut Elementary Education Center 800/K-6
4219 N Walnut Rd 95382 209-664-9907
Mark Holmes, prin. Fax 664-9970

Sacred Heart S - Turlock 200/PK-8
1225 Cooper Ave 95380 209-634-7787
Donna Noceti, prin. Fax 634-0156
Turlock Christian S 200/K-6
PO Box 1540 95381 209-632-6250
Pam Hanson, prin. Fax 632-5721

Tustin, Orange, Pop. 69,096
Tustin USD 20,500/K-12
300 S C St 92780 714-730-7305
Richard Bray, supt. Fax 730-7436
www.tustin.k12.ca.us
Benson ES 300/K-5
12712 Elizabeth Way 92780 714-730-7531
Kelly Fresch, prin. Fax 730-7368
Beswick ES 600/K-5
1362 Mitchell Ave 92780 714-730-7385
Fax 730-7387
Columbus Tustin MS 900/6-8
17952 Beneta Way 92780 714-730-7352
Dean Crow, prin. Fax 730-7512
Currie MS 800/6-8
1402 Sycamore Ave 92780 714-730-7360
David Mintz, prin. Fax 730-7593
Estock ES 500/K-5
14741 N B St 92780 714-730-7390
Gail Levy, prin. Fax 730-7562
Heideman ES 500/K-5
15571 Williams St 92780 714-730-7521
Norma Lemus, prin. Fax 558-3820
Ladera ES 300/K-5
2515 Rawlings Way 92782 714-730-7505
Ryan Bollenbach, prin. Fax 734-0193
Lambert ES 500/K-5
1151 San Juan St 92780 714-730-7457
Deanna Parks, prin. Fax 505-2736
Nelson ES 600/K-5
14392 Browning Ave 92780 714-730-7536
John Laurich, prin. Fax 730-7557
Peters Canyon ES 500/K-5
26900 Peters Canyon Rd 92782 714-730-7540
Janet Bittick, prin. Fax 838-3385
Pioneer MS 1,200/6-8
2700 Pioneer Rd 92782 714-730-7534
Mike Mattos, prin. Fax 730-5405
Thorman ES 700/K-5
1402 Sycamore Ave 92780 714-730-7364
Helen Chung, prin. Fax 730-7593
Tustin Ranch ES 500/K-5
12950 Robinson Dr 92782 714-730-7580
Dean Jennings, prin. Fax 508-1654
Utt MS 900/6-8
13601 Browning Ave 92780 714-730-7573
Christine Matos, prin. Fax 750-7576
Veeh ES 500/K-5
1701 San Juan St 92780 714-730-7544
Will Neddersen, prin. Fax 505-4615
Other Schools – See Irvine, Santa Ana

Grace Harbor Church S 100/PK-5
12881 Newport Ave 92780 714-544-4431
Kathleen DeSantis, prin. Fax 544-5738
Red Hill Lutheran S 400/PK-8
13200 Red Hill Ave 92780 714-544-3132
Cindy Jordan, prin. Fax 544-8176
St. Cecilia S 300/PK-8
1311 Sycamore Ave 92780 714-544-1533
Mary Alvarado, prin. Fax 544-0643
St. Jeanne De Lestonnac S 500/PK-8
16791 E Main St 92780 714-542-4271
Sr. Sharon Lemprecht, prin. Fax 542-0644
Spirit Academy 200/K-12
1372 Irvine Blvd 92780 714-731-2630
Joe Rispoli, admin. Fax 731-2639

Twain Harte, Tuolumne, Pop. 2,170
Twain Harte-Long Barn UESD 400/K-8
18995 Twain Harte Dr 95383 209-586-3772
John Keiter Ed.D., supt. Fax 586-9938
www.thsd.k12.ca.us
Black Oak ES 200/K-5
18995 Twain Harte Dr 95383 209-586-3266
Dan Mayers, prin. Fax 586-3975
Twain Harte MS 200/6-8
18995 Twain Harte Dr 95383 209-586-3266
Mike Woicicki, prin. Fax 586-3975
Other Schools – See Pinecrest

Twentynine Palms, San Bernardino, Pop. 28,409
Morongo USD 9,600/K-12
PO Box 1209 92277 760-367-9191
James Majchrzak, supt. Fax 367-7189
www.morongo.k12.ca.us
Condor ES 500/K-6
2551 Condor Rd 92277 760-367-0750
Gwen Dixon, prin. Fax 368-1144
Oasis ES 600/K-6
73175 El Paseo Dr 92277 760-367-3595
Randy Eigner, prin. Fax 367-2103
Palm Vista ES 400/K-6
74350 Baseline Rd 92277 760-367-7538
Cindy McVay, prin. Fax 367-6766
Twentynine Palms ES 700/K-6
74350 Playa Vista Dr 92277 760-367-3545
Pete Wood, prin. Fax 367-9801
Twentynine Palms JHS 600/7-8
5798 Utah Trl 92277 760-367-9507
Jolie Kelley, prin. Fax 367-0742
Other Schools – See Joshua Tree, Landers, Morongo Valley, Yucca Valley

---

Twentynine Palms SDA S 50/K-8
72070 Samarkand Dr 92277 760-367-7369
Dalaiah Wright, prin.

Twin Peaks, San Bernardino
Rim of the World USD
Supt. — See Lake Arrowhead
Grandview ES 600/K-6
180 Grandview Rd 92391 909-336-3420
Lauralea Hopper, prin. Fax 336-3430

Calvary Chapel Christian S 50/1-12
PO Box 1210 92391 909-337-2468
Frank Plummer, prin. Fax 337-9656

Ukiah, Mendocino, Pop. 15,463
Ukiah USD 6,000/K-12
925 N State St 95482 707-463-5200
Lois Nash Ed.D., supt. Fax 463-2120
www.uusd.net/
Calpella ES 300/K-2
151 W Moore St 95482 707-485-8701
Barbara Hopper, prin. Fax 485-0965
Hudson ES 400/K-7
251 Jefferson Ln 95482 707-463-3813
Diane Davidson, prin. Fax 463-3814
Nokomis ES 300/K-5
495 Washington Ave 95482 707-463-5242
John McCann, prin. Fax 468-3305
Oak Manor ES 400/K-6
400 Oak Manor Dr 95482 707-463-5249
David Warken, prin. Fax 462-6223
Pomolita MS 700/6-8
740 N Spring St 95482 707-463-5224
Diana Marshall, prin. Fax 463-5203
Yokayo ES 500/K-6
790 S Dora St 95482 707-463-5236
Carl Morgensen, prin. Fax 463-5297
Zeek ES 500/K-6
1060 N Bush St 95482 707-463-5245
Barbara Boyer, prin. Fax 468-3421
Other Schools – See Hopland, Redwood Valley

St. Mary of the Angels S 200/K-8
991 S Dora St 95482 707-462-3888
Mary Leittem-Thomas, prin. Fax 462-6014
Ukiah Junior Academy 100/K-10
180 Stipp Ln 95482 707-462-6350
Ken Nelson, prin. Fax 462-4026

Union City, Alameda, Pop. 69,176
New Haven USD 10,900/K-12
34200 Alvarado Niles Rd 94587 510-471-1100
David Pava, supt. Fax 471-7108
www.nhusd.k12.ca.us
Alvarado ES 600/K-5
31100 Fredi St 94587 510-471-1039
Tracie Noriega, prin. Fax 471-9414
Alvarado MS 1,200/6-8
31604 Alvarado Blvd 94587 510-489-0700
John Mattos, prin. Fax 475-3936
Chavez MS 1,200/6-8
725 Whipple Rd 94587 510-487-1700
Alberto Solorzano, prin. Fax 475-3938
Eastin ES 200/K-5
34901 Eastin Dr 94587 510-475-9630
Penny Loetterle, prin. Fax 475-9638
Emanuele ES 900/K-5
100 Decoto Rd 94587 510-471-2461
Heidi Green, prin. Fax 471-8799
Kitayama ES 700/K-5
1959 Sunsprite Dr 94587 510-475-3982
Lisa Metzinger, prin. Fax 475-3989
Pioneer ES 600/K-5
32737 Bel Aire St 94587 510-487-4530
Joanne Stanley, prin. Fax 487-0313
Searles ES 800/K-5
33629 15th St 94587 510-471-2772
Deborah Knoth, prin. Fax 471-8420
Other Schools – See Hayward

Our Lady of the Rosary S 200/K-8
678 B St 94587 510-471-3765
Gloria Galarsa, prin. Fax 471-4601

Upland, San Bernardino, Pop. 73,589
Upland USD 12,300/K-12
390 N Euclid Ave 91786 909-985-1864
Dr. Gary Rutherford, supt. Fax 949-7872
www.upland.k12.ca.us
Baldy View ES 700/K-6
979 W 11th St 91786 909-982-2564
Lorrie Buehler, prin. Fax 949-7712
Cabrillo ES 700/K-6
1562 W 11th St 91786 909-985-2619
Pam Chavira, prin. Fax 982-5511
Citrus ES 700/K-6
925 W 7th St 91786 909-949-7731
Dionthe Cusimano, prin. Fax 949-7733
Foothill Knolls ES 500/K-6
1245 Veterans Ct 91786 909-949-7740
Eileen Chavez, prin. Fax 949-7744
Magnolia ES 600/K-6
465 W 15th St 91786 909-949-7750
Deborah Davis, prin. Fax 949-7752
Pepper Tree ES 800/K-6
1045 W 18th St 91784 909-949-9635
Marilyn Ward, prin. Fax 949-7763
Pioneer JHS 1,100/7-8
245 W 18th St 91784 909-949-7770
Dr. Marge Ruffalo, prin. Fax 949-7778
Sierra Vista ES 500/K-6
253 E 14th St 91786 909-949-7780
Alison Benson, prin. Fax 982-2659
Sycamore ES 500/K-6
1075 W 13th St 91786 909-982-0347
Jeff Miller, prin. Fax 949-7792
Upland ES 600/K-6
601 5th Ave 91786 909-949-7800
Judy Lowrie, prin. Fax 946-9764
Upland JHS 1,000/7-8
444 E 11th St 91786 909-949-7810
Brad Cuff, prin. Fax 949-7817
Valencia ES 700/K-6
541 W 22nd St 91784 909-949-7830
Lori Thompson, prin. Fax 949-7837

Carden Arbor View S 200/K-8
1530 N San Antonio Ave 91786 909-982-9919
Cathy Edwards, hdmstr. Fax 981-3221
St. Joseph S 300/K-8
905 N Campus Ave 91786 909-920-5185
Sr. Mary Kelly, prin. Fax 920-5190
St. Mark's Episcopal S 200/PK-8
330 E 16th St 91784 909-920-5565
Brenda Hallock, hdmstr. Fax 920-5569
Upland Christian S 600/K-12
100 W 9th St 91786 909-920-5858
Susan Chiappone, hdmstr. Fax 920-5866

Upper Lake, Lake
Upper Lake UNESD 600/K-8
PO Box 36 95485 707-275-2357
Kurt Herndon, supt. Fax 275-2205
www.uluesd.lake.k12.ca.us/
Upper Lake Union ES 400/K-5
PO Box 36 95485 707-275-2357
Kurt Herndon, prin. Fax 275-2205
Upper Lake Union MS 200/6-8
PO Box 36 95485 707-275-0223
Rick Winer, prin. Fax 275-2911

Vacaville, Solano, Pop. 92,985
Travis USD
Supt. — See Fairfield
Cambridge ES 600/K-6
100 Cambridge Dr 95687 707-446-9494
Connie Green-Ownby, prin. Fax 448-4942
Foxboro ES 800/K-6
600 Morning Glory Dr 95687 707-447-7883
Lisa Eckhoff, prin. Fax 447-6055

Vacaville USD 12,400/K-12
751 School St 95688 707-453-6100
John Aycock, supt. Fax 453-6999
www.vacavilleusd.org
Alamo ES 600/K-6
500 S Orchard Ave 95688 707-453-6200
Kimberly Forrest, prin. Fax 446-2834
Browns Valley ES 900/K-6
333 Wrentham Dr 95688 707-453-6205
Valerie Rogers, prin. Fax 447-5307
Callison ES 800/K-6
6261 Vanden Rd 95687 707-453-6250
Alison Gardner, prin. Fax 446-3729
Cooper ES 800/K-6
750 Christine Dr 95687 707-453-6210
David Robertson, prin. Fax 447-5041
Hemlock ES 400/K-6
400 Hemlock St 95688 707-453-6245
Luci Del Rio, prin. Fax 448-7933
Jepson MS 1,000/7-8
580 Elder St 95688 707-453-6280
Kelley Birch, prin. Fax 447-7128
Markham ES 800/K-6
101 Markham Ave 95688 707-453-6230
Manolo Garcia, prin. Fax 453-0668
Orchard ES 400/K-6
805 N Orchard Ave 95688 707-453-6255
Christie Cochran, prin. Fax 453-7169
Padan ES 800/K-6
200 Padan School Rd 95687 707-453-6235
Sylvia Rodriguez, prin. Fax 448-3748
Sierra Vista ES 500/K-6
301 Bel Air Dr 95687 707-453-6260
Eldridge Glover, prin. Fax 449-1810
Vaca Pena MS 1,000/7-8
200 Keith Way 95687 707-453-6270
Janet Dietrich, prin. Fax 451-9501

Bethany Lutheran S 200/K-8
1011 Ulatis Dr 95687 707-451-6683
Kristopher Schneider, prin. Fax 359-2230
Notre Dame S 300/K-8
1781 Marshall Rd 95687 707-447-1460
Lee Yurkovic, prin. Fax 447-1498
Vacaville Christian S 1,500/PK-12
1117 Davis St 95687 707-446-1776
Paul Harrell, admin. Fax 446-1538
Vacaville SDA S 50/K-8
4740 Allendale Rd 95688 707-448-2842
Nancy Matthews, prin. Fax 448-9717

Valencia, See Santa Clarita
Castaic UNESD 3,400/K-8
28131 Livingston Ave 91355 661-257-4500
James Gibson, supt. Fax 257-3596
www.castaic.k12.ca.us/
Other Schools – See Castaic

Newhall ESD 7,000/K-6
25375 Orchard Village Rd 91355 661-291-4000
Dr. Marc Winger, supt. Fax 291-4001
www.newhallschooldistrict.net/
Meadows ES 700/K-6
25577 Fedala Rd 91355 661-291-4050
Chad Rose, prin. Fax 291-4051
Oak Hills ES 500/K-6
26730 Old Rock Rd, 661-291-4100
Wayne Abruzzo, prin. Fax 291-4102
Valencia Valley ES 700/K-6
23601 Carrizo Dr 91355 661-291-4060
Tammi Rainville, prin. Fax 291-4061
Other Schools – See Newhall, Santa Clarita, Stevenson Ranch

Saugus UNESD
Supt. — See Santa Clarita
Helmers ES 900/K-6
27300 Grandview Dr 91354 661-286-4399
Diane Miscione, prin. Fax 286-4391
North Park ES 900/K-6
23335 Sunset Hills Dr 91354 661-297-1476
Pete Bland, prin. Fax 297-1480
Tesoro del Valle ES 500/K-6
29171 Bernardo Way 91354 661-294-2600
Mary Post, prin. Fax 294-1461

William S. Hart UNHSD
Supt. — See Santa Clarita
Arroyo Seco JHS 1,200/7-8
27171 Vista Delgado Dr 91354 661-296-0991
Rhondi Durand, prin. Fax 296-3436
Rio Norte JHS 1,300/7-8
28771 Rio Norte Dr 91354 661-295-3700
John Costanzo, prin. Fax 257-1413

Legacy Christian Academy 300/K-7
27680 Dickason Dr 91355 661-257-7377
Timothy Borruel, supt. Fax 257-7370
Pinecrest S 200/K-5
25443 Orchard Village Rd 91355 661-255-8080
Vicki Lopez, admin. Fax 255-9734
Trinity Classical Academy 200/K-12
28310 Kelly Johnson Pkwy 91355 661-296-2601
Liz Caddow, hdmstr. Fax 296-2601

Valinda, Los Angeles, Pop. 18,735
Hacienda La Puente USD
Supt. — See City of Industry
Grandview ES 300/K-5
795 Grandview Ln, La Puente CA 91744
626-934-5800
David Purcey, prin. Fax 855-3824
Grandview MS 500/6-8
795 Grandview Ln, La Puente CA 91744
626-934-5801
David Purcey, prin. Fax 855-3824
Wing Lane ES 500/K-5
16605 Wing Ln, La Puente CA 91744 626-933-5900
Dr. Judy Devens-Seligman, prin. Fax 855-3797

Vallejo, Solano, Pop. 117,483
Napa Valley USD
Supt. — See Napa
Donaldson Way ES 500/K-5
430 Donaldson Way 94503 707-253-3524
Melissa Strongman, prin. Fax 253-6290

Vallejo City USD 16,500/K-12
665 Walnut Ave 94592 707-556-8921
Mary Bull Ph.D., supt. Fax 649-3907
www.vallejo.k12.ca.us
Beverly Hills ES 300/K-5
1450 Coronel Ave 94591 707-556-8400
Mary Dybdahl, prin. Fax 556-8407
Cave ES 400/K-5
770 Tregaskis Ave 94591 707-556-8410
Sandy Rhodes, prin. Fax 556-8415
Cooper ES 500/K-5
612 Del Mar Ave 94589 707-556-8420
Lucius McKelvy, prin. Fax 556-8423
Federal Terrace ES 500/K-5
415 Daniels Ave 94590 707-556-8460
Marisa Santoya, prin. Fax 556-8469
Franklin MS 900/6-8
501 Starr Ave 94590 707-556-8470
Michael David, prin. Fax 556-8475
Glen Cove ES 500/K-5
501 Glen Cove Pkwy 94591 707-556-8491
Greg Allison, prin. Fax 556-8494
Highland ES 700/K-5
1309 Ensign Ave 94590 707-556-8500
Alana Brown, prin. Fax 556-8504
Lincoln ES 200/K-5
620 Carolina St 94590 707-556-8540
Mitchell Romao, prin. Fax 556-8545
Loma Vista ES 400/K-5
146 Rainier Ave 94589 707-556-8550
Dolly McInnes, prin. Fax 556-8555
Mare Island ES 300/K-5
400 Rickover St 94592 707-556-8560
Margaret Clark, prin. Fax 556-8564
Mini ES 700/K-5
1530 Lorenzo Dr 94589 707-556-8570
Denise Hawke, prin. Fax 556-8573
Patterson ES 500/K-5
1080 Porter St 94590 707-556-8580
Elissa Stewart, prin. Fax 556-8589

Pennycook ES 600/K-5
3620 Fernwood St 94591 707-556-8590
Pat Andry-Jennings, prin. Fax 556-8595
Solano MS 800/6-8
1025 Corcoran Ave 94589 707-556-8600
Sheila Quintana, prin. Fax 556-8615
Springstowne MS 1,000/6-8
2833 Tennessee St 94591 707-556-8620
Jocelyn Hendrix, prin. Fax 556-8624
Steffan Manor ES 600/K-5
815 Cedar St 94591 707-556-8640
Dennis Gulbransen, prin. Fax 556-8649
Vallejo MS 800/6-8
1347 Amador St 94590 707-556-8650
Gigi Patrick, prin. Fax 556-8666
Wardlaw ES 800/K-5
1698 Oakwood Ave 94591 707-556-8730
Coreen Russell, prin. Fax 556-8739
Widenmann ES 600/K-5
100 Whitney Ave 94589 707-556-8740
Alexa Hauser, prin. Fax 556-8749

North Hills Christian S 600/PK-12
200 Admiral Callaghan Ln 94591 707-644-5284
Andrew Robinson, prin. Fax 644-5295
St. Basil S 300/PK-8
1230 Nebraska St 94590 707-642-7629
Neil Orlina, prin. Fax 642-8635
St. Catherine of Sienna S 300/K-8
3460 Tennessee St 94591 707-643-6691
Linda Mazzei, prin. Fax 647-4441
St. Vincent Ferrer S 300/K-8
420 Florida St 94590 707-642-4311
Tom Yurkovic, prin. Fax 642-1329
Sonshine K & Preschool 50/PK-K
210 Locust Dr 94591 707-643-4451
Beverly Herod, dir. Fax 644-4453

Valley Center, San Diego, Pop. 1,711
Valley Center-Pauma USD 3,800/K-12
28751 Cole Grade Rd 92082 760-749-0464
Dr. Lou Obermeyer, supt. Fax 749-1208
www.vcpusd.net/
Lilac ES 500/K-5
28751 Cole Grade Rd 92082 760-751-1042
Shannon Hargrave, prin. Fax 751-7407
Valley Center ES 400/3-5
28751 Cole Grade Rd 92082 760-749-1631
Wendy Heredia, prin. Fax 749-5501
Valley Center MS 700/6-8
28751 Cole Grade Rd 92082 760-751-4295
Jon Peterson, prin. Fax 751-4259
Valley Center PS 500/K-2
28751 Cole Grade Rd 92082 760-749-8282
Patty Christopher, prin. Fax 751-2654
Other Schools – See Pauma Valley

Valley Glen, Los Angeles

Laurence S 300/K-6
13639 Victory Blvd, 818-782-4001
Marvin Jacobson, hdmstr. Fax 782-4004

Valley Home, Stanislaus
Valley Home Joint SD 200/K-8
13231 Pioneer Ave 95361 209-847-0117
Kevin Hart, supt. Fax 848-9456
www.vhjsd.k12.ca.us/
Valley Home S 200/K-8
13231 Pioneer Ave 95361 209-847-0117
Kevin Hart, prin. Fax 848-9456

Valley Springs, Calaveras
Calaveras USD
Supt. — See San Andreas
Lind ES 700/K-6
5100 Driver Rd 95252 209-754-2168
Amy Hasselwander, prin. Fax 772-2566
Toyon MS 500/7-8
3412 Double Springs Rd 95252 209-754-2137
John Peckler, prin. Fax 754-5327
Valley Springs ES 500/K-6
240 Pine St 95252 209-754-2141
Tim Garrison, prin. Fax 772-1013

Valley Village, See Los Angeles

Adat Ari El Day S 200/K-6
12020 Burbank Blvd 91607 818-766-4992
Lana Marcus, hdmstr. Fax 766-1436

Van Nuys, See Los Angeles
Los Angeles USD
Supt. — See Los Angeles
Anatola Avenue ES 500/K-5
7364 Anatola Ave 91406 818-343-8733
Miriam King, prin. Fax 344-1550
Bassett Street ES 1,000/K-5
15756 Bassett St 91406 818-782-1340
Linda Barr, prin. Fax 782-8681
Chandler ES 500/K-5
14030 Weddington St 91401 818-789-6173
Kristine McIntire, prin. Fax 995-7095
Cohasset ES 700/K-5
15810 Saticoy St 91406 818-787-2113
Andrea Yahudian, prin. Fax 782-3522
Columbus Ave ES 600/K-5
6700 Columbus Ave 91405 818-779-5440
Barbara Thibodeau, prin. Fax 779-7947
Erwin Street ES 1,000/K-5
13400 Erwin St 91401 818-988-6292
Maria Awakian, prin. Fax 785-2674
Gault Street ES 500/K-5
17000 Gault St 91406 818-343-1933
William Albion, prin. Fax 776-0237
Hazeltine Avenue ES 1,000/K-5
7150 Hazeltine Ave 91405 818-781-1040
Susana Cuevas, prin. Fax 781-8613

Kester ES 800/K-5
5353 Kester Ave 91411 818-787-6751
Susan Goldberg, prin. Fax 787-5480
Kindergarten Learning Academy 200/K-K
6555 Sylmar Ave 91401 818-994-2904
Stannis Steinbeck, prin. Fax 994-8096
Kittridge Street ES 900/K-5
13619 Kittridge St 91401 818-786-7926
Joan Blair, prin. Fax 988-0692
LeMay ES 400/K-5
17520 Vanowen St 91406 818-343-4696
Elayne Elsky, prin. Fax 708-0549
Mulholland MS 1,900/6-8
17120 Vanowen St 91406 818-609-2500
John White, prin. Fax 345-1933
Stagg ES 500/K-5
7839 Amestoy Ave 91406 818-881-9850
Patricia Brandon, prin. Fax 609-8537
Sylvan Park ES 900/K-5
6238 Noble Ave 91411 818-988-4020
Lawrence Orozco, prin. Fax 997-7630
Valerio Primary Center 200/K-2
14935 Valerio St 91405 818-902-1851
Jacqueline Schneider, prin. Fax 902-0549
Valerio Street ES 1,100/K-5
15035 Valerio St 91405 818-785-8683
Anna Martinez, prin. Fax 786-8749
Van Nuys ES 800/1-5
6464 Sylmar Ave 91401 818-785-2195
Ada Yslas, prin. Fax 782-4173
Van Nuys MS 1,600/6-8
5435 Vesper Ave 91411 818-267-5900
Anita Barner, prin. Fax 909-7274
Vista MS 2,000/6-8
15040 Roscoe Blvd 91402 818-901-2727
Suzanne Blake, prin. Fax 901-2740

Childrens Community S 100/K-6
14702 Sylvan St 91411 818-780-6226
Neal Wrightson, prin. Fax 780-5834
Pacific S 100/K-12
15339 Saticoy St 91406 818-267-2600
Dee Brown, dir. Fax 988-9143
Pinecrest S 300/K-8
14111 Sherman Way 91405 818-988-5554
Kristine Hughes, prin. Fax 782-8837
St. Bridget of Sweden S 200/K-8
7120 Whitaker Ave 91406 818-785-4422
Robert Pawlak, prin. Fax 785-0490
St. Elisabeth S 300/PK-8
6635 Tobias Ave 91405 818-779-1766
Barbara Barreda, prin. Fax 779-1768
Valley S 200/PK-8
15700 Sherman Way 91406 818-786-4720
James Haddad, prin. Fax 786-2688
Valley Waldorf City S of Los Angeles 50/PK-8
17424 Sherman Way 91406 818-776-0011
Holly Baxter-Cunningham, admin. Fax 758-9151

Venice, See Los Angeles
Los Angeles USD
Supt. — See Los Angeles
Broadway ES 300/K-5
1015 Lincoln Blvd 90291 310-392-4944
Susan Wang, prin. Fax 314-7349
Coeur D'Alene ES 500/K-5
810 Coeur D Alene Ave 90291 310-821-7813
Rex Patton, prin. Fax 823-4486
Westminster ES 500/K-5
1010 Abbot Kinney Blvd 90291 310-392-3041
Karen Brown, prin. Fax 392-6506
Westside Leadership Magnet S 500/K-8
104 Anchorage St 90292 310-821-2039
Cyril Baird, prin. Fax 306-9730

First Lutheran S 100/K-8
815 Venice Blvd 90291 310-823-9367
David Rusch, prin. Fax 823-4822
St. Mark S 200/K-8
912 Coeur D Alene Ave 90291 310-821-6612
Mary Jo Aiken, prin. Fax 822-6101

Ventura, Ventura, Pop. 102,000
Ventura USD 17,200/K-12
255 W Stanley Ave Ste 100 93001 805-641-5000
Dr. Trudy Tuttle Arriaga, supt. Fax 653-7855
www.venturausd.org
Anacapa MS 1,000/6-8
100 S Mills Rd 93003 805-289-7900
Soledad Molinar, prin. Fax 289-7909
Balboa MS 1,400/6-8
247 S Hill Rd 93003 805-289-1800
Teresa Gern, prin. Fax 289-1806
Cabrillo MS 1,100/6-8
1426 E Santa Clara St 93001 805-641-5155
Glory Page, prin. Fax 641-5377
Citrus Glen ES 500/K-5
9655 Darling Rd 93004 805-672-0220
Shelley DuPratt, prin. Fax 672-0224
De Anza MS 500/6-8
2060 Cameron St 93001 805-641-5165
Anne Roundy-Harter, prin. Fax 641-5282
Elmhurst ES 600/K-5
5080 Elmhurst St 93003 805-289-1860
Patricia Kingsley, prin. Fax 289-1865
Foster ES 500/K-5
20 Pleasant Pl 93001 805-641-5420
Michael Tapia, prin. Fax 641-5390
Juanamaria ES 500/K-5
100 Crocker Ave 93004 805-672-0291
Gina Wolowicz, prin. Fax 659-3078
Junipero Serra ES 500/K-5
8880 Halifax St 93004 805-672-2717
Todd Tyner, prin. Fax 672-2716
Lincoln ES 300/K-5
1107 E Santa Clara St 93001 805-641-5438
Lee Warner, prin. Fax 641-5398

Loma Vista ES 400/K-5
300 Lynn Dr 93003 805-641-5443
Nancy Barker, prin. Fax 641-5334
Montalvo ES 400/K-5
2050 Grand Ave 93003 805-289-1872
Michele Dean, prin. Fax 289-1871
Mound ES 600/K-5
455 S Hill Rd 93003 805-289-1886
Tom Temprano, prin. Fax 289-1883
Pierpont ES 300/K-5
1254 Marthas Vineyard Ct 93001 805-641-5470
Larry Hardesty, prin. Fax 641-5283
Poinsettia ES 500/K-5
350 N Victoria Ave 93003 805-289-7971
Wes Wade, prin. Fax 289-7970
Portola ES 500/K-5
6700 Eagle St 93003 805-289-1734
Robert Ruiz, prin. Fax 289-9987
Reynolds ES 300/K-5
450 Valmore Ave 93003 805-289-1817
Paul Jablonowski, prin. Fax 289-1814
Rogers ES 400/K-5
316 Howard St 93003 805-641-5496
Patricia Short, prin. Fax 653-0625
Saticoy ES 400/K-5
760 Jazmin Ave 93004 805-672-2701
Jim Sather, prin. Fax 672-0296
Sheridan Way ES 500/K-5
573 Sheridan Way 93001 805-641-5491
Susan Eberhart, prin. Fax 641-5276
Other Schools – See Oak View

College Heights Christian S 200/K-8
6360 Telephone Rd 93003 805-658-2900
Jacquie Alderson, prin. Fax 658-2959
First Baptist Day S 100/PK-K
426 S Mills Rd 93003 805-642-1562
Julie Needham, admin. Fax 642-3246
Holy Cross S 300/PK-8
211 E Main St 93001 805-643-1500
Sr. Rachel Yourgul, prin. Fax 643-7831
Our Lady of the Assumption S 300/PK-8
3169 Telegraph Rd 93003 805-642-7198
Patricia Groff, prin. Fax 642-7110
Sacred Heart S 200/PK-8
10770 Henderson Rd 93004 805-647-6174
Laura Tellez, prin. Fax 647-2291
St. Paul's Parish Day S 50/K-8
3290 Loma Vista Rd 93003 805-648-5650
Victoria Cloninger, hdmstr. Fax 643-5946
Ventura County Christian S 100/K-12
96 MacMillan Ave 93001 805-641-0187
Fax 641-0252
Ventura Missionary S 400/PK-8
500 High Point Dr 93003 805-644-9515
Nancy Baker, prin. Fax 642-5197

Vernalis, San Joaquin
Patterson JUSD
Supt. — See Patterson
Rising Sun ES 50/K-5
PO Box 796 95385 209-835-0281
Arturo Duran, prin. Fax 839-1364

Vernon, Los Angeles, Pop. 92
Los Angeles USD
Supt. — See Los Angeles
Holmes Avenue ES 400/K-5
5108 Holmes Ave 90058 323-582-7238
Antonio Amparan, prin. Fax 582-0723
Vernon City ES 200/K-5
2360 E Vernon Ave 90058 323-582-3727
Martin Sandoval, prin. Fax 585-9957

Victor, San Joaquin
Lodi USD
Supt. — See Lodi
Victor ES 200/K-6
PO Box L 95253 209-331-7441
Carlos Villafana, prin. Fax 331-7530

Victorville, San Bernardino, Pop. 91,264
Adelanto ESD
Supt. — See Adelanto
Eagle Ranch ES 1,000/K-5
12545 Eagle Ranch Pkwy 92392 760-949-2100
Fax 949-2558
George Magnet S 500/K-8
17738 Nevada St 92394 760-246-8231
Jeff Youskievicz, prin. Fax 246-5821
Mesa Linda MS 1,100/6-8
13001 Mesa Linda Ave 92392 760-956-7355
Doug Newton, prin. Fax 956-7456
Morgan/Kincaid Prep S 600/K-5
13257 Mesa Linda Ave 92392 760-956-9006
Debra French, prin. Fax 956-2734
West Creek ES 300/K-5
15763 Cobalt Rd 92394 760-951-3628
Fax 955-7862

Hesperia USD
Supt. — See Hesperia
Hollyvale ES 600/K-6
11645 Hollyvale Ave 92392 760-947-3484
Matthew Fedders, prin. Fax 947-2048

Snowline JUSD
Supt. — See Phelan
Vista Verde ES 500/K-5
13403 Vista Verde St 92392 760-662-5650
Maria Hughes, prin. Fax 662-5659

Victor ESD 11,900/K-6
15579 8th St, 760-245-1691
Ralph Baker Ph.D., supt. Fax 245-6245
www.vesd.net
Academy ES 400/K-6
15579 8th St, 760-245-7961
Allen Miller, prin. Fax 245-2139

Brentwood ES 1,300/K-6
15579 8th St, 760-243-2301
Minda Stackelhouse, prin. Fax 243-4675
Challenger S of Sports and Fitness 1,000/K-6
15579 8th St, 760-843-6866
Audrey Howard, prin. Fax 843-5854
Del Rey ES 600/K-6
15579 8th St, 760-245-7941
Christa Robinson, prin. Fax 245-1627
Discovery S of the Arts 1,000/K-6
15579 8th St, 760-843-3577
Robert Hill, prin. Fax 843-1078
Endeavour S of Exploration 700/K-6
15579 8th St, 760-843-7303
Renee Thomas, prin. Fax 843-7348
Galileo 101 Academy 200/K-6
15579 8th St, 760-241-1799
Anita Campbell, prin. Fax 245-2524
Green Tree East ES 700/K-6
15579 8th St, 760-955-7600
Maureen Mills, prin. Fax 955-7550
Irwin ES 300/K-6
15579 8th St, 760-245-7691
Allen Miller, prin. Fax 245-2139
Liberty ES 900/K-6
15579 8th St, 760-241-1520
Ailene Cammon, prin. Fax 241-7674
Lomitas ES 800/K-6
15579 8th St, 760-243-2012
Denise Edge, prin. Fax 243-1291
Mojave Vista ES 1,000/K-6
15579 8th St, 760-241-2474
Martha McCarthy, prin. Fax 241-3606
Park View ES 900/K-6
15579 8th St, 760-241-7731
Paulina Ugo, prin. Fax 241-7269
Puesta Del Sol ES 600/K-6
15579 8th St, 760-243-2028
Gale Sakal, prin. Fax 243-4140
Village ES 1,000/K-6
15579 8th St, 760-243-1160
Christi Goodloe, prin. Fax 243-5752
West Palms Conservatory ES 500/K-6
15579 8th St, 760-245-3525
Melissa Theide, prin. Fax 245-3683

Victor Valley UNHSD 9,100/7-12
16350 Mojave Dr, 760-955-3200
Marilou Ryder Ed.D., supt. Fax 245-3128
www.vvuhsd.org
Cobalt MS 700/7-8
13801 Cobalt Rd 92392 760-955-2530
Lonnie Keeter, prin. Fax 955-2437
Hook JHS 1,100/7-8
15000 Hook Blvd 92394 760-955-3360
James Nason, prin. Fax 245-5839
Lakeview MS 7-8
12484 Tamarisk Rd, 760-955-3400
Greg Johnson, prin. Fax 955-1992

Victor Valley Christian S 500/PK-12
15260 Nisqually Rd, 760-241-8827
Dr. John Martin, supt. Fax 243-0654
Victor Valley SDA S 50/K-8
17137 Crestview Dr, 760-243-4176
Ralph Martinez, prin. Fax 245-5606
Zion Lutheran S 100/PK-6
15342 Jeraldo Dr 92394 760-243-3074
James Prill, prin. Fax 245-5945

Villa Park, Orange, Pop. 6,026
Orange USD
Supt. — See Orange
Cerro Villa MS 1,100/7-8
17852 Serrano Ave 92861 714-997-6251
Sue Baden, prin. Fax 921-9331
Serrano ES 500/K-6
17741 Serrano Ave 92861 714-997-6275
Roberta Lansman, prin. Fax 637-2051
Villa Park ES 600/K-6
10551 Center Dr 92861 714-997-6281
Debbie Larson, prin. Fax 532-5895

Vina, Tehama
Los Molinos USD
Supt. — See Los Molinos
Vina S 100/1-8
PO Box 230 96092 530-839-2182
Brad Wescoatt, prin. Fax 839-2743

Visalia, Tulare, Pop. 108,669
Liberty ESD 200/K-8
11535 Avenue 264 93277 559-686-1675
Al George, supt. Fax 686-2879
Liberty S 200/K-8
11535 Avenue 264 93277 559-686-1675
Al George, prin. Fax 686-2879

Outside Creek ESD 100/K-8
26452 Road 164 93292 559-747-0710
Elaine Brainard, supt. Fax 747-0398
www.tcoe.org/districts/outsidecreek.shtm
Outside Creek S 100/K-8
26452 Road 164 93292 559-747-0710
Elaine Brainard, prin. Fax 747-0398

Stone Corral ESD 100/K-8
15590 Avenue 383 93292 559-528-4455
Gabriel Perez, supt. Fax 528-3808
Stone Corral S 100/K-8
15590 Avenue 383 93292 559-528-4455
Gabriel Perez, prin. Fax 528-3808

Visalia USD 25,500/K-12
5000 W Cypress Ave 93277 559-730-7300
Stan Carrizosa, supt. Fax 730-7508
www.visalia.k12.ca.us
Conyer ES 500/K-6
814 S Sowell St 93277 559-730-7751
Kimberly Leon, prin. Fax 730-7380
Cottonwood Creek ES 400/K-6
4222 S Dans St 93277 559-735-3539
Clae Nave, prin. Fax 735-3541
Crestwood ES 800/K-6
3001 W Whitendale Ave 93277 559-730-7754
Jim Sullivan, prin. Fax 730-7744
Crowley ES 600/K-6
214 E Ferguson Ave 93291 559-730-7758
Jesse Sanchez, prin. Fax 730-7945
Divisadero MS 1,000/7-8
1200 S Divisadero St 93277 559-730-7661
Matt Shin, prin. Fax 730-7908
Elbow Creek ES 500/K-6
32747 Road 138 93292 559-730-7766
Shirley Williams, prin. Fax 730-7878
Fairview ES 600/K-6
1051 W Robin Dr 93291 559-730-7768
Felix Mata, prin. Fax 730-7439
Four Creeks ES 700/K-6
1844 N Burke St 93292 559-622-3115
Evaristo Trevino, prin. Fax 622-3118
Golden Oak ES 600/K-6
1700 N Lovers Ln 93292 559-730-7851
Susan Wallace-Sims, prin. Fax 730-7840
Goshen ES 500/K-6
6505 Avenue 308 93291 559-730-7847
Mimi Bonds, prin. Fax 730-7972
Green Acres MS 1,100/7-8
1147 N Mooney Blvd 93291 559-730-7671
Dave Tonini, prin. Fax 730-7918
Hernandez ES K-6
2133 N Leila St 93291 559-622-3199
Cheryl LaVerne, prin. Fax 622-3201
Highland ES 600/K-6
701 N Stevenson St 93291 559-730-7769
John Alvarez, prin. Fax 730-7980
Houston ES 600/K-6
1200 N Giddings St 93291 559-730-7772
Linda Barwick, prin. Fax 730-7721
Hurley ES 600/K-6
6600 W Hurley Ave 93291 559-730-7905
Julie Berk, prin. Fax 730-7458
La Joya MS 1,000/7-8
4711 W La Vida Ave 93277 559-730-7921
Melanie Stringer, prin. Fax 730-7505
Linwood ES 600/K-6
3129 S Linwood St 93277 559-730-7776
Jacqueline Gaebe, prin. Fax 730-7461
Mineral King ES 600/K-6
3333 E Kaweah Ave 93292 559-730-7779
Judy Burgess, prin. Fax 730-7781
Mitchell ES K-6
2121 E Laura Ave 93292 559-622-3195
Andy DiMeo, prin. Fax 622-3197
Mountain View ES 700/K-6
2021 S Encina St 93277 559-730-7783
Pam Merkel, prin. Fax 730-7407
Oak Grove ES 900/K-6
4445 W Ferguson Ave 93291 559-622-3105
Scott Wahab, prin. Fax 622-3108
Pinkham ES 600/K-6
2200 E Tulare Ave 93292 559-730-7853
Marty Frolli, prin. Fax 730-7982
Royal Oaks ES 600/K-6
1323 S Clover St 93277 559-730-7787
Samantha Tate, prin. Fax 730-7844
Valley Oak MS 1,000/7-8
2000 N Lovers Ln 93292 559-730-7681
Cindy Alonzo, prin. Fax 730-7822
Veva Blunt ES 700/K-6
1119 S Chinowth St 93277 559-730-7793
Doug Cardoza, prin. Fax 730-7893
Washington ES 300/K-6
500 S Garden St 93277 559-730-7795
Mary Kalashian, prin. Fax 730-7484
Willow Glen ES 600/K-6
310 N Akers St 93291 559-730-7798
Tammy Gonzales, prin. Fax 730-7788
Other Schools – See Ivanhoe

Central Valley Christian S 1,100/PK-12
5600 W Tulare Ave 93277 559-734-9481
Dr. John DeLeeuw, supt. Fax 734-7963
Grace Christian S 100/PK-6
1111 S Conyer St 93277 559-734-7694
Sandy Eitel, prin. Fax 734-0146
McCann Memorial Catholic S 200/K-8
200 E Race Ave 93291 559-732-5831
Sheila Rast, prin. Fax 741-1562
St. Paul's S 300/PK-9
6101 W Goshen Ave 93291 559-739-1619
Cathy Guadagni, dir. Fax 739-0950
Visalia Christian ES 200/K-6
3737 S Akers St 93277 559-733-9073
Tamara Olson, supt. Fax 733-1556

Vista, San Diego, Pop. 90,402
San Marcos USD
Supt. — See San Marcos
Leichtag ES K-5
653 Poinsettia Ave, 760-290-2888
Eric Forseth, prin. Fax 290-2855

Vista USD 24,000/K-12
1234 Arcadia Ave 92084 760-726-2170
Dr. Joyce Bales, supt. Fax 758-7838
www.vusd.k12.ca.us
Beaumont ES 600/K-5
550 Beaumont Dr 92084 760-726-4040
Peggy Fickes, prin. Fax 726-7961
Bobier ES 700/K-5
220 W Bobier Dr 92083 760-724-8501
David Lacey, prin. Fax 940-8695
Breeze Hill ES 700/K-5
1111 Melrose Way, 760-945-2373
Ron Arnold, prin. Fax 945-8259
Casita Center for Tech-Science & Math 800/K-5
260 Cedar Rd 92083 760-724-8442
Laura Smith, prin. Fax 758-4697
Crestview ES 600/K-5
510 Sunset Dr, 760-726-3240
Tracey Zachry, prin. Fax 726-0983
Foothill-Oak ES 600/K-5
1370 Oak Dr 92084 760-631-3458
Beth Graham, prin. Fax 631-3464
Grapevine ES 700/K-5
630 Grapevine Rd 92083 760-724-8329
Amy Illingworth, prin. Fax 724-1821
Hannalei ES 600/K-5
120 Hannalei Dr 92083 760-631-6248
Chuck Hoover, prin. Fax 631-6254
Maryland ES 500/K-5
700 North Ave 92083 760-631-6675
Karen Burke, prin. Fax 643-2668
Monte Vista ES 500/K-5
1720 Monte Vista Dr 92084 760-726-0410
Sue Orton, prin. Fax 726-0423
Olive ES 500/K-5
836 Olive Ave 92083 760-724-7129
Gina Zyburt, prin. Fax 724-3820
Rancho Minerva MS 900/6-8
2245 Foothill Dr 92084 760-631-4500
Steve Riehle, prin. Fax 643-2490
Vista Academy of Arts 1,100/K-8
600 N Santa Fe Ave 92083 760-941-0880
Mary Contreras, prin. Fax 945-3201
Vista Magnet MS 1,000/6-8
151 Escondido Ave 92084 760-726-5766
Jose Villarreal, prin. Fax 945-4273
Washington MS 1,100/6-8
740 Olive Ave 92083 760-724-7115
Michael Marcos, prin. Fax 941-6912
Other Schools – See Oceanside

Calvary Christian S 300/K-12
885 E Vista Way 92084 760-724-4590
Jess Hetherington, prin. Fax 560-0607
Faith Lutheran S 300/PK-8
700 E Bobier Dr 92084 760-724-7700
Joe Henkell, prin. Fax 724-6151
Memorial Christian S 50/PK-5
1830 Anna Ln 92083 760-941-1590
Kimberly Milligan, prin.
St. Francis of Assisi S 300/PK-8
525 W Vista Way 92083 760-630-7960
Linda McCotter, prin. Fax 726-2910
Tri City Christian S 1,100/PK-12
302 N Emerald Dr 92083 760-724-3016
Clark Gilbert, supt. Fax 724-6643
Vista Christian S 100/K-7
290 N Melrose Dr 92083 760-724-7353
Diane Nash, prin. Fax 724-9887

Walnut, Los Angeles, Pop. 31,424
Rowland USD
Supt. — See Rowland Heights
Oswalt Academy 700/K-8
19501 Shadow Oak Dr 91789 626-810-4109
Astrid Ramirez, prin. Fax 964-1372
Ybarra Academy of Arts and Technology 400/K-8
1300 Brea Canyon Cut Off Rd 91789 909-598-3744
Annette Lopez, prin. Fax 598-9264

Walnut Valley USD 15,400/K-12
880 S Lemon Ave 91789 909-595-1261
Cynthia Simms Ph.D., supt. Fax 444-3435
www.wvusd.k12.ca.us
Collegewood ES 700/K-5
20725 Collegewood Dr 91789 909-598-5308
Robert Chang, prin. Fax 598-2838
Morris ES 500/K-5
19875 Calle Baja 91789 909-594-0053
Susan Arzola, prin. Fax 595-9438
South Pointe MS 1,200/6-8
20671 Larkstone Dr 91789 909-595-8171
Scott Martinez, prin. Fax 468-5201
Suzanne MS 1,500/6-8
525 Suzanne Rd 91789 909-594-1657
Les Ojeda, prin. Fax 598-6741
Vejar ES 500/K-5
20222 Vejar Rd 91789 909-594-1434
Kaye Ekstrand, prin. Fax 594-7164
Walnut ES 500/K-5
841 Glenwick Ave 91789 909-594-1820
Nancy Stingley, prin. Fax 595-4680
Westhoff ES 600/K-5
20151 Amar Rd 91789 909-594-6483
Denise Rendon, prin. Fax 594-1393
Other Schools – See Diamond Bar

Southlands Christian S 600/PK-12
1920 Brea Canyon Cut Off Rd 91789 909-598-9733
Glenn Duncan, admin. Fax 468-9943

Walnut Creek, Contra Costa, Pop. 64,196
Mount Diablo USD
Supt. — See Concord
Bancroft ES 400/K-5
2200 Parish Dr 94598 925-933-3405
Linda Schuler, prin. Fax 943-1587
Foothill MS 1,100/6-8
2775 Cedro Ln 94598 925-939-8600
Linda Hutcherson, prin. Fax 256-4281
Valle Verde ES 600/K-5
3275 Peachwillow Ln 94598 925-939-5700
Carolyn Kreuscher, prin. Fax 930-7508
Walnut Acres ES 700/K-5
180 Cerezo Dr 94598 925-939-1333
Sandra Brickell, prin. Fax 939-1155

Walnut Creek ESD — 3,200/K-8
960 Ygnacio Valley Rd 94596 — 925-944-6850
Patricia Wool Ed.D., supt. — Fax 944-1768
www.wcsd.k12.ca.us
Buena Vista ES — 500/K-5
2355 San Juan Ave 94597 — 925-944-6822
Heather Duncan, prin. — Fax 934-8907
Indian Valley ES — 400/K-5
551 Marshall Dr 94598 — 925-944-6828
Nancy Weatherford, prin. — Fax 935-1091
Murwood ES — 400/K-5
2050 Vanderslice Ave 94596 — 925-943-2462
Fax 934-0356
Parkmead ES — 400/K-5
1920 Magnolia Way 94595 — 925-944-6858
Kathleen Scott Ed.D., prin. — Fax 939-2849
Walnut Creek IS — 1,100/6-8
2425 Walnut Blvd 94597 — 925-944-6840
Kevin Collins Ed.D., prin. — Fax 933-1922
Walnut Heights ES — 300/K-5
4064 Walnut Blvd 94596 — 925-944-6834
Susan Drews, prin. — Fax 934-0648

Contra Costa Christian S — 400/PK-12
2721 Larkey Ln 94597 — 925-934-4964
B. J. Huizenga, supt. — Fax 934-4966
Dorris-Eaton S — 300/K-8
1847 Newell Ave 94595 — 925-933-5225
Gerald Ludden, hdmstr. — Fax 256-9710
Legacy Academy — 100/1-12
1283 Boulevard Way 94595 — 925-262-4102
Bradley Smith, dir.
NorthCreek Academy — 600/PK-8
2303A Ygnacio Valley Rd 94598 — 925-954-6322
Greg Steele, admin. — Fax 954-6396
Palmer S for Boys & Girls — 300/K-8
2740 Jones Rd 94597 — 925-934-4888
Samuel Mendes, hdmstr. — Fax 932-4888
St. Mary S — 300/PK-8
1158 Bont Ln 94596 — 925-935-5054
Suzanne Edwards, prin. — Fax 935-5063
Seven Hills S — 400/PK-8
975 N San Carlos Dr 94598 — 925-933-0666
William Miller M.A., hdmstr. — Fax 933-6271
Trinity Lutheran Preschool — 50/PK-PK
2317 Buena Vista Ave 94597 — 925-935-3362
Stephanie Schmidt, dir. — Fax 935-7902
Walnut Creek Christian Academy — 300/PK-8
2336 Buena Vista Ave 94597 — 925-935-1587
Esther McClellan, prin. — Fax 934-1518

Walnut Grove, Sacramento
River Delta USD
Supt. — See Rio Vista
Walnut Grove ES — 200/K-6
PO Box 145 95690 — 916-776-1844
Debbie Evans, prin. — Fax 776-2074

Warner Springs, San Diego
Warner USD — 200/PK-12
PO Box 8 92086 — 760-782-3517
Ron Koenig Ph.D., supt. — Fax 782-9117
www.sdcoe.k12.ca.us/districts/warner/
Warner ES — 100/K-5
PO Box 8 92086 — 760-782-3517
Ron Koenig Ph.D., prin. — Fax 782-9117
Warner Preschool — PK-PK
PO Box 8 92086 — 760-782-3517
Ron Koenig Ph.D., prin. — Fax 782-9117

Wasco, Kern, Pop. 23,874
Semitropic ESD — 300/K-8
25300 Highway 46 93280 — 661-758-6412
Bryan Caples, supt. — Fax 758-4134
Semitropic S — 300/K-8
25300 Highway 46 93280 — 661-758-6412
Bryan Caples, prin. — Fax 758-4134

Wasco UNESD — 3,200/K-8
639 Broadway St 93280 — 661-758-7100
Paul Chounet, supt. — Fax 758-7110
www.wuesd.org
Burke ES — K-6
1301 Filburn St 93280 — 661-758-7480
Fax 758-3024
Clemens ES — 700/K-6
523 Broadway St 93280 — 661-758-7120
Danny Arellano, prin. — Fax 758-9200
Jefferson MS — 700/7-8
305 Griffith Ave 93280 — 661-758-7140
Kelly Richers, prin. — Fax 758-9366
Palm Avenue ES — 1,000/K-6
1017 Palm Ave 93280 — 661-758-7130
Rosalinda Chairez, prin. — Fax 758-9369
Prueitt ES — 800/K-6
3501 7th St 93280 — 661-758-7180
Joe Capilla, prin. — Fax 758-9361

North Kern Christian S — 100/PK-8
710 Peters St 93280 — 661-758-5997
Craig Haley, admin. — Fax 758-4370
St. John S — 100/PK-8
929 Broadway St 93280 — 661-758-6467
Jeanette White, prin. — Fax 758-6897

Washington, Nevada
Twin Ridges ESD
Supt. — See Nevada City
Washington S — 50/K-8
1 School St 95986 — 530-265-2880
Michelyn Brown, lead tchr. — Fax 265-6588

Waterford, Stanislaus, Pop. 8,161
Roberts Ferry UNESD — 100/K-8
101 Roberts Ferry Rd 95386 — 209-874-2331
George Johnson, supt. — Fax 874-4625
Roberts Ferry Union S — 100/K-8
101 Roberts Ferry Rd 95386 — 209-874-2331
George Johnson, prin. — Fax 874-4625

Waterford USD — 1,500/K-12
219 N Reinway Ave 95386 — 209-874-1809
Don Davis, supt. — Fax 874-3109
www.waterford.k12.ca.us
Moon PS — 500/K-2
319 N Reinway Ave 95386 — 209-874-2371
Steven Kuykendall, prin. — Fax 874-5910
Waterford MS — 400/6-8
12916 Bentley St 95386 — 209-874-2382
Paul Patterson, prin. — Fax 874-3652
Whitehead IS — 3-5
119 N Reinway Ave 95386 — 209-874-1080
Steve Kuyhendall, prin. — Fax 874-9018

Watsonville, Santa Cruz, Pop. 47,927
Pajaro Valley USD — 15,300/K-12
294 Green Valley Rd 95076 — 831-786-2100
Dorma Baker, supt. — Fax 728-4288
www.pvusd.net
Amesti ES — 600/K-5
25 Amesti Rd 95076 — 831-728-6250
Erin Haley, prin. — Fax 728-6276
Bradley ES — 600/K-6
321 Corralitos Rd 95076 — 831-728-6366
Kathy Arola, prin. — Fax 728-6946
Calabasas ES — 700/K-6
202 Calabasas Rd 95076 — 831-728-6368
Terry Eastman, prin. — Fax 761-6053
Hall District ES — 500/K-5
300 Sill Rd 95076 — 831-728-6371
Guillermo Ramos, prin. — Fax 761-6174
Hall MS — 700/6-8
201 Brewington Ave 95076 — 831-728-6270
Artemisa Cortez, prin. — Fax 761-6150
Hyde ES — 600/K-5
125 Alta Vista St 95076 — 831-728-6243
Brett Knupfer, prin. — Fax 728-6211
Lakeview MS — 700/6-8
2350 E Lake Ave 95076 — 831-728-6454
Ken Woods, prin. — Fax 728-6480
Landmark ES — 600/K-5
235 Ohlone Pkwy 95076 — 831-761-7940
Jennifer Wildman, prin. — Fax 761-6100
MacQuiddy ES — 500/K-5
330 Martinelli St 95076 — 831-728-6315
Jack Davidson, prin. — Fax 728-6466
Ohlone ES — 400/K-5
21 Bay Farms Rd 95076 — 831-728-6977
Gloria Miranda, prin. — Fax 761-6144
Pajaro MS — 500/6-8
250 Salinas Rd 95076 — 831-728-6238
Stella Moreno, prin. — Fax 728-6219
Rolling Hills MS — 500/6-8
130 Herman Ave 95076 — 831-728-6341
Rick Ito, prin. — Fax 724-7323
Soldo ES — 600/K-5
1140 Menasco Dr 95076 — 831-786-1310
Sylvia Mendez, prin. — Fax 786-1314
Starlight ES — 600/K-5
225 Hammer Dr 95076 — 831-728-6979
Dr. Mark Donnelly, prin. — Fax 761-6102
White ES — 500/K-5
515 Palm Ave 95076 — 831-728-6321
Olga De Santa Anna, prin. — Fax 728-6450
Other Schools – See Aptos, Freedom

Green Valley Christian S — 400/PK-12
376 S Green Valley Rd 95076 — 831-724-6505
Sharon Harris, prin. — Fax 724-1002
Moreland Notre Dame S — 300/K-8
133 Brennan St 95076 — 831-728-2051
Christine Grul, prin. — Fax 728-2052
Mount Madonna S — 200/PK-12
491 Summit Rd 95076 — 408-847-2717
Jivanti Rutansky, hdmstr. — Fax 847-5633

Weaverville, Trinity, Pop. 3,370
Trinity Alps USD — 900/K-12
PO Box 1227 96093 — 530-623-6104
Ed Traverso, supt. — Fax 623-3418
www.tausd.org/
Weaverville S — 400/K-8
PO Box 1000 96093 — 530-623-5533
Scott Payne, prin. — Fax 623-5548

Weed, Siskiyou, Pop. 3,114
Butteville UNESD — 200/K-8
24512 Edgewood Rd 96094 — 530-938-2255
Cynthia McConnell, supt. — Fax 938-3976
www.sisnet.ssku.k12.ca.us/~besftp/
Butteville Union S — 200/K-8
24512 Edgewood Rd 96094 — 530-938-2255
Cynthia McConnell, prin. — Fax 938-3976

Weed UNESD
Supt. — See Mount Shasta
Weed S — 400/K-8
575 White Ave 96094 — 530-938-2715
Gilbert Pimentel, prin. — Fax 938-2973

Weimar, Placer, Pop. 1,300
Placer Hills UNESD
Supt. — See Meadow Vista
Weimar Hills MS — 700/4-8
PO Box 255 95736 — 530-637-4121
Steve Schaumleffel, prin. — Fax 637-4054

Weldon, Kern
South Fork UNSD — 300/K-8
5225 S Kelso Valley Rd 93283 — 760-378-4000
Robin Shive, supt. — Fax 378-3046
www.southforkschool.org
South Fork ES — 200/K-5
6401 Fay Ranch Rd 93283 — 760-378-2211
Robin Shive, prin. — Fax 378-4369
South Fork MS — 200/6-8
5225 S Kelso Valley Rd 93283 — 760-378-1300
Robin Shive, prin. — Fax 378-9113

Weott, Humboldt
Southern Humboldt JUSD
Supt. — See Miranda
Johnson ES — 100/K-5
PO Box 280 95571 — 707-946-2347
Mike Leonard, prin. — Fax 946-2507

West Covina, Los Angeles, Pop. 108,185
Covina-Valley USD
Supt. — See Covina
Grovecenter ES — 400/K-5
775 N Lark Ellen Ave 91791 — 626-974-4400
Andrea Katanic, prin. — Fax 974-4415
Mesa ES — 600/K-5
409 S Barranca St 91791 — 626-974-4600
Debby Hodgson, prin. — Fax 974-4615
Rowland Avenue ES — 600/K-5
1355 E Rowland Ave 91790 — 626-974-4700
Judy Gonzales, prin. — Fax 974-4715
Traweek MS — 1,100/6-8
1941 E Rowland Ave 91791 — 626-974-7400
Rodney Zerbel, prin. — Fax 974-7415
Workman Avenue ES — 600/K-5
1941 E Workman Ave 91791 — 626-974-4900
Danielle Travieso, prin. — Fax 974-4915

Rowland USD
Supt. — See Rowland Heights
Giano IS — 800/7-8
3223 S Giano Ave 91792 — 626-965-2461
Helen Benavides, prin. — Fax 854-2212
Hollingworth ES — 700/K-6
3003 E Hollingworth St 91792 — 909-598-3661
Miriam Kim, prin. — Fax 468-9581
Rincon IS — 600/7-8
2800 E Hollingworth St 91792 — 626-965-1696
Debi Klotz, prin. — Fax 810-4916

West Covina USD — 9,200/K-12
1717 W Merced Ave 91790 — 626-939-4600
Liliam Leis-Castillo, supt. — Fax 939-4701
westcovina.ca.schoolwebpages.com/
California ES — 400/K-5
1125 W Bainbridge Ave 91790 — 626-939-4800
Cheryl Lisikar, prin. — Fax 939-4805
Cameron ES — 500/K-5
1225 E Cameron Ave 91790 — 626-931-1740
Will Mannion, prin. — Fax 931-1745
Edgewood MS — 1,400/6-8
1625 W Durness St 91790 — 626-939-4900
Marc Trovatore, prin. — Fax 939-4999
Hollencrest MS — 700/6-8
2101 E Merced Ave 91791 — 626-931-1760
Alejandro Ruvalcaba, prin. — Fax 931-1762
Merced ES — 400/K-5
1545 E Merced Ave 91791 — 626-931-1700
Gordon Pfitzer, prin. — Fax 931-1704
Merlinda ES — 500/K-5
1120 S Valinda Ave 91790 — 626-931-1720
Teresa Marquez, prin. — Fax 931-1726
Monte Vista ES — 500/K-5
1615 W Eldred Ave 91790 — 626-939-4830
Elizabeth Sims, prin. — Fax 939-4835
Orangewood ES — 500/K-5
1440 S Orange Ave 91790 — 626-939-4820
Mary Donielson, prin. — Fax 939-4825
Vine ES — 500/K-5
1901 E Vine Ave 91791 — 626-931-1790
William Bertrand, prin. — Fax 931-1795
Walnut Grove IS — 7-8
614 W Vine Ave 91790 — 626-919-7018
Rich Nambu, prin. — Fax 919-7207
Wescove ES — 400/K-5
1010 W Vine Ave 91790 — 626-939-4870
Dr. Elizabeth Quinn, prin. — Fax 939-4875

Christ Lutheran S — 300/K-8
311 S Citrus St 91791 — 626-967-7531
Carolyn Coffey, prin. — Fax 967-8513
Immanuel First Lutheran S — 200/PK-8
512 S Valinda Ave 91790 — 626-919-1072
Linda Redfox, prin. — Fax 919-5979
Jubilee Christian S — 200/PK-6
1211 E Badillo St 91790 — 626-858-8400
Jill Selak, prin. — Fax 858-8412
St. Christopher S — 300/PK-8
900 W Christopher St 91790 — 626-960-3079
Mary Bachman, prin. — Fax 338-7910
South Hills Academy — 400/PK-8
1600 E Francisquito Ave 91791 — 626-919-2000
Lorine Nunnally, hdmstr. — Fax 918-7730
West Covina Christian S — 400/PK-8
763 N Sunset Ave 91790 — 626-962-7080
Christine Petersen, prin. — Fax 962-1589
West Covina Hills Adventist S — 100/K-8
3528 E Temple Way 91791 — 626-859-5005
Angela Nair, prin.

West Hills, Los Angeles
Los Angeles USD
Supt. — See Los Angeles
Enadia ES — K-6
22944 Enadia Way 91307 — 818-595-3900
Robin Toder, prin. — Fax 716-7738
Haynes ES — 300/K-5
6624 Lockhurst Dr 91307 — 818-716-7310
Barbara A. Meade, prin. — Fax 716-7249

Kadima Hebrew Academy — 200/PK-8
7011 Shoup Ave 91307 — 818-346-0849
Dr. Barbara Gereboff, hdmstr. — Fax 346-0372
Shepherd of the Valley Lutheran S — 100/K-6
23838 Kittridge St 91307 — 818-347-6784
Diane Haskell, prin. — Fax 347-9944
West Valley Christian S — 400/PK-12
22450 Sherman Way 91307 — 818-884-4710
Louis Mann, admin. — Fax 884-4749

West Hollywood, Los Angeles, Pop. 36,732
Los Angeles USD
Supt. — See Los Angeles
West Hollywood ES 200/K-5
970 Hammond St 90069 310-274-5313
Jim Hum, prin. Fax 858-8139

Center for Early Education S 500/PK-6
563 N Alfred St 90048 323-651-0707
Reveta Bowers, hdmstr. Fax 651-0860

Westlake Village, Los Angeles, Pop. 8,585
Conejo Valley USD
Supt. — See Thousand Oaks
Westlake ES 500/K-5
1571 E Potrero Rd 91361 805-374-2150
Jeff Rickert, prin. Fax 496-4006
Westlake Hills ES 600/K-5
3333 Medicine Bow Ct 91362 805-497-9339
Sheila Carlson, prin. Fax 374-1162

Las Virgenes USD
Supt. — See Calabasas
White Oak ES 600/K-5
31761 Village School Rd 91361 818-889-1450
Abbe Irshay, prin. Fax 889-5904

Carden Conejo S 300/PK-8
975 Evenstar Ave 91361 805-497-7005
Holly Fleming, hdmstr. Fax 496-5628
Malibu Cove Private S 100/K-12
860 Hampshire Rd 91361 805-267-4818
Joanne Alfonso, dir.
St. Jude the Apostle S 300/PK-8
32036 Lindero Canyon Rd 91361 818-889-9483
Patrick Hayes, prin. Fax 889-1536

Westminster, Orange, Pop. 89,523
Garden Grove USD
Supt. — See Garden Grove
Anthony ES 500/K-6
15320 Pickford St 92683 714-663-6104
Dr. Andrew Heughins, prin. Fax 663-6017
Carrillo ES 700/K-6
15270 Bushard St 92683 714-663-6230
Michelle Askew, prin. Fax 663-6169
Marshall ES, 15791 Bushard St 92683 600/K-6
Dr. Jennifer Carter, prin. 714-663-6528
McGarvin IS, 9802 Bishop Pl 92683 700/7-8
Lila Jenkins, prin. 714-663-6218
Post ES, 14641 Ward St 92683 500/K-6
Rose Jansz Ed.D., prin. 714-663-6354

Ocean View SD
Supt. — See Huntington Beach
Westmont ES 400/K-5
8251 Heil Ave 92683 714-847-3561
Carol Parish Ed.D., prin. Fax 842-6051

Westminster ESD 9,900/PK-8
14121 Cedarwood St 92683 714-894-7311
Dr. Sharon Nordheim, supt. Fax 899-2781
www.wsd.k12.ca.us
Eastwood ES 500/PK-6
13552 University St 92683 714-894-7227
Donna Brush, prin. Fax 901-9104
Finley ES 500/PK-5
13521 Edwards St 92683 714-895-7764
Maria Gutierrez-Garcia, prin. Fax 901-7184
Fryberger ES 500/PK-5
6952 Hood Dr 92683 714-894-7237
Hiacynth Martinez, prin. Fax 896-8471
Johnson MS 900/6-8
13603 Edwards St 92683 714-894-7244
Heidi DeBritton, prin. Fax 379-0784
Land S PK-PK
15151 Temple St 92683 714-898-8389
Beverlee Mathenia, prin. Fax 895-6525
Schmitt ES 500/PK-5
7200 Trask Ave 92683 714-894-7264
Dr. Jerry Gargus, prin. Fax 890-9255
Sequoia ES 400/PK-6
5900 Iroquois Rd 92683 714-894-7271
Tammy Steel, prin. Fax 891-9164
Warner MS 900/6-8
14171 Newland St 92683 714-894-7281
Matthew Skoll, prin. Fax 895-2378
Webber ES 500/PK-6
14142 Hoover St 92683 714-894-7288
Orchid Rocha, prin. Fax 894-7301
Willmore ES 500/PK-5
7122 Maple St 92683 714-895-3765
Rob McKane, prin. Fax 901-0371
Other Schools – See Garden Grove, Huntington Beach, Midway City

Bethany Christian Academy 200/K-8
13431 Edwards St 92683 714-891-9783
Trish Harnish, prin. Fax 892-5379
Blessed Sacrament S 300/PK-8
14146 Olive St 92683 714-893-7701
Roisin McAree, prin. Fax 891-7186
Covenant Christian Academy 50/K-12
10101 Cunningham Ave 92683 714-531-9950
Nancy Gorrell, prin. Fax 531-9926
Westminster Lutheran K 100/PK-K
13841 Milton Ave 92683 714-893-8289
Iris McCray, dir.

Westmorland, Imperial, Pop. 2,266
Westmorland UNESD 400/K-8
PO Box 88 92281 760-344-4364
Linda Morse, supt. Fax 344-7294
www.wued.org
Westmorland S 400/K-8
PO Box 88 92281 760-344-4364
Linda Morse, prin. Fax 344-7294

West Point, Calaveras
Calaveras USD
Supt. — See San Andreas
West Point S 100/K-8
PO Box 96 95255 209-754-2255
Beverly Boone, prin. Fax 293-4727

West Sacramento, Yolo, Pop. 41,744
Washington USD 5,700/PK-12
930 Westacre Rd 95691 916-375-7600
Steven Lawrence Ph.D., supt. Fax 375-7619
www.wusd.k12.ca.us
Bridgeway Island S 700/K-8
3255 Half Moon Bay Cir 95691 916-375-7778
Grace Chin, prin. Fax 375-7794
Bryte ES 200/K-2
637 Todhunter Ave 95605 916-375-7660
Laura Twining, prin. Fax 375-7669
Elkhorn Village S 500/K-8
750 Cummins Way 95605 916-375-7670
Carmelita Goldsby, prin. Fax 375-7879
Norman Education Center PK-PK
1200 Anna St 95605 916-375-7650
Kerry Koerwitz, dir. Fax 375-7771
Riverbank IS 3-8
1100 Carrie St 95605 916-375-7700
Mike Woodcock, prin. Fax 375-7709
Southport S 700/K-8
2747 Linden Rd 95691 916-375-7890
Kendra Reynolds, prin. Fax 375-7894
Stonegate S 900/K-8
2500 La Jolla St 95691 916-375-0960
Marty Ofenham, prin. Fax 372-6057
Westfield Village ES 400/K-5
508 Poplar Ave 95691 916-375-7720
LaReisha Johnson, prin. Fax 375-7729
Westmore Oaks S 600/K-8
1504 Fallbrook St 95691 916-375-7730
Diane Smith, prin. Fax 375-7749

Holy Cross S 200/K-8
800 Todhunter Ave 95605 916-371-1313
Mollie Lashinsky, prin. Fax 371-4193
Our Lady of Grace S 200/K-8
1990 Linden Rd 95691 916-371-9416
Joshua Rucker, prin. Fax 371-1319

Westwood, Lassen, Pop. 2,017
Westwood USD 400/K-12
PO Box 1225 96137 530-256-2311
Henry Bietz, supt. Fax 256-3539
Walker ES 200/K-7
PO Box 1490 96137 530-256-3295
Adele Emershaw, prin. Fax 256-2949

Wheatland, Yuba, Pop. 3,638
Wheatland ESD 1,400/K-8
PO Box 818 95692 530-633-3130
Debra Pearson, supt. Fax 633-4807
www.wheatland.k12.ca.us/
Bear River MS 500/6-8
100 Wheatland Park Dr 95692 530-633-3135
Debbie Schoeppach, prin. Fax 633-3142
Wheatland ES 500/K-5
111 Hooper St 95692 530-633-3140
Angela Gouker, prin. Fax 633-2367
Other Schools – See Beale AFB

Whitethorn, Humboldt
Leggett Valley USD
Supt. — See Leggett
Whale Gulch S 50/K-8
76811 Usal Rd 95589 707-986-7131
Gordon Piffero, prin. Fax 986-1355

Southern Humbolt JUSD
Supt. — See Miranda
Whitethorn S 100/K-7
16851 Briceland Thorn Rd 95589 707-986-7420
Susie Jennings, prin.

Whitmore, Shasta
Whitmore UNESD 50/K-8
PO Box 10 96096 530-472-3243
Merle Stolz, supt. Fax 472-1127
www.shastalink.k12.ca.us/whitmore/Whitmore.htm
Whitmore S 50/K-8
PO Box 10 96096 530-472-3243
Merle Stolz, prin. Fax 472-1127

Whittier, Los Angeles, Pop. 84,473
East Whittier City ESD 8,700/K-8
14535 Whittier Blvd 90605 562-907-5959
Dr. Joe Gillentine, supt. Fax 696-9256
www.ewcsd.org/
Ceres ES 400/K-5
10601 Ceres Ave 90604 562-464-2200
Josephine Sanders, prin. Fax 946-0971
East Whittier MS 1,100/6-8
14421 Whittier Blvd 90605 562-789-7220
Richard Gebhard Ed.D., prin. Fax 945-3542
Evergreen ES 600/K-5
12915 Helmer Dr 90602 562-464-2300
Gabriela Tavitian, prin. Fax 698-6951
Granada MS 900/6-8
15337 Lemon Dr 90604 562-464-2330
Steve Dorsey, prin. Fax 943-5413
Hillview MS 1,000/6-8
10931 Stamy Rd 90604 562-789-2000
Toni Eannareno, prin. Fax 946-3066
La Colima ES 600/K-5
11225 Miller Rd 90604 562-789-7200
Carolyn Garcia, prin. Fax 944-0062
Laurel ES 900/K-5
13550 Lambert Rd 90605 562-789-2100
David Miyashiro Ed.D., prin. Fax 945-3698
Leffingwell ES 400/K-5
10625 Santa Gertrudes Ave 90603 562-907-6300
Dr. Scott Blackwell, prin. Fax 943-2445

Mulberry ES 600/K-5
14029 Mulberry Dr 90605 562-789-7100
Claudia Hamano, prin. Fax 693-2324
Murphy Ranch ES 400/K-5
16021 Janine Dr 90603 562-789-2150
Wendy Davio, prin. Fax 902-0267
Ocean View ES 700/K-5
14359 2nd St 90605 562-907-6400
Kathy Tryon, prin. Fax 693-7424
Orchard Dale ES 700/K-5
10625 Cole Rd 90604 562-789-7000
Diana Grant, prin. Fax 941-5197
Scott Avenue ES 600/K-5
11701 Scott Ave 90604 562-907-6440
Joan Weiss, prin. Fax 943-0454

Los Nietos ESD
Supt. — See Los Nietos
Aeolian ES 500/K-5
11600 Aeolian St 90606 562-699-0913
Amber Lee-Ruiz, prin. Fax 699-2545
Nelson ES 500/K-5
8140 Vicki Dr 90606 562-692-0615
Marla Duncan, prin. Fax 695-0484

Lowell JSD 3,100/K-8
11019 Valley Home Ave 90603 562-943-0211
Dr. Patricia Howell, supt. Fax 947-7874
www.ljsd.org
Jordan ES 500/K-6
10654 Jordan Rd 90603 562-902-4221
Cheree Montgomery, prin. Fax 947-9984
Meadow Green ES 500/K-6
12025 Grovedale Dr 90604 562-902-4241
Elizabeth Kaneshiro, prin. Fax 902-9208
Rancho-Starbuck IS 800/7-8
16430 Woodbrier Dr 90604 562-902-4261
Linda Takacs, prin. Fax 947-9911
Other Schools – See La Habra

South Whittier ESD 4,100/K-8
PO Box 3037 90605 562-944-6231
Dr. Erich Kwek, supt. Fax 944-9659
www.swhittier.k12.ca.us/
Carmela ES 600/K-6
13300 Lakeland Rd 90605 562-941-2132
Fax 941-5443
Graves MS 900/7-8
13243 Los Nietos Rd 90605 562-944-0135
Kathy Cardiff, prin. Fax 944-9433
Lake Marie ES 300/K-6
10001 Carmenita Rd 90605 562-944-0208
David Gunderman, prin. Fax 944-6784
Loma Vista ES 500/K-6
13463 Meyer Rd 90605 562-941-4712
Amin Oria, prin. Fax 941-5472
Los Altos ES 500/K-3
12001 Bonavista Ln 90604 562-941-3711
Francisco Meza, prin. Fax 941-5281
McKibben ES 400/K-6
10550 Mills Ave 90604 562-944-9878
Kathy Miyamoto, prin. Fax 944-4288
Monte Vista MS 500/3-6
12000 Loma Dr 90604 562-946-1494
Francisco Meza, prin. Fax 777-0914
Telechron ES 300/K-6
11200 Telechron Ave 90605 562-944-6467
Nathan Bellamy, prin. Fax 777-0939

Whittier City ESD 6,500/PK-8
7211 Whittier Ave 90602 562-789-3075
Dr. Ron Carruth, supt. Fax 698-6534
www.whittiercity.k12.ca.us
Andrews ES 500/K-6
1010 Caraway Dr 90601 562-789-3140
Alicia Aceves, prin. Fax 789-3145
Dexter MS 1,300/6-8
11532 Floral Dr 90601 562-789-3090
Diane Kinnart, prin. Fax 789-3095
Edwards MS 1,000/6-8
6812 Norwalk Blvd 90606 562-789-3120
Maria Ruiz, prin. Fax 789-3133
Hoover ES 400/K-5
6302 Alta Ave 90601 562-789-3150
Kathy Schmierer, prin. Fax 789-3155
Jackson ES 500/K-5
8015 Painter Ave 90602 562-789-3160
Mary Salcido, prin. Fax 789-3165
Longfellow ES 600/K-5
6005 Magnolia Ave 90601 562-789-3180
Jose Chavira, prin. Fax 789-3185
Mill ES 300/K-5
4030 Workman Mill Rd 90601 562-789-3190
Trudie Efstratios, prin. Fax 789-3195
Orange Grove ES 400/K-5
10626 Orange Grove Ave 90601 562-789-3200
Raquel Gasporra, prin. Fax 789-3205
Phelan ES 500/K-5
7150 Cully Ave 90606 562-789-3210
Kathy Marin, prin. Fax 789-3215
Sorensen ES 500/K-5
11493 Rose Hedge Dr 90606 562-789-3220
Dr. Debra Hokinson, prin. Fax 789-3225
Washington Preschool PK-PK
7804 Thornlake Ave 90606 562-789-3230
Fax 789-3235
West Whittier ES 500/K-5
6411 Norwalk Blvd 90606 562-789-3240
Erlinda Soltero-Ruiz, prin. Fax 789-3245

Broadoaks Children S of Whittier College 200/K-7
PO Box 634 90608 562-907-4250
Dr. Judith Wagner, dir. Fax 907-4960
Carden S of Whittier 400/K-8
11537 Grovedale Dr 90604 562-694-1879
Carol Tracy, dir. Fax 697-0668

Faith Lutheran S 100/PK-8
9920 Mills Ave 90604 562-941-0245
Harry Cypher, prin. Fax 941-4451
Palm View Christian S 100/PK-8
7106 Sorensen Ave 90606 562-693-3746
Marvin Miller, prin. Fax 782-7139
Plymouth Christian S 100/PK-6
12058 Beverly Blvd 90601 562-695-0745
Lindsay Frank, admin. Fax 699-3038
Remnant Christian S 50/K-12
7346 Painter Ave 90602 562-464-2554
James Turnbaugh, admin. Fax 464-2556
St. Bruno Parish S 300/PK-8
15700 Citrustree Rd 90603 562-943-8812
Peggy Vice, prin. Fax 943-2172
St. Gregory the Great S 300/K-8
13925 Telegraph Rd 90604 562-941-0750
Angela Ippolito, prin. Fax 903-7325
St. Mary of the Assumption S 200/K-8
7218 Pickering Ave 90602 562-698-0253
Maria Ortiz, prin. Fax 698-0206
Trinity Lutheran S 100/PK-8
11716 Floral Dr 90601 562-699-7431
Dennis Jacobson, prin. Fax 699-1821
Whittier Adventist S 50/PK-8
8841 Calmada Ave 90605 562-693-1211
Daniel Weston, prin. Fax 464-0266
Whittier Christian JHS 100/7-8
6548 Newlin Ave 90601 562-698-0527
Robert Sowell, prin. Fax 698-2859
Whittier Christian S 300/PK-6
6548 Newlin Ave 90601 562-698-0527
Claudia Schrock, prin. Fax 698-2859
Whittier Christian S 400/K-6
11700 Maybrook Ave 90604 562-947-3757
Michael Stovall, prin. Fax 902-9137
Whittier Friends S 50/PK-6
6726 Washington Ave 90601 562-945-1654
Laura Torres, hdmstr.

Wildomar, Riverside, Pop. 10,411
Lake Elsinore USD
Supt. — See Lake Elsinore
Brown MS 700/6-8
21861 Grand Ave 92595 951-678-8400
Karen Gaither, prin. Fax 678-8408
Collier ES 500/K-5
20150 Mayhall Dr 92595 951-678-8488
Gordon Wood, prin. Fax 678-8429
Graham ES 500/K-5
35450 Frederick St 92595 951-678-8450
James Judziewicz, prin. Fax 678-8456
Reagan ES 500/K-5
35445 Porras Rd 92595 951-253-7650
Nori Chandler, prin. Fax 253-7655
Wildomar ES 900/K-5
21575 Palomar St 92595 951-253-7555
Fernando Reyes, prin. Fax 678-0564

Bundy Canyon Christian S 200/PK-8
23411 Bundy Canyon Rd 92595 951-674-1254
Larry Walker, admin. Fax 674-2444
Cornerstone Christian S 300/PK-12
34570 Monte Vista Dr 92595 951-674-9381
Sharon Privett, hdmstr. Fax 674-8462
Faith Baptist Academy 200/K-12
PO Box 1030 92595 951-245-8748
Greg Beil, admin.
St. Frances of Rome Preschool 50/PK-PK
21591 Lemon St 92595 951-471-5144
Cathy Beck, dir. Fax 674-6443

Williams, Colusa, Pop. 4,755
Williams USD 1,200/K-12
PO Box 7 95987 530-473-2550
Dr. Judith Rossi, supt. Fax 473-5894
www.williamsusd.net
Williams ES 400/K-3
PO Box 7 95987 530-473-2885
Cyndee Engrahm, prin. Fax 473-3780
Williams JHS 200/7-8
PO Box 7 95987 530-473-3029
Rosa Villasenor, prin. Fax 473-2771
Williams MS 300/4-6
PO Box 7 95987 530-473-5304
Jennifer Foglesong, prin. Fax 473-5928

Willits, Mendocino, Pop. 5,066
Willits USD 2,000/K-12
120 Pearl St 95490 707-459-5314
Debra Kubin, supt. Fax 459-7862
www.willitsunified.net/
Baechtel Grove MS 400/6-8
1150 Magnolia St 95490 707-459-2417
Rick Jordan, prin. Fax 459-7881
Blosser Lane ES 400/3-5
1275 Blosser Ln 95490 707-459-3232
Michel Frey, prin. Fax 459-7621
Brookside ES 400/K-2
20 Spruce St 95490 707-459-5385
Olga O'Neill, prin. Fax 459-7857
Sherwood ES, 120 Pearl St 95490 100/K-5
Tawny Fernandez, prin. 707-984-6769

Willits SDA S, 22751 Bray Rd 95490 50/1-8
Dona Dunbar, prin. 707-459-4333

Willow Creek, Humboldt, Pop. 1,576
Klamath-Trinity JUSD
Supt. — See Hoopa
Trinity Valley S 200/K-8
PO Box 1229 95573 530-625-5600
Melanie Sanderson, prin. Fax 629-2452

Willow Creek Christian S 50/K-12
PO Box 1568 95573 530-629-3332
Jerry Nobles, prin. Fax 629-3332

Willows, Glenn, Pop. 6,296
Willows USD 1,700/K-12
823 W Laurel St 95988 530-934-6600
Steve Olmos, supt. Fax 934-6609
www.willowsunified.org/home.htm
Murdock ES 700/K-4
655 French St 95988 530-934-6640
Kathy Parsons, prin. Fax 934-6557
Willows IS 500/5-8
1145 W Cedar St 95988 530-934-6633
Steve Sailsbery, prin. Fax 934-6697

Wilmington, See Los Angeles
Los Angeles USD
Supt. — See Los Angeles
Broad Avenue ES 1,000/K-5
24815 Broad Ave 90744 310-835-3118
Deborah Evers Allen, prin. Fax 835-6012
Fries Avenue ES 800/K-5
1301 N Fries Ave 90744 310-834-6431
Blanca Cantu, prin. Fax 834-9238
Gulf ES 1,100/K-5
828 W L St 90744 310-835-3157
Nora Armenta, prin. Fax 549-7986
Hawaiian Avenue ES 800/K-5
540 Hawaiian Ave 90744 310-830-1151
Monica Friedman, prin. Fax 835-0028
Island ES 700/K-5
500 Island Ave 90744 310-847-1400
Irene Hinojosa, prin. Fax 834-9171
Wilmington MS 2,100/6-8
1700 Gulf Ave 90744 310-847-1500
Veronica Aragon, prin. Fax 549-5307
Wilmington Park ES 1,100/K-5
1140 Mahar Ave 90744 310-518-7460
Debra Bina, prin. Fax 830-8716

Holy Family S 200/PK-8
1122 E Robidoux St 90744 310-518-1440
Carmen Orinoco, prin. Fax 518-1257
Pacific Harbor Christian S 300/PK-8
1530 N Wilmington Blvd 90744 310-835-5665
Amie Gray, prin. Fax 835-6361
SS. Peter & Paul S 200/K-8
706 Bay View Ave 90744 310-834-5574
Nancy Kuria, prin. Fax 518-6100
Wilmington Christian S 100/K-8
24910 S Avalon Blvd 90744 310-834-1448
W. Paul Jameson, prin. Fax 834-0134

Wilton, Sacramento, Pop. 3,858
Elk Grove USD
Supt. — See Elk Grove
Dillard ES 500/K-6
9721 Dillard Rd 95693 916-687-6121
Clark Burke, prin. Fax 687-8183

Winchester, Riverside, Pop. 1,689
Hemet USD
Supt. — See Hemet
Winchester ES 600/K-5
28751 Winchester Rd 92596 951-926-0700
Mark Delano, prin. Fax 926-0706

Temecula Valley USD
Supt. — See Temecula
French Valley ES 900/K-5
36680 Cady Rd 92596 951-926-3643
Joe Mueller, prin. Fax 926-3683
LaVorgna ES 600/K-5
31777 Algarve Ave 92596 951-294-6385
Jona Hazlett, prin. Fax 294-6388

Windsor, Sonoma, Pop. 24,968
Windsor USD 4,100/K-12
9291 Old Redwood Hwy 95492 707-837-7700
Steven Herrington Ph.D., supt. Fax 838-4031
www.wusd.org
Brooks ES 500/4-5
750 Natalie Dr 95492 707-837-7717
Shannon Vehmeyer, prin. Fax 837-7722
Windsor Creek ES 500/2-3
8955 Conde Ln 95492 707-837-7757
Maureen Grafeld, prin. Fax 837-7760
Windsor MS 1,000/6-8
9500 Brooks Rd S 95492 707-837-7737
Lisa Saxon, prin. Fax 837-7743
Other Schools – See Santa Rosa

Windsor Christian Academy 300/PK-8
PO Box 1880 95492 707-838-3757
Tad Theiss, prin. Fax 838-3542

Winnetka, See Los Angeles

St. Joseph the Worker S 300/PK-8
19812 Cantlay St 91306 818-341-6616
Sr. Barbara Wilson, prin. Fax 341-3875
St. Martin-In-The-Fields S 100/PK-8
7136 Winnetka Ave 91306 818-340-5144
Rev. Christoper Eade, hdmstr. Fax 340-5882
West Valley Christian Academy 200/PK-6
7911 Winnetka Ave 91306 818-882-3242
Victoria Andrews, admin. Fax 882-3679

Winterhaven, Imperial
San Pasqual Valley USD 800/PK-12
676 Base Line Rd 92283 760-572-0222
David Schoneman, supt. Fax 572-0711
www.sanpasqual.k12.ca.us
San Pasqual Valley ES 400/K-5
676 Base Line Rd 92283 760-572-0222
Debbie Spain-Gibbs, prin. Fax 572-5600
San Pasqual Valley MS 200/PK-PK, 6-
676 Base Line Rd 92283 760-572-0222
Frances Franco, prin. Fax 572-0829

Winters, Yolo, Pop. 6,764
Winters JUSD 1,800/K-12
909 Grant Ave 95694 530-795-6100
Rebecca Gillespie Ed.D., supt. Fax 795-6114
winters.k12.ca.us
Rominger IS 200/4-5
502 Niemann St 95694 530-795-6320
Kate Helfrich, prin. Fax 795-6123
Waggoner ES 400/K-3
500 Edwards St 95694 530-795-6121
Suzen Holtemann, prin. Fax 795-6120
Winters MS 400/6-8
425 Anderson Ave 95694 530-795-6130
Pam Scheeline, prin. Fax 795-6137

Winters Community Christian S 50/PK-8
205 Russell St 95694 530-795-4682
Connie Badgley, admin. Fax 795-4682

Winton, Merced, Pop. 7,559
Merced River UNESD 200/K-8
4402 Oakdale Rd 95388 209-722-4581
Dr. Helio Brasil, supt. Fax 358-2855
www.mercedriver.k12.ca.us
Washington MS 100/4-8
4402 Oakdale Rd 95388 209-358-5679
Dr. Helio Brasil, prin. Fax 358-2855
Other Schools – See Snelling

Winton SD 2,700/K-8
PO Box 8 95388 209-357-6175
Michael Crass, supt. Fax 357-1994
www.winton.k12.ca.us
Crookham ES 600/K-5
PO Box 130 95388 209-357-6182
Kristie Warner, prin. Fax 357-6185
Sparkes ES 600/K-5
PO Box 1477 95388 209-357-6180
Marilyn Fauerbach, prin. Fax 357-6580
Winfield ES 900/K-5
PO Box 1839 95388 209-357-6891
Sherman Glenn, prin. Fax 357-6893
Winton MS 600/6-8
PO Box 1299 95388 209-357-6189
Ray Guerrero, prin. Fax 358-5889

Woodlake, Tulare, Pop. 7,215
Woodlake UNSD 2,400/K-12
300 W Whitney Ave 93286 559-564-8081
Tim Hire, supt. Fax 564-3831
www.woodlakepublicschools.org
Castle Rock ES 500/3-5
360 N Castle Rock St 93286 559-564-8001
Robert Gonzales, prin. Fax 564-8030
White Learning Center 500/K-2
700 N Cypress St 93286 559-564-8021
Nancy Stidman, prin. Fax 564-0901
Woodlake Valley MS 500/6-8
497 N Palm St 93286 559-564-8061
Lou Saephan, prin. Fax 564-0702

Woodland, Yolo, Pop. 51,020
Woodland JUSD 10,700/K-12
435 6th St 95695 530-662-0201
Fax 662-6956
www.wjusd.net
Beamer Park ES 400/K-6
525 Beamer St 95695 530-662-1769
Fax 668-5653
Dingle ES 400/K-6
625 Elm St 95695 530-662-7084
Juan Chaidez, prin. Fax 669-7101
Douglass MS 900/7-8
525 Granada Dr 95695 530-666-2191
Jonathan Brunson, prin. Fax 668-9217
Freeman ES 500/K-6
126 N West St 95695 530-662-1758
Maria Lewis, prin. Fax 662-9395
Gibson ES 600/K-6
312 Gibson Rd 95695 530-662-3944
Terry Ward, prin. Fax 662-0945
Lee MS 800/7-8
520 West St 95695 530-662-0251
Garth Lewis, prin. Fax 662-9423
Maxwell ES 500/K-6
50 Ashley Ave 95695 530-662-1784
Susan Alves, prin. Fax 662-1526
Plainfield ES 300/K-6
20450 County Road 97 95695 530-662-9301
Armando Olvera, prin. Fax 662-5043
Tafoya ES 900/K-6
720 Homestead Way 95776 530-666-4324
Denise Parnell, prin. Fax 666-3702
Whitehead ES 400/K-6
624 W Southwood Dr 95695 530-662-2824
Cyndee Ruiz, prin. Fax 662-7551
Willow Spring ES 300/K-6
1585 E Gibson Rd 95776 530-662-2452
Julieta Mendoza, prin. Fax 666-6854
Woodland Prairie ES 700/K-6
1444 Stetson St 95776 530-662-2898
Irene Oropeza-Enriquez, prin. Fax 666-3549
Zamora ES 400/K-6
1716 Cottonwood St 95695 530-666-3641
Monte Gregg, prin. Fax 668-0985
Other Schools – See Knights Landing

Holy Rosary S 200/PK-8
505 California St 95695 530-662-3494
Marianne Cates, prin. Fax 668-2442
Woodland Adventist Christian S 50/K-8
29 Elliot St 95695 530-666-6315
Woodland Christian S 500/PK-12
1616 West St 95695 530-666-6615
Dr. John Crandall, admin. Fax 666-3470
Woodland Montessori S 100/PK-6
1738 Cottonwood St 95695 530-662-1900
Pam Barrow-Lynn, dir.

Woodland Hills, See Los Angeles
Los Angeles USD
Supt. — See Los Angeles
Calabash ES 300/K-5
23055 Eugene St 91364 818-224-4430
Esther Gillis, prin. Fax 225-9385
Calvert ES 400/K-5
19850 Delano St 91367 818-347-2681
Roseanna Neustaedter, prin. Fax 347-5301
Hale MS 2,200/6-8
23830 Califa St 91367 818-313-7400
Neal Siegel, prin. Fax 346-7517
Lockhurst Drive ES 400/K-5
6170 Lockhurst Dr 91367 818-888-5280
Ann T. Teraoka, prin. Fax 346-0283
Serrania Avenue ES 700/K-5
5014 Serrania Ave 91364 818-340-6700
Vivian Cordoba, prin. Fax 592-0565
Woodlake ES 600/K-5
23231 Hatteras St 91367 818-347-7097
Kenneth McGee, prin. Fax 883-3953
Woodland Hills Academy 900/6-8
20800 Burbank Blvd 91367 818-226-2900
Allan Weiner, prin. Fax 716-0649
Woodland Hills ES 700/K-5
22201 San Miguel St 91364 818-347-9220
Stephen Bluestein, prin. Fax 347-2365

Pinecrest S, 5975 Shoup Ave 91367 400/K-8
Betty Monello, prin. 818-348-4314
St. Bernardine of Siena S 300/K-8
6061 Valley Circle Blvd 91367 818-340-2130
Margaret Hill, prin. Fax 340-3417
St. Mel S 500/PK-8
20874 Ventura Blvd 91364 818-340-1924
Mary Giordano, prin. Fax 347-4426
West Valley Hebrew Academy 100/PK-8
5850 Fallbrook Ave 91367 818-712-0365

Woodside, San Mateo, Pop. 5,463
Cabrillo USD
Supt. — See Half Moon Bay
Kings Mountain ES 100/K-5
211 Swett Rd 94062 650-712-7180
John Corry, prin. Fax 851-9370

Woodside ESD 500/K-8
3195 Woodside Rd 94062 650-851-1571
Diana Abbati, supt. Fax 851-5577
www.woodside.k12.ca.us/
Woodside S 500/K-8
3195 Woodside Rd 94062 650-851-1571
Diana Abbati, prin. Fax 851-5577

Woody, Kern
Blake ESD 50/K-8
PO Box 40 93287 661-636-4684
Bud Burrow, supt. Fax 636-4131
kcsos.kern.org/blakesd/
Blake S 50/K-8
PO Box 40 93287 661-536-8559
Dawn Carver, prin. Fax 536-9389

Wrightwood, San Bernardino, Pop. 3,308
Snowline JUSD
Supt. — See Phelan
Wrightwood ES 400/K-5
1175 State Hwy 2 92397 760-249-5828
Dale Levine, prin. Fax 249-5820

Yermo, San Bernardino
Silver Valley USD 2,700/PK-12
PO Box 847 92398 760-254-2916
Marc Jackson, supt. Fax 254-2091
www.silvervalley.k12.ca.us
Newberry Springs ES 200/K-5
PO Box 847 92398 760-257-3211
Sandra Schmidt, prin. Fax 257-4838
Powell Preschool PK-PK
PO Box 847 92398 760-386-7940
Fax 386-7980
Yermo S 400/K-8
PO Box 847 92398 760-254-2931
Derek Pinto, prin. Fax 254-2932
Other Schools – See Fort Irwin

Yorba Linda, Orange, Pop. 64,476
Placentia-Yorba Linda USD
Supt. — See Placentia
Bryant Ranch ES 800/K-5
24695 Paseo De Toronto 92887 714-986-7120
Debra Silverman, prin. Fax 694-0569
Fairmont ES 900/K-6
5241 Fairmont Blvd 92886 714-986-7130
Shawn Knutson, prin. Fax 970-7983
Glenknoll ES 500/K-6
6361 Glenknoll Dr 92886 714-970-0720
Douglas Slonkosky, prin. Fax 970-0721
Lakeview ES 500/K-5
17510 Lakeview Ave 92886 714-986-7190
Patrick Brown, prin. Fax 223-7509
Linda Vista ES 400/K-5
5600 Ohio St 92886 714-986-7200
Jackie Howland, prin. Fax 779-2138
Paine ES 400/K-5
4444 Plumosa Dr 92886 714-986-7210
Tamie Beeuwsaert, prin. Fax 777-4398
Rose Drive ES 300/K-5
4700 Rose Dr 92886 714-986-7250
Dorie Staack, prin. Fax 528-9406
Travis Ranch S 1,600/K-8
5200 Via De La Escuela 92887 714-986-7460
Larry Mauzey, prin. Fax 777-8312
Yorba Linda MS 800/6-8
4777 Casa Loma Ave 92886 714-986-7080
James Hardin, prin. Fax 996-2752
Yorba MS 900/7-8
5350 Fairmont Blvd 92886 714-986-7400
Cameron Malotte, prin. Fax 970-1647

Calvary Chapel Academy 300/PK-8
5401 Fairmont Blvd 92886 714-777-7131
Beth Holiday, prin. Fax 777-1766
Calvary Christian S 100/PK-7
18821 Yorba Linda Blvd 92886 714-777-3441
Cindy Gough, prin. Fax 701-1927
Discovery Depot Child Care Center 100/PK-K
16800 Imperial Hwy 92886 714-572-0522
Michele Nelson, dir. Fax 572-1687
Friends Christian MS 400/5-8
4231 Rose Dr 92886 714-524-5240
Larry Lewis, prin. Fax 524-5784
Friends Christian S 100/PK-K
5151 Lakeview Ave 92886 714-777-4356
Krista Slezak, dir. Fax 777-4028
Friends Christian S 400/1-4
5151 Lakeview Ave 92886 714-777-3009
Ron Ralston, prin. Fax 777-4028
Heritage Oak Private Education S 600/PK-8
16971 Imperial Hwy 92886 714-524-1350
Phyllis Cygan, dir.
Little Friends K 200/PK-K
4231 Rose Dr 92886 714-528-8402
Sandra Pierce, dir. Fax 528-2964
St. Francis of Assisi S 500/PK-8
5330 Eastside Cir 92887 714-695-3700
Kathleen Falcone, prin. Fax 695-3704

Yosemite National Park, Mariposa
Bass Lake JUNESD
Supt. — See Oakhurst
Wawona ES 50/K-6
PO Box 2068 95389 209-375-6383
Michelle Stauffer, prin. Fax 375-1029

Mariposa County USD
Supt. — See Mariposa
Yosemite Valley S 50/K-8
PO Box 485 95389 209-372-4791
Catherine Soria, prin. Fax 372-8791

Yountville, Napa, Pop. 3,307
Napa Valley USD
Supt. — See Napa
Yountville ES 200/K-5
6554 Yount St 94599 707-253-3485
Troy Knox, prin. Fax 253-6209

Yreka, Siskiyou, Pop. 7,295
Yreka UNESD 1,000/K-8
309 Jackson St 96097 530-842-1168
Dr. Vanston Shaw, supt. Fax 842-4576
www.sisnet.ssku.k12.ca.us/~yesftp
Evergreen ES 300/K-2
416 Evergreen Ln 96097 530-842-4912
Dave Parsons, prin. Fax 842-9438
Gold Street ES 200/3-4
321 N Gold St 96097 530-842-2438
Dave Parsons, prin. Fax 842-9436
Jackson Street MS 500/5-8
405 Jackson St 96097 530-842-3561
Paul McCoy, prin. Fax 842-1716

Yreka SDA Christian S 50/K-10
346 Payne Ln 96097 530-842-7071
Les Kelley, prin. Fax 842-7463

Yuba City, Sutter, Pop. 58,628
Franklin ESD 400/K-8
332 N Township Rd 95993 530-822-5151
Douglas Reeder, supt. Fax 822-5177
www.franklin.k12.ca.us/
Franklin S 400/K-8
332 N Township Rd 95993 530-822-5151
Douglas Reeder, prin. Fax 822-5177

Yuba City USD 12,600/K-12
750 N Palora Ave 95991 530-822-5200
Nancy Aaberg, supt. Fax 671-2454
www.ycusd.k12.ca.us
April Lane ES 600/K-5
800 April Ln 95991 530-822-5215
Angela Huerta, prin. Fax 822-5028
Barry S 800/K-8
1255 Barry Rd 95991 530-822-5220
Larry Bonds, prin. Fax 822-7262
Bridge Street ES 400/K-5
500 Bridge St 95991 530-822-5225
Louise McKray, prin. Fax 822-5002
Butte Vista ES 700/K-5
2195 Blevin Rd 95993 530-822-5034
Jas Peterson, prin. Fax 822-5008
Central-Gaither S 300/K-8
8403 Bailey Rd 95993 530-822-5230
Debbie Everett, prin. Fax 822-5004
Gray Avenue MS 900/6-8
808 Gray Ave 95991 530-822-5240
Brian Gault, prin. Fax 822-5057
Karperos S 1,000/K-8
1666 Camino De Flores 95993 530-822-5262
Lee McPeak, prin. Fax 671-5356
King Avenue ES 400/K-5
630 King Ave 95991 530-822-5250
Tom Walters, prin. Fax 822-5031
Lincoln ES 700/K-5
1582 Lincoln Rd 95993 530-822-5255
Lisa Shelton, prin. Fax 822-5303
Lincrest ES 800/K-5
1400 Phillips Rd 95991 530-822-5260
Elisabeth Miller, prin. Fax 674-9430
Park Avenue ES 600/K-5
100 Morton St 95991 530-822-5265
Linda Cohee, prin. Fax 822-5279
Riverbend S 900/K-8
301 Stewart Rd 95991 530-822-3100
Dave Morrow, prin. Fax 822-2520
Tierra Buena S 800/K-8
1794 Villa Ave 95993 530-822-5280
Steve Justus, prin. Fax 822-5024

Adventist Christian S 50/K-8
369 Harding Rd 95993 530-673-7645
Jennifer Higgins, prin. Fax 673-3458
Faith Christian ES 200/K-6
PO Box 1690 95992 530-674-3922
Bill Hannold, supt. Fax 674-0192
Grace Christian Academy 200/PK-8
1980 S Walton Ave 95993 530-674-7210
Russell Rohleder, prin. Fax 674-7291
St. Isidore S 200/PK-8
200 Clark Ave 95991 530-673-2217
Karen McDonald, prin. Fax 673-3673

Yucaipa, San Bernardino, Pop. 49,100
Yucaipa-Calimesa JUSD 9,800/K-12
12797 3rd St 92399 909-797-0174
Sherry Kendrick, supt. Fax 797-5751
www.yucaipaschools.com
Calimesa ES 600/K-6
13523 2nd St 92399 909-790-8570
Pam Cronk, prin. Fax 790-8576
Chapman Heights ES K-6
33692 Cramer Rd 92399 909-790-8080
Andy Anderson, prin. Fax 790-6177
Dunlap ES 500/K-6
32870 Avenue E 92399 909-797-5171
Frank Tucci, prin. Fax 790-6177
Meadow Creek ES 900/K-6
34450 Stonewood Dr 92399 909-790-3207
Janet Pasos, prin. Fax 790-8364
Mesa View MS 500/7-8
800 Mustang Way 92399 909-790-8008
Jim Stolze, prin.
Park View MS 1,200/7-8
34875 Tahoe Dr 92399 909-790-3285
Jeff Litel, prin. Fax 790-3295
Ridgeview ES 800/K-6
11021 Sunnyside Dr 92399 909-790-3270
Linda Moffatt, prin. Fax 790-3278
Valley ES 700/K-6
12333 8th St 92399 909-797-1125
Pam Whitehurst, prin. Fax 790-8560
Wildwood ES 800/K-6
35972 Susan St 92399 909-790-8521
James Cherry, prin. Fax 790-8525
Yucaipa ES 600/K-6
12375 California St 92399 909-797-9163
Tony Bennett, prin. Fax 797-9823

Yucaipa Christian S 300/PK-6
34784 Yucaipa Blvd 92399 909-790-9411
Jim Cochran, admin. Fax 797-5062

Yucca Valley, San Bernardino, Pop. 19,696
Morongo USD
Supt. — See Twentynine Palms
La Contenta JHS 800/7-8
7050 La Contenta Rd 92284 760-228-1802
Jean Johnson, prin. Fax 369-6324
Onaga ES 700/K-6
58001 Onaga Trl 92284 760-369-6333
Jesse Simpson, prin. Fax 369-6329
Yucca Mesa S 500/K-8
3380 Avalon Ave 92284 760-228-1777
Kyle Hannah, prin. Fax 365-2467
Yucca Valley ES 600/K-6
7601 Hopi Trl 92284 760-365-3381
John Lowe, prin. Fax 369-6303

Joshua Springs Christian S 300/PK-12
57373 Joshua Ln 92284 760-365-3599
Fem Ontiveros, admin. Fax 369-0315
Yucca Valley Adventist Team S 50/1-8
8035 Church St 92284 760-365-6637
Scott Bree, prin. Fax 365-4648

Zenia, Trinity
Southern Trinity JUSD
Supt. — See Bridgeville
Hoaglin-Zenia S 50/K-8
HC 62 Box 54 95595 707-923-9670
Roberta Drechsler, prin. Fax 923-4294

COLORADO

COLORADO DEPARTMENT OF EDUCATION
201 E Colfax Ave, Denver 80203-1799
Telephone 303-866-6600
Fax 303-830-0793
Website http://www.cde.state.co.us

Commissioner of Education Dwight Jones

COLORADO BOARD OF EDUCATION
201 E Colfax Ave, Denver 80203-1704

Chairperson Bob Schaffer

BOARDS OF COOPERATIVE EDUCATIONAL SERVICES (BOCES)

Adams County BOCES
Dave Carroll, dir. 303-286-7294
10290 Huron St, Northglenn 80260 Fax 853-1156
Centennial BOCES
Jack McCabe, dir. 303-772-4420
830 S Lincoln St, Longmont 80501 Fax 776-0504
www.cboces.org
East Central BOCES
Floyd Beard, dir. 719-775-2342
PO Box 910, Limon 80828 Fax 775-9714
www.ecboces.org
Expeditionary BOCES
Robert Stein, dir. 303-759-2076
1700 S Holly St, Denver 80222 Fax 757-7442
www.rmsel.org/
Front Range BOCES
Susan Sparks, dir. 303-556-6028
PO Box 173364, Denver 80217 Fax 556-6060
frontrangeboces.org/
Grand Valley BOCES
Marsha Arzy, dir. 970-255-2600
2508 Blichman Ave Fax 255-2626
Grand Junction 81505
www.coloradoboces.org/grandvalley.htm
Larimer BOCES
Jack Hale, dir. 970-613-5173
2880 Monroe Ave, Loveland 80538 Fax 613-5184
Mountain BOCES
Edward Vandertook, dir. 719-486-2603
1713 Mount Lincoln Dr W Fax 486-2109
Leadville 80461
www.mtnboces.org/
Mount Evans BOCES
Joyce Conrey, dir. 303-567-4467
PO Box 3399, Idaho Springs 80452 Fax 567-2208
Northeast Colorado BOCES
Tim Sanger, dir. 970-774-6152
PO Box 98, Haxtun 80731 Fax 774-6157
www.neboces.com
Northwest Colorado BOCES
Jane Toothaker, dir., PO Box 773390 970-879-0391
Steamboat Springs 80477 Fax 879-0442
www.nwboces.org/
Pikes Peak BOCES
Bob Selle, dir., 4825 Lorna Pl 719-570-7474
Colorado Springs 80915 Fax 380-9685
www.ppboces.org
Rio Blanco BOCES
Donna Day, dir. 970-675-2064
234 S Jones Ave, Rangely 81648 Fax 675-5738
www.rioblancoboces.org/
San Juan BOCES
Randy Boyer, dir. 970-247-3261
201 E 12th St, Durango 81301 Fax 247-8333
www.sjbocs.org/
San Luis Valley BOCES
John Tillman, dir. 719-589-5851
2261 Enterprise St, Alamosa 81101 Fax 589-5007
www.slvbocs.org
Santa Fe Trail BOCES
Sandy Malouff, dir. 719-383-2623
PO Box 980, La Junta 81050 Fax 383-2627
South Central BOCES
Cynthia Seidel, dir. 719-647-0023
323 S Purcell Blvd, Pueblo 81007 Fax 647-0136
www.scboces.k12.co.us
Southeastern BOCES
Jo Autrey, dir. 719-336-9046
PO Box 1137, Lamar 81052 Fax 336-9679
www.seboces.k12.co.us/
Southwest BOCES
Victor Bruce, dir. 970-565-8411
PO Box 1420, Cortez 81321 Fax 565-1203
Uncompahgre BOCS
Sharon Davarn, dir. 970-626-2977
PO Box 728, Ridgway 81432 Fax 626-2978
www.unbocs.org/
Ute Pass BOCES
Linda Murray, dir. 719-686-2012
PO Box 99, Woodland Park 80866 Fax 687-8408

PUBLIC, PRIVATE AND CATHOLIC ELEMENTARY SCHOOLS

Agate, Elbert, Pop. 100
Agate SD 300 100/PK-12
PO Box 118 80101 719-764-2741
Robin Purdy, supt. Fax 764-2751
www.agateschools.net/
Agate ES 50/PK-5
PO Box 118 80101 719-764-2741
Robin Purdy, prin. Fax 764-2751

Aguilar, Las Animas, Pop. 578
Aguilar RSD 6 200/PK-12
PO Box 567 81020 719-941-4188
Dr. Pam Siders, supt. Fax 941-4279
Aguilar ES 100/PK-6
PO Box 567 81020 719-941-4188
Dr. Pam Siders, prin. Fax 941-4279

Akron, Washington, Pop. 1,575
Akron SD R-1 400/K-12
PO Box 429 80720 970-345-2268
Bryce Monasmith, supt. Fax 345-6508
www.akronrams.net/homepage2.htm
Akron S 300/K-8
301 E 5th St 80720 970-345-2266
Rosemary Fetzer, prin. Fax 345-2827

Alamosa, Alamosa, Pop. 8,682
Alamosa SD RE-11J 2,100/PK-12
209 Victoria Ave 81101 719-587-1600
Rob Alejo, supt. Fax 587-1712
www.alamosa.k12.co.us/
Boyd ES 300/2-3
1107 Hunt Ave 81101 719-589-6791
Dianna Rodriguez, prin. Fax 589-5620
Evans IS 300/4-5
108 La Veta Ave 81101 719-589-3684
Jeff Bilderbeck, prin. Fax 589-1446
Ortega MS 500/6-8
401 Victoria Ave 81101 719-587-1650
Neil Seneff, prin. Fax 587-1721
Polston ES 300/PK-1
6935 State Highway 17 81101 719-589-6875
Lori Smith, prin. Fax 589-5632

Sunshine Christian S 50/1-8
315 Craft Dr 81101 719-589-2557
Clair James, lead tchr. Fax 589-9083
Trinity Lutheran S, PO Box 787 81101 100/PK-4
Mary Conner, prin. 719-589-3271

Anton, Washington, Pop. 40
Arickaree SD R-2 100/PK-12
12155 County Road NN 80801 970-383-2202
Gena Ramey, supt. Fax 383-2205
www.arickareeschool.info/
Arickaree ES 100/PK-6
12155 County Road NN 80801 970-383-2202
Gena Ramey, prin. Fax 383-2205

Antonito, Conejos, Pop. 850
South Conejos SD RE-10 300/PK-12
PO Box 398 81120 719-376-5512
Carlos Garcia, supt. Fax 376-5425
scsd.echalk.com/home.asp
Antonito JHS 50/7-8
PO Box 398 81120 719-376-5468
Erwin Romero, prin. Fax 376-5425
Guadalupe ES 100/PK-6
PO Box 398 81120 719-376-5407
Marcella Garcia, prin. Fax 376-5425

Arvada, Jefferson, Pop. 103,966
Adams County SD 50
Supt. — See Denver
Tennyson Knolls ES 400/K-5
6330 Tennyson St 80003 303-429-4090
Shayley Olson, prin. Fax 657-3877

Jefferson County SD R-1
Supt. — See Golden
Allendale ES 300/K-6
5900 Oak St 80004 303-982-1165
Cindy Charles, prin. Fax 982-1164
Arvada MS 300/7-8
5751 Balsam St 80002 303-982-1240
Rod Pugnetti, prin. Fax 982-1241
Arvada West Preschool PK-PK
6224 Johnson Way 80004 303-423-0798
Rita Rau, prin. Fax 423-0799
Campbell ES 500/PK-6
6500 Oak St 80004 303-982-1440
Rebecca Chao, prin. Fax 982-1441
Drake MS 700/7-8
12550 W 52nd Ave 80002 303-982-1510
Linda Rice, prin. Fax 982-1511
Fitzmorris ES 200/K-6
6250 Independence St 80004 303-982-1640
Barb Rodriguez, prin. Fax 982-1639
Foster ES 400/PK-6
5300 Saulsbury Ct 80002 303-982-1680
Leigh Hiester, prin. Fax 982-1679
Fremont ES 400/K-6
6420 Urban St 80004 303-982-1699
Deb Hines, prin. Fax 982-1698
Hackberry Hill ES 500/K-6
7300 W 76th Ave 80003 303-982-0260
Warren Blair, prin. Fax 982-0261
Lawrence ES 400/PK-6
5611 Zephyr St 80002 303-982-1825
Beth Morganfield, prin. Fax 982-1826
Little ES 400/K-6
8448 Otis Dr 80003 303-982-0310
Esther Valdez, prin. Fax 982-0309
Meiklejohn ES 200/PK-6
13405 W 83rd Pl 80005 303-982-5695
Kurt Braginetz, prin. Fax 982-5696
Moore MS 700/7-8
8455 W 88th Ave 80005 303-982-0400
John White, prin. Fax 982-0462
North Arvada MS 400/7-8
7285 Pierce St 80003 303-982-0528
George Sargent, prin. Fax 982-0529
Oberon MS 700/7-8
7300 Quail St 80005 303-982-2020
Dana Ellis, prin. Fax 982-2021
Parr ES 400/PK-6
5800 W 84th Ave 80003 303-982-9890
Troy Brickley, prin. Fax 982-9891
Peck ES 400/K-6
6495 Carr St 80004 303-982-0590
John Katsanis, prin. Fax 982-0591
Russell ES 300/K-6
5150 Allison St 80002 303-982-2145
Susan Chapla, prin. Fax 982-2122
Secrest ES 300/K-6
6875 W 64th Ave 80003 303-982-0760
Tim Chiles, prin. Fax 982-0759
Sierra ES 500/PK-6
7751 Oak St 80005 303-982-0821
Michelle McAteer, prin. Fax 982-0822
Stott ES 300/PK-6
6600 Yank Way 80004 303-982-2638
Gale Downing, prin. Fax 982-2639
Swanson ES 600/PK-6
6055 W 68th Ave 80003 303-982-0891
Andrew Schrant, prin. Fax 982-0892
Thompson ES 400/K-6
7750 Harlan St 80003 303-982-9935
Wendy Wyman, prin. Fax 982-9936
Van Arsdale ES 600/K-6
7535 Alkire St 80005 303-982-1080
Martha Tate, prin. Fax 982-1081

Vanderhoof ES 500/K-6
5875 Routt St 80004 303-982-2744
Ted Coberley, prin. Fax 982-2743
Warder ES 400/K-6
7840 Carr Dr 80005 303-982-0950
Becky Nelsen, prin. Fax 982-0949
Weber ES 500/K-6
8725 W 81st Pl 80005 303-982-1012
Matt Flores, prin. Fax 982-1013
West Woods ES 600/K-6
16650 W 72nd Ave 80007 303-982-5649
Ewa Chomka Campbell, prin. Fax 982-5650

Faith Christian Academy 400/K-5
6210 Ward Rd 80004 303-424-7310
Teresa Woodburn, prin. Fax 403-2710
Faith Christian Academy 300/6-8
6250 Wright St 80004 303-424-7310
Randy Ziemer, prin. Fax 403-2720
Maranatha Christian Center 400/PK-12
7180 Oak St 80004 303-431-5653
Sheryl Truesdell, dir. Fax 940-7474
Shrine of St. Anne S 400/K-8
7320 Grant Pl 80002 303-422-1800
Kathie Kuehl, prin. Fax 422-1011

Aspen, Pitkin, Pop. 5,804
Aspen SD 1 1,500/PK-12
235 High School Rd 81611 970-925-3760
Dr. Diana Sirko, supt. Fax 925-5721
www.aspenk12.net/
Aspen ES 500/K-4
235 High School Rd 81611 970-925-3760
Doreen Goldyn, prin. Fax 925-6878
Aspen MS 400/5-8
235 High School Rd 81611 970-925-3760
Tom Heald, prin. Fax 925-8374
Aspen Preschool 50/PK-PK
235 High School Rd 81611 970-925-3760
Betsy Anastas, prin.

Aspen Country Day S 200/PK-8
3 Music School Rd 81611 970-925-1909
John Suitor, hdmstr. Fax 925-7074

Ault, Weld, Pop. 1,425
Ault-Highland SD RE-9 900/K-12
PO Box 68 80610 970-834-1345
Robert Ring, supt. Fax 834-1347
www.weldre9.k12.co.us
Highland MS 200/6-8
PO Box 68 80610 970-834-2829
Todd Bissell, prin. Fax 834-2663
Other Schools – See Pierce

Aurora, Arapahoe, Pop. 297,235
Aurora SD 32,500/PK-12
1085 Peoria St 80011 303-344-8060
John Barry, supt. Fax 326-1280
www.aps.k12.co.us
Altura ES 500/PK-5
1650 Altura Blvd 80011 303-340-3500
Mary Ann Maddy, prin. Fax 326-1204
Arkansas ES 600/PK-5
17301 E Arkansas Ave 80017 303-755-0323
Dr. Alejandra Morales, prin. Fax 326-1205
Aurora Frontier S 600/K-8
3200 S Jericho Way 80013 303-693-1995
Cassie Parra, prin. Fax 326-1208
Aurora Hills MS 1,100/6-8
1009 S Uvalda St 80012 303-341-7450
Jinger Haberer, prin. Fax 326-1250
Aurora Public Schools Child Development 900/PK-PK
1420 Laredo St 80011 303-364-9371
Sheri Charles, dir. Fax 326-1215
Aurora Quest Academy 200/K-8
17315 E 2nd Ave 80011 303-343-3664
Nancy Williams, prin. Fax 326-1237
Boston S 200/K-8
1365 Boston St 80010 303-364-6878
Shawna Lyons, prin. Fax 326-1206
Century ES 400/PK-5
2500 S Granby Way 80014 303-745-4424
Cynthia Buchanan, prin. Fax 326-1207
Columbia MS 1,000/6-8
17600 E Columbia Ave 80013 303-690-6570
Steve Hamilton, prin. Fax 326-1251
Court ES 700/PK-5
395 S Troy St 80012 303-366-9594
Christine Fleming, prin. Fax 326-1244
Crawford ES 600/PK-5
1600 Florence St 80010 303-340-3290
Debbie Gerkin, prin. Fax 326-1210
Dalton ES 600/PK-5
17401 E Dartmouth Ave 80013 303-693-7561
Bonnie Hargrove, prin. Fax 326-1211
Dartmouth ES 400/PK-5
3050 S Laredo St 80013 303-690-1155
Jean Becker, prin. Fax 326-1212
East MS 1,000/6-8
1275 Fraser St 80011 303-340-0660
Fred Quinonez, prin. Fax 326-1252
Elkhart ES 600/K-5
1020 Eagle St 80011 303-340-3050
Maria Thomas, prin. Fax 326-1214
Fletcher ES 500/PK-5
10455 E 25th Ave 80010 303-343-1707
Lisa Nieto, prin. Fax 326-1219
Fulton ES 600/PK-5
755 Fulton St 80010 303-364-8078
Jill Cummings, prin. Fax 326-1216
Iowa ES 500/K-5
16701 E Iowa Ave 80017 303-751-3660
LuAnn Tallman, prin. Fax 326-1217
Jewell ES 500/PK-5
14601 E Jewell Ave 80012 303-751-8862
Mark Rodie, prin. Fax 326-1220
Kenton ES 500/K-5
1255 Kenton St 80010 303-364-0947
Linda Harvey, prin. Fax 326-1222
Knoll ES 300/K-5
12445 E 2nd Ave 80011 303-364-8455
Andrea Tucker, prin. Fax 326-1228
Lansing ES 300/K-5
551 Lansing St 80010 303-364-8297
Karen Hart, prin. Fax 326-1224
Laredo ES 400/K-5
1350 Laredo St 80011 303-366-0314
Quinn O'Keefe, prin. Fax 326-1226
Miller ES 500/PK-5
1701 Espana St 80011 303-364-7918
Kathleen Sullivan, prin. Fax 326-1209
Montview ES 400/PK-5
2055 Moline St 80010 303-364-8549
Michelle Barone, prin. Fax 326-1232
Mrachek MS 1,200/6-8
1955 S Telluride St 80013 303-750-2836
Edward Snyder, prin. Fax 326-1254
Murphy Creek S 400/K-8
1400 S Old Tom Morris Rd 80018 303-366-0579
Suzanne Morey, prin. Fax 326-1227
North MS 800/6-8
12095 Montview Blvd 80010 303-364-7411
Gerardo de la Garza, prin. Fax 326-1256
Paris ES 400/K-5
1635 Paris St 80010 303-341-1702
Lisa Jones, prin. Fax 326-1234
Park Lane ES 400/PK-5
13001 E 30th Ave 80011 303-343-8313
Jennifer Passchier, prin. Fax 326-1236
Peoria ES 200/PK-5
875 Peoria St 80011 303-340-0770
Harry Chan, prin. Fax 326-1235
Sable ES 500/PK-5
2601 Sable Blvd 80011 303-340-3140
James Scott, prin. Fax 326-1238
Side Creek ES 700/K-5
19191 E Iliff Ave 80013 303-755-1785
Suzanne Morris-Sherer, prin. Fax 326-1239
Sixth Avenue ES 600/K-5
560 Vaughn St 80011 303-366-6019
Dana McDonald, prin. Fax 326-1240
South MS 800/6-8
12310 E Parkview Dr 80011 303-364-7623
Yvonne Davis, prin. Fax 326-1258
Tollgate ES 700/K-5
701 S Kalispell Way 80017 303-696-0944
Laurie Godwin, prin. Fax 326-1221
Vassar ES 600/K-5
18101 E Vassar Pl 80013 303-752-3772
Stacey Stuart, prin. Fax 326-1241
Vaughn ES 600/PK-5
1155 Vaughn St 80011 303-366-8430
Judy Bleakley, prin. Fax 326-1242
West MS 800/6-8
10100 E 13th Ave 80010 303-366-2671
Dale Krueger, prin. Fax 326-1260
Wheeling ES 500/PK-5
472 S Wheeling St 80012 303-344-8670
Jan Lotter, prin. Fax 326-1246
Yale ES 600/PK-5
16001 E Yale Ave 80013 303-751-7470
Kerry Lord, prin. Fax 326-1248

Cherry Creek SD 5
Supt. — See Greenwood Village
Antelope Ridge ES 800/PK-5
5455 S Tempe St 80015 720-886-3300
Jennifer Perry, prin. Fax 886-3388
Arrowhead ES 700/PK-5
19100 E Bates Ave 80013 720-886-2800
Heidi Shriver, prin. Fax 886-2888
Aspen Crossing ES 500/PK-5
4655 S Himalaya St 80015 720-886-3700
Denise Maxwell, prin. Fax 886-4788
Buffalo Trail ES PK-5
24300 E Progress Dr 80016 720-886-4000
Tamara Speidel, prin. Fax 886-4088
Canyon Creek ES 700/PK-5
6070 S Versailles Way 80015 720-886-3600
Cheryl Fullmer, prin. Fax 886-3688
Cimarron ES 600/PK-5
17373 E Lehigh Pl 80013 720-886-8100
Kim Kenyon, prin. Fax 886-8188
Coyote Hills ES 400/PK-5
24605 E Davies Way 80016 720-886-3900
Jim McDevitt, prin. Fax 886-3988
Creekside ES 600/PK-5
19993 E Long Ave 80016 720-886-3500
David Gudridge, prin. Fax 886-3588
Dakota Valley ES 900/PK-5
3950 S Kirk Way 80013 720-886-3000
Thomas Kasper, prin. Fax 886-3088
Eastridge ES 900/PK-5
11777 E Wesley Ave 80014 720-747-2200
Marquetta Thomas, prin. Fax 747-2288
Falcon Creek MS 1,200/6-8
6100 S Genoa St 80016 720-886-7600
John Kennedy, prin.
Fox Hollow ES 800/PK-5
6363 S Waco St 80016 720-886-8700
Joleta Gallozzi, prin. Fax 886-8788
Fox Ridge MS 6-8
26301 E Arapahoe Pkwy N 80016 720-886-4700
Tracey Grant, prin.
Highline Community ES 600/PK-5
11000 E Exposition Ave 80012 720-747-2300
Stacey Peoples, prin. Fax 747-2388
Horizon Community MS 1,200/6-8
3981 S Reservoir Rd 80013 720-886-6100
Dr. Jeanette Patterson, prin. Fax 886-6253
Independence ES 500/PK-5
4700 S Memphis St 80015 720-886-8200
Matthew McDonald, prin. Fax 886-8288
Indian Ridge ES 600/PK-5
16501 E Progress Dr 80015 720-886-8400
Dee Bench, prin. Fax 886-8488
Laredo MS 1,300/6-8
5000 S Laredo St 80015 720-886-5000
Carla Stearns, prin. Fax 886-5298
Liberty MS 1,300/6-8
21500 E Dry Creek Rd 80016 720-886-2400
Katie Stahl, prin. Fax 886-2688
Meadow Point ES 600/PK-5
17901 E Grand Ave 80015 720-886-8600
John Cramer, prin. Fax 886-8688
Mission Viejo ES 700/PK-5
3855 S Alicia Pkwy 80013 720-886-8000
Andre Pearson, prin. Fax 886-8088
Peakview ES 700/PK-5
19451 E Progress Cir 80015 720-886-3100
Jeri Crispe, prin. Fax 886-3188
Polton Community ES 500/PK-5
2985 S Oakland St 80014 720-747-2600
Lisa Reddel, prin. Fax 747-2688
Ponderosa ES 600/PK-5
1885 S Lima St 80012 720-747-2800
Elizabeth Sloan, prin. Fax 747-2888
Prairie MS 1,500/6-8
12600 E Jewell Ave 80012 720-747-3000
Dr. Kandy Cassaday, prin. Fax 747-3113
Rolling Hills ES 800/PK-5
5756 S Biscay St 80015 720-886-3400
Darci Mickle, prin. Fax 886-3488
Sagebrush ES 600/PK-5
14700 E Temple Pl 80015 720-886-8300
Karen Liley, prin. Fax 886-8388
Sky Vista MS 800/6-8
4500 S Himalaya St 80015 720-886-4700
Dr. Tony Poole, prin. Fax 886-4788
Summit ES 500/PK-5
18201 E Quincy Ave 80015 720-886-6400
Mary Lams, prin. Fax 886-6488
Sunrise ES 700/PK-5
4050 S Genoa Way 80013 720-886-2900
Chris Hardy, prin. Fax 886-2988
Thunder Ridge MS 1,200/6-8
5250 S Picadilly St 80015 720-886-1500
Mark Sneden, prin. Fax 886-1582
Timberline ES 800/PK-5
5500 S Killarney St 80015 720-886-3200
Susan Snowdon, prin. Fax 886-3288
Trails West ES 600/PK-5
5400 S Waco St 80015 720-886-8500
Richie Strickland, prin. Fax 886-8588
Village East Community ES 700/PK-5
1433 S Oakland St 80012 720-747-2000
Toby Arritola, prin. Fax 747-2088

Bethel Christian S 100/PK-K
1450 Airport Blvd 80011 303-364-2541
CedarWood Christian Academy 100/K-12
PO Box 111389 80042 303-361-6456
Gene Oborny, admin. Fax 340-0971
Christ our Redeemer Lutheran S 100/PK-8
17700 E Iliff Ave 80013 303-337-3108
Dean Johnson, prin. Fax 671-9807
Crescent View Academy 200/PK-6
10958 E Bethany Dr 80014 303-745-2245
Fax 745-0347
Meadowood Christian S 100/PK-8
16051 E Dartmouth Ave 80013 303-690-2309
Harlan Humiston, admin. Fax 317-2978
Montessori S of Aurora 100/PK-K
18585 E Smoky Hill Rd 80015 303-617-0611
Lori Contreras, prin. Fax 617-3162
Mt. Olive Lutheran S 100/PK-K
11500 E Iliff Ave 80014 303-750-9856
JoAnn Stibrich, dir. Fax 745-5912
Peace with Christ Christian S 200/K-8
3290 S Tower Rd 80013 303-766-7116
Warren Paul, prin. Fax 672-6822
St. Marks Lutheran Preschool & K 100/PK-K
111 Del Mar Cir 80011 303-366-9702
Christine Geyer, dir. Fax 366-5089
St. Pius X S 400/PK-8
13680 E 14th Pl 80011 303-364-6515
Mark Strawbridge, prin. Fax 364-1822
St. Therese S 200/PK-8
1200 Kenton St 80010 303-364-7494
Laura Dement-Berger, prin. Fax 364-1340
Wood Adventist Christian S 50/PK-6
1159 S Moline St 80012 303-755-4483
Patricia Carpio, prin. Fax 755-1237

Avon, Eagle, Pop. 6,349
Eagle County SD RE-50
Supt. — See Eagle
Avon ES 300/PK-5
PO Box 7567 81620 970-328-2950
Melisa Rewold-Thuon, prin. Fax 845-6376

Vail Academy 100/PK-8
PO Box 1980 81620 970-845-0783
Dr. Robert Windel, prin. Fax 845-0784

Avondale, Pueblo, Pop. 1,798
Pueblo County SD 70
Supt. — See Pueblo
Avondale ES 200/PK-5
213 E US Highway 50 81022 719-947-3484
Carmen Avalos, prin. Fax 947-3403

Bailey, Park, Pop. 150
Platte Canyon SD 1 1,300/PK-12
57393 US Highway 285 80421 303-838-7666
Jim Walpole Ed.D., supt. Fax 679-7504
www.plattecanyonschools.org
Deer Creek ES 600/PK-5
1737 County Road 43 80421 303-838-7666
Paul Sandos, prin. Fax 816-0162
Fitzsimmons MS 300/6-8
57093 US Highway 285 80421 303-838-7666
Shannon Clarke, prin. Fax 679-7506

Basalt, Pitkin, Pop. 3,007
Roaring Fork SD RE-1
Supt. — See Glenwood Springs

Basalt ES 600/PK-4
151 Cottonwood Dr 81621 970-384-5800
Suzanne Wheeler, prin. Fax 385-5805
Basalt MS 400/5-8
51 School St 81621 970-384-5900
Jeremy Voss, prin. Fax 384-5905

Alpine Christian Academy 100/PK-12
20449 Highway 82 81621 970-927-9106
Zoe Stern, admin. Fax 927-3705

Bayfield, LaPlata, Pop. 1,639
Bayfield SD 10 JT-R 1,300/PK-12
24 S Clover Ln 81122 970-884-2496
Donald Magill, supt. Fax 884-4284
www.bayfield.k12.co.us
Bayfield ES 500/1-5
24 S Clover Ln 81122 970-884-9571
Brian Hanson, prin. Fax 884-9572
Bayfield K 100/PK-K
24 S Clover Ln 81122 970-884-0881
Brian Hanson, prin. Fax 884-0881
Bayfield MS 300/6-8
24 S Clover Ln 81122 970-884-9592
Michael Lister, prin. Fax 884-4110

Bellvue, Larimer, Pop. 300
Poudre SD R-1
Supt. — See Fort Collins
Stove Prairie ES 50/K-5
3891 Stove Prairie Rd 80512 970-488-6575
Patrick Kind, prin. Fax 488-6577

Bennett, Adams, Pop. 2,536
Bennett SD 29J 1,000/PK-12
615 7th St 80102 303-644-3234
Richard Coleman, supt. Fax 644-4121
www.bennett29j.k12.co.us
Bennett ES 300/K-5
462 8th St 80102 303-644-3234
Valerie Beard, prin. Fax 644-4679
Bennett MS 300/6-8
455 8th St 80102 303-644-3234
Amy Burns, prin. Fax 644-4398
Bennett Preschool, 455 8th St 80102 100/PK-PK
Patti Kopang, dir. 303-644-3234

Berthoud, Larimer, Pop. 5,055
Thompson SD R-2J
Supt. — See Loveland
Berthoud ES 400/K-5
560 Bunyan Ave 80513 970-613-7500
Camilla LoJeske, prin. Fax 613-7520
Stockwell ES 400/K-5
175 S 5th St 80513 970-613-6100
Rhonda Richer, prin. Fax 613-6120
Turner MS 400/6-8
950 Massachusetts Ave 80513 970-613-7400
Bill Siebers, prin. Fax 613-7420

Bethune, Kit Carson, Pop. 218
Bethune SD R-5 100/PK-12
PO Box 127 80805 719-346-7513
Shila Adolf, supt. Fax 346-5048
bethuneschool.com/
Bethune ES, PO Box 127 80805 100/PK-6
Shila Adolf, prin. 719-346-7513

Beulah, Pueblo, Pop. 600
Pueblo County SD 70
Supt. — See Pueblo
Beulah S 100/PK-8
8734 School House Ln W 81023 719-485-3127
Patrick Hyatt, prin. Fax 485-3701

Black Hawk, Gilpin, Pop. 107
Gilpin County SD RE-1 400/PK-12
10595 Highway 119 80422 303-582-3444
Ken Ladouceur, supt. Fax 582-3346
www.gilpinschool.org/
Gilpin County ES 200/PK-6
10595 Highway 119 80422 303-582-3444
Lisa Schell, prin. Fax 582-3346

Blanca, Costilla, Pop. 372
Sierra Grande SD R-30 300/PK-12
17523 E Highway 160 81123 719-379-3259
Darren Edgar, supt. Fax 379-2572
www.sierragrandeschool.net
Sierra Grande ES 100/PK-5
17523 E Highway 160 81123 719-379-3257
Christine Barela, prin. Fax 379-2572
Sierra Grande JHS 50/6-8
17523 E Highway 160 81123 719-379-3257
Christine Barela, prin. Fax 379-2572

Boulder, Boulder, Pop. 91,685
Boulder Valley SD RE-2 25,900/PK-12
PO Box 9011 80301 303-447-1010
Dr. Chris King, supt. Fax 561-5134
www.bvsd.org/default.aspx
Bear Creek ES 300/K-5
2500 Table Mesa Dr 80305 720-561-3500
Kent Crueger, prin. Fax 561-3501
Casey MS 300/6-8
2410 13th St 80304 720-561-5446
Alison Boggs, prin. Fax 561-2790
Centennial MS 600/6-8
2205 Norwood Ave 80304 720-561-5441
Cheryl Scott, prin. Fax 561-2090
Columbine ES 400/PK-5
3130 Repplier St 80304 303-443-0792
Marc Rodriguez, prin. Fax 443-0792
Community Montessori ES 300/PK-6
805 Gillaspie Dr 80305 720-561-3700
Marlene Skovsted, prin. Fax 561-3701
Community School of Integrated Studies 300/PK-5
3995 Aurora Ave 80303 303-494-1454
Phil Katsampes, prin. Fax 494-5533
Creekside ES 300/K-5
3740 Martin Dr 80305 720-561-3800
Alejandra Sotiros, prin. Fax 561-3801
Crest View ES 500/K-5
1897 Sumac Ave 80304 720-561-5461
Ned Levine, prin. Fax 561-2855
Douglass ES 500/K-5
840 75th St 80303 720-561-5541
Monica Draper, prin. Fax 561-6699
Eisenhower ES 400/K-5
1220 Eisenhower Dr 80303 303-443-4260
Charles Serns, prin. Fax 447-1605
Flatirons ES 300/K-5
1150 7th St 80302 303-442-7205
Scott Boesel, prin. Fax 442-7205
Foothill ES 500/K-5
1001 Hawthorn Ave 80304 303-443-1847
Melissa Potes, prin. Fax 443-1848
Heatherwood ES 300/K-5
7750 Concord Dr 80301 720-561-5586
Larry Orobona, prin. Fax 561-6965
High Peaks ES 300/PK-5
3995 Aurora Ave 80303 303-494-1454
Rosemary Lohndorf, prin. Fax 494-5533
Manhattan S of Arts and Academics 400/6-8
290 Manhattan Dr 80303 303-494-0335
Robbyn Fernandez, prin. Fax 494-0336
Mesa ES 400/K-5
1575 Lehigh St 80305 720-561-3000
Josh Baldner, prin. Fax 561-3001
Platt MS 500/6-8
6096 Baseline Rd 80303 720-561-5536
Kevin Gates, prin. Fax 561-6898
Southern Hills MS 500/6-8
1500 Knox Dr 80305 303-494-2866
Terry Gillach, prin. Fax 499-9251
University Hill ES 300/K-5
956 16th St 80302 720-561-5416
Leonora Velasquez, prin. Fax 561-2980
Whittier ES 300/K-5
2008 Pine St 80302 720-561-5416
Becky Escamilla, prin. Fax 561-2480
Other Schools – See Broomfield, Gold Hill, Jamestown, Lafayette, Louisville, Nederland, Superior

---

Bixby S 100/K-5
4760 Table Mesa Dr 80305 303-494-7508
Patricia Baker, dir. Fax 494-7519
Boulder Country Day S 300/PK-8
4820 Nautilus Ct N 80301 303-527-4931
Michael Shields, hdmstr. Fax 527-4944
Friends S 200/PK-5
5465 Pennsylvania Ave 80303 303-499-1999
Polly Talbot Donald, hdmstr. Fax 499-1365
Jarrow Montessori S 200/PK-6
3900 Orange Ct 80304 303-443-0511
Barbara Truan, prin. Fax 449-8811
Mountain Shadows Montessori 100/PK-6
4154 63rd St 80301 303-530-5353
Frank Vincent, dir. Fax 530-5230
Mt. Zion Lutheran S 50/PK-2
1680 Balsam Ave 80304 303-443-8477
Cheryl Wu, dir. Fax 448-9547
Sacred Heart of Jesus S 400/PK-8
1317 Mapleton Ave 80304 303-447-2362
Pam Jackimiec, prin. Fax 443-2466
Shining Mountain Waldorf S 300/PK-12
999 Violet Ave 80304 303-444-7697
Agaf Dancy, admin. Fax 444-7701

Branson, Las Animas, Pop. 79
Branson RSD 82 900/PK-12
PO Box 128 81027 719-946-5531
Dr. Larry Birden, supt. Fax 946-5619
www.bransonschoolonline.com
Branson ES 50/PK-6
PO Box 128 81027 719-946-5531
Vicki Goebel, prin. Fax 946-5620

Breckenridge, Summit, Pop. 2,680
Summit SD RE-1
Supt. — See Frisco
Breckenridge ES 200/K-5
PO Box 1213 80424 970-453-2845
Peg Connealy, prin. Fax 453-0156
Upper Blue ES 200/K-5
PO Box 1255 80424 970-547-9130
Kerry Buhler, prin. Fax 547-9134

Briggsdale, Weld, Pop. 225
Briggsdale SD RE-10 100/K-12
PO Box 125 80611 970-656-3417
Rick Mondt, supt. Fax 656-3479
www.briggsdaleschool.org/
Briggsdale ES 100/K-5
PO Box 125 80611 970-656-3417
Rick Mondt, prin. Fax 656-3479

Brighton, Adams, Pop. 28,013
Brighton SD 27J 9,400/PK-12
18551 E 160th Ave 80601 303-655-2900
Rod Blunck Ed.D., supt. Fax 655-2870
www.sd27j.org/
Northeast ES 600/K-5
1605 Longs Peak St 80601 303-655-2550
Michael Clow, prin. Fax 655-2575
North ES 500/PK-5
89 N 6th Ave 80601 303-655-2500
Ricky Bucher, prin. Fax 655-2548
Overland Trail MS 600/6-8
455 N 19th Ave 80601 303-655-4000
Joseph Libby, prin. Fax 655-2880
Pennock ES 700/K-5
3707 Estrella St 80601 720-685-7500
Valerie Ortega, prin. Fax 685-7504
Southeast ES 700/PK-5
1595 E Southern St 80601 303-655-2650
Brett Minne, prin. Fax 655-2893
South ES 500/K-5
305 S 5th Ave 80601 303-655-2600
Kay Collins, prin. Fax 655-2649
Vikan MS 500/6-8
879 Jessup St 80601 303-655-4050
Ana Mendoza, prin. Fax 655-2881
Other Schools – See Commerce City, Henderson, Thornton

Brighton Adventist Academy 100/PK-10
820 S 5th Ave 80601 303-659-1223
Kent Kast, prin. Fax 558-8837
Elmwood Baptist Academy 100/PK-12
13100 E 144th Ave 80601 303-659-3818
Josh Lehman, prin. Fax 685-9005
Meadowlark Montessori S 50/PK-4
15161 Shadow Wood St 80603 303-637-7556
Lynn Richards, prin.
Zion Lutheran S 400/PK-8
1400 Skeel St 80601 303-659-3443
Zach Brewer, prin. Fax 659-2342

Broomfield, Boulder, Pop. 43,478
Adams 12 Five Star SD
Supt. — See Thornton
Centennial ES 600/PK-5
13200 Westlake Dr 80020 720-972-5280
Warren Rudkin, prin. Fax 972-5299
Coyote Ridge ES 400/K-5
13770 Broadlands Dr, 720-972-5780
Kari Cocozzella, prin. Fax 972-5799
Meridian ES 500/K-5
14256 McKay Park Cir, 720-972-7880
Jennifer Weese, prin. Fax 972-7886
Mountain View ES 600/PK-5
12401 Perry St 80020 720-972-5520
Tracey Amend, prin. Fax 972-5539
Westlake MS 800/6-8
2800 W 135th Ave 80020 720-972-5200
Jessica Fiedler, prin. Fax 972-5239

Boulder Valley SD RE-2
Supt. — See Boulder
Aspen Creek S 900/K-8
5500 Aspen Creek Dr 80020 720-887-4537
Brett Livingston, prin. Fax 566-0125
Birch ES 400/K-5
1035 Birch St 80020 303-469-3397
Tracy Stegall, prin. Fax 887-3592
Broomfield Heights MS 600/6-8
1555 Daphne St 80020 303-466-2387
Nancy Vaughn, prin. Fax 466-2386
Emerald ES 400/K-5
755 W Elmhurst Pl 80020 303-466-2316
Larry Leatherman, prin. Fax 466-2316
Kohl ES 500/PK-5
1000 W 10th Ave 80020 303-466-5944
Cindy Kaier, prin. Fax 465-1071

Beautiful Savior Lutheran S 200/PK-8
PO Box 8 80038 303-469-2049
Julie Paschen, prin. Fax 469-6999
Nativity of Our Lord S 500/K-8
900 W Midway Blvd 80020 303-466-4177
Kathy Shadel, prin. Fax 469-5172

Brush, Morgan, Pop. 5,186
Brush SD RE-2(J) 1,600/PK-12
PO Box 585 80723 970-842-5176
Bret Miles, supt. Fax 842-4481
www.brushschools.org
Beaver Valley ES 300/3-5
PO Box 585 80723 970-842-4794
Rob Sanders, prin. Fax 842-3924
Brush MS 400/6-8
PO Box 585 80723 970-842-5035
Johan van Nieuwenhuizen, prin. Fax 842-3009
Thomson PS 400/PK-2
PO Box 585 80723 970-842-5139
Kendra Anderson, prin. Fax 842-2808

Riverview Christian S 100/PK-12
PO Box 665 80723 970-842-4604
Dave Mitchell, admin. Fax 842-4604

Buena Vista, Chaffee, Pop. 2,174
Buena Vista SD R-31 1,000/PK-12
PO Box 2027 81211 719-395-7000
Tina Goar, supt. Fax 395-7007
www.bvschools.org/
Avery/Parsons ES 300/PK-5
PO Box 2027 81211 719-395-7020
Stefani Franklin, prin. Fax 395-7015
McGinnis MS 300/6-8
PO Box 2027 81211 719-395-7060
Steve Goar, prin. Fax 395-7090

Patterson Christian Academy 200/PK-12
PO Box 1243 81211 719-395-6046
Erik Ritschard, admin. Fax 395-2055

Burlington, Kit Carson, Pop. 3,493
Burlington SD RE-6J 800/PK-12
PO Box 369 80807 719-346-8737
Don Anderson, supt. Fax 346-8541
www.burlingtonk12.org/
Burlington ES 300/PK-4
450 11th St 80807 719-346-8166
Deborah James, prin. Fax 346-8165
Burlington MS 200/5-8
2600 Rose Ave 80807 719-346-5440
Greg Swiatkowski, prin. Fax 346-7900

Byers, Arapahoe, Pop. 1,065
Byers SD 32J 500/PK-12
444 E Front St 80103 303-822-5292
Tom Turrell, supt. Fax 822-9592
www.byers32j.k12.co.us
Byers ES 300/PK-6
444 E Front St 80103 303-822-5292
Gloria Mitchell, prin. Fax 822-9511

Calhan, El Paso, Pop. 876
Calhan SD RJ-1 600/PK-12
PO Box 800 80808 719-347-2541
Tim Holt, supt. Fax 347-2144
calhanschool.org/
Calhan ES 300/PK-5
PO Box 800 80808 719-347-2766
Linda Miller, prin. Fax 347-2108
Calhan MS 100/6-8
PO Box 800 80808 719-347-2766
Linda Miller, prin. Fax 347-2108

Ellicott SD 22
Supt. — See Ellicott
Ellicott ES 300/K-5
399 S Ellicott Hwy 80808 719-683-2700
John Lawrence, prin. Fax 683-5432

Campo, Baca, Pop. 135
Campo SD RE-6 100/PK-12
PO Box 70 81029 719-787-2226
Nikki Johnson, supt. Fax 787-0140
Campo ES 50/PK-6
PO Box 70 81029 719-787-2226
Joe Patton, prin. Fax 787-0140

Canon City, Fremont, Pop. 16,000
Canon City SD RE-1 3,700/K-12
101 N 14th St 81212 719-276-5700
Dr. Robin Gooldy, supt. Fax 276-5739
www.canoncityschools.org/
Canon City MS 500/6-8
1215 Main St 81212 719-276-5740
Ken Trujillo, prin. Fax 276-5795
Harrison S 700/K-8
920 Field Ave 81212 719-276-5970
Larry Otte, prin. Fax 276-6005
Lincoln ES 200/K-5
420 Myrtle Ave 81212 719-276-5830
Tammy DeWolfe, prin. Fax 276-5865
McKinley ES 300/K-5
1240 McKinley St 81212 719-276-6010
Deb Chittenden, prin. Fax 276-6045
Skyline ES 200/K-5
2855 N 9th St 81212 719-276-6050
Marsha Harrington, prin. Fax 276-6080
Washington ES 400/K-5
606 N 9th St 81212 719-276-6090
Janice Zeiler, prin. Fax 276-6150

Four Mile Adventist S 50/PK-8
3180 E Main St 81212 719-275-6111

Carbondale, Garfield, Pop. 5,825
Roaring Fork SD RE-1
Supt. — See Glenwood Springs
Carbondale MS 200/5-8
180 Snowmass Dr 81623 970-384-5700
Rick Holt, prin. Fax 384-5705
Crystal River ES 500/PK-5
160 Snowmass Dr 81623 970-384-5620
Karen Olson, prin. Fax 384-5625

Waldorf S on the Roaring Fork 200/PK-8
16543 Highway 82 81623 970-963-1960
Harley Stroh, admin. Fax 963-1066

Castle Rock, Douglas, Pop. 35,745
Douglas County SD RE-1 45,200/PK-12
620 Wilcox St 80104 303-387-0100
Jim Christensen, supt. Fax 387-0107
www.dcsdk12.org
Buffalo Ridge ES 500/K-5
7075 Shoreham Dr, 303-387-5575
Ally Berggren, prin. Fax 387-5576
Castle Rock ES 800/K-6
1103 Canyon Dr 80104 303-387-5000
Christina Ciancio-Schor, prin. Fax 387-5001
Castle Rock MS 1,400/7-8
2575 Meadows Pkwy, 303-387-1300
Terry Olson, prin. Fax 387-1301
Clear Sky ES K-6
1470 Clear Sky Way, 303-387-5852
Tanya Carter, prin. Fax 387-5826
Flagstone ES 600/PK-6
104 Lovington St 80104 303-387-5225
Susan McConaghy, prin. Fax 387-5226
Meadow View ES 700/PK-6
3700 Butterfield Crossing, 303-387-5425
Patti Magby, prin. Fax 387-5426
Mesa MS 7-8
365 N Mitchell St 80104 303-387-4750
Karmen Smith, prin. Fax 387-4751
Renaissance Expeditionary Magnet S 300/PK-6
3960 Trail Boss Ln 80104 303-387-8000
Deborah Lemmer, prin. Fax 387-8001
Rock Ridge ES 600/K-6
400 Heritage Rd 80104 303-387-5150
Dennis Ingram, prin. Fax 387-5151
Soaring Hawk ES 800/K-6
4665 Tanglevine Dr, 303-387-5825
Laura Brinkman, prin. Fax 387-5826
South Street ES 600/K-6
1100 South St 80104 303-387-5075
Carrie Stephenson, prin. Fax 387-5076
Timber Trail ES 600/PK-5
690 Castle Pines Pkwy, 303-387-5700
Michele Radke, prin. Fax 387-5701
Other Schools – See Franktown, Highlands Ranch, Larkspur, Littleton, Lonetree, Parker, Sedalia

---

Montessori S of Castle Rock 50/PK-K
PO Box 34 80104 303-688-9553
Cynthia Oberdier, prin. Fax 688-0464

Cedaredge, Delta, Pop. 2,148
Delta County SD 50(J)
Supt. — See Delta
Cedaredge ES 400/K-5
230 NW Cedar Ave 81413 970-856-3885
Wayne Frazier, prin. Fax 856-3934
Cedaredge MS 200/6-8
845 SE Deer Creek Dr 81413 970-856-3118
Paul Rodriguez, prin. Fax 856-3235

Centennial, Arapahoe, Pop. 98,243
Cherry Creek SD 5
Supt. — See Greenwood Village
Heritage ES 300/PK-5
6867 E Heritage Pl S 80111 720-554-3500
Mary Pirog, prin. Fax 554-3588
Red Hawk Ridge ES 600/PK-5
16251 E Geddes Ave 80016 720-886-3800
Susan Heidemann, prin. Fax 886-3888

Littleton SD 6
Supt. — See Littleton
Franklin ES 400/K-5
1603 E Euclid Ave 80121 303-347-4500
Janie Youderian, prin. Fax 347-4524
Highland ES 400/K-5
711 E Euclid Ave 80121 303-347-4525
Debra March, prin. Fax 347-4240
Hopkins ES 300/K-5
7171 S Pennsylvania St 80122 303-347-4550
Drew Brueckner, prin. Fax 347-4570
Lenski ES 600/K-5
6350 S Fairfax Way 80121 303-347-4575
Barbara DeSpain, prin. Fax 347-4580
Newton MS 700/6-8
4001 E Arapahoe Rd 80122 303-347-7900
James O'Tremba, prin. Fax 347-7930
Peabody ES 300/K-5
3128 E Maplewood Ave 80121 303-347-4625
Kristin Ryan, prin. Fax 347-4630
Sandburg ES 500/K-5
6900 S Elizabeth St 80122 303-347-4675
Marj McDonald, prin. Fax 347-4680
Twain ES 400/K-5
6901 S Franklin St 80122 303-347-4700
Sarina Compoz, prin. Fax 347-4720

Centennial Christian Academy 100/K-6
4343 S Flanders St 80015 303-680-7402
Brent Johnson, admin. Fax 690-3318
Shepherd of the Hills Christian S 300/PK-8
7691 S University Blvd 80122 303-798-0711
Jim Krupski, prin. Fax 798-0718

Center, Saguache, Pop. 2,497
Center Consolidated SD 26JT 600/PK-12
550 Sylvester Ave 81125 719-754-3442
George Welsh, supt. Fax 754-3952
www.center.k12.co.us
Haskin ES 300/PK-5
550 Sylvester Ave 81125 719-754-3982
Katherine Kulp, prin. Fax 754-2857
Skoglund MS 100/6-8
550 Sylvester Ave 81125 719-754-2232
George Welsh, prin. Fax 754-2856

Cheraw, Otero, Pop. 212
Cheraw SD 31 200/PK-12
PO Box 160 81030 719-853-6655
Rick Lovato, supt. Fax 853-6322
cheraw.k12.co.us
Cheraw ES 100/PK-5
PO Box 160 81030 719-853-6655
Ryan Nesselhuf, prin. Fax 853-6322
Cheraw MS 50/6-8
PO Box 160 81030 719-853-6655
Ryan Nesselhuf, prin. Fax 853-6322

Cheyenne Wells, Cheyenne, Pop. 873
Cheyenne County SD RE-5 200/PK-12
PO Box 577 80810 719-767-5866
David Marx, supt. Fax 767-8773
www.cheyennesd.net/
Cheyenne Wells ES 100/PK-5
PO Box 577 80810 719-767-5656
Cheyenne Wells MS 100/6-8
PO Box 577 80810 719-767-5656

Chipita Park, El Paso, Pop. 1,479
Manitou Springs SD 14
Supt. — See Manitou Springs
Ute Pass ES 100/K-5
9230 Chipita Park Rd 80809 719-685-2227
Deb Yagmin, prin. Fax 685-2220

Clifton, Mesa, Pop. 12,671
Mesa County Valley SD 51
Supt. — See Grand Junction
Clifton ES 500/PK-5
3276 F Rd 81520 970-254-4760
Michelle Mansheim, prin. Fax 434-9725
Mt. Garfield MS 700/6-8
3475 Front St 81520 970-254-4720
Terrie Requa, prin. Fax 464-0536
Rocky Mountain ES 500/PK-5
3260 D 1/2 Rd 81520 970-254-4900
Patti Virden, prin. Fax 434-2804

Genesis Christian S 200/PK-6
615 I-70 Business Loop 81520 970-434-0205
Gladys Dial, admin. Fax 434-8225

Collbran, Mesa, Pop. 408
Plateau Valley SD 50 500/PK-12
56600 Highway 330 81624 970-487-3547
Gregory Randall, supt. Fax 487-3876
www.plateauvalley.k12.co.us/
Plateau Valley ES 100/PK-5
56600 Highway 330 81624 970-487-3547
Kristi Mease, prin. Fax 487-3876
Plateau Valley MS 100/6-8
56600 Highway 330 81624 970-487-3547
Leroy Gutierrez, prin. Fax 487-3876

Colorado City, Pueblo, Pop. 1,149
Pueblo County SD 70
Supt. — See Pueblo
Craver MS 200/6-8
PO Box 19369 81019 719-676-3030
Chuck Scott, prin. Fax 676-3511

Colorado Springs, El Paso, Pop. 369,815
Academy SD 20 18,100/PK-12
1110 Chapel Hills Dr 80920 719-234-1200
Dr. Mark Hatchell, supt. Fax 234-1299
www.asd20.org/
Academy Endeavour ES 500/K-5
3475 Hampton Park Dr 80920 719-234-5600
Bobbi Harper, prin. Fax 234-5699
Academy International ES 600/K-5
8550 Charity Dr 80920 719-234-4000
Peggy Healer, prin. Fax 234-4099
Antelope Trails ES 500/K-5
15280 Jessie Dr 80921 719-234-4100
Roy Getchell, prin. Fax 234-4199
Challenger MS 700/6-8
10215 Lexington Dr 80920 719-234-3000
Tony Scott, prin. Fax 234-3199
Chinook Trail ES K-5
11795 Grand Lawn Ct, 719-234-5700
Gail Kozhevnikov, prin. Fax 234-5799
Da Vinci Academy 500/K-5
1335 Bridle Oaks Ln 80921 719-234-5400
Kathy Griego, prin. Fax 234-5499
Discovery Canyon Campus 900/PK-12
1810 N Gate Blvd 80921 719-234-1800
Dr. Gary Batsell, prin. Fax 234-1899
Eagleview MS 900/6-8
1325 Vindicator Dr 80919 719-234-3400
Karon Cofield, prin. Fax 234-3599
Explorer ES 500/PK-5
4190 Bardot Dr 80920 719-234-4400
Maureen Lang, prin. Fax 234-4499
Foothills ES 400/K-5
825 Allegheny Dr 80919 719-234-4500
Rose Bergles, prin. Fax 234-4599
Frontier ES 400/K-5
3755 Meadow Ridge Dr 80920 719-234-4600
Belinda Lujan-Lindsey, prin. Fax 234-4699
High Plains ES 400/K-5
2248 Vintage Dr 80920 719-234-4700
Dr. Kim Hollm, prin. Fax 234-4799
Mountain Ridge MS 1,200/6-8
9150 Lexington Dr 80920 719-234-3200
Joy Porter, prin. Fax 234-3399
Mountain View ES 500/K-5
10095 Lexington Dr 80920 719-234-4800
Paula Mooney, prin. Fax 234-4899
Pioneer ES 500/K-5
3663 Woodland Hills Dr 80918 719-234-5000
Diane Naghi, prin. Fax 234-5099
Prairie Hills ES 600/K-5
8025 Telegraph Dr 80920 719-234-5100
Kathy Crawford, prin. Fax 234-5199
Ranch Creek ES K-5
9155 Tutt Blvd, 719-234-5500
Susan Paulson, prin. Fax 234-5599
Rockrimmon ES 400/K-5
195 Mikado Dr W 80919 719-234-5200
Barbara Barton, prin. Fax 234-5299
Timberview MS 1,000/6-8
8680 Scarborough Dr 80920 719-234-3600
Brett Smith, prin. Fax 234-3799
Wolford ES 500/K-5
13710 Black Forest Rd 80908 719-234-4300
Bob Wedel, prin. Fax 234-4399
Woodmen-Roberts ES 400/PK-5
8365 Orchard Path Rd 80919 719-234-5300
Susan Field, prin. Fax 234-5399
Other Schools – See USAF Academy

Cheyenne Mountain SD 12 4,000/PK-12
1775 LaClede St 80905 719-475-6100
Walter Cooper, supt. Fax 475-6106
www.cmsd.k12.co.us
Broadmoor ES 300/K-6
440 W Cheyenne Mountain Blv 80906 719-475-6130
Karen Fedorenchik, prin. Fax 475-6126
Canon ES 300/K-6
1201 W Cheyenne Rd 80906 719-475-6140
Joe Torrez, prin. Fax 475-6143
Cheyenne Mountain ES 300/K-6
5250 Farthing Dr 80906 719-576-3080
Jeri Crispe, prin. Fax 576-6834
Cheyenne Mountain JHS 700/7-8
1200 W Cheyenne Rd 80906 719-475-6120
Lori Smith, prin. Fax 475-6123
Gold Camp ES 300/PK-6
1805 Preserve Dr 80906 719-327-2820
Kallene Casias, prin. Fax 327-2825
Pinon Valley ES 400/PK-6
6205 Farthing Dr 80906 719-527-0300
Diane Wimp, prin. Fax 527-8018
Skyway Park ES 300/K-6
1100 Mercury Dr 80905 719-475-6150
Pat Webster, prin. Fax 630-4114

Colorado Springs SD 11 26,100/PK-12
1115 N El Paso St 80903 719-520-2000
Dr. Terry Bishop, supt. Fax 577-4546
www.d11.org/
Audubon ES 300/PK-5
2400 E Van Buren St 80909 719-328-2600
Nancy Smith, prin. Fax 630-0178
Bates ES 200/PK-5
702 Cragmor Rd 80907 719-328-5400
Judy McCollum, prin. Fax 260-8827
Bristol ES 200/K-5
890 N Walnut St 80905 719-328-4000
Steve Ferguson, prin. Fax 630-0182
Buena Vista ES 200/PK-5
924 W Pikes Peak Ave 80905 719-328-4100
Fax 630-0184

Carver ES 400/PK-5
4740 Artistic Cir 80917 719-328-7100
Cynthia Martinez, prin. Fax 596-3614
Chipeta ES 400/PK-5
2340 Ramsgate Ter 80919 719-328-5500
Lori Butler, prin. Fax 260-8825
Columbia ES 200/PK-5
835 E Saint Vrain St 80903 719-328-2700
Linda Schlagenhauf, prin. Fax 630-0235
Edison ES 200/PK-5
3125 N Hancock Ave 80907 719-328-2800
Steven Hesselberg, prin. Fax 630-0238
Freedom ES K-5
5280 Butterfield Dr, 719-228-0800
George Martin, prin. Fax 593-1749
Fremont ES 400/PK-5
5110 El Camino Dr 80918 719-328-5600
Chris Calrson, prin. Fax 260-8811
Galileo S of Math & Science 6-6
1600 N Union Blvd 80909 719-328-2200
Rusty Moomey, prin. Fax 448-0498
Grant ES 500/PK-5
3215 Westwood Blvd 80918 719-328-5700
Veronica Anderson, prin. Fax 260-8822
Henry ES 400/PK-5
1310 Lehmberg Blvd 80915 719-328-7200
Anne Howard, prin. Fax 596-0922
Holmes MS 700/6-8
2455 Mesa Rd 80904 719-328-3800
Robert Utter, prin. Fax 448-0358
Howbert ES 200/PK-5
1023 N 31st St 80904 719-328-4200
David Morris, prin. Fax 630-0187
Hunt ES 200/PK-5
917 E Moreno Ave 80903 719-328-2900
George Ewing, prin. Fax 630-2245
Ivywild S 100/PK-8
1604 S Cascade Ave 80905 719-328-4300
Libby Bailey, prin. Fax 630-0245
Jackson ES 200/PK-5
4340 Edwinstowe Ave 80907 719-328-5800
Anne Dancy, prin. Fax 260-8813
Jenkins MS 900/6-8
6410 Austin Bluffs Pkwy, 719-328-5300
Jason Ter Horst, prin. Fax 266-5276
Keller ES 500/PK-5
3730 Montebello Dr W 80918 719-328-5900
Bryan Relich, prin. Fax 260-8819
King ES 500/PK-5
6110 Sapporo Dr 80918 719-328-6000
Cordelia Stone, prin. Fax 260-8816
Lincoln ES 300/K-5
2727 N Cascade Ave 80907 719-328-4400
Dave Cook, prin. Fax 630-2289
Madison ES 400/PK-5
4120 Constitution Ave 80909 719-328-7300
Marcia Bader, prin. Fax 596-4323
Mann MS 700/6-8
1001 E Van Buren St 80907 719-328-2300
Scott Stanec, prin. Fax 488-0354
Martinez ES 600/PK-5
6460 Vickers Dr 80918 719-328-6100
Bobbie Long, prin. Fax 260-8806
McAuliffe ES PK-5
830 Hathaway Dr 80915 719-228-0900
Denise Rubio-Gurnett, prin. Fax 574-8372
Midland International ES 200/PK-5
2110 Broadway Ave 80904 719-328-4500
Fax 630-0247
Monroe ES 500/PK-5
15 S Chelton Rd 80910 719-328-7400
Karen Shaw, prin. Fax 596-4465
North MS 700/6-8
612 E Yampa St 80903 719-328-2400
David Bakalyan, prin. Fax 448-0268
Palmer ES 300/PK-5
1921 E Yampa St 80909 719-328-3200
Priscilla Barsotti, prin. Fax 630-7806
Penrose ES 400/PK-5
4285 S Nonchalant Cir 80917 719-328-7500
Kirsten Cortez, prin. Fax 596-0883
Pike ES 100/PK-5
2510 N Chestnut St 80907 719-328-4600
Manuel Ramsey, prin. Fax 630-0249
Rogers ES 400/PK-5
110 S Circle Dr 80910 719-328-3300
Bryan Casebeer, prin. Fax 630-7809
Rudy ES 500/PK-5
5370 Cracker Barrel Cir 80917 719-328-7600
Julie Foster, prin. Fax 596-0305
Russell MS 800/6-8
3825 E Montebello Dr 80918 719-328-5200
Jeanice Swift, prin. Fax 531-5520
Sabin MS 700/6-8
3605 N Carefree Cir 80917 719-328-7000
Sherry Kalbach, prin. Fax 573-4960
Scott ES 700/PK-5
6175 Whetstone Dr, 719-328-6200
Larry Howard, prin. Fax 260-9587
Steele ES 300/K-5
1720 N Weber St 80907 719-328-4700
Georganne Barnes, prin. Fax 630-0232
Stratton ES 300/PK-5
2460 Paseo Rd 80907 719-328-3400
Duane Helfer, prin. Fax 630-3382
Swigert Aerospace Academy 400/6-8
4220 E Pikes Peak Ave 80909 719-328-6900
Larry Bartel, prin. Fax 573-5094
Taylor ES 300/K-5
900 E Buena Ventura St 80907 719-328-3500
Mary Sullivan, prin. Fax 630-3397
Trailblazer ES 300/K-5
2015 Wickes Rd 80919 719-328-6300
Patricia Ring, prin. Fax 260-1049
Twain ES 500/PK-5
3402 E San Miguel St 80909 719-328-7700
Gail Smartt, prin. Fax 596-6889
West ES, 25 N 20th St 80904 K-5
Terry Martinez, prin. 719-328-4900

West MS 400/6-8
1920 W Pikes Peak Ave 80904 719-328-3900
Clay Gomez, prin. Fax 448-0141
Wilson ES 500/PK-5
1409 De Reamer Cir 80915 719-328-7800
Judy Hawkins, prin. Fax 596-7452

Falcon SD 49
Supt. — See Falcon
ECC PK-PK
6573 Shimmering Creek Dr, 719-494-8840
Barbara Johnson, dir.
Evans ES 700/K-5
1675 Winnebago Rd 80915 719-495-5299
Amber Whetstine, prin. Fax 495-5298
Horizon MS 700/6-8
1750 Piros Dr 80915 719-495-5210
Greg Moles, prin. Fax 495-5209
Odyssey ES 600/K-5
6275 Bridlespur Ave 80922 719-494-8622
Pam Weyer, prin. Fax 495-8623
Remington ES 500/K-5
2825 Pony Tracks Dr 80922 719-495-5266
Mark Brown, prin. Fax 495-5267
Ridgeview ES 600/K-5
6573 Shimmering Creek Dr, 719-494-8700
Vicki Axford, prin. Fax 494-8708
Skyview MS 1,000/6-8
6350 Windom Peak Blvd, 719-495-5566
Sandy Rivera, prin. Fax 495-5569
Springs Ranch ES 600/K-5
4350 Centerville Dr 80922 719-494-8600
Debbie Jones, prin. Fax 494-8612
Stetson ES 700/K-5
4910 Jedediah Smith Rd 80922 719-495-5252
Theresa Ritz, prin. Fax 495-5253

Hanover SD 28 300/K-12
17050 S Peyton Hwy 80928 719-683-2247
Darryl Webb, supt. Fax 683-4602
hanover.ppboces.org/
Hanover ES 100/K-5
17050 S Peyton Hwy 80928 719-683-2247
Mike Ferguson, prin. Fax 683-4602
Other Schools – See Pueblo

Harrison SD 2 9,500/PK-12
1060 Harrison Rd 80905 719-579-2000
F. Mike Miles, supt. Fax 579-2019
www.harrison.k12.co.us
Bricker ES 400/K-5
4880 Dover Dr 80916 719-579-2150
Amy McCord, prin. Fax 579-2808
Carmel MS 400/6-8
1740 Pepperwood Dr 80910 719-579-3210
Tina Vidovich, prin. Fax 579-2695
Centennial ES 400/K-5
1860 S Chelton Rd 80910 719-579-2155
Annette Ontiveros, prin. Fax 579-2864
Chamberlin ES 200/K-5
2400 Slater Ave 80905 719-579-2160
Sheryl Hobbs, prin. Fax 579-2886
Fox Meadow MS 600/6-8
1450 Cheyenne Meadows Rd 80906 719-527-7100
Cheryl Madrill, prin. Fax 527-7174
Giberson ES 400/K-6
2880 Ferber Dr 80916 719-579-2165
John Rogerson, prin. Fax 579-4994
Monterey ES 300/K-5
2311 Monterey Rd 80910 719-579-2170
Michael Claudio, prin. Fax 579-2954
Mountain Vista Community S 500/K-8
2550 Dorset Dr 80910 719-579-2067
Denise Garcia-Cooper, prin. Fax 527-3425
Oak Creek ES 300/PK-5
3333 Oak Creek Dr W 80906 719-579-2175
Karen Perea, prin. Fax 579-2991
Otero ES 400/K-6
1650 Charmwood Dr 80906 719-579-2110
Lorna Breske, prin. Fax 579-2002
Panorama MS 700/6-8
2145 S Chelton Rd 80916 719-579-3220
Teri Newbold, prin. Fax 579-2756
Pikes Peak ES 400/K-5
1520 Verde Dr 80910 719-579-2180
Brenda Matznick, prin. Fax 579-3565
Sand Creek ES 500/K-5
550 Sand Creek Dr 80916 719-579-3760
Tracy Killingsworth, prin. Fax 579-4943
Soaring Eagles ES 500/K-6
4710 Harrier Ridge Dr 80916 719-540-4000
Kelli Trausch, prin. Fax 540-4020
Stratmoor Hills ES 300/K-6
200 Loomis Ave 80906 719-579-2185
Pamela Robinson, prin. Fax 540-4030
Stratton Meadows ES 300/K-5
610 Brookshire Ave 80905 719-579-2190
Jeanette Garcia, prin. Fax 538-1400
Turman ES 300/K-5
3245 Springnite Dr 80916 719-579-2195
Michael Roth, prin. Fax 579-3699
Wildflower ES 300/K-5
1160 Keith Dr 80916 719-579-2115
Edward Knight, prin. Fax 579-3757

Lewis-Palmer SD 38
Supt. — See Monument
Kilmer ES 400/PK-5
4285 Walker Rd 80908 719-488-4740
David Young, prin. Fax 488-4744

Widefield SD 3 8,400/PK-12
1820 Main St 80911 719-391-3000
Stan Richardson, supt. Fax 390-4372
www.wsd3.org/
French ES 600/K-6
5225 Alturas Dr 80911 719-391-3495
Carlos Lopez, prin. Fax 391-9141
King ES 500/K-6
6910 Defoe Ave 80911 719-391-3455
Kim Jorgensen, prin. Fax 391-9324

North ES 300/K-6
209 Leta Dr 80911 719-391-3375
Paul Macrenato, prin. Fax 391-9425
Pinello ES 400/K-6
2515 Cody Dr 80911 719-391-3395
Maureen di Stasio, prin. Fax 392-1605
Sproul JHS 400/7-8
235 Sumac Dr 80911 719-391-3215
Larry Borchik, prin. Fax 391-3215
Sunrise ES 600/K-6
7070 Grand Valley Dr 80911 719-391-3415
Jill Strasheim, prin. Fax 391-9104
Talbott ES 400/K-6
401 Dean Dr 80911 719-391-3475
Carre Bonilla, prin. Fax 391-9414
Venetucci ES 500/K-6
405 Willis Dr 80911 719-391-3355
Joyce Cope, prin. Fax 391-7706
Watson JHS 400/7-8
136 Fontaine Blvd 80911 719-391-3255
Kirsten Toy, prin. Fax 392-3419
Webster ES 500/K-6
445 Jersey Ln 80911 719-391-3435
Connie Florell, prin. Fax 391-9166
Widefield ES 400/K-6
509 Widefield Dr 80911 719-391-3335
Tracy Vsetecka, prin. Fax 391-9416
Wilson Preschool 300/PK-PK
930 Leta Dr 80911 719-391-3050
Lisa Humberd, prin. Fax 391-9142
Other Schools – See Fountain

Colorado Springs Christian ES 500/K-5
4015 N Weber St 80907 719-535-8965
Doug Bray, prin. Fax 268-5508
Colorado Springs Christian MS 300/6-8
4845 Mallow Rd 80907 719-535-8968
Luke Butler, prin. Fax 268-2122
Colorado Springs S 500/PK-12
21 Broadmoor Ave 80906 719-475-9747
Kevin Reel, hdmstr. Fax 475-9864
Corpus Christi S 400/PK-8
2410 N Cascade Ave 80907 719-632-5092
Carole Johnson, prin. Fax 578-9124
Divine Redeemer S 300/PK-8
901 N Logan Ave 80909 719-471-7771
Jim Rigg, prin. Fax 234-0300
Evangelical Christian Academy 200/PK-6
2511 N Logan Ave 80907 719-634-7024
Pam Firks, prin. Fax 328-1554
Family of Christ Lutheran S 200/PK-K
675 E Baptist Rd 80921 719-481-0796
Amy Janisse, prin. Fax 481-1366
Heartland Christian Academy 50/PK-K
828 E Pikes Peak Ave 80903 719-636-3681
Marsha Whitted, prin. Fax 636-3995
Hilltop Baptist S 100/K-12
6915 Palmer Park Blvd 80915 719-597-1880
Jan Ocvirk, prin. Fax 597-8168
Holy Apostles Preschool 100/PK-PK
4925 N Carefree Cir 80917 719-591-1566
Mary Parsons, prin. Fax 591-1816
Hope Montessori Academy - East PK-8
6353 Stetson Hills Blvd, 719-573-5300
Norman Deeba, prin. Fax 955-0482
Hope Montessori Academy - West 200/PK-6
2041 Chuckwagon Rd 80919 719-388-8818
Norman Deeba, prin. Fax 590-1655
Pauline Memorial S 200/PK-8
1601 Mesa Ave 80906 719-632-1846
Larry Dorsey-Spitz, prin. Fax 632-0231
Pikes Peak Christian S 500/PK-12
5905 Flintridge Dr 80918 719-598-8610
Ken Preslar, dir. Fax 598-1491
Purple Mountain Academy 50/PK-12
1401 Potter Dr Ste 105 80909 719-216-7167
Randall Ferguson, prin.
St. Lukes Lutheran Children's Center 100/PK-K
5265 N Union Blvd 80918 719-598-7821
Michelle Brice, dir.
Salem Lutheran S 50/K-8
4318 N Chestnut St 80907 719-599-0200
Joseph Gumm, prin. Fax 593-7147
Springs Adventist Academy 100/K-9
5410 Palmer Park Blvd 80915 719-597-0155
Carol Miller, prin. Fax 574-2134

Commerce City, Adams, Pop. 34,189

Adams County SD 14 6,200/PK-12
5291 E 60th Ave 80022 303-853-3940
Susan Chandler, supt. Fax 286-9753
www.adams14.org/
Adams 14 Child Care Center 100/PK-K
5650 Bowen Ct 80022 303-853-5000
Kristen Speta, coord. Fax 853-5013
Adams City MS 600/6-8
4451 E 72nd Ave 80022 303-289-5881
Jennifer Skrobela, prin. Fax 288-8574
Alsup ES 500/PK-5
7101 Birch St 80022 303-288-6865
Teresa Benallo, prin. Fax 288-6866
Central ES 600/PK-5
6450 Holly St 80022 303-287-0327
Hollene Davis, prin. Fax 287-0328
Dupont ES 500/PK-5
7970 Kimberly St 80022 303-287-0189
Kathy Heronema, prin. Fax 287-0180
Hanson S 300/PK-8
7133 E 73rd Ave 80022 303-853-5800
Nelson Van Vranken, prin. Fax 288-5578
Kearney MS 600/6-8
6160 Kearney St 80022 303-287-0261
Shelli Robins, prin. Fax 287-0432
Kemp ES 400/PK-5
6775 Oneida St 80022 303-288-6633
Wanda Clark, prin. Fax 288-6634
Monaco ES 400/PK-5
7631 Monaco St 80022 303-287-0307
Jennifer Ikenouye, prin. Fax 287-0308

Rose Hill ES 400/PK-5
6900 E 58th Ave 80022 303-287-0163
Samara Williams, prin. Fax 287-0164
Sanville Preschool 100/PK-PK
5941 E 64th Ave 80022 303-853-5675
Kristen Speta, dir. Fax 287-2473

Brighton SD 27J
Supt. — See Brighton
Second Creek ES 800/K-5
9950 Laredo Dr 80022 720-685-7550
Evoice Sims, prin. Fax 685-7554
Stuart MS 6-8
15955 E 101st Way 80022 720-685-5500

Conifer, Jefferson, Pop. 600
Jefferson County SD R-1
Supt. — See Golden
West Jefferson ES 400/PK-5
26501 Barkley Rd 80433 303-982-2975
Debra O'Neill, prin. Fax 982-2976
West Jefferson MS 700/6-8
9449 Barnes Ave 80433 303-982-3056
Jean Kelley, prin. Fax 982-3057

Cortez, Montezuma, Pop. 8,244
Montezuma-Cortez SD RE-1 2,500/K-12
PO Box R 81321 970-565-7282
Stacy Houser, supt. Fax 565-2161
www.cortez.k12.co.us
Cortez MS 700/6-8
450 W 2nd St 81321 970-565-7824
Jamie Haukeness, prin. Fax 565-5120
Kemper ES 300/1-5
620 E Montezuma Ave 81321 970-565-3737
Theresa Spencer, prin. Fax 565-5158
Lewis-Arriola ES 100/K-5
21434 Road U 81321 970-882-4494
Dan Porter, prin. Fax 882-7617
Manaugh ES 300/1-5
300 E 4th St 81321 970-565-7691
Phil Kasper, prin. Fax 565-5142
Mesa ES 400/1-5
703 W 7th St 81321 970-565-3858
Jason Wayman, prin. Fax 565-5137
Other Schools – See Pleasant View

Cortez Adventist Christian S 50/K-8
540 W 4th St 81321 970-565-8257
Deirdre Franklin, prin. Fax 565-9740

Cotopaxi, Fremont, Pop. 130
Cotopaxi SD RE-3 300/PK-12
PO Box 385 81223 719-942-4131
Geoffrey Gerk, supt. Fax 942-4134
www.cotopaxire3.org/
Cotopaxi ES 100/PK-5
PO Box 385 81223 719-942-4131
Kristi Wilson, prin. Fax 942-4134

Craig, Moffat, Pop. 9,143
Moffat County SD RE-1 2,200/PK-12
775 Yampa Ave 81625 970-824-3268
Dr. Joe Petrone, supt. Fax 824-6655
moffatsd.org/
Craig MS 300/7-8
915 Yampa Ave 81625 970-824-3289
Bill Toovey, prin. Fax 824-3858
East ES 300/K-4
600 Texas Ave 81625 970-824-6042
Diana Cook, prin. Fax 824-3513
ECC, 775 Yampa Ave 81625 100/PK-PK
Sarah Hepworth, dir. 970-824-7457
Ridgeview ES 200/K-4
655 Westridge Rd 81625 970-824-7018
Julie Baker, prin. Fax 824-7010
Sandrock ES 100/PK-5
201 E 9th St 81625 970-824-3287
Kamisha Siminoe, prin. Fax 824-5278
Sunset ES 300/K-4
800 W 7th St 81625 970-824-5762
Zack Allen, prin. Fax 824-2816
Other Schools - See Maybell

Crawford, Delta, Pop. 386
Delta County SD 50(J)
Supt. — See Delta
Crawford S 100/K-8
PO Box 98 81415 970-921-4935
Helen Groome, prin. Fax 921-3671

Creede, Mineral, Pop. 412
Creede Consolidated SD 1 100/PK-12
PO Box 429 81130 719-658-2220
Buck Stroh, supt. Fax 658-2942
www.creedek12.net
Lamb ES 100/PK-6
PO Box 429 81130 719-658-2220
Lauren Sheldrake, prin. Fax 658-2942

Crested Butte, Gunnison, Pop. 1,546
Gunnison Watershed SD RE 1J
Supt. — See Gunnison
Crested Butte S 400/K-12
PO Box 339 81224 970-641-7720
Stephanie Niemi, prin. Fax 641-7729

Cripple Creek, Teller, Pop. 1,065
Cripple Creek-Victor SD RE-1 600/PK-12
PO Box 897 80813 719-689-2685
Susan Holmes, supt. Fax 689-2256
www.ccvschools.com/
Cresson ES 300/PK-6
PO Box 897 80813 719-689-9230
Martha DeJesus, prin. Fax 689-9236

De Beque, Mesa, Pop. 472
De Beque SD 49JT 200/PK-12
PO Box 70 81630 970-283-5418
Doug Pfau, supt. Fax 283-5213
De Beque ES 100/PK-6
PO Box 70 81630 970-283-5596
Sue Taylor, prin. Fax 283-5213

Deer Trail, Arapahoe, Pop. 577
Deer Trail SD 26J 200/PK-12
PO Box 129 80105 303-769-4421
Brad Caldwell, supt. Fax 769-4600
Deer Trail ES 100/PK-5
PO Box 129 80105 303-769-4421
Jeff Bollinger, prin. Fax 769-4600

Del Norte, Rio Grande, Pop. 1,569
Del Norte SD C-7 600/K-12
770 11th St 81132 719-657-4040
Michael Salvato, supt. Fax 657-2546
www.del-norte.k12.co.us/
Del Norte MS 100/6-8
770 11th St 81132 719-657-4030
Nathan Smith, prin. Fax 657-0329
Mesa ES 100/K-1
770 11th St 81132 719-657-4030
Lisa Masias-Hensley, prin. Fax 657-4020
Underwood ES 200/2-5
770 11th St 81132 719-657-4030
Lisa Masias-Hensley, prin. Fax 657-3084

Delta, Delta, Pop. 8,135
Delta County SD 50(J) 4,700/PK-12
7655 2075 Rd 81416 970-874-4438
Mike McMillan, supt. Fax 874-5744
www.deltaschools.com
Backpack Early Learning Academy 100/PK-PK
822 Grand Ave 81416 970-874-9517
Angela Fletcher, prin.
Delta MS 500/6-8
910 Grand Ave 81416 970-874-8046
Derek Carlson, prin. Fax 874-8049
Garnet Mesa ES 500/K-5
600 A St 81416 970-874-8003
Jim Farmer, prin. Fax 874-8303
Lincoln ES 500/K-5
1050 Hastings St 81416 970-874-3700
Doug Egging, prin. Fax 874-4714
Other Schools – See Cedaredge, Crawford, Hotchkiss, Paonia

Delta SDA S 50/K-8
PO Box 91 81416 970-874-9482

Denver, Denver, Pop. 557,917
Adams County SD 50 7,500/PK-12
2401 W 80th Ave 80221 303-428-3511
Dr. Roberta Selleck, supt. Fax 657-9450
www.adams50.org
Carpenter MS 500/6-8
7001 Lipan St 80221 303-428-8583
Kelly Williams, prin. Fax 657-3962
Clear Lake MS 600/6-8
1940 Elmwood Ln 80221 303-428-7526
Charisse Goza, prin. Fax 430-6465
Day ES 300/K-5
1740 Jordan Dr 80221 303-428-1330
Chadwick Anderson, prin. Fax 657-3835
Fairview ES 300/K-5
7826 Fairview Ave 80221 303-428-1405
Kathy Wiemer, prin. Fax 657-3838
Hodgkins ES PK-5
3475 W 67th Ave 80221 303-428-1121
Ricardo Concha, prin. Fax 657-3820
Metz ES 400/K-5
2341 Sherrelwood Dr 80221 303-428-1884
Shannon Willy, prin. Fax 657-3865
Sherrelwood ES 300/K-5
8095 Kalamath St 80221 303-428-5353
Cindy Davis, prin. Fax 657-3868
Skyline Vista ES 400/PK-5
7395 Zuni St 80221 303-428-2300
Stephanie Jackman, prin. Fax 657-3871
Other Schools – See Arvada, Westminster

Cherry Creek SD 5
Supt. — See Greenwood Village
Challenge S 500/PK-8
9659 E Mississippi Ave, 720-747-2100
Edie Alvarez, prin. Fax 747-2183
Holly Hills ES 300/3-5
6161 E Cornell Ave 80222 720-747-2500
Chad Gerity, prin. Fax 747-2588
Holly Ridge PS PK-2
3301 S Monaco Pkwy 80222 720-747-2400
Chad Gerity, prin. Fax 747-2488

Denver County SD 1 63,200/PK-12
900 Grant St 80203 720-423-3200
Michael Bennet, supt. Fax 423-3413
www.dpsk12.org/
Academia Ana Marie Sandoval Montessori 400/PK-6
3655 Wyandot St 80211 303-455-9326
JoAnn Trujillo-Hays, prin. Fax 424-4395
Amesse ES 500/PK-5
5440 Scranton St 80239 303-371-0940
Joyce Simmons, prin. Fax 424-9914
Archuleta ES 600/PK-5
16000 Maxwell Pl 80239 303-371-6363
Darlene LeDoux, prin. Fax 424-9834
Asbury ES 300/PK-5
1320 E Asbury Ave 80210 303-722-4695
Anita Theriot, prin. Fax 424-9775
Ashley ES 300/PK-5
1914 Syracuse St 80220 303-322-1853
Kenneth Hulslander, prin. Fax 424-9694
Barnum ES 500/PK-5
85 Hooker St 80219 303-935-3509
Myrella Goff, prin. Fax 424-9615
Barrett ES 200/PK-5
2900 Richard Allen Ct 80205 303-388-5841
Amy Green, prin. Fax 424-9555
Beach Court ES 300/PK-5
4950 Beach Ct 80221 303-455-3607
Frank Roti, prin. Fax 424-9495
Bradley International S 300/PK-5
3051 S Elm St 80222 303-756-8386
Heather Regan, prin. Fax 424-9414
Bromwell ES 300/K-5
2500 E 4th Ave 80206 303-388-5969
Jonathan Wolfer, prin. Fax 424-9355
Brown ES 400/PK-5
2550 Lowell Blvd 80211 303-477-1611
Suzanne Loughran, prin. Fax 424-9275
Bryant-Webster Dual Language S 500/PK-8
3635 Quivas St 80211 303-433-3336
Pam Linan, prin. Fax 424-9195
Carson ES 300/PK-5
5420 E 1st Ave 80220 303-355-7316
Gwendolyn Gathers, prin. Fax 424-9115
Castro ES 700/PK-5
845 S Lowell Blvd 80219 303-935-2458
Cheri Wrench, prin. Fax 424-9015
Centennial S 600/PK-8
4665 Raleigh St 80212 303-433-6489
Gail Page-Archambeau, prin. Fax 424-8925
Cheltenham ES 500/PK-5
1580 Julian St 80204 303-825-3323
Claudia Salvestrin, prin. Fax 424-8836
Cole Arts and Science Academy 100/PK-7
3240 Humboldt St 80205 303-423-9120
Julie Murgel, prin.
Colfax ES 300/PK-5
1526 Tennyson St 80204 303-623-6148
Joanna Martinez, prin. Fax 424-8765
College View ES 400/PK-5
2675 S Decatur St 80219 720-424-8660
Richard Vigil, prin. Fax 424-8685
Columbian ES 300/PK-5
2925 W 40th Ave 80211 303-433-2539
Deborah Tu-Tygrs, prin. Fax 424-8605
Columbine ES 300/PK-6
2540 E 29th Ave 80205 303-388-3617
Stephen Wera, prin. Fax 424-8535
Cory ES 400/PK-5
1550 S Steele St 80210 303-744-2726
Julia Shepherd, prin. Fax 424-8405
Cowell ES 500/PK-5
4540 W 10th Ave 80204 303-571-0617
Thomas Elliott, prin. Fax 424-8325
Denison Montessori ES 400/PK-6
1821 S Yates St 80219 303-934-7805
Bethany Hamilton, prin. Fax 424-8105
Doull ES 500/PK-5
2520 S Utica St 80219 303-935-2489
Dan Villescas, prin. Fax 424-8025
Eagleton ES 400/PK-5
880 Hooker St 80204 303-623-0181
Erica Ramlow, prin. Fax 424-7955
Edison ES 500/PK-5
3350 Quitman St 80212 303-455-3615
Ann Christy, prin. Fax 424-7805
Ellis ES 500/PK-5
1651 S Dahlia St 80222 303-756-8363
Khoa Nguyen, prin. Fax 424-7725
Fairmont Dual Language Immersion Academy 400/PK-8
520 W 3rd Ave 80223 303-893-1957
Elizabeth Tencate, prin. Fax 424-7645
Fairview ES 300/PK-5
2715 W 11th Ave 80204 303-623-7193
Norma Giron, prin. Fax 424-7565
Force ES 500/PK-5
1550 S Wolff St 80219 303-935-3595
Rachel Starks, prin. Fax 424-7425
Ford ES 600/PK-5
14500 Maxwell Pl 80239 303-371-6990
Gilberto Marin, prin. Fax 424-7325
Garden Place ES 400/PK-6
4425 Lincoln St 80216 303-295-7785
Monica Dilts, prin. Fax 424-7245
Gilpin S 400/PK-8
2949 California St 80205 303-297-0313
Catherine Gonzales, prin. Fax 424-7165
Godsman ES 500/PK-5
2120 W Arkansas Ave 80223 303-936-3466
Patricia Hurrieta, prin. Fax 424-7085
Goldrick ES 600/PK-5
1050 S Zuni St 80223 303-935-3544
Maria Uribe, prin. Fax 424-7005
Grant MS 400/6-8
1751 S Washington St 80210 720-423-9360
Greta Martinez, prin. Fax 423-9385
Grant Ranch S 700/PK-8
5400 S Jay Cir 80123 720-424-6880
Sandra Blomeyer, prin. Fax 424-6905
Greenlee S 400/PK-8
1150 Lipan St 80204 303-629-6364
Josephine Garcia, prin. Fax 424-6825
Green Valley ES 700/PK-5
4100 Jericho St 80249 303-307-1659
Andrew Hoffer, prin. Fax 424-6735
Greenwood S 600/PK-8
5130 Durham Ct 80239 303-371-0247
Devin Dillon, prin. Fax 424-6655
Gust ES 500/PK-5
3440 W Yale Ave 80219 303-935-4613
Jamie Roybal, prin. Fax 424-6585
Hamilton MS 1,000/6-8
8600 E Dartmouth Ave 80231 720-423-9500
Reina Gutierrez, prin. Fax 423-9445
Harrington ES 500/PK-6
2401 E 37th Ave 80205 303-333-4293
Sally Edwards, prin. Fax 424-6445
Henry MS 900/6-8
3005 S Golden Way 80227 720-423-9560
Wendy Lanier, prin. Fax 423-9585
Hill MS 600/6-8
451 Clermont St 80220 720-423-9680
Don Roy, prin. Fax 423-9705
Holm ES 500/PK-5
3185 S Willow St 80231 303-751-3157
James Metcalfe, prin. Fax 424-6375

Howell S 500/K-8
14250 Albrook Dr 80239 720-424-2740
Keith Mills, prin. Fax 424-2765
Johnson ES 400/PK-5
1850 S Irving St 80219 303-935-4659
Cora Gonzales, prin. Fax 424-6315
Kaiser ES 400/PK-6
4500 S Quitman St 80236 303-795-6014
Elinor Roller, prin. Fax 424-6235
Kepner MS 1,000/6-8
911 S Hazel Ct 80219 720-424-0000
Frank Gonzales, prin. Fax 424-0023
Knapp ES 700/PK-5
500 S Utica St 80219 303-935-4663
Christina Bansch-Schott, prin. Fax 424-6155
Knight Fundamental Academy 300/K-5
3245 E Exposition Ave 80209 303-722-4681
Charmaine Keeton, prin. Fax 424-6095
Kunsmiller MS 700/6-8
2250 S Quitman Way 80219 720-424-0200
Jorge Loera, prin. Fax 424-0145
Lake MS 600/6-8
1820 Lowell Blvd 80204 720-424-0260
Hans Keyser, prin. Fax 424-0380
Lincoln ES 200/PK-5
710 S Pennsylvania St 80209 303-744-1785
Diane Smith, prin. Fax 424-6015
Lowry ES 400/PK-5
8001 E Cedar Ave 80230 303-340-0179
Carolyn Riedlin, prin. Fax 424-5935
Marrama ES 600/PK-5
19100 E 40th Ave 80249 303-371-3780
Merida Fraguada, prin. Fax 424-5845
Maxwell ES 600/PK-5
14390 Bolling Dr 80239 303-576-6557
Mikel Royal, prin. Fax 424-5765
McGlone ES 600/PK-5
4500 Crown Blvd 80239 303-373-5080
Ann Ally-Walker, prin. Fax 424-5685
McKinley-Thatcher ES 200/PK-5
1230 S Grant St 80210 303-777-8816
Brette Scott, prin. Fax 424-5625
McMeen ES 500/PK-5
1000 S Holly St 80246 303-388-5649
Michael Deguire, prin. Fax 424-5545
Merrill MS 600/6-8
1551 S Monroe St 80210 720-424-0600
Stacy Miller, prin. Fax 424-0625
Montclair S of Academics/Enrichment 300/PK-5
1151 Newport St 80220 303-333-5497
Shannon Hagerman, prin. Fax 424-5405
Moore S 400/PK-8
846 Corona St 80218 303-831-7044
Joan Wamsley, prin. Fax 424-5325
Morey MS 800/6-8
840 E 14th Ave 80218 720-424-0700
Doris Claunch, prin. Fax 424-0727
Munroe ES 600/PK-5
3440 W Virginia Ave 80219 303-934-5547
Jody Cohn, prin. Fax 424-5255
Newlon ES 500/PK-5
361 Vrain St 80219 303-934-2441
Debra Lucero-Kraft, prin. Fax 424-5175
Noel MS 800/6-8
5290 Kittredge St 80239 720-424-0800
Amanda DeBell, prin. Fax 424-0945
Oakland ES 500/PK-5
4580 Dearborn St 80239 303-371-2960
Reggie Robinson, prin. Fax 424-5095
Palmer ES 300/PK-5
995 Grape St 80220 303-388-5929
Elizabeth Trujillo, prin. Fax 424-5025
Park Hill S 700/PK-8
5050 E 19th Ave 80220 303-322-1811
Tonda Potts, prin. Fax 424-4935
Philips Preparatory ES 200/PK-5
6550 E 21st Ave 80207 303-388-5313
Margaret Clinkscales, prin. Fax 424-4865
Place Bridge Academy 400/PK-8
7125 Cherry Creek North Dr 80224 720-424-0960
Brenda Kazin, prin. Fax 424-0985
Polaris S at Ebert 300/K-5
410 Park Ave W 80205 303-292-4629
Karin Johnson, prin. Fax 424-7885
Rishel MS 700/6-8
451 S Tejon St 80223 720-424-1260
Sylvia Bookhardt, prin. Fax 424-1350
Roberts S PK-8
2100 Akron Way 80238 720-424-2640
Patricia Lea, prin. Fax 424-2665
Sabin International ES 600/PK-5
3050 S Vrain St 80236 303-936-3413
Wendy Pierce, prin. Fax 424-4545
Samuels ES 500/PK-5
3985 S Vincennes Ct 80237 303-770-2215
Jim Kimbrough, prin. Fax 424-4475
Schenck ES 600/PK-5
1300 S Lowell Blvd 80219 303-935-4606
Kristin Nelson-Steinhoff, prin. Fax 424-4325
Schmitt ES 400/PK-5
1820 S Vallejo St 80223 303-935-4651
Anne Dalton, prin. Fax 424-4255
Skinner MS 500/6-8
3435 W 40th Ave 80211 720-424-1420
Nicole Veltze, prin. Fax 424-1446
Slavens S 500/PK-8
3000 S Clayton St 80210 720-424-4150
Kurt Siebold, prin. Fax 424-4175
Smiley MS 400/6-8
2540 Holly St 80207 720-424-1540
Nathaniel Howard, prin. Fax 424-1565
Smith Renaissance S of the Arts 400/PK-5
3590 Jasmine St 80207 303-388-1658
Betty Johnson, prin. Fax 424-4025
Southmoor ES 400/PK-5
3755 S Magnolia Way 80237 303-756-0392
Kenton Burger, prin. Fax 424-3955

Steck ES 300/PK-5
450 Albion St 80220 303-355-7314
LaDawn Baity, prin. Fax 424-3895
Stedman ES 300/PK-5
2940 Dexter St 80207 303-322-7781
Deborah Johnson-Graham, prin. Fax 424-3825
Steele ES 400/PK-5
320 S Marion Pkwy 80209 303-744-1717
Charles Raisch, prin. Fax 424-3745
Swansea ES 600/PK-6
4650 Columbine St 80216 303-296-8429
Mary Sours, prin. Fax 424-3655
Teller ES 200/PK-5
1150 Garfield St 80206 303-333-4285
Jennifer Barton, prin. Fax 424-3585
Traylor Academy 600/PK-5
2900 S Ivan Way 80227 303-985-1535
Patricia Castro, prin. Fax 424-3505
Trevista S at Horace Mann 300/PK-8
4130 Navajo St 80211 720-423-9800
Veronica Benavidez, prin. Fax 423-9850
University Park ES 300/PK-5
2300 S Saint Paul St 80210 303-756-9407
Dana Williams, prin. Fax 424-3435
Valdez S 400/PK-8
2525 W 29th Ave 80211 303-433-2581
Peter Sherman, prin. Fax 424-3335
Valverde ES 400/PK-5
2030 W Alameda Ave 80223 303-722-4697
Ardell Francis, prin. Fax 424-3275
Waller S PK-8
21601 E 51st Pl 80249 720-424-2840
Charles Babb, prin. Fax 424-2866
Westerly Creek ES 300/PK-2
8800 E 28th Ave 80238 303-322-5877
Jill Corcoran, prin. Fax 424-3185
Whittier S 200/PK-7
2480 Downing St 80205 303-861-1310
Jai Palmer, prin. Fax 424-3065

Mapleton SD 1 6,300/PK-12
591 E 80th Ave 80229 303-853-1000
Charlotte Ciancio, supt. Fax 853-1087
www.mapleton.us
Adventure ES at Western Hills 300/K-6
7700 Delta St 80221 303-853-1410
Erica Branscum, dir. Fax 853-1456
Enrichment Academy at Western Hills 600/K-6
7700 Delta St 80221 303-853-1400
Lisa Marchi, dir. Fax 853-1456
Explore ES at Bertha Heid 900/K-6
9100 Poze Blvd 80229 303-853-1311
Kevin King, dir. Fax 853-1356
Global Leadership Academy 300/K-12
7480 Conifer Rd 80221 303-853-1930
Richard Sinclair, dir. Fax 853-1956
Mapleton Early Learning Center 300/PK-K
602 E 64th Ave 80229 303-853-1100
Jill Fuller, dir. Fax 853-1145
Meadow Community S 500/K-8
9150 Monroe St 80229 303-853-1500
Jeff Park, dir. Fax 853-1556
Monterey Community S 400/K-8
2201 McElwain Blvd 80229 303-853-1360
Johnny Terrell, dir. Fax 853-1396
Valley View S 400/K-8
660 W 70th Ave 80221 303-853-1560
Susan Gerhart, dir. Fax 853-1596
York International S 500/K-12
9200 York St 80229 303-853-1600
Paul Frank, dir. Fax 853-1656
Other Schools – See Thornton

Sheridan SD 2
Supt. — See Sheridan
Early Childhood Education Center 100/PK-K
4000 S Lowell Blvd 80236 720-833-6991
Aimee Chapman, prin. Fax 833-6649
Ft. Logan ES 300/3-5
3700 S Knox Ct 80236 720-833-6989
Susan Resnick, prin. Fax 833-6746

Accelerated Schools Foundation 50/K-12
2160 S Cook St 80210 303-758-2003
Fax 757-4336
Annunciation S 200/K-8
3536 Lafayette St 80205 303-295-2515
Sr. Jean Panisko, prin. Fax 295-2516
Assumption S 200/PK-8
2341 E 78th Ave 80229 303-288-2159
Gene Chavez, prin. Fax 288-4716
Blessed Sacrament S 200/PK-8
1973 Elm St 80220 303-377-8835
Greg Kruthaupt, prin. Fax 321-7765
Christ Lutheran S 50/PK-K
2695 S Franklin St 80210 303-722-1424
Fax 722-0933
Christ the King S 300/PK-8
860 Elm St 80220 303-321-2123
James Feldewerth, prin. Fax 321-2191
Colorado Academy 900/PK-12
3800 S Pierce St 80235 303-986-1501
Michael Davis Ph.D., hdmstr. Fax 914-2583
Denver Academy 500/1-12
4400 E Iliff Ave 80222 303-777-5870
Kevin Smith, hdmstr. Fax 777-5893
Denver Academy of Torah 100/PK-9
6825 E Alameda Ave 80224 720-859-6806
Rabbi Daniel Alter, hdmstr. Fax 859-6847
Denver Christian S Van Dellen Campus 300/PK-8
4200 E Warren Ave 80222 303-757-8501
Richard Schemper, prin. Fax 753-6028
Denver International S 200/PK-5
1958 Elm St 80220 303-756-0381
Adam Sexton, dir. Fax 753-9426
Denver Waldorf S 300/PK-12
940 Fillmore St 80206 303-777-0531
Fax 744-1216

Emmaus Lutheran S 50/PK-8
3120 Irving St 80211 303-477-0080
Jeff Burkee, prin. Fax 433-2280
Escuela de Guadalupe S K-6
3401 Pecos St 80211 303-964-8456
Vernita Vellez, prin. Fax 964-0755
Good Shepherd S 400/PK-8
620 Elizabeth St 80206 303-321-6231
Mary Bartek, prin. Fax 261-1059
Graland Country Day S 600/K-8
30 Birch St 80220 303-399-0390
Bill Waskowitz, hdmstr. Fax 388-2803
Guardian Angels S 200/PK-8
1843 W 52nd Ave 80221 303-480-9005
Mary Gold, prin. Fax 480-3527
Herzl/RMHA at the Denver Campus 400/K-12
2450 S Wabash St 80231 303-369-0663
Avi Halzel, pres. Fax 369-0664
Hillel Academy 200/PK-8
450 S Hudson St 80246 303-333-1511
La Esperanza Adventist S K-5
2005 S Lincoln St 80210 720-982-4271
Logan S for Creative Learning 200/K-8
1005 Yosemite St 80230 303-340-2444
Andrew Slater, hdmstr. Fax 340-2041
Loyola S 100/K-6
2350 Gaylord St 80205 303-355-9900
Sr. Mary Roach, prin. Fax 355-9911
Mile High Adventist Academy 200/PK-12
711 E Yale Ave 80210 303-744-1069
Brent Baldwin, prin. Fax 744-1060
Montclair Academy 100/PK-8
206 Red Cross Way 80230 303-366-7588
Esther Tipton, hdmstr. Fax 367-2530
Montessori at the Marina 100/PK-6
8101 E Belleview Ave 80237 303-290-8843
Dana Hill, prin. Fax 302-2852
Montessori Children's House of Denver PK-4
1467 Birch St 80220 303-322-8324
Rachel Averch, prin. Fax 355-8629
Montessori S of Denver 300/PK-6
1460 S Holly St 80222 303-756-9441
Stephanie Flanigan, hdmstr. Fax 757-6145
Most Precious Blood S 300/PK-8
3959 E Iliff Ave 80210 303-757-1279
Colleen McManamon, prin. Fax 757-1270
Notre Dame S 400/PK-8
2165 S Zenobia St 80219 303-935-3549
Charlene Molis, prin. Fax 937-4868
Our Lady of Lourdes S 100/K-8
2256 S Logan St 80210 303-722-7525
Bob Sickles, prin. Fax 765-5305
Our Lady of the Rosary Academy 100/K-12
4165 Eaton St 80212 303-424-1531
Fax 424-9064
Presentation of Our Lady S 100/PK-8
660 Julian St 80204 303-629-6562
Sandra Howard, prin. Fax 893-5056
Redeemer Lutheran S 100/1-8
3400 W Nevada Pl 80219 303-934-0422
Mark Kehr, prin. Fax 935-9256
Ricks Center for Gifted Children 200/PK-8
2040 S York St 80210 303-871-2982
Dr. Norma Hafenstein, dir. Fax 871-3197
St. Andrew Lutheran S 100/PK-4
12150 Andrews Dr 80239 303-371-7014
Lucille Foglesong, prin. Fax 371-1099
St. Anne's Episcopal S 400/PK-8
2701 S York St 80210 303-756-9481
Alan Smiley, hdmstr. Fax 756-5512
St. Catherine of Siena S 200/PK-8
4200 Federal Blvd 80211 303-477-8035
Diana Bennett, prin. Fax 477-0110
St. Elizabeth's S 50/K-1
3605 Martin L King Blvd 80205 303-322-4209
Walter McCoy, hdmstr. Fax 322-4210
St. Francis de Sales S 200/PK-8
235 S Sherman St 80209 303-744-7231
Sr. Eleanor O'Hearn, prin. Fax 744-1028
St. James S 200/PK-8
1250 Newport St 80220 303-333-8275
Carol Hovell-Genth, prin. Fax 780-0137
St. John's Lutheran S 300/PK-8
700 S Franklin St 80209 303-733-3777
Loren Otte, prin. Fax 778-6070
St. Rose of Lima S 200/PK-8
1345 W Dakota Ave 80223 303-733-5806
Jeannie Courchene, prin. Fax 733-0125
St. Vincent De Paul S 500/PK-8
1164 S Josephine St 80210 303-777-3812
Sr. Mary Gertrude, prin. Fax 733-9528
Stanley British PS 400/K-8
350 Quebec Ct 80230 303-360-0803
Tim Barrier, prin. Fax 360-0353
Trinity Lutheran Early Child Lrng Center 100/PK-K
4225 W Yale Ave 80219 303-934-6160
Gwen Marshall, prin. Fax 934-9327
Zion Evangelical Lutheran S 50/PK-PK
2600 S Wadsworth Blvd 80227 303-985-2334
Earle Treptow, prin. Fax 985-2466

Dillon, Summit, Pop. 774
Summit SD RE-1
Supt. — See Frisco
Dillon Valley ES 300/PK-5
PO Box 4788 80435 970-468-6836
Gayle Jones-Westerberg, prin. Fax 468-9026
Summit Cove ES 200/PK-5
727 Cove Blvd 80435 970-513-0083
Crystal Miller, prin. Fax 513-0243

Summit County Christian S 100/PK-9
371 E La Bonte St 80435 970-547-7150
Deborah Russell, admin. Fax 547-7155

Divide, Teller, Pop. 600
Woodland Park SD RE-2
Supt. — See Woodland Park

Summit ES 400/PK-5
PO Box 339 80814 719-686-2401
Eric Owen, prin. Fax 687-8469

Dolores, Montezuma, Pop. 863
Dolores SD RE-4A 800/PK-12
17631 Highway 145 81323 970-882-7255
Mark MacHale, supt. Fax 882-7685
www.dolores.k12.co.us
Dolores ES 300/K-5
17631 Highway 145 81323 970-882-4688
Sherri Maxwell, prin. Fax 882-7669
Dolores MS 200/6-8
17631 Highway 145 81323 970-882-7288
Quinn Swope, prin. Fax 882-7289
Teddy Bear Preschool 100/PK-PK
17631 Highway 145 81323 970-882-7277
Valiena Rosenkrance, dir. Fax 882-7277

Dove Creek, Dolores, Pop. 683
Dolores County SD RE-2J 300/PK-12
PO Box 459 81324 970-677-2522
Steve Strong, supt. Fax 677-2712
Seventh Street ES 100/PK-6
PO Box 459 81324 970-677-2296
Ty Gray, prin. Fax 677-2712
Other Schools – See Rico

Durango, LaPlata, Pop. 15,501
Durango SD 9-R 4,600/PK-12
201 E 12th St 81301 970-247-5411
Dr. Keith Owen, supt. Fax 247-9581
www.durangoschools.org
Animas Valley ES 200/PK-5
373 Hermosa Meadows Camper 81301
970-247-0124
Lisa Schuba, prin. Fax 385-1183
Escalante MS 500/6-8
141 Baker Ln 81303 970-247-9490
Amy Kendziorski, prin. Fax 385-1194
Florida Mesa ES 300/PK-5
216 Highway 172 81303 970-247-4250
Cindy Smart, prin. Fax 385-7453
Miller MS 500/6-8
2608 Junction St 81301 970-247-1418
Tam Smith, prin. Fax 385-1191
Needham ES 500/PK-5
2425 W 3rd Ave 81301 970-247-4791
Pete Harter, prin. Fax 247-3388
Park ES 400/PK-5
623 E 5th St 81301 970-247-3718
Scott Cooper, prin. Fax 385-1492
Riverview ES 400/PK-5
2900 Mesa Ave 81301 970-247-3862
Diane Chambers, prin. Fax 247-4761
Sunnyside ES 100/PK-5
75 County Road 218 81303 970-259-5249
Lauri Kloepfer, prin. Fax 382-2953
Other Schools – See Hesperus

Columbine Christian S 100/PK-8
1775 Florida Rd 81301 970-259-1189
May Oles, prin.
St. Columba S 200/PK-8
1801 E 3rd Ave 81301 970-247-5527
Sr. Edith Hauser, prin. Fax 382-9355

Eads, Kiowa, Pop. 651
Eads SD RE-1 200/PK-12
210 W 10th St 81036 719-438-2218
Glenn Smith, supt. Fax 438-5499
www.eadseagles.com
Eads ES 100/PK-5
900 Maine St 81036 719-438-2216
Glenn Smith, prin. Fax 438-2090
Eads JHS 50/6-8
900 Maine St 81036 719-438-2216
Glenn Smith, prin. Fax 438-2090

Eagle, Eagle, Pop. 4,276
Eagle County SD RE-50 5,100/PK-12
PO Box 740 81631 970-328-6321
Sandra Smyser, supt. Fax 328-1024
www.eagleschools.net
Brush Creek ES 400/PK-5
PO Box 4630 81631 970-328-8930
Anne Heckman, prin. Fax 328-4011
Eagle Valley ES 300/K-5
PO Box 780 81631 970-328-6981
Monica Lammers, prin. Fax 328-5665
Eagle Valley MS 200/6-8
PO Box 1019 81631 970-328-6224
John Trinca, prin. Fax 328-6430
Meadow Mountain ES 200/K-5
650 Eagle Rd 81631 970-328-2940
Melissa Carpenter, prin. Fax 949-1536
Other Schools – See Avon, Edwards, Gypsum, Minturn, Vail

Eaton, Weld, Pop. 3,932
Eaton SD RE-2 1,700/K-12
200 Park Ave 80615 970-454-3402
Randy Miller Ed.D., supt. Fax 454-5193
www.eaton.k12.co.us
Eaton ES 300/K-2
25 Cheyenne Ave 80615 970-454-3331
Deb Campbell, prin. Fax 454-5123
Eaton ES 300/3-5
100 S Mountain View Dr 80615 970-454-5200
Diane Eussen, prin. Fax 454-5217
Eaton MS 400/6-8
225 Juniper Ave 80615 970-454-3358
Jim Orth, prin. Fax 454-1337
Other Schools – See Galeton

Edgewater, Jefferson, Pop. 5,211
Jefferson County SD R-1
Supt. — See Golden
Edgewater ES 400/PK-6
5570 W 24th Ave 80214 303-982-6050
Celeste Sultze, prin. Fax 982-6044

Lumberg ES 500/K-6
6705 W 22nd Ave 80214 303-982-6182
Shatta Mejia, prin. Fax 982-6183

Edwards, Eagle, Pop. 500
Eagle County SD RE-50
Supt. — See Eagle
Berry Creek MS 300/6-8
PO Box 1416 81632 970-328-2960
Robert Cuevas, prin. Fax 926-4137
Edwards ES 400/K-5
22 Meile Ln 81632 970-328-2970
Heidi Hanssen, prin. Fax 926-2911
June Creek ES PK-5
1121 Miller Ranch Rd 81632 970-328-2980
Tracy Barber, prin. Fax 328-2985

St. Clare of Assisi S 200/K-8
PO Box 667 81632 970-926-8980
Sr. Rita Schneider, prin. Fax 926-8073

Elbert, Elbert, Pop. 150
Elbert SD 200 300/PK-12
PO Box 38 80106 303-648-3030
Kelli Loflin, supt. Fax 648-3652
elbertschool.org
Elbert ES 100/PK-6
PO Box 38 80106 303-648-3030
Kelli Loflin, prin. Fax 648-3652

Elizabeth, Elbert, Pop. 1,513
Elizabeth SD C-1 2,500/PK-12
PO Box 610 80107 303-646-4441
Fax 646-0337
elizabeth.k12.co.us/
Elizabeth MS 600/6-8
PO Box 369 80107 303-646-4520
Robert McMullen, prin. Fax 646-0980
Elizabeth Running Creek Preschool 100/PK-PK
PO Box 610 80107 303-646-1848
Christine Logue, dir. Fax 646-1329
Running Creek ES 500/K-5
PO Box 550 80107 303-646-4620
Jim Wilson, prin. Fax 688-5305
Other Schools – See Parker

Ellicott, El Paso
Ellicott SD 22 900/K-12
395 S Ellicott Hwy 80808 719-683-2700
Terry Ebert, supt. Fax 683-4442
www.ellicottschools.org
Ellicott MS 200/6-8
350 S Ellicott Hwy 80808 719-683-2700
Chris Smith, prin. Fax 683-5430
Other Schools – See Calhan

Englewood, Arapahoe, Pop. 32,350
Cherry Creek SD 5
Supt. — See Greenwood Village
Belleview ES 600/PK-5
4851 S Dayton St 80111 720-554-3100
Amanda Waleski, prin. Fax 554-3109
Campus MS 1,300/6-8
4785 S Dayton St 80111 720-554-2700
Jane Miller, prin. Fax 554-2782
Cherry Hills Village ES 500/PK-5
2400 E Quincy Ave, 720-747-2700
Pam Livingston, prin. Fax 747-2788
Cottonwood Creek ES 600/PK-5
11200 E Orchard Rd 80111 720-554-3200
Mary Shay, prin. Fax 554-3288
Dry Creek ES 400/PK-5
7686 E Hinsdale Ave 80112 720-554-3300
Diana Roybal, prin. Fax 554-3388
High Plains ES 500/PK-5
6100 S Fulton St 80111 720-554-3600
Lisa Morris, prin. Fax 554-3688
Homestead ES 500/PK-5
7451 S Homestead Pkwy 80112 720-554-3700
Scott Schleich, prin. Fax 554-3788
Walnut Hills Community ES 400/PK-5
8195 E Costilla Blvd 80112 720-554-3800
Cyndi Burdick, prin. Fax 554-3888
Willow Creek ES 500/PK-5
7855 S Willow Way 80112 720-554-3900
Mike Chipman, prin. Fax 554-3988

Englewood SD 1 3,100/PK-12
4101 S Bannock St 80110 303-761-7050
Sean McDaniel, supt. Fax 806-2064
www.englewood.k12.co.us
Bishop ES 200/K-5
3100 S Elati St 80110 303-761-1496
Linda McCaslin, prin. Fax 761-5994
Cherrelyn ES 300/K-5
4500 S Lincoln St, 303-761-2102
Eva Pasiewicz, prin. Fax 761-1498
Clayton ES 300/PK-5
4600 S Fox St 80110 303-781-7831
Jon Fore, prin. Fax 806-2500
Englewood MS 300/6-8
300 W Chenango Ave 80110 303-781-7817
Mandy Braun, prin. Fax 806-2399
Hay ES 200/K-5
3195 S Lafayette St, 303-761-2433
Chris Laney-Barnes, prin. Fax 761-8156
Lowell Pre-Kindergarten 200/PK-PK
3794 S Logan St, 303-781-7585
Beth Engle, prin. Fax 806-2535
Maddox ES 200/K-5
700 W Mansfield Ave 80110 303-761-2331
Marsha Harrington, prin. Fax 806-2416

All Souls S 500/PK-8
4951 S Pennsylvania St, 303-789-2155
William Moore, prin. Fax 833-2778
St. Louis S 100/K-8
3301 S Sherman St, 303-762-8307
Pattie Hagen, prin. Fax 762-0156

St. Mary's Academy 300/PK-5
4545 S University Blvd, 303-762-8300
Mary Jane Frederick, prin. Fax 783-6201
St. Mary's Academy 200/6-8
4545 S University Blvd, 303-762-8300
Marsha Ashley, prin. Fax 783-6201
St. Thomas More S 700/PK-8
7071 E Otero Ave 80112 303-770-0441
Paul Mott, prin. Fax 267-1899

Erie, Weld, Pop. 12,351
St. Vrain Valley SD RE-1J
Supt. — See Longmont
Black Rock ES PK-5
2000 Mountain View Blvd 80516 720-890-3995
Cathy O'Donnell, prin. Fax 652-8195
Erie ES 700/PK-5
PO Box 700 80516 303-828-3395
Larry Shores, prin. Fax 828-4501
Erie MS 400/6-8
650 Main St 80516 303-828-3391
Todd Bissell, prin. Fax 828-3817

Vista Ridge Academy 100/K-12
3100 Ridgeview Dr 80516 303-828-4944
Carol Schneider, prin. Fax 828-1525

Estes Park, Larimer, Pop. 5,812
Park SD R-3 1,300/PK-12
1605 Brodie Ave 80517 970-586-2361
Linda Chapman, supt. Fax 586-1108
www.psdr3.k12.co.us/
Estes Park ES 500/PK-5
1505 Brodie Ave 80517 970-586-7406
John Bryant, prin. Fax 586-7407
Estes Park MS 300/6-8
1500 Manford Ave 80517 970-586-4439
Robin Weidemueller, prin. Fax 586-1100

Evans, Weld, Pop. 17,470
Weld County SD 6
Supt. — See Greeley
Centennial ES 600/PK-5
1400 37th St 80620 970-348-1100
Jan Jervis, prin. Fax 348-1130
Chappelow Arts & Literacy Magnet S 700/K-8
2001 34th St 80620 970-348-1200
Cheryl Gregg, prin. Fax 348-1230
Dos Rios ES 500/PK-5
2201 34th St 80620 970-348-1300
Lydia McCabe, prin. Fax 348-1330
Heiman ES 600/K-5
3500 Palermo Ave 80620 970-348-2400
Terry Zubler, prin. Fax 348-2430

Evergreen, Jefferson, Pop. 7,582
Clear Creek SD RE-1
Supt. — See Idaho Springs
King-Murphy ES 200/PK-6
425 Circle K Ranch Rd 80439 303-670-0005
Colleen Larson, prin. Fax 674-6735

Jefferson County SD R-1
Supt. — See Golden
Bergen Meadow ES 400/PK-2
1892 Bergen Pkwy 80439 303-982-4890
Peggy Miller, prin. Fax 982-4891
Bergen Valley ES 300/3-5
1422 Sugarbush Dr 80439 303-982-4964
Bethany Elmgreen, prin. Fax 982-4965
Evergreen MS 700/6-8
2059 Hiwan Dr 80439 303-982-5020
Kristopher Schuh, prin. Fax 982-5021
Marshdale ES 400/K-5
26663 N Turkey Creek Rd 80439 303-982-5188
Christie Frost, prin. Fax 982-5187
Wilmot ES 500/PK-5
5124 S Hatch Dr 80439 303-982-5370
Dannae McReynolds, prin. Fax 982-5371

Evergreen Academy 50/K-8
27826 Alabraska Ln 80439 303-670-1721
Chris Lierheimer, hdmstr. Fax 674-4231
Evergreen Country Day S 100/PK-8
1093 Swede Gulch Rd 80439 303-674-3400
Ben Jackson, hdmstr.
Montessori School of Evergreen PK-4
PO Box 2468 80437 303-670-8540
Betsy Hoke, dir. Fax 670-6563
Montessori School of Evergreen 300/PK-8
PO Box 2468 80437 303-674-0093
Betsy Hoke, dir. Fax 670-6993

Fairplay, Park, Pop. 677
Park County SD RE-2 500/PK-12
PO Box 189 80440 719-836-3114
Charles Soper, supt. Fax 836-2275
www.parkcountyre2.org/
Silverheels MS 100/6-8
PO Box 189 80440 719-836-4406
Jane Newman, prin. Fax 836-2275
Teter ES 300/PK-5
PO Box 189 80440 719-836-2949
Cindy Peratt, prin. Fax 836-2275

Falcon, El Paso, Pop. 200
Falcon SD 49 10,900/PK-12
10850 E Woodmen Rd 80831 719-495-3601
Grant Schmidt, supt. Fax 495-0832
www.d49.org
Falcon ES 400/K-6
12050 Falcon Hwy 80831 719-495-5272
Nancy Valdez, prin. Fax 495-5282
Meridian Ranch ES 600/K-6
10480 Rainbow Bridge Dr 80831 719-494-2909
Fax 494-2912
Woodmen Hills ES 800/K-6
8308 Del Rio Rd 80831 719-495-5500
Monty Lammers, prin. Fax 495-5501
Other Schools – See Colorado Springs, Peyton

Federal Heights, Adams, Pop. 11,706
Adams 12 Five Star SD
Supt. — See Thornton
Federal Heights ES 500/PK-5
2500 W 96th Ave 80260 720-972-5360
Kim Walsh, prin. Fax 972-5379

Cornerstone Christian Academy 100/K-12
2300 W 90th Ave 80260 303-451-1421
Larry Zimbelman, admin. Fax 280-0361

Firestone, Weld, Pop. 6,410
St. Vrain Valley SD RE-1J
Supt. — See Longmont
Centennial ES PK-5
10290 Neighbors Pkwy 80504 720-652-8240
Keith Liddle, prin. Fax 652-8255
Coal Ridge MS 800/6-8
6201 Booth Dr 80504 303-833-4176
Paul Talafuse, prin. Fax 833-4192
Prairie Ridge ES 700/PK-5
6632 St Vrain Ranch Blvd 80504 720-494-3641
Kirsten McNeill, prin. Fax 833-4972

Flagler, Kit Carson, Pop. 590
Arriba-Flagler SD C-20 100/PK-12
PO Box 218 80815 719-765-4684
Thomas Arensdorf, supt. Fax 765-4418
www.arriba-flaglercsd20.net
Flagler S 100/PK-8
PO Box 218 80815 719-765-4684
Daniel Harris, prin. Fax 765-4418

Fleming, Logan, Pop. 444
Frenchman SD RE-3 200/PK-12
506 N Fremont Ave 80728 970-265-2111
Jim Copeland, supt. Fax 265-2815
www.flemingschools.org
Fleming ES 100/PK-6
506 N Fremont Ave 80728 970-265-2022
Dustin Seger, prin. Fax 265-2029

Florence, Fremont, Pop. 3,685
Florence SD RE-2 1,700/K-12
403 W 5th St 81226 719-784-6312
Cyndy Scriven, supt. Fax 784-4140
www.re-2.org/
Fremont ES 500/K-5
500 W 5th St 81226 719-784-6303
Sue Hall, prin. Fax 784-4060
Fremont MS 400/6-8
215 Maple St 81226 719-784-4856
Dominic Carochi, prin. Fax 784-4060
Other Schools – See Penrose

Florence Christian S 50/PK-12
303 E 3rd St 81226 719-784-6352

Fort Carson, El Paso, Pop. 11,309
Fountain-Fort Carson SD 8
Supt. — See Fountain
Abrams ES 600/PK-5
600 Chiles Ave, 719-382-1490
Janet Liddle, prin. Fax 382-8572
Carson MS 400/6-8
6200 Prussman Blvd, 719-382-1610
Steve Jerman, prin. Fax 382-8526
Mountainside ES 500/PK-5
5506 Harr Ave, 719-382-1430
Lynn Zupans, prin. Fax 527-9273
Patriot ES 500/PK-5
7010 Harr Ave, 719-382-1460
Gary Duncan, prin. Fax 576-4237

Fort Collins, Larimer, Pop. 128,026
Poudre SD R-1 20,400/PK-12
2407 Laporte Ave 80521 970-490-3607
Dr. Jerry Wilson, supt. Fax 490-3514
www.psdschools.org
Bacon ES 400/K-5
5844 S Timberline Rd 80528 970-488-5300
Joe Horky, prin. Fax 488-5306
Barton ECC 600/PK-PK
703 E Prospect Rd 80525 970-490-3204
Kim Bloemen, coord. Fax 490-3203
Bauder ES 300/K-5
2345 W Prospect Rd 80526 970-488-4150
Brian Carpenter, prin. Fax 488-4152
Beattie ES 300/PK-5
3000 Meadowlark Ave 80526 970-488-4225
Sam Aldern, prin. Fax 488-4227
Bennett ES 400/K-5
1125 Bennett Rd 80521 970-488-4750
Michael Schooler, prin. Fax 488-4752
Blevins MS 300/6-8
2102 S Taft Hill Rd 80526 970-488-4000
David Linehan, prin. Fax 488-4011
Boltz MS 400/6-8
720 Boltz Dr 80525 970-472-3700
Dana Calkins, prin. Fax 472-3730
Dunn ES 400/K-5
501 S Washington Ave 80521 970-488-4825
Deb Ellis, prin. Fax 488-4827
Fullana Learning Center PK-PK
220 N Grant Ave 80521 970-490-3160
Kim Bloemen, coord. Fax 490-3134
Harris Bilingual ES 300/K-5
501 E Elizabeth St 80524 970-488-5200
Julie Schiola, prin. Fax 488-5203
Irish ES 300/PK-5
515 Irish Dr 80521 970-488-6900
Guillermo Medina, prin. Fax 488-6902
Johnson ES 400/K-5
4101 Seneca St 80526 970-488-5000
Will Allen, prin. Fax 488-5007
Kinard MS 500/6-8
3002 E Trilby Rd 80528 970-488-5400
Joe Cuddemi, prin. Fax 488-5402
Kruse ES 400/K-5
4400 McMurry Ave 80525 970-488-5625
Sean Gorman, prin. Fax 488-5627
Lab S 100/K-6
223 S Shields St 80521 970-482-2506
Brian Carpenter, prin. Fax 484-5037
Laurel ES 300/PK-5
1000 Locust St 80524 970-488-5925
Tommi Sue Cox, prin. Fax 488-5927
Lesher MS 400/6-8
1400 Stover St 80524 970-472-3800
Thomas Dodd, prin. Fax 472-3880
Lincoln MS 300/6-8
1600 Lancer Dr 80521 970-488-5700
Monique Flickinger, prin. Fax 488-5752
Linton ES 400/K-5
4100 Caribou Dr 80525 970-488-5850
Kristin Stolte, prin. Fax 488-5852
Lopez ES 400/K-5
637 Wabash St 80526 970-488-8800
Anthony Asmus, prin. Fax 488-8802
McGraw ES 400/PK-5
4800 Hinsdale Dr 80526 970-488-8335
Bob Kulovany, prin. Fax 488-8337
Moore ES 300/K-5
1905 Orchard Pl 80521 970-488-8260
Amy Smith, prin. Fax 488-8262
O'Dea ES 300/K-5
312 Princeton Rd 80525 970-488-4450
Laurie Corso, prin. Fax 484-4120
Olander ES 300/K-5
3401 Auntie Stone St 80526 970-488-8410
Brian Oliver, prin. Fax 488-8412
Preston MS 500/6-8
4901 Corbett Dr 80528 970-488-7300
Scott Nielsen, prin. Fax 488-7307
Putnam ES 300/PK-5
1400 Maple St 80521 970-488-7700
Steve Apodaca, prin. Fax 488-7702
Riffenburgh ES 300/K-5
1320 E Stuart St 80525 970-488-7935
Marc Ryby, prin. Fax 488-7937
Shepardson ES 400/K-5
1501 Springwood Dr 80525 970-488-4525
Mary Kay Sommers, prin. Fax 488-4527
Tavelli ES 500/K-5
1118 Miramont Dr 80524 970-488-6725
Christine Hendricks, prin. Fax 488-6727
Traut ES 500/K-5
2515 Timberwood Dr 80528 970-488-7500
Mark Wertheimer, prin. Fax 488-7504
Webber MS 600/6-8
4201 Seneca St 80526 970-488-7800
Sandra Bickel, prin. Fax 488-7811
Werner ES 400/K-5
5400 Mail Creek Ln 80525 970-488-5550
Hayden Camp, prin. Fax 488-5552
Zach ES 600/K-5
3715 Kechter Rd 80528 970-488-5100
Don Rangel, prin. Fax 488-5106
Other Schools – See Bellvue, Laporte, Livermore, Red Feather Lakes, Timnath, Wellington

Thompson SD R-2J
Supt. — See Loveland
Cottonwood Plains ES 500/K-5
525 Turman Dr 80525 970-613-5900
David Patterson, prin. Fax 613-5920
Coyote Ridge ES K-5
7115 Avondale Rd 80525 970-679-9400
Diane Spearnak, prin. Fax 679-9420

Beebe Christian S 50/K-8
821 W Lake St 80521 970-482-4409
Keiko Nagasawa, prin.
Front Range Baptist Academy 100/PK-12
625 E Harmony Rd 80525 970-223-2173
Jamison Coppola, prin. Fax 223-5826
Heritage Christian Academy 200/K-12
2506 Zurich Dr 80524 970-494-1022
Mike Cuckler, admin. Fax 494-1025
Rivendell S of Northern Colorado 200/PK-5
1800 E Prospect Rd 80525 970-493-9052
Kate Duncan, prin. Fax 493-9056
St. Joseph S 400/K-9
PO Box 502 80522 970-484-1171
Barbara Bullock, prin. Fax 482-5291
Spring Creek Country Day S 200/PK-K
1900 Remington St 80525 970-224-4240
Rhonda Barlow, dir. Fax 224-2969

Fort Lupton, Weld, Pop. 7,121
Weld County SD RE-8 2,500/PK-12
301 Reynolds St 80621 303-857-3200
Mark Payler, supt. Fax 857-3219
www.ftlupton.k12.co.us
Butler ES 600/PK-5
411 McKinley Ave 80621 303-857-7300
Cindy Kusuno, prin. Fax 857-7340
Fort Lupton MS 500/6-8
201 S McKinley Ave 80621 303-857-7200
Melanie Patterson, prin. Fax 857-7287
Twombly ES 700/PK-5
1600 9th St 80621 303-857-7400
Gayle Dunlap, prin. Fax 857-7497

Fort Morgan, Morgan, Pop. 10,844
Ft. Morgan SD RE-3 3,300/PK-12
715 W Platte Ave 80701 970-867-5633
Greg Wagers, supt. Fax 867-0262
www.morgan.k12.co.us
Baker Central ES 500/5-6
300 Lake St 80701 970-867-8422
Cynthia Price, prin. Fax 867-8498
Columbine ES 300/1-4
815 West St 80701 970-867-7418
Nancy Hopper, prin. Fax 867-2369
Fort Morgan MS 500/7-8
300 Deuel St 80701 970-867-8253
Ben Bauman, prin. Fax 867-4876
Green Acres ES 300/1-4
930 Sherman St 80701 970-867-5460
Denise Hayden, prin. Fax 867-9408
Pioneer ES 400/1-4
415 Spruce St 80701 970-867-2080
Mike Mares, prin. Fax 867-9365
Sherman ECC 500/PK-K
300 Sherman St 80701 970-867-2998
Henry Taylor, prin. Fax 542-0728

Trinity Lutheran S 100/PK-8
1215 W 7th Ave 80701 970-867-4931
Karen Freidenberger, prin. Fax 867-9384

Fountain, El Paso, Pop. 19,081
Fountain-Fort Carson SD 8 6,200/PK-12
10665 Jimmy Camp Rd 80817 719-382-1300
Cheryl Serrano, supt. Fax 382-7338
www.ffc8.org
Aragon ES 500/PK-5
211 S Main St 80817 719-382-1340
Clint Allison, prin. Fax 382-8594
Eagleside ES PK-5
9750 Sentry Dr 80817 719-382-1520
Jason Crow, prin. Fax 382-7656
Fountain MS 800/6-8
515 N Santa Fe Ave 80817 719-382-1580
Debra Keiley, prin. Fax 382-9065
Jordahl ES 600/PK-5
800 Progress Dr 80817 719-382-1400
Laurie Noblitt, prin. Fax 382-3556
Mesa ES 600/K-5
400 Camino Del Rey 80817 719-382-1370
Coleman Onkle, prin. Fax 382-8520
Other Schools – See Fort Carson

Widefield SD 3
Supt. — See Colorado Springs
Janitell JHS 500/7-8
7635 Fountain Mesa Rd 80817 719-391-3295
Aaron Hoffman, prin. Fax 390-7869

Fowler, Otero, Pop. 1,138
Fowler SD R-4J 400/K-12
PO Box 218 81039 719-263-4224
Larry Vibber Ed.D., supt. Fax 263-4625
www.fowler.k12.co.us/
Fowler ES 200/K-6
PO Box 218 81039 719-263-4364
Steven Grasmick, prin. Fax 263-4625
Fowler JHS 100/7-8
PO Box 218 81039 719-263-4224
Russell Bates, prin. Fax 263-4625

Franktown, Douglas, Pop. 350
Douglas County SD RE-1
Supt. — See Castle Rock
Cherry Valley ES 100/K-6
9244 S Highway 83 80116 303-688-3211
Mark Harrell, prin. Fax 688-8096
Franktown ES 300/PK-6
PO Box 308 80116 303-387-5300
Mark Harrell, prin. Fax 387-5301

Castlewood Christian S 50/PK-8
7086 E Park Dr 80116 303-688-5353
Fax 688-0547
Trinity Lutheran S 200/PK-8
4740 N Highway 83 80116 303-841-4660
LuAnn Larrabee, prin. Fax 841-2761

Fraser, Grand, Pop. 899
East Grand SD 2
Supt. — See Granby
Fraser Valley ES 300/PK-5
PO Box 128 80442 970-726-8033
Penny Suazo, prin. Fax 726-8340

Frederick, Weld, Pop. 6,620
St. Vrain Valley SD RE-1J
Supt. — See Longmont
Frederick ES 600/PK-5
555 8th St 80530 303-833-2456
Karen Musick, prin. Fax 833-2549

Frisco, Summit, Pop. 2,418
Summit SD RE-1 3,000/PK-12
PO Box 7 80443 970-668-3011
Dr. Millie Hamner, supt. Fax 668-0361
summit.k12.co.us
Frisco ES 200/PK-5
PO Box 4820 80443 970-668-3282
Renea Hill, prin. Fax 668-5328
Summit MS 600/6-8
PO Box 7 80443 970-668-5037
Iva Katz-Hesse, prin. Fax 668-5038
Other Schools – See Breckenridge, Dillon, Silverthorne

Fruita, Mesa, Pop. 6,878
Mesa County Valley SD 51
Supt. — See Grand Junction
Fruita MS 500/6-7
239 N Maple St 81521 970-254-6570
Irene Almond, prin. Fax 858-0486
Rim Rock ES 500/PK-5
1810 J 6/10 Rd 81521 970-254-6770
Tami Kramer, prin. Fax 858-7654
Shelledy ES 600/PK-5
363 N Mesa St 81521 970-254-6460
Steven States, prin. Fax 858-9693

Galeton, Weld, Pop. 200
Eaton SD RE-2
Supt. — See Eaton
Galeton ES 100/K-5
PO Box 759 80622 970-454-3421
Kathryn Friesen, prin. Fax 454-2926

Gardner, Huerfano, Pop. 200
Huerfano SD RE-1
Supt. — See Walsenburg
Gardner S 100/PK-8
PO Box 191 81040 719-746-2446
Julia Marchant, prin. Fax 746-2066

Gateway, Mesa, Pop. 7,510
Mesa County Valley SD 51
Supt. — See Grand Junction
Gateway S 50/K-12
PO Box 240 81522 970-254-7080
Pat Chapin, prin. Fax 931-2883

Gilcrest, Weld, Pop. 1,149
Weld County SD RE-1 1,900/PK-12
PO Box 157 80623 970-737-2403
Jo Barbie, supt. Fax 737-2516
www.weld-re1.k12.co.us
Gilcrest ES 200/PK-5
PO Box 158 80623 970-737-2409
Darron Diemert, prin. Fax 737-2400
Other Schools – See La Salle, Platteville

Glenwood Springs, Garfield, Pop. 8,564
Roaring Fork SD RE-1 4,900/PK-12
1405 Grand Ave 81601 970-384-6000
Judy Haptonstall, supt. Fax 384-6005
www.rfsd.k12.co.us
Glenwood Springs ES 500/K-5
915 School St 81601 970-384-5450
Sonya Hemmen, prin. Fax 384-5455
Glenwood Springs MS 500/6-8
120 Soccer Field Rd 81601 970-384-5500
Brad Ray, prin. Fax 384-5505
Sopris ES 600/PK-5
1150 Mount Sopris Dr 81601 970-384-5400
Howard Jay, prin. Fax 384-5405
Other Schools – See Basalt, Carbondale

Columbine Christian S 50/1-8
2314 Blake Ave 81601 970-945-7630
St. Stephens S 200/PK-8
414 Hyland Park Dr 81601 970-945-7746
Thomas Alby Ph.D., prin. Fax 945-1208

Golden, Jefferson, Pop. 17,366
Jefferson County SD R-1 80,200/PK-12
PO Box 4001 80401 303-982-6500
Dr. Cindy Stevenson, supt. Fax 982-6814
www.jeffcopublicschools.org/
Bell MS 700/7-8
1001 Ulysses St 80401 303-982-4280
Bridget Jones, prin. Fax 982-4281
Coal Creek Canyon S 100/K-8
11719 Ranch Elsie Rd 80403 303-982-3409
Chuck Clark, prin. Fax 982-3408
Fairmount ES 500/K-6
15975 W 50th Ave 80403 303-982-5422
Brady Stroup, prin. Fax 982-5423
Kyffin ES 600/K-6
205 Flora Way 80401 303-982-5760
Val Braginetz, prin. Fax 982-5761
Litz Preschool, PO Box 4001 80401 100/PK-PK
Veronica Tennal, dir. 303-982-5928
Maple Grove ES 400/K-6
3085 Alkire St 80401 303-982-5808
Mike Maffoni, prin. Fax 982-5815
Mitchell ES 500/K-6
201 Rubey Dr 80403 303-982-5875
Kim Summeril, prin. Fax 982-5874
Pleasant View ES 300/PK-6
15920 W 10th Ave 80401 303-982-5921
Connie Brakken, prin. Fax 982-5922
Ralston ES 300/K-6
25856 Columbine Glen Ave 80401 303-982-4386
Karen Quanbeck, prin. Fax 982-4387
Shelton ES 400/K-6
420 Crawford St 80401 303-982-5686
Peggy Griebenow, prin. Fax 982-5685
Welchester ES 300/K-6
13000 W 10th Ave 80401 303-982-7450
James Younger, prin. Fax 982-7451
Other Schools – See Arvada, Conifer, Edgewater, Evergreen, Indian Hills, Lakewood, Littleton, Morrison, Pine, Westminster, Wheat Ridge

Gold Hill, Boulder, Pop. 180
Boulder Valley SD RE-2
Supt. — See Boulder
Gold Hill ES 50/K-5
890 Main St, Boulder CO 80302 303-245-5940
Kelley King, prin. Fax 449-2043

Granada, Prowers, Pop. 611
Granada SD RE-1 300/PK-12
PO Box 259 81041 719-734-5492
Leo Laprarie, supt. Fax 734-5495
www.granadaschool.com
Granada ES 100/PK-6
PO Box 259 81041 719-734-5492
Ty Kemp, prin. Fax 734-5495

Granby, Grand, Pop. 1,685
East Grand SD 2 1,300/PK-12
PO Box 125 80446 970-887-2581
Nancy Karas, supt. Fax 887-2635
www.egsd.org
East Grand MS 300/6-8
PO Box 2210 80446 970-887-3382
Jeff Verosky, prin. Fax 887-9234
Granby ES 300/PK-5
PO Box 2240 80446 970-887-3312
Andrea Verosky, prin. Fax 887-9565
Other Schools – See Fraser, Grand Lake

Grand Junction, Mesa, Pop. 45,299
Mesa County Valley SD 51 20,600/PK-12
2115 Grand Ave 81501 970-254-5100
Steven Schultz, supt. Fax 254-5282
www.mesa.k12.co.us
Appleton ES 400/PK-5
2358 H Rd 81505 970-254-6400
Mark Schmalz, prin. Fax 243-6604
Bookcliff MS 500/6-8
540 29 1/4 Rd 81504 970-254-6220
Catherine Drake, prin. Fax 245-7812
Broadway ES 300/PK-5
2248 Broadway, 970-254-6430
Sharon Kallus, prin. Fax 242-6292
Chatfield ES 400/PK-5
3188 D 1/2 Rd 81504 970-254-4930
Jackie Wilson, prin. Fax 434-1856
Chipeta ES K-5
950 Chipeta Ave 81501 970-254-6825
Pat Buckley, prin. Fax 242-6386
Dos Rios ES 400/PK-5
265 Linden Ave 81503 970-254-7910
Vernann Raney, prin. Fax 255-8504
East MS 400/6-8
830 Gunnison Ave 81501 970-254-5020
Leigh Grasso, prin. Fax 242-0513
Fruitvale ES 500/PK-5
585 30 Rd 81504 970-254-5930
Kathy Hays, prin. Fax 245-9143
Grand Mesa MS 700/6-8
585 31 1/2 Rd 81504 970-254-6270
Mark Vana, prin. Fax 254-6307
Hawthorne Preschool 50/PK-PK
410 Hill Ave 81501 970-254-5400
Jackie Howard, prin. Fax 245-0825
Lincoln Orchard Mesa ES 400/PK-5
2888 B 1/2 Rd 81503 970-254-7940
Meri Nofzinger, prin. Fax 243-8341
Mesa View ES 400/PK-5
2967 B Rd 81503 970-254-7970
Mary Biagini, prin. Fax 243-1449
New Emerson ES 100/K-5
2660 Unaweep Ave 81503 970-254-6500
Terry Schmalz, prin. Fax 256-9868
Nisley ES 500/PK-5
543 28 3/4 Rd 81501 970-254-5900
Curry Newton, prin. Fax 243-3065
Orchard Avenue ES 400/PK-5
1800 Orchard Ave 81501 970-254-7560
Denise Hoctor, prin. Fax 244-8650
Orchard Mesa MS 500/6-8
2736 C Rd 81503 970-254-6320
John Murtell, prin. Fax 245-7343
Pear Park ES 400/PK-5
432 30 1/4 Rd 81504 970-254-5960
Cheryl Taylor, prin. Fax 434-7415
Pomona ES 500/K-5
588 25 1/2 Rd 81505 970-254-4990
Emma-Leigh Larson, prin. Fax 242-2613
Redlands MS 600/6-8
2200 Broadway, 970-254-7000
Kelly Reed, prin. Fax 245-1985
Scenic ES 300/K-5
451 W Scenic Dr, 970-254-6370
Doug Levinson, prin. Fax 245-8605
Thunder Mountain ES 600/PK-5
3063 F 1/2 Rd 81504 970-254-5870
Diane Carver, prin. Fax 434-4457
Tope ES 500/PK-5
2220 N 7th St 81501 970-254-7070
Jeannie Dunn, prin. Fax 241-0687
West MS 400/6-8
123 W Orchard Ave 81505 970-254-5090
Vernan Walker, prin. Fax 243-0574
Wingate ES 400/K-5
351 S Camp Rd, 970-254-4960
Carol Wethington, prin. Fax 245-0748
Other Schools – See Clifton, Fruita, Gateway, Loma, Palisade

Bookcliff Christian S 100/K-9
2702 Patterson Rd 81506 970-243-2999
Douglas McClaskey, admin. Fax 263-4028
Holy Family S 400/PK-8
786 26 1/2 Rd 81506 970-242-6168
Ann Ashwood-Piper, prin. Fax 242-4244
Intermountain Adventist Academy 50/PK-10
1704 N 8th St 81501 970-242-5116
Ed Harlan, prin. Fax 242-5659
Life Academy 100/PK-12
636 29 Rd 81504 970-242-9431
Messiah Lutheran S 100/PK-8
840 N 11th St 81501 970-245-2838
Neal Kaspar, prin. Fax 245-8145

Grand Lake, Grand, Pop. 438
East Grand SD 2
Supt. — See Granby
Grand Lake ES 100/K-5
PO Box 1019 80447 970-627-3466
Phyllis Price, prin. Fax 627-3476

Greeley, Weld, Pop. 87,596
Weld County SD 6 15,700/PK-12
1025 9th Ave 80631 970-348-6000
Dr. Ranelle Lang, supt. Fax 348-6231
www.greeleyschools.org
Brentwood MS 600/6-8
2600 24th Avenue Ct 80634 970-348-3000
John Diebold, prin. Fax 348-3030
Cameron ES 400/K-5
1424 13th Ave 80631 970-348-1000
Juan Verdugo, prin. Fax 348-1030
East Memorial ES 500/PK-5
614 E 20th St 80631 970-348-1400
Dr. Mark Thompson, prin. Fax 348-1430
Evans MS 700/6-8
2900 15th Ave 80631 970-348-3600
Dr. Margaret Crespo, prin. Fax 348-3630
Franklin MS 600/6-8
818 35th Ave 80634 970-348-3200
Steven Linkous, prin. Fax 348-3230
Heath MS 800/6-8
2223 16th St 80631 970-348-3400
Arnold Jahnke, prin. Fax 348-3430
Jackson ES 400/PK-5
2002 25th St 80631 970-348-1500
Ingrid Dillehay, prin. Fax 348-1530
Jefferson ES 300/PK-5
1315 4th Ave 80631 970-348-1600
Maury Darnell, prin. Fax 348-1630
Madison ES 400/PK-5
500 24th Ave 80634 970-348-1700
Val Smythe, prin. Fax 348-1730
Maplewood MS 500/6-8
1201 21st Ave 80631 970-348-3800
Margo Walsh, prin. Fax 348-3830
Martinez ES 500/PK-5
341 14th Ave 80631 970-348-1800
Monica Draper, prin. Fax 348-1830
McAuliffe ES 600/PK-5
600 51st Ave 80634 970-348-1900
Sandra Cosner, prin. Fax 348-1930
Meeker ES 500/PK-5
2221 28th Ave 80634 970-348-2000
Wes Tuttle, prin. Fax 348-2030
Monfort ES 500/PK-5
2101 47th Ave 80634 970-348-2100
Amie Cieminski, prin. Fax 348-2130
Romero ES 400/K-5
1400 E 20th St 80631 970-348-2500
Jonathan Cooney, prin. Fax 348-2530
Scott ES 500/PK-5
3000 W 13th St 80634 970-348-2200
Dr. Blakely Wallace, prin. Fax 348-2230
Shawsheen ES 500/PK-5
4020 W 7th St 80634 970-348-2300
Steven Isenhour, prin. Fax 348-2330
Winograd S 300/K-8
320 N 71st Ave 80634 970-348-2600
Holly Bressler, prin. Fax 348-2630
Other Schools – See Evans

Dayspring Christian Academy 300/PK-12
3734 W 20th St 80634 970-330-1151
Del Groen, dir. Fax 330-0565
Greeley Adventist Christian S 50/K-8
612 23rd Ave 80634 970-353-2770
St. Mary's S 200/K-8
2351 22nd Ave 80631 970-353-8100
Sr. Anno Lamere, prin. Fax 353-8700
Shepherd of the Hills S 50/PK-5
950 43rd Ave 80634 970-353-6582
Jeffry Sell, prin. Fax 304-9242
Trinity Lutheran S 100/PK-8
3000 35th Ave 80634 970-330-2485
Larry Whitney, prin. Fax 330-2844

Greenwood Village, Arapahoe, Pop. 12,817
Cherry Creek SD 5 48,800/PK-12
4700 S Yosemite St 80111 303-773-1184
Mary Chesley, supt. Fax 773-9370
www.ccsd.k12.co.us
Greenwood ES 400/PK-5
5550 S Holly St 80111 720-554-3400
Midge Eidson, prin. Fax 554-3488
Other Schools – See Aurora, Centennial, Denver, Englewood, Littleton

---

Aspen Academy 200/PK-9
5859 S University Blvd 80111 303-346-3500
Kristina Scala, prin. Fax 379-7744
Beacon Country Day S 100/PK-8
6100 E Belleview Ave 80111 303-771-3990
Dr. Cynthia Wallace, prin. Fax 290-6462

Grover, Weld, Pop. 155
Pawnee SD RE-12 100/PK-12
PO Box 220 80729 970-895-2222
Phillip Graham, supt. Fax 895-2221
www.pawneeschool.com
Pawnee ES 100/PK-6
PO Box 220 80729 970-895-2222
Phillip Graham, prin. Fax 895-2221

Gunnison, Gunnison, Pop. 5,298
Gunnison Watershed SD RE 1J 1,700/PK-12
800 N Boulevard St 81230 970-641-7760
Jon Nelson, supt. Fax 641-7777
www.gunnisonschools.net/
Gunnison ES 500/K-5
1099 N 11th St 81230 970-641-7710
Marta Smith, prin. Fax 641-7739
Gunnison MS 300/6-8
1099 N 11th St 81230 970-641-7710
Doug Tredway, prin. Fax 641-7739
Gunnison Preschool 100/PK-PK
800 N Boulevard St 81230 970-641-7751
Sally Hensley, prin. Fax 641-7777
Other Schools – See Crested Butte

Gypsum, Eagle, Pop. 4,964
Eagle County SD RE-50
Supt. — See Eagle
Gypsum Creek MS 300/6-8
PO Box 5129 81637 970-328-8980
Steve Smith, prin. Fax 524-7393
Gypsum ES 300/PK-5
PO Box 570 81637 970-328-8940
Mitch Forsberg, prin. Fax 524-7054
Red Hill ES 400/K-5
PO Box 1009 81637 970-328-8970
Jill Pappas, prin. Fax 524-7374
Red Table Early Learning Center PK-PK
500 Red Table Rd 81637 970-328-2910
Shelley Smith, prin. Fax 476-4769

Haxtun, Phillips, Pop. 995
Haxtun SD RE-2J 300/PK-12
201 W Powell St 80731 970-774-6111
Darcy Garretson, supt. Fax 774-7568
Haxtun S 200/PK-8
601 N Colorado Ave 80731 970-774-6111
Becky Heinz, prin. Fax 774-3260

Hayden, Routt, Pop. 1,539
Hayden SD RE-1 400/PK-12
PO Box 70 81639 970-276-3864
Greg Rockhold, supt. Fax 276-4217
www.haydensd.org

Hayden MS 100/6-8
PO Box 70 81639 970-276-3762
Regina Zabel, prin. Fax 276-7235
Hayden Valley ES 200/PK-5
PO Box 70 81639 970-276-3756
Rhonda Sweetser, prin. Fax 276-4468

Henderson, Adams, Pop. 500
Brighton SD 27J
Supt. — See Brighton
Henderson ES 700/PK-5
12301 E 124th Ave 80640 303-655-2700
David Felten, prin. Fax 655-2704
Prairie View MS 6-8
12915 E 120th Ave 80640 720-685-5400
Tom Delgado, prin. Fax 685-5404
Thimmig ES 600/K-5
11453 Oswego St 80640 303-655-2750
Justin McMillin, prin. Fax 655-2754

Hesperus, LaPlata
Durango SD 9-R
Supt. — See Durango
Ft. Lewis Mesa ES 200/PK-5
11274 Highway 140 81326 970-588-3331
Dr. John Marchino, prin. Fax 588-3629

Highlands Ranch, Douglas, Pop. 10,181
Douglas County SD RE-1
Supt. — See Castle Rock
Arrowwood ES 600/PK-6
10345 Arrowwood Dr 80130 303-387-6875
Staci McCormack, prin. Fax 387-6876
Bear Canyon ES 600/K-6
9660 Salford Ln 80126 303-387-6475
Mike Weaver, prin. Fax 387-6476
Copper Mesa ES 500/K-6
3501 Poston Pkwy 80126 303-387-7375
Luan Ezra, prin. Fax 387-7376
Cougar Run ES 600/K-6
8780 Venneford Ranch Rd 80126 303-387-6675
John Gutierrez, prin. Fax 387-6676
Coyote Creek ES 600/PK-6
2861 Baneberry Ct 80129 303-387-6175
Jan Dow, prin. Fax 387-6176
Cresthill MS 900/7-8
9195 Cresthill Ln 80130 303-387-2800
Sid Rundle, prin. Fax 387-2801
Eldorado ES 700/PK-6
1305 Timbervale Trl 80129 303-387-6325
John Melkonian, prin. Fax 387-6326
Fox Creek ES 600/K-6
6585 Collegiate Dr 80130 303-387-7000
Brian Rodda, prin. Fax 387-7001
Heritage ES 600/PK-6
3350 Summit View Pkwy 80126 303-387-6725
Mary Lams, prin. Fax 387-6726
Mountain Ridge MS 900/7-8
10590 Mountain Vista Rdg 80126 303-387-1800
Kara Shepherd, prin. Fax 387-1801
Northridge ES 700/K-6
555 Southpark Rd 80126 303-387-6525
Elizabeth Morris, prin. Fax 387-6526
Ranch View MS 900/7-8
1731 W Wildcat Reserve Pkwy 80129 303-387-2300
Bryan Breuer, prin. Fax 387-2301
Redstone ES 600/K-6
9970 Glenstone Cir 80130 303-387-7300
Laura Wilson, prin. Fax 387-7301
Saddle Ranch ES 800/PK-6
805 English Sparrow Trl 80129 303-387-6400
Fred Rundle, prin. Fax 387-6401
Sand Creek ES 600/K-6
8898 Maplewood Dr 80126 303-387-6600
Chris Smith, prin. Fax 387-6601
Stone Mountain ES K-6
10635 Weathersfield Way 80129 303-387-7525
Marie Unger, prin. Fax 387-7526
Summit View ES 700/K-6
10200 Piedmont Dr 80126 303-387-6800
Ron Schumacher, prin. Fax 387-6801
Trailblazer ES 700/K-6
9760 S Hackberry St 80129 303-387-6250
Linda Schneider, prin. Fax 387-6251

Cherry Hills Christian S 1,200/PK-8
3900 Grace Blvd 80126 303-791-5500
Robert Bignell, supt. Fax 683-5252
Denver Christian S Highlands Ranch 800/PK-8
1733 Dad Clark Dr 80126 303-791-3243
Kati Melton, prin. Fax 791-7083

Hoehne, Las Animas, Pop. 150
Hoehne RSD 3 400/PK-12
PO Box 91 81046 719-846-4457
Reid Straabe, supt. Fax 846-4450
Hoehne ES, PO Box 91 81046 200/PK-6
Kay Maes, prin. 719-846-4457
Hoehne JHS, PO Box 91 81046 100/7-8
Kay Maes, prin. 719-846-4457

Holly, Prowers, Pop. 997
Holly SD RE-3 300/PK-12
PO Box 608 81047 719-537-6616
Carlyn Yokum, supt. Fax 537-0315
www.hollyschools.org
Shanner ES 200/PK-6
PO Box 608 81047 719-537-6662
Heather Flint, prin. Fax 537-0822

Holyoke, Phillips, Pop. 2,289
Holyoke SD RE-1J 500/K-12
435 S Morlan Ave 80734 970-854-3634
Stephen Bohrer, supt. Fax 854-4049
www.hcosd.org
Holyoke ES 300/K-5
326 E Kellogg St 80734 970-854-3511
Jennifer Kral, prin. Fax 854-2703
Holyoke JHS 100/6-8
545 E Hale St 80734 970-854-2284
Susan Ortner, prin. Fax 854-2441

Hooper, Alamosa, Pop. 128
Sangre De Cristo SD RE-22J
Supt. — See Mosca
Sangre De Cristo ES 200/PK-6
PO Box 27 81136 719-378-2381
Dixie Rogers, prin. Fax 378-2382

Hotchkiss, Delta, Pop. 1,043
Delta County SD 50(J)
Supt. — See Delta
Hotchkiss S 400/K-8
465 Lorah Ln 81419 970-872-3325
Carrie Coats, prin. Fax 872-3808
North Fork Montessori S 100/PK-6
397 Bulldog St 81419 970-872-5910
William Eyler, prin.

Hudson, Weld, Pop. 1,587
Weld County SD RE-3J
Supt. — See Keenesburg
Hudson ES 300/PK-6
PO Box 278 80642 303-536-2200
Gregory Dent, prin. Fax 536-2210

Hugo, Lincoln, Pop. 799
Genoa-Hugo SD C113 200/PK-12
PO Box 247 80821 719-743-2428
Dan Schmidt, supt. Fax 743-2194
www.genoahugo.org/
Genoa-Hugo ES 100/PK-5
PO Box 247 80821 719-743-2428
Ellen Froman, prin. Fax 743-2194
Genoa-Hugo MS 100/6-8
PO Box 247 80821 719-743-2428
Ellen Froman, prin. Fax 743-2194

Idaho Springs, Clear Creek, Pop. 1,807
Clear Creek SD RE-1 900/PK-12
PO Box 3399 80452 303-567-3850
Bill Patterson, supt. Fax 567-3861
www.ccsdre1.org/
Carlson ES 300/PK-6
PO Box 3339 80452 303-567-4431
Marcia Jochim, prin. Fax 567-9135
Clear Creek MS 200/7-8
PO Box 3369 80452 303-567-4461
Roslin Marshall, prin. Fax 567-3856
Other Schools – See Evergreen

Idalia, Yuma, Pop. 100
Idalia SD RJ-3 200/PK-12
PO Box 40 80735 970-354-7298
Jim Poole, supt. Fax 354-7416
www.idaliaco.us/
Idalia ES 100/PK-6
PO Box 40 80735 970-354-7298
Tim Krause, prin. Fax 354-7416

Ignacio, LaPlata, Pop. 679
Ignacio SD 11 JT 800/K-12
PO Box 460 81137 970-563-0500
Juvie Jones, supt. Fax 563-4524
www.ignacio.k12.co.us
Ignacio ES 200/K-3
PO Box 460 81137 970-563-0675
Karl Herr, prin. Fax 563-4208
Ignacio IS 100/4-6
PO Box 460 81137 970-563-0650
Kathy Pokorney, prin. Fax 563-4537
Ignacio JHS 100/7-8
PO Box 460 81137 970-563-0600
Beverly Lyons, prin. Fax 563-1030

Southern Ute Indian Montessori Academy 100/PK-6
PO Box 737 81137 970-563-0253
Carol Baker Olguin, dir. Fax 563-3695

Iliff, Logan, Pop. 218
Valley SD RE-1
Supt. — See Sterling
Caliche ES 200/PK-6
26308 County Road 65 80736 970-522-8330
Helen Duncan, prin. Fax 522-8331

Indian Hills, Jefferson, Pop. 1,500
Jefferson County SD R-1
Supt. — See Golden
Parmalee ES 200/K-5
PO Box 58 80454 303-982-8014
Ingrid Mielke, prin. Fax 982-8013

Jamestown, Boulder, Pop. 233
Boulder Valley SD RE-2
Supt. — See Boulder
Jamestown ES 50/K-5
PO Box 309 80455 303-442-6613
Kelley King, prin. Fax 447-0459

Joes, Yuma, Pop. 75
Liberty SD J-4 100/PK-12
PO Box 112 80822 970-358-4288
David Eastin, supt. Fax 358-4282
www.libertyschoolj4.com
Liberty ES 50/PK-6
PO Box 112 80822 970-358-4288
David Eastin, prin. Fax 358-4282

Johnstown, Weld, Pop. 7,250
Weld County SD RE-5J
Supt. — See Milliken
Letford ES 400/K-5
2 Jay Ave 80534 970-587-6150
Kerry Boren, prin. Fax 587-0115
Pioneer Ridge ES 500/K-5
2300 Cinnamon Teal Ave 80534 970-587-8100
Rick Baldino, prin. Fax 587-8169

Julesburg, Sedgwick, Pop. 1,335
Julesburg SD RE-1 300/PK-12
102 W 6th St 80737 970-474-3365
Shawn Ehnes, supt. Fax 474-3742
www.julesburg.org/
Julesburg ES 200/PK-6
525 Spruce St 80737 970-474-3319
Mary Rice, prin. Fax 474-3319

Karval, Lincoln, Pop. 50
Karval SD RE-23 100/PK-12
PO Box 5 80823 719-446-5311
Martin Adams, supt. Fax 446-5332
Karval ES 50/PK-5
PO Box 5 80823 719-446-5311
Martin Adams, prin. Fax 446-5332

Keenesburg, Weld, Pop. 1,141
Weld County SD RE-3J 1,900/PK-12
PO Box 269 80643 303-536-2000
Susan Townsend, supt. Fax 536-2010
www.re3j.com/
Hoff ES 300/PK-6
7558 County Road 59 80643 303-536-2300
David Miller, prin. Fax 536-2310
Weld Central JHS 300/7-8
4977 County Road 59 80643 303-536-2700
Karla Schriner, prin. Fax 536-2710
Other Schools – See Hudson, Lochbuie

Kersey, Weld, Pop. 1,401
Weld County SD RE-7 1,100/PK-12
PO Box 485 80644 970-336-8500
E. Glenn McClain, supt. Fax 336-8511
www.plattevalley.k12.co.us
Platte Valley ES 500/PK-5
PO Box 486 80644 970-336-8520
Don Beard, prin. Fax 336-8538
Platte Valley MS 300/6-8
PO Box 515 80644 970-336-8610
George Clear, prin. Fax 336-8635

Kim, Las Animas, Pop. 67
Kim RSD 88 100/PK-12
PO Box 100 81049 719-643-5295
Art Dowell, supt. Fax 643-5299
www.kim.k12.co.us/
Kim ES 50/PK-6
PO Box 100 81049 719-643-5295
Art Dowell, prin. Fax 643-5299

Kiowa, Elbert, Pop. 596
Kiowa SD C-2 400/PK-12
PO Box 128 80117 303-621-2220
Bret Robinson, supt. Fax 621-2239
www.kiowaschool.org
Kiowa ES 200/PK-5
PO Box 128 80117 303-621-2042
Brenda Wham, prin. Fax 621-2566
Kiowa MS 100/6-8
PO Box 128 80117 303-621-2785
Lance Luitjens, prin. Fax 621-2566

Kit Carson, Cheyenne, Pop. 225
Kit Carson SD R-1 100/K-12
PO Box 185 80825 719-962-3219
Gerald Keefe, supt. Fax 962-3317
www.kcsdr1.org
Carson ES 50/K-5
PO Box 185 80825 719-962-3219
Kathy Fabrizius, prin. Fax 962-3317

Kremmling, Grand, Pop. 1,554
West Grand SD 1-JT 400/K-12
PO Box 515 80459 970-724-3217
Dr. Jeff Perry, supt. Fax 724-9373
www.westgrand.k12.co.us/
West Grand S 200/K-8
PO Box 515 80459 970-724-3656
Kelly Farrell, prin. Fax 724-0538

Lafayette, Boulder, Pop. 23,884
Boulder Valley SD RE-2
Supt. — See Boulder
Angevine MS 500/6-8
1150 W South Boulder Rd 80026 303-665-5540
Mike Medina, prin. Fax 661-0354
Lafayette ES 400/PK-5
101 N Bermont Ave 80026 720-561-8900
Dr. Holly Hultgren, prin. Fax 561-8901
Pioneer Bilingual ES 400/PK-5
101 E Baseline Rd 80026 303-666-4971
Miguel Villalon, prin. Fax 665-3713
Ryan ES 400/K-5
1405 Centaur Village Dr 80026 720-561-7000
Cyrus Weinberger, prin. Fax 561-7001
Sanchez ES 300/PK-5
655 Sir Galahad Dr 80026 303-665-2044
Doris Candelarie, prin. Fax 665-2044

Dawson S 400/K-12
10455 Dawson Dr 80026 303-665-6679
Brian Johnson, hdmstr. Fax 665-0757

La Jara, Conejos, Pop. 831
North Conejos SD RE-1J 1,200/PK-12
PO Box 72 81140 719-274-5174
Rick Ivers, supt. Fax 274-5621
north.co.schoolwebpages.com/
Centauri MS 200/6-8
PO Box 72 81140 719-274-4301
Susan Hamilton, prin. Fax 274-4301
La Jara ES 300/PK-5
PO Box 470 81140 719-274-5791
W. Brian Crowther, prin. Fax 274-3147
Other Schools – See Manassa

La Junta, Otero, Pop. 7,260
East Otero SD R-1 1,400/K-12
1802 Colorado Ave Ste 200 81050 719-384-6900
Jim Sullivan, supt. Fax 384-6910
www.lajunta.k12.co.us
La Junta IS, 1401 E 6th St 81050 300/3-5
Ellen Schreivogel, prin. 719-384-9151
La Junta MS 400/6-8
901 Smithland Ave 81050 719-384-4371
Paul Jebe, prin.

La Junta PS, 600 Topeka Ave 81050 300/K-2
Sue Barbee, prin. 719-384-2991

Lake City, Hinsdale, Pop. 359
Hinsdale County SD RE 1 100/PK-12
PO Box 39 81235 970-944-2314
Karen Thormalen, supt. Fax 944-2662
www.lakecityschool.org/
Lake City Community S 100/PK-12
PO Box 39 81235 970-944-2314
Karen Thormalen, prin. Fax 944-2662

Lakewood, Jefferson, Pop. 140,671
Jefferson County SD R-1
Supt. — See Golden
Bear Creek S 1,100/K-8
9601 W Dartmouth Pl 80227 303-982-8714
Victoria Kaye, prin. Fax 982-8715
Belmar ES 300/K-6
885 S Garrison St 80226 303-982-8220
Peter Ludwig, prin. Fax 982-8221
Carmody MS 700/7-8
2050 S Kipling St 80227 303-982-8930
Heather Beck, prin. Fax 982-8931
Creighton MS 600/7-8
75 Independence St 80226 303-982-6282
Patty DeLorenzo, prin. Fax 982-6283
Deane ES 500/K-6
580 S Harlan St 80226 303-982-9655
Charlene White, prin. Fax 982-9660
DeVinny ES 600/K-6
1725 S Wright St 80228 303-982-9200
Michelle Stansbury, prin. Fax 982-9201
Dunstan MS 800/7-8
1855 S Wright St 80228 303-982-9270
Kevin Carroll, prin. Fax 982-9269
Eiber ES 400/K-6
1385 Independence St 80215 303-982-6406
Bing Peng, prin. Fax 982-6407
Foothills ES 400/PK-6
13165 W Ohio Ave 80228 303-982-9324
Barbara Donahue, prin. Fax 982-9325
Glennon Heights ES 300/K-6
11025 W Glennon Dr 80226 303-982-8240
Mike Collins, prin. Fax 982-8241
Green Gables ES 400/K-6
8701 W Woodard Dr 80227 303-982-8314
Kathy Chandler, prin. Fax 982-8315
Green Mountain ES 400/PK-6
12250 W Kentucky Dr 80228 303-982-9380
Brenda Somerville, prin. Fax 982-9381
Hutchinson ES 400/K-6
12900 W Utah Ave 80228 303-982-9561
Beth Bacon, prin. Fax 982-9562
Irwin Preschool PK-PK
1505 S Pierson St 80232 303-969-9704
Joette Stewart, dir. Fax 763-5635
Jefferson County Open S 300/PK-12
7655 W 10th Ave 80214 303-982-7045
Wendy Wheaton, prin. Fax 982-7046
Kendrick Lakes ES 400/K-6
1350 S Hoyt St 80232 303-982-8324
Barbara Gunther, prin. Fax 982-8325
Lasley ES 700/K-6
1401 S Kendall St 80232 303-982-9720
Debra Williamson, prin. Fax 982-9721
Molholm ES 500/PK-6
6000 W 9th Ave 80214 303-982-6240
John D'Orazio, prin. Fax 982-6238
O'Connell MS 500/7-8
1275 S Teller St 80232 303-982-8370
Pati Montgomery, prin. Fax 982-8371
Patterson ES 500/PK-6
1263 S Dudley St 80232 303-982-8470
Susie D'Amanti, prin. Fax 982-8467
Rooney Ranch ES 400/K-6
2200 S Coors St 80228 303-982-9620
Ellyn Martinez, prin. Fax 982-9619
Slater ES 300/PK-6
8605 W 23rd Ave 80215 303-982-7575
Nick Kemmer, prin. Fax 982-7574
South Lakewood ES 500/K-6
8425 W 1st Ave 80226 303-982-7325
Anne Chenoweth, prin. Fax 982-7324
Stein ES 700/PK-6
80 S Teller St 80226 303-982-7407
Socorro Alarcon, prin. Fax 982-7408
Stober ES 300/K-6
2300 Urban St 80215 303-982-7610
Susan Borzych, prin. Fax 982-7609
Vivian ES 200/PK-6
10500 W 25th Ave 80215 303-982-7670
Rita Throckmorton, prin. Fax 982-7666
Westgate ES 600/K-6
8550 W Vassar Dr 80227 303-982-9130
Robert Linton, prin. Fax 982-9131

Bethlehem Lutheran S 300/PK-8
2100 Wadsworth Blvd 80214 303-233-0401
Kenneth Palmreuter, prin. Fax 237-4011
Concordia Lutheran S 100/PK-K
13371 W Alameda Pkwy 80228 303-989-5260
Fax 988-3136
Front Range Waldorf S 50/PK-K
12755 W Cedar Dr 80228 303-384-0139
Carla Abate, prin. Fax 215-0318
Our Lady of Fatima S 300/PK-8
10530 W 20th Ave 80215 303-233-2500
Lisa Taylor, prin. Fax 205-1567
St. Bernadette S 200/PK-8
1100 Upham St 80214 303-237-0401
Debra Roberts, prin. Fax 237-0608

Lamar, Prowers, Pop. 8,414
Lamar SD RE-2 1,100/PK-12
210 W Pearl St 81052 719-336-3251
Wayne Graybeal, supt. Fax 336-2817
www.lamar.k12.co.us
Hendrickson Development Center 100/PK-PK
510 Savage Ave 81052 719-336-2022
Fax 336-4725
Lamar MS 200/7-8
104 W Park St 81052 719-336-7436
David Tecklenburg, prin. Fax 336-5457
Lincoln ES 50/5-6
200 N 10th St 81052 719-336-7741
Kermit Snyder, prin. Fax 336-4445
Parkview ES 100/3-4
1105 Parkview Ave 81052 719-336-7413
Matt Snyder, prin. Fax 336-0183
Washington ES 200/K-2
510 S 9th St 81052 719-336-7764
Steve Banker, prin. Fax 336-4458

Laporte, Larimer, Pop. 1,500
Poudre SD R-1
Supt. — See Fort Collins
Cache-La Poudre ES 300/PK-5
3511 W County Road 54G 80535 970-488-7600
Roxann Hall, prin. Fax 488-7676
Cache La Poudre MS 300/6-8
3515 W County Road 54G 80535 970-488-7400
Skip Caddoo, prin. Fax 488-7433

Larkspur, Douglas, Pop. 306
Douglas County SD RE-1
Supt. — See Castle Rock
Larkspur ES 400/K-6
1103 Perry Park Ave 80118 303-387-5375
Darryl Sigman, prin. Fax 387-5376

La Salle, Weld, Pop. 1,895
Weld County SD RE-1
Supt. — See Gilcrest
Mirich ES 300/PK-5
PO Box 268 80645 970-284-5513
John Steckel, prin. Fax 284-6913
North Valley MS 300/6-8
PO Box 248 80645 970-284-5508
Richard Dolgliesh, prin. Fax 284-6595

Las Animas, Bent, Pop. 2,543
Las Animas SD RE-1 600/PK-12
1021 2nd St 81054 719-456-0161
Scott Cuckow, supt. Fax 456-1117
www.lasanimas.k12.co.us
Jump Start Learning Center 50/PK-PK
138 6th St 81054 719-456-1990
Vivian Noble, dir. Fax 456-1990
Las Animas ES 200/K-5
530 Poplar Ave 81054 719-456-1862
Libby Hiza, prin. Fax 456-1201
Las Animas MS 100/6-8
1021 2nd St 81054 719-456-0228
Elsie Goines, prin. Fax 456-0241

La Veta, Huerfano, Pop. 887
La Veta SD RE-2 300/PK-12
PO Box 85 81055 719-742-3562
Dave Seaney, supt. Fax 742-3959
www.laveta.k12.co.us
La Veta ES 100/PK-6
PO Box 85 81055 719-742-3621
Betty Trahern, prin. Fax 742-5796

Leadville, Lake, Pop. 2,688
Lake County SD R-1 1,200/PK-12
107 Spruce St 80461 719-486-6800
Dr. Bette Bullock, supt. Fax 486-2048
www.lakecountyschools.net/
Lake County MS 300/5-8
1000 W 6th St 80461 719-486-6830
Deb Forkner, prin. Fax 486-6880
Pitts ES 300/PK-1
315 W 6th St 80461 719-486-6920
Emily Bordogna, prin. Fax 486-9992
Westpark ES 300/1-4
130 W 12th St 80461 719-486-6890
Linda Adams, prin. Fax 486-3421

Limon, Lincoln, Pop. 1,879
Limon SD RE-4J 500/K-12
PO Box 249 80828 719-775-2350
Scott Vratil, supt. Fax 775-9052
www.limonbadgers.com/
Limon ES 200/K-5
PO Box 249 80828 719-775-2350
Joel Albers, prin. Fax 775-9052

Littleton, Arapahoe, Pop. 40,396
Cherry Creek SD 5
Supt. — See Greenwood Village
West MS 1,200/6-8
5151 S Holly St 80121 720-554-5100
David Strohfus, prin. Fax 554-5181

Douglas County SD RE-1
Supt. — See Castle Rock
Acres Green ES 700/PK-6
13524 Acres Green Dr 80124 303-387-7125
Karen Moore, prin. Fax 387-7126
Rocky Heights MS 1,000/6-8
11033 Monarch Blvd 80124 303-387-3300
Pat Dierberger, prin. Fax 387-3301
Roxborough IS 500/3-6
7370 E Village Cir 80125 303-387-7600
Karen Brofft, prin. Fax 387-7601
Roxborough PS 400/K-2
8000 Village Cir W 80125 303-387-6000
Karen Brofft, prin. Fax 387-6001
Wildcat Mountain ES 500/PK-6
6585 Lionshead Pkwy 80124 303-387-6925
Gary Poole, prin. Fax 387-6926

Jefferson County SD R-1
Supt. — See Golden
Blue Heron ES 500/PK-6
5987 W Dorado Dr 80123 303-982-2770
Joe Turnage, prin. Fax 982-2771
Bradford IS 400/4-6
2 Woodruff Dr 80127 303-982-4882
Sam Palamara, prin. Fax 982-4883
Bradford PS 500/K-3
1 White Oak Dr 80127 303-982-3480
Eugene Lewis, prin. Fax 982-3481
Colorow ES 300/K-6
6317 S Estes St 80123 303-982-5480
Sandy Burch, prin. Fax 982-5479
Columbine Hills ES 400/PK-6
6005 W Canyon Ave 80128 303-982-5540
Connie Brasher, prin. Fax 982-5541
Columbine Preschool PK-PK
5977 W Elmhurst Ave 80128 303-979-5230
Kelly Kennelly, dir. Fax 973-5574
Coronado ES 500/PK-6
7922 S Carr St 80128 303-982-3737
Nancy Graeve, prin. Fax 982-3738
Deer Creek MS 600/7-8
9201 W Columbine Dr 80128 303-982-3820
Rob Hoover, prin. Fax 982-3821
Dutch Creek ES 400/K-6
7304 W Roxbury Pl 80128 303-982-4565
Jennifer Pennell, prin. Fax 982-4566
Falcon Bluffs MS 700/6-8
8449 S Garrison St 80128 303-982-9900
Wendy Rubin, prin. Fax 982-9901
Governors Ranch ES 500/K-6
5354 S Field St 80123 303-982-4625
Annette Zambrano, prin. Fax 982-4626
Ken Caryl MS 700/7-8
6509 W Ken Caryl Ave 80128 303-982-4710
Patrick Sandos, prin. Fax 982-4711
Leawood ES 400/PK-6
6155 W Leawood Dr 80123 303-982-7860
Ari Goldberg, prin. Fax 982-7861
Mortensen ES 400/PK-6
8006 S Iris Way 80128 303-982-0022
Karla Hankins, prin. Fax 982-0021
Mount Carbon ES 400/K-6
12776 W Cross Ave 80127 303-982-7900
Tracy Haschker, prin. Fax 982-7901
Normandy ES 700/K-6
6750 S Kendall Blvd 80128 303-982-4766
Liz Costello, prin. Fax 982-4767
Peiffer ES 400/K-6
4997 S Miller Way 80127 303-982-4800
Robin Weikel, prin. Fax 982-4801
Powderhorn ES 600/K-6
12109 W Coal Mine Ave 80127 303-982-0074
Mike Freeman, prin. Fax 982-0066
Shaffer ES 600/K-5
7961 Sangre De Cristo Rd 80127 303-982-3901
Anne Sterrett, prin. Fax 982-3899
Stony Creek ES 800/PK-6
7203 S Everett St 80128 303-982-4120
John de la Garza, prin. Fax 982-4121
Summit Ridge MS 900/7-8
11809 W Coal Mine Ave 80127 303-982-9013
Lisa Myles, prin. Fax 982-8998
Ute Meadows ES 500/K-6
11050 W Meadows Dr 80127 303-982-4044
Steve Weigum, prin. Fax 982-4045
Westridge ES 600/PK-6
10785 W Alamo Pl 80127 303-982-3975
Barbara Boillot, prin. Fax 982-3976

Littleton SD 6 14,500/PK-12
5776 S Crocker St 80120 303-347-3300
Scott Murphy, supt. Fax 347-3439
www.littletonpublicschools.net
Centennial Academy of Fine Arts 400/K-5
3306 W Berry Ave 80123 303-347-4425
Mary Ellen Dillman, prin. Fax 347-4430
East ES 200/K-5
5933 S Fairfield St 80120 303-347-4450
Greg Sumlin, prin. Fax 347-4470
Euclid MS 800/6-8
777 W Euclid Ave 80120 303-347-7800
Gary Hein, prin. Fax 347-7830
Field ES 500/K-5
5402 S Sherman Way 80121 303-347-4475
Mike Montgomery, prin. Fax 347-4490
Goddard MS 900/6-8
3800 W Berry Ave 80123 303-347-7850
Kathleen Ambron, prin. Fax 347-7880
Moody ES 300/K-5
6390 S Windermere St 80120 303-347-4600
Doug Andrews, prin. Fax 347-4620
Powell MS 900/6-8
8000 S Corona Way 80122 303-347-7950
Steve Wolf, prin. Fax 347-3975
Runyon ES 400/K-5
7455 S Elati St 80120 303-347-4650
David Hilliard, prin. Fax 347-4670
Village at North 300/PK-PK
1907 W Powers Ave 80120 303-347-6985
Phyllis Dornseit, dir. Fax 347-6981
Wilder ES 600/K-5
4300 W Ponds Cir 80123 303-347-4750
Trish Cook, prin. Fax 347-4755
Other Schools – See Centennial

Abiding Hope K 100/PK-K
6337 S Robb Way 80127 303-932-9160
Fax 972-0424
Front Range Christian S 200/K-6
6657 W Ottawa Ave Ste A18 80128 303-531-4512
Julie Melton, admin. Fax 531-4527
Hope Christian Academy 100/K-8
PO Box 621087 80162 303-979-6839
Nancy Thurston, prin. Fax 979-6907
Mackintosh Academy 100/PK-8
7018 S Prince St 80120 303-794-6222
Renu Rose, hdmstr. Fax 794-2286
St. Marys S 500/PK-8
6833 S Prince St 80120 303-798-2375
Mary Cohen, prin. Fax 283-4756

Truth Christian Academy 50/PK-10
PO Box 621961 80162 303-670-3360
Stanley Silverman, admin. Fax 670-8069

Livermore, Larimer, Pop. 200
Poudre SD R-1
Supt. — See Fort Collins
Livermore ES 100/K-5
360 Red Feather Lakes Rd 80536 970-488-6520
Patrick Kind, prin. Fax 488-6522

Lochbuie, Weld, Pop. 3,588
Weld County SD RE-3J
Supt. — See Keenesburg
Lochbuie ES 400/PK-6
201 Bonanza Blvd 80603 303-536-2400
John Reimers, prin. Fax 536-2410

Loma, Mesa, Pop. 350
Mesa County Valley SD 51
Supt. — See Grand Junction
Loma ES 300/PK-5
1360 13 Rd 81524 970-254-6520
Karen Rigg, prin. Fax 858-7909

Lonetree, See Littleton
Douglas County SD RE-1
Supt. — See Castle Rock
Eagle Ridge ES 600/K-6
7716 Timberline Rd 80124 303-387-7075
Kathy Truglio, prin. Fax 387-7076
Lonetree ES PK-6
9375 Heritage Hills Cir 80124 303-387-7450
Karen Moore, prin. Fax 387-7451

Longmont, Boulder, Pop. 81,818
St. Vrain Valley SD RE-1J 22,300/PK-12
395 S Pratt Pkwy 80501 303-776-6200
Don Haddad, supt. Fax 682-7343
www.stvrain.k12.co.us
Alpine ES 500/PK-5
2005 Alpine St 80504 720-652-8140
DeDe Frothingham, prin. Fax 652-8141
Altona MS 500/6-8
4600 Clover Basin Dr 80503 720-494-3980
Joe Mehsling, prin. Fax 494-3989
Blue Mountain ES PK-5
1260 Mountain Dr 80503 720-652-8220
Kristie Venrick, prin. Fax 652-8235
Burlington ES 500/PK-5
1051 S Pratt Pkwy 80501 303-776-8861
Janis Hughes, prin. Fax 772-8414
Central ES 400/PK-5
1020 4th Ave 80501 303-776-3236
Jim Hecocks, prin. Fax 772-8566
Columbine ES 400/PK-5
111 Longs Peak Ave 80501 303-776-2840
Eddie Cloke, prin. Fax 772-8837
Eagle Crest ES 600/PK-5
4444 Clover Basin Dr 80503 303-485-6073
Ryan Ball, prin. Fax 485-6094
Fall River ES 600/PK-5
1400 Deerwood Dr 80504 720-652-7920
Jennifer Guthals, prin. Fax 494-9868
Heritage MS 500/6-8
233 E Mountain View Ave 80504 303-772-7900
Karrie Borski, prin. Fax 776-4376
Hygiene ES 400/K-5
11968 N 75th St 80503 720-652-8021
Michael O'Donnell, prin. Fax 772-9158
Indian Peaks ES 400/PK-5
1335 S Judson St 80501 303-772-7240
Judy Orbanosky, prin. Fax 772-9145
Legacy ES 500/PK-5
7701 Eagle Blvd 80504 720-652-8160
Sean Corey, prin. Fax 652-4192
Loma Linda ES 500/PK-5
333 E Mountain View Ave 80501 303-772-4280
Dina Perfetti-Deany, prin. Fax 772-9020
Longmont Estates ES 400/K-5
1601 Northwestern Rd 80503 720-652-8101
Brian Childress, prin. Fax 772-9402
Longs Peak MS 500/6-8
1500 14th Ave 80501 303-776-5611
Matt Buchler, prin. Fax 651-3144
Mountain View ES 300/PK-5
1415 14th Ave 80501 720-652-8261
Nancy Pitz, prin. Fax 772-9494
Niwot ES 500/PK-5
8778 Morton Rd 80503 303-652-2828
Mike Keppler, prin. Fax 652-2648
Northridge ES 400/PK-5
1200 19th Ave 80501 303-772-3040
Rob Orbanosky, prin. Fax 772-9018
Rocky Mountain ES 500/PK-5
800 E 5th Ave 80501 303-772-6750
Stephen Hoel, prin. Fax 772-9507
Sanborn ES 400/K-5
2235 Vivian St 80501 303-772-3838
John Wahler, prin. Fax 678-0742
Spangler ES 400/PK-5
1440 Collyer St 80501 720-494-3761
Michelle Johnstone, prin. Fax 772-8850
Sunset MS 600/6-8
1300 S Sunset St 80501 303-776-3963
Dawn Macy, prin. Fax 772-2875
Trail Ridge MS 600/6-8
1000 Button Rock Dr 80504 720-494-3820
Tim Root, prin. Fax 494-3829
Westview MS 600/6-8
1651 Airport Rd 80503 303-772-3134
Mark Spencer, prin. Fax 772-0596
Other Schools – See Erie, Firestone, Frederick, Lyons, Mead

Aspen Christian S 50/K-8
316 15th Ave 80501 303-776-5866
Lloyd Petersen, prin. Fax 776-5866
Faith Baptist S 200/K-12
833 15th Ave 80501 303-776-5677
Dan Perryman, prin. Fax 682-5359
Longmont Christian S 400/PK-12
550 Coffman St 80501 303-776-3254
Donnie Bennett, prin. Fax 485-6937
Messiah Lutheran S 100/PK-5
1335 Francis St 80501 303-776-3466
Angela Sitz, prin. Fax 776-2599
Our Savior Lutheran S 50/K-8
1219 17th Ave 80501 303-776-1688
Dane Mattes, prin. Fax 776-1688
Rocky Mountain Christian Academy 500/PK-8
9447 Niwot Rd 80503 303-652-9162
Dr. Sylvia Robinson, prin. Fax 652-8072
St. John the Baptist S 400/PK-8
350 Emery St 80501 303-776-8760
Julie Rossi, prin. Fax 772-5636

Louisville, Boulder, Pop. 18,358
Boulder Valley SD RE-2
Supt. — See Boulder
Coal Creek ES 500/K-5
801 W Tamarisk St 80027 303-666-4843
John Kiemele, prin. Fax 661-9892
Fireside ES 400/PK-5
845 W Dahlia St 80027 720-561-7900
Pat Heinz-Pribyl, prin. Fax 561-7901
Louisville ES 400/K-5
400 Hutchinson St 80027 303-666-6562
Jennifer Rocke, prin. Fax 890-7281
Louisville MS 600/6-8
1341 Main St 80027 303-666-6503
Adam Fels, prin. Fax 665-3703
Monarch S 700/K-8
263 Campus Dr 80027 720-561-4000
Richard Glaab, prin. Fax 561-4001
Superior ES 700/K-5
1800 S Indiana St 80027 303-543-9330
Mary Hausermann, prin. Fax 543-9611

Louisville Montessori S 100/PK-K
461 Tyler Ave 80027 303-665-2002
Judith Cole, dir. Fax 666-2146
St. Louis S 300/PK-8
925 Grant Ave 80027 303-666-6220
Annette Canfield, prin. Fax 666-0826

Loveland, Larimer, Pop. 59,563
Thompson SD R-2J 14,600/K-12
800 S Taft Ave 80537 970-613-5000
Dr. Ron Cabrera, supt. Fax 613-5095
www.thompson.k12.co.us
Ball MS 800/6-8
2660 Monroe Ave 80538 970-613-7300
Sheila Pottorff, prin. Fax 613-7341
Big Thompson ES 200/K-5
7702 W US Highway 34 80537 970-613-5600
Kendrick White, prin. Fax 613-5620
Blair ES 500/K-5
860 E 29th St 80538 970-613-6400
Traci Gile, prin. Fax 613-6420
Centennial ES 300/K-5
1555 W 37th St 80538 970-613-5800
Anne Sanchez, prin. Fax 613-5820
Clark MS 700/6-8
2605 Carlisle Dr 80537 970-613-5400
Martha Gustafson, prin. Fax 613-5420
Edmondson ES 300/K-5
307 W 49th St 80538 970-613-6300
Georgianna Dawson, prin. Fax 613-6320
Erwin MS 800/6-8
4700 Lucerne Ave 80538 970-613-7600
Diane Worner, prin. Fax 613-7619
Garfield ES 300/K-5
720 Colorado Ave 80537 970-613-6000
Celeste Hyland, prin. Fax 613-6020
Kitchen ES 200/K-5
915 Deborah Dr 80537 970-613-5500
Kandi Smith, prin. Fax 613-5520
Lincoln ES 400/K-5
3312 Douglas Ave 80538 970-613-6200
Joan Brockway, prin. Fax 613-6220
Martin ES 300/K-5
4129 Joni Ln 80537 970-613-5700
Sheryl Weitzel, prin. Fax 613-5720
Milner ES 400/K-5
743 Jocelyn Dr 80537 970-613-6700
Dale Bryant, prin. Fax 613-6720
Monroe ES 400/K-5
1500 Monroe Ave 80538 970-613-6500
Susan Goppert, prin. Fax 613-6520
Namaqua ES 500/K-5
209 N County Road 19 E 80537 970-613-6600
Rick Bowles, prin. Fax 613-6620
Reed MS 600/6-8
370 W 4th St 80537 970-613-7200
Todd Ball, prin. Fax 613-7287
Stansberry ES 200/K-5
407 E 42nd St 80538 970-613-6800
Grant Waaler, prin. Fax 613-6820
Truscott ES 300/K-5
211 W 6th St 80537 970-613-6900
Wendy Fothergill, prin. Fax 613-6920
Van Buren ES 300/K-5
1811 W 15th St 80538 970-613-7000
Lamb Caro, prin. Fax 613-7020
Winona ES 400/K-5
201 S Boise Ave 80537 970-613-7100
Lori Garcia-Sander, prin. Fax 613-7120
Other Schools – See Berthoud, Fort Collins

HMS Richards SDA S 50/PK-8
342 42nd St SW 80537 970-667-2427
Fax 667-2427
Immanuel Lutheran S 300/PK-8
4650 Sunview Dr 80538 970-667-7606
Mark L'Heureux, prin. Fax 624-3422
Resurrection Christian S 600/K-12
6508 E Crossroads Blvd 80538 970-612-0674
Allen Howlett, supt. Fax 612-0975
St. John the Evangelist S 300/PK-8
1730 W 12th St 80537 970-635-5830
Dr. Sara Amodio, prin.

Lyons, Boulder, Pop. 1,624
St. Vrain Valley SD RE-1J
Supt. — See Longmont
Lyons ES 200/PK-5
PO Box 559 80540 303-823-6915
Christa Keppler, prin. Fax 823-6959

Mc Clave, Bent, Pop. 150
McClave SD RE-2 300/PK-12
PO Box 1 81057 719-829-4517
Terry Webber, supt. Fax 829-4430
www.mcclaveschools.org/
Mc Clave ES 100/PK-6
PO Box 1 81057 719-829-4517
Terry Webber, prin. Fax 829-4430

Manassa, Conejos, Pop. 1,024
North Conejos SD RE-1J
Supt. — See La Jara
Manassa ES 300/K-5
PO Box 430 81141 719-843-5277
Denny Fringer, prin. Fax 843-5080

Mancos, Montezuma, Pop. 1,183
Mancos SD RE-6 400/PK-12
395 Grand Ave 81328 970-533-7748
Brian Hanson, supt. Fax 533-7954
www.mancosre6.edu
Mancos ES 200/PK-5
301 Grand Ave 81328 970-533-7744
Jeanette Allen, prin. Fax 533-1165
Mancos MS 100/6-8
100 S Beech St 81328 970-533-9143
Laura Harper, prin. Fax 533-1463

Manitou Springs, El Paso, Pop. 5,039
Manitou Springs SD 14 1,400/PK-12
405 El Monte Pl 80829 719-685-2024
Roy Crawford, supt. Fax 685-4536
www.mssd14.org/
Manitou Springs ES 400/PK-5
110 Pawnee Ave 80829 719-685-2195
Russ Vogel, prin. Fax 685-2185
Manitou Springs MS 300/6-8
415 El Monte Pl 80829 719-685-2127
Steve Paterson, prin. Fax 685-4552
Other Schools – See Chipita Park

Manzanola, Otero, Pop. 496
Manzanola SD 3J 200/K-12
PO Box 148 81058 719-462-5527
Todd Werner, supt. Fax 462-5708
www.manzanola.k12.co.us/
Manzanola ES 100/K-6
PO Box 148 81058 719-462-5578
Glen Bradshaw, prin. Fax 462-5708

Maybell, Moffat, Pop. 100
Moffat County SD RE-1
Supt. — See Craig
Maybell ES 50/1-4
PO Box 9 81640 970-272-3266
Julie Baker, prin. Fax 272-3267

Mead, Weld, Pop. 2,663
St. Vrain Valley SD RE-1J
Supt. — See Longmont
Mead ES 500/K-5
520 Welker Ave 80542 970-535-4488
Connie Brodt, prin. Fax 535-4648
Mead MS 300/6-8
620 Welker Ave 80542 970-535-4446
Joshua Barnett, prin. Fax 535-4434

Meeker, Rio Blanco, Pop. 2,222
Meeker SD RE-1 700/PK-12
PO Box 1089 81641 970-878-9040
Dan Evig, supt. Fax 878-3682
www.meeker.k12.co.us
Barone MS 100/6-8
PO Box 690 81641 970-878-9060
Jim Hanks, prin. Fax 878-4291
Meeker ES 400/PK-5
PO Box 988 81641 970-878-9050
Jason Hightower, prin. Fax 878-0016

Merino, Logan, Pop. 279
Merino SD RE-4J 300/K-12
PO Box 198 80741 970-522-7424
Nathan Lightle, supt. Fax 522-1541
www.merino-sd.schoolfusion.us/
Merino ES 200/K-6
PO Box 198 80741 970-522-7229
Kyle Stumpf, prin. Fax 522-2547

Milliken, Weld, Pop. 5,593
Weld County SD RE-5J 2,400/K-12
110 Centennial Dr Ste A 80543 970-587-6050
Dr. Marti Foster, supt. Fax 587-2607
www.weldre5j.k12.co.us
Milliken ES 400/K-5
100 Broad St 80543 970-587-6200
Paul Dillehay, prin. Fax 587-2855
Milliken MS 500/6-8
PO Box 339 80543 970-587-6300
Trevor Long, prin. Fax 587-5749
Other Schools – See Johnstown

Minturn, Eagle, Pop. 1,097
Eagle County SD RE-50
Supt. — See Eagle
Minturn MS 200/6-8
PO Box 280 81645 970-328-2920
Toni Boush, prin. Fax 827-5805

Moffat, Saguache, Pop. 121
Moffat SD 2 100/PK-12
PO Box 428 81143 719-256-4710
Charles Warren, supt. Fax 256-4730
www.moffat.k12.co.us

Moffat MS 50/6-8
PO Box 428 81143 719-256-4710
Michelle Hashbarger, prin. Fax 256-4730
Moffat S 100/PK-5
PO Box 428 81143 719-256-4710
Michelle Hashbarger, prin. Fax 256-4730

Monte Vista, Rio Grande, Pop. 4,212
Monte Vista SD C-8 1,100/PK-12
345 E Prospect Ave 81144 719-852-5996
Dwayne Newman, supt. Fax 852-6184
www.monte.k12.co.us
Marsh ES 200/PK-1
215 Lyell St 81144 719-852-3231
Kristin Steed, prin. Fax 852-5870
Metz ES 300/2-5
545 2nd Ave 81144 719-852-4041
Gesine Skaggs, prin. Fax 852-6196
Monte Vista MS 200/6-8
3720 Sherman Ave 81144 719-852-5984
Philip Trejo, prin. Fax 852-6199

Sargent SD RE-33J 400/K-12
7090 N County Road 2 E 81144 719-852-4023
Lauren Sheldrake, supt. Fax 852-9890
www.sargent.k12.co.us
Sargent ES 200/K-6
7090 N County Road 2 E 81144 719-852-4024
Laura Kelso, prin. Fax 852-0399

St. Peter Lutheran S 50/K-8
330 Faraday St 81144 719-852-5449
Linda Navo, prin.

Montrose, Montrose, Pop. 15,479
Montrose County SD RE-1J 6,000/PK-12
PO Box 10000 81402 970-249-7726
Dr. George Voorhis, supt. Fax 249-7173
www.mcsd.org
Centennial MS 500/6-8
PO Box 10000 81402 970-249-2576
Nancy Alex, prin. Fax 240-6461
Columbine MS 500/6-8
PO Box 10000 81402 970-249-2581
Ben Stephenson, prin. Fax 240-6404
Cottonwood ES 500/K-5
PO Box 10000 81402 970-249-2539
Russell Tomlin, prin. Fax 240-6407
ECC 200/PK-PK
PO Box 10000 81402 970-249-5858
Cathy Crane, dir. Fax 249-7537
Johnson ES 500/K-5
PO Box 10000 81402 970-249-2584
Laura Burris, prin. Fax 240-6408
Northside ES 400/K-5
PO Box 10000 81402 970-249-2554
Cara Godbe, prin. Fax 240-6403
Oak Grove ES 400/K-5
PO Box 10000 81402 970-249-6867
Laurel Pascoe, prin. Fax 240-6409
Pomona ES 500/K-5
PO Box 10000 81402 970-249-2514
Don Davidson, prin. Fax 240-6406
Other Schools – See Olathe

Colorado West Christian S 200/K-10
2705 Sunnyside Rd 81401 970-249-1094
Raymond Fell, admin. Fax 249-7988
Spring Creek Christian S 50/K-8
14488 6175 Rd, 970-249-5500

Monument, El Paso, Pop. 2,508
Lewis-Palmer SD 38 5,300/PK-12
PO Box 40 80132 719-488-4700
Raymond Blanch, supt. Fax 488-5951
www.lewispalmer.org
Best ES 500/PK-5
66 Jefferson St 80132 719-488-4770
Peggy Parsley, prin. Fax 488-4774
Creekside MS 700/6-8
1330 Creekside Dr 80132 719-481-1099
Caryn Collette, prin. Fax 481-0681
Lewis-Palmer ES 500/PK-5
1315 Lake Woodmoor Dr 80132 719-488-4750
Lois Skaggs, prin. Fax 488-4752
Lewis-Palmer MS 600/6-8
1776 Woodmoor Dr 80132 719-488-4776
Terry Miller, prin. Fax 488-4780
Prairie Winds ES 400/PK-5
790 E Kings Deer Pt 80132 719-559-0800
Aileen Finnegan, prin. Fax 559-0805
Other Schools – See Colorado Springs, Palmer Lake

Hope & Andrews Montsr Acad - North 100/PK-6
18075 Minglewood Trl 80132 719-488-8723
Norman Deeba, prin. Fax 488-1310
St. Peters Catholic S 100/PK-3
PO Box 827 80132 719-481-1855
Peggy McFarland, prin. Fax 481-9606

Morrison, Jefferson, Pop. 410
Jefferson County SD R-1
Supt. — See Golden
Kendallvue ES 500/PK-6
13658 W Marlowe Ave 80465 303-982-7990
Marc Nestorick, prin. Fax 982-7991
Red Rocks ES 300/PK-6
17199 Highway 74 80465 303-982-8063
Wanda Hamilton, prin. Fax 982-8064

Silver State Baptist S 200/PK-12
PO Box 463 80465 303-922-8850
Daniel Brock, admin. Fax 922-4573

Mosca, Alamosa, Pop. 180
Sangre De Cristo SD RE-22J 300/PK-12
PO Box 145 81146 719-378-2321
Lynn Howard, supt. Fax 378-2327
www.sangreschools.org/
Other Schools – See Hooper

Naturita, Montrose, Pop. 665
West End SD RE-2 300/PK-12
PO Box 190 81422 970-865-2290
Gary Gazaway, supt. Fax 865-2573
www.westendschools.org
Naturita ES 200/PK-6
PO Box 400 81422 970-865-2204
Mike Epright, prin. Fax 865-2850

Nederland, Boulder, Pop. 1,337
Boulder Valley SD RE-2
Supt. — See Boulder
Nederland ES 300/PK-5
1 Sundown Trl 80466 303-258-7092
Debra Benitez, prin. Fax 258-8696

New Castle, Garfield, Pop. 3,017
Garfield SD RE-2
Supt. — See Rifle
Elk Creek ES K-4
804 Main Dr 81647 970-665-7800
Carrie Close, prin. Fax 665-7846
Riverside MS 5-8
215 Alder Ave 81647 970-665-7800
Lacey Moser, prin. Fax 665-7846
Senor ES 500/PK-4
PO Box 950 81647 970-665-7700
Dave Lindenberg, prin. Fax 665-7722

New Raymer, Weld, Pop. 109
Prairie SD RE-11 200/PK-12
PO Box 68 80742 970-437-5351
R. Joe Kimmel, supt. Fax 437-5732
www.prairieschool.org/
Prairie ES 100/PK-6
PO Box 68 80742 970-437-5351
Rick Price, prin. Fax 437-5732

Niwot, Boulder, Pop. 2,666

Shepherd Valley Waldorf S 100/PK-8
6500 Dry Creek Pkwy 80503 303-652-0130
Linda Abelkis, admin. Fax 652-0133

Northglenn, Adams, Pop. 32,906
Adams 12 Five Star SD
Supt. — See Thornton
Hillcrest ES 400/K-5
10335 Croke Dr 80260 720-972-5380
Tanya Garcia, prin. Fax 972-5399
Hulstrom Options S 600/K-8
11551 Wyco Dr 80233 720-972-5400
Kym LeBlanc, prin. Fax 972-5419
Leroy Drive ES 400/PK-5
1451 Leroy Dr 80233 720-972-5460
Jill Roth, prin. Fax 972-5479
Malley Drive ES 300/K-5
1300 Malley Dr 80233 720-972-5480
Anne Wesley, prin. Fax 972-5499
Northglenn MS 700/6-8
1123 Muriel Dr 80233 720-972-5080
Paula Redig, prin. Fax 972-5119
North Mor ES 500/PK-5
9580 Damon Dr 80260 720-972-5540
Betsy Miller, prin. Fax 972-5559
Studio S K-2
10604 Grant Dr 80233 720-972-3620
Roberta Mantione, prin. Fax 972-3719
Stukey ES 500/K-5
11080 Grant Dr 80233 720-972-5420
Jacob Murphey, prin. Fax 972-5439
Westview ES 500/PK-5
1300 Roseanna Dr 80234 720-972-5680
Amy Bruce, prin. Fax 972-5699

Community Christian S 300/K-12
11980 Irma Dr 80233 303-452-7514
John Reynolds, admin. Fax 452-4904
Gethsemane Lutheran S 200/PK-8
10675 Washington St 80233 303-451-6908
David Meineke, prin. Fax 451-1067
Lord of Life Lutheran S 100/PK-8
11700 Irma Dr 80233 303-452-3656
Joshua Glowicki, prin. Fax 920-9591

Norwood, San Miguel, Pop. 460
Norwood SD R-2J 200/PK-12
PO Box 448 81423 970-327-4336
David Crews, supt. Fax 327-4116
www.norwoodpublicschoolr2-jt.com
Norwood S 100/PK-8
PO Box 448 81423 970-327-4336
James Hoffman, prin. Fax 327-4116

Oak Creek, Routt, Pop. 797
South Routt SD RE-3 400/PK-12
PO Box 158 80467 970-736-2313
Scott Mader, supt. Fax 736-2458
www.southroutt.k12.co.us
Soroco MS 100/6-8
PO Box 158 80467 970-736-8531
Dennis Alt, prin. Fax 736-0182
South Routt Early Learning Center 50/PK-PK
PO Box 187 80467 970-736-2434
Lisa Constine, prin. Fax 736-8246
Other Schools – See Yampa

Olathe, Montrose, Pop. 1,679
Montrose County SD RE-1J
Supt. — See Montrose
Olathe ES 500/K-5
211 North Roberts 81425 970-252-7940
Joe Brummitt, prin. Fax 323-6339
Olathe MS 300/6-8
410 Highway 50 81425 970-252-7950
Scot Brown, prin. Fax 323-5947

Ordway, Crowley, Pop. 1,178
Crowley County SD RE-1-J 500/K-12
PO Box 338 81063 719-267-3117
John McCleary, supt. Fax 267-3130
www.cck12.net/
Crowley County ES 200/K-5
PO Box 338 81063 719-267-3558
Pam Arbuthnot, prin. Fax 267-4195
Crowley County MS 100/6-8
PO Box 338 81063 719-267-9880
Jim Trainor, prin. Fax 267-9881

Otis, Washington, Pop. 512
Lone Star SD 101 100/K-12
44940 County Road 54 80743 970-848-2778
Laurie Kjosness, supt. Fax 848-0340
www.lonestar.k12.co.us/
Lone Star ES 50/K-6
44940 County Road 54 80743 970-848-2778
Laurie Kjosness, prin. Fax 848-0340

Otis SD R-3 200/PK-12
518 Dungan St 80743 970-246-3413
Jeff Durbin, supt. Fax 246-0518
www.osdco.com
Otis ES 100/PK-6
518 Dungan St 80743 970-246-3366
Michael Warren, prin. Fax 246-0518

Ouray, Ouray, Pop. 877
Ouray SD R-1 300/PK-12
PO Box N 81427 970-325-4505
Sandy Kern, supt. Fax 325-7343
www.ouray.k12.co.us/
Ouray ES 100/PK-6
PO Box N 81427 970-325-4505
Tim Finkbeiner, prin. Fax 325-7343
Ouray MS 50/7-8
PO Box N 81427 970-325-4505
Tim Finkbeiner, prin. Fax 325-7343

Ovid, Sedgwick, Pop. 316
Platte Valley SD RE-3 100/PK-12
PO Box 369 80744 970-463-5414
William Pile, supt. Fax 463-5493
www.plattevsd.k12.co.us/
Other Schools – See Sedgwick

Pagosa Springs, Archuleta, Pop. 1,628
Archuleta SD 50 JT 1,700/K-12
PO Box 1498 81147 970-264-2228
Mark DeVoti, supt. Fax 264-4631
www.pagosa.k12.co.us
Pagosa Springs ES 600/K-4
PO Box 1498 81147 970-264-2229
Kate Lister, prin. Fax 264-4871
Pagosa Springs IS 200/5-6
PO Box 1498 81147 970-264-2256
Lisa Hudson, prin. Fax 264-2257
Pagosa Springs JHS 300/7-8
PO Box 1498 81147 970-264-2794
Chris Hinger, prin. Fax 264-6112

Our Savior Lutheran S 100/PK-4
56 Meadows Dr 81147 970-731-5910
Fax 731-4668
Pagosa Springs SDA S 50/K-8
40 Oren Rd 81147 970-731-1005
Kathy Goley, prin.

Palisade, Mesa, Pop. 2,683
Mesa County Valley SD 51
Supt. — See Grand Junction
Taylor ES 400/PK-5
689 Brentwood Dr 81526 970-254-4870
Corey Hafey, prin. Fax 464-7503

Palmer Lake, El Paso, Pop. 2,271
Lewis-Palmer SD 38
Supt. — See Monument
Palmer Lake ES 300/PK-5
PO Box 10 80133 719-488-4760
Julie Jadomski, prin. Fax 488-4764

Paonia, Delta, Pop. 1,584
Delta County SD 50(J)
Supt. — See Delta
Paonia ES 300/K-6
PO Box 1179 81428 970-527-3639
Greg Figenser, prin. Fax 527-3339

Parachute, Garfield, Pop. 1,094
Garfield County SD 16 1,100/PK-12
PO Box 68 81635 970-285-5701
Ken Haptonstall, supt. Fax 285-5711
www.garcoschools.org
Grand Valley ECC 200/PK-K
PO Box 68 81635 970-285-5702
Rebecca Ruland, prin. Fax 285-5712
L.W. St. John MS 200/6-8
PO Box 68 81635 970-285-5704
Scott Pankow, prin. Fax 285-5714
Underwood ES 400/1-5
PO Box 68 81635 970-285-5703
Brian Berg, prin. Fax 285-5713

Parker, Douglas, Pop. 38,428
Douglas County SD RE-1
Supt. — See Castle Rock
Cherokee Trail ES 700/PK-6
17302 Clarke Farms Dr 80134 303-387-8125
Regina Renaldi, prin. Fax 387-8126
Cimarron MS 7-8
22219 Hilltop Dr 80138 303-387-4500
Karen Tarbell, prin. Fax 387-4501
Frontier Valley ES 700/PK-6
23919 Canterberry Pkwy 80138 303-387-8475
Pam McEwen, prin. Fax 387-8476
Gold Rush ES K-6
12021 S Swift Fox Way 80134 303-387-0708
Patty Hanrahan, prin. Fax 805-1014
Iron Horse ES 700/PK-6
20151 Tallman Dr 80138 303-387-8525
Steve Getchell, prin. Fax 387-8526
Legacy Point ES 500/K-6
12736 Red Rosa Cir 80134 303-387-8725
Sheila Beving, prin. Fax 387-8726

Mammoth Heights ES PK-6
9500 Stonegate Pkwy 80134 303-387-8925
David Ray, prin. Fax 387-8926
Mountain View ES 600/K-3
8502 E Pinery Pkwy 80134 303-387-8675
Nancy Wortmann, prin. Fax 387-8676
Northeast ES 500/4-6
6598 N Highway 83 80134 303-387-8600
Darren Knox, prin. Fax 387-8601
Pine Grove ES 700/K-6
10450 Stonegate Pkwy 80134 303-387-8075
Dave Minter, prin. Fax 387-8076
Pine Lane IS 600/4-6
6485 E Ponderosa Dr 80138 303-387-8275
Jean Bartlett, prin. Fax 387-8276
Pine Lane PS 800/PK-3
6475 E Ponderosa Dr 80138 303-387-8325
Ginny Reed, prin. Fax 387-8326
Pioneer ES 700/PK-6
10881 Riva Ridge St 80138 303-387-8400
Tim Krabacher, prin. Fax 387-8401
Prairie Crossing ES 700/PK-6
11605 S Bradbury Ranch Dr 80134 303-387-8200
Tom McDowell, prin. Fax 387-8201
Sagewood MS 1,100/7-8
4725 Fox Sparrow Rd 80134 303-387-4300
Ralph Montgomery, prin. Fax 387-4301
Sierra MS 1,200/7-8
6651 E Pine Ln 80138 303-387-3800
Michelle Davis, prin. Fax 387-3801

Elizabeth SD C-1
Supt. — See Elizabeth
Singing Hills ES 400/PK-5
41012 Madrid Dr 80138 303-646-1858
Danelle Hiatt, prin. Fax 841-9732

Ave Maria S 500/PK-8
9056 E Parker Rd 80138 720-842-5400
Erlene Madsen, prin. Fax 842-5402
Parker Montessori S 200/PK-3
10750 Victorian Dr 80138 303-841-4325
Anitha Harshan, dir. Fax 841-5878
Southeast Christian S 700/PK-8
9650 Jordan Rd 80134 303-841-5988
Dr. Vern Walters, hdmstr. Fax 831-9594

Peetz, Logan, Pop. 225
Plateau SD RE-5 100/PK-12
PO Box 39 80747 970-334-2435
Dean Koester, supt. Fax 334-2360
www.plateau.k12.co.us/
Peetz S 100/PK-8
PO Box 39 80747 970-334-2361
Robert Long, prin. Fax 334-2360

Penrose, Fremont, Pop. 2,235
Florence SD RE-2
Supt. — See Florence
Penrose ES 300/K-5
100 Illinois St 81240 719-372-6777
Judy Blackwell, prin. Fax 372-0719

Peyton, El Paso, Pop. 200
Falcon SD 49
Supt. — See Falcon
Falcon MS 600/7-8
9755 Towner Ave 80831 719-495-5232
Robert Felice, prin. Fax 495-5237

Peyton SD 23 JT 700/PK-12
13990 Bradshaw Rd 80831 719-749-2330
Tim Kistler, supt. Fax 749-2368
www.peyton.k12.co.us/
Peyton ES 300/PK-5
13550 Bradshaw Rd 80831 719-749-0170
Michael Auclaire, prin. Fax 749-0060
Peyton MS 200/6-8
18220 Main St 80831 719-749-2244
Brian Rea, prin. Fax 749-2567

Pierce, Weld, Pop. 872
Ault-Highland SD RE-9
Supt. — See Ault
Highland ES 400/K-5
PO Box 39 80650 970-834-2853
Bev Menke, prin. Fax 834-1294

Pine, Jefferson, Pop. 600
Jefferson County SD R-1
Supt. — See Golden
Elk Creek ES 400/K-5
13304 US Highway 285 80470 303-982-2900
Joann Marion, prin. Fax 982-2901

Platteville, Weld, Pop. 2,598
Weld County SD RE-1
Supt. — See Gilcrest
Platteville ES, PO Box 427 80651 400/PK-5
Dan Barney, prin. 970-785-2271
South Valley MS 200/6-8
1004 Main St 80651 970-785-2205
Jeff Angus, prin. Fax 785-2180

Pleasant View, Montezuma
Montezuma-Cortez SD RE-1
Supt. — See Cortez
Pleasant View ES 50/K-5
PO Box 329 81331 970-562-2491
Dan Porter, prin. Fax 562-4287

Pritchett, Baca, Pop. 124
Pritchett SD RE-3 100/PK-12
PO Box 7 81064 719-523-4045
Stephanie Hund, supt. Fax 523-6991
Pritchett ES 50/PK-5
PO Box 7 81064 719-523-4045
Stephanie Hund, prin. Fax 523-6991
Pritchett JHS 50/6-8
PO Box 7 81064 719-523-4045
Stephanie Hund, prin. Fax 523-6991

Pueblo, Pueblo, Pop. 103,495
Hanover SD 28
Supt. — See Colorado Springs
Prairie Heights ES K-5
7930 Indian Village Hts 81008 719-382-1260
Mike Ferguson, prin. Fax 382-9589

Pueblo CSD 60 16,000/PK-12
315 W 11th St 81003 719-549-7100
Dr. John Covington, supt. Fax 549-7112
pueblocityschools.us/
Baca ES 200/PK-5
2800 E 17th St 81001 719-549-7530
Rosa Saenz, prin. Fax 583-1943
Belmont ES 500/PK-5
31 MacNaughton Rd 81001 719-549-7500
Stephanie Smith, prin. Fax 545-2956
Bessemer Academy 500/PK-8
1125 E Routt Ave 81004 719-549-7505
Karen Ortiz, prin. Fax 545-2997
Beulah Heights ES 300/PK-5
2670 Delphinium St 81005 719-549-7510
Gina Gallegos, prin. Fax 564-3257
Bradford ES 300/PK-5
107 S La Crosse Ave 81001 719-549-7515
Sandra Alvarez, prin. Fax 544-7639
Carlile ES 300/PK-5
736 W Evans Ave 81004 719-549-7520
Elaine Madrid, prin. Fax 549-7990
Columbian ES 300/PK-5
1203 Palmer Ave 81004 719-549-7525
Cindy Muckel, prin. Fax 545-0439
Corwin International Magnet MS 300/4-8
1500 Lakeview Ave 81004 719-549-7400
Julie Shue, prin. Fax 564-2773
Fountain International Magnet ES 200/PK-3
925 N Glendale Ave 81001 719-549-7535
Aida Andrews, prin. Fax 562-0417
Franklin ES 500/PK-5
1315 Horseshoe Dr 81001 719-549-7540
Keith Johnson, prin. Fax 562-0428
Freed MS 500/6-8
715 W 20th St 81003 719-549-7410
Danielle Romero, prin. Fax 562-0816
Goodnight S 600/PK-8
624 Windy Way 81005 719-549-7545
Marne Milyard, prin. Fax 560-9323
Haaff ES 400/PK-5
15 Chinook Ln 81001 719-549-7550
Rhonda Holcomb, prin. Fax 562-0433
Heaton MS 700/6-8
6 Adair Rd 81001 719-549-7420
Tharyn Mulberry, prin. Fax 549-7838
Hellbeck ES 300/PK-5
3000 Lakeview Ave 81005 719-549-7555
Jackie Henderson, prin. Fax 566-0953
Heritage ES 400/PK-5
625 Brown Ave 81004 719-549-7575
Alan Berry, prin. Fax 583-0240
Highland Park ES 500/PK-5
2701 Vinewood Ln 81005 719-549-7560
Ted Johnson, prin. Fax 564-3282
Irving ES 400/K-5
1629 W 21st St 81003 719-549-7570
Joseph Caruselle, prin. Fax 543-5329
Minnequa ES 300/PK-5
1708 E Orman Ave 81004 719-549-7580
Twila Jessen, prin. Fax 564-3423
Morton ES 500/PK-5
1900 W 31st St 81008 719-549-7585
Floyd Gallegos, prin. Fax 595-4200
Park View ES 400/PK-5
1327 E 9th St 81001 719-549-7590
Sheila Perez, prin. Fax 562-0673
Pitts MS 600/6-8
29 Lehigh Ave 81005 719-549-7430
John Huff, prin. Fax 549-7878
Risley MS 400/6-8
625 N Monument Ave 81001 719-549-7440
Rena Jimenez, prin. Fax 549-7926
Roncalli MS 700/6-8
4202 W State Highway 78 81005 719-549-7450
Bradley Farbo, prin. Fax 549-7469
Somerlid ES 300/PK-5
2717 West St 81003 719-549-7595
Doug Ferguson, prin. Fax 583-0756
South Park ES 400/PK-5
3100 Hollywood Dr 81005 719-549-7600
Cary Palumbo, prin. Fax 564-3447
Spann ES 300/PK-5
2300 E 10th St 81001 719-253-6115
Carrie Cook, prin. Fax 544-3604
Sunset Park ES 500/PK-5
110 University Cir 81005 719-549-7610
John Hull, prin. Fax 566-1759

Pueblo County SD 70 8,300/PK-12
24951 E US Highway 50 81006 719-542-0220
Daniel Lere Ed.D., supt. Fax 542-0225
www.district70.org/
North Mesa ES 400/PK-5
28881 Gale Rd 81006 719-948-3303
Jeff Howes, prin. Fax 948-0178
Pleasant View MS 400/6-8
23600 Everett Rd 81006 719-542-7813
Ted Shepard, prin. Fax 545-6291
Sierra Vista ES 600/PK-5
500 S Spaulding Ave 81007 719-547-2878
Merry Martin, prin. Fax 547-2920
South Mesa ES 300/PK-5
23701 Preston Rd 81006 719-543-6444
Manuel Calderon, prin. Fax 545-6191
Vineland ES 300/PK-5
35777 Iris Rd 81006 719-948-3331
Laurie Stratman, prin. Fax 948-0179
Vineland MS 300/6-8
1132 36th Ln 81006 719-948-3336
Laurie Stratman, prin. Fax 948-2323
Other Schools – See Avondale, Beulah, Colorado City, Pueblo West, Rye

---

Daystar Christian S 50/1-8
3912 Oneal Ave 81005 719-561-9120
McClelland S 200/PK-8
415 E Abriendo Ave 81004 719-543-5271
Edward Mercer, hdmstr. Fax 584-2793
Park Hill Christian Academy 100/PK-12
PO Box 8147 81008 719-544-6174
St. John Neuman Catholic S 200/PK-8
2415 E Orman Ave 81004 719-561-9419
Joyce Anderson, admin. Fax 561-4718
St. Therese Catholic S 200/PK-8
320 Goodnight Ave 81004 719-561-1121
John Brainard, prin. Fax 561-2252
Trinity Evangelical Lutheran S 200/K-8
701 W Evans Ave 81004 719-542-1864
Fax 542-1864

Pueblo West, Pueblo, Pop. 4,386
Pueblo County SD 70
Supt. — See Pueblo
Cedar Ridge ES 300/PK-5
1267 W Oro Grande Dr 81007 719-547-8268
Marty Rahl, prin. Fax 547-8310
Desert Sage ES 500/PK-5
935 S Palomar Dr 81007 719-647-8878
Robin Reinstema, prin. Fax 647-9034
Prairie Winds ES 400/PK-5
579 E Earl Dr 81007 719-647-9732
Stephanie Russell, prin. Fax 647-9730
Pueblo West ES 400/PK-5
386 E Hahns Peak Ave 81007 719-547-2191
Cheryl Vincent, prin. Fax 547-0677
Pueblo West MS 500/6-8
484 S Maher Dr 81007 719-547-3752
Terri Tafoya, prin. Fax 547-0499
Sky View MS 600/6-8
1047 S Camino De Bravo 81007 719-547-1175
Robert DiPietro, prin. Fax 647-9667

Pueblo West Christian Academy 100/PK-3
434 S Conquistador Ave 81007 719-647-2868
Joy Cress, dir. Fax 547-0320

Rangely, Rio Blanco, Pop. 2,038
Rangely SD RE-4 500/PK-12
550 River Rd 81648 970-675-2207
Dwayne Newman, supt. Fax 675-5143
www.rangelyk12.org/
Parkview ES 200/PK-5
609 S Stanolind Ave 81648 970-675-2267
Mary Lansing, prin. Fax 675-5032
Rangely MS 100/6-8
550 River Rd 81648 970-675-5021
Dwayne Newman, prin. Fax 675-5143

Red Feather Lakes, Larimer, Pop. 200
Poudre SD R-1
Supt. — See Fort Collins
Red Feather Lakes ES 50/K-5
505 N County Road 73C 80545 970-488-6550
Patrick Kind, prin. Fax 488-6552

Rico, Dolores, Pop. 225
Dolores County SD RE-2J
Supt. — See Dove Creek
Rico ES, PO Box 250 81332 50/K-6
Ty Gray, prin. 970-967-3540

Ridgway, Ouray, Pop. 752
Ridgway SD R-2 300/PK-12
1115 Clinton St 81432 970-626-4320
Douglas Bissonette, supt. Fax 626-4337
www.ridgway.k12.co.us/
Ridgway ES 200/PK-5
1115 Clinton St 81432 970-626-5468
Mary DeZeeuw, prin. Fax 626-5597
Ridgway MS 100/6-8
1200 Green St 81432 970-626-5788
Emma Brockman, prin. Fax 626-3249

Rifle, Garfield, Pop. 8,038
Garfield SD RE-2 3,400/PK-12
839 Whiteriver Ave 81650 970-665-7600
David Smucker, supt. Fax 665-7623
www.garfieldre2.k12.co.us
Graham Mesa ES 100/K-4
1575 Farmstead Pkwy 81650 970-665-7500
Shawnda Zahara-Harris, prin.
Highland ES 500/K-4
1500 E 7th St 81650 970-665-6800
Allan Dillon, prin. Fax 665-6801
Rifle MS 700/5-8
753 Railroad Ave 81650 970-665-7900
Shane Bostic, prin. Fax 665-7930
Wamsley ES 500/PK-4
225 E 30th St 81650 970-665-7950
Desha Bierbaum, prin. Fax 665-7985
Other Schools – See New Castle, Silt

Rocky Ford, Otero, Pop. 4,121
Rocky Ford SD R-2 800/PK-12
601 S 8th St 81067 719-254-7423
Nancy Aschermann, supt. Fax 254-7425
www.rockyford.k12.co.us/
Jefferson MS 200/6-8
901 S 11th St 81067 719-254-7669
Monica Johnson, prin. Fax 254-4307
Liberty ES 200/3-5
608 N 11th St 81067 719-254-7851
Toni Cook, prin. Fax 254-7862
Washington PS 200/PK-2
709 S 11th St 81067 719-254-7681
Roxann Hall, prin. Fax 254-7789

Rush, El Paso, Pop. 100
Miami-Yoder SD 60 JT 300/PK-12
420 S Rush Rd 80833 719-478-2186
Rick Walter, supt. Fax 478-2205
www.miamiyoder.org

Miami-Yoder ES 200/PK-5
420 S Rush Rd 80833 719-478-2186
Sharon Webb, prin. Fax 478-5380

Rye, Pueblo, Pop. 205
Pueblo County SD 70
Supt. — See Pueblo
Rye ES 300/PK-5
PO Box 220 81069 719-489-2272
Sue Moore, prin. Fax 489-2275

Saguache, Saguache, Pop. 606
Mountain Valley SD RE-1 100/PK-12
PO Box 127 81149 719-655-0268
Corey Doss, supt. Fax 655-0269
www.valley.k12.co.us
Mountain Valley ES 100/PK-5
PO Box 127 81149 719-655-2578
John Stephens, prin. Fax 655-2875
Mountain Valley MS 50/6-8
PO Box 127 81149 719-655-2578
John Stephens, prin. Fax 655-2875

Salida, Chaffee, Pop. 5,476
Salida SD R-32 1,100/K-12
310 E 9th St 81201 719-530-5252
John Rouse, supt. Fax 539-6220
www.salida.k12.co.us/
Longfellow ES 400/K-4
350 W 8th St 81201 719-530-5260
Dan Estell, prin. Fax 539-5072
Salida MS 300/5-8
520 Milford St 81201 719-530-5300
Rose Ley, prin. Fax 530-5364

Salida Christian S 200/PK-8
PO Box 923 81201 719-539-1693
Treva Dominguez, dir. Fax 539-1693

Sanford, Conejos, Pop. 802
Sanford SD 6J 300/PK-12
PO Box 39 81151 719-274-5167
Kevin Edgar, supt. Fax 274-5830
sanford.co.schoolwebpages.com/
Sanford ES 200/PK-6
PO Box 39 81151 719-274-5167
Luella Crowther, prin. Fax 274-5830

San Luis, Costilla, Pop. 697
Centennial SD R-1 200/PK-12
PO Box 350 81152 719-672-3322
Emily Romero, supt. Fax 672-3345
www.centennialsd.org/
Centennial ES, PO Box 350 81152 100/PK-6
David Judd, prin. 719-672-3322
Centennial JHS, PO Box 350 81152 50/7-8
David Judd, prin. 719-672-3322

Sedalia, Douglas, Pop. 400
Douglas County SD RE-1
Supt. — See Castle Rock
Sedalia ES 300/PK-6
5449 Huxtable St 80135 303-387-5500
Robin Stranahan, prin. Fax 387-5501

Sedgwick, Sedgwick, Pop. 174
Platte Valley SD RE-3
Supt. — See Ovid
Platte Valley ES 100/PK-6
PO Box 128 80749 970-463-5650
Sharon Green, prin. Fax 463-9925

Sheridan, Arapahoe, Pop. 5,483
Sheridan SD 2 1,600/PK-12
4000 S Lowell Blvd 80110 720-833-6617
Michael Clough, supt. Fax 833-6617
www.sheridank12.org
Sheridan MS 400/6-8
4107 S Federal Blvd 80110 720-833-6988
William Wooddell, prin. Fax 833-6903
Terry ES 300/K-2
4485 S Irving St 80110 720-833-6990
Lyn Bajaj, prin. Fax 833-6698
Other Schools – See Denver

Sheridan Lake, Kiowa, Pop. 61
Plainview SD RE-2 100/K-12
13997 County Road 71 81071 719-729-3331
Garry Coulter, supt. Fax 727-4471
www.plainview.k12.co.us/
Plainview ES 50/K-5
13997 County Road 71 81071 719-729-3331
Garry Coulter, prin. Fax 727-4471

Silt, Garfield, Pop. 2,260
Garfield SD RE-2
Supt. — See Rifle
Cactus Valley ES PK-5
222 Grand Ave 81652 970-665-7850
Lisa Whitmore, prin. Fax 665-7884

Silverthorne, Summit, Pop. 3,610
Summit SD RE-1
Supt. — See Frisco
Silverthorne ES 300/K-5
PO Box 1039 80498 970-468-6700
Dianna Hulbert, prin. Fax 262-1419

Silverton, San Juan, Pop. 548
Silverton SD 1 50/K-12
PO Box 128 81433 970-387-5543
Kim White, supt. Fax 387-5791
www.silvertonschool.org
Silverton ES 50/K-5
PO Box 128 81433 970-387-5543
Kim White, prin. Fax 387-5791

Simla, Elbert, Pop. 728
Big Sandy SD 100J 200/K-12
PO Box 68 80835 719-541-2292
Steve Wilson, supt. Fax 541-2186
bigsandy.ppboces.org
Simla ES 100/K-5
PO Box 68 80835 719-541-2291
Greg Mitchell, prin. Fax 541-2443

Springfield, Baca, Pop. 1,363
Springfield SD RE-4 300/PK-12
389 Tipton St 81073 719-523-6654
Michael Page, supt. Fax 523-4192
www.springfield.k12.co.us/
Springfield ES 200/PK-6
389 Tipton St 81073 719-523-4391
Michael Page, prin. Fax 523-4192
Springfield JHS 50/7-8
389 Tipton St 81073 719-523-6522
Richard Hargrove, prin. Fax 523-4361

Steamboat Springs, Routt, Pop. 9,354
Steamboat Springs SD RE-2 2,000/K-12
PO Box 774368 80477 970-879-1530
Shalee Cunningham, supt. Fax 879-3943
www.sssd.k12.co.us
Soda Creek ES 400/K-5
PO Box 774368 80477 970-879-0652
Judy Harris, prin. Fax 879-7834
Steamboat Springs MS 500/6-8
PO Box 774368 80477 970-879-1058
Tim Bishop, prin. Fax 870-0368
Strawberry Park ES 500/K-5
PO Box 774368 80477 970-879-7550
Michele Miller, prin. Fax 879-6217

Christian Heritage S 100/K-12
27285 Brandon Cir 80487 970-879-1760
Tim Calkins, prin. Fax 879-5511
Whiteman PS 100/K-8
PO Box 770723 80477 970-879-8081
Nancy Spillane, hdmstr. Fax 879-9332

Sterling, Logan, Pop. 12,589
Valley SD RE-1 2,000/PK-12
301 Hagen St 80751 970-522-0792
Dr. Betty Summers, supt. Fax 522-0525
www.re1valleyschools.org/
Ayres ES 200/K-2
1812 Robin Rd 80751 970-522-1409
Susan Sonnenberg, prin. Fax 522-5908
Campbell ES 300/3-5
902 Clark St 80751 970-522-2514
Dianna Chrisman, prin. Fax 522-2516
Hagen Early Education Center 100/PK-PK
301 Hagen St 80751 970-522-0432
Georgia Sanders, coord. Fax 522-5439
Sterling MS 500/6-8
1177 Pawnee Ave 80751 970-522-1041
Robert Hall, prin. Fax 522-0209
Other Schools – See Iliff

St. Anthony S 200/PK-8
324 S 3rd St 80751 970-522-7567
Joseph Skerjanec, prin. Fax 522-6442

Strasburg, Adams, Pop. 1,200
Strasburg SD 31J 900/PK-12
PO Box 207 80136 303-622-9211
Dr. David VanSant, supt. Fax 622-9224
www.strasburg31j.com
Hemphill MS, PO Box 207 80136 200/6-8
Larry Deffenbaugh, prin. 303-622-9213
Strasburg ES 500/PK-5
PO Box 207 80136 303-622-9215
Joanne Brummel, prin. Fax 622-4891

Stratton, Kit Carson, Pop. 626
Stratton SD R-4 200/PK-12
219 Illinois Ave 80836 719-348-5369
Eric Moser, supt. Fax 348-5555
www.strattonschools.org
Stratton ES 100/PK-5
6 Main St 80836 719-348-5521
Steven Sanchez, prin. Fax 348-5555
Stratton MS 50/6-8
219 Illinois Ave 80836 719-348-5369
Steven Sanchez, prin. Fax 348-5555

Superior, Boulder, Pop. 10,308
Boulder Valley SD RE-2
Supt. — See Boulder
Eldorado S 1,000/K-8
3351 S Indiana St 80027 720-561-4400
Robyn Hamasaki, prin. Fax 561-4401

Swink, Otero, Pop. 683
Swink SD 33 400/K-12
PO Box 487 81077 719-384-8103
Dr. Rocco Fuschetto, supt. Fax 384-5471
www.swink.k12.co.us/
Swink ES 200/K-6
PO Box 487 81077 719-384-8103
Randy Bohlander, prin. Fax 384-5471

Tabernash, Grand

Winter Park Christian S 100/1-12
PO Box 518 80478 970-887-9784
Ron Widdifield, prin. Fax 887-9785

Telluride, San Miguel, Pop. 2,303
Telluride SD R-1 700/PK-12
725 W Colorado Ave 81435 970-728-6617
Mary Rubadeau, supt. Fax 728-9490
www.tellurideschool.org
Telluride ES 400/PK-6
447 W Columbia Ave 81435 970-728-6615
Trish Scherner, prin. Fax 728-5035
Telluride MS 100/7-8
721 W Colorado Ave 81435 970-369-4719
Steve Smith, prin. Fax 728-0257

Telluride Mountain S 100/PK-12
200 San Miguel River Dr 81435 970-728-1969
Ernie Patterson, hdmstr. Fax 369-4412

Thornton, Adams, Pop. 105,182
Adams 12 Five Star SD 32,100/PK-12
1500 E 128th Ave 80241 720-972-4000
Dr. Mike Paskewicz, supt. Fax 972-4169
www.adams12.org
Century MS 1,000/6-8
13000 Lafayette St 80241 720-972-5240
Larry Pohlit, prin. Fax 972-5279
Cherry Drive ES 600/K-5
11500 Cherry Dr 80233 720-972-5300
David Knapp, prin. Fax 972-5319
Coronado Hills ES 500/PK-5
8300 Downing Dr 80229 720-972-5320
Barry Buck, prin. Fax 972-5339
Eagleview ES 600/K-5
4601 Summit Grove Pkwy 80241 720-972-5760
Frank Saponaro, prin. Fax 972-5779
Glacier Peak ES 600/K-5
12060 Jasmine St 80602 720-972-5940
Beau Foubert, prin. Fax 972-5999
Hunters Glen ES 700/K-5
13222 Corona St 80241 720-972-5440
Kathy Hatz, prin. Fax 972-5459
McElwain ES 400/PK-5
1020 Dawson Dr 80229 720-972-5500
Tammy Stewart, prin. Fax 972-5519
Niver Creek MS 800/6-8
9450 Pecos St 80260 720-972-5120
Jacque Kerr, prin. Fax 972-5159
North Star ES 500/PK-5
8740 Northstar Dr 80260 720-972-5560
Barb Stallings, prin. Fax 972-5579
Prairie Hills ES 400/K-5
13801 Garfield Pl 80602 720-972-8780
Kathy Hastings, prin. Fax 972-8800
Riverdale ES 500/PK-5
10724 Elm Dr 80233 720-972-5580
Terry Terrill, prin. Fax 972-5599
Rocky Top MS 900/6-8
14150 York St 80602 720-972-2200
Chelsea Behana, prin. Fax 972-2303
Shadow Ridge MS 1,300/6-8
12551 Holly St 80241 720-972-5040
Susie Wickham, prin. Fax 972-5079
Silver Creek ES 600/K-5
15101 Fillmore St 80602 720-972-3940
Judi Madsen, prin. Fax 972-3999
Skyview ES 600/PK-5
5021 E 123rd Ave 80241 720-972-5620
Jim Palmer, prin. Fax 972-5639
Stellar ES K-5
3901 E 124th Ave 80241 720-972-2340
Judi Dauman, prin. Fax 972-2399
Tarver ES 700/PK-5
3500 Summit Grove Pkwy 80241 720-972-5640
David Edinger, prin. Fax 972-5659
Thornton ES 600/PK-5
991 Eppinger Blvd 80229 720-972-5660
Carol Sorvig, prin. Fax 972-5679
Thornton MS 700/6-8
9451 Hoffman Way 80229 720-972-5160
Bobby Ortega, prin. Fax 972-5199
Woodglen ES 700/PK-5
11717 Madison St 80233 720-972-5700
Brett Drobney, prin. Fax 972-5719
Other Schools – See Broomfield, Federal Heights, Northglenn, Westminster

Brighton SD 27J
Supt. — See Brighton
West Ridge ES K-5
13102 Monaco St 80602 720-685-5300
William Pierce, prin. Fax 685-5304

Mapleton SD 1
Supt. — See Denver
Achieve Academy at Bertha Heid 400/K-8
9100 Poze Blvd 80229 303-853-1300
Jim Hamilton, dir. Fax 853-1356
Clayton Partnership S 400/K-8
2410 Poze Blvd 80229 303-901-1595
Sue-Lin Toussaint, dir. Fax 853-1496
Highland Montessori S 100/PK-6
8990 York St 80229 303-853-1700
Rhonda Ronczka, dir. Fax 853-1726

Timnath, Larimer, Pop. 214
Poudre SD R-1
Supt. — See Fort Collins
Bethke ES K-5
5100 School House Dr 80547 970-488-4300
Ann Alfonso, prin. Fax 488-4302
Timnath ES 500/K-5
PO Box 10 80547 970-488-6825
Ron Bowen, prin. Fax 488-6827

Trinidad, Las Animas, Pop. 9,077
Trinidad SD 1 1,600/PK-12
215 S Maple St 81082 719-846-3324
Mike Tranter, supt. Fax 846-2957
www.trinidad.k12.co.us/
Eckhart ES 400/PK-1
1021 Pierce St 81082 719-846-6995
Linda Covington, prin. Fax 846-2775
Fisher's Peak ES 400/2-5
900 Moores Canyon Rd 81082 719-846-2513
Shonie Pachelli, prin. Fax 846-2519
Trinidad MS 300/6-8
614 Park St 81082 719-846-4411
Deana Dunford, prin. Fax 846-4740

Grace Christian Center S 50/K-9
1001 Obregon St 81082 719-846-6133
Jean Griffis, prin.

USAF Academy, El Paso, Pop. 9,062
Academy SD 20
Supt. — See Colorado Springs
Douglass Valley ES 300/PK-5
4610 E Douglass Dr, 719-234-4200
Doug Piper, prin. Fax 234-4299

Vail, Eagle, Pop. 4,589
Eagle County SD RE-50
Supt. — See Eagle
Red Sandstone ES 200/PK-5
551 N Frontage Rd 81657 970-328-2910
Nancy Ricci, prin. Fax 476-4769

Vail Mountain S 400/K-12
3000 Booth Falls Rd 81657 970-476-3850
Peter Abuisi, prin. Fax 476-3860

Vilas, Baca, Pop. 100
Vilas SD RE-5 600/PK-12
PO Box 727 81087 719-523-6738
Joseph Shields, supt. Fax 523-4818
www.vilashi.com
Vilas ES 50/PK-6
PO Box 727 81087 719-523-6738
Dennis Hoyt, prin. Fax 523-4818

Vona, Kit Carson, Pop. 91
Hi-Plains SD R-23 100/PK-12
PO Box 9 80861 970-664-2636
Steven McCracken, supt. Fax 664-2283
www.hp-patriots.com/
Hi-Plains ES 100/PK-6
PO Box 9 80861 970-664-2636
Dale Oliver, prin. Fax 664-2283

Walden, Jackson, Pop. 646
North Park SD R-1 200/PK-12
PO Box 798 80480 970-723-3300
Jim Anderson, supt. Fax 723-8486
www.northpark.k12.co.us
Walden ES 100/PK-5
PO Box 798 80480 970-723-3300
Jim Anderson, prin. Fax 723-4417

Walsenburg, Huerfano, Pop. 3,946
Huerfano SD RE-1 500/PK-12
201 E 5th St 81089 719-738-1520
Michael Doyle, supt. Fax 738-3148
www.huerfano.k12.co.us/
Peakview ES 200/PK-7
375 W Pine St 81089 719-738-2190
Patricia Martinez, prin. Fax 738-5746
Other Schools – See Gardner

Walsh, Baca, Pop. 682
Walsh SD RE-1 200/PK-12
PO Box 68 81090 719-324-5632
Kyle Hebberd, supt. Fax 324-5426
www.walsheagles.com
Walsh ES 100/PK-6
PO Box 68 81090 719-324-5400
Kyle Hebberd, prin. Fax 324-5426

Weldona, Morgan, Pop. 325
Weldon Valley SD RE-20(J) 200/PK-12
911 North Ave 80653 970-645-2411
Robert Petterson, supt. Fax 645-2377
www.weldonvalley.org/
Weldon Valley ES 100/PK-6
911 North Ave 80653 970-645-2411
Fran Covelli, prin. Fax 645-2377
Weldon Valley JHS 50/7-8
911 North Ave 80653 970-645-2411
Fran Covelli, prin. Fax 645-2377

Wellington, Larimer, Pop. 3,469
Poudre SD R-1
Supt. — See Fort Collins
Eyestone ES 600/PK-5
PO Box 69 80549 970-488-8600
David Sobson, prin. Fax 488-8602
Rice ES K-5
7000 3rd St 80549 970-488-8700
Karen Koehn, prin. Fax 488-8702
Wellington MS 200/6-8
PO Box 440 80549 970-488-6600
Alicia Durand, prin. Fax 488-6602

Westcliffe, Custer, Pop. 456
Custer County SD 1 500/PK-12
PO Box 730 81252 719-783-2357
Lance Villers, supt. Fax 783-2334
www.ccbobcats.net
Custer County ES 200/PK-5
PO Box 730 81252 719-783-2291
Michael Norris, prin. Fax 783-4944
Custer County JHS 100/6-8
PO Box 730 81252 719-783-2291
Barb Jones, prin. Fax 783-4944

Westminster, Adams, Pop. 105,084
Adams 12 Five Star SD
Supt. — See Thornton
Arapahoe Ridge ES 600/K-5
13095 Pecos St 80234 720-972-5740
Trena Speirs, prin. Fax 972-5759
Cotton Creek ES 600/PK-5
11100 Vrain St 80031 720-972-5340
Bill Kempsell, prin. Fax 972-5355
Rocky Mountain ES 500/PK-5
3350 W 99th Ave 80031 720-972-5600
David Knapp, prin. Fax 972-5619
Silver Hills MS 700/6-8
12400 Huron St 80234 720-972-5000
Jami Miller, prin. Fax 972-5039

Adams County SD 50
Supt. — See Denver
ECC 300/PK-PK
8030 Irving St 80031 303-428-1560
Mathieu Aubuchon, prin. Fax 657-3846
Flynn ES 300/K-5
8731 Lowell Blvd 80031 303-428-2161
Anthony Matthews, prin. Fax 657-3843
Harris Park ES 300/K-5
4300 W 75th Ave 80030 303-428-1721
Chris Benisch, prin. Fax 657-3849
Mesa ES 300/K-5
9100 Lowell Blvd 80031 303-428-2891
Mike Nolan, prin. Fax 657-3856
Shaw Heights MS 700/6-8
8780 Circle Dr 80031 303-428-9533
Fax 650-6859
Sunset Ridge ES 300/K-5
9451 Hooker St 80031 303-426-8907
Roger Vadeen, prin. Fax 657-3874
Westminster ES 300/K-5
7482 Irving St 80030 303-428-2494
Lorynda Sampson, prin. Fax 657-3883

Jefferson County SD R-1
Supt. — See Golden
Adams ES 500/PK-6
6450 W 95th Pl 80021 303-982-9790
Brendan Feely, prin. Fax 982-9791
Carle MS 300/7-8
10200 W 100th Ave 80021 303-982-9070
Greg Bushey, prin. Fax 982-9071
Lukas ES 500/K-6
9650 W 97th Ave 80021 303-982-0368
Jef Fugita, prin. Fax 982-0369
Mandalay MS 400/7-8
9651 Pierce St 80021 303-982-9802
John Schalk, prin. Fax 982-9813
Ryan ES 600/K-6
5851 W 115th Ave 80020 303-982-3105
Robin Techmanski, prin. Fax 982-3106
Semper ES 500/K-6
7575 W 96th Ave 80021 303-982-6460
Judy Lynn, prin. Fax 982-6461
Sheridan Green ES 400/K-6
10951 Harlan St 80020 303-982-3182
Kurt Freeman, prin. Fax 982-3183
Witt ES 300/PK-6
10255 W 104th Dr 80021 303-982-3380
Christine Mayer, prin. Fax 982-3381
Zerger ES 300/K-6
9050 Field St 80021 303-982-1075
Tria Dassler, prin. Fax 982-1074

Belleview Christian S 300/PK-12
3455 W 83rd Ave 80031 303-427-5459
Dr. Peggy Polson, prin. Fax 426-6768
Devereux Cleo Wallace 100/3-12
8405 Church Ranch Blvd 80021 303-466-7391
Dana Dosik, prin. Fax 466-0904
Holy Trinity S 300/PK-8
3050 W 76th Ave 80030 303-427-5632
David Baker, prin. Fax 427-4125
Hyland Christian S 100/K-12
5255 W 98th Ave 80020 303-466-1673
LIFE Christian Academy 200/PK-12
11500 Sheridan Blvd 80020 303-438-1260
Kenneth Walsh, supt. Fax 438-1866
Shepherd of the Valley S 100/PK-8
8820 Field St 80021 303-424-1306
Matthew Foley, prin. Fax 996-2995

Weston, Las Animas, Pop. 200
Primero RSD RE-2 200/PK-12
20200 State Highway 12 81091 719-868-2715
Gerald Gabbard, supt. Fax 868-2241
www.primeroschool.org/
Primero ES 100/PK-5
20200 State Highway 12 81091 719-868-2715
Bill Naccarato, prin. Fax 868-2241

Wheat Ridge, Jefferson, Pop. 31,242
Jefferson County SD R-1
Supt. — See Golden
Anderson Preschool 100/PK-PK
10801 W 44th Ave 80033 303-982-1740
Fax 982-1742
Everitt MS 500/7-8
3900 Kipling St 80033 303-982-1580
Steve Wiersma, prin. Fax 982-1581
Kullerstrand ES 300/K-6
12225 W 38th Ave 80033 303-982-1780
Bill Blandon, prin. Fax 982-1782
Martensen ES 200/PK-6
6625 W 45th Pl 80033 303-982-1870
Rhonda Hatch-Rivera, prin. Fax 982-1871
Pennington ES 200/PK-6
4645 Independence St 80033 303-982-2083
Matt Cormier, prin. Fax 982-2082
Prospect Valley ES 500/K-6
3400 Pierson St 80033 303-982-7535
Brenda Carlson, prin. Fax 982-7536
Stevens ES 400/K-6
4001 Reed St 80033 303-982-2198
Marie Norby-Loud, prin. Fax 982-2163
Wheat Ridge MS 400/7-8
7101 W 38th Ave 80033 303-982-2833
Joan Chavez, prin. Fax 982-2834
Wilmore-Davis ES 300/K-6
7975 W 41st Ave 80033 303-982-2890
Jeff Gomez, prin. Fax 982-2891

Beth Eden Baptist S 200/K-12
2600 Wadsworth Blvd 80033 303-232-2313
Fax 233-3027
Foothills Academy 200/PK-12
4725 Miller St 80033 303-431-0920
Mary Lou Faddick, hdmstr. Fax 431-9505
SS. Peter & Paul S 400/PK-8
3920 Pierce St 80033 303-424-0402
Kathleen Byrnes, prin. Fax 456-1888

Wiggins, Morgan, Pop. 951
Wiggins SD RE-50(J) 600/PK-12
320 Chapman St 80654 970-483-7762
Dr. Sharol Little, supt. Fax 483-6205
www.wiggins50.k12.co.us/
Wiggins ES 300/PK-5
415 Main St 80654 970-483-7784
Gary Bruntz, prin. Fax 483-7227

Wiley, Prowers, Pop. 476
Wiley SD RE-13 JT 200/PK-12
PO Box 247 81092 719-829-4806
Randy Holmen, supt. Fax 829-4422
www.wiley.k12.co.us
Wiley S 200/PK-12
PO Box 247 81092 719-829-4806
Curtis Turner, prin. Fax 829-4805

Windsor, Weld, Pop. 14,874
Weld County SD RE-4 3,400/PK-12
PO Box 609 80550 970-686-8000
Karen Trusler, supt. Fax 686-5280
www.weldre4.k12.co.us/
Grandview ES 400/PK-5
1583 Grand Ave 80550 970-686-8600
David Grubbs, prin. Fax 686-8601
Mountain View ES 400/3-5
810 3rd St 80550 970-686-8300
Dan Cox, prin. Fax 686-5262
Severance MS 6-8
1801 Avery Plaza St 80550 970-674-5200
Jay Tapia, prin.
Skyview ES 400/PK-5
1000 Stone Mountain Dr 80550 970-686-8500
Tammy Seib, prin. Fax 686-5232
Tozer PS 500/PK-2
501 Oak St 80550 970-686-8400
Shelly Prenger, prin. Fax 686-0866
Windsor MS 800/6-8
900 Main St 80550 970-686-8200
Douglas Englert, prin. Fax 686-7122

Woodland Park, Teller, Pop. 6,660
Woodland Park SD RE-2 3,000/PK-12
PO Box 99 80866 719-686-2000
Guy Arseneau, supt. Fax 687-8408
www.wpsdk12.org/
Columbine ES 400/PK-5
PO Box 6700 80866 719-686-2300
Cris Gammill, prin. Fax 687-8473
Gateway ES 300/PK-5
PO Box 6670 80866 719-686-2051
KayLynn Waddell, prin. Fax 687-8475
Woodland Park MS 700/6-8
PO Box 6790 80866 719-686-2200
John Jamison, prin. Fax 687-8458
Other Schools – See Divide

Colorado Springs Christian S 100/K-8
1003 Tamarac Pkwy 80863 719-686-0706
Diane Hathaway, prin. Fax 686-0081

Woodrow, Washington, Pop. 20
Woodlin SD R-104 100/PK-12
PO Box 185 80757 970-386-2223
Rose Cronk, supt. Fax 386-2241
www.woodlinschool.com
Woodlin ES 100/PK-6
PO Box 185 80757 970-386-2223
Rose Cronk, prin. Fax 386-2241

Wray, Yuma, Pop. 2,147
Wray SD RD-2 700/PK-12
30222 County Road 35 80758 970-332-5764
Ron Howard, supt. Fax 332-5773
www.wrayschools.org
Buchanan MS 200/5-8
620 W 7th St 80758 970-332-4723
Jennifer Witzel, prin. Fax 332-3356
Wray ES 300/PK-4
30204 County Road 35 80758 970-332-4347
Gregory Fruhwirth, prin. Fax 332-5408

Yampa, Routt, Pop. 416
South Routt SD RE-3
Supt. — See Oak Creek
South Routt ES 200/K-5
PO Box 97 80483 970-638-4558
Michael Young, prin. Fax 638-4530

Yoder, El Paso, Pop. 40
Edison SD 54 JT 100/PK-12
14550 Edison Rd 80864 719-478-2125
David Grosche, supt. Fax 478-3000
www.edison54jt.org
Edison ES 50/PK-5
14550 Edison Rd 80864 719-478-2125
Rachel Paul, prin. Fax 478-3000

Yuma, Yuma, Pop. 3,231
Yuma SD 1 900/PK-12
PO Box 327 80759 970-848-5831
Dennis Veal, supt. Fax 848-2256
www.yumaschools.org
Little Indians Preschool 100/PK-PK
709 W 3rd Ave 80759 970-848-4572
Tiffany Roundtree, dir. Fax 848-4291
Morris ES 300/K-8
416 S Elm St 80759 970-848-5738
Donna Fields, prin. Fax 848-5400
Yuma MS 200/5-8
500 S Elm St 80759 970-848-2000
Donna Fields, prin. Fax 848-4261

CONNECTICUT

CONNECTICUT DEPARTMENT OF EDUCATION
PO Box 2219, Hartford 06145-2219
Telephone 860-713-6500
Fax 860-713-7001
Website http://www.state.ct.us/sde

Commissioner of Education Mark McQuillan

CONNECTICUT BOARD OF EDUCATION
165 Capitol Ave, Hartford 06106-1630

Chairperson Allan Taylor

REGIONAL EDUCATIONAL SERVICE CENTERS

Area Coop. Educational Services RESC
Craig Edmondson Ed.D., dir. 203-498-6800
350 State St, North Haven 06473 Fax 498-6890
www.aces.org

Capitol Region Education Council RESC
Dr. Bruce Douglas, dir. 860-524-4063
111 Charter Oak Ave Fax 548-9924
Hartford 06106
www.crec.org

Cooperative Educational Services RESC
Evan Pitkoff, dir. 203-365-8803
40 Lindeman Dr, Trumbull 06611 Fax 365-8804
www.ces.k12.ct.us

Eastconn RESC
Paula Colen, dir. 860-455-0707
376 Hartford Tpke, Hampton 06247 Fax 455-0691
www.eastconn.org

Education Connection RESC
Danuta Thibodeau Ph.D., dir. 860-567-0863
PO Box 909, Litchfield 06759 Fax 567-3381
www.educationconnection.org

Learn RESC
Virginia Seccombe, dir. 860-434-4800
44 Hatchetts Hill Rd Fax 434-4837
Old Lyme 06371
www.learn.k12.ct.us

PUBLIC, PRIVATE AND CATHOLIC ELEMENTARY SCHOOLS

Andover, Tolland
Andover SD 300/PK-6
35 School Rd 06232 860-742-7339
Andrew Maneggia, supt. Fax 742-8288
www.andoverelementary.com
Andover ES 300/PK-6
35 School Rd 06232 860-742-7339
Dr. David Griffin, prin. Fax 742-8288

Ansonia, New Haven, Pop. 18,744
Ansonia SD 2,400/K-12
42 Grove St 06401 203-736-5095
Carol Merlone, supt. Fax 736-5098
www.ansonia.org
Ansonia MS 400/7-8
115 Howard Ave 06401 203-736-5070
Lynn Bennett-Wallick, prin. Fax 736-1044
Mead ES 600/K-6
75 Ford St 06401 203-736-5090
Terri Goldson, prin. Fax 736-1042
Prendergast ES 700/K-6
59 Finney St 06401 203-736-5080
Lawrence DiPalma, prin. Fax 736-1045

Assumption S 300/PK-8
51 N Cliff St 06401 203-734-0855
Kathleen Molner, prin. Fax 734-5521

Ashford, Windham
Ashford SD 500/PK-8
440 Westford Rd 06278 860-429-1927
Arthur Breault, supt. Fax 429-3651
www.ashfordct.org/
Ashford S 500/PK-8
440 Westford Rd 06278 860-429-6419
Nancy Johndrow, prin. Fax 429-3651

Avon, Hartford
Avon SD 3,500/PK-12
34 Simsbury Rd 06001 860-404-4700
David Erwin, supt. Fax 404-4702
www.avon.k12.ct.us
Avon MS 600/7-8
375 W Avon Rd 06001 860-404-4770
Marco Famiglietti, prin. Fax 404-4773
Pine Grove ES 600/K-4
151 Scoville Rd 06001 860-404-4790
Gail Dahling-Hench, prin. Fax 404-4793
Roaring Brook ES 800/PK-4
30 Old Wheeler Ln 06001 860-404-4810
Crisanne Colgan, prin. Fax 404-4813
Thompson Brook S 600/5-6
150 Thompson Rd 06001 860-404-4870
Anne Watson, prin. Fax 404-4873

Capitol Region Education Council RESC
Supt. — See Hartford
Reggio Magnet School of the Arts PK-5
150 Fisher Dr 06001 860-674-8549
Kerri-Lynn Faselle, prin.

Farmington Valley Academy Montessori 100/PK-8
150 Fisher Dr 06001 860-677-2403
Sharon Healy, prin. Fax 215-4638

Baltic, New London
Sprague SD 300/PK-8
25 Scotland Rd 06330 860-822-8264
Edmund Senesac Ed.D., supt. Fax 822-1347
www.saylesschool.org
Sayles S 300/PK-8
25 Scotland Rd 06330 860-822-8264
Jean Wierzbinski, prin. Fax 822-1347

St. Joseph S 100/PK-8
10 School Hill Rd 06330 860-822-6141
Sr. Mary Mulready, prin. Fax 842-1479

Barkhamsted, Litchfield
Barkhamsted SD 300/PK-6
65 Ripley Hill Rd 06063 860-379-2729
Jeff Linton, supt. Fax 379-4412
www.barkhamstedschool.org
Barkhamsted ES 300/PK-6
65 Ripley Hill Rd 06063 860-379-2729
Joanne Sciola, prin. Fax 379-4412

Beacon Falls, New Haven
Regional SD 16
Supt. — See Prospect
Laurel Ledge ES 500/PK-5
30 Highland Ave 06403 203-729-5355
Regina Murzak, prin. Fax 729-7349

Berlin, Hartford
Berlin SD 3,300/PK-12
238 Kensington Rd 06037 860-828-6581
Dr. Michael Cicchetti, supt. Fax 829-0832
www.berlinschools.org
McGee MS 800/6-8
899 Norton Rd 06037 860-828-0323
Brian Benigni, prin. Fax 828-0676
Willard ES 600/PK-5
1088 Norton Rd 06037 860-828-4151
Salvatore Urso, prin. Fax 828-4178
Other Schools – See East Berlin, Kensington

St. Paul S 300/PK-8
461 Alling St 06037 860-828-4343
Robert Biancamano, prin. Fax 828-1226

Bethany, New Haven
Bethany SD 600/PK-6
44 Peck Rd 06524 203-393-3350
Timothy Connellan, supt. Fax 393-0239
www.bethany-ed.org
Bethany Community ES 600/PK-6
44 Peck Rd 06524 203-393-3350
Mary Federico, prin. Fax 393-3849

Regional SD 5
Supt. — See Woodbridge
Amity Regional MS 400/7-8
190 Luke Hill Rd 06524 203-393-3102
Richard Dellinger, prin. Fax 393-0583

Bethel, Fairfield, Pop. 8,835
Bethel SD 3,200/PK-12
PO Box 253 06801 203-794-8601
Gary Chesley, supt. Fax 794-8723
www.bethel.k12.ct.us
Berry ES 500/PK-3
200 Whittlesey Dr 06801 203-794-8680
Kristen Brooks, prin. Fax 794-8783
Bethel MS 800/6-8
600 Whittlesey Dr 06801 203-794-8663
Kevin Smith, prin. Fax 830-7318
Johnson ES 500/4-5
500 Whittlesey Dr 06801 203-794-8700
Kathleen Gombos, prin. Fax 794-8716
Rockwell ES 400/K-3
400 Whittlesey Dr 06801 203-794-8688
Brian Kirmil, prin. Fax 794-8687

St. Mary S 200/K-8
24 Dodgingtown Rd 06801 203-744-2922
Sr. Anne McCarthy, prin. Fax 798-8803

Bethlehem, Litchfield
Regional SD 14
Supt. — See Woodbury
Bethlehem ES 200/K-2
92 East St 06751 203-266-7506
Melinda McKenna, prin. Fax 266-7876

Bloomfield, Hartford, Pop. 7,200
Bloomfield SD 2,200/PK-12
1133 Blue Hills Ave 06002 860-769-4200
David Title, supt. Fax 769-4215
www.bloomfieldschools.org/
Arace IS 300/5-6
390 Park Ave 06002 860-286-2626
Tracy Youngberg, prin. Fax 242-8939
Arace MS 400/7-8
390 Park Ave 06002 860-286-2622
Trevor Ellis, prin. Fax 242-0347
Laurel ES 300/K-4
1 Filley St 06002 860-286-2675
Jill Naraine, prin. Fax 769-5517
Metacomet ES 300/K-4
185 School St 06002 860-286-2660
Paul Guzzo, prin. Fax 769-5296
Vincent ES 300/PK-4
11 Turkey Hill Rd 06002 860-286-2640
Sheila Way, prin. Fax 769-5512
Wintonbury Early Childhood Magnet School PK-K
44 Brown St 06002 860-769-4200
Jenna Tenore, prin.

Sigel Hebrew Academy 100/PK-8
53 Gabb Rd 06002 860-243-8333
Rabbi Mordechai Weiss, prin. Fax 243-3986

Bolton, Tolland
Bolton SD 900/K-12
108 Notch Rd 06043 860-643-1569
Mark Winzler, supt. Fax 647-8452
www.boltonpublicschools.com/
Bolton Center S 600/K-8
108 Notch Rd 06043 860-643-2411
Mary Grande, prin. Fax 646-4860

Holy Seed Christian Academy 50/K-8
104 Notch Rd 06043 860-533-9483
Henrietta Creighton, admin. Fax 649-8391

Bozrah, New London, Pop. 2,297
Bozrah SD 300/PK-8
PO Box 185 06334 860-887-2561
Mary Lou Bargnesi Ph.D., supt. Fax 889-2715
www.bozrah.org
Fields Memorial S 300/PK-8
PO Box 185 06334 860-887-2561
Karen Scopino, prin. Fax 889-2715

Branford, New Haven, Pop. 27,603
Branford SD 3,600/PK-12
1111 Main St 06405 203-488-7276
Dr. Kathleen Halligan, supt. Fax 315-3505
www.branford.k12.ct.us

Indian Neck Preschool 100/PK-PK
12 Melrose Ave 06405 203-315-3540
Dr. Dianibel Aviles, prin. Fax 315-4143
Murphy ES 400/K-4
14 Brushy Plain Rd 06405 203-483-1832
Anthony Buono, prin. Fax 483-5189
Sliney ES 400/K-4
23 Eades St 06405 203-481-5386
Kathleen Higgins, prin. Fax 483-0749
Tisko ES 500/K-4
118 Damascus Rd 06405 203-483-1826
Mark Rabinowitz, prin. Fax 483-7528
Walsh IS 1,100/5-8
185 Damascus Rd 06405 203-488-8317
Robin Goeler, prin. Fax 481-2785

Pine Brook S 100/PK-6
56 Stony Creek Rd 06405 203-481-0363
Christine Aulicino Ph.D., prin. Fax 488-3985
St. Mary S 200/PK-8
62 Cedar St 06405 203-488-8386
Donna Binkowski, prin. Fax 488-2347

Bridgeport, Fairfield, Pop. 139,008
Bridgeport SD 19,400/PK-12
45 Lyon Ter Rm 203 06604 203-275-1000
John Ramos Ed.D., supt. Fax 337-0150
www.bridgeportedu.com
Barnum S 300/PK-8
495 Waterview Ave 06608 203-275-2300
Lourdes Delgado, prin. Fax 275-2302
Batalla S PK-8
606 Howard Ave 06605 203-579-8500
Hector Sanchez, prin. Fax 337-0196
Beardsley ES 600/PK-6
500 Huntington Rd 06610 203-576-7184
Amy Marshall, prin. Fax 576-8078
Blackham S 1,100/PK-8
425 Thorme St 06606 203-576-7951
Anne Engelson, prin. Fax 365-8330
Black Rock ES 300/K-6
545 Brewster St 06605 203-576-7500
Danuta Bristol, prin. Fax 339-8856
Bryant ES 400/PK-6
230 Poplar St 06605 203-576-7303
Gladys Walker-Jones, prin. Fax 330-2442
Classical Studies Academy 400/K-6
240 Linwood Ave 06604 203-576-7188
Helen Giles, prin. Fax 337-0195
Columbus S 800/PK-8
160 Iranistan Ave 06604 203-275-2100
Manuel Rocha, prin. Fax 576-7195
Cross S 400/K-8
1775 Reservoir Ave 06606 203-576-7553
Dyrene Meekins, prin. Fax 337-0136
Curiale S 700/K-8
300 Laurel Ave 06605 203-576-8437
Audrey Skoda, prin. Fax 576-7565
Dunbar S 500/K-8
445 Union Ave 06607 203-576-7194
Fax 337-0112
Edison ES 400/PK-6
115 Boston Ter 06610 203-275-2253
Donna Falat, prin. Fax 337-2534
Hall ES 300/K-6
290 Clermont Ave 06610 203-576-7560
Veronica Thomas, prin. Fax 337-0166
Hallen ES 400/PK-6
68 Omega Ave 06606 203-576-8216
Lucille Sekara, prin. Fax 339-8828
High Horizons Magnet S 400/K-8
700 Palisade Ave 06610 203-576-7807
Melissa Jenkins, prin. Fax 337-0178
Hooker S 500/K-8
138 Roger Williams Rd 06610 203-576-7185
Andrew Cimmino, prin. Fax 576-7517
Johnson S PK-8
475 Lexington Ave 06604 203-275-2500
Marlene Roberts, prin. Fax 337-0191
Longfellow S 500/PK-8
139 Ocean Ter 06605 203-576-8036
James Adams, prin. Fax 337-0184
Madison ES 700/K-6
376 Wayne St 06606 203-576-7186
Giovanna DeNitto, prin. Fax 337-0180
Marin S 900/PK-8
479 Helen St 06608 203-576-8202
Steven Douglas, prin. Fax 337-0183
Multicultural Magnet S 500/K-8
700 Palisade Ave 06610 203-576-7505
Helen Moran, prin. Fax 337-0184
Park City Magnet S 500/PK-8
1526 Chopsey Hill Rd 06606 203-576-7547
Alana Callahan, prin. Fax 337-0186
Read S 900/PK-8
130 Ezra St 06606 203-576-8030
Sandra McLeod, prin. Fax 337-0187
Roosevelt S 800/PK-8
680 Park Ave 06604 203-576-8032
Carmen Perez-Dickson, prin. Fax 576-7085
Tisdale S PK-8
250 Hollister Ave 06607 203-275-2089
William Rice, prin. Fax 337-0108
Waltersville S 400/PK-8
150 Hallett St 06608 203-275-2401
Ann de Bernard, prin. Fax 330-5935
Winthrop S 800/K-8
85 Eckart St 06606 203-576-7769
Randolph Dixon, prin. Fax 337-0192

Fairfield County SDA S 50/K-8
827 Trumbull Ave 06606 203-374-3203
J. Sargeant, prin. Fax 374-3203
St. Ambrose S 300/PK-8
461 Mill Hill Ave 06610 203-368-2835
Margaret Carabelli, prin. Fax 366-0599
St. Andrew S 200/K-8
395 Anton St 06606 203-373-1552
Maria O'Neill, prin. Fax 396-0378
St. Ann S 200/PK-8
521 Brewster St 06605 203-334-5856
Theresa Tillinger, prin. Fax 333-8263
St. Augustine Cathedral S 200/PK-8
63 Pequonnock St 06604 203-366-6500
Mary Daley, prin. Fax 366-6505
St. Peter S 200/K-8
659 Beechwood Ave 06605 203-333-2048
Suzanna Zello, prin. Fax 333-2878
St. Raphael S 200/PK-8
324 Frank St 06604 203-333-6818
Sr. Veronica Beato, prin. Fax 336-9205

Bridgewater, Litchfield
Regional SD 12
Supt. — See Washington Depot
Burnham ES 100/K-5
80 Main St S 06752 860-354-5559
Cathy Colella, prin. Fax 350-1597

Bristol, Hartford, Pop. 61,353
Bristol SD 8,900/PK-12
PO Box 450 06011 860-584-7002
Philip Streifer Ph.D., supt. Fax 584-7611
www.bristol.k12.ct.us
Bingham ES 300/K-5
3 North St 06010 860-584-7807
Steven Bent, prin. Fax 584-7808
Chippins Hill MS 900/6-8
551 Peacedale St 06010 860-584-3881
Catherine Carbone, prin. Fax 584-4833
Edgewood ES 400/K-5
345 Mix St 06010 860-584-7828
Angela Rossbach, prin. Fax 584-7827
Greene-Hills ES 400/K-5
718 Pine St 06010 860-584-7822
P. Scott Gaudet, prin. Fax 314-4632
Hubbell ES 500/PK-5
90 W Washington St 06010 860-584-7842
Rochelle Schwartz, prin. Fax 584-7842
Ivy Drive ES 400/K-5
160 Ivy Dr 06010 860-584-7844
RoseAnn Vojtek, prin. Fax 584-3876
Jennings ES 400/K-5
291 Burlington Ave 06010 860-584-7804
Steven Woznicki, prin. Fax 314-4633
Memorial Boulevard MS 500/6-8
70 Memorial Blvd 06010 860-584-7882
Marciann Jones, prin. Fax 584-3889
Mountain View ES 400/PK-5
71 Vera Rd 06010 860-584-7726
Dennis Bieu, prin. Fax 314-4629
Northeast MS 600/6-8
530 Stevens St 06010 860-584-7839
Robert Garry, prin. Fax 584-7837
O'Connell ES 400/PK-5
120 Park St 06010 860-584-7815
Michael Audette, prin. Fax 584-7814
South Side ES 600/PK-5
Tuttle Rd 06010 860-584-7812
Gary Maynard, prin. Fax 584-7810
Stafford ES 400/PK-5
212 Louisiana Ave 06010 860-584-7824
Catherine Cassin, prin. Fax 314-4631

Immanuel Lutheran S 200/PK-8
154 Meadow St 06010 860-583-5631
Claire Neagley, prin. Fax 585-4785
St. Anthony S 200/PK-8
30 Pleasant St 06010 860-582-7874
Virginia Gore, prin. Fax 582-2440
St. Joseph S 300/PK-8
335 Center St 06010 860-582-8696
Mark Monnerat, prin. Fax 584-9907
St. Matthew S 300/PK-8
33 Welch Dr 06010 860-583-5214
Sr. Christina Joseph Dolan, prin. Fax 314-1541

Broad Brook, Hartford, Pop. 3,585
East Windsor SD
Supt. — See East Windsor
Broad Brook ES 600/PK-4
14 Rye St 06016 860-623-2433
Jeanne McCarroll, prin. Fax 623-0717
East Windsor MS 400/5-8
38 Main St 06016 860-623-4488
James Slattery, prin. Fax 654-1915

Brookfield, Fairfield
Brookfield SD 3,000/PK-12
PO Box 5194 06804 203-775-7620
Anthony Bivona, supt. Fax 740-9008
www.brookfield.k12.ct.us/
Center ES 400/PK-1
8 Obtuse Hill Rd 06804 203-775-7650
June Gordon, prin. Fax 775-7672
Huckleberry Hill ES 600/2-4
100 Candlewood Lake Rd 06804 203-775-7675
Sharon Beitel, prin. Fax 775-7684
Whisconier MS 1,000/5-8
17 W Whisconier Rd 06804 203-775-7710
Eugenia Slone, prin. Fax 775-7615

Christian Life Academy 100/PK-8
133 Junction Rd 06804 203-775-5191
Cheryl Jenkins, prin. Fax 775-5567
St. Joseph S 200/PK-8
5 Obtuse Hill Rd 06804 203-775-2774
Rosemarie Forte, prin. Fax 775-5810

Brooklyn, Windham
Brooklyn SD 1,000/PK-8
119 Gorman Rd 06234 860-774-9153
Louise Berry, supt. Fax 774-6938
www.brooklyn.ctschool.net
Brooklyn ES 600/PK-4
119 Gorman Rd 06234 860-774-7577
Fax 779-1162
Brooklyn MS 400/5-8
119 Gorman Rd 06234 860-774-9153
Alan Yanku, prin. Fax 774-6938

Burlington, Hartford
Regional SD 10 2,600/PK-12
24 Lyon Rd 06013 860-673-2538
Alan Beitman, supt. Fax 675-4976
www.region10ct.org
Har-Bur MS 700/5-8
26 Lyon Rd 06013 860-673-6163
Kenneth Platz, prin. Fax 673-3481
Lake Garda ES 600/PK-4
61 Monce Rd 06013 860-673-2511
Robert Choiniere, prin. Fax 673-3721
Other Schools – See Harwinton

Canaan, Litchfield, Pop. 1,194
North Canaan SD
Supt. — See Falls Village
North Canaan S 400/PK-8
PO Box 758 06018 860-824-5149
Rosemary Keilty, prin. Fax 824-4879

Canterbury, Windham
Canterbury SD 500/PK-8
45 Westminster Rd 06331 860-546-6950
Janet Tyler, supt. Fax 546-6423
www.canterburypublicschools.org/
Baldwin MS 300/5-8
45 Westminster Rd 06331 860-546-9421
Kathleen Boyhan-Maus, prin. Fax 546-6289
Canterbury ES 300/PK-4
67 Kitt Rd 06331 860-546-6744
A. Catherine Ferguson, prin. Fax 546-6742

Canton, Hartford
Canton SD
Supt. — See Collinsville
Cherry Brook PS 500/PK-3
4 Barbourtown Rd 06019 860-693-7721
Andrew Robbin, prin. Fax 693-7647

Centerbrook, Middlesex
Essex SD
Supt. — See Deep River
Essex ES 600/PK-6
108 Main St 06409 860-767-8215
Joanne Beekley, prin. Fax 767-1476

Chaplin, Windham
Chaplin SD 200/PK-6
304 Parish Hill Rd 06235 860-455-9306
Kenneth Henrici, supt. Fax 455-1263
www.chaplinschool.org
Chaplin ES 200/PK-6
240 Palmer Rd 06235 860-455-9593
Daniel White, prin. Fax 455-0742

Cheshire, New Haven, Pop. 25,684
Cheshire SD 5,200/PK-12
29 Main St 06410 203-250-2420
Greg Florio Ed.D., supt. Fax 250-2453
www.cheshire.k12.ct.us/
Chapman ES 300/1-6
38 Country Club Rd 06410 203-272-3591
Russell Hinckley, prin. Fax 271-9833
Darcey K 400/PK-K
1686 Waterbury Rd 06410 203-272-3577
Barbara Stern, prin. Fax 271-2554
Dodd MS 800/7-8
100 Park Pl 06410 203-272-3249
Jeffrey Solan, prin. Fax 250-7614
Doolittle ES 500/1-6
735 Cornwall Ave 06410 203-272-3549
Sharon Weirsman, prin. Fax 272-0546
Highland ES 900/1-6
490 Highland Ave 06410 203-272-0335
Beverly Scully, prin. Fax 272-9003
Norton ES 500/1-6
414 N Brooksvale Rd 06410 203-272-7283
Mary Karas, prin. Fax 250-0654

St. Bridget S 400/PK-8
171 Main St 06410 203-272-5860
Margaret Whalen, prin. Fax 271-7031

Chester, Middlesex, Pop. 1,563
Chester SD
Supt. — See Deep River
Chester ES 300/PK-6
23 Ridge Rd 06412 860-526-5797
Henry Stockmal, prin. Fax 526-3570

Clinton, Middlesex, Pop. 3,439
Clinton SD 2,100/PK-12
137B Glenwood Rd 06413 860-664-6500
Albert Coviello, supt. Fax 664-6580
www.clintonpublic.org
Eliot MS 500/6-8
69 Fairy Dell Rd 06413 860-664-6503
Linda Tucker, prin. Fax 664-6583
Joel ES 700/PK-3
137 Glenwood Rd 06413 860-664-6501
Jack Gedney, prin. Fax 664-6581
Pierson ES 300/4-5
75 E Main St 06413 860-664-6502
Angela Guarascio, prin. Fax 664-6582

Colchester, New London, Pop. 3,212
Colchester SD 3,200/PK-12
127 Norwich Ave Ste 202 06415 860-537-7260
Karen Loiselle, supt. Fax 537-1252
www.colchesterct.org/
Colchester ES 700/PK-2
315 Halls Hill Rd 06415 860-537-0717
Jacqueline Somberg, prin. Fax 537-6573
Jackter IS 700/3-5
215 Halls Hill Rd 06415 860-537-9421
Deborah Sandberg, prin. Fax 537-0349

Johnston MS 800/6-8
360 Norwich Ave 06415 860-537-2313
Christopher Bennett, prin. Fax 537-6391

Colebrook, Litchfield
Colebrook SD 100/K-6
PO Box 9 06021 860-379-2179
James Chittum, supt. Fax 379-9506
www.colebrookschool.org/
Colebrook Consolidated ES 100/K-6
PO Box 9 06021 860-379-2179
Elizabeth Driscoll, prin. Fax 379-9506

Collinsville, Hartford, Pop. 2,591
Canton SD 1,700/PK-12
4 Market St Ste 100 06019 860-693-7704
Kevin Case, supt. Fax 693-7706
www.cantonschools.org
Canton IS 400/4-6
39 Dyer Ave 06019 860-693-7717
Jordan Grossman, prin. Fax 693-7814
Canton MS 300/7-8
76 Simonds Ave 06019 860-693-7712
Joseph Scheideler, prin. Fax 693-7812
Other Schools – See Canton

Columbia, Tolland
Columbia SD 600/PK-8
PO Box 166 06237 860-228-8590
Dr. Richard Saddlemire, supt. Fax 228-7608
www.hwporter.org
Porter S 600/PK-8
PO Box 166 06237 860-228-9493
Francine Coss, prin. Fax 228-8592

Lighthouse Christian S 50/PK-PK
195 Route 6 06237 860-228-2891
Susan Granniss, dir. Fax 228-4090

Cos Cob, Fairfield
Greenwich SD
Supt. — See Greenwich
Cos Cob ES 400/K-5
300 E Putnam Ave 06807 203-869-4670
Kimberly Beck, prin. Fax 869-7640

Coventry, Tolland, Pop. 10,063
Coventry SD 2,000/K-12
1700 Main St 06238 860-742-7317
Donna Bernard, supt. Fax 742-4567
www.coventrypublicschools.org/
Coventry Grammar S 400/K-2
3453 Main St 06238 860-742-7313
Marybeth Moyer, prin. Fax 742-4555
Hale MS 500/6-8
1776 Main St 06238 860-742-7334
Michele Mullaly, prin. Fax 742-4565
Robertson IS 500/3-5
227 Cross St 06238 860-742-7341
David Petrone, prin. Fax 742-4582

Cromwell, Middlesex
Cromwell SD 2,000/PK-12
9 Mann Memorial Dr 06416 860-632-4830
Dr. Matt Bisceglia, supt. Fax 632-4865
www.cromwell.k12.ct.us/
Cromwell MS 500/6-8
6 Mann Memorial Dr 06416 860-632-4853
John Maloney, prin. Fax 632-4863
Stevens ES 500/PK-2
25 Court St 06416 860-632-4866
Lucille DiTunno, prin. Fax 632-4881
Woodside IS 500/3-5
30 Woodside Rd 06416 860-632-3564
Bo Ryan, prin. Fax 613-3970

Danbury, Fairfield, Pop. 78,736
Danbury SD 9,400/PK-12
63 Beaver Brook Rd 06810 203-797-4701
Sal Pascavella Ed.D., supt. Fax 830-6560
www.danbury.k12.ct.us
Broadview MS 1,100/6-8
72 Hospital Ave 06810 203-797-4861
Edward Robbs, prin. Fax 790-2856
Ellsworth Avenue ES 300/K-5
53 Ellsworth Ave 06810 203-797-4740
Anna Rocco, prin. Fax 830-6527
Great Plain ES 300/PK-5
10 Stadley Rough Rd 06811 203-797-4749
Keisha Smith, prin. Fax 830-6581
Hayestown Avenue ES 400/PK-5
42 Tamarack Ave 06811 203-797-4771
Laura Kaddis, prin. Fax 830-6505
King Street IS 300/3-5
151 S King St 06811 203-797-4761
Linda Schreiner, prin. Fax 830-6515
King Street PS 300/PK-2
151 S King St 06811 203-797-4744
Jackie Bacon, prin. Fax 830-6596
Mill Ridge IS 300/3-5
1 School Ridge Rd 06811 203-797-4722
Greg Scails, prin. Fax 830-6513
Mill Ridge PS 300/PK-2
49A High Ridge Rd 06811 203-797-4781
Mary Cronin, prin. Fax 830-6583
Morris Street ES 400/PK-5
28 Morris St 06810 203-797-4809
William Santarsiero, prin. Fax 830-6514
Park Avenue ES 400/K-5
82 Park Ave 06810 203-797-4763
David Krafick, prin. Fax 790-2608
Pembroke ES 300/PK-5
34 1/2 Pembroke Rd 06811 203-797-4751
Edie Thomas, prin. Fax 830-6585
Rogers Park MS 1,000/6-8
21 Memorial Dr 06810 203-797-4881
Patricia Joaquim, prin. Fax 790-2829
Shelter Rock ES 300/K-5
2 Crows Nest Ln 06810 203-797-4777
Julia Horne, prin. Fax 830-6586
South Street ES 300/K-5
129 South St 06810 203-797-4787
Marnie Schork, prin. Fax 830-6587
Stadley Rough ES 400/K-5
25 Karen Rd 06811 203-797-4773
Mary Johnson, prin. Fax 830-6520
Western CT Acad of International Studies K-5
201 University Blvd 06811 203-778-7462
Helena Nitowski, prin. Fax 778-7467

Hudson Country Montessori S 200/PK-8
44A Shelter Rock Rd 06810 203-744-8088
Mark Meyer, admin. Fax 748-3403
Immanuel Lutheran S 100/PK-8
18 Clapboard Ridge Rd 06811 203-748-7823
Nate Palkewick, prin. Fax 748-5022
Sacred Heart S 100/K-8
17 Cottage St 06810 203-792-6194
Mary McCormack, prin. Fax 778-4025
St. Gregory the Great S 300/PK-8
85 Great Plain Rd 06811 203-748-1217
Sr. Mary O'Rourke, prin. Fax 778-0414
St. Joseph S 300/K-8
370 Main St 06810 203-748-6615
Gerianne O'Rourke, prin. Fax 748-6508
St. Peter S 100/PK-8
98 Main St 06810 203-748-2895
Mary McCormack, prin. Fax 748-5684
Wooster S 300/K-12
91 Miry Brook Rd 06810 203-830-3900
Timothy Golding, hdmstr. Fax 790-7147

Danielson, Windham, Pop. 4,285
Killingly SD 2,700/K-12
PO Box 210 06239 860-779-6600
William Silver, supt. Fax 779-3798
www.killingly.k12.ct.us
Killingly Memorial S 600/K-4
339 Main St 06239 860-779-6680
Marilyn Oat, prin. Fax 774-6028
Other Schools – See Dayville

St. James S 200/PK-8
120 Water St 06239 860-774-3281
Cheryl Veilleux, prin. Fax 779-2137

Darien, Fairfield, Pop. 18,130
Darien SD 4,600/K-12
PO Box 1167 06820 203-656-7412
Donald Fiftal, supt. Fax 656-3052
www.darienps.org/boe/default.php
Hindley ES 500/K-5
10 Nearwater Ln 06820 203-655-1323
Anthony Timpanelli, prin. Fax 655-7024
Holmes ES 500/K-5
18 Hoyt St 06820 203-353-4371
Geraldine Petrizzi, prin. Fax 359-2533
Middlesex MS 1,100/6-8
204 Hollow Tree Ridge Rd 06820 203-655-2518
Debi Boccanfuso, prin. Fax 655-1627
Ox Ridge ES 500/K-5
395 Mansfield Ave 06820 203-655-2579
John Rechi, prin. Fax 655-9012
Royle ES 500/K-5
133 Mansfield Ave 06820 203-655-0044
Neal Gallub, prin. Fax 655-9920
Tokeneke ES 400/K-5
7 Old Farm Rd 06820 203-655-9666
Mary Fisher, prin. Fax 655-7084

Pear Tree Point S 200/PK-5
90 Pear Tree Point Rd 06820 203-655-0030
David Trigaux, hdmstr. Fax 655-3164

Dayville, Windham
Killingly SD
Supt. — See Danielson
Killingly Central S 400/K-4
60 Soap St 06241 860-779-6750
Joan Gardner, prin. Fax 774-3299
Killingly IS 800/5-8
1599 Upper Maple St 06241 860-779-6700
Sheryl Kempain, prin. Fax 779-9639

Deep River, Middlesex, Pop. 2,520
Chester SD 300/PK-6
PO Box 187 06417 860-526-2417
Kim Caron, supt. Fax 526-5469
www.reg4.k12.ct.us/
Other Schools – See Chester

Deep River SD 400/PK-6
PO Box 187 06417 860-526-2417
Kim Caron, supt. Fax 526-5469
www.dres.k12.ct.us/
Deep River ES 400/PK-6
12 River St 06417 860-526-5319
John Pietrick, prin. Fax 526-4208

Essex SD 600/PK-6
PO Box 187 06417 860-526-2417
Kim Caron, supt. Fax 526-5469
www.reg4.k12.ct.us
Other Schools – See Centerbrook

Regional SD 4 900/7-12
PO Box 187 06417 860-526-2417
Kim Caron, supt. Fax 526-5469
www.reg4.k12.ct.us
Winthrop MS 400/7-8
PO Box 187 06417 860-526-9546
David Russell, prin. Fax 526-3721

Derby, New Haven, Pop. 12,536
Derby SD 1,500/PK-12
PO Box 373 06418 203-736-5027
Stephen Tracy, supt. Fax 736-5031
www.derbyps.org/
Bradley ES 300/K-6
155 David Humphrey Rd 06418 203-736-5040
Linda Coppola, prin. Fax 736-5041
Irving ES 400/PK-6
9 Garden Pl 06418 203-736-5043
Francis Gallo, prin. Fax 736-5045

SS. Mary & Michael S 100/K-3
14 Seymour Ave 06418 203-735-6471
Donna Doherty, prin. Fax 734-8166
SS. Mary & Michael S 100/4-8
73 Derby Ave 06418 203-734-2017
Donna Doherty, prin.

Durham, Middlesex, Pop. 2,650
Regional SD 13 2,200/PK-12
135A Pickett Ln 06422 860-349-7200
Susan Viccaro, supt. Fax 349-7203
www.rsd13ct.org/
Brewster ES 300/PK-2
126 Tuttle Rd 06422 860-349-7227
Nancy Heckler, prin. Fax 349-7232
Korn ES 200/3-4
144 Pickett Ln 06422 860-349-7210
Laurie Sinder, prin. Fax 349-7213
Strong MS 400/7-8
PO Box 435 06422 860-349-7222
Scott Nicol, prin. Fax 349-7225
Other Schools – See Middlefield

East Berlin, Hartford
Berlin SD
Supt. — See Berlin
Hubbard ES 300/K-5
139 Grove St 06023 860-828-4119
Alfred Souza, prin. Fax 828-6324

Eastford, Windham
Eastford SD 200/PK-8
PO Box 158 06242 860-974-1130
Guy DiBiasio Ed.D., supt. Fax 974-0837
Eastford S 200/PK-8
PO Box 158 06242 860-974-1130
Linda Loretz, prin. Fax 974-0837

East Granby, Hartford
East Granby SD 900/PK-12
PO Box 674 06026 860-653-6486
Dr. Christine Mahoney, supt. Fax 413-9075
www.eastgranby.k12.ct.us/
Allgrove ES 300/PK-3
33 Turkey Hills Rd 06026 860-653-2505
Leonard Strauss, prin. Fax 413-9080
East Granby MS 200/6-8
95 S Main St 06026 860-653-7113
Thomas Russo, prin. Fax 413-9126
Seymour ES 100/4-5
185 Hartford Ave 06026 860-653-7214
Scott Lawrence, prin. Fax 413-9084

East Hampton, Middlesex, Pop. 2,167
East Hampton SD 2,100/PK-12
94 Main St 06424 860-365-4000
Dr. Judith Golden, supt. Fax 365-4004
Center ES 300/4-5
7 Summit St 06424 860-365-4050
Donna Turchi, prin. Fax 365-4054
East Hampton MS 500/6-8
19 Childs Rd 06424 860-365-4060
John Fidler, prin. Fax 365-4064
Memorial ES 700/PK-3
20 Smith St 06424 860-365-4020
Karen Fitzsimmons, prin. Fax 365-4024

East Hartford, Hartford, Pop. 49,400
Capitol Region Education Council RESC
Supt. — See Hartford
East Hartford Glastonbury Magnet ES 300/K-5
305 May Rd 06118 860-622-5400
Glen Peterson, prin. Fax 622-5419
International S for Global Citizenship PK-5
656 Silver Ln 06118 860-895-9144
Cindy Rigling, prin.
Two Rivers Magnet MS 600/6-8
337 E River Dr 06108 860-290-5320
Tom Scarice, prin. Fax 509-3609

East Hartford SD 7,600/PK-12
1110 Main St 06108 860-622-5107
Mark Zito, supt. Fax 622-5119
www.easthartford.org
East Hartford MS 1,000/7-8
777 Burnside Ave 06108 860-622-5600
Nathan Quesnel, prin. Fax 622-5619
Goodwin ES 300/K-5
1235 Forbes St 06118 860-622-5420
Daniel Brodeur, prin. Fax 622-5439
Hockanum ES 400/PK-5
191 Main St 06118 860-622-5440
Lisa Beauchamp, prin. Fax 622-5459
Langford ES 400/K-5
61 Alps Dr 06108 860-622-5701
Gregory Fox, prin. Fax 622-5719
Mayberry ES 400/K-5
101 Great Hill Rd 06108 860-622-5720
Jenny Correa, prin. Fax 622-5739
Norris ES 300/K-5
40 Remington Rd 06108 860-622-5740
Pietro Cerone, prin. Fax 622-5759
O'Brien ES 500/K-5
56 Farm Dr 06108 860-622-5761
Lesley Morgan-Thompson, prin. Fax 622-5779
Pitkin ES 400/K-5
330 Hills St 06118 860-622-5481
Fax 568-7657
Silver Lane ES 300/K-5
15 Mercer Ave 06118 860-622-5501
Catherine Ciccomascolo, prin. Fax 622-5519
Sunset Ridge ES 500/6-6
450 Forbes St 06118 860-622-5800
David Flanagan, prin. Fax 622-5819
Willowbrook ECC 100/PK-PK
95 Willowbrook Rd 06118 860-622-5520
Nancy Moriarty, admin. Fax 568-6946

Other Schools – See Hartford

New Testament Baptist Church S 100/PK-12
111 Ash St 06108 860-290-6696
Mark Davis, prin. Fax 290-6698
St. Christopher S 300/PK-8
570 Brewer St 06118 860-568-4100
Kathleen Madej, prin. Fax 568-1070
St. Rose S 100/K-8
21 Church St 06108 860-528-4169
Mary Macunas, prin. Fax 528-4160

East Hartland, Hartford
Hartland SD 200/PK-8
30 South Rd 06027 860-653-0295
Dr. Robert Fish, supt. Fax 844-8528
www.hartlandschool.com/
Hartland S 200/PK-8
30 South Rd 06027 860-653-7207
Joanne St. Peter, prin. Fax 844-8528

East Haven, New Haven, Pop. 28,600
East Haven SD 3,700/PK-12
35 Wheelbarrow Ln 06513 203-468-3261
Anthony Serio, supt. Fax 468-3918
www.east-haven.k12.ct.us/ehsd/
Carbone ES 300/1-6
67 Hudson St 06512 203-468-3880
Suzanne Goodison, prin. Fax 468-3958
Deer Run ES 400/1-6
311 Foxon Rd 06513 203-468-3324
William Grimm, prin. Fax 468-3246
East Haven Academy 200/3-8
200 Tyler St 06512 203-468-3219
Marianne Johnson, prin. Fax 468-3961
Ferrara ES 200/1-6
22 Maynard Rd 06513 203-468-3318
Stan Mendygral, prin. Fax 468-3875
Hays Early Learning Center 200/PK-K
1 Maple St 06512 203-468-3268
Karen Schmidt, prin. Fax 468-3919
Melillo MS 500/7-8
67 Hudson St 06512 203-468-3227
John Prato, prin. Fax 468-3866
Momauguin ES 200/1-6
99 Cosey Beach Rd 06512 203-468-3321
Karen Goodale, prin. Fax 468-3313
Moore ES 200/1-6
82 Elliot St 06512 203-468-3316
Domenic Santilli, prin. Fax 468-3809
Overbrook Early Learning Center 200/PK-K
54 Gerrish Ave 06512 203-468-3305
Karen Schmidt, prin. Fax 468-3306
Tuttle ES 200/1-6
108 Prospect Rd 06512 203-467-3315
Anita Ruff, prin. Fax 467-8861

St. Vincent De Paul S 200/PK-8
35 Bishop St 06512 203-467-1606
Pasquale Guido, prin. Fax 467-8851

East Lyme, New London
East Lyme SD 3,200/PK-12
PO Box 176 06333 860-739-3966
Paul Smotas, supt. Fax 739-1215
www.eastlymeschools.org
Flanders ES 400/K-4
PO Box 32 06333 860-739-8475
Kathryn Sassu, prin. Fax 739-1242
Other Schools – See Niantic

Easton, Fairfield
Easton SD 1,100/PK-8
PO Box 500 06612 203-261-2513
Dr. Allen Fossbender, supt. Fax 261-4549
www.er9.org
Keller MS 400/6-8
360 Sport Hill Rd 06612 203-268-8651
Joan Parker, prin. Fax 268-6105
Staples ES 800/PK-5
515 Morehouse Rd 06612 203-261-3607
Kimberly Fox-Santora, prin. Fax 452-8403

Redding SD 1,200/K-8
PO Box 500 06612 203-261-2513
Dr. Allen Fossbender, supt. Fax 261-4549
www.er9.org
Other Schools – See Redding, West Redding

East Windsor, Hartford
East Windsor SD 1,500/PK-12
70 S Main St 06088 860-623-3346
Timothy Howes, supt. Fax 292-6817
www.eastwindsorschools.org/boe/boemem.htm
Other Schools – See Broad Brook

Ellington, Tolland
Canaan SD
Supt. — See Falls Village
Kellogg S 100/PK-8
47 Main St 06029 860-824-7791
Maria Bulson, prin. Fax 824-7892

Ellington SD 2,500/PK-12
PO Box 179 06029 860-896-2300
Stephen Cullinan, supt. Fax 896-2312
www.ellingtonschools.org
Center ES 400/PK-4
49 Main St 06029 860-896-2315
Trudie Roberts, prin. Fax 896-2321
Crystal Lake ES 200/K-4
284 Sandy Beach Rd 06029 860-896-2322
Michael Larkin, prin. Fax 896-2328
Ellington MS 400/7-8
46 Middle Butcher Rd 06029 860-896-2339
David Pearson, prin. Fax 896-2351
Windermere ES 800/K-6
2 Abbott Rd 06029 860-896-2329
Steven Moccio, prin. Fax 896-2338

Enfield, Hartford, Pop. 45,500
Enfield SD 6,400/PK-12
27 Shaker Rd 06082 860-253-6531
John Gallacher, supt. Fax 253-6515
www.enfieldschools.org
Alcorn ES 300/K-6
1010 Enfield St 06082 860-253-6505
Deborah Berger, prin. Fax 253-6506
Barnard ES 400/K-6
27 Shaker Rd 06082 860-253-6540
Nancy Hayes, prin. Fax 253-6545
Crandall ES 400/K-6
150 Brainard Rd 06082 860-253-6464
Bonnie Mazzoli, prin. Fax 253-6467
Enfield Street ES 300/PK-6
1318 Enfield St 06082 860-253-6565
Sandra Ingalls, prin. Fax 253-6568
Hale ES 300/K-6
5 Taylor Rd 06082 860-763-8899
LeAnn Beaulieu, prin. Fax 763-8897
Hazardville Memorial ES 400/K-6
68 N Maple St 06082 860-763-7500
Altressa Cox-Blackwell, prin. Fax 763-7507
Kennedy MS 1,000/7-8
155 Raffia Rd 06082 860-763-8855
Timothy Neville, prin. Fax 763-8888
Parkman ES 400/K-6
165 Weymouth Rd 06082 860-253-6570
Maureen Sampl, prin. Fax 253-6577
Stowe ES 300/K-6
117 Post Office Rd 06082 860-253-6580
Robert Fenton, prin. Fax 253-6585
Whitney ES 400/K-6
94 Middle Rd 06082 860-763-7540
Timothy VanTasel, prin. Fax 763-7547

Enfield Montessori S 100/PK-6
1370 Enfield St 06082 860-745-5847
Sr. Francine Sousa, prin. Fax 745-2010
Little Angels Preschool PK-PK
90 Alden Ave 06082 860-745-6135
Sr. Marie Lewko, prin. Fax 741-7358
St. Bernard S 300/K-8
232 Pearl St 06082 860-745-5275
Sr. Marie Lewko, prin. Fax 745-0167
St. Martha S 200/K-8
214 Brainard Rd 06082 860-745-3833
Sr. Theresa Grochowski, prin. Fax 745-3329

Fairfield, Fairfield, Pop. 54,400
Fairfield SD 9,500/PK-12
PO Box 320189, 203-255-8371
Ann Clark, supt. Fax 255-8245
www.fairfield.k12.ct.us
Burr ES 500/K-5
1960 Burr St, 203-255-7385
Gary Kass, prin. Fax 255-8244
Dwight ES 300/K-5
1600 Redding Rd, 203-255-8312
Brenda Anziano, prin. Fax 255-8201
Early Childhood Education Center 100/PK-PK
755 Melville Ave, 203-255-8380
Marlene Cavagnuolo, prin. Fax 255-8247
Fairfield Woods MS 600/6-8
1115 Fairfield Woods Rd, 203-255-8334
Greg Hatzis, prin. Fax 255-8210
Holland Hill ES 300/K-5
105 Meadowcroft Rd, 203-255-8314
Frank Arnone, prin. Fax 255-8202
Jennings ES 300/K-5
31 Palm Dr, 203-255-8316
Anthony Vuolo, prin. Fax 255-8203
Ludlowe MS 800/6-8
689 Unquowa Rd, 203-255-8345
Glenn Mackno, prin. Fax 255-8214
McKinley ES 400/K-5
60 Thompson St, 203-255-8318
Dr. Dale Bernardoni, prin. Fax 255-8204
North Stratfield ES 500/K-5
190 Putting Green Rd, 203-255-8322
Deborah Jackson, prin. Fax 255-8206
Osborn Hill ES 500/K-5
760 Stillson Rd, 203-255-8340
Alan Lipman, prin. Fax 255-8213
Riverfield ES 500/K-5
1625 Mill Plain Rd, 203-255-8328
Paul Toaso, prin. Fax 255-8207
Sherman ES 400/K-5
250 Fern St, 203-255-8330
Eileen O. Roxbee, prin. Fax 255-8208
Stratfield ES 500/K-5
1407 Melville Ave, 203-255-8332
Thomas Pesce, prin. Fax 255-8209
Tomlinson MS 700/6-8
200 Unquowa Rd, 203-255-8336
Connee Dawson, prin. Fax 255-8211
Other Schools – See Southport

Fairfield Country Day S 300/K-9
2970 Bronson Rd, 203-259-2723
Christian Sullivan, hdmstr. Fax 259-3249
Hillel Academy 50/PK-8
1571 Stratfield Rd, 203-374-6147
Nancy Fitzpatrick, admin. Fax 374-2162
Holy Family S 200/PK-8
140 Edison Ave, 203-367-5409
Larry Fitzgerald, prin. Fax 335-7317
Our Lady of Assumption S 200/PK-8
605 Stratfield Rd, 203-334-6271
Gerrie Desio, prin. Fax 382-0399
St. Thomas Aquinas S 400/PK-8
118 Ruane St, 203-255-0556
Patricia Brady, prin. Fax 255-0596
Unquowa S 200/PK-8
981 Stratfield Rd, 203-336-3801
Sharon Lauer, hdmstr. Fax 336-3479

Falls Village, Litchfield
Canaan SD 100/PK-8
246 Warren Tpke 06031 860-824-0855
Patricia Chamberlain, supt. Fax 824-1271
www.region1schools.org/
Other Schools – See Ellington

Cornwall SD 100/K-8
246 Warren Tpke 06031 860-824-0855
Patricia Chamberlain, supt. Fax 824-1271
www.region1schools.org/
Other Schools – See West Cornwall

Kent SD 300/PK-8
246 Warren Tpke 06031 860-824-0855
Patricia Chamberlain, supt. Fax 824-1271
Other Schools – See Kent

North Canaan SD 400/PK-8
246 Warren Tpke 06031 860-824-0855
Patricia Chamberlain, supt. Fax 824-1271
www.region1schools.org/
Other Schools – See Canaan

Salisbury SD 300/PK-8
246 Warren Tpke 06031 860-824-0855
Patricia Chamberlain, supt. Fax 824-1271
www.region1schools.org/
Other Schools – See Lakeville

Sharon SD 200/PK-8
246 Warren Tpke 06031 860-824-0855
Patricia Chamberlain, supt. Fax 824-1271
www.region1schools.org
Other Schools – See Sharon

Farmington, Hartford, Pop. 2,500
Farmington SD 4,200/PK-12
1 Monteith Dr 06032 860-673-8268
Robert Villanova, supt. Fax 673-8224
www.fpsct.org
East Farms ES 400/PK-4
25 Wolf Pit Rd 06032 860-674-9519
Michael Galluzzo, prin. Fax 677-7915
Robbins MS 700/7-8
20 Wolf Pit Rd 06032 860-677-2683
Kelly Lyman, prin. Fax 676-0697
Wallace ES 400/K-4
2 School St 06032 860-677-1659
Dr. Diane Cloud, prin. Fax 677-8024
West Woods Upper ES 700/5-6
50 Judson Ln 06032 860-284-1230
Dr. Peter Cummings, prin. Fax 284-1240
Other Schools – See Unionville

Gales Ferry, New London
Ledyard SD
Supt. — See Ledyard
Gales Ferry ES 200/K-2
1858 Route 12 06335 860-464-7664
Mary Porter-Price, prin. Fax 464-5138
Gallup Hill ES 300/PK-6
169 Gallup Hill Rd 06339 860-536-9477
Jennifer Byars, prin. Fax 572-2788
Ledyard Center ES 400/K-6
740 Colonel Ledyard Hwy 06339 860-464-8080
Mary Fort Boyle, prin. Fax 464-5140
Ledyard MS 400/7-8
1860 Route 12 06335 860-464-0200
Joseph Chella, prin. Fax 464-2155
Long ES 400/3-6
1854 Route 12 06335 860-464-2780
Mary Porter-Price, prin. Fax 464-5139

Glastonbury, Hartford, Pop. 27,901
Glastonbury SD 6,500/PK-12
PO Box 191 06033 860-652-7961
Alan Bookman, supt. Fax 652-7979
www.glastonburyus.org
Buttonball Lane ES 700/K-5
376 Buttonball Ln 06033 860-652-7276
Margaret McQuillan, prin. Fax 652-7285
Eastbury ES 600/K-5
1389 Neipsic Rd 06033 860-652-7858
Sheryl Harriman, prin. Fax 652-7866
Hebron Avenue ES 500/K-5
1323 Hebron Ave 06033 860-652-7875
Linda Provost, prin. Fax 652-7887
Naubuc ES 500/PK-5
84 Griswold St 06033 860-652-7918
Kent Hurlburt, prin. Fax 652-7630
Smith MS 1,000/7-8
216 Addison Rd 06033 860-652-7040
Donna Schilke, prin. Fax 652-4450
Welles S 500/6-6
1029 Neipsic Rd 06033 860-652-7800
James Gregorski, prin. Fax 652-7825
Other Schools – See South Glastonbury

Goshen, Litchfield
Regional SD 6
Supt. — See Litchfield
Goshen Center ES 200/K-6
50 North St 06756 860-491-6020
Sherri Turner, prin. Fax 491-6025

Granby, Hartford
Granby SD 2,300/K-12
15B N Granby Rd 06035 860-844-5250
Alan Addley, supt. Fax 844-6081
www.granby.k12.ct.us
Granby Memorial MS 400/7-8
321 Salmon Brook St 06035 860-844-3029
Paul Osypuk, prin. Fax 844-3039
Kearns PS 500/K-2
5 Canton Rd 06035 860-844-3044
Kimberly Dessert, prin. Fax 844-3047
Kelly Lane IS 400/3-6
60 Kelly Ln 06035 860-844-3041
Robert Gilbert, prin. Fax 413-9295

Wells Road IS 400/3-6
134 Wells Rd 06035 860-844-3048
Virginia Austin, prin. Fax 844-6180

Greens Farms, Fairfield

Greens Farms Academy 600/K-12
PO Box 998, 203-256-0717
Janet Hartwell, hdmstr. Fax 256-7501

Greenwich, Fairfield, Pop. 57,100
Greenwich SD 8,800/K-12
290 Greenwich Ave 06830 203-625-7400
Dr. Betty Sternberg, supt. Fax 618-9379
www.greenwichschools.org
Central MS 700/6-8
9 Indian Rock Ln 06830 203-661-8500
Carol Walsh, prin. Fax 661-2576
Curtiss ES 400/K-5
180 E Elm St 06830 203-869-1896
Nancy Carbone, prin. Fax 869-5101
Glenville ES 400/K-5
33 Riversville Rd 06831 203-531-9287
Marc D'Amico, prin. Fax 531-9285
Hamilton Avenue ES 300/K-5
1 Western Junior Hwy 06830 203-869-1685
Damaris Rau, prin. Fax 869-1702
New Lebanon ES 200/K-5
25 Mead Ave 06830 203-531-9139
Gene Nyitray, prin. Fax 531-3457
North Street ES 500/K-5
381 North St 06830 203-869-6756
Charles Smith, prin. Fax 869-1052
Parkway ES 300/K-5
141 Lower Cross Rd 06831 203-869-7466
Paula Bleakley, prin. Fax 869-9352
Western MS 500/6-8
1 Western Junior Hwy 06830 203-531-5700
Stacey Gross, prin. Fax 531-5220
Other Schools – See Cos Cob, Old Greenwich, Riverside

Brunswick S 900/PK-12
100 Maher Ave 06830 203-625-5800
Thomas Philip, hdmstr. Fax 625-5889
Convent of Sacred Heart S 700/PK-12
1177 King St 06831 203-531-6500
Sr. Joan Magnetti, hdmstr. Fax 531-5206
Greenwich Academy 800/PK-12
200 N Maple Ave 06830 203-625-8900
Molly King, hdmstr. Fax 869-6580
Greenwich Catholic S 400/PK-8
471 North St 06830 203-869-4000
Genevieve Madonna, prin. Fax 869-3405
Greenwich Country Day S 800/PK-9
PO Box 623 06836 203-863-5600
Adam Rohdie, hdmstr. Fax 622-6046
Stanwich S 500/PK-9
257 Stanwich Rd 06830 203-542-0000
Patricia Young, hdmstr. Fax 542-0025
Whitby S 300/PK-8
969 Lake Ave 06831 203-869-8464
Douglas Fainelli, hdmstr. Fax 869-2215

Griswold, See Jewett City
Griswold SD
Supt. — See Jewett City
Griswold ES 900/PK-5
303 Slater Ave 06351 860-376-7610
Susan Rourke, prin. Fax 376-7612
Griswold MS 500/6-8
211 Slater Ave 06351 860-376-7630
Thanh Nguyen, prin. Fax 376-7631

Groton, New London, Pop. 9,493
Groton SD
Supt. — See Mystic
Barnum ES 300/PK-5
68 Briar Hill Rd 06340 860-449-5640
Valerie Nelson, prin. Fax 449-5642
Chester ES 400/PK-5
1 Harry Day Dr 06340 860-449-5636
Carol Glaude Ed.D., prin. Fax 449-5638
Fitch MS 500/6-8
61 Fort Hill Rd 06340 860-449-5620
Robert Pendolphi, prin. Fax 449-5623
Kolnaski Magnet S PK-5
500 Poquonnock Rd 06340 860-449-5612
Dominick Bassi, prin. Fax 449-5616
Morrisson ES 400/PK-5
154 Toll Gate Rd 06340 860-449-5655
Susan Morehouse, prin. Fax 449-5654
Pleasant Valley ES 200/PK-5
380 Pleasant Valley Rd S 06340 860-449-5600
Fax 449-5602
West Side MS 300/6-8
250 Brandegee Ave 06340 860-449-5630
John Jones, prin. Fax 449-5628

Sacred Heart S 200/PK-8
58 Sacred Heart Dr 06340 860-445-0611
David Young, prin. Fax 448-4999

Guilford, New Haven, Pop. 19,848
Guilford SD 3,800/PK-12
PO Box 367 06437 203-453-8200
Dr. Thomas Forcella, supt. Fax 453-8211
www.guilford.k12.ct.us/
Adams MS 600/7-8
233 Church St 06437 203-453-2755
Catherine Walker, prin. Fax 453-8446
Baldwin MS 600/5-6
68 Bullard Dr 06437 203-457-0222
Anne Snurkowski, prin. Fax 457-9502
Cox ES 300/K-4
143 Three Mile Crse 06437 203-453-5291
Merry Leventhal, prin. Fax 453-8552
Guilford Lakes ES 500/PK-4
40 Maupas Rd 06437 203-453-5201
Michael Biddle, prin. Fax 453-9507

Jones ES 300/K-4
181 Ledge Hill Rd 06437 203-457-0773
Paula McCarthy, prin. Fax 457-9263
Leete ES 300/K-4
280 S Union St 06437 203-453-2726
Nancy Bishop, prin. Fax 458-2468

Hamden, New Haven, Pop. 52,600
Area Coop. Educational Services RESC
Supt. — See North Haven
Wintergreen Magnet S 600/K-8
670 Wintergreen Ave 06514 203-281-9668
Sharyn Esdaile, prin. Fax 281-7946

Hamden SD 6,200/K-12
60 Putnam Ave 06517 203-407-2000
Fran Rabinowitz, supt. Fax 407-2001
www.hamden.org
Bear Path ES 500/K-6
10 Kirk Rd 06514 203-407-2015
Susan Smey, prin. Fax 407-5102
Church Street ES 400/K-6
95 Church St 06514 203-407-2020
Joyce Kossman, prin. Fax 407-5860
Dunbar Hill ES 400/K-6
315 Lane St 06514 203-407-2025
Stephen Bergin, prin. Fax 407-2027
Hamden MS 1,000/7-8
2623 Dixwell Ave 06518 203-407-3140
James O'Conner, prin. Fax 407-3141
Helen Street ES 300/K-6
285 Helen St 06514 203-407-2030
Lynette Kelleher, prin. Fax 407-2052
Ridge Hill ES 300/K-6
120 Carew Rd 06517 203-407-2035
Karen Butler, prin. Fax 407-2012
Shepherd Glen ES 300/K-6
1 Skiff Street Ext 06514 203-407-2070
Christopher Melillo, prin. Fax 407-2072
Spring Glen ES 300/K-6
1908 Whitney Ave 06517 203-407-2045
Vanessa Ditta, prin. Fax 407-2048
West Woods ES 500/K-6
350 W Todd St 06518 203-407-2050
Barbara Nana, prin. Fax 407-5863

New Haven SD
Supt. — See New Haven
Clemente Leadership Academy 600/K-8
130B Leeder Hill Dr 06517 203-946-8886
Dr. Leroy Williams, prin. Fax 946-6635
Fair Haven S 700/K-8
164 Grand Ave 06517 203-691-2600
Kim Johnsky, prin. Fax 691-2697
Troup Magnet Academy of Science 400/K-8
130 Leeder Hill Dr 06517 203-691-3000
Richard Kaliszewski, prin. Fax 691-7276

Hamden Hall Country Day S 600/PK-12
1108 Whitney Ave 06517 203-752-2600
Robert Izzo, hdmstr. Fax 752-2651
Laurel Oaks SDA S 50/1-8
14 W Shepard Ave 06514 203-248-3251
Fax 248-3251
St. Rita S 500/PK-8
1601 Whitney Ave 06517 203-248-3114
Sr. Maureen Fitzgerald, prin. Fax 248-1016
St. Stephen S 200/PK-8
418 Ridge Rd 06517 203-288-6792
Maria Testa, prin. Fax 287-9158
West Woods Christian Academy 100/K-12
2105 State St 06517 203-562-9922
William Kane, prin. Fax 786-4730

Hampton, Windham
Hampton SD, 380 Main St 06247 200/PK-6
Marsha Willhoit, supt. 860-455-9409
Hampton ES 200/PK-6
380 Main St 06247 860-455-9409
Marsha Willhoit, prin. Fax 455-9397

Hartford, Hartford, Pop. 124,397
Capitol Region Education Council RESC 2,500/
111 Charter Oak Ave 06106 860-524-4063
Dr. Bruce Douglas, dir. Fax 548-9924
www.crec.org
Montessori Magnet S 300/PK-6
1460 Broad St 06106 860-757-6100
Jackie Cossentino, prin. Fax 757-6144
University of Hartford Magnet S 400/PK-5
196 Bloomfield Ave 06117 860-236-2899
Dr. Elaina Brachman, prin. Fax 236-2062
Other Schools – See Avon, East Hartford

East Hartford SD
Supt. — See East Hartford
O'Connell ES 300/K-5
301 May Rd 06118 860-622-5461
Scott Nozik, prin. Fax 622-5479

Hartford SD 17,600/PK-12
960 Main St 06103 860-695-8000
Steven Adamowski, supt. Fax 722-8650
www.hartfordschools.org
Batchelder S 500/PK-8
757 New Britain Ave 06106 860-695-2720
James Pappas, prin. Fax 953-4604
Belizzi MS 500/5-8
215 South St 06114 860-695-2400
Angela Thomas, prin. Fax 956-9993
Betances ES 400/PK-5
42 Charter Oak Ave 06106 860-695-2840
Josephine Smith, prin. Fax 278-0126
Breakthrough II ES PK-3
150 Tower Ave 06120 860-695-6380
Tammy Kyparidis, prin.
Breakthrough Magnet S 300/PK-8
290 Brookfield St 06106 860-695-5700
Norma Neumann-Johnson, prin. Fax 722-6817

Burr S 500/K-8
400 Wethersfield Ave 06114 860-695-3080
Donna Caldeira, prin. Fax 296-0717
Clark ES 400/PK-8
75 Clark St 06120 860-695-3240
Dr. Beryl Bailey, prin. Fax 560-1137
Core Knowledge Academy 400/PK-8
104 Vine St 06112 860-695-4380
Tyrone Richardson, prin. Fax 278-4694
Dwight ES 400/PK-4
585 Wethersfield Ave 06114 860-695-3400
Stacey McCann, prin. Fax 296-2938
Fisher Magnet S 500/PK-6
280 Plainfield St 06112 860-695-3560
John Freeman, prin. Fax 722-8443
Fox CommPACT ES 800/PK-6
470 Maple Ave 06114 860-695-3600
Michael Lorenzo, prin. Fax 724-5855
Global Communications Academy K-12
150 Tower Ave 06120 860-695-1960
Darlene Pugnali, prin.
Hartford Magnet MS 600/6-8
53 Vernon St 06106 860-757-6200
Sally Biggs, prin. Fax 947-9935
Hooker Environmental Studies S 400/PK-8
200 Sherbrooke Ave 06106 860-695-3760
Raul Montanez-Pitre, prin. Fax 522-7590
Kennelly S 800/PK-8
180 White St 06114 860-695-3860
Mark Levy, prin. Fax 522-9372
King ES 700/PK-6
25 Ridgefield St 06112 860-695-3980
Baxter Atkinson, prin. Fax 722-8342
Kinsella Sch of Performing Arts 500/PK-8
65 Van Block Ave 06106 860-695-4140
Pamela Totten-Alvarado, prin. Fax 522-0004
Latino Studies Academy PK-7
195 Putnam St 06106 860-698-2980
Dr. Lourdes Soto, prin.
Little Owls Learning Center 50/PK-PK
55 Forest St 06105 860-695-1462
Julie Wacht, coord.
McDonough ES 500/PK-6
111 Hillside Ave 06106 860-695-4260
Dr. Tina Jeter, prin. Fax 722-8825
Moylan S 600/PK-8
101 Catherine St 06106 860-695-4500
Irene Coe, prin. Fax 722-8133
Naylor S 600/PK-8
639 Franklin Ave 06114 860-695-4620
Robert Travaglini, prin. Fax 296-2595
Parkville Community ES 500/K-6
1755 Park St 06106 860-695-4720
Elizabeth Michaelis, prin. Fax 232-7350
Quirk MS 400/8-8
85 Edwards St 06120 860-695-2140
William Chambers, prin. Fax 527-0346
Rawson ES 400/PK-8
260 Holcomb St 06112 860-695-4840
Gerald Martin, prin. Fax 242-3238
Sanchez ES 500/PK-6
176 Babcock St 06106 860-695-4940
Myrella Lara, prin. Fax 560-3493
Sand ES 400/PK-6
1750 Main St 06120 860-695-5040
Carol Wright, prin. Fax 722-8377
Simpson-Waverly Classical Magnet S 400/PK-6
55 Waverly St 06112 860-695-5160
Nicolas Jones, prin. Fax 724-3548
Webster MicroSociety S 600/PK-8
5 Cone St 06105 860-695-5380
Delores Cole, prin. Fax 722-8786
West S 700/PK-8
927 Asylum Ave 06105 860-695-5480
Sheilda Garrison, prin. Fax 724-5506
Wish ES 400/PK-8
350 Barbour St 06120 860-695-5600
Lynne Lanier, prin. Fax 722-8326
Young Men's Leadership Academy 6-7
875 Asylum Ave 06105

Hartford Area SDA S 100/K-10
474 Woodland St 06112 860-724-5777
St. Augustine S 200/PK-8
20 Clifford St 06114 860-249-5661
Sharon Roberts, prin. Fax 293-2981
Shiloh Christian Academy 50/K-6
185 Bellevue St 06120 860-729-2703
Manirah Agans, prin.
SS. Cyril & Methodius S 200/PK-8
35 Groton St 06106 860-522-8490
Sr. Dolores Ungerer, prin. Fax 493-7409

Harwinton, Litchfield, Pop. 5,228
Regional SD 10
Supt. — See Burlington
Harwinton Consolidated ES 500/PK-4
115 Litchfield Rd 06791 860-485-9029
Maureen Dodd, prin. Fax 485-9237

Hebron, Tolland
Hebron SD 1,200/PK-6
580 Gilead St 06248 860-228-2577
Eleanor Cruz, supt. Fax 228-2912
www.hebron.k12.ct.us
Gilead Hill ES 500/PK-2
580 Gilead St 06248 860-228-9458
Kathryn Veronesi, prin. Fax 228-1106
Hebron ES 700/3-6
92 Church St 06248 860-228-9465
Joanne Collins, prin. Fax 228-1378

Regional SD 8 1,600/7-12
PO Box 1438 06248 860-228-2115
Robert Siminski Ed.D., supt. Fax 228-4346
www.reg8.k12.ct.us/
RHAM MS 600/7-8
25 RHAM Rd 06248 860-228-9423
Michael Seroussi, prin. Fax 228-2471

Higganum, Middlesex, Pop. 1,692
Regional SD 17 2,100/PK-12
PO Box 568 06441 860-345-4534
Gary Mala, supt. Fax 345-2817
rsd17.org
Burr District ES 300/PK-4
PO Box 570 06441 860-345-4584
Eric Larson, prin. Fax 345-7963
Haddam ES 300/K-4
PO Box 439 06441 860-345-4551
Janice Harris, prin. Fax 345-8709
Other Schools – See Killingworth

Jewett City, New London, Pop. 3,001
Griswold SD 2,200/PK-12
2 N Main St 06351 860-376-7600
Colette Trailor Ph.D., supt. Fax 376-2071
griswold.k12.ct.us
Other Schools – See Griswold

St. Mary S 50/PK-8
34 N Main St 06351 860-376-0446
Richard Woodworth, prin. Fax 376-4200

Kensington, Hartford, Pop. 8,306
Berlin SD
Supt. — See Berlin
Griswold ES 600/K-5
133 Heather Ln 06037 860-828-6336
Laurie Gjerpen, prin. Fax 829-2923

Mooreland Hill S 50/5-8
166 Lincoln St 06037 860-223-6428
Michael Dooman, hdmstr. Fax 223-3318

Kent, Litchfield
Kent SD
Supt. — See Falls Village
Kent Center S 300/PK-8
PO Box 219 06757 860-927-3537
Dr. Rima Zelvis, prin. Fax 927-3925

Killingworth, Middlesex
Regional SD 17
Supt. — See Higganum
Haddam-Killingworth MS 400/5-8
451 Route 81 06419 860-663-1241
Miriam Wagner, prin. Fax 663-2071
Killingworth ES 400/K-4
PO Box 609 06419 860-663-1121
Rita Peretto, prin. Fax 663-3827

Lakeville, Litchfield
Salisbury SD
Supt. — See Falls Village
Salisbury Central S 300/PK-8
PO Box 1808 06039 860-435-9871
Christopher Butwill, prin. Fax 435-3925

Indian Mountain S 200/PK-9
211 Indian Mountain Rd 06039 860-435-0871
Mark Devey, hdmstr. Fax 435-0641

Lebanon, New London
Lebanon SD 1,500/PK-12
891 Exeter Rd 06249 860-642-3560
Robert McGray, supt. Fax 642-4589
www.lebanonct.org/default.htm
Lebanon ES 500/PK-4
479 Exeter Rd 06249 860-642-7593
Sandye Simon, prin. Fax 642-3548
Lebanon MS 400/5-8
891 Exeter Rd 06249 860-642-4702
Robert Laskarzewski, prin. Fax 642-3534

Ledyard, New London
Ledyard SD 2,900/PK-12
4 Blonder Park Rd 06339 860-464-9255
Michael Graner, supt. Fax 464-8589
ledyard.net/
Other Schools – See Gales Ferry

Lisbon, New London, Pop. 3,790
Lisbon SD 600/PK-8
15 Newent Rd 06351 860-376-5565
Julius D'Agostino, supt. Fax 376-1102
www.lisboncentralschool.com
Lisbon Central S 600/PK-8
15 Newent Rd 06351 860-376-2403
Fax 376-1102

Litchfield, Litchfield, Pop. 1,340
Litchfield SD 1,300/PK-12
PO Box 110 06759 860-567-7500
Dr. William Papallo, supt. Fax 567-7508
www.litchfieldschools.org
Center ES 400/PK-3
PO Box 110 06759 860-567-7510
Adrienne Longobucco, prin. Fax 567-7518
Litchfield IS 200/4-6
PO Box 110 06759 860-567-7520
Jennifer Marinelli, prin. Fax 567-7528

Regional SD 6 1,100/K-12
98 Wamogo Rd 06759 860-567-7400
Craig Drezek Ph.D., supt. Fax 567-6652
rsd6.org
Other Schools – See Goshen, Morris, Warren

Lyme, New London
Regional SD 18
Supt. — See Old Lyme
Lyme Consolidated ES 200/K-5
478 Hamburg Rd 06371 860-434-1233
James Cavalieri, prin. Fax 434-5735

Madison, New Haven, Pop. 15,485
Madison SD 3,800/K-12
PO Box 71 06443 203-245-6300
David Klein, supt. Fax 245-6336
www.madison.k12.ct.us
Brown MS 600/5-6
980 Durham Rd 06443 203-245-6400
Julianne Phelps, prin. Fax 245-6425
Island Avenue ES 300/1-4
20 Island Ave 06443 203-245-6450
Kathy Nutley, prin. Fax 245-6456
Jeffrey ES 600/K-4
331 Copse Rd 06443 203-245-6460
Mona Goodman, prin. Fax 245-6466
Polson MS 600/7-8
302 Green Hill Rd 06443 203-245-6480
Frank Henderson, prin. Fax 245-6494
Ryerson ES 400/1-4
982 Durham Rd 06443 203-245-6440
Paul Sinicrope, prin. Fax 245-6446

Country S 300/PK-8
341 Opening Hill Rd 06443 203-421-3113
William Powers, hdmstr. Fax 421-4390
Our Lady of Mercy S 200/PK-8
149 Neck Rd 06443 203-245-4393
Dr. John Alfone, prin. Fax 245-3498
Shoreline Christian S 100/K-8
1185 Durham Rd 06443 203-421-4626
Dana Bittner, admin. Fax 421-5827

Manchester, Hartford, Pop. 52,500
Manchester SD 6,500/PK-12
45 N School St, 860-647-3441
Kathleen Ouellette Ed.D., supt. Fax 647-5042
boe.townofmanchester.org/
Bennet Academy 6-6
1151 Main St 06040 860-647-3571
David Welch, prin. Fax 647-3577
Bowers ES 400/K-5
141 Princeton St, 860-647-3313
Mary Lou Ruggiero, prin. Fax 647-3320
Buckley ES 300/PK-5
250 Vernon St, 860-647-3302
Holly Maiorano, prin. Fax 647-5007
Hale ES 300/K-5
160 Spruce St 06040 860-647-3346
Kate England, prin. Fax 647-6379
Highland Park ES 300/K-5
397 Porter St 06040 860-647-3430
Katherine Colavecchio, prin. Fax 647-6376
Illing MS 1,000/7-8
229 Middle Tpke E 06040 860-647-3400
Troy Monroe, prin. Fax 647-5008
Keeney ES 400/PK-5
179 Keeney St 06040 860-647-3354
Mary Luce, prin. Fax 647-5043
Martin ES 200/K-5
140 Dartmouth Rd 06040 860-647-3367
Donna Fitzgerald, prin. Fax 647-3492
Robertson ES 400/K-5
65 N School St, 860-647-3372
Stuart Wolf, prin. Fax 647-6378
Verplanck ES 400/PK-5
126 Olcott St 06040 860-647-3383
Mike Saimond, prin. Fax 647-5029
Waddell ES 300/K-5
163 Broad St, 860-647-3392
Roland Axelson, prin. Fax 647-6377
Washington ES 300/PK-5
94 Cedar St 06040 860-647-3332
Cynthia Womack, prin. Fax 647-5026

Assumption S 100/PK-5
27 Adams St S 06040 860-649-0889
Marguerite Ouellette, prin. Fax 643-0559
Assumption S East Campus 50/6-8
45 Ludlow Rd 06040 860-645-0637
Marguerite Ouellette, prin.
Cornerstone Christian S 200/PK-12
236 Main St, 860-643-0792
Barbara Fish, hdmstr. Fax 647-9291
St. Bridget S 200/PK-8
74 Main St 06040 860-649-7731
Rita Barry, prin. Fax 646-6936
St. James S 500/PK-8
73 Park St 06040 860-643-5088
Patricia Kanute, prin. Fax 649-6462

Mansfield Center, Tolland
Mansfield SD
Supt. — See Storrs
Southeast ES 300/PK-4
134 Warrenville Rd 06250 860-423-1611
Norma Fisher-Doiron, prin. Fax 423-0610
Vinton ES 300/PK-4
306 Stafford Rd 06250 860-423-3086
James Palmer, prin. Fax 456-4694

Oak Grove Montessori S 100/PK-6
132 Pleasant Valley Rd 06250 860-456-1031
Karen Drazen, prin. Fax 456-2907

Marlborough, Hartford
Marlborough SD 700/PK-6
25 School Dr 06447 860-295-6236
Salvatore Menzo, supt. Fax 295-6153
www.marlborough.k12.ct.us
Thienes-Hall ES 700/PK-6
25 School Dr 06447 860-295-6220
Loraine Giannini, prin. Fax 295-6223

Meriden, New Haven, Pop. 59,653
Area Coop. Educational Services RESC
Supt. — See North Haven
Edison MS 800/6-8
1355 N Broad St 06450 203-639-8403
Karen Habegger, prin. Fax 639-8323
Meriden SD 8,800/PK-12
22 Liberty St 06450 203-630-4171
Mary Cortright, supt. Fax 630-0110
www.meriden.k12.ct.us
Barry ES 600/PK-5
124 Columbia St 06451 203-237-8831
Karen Dahn, prin. Fax 630-4212
Franklin ES 400/K-5
426 W Main St 06451 203-235-7997
Daniel Coffey, prin. Fax 630-4055
Hale ES 600/K-5
277 Atkins Street Ext 06450 203-237-7486
Judy Seldner, prin. Fax 630-4216
Hanover ES 600/PK-5
208 Main St 06451 203-235-6359
Miguel Cardona, prin. Fax 630-4099
Hooker ES 500/K-5
70 Overlook Dr 06450 203-237-8839
James Quinn, prin. Fax 630-4114
Lincoln MS 800/6-8
164 Centennial Ave 06451 203-238-2381
Leo Lavallee, prin. Fax 238-7258
Pulaski ES 700/K-5
100 Clearview Ave 06450 203-238-1273
Thomas Brown, prin. Fax 630-4144
Putnam ES 600/K-5
133 Parker Ave 06450 203-237-8493
Dr. Anne Jellison, prin. Fax 630-4189
Sherman ES 600/PK-5
64 N Pearl St 06450 203-238-1286
Louise Moss, prin. Fax 630-4199
Washington MS 900/6-8
1225 N Broad St 06450 203-235-6606
Jean Privitera, prin. Fax 235-6040

Our Lady Mt. Carmel S 200/PK-8
115 Lewis Ave 06451 203-235-2959
Norine McDermott, prin. Fax 238-3629
St. Joseph S 200/K-8
159 W Main St 06451 203-237-6800
Katherine Spencer, prin. Fax 238-2963
St. Mary S 100/K-8
97 Grove St 06451 203-237-2931
Robert Biancamano, prin. Fax 237-9013
St. Stanislaus S 200/PK-8
81 Akron St 06450 203-237-1005
George Claffey, prin. Fax 630-3424

Middlebury, New Haven, Pop. 4,100
Regional SD 15 4,600/PK-12
PO Box 395 06762 203-758-8258
Dr. Frank Sippy, supt. Fax 758-1908
www.region15.org
Long Meadow ES 600/PK-5
65 N Benson Rd 06762 203-758-1144
Richard Gusenburg, prin. Fax 758-1934
Memorial MS 500/6-8
PO Box 903 06762 203-758-2496
John Sieller, prin. Fax 758-9594
Middlebury ES 500/PK-5
PO Box 1093 06762 203-758-2401
Jack Zamary, prin. Fax 758-9918
Other Schools – See Southbury

Middlefield, Middlesex
Regional SD 13
Supt. — See Durham
Lyman ES 300/K-4
106 Way Rd 06455 860-349-7240
Karen Brimecombe, prin. Fax 349-7242
Middlefield Memorial MS 400/5-6
124 Hubbard St 06455 860-349-7235
Kevin Brough, prin. Fax 349-7246

Independent Day S 200/PK-8
115 Laurel Brook Rd 06455 860-347-7235
John Barrengos Ed.D., hdmstr. Fax 347-8852

Middletown, Middlesex, Pop. 47,438
Middletown SD 5,100/PK-12
311 Hunting Hill Ave 06457 860-638-1401
Michael Frechette Ph.D., supt. Fax 638-1495
www.middletownschools.org
Bielefield ES 400/PK-5
70 Maynard St 06457 860-347-4124
Renata Lantos, prin. Fax 347-4284
Farm Hill ES 300/K-5
390 Ridge Rd 06457 860-346-1225
Patricia Girard, prin. Fax 346-1314
Keigwin MS 300/6-6
99 Spruce St 06457 860-632-2433
Tracey Koff, prin. Fax 632-2032
Lawrence ES 300/K-5
Kaplan Dr 06457 860-632-2158
Enza Macri, prin. Fax 632-0738
Macdonough ES 200/K-5
66 Spring St 06457 860-347-8553
Jon Romeo, prin. Fax 346-7684
Moody ES 400/K-5
300 Country Club Rd 06457 860-347-2561
Yolande Eldridge, prin. Fax 347-5688
Snow ES 300/PK-5
299 Wadsworth St 06457 860-347-2579
James Gaudreau, prin. Fax 638-3748
Spencer ES 400/K-5
207 Westfield St 06457 860-344-0711
Amy Clarke, prin. Fax 344-0490
Wesley ES 300/K-5
10 Wesleyan Hills Rd 06457 860-344-0381
Joseph Cassella, prin. Fax 346-5653
Wilson MS 700/7-8
370 Hunting Hill Ave 06457 860-347-8594
Eugene Nocera, prin. Fax 347-2158

Connecticut Christian Academy 50/K-8
30 Brooks Rd 06457 860-347-6757
Rev. James Rodriguez, hdmstr. Fax 344-0598

St. John S 200/PK-8
5 Saint Johns Sq 06457 860-347-3202
Kathleen King, prin. Fax 347-3537

St. Mary S 200/PK-8
87 S Main St 06457 860-347-2978
Kathleen Dutil, prin. Fax 347-7267

St. Sebastian S 100/PK-8
61 Durant Ter 06457 860-347-3438
Bohdan Cuprak, prin. Fax 343-0543

Milford, New Haven, Pop. 51,734

Milford SD 7,500/PK-12
70 W River St 06460 203-783-3402
Harvey Polansky Ph.D., supt. Fax 783-3475
www.milforded.org

Calf Pen Meadow ES 400/PK-5
395 Welchs Point Rd 06460 203-783-3521
Carrie Keramis, prin. Fax 783-3680

East Shore MS 600/6-8
240 Chapel St 06460 203-783-3559
Catherine Williams, prin. Fax 301-5060

Harborside MS 600/6-8
175 High St 06460 203-783-3523
Ken Saranich, prin. Fax 783-3687

Kennedy ES 400/K-5
404 West Ave, 203-783-3568
Sean Smyth, prin. Fax 783-3688

Live Oaks ES 400/K-5
575 Merwin Ave 06460 203-783-3564
Rose Lacobelle, prin. Fax 783-3616

Mathewson ES 600/K-5
466 W River St, 203-783-3527
Clifford Dudley, prin. Fax 783-3563

Meadowside ES 400/K-5
80 Seemans Ln 06460 203-783-3555
Robert Davis, prin. Fax 783-4826

Orange Avenue ES 500/K-5
260 Orange Ave, 203-783-3537
Steven Madancy, prin. Fax 783-3619

Orchard Hills ES 400/K-5
185 Marino Dr 06460 203-783-3566
Michelle Dixon, prin. Fax 783-3716

Pumpkin Delight ES 300/PK-5
27 Art St 06460 203-783-3531
Deborah Herbst, prin. Fax 783-3696

Simon Lake ES 300/PK-5
59 Devonshire Rd 06460 203-783-3533
Donald Busca, prin. Fax 783-4825

West Shore MS 500/6-8
70 Kay Ave 06460 203-783-3553
Vince Scarpetti, prin. Fax 783-3696

New England S of Montessori 100/PK-5
301 Brewster Rd Ste A 06460 203-878-9822
Maria Zullo, prin. Fax 878-9833

St. Ann S 100/PK-8
64 Ridge St 06460 203-878-2738
Carol Schweitzer, prin. Fax 878-5473

St. Gabriel S 200/PK-8
1 Tudor Rd 06460 203-874-3811
Dr. Gail Kingston, prin. Fax 874-0416

St. Mary S 300/PK-8
72 Gulf St 06460 203-878-6539
Frank Lacerenza, prin. Fax 878-1866

Monroe, Fairfield

Monroe SD 4,400/PK-12
375 Monroe Tpke 06468 203-452-2860
Dr. Colleen Palmer, supt. Fax 452-5818
www.monroeps.org

Chalk Hill S 700/5-6
375 Fan Hill Rd 06468 203-452-2914
Bruce Lazar, prin. Fax 452-5844

Fawn Hollow ES 600/K-4
345 Fan Hill Rd 06468 203-452-2923
Rebecca Kosisko, prin. Fax 452-2444

Jockey Hollow S 700/7-8
365 Fan Hill Rd 06468 203-452-2905
John Ceccolini, prin. Fax 452-2444

Monroe ES 400/PK-4
375 Monroe Tpke 06468 203-452-2870
Debra Kovachi, prin. Fax 452-5868

Stepney ES 500/K-4
180 Old Newtown Rd 06468 203-452-2885
Susan Austin, prin. Fax 452-5873

St. Jude S 200/PK-8
707 Monroe Tpke 06468 203-261-3619
Linda Dunn, prin. Fax 268-8748

Moodus, Middlesex, Pop. 1,170

East Haddam SD 1,300/PK-12
PO Box 401 06469 860-873-5090
Ellen Solek, supt. Fax 873-5092
www.easthaddamschools.org

East Haddam ES 400/PK-3
PO Box 425 06469 860-873-5076
Joanne Collins, prin. Fax 873-5155

Hale-Ray MS 500/4-8
PO Box 363 06469 860-873-5081
Jason Peacock, prin. Fax 873-5086

Moosup, Windham, Pop. 3,289

Plainfield SD
Supt. — See Plainfield

Moosup ES 300/1-3
35 Church St 06354 860-564-6430
Susan Chamie, prin. Fax 564-6175

Plainfield Catholic S 100/PK-8
120 Prospect St 06354 860-564-3476
Sr. Anne Landry, prin. Fax 564-8303

Morris, Litchfield

Regional SD 6
Supt. — See Litchfield

Morris ES 200/K-6
10 East St 06763 860-567-7420
Guy Weik, prin. Fax 567-7425

Mystic, New London, Pop. 2,618

Groton SD 4,600/PK-12
1300 Flanders Rd 06355 860-572-2100
Paul Kadri, supt. Fax 572-2107
www.groton.k12.ct.us

Butler ES 300/PK-5
155 Ocean View Ave 06355 860-572-5825
Fax 572-5827

Cutler MS 400/6-8
160 Fishtown Rd 06355 860-572-5830
Monson Lane, prin. Fax 572-5834

Northeast Academy 400/PK-5
115 Oslo St 06355 860-572-5852
Carolyn Doutre, prin.
Other Schools – See Groton

Stonington SD
Supt. — See Old Mystic

Mystic MS 500/5-8
204 Mistuxet Ave 06355 860-536-9613
Stafford Thomas, prin. Fax 536-4508

Naugatuck, New Haven, Pop. 31,864

Naugatuck SD 4,900/K-12
380 Church St 06770 203-720-5265
John Tindall-Gibson Ph.D., supt. Fax 720-5272
www.naugy.net

Andrew Avenue ES 200/K-4
140 Andrew Ave 06770 203-720-5221
Theresa Forish, prin. Fax 720-5213

Central Avenue ES 300/K-4
28 Central Ave 06770 203-720-5224
Evelyn Gobstein, prin. Fax 720-5214

City Hill MS 500/7-8
441 City Hill St 06770 203-720-5246
Christine Zockoff, prin. Fax 720-5256

Cross Street IS 400/5-6
120 Cross St 06770 203-720-5227
Christopher Montini, prin. Fax 720-5215

Hillside MS 300/7-8
51 Hillside Ave 06770 203-720-5260
Brian Sullivan, prin. Fax 720-5209

Hop Brook IS 400/5-6
75 Crown St 06770 203-720-5231
Lori Ferreira, prin. Fax 720-5234

Maple Hill ES 400/K-4
641 Maple Hill Rd 06770 203-720-5236
Cheryl Kane, prin. Fax 720-5217

Prospect Street ES 300/K-4
100 Prospect St 06770 203-720-5239
Barbara Mechler, prin. Fax 720-5218

Salem ES 300/K-4
124 Meadow St 06770 203-720-5242
Jennifer Kruge, prin. Fax 720-5219

Western ES 300/K-4
100 Pine St 06770 203-720-5244
Melissa D'Alessandro, prin. Fax 720-5220

St. Francis S 200/PK-8
294 Church St 06770 203-729-2247
Thomas Fuller, prin. Fax 729-0512

St. Hedwig S 200/PK-8
32 Golden Hill St 06770 203-729-2403
John Salatto, prin. Fax 723-7954

Salem Community Childcare Center 50/PK-PK
14 Salem St 06770 203-723-4820

New Britain, Hartford, Pop. 71,254

New Britain SD 10,600/PK-12
PO Box 1960 06050 860-827-2204
Dr. Doris Kurtz, supt. Fax 612-1533
www.csdnb.org/

Chamberlain ES 600/K-5
120 Newington Ave 06051 860-832-5691
Jane Perez, prin. Fax 224-1597

DiLoreto Magnet ES 600/K-5
732 Slater Rd 06053 860-223-2885
Marina Taverner, prin. Fax 832-5685

Gaffney ES 500/PK-5
322 Slater Rd 06053 860-225-6247
Lisa Eells, prin. Fax 225-1128

HALS Academy 6-8
30 Pendleton Rd 06053 860-826-1866
Elaine Zottola, prin. Fax 826-1867

Holmes ES 400/K-5
2150 Stanley St 06053 860-223-8294
Glenn Horter, prin. Fax 832-9666

Jefferson ES 400/K-5
140 Horseplain Rd 06053 860-223-8007
Nancy Sarra, prin. Fax 225-1646

Lincoln ES 600/K-5
145 Steele St 06052 860-229-2564
Cynthia Cassada, prin. Fax 225-1638

Northend ES 300/K-5
160 Bassett St 06051 860-223-3819
Elsa Saavedra-Rodriguez, prin. Fax 225-1660

Pulaski MS 900/6-8
757 Farmington Ave 06053 860-225-7665
Vonetta Romeo-Rivers, prin. Fax 223-3840

Roosevelt MS 600/6-8
40 Goodwin St 06051 860-612-3334
Brenda Lewis-Collins, prin. Fax 826-1162

Slade MS 700/6-8
183 Steele St 06052 860-225-6395
Mark Fernandes, prin. Fax 826-7894

Smalley Academy 700/PK-5
175 West St 06051 860-225-8647
Sharon O'Brien, prin. Fax 225-8044

Smith ES 600/K-5
142 Rutherford St 06051 860-223-1574
Paula Eshoo, prin. Fax 832-5682

Vance ES 500/K-5
183 Vance St 06052 860-225-8731
Mary Beth Iacobelli, prin. Fax 225-1019

Pope John Paul II S 200/PK-8
221 Farmington Ave 06053 860-225-4275
Donald Bellizzi, prin. Fax 225-5073

Sacred Heart S 500/PK-8
35 Orange St 06053 860-229-7663
Sr. Alma Sakowicz, prin. Fax 832-6098

St. Matthew Lutheran S 50/PK-5
87 Franklin Sq 06051 860-223-7829
Martin Boettner, prin. Fax 223-7829

New Canaan, Fairfield, Pop. 17,864

New Canaan SD 4,100/PK-12
39 Locust Ave 06840 203-594-4000
Dr. David Abbey, supt. Fax 594-4035
www.newcanaan.k12.ct.us

East ES 500/K-4
54 Little Brook Rd 06840 203-594-4200
Alexandra Potts, prin. Fax 594-4215

Saxe MS 1,300/5-8
468 South Ave 06840 203-594-4500
Greg Macedo, prin. Fax 594-4565

South ES 500/PK-4
8 Farm Rd 06840 203-594-4300
Joanne Rocco, prin. Fax 594-4314

West ES 500/PK-4
769 Ponus Rdg 06840 203-594-4400
Dr. Jill Correnty, prin. Fax 594-4412

New Canaan Country S 600/PK-9
PO Box 997 06840 203-972-0771
Timothy Bazemore, hdmstr. Fax 966-5924

St. Aloysius S 200/K-8
33 South Ave 06840 203-966-0786
Dr. Donald Howard, prin. Fax 972-6960

New Fairfield, Fairfield, Pop. 12,911

New Fairfield SD 3,100/PK-12
3 Brush Hill Rd 06812 203-312-5770
Dr. Joseph Castagnola, supt. Fax 312-5609
www.newfairfieldschools.org

Consolidated ES 700/PK-2
12 Gillotti Rd 06812 203-312-5940
Wendy Seeley, prin. Fax 312-5942

Meeting House Hill ES 700/3-5
24 Gillotti Rd 06812 203-312-5905
Sarah McLain, prin. Fax 312-5907

New Fairfield MS 800/6-8
56 Gillotti Rd 06812 203-312-5886
Diane Hartman-Chesley, prin. Fax 312-5887

New Hartford, Litchfield, Pop. 5,769

New Hartford SD 600/PK-6
PO Box 315 06057 860-379-8546
Dr. Philip O'Reilly, supt. Fax 738-1766
www.newhtfd.org

Antolini ES 300/3-6
30 Antolini Rd 06057 860-489-4169
Katherine Rieger, prin. Fax 489-0392

Bakerville Consolidated ES 200/K-2
51 Cedar Ln 06057 860-482-0288
Stephen Nadeau, prin. Fax 482-1905

New Hartford ES 100/PK-2
PO Box 367 06057 860-379-1653
Stephen Nadeau, prin. Fax 379-6762

New Haven, New Haven, Pop. 124,791

New Haven SD 18,100/PK-12
54 Meadow St 06519 203-946-8888
Dr. Reginald Mayo, supt. Fax 946-7300
www.nhps.net

Barnard Envioronmental Studies Magnet S 300/PK-8
170 Derby Ave 06511 203-691-3500
Michael Crocco, prin. Fax 691-3505

Beecher S 300/PK-8
100 Jewell St 06515 203-691-3800
Kathy Russell-Beck, prin. Fax 691-3805

Bishop Woods ES 200/K-4
460 Lexington Ave 06513 203-946-8623
Barbara Chock, prin. Fax 946-7328

Bishop Woods MS 5-7
375 Quinnipiac Ave 06513 203-946-8623
Barbara Chock, prin. Fax 946-7328

Brennan S 200/3-8
200 Wilmot Rd 06515 203-946-8640
Celeste Davis, prin. Fax 946-7516

Celentano Museum Academy 400/PK-8
400 Canner St 06511 203-691-3400
Fax 691-5064

Clinton Avenue S 500/K-8
293 Clinton Ave 06513 203-691-3300
Carmen Rodriguez Robles, prin. Fax 946-5034

Columbus Family Academy 300/K-7
255 Blatchley Ave 06513 203-946-8620
Dr. Abie Benitez, prin. Fax 946-8384

Conte/West Hills Magnet S 600/K-8
511 Chapel St 06511 203-946-8613
Dianne Spence, prin. Fax 946-8802

Daniels S PK-8
569 Congress Ave 06519 203-691-3600
Gina Wells, prin. Fax 691-3605

Davis Street Magnet ES 400/PK-5
35 Davis St 06515 203-946-8660
Lola Nathan, prin. Fax 946-7776

East Rock Global Studies Magnet S 700/K-8
133 Nash St 06511 203-946-8867
Dr. Michael Conte, prin. Fax 946-7310

Edgewood Magnet S 400/K-8
737 Edgewood Ave 06515 203-946-8611
Bonnie Pachesa, prin. Fax 946-8957

Hale S 600/PK-8
480 Townsend Ave 06512 203-946-8669
Lucia Paolella, prin. Fax 946-7331

Hill Central Music Academy 500/PK-8
140 Dewitt St 06519 203-946-8680
Glen Worthy, prin. Fax 946-7339

Hooker ES 100/K-2
180 Canner St 06511 203-691-3700
Robert Rifenburg, prin. Fax 691-3705

Hooker MS 200/3-8
804 State St 06511 203-946-6610
Robert Rifenburg, prin. Fax 946-6376

Jepson Magnet S 300/PK-8
15 Lexington Ave 06513 203-691-2900
Peggy Pelley, prin. Fax 691-2905
King/Robinson Magnet S 300/PK-8
150 Fournier St 06511 203-691-2700
Illine Tracey, prin. Fax 946-2786
Lincoln-Bassett S 500/K-8
130 Bassett St 06511 203-946-8839
Ramona Gatison, prin. Fax 946-5607
Martinez S 600/PK-8
100 James St 06513 203-691-2000
Sequella Coleman, prin. Fax 691-2095
Mauro Magnet ES 400/PK-6
130 Orchard St 06519 203-946-5970
Denise Coles-Cross, prin. Fax 946-7341
MicroSociety Magnet S 200/PK-8
103 Hallock Ave 06519 203-946-7761
Laura Russo, prin. Fax 946-5794
Rogers S 100/K-2
199 Wilmot Rd 06515 203-946-5400
Celeste Davis, prin. Fax 946-5404
Ross Arts MS 500/5-8
150 Kimberly Ave 06519 203-946-8974
Peggy Moore, prin. Fax 946-5824
Ross/Woodward S 700/PK-8
185 Barnes Ave 06513 203-691-3100
Cheryl Brown, prin. Fax 691-3170
Sheridan Communications & Tech Magnet S 300/5-8
311 Valley St 06515 203-946-8828
Eleanor Turner, prin. Fax 946-5661
Strong Kindergarten K-K
69 Grand Ave 06513 203-946-8620
Gregory Huff, admin. Fax 946-8384
Truman S 500/K-8
114 Truman St 06519 203-691-2100
Roy Araujo, prin. Fax 691-2193
Wexler/Grant S 500/PK-8
55 Foote St 06511 203-946-8689
Fax 946-2363
Other Schools – See Hamden

Cold Spring S 100/K-6
263 Chapel St 06513 203-787-1584
Jeff Jonathan, hdmstr. Fax 787-9444
Foote S 500/K-9
50 Loomis Pl 06511 203-777-3464
Dary Dunham, prin. Fax 777-2809
St. Aedan S 200/PK-8
351 McKinley Ave 06515 203-387-5693
Catherine Fiorino, prin. Fax 387-1609
St. Bernadette S 200/PK-8
20 Burr St 06512 203-469-2271
Dr. Peter Barile, prin. Fax 469-4615
St. Brendan S 200/K-8
342 Ellsworth Ave 06511 203-562-6128
Catherine Fiorino, prin. Fax 562-6129
St. Francis S 200/PK-8
423 Ferry St 06513 203-777-5352
Dennis Beaupre, prin. Fax 865-1271
St. Martin dePorres Academy 100/5-8
208 Columbus Ave 06519 203-777-8137
Mary Surowiecki, prin. Fax 776-5018
St. Rose of Lima S 100/PK-8
12 Richard St 06513 203-624-5075
Sr. Marialice Ackermann, prin. Fax 624-1586
St. Thomas's Day S 200/PK-6
830 Whitney Ave 06511 203-776-2123
Fred Acquavita, hdmstr. Fax 776-3467
Yeshiva S 50/PK-8
765 Elm St 06511 203-777-2200
Sarah Greer, prin. Fax 777-7198

Newington, Hartford, Pop. 29,300
Newington SD 4,600/PK-12
131 Cedar St 06111 860-665-8610
Ernest Perlini, supt. Fax 665-8616
www.newington-schools.org
Chaffee ES 400/K-4
160 Superior Ave 06111 860-666-4687
Richard DeBellis, prin. Fax 667-5847
Green ES 300/PK-4
30 Thomas St 06111 860-666-3394
Anne-Marie Sladewski, prin. Fax 667-5843
Kellogg MS 700/5-8
155 Harding Ave 06111 860-666-5418
Jason Lambert, prin. Fax 666-5925
Paterson ES 500/PK-4
120 Church St 06111 860-666-4657
Stephen Foresi, prin. Fax 667-5853
Reynolds ES 500/PK-4
85 Reservoir Rd 06111 860-521-7830
Ellen Miller, prin. Fax 561-9725
Wallace MS 800/5-8
71 Halleran Dr 06111 860-667-5888
David Milardo, prin. Fax 667-5893

St. Mary S 300/PK-8
652 Willard Ave 06111 860-666-3844
Thomas Maynard, prin. Fax 666-5570

New London, New London, Pop. 26,174
Learn RESC
Supt. — See Old Lyme
Regional Multicultural Magnet S 500/K-5
1 Bulkeley Pl 06320 860-437-7775
Paul Carolan, dir. Fax 437-1475

New London SD 2,900/PK-12
134 Williams St 06320 860-447-6000
Christopher Clouet, supt. Fax 447-6016
www.newlondon.org
Hale ES 400/PK-5
37 Beech Dr 06320 860-447-6060
Donna Slate, prin. Fax 447-6066
Harbor ES 400/K-5
432 Montauk Ave 06320 860-447-6040
Susan Stambler, prin. Fax 447-6046
Jackson MS 700/6-8
36 Waller St 06320 860-437-6480
Tracy Barber, prin. Fax 437-6494
Jennings ES 400/K-5
50 Mercer St 06320 860-447-6040
Laurelle Texidor, prin. Fax 447-6046
Winthrop ES 300/PK-5
74 Grove St 06320 860-447-6070
Jaye Wilson, prin. Fax 447-6076

St. Joseph S 200/K-8
25 Squire St 06320 860-442-1720
Marianne Cote, prin. Fax 443-5247
St. Mary Star of Sea S 100/PK-8
10 Huntington St 06320 860-443-7758
Regina Ferrante, prin. Fax 444-2465
Solomon Schecter Academy 50/K-6
660 Ocean Ave 06320 860-443-5589
Karen Rosenberg, prin. Fax 437-1489

New Milford, Litchfield, Pop. 5,775
New Milford SD 5,000/PK-12
50 East St 06776 860-355-8406
JeanAnn Paddyfote Ph.D., supt. Fax 210-4132
www.newmilfordps.org
Hill & Plain ES 500/PK-3
60 Old Town Park Rd 06776 860-354-5430
Sandra Nadeau Ed.D., prin. Fax 355-3568
Noble IS 1,200/4-6
25 Sunny Valley Rd 06776 860-210-4020
Les Weintraub, prin. Fax 210-4030
Northville ES 500/PK-3
22 Hipp Rd 06776 860-355-3713
Susan Murray, prin. Fax 350-4234
Pettibone ES 500/PK-3
2 Pickett District Rd 06776 860-354-3218
Paula Kelleher, prin. Fax 355-8264
Schaghticoke MS 800/7-8
23 Hipp Rd 06776 860-354-2204
Dana Ford, prin. Fax 210-2217

Faith Academy/Faith Prep S 200/K-12
600 Danbury Rd Ste 2 06776 860-210-3677
Josephine DuBois, prin. Fax 210-3685

New Preston, Litchfield, Pop. 1,217

Washington Montessori S 300/PK-8
240 Litchfield Tpke 06777 860-868-0551
Patricia Werner, hdmstr. Fax 868-1362

Newtown, Fairfield, Pop. 1,835
Newtown SD 5,700/PK-12
31 Pecks Ln 06470 203-426-7621
Janet Robinson, supt. Fax 270-6199
www.newtown.k12.ct.us
Hawley ES 400/K-4
29 Church Hill Rd 06470 203-426-7666
Jo Ann Peters, prin. Fax 270-6543
Head O'Meadow ES 500/K-4
94 Boggs Hill Rd 06470 203-426-7670
William Bircher, prin. Fax 270-9610
Middle Gate ES 500/K-4
7 Cold Spring Rd 06470 203-426-7662
Judith Liestman, prin. Fax 426-7896
Newtown MS 900/7-8
11 Queen St 06470 203-426-7638
Diane Sherlock, prin. Fax 270-6102
Newtown Preschool 100/PK-PK
3 Trades Ln 06470 203-426-7683
Donna Denniston, prin. Fax 270-4899
Reed IS 900/5-6
3 Trades Ln 06470 203-270-4880
Donna Denniston, prin. Fax 270-4899
Other Schools – See Sandy Hook

Fraser-Woods S 200/PK-8
173 S Main St 06470 203-426-3390
Myriam Woods, hdmstr. Fax 426-0692
Housatonic Valley Waldorf S 100/PK-8
40 Dodgingtown Rd 06470 203-364-1113
Fax 364-0630
St. Rose S 400/PK-8
40 Church Hill Rd 06470 203-426-5102
Mary Maloney, prin. Fax 426-5374

Niantic, New London, Pop. 3,048
East Lyme SD
Supt. — See East Lyme
East Lyme MS 900/5-8
31 Society Rd 06357 860-739-4491
Judy DeLeeuw, prin. Fax 691-5400
Haynes ES 300/PK-4
29 Society Rd 06357 860-739-2922
David Miko, prin. Fax 739-1527
Niantic Center ES 200/K-4
7 W Main St 06357 860-739-3961
Lucy Schuman, prin. Fax 739-1258

Norfolk, Litchfield
Norfolk SD 200/PK-6
128 Greenwoods Rd E 06058 860-542-5553
George Counter, supt.
Botelle ES 200/PK-6
128 Greenwoods Rd E 06058 860-542-5286
Peter Michelson, prin.

North Branford, New Haven, Pop. 12,996
North Branford SD
Supt. — See Northford
Harrison ES 400/PK-3
335 Foxon Rd 06471 203-484-1235
Shawn Parkhurst, prin. Fax 484-1237
North Branford IS 600/6-8
654 Foxon Rd 06471 203-484-1500
Alan Davis, prin. Fax 484-1505

Northfield, Litchfield

Litchfield Montessori S 100/PK-6
5 Knife Shop Rd 06778 860-283-5920
Anne Marie Fenn, prin. Fax 283-0552

Northford, New Haven, Pop. 3,200
North Branford SD 2,400/PK-12
PO Box 129 06472 203-484-1440
M. Scott Schoonmaker, supt. Fax 484-1445
www.northbranfordschools.org
Totoket Valley ES 500/3-5
1388 Middletown Ave 06472 203-484-1455
Kris Lindsay, prin. Fax 484-6090
Williams ES 300/K-2
1332 Middletown Ave 06472 203-484-1240
Doug Hammel, prin. Fax 484-1245
Other Schools – See North Branford

North Franklin, New London
Franklin SD 200/PK-8
206 Pond Rd 06254 860-642-6113
A. Rodger Wutzl, supt. Fax 642-7256
www.franklin.k12.ct.us/
Franklin S 200/PK-8
206 Pond Rd 06254 860-642-7063
Amy Drowne, prin. Fax 642-7241

North Grosvenordale, Windham, Pop. 1,705
Thompson SD 1,500/PK-12
785 Riverside Dr 06255 860-923-9581
Michael Jolin Ph.D., supt. Fax 923-9638
www.thompson.ctschool.net
Fisher ES 600/PK-4
785 Riverside Dr 06255 860-923-9142
Noveline Beltram, prin. Fax 923-2062
Thompson MS 500/5-8
785 Riverside Dr 06255 860-923-9380
Ron Springer, prin. Fax 923-9638

St. Joseph S 100/PK-8
PO Box 137 06255 860-923-2090
Sharon Briere, prin. Fax 923-3609

North Haven, New Haven, Pop. 22,249
Area Coop. Educational Services RESC 1,800/
350 State St 06473 203-498-6800
Craig Edmondson Ed.D., dir. Fax 498-6890
www.aces.org
Other Schools – See Hamden, Meriden

North Haven SD 4,000/PK-12
5 Linsley St 06473 203-239-2581
Sara-Jane Querfeld, supt. Fax 234-9811
www.north-haven.k12.ct.us/
Clintonville ES 400/K-5
456 Clintonville Rd 06473 203-239-5865
Lauretta Dowling, prin. Fax 239-4009
Green Acres ES 500/PK-5
146 Upper State St 06473 203-239-5387
Linda Cahill, prin. Fax 239-4773
Montowese ES 400/K-5
145 Fitch St 06473 203-239-2564
Anthony Mancini, prin. Fax 234-7205
North Haven MS 900/6-8
55 Bailey Rd 06473 203-239-1683
Philip Piazza, prin. Fax 234-2846
Ridge Road ES 500/K-5
1341 Ridge Rd 06473 203-248-4050
Kathleen Peters-Durrigan, prin. Fax 407-1816

North Stonington, New London
North Stonington SD 800/PK-12
297 Norwich Westerly Rd 06359 860-535-2800
Natalie Pukas, supt. Fax 535-1470
www.northstonington.k12.ct.us
North Stonington ES 400/PK-5
311 Norwich Westerly Rd 06359 860-535-2805
Veronica Wilkison, prin. Fax 535-4641
Wheeler MS 200/6-8
298 Norwich Westerly Rd 06359 860-535-0377
Michael Susi, prin. Fax 535-2536

North Stonington Christian Academy 100/PK-12
12 Stillman Rd 06359 860-599-5071
Pamela Wilkinson, dir. Fax 599-2815

North Windham, Windham
Windham SD
Supt. — See Willimantic
North Windham ES 400/K-4
112 Jordan Ln 06256 860-465-2400
Betsy Fernandez, prin. Fax 465-2403

Norwalk, Fairfield, Pop. 84,437
Norwalk SD 10,700/PK-12
PO Box 6001 06852 203-854-4000
Dr. Salvatore Corda, supt. Fax 838-3299
www.norwalk.k12.ct.us
Brookside ES 400/K-5
382 Highland Ave 06854 203-899-2830
David Hay, prin. Fax 899-2834
Columbus ES 400/K-5
46 Concord St 06854 203-899-2840
Emily Lopez, prin. Fax 899-2844
Cranbury ES 500/PK-5
5 Knowalot Ln 06851 203-846-3600
Robin Ives, prin. Fax 899-2854
Fox Run ES 400/PK-5
228 Fillow St 06850 203-899-2860
Patricia Dielman, prin. Fax 899-2864
Hale MS 500/6-8
176 Strawberry Hill Ave 06851 203-899-2910
Robert McCain, prin. Fax 899-2914
Jefferson ES 400/K-5
75 Van Buren Ave 06850 203-899-2870
John Reynolds, prin. Fax 899-2874
Kendall ES 500/PK-5
57 Fillow St 06850 203-899-2880
Tony Ditrio, prin. Fax 899-2884
Marvin ES 500/PK-5
15 Calf Pasture Beach Rd 06855 203-899-2890
Myrna Tortorello, prin. Fax 899-2894
Naramake ES 400/K-5
16 King St 06851 203-899-2900
Robert Henry, prin. Fax 899-2904

Ponus Ridge MS 600/6-8
21 Hunters Ln 06850 203-847-3557
Linda Sumpter, prin. Fax 899-2924
Roton MS 400/6-8
201 Highland Ave 06853 203-899-2930
Joseph Vellucci, prin. Fax 899-2934
Rowayton ES 400/K-5
1 Roton Ave 06853 203-899-2940
Sara Reilly, prin. Fax 899-2944
Silvermine ES 400/K-5
157 Perry Ave 06850 203-899-2950
Ivette Ellis, prin. Fax 899-2954
Tracey ES 400/K-5
20 Camp St 06851 203-899-2960
Paul Krasnavage, prin. Fax 899-2964
West Rocks MS 800/6-8
81 W Rocks Rd 06851 203-899-2970
Lynne Moore, prin. Fax 899-2974
Wolfpit ES 300/PK-5
1 Starlight Dr 06851 203-899-2980
Frances Mahoney, prin. Fax 899-2984

All Saints S 700/PK-8
139 W Rocks Rd 06851 203-847-3881
Nancy DiBuono, prin. Fax 847-8055

Norwich, New London, Pop. 36,598
Norwich SD 3,900/PK-8
90 Town St 06360 860-823-4245
Pamela Aubin, supt. Fax 823-1880
www.norwichpublicschools.org
Bishop ES 100/PK-5
526 E Main St 06360 860-823-4201
Cheryl Vocatura, prin. Fax 823-4220
Greeneville ES 300/K-5
165 Golden St 06360 860-823-4203
Marianne Nardone, prin. Fax 823-4288
Huntington ES 400/PK-5
80 W Town St 06360 860-823-4204
Rebecca Pellerin, prin. Fax 823-4241
Kelly MS 700/6-8
25 Mahan Dr 06360 860-823-4211
Michael Cain, prin. Fax 892-4302
Mahan ES 300/PK-5
94 Salem Tpke 06360 860-823-4205
Rose Herrick, prin. Fax 823-4235
Moriarty ES 400/PK-5
20 Lawler Ln 06360 860-823-4206
Linda Demikat, prin. Fax 823-4246
Stanton ES 300/PK-5
386 New London Tpke 06360 860-823-4207
Janis Sawicki, prin. Fax 823-4250
Teachers Memorial MS 500/6-8
15 Teachers Dr 06360 860-823-4212
William Peckham, prin. Fax 823-4277
Uncas ES 200/K-5
280 Elizabeth Street Ext 06360 860-823-4208
Christie Gilluly, prin. Fax 823-4251
Veterans Memorial ES 300/PK-5
80 Crouch Ave 06360 860-823-4209
Susan Lacy, prin. Fax 823-4252
Other Schools – See Taftville

Montessori Discovery S 100/PK-6
218 Dudley St 06360 860-889-0340
Patrice Champagne, hdmstr. Fax 889-7949
St. Joseph S 100/PK-8
120 Cliff St 06360 860-887-4565
Sr. Rafael Allen, prin. Fax 886-6468
St. Patrick Cathedral S 200/K-8
211 Broadway 06360 860-889-4174
Catherine Reed, prin. Fax 889-0040
Wildwood Christian S 100/PK-8
35 Wawecus Hill Rd 06360 860-887-7830
Katherine Anderson, prin. Fax 887-5678

Oakdale, New London
Montville SD 2,900/PK-12
800 Old Colchester Rd 06370 860-848-1228
David Erwin, supt. Fax 848-0589
www.montvilleschools.org
Murphy ES 400/K-5
500 Chesterfield Rd 06370 860-848-9241
Jeffrey Newton, prin. Fax 848-1703
Oakdale ES 500/PK-5
30 Indiana Cir 06370 860-859-1800
Mark Johnson, prin. Fax 859-2170
Tyl MS 700/6-8
166 Chesterfield Rd 06370 860-848-2822
Thomas Girard, prin. Fax 848-8854
Other Schools – See Uncasville

Oakville, Litchfield, Pop. 8,741
Watertown SD
Supt. — See Watertown
Polk ES 400/3-5
435 Buckingham St 06779 860-945-4840
Emily Judd, prin. Fax 945-7113
Swift MS 600/6-8
250 Colonial St 06779 860-945-4830
Marylu Lerz, prin. Fax 945-6449
Trumbull PS 800/PK-2
779 Buckingham St 06779 860-945-2776
Kathy Scully, prin. Fax 945-2781

St. Mary Magdalen S 300/PK-8
140 Buckingham St 06779 860-945-0621
Julie Pion, prin. Fax 945-6162

Old Greenwich, Fairfield
Greenwich SD
Supt. — See Greenwich
Old Greenwich ES 400/K-5
285 Sound Beach Ave 06870 203-637-0150
Patricia Raineri, prin. Fax 637-4666

Old Lyme, New London
Learn RESC 600/
44 Hatchetts Hill Rd 06371 860-434-4800
Virginia Seccombe, dir. Fax 434-4837
www.learn.k12.ct.us
Other Schools – See New London, Waterford

Regional SD 18 1,500/PK-12
4 Davis Rd W 06371 860-434-7238
Dr. Elizabeth Osga, supt. Fax 434-9959
www.region18.org
Center IS 200/3-5
49 Lyme St 06371 860-434-7838
Christopher Pomroy, prin. Fax 434-6901
Lyme-Old Lyme MS 400/6-8
53 Lyme St 06371 860-434-2568
Jeffrey Ostroff, prin. Fax 434-0717
Mile Creek ES 300/PK-2
205 Mile Creek Rd 06371 860-434-2209
Patricia Downes, prin. Fax 434-8347
Other Schools – See Lyme

Old Mystic, New London
Stonington SD 2,500/K-12
PO Box 479 06372 860-572-0506
Michael McKee, supt. Fax 572-1470
www.stoningtonschools.org
Other Schools – See Mystic, Pawcatuck, Stonington

Old Saybrook, Middlesex, Pop. 9,552
Old Saybrook SD 1,600/PK-12
50 Sheffield St 06475 860-395-3157
Joseph Onofrio, supt. Fax 395-3162
www.oldsaybrook.k12.ct.us
Goodwin ES 500/PK-3
80 Old Boston Post Rd 06475 860-395-3165
Sheila Brown, prin. Fax 395-3360
Old Saybrook MS 600/4-8
60 Sheffield St 06475 860-395-3168
Michael Rafferty, prin. Fax 395-3350

Children's Tree Montessori S 100/PK-6
96 Essex Rd 06475 860-388-3536
Marci Martindale, hdmstr. Fax 388-4756
St. John S 200/PK-8
42 Maynard Rd 06475 860-388-0849
Mother Martin LeClair, prin. Fax 388-6265

Orange, New Haven, Pop. 12,830
Orange SD 1,400/PK-6
637 Orange Center Rd 06477 203-891-8020
Tim James, supt. Fax 891-8025
www.oess.org/
Peck Place ES 500/1-6
500 Peck Ln 06477 203-891-8034
Albert deCant, prin. Fax 891-8038
Race Brook ES 400/1-6
107 Grannis Rd 06477 203-891-8030
Michael Gray, prin. Fax 891-8044
Tracy S 200/PK-K
650 Schoolhouse Ln 06477 203-891-8028
Ralph Nuzzo, prin. Fax 795-2119
Turkey Hill ES 300/1-6
441 Turkey Hill Rd 06477 203-891-8040
Colleen Murray, prin. Fax 891-8043

Regional SD 5
Supt. — See Woodbridge
Amity Regional MS 400/7-8
100 Ohman Ave 06477 203-392-3200
Robert Slie, prin. Fax 387-7603

Southern Connecticut Hebrew Academy 200/K-12
261 Derby Ave 06477 203-795-5261
Rabbi Sheya Hecht, hdmstr. Fax 891-9719

Oxford, New Haven
Oxford SD 1,600/PK-12
1 Great Hill Rd 06478 203-888-7754
Judith Palmer, supt. Fax 888-5955
www.oxfordpublicschools.org
Great Oak MS 500/6-8
50 Great Oak Rd 06478 203-888-5418
Brian Murphy, prin. Fax 888-7798
Oxford Center IS 500/3-5
462 Oxford Rd 06478 203-888-6492
Heath Hendershot, prin. Fax 888-1216
Quaker Farms ES 600/PK-2
30 Great Oak Rd 06478 203-888-5842
Rachael Cacace, prin. Fax 888-6813

Pawcatuck, New London, Pop. 5,289
Stonington SD
Supt. — See Old Mystic
Pawcatuck MS 300/5-8
40 Field St 06379 860-599-5696
Jane Giulini, prin. Fax 599-8948
West Broad Street ES 200/3-4
131 W Broad St 06379 860-599-5633
Theresa Jordan, prin. Fax 599-0611
West Vine Street ES 200/K-2
17 W Vine St 06379 860-599-5832
Virginia Brown, prin. Fax 599-1560

St. Michael S 100/K-8
63 Liberty St 06379 860-599-1084
Doris Messina, prin. Fax 599-2817

Plainfield, Windham, Pop. 14,363
Plainfield SD 2,800/PK-12
651 Norwich Rd 06374 860-564-6403
Dr. Mary Conway, supt. Fax 564-6412
www.plainfieldschools.org/
ECC 300/PK-K
651 Norwich Rd 06374 860-564-6400
William Nagel, prin. Fax 564-6409
Plainfield Central MS 600/6-8
75 Canterbury Rd 06374 860-564-6437
Jerry Davis, prin. Fax 564-1147
Plainfield Memorial ES 400/4-5
95 Canterbury Rd 06374 860-564-6440
Lyn Gandolf, prin. Fax 564-6076
Shepard Hill ES 300/1-3
234 Shepard Hill Rd 06374 860-564-6432
Mark Levanto, prin. Fax 564-6060
Other Schools – See Moosup

Plainville, Hartford, Pop. 17,932
Plainville SD 2,600/PK-12
1 Central Sq 06062 860-793-3200
Kathleen Binkowski, supt. Fax 747-6790
www.plainvilleschools.org
Linden Street ES 400/PK-5
69 Linden St 06062 860-793-3270
Suzanne Greenbacker, prin. Fax 793-3269
MS of Plainville 700/6-8
150 Northwest Dr 06062 860-793-3250
Matthew Guarino, prin. Fax 793-3265
Toffolon ES 300/K-5
145 Northwest Dr 06062 860-793-3280
Lynn Logoyke, prin. Fax 793-6302
Wheeler ES 300/K-5
15 Cleveland Memorial Dr 06062 860-793-3290
Catherine Frayler, prin. Fax 793-3288

Plantsville, Hartford, Pop. 7,000
Southington SD
Supt. — See Southington
Kennedy MS 800/6-8
1071 S Main St 06479 860-628-3275
Angelo Campagnano, prin. Fax 628-3404
South End ES 200/K-5
514 S End Rd 06479 860-628-3320
Sally Kamerbeek, prin. Fax 620-1667
Strong ES 400/K-5
820 Marion Ave 06479 860-628-3314
Linda Lackner, prin. Fax 628-3322

Plymouth, Litchfield
Plymouth SD
Supt. — See Terryville
Plymouth Center ES 500/PK-5
107 North St 06782 860-283-6321
Chrystal Collins, prin. Fax 283-6981

Pomfret, Windham

Rectory S 200/K-9
PO Box 68 06258 860-928-7759
Thomas Army, hdmstr. Fax 963-2355

Pomfret Center, Windham
Pomfret SD 500/PK-8
20 Pomfret St 06259 860-928-2718
Richard Packman, supt. Fax 928-3839
www.pomfret.ctschool.net
Pomfret Community S 500/PK-8
20 Pomfret St 06259 860-928-2718
Jane Dion, prin. Fax 928-3839

Portland, Middlesex, Pop. 5,645
Portland SD 1,500/PK-12
33 E Main St 06480 860-342-6790
Dr. Sally Doyen, supt. Fax 342-6791
www.portlandct.org
Brownstone IS 300/5-6
314 Main St 06480 860-342-6765
Laurie Boske, prin. Fax 342-6766
Gildersleeve ES 200/3-4
575 1/2 Main St 06480 860-342-0411
Eileen Katz, prin. Fax 342-3194
Portland MS 200/7-8
93 High St 06480 860-342-1880
Scott Giegerich, prin. Fax 342-3934
Valley View ES 400/PK-2
81 High St 06480 860-342-3131
Deborah Graner, prin. Fax 342-3138

Preston, New London
Preston SD 500/PK-8
325 Shetucket Tpke 06365 860-889-6098
Dr. John Welch, supt. Fax 889-8685
www.prestonschools.org/
Preston Plains MS 200/6-8
1 Route 164 06365 860-889-3831
Raymond Bernier, prin. Fax 889-8685
Preston Veteran's Memorial S 300/PK-5
325 Shetucket Tpke 06365 860-887-3113
Dr. Kathryn Walsh, prin. Fax 889-5478

Prospect, New Haven, Pop. 7,775
Regional SD 16 2,700/PK-12
207 New Haven Rd 06712 203-758-6671
James Agostine, supt. Fax 758-5797
www.region16ct.org
Algonquin ES 500/PK-3
30 Coer Rd 06712 203-758-4408
Lynn Patterson, prin. Fax 758-7505
Community ES 200/4-5
12 Center St 06712 203-758-6674
Joseph Nuzzo, prin. Fax 758-7543
Long River MS 600/6-8
Columbia Ave 06712 203-758-4421
Jayne Lanphear, prin. Fax 758-6948
Other Schools – See Beacon Falls

Putnam, Windham, Pop. 9,031
Putnam SD 1,300/PK-12
126 Church St 06260 860-963-6900
William Hull, supt. Fax 963-6903
www.putnam.k12.ct.us/
Putnam ES 700/PK-5
33 Wicker St 06260 860-963-6925
Georgeann Farrah, prin. Fax 963-5364
Putnam MS 300/6-8
35 Wicker St 06260 860-963-6920
Joseph Morris, prin. Fax 963-6921

St. Mary S 100/PK-8
23 Marshall St 06260 860-928-7046
Michael Ryba, prin. Fax 928-9379

Tri-State Christian Academy 50/K-8
250 E Putnam Rd 06260 860-963-3787
Linda Filteau, admin. Fax 963-0623

Quaker Hill, New London

Waterford SD
Supt. — See Waterford
Quaker Hill ES 200/K-5
285 Bloomingdale Rd 06375 860-442-1095
Dr. Glenda Dexter, prin.

Redding, Fairfield

Redding SD
Supt. — See Easton
Redding ES 700/K-4
33 Lonetown Rd 06896 203-938-2519
Stephanie Ugol, prin. Fax 938-3251

Ridgefield, Fairfield, Pop. 6,363

Ridgefield SD 5,600/PK-12
70 Prospect St 06877 203-431-2800
Deborah Low, supt. Fax 431-2810
www.ridgefield.org
Barlow Mountain ES 500/PK-5
115 Barlow Mountain Rd 06877 203-431-2800
Rebecca Pembrook, prin. Fax 894-7701
Branchville ES 400/K-5
40 Florida Rd 06877 203-544-7980
Jason McKinnon, prin. Fax 544-7984
East Ridge MS 700/6-8
10 E Ridge Rd 06877 203-438-3744
Martin Fiedler, prin. Fax 431-2843
Farmingville ES 400/K-5
324 Farmingville Rd 06877 203-431-2830
Susan Gately, prin. Fax 431-2835
Ridgebury ES 500/K-5
112 Bennetts Farm Rd 06877 203-438-6555
Elizabeth Smith, prin. Fax 431-2853
Scotland ES 400/K-5
111 Barlow Mountain Rd 06877 203-438-6563
Mark Solomon, prin. Fax 431-2861
Scotts Ridge MS 600/6-8
750 N Salem Rd 06877 203-894-3400
Marie Doyon, prin. Fax 894-3411
Veterans Park ES 300/K-5
8 Governor St 06877 203-438-6571
Julie Droller, prin. Fax 431-2875

Ridgefield Academy 400/PK-8
223 W Mountain Rd 06877 203-894-1800
James Heus, hdmstr. Fax 894-1810
St. Mary S 300/PK-8
183 High Ridge Ave 06877 203-438-4638
Edward Brennan, prin. Fax 431-8742

Riverside, Fairfield

Greenwich SD
Supt. — See Greenwich
Eastern MS 700/6-8
51 Hendrie Ave 06878 203-637-1744
Ralph Mayo, prin. Fax 637-3567
International S at Dundee 400/K-5
55 Florence Rd 06878 203-637-3800
Terri Ricci, prin. Fax 637-5423
North Mianus ES 400/K-5
309 Palmer Hill Rd 06878 203-637-9730
Bonnie Butera, prin. Fax 637-9387
Riverside ES 500/K-5
90 Hendrie Ave 06878 203-637-1440
John Grasso, prin. Fax 637-1004

Rocky Hill, Hartford, Pop. 16,554

Rocky Hill SD 2,600/PK-12
PO Box 627 06067 860-258-7701
Jeffrey Villar Ph.D., supt. Fax 258-7710
Griswold MS 600/6-8
144 Bailey Rd 06067 860-258-7741
Richard Watson, prin. Fax 258-7746
Moser ES 100/K-2
10 School St 06067 860-258-7771
Audrey Boutaugh, prin. Fax 258-7773
Stevens ES 500/PK-5
322 Orchard St 06067 860-258-7751
Audrey Boutaugh, prin. Fax 258-7753
West Hill ES 600/PK-5
95 Cronin Dr 06067 860-258-7761
Cori-Ann DiMaggio, prin. Fax 258-7764

Roxbury, Litchfield

Regional SD 12
Supt. — See Washington Depot
Booth Free ES 100/K-5
14 South St 06783 860-354-9391
Cathy Colella, prin. Fax 350-6563

Salem, New London, Pop. 3,310

Salem SD 500/PK-8
200 Hartford Rd 06420 860-892-1223
Dr. Donna Leake, supt. Fax 859-2130
www.salemschools.org
Salem S 500/PK-8
200 Hartford Rd 06420 860-859-0267
Nikki Gullickson, prin. Fax 859-2130

Sandy Hook, Fairfield

Newtown SD
Supt. — See Newtown
Sandy Hook ES 700/K-4
12 Dickenson Dr 06482 203-426-7657
Donna Page, prin. Fax 426-2649

Scotland, Windham

Scotland SD 200/PK-6
68 Brook Rd 06264 860-423-0064
Dr. Paul Blackstone, supt. Fax 423-0390
www.scotlandschool.org/
Scotland ES 200/PK-6
68 Brook Rd 06264 860-423-0064
Dr. Paul Blackstone, prin. Fax 423-0390

Seymour, New Haven, Pop. 14,288

Seymour SD 2,700/PK-12
98 Bank St 06483 203-888-4565
MaryAnne Mascolo, supt. Fax 888-1704
www.seymourschools.org
Bungay ES 600/PK-5
35 Bungay Rd 06483 203-881-7500
Mary Sue Feige, prin. Fax 881-7506
Chatfield ES 300/K-5
51 Skokorat St 06483 203-888-4640
Jamie Giordano, prin. Fax 888-5492
Lopresti ES 300/K-5
29 Maple St 06483 203-888-2009
Monica Briggs, prin. Fax 888-1932
Seymour MS 600/6-8
211 Mountain Rd 06483 203-888-4513
Bernadette Hamad, prin. Fax 881-7535

Sharon, Litchfield

Sharon SD
Supt. — See Falls Village
Sharon Center S 200/PK-8
80 Hilltop Rd 06069 860-364-5153
Karen Manning, prin. Fax 364-5473

Shelton, Fairfield, Pop. 39,477

Shelton SD 5,700/PK-12
382 Long Hill Ave 06484 203-924-1023
Freeman Burr, supt. Fax 924-5894
www.sheltonpublicschools.org
Booth Hill ES 500/K-6
544 Booth Hill Rd 06484 203-929-5625
Kathleen Sheehy, prin. Fax 225-1587
Lafayette ES 400/PK-6
54 Grove St 06484 203-924-2533
Darlene Tickey, prin. Fax 922-3019
Long Hill ES 600/PK-6
565 Long Hill Ave 06484 203-929-4077
Susan Arpin, prin. Fax 929-8250
Mohegan ES 600/K-6
47 Mohegan Rd 06484 203-929-4121
Lorraine Williams, prin. Fax 929-8246
Shelton ES 600/K-6
138 Willoughby Rd 06484 203-929-1330
Beverly Belden, prin. Fax 225-1574
Shelton IS 900/7-8
675 Constitution Blvd N 06484 203-926-2000
Kenneth Saranich, prin. Fax 926-2017
Sunnyside ES 400/K-6
418 River Rd 06484 203-922-3021
Anne Hamilton, prin. Fax 924-7581

St. Joseph S 200/PK-8
430 Coram Ave 06484 203-924-4669
Arlene Clancy, prin. Fax 922-0161
St. Lawrence S 300/PK-8
503 Shelton Ave 06484 203-929-4422
Martha Reitman, prin. Fax 929-3669

Sherman, Fairfield

Sherman SD 500/PK-8
2 Route 37 E 06784 860-355-3793
Joseph Reardon, supt. Fax 355-9023
www.shermanschool.com
Sherman S 500/PK-8
2 Route 37 E 06784 860-355-3793
Mary Boylan, prin. Fax 355-9023

Simsbury, Hartford, Pop. 22,023

Simsbury SD 5,000/PK-12
933 Hopmeadow St 06070 860-651-3361
Diane Ullman, supt. Fax 651-4343
www.simsbury.k12.ct.us
Central ES 500/PK-6
29 Massaco St 06070 860-658-4732
Edie Balkun, prin. Fax 658-3620
James Memorial MS 800/7-8
155 Firetown Rd 06070 860-651-3341
Susan Homrok, prin. Fax 658-3629
Squadron Line ES 800/K-6
44 Squadron Line Rd 06070 860-658-2251
Matt Curtis, prin. Fax 658-3627
Other Schools – See Tariffville, Weatogue, West Simsbury

Cobb S 100/PK-6
112 Sand Hill Rd 06070 860-658-1144
Mary Lou Cobb, admin. Fax 651-4900
St. Mary S 300/PK-8
946 Hopmeadow St 06070 860-658-9412
Marie Gannatti, prin. Fax 658-1737

Somers, Tolland

Somers SD 1,700/PK-12
47 9th District Rd 06071 860-749-2270
Dr. Maynard Suffredini, supt. Fax 763-0748
www.somers.k12.ct.us
Avery MS 400/6-8
47 9th District Rd 06071 860-749-2270
Nancy Barry, prin. Fax 763-2073
Somers ES 700/PK-5
55 9th District Rd 06071 860-749-2270
Ralph Riola, prin. Fax 763-0620

Southbury, New Haven, Pop. 15,818

Regional SD 15
Supt. — See Middlebury
Gainfield ES 500/K-5
307 Old Field Rd 06488 203-264-5312
Dr. Leonard Tomasello, prin. Fax 264-6439
Pomperaug ES 500/K-5
607 Main St S 06488 203-264-8283
Carissa Keepin, prin. Fax 264-7387
Rochambeau MS 600/6-8
100 Peter Rd 06488 203-264-2711
Anthony Salutari, prin. Fax 264-6638

South Glastonbury, Hartford

Glastonbury SD
Supt. — See Glastonbury
Hopewell ES 700/K-5
1068 Chestnut Hill Rd 06073 860-652-7897
Kathleen Murphy, prin. Fax 652-7904
Nayaug ES K-5
222 Old Maids Ln 06073 860-652-4949
Kate Carter, prin. Fax 652-4950

Southington, Hartford, Pop. 39,200

Southington SD 6,900/PK-12
49 Beecher St 06489 860-628-3202
Dr. Joseph Erardi, supt. Fax 628-3205
www.southingtonschools.org
DePaolo MS 800/6-8
385 Pleasant St 06489 860-628-3260
Frank Pepe, prin. Fax 628-3403
Derynoski ES 700/K-5
240 Main St 06489 860-628-3286
Karen Smith, prin. Fax 628-3381
Flanders ES 300/K-5
100 Victoria Dr 06489 860-628-3372
Patricia Mazzarella, prin. Fax 628-3253
Hatton ES 400/PK-5
50 Spring Lake Rd 06489 860-628-3377
Roberta McAloon, prin. Fax 628-3210
Kelley ES 400/K-5
501 Ridgewood Rd 06489 860-628-3310
Elizabeth Lutz, prin. Fax 628-3335
Plantsville ES 200/K-5
200 N Main St 06489 860-628-3379
Patricia Corvello, prin. Fax 628-3418
Thalberg ES 400/K-5
145 Dunham St 06489 860-628-3370
Beecher Lajoie, prin. Fax 628-3308
Other Schools – See Plantsville

St. Dominic S 200/PK-5
1050 Flanders Rd 06489 860-628-4678
Patricia Tiezzi, prin. Fax 628-6572
St. Thomas S 100/PK-5
133 Bristol St 06489 860-628-2485
Joan Murphy, prin. Fax 628-7341

Southport, Fairfield

Fairfield SD
Supt. — See Fairfield
Mill Hill ES 400/K-5
635 Mill Hill Ter, 203-255-8320
Kevin Chase, prin. Fax 255-8205

South Windsor, Hartford, Pop. 22,090

South Windsor SD 5,000/K-12
1737 Main St 06074 860-291-1205
Dr. Robert Kozaczka, supt. Fax 291-1291
www.swindsor.k12.ct.us
Edwards MS 1,200/6-8
100 Arnold Way 06074 860-648-5030
Kristin Heckt, prin. Fax 648-5029
Orchard Hill ES 500/K-5
350 Foster St 06074 860-648-5015
Michael Tortora, prin. Fax 648-0141
Pleasant Valley ES 500/K-5
591 Ellington Rd 06074 860-291-1280
Michael Seal, prin. Fax 282-2287
Smith ES 500/K-5
949 Avery St 06074 860-648-5025
Laura Stuart-Wonderlie, prin. Fax 648-5014
Terry ES 400/K-5
569 Griffin Rd 06074 860-648-5020
Marilyn Sevick, prin. Fax 648-0142
Wapping ES 300/K-5
91 Ayers Rd 06074 860-648-5010
Laura Hickson, prin. Fax 648-5802

Stafford Springs, Tolland, Pop. 4,100

Stafford SD 1,300/PK-12
PO Box 147 06076 860-684-4211
Therese Fishman, supt. Fax 684-5172
www.stafford.ctschool.net/
Stafford ES 2-5
PO Box 586 06076 860-684-6677
Henry Skala, prin. Fax 684-3925
Stafford MS 500/6-8
PO Box 106 06076 860-684-2785
Kenneth Valentine, prin. Fax 684-4671
West Stafford ES 200/PK-1
153 W Stafford Rd 06076 860-684-3181
Marcia Elliott Ed.D., prin. Fax 684-0328
Other Schools – See Staffordville

St. Edward S 100/PK-8
25 Church St 06076 860-684-2600
MaryAnne Pelletier, prin. Fax 684-4030

Staffordville, Tolland

Stafford SD
Supt. — See Stafford Springs
Staffordville ES 100/PK-1
PO Box 216 06077 860-684-3298
Paula Kuenzler, prin. Fax 684-7088

Stamford, Fairfield, Pop. 120,045

Stamford SD 15,000/PK-12
888 Washington Blvd Fl 5 06901 203-977-4543
Dr. Joshua Starr, supt. Fax 977-5964
www.stamfordpublicschools.org/
Cloonan MS 600/6-8
11 W North St 06902 203-977-4544
David Rudolph, prin. Fax 977-4867
Davenport Ridge ES 600/K-5
1300 Newfield Ave 06905 203-977-4291
Cheryl Dwyer, prin. Fax 977-5116
Dolan MS 600/6-8
51 Toms Rd 06906 203-977-4441
Charmaine Tourse, prin. Fax 977-4880
Hart Magnet ES 500/K-5
61 Adams Ave 06902 203-977-5082
Linda Darling, prin. Fax 977-5084
International S @ Rogers Magnet 600/K-5
83 Lockwood Ave 06902 203-977-4560
Cathy Cummings, prin. Fax 977-5732

Murphy ES 500/K-5
19 Horton St 06902 203-977-4516
Barbara Friedman, prin. Fax 977-5103
Newfield ES 600/K-5
345 Pepper Ridge Rd 06905 203-977-4282
Miriam Arango, prin. Fax 977-4818
Northeast ES 800/K-5
82 Scofieldtown Rd 06903 203-977-4469
Dr. Ethan Margolis, prin. Fax 977-4312
Rippowam MS 800/6-8
381 High Ridge Rd 06905 203-977-5255
George Giberti, prin. Fax 977-5154
Roxbury ES 700/K-5
751 W Hill Rd 06902 203-977-4287
Gail Flaster, prin. Fax 977-4615
Scofield Magnet MS 600/6-8
641 Scofieldtown Rd 06903 203-977-2750
Jan Rossman, prin. Fax 977-2766
Springdale ES 600/K-5
1127 Hope St 06907 203-977-4575
Roshelley Woodson, prin. Fax 977-4058
Stark ES 600/PK-5
398 Glenbrook Rd 06906 203-977-4583
Mary Savage, prin. Fax 977-5426
Stillmeadow ES 600/PK-5
800 Stillwater Rd 06902 203-977-4507
Dr. Michael Sanders, prin. Fax 977-4506
Toquam Magnet ES 500/K-5
123 Ridgewood Ave 06907 203-977-4556
Louise Spolowitz, prin. Fax 977-5055
Turn of River MS 600/6-8
117 Vine Rd 06905 203-977-4284
Dr. Michael Fernandes, prin. Fax 977-5037
Westover ES 600/PK-5
412 Stillwater Ave 06902 203-977-4572
Kathy Wunder, prin. Fax 977-5180

Bi-Cultural Day S 400/PK-8
2186 High Ridge Rd 06903 203-329-2186
Dr. Gerald Kirshenbaum, hdmstr. Fax 329-0464
Children's S 100/PK-3
118 Scofieldtown Rd 06903 203-329-8815
Maureen Murphy, hdmstr. Fax 329-9443
Grace Christian S 100/PK-7
602 High Ridge Rd 06905 203-329-1482
Elizabeth Nolan, hdmstr. Fax 329-0458
Holy Spirit S 100/PK-5
403 Scofieldtown Rd 06903 203-329-7148
Patricia Torchen, prin. Fax 595-0858
King Low Heywood Thomas S 700/PK-12
1450 Newfield Ave 06905 203-322-3496
Thomas Main, hdmstr. Fax 329-0291
Long Ridge S 100/PK-5
478 Erskine Rd 06903 203-322-7693
Kris Bria, hdmstr. Fax 322-0406
Mead S 100/PK-8
1095 Riverbank Rd 06903 203-595-9500
Karen Biddulph, dir. Fax 595-0735
Our Lady Star of the Sea S 100/PK-5
1170 Shippan Ave 06902 203-348-1155
Gail Ryan, prin. Fax 324-6150
Sacred Heart S PK-PK
1 Schuyler Ave 06902 203-323-4844
Fax 359-9859
St. Cecilia S 300/PK-5
1186 Newfield Ave 06905 203-322-6505
Dr. Joann Borchetta, prin. Fax 322-6835
Trinity Catholic MS 200/6-8
948 Newfield Ave 06905 203-322-7383
Richard Fox, prin. Fax 324-4435

Sterling, Windham
Sterling SD 500/PK-8
251 Sterling Rd 06377 860-564-4219
Richard Spurling Ph.D., supt. Fax 564-1989
Sterling Community S 500/PK-8
251 Sterling Rd 06377 860-564-2728
Vincent Agostine, prin. Fax 564-1989

Stonington, New London, Pop. 1,054
Stonington SD
Supt. — See Old Mystic
Deans Mill ES 500/K-4
35 Deans Mill Rd 06378 860-535-2235
Kelly Spooner, prin. Fax 535-1417

Pine Point S 300/PK-9
89 Barnes Rd 06378 860-535-0606
Paul Geise, hdmstr. Fax 535-8033

Storrs, Tolland, Pop. 12,198
Mansfield SD 1,300/PK-8
4 S Eagleville Rd 06268 860-429-3350
Frederick Baruzzi, supt. Fax 429-3379
www.mansfieldct.org
Goodwin ES 200/PK-4
321 Hunting Lodge Rd 06268 860-429-4630
Debra Adamczyk, prin. Fax 487-5641
Mansfield MS 600/5-8
205 Spring Hill Rd 06268 860-429-9341
Jeffrey Cryan, prin. Fax 429-1020
Other Schools – See Mansfield Center

Stratford, Fairfield, Pop. 50,100
Stratford SD 7,400/PK-12
1000 E Broadway 06615 203-385-4210
Irene Cornish, supt. Fax 381-2012
www.stratfordk12.org
Chapel ES 500/K-6
380 Chapel St 06614 203-385-4192
Mary Ann Craig, prin. Fax 381-6964
Flood MS 600/7-8
490 Chapel St 06614 203-385-4280
John Dellapiano, prin. Fax 381-2033
Franklin ES 400/K-6
1895 Barnum Ave 06614 203-385-4190
Lea Ann Blackwell, prin. Fax 385-4116
Lordship ES 200/K-6
254 Crown St 06615 203-385-4170
Melissa Bilotta, prin. Fax 385-4118
Nichols ES 400/K-6
396 Nichols Ave 06614 203-385-4294
Elizabeth McGoey, prin. Fax 381-6913
Second Hill Lane ES 700/PK-6
65 2nd Hill Ln 06614 203-385-4292
James Noga, prin. Fax 385-4291
Stratford Academy - Johnson House 500/3-6
719 Birdseye St 06615 203-385-4180
Mary Bolton, prin. Fax 385-4185
Stratford Acad - Honeyspot House ES 300/K-2
55 Fotch St 06615 203-385-4188
Diana Dilorio, prin. Fax 381-2006
Whitney ES 500/K-6
1130 Huntington Rd 06614 203-385-4198
Donna Seidell, prin. Fax 381-6950
Wilcoxson ES 400/K-6
600 Wilcoxson Ave 06614 203-385-4196
Deborah Dayo, prin. Fax 381-6912
Wooster MS 500/7-8
150 Lincoln St 06614 203-385-4275
Jack Lynch, prin. Fax 381-6918

St. James S 400/PK-8
1 Monument Pl 06615 203-375-5994
Kathleen Lainey, prin. Fax 380-0749
St. Mark S 200/K-8
500 Wigwam Ln 06614 203-375-4291
Phillip Adzima, prin. Fax 375-4833

Suffield, Hartford
Suffield SD 2,600/PK-12
350 Mountain Rd 06078 860-668-3800
Jack Reynolds, supt. Fax 668-3805
www.suffield.org
McAlister IS 600/3-5
260 Mountain Rd 06078 860-668-3830
Karen Carpenter, prin. Fax 668-3809
Suffield MS 600/6-8
350 Mountain Rd 06078 860-668-3820
John Warrington, prin. Fax 668-3088
Other Schools – See West Suffield

Taftville, See Norwich
Norwich SD
Supt. — See Norwich
Wequonnoc ES 200/PK-5
155 Providence St 06380 860-823-4210
Scott Fain, prin. Fax 823-4253

Sacred Heart S 200/K-8
15 Hunters Ave 06380 860-887-1757
Sr. Mary Riquier, prin. Fax 889-7276

Tariffville, Hartford, Pop. 1,477
Simsbury SD
Supt. — See Simsbury
Tariffville ES 300/1-6
42 Winthrop St 06081 860-658-5825
Kristine Murdick, prin. Fax 658-3626

Terryville, Litchfield, Pop. 5,426
Plymouth SD 1,100/PK-12
77 Main St 06786 860-314-8005
Anthony Distasio Ph.D., supt. Fax 314-2766
www.plymouth.k12.ct.us/
Fisher ES PK-5
79 N Main St 06786 860-314-2777
Phyllis Worhunsky, prin. Fax 314-8008
Terry MS 6-8
21 N Main St 06786 860-314-2790
Gary Travers, prin. Fax 314-2768
Other Schools – See Plymouth

Thomaston, Litchfield, Pop. 6,947
Thomaston SD 1,300/PK-12
PO Box 166 06787 860-283-4796
Lynda Mitchell, supt. Fax 283-6708
www.thomastonschools.net/
Black Rock ES 400/PK-3
57 Branch Rd 06787 860-283-3040
Paul Johnson, prin. Fax 283-3043
Thomaston Center S 300/4-6
1 Thomas Ave 06787 860-283-3036
James Diorio, prin. Fax 283-3048

Tolland, Tolland
Tolland SD 2,400/PK-12
51 Tolland Grn 06084 860-870-6850
William Guzman, supt. Fax 870-7737
www.tolland.k12.ct.us
Birch Grove PS 800/PK-2
247 Rhodes Rd 06084 860-870-6750
Patricia Wahlberg, prin. Fax 870-6754
Tolland IS 3-5
96 Old Post Rd 06084 860-870-6885
James Dineen, prin. Fax 872-7126
Tolland MS 700/6-8
1 Falcon Way 06084 860-870-6860
Walt Willett, prin. Fax 870-5737

Torrington, Litchfield, Pop. 35,995
Torrington SD 4,800/K-12
355 Migeon Ave 06790 860-489-2327
Edward Arum, supt. Fax 489-2391
www.torrington.org
East ES 500/K-5
215 Hogan Dr 06790 860-489-2303
Susan Fergusson, prin. Fax 489-2308
Forbes ES 500/K-5
500 Migeon Ave 06790 860-489-2500
Susan Lubomski, prin. Fax 489-2555
Southwest ES 200/K-5
340 Litchfield St 06790 860-489-2311
Judith Theeb, prin. Fax 489-2324
Torringford ES 500/K-5
800 Charles St 06790 860-489-2300
Cathleen Todor, prin. Fax 489-2325
Torrington MS 1,200/6-8
200 Middle School Dr 06790 860-496-4050
Matthew Harnett, prin. Fax 496-1089
Vogel-Wetmore ES 500/1-5
68 Church St 06790 860-489-2570
Pamela Dzurilla, prin. Fax 489-2577

St. Peter & St. Francis of Assisi S 200/PK-8
360 Prospect St 06790 860-489-4177
Jo Anne Gauger, prin. Fax 489-1590

Trumbull, Fairfield, Pop. 34,600
Trumbull SD 6,700/PK-12
6254 Main St 06611 203-452-4301
Ralph Iassogna, supt. Fax 452-4305
www.trumbullps.org
Booth Hill ES 500/K-5
545 Booth Hill Rd 06611 203-452-4377
Dana Pierce, prin. Fax 452-4375
Daniels Farm ES 500/K-5
710 Daniels Farm Rd 06611 203-452-4388
Gail Karwoski, prin. Fax 452-4387
Frenchtown ES 600/K-5
30 Frenchtown Rd 06611 203-452-4227
Jacqueline Norcel, prin. Fax 452-4226
Hillcrest MS 700/6-8
530 Daniels Farm Rd 06611 203-452-4466
Rosemary Seaman, prin. Fax 452-4479
Madison MS 900/6-8
4630 Madison Ave 06611 203-452-4499
Valerie Forshaw, prin. Fax 452-4490
Middlebrook ES 500/PK-5
220 Middlebrooks Ave 06611 203-452-4411
Patricia Colello, prin. Fax 452-4426
Ryan ES 400/K-5
190 Park Ln 06611 203-452-4400
Robert Gabriel, prin. Fax 452-4409
Tashua ES 500/K-5
401 Stonehouse Rd 06611 203-452-4433
Charlotte Janis, prin. Fax 452-4432
Trumbull ECC PK-PK
240 Middlebrooks Ave 06611 203-452-4422
Matthew Wheeler, prin. Fax 452-4419

Christian Heritage S 500/K-12
575 White Plains Rd 06611 203-261-6230
Barry Giller, hdmstr. Fax 452-1531
St. Catherine of Siena S 300/PK-8
190 Shelton Rd 06611 203-375-1947
Sr. Anne Marie Dorff, prin. Fax 378-3935
St. Theresa S 200/PK-8
55 Rosemond Ter 06611 203-268-7966
Salvatore Vittoria, prin. Fax 378-3935

Uncasville, New London, Pop. 2,975
Montville SD
Supt. — See Oakdale
Mohegan ES 400/K-5
49 Golden Rd 06382 860-848-9261
Lorilyn Caron, prin. Fax 848-1603

St. Bernard Academy 100/6-8
1593 Norwich New London Tpk 06382
860-848-3007
Mary Dillman, prin. Fax 848-0261

Union, Tolland
Union SD 100/K-8
18 Kinney Hollow Rd 06076 860-684-3146
William Oros, supt. Fax 684-9385
Union S 100/K-8
18 Kinney Hollow Rd 06076 860-684-3146
Stephen Schachner, prin. Fax 684-9385

Unionville, Hartford, Pop. 3,500
Farmington SD
Supt. — See Farmington
Union ES 300/K-4
173 School St 06085 860-673-2575
Lynn Katz, prin. Fax 675-4264
West District ES 300/K-4
114 W District Rd 06085 860-673-2579
Sharon Lowery, prin. Fax 675-4103

Vernon Rockville, Tolland, Pop. 28,900
Vernon SD 3,800/PK-12
PO Box 600 06066 860-870-6000
Richard Paskiewicz, supt. Fax 870-6005
www.vernonschools.com
Center Road ES 500/PK-5
20 Center Rd 06066 860-870-6300
Mary Jo Myslinski, prin. Fax 870-6309
Lake Street ES 300/K-5
201 Lake St 06066 860-870-6085
Robert Testa, prin. Fax 870-6084
Maple Street ES 300/K-5
20 Maple St 06066 860-870-6175
Dr. Lois Possell, prin. Fax 870-6181
Northeast ES 300/PK-5
69 East St 06066 860-870-6080
Melissa DeLoreto, prin. Fax 870-6095
Skinner Road ES 300/PK-5
90 Skinner Rd 06066 860-870-6180
Matthew Wlodarczyk, prin. Fax 870-6187
Vernon Center MS 900/6-8
777 Hartford Tpke 06066 860-870-6070
Dr. Beth Katz, prin. Fax 870-6318

St. Bernard S 100/K-8
PO Box 177 06066 860-875-0475
Ann Aulerich, prin. Fax 872-2444
St. Joseph S 200/PK-8
41 West St 06066 860-875-4943
Lucia Trudeau, prin. Fax 870-4532

Voluntown, New London
Voluntown SD 300/PK-8
PO Box 129 06384 860-376-9167
Adam Burrows, supt. Fax 376-3185
www.voluntownct.org
Voluntown S 300/PK-8
PO Box 129 06384 860-376-2325
Mary Chinigo, prin. Fax 376-6690

Wallingford, New Haven, Pop. 41,700
Wallingford SD 6,900/PK-12
142 Hope Hill Rd 06492 203-949-6500
Dale Wilson, supt. Fax 949-6550
www.wallingford.k12.ct.us
Beach ES 300/PK-5
340 N Main St 06492 203-949-0343
Kathryn Hile, prin. Fax 284-8226
Cook Hill ES 400/PK-5
57 Hall Rd 06492 203-284-5400
Janet Murphy, prin. Fax 284-5439
Hammarskjold MS 800/6-8
106 Pond Hill Rd 06492 203-294-5340
Enrico Buccilli, prin. Fax 294-5322
Highland ES 300/K-5
200 Highland Ave 06492 203-949-0121
Victoria Reed, prin. Fax 284-8287
Moran MS 900/6-8
141 Hope Hill Rd 06492 203-741-2900
Robert Cyr, prin. Fax 741-2939
Parker Farms ES 300/K-5
30 Parker Farms Rd 06492 203-949-0349
Patricia Crowley, prin. Fax 284-8370
Pond Hill ES 300/K-5
299 Pond Hill Rd 06492 203-949-0109
Richard Pizzonia, prin. Fax 284-8355
Rock Hill ES 300/K-5
911 Durham Rd 06492 203-949-0115
Alysson Glass, prin. Fax 284-8242
Stevens ES 400/K-5
18 Kondracki Ln 06492 203-284-5330
Doreen Duren, prin. Fax 294-5312
Yalesville ES 500/PK-5
415 Church St 06492 203-265-1498
Carol Mikulski, prin. Fax 265-1848

Holy Trinity S 200/K-8
11 N Whittlesey Ave 06492 203-269-4476
Sr. Kathleen Kelly, prin. Fax 294-4983

Warren, Litchfield
Regional SD 6
Supt. — See Litchfield
Warren ES 100/K-6
21 Sackett Hill Rd 06754 860-868-2223
Anthony Hibbert, prin. Fax 868-7375

Washington, Litchfield
Regional SD 12
Supt. — See Washington Depot
Reach ECC 50/PK-PK
159 South St 06793 860-868-6233
Joseph Boyle, dir. Fax 868-6233
Shepaug Valley MS 200/6-8
159 South St 06793 860-868-6208
Teresa DeBrito, prin. Fax 868-0622

Glenholme S Devereux Center 100/3-12
81 Sabbaday Ln 06793 860-868-7377
Maryann Campbell, dir. Fax 868-7413

Washington Depot, Litchfield
Regional SD 12 1,100/PK-12
PO Box 386 06794 860-868-6100
Dr. Bruce Storm, supt. Fax 868-6103
www.region-12.org
Washington ES 200/K-5
11 School St 06793 860-868-7331
Gail Prelli, prin. Fax 868-2975
Other Schools – See Bridgewater, Roxbury, Washington

Rumsey Hall S 300/K-9
201 Romford Rd 06794 860-868-0535
Thomas Farmen, hdmstr. Fax 868-7907

Waterbury, New Haven, Pop. 107,902
Waterbury SD 17,700/PK-12
236 Grand St 06702 203-574-8000
Dr. David Snead, supt. Fax 574-8010
www.waterbury.k12.ct.us/
Barnard ES 300/K-5
11 Draher Ave 06708 203-574-8181
Thomas Pannone, prin. Fax 573-6650
Brooklyn ES 200/K-5
29 John St 06708 203-346-3931
Dr. Frank Zillo, prin. Fax 346-3934
Bucks Hill ES 600/PK-5
330 Bucks Hill Rd 06704 203-574-8182
Ann Begley, prin. Fax 573-6643
Bunker Hill ES 500/PK-5
170 Bunker Hill Ave 06708 203-574-8183
Brian Goggin, prin. Fax 574-8007
Carrington ES 600/K-5
24 Kenmore Ave 06708 203-574-8184
Fax 574-6728
Chase ES 800/K-5
40 Woodtick Rd 06705 203-574-8188
Celia Piccochi, prin. Fax 573-6652
Cross ES 400/K-5
1255 Hamilton Ave 06706 203-574-8171
Joseph Amato, prin. Fax 574-0719
Driggs ES 600/PK-5
77 Woodlawn Ter 06710 203-574-8160
Mark Ladin, prin. Fax 574-8299
Generali ES 600/K-5
3196 E Main St 06705 203-574-8174
Kathy Stamp, prin. Fax 574-6719
Gilmartin ES 200/K-5
289 Willow St 06710 203-574-8175
Fax 573-6649
Hopeville ES 500/K-5
2 Cypress St 06706 203-574-8173
Fax 597-3419
Kingsbury ES 500/K-5
220 Columbia Blvd 06710 203-574-8172
Pamela Baim, prin. Fax 573-6644
Maloney Interdistrict Magnet ES 600/PK-5
233 S Elm St 06706 203-574-8162
Fax 574-8389
North End MS 1,300/6-8
534 Bucks Hill Rd 06704 203-574-8097
Hattie Beauchamp, prin. Fax 574-8203
Regan ES 300/K-5
2780 N Main St 06704 203-574-8187
Dr. Patricia Frageau, prin. Fax 573-6647
Rotella Interdistict Magnet ES 600/PK-5
380 Pierpont Rd 06705 203-574-8168
Gina Calabrese, prin. Fax 574-8045
Special Education Preschool 200/PK-PK
330 Bucks Hill Rd 06704 203-574-8053
Mary Ann Daukas, admin. Fax 574-8067
Sprague ES 500/PK-5
1443 Thomaston Ave 06704 203-574-8189
Donna Perreault, prin. Fax 573-6622
Tinker ES 500/K-5
809 Highland Ave 06708 203-574-8186
Lauren Elias, prin. Fax 597-3440
Wallace MS 1,300/6-8
3465 E Main St 06705 203-574-8140
Dr. Louis Padua, prin. Fax 574-8141
Walsh ES 500/PK-5
55 Dikeman St 06704 203-574-8164
Erik Brown, prin. Fax 597-3488
Washington ES 300/K-5
685 Baldwin St 06706 203-574-8177
Roxanne Augelli, prin. Fax 573-6645
West Side MS 1,100/6-8
483 Chase Pkwy 06708 203-574-8120
Charles Nappi, prin. Fax 574-8130
Wilson ES 400/PK-5
235 Birch St 06704 203-573-6660
Dr. Susie DaSilva, prin. Fax 573-6663

Blessed Sacrament S 300/K-8
386 Robinwood Rd 06708 203-756-5313
Debora Mainstruck, prin. Fax 756-5313
Chase Collegiate S 500/PK-12
565 Chase Pkwy 06708 203-236-9560
John Fixx, hdmstr. Fax 236-9503
Children's Community S 100/PK-5
31 Wolcott St 06702 203-575-0659
Barbara Roggiero Ph.D., prin. Fax 754-7825
Lighthouse Christian Academy 100/PK-8
1245 Thomaston Ave 06704 203-575-1385
Mark Cenaro, prin. Fax 755-1088
Our Lady of Mt. Carmel S 200/PK-8
645 Congress Ave 06708 203-755-6809
Joaquim Tavares, prin. Fax 755-5850
St. Francis Xavier S 200/PK-8
605 Baldwin St 06706 203-753-3197
Henry Schnakenberg, prin. Fax 574-0128
St. Mary S 400/K-8
55 Cole St 06706 203-753-2574
Joseph Kenny, prin. Fax 596-2498
SS. Peter & Paul S 300/PK-8
116 Beecher Ave 06705 203-755-0881
Janet Curry, prin. Fax 755-3535
Yeshiva Ketana of Waterbury 200/PK-7
47 Buckingham St 06710 203-756-1800

Waterford, New London, Pop. 17,930
Learn RESC
Supt. — See Old Lyme
Friendship S PK-PK
24 Rope Ferry Rd 06385 860-447-4049
Kathy Suprin, prin. Fax 447-4056

Waterford SD 2,500/K-12
15 Rope Ferry Rd 06385 860-444-5801
Randall Collins, supt. Fax 444-5870
www.waterfordschools.org
Clark Lane MS 800/6-8
105 Clark Ln 06385 860-443-2837
Michael Lovetere, prin. Fax 437-6985
Oswegatchie ES 300/K-5
470 Boston Post Rd 06385 860-442-4331
Nancy Macione, prin. Fax 447-6261
Southwest ES 200/K-5
51 Daniels Ave 06385 860-443-3210
Patricia Fedor, prin. Fax 447-7922
Other Schools – See Quaker Hill

Watertown, Litchfield, Pop. 6,000
Watertown SD 3,200/PK-12
10 Deforest St 06795 860-945-4801
Karen Baldwin, supt. Fax 945-2775
www.watertownctschools.org
Judson ES 400/3-5
124 Hamilton Ln 06795 860-945-4850
Lisa Rommel, prin. Fax 945-7108
Other Schools – See Oakville

St. John the Evangelist S 200/K-8
760 Main St 06795 860-274-9208
John Petto, prin. Fax 945-1082

Weatogue, Hartford, Pop. 2,521
Simsbury SD
Supt. — See Simsbury
Latimer Lane ES 600/K-6
33 Mountain View Dr 06089 860-658-4774
Grace Morris, prin. Fax 658-3618

Westbrook, Middlesex, Pop. 2,060
Westbrook SD 900/PK-12
158 McVeagh Rd 06498 860-399-6432
Patricia Charles, supt. Fax 399-8817
www.westbrookctschools.org/
Ingraham ES 400/PK-5
105 Goodspeed Dr 06498 860-399-7925
Katharine Bishop, prin. Fax 399-2002
Westbrook MS 200/6-8
154 McVeagh Rd 06498 860-399-2010
Philip House, prin. Fax 399-2007

West Cornwall, Litchfield
Cornwall SD
Supt. — See Falls Village
Cornwall Consolidated S 100/K-8
5 Cream Hill Rd 06796 860-672-6617
Dr. Kathleen Fitzgibbons, prin. Fax 672-4879

West Hartford, Hartford, Pop. 64,300
West Hartford SD 9,600/PK-12
50 S Main St, 860-561-6600
Karen List, supt. Fax 561-6910
www.whps.org
Aiken ES 400/K-5
212 King Philip Dr, 860-233-6994
Kathleen McKay, prin. Fax 236-9184
Braeburn ES 400/K-5
45 Braeburn Rd, 860-561-2200
Natalie Simpson, prin. Fax 521-8416
Bristow MS 6-8
34 Highland St, 860-231-2100
Andrew Murrow, prin. Fax 231-2107
Bugbee ES 400/K-5
1943 Asylum Ave, 860-233-1234
Margaret Beecher, prin. Fax 236-2486
Charter Oak ES 300/K-5
425 Oakwood Ave, 860-233-8506
Mary Thompson, prin. Fax 231-9654
Duffy ES 500/K-5
95 Westminster Dr, 860-521-0110
Kathleen Tracy, prin. Fax 561-1492
King Philip MS 900/6-8
100 King Philip Dr, 860-233-8236
Michael Renkawitz, prin. Fax 233-0812
Morley ES 400/K-5
77 Bretton Rd, 860-233-8535
Ellen Rosow-Stokoe, prin. Fax 233-7705
Norfeldt ES 400/K-5
35 Barksdale Rd, 860-233-4421
Caryn Falvey, prin. Fax 232-4732
Sedgwick MS 900/6-8
128 Sedgwick Rd, 860-521-0610
Ben Skaught, prin. Fax 521-7502
Smith ES 400/K-5
64 Saint James St, 860-236-3317
Delores Bolton, prin. Fax 236-3342
Webster Hill ES 500/K-5
125 Webster Hill Blvd, 860-521-0320
Jeffrey Wallowitz, prin. Fax 561-1230
Whiting Lane ES 500/PK-5
47 Whiting Ln, 860-233-8541
Nancy DePalma, prin. Fax 236-9367
Wolcott ES 500/K-5
71 Wolcott Rd, 860-561-2300
Plato Karafelis, prin. Fax 521-7545

Montessori S of Greater Hartford 200/PK-6
141 N Main St, 860-236-4565
Una Barry, hdmstr. Fax 586-7420
Renbrook S 500/PK-9
2865 Albany Ave, 860-236-1661
Jane Shipp, hdmstr. Fax 231-8206
St. Brigid S 300/PK-8
100 Mayflower St, 860-561-2130
Patricia Wirkus, prin. Fax 561-0011
St. Thomas the Apostle S 200/PK-5
25 Dover Rd, 860-236-6257
Colleen DiSanto, prin. Fax 236-8865
St. Timothy MS 100/6-8
225 King Philip Dr, 860-236-0614
Dr. Stephen Balkun, prin. Fax 920-0293
Solomon Schechter Day S 200/PK-8
26 Buena Vista Rd, 860-561-0700
Behzad Dayanim, dir. Fax 561-2329

West Haven, New Haven, Pop. 52,923
West Haven SD 6,700/PK-12
25 Ogden St 06516 203-937-4310
Neil Cavallaro, supt. Fax 937-4315
www.whschools.org
Bailey MS 800/6-8
106 Morgan Ln 06516 203-937-4380
Anthony Cordone, prin. Fax 937-4385
Carrigan MS 900/6-8
2 Tetlow St 06516 203-937-4390
Patricia Libero, prin. Fax 937-4393
Forest ES 500/K-5
95 Burwell Rd 06516 203-931-6800
Thomas Hunt, prin. Fax 931-6803
Haley ES 500/K-5
148 South St 06516 203-931-6810
Ronald Stancil, prin. Fax 931-6813
Mackrille ES 400/PK-5
806 Jones Hill Rd 06516 203-931-6820
Catherine Biagetti, prin. Fax 931-6823
Molloy ES 300/K-5
225 Meloy Rd 06516 203-931-6830
Steven Lopes, prin. Fax 931-6833
Pagels ES 400/K-5
26 Benham Hill Rd 06516 203-931-6840
Gina Prisco, prin. Fax 931-6844
Savin Rock Community ES 500/K-5
50 Park St 06516 203-931-6850
Gary Palermo, prin. Fax 931-6853
Thompson ES 300/K-5
165 Richards St 06516 203-931-6870
Frank Paolino, prin. Fax 931-6873
Washington ES 400/K-5
369 Washington Ave 06516 203-931-6880
Timothy Van Winkle, prin. Fax 931-6883

Living Word Christian Academy 200/PK-12
225 Meloy Rd 06516 203-931-7750
Alden Hall, prin. Fax 931-7540
Our Lady of Victory S 200/PK-8
620 Jones Hill Rd 06516 203-932-6457
Ardell Bartolotta, prin. Fax 932-6456
St. Lawrence S 200/PK-8
231 Main St 06516 203-933-2518
Paul DeFonzo, prin. Fax 933-2058

Weston, Fairfield
Weston SD 2,000/PK-12
24 School Rd 06883 203-291-1401
Jerome Belair, supt. Fax 291-1415
www.westonk12-ct.org
Hurlbutt ES 600/PK-2
9 School Rd 06883 203-291-1444
Joanna Genovese, prin. Fax 291-1452
Weston IS 3-5
95 School Rd 06883 203-291-2701
Mark Ribbens, prin. Fax 291-2707
Weston MS 600/6-8
135 School Rd 06883 203-291-1500
Kenneth Craw, prin. Fax 291-1516

Westport, Fairfield, Pop. 24,407
Westport SD 5,500/PK-12
110 Myrtle Ave 06880 203-341-1025
Elliott Landon, supt. Fax 341-1029
www.westport.k12.ct.us/
Bedford MS 800/6-8
88 North Ave 06880 203-341-1510
Carol Stephens-Klipp, prin. Fax 341-1508
Coleytown ES 500/PK-4
65 Easton Rd 06880 203-341-1710
Melissa Poalini, prin. Fax 341-1700
Coleytown MS 500/6-8
255 North Ave 06880 203-341-1610
Kris Bienkowski, prin. Fax 341-1603
Green's Farms ES 500/K-5
17 Morningside Dr S 06880 203-222-3600
John Bayers, prin. Fax 222-3668
Kings Highway ES 500/K-5
125 Post Rd W 06880 203-341-1810
Maria Castelluccio, prin. Fax 341-1808
Long Lots ES 600/K-5
13 Hyde Ln 06880 203-341-1910
Rex Jones, prin. Fax 341-1905
Saugatuck ES 500/K-5
170 Riverside Ave 06880 203-221-2910
Robert Buckley, prin. Fax 221-2952
Stepping Stones Preschool PK-PK
65 Easton Rd 06880 203-341-1712
Lynda Codeghini, dir. Fax 341-1714

Landmark of Ridgefield Academy PK-K
11 Burr Rd 06880 203-226-6982
Fax 226-7195
St. Paul Lutheran S 100/PK-K
41 Easton Rd 06880 203-227-7920
Lesley Troup, prin. Fax 227-1886

West Redding, Fairfield
Redding SD
Supt. — See Easton
Read MS 500/5-8
486 Redding Rd 06896 203-938-2533
Dianne Martin, prin. Fax 938-8667

West Simsbury, Hartford, Pop. 2,149
Simsbury SD
Supt. — See Simsbury
Tootin Hills ES 600/PK-6
25 Nimrod Rd 06092 860-658-7629
Ronald Perrault, prin. Fax 658-3624

Master's S 400/PK-12
36 Westledge Rd 06092 860-651-9361
Jon Holley, hdmstr. Fax 651-9363

West Suffield, Hartford
Suffield SD
Supt. — See Suffield
Spaulding ES 500/PK-2
945 Mountain Rd 06093 860-668-3826
Angie Roman, prin. Fax 668-3087

Wethersfield, Hartford, Pop. 26,400
Wethersfield SD 3,800/K-12
127 Hartford Ave 06109 860-571-8110
Michael Kohlhagen, supt. Fax 571-8130
www.wethersfield.k12.ct.us/
Deane MS 600/7-8
551 Silas Deane Hwy 06109 860-571-8300
Steven Cook, prin. Fax 563-0563
Emerson-Williams ES 400/K-6
461 Wells Rd 06109 860-571-8360
Elizabeth Catarius, prin. Fax 721-0044
Hanmer ES 400/K-6
50 Francis St 06109 860-571-8370
Margaret Zacchei, prin. Fax 257-1629
Highcrest ES 400/K-6
95 Highcrest Rd 06109 860-571-8380
Maresa Harvey, prin. Fax 563-9193
Webb ES 400/K-6
51 Willow St 06109 860-571-8340
Elise Guari, prin. Fax 257-1668
Wright ES 300/K-6
186 Nott St 06109 860-571-8350
Fax 563-2198

Corpus Christi S 400/PK-8
581 Silas Deane Hwy 06109 860-529-5487
Eileen Sampiere, prin. Fax 257-9106

Willimantic, Windham, Pop. 14,746
Windham SD 3,500/PK-12
322 Prospect St 06226 860-465-2310
Doreen Fuller, supt. Fax 456-2311
www.windham.k12.ct.us/
Natchaug ES 300/K-4
123 Jackson St 06226 860-465-2380
Joseph Janisaitis, prin. Fax 465-2383
Sweeney ES 300/K-4
60 Oak Hill Dr 06226 860-465-2420
Angela Kiss, prin. Fax 465-2423
Windham ECC 200/PK-PK
322 Prospect St 06226 860-465-2627
Mary Jane Crotty, dir. Fax 465-2605
Windham MS 1,000/5-8
123 Quarry St 06226 860-465-2351
Madeline Negron, prin. Fax 465-2353
Other Schools – See North Windham, Windham

Maranatha SDA Regional S 50/1-8
126 Quarry St 06226 860-456-4984
SS. Mary & Joseph S 100/PK-8
35 Valley St 06226 860-423-8479
Sr. Elaine Moorcroft, prin. Fax 423-8365
Windham Christian Academy 50/1-8
143 Windham Rd 06226 860-423-0172
Wanda Harper, admin. Fax 423-1883

Willington, Tolland
Willington SD 600/PK-8
40 Old Farms Rd Ste A 06279 860-487-3130
David Harding, supt. Fax 487-3132
www.willingtonpublicschools.org
Center ES 200/PK-3
12 Old Farms Rd 06279 860-429-9367
Colin McNamara, prin. Fax 429-8768
Hall Memorial MS 400/4-8
111 River Rd 06279 860-429-9391
Deborah Sullivan, prin. Fax 429-5682

Wilton, Fairfield, Pop. 7,200
Wilton SD 4,400/PK-12
PO Box 277 06897 203-762-3381
Gary Richards, supt. Fax 762-2177
www.wilton.k12.ct.us/
Cider Mill ES 1,100/3-5
240 School Rd 06897 203-762-3351
Virginia Rico, prin. Fax 761-0382
Driscoll ES 500/PK-2
336 Belden Hill Rd 06897 203-762-3374
Lynette Tinacci, prin. Fax 761-1570
Middlebrook MS 1,000/6-8
131 School Rd 06897 203-762-8388
Julia Harris, prin. Fax 762-1716
Miller ES 500/PK-2
217 Wolfpit Rd 06897 203-762-8678
Cheryl Jensen, prin. Fax 761-1570

Connecticut Friends S 50/K-8
317A New Canaan Rd 06897 203-762-9860
Kim Tsocanos, hdmstr. Fax 834-9640
Montessori S 200/PK-8
34 Whipple Rd 06897 203-834-0440
Mary Zeman, hdmstr. Fax 761-9386
Our Lady of Fatima S 200/PK-8
225 Danbury Rd 06897 203-762-8100
Joseph Carmen, prin. Fax 834-0614

Windham, Windham
Windham SD
Supt. — See Willimantic
Windham Center ES 300/K-4
PO Box 138 06280 860-465-2440
Nivea Torres, prin. Fax 465-2343

Windsor, Hartford, Pop. 27,817
Windsor SD 4,100/PK-12
601 Matianuck Ave 06095 860-687-2000
Elizabeth Feser Ed.D., supt. Fax 687-2009
www.windsorct.org
Clover Street ES 300/1-5
57 Clover St 06095 860-687-2050
Michelle Williams, prin. Fax 687-2059
Ellsworth ES 500/1-5
730 Kennedy Rd 06095 860-687-2070
Patricia Phelan, prin. Fax 687-2079
Kennedy ES 400/1-5
530 Park Ave 06095 860-687-2060
Tangular Irby, prin. Fax 687-2069
Poquonock ES 300/1-5
1760 Poquonock Ave 06095 860-687-2080
R.J. Sullivan, prin. Fax 687-2089
Sage Park MS 1,000/6-8
25 Sage Park Rd 06095 860-687-2030
Paul Cavaliere, prin. Fax 687-2039
Wolcott ECC 300/PK-K
57 E Wolcott Ave 06095 860-246-9032
Ronda Lezberg, prin. Fax 728-1206

Praise Power & Prayer Christian S 100/K-12
PO Box 474 06095 860-285-8898
Rev. Raymond McMahon, prin.
St. Gabriel S 200/K-8
77 Bloomfield Ave 06095 860-688-6401
Patricia Martin, prin. Fax 298-8668

Trinity Christian S 200/PK-8
180 Park Ave 06095 860-688-2008
Malcolm McGuire, hdmstr. Fax 687-9737
Windsor Montessori S 50/K-K
114 Palisado Ave 06095 860-285-1420
Anne Wakelin, prin. Fax 298-9036

Windsor Locks, Hartford, Pop. 12,358
Windsor Locks SD 1,900/PK-12
58 S Elm St 06096 860-292-5000
Dr. Greg W. Little, supt. Fax 292-5003
www.wlps.org
North Street ES 400/PK-2
325 North St 06096 860-292-5027
Jeff Ferreira, prin. Fax 292-8191
South ES 500/3-5
87 South St 06096 860-292-5021
Jim Moriarty, prin. Fax 292-5026
Windsor Locks MS 400/6-8
7 Center St 06096 860-292-5012
Gregory Blanchfield, prin. Fax 292-5017

Winsted, Litchfield, Pop. 8,254
Regional SD 7 1,100/7-12
PO Box 656 06098 860-379-1084
Clint Montgomery, supt. Fax 379-0618
www.nwr7.com
Northwestern Regional MS 400/7-8
100 Battistoni Rd 06098 860-379-7243
Candy Perez, prin. Fax 738-6205

Winchester SD 1,000/PK-8
30 Elm St 06098 860-379-0706
Blaise Salerno, supt. Fax 379-6521
www.winchesterschools.org/
Batcheller ES 300/PK-5
201 Pratt St 06098 860-379-5423
Matthew O'Connell, prin. Fax 379-1301
Hinsdale ES 400/K-5
15 Hinsdale Ave 06098 860-379-5956
Deborah Alduini, prin. Fax 379-3840
Pearson MS 300/6-8
2 Wetmore Ave 06098 860-379-7588
Clay Krevolin, prin. Fax 379-0406

St. Anthony S 200/PK-8
55 Oak St 06098 860-379-7521
Patricia Devanney, prin. Fax 379-7522

Wolcott, New Haven, Pop. 13,700
Wolcott SD 2,900/PK-12
154 Center St 06716 203-879-8183
Dr. Thomas Smyth, supt. Fax 879-8182
www.wolcottps.org
Alcott ES 400/PK-5
1490 Woodtick Rd 06716 203-879-8160
Holly Wrenn, prin. Fax 879-8163
Frisbie ES 400/K-5
24 Todd Rd 06716 203-879-8146
Richard Dorval, prin. Fax 879-8148
Tyrrell MS 700/6-8
500 Todd Rd 06716 203-879-8151
Arline Tansley, prin. Fax 879-8419
Wakelee ES 500/K-5
12 Hemple Dr 06716 203-879-8154
Thomas Buzzelli, prin. Fax 879-8035

Woodbridge, New Haven, Pop. 7,924
Regional SD 5 2,500/7-12
25 Newton Rd 06525 203-392-2106
Dr. John Brady, supt. Fax 397-4864
www.amityregion5.org
Other Schools – See Bethany, Orange

Woodbridge SD 800/PK-6
40 Beecher Rd 06525 203-387-6631
Dr. Gaeton Stella, supt. Fax 397-0724
www.woodbridgesd.org
Beecher Road IS 500/3-6
40 Beecher Rd 06525 203-389-3542
MaryLou Torre, prin. Fax 389-2196
Beecher Road PS 300/PK-2
40 Beecher Rd 06525 203-389-2195
Carol Bequary, prin. Fax 389-2196

Ezra Academy 200/K-8
75 Rimmon Rd 06525 203-389-5500
Amanda Brodie, prin. Fax 387-5607

Woodbury, Litchfield, Pop. 8,131
Regional SD 14 2,000/K-12
PO Box 469 06798 203-263-4330
Robert Cronin Ph.D., supt. Fax 263-0372
www.ctreg14.org
Mitchell ES 500/K-5
14 School St 06798 203-263-4314
Dawn Hochsprung, prin. Fax 263-4244
Woodbury MS 500/6-8
67 Washington Ave 06798 203-263-4306
Alice Jones, prin. Fax 263-0825
Other Schools – See Bethlehem

Woodstock, Windham
Woodstock SD 1,000/PK-8
147A Route 169 06281 860-928-7453
Dr. Francis Baran, supt. Fax 928-0206
www.woodstockschools.net
Woodstock ES 500/PK-4
24 Frog Pond Rd 06281 860-928-0471
Viktor Toth, prin. Fax 928-1220
Woodstock MS 500/5-8
147B Route 169 06281 860-963-6575
Paul Gamache, prin. Fax 963-6577

DELAWARE

DELAWARE DEPARTMENT OF EDUCATION
401 Federal St Ste 2, Dover 19901-3639
Telephone 302-735-4000
Fax 302-739-4654
Website http://www.doe.k12.de.us

Secretary of Education Lillian Lowery

DELAWARE BOARD OF EDUCATION
1006 Tulip Tree Ln, Newark 19713-1128

President Teri Quinn Gray

PUBLIC, PRIVATE AND CATHOLIC ELEMENTARY SCHOOLS

Bear, New Castle
Appoquinimink SD
Supt. — See Odessa
Loss ES 600/1-5
200 Brennan Blvd 19701 302-832-1343
Lorraine Lybarger, prin. Fax 832-3213

Christina SD
Supt. — See Wilmington
Porter Road ES K-5
500 Caledonia Way 19701 302-834-5910
Richelle Talbert, prin.

Colonial SD
Supt. — See New Castle
Wilbur ES K-5
4050 Wrangle Hill Rd 19701 302-832-6330
Beth Howell, prin. Fax 832-6335

Caravel Academy 1,100/PK-12
2801 Del Laws Rd 19701 302-834-8938
Donald Keister, hdmstr. Fax 834-3658
Fairwinds Christian S 200/PK-12
801 Seymour Rd 19701 302-328-7404
Neil Webster, prin. Fax 328-0190
Red Lion Christian Academy 900/PK-12
1390 Red Lion Rd 19701 302-834-2526
Dr. Rob Brown, hdmstr. Fax 836-6346

Blades, Sussex, Pop. 999
Seaford SD
Supt. — See Seaford
Blades ES 500/K-5
900 S Arch St 19973 302-628-4416
Susan Nancarrow, prin. Fax 628-4480

Bridgeville, Sussex, Pop. 1,578
Woodbridge SD 1,900/PK-12
16359 Sussex Hwy 19933 302-337-7990
Kevin Carson Ed.D., supt. Fax 337-7998
www.wsd.k12.de.us
Wheatley MS 700/5-8
48 Church St 19933 302-337-3469
Delores Tunstall, prin. Fax 337-6016
Other Schools – See Greenwood

Camden, Kent, Pop. 2,281
Caesar Rodney SD 7,000/K-12
219 Old North Rd 19934 302-697-2173
Dr. Kevin Fitzgerald, supt. Fax 697-3406
www.cr.k12.de.us
Simpson ES 500/K-5
5 Old North Rd 19934 302-697-3207
Joseph Birch Ed.D., prin. Fax 697-4963
Other Schools – See Camden Wyoming, Dover, Magnolia

Camden Wyoming, Kent, Pop. 1,045
Caesar Rodney SD
Supt. — See Camden
Fifer MS 800/6-8
109 E Camden Wyoming Ave 19934 302-698-8400
Josette McCullough Ed.D., prin. Fax 698-8409
Frear ES 600/K-5
238 Sorghum Mill Rd 19934 302-697-3279
Ken Goodwin, prin. Fax 697-4056
Postlethwait MS 800/6-8
2841 S State St 19934 302-698-8410
Michael Noel Ed.D., prin. Fax 698-8419

Christiana, New Castle
Christina SD
Supt. — See Wilmington
Jones ES 400/K-5
35 W Main St 19702 302-454-2131
Merridith Murray, prin. Fax 454-3481

Claymont, New Castle, Pop. 9,800
Brandywine SD 10,300/K-12
1000 Pennsylvania Ave 19703 302-793-5000
Dr. James Scanlon, supt. Fax 792-3823
www.bsd.k12.de.us
Claymont ES 900/4-6
3401 Green St 19703 302-792-3880
Betty Pinchin, prin. Fax 792-3877
Darley Road ES 300/K-3
500 Darley Rd 19703 302-792-3916
James Grant, prin. Fax 792-3944
Maple Lane ES 300/K-3
100 Maple Ln 19703 302-792-3906
Julianne Pecorella, prin. Fax 792-3941
Other Schools – See Wilmington

Clayton, Kent, Pop. 1,400
Smyrna SD
Supt. — See Smyrna
Clayton ES 500/K-4
510 Main St 19938 302-653-8587
Mike Dulin, prin. Fax 653-3421

Dagsboro, Sussex, Pop. 555

Lighthouse Christian S 200/PK-8
28157 Lighthouse Xing 19939 302-732-3309
Terri Menoche, admin. Fax 732-1253

Delmar, Sussex, Pop. 1,483
Delmar SD 1,100/6-12
200 N 8th St 19940 302-846-9544
Dr. David Ring, supt. Fax 846-2793
www.k12.de.us/delmar
Delmar MS 500/6-8
200 N 8th St 19940 302-846-9544
Cathy Townsend, prin. Fax 846-2793

Dover, Kent, Pop. 34,288
Caesar Rodney SD
Supt. — See Camden
Brown ES 500/K-5
360 Webbs Ln 19904 302-697-2101
Craig Wearden, prin. Fax 697-4973
Dover AFB MS 200/6-8
3100 Hawthorne Dr 19901 302-674-3284
Ernestine Adams, prin. Fax 730-4283
Star Hill ES 500/K-5
594 Voshells Mill Star Hill 19901 302-697-6117
Chester Cox, prin. Fax 697-4983
Stokes ES 500/K-5
3874 Upper King Rd 19904 302-697-3205
Christine Alois, prin. Fax 697-4029
Welch ES 400/K-5
3100 Hawthorne Dr 19901 302-674-9080
Alane Brown, prin. Fax 674-0682

Capital SD 6,100/PK-12
945 Forest St 19904 302-672-1500
Michael Thomas Ed.D., supt. Fax 672-1714
www.capital.k12.de.us/
Central MS 1,000/7-8
211 Delaware Ave 19901 302-672-1772
Darren Guido, prin. Fax 672-1733
East Dover ES 300/PK-4
852 S Little Creek Rd 19901 302-672-1655
Colleen Rinker, prin. Fax 672-1663
Fairview ES 400/PK-4
700 Walker Rd 19904 302-672-1645
Marcia Harrison, prin. Fax 672-1654
Henry MS 900/5-6
65 Carver Rd 19904 302-672-1622
Eric Niebrzydowski, prin. Fax 672-1633
North Dover ES 400/K-4
855 State College Rd 19904 302-672-1980
Eleanor Marine, prin. Fax 672-1985
South Dover ES 400/K-4
955 S State St 19901 302-672-1690
Marian Wolak, prin. Fax 672-1697
Towne Point ES 300/K-4
629 Buckson Dr 19901 302-672-1590
Gene Capers, prin. Fax 672-1595
Washington ES 400/K-4
901 Forest St 19904 302-672-1900
Marcia Johnson, prin. Fax 672-1902
Other Schools – See Hartly

Calvary Christian Academy 300/PK-12
1143 E Lebanon Rd 19901 302-697-7860
Aaron Coon, admin. Fax 697-0284
Central Delaware Christian Academy 100/PK-9
4698 S duPont Hwy 19901 302-697-8407
Robert Draper, admin. Fax 697-8607
Holy Cross S 600/PK-8
631 S State St 19901 302-674-5784
Denise Jacono, prin. Fax 674-5782
Kingdom Christian Academy 50/PK-8
PO Box 924 19903 302-741-2467
Angela Wilson, dean Fax 741-2469
St. John Lutheran S 100/PK-6
1156 Walker Rd 19904 302-734-3767
Dina Vendetti, prin. Fax 734-8809

Felton, Kent, Pop. 838
Lake Forest SD 3,300/PK-12
5423 Killens Pond Rd 19943 302-284-3020
Dr. Daniel Curry, supt. Fax 284-4491
www.lf.k12.de.us
Lake Forest Central ES 300/4-5
5424 Killens Pond Rd 19943 302-284-5810
Cathy Zimmerman, prin. Fax 284-5819
Lake Forest North ES 500/PK-3
319 E Main St 19943 302-284-9611
Brenda Wynder, prin. Fax 284-5820
Other Schools – See Frederica, Harrington

Frankford, Sussex, Pop. 754
Indian River SD
Supt. — See Selbyville
Frankford ES 500/PK-5
30207 Frankford School Rd 19945 302-732-3808
Duncan Smith, prin. Fax 732-3811

Frederica, Kent, Pop. 697
Lake Forest SD
Supt. — See Felton
Lake Forest East ES 300/K-3
124 W Front St 19946 302-335-5261
Martha Clark, prin. Fax 335-5273

Georgetown, Sussex, Pop. 4,911
Indian River SD
Supt. — See Selbyville
Georgetown ES 600/PK-5
301 W Market St 19947 302-856-1940
Lesia Jones, prin. Fax 855-2479
Georgetown MS 1,100/6-8
301 W Market St 19947 302-856-1900
Mike Williams, prin. Fax 856-1915
North Georgetown ES 600/PK-5
664 N Bedford St 19947 302-855-2430
Belinda Waples, prin. Fax 855-2439

Jefferson S 100/PK-8
22051 Wilson Rd 19947 302-856-3300
Theresa McManaman, hdmstr. Fax 856-1750

Greenville, New Castle
Red Clay Consolidated SD
Supt. — See Wilmington
DuPont MS 500/6-8
3130 Kennett Pike 19807 302-651-2690
Theodore Boyer, prin. Fax 425-4585

Greenwood, Sussex, Pop. 883
Woodbridge SD
Supt. — See Bridgeville
Woodbridge ES 800/PK-4
PO Box 2007 19950 302-349-4539
Corey Miklus M.Ed., prin. Fax 349-1413

Greenwood Mennonite S 200/K-12
12802 Mennonite School Rd 19950 302-349-4131
Larry Crossgrove, admin. Fax 349-5076

Harrington, Kent, Pop. 3,236
Lake Forest SD
Supt. — See Felton
Chipman MS 600/7-8
101 W Center St 19952 302-398-8197
James Cave, prin. Fax 398-8375
ECC PK-PK
100 W Mispillion St 19952 302-398-8945
Janet Cornwell Ph.D., dir. Fax 398-8983
Lake Forest South ES 500/K-3
301 Dorman St 19952 302-398-8011
Dr. Judy Craig, prin. Fax 398-8492

Hartly, Kent, Pop. 84
Capital SD
Supt. — See Dover
Hartly ES 400/PK-4
PO Box 25 19953 302-672-1670
Tammy Augustus, prin. Fax 672-1750

Hockessin, New Castle
Red Clay Consolidated SD
Supt. — See Wilmington
DuPont MS 900/6-8
735 Meeting House Rd 19707 302-239-3420
Chad Carmack, prin. Fax 239-3450
North Star ES 600/K-5
1340 Little Baltimore Rd 19707 302-234-7200
Andrea Lanciault, prin. Fax 234-7212

CACC Montessori S 100/PK-K
PO Box 1599 19707 302-239-2917
Elizabeth Simon, dir. Fax 239-0184
Hockessin Montessori S 200/PK-8
1000 Old Lancaster Pike 19707 302-234-1240
Marcia Kinnamen, hdmstr. Fax 234-6950
Sanford S 700/PK-12
PO Box 888 19707 302-239-5263
Douglas MacKelcan, hdmstr. Fax 239-5389
Towle Institute 200/K-12
PO Box 580 19707 302-993-1408
Kathleen Todd, prin. Fax 993-1409
Wilmington Christian S 500/K-12
825 Loveville Rd 19707 302-239-2121
William Stevens, hdmstr. Fax 239-2778

Laurel, Sussex, Pop. 3,822
Laurel SD 2,100/PK-12
1160 S Central Ave 19956 302-875-6100
Dr. John McCoy, supt. Fax 875-6106
www.laurel.k12.de.us
Dunbar ES 300/PK-1
499 W 6th St 19956 302-875-6140
Judy Noll, prin. Fax 875-6143
Laurel IS 300/5-6
801 S Central Ave 19956 302-875-6113
Julie Bradley, prin. Fax 875-6109
Laurel MS 400/7-8
801 S Central Ave 19956 302-875-6110
Jennifer Givens, prin. Fax 875-6148
North Laurel ES 500/2-4
300 Wilson St 19956 302-875-6130
Cristy Greaves Ed.D., prin. Fax 875-6133

Epworth Christian S 200/PK-8
14511 Sycamore Rd 19956 302-875-4488
Ivy Ulrich-Bonk, admin. Fax 875-7207

Lewes, Sussex, Pop. 3,116
Cape Henlopen SD 4,400/K-12
1270 Kings Hwy 19958 302-645-6686
George Stone Ed.D., supt. Fax 645-6684
www.k12.de.us/capehenlopen
Beacon MS 500/6-8
19483 John J Williams Hwy 19958 302-645-6288
T.S. Buckmaster, prin. Fax 644-6118
Shields ES 500/K-5
910 Shields Ave 19958 302-645-7748
Patricia Magee Ph.D., prin. Fax 644-7924
Other Schools – See Milton, Rehoboth Beach

Lincoln, Sussex
Milford SD
Supt. — See Milford
Morris ECC 700/PK-1
8609 3rd St 19960 302-422-1650
Susan Donahue, prin. Fax 424-5447

Christian Tabernacle Academy 100/PK-12
PO Box 148 19960 302-422-6471
Ronald Hill, admin. Fax 422-9207

Magnolia, Kent, Pop. 239
Caesar Rodney SD
Supt. — See Camden
McIlvaine ECC 100/K-K
PO Box 258 19962 302-335-5039
Sherry Kijowski, prin. Fax 335-3705

Middletown, New Castle, Pop. 9,121
Appoquinimink SD
Supt. — See Odessa
Appoquinimink ECC 200/PK-K
502 S Broad St 19709 302-376-4400
Rene Nolan, prin. Fax 378-5696
Brick Mill ES, 378 Brick Mill Rd 19709 800/1-5
Don Davis, prin. 302-378-5045
Cedar Lane ECC 300/PK-K
1221 Cedar Lane Rd 19709 302-449-5873
Sandra Cohee Ed.D., prin.
Cedar Lane ES 700/1-5
1259 Cedar Lane Rd 19709 302-378-5045
Donna Kolakowski, prin. Fax 378-5091
Meredith MS 1,100/6-8
504 S Broad St 19709 302-378-5001
Dr. Claude McAllister, prin. Fax 378-5008
Redding MS 800/6-8
201 New St 19709 302-378-5030
Matthew Burrowss, prin. Fax 378-5080
Silver Lake ES 600/1-5
200 E Cochran St 19709 302-378-5023
Dr. Sharon Pepukayi, prin. Fax 378-5092
Waters MS 6-8
1235 Cedar Lane Rd 19709 302-449-3490
James Comegys, prin.

St. Anne's Episcopal S 300/PK-8
211 Silver Lake Rd 19709 302-378-3179
Peter Thayer, hdmstr. Fax 449-0957

Milford, Sussex, Pop. 7,201
Milford SD 3,900/PK-12
906 Lakeview Ave 19963 302-422-1600
Fax 422-1608
www.milfordschooldistrict.org/
Banneker ES 600/2-5
449 North St 19963 302-422-1630
Jean Wylie, prin. Fax 424-5487
Milford MS 1,000/6-8
612 Lakeview Ave 19963 302-422-1620
Nicole Durkin Ed.D., prin. Fax 424-5466
Ross ES 600/2-5
310 Lovers Ln 19963 302-422-1640
Sylvia Henderson Ed.D., prin. Fax 424-5453
Other Schools – See Lincoln

Milford Christian S 100/PK-12
6062 Old Shawnee Rd 19963 302-422-4263
Rev. David Perdue, admin. Fax 422-6379

Millsboro, Sussex, Pop. 2,505
Indian River SD
Supt. — See Selbyville
East Millsboro ES 700/PK-5
29346 Iron Branch Rd 19966 302-934-3222
Mary Bixler, prin. Fax 934-3227
Long Neck ES 500/K-5
26064 School Ln 19966 302-945-6200
Charlynne Hopkins Ed.D., prin. Fax 945-6203
Millsboro MS 6-8
302 E State St 19966 302-934-3200
LouAnn Hudson, prin. Fax 934-3215

Milton, Sussex, Pop. 1,791
Cape Henlopen SD
Supt. — See Lewes
Brittingham ES 500/K-5
400 Mulberry St 19968 302-684-8522
Cathy Petitgout, prin. Fax 684-2043
Mariner MS 500/6-8
16391 Harbeson Rd 19968 302-684-8516
Brian Donahue, prin. Fax 684-5606
Milton ES 500/K-5
512 Federal St 19968 302-684-2516
Kevin Mumford, prin. Fax 684-8565

Eagle's Nest Christian Academy 500/PK-8
PO Box 129 19968 302-684-4983
Lucy Dutton, dir. Fax 684-2905

Newark, New Castle, Pop. 30,060
Christina SD
Supt. — See Wilmington
Brader ES 700/K-5
107 Four Seasons Pkwy 19702 302-454-5959
Heather Maldonado, prin. Fax 454-5459
Brookside ES 500/K-5
800 Marrows Rd 19713 302-454-5454
Eric Stephens, prin. Fax 454-3480
Downes ES 500/K-5
220 Casho Mill Rd 19711 302-454-2133
Denise Schwartz, prin. Fax 454-3483
Gallaher ES 500/K-5
800 N Brownleaf Rd 19713 302-454-2464
Michael Kijowski, prin. Fax 454-3484
Gauger/Cobbs MS 1,000/6-8
50 Gender Rd 19713 302-454-2358
Amy Levitz-Grundy, prin. Fax 454-3482
Keene ES 700/K-5
200 LaGrange Ave 19702 302-454-2018
Beatrice Speir, prin. Fax 454-5969
Kirk MS 900/6-8
140 Brennen Dr 19713 302-454-2164
William Clifton, prin. Fax 454-3491
Leasure ES 700/K-5
1015 Church Rd 19702 302-454-2103
Deirdra Aikens, prin. Fax 454-2109
MacLary ES 400/PK-5
300 Saint Regis Dr 19711 302-454-2142
Margaret Mason, prin. Fax 454-3485
Marshall ES 800/K-5
101 Barrett Run Dr 19702 302-454-4700
Patrice Buchanan, prin. Fax 454-4701
McVey ES 500/K-5
908 Janice Dr 19713 302-454-2145
Heather Bordas, prin. Fax 454-3486
Shue-Medill MS 1,200/6-8
1550 Capitol Trl 19711 302-454-2171
Jason de Jonghe, prin. Fax 454-3492
Smith ES 500/PK-5
142 Brennen Dr 19713 302-454-2174
Daniel Shelton, prin. Fax 454-3487
West Park Place ES 400/PK-5
193 W Park Pl 19711 302-454-2290
Kalia Reynolds, prin. Fax 454-3488
Wilson ES 500/K-5
14 Forge Rd 19711 302-454-2180
Helen Spacht, prin. Fax 454-3489

Red Clay Consolidated SD
Supt. — See Wilmington
Forest Oak ES 500/K-5
55 S Meadowood Dr 19711 302-454-3420
Diane Dambach, prin. Fax 454-3423

Aletheia Christian S 100/PK-8
91 Salem Church Rd 19713 302-737-7048
Richard Duzan, prin. Fax 737-4571
Christ the Teacher Catholic S 600/PK-8
2451 Frazer Rd 19702 302-838-8850
Sr. LaVerne King, prin. Fax 838-8854
Holy Angels S 500/K-8
82 Possum Park Rd 19711 302-731-2210
Denise Winterberger, prin. Fax 731-2211
Independence S 800/PK-8
1300 Paper Mill Rd 19711 302-239-0330
Victoria Yatzus, hdmstr. Fax 239-3696

Mount Sophia Academy 200/K-12
PO Box 9925 19714 302-398-7116
Vicki Tillman, contact
Pike Creek Christian S 300/PK-8
199 Polly Drummond Hill Rd 19711 302-731-7773
Steve Taylor, prin. Fax 731-8554
St. John Lutheran S 50/PK-8
135 Old Baltimore Pike 19702 302-738-6806
Andrew Monday, prin. Fax 368-7394
St. Pauls Lutheran S 100/PK-K
701 S College Ave 19713 302-368-0064
Katherine Johnston, dir. Fax 368-0064
Tall Oaks Classical S 100/K-12
181 Stanton Christiana Rd 19702 302-738-3337
Donald Post, hdmstr. Fax 737-3369

New Castle, New Castle, Pop. 4,836
Colonial SD 8,800/K-12
318 E Basin Rd 19720 302-323-2700
George Meney Ed.D., supt. Fax 323-2748
www.colonial.k12.de.us
Bedford MS 1,200/6-8
801 Coxneck Rd 19720 302-832-6280
Paul Walmsley Ed.D., prin. Fax 834-6729
Castle Hills ES 700/K-5
502 Moores Ln 19720 302-323-2915
Raquel Johnson, prin. Fax 323-2921
Colwyck ES 400/K-5
12 Landers Ln 19720 302-429-4085
Jennifer Alexander, prin. Fax 429-4097
Downie ES 400/K-5
1201 Delaware St 19720 302-323-2926
Nneka Jones, prin. Fax 323-2929
Eisenberg ES 500/K-5
27 Landers Ln 19720 302-429-4074
Jacob Getty, prin. Fax 429-4081
McCullough MS 6-8
20 Chase Ave 19720 302-429-4000
Elizabeth Fleetwood, prin. Fax 429-4005
Pleasantville ES 600/K-5
16 Pleasant Pl 19720 302-323-2935
Peter Leida, prin. Fax 323-2943
Read MS 1,100/6-8
314 E Basin Rd 19720 302-323-2760
Holly Sage, prin. Fax 323-2763
Southern ES 1,100/K-5
795 Coxneck Rd 19720 302-832-6300
Deborah Sweeney, prin. Fax 832-6305
Wilmington Manor ES 400/K-5
200 E Roosevelt Ave 19720 302-323-2901
Michael Rees, prin. Fax 323-2908
Other Schools – See Bear

New Castle Christian Academy 200/PK-12
901 E Basin Rd 19720 302-328-7026
Mark Unruh, admin. Fax 328-7886
Our Lady of Fatima S 400/PK-8
801 N Dupont Hwy 19720 302-328-2803
Kathleen Kenney, prin. Fax 328-1572
St. Peter S 200/PK-8
515 Harmony St 19720 302-328-1191
Paula Ryan, prin. Fax 328-8049

Newport, New Castle, Pop. 1,106
Red Clay Consolidated SD
Supt. — See Wilmington
Richey ES 400/K-5
105 E Highland Ave 19804 302-992-5535
Dorothy Johnson, prin. Fax 892-3242

Ocean View, Sussex, Pop. 1,094
Indian River SD
Supt. — See Selbyville
Baltimore ES 600/PK-5
PO Box 21 19970 302-537-2700
Janet Hickman, prin. Fax 537-2708

Odessa, New Castle, Pop. 322
Appoquinimink SD 7,700/PK-12
PO Box 4010 19730 302-376-4128
Dr. Tony Marchio, supt. Fax 378-5016
www.apposchooldistrict.com
Other Schools – See Bear, Middletown, Townsend

Rehoboth Beach, Sussex, Pop. 1,556
Cape Henlopen SD
Supt. — See Lewes
Rehoboth ES 600/K-5
500 Stockley St 19971 302-227-2571
Michael Dmiterchik, prin. Fax 227-5178

Seaford, Sussex, Pop. 6,997
Seaford SD 3,300/K-12
390 N Market St 19973 302-629-4587
Dr. Russell Knorr, supt. Fax 629-2619
www.seaford.k12.de.us
Douglass ES 500/K-5
1 Swain Rd 19973 302-628-4413
Travis Moorman, prin. Fax 628-4486
Seaford Central ES 400/K-5
1 Delaware Pl 19973 302-629-4587
Rob Zachry, prin. Fax 628-4380
Seaford MS 800/6-8
500 E Stein Hwy 19973 302-629-4587
Stephanie Smith, prin. Fax 628-4485
West Seaford ES 400/K-5
511 Sussex Ave 19973 302-628-4414
Patricia Harris Ed.D., prin. Fax 628-4487
Other Schools – See Blades

Seaford Christian Academy 200/PK-12
110 Holly St 19973 302-629-7161
Larry Snyder, admin. Fax 629-7726

Selbyville, Sussex, Pop. 1,742
Indian River SD 8,100/PK-12
31 Hosier St 19975 302-436-1000
Susan Bunting Ed.D., supt. Fax 436-1034
www.irsd.net/

Selbyville MS 700/6-8
80 Bethany Rd 19975 302-436-1020
Brice Reed, prin. Fax 436-1035
Showell ES 300/PK-5
41 Bethany Rd 19975 302-436-1040
Laura Schneider, prin. Fax 436-1053
Southern Delaware S of the Arts 400/1-8
27 Hosier St 19975 302-436-1066
Neil Beahan, prin. Fax 436-1068
Other Schools – See Frankford, Georgetown, Millsboro, Ocean View

Smyrna, Kent, Pop. 7,413
Smyrna SD 4,100/K-12
82 Monrovia Ave 19977 302-653-8585
Deborah Wicks, supt. Fax 653-3429
www.smyrna.k12.de.us
Moore MS 700/5-6
20 W Frazier St 19977 302-659-6297
Derek Prillaman, prin. Fax 659-6299
North Smyrna ES 500/K-4
365 N Main St 19977 302-653-8589
Cynthia Allen, prin. Fax 653-3146
Smyrna ES 500/K-4
121 S School Ln 19977 302-653-8588
David Morrison, prin. Fax 653-3411
Smyrna MS 800/7-8
700 Duck Creek Pkwy 19977 302-653-8584
Patrik Williams, prin. Fax 653-3424
Sunnyside ES K-4
123 Rabbit Chase Ln 19977 302-653-2808
Kathleen Castro, prin.
Other Schools – See Clayton

Smyrna Christian S 100/PK-10
PO Box 159 19977 302-653-2538
William Kidwell, admin. Fax 653-8467

Townsend, New Castle, Pop. 373
Appoquinimink SD
Supt. — See Odessa
Townsend ECC 200/PK-K
10 Brook Ramble Ln 19734 302-378-9960
Lucia Weathers, admin.
Townsend ES 400/1-5
PO Box 369 19734 302-378-5020
Charles Sheppard, prin. Fax 378-5088

Wilmington, New Castle, Pop. 72,786
Brandywine SD
Supt. — See Claymont
Brandywood ES 400/K-3
2115 Anson Rd 19810 302-475-3966
Veronica Wilkie, prin. Fax 529-3090
Carrcroft ES 400/K-3
503 Crest Rd 19803 302-762-7165
Carol Norman, prin. Fax 762-7106
DuPont ES 800/K-K, 4-6
701 W 34th St 19802 302-762-7146
Lincoln Hohler, prin. Fax 762-7196
Forwood ES 300/K-3
1900 Westminster Dr 19810 302-475-3956
Enid Van Such, prin. Fax 529-3092
Hanby MS 700/7-8
2523 Berwyn Rd 19810 302-479-1631
Ronald Mendenhall, prin. Fax 479-1643
Harlan ES 600/4-6
3601 N Jefferson St 19802 302-762-7156
Dorrell Green, prin. Fax 762-7117
Lancashire ES 300/K-3
2000 Naamans Rd 19810 302-475-3990
Peter Barry, prin. Fax 475-3999
Lombardy ES 300/K-3
412 Foulk Rd 19803 302-762-7190
Lynn Sharps, prin. Fax 762-7108
Mt. Pleasant ES 500/K-3
500 Duncan Rd 19809 302-762-7120
Joyce Skrobot, prin. Fax 762-7040

Springer MS 600/7-8
2220 Shipley Rd 19803 302-479-1621
Michael Gliniak, prin. Fax 479-1628
Talley MS 400/7-8
1110 Cypress Rd 19810 302-475-3976
Richard Carter, prin. Fax 475-3998

Christina SD 16,400/PK-12
600 N Lombard St 19801 302-552-2600
Marcia Lyles, supt. Fax 429-4109
www.christina.k12.de.us/
Bancroft ES 600/K-5
700 N Lombard St 19801 302-429-4102
Jackie Lee, prin. Fax 429-3956
Bayard MS 300/6-8
200 S Dupont St 19805 302-429-4118
Donald Patton, prin. Fax 429-4153
Elbert-Palmer ES 200/K-5
1210 Lobdell St 19801 302-429-4188
Patricia Thomas, prin. Fax 429-3957
Pulaski ES 200/K-5
1300 Cedar St 19805 302-429-4136
Tracey Roberts, prin. Fax 429-3955
Stubbs ES 100/K-5
1100 N Pine St 19801 302-429-4175
Mae Gaskins, prin. Fax 429-3958
Other Schools – See Bear, Christiana, Newark

Red Clay Consolidated SD 15,400/K-12
4550 New Linden Hill Rd 19808 302-552-3700
Dr. Robert Andrzejewski, supt. Fax 992-7820
www.redclay.k12.de.us
Baltz ES 600/K-6
1500 Spruce Ave 19805 302-992-5560
Jennifer Sheilds-Russell, prin. Fax 992-5518
Brandywine Springs S 900/K-8
2916 Duncan Rd 19808 302-636-5681
William Cooke, prin. Fax 636-5683
Heritage ES 500/K-5
2815 Highlands Ln 19808 302-454-3424
Linda Ennis, prin. Fax 454-3427
Highlands ES 400/K-5
2100 Gilpin Ave 19806 302-651-2715
Robert Farr, prin. Fax 425-4599
Lewis ES 500/K-5
920 N Van Buren St 19806 302-651-2695
Myron Cornish, prin. Fax 651-2759
Linden Hill ES 700/K-5
3415 Skyline Dr 19808 302-454-3406
Dr. Mary Bradley, prin. Fax 454-3549
Marbrook ES 400/K-5
2101 Centerville Rd 19808 302-992-5555
Bradford Holstein, prin. Fax 892-3253
Mote ES 500/K-5
2110 Edwards Ave 19808 302-992-5565
Aaron Selekman, prin. Fax 892-3251
Richardson Park ES 400/K-5
16 Idella Ave 19804 302-992-5570
Angela Frey, prin. Fax 892-3255
Shortlidge Academy 400/K-5
100 W 18th St 19802 302-651-2710
Linda Thomas, prin. Fax 425-3385
Skyline MS 700/6-8
2900 Skyline Dr 19808 302-454-3410
Janet Basara, prin. Fax 454-3541
Stanton MS 600/6-8
1800 Limestone Rd 19804 302-992-5540
Michael Hanley, prin. Fax 992-5586
Warner ES 700/K-5
801 W 18th St 19802 302-651-2740
Meg Hoefer, prin. Fax 651-2661
Other Schools – See Greenville, Hockessin, Newark, Newport

Centreville S 100/K-8
6201 Kennett Pike 19807 302-571-0230
Denise Orenstein, hdmstr. Fax 571-0270
Children's House Montessori S 100/PK-3
2848 Grubb Rd 19810 302-529-9259
Cathy Lopez-Cooling, hdmstr. Fax 529-9257

Concord Christian Academy 200/PK-12
2510 Marsh Rd 19810 302-475-3247
Jeffrey Bergey, prin. Fax 475-6462
Corpus Christi S 400/K-8
907 New Rd 19805 302-995-2231
Kathleen Connor, prin. Fax 993-0767
Einstein Academy 100/K-6
101 Garden of Eden Rd 19803 302-478-5026
Dr. Jack Sparks, hdmstr. Fax 478-0664
Elementary Workshop Montessori S 100/PK-6
502 N Pine St 19801 302-656-1498
E. McCrae Harrison, dir. Fax 656-1905
Immaculate Heart of Mary S 500/PK-8
1000 Shipley Rd 19803 302-764-0977
Jan Chapdelaine, prin. Fax 764-0375
Nativity Preparatory S 50/5-8
1515 Linden St 19805 302-777-1015
Fr. Joseph DiMauro, prin. Fax 777-1225
Pilot School 200/K-8
100 Garden Of Eden Rd 19803 302-478-1740
Kathleen Craven, dir.
Pope John Paul II S 200/PK-8
210 Bellefonte Ave 19809 302-762-5595
Monica Malseed, prin. Fax 762-6329
St. Ann's S 300/PK-8
2006 Shallcross Ave 19806 302-652-6567
Sr. Virginia Pfau, prin. Fax 652-4156
St. Anthony of Padua S 400/PK-8
1715 W 9th St 19805 302-421-3743
Patricia O'Donnell, prin. Fax 421-3796
St. Catherine of Siena S 200/K-8
2501 Centerville Rd 19808 302-633-4901
Deborah Ruff, prin. Fax 633-4902
St. Edmond's Academy 300/K-8
2120 Veale Rd 19810 302-475-5370
Dr. Michael Marinelli, hdmstr. Fax 475-2256
St. Elizabeth S 400/K-8
1500 Cedar St 19805 302-655-8208
William Beliveau, prin. Fax 655-5457
St. John the Beloved S 600/K-8
905 Milltown Rd 19808 302-998-5525
Richard Hart, prin. Fax 998-1923
St. Mary Magdalen S 500/PK-8
9 Sharpley Rd 19803 302-656-2745
Barbara Wanner, prin. Fax 656-7889
St. Matthew S 400/PK-8
1 Fallon Ave 19804 302-633-5860
Bernard Fisher, prin. Fax 633-5860
St. Paul S 200/PK-8
312 N Van Buren St 19805 302-656-1372
Alexandria Cirko, prin. Fax 656-5238
St. Peter Cathedral S 200/K-8
310 W 6th St 19801 302-656-5234
Sr. Barbara Curran, prin. Fax 658-6489
Serviam Girls Academy 50/5-6
PO Box 7907 19803 302-438-0004
Anne Weber, pres.
Sharon Temple Junior Academy 50/K-8
2001 N Washington St 19802 302-428-0216
Gloria Perry, prin. Fax 428-3816
Tatnall S 700/PK-12
1501 Barley Mill Rd 19807 302-998-2292
Eric Ruoss, hdmstr. Fax 892-4389
Tower Hill S 700/PK-12
2813 W 17th St 19806 302-575-0550
Dr. Christopher Wheeler, hdmstr. Fax 657-8373
Ursuline Academy 600/PK-12
1106 Pennsylvania Ave 19806 302-658-7158
Cathie Field-Lloyd, pres. Fax 658-4297
Wilmington Friends S 800/PK-12
101 School Rd 19803 302-576-2900
Bryan Garman, hdmstr. Fax 576-2939
Wilmington Junior Academy 50/K-8
3001 Millcreek Rd 19808 302-998-0530
Mike Marinkovic, prin. Fax 998-7413
Wilmington Montessori S 400/PK-6
1400 Harvey Rd 19810 302-475-0555
Linda Zankowsky, hdmstr. Fax 529-7004
Zion Early Education Center 100/PK-K
2101 Lancaster Ave 19805 302-655-7874
Saralee Hawk, dir. Fax 658-2335

DISTRICT OF COLUMBIA

DISTRICT OF COLUMBIA PUBLIC SCHOOLS

825 N Capitol St NE, Washington 20002
Telephone 202-442-5885
Fax 202-442-5026
Website http://www.k12.dc.us

Chancellor Michelle Rhee

DISTRICT OF COLUMBIA BOARD OF EDUCATION

825 N Capitol St NE, Washington 20002-8207

President Lisa Raymond

PUBLIC, PRIVATE AND CATHOLIC ELEMENTARY SCHOOLS

Washington, District of Columbia, Pop. 550,521

District of Columbia SD 41,500/PK-12
825 N Capitol St NE 20002 202-442-5885
Michelle Rhee, chncllr. Fax 442-5026
www.k12.dc.us/

Aiton ES 400/PK-5
533 48th Pl NE 20019 202-724-4627
Peggy Mussenden, prin. Fax 724-4630

Amidon-Bowen ES 200/PK-5
401 I St SW 20024 202-724-4867
Almeta Hawkins, prin. Fax 724-4868

Bancroft ES 400/PK-6
1755 Newton St NW 20010 202-673-7280
Fay Thompson, prin. Fax 673-6991

Barnard ES 300/PK-5
430 Decatur St NW 20011 202-576-1100
Shirley Hopkinson, prin. Fax 541-6010

Beers ES 300/PK-5
3600 Alabama Ave SE 20020 202-645-3240
Gwendolyn Payton, prin. Fax 645-3225

Birney ES 300/PK-5
2501 Mrtn Lthr Kng Jr Av SE 20020 202-698-1133
Charles Webb, prin. Fax 698-1141

Brent ES 200/PK-5
301 N Carolina Ave SE 20003 202-698-3363
Cheryl Wilhoyte, prin. Fax 698-3369

Brightwood S 400/PK-8
1300 Nicholson St NW 20011 202-722-5670
Wanda Fox, prin. Fax 576-6168

Brookland S 200/PK-8
1401 Michigan Ave NE 20017 202-576-6095
Donna Pressley, prin. Fax 576-4632

Browne S 200/PK-8
850 26th St NE 20002 202-724-4547
Keith Stephenson, prin. Fax 724-1530

Bruce-Monroe S 200/PK-5
3560 Warder St NW 20010 202-576-6222
Marta Palacios, prin. Fax 576-6225

Burroughs S 300/PK-8
1820 Monroe St NE 20018 202-576-6039
Linda Little, prin. Fax 541-6477

Burrville ES 400/PK-5
801 Division Ave NE 20019 202-724-4598
Donnie Rutledge, prin. Fax 724-5578

Cleveland ES 200/PK-5
1825 8th St NW 20001 202-939-4380
Annie Mair, prin. Fax 673-6461

Cooke ES 300/PK-6
300 Bryant St NW 20001 202-671-1788
Kathleen Black, prin. Fax 671-0086

Davis ES 300/PK-5
4430 H St SE 20019 202-645-3220
Joyce Thompson, prin. Fax 645-3215

Deal JHS 500/7-8
3815 Fort Dr NW 20016 202-282-0100
Melissa Kim, prin. Fax 282-1116

Draper ES 100/PK-6
908 Wahler Pl SE 20032 202-645-3309
Sandra Coates, prin. Fax 645-3315

Drew ES 300/PK-5
5600 Eads St NE 20019 202-724-4922
Kimberly Davis, prin. Fax 724-4924

Eaton ES 400/PK-6
3301 Lowell St NW 20008 202-282-0103
Jacqueline Gartrell, prin. Fax 282-0074

Eliot-Hine MS 200/6-8
1830 Constitution Ave NE 20002 202-673-8666
Willie Jackson, prin. Fax 543-4500

Emery S 200/PK-8
1720 1st St NE 20002 202-576-6034
Ronald Taylor, prin. Fax 576-7365

Ferebee-Hope ES 300/PK-5
3999 8th St SE 20032 202-645-3100
Sharron Stroman, prin. Fax 645-3104

Fillmore Arts Center-East PK-8
915 Spring Rd NW Fl 3 20010 202-576-6236
Katherine Latterner, prin.

Fillmore Arts Center-West PK-8
1819 35th St NW 20007 202-729-3796
Katherine Latterner, prin. Fax 333-8340

Francis-Stevens S 200/PK-8
2425 N St NW 20037 202-724-4841
Maurice Kennard, prin. Fax 724-3957

Garfield ES 300/PK-5
2435 Alabama Ave SE 20020 202-698-1600
Tammy Thomas, prin. Fax 698-1614

Garrison ES 200/PK-5
1200 S St NW 20009 202-673-7263
Geneva Williams, prin. Fax 673-6828

Hardy MS 300/6-8
1819 35th St NW 20007 202-729-4350
Patrick Pope, prin. Fax 673-8123

Harris ES 300/PK-5
301 53rd St SE 20019 202-645-3188
Shirley Ambush, prin. Fax 645-3190

Hart MS 600/6-8
601 Mississippi Ave SE 20032 202-645-3420
Kisha Webster, prin. Fax 645-3426

Hearst ES 200/PK-3
3950 37th St NW 20008 202-282-0106
Bernarda Tally, prin. Fax 282-2303

Hendley ES 200/PK-6
425 Chesapeake St SE 20032 202-645-3450
Barbara Green, prin. Fax 645-7098

Houston ES 300/PK-5
1100 50th Pl NE 20019 202-724-4622
Charlotte Watkins, prin. Fax 724-4625

Hyde ES 200/PK-5
3219 O St NW 20007 202-282-0170
Dana Nerenberg, prin. Fax 282-0087

Janney ES 500/PK-6
4130 Albemarle St NW 20016 202-282-0110
Karen Crews, prin. Fax 282-0112

Jefferson MS 400/6-8
801 7th St SW 20024 202-729-3270
Stephanie Patton, prin. Fax 724-2459

Johnson MS 300/6-8
1400 Bruce Pl SE 20020 202-698-1017
Robert Saunders, prin. Fax 698-1066

Kenilworth ES 300/PK-6
1300 44th St NE 20019 202-724-4643
Fatima Johnson, prin. Fax 724-3890

Ketcham ES 300/PK-5
1919 15th St SE 20020 202-698-1122
Joyce Goche-Grimes, prin. Fax 698-1113

Key ES 300/PK-5
5001 Dana Pl NW 20016 202-282-3800
David Landeryou, prin. Fax 282-0188

Kimball ES 300/PK-5
3375 Minnesota Ave SE 20019 202-645-3150
Sheila Miller, prin. Fax 645-3147

King ES 400/PK-5
3200 6th St SE 20032 202-645-3440
Valoria Baylor, prin. Fax 645-7308

Kramer MS 400/6-8
1700 Q St SE 20020 202-698-1188
Kenneth Parker, prin. Fax 698-1171

LaFayette ES 600/PK-6
5701 Broad Branch Rd NW 20015 202-282-0116
G. Lynn Main, prin. Fax 282-1126

Langdon S 500/PK-8
1900 Evarts St NE 20018 202-576-6048
Barbara Campbell, prin. Fax 576-7976

LaSalle-Backus S 300/PK-8
501 Riggs Rd NE 20011 202-576-6120
Richard Rogers, prin. Fax 541-3859

Leckie ES 300/PK-6
4201 Martin Luther King Jr 20032 202-645-3330
Clementine Homesley, prin. Fax 645-3331

Ludlow-Taylor ES 200/PK-5
659 G St NE 20002 202-698-3244
Carolyn Cobbs, prin. Fax 698-3250

MacFarland MS 300/6-8
4400 Iowa Ave NW 20011 202-576-6207
Harold Barber, prin. Fax 576-6212

Malcolm X ES 400/PK-5
1351 Alabama Ave SE 20032 202-645-3409
Darwin Bobbitt, prin. Fax 645-7219

Mann ES 200/PK-6
4430 Newark St NW 20016 202-282-0126
Elizabeth Whisnant, prin. Fax 282-0128

Marshall S 300/PK-8
3100 Fort Lincoln Dr NE 20018 202-576-6900
Margaret Blake, prin. Fax 576-7932

Maury ES 200/PK-5
1250 Constitution Ave NE 20002 202-698-3838
Michael Wilson, prin. Fax 698-3844

Miller MS 400/6-8
301 49th St NE 20019 202-388-6870
Laureal Robinson, prin. Fax 727-8330

Miner ES 400/PK-5
601 15th St NE 20002 202-397-3960
Lavonne Taliaferro-Bunch, prin. Fax 724-4957

Montgomery ES 200/PK-4
421 P St NW 20001 202-673-7245
Melissa Martin, prin. Fax 673-7247

Murch ES 500/PK-6
4810 36th St NW 20008 202-282-0130
Brenda Lewis, prin. Fax 282-0132

Nalle ES 400/PK-5
219 50th St SE 20019 202-645-7300
Kim Burke, prin. Fax 645-3196

Noyes S 300/PK-8
2725 10th St NE 20018 202-281-2580
Wayne Ryan, prin. Fax 576-7397

Orr ES 300/PK-5
2200 Minnesota Ave SE 20020 202-645-3288
Michelle Edwards, prin. Fax 645-3292

Oyster-Adams Bilingual ES 400/PK-8
2801 Calvert St NW 20008 202-671-3111
Monica Aguirre, prin. Fax 671-3087

Patterson ES 300/PK-6
4399 S Capitol Ter SW 20032 202-574-7600
Linda Williams, prin. Fax 645-3758

Payne ES 200/PK-5
305 15th St SE 20003 202-698-3262
Vielka Scott, prin. Fax 698-3263

Peabody ECC 100/PK-K
425 C St NE 20002 202-698-3277
Brandon Eatman, prin. Fax 698-3275

Plummer ES 300/PK-5
4601 Texas Ave SE 20019 202-645-3179
Christopher Gray, prin. Fax 645-3176

Powell S 300/PK-8
1350 Upshur St NW 20011 202-576-6247
Jose Belloso, prin. Fax 576-7155

Randle Highlands ES 400/PK-5
1650 30th St SE 20020 202-645-3282
Sheron Colston, prin. Fax 645-3911

Raymond S 200/PK-8
915 Spring Rd NW 20010 202-576-6236
LaShada Ham, prin. Fax 576-7275

Reed Learning Center 400/PK-6
2200 Champlain St NW 20009 202-673-7308
Dayo Akinsheye, prin. Fax 673-3410

River Terrace ES 200/PK-5
420 34th St NE 20019 202-724-4589
Shannon Foster, prin. Fax 724-5606

Ross ES 200/PK-6
1730 R St NW 20009 202-673-7200
Amanda Alexander, prin. Fax 673-6644

Savoy ES 300/PK-5
2501 M L King Jr Ave SE 20020 202-698-1134
Anne Evans, prin. Fax 645-9888

School Within School at Peabody PK-K
425 C St NE 20002 202-698-3283
John Burst, dir. Fax 727-9276

Seaton ES 300/PK-5
1503 10th St NW 20001 202-673-7215
H. Douglas Rice, prin. Fax 673-7216

Shaed S 200/PK-8
301 Douglas St NE 20002 202-576-6052
Cheryl Taylor, prin. Fax 576-6455

Shaw MS 200/6-8
2001 10th St NW 20001 202-673-7329
Brian Betts, prin. Fax 673-6543

Shepherd ES 300/PK-6
7800 14th St NW 20012 202-576-6140
Galeet BenZion, prin. Fax 576-7578

Simon ES 300/PK-5
401 Mississippi Ave SE 20032 202-645-3360
Adelaide Flamer, prin. Fax 645-3359

Smothers ES 200/PK-5
4400 Brooks St NE 20019 202-724-4640
Angela Morton, prin. Fax 724-2377

Sousa MS 300/6-8
3650 Ely Pl SE 20019 202-729-3260
Dwan Jordon, prin. Fax 645-6331

Stanton ES 400/PK-5
2701 Naylor Rd SE 20020 202-645-3255
Donald Presswood, prin. Fax 645-3264

Stoddert ES 200/PK-5
4001 Calvert St NW 20007 202-282-0143
Andriana Kalapothakos, prin. Fax 282-0145
Stuart-Hobson MS 400/5-8
410 E St NE 20002 202-698-4700
Brandon Eatman, prin. Fax 698-4720
Takoma S 400/PK-8
7010 Piney Branch Rd NW 20012 202-576-6127
Rikki Taylor, prin. Fax 576-7592
Terrell/McGogney ES 400/PK-6
3301 Wheeler Rd SE 20032 202-645-3740
Tanya Deskins, prin. Fax 645-7322
Thomas ES 300/PK-5
650 Anacostia Ave NE 20019 202-724-4593
Ruth Barnes, prin. Fax 724-5053
Thomson ES 300/PK-6
1200 L St NW 20005 202-898-4660
Gladys Camp, prin. Fax 442-8706
Truesdale S 300/PK-8
800 Ingraham St NW 20011 202-576-6202
Brearn Wright, prin. Fax 576-6205
Tubman ES 400/PK-6
3101 13th St NW 20010 202-673-7285
Harry Hughes, prin. Fax 673-7287
Turner ES 300/PK-5
1500 Mississippi Ave SE 20032 202-645-3470
Robert Gregory, prin. Fax 645-3467
Tyler ES 200/PK-5
1001 G St SE 20003 202-698-3577
Terry Dade, prin. Fax 698-3848
Walker-Jones/Terrell S 400/PK-8
100 L St NW 20001 202-535-1222
Jeffrey Grant, prin. Fax 535-0373
Watkins ES 500/PK-4
420 12th St SE 20003 202-698-3355
Brandon Eatman, prin. Fax 698-3340
Webb/Wheatley ES 300/PK-6
1375 Mount Olivet Rd NE 20002 202-724-4543
Scott Cartland, prin. Fax 724-4545
West S 200/PK-8
1338 Farragut St NW 20011 202-576-6226
Marlen Moses, prin. Fax 541-6087
Whittier S 400/PK-8
6201 5th St NW 20011 202-576-6156
Nicole Clifton, prin. Fax 576-6158
Wilson ES 300/PK-5
660 K St NE 20002 202-698-4733
Cheryl Warley, prin. Fax 698-4727
Winston Education Center 300/PK-8
3100 Erie St SE 20020 202-645-3300
Katie Jones, prin. Fax 645-5941

Academia de la Recta Porta Christian S 50/K-12
7614 Georgia Ave NW 20012 202-726-8737
Annette Miles, admin. Fax 726-8759
Aidan Montessori S 200/PK-6
2700 27th St NW 20008 202-387-2700
Kathleen Minardi, hdmstr. Fax 387-0346
Ambassador Christian S 100/K-8
PO Box 6943 20032 202-678-1993
Sheryl Jenifer, prin. Fax 678-0550
Annunciation S 100/PK-8
3825 Klingle Pl NW 20016 202-362-1408
K. Marguerite Conley, prin. Fax 363-4057
Beauvoir S 400/PK-3
3500 Woodley Rd NW 20016 202-537-6485
Paula Carreiro, hdmstr. Fax 537-6512
Blessed Sacrament S 500/K-8
5841 Chevy Chase Pkwy NW 20015 202-966-6682
Chris Kelly, prin. Fax 966-4938
Burroughs S 100/PK-6
601 50th St NE 20019 202-398-5266
Rita Johnson, prin. Fax 398-5652
Calvary Christian Academy 200/PK-8
806 Rhode Island Ave NE 20018 202-526-5176
Bernard Perry, prin. Fax 526-2672
Capitol Hill Day S 200/PK-8
210 S Carolina Ave SE 20003 202-547-2244
M. Shepheardson-Killem, hdmstr. Fax 543-4597
Cornerstone S 100/K-8
3740 Ely Pl SE 20019 202-842-0490
Joanna Lange, prin. Fax 842-0492
Dupont Park Adventist S 300/PK-10
3942 Alabama Ave SE 20020 202-583-8500
Lafese Quinnonez, prin. Fax 583-0650
Fears Boys Academy 50/K-10
1544 5th St NW 20001 202-232-2860
David Spruill, hdmstr. Fax 232-2860
First Rock Baptist Church Christian S 50/K-5
834 Hilltop Ter SE 20019 202-583-0992
Fax 583-0991
Georgetown Day S 600/PK-8
4530 MacArthur Blvd NW 20007 202-295-6200
Peter Branch, hdmstr. Fax 295-6221
Holy Redeemer S 300/PK-8
1135 New Jersey Ave NW 20001 202-638-5789
Ben Ketchum, prin. Fax 628-0401
Holy Trinity S 300/PK-8
1325 36th St NW 20007 202-337-2339
Mary Shannon, prin. Fax 337-0368
Jewish Primary Day S 200/PK-6
6045 16th St NW 20011 202-291-5737
Naomi Reem, hdmstr. Fax 291-9750
Kendall Demonstration S 100/PK-8
800 Florida Ave NE 20002 202-651-5045
Ed Bosso, dean Fax 651-5646
Lab S of Washington 300/1-12
4759 Reservoir Rd NW 20007 202-965-6600
Sally Seawright, dir. Fax 454-2270
Lowell S 300/PK-6
1640 Kalmia Rd NW 20012 202-577-2000
Debbie Gibbs, dir. Fax 577-2001
Maret S 600/K-12
3000 Cathedral Ave NW 20008 202-939-8800
Marjo Talbott, hdmstr. Fax 939-8884
Metropolitan Day S 100/PK-5
1240 Randolph St NE 20017 202-234-3210
Dr. Patricia Daniels, prin. Fax 234-3214
National Presbyterian S 200/PK-6
4121 Nebraska Ave NW 20016 202-537-7500
Jim Neill, hdmstr. Fax 537-7568
New Macedonia Christian Academy 50/PK-1
4115 Alabama Ave SE 20019 202-575-0856
Yvonne Pettiford, dir. Fax 575-0312
Our Lady of Victory S 200/PK-8
4755 Whitehaven Pkwy NW 20007 202-337-1421
Sheila Martinez, prin. Fax 337-2068
Sacred Heart S 200/PK-8
1625 Park Rd NW 20010 202-265-4828
Sandra Rojas, prin. Fax 265-0595
St. Anns Academy 200/PK-8
4404 Wisconsin Ave NW 20016 202-363-4460
Barbara Kelley, prin. Fax 362-6560
St. Anthony S 200/PK-8
12th & Lawrence Streets NE 20017 202-526-4657
William Eager, prin. Fax 832-5567
St. Augustine S 200/PK-8
1421 V St NW 20009 202-667-2608
Sr. Gloriamary Agumagu, prin. Fax 667-2610
St. Francis Xavier S 200/PK-8
2700 O St SE 20020 202-581-2010
Harold Thomas, prin. Fax 581-1142
St. Patrick's Episcopal Day S 500/PK-8
4700 Whitehaven Pkwy NW 20007 202-342-2805
Peter Barrett, hdmstr. Fax 342-7001
St. Peters Interparish S 200/PK-8
422 3rd St SE 20003 202-544-1618
Jennifer Ketchum, prin. Fax 547-5101
St. Thomas More S 200/PK-8
4265 4th St SE 20032 202-561-1189
Bridget Coates, prin. Fax 562-2336
San Miguel MS 100/6-8
1525 Newton St NW 20010 202-232-8345
Br. Francis Eells, prin. Fax 232-3987
Sheridan S 200/K-8
4400 36th St NW 20008 202-362-7900
C.R. Plummer, prin. Fax 244-9696
Sidwell Friends S 1,100/PK-12
3825 Wisconsin Ave NW 20016 202-537-8100
Bruce Stewart, hdmstr. Fax 537-8138
Walker S for Boys 600/PK-K
Mount Saint Alban 20016 202-257-9020
Rev. Kwasi Thornell, admin.
Washington International S 400/PK-5
1690 36th St NW 20007 202-243-1700
Clayton Lewis, hdmstr. Fax 243-1797
Washington Jesuit Academy 100/6-8
900 Varnum St NE 20017 202-832-7679
Joseph Powers, hdmstr. Fax 832-8098

FLORIDA

FLORIDA DEPARTMENT OF EDUCATION
325 W Gaines St, Tallahassee 32399-0400
Telephone 850-245-0505
Fax 850-245-9667
Website http://www.fldoe.org/

Commissioner of Education Eric Smith

FLORIDA BOARD OF EDUCATION
325 W Gaines St, Tallahassee 32399-0400

Chairperson T. Willard Fair

PUBLIC, PRIVATE AND CATHOLIC ELEMENTARY SCHOOLS

Alachua, Alachua, Pop. 7,557
Alachua County SD
Supt. — See Gainesville
Alachua ES 400/3-5
13800 NW 152nd Pl 32615 386-462-1841
Jim Brandenburg, prin. Fax 462-0133
Irby ES 500/PK-2
13505 NW 140th St 32615 386-462-5002
Lina Burklew, prin. Fax 462-5731
Mebane MS 500/6-8
16401 NW 140th St 32615 386-462-1648
Veita Jackson-Carter, prin. Fax 462-9094

Altamonte Springs, Seminole, Pop. 41,057
Seminole County SD
Supt. — See Sanford
Altamonte ES 900/PK-5
525 Pineview St 32701 407-746-2950
Fran Duvall, prin. Fax 746-2999
Forest City ES 900/PK-5
1010 Sand Lake Rd 32714 407-746-1050
Frank Haynie, prin. Fax 746-1099
Lake Orienta ES 700/PK-5
612 Newport Ave 32701 407-746-2650
Ines Schmook, prin. Fax 320-2699
Spring Lake ES 800/PK-5
695 Orange Ave 32714 407-746-1650
Alexis Agosto, prin. Fax 746-1699
Teague MS 1,600/6-8
1350 Mcneil Rd 32714 407-320-1550
Adrienne DeRienzo, prin. Fax 320-1545

Altamonte Christian S 200/K-12
601 Palm Springs Dr 32701 407-831-0950
Rev. Scott Carlson, dir. Fax 831-6840
Annunciation Academy 500/PK-8
593 Jamestown Blvd 32714 407-774-2801
Dr. Margaret Curran, prin. Fax 774-2826
Champion Preparatory Academy 300/K-12
931 N State Road 434 # 1201 32714 407-788-0018
Vicki Falco, dir. Fax 788-7625
Forest City Adventist S 100/K-8
1238 Bunnell Rd 32714 407-299-0703
Alipia Gonzalez, prin. Fax 299-9481
St. Mark's S 100/PK-8
1021 Palm Springs Dr 32701 407-830-9298
Carol Czwornog, prin. Fax 830-0748
St. Mary Magdalen S 500/PK-8
869 Maitland Ave 32701 407-339-7301
Lloyd Kinderknecht, prin. Fax 339-9556

Altha, Calhoun, Pop. 511
Calhoun County SD
Supt. — See Blountstown
Altha S 600/PK-12
PO Box 67 32421 850-762-3121
Ladonna Kelley, prin. Fax 762-9502

Alturas, Polk
Polk County SD
Supt. — See Bartow
Alturas ES 300/PK-5
PO Box 97 33820 863-519-3917
Dodie Haynes, prin. Fax 519-3923

Alva, Lee, Pop. 1,036
Lee County SD
Supt. — See Fort Myers
Alva ES 500/PK-5
17500 Church Ave 33920 239-728-2494
Callie Lawrence, prin. Fax 728-3259
Alva MS 500/6-8
21219 N River Rd 33920 239-728-2525
Stephen Hutnik, prin. Fax 728-2835
River Hall ES 700/PK-5
2800 River Hall Pkwy 33920 239-693-0349
Allen Humfleet, prin. Fax 693-5307

Anthony, Marion
Marion County SD
Supt. — See Ocala
Anthony ES 300/PK-5
9501 NE Jacksonville Rd 32617 352-671-6000
Jerome Brown, prin. Fax 671-6001

Apollo Beach, Hillsborough, Pop. 6,025
Hillsborough County SD
Supt. — See Tampa
Apollo Beach ES 600/K-5
501 Apollo Beach Blvd 33572 813-671-5172
Jamie Gerding, prin. Fax 672-5075
Doby ES 400/K-5
6720 Covington Garden Dr 33572 813-672-5388
Catherine Ferguson, prin. Fax 672-5392

Apopka, Orange, Pop. 34,728
Orange County SD
Supt. — See Orlando
Apopka ES 500/PK-5
675 Old Dixie Hwy 32712 407-884-2200
Roxann Paulsen, prin. Fax 884-2296
Apopka MS 900/6-8
425 N Park Ave 32712 407-884-2208
Christopher Camacho, prin. Fax 884-2217
Clarcona ES 1,000/PK-5
3607 Damon Rd 32703 407-884-2220
Dr. Bruce Suther, prin. Fax 884-6314
Clay Springs ES 800/PK-5
555 N Wekiwa Springs Rd 32712 407-884-2275
Nancy Schroeder, prin. Fax 884-2289
Dream Lake ES 800/PK-5
500 N Park Ave 32712 407-884-2227
Gary Schadow, prin. Fax 884-2298
Lakeville ES 900/K-5
2015 Lakeville Rd 32703 407-814-6110
Kim Stutsman, prin. Fax 814-6120
Lovell ES 800/PK-5
815 Roger Williams Rd 32703 407-884-2235
Oscar Aguirre, prin. Fax 884-6302
Piedmont Lakes MS 1,400/6-8
2601 Lakeville Rd 32703 407-884-2265
David Magee, prin. Fax 884-2287
Rock Springs ES 800/PK-5
2400 Rock Springs Rd 32712 407-884-2242
Dr. Nancy Pender, prin. Fax 884-6225
Wheatley ES 500/PK-5
2 W 18th St 32703 407-884-2250
Jackie Massey, prin. Fax 884-3102
Wolf Lake ES 900/PK-5
1771 W Ponkan Rd 32712 407-464-3342
Fax 464-3366
Wolf Lake MS 1,000/6-8
1725 W Ponkan Rd 32712 407-464-3317
Dr. Cathy Thornton, prin. Fax 464-3336

Seminole County SD
Supt. — See Sanford
Bear Lake ES 1,100/K-5
3399 Gleaves Ct 32703 407-746-5550
Gayle Bennett, prin. Fax 746-5599

Starchild Academy 200/PK-2
1550 N Wekiwa Springs Rd 32712 407-880-6060
Cindy Zimmerman, admin. Fax 880-7688
Trinity Christian S 400/K-8
1022 S Orange Blossom Trl 32703 407-886-0212
Beverly Smith, admin. Fax 886-3052

Arcadia, DeSoto, Pop. 7,151
De Soto County SD 4,700/PK-12
PO Box 2000 34265 863-494-4222
Adrian Cline, supt. Fax 494-9675
www.desotoschools.com
Desoto ECC 100/PK-PK
318 N Wilson Ave 34266 863-494-9303
Sharon Goodman, prin. Fax 494-9030
DeSoto MS 1,000/6-8
420 E Gibson St 34266 863-494-4133
Dave Bremer, prin. Fax 494-6263
Memorial ES 900/K-5
851 E Hickory St 34266 863-494-2736
Debra Hall, prin. Fax 993-2202
West ES 700/K-5
304 W Imogene St 34266 863-494-3155
Robert Shayman, prin. Fax 494-3689
Other Schools – See Nocatee

First Assembly Christian Academy 50/PK-PK
201 N 11th Ave 34266 863-494-9442
Lucy Garcia, dir. Fax 494-9657

Archer, Alachua, Pop. 1,288
Alachua County SD
Supt. — See Gainesville
Archer Community ES 300/PK-5
14533 SW 170th St 32618 352-495-2111
Jerry Douglas, prin. Fax 495-1796

Jordan Glen S 100/PK-8
12425 SW 154th St 32618 352-495-2728
Fax 495-1539

Astatula, Lake, Pop. 1,629
Lake County SD
Supt. — See Tavares
Astatula ES 800/PK-5
13925 Florida Ave 34705 352-343-1334
Kathy Tatro, prin. Fax 343-1457

Atlantic Beach, Duval, Pop. 13,436
Duval County SD
Supt. — See Jacksonville
Atlantic Beach ES 500/K-5
298 Sherry Dr 32233 904-247-5924
Kimberly Wright, prin. Fax 270-1894
Finegan ES 500/PK-5
555 Wonderwood Dr 32233 904-247-5996
David Pinter, prin. Fax 270-1858
Mayport ES 600/PK-5
2753 Shangri La Dr 32233 904-247-5988
Yvonne Ferguson, prin. Fax 247-5990
Mayport MS 700/6-8
2600 Mayport Rd 32233 904-247-5977
Katrina McCray, prin. Fax 247-5987

Community Presbyterian S 100/PK-K
150 Sherry Dr 32233 904-241-7335
Barbara Lynn, dir. Fax 246-1522

Auburndale, Polk, Pop. 12,381
Polk County SD
Supt. — See Bartow
Auburndale Central ES 400/PK-5
320 Lemon St 33823 863-965-5450
Virginia Cummings-Lang, prin. Fax 965-6390
Boswell ES 500/K-5
2820 K Ville Ave 33823 863-499-2990
Pamela Wingate, prin. Fax 284-4251
Caldwell ES 800/PK-5
141 Dairy Rd 33823 863-965-5470
Deron Williams, prin. Fax 965-5473
Lena Vista ES 800/PK-5
925 Berkley Rd 33823 863-965-5464
Mary Payne, prin. Fax 965-6274
Stambaugh MS 900/6-8
226 N Main St 33823 863-965-5494
Allison Kalbfleisch, prin. Fax 965-5496

Aventura, Miami-Dade, Pop. 29,391

Cheder Yesod Hadas PK-3
2956 Aventura Blvd 33180 305-933-1177
Tauber Academy 100/PK-K
20400 NE 30th Ave 33180 305-931-0010
Judy Baratta, admin. Fax 931-2190

Avon Park, Highlands, Pop. 8,872
Highlands County SD
Supt. — See Sebring
Avon ES 700/PK-5
705 Winthrop St 33825 863-452-4355
Pam Burnham, prin. Fax 452-4352
Avon Park MS 700/6-8
401 S Lake Ave 33825 863-452-4333
Dan Johnson, prin. Fax 452-4341
Memorial ES K-5
867 Memorial Dr 33825 863-471-5555
Ruby Handley, prin. Fax 784-0200
Park ES 700/PK-5
327 E Palmetto St 33825 863-452-4373
Brenda Longshore, prin. Fax 452-4376

Walker Memorial Academy 200/PK-12
1525 W Avon Blvd 33825 863-453-3131
William Farmer, dir. Fax 453-4925

Baker, Okaloosa
Okaloosa County SD
Supt. — See Fort Walton Beach
Baker S 1,400/PK-12
1369 14th St 32531 850-689-7279
Tom Shipp, prin. Fax 689-7416

Baldwin, Duval, Pop. 1,589
Duval County SD
Supt. — See Jacksonville
Jones ES 400/PK-5
700 Orange Ave 32234 904-266-1214
Skip Hatcher, prin. Fax 266-1222

Bartow, Polk, Pop. 16,278
Polk County SD 84,700/PK-12
PO Box 391 33831 863-534-0500
Dr. Gail McKinzie, supt. Fax 519-8231
www.polk-fl.net/
Bartow ES 400/K-5
590 S Wilson Ave 33830 863-534-7410
Carol Borders, prin. Fax 534-7218
Bartow MS 800/6-8
550 E Clower St 33830 863-534-7415
Danny Adams, prin. Fax 534-7418
Floral Avenue ES 600/K-5
1530 S Floral Ave 33830 863-534-7420
Sheila Dyer, prin. Fax 534-5003
Gibbons Street ES 400/PK-5
1860 E Gibbons St 33830 863-534-7430
Ava Brown, prin. Fax 534-7472
Stephens ES 500/PK-5
1350 N Maple Ave 33830 863-534-7455
April Sumner, prin. Fax 534-0438
Union Academy 400/6-8
1795 E Wabash St 33830 863-534-7435
Steve Petrie, prin. Fax 534-7487
Other Schools – See Alturas, Auburndale, Davenport, Dundee, Eagle Lake, Eaton Park, Fort Meade, Frostproof, Haines City, Highland City, Lake Alfred, Lakeland, Lake Wales, Mulberry, Poinciana, Polk City, Winter Haven

---

First Methodist S 200/PK-8
455 S Broadway Ave 33830 863-533-0905
Jacqueline Stoltz, prin. Fax 533-9023

Bay Harbor Islands, Miami-Dade, Pop. 5,093
Miami-Dade County SD
Supt. — See Miami
Broad-Bay Harbor ES 1,300/PK-6
1155 93rd St 33154 305-865-7912
Arlene Ortenzo, prin. Fax 864-1396

Bell, Gilchrist, Pop. 390
Gilchrist County SD
Supt. — See Trenton
Bell ES 600/PK-5
2771 E Bell Ave 32619 352-463-3275
Michelle Smith, prin. Fax 463-3456

Belle Glade, Palm Beach, Pop. 15,423
Palm Beach County SD
Supt. — See West Palm Beach
Belle Glade ES 600/PK-5
500 NW Avenue L 33430 561-829-4800
Roxanne Curtiss, prin. Fax 829-4850
Glade View ES 400/PK-5
1100 SW Avenue G 33430 561-993-8800
Sheila Henry, prin. Fax 993-8850
Gove ES 900/K-6
900 SE Avenue G 33430 561-993-8700
Anne Turner, prin. Fax 993-8750
Lake Shore MS 1,000/6-8
425 W Canal St N 33430 561-829-1100
Floyd Henry, prin. Fax 829-1190
Pioneer Park ES 500/K-5
39500 Pioneer Park Rd 33430 561-993-8600
Peggy Back-Nelson, prin. Fax 993-8650

Glades Day S 600/PK-12
400 Gator Blvd 33430 561-996-6769
James Teets, hdmstr. Fax 992-9274

Belleview, Marion, Pop. 3,856
Marion County SD
Supt. — See Ocala
Belleview ES 700/PK-5
5556 SE Agnew Rd 34420 352-671-6100
Brenda Conner, prin. Fax 671-6105
Belleview MS 1,200/6-8
10500 SE 36th Ave 34420 352-671-6235
Lisa Krysalka, prin. Fax 671-6239
Belleview-Santos ES 900/K-5
9600 SE US Highway 441 34420 352-671-6260
Troy Sanford, prin. Fax 671-6261

Little Friends Christian S 100/PK-5
6107 SE Agnew Rd 34420 352-245-9106
Julie Judy, dir. Fax 245-3710

Beverly Hills, Citrus, Pop. 6,163

St. Paul Lutheran S 50/PK-8
6150 N Lecanto Hwy 34465 352-489-3027
Kyle Bender, prin. Fax 489-1062

Blountstown, Calhoun, Pop. 2,433
Calhoun County SD 2,200/PK-12
20859 Central Ave E Ste G20 32424 850-674-5927
Wilson McClellan, supt. Fax 674-5814
www.calhounflschools.org
Blountstown ES 600/PK-5
20883 NE Fuller Warren Dr 32424 850-674-8169
Pam Bozeman, prin. Fax 674-8844
Blountstown MS 300/6-8
21089 SE Mayhaw Dr 32424 850-674-8234
Neva Miller, prin. Fax 674-6480
Other Schools – See Altha, Clarksville

Boca Raton, Palm Beach, Pop. 86,632
Palm Beach County SD
Supt. — See West Palm Beach
Boca Raton Community MS 1,100/6-8
1251 NW 8th St 33486 561-416-8700
Jack Thompson, prin. Fax 416-8777
Boca Raton ES 400/K-5
103 SW 1st Ave 33432 561-338-1454
Bradley Henry, prin. Fax 362-4552
Calusa ES 800/K-5
2051 Clint Moore Rd 33496 561-989-7500
Catherine Lewis, prin. Fax 989-7550
Coral Sunset ES 800/K-5
22400 Hammock St 33428 561-477-2100
Gary Hagermann, prin. Fax 477-2150
Del Prado ES 900/K-5
7900 Del Prado Cir N 33433 561-338-1490
Sandra Rhategan, prin. Fax 338-1496
Eagles Landing MS 1,200/6-8
19500 Coral Ridge Dr 33498 561-470-7000
Anthony Anderson, prin. Fax 470-7030
Estridge High Tech MS 1,200/6-8
1798 NW Spanish River Blvd 33431 561-989-7800
Karen Whetsell, prin. Fax 989-7810
Hammock Pointe ES 700/K-5
8400 SW 8th St 33433 561-477-2200
Carole Crilley, prin. Fax 477-2250
Loggers Run Community MS 1,000/6-8
11584 W Palmetto Park Rd 33428 561-883-8000
Carol Blacharski, prin. Fax 883-8027
Mitchell ES 600/K-5
2470 NW 5th Ave 33431 561-750-4900
Linda Nelson, prin. Fax 750-4906
Mizner ES 900/K-5
199 SW 12th Ave 33486 561-338-1450
Donna C. Binninger, prin. Fax 338-1453
Omni MS 1,300/6-8
5775 Jog Rd 33496 561-989-2800
Mark Stenner, prin. Fax 989-2851
Sandpiper Shores ES 700/K-5
11201 Glades Rd 33498 561-883-4000
Pamela Popaca, prin. Fax 883-4050
Sunrise Park ES 1,000/K-5
19400 Coral Ridge Dr 33498 561-477-4300
Laura Riopelle, prin. Fax 477-4350
Verde ES 800/K-5
6590 Verde Trl 33433 561-218-6800
Walter Cornnell, prin. Fax 218-6850
Waters Edge ES 1,000/K-5
21601 Shorewind Dr 33428 561-852-2400
Patricia Brehm, prin. Fax 852-2450
Whispering Pines ES 600/K-5
9090 Spanish Isles Blvd 33496 561-672-2700
Donald Messing, prin. Fax 672-2750

Advent Lutheran S 300/K-8
300 E Yamato Rd 33431 561-395-3631
Paul Humphreys, hdmstr. Fax 750-3632
Boca Prep International S 100/PK-12
10333 Diego Dr S 33428 561-852-1410
Graham Hurrell, prin. Fax 470-6124
Boca Raton Christian S 600/PK-12
315 NW 4th St 33432 561-391-2727
Robert Tennies Ed.D., hdmstr. Fax 367-6808
Claremont Montessori S 100/1-8
2450 NW 5th Ave 33431 561-394-7674
Harvey Hallenberg, prin. Fax 394-9792
Grandview Preparatory S 200/PK-12
336 NW Spanish River Blvd 33431 561-416-9737
Jacqueline Westerfield, prin. Fax 416-9739
Hillel S of Boca Raton 400/PK-8
21011 95th Ave S 33428 561-470-5000
Rabbi Samuel Levine, hdmstr. Fax 470-5005
Klein Jewish Academy 700/K-12
9701 Donna Klein Blvd 33428 561-852-3300
Karen Feller, hdmstr. Fax 852-3327
Pine Crest S at Boca Raton 900/PK-8
2700 Saint Andrews Blvd 33434 561-852-2800
Dale Smith, hdmstr. Fax 852-2832
St. Andrew's S 1,200/PK-12
3900 Jog Rd 33434 561-210-2000
AnnMarie Krejcarek Ed.D., hdmstr. Fax 210-2007
St. Joan of Arc S 600/PK-8
510 SW 3rd Ave 33432 561-392-7974
Sr. Ellen Murphy, prin. Fax 368-6671
St. Jude S 400/K-8
21689 Toledo Rd 33433 561-392-9160
Deborah Armstrong, prin. Fax 392-5815
St. Paul Lutheran S 500/PK-8
701 W Palmetto Park Rd 33486 561-395-8548
Jeffery Krempler, prin. Fax 395-2902
Spanish River Christian S 600/PK-8
2400 NW 51st St 33431 561-994-5006
Sharon Demko, hdmstr. Fax 994-1160
Summit Private S 200/PK-6
3881 NW 3rd Ave 33431 561-338-5020
Dr. John Mike, dir. Fax 338-5021
Torah Academy of Boca Raton 100/PK-8
447 NW Spanish River Blvd 33431 561-347-1821
West Glades Montessori S 100/PK-3
20400 Cain Blvd 33498 561-479-4629
Gail Carmean, prin. Fax 479-1736

Bokeelia, Lee
Lee County SD
Supt. — See Fort Myers
Pine Island ES 400/PK-5
5360 Ridgewood Dr 33922 239-283-0505
Robert Mazzoli, prin. Fax 283-1748

Bonifay, Holmes, Pop. 2,711
Holmes County SD 3,300/PK-12
701 E Pennsylvania Ave 32425 850-547-9341
Gary Galloway, supt. Fax 547-0381
www.hdsb.org
Bethlehem S 500/PK-12
2676 Highway 160 32425 850-547-3621
Jerry Dixon, prin. Fax 547-4856
Bonifay ES 700/PK-4
307 W North Ave 32425 850-547-3631
Rodd Jones, prin. Fax 547-4026
Bonifay MS 500/5-8
401 Mclaughlin Ave 32425 850-547-2754
Donald Etheridge, prin. Fax 547-3685
Other Schools – See Graceville, Ponce de Leon

Bonita Springs, Lee, Pop. 37,992
Lee County SD
Supt. — See Fort Myers
Bonita Springs ES 400/PK-5
10701 Dean St 34135 239-992-0801
David Short, prin. Fax 992-9118
Bonita Springs MS 600/6-8
10141 W Terry St 34135 239-992-4422
Dr. Ruthie Lohmeyer, prin. Fax 992-9157
Spring Creek ES 800/PK-5
25571 Elementary Way 34135 239-947-0001
Karen Leonardi, prin. Fax 947-4690

Grace Community S 100/PK-K
8971 Brighton Ln 34135 239-948-7878
Fax 949-1597

Bowling Green, Hardee, Pop. 2,928
Hardee County SD
Supt. — See Wauchula
Bowling Green ES 400/PK-5
PO Box 158 33834 863-375-2288
Kathy Clark, prin. Fax 375-3501

Boynton Beach, Palm Beach, Pop. 66,885
Palm Beach County SD
Supt. — See West Palm Beach
Citrus Cove ES 800/K-5
8400 Lawrence Rd 33436 561-292-7000
Judy Asbury, prin. Fax 292-7050
Congress MS 1,000/6-8
101 S Congress Ave 33426 561-374-5600
Kathy Harris, prin. Fax 374-5642
Crosspointe ES 800/K-5
3015 S Congress Ave 33426 561-292-4100
Cheryl McKeever, prin. Fax 292-4150
Crystal Lakes ES 600/K-5
6050 Gateway Blvd, 561-292-6600
Diane Curcio-Greaves, prin. Fax 292-6650
Forest Park ES 500/K-5
1201 SW 3rd St 33435 561-292-6900
Sharon Brannon, prin. Fax 292-6950
Freedom Shores ES 1,000/K-5
3400 Hypoluxo Rd 33436 561-804-3100
Valerie Haines, prin. Fax 804-3150
Galaxy ES 500/K-5
301 Galaxy Way 33435 561-739-5600
Joseph Schneider, prin. Fax 739-5650
Hagen Road ES 600/PK-5
10565 Hagen Ranch Rd 33437 561-292-6700
Richard Hughes, prin. Fax 292-6750
McAuliffe MS 1,300/6-8
6500 Le Chalet Blvd, 561-374-6600
Faith Cheek, prin. Fax 374-6636
Odyssey MS 1,100/6-8
6161 W Woolbright Rd 33437 561-752-1300
Bonnie Fox, prin. Fax 752-1305
Poinciana ES 600/K-5
1203 N Seacrest Blvd 33435 561-739-5700
Peter Slack, prin. Fax 739-5750
Rolling Green ES 700/K-5
550 Miner Rd 33435 561-202-9500
Sandra Sanchez, prin. Fax 202-9550
Sunset Palms ES K-5
8650 Boynton Beach Blvd, 561-752-1100
Karen Riddle, prin. Fax 752-1150

Gold Coast Junior Academy 50/K-8
138 SE 27th Ave 33435 561-364-7388
Lake Worth Christian S 400/PK-12
7592 High Ridge Rd 33426 561-586-8216
Robert Hook, supt. Fax 586-4382
St. Joseph's Episcopal S 200/PK-8
3300B S Seacrest Blvd 33435 561-732-2045
Tami Pleasanton, prin. Fax 732-1315
St. Mark S 300/PK-8
730 NE 6th Ave 33435 561-732-9934
Dr. Joseph Finley, prin. Fax 732-0501
St. Thomas More Preschool 100/PK-PK
10935 S Military Trl 33436 561-737-3770
Adriana Palazzi, dir. Fax 737-8128
Schechter S of Palm Beach Co. 50/K-5
8600 S Jog Rd, 561-364-5533
Allison Oakes M.Ed., hdmstr. Fax 364-5756

Bradenton, Manatee, Pop. 53,917
Manatee County SD 40,200/PK-12
PO Box 9069 34206 941-708-8770
Tim McGonegal, supt. Fax 708-8686
www.manatee.k12.fl.us
Ballard ES 500/K-5
912 18th St W 34205 941-708-8400
Mary Bidwell, prin. Fax 708-8408
Bashaw ES 700/PK-5
3515 Morgan Johnson Rd 34208 941-741-3307
Ron Hirst, prin. Fax 741-3559
Bayshore ES 700/PK-5
6120 26th St W 34207 941-751-7000
Annette Codelia, prin. Fax 753-0802
Braden River ES 600/K-5
6125 River Club Blvd 34202 941-751-7012
Randy Mungillo, prin. Fax 753-0911
Braden River MS 900/6-8
6215 River Club Blvd 34202 941-751-7080
Randy Petrilla, prin. Fax 751-7085
Daughtrey ES 700/PK-5
515 63rd Ave E 34203 941-751-7023
Monica Hankerson, prin. Fax 753-0849
Freedom ES 800/PK-5
9515 E State Road 64 34212 941-708-4990
James Mennes, prin. Fax 708-4919

Gullet ES PK-5
12125 44th Ave E 34211 941-727-2067
Kathy Hayes, prin. Fax 727-2094
Haile MS 1,000/6-8
9501 E State Road 64 34212 941-714-7240
Janet Kerley, prin. Fax 714-7245
Harllee MS 800/6-8
6423 9th St E 34203 941-751-7027
James Hird, prin. Fax 751-7030
Johnson MS 800/6-8
2121 26th Ave E 34208 941-741-3344
Ann McDonald, prin. Fax 741-3345
King MS 900/6-8
600 75th St NW 34209 941-798-6820
Robin Hardy, prin. Fax 798-6835
Lee MS 900/6-8
4000 53rd Ave W 34210 941-727-6500
Scot Boice, prin. Fax 727-6513
Manatee ES 400/K-5
1609 6th Ave E 34208 941-741-3319
Helen Abernathy, prin. Fax 741-3507
McNeal ES 700/PK-5
6325 Lorraine Rd 34202 941-751-8165
Norma Scott, prin. Fax 751-8155
Miller ES 700/PK-5
601 43rd St W 34209 941-741-3300
Chuck Banks, prin. Fax 741-3415
Moody ES 700/K-5
5425 38th Ave W 34209 941-741-3170
Tom Wailand, prin. Fax 741-3555
Nolan MS 800/6-8
6615 Greenbrook Blvd 34202 941-751-8200
Nancy High, prin. Fax 751-8210
Oneco ES 700/PK-5
5214 22nd Street Ct E 34203 941-751-7018
Marian Summers, prin. Fax 753-0926
Orange Ridge-Bullock ES 800/PK-5
400 30th Ave W 34205 941-741-3325
Doug DuPouy, prin. Fax 708-5511
Palma Sola ES 600/PK-5
6806 5th Ave NW 34209 941-741-3179
Kathy Redmond, prin. Fax 741-3181
Prine ES 800/PK-5
3801 Southern Pkwy W 34205 941-751-7006
Guy Grimes, prin. Fax 753-0924
Rogers Garden ES PK-5
513 13th Ave W 34205 941-209-7540
Wendy Herrera, prin. Fax 209-7550
Rowlett Magnet ES 800/K-5
3500 9th St E 34208 941-708-6100
Brian Flynn, prin. Fax 708-6109
Samoset ES 500/PK-5
3300 19th St E 34208 941-708-6400
Scott Boyes, prin. Fax 708-6408
Sea Breeze ES 700/K-5
3601 71st St W 34209 941-741-3190
Jackie West, prin. Fax 741-3614
Stewart ES 500/K-5
7905 15th Ave NW 34209 941-741-3176
Jackie Featherston, prin. Fax 741-3467
Sugg MS 900/6-8
3801 59th St W 34209 941-741-3157
Sharon Scarbrough, prin. Fax 741-3514
Tara ES 800/PK-5
6950 Linger Lodge Rd E 34203 941-751-7660
Linda Fouse, prin. Fax 753-0975
Wakeland ES 400/PK-5
1812 27th St E 34208 941-741-3358
Chuck Fradley, prin. Fax 741-3549
Willis ES 500/PK-5
14705 the Masters Ave 34202 941-316-8245
Bill Stenger, prin. Fax 316-8259
Witt ES 900/PK-5
200 Rye Rd E 34212 941-741-3628
Myra Russell, prin. Fax 741-3630
Other Schools – See Duette, Holmes Beach, Myakka City, Palmetto, Parrish, Sarasota

---

Bradenton Christian S 600/PK-12
3304 43rd St W 34209 941-792-5454
Dan van der Kooy, supt. Fax 795-7190
Bradenton Preparatory Academy 400/K-12
7900 40th Ave W 34209 941-792-7838
Susan Hedgcock, prin. Fax 798-9920
Center for Education Montessori S 200/PK-8
6024 26th St W 34207 941-753-4987
Janice Mattina, dir. Fax 756-4985
Community Christian S 300/PK-12
5500 18th St E 34203 941-756-8748
Charles Sartor, prin. Fax 753-7057
Edison Academic Center 300/K-12
7431 Manatee Ave W 34209 941-794-3630
Fax 794-3955
Gulfcoast Christian Academy 50/K-12
1700 51st Ave E 34203 941-755-0332
Jimmy Brown, admin. Fax 755-0332
Peace Lutheran S 50/K-8
1611 30th Ave W 34205 941-747-6753
Nathan Nolte, prin. Fax 747-6753
Pendleton S 400/PK-12
5500 34th St W 34210 941-739-3964
Richard Odell, hdmstr. Fax 739-6483
Providence Community S 100/PK-12
5512 26th St W 34207 941-727-6860
Barry Batson, admin. Fax 756-5656
St. Joseph S 300/PK-8
2990 26th St W 34205 941-755-2611
Robert Siccone, prin. Fax 753-6339
St. Stephen's Episcopal S 800/PK-12
315 41st St W 34209 941-746-2121
Jan Pullen, hdmstr. Fax 746-5699
Sunshine Academy 100/PK-5
2520 43rd St W 34209 941-794-3143
Kristin Lamphron, prin. Fax 794-1819
West Coast Christian Academy 50/PK-8
1112 49th Ave E 34203 941-755-9667
Rodney Ramey, prin. Fax 755-4530

Brandon, Hillsborough, Pop. 83,200
Hillsborough County SD
Supt. — See Tampa
Brooker ES 1,000/PK-5
812 Dewolf Rd 33511 813-744-8184
Julie Lacy, prin. Fax 740-3621
Burns MS 1,500/6-8
615 Brooker Rd 33511 813-744-8383
Brenda Nolte, prin. Fax 740-3623
Kingswood ES 600/PK-5
3102 S Kings Ave 33511 813-744-8234
Amber Craft, prin. Fax 744-8150
Limona ES 600/PK-5
1115 Telfair Rd 33510 813-744-8200
Karen Pierson, prin. Fax 744-8147
Mann MS 900/6-8
409 E Jersey Ave 33510 813-744-8400
Nancy Trathowen, prin. Fax 744-6707
McLane MS 1,100/6-8
306 N Knights Ave 33510 813-744-8100
James Elliott, prin. Fax 744-8135
Mintz ES 900/PK-5
1510 Heather Lakes Blvd 33511 813-744-8353
Catherine Shields, prin. Fax 744-6755
Schmidt ES 700/K-5
1250 Williams Rd 33510 813-651-2110
Cindy Malone, prin. Fax 651-2114
Yates ES 700/K-5
301 Kingsway Rd 33510 813-744-8177
Richard Shields, prin. Fax 744-8179

Bell Shoals Baptist Academy 600/PK-8
2102 Bell Shoals Rd 33511 813-689-9183
Sandra Carnley, prin. Fax 643-1649
Brandon Academy 300/PK-8
801 Limona Rd 33510 813-689-1952
Robert Rudolph, hdmstr. Fax 651-4278
Central Baptist Christian S 500/PK-8
402 E Windhorst Rd 33510 813-689-6133
David O'Hara, admin. Fax 689-0011
Faith Baptist Christian S 100/PK-12
1118 N Parsons Ave 33510 813-654-4936
Anthony Perry, prin. Fax 654-7239
First Baptist Brandon Christian Academy 200/PK-2
216 N Parsons Ave 33510 813-689-9435
Paul Pucciarelli, prin. Fax 685-3853
Immanuel Lutheran S 200/K-8
2913 John Moore Rd 33511 813-685-1978
David Geidel, prin. Fax 681-6852
Kings Avenue Christian S 100/PK-5
2602 S Kings Ave 33511 813-684-9453
Rita Woodard, admin. Fax 651-0032
Nativity S 800/PK-8
705 E Brandon Blvd 33511 813-689-3395
Bernadette Kunnen, prin. Fax 681-5406
Tampa Bay Christian S 100/PK-9
3920 S Kings Ave 33511 813-685-8336
Scott Schwind, prin. Fax 653-2676

Branford, Suwannee, Pop. 756
Suwannee County SD
Supt. — See Live Oak
Branford ES 600/PK-5
26801 State Road 247 32008 386-935-6300
Carol Risk, prin. Fax 935-6311

Bristol, Liberty, Pop. 910
Liberty County SD 1,200/PK-12
PO Box 429 32321 850-643-2275
Sue Summers, supt. Fax 643-2533
www.lcsbonline.org/
Tolar S 600/PK-8
PO Box 609 32321 850-643-2426
Kathy Nobles, prin. Fax 643-4168
Other Schools – See Hosford

Bronson, Levy, Pop. 1,041
Levy County SD 6,100/PK-12
PO Box 129 32621 352-486-5231
Robert Hastings, supt. Fax 486-5237
www.levy.k12.fl.us
Bronson ES 700/PK-5
PO Box 220 32621 352-486-5281
Cheryl Beachamp, prin. Fax 486-5285
Other Schools – See Cedar Key, Chiefland, Williston, Yankeetown

Brooker, Bradford, Pop. 366
Bradford County SD
Supt. — See Starke
Brooker ES 100/PK-5
PO Box 7 32622 904-966-6887
Lynn Melvin, prin. Fax 966-6889

Brooksville, Hernando, Pop. 7,637
Hernando County SD 22,100/PK-12
919 N Broad St 34601 352-797-7000
Wayne Alexander Ed.D., supt. Fax 797-7101
www.hcsb.k12.fl.us
Brooksville ES 800/PK-5
885 N Broad St 34601 352-797-7014
Mary LeDoux, prin. Fax 797-7114
Chocachatti ES 900/PK-5
4135 California St 34604 352-797-7067
Maria Rybka, prin. Fax 797-7167
Eastside ES 700/PK-5
27151 Roper Rd 34602 352-797-7045
Beverly Chapin, prin. Fax 797-7145
Moton ES 700/PK-5
7175 Emerson Rd 34601 352-797-7065
Debi Vermette, prin. Fax 797-7165
Parrott MS 900/6-8
19220 Youth Dr 34601 352-797-7075
Leechele Booker, prin. Fax 797-7175
Pine Grove ES 1,200/PK-5
14411 Ken Austin Pkwy 34613 352-797-7090
Earl Deen, prin. Fax 797-7190
Powell MS 1,200/6-8
4100 Barclay Ave 34609 352-797-7095
Dave Dannemiller, prin. Fax 797-7195
West Hernando MS 1,100/6-8
14325 Ken Austin Pkwy 34613 352-797-7035
Toni Noyes, prin. Fax 797-7135
Other Schools – See Spring Hill

Eden Christian S 100/PK-K
22308 Lake Lindsey Rd 34601 352-797-1619
First United Methodist S 200/PK-8
109 S Broad St 34601 352-796-3496
Hernando Christian Academy 400/PK-12
7200 Emerson Rd 34601 352-796-0616
Ronald Watford, supt. Fax 799-3400

Bryceville, Nassau
Nassau County SD
Supt. — See Fernandina Beach
Bryceville ES 300/K-5
6504 Church Ave 32009 904-491-7932
Misty Mathis, prin. Fax 266-2155

Bunnell, Flagler, Pop. 1,479
Flagler County SD 11,800/PK-12
PO Box 755 32110 386-437-7526
Bill Delbrugge, supt. Fax 437-7577
www.flaglerschools.com
Bunnell ES 900/PK-5
305 N Palmetto St 32110 386-437-7533
Richard DuPont, prin. Fax 437-7591
Other Schools – See Flagler Beach, Palm Coast

Bushnell, Sumter, Pop. 2,119
Sumter County SD 4,600/PK-12
2680 W C 476 33513 352-793-2315
Richard Shirley, supt. Fax 793-4180
www.sumter.k12.fl.us
Bushnell ES 700/K-5
218 W Flannery Ave 33513 352-793-3501
Helen Christian, prin. Fax 793-1336
Other Schools – See Lake Panasoffkee, Webster, Wildwood

Callahan, Nassau, Pop. 951
Nassau County SD
Supt. — See Fernandina Beach
Callahan ES 700/PK-2
449618 US Highway 301 32011 904-491-7933
Susan Howard, prin. Fax 879-5560
Callahan IS 600/3-5
34586 Ball Park Rd 32011 904-491-7934
Lee Ann Jackson, prin. Fax 879-5288
Callahan MS 800/6-8
450121 Old Dixie Hwy 32011 904-491-7935
Ellen Ryan, prin. Fax 879-2860

Sonshine Christian Academy 200/PK-10
PO Box 5026 32011 904-879-1260
Lorie Johnson, prin. Fax 879-2640

Canal Point, Palm Beach
Palm Beach County SD
Supt. — See West Palm Beach
Cunningham/Canal Point ES 500/K-6
37000 Main St 33438 561-924-9800
LaVoise Taylor-Smith, prin. Fax 924-9850

Cantonment, Escambia, Pop. 4,500
Escambia County SD
Supt. — See Pensacola
Allen ES 600/K-5
1051 N Highway 95A 32533 850-937-2260
Rachel Watts, prin. Fax 937-2269
Nelson Preschool 100/PK-PK
648 Muscogee Rd 32533 850-937-2280
Dr. Patrice Moody, prin. Fax 937-2284
Ransom MS 1,400/6-8
1000 W Kingsfield Rd 32533 850-937-2220
Jeff Pomeroy, prin. Fax 937-2232

Cape Canaveral, Brevard, Pop. 10,523
Brevard County SD
Supt. — See Melbourne
Cape View ES 400/PK-6
8440 Rosalind Ave 32920 321-784-0284
Kelli Dufresne, prin. Fax 868-6690

Cape Coral, Lee, Pop. 140,010
Lee County SD
Supt. — See Fort Myers
Cafferata ES 800/K-5
250 Santa Barbara Blvd N 33993 239-458-7391
Donald Hopper, prin. Fax 772-0749
Caloosa ES 1,000/PK-5
620 Del Prado Blvd S 33990 239-574-3113
Cheryl Curry, prin. Fax 574-1449
Caloosa MS 1,100/6-8
610 Del Prado Blvd S 33990 239-574-3232
Brian Mangan, prin. Fax 574-2660
Cape ES 800/K-5
4519 Vincennes Blvd 33904 239-542-3551
Toni Sindler, prin. Fax 542-3264
Challenger MS 300/6-8
624 SW Trafalgar Pkwy 33991 239-242-4341
Teri Cannady, prin. Fax 242-7217
Diplomat ES 900/PK-5
1115 NE 16th Ter 33909 239-458-0033
Linda Caruso, prin. Fax 458-1697
Diplomat MS 1,000/6-8
1039 NE 16th Ter 33909 239-574-5257
Angela Roles, prin. Fax 574-4008
Gulf ES 1,400/K-5
3400 SW 17th Pl 33914 239-549-2726
Martin Mesch, prin. Fax 549-2117
Gulf MS 1,100/6-8
1809 SW 36th Ter 33914 239-549-0606
William Lane, prin. Fax 549-2806
Mariner MS 1,000/6-8
425 Chiquita Blvd N 33993 239-772-1848
Richard Hagy, prin. Fax 242-1256
Patriot ES 800/K-5
711 SW 18th St 33991 239-242-1023
Carol Bromby, prin. Fax 242-1238

Pelican ES 1,100/K-5
3525 SW 3rd Ave 33914 239-549-4966
Richard Ivill, prin. Fax 549-4973
Skyline ES 1,100/PK-5
620 SW 19th St 33991 239-772-3223
Charles Vilardi, prin. Fax 772-8934
Trafalgar ES 900/PK-5
1850 SW 20th Ave 33991 239-283-3043
Marie Vetter, prin. Fax 282-5595
Trafalgar MS 1,300/6-8
2120 SW Trafalgar Pkwy 33991 239-283-2001
Dr. Angela Pruitt, prin. Fax 283-5620

Cape Coral Christian S 200/PK-12
811 Santa Barbara Blvd 33991 239-574-3707
Christopher Roy, prin. Fax 574-0947
Christ Lutheran S 200/PK-8
2911 Del Prado Blvd S 33904 239-542-8768
Iris Mitchell, prin. Fax 542-3702
Providence Christian S 200/PK-8
701 Mohawk Pkwy 33914 239-549-8024
Dodie Jeter, hdmstr. Fax 549-4465
St. Andrew S 400/PK-8
1509 SE 27th St 33904 239-772-3922
Sr. Elizabeth Meegan, prin. Fax 772-7182
Sonrise Academy 50/PK-6
1403 SE 16th Pl 33990 239-573-6433
Rev. Paul Welch, dir. Fax 573-6584
Trinity Lutheran S 100/PK-K
706 SW 6th Ave 33991 239-772-1549
Christina Dennis, dir. Fax 573-6336

Casselberry, Seminole, Pop. 24,298
Seminole County SD
Supt. — See Sanford
Casselberry ES 800/PK-5
1075 Crystal Bowl Cir 32707 407-746-2550
Janet Beth Ransom, prin. Fax 746-2599
Red Bug ES 800/PK-5
4000 Red Bug Lake Rd 32707 407-746-8350
Dr. Heidi Gooch, prin. Fax 746-8399
South Seminole MS 1,200/6-8
101 S Winter Park Dr 32707 407-746-1350
Patricia Bowman, prin. Fax 746-1420
Sterling Park ES 700/PK-5
905 Eagle Cir S 32707 407-746-8250
Irene Kelleher, prin. Fax 746-8299

Regent Academy 100/K-12
910 S Winter Park Dr 32707 407-740-0561

Cedar Key, Levy, Pop. 958
Levy County SD
Supt. — See Bronson
Cedar Key S 200/PK-12
951 Whiddon Ave 32625 352-543-5223
Sue Ice, prin. Fax 543-5988

Celebration, Osceola
Osceola County SD
Supt. — See Kissimmee
Celebration S 1,200/K-8
510 Campus St 34747 407-566-2300
Wayne Kennedy, prin. Fax 566-2354

Montessori S of Celebration 100/PK-9
901 Begonia Rd 34747 407-566-1561
Karen Simon, prin. Fax 566-1544

Century, Escambia, Pop. 1,799
Escambia County SD
Supt. — See Pensacola
Bratt ES 400/PK-5
5721 Highway 99 32535 850-327-6137
Sheryl Pomeroy, prin. Fax 327-4879
Carver/Century S 300/PK-8
440 E Hecker Rd 32535 850-256-6380
Jeff Garthwaite, prin. Fax 256-6384

Chattahoochee, Gadsden, Pop. 3,720
Gadsden County SD
Supt. — See Quincy
Chattahoochee ES 200/PK-6
335 Maple St 32324 850-663-4373
Annette Harris, prin. Fax 663-2236

Chiefland, Levy, Pop. 2,095
Levy County SD
Supt. — See Bronson
Chiefland ES 800/PK-5
1205 NW 4th Ave 32626 352-493-6040
Patrice McCully, prin. Fax 493-6042
Chiefland MS 400/6-8
811 NW 4th Dr 32626 352-493-6025
Bobbie Turnipseed, prin. Fax 493-6048

Chipley, Washington, Pop. 3,682
Washington County SD 3,700/PK-12
652 3rd St 32428 850-638-6222
Dr. Sandra Cook, supt. Fax 638-6226
wcsb.paec.org/
Roulhac MS 700/5-8
1535 Brickyard Rd 32428 850-638-6170
Mike Park, prin. Fax 638-6319
Smith ES 900/PK-4
750 Sinclair St 32428 850-638-6220
Jerry Register, prin. Fax 638-6279
Other Schools – See Vernon

Washington County Christian S 100/PK-12
1405 Brickyard Rd 32428 850-638-9227
Jason Haddock, admin. Fax 638-9234

Chuluota, Seminole, Pop. 1,441
Seminole County SD
Supt. — See Sanford
Walker ES 900/K-5
3101 Snow Hill Rd 32766 407-871-7350
Kathy Phillips, prin. Fax 871-7399

Double R Private S 200/PK-8
725 Country School Rd 32766 407-365-6856
Fax 365-0543

Citra, Marion
Marion County SD
Supt. — See Ocala
North Marion MS 900/6-8
2085 W Highway 329 32113 352-671-6035
John Williams, prin. Fax 671-6044

Citrus Springs, Citrus, Pop. 2,213
Citrus County SD
Supt. — See Inverness
Central Ridge ES PK-5
185 W Citrus Springs Blvd 34434 352-344-3833
Nancy Simon, prin.
Citrus Springs ES 1,000/PK-5
3570 W Century Blvd 34433 352-344-4079
Trish Douglas, prin. Fax 489-3134
Citrus Springs MS 800/6-8
150 W Citrus Springs Blvd 34434 352-344-2244
David Roland, prin. Fax 489-1050

Clarksville, Calhoun
Calhoun County SD
Supt. — See Blountstown
Carr S 300/PK-8
18987 NW State Road 73 32430 850-674-5395
Darryl Taylor, prin. Fax 674-5421

Clearwater, Pinellas, Pop. 108,687
Pinellas County SD
Supt. — See Largo
Belcher ES 700/K-5
1839 S Belcher Rd 33764 727-538-7437
Lisa Roth, prin. Fax 538-7255
Belleair ES 500/PK-5
1156 Lakeview Rd 33756 727-469-5983
Robert Ovalle, prin. Fax 469-5972
Coachman Fundamental MS 500/6-8
2235 NE Coachman Rd 33765 727-669-1190
David Rosenberger, prin. Fax 669-1194
Davis ES 700/K-5
2630 Landmark Dr 33761 727-725-7972
Carol Hughes, prin. Fax 725-7975
De Leon ES 700/PK-5
1301 Ponce De Leon Blvd 33756 727-588-3573
Thea Saccasyn, prin. Fax 588-3700
Eisenhower ES 700/PK-5
2800 Drew St 33759 727-725-7978
Sandra Downs, prin. Fax 725-7981
Frontier ES 800/PK-5
6995 Hopedale Ln 33764 727-538-7335
Wendy Bryan, prin. Fax 538-7444
High Point ES 600/K-5
5921 150th Ave N 33760 727-538-7440
Kevin Gordon, prin. Fax 538-7442
Kennedy MS 600/6-8
1660 Palmetto St 33755 727-298-1609
Susan W. Keller, prin. Fax 298-1614
Kings Highway ES 400/K-5
1715 Kings Hwy 33755 727-469-5963
Margaret Drizd, prin. Fax 298-2540
McMullen-Booth ES 700/PK-5
3025 Union St 33759 727-669-1800
Katherine Wickett, prin. Fax 669-1803
North Ward ES 300/K-5
900 N Fort Harrison Ave 33755 727-469-5982
Sandra Cowley, prin. Fax 298-2626
Oak Grove MS 1,000/6-8
1370 S Belcher Rd 33764 727-524-4430
Dawn Coffin, prin. Fax 524-4416
Plumb ES 800/PK-5
1920 Lakeview Rd 33764 727-469-5976
Lisa Bultmann, prin. Fax 469-5728
Sandy Lane ES 400/K-5
1360 Sandy Ln 33755 727-469-5974
Delores Milton, prin. Fax 469-5986
Skycrest ES 600/K-5
10 N Corona Ave 33765 727-469-5987
Angelean Bing, prin. Fax 469-4186

Allendale Academy Private S 800/K-12
7208 Amhurst Way 33764 727-531-2481
Pat Carter, prin. Fax 531-6491
Christ the Lord Lutheran S 50/K-8
2045 N Hercules Ave 33763 727-441-8239
Jonathan Ross, prin. Fax 441-8239
Clearwater Academy International 300/PK-12
801 Drew St 33755 727-446-1722
Joan Spencer, dir. Fax 443-5252
Clearwater Jr. Academy 50/1-8
1435 Lakeview Rd 33756 727-442-7080
Countryside Christian Academy 200/PK-8
1850 N McMullen Booth Rd 33759 727-799-1618
Crystal Mascaro, prin. Fax 499-1841
First Lutheran S 200/PK-8
1644 Nursery Rd 33756 727-462-8000
Elaine Popp, prin. Fax 442-7473
Guardian Angels S 400/K-8
2270 Evans Rd 33763 727-799-6724
Cindy Malinski, admin. Fax 724-9018
Lakeside Christian S 200/K-12
1897 Sunset Point Rd 33765 727-461-3311
Jim Jensen, prin. Fax 445-1835
Light of Christ ECC 100/PK-PK
2176 Marilyn St 33765 727-442-4797
Becky Daschbach, dir. Fax 441-8771
Little Nazareth ECC 50/PK-PK
820 Jasmine Way 33756 727-447-3494
Sandra Barbeau, dir. Fax 442-4810
Northbay Christian Academy 100/PK-8
1625 Union St 33755 727-462-0134
Robin Isham, dir. Fax 724-1191
Pinellas County Jewish Day S 200/PK-8
1775 S Highland Ave 33756 727-588-0100
Brian Siegel, hdmstr. Fax 588-4468

Safety Harbor Montessori Academy 200/PK-8
2669 N McMullen Booth Rd 33761 727-724-1767
Melinda Robinson, prin. Fax 724-0289
St. Cecelia S 500/PK-8
400 S Hillcrest Ave 33756 727-461-1200
Mary Beth Scanlon, prin. Fax 446-9140
St. Paul's S 500/PK-8
1600 Saint Pauls Dr 33764 727-536-2756
Dr. Angel Kytle, hdmstr. Fax 531-2276
Skycrest Christian S 400/PK-8
129 N Belcher Rd 33765 727-797-1186
Steven Clagg, prin. Fax 797-8516

Clermont, Lake, Pop. 11,617
Lake County SD
Supt. — See Tavares
Clermont ES 800/PK-5
680 E Highland Ave 34711 352-394-2706
Cleamstine Caple, prin. Fax 394-5081
Clermont MS 900/6-8
301 East Ave 34711 352-243-2460
Dave Coggshall, prin. Fax 243-1407
Cypress Ridge ES 600/K-5
350 East Ave 34711 352-394-6633
Robert McCue, prin. Fax 394-1170
East Ridge MS 6-8
13201 Excalibur Rd 34711 352-536-8020
Charlie McDaniel, prin. Fax 536-8039
Lost Lake ES 1,500/PK-5
1901 Johns Lake Rd 34711 352-243-2433
Barbara Longo, prin. Fax 243-3541
Pine Ridge ES 1,300/PK-5
10245 County Road 561 34711 352-242-2223
Amy Cockcroft, prin. Fax 242-2818
Saw Grass Bay ES 1,000/K-5
16325 Superior Blvd, 352-243-1845
Julio Valle, prin. Fax 394-5732
Windy Hill MS 1,400/6-8
3575 Hancock Rd 34711 352-394-2123
David Tucker, prin. Fax 394-7901

Orlando Christian S 100/PK-5
100 N Grand Hwy 34711 352-243-1228
Real Life Christian Academy 200/PK-10
1501 Steves Rd 34711 352-394-5575
Dr. Steven Long, admin. Fax 394-7860
South Lake Montessori S 100/PK-6
983 W Desoto St 34711 352-365-7212
Janis Sheldon, dir.

Clewiston, Hendry, Pop. 7,173
Hendry County SD
Supt. — See La Belle
Central ES 600/PK-5
1000 S Deane Duff Ave 33440 863-983-1550
Anna Jo Springfield, prin. Fax 983-1558
Clewiston MS 800/6-8
601 W Pasadena Ave 33440 863-983-1530
Garry Ensor, prin. Fax 983-1541
Eastside ES 600/PK-5
201 Arroyo Ave 33440 863-983-1560
Lori Duckstein, prin. Fax 983-2123
Westside ES 600/PK-5
205 Arroyo Ave 33440 863-983-1570
Richard Shearer, prin. Fax 902-4232

Clewiston Christian S 100/PK-8
PO Box 129 33440 863-983-5388
Brenda Braddock, admin. Fax 983-5027

Cocoa, Brevard, Pop. 16,898
Brevard County SD
Supt. — See Melbourne
Atlantis ES 800/K-6
7300 Briggs Ave 32927 321-633-6143
Sherry Tomlinson, prin. Fax 633-6038
Cambridge ES 600/PK-6
2000 Cambridge Dr 32922 321-633-3550
Hilah Mercer, prin. Fax 633-3420
Challenger 7 ES 500/K-6
6135 Rena Ave 32927 321-636-5801
Carol Mela, prin. Fax 631-3208
Clearlake MS 400/7-8
1225 Clearlake Rd 32922 321-633-3660
Mark Mullins, prin. Fax 617-7731
Endeavour ES 600/PK-6
905 Pineda St 32922 321-633-3545
Mecheall Giombetti, prin. Fax 633-3546
Enterprise ES 900/K-6
7000 Enterprise Rd 32927 321-633-3434
Teresa Lee, prin. Fax 633-3438
Fairglen ES 800/PK-6
201 Indian Trl 32927 321-631-1993
Kathryn Cline, prin. Fax 631-3011
Saturn ES 700/PK-6
880 N Range Rd 32926 321-633-3535
Michael Miller, prin. Fax 633-3539

Cocoa Adventist S 50/PK-8
1500 Cox Rd 32926 321-636-2551
Fax 636-2551
Friendship Christian Academy 50/PK-6
385 S Burnett Rd 32926 321-636-6980
Edward Buckner, admin. Fax 636-3082
St. Mark's Episcopal Academy 100/PK-6
2 Church St 32922 321-639-5771
Ruth Casey, admin. Fax 639-5774

Cocoa Beach, Brevard, Pop. 12,435
Brevard County SD
Supt. — See Melbourne
Freedom 7 ES of International Studies 400/PK-6
400 S 4th St 32931 321-868-6610
Dorine Zimmerman, prin. Fax 868-6615
Roosevelt ES 500/PK-6
1400 Minutemen Cswy 32931 321-868-6660
Dorothy Richardson, prin. Fax 783-2331

Cocoa Beach Christian S 50/PK-6
830 S Atlantic Ave 32931 321-799-0577

Our Saviour S 200/PK-8
5301 N Atlantic Ave 32931 321-783-2330
Lauren Longa, prin. Fax 784-6330

Coconut Creek, Broward, Pop. 49,017
Broward County SD
Supt. — See Fort Lauderdale
Coconut Creek ES 900/K-5
500 NW 45th Ave 33066 754-322-5800
William Roach, prin. Fax 322-5840
Lyons Creek MS 2,000/6-8
4333 Sol Press Blvd 33073 754-322-3700
Washington Collado, prin. Fax 322-3785
Tradewinds ES 1,100/PK-5
5400 Johnson Rd 33073 754-322-8700
Dr. Susan Whiting, prin. Fax 322-8740
Winston Park ES 1,200/K-5
4000 Winston Park Blvd 33073 754-322-9000
Carolyn Eggelletion, prin. Fax 322-9040

North Broward Preparatory Schools 1,800/PK-12
7600 Lyons Rd 33073 954-247-0011
Dr. Tom Marcy, hdmstr. Fax 247-0042
Randazzo S 200/PK-12
2251 NW 36th Ave 33066 954-968-1750
Dr. Ronald Simon, hdmstr. Fax 968-1857

Coconut Grove, See Miami
Miami-Dade County SD
Supt. — See Miami
Carver MS 1,000/6-8
4901 Lincoln Dr 33133 305-444-7388
Libia Gonzalez, prin. Fax 529-5148
Coconut Grove ES 200/PK-3
3351 Matilda St 33133 305-445-7876
Eva Ravelo, prin. Fax 443-6748

Carrollton S of the Sacred Heart 700/PK-12
3747 Main Hwy 33133 305-446-5673
Sr. Suzanne Cooke, hdmstr. Fax 592-6533
St. Hugh S 300/PK-8
3460 Royal Rd 33133 305-448-5602
Sr. Kathleen Donnelly, prin. Fax 444-4299
St. Stephen's Episcopal S 300/PK-6
3439 Main Hwy 33133 305-445-2606
Silvia Larrauri, hdmstr. Fax 445-7320

Cooper City, Broward, Pop. 30,022
Broward County SD
Supt. — See Fort Lauderdale
Cooper City ES 900/PK-5
5080 SW 92nd Ave 33328 754-323-5200
Dennis Sciullo, prin. Fax 323-5240
Embassy Creek ES 900/K-5
10905 SE Lake Blvd 33026 754-323-5550
Robert Becker, prin. Fax 323-5590
Griffin ES 600/K-5
5050 SW 116th Ave 33330 754-323-5900
Cynthia Novotny, prin. Fax 323-5940
Pioneer MS 1,700/6-8
5350 SW 90th Ave 33328 754-323-4100
Linda Arnold, prin. Fax 323-4185

Flamingo Road Christian Academy 200/PK-5
12401 Stirling Rd 33330 954-434-1550
William Hewlett, hdmstr. Fax 318-0077
Lycee Franco-Americain International S 100/PK-5
8950 Sterling Rd 33024 954-237-0356
Dr. Jacquelyne Hoy, prin. Fax 237-0366
Nur Ul-Islam Academy 300/PK-12
10600 SW 59th St 33328 954-434-3288
Kem Hussain, prin. Fax 434-9333

Coral Gables, Miami-Dade, Pop. 42,871
Miami-Dade County SD
Supt. — See Miami
Carver ES 500/PK-5
238 Grand Ave 33133 305-443-5286
Dr. Cheryl Johnson, prin. Fax 567-3531
Coral Gables ES 700/PK-5
105 Minorca Ave 33134 305-448-1731
Graciela Cerra, prin. Fax 442-2075
Ponce De Leon MS 1,200/6-8
5801 Augusto St 33146 305-661-1611
Anna Rodriguez, prin. Fax 666-3140
West Laboratory ES 300/K-6
5300 Carillo St 33146 305-661-7661
Barbara Soto, prin. Fax 662-2935

French American S of Miami 100/PK-5
6565 SW 57th Ave 33143 786-268-1914
Lena McLorin-Slavant, prin. Fax 268-1941
Granada Day S 200/PK-K
900 University Dr 33134 305-444-2028
Elizabeth Travis, dir. Fax 444-3193
Gulliver Academy 1,000/PK-8
12595 SW 57th Ave 33156 305-665-3593
John Krutulis, hdmstr. Fax 669-1569
Riviera Day and Preparatory S 400/PK-8
6800 Nervia St 33146 305-666-1856
Alvin Glicksberg, prin. Fax 661-5437
St. Philip's Episcopal S 200/PK-6
1142 Coral Way 33134 305-444-6366
Jeff Devin, hdmstr. Fax 442-0236
St. Theresa S 1,000/PK-8
2701 Indian Mound Trl 33134 305-446-1738
Sr. Rosalie Nagy, prin. Fax 446-2877
St. Thomas Episcopal Parish S 400/PK-5
5692 N Kendall Dr 33156 305-665-4851
Kris Matteson Charlton, hdmstr. Fax 669-9449

Coral Springs, Broward, Pop. 128,804
Broward County SD
Supt. — See Fort Lauderdale
Coral Park ES 700/K-5
8401 Westview Dr 33067 754-322-5850
Dr. Amanda Miles, prin. Fax 322-5890
Coral Springs ES 800/K-5
3601 NW 110th Ave 33065 754-322-5900
Dr. Frances Shaw, prin. Fax 322-5940
Coral Springs MS 1,300/6-8
10300 Wiles Rd 33076 754-322-3000
Ian Murray, prin. Fax 322-3085
Country Hills ES 1,000/K-5
10550 Westview Dr 33076 754-322-5950
Donna Morrison, prin. Fax 322-5990
Eagle Ridge IS 400/4-6
11500 Westview Dr 33076 754-322-6300
Marina Rashid, prin. Fax 322-6340
Forest Glen MS 1,400/6-8
6501 Turtle Run Blvd 33067 754-322-3400
James McDermott, prin. Fax 322-3485
Forest Hills ES 700/K-5
3100 NW 85th Ave 33065 754-322-6400
Elise Portman, prin. Fax 322-6440
Hunt ES 900/PK-5
7800 NW 35th Ct 33065 754-322-6500
Deborah Braly, prin. Fax 322-6540
Maplewood ES 900/PK-5
9850 Ramblewood Dr 33071 754-322-6850
Sherry Bees, prin. Fax 322-6890
Parkside ES 900/K-5
10257 NW 29th St 33065 754-322-7850
Susan Colton, prin. Fax 322-7890
Park Springs ES 1,000/PK-5
5800 NW 66th Ter 33067 754-322-7750
Camille Pontillo, prin. Fax 322-7790
Ramblewood ES 900/K-5
8950 Shadow Wood Blvd 33071 754-322-8150
Betty Colyer, prin. Fax 322-8190
Ramblewood MS 1,300/6-8
8505 W Atlantic Blvd 33071 754-322-4300
Christine Recchi, prin. Fax 322-4385
Riverside ES 900/K-5
11450 Riverside Dr 33071 754-322-8250
Julianne Smith, prin. Fax 322-8290
Sawgrass Springs MS 1,400/6-8
12500 W Sample Rd 33065 754-322-4500
Adeline Andreano, prin. Fax 322-4585
Westchester ES 1,100/K-5
12405 Royal Palm Blvd 33065 754-322-8900
Raymond LeFevre, prin. Fax 322-8940

Academy HS - Davie Campus 400/3-12
11411 NW 56th Dr 33076 954-752-5038
Nina Kaufman, pres. Fax 752-1470
Coral Springs Christian Academy 800/PK-12
2251 Riverside Dr 33065 954-752-2870
Robert Clampett, hdmstr. Fax 346-1112
Glades Christian Academy 100/PK-6
400 Lakeview Dr 33071 954-755-6405
Rod Evans, hdmstr. Fax 825-0872
North Broward Preparatory Schools 200/PK-5
3251 NW 101st Ave 33065 954-752-3020
David Hicks, hdmstr. Fax 757-7590
Parkridge Christian Academy 100/PK-4
5600 Coral Ridge Dr 33076 954-346-0236
Jenniffer Wood, prin. Fax 346-0016
St. Andrew S 500/PK-8
9990 NW 29th St 33065 954-753-1280
Lois Lawlor, prin. Fax 753-1933

Cottondale, Jackson, Pop. 879
Jackson County SD
Supt. — See Marianna
Cottondale ES 500/PK-5
2766 Levy St 32431 850-482-9820
Diane Long, prin. Fax 482-9825

Crawfordville, Wakulla
Wakulla County SD 4,600/PK-12
PO Box 100 32326 850-926-0065
David Miller, supt. Fax 926-0123
wakulla.fl.schoolwebpages.com/
Crawfordville ES 800/K-5
379 Arran Rd 32327 850-926-3641
Angie Walker, prin. Fax 926-4303
Medart ES 700/K-5
2558 Coastal Hwy 32327 850-926-4881
Robert Pearce, prin. Fax 962-3953
Riversink ES K-5
530 Lonnie Raker Ln 32327 850-926-2664
Jackie High, prin. Fax 926-9462
Riversprings MS 500/6-8
800 Spring Creek Hwy 32327 850-926-2300
Dod Walker, prin. Fax 926-2111
Shadeville ES 700/K-5
45 Warrior Way 32327 850-926-7155
Susan Brazier, prin. Fax 926-5044
Wakulla MS 500/6-8
22 Jean Dr 32327 850-926-7143
JoAnn Daniels, prin. Fax 926-3752
Wakulla Preschool PK-PK
87 Andrew J Hargrett Sr Rd 32327 850-926-8111
Kim Dutton, prin. Fax 926-1694

Crescent City, Putnam, Pop. 1,817
Putnam County SD
Supt. — See Palatka
Middleton-Burney ES 700/PK-3
1020 Huntington Rd 32112 386-698-1238
Carolyn Radtke, prin. Fax 698-4364
Miller IS 500/4-6
101 S Prospect St 32112 386-698-1360
Tom Bolling, prin. Fax 698-1973

Crestview, Okaloosa, Pop. 17,707
Okaloosa County SD
Supt. — See Fort Walton Beach
Antioch ES 900/K-5
4700 Whitehurst Ln 32536 850-683-7540
Glenda Robinson, prin. Fax 683-7561
Davidson MS 900/6-8
6261 Old Bethel Rd 32536 850-683-7500
Beth Walthall, prin. Fax 683-7523
Northwood ES 700/PK-5
501 4th Ave 32536 850-689-7252
Jacqueline Craig, prin. Fax 689-7488
Richbourg MS 700/6-8
500 Alabama St 32536 850-689-7229
Bob Jones, prin. Fax 689-7245
Sikes ES 700/K-5
425 Adams Dr 32536 850-689-7268
Gary Massey, prin. Fax 689-7263
Southside ES 600/PK-5
650 S Pearl St 32539 850-689-7203
Donna Holloway, prin. Fax 689-7401
Walker ES 700/PK-5
2988 Stillwell Blvd 32539 850-689-7220
Jeanine Kirkland, prin. Fax 689-7654

Crossroads Christian S 300/K-12
PO Box 295 32536 850-423-1291
Fax 423-1291

Cross City, Dixie, Pop. 1,808
Dixie County SD 2,200/PK-12
PO Box 890 32628 352-498-6131
Mark Rains, supt. Fax 498-1308
www.dixie.k12.fl.us/
Anderson ES 600/PK-5
PO Box 5050 32628 352-498-1333
Denee Hurst, prin. Fax 498-1342
Rains MS 500/6-8
PO Box 2159 32628 352-498-1346
Beverly Baumer, prin. Fax 498-1283
Other Schools – See Old Town

Crystal River, Citrus, Pop. 3,600
Citrus County SD
Supt. — See Inverness
Crystal River ES 700/PK-5
947 NE 6th St 34428 352-795-2211
Edie Speight, prin. Fax 795-1705
Crystal River MS 1,000/6-8
344 NE Crystal St 34428 352-795-2116
Mark McCoy, prin. Fax 795-2378

Westcoast Christian S 50/K-12
718 NW 1st Ave 34428 352-795-1619

Cutler Bay, Miami-Dade
Miami-Dade County SD
Supt. — See Miami
Bel-Aire ES 400/PK-4
10205 SW 194th St, 305-233-5401
Dr. Columbus Williams, prin. Fax 256-3101
Centennial MS 900/6-8
8601 SW 212th St, 305-235-1581
Yamila Carballo, prin. Fax 234-8071
Gulfstream ES 700/PK-6
20900 SW 97th Ave, 305-235-6811
Susan Lyle, prin. Fax 254-1721
Whigham ES 1,100/PK-5
21545 SW 87th Ave, 305-234-4840
Kimberly Davis, prin. Fax 234-4837
Whigham Primary Learning Center PK-K
8035 SW 196th St, 305-252-5050
Fax 252-5798

Cutler Ridge, Miami-Dade, Pop. 21,268
Miami-Dade County SD
Supt. — See Miami
Cutler Ridge ES 1,000/PK-5
20210 Coral Sea Rd 33189 305-235-4611
Adrienne Wright-Mullings, prin. Fax 232-6740
Cutler Ridge MS 1,100/6-8
19400 Gulfstream Rd 33157 305-235-4761
Eduardo Alonso, prin. Fax 254-3746

Cutler Ridge Christian Academy 200/PK-10
10301 Caribbean Blvd 33189 305-251-1534
Stephen Hager, prin. Fax 255-6978

Dade City, Pasco, Pop. 6,823
Pasco County SD
Supt. — See Land O Lakes
Centennial ES 700/K-5
38501 Centennial Rd 33525 352-524-5000
J. Scott Mitchell, prin. Fax 524-5091
Centennial MS 700/6-8
38505 Centennial Rd 33525 352-524-9700
Thomas Rulison, prin. Fax 524-9791
Cox ES 500/PK-5
37615 Martin Luther King Bl 33523 352-524-5100
Leila Mizer, prin. Fax 524-5191
LaCoochee ES 400/PK-5
38815 Cummer Rd 33523 352-524-5600
Karen Marler, prin. Fax 524-5691
Pasco ES 700/PK-5
37350 Florida Ave 33525 352-524-5200
Barbara Munz, prin. Fax 524-5291
Pasco MS 800/6-8
13925 14th St 33525 352-524-8400
Jim Lane, prin. Fax 524-8491
San Antonio ES 700/PK-5
32416 Darby Rd 33525 352-524-5300
Vanessa Hilton, prin. Fax 524-5391

East Pasco Adventist Academy 100/PK-10
38434 Centennial Rd 33525 352-567-3646
Tracy Arnett, prin. Fax 567-1907
Sacred Heart ECC 200/PK-PK
32245 Saint Joe Rd 33525 352-588-4060
Toni Watkins, dir. Fax 588-4871

Dania, Broward, Pop. 14,456
Broward County SD
Supt. — See Fort Lauderdale
Collins ES 400/PK-5
1050 NW 2nd St 33004 754-323-5150
Lincoln Pasteur, prin. Fax 323-5190
Dania ES 600/PK-5
300 SE 2nd Ave 33004 754-323-5350
Donna Patton, prin. Fax 323-5390
Olsen MS 1,300/6-8
330 SE 11th Ter 33004 754-323-3800
Kim Flynn, prin. Fax 323-3885

Davenport, Polk, Pop. 2,017
Polk County SD
Supt. — See Bartow
Davenport S of the Arts 600/PK-8
PO Box 728 33836 863-421-3247
Brian Kier, prin. Fax 421-3662
Horizons ES K-5
1700 Forest Lake Dr 33837 863-419-3430
Leshelle Seay, prin. Fax 419-3432
Loughman Oaks ES 1,100/PK-5
4600 US Highway 17 92 N 33837 863-421-3309
Jodi Lamb, prin. Fax 421-3333

Ridge Christian Academy 100/PK-5
41219 Highway 27 33837 863-420-2885
Deborah Keaton, dir. Fax 420-7117

Davie, Broward, Pop. 84,204
Broward County SD
Supt. — See Fort Lauderdale
Davie ES 900/PK-5
7025 SW 39th St 33314 754-323-5400
Robert Schneider, prin. Fax 323-5440
Flamingo ES 800/PK-5
1130 SW 133rd Ave 33325 754-323-5700
Lee Ann Jones, prin. Fax 323-5740
Fox Trail ES 1,200/K-5
1250 S Nob Hill Rd 33324 754-323-5800
Lynn Burgess, prin. Fax 323-5840
Hawkes Bluff ES 1,000/PK-5
5900 SW 160th Ave 33331 754-323-6100
Deborah Sheats, prin. Fax 323-6140
Indian Ridge MS 700/6-6
1355 S Nob Hill Rd 33324 754-323-3300
Frank Zagari, prin. Fax 323-3385
Nova Blanche Forman ES 800/K-5
3521 Davie Rd 33314 754-323-6600
Chuck McCanna, prin. Fax 323-6640
Nova Eisenhower ES 800/K-5
6501 SW 39th St 33314 754-323-6650
Carol Lesser, prin. Fax 323-6690
Nova MS 1,200/6-8
3602 College Ave 33314 754-323-3700
Dr. Ricardo Garcia, prin. Fax 323-3785
Silver Ridge ES 1,000/K-5
9100 SW 36th St 33328 754-323-7500
Marion Gundling, prin. Fax 323-7540

Apple Tree Montessori S 300/PK-8
6301 SW 160th Ave 33331 954-252-9250
Susan Levine, prin. Fax 252-9230
Gloria Dei Lutheran Academy 200/PK-8
7601 SW 39th St 33328 954-475-8584
Larry Ueltzen, prin. Fax 475-2232
Kentwood Preparatory S 100/1-12
4650 SW 61st Ave 33314 954-581-8222
Lynette Vanheyzen, prin. Fax 797-0700
Montessori Institute of Broward PK-5
12425 Orange Dr 33330 954-472-9620
Graciela Covarrubias, dir. Fax 424-2898
Parkway Christian S 300/PK-8
1200 S Flamingo Rd 33325 954-424-6425
Nicole Koski, prin. Fax 424-6761
St. Bonaventure S 600/PK-8
1301 SW 136th Ave 33325 954-476-5200
Nydia Claudio, prin. Fax 476-5203
St. David S 600/PK-8
3900 S University Dr 33328 954-472-7086
Mariann Kiar, prin. Fax 452-8243
Summit-Questa Montessori S 200/PK-8
5451 SW 64th Ave 33314 954-584-3466
Judy Dempsey, dir. Fax 584-7816

Daytona Beach, Volusia, Pop. 64,421
Volusia County SD
Supt. — See De Land
Campbell MS, 625 S Keech St 32114 800/6-8
Vickie Presley, prin. 386-258-4661
Hinson MS 1,000/6-8
1860 N Clyde Morris Blvd 32117 386-258-4682
Ted Petrucciani, prin.
Longstreet ES 400/K-5
2745 S Peninsula Dr 32118 386-322-6172
Bonnie Gyarfas, prin. Fax 756-7281
Ortona ES 300/K-5
1265 N Grandview Ave 32118 386-258-4668
Juanita Collins, prin. Fax 239-6386
Palm Terrace ES 600/PK-5
1825 Dunn Ave 32114 386-258-4670
John Cash, prin. Fax 274-3448
Small ES 400/PK-5
800 South St 32114 386-258-4675
Betty Powers, prin. Fax 239-6346
Westside ES 500/PK-5
1210 Jimmy Ann Dr 32117 386-258-4678
Judi Winch, prin. Fax 274-3417

Basilica S of St. Paul 200/PK-8
317 Mullally St 32114 386-252-7915
Yvonne Toro, prin. Fax 238-7903
Daytona Beach Christian S 200/PK-8
1851 S Clyde Morris Blvd 32119 386-760-4808
Dr. Randolph Price, prin. Fax 760-1357
Indigo Christian Jr. Academy 50/K-8
401 N Williamson Blvd 32114 386-255-5917
Lourdes Academy 300/PK-8
1014 N Halifax Ave 32118 386-252-0391
Peter Randlov, prin. Fax 238-1175
Mount Calvary Academy 100/PK-6
PO Box 9358 32120 386-255-8654

De Bary, Volusia, Pop. 16,413
Volusia County SD
Supt. — See De Land
De Bary ES 800/PK-5
88 W Highbanks Rd 32713 386-575-4230
Joseph Rawlings, prin. Fax 668-3538

Deerfield Beach, Broward, Pop. 76,348
Broward County SD
Supt. — See Fort Lauderdale
Deerfield Beach ES 800/PK-5
650 NE 1st St 33441 754-322-6100
Michael Breslaw, prin. Fax 322-6140
Deerfield Beach MS 1,400/6-8
701 SE 6th Ave 33441 754-322-3300
Vincent Alessi, prin. Fax 322-3385
Deerfield Park ES 700/PK-5
650 SW 3rd Ave 33441 754-322-6150
Constantina Pettis, prin. Fax 322-6190
Quiet Waters ES 1,200/PK-5
4150 W Hillsboro Blvd 33442 754-322-8100
Lori McConaughey, prin. Fax 322-8140

Deerfield Christian Academy 100/PK-8
747 S Federal Hwy 33441 954-428-8910
Anthony Guadagnino, admin. Fax 480-9755
St. Ambrose S 300/PK-8
PO Box 999 33443 954-427-2226
Anita Gentile, prin. Fax 427-2293
Zion Lutheran Christian S 600/PK-12
959 SE 6th Ave 33441 954-421-3146
Joe Kemp, prin. Fax 421-5465

De Funiak Springs, Walton, Pop. 5,038
Walton County SD 6,400/PK-12
145 S Park St Ste 2 32435 850-892-1100
Carlene Anderson, supt. Fax 892-1191
www.walton.k12.fl.us
Mossy Head S K-5
13270 US Highway 90 W 32433 850-892-1290
Ronda Hinote, prin. Fax 892-1291
Saunders ES 700/PK-5
416 John Baldwin Rd 32433 850-892-1260
Tracey Dickey, prin. Fax 892-1269
Walton MS 700/6-8
625 Park Ave 32435 850-892-1280
Tripp Hope, prin. Fax 892-1289
West DeFuniak ES 700/PK-5
815 Lincoln Ave 32435 850-892-1250
Darlene Paul, prin. Fax 892-1259
Other Schools – See Freeport, Paxton, Santa Rosa Beach

First Christian Academy 50/K-5
216 Live Oak Ave E 32435 850-892-2722
Jennifer Wilkerson, dir. Fax 892-2381
Galilean Academy 50/K-7
PO Box 1488 32435 850-892-3421
Nell Vogel, admin.

De Land, Volusia, Pop. 24,375
Volusia County SD 64,300/PK-12
PO Box 2118 32721 386-734-7190
Margaret Smith, supt. Fax 943-3423
www.volusia.k12.fl.us
Blue Lake ES 700/PK-5
282 N Blue Lake Ave 32724 386-822-4070
Carol Thames, prin. Fax 822-6765
DeLand MS 1,700/6-8
1400 Aquarius Ave 32724 386-822-5678
Matt Krajewski, prin. Fax 822-6583
Freedom ES 700/PK-5
1395 S Blue Lake Ave 32724 386-943-4375
Claire Beth Link, prin. Fax 943-7680
Marks ES 900/PK-5
1000 N Garfield Ave 32724 386-822-6986
Kate Godbee, prin. Fax 822-6636
Southwestern MS 700/6-8
605 W New Hampshire Ave 32720 386-822-6815
Mamie Oatis, prin. Fax 822-6708
Starke ES 400/PK-5
730 S Parsons Ave 32720 386-943-9651
Barbara Head, prin. Fax 943-7957
Woodward Avenue ES 900/PK-5
1201 S Woodward Ave 32720 386-740-7910
Dr. Deedara Hicks, prin. Fax 943-7921
Other Schools – See Daytona Beach, De Bary, De Leon Springs, Deltona, Edgewater, Enterprise, Holly Hill, Lake Helen, New Smyrna Beach, Oak Hill, Orange City, Ormond Beach, Osteen, Pierson, Port Orange, South Daytona

---

Childrens House Montessori S 100/PK-6
509 E Pennsylvania Ave 32724 386-736-3632
Dora Mallett, admin. Fax 736-3667
First Presbyterian Church Day S 100/PK-5
724 N Woodland Blvd 32720 386-734-6214
Jennifer Rogers, dir. Fax 736-7878
Lighthouse Christian Academy 200/PK-5
126 S Ridgewood Ave 32720 386-734-4631
Ruth Dormire, prin. Fax 734-5627
St. Barnabas Episcopal S 400/PK-8
322 W Michigan Ave 32720 386-734-3005
Karen Lyon, prin. Fax 822-9417
St. Peters S 300/PK-8
421 W New York Ave 32720 386-822-6010
Mary Martin, prin. Fax 822-6013
Stetson Baptist Christian S 300/PK-8
1025 W Minnesota Ave 32720 386-734-7791
Sheryl Jackson, dir. Fax 734-7109

De Leon Springs, Volusia, Pop. 1,481
Volusia County SD
Supt. — See De Land
McInnis ES 500/K-5
5175 US Highway 17 32130 386-943-6384
Alba Perez, prin. Fax 985-6710

Delray Beach, Palm Beach, Pop. 64,757
Palm Beach County SD
Supt. — See West Palm Beach
Banyan Creek ES 900/PK-5
4243 Sabal Lakes Rd 33445 561-894-7100
William Fay, prin. Fax 894-7150
Carver Community MS 1,000/6-8
101 Barwick Rd 33445 561-638-2100
Lena Roundtree, prin. Fax 638-2181
Morikami Park ES 1,000/K-5
6201 Morikami Park Rd 33484 561-865-3960
Renee Elfe, prin. Fax 865-3965
Orchard View ES 600/K-5
4050 Germantown Rd 33445 561-894-7400
Gerald Riopelle, prin. Fax 894-7450
Pine Grove ES 500/K-5
400 SW 10th St 33444 561-243-1554
Marline Campbell, prin. Fax 243-1548
Plumosa ES 400/K-5
1712 NE 2nd Ave 33444 561-243-1562
Priscilla Bowers-Maloney, prin. Fax 279-1701
Spady ES 600/PK-6
901 NW 3rd St 33444 561-454-7800
Martha O'Hare, prin. Fax 454-7801
Village Academy 600/K-12
400 SW 12th Ave 33444 561-243-6100
Tammy Ferguson, prin. Fax 243-6154

American Heritage S of Boca/Delray 1,000/PK-12
6200 Linton Blvd 33484 561-495-7272
Robert Stone, hdmstr. Fax 495-6106
Daughter of Zion Junior Academy 100/PK-8
250 NW 3rd Ave 33444 561-243-0715
Audrey Wainwright, prin. Fax 243-0919
St. Vincent Ferrer S 300/PK-8
810 George Bush Blvd 33483 561-278-3868
Maria Delgado, prin. Fax 279-9508
Trinity Lutheran S 400/PK-8
400 N Swinton Ave 33444 561-276-8458
Tim Guelzow, prin. Fax 272-3215
Unity S 400/PK-8
101 NW 22nd St 33444 561-276-4414
Maria Barber, hdmstr. Fax 265-0990

Deltona, Volusia, Pop. 82,788
Volusia County SD
Supt. — See De Land
Deltona Lakes ES 1,000/PK-5
2022 Adelia Blvd 32725 386-575-4115
Judith Rivera-Hilaire, prin. Fax 789-7018
Deltona MS 1,500/6-8
250 Enterprise Rd 32725 386-575-4150
James Bambrick, prin. Fax 860-3383
Discovery ES 900/PK-5
975 Abagail Dr 32725 386-575-4133
Susie Williamson, prin. Fax 860-3316
Forest Lake ES, 1600 Doyle Rd 32725 700/K-5
David Fisher, prin. 386-575-4166
Friendship ES 800/PK-5
2746 Fulford St 32738 386-575-4130
Maria Martoral, prin. Fax 789-7032
Galaxy MS 1,800/6-8
2400 Eustace Ave 32725 386-575-4144
Julian Jones, prin. Fax 789-7058
Heritage MS, 1001 Parnell Ct 32738 1,500/6-8
Dennis Neal, prin. 386-575-4113
Pride ES, 1100 Learning Ln 32738 K-5
Leslie Frazee, prin. 386-968-0010
Spirit ES, 1500 Meadowlark Dr 32725 800/K-5
Dr. Donald Travis, prin. 386-575-4080
Sunrise ES, 3155 Phonetia Dr 32738 1,000/K-5
Sandra Kaye, prin. 386-575-4103
Timbercrest ES 900/K-5
2401 Eustace Ave 32725 386-575-4221
Dr. Mary Cool, prin. Fax 775-5412

Deltona Adventist S 100/PK-8
1725 Catalina Blvd 32738 386-532-9333
Loralee Muhlenbeck, prin. Fax 532-9633
Deltona Christian S 200/PK-12
1200 Providence Blvd 32725 386-574-1971
Trinity Christian Academy 600/PK-12
875 Elkcam Blvd 32725 386-789-4515
Dennis Robinson, prin. Fax 789-0210

Destin, Okaloosa, Pop. 12,423
Okaloosa County SD
Supt. — See Fort Walton Beach
Destin ES 900/PK-5
630 Kelly St 32541 850-833-4360
Marti Gardner, prin. Fax 833-4370
Destin MS 600/6-8
4608 Legendary Marina Dr 32541 850-833-7655
Tommy Britt, prin. Fax 833-7677

Destin Christian Academy 100/K-5
201 Beach Dr 32541 850-837-7247
Dean DeMarra, admin. Fax 654-6090
First Baptist Academy 100/K-5
201 Beach Dr 32541 850-837-6515

Doral, Miami-Dade, Pop. 21,895
Miami-Dade County SD
Supt. — See Miami
Espinosa K-8 Center 1,200/K-8
11250 NW 86th St, 305-889-5757
Reva Vangates, prin. Fax 889-5758

Divine Savior Lutheran Academy 200/PK-7
10311 NW 58th St, 305-597-4545
Benjamin Troge, prin. Fax 597-4077

Dover, Hillsborough, Pop. 2,606
Hillsborough County SD
Supt. — See Tampa
Dover ES 800/PK-5
3035 Nelson Ave 33527 813-757-9457
Marie Caracciola, prin. Fax 707-7161
Nelson ES 900/K-5
5413 Durant Rd 33527 813-651-2120
Cindy Guy, prin. Fax 651-2124

Duette, Manatee
Manatee County SD
Supt. — See Bradenton
Duette ES 50/K-5
40755 State Road 62, 941-721-6674
David Marshall, prin. Fax 721-6675

Dundee, Polk, Pop. 3,064
Polk County SD
Supt. — See Bartow
Dundee ES 500/PK-5
215 E Frederick Ave 33838 863-421-3316
Constance Jones, prin. Fax 421-3317
Dundee Ridge MS 1,100/6-8
5555 Lake Trask Rd 33838 863-419-3088
Kathryn Blackburn, prin. Fax 419-3157

Dunedin, Pinellas, Pop. 36,690
Pinellas County SD
Supt. — See Largo
Curtis Fundamental ES 400/K-5
531 Beltrees St 34698 727-738-6483
Kathy Duncan, prin. Fax 738-6488
Dunedin ES 600/K-5
900 Union St 34698 727-738-2990
Kathy Brickley, prin. Fax 738-2994
Dunedin Highland MS 1,100/6-8
70 Patricia Ave 34698 727-469-4112
Margaret Landers, prin. Fax 469-4115
Garrison-Jones ES 700/PK-5
3133 Garrison Rd 34698 727-469-5716
Karen Buckles, prin. Fax 469-5725
San Jose ES 500/PK-5
1670 San Helen Dr 34698 727-469-5956
Monika Wolcott, prin. Fax 469-5960

Dunedin Academy 200/PK-12
1408 County Road 1 34698 727-733-9148
Kathleen Porter, dir. Fax 733-6696
Dunedin Montessori Academy 50/PK-K
637 Michigan Blvd 34698 727-734-0332
Ann Dietz, prin. Fax 734-0332
Our Lady of Lourdes S 300/PK-8
730 San Salvador Dr 34698 727-733-3776
Kathy Bogataj, prin. Fax 733-4333

Dunnellon, Marion, Pop. 1,971
Marion County SD
Supt. — See Ocala
Dunnellon ES 700/PK-5
10235 SW 180th Avenue Rd 34432 352-465-6710
Patricia Hornsby, prin. Fax 465-6711
Dunnellon MS 1,100/6-8
21005 Chestnut St 34431 352-465-6720
Jane Ashman, prin. Fax 465-6721
Romeo ES 800/K-5
19550 SW 36th St 34431 352-465-6700
Kathy Hultman, prin. Fax 465-6701

Dunnellon Christian Academy 200/PK-12
20831 Powell Rd 34431 352-489-7716
Rev. Russell Randall, admin. Fax 489-0337

Eagle Lake, Polk, Pop. 2,489
Polk County SD
Supt. — See Bartow
Eagle Lake ES 600/K-5
400 W Crystal Beach Rd 33839 863-291-5357
Jodie Bailey, prin. Fax 291-5360
Pinewood ES 500/K-5
1400 Gilbert St 33839 863-298-7977
Brenda Johnson, prin. Fax 298-7978

Eastpoint, Franklin, Pop. 1,577
Franklin County SD 600/K-12
85 School Rd Ste 1 32328 850-670-2810
Jo Ann Gander, supt. Fax 670-2811
www.franklincountyschools.org/
Franklin County S 600/K-12
1250 US Highway 98 32328 850-670-2800
Freddie Hargett, prin.

Eaton Park, Polk
Polk County SD
Supt. — See Bartow
Pope ES 400/PK-5
PO Box 1596 33840 863-499-2992
Janel Barber, prin. Fax 499-2996

Eatonville, Orange, Pop. 2,390
Orange County SD
Supt. — See Orlando
Hungerford ES 200/PK-5
230 S College Ave 32751 407-623-1430
Jenell Bovis, prin. Fax 623-1498

Life Academy of Excellence 100/K-8
107 Wymore Rd 32751 407-622-1330
Danton Thomas, prin. Fax 622-1329

Edgewater, Volusia, Pop. 21,132
Volusia County SD
Supt. — See De Land
Edgewater ES 600/K-5
801 S Old County Rd 32132 386-424-2573
Lynda Moore, prin. Fax 426-7349
Indian River ES 700/PK-5
650 Roberts Rd 32141 386-424-2650
Susan Persis, prin.

Discovery Days Institute of Learning 200/PK-8
227 N Ridgewood Ave 32132 386-428-0860
Nancy Solman, admin. Fax 427-9400

Eglin AFB, Okaloosa, Pop. 8,347
Okaloosa County SD
Supt. — See Fort Walton Beach
Elgin ES 300/PK-4
200 Gaffney Rd 32542 850-833-4320
Dr. Karyn Combs, prin. Fax 833-3671

Elkton, Saint Johns
St. Johns County SD
Supt. — See Saint Augustine
South Woods ES 600/K-5
4750 State Road 206 W 32033 904-547-8611
Brian McElhone, prin. Fax 547-8615

Englewood, Sarasota, Pop. 15,025
Sarasota County SD
Supt. — See Sarasota
Englewood ES 500/K-5
150 N Mccall Rd 34223 941-474-3247
Pamela Buchanan, prin. Fax 474-0872

Heritage Christian Academy 100/PK-12
75 Pine St 34223 941-474-5884
Dawn Johnson, admin. Fax 473-1797

Enterprise, Volusia
Volusia County SD
Supt. — See De Land
Enterprise ES, 211 Main St 32725 700/PK-5
Dr. Virginia Abernathy, prin. 386-575-4135

Estero, Lee, Pop. 3,177
Lee County SD
Supt. — See Fort Myers
Pinewoods ES 900/PK-5
11900 Stoneybrook Golf Dr 33928 239-947-7500
Dr. Denise Carlin, prin. Fax 947-0834

Eustis, Lake, Pop. 17,683
Lake County SD
Supt. — See Tavares
Eustis ES 500/K-5
714 E Citrus Ave 32726 352-357-2779
Rusty Dosh, prin. Fax 357-4179
Eustis Heights ES 700/K-5
310 W Taylor Ave 32726 352-357-2447
Douglas Kroulik, prin. Fax 357-3602
Eustis MS 1,100/6-8
18725 Bates Ave 32736 352-357-3366
Julie Robinson-Lueallen, prin. Fax 357-5963
Seminole Springs ES 800/PK-5
26200 W Huff Rd 32736 352-589-1117
Adrian Boyd, prin. Fax 589-1749

Blue Lake Academy 200/PK-12
PO Box 1947 32727 352-357-8655
Gail Hatmaker, prin. Fax 357-6956
Faith Lutheran S 300/PK-8
2727 S Grove St 32726 352-589-5683
Corinne Hoffert, prin. Fax 589-1328

Everglades City, Collier
Collier County SD
Supt. — See Naples
Everglades City S 100/PK-12
PO Box 170 34139 239-377-9800
Bobby Jones, prin. Fax 377-9801

Fellsmere, Indian River, Pop. 4,800
Indian River County SD
Supt. — See Vero Beach
Fellsmere ES 600/PK-5
50 N Cypress St 32948 772-564-5970
Barry Sesack, prin. Fax 564-6020

Fernandina Beach, Nassau, Pop. 11,264
Nassau County SD 10,500/PK-12
1201 Atlantic Ave 32034 904-491-9900
John Ruis, supt. Fax 277-9042
www.nassau.k12.fl.us
Fernandina Beach MS 600/6-8
315 Citrona Dr 32034 904-491-7938
John Mazzella, prin. Fax 261-8919
Hardee ES 400/3-5
2200 Susan Dr 32034 904-491-7936
Eric Larsen, prin. Fax 321-5890
Southside ES 400/PK-2
1112 Jasmine St 32034 904-491-7941
Cindy Olson, prin. Fax 321-5873
Other Schools – See Bryceville, Callahan, Hilliard, Yulee

Amelia Island Montessori S 100/PK-6
PO Box 3000 32035 904-261-6610
Renee Crane, hdmstr. Fax 261-6196
Faith Christian Academy 200/PK-8
96282 Brady Point Rd 32034 904-321-2137
Bryan Alvare, prin. Fax 321-1707
St. Michael Academy 200/PK-8
228 N 4th St 32034 904-321-2102
Sr. Martha Rohde, prin. Fax 321-2330

Fern Park, Seminole, Pop. 8,294
Seminole County SD
Supt. — See Sanford
English Estates ES 800/PK-5
299 Oxford Rd 32730 407-746-2850
Beth Sharpe, prin. Fax 746-2858

Flagler Beach, Flagler, Pop. 3,179
Flagler County SD
Supt. — See Bunnell
Old Kings ES 1,100/K-5
301 Old Kings Rd S 32136 386-517-2060
Denise Haymes, prin. Fax 517-2074

Florahome, Putnam
Putnam County SD
Supt. — See Palatka
Roberts MS 300/6-8
901 State Road 100 32140 386-659-1737
Debra Buckles, prin. Fax 659-1986

Floral City, Citrus, Pop. 2,609
Citrus County SD
Supt. — See Inverness
Floral City ES 400/PK-5
PO Box 340 34436 352-726-1554
Janet Reed, prin. Fax 726-5270

Florida City, Miami-Dade, Pop. 8,913
Miami-Dade County SD
Supt. — See Miami
Florida City ES 800/PK-5
364 NW 6th Ave 33034 305-247-4676
Gloria Arazoza, prin. Fax 248-8317

Bethel SDA ES K-3
32900 SW 187th Ave 33034 305-248-5075

Fort Lauderdale, Broward, Pop. 167,380
Broward County SD 240,200/PK-12
600 SE 3rd Ave 33301 754-321-0000
James Notter, supt. Fax 321-2701
www.browardschools.com
Ashe MS 900/6-8
1701 NW 23rd Ave 33311 754-322-2800
Andrew Luciani, prin. Fax 322-2880
Bayview ES 500/K-5
1175 Middle River Dr 33304 754-322-5400
JoEllen Scott, prin. Fax 322-5440
Bennett ES 400/PK-5
1755 NE 14th St 33304 754-322-5450
Chris Carney, prin. Fax 322-5490
Broward Estates ES 700/PK-5
441 NW 35th Ave 33311 754-322-5550
Stephanie Beville, prin. Fax 322-5590
Croissant Park ES 700/PK-5
1800 SW 4th Ave 33315 754-323-5300
Cheri Zahn, prin. Fax 323-5340
Dandy MS 1,300/6-8
2400 NW 26th St 33311 754-322-3200
Casandra Robinson, prin. Fax 322-3285
Dillard ES 800/PK-5
2330 NW 12th Ct 33311 754-322-6200
Angela Fulton, prin. Fax 322-6240
Floranada ES 700/PK-5
5251 NE 14th Way 33334 754-322-6350
Brian Kohli, prin. Fax 322-6390
Foster ES 700/PK-5
3471 SW 22nd St 33312 754-323-5750
Michael Cassaw, prin. Fax 323-5790
Harbordale ES 400/PK-5
900 SE 15th St 33316 754-323-6050
Theresa Bucolo, prin. Fax 323-6090
King ES 600/PK-5
591 NW 31st Ave 33311 754-322-6550
Marvis Ward, prin. Fax 322-6590
Larkdale ES 500/PK-5
3250 NW 12th Pl 33311 754-322-6600
Dr. Valoria Latson, prin. Fax 322-6640
Lauderdale Manors ES 600/PK-5
1400 NW 14th Ct 33311 754-322-6650
Heather Hedman-Devaughn, prin. Fax 322-6690
Marshall ES 600/PK-5
800 NW 13th St 33311 754-322-7000
Oliva Vega, prin. Fax 322-7040
Meadowbrook ES 600/PK-5
2300 SW 46th Ave 33317 754-323-6500
Dr. Dorothy Cook, prin. Fax 323-6540
New River MS 1,500/6-8
3100 Riverland Rd 33312 754-323-3600
Kathrine Hinden, prin. Fax 323-3685
North Andrews Gardens ES 800/K-5
345 NE 56th St 33334 754-322-7300
Davida Shacter, prin. Fax 322-7340
North Fork ES 600/PK-5
101 NW 15th Ave 33311 754-322-7350
Rendolyn Amaker, prin. Fax 322-7390
North Side ES 500/PK-5
120 NE 11th St 33304 754-322-7450
Camille LaChance, prin. Fax 322-7490
Parkway MS 1,300/6-8
3600 NW 5th Ct 33311 754-322-4000
Bradford Mattair, prin. Fax 322-4085
Riverland ES 600/PK-5
2600 SW 11th Ct 33312 754-323-7200
Millicent Thorpe, prin. Fax 323-7240
Rock Island ES 600/PK-5
2350 NW 19th St 33311 754-322-8300
James Griffin, prin. Fax 322-8340
Sunland Park ES 500/PK-5
919 NW 13th Ave 33311 754-322-8550
Mattie Benson, prin. Fax 322-8590
Sunrise MS 1,300/6-8
1750 NE 14th St 33304 754-322-4700
Oslay Gil, prin. Fax 322-4790
Walker ES 800/PK-5
1001 NW 4th St 33311 754-322-8800
Dr. Eric Miller, prin. Fax 322-8840
Westwood Heights ES 800/PK-5
2861 SW 9th St 33312 754-323-7900
Gwendolyn Burney, prin. Fax 323-7940
Wilton Manors ES 600/PK-5
2401 NE 3rd Ave 33305 754-322-8950
Mark Narkier, prin. Fax 322-8990
Young ES 800/PK-5
101 NE 11th Ave 33301 754-322-9050
Dr. Mark Strauss, prin. Fax 322-9090
Other Schools – See Coconut Creek, Cooper City, Coral Springs, Dania, Davie, Deerfield Beach, Hallandale, Hollywood, Lauderdale Lakes, Lauderhill, Margate, Miramar, North Lauderdale, Oakland Park, Parkland, Pembroke Park, Pembroke Pines, Plantation, Pompano Beach, Sunrise, Tamarac, Weston

---

Bethany Christian S 200/PK-8
615 SE 9th St 33316 954-522-2554
Jean Boer, hdmstr. Fax 522-3406
Brauser Maimonides Academy 400/PK-8
5300 SW 40th Ave 33314 954-989-6886
Rabbi Avram Skurowitz Ed.D., prin. Fax 989-4548
Calvary Christian Academy 1,300/PK-12
2401 W Cypress Creek Rd 33309 954-905-5100
David Salvatelli, dir. Fax 556-4650
Christ Church S 300/PK-5
4845 NE 25th Ave 33308 954-771-7700
Tane Bonham, prin. Fax 776-4553
Faith Lutheran S 100/PK-8
1161 SW 30th Ave 33312 954-581-2918
Fax 581-2918
Fort Lauderdale Christian S 300/PK-12
6330 NW 31st Ave 33309 954-972-3444
Gerald Mitchell, hdmstr. Fax 977-2681

Fort Lauderdale Preparatory S 100/PK-12
3275 W Oakland Park Blvd 33311 954-485-7500
Anita Lonstein, prin. Fax 485-1732
Gateway Christian Academy 100/PK-5
2130 NW 26th St 33311 954-485-7012
Holy Temple Christian Academy 200/PK-12
1800 NW 9th Ave 33311 954-467-0758
Margaret Johnson, prin. Fax 467-0748
Master's Academy 300/PK-8
13900 Griffin Rd 33330 954-434-2960
Dr. James Virtue, supt. Fax 434-4719
Mt. Olivet SDA S 100/PK-8
3013 NW 11th St 33311 954-792-6010
Kalisha Waldon M.Ed., prin. Fax 792-2248
New Hope SDA S PK-5
545 E Campus Cir 33312 954-587-3842
Our Lady Queen of Martyrs S 300/PK-8
2785 Happy Hoyer St 33312 954-583-8112
Althea Mossop, prin. Fax 797-4984
Pine Crest S 1,700/PK-12
1501 NE 62nd St 33334 954-492-4100
Lourdes Cowgill, pres. Fax 492-4109
Redeeming Word Christian Academy 100/PK-5
2800 W Prospect Rd 33309 954-485-1435
Fax 485-6023
St. Anthony S 300/PK-8
820 NE 3rd St 33301 954-467-7747
Norma Kramer, prin. Fax 467-9908
St. Clement S 100/PK-8
225 NW 29th St 33311 954-563-5608
Mary McKinney, prin. Fax 563-1355
St. Helen S 200/PK-8
3340 W Oakland Park Blvd 33311 954-739-7094
Barbara Wilson Ed.D., prin. Fax 739-0797
St. Jerome S 300/PK-8
2601 SW 9th Ave 33315 954-524-1990
Sr. Vivian Gomez, prin. Fax 524-7439
St. Mark's Episcopal S 600/PK-8
1750 E Oakland Park Blvd 33334 954-563-4508
Rev. William Brooks, hdmstr. Fax 563-0487
Shepherd of the Coast Lutheran S 50/PK-8
1901 E Commercial Blvd 33308 954-772-5468
Dr. Daniel Czaplewski, prin. Fax 772-2232
Trinity Lutheran Academy 100/K-8
11 SW 11th St 33315 954-463-7471
Candace Church, prin. Fax 463-3928
University S of Nova Southeastern Univ 1,900/PK-12
3301 College Ave 33314 954-262-4400
Dr. Jerome Chermak, hdmstr. Fax 262-3971
West Broward Christian S 50/PK-PK
17950 Griffin Rd 33331 954-680-5577
Kimberly Warters, dir. Fax 434-9215
Westminster Academy 1,000/PK-12
5601 N Federal Hwy 33308 954-771-4600
LeRoy Schwab, hdmstr. Fax 491-3021

Fort Mc Coy, Marion
Marion County SD
Supt. — See Ocala
Fort Mc Coy S 1,100/PK-8
16160 NE Highway 315 32134 352-671-6325
Robert Hensel, prin. Fax 671-6326

Fort Meade, Polk, Pop. 5,742
Polk County SD
Supt. — See Bartow
Woodbury ES - Lewis Campus 600/PK-3
115 S Oak Ave 33841 863-285-1150
Thaddeus Davis, prin. Fax 285-1155
Woodbury ES - Woodbury Campus 200/4-5
610 S Charleston Ave 33841 863-285-1133
Thaddeus Davis, prin. Fax 285-1138

Fort Myers, Lee, Pop. 58,428
Lee County SD 73,400/PK-12
2855 Colonial Blvd 33966 239-337-8300
Dr. James Browder, supt. Fax 337-8378
www.leeschools.net
Allen Park ES 900/PK-5
3345 Canelo Dr 33901 239-936-1459
Gini Moore, prin. Fax 936-3470
Colonial ES 800/PK-5
3800 Schoolhouse Rd E 33916 239-939-2242
Sandra Strausser, prin. Fax 939-5143
Cypress Lake MS 800/6-8
8901 Cypress Lake Dr 33919 239-481-1533
Jeananne Folaros, prin. Fax 481-3121
Dunbar MS 900/6-8
4750 Winkler Avenue Ext, 239-334-1357
Beth Ellen Bolger, prin. Fax 334-7633
Edgewood Academy 700/PK-5
3464 Edgewood Ave 33916 239-334-6205
Nancy Durham, prin. Fax 334-6776
Edison Park Creative/Expressive Arts ES 400/K-5
2401 Euclid Ave 33901 239-334-6232
Jamie Kirschner, prin. Fax 332-3474
Fort Myers Middle Academy 800/6-8
3050 Central Ave 33901 239-936-1759
Brian Botts, prin. Fax 936-4350
Franklin Park Magnet ES 500/PK-5
2323 Ford St 33916 239-332-1969
Yvonne Bryan, prin. Fax 337-1127
Gateway Magnet ES 900/K-5
13280 Griffin Dr 33913 239-768-3737
Nancy Adams, prin. Fax 768-2967
Hancock Creek ES 1,000/PK-5
1601 Skyline Dr 33903 239-995-3600
Kelly Vaughn, prin. Fax 995-7674
Heights ES 700/K-5
15200 Alexandria Ct 33908 239-481-1761
Diane Salko, prin. Fax 481-3154
Lee MS 700/6-8
1333 Marsh Ave 33905 239-337-1333
Vivian Smith, prin. Fax 334-4144
Lexington MS 900/6-8
16351 Summerlin Rd 33908 239-454-6130
Linda Caprarotta, prin. Fax 489-3419
Littleton ES 700/PK-5
700 Hutto Rd 33903 239-995-3800
Monica Broughton, prin. Fax 995-6551
Manatee ES 800/K-5
5301 Tice St 33905 239-694-2097
Jill Louzao, prin. Fax 694-4282
Michigan International Academy 700/PK-8
4312 Michigan Ave 33905 239-334-8411
Denise Phillips-Luster, prin. Fax 334-8262
Oak Hammock MS 6-8
5321 Tice St 33905 239-693-0469
Clayton Simmons, prin. Fax 694-4089
Orange River ES 900/PK-5
4501 Underwood Dr 33905 239-694-1258
Holly Bell, prin. Fax 694-8680
Orangewood ES 700/PK-5
4001 Deleon St 33901 239-936-2950
Michelle Pescatrice, prin. Fax 936-2134
Page ES 700/K-5
17000 S Tamiami Trl 33908 239-432-2737
Susan Caputo, prin. Fax 432-2749
Pottorf ES 800/K-5
4600 Challenger Blvd, 239-274-3932
Dorothy Whittaker, prin. Fax 275-3381
San Carlos Park ES 900/PK-5
17282 Lee Rd, 239-267-7177
Jill Van Waus, prin. Fax 267-0057
Tanglewood/Riverside ES 700/PK-5
1620 Manchester Blvd 33919 239-936-0891
Alane Adams, prin. Fax 939-0411
Three Oaks ES 900/PK-5
19600 Cypress View Dr, 239-267-8020
Dr. Vicki Parks, prin. Fax 267-9559
Three Oaks MS 800/6-8
18500 3 Oaks Pkwy, 239-267-5757
Mike Carson, prin. Fax 267-4007
Tice ES 700/PK-5
4524 Tice St 33905 239-694-1257
James Jackson, prin. Fax 694-8745
Treeline ES 700/K-5
10900 Treeline Ave 33913 239-768-5208
Dana Folsom, prin. Fax 768-5415
Villas ES 900/PK-5
8385 Beacon Blvd 33907 239-936-3776
Linda Buckley, prin. Fax 936-6884
Other Schools – See Alva, Bokeelia, Bonita Springs, Cape Coral, Estero, Fort Myers Beach, Lehigh Acres, North Fort Myers, Sanibel

---

Canterbury S 700/PK-12
8141 College Pkwy 33919 239-481-4323
John Paulus, hdmstr. Fax 481-8339
Crestwell S 200/PK-8
1901 Park Meadows Dr 33907 239-481-4478
Cindy Butterfield, prin. Fax 481-8125
Evangelical Christian S 1,000/PK-12
8237 Beacon Blvd 33907 239-936-3319
John Hunte, hdmstr. Fax 939-1445
Florida Christian Institute 200/K-12
940 Tarpon St Bldg E 33916 239-274-5935
Fort Myers Christian S 500/PK-8
1550 Colonial Blvd 33907 239-939-4642
Mel Mitchell, prin. Fax 936-5016
Mount Hermon Christian S 100/PK-6
2856 Douglas Ave 33916 239-334-8075
Eartha Oni, dir. Fax 334-3470
Noonan Elementary Academy 200/PK-8
6401 Techster Blvd, 239-561-7755
Nancy Sain, prin. Fax 561-0619
Renaissance S 100/PK-8
37 Barkley Cir 33907 239-275-2022
Kathleen Leitch, hdmstr. Fax 275-8638
St. Francis Xavier S 600/PK-8
2055 Heitman St 33901 239-334-7707
Janet Ortenzo, prin. Fax 334-8605
St. Michael Lutheran S 500/PK-8
3595 Broadway 33901 239-939-1218
Robert Ziegler, prin. Fax 939-1839
Sonshine Chistian Academy 100/PK-12
12925 Palm Beach Blvd 33905 239-694-8882
Ken Norvell, prin. Fax 694-8885
Southwest Florida Christian Academy 600/K-12
3750 Colonial Blvd, 239-936-8865
Dr. Phil Tingle, hdmstr. Fax 936-7095
Summit Christian S 100/PK-8
9065 Ligon Ct 33908 239-482-7007
Mary Lou Capan, hdmstr. Fax 454-7042

Fort Myers Beach, Lee, Pop. 6,834
Lee County SD
Supt. — See Fort Myers
Fort Myers Beach ES 200/K-5
2751 Oak St 33931 239-463-6356
Larry Wood, prin. Fax 463-3592

Fort Pierce, Saint Lucie, Pop. 38,552
St. Lucie County SD 37,200/PK-12
4204 Okeechobee Rd 34947 772-429-3600
Michael Lannon, supt. Fax 429-3916
www.stlucie.k12.fl.us/
Fairlawn ES 700/PK-5
3203 Rhode Island Ave 34947 772-468-5345
Susan Lyle, prin. Fax 467-4223
Forest Grove MS 1,000/6-8
3201 S 25th St 34981 772-468-5885
Charles Cuomo, prin. Fax 595-1187
Fort Pierce Magnet S of the Arts 400/K-12
1100 Delaware Ave 34950 772-467-4278
Dr. David Washington, prin. Fax 460-3094
Lakewood Park ES 700/K-5
7800 Indrio Rd 34951 772-468-5830
Scott Neil, prin. Fax 468-5833
Lawnwood ES 700/K-5
1900 S 23rd St 34950 772-468-5740
Felicia Nixon, prin. Fax 468-5204
McCarty MS 1,100/6-8
1201 Mississippi Ave 34950 772-468-5700
Kerry Padrick, prin. Fax 595-1124
Moore ES 600/PK-5
827 N 29th St 34947 772-468-5315
Keith Davis, prin. Fax 435-5896
Parkway ES 600/PK-5
7000 NW Selvitz Rd 34983 772-340-4800
Ucola Barrett-Baxter, prin. Fax 340-4807
Port St. Lucie ES 800/K-5
198 NW Marion Ave 34983 772-340-4820
Glenn Rustay, prin. Fax 340-4821
St. Lucie ES 800/PK-5
2020 S 13th St 34950 772-468-5213
Cindy Cobb, prin. Fax 468-5823
Sweet ES 700/PK-5
1400 Avenue Q 34950 772-468-5330
Juanita Wright, prin. Fax 468-5334
Weatherbee ES 600/PK-5
800 E Weatherbee Rd 34982 772-468-5300
Michael Hitsman, prin. Fax 468-4033
White City ES 600/K-5
905 W 2nd St 34982 772-468-5840
Jackie Lynch, prin. Fax 468-4067
Other Schools – See Port Saint Lucie

Bible Baptist S 100/PK-12
4401 S 25th St 34981 772-461-6630
Anita Hibbard, dir. Fax 461-7215
Faith Baptist S 300/PK-12
3607 Oleander Ave 34982 772-461-3607
Scott Birt, admin. Fax 461-4732
Liberty Baptist Academy 400/PK-12
3660 W Midway Rd 34981 772-461-2731
Dan Bousquet, prin. Fax 461-2542
Orange Avenue Baptist S 100/PK-12
100 Cyclone Dr 34945 772-461-1225
St. Anastasia S 700/PK-8
401 S 33rd St 34947 772-461-2232
Kevin Hoeffner, prin. Fax 468-2037
St. Andrew's Episcopal S 200/PK-8
210 S Indian River Dr 34950 772-461-7689
Gary Peirce, hdmstr. Fax 461-4683
Sampson Memorial SDA S 50/K-8
3201 Memory Ln 34981 772-465-8386
Deborah Dahl, prin. Fax 489-7858
Sun Grove Montessori S 100/PK-8
5610 Oleander Ave 34982 772-464-5436
Fax 464-0834

Fort Walton Beach, Okaloosa, Pop. 19,817
Okaloosa County SD 27,200/PK-12
120 Lowery Pl SE 32548 850-833-3100
Dr. Alexis Tibbetts, supt. Fax 833-3401
www.okaloosaschools.com/
Bruner MS 1,000/6-8
322 Holmes Blvd NW 32548 850-833-3266
John Spolski, prin. Fax 833-3434
Edwins ES 400/PK-5
7 Wright Pkwy SW 32548 850-833-3333
Dr. Connie Hall, prin. Fax 833-3480
Elliott Point ES 600/PK-5
301 Hughes St NE 32548 850-833-3355
Janet Stein, prin. Fax 833-3473
Kenwood ES 600/PK-5
15 Eagle St NE 32547 850-833-3570
Alan Lambert, prin. Fax 833-3597
Pryor MS 700/6-8
201 Racetrack Rd NW 32547 850-833-3613
Marcus Chambers, prin. Fax 833-4276
Wright ES 600/PK-5
305 Lang Rd 32547 850-833-3580
Cathy Hubeli, prin. Fax 833-3584
Other Schools – See Baker, Crestview, Destin, Eglin AFB, Laurel Hill, Mary Esther, Niceville, Shalimar, Valparaiso

---

Calvary Christian Academy 400/PK-12
535 Clifford St 32547 850-862-1414
Jon Gross, admin. Fax 862-9826
Cinco Baptist S 200/PK-5
26 Yacht Club Dr NE 32548 850-243-7515
Janet Zbydniewski, prin. Fax 243-1792
Emerald Coast Christian S 50/K-8
119 Saint Mary Ave SW 32548 850-243-1970
St. Mary S 400/PK-8
110 Robinwood Dr SW 32548 850-243-8913
Regina Nadicksbernd, prin. Fax 243-7895

Fort White, Columbia, Pop. 454
Columbia County SD
Supt. — See Lake City
Fort White ES 700/PK-5
18119 SW State Road 47 32038 386-497-2301
Wanda Conner, prin. Fax 497-4684

Freeport, Walton, Pop. 1,474
Walton County SD
Supt. — See De Funiak Springs
Freeport ES 600/PK-5
15381 331 Business 32439 850-892-1210
Pam Jones, prin. Fax 892-1219
Freeport MS 300/6-8
360 Kylea Laird Dr 32439 850-892-1220
Beth Tucker, prin. Fax 892-1229

Frostproof, Polk, Pop. 2,950
Polk County SD
Supt. — See Bartow
Frostproof ES 500/PK-2
118 W 3rd St 33843 863-635-7802
Kimberly Van Hook, prin. Fax 635-8501
Griffin ES 400/3-5
501 McCloud Rd 33843 863-635-7820
Patti McGill, prin. Fax 635-8500

Fruitland Park, Lake, Pop. 3,578
Lake County SD
Supt. — See Tavares
Fruitland Park ES 700/PK-5
304 W Fountain St 34731 352-787-2693
Melissa DeJarlais, prin. Fax 787-9402

Gainesville, Alachua, Pop. 108,184
Alachua County SD 27,000/PK-12
620 E University Ave 32601 352-955-7300
Dr. W. Daniel Boyd, supt. Fax 955-6700
www.sbac.edu/
Bishop MS 900/6-8
1901 NE 9th St 32609 352-955-6701
Mike Thorne, prin. Fax 955-6966
Chiles ES 800/PK-5
2525 School House Rd 32608 352-333-2825
Judy Black, prin. Fax 333-2826
Duval ES 500/PK-5
2106 NE 8th Ave 32641 352-955-6703
Dr. Leanetta McNealy, prin. Fax 955-6967
Fearnside Family Services Center 50/PK-PK
3600 NE 15th St 32609 352-955-6875
Ann Crowell, prin. Fax 955-6965
Finley ES 400/PK-5
1912 NW 5th Ave 32603 352-955-6705
Donna Jones, prin. Fax 955-7128
Ft. Clarke MS 900/6-8
9301 NW 23rd Ave 32606 352-333-2800
Donna Kidwell, prin. Fax 333-2806
Foster ES 400/PK-5
3800 NW 6th St 32609 352-955-6706
Dr. Darla Boyd, prin. Fax 955-6746
Glen Springs ES 400/PK-5
2826 NW 31st Ave 32605 352-955-6708
Dr. Leon Henderson, prin. Fax 955-7304
Hidden Oak ES 800/PK-5
9205 NW 23rd Ave 32606 352-333-2801
Frank Burns, prin. Fax 333-2805
Idylwild ES 600/PK-5
4601 SW 20th Ter 32608 352-955-6709
Dr. John Fielding, prin. Fax 955-7123
Kanapaha MS 900/6-8
5005 SW 75th St 32608 352-955-6960
Jennifer Wise, prin. Fax 955-6858
Lake Forest ES 400/PK-5
4401 SE 4th Ave 32641 352-955-6710
Diane Hill, prin. Fax 955-6750
Lincoln MS 800/6-8
1001 SE 12th St 32641 352-955-6711
Don Lewis, prin. Fax 955-7133
Littlewood ES 600/PK-5
812 NW 34th St 32605 352-955-6712
Katherine Munn, prin. Fax 955-7149
Metcalfe ES 400/PK-5
1250 NE 18th Ave 32609 352-955-6713
Felecia Moss, prin. Fax 955-6753
Norton ES 700/PK-5
2200 NW 45th Ave 32605 352-955-6765
Gail Hamilton, prin. Fax 955-7126
Rawlings ES 400/PK-5
3500 NE 15th St 32609 352-955-6715
Emory Bishop, prin. Fax 955-7137
Talbot ES 700/PK-5
5701 NW 43rd St 32653 352-955-6716
Brad Burklew, prin. Fax 955-7132
Terwilliger ES 600/PK-5
301 NW 62nd St 32607 352-955-6717
Dr. Beth LeClear, prin. Fax 955-7134
Westwood MS 900/6-8
3215 NW 15th Ave 32605 352-955-6718
James Tenbieg, prin. Fax 955-6897
Wiles ES 700/PK-5
4601 SW 75th St 32608 352-955-6955
Dr. Barbara Buys, prin. Fax 955-7124
Williams ES 500/PK-5
1245 SE 7th Ave 32641 352-955-6719
Katherine Dixon, prin. Fax 955-6759
Other Schools – See Alachua, Archer, Hawthorne, High Springs, Newberry, Waldo

---

Brentwood S 300/PK-5
1111 NW 55th St 32605 352-373-3222
Robert Schackow, prin. Fax 378-7848
Compassionate Outreach Ministries Acad 50/K-5
PO Box 143116 32614 352-373-1888
Margaret Dennison, prin. Fax 335-9684
Cornerstone Academy 200/PK-12
PO Box 357430 32635 352-378-9337
Doug Lawson, hdmstr. Fax 378-7708
Countryside Christian S 100/PK-12
10926 NW 39th Ave 32606 352-332-9731
Gainesville Country Day S 300/PK-5
6801 SW 24th Ave 32607 352-332-7783
Nancy Childers, prin. Fax 331-7613
Millhopper Montessori S 200/PK-8
8505 NW 39th Ave 32606 352-375-6773
Christina Miller, prin. Fax 374-7125
Oak Hall Lower S 400/PK-5
7715 SW 14th Ave 32607 352-332-1452
Richard Gehman, hdmstr. Fax 332-4945
Queen of Peace Academy 300/PK-8
10900 SW 24th Ave 32607 352-332-8808
Sr. Nancy Elder, prin. Fax 331-7347
Rock S 200/PK-12
9818 SW 24th Ave 32607 352-331-7625
Bob Carter, prin. Fax 331-9760
St. Patrick Interparish S 500/PK-8
550 NE 16th Ave 32601 352-376-9878
Sandra Vahl, prin. Fax 371-6177
Star Christian Academy 50/PK-9
6702 NW 28th Ter 32653 352-336-5300
Phyllis Thomas-Dykes, prin. Fax 372-2994
Sung SDA S 50/K-12
2115 NW 39th Ave 32605 352-376-6040
Westwood Hills Christian S 200/PK-12
1520 NW 34th St 32605 352-378-5190
Jay Jethro, prin. Fax 371-6782
Windsor Christian Academy 50/1-12
918 SE County Road 234 32641 352-375-7316
Mike Redmond, admin. Fax 375-7316

Geneva, Seminole
Seminole County SD
Supt. — See Sanford
Geneva ES 500/PK-5
275 1st St 32732 407-320-4950
Dr. Tina Erwin, prin. Fax 320-4981

Gibsonton, Hillsborough, Pop. 7,706
Hillsborough County SD
Supt. — See Tampa
Corr ES 600/K-5
13020 Kings Lake Dr 33534 813-672-5345
Sylvia Hastings, prin. Fax 672-5349
Eisenhower MS 1,500/6-8
7620 Old Big Bend Rd 33534 813-671-5121
Dena Collins, prin. Fax 671-5039
Gibsonton ES 800/PK-5
7723 Gibsonton Dr 33534 813-671-5100
Donna Marra, prin. Fax 672-5003

Glen Saint Mary, Baker, Pop. 537
Baker County SD
Supt. — See Macclenny
Westside ES 700/1-3
1 Panther Cir 32040 904-259-2216
Lynne Fort, prin. Fax 259-5172

Gotha, Orange

Central Florida Preparatory S 400/PK-12
PO Box 817 34734 407-290-8073
Rowena Flanders-Ramos, dir. Fax 298-6443

Goulds, Miami-Dade, Pop. 7,284
Miami-Dade County SD
Supt. — See Miami
Mays MS 800/6-8
11700 SW 216th St 33170 305-233-2300
Kenneth Cooper, prin. Fax 251-5462

Graceville, Jackson, Pop. 2,423
Holmes County SD
Supt. — See Bonifay
Poplar Springs S 300/PK-12
3726 Atomic Dr 32440 850-263-6260
Gordon Wells, prin. Fax 263-1252

Jackson County SD
Supt. — See Marianna
Graceville ES 300/PK-5
5331 Alabama St 32440 850-263-4402
Barbara Mixson, prin. Fax 263-3304

Grand Ridge, Jackson, Pop. 802
Jackson County SD
Supt. — See Marianna
Grand Ridge S 600/PK-12
6925 Florida St 32442 850-482-9835
Randy Ward, prin. Fax 482-9834

Greenacres, Palm Beach, Pop. 32,525
Palm Beach County SD
Supt. — See West Palm Beach
Cholee Lake ES 1,100/K-5
6680 Dillman Rd 33413 561-383-9600
Eugina Smith-Feaman Ed.D., prin. Fax 383-9650
Diamond View ES 900/K-5
5300 Haverhill Rd 33463 561-304-4200
Carolyn Seal, prin. Fax 304-4210
Greenacres ES 600/K-5
405 Jackson Ave 33463 561-434-8197
Patricia Lucas, prin. Fax 434-8948
Heritage ES 800/K-5
5100 Melaleuca Ln 33463 561-804-3200
Seth Moldovan, prin. Fax 804-3250
Liberty Park ES 800/K-5
6601 Constitution Way 33413 561-804-3400
Miriam Williams, prin. Fax 804-3450
Swain MS 1,100/6-8
5332 Lake Worth Rd 33463 561-649-6900
Edward Harris, prin. Fax 649-6910

Greenacres Christian Academy 100/PK-12
4982 Cambridge St 33463 561-965-0363
Billy Fritsch, prin. Fax 439-7149

Green Cove Springs, Clay, Pop. 6,085
Clay County SD 35,200/PK-12
900 Walnut St 32043 904-284-6500
Ben Wortham, supt. Fax 284-6525
www.clay.k12.fl.us/
Bennett ES 700/PK-6
1 S Oakridge Ave 32043 904-529-2126
Evelyn Chastain, prin. Fax 529-2133
Green Cove Springs JHS 900/7-8
1220 Bonaventure Ave 32043 904-529-2140
Dr. Saryn Hatcher, prin. Fax 529-2144
Lake Asbury ES 1,400/K-6
2901 Sandridge Rd 32043 904-291-5440
Jackie Cory, prin. Fax 291-5444
Lake Asbury JHS 1,100/7-8
2851 Sandridge Rd 32043 904-291-5582
Cathy Richardson, prin. Fax 291-5593
Shadowlawn ES PK-6
2945 County Road 218 32043 904-529-1007
Dale Eichhorn, prin.
Other Schools – See Jacksonville, Keystone Heights, Middleburg, Orange Park

Greenville, Madison, Pop. 829
Madison County SD
Supt. — See Madison
Greenville ES 100/PK-5
729 SW Overstreet Ave 32331 850-973-5033
Davis Barclay, prin. Fax 973-5040

Gretna, Gadsden, Pop. 1,699
Gadsden County SD
Supt. — See Quincy
Gretna ES 400/PK-5
706 M L King Blvd 32332 850-856-5249
Lisa Robinson, prin. Fax 856-9415

Groveland, Lake, Pop. 5,205
Lake County SD
Supt. — See Tavares
Gray MS 1,300/6-8
205 E Magnolia St 34736 352-429-3322
Janice Boyd, prin. Fax 429-0133
Groveland ES 1,000/PK-5
930 Parkwood Ave 34736 352-429-2472
Dale Delpit, prin. Fax 429-2516

Bright Horizons Christian Academy K-5
21800 Groveland Ave 34736 352-429-8059

Gulf Breeze, Santa Rosa, Pop. 6,455
Santa Rosa County SD
Supt. — See Milton
Gulf Breeze ES 700/K-5
549 Gulf Breeze Pkwy 32561 850-934-5185
Karen Murray, prin. Fax 934-5189
Gulf Breeze MS 900/6-8
649 Gulf Breeze Pkwy 32561 850-934-4080
Jennifer Granse, prin. Fax 934-4085
Oriole Beach ES 800/PK-5
1260 Oriole Beach Rd 32563 850-934-5160
Dawn Alt, prin. Fax 934-5166
Woodlawn Beach MS 900/6-8
1500 Woodlawn Way 32563 850-934-4010
Victor Lowrimore, prin. Fax 934-4015

Good Shepherd Lutheran S 50/PK-8
4257 Gulf Breeze Pkwy 32563 850-932-9127
Connie Omelian, prin. Fax 932-7830
St. Ann Discovery S 100/PK-PK
PO Box 1057 32562 850-932-9330
Jean Jones, dir. Fax 934-2804

Gulfport, Pinellas, Pop. 12,661
Pinellas County SD
Supt. — See Largo
Gulfport ES 500/PK-5
2014 52nd St S 33707 727-893-2643
Lisa Grant, prin. Fax 552-1574

Most Holy Name of Jesus ECC 100/PK-PK
1508 59th St S 33707 727-347-1774
Carrie Eveland, dir. Fax 343-6420

Gulf Stream, Palm Beach, Pop. 751

Gulf Stream S 300/PK-8
3600 Gulfstream Rd 33483 561-276-5225
Joseph Zaluski, hdmstr. Fax 276-7115

Haines City, Polk, Pop. 16,371
Polk County SD
Supt. — See Bartow
Alta Vista ES 1,000/PK-5
801 Scenic Hwy 33844 863-421-3235
Victor Duncan, prin. Fax 421-3344
Bethune Academy 500/K-5
900 Avenue F 33844 863-421-3334
Sharon Knowles, prin. Fax 421-3243
Boone MS 1,000/6-8
225 S 22nd St 33844 863-421-3302
Nancy Leonard, prin. Fax 421-3305
Eastside ES 1,100/PK-5
1820 E Johnson Ave 33844 863-421-3254
Sharon Hartwig, prin. Fax 421-3256
Sandhill ES 1,000/PK-5
1801 Tyner Rd 33844 863-419-3166
Sue Buckner, prin. Fax 419-3167

Landmark Christian S 300/PK-12
2020 E Hinson Ave 33844 863-422-2037
Wallace Hill, admin. Fax 419-1256
Northridge Christian Academy 300/PK-10
2250 State Road 17 S 33844 863-422-3473
Misty Rutledge, prin. Fax 421-2582

Hallandale, Broward, Pop. 31,163
Broward County SD
Supt. — See Fort Lauderdale
Gulfstream MS 300/6-8
120 SW 4th Ave 33009 754-323-4700
Debra Patterson, prin. Fax 323-4785
Hallandale ES 1,200/PK-5
900 SW 8th St 33009 754-323-5950
Sharon Ludwig, prin. Fax 323-5990

Hampton, Bradford, Pop. 448
Bradford County SD
Supt. — See Starke
Hampton ES 200/PK-5
PO Box 200 32044 904-966-6884
Rick Stephens, prin. Fax 966-6883

Havana, Gadsden, Pop. 1,701
Gadsden County SD
Supt. — See Quincy
Havana ES 600/PK-5
705 S US Highway 27 32333 850-539-2877
Hilda Jackson, prin. Fax 539-2878
Havana MS 300/6-8
1210 Kemp Rd 32333 850-539-2822
Dr. Verna Norris, prin. Fax 539-2866

Metropolitan Christian Acad of the Arts 100/PK-7
1110 Rich Bay Rd 32333 850-539-3718
Mary Colson-Clayton, admin. Fax 539-3721
Tallavana Christian S 200/PK-12
5840 Havana Hwy 32333 850-539-5300

Hawthorne, Alachua, Pop. 1,443
Alachua County SD
Supt. — See Gainesville
Shell ES 200/PK-5
21633 SE 65th Ave 32640 352-481-1901
Dr. Gladys Wright, prin. Fax 481-1911

Putnam County SD
Supt. — See Palatka
Ochwilla ES 500/PK-5
299 N State Road 21 32640 352-481-0204
Neil Stephenson, prin. Fax 481-5541

Hernando, Citrus, Pop. 2,103
Citrus County SD
Supt. — See Inverness
Forest Ridge ES 800/PK-5
2927 N Forest Ridge Blvd 34442 352-527-1808
Donnie Brown, prin. Fax 527-1809
Hernando ES 700/PK-5
2975 E Trailblazer Ln 34442 352-726-1833
Belinda Woythaler, prin. Fax 726-3380

Hialeah, Miami-Dade, Pop. 220,485
Miami-Dade County SD
Supt. — See Miami
Bright ES 800/K-6
2530 W 10th Ave 33010 305-885-1683
Maritza Garcia, prin. Fax 888-7059
Dupuis ES 900/PK-5
1150 W 59th Pl 33012 305-821-6361
Claudine Winsor, prin. Fax 825-2433
Earhart ES 600/PK-6
5987 E 7th Ave 33013 305-688-9619
Dr. Ada Hernandez, prin. Fax 769-9038
Filer MS 1,200/6-8
531 W 29th St 33012 305-822-6601
Julian Cazanas, prin. Fax 822-2063
Flamingo ES 900/PK-6
701 E 33rd St 33013 305-691-5531
Claudia James, prin. Fax 835-8525
Good ES 1,500/PK-5
6350 NW 188th Ter 33015 305-625-2008
Lizette O'Halloran, prin. Fax 628-0460
Graham ES 2,200/PK-6
7330 W 32nd Ave 33018 305-825-2122
Mayra Alfaro, prin. Fax 557-5739
Graham Primary Learning Center PK-K
8875 NW 143rd St 33018 305-231-8778
Fax 231-9034
Hialeah ES 900/PK-5
550 E 8th St 33010 305-888-6709
Carolina Naveiras, prin. Fax 884-6503
Hialeah Gardens ES 1,500/PK-5
9702 NW 130th St 33018 305-827-8830
Ivette Bernal-Pino, prin. Fax 818-7970
Hialeah Gardens Primary Learning Center PK-K
9749 NW 127th St 33018 305-818-7976
Fax 818-7978
Hialeah MS 1,100/6-8
6027 E 7th Ave 33013 305-681-3527
Lourdes Diaz, prin. Fax 681-6225
Johnson ES 100/PK-5
735 W 23rd St 33010 305-883-1357
Maritza Garcia, prin. Fax 883-9462
Marti MS 1,300/6-8
5701 W 24th Ave 33016 305-557-5931
Jose Enriquez, prin. Fax 556-6917
Meadowlane ES 1,200/PK-5
4280 W 8th Ave 33012 305-822-0660
Dr. Kevin Hart, prin. Fax 362-9904
Miami Lakes MS 1,200/6-8
6425 Miami Lakeway N 33014 305-557-3900
Joaquin Hernandez, prin. Fax 828-6753
Miami Lakes Preschool PK-PK
14250 NW 67th Ave 33014 305-822-7757
Fax 557-6595
Miami Lakes S 1,300/PK-8
14250 NW 67th Ave 33014 305-822-7757
Rosa Calvo, prin. Fax 557-6595
Milam K-8 Center 1,400/PK-8
6020 W 16th Ave 33012 305-822-0301
Anna Hernandez, prin. Fax 556-1388
North Hialeah ES 700/PK-6
4251 E 5th Ave 33013 305-681-4611
John Schoeck, prin. Fax 688-6652
North Twin Lakes ES 700/PK-5
625 W 74th Pl 33014 305-822-0721
Robert Kalinsky, prin. Fax 558-1697
Palm Lakes ES 900/PK-5
7450 W 16th Ave 33014 305-823-6970
Alina Iglesias, prin. Fax 828-6136
Palm Springs ES 900/PK-6
6304 E 1st Ave 33013 305-822-0911
Roxana Herrera, prin. Fax 828-5802
Palm Springs North ES 1,700/PK-5
17615 NW 82nd Ave 33015 305-821-4631
Dr. Manuel Sanchez, prin. Fax 825-0422
Sheppard ES 1,400/K-5
5700 W 24th Ave 33016 305-556-2204
Dr. Georgette Menocal, prin. Fax 822-0558
Sheppard Primary Learning Center PK-K
5601 W 24th Ave 33016 305-818-7984
Fax 818-7986
South Hialeah ES 1,100/PK-5
265 E 5th St 33010 305-885-4556
Dr. Julio Carrera, prin. Fax 888-7730
Twin Lakes ES 700/PK-6
6735 W 5th Pl 33012 305-822-0770
Maria DeLeon, prin. Fax 824-0915
Walters ES 900/PK-5
650 W 33rd St 33012 305-822-4600
Yolanda Valls, prin. Fax 827-4465

Asbury Christian S 200/PK-5
5559 Palm Ave 33012 305-823-5313
Champagnat Catholic S 300/PK-12
369 E 10th St 33010 305-888-3760
Maria Alonso, prin. Fax 883-1174
Edison Private S 400/PK-12
3720 E 4th Ave 33013 305-824-0303
Fax 822-4205
Faith Lutheran S 100/PK-8
293 Hialeah Dr 33010 305-885-2845
Ruth Wessling, prin. Fax 885-2845
Horeb Christian S 300/PK-12
795 W 68th St 33014 305-557-6811
Jesus Perez, prin. Fax 821-5048
Immaculate Conception S 900/PK-8
125 W 45th St 33012 305-822-6461
Eddy Garcia, prin. Fax 822-0289
Lincoln-Marti S 100/PK-8
90 W 11th St 33010 305-883-1222
Lincoln-Marti S 300/PK-12
1750 E 4th Ave 33010 305-884-1570
Lincoln-Marti S 500/PK-8
7675 W 32nd Ave 33018 305-826-4214
North Hialeah Christian S 50/PK-5
5800 Palm Ave 33012 305-557-2821
Rev. Dan Ramos, prin. Fax 821-4022
Nuestra Senora De Lourdes S 200/PK-1
1164 W 71st St 33014 305-822-2645
St. John the Apostle S 400/PK-8
479 E 4th St 33010 305-888-6819
Lyn Bymonte, prin. Fax 887-1256
St. Luke Christian S 50/PK-5
660 E 41st St 33013 305-836-3623
Thumbelina Learning Center #4 200/PK-8
3580 W 84th St 33018 305-556-8116
Ubaldo Interian, prin. Fax 556-8589
Trinity Christian Academy 100/PK-12
1498 W 84th St 33014 305-819-8999
Joseph Jimenez, prin. Fax 819-2554

Hialeah Gardens, Miami-Dade, Pop. 19,930
Miami-Dade County SD
Supt. — See Miami
Hialeah Gardens MS 6-8
11690 NW 92nd Ave 33018 305-817-0017
Martha Montiel, prin. Fax 817-0018
West Hialeah Gardens ES 700/PK-5
11990 NW 92nd Ave 33018 305-818-4000
Sharon Gonzalez, prin. Fax 818-4001

Highland City, Polk, Pop. 1,919
Polk County SD
Supt. — See Bartow
Highland City ES 600/K-5
PO Box 1327 33846 863-648-3540
Chris Roberts, prin. Fax 648-3542

High Springs, Alachua, Pop. 4,157
Alachua County SD
Supt. — See Gainesville
High Springs Community S 1,000/K-8
1015 N Main St 32643 386-454-1958
Jeffrey Means, prin. Fax 454-2298

First Christian Academy 100/PK-4
24530 NW 199th Ln 32643 386-454-1641
Juli Marcus, admin. Fax 454-9727
Living Springs Academy 50/1-12
23901 NW 212th Ave 32643 386-454-2777
Jerry Kiernan, admin. Fax 454-2767

Hilliard, Nassau, Pop. 2,913
Nassau County SD
Supt. — See Fernandina Beach
Hilliard ES 700/PK-5
27568 Ohio St 32046 904-491-7939
Kristi Simpkins, prin. Fax 845-7427

Hobe Sound, Martin, Pop. 11,507
Martin County SD
Supt. — See Stuart
Hobe Sound ES 600/K-5
11550 SE Gomez Ave 33455 772-219-1540
Joan Gibbons, prin. Fax 219-1546
SeaWind ES 600/K-5
3700 SE Seabranch Blvd 33455 772-219-1625
Larry Green, prin. Fax 219-1631

Florida Unschoolers 200/K-12
8680 SE Eagle Ave 33455 772-486-6146
Nance Confer, dir.
Hobe Sound Christian Academy 200/K-12
PO Box 1065 33475 772-545-1455
Dr. Randall McElwan, prin. Fax 545-1454

Holiday, Pasco, Pop. 19,360
Pasco County SD
Supt. — See Land O Lakes
Gulfside ES 600/K-5
2329 Anclote Blvd 34691 727-774-6000
Chris Clayton, prin. Fax 774-6091
Gulf Trace ES 200/K-5
3303 Gulf Trace Blvd 34691 727-246-3600
Hope Schooler, prin. Fax 246-3691
Smith MS 900/6-8
1410 Sweetbriar Dr 34691 727-246-3200
Dr. Chris Dunning, prin. Fax 246-3291
Sunray ES 900/K-5
4815 Sunray Dr 34690 727-774-9100
Yvonne Reins, prin. Fax 774-9191

New Covenant Academy 50/K-8
4923 Darlington Rd 34690 727-939-2400
Dr. Joseph Cerreta, admin. Fax 937-7182
World of Knowledge A Montessori S 100/PK-9
1935 Abacus Rd 34690 727-934-3028
Gail Gilmore, dir. Fax 937-0642

Holly Hill, Volusia, Pop. 12,630
Volusia County SD
Supt. — See De Land
Holly Hill ES, 1500 Center Ave 32117 600/PK-5
Julie Roseboom, prin. 386-258-4662
Holly Hill MS 600/6-8
1200 Center Ave 32117 386-258-4663
John Polsinelli, prin. Fax 239-6314
Hurst ES 400/PK-5
1340 Wright St 32117 386-258-4664
Maryann Bull, prin. Fax 239-6240

Trinity Lutheran S 100/PK-5
1205 Ridgewood Ave 32117 386-255-7580
Barbara Phillips, prin. Fax 323-1691

Hollywood, Broward, Pop. 145,629
Broward County SD
Supt. — See Fort Lauderdale
Apollo MS 1,200/6-8
6800 Arthur St 33024 754-323-2900
Aimee Zekofsky, prin. Fax 323-2985
Attucks MS 1,000/6-8
3500 N 22nd Ave 33020 754-323-3000
Carletha Shaw, prin. Fax 323-3085
Bethune ES 800/PK-5
2400 Meade St 33020 754-323-4900
Mary Lou Ridge, prin. Fax 323-4940
Boulevard Heights ES 900/PK-5
7201 Johnson St 33024 754-323-4950
Linda Pazos, prin. Fax 323-4990
Colbert ES 700/PK-5
2701 Plunkett St 33020 754-323-5100
Dr. Michael Cosimano, prin. Fax 323-5140
Driftwood ES 700/PK-5
2700 NW 69th Ave 33024 754-323-5450
Gladys Donovan, prin. Fax 323-5490
Driftwood MS 1,600/6-8
2751 NW 70th Ter 33024 754-323-3100
Jody Perry, prin. Fax 323-3185
Hollywood Central ES 700/K-5
1700 Monroe St 33020 754-323-6150
Frances Merenstein, prin. Fax 323-6190
Hollywood Hills ES 800/K-5
3501 Taft St 33021 754-323-6200
Vered Roberts, prin. Fax 323-6240
Hollywood Park ES 600/PK-5
901 NW 69th Way 33024 754-323-6250
Wendy Galinsky, prin. Fax 323-6290
Lake Forest ES 900/PK-5
3550 SW 48th Ave 33023 754-323-6350
Dr. Pamela Garwood, prin. Fax 323-6390
McNicol MS 1,100/6-8
1602 S 27th Ave 33020 754-323-3400
Darren Jones, prin. Fax 323-3485
Oakridge ES 800/PK-5
1507 N 28th Ave 33020 754-323-6700
Alan Gatzke, prin. Fax 323-6740
Orange-Brook ES 800/PK-5
715 S 46th Ave 33021 754-323-6750
Dr. Joanne Nitti, prin. Fax 323-6790
Sheridan Hills ES 700/PK-5
5001 Thomas St 33021 754-323-7300
Donald Fitz, prin. Fax 323-7340
Sheridan Park ES 800/PK-5
2310 NW 70th Ter 33024 754-323-7350
Maria Calzadilla-Tracy, prin. Fax 323-7390
Stirling ES 700/PK-5
5500 Stirling Rd 33021 754-323-7600
Alfred Dobronz, prin. Fax 323-7640
West Hollywood ES 700/PK-5
6301 Hollywood Blvd 33024 754-323-7850
Marisol Smith, prin. Fax 323-7890

Aukela Christian Military Academy 100/PK-12
2835 Madison St 33020 954-929-7010
Audrey Rodriguez, prin. Fax 927-2523
Beacon Hill S 200/PK-8
7600 Davie Road Ext 33024 954-963-2600
Andrew Liss, dir. Fax 963-2878
Hollywood Christian Academy 500/PK-12
1708 N State Road 7 33021 954-966-2350
Dr. Michael Chivalette, hdmstr. Fax 966-0097
Little Flower S 300/PK-8
1843 Pierce St 33020 954-922-1217
Maureen McNulty, prin. Fax 927-8962
Nativity S 900/PK-8
5200 Johnson St 33021 954-987-3300
Elena Ortiz, prin. Fax 987-6368
St. Bernadette S 300/PK-8
7450 Stirling Rd 33024 954-432-7022
Michelle Sanders, prin. Fax 443-8030
St. Mark's Lutheran Church S 200/PK-8
502 N 28th Ave 33020 954-922-7572
Rev. George Poulos, prin. Fax 925-5388
Sheridan Hills Christian S 600/PK-12
3751 Sheridan St 33021 954-966-7995
Roy Johnson, hdmstr. Fax 961-1359

Holmes Beach, Manatee, Pop. 5,100
Manatee County SD
Supt. — See Bradenton
Anna Maria ES 300/K-5
4700 Gulf Dr 34217 941-708-5525
Tom Levengood, prin. Fax 708-5529

Homestead, Miami-Dade, Pop. 44,494
Miami-Dade County SD
Supt. — See Miami
Air Base ES 700/PK-5
12829 SW 272nd St 33032 305-258-3676
Raul Calzadilla, prin. Fax 258-7241
Avocado ES 1,100/K-5
16969 SW 294th St 33030 305-247-4942
Cory Rodriguez, prin. Fax 246-9603
Campbell Drive MS 1,100/6-8
900 NE 23rd Ave 33033 305-248-7911
Evonne Alvarez, prin. Fax 248-3518
Chapman ES 900/PK-5
27190 SW 140th Ave 33032 305-245-1055
Carzell Morris, prin. Fax 245-1187
Coconut Palm K-8 Academy K-8
24400 SW 124th Ave 33032 305-257-0500
Dr. Linda Roberts, prin. Fax 257-0501
Goulds ES 500/PK-5
23555 SW 112th Ave 33032 305-257-4400
Crystal Coffey, prin. Fax 257-4401
Homestead MS 1,200/6-8
650 NW 2nd Ave 33030 305-247-4221
Nikolai Vitti, prin. Fax 247-1098

Leisure City S 1,500/PK-8
14950 SW 288th St 33033 305-247-5431
Kelli Hunter, prin. Fax 247-5179
Mandarin Lakes K-8 Academy 1,200/K-8
12225 SW 280th St 33032 305-257-0377
Angeles Fleites, prin. Fax 257-0378
Peskoe ES 1,300/K-5
29035 SW 144th Ave 33033 305-242-8340
Maria Acosta, prin. Fax 242-8351
Redland ES 1,100/K-5
24501 SW 162nd Ave 33031 305-247-8141
Eileen Medina, prin. Fax 242-4698
Redland MS 1,500/6-8
16001 SW 248th St 33031 305-247-6112
Craig DePriest, prin. Fax 248-0628
Redondo ES 900/PK-5
18480 SW 304th St 33030 305-247-5943
Dr. Rene Baly, prin. Fax 242-0318
Saunders ES 900/PK-5
505 SW 8th St 33030 305-247-3933
Suzet Hernandez, prin. Fax 247-8522
South Dade MS 900/4-8
29100 SW 194th Ave 33030 305-224-5200
Brian Hamilton, prin. Fax 224-5201
West Homestead ES 800/PK-5
1550 SW 6th St 33030 305-248-0812
Prudence Ingraham, prin. Fax 247-3205

Colonial Christian S 200/PK-12
17105 SW 296th St 33030 305-246-8608
Terri Morrissey, prin. Fax 246-1542
Faith Fellowship S 50/1-9
28945 SW 187th Ave 33030 305-246-5534
Melissa Muniz, prin. Fax 246-5586
First United Methodist Christian S 200/PK-5
622A N Krome Ave 33030 305-248-7992
Mercy Nyman, dir. Fax 243-2512
Kingswood Montessori S 100/PK-8
20130 SW 304th St 33030 305-248-2308
David Calabrese, admin. Fax 248-4484
Redland Christian Academy 200/PK-12
17700 SW 280th St 33031 305-247-7399
Sharon Waldbillig, dir. Fax 247-1147
Sacred Heart S 200/PK-8
300 SE 1st Dr 33030 305-247-2678
August Silva, prin. Fax 248-6794
St. John's Episcopal S 200/PK-8
145 NE 10th St 33030 305-247-5445
Fr. George Ronkowitz, hdmstr. Fax 245-4063

Homosassa, Citrus, Pop. 2,113
Citrus County SD
Supt. — See Inverness
Homosassa ES 400/PK-5
PO Box 498 34487 352-628-2953
Scott Hebert, prin. Fax 628-5408
Rock Crusher ES 700/PK-5
814 S Rock Crusher Rd 34448 352-795-2010
John Weed, prin. Fax 795-4742

Hosford, Liberty
Liberty County SD
Supt. — See Bristol
Hosford S 300/PK-8
PO Box 10 32334 850-379-8480
Hal Summers, prin. Fax 379-8703

Hudson, Pasco, Pop. 7,344
Pasco County SD
Supt. — See Land O Lakes
Hudson ES 800/PK-5
7229 Hudson Ave 34667 727-774-4000
Linda McCarthy, prin. Fax 774-4091
Hudson MS 1,200/6-8
14540 Cobra Way 34669 727-774-8200
Steve Van Gorden, prin. Fax 774-8291
Northwest ES 700/PK-5
14302 Cobra Way 34669 727-774-4700
Tracy Graziaplene, prin. Fax 774-4791

Grace Christian S 200/PK-12
9403 Scot St 34669 727-863-1825
Glenwood Pratt, prin. Fax 862-4484

Immokalee, Collier, Pop. 14,120
Collier County SD
Supt. — See Naples
Eden Park ES K-5
3655 Westclox St 34142 239-377-9200
Melba Meriwether, prin. Fax 377-9201
Highlands ES 700/K-5
1101 Lake Trafford Rd 34142 239-377-7100
Sean Kinsley, prin. Fax 377-7101
Immokalee MS 1,100/6-8
401 N 9th St 34142 239-377-4200
Lisa Rivera-Scallan, prin. Fax 377-4201
Lake Trafford ES 900/PK-5
3500 Lake Trafford Rd 34142 239-377-7300
Robert Murray, prin. Fax 377-7301
Pinecrest ES 600/K-5
313 S 9th St 34142 239-377-8000
Dr. Connie Helton, prin. Fax 377-8001
Village Oaks ES 600/K-5
1601 State Road 29 S 34142 239-377-8600
Dorcas Howard, prin. Fax 377-8601

Indialantic, Brevard, Pop. 3,076
Brevard County SD
Supt. — See Melbourne
Hoover MS 500/7-8
2000 Hawk Haven Dr 32903 321-727-1611
Barbara Rodrigues, prin. Fax 725-0076
Indialantic ES 800/PK-6
1050 N Palm Ave 32903 321-723-2811
Mary Cassidy, prin. Fax 952-5848

Holy Name Jesus S 500/PK-8
3060 N Highway A1A 32903 321-773-1630
Mary Massey, prin. Fax 773-7148

Indian Harbor Beach, Brevard, Pop. 7,530
Brevard County SD
Supt. — See Melbourne
Ocean Breeze ES 500/PK-6
1101 Cheyenne Dr 32937 321-779-2040
Colleen Skinner, prin. Fax 779-2045

Indian Harbour Montessori S 200/PK-6
1230 Banana River Dr 32937 321-777-1480
Denise Johnson, prin. Fax 777-9566

Indiantown, Martin, Pop. 4,794
Martin County SD
Supt. — See Stuart
Indiantown MS 400/5-8
16303 SW Farm Rd 34956 772-597-2146
Debbie Henderson, prin. Fax 597-5854
Warfield ES 600/K-4
15260 SW 150th St 34956 772-597-2551
Loreen Francescani, prin. Fax 597-2119

Hope Rural S 100/PK-5
15929 SW 150th St 34956 772-597-2203
Sr. Katherine Kinnally, prin. Fax 597-2259

Interlachen, Putnam, Pop. 1,518
Putnam County SD
Supt. — See Palatka
Interlachen ES 800/PK-5
251 S County Road 315 32148 386-684-2130
Suzanne Mathe, prin. Fax 684-3909
Price MS 600/6-8
140 N County Road 315 32148 386-684-2113
Leah Lundy, prin. Fax 684-3908

Inverness, Citrus, Pop. 7,295
Citrus County SD 15,900/PK-12
1007 W Main St 34450 352-726-1931
Sandra Himmel, supt. Fax 726-4418
www.citrus.k12.fl.us
Inverness ES 800/PK-5
206 S Line Ave 34452 352-726-2632
Marlise Bushman, prin. Fax 726-1883
Inverness MS 1,200/6-8
1950 Highway 41 N 34450 352-726-1471
Bill Farrell, prin. Fax 726-4535
Pleasant Grove ES 700/PK-5
630 Pleasant Grove Rd 34452 352-637-4400
Lynne Kirby, prin. Fax 637-5087
Other Schools – See Citrus Springs, Crystal River, Floral City, Hernando, Homosassa, Lecanto

Islamorada, Monroe, Pop. 1,220

Island Christian S 200/PK-12
83400 Overseas Hwy 33036 305-664-4933
James Roper, prin. Fax 664-8170

Jacksonville, Duval, Pop. 782,623
Clay County SD
Supt. — See Green Cove Springs
Clay Hill ES 500/K-6
6345 County Road 218 32234 904-289-7193
Larry Davis, prin. Fax 289-9667

Duval County SD 122,800/PK-12
1701 Prudential Dr 32207 904-390-2000
Ed Pratt-Dannals, supt. Fax 390-2586
www.duvalschools.org/
Abess Park ES 800/K-5
12731 Abess Blvd 32225 904-220-1260
Caroline Wells, prin. Fax 220-1264
Alimacani ES 1,100/PK-5
2051 San Pablo Rd S 32224 904-221-7101
Kathy Stalls, prin. Fax 221-8823
Arlington ES 300/PK-5
1201 University Blvd N 32211 904-745-4900
Paula Smith, prin. Fax 745-4946
Arlington Heights ES 600/PK-5
1520 Sprinkle Dr 32211 904-745-4923
Robert Snyder, prin. Fax 745-4944
Arlington MS 900/6-8
8141 Lone Star Rd 32211 904-720-1680
Dr. Linda Lisella, prin. Fax 720-1702
Axson ES 500/PK-5
4763 Sutton Park Ct 32224 904-992-3600
Paula Renfro, prin. Fax 992-3605
Bank of America Learning Academy 200/K-5
9000 Southside Blvd 32256 904-464-3895
Sherry Adams, prin. Fax 464-4465
Bayview ES 400/K-5
3257 Lake Shore Blvd 32210 904-381-3920
Susan Hamner, prin. Fax 381-3919
Beauclerc ES 1,300/K-5
4555 Craven Rd W 32257 904-739-5226
Annetta Kornblum, prin. Fax 739-5317
Biltmore ES 400/PK-5
2101 W Palm Ave 32254 904-693-7569
Helen Dunbar, prin. Fax 693-7574
Biscayne ES 500/K-5
12230 Biscayne Blvd 32218 904-714-4650
Crystal Lewis, prin. Fax 714-4655
Brentwood ES 300/PK-5
3750 Springfield Blvd 32206 904-630-6630
Angela Kasper, prin. Fax 630-6638
Brewer ES 600/3-5
3385 Hartsfield Rd 32277 904-745-4990
Marianne Lee, prin. Fax 745-4986
Brookview ES 700/K-5
10450 Theresa Dr 32246 904-565-2720
Shana Adams, prin. Fax 565-2734
Brown ES 700/K-5
1535 Milnor St 32206 904-630-6570
Sabrina Session-Jones, prin. Fax 630-6576
Butler MS 500/6-8
900 Acorn St 32209 904-630-6900
Sylvia Johnson, prin. Fax 630-6913
Carver ES 500/PK-5
2854 W 45th St 32209 904-924-3122
Timothy Warren, prin. Fax 924-3280

Cedar Hills ES 400/K-5
6534 Ish Brant Rd 32210 904-573-1050
Laverne Hamilton, prin. Fax 573-1051
Central Riverside ES 400/K-5
2555 Gilmore St 32204 904-381-7495
David Theus, prin. Fax 381-7423
Chaffee Trail ES 600/PK-5
11400 Sam Caruso Way 32221 904-693-7510
Beverly Walker, prin. Fax 693-7932
Chet's Creek ES 1,100/K-5
13200 Chets Creek Blvd 32224 904-992-6390
Susan Phillips, prin. Fax 992-6398
Chimney Lakes ES 1,100/K-5
9353 Staples Mill Dr 32244 904-573-1100
Janet Knott, prin. Fax 573-1109
Crown Point ES 1,300/K-5
3800 Crown Point Rd 32257 904-260-5808
Kathy Cooley, prin. Fax 260-5839
Crystal Springs ES 1,300/PK-5
1200 Hammond Blvd 32221 904-693-7645
Jacqueline Davis, prin. Fax 693-7658
Daniels ES 400/K-2
1951 W 15th St 32209 904-630-6872
Kimberly Dennis, prin. Fax 630-6875
Davis MS 1,500/6-8
7050 Melvin Rd 32210 904-573-1060
Addison Davis, prin. Fax 573-1066
Dinsmore ES 500/K-5
7126 Civic Club Dr 32219 904-924-3126
Christina Lord, prin. Fax 924-3142
DuPont MS 1,000/6-8
2710 Dupont Ave 32217 904-739-5200
Teresa Mowbray, prin. Fax 739-5321
Englewood ES 400/PK-5
4359 Spring Park Rd 32207 904-739-5280
Gail Brinson, prin. Fax 739-5316
Enterprise Learning Academy 1,100/PK-5
8085 Old Middleburg Rd S 32222 904-573-3260
Sheridan Brown, prin. Fax 573-3270
Fishweir ES 300/PK-5
3977 Herschel St 32205 904-381-3910
Andrea Akers, prin. Fax 381-3916
Ford S 800/K-8
1137 Cleveland St 32209 904-630-6540
Nan Brooks-Hoyle, prin. Fax 630-6548
Ft. Caroline ES 700/K-5
3925 Athore Dr 32277 904-745-4904
Tammy Boyd, prin. Fax 745-4945
Ft. Caroline MS 900/6-8
3787 University Club Blvd 32277 904-745-4927
Kathy Kassees, prin. Fax 745-4937
Garden City ES 700/K-5
2814 Dunn Ave 32218 904-924-3130
Debbie Sapp, prin. Fax 924-3178
Gilbert MS 600/6-8
1424 Franklin St 32206 904-630-6700
Jackie Simmons, prin. Fax 630-6713
Greenfield ES 600/K-5
6343 Knights Ln N 32216 904-739-5249
Maren Firment, prin. Fax 739-5299
Greenland Pines ES 1,100/K-5
5050 Greenland Rd 32258 904-260-5450
Chiquita Maxwell-Rivers, prin. Fax 260-5455
Gregory Drive ES 800/PK-5
7800 Gregory Dr 32210 904-573-1190
Andrea Williams-Scott, prin. Fax 573-3218
Hendricks Avenue ES 600/K-5
3400 Hendricks Ave 32207 904-346-5610
Jayne Owens-Thompson, prin. Fax 346-5616
Highlands ES 400/PK-5
1000 Depaul Dr 32218 904-696-8754
Kerwyn Neal, prin. Fax 696-8787
Highlands MS 1,200/6-8
10913 Pine Estates Rd E 32218 904-696-8771
Dr. Catherine Barnes, prin. Fax 696-8782
Hogan-Spring Glen ES 500/PK-5
6736 Beach Blvd 32216 904-720-1640
Jacquelyn Christopher, prin. Fax 720-1706
Holiday Hill ES 600/K-5
6900 Altama Rd 32216 904-720-1676
Susan Chick, prin. Fax 720-1731
Hull ES 300/PK-5
7528 Hull St 32219 904-924-3136
Randall Strickland, prin. Fax 924-3139
Hyde Grove ES 500/K-5
2056 Lane Ave S 32210 904-693-7562
Nancy Carter, prin. Fax 693-7565
Hyde Park ES 500/K-5
5300 Park St 32205 904-381-3950
Tarsha Mitchell, prin. Fax 381-3954
Jackson ES 300/K-5
6127 Cedar Hills Blvd 32210 904-573-1020
Angela Lott, prin. Fax 573-1059
Jacksonville Heights ES 900/K-5
7750 Tempest St S 32244 904-573-1120
Marcy Dunavant, prin. Fax 573-1043
Jefferson ES 600/K-5
8233 Nevada St 32220 904-693-7500
Lori Turner, prin. Fax 693-7507
Johnson MS 1,100/6-8
1840 W 9th St 32209 904-630-6640
Sharwonda Peek, prin. Fax 630-6653
Justina Road ES 400/PK-5
3101 Justina Rd 32277 904-745-4909
Angela Maxey, prin. Fax 745-4947
Kernan MS 1,200/6-8
2271 Kernan Blvd S 32246 904-220-1350
David Gilmore, prin. Fax 220-1355
Kernan Trail ES 700/K-5
2281 Kernan Blvd S 32246 904-220-1310
David Gilmore, prin. Fax 220-1315
King ES 500/PK-5
8801 Lake Placid Dr E 32208 904-924-3027
Carolyn Blackshear, prin. Fax 766-9031
Kings Trail ES 500/K-5
7401 Old Kings Rd S 32217 904-739-5254
Diane Clark, prin. Fax 739-5326
Kirby-Smith MS 1,000/6-8
2034 Hubbard St 32206 904-630-6600
June Marshall, prin. Fax 630-6605

Kite ES 400/PK-5
9430 Lem Turner Rd 32208 904-924-3031
Erdine Johnson, prin. Fax 924-3473
Lake Forest ES 500/PK-5
901 Kennard St 32208 904-924-3024
Kim Bays, prin. Fax 924-3194
Lake Lucina ES 500/PK-5
6527 Merrill Rd 32277 904-745-4916
Jana Grenier, prin. Fax 745-4917
Lake Shore MS 1,100/6-8
2519 Bayview Rd 32210 904-381-7440
Ronda Cotter, prin. Fax 381-7437
Landmark MS 1,300/6-8
101 Kernan Blvd N 32225 904-221-7125
Michael Henry, prin. Fax 221-8847
Landon MS 600/6-8
1819 Thacker Ave 32207 904-346-5650
Kelly Coker-Daniel, prin. Fax 346-5657
LaVilla S of the Arts 1,100/6-8
501 N Davis St 32202 904-633-6069
Janelle Wagoner, prin. Fax 633-8089
Livingston ES 600/PK-5
1128 Barber St 32209 904-630-6580
Jermall Wright, prin. Fax 630-6587
Lone Star ES 800/K-5
10400 Lone Star Rd 32225 904-565-2711
Elizabeth Kavanagh, prin. Fax 565-2733
Long Branch ES 300/PK-5
3723 Franklin St 32206 904-630-6620
Marva McKinney, prin. Fax 630-6639
Loretto ES 1,200/K-5
3900 Loretto Rd 32223 904-260-5800
Christopher Begley, prin. Fax 260-5835
Love ES 300/PK-5
1531 Winthrop St 32206 904-630-6790
Michelle Quarles, prin. Fax 630-6793
Love Grove ES 500/K-5
2446 University Blvd S 32216 904-720-1645
Bill Permenter, prin. Fax 720-1742
Mandarin MS 1,600/6-8
5100 Hood Rd 32257 904-292-0555
Joy Recla, prin. Fax 260-5415
Mandarin Oaks ES 1,200/K-5
10600 Hornets Nest Rd 32257 904-260-5820
Patti Carson, prin. Fax 260-5846
Mathis ES 300/PK-5
3501 Winton Dr 32208 904-924-3086
Gwen Crutchfield, prin. Fax 924-3193
Merrill Road ES 500/K-2
8239 Merrill Rd 32277 904-745-4919
Julie Hudson, prin. Fax 745-4943
Morgan ES 500/PK-5
964 Saint Clair St 32254 904-381-3970
Donna Frank, prin. Fax 381-3998
New Berlin ES 700/K-5
3613 New Berlin Rd 32226 904-714-4601
Deidra Johnson, prin. Fax 714-4610
Normandy Village ES 600/K-5
8257 Herlong Rd 32210 904-693-7548
Clemijene Alexander, prin. Fax 693-7553
North Shore Magnet S 400/PK-8
5701 Silver Plz 32208 904-924-3081
Deidra McDowell-Sutton, prin. Fax 924-3191
Northwestern MS 800/6-8
2100 W 45th St 32209 904-924-3100
Robert Gresham, prin. Fax 924-3284
Oak Hill ES 500/K-5
6910 Daughtry Blvd S 32210 904-573-1030
Rebecca Rhoden, prin. Fax 573-3214
Oceanway ES 600/K-5
12555 Gillespie Ave 32218 904-696-8762
Michael Cobb, prin. Fax 696-8788
Oceanway MS 1,200/6-8
143 Oceanway Ave 32218 904-714-4680
John Cochran, prin. Fax 714-4685
Ortega ES 300/K-5
4010 Baltic St 32210 904-381-7460
Jennifer Brown, prin. Fax 381-7484
Parkwood Heights ES 500/K-5
1709 Lansdowne Dr 32211 904-720-1670
Ashton Price, prin. Fax 720-1674
Paxon MS 800/6-8
3276 Norman E Thagard Blvd 32254 904-693-7600
Darrell Perry, prin. Fax 693-7661
Payne ES 400/PK-5
6725 Hema Rd 32209 904-924-3020
Pearl Roziers, prin. Fax 924-3181
Pearson ES 300/PK-5
4346 Roanoke Blvd 32208 904-924-3077
Debra Crotty, prin. Fax 924-3160
Pickett ES 300/PK-5
6305 Old Kings Rd 32254 904-693-7555
Carolyn Laws, prin. Fax 693-7558
Pinedale ES 500/PK-5
4229 Edison Ave 32254 904-381-7490
Alan Due, prin. Fax 381-7466
Pine Estates ES 300/PK-5
10741 Pine Estates Rd E 32218 904-696-8767
Violetra Ward, prin. Fax 696-8745
Pine Forest ES 500/PK-5
3929 Grant Rd 32207 904-346-5600
Denise Ahearn, prin. Fax 346-5632
Ramona Boulevard ES 600/PK-5
5540 Ramona Blvd 32205 904-693-7576
Lisa Brady, prin. Fax 693-7582
Reynolds Lane ES 400/PK-5
840 Reynolds Ln 32254 904-381-3960
Todd Simpson, prin. Fax 381-3964
Ribault MS 700/6-8
3610 Ribault Scenic Dr 32208 904-924-3062
George Maxey, prin. Fax 924-3167
Robinson ES 800/PK-5
101 W 12th St 32206 904-630-6550
Louise Hill, prin. Fax 630-6555
Sabal Palm ES 1,300/PK-5
1201 Kernan Blvd N 32225 904-221-7169
Mary Mickel, prin. Fax 221-8811
Saint Clair Evans Academy 500/PK-5
5443 Moncrief Rd 32209 904-924-3035
Edward Robinson, prin. Fax 924-3038

San Jose ES 700/PK-5
5805 Saint Augustine Rd 32207 904-739-5260
Deborah Cobbin, prin. Fax 739-5327
San Mateo ES 600/K-5
600 Baisden Rd 32218 904-696-8750
Kristie Kemp, prin. Fax 696-8748
Sheffield ES 700/K-5
13333 Lanier Rd 32226 904-696-8758
Art Lauzon, prin. Fax 696-8791
Southside Estates ES 600/PK-5
9775 Ivey Rd 32246 904-565-2706
Patricia Latimer, prin. Fax 565-2737
Southside MS 1,000/6-8
2948 Knights Ln E 32216 904-739-5238
LaTanya McNeal, prin. Fax 739-5244
Spring Park ES 300/PK-5
2250 Spring Park Rd 32207 904-346-5640
Pam Bradley-Pierce, prin. Fax 346-5646
Stilwell MS 1,200/6-8
7840 Burma Rd 32221 904-693-7523
Vincent Hall, prin. Fax 693-7539
Stockton ES 600/K-5
4827 Carlisle Rd 32210 904-381-3955
Lacy Healy, prin. Fax 381-7408
Stuart MS 1,100/6-8
4815 Wesconnett Blvd 32210 904-573-1000
Gregory Bostic, prin. Fax 573-3213
Tillis ES 500/PK-5
6084 Morse Ave 32244 904-573-1090
Tangela Johnson, prin. Fax 573-1169
Timucuan ES 700/PK-5
5429 110th St 32244 904-573-1130
Kimberly Harrison, prin. Fax 573-1136
Tolbert ES 400/3-5
1925 W 13th St 32209 904-630-6860
Terry Boatman, prin. Fax 630-6868
Twin Lakes Academy 1,400/6-8
8050 Point Meadows Dr 32256 904-538-0825
Don Nelson, prin. Fax 538-0840
Twin Lakes Academy ES 1,100/K-5
8000 Point Meadows Dr 32256 904-538-0238
Denise Robertson, prin. Fax 538-0241
Upson ES 400/K-5
1090 Dancy St 32205 904-381-7485
Peggy Kring, prin. Fax 381-3976
Venetia ES 400/PK-5
4300 Timuquana Rd 32210 904-381-3990
Ellen Rubens, prin. Fax 381-7451
Wesconnett ES 300/PK-5
5710 Wesconnett Blvd 32244 904-573-1140
Michael Akers, prin. Fax 573-1144
West Jacksonville ES 200/PK-5
2115 Commonwealth Ave 32209 904-630-6592
Michele Floyd-Hatcher, prin. Fax 630-6597
West Riverside ES 400/K-5
2801 Herschel St 32205 904-381-3900
Christopher Smith, prin. Fax 381-3905
Whitehouse ES 800/K-5
11160 General Ave 32220 904-693-7542
Marie Kite, prin. Fax 693-7544
Windy Hill ES 700/PK-5
3831 Forest Blvd 32246 904-565-2700
Sharon Sanders, prin. Fax 565-2702
Woodland Acres ES 500/PK-5
328 Bowlan St N 32211 904-720-1663
Marianne Simon, prin. Fax 720-1730
Woodson ES 500/PK-5
2334 Butler Ave 32209 904-924-3004
Cheryl Quarles-Gaston, prin. Fax 924-3442
Other Schools – See Atlantic Beach, Baldwin, Jacksonville Beach, Neptune Beach

---

ABC Christian Academy 200/PK-6
2360 Kings Rd 32209 904-353-4471
Lois Diamond, prin. Fax 355-0567
Academie De Montessori 50/PK-4
1216 LaSalle St 32207 904-398-3830
Mary Saltmarsh, prin. Fax 398-0992
All Saints Early Learning Center 100/PK-2
4171 Hendricks Ave 32207 904-737-7800
Fax 737-0646
Argyle Christian K 100/PK-K
6823 Argyle Forest Blvd 32244 904-778-4838
Terri Johnson, dir. Fax 779-1225
Arlington Country Day S 400/K-12
5725 Fort Caroline Rd 32277 904-762-0123
Deborah Condit, dir. Fax 762-0125
Assumption S 500/PK-8
2431 Atlantic Blvd 32207 904-398-1774
Angie Fuller, prin. Fax 398-6712
Baymeadows Baptist Day S 300/PK-7
4826 Baymeadows Rd 32217 904-733-3400
Garry Broward, admin. Fax 733-5003
Blessed Trinity S 300/PK-8
10472 Beach Blvd 32246 904-641-6458
Marie Davis, prin. Fax 645-3762
Bolles S 1,800/PK-12
7400 San Jose Blvd 32217 904-733-9292
Dr. John E. Trainer, pres. Fax 739-9363
Bolles S - Bartrum Campus 400/6-8
2264 Bartram Rd 32207 904-724-8850
Dr. John Trainer, hdmstr. Fax 724-8862
Broach S - Westside 100/1-12
440 Lenox Sq 32254 904-389-5106
Darrell Lewis, dir. Fax 388-1077
Cedar Creek Christian S 200/PK-12
1372 Lane Ave S 32205 904-781-9151
Lisa Pearson, prin. Fax 781-9182
Cedar Hills Baptist Christian S 200/PK-8
4200 Jammes Rd 32210 904-772-0812
Judy Pugh, prin. Fax 771-1699
Christian Heritage Academy 200/PK-8
3930 University Blvd S 32216 904-733-4722
James Stephens, admin. Fax 338-9977
Christ the King S 400/PK-8
6822 Larkin Rd 32211 904-724-2954
Stephanie Chinault, prin. Fax 721-8004
Cornerstone Christian S 200/PK-12
4000 Spring Park Rd 32207 904-730-5500
Deborah Wagner, prin. Fax 730-5502

Eagle Academy 200/PK-8
8985 Lone Star Rd 32211 904-722-9223
Eunice Jones, prin. Fax 854-0907
Eagle's View Academy 400/K-12
7788 Ramona Blvd W 32221 904-786-1411
Scott Kinlaw, admin. Fax 786-1445
Ephesus Jr. Academy 100/K-9
2760 Edgewood Ave W 32209 904-765-3225
Esprit De Corps Center for Learning 100/PK-12
9840 Wagner Rd 32219 904-924-2000
Betty White, prin. Fax 766-8870
First Coast Christian S 500/PK-12
7587 Blanding Blvd 32244 904-777-3040
Morry Kemple, admin. Fax 777-3045
Fort Caroline Baptist Academy 100/PK-4
11428 McCormick Rd 32225 904-642-3210
Evelynn Livingston, dir. Fax 642-8694
Foundation Academy 200/K-12
3675 San Pablo Rd S 32224 904-493-7300
Nadia Hionides, prin. Fax 821-1247
Good Shepherd S 200/PK-5
1656 Edgewood Ave W 32208 904-768-1580
Gottlieb Day S 100/K-8
3662 Crown Point Rd 32257 904-268-4200
Carole Goldberg, hdmstr. Fax 268-5292
Grace Lutheran S 200/PK-8
12200 Mccormick Rd 32225 904-928-9136
Rod Jackson, prin. Fax 928-0181
Guardian Lutheran S 200/PK-8
4911 Losco Rd 32257 904-262-7887
Mary Tereszkiewicz, prin. Fax 421-4932
Harvest Community S 300/PK-12
2360 Saint Johns Bluff Rd S 32246 904-997-1882
Patty Wilcox, admin. Fax 997-1862
Hendricks Day S of Jacksonville 300/PK-8
1824 Dean Rd 32216 904-720-0398
Sally Lott, dir. Fax 720-0435
Holy Family S 400/PK-8
9800 Baymeadows Rd Ste 3 32256 904-645-9875
Rosemary Nowotny, prin. Fax 899-6060
Holy Rosary S 200/K-8
4920 Brentwood Ave 32206 904-765-6522
Sr. Dianne Rumschlag, prin. Fax 765-9486
Holy Spirit S 300/PK-8
11665 Fort Caroline Rd 32225 904-642-9165
Dr. John Luciano, prin. Fax 642-1047
Jacksonville Adventist Academy 100/PK-8
4298 Livingston Rd 32257 904-268-2433
Richard Butterfield, dir. Fax 268-7770
Jacksonville Country Day S 500/PK-6
10063 Baymeadows Rd 32256 904-641-6644
Terry Bartow, hmdstr. Fax 641-1494
Joshua Christian Academy 200/K-9
924 Saint Clair St 32254 904-388-2227
Lisa Harris, dir. Fax 388-2262
Mandarin Christian S 600/K-12
10850 Old St Augustine Rd 32257 904-268-8667
Dr. Milton Threadcraft, hdmstr. Fax 880-3251
Parsons Christian Academy 200/PK-12
5705 Fort Caroline Rd 32277 904-745-4588
Grace Williams, prin. Fax 745-6366
Potters House Christian Academy 600/PK-12
5732 Normandy Blvd 32205 904-786-0028
Belinda Slater, admin. Fax 693-6426
Promise Land Academy 100/K-6
3990 Loretto Rd 32223 904-268-2422
Kimberly Johnson, prin. Fax 268-5321
Providence S 1,500/PK-12
2701 Hodges Blvd 32224 904-223-5270
Don Barfield, hdmstr. Fax 223-4930
Resurrection S 200/PK-8
3406 Justina Rd 32277 904-744-1266
Patricia Sevilla, prin. Fax 744-5800
Riverside Presbyterian Day S 500/PK-6
830 Oak St 32204 904-353-5511
H. Palmer Bell, hdmstr. Fax 634-1739
Sacred Heart S 500/PK-8
5752 Blanding Blvd 32244 904-771-5800
Marybeth O'Neill, prin. Fax 771-5323
St. Joseph S 500/K-8
11600 Old St Augustine Rd 32258 904-268-6688
Rhonda Rose, prin. Fax 268-8989
St. Mark's Episcopal Day S 500/PK-6
4114 Oxford Ave 32210 904-388-2632
Cathy Hardage, hdmstr. Fax 387-5647
St. Matthew S 300/PK-8
1767 Blanding Blvd 32210 904-387-4401
Katherine Tuerk, prin. Fax 388-4404
St. Patrick S 200/PK-8
1429 Broward Rd 32218 904-768-6323
Sr. Carmel O'Callaghan, prin. Fax 768-2144
St. Paul S 300/PK-8
2609 Park St 32204 904-387-2841
Joann Leskanic, prin. Fax 388-1781
St. Pius V S 200/PK-8
1470 W 13th St 32209 904-354-2613
Sr. Elise Kennedy, prin. Fax 356-4522
St. Stephen Learning Center 200/PK-1
1525 N Davis St 32209 904-358-2799
Fax 359-0055
San Jose Episcopal S 500/PK-6
7423 San Jose Blvd 32217 904-733-0352
Rev. Jean Dodd, prin. Fax 733-2582
San Jose S 500/PK-8
3619 Toledo Rd 32217 904-733-2313
Janice Magiera, prin. Fax 731-7169
San Juan Del Rio S 200/PK-8
1714 State Road 13 32259 904-287-8081
Jeanne Brown, prin. Fax 287-4574
Seacoast Christian Academy 500/PK-12
9570 Regency Square Blvd 32225 904-725-5544
Cynthia Stremmel, admin. Fax 727-6748
Shekinah Christian Academy 100/K-12
10551 Beach Blvd 32246 904-421-1015
CoSundra Fanner, prin. Fax 421-1022
Success Academy 200/PK-12
2103 Grand St 32208 904-766-6212
Torah Academy 50/PK-5
10167 San Jose Blvd 32257 904-268-7719

Trinity Christian Academy 1,700/PK-12
800 Hammond Blvd 32221 904-596-2400
Fax 596-2531

University Christian S 1,000/PK-12
5520 University Blvd W 32216 904-737-6330
Heath Nivens, dir. Fax 737-3359

Victory Christian Academy 300/PK-12
10613 Lem Turner Rd 32218 904-764-7781
David Wright, dir. Fax 764-7297

West Meadows Baptist Academy 50/K-12
11711 Normandy Blvd 32221 904-786-2711
Dr. Bruce Armstrong, admin. Fax 786-2712

Jacksonville Beach, Duval, Pop. 21,770

Duval County SD
Supt. — See Jacksonville

Fletcher MS 1,300/6-8
2000 3rd St N 32250 904-247-5929
Laurie Flynn, prin. Fax 247-5940

Jacksonville Beach ES 600/K-5
315 10th St S 32250 904-247-5942
Jill Leinhauser, prin. Fax 270-1825

San Pablo ES 500/K-5
801 18th Ave N 32250 904-247-5947
Linda Graham, prin. Fax 270-1860

Seabreeze ES 500/PK-5
1400 Seabreeze Ave 32250 904-247-5900
William Dutter, prin. Fax 270-1850

Beaches Episcopal S 300/PK-6
1150 5th St N 32250 904-246-2466
Jackie Busse, hdmstr. Fax 246-1626

Discovery Montessori S 100/PK-5
102 15th St S 32250 904-247-4577
Dr. Mary-Beth Sullivan, dir. Fax 247-5626

Montessori Tides S 100/PK-4
1550 Penman Rd 32250 904-241-1139
Kathy Graham, prin. Fax 241-0971

St. Paul S 500/K-8
428 2nd Ave N 32250 904-249-5934
Katherine Boice, prin. Fax 241-2911

Jasper, Hamilton, Pop. 1,817

Hamilton County SD 2,000/PK-12
4280 SW County Road 152 32052 386-792-1228
Harry Pennington, supt. Fax 792-3681
www.hamiltonfl.com/

Central Hamilton ES 500/K-6
553 Chan Bridge Dr 32052 386-792-6530
Marjorie Cooks, prin. Fax 792-6512

Other Schools – See Jennings, White Springs

Jay, Santa Rosa, Pop. 665

Santa Rosa County SD
Supt. — See Milton

Chumuckla ES 300/PK-6
2312 Highway 182 32565 850-995-3690
Dr. Karen Barber, prin. Fax 995-3695

Jay ES 600/PK-6
13833 Alabama St 32565 850-675-4554
Danny Carnley, prin. Fax 675-3362

Jennings, Hamilton, Pop. 830

Hamilton County SD
Supt. — See Jasper

North Hamilton ES 400/PK-6
1291 Florida St 32053 386-938-1400
Lee Wetherington-Zamora, prin. Fax 938-1411

Jensen Beach, Martin, Pop. 9,884

Martin County SD
Supt. — See Stuart

Jensen Beach ES 600/K-5
2525 NE Savannah Rd 34957 772-219-1555
Don Merritt, prin. Fax 219-1558

Juno Beach, Palm Beach, Pop. 3,395

Batt Private S 100/PK-12
13205 US Highway 1 Ste 202 33408 561-630-9980
Kate Brannum, hdmstr. Fax 776-7292

Jupiter, Palm Beach, Pop. 47,909

Palm Beach County SD
Supt. — See West Palm Beach

Beacon Cove IS 1,000/3-5
150 Schoolhouse Rd 33458 561-366-6400
Una Hukill, prin. Fax 366-6450

Independence MS 1,200/6-8
4001 Greenway Dr 33458 561-799-7500
Lori Bonino, prin. Fax 799-7505

Jupiter ES 600/K-5
200 S Loxahatchee Dr 33458 561-741-5300
Daniel Smith, prin. Fax 741-5350

Jupiter Farms ES 700/K-5
17400 Haynie Ln 33478 561-741-5400
Marilyn Weisgerber, prin. Fax 741-5450

Jupiter MS 1,200/6-8
15245 Military Trl 33458 561-745-7200
David Culp, prin. Fax 745-7246

Lighthouse ES 900/K-2
4750 Dakota Dr 33458 561-741-9400
Eric Gross, prin. Fax 741-9450

Limestone Creek ES 900/K-5
6701 Church St 33458 561-741-9200
Suzanne Gibbs, prin. Fax 741-9250

Thomas ES 800/K-5
800 Maplewood Dr 33458 561-741-9100
Sharon Barwick, prin. Fax 741-9150

ABC Montessori Academy PK-6
700 S Orange Ave 33458 561-575-4331
Michele Kinard, prin. Fax 744-2988

All Saints Catholic S 600/PK-8
1759 Indian Creek Pkwy 33458 561-748-8994
Mary Beth Quick, prin. Fax 748-8979

Jupiter Christian S 600/PK-12
700 S Delaware Blvd 33458 561-746-7800
Leslie Downs, pres. Fax 748-9528

Turtle River Montessori S 100/PK-5
100 Intracoastal Pointe Dr 33477 561-745-1995
Bharati Dandiya, prin. Fax 745-1313

Key Biscayne, Miami-Dade, Pop. 10,158

Miami-Dade County SD
Supt. — See Miami

Key Biscayne S 1,100/PK-8
150 W McIntyre St 33149 305-361-5418
Silvia Tarafa, prin. Fax 361-8120

St. Agnes Academy 500/PK-8
122 Harbor Dr 33149 305-361-3245
Sheila Cruse, prin. Fax 361-6329

St. Christophers By-The-Sea S 100/PK-6
95 Harbor Dr 33149 305-361-5080
Rev. Burt Froehlich, hdmstr. Fax 361-0355

Key Largo, Monroe, Pop. 11,336

Monroe County SD
Supt. — See Key West

Key Largo S 1,000/PK-8
104801 Overseas Hwy 33037 305-453-1255
Annette Martinson, prin. Fax 453-1248

Academy at Ocean Reef 50/PK-8
395 S Harbor Dr 33037 305-367-2409
Melba Hardy, hdmstr. Fax 367-2055

Keystone Heights, Clay, Pop. 1,427

Clay County SD
Supt. — See Green Cove Springs

Keystone Heights ES 800/PK-6
335 SW Pecan St 32656 352-473-4844
Mary Mimbs, prin. Fax 473-4110

McRae ES 600/PK-6
6770 County Road 315 32656 352-473-5686
Marcus Dooley, prin. Fax 473-5148

Community Christian S 200/PK-8
345 SE Palmetto Ave 32656 352-473-6600
Gracie Lesch, prin. Fax 473-5103

Key West, Monroe, Pop. 23,935

Monroe County SD 7,900/PK-12
241 Trumbo Rd 33040 305-293-1400
Randy Acevedo, supt. Fax 293-1408
www.keysschools.com

Adams ES 500/PK-5
5855 College Rd 33040 305-293-1609
Frannie Herrin, prin. Fax 293-1608

Archer ES 300/PK-5
1302 White St 33040 305-293-1601
Henry Boza, prin. Fax 293-1662

O'Bryant MS 700/6-8
1105 Leon St 33040 305-296-5628
Marian Smith, prin. Fax 293-1644

Poinciana ES 500/K-5
1407 Kennedy Dr 33040 305-293-1630
Amber Bosco, prin. Fax 293-1667

Sigsbee ES 300/PK-5
939 Felton Rd 33040 305-294-1861
Henry Boza, prin. Fax 292-6869

Other Schools – See Key Largo, Marathon, Summerland Key, Tavernier

---

Grace Lutheran S 100/PK-K
2713 Flagler Ave 33040 305-296-8262
Sue Heidle, dir. Fax 296-0622

Mary Immaculate Star of the Sea S 100/PK-8
700 Truman Ave 33040 305-294-1031
Beth Harris, prin. Fax 294-2095

Kissimmee, Osceola, Pop. 59,364

Osceola County SD 50,600/PK-12
817 Bill Beck Blvd 34744 407-870-4600
Michael Grego, supt. Fax 870-4010
www.osceola.k12.fl.us

Boggy Creek ES 900/PK-5
810 Florida Pkwy 34743 407-344-5060
Linda Caswell-Johnson, prin. Fax 344-5070

Central Avenue ES 900/K-5
500 W Columbia Ave 34741 407-343-7330
Kay Wong, prin. Fax 343-7332

Chestnut ES 1,100/PK-5
4300 Chestnut St 34759 407-870-4862
Randy Shuttera, prin. Fax 870-4864

Cypress ES 900/PK-5
2251 Lakeside Dr 34743 407-344-5000
Stacy Burdette, prin. Fax 344-5006

Deerwood ES 1,100/K-5
3701 Marigold Ave 34758 407-870-2400
Jimmy Hendrix, prin. Fax 870-2648

Denn John MS 1,200/6-8
2001 Denn John Ln 34744 407-935-3560
Rob Paswaters, prin. Fax 935-3572

Discovery IS 1,600/6-8
5350 San Miguel Rd 34758 407-343-7300
Larry Meadows, prin. Fax 343-7310

Flora Ridge ES 700/PK-5
2900 Dyer Blvd 34741 407-933-3999
Mike Vondracek, prin. Fax 933-3998

Highlands ES 800/PK-5
800 W Donegan Ave 34741 407-935-3620
Susan Godman, prin. Fax 935-3629

Horizon MS 1,600/6-8
2020 Ham Brown Rd 34746 407-943-7240
Michael Allen, prin. Fax 943-7250

Kissimmee ES 1,100/PK-5
3700 W Donegan Ave 34741 407-935-3640
Kenneth Meyers, prin. Fax 935-3651

Kissimmee MS 1,000/6-8
2410 Dyer Blvd 34741 407-870-0857
Paula Evans, prin. Fax 870-5669

Mill Creek ES 1,000/PK-5
1700 Mill Slough Rd 34744 407-935-3660
Holly Willis, prin. Fax 935-3667

Neptune MS 1,500/6-8
2727 Neptune Rd 34744 407-935-3500
Cindy Mohen, prin. Fax 935-3519

Parkway MS 1,000/6-8
857 Florida Pkwy 34743 407-344-7000
Fax 348-2797

Partin Settlement ES 1,000/K-5
2434 Remington Blvd 34744 407-518-2000
David Groover, prin. Fax 518-2019

Pleasant Hill ES 1,100/PK-5
1253 Pleasant Hill Rd 34741 407-935-3700
Rene Clayton, prin. Fax 935-3705

Poinciana ES 1,100/K-5
4201 Rhododendron Ave 34758 407-343-4500
Sheri Turchi, prin. Fax 343-4519

Reedy Creek ES 1,000/PK-5
5100 Eagles Trl 34758 407-935-3580
Diane Crook-Nichols, prin. Fax 935-3590

Sunrise ES 1,000/PK-5
1925 Ham Brown Rd 34746 407-870-4866
John Campbell, prin. Fax 933-9975

Thacker Avenue ES 700/PK-5
301 N Thacker Ave 34741 407-935-3540
Mark Ferguson, prin. Fax 935-3549

Ventura ES 1,200/PK-5
275 Waters Edge Dr 34743 407-344-5040
Janice Castro-Franceschi, prin. Fax 344-5046

Other Schools – See Celebration, Saint Cloud

City of Life Christian Academy 300/PK-12
2874 E Irlo Bronson Mem Hwy 34744 407-847-5184
Kathy Harkema, prin. Fax 870-2678

First United Methodist Church S 200/PK-5
122 W Sproule Ave 34741 407-847-8805
Debby Jones, dir. Fax 847-7952

Heritage Christian S 500/K-12
1500 E Vine St 34744 407-847-4087
Fax 932-2806

Holy Redeemer S 300/PK-8
1800 W Columbia Ave 34741 407-870-9055
Colleen Ehlenbeck, prin. Fax 870-2214

Life Academy 200/K-12
2269 Partin Settlement Rd 34744 407-847-8222
Sam Velazquez, prin. Fax 932-4431

North Kissimmee Christian S 200/PK-12
425 W Donegan Ave 34741 407-847-2877
Yvonne Johnson, prin. Fax 847-5372

Osceola Adventist Christian Academy 50/1-8
2391 Fortune Rd 34744 407-348-2226
Fax 348-2226

Pleasant Hill Academy 200/PK-12
601 Walnut St 34759 863-427-6760
Carmen Caban-Ruiz, prin. Fax 427-6763

Shady Oaks Private S 200/PK-5
2355 N Orange Blossom Trl 34744 407-847-6465
Fax 933-2007

Trinity Lutheran S 200/PK-8
3016 W Vine St 34741 407-847-5377
Jake Morrow, prin. Fax 944-0805

La Belle, Hendry, Pop. 3,302

Glades County SD
Supt. — See Moore Haven

West Glades S 400/K-8
2586 County Road 731 33935 863-675-3490
Debra Davis, prin. Fax 675-3890

Hendry County SD 7,300/PK-12
PO Box 1980 33975 863-674-4550
Richard Murphy, supt. Fax 674-4090
www.hendry-schools.org

Country Oaks ES 800/K-5
2052 NW Eucalyptus Blvd 33935 863-674-4140
James Sealey, prin. Fax 674-4129

La Belle ES 600/PK-5
150 W Cowboy Way 33935 863-674-4150
John Baker, prin. Fax 674-4155

La Belle MS 800/6-8
8000 E Cowboy Way 33935 863-674-4646
Gary White, prin. Fax 674-4645

Upthegrove ES 400/K-5
280 N Main St 33935 863-612-0750
Larry Luckey, prin. Fax 612-0753

Other Schools – See Clewiston

Community Christian S 200/PK-8
1092 E Cowboy Way 33935 863-675-3277
Shelton Gwaltney, admin. Fax 675-9212

Lady Lake, Lake, Pop. 13,244

Lake County SD
Supt. — See Tavares

Villages ES 900/PK-5
695 Rolling Acres Rd 32159 352-751-0111
Ted Wolf, prin. Fax 751-0117

Lake Alfred, Polk, Pop. 3,930

Polk County SD
Supt. — See Bartow

Lake Alfred-Addair MS 600/6-8
925 N Buena Vista Dr 33850 863-295-5988
Asonja Corbett, prin. Fax 295-5989

Lake Alfred ES 600/PK-5
550 E Cummings St 33850 863-295-5985
Eileen Castle, prin. Fax 295-5987

Lake Butler, Union, Pop. 1,967

Union County SD 2,200/PK-12
55 SW 6th St 32054 386-496-2045
Carlton Faulk, supt. Fax 496-2580
www.union.k12.fl.us/

Lake Butler ES 1,000/PK-4
800 SW 6th St 32054 386-496-3047
Lynn Bishop, prin. Fax 496-4395

Lake Butler MS 700/5-8
150 SW 6th St 32054 386-496-3046
Russell Larramore, prin. Fax 496-4352

Lake City, Columbia, Pop. 10,970

Columbia County SD 10,100/PK-12
372 W Duval St 32055 386-755-8000
Mike Millikin, supt. Fax 755-8029
www.columbia.k12.fl.us

Columbia City ES 700/PK-5
7438 SW State Road 47 32024 386-758-4850
Lana Boone, prin. Fax 758-4857
Eastside ES 600/PK-5
256 SE Beech St 32025 386-755-8220
Todd Widergren, prin. Fax 758-4885
Five Points ES 600/PK-5
303 NW Johnson St 32055 386-755-8230
Michael Allen, prin. Fax 755-8240
Lake City MS 1,100/6-8
843 SW Arlington Blvd 32025 386-758-4800
Sonja Knight-Judkins, prin. Fax 758-4839
Melrose Park ES 500/PK-5
820 SE Putnam St 32025 386-755-8260
Joe Adkins, prin. Fax 755-8276
Niblack ES 300/PK-5
837 NE Broadway Ave 32055 386-755-8200
William Murphy, prin. Fax 755-8218
Pinemount ES PK-5
324 SW Gabriel Pl 32024 386-755-8179
Donna McAdams, prin.
Richardson MS 700/6-8
646 SE Pennsylvania St 32025 386-755-8130
Keith Couey, prin. Fax 755-8154
Summers ES 900/PK-5
1388 SW McFarlane Ave 32025 386-755-8250
Terri Metrick, prin. Fax 758-4916
Westside ES 800/PK-5
1956 SW County Road 252B 32024 386-755-8280
Cherie Hill, prin. Fax 755-8285
Other Schools – See Fort White

Covenant Community S 100/K-9
2019 SW Main Blvd 32025 386-755-3636
Cindy Soucinek, admin. Fax 755-3609
Epiphany S 100/K-8
1937 SW Epiphany Ct 32025 386-752-2320
Carol Ghionzoli, prin. Fax 752-2364
Lake City Christian Academy 100/K-12
3035 SW Pinemount Rd 32024 386-758-0055

Lake Helen, Volusia, Pop. 2,816
Volusia County SD
Supt. — See De Land
Volusia Pines ES 700/K-5
500 E Kicklighter Rd 32744 386-575-4125
Dorothy Taylor, prin. Fax 228-1144

Lakeland, Polk, Pop. 88,713
Polk County SD
Supt. — See Bartow
Blake Academy 600/PK-7
510 Hartsell Ave 33815 863-499-2870
Dr. Gwen Kessell, prin. Fax 284-4521
Chiles MS Academy 600/6-8
400 N Florida Ave 33801 863-499-2742
Sharon Neuman, prin. Fax 499-2774
Churchwell ES 700/PK-5
8201 Park Byrd Rd 33810 863-853-6011
Betty Fitzgerald, prin. Fax 815-6538
Cleveland Court ES 500/K-5
328 E Edgewood Dr 33803 863-499-2929
Daniel Lunn, prin. Fax 499-2625
Combee ES 700/PK-5
2805 Morgan Combee Rd 33801 863-499-2960
Steven Comparato, prin. Fax 284-4421
Crystal Lake ES 600/PK-5
700 Galvin Dr 33801 863-499-2966
Joseph Griffin, prin. Fax 603-6329
Crystal Lake MS 800/6-8
2410 N Crystal Lake Dr 33801 863-499-2970
Christopher Canning, prin. Fax 603-6267
Dixieland ES 500/K-5
416 Ariana St 33803 863-499-2930
Deborah Henderson, prin. Fax 499-2932
Griffin ES 600/PK-5
3315 Kathleen Rd 33810 863-853-6020
Terry Broadnax, prin. Fax 853-6189
Highlands Grove ES 700/PK-5
4510 Lakeland Highlands Rd 33813 863-648-3002
Cindy Franks, prin. Fax 648-3005
Kathleen ES 600/PK-5
3515 Sherertz Rd 33810 863-853-6030
Lana Tatom, prin. Fax 853-6033
Kathleen MS 800/6-8
3627 Kathleen Pnes 33810 863-853-6040
Brett Butler, prin. Fax 853-6037
Keen ES 600/PK-5
815 Plateau Ave 33815 863-499-2880
Faye Wilson, prin. Fax 413-2506
Lake Gibson MS 1,100/6-8
6901 N Socrum Loop Rd 33809 863-853-6151
John Barber, prin. Fax 853-6171
Lakeland Highlands MS 1,200/6-8
740 Lake Miriam Dr 33813 863-648-3500
Robert Hartley, prin. Fax 648-3580
Lincoln Avenue Academy 500/K-5
1330 N Lincoln Ave 33805 863-499-2955
Evelyn Hollen, prin. Fax 499-2959
Medulla ES 800/PK-5
850 Schoolhouse Rd 33813 863-648-3515
Jill Cheatham, prin. Fax 648-3214
North Lakeland ES 700/PK-5
410 W Robson St 33805 863-499-2850
Gregory Deal, prin. Fax 499-2760
O'Brien ES 600/K-5
1225 E Lime St 33801 863-499-2950
Merri Crawford, prin. Fax 688-8774
Padgett ES 700/PK-5
110 Leelon Rd 33809 863-853-6044
Tanya Matthews, prin. Fax 853-6092
Palmore ES 700/K-5
3725 Cleveland Heights Blvd 33803 863-648-3510
Lori Morrison, prin. Fax 648-3122
Roberts ES 1,000/K-5
6600 Green Rd 33810 863-815-6633
Tonia Howe, prin. Fax 815-6640
Rochelle S of the Arts 900/PK-8
1501 Martin L King Jr Ave 33805 863-499-2810
Jacqueline Moore, prin. Fax 499-2797
Scott Lake ES 900/K-5
1140 E County Road 540A 33813 863-648-3520
Janet Wizda, prin. Fax 701-1076
Sikes ES 800/K-5
2727 Shepherd Rd 33811 863-648-3525
Corey Swindler, prin. Fax 648-3187
Sleepy Hill ES 600/PK-5
2285 Sleepy Hill Rd 33810 863-815-6768
Julie Grice, prin. Fax 815-6775
Sleepy Hill MS 1,200/6-8
2215 Sleepy Hill Rd 33810 863-815-6577
Mark Thomas, prin. Fax 815-6586
Socrum ES 600/K-5
9400 Old Dade City Rd 33810 863-853-6050
Jack Cline, prin. Fax 853-6059
Southwest ES 500/K-5
2650 Southwest Ave 33803 863-499-2830
Ellen Andersen, prin. Fax 499-2943
Southwest MS 1,000/6-8
2815 Eden Pkwy 33803 863-499-2840
John Wilson, prin. Fax 499-2762
Valleyview ES 1,100/K-5
2900 E County Road 540A 33813 863-648-3535
Ann Wellman, prin. Fax 648-3598
Wagner ES 700/PK-5
5500 Yates Rd 33811 863-701-1450
Julie Ward, prin. Fax 701-1457
Watson ES 900/K-5
6800 Walt Williams Rd 33809 863-853-6060
Kathy Giroux, prin. Fax 853-6056
Winston ES 600/PK-5
3415 Swindell Rd 33810 863-499-2890
Terry Strong, prin. Fax 499-2894

Families of Faith Christian Academy 300/K-12
4404 S Florida Ave Ste 11 33813 863-686-7755
James Lawson, prin. Fax 248-4128
Geneva Classical Academy 200/PK-12
4410 E County Road 540A 33813 863-644-1408
Charles Clendinen, hdmstr. Fax 619-5841
Highlands Christian Academy 100/PK-12
4210 Lakeland Highlands Rd 33813 863-646-5031
Mike Odum, admin. Fax 646-2267
Lakeland Christian S 1,000/PK-12
1111 Forest Park St 33803 863-688-2771
Michael Sligh, hdmstr. Fax 682-5637
Lakewire/Excel Christian Academy 300/PK-7
6505 Odom Rd 33809 863-853-9235
Resurrection S 500/PK-8
3720 Old Rd 37 33813 863-644-3931
Nancy Genzel, prin. Fax 648-0625
St. Anthony S 200/PK-8
924 Marcum Rd 33809 863-858-0671
Janet Peddecord, prin. Fax 858-0876
St. Joseph Academy 200/PK-8
310 McDonald St 33803 863-686-6415
Lana Swartzwelder, prin. Fax 687-8074
St. Paul Lutheran S 500/PK-8
4450 Harden Blvd 33813 863-644-7710
Leo Raschke, prin. Fax 644-7491
Sonrise Christian S 200/PK-12
3151 Hardin Combee Rd 33801 863-665-4187
Scott Skeans, dir. Fax 665-6065
Victory Christian Academy 500/PK-12
PO Box 90489 33804 863-858-5614
Lisa Coscia, prin. Fax 858-4268

Lake Mary, Seminole, Pop. 14,638
Seminole County SD
Supt. — See Sanford
Crystal Lake ES 600/K-5
231 Rinehart Rd 32746 407-871-8150
Jo Leblanc, prin. Fax 871-8199
Greenwood Lakes MS 1,200/6-8
601 Lake Park Dr 32746 407-320-7650
Corbet Wilson, prin. Fax 320-7699
Heathrow ES 1,100/PK-5
5715 Markham Woods Rd 32746 407-320-6850
Barbara Nixon, prin. Fax 320-6890
Lake Mary ES 600/PK-5
132 S Country Club Rd 32746 407-320-5650
Deborah Wright, prin. Fax 320-5699
Markham Woods MS 900/6-8
6003 Markham Woods Rd 32746 407-871-1750
Roger Gardner, prin. Fax 871-1799

Lake Mary Montessori Academy 100/PK-4
3551 W Lake Mary Blvd 32746 407-324-2304
Sheila Linville, prin. Fax 699-9323
Lake Mary Preparatory S 600/PK-12
650 Rantoul Ln 32746 407-805-0095
Donna Montague-Russell, hdmstr. Fax 322-3872
St. Peters Episcopal Preschool & K 100/PK-K
700 Rinehart Rd 32746 407-333-1707
Jeri Graumlich, dir. Fax 333-9342

Lake Panasoffkee, Sumter, Pop. 2,705
Sumter County SD
Supt. — See Bushnell
Lake Panasoffkee ES 500/PK-5
790 CR 482N 33538 352-793-1093
Donna Wells, prin. Fax 568-8080

Lake Park, Palm Beach, Pop. 9,039
Palm Beach County SD
Supt. — See West Palm Beach
Grove Park ES 700/K-5
8330 N Military Trl 33410 561-904-7700
Leslie Bolte, prin. Fax 904-7750
Lake Park ES 400/K-5
410 3rd St 33403 561-494-1300
Valerie Reddick-Mason, prin. Fax 494-1350

Lake Park Baptist S 300/PK-8
625 Park Ave 33403 561-844-2747
Dr. Bonnie Arnone, prin. Fax 881-5367

Lake Placid, Highlands, Pop. 1,784
Highlands County SD
Supt. — See Sebring
Lake Country ES 600/PK-5
516 County Road 29 33852 863-699-5050
Majel Bowerman, prin. Fax 699-5058
Lake Placid ES 800/PK-5
101 Green Dragon Dr 33852 863-699-5070
Carole Disler, prin. Fax 699-5079
Lake Placid MS 600/6-8
201 S Tangerine Ave 33852 863-699-5030
Derrel Bryan, prin. Fax 699-5029

Lake Suzy, Desoto

Laurel Oaks Academy 100/PK-9
12100 SW Academy Dr 34269 941-764-0456
Sheri Glastonbury, hdmstr. Fax 255-3731

Lake Wales, Polk, Pop. 12,964
Polk County SD
Supt. — See Bartow
McLaughlin MS 900/6-8
800 S 4th St 33853 863-678-4233
Matt Burkett, prin. Fax 678-4033
Spook Hill ES 400/K-5
321 Dr J A Wiltshire Ave E 33853 863-678-4262
Eric Edwards, prin. Fax 678-4210

Endtime Christian S of Excellence 50/1-8
200 S 3rd St 33853 863-676-8299
Betty Hill, prin. Fax 678-1193
Lake Wales Lutheran S 100/PK-5
640 S Scenic Hwy 33853 863-676-7300
Barbara Fackender, prin. Fax 676-8484

Lake Worth, Palm Beach, Pop. 36,342
Palm Beach County SD
Supt. — See West Palm Beach
Barton ES 600/K-5
1700 Barton Rd 33460 561-540-9100
Aurora Francois, prin. Fax 540-9128
Coral Reef ES 1,100/K-5
6151 Hagen Ranch Rd 33467 561-804-3700
Bobbi Moretto, prin. Fax 804-3750
Discovery Key ES 1,200/K-5
3550 Lyons Rd 33467 561-491-8200
Stephen Sills, prin. Fax 491-8250
Hidden Oaks ES 900/K-5
7685 S Military Trl 33463 561-804-3800
Sari Myers, prin. Fax 804-3850
Highland ES 700/K-5
500 Highland Ave 33460 561-202-0500
Brian Killeen, prin. Fax 202-0550
Indian Pines ES 900/K-5
6000 Oak Royal Dr 33463 561-804-3300
Laura Lougee, prin. Fax 804-3350
Lake Worth MS 800/6-8
1300 Barnett Dr 33461 561-540-5500
Jesus Armas, prin. Fax 540-5559
Manatee ES 1,200/K-5
7001 Charleston Shores Blvd 33467 561-649-6827
Mary Churchill-Jones, prin. Fax 434-7484
North Grade ES 800/K-5
824 N K St 33460 561-202-9300
Debbie Battles, prin. Fax 202-9350
Palm Springs ES 800/K-5
101 Davis Rd 33461 561-804-3000
Denise O'Connor, prin. Fax 804-3050
Panther Run ES 800/K-5
10775 Lake Worth Rd, 561-804-3900
Pierre D'Aoust, prin. Fax 804-3950
South Grade ES 800/K-5
716 S K St 33460 561-202-9400
Michael Riley, prin. Fax 202-9450
Tradewinds MS 1,200/6-8
5090 Haverhill Rd 33463 561-493-6400
Kirk Howell, prin. Fax 493-6410
Woodlands MS 1,600/6-8
5200 Lyons Rd 33467 561-357-0300
Larry Clawson, prin. Fax 357-0307

Our Savior Lutheran S 100/PK-5
1615 Lake Ave 33460 561-582-8624
Fax 582-1074
Sacred Heart S 200/PK-8
410 N M St 33460 561-582-2242
Candace Tamposi, prin. Fax 547-9699
Suncoast Christian Academy 100/PK-5
5561 Hypoluxo Rd 33463 561-641-1446
Fax 965-7245
Trinity Christian Academy 700/PK-12
7259 S Military Trl 33463 561-967-1900
Cindy Ansell, prin. Fax 965-4347

Land O Lakes, Pasco, Pop. 7,892
Pasco County SD 67,800/PK-12
7227 Land O Lakes Blvd 34638 813-794-2000
Heather Fiorentino Ph.D., supt. Fax 794-2716
www.pasco.k12.fl.us
Lake Myrtle ES 800/K-5
22844 Weeks Blvd 34639 813-794-1000
Kara McComeskey, prin. Fax 794-1091
Oakstead ES 700/K-5
19925 Lake Patience Rd, 813-346-1500
Tammy Kimpland, prin. Fax 346-1591
Pine View ES 700/K-5
5333 Parkway Blvd 34639 813-794-0600
Cortney Gantt, prin. Fax 794-0691
Pine View MS 1,900/6-8
5334 Parkway Blvd 34639 813-794-4800
Kim Anderson, prin. Fax 794-4891
Rushe MS 1,200/6-8
18654 Mentmore Blvd, 813-346-1200
Dave Estabrook, prin. Fax 346-1291
Sanders Memorial ES 700/PK-5
5126 School Rd, 813-794-1500
Jill Middleton, prin. Fax 794-1591
Other Schools – See Dade City, Holiday, Hudson, Lutz, New Port Richey, Port Richey, Spring Hill, Wesley Chapel, Zephyrhills

Academy at the Lakes 400/PK-12
2331 Collier Pkwy 34639 813-948-7600
Mark Heller, hdmstr. Fax 949-0563
Land O'Lakes Christian S 200/PK-12
5105 School Rd, 813-995-9040
David Nichols, admin. Fax 996-6106
Mary's House PK-PK
2348 Collier Pkwy 34639 813-948-5999
Corrine Ertl, dir. Fax 948-5998

Lantana, Palm Beach, Pop. 10,498
Palm Beach County SD
Supt. — See West Palm Beach
Lantana Community MS 800/6-8
1225 W Drew St 33462 561-540-3400
Edward Burke, prin. Fax 540-3435
Lantana ES 500/PK-5
710 W Ocean Ave 33462 561-202-0300
Elaine Persek, prin. Fax 202-0350
Starlight Cove ES 800/K-5
6300 Seminole Dr 33462 561-804-3600
Susan St. John, prin. Fax 804-3650

Kentwood Preparatory S 100/3-12
6210 S Congress Ave 33462 561-649-6141
Adrian Thomas, dir. Fax 649-6142

Largo, Pinellas, Pop. 74,473
Pinellas County SD 105,200/PK-12
301 4th St SW 33770 727-588-6000
Julie Janssen Ed.D., supt. Fax 588-6200
www.pcsb.org
Anona ES 400/K-5
12301 Indian Rocks Rd 33774 727-588-4730
Marsha Jordan, prin. Fax 588-4733
Fitzgerald MS 1,200/6-8
6410 118th Ave 33773 727-547-4526
Bill Corbett, prin. Fax 547-6631
Fuguitt ES 600/PK-5
13010 101st St 33773 727-588-3576
Michael Moss, prin. Fax 588-4630
Helms ES 700/PK-5
561 Clearwater Largo Rd S 33770 727-588-3569
Joyce Spencer, prin. Fax 588-3603
Largo MS 1,100/6-8
155 8th Ave SE 33771 727-588-4600
Fred Ulrich, prin. Fax 588-3720
Oakhurst ES 700/K-5
10535 137th St 33774 727-588-6801
Nanci Wilson, prin. Fax 588-6811
Ridgecrest ES 700/PK-5
1901 119th St 33778 727-588-3580
Donna Benkert, prin. Fax 588-4608
Southern Oak ES 600/PK-5
9101 Walsingham Rd 33773 727-588-4654
Randall Rozelle, prin. Fax 588-4656
Walsingham ES 700/PK-5
9099 Walsingham Rd 33773 727-588-3519
William Nordmark, prin. Fax 588-6990
Other Schools – See Clearwater, Dunedin, Gulfport, Madeira Beach, Oldsmar, Palm Harbor, Pinellas Park, Safety Harbor, Saint Petersburg, Saint Petersburg Beach, Seminole, Tarpon Springs

Country Day S 200/PK-8
11499 Vonn Rd 33774 727-596-1902
Ted Gillette, prin. Fax 596-5479
Indian Rocks Christian S 900/PK-12
12685 Ulmerton Rd 33774 727-596-4321
Don Mayes, supt. Fax 593-5485
St. Jerome ECC 100/PK-PK
10895 Hamlin Blvd 33774 727-596-9491
Denise Roach, dir. Fax 596-8953
St. Patrick S 200/PK-8
1501 Trotter Rd 33770 727-581-4865
Sr. Veronica Visceglia, prin. Fax 581-7842
Veritas Preparatory Academy 100/K-12
12685 Ulmerton Rd 33774 727-593-8791
Kira Wilson, prin.
Westside Christian S 100/K-12
11633 137th St 33774 727-517-2153
Dr. Vicky Jones, admin. Fax 593-7700

Lauderdale Lakes, Broward, Pop. 31,826
Broward County SD
Supt. — See Fort Lauderdale
Lauderdale Lakes MS 1,000/6-8
3911 NW 30th Ave 33309 754-322-3500
Angela Jackson, prin. Fax 322-3585
Oriole ES 800/PK-5
3081 NW 39th St 33309 754-322-7550
Deborah Peeples, prin. Fax 322-7590
Park Lakes ES 1,100/K-5
3925 N State Road 7 33319 754-322-7650
Jeannie Floyd, prin. Fax 322-7690

Phyl's Academy 200/1-8
4645 N State Road 7 33319 954-731-7524
Afua Baptiste, dir. Fax 777-9960

Lauderhill, Broward, Pop. 59,621
Broward County SD
Supt. — See Fort Lauderdale
Castle Hill ES 800/PK-5
2640 NW 46th Ave 33313 754-322-5600
Frances Fuce-Ollivierre, prin. Fax 322-5640
Endeavour Primary Learning Center 500/PK-3
2701 NW 56th Ave 33313 754-321-6600
Vera Groover, prin. Fax 321-6640
Lauderhill MS 800/6-8
1901 NW 49th Ave 33313 754-322-3600
Leo Nesmith, prin. Fax 322-3685
Lauderhill Paul Turner ES 700/PK-5
1500 NW 49th Ave 33313 754-322-6700
Lisa George, prin. Fax 322-6740
Royal Palm ES 900/PK-5
1951 NW 56th Ave 33313 754-322-8350
Robin David, prin. Fax 322-8390

Laurel Hill, Okaloosa, Pop. 577
Okaloosa County SD
Supt. — See Fort Walton Beach
Laurel Hill S 400/PK-12
8078 4th St 32567 850-652-4111
Susan Lowrey-Sexton, prin. Fax 652-4659

Lawtey, Bradford, Pop. 684
Bradford County SD
Supt. — See Starke
Lawtey S 400/PK-8
22703 Park St 32058 904-966-6796
David Tew, prin. Fax 966-6748

Lecanto, Citrus, Pop. 1,243
Citrus County SD
Supt. — See Inverness
Lecanto ES 800/PK-5
3790 W Educational Path 34461 352-746-2220
Rick Kenney, prin. Fax 746-3803
Lecanto MS 800/6-8
3800 W Educational Path 34461 352-746-2050
James Kusmaul, prin. Fax 746-3639

Pope John Paul II Catholic S 200/PK-8
4341 W Homosassa Trl 34461 352-746-2020
Dr. Lou Whitaker, prin. Fax 746-3448
Seven Rivers Christian S 400/PK-12
4221 W Gulf to Lake Hwy 34461 352-746-5696
Joel Satterly, hdmstr. Fax 746-5520

Lee, Madison, Pop. 360
Madison County SD
Supt. — See Madison
Lee ES 200/PK-5
7731 E US Highway 90 32059 850-973-5030
Jack McClellan, prin. Fax 973-5032

Leesburg, Lake, Pop. 19,086
Lake County SD
Supt. — See Tavares
Beverly Shores ES 700/K-5
1108 Griffin Rd 34748 352-787-4175
Mollie Cunningham, prin. Fax 787-1760
Carver MS 800/6-8
1200 Beecher St 34748 352-787-7868
Linda Shepherd-Miller, prin. Fax 787-1339
Leesburg ES 900/K-5
2229 South St 34748 352-365-6308
Durenda McKinney, prin. Fax 365-9018
Oak Park MS 600/6-8
2101 South St 34748 352-787-3232
Letizia Haugabrook, prin. Fax 326-2177
Rimes Early Learning Center 200/PK-2
3101 Schoolview St 34748 352-787-5757
Kathy Cantwell, admin. Fax 787-5615
Treadway ES 900/PK-5
10619 Treadway School Rd 34788 352-742-2291
Robin Neeld, prin. Fax 742-8343

First Academy 400/K-12
219 N 13th St 34748 352-787-7762
Gregory Frescoln, admin. Fax 323-1773
Lake Montessori and Learning Institute 100/PK-8
415 Lee St 34748 352-787-5333
Dr. Hilary Bowman, dir. Fax 787-6517
St. Paul S 200/PK-8
1320 Sunshine Ave 34748 352-787-4657
Lynn Greene, prin. Fax 787-0324

Lehigh Acres, Lee, Pop. 13,611
Lee County SD
Supt. — See Fort Myers
Harns Marsh ES 900/K-5
1800 Unice Ave N 33971 239-690-1249
Charles Luckey, prin. Fax 694-1325
Lehigh Acres MS 1,000/6-8
104 Arthur Ave 33936 239-369-6108
Joe Pitura, prin. Fax 369-8808
Lehigh ES 1,000/PK-5
1200 Homestead Rd N 33936 239-369-2477
Dwayne Courtney, prin. Fax 369-4506
Mirror Lakes ES 1,100/PK-5
525 Charwood Ave S, 239-369-2200
Karen Holliday, prin. Fax 369-0542
Sunshine ES 1,100/PK-5
601 Sara Ave N 33971 239-369-5836
Jeff Dobbins, prin. Fax 369-1455
Varsity Lakes MS 1,000/6-8
801 Gunnery Rd N 33971 239-694-3464
Scott Cook, prin. Fax 694-7093
Veterans Park Academy for the Arts 1,500/K-8
49 Homestead Rd S 33936 239-303-3003
Dale Houchin, prin. Fax 303-3075

Leisure City, Miami-Dade, Pop. 19,379
Miami-Dade County SD
Supt. — See Miami
Campbell Drive ES 1,200/PK-5
15790 SW 307th St 33033 305-245-0270
Annette Diaz, prin. Fax 247-7903

Lithia, Hillsborough
Hillsborough County SD
Supt. — See Tampa
Bevis ES 800/K-5
5720 Osprey Ridge Dr 33547 813-740-4000
Tricia Simonsen, prin. Fax 740-4004
Fishhawk Creek ES 900/K-5
16815 Dorman Rd 33547 813-651-2150
Pam Bush, prin. Fax 651-2154
Pinecrest ES 700/PK-5
7950 Lithia Pinecrest Rd 33547 813-744-8164
Vicki Dotson, prin. Fax 740-4456
Randall MS 1,500/6-8
16510 Fishhawk Blvd 33547 813-740-3900
Marcia Elliott, prin. Fax 740-3910

Live Oak, Suwannee, Pop. 6,922
Suwannee County SD 5,900/PK-12
702 2nd St NW 32064 386-364-2601
Jerry Scarborough, supt. Fax 364-2635
www.suwannee.k12.fl.us
Suwannee ES 700/2-3
1748 Ohio Ave S 32064 386-330-1201
Donna Long, prin. Fax 330-1215
Suwannee IS 600/4-5
1419 Walker Ave SW 32064 386-364-2670
Betty Ann Sumner, prin. Fax 364-2680
Suwannee MS 1,100/6-8
1730 Walker Ave SW 32064 386-364-2730
Norri Steele, prin. Fax 208-1474
Suwannee PS 900/PK-1
1625 Walker Ave SW 32064 386-364-2650
Melissa Moseley, prin. Fax 364-2667
Other Schools – See Branford

Melody Christian Academy 200/PK-12
PO Box 100 32064 386-364-4800
Amanda Davis, prin. Fax 364-1889
Westwood Christian S 100/PK-6
920 11th St SW 32064 386-362-3735
Phyllis Peace, admin. Fax 364-6486

Longwood, Seminole, Pop. 13,580
Seminole County SD
Supt. — See Sanford
Longwood ES 700/PK-5
840 Orange Ave 32750 407-746-3350
Ginny Fisher, prin. Fax 746-3349
Milwee MS 1,100/6-8
1341 S Ronald Reagan Blvd 32750 407-746-3850
Michelle Walsh, prin. Fax 746-3899
Rock Lake MS 1,100/6-8
250 Slade Dr 32750 407-746-9350
Pamela Shellman-Ross, prin. Fax 746-9399
Sabal Point ES 800/PK-5
960 Wekiva Springs Rd 32779 407-746-3050
Angela Zambaux, prin. Fax 746-3058
Wekiva ES 900/PK-5
1450 E Wekiva Trl 32779 407-746-3150
Mike Pfeiffer, prin. Fax 746-3163
Woodlands ES 800/PK-5
1420 EE Williamson Rd 32750 407-746-2750
Barry Liebovitz, prin. Fax 746-2799

Forest Lake Education Center 600/PK-8
1275 Learning Loop 32779 407-862-7688
Janet Ledesma, prin. Fax 774-7723
Sweetwater Episcopal Academy 200/PK-5
251 E Lake Brantley Dr 32779 407-862-1882
Janet Stroup, hdmstr. Fax 788-1714
Wekiva Christian S 200/PK-8
1675 Dixon Rd 32779 407-774-0168

Loxahatchee, Palm Beach
Palm Beach County SD
Supt. — See West Palm Beach
Acreage Pines ES 500/K-5
14200 Orange Blvd 33470 561-904-9500
James Campbell, prin. Fax 904-9550
Frontier ES 900/K-5
6701 180th Ave N 33470 561-784-4100
Dwan Moore-Ross, prin. Fax 784-4105
Loxahatchee Groves ES 700/K-5
16020 Okeechobee Blvd 33470 561-795-4961
Richard Myerson, prin. Fax 791-9318
Osceola Creek MS 900/6-8
6775 180th Ave N 33470 561-422-2500
David Alfonso, prin. Fax 422-2510
Pierce Hammock ES 700/K-5
14255 Hamlin Blvd 33470 561-651-0400
Jeffrey Eassa, prin. Fax 651-0410

Lutz, Hillsborough, Pop. 10,552
Hillsborough County SD
Supt. — See Tampa
Lutz ES 800/PK-5
202 5th Ave SE 33549 813-949-1452
Mary Fernandez, prin. Fax 948-2982
Maniscalco ES 700/PK-5
939 Debuel Rd 33549 813-949-0337
Annette Gaddy, prin. Fax 948-3270
Martinez MS 1,100/6-8
5601 W Lutz Lake Fern Rd 33558 813-558-1190
Shaylia Hall, prin. Fax 558-1226
McKitrick ES 1,100/K-5
5503 W Lutz Lake Fern Rd 33558 813-558-5427
Lisa Yost, prin. Fax 558-5431
Schwarzkopf ES 700/K-5
18333 Calusa Trace Blvd 33558 813-975-6945
Cheryl Holley, prin. Fax 975-6948

Pasco County SD
Supt. — See Land O Lakes
Denham Oaks ES 900/K-5
1422 Oak Grove Blvd 33559 813-794-1600
Mardee Powers, prin. Fax 794-1691

Berean Academy 200/K-12
17951 N US Highway 41 33549 813-932-0552
Bruce Kirby, hdmstr. Fax 930-2134
St. Timothy ECC 100/PK-PK
17512 Lakeshore Rd 33558 813-960-4857
Daisy Cintron, dir. Fax 961-9429

Lynn Haven, Bay, Pop. 15,677
Bay County SD
Supt. — See Panama City
Lynn Haven ES 900/PK-5
301 W 9th St 32444 850-265-2131
Lee Anne Stafford, prin. Fax 271-3685
Mowat MS 1,000/6-8
1903 W Highway 390 32444 850-271-6140
Shirley Baker, prin. Fax 265-2179

Macclenny, Baker, Pop. 5,186
Baker County SD 5,000/PK-12
392 South Blvd E 32063 904-259-6251
Sherrie Raulerson, supt. Fax 259-2825
www.baker.k12.fl.us
Baker County MS 1,100/6-8
211 E Jonathan St 32063 904-259-2226
David Davis, prin. Fax 259-7955
Baker County PK/K Center 600/PK-K
362 South Blvd E 32063 904-259-0405
Debbie Fraser, prin. Fax 259-0379
Keller IS 700/4-5
420 S 8th St 32063 904-259-4244
Gail Griffis, prin. Fax 259-3771
Macclenny ES 500/1-3
1 Wild Kitten Dr 32063 904-259-2551
Luanne Williams, prin. Fax 259-5171
Other Schools – See Glen Saint Mary

MacDill AFB, See Tampa
Hillsborough County SD
Supt. — See Tampa
Tinker ES 600/PK-5
8207 Tinker St 33621 813-840-2043
Cheryl Tyo, prin. Fax 233-3664

Madeira Beach, Pinellas, Pop. 4,464
Pinellas County SD
Supt. — See Largo
Madeira Beach ES 500/PK-5
749 Madeira Beach Cswy 33708 727-547-7838
Susan Kotchman, prin. Fax 545-6432
Madeira Beach MS 1,100/6-8
591 Tom Stuart Cswy 33708 727-547-7697
Brenda Poff, prin. Fax 547-7528

Madison, Madison, Pop. 3,190
Madison County SD 2,700/PK-12
210 NE Duval Ave 32340 850-973-5022
Lou Miller, supt. Fax 973-5027
www.madison.k12.fl.us
Madison County Central S 1,300/PK-8
2093 W US 90 32340 850-973-5192
Sam Stalnaker, prin. Fax 973-5194
Other Schools – See Greenville, Lee, Pinetta

Madison Academy 200/PK-8
PO Box 690 32341 850-973-2529
Janna Barrs, hdmstr. Fax 973-8974

Maitland, Orange, Pop. 14,125
Orange County SD
Supt. — See Orlando
Dommerich ES 700/PK-5
1900 Choctaw Trl 32751 407-623-1407
Robin Matthes, prin. Fax 623-5738
Lake Sybelia ES 500/PK-5
600 Sandspur Rd 32751 407-623-1445
John Rowland, prin. Fax 623-1452
Maitland MS 1,000/6-8
1901 Choctaw Trl 32751 407-623-1462
Eric Lundman, prin. Fax 623-1474

Hebrew Day S 200/K-8
851 N Maitland Ave 32751 407-647-0713
Lynne Shefsky, dir. Fax 647-1223
King of Kings Lutheran S 100/PK-8
1101 N Wymore Rd 32751 407-628-5696
Martin Plocher, prin. Fax 628-5230
Lake Forrest Preparatory S 200/PK-5
866 Lake Howell Rd 32751 407-331-5144
Michele Purvis, prin. Fax 331-1849
Maitland Montessori S 100/PK-6
200 N Swoope Ave 32751 407-628-0019
Adele Fondo, prin. Fax 628-9796
Orangewood Christian S 700/PK-12
1300 W Maitland Blvd 32751 407-339-0223
LuAnne Schendel, hdmstr. Fax 339-4148
Park Maitland S 700/PK-6
1450 S Orlando Ave 32751 407-647-3038
Carolyn Cappleman, prin. Fax 645-4755

Malone, Jackson, Pop. 2,012
Jackson County SD
Supt. — See Marianna
Malone S 600/PK-12
PO Box 68 32445 850-482-9950
Linda Hall, prin. Fax 482-9981

Marathon, Monroe, Pop. 9,822
Monroe County SD
Supt. — See Key West
Switlik ES 500/PK-5
3400 Overseas Hwy 33050 305-289-2490
Barbara Wright, prin. Fax 289-2496

Marathon Lutheran S 50/K-6
325 122nd Street Gulf 33050 305-289-0700
Paula Roberts, prin. Fax 289-0700

Marco Island, Collier, Pop. 16,109
Collier County SD
Supt. — See Naples
Barfield ES 700/K-5
101 Kirkwood St 34145 239-377-8500
Dr. Jory Westberry, prin. Fax 377-8501

Island Montessori Academy 50/PK-4
PO Box 224 34146 239-642-2020
Lisa Baldwin, prin. Fax 394-6570

Margate, Broward, Pop. 56,002
Broward County SD
Supt. — See Fort Lauderdale
Atlantic West ES 1,000/K-5
301 NW 69th Ter 33063 754-322-5300
Dr. Sharon Moffitt, prin. Fax 322-5340
Liberty ES 1,100/K-5
2450 Banks Rd 33063 754-322-6750
David Levine, prin. Fax 322-6790
Margate ES 1,000/K-5
6300 NW 18th St 33063 754-322-6900
Sharon Schmidt, prin. Fax 322-6940
Margate MS 1,200/6-8
500 NW 65th Ave 33063 754-322-3800
Hudson Thomas, prin. Fax 322-3885

Abundant Life Christian Academy 400/PK-8
1494 Banks Rd 33063 954-979-2665
Stacy Angier, admin. Fax 979-1983
Faith Christian S 100/PK-12
6950 Royal Palm Blvd 33063 954-974-2404
Michael Linder, prin. Fax 974-0139
Hebrew Academy Community S 400/PK-8
1500 N State Road 7 33063 954-978-6341
Carol Stav, admin. Fax 333-3913

Marianna, Jackson, Pop. 6,275
Jackson County SD 7,200/PK-12
PO Box 5958 32447 850-482-1200
Lee Miller, supt. Fax 482-1299
web.jcsb.org
Golson ES 1,000/PK-2
4258 2nd Ave 32446 850-482-9607
Don Wilson, prin. Fax 482-1203
Marianna MS 700/6-8
4144 South St 32448 850-482-9609
Dr. Gayle Westbrook, prin. Fax 482-9795
Riverside ES 700/3-5
2958 Cherokee St 32446 850-482-9611
John Ellerbee, prin. Fax 482-9300
Other Schools – See Cottondale, Graceville, Grand Ridge, Malone, Sneads

---

Dayspring Christian Academy 100/PK-8
4685 Meadowview Rd 32446 850-526-4919
Marianna Adventist Academy K-6
PO Box 159 32447 850-482-2659

Mary Esther, Okaloosa, Pop. 4,086
Okaloosa County SD
Supt. — See Fort Walton Beach
Florosa ES 600/PK-5
1700 W Highway 98 32569 850-833-4381
Carolyn Lulue, prin. Fax 833-4391
Mary Esther ES 500/PK-5
320 E Miracle Strip Pkwy 32569 850-833-3371
Annette Maldonado, prin. Fax 833-3474

Mayo, Lafayette, Pop. 1,032
LaFayette County SD 1,100/PK-12
363 NE Crawford St 32066 386-294-1351
Thomas Lashley, supt. Fax 294-3072
hornet.lafayette.k12.fl.us
LaFayette ES 600/PK-5
811 E Main St 32066 386-294-4112
Gina Hart, prin. Fax 294-4320

Lighthouse Christian Academy 100/PK-12
PO Box 458 32066 386-294-2994
Jennifer Roberts, prin. Fax 294-3449

Melbourne, Brevard, Pop. 76,646
Brevard County SD 69,600/PK-12
2700 Jdge Fran Jamieson Way 32940 321-633-1000
Dr. Richard DiPatri, supt. Fax 633-3432
www.brevard.k12.fl.us
Allen ES 800/PK-6
2601 Fountainhead Blvd 32935 321-242-6450
Carol Carmichael, prin. Fax 242-6453
Creel ES 900/PK-6
2000 Glenwood Dr 32935 321-259-3233
Kathryn Eward, prin. Fax 259-3844
Croton ES 600/PK-6
1449 Croton Rd 32935 321-259-3818
Linda Rinehart, prin. Fax 242-6477
Harbor City ES 400/K-6
1377 Sarno Rd 32935 321-254-5534
Barbara Belanger, prin. Fax 242-6468
Johnson MS 1,000/7-8
2155 Croton Rd 32935 321-242-6430
Robert Fish, prin. Fax 242-6436
Longleaf ES 600/K-6
4290 N Wickham Rd 32935 321-242-4700
Marilyn Sylvester, prin. Fax 242-4708
Manatee ES 800/PK-6
3425 Viera Blvd 32940 321-433-0050
Carl Brown, prin. Fax 433-9927
Meadowlane IS 500/4-6
2700 Wingate Blvd 32904 321-722-5539
Kerri Nash, prin. Fax 722-4719
Quest ES 700/PK-6
8751 Trafford Dr 32940 321-242-1411
Elia Lea, prin. Fax 242-1719
Sabal ES 600/PK-6
1401 N Wickham Rd 32935 321-254-7261
Stephanie Hall, prin. Fax 242-6475
Sherwood ES 700/PK-6
2541 Post Rd 32935 321-254-6424
Cindy Wilson, prin. Fax 242-6478
Stone MS 700/7-8
1101 E University Blvd 32901 321-723-0741
Andrew Johnson, prin. Fax 951-1497
Suntree ES 800/PK-6
900 Jordan Blass Dr 32940 321-242-6480
Lisa Larkin, prin. Fax 242-6485
University Park ES 600/PK-6
500 W University Blvd 32901 321-723-2566
Donna Entsminger, prin. Fax 952-5971
Other Schools – See Cape Canaveral, Cocoa, Cocoa Beach, Indialantic, Indian Harbor Beach, Melbourne Beach, Merritt Island, Mims, Palm Bay, Rockledge, Satellite Beach, Titusville, West Melbourne

---

Ascension Catholic S 500/PK-8
2950 N Harbor City Blvd 32935 321-254-5495
Douglas Workman, prin. Fax 259-0993
Community Christian S 100/PK-12
1616 Ferndale Ave 32935 321-259-1590
Laurel Earls, prin. Fax 259-5301
Faith Fellowship Academy 200/PK-PK
2820 Business Center Blvd 32940 321-259-7200
Carissa Reynolds, dir.
Holy Trinity Episcopal Academy 900/PK-12
5625 Holy Trinity Dr 32940 321-723-8323
Catherine Ford, hdmstr. Fax 308-9077
Melbourne-Palm Bay Christian S 50/PK-8
210 W New Haven Ave 32901 321-727-8877
New Covenant Christian S 100/K-12
1926 S Babcock St 32901 321-724-9603
Sandra Hancock, prin. Fax 724-6932
Our Lady of Lourdes S 200/PK-8
420 E Fee Ave 32901 321-723-3631
Lourdes Wyatt, prin. Fax 723-7408
R.F.M Christian Academy 100/K-12
777 S Apollo Blvd 32901 321-952-3787
Ezella Parker, prin. Fax 952-8171
Wade Christian Academy 100/K-12
4300 N Wickham Rd 32935 321-259-6788
Jack Snyder, prin. Fax 259-0399
West Melbourne Christian Academy 200/PK-12
3150 Milwaukee Ave 32904 321-725-3743
Mark Siler, prin. Fax 725-6661

Melbourne Beach, Brevard, Pop. 3,314
Brevard County SD
Supt. — See Melbourne
Gemini ES 600/PK-6
2100 Oak St 32951 321-727-3090
Joan Holliday, prin. Fax 725-7481

Melrose, Putnam
Putnam County SD
Supt. — See Palatka
Melrose Community ES 300/PK-5
401 State Road 26 32666 352-475-2060
Montez Wynn, prin. Fax 475-1049

Merritt Island, Brevard, Pop. 36,800
Brevard County SD
Supt. — See Melbourne
Audubon ES 600/PK-6
1201 N Banana River Dr 32952 321-452-2085
Lynn Francisco, prin. Fax 454-1055
Carroll ES 900/K-6
1 Skyline Blvd 32953 321-452-1234
Pennie Farrell-Wade, prin. Fax 454-1064
Gardendale ES 500/PK-6
301 Grove Blvd 32953 321-452-1411
Terri Moeller, prin. Fax 454-1094
Jefferson MS 700/7-8
1275 S Courtenay Pkwy 32952 321-453-5154
Sherri Bowman, prin. Fax 459-2854
Mila ES 400/PK-6
288 W Merritt Ave 32953 321-454-1070
Dr. Betsy Butler, prin. Fax 454-1071
Stevenson S of the Arts 300/PK-6
1450 Martin Blvd 32952 321-454-3550
Michael Corneau, prin. Fax 454-3553
Tropical ES 800/PK-6
885 S Courtenay Pkwy 32952 321-454-1080
Jane Respess, prin. Fax 454-1087

Divine Mercy Catholic S 200/PK-8
1940 N Courtenay Pkwy 32953 321-452-0263
Ronald Gagnon, prin. Fax 453-7573
Merritt Island Christian S 700/PK-12
140 Magnolia Ave 32952 321-453-2710
Dr. David Piccolo, hdmstr. Fax 452-6580

Miami, Miami-Dade, Pop. 386,417
Miami-Dade County SD 338,000/PK-12
1450 NE 2nd Ave 33132 305-995-1000
Dr. Rudolph Crew, supt. Fax 995-1488
www.dadeschools.net/
Allapattah MS 800/6-8
1331 NW 46th St 33142 305-634-9787
Adolfo Costa, prin. Fax 638-8254
Ammons MS 1,200/6-8
17990 SW 142nd Ave 33177 305-971-0158
Irwin Adler, prin. Fax 971-0179
Andover MS 6-8
121 NE 207th St 33179 305-654-2727
Arnold Montgomery, prin. Fax 654-2728
Angelou ES 700/PK-5
1850 NW 32nd St 33142 305-636-3480
Dr. Linda Whye, prin. Fax 636-3486
Arcola Lake ES 600/PK-6
1037 NW 81st St 33150 305-836-2820
Vanady Daniels, prin. Fax 694-2340
Arvida MS 1,600/6-8
10900 SW 127th Ave 33186 305-385-7144
Nancy Aragon, prin. Fax 383-9472
Ashe ES 1,300/PK-5
6601 SW 152nd Ave 33193 305-386-6667
Dr. Kamela Patto, prin. Fax 385-6408
Ashe Primary Learning Center PK-K
16251 SW 72nd St 33193 305-380-1927
Fax 380-1930
Auburndale ES 1,000/PK-5
3255 SW 6th St 33135 305-445-3587
Liliana Salazar, prin. Fax 446-4709
Aventura Waterways K-8 Center 1,300/K-8
21101 NE 26th Ave 33180 305-933-5200
Luis Bello, prin. Fax 933-5201
Banyan ES 300/K-5
3060 SW 85th Ave 33155 305-221-4011
Carolyn McCalla, prin. Fax 225-4602
Barreiro ES K-5
5125 SW 162nd Pl 33185 305-229-4800
Patricia Morales, prin. Fax 229-4801
Beckford/Richmond ES 400/PK-5
16929 SW 104th Ave 33157 305-238-5194
Dr. Sharon Lee, prin. Fax 238-0397
Beckham ES 800/PK-5
4702 SW 143rd Ct 33175 305-222-8161
Maria Visiedo, prin. Fax 222-4900
Bell MS 1,300/6-8
11800 NW 2nd St 33182 305-220-2075
Ingrid Soto, prin. Fax 229-0798

Bent Tree ES 600/K-5
4861 SW 140th Ave 33175 305-221-0461
Esther Visiedo, prin. Fax 551-2661

Biscayne Gardens ES 900/K-6
560 NW 151st St 33169 305-681-5721
Maria Lacavalla, prin. Fax 685-8036

Blanton ES 600/PK-5
10327 NW 11th Ave 33150 305-696-9241
Tangela Goa, prin. Fax 693-5375

Blue Lakes ES 500/PK-5
9250 SW 52nd Ter 33165 305-271-7411
Aida Marrero, prin. Fax 279-5103

Boone-Highland Oaks ES 1,000/PK-6
20500 NE 24th Ave 33180 305-931-1770
Dr. Kim Rubin, prin. Fax 936-5722

Bossard ES 600/K-5
15950 SW 144th St 33196 305-254-5200
Charmyn Kirton, prin. Fax 254-5201

Broadmoor ES 500/PK-5
3401 NW 83rd St 33147 305-691-0861
Linda Klein, prin. Fax 696-7908

Calusa ES 800/PK-5
9580 W Calusa Club Dr 33186 305-385-0589
Carmen Fuentes, prin. Fax 383-3829

Canosa MS 1,300/6-8
15735 SW 144th St 33196 305-252-5900
Dr. Pablo Ortiz, prin. Fax 252-5901

Caribbean ES 900/PK-5
11990 SW 200th St 33177 305-233-7131
Christina Guerra, prin. Fax 238-7082

Chiles MS 1,600/6-8
8190 NW 197th St 33015 305-816-9101
John Messersmith, prin. Fax 816-9248

Citrus Grove ES 1,100/PK-5
2121 NW 5th St 33125 305-642-4141
Gwendolyn Haynes, prin. Fax 649-3789

Citrus Grove MS 1,100/6-8
2153 NW 3rd St 33125 305-642-5055
Emirce Ladaga, prin. Fax 642-9349

Colonial Drive ES 400/PK-5
10755 SW 160th St 33157 305-238-2392
Henry Fernandez, prin. Fax 232-9405

Comstock ES 700/PK-5
2420 NW 18th Ave 33142 305-635-7341
Deborah Wilson, prin. Fax 636-1740

Coral Park ES 900/K-5
1225 SW 97th Ave 33174 305-221-5632
Maria Nunez, prin. Fax 227-5734

Coral Reef ES 800/PK-5
7955 SW 152nd St 33157 305-235-1464
Dr. Fred Albion, prin. Fax 254-3725

Coral Terrace ES 500/PK-5
6801 SW 24th St 33155 305-262-8300
Jorge Sotolongo, prin. Fax 267-1526

Coral Way S 1,600/PK-8
1950 SW 13th Ave 33145 305-854-0515
Alejandro Perez, prin. Fax 285-9632

Country Club MS 400/6-8
18305 NW 75th Pl 33015 305-820-8800
Jose Bueno, prin. Fax 820-8801

Crowder ES 200/PK-3
757 NW 66th St 33150 305-836-0012
Avis Bembry, prin. Fax 836-6910

Curry MS 1,700/6-8
15750 SW 47th St 33185 305-222-2775
Wandarece Ruan, prin. Fax 229-1521

Cypress ES 400/PK-5
5400 SW 112th Ct 33165 305-271-1611
Melanie Visnich, prin. Fax 279-3622

Dario MS 900/6-8
350 NW 97th Ave 33172 305-226-0179
Barbara Mendizabal, prin. Fax 559-0919

De Diego MS 900/6-8
3100 NW 5th Ave 33127 305-573-7229
Jerry Clay, prin. Fax 573-6415

Devon Aire K-8 Center 1,100/PK-8
10501 SW 122nd Ave 33186 305-274-7100
Andy Pierre-Louis, prin. Fax 270-1826

Doolin MS 1,000/6-8
6401 SW 152nd Ave 33193 305-386-6656
Eduardo Tillet, prin. Fax 408-3068

Doral MS 1,400/6-8
5005 NW 112th Ct 33178 305-592-2822
Tatiana De Miranda, prin. Fax 597-3853

Douglas ES 1,100/PK-5
11901 SW 2nd St 33184 305-226-4356
Rodolfo Rodriguez, prin. Fax 553-0001

Douglas Primary Learning Ctr PK-K
650 NW 132nd Ave 33182 305-222-4822
Fax 227-3602

Douglass ES 500/PK-5
314 NW 12th St 33136 305-371-4687
Regina Lowe-Smith, prin. Fax 350-7590

Drew ES 600/PK-5
1775 NW 60th St 33142 305-691-8021
Cathy Williams, prin. Fax 691-3960

Drew MS 800/6-8
1801 NW 60th St 33142 305-633-6057
Dr. Henry Crawford, prin. Fax 638-1307

Dunbar ES 500/PK-6
505 NW 20th St 33127 305-573-2344
Ann Gary, prin. Fax 573-8482

Earlington Heights ES 500/PK-5
4750 NW 22nd Ave 33142 305-635-7505
Dr. Thalya Watkins, prin. Fax 634-4973

Edison Park ES 400/PK-5
500 NW 67th St 33150 305-758-3658
Yecenia Lopez, prin. Fax 758-5732

Emerson ES 400/PK-5
8001 SW 36th St 33155 305-264-5757
Liliana Albuerne, prin. Fax 267-2476

Evans ES 300/PK-5
1895 NW 75th St 33147 305-691-4973
Reggie Johnson, prin. Fax 691-4867

Eve ES 800/PK-5
16251 SW 99th St 33196 305-383-9392
Carlos Diaz, prin. Fax 380-1919

Everglades S 1,200/PK-8
8375 SW 16th St 33155 305-264-4154
Dr. Doylene Tarver, prin. Fax 261-8179

Fairchild ES 600/PK-5
5757 SW 45th St 33155 305-665-5483
William Kinney, prin. Fax 669-5401

Fairlawn ES 700/PK-5
444 SW 60th Ave 33144 305-261-8880
Amelia Leth, prin. Fax 267-9174

Fascell ES 1,000/PK-5
15625 SW 80th St 33193 305-380-1901
Estela Santiago, prin. Fax 380-1912

Finlay ES 700/PK-5
851 SW 117th Ave 33184 305-552-7122
Cecelia Sanchez, prin. Fax 480-7652

Flagami ES 500/PK-5
920 SW 76th Ave 33144 305-261-2031
Dr. Kathleen Caballero, prin. Fax 267-2980

Flagler ES 800/PK-5
5222 NW 1st St 33126 305-443-2529
Maria Izquierdo, prin. Fax 448-8508

Floyd ES 700/PK-5
12650 SW 109th Ave 33176 305-255-3934
Eliseo Hernandez, prin. Fax 234-0484

Glades MS 1,400/6-8
9451 SW 64th Ter 33173 305-271-3342
Elio Falcon, prin. Fax 271-0402

Glazer MS 6-8
15015 SW 24th St 33185 305-485-2323
Melba Brito, prin. Fax 485-2324

Gordon ES 1,100/PK-PK, 2-
14600 Country Walk Dr 33186 305-234-4805
Ruth Alperin, prin. Fax 234-4815

Gordon Panther Primary Learning Center K-1
15001 SW 127th Ave 33186 305-234-4855
Fax 234-4858

Gratigny ES 700/PK-6
11905 N Miami Ave 33168 305-681-6685
Dr. Aaron Enteen, prin. Fax 687-3321

Greenglade ES 700/PK-5
3060 SW 127th Ave 33175 305-223-5330
Dr. Maria Tercilla, prin. Fax 222-8141

Hadley ES 1,200/PK-5
8400 NW 7th St 33126 305-261-3719
Maria Menchero, prin. Fax 267-2984

Hall ES 800/PK-5
1901 SW 134th Ave 33175 305-223-9823
Cathay Abreu, prin. Fax 220-9758

Hammocks MS 2,200/6-8
9889 Hammocks Blvd 33196 305-385-0896
Peter Cabrera, prin. Fax 382-0861

Hartner ES 800/PK-5
401 NW 29th St 33127 305-573-8181
Dr. Orlando Gonzalez, prin. Fax 571-2511

Hibiscus ES 600/K-5
18701 NW 1st Ave 33169 305-652-3018
Dyona McLean, prin. Fax 654-5700

Holmes ES 300/PK-6
1175 NW 67th St 33150 305-836-3421
Dahlia Gonzalez, prin. Fax 696-4517

Hoover ES 1,100/PK-5
9050 Hammocks Blvd 33196 305-385-4382
Neyda Navarro, prin. Fax 380-9609

Hoover Preschool PK-PK
15700 SW 96th St 33196 305-383-0915
Fax 385-2717

Howard Drive ES 600/PK-5
7750 SW 136th St 33156 305-235-1412
Deanna Dalby, prin. Fax 256-3105

Hurston ES 800/PK-5
13137 SW 26th St 33175 305-222-8152
Dr. Lilia Dobao, prin. Fax 222-4923

Kendale ES 500/PK-5
10693 SW 93rd St 33176 305-274-2735
Dr. Jeanethe Thompson, prin. Fax 274-4792

Kendale Lakes ES 900/PK-5
8000 SW 142nd Ave 33183 305-385-2575
Margaret Ferrarone, prin. Fax 386-2718

Kensington Park ES 1,300/PK-5
711 NW 30th Ave 33125 305-649-2811
Genaro Navarro, prin. Fax 642-9346

Kensington Park Primary Learning Center PK-K
1025 NW 30th Ave 33125 305-649-4301
Fax 649-2316

Kenwood S 1,100/PK-8
9300 SW 79th Ave 33156 305-271-5061
Moraima Perez, prin. Fax 273-2132

King ES 300/PK-3
7124 NW 12th Ave 33150 305-836-0928
Tamme Williams, prin. Fax 691-0638

Kinloch Park ES 900/PK-5
4275 NW 1st St 33126 305-445-1351
Ana Casas, prin. Fax 567-3530

Kinloch Park MS 1,200/6-8
4340 NW 3rd St 33126 305-445-5467
Scott Weiner, prin. Fax 445-3110

Lakeview ES 600/PK-5
1290 NW 115th St 33167 305-757-1535
Dr. Sharon Lewis, prin. Fax 754-0657

Leewood K-8 Center 600/K-8
10343 SW 124th St 33176 305-233-7430
Bart Christie, prin. Fax 256-3104

Lehman ES 800/PK-5
10990 SW 113th Pl 33176 305-273-2140
Maria Cruz, prin. Fax 273-2228

Liberty City ES 200/PK-5
1855 NW 71st St 33147 305-691-8532
Cheri Davis, prin. Fax 696-7842

Little River ES 600/PK-5
514 NW 77th St 33150 305-754-7531
Fernando Diaz, prin. Fax 756-8768

Lorah Park ES 500/PK-5
5160 NW 31st Ave 33142 305-633-1424
Mattye Jones, prin. Fax 636-3075

L'Ouverture ES 500/PK-5
120 NE 59th St 33137 305-758-2600
Dr. Liliane Delbor, prin. Fax 751-6764

Mack/West Little River ES 200/PK-K, 4-6
2450 NW 84th St 33147 305-691-6491
Sandra Banky, prin. Fax 693-1960

Madison MS 800/6-8
3400 NW 87th St 33147 305-836-2610
Dr. Tonya Dillard, prin. Fax 696-5249

Mann MS 900/6-8
8950 NW 2nd Ave 33150 305-757-9537
Carmen Jones-Carey, prin. Fax 754-0724

Martin S 900/PK-8
14250 Boggs Dr 33176 305-238-3688
Pamela Brown, prin. Fax 232-4068

Matthews ES 900/PK-5
12345 SW 18th Ter 33175 305-222-8150
John Lengomin, prin. Fax 222-8168

McMillan MS 1,200/6-8
13100 SW 59th St 33183 305-385-6877
Hilca Thomas, prin. Fax 387-9641

Meek/Westview ES 500/PK-5
2101 NW 127th St 33167 305-688-9641
Tracey Crews, prin. Fax 769-0166

Melrose ES 600/PK-5
3050 NW 35th St 33142 305-635-8676
Sergio Munoz, prin. Fax 635-4006

Merritt S 600/PK-8
660 SW 3rd St 33130 305-326-0791
Carmen Garcia, prin. Fax 326-0749

Miami Edison MS 600/6-8
6101 NW 2nd Ave 33127 305-754-4683
Richelle Lumpkin, prin. Fax 757-2219

Miami Heights ES 1,400/PK-5
17661 SW 117th Ave 33177 305-238-3602
John Lux, prin. Fax 233-0991

Miami Park ES 600/PK-5
2225 NW 103rd St 33147 305-691-6361
Sandra Pelham, prin. Fax 694-8328

Morningside ES 500/PK-5
6620 NE 5th Ave 33138 305-758-6741
Kathleen Louissaint, prin. Fax 751-2980

Norland ES 700/PK-5
19340 NW 8th Ct 33169 305-652-6074
Karen Powers, prin. Fax 651-4553

Norland MS 1,500/6-8
1235 NW 192nd Ter 33169 305-653-1210
Cheryl Nelson, prin. Fax 654-1237

Norwood ES 500/PK-6
19810 NW 14th Ct 33169 305-653-0068
Frances Daddario, prin. Fax 654-5702

Ojus ES 800/K-5
18600 W Dixie Hwy 33180 305-931-4881
Dr. Marta Mejia, prin. Fax 933-8592

Olinda ES 400/K-5
5536 NW 21st Ave 33142 305-633-0308
Adrian Montes, prin. Fax 635-8919

Olympia Heights ES 600/PK-5
9797 SW 40th St 33165 305-221-3821
Francisca Nobregas, prin. Fax 221-5195

Orchard Villa ES 600/PK-5
5720 NW 13th Ave 33142 305-754-0607
Patricia Duncan, prin. Fax 754-0929

Palmetto ES 600/PK-6
12401 SW 74th Ave 33156 305-238-4306
Mirta Segredo, prin. Fax 254-7774

Parkway ES 600/PK-5
1320 NW 188th St 33169 305-653-0066
Tracie Abner, prin. Fax 654-5701

Pepper ES 1,000/PK-5
14550 SW 96th St 33186 305-386-5244
Deborah Roberts, prin. Fax 382-7150

Pharr ES 200/PK-K, 4-6
2000 NW 46th St 33142 305-633-0429
Dr. Sandra Clark, prin. Fax 634-8487

Pinecrest ES 800/PK-5
10250 SW 57th Ave 33156 305-667-5579
Marisol Diaz, prin. Fax 662-7163

Pine Lake ES 600/PK-5
16700 SW 109th Ave 33157 305-233-7018
Caleb Lopez, prin. Fax 233-4042

Pine Villa ES 800/PK-5
21799 SW 117th Ct 33170 305-258-5366
Tamela Brown, prin. Fax 258-5848

Poinciana Park ES 400/PK-5
6745 NW 23rd Ave 33147 305-691-5640
Kimberly Emmanuel, prin. Fax 696-8624

Porter ES 1,000/PK-5
15851 SW 112th St 33196 305-382-0792
Raul Gutierrez, prin. Fax 383-2761

Reeves ES 900/K-5
2005 NW 111th St 33167 305-953-7243
Julian Gibbs, prin. Fax 953-7251

Richmond Heights MS 1,300/6-8
15015 SW 103rd Ave 33176 305-238-2316
Carol Wright, prin. Fax 251-3712

Riverside ES 1,100/PK-5
1190 SW 2nd St 33130 305-547-1520
Sharon Lopez, prin. Fax 547-4102

Riviera MS 700/6-8
10301 SW 48th St 33165 305-226-4286
Valerie Carrier, prin. Fax 226-1025

Roberts K-8 Center 1,300/PK-8
14850 Cottonwood Cir 33185 305-220-8254
Ana Othon, prin. Fax 226-8345

Rockway ES 500/PK-5
2790 SW 93rd Ct 33165 305-221-1192
Debbie Saumell, prin. Fax 223-5794

Rockway MS 1,300/6-8
9393 SW 29th Ter 33165 305-221-8212
Maria Cedeno, prin. Fax 221-5940

Royal Green ES 800/K-5
13047 SW 47th St 33175 305-221-4452
Alba Misas, prin. Fax 220-6238

Royal Palm ES 600/PK-5
4200 SW 112th Ct 33165 305-221-7961
Carlos Fernandez, prin. Fax 222-8145

Santa Clara ES 600/PK-5
1051 NW 29th Ter 33127 305-635-1417
Marie Caceres, prin. Fax 637-1705

Scott Lake ES 700/PK-5
1160 NW 175th St 33169 305-624-1443
Valerie Ward, prin. Fax 625-2567

Seminole ES 600/PK-5
121 SW 78th Pl 33144 305-261-7071
Cynthia Flanagan, prin. Fax 262-8740

Shadowlawn ES 300/PK-5
149 NW 49th St 33127 305-758-3673
Cathleen McGinn, prin. Fax 759-9352

Shenandoah ES 1,000/PK-5
1023 SW 21st Ave 33135 305-643-4433
Martha Rodriguez, prin. Fax 643-3745
Shenandoah MS 1,100/6-8
1950 SW 19th St 33145 305-856-8282
Lourdes Delgado, prin. Fax 285-4792
Sibley ES 900/K-5
255 NW 115th St 33168 305-953-3737
Michael Charlot, prin. Fax 953-5447
Silver Bluff ES 600/PK-5
2609 SW 25th Ave 33133 305-856-5197
Dr. Brenda Dawkins, prin. Fax 854-9671
Smith ES 1,300/PK-5
10415 NW 52nd St 33178 305-406-0220
Gwendolyn Hines, prin. Fax 406-0225
Smith ES 600/PK-5
4700 NW 12th Ave 33127 305-635-0873
Wanda Heidelberg, prin. Fax 637-1124
Snapper Creek ES 600/PK-5
10151 SW 64th St 33173 305-271-2111
Eric Torres, prin. Fax 596-2475
South Miami Heights ES 800/PK-5
12231 SW 190th Ter 33177 305-238-6610
Dr. Maria Pabellon, prin. Fax 233-7632
Southside ES 400/PK-5
45 SW 13th St 33130 305-371-3311
Salvatore Schiavone, prin. Fax 381-6237
Spanish Lake ES 1,300/PK-5
7940 NW 194th St 33015 305-816-0300
Jacqueline Gonzalez, prin. Fax 816-0301
Stirrup ES 900/PK-5
330 NW 97th Ave 33172 305-226-7001
Dr. Marisel Elias, prin. Fax 220-6737
Sunset Park ES 700/PK-5
10235 SW 84th St 33173 305-279-3222
Sara Martin, prin. Fax 273-2130
Sweetwater ES 1,000/PK-5
10655 SW 4th St 33174 305-559-1101
Delio Diaz, prin. Fax 485-9396
Sylvania Heights ES 600/PK-5
5901 SW 16th St 33155 305-266-3511
Maria Llerena, prin. Fax 266-4435
Thomas K-8 Center 1,700/K-8
5950 NW 114th Ave 33178 305-592-7914
Mayra Falcon, prin. Fax 463-7241
Thomas MS 1,100/6-8
13001 SW 26th St 33175 305-995-3800
Lisa Pizzimenti, prin. Fax 995-3537
Tropical ES 500/PK-5
4545 SW 104th Ave 33165 305-221-0284
Yubeda Miah, prin. Fax 220-4902
Tucker ES 400/PK-5
3500 S Douglas Rd 33133 305-567-3533
Annette Degoti, prin. Fax 529-0409
Village Green ES 500/PK-5
12265 SW 34th St 33175 305-226-0441
Maria Chappotin, prin. Fax 222-8140
Vineland ES 600/K-8
8455 SW 119th St 33156 305-238-7931
Maryann MacLaren, prin. Fax 378-0776
West Miami MS 1,200/6-8
7525 SW 24th St 33155 305-261-8383
Jacques Bentolila, prin. Fax 267-8204
Westview MS 700/6-8
1901 NW 127th St 33167 305-681-6647
Robin Atkins, prin. Fax 685-3192
Wheatley ES 300/PK-6
1801 NW 1st Pl 33136 305-573-2638
Deloise Brown, prin. Fax 573-2423
Whispering Pines ES 800/K-5
18929 SW 89th Rd 33157 305-238-7382
W.J. Roberson, prin. Fax 251-3615
Winston Park K-8 Center 1,100/PK-8
13200 SW 79th St 33183 305-386-7622
Noreen Virgin, prin. Fax 386-5684
Other Schools – See Bay Harbor Islands, Coconut Grove, Coral Gables, Cutler Bay, Cutler Ridge, Doral, Florida City, Goulds, Hialeah, Hialeah Gardens, Homestead, Key Biscayne, Leisure City, Miami Beach, Miami Gardens, Miami Lakes, Miami Shores, Miami Springs, Naranja, North Bay Village, North Miami, North Miami Beach, Opa Locka, Palmetto Bay, Perrine, South Miami, Sunny Isles

---

Atlantis Academy 200/K-12
9600 SW 107th Ave 33176 305-271-9771
Carlos Aballi, prin. Fax 271-7078
Bet Breira S 200/PK-5
9400 SW 87th Ave 33176 305-595-3008
Dr. Francine Hamel, prin. Fax 279-4147
Brito Miami Private S 300/PK-12
2732 SW 32nd Ave 33133 305-448-1463
Beatrice Brito-Ferrer, dir. Fax 448-0181
Calusa Preparatory S 200/K-12
12515 SW 72nd St 33183 305-596-3787
Cattoria Montessori S PK-6
9385 SW 79th Ave 33156 305-274-6509
Carlos Cattoira, admin. Fax 274-4741
Champagnat Catholic S 200/PK-12
2609 NW 7th St 33125 305-642-4132
Fax 642-8624
Christian Learning Center 200/PK-5
8755 SW 16th St 33165 305-559-9409
Carmen Comesanas, admin. Fax 559-0237
Coconut Grove Montessori S 50/PK-3
2850 SW 27th Ave 33133 305-444-4484
Maria Arencibia, prin. Fax 444-4484
Coral Villa Christian Academy 50/PK-K
3201 SW 67th Ave 33155 305-661-4998
Corpus Christi S 200/PK-8
795 NW 32nd St 33127 305-635-8571
Beatriz Perez, prin. Fax 636-4421
Cushman S 500/PK-8
592 NE 60th St 33137 305-757-1966
Dr. Joan Lutton, hdmstr. Fax 757-1632
Dade Christian S 1,300/PK-12
6601 NW 167th St 33015 305-822-7690
Dr. Jim Virtue, admin. Fax 826-4072
Ebenezer Christian Academy 100/PK-12
3901 NW 2nd Ave 33127 305-573-2867

Epiphany S 1,000/PK-8
5557 SW 84th St 33143 305-667-5251
Sr. Margaret Fagan, prin. Fax 667-6828
Espinosa Academy 600/K-8
12975 SW 6th St 33184 305-227-1149
Maribel Diaz, dir. Fax 225-0184
Florida Christian S 1,400/PK-12
4200 SW 89th Ave 33165 305-226-8152
Dr. Robert Andrews, dir. Fax 226-8166
Gateway Christian S 200/PK-6
6500 SW 97th Ave 33173 305-271-1213
Nava Hector, prin. Fax 271-9125
Gladeview Christian S 200/PK-8
12201 SW 26th St 33175 305-551-6143
Luis Couvertier, prin. Fax 225-1632
Glendale Christian Academy 100/PK-2
14580 SW 117th Ave 33186 305-235-5347
Lois Reittie, dir. Fax 254-6321
Good Shepherd S 200/PK-7
14187 SW 72nd St 33183 305-385-7002
Susan Del Riego, prin. Fax 385-7026
Greater Miami Adventist Academy 300/PK-12
500 NW 122nd Ave 33182 305-220-5955
Luis Cortes, prin. Fax 220-5970
Greenfield Day S 100/K-8
11155 SW 112th Ave 33176 305-595-4868
Dr. Lee Binder, prin. Fax 595-4162
Heritage S 200/PK-8
13300 SW 120th St 33186 305-232-2222
Robert Stephens, prin. Fax 232-4272
Highpoint Academy 300/PK-8
12101 SW 34th St 33175 305-552-0202
Alicia Casanova, dir. Fax 559-8253
Jesus Fellowship Christian S 100/PK-2
9775 SW 87th Ave 33176 305-595-5314
Pam Woodruff, dir. Fax 675-2393
Joy of Learning 200/PK-K
3601 NW 114th Ave 33178 305-597-5665
Georgina Prats, admin. Fax 594-7355
Kendall Christian S 100/PK-5
8485 SW 112th St 33156 305-271-3723
Janet Powell, prin. Fax 274-0648
Kids Learning Center of Miami Dade 100/PK-1
16237 SW 88th St 33196 305-385-3761
Killian Oaks Academy 100/PK-12
10545 SW 97th Ave 33176 305-274-2221
Fax 279-5460
Kings Christian S 200/PK-8
8951 SW 44th St 33165 305-221-2008
Debbie Hew, prin. Fax 223-3823
Landow Yeshiva/Bais Chana HS 500/PK-12
17330 NW 7th Ave 33169 305-653-8770
Fax 653-6790
La Progressiva Presbyterian S 300/PK-12
2480 NW 7th St 33125 305-642-8600
Ailynn Hernandez, prin. Fax 642-2169
Lincoln-Marti S 100/PK-PK
904 SW 23rd Ave 33135 305-643-4888
Fax 649-2767
Lincoln-Marti S 100/K-9
1521 NW 13th Ct 33125 305-643-4888
Fax 649-2767
Lincoln-Marti S 1,100/PK-12
931 SW 1st St 33130 305-324-4060
Lincoln-Marti S 400/PK-8
1001 SW 1st St 33130 305-324-7322
Fax 649-2767
Marti S 100/PK-3
2660 SW 17th St 33145 305-856-9044
Fax 858-0858
Miami Christian S 400/PK-12
200 NW 109th Ave 33172 305-221-7754
Dr. Lorena Morrison, hdmstr. Fax 221-7783
Miami Country Day S 1,000/PK-12
PO Box 380608 33238 305-759-2843
John Davies Ed.D., hdmstr. Fax 759-4871
Mother of Christ S 200/PK-8
14141 SW 26th St 33175 786-497-6111
Rita Rodriguez, prin. Fax 497-6113
Mother of Our Redeemer S 200/PK-8
8445 NW 186th St 33015 305-829-3988
Evelyn Salinas, prin. Fax 829-3019
New Jerusalem Christian Academy 100/K-6
777 NW 85th St 33150 305-691-1291
Edward Bethel, admin. Fax 691-1176
Northwest Christian Academy 400/PK-12
951 NW 136th St 33168 305-685-8734
L.J. Nelson, admin. Fax 685-5341
Our Lady of Divine Providence S 100/PK-8
10207 W Flagler St 33174 305-552-7974
Anna Casariego, prin. Fax 551-7466
Our Lady of Lourdes S 600/PK-8
14000 SW 112th St 33186 305-386-8446
Thomas Halfker, prin. Fax 386-6694
Our Lady of the Holy Rosary S 400/PK-8
18455 Franjo Rd 33157 305-235-5442
Emma Ventura Ed.D., prin. Fax 235-5670
Pentab Academy 100/PK-7
18415 NW 7th Ave 33169 305-405-0088
Perrine SDA S 50/PK-8
9750 W Datura St 33157 305-378-2192
Rosalee Carter, prin. Fax 232-8073
Pinewood Acres Private S 200/PK-6
9500 SW 97th Ave 33176 305-271-3211
Fax 271-3212
Rainbow Christian Academy 300/PK-8
PO Box 700762 33170 305-258-0194
Delores Ward, dir. Fax 258-2167
St. Agatha S 600/PK-8
1125 SW 107th Ave 33174 305-222-8751
Maria Glass, prin. Fax 222-1517
St. Brendan S 600/PK-8
8755 SW 32nd St 33165 305-221-2722
Antonio Cejas, prin. Fax 554-6726
St. Francis Xavier S 100/K-8
1682 NW 4th Ave 33136 305-573-8532
Brenda Dawson, prin. Fax 573-0263
St. John Neumann S 400/PK-8
12115 SW 107th Ave 33176 305-255-7315
Maria Vilas, prin. Fax 255-7316

St. Kevin S 700/PK-8
4001 SW 127th Ave 33175 305-227-7571
Mayra Constantino Ed.D., prin. Fax 227-7574
St. Mary Cathedral S 300/PK-8
7485 NW 2nd Ave 33150 305-795-2000
Sr. Jane Stoecker, prin. Fax 795-2013
St. Matthew Lutheran S 100/PK-8
621 Beacom Blvd 33135 305-642-4177
Luis Santana, prin. Fax 642-3477
St. Michael the Archangel S 400/PK-8
300 NW 28th Ave 33125 305-642-6732
Carmen Alfonso, prin. Fax 649-5867
St. Paul Lutheran S 300/PK-8
10700 SW 56th St 33165 305-271-3109
Maria Saunders, prin. Fax 271-5315
St. Thomas the Apostle S 800/PK-8
7303 SW 64th St 33143 305-661-8591
Lisa Figueredo, prin. Fax 661-2181
St. Timothy S 700/PK-8
5400 SW 102nd Ave 33165 305-274-8229
Richard Jean, prin. Fax 598-7107
Sierra Norwood Calvary Child Dev Center 100/PK-3
495 NW 191st St 33169 305-770-3733
Vorst Ledgister, prin. Fax 652-7763
SS. Peter & Paul S 500/PK-8
1435 SW 12th Ave 33129 305-858-3722
Carlota Morales Ed.D., prin. Fax 856-4322
Sunflowers Academy 200/PK-6
2901 SW 7th St 33135 305-631-1284
Fax 649-0084
Sunrise S of Miami PK-8
8795 SW 112th St 33176 305-274-6562
Sunset Christian Academy 300/PK-8
9393 SW 72nd St 33173 305-595-7558
Douglas Flores, prin. Fax 271-3752
Temple Beth Am Day S 300/PK-5
5950 N Kendall Dr 33156 305-667-6667
Dr. Mindy Pincus, prin. Fax 668-6340
Town Center S 200/PK-2
10201 Hammocks Blvd Ste 149 33196
305-385-9981
Tropical Christian S 100/PK-8
12001 SW 72nd St 33183 305-595-2147
Julie Bergman, prin. Fax 596-3801
Village Pines S 100/PK-5
15000 SW 92nd Ave 33176 305-235-6621
Lucille Frazier, admin. Fax 253-1445
Westminster Christian ES 400/K-5
15000 SW 67 Avenue 33193 305-233-2030
Jean Boer, prin. Fax 232-4547
Westwood Christian S 300/K-6
4301 SW 107th Ave 33165 305-221-8381
Dr. Edwin Oksanen, hdmstr. Fax 305-5957
World Hope Academy 3,000/PK-12
10691 N Kendall Dr Ste 105 33176 305-270-9830
Dr. Alan Goldstein, prin. Fax 270-9780

Miami Beach, Miami-Dade, Pop. 87,925
Miami-Dade County SD
Supt. — See Miami
Biscayne ES 1,000/PK-6
800 77th St 33141 305-402-9448
Maria Rodriguez, prin. Fax 864-5543
Fienberg-Fisher K-8 Center 700/PK-8
1420 Washington Ave 33139 305-531-0419
Olga Figueras, prin. Fax 534-3925
Nautilus MS 1,100/7-8
4301 N Michigan Ave 33140 305-532-3481
Dr. Allyn Sachtle, prin. Fax 532-8906
North Beach ES 1,100/PK-6
4100 Prairie Ave 33140 305-531-7666
Dr. Alice Quarles, prin. Fax 674-8425
South Pointe ES 500/PK-6
1050 4th St 33139 305-531-5437
Melanie Fishman, prin. Fax 532-6096

Casa Dei Bambini Montessori S 100/PK-5
4025 Pine Tree Dr 33140 305-534-8911
Rachel Redington, prin. Fax 531-6667
Lehrman Community Day S 300/PK-8
727 77th St 33141 305-866-2771
Rabbi Seth Linfield, hdmstr. Fax 865-6575
Le Petit Papillon Montessori S 100/PK-5
PO Box 416493 33141 305-867-4244
Damarys Zarling, dir. Fax 867-4279
RASG Hebrew Academy 600/PK-12
2400 Pine Tree Dr 33140 305-532-6421
Fax 672-6191
St. Joseph S 200/PK-8
8625 Byron Ave 33141 305-866-1471
Maria Chelala Ed.D., prin. Fax 866-3175
St. Patrick S 200/PK-8
3700 Garden Ave 33140 305-534-4616
Bertha Moro, prin. Fax 538-5463
Yeshiva S 300/PK-6
7902 Carlyle Ave 33141 305-867-3322
Rabbi Yisroel Janowski, prin. Fax 867-3388

Miami Gardens, Miami-Dade, Pop. 99,438
Miami-Dade County SD
Supt. — See Miami
Brentwood ES 1,000/PK-5
3101 NW 191st St, 305-624-2657
Dr. Sharon Jackson, prin. Fax 625-4981
Carol City ES 700/PK-6
4375 NW 173rd Dr, 305-621-0509
Patricia Bloodworth, prin. Fax 620-5638
Carol City MS 1,000/6-8
3737 NW 188th St, 305-624-2652
Nelson Izquierdo, prin. Fax 623-2955
Crestview ES 900/PK-5
2201 NW 187th St, 305-624-1495
Melissa Mesa, prin. Fax 628-3198
Hawkins ES 400/PK-5
19010 NW 37th Ave, 305-624-2615
Evelyn Harrison, prin. Fax 621-9839
Lake Stevens ES 500/PK-5
5101 NW 183rd St, 305-625-6536
Stephanie Goree, prin. Fax 624-0437

Lake Stevens MS 1,200/6-8
18484 NW 48th Pl, 305-620-1294
Derick McKoy, prin. Fax 620-1345
Miami Gardens ES 400/PK-5
4444 NW 195th St, 305-625-5321
Ms. Johnnie Brown, prin. Fax 628-5764
Myrtle Grove ES 500/PK-5
3125 NW 176th St, 305-624-8431
Dr. Barbara Johnson, prin. Fax 624-3015
North County ES 400/PK-5
3250 NW 207th St, 305-624-9648
Dr. Lucille Collins, prin. Fax 620-2372
North Glade ES 600/PK-6
5000 NW 177th St, 305-624-3608
Dr. Thomas Frederick, prin. Fax 621-3606
Parkview ES 500/PK-5
17631 NW 20th Ave, 305-625-1591
Dr. Edith Hall, prin. Fax 621-5027
Parkway MS 500/6-8
2349 NW 175th St, 305-624-9613
Paulette Fredrik, prin. Fax 623-9756
Skyway ES 700/PK-5
4555 NW 206th Ter, 305-621-5838
Linda Harrison, prin. Fax 621-0919
Wyche ES 1,100/K-5
5241 NW 195th Dr, 305-628-5776
Dianne Jones, prin. Fax 628-5775

Beacon Hill S 300/PK-8
18001 NW 22nd Ave, 305-624-1600
Susan Liss-Hyman, dir. Fax 628-4390
Emmanuel S 200/PK-6
3001 NW 167th Ter, 305-474-0658
Kirlew Jr. Academy 200/K-8
18900 NW 32nd Ave, 305-474-4760
New Life Christian S 100/PK-4
5005 NW 173rd Dr, 305-624-2339

Miami Lakes, Miami-Dade, Pop. 22,321
Miami-Dade County SD
Supt. — See Miami
Graham Education Center 2,100/PK-8
15901 NW 79th Ave 33016 305-557-3303
Dr. Robin Behrman, prin. Fax 826-5434

Miami Lake Christian Academy 100/PK-12
6250 Miami Lakes Dr E 33014 305-823-3888
Miriam Nunez, prin. Fax 823-7219
Montessori Christian Ctr of Miami Lakes 100/PK-6
6381 Miami Lakeway N 33014 305-823-5632
Paul Thibodeau, prin. Fax 823-5436
Our Lady of the Lakes S 500/PK-8
6600 Miami Lakeway N 33014 305-362-5315
Ricardo Briz, prin. Fax 362-4573

Miami Shores, Miami-Dade, Pop. 10,040
Miami-Dade County SD
Supt. — See Miami
Miami Shores ES 800/PK-5
10351 NE 5th Ave 33138 305-758-5525
Sherry Krubitch, prin. Fax 756-3805
Miller ES 800/PK-5
840 NE 87th St 33138 305-756-3800
Verdell King, prin. Fax 756-3804

Miami Shores Presbyterian S 300/PK-5
9405 Park Dr 33138 305-751-5417
Sandi Busta, prin. Fax 756-7165
St. Rose of Lima S 600/PK-8
425 NE 105th St 33138 305-751-4257
Sr. Bernadette Keane, prin. Fax 751-5034

Miami Springs, Miami-Dade, Pop. 13,170
Miami-Dade County SD
Supt. — See Miami
Miami Springs ES 700/K-5
51 Park St 33166 305-888-4558
Sally Hutchings, prin. Fax 882-0521
Miami Springs MS 1,800/6-8
150 S Royal Poinciana Blvd 33166 305-888-6457
Maria Mason, prin. Fax 887-5281
Springview ES 700/PK-5
1122 Bluebird Ave 33166 305-885-6466
Mayte Dovale, prin. Fax 883-8391

All Angels Academy 100/PK-8
1801 Ludlam Dr 33166 305-888-9483
Debra Peacock, prin. Fax 885-3887
Blessed Trinity S 300/PK-8
4020 Curtiss Pkwy 33166 305-871-5766
Maria Teresa Perez, prin. Fax 876-1755
Grace Lutheran Learning Center 50/PK-K
254 Curtiss Pkwy 33166 305-888-3220
Ligia Estrada, dir. Fax 888-4489
Miami Springs SDA S 100/PK-8
701 Curtiss Pkwy 33166 305-888-2244
Eugenia Vega, dir. Fax 888-5149

Middleburg, Clay, Pop. 6,223
Clay County SD
Supt. — See Green Cove Springs
Coppergate ES 600/K-6
2250 County Road 209 N 32068 904-291-5594
David Nix, prin.
Doctors Inlet ES 1,000/PK-6
2634 County Road 220 32068 904-213-3000
Anne Miller, prin. Fax 213-3011
Middleburg ES 700/K-6
3958 Main St 32068 904-291-5485
Becky Wilkerson, prin. Fax 291-5491
RideOut ES 1,100/PK-6
3065 Apalachicola Blvd 32068 904-291-5430
Laura Johnson, prin. Fax 291-5434
Swimming Pen Creek ES 600/PK-6
1630 Woodpecker Ln 32068 904-278-5707
Lenore Paulk, prin. Fax 278-5720
Tynes ES 800/PK-6
1550 Tynes Blvd 32068 904-291-5400
Jenny Newhall, prin. Fax 291-5403
Wilkinson ES 900/PK-6
4965 County Road 218 32068 904-291-5420
Jeff Umbaugh, prin. Fax 291-5425
Wilkinson JHS 800/7-8
5025 County Road 218 32068 904-291-5500
Dr. David McDonald, prin. Fax 291-5510

Annunciation S 400/PK-8
1610 Blanding Blvd 32068 904-282-0504
Susan Altieri, prin. Fax 282-6808
Calvary Christian Academy 50/K-12
1532 Long Bay Rd 32068 904-282-0407
Dr. Ken Pledger, prin. Fax 282-6212
Madeira Christian Academy 100/K-8
1650 Blanding Blvd 32068 904-291-1875
Pinewood Christian Academy 300/PK-8
198 Knight Boxx Rd 32068 904-272-6408
Karan Jennings, prin. Fax 644-0566

Milton, Santa Rosa, Pop. 8,131
Santa Rosa County SD 25,800/PK-12
5086 Canal St 32570 850-983-5000
John Rogers, supt. Fax 983-5011
www.santarosa.k12.fl.us/
Avalon MS 800/6-8
5445 King Arthurs Way 32583 850-983-5540
Erma Fillingim, prin. Fax 983-5545
Bagdad ES 500/K-5
4512 Forsyth St 32583 850-983-5680
Linda Gooch, prin. Fax 983-5687
Berryhill ES 1,000/K-5
4900 Berryhill Rd 32570 850-983-5690
Roger Golden, prin. Fax 983-5694
East Milton ES 800/K-5
5156 Ward Basin Rd 32583 850-983-5620
David Johnson, prin. Fax 983-5625
Hobbs MS 700/6-8
5317 Glover Ln 32570 850-983-5630
Stephen Shell, prin. Fax 983-5635
Jackson Preschool 300/PK-PK
4950 Susan St 32570 850-983-5720
Bettie Washington, prin. Fax 983-5722
King MS 600/6-8
5928 Stewart St 32570 850-983-5660
David Gunter, prin. Fax 983-5665
Munson ES 100/K-5
11550 Munson Hwy 32570 850-957-6130
Sherry Smith, prin. Fax 957-6132
Rhodes ES 1,000/K-5
5563 Byrom St 32570 850-983-5670
Tom Kennell, prin. Fax 983-5672
Russell ES 700/K-5
3740 Excalibur Way 32583 850-983-7000
Pam Smith, prin. Fax 983-7007
Other Schools – See Gulf Breeze, Jay, Navarre, Pace

Santa Rosa Christian S 300/PK-12
6331 Chestnut St 32570 850-623-4671
Doris Peppard, prin. Fax 623-9559
West Florida Baptist Academy 300/K-12
5621 Highway 90 32583 850-623-9306
Fax 623-8313

Mims, Brevard, Pop. 9,412
Brevard County SD
Supt. — See Melbourne
Mims ES 600/PK-6
2582 US Highway 1 32754 321-264-3020
Debra Crannell, prin. Fax 264-3026
Pinewood ES 400/PK-6
3757 Old Dixie Hwy 32754 321-269-4530
Donna Neill, prin. Fax 264-3030

Indian River Academy 100/PK-12
10361 Epiphyte Rd 32754 321-536-3240
David Amstadt, prin. Fax 349-9743

Minneola, Lake, Pop. 8,665
Lake County SD
Supt. — See Tavares
Grassy Lake ES 1,000/K-5
1100 Fosgate Rd, 352-242-0313
Doreathe Cole, prin. Fax 242-1504

Miramar, Broward, Pop. 106,623
Broward County SD
Supt. — See Fort Lauderdale
Coconut Palm ES 1,100/K-5
13601 Monarch Lakes Blvd 33027 754-323-5050
Teresa Thelmas, prin. Fax 323-5090
Coral Cove ES 900/K-5
5100 SW 148th Ave 33027 754-323-7950
Marilyn Holmes, prin. Fax 323-7990
Dolphin Bay ES 600/K-5
16450 Miramar Pkwy 33027 754-323-8000
Irene Cejka, prin. Fax 323-8040
Fairway ES 900/K-5
7850 Fairway Blvd 33023 754-323-5650
Josetta Campbell, prin. Fax 323-5690
Glades MS 1,700/6-8
16700 SW 48th Ct 33027 754-323-4600
Krista Herrera, prin. Fax 323-4685
Miramar ES 900/PK-5
6831 SW 26th St 33023 754-323-6550
Phillip Bullock, prin. Fax 323-6590
New Renaissance MS 1,700/6-8
10701 Miramar Blvd 33025 754-323-3500
Janet Morales, prin. Fax 323-3585
Perry ES 700/PK-5
6850 SW 34th St 33023 754-323-7050
Davida Johnson, prin. Fax 323-7090
Perry MS 1,200/6-8
3400 Wildcat Way 33023 754-323-3900
Steven Frazier, prin. Fax 323-3985
Sea Castle ES 1,000/K-5
9600 Miramar Blvd 33025 754-323-7250
Estella Eckhardt, prin. Fax 323-7290
Silver Lakes ES 900/K-5
2300 SW 173rd Ave 33029 754-323-7400
Tammy Gilbert, prin. Fax 323-7440
Silver Shores ES 700/K-5
1701 SW 160th Ave 33027 754-323-7550
Angela Iudica, prin. Fax 323-7590
Sunset Lakes ES 1,000/K-5
18400 SW 25th St 33029 754-323-7650
Dr. Linda McDaniels, prin. Fax 323-7690
Sunshine ES 900/PK-5
7737 Lasalle Blvd 33023 754-323-7700
Lewis Jackson, prin. Fax 323-7740

Florida Bible Christian S 600/PK-12
9300 Pembroke Rd 33025 954-431-6770
Tony Fajardo, prin. Fax 431-5475
St. Bartholomew S 200/PK-8
8001 Miramar Pkwy 33025 954-431-5253
Christine Gonzalez, prin. Fax 431-3385
St. Stephen S 200/PK-8
2000 S State Road 7 33023 954-983-2636
Sr. Mary David, prin. Fax 986-8557

Miramar Beach, Walton, Pop. 1,644

Gateway Academy 100/PK-2
122 Poinciana Blvd 32550 850-654-9095
Jeri Michie, prin. Fax 654-1888

Molino, Escambia, Pop. 1,207
Escambia County SD
Supt. — See Pensacola
Molino Park ES 500/PK-5
899 Highway 97 32577 850-587-5265
Alice Woodward, prin. Fax 587-2340

Monticello, Jefferson, Pop. 2,546
Jefferson County SD 900/PK-12
1490 W Washington St 32344 850-342-0100
Bill Brumfield, supt. Fax 342-0108
www.edline.net/pages/jcsb
Jefferson County ES 700/PK-5
960 Rocky Branch Rd 32344 850-342-0115
Dr. Melvin Roberts, prin. Fax 342-0123

Aucilla Christian Academy 400/PK-12
7803 Aucilla Rd 32344 850-997-3597
Richard Finlayson, dir. Fax 997-3598

Montverde, Lake, Pop. 956

Montverde Academy 600/PK-12
17235 7th St 34756 407-469-2561
Kasey Kesselring M.Ed., hdmstr. Fax 469-3711
Woodlands Lutheran S 100/PK-5
15333 County Road 455 34756 407-469-3355
Jim Essig, prin. Fax 469-3199

Moore Haven, Glades, Pop. 1,751
Glades County SD 1,200/K-12
PO Box 459 33471 863-946-2083
Wayne Aldrich, supt. Fax 946-1529
www.glades-schools.org
Moore Haven ES 400/K-6
PO Box 160 33471 863-946-0737
Jim Brickel, prin. Fax 946-1670
Other Schools – See La Belle

Mount Dora, Lake, Pop. 11,474
Lake County SD
Supt. — See Tavares
Mount Dora MS 700/6-8
1405 Lincoln Ave 32757 352-383-6101
Thomas Sanders, prin. Fax 383-4949
Triangle ES 700/PK-5
1707 Eudora Rd 32757 352-383-6176
Kathy Billar, prin. Fax 383-6674

Christian Home & Bible S 800/PK-12
301 W 13th Ave 32757 352-383-2155
Patrick Todd, hdmstr. Fax 383-3112
Life Changing Christian Academy 100/PK-10
2705 Robie Ave 32757 352-383-9920
Fred Armstrong, prin. Fax 383-9921
Montessori N.E.S.T. 100/PK-6
751 E 5th Ave 32757 352-735-2324
Merry Hadden, hdmstr. Fax 735-2911

Mulberry, Polk, Pop. 3,233
Polk County SD
Supt. — See Bartow
Kingsford ES 500/PK-5
1400 Dean St 33860 863-701-1054
Brad Knopp, prin. Fax 701-1059
Mulberry MS 900/6-8
500 Dr Mlk Jr Ave 33860 863-701-1066
Michael Young, prin. Fax 701-1068
Purcell ES 500/PK-5
305 NE 1st Ave 33860 863-701-1061
Ellistine Smith, prin. Fax 701-1064

Calvary Academy 50/K-12
5400 Bethlehem Rd 33860 863-428-2071
Carlton Weisheim, prin. Fax 428-2584

Myakka City, Manatee
Manatee County SD
Supt. — See Bradenton
Myakka City ES 400/PK-5
PO Box 38 34251 941-708-5515
Roy Shaw, prin. Fax 708-5517

Naples, Collier, Pop. 21,709
Collier County SD 43,300/PK-12
5775 Osceola Trl 34109 239-377-0001
Dr. Dennis Thompson, supt. Fax 377-0336
www.collier.k12.fl.us
Avalon ES 500/K-5
3300 Thomasson Dr 34112 239-377-6200
Dr. Suzette Nolan, prin. Fax 377-6201
Big Cypress ES 900/K-5
3250 Golden Gate Blvd W 34120 239-377-6300
Angela Lettiere, prin. Fax 377-6301

Calusa Park ES — 1,100/K-5
4600 Santa Barbara Blvd 34104 — 239-377-6400
Dr. Terrie Mitev, prin. — Fax 377-6401
Corkscrew ES — 900/PK-5
1065 County Road 858 34120 — 239-377-6500
Terri Lonneman, prin. — Fax 377-6501
Corkscrew MS — 1,500/6-8
1165 County Road 858 34120 — 239-377-3400
Dennis Snider, prin. — Fax 377-3401
Cypress Palm MS — 800/6-8
4255 18th Ave NE 34120 — 239-377-5200
John Kasten, prin. — Fax 377-5201
Davis ES — K-5
3215 Magnolia Pond Dr 34116 — 239-377-9000
Bob Spano, prin. — Fax 377-8601
East Naples MS — 1,200/6-8
4100 Estey Ave 34104 — 239-377-3600
Tammy Caraker, prin. — Fax 377-3601
Estates ES — 700/K-6
5945 Everglades Blvd N 34120 — 239-377-6600
Oliver Phipps, prin. — Fax 377-6601
Golden Gate IS — 3-5
5055 20th Pl SW 34116 — 239-377-6700
Marilou Andrews, prin. — Fax 377-6701
Golden Gate MS — 800/6-8
2701 48th Ter SW 34116 — 239-377-3800
Mary Murray, prin. — Fax 377-3801
Golden Gate PS — 500/PK-2
4911 20th Pl SW 34116 — 239-377-6900
Marilou Andrews, prin. — Fax 377-6901
Golden Terrace IS — 300/4-5
2965 44th Ter SW 34116 — 239-377-6800
Dr. David Glennon, prin. — Fax 377-6801
Golden Terrace PS — 700/K-3
2711 44th Ter SW 34116 — 239-377-7000
Dr. David Glennon, prin. — Fax 377-7001
Gulfview MS — 600/6-8
255 6th St S 34102 — 239-377-4000
Kevin Huelsman, prin. — Fax 377-4001
Lake Park ES — 500/K-5
1295 14th Ave N 34102 — 239-377-7200
Tamie Stewart, prin. — Fax 377-7201
Laurel Oak ES — 1,200/K-5
7800 Immokalee Rd 34119 — 239-377-7400
Charles Frontz, prin. — Fax 377-7401
Lely ES — 800/PK-5
8125 Lely Cultural Pkwy 34113 — 239-377-7500
Dr. Karey Stewart, prin. — Fax 377-7501
Manatee ES — 800/PK-3
1880 Manatee Rd 34114 — 239-377-7600
Wendy Crawford, prin. — Fax 377-7601
Manatee MS — 500/6-8
1920 Manatee Rd 34114 — 239-377-4400
Scholastica Choi, prin. — Fax 377-4401
Naples Park ES — 900/K-5
685 111th Ave N 34108 — 239-377-7700
Beverly Budzynski, prin. — Fax 377-7701
North Naples MS — 900/6-8
16165 Learning Ln 34110 — 239-377-4600
Frank Zencuch, prin. — Fax 377-4601
Oakridge MS — 1,100/6-8
14975 Collier Blvd 34119 — 239-377-4800
Kevin Saba, prin. — Fax 377-4801
Osceola ES — 900/K-5
5770 Osceola Trl 34109 — 239-377-7800
Jody Jordan, prin. — Fax 377-7801
Palmetto ES — PK-5
3000 10th Ave SE 34117 — 239-377-9100
Dr. Marilyn Moser, prin. — Fax 377-9101
Parkside ES — 800/K-5
5322 Texas Ave 34113 — 239-377-8900
Dr. Jan Messer, prin. — Fax 377-8901
Pelican Marsh ES — 800/PK-5
9480 Airport Pulling Rd N 34109 — 239-377-7900
Dr. James Gasparino, prin. — Fax 377-7901
Pine Ridge MS — 1,100/6-8
1515 Pine Ridge Rd 34109 — 239-377-5000
George Brenco, prin. — Fax 377-5001
Poinciana ES — 700/K-5
2825 Airport Rd S 34105 — 239-377-8100
Dr. Susan Barcellino, prin. — Fax 377-8101
Sabal Palm ES — 1,000/PK-5
4095 18th Ave NE 34120 — 239-377-8200
Tammy Brown, prin. — Fax 377-8201
Sea Gate ES — 700/K-5
650 Seagate Dr 34103 — 239-377-8300
Brian Castellani, prin. — Fax 377-8301
Shadowlawn ES — 600/PK-5
2161 Shadowlawn Dr 34112 — 239-377-8400
Nicole Stocking, prin. — Fax 377-8401
Veterans Memorial ES — 900/K-5
15960 Veterans Memorial Blv 34110 — 239-377-8800
Tim Ferguson, prin. — Fax 377-8801
Vineyards ES — 1,000/PK-5
6225 Arbor Blvd W 34119 — 239-377-8700
Mary Smith, prin. — Fax 377-8701
Other Schools – See Everglades City, Immokalee, Marco Island

Community S of Naples — 800/PK-12
13275 Livingston Rd 34109 — 239-597-7575
John Zeller, hdmstr. — Fax 598-2973
Eagle's Nest Christian Academy — 100/PK-PK
6920 Immokalee Rd 34119 — 239-593-0060
Kathryn Canfield, dir. — Fax 593-3565
First Baptist Academy Naples — 500/PK-12
3000 Orange Blossom Dr 34109 — 239-597-2233
Thomas Rider, admin. — Fax 597-4187
Naples Christian Academy — 200/PK-8
3161 Santa Barbara Blvd 34116 — 239-455-1087
Scott Jones, hdmstr. — Fax 455-5225
Naples SDA S — 50/PK-8
1055 Pine Ridge Rd 34108 — 239-597-2033
Julie Mowry, prin. — Fax 597-7229
Nicaea Academy — 200/PK-12
14785 Collier Blvd 34119 — 239-353-9099
Rev. Barton McIntyre, admin. — Fax 348-0499
Royal Palm Academy — 200/PK-8
16100 Livingston Rd 34110 — 239-594-9888
Dr. Margaret Richardson, prin. — Fax 594-9898

St. Ann S — 300/PK-8
542 8th Ave S 34102 — 239-262-4110
James Bridges, prin. — Fax 262-3991
St. Elizabeth Seton S — 200/PK-8
2730 53rd Ter SW 34116 — 239-455-2262
Dr. Denny Denison, prin. — Fax 455-0549
Seacrest Country Day S — 600/PK-12
7100 Davis Blvd 34104 — 239-793-1986
Lynne Powell Ed.D., prin. — Fax 793-1460
Village S — 300/PK-8
6000 Goodlette Rd N 34109 — 239-593-7686
Ginger Sauter, hdmstr. — Fax 593-6599

Naranja, Miami-Dade, Pop. 5,790
Miami-Dade County SD
Supt. — See Miami
Naranja ES — 600/PK-5
13990 SW 264th St 33032 — 305-258-3401
Fax 258-7240

Navarre, Santa Rosa
Santa Rosa County SD
Supt. — See Milton
Holley-Navarre IS — 700/3-5
1936 Navarre School Rd 32566 — 850-936-6020
Elizabeth West, prin. — Fax 936-6026
Holley-Navarre MS — 700/6-8
1976 Williams Creek Dr 32566 — 850-936-6040
Donald Bowersox, prin. — Fax 936-6049
Holley-Navarre PS — 800/K-2
8019 Escola St 32566 — 850-936-6130
Jacque Cooke, prin. — Fax 936-6132
West Navarre IS — 700/3-5
1970 Cotton Bay Ln 32566 — 850-936-6060
Anna Ratliff, prin. — Fax 936-6067
West Navarre PS — 800/PK-2
1955 Lowe Rd 32566 — 850-936-6000
Sandy Eubanks, prin. — Fax 963-6010

Montessori S of Navarre — 50/PK-4
6885 Gordon Evans Rd 32566 — 850-515-1255
Yolonda Washington, dir. — Fax 939-4893

Neptune Beach, Duval, Pop. 7,018
Duval County SD
Supt. — See Jacksonville
Neptune Beach ES — 1,000/K-5
1515 Florida Blvd 32266 — 904-247-5954
Stephanie Manabat, prin. — Fax 247-5969

Beaches Chapel Christian S — 200/K-9
610 Florida Blvd 32266 — 904-241-4211
Vicki McDonald, prin. — Fax 249-2046

Newberry, Alachua, Pop. 3,804
Alachua County SD
Supt. — See Gainesville
Newberry ES — 500/PK-4
25705 SW 15th Ave 32669 — 352-472-1100
Lacy Redd, prin. — Fax 472-1120
Oak View MS — 400/5-8
1203 SW 250th St 32669 — 352-472-1102
Karen Clarke, prin. — Fax 472-1131

New Port Richey, Pasco, Pop. 16,928
Pasco County SD
Supt. — See Land O Lakes
Anclote ES — 600/PK-5
3610 Madison St 34652 — 727-774-3200
Carole Baird, prin. — Fax 774-3291
Bayonet Point MS — 1,000/6-8
11125 Little Rd 34654 — 727-774-7400
Michael Asbell, prin. — Fax 774-7491
Calusa ES — 700/K-5
7520 Orchid Lake Rd 34653 — 727-774-3700
Deanna DeCubellis, prin. — Fax 794-3791
Cotee River ES — 800/K-5
7515 Plathe Rd 34653 — 727-774-3000
Barbara Kleinsorge, prin. — Fax 774-3091
Cypress ES — 900/K-5
10055 Sweet Bay Ct 34654 — 727-774-4500
Teresa Love, prin. — Fax 774-4591
Deer Park ES — 600/K-5
8636 Trouble Creek Rd 34653 — 727-774-8900
John Shafchuk, prin. — Fax 774-8991
Gulf MS — 1,000/6-8
6419 Louisiana Ave 34653 — 727-774-8000
Stan Trapp, prin. — Fax 774-8091
Locke ES — 900/PK-5
4339 Evans Ave 34652 — 727-774-3100
Tammy Berryhill, prin. — Fax 774-3191
Longleaf ES — 800/K-5
3253 Town Ave 34655 — 727-774-0800
Arlene Moreno-Bodden, prin. — Fax 774-0891
Marlowe ES — 600/K-5
5642 Cecelia Dr 34652 — 727-774-8600
Terri Mutell, prin. — Fax 774-8691
Moon Lake ES — 600/PK-5
12019 Tree Breeze Dr 34654 — 727-774-4600
Cara Allen, prin. — Fax 774-4691
Richey ES — 700/PK-5
6807 Madison St 34652 — 727-774-3500
Ken Miesner, prin. — Fax 774-3591
River Ridge MS — 1,500/6-8
11646 Town Center Rd 34654 — 727-774-7200
Jason Joens, prin. — Fax 774-7291
Schrader ES — 600/PK-5
11041 Little Rd 34654 — 727-774-5900
Mary Ellen Stelnicki, prin. — Fax 774-5991
Seven Springs ES — 700/K-5
8025 Mitchell Ranch Rd 34655 — 727-774-9600
Vicki Garner, prin. — Fax 774-9691
Seven Springs MS — 1,300/6-8
2441 Little Rd 34655 — 727-774-6700
David Salerno, prin. — Fax 774-6791
Trinity ES — 600/K-5
2209 Duck Slough Blvd 34655 — 727-774-9900
Kathryn Rushe, prin. — Fax 774-9991
Trinity Oaks ES — 500/K-5
1827 Trinity Oaks Blvd 34655 — 727-774-0900
Allison Hoskins, prin. — Fax 774-0991

Elfers Christian S — 200/PK-12
5630 Olympia St 34652 — 727-845-0235
Fax 848-5135
Genesis S - West Campus — 300/PK-5
6609 River Rd 34652 — 727-845-1111
Joan Houck, prin. — Fax 845-0089
Gulf Coast Christian S — 50/PK-8
10534 Little Rd 34654 — 727-862-3852
Linda Arnold, admin. — Fax 862-8098
New Port Richey SDA S — 50/PK-8
4416 Thys Rd 34653 — 727-842-8919
Fax 842-8919
St. Thomas Aquinas ECC — 100/PK-PK
8320 Old County Road 54 34653 — 727-376-2330
Cynthia McKallip, dir. — Fax 376-7204

New Smyrna Beach, Volusia, Pop. 22,356
Volusia County SD
Supt. — See De Land
Chisholm ES — 400/PK-5
557 Ronnoc Ln 32168 — 386-424-2540
William Mead, prin. — Fax 426-7332
Coronado Beach ES — 300/K-5
3550 Michigan Ave 32169 — 386-424-2525
Jeri Murphy, prin. — Fax 426-7438
New Smyrna Beach MS — 1,500/6-8
1200 S Myrtle Ave 32168 — 386-424-2550
Jim Tager, prin. — Fax 426-7476
Read-Pattilo ES — 500/PK-5
400 6th St 32168 — 386-424-2600
Marilyn Travis, prin. — Fax 426-7409

Glencoe Classical Academy — 100/PK-5
PO Box 702938 32170 — 386-428-3959
Kellie Conley, admin. — Fax 428-8981
Sacred Heart S — 200/PK-8
1003 Turnbull St 32168 — 386-428-4732
Lynn Abboud, prin. — Fax 428-4087

Niceville, Okaloosa, Pop. 12,582
Okaloosa County SD
Supt. — See Fort Walton Beach
Bluewater ES — 700/PK-5
4545 Range Rd 32578 — 850-833-4240
Janet Norris, prin. — Fax 833-4232
Edge ES — 500/PK-5
300 Highway 85 N 32578 — 850-833-4138
Shelly Arneson, prin. — Fax 833-3496
Plew ES — 600/PK-5
220 Pine Ave 32578 — 850-833-4100
David Larrimore, prin. — Fax 833-4103
Ruckel MS — 800/6-8
201 Partin Dr N 32578 — 850-833-4142
Debbie Culbreth, prin. — Fax 833-3291

Agape Christian Academy — 50/PK-5
801 John Sims Pkwy E 32578 — 850-678-8061
Rocky Bayou Christian S — 700/PK-12
2101 Partin Dr N 32578 — 850-678-7358
Don Larson, supt. — Fax 729-2513

Nocatee, DeSoto
De Soto County SD
Supt. — See Arcadia
Nocatee ES — 700/K-5
PO Box 188 34268 — 863-494-4511
Linda Waters, prin. — Fax 494-3264

Nokomis, Sarasota, Pop. 3,448
Sarasota County SD
Supt. — See Sarasota
Laurel Nokomis S — 1,200/K-8
1900 Laurel Rd E 34275 — 941-486-2171
Nancy Dubin, prin. — Fax 486-2013

North Bay Village, Miami-Dade, Pop. 7,615
Miami-Dade County SD
Supt. — See Miami
Treasure Island ES — 800/PK-6
7540 E Treasure Dr, — 305-865-3141
Gloria Barnes, prin. — Fax 864-1729

North Fort Myers, Lee, Pop. 42,900
Lee County SD
Supt. — See Fort Myers
Bayshore ES — 600/PK-5
17050 Williams Rd 33917 — 239-543-3663
Lynn Herrell, prin. — Fax 543-4040
English ES — 600/PK-5
120 Pine Island Rd 33903 — 239-995-2258
Joe Williams, prin. — Fax 995-5681
North Fort Myers Academy for the Arts — 1,200/PK-8
1856 Arts Way 33917 — 239-997-2131
Dr. Douglas Santini, prin. — Fax 997-6762
Tropic Isles ES — 1,000/PK-5
5145 Orange Grove Blvd 33903 — 239-995-4704
Donald Bryant, prin. — Fax 997-2422

First Baptist Church S — 100/PK-PK
75 Evergreen Rd 33903 — 239-995-8414
Good Shepherd Lutheran S — 200/PK-8
4770 Orange Grove Blvd 33903 — 239-995-7711
Fax 995-0473
Grace Community S — 100/PK-1
4735 Orange Grove Blvd 33903 — 239-997-3727
Fax 997-7996
Temple Christian S — 100/PK-12
18841 State Road 31 33917 — 239-543-3222
Maribeth Singleton, prin. — Fax 543-6112

North Lauderdale, Broward, Pop. 42,262
Broward County SD
Supt. — See Fort Lauderdale
Morrow ES — 700/PK-5
408 SW 76th Ter 33068 — 754-322-7150
Victoria Thurston, prin. — Fax 322-7190
North Lauderdale ES — 1,000/PK-5
7500 Kimberly Blvd 33068 — 754-322-7400
Stephanie Shipe, prin. — Fax 322-7440

Pinewood ES 1,000/PK-5
1600 SW 83rd Ave 33068 754-322-7950
Marie Johnson, prin. Fax 322-7990
Silver Lakes MS 1,000/6-8
7600 Tam Oshanter Blvd 33068 754-322-4600
Kathryn Sullivan, prin. Fax 322-4685

North Miami, Miami-Dade, Pop. 57,654
Miami-Dade County SD
Supt. — See Miami
Arch Creek ES K-6
700 NE 137th St 33161 305-892-4000
Marie Bazile, prin. Fax 892-4001
Bryan ES 800/PK-6
1201 NE 125th St 33161 305-891-0602
Milagros Maytin, prin. Fax 895-4708
Bryan Primary Learning Ctr PK-K
12175 NE 12th Ct 33161 305-892-7080
Fax 892-7083
Franklin ES 700/PK-5
13100 NW 12th Ave 33168 305-681-3547
Mary Gil-Alonso, prin. Fax 769-2845
Lawrence S 900/K-8
15000 Bay Vista Blvd 33181 305-354-2600
Bernard Osborn, prin. Fax 354-2601
Lentin K-8 Center 1,200/K-8
14312 NE 2nd Ct 33161 305-891-4011
Agenoria Powell, prin. Fax 895-0545
Natural Bridge ES 800/PK-5
1650 NE 141st St 33181 305-891-8649
Janice Hutson, prin. Fax 899-9695
North Miami ES 900/PK-6
655 NE 145th St 33161 305-949-6156
Debra Dubin, prin. Fax 949-3153

Holy Cross Lutheran S 300/PK-8
650 NE 135th St 33161 305-893-0851
Sherri Blizzard, prin. Fax 893-3044
Holy Family S 200/PK-8
14650 NE 12th Ave 33161 305-947-6535
Sr. Milagros, prin. Fax 947-1826
Miami Union Academy 300/PK-12
12600 NW 4th Ave 33168 305-953-9907
Regina Harris, prin. Fax 953-3602
Montessori S of North Miami 100/PK-8
695 NE 123rd St 33161 305-893-5994
Evelyn Lopez-Cuoto, prin. Fax 893-1551
St. James S 300/PK-8
601 NW 131st St 33168 305-681-3822
Sr. Kathleen Carr, prin. Fax 681-6435
Von Wedel Montessori S 100/PK-3
11820 NE 13th Ave 33161 305-893-9876
Rene Martinez, hdmstr. Fax 893-1893

North Miami Beach, Miami-Dade, Pop. 39,442
Miami-Dade County SD
Supt. — See Miami
Edelman / Sabal Palm ES 800/K-5
17101 NE 7th Ave 33162 305-651-2411
Susan Blount, prin. Fax 654-7219
Fulford ES 700/PK-5
16140 NE 18th Ave 33162 305-949-3425
Rhonda Turner, prin. Fax 949-2243
Greynolds Park ES 1,300/PK-5
1536 NE 179th St 33162 305-949-2129
Dr. Eduardo Rivas, prin. Fax 949-0899
Greynolds Park Primary Learning Center PK-K
1575 NE 177th St 33162 305-354-3208
Fax 354-3207
Highland Oaks MS 2,200/6-8
2375 NE 203rd St, Miami FL 33180 305-932-3810
Dawn Baglos, prin. Fax 932-0676
Ives ES 800/2-5
20770 NE 14th Ave 33179 305-651-3155
Dr. Tanya Brown-Major, prin. Fax 770-3740
Ives PS 400/PK-1
1351 Ives dairy Rd 33179 305-651-3155
Fax 770-3740
Kennedy MS 2,000/6-8
1075 NE 167th St 33162 305-947-1451
Karen Robinson, prin. Fax 949-9046
Oak Grove ES 900/PK-6
15640 NE 8th Ave 33162 305-945-1511
Steffond Cone, prin. Fax 949-4090

Aventura Learning Center 100/PK-2
2221 NE 171st St 33160 305-940-0408
Eileen Otero, prin. Fax 947-7343
Hillel Community Day S 1,100/PK-12
19000 NE 25th Ave, Miami FL 33180 305-931-2831
Dr. Adam Holden, hdmstr. Fax 932-7463
Hochberg Preparatory S 100/K-8
20350 NE 26th Ave, Miami FL 33180 305-933-6946
Dr. Richard Cuenca, prin. Fax 933-6955
Jacobson Sinai Academy 200/K-8
18801 NE 22nd Ave, Miami FL 33180 305-932-9011
David Prashker, dir. Fax 932-5153
Rohr MS 100/6-8
1051 N Miami Beach Blvd 33162 305-947-7779
St. Lawrence S 200/K-8
2200 NE 191st St, Miami FL 33180 305-932-4912
Dian Hyatt, prin. Fax 932-7898
Toras Emes Academy 400/PK-5
1051 N Miami Beach Blvd 33162 305-947-6000

North Palm Beach, Palm Beach, Pop. 12,633
Palm Beach County SD
Supt. — See West Palm Beach
North Palm Beach ES 500/K-5
401 Anchorage Dr 33408 561-494-1800
Maria Bishop, prin. Fax 494-1850

Benjamin S 1,300/PK-12
11000 Ellison Wilson Rd 33408 561-626-3747
Robert Goldberg, hdmstr. Fax 626-8752
St. Clare S 500/K-8
821 Prosperity Farms Rd 33408 561-622-7171
Andrew Houvouras, prin. Fax 627-4426

North Port, Sarasota, Pop. 42,253
Sarasota County SD
Supt. — See Sarasota
Atwater ES K-5
4701 Huntsville Ave 34288 941-257-2317
Kirk Hutchinson, prin. Fax 257-2319
Cranberry ES 800/K-5
2775 Shalimar Ter 34286 941-480-3400
Linda Daniels, prin. Fax 480-3401
Glenallen ES 900/K-5
7050 Glenallen Blvd 34287 941-426-9517
Amy Archer, prin. Fax 423-8131
Heron Creek MS 2,000/6-8
6501 W Price Blvd, 941-480-3371
William Bolander, prin. Fax 480-3398
Lamarque ES 1,000/K-5
3415 Lamarque Ave 34286 941-426-6371
Sally Mancheno, prin. Fax 426-6392
Toledo Blade ES 1,400/K-5
1201 Geranium Ave 34288 941-426-6100
Chris Renouf, prin. Fax 426-9340
Woodland MS 6-8
2700 Panacea Blvd 34289 941-240-8590
Kristine Lawrence, prin. Fax 240-8589

Oak Hill, Volusia, Pop. 1,484
Volusia County SD
Supt. — See De Land
Burns - Oak Hill ES 200/K-5
160 Ridge Rd 32759 386-424-2545
Torrence Broxton, prin. Fax 345-5409

Oakland Park, Broward, Pop. 31,713
Broward County SD
Supt. — See Fort Lauderdale
Lloyd Estates ES 500/PK-5
750 NW 41st St 33309 754-322-6800
Pamela Govoni, prin. Fax 322-6840
Oakland Park ES 700/PK-5
936 NE 33rd St 33334 754-322-7500
Joanne Krisel, prin. Fax 322-7540
Rickards MS 1,000/6-8
6000 NE 9th Ave 33334 754-322-4400
Ronald Forsman, prin. Fax 322-4485

Ocala, Marion, Pop. 49,745
Marion County SD 40,500/PK-12
PO Box 670 34478 352-671-7700
James Yancey, supt. Fax 671-7581
www.marion.k12.fl.us/
Bowen ES 800/K-5
4397 SW 95th St 34476 352-291-7900
Leanna Dixon, prin. Fax 291-7901
College Park ES 700/PK-5
1330 SW 33rd Ave 34474 352-291-4040
Patricia Stout, prin. Fax 291-4042
Eighth Street ES 400/K-5
513 SE 8th St 34471 352-671-7125
John McCollum, prin. Fax 671-7126
Emerald Shores ES 700/PK-5
404 Emerald Rd 34472 352-671-4800
Jaycee Oliver, prin. Fax 671-4805
Evergreen ES 800/PK-5
4000 W Anthony Rd 34475 352-671-4925
Cassandra Boston, prin. Fax 671-4931
Fessenden ES 500/PK-5
4200 NW 89th Pl 34482 352-671-4935
Anna DeWese, prin. Fax 671-4936
Fort King MS 1,000/6-8
545 NE 17th Ave 34470 352-671-4725
Wayne Livingston, prin. Fax 671-4726
Greenway ES 1,000/PK-5
207 Midway Rd 34472 352-671-4845
Erin Quainton, prin. Fax 671-4853
Horizon Academy - Marion Oak 500/4-8
365 Marion Oaks Dr 34473 352-671-6290
Juan Cordova, prin. Fax 671-6291
Howard MS 1,100/6-8
1108 NW M L King Jr 34475 352-671-7225
Kathy Collins, prin. Fax 671-7226
Jones ES 800/PK-5
1900 SW 5th St 34471 352-671-7260
Don Raymond, prin. Fax 671-7266
Liberty MS 6-8
4773 SW 95th St 34476 352-291-7930
Gregg Dudley, prin. Fax 291-7931
Madison Street Academy 500/K-5
401 NW Mrtn Lthr Kng Jr Ave 34475 352-671-7250
Phillip Leppert, prin. Fax 671-7252
Maplewood ES 900/PK-5
4751 SE 24th St 34471 352-671-6820
Barbara Dobbins, prin. Fax 671-6821
Oakcrest ES 500/PK-5
1112 NE 28th St 34470 352-671-6350
Jeannine Mills, prin. Fax 671-6357
Ocala Springs ES 600/K-5
5757 NE 40th Avenue Rd 34479 352-671-6360
Penny McKee, prin. Fax 671-6368
Osceola MS 1,200/6-8
526 SE Tuscawilla Ave 34471 352-671-7100
John McCollum, prin. Fax 671-7101
Saddlewood ES 600/PK-5
3700 SW 43rd Ct 34474 352-291-4075
Cheryl Laffey, prin. Fax 291-4079
Shady Hill ES 600/PK-5
5959 S Magnolia Ave 34471 352-291-4085
Carol Ely, prin. Fax 291-4087
South Ocala ES 500/PK-5
2831 SE Lake Weir Ave 34471 352-671-4750
Laura Burgess, prin. Fax 671-4759
Sunrise ES 1,200/PK-5
375 Marion Oaks Crse 34473 352-671-6200
Isaac Burgess, prin. Fax 671-6206
Ward-Highlands ES 900/PK-5
537 SE 36th Ave 34471 352-671-6810
Gary Smallridge, prin. Fax 671-6813
Wyomina Park ES 600/PK-5
511 NE 12th Ave 34470 352-671-6370
Mike Graff, prin. Fax 671-6372

Other Schools – See Anthony, Belleview, Citra, Dunnellon, Fort Mc Coy, Reddick, Silver Springs, Sparr, Summerfield, Weirsdale

---

Blessed Trinity S 700/PK-8
5 SE 17th St 34471 352-622-5808
Jason Halstead, prin. Fax 622-1660
Cornerstone S 200/PK-8
2313 SE Lake Weir Ave 34471 352-351-8840
Ingrid Wasserfall, dir. Fax 351-4226
First Assembly Christian S 300/PK-8
1827 NE 14th St 34470 352-351-1913
Saundra McCallister, dir. Fax 351-5170
Grace Building Blocks 100/PK-2
2255 SE 38th St 34480 352-629-4523
Ruth Bell, prin. Fax 629-3383
Grace Episcopal S 300/PK-8
4410 SE 3rd Ave 34480 352-387-3090
Edward England, hdmstr. Fax 629-7724
Hale Academy 100/PK-12
3443 SW 20th St 34474 352-854-8835
Melissa Cook, hdmstr. Fax 861-8822
Heritage Jr Academy 50/1-8
415 NE 41st Ave 34470 352-236-2420
Linda Westbrook, prin. Fax 236-2420
Meadowbrook Academy 300/K-12
4741 SW 20th St Ste 1 34474 352-861-0700
James Watts, dir. Fax 861-0533
Ocala Christian Academy 400/PK-12
1714 SE 36th Ave 34471 352-694-4178
Randy Swartz, admin. Fax 694-7192
Redeemer Christian S 300/PK-8
155 SW 87th Pl 34476 352-854-2999
Bruce Hawk, prin. Fax 291-9196
St. John Lutheran S 500/PK-12
1915 SE Lake Weir Ave 34471 352-622-7275
Deborah Heath, dir. Fax 622-5564
Shiloh SDA S 100/PK-8
500 SW 17th Ave 34471 352-629-6857
Murray Ramnarine, dir. Fax 629-6857
Shores Christian Academy 300/PK-12
10515 SE 115th Ave 34472 352-687-4454
Rev. Stephen Davison, admin. Fax 687-1462

Ocoee, Orange, Pop. 29,849
Orange County SD
Supt. — See Orlando
Citrus ES 900/K-5
87 N Clarke Rd 34761 407-445-5475
Cynthia Drayton, prin. Fax 445-5499
Ocoee ES 700/PK-5
400 S Lakewood Ave 34761 407-877-5027
Sheila Johnson, prin. Fax 877-8583
Ocoee MS 1,700/6-8
300 S Bluford Ave 34761 407-877-5035
Sharyn Gabriel, prin. Fax 877-5045
Spring Lake ES 600/PK-5
115 Spring Lake Cir 34761 407-877-5047
Dr. Angela Murphy-Osborne, prin. Fax 877-5062
Thornebrooke ES 900/K-5
601 Thornebrooke Dr 34761 407-909-1301
Christopher Daniels, prin. Fax 909-1318
Westbrooke ES 600/PK-5
500 Tomyn Blvd 34761 407-656-6228
Robert Bixler, prin. Fax 656-6741

Victory Christian Academy 100/K-8
1601 A D Mims Rd 34761 407-656-1295
Bradley Phillips, admin. Fax 656-6895

Odessa, Hillsborough, Pop. 1,200
Hillsborough County SD
Supt. — See Tampa
Hammond ES 600/K-5
8008 N Mobley Rd 33556 813-792-5120
Karen Zielinski, prin. Fax 792-5124
Walker MS 1,100/6-8
8282 N Mobley Rd 33556 813-631-4726
Kathleen Hoffman, prin. Fax 631-4738

Odessa Christian S K-12
19521 Michigan Ave 33556 813-792-1825
Erin Ciulla, prin. Fax 712-9044

Okeechobee, Okeechobee, Pop. 5,900
Okeechobee County SD 6,700/PK-12
700 SW 2nd Ave 34974 863-462-5000
Dr. Patricia Cooper, supt. Fax 462-5151
www.okee.k12.fl.us/web.nsf
Central ES 600/PK-4
610 SW 5th Ave 34974 863-462-5077
Randy Paulson, prin. Fax 462-5082
Everglades ES 700/PK-5
3725 SE 8th St 34974 863-462-5108
Cynthia Weigum, prin. Fax 462-5113
North ES 700/PK-5
3000 NW 10th Ter 34972 863-462-5100
Pat McCoy, prin. Fax 462-5107
Osceola MS 800/5-8
825 SW 28th St 34974 863-462-5070
Theda Bass, prin. Fax 462-5076
Seminole ES 600/PK-5
2690 NW 42nd Ave 34972 863-462-5116
Brian Greseth, prin. Fax 462-5119
South ES 500/PK-4
2468 SW 7th Ave 34974 863-462-5087
Renee Geeting, prin. Fax 462-5094
Yearling MS 800/6-8
925 NW 23rd Ln 34972 863-462-5056
Andy Brewer, prin. Fax 462-5062

Okeechobee Christian Academy 100/PK-12
701 S Parrott Ave 34974 863-763-3072
Rev. Joshua Strunk, hdmstr. Fax 213-1339

Oldsmar, Pinellas, Pop. 13,552
Pinellas County SD
Supt. — See Largo

Forest Lakes ES 800/PK-5
301 Pine Ave N 34677 813-891-0785
Karen Aspen, prin. Fax 891-9178
Oldsmar ES 600/K-5
302 Dartmouth Ave W 34677 813-855-7316
David Schmitt, prin. Fax 855-5136

Oldsmar Christian S 300/PK-12
650 Burbank Rd 34677 813-855-5746
Eddie Preston, prin. Fax 855-4476

Old Town, Dixie
Dixie County SD
Supt. — See Cross City
Old Town ES 600/PK-5
PO Box 940 32680 352-542-7818
Karen Tillis, prin. Fax 542-8797

Dixie County Learning Academy 100/K-12
1357 NE 82 Ave 32680 352-542-3306
Dr. Sylvia Lamenta, prin. Fax 542-7291

Opa Locka, Miami-Dade, Pop. 15,081
Miami-Dade County SD
Supt. — See Miami
Bunche Park ES 300/PK-6
16001 Bunche Park School Dr 33054 305-621-1469
Dr. Viola Irons, prin. Fax 628-1416
Golden Glades ES 400/PK-6
16520 NW 28th Ave 33054 305-624-9641
Theron Clark, prin. Fax 628-5760
Ingram ES 500/PK-6
600 Ahmad St 33054 305-688-4605
Dr. Susan McEachin, prin. Fax 688-3971
North Dade Center for Modern Language 500/1-5
1840 NW 157th St 33054 305-625-3885
Dr. Maria Castaigne, prin. Fax 625-6069
North Dade MS 800/6-8
1840 NW 157th St 33054 305-624-8415
Lowell Crawford, prin. Fax 628-2954
Rainbow Park ES 600/PK-5
15355 NW 19th Ave 33054 305-688-4631
Robin Armstrong, prin. Fax 685-0693
Young ES 500/PK-5
14120 NW 24th Ave 33054 305-685-7204
Apryle Kirnes, prin. Fax 688-6465

Betesda Christian S 100/K-12
3300 NW 135th St 33054 305-685-8255
Jose Bello, hdmstr. Fax 685-5338
North Dade Academy 100/PK-10
13850 NW 26th Ave 33054 305-725-4755
Fax 687-0098

Orange City, Volusia, Pop. 7,862
Volusia County SD
Supt. — See De Land
Manatee Cove ES 800/K-5
734 W Ohio Ave 32763 386-968-0004
Alice Gonzalez, prin.
Orange City ES 700/K-5
555 E University Ave 32763 386-575-4215
Lisa Buchanan, prin. Fax 775-5227
River Springs MS 6-8
900 W Ohio Ave 32763 386-968-0011
John Atkinson, prin. Fax 456-5355

Orange Park, Clay, Pop. 9,205
Clay County SD
Supt. — See Green Cove Springs
Argyle ES 1,000/K-6
2625 Spencer Plantation Blv 32073 904-573-2357
Theresa Roman, prin. Fax 573-2768
Cherry ES 600/K-6
420 Edson Dr 32073 904-278-2050
Angela Whiddon, prin. Fax 278-2056
Fleming Island ES 1,100/PK-6
4425 Lakeshore Dr 32003 904-278-2020
Sandra Mead, prin. Fax 278-2026
Grove Park ES 600/PK-6
1643 Miller St 32073 904-278-2010
Lynda Braxton, prin. Fax 278-2015
Jennings ES 600/PK-6
215 Corona Dr 32073 904-213-3021
Dana Archibald, prin. Fax 213-3014
Lakeside ES 600/K-6
2752 Moody Ave 32073 904-213-2966
John Schlichtman, prin. Fax 213-2965
Lakeside JHS 1,000/7-8
2750 Moody Ave 32073 904-213-2980
Randy Oliver, prin. Fax 213-2987
Montclair ES 600/K-6
2398 Moody Ave 32073 904-278-2030
Bill Miller, prin. Fax 278-2090
Oakleaf JHS 600/7-8
4085 Plantation Oaks Blvd 32065 904-213-5500
Nancy Crowder, prin. Fax 291-2549
Oakleaf Village ES PK-5
410 Oakleaf Village Pkwy 32065 904-291-5458
Colette Wyant, prin. Fax 291-5471
Orange Park ES 500/K-6
1401 Plainfield Ave 32073 904-278-2040
Jane Bromagen, prin. Fax 278-2045
Orange Park JHS 900/7-8
1500 Gano Ave 32073 904-278-2000
Joyce Orsi, prin. Fax 278-2009
Paterson ES 1,100/K-6
5400 Pine Ave 32003 904-278-2078
Terry Grieninger, prin. Fax 278-2093
Ridgeview ES 800/K-6
421 Jefferson Ave 32065 904-213-2952
Ruth Casias, prin. Fax 213-2960
Thunderbolt ES 1,200/PK-6
2020 Thunderbolt Rd 32003 904-278-5630
Dee Dee Phillips, prin. Fax 278-5633

Berean Christian Academy 100/PK-12
4459 US Highway 17 32003 904-264-5333
David Wright, prin. Fax 264-9185
Grace Episcopal Day S 300/PK-6
156 Kingsley Ave 32073 904-269-3718
Martha Milton, hdmstr. Fax 269-9183
Lighthouse Christian S 400/1-12
1542 Kingsley Ave Ste 143 32073 904-637-0637
Elaine Ludwig, dir. Fax 637-0638
St. Johns Country Day S 800/PK-12
3100 Doctors Lake Dr 32073 904-264-9572
Gregory Foster, hdmstr. Fax 264-0375

Orlando, Orange, Pop. 213,223
Orange County SD 176,100/PK-12
445 W Amelia St 32801 407-317-3200
Ronald Blocker, supt. Fax 317-3401
www.ocps.k12.fl.us
Andover ES 500/PK-5
3100 Sanctuary Point Blvd 32825 407-658-6800
Matthew Pritts, prin. Fax 658-6801
Arbor Ridge S 800/K-8
2900 Logandale Dr 32817 407-672-3110
Laura Tracy, prin. Fax 672-1310
Audubon Park ES 600/PK-5
1750 Common Way Rd 32814 407-897-6400
Trevor Honohan, prin. Fax 897-2415
Avalon ES 800/K-5
13500 Tanja King Blvd 32828 407-207-3825
Pamela Sanders, prin. Fax 207-3828
Avalon MS 1,200/6-8
13914 Mailer Blvd 32828 407-207-7839
Judith Frank, prin. Fax 207-7872
Azalea Park ES 1,000/PK-5
1 Carol Ave 32807 407-249-6280
James Leslie, prin. Fax 207-7470
Bay Meadows ES 500/PK-5
9150 S Apopka Vineland Rd 32836 407-876-7500
Dr. Diane Gullett, prin. Fax 876-7509
Blankner S 900/PK-8
2500 S Mills Ave 32806 407-245-1720
Polly Roper, prin. Fax 245-1725
Bonneville ES 600/PK-5
14700 Sussex Dr 32826 407-249-6290
Kimberly Bias, prin. Fax 249-4661
Camelot ES 700/K-5
14501 Waterford Chase Pkwy 32828 407-207-3875
Janet Medina-Maestre, prin. Fax 207-3881
Carver MS 1,000/6-8
4500 Columbia St 32811 407-296-5110
Wayne Green, prin. Fax 296-6407
Castle Creek ES 600/PK-5
1245 Avalon Park North Blvd 32828 407-207-7428
Joy Taylor, prin. Fax 207-7723
Catalina ES 700/PK-5
2448 29th St 32805 407-245-1735
Sharon Jenkins, prin. Fax 245-2744
Chain of Lakes MS 1,300/6-8
8720 Conroy Windermere Rd 32835 407-909-5400
Carol Kindt, prin. Fax 909-5410
Cheney ES 700/PK-5
2000 N Forsyth Rd 32807 407-672-3120
Lorrie Butler, prin. Fax 672-3126
Chickasaw ES 800/PK-5
6900 Autumnvale Dr 32822 407-249-6300
Margarita Vega, prin. Fax 249-4407
Chiles ES 800/K-5
11001 Bloomfield Dr 32825 407-737-1470
Ian Gesundheit, prin. Fax 737-1471
Columbia ES 800/PK-5
18501 Cypress Lake Glen 32820 407-568-2921
Karen Finkelstein, prin. Fax 568-7330
Conway ES 600/PK-5
4100 Lake Margaret Dr 32812 407-249-6310
Karen Babb, prin. Fax 249-6319
Conway MS 1,300/6-8
4600 Anderson Rd 32812 407-249-6420
Claudia Vogt, prin. Fax 249-6429
Corner Lake MS 1,400/6-8
1700 Chuluota Rd 32820 407-568-0510
Fax 568-0920
Cypress Park ES 400/PK-5
9601 11th Ave 32824 407-858-3100
Catherine Roach, prin. Fax 858-4633
Cypress Springs ES 800/K-5
10401 Cypress Springs Pkwy 32825 407-249-6950
Ruthie Haniff, prin. Fax 249-6951
Deerwood ES 700/PK-5
1356 S Econlockhatchee Trl 32825 407-249-6320
Margarete Talbert-Irving, prin. Fax 249-4422
Discovery MS 1,000/6-8
601 Woodbury Rd 32828 407-384-1555
Gloria Fernandez, prin. Fax 384-1580
Dover Shores ES 700/PK-5
1200 Gaston Foster Rd 32812 407-249-6330
Randall Hart, prin. Fax 249-4401
Durrance ES 500/PK-5
8101 Benrus St 32827 407-858-3110
Susan Abbe, prin. Fax 858-2225
Eagle's Nest ES 700/K-5
5353 Metrowest Blvd 32811 407-521-2795
Gladys White, prin. Fax 521-2797
East Lake ES 900/PK-5
3971 N Tanner Rd 32826 407-658-6825
Marc Rummler, prin. Fax 658-6830
Eccleston ES 500/PK-5
1500 Aaron Ave 32811 407-296-6400
Wendy Ivory, prin. Fax 521-3321
Endeavor ES 800/K-5
13501 Balcombe Rd 32837 407-251-2560
Myrlene Jackson-Kimble, prin. Fax 251-2561
Engelwood ES 500/PK-5
900 Engel Dr 32807 407-249-6340
Kelly Pelletier, prin. Fax 249-6344
Fern Creek ES 400/PK-5
1121 N Ferncreek Ave 32803 407-897-6410
Julie Paradise, prin. Fax 897-2417
Frangus ES 700/PK-5
380 Killington Way 32835 407-296-6469
Dr. Jeffrey Bauer, prin. Fax 521-3323
Freedom MS 1,100/6-8
2850 W Taft Vineland Rd 32837 407-858-6130
Timothy Smith, prin. Fax 858-6132
Glenridge MS 1,300/6-8
2900 Upper Park Rd 32814 407-623-1415
Michele Erickson, prin. Fax 623-1427
Grand Avenue Primary Learning Center 200/PK-2
800 Grand St 32805 407-245-1750
Lino Rodriguez, prin. Fax 245-1760
Hiawassee ES 700/PK-5
6800 Hennepin Blvd 32818 407-296-6410
Althea Tucker Jackson, prin. Fax 521-3340
Hidden Oaks ES 600/PK-5
9051 Suburban Dr 32829 407-249-6350
Kevin Storch, prin. Fax 249-4406
Hillcrest ES 400/PK-5
1010 E Concord St 32803 407-245-1770
Ana Gonzalez, prin. Fax 245-1779
Howard MS 700/6-8
800 E Robinson St 32801 407-245-1780
Dr. Carl Cartwright, prin. Fax 245-1785
Hunters Creek ES 600/PK-5
4650 Town Center Blvd 32837 407-858-4610
Anne Geisler, prin. Fax 858-4611
Hunters Creek MS 1,100/6-8
13400 Town Loop Blvd 32837 407-858-4620
Anne Carcara, prin. Fax 858-4621
Ivey Lane ES 400/PK-5
209 Silverton St 32811 407-296-6420
Joscelyn Harold, prin. Fax 521-3324
Jackson MS 1,000/6-8
6000 Stonewall Jackson Rd 32807 407-249-6430
Dr. Joseph Miller, prin. Fax 249-6438
Kaley ES 300/PK-5
1600 E Kaley St 32806 407-897-6420
Sandra Daves, prin. Fax 897-2407
Lake Como ES 300/PK-5
901 S Bumby Ave 32806 407-897-6430
Carmen Carrasco-Thompson, prin. Fax 897-2409
Lake Gem ES 800/K-5
4801 Bloodhound St 32818 407-532-7900
Patty Harrelson, prin. Fax 532-7911
Lake George ES 600/K-5
4101 Gatlin Ave 32812 407-737-1430
Debra Brown, prin. Fax 623-1440
Lake Silver ES 500/PK-5
2401 N Rio Grande Ave 32804 407-245-1850
Cynthia Dodge, prin. Fax 245-1865
Lake Weston ES 600/PK-5
5500 Milan Dr 32810 407-296-6430
John Dobbs, prin. Fax 521-3341
Lancaster ES 1,000/PK-5
6700 Sheryl Ann Dr 32809 407-858-3130
Belinda Reyes, prin. Fax 858-2202
Lee MS 1,000/6-8
1201 Maury Rd 32804 407-245-1800
William Pylant, prin. Fax 245-1809
Legacy MS 1,000/6-8
11398 Lake Underhill Rd 32825 407-658-5330
Wesley Trimble, prin. Fax 658-5334
Liberty MS 1,100/6-8
3405 S Chickasaw Trl 32829 407-249-6440
Frederick Heid, prin. Fax 249-6449
Little River ES 1,100/PK-5
100 Caswell Dr 32825 407-249-6360
Dr. Norma Masterson, prin. Fax 249-4409
Lockhart ES 600/PK-5
7500 Edgewater Dr 32810 407-296-6440
Donna Smith, prin. Fax 521-3342
Lockhart MS 1,000/6-8
3411 Dr Love Rd 32810 407-296-5120
Eric Hollinhead, prin. Fax 296-6549
McCoy ES 900/PK-5
5225 S Semoran Blvd 32822 407-249-6370
Ruth Ortega, prin. Fax 249-4423
Meadowbrook MS 1,200/6-8
6000 North Ln 32808 407-296-5130
Dr. Chuck Rivers, prin. Fax 296-5139
Meadow Woods ES 800/PK-5
500 Rhode Island Woods Cir 32824 407-858-3140
Sandra Pipkin, prin. Fax 858-2200
Meadow Woods MS 1,400/6-8
1800 Rhode Island Woods Cir 32824 407-850-5180
Dr. Isom Rivers, prin. Fax 850-5190
Memorial MS 800/6-8
2510 Gulfstream Rd 32805 407-245-1810
Dr. Stefanie Shames, prin. Fax 245-1820
Metrowest ES 1,200/PK-5
1801 Lake Vilma Dr 32835 407-296-6450
Patricia Smith, prin. Fax 445-5492
Millennia ES 600/K-5
5301 Cypress Creek Dr 32811 407-355-5730
Fax 355-5711
Moss Park ES 800/K-5
9301 N Shore Golf Club Blvd 32832 407-249-4747
Fax 249-4469
Northlake Park Community ES 1,100/PK-5
9055 Northlake Pkwy 32827 407-852-3500
Wendy Wagner, prin. Fax 850-5173
Oak Hill ES 500/PK-5
11 S Hiawassee Rd 32835 407-296-6470
Dr. June Jones, prin. Fax 521-3343
Oakshire ES 800/K-5
14501 Oakshire Blvd 32824 407-251-2500
Gonzalo La Cava, prin. Fax 251-2514
Odyssey MS 1,400/6-8
9290 Lee Vista Blvd 32829 407-207-3850
Patricia Bowen-Painter, prin. Fax 207-3873
Orange Center ES 400/PK-5
621 S Texas Ave 32805 407-296-6480
Dr. Ginny Kennerly, prin. Fax 521-3344
Orlo Vista ES 600/PK-5
3 N Hastings St 32835 407-296-6490
Mindi Smith, prin. Fax 521-3315
Palmetto ES 1,300/PK-5
2015 Duskin Ave 32839 407-858-3150
Pamela Angelo, prin. Fax 858-3159
Palm Lake ES 700/PK-5
8000 Pin Oak Dr 32819 407-354-2610
Carol Dorsey, prin. Fax 354-2618
Pershing ES 400/PK-5
1800 Pershing Ave 32806 407-858-3160
Dr. Jennifer Cupid-McCoy, prin. Fax 858-2226

Phillips ES 600/PK-5
6909 Dr Phillips Blvd 32819 407-354-2600
Daniel Merchant, prin. Fax 354-2606
Pinar ES 500/PK-5
3701 Anthony Ln 32822 407-249-6380
Elaine Martinez, prin. Fax 249-4424
Pine Castle ES 500/PK-5
905 Waltham Ave 32809 407-858-3170
Janice Quint, prin. Fax 858-2227
Pine Hills ES 900/PK-5
1006 Ferndell Rd 32808 407-296-6500
Debra Gore, prin. Fax 296-6436
Pineloch ES 700/PK-5
3101 Woods Ave 32805 407-245-1825
Dr. Janice Choice, prin. Fax 245-1830
Pinewood ES 700/K-5
3005 N Apopka Vineland Rd 32818 407-532-7930
Kandace Goshe, prin. Fax 532-7933
Princeton ES 500/PK-5
311 W Princeton St 32804 407-245-1840
Shayne Grove, prin. Fax 245-1849
Ray ES 700/PK-5
2000 Beecher St 32808 407-296-6460
Kathryn Shuler, prin. Fax 521-3327
Richmond Heights ES 400/PK-5
2500 Bruton Blvd 32805 407-245-1870
Dr. Shelia Windom, prin. Fax 245-1876
Ridgewood Park ES 800/PK-5
3401 Pioneer Rd 32808 407-296-6510
Edward Thompson, prin. Fax 521-3345
Riverdale ES 800/K-5
11301 Lokanotosa Trl 32817 407-737-1400
Sylvia Boyd, prin. Fax 737-1414
Riverside ES 600/PK-5
3125 Pembrook Dr 32810 407-296-6520
Debra Knerr, prin. Fax 521-3346
Robinswood MS 1,200/6-8
6305 Balboa Dr 32818 407-296-5140
Harrison Peters, prin. Fax 296-5148
Rock Lake ES 300/PK-5
408 N Tampa Ave 32805 407-245-1880
Brenda Martin-Smith, prin. Fax 245-1885
Rolling Hills ES 800/PK-5
4903 Donovan St 32808 407-296-6530
Patrick Galatowitsch, prin. Fax 521-3347
Rosemont ES 1,000/PK-5
4650 Point Lookout Rd 32808 407-522-6050
Mary Hodges, prin. Fax 522-6064
Sadler ES 900/PK-5
4000 W Oak Ridge Rd 32809 407-354-2620
Milagros Rivera, prin. Fax 354-2665
Sand Lake ES 500/PK-5
8301 Buenavista Woods Blvd 32836 407-903-7400
Mary Hool, prin. Fax 903-7411
Shenandoah ES 700/PK-5
4827 S Conway Rd 32812 407-858-3180
Belinda Vitale, prin. Fax 858-2208
Shingle Creek ES 1,000/PK-5
5620 Harcourt Ave 32839 407-354-2650
Laura Suprenard, prin. Fax 354-2657
South Creek MS 800/6-8
3901 Wetherbee Rd 32824 407-251-2413
Gregory Moody, prin. Fax 251-2464
Southwest MS 1,200/6-8
6450 Dr Phillips Blvd 32819 407-370-7200
Mark Brown, prin. Fax 370-7210
Southwood ES 800/PK-5
12600 Bisted Dr 32824 407-858-2230
Laurie Welch-Storch, prin. Fax 858-4698
Stone Lakes ES 1,000/PK-5
15200 Stoneybrook Blvd 32828 407-207-7793
Dr. Margaret Osteen, prin. Fax 207-7796
Sunrise ES 600/PK-5
101 Lone Palm Rd 32828 407-384-1585
Dr. Delores Inniss, prin. Fax 384-1599
Tangelo Park ES 400/PK-5
5115 Anzio St 32819 407-354-2630
Tashanda Brown-Cannon, prin. Fax 354-2663
Three Points ES 800/PK-5
4001 S Goldenrod Rd 32822 407-207-3800
Magali Rassel, prin. Fax 207-3803
Timber Lakes ES 600/K-5
2149 Crown Hill Blvd 32828 407-249-6177
Arlene Carlock, prin. Fax 249-6172
Union Park ES 800/PK-5
1600 N Dean Rd 32825 407-249-6390
Stacey Merritt, prin. Fax 249-4416
Union Park MS 1,300/6-8
1844 Westfall Dr 32817 407-249-6309
Kris Viles, prin. Fax 249-4404
Ventura ES 800/PK-5
4400 Woodgate Blvd 32822 407-249-6400
Lisa Suggs, prin. Fax 249-4417
Vista Lakes ES 800/PK-5
6050 Lake Champlain Dr 32829 407-207-4991
Linda Shear, prin. Fax 207-7701
Walker MS 1,100/6-8
150 Amidon Ln 32809 407-858-3210
Stephen Frankenstein, prin. Fax 858-3218
Washington Shores ES 500/PK-5
944 W Lake Mann Dr 32805 407-296-6540
Jeraldine Sims, prin. Fax 521-3348
Waterbridge ES 1,000/PK-5
11100 Galvin Dr 32837 407-858-3190
Mary Boyd, prin. Fax 858-2205
Waterford ES 900/PK-5
12950 Lake Underhill Rd 32828 407-249-6410
Dr. Brenda Cunningham, prin. Fax 249-4425
West Creek ES 800/K-5
5056 Tacon Dr 32837 407-858-5920
Dr. Patricia Fritzler, prin. Fax 858-5922
West Oaks ES 700/K-5
905 Dorscher Rd 32818 407-532-3875
Donald Richardson, prin. Fax 532-3878
Westridge MS 1,100/6-8
3800 W Oak Ridge Rd 32809 407-354-2640
Gabriel Berrio, prin. Fax 354-2637
Windy Ridge S 1,100/K-8
3900 Beech Tree Dr 32835 407-296-5100
Sarah Concepcion, prin. Fax 296-5107

Winegard ES 700/PK-5
7055 Winegard Rd 32809 407-858-3200
Dr. Ella Barnes, prin. Fax 858-2215
Wyndham Lakes ES 900/PK-5
14360 Wyndham Lakes Blvd 32824 407-251-2347
Bonita Glester, prin. Fax 251-2376
Young ES 1,000/PK-5
12550 Marsfield Ave 32837 407-858-3120
Regina Ponce, prin. Fax 858-2224
Other Schools – See Apopka, Eatonville, Maitland, Ocoee, Windermere, Winter Garden, Winter Park, Zellwood

---

Agape Christian Academy 600/PK-12
2425 N Hiawassee Rd 32818 407-298-1111
Avalon S 100/1-12
5002 Andrus Ave 32804 407-297-4353
Azalea Park Baptist S 200/PK-8
5725 Dahlia Dr 32807 407-277-4056
Linda Wolfe, dir. Fax 277-4068
Baldwin Oaks Academy 100/PK-8
1862 E Winter Park Rd 32803 407-647-0119
Roberta Hermann, dir. Fax 647-2590
Beryl Wisdom Adventist S 100/PK-8
4955 Rose Ave 32808 407-291-3073
Val Dixon, prin. Fax 291-6149
Brush Arbor Christian S 200/PK-8
2304 N Goldenrod Rd 32807 407-671-9774
Gary Carroll, dir. Fax 678-4807
Central Florida Christian Academy 500/PK-12
700 Good Homes Rd 32818 407-293-8062
Edward Gamble, hdmstr. Fax 290-1579
Christian Victory Academy 100/K-12
PO Box 721436 32872 407-281-6244
Paula Williamson, pres. Fax 281-6610
Christ S 400/K-8
106 E Church St 32801 407-849-1665
Jason Powell, hdmstr. Fax 481-2325
Downey Christian S 300/PK-12
10201 E Colonial Dr 32817 407-275-0340
Dr. Charles Dees, prin. Fax 275-1481
Eastland Christian S 300/PK-12
9000 Lake Underhill Rd 32825 407-277-5858
Fax 658-1013
Faith Christian Academy 700/PK-12
2008 N Goldenrod Rd 32807 407-275-8031
Dr. Chuck Smith, admin. Fax 281-3710
First Academy 1,000/PK-12
2667 Bruton Blvd 32805 407-206-8600
Dr. Steve Whitaker, hdmstr. Fax 206-8771
Good Shepherd S 700/PK-8
5902 Oleander Dr 32807 407-277-3973
Patricia McNamee, prin. Fax 277-2605
Heritage Prep S 300/PK-12
6000 W Colonial Dr 32808 407-293-6000
Dr. Steve Ware, pres. Fax 292-7246
Holy Family S 700/PK-8
5129 S Apopka Vineland Rd 32819 407-876-9344
Sr. Dorothy Sayers, prin. Fax 876-8775
Kingsway Christian Academy 500/PK-8
4161 N Powers Dr 32818 407-295-8901
Thomas Copeland, pres. Fax 295-9651
Lake Highland Prep S 2,100/PK-12
901 Highland Ave 32803 407-206-1900
Warren Hudson, pres. Fax 206-1933
Leaders Preparatory S 200/PK-12
1021 N Goldenrod Rd 32807 407-382-9900
Fax 277-4190
Living Word Academy 100/PK-5
653 Wetherbee Rd 32824 407-851-9800
Michelle Nieves, prin. Fax 447-7638
Montessori S of East Orlando 50/PK-4
2526 Percival Rd 32826 407-447-5860
Marci Hurlbutt, dir. Fax 737-1087
Montessori World S 100/PK-6
11659 Ruby Lake Rd 32836 407-239-6024
W. Nora Yee, prin. Fax 239-6582
Mount Sinai Jr Academy 100/K-8
2610 Orange Center Blvd 32805 407-298-7871
Toni Drummond, prin. Fax 298-7874
Orlando Christian Prep S 300/PK-12
500 S Semoran Blvd 32807 407-823-9744
Dexter Costin, admin. Fax 380-1186
Orlando Junior Academy 200/PK-8
30 E Evans St 32804 407-898-1251
Beth Bursey, prin. Fax 894-6213
Page Private S 400/PK-8
10250 University Blvd 32817 407-678-0333
Patricia Klindworth, dir. Fax 657-7288
Pathways Private S 300/PK-8
1877 W Oak Ridge Rd 32809 407-816-2040
Christina James, prin. Fax 816-2080
Pine Castle Christian Academy 700/PK-12
5933 Randolph Ave 32809 407-438-2737
Dr. Lorne Wenzel, hdmstr. Fax 438-2739
Prince of Peace Lutheran Preschool 100/PK-PK
1515 S Semoran Blvd 32807 407-275-6703
Fax 380-1802
Radiant Life Academy 100/PK-8
8151 Clarcona Ocoee Rd 32818 407-299-7460
Stacia Cromwell, prin. Fax 299-7462
Regency Christian Academy 200/PK-5
11513 S Orange Blossom Trl 32837 407-851-7270
Tim Cartwright, prin. Fax 859-1130
St. Andrew S 300/PK-8
877 N Hastings St 32808 407-295-4230
Dr. Kathleen Kiley, prin. Fax 290-0959
St. Charles Borromeo S 500/PK-8
4005 Edgewater Dr 32804 407-293-7691
Mary Agnew, prin. Fax 295-9839
St. James Cathedral S 500/PK-8
505 E Ridgewood St 32803 407-841-4432
Geraldine Gendall, prin. Fax 648-4603
St. John Vianney S 700/PK-8
6200 S Orange Blossom Trl 32809 407-855-4660
Sr. Elizabeth Murphy, prin. Fax 857-7932
South Orlando Christian Academy 200/PK-12
PO Box 592929 32859 407-859-9511

Teachers Hands Academy 400/PK-12
3001 Curry Ford Rd 32806 407-897-7477
Barbara Serianni, prin. Fax 897-6690
Trinity Lutheran S 300/PK-8
123 E Livingston St 32801 407-843-4896
Melissa Wittcop, prin. Fax 488-1230
University SDA Church S 50/1-8
9191 University Blvd 32817 407-657-6904
Victory Christian Academy 100/K-9
240 N Ivey Ln 32811 407-295-3332
Lakisha Robinson, prin. Fax 523-0443
West Oaks Academy 100/K-12
8624 A D Mims Rd 32818 407-292-8481

Ormond Beach, Volusia, Pop. 38,613
Volusia County SD
Supt. — See De Land
Ormond Beach ES 300/K-5
100 Corbin Ave 32174 386-258-4666
Marie Stratton, prin.
Ormond Beach MS 1,000/6-8
151 Domicilio Ave 32174 386-258-4667
Carl Persis, prin. Fax 676-1258
Osceola ES 400/PK-5
100 Osceola Ave 32176 386-258-4669
Earl Johnson, prin. Fax 676-1233
Pathways ES, 2100 Airport Rd 32174 600/K-5
Joe Ronca, prin. 386-258-4671
Pine Trail ES 800/K-5
300 Airport Rd 32174 386-258-4672
Barbara Paranzino, prin. Fax 676-5308
Tomoka ES 800/K-5
999 Old Tomoka Rd 32174 386-258-4676
Julie Johnson, prin. Fax 676-1215

Calvary Christian Academy 400/PK-12
1687 W Granada Blvd 32174 386-672-2081
Anthony Arnett, prin. Fax 615-3736
Riverbend Academy 200/PK-12
2080 W Granada Blvd 32174 386-615-0986
Jason Karr, admin. Fax 672-7945
St. Brendan S 200/PK-8
1000 Ocean Shore Blvd 32176 386-441-1331
Marybeth Boyle, prin. Fax 441-0774
St. James Episcopal S 200/PK-8
38 S Halifax Dr 32176 386-677-1811
Harry Demontmollin, prin. Fax 677-9187

Osprey, Sarasota, Pop. 2,597

Victory Baptist Academy 50/PK-10
241 Burney Rd 34229 941-966-4716
Rene Kelly, admin. Fax 966-4716

Osteen, Volusia
Volusia County SD
Supt. — See De Land
Osteen ES, 500 Doyle Rd 32764 700/K-5
Robert Ouellette, prin. 386-575-4255

Oviedo, Seminole, Pop. 29,848
Seminole County SD
Supt. — See Sanford
Carillon ES 800/PK-5
3200 Lockwood Blvd 32765 407-320-4650
Marian Cummings, prin. Fax 320-4699
Chiles MS 1,400/6-8
1240 Sanctuary Dr 32766 407-871-7050
Robin Dehlinger, prin. Fax 871-7099
Evans ES 900/PK-5
100 E Chapman Rd 32765 407-320-9850
Kay Winger, prin. Fax 320-9899
Jackson Heights MS 1,300/6-8
141 Academy Ave 32765 407-320-4550
Winston Bailey, prin. Fax 320-4599
Lawton ES 900/PK-5
151 Graham Ave 32765 407-320-6350
Rick Carver, prin. Fax 320-6399
Partin ES 800/PK-5
1500 Twin Rivers Blvd 32766 407-320-4850
Kristy Marshall, prin. Fax 320-4899
Stenstrom ES 700/K-5
1800 Alafaya Woods Blvd 32765 407-320-2450
Sharon O'Rear, prin. Fax 320-2488
Tuskawilla MS 1,200/6-8
1801 Tuskawilla Rd 32765 407-746-8550
Michael Mizwicki, prin. Fax 746-8599

First Years K 200/PK-K
45 W Broadway St 32765 407-366-5070
Shannon Chambley, admin. Fax 365-2712
Master's Academy 1,100/K-12
1500 Lukas Ln 32765 407-971-2221
Dr. William Harris, supt. Fax 706-0254
St. Luke's Lutheran S 900/PK-8
2025 W State Road 426 32765 407-365-3228
Patrick Leupold, prin. Fax 365-7285
Tuskawilla Montessori S 200/PK-8
1625 Tuskawilla Rd 32765 407-678-3879
Lois Phillis, dir. Fax 678-3987

Pace, Santa Rosa, Pop. 6,277
Santa Rosa County SD
Supt. — See Milton
Dixon IS 800/3-5
5540 Education Dr 32571 850-995-3650
Judy Friery, prin. Fax 995-3655
Dixon PS 800/PK-2
4585 S S Dixon St 32571 850-995-3660
Debbie Bagley, prin. Fax 995-3675
Pea Ridge ES 900/K-5
4775 School Ln 32571 850-995-3680
Rick Hunsucker, prin. Fax 995-3688
Sims MS 900/6-8
5500 Education Dr 32571 850-995-3676
Wanda Knowles, prin. Fax 995-3696

Pahokee, Palm Beach, Pop. 6,554
Palm Beach County SD
Supt. — See West Palm Beach

Pahokee ES 500/K-6
560 E Main Pl 33476 561-924-9700
Vivian Green, prin. Fax 924-9751

Palatka, Putnam, Pop. 10,942
Putnam County SD 11,700/PK-12
200 S 7th St 32177 386-329-0510
Tom Townsend, supt. Fax 329-0520
www.putnamschools.org
Beasley MS 600/6-8
1100 S 18th St 32177 386-329-0569
Sandra Gilyard, prin. Fax 329-0670
Jenkins MS 700/6-8
1100 N 19th St 32177 386-329-0588
Rick Surrency, prin. Fax 329-0636
Long ES 500/PK-5
1400 Old Jacksonville Rd 32177 386-329-0575
Libby Weaver, prin. Fax 329-0675
Mellon ES 500/PK-5
301 Mellon Rd 32177 386-329-0593
Kelley Prince, prin. Fax 329-0594
Moseley ES 500/K-5
1100 Husson Ave 32177 386-329-0562
Laura France, prin. Fax 329-0563
Smith Community ES 700/PK-5
141 Kelley Smith School Rd 32177 386-329-0568
Rodney Symonds, prin. Fax 329-0629
Other Schools – See Crescent City, Florahome, Hawthorne, Interlachen, Melrose, San Mateo

---

First Baptist Preschool 100/PK-PK
501 Oak St 32177 386-325-1363
Peniel Baptist Academy 300/PK-12
110 Peniel Church Rd 32177 386-328-1707
Lester Jenkins, prin. Fax 328-0950

Palm Bay, Brevard, Pop. 92,833
Brevard County SD
Supt. — See Melbourne
Columbia ES 600/PK-6
1225 Waco Blvd SE 32909 321-676-1319
Linda Jennings, prin. Fax 952-5854
Discovery ES 1,000/PK-6
1275 Glendale Ave NW 32907 321-951-4920
Dawna Bobersky, prin. Fax 952-5870
Jupiter ES 800/PK-6
950 Tupelo Rd SW 32908 321-952-5990
Cynthia Harris, prin. Fax 952-5992
Lockmar ES 700/PK-6
525 Pepper St NE 32907 321-676-3730
Norma Hostetler, prin. Fax 952-5879
McAuliffe ES 900/PK-6
155 Del Mundo St NW 32907 321-768-0465
Carol Roddenberry, prin. Fax 952-5985
Palm Bay ES 700/PK-6
1200 Alamanda Rd NE 32905 321-723-1055
Lori Migliore, prin. Fax 952-5924
Port Malabar ES 800/PK-6
301 Pioneer Ave NE 32907 321-725-0070
Joseph Loffek, prin. Fax 952-5949
Riviera ES 600/PK-6
351 Riviera Dr NE 32905 321-676-4237
Linda Piccolella, prin. Fax 952-5957
Southwest MS 1,500/7-8
451 Eldron Blvd SE 32909 321-952-5800
Todd Scheuerer, prin. Fax 952-5819
Sunrise ES 600/K-6
1651 Mara Loma Blvd SE 32909 321-674-6145
Barry Pichard, prin. Fax 674-6147
Turner ES 700/PK-6
3175 Jupiter Blvd SE 32909 321-676-5700
Ana Diaz, prin. Fax 952-5964
Westside ES 800/K-6
2175 Degroodt Rd SW 32908 321-956-5050
Elaine Passanisi, prin. Fax 956-5053

Covenant Christian S 400/K-12
720 Emerson Dr NE 32907 321-727-2661
Paul Rumbley, hdmstr. Fax 728-9574
St. Joseph Parish S 300/PK-8
5320 Babcock St NE 32905 321-723-8866
Anna Adam, prin. Fax 727-1181

Palm Beach, Palm Beach, Pop. 9,852
Palm Beach County SD
Supt. — See West Palm Beach
Palm Beach ES 400/K-5
239 Cocoanut Row 33480 561-822-0700
Sharon Stevens, prin. Fax 822-0750

Palm Beach Day Academy 200/4-9
241 Seaview Ave 33480 561-655-1188
Dr. Becky van der Bogert, hdmstr. Fax 655-5794

Palm Beach Gardens, Palm Beach, Pop. 48,989
Palm Beach County SD
Supt. — See West Palm Beach
Allamanda ES 500/K-5
10300 Allamanda Dr 33410 561-803-7200
Marilu Garcia, prin. Fax 803-7250
Duncan MS 1,200/6-8
5150 117th Ct N 33418 561-776-3500
Jose Garcia, prin. Fax 776-3550
Eisenhower ES 400/PK-5
2926 Lone Pine Rd 33410 561-366-6000
James Pegg, prin. Fax 366-6050
Marsh Pointe ES K-5
12649 Ibiza Dr 33418 561-366-6800
Maureen Werner, prin. Fax 366-6850
Palm Beach Gardens ES 500/K-5
10060 Riverside Dr 33410 561-366-6500
Linda Brown, prin. Fax 366-6550
Timber Trace ES 900/K-5
5200 117th Ct N 33418 561-366-6200
Sue Slone, prin. Fax 366-6250
Watkins MS 1,000/6-8
9480 MacArthur Blvd 33403 561-776-3600
Ann Wark, prin. Fax 776-3603

Maranatha Christian Academy 100/PK-8
PO Box 31149 33420 561-622-8377
Richard Rimes, hdmstr. Fax 622-8362
St. Mark's Episcopal S 600/PK-8
3395 Burns Rd 33410 561-622-1504
Kay Carnes, hdmstr. Fax 622-6801
Trinity Christian S 300/PK-4
9625 N Military Trl 33410 561-253-3950
Maryanne Puglisi, prin. Fax 253-3953
Weiss S 300/PK-8
4176 Burns Rd 33410 561-627-0740
Dr. Rosemary Daniels, prin. Fax 775-7794

Palm City, Martin, Pop. 3,925
Martin County SD
Supt. — See Stuart
Bessey Creek ES 800/K-5
2201 SW Matheson Ave 34990 772-219-1500
Victoria Defenthaler, prin. Fax 219-1506
Citrus Grove ES K-5
2527 SW Citrus Blvd 34990 772-223-2513
Tyson Villwock, prin. Fax 223-2535
Hidden Oaks MS 1,100/6-8
2801 SW Martin Hwy 34990 772-219-1655
Jenny Lambdin, prin. Fax 219-1663
Palm City ES 900/K-5
1951 SW 34th St 34990 772-219-1565
Nancy Marin, prin. Fax 219-1570

Peace Christian Academy 100/K-12
1484 SW 34th St 34990 772-287-0311
Robert Watts, hdmstr. Fax 287-0321

Palm Coast, Flagler, Pop. 60,952
Flagler County SD
Supt. — See Bunnell
Belle Terre ES 1,400/K-5
5545 Belle Terre Pkwy 32137 386-447-1500
Steven Hinson, prin. Fax 447-1516
Indian Trails MS 1,600/6-8
5505 Belle Terre Pkwy 32137 386-446-6732
Michele Crosby, prin. Fax 445-7662
Rymfire ES 1,100/K-5
1425 Rymfire Dr 32164 386-206-4600
Paula St. Francis, prin. Fax 586-2305
Taylor MS 1,200/6-8
4500 Belle Terre Pkwy 32164 386-446-6700
Winnie Oden, prin. Fax 446-6711
Wadsworth ES 900/PK-5
4550 Belle Terre Pkwy 32164 386-446-6700
Stewart Maxcy, prin. Fax 446-7681

St. Elizabeth Ann Seton S 300/PK-8
4600 Belle Terre Pkwy Ste B 32164 386-445-2411
Kathleen Falk, prin. Fax 445-2522

Palmetto, Manatee, Pop. 13,510
Manatee County SD
Supt. — See Bradenton
Blackburn ES 700/PK-5
3904 17th St E 34221 941-723-4800
David Marshall, prin. Fax 721-6647
Buffalo Creek MS 700/6-8
7320 69th St E 34221 941-721-2260
Matthew Gruhl, prin. Fax 721-2275
Lincoln MS 1,200/6-8
305 17th St E 34221 941-721-6840
Curtis Davis, prin. Fax 721-6853
Mills ES 1,000/K-5
7200 69th St E 34221 941-721-2140
Mike Rio, prin. Fax 721-2152
Palmetto ES 800/K-5
834 7th St W 34221 941-723-4822
Eddie Hundley, prin. Fax 723-4607
Palm View ES 600/PK-5
6025 Bayshore Rd 34221 941-723-4812
Frank Pistella, prin. Fax 723-4532
Tillman ES 400/PK-K, 3-5
1415 29th St E 34221 941-723-4833
Diane Nichols, prin. Fax 723-4530

Palmetto Christian S 200/K-8
1601 17th St W 34221 941-723-3711
Brian Bustle, hdmstr. Fax 729-5805

Palmetto Bay, Miami-Dade
Miami-Dade County SD
Supt. — See Miami
Southwood MS 1,800/6-8
16301 SW 80th Ave, 305-251-5361
Deborah Leal, prin. Fax 251-7464

Alexander Montessori S 600/PK-6
14850 SW 67th Ave, 305-665-6274
James McGhee, dir. Fax 665-7726
Christ Fellowship Academy 400/PK-6
8900 SW 168th St, 305-238-1833
Pam Armstrong, dir. Fax 232-3518
Westminster Christian MS 300/6-8
6855 SW 152nd St, 305-233-2030
John Manoogian, prin. Fax 233-5737

Palm Harbor, Pinellas, Pop. 61,400
Pinellas County SD
Supt. — See Largo
Carwise MS 1,300/6-8
3301 Bentley Dr 34684 727-724-1442
Garrison Linder, prin. Fax 724-1446
Curlew Creek ES 600/K-5
3030 Curlew Rd 34684 727-724-1423
John Burwell, prin. Fax 724-1426
Cypress Woods ES 800/PK-5
4900 Cypress Woods Blvd 34685 727-538-7325
Randall DeVries, prin. Fax 725-7988
Highland Lakes ES 700/PK-5
1230 Highlands Blvd 34684 727-724-1429
Dr. Susan Taylor, prin. Fax 724-1435
Lake St. George ES 600/K-5
2855 County Road 95 34684 727-669-1161
Lon Jensen, prin. Fax 669-1165
Ozona ES 700/PK-5
601 Tampa Rd 34683 727-724-1589
Kerry Apuzzo, prin. Fax 724-1591
Palm Harbor ES 400/K-5
415 15th St 34683 727-669-1156
Robert McFadden, prin. Fax 669-1159
Palm Harbor MS 1,400/6-8
1800 Tampa Rd 34683 727-669-1146
Victoria Hawkins, prin. Fax 669-1244
Sutherland ES 600/PK-5
3150 N Belcher Rd 34683 727-724-1466
Marilyn Cromwell, prin. Fax 724-1469

New Horizons Country Day S 200/PK-5
2060 Nebraska Ave 34683 727-785-8591
Kim Trocin, prin. Fax 786-8591
Palm Harbor Montessori Academy 200/PK-8
2355 Nebraska Ave 34683 727-786-1854
Christine Varkas, hdmstr. Fax 786-5160
St. Luke ECC 100/PK-PK
2757 Alderman Rd 34684 727-787-2914
Bonnie Faucher, dir. Fax 786-8648
Suncoast Waldorf S 100/PK-8
1857 Curlew Rd 34683 727-786-8311
Deborah Richardson, admin. Fax 789-8265
Westlake Christian S 300/K-8
1551 Belcher Rd 34683 727-781-3808
Rick Pucci, prin. Fax 785-2608

Palm Springs, Palm Beach, Pop. 15,267
Palm Beach County SD
Supt. — See West Palm Beach
Taylor/Kirklane ES 1,000/K-5
4200 Purdy Ln 33461 561-804-3500
Agartha Gragg, prin. Fax 804-3550

St. Luke S 200/PK-8
2896 S Congress Ave 33461 561-965-8190
Suzanne Sandelier, prin. Fax 965-2404

Panama City, Bay, Pop. 37,188
Bay County SD 25,400/PK-12
1311 Balboa Ave 32401 850-872-4100
Bill Husfeldt, supt. Fax 872-4367
www.bay.k12.fl.us
Bozeman S 1,200/K-12
13410 Highway 77 32409 850-265-9887
Peggy Bunch, prin. Fax 265-5377
Breakfast Point Academy PK-6
601 Beckritch Rd 32407 850-236-0074
Denise Kelley, prin. Fax 230-1006
Brown MS 800/6-8
5044 Merritt Brown Way 32404 850-872-4740
Charlotte Marshall, prin. Fax 872-7625
Callaway ES 600/PK-5
7115 E Highway 22 32404 850-871-2645
Bobby Hooper, prin. Fax 871-2865
Cedar Grove ES 600/PK-5
2826 E 15th St 32405 850-872-4550
Billy May, prin. Fax 747-5649
Everitt MS 700/6-8
608 School Ave 32401 850-872-4790
Linda Landen, prin. Fax 872-7721
Hiland Park ES 900/PK-5
2507 E Baldwin Rd 32405 850-872-4685
Angela Hutchinson, prin. Fax 747-5307
Hutchison Beach ES 800/PK-5
12900 Hutchison Blvd 32407 850-233-5195
Shirley Ramsey, prin. Fax 233-5178
Jinks MS 600/6-8
600 W 11th St 32401 850-872-4695
James McCalister, prin. Fax 872-7612
Merriam Cherry Street ES 400/PK-5
1125 Cherry St 32401 850-872-4780
Dr. Jean Olson, admin. Fax 747-5499
Millville ES 400/PK-5
203 N East Ave 32401 850-872-4765
Ann Walsingham, prin. Fax 872-4727
Moore ES 600/PK-5
1900 Michigan Ave 32405 850-872-4770
Kathleen Schmidt, prin. Fax 747-5686
Northside ES 700/PK-5
2001 Northside Dr 32405 850-872-4760
Ann Tyree, prin. Fax 747-5315
Oakland Terrace S for Visual/Perfrmg Art 400/PK-5
2010 W 12th St 32401 850-872-4565
Dr. Stefanie Gall, prin. Fax 872-7613
Parker ES 700/PK-5
640 S Highway 22 A 32404 850-872-4570
Ed Sheffield, prin. Fax 747-5197
Patronis ES 900/PK-5
7400 Patronis Dr 32408 850-233-5075
Ellie Spivey, prin. Fax 233-5077
Patterson ES 400/PK-5
1025 Redwood Ave 32401 850-872-4675
Dr. Linward Barnes, prin. Fax 747-5478
Rosenwald MS 900/6-8
924 Bay Ave 32401 850-872-4580
Mike Riley, prin. Fax 872-7615
Smith ES 900/PK-5
5044 Tommy Smith Dr 32404 850-872-7540
Lynn Stryker, prin. Fax 747-5339
Springfield ES 400/K-5
520 School Ave 32401 850-872-4575
Harriet Taylor, prin. Fax 747-5386
Surfside MS 1,100/6-8
300 Nautilus St 32413 850-233-5180
Sue Harrell, prin. Fax 233-5193
West Bay ES 300/PK-5
14813 School Dr 32413 850-233-5135
Wanda Robbins, prin. Fax 233-5138
Other Schools – See Lynn Haven, Southport, Tyndall AFB, Youngstown

Covenant Christian S 300/PK-12
2350 Frankford Ave 32405 850-769-7448
Fax 763-2104
Holy Nativity Episcopal S 400/PK-8
1009 E 2nd Plz 32401 850-747-4774
Joanne Mallary, prin. Fax 747-1009
Panama City Christian S 300/PK-12
1104 Balboa Ave 32401 850-769-6000
Debbie Jones, prin. Fax 785-5212
Panama City SDA S 50/K-9
2700 Lisenby Ave 32405 850-769-3405
Sandra Pinkard, prin.
St. John the Evangelist S 200/PK-8
1005 Fortune Ave 32401 850-763-1775
Dr. Kathryn Kidd, prin. Fax 784-4461

Panama City Beach, Bay, Pop. 11,477

St. Bernadette Child Development Center 100/PK-PK
1214 Moylan Rd 32407 850-230-0009
Julie Roock, dir. Fax 230-6989

Parkland, Broward, Pop. 22,145
Broward County SD
Supt. — See Fort Lauderdale
Park Trails ES 1,300/K-5
10700 Trails End 33076 754-322-7800
Fran Renguso, prin. Fax 322-7840
Riverglades ES 900/K-5
7400 Parkside Dr 33067 754-322-8200
Shelly Isenberg, prin. Fax 322-8240
Westglades MS 1,400/6-8
11000 Holmberg Rd 33076 754-322-4800
Christine Flynn, prin. Fax 322-4885

Mary Help of Christians S 100/K-2
6000 N University Dr 33067 954-323-8006
Robert Messina, prin. Fax 323-8012

Parrish, Manatee
Manatee County SD
Supt. — See Bradenton
Williams ES PK-5
3404 Fort Hamer Rd 34219 941-776-4040
Nancy Beal, prin. Fax 776-4080

Paxton, Walton, Pop. 772
Walton County SD
Supt. — See De Funiak Springs
Paxton S 600/PK-12
PO Box 1168 32538 850-892-1230
Sonya Alford, prin. Fax 892-1239

Pembroke Park, Broward, Pop. 5,487
Broward County SD
Supt. — See Fort Lauderdale
Watkins ES 800/PK-5
3520 SW 52nd Ave 33023 754-323-7800
Cynthia Hanna, prin. Fax 323-7840

Pembroke Pines, Broward, Pop. 150,380
Broward County SD
Supt. — See Fort Lauderdale
Chapel Trail ES 1,100/K-5
19595 Taft St 33029 754-323-5000
Joseph Balchunas, prin. Fax 323-5040
Lakeside ES 900/K-5
900 NW 136th Ave 33028 754-323-6400
Marion Fee, prin. Fax 323-6440
Palm Cove ES 1,000/K-5
11601 Washington St 33025 754-323-6800
Dorothy Cain, prin. Fax 323-6840
Panther Run ES 800/PK-5
801 NW 172nd Ave 33029 754-323-6850
Elaine Saef, prin. Fax 323-6890
Pasadena Lakes ES 800/K-5
8801 Pasadena Blvd 33024 754-323-6900
Jill Wilson, prin. Fax 323-6940
Pembroke Lakes ES 800/K-5
11251 Taft St 33026 754-323-6950
Rosemary Lester, prin. Fax 323-6990
Pembroke Pines ES 700/K-5
6700 SW 9th St 33023 754-323-7000
Marc Charpentier, prin. Fax 323-7040
Pines Lakes ES 800/PK-5
10300 Johnson St 33026 754-323-7100
Patricia Yackel, prin. Fax 323-7140
Pines MS 1,300/6-8
200 N Douglas Rd 33024 754-323-4000
Carlton Campbell, prin. Fax 323-4085
Silver Palms ES 1,000/PK-5
1209 NW 155th Ave 33028 754-323-7450
Amada Walker, prin. Fax 323-7490
Silver Trail MS 600/6-6
18300 Sheridan St 33331 754-323-4300
Steven Williams, prin. Fax 323-4385
Young Resource Center MS 1,900/6-8
901 NW 129th Ave 33028 754-323-4500
Diane Hall, prin. Fax 323-4585

Montessori Academy 500/PK-5
19620 Pines Blvd 33029 954-437-2329
Monica Gargillo-Benitz, prin. Fax 437-3367
Tanglewood Academy 200/PK-1
9860 Pines Blvd 33024 954-431-8805
Fax 431-3840

Pensacola, Escambia, Pop. 54,055
Escambia County SD 38,900/PK-12
215 W Garden St 32502 850-469-6121
Malcolm Thomas, supt. Fax 469-6379
www.escambia.k12.fl.us
Bailey MS 1,500/6-8
4110 Bauer Rd 32506 850-492-6136
Dr. Judy Pippin, prin. Fax 492-9860
Bellview ES 800/K-5
4425 Bellview Ave 32526 850-941-6060
Rebecca Hewitt, prin. Fax 941-6062
Bellview MS 1,200/6-8
6201 Mobile Hwy 32526 850-941-6080
Vicki Gibowksi, prin. Fax 941-6089
Beulah ES 700/K-5
6201 Helms Rd 32526 850-941-6180
Pam Thompson, prin. Fax 941-6183
Bibbs ES 400/K-5
2005 N 6th Ave 32503 850-595-6875
Debra Simpkins, prin. Fax 595-6879
Blue Angels ES 800/K-5
1551 Dog Track Rd 32506 850-457-6356
Karen Montgomery, prin. Fax 457-6954
Brentwood ES 500/PK-5
4820 N Palafox St 32505 850-595-6800
Brian Alaback, prin. Fax 595-6802
Brown Barge MS 500/6-8
201 Hancock Ln 32503 850-494-5640
Dr. Patricia Kerrigan, prin. Fax 494-5699
Caro ES 900/PK-5
12551 Meadson Rd 32506 850-492-0531
Sandra Moore, prin. Fax 492-3592
Cook ES 600/K-5
1310 N 12th Ave 32503 850-595-6826
Dr. Karen Owen, prin. Fax 595-6823
Cordova Park ES 600/K-5
2250 Semur Rd 32503 850-595-6830
Aggie Bauer, prin. Fax 595-6835
Edgewater ES 400/PK-5
100 Boeing St 32507 850-453-7400
Steve Schubert, prin. Fax 453-7574
Ensley ES 400/PK-5
501 E Johnson Ave 32514 850-494-5600
Patricia McElfresh, prin. Fax 494-5603
Ferry Pass ES 700/PK-5
8310 N Davis Hwy 32514 850-494-5605
Rhonda Shuford, prin. Fax 494-7480
Ferry Pass MS 900/6-8
8355 Yancey Ave 32514 850-494-5650
Ann Bookout, prin. Fax 494-5653
Hallmark ES 200/PK-3
115 S E St 32502 850-595-6950
Dr. Sheree Cagle Mauldin, prin. Fax 595-6961
Holm ES 600/PK-5
6101 Lanier Dr 32504 850-494-5610
Nettie Eaton, prin. Fax 494-7290
Lincoln Park ES 400/PK-5
7600 Kershaw St 32534 850-494-5620
Carol McIntosh, prin. Fax 494-7481
Lipscomb ES 900/K-5
10200 Ashton Brosnaham Rd 32534 850-494-5760
Dale Cooey, prin. Fax 494-5722
Longleaf ES 800/K-5
2600 Longleaf Dr 32526 850-941-6110
Patricia Reynolds, prin. Fax 941-6112
McArthur ES 700/K-5
330 E Ten Mile Rd 32534 850-494-5625
Dr. Tama Vaughn, prin. Fax 494-5707
McMillan Preschool 200/PK-PK
1403 W Saint Joseph Ave 32501 850-595-6910
Dr. Patrice Moody, prin. Fax 595-6944
Montclair ES 300/PK-5
820 Massachusetts Ave 32505 850-595-6969
Sandra Rush, prin. Fax 595-6968
Myrtle Grove ES 700/K-5
6115 Lillian Hwy 32506 850-453-7410
Edwinna Williams, prin. Fax 453-7740
Navy Point ES 400/K-5
1321 Patton Dr 32507 850-453-7415
Linda Brown, prin. Fax 453-7419
Oakcrest ES 500/PK-5
1820 Hollywood Ave 32505 850-595-6980
Denny Wilson, prin. Fax 595-6988
Pine Meadow ES 800/PK-5
10001 Omar Ave 32534 850-494-5630
Dr. Patti Burt Thomas, prin. Fax 494-7318
Pleasant Grove ES 600/PK-5
3000 Owen Bell Ln 32507 850-492-0233
Linda Maletsidis, prin. Fax 492-6691
Scenic Heights ES 800/K-5
3801 Cherry Laurel Dr 32504 850-494-5635
Mary Ellen Wiggins, prin. Fax 494-5624
Semmes ES 300/K-5
1250 E Texar Dr 32503 850-595-6975
Larry Knight, prin. Fax 595-6977
Sherwood ES 500/PK-5
501 Cherokee Trl 32506 850-453-7420
Sabrena Cunningham, prin. Fax 453-7466
Suter ES 400/K-5
501 Pickens Ave 32503 850-595-6810
Pam Lewis, prin. Fax 595-6819
Warrington ES 500/PK-5
220 N Navy Blvd 32507 850-453-7425
Peggy Tucker, prin. Fax 453-7519
Weis ES 500/PK-5
2701 N Q St 32505 850-595-6888
Ann Smith, prin. Fax 595-6893
West Pensacola ES 500/K-5
801 N 49th Ave 32506 850-453-7470
Russell Queen, prin. Fax 453-7717
Woodham MS 1,300/6-8
150 E Burgess Rd 32503 850-494-7140
Marsha Higgins, prin. Fax 494-7484
Workman MS 800/6-8
6299 Lanier Dr 32504 850-494-5665
Juanita Edwards, prin. Fax 494-5697
Yniestra ES 400/PK-5
2315 W Jackson St 32505 850-595-1535
Nancy Reese, prin. Fax 595-1536
Other Schools – See Cantonment, Century, Molino, Walnut Hill, Warrington

Aletheia Christian Academy 200/PK-12
1700 Woodchuck Ave 32504 850-969-0088
Jeff Caulfield-James, admin. Fax 969-0906
Christian Institute of Arts and Sciences 100/K-12
6100 W Fairfield Dr Ste H 32506 850-457-4058
Creative Learning Academy 200/PK-8
3151 Hyde Park Rd 32503 850-432-1768
Michelle White, hdmstr. Fax 432-1896
East Hill Christian S 300/PK-12
1301 E Gonzalez St 32501 850-432-2321
Angie Wood, hdmstr. Fax 432-7679
Episcopal Day S of Christ Church Parish 400/PK-8
223 N Palafox St 32502 850-434-6474
Beverly Patteson, prin. Fax 434-6560
Escambia Christian S 200/PK-8
PO Box 17449 32522 850-433-8476
Frank Thomann, prin. Fax 433-8333
Jubilee Christian Academy 200/PK-8
5910 N W St 32505 850-494-2477
Dan Mendoza, hdmstr. Fax 494-2900
Little Flower S 200/K-8
PO Box 3009 32516 850-455-4851
Sr. Barbara Zipoli, prin. Fax 457-8982
Marcus Pointe Christian S 200/PK-5
6205 N W St 32505 850-479-1605
Sue Sanders, lead tchr. Fax 479-0743
Montessori S of Pensacola 100/PK-PK
1010 N 12th Ave Ste 138 32501 850-469-8138
Mary Gaudet, admin. Fax 433-0794
Montessori S of Pensacola 300/PK-8
4100 Montessori Dr 32504 850-433-4155
Mary Gaudet, admin. Fax 433-5613
Pensacola Christian Academy 2,600/PK-12
10 Brent Ln 32503 850-478-8483
Fax 479-6572
Pensacola SDA Jr Academy 50/K-8
8751 University Pkwy 32514 850-478-8838
Gwen Stinson B.A., dir. Fax 477-9513
Redeemer Lutheran S 200/PK-8
333 Commerce St 32507 850-455-0330
John Price, prin. Fax 455-3083
Sacred Heart Cathedral S 300/K-8
1603 N 12th Ave 32503 850-436-6440
Sr. Elizabeth Knight, prin. Fax 436-6444
St. John the Evangelist S 200/PK-8
325 S Navy Blvd 32507 850-456-5218
Sr. Isabel Garza, prin. Fax 456-5956
St. Paul S 300/K-8
3121 Hyde Park Rd 32503 850-436-6435
Louise West, prin. Fax 436-6437
Trinitas Christian S 100/K-12
3301 E Johnson Ave 32514 850-484-3515
Kenneth Trotter, admin. Fax 484-3590

Perrine, Miami-Dade, Pop. 15,576
Miami-Dade County SD
Supt. — See Miami
Moton ES 100/5-6
18050 Homestead Ave 33157 305-235-3612
Todd Morrow, prin. Fax 256-3128
Perrine ES 800/K-5
8851 SW 168th St 33157 305-235-2442
Maileen Ferrer, prin. Fax 253-6817

Perry, Taylor, Pop. 6,734
Taylor County SD 3,300/PK-12
318 N Clark St 32347 850-838-2500
Paul Dyal, supt. Fax 838-2501
www.taylor.k12.fl.us
Perry PS 800/K-2
400 N Clark St 32347 850-838-2506
George Clayton, prin. Fax 838-2556
Taylor County ES 700/3-5
1600 E Green St 32347 850-838-2530
Jan Walker, prin. Fax 838-1379
Taylor County MS 700/6-8
601 E Lafayette St 32347 850-838-2516
Kiki Puhl, prin. Fax 838-2559
Taylor County Pre K 300/PK-PK
502 E Lafayette St 32347 850-838-2535
Sharon Hathcock, coord. Fax 838-2575
Other Schools – See Steinhatchee

Pierson, Volusia, Pop. 2,604
Volusia County SD
Supt. — See De Land
Pierson ES 500/PK-5
1 W 1st Ave 32180 386-740-0850
Carolyn Solomon, prin. Fax 749-6870

Pinecrest, Miami-Dade

Gulliver S-Pinecrest MS 100/5-8
7500 SW 120th St 33156 305-238-3424
Ken Loughry, prin. Fax 255-5037
St. Louis Covenant S 300/PK-5
7270 SW 120th St 33156 305-238-7562
Christine Mathisen, prin. Fax 238-4296

Pinellas Park, Pinellas, Pop. 47,352
Pinellas County SD
Supt. — See Largo
Cross Bayou ES 600/PK-5
6886 102nd Ave 33782 727-547-7834
Marcia Stone, prin. Fax 547-7837
Pinellas Central ES 600/PK-5
10501 58th St 33782 727-547-7853
Randi Latzke, prin. Fax 547-7856
Pinellas Park ES 700/K-5
7520 52nd St 33781 727-547-7888
Alicia Urbano, prin. Fax 547-7892
Pinellas Park MS 1,000/6-8
6940 70th Ave 33781 727-545-6400
Robyn Witcher, prin. Fax 547-7894
Rawlings ES 700/PK-5
6505 68th St 33781 727-547-7828
Sharon Porter, prin. Fax 547-7777
Skyview ES 600/PK-5
8601 60th St 33782 727-547-7857
Douglas Cowley, prin. Fax 545-7521

Classical Christian S for the Arts 100/K-8
4981 78th Ave 33781 727-547-6820
Daniel Baker, pres. Fax 545-3579
Creative Learning Center 100/PK-1
4970 82nd Ave 33781 727-544-8416
Stephanie Powers, prin. Fax 541-4498

First Baptist Preschool | 200/PK-PK
5495 Park Blvd 33781 | 727-544-9465
Irene Robison, dir. | Fax 545-3949
Sacred Heart Interparochial S | 200/PK-8
7951 46th Way 33781 | 727-544-1106
Andy Shannon, prin. | Fax 548-9606

Pinetta, Madison
Madison County SD
Supt. — See Madison
Pinetta ES | 200/PK-5
PO Box 98 32350 | 850-973-5028
Elizabeth Moore, prin. | Fax 973-5147

Plantation, Broward, Pop. 85,989
Broward County SD
Supt. — See Fort Lauderdale
Central Park ES | 1,200/K-5
777 N Nob Hill Rd 33324 | 754-322-5700
Muriel Knabb, prin. | Fax 322-5740
Mirror Lake ES | 600/PK-5
1200 NW 72nd Ave 33313 | 754-322-7100
Mary Vos, prin. | Fax 322-7140
Peters ES | 700/K-5
851 NW 68th Ave 33317 | 754-322-7900
Kathy Sedlack, prin. | Fax 322-7940
Plantation ES | 800/PK-5
651 NW 42nd Ave 33317 | 754-322-8000
Susan Walton, prin. | Fax 322-8040
Plantation MS | 1,100/6-8
6600 W Sunrise Blvd 33313 | 754-322-4100
Patricia Hague, prin. | Fax 322-4185
Plantation Park ES | 500/K-5
875 SW 54th Ave 33317 | 754-323-7150
Julie Gittelman, prin. | Fax 323-7190
Seminole MS | 1,300/6-8
6200 SW 16th St 33317 | 754-323-4200
Dr. Kris Black, prin. | Fax 323-4285
Tropical ES | 800/PK-5
1500 SW 66th Ave 33317 | 754-323-7750
Eric Anderson, prin. | Fax 323-7790

American Heritage S | 2,000/PK-12
12200 W Broward Blvd 33325 | 954-472-0022
Peter Gulotta, hdmstr. | Fax 472-3088
Broward Junior Academy | 100/K-8
201 NW 46th Ave 33317 | 954-316-8301
Fax 316-8308
Jacaranda S | 200/PK-5
8250 Peters Rd 33324 | 954-473-4400
Idali Medina, dir. | Fax 473-4433
LASER Christian Academy | 100/PK-5
4537 W Broward Blvd 33317 | 954-583-8968
Our Savior Lutheran S | 200/PK-8
8001 NW 5th St 33324 | 954-370-2161
Jane Nicklas, prin. | Fax 473-0395
Posnack Hebrew Day S | 500/K-12
6511 W Sunrise Blvd 33313 | 954-583-6100
Dr. Laurence Kutler, hdmstr. | Fax 791-5463
St. Gregory the Great S | 800/PK-8
200 N University Dr 33324 | 954-473-8169
Caridad Canino, prin. | Fax 472-1638
Sawgrass Adventist S | 100/PK-8
11701 NW 4th St 33325 | 954-473-4622
Sueli Menezes, prin. | Fax 370-8041
Temple Kol Ami Emanu-El Day S | 200/PK-5
8200 Peters Rd 33324 | 954-358-4200
Toni Weissberg, prin. | Fax 472-4439

Plant City, Hillsborough, Pop. 31,450
Hillsborough County SD
Supt. — See Tampa
Bryan ES | 800/K-5
2006 W Oak Ave, | 813-757-9300
Cheryl Boddie, prin. | Fax 707-7075
Burney ES | 400/PK-5
901 S Evers St, | 813-707-7334
Sally Stephens, prin. | Fax 707-7339
Cork ES | 900/K-5
3501 Cork Rd 33565 | 813-757-9353
Melody Murphy, prin. | Fax 707-7076
Jackson ES | 600/PK-5
502 E Gilchrist St, | 813-757-9341
Dora Madison, prin. | Fax 757-9343
Knights ES | 800/PK-5
4815 Keene Rd 33565 | 813-757-9333
Janine Hall, prin. | Fax 757-9319
Lincoln Magnet ES | 400/PK-5
1207 E Renfro St, | 813-757-9329
Susan Raburn, prin. | Fax 757-9077
Marshall MS | 1,000/6-8
18 S Maryland Ave, | 813-757-9360
Faychone Durant, prin. | Fax 707-7385
Robinson ES | 600/PK-5
4801 Turkey Creek Rd 33567 | 813-757-9424
Jane Morgan, prin. | Fax 757-9074
Springhead ES | 900/PK-5
3208 Nesmith Rd 33566 | 813-757-9321
Ann Rushing, prin. | Fax 757-9500
Tomlin MS | 1,500/6-8
501 N Woodrow Wilson St, | 813-757-9400
Dr. Beverly Carbaugh, prin. | Fax 707-7024
Trapnell ES | 600/PK-5
1605 W Trapnell Rd 33566 | 813-757-9313
Rhonda Pulling, prin. | Fax 757-9129
Turkey Creek MS | 1,100/6-8
5005 Turkey Creek Rd 33567 | 813-757-9442
Dennis Mayo, prin. | Fax 757-9451
Walden Lake ES | 900/K-5
2800 Turkey Creek Rd 33566 | 813-757-9433
Dina Wyatt, prin. | Fax 707-7170
Wilson ES | 400/PK-5
702 W English St, | 813-757-9307
Gina Becker, prin. | Fax 757-9310

Hope Christian Academy | 100/K-12
1109 W Grant St, | 813-752-1000
Michelle Hagel, admin. | Fax 752-1367

St. Clement ECC | 50/PK-PK
1104 N Alexander St, | 813-754-1237
Maureen Ringley, dir. | Fax 759-2721

Poinciana, Osceola, Pop. 3,618
Polk County SD
Supt. — See Bartow
Lake Marion Creek ES | 1,200/K-5
3055 Lake Marion Creek Dr 34759 | 863-427-1471
Albert Pido, prin.
Laurel ES | 600/PK-5
1851 Laurel Ave 34759 | 863-427-1375
Julia Allen, prin. | Fax 427-1303
Palmetto ES | 700/PK-5
315 Palmetto St 34759 | 863-427-6012
Luis Alvarez, prin. | Fax 427-6013

Polk City, Polk, Pop. 1,522
Polk County SD
Supt. — See Bartow
Polk City ES | 600/PK-5
125 S Bougainvillea Ave 33868 | 863-965-6338
Martin Young, prin. | Fax 965-6340

Pompano Beach, Broward, Pop. 104,179
Broward County SD
Supt. — See Fort Lauderdale
Broadview ES | 900/PK-5
1800 SW 62nd Ave 33068 | 754-322-5500
Donald Cottrell, prin. | Fax 322-5540
Cresthaven ES | 700/PK-5
801 NE 25th St 33064 | 754-322-6000
Joshua Kisten, prin. | Fax 322-6040
Crystal Lake Community MS | 1,500/6-8
3551 NE 3rd Ave 33064 | 754-322-3100
James Neer, prin. | Fax 322-3185
Cypress ES | 800/PK-5
851 SW 3rd Ave 33060 | 754-322-6050
Paulette Samai, prin. | Fax 322-6090
Drew ES | 600/K-5
1000 NW 31st Ave 33069 | 754-322-6250
Angeline Flowers, prin. | Fax 322-6290
Markham ES | 600/PK-5
1501 NW 15th Ave 33069 | 754-322-6950
Dr. Theodore Toomer, prin. | Fax 322-6990
McNab ES | 700/PK-5
1350 SE 9th Ave 33060 | 754-322-7050
Kellee Stroup, prin. | Fax 322-7090
Norcrest ES | 700/K-5
3951 NE 16th Ave 33064 | 754-322-7250
Roberta Ray, prin. | Fax 322-7290
Palmview ES | 700/PK-5
2601 N Cypress Rd 33064 | 754-322-7600
Robert Gibson, prin. | Fax 322-7640
Park Ridge ES | 500/PK-5
5200 NE 9th Ave 33064 | 754-322-7700
Arlene Klaasen, prin. | Fax 322-7740
Pompano Beach ES | 600/PK-5
700 NE 13th Ave 33060 | 754-322-8050
Michelle Garcia, prin. | Fax 322-8090
Pompano Beach MS | 1,100/6-8
310 NE 6th St 33060 | 754-322-4200
Sonja Braziel, prin. | Fax 322-4285
Sanders Park ES | 500/K-5
800 NW 16th St 33060 | 754-322-8400
Dr. Fabian Cone, prin. | Fax 322-8440
Tedder ES | 700/PK-5
4157 NE 1st Ter 33064 | 754-322-8650
Fran Rubinstein, prin. | Fax 322-8690

Highlands Christian Academy | 700/PK-12
501 NE 48th St 33064 | 954-421-1747
Ken Lopez, admin. | Fax 421-2429
Lighthouse Christian S | 100/K-8
2331 NE 26th Ave 33062 | 954-941-7501
Rita O'Leary, admin. | Fax 788-7311
St. Coleman S | 600/PK-8
2250 SE 12th St 33062 | 954-942-3500
Dr. Lori St. Thomas, prin. | Fax 785-0603
St. Elizabeth of Hungary S | 200/PK-8
901 NE 33rd St 33064 | 954-942-2161
Craig Mousseau, prin. | Fax 942-7551

Ponce de Leon, Holmes, Pop. 469
Holmes County SD
Supt. — See Bonifay
Ponce De Leon ES | 400/PK-5
1473 Ammons Rd 32455 | 850-836-4296
Woodrow Vaughan, prin. | Fax 836-5325

Ponte Vedra Beach, Saint Johns
St. Johns County SD
Supt. — See Saint Augustine
Landrum MS | 1,100/6-8
230 Landrum Ln 32082 | 904-547-8410
Wayne King, prin. | Fax 547-8415
Ocean Palms ES | 800/K-5
355 Landrum Ln 32082 | 904-547-3760
Michael Parrish, prin. | Fax 547-3775
Ponte Vedra-Palm Valley/Rawlings ES | 1,100/K-5
630 A1A N 32082 | 904-547-3820
Kathleen Furness, prin. | Fax 547-3825

Accotink Academy By The Sea | 200/PK-5
171 Canal Blvd 32082 | 904-273-4267
Mary Kay Rodgers, dir. | Fax 273-1427
Bolles S - Ponte Vedra Beach | PK-5
200 ATP Tour Blvd 32082 | 904-733-9292
Christ Church Episcopal S | 200/PK-K
PO Box 1558 32004 | 904-285-6371
Fax 285-0412
Little Stars Preschool | PK-PK
545 A1A N 32082 | 904-285-2698
Chris Saliba, dir. | Fax 273-9740
New Beginnings Preschool | 100/PK-K
PO Box 1279 32004 | 904-285-2965
Palmer Catholic Academy | 500/K-8
4889 Palm Valley Rd 32082 | 904-543-8515
Linda Earp, prin. | Fax 543-8750

Port Charlotte, Charlotte, Pop. 47,600
Charlotte County SD | 17,800/PK-12
1445 Education Way 33948 | 941-255-0808
Dr. David Gayler, supt. | Fax 255-0413
www.ccps.k12.fl.us
Armstrong ES | 600/PK-5
22100 Breezeswept Ave 33952 | 941-255-7450
Kathleen Rooker, prin. | Fax 255-7456
Kingsway ES | 900/K-5
23300 Quasar Blvd 33980 | 941-255-7590
Lori Davis, prin. | Fax 255-7591
Liberty ES | 800/PK-5
370 Atwater St 33954 | 941-255-7515
Thomas Gifford, prin. | Fax 255-7519
Meadow Park ES | 800/PK-5
3131 Lake View Blvd 33948 | 941-255-7470
John Leclair, prin. | Fax 255-7477
Murdock MS | 900/6-8
17325 Mariner Way 33948 | 941-255-7525
Maria Gifford, prin. | Fax 255-7533
Myakka River ES | 700/PK-5
12650 Willmington Blvd 33981 | 941-697-7111
Jeffrey Harvey, prin. | Fax 697-6326
Peace River ES | 500/PK-5
4070 Beaver Ln 33952 | 941-255-7622
Bertie Alvarez, prin. | Fax 255-7626
Port Charlotte MS | 1,000/6-8
23000 Midway Blvd 33952 | 941-255-7460
Demetrius Revelas, prin. | Fax 255-7469
Other Schools – See Punta Gorda, Rotonda West

Charlotte Academy | 200/PK-8
365 Orlando Blvd 33954 | 941-764-7673
Christine Gerofsky, hdmstr. | Fax 764-0342
Community Christian S | 300/PK-12
20035 Quesada Ave 33952 | 941-625-8977
Dr. David Stone, admin. | Fax 625-1735
Genesis Christian S | 100/PK-8
19150 Helena Ave 33948 | 941-627-4849
Mary Bradshaw, dir. | Fax 627-5890
Port Charlotte Adventist S | 100/K-12
2100 Loveland Blvd 33980 | 941-625-5237
Fax 625-8460
Port Charlotte Christian S | 50/K-12
3279 Sherwood Rd 33980 | 941-625-4450
Elizabeth Kolenda, prin. | Fax 243-0586
St. Charles Borromeo S | 200/PK-8
21505 Augusta Ave 33952 | 941-625-5533
Michael O'Loughlin, prin. | Fax 625-7359

Port Orange, Volusia, Pop. 53,746
Volusia County SD
Supt. — See De Land
Creekside MS | 1,200/6-8
6801 Airport Rd 32128 | 386-322-6155
Kevin Tucker, prin. | Fax 304-5508
Cypress Creek ES | 600/K-5
6100 S Williamson Blvd 32128 | 386-322-6101
David Butler, prin.
Horizon ES | 900/K-5
4751 Hidden Lake Dr 32129 | 386-322-6150
Dr. Margot May, prin. | Fax 756-7162
Port Orange ES | 500/K-5
402 Dunlawton Ave 32127 | 386-322-6271
Jim Bishop, prin. | Fax 756-7117
Silver Sands MS | 1,200/6-8
1300 Herbert St 32129 | 386-322-6175
Dr. Leslie Potter, prin. | Fax 322-7574
Spruce Creek ES | 800/PK-5
642 Taylor Rd 32127 | 386-322-6200
Bonnie Lane, prin.
Sugar Mill ES | 800/PK-5
1101 Charles St 32129 | 386-322-6171
Richard Inge, prin. | Fax 756-7140
Sweetwater ES | 1,000/K-5
5800 Victoria Gardens Blvd 32127 | 386-322-6230
Pat Miller, prin. | Fax 322-7526

Port Richey, Pasco, Pop. 3,333
Pasco County SD
Supt. — See Land O Lakes
Chasco ES | 600/K-5
7906 Ridge Rd 34668 | 727-774-1200
Delores Gauvey, prin. | Fax 774-1291
Chasco MS | 900/6-8
7702 Ridge Rd 34668 | 727-774-1300
Christine Wolff, prin. | Fax 774-1391
Fox Hollow ES | 700/PK-5
8309 Fox Hollow Dr 34668 | 727-774-7600
Lisa Miller, prin. | Fax 774-7691
Gulf Highlands ES | 600/K-5
8019 Gulf Highlands Dr 34668 | 727-774-7700
Margie Polen, prin. | Fax 774-7791

Bishop Larkin S | 300/K-8
8408 Monarch Dr 34668 | 727-862-6981
Sr. Regina Ozuzu, prin. | Fax 869-9893
Renaissance Academy | 100/K-12
5844 Pine Hill Rd 34668 | 727-845-8150
Lori Ekblad, hdmstr. | Fax 844-5424

Port Saint Joe, Gulf, Pop. 4,150
Gulf County SD | 2,200/PK-12
150 Middle School Rd 32456 | 850-229-8256
Tim Wilder, supt. | Fax 229-6089
www.gulf.k12.fl.us
Port Saint Joe ES | 500/PK-5
2201 Long Ave 32456 | 850-227-1221
Melissa Ramsey, prin. | Fax 227-3422
Port Saint Joe MS | 300/6-8
191 Middle School Rd 32456 | 850-227-3211
Juanise Griffin, prin. | Fax 229-9078
Other Schools – See Wewahitchka

Faith Christian S | 100/PK-12
801 20th St 32456 | 850-229-6707
Mike Chisholm, chrpsn. | Fax 227-1307

Port Saint Lucie, Saint Lucie, Pop. 98,538
St. Lucie County SD
Supt. — See Fort Pierce
Bayshore ES 1,100/PK-5
1661 SW Bayshore Blvd 34984 772-340-4720
Carolyn Wilkins, prin. Fax 340-4726
Floresta ES 700/K-5
1501 SE Floresta Dr 34983 772-340-4755
Fax 340-4756
Manatee ES 1,200/K-5
1450 SW Heatherwood Blvd 34986 772-340-4745
Mary Hoffman, prin. Fax 340-4775
Mariposa ES 900/PK-5
2620 SE Mariposa Ave 34952 772-337-5960
Craig Logue, prin. Fax 337-5976
Morningside ES 700/K-5
2300 SE Gowin Dr 34952 772-337-6730
Marcia Cully, prin. Fax 337-5976
Northport S 1,300/K-8
250 NW Floresta Dr 34983 772-340-4700
Eric Seymour, prin. Fax 340-7116
Oak Hammock S 1,800/K-8
1251 SW California Blvd 34953 772-344-4490
Carmen Peterson, prin. Fax 621-4907
Rivers Edge ES 900/PK-5
5600 NE Saint James Dr 34983 772-785-5600
Debra Caudill, prin. Fax 785-5625
St. Lucie West MS 1,400/6-8
1501 SW Cashmere Blvd 34986 772-785-6630
Pam Frederick, prin. Fax 785-6632
Savanna Ridge ES 600/PK-5
6801 SE Lennard Rd 34952 772-460-3050
Barbara Kelley, prin. Fax 460-3058
Southern Oaks MS 900/6-8
5500 NE Saint James Dr 34983 772-785-5640
Fax 785-5660
Southport MS 1,100/6-8
2420 SE Morningside Blvd 34952 772-337-5900
Dr. Mary Mosley, prin. Fax 337-5903
Village Green ES 600/K-5
1700 SE Lennard Rd 34952 772-337-6750
Fax 337-6764
Westgate S 1,700/K-8
1050 NW Cashmere Blvd 34986 772-807-7600
Robert Cranmer, prin. Fax 807-7601
Windmill Point ES 1,100/K-5
700 SW Darwin Blvd 34953 772-336-6980
Fax 336-6962

Morningside Academy 400/K-5
2180 SE Morningside Blvd 34952 772-335-3231
Kim Adams, prin. Fax 335-7323
Treasure Coast Christian Academy 200/PK-12
590 NW Peacock Blvd Ste 4 34986 772-343-8088
Cynthia Netwig, prin. Fax 879-6975

Princeton, Miami-Dade, Pop. 7,073

Princeton Christian S 400/PK-12
PO Box 924916 33092 305-258-3107
Cynthia Stone, admin. Fax 258-6747

Punta Gorda, Charlotte, Pop. 17,111
Charlotte County SD
Supt. — See Port Charlotte
Baker Pre-K Center 100/PK-PK
311 E Charlotte Ave 33950 941-575-5470
Janesy Gravelin, coord. Fax 255-5474
Deep Creek ES 800/PK-5
26900 Harbor View Rd 33983 941-255-7535
Deborah Carney, prin. Fax 255-7541
East ES 600/PK-5
27050 Fairway Dr 33982 941-575-5475
Dr. Lauralee Carr, prin. Fax 575-5482
Jones ES 800/PK-5
1230 Narranja St 33950 941-575-5440
Carmel Kisiday, prin. Fax 575-5444
Punta Gorda MS 1,000/6-8
1001 Education Ave 33950 941-575-5485
Cathy Corsaletti, prin. Fax 575-5491

Good Shepherd Day S 200/PK-8
1800 Shreve St 33950 941-639-5454
Rae Konjoian, prin. Fax 575-2139

Quincy, Gadsden, Pop. 6,993
Gadsden County SD 6,300/PK-12
35 Martin Luther King Jr Bl 32351 850-627-9651
Reginald James, supt. Fax 627-2760
www.gcps.k12.fl.us
Gadsden Magnet Center 100/PK-5
500 W King St 32351 850-627-7557
Delshauna Jackson, prin. Fax 875-6695
Greensboro ES 400/PK-5
559 Greensboro Hwy 32351 850-442-6327
Ella Ponder, prin. Fax 442-9524
Munroe ES 800/PK-5
1830 W King St 32351 850-875-8800
Joe Lewis, prin. Fax 875-8805
St. John ES 400/PK-5
4463 Bainbridge Hwy 32352 850-627-3442
Alyson Davis, prin. Fax 875-7270
Shanks MS 700/6-8
1400 W King St 32351 850-875-8737
Pauline Gunn, prin. Fax 875-8775
Stewart Street ES 600/PK-5
749 S Stewart St 32351 850-627-3145
Juanita Ellis, prin. Fax 875-8750
Other Schools – See Chattahoochee, Gretna, Havana

Community Learning Institute 200/PK-12
523 S Pat Thomas Pkwy 32351 850-627-8150
Munroe Day S 300/PK-12
91 Old Mt Pleasant Rd 32352 850-856-5500
James Harris, prin. Fax 856-5856

Reddick, Marion, Pop. 640
Marion County SD
Supt. — See Ocala
Reddick-Collier ES 400/PK-5
4595 W Highway 316 32686 352-671-6070
Vernon Chisholm, prin. Fax 671-6075

Riverview, Hillsborough, Pop. 6,478
Hillsborough County SD
Supt. — See Tampa
Boyette Springs ES 1,100/K-5
10141 Sedgebrook Dr 33569 813-671-5060
Nancy Dukes, prin. Fax 672-5077
Collins ES 1,000/K-5
12424 Summerfield Blvd, 813-672-5400
Ellen Cyr, prin. Fax 672-5404
Frost ES 800/K-5
3950 S Falkenburg Rd, 813-740-4900
Pam Locke, prin. Fax 740-4904
Giunta MS 1,200/6-8
4202 S Falkenburg Rd, 813-740-4888
Arlene Castelli, prin. Fax 740-4892
Ippolito ES 700/PK-5
6874 S Falkenburg Rd, 813-672-5180
Susan Brill, prin. Fax 672-5184
Riverview ES 600/PK-5
10809 Hannaway Dr, 813-671-5105
JoAnn Collings, prin. Fax 671-5087
Rodgers MS 1,100/6-8
11910 Tucker Rd 33569 813-671-5288
Clara Davis, prin. Fax 671-5245
Sessums ES 900/K-5
11525 Ramble Creek Dr 33569 813-672-5230
Winnie McCandless, prin. Fax 672-5234
Summerfield Crossings ES 700/K-5
11050 Fairway Meadow Dr, 813-672-5621
Margo Michalak, prin. Fax 672-5625
Summerfield ES 900/PK-5
11990 Big Bend Rd, 813-671-5115
Margaret Michalak, prin. Fax 672-5221
Symmes ES 600/K-5
6280 Watson Rd, 813-740-4182
Susan Marohnic, prin. Fax 740-4186

East Bay Christian S 200/PK-12
10102 Old Big Bend Rd, 813-677-5236
Providence Christian S 300/K-12
5416 Providence Rd, 813-661-0588
Robert Hewitt, dir. Fax 681-3852
Resurrection ECC 50/PK-PK
6819 Krycul Ave, 813-672-0077
Ivonne Cortes, dir. Fax 671-7844
St. Stephen S 400/PK-8
10424 Saint Stephen Cir 33569 813-741-9203
Therese Jackson, prin. Fax 741-9622
Tropical Acres Baptist S 50/K-10
12107 Rhodine Rd, 813-677-8036

Riviera Beach, Palm Beach, Pop. 33,772
Palm Beach County SD
Supt. — See West Palm Beach
Bethune ES 500/K-5
1501 Avenue U 33404 561-882-7600
Glenda Sheffield, prin. Fax 882-7650
Kennedy MS 1,000/6-8
1901 Avenue S 33404 561-845-4500
Donald Greene, prin. Fax 845-4537
Lincoln ES 500/PK-5
1160 Avenue N 33404 561-494-1400
Jo Anne Rogers, prin. Fax 494-1450
Washington ES 400/K-5
1709 W 30th St 33404 561-494-1200
Olivia Butler, prin. Fax 494-1250
West Riviera ES 600/K-5
1057 W 6th St 33404 561-494-1900
Gayle Harper, prin. Fax 494-1950

Hendley Christian Education Center 300/PK-12
2800 R J Henley Ave 33404 561-881-8015
Palm Beach SDA Bilingual S 100/PK-8
2850 Avenue F 33404 561-881-0130

Rockledge, Brevard, Pop. 24,245
Brevard County SD
Supt. — See Melbourne
Andersen ES 500/PK-5
3011 Fiske Blvd 32955 321-633-3610
Denise Johnson, prin. Fax 633-3619
Golfview ES 600/PK-6
1530 Fiske Blvd 32955 321-633-3570
Jacqueline Feagin, prin. Fax 633-3579
Kennedy MS 600/6-8
2100 Fiske Blvd 32955 321-633-3500
Richard Myers, prin. Fax 633-3509
McNair Magnet MS 500/6-8
1 Challenger Dr 32955 321-633-3630
Rosette Brown, prin. Fax 633-3639
Williams ES 800/K-6
1700 Clubhouse Dr 32955 321-617-7700
Cynthia Ford, prin. Fax 617-7703

Rockledge Christian S 100/K-8
2175 Fiske Blvd 32955 321-632-6966
Kenneth Kerstetter, prin. Fax 632-8951
Rockledge Montessori S 50/K-K
3260 Fiske Blvd 32955 321-639-2266
Cynthia Maslin, prin. Fax 433-3686
St. Mary S 400/PK-8
1152 Seminole Dr 32955 321-636-4208
Nancie Rowan, prin. Fax 636-0591
Trinity Lutheran S 200/PK-8
1330 Fiske Blvd 32955 321-636-5431
Jon Wareham, prin. Fax 638-4498

Rotonda West, Charlotte
Charlotte County SD
Supt. — See Port Charlotte
Ainger MS 1,000/6-8
245 Cougar Way 33947 941-697-5800
Marcia Louden, prin. Fax 697-5470
Vineland ES 900/PK-5
467 Boundary Blvd 33947 941-697-6600
Laura Blunier, prin. Fax 697-5902

Royal Palm Beach, Palm Beach, Pop. 30,886
Palm Beach County SD
Supt. — See West Palm Beach
Crestwood MS 1,300/6-8
64 Sparrow Dr 33411 561-753-5000
Stephanie Nance, prin. Fax 753-5035
Cypress Trails ES 900/K-5
133 Park Rd N 33411 561-795-4950
Gale Fulford, prin. Fax 791-9305
Johnson ES 900/PK-5
1000 Crestwood Blvd N 33411 561-795-4955
Sharon Hench, prin. Fax 795-4937
Royal Palm Beach ES 900/K-5
11911 Okeechobee Blvd 33411 561-784-4140
Suzanne Watson, prin. Fax 784-4145

Ideal S 300/PK-8
400 Royal Commerce Rd 33411 561-791-2881
Fax 791-2117

Ruskin, Hillsborough, Pop. 6,046
Hillsborough County SD
Supt. — See Tampa
Cypress Creek ES 900/K-5
4040 19th Ave NE 33573 813-671-5167
Lisa Tierney-Jackson, prin. Fax 671-5204
Ruskin ES 1,000/PK-5
101 College Ave E 33570 813-671-5177
Donna Ippolito, prin. Fax 671-5182
Shields MS 1,100/6-8
15732 Beth Shields Way 33573 813-672-5338
Tom Scott, prin. Fax 672-5342

First Baptist/Ruskin Christian S 300/PK-12
820 College Ave W 33570 813-645-6441
Dr. Barry Rumsey, supt. Fax 641-2073

Safety Harbor, Pinellas, Pop. 17,517
Pinellas County SD
Supt. — See Largo
Safety Harbor ES 700/K-5
535 5th Ave N 34695 727-724-1462
Robert Kalach, prin. Fax 724-1461
Safety Harbor MS 1,300/6-8
901 1st Ave N 34695 727-724-1400
Alison Kennedy, prin. Fax 724-1407

Espiritu Santos Catholic S 500/PK-8
2405A Phillippe Pkwy 34695 727-812-4650
Margaret Penn, prin. Fax 812-4658

Saint Augustine, Saint Johns, Pop. 11,915
St. Johns County SD 27,600/PK-12
40 Orange St 32084 904-547-7500
Joseph Joyner Ed.D., supt. Fax 547-7515
www.stjohns.k12.fl.us
Crookshank ES 500/K-5
1455 N Whitney St 32084 904-547-7840
Jay Willets, prin. Fax 547-7845
Hartley ES 600/K-5
260 Cacique Dr 32086 904-547-8400
Mary Seymour, prin. Fax 547-8385
Hunt ES 600/K-5
125 Magnolia Dr 32080 904-547-7960
Don Steele, prin. Fax 547-7955
Ketterlinus ES 500/K-5
67 Orange St 32084 904-547-8540
Wayne Jenkins, prin. Fax 547-8554
Mason ES 500/K-5
207 Mason Manatee Way 32086 904-547-8440
Theresa Grady, prin. Fax 547-8445
Mill Creek ES 1,200/K-5
3750 International Golf Pkw 32092 904-547-3720
Mary Ford, prin. Fax 547-3730
Murray MS 900/6-8
150 N Holmes Blvd 32084 904-547-8470
Tom Schwarm, prin. Fax 547-8475
Osceola ES 600/K-5
1605 Osceola Elementary Rd 32084 904-547-3780
Nancy Little, prin. Fax 547-3795
Pacetti Bay MS 600/6-8
245 Meadowlark Ln 32092 904-547-8760
Sue Sparkman, prin. Fax 547-8765
Rogers MS 900/6-8
6250 US Highway 1 S 32086 904-547-8700
Beverly Gordon, prin. Fax 547-8705
Sebastian MS 700/6-8
2955 Lewis Speedway 32084 904-547-3840
Kelly Battel, prin. Fax 547-3845
Timberlin Creek ES 1,200/K-5
555 Pine Tree Ln 32092 904-547-7400
Cathy Hutchins, prin. Fax 547-7405
Wards Creek ES 700/K-5
6555 State Road 16 32092 904-547-8730
Don Campbell, prin. Fax 547-8735
Webster S 700/PK-12
420 N Orange St 32084 904-547-3860
George Leidigh, prin. Fax 547-3865
Other Schools – See Elkton, Ponte Vedra Beach, Saint Johns

Beacon of Hope Christian S 200/K-12
1230 Kings Estate Rd 32086 904-797-6996
Mary Whitfield, prin. Fax 797-6997
Cathedral Parish Early Ed Center 100/PK-PK
10 Sebastian Ave 32084 904-829-2933
Jill Valley, dir. Fax 829-9339
Cathedral Parish S 400/K-8
259 Saint George St 32084 904-824-2861
Janet Morton, prin. Fax 829-2059
St. John's Academy 100/PK-12
1533 Wildwood Dr 32086 904-824-9224
Wallis Brooks, prin. Fax 823-1145

Saint Cloud, Osceola, Pop. 21,480
Osceola County SD
Supt. — See Kissimmee
Hickory Tree ES 800/K-5
2355 Old Hickory Tree Rd 34772 407-891-3120
Scott Knoebel, prin. Fax 891-3129

Lakeview ES 1,000/PK-5
2900 5th St 34769 407-891-3220
Frank Telemko, prin. Fax 891-3228
Michigan Avenue ES 1,000/PK-5
2015 Michigan Ave 34769 407-891-3140
Bettye Hobbs, prin. Fax 891-3149
Narcoossee Community S 1,600/PK-8
2700 N Narcoossee Rd 34771 407-891-6600
Tom Phelps, prin. Fax 891-6610
Neptune ES 700/PK-5
1200 Betsy Ross Ln 34769 407-892-8387
Linda Harwood, prin. Fax 957-2683
Saint Cloud ES 1,000/K-5
2701 Budinger Ave 34769 407-891-3160
William Coffman, prin. Fax 891-3169
Saint Cloud MS 1,300/6-8
1975 Michigan Ave 34769 407-891-3200
Terry Andrews, prin. Fax 891-3206

St. Thomas Aquinas S 400/PK-8
800 Brown Chapel Rd 34769 407-957-1772
Maura Cox, prin. Fax 957-8700
Southland Christian S 400/PK-12
2901 17th St 34769 407-891-7723
Rob Ennis, prin. Fax 891-7734

Saint Johns, Saint Johns
St. Johns County SD
Supt. — See Saint Augustine
Cunningham Creek ES 800/K-5
1205 Roberts Rd, 904-547-7860
Betsy Wierda, prin. Fax 547-7854
Durbin Creek ES 800/K-5
4100 Race Track Rd, 904-547-3880
Dr. Patricia Falaney, prin. Fax 547-3885
Fruit Cove MS 1,200/6-8
3180 Race Track Rd, 904-547-7880
Steve McCormick, prin. Fax 547-7885
Hickory Creek ES 700/K-5
235 Hickory Creek Trl, 904-547-7450
Dr. Paul Gorcki, prin. Fax 547-7455
Julington Creek ES 1,000/K-5
2316 Race Track Rd, 904-547-7980
Michael Story, prin. Fax 547-7985
Liberty Pines Academy K-8
10901 Russell Sampson Rd, 904-547-7900
Randy Kelley, prin.
Switzerland Point MS 1,300/6-8
777 Greenbriar Rd, 904-547-8650
Lisa Kunze, prin. Fax 547-8645

Saint Petersburg, Pinellas, Pop. 247,610
Pinellas County SD
Supt. — See Largo
Azalea ES 600/PK-5
1680 74th St N 33710 727-893-2187
Susan Boyd, prin. Fax 893-2190
Azalea MS 1,200/6-8
7855 22nd Ave N 33710 727-893-2606
Teresa Anderson, prin. Fax 893-2624
Bay Point ES 700/K-5
5800 22nd St S 33712 727-552-1449
Gaye Lively, prin. Fax 552-1457
Bay Point MS 1,200/6-8
2151 62nd Ave S 33712 727-893-1153
Ann Marie Clarke, prin. Fax 893-1181
Bay Vista Fundamental ES 600/K-5
5900 Dr Martin L King St S 33705 727-893-2335
Kristen Sulte, prin. Fax 893-1800
Bear Creek ES 500/PK-5
350 61st St S 33707 727-893-2332
Paula Texel, prin. Fax 893-2334
Blanton ES 600/PK-5
6400 54th Ave N 33709 727-547-7820
Deborah Turner, prin. Fax 545-6562
Campbell Park ES 600/PK-5
1051 7th Ave S 33705 727-893-2650
Tijuana Bigham, prin. Fax 893-2652
Clearview Avenue ES 400/K-5
3815 43rd St N 33714 727-570-3059
Karen Russell, prin. Fax 570-3062
Fairmount Park ES 600/PK-5
575 41st St S 33711 727-893-2132
Karen Moseley, prin. Fax 893-5451
Hopkins MS 1,300/6-8
701 16th St S 33705 727-893-2400
Maureen Thornton, prin. Fax 893-1600
Jamerson ES 600/K-5
1200 37th St S 33711 727-552-1703
Mary Jane Dann, prin. Fax 552-1704
Lakeview Fundamental ES 300/K-5
2229 25th St S 33712 727-893-2139
Christopher Ateek, prin. Fax 893-1359
Lakewood ES 500/PK-5
4151 6th St S 33705 727-893-2196
Kathleen Young, prin. Fax 893-9152
Lealman Avenue ES 500/PK-5
4001 58th Ave N 33714 727-570-3020
Bonita Paquette, prin. Fax 570-3300
Lynch ES 600/PK-5
1901 71st Ave N 33702 727-570-3170
Lorraine Bigelow, prin. Fax 570-3186
Marshall Fundamental MS 600/6-8
3901 22nd Ave S 33711 727-552-1737
Dr. Dallas Jackson, prin. Fax 552-1741
Maximo ES 700/PK-5
4850 31st St S 33712 727-893-2191
Seymour Brown, prin. Fax 893-5525
Meadowlawn MS 1,100/6-8
6050 16th St N 33703 727-570-3097
Valencia Walker, prin. Fax 570-3396
Melrose ES 500/K-5
1752 13th Ave S 33712 727-893-2175
Oscar Robinson, prin. Fax 893-1884
Mt. Vernon ES 500/K-5
4629 13th Ave N 33713 727-893-1815
Peggy Pearson, prin. Fax 550-4149
New Heights ES 600/PK-5
3901 37th St N 33714 727-893-2135
Sandra Kemp, prin. Fax 893-1349
North Shore ES 500/K-5
200 35th Ave NE 33704 727-893-2181
Juanita Deason, prin. Fax 893-5483
Northwest ES 700/K-5
5601 22nd Ave N 33710 727-893-2147
Benigna Pollauf, prin. Fax 893-1888
Pasadena Fundamental ES 400/K-5
95 72nd St N 33710 727-893-2646
Busara Pitts, prin. Fax 893-2408
Perkins ES 600/PK-5
2205 18th Ave S 33712 727-893-2117
Robert Lister, prin. Fax 893-1113
Rio Vista ES 400/K-5
8131 Macoma Dr NE 33702 727-570-3178
Wayne Whitney, prin. Fax 570-3177
Sanderlin ES 500/K-5
2350 22nd Ave S 33712 727-552-1700
Dr. Denise Miller, prin. Fax 552-1701
Sawgrass Lake ES 700/PK-5
1815 77th Ave N 33702 727-570-3121
Jean Charles-Marks, prin. Fax 217-7251
Seventy-Fourth Street ES 600/PK-5
3801 74th St N 33709 727-893-2120
Cooper Dawson, prin. Fax 893-2143
Sexton ES 800/PK-5
1997 54th Ave N 33714 727-570-3400
Patricia Davey, prin. Fax 217-7236
Shore Acres ES 600/PK-5
1800 62nd Ave NE 33702 727-570-3173
Timothy Owens, prin. Fax 570-3175
Southside Fundamental MS 600/6-8
1701 10th St S 33705 727-893-2742
Michael Miller, prin. Fax 893-2129
Tyrone MS 900/6-8
6421 22nd Ave N 33710 727-893-1819
Stephanie Adkinson, prin. Fax 893-1946
Westgate ES 800/K-5
3560 58th St N 33710 727-893-2144
Cara Walsh, prin. Fax 893-2146
Woodlawn ES 500/K-5
1600 16th St N 33704 727-893-1857
Kathleen Proper, prin. Fax 893-5482

Admiral Farragut Academy 400/PK-12
501 Park St N 33743 727-384-5500
Robert Fine, hdmstr. Fax 384-5507
Alegria Montessori S 50/PK-6
3200 58th Ave S 33712 727-866-1901
Sarah Madle, prin.
Canterbury S - Hough Campus PK-4
1200 Snell Isle Blvd NE 33704 727-823-5515
Dr. Margaret Scot Smith, prin. Fax 525-2545
Cathedral School of St. Jude 500/PK-8
600 58th St N 33710 727-347-8622
Thomas Prendergast, prin. Fax 343-0305
Elim Jr. Academy 50/PK-8
4824 2nd Ave S 33711 727-327-8651
Renee White, prin. Fax 323-1370
Garden of Peace Lutheran S 100/PK-PK
6161 22nd Ave N 33710 727-384-9119
Fax 384-3444
Grace Lutheran S 300/PK-8
4301 16th St N 33703 727-527-6213
Mary Lou Wells, prin. Fax 522-4535
Gulf Coast Christian S 100/PK-8
6355 38th Ave N 33710 727-345-3448
Linda Smock, dir. Fax 384-2237
Gulfcoast SDA S 50/K-8
6001 7th Ave S 33707 727-345-2141
A. Peoples, dir. Fax 384-1611
Holy Family S 200/PK-8
250 78th Ave NE 33702 727-526-8194
Sr. Florence Marino, prin. Fax 527-6567
Immaculate Conception ECC 200/PK-PK
2100 26th Ave S 33712 727-822-2156
Rita Jackson, dir. Fax 553-9133
Keswick Christian S 600/PK-12
10101 54th Ave N 33708 727-393-9100
David Holtzhouse, supt. Fax 397-5378
Liberty Christian S 100/PK-5
9401 4th St N 33702 727-576-9635
Helen Wilson, prin. Fax 576-4992
Lutheran Church of the Cross Day S 400/PK-8
4400 Chancellor St NE 33703 727-522-8331
Holly Carlson, dir. Fax 527-3252
Northside Christian S 800/PK-12
7777 62nd Ave N 33709 727-541-7593
Mary Brandes, hdmstr. Fax 546-5836
Our Savior Lutheran S 200/PK-8
5843 4th Ave S 33707 727-344-1026
Jesse Crosmer, prin. Fax 381-3980
Reed Christian S 100/K-5
3455 26th Ave S 33711 727-321-2999
Riviera Day S 100/PK-K
175 62nd Ave N 33702 727-525-8866
Sharon Carder, prin. Fax 522-4096
St. Paul Children's Center 300/PK-PK
1800 12th St N 33704 727-822-3481
Valerie Gervais, dir. Fax 822-1754
St. Paul S 300/PK-8
1900 12th St N 33704 727-823-6144
Elizabeth Fulham, prin. Fax 896-0609
St. Petersburg Christian S 500/1-8
2021 62nd Ave N 33702 727-522-3000
Sheila Cornea, admin. Fax 525-0998
St. Raphael S 200/PK-8
1376 Snell Isle Blvd NE 33704 727-821-9663
Valerie Wostbrock, prin. Fax 502-9594
Shorecrest Preparatory S 1,000/PK-12
5101 1st St NE 33703 727-522-2111
Michael Murphy, hdmstr. Fax 527-4191
Southside Christian Academy 100/PK-5
3624 Queensboro Ave S 33711 727-327-2691
Richard Jackson, prin. Fax 321-2981
Transfiguration ECC 50/PK-PK
4000 43rd St N 33714 727-527-2880
Amy Lounsbury, dir. Fax 526-7794
Wellington S - St. Petersburg Campus 300/K-8
5175 45th St N 33714 727-528-8717
Lorraine Pelosi, hdmstr. Fax 528-8915

Saint Petersburg Beach, Pinellas, Pop. 9,756
Pinellas County SD
Supt. — See Largo
Gulf Beaches ES 400/K-5
8600 Boca Ciega Dr 33706 727-893-2630
Tony Pleshe, prin. Fax 893-2996

Montessori by the Sea 100/PK-4
1603 Gulf Way 33706 727-360-7621
Dorothy Cox, prin.
St. John Vianney S 200/PK-8
500 84th Ave 33706 727-360-1113
Dr. Kristy Swol, prin. Fax 367-8734

San Antonio, Pasco, Pop. 975

St. Anthony S 200/PK-8
PO Box 847 33576 352-588-3041
Sr. Roberta Bailey, prin. Fax 588-3142

Sanford, Seminole, Pop. 47,257
Seminole County SD 65,100/PK-12
400 E Lake Mary Blvd 32773 407-320-0000
Dr. Bill Vogel, supt. Fax 320-0281
www.scps.k12.fl.us
Bentley ES 1,000/PK-5
2190 S Oregon Ave 32771 407-871-9950
Ron Nathan, prin. Fax 871-9996
Goldsboro Magnet ES 700/PK-5
1300 W 20th St 32771 407-320-5850
Cheryl Nicholas, prin. Fax 320-5896
Hamilton ES 800/PK-5
1501 E 8th St 32771 407-320-6050
Peter Gaffney, prin. Fax 320-6005
Idyllwilde ES 900/PK-5
430 Vihlen Rd 32771 407-320-3750
CarolAnn Darnell, prin. Fax 320-3799
Midway ES 400/PK-5
2251 Jitway Ave 32771 407-320-5950
Sharon Tanner, prin. Fax 320-5961
Millennium MS 1,700/6-8
21 Lakeview Ave 32773 407-320-6550
Kate Eglof, prin. Fax 320-6599
Pine Crest ES 900/PK-5
405 W 27th St 32773 407-320-5450
Dianne Lebruto, prin. Fax 320-5499
Sanford MS 1,300/6-8
1700 S French Ave 32771 407-320-6150
Mark Russi, prin. Fax 320-6265
Wicklow ES 800/K-5
100 Placid Lake Dr 32773 407-320-1250
Greg Turner, prin. Fax 320-1215
Wilson ES 900/PK-5
985 S Orange Blvd 32771 407-320-6950
Sallie Jenkins, prin. Fax 320-6999
Other Schools – See Altamonte Springs, Apopka, Casselberry, Chuluota, Fern Park, Geneva, Lake Mary, Longwood, Oviedo, Winter Park, Winter Springs

---

All Souls Catholic S 300/PK-8
810 S Oak Ave 32771 407-322-7090
Thomas Doyle, prin. Fax 321-7255
Holy Cross Academy 400/PK-8
5450 Holy Cross Ct 32771 407-936-3636
Betty Hoyer, prin. Fax 936-0041
Lake Monroe Christian Academy 50/K-8
1000 E 1st St 32771 407-547-2408
Roger Dockum, admin. Fax 330-0376
Liberty Christian S 200/K-12
2626 S Palmetto Ave 32773 407-323-1583
Fax 323-1588
Page Private S 300/PK-8
100 Aero Ln 32771 407-324-1144
Laura Porter, dir. Fax 324-4513
Riverwalk Christian Academy 100/PK-8
801 W 22nd St 32771 407-322-3942
Dwayne Harris, dir. Fax 322-7627

Sanibel, Lee, Pop. 6,072
Lee County SD
Supt. — See Fort Myers
Sanibel S 400/K-8
3840 Sanibel Captiva Rd 33957 239-472-1617
Barbara Von Harten, prin. Fax 472-6544

San Mateo, Putnam
Putnam County SD
Supt. — See Palatka
Browning-Pearce Community ES 900/PK-5
100 Bear Blvd 32187 386-329-0557
Verlene Bennett, prin. Fax 329-0623

Santa Rosa Beach, Walton
Walton County SD
Supt. — See De Funiak Springs
Bay ES 300/PK-5
118 Gilmore Rd 32459 850-622-5050
Dr. Gail Pettus, prin. Fax 622-5059
Butler ES 600/PK-5
6694 W County Highway 30A 32459 850-622-5040
Tammy Smith, prin. Fax 622-5048
Emerald Coast MS 300/6-8
6694 W County Highway 30A 32459 850-622-5025
Gail Smith, prin. Fax 622-5027

St. Rita Preschool PK-PK
137 Moll Dr 32459 850-267-1145
Ali Barrett, dir. Fax 267-3711
South Walton Montessori Academy 50/PK-5
101 Eden Gardens Rd 32459 850-231-5955
Catherine Beall, hdmstr. Fax 231-5955

Sarasota, Sarasota, Pop. 53,711
Manatee County SD
Supt. — See Bradenton
Abel ES 600/K-5
7100 Madonna Pl 34243 941-751-7040
Judy Bayer, prin. Fax 753-0919

Kinnan ES 800/K-5
3415 Tallevast Rd 34243 941-358-2888
Kris Bayer, prin. Fax 358-2956

Sarasota County SD 39,400/K-12
1960 Landings Blvd 34231 941-927-9000
Lori White, supt. Fax 927-4009
www.sarasota.k12.fl.us
Alta Vista ES 700/K-5
1050 S Euclid Ave 34237 941-361-6400
Dr. Barbara Shirley, prin. Fax 361-6956
Ashton ES 900/K-5
5110 Ashton Rd 34233 941-361-6440
Bill Muth, prin. Fax 361-6444
Bay Haven S of Basics Plus 600/K-5
2901 W Tamiami Cir 34234 941-359-5800
Betsy Asheim-Dein, prin. Fax 359-5694
Booker ES 600/K-5
2350 Dr Martin Luther King 34234 941-361-6480
Dawn Clayton, prin. Fax 361-6484
Booker MS 900/6-8
2250 Myrtle St 34234 941-359-5824
Joe Bazenas, prin. Fax 359-5898
Brentwood ES 700/K-5
2500 Vinson Ave 34232 941-361-6230
Michelle Henderson, prin. Fax 361-6381
Brookside MS 1,100/6-8
3636 S Shade Ave 34239 941-361-6472
Jack Turgeon, prin. Fax 361-6508
Fruitville ES 600/K-5
601 Honore Ave 34232 941-361-6200
Dr. Laura Kingsley, prin. Fax 361-6203
Gocio ES 900/K-5
3450 Gocio Rd 34235 941-361-6405
Steven Dragon, prin. Fax 361-6793
Gulf Gate ES 800/K-5
6500 S Lockwood Ridge Rd 34231 941-361-6499
Robin Magac, prin. Fax 361-6799
Lakeview ES 800/K-5
7299 Proctor Rd 34241 941-361-6571
Joan Bower, prin. Fax 361-6573
McIntosh MS 1,100/6-8
701 Mcintosh Rd 34232 941-361-6520
George Neville, prin. Fax 361-6340
Philippi Shores ES 500/K-5
4747 S Tamiami Trl 34231 941-361-6424
Allison Stewart, prin. Fax 361-6814
Sarasota MS 1,200/6-8
4826 Ashton Rd 34233 941-361-6464
Karen Rose, prin. Fax 361-6798
Southside ES 600/K-5
1901 Webber St 34239 941-361-6420
Sharon Marks, prin. Fax 361-6866
Tatum Ridge ES 800/K-5
4100 Tatum Rd 34240 941-316-8188
Sandra Russell, prin. Fax 316-8189
Tuttle ES 800/K-5
2863 8th St 34237 941-361-6433
Thomas Buchanan, prin. Fax 361-6530
Wilkinson ES 700/K-5
3400 Wilkinson Rd 34231 941-361-6477
Ruth Thomas, prin. Fax 361-1877
Other Schools – See Englewood, Nokomis, North Port, Venice

Ascension Lutheran S 100/PK-8
800 McIntosh Rd 34232 941-371-5909
Kurt Rosenbaum, prin. Fax 377-9670
Calvary Chapel S 200/PK-8
3800 27th Pkwy 34235 941-366-6522
Nicholas Sommer, prin. Fax 955-3081
Feldman Academy 300/PK-8
1050 S Tuttle Ave 34237 941-552-2770
Kavita Vasil, dir. Fax 552-2771
Incarnation S 300/PK-8
2911 Bee Ridge Rd 34239 941-924-8588
Regina Housel, prin. Fax 925-1248
New Gate S 300/PK-12
5237 Ashton Rd 34233 941-922-4949
Paul Wenninger, hdmstr. Fax 922-7660
Out of Door Academy 300/PK-6
444 Reid St 34242 941-349-3223
David Mahler, hdmstr. Fax 349-8133
Potter's Wheel Academy 100/K-12
PO Box 50203 34232 866-335-1098
Reed Palmer, dir. Fax 335-1098
Rohr Academy 300/PK-8
4466 Fruitville Rd 34232 941-371-4979
Julie Rohr McHugh, prin. Fax 379-5816
St. Martha S 500/PK-8
4380 Fruitville Rd 34232 941-953-4181
Dr. Elizabeth Bowman, prin. Fax 366-5580
Sarasota Christian S 500/K-12
5415 Bahia Vista St 34232 941-371-6481
Eugene Miller, supt. Fax 371-0898
Sarasota Lutheran S 100/PK-8
5651 Honore Ave 34233 941-922-8164
Jonna Owens, prin. Fax 923-6512
Sarasota Waldorf S 100/PK-5
6124 Crestwood Ave 34231 941-927-3711
Linda Bounds, admin. Fax 927-2006
Sonhaven Preparatory Academy 50/PK-12
PO Box 50517 34232 941-926-7472
Dr. Carolyn Hilt, prin. Fax 355-6127
Tabernacle Christian S 300/PK-8
4141 Desoto Rd 34235 941-365-1050
Bill Medred, dir. Fax 358-7051
West Florida Christian S 200/PK-12
4311 Wilkinson Rd 34233 941-921-6311
Rick McGowan, prin. Fax 921-4046

Satellite Beach, Brevard, Pop. 9,811
Brevard County SD
Supt. — See Melbourne
DeLaura MS 700/7-8
300 Jackson Ave 32937 321-773-7581
Jeremy Salmon, prin. Fax 773-0702
Holland ES 400/PK-6
50 Holland Ct 32937 321-773-7591
Larry Kuhn, prin. Fax 773-6315

Sea Park ES 300/PK-6
300 Sea Park Blvd 32937 321-779-2050
Ena Leiba, prin. Fax 779-2052
Surfside ES 400/PK-6
475 Cassia Blvd 32937 321-773-2818
Susan Murray, prin. Fax 777-1841

Sebastian, Indian River, Pop. 19,643
Indian River County SD
Supt. — See Vero Beach
Pelican Island ES 500/PK-5
1355 Schumann Dr 32958 772-564-6500
Jody Bennett, prin. Fax 564-6493
Sebastian ES 600/K-5
400 Sebastian Blvd 32958 772-978-8200
Letitia Whitfield-Hart, prin. Fax 978-8205
Sebastian River MS 1,400/6-8
9400 County Road 512 32958 772-564-5111
Todd Racine, prin. Fax 564-5113
Treasure Coast ES 700/K-5
8955 85th St 32958 772-978-8550
Mark Dugan, prin. Fax 978-8530

Sebring, Highlands, Pop. 10,431
Highlands County SD 12,300/PK-12
426 School St 33870 863-471-5555
Wally Cox, supt. Fax 471-5622
www.highlands.k12.fl.us
Cracker Trail ES 800/PK-5
8200 Sparta Rd 33875 863-471-5777
Richard Demeri, prin. Fax 471-5785
Hill-Gustat MS 700/6-8
4700 Schumacher Rd 33872 863-471-5437
Chris Doty, prin. Fax 314-5245
Sebring MS 800/6-8
500 E Center Ave 33870 863-471-5700
Sandi Whidden, prin. Fax 471-5710
Sun N Lake ES 900/K-5
4515 Ponce De Leon Blvd 33872 863-471-5464
Diane Lethbridge, prin. Fax 471-5466
Wild ES 800/PK-5
3550 Youth Care Ln 33870 863-471-5400
Laura Waldron, prin. Fax 471-5426
Woodlawn ES 800/PK-5
817 Woodlawn Dr 33870 863-471-5444
Kaye Bowers, prin. Fax 471-5446
Other Schools – See Avon Park, Lake Placid

Heartland Christian S 200/PK-12
1160 Persimmon Ave 33870 863-385-3850
David Kaser, hdmstr. Fax 385-6926
Kenilworth S 100/PK-5
2835 Kenilworth Blvd 33870 863-471-0203
Liberty Christian Academy 50/K-12
420 S Pine St 33870 863-385-0400
Anna Beasley, admin. Fax 385-3901
St. Catherine S PK-3
747 S Franklin St 33870 863-385-0049
Fax 385-5169

Seffner, Hillsborough, Pop. 5,371
Hillsborough County SD
Supt. — See Tampa
Burnett MS 1,000/6-8
1010 N Kingsway Rd 33584 813-744-6745
Herbert Peeples, prin. Fax 744-8973
Colson ES 700/K-5
1520 Lakeview Ave 33584 813-744-8031
Karen Lynch, prin. Fax 744-8439
Jennings MS 1,000/6-8
9325 Governors Run Dr 33584 813-740-4575
Joann Johnson, prin. Fax 740-4579
Lopez ES 800/PK-5
200 N Kingsway Rd 33584 813-744-8000
Michael Engle, prin. Fax 744-8005
Mango ES 700/PK-5
4220 County Road 579 33584 813-744-8208
Patricia Jones, prin. Fax 744-8211
McDonald ES 600/PK-5
501 Pruett Rd 33584 813-744-8154
Dave McMeen, prin. Fax 744-8012
Seffner ES 700/PK-5
109 Cactus Rd 33584 813-744-8171
Sharon Whitworth, prin. Fax 740-3984

Hillsborough Baptist S 100/PK-12
6021 Williams Rd 33584 813-620-0683
Fax 663-9776
New Jerusalem Christian Academy 100/PK-8
PO Box 1238 33583 813-684-2754
Rev. Miriam Gonzalez, prin. Fax 684-0051
Seffner Christian Academy 700/PK-12
11605 E US Highway 92 33584 813-626-0001
Roger Duncan, dir. Fax 627-0330

Seminole, Pinellas, Pop. 18,505
Pinellas County SD
Supt. — See Largo
Bardmoor ES 600/PK-5
8900 Greenbriar Rd 33777 727-547-7824
Linda Emanuel, prin. Fax 545-6593
Bauder ES 800/PK-5
12755 86th Ave 33776 727-547-7829
Janet Johnston, prin. Fax 547-4564
Orange Grove ES 400/K-5
10300 65th Ave 33772 727-547-7845
Nanette Grasso, prin. Fax 547-7505
Osceola MS 1,200/6-8
9301 98th St 33777 727-547-7689
Bob Vicari, prin. Fax 547-7667
Seminole ES 700/K-5
10950 74th Ave 33772 727-547-7668
Dr. Bonnie Cangelosi, prin. Fax 545-6585
Seminole MS 1,200/6-8
8701 131st St 33776 727-547-4520
Thomas Lechner, prin. Fax 547-7741
Starkey ES 600/K-5
9300 86th Ave 33777 727-547-7841
Kenneth Mackenzie, prin. Fax 545-7550

Bay Pines Lutheran S 100/K-8
7589 113th Ln 33772 727-397-3204
Mark Boehme, prin. Fax 391-6823
Blessed Sacrament S 200/K-8
11501 66th Ave 33772 727-391-4060
Cindy Yevich, prin. Fax 391-5638
Wellington S - Seminole Campus 200/PK-4
8000 Starkey Rd 33777 727-397-4565
Lorraine Pelosi, hdmstr. Fax 397-4086

Shalimar, Okaloosa, Pop. 733
Okaloosa County SD
Supt. — See Fort Walton Beach
Longwood ES 400/PK-5
50 Holly Ave 32579 850-833-4329
Fax 833-4336
Meigs MS 700/6-8
150 Richbourg Ave 32579 850-833-4301
Dr. Lamar White, prin. Fax 833-9392
Shalimar ES 500/PK-5
1350 Joe Martin Cir 32579 850-833-4339
Sheila Lightbourne, prin. Fax 833-4357

Silver Springs, Marion
Marion County SD
Supt. — See Ocala
East Marion ES 800/PK-5
14550 NE 14th Street Rd 34488 352-671-4810
Mike Hearn, prin. Fax 671-4811

Sneads, Jackson, Pop. 1,943
Jackson County SD
Supt. — See Marianna
Sneads ES 500/PK-5
1961 Lockey Dr 32460 850-482-9003
Cheryl McDaniel, prin. Fax 482-9590

Victory Christian Academy 100/PK-12
2271 River Rd 32460 850-593-6699
Dr. David Pipping, admin. Fax 593-3341

South Bay, Palm Beach, Pop. 4,059
Palm Beach County SD
Supt. — See West Palm Beach
Rosenwald ES 300/K-5
1321 W Palm Beach Rd 33493 561-993-8900
Shundra Dowers, prin. Fax 993-8950

South Daytona, Volusia, Pop. 13,733
Volusia County SD
Supt. — See De Land
South Daytona ES 800/PK-5
600 Elizabeth Pl 32119 386-322-6180
Dr. Carolyn Burhans, prin.

Warner Christian Academy 600/PK-12
1730 S Ridgewood Ave 32119 386-767-5451
Mark Tress, hdmstr. Fax 760-6834

South Miami, Miami-Dade, Pop. 11,147
Miami-Dade County SD
Supt. — See Miami
Ludlam ES 600/PK-5
6639 SW 74th St 33143 305-667-5551
Pamela Sanders, prin. Fax 669-5406
South Miami K-8 Ctr 600/PK-8
6800 SW 60th St 33143 305-667-8847
Anamarie Moreiras, prin. Fax 665-3217
South Miami MS 800/7-8
6750 SW 60th St 33143 305-661-3481
Dr. Lisa Robertson, prin. Fax 665-6728
Sunset ES 1,100/PK-5
5120 SW 72nd St 33143 305-661-8527
Aline Sarria, prin. Fax 666-2327

Gulliver S - South Miami Campus 50/K-K
8530 SW 57th Ave 33143 305-669-5497
Marian Krutulis, dir. Fax 663-9349
South Miami Christian S 200/PK-12
6767 Sunset Dr 33143 305-666-5171

Southport, Bay, Pop. 1,700
Bay County SD
Supt. — See Panama City
Southport ES 400/PK-5
1835 Bridge St 32409 850-265-2810
Dianne Miller, prin. Fax 265-3703

Southwest Ranches, Broward, Pop. 7,388

St. Mark S 700/PK-8
5601 S Flamingo Rd, 954-434-3887
Shirley Sandusky, prin. Fax 434-3595

Sparr, Marion
Marion County SD
Supt. — See Ocala
Sparr ES 400/PK-5
PO Box 539 32192 352-671-6060
Woody Clymer, prin. Fax 671-6061

Spring Hill, Hernando, Pop. 85,900
Hernando County SD
Supt. — See Brooksville
Challenger S of Science and Mathematics 1,500/K-8
13400 Elgin Blvd 34609 352-797-7024
Sue Stoops, prin. Fax 797-7124
Deltona ES 1,000/PK-5
2055 Deltona Blvd 34606 352-797-7040
Betty Harper, prin. Fax 797-7140
Explorer K-8 S K-8
10252 Northcliffe Blvd 34608 352-797-7094
Dominick Ferello, prin. Fax 797-7194
Floyd ES 1,300/PK-5
3139 Dumont Ave 34609 352-797-7055
Joe Clifford, prin. Fax 797-7155
Fox Chapel MS 1,000/6-8
9412 Fox Chapel Ln 34606 352-797-7025
Ray Pinder, prin. Fax 797-7125

Spring Hill ES 1,000/PK-5
6001 Mariner Blvd 34609 352-797-7030
Marvin Gordon, prin. Fax 797-7130
Suncoast ES 1,000/PK-5
11135 Quality Dr 34609 352-797-7085
Jean Ferris, prin. Fax 797-7185
Westside ES 1,000/PK-5
5400 Applegate Dr 34606 352-797-7080
Charles Johnson, prin. Fax 797-7180

Pasco County SD
Supt. — See Land O Lakes
Crews Lake MS 700/6-8
15144 Shady Hills Rd 34610 727-246-1600
Chris Christoff, prin. Fax 246-1691
Giella ES 600/PK-5
14710 Shady Hills Rd 34610 727-774-5800
Katherine Lail, prin. Fax 774-5891
Shady Hills ES 600/PK-5
18000 Shady Hills Rd 34610 813-794-4100
Tom Barker, prin. Fax 794-4191

Faith Christian Academy 100/PK-6
185 Spring Time St 34608 352-686-9350
Claudia Tassey, admin. Fax 686-9350
Notre Dame S 200/PK-8
1095 Commercial Way 34606 352-683-0755
Sr. Eileen Marie Woodbury, prin. Fax 683-3924
Spring Hill Christian Academy 300/PK-12
3140 Mariner Blvd 34609 352-683-8485
Michael Willis, prin. Fax 683-5087
West Hernando Christian S 300/PK-12
2250 Osowaw Blvd 34607 352-688-9918
Marti Covert, admin. Fax 683-1184
Wider Horizons S 200/PK-12
4060 Castle Ave 34609 352-686-1934
Dr. Domenick Maglio, prin. Fax 688-4371

Starke, Bradford, Pop. 5,844
Bradford County SD 3,600/PK-12
501 W Washington St 32091 904-966-6800
Beth Moore, supt. Fax 966-6030
www.mybradford.us/
Bradford MS 700/6-8
527 N Orange St 32091 904-966-6704
Jeff Cable, prin. Fax 966-6714
Rainbow Center 50/PK-PK
501 W Washington St 32091 904-966-6039
Cindy Devalerio, prin. Fax 966-6081
Southside ES 600/PK-5
823 Stansbury St 32091 904-966-6066
Bill McRae, prin. Fax 964-8881
Starke ES 500/K-5
1000 W Weldon St 32091 904-966-6047
Christy Reddish, prin. Fax 966-6868
Other Schools – See Brooker, Hampton, Lawtey

Hope Christian Academy 200/PK-12
3900 SE State Road 100 32091 352-473-4040
Angie Davis, prin. Fax 473-2024
Northside Christian Academy 200/PK-12
7415 NW County Road 225 32091 904-964-7124
David Coxe, admin. Fax 964-7141

Steinhatchee, Taylor
Taylor County SD
Supt. — See Perry
Steinhatchee S 100/K-8
1209 Southeast First Ave 32359 352-498-3304
Sandy Hendry, prin. Fax 498-6050

Stuart, Martin, Pop. 15,764
Martin County SD 17,500/PK-12
500 SE Ocean Blvd 34994 772-219-1200
Dr. Sara Wilcox, supt. Fax 219-1231
www.sbmc.org
Anderson MS 800/6-8
7000 SE Atlantic Ridge Dr 34997 772-221-7100
Dr. Larthenia Howard, prin. Fax 221-7149
Crystal Lake ES 700/K-5
2095 SW 96th St 34997 772-219-1525
Xenobia Anderson, prin. Fax 219-1529
Murray MS 800/6-8
4400 SE Murray St 34997 772-219-1670
Kit Weir, prin. Fax 219-1677
Parker ES 600/K-5
1050 SE 10th St 34996 772-219-1580
Mary White, prin. Fax 219-1583
Pinewood ES 900/K-5
5200 SE Willoughby Blvd 34997 772-219-1595
Brenda Watkins, prin. Fax 219-1603
Port Salerno ES 700/K-5
3260 SE Lionel Ter 34997 772-219-1610
Tracey Miller, prin. Fax 219-1615
Stuart MS 1,000/6-8
575 SE Georgia Ave 34994 772-219-1685
Sigrid George, prin. Fax 219-1690
Williams ES 700/PK-5
401 NW Baker Rd 34994 772-219-1640
Gail Olsen, prin. Fax 219-1646
Other Schools – See Hobe Sound, Indiantown, Jensen Beach, Palm City

---

Bridges Montessori S 200/PK-6
51 SE Central Pkwy 34994 772-221-9490
Tracey Etelson, hdmstr. Fax 221-9787
Community Christian Academy 200/PK-12
777 SE Salerno Rd 34997 772-288-7227
Kenny Kotouc, hdmstr. Fax 600-2728
First Baptist Christian S 200/PK-8
201 SW Ocean Blvd 34994 772-287-5161
Michael Casey, hdmstr. Fax 287-7735
Pine S 300/PK-6
1300 SE 10th St 34996 772-283-1222
Stephen Mandell Ed.D., hdmstr. Fax 220-9149
Redeemer Lutheran S 200/PK-8
2450 SE Ocean Blvd 34996 772-286-0932
Fax 287-0434

St. Joseph S 400/PK-8
1200 SE 10th St 34996 772-287-6975
Mary Preston, prin. Fax 287-4733

Summerfield, Marion
Marion County SD
Supt. — See Ocala
Harbour View ES 700/PK-5
8445 SE 147th Pl 34491 352-671-6110
Marlene Bjork, prin. Fax 671-6111
Lake Weir MS 1,400/6-8
10220 SE Sunset Harbor Rd 34491 352-671-6120
Mike Kelly, prin. Fax 671-6121

Summerland Key, Monroe
Monroe County SD
Supt. — See Key West
Sugarloaf S 700/PK-8
255 Crane Blvd 33042 305-745-3282
Theresa Axford, prin. Fax 745-2019

Sunny Isles, Miami-Dade, Pop. 11,772
Miami-Dade County SD
Supt. — See Miami
Sunny Isles Beach S K-8
201 182nd Dr 33160 305-933-6161
Dr. Annette Weissman, prin. Fax 933-6162

Sunrise, Broward, Pop. 90,589
Broward County SD
Supt. — See Fort Lauderdale
Bair MS 1,200/6-8
9100 NW 21st Mnr 33322 754-322-2900
Ellen Etling, prin. Fax 322-2985
Banyan ES 900/K-5
8800 NW 50th St 33351 754-322-5350
Bruce Voelkel, prin. Fax 322-5390
Horizon ES 900/K-5
2101 N Pine Island Rd 33322 754-322-6450
Nora Chiet, prin. Fax 322-6490
Nob Hill ES 800/K-5
2100 NW 104th Ave 33322 754-322-7200
Dr. Patricia Patterson, prin. Fax 322-7240
Sandpiper ES 900/K-5
3700 N Hiatus Rd 33351 754-322-8450
Dr. Deloris Johnson, prin. Fax 322-8490
Sawgrass ES 1,000/PK-5
12655 NW 8th St 33325 754-322-8500
Charles Radkowski, prin. Fax 322-8540
Village ES 900/PK-5
2100 NW 70th Ave 33313 754-322-8750
Lee Dollar, prin. Fax 322-8790
Welleby ES 900/PK-5
3230 N Nob Hill Rd 33351 754-322-8850
Margaret Roberts, prin. Fax 322-8890
Westpine MS 1,400/6-8
9393 NW 50th St 33351 754-322-4900
Paula Meadows, prin. Fax 322-4985

All Saints S 300/PK-8
10900 W Oakland Park Blvd 33351 954-742-4842
Antoinette McNamara, prin. Fax 742-4871
Tawfik S 200/PK-8
5457 NW 108th Ave 33351 954-741-8130
Dr. Rassem Amash, prin. Fax 741-8788

Switzerland, Saint Johns

St. Johns Grammar S 100/PK-8
2353 State Road 13 32259 904-287-8760
Jeannine Decker, hdmstr. Fax 287-6266

Tallahassee, Leon, Pop. 158,500
Leon County SD 31,100/PK-12
2757 W Pensacola St 32304 850-487-7100
Jackie Pons, supt. Fax 487-7141
www.leon.k12.fl.us
Apalachee ES 700/PK-5
650 Trojan Trl 32311 850-488-7110
Ross Witherspoon, prin. Fax 922-0202
Astoria Park ES 600/PK-5
2465 Atlas Rd 32303 850-488-4673
Desmond Cole, prin. Fax 922-4174
Bond ES 700/PK-5
2204 Saxon St 32310 850-488-7676
Pam Hightower, prin. Fax 922-5206
Buck Lake ES 900/PK-5
1600 Pedrick Rd 32317 850-488-6133
Eydie Sands, prin. Fax 922-4161
Canopy Oaks ES 700/PK-5
3250 Point View Dr 32303 850-488-3301
Carol Barineau, prin. Fax 414-7356
Chaires ES 700/PK-5
4774 Chaires Cross Rd 32317 850-878-8534
Michelle Prescott, prin. Fax 922-6462
Cobb MS 900/6-8
915 Hillcrest St 32308 850-488-3364
Shelly Bell, prin. Fax 922-2452
Conley ES 600/PK-5
2400 Orange Ave E 32311 850-414-5610
Laura Brooks, prin. Fax 414-8163
Deerlake MS 1,300/6-8
9902 Deer Lk W 32312 850-922-6545
Shane Syfrett, prin. Fax 488-3275
DeSoto Trail ES 600/PK-5
5200 Tredington Park Dr 32309 850-488-4511
Michele Keltner, prin. Fax 487-1623
Fairview MS 800/6-8
3415 Zillah St 32305 850-488-6880
Scott Hansen, prin. Fax 922-6326
Ft. Braden S 600/PK-8
15100 Blountstown Hwy 32310 850-488-9374
Jim Jackson, prin. Fax 488-5948
Gilchrist ES 900/PK-5
1301 Timberlane Rd 32312 850-893-4310
David Solz, prin. Fax 487-0959
Griffin MS 700/6-8
800 Alabama St 32304 850-488-8436
Gwendolyn Lynn, prin. Fax 922-4226

Hartsfield ES 600/PK-5
1414 Chowkeebin Nene 32301 850-488-7322
Cora Franklin, prin. Fax 922-2372
Hawks Rise ES 900/PK-5
205 Meadow Ridge Dr 32312 850-487-4733
Penny Brinson, prin. Fax 488-6971
Killearn Lakes ES 900/PK-5
8037 Deer Lk E 32312 850-893-1265
Brenda McGalliard, prin. Fax 922-2566
Montford MS 6-8
5789 Pimlico Dr 32309 850-922-6011
Doug Cook, prin. Fax 922-7974
Moore ES 700/PK-5
1706 Dempsey Mayo Rd 32308 850-877-6158
Sue Kraul, prin. Fax 922-6658
Nims MS 400/6-8
723 W Orange Ave 32310 850-488-5960
Kay Collins, prin. Fax 922-0203
Oak Ridge ES 500/PK-5
4530 Shelfer Rd 32305 850-488-3124
D.J. Wright, prin. Fax 922-7145
Pineview ES 600/PK-5
2230 Lake Bradford Rd 32310 850-488-2819
Marilyn Rahming, prin. Fax 487-1239
Raa MS 800/6-8
401 W Tharpe St 32303 850-488-6287
Donna Callaway, prin. Fax 922-5835
Riley ES 500/PK-5
1400 Indiana St 32304 850-488-5840
Karwynn Paul, prin. Fax 922-4227
Roberts ES 800/K-5
5777 Centerville Rd 32309 850-488-0923
Kim McFarland, prin. Fax 487-2416
Ruediger ES 600/PK-5
526 W 10th Ave 32303 850-488-1074
Melissa Fullmore, prin. Fax 487-0007
Sabal Palm ES 700/PK-5
2813 Ridgeway St 32310 850-488-0167
Ann Johnson, prin. Fax 922-8481
Sealey ES 500/K-5
2815 Allen Rd 32312 850-488-5640
Demetria Clemons, prin. Fax 488-1239
Springwood ES 600/K-5
3801 Fred George Rd 32303 850-488-6225
Claire Frick, prin. Fax 922-8932
Sullivan ES 800/K-5
927 Miccosukee Rd 32308 850-487-1216
Pam Stevens, prin. Fax 487-0005
Swift Creek MS 1,000/6-8
2100 Pedrick Rd 32317 850-487-4868
Joe Burgess, prin. Fax 414-2650
Woodville ES 500/PK-5
9373 Woodville Hwy 32305 850-487-7043
Nancy Stokely, prin. Fax 921-4281

Advent Parish Day S 200/PK-K
815 Piedmont Dr 32312 850-386-5100
Christine York, dir. Fax 385-7225
Betton Hills Preparatory S 300/PK-8
2205 Thomasville Rd 32308 850-422-2464
Ilona Faust, prin. Fax 422-1369
Christ Classical Academy 100/1-12
1983 Mahan Dr 32308 850-656-2373
Paul Shackelford, hdmstr. Fax 656-6373
Community Christian S 300/PK-12
4859 Kerry Forest Pkwy 32309 850-893-6628
Tom Argersinger, hdmstr. Fax 668-3966
Cornerstone Learning Community 200/PK-8
2524 Hartsfield Rd 32303 850-386-5550
Beverly Wells, dir. Fax 386-5421
Epiphany Lutheran S 50/PK-PK
8300 Deerlake Rd W 32312 850-385-9822
Dewey Rykard, prin. Fax 422-0984
Holy Comforter Episcopal S 700/PK-8
2001 Fleischmann Rd 32308 850-383-1007
Dr. Barbara Hodges, hdmstr. Fax 383-1021
Innovation S of Excellence 200/K-8
329 Ausley Rd 32304 850-575-5580
Otis Young, prin. Fax 575-0833
Maclay S 1,000/PK-12
3737 N Meridian Rd 32312 850-893-2138
William Jablon, hdmstr. Fax 893-7434
Maranatha Christian S 200/PK-12
2532 W Tharpe St 32303 850-385-5920
Alan Risk, admin. Fax 386-7785
North Florida Christian S 1,100/PK-12
3000 N Meridian Rd 32312 850-386-6327
Dr. Rick Fielding, admin. Fax 386-7163
Seven Hills Academy 100/1-12
1500 Miccosukee Rd 32308 850-656-9211
Duwayne Baum, prin. Fax 893-4464
Tallahassee Adventist Christian Academy 50/PK-8
618 Capital Cir NE 32301 850-656-1259
Trinity Catholic S 500/PK-8
706 E Brevard St 32308 850-222-0444
Janet Gendusa, prin. Fax 224-5067

Tamarac, Broward, Pop. 59,923
Broward County SD
Supt. — See Fort Lauderdale
Challenger ES 1,200/K-5
5703 NW 94th Ave 33321 754-322-5750
Maria Bach, prin. Fax 322-5790
Millennium MS 1,400/6-8
5803 NW 94th Ave 33321 754-322-3900
Dr. Cheryl Cendan, prin. Fax 322-3985
Tamarac ES 1,100/K-5
7601 N University Dr 33321 754-322-8600
Nancy Seiler, prin. Fax 322-8640

Alazhar S 100/PK-8
7201 W McNab Rd 33321 954-722-1555
Heba Hussein, prin. Fax 722-4066
Excelsior Preparatory S 100/PK-8
8197 N University Dr Ste 13 33321 954-721-3471
Kayann Baugh, prin. Fax 721-3872
St. Malachy S 100/PK-8
7595 NW 61st St 33321 954-722-3130
Annette Giuliano, prin. Fax 722-7233

Tampa, Hillsborough, Pop. 325,989
Hillsborough County SD 188,300/PK-12
PO Box 3408 33601 813-272-4000
Mary Ellen Elia, supt. Fax 272-4510
www.sdhc.k12.fl.us/
Adams MS 1,200/6-8
10201 N Boulevard 33612 813-975-7665
Odalys Pritchard, prin. Fax 632-6889
Alexander ES 600/PK-5
5602 N Lois Ave 33614 813-872-5395
Kristina Alvarez, prin. Fax 356-1121
Anderson ES 400/K-5
3910 W Fair Oaks Ave 33611 813-272-3075
Betty Lou Turner, prin. Fax 276-5919
Ballast Point ES 400/K-5
2802 W Ballast Point Blvd 33611 813-272-3070
Sherri Frick, prin. Fax 276-5923
Bartels MS 700/6-8
9020 Imperial Oak Blvd 33647 813-907-6801
Maribeth Franklin, prin. Fax 907-6805
Bay Crest ES 800/PK-5
4925 Webb Rd 33615 813-872-5382
Dr. Susan Parks, prin. Fax 356-1153
Bellamy ES 800/PK-5
9720 Wilsky Blvd 33615 813-872-5387
Lynn Rattray, prin. Fax 873-4877
Benito MS 1,200/6-8
10101 Cross Creek Blvd 33647 813-631-4694
Dr. Bobby Smith, prin. Fax 631-4706
Bing ES 600/K-5
6409 36th Ave S 33619 813-744-8088
Roger Stanley, prin. Fax 740-3620
Broward ES 500/PK-5
400 W Osborne Ave 33603 813-276-5592
Kathy Moore, prin. Fax 276-5887
Bryant ES 800/K-5
13910 Nine Eagles Dr 33626 813-356-1645
Karen Bass, prin. Fax 356-1649
Buchanan MS 700/6-8
1001 W Bearss Ave 33613 813-975-7600
Dr. Dwight Raines, prin. Fax 975-7610
Cahoon ES 400/PK-5
2312 E Yukon St 33604 813-975-7647
Joanne Griffiths, prin. Fax 975-7651
Cannella ES 900/K-5
10707 Nixon Rd 33624 813-975-6941
Sue Whitinger, prin. Fax 631-5328
Carrollwood ES 700/K-5
3516 McFarland Rd 33618 813-975-7640
Susan Avery, prin. Fax 631-5364
Chiaramonte ES 300/K-5
6001 S Himes Ave 33611 813-272-3066
Marie Valenti, prin. Fax 272-3284
Chiles ES 800/K-5
16541 Tampa Palms Blvd W 33647 813-558-5422
Kim Pietsch, prin. Fax 558-5426
Citrus Park ES 800/PK-5
7700 Gunn Hwy 33625 813-558-5356
Joan Bookman, prin. Fax 558-5111
Clair-Mel ES 800/PK-5
1025 S 78th St 33619 813-744-8080
Shelly Hermann, prin. Fax 744-8083
Clark ES 600/K-5
19002 Wood Sage Dr 33647 813-631-4333
Brenda Griffin, prin. Fax 631-4349
Claywell ES 900/PK-5
4500 Northdale Blvd 33624 813-975-7300
Lisa Maltezos, prin. Fax 631-4536
Cleveland ES 400/PK-5
723 E Hamilton Ave 33604 813-276-5583
Peter Russo, prin. Fax 276-5586
Coleman MS 900/6-8
1724 S Manhattan Ave 33629 813-872-5335
Michael Hoskinson, prin. Fax 872-5338
Crestwood ES 1,000/K-5
7824 N Manhattan Ave 33614 813-872-5374
Dianna Smith, prin. Fax 871-7788
Davidsen MS 1,200/6-8
10501 Montague St 33626 813-558-5300
Michael Miranda, prin. Fax 558-5299
Davis ES 900/K-5
10907 Memorial Hwy 33615 813-854-6010
Cecilia Troutt, prin. Fax 854-6014
Deer Park ES 400/K-5
11605 Citrus Park Dr 33626 813-854-6031
Lou Cerreta, prin. Fax 854-6041
DeSoto ES 400/PK-5
2618 Corrine St 33605 813-276-5779
Gilda Garcia, prin. Fax 233-2475
Dickenson ES 600/PK-5
4720 Kelly Rd 33615 813-873-4732
Felicia Williams, prin. Fax 356-1156
Dowdell MS 800/6-8
1208 Wishing Well Way 33619 813-744-8322
Robert Lawson, prin. Fax 740-3616
Dunbar Magnet ES 300/K-5
1730 W Union St 33607 813-276-5677
Krystal Carson, prin. Fax 272-2254
Early Learning Childhood Program PK-PK
207 Kelsey Ln Ste K 33619 813-744-8941
Susan Morris, prin. Fax 740-3743
Edison ES 500/K-5
1607 E Curtis St 33610 813-276-5579
Julie Scardino, prin. Fax 276-5582
Egypt Lake ES 500/PK-5
6707 N Glen Ave 33614 813-872-5225
Lydia Sierra, prin. Fax 554-2358
Essrig ES 800/K-5
13131 Lynn Rd 33624 813-975-7307
Teresa Campbell, prin. Fax 558-5104
Farnell MS 1,300/6-8
13912 Nine Eagles Dr 33626 813-356-1640
John Cobb, prin. Fax 356-1644
Ferrell Magnet MS 600/6-8
4302 N 24th St 33610 813-276-5608
Larry Sykes, prin. Fax 276-5615
Forest Hills ES 1,100/PK-5
10112 N Ola Ave 33612 813-975-7633
Sandra Thrower, prin. Fax 975-4812
Foster ES 500/K-5
2014 E Diana St 33610 813-276-5573
Debra Mills, prin. Fax 276-5731
Franklin MS 600/6-8
3915 E 21st Ave 33605 813-744-8108
Joe Brown, prin. Fax 744-8579
Gorrie ES 600/K-5
705 W De Leon St 33606 813-276-5673
Marjorie Sandler, prin. Fax 276-5880
Grady ES 400/PK-5
3910 W Morrison Ave 33629 813-872-5325
Melanie Palmeri, prin. Fax 356-1476
Graham ES 400/K-5
2915 N Massachusetts Ave 33602 813-276-5408
Sherry Orr, prin. Fax 276-5534
Heritage ES 500/K-5
18201 E Meadow Rd 33647 813-740-4580
Shirley Porebski, prin. Fax 740-4584
Hill MS 1,100/6-8
5200 Ehrlich Rd 33624 813-975-7325
Barry Davis, prin. Fax 975-4819
Hunter's Green ES 900/K-5
9202 Highland Oak Dr 33647 813-973-7394
Kristin Tonelli, prin. Fax 631-4525
James ES 400/K-5
4302 E Ellicott St 33610 813-740-4800
Dr. Patricia Royal, prin. Fax 740-4804
Just ES 700/K-5
1315 W Spruce St 33607 813-276-5708
Tricia McManus, prin. Fax 272-2379
Kenly ES 500/PK-5
2909 N 66th St 33619 813-744-8074
Shirlean Cobb, prin. Fax 744-8077
Kimbell ES K-5
8406 N 46th St 33617 813-983-3900
Sheryl Marceaux, prin. Fax 983-3974
Lake Magdalene ES 900/K-5
2002 Pine Lake Dr 33612 813-975-7625
Darlene Choe, prin. Fax 558-1209
Lanier ES 400/PK-5
4704 W Montgomery Ave 33616 813-272-3060
Sarah Jacobsen Capps, prin. Fax 272-3065
Lee ES 400/K-5
305 E Columbus Dr 33602 813-276-5405
Mamie Buzzetti, prin. Fax 272-3228
Liberty MS 1,200/6-8
17400 Commerce Park Blvd 33647 813-558-1180
James Ammirati, prin. Fax 558-1184
Lockhart ES 500/PK-5
3719 N 17th St 33610 813-276-5727
Mary Cunningham, prin. Fax 233-3565
Lomax ES 400/K-5
4207 N 26th St 33610 813-276-5569
Lynn Roberts, prin. Fax 272-2803
Lowry ES 900/PK-5
11505 Country Hollow Dr 33635 813-855-8178
Kathy Coto, prin. Fax 356-1597
Mabry ES 700/K-5
4201 W Estrella St 33629 813-872-5364
Scott Weaver, prin. Fax 554-2252
MacFarlane Park Magnet ES 400/K-5
1721 N MacDill Ave 33607 813-356-1760
Dr. M. Denyse Riviero, prin. Fax 356-1764
Madison MS 800/6-8
4444 W Bay Vista Ave 33611 813-272-3050
John Haley, prin. Fax 233-2796
Memorial MS 800/6-8
4702 N Central Ave 33603 813-872-5230
Arthur Atkins, prin. Fax 872-5238
Mendenhall ES 600/K-5
5202 N Mendenhall Dr 33603 813-872-5221
Patricia Orta, prin. Fax 872-5224
Miles ES 700/K-5
317 E 124th Ave 33612 813-975-7337
Dr. Deborah Coyle, prin. Fax 975-7099
Mitchell ES 500/PK-5
205 S Bungalow Park Ave 33609 813-872-5216
Joanne Baumgartner, prin. Fax 356-1662
Monroe MS 800/6-8
4716 W Montgomery Ave 33616 813-272-3020
Juanita Underwood, prin. Fax 272-3027
Morgan Woods ES 500/PK-5
7001 Armand Dr 33634 813-872-5369
Susan Kuhn, prin. Fax 873-4869
Mort ES 900/PK-5
1806 E Bearss Ave 33613 813-975-7373
Beny Peretz Ed.D., prin. Fax 558-5489
MOSI Partnership S K-5
4801 E Fowler Ave Ste 100 33617 813-983-3989
Cheryl Dafeldecker, prin. Fax 983-3998
Muller ES 400/K-5
13615 N 22nd St 33613 813-558-1355
Bonnye Taylor, prin. Fax 558-1359
Northwest ES 800/K-5
16438 Hutchison Rd 33625 813-975-7315
Darlene Carter, prin. Fax 975-7322
Oak Grove ES 800/K-5
6315 N Armenia Ave 33604 813-356-1532
Pamela Roberts, prin. Fax 356-1536
Oak Park ES 400/PK-5
2716 N 46th St 33605 813-740-7733
Joyce Miles, prin. Fax 740-7744
Orange Grove Magnet MS 700/6-8
3415 N 16th St 33605 813-276-5717
Linda Denison, prin. Fax 276-5857
Palm River ES 600/K-5
805 Maydell Dr 33619 813-744-8066
William Johnson, prin. Fax 744-8069
Pierce MS 1,100/6-8
5511 N Hesperides St 33614 813-872-5344
Victor Fernandez, prin. Fax 871-7978
Pizzo ES 900/PK-5
11701 USF Bull Run St 33617 813-987-6500
Pamela Wilkins, prin. Fax 987-6516
Potter ES 800/K-5
3224 E Cayuga St 33610 813-276-5564
Tracye Brown, prin. Fax 233-3693
Pride ES 900/K-5
10310 Lions Den Dr 33647 813-558-5400
Jamie Dunnam, prin. Fax 558-5404
Progress Village MS 900/6-8
8113 Zinnia Dr 33619 813-671-5110
Walt Shaffner, prin. Fax 671-5240
Rampello Downtown S 700/K-8
802 E Washington St 33602 813-233-2333
Liz Uppercue, prin. Fax 233-2337
Robles ES 700/K-5
4405 E Sligh Ave 33610 813-744-8033
Bonnie McDaniel, prin. Fax 744-8350
Roland Park S 800/K-8
1510 N Manhattan Ave 33607 813-872-5212
Dave Burgess, prin. Fax 673-4388
Roosevelt ES 500/PK-5
3205 S Ferdinand Ave 33629 813-272-3090
Colleen Faucett, prin. Fax 272-3577
Seminole ES 500/PK-5
6201 N Central Ave 33604 813-276-5556
Jackie Masters, prin. Fax 272-2279
Shaw ES 1,100/PK-5
11311 N 15th St 33612 813-975-7366
Holly Saia, prin. Fax 558-5025
Sheehy ES 500/K-5
6402 N 40th St 33610 813-233-3800
Fontaine Marion, prin. Fax 233-3804
Shore ES 400/K-5
1908 E 2nd Ave 33605 813-276-5712
Barbara Mercer, prin. Fax 272-0426
Sligh MS 900/6-8
2011 E Sligh Ave 33610 813-276-5596
Barbara Fillhart, prin. Fax 276-5606
Smith MS 6-8
14303 Citrus Pointe Dr 33625 813-792-5125
Kathleen Flanagan, prin. Fax 792-5129
Stewart MS 900/6-8
1125 W Spruce St 33607 813-276-5691
Baretta Wilson, prin. Fax 276-5698
Sulphur Springs ES 700/K-5
8412 N 13th St 33604 813-975-7305
Christi Buell, prin. Fax 975-7398
Tampa Bay Boulevard ES 800/PK-5
3111 W Tampa Bay Blvd 33607 813-872-5208
Arlene Babanats, prin. Fax 871-7586
Tampa Palms ES 800/PK-5
6100 Tampa Palms Blvd 33647 813-975-7390
Kimberly Keenan, prin. Fax 975-6654
Town and Country ES 500/PK-5
6025 Hanley Rd 33634 813-871-7500
Jenilda Gallo, prin. Fax 554-2378
Turner ES 600/K-5
9190 Imperial Oak Blvd 33647 813-907-9066
Donna Ares, prin. Fax 907-9546
Twin Lakes ES 700/K-5
8507 N Habana Ave 33614 813-975-7380
Edith Lefler, prin. Fax 631-4153
Van Buren MS 800/6-8
8715 N 22nd St 33604 813-975-7652
JoAnn Redden, prin. Fax 631-4312
Washington ES 600/K-5
1407 Estelle St 33605 813-233-3720
Jason Pepe, prin. Fax 233-3724
Webb MS 700/6-8
6035 Hanley Rd 33634 813-872-5351
Brent McBrien, prin. Fax 872-5359
Westchase ES 1,000/K-5
9517 W Linebaugh Ave 33626 813-631-4600
Joyce Wieland, prin. Fax 631-4617
West Shore ES 400/PK-5
7110 S West Shore Blvd 33616 813-272-3080
Elizabeth Calleri, prin. Fax 233-2443
West Tampa ES 500/K-5
2700 W Cherry St 33607 813-872-5200
Linda Geller, prin. Fax 356-1452
Williams MS 900/6-8
5020 N 47th St 33610 813-744-8600
Patricia Harrell, prin. Fax 744-8665
Wilson MS 600/6-8
1005 W Swann Ave 33606 813-276-5682
Stephanie Woodford, prin. Fax 233-2540
Witter ES 800/K-5
10801 N 22nd St 33612 813-975-7383
Anna Brown, prin. Fax 631-4447
Woodbridge ES 600/K-5
8301 Woodbridge Blvd 33615 813-871-7460
Diane Farmer, prin. Fax 871-7063
Young Magnet MS 800/6-8
1807 E Dr Martn Lthr King 33610 813-276-5739
Dr. Angela Oliver-Chaniel, prin. Fax 276-5893
Other Schools – See Apollo Beach, Brandon, Dover, Gibsonton, Lithia, Lutz, MacDill AFB, Odessa, Plant City, Riverview, Ruskin, Seffner, Temple Terrace, Thonotosassa, Valrico, Wimauma

---

Academy of the Holy Names S 500/PK-8
3319 Bayshore Blvd 33629 813-839-5371
Darcy Devrnja, prin. Fax 839-1486
American Youth Academy 300/PK-12
5905 E 130th Ave 33617 813-987-9282
Fax 987-9262
Bayshore Christian S 400/PK-12
3909 S MacDill Ave 33611 813-839-4297
Dr. Wendell Murray, hdmstr. Fax 835-1404
Berkeley Preparatory S 1,200/PK-12
4811 Kelly Rd 33615 813-885-1673
Joseph Merluzzi, prin. Fax 886-6933
Cambridge S 600/PK-12
6101 N Habana Ave 33614 813-872-6744
Boyd Chitwood, hdmstr. Fax 872-6013
Carrollwood Day S 200/PK-K
12606 Casey Rd 33618 813-963-2388
Mary Kanter, hdmstr. Fax 968-1275
Carrollwood Day S 700/PK-12
1515 W Bearss Ave 33613 813-920-2288
Mary Kanter, hdmstr. Fax 920-8237
Christ the King S 500/PK-8
3809 W Morrison Ave 33629 813-876-8770
Jane Forbus, prin. Fax 879-0315
Church of Our Saviour Preschool 100/PK-PK
8401 W Hillsborough Ave 33615 813-885-2263
Fax 889-7577

Citrus Park Christian S 400/PK-12
7705 Gunn Hwy 33625 813-920-3960
Karen Jeffers, admin. Fax 926-1240
Concordia Lutheran S 100/PK-8
5601 Hanley Rd 33634 813-806-9199
Fax 886-4155
Faith Outreach Academy 200/PK-12
7607 Sheldon Rd 33615 813-887-5546
Julie Sierra, prin. Fax 249-6896
Family of Christ Christian S 100/PK-8
16190 Bruce B Downs Blvd 33647 813-558-9343
Jennifer Snow, prin. Fax 977-0549
Florida College Academy 200/PK-9
7032 Temple Terrace Hwy 33637 813-899-6800
Lynn Wade, prin. Fax 984-8301
Harvest Time Christian S 100/PK-8
1511 S US Highway 301 33619 813-626-4600
Allen Sayers, prin. Fax 622-8085
Hebrew Academy of Tampa Bay 50/PK-8
14908 Pennington Rd 33624 813-963-0706
Sulha Dubrowski, dir. Fax 265-8543
Hillel S of Tampa 200/PK-8
2020 W Fletcher Ave 33612 813-963-2242
Amy Wasser, hdmstr. Fax 264-0544
Hillsdale Academy 100/PK-5
6201 Ehrlich Rd 33625 813-884-8250
Tanya Henry, dir. Fax 886-5251
Holy Trinity Lutheran S 100/PK-5
3712 W El Prado Blvd 33629 813-839-0665
Robert Reed, prin. Fax 839-2706
Incarnation Catholic S 400/K-8
5111 Webb Rd 33615 813-884-4502
Carolyn Goslee, prin. Fax 885-3734
Independent Day S 50/PK-8
12015 Orange Grove Dr 33618 813-961-3087
Dr. Joyce Burick Swarzman, hdmstr. Fax 963-0846
Kings Kids Christian Academy 200/PK-5
3000 N 34th St 33605 813-248-6548
Marva Scott, prin. Fax 247-4337
Land of Learning Academy 300/PK-PK
8809 W Robson St 33615 813-886-6494
Sherry Brown, dir. Fax 886-6499
Montessori Academy of Tampa Bay 100/PK-6
1901 W Waters Ave 33604 813-933-4782
Montessori Children's House of Hyde Park 100/PK-6
2416 W Cleveland St 33609 813-354-9511
Amanda Linton-Evans, admin. Fax 354-1902
Montessori House Day S 100/PK-6
5117 Ehrlich Rd 33624 813-961-9295
Kay Murrell, hdmstr. Fax 961-8639
Montessori House Day S 50/PK-6
7010 Hanley Rd 33634 813-884-7220
Kay Murrell, hdmstr. Fax 886-7552
Montessori Preparatory S 200/PK-5
11302 N 53rd St 33617 813-899-2345
Sonia Johnson, dir. Fax 989-9870
Most Holy Redeemer S 300/K-8
302 E Linebaugh Ave 33612 813-933-4750
Fred Coffaro, prin. Fax 933-3181
Mt. Calvary SDA S 100/K-8
3111 E Wilder Ave 33610 813-238-0433
Paideia S of Tampa Bay 100/K-12
7834 N 56th St 33617 813-988-7700
Conrad Bray, hdmstr. Fax 988-7740
R T M Academy 100/PK-4
5201 N Armenia Ave 33603 813-348-0878
D.J. McCray, admin. Fax 673-8695
Sacred Heart Academy 200/PK-8
3515 N Florida Ave 33603 813-229-0618
Margaret Ruiz-Carus, prin. Fax 223-7667
St. John Greek Orthodox S 200/PK-8
2418 W Swann Ave 33609 813-876-4569
James Larkin, hdmstr. Fax 877-4923
St. John's Episcopal S 500/K-8
906 S Orleans Ave 33606 813-849-5200
Gordon Rode, hdmstr. Fax 258-2548
St. John's Episcopal S 100/5-8
240 S Plant Ave 33606 813-849-4200
Gordon Rode, hdmstr. Fax 849-1026
St. Joseph S 200/PK-8
2200 N Gomez Ave 33607 813-879-7720
Sr. Lou Ann Fantauzza, prin. Fax 873-0804
St. Lawrence S 600/PK-8
5223 N Himes Ave 33614 813-879-5090
Therese Hernandez, prin. Fax 879-6886
St. Mary's Episcopal Day S 400/PK-8
2101 S Hubert Ave 33629 813-258-5508
Scott Laird, hdmstr. Fax 258-5603
St. Paul Child Enrichment Center 200/PK-PK
12708 N Dale Mabry Hwy 33618 813-264-3314
Joanne Ruddy, dir. Fax 962-8780
St. Peter Claver S 100/PK-8
1401 N Governor St 33602 813-224-0865
Sr. Maria Babatunde, prin. Fax 223-6726
Tampa Adventist Academy 100/PK-10
3205 N Boulevard 33603 813-228-7950
David Matthews, prin. Fax 228-0170
Tampa Bay Christian Academy 300/PK-12
300 E Sligh Ave 33604 813-238-3229
Dr. Barbara Bode, hdmstr. Fax 237-3426
Tampa Christian Community S 100/PK-8
PO Box 341193 33694 813-872-8227
Melissa Walker, prin. Fax 877-3111
Temple Heights Christian S 200/PK-9
5020 Puritan Rd 33617 813-988-5143
Universal Academy of Florida 400/PK-12
6801 Orient Rd 33610 813-664-0695
Dr. Moosa Yahya, prin. Fax 664-4506
Villa Madonna S 500/PK-8
315 W Columbus Dr 33602 813-229-1322
Sr. Helene Godin, prin. Fax 223-4812
West Gate Christian S 400/PK-12
5121 Kelly Rd 33615 813-884-3698
Charles Shaw, prin. Fax 888-5368

Tarpon Springs, Pinellas, Pop. 22,651
Pinellas County SD
Supt. — See Largo
Brooker Creek ES 600/K-5
3130 Forelock Rd 34688 727-943-4600
Donna Gehringer, prin. Fax 943-4603
Sunset Hills ES 600/K-5
1347 Gulf Rd 34689 727-943-5523
Arthur Steullet, prin. Fax 943-4939
Tarpon Springs ES 500/K-5
555 Pine St 34689 727-943-5500
Leah Pappas, prin. Fax 943-5580
Tarpon Springs Fundamental ES 300/K-5
400 E Harrison St 34689 727-943-5508
Dr. Elaine Meils, prin. Fax 942-5443
Tarpon Springs MS 1,300/6-8
501 N Florida Ave 34689 727-943-5511
Felita Lott, prin. Fax 943-5519

First Christian Academy 200/PK-8
2795 Keystone Rd 34688 727-943-7411
Ramita Buckley, admin. Fax 942-3451
St. Ignatius ECC 100/PK-PK
PO Box 1306 34688 727-937-5427
Nancy Gorby, dir. Fax 722-9000

Tavares, Lake, Pop. 11,621
Lake County SD 37,200/PK-12
201 W Burleigh Blvd 32778 352-253-6500
Susan Moxley Ed.D., supt. Fax 343-0198
www.lake.k12.fl.us/
Tavares ES 700/PK-5
720 E Clifford St 32778 352-343-2861
Caroline Burnsed, prin. Fax 343-6618
Tavares MS 1,100/6-8
13032 Lane Park Cutoff 32778 352-343-4545
Trella Mott, prin. Fax 343-7212
Other Schools – See Astatula, Clermont, Eustis, Fruitland Park, Groveland, Lady Lake, Leesburg, Minneola, Mount Dora, Umatilla

Adventure Christian Academy 100/PK-8
3800 State Road 19 32778 352-343-9020
Jacqueline Overton, admin. Fax 343-3444
Liberty Christian Academy 300/PK-12
2451 Dora Ave 32778 352-343-0061
Debra Zischke, prin. Fax 343-2424

Tavernier, Monroe, Pop. 2,433
Monroe County SD
Supt. — See Key West
Plantation Key S 600/PK-8
100 Lake Rd 33070 305-853-3281
Vanessa Strickland, prin. Fax 853-3279

Temple Terrace, Hillsborough, Pop. 21,978
Hillsborough County SD
Supt. — See Tampa
Greco MS 1,000/6-8
6925 E Fowler Ave 33617 813-987-6926
Dr. Judith Kennedy, prin. Fax 987-6863
Lewis ES 800/K-5
6700 Whiteway Dr 33617 813-987-6947
Loretta Campo, prin. Fax 987-6920
Riverhills ES 500/K-5
405 S Riverhills Dr 33617 813-987-6911
Dr. Jackie Scaglione, prin. Fax 987-6962
Temple Terrace ES 700/PK-5
124 Flotto Ave 33617 813-987-6903
Mary Frances Ledo, prin. Fax 987-6406

Christ Our Redeemer Lutheran S 200/PK-8
304 Druid Hills Rd 33617 813-988-4025
Beth Gray, prin. Fax 989-0461
Corpus Christi S 300/PK-8
9715 N 56th St 33617 813-988-1722
Dr. Carmen Caltagirone, prin. Fax 989-2665

Tequesta, Palm Beach, Pop. 5,989

Good Shepherd Episcopal S 100/PK-5
402 Seabrook Rd 33469 561-746-5507
C. Vanderwesthuizen, prin. Fax 746-2870

Thonotosassa, Hillsborough
Hillsborough County SD
Supt. — See Tampa
Folsom ES 600/K-5
9855 Harney Rd 33592 813-987-6755
Cora-Lynne Wimberly, prin. Fax 987-6970
Thonotosassa ES 400/PK-5
10050 Skewlee Rd 33592 813-987-6987
Michele Gregory, prin. Fax 987-6865

Titusville, Brevard, Pop. 43,767
Brevard County SD
Supt. — See Melbourne
Apollo ES 700/PK-6
3085 Knox Mcrae Dr 32780 321-267-7890
Dr. Pamela O'Kell, prin. Fax 269-3838
Coquina ES 400/K-6
850 Knox Mcrae Dr 32780 321-264-3060
Andrea Townsend, prin. Fax 264-3062
Imperial Estates ES 600/PK-6
900 Imperial Estates Ln 32780 321-267-1773
Stephanie Green, prin. Fax 264-3038
Jackson MS 700/7-8
1515 Knox Mcrae Dr 32780 321-269-1812
James Hickey, prin. Fax 269-7811
Madison MS 700/7-8
3375 Dairy Rd 32796 321-264-3120
Joan Sparks, prin. Fax 264-3124
Oak Park ES 700/PK-6
3395 Dairy Rd 32796 321-269-3252
Ronald Dedmon, prin. Fax 264-3080
Riverview ES 500/PK-6
3000 Jolly St 32780 321-269-2326
Vicki Sacco, prin. Fax 264-3092
South Lake ES 500/PK-6
3755 Garden St 32796 321-269-1022
Nancy Nichols, prin. Fax 264-3047

Park Avenue Christian Academy 400/PK-8
2600 S Park Ave 32780 321-267-1871
Enrico Pucci, admin. Fax 268-4057
St. Teresa Catholic S 300/PK-8
207 Ojibway Ave 32780 321-267-1643
Jacqueline Zackel, prin. Fax 268-5124
Temple Christian S 200/PK-12
1400 N US Highway 1 32796 321-269-2837
Dr. Ted Hollingsworth, admin. Fax 383-9101

Trenton, Gilchrist, Pop. 1,793
Gilchrist County SD 2,900/PK-12
310 NW 11th Ave 32693 352-463-3200
James Vickers, supt. Fax 463-3276
www.gilchristschools.org
Trenton ES 700/PK-4
1350 SW State Rd 26 32693 352-463-3224
Riley Deen, prin. Fax 463-3299
Other Schools – See Bell

Tyndall AFB, Bay, Pop. 4,318
Bay County SD
Supt. — See Panama City
Tyndall ES 800/PK-5
7800 Tyndall Pkwy 32403 850-286-6481
Libbie Pippin, prin. Fax 286-6484

Umatilla, Lake, Pop. 2,647
Lake County SD
Supt. — See Tavares
Umatilla ES 800/PK-5
401 Lake St 32784 352-669-3181
Susan Learned, prin. Fax 669-8740
Umatilla MS 700/6-8
305 E Lake St 32784 352-669-3171
Bonnie McKee, prin. Fax 669-5424

Living Word Academy 300/PK-12
19624 Quails Nest Run 32784 352-350-0244

Valparaiso, Okaloosa, Pop. 6,365
Okaloosa County SD
Supt. — See Fort Walton Beach
Lewis MS 500/6-8
281 Mississippi Ave 32580 850-833-4130
Billy Mikel, prin. Fax 833-4197
Valparaiso ES 400/PK-5
379 Edge Ave 32580 850-833-4120
Mike Fantaski, prin. Fax 833-4177

Valrico, See Brandon
Hillsborough County SD
Supt. — See Tampa
Alafia ES 700/K-5
3535 Culbreath Rd, 813-744-8190
Ellyn Smith, prin. Fax 744-8207
Buckhorn ES 700/K-5
2420 Buckhorn School Ct 33594 813-744-8240
Amy Zilbar, prin. Fax 740-3622
Cimino ES 1,000/K-5
4329 Culbreath Rd, 813-740-4450
Deborah Talley, prin. Fax 740-4454
Lithia Springs ES 700/K-5
4332 Lynx Paw Trl, 813-744-8016
MaryAnn Keene, prin. Fax 744-4462
Mulrennan MS 1,400/6-8
4215 Durant Rd, 813-651-2100
Tim Ducker, prin. Fax 651-2104
Valrico ES 900/K-5
609 S Miller Rd 33594 813-744-6777
Mary Knox Ed.D., prin. Fax 740-3535

Grace Christian S 300/K-12
1425 N Valrico Rd 33594 813-689-8815
Bob Gustafson, dir. Fax 681-7396

Venice, Sarasota, Pop. 20,974
Sarasota County SD
Supt. — See Sarasota
Garden ES 600/K-5
700 Center Rd 34285 941-486-2110
John McQueen, prin. Fax 486-2610
Taylor Ranch ES 900/K-5
2500 Taylor Ranch Trl 34293 941-486-2000
Kelly Ellington, prin. Fax 486-2129
Venice Area MS 900/6-8
1900 Center Rd 34292 941-486-2100
Karin Schmidt, prin. Fax 486-2108
Venice ES 600/K-5
150 Miami Ave E 34285 941-486-2111
Theresa Baus, prin. Fax 486-2117

Epiphany Cathedral S 300/PK-8
316 Sarasota St 34285 941-488-2215
Irene Lynch, prin. Fax 480-1565
Venice Christian S 200/K-10
1200 Center Rd 34292 941-496-4411
Jerry Frimmel, admin. Fax 408-8362
Venice SDA S 50/1-8
2375 Seaboard Ave 34293 941-493-0997

Vernon, Washington, Pop. 766
Washington County SD
Supt. — See Chipley
Vernon ES 600/PK-4
3665 Roche Ave 32462 850-535-2486
Peggy Adams, prin. Fax 535-1437
Vernon MS 400/5-8
3206 Moss Hill Rd 32462 850-535-2807
Arthur Beard, prin. Fax 535-1683

Vero Beach, Indian River, Pop. 17,078
Indian River County SD 16,500/PK-12
1990 25th St 32960 772-564-3000
Harry LaCava Ed.D., supt. Fax 564-3128
www.indian-river.k12.fl.us/
Beachland ES 500/K-5
3550 Indian River Dr E 32963 772-564-3300
Carol Wilson, prin. Fax 564-3350

Citrus ES 500/K-5
2771 4th Pl 32968 772-978-8350
Jon Teske, prin. Fax 978-8351
Dodgertown ES 600/K-5
4350 43rd Ave 32967 772-564-4100
Ramon Echeverria, prin. Fax 564-4093
Gifford MS 1,300/6-8
4530 28th Ct 32967 772-564-3550
Dave Kramek, prin. Fax 564-3561
Glendale ES 600/PK-5
4940 8th St 32968 772-978-8050
Mary Ellen Schneider, prin. Fax 978-8098
Highlands ES 600/PK-5
500 20th St SW 32962 772-564-3390
Dr. Lillian Torres-Martinez, prin. Fax 564-3373
Liberty Magnet ES 500/K-5
6850 81st St 32967 772-564-5350
Dale Klaus, prin. Fax 564-5303
Osceola Magnet ES 500/K-5
665 20th St 32960 772-564-5821
Susan Roberts, prin. Fax 564-5827
Oslo MS 1,100/6-8
480 20th Ave SW 32962 772-564-3980
Deborah Long, prin. Fax 564-4029
Rosewood Magnet ES 500/PK-5
3850 16th St 32960 772-564-3840
Deborah Dillon, prin. Fax 564-3888
Storm Grove MS, 6400 57th St 32967 100/6-8
Shawn O'Keefe, prin. 772-564-6329
Thompson Magnet ES 400/PK-5
1110 18th Ave SW 32962 772-564-3240
Onesha McIntosh, prin. Fax 564-3295
Vero Beach ES 500/PK-5
1770 12th St 32960 772-564-4550
Bonnie Swanson, prin. Fax 564-4552
Other Schools – See Fellsmere, Sebastian

Glendale Christian S 100/PK-8
790 27th Ave 32968 772-569-1095
Denise Macdonald, dir. Fax 562-4919
Indian River Christian Preschool 100/PK-PK
6767 20th St 32966 772-562-9623
Larry Boan, admin. Fax 562-4892
Master's Academy 300/PK-12
1105 58th Ave 32966 772-794-4655
Dr. H. Grant Powell, hdmstr. Fax 562-9808
Redeemer Lutheran S 100/PK-PK
900 27th Ave 32960 772-770-0021
Patricia Willenbrock, prin. Fax 567-8109
St. Edward's S 900/PK-12
1895 Saint Edwards Dr 32963 772-231-4136
Bruce Wachter, hdmstr. Fax 231-2427
St. Helen S 300/K-8
2050 Vero Beach Ave 32960 772-567-5457
Howard Avril, prin. Fax 567-4823

Waldo, Alachua, Pop. 776
Alachua County SD
Supt. — See Gainesville
Waldo Community ES 200/PK-5
PO Box 190 32694 352-468-1451
Bill Powell, prin. Fax 468-2097

Walnut Hill, Escambia
Escambia County SD
Supt. — See Pensacola
Ward MS 500/6-8
7650 Highway 97 32568 850-327-4283
Nancy Perry, prin. Fax 327-4991

Warrington, Escambia, Pop. 16,040
Escambia County SD
Supt. — See Pensacola
Warrington MS 600/6-8
450 S Old Corry Field Rd, Pensacola FL 32507
850-453-7440
Christine Nixon, prin. Fax 453-7572

Wauchula, Hardee, Pop. 4,450
Hardee County SD 5,000/PK-12
PO Box 1678 33873 863-773-9058
David Durastanti, supt. Fax 773-0069
www.hardee.k12.fl.us
Hardee JHS 1,100/6-8
2401 US Highway 17 N 33873 863-773-3147
Doug Herron, prin. Fax 773-3167
Hilltop ES 400/K-5
2401 US Highway 17 N 33873 863-773-2750
Doug Herron, prin. Fax 773-2751
North Wauchula ES 500/K-5
1120 N Florida Ave 33873 863-773-2183
Tracey Nix, prin. Fax 773-3514
Wauchula ES 600/PK-5
400 S Florida Ave 33873 863-773-3141
Sonja Bennett, prin. Fax 773-0416
Other Schools – See Bowling Green, Zolfo Springs

Webster, Sumter, Pop. 838
Sumter County SD
Supt. — See Bushnell
South Sumter MS 900/6-8
773 NW 10th Ave 33597 352-793-2232
Kathy Dustin, prin. Fax 793-3976
Webster ES 600/PK-5
349 S Market Blvd 33597 352-793-2828
Eileen Goodson, prin. Fax 793-6785

Weirsdale, Marion
Marion County SD
Supt. — See Ocala
Stanton-Weirsdale ES 500/PK-5
16700 SE 134th Ter 32195 352-671-6150
Brent Carson, prin. Fax 671-6155

Wellington, Palm Beach, Pop. 53,583
Palm Beach County SD
Supt. — See West Palm Beach
Binks Forest ES 1,200/K-5
15101 Bent Creek Rd 33414 561-792-5250
Julie Hopkins, prin. Fax 792-5255
Emerald Cove MS 1,100/6-8
9950 Stribling Way 33414 561-803-8000
Nancy Lucas, prin. Fax 803-8050
Equestrian Trails ES 1,000/K-5
9720 Stribling Way 33414 561-791-9300
Sandra Gero, prin. Fax 791-9322
Gale ES 800/K-5
1915 Royal Fern Dr 33414 561-422-9300
Gail Pasterczyk, prin. Fax 422-9310
New Horizons ES 700/K-5
13900 Greenbriar Blvd 33414 561-795-4966
Elizabeth Cardozo, prin. Fax 795-4988
Polo Park MS 1,600/6-8
11901 Lake Worth Rd 33414 561-333-5500
William Latson, prin. Fax 333-5505
Wellington ES 900/K-5
13000 Paddock Dr 33414 561-795-4969
Michael Borowski, prin. Fax 795-4974
Wellington Landings MS 1,100/6-8
1100 Aero Club Dr 33414 561-792-8100
Eric Paul, prin. Fax 792-8106

St. David's Episcopal S 100/PK-1
465 W Forest Hill Blvd 33414 561-793-1272
Kathy Vandamas, hdmstr. Fax 793-2301
Wellington Christian S 700/PK-12
1000 Wellington Trce 33414 561-793-1017
Don Stimely, admin. Fax 798-9622

Wesley Chapel, Pasco, Pop. 1,200
Pasco County SD
Supt. — See Land O Lakes
Double Branch ES 700/PK-5
31500 Chancey Rd 33543 813-346-0400
Peggy Lewis, prin. Fax 346-0491
Long MS 1,200/6-8
2025 Mansfield Blvd 33543 813-346-6200
Beth Brown, prin. Fax 346-6291
New River ES 300/K-5
4710 River Glen Blvd, 813-346-0500
Lynn Pabst, prin. Fax 346-0591
Quail Hollow ES 900/PK-5
7050 Quail Hollow Blvd 33544 813-794-1100
Michelle Berger, prin. Fax 794-1191
Sand Pine ES 1,000/K-5
29040 County Line Rd 33543 813-794-1900
Ginny Yanson, prin. Fax 794-1991
Seven Oaks ES 1,000/K-5
27633 Mystic Oak Blvd 33544 813-794-0700
B. J. Smith, prin. Fax 794-0791
Veterans ES 800/K-5
26940 Progress Pkwy 33544 813-346-1400
Donna Busby, prin. Fax 346-1400
Weightman MS 1,100/6-8
30649 Wells Rd, 813-794-0200
Shae Davis, prin. Fax 794-0291
Wesley Chapel HS 1,300/PK-5
30243 Wells Rd, 813-794-0100
John Abernathy, prin. Fax 794-0191

Faith Baptist Academy 50/PK-8
6300 Oakley Blvd 33544 813-907-9462
Travis Hartsfield, admin. Fax 907-9986
New River Academy 50/PK-8
4210 Ernest Dr 33543 813-783-1350
Melanie Gasbarro, prin. Fax 783-2225
Saddlebrook Preparatory S 100/3-12
5700 Saddlebrook Way 33543 813-907-4200
Larry Robison, dir. Fax 991-4713
Victorious Life Academy 200/PK-5
6224 Old Pasco Rd 33544 813-994-8456
Dr. Jerry Forrester, prin.

West Hollywood, See Hollywood

Annunciation S 300/PK-8
3751 SW 39th St 33023 954-989-8287
Nestor Pereira, prin. Fax 989-0660

West Melbourne, Brevard, Pop. 15,054
Brevard County SD
Supt. — See Melbourne
Central MS 1,000/7-8
2600 Wingate Blvd 32904 321-722-4150
Pamela Mitchell, prin. Fax 722-4165
Meadowlane PS 700/PK-3
2800 Wingate Blvd 32904 321-723-6354
Karen Kise, prin. Fax 952-5948
West Melbourne ES of Science 400/PK-6
2255 Meadowlane Ave 32904 321-956-5040
Tom Westermeyer, prin. Fax 956-5043

Brevard Christian S 300/PK-12
1100 Dorchester Ave 32904 321-727-2038
Ric Speigner, admin. Fax 729-4212
Calvary Chapel Christian S 300/PK-8
2955 Minton Rd 32904 321-729-9922
Lynn Salberg, prin. Fax 952-1329
Country Day S for Children 50/PK-K
1281 S Wickham Rd 32904 321-951-8005
Michelle Sutton, admin. Fax 951-8005
New Hope Lutheran Academy 50/PK-10
PO Box 120208 32912 321-768-1500
Dale Raether, prin. Fax 727-2320

Weston, Broward, Pop. 65,679
Broward County SD
Supt. — See Fort Lauderdale
Country Isles ES 1,000/K-5
2300 Country Isles Rd 33326 754-323-5250
Tonya Frost, prin. Fax 323-5290
Eagle Point ES 1,300/K-5
100 Indian Trce 33326 754-323-5500
Linda Chuckman, prin. Fax 323-5540
Everglades ES 1,000/K-5
2900 Bonaventure Blvd 33331 754-323-5600
Eliot Tillinger, prin. Fax 323-5640
Falcon Cove MS 2,300/6-8
4251 Bonaventure Blvd 33332 754-323-3200
Mark Kaplan, prin. Fax 323-3285
Gator Run ES 1,200/K-5
1101 Glades Pkwy 33327 754-323-5850
Susan Sasse, prin. Fax 323-5890
Indian Trace ES 800/K-5
400 Indian Trce 33326 754-323-6300
Wanda Ross, prin. Fax 323-6340
Manatee Bay ES 1,400/PK-5
19200 Manatee Isles Dr 33332 754-323-6450
Donna McCann, prin. Fax 323-6490
Tequesta Trace MS 1,600/6-8
1800 Indian Trce 33326 754-323-4400
Paul Micensky, prin. Fax 323-4485

Sagemont S - Lower Campus 300/PK-5
1570 Sagemont Way 33326 954-384-5454
JoAnn Laskin, prin. Fax 384-0053
Weston Christian Academy 200/PK-8
1420 Indian Trce 33326 954-349-9224
Julia Elliott, dir. Fax 349-0678

West Palm Beach, Palm Beach, Pop. 97,498
Palm Beach County SD 161,200/PK-12
3300 Forest Hill Blvd 33406 561-434-8000
Arthur Johnson Ph.D., supt. Fax 434-8571
www.palmbeach.k12.fl.us
Bak MS of the Arts 1,400/6-8
1725 Echo Lake Dr 33407 561-882-3870
Elizabeth Kennedy, prin. Fax 882-3879
Bear Lakes MS 900/6-8
3505 Shenandoah Rd 33409 561-615-7700
Anthony Lockhart, prin. Fax 615-7756
Belvedere ES 600/K-5
3000 Parker Ave 33405 561-838-5900
Diane Mahar, prin. Fax 838-5950
Benoist Farms ES 500/K-5
1765 Benoist Farms Rd 33411 561-383-9700
Ruthann Miller, prin. Fax 383-9750
Berkshire ES 600/K-5
1060 Kirk Rd 33406 561-304-2000
Teresa Stoupas, prin. Fax 304-2050
Conniston Community MS 900/6-8
3630 Parker Ave 33405 561-802-5400
Mary Stratos, prin. Fax 802-5409
Egret Lake Community ES 500/K-5
5115 47th Pl N 33417 561-688-5314
Rebecca Subin, prin. Fax 688-5381
Forest Hill ES 1,200/K-5
5555 Purdy Ln 33415 561-434-8483
Ana Arce-Gonzalez, prin. Fax 434-8647
Golden Grove ES 800/K-5
5959 140th Ave N 33411 561-792-5200
Kathryn Koerner, prin. Fax 792-5226
Grassy Waters ES 1,000/K-5
3550 N Jog Rd 33411 561-383-9000
Amy Wilkinson, prin. Fax 383-9050
Jeaga MS 1,200/6-8
3777 N Jog Rd 33411 561-242-8000
Joseph DePasquale, prin. Fax 242-8005
Kinsey/Palmview ES 600/K-5
800 11th St 33401 561-671-6500
Adrienne Howard, prin. Fax 671-6550
Meadow Park ES 600/K-5
956 Florida Mango Rd 33406 561-357-2800
Pamela Arnette, prin. Fax 357-2828
Melaleuca ES 900/K-5
5759 Gun Club Rd 33415 561-640-5071
Jamie Wyatt, prin. Fax 688-5222
Northboro ES 800/PK-5
2936 Lone Pine Rd 33410 561-494-1600
Moneek McTier, prin. Fax 494-1650
Northmore ES 500/K-5
4111 N Terrace Dr 33407 561-494-1700
Nancy Robinson, prin. Fax 494-1750
Okeeheelee MS 1,200/6-8
2200 Pinehurst Dr 33413 561-434-3200
David Samore, prin. Fax 434-3244
Palmetto ES 600/K-5
5801 Parker Ave 33405 561-202-0400
Raul Iribarren, prin. Fax 202-0450
Palm Springs Community MS 1,400/6-8
1560 Kirk Rd 33406 561-434-3300
Sandra Jinks, prin. Fax 434-3303
Pine Jog ES K-5
6315 Summit Blvd 33415 561-656-5400
Fred Barch, prin. Fax 656-5450
Pleasant City ES 300/K-5
2222 Spruce Ave 33407 561-838-5800
Jacqueline Perkins, prin. Fax 838-5850
Roosevelt Community MS 1,400/6-8
1900 N Australian Ave 33407 561-822-0200
George Lockhart, prin. Fax 882-0222
Roosevelt ES 600/K-5
1220 L A Kirksey St 33401 561-653-5100
Glenda Garrett, prin. Fax 653-5150
Seminole Trails ES 800/K-5
4075 Willow Pond Rd 33417 561-640-5051
Judith Garrard, prin. Fax 688-5223
South Olive ES 700/K-5
7101 S Olive Ave 33405 561-202-0200
Hank Smith, prin. Fax 202-0250
Western Pines MS 1,300/6-8
5949 140th Ave N 33411 561-792-2500
Robert Hatcher, prin. Fax 792-2530
West Gate ES 1,000/K-5
1545 Loxahatchee Dr 33409 561-684-7100
Francisco Rodriguez, prin. Fax 684-7150
Westward ES 500/K-5
1101 Golf Ave 33401 561-653-5200
Melvis Pender, prin. Fax 653-5250
Wynnebrook ES 800/PK-5
1167 Drexel Rd 33417 561-640-5086
Jeffrey Pegg, prin. Fax 688-5297
Other Schools – See Belle Glade, Boca Raton, Boynton Beach, Canal Point, Delray Beach, Greenacres, Jupiter, Lake Park, Lake Worth, Lantana, Loxahatchee, North Palm Beach, Pahokee, Palm Beach, Palm Beach Gardens, Palm Springs, Riviera Beach, Royal Palm Beach, South Bay, Wellington

ABC Children's Learning Academy 200/PK-2
4330 Summit Blvd 33406 561-964-2800
Alethea Brown, prin. Fax 642-2314
Atlantis Academy 100/K-12
1950 Prairie Rd 33406 561-642-3100
Dennis Kelley, dir. Fax 969-1950
Berean Christian S 800/PK-12
8350 Okeechobee Blvd 33411 561-798-9300
Timothy Hays, hdmstr. Fax 792-3073
Ephesus Junior Academy 50/PK-9
4011 N Shore Dr 33407 561-841-0033
Robin Young, prin. Fax 841-0087
Haverhill Baptist S 200/PK-3
671 Haverhill Rd N 33415 561-683-1780
Diana Atwell, admin. Fax 683-1803
Holy Cross Preschool 100/PK-PK
930 Southern Blvd 33405 561-366-8026
Ana Fundora, dir. Fax 366-8577
Holy Name of Jesus S 300/PK-8
345 S Military Trl 33415 561-683-2990
Sr. Kathleen Cummins, prin. Fax 683-0803
King's Academy 1,400/PK-12
8401 Belvedere Rd 33411 561-686-4244
Jeffrey Loveland, pres. Fax 686-8017
Meyer Jewish Academy 400/K-8
3261 N Military Trl 33409 561-686-6520
Barbara Steinberg, hdmstr. Fax 686-8522
Palm Beach Day Academy 300/PK-3
1901 S Flagler Dr 33401 561-832-8815
Dr. Becky van der Bogert, hdmstr. Fax 832-3343
Rosarian Academy 500/PK-8
807 N Flagler Dr 33401 561-832-5131
Sr. Corinne Sanders Ed.D., prin. Fax 820-8750
St. Ann S 300/PK-8
324 N Olive Ave 33401 561-832-3676
Patricia Scheffler, prin. Fax 832-1791
St. Juliana S 500/PK-8
4355 S Olive Ave 33405 561-655-1922
Serena Brasco, prin. Fax 655-8552
Summit Christian S 700/PK-12
4900 Summit Blvd 33415 561-686-8081
Sam Skelton, hdmstr. Fax 640-7613
West Palm Beach Junior Academy 50/PK-8
6300 Summit Blvd 33415 561-689-9575
Glenn Timmons, prin. Fax 689-6183

Wewahitchka, Gulf, Pop. 1,691
Gulf County SD
Supt. — See Port Saint Joe
Wewahitchka ES 400/PK-5
514 E River Rd 32465 850-639-2476
Lori Price, prin. Fax 639-3298
Wewahitchka MS 200/6-8
190 Aligator Aly 32465 850-639-6840
Pam Lister, prin. Fax 639-6929

White Springs, Hamilton, Pop. 815
Hamilton County SD
Supt. — See Jasper
South Hamilton ES 200/PK-6
16693 Springs St 32096 386-397-4400
Waylon Bush, prin. Fax 397-4410

Wildwood, Sumter, Pop. 3,428
Sumter County SD
Supt. — See Bushnell
Wildwood ES 300/K-5
300 Huey St 34785 352-748-3353
Dana Williams, prin. Fax 748-4788

Williston, Levy, Pop. 2,508
Levy County SD
Supt. — See Bronson
Bullock ES 600/PK-2
130 SW 3rd St 32696 352-528-3341
Jaime Handlin, prin. Fax 528-5541
Williston ES 500/3-5
801 S Main St 32696 352-528-6030
Cynthia Lewis, prin. Fax 528-5458
Williston MS 600/6-8
20550 NE 42nd Pl 32696 352-528-2941
Ernst Kordgien, prin. Fax 528-2941

Wimauma, Hillsborough, Pop. 2,932
Hillsborough County SD
Supt. — See Tampa
Reddick ES, 325 W Lake Dr 33598 K-5
J. Thomas Roth, prin. 813-634-0809
Wimauma ES 600/K-5
5709 Hickman St 33598 813-671-5159
Roy Moral, prin. Fax 672-5222

Windermere, Orange, Pop. 2,003
Orange County SD
Supt. — See Orlando
Gotha MS 1,600/6-8
9155 Gotha Rd 34786 407-521-2360
Daniel Axtell, prin. Fax 521-2361
Sunset Park ES 1,000/K-5
12050 Overstreet Rd 34786 407-905-3724
Fax 905-3815
Windermere ES 1,100/PK-5
11125 Park Ave 34786 407-876-7520
Dr. Connie Chisena, prin. Fax 876-7523

Premier Academy 100/PK-1
PO Box 828 34786 407-290-3277
Windemere Preparatory S 700/PK-12
6189 State Road 535 34786 407-905-7737
William Ford, hdmstr. Fax 905-7710

Winter Garden, Orange, Pop. 25,500
Orange County SD
Supt. — See Orlando
Bridgewater MS 1,000/6-8
5600 Tiny Rd 34787 407-905-3710
Fax 905-3858
Dillard Street ES 700/PK-5
310 N Dillard St 34787 407-877-5000
Mark Shanoff, prin. Fax 877-5009
Lakeview MS 1,800/6-8
1200 W Bay St 34787 407-877-5010
Shirley Fox, prin. Fax 877-5019
Lake Whitney ES 1,000/PK-5
1351 Windermere Rd 34787 407-877-8888
Elizabeth Prince, prin. Fax 877-1181
Maxey ES 300/PK-5
1100 E Maple St 34787 407-877-5020
Belinda Davis, prin. Fax 877-2580
Tildenville ES 600/PK-5
1221 Brick Rd 34787 407-877-5054
Carmen Balgobin, prin. Fax 877-5060
Whispering Oak ES 1,400/PK-5
15300 Stoneybrook West Pkwy 34787 407-656-7773
Anne Ramsey, prin. Fax 905-3566

Crenshaw S 200/PK-12
305 Beulah Rd 34787 407-877-7412
Tamie Shuster, prin. Fax 877-7657
Family Christian S 200/PK-12
PO Box 770698 34777 407-656-7904
Terri Schneberger, prin. Fax 656-7904
Foundation Academy 600/PK-12
125 E Plant St 34787 407-656-3677
Shawn Minks, hdmstr. Fax 656-0118

Winter Haven, Polk, Pop. 29,501
Polk County SD
Supt. — See Bartow
Brigham Academy 600/K-5
601 Avenue C SE 33880 863-291-5300
Bill Londeree, prin. Fax 298-7913
Chain of Lakes ES 800/PK-5
7001 County Road 653 33884 863-326-5388
Lynn Boland, prin. Fax 326-5391
Denison MS 1,000/6-8
400 Avenue A SE 33880 863-291-5353
Linda Williams, prin. Fax 291-5347
Elbert ES 600/PK-5
205 15th St NE 33881 863-291-5364
William Dawson, prin. Fax 291-5363
Garden Grove ES 700/K-5
4599 Cypress Gardens Rd 33884 863-291-5396
Deborah Compton, prin. Fax 297-3061
Garner ES 800/PK-5
2500 Havendale Blvd NW 33881 863-965-5455
J. Dart Meyers, prin. Fax 965-5459
Inwood ES 500/K-5
2200 Avenue G NW 33880 863-291-5369
Rena Wood, prin. Fax 291-5370
Jewett Academy 600/6-8
601 Avenue T NE 33881 863-291-5320
Linda Ray, prin. Fax 297-3049
Jewett S of the Arts 700/PK-8
2250 8th St NE 33881 863-291-5373
Edith Henderson, prin. Fax 295-5963
Lake Shipp ES 500/PK-5
250 Camellia Dr 33880 863-291-5384
Vicki Stangle, prin. Fax 298-7511
Snively ES 400/PK-5
1004 Snively Ave 33880 863-291-5325
Dr. JoAnn McKinney, prin. Fax 297-3080
Wahneta ES 500/PK-5
205 4th Wahneta St E 33880 863-291-5392
Lisa Myers, prin. Fax 295-5962
Westwood MS 1,000/6-8
3520 Avenue J NW 33881 863-965-5484
Jose Perez, prin. Fax 965-5585

All Saints' Academy 700/PK-12
5001 State Road 540 W 33880 863-293-5980
Anthony Jordan, hdmstr. Fax 294-2819
Grace Lutheran S 600/PK-8
320 Bates Ave SE 33880 863-293-9744
Roger Walker, prin. Fax 595-0106
Haven Christian Academy 300/PK-12
2105 King Rd 33880 863-293-0930
Dr. Joseph Fox, admin. Fax 293-0429
Heritage Christian Academy 100/PK-8
PO Box 819 33882 863-293-0690
John Scott, admin. Fax 299-4146
St. Joseph S 400/PK-8
535 Avenue M NW 33881 863-293-3311
Deborah Schwope, prin. Fax 299-7894
Winter Haven Adventist Academy 50/1-8
401 Avenue K SE 33880 863-299-7984
Sheila Clinite, prin. Fax 299-9322
Winter Haven Christian S 100/PK-8
1700 Buckeye Loop Rd 33881 863-294-4135
Joseph Klein, dir. Fax 299-8871

Winter Park, Orange, Pop. 28,179
Orange County SD
Supt. — See Orlando
Aloma ES 500/PK-5
2949 Scarlet Rd 32792 407-672-3100
Rahim Jones, prin. Fax 672-0391
Brookshire ES 500/PK-5
400 Greene Dr 32792 407-623-1400
Jeremy Moore, prin. Fax 623-5739
Killarney ES 500/PK-5
2401 Wellington Blvd 32789 407-623-1438
Letecia Foster, prin. Fax 623-1437
Lakemont ES 700/PK-5
901 N Lakemont Ave 32792 407-623-1453
Dr. Susan Stephens, prin. Fax 623-5737

Seminole County SD
Supt. — See Sanford
Eastbrook ES 800/PK-5
5525 Tangerine Ave 32792 407-746-7950
Maria Katz, prin. Fax 746-7999

Alpha Christian Academy 100/PK-8
1550 S Lakemont Ave 32792 407-647-4222
Linda Andriano, admin. Fax 647-8222
Central Christian Academy 800/1-12
PO Box 6000 32793 407-332-6988
Leslie Rawle, dir. Fax 332-4413
Geneva S 500/PK-12
2025 State Road 436 32792 407-332-6363
Robert Ingram, hdmstr. Fax 332-1664
International Community S 400/PK-12
1021 N New York Ave 32789 407-645-2343
Robyn Terwilleger, prin. Fax 645-2366
Learning Tree S 100/PK-K
1021 N New York Ave 32789 407-628-1761
Sandra Varnell, prin. Fax 628-1761
Parke House Academy 200/PK-5
1776 Minnesota Ave 32789 407-647-1121
Frank Rosato, prin. Fax 647-1134
St. Margaret Mary S 600/PK-8
142 E Swoope Ave 32789 407-644-7537
Kathleen Walsh, prin. Fax 644-7357

Winter Springs, Seminole, Pop. 32,583
Seminole County SD
Supt. — See Sanford
Highlands ES 500/PK-5
1600 Shepard Rd 32708 407-746-6650
Donna Weaver, prin. Fax 746-6700
Indian Trails MS 1,400/6-8
415 Tuskawilla Rd 32708 407-320-4350
Lois Chavis, prin. Fax 320-4399
Keeth ES 800/K-5
425 Tuskawilla Rd 32708 407-320-5350
Paul Senko, prin. Fax 320-5399
Layer ES 600/PK-5
4201 State Road 419 32708 407-871-8050
Gloria Staats, prin. Fax 871-8099
Rainbow ES 900/K-5
1412 Rainbow Trl 32708 407-320-8450
Patricia Milliot, prin. Fax 320-8499
Winter Springs ES 600/PK-5
701 W State Road 434 32708 407-320-0650
Michelle Morrison, prin. Fax 320-0600

Yankeetown, Levy, Pop. 678
Levy County SD
Supt. — See Bronson
Yankeetown S 300/PK-8
4500 Highway 40 W 34498 352-447-2372
Ann Hayes, prin. Fax 447-3961

Youngstown, Bay
Bay County SD
Supt. — See Panama City
Waller ES 700/PK-5
11332 E Highway 388 32466 850-722-4341
Patti Fowler, prin. Fax 722-0988

Yulee, Nassau, Pop. 6,915
Nassau County SD
Supt. — See Fernandina Beach
Yulee ES 700/3-5
86063 Felmor Rd 32097 904-491-7943
Scott Hodges, prin. Fax 225-9993
Yulee MS 700/6-8
85439 Miner Rd 32097 904-491-7944
James Rodeffer, prin. Fax 225-0104
Yulee PS 800/PK-2
86426 Goodbread Rd 32097 904-491-7945
Mary Ann Bennett, prin. Fax 225-8269

Zellwood, Orange
Orange County SD
Supt. — See Orlando
Zellwood ES 600/PK-5
3551 N Washington St 32798 407-884-2258
Deborah Duda, prin. Fax 884-3100

Zephyrhills, Pasco, Pop. 12,258
Pasco County SD
Supt. — See Land O Lakes
Stewart MS 1,000/6-8
38505 10th Ave, 813-794-6500
Jackson Johnson, prin. Fax 794-6591
Taylor ES 800/K-5
3638 Morris Bridge Rd 33543 813-794-6900
Eva Hunsberger, prin. Fax 794-6991
West Zephyrhills ES 900/PK-5
37900 14th Ave, 813-794-6300
Emily Keene, prin. Fax 794-6391
Woodland ES 1,000/PK-5
38203 Henry Dr, 813-794-6400
Kim Poe, prin. Fax 794-6491

Heritage Academy 100/PK-8
35636 State Road 54 33541 813-782-7848
Dawn Haas, prin. Fax 782-5909

Zolfo Springs, Hardee, Pop. 1,666
Hardee County SD
Supt. — See Wauchula
Zolfo Springs ES 600/PK-5
3215 School House Rd 33890 863-735-1221
Jan Beckley, prin. Fax 735-1788

GEORGIA

GEORGIA DEPARTMENT OF EDUCATION
2066 Twin Towers E, Atlanta 30334-9050
Telephone 404-656-2800
Fax 404-651-6867
Website http://www.doe.k12.ga.us

State Superintendent of Schools Kathy Cox

GEORGIA BOARD OF EDUCATION
2053 Twin Towers East, Atlanta 30334

Chief Executive Officer Kathy Cox

REGIONAL EDUCATIONAL SERVICE AGENCIES (RESA)

Central Savannah River Area RESA
Dr. Terry Nelson, dir. 706-556-6225
4683 Augusta Hwy, Dearing 30808 Fax 556-8891
www.csraresa.org/

Chattahoochee-Flint RESA
Norman Carter, dir. 229-937-5341
PO Box 1150, Ellaville 31806 Fax 937-5754
www.cfresa.org/

Coastal Plains RESA
Harold Chambers, dir. 229-546-4094
245 N Robinson St, Lenox 31637 Fax 546-4167
www.cpresa.org

First District RESA
Shelly Smith, dir. 912-842-5000
PO Box 780, Brooklet 30415 Fax 842-5161
www.fdresa.org/

Griffin RESA
Dr. Stephanie Gordy, dir. 770-229-3247
PO Box H, Griffin 30224 Fax 228-7316
www.griffinresa.net/

Heart of Georgia RESA
Dr. Charlotte Pipkin, dir. 478-374-2240
1141 Cochran Hwy Fax 374-1524
Eastman 31023
www.hgresa.org/

Metro RESA
Dr. Fran Davis Perkins, dir. 770-432-2404
1870 Teasley Dr SE, Smyrna 30080 Fax 432-6105
www.ciclt.net/mresa

Middle Georgia RESA
Carolyn Williams, dir. 478-475-8630
100 College Station Dr Fax 475-8623
Macon 31206
www.mgresa.org/

Northeast Georgia RESA
Dr. Russell Cook, dir. 706-742-8292
375 Winter St, Winterville 30683 Fax 742-8928
www.negaresa.org

North Georgia RESA
Larry Harmon, dir. 706-276-1111
4731 Old Highway 5 S Fax 276-1114
Ellijay 30540
www.ngresa.org/

Northwest Georgia RESA
Mona Tucker, dir. 706-295-6189
3167 Cedartown Hwy SE Fax 295-6098
Rome 30161
www.nwgaresa.com/

Oconee RESA
Linda Cowan, dir. 478-552-5178
206 S Main St, Tennille 31089 Fax 552-6499
www.oconeeresa.org

Okefenokee RESA
Dr. Teresa Pack, dir. 912-285-6151
1450 N Augusta Ave Fax 287-6650
Waycross 31503
www.okresa.org

Pioneer RESA
Dr. Sandy Addis, dir. 706-865-2141
PO Box 1789, Cleveland 30528 Fax 865-6748
www.pioneerresa.org/

Southwest Georgia RESA
Dr. Larry Green, dir. 229-294-6750
118 McLaughlin St SW Fax 294-6777
Pelham 31779
www.sw-georgia.resa.k12.ga.us

West Georgia RESA
Dr. Ronnie Williams, dir. 770-583-2528
99 Brown School Dr Fax 583-3223
Grantville 30220
www.garesa.org/

PUBLIC, PRIVATE AND CATHOLIC ELEMENTARY SCHOOLS

Abbeville, Wilcox, Pop. 2,471
Wilcox County SD 1,400/PK-12
103 Broad St N 31001 229-467-2141
Charles Bloodsworth, supt. Fax 467-2302
www.wilcox.k12.ga.us/
Other Schools – See Rochelle

Acworth, Cobb, Pop. 18,428
Bartow County SD
Supt. — See Cartersville
Allatoona ES 600/K-5
4150 New Hope Church Rd SE 30102 770-606-5843
Dr. Marvin Bynes, prin. Fax 975-4173

Cherokee County SD
Supt. — See Canton
Oak Grove ES 800/PK-4
6118 Woodstock Rd 30102 770-974-6682
Dr. Jennifer Scrivner, prin. Fax 975-9292

Cobb County SD
Supt. — See Marietta
Acworth ES 800/2-5
4220 Cantrell Rd NW 30101 770-975-6600
Kathleen Curran, prin. Fax 975-6602
Baker ES 800/PK-5
2361 Baker Rd NW 30101 770-975-6629
Dr. Phyllis Jones, prin. Fax 975-6631
Barber MS 900/6-8
4222 Cantrell Rd NW 30101 770-975-6764
Lisa Williams, prin. Fax 529-0325
Durham MS 1,100/6-8
2891 Mars Hill Rd NW 30101 770-975-6641
Georganne Young, prin. Fax 975-6643
Ford ES 1,000/K-5
1345 Mars Hill Rd NW 30101 678-594-8092
Peggy Pepper, prin. Fax 594-8094
Frey ES 900/PK-5
2865 Mars Hill Rd NW 30101 770-975-6655
Joyce Piket, prin. Fax 975-6657
McCall ES 400/K-1
4496 Dixie Ave 30101 770-975-6775
JoAnn Kevins, prin. Fax 529-1580
Picketts Mill ES K-5
6400 Old Stilesboro Rd NW 30101 770-975-7172
Shelia Chesser, prin. Fax 975-7121
Pitner ES 1,100/PK-5
4575 Wade Green Rd NW 30102 678-594-8320
Sherri Hill, prin. Fax 594-8319

Brookwood Christian Language S 50/1-12
4728 Wood St 30101 678-401-5855
Kim Wigington, prin.
St. Laurence Education 5-8
PO Box 801127 30101 770-442-3826
Alen Brown, dir.

Adairsville, Bartow, Pop. 3,090
Bartow County SD
Supt. — See Cartersville
Adairsville ES 600/K-5
122 King St 30103 770-606-5840
Melissa Zarefoos, prin. Fax 773-7755
Adairsville MS 700/6-8
100 College St 30103 770-606-5842
Bruce Mulkey, prin. Fax 606-5842

Adel, Cook, Pop. 5,434
Cook County SD 3,200/PK-12
1109 N Parrish Ave 31620 229-896-2294
Dr. Fred Rayfield, supt. Fax 896-3443
www.cook.k12.ga.us/
Cook PS 900/PK-2
1531 Patterson St 31620 229-549-7715
Timmie Baker, prin. Fax 549-8312
Other Schools – See Sparks

Adrian, Emanuel, Pop. 574
Emanuel County SD
Supt. — See Swainsboro
Adrian S of Performing Arts 200/PK-8
PO Box 247 31002 478-668-3206
Maria Daniels, prin. Fax 668-4317

Ailey, Montgomery, Pop. 540
Montgomery County SD
Supt. — See Mount Vernon
Montgomery County ES 700/PK-5
900 Martin Luther King Dr 30410 912-583-2279
Randy Rodgers, prin. Fax 583-4560

Alamo, Wheeler, Pop. 2,451
Wheeler County SD 1,100/PK-12
404 McRae St 30411 912-568-7198
Mark Davidson, supt. Fax 568-1985
www.wheelercountyschools.org
Wheeler County ES 500/PK-5
RR 2 Box 5 30411 912-568-7159
Dr. Susan White, prin. Fax 568-1935

Albany, Dougherty, Pop. 75,394
Dougherty County SD 15,700/PK-12
PO Box 1470 31702 229-431-1285
Dr. Sally Whatley, supt. Fax 431-1276
www.docoschools.org
Albany MS 600/6-8
1700 Cordell Ave 31705 229-431-3325
Gloria Jones-Baker, prin. Fax 431-3474
Coachman ES 500/K-5
1425 W Oakridge Dr 31707 229-431-3488
Patricia Victor, prin. Fax 431-3490
Cross MS 600/6-8
324 Lockett Station Rd, 229-431-3362
Dr. Sammie Pringle, prin. Fax 431-3476
Dougherty MS 700/6-8
1800 Massey Dr 31705 229-431-3328
Thelma Chunn, prin. Fax 431-3475
Jackson Heights ES 300/3-5
1305 E 2nd Ave 31705 229-431-3367
Dr. LaZoria Walker-Brown, prin. Fax 431-3355
King ES 400/K-5
3125 Mrtn Luther King Jr Dr 31701 229-438-3502
Carolyn Scott, prin. Fax 438-3504
Lake Park ES 700/PK-5
605 Meadowlark Dr 31707 229-431-3370
Catherine Whitfield, prin. Fax 431-3356
Lincoln Magnet ES 700/K-5
518 W Society Ave 31701 229-431-3373
Sheryl Holmes, prin. Fax 431-3357
Live Oak ES 600/K-5
4529 Gillionville Rd, 229-431-1209
Ellen Lane, prin. Fax 431-1237
Magnolia ES 800/PK-5
1700 Samford Ave 31707 229-431-3376
Dr. Jackie Frazier, prin. Fax 431-3358
Merry Acres MS 800/6-8
1601 Florence Dr 31707 229-431-3338
Dr. Ufot Inyang, prin. Fax 431-1204
Morningside ES 300/PK-2
120 Sunset Ln 31705 229-431-3387
Jose Roguemore, prin. Fax 431-3383
Northside ES 400/PK-5
901 14th Ave 31701 229-431-3390
Dr. Angela Shumate, prin. Fax 431-3383
Radium Springs ES 600/PK-5
2400 Roxanna Rd 31705 229-431-3395
Gail Griffin, prin. Fax 431-3444
Radium Springs MS 600/6-8
2600 Radium Springs Rd 31705 229-431-3346
Geraldine Hudley, prin. Fax 431-3552
Reese ES 500/K-5
1215 Lily Pond Rd 31701 229-431-3495
Dr. Valerie Thomas, prin. Fax 431-3497
Sherwood Acres ES 700/PK-5
2201 Doncaster Dr 31707 229-431-3397
Eddie Johnson, prin. Fax 431-3446
Southside MS 500/6-8
1615 Newton Rd 31701 229-431-3351
Joey James, prin. Fax 431-1209
Sylvester Road ES 300/3-5
2600 Trenton Ln 31705 229-431-3403
Deborah Jones, prin. Fax 431-3471
Turner ES 600/PK-5
2001 Leonard Ave 31705 229-431-3406
Dr. Gail Solomon, prin. Fax 431-3472
West Town ES 400/PK-5
1113 University St 31707 229-431-3409
Alene Pringle, prin. Fax 431-3470

Byne Christian S 200/K-12
2832 Ledo Rd 31707 229-436-0173
David Bess, hdmstr. Fax 434-0039
Deerfield-Windsor S 900/PK-12
PO Box 71149 31708 229-435-1301
W.T. Henry, hdmstr. Fax 888-6085
Emmanuel SDA Jr. Academy 50/1-8
1534 E Broad Ave 31705 229-420-9823
Victoria Robinzine, prin. Fax 878-6167
St. Teresa S 200/PK-8
417 Edgewood Ln 31707 229-436-0134
MaryLou Gamache, prin. Fax 436-0135
Sherwood Christian Academy 500/PK-12
1418 Old Pretoria Rd, 229-883-5677
Glen Schultz, hdmstr. Fax 883-5794

Alma, Bacon, Pop. 3,361
Bacon County SD 1,900/PK-12
102 W 4th St 31510 912-632-7363
Phillip Murphy, supt. Fax 632-2454
www.bcraiders.com/
Bacon County ES 400/3-5
523 E 16th St 31510 912-632-4133
Teresa Sermons, prin. Fax 632-5414
Bacon County MS 400/6-8
901 N Pierce St 31510 912-632-4662
Stephanie Deen, prin. Fax 632-6603
Bacon County PS 600/PK-2
251 Cumberland Rd 31510 912-632-4765
Jara Merritt, prin. Fax 632-6611

Alpharetta, Fulton, Pop. 40,128
Forsyth County SD
Supt. — See Cumming
Midway ES 600/PK-5
4805 Atlanta Hwy 30004 770-475-6670
Todd Smith, prin. Fax 521-1866

Fulton County SD
Supt. — See Atlanta
Alpharetta ES 700/PK-5
192 Mayfield Rd 30009 770-740-7015
Patricia Reed, prin. Fax 667-2840
Autrey Mill MS 1,200/6-8
4110 Old Alabama Rd 30022 770-521-7622
Dr. Ann Ferrell, prin. Fax 521-7630
Barnwell ES 700/PK-5
9425 Barnwell Rd 30022 770-552-4960
Doug Brown, prin. Fax 643-3330
Cogburn Woods ES 900/K-5
13080 Cogburn Rd 30004 770-667-2845
John Anderson, prin. Fax 667-2854
Crabapple Crossing ES 800/K-5
12775 Birmingham Hwy 30004 770-740-7055
Sonia Terry, prin. Fax 667-2841
Creek View ES 1,000/K-5
3995 Webb Bridge Rd 30005 770-667-2932
Ronald Trussell, prin. Fax 667-2936
Dolvin ES 900/K-5
10495 Jones Bridge Rd 30022 770-740-7020
Marie Shelton, prin. Fax 740-7025
Haynes Bridge MS 700/6-8
10665 Haynes Bridge Rd 30022 770-740-7030
Debbie Reeves, prin. Fax 667-2842
Holcomb Bridge MS 700/6-8
2700 Holcomb Bridge Rd 30022 770-594-5280
Joy Schroerlucke, prin. Fax 643-3333
Hopewell MS 1,000/6-8
13060 Cogburn Rd 30004 678-297-3240
Bill Thompson, prin. Fax 297-3250
Lake Windward ES 900/PK-5
11770 E Fox Ct 30005 770-740-7050
Martha Messina, prin. Fax 740-7069
Manning Oaks ES 900/PK-5
405 Cumming St 30004 770-667-2912
Sharon Reinig, prin. Fax 667-2916
Medlock Bridge ES 700/PK-5
10215 Medlock Bridge Pkwy 30022 770-623-2980
Margaret Pupillo, prin. Fax 623-2988
New Prospect ES 700/K-5
3055 Kimball Bridge Rd 30022 770-667-2800
Charlia Faulkner, prin. Fax 667-2843
Northwestern MS 1,200/6-8
12805 Birmingham Hwy 30004 770-667-2870
Bruce Fraser, prin. Fax 667-2878
Ocee ES 800/PK-5
4375 Kimball Bridge Rd 30022 770-667-2960
Debra Pernice, prin. Fax 667-2964
State Bridge Crossing ES 700/PK-5
5530 State Bridge Rd 30022 770-497-3850
Trey Martin, prin. Fax 497-3856
Summit Hill ES 1,100/PK-5
13855 Providence Rd 30004 770-667-2830
Nancy Murphy, prin. Fax 667-2834
Taylor Road MS 900/6-8
5150 Taylor Rd 30022 770-740-7090
Ed Williamson, prin. Fax 619-5609
Webb Bridge MS 1,300/6-8
4455 Webb Bridge Rd 30005 770-667-2940
Elizabeth Fogartie, prin. Fax 667-2948

Academy 200/PK-6
89 Cumming St 30009 770-518-1652
Mary Dean Townsend, hdmstr. Fax 569-5548
Bridgeway Christian Academy 300/PK-12
4755 Kimball Bridge Rd 30005 770-751-1972
Rob Starner, hdmstr. Fax 942-1159
Holy Redeemer S 500/K-8
3380 Old Alabama Rd 30022 770-410-4056
Dr. Eric Westley, prin. Fax 410-1454
King's Ridge Christian S 600/K-12
2765 Bethany Bnd 30004 770-754-5738
David Rhodes, hdmstr. Fax 573-3327
Mill Springs Academy 300/1-12
13660 New Providence Rd 30004 770-360-1336
Robert Moore, pres. Fax 360-1341

Ambrose, Coffee, Pop. 328
Coffee County SD
Supt. — See Douglas
Ambrose ES 400/PK-5
3753 Vickers Xing 31512 912-359-2303
Mary Vickers, prin. Fax 359-5565

Americus, Sumter, Pop. 16,873
Sumter County SD 5,500/PK-12
100 Learning Ln, 229-931-8500
Dr. Dennis McMahon, supt. Fax 931-8555
www.sumterschools.org
Cherokee ES 700/PK-2
300 Cherokee St 31709 229-924-3522
Dr. Wanda Jackson, prin. Fax 924-6406
Cobb S 500/3-5
63 Valley Dr 31709 229-924-4888
Thelma Owens, prin. Fax 928-9277
Staley MS 400/6-8
915 N Lee St, 229-924-3168
Victoria Harris, prin. Fax 928-2135
Sumter County ES 800/3-5
438 Bumphead Rd, 229-924-7835
Sharron Marcus, prin. Fax 924-8831
Sumter County MS 700/6-8
439 Bumphead Rd, 229-924-1010
Kimothy Hadley, prin. Fax 928-5571
Sumter County PS - Fine Arts Academy 900/PK-2
123 Learning Ln, 229-924-1012
Valerie Duff, prin. Fax 931-0662

Southland Academy 600/PK-12
PO Box 1127 31709 229-924-4406
William Stubbs, hdmstr. Fax 924-2996

Appling, Columbia
Columbia County SD
Supt. — See Evans
North Columbia ES 400/PK-5
2874 Ray Owens Rd 30802 706-541-1158
Kay Sanders, prin. Fax 854-5833

Arlington, Calhoun, Pop. 1,505
Calhoun County SD
Supt. — See Morgan
Calhoun County ES 400/PK-5
18904 Morgan Rd, 229-725-4985
JoAnn Wims, prin. Fax 725-4020

Armuchee, Floyd
Floyd County SD
Supt. — See Rome
Armuchee MS 500/6-8
471 Floyd Springs Rd NE 30105 706-378-7924
Albert Watters, prin. Fax 378-7983

Ashburn, Turner, Pop. 4,397
Turner County SD 1,700/K-12
PO Box 609 31714 229-567-3338
Ray Jordan, supt. Fax 567-3285
www.turner.k12.ga.us/
Turner County ES 800/K-5
705 Hudson Ave 31714 229-567-3611
Tim Huff, prin. Fax 567-2546
Turner County MS 400/6-8
316 Lamar St 31714 229-567-4343
David Wheeler, prin. Fax 567-9243

Athens, Clarke, Pop. 102,663
Clarke County SD 11,800/PK-12
PO Box 1708 30603 706-546-7721
Philip Lanoue, supt. Fax 369-1804
www.clarke.k12.ga.us
Alps Road ES 500/PK-5
205 Alps Rd 30606 706-548-2261
Anita Lumpkin-Barnett, prin. Fax 227-7818
Barnett Shoals ES 600/PK-5
3220 Barnett Shoals Rd 30605 706-357-5334
Sharon White, prin. Fax 208-8835
Barrow ES 400/PK-5
100 Pinecrest Dr 30605 706-543-2676
Theodore MacMillan, prin. Fax 357-5279
Burney-Harris-Lyons MS 600/6-8
1600 Tallassee Rd 30606 706-548-7208
Melanie Sigler, prin. Fax 357-5263
Chase Street ES 300/PK-5
757 N Chase St 30601 706-543-1081
Adam Kurtz, prin. Fax 357-5249
Clarke MS 600/6-8
1235 Baxter St 30606 706-543-6547
Dr. Kelley Castlin-Gacutan, prin. Fax 548-0257
Coile MS 600/6-8
110 Old Elberton Rd 30601 706-357-5318
Dwight Manzy, prin. Fax 357-5321
Fourth Street ES 400/PK-5
715 Fourth St 30601 706-369-1893
Toni Pickett, prin. Fax 357-5254
Fowler Drive ES 500/PK-5
400 Fowler Dr 30601 706-357-5330
Dr. Dale Rogers, prin. Fax 357-5329
Gaines ES 600/PK-5
900 Gaines School Rd 30605 706-357-5338
Phyllis Stewart, prin. Fax 357-5297
Hilsman MS 700/6-8
870 Gaines School Rd 30605 706-548-7281
Dr. Tony Price, prin. Fax 357-5295
Oglethorpe Avenue ES 500/PK-5
1150 Oglethorpe Ave 30606 706-549-0762
Scarlett Dunne, prin. Fax 227-7813
Timothy ES 500/PK-5
1900 Timothy Rd 30606 706-549-0107
Angela Nowell, prin. Fax 357-5255
Whit Davis Road ES 600/K-5
1450 Whit Davis Rd 30605 706-369-1036
Katrina Daniel, prin. Fax 357-5298
Whitehead Road ES 500/PK-5
500 Whitehead Rd 30606 706-548-7296
Luther McDaniel, prin. Fax 357-5282
Other Schools – See Bogart, Winterville

Jackson County SD
Supt. — See Jefferson
Kings Bridge MS 400/6-8
1630 New Kings Bridge Rd 30607 706-208-3552
Debra Morris, prin. Fax 208-3555
South Jackson ES 500/PK-5
8144 Jefferson Rd 30607 706-543-8798
Pam Johns, prin. Fax 543-4032

Athens Academy 900/PK-12
PO Box 6548 30604 706-549-9225
Robert Chambers, hdmstr. Fax 354-3775
Athens Christian S 700/K-12
1270 Highway 29 N 30601 706-549-7586
Steve Cummings, hdmstr. Fax 549-2899
Athens Montessori S 300/PK-8
3145 Barnett Shoals Rd 30605 706-549-8490
Fax 355-8479
St. Joseph S 300/K-8
134 Prince Ave 30601 706-543-1621
Donavan Yarnall, prin. Fax 543-0149

Atlanta, Fulton, Pop. 470,688
Atlanta CSD 46,400/PK-12
130 Trinity Ave SW 30303 404-802-2700
Dr. Beverly Hall, supt. Fax 802-1803
www.atlanta.k12.ga.us
Adamsville ES 400/K-5
286 Wilson Mill Rd SW 30331 404-802-4300
Sharon Suitt, prin.
Beecher Hills ES 300/K-5
2257 Bolling Brook Dr SW 30311 404-802-8300
Dr. Robin Hall, prin. Fax 752-0828
Benteen ES 400/K-5
200 Cassanova St SE 30315 404-802-7300
Dr. Diana Quisenberry, prin.
Bethune ES 400/K-5
220 Northside Dr NW 30314 404-802-8200
RoseMary Hamer, prin. Fax 330-4103
Blalock ES 300/K-5
1445 Maynard Rd NW 30331 404-802-8250
Frances Thompson, prin. Fax 505-5119
Bolton Academy 400/PK-5
2268 Adams Dr NW 30318 404-802-8350
Laura Strickling, prin.
Boyd ES 300/K-5
1891 Johnson Rd NW 30318 404-802-8150
Emalyn Foreman, prin. Fax 792-5763
Brandon ES 700/K-5
2741 Howell Mill Rd NW 30327 404-802-7250
Karen Evans, prin. Fax 350-2826
Brown MS, 765 Peeples St SW 30310 700/6-8
Donell Underdue, prin. 404-802-6800
Bunche MS 800/6-8
1925 Niskey Lake Rd SW 30331 404-802-6700
Aaron Fernander, prin.
Burgess/Peterson ES 400/PK-5
480 Clifton St SE 30316 404-802-3400
Robin Robbins, prin.
Capitol View ES 200/K-5
1442 Metropolitan Pkwy SW 30310 404-802-7200
Arlene Snowden, prin.
Carson Honors Prep MS 600/6-8
2210 Perry Blvd NW 30318 404-802-4900
Dr. Flora Goolsby, prin.
Cascade ES 500/K-5
2326 Venetian Dr SW 30311 404-802-8100
Dr. Alfonso Jessie, prin. Fax 752-0798
Centennial Place ES 600/K-5
531 Luckie St NW 30313 404-802-8550
Alison Shelton, prin. Fax 853-4089
Cleveland Avenue ES 400/K-5
2672 Old Hapeville Rd SW 30315 404-802-8400
Rhonda Ware-Brazier, prin. Fax 669-2725
Coan MS 400/6-8
1550 Hosea L Williams Dr NE 30317 404-802-6600
Dr. Andre Williams, prin. Fax 371-7135
Connally ES 400/K-5
1654 S Alvarado Ter SW 30311 404-802-8450
Mimi Robinson, prin. Fax 752-0807
Continental Colony ES 300/K-5
3181 Hogan Rd SW 30331 404-802-8000
Sandra Sessoms, prin. Fax 346-2354
Cook ES 300/K-5
211 Memorial Dr SE 30312 404-802-8500
LaPaul Shelton, prin. Fax 330-4104
Deerwood Academy 500/K-5
3070 Fairburn Rd SW 30331 404-802-3300
Lisa Smith, prin.
Dobbs ES 500/K-5
2025 Jonesboro Rd SE 30315 404-802-8050
Dana Evans, prin.
Dunbar ES 200/K-5
660 McWilliams Rd SE 30315 404-802-7950
Betty Greene, prin. Fax 525-2778
East Lake ES 300/PK-5
145 4th Ave SE 30317 404-802-7900
Gwendolyn Benton, prin. Fax 371-7153
Fain ES 500/K-5
101 Hemphill School Rd NW 30331 404-802-8600
Marcus Stallworth, prin. Fax 699-4579
Fickett ES 500/PK-5
3935 Rux Rd SW 30331 404-802-7850
Anthony Dorsey, prin. Fax 346-2358
Finch, 1114 Avon Ave SW 30310 500/K-5
Dr. Linda Paden, prin. 404-802-4000
Garden Hills ES 600/PK-5
285 Sheridan Dr NE 30305 404-802-7800
Amy Wilson, prin. Fax 842-3050
Gideons ES 500/PK-5
897 Welch St SW 30310 404-802-7700
Armstead Salters, prin. Fax 330-4103
Grove Park ES 500/PK-5
20 Evelyn Way NW 30318 404-802-7750
Caitlin Sims, prin. Fax 799-7519
Harper-Archer MS 800/6-8
3399 Collier Dr NW 30331 404-802-6500
Michael Milstead, prin. Fax 699-4569
Heritage Academy 500/PK-5
370 Blair Villa Dr SE 30354 404-802-8650
Dr. Yvonne Bernal, prin. Fax 608-8321
Herndon ES 400/K-5
350 Temple St NW 30314 404-802-8700
Dr. Betty Tinsley, prin.
Hill ES 400/PK-5
386 Pine St NE 30308 404-802-7150
Yolanda Brown, prin. Fax 853-4014

Hope ES, 112 Boulevard NE 30312 300/K-5
Dr. Cassandra Miller-Ashley, prin. 404-802-7450
Humphries ES 300/PK-5
3029 Humphries Dr SE 30354 404-802-8750
Don Clark, prin. Fax 362-2408
Hutchinson ES 500/PK-5
650 Cleveland Ave SW 30315 404-802-7650
R. Dashiell-Mitchell, prin. Fax 768-5690
Inman MS 800/6-8
774 Virginia Ave NE 30306 404-802-3200
Dr. Betsy Bockman, prin. Fax 853-4085
Jackson ES 600/1-5
1325 Mount Paran Rd NW 30327 404-802-8800
Dr. Lorraine Reich, prin. Fax 842-1177
Jones ES, 1040 Fair St SW 30314 500/K-5
Margul Woolfolk, prin. 404-802-3900
Kennedy MS 500/6-8
225 James P Brawley Dr NW 30314 404-802-3600
Lucious Brown, prin.
Kimberly ES 400/PK-5
3090 McMurray Dr SW 30311 404-802-7600
Carolyn Hall, prin. Fax 346-2546
King MS, 545 Hill St SE 30312 600/6-8
Danielle Battle, prin. 404-802-5400
Lin ES 500/K-5
586 Candler Park Dr NE 30307 404-802-8850
Brian Mitchell, prin. Fax 371-7168
Long MS 500/6-8
3200 Latona Dr SW 30354 404-802-4800
Dr. Elizabeth Harris, prin. Fax 802-4899
Miles ES 400/PK-5
4215 Bakers Ferry Rd SW 30331 404-802-8900
Christopher Estes, prin.
Morningside ES 900/PK-5
1053 E Rock Springs Rd NE 30306 404-802-8950
Rebecca Pruitt, prin. Fax 853-4043
Parkside ES 500/K-5
685 Mercer St SE 30312 404-802-4100
Phillip Luck, prin. Fax 624-9855
Parks MS, 1090 Windsor St SW 30310 500/6-8
Christopher Waller, prin. 404-802-6400
Perkerson ES 400/K-5
2040 Brewer Blvd SW 30310 404-802-3950
Dr. Mable Johnson, prin. Fax 756-3996
Peyton Forest ES 500/K-5
301 Peyton Rd SW 30311 404-802-7100
Karen Barlow-Brown, prin.
Price MS 700/6-8
1670 Benjamin W Bickers SE 30315 404-802-6300
Sterling Christy, prin. Fax 624-2118
Rivers ES 500/PK-5
8 Peachtree Battle Ave NW 30305 404-802-7050
David White, prin. Fax 350-2831
Scott ES 400/PK-5
1752 Hollywood Rd NW 30318 404-802-7000
Roxianne Smith, prin.
Slater ES 500/PK-5
1320 Pryor Rd SW 30315 404-802-4050
Dr. Selina Dukes-Walton, prin. Fax 624-2045
Smith ES 800/K-5
370 Old Ivy Rd NE 30342 404-802-3850
Dr. Sidney Baker, prin. Fax 842-3046
Stanton ES, 970 Martin St SE 30315 400/K-5
Dr. Willie Davenport, prin. 404-802-4200
Stanton ES 300/K-5
1625 Martin Luther King NW 30314 404-802-7500
Dr. Marlo Barber, prin.
Sutton MS 800/6-8
4360 Powers Ferry Rd NW 30327 404-802-5600
Audrey Sofianos, prin.
Sylvan Hills MS 500/6-8
1461 Sylvan Rd SW 30310 404-802-6200
Gwendolyn Atkinson, prin.
Thomasville Heights ES 600/PK-5
1820 Henry Thomas Dr SE 30315 404-802-5750
Janice Kelsey, prin. Fax 624-2048
Toomer ES 200/PK-5
65 Rogers St NE 30317 404-802-3450
Tonya Saunders, prin. Fax 687-7992
Towns ES 400/PK-5
760 Bolton Rd NW 30331 404-802-7400
Carla Pettis, prin. Fax 505-6519
Turner MS 400/6-8
98 Anderson Ave NW 30314 404-802-6100
Karen Riggins, prin.
Usher ES, 631 Harwell Rd NW 30318 400/K-5
Dr. Gwen Rogers, prin. 404-802-5700
Venetian Hills ES 400/K-5
1910 Venetian Dr SW 30311 404-802-4550
Clarietta Davis, prin. Fax 752-0028
West Manor ES 300/K-5
570 Lynhurst Dr SW 30311 404-802-3350
Cheryl Twyman, prin. Fax 699-6784
White ES 400/K-5
1890 Detroit Ave NW 30314 404-802-2950
Tamarah Larkin-Currie, prin. Fax 799-0191
Whitefoord ES 400/K-5
35 Whitefoord Ave SE 30317 404-802-6900
Patricia Lavant, prin.
Williams ES 500/PK-5
1065 Wilkes Cir NW 30318 404-802-2900
Joyce Harris, prin. Fax 792-5798
Woodson ES 400/PK-5
1605 Donald L Hollowell Pky 30318 404-802-7350
Dr. Viola Blackshear, prin. Fax 792-5761
Young MS, 2250 Perry Blvd NW 30318 1,000/6-8
Thomas Kenner, prin. 404-802-5900

DeKalb County SD
Supt. — See Decatur
Ashford Park ES 300/PK-5
2968 Cravenridge Dr NE 30319 678-676-6700
Toni Fallon, prin. Fax 676-6710
Briar Vista ES 400/PK-5
1131 Briar Vista Ter NE 30324 678-874-5900
Augretta Tutson, prin. Fax 874-5910
Chamblee MS 1,000/6-8
3601 Sexton Woods Dr 30341 678-874-8200
Cynthia Jackson, prin. Fax 874-8210
Clifton ES 500/PK-5
3132 Clifton Church Rd SE 30316 678-874-4400
Sandra Clay, prin. Fax 874-4410

Fernbank ES 500/PK-5
157 Heaton Park Dr NE 30307 678-874-9300
Jason Marshall, prin. Fax 874-9310
Gresham Park ES 300/PK-5
1848 Vicki Ln SE 30316 678-874-4700
Lucille Sharper, prin. Fax 874-4710
Hawthorne ES 400/PK-5
2535 Caladium Dr NE 30345 678-874-2800
Jennifer Pittman, prin. Fax 874-2810
Henderson Mill ES 500/PK-5
2408 Henderson Mill Rd NE 30345 678-874-3100
Rebecca Jackson Ph.D., prin. Fax 874-3110
Kittredge Magnet ES 400/4-6
1663 E Nancy Creek Dr NE 30319 678-874-6600
Gail Humble, prin. Fax 874-6610
Meadowview ES 400/PK-5
1879 Wee Kirk Rd SE 30316 678-874-5300
Carolyn English, prin. Fax 874-5310
Montclair ES 800/PK-5
1680 Clairmont Pl NE 30329 678-874-7300
Kathy Wells, prin. Fax 874-7310
Montgomery ES 400/PK-5
3995 Ashford Dunwoody Rd NE 30319
678-676-7500
Esther Silvers, prin. Fax 676-7510
Oak Grove ES 600/PK-5
1857 Oak Grove Rd NE 30345 678-874-7400
Charlene Burger, prin. Fax 874-7410
Sagamore Hills ES 500/PK-5
1865 Alderbrook Rd NE 30345 678-874-7500
Julie Martin, prin. Fax 874-7510
Sky Haven ES 500/PK-5
1372 Skyhaven Rd SE 30316 678-874-0102
Dr. Jeanette Roberts, prin. Fax 874-0110
Woodward ES 600/PK-5
3034 Curtis Dr NE 30319 678-874-7800
Ken Bradshaw, prin. Fax 874-7810

Fulton County SD 79,700/PK-12
786 Cleveland Ave SW 30315 404-768-3600
Dr. Cindy Loe, supt. Fax 763-6798
www.fultonschools.org
Heards Ferry ES 500/PK-5
1050 Heards Ferry Rd NW 30328 770-933-6190
Susan Dorenkamp, prin. Fax 933-6195
High Point ES 800/PK-5
520 Greenland Rd NE 30342 404-843-7716
Lisa Nash, prin. Fax 847-3294
Lake Forest ES PK-5
5920 Sandy Springs Cir NE 30328 770-256-8740
Dara Wilson, prin. Fax 256-8746
Randolph ES 800/PK-5
5320 Campbellton Rd SW 30331 404-346-6520
Sara Glynn, prin. Fax 346-6526
Sandtown MS 1,600/6-8
5400 Campbellton Rd SW 30331 404-346-6500
Kine Geathers, prin. Fax 346-6510
Sandy Springs MS 700/6-8
8750 Colonel Dr 30350 770-552-4970
Kay Walker, prin. Fax 643-3334
Other Schools – See Alpharetta, College Park, Duluth, East Point, Fairburn, Hapeville, Milton, Palmetto, Roswell, Sandy Springs, Union City

---

Apostles Lutheran Child Development Ctr 100/PK-PK
6025 Glenridge Dr NE 30328 404-256-3091
Fax 250-1775
Atlanta International S 900/PK-12
2890 N Fulton Dr NE 30305 404-841-3840
Robert Brindley, hdmstr. Fax 841-3873
Atlanta North SDA S 100/PK-8
5123 Chamblee Dunwoody Rd 30338 770-512-8456
April Schander, prin. Fax 512-8298
Atlanta Speech S 300/PK-6
3160 Northside Pkwy NW 30327 404-233-5332
Comer Yates, dir. Fax 266-2175
Atlanta Youth Academy 100/PK-8
PO Box 18237 30316 404-370-1960
Derrick Lockwood, prin. Fax 370-1210
Berean Christian Junior Academy 200/K-8
401 Hamilton E Holmes Dr NW 30318 404-799-0337
Shirley Johnson, prin. Fax 799-0977
Children's Christian S 50/K-3
4380 Danforth Rd SW 30331 404-691-1812
Bertha Furcron, admin.
Children's S 400/PK-6
345 10th St NE 30309 404-873-6985
Marcia Prewitt-Spiller, hdmstr. Fax 607-8565
Christ the King S 500/K-8
46 Peachtree Way NE 30305 404-233-0383
Peggy Warner, prin. Fax 266-0704
Cliff Valley S 300/PK-5
2426 Clairmont Rd NE 30329 678-302-1302
Michael Edwards, hdmstr.
Davis Academy 700/K-8
8105 Roberts Dr 30350 770-671-0085
Sidney Kirschner, hdmstr. Fax 671-8838
Epstein Solomon Schecter S 600/PK-8
335 Colewood Way NW 30328 404-250-5600
Stan Beiner, hdmstr. Fax 250-5585
First Montessori S of Atlanta 300/PK-8
5750 Long Island Dr NW 30327 404-252-3910
Jerri King, hdmstr. Fax 843-9815
Galloway S 700/PK-12
215 W Wieuca Rd NW 30342 404-252-8389
Thomas Brereton, hdmstr. Fax 252-7770
Greenfield Hebrew Academy 400/PK-8
5200 Northland Dr NE 30342 404-843-9900
Kevin King, dir. Fax 252-0934
Heiskell S 300/PK-8
3260 Northside Dr NW 30305 404-262-2233
Cyndie Heiskell, dir. Fax 262-2575
Heritage Preparatory S 100/PK-8
1700 Piedmont Ave NE 30324 404-815-7711
Dr. W. Davies Owens, hdmstr. Fax 815-7737
Holy Innocents' Episcopal S 1,300/PK-12
805 Mount Vernon Hwy NW 30327 404-255-4026
Kirk Duncan, hdmstr. Fax 250-0815
Holy Spirit Preparatory S 700/PK-12
4449 Northside Dr NW 30327 678-904-2811
Gareth Genner, pres. Fax 904-4983

Horizons S 100/K-12
1900 DeKalb Ave NE 30307 404-378-2219
Les Garber, hdmstr. Fax 378-8946
Howard S 200/K-12
1192 Foster St NW 30318 404-377-7436
Marifred Cilella, hdmstr. Fax 377-0884
Imhotep Center of Education 200/PK-8
541 Harwell Rd NW 30318 404-696-8777
Fax 696-0693
Immaculate Heart of Mary S 500/K-8
2855 Briarcliff Rd NE 30329 404-636-4488
Tricia DeWitt, prin. Fax 636-1853
Intown Community S 200/K-8
2059 Lavista Rd NE 30329 404-633-8081
Pamela Stegall, prin. Fax 329-7144
Light of the World of Atlanta S 100/K-12
542 Moreland Ave SE 30316 404-635-1199
Marilyn Bryant, dir. Fax 635-1188
Lovett S 1,600/K-12
4075 Paces Ferry Rd NW 30327 404-262-3032
William Peebles, hdmstr. Fax 261-1967
Mohammed Schools of Atlanta 200/PK-12
735 Fayetteville Rd SE 30316 404-378-4219
Fax 378-4600
Mount Nebo Christian Academy 100/PK-6
1025 McDonough Blvd SE 30315 404-622-3161
Brenda McMichael, admin. Fax 627-9065
Mt. Vernon Presbyterian S 900/PK-12
471 Mount Vernon Hwy NE 30328 404-252-3448
Dr. Jeff Jackson, hdmstr. Fax 252-6777
North Peachtree Academy 100/PK-9
4805 Tilly Mill Rd 30360 770-457-8963
Dr. Tony Romans, hdmstr. Fax 457-2387
Our Lady of the Assumption S 500/PK-8
1320 Hearst Dr NE 30319 404-364-1902
Anita Nagel, prin. Fax 364-1914
Pace Academy 900/K-12
966 W Paces Ferry Rd NW 30327 404-262-1345
Fred Assaf, hdmstr. Fax 264-9376
Paideia S 900/PK-12
1509 Ponce De Leon Ave NE 30307 404-377-3491
Paul Bianchi, hdmstr. Fax 377-0032
Renaissance Montessori S 50/PK-6
2407 Cascade Rd SW 30311 404-755-1915
Rita Merk, prin. Fax 755-1915
Rivercliff Lutheran S 50/K-4
8750 Roswell Rd 30350 770-993-4316
Kris Hoffman, prin. Fax 518-6027
St. Anne's Day S 100/PK-K
3098 Saint Annes Ln NW 30327 404-237-7024
Fax 237-9226
St. Jude the Apostle S 500/K-8
7171 Glenridge Dr NE 30328 770-394-2880
Patty Childs, prin. Fax 804-9248
St. Martin's Episcopal S 600/PK-8
3110 Ashford Dunwoody Rd NE 30319
404-237-4260
Rev. James Hamner, hdmstr. Fax 237-9311
Schenck S 300/K-6
282 Mount Paran Rd NW 30327 404-252-2591
Gena Calloway, hdmstr. Fax 252-7615
Seeds of Faith Christian Academy 100/PK-5
1581 Fairburn Rd SW 30331 404-344-3985
Wanda Kimbrough, admin. Fax 349-4616
Solidarity S K-8
120 Northwood Dr NE 30342 404-236-0868
Jamie Arthur, hdmstr.
Sophia Academy 100/K-8
2880 Dresden Dr 30341 404-303-8722
Marie Corrigan, dir. Fax 303-8883
Southwest Atlanta Christian Academy 300/PK-12
PO Box 310750 31131 404-346-2080
Geraldine Thompson, hdmstr. Fax 346-2085
Torah S of Atlanta 300/K-8
1985 Lavista Rd NE 30329 404-982-0800
Rabbi Kalmen Rosenbaum, hdmstr. Fax 248-1039
Trinity S 600/PK-6
4301 Northside Pkwy NW 30327 404-231-8100
Stephen Kennedy, hdmstr. Fax 231-8111
Westminster S 1,800/K-12
1424 W Paces Ferry Rd NW 30327 404-355-8673
William Clarkson, pres. Fax 355-6606
Worthy's Christian Academy 50/PK-6
330 Lynhurst Dr SW 30311 404-691-9368
Earnestine Worthy, admin. Fax 691-7788

Attapulgus, Decatur, Pop. 481
Decatur County SD
Supt. — See Bainbridge
Williams ES 200/K-5
114 McGriff Ave, 229-465-3306
Dr. Florence Harrell, prin. Fax 465-3307

Auburn, Barrow, Pop. 7,134
Barrow County SD
Supt. — See Winder
Auburn ES 400/K-5
1334 6th Ave 30011 770-963-7887
Shawn Williams, prin. Fax 963-2923
Bramlett ES 800/K-5
622 Freeman Brock Rd 30011 770-307-1627
Cindy Propst, prin. Fax 868-1442

Gwinnett County SD
Supt. — See Suwanee
Mulberry ES 500/PK-5
442 E Union Grove Cir 30011 678-226-7460
Vivian Stranahan, prin.

Old Peachtree Montessori S 100/PK-12
33 Hills Shop Rd 30011 770-963-3052
Gus Garcia, admin. Fax 963-5523

Augusta, Richmond, Pop. 193,101
Columbia County SD
Supt. — See Evans
Stallings Island MS 6-8
3830 Blackstone Camp Rd 30907 706-447-2106
Don Putnam, prin. Fax 447-2103
Stevens Creek ES 900/PK-5
3780 Evans To Locks Rd 30907 706-868-3705
Michelle Paschal, prin. Fax 854-5837

Richmond County SD 31,900/PK-12
864 Broad St 30901 706-826-1000
Dr. Dana Bedden, supt. Fax 826-4613
www.rcboe.org
Barton Chapel Road ES 600/PK-5
2329 Barton Chapel Rd 30906 706-796-4955
Joretta Akpo-Sanni, prin. Fax 796-4774
Bayvale ES 300/PK-5
3309 Milledgeville Rd 30909 706-737-7255
Dr. Dana Harris, prin. Fax 737-7256
Collins ES 500/PK-6
1321 Swanee Quintet Blvd 30901 706-823-6922
Frails Beasley, prin. Fax 823-4381
Copeland ES 400/PK-5
1440 Jackson Rd 30909 706-737-7228
Dr. Anita Evans, prin. Fax 731-7656
Craig-Houghton ES 500/PK-5
1001 4th St 30901 706-823-6946
Brenda Taylor, prin. Fax 823-6988
East Augusta MS 400/6-8
320 Kentucky Ave 30901 706-823-6960
Dr. Verma Curtis, prin. Fax 823-6963
Garrett ES 300/PK-5
1100 Eisenhower Dr 30904 706-737-7222
Paula Kaminski, prin. Fax 737-1166
Glenn Hills ES 500/K-5
2838 Glenn Hills Dr 30906 706-796-4942
Pamela Ward, prin. Fax 796-4701
Glenn Hills MS 900/6-8
2941 Glenn Hills Dr 30906 706-796-4705
Glenn Andrews, prin. Fax 796-4716
Goshen ES 500/PK-5
4040 Old Waynesboro Rd 30906 706-796-4646
Dr. Lisa Schoer, prin. Fax 796-4676
Gracewood ES 500/PK-5
2032 Tobacco Rd 30906 706-796-4969
Baxton Garland, prin. Fax 796-4677
Hains ES 200/PK-K, 4-5
1820 Windsor Spring Rd 30906 706-796-4918
Sophia Cogle, prin. Fax 796-4668
Hornsby ES 300/PK-5
310 Kentucky Ave 30901 706-823-6928
Ruby Stewart, prin. Fax 823-4372
Lake Forest Hills ES 400/PK-5
3140 Lake Forest Dr 30909 706-737-7317
Sonya Bailey, prin. Fax 737-7318
Lamar ES 300/PK-6
970 Baker Ave 30904 706-737-7262
Benjamin Motley, prin. Fax 737-7261
Langford MS 700/6-8
3019 Walton Way Ext 30909 706-737-7301
Cheryl Fry, prin. Fax 737-7302
Meadowbrook ES 600/PK-5
3630 Goldfinch Dr 30906 706-796-4915
Victoria Reese, prin. Fax 796-4681
Merry ES 300/PK-5
415 Boy Scout Rd 30909 706-737-7185
Elizabeth Schad, prin. Fax 731-7653
Milledge ES 300/PK-6
510 Eve St 30904 706-737-7260
Raye Robinson, prin. Fax 729-5223
Monte Sano ES 300/PK-6
2164 Richmond Ave 30904 706-481-1813
Kathryn Perrin, prin. Fax 481-1814
National Hills ES 200/PK-5
1215 Northwood Rd 30909 706-737-7266
Dr. Charles Thompson, prin. Fax 737-7481
Reynolds ES 700/PK-5
3840 Wrightsboro Rd 30909 706-855-2540
Dr. Melissa Jones, prin. Fax 855-2546
Rollins ES 400/PK-5
2160 Mura Dr 30906 706-796-4972
Cheri Ogden, prin. Fax 796-4971
Sego MS 800/6-8
3420 Julia Ave 30906 706-796-4944
Sonya Jefferson, prin. Fax 796-4670
Southside ES 400/PK-5
3310 Old Louisville Rd 30906 706-796-4952
Dr. Tujuana Wiggins, prin. Fax 772-8117
Terrace Manor ES 300/PK-5
3110 Tate Rd 30906 706-796-4910
Hartley Gibbons, prin. Fax 796-4686
Tobacco Road ES 500/PK-5
2397 Tobacco Rd 30906 706-796-4658
Geoclyn Williams, prin. Fax 796-4663
Tubman MS 400/7-8
1740 Walton Way 30904 706-737-7250
Dr. Wayne Frazier, prin. Fax 737-7246
Tutt MS 500/6-8
495 Boy Scout Rd 30909 706-737-7288
Dr. Debbie Alexander, prin. Fax 481-1620
Walker Magnet S 700/K-8
1301 Wrightsboro Rd 30901 706-823-6950
Beverly Hite, prin. Fax 823-6954
Warren Road ES 500/PK-5
311 Warren Rd 30907 706-868-4022
Dr. Connie Ryals, prin. Fax 868-3647
Wheeless Road ES 400/PK-5
2530 Wheeless Rd 30906 706-796-4985
Joe Moore, prin. Fax 796-4771
Wilkinson Gardens ES 500/PK-5
1925 Kratha Dr 30906 706-737-7219
Rickey Lumpkin, prin. Fax 731-8803
Windsor Spring Road ES 500/PK-5
2534 Windsor Spring Rd 30906 706-796-4939
Lori Johnson, prin. Fax 796-4702
Other Schools – See Blythe, Fort Gordon, Hephzibah

Alleluia Community S 200/K-12
2819 Peach Orchard Rd 30906 706-793-9663
Fax 560-2759
Augusta SDA S 50/K-8
4299 Wheeler Rd 30907 706-651-0491
Curtis Baptist S 300/PK-12
1326 Broad St 30901 706-722-5252
William Pevey, admin. Fax 722-1881
Ebenezer Adventist Academy 50/K-8
1699 Olive Rd 30904 706-736-7044
Equilla Wright, prin. Fax 798-7225
Episcopal Day S 500/PK-8
2248 Walton Way 30904 706-733-1192
Ned Murray, hdmstr. Fax 733-1388
Heritage Academy 100/K-7
333 Greene St 30901 706-821-0034
Dr. Linda Tucciarone, admin. Fax 821-0122
Hillcrest Baptist S 200/PK-8
3045 Deans Bridge Rd 30906 706-798-5600
David Smith, prin. Fax 796-1544
Immaculate Conception S 100/K-8
PO Box 2446 30903 706-722-9964
Jon Pike, prin. Fax 722-9994
New Life Christian Academy 100/PK-12
3336 Wrightsboro Rd 30909 706-738-2526
Stacy Wilson, admin. Fax 738-2560
St. Mary on the Hill S 500/K-8
1220 Monte Sano Ave 30904 706-733-6193
Keith Darr, prin. Fax 737-7985
Westminster S of Augusta 500/PK-12
3067 Wheeler Rd 30909 706-731-5260
Stephen O'Neil, hdmstr. Fax 731-5274

Austell, Cobb, Pop. 6,566
Cobb County SD
Supt. — See Marietta
Austell PS 300/K-1
5600 Mulberry St 30106 770-819-5804
Betty Jo Jackson, prin. Fax 398-0041
Clarkdale ES 400/PK-5
4455 Wesley Dr 30106 770-819-2422
Marjorie Bickerstaff, prin. Fax 819-2424
Cooper MS 1,000/6-8
4605 Ewing Rd 30106 770-819-2438
Peggy Martin, prin. Fax 819-2440
Garrett MS 900/6-8
5235 Austell Pwdr Sprgs Rd 30106 770-819-2466
Dr. Phillip Page, prin. Fax 819-2468
Sanders IS 400/3-5
1550 Anderson Mill Rd 30106 770-819-2568
Pamela Dingle, prin. Fax 819-2570
Sanders PS 900/PK-2
1550 Anderson Mill Rd 30106 770-819-2568
Rebecca Jenkins, prin. Fax 819-2582

Cumberland Christian Academy 200/PK-5
2356 Clay Rd 30106 770-819-6443
Larry Kendrick, hdmstr. Fax 945-0224
Good Shepherd Learning Center 100/PK-7
3950 Hicks Rd 30106 770-803-6475
Teresa Sigman, prin. Fax 432-1050

Avondale Estates, DeKalb, Pop. 2,623
DeKalb County SD
Supt. — See Decatur
Avondale ES 400/PK-5
10 Lakeshore Dr 30002 678-676-5200
Rosemary Malone, prin. Fax 676-5210
Avondale MS 700/6-8
3131 Old Rockbridge Rd 30002 678-875-0100
Bernetta Jordan, prin. Fax 875-0110

Bainbridge, Decatur, Pop. 11,874
Decatur County SD 5,800/PK-12
100 S West St 39817 229-248-2200
Ralph Jones, supt. Fax 248-2252
www.dcboe.com
Elcan-King ES 600/PK-5
725 E Louise St, 229-248-2212
Pam Lunsford, prin. Fax 248-2263
Hutto MS 700/6-8
1201 Martin Luther King Jr, 229-248-2224
Dr. Marvin Thomas, prin. Fax 243-5303
Johnson ES 500/PK-5
1947 S West St, 229-248-2215
Kathy Varner, prin. Fax 248-2272
Jones-Wheat ES 500/PK-5
1400 E Broughton St, 229-248-2218
Dr. Larry Clark, prin. Fax 248-2265
Potter Street ES 500/PK-5
725 Potter St, 229-248-2253
Dr. Lillie Brown, prin. Fax 248-2255
West Bainbridge ES 500/PK-5
915 Zorn Rd, 229-248-2821
Allyson Key, prin. Fax 248-2820
West Bainbridge MS 600/6-8
1417 Dothan Rd, 229-248-2206
Steven Dupree, prin. Fax 248-2270
Other Schools – See Attapulgus

Grace Christian Academy 300/PK-12
1302 Lake Douglas Rd, 229-243-8851
Joan Shiver, prin. Fax 243-0515

Baldwin, Banks, Pop. 2,818
Habersham County SD
Supt. — See Clarkesville
Baldwin ES 400/K-5
894 Willingham Ave 30511 706-778-6435
Karle Maxwell, prin. Fax 776-5946

Ball Ground, Cherokee, Pop. 811
Cherokee County SD
Supt. — See Canton
Ball Ground ES 400/PK-6
480 Old Canton Rd 30107 770-735-3366
Doug Knott, prin. Fax 735-4182

Barnesville, Lamar, Pop. 5,808
Lamar County SD 2,500/PK-12
3 Trojan Way 30204 770-358-5891
Dr. Bill Truby, supt. Fax 358-5897
www.lamar.k12.ga.us
Lamar County ES 500/3-5
228 Roberta Dr 30204 770-358-5556
Andrea Scandrett, prin. Fax 358-5560
Lamar County MS 600/6-8
100 Burnette Rd 30204 770-358-8652
Diane Harvey, prin. Fax 358-8657
Lamar County PS 700/PK-2
154 Burnette Rd 30204 770-358-8661
Julie Steele, prin. Fax 358-8666

Liberty Christian Academy 50/PK-12
619 Old Milner Rd 30204 770-358-7300
Jonathan English, prin.

Baxley, Appling, Pop. 4,402
Appling County SD 3,400/PK-12
249 Blackshear Hwy 31513 912-367-8600
Gene Herndon, supt. Fax 367-1011
www.appling.k12.ga.us
Altamaha ES 400/PK-5
344 Altamaha School Rd 31513 912-367-3713
Beth Boone-Davis, prin. Fax 367-2609
Appling County ES 500/3-5
680 Blackshear Hwy 31513 912-367-8640
Dr. Areatha Virgil, prin. Fax 367-8649
Appling County MS 700/6-8
2997 Blackshear Hwy 31513 912-367-8630
Dr. Keith Johnson, prin. Fax 367-8803
Appling County PS 700/PK-2
678 Blackshear Hwy 31513 912-367-8642
Scarlett Copeland, prin. Fax 367-8141
Other Schools – See Surrency

Bellville, Evans, Pop. 139

Pinewood Christian Academy 600/K-12
PO Box 7 30414 912-739-1272
Jon Dorminey, hdmstr. Fax 739-2321

Berkeley Lake, Gwinnett, Pop. 2,071
Gwinnett County SD
Supt. — See Suwanee
Berkeley Lake ES 1,200/PK-5
4300 S Berkeley Lake Rd NW, 770-446-0947
Dr. Florence McLeod, prin. Fax 582-7514

Bethlehem, Barrow, Pop. 938
Barrow County SD
Supt. — See Winder
Barrow County Early Learning Center PK-PK
54 Star St W 30620 770-868-1520
Tonya Royal, prin. Fax 868-1869
Bethlehem ES 700/K-5
47 McElhannon Rd SW 30620 770-867-2238
Marisa Grant, prin. Fax 307-0529

Bethlehem Christian Academy 300/PK-8
PO Box 187 30620 770-307-1574
Rhonda Whiting, prin. Fax 307-1589

Bishop, Oconee, Pop. 158
Oconee County SD
Supt. — See Watkinsville
High Shoals ES K-5
401 Hopping Rd 30621 706-310-1985
Tom Brown, prin. Fax 310-1986

Blackshear, Pierce, Pop. 3,421
Pierce County SD 3,400/PK-12
PO Box 349 31516 912-449-2044
Dr. Joy Williams, supt. Fax 449-2046
www.pierce.k12.ga.us/
Blackshear ES 1,200/PK-5
5217 GA Highway 121 31516 912-449-2088
Dr. Tammy Theologus, prin. Fax 449-2081
Pierce County MS 800/6-8
5216 County Farm Rd 31516 912-449-2077
Terri DeLoach, prin. Fax 449-2075
Other Schools – See Patterson

Blairsville, Union, Pop. 683
Union County SD 2,700/K-12
10 Hughes St 30512 706-745-2322
Tommy Stephens, supt. Fax 745-5025
www.union.k12.ga.us
Union County ES 600/3-5
446 Wellborn St 30512 706-745-9615
Trish Cook, prin. Fax 745-6081
Union County MS 600/6-8
401 Wellborn St 30512 706-745-2483
Donnie Kelley, prin. Fax 745-3920
Union County PS 600/K-2
450 School Cir 30512 706-745-5450
Bobby Kelley, prin. Fax 745-8391
Other Schools – See Suches

Blakely, Early, Pop. 5,476
Early County SD 2,500/PK-12
11927 Columbia St, 229-723-4337
Kenneth Hall, supt. Fax 723-8183
www.early.k12.ga.us
Early County ES 1,200/PK-5
283 Martin Luther King Jr, 229-723-4101
David Ferry, prin. Fax 723-6072
Early County MS 600/6-8
12053 Columbia St, 229-723-3746
Anthony Yarbrough, prin. Fax 723-3942

Bloomingdale, Chatham, Pop. 2,677
Savannah-Chatham County SD
Supt. — See Savannah
Bloomingdale ES 600/K-5
101 E Main St 31302 912-395-3680
John King, prin. Fax 748-3690

Blue Ridge, Fannin, Pop. 1,089
Fannin County SD 3,200/K-12
2290 E First St 30513 706-632-3771
Mark Henson, supt. Fax 632-7583
www.fannin.k12.ga.us
Blue Ridge ES 500/K-5
224 E Highland St 30513 706-632-5772
Brenda Payne, prin. Fax 632-6069
Fannin County MS 800/6-8
4560 Old Highway 76 30513 706-632-6100
Lori Chastain, prin. Fax 632-0461
West Fannin ES 500/K-5
5060 Blue Ridge Dr 30513 706-492-3644
Robert Ensley, prin. Fax 492-4523
Other Schools – See Morganton

Blythe, Richmond, Pop. 788
Richmond County SD
Supt. — See Augusta
Blythe ES 400/PK-5
290 Church St 30805 706-592-4090
Donald Williams, prin. Fax 592-3708

Bogart, Clarke, Pop. 1,094
Clarke County SD
Supt. — See Athens
Cleveland Road ES 300/PK-5
1700 Cleveland Rd 30622 770-725-1664
Tanya Long, prin. Fax 725-2704

Oconee County SD
Supt. — See Watkinsville
Malcom Bridge ES 500/K-5
2600 Malcom Bridge Rd 30622 770-725-6700
Andrea Roper, prin. Fax 725-6725
Malcom Bridge MS 600/6-8
2500 Malcom Bridge Rd 30622 770-725-2319
Tom Odom, prin. Fax 725-0961

Prince Avenue Christian S 500/K-12
2201 Ruth Jackson Rd 30622 678-753-3000
Danny Howell, hdmstr. Fax 753-3028

Bonaire, Houston
Houston County SD
Supt. — See Perry
Bonaire ES 800/PK-5
101 Elm St 31005 478-929-7826
Eric Payne, prin. Fax 542-2281
Bonaire MS 800/6-8
125 GA Highway 96 E 31005 478-929-6236
Cindy Randall, prin. Fax 929-6245
Hilltop ES 600/PK-5
301 Robert Bryson Smith Pky 31005 478-929-6113
Ed Mashburn, prin. Fax 929-6109

Bowdon, Carroll, Pop. 1,963
Carroll County SD
Supt. — See Carrollton
Bowdon ES 700/PK-5
223 Kent Ave 30108 770-258-2161
Rebecca Waldrep, prin. Fax 258-8204
Jonesville MS 400/6-8
129 N Jonesville Rd 30108 770-258-1778
Dana Harman, prin. Fax 258-4374

Bowersville, Hart, Pop. 341
Hart County SD
Supt. — See Hartwell
North Hart ES 600/K-5
124 Ankerich Rd 30516 706-856-7369
Sam Gray, prin. Fax 856-7372

Bowman, Elbert, Pop. 987
Elbert County SD
Supt. — See Elberton
Bowman ES 300/PK-5
PO Box 489 30624 706-213-4500
Jon Jarvis, prin. Fax 245-2618

Braselton, Jackson, Pop. 2,294
Jackson County SD
Supt. — See Jefferson
West Jackson PS 700/PK-2
4825 Highway 53 30517 706-654-2243
Denny Turner, prin. Fax 654-1560

Bremen, Haralson, Pop. 5,350
Bremen CSD 1,800/PK-12
504 Laurel St 30110 770-537-5508
Dr. Stanley McCain, supt. Fax 537-0610
www.bremencs.com
Bremen MS 400/6-8
515 Laurel St 30110 770-537-4874
Christa Smith, prin. Fax 537-5043
Jones ES 900/PK-5
206 Lakeview Dr 30110 770-537-4352
Bill Garrett, prin. Fax 537-1280

Brooklet, Bulloch, Pop. 1,176
Bulloch County SD
Supt. — See Statesboro
Brooklet ES 600/PK-5
600 W Lane St 30415 912-842-2735
Marlin Baker, prin. Fax 842-9413
Southeast Bulloch MS 700/6-8
9124 Brooklet Denmark Rd 30415 912-842-9555
Donna Clifton, prin. Fax 842-9559
Stilson ES 400/PK-5
15569 GA Highway 119 30415 912-823-3150
Eileen Bayens, prin. Fax 823-9057

Brooks, Fayette, Pop. 643
Fayette County SD
Supt. — See Fayetteville
Brooks ES 300/K-5
PO Box 1 30205 770-719-8150
Sue Cleek, prin. Fax 719-8100

Broxton, Coffee, Pop. 1,468
Coffee County SD
Supt. — See Douglas
Broxton ES 300/PK-5
102 Little Ave W 31519 912-359-2391
Lee Mobley, prin. Fax 359-3968

Brunswick, Glynn, Pop. 15,956
Glynn County SD, PO Box 1677 31521 12,400/PK-12
Howard Mann, supt. 912-267-4100
www.glynn.k12.ga.us
Altama ES 700/PK-5
5505 Altama Ave 31525 912-264-3563
Dr. Juliann Rogers, prin. Fax 267-4111
Burroughs-Molette ES 600/PK-5
1900 Lee St 31520 912-267-4130
Joseph Lanham, prin. Fax 267-4178
FACES PK-PK
1900 Lee St 31520 912-267-4229
Stephanie Thompson, prin. Fax 267-4195
Glyndale ES 700/PK-5
1785 Old Jesup Rd 31525 912-264-8740
Debbie Baylor, prin. Fax 267-4129
Glynn MS 700/6-8
901 George St 31520 912-267-4150
Ricky Rentz, prin. Fax 267-4158
Golden Isles ES 1,000/PK-5
1350 Cate Rd 31525 912-264-6822
Sung Hui Lewis, prin. Fax 264-6110
Goodyear ES 600/PK-5
3000 Roxboro Rd 31520 912-267-4170
Dr. Karen Smith, prin. Fax 261-4443
Greer ES 800/PK-5
695 Harry Driggers Blvd 31525 912-267-4135
Dr. Camille Shirah, prin. Fax 267-4139
Macon MS 800/6-8
3885 Altama Ave 31520 912-265-3337
Scott Spence, prin. Fax 267-4118
Needwood MS 900/6-8
669 Harry Driggers Blvd 31525 912-261-4488
Marty Simmons, prin. Fax 261-4491
Satilla Marsh ES 700/PK-5
360 S Port Pkwy 31523 912-265-3675
Kathryn Matthews, prin. Fax 267-4197
Sterling ES 600/K-5
200 McKenzie Dr 31523 912-267-4100
Kelly Howe, prin. Fax 278-1738
Other Schools – See Saint Simons Island

Agape Christian Academy and the Arts 50/PK-7
2308 Parkwood Dr 31520 912-554-1566
Chante Roberts, admin. Fax 554-1567
Brunswick Christian Academy 200/PK-12
4231 US Highway 17 N 31525 912-264-4546
Fax 264-0851
Emmanuel Christian S 100/K-12
1010 Old Jesup Rd 31520 912-265-9647
Keith Mitchell, prin. Fax 265-9647
Heritage Christian Academy 200/PK-12
4265 Norwich Street Ext 31520 912-264-5491
Jill Geary, admin. Fax 264-0799
St. Francis Xavier S 300/PK-8
1121 Union St 31520 912-265-9470
Erin Finn, prin. Fax 261-9950

Buchanan, Haralson, Pop. 1,018
Haralson County SD 3,900/PK-12
10 Van Wert St 30113 770-646-3882
Brett Stanton, supt. Fax 646-8628
www.haralson.k12.ga.us
Buchanan ES 400/3-5
215 College Cir 30113 770-646-5140
Larry Parker, prin. Fax 646-5140
Buchanan PS 600/PK-2
271 Van Wert St 30113 770-646-5523
Gail Ray, prin. Fax 646-8309
Other Schools – See Tallapoosa

Buena Vista, Marion, Pop. 1,697
Marion County SD 1,600/PK-12
PO Box 391 31803 229-649-2234
Richard McCorkle, supt. Fax 649-7423
www.marion.k12.ga.us/
Marion MS 500/5-8
PO Box 16 31803 229-649-2145
Janie Downer, prin. Fax 649-5570
Moss PS 600/PK-4
PO Box 578 31803 229-649-5567
Michelle Rigdon, prin. Fax 649-5565

Buford, Gwinnett, Pop. 10,972
Buford CSD 2,500/K-12
70 Wiley Dr Ste 200 30518 770-945-5035
Dr. Geye Hamby, supt. Fax 945-4629
www.bufordcityschools.org
Buford Academy 600/2-5
2705 Robert Bell Pkwy 30518 678-482-6960
Joy Davis, prin. Fax 482-6969
Buford ES 500/K-1
2500 Sawnee Ave 30518 770-945-5248
Melanie Reed, prin. Fax 932-7579
Buford MS 600/6-8
2700 Robert Bell Pkwy 30518 770-904-3690
Rachel Adams, prin. Fax 904-3689

Gwinnett County SD
Supt. — See Suwanee
Buice S 100/PK-PK
1160 Level Creek Rd 30518 770-271-5060
Kim Holland, prin. Fax 271-5066
Harmony ES 1,300/K-5
3946 S Bogan Rd 30519 770-945-7272
Anne Marie Keskonis, prin. Fax 932-7497
Ivy Creek ES 1,300/K-5
3443 Ridge Rd 30519 678-714-3655
Yvonne Frey, prin. Fax 714-3680
Jones MS 1,200/6-8
3575 Ridge Rd 30519 770-904-5450
Dr. Richard Holland, prin. Fax 904-5452
Lanier MS 2,500/6-8
6482 Suwanee Dam Rd 30518 770-945-8419
Jaime Espinosa, prin. Fax 271-5108
Patrick ES, 2707 Kilgore Rd 30519 800/K-5
Margaret Ackerman, prin. 678-765-5260
Sugar Hill ES 1,100/K-5
939 Level Creek Rd 30518 770-945-5735
Sandra Levent, prin. Fax 932-7421
Twin Rivers MS 1,400/6-8
2300 Braselton Hwy 30519 678-407-7550
Linda Boyd, prin.
White Oak ES K-5
6442 Suwanee Dam Rd 30518 678-546-5550
Jean Loethen-Payne, prin.

Hall County SD
Supt. — See Gainesville
Friendship ES 800/K-5
4450 Friendship Rd 30519 770-932-1223
Berry Walton, prin. Fax 932-2162

Butler, Taylor, Pop. 1,888
Taylor County SD 1,400/PK-12
PO Box 1930 31006 478-862-5224
Wayne Smith, supt. Fax 862-5818
www.taylor.k12.ga.us
Taylor County MS 300/6-8
PO Box 580 31006 478-862-5285
Anzy Hardman, prin. Fax 862-5368
Taylor County PS 400/PK-2
PO Box 1946 31006 478-862-4855
Debi Nagy, prin. Fax 862-4856
Taylor County Upper ES 400/PK-PK, 3-
PO Box 428 31006 478-862-5690
Craig Lockhart, prin. Fax 862-9122

Byron, Peach, Pop. 3,251
Houston County SD
Supt. — See Perry
Eagle Springs ES 800/PK-5
3591 US Highway 41 N 31008 478-953-0450
Andrea McGee, prin. Fax 953-0444

Peach County SD
Supt. — See Fort Valley
Byron ES 900/K-5
202 New Dunbar Rd 31008 478-956-5020
Dannelly Martin, prin. Fax 956-5910
Byron MS 500/6-8
201 Linda Dr 31008 478-956-4999
Dr. Ken Banter, prin. Fax 956-3916

Cairo, Grady, Pop. 9,389
Grady County SD 4,400/PK-12
122 N Broad St 229-377-3701
Tommy Pharis, supt. Fax 377-3437
www.grady.k12.ga.us
Eastside ES 600/PK-5
1201 20th St NE, 229-377-8441
Shelia Cain, prin. Fax 377-7816
Northside ES 400/PK-5
985 1st St NW, 229-377-2422
Gloria Fuller, prin. Fax 378-1133
Southside ES 600/PK-5
491 3rd St SE, 229-377-3723
Cheryl Harrison, prin. Fax 377-5939
Washington MS 600/6-8
1277 Booker Hill Blvd SW, 229-377-2106
Kermit Gilliard, prin. Fax 377-7779
Other Schools – See Pelham, Whigham

Calhoun, Gordon, Pop. 13,570
Calhoun CSD 3,300/PK-12
380 Barrett Rd 30701 706-629-2900
Dr. Michele Taylor, supt. Fax 629-3235
www.calhounschools.org
Calhoun ES 700/3-5
101 Raymond King Dr 30701 706-629-7130
Wesley Roach, prin. Fax 602-6689
Calhoun MS 800/6-8
399 S River St 30701 706-629-3340
Greg Green, prin. Fax 629-0236
Calhoun Preschool PK-PK
380 Barrett Rd 30701 706-602-6601
Michelle Knight, prin. Fax 629-3235
Calhoun PS 1,000/PK-2
101 Raymond King Dr 30701 706-629-8323
Sherry Campbell, prin. Fax 602-6701

Gordon County SD 6,800/PK-12
PO Box 12001 30703 706-629-7366
Dr. Bill McCown, supt. Fax 625-5671
www.gcbe.org
Ashworth MS 700/6-8
PO Box 12001 30703 706-625-9545
Scott McClanahan, prin. Fax 625-0114
Belwood ES 700/PK-5
PO Box 12001 30703 706-629-9547
Kelly Bumgardner, prin. Fax 629-2095
Red Bud ES 900/PK-5
PO Box 12001 30703 706-625-2111
Beth Holcomb, prin. Fax 625-2730
Sonoraville East MS 800/6-8
PO Box 12001 30703 706-629-0793
Allen Bowen, prin. Fax 629-2983
Other Schools – See Fairmount, Plainville, Resaca

Coble SDA S 100/K-8
450 Academy Dr SW 30701 706-629-1578
Fax 629-2203

Camilla, Mitchell, Pop. 5,616
Mitchell County SD 2,100/PK-12
108 S Harney St 31730 229-336-2100
Beauford Hicks, supt. Fax 336-1615
www.mitchell.k12.ga.us
Mitchell County MS 500/6-8
55 Griffin Rd 31730 229-336-0980
Rodney Bullard, prin. Fax 336-2139
Mitchell County PS 600/PK-2
50 Griffin Rd 31730 229-336-8250
Vicki Hicks-Jackson, prin. Fax 336-2135
Walker-Inman ES 500/3-5
550 Mrtin Luther King Jr Rd 31730 229-336-2118
Jacquelyn White, prin. Fax 336-2103

Westwood S 300/PK-12
255 Fuller St 31730 229-336-7992
Ross Worsham, hdmstr. Fax 336-0982

Canton, Cherokee, Pop. 17,685
Cherokee County SD 34,100/PK-12
PO Box 769 30169 770-479-1871
Dr. Frank Petruzielo, supt. Fax 479-7758
www.cherokeek12.org/
Avery ES, 6391 E Cherokee Dr 30115 K-6
Dr. Georgann Toop, prin. 770-479-6200
Bunche Center 100/PK-PK
400 Belletta Dr 30114 770-479-4744
Dr. Gayle McLaurin, admin. Fax 720-3552
Canton ES K-6
712 Marietta Hwy 30114 770-720-6100
Gwen Lince, prin. Fax 720-6328

Clayton ES 400/PK-6
221 Upper Burris Rd 30114 770-479-2550
Barbara Parisi, prin. Fax 479-6796
Creekland MS 1,200/6-8
1555 Owens Store Rd 30115 770-479-3200
Dr. Deborah Wiseman, prin. Fax 479-3210
Freedom MS 600/7-8
10550 Bells Ferry Rd 30114 770-345-4100
Karen Hawley, prin. Fax 345-4140
Free Home ES 200/K-4
12525 Cumming Hwy 30115 770-887-5738
Les Conley, prin. Fax 781-8095
Hasty ES 1,300/K-6
205 Brown Industrial Pkwy 30114 770-479-1600
Izell McGruder, prin.
Hickory Flat ES 1,300/K-6
2755 E Cherokee Dr 30115 770-345-6841
Dr. Keith Ingram, prin. Fax 345-2689
Holly Springs ES 1,000/K-6
1965 Hickory Rd 30115 770-345-5035
Jonathan Hall, prin. Fax 345-5913
Knox ES, 151 River Bend Way 30114 K-6
Dr. Kelly Brooks, prin. 770-345-4307
Liberty ES 1,400/K-6
10500 Bells Ferry Rd 30114 770-345-6411
Dr. Nicole Holmes, prin.
Macedonia ES 900/K-4
10370 E Cherokee Dr 30115 770-479-3429
Catherine Elliott, prin. Fax 479-4026
Rusk MS 900/7-8
4695 Hickory Rd 30115 770-345-2832
Dr. Adrian Thomason, prin. Fax 345-5073
Sixes ES 1,000/K-6
20 Ridge Rd 30114 770-345-3070
John Hultquist, prin. Fax 345-0417
Teasley MS 800/7-8
8871 Knox Bridge Hwy 30114 770-479-7077
Lory Hill, prin. Fax 479-3275
Other Schools – See Acworth, Ball Ground, Waleska, Woodstock

Carnesville, Franklin, Pop. 617
Franklin County SD 3,800/K-12
PO Box 99 30521 706-384-4554
Dr. Ruth O'Dell, supt. Fax 384-7472
www.franklin.k12.ga.us
Carnesville ES 400/K-5
PO Box 39 30521 706-384-4523
Jennifer Gaines, prin. Fax 384-2226
Central Franklin ES 400/K-5
PO Box 189 30521 706-384-7326
David Gailer, prin. Fax 384-7326
Franklin County MS 900/6-8
PO Box 544 30521 706-384-4581
Lucy Floyd, prin. Fax 384-2284
Other Schools – See Lavonia, Royston

Carrollton, Carroll, Pop. 21,837
Carroll County SD 15,000/PK-12
164 Independence Dr 30116 770-832-3568
John Zauner, supt. Fax 834-6399
www.carrollcountyschools.com/
Central ES 1,000/PK-5
633 Stripling Chapel Rd 30116 770-832-6466
Tony Childers, prin. Fax 830-5017
Central MS 900/6-8
155 Whooping Creek Rd 30116 770-832-8114
Shannon Christian, prin. Fax 836-2782
Mount Zion ES 600/PK-5
260 Eureka Church Rd 30117 770-832-8588
Scott Estes, prin. Fax 832-0326
Sand Hill ES 800/PK-5
45 Sandhill School Rd 30116 770-832-8541
Cindy Parker, prin. Fax 830-5034
Sharp Creek ES 700/PK-5
115 Old Muse Rd 30116 770-214-8848
Deaidra Wilson, prin. Fax 836-2734
Other Schools – See Bowdon, Roopville, Temple, Villa Rica, Whitesburg

Carrollton CSD 3,800/K-12
106 Trojan Dr 30117 770-832-9633
Thomas Wilson, supt. Fax 836-2830
www.carrolltoncityschools.net/
Carrollton ES 1,200/K-3
401 Ben Scott Blvd 30117 770-832-2120
Sherry Goodson, prin. Fax 214-2079
Carrollton JHS 900/6-8
510 Ben Scott Blvd 30117 770-832-6535
Todd Simpson, prin. Fax 832-7003
Carrollton MS 600/4-5
151 Tom Reeves Dr 30117 770-830-0997
Trent North, prin. Fax 834-5391

Oak Grove Montessori S 100/PK-3
180 Oak Grove Rd 30117 770-214-0112
Laura Gayle McCord, prin. Fax 214-0113
Oak Mountain Academy 300/K-12
222 Cross Plains Rd 30116 770-834-6651
Ricky Parmer, hdmstr. Fax 834-6785

Cartersville, Bartow, Pop. 17,653
Bartow County SD 14,200/PK-12
PO Box 200007 30120 770-606-5800
John Harper Ed.D., supt. Fax 606-5857
www.bartow.k12.ga.us
Cass MS 1,000/6-8
195 Fire Tower Rd NW 30120 770-606-5846
Kristy Arnold, prin. Fax 606-3835
Clear Creek ES 600/K-5
50 Pleasant Valley Rd NW 30121 770-606-5886
Sherry Glaze, prin. Fax 386-4450
Cloverleaf ES 700/K-5
71 W Felton Rd 30120 770-606-5847
Melinda Moe, prin. Fax 606-3842
Hamilton Crossing ES 600/K-5
116 Hamilton Crossing Rd NW 30120 770-606-5849
Lynn Robertson, prin. Fax 606-3852
Mission Road ES 500/K-5
1100 Mission Rd SW 30120 770-606-5863
Sherrie Hughes, prin. Fax 606-3862
STARS Pre-K Center PK-PK
1653 Cassville Rd NW 30121 770-606-5866
Phyllis Henry, prin. Fax 606-2059
Other Schools – See Acworth, Adairsville, Emerson, Euharlee, Kingston, Rydal, Taylorsville, White

Cartersville CSD 3,800/PK-12
PO Box 3310 30120 770-382-5880
Dr. J. Howard Hinesley, supt. Fax 387-7476
www.cartersville.k12.ga.us
Cartersville ES 900/3-5
340 Old Mill Rd 30120 770-382-0983
Ken Mackenzie, prin. Fax 387-7497
Cartersville MS 900/6-8
825 Douthit Ferry Rd 30120 770-382-3666
Jeff Hogan, prin. Fax 387-7495
Cartersville PS 1,000/K-2
315 Etowah Dr 30120 770-382-1733
Walter Gordon, prin. Fax 387-7493
Kids & Company Preschool PK-PK
323 S Erwin St 30120 678-535-6330
Kathy Dixon-Anderson, prin. Fax 387-7476

Excel Christian Academy 400/K-12
325 Old Mill Rd 30120 770-382-9488
A. Tommy Harris, hdmstr. Fax 606-9884

Cataula, Harris
Harris County SD
Supt. — See Hamilton
Creekside MS 5-6
8403 GA Highway 315 31804 706-596-1300
Dr. Dan Lomax, prin.
Mulberry Creek ES 500/PK-4
8405 GA Highway 315 31804 706-320-9397
Jeff Branham, prin. Fax 322-4569

Cave Spring, Floyd, Pop. 997
Floyd County SD
Supt. — See Rome
Cave Spring ES 300/PK-5
13 Rome Rd SW 30124 706-777-3371
Susan Childers, prin. Fax 777-9943

Cedartown, Polk, Pop. 9,771
Polk County SD 6,300/PK-12
PO Box 128 30125 770-748-3821
Marvin Williams, supt. Fax 748-5131
www.polk.k12.ga.us/
Cedartown MS 1,000/6-8
1664 W Syble Brannon Pkwy 30125 770-749-8850
Fax 749-2795
Cherokee ES 800/PK-5
191 Evergreen Ln 30125 770-748-5614
Dale Freeman, prin. Fax 748-5607
Northside ES 500/PK-5
100 N Philpot St 30125 770-748-4932
Brinda Morris, prin. Fax 748-8318
Westside ES 800/PK-5
51 Frank Lott Dr 30125 770-748-0831
Greg McElwee, prin. Fax 748-5859
Other Schools – See Rockmart

Centerville, Houston, Pop. 6,624
Houston County SD
Supt. — See Perry
Centerville ES 600/PK-5
450 N Houston Lake Blvd 31028 478-953-0400
Cindy Flesher, prin. Fax 953-0411
Thomson MS 800/6-8
301 Thomson Rd 31028 478-953-0489
Tammy Dunn, prin. Fax 953-0484

Chamblee, DeKalb, Pop. 9,763
DeKalb County SD
Supt. — See Decatur
Dresden ES 700/PK-5
2449 Dresden Dr 30341 678-676-7200
Anquinette Guthrie, prin. Fax 676-7210
Henderson MS 1,200/6-8
2830 Henderson Mill Rd 30341 678-874-2900
Terese Allen, prin. Fax 874-2910
Huntley Hills ES 300/PK-5
2112 Seaman Cir 30341 678-676-7400
Angela Leissa Ph.D., prin. Fax 676-7410

Cross & Crown S 100/PK-5
4276A Chamblee Dunwoody Rd 30341
770-458-5274
Steve Mayo, hdmstr. Fax 458-7087

Chatsworth, Murray, Pop. 3,924
Murray County SD 8,000/PK-12
PO Box 40 30705 706-695-4531
Dr. Vickie Reed, supt. Fax 695-8425
www.murray.k12.ga.us
Bagley MS 1,100/6-8
4600 Highway 225 N 30705 706-695-1115
Spencer Gazaway, prin. Fax 695-7289
Chatsworth ES 700/PK-5
500 Green Rd 30705 706-695-2434
Mike Pritchett, prin. Fax 695-7735
Coker ES 800/PK-5
1733 Leonard Bridge Rd 30705 706-695-0888
Donna Standridge, prin. Fax 695-0863
Eton ES 600/PK-5
829 Highway 286 30705 706-695-3207
Judy Redmond, prin. Fax 517-1414
Gladden MS 700/6-8
700 Old Dalton Ellijay Rd 30705 706-695-7448
Ardith Bates, prin. Fax 517-2479
Northwest ES 600/PK-5
110 McEntire Cir 30705 706-695-2262
Dr. C.L. Dunn, prin. Fax 695-7751
Spring Place ES 700/PK-5
2795 Leonard Bridge Rd 30705 706-695-2525
Emma Long, prin. Fax 517-0184
Woodlawn ES 800/PK-5
4580 Highway 225 N 30705 706-517-5213
Jackie Townsend, prin. Fax 517-5147

Chickamauga, Walker, Pop. 2,497
Chickamauga CSD 1,300/K-12
402 Cove Rd 30707 706-382-3100
Melody Day, supt. Fax 375-5364
www.chickamaugacityschools.org/
Chickamauga ES 500/K-5
210 Crescent Ave 30707 706-382-3100
Kristen Bradley, prin. Fax 375-7995
Lee MS 300/6-8
300 Crescent Ave 30707 706-382-3100
Benny Ashley, prin. Fax 375-7988

Walker County SD
Supt. — See La Fayette
Cherokee Ridge ES 800/K-5
2423 Johnson Rd 30707 706-375-9831
Lori Vann, prin. Fax 375-9834

Chula, Tift

Tiftarea Academy 500/PK-12
PO Box 10 31733 229-382-0436
Ron Drummonds, hdmstr. Fax 382-7742

Clarkesville, Habersham, Pop. 1,505
Habersham County SD 6,000/PK-12
PO Box 70 30523 706-754-2118
Robert Costley, supt. Fax 754-1549
www.habershamschools.com/
Clarkesville ES 500/K-5
6539 Highway 115 30523 706-754-2442
Susan Turpin, prin. Fax 754-5964
North Habersham MS 500/7-8
1500 Wall Bridge Rd 30523 706-754-2915
B. Tuck, prin. Fax 754-8218
Woodville ES 200/K-5
911 Historic Old Hwy 441 30523 706-754-4225
Alison Anglin, prin. Fax 754-1812
Other Schools – See Baldwin, Cornelia, Demorest, Mount Airy

Clarkston, DeKalb, Pop. 7,078
DeKalb County SD
Supt. — See Decatur
Dunwoody Are 4/5 ES 700/4-5
955 N Indian Creek Dr 30021 678-676-2802
Johnathan Clark, prin. Fax 676-2840
Indian Creek ES 700/PK-5
724 N Indian Creek Dr 30021 678-676-5700
James Hearn, prin. Fax 676-5710
Jolly ES 500/PK-5
1070 Otello Ave 30021 678-676-5800
Ruth Johnson-Floyd, prin. Fax 676-5810

Claxton, Evans, Pop. 2,400
Evans County SD 1,700/PK-12
613 W Main St 30417 912-739-3544
Dr. Joy Collins, supt. Fax 739-2492
www.evans.k12.ga.us
Claxton ES 800/K-5
6463 US Highway 301 30417 912-739-2714
Marty Todd, prin. Fax 739-0834
Claxton MS 400/6-8
4 N College St 30417 912-739-3646
Diane Holland, prin. Fax 739-7217
Evans County Pre-Kindergarten PK-PK
6461 US Highway 301 30417 912-739-2278
Janet Massey, dir. Fax 739-8255

Clayton, Rabun, Pop. 2,100
Rabun County SD 2,300/PK-12
41 Education St 30525 706-746-5376
Robert Arthur, supt. Fax 746-3084
www.rabun.k12.ga.us
Other Schools – See Rabun Gap, Tiger

Cleveland, White, Pop. 2,360
White County SD 3,500/PK-12
113 N Brooks St 30528 706-865-2315
Dr. Paul Shaw, supt. Fax 865-7784
www.white.k12.ga.us
Mossy Creek ES K-6
128 Horace Fitzpatrick Dr 30528 706-865-5000
Roger Fitzpatrick, prin. Fax 865-5001
Nix PS 700/K-2
342 W Kytle St 30528 706-865-6935
Jennifer King, prin. Fax 865-5569
White County Headstart PK-PK
PO Box 842 30528 706-865-4947
Janice Allison, dir. Fax 219-3073
White County IS 600/3-6
2696 Tesnatee Gap Valley Rd 30528 706-865-1037
Shann Cash, prin. Fax 219-3141
White County MS 600/7-8
283 Old Blairsville Rd 30528 706-865-4060
Dr. Kristi Smith, prin. Fax 865-1947
Other Schools – See Sautee

Cochran, Bleckley, Pop. 4,721
Bleckley County SD 2,300/PK-12
PO Box 516 31014 478-934-2821
Dr. Charlotte Pipkin, supt. Fax 934-9595
www.bleckley.k12.ga.us
Bleckley County ES 500/3-5
470 GA Highway 26 E 31014 478-934-3600
Janet DeLoach, prin. Fax 934-0309
Bleckley County Learning Center PK-PK
242 E Dykes St 31014 478-934-9094
Jan Evans, dir. Fax 934-6713
Bleckley County MS 600/6-8
590 GA Highway 26 E 31014 478-934-7270
Anthony Jenkins, prin. Fax 934-6502
Bleckley County PS 500/K-2
259 E Peter St 31014 478-934-2280
Quent Floyd, prin. Fax 934-2006

Cohutta, Whitfield, Pop. 597
Whitfield County SD
Supt. — See Dalton
Cohutta ES 300/PK-5
254 Wolfe St 30710 706-694-8812
Cindy Dobbins, prin. Fax 694-8390

Colbert, Madison, Pop. 515
Madison County SD
Supt. — See Danielsville
Colbert ES 400/K-5
255 Colbert School Rd 30628 706-788-2341
Billy Heaton, prin. Fax 788-3619

College Park, Fulton, Pop. 20,181
Clayton County SD
Supt. — See Jonesboro
King ES 1,000/PK-5
5745 W Lees Mill Rd, 770-991-4651
Dr. Machelle Matthews, prin. Fax 991-4679
North Clayton MS 1,000/6-8
5517 W Fayetteville Rd, 770-994-4025
Clarence Jackson, prin. Fax 994-4028
Northcutt ES 600/PK-5
5451 W Fayetteville Rd, 770-994-4020
Cynthia James, prin. Fax 994-4479
West Clayton ES 500/PK-5
5580 Riverdale Rd, 770-994-4005
Lisa Adams, prin. Fax 994-4009

Fulton County SD
Supt. — See Atlanta
Bethune ES 700/PK-5
5925 Old Carriage Dr, 770-991-7940
Gwendolyn Miller, prin. Fax 991-7945
Camp Creek MS 900/6-8
4345 Welcome All Rd SW, 404-669-8030
Minnie Miller, prin. Fax 669-8228
College Park ES 300/PK-5
2075 Princeton Ave 30337 404-669-8040
Gretchen Thornton, prin. Fax 669-8231
Heritage ES 1,000/PK-5
2600 Jolly Rd, 404-669-8144
Joyce Mahomes, prin. Fax 669-8148
Lee ES 600/PK-5
4600 Scarborough Rd, 404-669-8025
Emily Massey, prin. Fax 669-8229
Lewis ES 700/PK-5
6201 Connell Rd, 770-969-3450
Josephine Richmond, prin. Fax 306-3581
McNair MS 800/6-8
2800 Burdett Rd, 770-991-4160
Ronald Taylor, prin. Fax 991-4165
Nolan ES 700/PK-5
2725 Creel Rd, 770-991-7950
Chandra Lemons, prin. Fax 991-7955
Stonewall Tell ES 900/PK-5
3310 Stonewall Tell Rd, 770-306-3500
Shannon Flounnory, prin. Fax 306-3504
Tubman ES 500/PK-5
2861 Lakeshore Dr 30337 404-669-8115
Gregory Middleton, prin. Fax 669-8120
West Stubbs Road ES PK-5
3340 W Stubbs Rd, 404-768-3600
Tony Wilcher, prin.

Woodward Academy 2,900/PK-12
1662 Rugby Ave 30337 404-765-4000
Dr. Stuart Gulley, pres. Fax 765-4009

Collins, Tattnall, Pop. 552
Tattnall County SD
Supt. — See Reidsville
Collins ES 300/PK-5
720 N Main St 30421 912-693-2455
Jeannie Burkhalter, prin. Fax 693-9046
Collins MS 100/6-8
720 N Main St 30421 912-693-2455
Chris Freeman, prin. Fax 693-9046

Colquitt, Miller, Pop. 1,889
Miller County SD 1,100/PK-12
PO Box 188, 229-758-5592
Robert Phillips, supt. Fax 758-4138
www.miller.k12.ga.us/
Miller County ES 500/PK-5
100 Pirate Dr, 229-758-4140
Beth Mithen, prin. Fax 758-4139
Miller County MS 200/6-8
96 Perry St, 229-758-4131
Frank Killingsworth, prin. Fax 758-4152

Columbus, Muscogee, Pop. 185,271
Muscogee County SD 33,400/PK-12
PO Box 2427 31902 706-748-2000
Dr. Susan Andrews, supt. Fax 748-2001
www.mcsdga.net
Allen ES 400/K-5
5201 23rd Ave 31904 706-748-2418
Angela Jackson, prin. Fax 748-2415
Arnold Magnet Academy 800/6-8
2011 51st St 31904 706-748-2436
Lura Reed, prin. Fax 748-2435
Baker MS 500/6-8
1215 Benning Dr 31903 706-683-8721
Dr. Marvin Crumbs, prin. Fax 683-8731
Benning Hills ES 200/PK-5
190 Munson Dr 31903 706-683-8752
Pam McCoy, prin. Fax 683-8757
Blackmon Road MS 1,000/6-8
7251 Blackmon Rd 31909 706-565-2998
Michael Barden, prin. Fax 565-3006
Blanchard ES 700/PK-5
3512 Weems Rd 31909 706-748-2461
Tim Smith, prin. Fax 748-2466
Brewer ES 500/PK-5
2951 Mrtn Lthr King Jr Blvd 31906 706-748-2479
Jan Grogan, prin. Fax 748-2481
Cusseta Road ES 500/PK-5
4150 Cusseta Rd 31903 706-683-8760
Linda Sessions, prin. Fax 683-8764
David Computer Magnet Academy 500/K-5
5801 Armour Rd 31909 706-748-2617
Ronie Collins, prin. Fax 748-2620
Davis ES 400/PK-5
1822 Shepherd Dr 31906 706-748-2638
Joe Myles, prin. Fax 748-2635
Dawson ES 300/PK-5
180 Northstar Dr 31907 706-683-8732
Denise Perryman, prin. Fax 683-8737
Dimon Magnet ES 500/K-5
480 Dogwood Dr 31907 706-683-8772
Valerie Williams, prin. Fax 683-8776
Double Churches ES 500/PK-5
1213 Double Churches Rd 31904 706-748-2660
Dr. Paula Shaw Powell, prin. Fax 748-2663
Double Churches MS 800/6-8
7611 Whitesville Rd 31904 706-748-2678
Molly Hart, prin. Fax 748-2682
Downtown Magnet Academy 500/PK-5
1400 1st Ave 31901 706-748-2702
Tonya Douglass, prin. Fax 748-2708
Eagle Ridge Academy 400/PK-5
7601 Schomburg Rd 31909 706-569-3746
Joanna Culbreth, prin. Fax 569-3753
East Columbus Magnet Academy 800/6-8
6100 Georgetown Dr 31907 706-565-3026
Kevin Scott, prin. Fax 565-3031
Eddy MS 600/6-8
2100 S Lumpkin Rd 31903 706-683-8782
Alonzo James, prin. Fax 683-8789
Edgewood ES 500/K-5
3835 Forest Rd 31907 706-565-3048
Melana Cassell, prin. Fax 565-3053
Forrest Road ES 400/PK-5
6400 Forest Rd 31907 706-565-3062
Beatrice Riley, prin. Fax 565-3066
Fort MS 500/6-8
2900 Woodruff Farm Rd 31907 706-569-3740
Sonja Coaxum, prin. Fax 569-3616
Fox ES 500/K-5
600 38th St 31904 706-748-2723
Penny Thornton, prin. Fax 748-2726
Gentian ES 500/PK-5
4201 Primrose Rd 31907 706-569-3625
Rodney Harrison, prin. Fax 569-3628
Georgetown ES 500/PK-5
954 High Ln 31907 706-565-2980
Dr. LaVerne Brown, prin. Fax 565-2985
Hannan Magnet Academy 300/K-5
1338 Talbotton Rd 31901 706-748-2744
Dr. Ann Robison, prin. Fax 748-2749
Jackson Academy 500/K-5
4601 Buena Vista Rd 31907 706-565-3039
Ramona Jones, prin. Fax 565-3046
Johnson ES 400/PK-5
3700 Woodlawn Ave 31904 706-748-2795
Mark Hanner, prin. Fax 748-2799
Key ES 300/PK-5
2520 Broadmoor Dr 31903 706-683-8797
Donna Hart, prin. Fax 683-8802
King ES 500/PK-5
350 30th Ave 31903 706-683-8815
Terry Baker, prin. Fax 683-8819
Marshall MS 500/6-8
1830 Shepherd Dr 31906 706-748-2900
Melvin Blackwell, prin. Fax 748-2908
Muscogee ES 400/PK-5
3900 Baker Plaza Dr 31903 706-683-8822
Dr. Mary Avery, prin. Fax 683-8829
North Columbus ES 500/K-5
2006 Old Guard Rd 31909 706-748-3183
Dawn Upshaw, prin. Fax 748-3189
Reese Road ES 500/PK-5
3100 Reese Rd 31907 706-569-3684
Jeanella Pendleton, prin. Fax 569-3688
Richards MS 800/6-8
2892 Edgewood Rd 31906 706-569-3697
Mike Johnson, prin. Fax 569-3704
Rigdon Road ES 200/K-5
1320 Rigdon Rd 31906 706-565-2989
Charleen Robinson, prin. Fax 565-2994
River Road ES 400/PK-5
516 Heath Dr 31904 706-748-3072
Patrick Knopf, prin. Fax 748-3074
Rothschild MS 600/6-8
1136 Hunt Ave 31907 706-569-3709
Chris Cox, prin. Fax 569-3717
St. Elmo Center for Gifted Education K-12
2101 18th Ave 31901 706-748-3115
Elizabeth Housand, prin. Fax 748-3118
St. Marys Magnet Academy 500/K-5
4408 Saint Marys Rd 31907 706-683-8841
Brenda Byrd, prin. Fax 683-8847
South Columbus ES 500/PK-5
1964 Torch Hill Rd 31903 706-683-8833
Dr. Burl Levins, prin. Fax 683-8838
Thirtieth Avenue Preschool Center PK-PK
151 30th Ave 31903 706-683-8863
Karen Wilson, lead tchr. Fax 683-8862
Veterans Memorial MS 600/6-8
2008 Old Guard Rd 31909 706-748-3203
Melanie Knight, prin. Fax 748-3211
Waddell ES 600/K-5
6101 Miller Rd 31907 706-569-3722
Carolyn Ambrose, prin. Fax 569-3727
Wesley Heights ES 400/PK-5
1801 Amber Dr 31907 706-569-3733
Donna Kemp, prin. Fax 569-3737
Wynnton ES 400/K-5
2303 Wynnton Rd 31906 706-748-3147
Nancy Johnson, prin. Fax 748-3151
Other Schools – See Midland

Brookstone S 800/PK-12
440 Bradley Park Dr 31904 706-324-1392
Scott Wilson, hdmstr. Fax 571-0178
Calvary Christian S 600/PK-12
7556 Old Moon Rd 31909 706-323-0467
Len McWilliams, hdmstr. Fax 323-1941
Columbus First SDA S 50/1-7
7880 Schomburg Rd 31909 706-561-7601
Marleen Young, prin. Fax 561-7601
Grace Christian S 200/PK-12
2915 14th Ave 31904 706-323-9161
Jeff Amsbaugh, prin. Fax 323-8554
New Bethel Christian S 50/K-8
2423 Woodruff Farm Rd 31907 706-569-0004
Our Lady of Lourdes S 100/PK-8
1973 Torch Hill Rd 31903 706-689-5644
Diana Hankins, prin. Fax 689-0671
Pinehurst Christian S 200/PK-5
4217 Saint Marys Rd 31907 706-689-8044
Linda Phillips, prin. Fax 689-3027
St. Anne Pacelli S 400/PK-12
2020 Kay Cir 31907 706-561-8232
Danni Harris, pres. Fax 563-0211
Wynnbrook Christian S 100/K-6
500 River Knoll Way 31904 706-323-0795
Oliver Boone, prin. Fax 322-3688

Comer, Madison, Pop. 1,156
Madison County SD
Supt. — See Danielsville
Comer ES 400/K-5
PO Box 97 30629 706-783-2797
Christine Register, prin. Fax 783-3138
Madison County MS 1,100/6-8
3215 Highway 172 30629 706-783-2400
Matt Boggs, prin. Fax 783-4390

Commerce, Jackson, Pop. 5,856
Commerce CSD 1,500/PK-12
270 Lakeview Dr 30529 706-335-5500
Dr. James McCoy, supt. Fax 335-5214
www.commerce-city.k12.ga.us
Commerce ES 200/3-4
825 Lakeview Dr 30529 706-335-1801
David Cash, prin.
Commerce MS 500/5-8
7690 Jefferson Rd 30529 706-335-5594
Chuck Bell, prin. Fax 335-6222
Commerce PS 400/PK-2
395 Minish Dr 30529 706-335-5587
Kim Savage, prin. Fax 335-7382

Jackson County SD
Supt. — See Jefferson
East Jackson ES 400/PK-5
1531 Hoods Mill Rd 30529 706-336-7900
Jennifer Halley, prin. Fax 336-7919
East Jackson MS 600/6-8
1880 Hoods Mill Rd 30529 706-335-2083
Heidi Hill, prin. Fax 335-0935

Conley, Clayton, Pop. 5,528
Clayton County SD
Supt. — See Jonesboro
Anderson ES 500/PK-5
4199 Old Rock Cut Rd 30288 404-362-3820
Marsha Hood, prin. Fax 362-4089

Conyers, Rockdale, Pop. 12,205
Rockdale County SD 15,300/PK-12
PO Box 1199 30012 770-860-4211
Samuel King, supt. Fax 860-4285
www.rockdale.k12.ga.us
Barksdale ES 600/K-5
596 Oglesby Bridge Rd SE 30094 770-483-9514
Jana O'Kelley, prin. Fax 483-0665
Conyers MS 1,100/6-8
400 Sigman Rd NW 30012 770-483-3371
Maryland Nesmith, prin. Fax 483-9448
Edwards MS 900/6-8
2633 Stanton Rd SE 30094 770-483-3255
Tonya Bloodworth, prin. Fax 483-3676
Flat Shoals ES 800/PK-5
1455 Flat Shoals Rd SE 30013 770-483-5136
Georgi Brown, prin. Fax 483-3579
Hicks ES 600/PK-5
930 Rowland Rd NE 30012 770-483-4410
Sherrod Willaford, prin. Fax 483-0592
Hightower Trail ES 600/K-5
2510 Highway 138 NE 30013 770-388-0751
Laura Bates, prin. Fax 918-9620
Honey Creek ES 600/K-5
700 Honey Creek Rd SE 30094 770-483-5706
Dr. Carolyn Ormsby, prin. Fax 483-9433
House ES 600/PK-5
2930 Highway 20 NE 30012 770-483-9504
Carolyn Poole, prin. Fax 483-0397
Memorial MS 900/6-8
3205 Underwood Rd SE 30013 770-922-0139
Emilio Garza, prin. Fax 922-6192
Peeks Chapel ES 600/PK-5
2800 Avalon Pkwy 30013 770-761-1842
Shirley Chesser, prin. Fax 761-1843
Pine Street ES 500/PK-5
960 Pine St NE 30012 770-483-8713
Tammy Smith, prin. Fax 483-0158
Shoal Creek ES 600/K-5
1300 McWilliams Rd SW 30094 770-929-1430
Blake Craft, prin. Fax 483-8676
Sims ES 500/K-5
1821 Walker Rd SW 30094 770-922-0666
Carol Buhler, prin. Fax 922-2499
Other Schools – See Stockbridge

Peachtree Academy 200/PK-7
1801 Ellington Rd SE 30013 770-860-8900
Jenna Johnson, admin. Fax 761-0883
Victory Christian S 300/PK-12
1151 Flat Shoals Rd SE 30013 770-929-3758
Fax 929-8848
Young Americans Christian S 500/PK-12
1701 Honey Creek Rd SE 30013 770-760-7902
David Taylor, admin. Fax 760-7981

Cordele, Crisp, Pop. 11,493
Crisp County SD 4,100/PK-12
PO Box 729 31010 229-276-3400
Judy Bean Ed.D., supt. Fax 276-3406
www.crisp.k12.ga.us
Blackshear Trail ES 500/K-2
1001 Blackshear Rd 31015 229-276-3415
Freddie Gilliam, prin. Fax 276-3417
Clark ES 400/3-5
401 S 15th St 31015 229-276-3425
Kay Mathews, prin. Fax 276-3426
Crisp County MS 1,000/6-8
1116 E 24th Ave 31015 229-276-3460
David Mims, prin. Fax 276-3466

O'Neal Pre-Kindergarten PK-PK
500 E 14th Ave 31015 229-276-3444
Carol Harris, prin. Fax 297-3414
Pate ES 600/K-2
802 E 24th Ave 31015 229-276-3410
Gail Nesbitt, prin. Fax 276-3409
Southwestern ES 500/3-5
1001 W 24th Ave 31015 229-276-3420
Suzie Giannoni, prin. Fax 276-3421

Crisp Academy 300/PK-12
150 Crisp Academy Dr 31015 229-273-6330
Adam Smith, prin. Fax 273-4141

Cornelia, Habersham, Pop. 3,771
Habersham County SD
Supt. — See Clarkesville
Cornelia ES 600/K-5
375 Old Cleveland Rd 30531 706-778-6526
Renee Smith, prin. Fax 776-7828
Level Grove ES 500/PK-5
2525 Level Grove Rd 30531 706-778-3087
Tony Reabold, prin. Fax 778-3731
South Habersham MS 500/7-8
237 Old Athens Hwy 30531 706-778-7121
Constance Franklin, prin. Fax 778-2110
South Habersham Sixth Grade Academy 6-6
427 Cash St 30531 706-776-1600
Darlene Hudson, prin. Fax 776-1602

Covington, Newton, Pop. 13,856
Newton County SD 18,300/PK-12
PO Box 1469 30015 770-787-1330
Dr. R. Steven Whatley, supt. Fax 784-2950
www.newtoncountyschools.org
Clements Theme S 1,100/4-8
66 Jack Neely Rd 30016 770-784-2934
Dr. Jill Adams, prin. Fax 784-2992
Cousins MS 800/6-8
8187 Carlton Trl NW 30014 770-786-7311
Scott Sauls, prin. Fax 784-2991
East Newton ES 600/PK-5
2286 Dixie Rd 30014 770-784-2973
Dr. Kim Coady, prin. Fax 784-2976
Fairview Theme S 600/K-3
3325 Fairview Rd 30016 770-784-2959
Dr. RuthAnne Smith, prin. Fax 784-2963
Ficquett ES 700/PK-5
2207 Williams St NE 30014 770-786-2636
Miriam Wilkins, prin. Fax 784-2938
Heard-Mixon ES 500/PK-5
14110 Highway 36 30014 770-784-2980
Lee Peck, prin. Fax 784-2984
Indian Creek MS 1,100/6-8
11051 S by Pass Rd 30014 770-385-6453
Dr. Renee Mallard, prin. Fax 385-6456
Liberty MS 100/6-8
5225 Salem Rd 30016 678-625-6617
Victor Lee, prin. Fax 625-6200
Live Oak ES 100/PK-5
500 Kirkland Rd 30016 678-625-6654
Ericka Anderson, prin. Fax 625-6201
Livingston ES 900/PK-5
3657 Highway 81 S 30016 770-784-2930
Wendy Hughes, prin. Fax 784-2996
Middle Ridge ES 500/PK-5
11649 S by Pass Rd 30014 770-385-6463
Alan Satterfield, prin. Fax 385-6466
Oak Hill ES 900/PK-5
6243 Highway 212 30016 770-385-6906
Dr. Brenda Gammans, prin. Fax 385-6909
Porterdale ES 900/PK-5
45 Ram Dr 30014 770-784-2928
Lizzella Dodson, prin. Fax 784-2993
Rocky Plains ES 900/PK-5
5300 Highway 162 S 30016 770-784-4987
Dr. Miranda Jones, prin. Fax 784-4988
South Salem ES PK-5
5335 Salem Rd 30016 678-342-5907
Holly Dubois, prin. Fax 342-5908
Veterans Memorial MS 1,300/6-8
13357 Brown Bridge Rd 30016 770-385-6893
James Peek, prin. Fax 385-6899
West Newton ES 1,100/PK-5
13387 Brown Bridge Rd 30016 770-385-6472
Takila Curry, prin. Fax 385-6475
Other Schools – See Mansfield, Oxford

Walton County SD
Supt. — See Monroe
Walnut Grove ES 500/PK-5
460 Highway 81 SW 30014 770-784-0046
Dr. Cindy Callaway, prin. Fax 784-5599

Woodlee's Christian Academy 200/K-12
3915 Highway 162 30016 770-788-2770
Terri Knight, dir. Fax 788-1883

Cumming, Forsyth, Pop. 5,802
Forsyth County SD 30,900/PK-12
1120 Dahlonega Hwy 30040 770-887-2461
Dr. L.C. Evans, supt. Fax 781-6632
www.forsyth.k12.ga.us
Big Creek ES 900/K-5
1994 Peachtree Pkwy 30041 770-887-4584
Dr. Thomas Davis, prin. Fax 781-2247
Chattahoochee ES 900/K-5
2800 Holtzclaw Rd 30041 770-781-2240
David Culpepper, prin. Fax 781-2244
Coal Mountain ES 800/K-5
3455 Coal Mountain Dr 30028 770-887-7705
Ann Reid, prin. Fax 781-2286
Cumming ES 1,100/K-5
540 Dahlonega St 30040 770-887-7749
Dr. Lynne Castleberry, prin. Fax 888-1233
Daves Creek ES 1,100/K-5
3740 Melody Mizer Ln 30041 770-888-1222
Eric Ashton, prin. Fax 888-1223
Liberty MS 900/6-8
7465 Wallace Tatum Rd 30028 770-781-4889
Connie Stovall, prin. Fax 513-3877
Little Mill MS 700/6-8
6800 Little Mill Rd 30041 678-965-5000
Connie McCrary, prin. Fax 965-5001
Mashburn ES 700/K-5
3777 Samples Rd 30041 770-889-1630
Kathie Braswell, prin. Fax 888-1202
Matt ES 900/K-5
7455 Wallace Tatum Rd 30028 678-455-4500
Charley Stadler, prin. Fax 455-4514
North Forsyth MS 1,100/6-8
3645 Coal Mountain Dr 30028 770-889-0743
Jeff Hunt, prin. Fax 888-1210
Otwell MS 900/6-8
605 Tribble Gap Rd 30040 770-887-5248
Steve Miller, prin. Fax 888-1214
Piney Grove MS 800/6-8
8135 Majors Rd 30041 678-965-5010
Terri North, prin. Fax 965-5011
Sawnee ES 600/3-5
1616 Canton Hwy 30040 770-887-6161
Dr. Eileen Nix, prin. Fax 781-2254
Shiloh Point ES 1,100/K-5
8145 Majors Rd 30041 678-341-6481
Sharon Ericson, prin. Fax 341-6491
Silver City ES 700/K-5
6200 Dahlonega Hwy 30028 678-965-5020
Kristen Morse, prin. Fax 965-5021
South Forsyth MS 1,000/6-8
2865 Old Atlanta Rd 30041 770-888-3170
Debbie Sarver, prin. Fax 888-3179
Vickery Creek ES 1,100/K-5
6280 Post Rd 30040 770-346-0040
Ron McAllister, prin. Fax 346-0045
Vickery Creek MS 1,100/6-8
6240 Post Rd 30040 770-667-2580
Kathy Rohacek, prin. Fax 667-2593
Other Schools – See Alpharetta, Gainesville, Suwanee

Covenant Christian Academy 200/PK-12
6905 Post Rd 30040 770-674-2990
Johnathan Arnold, hdmstr. Fax 674-2989
Fideles Christian S 100/K-12
1390 Weber Industrial Dr 30041 770-888-6705
Jonny Whisenant, dir. Fax 888-9720
Horizon Christian Academy 300/K-12
PO Box 2715 30028 678-947-3583
Garin Berry, admin. Fax 947-0721
Ivy League Montessori 100/PK-6
1791 Kelly Mill Rd 30040 770-781-5586
Becky Carty, dir. Fax 205-7180
Montessori Academy at Sharon Springs 200/PK-8
2830 Old Atlanta Rd 30041 770-205-6277
Katherine Lindaman, prin. Fax 887-0081
Pinecrest Academy 800/PK-12
955 Peachtree Pkwy 30041 770-888-4477
John Tarpley, pres. Fax 888-0404

Cusseta, Chattahoochee, Pop. 1,258
Chattahoochee County SD 800/PK-12
326 Broad St 31805 706-989-3774
Jimmy Martin, supt. Fax 989-3776
www.chattahoochee.k12.ga.us/
Chattahoochee County ES 300/PK-5
140 Merrell St 31805 706-989-3648
Tabitha Walton, prin. Fax 989-3103
Chattahoochee County MS 200/6-8
360 GA Highway 26 31805 706-989-3678
Lane Lindsay, prin. Fax 989-0694

Cuthbert, Randolph, Pop. 3,491
Randolph County SD 1,500/PK-12
98 School Dr, 229-732-3601
Bobby Jenkins, supt. Fax 732-3840
www.sowegak12.org/
Randolph-Clay MS 300/6-8
3451 GA Highway 266, 229-732-2101
Shirlette Morris, prin. Fax 732-5633
Randolph County ES 700/PK-5
200 Highland Ave, 229-732-3794
Larry Calloway, prin. Fax 732-6027

Dacula, Gwinnett, Pop. 4,425
Gwinnett County SD
Supt. — See Suwanee
Alcova ES 900/K-5
770 Ewing Chapel Rd 30019 678-376-8500
Dr. Carolyn Ford, prin. Fax 376-8502
Dacula ES 2,000/K-5
2500 Fence Rd 30019 770-963-7174
Mary Lou Enright, prin. Fax 277-4448
Dacula MS 1,900/6-8
137 Dacula Rd 30019 770-963-1110
Dr. Kellye Riggins, prin. Fax 338-4632
Fort Daniel ES 1,200/PK-5
1725 Auburn Rd 30019 770-932-7400
Carolyn Madsen, prin. Fax 271-5194
Harbins ES 1,000/K-5
3550 New Hope Rd 30019 770-682-4270
Dr. Cindy Truett, prin. Fax 682-4285
Puckett's Mill ES K-5
2442 S Pucketts Mill Rd 30019 678-765-5110
Michelle Farmer, prin. Fax 765-5240

Hebron Christian Academy 500/K-5
PO Box 1028 30019 770-962-5423
Esther Birge, prin. Fax 339-5683

Dahlonega, Lumpkin, Pop. 4,519
Lumpkin County SD 3,800/PK-12
56 Indian Dr 30533 706-864-3611
Dewey Moye, supt. Fax 864-3755
www.lumpkin.k12.ga.us
Long Branch ES 500/K-5
4518 Highway 52 E 30533 706-864-5361
Sharon Head, prin. Fax 864-5477
Lumpkin County ES 600/PK-5
153 School Dr 30533 706-864-3254
Tony Herrington, prin. Fax 864-2103
Lumpkin County MS 900/6-8
44 School Dr 30533 706-864-6180
Rick Conner, prin. Fax 864-0199
Other Schools – See Dawsonville

Dallas, Paulding, Pop. 8,667
Paulding County SD 26,900/PK-12
3236 Atlanta Hwy 30132 770-443-8000
Larry Ragsdale, supt. Fax 443-8089
www.paulding.k12.ga.us
Abney ES 600/K-5
4555 Dallas Acworth Hwy 30132 770-445-2656
Amy Durham, prin. Fax 443-7006
Allgood ES 800/PK-5
312 Hart Rd 30157 770-443-8070
Sheral Threadgill, prin. Fax 443-8071
Burnt Hickory ES K-5
80 N Paulding Dr 30132 678-363-0970
Dr. Mark Crowe, prin. Fax 505-0640
Dallas ES 600/PK-5
520 Hardee St 30132 770-443-8018
Joyce Gladden, prin. Fax 443-8020
East Paulding MS 1,100/6-8
2945 Hiram Acworth Hwy 30157 770-443-7000
Stan Ingram, prin. Fax 443-0116
Jones MS 1,100/6-8
100 Stadium Dr 30132 770-443-8024
Craig Wilcox, prin. Fax 443-8026
McClure MS 800/6-8
315 Bob Grogan Dr 30132 770-505-3700
Richard Hutnick, prin. Fax 505-7253
Moses MS 1,400/6-8
1066 Old County Farm Rd 30132 770-443-8727
Dr. Tracey Bennett, prin. Fax 443-8078
Nebo ES 800/PK-5
2843 Nebo Rd 30157 770-443-8777
Karla Dodgen, prin. Fax 445-6465
Northside ES 800/PK-5
2223 Cartersville Hwy 30132 770-443-7008
Jan Sholder, prin. Fax 443-7010
Poole ES 900/PK-5
1002 Wayside Ln 30132 770-505-5541
Angie Capobianco, prin. Fax 505-5540
Roberts ES 800/PK-5
1833 Mount Tabor Church Rd 30157 770-443-8060
Jason Gregaydis, prin. Fax 443-2624
Russom ES 800/PK-5
44 Russom Elementary School 30132 678-574-3480
Gina King, prin. Fax 574-5893
Scoggins MS 6-8
1663 Mulberry Rock Rd 30157 770-456-4188
Tammy Allen, prin. Fax 456-4189
Shelton ES 1,200/PK-5
1531 Cedarcrest Rd 30132 770-443-4244
Penney Noel, prin. Fax 975-9172
South Paulding MS 800/6-8
592 Nebo Rd 30157 770-445-8500
Jim Gottwald, prin. Fax 445-9989
Other Schools – See Douglasville, Hiram, Powder Springs, Rockmart, Temple, Villa Rica

Dalton, Whitfield, Pop. 32,140
Dalton CSD 6,400/PK-12
PO Box 1408 30722 706-278-8766
Jim Hawkins, supt. Fax 226-4583
www.daltonpublicschools.com/
Blue Ridge ES 600/PK-5
100 Bogle St 30721 706-260-2700
Dr. Lisa Goode, prin. Fax 260-2848
Brookwood ES 400/PK-5
501 Central Ave 30720 706-278-9202
Will Esters, prin. Fax 278-8224
City Park ES 800/K-5
405 School St 30720 706-278-8859
Dr. Rick Little, prin. Fax 226-5457
Dalton MS 1,300/6-8
1250 Cross Plains Trl 30721 706-278-3903
Brian Suits, prin. Fax 428-7852
Park Creek ES 600/PK-5
1500 Hale Bowen Dr 30721 706-428-7700
Dr. Phil Jones, prin. Fax 428-7725
Roan ES 600/PK-5
1116 Roan St 30721 706-226-3225
Cindy Parrott, prin. Fax 278-0979
Westwood ES 500/K-5
708 Trammell St 30720 706-278-2809
Angela Garrett, prin. Fax 278-1379

Whitfield County SD 13,500/PK-12
PO Box 2167 30722 706-217-6780
Dr. Katie Brochu, supt. Fax 278-5042
www.astihosted.com/WHITFIELDDCP/
Antioch ES 700/PK-5
1819 Riverbend Rd 30721 706-278-7550
Lisa Jones, prin. Fax 226-9674
Beaverdale ES 400/PK-5
1350 Prater Mill Rd NE 30721 706-275-4414
Joe Barnett, prin. Fax 259-2562
Cedar Ridge ES 200/PK-5
285 Cedar Ridge Rd SE 30721 706-712-8400
Allyson Millican, prin.
Dawnville ES 700/K-5
1380 Dawnville Rd NE 30721 706-259-3914
Sherri Travisano, prin. Fax 259-7462
Dug Gap ES 500/PK-5
2032 Dug Gap Rd 30720 706-226-3919
Mandy Locke, prin. Fax 226-9753
Eastbrook MS 800/6-8
700 Hill Rd 30721 706-278-6135
Brian Satterfield, prin. Fax 226-9859
Eastside ES 600/PK-5
102 Hill Rd 30721 706-278-3074
Ty Snyder, prin. Fax 226-9951
New Hope ES 600/K-5
1175 New Hope Rd NW 30720 706-673-3180
Brinda Clayton, prin. Fax 673-3182
New Hope MS 500/6-8
1325 New Hope Rd NW 30720 706-673-2295
George Kopcsak, prin. Fax 673-2086
North Whitfield MS 700/6-8
3264 Cleveland Rd 30721 706-259-3381
Andrea Bradley, prin. Fax 259-8168
Pleasant Grove ES 600/PK-5
2725 Cleveland Hwy 30721 706-259-3920
Richard Knox, prin. Fax 259-6271

Valley Point ES 600/PK-5
3798 S Dixie Rd 30721 706-277-3259
Karey Williams, prin. Fax 277-7721
Valley Point MS 400/6-8
3796 S Dixie Rd 30721 706-277-9662
Britt Adams, prin. Fax 277-7035
Varnell ES 500/K-5
3900 Cleveland Rd 30721 706-694-3471
Ellen Thompson, prin. Fax 694-3289
Other Schools – See Cohutta, Rocky Face, Tunnel Hill

Christian Heritage S 400/K-12
1600 Martin Luther King Jr 30721 706-277-1198
Renny Scott, hdmstr. Fax 277-2300
Learning Tree S 100/PK-8
300 S Tibbs Rd 30720 706-278-2736
Vicky Lauritzen, prin. Fax 278-6731

Damascus, Early, Pop. 265

Southwest Georgia Academy 400/PK-12
14105 GA Highway 200, 229-725-4792
Doug Dease, prin. Fax 725-5476

Danielsville, Madison, Pop. 508
Madison County SD 4,700/K-12
PO Box 37 30633 706-795-2191
Mitch McGee, supt. Fax 795-5104
www.madison.k12.ga.us
Danielsville ES 500/K-5
900 Madison St 30633 706-795-2181
Angie Waggoner, prin. Fax 795-5420
Other Schools – See Colbert, Comer, Hull, Ila

Darien, McIntosh, Pop. 1,713
McIntosh County SD 2,000/PK-12
200 Pine St SE 31305 912-437-6645
Dr. William Hunter, supt. Fax 437-2140
www.mcintosh.k12.ga.us/
McIntosh County MS 500/6-8
500 Greene St 31305 912-437-6685
Merwan Massa, prin. Fax 437-5676
Oak Grove IS 300/4-5
500 Greene St 31305 912-437-6655
Carolyn Smith, prin. Fax 437-2719
Todd-Grant ES 700/PK-3
1102 CA Devillars Rd 31305 912-437-6675
Cassandra Noble, prin. Fax 437-5296

Dawson, Terrell, Pop. 4,859
Terrell County SD 1,700/PK-12
PO Box 151, 229-995-4425
Robert Aaron, supt. Fax 995-4632
www.terrellcounty-ga.com/schools/boe/
Carver ES 400/3-5
PO Box 151, 229-995-5451
Fax 995-6020
Cooper PS 500/PK-2
PO Box 151, 229-995-2843
Fax 995-4454

Terrell Academy 300/K-12
602 Academy Dr SE, 229-995-4242
Bill Murdock, hdmstr. Fax 995-6149

Dawsonville, Dawson, Pop. 1,066
Dawson County SD 4,100/K-12
517 Allen St 30534 706-265-3246
Nicky Gilleland, supt. Fax 265-1226
www.dawsoncountyschools.org/
Black's Mill ES 500/K-5
1860 Dawson Forest Rd E 30534 706-216-3300
Julia Mashburn, prin. Fax 216-6822
Dawson County MS 800/6-8
332 Highway 9 N 30534 706-216-5801
Dr. Mark Merges, prin. Fax 265-7252
Kilough ES 500/K-5
1063 Kilough Church Rd 30534 706-216-8595
Lois Zangara, prin. Fax 216-7424
Riverview MS 800/6-8
5126 Highway 9 S 30534 706-216-4849
William Zadernak, prin. Fax 265-1426
Robinson ES 700/K-5
1150 Perimeter Rd 30534 706-265-6544
Roxanne Fausett, prin. Fax 265-1529

Lumpkin County SD
Supt. — See Dahlonega
Blackburn ES 700/K-5
45 Blackburn Rd 30534 706-864-8180
Susan Burrell, prin. Fax 864-8176

Dearing, McDuffie, Pop. 446
McDuffie County SD
Supt. — See Thomson
Dearing ES 400/PK-5
500 Main St N 30808 706-986-4900
Dr. Laura Hughes, prin. Fax 986-4901

Decatur, DeKalb, Pop. 17,884
DeKalb County SD 97,700/PK-12
3770 N Decatur Rd 30032 678-676-1200
Dr. Crawford Lewis, supt. Fax 676-0785
www.dekalb.k12.ga.us
Alexander ES 500/K-7
3414 Memorial Dr 30032 678-874-1300
Thomas Powell, prin. Fax 874-1310
Atherton ES 400/PK-5
1674 Atherton Dr 30035 678-874-0300
Dr. James Berry, prin. Fax 874-0310
Bethune MS 1,200/6-8
5200 Covington Hwy 30035 678-875-0300
Dr. Terry McMullen, prin. Fax 875-0310
Briarlake ES 400/PK-5
3590 Lavista Rd 30033 678-874-2500
Dr. Ann Culbreath, prin. Fax 874-2510
Canby Lane ES 700/PK-5
4150 Green Hawk Trl 30035 678-874-0600
Dr. Anita Stokes-Brown, prin. Fax 874-0610
Cedar Grove MS 1,200/6-8
2300 Wildcat Rd 30034 678-874-4200
Dr. Agnes Flanagan, prin. Fax 874-4210
Chapel Hill ES 700/PK-5
3536 Radcliffe Blvd 30034 678-676-8400
Michael Williamson, prin. Fax 676-8410
Chapel Hill MS 1,000/6-8
3535 Dogwood Farm Rd 30034 678-676-8500
Carlus Daniel, prin. Fax 676-8510
Columbia ES 500/PK-5
3230 Columbia Woods Dr 30032 678-874-0700
Leroy Jenkins, prin. Fax 874-0710
Columbia MS 1,000/6-8
3001 Columbia Dr 30034 678-875-0500
Stephanie Amey, prin. Fax 875-0510
Flat Shoals ES 400/PK-5
3226 Flat Shoals Rd 30034 678-874-4600
Keith Reynolds, prin. Fax 874-4610
Glenhaven ES 500/PK-5
1402 Austin Dr 30032 678-874-1200
Beverly Jackson, prin. Fax 874-1210
Harris ES 1,000/PK-5
3981 Mcgill Dr 30034 678-676-9200
Dr. Sean Tartt, prin. Fax 676-9210
Kelley Lake ES 400/PK-5
2590 Kelly Lake Rd 30032 678-874-4800
Howard Harvey, prin. Fax 874-4810
Knollwood ES 500/PK-5
3039 Santa Monica Dr 30032 678-874-1400
Dr. Sheila Hollins, prin. Fax 874-1410
Laurel Ridge ES 300/PK-5
1215 Balsam Dr 30033 678-874-6900
Mark Gordon, prin. Fax 874-6910
Mathis ES 400/PK-5
3505 Boring Rd 30034 678-874-5800
Dr. Willa Blalock, prin. Fax 874-5810
McLendon ES 500/PK-5
3169 Hollywood Dr 30033 678-676-5900
Lloyd McFarlane, prin. Fax 676-5910
McNair Discovery Learning Academy 800/PK-5
2162 Second Ave 30032 678-875-3402
Dr. Marchell Boston, prin. Fax 875-3410
McNair MS 1,000/6-8
2190 Wallingford Dr 30032 678-874-5100
Susan Freeman, prin. Fax 874-5110
Medlock ES 300/PK-5
2418 Wood Trail Ln 30033 678-874-7200
Fred Hammonds, prin. Fax 874-7210
Midway ES 400/PK-5
3318 Midway Rd 30032 678-874-1500
Dr. Denise Mapp, prin. Fax 874-1510
Miller Grove MS 1,200/6-8
2215 Miller Rd 30035 678-676-8900
Dr. Triscilla Weaver, prin. Fax 676-8910
Oak View ES 900/PK-5
3574 Oakvale Rd 30034 678-875-1300
Sandra Wilson, prin. Fax 875-1310
Peachcrest ES 300/PK-5
1530 Joy Ln 30032 678-874-1600
Dr. Jeffrey Jenkins, prin. Fax 874-1610
Shamrock MS 1,100/6-8
3100 Mount Olive Dr 30033 678-874-7600
Robert Thorpe, prin. Fax 874-7610
Snapfinger ES 600/PK-5
1365 Snapfinger Rd 30032 678-874-1800
Sylvia Reddick, prin. Fax 874-1810
Toney ES 300/PK-5
2701 Oakland Ter 30032 678-874-2100
Oliver Dean, prin. Fax 874-2110
Wadsworth ES 100/4-6
2084 Green Forrest Dr 30032 678-874-2400
Dr. Cornellia Crum, prin. Fax 874-2410
Other Schools – See Atlanta, Avondale Estates, Chamblee, Clarkston, Doraville, Dunwoody, Ellenwood, Lithonia, Scottdale, Stone Mountain, Tucker

Decatur CSD 2,400/PK-12
758 Scott Blvd 30030 404-370-4400
Dr. Phyllis Edwards, supt. Fax 370-3843
www.decatur-city.k12.ga.us
Clairemont ES 300/K-3
155 Erie Ave 30030 404-370-4450
Dr. Graneze Scott, prin. Fax 370-4453
College Heights ECLC PK-PK
917 S McDonough St 30030 404-370-4480
Suzanne Kennedy, dir. Fax 370-4482
Glennwood Academy 300/4-5
440 E Ponce de Leon Ave 30030 404-370-4435
Dr. Gloria Lee, prin. Fax 370-4489
Oakhurst ES 200/K-3
175 Mead Rd 30030 404-370-4470
Mary Mack, prin. Fax 370-4467
Renfroe MS 500/6-8
220 W College Ave 30030 404-370-4440
Bruce Roaden, prin. Fax 370-4449
Winnona Park ES 300/K-3
510 Avery St 30030 404-370-4490
Greg Wiseman, prin. Fax 370-4493

Arbor Montessori S 300/PK-8
2998 Lavista Rd 30033 404-321-9304
Jan Deason, hdmstr. Fax 636-2700
Augustine Preparatory Academy of Atlanta 200/PK-8
4650 Flat Shoals Pkwy 30034 404-326-5132
Vickie Turner, hdmstr. Fax 207-1352
Friends S of Atlanta 100/PK-8
862 Columbia Dr 30030 404-373-8746
Waman French, hdmstr. Fax 990-1318
Greenforest/McCalep Christian Academy 600/PK-12
3250 Rainbow Dr 30034 404-486-6737
Leonard Fritz, prin. Fax 486-1127
Green Pastures Christian S 200/PK-12
5455 Flat Shoals Pkwy 30034 770-987-8121
Samuel Mosteller, admin. Fax 987-7475
Montessori School at Emory 100/PK-6
3021 N Decatur Rd 30033 404-634-5777
Trayce Marino, dir. Fax 633-5373
St. Peter Claver Regional S 100/PK-8
2560 Tilson Rd 30032 404-241-3063
Catherine Spencer, prin. Fax 241-4382
St. Thomas More S 500/K-8
630 W Ponce De Leon Ave 30030 404-373-8456
Terry Collis, prin. Fax 377-8554

Waldorf S of Atlanta 200/PK-8
827 Kirk Rd 30030 404-377-1315
Beatrice Meyer-Parsons, admin. Fax 377-5013
Wings of a Dove Christian Academy 50/K-2
6038 Covington Hwy 30035 678-418-3209
Sharon Boddie, dir. Fax 418-3290

Demorest, Habersham, Pop. 1,777
Habersham County SD
Supt. — See Clarkesville
Demorest ES 500/K-5
3116 Demorest Mt Airy Hwy 30535 706-778-4126
Jamie Spinks, prin. Fax 776-6691
Fairview ES 300/K-5
2925 Cannon Bridge Rd 30535 706-778-2030
Ricky Williams, prin. Fax 778-2033
North Habersham Sixth Grade Academy 6-6
250 Alabama St 30535 706-778-7978
Marybeth Thomas, prin. Fax 776-8743

Doerun, Colquitt, Pop. 848
Colquitt County SD
Supt. — See Moultrie
Doerun ES 200/PK-5
111 Mathis Ave 31744 229-782-5276
Charles Jones, prin. Fax 782-5495

Donalsonville, Seminole, Pop. 2,702
Seminole County SD 1,700/PK-12
800 S Woolfork Ave, 229-524-2433
Monroe Bonner, supt. Fax 524-2212
www.seminole.k12.ga.us
Seminole County ES 900/PK-5
800 Marianna Hwy, 229-524-5235
Renea Moody, prin. Fax 524-8638

Doraville, DeKalb, Pop. 9,872
DeKalb County SD
Supt. — See Decatur
Evansdale ES 500/PK-5
2914 Evans Woods Dr 30340 678-874-2700
Joe D'Ambra, prin. Fax 874-2710
Hightower ES 600/PK-5
4236 Tilly Mill Rd, Atlanta GA 30360 678-676-7300
Oliver Lewis, prin. Fax 676-7310
Oakcliff ES 600/PK-5
3150 Willow Oak Way 30340 678-676-3100
Ardell Saleem, prin. Fax 676-3110
Pleasantdale ES 700/PK-5
3695 Northlake Dr 30340 678-874-3500
Karen Boswell, prin. Fax 874-3510
Reynolds ES 700/PK-5
3498 Pine St 30340 678-676-6802
Melanie Pearch, prin. Fax 676-6810
Sequoyah MS 800/6-8
3456 Aztec Rd 30340 678-676-7900
Trenton Arnold, prin. Fax 676-7910

Northwoods Montessori S 200/PK-6
3340 Chestnut Dr 30340 770-457-7261
Elizabeth Samples, dir. Fax 455-9211

Douglas, Coffee, Pop. 10,978
Coffee County SD 7,800/PK-12
PO Box 1290 31534 912-384-2086
Dr. Steve Wilmoth, supt. Fax 383-5333
coffee.k12.ga.us
Coffee MS 1,000/6-8
901 GA Connector 206 NW 31533 912-720-1001
Phil Dockery, admin. Fax 720-1032
Eastside ES 700/PK-5
603 Mcdonald Ave N 31533 912-384-3187
Michael Davis, prin. Fax 383-0520
Indian Creek ES 900/PK-5
2033 GA Highway 158 W 31535 912-393-1300
Wendell Stone, prin. Fax 393-3040
Pre K Center PK-PK
1303 Peterson Ave S 31533 912-383-4100
Bob McCulley, prin. Fax 383-4114
Satilla ES 600/PK-5
5325 Old Axson Rd 31535 912-384-2602
Scott Gillis, prin. Fax 383-5492
Westside ES 600/PK-5
311 Westside Dr 31533 912-384-5506
Kim Harper, prin. Fax 383-7833
Other Schools – See Ambrose, Broxton, Nicholls, West Green

Citizens Christian Academy 300/PK-12
PO Box 1064 31534 912-384-8862
William Rish, hdmstr. Fax 384-8426

Douglasville, Douglas, Pop. 27,568
Douglas County SD 24,700/K-12
PO Box 1077 30133 770-651-2000
Donald Remillard, supt. Fax 920-4159
www.douglas.k12.ga.us
Arbor Station ES 600/K-5
9999 Parkway S 30135 770-651-3000
Melissa Joe, prin. Fax 920-4314
Arp ES 800/K-5
6550 Alexander Pkwy 30135 770-651-3200
Donna Pritchard, prin. Fax 920-4213
Beulah ES 500/K-5
1150 S Burnt Hickory Rd 30134 770-651-3300
Sheila Miller, prin. Fax 920-4331
Bright Star ES 500/K-5
6300 John West Rd 30134 770-651-3400
Dale McGill, prin. Fax 920-4124
Burnett ES 400/K-5
8277 Connally Dr 30134 770-651-3500
Joyce Bass, prin. Fax 920-4348
Chapel Hill ES 600/K-5
4433 Coursey Lake Rd 30135 770-651-3600
Yvonne Kidney, prin. Fax 920-4254
Chapel Hill MS 1,200/6-8
3989 Chapel Hill Rd 30135 770-651-5000
William Foster, prin. Fax 920-4242
Chestnut Log MS 900/6-8
2544 Pope Rd 30135 770-651-5100
Nicole Keith, prin. Fax 920-4557

Dorsett Shoals ES 500/K-5
5866 Dorsett Shoals Rd 30135 770-651-3700
Kacia Thompson, prin. Fax 920-4263
Eastside ES 500/K-5
8266 Connally Dr 30134 770-651-3800
Lisa Dunnigan, prin. Fax 920-4086
Factory Shoals ES 500/K-5
2300 Shoals School Rd 30135 770-651-3900
Tommy Shadinger, prin. Fax 920-4377
Factory Shoals MS 800/6-8
3301 Shoals School Rd 30135 770-651-5800
James Allen, prin. Fax 920-4356
Fairplay MS 1,000/6-8
8311 Highway 166 30135 770-651-5300
Monte Beaver, prin. Fax 920-4599
Holly Springs ES 700/K-5
4909 W Chapel Hill Rd 30135 770-651-4000
Stefanie Cosper, prin. Fax 947-7615
Mt. Carmel ES 400/K-5
2356 Fairburn Rd 30135 770-651-4200
John McGill, prin. Fax 920-4471
New Manchester ES 900/K-5
2242 Old Lower River Rd 30135 770-651-4400
Sandra Shuler, prin. Fax 947-3830
North Douglas ES 500/K-5
1630 Dorris Rd 30134 770-651-4800
Fran Davis, prin. Fax 920-4590
South Douglas ES 500/K-5
8299 Highway 166 30135 770-651-4500
Casey Duffey, prin. Fax 920-4477
Stewart MS 700/6-8
8138 Malone St 30134 770-651-5400
Dewayne Jackson, prin. Fax 920-4229
Yeager MS 1,100/6-8
4000 Kings Hwy 30135 770-651-5600
Garrick Askew, prin. Fax 947-7374
Other Schools – See Lithia Springs, Villa Rica, Winston

Paulding County SD
Supt. — See Dallas
Austin MS 1,000/6-8
3490 Ridge Rd 30134 770-942-0316
Joel Slater, prin. Fax 942-0548
Dugan ES 1,000/PK-5
1362 Winn Rd 30134 770-949-5261
Kelli Day, prin. Fax 949-5423
Hutchens ES, 586 Clonts Rd 30134 K-5
Cassandra Dobbs, prin. 678-838-2683

Douglasville SDA S 50/1-9
2836 Bright Star Rd 30134 770-949-6734
Fax 949-2954
Harvester Christian Academy 400/PK-12
4241 Central Church Rd 30135 770-942-1583
Jack North, hdmstr. Fax 942-9332
Heirway Christian Academy 200/PK-12
6758 Spring St 30134 770-489-4392
Timothy Thomas, prin. Fax 489-4318
Inner Harbour S 100/K-12
4685 Dorsett Shoals Rd 30135 770-942-2391
Dr. Penny Honeycutt, prin. Fax 489-0406
Kings Way Christian S 400/PK-12
6456 The Kings Way 30135 770-949-0812
Dr. Ray Conway, admin. Fax 949-1045

Dublin, Laurens, Pop. 16,924
Dublin CSD 2,700/PK-12
207 Shamrock Dr 31021 478-272-3440
Dr. Elaine Connell, supt. Fax 272-1249
echalk.dublinirish.org
Dasher ES 500/K-1
911 Martin Luther King Jr D 31021 478-277-9807
Fred Williams, prin. Fax 277-9846
Dublin MS 600/6-8
1501 N Jefferson St 31021 478-272-8122
Dr. Larry Moore, prin. Fax 277-9828
Hillcrest Preschool Center PK-PK
1100 Edgewood Dr 31021 478-277-9833
Ellen Smith, prin. Fax 277-9809
Moore Street ES 400/4-5
1405 W Moore St 31021 478-277-9817
John Strickland, prin. Fax 277-9840
Saxon Heights ES 400/2-3
717 Smith St 31021 478-277-9820
Dr. Marie Hooks, prin. Fax 277-9814

Laurens County SD 6,400/PK-12
467 Firetower Rd 31021 478-272-4767
Jerry Hatcher, supt. Fax 277-2619
www.lcboe.net
East Laurens ES 500/3-5
960 US Highway 80 E 31027 478-272-8612
Eddie Morris, prin. Fax 277-2641
East Laurens MS 600/6-8
920 US Highway 80 E 31027 478-272-1201
Dianne Jones, prin. Fax 275-1627
East Laurens PS 600/PK-2
950 US Highway 80 E 31027 478-272-4440
Julie Alligood, prin. Fax 272-7815
West Laurens MS 900/6-8
332 W Laurens School Rd 31021 478-272-8452
Fax 275-0848
Other Schools – See Dudley, Rentz

Trinity Christian S 400/K-12
200 Trinity Rd 31021 478-272-7699
Rick Johnson, prin. Fax 272-7685

Dudley, Laurens, Pop. 468
Laurens County SD
Supt. — See Dublin
Northwest Laurens ES 1,000/PK-5
3330 US Highway 80 W 31022 478-676-3475
John Warren, prin. Fax 676-2246

Duluth, Gwinnett, Pop. 24,482
Fulton County SD
Supt. — See Atlanta
Abbotts Hill ES 700/K-5
5575 Abbotts Bridge Rd 30097 770-667-2860
Roytunda Stabler, prin. Fax 667-2864
Findley Oaks ES 900/K-5
5880 Findley Chase Dr 30097 770-497-3800
Steven Curry, prin. Fax 497-3810
River Trail MS 1,400/6-8
10795 Rogers Cir 30097 770-497-3860
Dawn Melin, prin. Fax 497-3866
Shakerag ES 800/PK-5
10885 Rogers Cir 30097 770-497-3880
Martin Neuhaus, prin. Fax 497-3886
Wilson Creek ES 900/K-5
6115 Wilson Rd 30097 770-497-3811
Jimmy Zoll, prin. Fax 497-3819

Gwinnett County SD
Supt. — See Suwanee
Chattahoochee ES 1,200/K-5
2930 Albion Farm Rd 30097 770-497-9907
Jeff Lee, prin. Fax 232-3272
Chesney ES 800/K-5
3878 Old Norcross Rd 30096 678-542-2300
Carlotta Rozzi, prin. Fax 542-2304
Duluth MS 1,900/6-8
3200 Pleasant Hill Rd 30096 770-476-3372
Deborah Fusi, prin. Fax 232-3295
Harris ES 700/K-5
3123 Claiborne Dr 30096 770-476-2241
Dr. Lauri Burton, prin. Fax 232-3258
Hull MS 2,200/6-8
1950 Old Peachtree Rd 30097 770-232-3200
Denise Showell, prin. Fax 232-3203
Mason ES 1,400/PK-5
3030 Bunten Rd 30096 770-232-3370
Paula Deweese, prin. Fax 232-3372
Radloff MS 1,100/6-8
3939 Shackleford Rd 30096 678-245-3400
Dr. Patty Heitmuller, prin. Fax 245-3403

Duluth Adventist Christian S 100/PK-8
2959 Duluth Highway 120 30096 770-497-8607
David Forsey, prin. Fax 476-2133
Duluth Montessori S 200/PK-6
1768 Old Peachtree Rd 30097 770-476-9307
Edith Overholser, dir. Fax 476-9792
Notre Dame Academy 500/PK-8
4635 River Green Pkwy 30096 678-387-9385
Debra Orr, pres. Fax 990-9353
Woodward North Academy 400/PK-6
6565 Boles Rd 30097 404-765-4490
Lee Vincent, prin. Fax 765-4499

Dunwoody, DeKalb, Pop. 34,400
DeKalb County SD
Supt. — See Decatur
Austin ES 700/PK-5
5435 Roberts Dr 30338 678-874-8100
Beth Fogletree, prin. Fax 874-8110
Vanderlyn ES 900/PK-5
1877 Vanderlyn Dr 30338 678-874-9000
Noel Maloof, prin. Fax 874-9010

Eastanollee, Stephens
Stephens County SD
Supt. — See Toccoa
Big A ES 600/PK-5
289 Sorrells Dr 30538 706-886-2987
George Sanders, prin. Fax 282-4698
Eastanollee ES 500/PK-5
50 Eastanollee Livestock Rd 30538 706-779-2216
Susan Crawford, prin. Fax 779-3801

Eastman, Dodge, Pop. 5,441
Dodge County SD 3,500/PK-12
720 College St 31023 478-374-3783
Dr. Lynn Rogers, supt. Fax 374-6697
www.dodge.k12.ga.us
Dodge County MS 800/6-8
5911 Oak St 31023 478-374-6492
Davey Sheffield, prin. Fax 374-6484
North Dodge ES 800/K-5
167 Orphans Cemetery Rd 31023 478-374-6690
Mike Hilliard, prin. Fax 374-6486
South Dodge ES 900/PK-5
1118 McRae Hwy 31023 478-374-6691
Elvis Davis, prin. Fax 374-6750

East Point, Fulton, Pop. 40,680
Fulton County SD
Supt. — See Atlanta
Brookview ES 600/PK-5
3250 Hammarskjold Dr 30344 404-669-8020
Paul Brown, prin. Fax 669-8046
Conley Hills ES 600/PK-5
2580 Delowe Dr 30344 404-669-8170
Serena Lowe, prin. Fax 669-8175
Holmes ES 600/PK-5
2301 Connally Dr 30344 404-767-3092
LaRoyce Sublett, prin. Fax 767-5439
Mt. Olive ES 600/PK-5
3353 Mount Olive Rd 30344 404-669-8050
Darryl Felker, prin. Fax 669-8230
Oak Knoll ES 600/PK-5
2626 Hogan Rd 30344 404-669-8060
Cheree Turner, prin. Fax 669-8227
Parklane ES 400/PK-5
2809 Blount St 30344 404-669-8070
Lee Adams, prin. Fax 669-8079
West MS 1,000/6-8
2376 Headland Dr 30344 404-669-8130
Dan Sims, prin. Fax 669-8121
Woodland MS 700/6-8
2745 Stone Rd 30344 404-305-2182
Andre Wright, prin. Fax 305-2190

Christ Lutheran S 100/PK-6
2719 Delowe Dr 30344 404-767-2892
Aaron Dickerson, prin. Fax 767-0516
Pathway Christian S 100/PK-12
1706 Washington Ave 30344 404-763-3216
Dr. Hoyt Johnson, prin. Fax 767-2707

Eatonton, Putnam, Pop. 6,758
Putnam County SD 2,800/PK-12
158 Old Glenwood Springs Rd 31024 706-485-5381
Dr. Jim Willis, supt. Fax 485-3820
www.putnam.k12.ga.us/boe/
Putnam County ES 1,400/PK-5
162 Old Glenwood Springs Rd 31024 706-485-5141
Dr. Susan Usry, prin. Fax 485-4147
Putnam County MS 600/6-8
314 S Washington Ave 31024 706-485-8547
Fernando Aker, prin. Fax 485-7090

Gatewood S 500/PK-12
139 Phillips Dr 31024 706-485-8231
Laura Thompson, hdmstr. Fax 485-2455
Redeemer Episcopal Academy 50/PK-3
680 Old Phoenix Rd 31024 706-484-1238
Dr. Trish Klein, prin. Fax 991-1502

Elberton, Elbert, Pop. 4,714
Elbert County SD 3,600/PK-12
50 Laurel Dr 30635 706-213-4000
Abe Plummer, supt. Fax 283-6674
www.elbert.k12.ga.us
Beaverdam ES 400/PK-5
1088 Ruckersville Rd 30635 706-213-4300
Barbara Gailey, prin. Fax 283-1165
Blackwell ES 300/PK-5
373 Campbell St 30635 706-213-4400
Vickie Smith, prin. Fax 283-1162
Doves Creek ES 400/PK-5
1150 Athens Tech Rd 30635 706-213-4600
Connie Spivey, prin. Fax 283-1180
Elbert County MS 800/6-8
1108 Athens Tech Rd 30635 706-213-4200
Paul Garrett, prin. Fax 283-1117
Falling Creek ES 400/PK-5
1019 Falling Creek Dr 30635 706-213-4700
Sandra Guest, prin. Fax 283-8878
Other Schools – See Bowman

Ellaville, Schley, Pop. 1,758
Schley County SD 1,300/PK-12
PO Box 66 31806 229-937-2405
William Johnson, supt. Fax 937-5180
www.schleyk12.org/
Schley County ES 700/PK-5
PO Box 900 31806 229-937-0550
Melody Murray, prin. Fax 937-5318

Ellenwood, Clayton
Clayton County SD
Supt. — See Jonesboro
East Clayton ES 600/PK-5
2750 Forest Pkwy 30294 404-362-3885
Connie Tyler, prin. Fax 362-8895

DeKalb County SD
Supt. — See Decatur
Cedar Grove ES 700/PK-5
2330 River Rd 30294 678-874-3902
Valerie Swinton, prin. Fax 874-3910

Anointed Word Christian S International 100/PK-8
3800 Linecrest Rd 30294 404-241-8200
Chrislyn Davis, admin. Fax 328-9801

Ellerslie, Harris
Harris County SD
Supt. — See Hamilton
Pine Ridge ES 500/PK-4
PO Box 129 31807 706-568-6578
Debbie Korytoski, prin. Fax 562-9576

Ellijay, Gilmer, Pop. 1,519
Gilmer County SD 4,800/PK-12
497 Bobcat Trl 30540 706-276-5000
Randy Parson, supt. Fax 276-5005
www.gilmerschools.com/
Clear Creek MS 600/6-8
1020 Clear Creek Rd, 706-276-5150
David Ueltzen, prin.
Ellijay ES 600/3-5
32 McCutchen St 30540 706-276-5020
Sandy Layman, prin. Fax 276-5022
Ellijay PS 600/PK-2
196 Mccutchen St 30540 706-276-5010
Sandra Davenport, prin. Fax 276-5013
Gilmer MS 1,000/6-8
1860 S Main St 30540 706-276-5030
Jason Kouns, prin. Fax 276-5035
Mountain View ES 600/K-5
350 Calvin Jackson Dr 30540 706-276-5100
Kim Cagle, prin. Fax 276-5102
Oakland ES 300/K-5
8264 Highway 52 E, 706-276-5040
James Parmer, prin. Fax 276-5041

Edwards Christian S 50/K-8
12472 Highway 515 N, 706-635-2644
Del Leeds, prin. Fax 635-2644
North Georgia Christian Academy 100/PK-10
191 Harold Pritchett Rd 30540 706-635-6422
Sharla Reynolds, admin. Fax 635-6425

Emerson, Bartow, Pop. 1,302
Bartow County SD
Supt. — See Cartersville
Emerson ES 400/K-5
54 7th St 30137 770-606-5848
Denise Welker, prin. Fax 606-3847
South Central MS 600/6-8
224 Old Old Alabama Rd SE 30137 770-606-5865
Pat Phillips, prin. Fax 606-3872

Euharlee, Bartow, Pop. 3,859
Bartow County SD
Supt. — See Cartersville
Euharlee ES 800/K-5
1058 Euharlee Rd, 770-606-5900
Walter Gordon, prin. Fax 721-4266

Evans, Columbia, Pop. 13,713
Columbia County SD — 22,900/PK-12
4781 Hereford Farm Rd 30809 — 706-541-0650
Charles Nagle, supt. — Fax 541-2723
www.ccboe.net
Bel Air ES — 500/PK-5
325 N Belair Rd 30809 — 706-868-3698
Dr. Mark Boyd, prin. — Fax 854-5826
Blue Ridge ES — 700/PK-5
550 Blue Ridge Dr 30809 — 706-868-0894
Jeff Collman, prin. — Fax 854-5827
Evans ES — 500/PK-5
628 Gibbs Rd 30809 — 706-863-1202
Scott Weinand, prin. — Fax 854-5812
Evans MS — 900/6-8
4785 Hereford Farm Rd 30809 — 706-863-2275
Michael Johnson, prin. — Fax 854-5810
Greenbrier ES — 600/PK-5
5116 Riverwood Pkwy 30809 — 706-650-6060
Dr. Judy Holton, prin. — Fax 855-3889
Greenbrier MS — 900/6-8
5120 Riverwood Pkwy 30809 — 706-650-6080
Sharon Carson, prin. — Fax 854-5800
Lakeside MS — 800/6-8
527 Blue Ridge Dr 30809 — 706-855-6900
Felicia Turner, prin. — Fax 854-5805
Lewiston ES — 800/PK-5
5426 Hereford Farm Rd 30809 — 706-650-6064
Dr. Mike Doolittle, prin. — Fax 854-5831
River Ridge ES — 700/K-5
4109 Mullikin Rd 30809 — 706-447-1016
Revelle Cox, prin. — Fax 854-5835
Riverside ES — 800/K-5
4431 Hardy Mcmanus Rd 30809 — 706-868-3736
Judy Bonadio, prin. — Fax 854-5834
Riverside MS — 1,000/6-8
1095 Furys Ferry Rd 30809 — 706-868-3712
Chris Segraves, prin. — Fax 854-5824
Other Schools – See Appling, Augusta, Grovetown, Harlem, Martinez

Fairburn, Fulton, Pop. 8,564
Fulton County SD
Supt. — See Atlanta
Bear Creek MS — 1,600/6-8
7415 Herndon Rd 30213 — 770-969-6080
Darron Franklin, prin. — Fax 306-3584
Campbell ES — 1,000/PK-5
91 Elder St 30213 — 770-969-3430
Denine Cadet, prin. — Fax 306-3522
Renaissance ES — 800/PK-5
7250 Hall Rd 30213 — 770-306-4320
Sandra DeShazier, prin. — Fax 306-4327
Renaissance MS — 1,000/6-8
7155 Hall Rd 30213 — 770-306-4330
George Weathers, prin. — Fax 306-4338
West ES — 1,000/PK-5
7040 Rivertown Rd 30213 — 770-969-3460
Tony Wilcher, prin. — Fax 306-3583

Arlington Christian S — 400/K-12
4500 Ridge Rd 30213 — 770-964-9871
Chris King, hdmstr. — Fax 306-3630
Landmark Christian S — 800/PK-12
50 SE Broad St 30213 — 770-306-0647
Matthew Skinner, hdmstr. — Fax 969-6551

Fairmount, Gordon, Pop. 785
Gordon County SD
Supt. — See Calhoun
Fairmount ES — 600/PK-5
130 Peachtree St 30139 — 706-337-5321
Sherry Walraven, prin. — Fax 337-4481

Fayetteville, Fayette, Pop. 14,363
Clayton County SD
Supt. — See Jonesboro
Rivers Edge ES — 1,200/PK-5
205 Northbridge Rd 30215 — 770-460-2340
Alisha Mohr, prin. — Fax 460-2343

Fayette County SD — 22,900/PK-12
PO Box 879 30214 — 770-460-3535
Dr. John DeCotis, supt. — Fax 460-8191
www.fcboe.org
Bennetts Mill MS — 500/6-8
210 Lester Rd 30215 — 770-716-3982
Rae Presley-King, prin. — Fax 716-3983
Cleveland ES — 500/K-5
190 Lester Rd 30215 — 770-716-3905
Jeanie Miller, prin. — Fax 716-3909
Fayette MS — 1,000/6-8
450 Grady Ave 30214 — 770-460-3550
Sharlene Patterson, prin. — Fax 460-3882
Fayetteville IS — 500/3-5
440 Hood Ave 30214 — 770-460-3555
Kim Herron, prin. — Fax 460-3419
Hood Avenue PS — 400/PK-2
490 Hood Ave 30214 — 770-460-3560
Dr. Kiawana Kennedy, prin. — Fax 460-3402
Inman ES — 600/PK-5
677 Inman Rd 30215 — 770-460-3565
Louis Robinson, prin. — Fax 460-3563
Minter ES — 700/K-5
1650 Highway 85 S 30215 — 770-716-3910
Mike Smith, prin. — Fax 716-3914
North Fayette ES — 500/PK-5
609 Kenwood Rd 30214 — 770-460-3570
Jade Bolton, prin. — Fax 460-3581
Peeples ES — 900/K-5
153 Panther Path 30215 — 770-486-2734
Erin Roberson, prin. — Fax 486-2731
Rising Starr MS — 1,100/6-8
183 Panther Path 30215 — 770-486-2721
Len Patton, prin. — Fax 486-2727
Rivers ES — K-5
361 Sandy Creek Rd 30214 — 770-460-3535
Spring Hill ES — 600/K-5
100 Bradford Sq 30215 — 770-460-3432
Randy Hudson, prin. — Fax 460-3433
Whitewater MS — 1,200/6-8
1533 Highway 85 S 30215 — 770-460-3450
Connie Baldwin, prin. — Fax 460-0362
Other Schools – See Brooks, Peachtree City, Tyrone

Counterpane S — 100/PK-12
PO Box 898 30214 — 770-461-2304
Brenda Erickson, prin. — Fax 460-7016
Fayette Montessori S — 100/PK-6
190 Weatherly Dr 30214 — 770-460-6790
Margaret Sisson, dir. — Fax 460-5578
Grace Christian Academy — 200/PK-12
355 McDonough Rd 30214 — 770-461-0137
Brian Fourman, prin. — Fax 461-1190

Fitzgerald, Ben Hill, Pop. 8,920
Ben Hill County SD — 3,300/K-12
509 W Palm St 31750 — 229-409-5500
Dr. John Key, supt. — Fax 409-5513
www.ben-hill.k12.ga.us
Ben Hill County ES — 700/3-5
327 Dewey McGlamry Rd 31750 — 229-409-5586
Tracy McCray, prin. — Fax 409-5590
Ben Hill County MS — 700/6-8
134 JC Hunter Rd 31750 — 229-409-5578
Patti Barwick, prin. — Fax 409-5580
Ben Hill County PS — 900/K-2
221 JC Hunter Rd 31750 — 229-409-5592
Steve Harden, prin. — Fax 409-5595

Flintstone, Walker
Walker County SD
Supt. — See La Fayette
Chattanooga Valley ES — 600/PK-5
3420 Chattanooga Valley Rd 30725 — 706-820-2511
Jennifer Genter, prin. — Fax 820-7921
Chattanooga Valley MS — 600/6-8
847 Allgood Rd 30725 — 706-820-0735
Eugene Ward, prin. — Fax 820-0736

Flowery Branch, Hall, Pop. 2,087
Hall County SD
Supt. — See Gainesville
Chestnut Mountain ES — 500/K-5
4841 Union Church Rd 30542 — 770-967-3121
Sabrina May, prin. — Fax 967-4891
Davis MS — 1,200/6-8
4335 Falcon Pkwy 30542 — 770-965-3020
Eddie Millwood, prin. — Fax 965-3025
Flowery Branch ES — 600/K-5
5544 Radford Rd 30542 — 770-967-6621
Susan Miller, prin. — Fax 967-4880
Martin ES — 700/K-5
4216 Martin Rd 30542 — 770-965-1578
Tamara Seymour, prin. — Fax 965-1668
Spout Springs ES — 900/K-5
6640 Spout Springs Rd 30542 — 770-967-4860
Steve McDaniel, prin. — Fax 967-4883

Folkston, Charlton, Pop. 3,270
Charlton County SD — 1,900/PK-12
500 S 3rd St 31537 — 912-496-2596
Steve McQueen, supt. — Fax 496-2595
www.charlton.k12.ga.us
Bethune ES — 400/PK-2
204 Mary M Bethune Dr 31537 — 912-496-7369
Mike Walker, prin. — Fax 496-4291
Folkston ES — 400/3-6
34574 Okefenokee Dr 31537 — 912-496-2360
Nora Nettles, prin. — Fax 496-3766
Other Schools – See Saint George

Forest Park, Clayton, Pop. 22,201
Clayton County SD
Supt. — See Jonesboro
Babb MS — 900/6-8
5500 Reynolds Rd 30297 — 404-362-3880
Felicia Brown, prin. — Fax 362-4087
Edmonds ES — 500/PK-5
4495 Simpson Rd 30297 — 404-362-3830
Rebecca Harrison, prin. — Fax 608-7573
Forest Park MS — 600/6-8
930 Finley Dr 30297 — 404-362-3840
Jamille Brown, prin. — Fax 362-8899
Fountain ES — 500/PK-5
5215 West St 30297 — 404-362-3875
Dr. Tonya Mahone-Williams, prin. — Fax 362-4083
Hendrix Drive ES — 200/3-5
4475 Hendrix Dr 30297 — 404-362-3835
Nancy Said, prin. — Fax 362-8898
Huie ES — 600/PK-5
1260 Rockcut Rd 30297 — 404-362-3825
Baxter Harper, prin. — Fax 608-7589

Rising SON Academy — 100/PK-5
5880 Old Dixie Hwy 30297 — 404-361-0812
Kathy Bowen, dir. — Fax 631-0422

Forsyth, Monroe, Pop. 4,259
Monroe County SD — 3,900/PK-12
PO Box 1308 31029 — 478-994-2031
Anthony Pack, supt. — Fax 994-3364
www.monroe.k12.ga.us
Hubbard ES — 900/PK-5
558 GA Highway 83 S 31029 — 478-994-7066
Angie Dillon, prin. — Fax 994-7068
Hubbard MS — 400/6-8
500 Highway 83 S 31029 — 478-994-6803
Steve Edwards, prin. — Fax 994-3061
Scott ES — 900/PK-5
70 Thornton Rd 31029 — 478-994-3495
Dr. Richard Bazemore, prin. — Fax 994-2860
Stephens MS — 500/6-8
66 Thornton Rd 31029 — 478-994-6186
Dr. Mike Hickman, prin. — Fax 994-7061

Monroe Academy — 200/PK-12
433 Highway 41 S 31029 — 478-994-5986
Martha Krepps, hdmstr. — Fax 994-1942

Fort Gaines, Clay, Pop. 1,059
Clay County SD — 400/PK-8
PO Box 219, — 229-768-2232
Johnnie Grimsley, supt. — Fax 768-3654
www.clay.k12.ga.us/
Clay County ES — 300/PK-5
200 Hobbs Ln, — 229-768-2234
Michael Johnson, prin. — Fax 768-2363
Clay County MS — 100/6-8
200 Hobbs Ln, — 229-768-2234
Michael Johnson, prin. — Fax 768-2363

Fort Gordon, Richmond, Pop. 9,140
Richmond County SD
Supt. — See Augusta
Freedom Park S — 500/PK-8
345 42nd St Bldg 43400 30905 — 706-796-8428
Rita Bradley, prin. — Fax 796-2265

Fort Oglethorpe, Catoosa, Pop. 8,964
Catoosa County SD
Supt. — See Ringgold
Battlefield ES — 400/3-5
2206 Battlefield Pkwy 30742 — 706-866-9183
Dr. Becky Howard, prin. — Fax 861-6640
Battlefield PS — 500/K-2
2204 Battlefield Pkwy 30742 — 706-861-5778
Dr. Sandy Boyles, prin. — Fax 861-5798

Fortson, Muscogee
Harris County SD
Supt. — See Hamilton
New Mountain Hill ES — 400/PK-4
33 Mountain Hill Rd 31808 — 706-323-1144
Garnett Ray, prin. — Fax 324-0296

Fort Valley, Peach, Pop. 8,197
Peach County SD — 4,200/K-12
523 Vineville St 31030 — 478-825-5933
Dr. Susan Clark, supt. — Fax 825-9970
www.peachschools.org
Fort Valley MS — 500/6-8
712 Peggy Dr 31030 — 478-825-2413
Joy Warren, prin. — Fax 825-1332
Hunt ES — 500/K-2
801 Chamlee Dr 31030 — 478-825-8893
Dr. Stanley Messer, prin. — Fax 825-1071
Hunt ES — 500/3-5
1000 Tulip Dr 31030 — 478-825-5296
Janice Flowers, prin. — Fax 825-1123
Other Schools – See Byron

Franklin, Heard, Pop. 897
Heard County SD — 2,200/PK-12
PO Box 1330 30217 — 706-675-3320
Benjamin Hyatt, supt. — Fax 675-3357
www.heard.k12.ga.us
Centralhatchee ES — 200/PK-5
315 Centralhatchee Pkwy 30217 — 770-854-4002
Carol Thomas, prin. — Fax 854-4124
Heard County ES — 700/PK-5
4647 Pearidge Rd 30217 — 706-675-3687
William Lipham, prin. — Fax 675-0999
Heard County MS — 500/6-8
269 Old Field Rd 30217 — 706-675-9247
Marti Robinson, prin. — Fax 675-9255
Other Schools – See Roopville

Funston, Colquitt, Pop. 426
Colquitt County SD
Supt. — See Moultrie
Funston ES — 400/PK-5
PO Box 40 31753 — 229-941-2626
Ricky Reynolds, prin. — Fax 941-5039

Gainesville, Hall, Pop. 32,444
Forsyth County SD
Supt. — See Cumming
Chestatee ES — 1,000/PK-5
6945 Keith Bridge Rd 30506 — 770-887-2341
Dr. Amy Davis, prin. — Fax 781-2281

Gainesville CSD — 5,700/PK-12
508 Oak St 30501 — 770-536-5275
Dr. Merrianne Dyer, supt. — Fax 287-2004
www.gcssk12.net/
Centennial ES — 800/PK-5
852 Century Pl 30501 — 770-287-2044
Susan Gilliam, prin. — Fax 287-2047
Enota ES — 700/PK-5
1340 Enota Ave NE 30501 — 770-532-7711
Susan Culbreth, prin. — Fax 287-2011
Fair Street ES — 600/PK-5
695 Fair St 30501 — 770-536-5295
William Campbell, prin. — Fax 287-2016
Gainesville ES — 700/PK-5
1145 McEver Rd 30504 — 770-287-1223
Priscilla Collins, prin. — Fax 535-3798
Gainesville MS — 1,200/6-8
715 Woodsmill Rd 30501 — 770-534-4237
Audrey Simmons, prin. — Fax 287-2022
New Holland ES — 600/PK-5
170 Barn St 30501 — 770-536-5275
Jill Goforth, prin. — Fax 718-9935

Hall County SD — 24,800/PK-12
711 Green St NW Ste 100 30501 — 770-534-1080
Will Schofield, supt. — Fax 535-7404
www.hallco.org
Chestatee MS — 900/6-8
2740 Fran Mar Dr 30506 — 770-297-6270
Suzanne Jarrad, prin. — Fax 297-6275
Chicopee Woods ES — 600/K-5
2029 Calvary Church Rd 30507 — 770-536-2057
Janet Adams, prin. — Fax 536-2175
East Hall MS — 900/6-8
4120 E Hall Rd 30507 — 770-531-9457
Kevin Bales, prin. — Fax 531-2327
Jones ES — 500/K-5
50 Sixth St 30504 — 770-534-3939
Hank Ramey, prin. — Fax 531-2346
Lanier ES — 700/K-5
4782 Thompson Bridge Rd 30506 — 770-532-8781
John Wiggins, prin. — Fax 532-3017

Lyman Hall ES 700/K-5
2150 Memorial Park Dr 30504 770-534-7044
Pat Tilson, prin. Fax 531-2321
McEver ES 400/K-5
3265 Montgomery Dr 30504 770-534-7473
Dr. Catherine Rosa, prin. Fax 531-3055
Mount Vernon ES 800/K-5
4844 Jim Hood Rd 30506 770-983-1759
Connie Daniels, prin. Fax 983-1663
Myers ES 700/K-5
2676 Candler Rd 30507 770-536-0814
Beth Hudgins, prin. Fax 531-2323
North Hall MS 800/6-8
4856 Rilla Rd 30506 770-983-9749
Brad Brown, prin. Fax 983-9993
Riverbend ES 400/K-5
1742 Cleveland Hwy 30501 770-534-4141
Dr. Debra Smith, prin. Fax 531-3054
Sardis ES 600/K-5
2805 Sardis Rd 30506 770-532-0104
Jan Hughes, prin. Fax 531-3057
South Hall MS 900/6-8
3215 Poplar Springs Rd 30507 770-532-4416
Paula Stubbs, prin. Fax 531-2348
Sugar Hill ES 700/K-5
3259 Athens Hwy 30507 770-503-1749
Dr. Richard Quarles, prin. Fax 503-9686
Tadmore ES 600/K-5
3278 Gillsville Hwy 30507 770-536-9929
Joseph Gonsalves, prin. Fax 531-2325
Wauka Mountain ES 500/PK-5
5850 Brookton Lula Rd 30506 770-983-3221
Jo Dinnan, prin. Fax 983-1019
White Sulphur ES 600/K-5
2480 Old Cornelia Hwy 30507 770-532-0945
Donald Watson, prin. Fax 531-2324
Other Schools – See Buford, Flowery Branch, Lula, Oakwood

Lakeview Academy 600/PK-12
796 Lakeview Dr 30501 770-532-4383
James Curry Robison, hdmstr. Fax 536-6142
North Georgia Christian S 300/PK-12
1397 Thompson Bridge Rd 30501 770-534-1081
Carol Cox, prin. Fax 534-1025

Garden City, Chatham, Pop. 9,550
Savannah-Chatham County SD
Supt. — See Savannah
Garden City ES 600/PK-5
4037 Kessler Ave 31408 912-395-6820
Dr. Jane Ford-Brocato, prin. Fax 965-6823

Georgetown, Quitman, Pop. 912
Quitman County SD 300/PK-8
PO Box 248, 229-334-4189
William Burns, supt. Fax 334-2109
www.quitman.k12.ga.us/
Quitman County S 300/PK-8
173 Kaigler Rd, 229-334-4298
Martin Wright, prin. Fax 334-4700

Gibson, Glascock, Pop. 741
Glascock County SD 600/PK-12
PO Box 205 30810 706-598-2291
James Holton, supt. Fax 598-2611
www.glascock.k12.ga.us
Glascock County Consolidated S 600/PK-12
1230 Panther Way 30810 706-598-2121
Sarah Garrett, prin. Fax 598-2621

Glennville, Tattnall, Pop. 5,031
Tattnall County SD
Supt. — See Reidsville
Glennville ES 700/PK-5
525 Sylvester Ashford Dr 30427 912-654-3931
Denise Bargeron, prin. Fax 654-4998
Glennville MS 300/6-8
721 E Barnard St 30427 912-654-1467
Lisa Trim, prin. Fax 654-1300

Grantville, Coweta, Pop. 2,407
Coweta County SD
Supt. — See Newnan
Glanton ES 400/PK-5
5725 Highway 29 30220 770-583-2873
Kattie Garrett, prin. Fax 254-2807

Gray, Jones, Pop. 2,109
Jones County SD 5,400/PK-12
125 Stewart Ave 31032 478-986-3032
Jim LeBrun, supt. Fax 986-4412
www.edline.net/pages/Jones_County_BOE
Dames Ferry ES 900/PK-5
545 GA Highway 18 W 31032 478-986-2023
Estelle Jacobs, prin. Fax 986-2027
Gray ES 1,000/PK-5
273 Railroad St 31032 478-986-6295
Cecil Patterson, prin. Fax 986-3911
Gray Station MS 700/6-8
324 GA Highway 18 E 31032 478-986-2090
Johnny Holliday, prin. Fax 986-2099
Other Schools – See Macon

Grayson, Gwinnett, Pop. 1,314
Gwinnett County SD
Supt. — See Suwanee
Bay Creek MS, 821 Cooper Rd 30017 6-8
Dana Pugh, prin. 678-344-7570
Couch MS, 1777 Grayson Hwy 30017 6-8
Devon Williams, prin. 678-407-7272
Grayson ES 1,500/K-5
460 Grayson Pkwy 30017 770-963-7189
Christopher Ray, prin. Fax 682-4151
Starling ES, 1725 Grayson Hwy 30017 K-5
Donna Ledford, prin. 678-344-6100
Trip ES K-5
841 Cooper Rd 30017 678-639-3850
Marci Resnick, prin. Fax 639-3870

Garden of Discovery Montessori S 100/PK-6
420 Pine Grove Ave 30017 678-377-5777
Stephanie Michielsen, admin. Fax 339-1587

Harbour Oaks Montessori S 200/PK-9
1741 Athens Hwy 30017 770-979-8900
Anna Robichaux, prin. Fax 979-5949

Graysville, Catoosa, Pop. 500
Catoosa County SD
Supt. — See Ringgold
Graysville ES 500/K-5
PO Box 10 30726 706-937-3147
Paula Crosby, prin. Fax 937-2812

Greensboro, Greene, Pop. 3,303
Greene County SD 2,000/PK-12
101 E Third St 30642 706-453-7688
Barbara Pulliam, supt. Fax 454-1058
www.greene.k12.ga.us
Carson MS 500/6-8
1010 S Main St 30642 706-453-3308
Dr. Zheadric Barbra, prin. Fax 453-4674
Greensboro ES 600/K-5
1441 Martin Luther King Jr 30642 706-453-2214
Dr. Joan Antone, prin. Fax 453-3316
Other Schools – See Union Point

Greenville, Meriwether, Pop. 938
Meriwether County SD 3,700/PK-12
PO Box 70 30222 706-672-4297
Carol Lane, supt. Fax 672-1618
www.meriwether.k12.ga.us
Greenville MS 400/6-8
PO Box 190 30222 706-672-3115
Robert Johnson, prin. Fax 672-3119
Other Schools – See Luthersville, Manchester, Woodbury

Griffin, Spalding, Pop. 23,286
Griffin-Spalding County SD 10,700/PK-12
PO Box N 30224 770-229-3700
Dr. Curtis Jones, supt. Fax 229-3708
www.spalding.k12.ga.us
Anne Street ES 500/PK-5
802 Anne St 30224 770-229-3746
Evelyn Jones, prin. Fax 467-4636
Atkinson ES 500/PK-5
307 Atkinson Dr 30223 770-229-3715
Aveory Allen, prin. Fax 229-3713
Beaverbrook ES 500/PK-5
251 Birdie Rd 30223 770-229-3750
Ken Bozeman, prin. Fax 467-5006
Carver Road MS 500/6-8
2185 Carver Rd 30224 770-229-3739
Eclan David, prin. Fax 229-3712
Cowan Road ES 700/PK-5
1233 Cowan Rd 30223 770-229-3790
Natalie Wood, prin. Fax 229-3749
Cowan Road MS 700/6-8
1185 Cowan Rd 30223 770-229-3722
Rachelle Holloway, prin. Fax 227-8583
Crescent Road ES 400/PK-5
201 Crescent Rd 30224 770-229-3719
Beth Gaff, prin. Fax 467-4633
Jackson Road ES 500/PK-5
1233 Jackson Rd 30223 770-229-3717
Sara Jones, prin. Fax 229-3717
Jordan Hill Road ES 400/PK-5
75 Jordan Hill Rd 30223 770-229-3777
Ellen Lee, prin. Fax 229-1929
Kennedy Road MS 600/6-8
280 Kennedy Rd 30223 770-229-3760
Brenda Ford, prin. Fax 467-4626
Moore ES 400/PK-5
201 Cabin Creek Dr 30223 770-229-3756
Dr. Martha Taylor, prin. Fax 229-3785
Moreland Road ES 500/PK-5
455 Moreland Rd 30224 770-229-3755
Stan Mangham, prin. Fax 229-4022
Orrs ES 600/PK-5
1553 Flynt St 30223 770-229-3743
Dexter Martin, prin. Fax 467-4629
Rehoboth Road MS 700/6-8
1500 Rehoboth Rd 30224 770-229-3727
Lindy Pruitt, prin. Fax 229-3770

Griffin Christian Academy 300/PK-6
2000 W McIntosh Rd 30223 770-228-2711
Michael Pendleton, prin. Fax 228-2216

Grovetown, Columbia, Pop. 7,483
Columbia County SD
Supt. — See Evans
Brookwood ES 600/PK-5
455 S Old Belair Rd 30813 706-855-7538
Brenda Jones, prin. Fax 854-5828
Cedar Ridge ES 800/PK-5
1000 Trudeau Trl 30813 706-447-2100
Dr. Sarah Walls, prin. Fax 854-5839
Columbia MS 700/6-8
6000 Columbia Rd 30813 706-541-1252
Dr. Donna Anderson, prin. Fax 854-5820
Euchee Creek ES 600/PK-5
795 Louisville Rd 30813 706-556-4000
Wanda Golosky, prin. Fax 854-5829
Grovetown ES 800/PK-5
300 Ford Ave 30813 706-863-0800
Bob Boyd, prin. Fax 854-5830
Grovetown MS 600/6-8
5463 Harlem Grovetown Rd 30813 706-855-2514
Tom Smallwood, prin. Fax 854-5822

New Hope Christian S 100/PK-8
715 S Old Belair Rd 30813 706-868-7249
Wayne Gaines, admin. Fax 650-3107

Guyton, Effingham, Pop. 1,707
Effingham County SD
Supt. — See Springfield
Guyton ES 800/PK-5
4752 GA Highway 17 S 31312 912-772-3384
H. Beacham, prin. Fax 772-5523
Marlow ES 800/PK-5
5160 GA Highway 17 S 31312 912-728-3262
Betty Ferguson, prin. Fax 728-4477

Marlow Learning Center PK-PK
4752 GA Highway 17 S 31312 912-728-9080
Fax 728-9084
Sand Hill ES 500/PK-5
199 Stagecoach Ave 31312 912-728-5112
Kristin Richards, prin. Fax 728-5125
South Effingham ES 600/PK-5
767 Kolic Helmey Rd 31312 912-728-3801
Cheryl Christain, prin. Fax 728-4487
South Effingham MS 900/6-8
1200 Noel C Conaway Rd 31312 912-728-7500
Dr. Mark Winters, prin. Fax 728-7508

Hahira, Lowndes, Pop. 1,915
Lowndes County SD
Supt. — See Valdosta
Hahira ES 700/PK-5
350 Claudia Dr 31632 229-794-2626
Suzanne Tanner, prin. Fax 794-1849
Hahira MS 1,300/6-8
101 S Nelson St 31632 229-794-2838
Kip McLeod, prin. Fax 794-3564

Valwood S 400/PK-12
4380 Old US 41 N 31632 229-242-8491
Cobb Atkinson, hdmstr. Fax 245-7894

Hamilton, Harris, Pop. 527
Harris County SD 4,200/PK-12
132 Barnes Mill Rd 31811 706-628-4206
Craig Dowling, supt. Fax 628-5609
www.harris.k12.ga.us
Harris County - Carver MS 800/7-8
184 S College St 31811 706-628-4951
Stacey Carlisle, prin. Fax 628-5737
Park ES 500/PK-4
13185 US Highway 27 N 31811 706-628-4997
Mark Gilreath, prin. Fax 628-5413
Other Schools – See Cataula, Ellerslie, Fortson

Hampton, Henry, Pop. 4,743
Clayton County SD
Supt. — See Jonesboro
Hawthorne ES 800/K-5
10750 English Rd 30228 770-472-7669
Wynton Walker, prin. Fax 472-7663
Kemp ES 700/3-5
10990 Folsom Rd 30228 770-473-2870
Janice Sills, prin. Fax 473-5058
Kemp PS 700/K-2
1090 McDonough Rd 30228 678-610-4300
Lisa Hightower, prin. Fax 610-4321
Lovejoy MS 1,300/6-8
1588 Lovejoy Rd 30228 770-473-2933
Keith Colbert, prin. Fax 603-5777

Henry County SD
Supt. — See Mc Donough
Dutchtown ES 500/K-5
159 Mitchell Rd 30228 770-471-0844
Dr. Winnie Johnson, prin. Fax 471-8066
Dutchtown MS 1,200/6-8
155 Mitchell Rd 30228 770-515-7500
Susan Downs, prin. Fax 515-7505
Hampton ES 600/PK-5
10 Central Ave 30228 770-946-4345
Debbie Collins, prin. Fax 946-3472
Mt. Carmel ES 700/K-5
2450 Mount Carmel Rd 30228 770-897-9799
Martin Gore, prin. Fax 897-9806

Bible Baptist Christian S 200/PK-12
2780 Mount Carmel Rd 30228 770-946-4700
Timothy Lee, prin. Fax 946-4715

Hapeville, Fulton, Pop. 6,085
Fulton County SD
Supt. — See Atlanta
Hapeville ES 700/PK-5
3440 N Fulton Ave 30354 404-669-8220
Juanita Nelson, prin. Fax 669-8226

St. John the Evangelist S 300/PK-8
240 Arnold St 30354 404-767-4312
Karen Votgner, prin. Fax 767-0359

Harlem, Columbia, Pop. 1,818
Columbia County SD
Supt. — See Evans
Harlem MS 400/6-8
375 W Forrest St 30814 706-556-5990
Carla Shelton, prin. Fax 854-5816
North Harlem ES 600/PK-5
525 S Fairview Dr 30814 706-556-5995
Kirk Wright, prin. Fax 854-5818

Hartsfield, Colquitt
Colquitt County SD
Supt. — See Moultrie
Hamilton ES 300/PK-5
5110 GA Highway 111 31756 229-941-5594
Brenda DeMott, prin. Fax 941-5818

Hartwell, Hart, Pop. 4,288
Hart County SD 3,600/K-12
PO Box 696 30643 706-376-5141
Dr. David Hicks, supt. Fax 376-7046
www.hart.k12.ga.us
Hart County MS 800/6-8
176 Powell Rd 30643 706-376-5431
Dr. Veronica Johnson, prin. Fax 376-2207
Hartwell ES 500/K-5
147 S College Ave 30643 706-376-4425
Dana White, prin. Fax 856-7317
South Hart ES 600/K-5
121 EM Dairy Rd 30643 706-856-7383
Beth Hendrick, prin. Fax 856-7386
Other Schools – See Bowersville

Hawkinsville, Pulaski, Pop. 4,212
Pulaski County SD 1,600/PK-12
47 McCormick Ave 31036 478-783-7200
Janis Sparrow, supt. Fax 783-7204
www.pulaski.k12.ga.us
L.I.T.T.L.E. Children Growing Preschool PK-PK
Academy St 31036 478-783-7205
Natasha Kilgore, dir. Fax 783-7207
Pulaski County ES 700/K-5
280 Broad St 31036 478-783-7275
Dale Garnto, prin. Fax 783-4918
Pulaski County MS 300/6-8
8 Red Devil Dr 31036 478-892-7215
Larry Faulk, prin. Fax 783-7297

Hazlehurst, Jeff Davis, Pop. 3,729
Jeff Davis County SD 2,700/K-12
PO Box 1780 31539 912-375-6700
Dr. Lula Mae Perry, supt. Fax 375-6703
www.jeff-davis.k12.ga.us
Davis ES 600/3-5
81 Pat Dixon Rd 31539 912-375-6730
Chuck Crosby, prin. Fax 375-7604
Davis MS 600/6-8
96 W Jefferson St 31539 912-375-6750
David Stapleton, prin. Fax 375-6756
Davis PS 700/K-2
71 Burketts Ferry Rd 31539 912-375-6720
Julia Swanson, prin. Fax 375-0820

Hephzibah, Richmond, Pop. 4,210
Richmond County SD
Supt. — See Augusta
Deer Chase ES 600/PK-5
1780 Deer Chase Ln 30815 706-772-6240
Rachel McRae, prin. Fax 772-6244
Diamond Lakes ES 500/PK-5
4153 Windsor Spring Rd 30815 706-771-2881
Glenda Collingsworth, prin. Fax 771-2885
Foreman ES 400/PK-5
2413 Willis Foreman Rd 30815 706-592-3991
Dorothy Beck, prin. Fax 592-3706
Hephzibah ES 500/PK-5
2542 GA Highway 88 30815 706-592-4561
Dr. Mary Ellison, prin. Fax 592-3703
Hephzibah MS 900/6-8
PO Box 70 30815 706-592-4534
Dr. Deborah Shepherd, prin. Fax 592-3979
Jamestown ES 400/PK-5
3637 Hiers Blvd 30815 706-796-4760
Dr. Marion Furr, prin. Fax 796-4703
McBean ES 500/PK-5
1165 Hephzibah McBean Rd 30815 706-592-3723
Dr. Janina Dallas, prin. Fax 592-3729
Morgan Road MS 700/6-8
3635 Hiers Blvd 30815 706-796-4992
Dr. LaMonica Lewis, prin. Fax 560-3947
Spirit Creek MS 900/6-8
115 Dolphin Way 30815 706-592-3987
Mary Braswell, prin. Fax 592-3999

Hiawassee, Towns, Pop. 844
Towns County SD 1,200/PK-12
67 Lakeview Cir Ste C 30546 706-896-2279
Dr. Richard Behrens, supt. Fax 896-2632
www.towns.k12.ga.us
Towns County ES 600/PK-5
1150 Konahetah Rd 30546 706-896-4131
Donald Dermody, prin. Fax 896-9872
Towns County MS 300/6-8
1400 Highway 76 E 30546 706-896-4131
Dr. Marian Sumner, prin. Fax 896-6628

Hinesville, Liberty, Pop. 28,615
Liberty County SD 11,000/PK-12
200 Bradwell St 31313 912-876-2161
Dr. Judy Scherer, supt. Fax 368-6201
www.liberty.k12.ga.us/
Bacon ES 500/K-5
100 Deen St 31313 912-876-3959
Dr. James Johnson, prin. Fax 876-3012
Frasier MS 800/6-8
910 Long Frasier Dr 31313 912-877-5367
Tom Alexander, prin. Fax 877-3291
Gwinnett ES 1,000/PK-5
635 Taylor Rd 31313 912-876-0146
Dr. LaVerne Halliburton, prin. Fax 876-0256
Hall ES 500/K-5
1396 Shaw Rd 31313 912-368-3348
Claire Blanchard, prin. Fax 368-3402
Long ES 600/K-5
920 Long Frasier Dr 31313 912-368-3595
Scott Carrier, prin. Fax 368-3512
Martin ES 600/K-5
1000 Joseph Martin Rd 31313 912-368-3114
Sue Tolley, prin. Fax 368-5449
Pafford ES 600/K-5
2550 15th St 31313 912-877-4188
Dorothy Cottom, prin. Fax 877-5249
Pre-K Program PK-PK
206 Bradwell St 31313 912-876-0773
Dr. Shelby Bush, prin. Fax 876-6966
Snelson Golden MS 1,000/6-8
465 Coates Rd 31313 912-877-3112
Dr. Chris Garretson, prin. Fax 368-5342
Taylors Creek ES 700/K-5
378 Airport Rd 31313 912-369-0378
Dr. Debbie Rodriguez, prin. Fax 369-0377
Other Schools – See Midway

Hiram, Paulding, Pop. 1,762
Paulding County SD
Supt. — See Dallas
Hiram ES 600/PK-5
200 Seaboard Ave 30141 770-443-3392
Paul Wilder, prin. Fax 943-0636
McGarity ES 700/PK-5
262 Rakestraw Mill Rd 30141 770-445-9007
Barbara Cook, prin. Fax 445-6691
Panter ES 600/K-5
190 Panter School Rd 30141 770-443-4303
Priscilla Smith, prin. Fax 222-9775
Ritch ES 600/PK-5
140 Bethel Church Rd 30141 770-443-4269
Deryl Dennis, prin. Fax 920-7022

Grace Baptist Christian S 500/PK-12
5790 Powder Springs/Dallas 30141 770-222-3330
Jeremiah Boyle, admin. Fax 222-3321

Hoboken, Brantley, Pop. 512
Brantley County SD
Supt. — See Nahunta
Hoboken ES 600/PK-6
224 Church St N 31542 912-458-2135
Kim Morgan, prin. Fax 458-2133

Hogansville, Troup, Pop. 2,823
Troup County SD
Supt. — See La Grange
Hogansville ES 400/PK-5
611 E Main St 30230 706-812-7990
Bret Bryant, prin. Fax 812-7996

Homer, Banks, Pop. 1,085
Banks County SD 2,700/PK-12
102 Highway 51 S 30547 706-677-2224
Christopher Erwin, supt. Fax 677-2223
www.banks.k12.ga.us
Banks County ES 600/3-5
180 Highway 51 S 30547 706-677-2308
Jan Bertrang, prin. Fax 677-4346
Banks County MS 600/6-8
712 Thompson St 30547 706-677-2277
Matthew Cooper, prin. Fax 677-5227
Banks County PS 700/PK-2
266 Highway 51 S 30547 706-677-2355
Janice Reiselt, prin. Fax 677-4797

Homerville, Clinch, Pop. 2,811
Clinch County SD 1,300/K-12
46 S College St 31634 912-487-5321
Dr. Gayle Hughes, supt. Fax 487-5068
www.clinchcounty.com/
Clinch County ES 400/4-7
575 Woodlake Dr 31634 912-487-5385
Dr. Randy Jones, prin. Fax 487-1732
Clinch County PS 400/K-3
575 Woodlake Dr 31634 912-487-5385
Nancy Mikell, prin. Fax 487-1732

Hoschton, Jackson, Pop. 1,455
Gwinnett County SD
Supt. — See Suwanee
Duncan Creek ES 1,600/K-5
4500 Braselton Hwy 30548 678-714-5800
Chris Emsley, prin. Fax 714-5804
Osborne MS 2,000/6-8
4404 Braselton Hwy 30548 770-904-5400
John Campbell, prin. Fax 904-5408

Jackson County SD
Supt. — See Jefferson
West Jackson IS 600/3-5
391 E Jefferson St 30548 706-654-2044
Diane Carr, prin. Fax 824-9911

Hull, Madison, Pop. 163
Madison County SD
Supt. — See Danielsville
Hull-Sanford ES 500/K-5
9193 Fortson Store Rd 30646 706-353-7888
Cathy Gruetter, prin. Fax 546-0303

Ila, Madison, Pop. 328
Madison County SD
Supt. — See Danielsville
Ila ES 400/K-5
PO Box 48 30647 706-789-3445
Lynne Jeffers, prin. Fax 789-2528

Irwinton, Wilkinson, Pop. 584
Wilkinson County SD 1,700/PK-12
PO Box 206 31042 478-946-5521
Aaron Geter, supt. Fax 946-3275
www.wilkinson.k12.ga.us/
Wilkinson County ES 400/3-5
PO Box 570 31042 478-946-5527
Dr. Paul Smith, prin. Fax 946-7153
Wilkinson County MS 300/6-8
PO Box 527 31042 478-946-2541
Ginger Jackson, prin. Fax 946-8981
Wilkinson County PS 500/PK-2
PO Box 570 31042 478-946-2161
Dr. Paul Smith, prin. Fax 946-3678

Jackson, Butts, Pop. 4,358
Butts County SD 3,500/K-12
181 N Mulberry St 30233 770-504-2300
Lynda White, supt. Fax 504-2305
www.butts.k12.ga.us
Daughtry ES 500/K-5
150 Shiloh Rd 30233 770-504-2356
Joyce Rowe, prin. Fax 504-2474
Henderson MS 800/6-8
494 George Tate Dr 30233 770-504-2310
Jay Homan, prin. Fax 504-2315
Jackson ES 600/K-5
218 Woodland Way 30233 770-504-2320
Sharon Ohonba, prin. Fax 504-2324
North Mulberry Academy 600/K-5
820 N Mulberry St 30233 770-504-2330
Keith Benton, prin. Fax 504-2333
Stark ES K-5
209 Stark Rd 30233 770-775-9470
Dr. Melinda Ellis, prin. Fax 775-9478

Jasper, Pickens, Pop. 2,837
Pickens County SD 4,300/K-12
159 Stegall Dr 30143 706-253-1700
Michael Ballew, supt. Fax 253-1705
www.pickens.k12.ga.us/
Harmony ES 600/K-5
550 Harmony School Rd 30143 706-253-1840
Sherry Mullins, prin. Fax 253-1845
Hill City ES 600/K-5
600 Hill Cir 30143 706-253-1880
Carlton Wilson, prin. Fax 253-1885
Jasper ES 500/K-5
158 Stegall Dr 30143 706-253-1730
Nonnie Weeks, prin. Fax 253-1735
Jasper MS 500/6-8
339 W Church St 30143 706-253-1760
Neil Howell, prin. Fax 253-1765
Pickens County MS 500/6-8
1802 Refuge Rd 30143 706-253-1830
Chris LeMieux, prin. Fax 253-1835
Other Schools – See Tate

Jasper SDA S 50/1-8
600 Burnt Mountain Rd 30143 706-253-2782

Jefferson, Jackson, Pop. 5,599
Jackson County SD 7,900/PK-12
1660 Winder Hwy 30549 706-367-5151
Dr. Shannon Adams, supt. Fax 367-9457
www.jackson.k12.ga.us
Gum Springs ES PK-5
1660 Winder Hwy 30549 706-367-5151
Alisa Hanley, prin. Fax 654-1255
West Jackson MS 900/6-8
400 Gum Springs Church Rd 30549 706-654-2775
Rise Hawley, prin. Fax 824-1969
Other Schools – See Athens, Braselton, Commerce, Hoschton, Maysville, Nicholson, Talmo

Jefferson CSD 2,400/PK-12
575 Washington St 30549 706-367-2880
Dr. John Jackson, supt. Fax 367-2291
www.jeffcityschools.org/
Jefferson ES 1,200/PK-5
415 Hoschton St 30549 706-367-8242
Diane Oliver, prin. Fax 367-5405
Jefferson MS 600/6-8
100 Dragon Dr 30549 706-367-2882
Howard McGlennen, prin. Fax 367-5207

Jeffersonville, Twiggs, Pop. 1,219
Twiggs County SD 1,200/PK-12
PO Box 232 31044 478-945-3127
Dr. Carol Brown, supt. Fax 945-3078
www.twiggs.k12.ga.us
Jeffersonville ES 400/PK-4
675 Bullard Rd 31044 478-945-3114
Dr. Brenda Scruggs, prin. Fax 945-3228
Twiggs County MS 400/5-8
375 Watson Dr 31044 478-945-3113
Lindsey Napier, prin. Fax 945-3140

Twiggs Academy 100/PK-12
961 Hamlin Floyd Rd 31044 478-945-3175

Jesup, Wayne, Pop. 9,851
Wayne County SD 5,200/PK-12
555 Sunset Blvd 31545 912-427-1000
Dr. Morris Leis, supt. Fax 427-1004
www.wayne.k12.ga.us
Bacon ES 600/K-5
1425 W Orange St 31545 912-427-1077
Kathy Carter, prin. Fax 427-1079
Jesup ES 600/K-5
642 E Plum St 31546 912-427-1033
Brenda Edenfield, prin. Fax 427-1037
Puckett MS 600/6-8
475 Durrence Rd 31545 912-427-1061
Pam Shuman, prin. Fax 427-1069
Ritch Preschool PK-PK
420 Cedar St 31546 912-427-1022
Raeghan Given, prin. Fax 427-1024
Smith ES 600/K-5
710 W Pine St 31545 912-427-1044
Roger Lewis, prin. Fax 427-1043
Williams MS 600/6-8
1175 S US Highway 301 31546 912-427-1025
James Burgess, prin. Fax 427-1032
Other Schools – See Odum, Screven

Johns Creek, Fulton

Mt. Pisgah Christian S 700/PK-12
9820 Nesbit Ferry Rd, 678-336-3000
Scott Barron, hdmstr. Fax 336-3399

Jonesboro, Clayton, Pop. 3,922
Clayton County SD 51,500/PK-12
1058 5th Ave 30236 770-473-2700
John Thompson Ph.D., supt. Fax 473-2706
www.clayton.k12.ga.us/
Arnold ES 500/K-5
216 Stockbridge Rd 30236 770-473-2800
Faith Duncan, prin. Fax 473-5057
Brown ES 800/PK-5
9771 Poston Rd 30238 770-473-2785
Jocelyn Wright, prin. Fax 603-5799
Callaway ES 900/PK-5
120 Oriole Dr 30238 678-479-2600
Marcus Fuller, prin. Fax 479-2613
Jackson ES 900/PK-5
7711 Mount Zion Blvd 30236 678-610-4401
Dr. Donna Jackson, prin. Fax 610-4422
Jonesboro MS 900/6-8
1308 Arnold St 30236 678-610-4331
Freda Givens, prin. Fax 610-4347
Kendrick MS 900/6-8
7971 Kendrick Rd 30238 770-472-8400
Steve Hughes, prin. Fax 472-8413
Kilpatrick ES 600/PK-5
7534 Tara Rd 30236 770-473-2790
Dr. Donna Vining, prin. Fax 603-5198
Lee Street ES 600/PK-5
178 Lee St 30236 770-473-2815
Marcy Perry, prin. Fax 603-5771
Mt. Zion ES 500/3-5
2984 Mount Zion Rd 30236 770-968-2935
Charles Wilkerson, prin. Fax 968-2939

Mt. Zion PS PK-2
2920 Mount Zion Rd 30236 770-473-2700
Denise Thompson, prin.
Mundy's Mill MS 1,000/6-8
1251 Mundys Mill Rd 30238 770-473-2880
Nash Alexander, prin. Fax 603-5779
Pointe South MS 1,000/6-8
8495 Thomas Rd 30238 770-473-2890
Dean Lillard, prin. Fax 477-4603
Roberts MS 800/6-8
1905 Walt Stephens Rd 30236 678-479-0100
Charmine Johnson, prin. Fax 479-0114
Suder ES 800/PK-5
1400 Lake Jodeco Rd 30236 770-473-2820
Ernestine Hyche, prin. Fax 603-5197
Swint ES 600/K-5
500 Highway 138 W 30238 770-473-2780
Fax 603-5778
Other Schools – See College Park, Conley, Ellenwood, Fayetteville, Forest Park, Hampton, Lake City, Morrow, Rex, Riverdale

---

Atlanta Adventist International S K-8
9940 Dixon Industrial Blvd 30236 678-361-2912
DFMI Christian Academy 50/1-9
9800 Tara Blvd 30236 770-210-9717
Joyce Clarke, admin. Fax 603-9690
HOPE Christian Academy 100/PK-12
455 Highway 138 W Ste H 30238 770-472-9957
Arlecia Taylor, admin. Fax 473-7765
Mt. Zion Christian Academy 400/PK-12
7102 Mount Zion Blvd 30236 770-478-9842
Robert Wilson, admin. Fax 478-4817

Kathleen, Houston
Houston County SD
Supt. — See Perry
Arthur ES 800/PK-5
2500 GA Highway 127 31047 478-988-6170
Jolie Hardin, prin. Fax 988-6178
Mossy Creek MS 600/6-8
200 Danny Carpenter Dr 31047 478-988-6171
Paige Busbee, prin. Fax 218-7538

Kennesaw, Cobb, Pop. 30,522
Cobb County SD
Supt. — See Marietta
Awtrey MS 800/6-8
3601 Nowlin Rd NW 30144 770-975-6615
Jeffrey Crawford, prin. Fax 975-6617
Big Shanty ES 800/PK-5
1575 Ben King Rd NW 30144 678-594-8023
Lynne Hutnik, prin. Fax 594-8026
Bullard ES 1,200/K-5
3656 Old Stilesboro Rd NW 30152 678-594-8720
Sharon Hardin, prin. Fax 594-8727
Chalker ES 900/K-5
325 N Booth Rd NW 30144 678-494-7621
Dr. Carla Jones, prin. Fax 494-7623
Hayes ES 1,100/PK-5
1501 Kennesaw Due West Rd 30152 678-594-8127
David Pearce, prin. Fax 594-8129
Kennesaw ES 900/PK-5
3155 Jiles Rd NW 30144 678-594-8172
Dr. Kathie Elliott, prin. Fax 594-8174
Lewis ES 1,100/PK-5
4179 Jim Owens Rd NW 30152 770-975-6673
Kristi Kee, prin. Fax 975-6675
Lost Mountain MS 1,200/6-8
700 Old Mountain Rd NW 30152 678-594-8224
Dr. Terry Poor, prin. Fax 594-8226
McClure MS 1,000/6-8
3660 Old Stilesboro Rd NW 30152 678-331-8131
Susan Wing, prin. Fax 331-8132
Palmer MS 1,200/6-8
690 N Booth Rd NW 30144 770-591-5020
Geraldine Ray, prin. Fax 591-5032
Pine Mountain MS 800/6-8
2720 Pine Mountain Cir NW 30152 678-594-8252
Lisa Jackson, prin. Fax 594-8254

First Baptist Christian S 200/PK-5
2958 N Main St NW 30144 770-422-3254
Kim Dahnke, prin. Fax 427-2332
Mount Paran Christian S 1,200/PK-12
1275 Stanley Rd NW 30152 770-578-0182
Dr. David Tilley, hdmstr. Fax 977-9284
North Cobb Christian S 1,000/PK-12
4500 Lakeview Dr NW 30144 770-975-0252
Todd Clingman, hdmstr. Fax 975-8446
St. Catherine of Siena S 200/PK-8
1618 Ben King Rd NW 30144 770-419-8601
Sr. Mary Jacinta, prin. Fax 626-0000
Shiloh Hills Christian S 400/K-12
260 Hawkins Store Rd NE 30144 770-926-7729
John Ward, admin. Fax 926-3762

Kingsland, Camden, Pop. 12,063
Camden County SD 9,700/PK-12
311 S East St 31548 912-729-5687
Dr. William Hardin, supt. Fax 729-1489
www.camden.k12.ga.us/
Camden MS 1,200/6-8
1300 Middle School Rd 31548 912-729-3113
Mark Durham, prin. Fax 729-7489
Harris ES 500/PK-5
1100 The Lakes Blvd 31548 912-729-2940
Dr. Joey Goble, prin. Fax 729-2223
Kingsland ES 500/PK-5
900 W King Ave 31548 912-729-5246
Charles Curry, prin. Fax 729-8431
Rainer ES 600/PK-5
850 May Creek Dr 31548 912-729-9071
Dr. Joseph LaBelle, prin. Fax 576-8991
Other Schools – See Saint Marys, Woodbine

Kingston, Bartow, Pop. 668
Bartow County SD
Supt. — See Cartersville
Kingston ES 600/K-5
240 Hardin Bridge Rd 30145 770-606-5850
Donald Rucker, prin. Fax 336-5591

Woodland MS at Euharlee 1,000/6-8
1061 Euharlee Rd 30145 770-606-5871
Lamar Barnes, prin. Fax 606-2092

La Fayette, Walker, Pop. 6,753
Walker County SD 9,300/PK-12
201 S Duke St 30728 706-638-1240
Melissa Mathis, supt. Fax 638-7827
www.walkerschools.org
Gilbert ES 500/PK-5
87 S Burnt Mill Rd 30728 706-638-2432
Brad Hayes, prin. Fax 638-0122
La Fayette MS 900/6-8
419 Roadrunner Blvd 30728 706-638-6440
Mike Culberson, prin. Fax 638-7616
Naomi ES 500/PK-5
4038 E Highway 136 30728 706-638-2443
John Parker, prin. Fax 638-2446
North LaFayette ES 600/PK-5
610 N Duke St 30728 706-638-1869
Kim Cardwell, prin. Fax 638-7046
Other Schools – See Chickamauga, Flintstone, Lookout Mountain, Rock Spring, Rossville

La Grange, Troup, Pop. 26,424
Troup County SD 12,300/PK-12
100 N Davis Rd Bldg C 30241 706-812-7900
Dr. Edwin Smith, supt. Fax 812-7904
www.troup.org/
Callaway ES PK-5
2200 Hammett Rd, 706-845-2059
Sequita Freeman, prin. Fax 812-2295
Callaway MS 600/6-8
2244 Hammett Rd, 706-845-2080
Tina Johnson, prin. Fax 845-2081
Cannon Street ES 400/PK-5
115 E Cannon St, 706-883-1540
Candace McGhee, prin. Fax 883-1543
Franklin Forest ES 500/PK-5
1 Scholar Ln, 706-845-7556
Carol Montgomery, prin. Fax 845-7572
Gardner-Newman MS 1,000/6-8
101 Shannon Dr, 706-883-1535
Ernest Ward, prin. Fax 883-1562
Hand ES 400/PK-5
641 Country Club Rd, 706-883-1580
Jack Morman, prin. Fax 883-1582
Hillcrest ES 400/PK-5
3116 New Franklin Rd, 706-812-7940
Pam Doig, prin. Fax 812-7942
Kight Magnet S 500/PK-5
80 N Kight Dr, 706-812-7943
Anne Cook, prin. Fax 812-7945
Long Cane ES 500/PK-5
238 Long Cane Rd, 706-812-7948
Patty Lee, prin. Fax 812-7950
Long Cane MS 1,100/6-8
326 Long Cane Rd, 706-845-2085
Chip Giles, prin. Fax 845-2086
Mountville ES 500/PK-5
4117 Greenville Rd, 706-812-7951
Jan Franks, prin. Fax 812-7953
Rosemont ES 400/PK-5
4679 Hamilton Rd, 706-812-7954
Natalie Givins, prin. Fax 812-7956
Unity ES 400/PK-5
525 Park Ave, 706-883-1555
Micki Wallace, prin. Fax 883-1565
Weathersbee ES 400/PK-5
1200 Forrest Ave, 706-883-1570
Dr. Lorraine Jackson, prin. Fax 883-1573
West Side Magnet S 500/3-8
301 Forrest Ave, 706-883-1550
Dr. Cynthia McCloud, prin. Fax 883-1563
Whitesville Road ES 500/PK-5
1700 Whitesville Rd, 706-812-7968
Gretta Wright, prin. Fax 812-7970
Other Schools – See Hogansville, West Point

Lafayette Christian S 200/PK-12
1904 Hamilton Rd, 706-884-6684
John Cipolla, hdmstr. Fax 882-2515
LaGrange Academy 300/K-12
1501 Vernon Rd, 706-882-8097
Matthew Walsh, hdmstr. Fax 882-8640
Lagrange SDA S 50/K-8
PO Box 628, 706-884-8572
St. Marks K 100/PK-K
207 N Greenwood St, 706-884-1568
Fax 884-8801

Lake City, Clayton, Pop. 2,776
Clayton County SD
Supt. — See Jonesboro
Lake City ES 500/K-5
5354 Phillips Dr 30260 404-362-3855
Kelly Veal, prin. Fax 362-8897

Lakeland, Lanier, Pop. 2,769
Lanier County SD 1,600/PK-12
247 S Highway 221 31635 229-482-3966
Dr. Keith Humphrey, supt. Fax 482-3020
www.lanier.k12.ga.us/
Lanier County ES 800/PK-5
242 S Valdosta Rd 31635 229-482-3580
Reada Hamm, prin. Fax 482-8339
Lanier County MS 300/6-8
325 W Patten Ave 31635 229-482-8247
Gene Culpepper, prin. Fax 482-3643

Lakeland Adventist S 50/1-8
842 W Thigpen Ave 31635 229-482-2418

Lake Park, Lowndes, Pop. 560
Lowndes County SD
Supt. — See Valdosta
Lake Park ES 600/PK-5
604 W Marion Ave 31636 229-559-5153
Cathie Felix, prin. Fax 559-3117

Lavonia, Franklin, Pop. 1,982
Franklin County SD
Supt. — See Carnesville
Lavonia ES 400/K-5
818 Hartwell Rd 30553 706-356-8209
Brad Roberts, prin. Fax 356-2966

Lawrenceville, Gwinnett, Pop. 28,393
Gwinnett County SD
Supt. — See Suwanee
Alford ES 1,000/K-5
2625 Lawrenceville Hwy 30044 678-924-5300
Monica Batiste, prin.
Benefield ES 1,200/PK-5
1221 Old Norcross Rd 30046 770-962-3771
Ron Boyd, prin. Fax 682-4187
Bethesda ES 1,100/PK-5
525 Bethesda School Rd 30044 770-921-2000
Deborah Harris, prin. Fax 931-5690
Cedar Hill ES 1,300/K-5
3615 Sugarloaf Pkwy 30044 770-962-5015
Dr. Beverly Smith, prin. Fax 377-8980
Corley ES 1,200/K-5
1331 Pleasant Hill Rd 30044 678-924-5330
Paula Cobb, prin.
Craig ES 1,200/PK-5
1075 Rocky Rd 30044 770-978-5560
Angie Wright, prin. Fax 978-5567
Creekland MS 2,900/6-8
170 Russell Rd 30043 770-338-4700
Dr. William Kruskamp, prin. Fax 338-4703
Crews MS 1,300/6-8
1000 Old Snellville Hwy 30044 770-982-6940
Dr. Vince Botta, prin. Fax 982-6942
Dyer ES 600/K-5
713 Hi Hope Rd 30043 770-963-6214
Donna Torbush, prin. Fax 338-4775
Five Forks MS 1,200/6-8
3250 River Dr 30044 770-972-1506
Dr. Mary Hensien, prin. Fax 736-4547
Freeman's Mill ES 1,200/K-5
2303 Old Peachtree Rd NE 30043 770-377-8955
Marian Hicks, prin. Fax 377-8958
Gwin Oaks ES 1,000/K-5
400 Gwin Oaks Dr 30044 770-972-3110
Peggy Goodman, prin. Fax 982-6901
Holt ES 1,500/K-5
588 Old Snellville Hwy 30046 678-376-8600
Dr. James Curtiss, prin. Fax 376-8611
Jackson ES 1,800/K-5
1970 Sever Rd 30043 770-682-4200
Ruth Markham, prin. Fax 225-7639
Kanoheda ES 1,100/K-5
1025 Herrington Rd 30044 770-682-4221
Terry Ann Watlington, prin. Fax 682-4266
Lawrenceville ES 1,000/PK-5
122 Gwinnett Dr 30046 770-963-1813
Dorothy Hines, prin. Fax 513-6741
Lovin ES, 1705 New Hope Rd 30045 500/PK-5
Laurie Allison, prin. 678-518-6940
McKendree ES 1,100/K-5
1600 Riverside Pkwy 30043 678-377-8933
Cindy Antrim, prin. Fax 377-8915
Richards MS 2,500/6-8
3555 Sugarloaf Pkwy 30044 770-995-7133
Reginald Kirkland, prin. Fax 338-4791
Rock Springs ES 1,100/PK-5
888 Rock Springs Rd 30043 770-932-7474
Angie Pacholke, prin. Fax 932-7476
Simonton ES 1,500/K-5
275 Simonton Rd SW 30045 770-513-6637
Dr. Dot Schoeller, prin. Fax 682-4197
Sweetwater MS 1,700/6-8
3500 Cruse Rd 30044 770-923-4131
Georgann Eaton, prin. Fax 931-7077
Taylor ES 1,200/K-5
600 Taylor School Dr 30043 770-338-4680
Sandra Williams, prin. Fax 338-4685
Woodward Mill ES K-5
2020 Buford Dr 30043 678-407-7590
Barbara Ergle, prin. Fax 407-7827

Branch Christian Academy 100/PK-8
1288 Braselton Hwy 30043 770-277-4722
Janice Sinclair, prin. Fax 277-4365
Sola Fide Lutheran S 50/K-8
1307 Webb Gin House Rd 30045 770-972-1771
Luke Hartzell, prin. Fax 972-6079

Leesburg, Lee, Pop. 2,777
Lee County SD 5,800/PK-12
PO Box 399 31763 229-903-2100
Dr. Lawrence Walters, supt. Fax 903-2130
www.lee.k12.ga.us
Kinchafoonee PS 700/K-2
295 Leslie Hwy 31763 229-903-2200
Dr. Mary Beth Tedder, prin. Fax 903-2218
Lee County ES 700/3-5
185 Firetower Rd 31763 229-903-2220
Donna Ford, prin. Fax 903-2237
Lee County MS 1,400/6-8
190 Smithville Rd N 31763 229-903-2140
Susan Manry, prin. Fax 903-2160
Lee County PreK Center PK-PK
116 Starksville Ave N 31763 229-903-2136
Jan Duke, dir. Fax 903-2130
Lee County PS 700/K-2
282 Magnolia Ave 31763 229-903-2180
Dr. Jeannie Johnson, prin. Fax 903-2196
Twin Oaks ES 600/3-5
240 Smithville Rd N 31763 229-903-2240
Dr. Jason Miller, prin. Fax 903-2257

Lexington, Oglethorpe, Pop. 236
Oglethorpe County SD 2,500/PK-12
735 Athens Rd 30648 706-743-8128
Raymond Akridge, supt. Fax 743-3211
www.oglethorpe.k12.ga.us
Oglethorpe County ES 600/3-5
15 Fairground Rd 30648 706-743-8750
Kimberly Lord, prin. Fax 743-3092
Oglethorpe County MS 600/6-8
757 Athens Rd 30648 706-743-8146
Beverley Levine, prin. Fax 743-3536

Oglethorpe County PS 600/PK-2
300 Comer Rd 30648 706-743-8194
Katie Coyne, prin. Fax 743-5720

Lilburn, Gwinnett, Pop. 11,416
Gwinnett County SD
Supt. — See Suwanee
Arcado ES 900/K-5
5150 Arcado Rd SW 30047 770-925-2100
Joe Ahrens, prin. Fax 931-7026
Berkmar MS 1,000/6-8
4355 Lawrenceville Hwy NW 30047 770-638-2300
Kenney Wells, prin. Fax 638-2309
Camp Creek ES 1,000/PK-5
958 Cole Rd SW 30047 770-921-1626
Kathy Jones, prin. Fax 806-3784
Head ES 600/K-5
1801 Hewatt Rd SW 30047 770-972-8050
Leigh Westcott, prin. Fax 736-4498
Hopkins ES 1,800/PK-5
1315 Dickens Rd NW 30047 770-564-2661
Paige Ryals, prin. Fax 931-7010
Knight ES 700/K-5
401 N River Dr SW 30047 770-921-2400
Mona Roberts, prin. Fax 806-3876
Lilburn ES 1,300/K-5
531 Lilburn School Rd NW 30047 770-921-7707
Wandy Taylor, prin. Fax 931-5627
Lilburn MS 1,300/6-8
4994 Lawrenceville Hwy NW 30047 770-921-1776
Dr. Gene Taylor, prin. Fax 806-3866
Mountain Park ES 600/K-5
1500 Pounds Rd SW 30047 770-921-2224
Valerie Robinett, prin. Fax 931-7071
Trickum MS 1,800/6-8
130 Killian Hill Rd SW 30047 770-921-2705
Kay Sands, prin. Fax 806-3742

Calvary Chapel Christian S 100/K-8
1969 McDaniels Bridge Rd SW 30047 770-736-2828
James Chapman, prin. Fax 736-2830
Killian Hill Christian S 500/K-12
151 Arcado Rd SW 30047 770-921-3224
Paul Williams, prin. Fax 921-9395
Providence Christian Academy 800/PK-12
4575 Lawrenceville Hwy NW 30047 770-279-7200
James Vaught, hdmstr. Fax 279-8258
St. John Neumann Regional Catholic S 600/K-8
791 Tom Smith Rd SW 30047 770-381-0557
James Anderson, prin. Fax 381-0276

Lincolnton, Lincoln, Pop. 1,515
Lincoln County SD 1,400/PK-12
PO Box 39 30817 706-359-3742
Dr. G. R. Edmunds, supt. Fax 359-7938
www.lincolncountyschools.org
Lincoln County ES 600/PK-5
175 Rowland York Dr 30817 706-359-3449
Marilyn Bell, prin. Fax 359-6996
Lincoln County MS 300/6-8
PO Box 550 30817 706-359-3069
Pam Carmichael, prin. Fax 359-2200

Lindale, Floyd, Pop. 4,187
Floyd County SD
Supt. — See Rome
Pepperell ES 500/4-5
270 Hughes Dairy Rd SE 30147 706-290-8527
Kathy Steinbruegge, prin. Fax 290-8530
Pepperell MS 800/6-8
200 Hughes Dairy Rd SE 30147 706-236-1849
Trevor Hubbard, prin. Fax 802-6776
Pepperell PS 500/PK-3
1 Dragon Dr SE 30147 706-236-1835
Carmen Jones, prin. Fax 236-1843

Lithia Springs, Douglas, Pop. 11,403
Douglas County SD
Supt. — See Douglasville
Lithia Springs ES 600/K-5
6946 Florence Dr 30122 770-651-4100
William Marchant, prin. Fax 732-2699
Sweetwater ES 500/K-5
2505 E County Line Rd 30122 770-651-4600
Teresa Martin, prin. Fax 732-5972
Turner MS 800/6-8
7101 Turner Dr 30122 770-651-5500
Eric Collins, prin. Fax 732-2698
Winn ES 500/K-5
3536 Bankhead Hwy 30122 770-651-3100
Mary Woodfin, prin. Fax 732-5625

Colonial Hills Christian S 500/PK-12
7131 Mount Vernon Rd 30122 770-941-6342
Westley Smith, hdmstr. Fax 941-2090
Lithia Christian Academy 100/PK-12
2548 Vulcan Dr 30122 770-941-5406
Lanier Motes, admin. Fax 941-9944

Lithonia, DeKalb, Pop. 2,197
DeKalb County SD
Supt. — See Decatur
Bouie ES 900/PK-5
5100 Rock Springs Rd 30038 678-676-8200
Dr. Veronica Allen, prin. Fax 676-8210
Browns Mill ES 1,000/PK-6
4863 Browns Mill Rd 30038 678-676-8300
Dr. Yvonne Butler, prin. Fax 676-8310
Candler ES 900/PK-5
6775 S Goddard Rd 30038 678-676-9100
Dr. Yolanda Turner, prin. Fax 676-9110
Fairington ES 1,100/PK-5
5505 Philip Bradley Dr 30038 678-676-8700
JoAnne Doute-Cooper, prin. Fax 676-8710
Flat Rock ES 1,100/PK-5
4603 Evans Mill Rd 30038 678-875-3202
Dr. Shelton Wright, prin. Fax 875-3210
Lithonia MS 1,500/6-8
2451 Randall Ave 30058 678-875-0700
Patricia May, prin. Fax 875-0710
Marbut ES 900/PK-5
5776 Marbut Rd 30058 678-676-8800
Rachel Zeigler, prin. Fax 676-8810
Panola Way ES 900/PK-5
2170 Panola Way Ct 30058 678-676-9300
Dr. Yolanda Beavers, prin. Fax 676-9310
Princeton ES 900/PK-5
1321 S Deshon Rd 30058 678-875-3000
Juanita Letcher, prin. Fax 875-3010
Redan ES 1,000/PK-5
1914 Stone Mtn Lithonia Rd 30058 678-676-3500
Tawni Taylor, prin. Fax 676-3510
Redan MS 1,000/6-8
1775 Young Rd 30058 678-874-7900
Matthew Priester, prin. Fax 874-7910
Rock Chapel ES 900/PK-5
1130 Rock Chapel Rd 30058 678-676-3800
Angela Jennings, prin. Fax 676-3810
Salem MS 1,200/6-8
5333 Salem Rd 30038 678-676-9400
Donald Mason, prin. Fax 676-9410
Shadow Rock ES 800/PK-5
1040 King Way Dr 30058 678-676-3902
Alice Stewart-Reese, prin. Fax 676-3910
Stoneview ES 900/PK-5
2629 Huber St 30058 678-676-3200
Dr. Farrell Young, prin. Fax 676-3210

Glenn Nova Christian Academy 50/PK-8
5241 Rock Springs Rd 30038 770-322-2337
Rufus Lawrence, admin. Fax 322-8480
Lithonia Adventist Academy 50/K-10
3533 Ragsdale Rd 30038 770-482-0294
Pearl Carrington, prin. Fax 482-6224
New Birth Christian Academy 200/PK-12
PO Box 610 30058 770-696-9678
Dr. M.O. Clarke, hdmstr. Fax 696-9674

Lizella, Bibb
Bibb County SD
Supt. — See Macon
Skyview ES 800/PK-5
5700 Fulton Mill Rd 31052 478-779-4000
Richard Key, prin. Fax 779-3958

Locust Grove, Henry, Pop. 3,434
Henry County SD
Supt. — See Mc Donough
Bethlehem ES K-5
1000 Academic Pkwy 30248 770-957-6601
Jessalyn Askew, prin. Fax 288-8577
Locust Grove ES 700/PK-5
95 L G Griffin Rd 30248 770-957-5416
Christi Peterman, prin. Fax 957-4775
Luella ES 1,300/K-5
575 Walker Dr 30248 770-288-2035
Dr. Lois Wolfe, prin. Fax 288-2040
Luella MS 1,600/6-8
2075 Hmpton Locust Grove Rd 30248 678-583-8919
Aaryn Schmuhl, prin. Fax 583-8920
New Hope ES 800/K-5
1655 New Hope Rd 30248 770-898-7362
Tim Tilley, prin. Fax 898-7370
Unity Grove ES 800/K-5
1180 LeGuin Mill Rd 30248 770-898-8886
Anne Roper-Wilson, prin. Fax 898-8834

Strong Rock Christian S 600/PK-12
4200 Strong Rock Pkwy 30248 770-833-1200
David Mann, pres. Fax 833-1396

Loganville, Walton, Pop. 8,881
Gwinnett County SD
Supt. — See Suwanee
Cooper ES, 555 Ozora Rd 30052 1,800/K-5
Dr. Donna Bishop, prin. 770-554-7050
Magill ES 1,700/K-5
3900 Brushy Fork Rd 30052 770-554-1030
Donna Ledford, prin. Fax 554-1048
McConnell MS 2,500/6-8
550 Ozora Rd 30052 770-554-1000
Paula Truppi, prin. Fax 554-1003
Rosebud ES K-5
4151 Rosebud Rd 30052 678-639-3800
Tarsha Chambers, prin. Fax 639-3804

Walton County SD
Supt. — See Monroe
Bay Creek ES 700/PK-5
100 Homer Moon Rd 30052 678-684-2800
Nancy Strawbridge, prin. Fax 684-2801
Loganville ES 600/PK-5
4303 Lawrenceville Rd 30052 678-684-2840
Shannon LaChappelle, prin. Fax 684-2839
Loganville MS 1,000/6-8
152 Clark McCullers Dr 30052 678-684-2960
Dr. Russell Brock, prin. Fax 684-2983
Sharon ES 800/PK-5
2700 White Rd 30052 678-684-2850
Dr. Sean Callahan, prin. Fax 684-2849
Youth ES 1,100/PK-5
4009 Centerhill Church Rd 30052 770-554-0172
Denise Cobb, prin. Fax 466-7069
Youth MS 1,100/6-8
1804 Highway 81 30052 770-466-6849
Bridget Lynch, prin. Fax 466-8596

Bright Beginnings Preschool 100/PK-K
680 Tom Brewer Rd 30052 770-466-2770
Tracey Means, dir. Fax 466-9499
Covenant Christian Academy 400/PK-12
3425 Loganville Hwy 30052 770-466-7890
Emmaline McKinnon, admin. Fax 466-2833
Integrity Christian Academy 100/PK-9
781 Athens Hwy 30052 770-554-0909
Djuana Ferguson, admin. Fax 554-0901
Loganville Christian Academy 500/PK-12
2575 Highway 81 30052 770-554-9888
Christy Monda, admin. Fax 554-9881

Lookout Mountain, Walker, Pop. 1,570
Walker County SD
Supt. — See La Fayette
Fairyland ES 300/PK-5
1306 Lula Lake Rd 30750 706-820-1171
Dr. Terry Stevenson, prin. Fax 820-9199

Louisville, Jefferson, Pop. 2,643
Jefferson County SD 3,200/PK-12
1001 Peachtree St 30434 478-625-7626
Carl Bethune, supt. Fax 625-7459
www.jefferson.k12.ga.us
Louisville Academy ES 600/PK-5
901 Mimosa Dr 30434 478-625-7794
Hulet Kitterman, prin. Fax 625-3548
Louisville MS 400/6-8
1200 School St 30434 478-625-7764
Samuel Dasher, prin. Fax 625-3120
Other Schools – See Wadley, Wrens

Jefferson Academy 200/K-12
2264 US Highway 1 N 30434 478-625-8861
Chuck Wimberley, prin. Fax 625-9196

Ludowici, Long, Pop. 1,558
Long County SD 2,200/PK-12
PO Box 428 31316 912-545-2367
Dr. Robert Waters, supt. Fax 545-2380
www2.long.k12.ga.us
Smiley ES 700/K-3
1530 GA Highway 57 31316 912-545-2147
David Edwards, prin. Fax 545-2639
Walker MS 900/PK-PK, 4-
PO Box 579 31316 912-545-2069
Vicky Wells, prin. Fax 545-2775

Lula, Hall, Pop. 1,878
Hall County SD
Supt. — See Gainesville
Lula ES 500/K-5
6130 Chattahoochee St 30554 770-869-3261
Matthew Alexander, prin. Fax 869-1961

Lumpkin, Stewart, Pop. 1,265
Stewart County SD 700/PK-12
PO Box 547 31815 229-838-4329
Floyd Fort, supt. Fax 838-6984
www.stewart.k12.ga.us/
Stewart County ES 300/PK-5
PO Box 37 31815 229-838-4374
Joann Chester, prin. Fax 838-6750
Stewart County MS 200/6-8
PO Box 706 31815 229-838-4532
Viola Fedd, prin. Fax 838-4352

Luthersville, Meriwether, Pop. 844
Meriwether County SD
Supt. — See Greenville
Unity ES 500/PK-5
PO Box 160 30251 770-927-6488
Tracy Sims, prin. Fax 927-1358

Lyerly, Chattooga, Pop. 513
Chattooga County SD
Supt. — See Summerville
Lyerly S 400/PK-8
150 Oak Hill Rd 30730 706-895-3323
William Robinson, prin. Fax 895-2848

Lyons, Toombs, Pop. 4,384
Toombs County SD 2,900/PK-12
117 E Wesley Ave 30436 912-526-3141
Dr. Kendall Brantley, supt. Fax 526-3291
www.toombs.k12.ga.us
Lyons PS 600/PK-2
298 N Lexington St 30436 912-526-8391
Tim Young, prin. Fax 526-3666
Lyons Upper ES 500/3-5
830 S State St 30436 912-526-5816
Dr. Sabrina Calhoun, prin. Fax 526-5555
Toombs Central ES 500/PK-5
6287 US Highway 1 S 30436 912-565-7781
Dr. Renee Stanley, prin. Fax 565-9069
Toombs County MS 600/6-8
701 Bulldog Rd 30436 912-526-8363
Pam Sears, prin. Fax 526-0240

Toombs Christian Academy 300/PK-12
PO Box 227 30436 912-526-8938
John Sharpe, hdmstr. Fax 526-0571

Mableton, Cobb, Pop. 30,600
Cobb County SD
Supt. — See Marietta
Bryant IS 3-5
6800 Factory Shoals Rd SW 30126 770-819-2402
Alfreda Williams, prin. Fax 819-2404
Bryant PS 400/PK-2
6800 Factory Shoals Rd SW 30126 770-819-2402
Dr. Patrice Moore, prin. Fax 819-2404
Clay ES 500/PK-5
730 Boggs Rd SW 30126 770-819-2430
Florence Williams, prin. Fax 819-2432
Floyd MS 900/6-8
4803 Floyd Rd SW 30126 770-819-2453
Teresa Hargrett, prin. Fax 819-2455
Harmony-Leland ES 600/PK-5
5891 Dodgen Rd SW 30126 770-819-2483
Hermia Deveaux, prin. Fax 819-2485
Lindley 6th Grade Academy 500/6-6
1550 Pebblebrook Cir SE 30126 770-819-2414
Landon Brown, prin. Fax 819-2418
Lindley MS 1,300/7-8
50 Veterans Memorial Hwy SE 30126 770-819-2496
Sandra Ervin, prin. Fax 819-2498
Mableton ES 400/PK-5
5220 Church St SW 30126 770-819-2513
Kym Eisgruber, prin. Fax 819-2515
Riverside IS 800/2-5
285 S Gordon Rd SW 30126 770-819-2553
Althea Singletary, prin. Fax 819-2643

Riverside PS 500/K-1
461 S Gordon Rd SW 30126 770-819-5851
Dr. Doris Billups-McClure, prin. Fax 398-0040
Sky View ES 400/PK-5
5805 Dunn Rd SW 30126 770-819-2584
Cynthia Cutler, prin. Fax 819-2586

Cumberland Christian Academy 100/6-8
4900 Floyd Rd SW 30126 770-819-9942
Larry Kendrick, hdmstr. Fax 819-9091
Whitefield Academy 700/PK-12
1 Whitefield Dr SE 30126 678-305-3000
John Lindsell, hdmstr. Fax 305-3010

Mc Donough, Henry, Pop. 3,773
Henry County SD 39,900/PK-12
33 N Zack Hinton Pkwy 30253 770-957-6601
Michael Surma, supt. Fax 914-6178
www.henry.k12.ga.us
Eagle's Landing MS 900/6-8
295 Tunis Rd 30253 770-914-8189
James Davis, prin. Fax 914-2989
East Lake ES 800/K-5
199 E Lake Rd, 678-583-8947
Virgil Cole, prin. Fax 583-8927
Flippen ES 900/K-5
425 Peach Dr 30253 770-954-3522
Joe Landerman, prin. Fax 954-3525
Henry County MS 800/6-8
166 Holly Smith Dr 30253 770-957-3945
Larry Monk, prin. Fax 957-0368
Hickory Flat ES 800/PK-5
841 Brannan Rd 30253 770-898-0107
Paula Crumbley, prin. Fax 898-0114
Mc Donough ES 900/PK-5
330 Tomlinson St 30253 770-957-4101
Legena Williams, prin. Fax 957-0372
Oakland ES 500/PK-5
551 Highway 81 W 30253 770-954-1901
Dr. Sheila Korvayan, prin. Fax 914-5565
Ola ES 1,100/PK-5
278 N Ola Rd, 770-957-5777
Anne Wyatt, prin. Fax 957-7031
Ola MS 1,500/6-8
353 N Ola Rd, 770-288-2108
Louann Jones, prin. Fax 288-2114
Rock Spring ES K-5
1550 Stroud Rd, 770-957-6851
Mike Hightower, prin. Fax 957-2238
Timber Ridge ES 600/K-5
2825 Highway 20 E, 770-288-3237
Dr. Pam Consolie, prin. Fax 288-3316
Tussahaw ES K-5
225 Coan Dr, 770-957-0164
Carl Knowlton, prin. Fax 957-0546
Union Grove MS 1,600/6-8
210 E Lake Rd, 678-583-8978
Robyn Mullis, prin. Fax 583-8580
Walnut Creek ES 500/K-5
3535 McDonough Pkwy 30253 770-288-8561
Terry Hall, prin. Fax 288-8566
Wesley Lakes ES 800/K-5
685 McDonough Pkwy 30253 770-914-1889
Lori Squires, prin. Fax 914-1989
Other Schools – See Hampton, Locust Grove, Stockbridge

Creekside Christian Academy 200/PK-9
175 Foster Dr 30253 770-961-9300
Rodney Knox, hdmstr. Fax 960-1875
Eagle's Landing Christian Academy 1,300/PK-12
2400 Highway 42 N 30253 770-957-2927
Marshall Chambers, admin. Fax 957-2290
Mc Donough Christian Academy 200/PK-8
2000 Jonesboro Rd 30253 770-898-5530
Scott Gregory, admin. Fax 954-0940

Macon, Bibb, Pop. 94,316
Bibb County SD 24,400/PK-12
484 Mulberry St 31201 478-765-8711
Sharon Patterson, supt. Fax 765-8549
www.bibb.k12.ga.us/
Alexander II Magnet ES 500/K-5
1156 College St 31201 478-779-2700
Dr. Linda Bivins, prin. Fax 779-2670
Appling MS 800/6-8
1210 Shurling Dr 31211 478-779-2200
Robert Stevenson, prin. Fax 779-2202
Ballard-Hudson MS 400/6-8
1070 Anthony Rd 31204 478-779-3400
Dr. Benjy Morgan, prin. Fax 779-3396
Barden ES 400/PK-5
2521 Anderson Dr 31206 478-779-3300
Dr. Jacquelyn Jackson, prin. Fax 779-3271
Bernd ES 500/PK-5
4160 Ocmulgee East Blvd 31217 478-779-2750
Laura Holder, prin. Fax 779-2731
Bloomfield MS 500/6-8
4375 Bloomfield Drive Ext 31206 478-779-4800
David Dillard, prin. Fax 779-4760
Brookdale ES 500/PK-5
3600 Brookdale Ave 31204 478-779-2800
Vicki Williams, prin. Fax 779-2770
Bruce ES 600/PK-5
3660 Houston Ave 31206 478-779-4550
Dr. Ramon Johnson, prin. Fax 779-4562
Burdell-Hunt Magnet ES 400/K-5
972 Fort Hill St 31217 478-779-2950
Tanya Allen, prin. Fax 779-2940
Burghard ES 400/PK-5
6020 Bloomfield Rd 31206 478-779-2900
Lynne Donehoo, prin. Fax 779-2882
Burke ES 400/PK-5
2051 2nd St 31201 478-779-2850
Emanuel Frazier, prin. Fax 779-2829
Butler ECC 100/PK-K
3705 Earl St 31204 478-779-3200
Dr. Lisa Garrett, prin. Fax 779-3202
Carter ES 500/PK-5
5910 Zebulon Rd 31210 478-779-3350
Kelly Causey, prin. Fax 779-3328
Hartley ES 300/PK-5
2230 Anthony Rd 31204 478-779-2500
Dr. Deotha Campbell, prin. Fax 779-2485
Heard ES 500/PK-5
6515 Houston Rd 31216 478-779-4250
Sandra Stanley, prin. Fax 779-4219
Heritage ES 800/PK-5
6050 Thomaston Rd 31220 478-779-4700
Donna Jackson, prin. Fax 779-4721
Howard MS 1,100/6-8
6600 Forsyth Rd 31210 478-779-3500
Matt Adams, prin. Fax 779-3458
Ingram/Pye ES 300/PK-5
855 Anthony Rd 31204 478-779-3000
Beheejah Hasan, prin. Fax 779-2989
Jones ES 500/PK-5
2350 Alandale Dr 31211 478-779-3600
Dr. K. Malone, prin. Fax 779-3614
King-Danforth ES 400/PK-5
1301 Shurling Dr 31211 478-779-2100
Dr. La Quanda Brown, prin. Fax 779-2112
Lane ES 500/PK-5
990 Newport Rd 31210 478-779-3150
Dr. Sherri Flagg, prin. Fax 779-3151
Miller Magnet MS 600/6-8
751 Hendley St 31204 478-779-4050
Steven Jones, prin. Fax 779-4032
Morgan ES 500/PK-5
4901 Faubus Ave 31204 478-779-2400
Mary Sams, prin. Fax 779-2411
Porter ES 500/PK-5
5802 School Rd 31216 478-779-4350
Dr. Russ Chesser, prin. Fax 779-4320
Rice ES 400/PK-5
3750 Jessie Rice St 31206 478-779-4300
Dr. Teresa Yarser, prin. Fax 779-4270
Riley ES 400/PK-5
3522 Greenbriar Rd 31204 478-779-2050
Dr. Jacquelyn Walden, prin. Fax 779-2066
Rutland MS 1,100/6-8
6260 Skipper Rd 31216 478-779-4400
Dr. Jerri Hall, prin. Fax 779-4373
Springdale ES 600/PK-5
4965 Northside Dr 31210 478-779-3750
Dr. Amy Duke, prin. Fax 779-3742
Taylor ES 500/PK-5
2976 Crestline Dr 31204 478-779-3550
Dr. Susan Simpson, prin. Fax 779-3569
Union ES 400/PK-5
4831 Mamie Carter Dr 31210 478-779-2650
Dr. Efram Yarber, prin. Fax 779-2631
Vineville Academy 400/K-5
2260 Vineville Ave 31204 478-779-3250
Paulette Winters, prin. Fax 779-3228
Weaver MS 900/6-8
2570 Heath Rd 31206 478-779-4650
Dr. Pam Carswell, prin. Fax 779-4627
Williams ES 300/PK-5
325 Pursley St 31201 478-779-3650
S. Griffin-Stewart, prin. Fax 779-3661
Other Schools – See Lizella

Jones County SD
Supt. — See Gray
Clifton Ridge MS 600/6-8
169 Dusty Ln 31211 478-743-5182
Wes Cavender, prin. Fax 743-8282
Wells ES 400/3-5
512 GA Highway 49 31211 478-746-7335
Kevin Sterling, prin. Fax 746-5441
Wells PS 400/PK-2
101 Mattie Wells Dr 31217 478-742-5959
Janne Childs, prin. Fax 742-5930

Bethany Christian Academy 50/1-8
2742 Millerfield Rd 31217 478-746-0009
Robert Williams, prin. Fax 746-8481
Central Fellowship Christian Academy 500/PK-12
8460 Hawkinsville Rd 31216 478-788-6909
Truitt Franklin, hdmstr. Fax 788-1614
Covenant Academy 200/PK-12
4652 Ayers Rd 31210 478-471-0285
Dr. Jake Walters, hdmstr. Fax 471-8884
First Presbyterian Day S 900/PK-12
5671 Calvin Dr 31210 478-477-6505
Gregg Thompson, hdmstr. Fax 477-2804
Middle Georgia Christian S 100/PK-12
5859 Thomaston Rd 31220 478-757-9585
Stan Frank, dir. Fax 757-9587
Montessori of Macon 100/PK-8
436 Forest Hill Rd 31210 478-757-8927
Tanya Melville, prin. Fax 757-9304
Progressive Christian Academy 300/PK-8
151 Madison St 31201 478-742-3134
Dr. Betty Tolbert, prin. Fax 742-3160
St. Joseph S 300/K-6
905 High St 31201 478-742-0636
Dr. Kaye Hlavaty, prin. Fax 746-7685
St. Peter Claver S 300/PK-8
133 Ward St 31204 478-743-3985
Sr. Ellen Hagar, prin. Fax 743-0054
Stratford Academy 900/PK-12
6010 Peake Rd 31220 478-477-8073
Dr. Robert Veto, hdmstr. Fax 477-0299
Tattnall Square Academy 700/PK-12
111 Trojan Trl 31210 478-477-6760
Barney Hester, hdmstr. Fax 474-7887
Wimbish Adventist S 50/1-9
640 Wimbish Rd 31210 478-477-4600
RuthAnn Fillman, prin. Fax 477-4875
Windsor Academy 300/K-12
4150 Jones Rd 31216 478-781-1621
John Cranford, hdmstr. Fax 781-0757

Mc Rae, Telfair, Pop. 3,041
Telfair County SD 1,900/PK-12
PO Box 240 31055 229-868-5661
Cary Clark, supt. Fax 868-5549
www.telfair.k12.ga.us
Telfair County ES 900/K-5
532 E Oak St 31055 229-868-7483
Anthony McIver, prin. Fax 868-7578
Telfair County MS 400/6-8
101 GA Highway 280 W 31055 229-868-7465
Coleen McIver, prin. Fax 868-2616
Telfair County Preschool 100/PK-PK
212 Huckabee St 31055 229-868-5414
Shirley Martin, dir. Fax 868-5549

Madison, Morgan, Pop. 3,833
Morgan County SD 3,300/PK-12
1065 East Ave 30650 706-752-4600
Dr. Stan DeJarnett, supt. Fax 752-4601
www.morgan.k12.ga.us
Morgan County ES 700/3-5
1640 Buckhead Rd 30650 706-342-5039
Jean Triplett, prin. Fax 342-5050
Morgan County MS 800/6-8
920 Pearl St 30650 706-342-0556
Dr. Joe Hutcheson, prin. Fax 342-5048
Morgan County PS 800/PK-2
993 East Ave 30650 706-342-3475
Betsy Short, prin. Fax 342-9184

Manchester, Meriwether, Pop. 3,719
Meriwether County SD
Supt. — See Greenville
Even Start PK-PK
JD Parham St 31816 706-846-2311
Chris Wilson, prin. Fax 846-2354
Manchester MS 400/6-8
231 W Perry St 31816 706-846-2846
Edward Boswell, prin. Fax 846-8111
Mountain View ES 900/PK-5
2600 Judson Bulloch Rd 31816 706-655-3969
William Edgar, prin. Fax 655-3962

Manor, Ware
Ware County SD
Supt. — See Waycross
Ware County Magnet S 500/K-12
4650 Manor Millwood Rd S 31550 912-287-2338
Dr. Darlene Tanner, prin. Fax 287-2337

Mansfield, Newton, Pop. 503
Newton County SD
Supt. — See Covington
Mansfield ES 500/PK-5
45 E Third Ave 30055 770-784-2948
G.W. Davis, prin. Fax 784-2995

Marietta, Cobb, Pop. 61,261
Cobb County SD 101,900/PK-12
514 Glover St SE 30060 770-426-3300
Fred Sanderson, supt. Fax 426-3329
www.cobb.k12.ga.us
Bells Ferry ES 600/PK-5
2600 Bells Ferry Rd 30066 678-594-8950
Ladonna Starnes, prin. Fax 594-8952
Birney ES 900/PK-5
775 Smyrn Pdr Spgs Rd SW 30060 678-842-6824
Rattana Inthirathvongsy, prin. Fax 842-6826
Blackwell ES 700/PK-5
3470 Canton Rd 30066 678-494-7600
Dr. Maurine Kozol, prin. Fax 494-7602
Brumby ES 900/K-5
1306 Powers Ferry Rd SE 30067 770-916-7070
Joshua Morreale, prin. Fax 916-7072
Cheatham Hill ES 1,100/PK-5
1350 John Ward Rd SW 30064 678-594-8034
Belinda Walters-Brazile, prin. Fax 594-8036
Daniell MS 1,000/6-8
2900 Scott Rd 30066 678-594-8048
David Nelson, prin. Fax 594-8050
Davis ES 600/PK-5
2433 Jamerson Rd 30066 678-494-7636
Dr. Dee Mobley, prin. Fax 494-7638
Dickerson MS 1,300/6-8
855 Woodlawn Dr NE 30068 770-578-2710
Carole Brink, prin. Fax 578-2712
Dodgen MS 1,100/6-8
1725 Bill Murdock Rd 30062 770-578-2726
James Snell, prin. Fax 578-2728
Dowell ES 1,000/PK-5
2121 W Sandtown Rd SW 30064 678-594-8059
Dr. Jami Frost, prin. Fax 594-8061
Due West ES 400/K-5
3900 Due West Rd NW 30064 678-594-8071
Cynthia Hanauer, prin. Fax 594-8073
East Cobb MS 1,200/6-8
380 Holt Rd NE 30068 770-578-2740
David Chiprany, prin. Fax 578-2742
East Side ES 900/K-5
3850 Roswell Rd 30062 770-578-7200
Elizabeth Mavity, prin. Fax 578-7202
Eastvalley ES 600/K-5
2570 Lower Roswell Rd 30068 770-578-7214
Karen Wacker, prin. Fax 578-7216
Fair Oaks ES 800/PK-5
407 Barber Rd SE 30060 678-594-8080
Dr. Cindy Szwec, prin. Fax 594-8082
Garrison Mill ES 600/PK-5
4111 Wesley Chapel Rd 30062 770-642-5600
Paula Huffman, prin. Fax 642-5602
Hightower Trail MS 1,000/6-8
3905 Post Oak Tritt Rd 30062 770-578-7225
Dr. Hilda Wilkins, prin. Fax 578-7227
Hollydale ES 800/PK-5
2901 Bay Berry Dr SW 30008 678-594-8143
Wanda Floyd, prin. Fax 594-8145
Keheley ES 500/PK-5
1985 Kemp Rd 30066 678-494-7836
Liz Jackson, prin. Fax 494-7838
Kincaid ES 600/PK-5
1410 Kincaid Rd 30066 770-578-7238
Cheryl Mauldin, prin. Fax 578-7240
LaBelle ES 400/PK-5
230 Cresson Dr SW 30060 678-842-6955
Lisa Hogan, prin. Fax 842-6957
Mabry MS 900/6-8
2700 Jims Rd NE 30066 770-928-5546
Merrilee Heflin, prin. Fax 928-5548
McCleskey MS 800/6-8
4080 Maybreeze Rd 30066 770-928-5560
Dr. Chris Richie, prin. Fax 928-5562

Milford ES 600/K-5
2390 Austell Rd SW 30008 678-842-6966
Denise Feezor, prin. Fax 842-6968
Mountain View ES 800/PK-5
3448 Sandy Plains Rd 30066 770-578-7265
Angela Huff, prin. Fax 578-7267
Mt. Bethel ES 900/PK-5
1210 Johnson Ferry Rd 30068 770-578-7248
Robin Lattizori, prin. Fax 578-7250
Murdock ES 800/PK-5
2320 Murdock Rd 30062 770-509-5071
Natalie Richman, prin. Fax 509-5217
Nicholson ES 500/PK-5
1599 Shallowford Rd 30066 770-928-5573
Lynn McWhorter, prin. Fax 928-5575
Powers Ferry ES 500/K-5
403 Powers Ferry Rd SE 30067 770-578-7936
Dr. Joan Mills, prin. Fax 578-7938
Rocky Mount ES 600/PK-5
2400 Rocky Mountain Rd NE 30066 770-591-5050
Gail May, prin. Fax 591-5041
Shallowford Falls ES 600/K-5
3529 Lassiter Rd 30062 770-642-5610
Dr. Doreen Griffeth, prin. Fax 642-5612
Simpson MS 800/6-8
3340 Trickum Rd NE 30066 770-971-4711
Andrew Bristow, prin. Fax 971-4507
Smitha MS 1,000/6-8
2025 Powder Springs Rd SW 30064 678-594-8267
Sharon Tucker, prin. Fax 594-8269
Sope Creek ES 1,100/PK-5
3320 Paper Mill Rd SE 30067 770-916-7085
Martha Whalen, prin. Fax 916-7087
Timber Ridge ES 500/PK-5
5000 Timber Ridge Rd 30068 770-642-5621
Dr. Tracie Doe, prin. Fax 642-5623
Tritt ES 800/PK-5
4435 Post Oak Tritt Rd 30062 770-642-5630
Dr. Rebecca Rutledge, prin. Fax 642-5632
Other Schools – See Acworth, Austell, Kennesaw, Mableton, Powder Springs, Smyrna

Marietta CSD 6,900/K-12
250 Howard St NE 30060 770-422-3500
Dr. Emily Lembeck, supt. Fax 425-4095
www.marietta-city.org
Burruss ES 300/K-5
325 Manning Rd SW 30064 770-429-3144
Julie King, prin. Fax 429-3146
Dunleith ES 500/K-5
120 Saine Dr SW 30008 770-429-3190
Tiffany Pollock, prin. Fax 429-3193
Hickory Hills ES 300/K-5
500 Redwood Dr SW 30064 770-429-3125
Diana Mills, prin. Fax 429-3126
Lockheed ES 800/K-5
1205 Merritt Rd 30062 770-429-3196
Gabe Carmona, prin. Fax 429-3184
Marietta Center for Advanced Academics 200/K-5
311 Aviation Rd SE 30060 770-420-0822
Dr. Karen Smits, prin. Fax 420-0839
Marietta MS 1,100/7-8
121 Winn St NW 30064 770-422-0311
Dr. Darlene Darby, prin. Fax 429-3162
Marietta Sixth Grade Academy 500/6-6
340 Aviation Rd SE 30060 770-429-3115
Dayton Hibbs, prin. Fax 429-3118
Park Street ES 700/K-5
105 Park St SE 30060 770-429-3180
Corey Lawson, prin. Fax 429-3182
West Side ES 400/K-5
344 Polk St NW 30064 770-429-3172
Jennifer Lawson, prin. Fax 429-3173

Carman Adventist S 100/K-8
1330 Cobb Pkwy N 30062 770-424-0606
Steve Wilson, prin. Fax 420-9145
Casa Dei Bambini of East Marietta 300/PK-6
150 Powers Ferry Rd SE 30067 770-973-2731
Florence Johnson, dir. Fax 973-1450
Cobb County Christian S 50/PK-12
545 Lorene Dr SW 30060 770-434-1320
Gloria Kelly, dir. Fax 434-1442
Covenant Christian Ministries Academy 200/PK-12
PO Box 4065 30061 770-919-0022
Vanessa Anderson, supt. Fax 919-2098
Eastside Christian S 300/K-8
2450 Lower Roswell Rd 30068 770-971-2332
Judith Cripps, prin. Fax 578-7967
Faith Lutheran S 200/PK-8
2111 Lower Roswell Rd 30068 770-973-8921
Jack Hibbs, prin. Fax 971-7796
Mt. Bethel Christian Academy 500/K-8
4385 Lower Roswell Rd 30068 770-971-0245
Dr. Bob Burris, hdmstr. Fax 971-3770
Riverstone Montessori Academy PK-6
455 Casteel Rd SW 30064 770-422-9194
Cindy Neck, admin. Fax 422-9454
St. Joseph Catholic S 500/K-8
81 Lacy St NW 30060 770-428-3328
Patricia Allen, prin. Fax 424-2960
Shreiner Academy 200/PK-8
1340 Terrell Mill Rd SE 30067 770-953-1340
David Shreiner, hdmstr. Fax 953-1415
Walker S 1,100/PK-12
700 Cobb Pkwy N 30062 770-427-2689
Donald Robertson, hdmstr. Fax 514-8122

Martinez, Columbia, Pop. 27,700
Columbia County SD
Supt. — See Evans
Martinez ES 500/PK-5
213 Flowing Wells Rd 30907 706-863-8308
Cory Ellis, prin. Fax 868-2185
South Columbia ES 500/PK-5
325 McCormick Rd 30907 706-863-3220
Lisa Reeder, prin. Fax 854-5836
Westmont ES 600/PK-5
4558 Oakley Pirkle Rd 30907 706-863-0992
Dr. Tami Flowers, prin. Fax 854-5838

Augusta Christian S 600/K-12
313 Baston Rd 30907 706-863-2905
John Bartlett, hdmstr. Fax 860-6618
Augusta Preparatory Day S 600/PK-12
285 Flowing Wells Rd 30907 706-863-1906
Jack Hall, hdmstr. Fax 863-6198

Maysville, Jackson, Pop. 1,520
Jackson County SD
Supt. — See Jefferson
Maysville ES 400/PK-5
9270 Highway 82 Spur 30558 706-652-2241
Dr. Jane Scales, prin. Fax 652-3185

Menlo, Chattooga, Pop. 509
Chattooga County SD
Supt. — See Summerville
Menlo S 400/PK-8
2430 Highway 337 30731 706-862-2323
Mike Martin, prin. Fax 862-2360

Metter, Candler, Pop. 4,143
Candler County SD 1,900/PK-12
210 S College St 30439 912-685-5713
Dr. Thomas Bigwood, supt. Fax 685-3068
www.metter.org
Metter ES 700/PK-3
805 E Lillian St 30439 912-685-2058
Charlotte Coursey, prin. Fax 685-3477
Metter IS 300/4-5
423 W Vertia St 30439 912-685-7400
Lesa Brown, prin. Fax 685-2076
Metter MS 400/6-8
431 W Vertia St 30439 912-685-5580
Robbie Dollar, prin. Fax 685-4970

Midland, Muscogee
Muscogee County SD
Supt. — See Columbus
Mathews ES 600/K-5
7533 Lynch Rd 31820 706-569-3656
Kaw Dowis, prin. Fax 569-3663
Midland Academy 700/K-5
7373 Psalmond Rd 31820 706-569-3664
Janice Miley, prin. Fax 569-3668
Midland MS 1,000/6-8
6990 Warm Springs Rd 31820 706-569-3673
Richard Green, prin. Fax 569-3678

Midway, Liberty, Pop. 1,008
Liberty County SD
Supt. — See Hinesville
Liberty ES 700/PK-5
600 Edgewater Dr 31320 912-884-3326
Chris Anderson, prin. Fax 884-3631
Midway MS 900/6-8
425 Edgewater Dr 31320 912-884-6677
Debra Frazier, prin. Fax 884-5944

Milledgeville, Baldwin, Pop. 19,397
Baldwin County SD 5,900/PK-12
PO Box 1188 31059 478-453-4176
Geneva Braziel, supt. Fax 457-3327
www.baldwin-county-schools.com
Blandy Hills ES 700/K-5
375 Blandy Rd NW 31061 478-457-2495
Dr. Runee Sallad, prin. Fax 457-2499
Creekside ES 700/K-5
372 Blandy Rd NW 31061 478-457-3301
Dianne Becker, prin. Fax 457-3340
Eagle Ridge ES 1,200/PK-5
220 N ABC Dr 31061 478-457-2967
Jeanette Scott, prin. Fax 457-2924
Midway ES 600/K-5
101 Carl Vinson Rd SE 31061 478-457-2440
Carol Goings, prin. Fax 453-2680
Oak Hill MS 1,400/6-8
356 Blandy Rd NW 31061 478-457-3370
Dr. Linda Ramsey, prin. Fax 457-2422

Milledge Academy 600/PK-12
197 Log Cabin Rd NE 31061 478-452-5570
Larry Prestridge, hdmstr. Fax 452-5000

Millen, Jenkins, Pop. 3,526
Jenkins County SD 1,700/PK-12
PO Box 660 30442 478-982-6000
Melissa Williams, supt. Fax 982-6002
www.jchs.com/
Jenkins County ES 900/PK-5
220 Landrum Dr 30442 478-982-5503
Jim Jarvis, prin. Fax 982-6027
Jenkins County MS 400/6-8
409 Barney Ave 30442 478-982-1063
Charre Moulton, prin. Fax 982-6015

Milner, Lamar, Pop. 497

Rock Springs Christian Academy 100/PK-3
219 Rock Springs Rd 30257 678-692-0192
Lee Nelson, dir. Fax 229-6126
St. George's Episcopal S 200/PK-8
103 Birch St 30257 770-358-9432
Donna Mallett, hdmstr. Fax 358-9495

Milton, Fulton
Fulton County SD
Supt. — See Atlanta
Birmingham Falls ES PK-5
14865 Birmingham Hwy, 404-768-3600
Ronald Trussell, prin.

Monroe, Walton, Pop. 12,329
Walton County SD 12,900/PK-12
200 Double Springs Church R 30656 770-266-4417
Gary Hobbs, supt. Fax 266-4420
www.walton.k12.ga.us
Atha Road ES 1,300/PK-5
821 H D Atha Rd 30655 770-266-5995
Madenna Landers, prin. Fax 266-5965
Blaine Street ES 700/PK-5
109 Blaine St 30655 770-267-6574
Melissa Clarke, prin. Fax 207-3300
Carver MS 700/6-8
1095 Good Hope Rd 30655 770-207-3333
Dr. Dawn Spruill, prin. Fax 207-3332
Monroe ES 600/PK-5
140 Dillard Dr 30656 770-207-3205
Dr. Zeester Swint, prin. Fax 207-3207
Walker Park ES 700/PK-5
333 Carl Davis Rd NW 30656 770-207-3240
Dr. Seabrook Royal, prin. Fax 207-3241
Other Schools – See Covington, Loganville

Walton Academy 1,000/PK-12
1 Bulldog Dr 30655 770-267-7578
William Nicholson, hdmstr. Fax 267-4023

Montezuma, Macon, Pop. 3,997
Macon County SD
Supt. — See Oglethorpe
Macon County MS 500/6-8
615 Vienna Rd 31063 478-472-7045
Issiah Ross, prin. Fax 472-2549

Monticello, Jasper, Pop. 2,565
Jasper County SD 2,200/PK-12
1125 Fred Smith St Ste A 31064 706-468-6350
Jay Brinson, supt. Fax 468-0045
www.jasper.k12.ga.us
Jasper County MS 500/6-8
1289 College St 31064 706-468-2227
Monica McWhorter, prin. Fax 468-4991
Jasper County PS 600/PK-2
495 GA Highway 212 W 31064 706-468-4968
Cindy Hughes, prin. Fax 468-4985
Washington Park ES 500/3-5
721 GA Highway 212 W 31064 706-468-6284
Anthony Tanner, prin. Fax 468-4984

Piedmont Academy 400/PK-12
PO Box 231 31064 706-468-8818
Dr. Michael Rossi, hdmstr. Fax 468-2409

Moreland, Coweta, Pop. 420
Coweta County SD
Supt. — See Newnan
Moreland ES 500/PK-5
145 Railroad St 30259 770-254-2875
Beverly Yeager, prin. Fax 304-5920

Morgan, Calhoun, Pop. 1,470
Calhoun County SD 700/PK-12
PO Box 39 39866 229-849-2765
Jewell Howard, supt. Fax 849-2113
www.calhoun.k12.ga.us/
Other Schools – See Arlington

Morganton, Union, Pop. 265
Fannin County SD
Supt. — See Blue Ridge
East Fannin ES 500/K-5
1 Elementary Cir 30560 706-374-6418
Bonnie Angel, prin. Fax 374-2470

Mountain Area Christian Academy 200/PK-12
14090 Old Highway 76 30560 706-374-6222
Keith Scott, admin. Fax 374-4831

Morrow, Clayton, Pop. 5,283
Clayton County SD
Supt. — See Jonesboro
Haynie ES 800/K-5
1169 Morrow Rd 30260 770-968-2905
Erica Johnson, prin. Fax 968-2904
Marshall ES 900/K-5
5885 Maddox Rd 30260 404-675-8019
Dr. Velma Mobley, prin. Fax 675-8047
McGarrah ES 700/PK-5
2201 Lake Harbin Rd 30260 770-968-2910
Tammy Burroughs, prin. Fax 968-2920
Morrow ES 500/PK-5
6115 Reynolds Rd 30260 770-968-2900
Lee Casey, prin. Fax 968-2903
Morrow MS 800/6-8
5968 Maddox Rd 30260 404-362-3860
Greg Curry, prin. Fax 608-2557
Tara ES 600/PK-5
937 Mount Zion Rd 30260 770-968-2915
Cynthia Dickerson, prin. Fax 968-2919

Morven, Brooks, Pop. 623
Brooks County SD
Supt. — See Quitman
North Brooks ES 500/PK-5
10295 Coffee Rd 31638 229-775-2414
Ervin Sloan, prin. Fax 775-2879

Moultrie, Colquitt, Pop. 14,913
Colquitt County SD 7,200/PK-12
PO Box 2708 31776 229-890-6200
Leonard McCoy, supt. Fax 890-6206
www.colquitt.k12.ga.us/
Cox ES 600/PK-5
1275 11th Ave SE 31768 229-890-6190
Laura Whitfield, prin. Fax 890-6127
Odom ES 600/PK-5
2902 Sardis Church Rd, 229-324-3313
James Harrell, prin. Fax 324-3317
Okapilco ES 400/PK-5
3300 GA Highway 33 N 31768 229-890-6191
Eric Croft, prin. Fax 890-6248
Stringfellow ES 400/PK-5
200 5th Ave SW 31768 229-890-6111
Darlene Reynolds, prin. Fax 890-5007
Sunset ES 700/PK-5
698 US Highway 319 S 31768 229-890-6184
Bruce Owen, prin. Fax 873-3306
Williams MS 600/6-7
950 4th St SW 31768 229-890-6183
Doug Howell, prin. Fax 890-6258
Wright ES 500/PK-5
1812 2nd St SE 31768 229-890-6186
Marcus Bell, prin. Fax 890-5002
Other Schools – See Doerun, Funston, Hartsfield, Norman Park

Moultrie SDA S 50/K-8
1022 2nd St SE 31768 229-985-0940

Mount Airy, Habersham, Pop. 665
Habersham County SD
Supt. — See Clarkesville
Hazel Grove ES 300/K-5
6390 Dicks Hill Pkwy 30563 706-754-2942
Tim Goss, prin. Fax 754-3308

Mount Berry, Floyd

Berry College S 100/K-8
2277 Martha Berry Hwy NW 30149 706-232-5374
Paul Atkinson, dir. Fax 238-7732

Mount Vernon, Montgomery, Pop. 2,162
Montgomery County SD 1,300/PK-12
PO Box 315 30445 912-583-2301
Dr. Lynn Batten, supt. Fax 583-4822
www.montgomery.k12.ga.us
Montgomery County MS 300/6-8
701 Dobbins St 30445 912-583-2351
Dr. Marvin Howard, prin. Fax 583-4469
Other Schools – See Ailey

Nahunta, Brantley, Pop. 1,044
Brantley County SD 3,600/PK-12
272 School Cir 31553 912-462-6176
Drew Sauls, supt. Fax 462-6731
www.brantley.k12.ga.us/
Brantley County MS 500/7-8
10990 Highway 82 31553 912-462-7092
Dr. Shelli Tyre, prin. Fax 462-6785
Nahunta ES 300/4-6
9110 Main St S 31553 912-462-5166
Tim Sawyer, prin. Fax 462-7330
Nahunta PS 400/PK-3
479 School Cir 31553 912-462-5179
Evon Griffin, prin. Fax 462-7118
Other Schools – See Hoboken, Waynesville

Nashville, Berrien, Pop. 4,841
Berrien County SD 3,000/PK-12
PO Box 625 31639 229-686-2081
Paula Raley, supt. Fax 686-9002
www.berrien.k12.ga.us
Berrien ES 700/3-5
802 Middle School Cir 31639 229-686-2939
Angie Lovein, prin. Fax 686-5500
Berrien MS 700/6-8
800 Tifton Rd 31639 229-686-2021
Ross New, prin. Fax 686-6546
Berrien PS 800/PK-2
1427 N Davis St 31639 229-686-7438
Gail Melton, prin. Fax 686-6211

Newnan, Coweta, Pop. 24,654
Coweta County SD 21,300/PK-12
PO Box 280 30264 770-254-2801
Blake Bass, supt. Fax 254-2807
www.cowetaschools.org
Arbor Springs ES 600/PK-5
4840 Highway 29 N 30265 770-463-5903
Dr. Patricia Falk, prin. Fax 463-5937
Arnall MS 900/6-8
700 Lora Smith Rd 30265 770-254-2765
Dr. Jan Franks, prin. Fax 254-2770
Arnco-Sargent ES 500/PK-5
2449 Highway 16 W 30263 770-254-2830
Dr. Monica Hughes, prin. Fax 304-5916
Atkinson ES 400/PK-5
14 Nimmons St 30263 770-254-2835
Melissa Wimbish, prin. Fax 304-5917
Elm Street ES 400/PK-5
46 Elm St 30263 770-254-2865
Dr. Julie Raschen, prin. Fax 304-5918
Evans MS 800/6-8
41 Evans Dr 30263 770-254-2780
Vince Bass, prin. Fax 254-2783
Hill ES 400/PK-5
57 Sunset Ln 30263 770-254-2895
Valerie Mathura, prin. Fax 304-5923
Jefferson Parkway ES 500/PK-5
154 Millard Farmer Ind Blvd 30263 770-254-2771
Bill Sanborn, prin. Fax 254-2775
Madras MS 1,000/6-8
240 Edgeworth Rd 30263 770-254-2744
Lorraine Johnson, prin. Fax 304-5928
Newnan Crossing ES 600/PK-5
1267 Lower Fayetteville Rd 30265 770-254-2872
Terri Lassetter, prin. Fax 304-5921
Northside ES 500/PK-5
720 Country Club Rd 30263 770-254-2890
Dr. Dana Ballou, prin. Fax 304-5922
Smokey Road MS 900/6-8
965 Smokey Rd 30263 770-254-2840
Dr. Laurie Barron, prin. Fax 304-5933
Welch ES 800/K-5
240 Mary Freeman Rd 30265 770-254-2597
Becky Darrah, prin. Fax 251-0986
Western ES 500/PK-5
1730 Welcome Rd 30263 770-254-2790
Denise Pigatt, prin. Fax 304-5925
White Oak ES 700/PK-5
770 Lora Smith Rd 30265 770-254-2860
Cheryl Sanborn, prin. Fax 304-5927
Other Schools – See Grantville, Moreland, Senoia, Sharpsburg

Barron Montessori S 200/PK-8
195 Jackson St 30263 770-253-2135
Kathleen Winters, prin. Fax 253-4433
Heritage S 400/PK-12
2093 Highway 29 N 30263 770-253-9898
Judith Griffith, hdmstr. Fax 253-4850
Newnan Christian S 100/PK-12
1608 Highway 29 N 30263 770-253-7175
Fax 253-4776
Orchard Hills Academy 50/K-10
171 Gordon Rd 30263 678-854-9188
Angie Gruner, prin. Fax 854-9199

Newton, Baker, Pop. 867
Baker County SD 400/PK-10
PO Box 40, 229-734-5346
Thomas Rogers, supt. Fax 734-3064
www.baker.k12.ga.us/
Baker County S 400/PK-10
348 State Route 37, 229-734-5274
Robert Graper, prin. Fax 734-3071

Nicholls, Coffee, Pop. 2,557
Coffee County SD
Supt. — See Douglas
Nicholls ES 400/PK-5
704 Van Streat Hwy 31554 912-345-2429
Sherri Berry, prin. Fax 345-5455

Nicholson, Jackson, Pop. 1,452
Jackson County SD
Supt. — See Jefferson
Benton ES 300/PK-5
5488 Highway 441 30565 706-757-2211
Pam Sheilds, prin. Fax 757-3097

Norcross, Gwinnett, Pop. 9,887
Gwinnett County SD
Supt. — See Suwanee
Beaver Ridge ES 1,100/PK-5
1978 Beaver Ruin Rd 30071 770-447-6307
Esther Adames-Jimenez, prin. Fax 447-2688
Meadowcreek ES 1,000/PK-5
5025 Georgia Belle Ct 30093 770-931-5701
Kelli McCain, prin. Fax 931-5705
Norcross ES 1,000/K-5
150 Hunt St 30071 770-448-2188
Dr. Dora Hill, prin. Fax 417-2492
Peachtree ES 1,400/K-5
5995 Crooked Creek Rd 30092 770-448-8710
Jean Loethen-Payne, prin. Fax 417-2451
Pinckneyville MS 1,200/6-8
5440 W Jones Bridge Rd 30092 770-263-0860
Nancy Martin, prin. Fax 447-2617
Rockbridge ES 800/K-5
6066 Rockbridge School Rd 30093 770-448-9363
Dion Jones, prin. Fax 417-2437
Simpson ES 1,000/K-5
4525 E Jones Bridge Rd 30092 770-417-2400
Bron Gayna Schmit, prin. Fax 417-2406
Stripling ES 1,000/PK-5
6155 Atlantic Blvd 30071 770-582-7577
Clay Hunter, prin. Fax 582-7586
Summerour MS 1,000/6-8
585 Mitchell Rd 30071 770-448-3045
Dana Pugh, prin. Fax 417-2476

Cornerstone Christian Academy 100/K-8
5295 Triangle Pkwy 30092 770-441-9222
De Ann Crawford, hdmstr. Fax 441-9380
Country Brook Montessori S 100/PK-4
2175 N Norcross Tucker Rd 30071 770-446-2397
Jim Parsons, dir. Fax 446-5610
Greater Atlanta Christian S 1,900/PK-12
1575 Indian Trail Rd 30093 770-243-2000
Dr. David Fincher, pres. Fax 243-2213
Hopewell Christian Academy 200/PK-12
182 Hunter St 30071 770-903-3387
Beauty Baldwin, admin. Fax 449-8316
Norcross Christian Academy 50/PK-1
706 N Peachtree St 30071 770-446-9559
Carolanne Eaves, dir. Fax 417-1738
Victory World Christian S 100/PK-5
5905 Brook Hollow Pkwy 30071 678-684-2030
Irene Prue Ph.D., prin. Fax 684-2031
Wesleyan S 1,100/K-12
5405 Spalding Dr 30092 770-448-7640
Zach Young, hdmstr. Fax 448-3699

Norman Park, Colquitt, Pop. 859
Colquitt County SD
Supt. — See Moultrie
Norman Park ES 600/PK-5
249 Weeks Ave 31771 229-769-3612
Keith Adams, prin. Fax 769-5003

Oakwood, Hall, Pop. 3,408
Hall County SD
Supt. — See Gainesville
Oakwood ES 500/K-5
4500 Allen St 30566 770-532-1656
Karla Swafford, prin. Fax 531-2326
West Hall MS 900/6-8
5470 Mcever Rd 30566 770-967-4871
Dr. Sarah Justus, prin. Fax 967-4874

Maranatha Christian Academy 100/PK-12
PO Box 877 30566 770-536-6334
Fax 531-9625

Ocilla, Irwin, Pop. 3,417
Irwin County SD 1,700/PK-12
PO Box 225 31774 229-468-7485
Betty Sue Stripling, supt. Fax 468-7220
www.irwin.k12.ga.us/
Irwin County ES 900/PK-5
521 Lax Hwy 31774 229-468-9476
Donna Barker, prin. Fax 468-9478
Irwin County MS 400/6-8
149 Chieftain Cir 31774 229-468-5517
Heather Purvis, prin. Fax 468-3134

Odum, Wayne, Pop. 447
Wayne County SD
Supt. — See Jesup
Odum ES 400/PK-5
322 Walter St 31555 912-586-2225
James Brinson, prin. Fax 586-6906

Oglethorpe, Macon, Pop. 1,157
Macon County SD 2,000/PK-12
PO Box 488 31068 478-472-8188
Dr. Carolyn Medlock, supt. Fax 472-2042
www.macon.k12.ga.us/
Macon County ES 1,000/PK-5
400 GA Highway 128 31068 478-472-6563
Gail Smith, prin. Fax 472-2591
Other Schools – See Montezuma

Oglethorpe SDA S 50/1-8
PO Box 1088 31068 478-472-2388

Omega, Tift, Pop. 1,360
Tift County SD
Supt. — See Tifton
Omega ES, 150 College St 31775 400/K-6
Glenda Huggins, prin. 229-387-2418

Oxford, Newton, Pop. 2,214
Newton County SD
Supt. — See Covington
Stone ES 700/PK-5
1110 Emory St 30054 770-784-2969
Dr. Lori Thomas, prin. Fax 784-2994

Providence Christian S 100/1-12
252 Byrd Rd 30054 770-788-6618
Justin Hornsby, hdmstr. Fax 385-4988

Palmetto, Fulton, Pop. 4,676
Fulton County SD
Supt. — See Atlanta
Palmetto ES 600/PK-5
505 Carlton Rd 30268 770-463-6100
Maureen Wheeler, prin. Fax 463-6105

Patterson, Pierce, Pop. 662
Pierce County SD
Supt. — See Blackshear
Patterson ES 500/PK-5
3414 Drawdy St 31557 912-647-5373
Stephany Smith, prin. Fax 647-5523

Peachtree City, Fayette, Pop. 34,524
Fayette County SD
Supt. — See Fayetteville
Booth MS 1,200/6-8
250 S Peachtree Pkwy 30269 770-631-3240
Ted Lombard, prin. Fax 631-3245
Braelinn ES 500/K-5
975 Robinson Rd 30269 770-631-5410
Wenonah Bell, prin. Fax 631-5430
Crabapple Lane ES 500/K-5
450 Crabapple Ln 30269 770-487-5425
Doe Evans, prin. Fax 487-6590
Huddleston ES 600/PK-5
200 Mcintosh Trl 30269 770-631-3255
Rebekah Maddox, prin. Fax 631-3252
Kedron ES 500/PK-5
200 Kedron Dr 30269 770-486-2700
Mary Bivings, prin. Fax 486-2707
Oak Grove ES 500/PK-5
101 Crosstown Dr 30269 770-631-3260
Bonnie Hancock, prin. Fax 631-5431
Peachtree City ES 500/PK-5
201 Wisdom Rd 30269 770-631-3250
Kristen Berryman, prin. Fax 631-3249

Footprints Christian Academy 50/K-12
255 Clover Reach 30269 770-487-2345
Chandra Horne, dir. Fax 487-2422
St. Paul Lutheran S 200/PK-8
700 Ardenlee Pkwy 30269 770-486-3545
James Richards, prin. Fax 692-6389

Pearson, Atkinson, Pop. 1,901
Atkinson County SD 1,800/PK-12
98 Roberts Ave E 31642 912-422-7373
Don Spence, supt. Fax 422-7369
www.atkinson.k12.ga.us/
Pearson ES 900/PK-7
563 King St N 31642 912-422-3882
Janice Tillman, prin. Fax 422-7024
Other Schools – See Willacoochee

Pelham, Mitchell, Pop. 3,914
Grady County SD
Supt. — See Cairo
Shiver S 600/PK-8
1847 GA Highway 93 N 31779 229-377-2325
Patsy Clark, prin. Fax 377-4366

Pelham CSD 1,600/PK-12
188 W Railroad St S 31779 229-294-8715
Dr. Paul Fanning, supt. Fax 294-2760
www.pelham-city.k12.ga.us/
Pelham City MS 300/6-8
209 Mathewson Ave SW 31779 229-294-6063
Laron Smith, prin. Fax 294-6046
Pelham ES 800/PK-5
534 Barrow Ave SW 31779 229-294-8170
Dr. Torrence Choates, prin. Fax 294-7454

Pembroke, Bryan, Pop. 2,503
Bryan County SD 6,400/PK-12
66 S Industrial Blvd 31321 912-626-5000
John Oliver, supt. Fax 653-4386
www.bryan.k12.ga.us/
Bryan County ES 400/3-5
104 Ash Branch Rd 31321 912-626-5033
Debra Laing, prin. Fax 653-4350
Bryan County MS 400/6-8
600 Payne Dr 31321 912-626-5050
Deborah Hamm, prin. Fax 653-2705
Bryan Preschool - Pembroke PK-PK
66 S Industrial Blvd 31321 912-653-4308
Fax 653-4386
Bryan Preschool - Richmond PK-PK
66 S Industrial Blvd 31321 912-756-3335
Fax 653-4386
Lanier PS 400/K-2
6024 US Highway 280 E 31321 912-626-5020
Dr. Patti Newman, prin. Fax 858-4350
Other Schools – See Richmond Hill

Perry, Houston, Pop. 11,018
Houston County SD 25,900/PK-12
PO Box 1850 31069 478-988-6200
David Carpenter, supt. Fax 988-6259
www.hcbe.net
Kings Chapel ES 300/PK-5
460 Arena Rd 31069 478-988-6273
Paulette Tompkins, prin. Fax 988-6346
Morningside ES 400/2-5
1206 Morningside Dr 31069 478-988-6261
Pat Witt, prin. Fax 988-6265
Perry MS 900/6-8
495 Perry Pkwy 31069 478-988-6285
Thomas Moore, prin. Fax 988-6345
Perry PS 700/PK-1
1530 Sunshine Ave 31069 478-988-6160
Elgin Mayfield, prin. Fax 988-6166
Tucker ES 400/2-5
1300 Tucker Rd 31069 478-988-6278
Dr. Kim Halstead, prin. Fax 988-6379
Other Schools – See Bonaire, Byron, Centerville, Kathleen, Warner Robins

Westfield S 600/PK-12
PO Box 2300 31069 478-987-0547
Janette Anderson, prin. Fax 987-7379

Pinehurst, Dooly, Pop. 335
Dooly County SD
Supt. — See Vienna
Dooly County ES 800/PK-5
11949 US Highway 41 31070 229-645-3421
Dr. Sandra Ferguson, prin. Fax 268-6148
Dooly County MS 300/6-8
11949 US Highway 41 31070 229-645-3421
Dr. Daniel Sturdivant, prin. Fax 268-1916

Fullington Academy 300/PK-12
PO Box B 31070 229-645-3383
Mike Cason, hdmstr. Fax 645-3386

Plainville, Gordon, Pop. 270
Gordon County SD
Supt. — See Calhoun
Swain ES 600/PK-5
2505 Rome Rd SW 30733 706-629-0141
Dr. Gina Daniel, prin. Fax 629-6815

Pooler, Chatham, Pop. 10,019
Savannah-Chatham County SD
Supt. — See Savannah
Pooler ES 400/K-5
308 Holly Ave 31322 912-748-3625
Caroline Gordon-Jelks, prin. Fax 748-3636
West Chatham ES 700/K-5
820 Pine Barren Rd 31322 912-748-3600
Peter Ulrich, prin. Fax 748-3615
West Chatham MS 900/6-8
800 Pine Barren Rd 31322 912-748-3650
Stascia Hardy, prin. Fax 748-3669

Savannah Adventist Christian S 50/K-9
50 Godley Way 31322 912-748-5977
Cindy Morrison, prin. Fax 748-5977

Portal, Bulloch, Pop. 595
Bulloch County SD
Supt. — See Statesboro
Portal ES 400/PK-5
328 Grady St S 30450 912-865-9550
Paul Hudson, prin. Fax 865-9553

Port Wentworth, Chatham, Pop. 3,238
Savannah-Chatham County SD
Supt. — See Savannah
Port Wentworth ES 400/PK-5
507 S Coastal Hwy 31407 912-965-6742
Julie Newton, prin. Fax 965-6734

Powder Springs, Cobb, Pop. 14,507
Cobb County SD
Supt. — See Marietta
Austell IS 600/2-5
5243 Meadows Rd 30127 770-819-2387
Clint Terza, prin. Fax 819-2389
Compton ES 600/K-5
3450 New Macland Rd 30127 770-222-3700
Elizabeth Murphy, prin. Fax 222-3702
Kemp ES 900/K-5
865 Corner Rd 30127 678-594-8158
Kristina Mason, prin. Fax 594-8160
Lovinggood MS 1,300/6-8
3825 Luther Ward Rd 30127 678-331-3015
Zinta Perkins, prin. Fax 331-3016
Powder Springs ES 900/PK-5
4570 Grady Grier Dr 30127 770-222-3746
Darlene Mitchell, prin. Fax 222-3748
Still ES 600/K-5
870 Casteel Rd 30127 678-594-8287
Grace Manharth, prin. Fax 594-8289
Tapp MS 900/6-8
3900 Macedonia Rd 30127 770-222-3758
Dr. Jerry Dority, prin. Fax 222-3760
Varner ES 800/PK-5
4761 Gaydon Rd 30127 770-222-3775
Ana Crommett, prin. Fax 222-3777
Vaughan ES 1,100/K-5
5950 Nichols Rd 30127 678-594-8298
Barbara Swinney, prin. Fax 594-8300

Paulding County SD
Supt. — See Dallas
Baggett ES 900/PK-5
948 Williams Lake Rd 30127 678-460-1570
Jeffrey Robinson, prin. Fax 943-6255
Dobbins MS 700/6-8
637 Williams Lake Rd 30127 770-443-4835
Cartess Ross, prin. Fax 439-1672

Midway Covenant Christian S 300/PK-8
4635 Dallas Hwy 30127 770-590-1866
Barbara Kline, admin. Fax 422-6416

Praise Academy 300/PK-12
4052 Hiram Lithia Springs 30127 770-943-2484
Georgia White, prin. Fax 943-9458
Youth Christian S 200/PK-12
4967 Brownsville Rd 30127 770-943-1394
Michele Jones, prin. Fax 943-0756

Preston, Webster, Pop. 438
Webster County SD 400/PK-12
7168 Washington St 31824 229-828-3365
James Stevens, supt. Fax 828-3206
www.webstereagles.net/
Webster County S 400/PK-8
7168 Washington St 31824 229-828-3365
James Stevens, prin. Fax 828-2014

Quitman, Brooks, Pop. 4,520
Brooks County SD 2,400/PK-12
PO Box 511 31643 229-263-7531
Debra Folsom, supt. Fax 263-5206
www.brookscountyschools.com/
Brooks County MS 600/6-8
2171 Moultrie Hwy 31643 229-263-7521
Al Williams, prin. Fax 263-9038
Quitman ES 800/PK-5
2200 Moultrie Hwy 31643 229-263-9302
Irma Hall, prin. Fax 263-4169
Other Schools – See Morven

Rabun Gap, Rabun
Rabun County SD
Supt. — See Clayton
Rabun Gap ES 200/K-2
1411 Bettys Creek Rd 30568 706-746-2273
Judith Ross, prin. Fax 746-5922

Reidsville, Tattnall, Pop. 2,400
Tattnall County SD 3,300/PK-12
PO Box 157 30453 912-557-4726
Gina Williams, supt. Fax 557-3036
www.tattnallschools.org/home.asp
Reidsville ES 700/PK-5
PO Box 428 30453 912-557-6711
Joy Pinckard, prin. Fax 557-3265
Reidsville MS 300/6-8
PO Box 369 30453 912-557-3993
Gwenda Johnson, prin. Fax 557-4124
Other Schools – See Collins, Glennville

Rentz, Laurens, Pop. 318
Laurens County SD
Supt. — See Dublin
Southwest Laurens ES 1,000/PK-5
1799 GA Highway 117 31075 478-984-4276
Pattii Rowe, prin. Fax 984-4711

Resaca, Gordon, Pop. 864
Gordon County SD
Supt. — See Calhoun
Tolbert ES 700/PK-5
1435 Hall Memorial Rd NW 30735 706-629-4404
Kim Muse, prin. Fax 629-6720

Rex, Clayton
Clayton County SD
Supt. — See Jonesboro
Adamson MS 800/6-8
3187 Rex Rd 30273 770-968-2925
Lonnie White, prin. Fax 968-2949
Rex Mill MS 600/6-8
6380 Evans Dr 30273 770-474-0702
Susan Patrick, prin. Fax 474-5812
Smith ES 900/PK-5
6340 Highway 42 30273 770-960-5750
Cindy Brictson, prin. Fax 960-5764

Richmond Hill, Bryan, Pop. 9,187
Bryan County SD
Supt. — See Pembroke
Carver ES 700/4-5
476 Frances Meeks Way 31324 912-459-5111
Crystal Morales, prin. Fax 756-5872
Richmond Hill ES 700/2-3
120 Constitution Way 31324 912-459-5100
Walt Barnes, prin. Fax 756-3916
Richmond Hill MS 1,100/6-8
665 Harris Trail Rd 31324 912-459-5130
Helen Herndon, prin. Fax 756-5369
Richmond Hill PS 800/PK-1
471 Frances Meeks Way 31324 912-459-5080
MaryAnn Tiedeman, prin. Fax 756-5153

Rincon, Effingham, Pop. 6,349
Effingham County SD
Supt. — See Springfield
Blandford ES 700/PK-5
4650 McCall Rd 31326 912-826-4200
Karen Durkin, prin. Fax 826-4747
Ebenezer ES 600/PK-5
1198 Ebenezer Rd 31326 912-754-5522
Beth Kight, prin. Fax 754-5527
Ebenezer MS 900/6-8
1100 Ebenezer Rd 31326 912-754-7757
Ramona Lovett, prin. Fax 754-4012
Rincon ES 600/PK-5
501 Richland Ave 31326 912-826-5523
Paige Dickey, prin. Fax 826-4052

Effingham Christian S 100/PK-9
PO Box 370 31326 912-826-3327
Ted Trainor, hdmstr. Fax 826-6555

Ringgold, Catoosa, Pop. 2,793
Catoosa County SD 10,600/PK-12
PO Box 130 30736 706-965-2297
Denia Reese, supt. Fax 965-8913
www.catoosa.k12.ga.us
Boynton ES 600/K-5
3938 Boynton Dr 30736 706-866-1521
Belinda Crisman, prin. Fax 861-6641
Heritage MS 900/6-8
4005 Poplar Springs Rd 30736 706-937-3568
Chris Lusk, prin. Fax 937-2583
Ringgold ES 500/3-5
322 Evitt Ln 30736 706-935-2912
Kim Erwin, prin. Fax 965-8907
Ringgold MS 900/6-8
217 Tiger Trl 30736 706-935-3381
Mike Sholl, prin. Fax 965-8908
Ringgold PS 600/PK-2
340 Evitt Ln 30736 706-937-5437
Nancy Gurganus, prin. Fax 937-8383
Other Schools – See Fort Oglethorpe, Graysville, Rock Spring, Rossville, Tunnel Hill

Riverdale, Clayton, Pop. 15,475
Clayton County SD
Supt. — See Jonesboro
Church Street ES 900/K-5
7013 Church St 30274 770-994-4000
Debra Smith, prin. Fax 994-4469
Harper ES 800/K-5
93 Valley Hill Rd SW 30274 678-479-2654
Lynda Daniel, prin. Fax 479-2673
Lake Ridge ES 900/PK-5
7900 Lake Ridge Cir 30296 770-907-5170
Dr. Brenda Cloud, prin. Fax 907-5185
Oliver ES 900/PK-5
1725 Cheryl Leigh Dr 30296 770-994-4010
Dr. Ronald Boykins, prin. Fax 994-4014
Pointe South ES 800/PK-5
631 Flint River Rd SW 30274 770-473-2900
Frank Tanner, prin. Fax 603-5774
Riverdale ES 600/K-5
6630 Camp St 30274 770-994-4015
April Madden, prin. Fax 994-4018
Riverdale MS 900/6-8
400 Roberts Dr 30274 770-994-4045
Dr. Mildred McCoy, prin. Fax 994-4467
Sequoyah MS 900/6-8
95 Valley Hill Rd SW 30274 770-515-7524
Stephanie Johnson, prin. Fax 515-7540

Roberta, Crawford, Pop. 776
Crawford County SD 2,000/PK-12
PO Box 8 31078 478-836-3131
John Douglas, supt. Fax 836-3114
www.crawford.k12.ga.us
Crawford County ES 900/PK-5
PO Box 308 31078 478-836-3171
Donald Spinks, prin. Fax 836-9228
Crawford County MS 500/6-8
PO Box 335 31078 478-836-3181
Anthony English, prin. Fax 836-3795

Rochelle, Wilcox, Pop. 1,418
Wilcox County SD
Supt. — See Abbeville
Wilcox County ES 700/PK-5
104 Gordon St 31079 229-365-2441
Dianne Walker, prin. Fax 365-2553
Wilcox County MS 300/6-8
114 7th Ave 31079 229-365-2331
Valentina Sutton, prin. Fax 365-2641

Rockmart, Polk, Pop. 4,310
Paulding County SD
Supt. — See Dallas
Ragsdale ES K-5
528 Holly Springs Rd 30153 770-443-2140
Ashley Anderson, prin.

Polk County SD
Supt. — See Cedartown
Eastside ES 800/1-5
425 Prospect Rd 30153 770-684-5335
Mark Lumpkin, prin. Fax 684-1335
Rockmart MS 600/6-8
60 Knox Mountain Rd 30153 678-757-1479
Shannon Hulsey, prin. Fax 757-9868
Van Wert ES, 370 Atlanta Hwy 30153 PK-5
Sherri Cox, prin. 770-684-6924

Rock Spring, Walker
Catoosa County SD
Supt. — See Ringgold
Woodstation ES 400/K-5
3404 Colbert Hollow Rd 30739 706-935-6700
Doug Suits, prin. Fax 935-3377

Walker County SD
Supt. — See La Fayette
Rock Spring ES 400/PK-5
372 Highway 95 30739 706-764-1383
Angie Ingram, prin. Fax 764-2248

Rocky Face, Whitfield
Whitfield County SD
Supt. — See Dalton
West Side ES 800/K-5
1815 Utility Rd 30740 706-673-6531
Tracy Mardis, prin. Fax 673-5556
Westside MS 600/6-8
580 Lafayette Rd 30740 706-673-2611
Stan Stewart, prin. Fax 673-5349

Rome, Floyd, Pop. 35,816
Floyd County SD 10,700/PK-12
600 Riverside Pkwy NE 30161 706-234-1031
Lynn Plunkett Ed.D., supt. Fax 236-1824
www.floydboe.net
Alto Park ES 500/PK-5
525 Burnett Ferry Rd SW 30165 706-236-1892
Dr. Aaron Anderson, prin. Fax 236-1894
Armuchee ES 500/3-5
5075 Martha Berry Hwy NW 30165 706-802-6758
Rodney Stewart, prin. Fax 802-6761
Coosa MS 600/6-8
212 Eagle Dr NW 30165 706-236-1856
Dr. Lisa Landrum, prin. Fax 802-6766
Garden Lakes ES 500/K-5
2903 Garden Lakes Blvd NW 30165 706-236-1865
Mary Alcorn, prin. Fax 802-6773
Glenwood PS 600/PK-2
75 Glenwood School Rd NE 30165 706-236-1855
Terri Snelling, prin. Fax 290-8156

Johnson ES 500/PK-5
1839 Morrison Campground Rd 30161 706-236-1830
LaDonna Turrentine, prin. Fax 290-8152
McHenry PS 300/PK-3
100 McHenry Dr SW 30161 706-236-1833
Jenni Cunningham, prin. Fax 290-8166
Model ES 600/PK-5
3200 Calhoun Rd NE 30161 706-236-1827
Tony Bethune, prin. Fax 290-8162
Model MS 500/6-8
164 Barron Rd NE 30161 706-290-8150
David Tucker, prin. Fax 802-6775
Other Schools – See Armuchee, Cave Spring, Lindale, Silver Creek

Rome CSD 5,400/PK-12
508 E 2nd St 30161 706-236-5050
Dr. Gayland Cooper, supt. Fax 802-4311
www.rcs.rome.ga.us
Davie ES 200/PK-6
301 Nixon Ave SW 30161 706-234-4118
Kelvin Portis, prin. Fax 234-5059
East Central ES 400/K-6
1502 Dean Ave SE 30161 706-232-8310
Tonya Wood, prin. Fax 234-5374
Elm Street ES 500/K-6
8 S Elm St SW 30165 706-232-5313
Dr. JoAnn Moss, prin. Fax 802-4315
Main ES 200/PK-6
3 Watters St SE 30161 706-295-7180
Parke Wilkinson, prin. Fax 235-4930
North Heights ES 200/PK-6
26 Atteiram Dr NE 30161 706-295-4442
Gordon Scoggins, prin. Fax 234-5727
Rome MS 800/7-8
1020 Veterans Memorial NE 30161 706-235-4695
Greg Christian, prin. Fax 234-5903
Southeast ES 200/PK-6
1400 Crane St SW 30161 706-232-4913
Doug Long, prin. Fax 235-3772
West Central ES 600/PK-6
409 Lavender Dr NW 30165 706-235-8836
Dr. Janice Merritt, prin. Fax 234-5854
West End ES 700/PK-6
5 Brown Fox Dr SW 30165 706-234-9366
Buffi Murphy, prin. Fax 234-5869

Darlington S 900/PK-12
1014 Cave Spring Rd SW 30161 706-235-6051
Thomas Whitworth, hdmstr. Fax 232-3600
St. Mary S 400/PK-8
401 E 7th St SE 30161 706-234-4953
Alex Porto, prin. Fax 234-3030
Unity Christian S 400/PK-12
2960 New Calhoun Hwy NE 30161 706-292-0700
Glenn Getchell, hdmstr. Fax 292-0772

Roopville, Carroll, Pop. 196
Carroll County SD
Supt. — See Carrollton
Roopville ES 400/PK-5
60 Old Carrollton Rd 30170 770-854-4421
Anna Clifton, prin. Fax 854-3001

Heard County SD
Supt. — See Franklin
Ephesus ES 200/PK-5
24414 Georgia Highway 100 30170 770-854-4400
Rebecca Carlisle, prin. Fax 854-6555

Rossville, Walker, Pop. 3,416
Catoosa County SD
Supt. — See Ringgold
Cloud Springs ES 500/PK-5
163 Fernwood Dr 30741 706-866-6640
Cliff Brittingham, prin. Fax 861-6642
Lakeview MS 800/6-8
416 Cross St 30741 706-866-1040
Steve McClure, prin. Fax 861-6644
West Side ES 400/K-5
72 Braves Ln 30741 706-866-9211
Chris Byrum, prin. Fax 861-6647

Walker County SD
Supt. — See La Fayette
Rossville ES 500/PK-5
1250 Wilson Rd 30741 706-866-5901
Robin Samples, prin. Fax 866-6169
Rossville MS 500/6-8
316 Bull Dog Trl 30741 706-820-0638
Wanda Janeway, prin. Fax 820-0696
Stone Creek ES 400/PK-5
1600 Happy Valley Rd 30741 706-866-3600
Brandon Mosgrove, prin. Fax 861-4325

Roswell, Fulton, Pop. 85,920
Fulton County SD
Supt. — See Atlanta
Crabapple MS 900/6-8
10700 Crabapple Rd 30075 770-552-4520
Dr. Kimothy Jarrett, prin. Fax 552-4524
Elkins Pointe MS 900/6-8
11290 Elkins Rd 30076 770-667-2892
Vivian Bankston, prin. Fax 667-2898
Hembree Springs ES 800/PK-5
815 Hembree Rd 30076 770-667-2902
Kalpana Raju, prin. Fax 667-2906
Hillside ES 700/PK-5
9250 Scott Rd 30076 770-552-6362
Lori Fanning, prin. Fax 552-6366
Jackson ES 700/PK-5
1400 Martin Rd 30076 770-594-5290
Constance Coles, prin. Fax 643-3332
Mimosa ES 800/PK-5
1550 Warsaw Rd 30076 770-552-4540
Cheryl Williams, prin. Fax 552-6346
Mountain Park ES 800/K-5
11895 Mountain Park Rd 30075 770-552-4530
Stacy Perlman, prin. Fax 643-3331
Northwood ES 900/K-5
10200 Wooten Rd 30076 770-552-6390
Sheila Michael, prin. Fax 552-6397
River Eves ES 700/K-5
9000 Eves Rd 30076 770-552-4550
Neil Pinnock, prin. Fax 552-4557
Roswell North ES 800/PK-5
10525 Woodstock Rd 30075 770-552-6320
Jerome Huff, prin. Fax 552-6326
Sweet Apple ES 900/K-5
12025 Etris Rd 30075 770-643-3310
Lenny Forti, prin. Fax 643-3316

Cross of Life Montessori S 100/PK-K
1000 Hembree Rd 30076 770-475-3812
Kim Colburn, dir. Fax 751-5726
Fellowship Christian S 700/PK-12
10965 Woodstock Rd 30075 770-992-4975
Eric Munn, hdmstr. Fax 993-9262
High Meadows S 400/PK-8
1055 Willeo Rd 30075 770-993-2940
Liz Gembecki, hdmstr. Fax 993-8331
Queen of Angels S 500/K-8
11340 Woodstock Rd 30075 770-518-1804
Dr. Kathy Wood, prin. Fax 518-0945
Village Montessori S 100/PK-6
1610 Woodstock Rd 30075 770-552-0834
Cara Friedline, admin. Fax 645-6425

Royston, Franklin, Pop. 2,678
Franklin County SD
Supt. — See Carnesville
Royston ES 500/K-5
660 College St 30662 706-245-9252
Jimmy Truitt, prin. Fax 245-0903

Rutledge, Morgan, Pop. 752

Philadelphia Christian S 200/PK-12
4031 Davis Academy Rd 30663 706-557-7995
Dr. Jerry Kramer, prin. Fax 557-7749

Rydal, Bartow
Bartow County SD
Supt. — See Cartersville
Pine Log ES 400/K-5
3370 Pine Log Rd NE 30171 770-606-5864
Nancy Summey, prin. Fax 606-3866

Saint George, Charlton
Charlton County SD
Supt. — See Folkston
Saint George ES 200/PK-6
PO Box 298, 912-843-2383
Joan Crews, prin. Fax 843-8287

Saint Marys, Camden, Pop. 15,811
Camden County SD
Supt. — See Kingsland
Clark ES 600/PK-5
318 Mickler Dr 31558 912-882-4373
Dr. Angela McManigal, prin. Fax 576-5126
Crooked River ES 500/PK-5
3570 Charlie Smith Sr Hwy 31558 912-673-6995
Dr. Sheila Sapp, prin. Fax 882-2761
Saint Marys ES 600/PK-5
510 Osborne St 31558 912-882-4839
Thomas McClendon, prin. Fax 882-9200
Saint Marys MS 1,100/6-8
205 Martha Dr 31558 912-882-8626
Michael Wooden, prin. Fax 882-5473
Sugarmill ES 600/PK-5
2885 Winding Rd 31558 912-882-8191
Dr. Michael Hunter, prin. Fax 882-8681

Saint Simons Island, Glynn, Pop. 12,026
Glynn County SD
Supt. — See Brunswick
Oglethorpe Point ES 600/PK-5
6200 Frederica Rd 31522 912-638-6200
Susan Arnold, prin. Fax 634-1289
St. Simons Island ES 400/PK-5
805 Ocean Blvd 31522 912-638-2851
Suzanne Clements, prin. Fax 638-1783

Christian Montessori S 100/PK-6
111 Menendez Ave 31522 912-638-1692
Sidneye Henderson, prin. Fax 638-8171
Frederica Academy 400/PK-12
200 Hamilton Rd 31522 912-638-9981
Ellen Fleming, hdmstr. Fax 638-1442
Whitefield S 100/PK-7
46 Hampton Point Dr 31522 912-634-8177
Karl Graustein, hdmstr. Fax 634-2900

Sandersville, Washington, Pop. 6,031
Washington County SD 3,300/PK-12
PO Box 716 31082 478-552-3981
Donna Hinton, supt. Fax 552-3128
www.washington.k12.ga.us/
Elder MS 800/6-8
PO Box 816 31082 478-552-2007
Manzie Broxton, prin. Fax 552-7388
Elder PS 500/PK-2
PO Box 856 31082 478-552-6047
Dexter Wansley, prin. Fax 552-9020
Sandersville ES 500/3-5
514 N Harris St 31082 478-552-2245
Carla Hutchings, prin. Fax 552-0870
Other Schools – See Tennille

Brentwood S 400/PK-12
PO Box 955 31082 478-552-5136
Jackie Holton, prin. Fax 552-2947

Sandy Springs, Fulton, Pop. 90,300
Fulton County SD
Supt. — See Atlanta
Ison Road ES, 8261 Ison Rd 30350 PK-5
Sara Glynn, prin. 404-768-3600

Sardis, Burke, Pop. 1,217
Burke County SD
Supt. — See Waynesboro
S.G.A. ES 400/PK-5
1265 Charles Perry Ave 30456 478-569-4322
Sam Adkins, prin. Fax 569-4065

Sautee, White
White County SD
Supt. — See Cleveland
Mount Yonah ES 500/K-6
1161 Duncan Bridge Rd, 706-865-3514
Dana Magill, prin. Fax 865-1466

Savannah, Chatham, Pop. 128,453
Savannah-Chatham County SD 32,500/PK-12
208 Bull St 31401 912-201-5600
Dr. Thomas Lockamy, supt. Fax 201-5628
www.savannah.chatham.k12.ga.us/
Bartlett MS 600/6-8
207 E Montgomery Xrd 31406 912-961-3500
Drema Jackson, prin. Fax 961-3515
Bartow ES 500/PK-5
1804 Stratford St 31415 912-395-5300
Maggie Walker-Zeigler, prin. Fax 201-5302
Butler ES 800/PK-5
1909 Cynthia St 31415 912-395-2525
Lynette Ward, prin. Fax 201-7578
Coastal MS 700/6-8
170 Whitemarsh Island Rd 31410 912-898-3950
Kerry Coursey, prin. Fax 898-3951
DeRenne MS 900/6-8
3609 Hopkins St 31405 912-201-5900
Pat Rossiter, prin. Fax 201-5903
East Broad Street ES 600/PK-5
400 E Broad St 31401 912-201-5500
Dr. Charlene Ford, prin. Fax 201-5503
Ellis Montessori Academy 500/PK-8
220 E 49th St 31405 912-201-5470
Charles Wooten, prin. Fax 201-5473
Gadsden ES 600/PK-5
919 May St 31415 912-201-5940
Dr. Deborah Jones, prin. Fax 201-5943
Garrison ES 400/PK-5
649 W Jones St 31401 912-201-5975
Renae Miller-McCullough, prin. Fax 201-5978
Georgetown ES 600/K-5
1516 King George Blvd 31419 912-961-3475
Joseph Thomas, prin. Fax 961-3479
Gould ES 600/PK-5
4910 Pineland Dr 31405 912-201-5400
Vernon Cole, prin. Fax 201-5403
Haven ES 400/PK-5
5111 Dillon Ave 31405 912-395-6501
Megan Kicklighter, prin. Fax 303-6509
Heard ES 700/PK-5
414 Lee Blvd 31405 912-303-6630
James Heater, prin. Fax 303-6637
Hesse ES 500/PK-5
9116 Whitfield Ave 31406 912-303-6440
Lawrence Butler, prin. Fax 303-6450
Hodge ES 400/PK-5
1101 W Victory Dr 31405 912-395-5200
Donna Myers, prin. Fax 201-5213
Howard ES 700/PK-5
115 Wilmington Island Rd 31410 912-898-3925
Dr. Ethel Bowles, prin. Fax 898-3934
Hubert MS 500/6-8
768 Grant St 31401 912-201-5235
Dr. Gequetta Jenkins, prin. Fax 201-5238
Islands ES 700/PK-5
4595 US Highway 80 E 31410 912-898-3900
Diane Towles, prin. Fax 898-3911
Isle of Hope ES 500/PK-5
100 Parkersburg Rd 31406 912-303-6555
Julie Gannan, prin. Fax 303-6572
Largo-Tibet ES 500/PK-5
430 Tibet Ave 31406 912-961-3450
Dr. Andrea DeShazo, prin. Fax 961-3460
Low ES 500/PK-5
15 Blue Ridge Ave 31404 912-303-6380
Dr. Linda Canady, prin. Fax 303-6386
Marshpoint ES 900/PK-5
135 Whitemarsh Island Rd 31410 912-898-4000
Kaye Aikens, prin. Fax 898-4001
Myers MS 700/6-8
2025 E 52nd St 31404 912-303-6600
Dora Myles, prin. Fax 303-6604
Pulaski ES 500/PK-5
5330 Montgomery St 31405 912-395-6466
Kamal Piankhi, prin. Fax 303-6473
Shuman MS 900/6-8
415 Goebel Ave 31404 912-201-7500
Karyta Byers, prin. Fax 201-7503
Smith ES 400/K-5
210 Lamara Dr 31405 912-395-6530
Jane Tyler, prin. Fax 303-6538
Southwest ES 800/K-5
6020 Ogeechee Rd 31419 912-961-3301
Kimberly Hancock, prin. Fax 961-3312
Southwest MS 900/6-8
6030 Ogeechee Rd 31419 912-961-3540
Kimsherion Reid, prin. Fax 961-3548
Spencer ES 600/PK-5
100 Bouhan Ave 31404 912-201-7525
Andrea Williams, prin. Fax 201-7528
White Bluff ES 700/PK-5
9902 White Bluff Rd 31406 912-961-3325
Jerry Wichman, prin. Fax 961-3334
Windsor Forest ES 500/PK-5
414 Briarcliff Cir 31419 912-961-3353
Marcia McManus, prin. Fax 961-3359
Other Schools – See Bloomingdale, Garden City, Pooler, Port Wentworth, Thunderbolt

---

Bible Baptist S 400/PK-12
4700 Skidaway Rd 31404 912-352-3067
Steven Kyle, admin. Fax 352-9830
Blessed Sacrament S 400/PK-8
1003 E Victory Dr 31405 912-356-6987
Lynn Brown, prin. Fax 356-6988
Calvary Day S 1,000/PK-12
4625 Waters Ave 31404 912-351-2299
Ralph Finnegan, hdmstr. Fax 351-2280

Chatham Academy 100/1-12
4 Oglethorpe Prfssonal Blvd 31406 912-354-4047
Carolyn Hannaford, prin. Fax 354-4633
Hancock S 200/PK-5
6600 Howard Foss Dr 31406 912-351-4500
Francine Wright, prin. Fax 351-4550
Memorial Day S 200/PK-12
6500 Habersham St 31405 912-352-4535
Gary Lackey, hdmstr. Fax 352-4536
Notre Dame Academy 100/PK-8
1709 Bull St 31401 912-232-5473
Carol Foran, prin. Fax 232-3352
Providence Christian S 200/PK-12
2417 Louis Mills Blvd 31405 912-335-7976
David Osborne, hdmstr. Fax 335-7981
Ramah SDA Junior Academy 100/PK-8
3400 Florance St 31405 912-233-3101
Sheridan Albert, prin. Fax 233-1664
Rambam Day S 100/PK-8
5111 Abercorn St 31405 912-352-7994
Ester Rabhan, prin. Fax 352-1920
St. Andrew's S on the Marsh 500/PK-12
601 Penn Waller Rd 31410 912-897-4941
Gilbert Webb, hdmstr. Fax 897-4943
St. Francis Cabrini S 100/PK-2
11500 Middleground Rd 31419 912-925-6249
Cary Jane Williamson, prin. Fax 925-5661
St. James S 400/PK-8
8412 Whitfield Ave 31406 912-355-3132
Pam Dufrain, prin. Fax 355-1996
St. Paul's Lutheran S 100/PK-PK
10 W 31st St 31401 912-234-4255
St. Peter the Apostle S 300/PK-8
PO Box 30460 31410 912-897-5224
Kelly Ryan, prin. Fax 897-0801
Savannah Christian Preparatory S 1,400/PK-12
PO Box 2848 31402 912-234-1653
Roger Yancey, hdmstr. Fax 234-0491
Savannah Country Day S 1,000/PK-12
824 Stillwood Dr 31419 912-925-8800
Thomas Bonnell, hdmstr. Fax 920-7800

Scottdale, DeKalb, Pop. 8,636
DeKalb County SD
Supt. — See Decatur
Shaw Theme ES 500/PK-5
385 Glendale Rd 30079 678-676-6000
Millicent Frieson, prin. Fax 676-6010

Screven, Wayne, Pop. 756
Wayne County SD
Supt. — See Jesup
Screven ES 300/PK-5
PO Box 159 31560 912-579-2261
Dr. Mark Priester, prin. Fax 579-2225

Senoia, Coweta, Pop. 2,719
Coweta County SD
Supt. — See Newnan
East Coweta MS 600/6-8
6291 Highway 16 30276 770-599-6607
Dr. Nancy Cook, prin. Fax 599-1051
Eastside ES 600/PK-5
1225 Eastside School Rd 30276 770-599-6621
Sandra Hinton, prin. Fax 599-8530

Sharpsburg, Coweta, Pop. 328
Coweta County SD
Supt. — See Newnan
Canongate ES 800/PK-5
200 Pete Rd 30277 770-463-8010
Julie Lutz, prin. Fax 463-8012
Lee MS 800/6-8
370 Willis Rd 30277 770-251-1547
Dr. Bob Heaberlin, prin. Fax 253-8381
Poplar Road ES 700/PK-5
2925 Poplar Rd 30277 770-254-2740
Lesley Goodwin, prin. Fax 304-5926
Thomas Crossroads ES 500/PK-5
3530 Highway 34 E 30277 770-254-2751
Dr. Fate Simmons, prin. Fax 304-5924
Willis Road ES 800/PK-5
430 Willis Rd 30277 770-304-7995
Dr. Charles Smith, prin. Fax 304-7999

Heritage Christian S 100/K-12
3613 Highway 34 E 30277 770-252-1234
Roy Davis, prin. Fax 304-9576
Shoal Creek SDA S 100/PK-8
4957 Highway 34 E 30277 770-251-1464
Tiffany Swinney, prin. Fax 251-1973

Shellman, Randolph, Pop. 1,084

Randolph Southern S 200/K-12
PO Box 300, 229-679-5324
Dr. Terry Tedder, hdmstr. Fax 679-5325

Siloam, Greene, Pop. 344

Greene Academy 300/PK-12
PO Box 109 30665 706-467-2147
John Arnold, hdmstr. Fax 467-2147

Silver Creek, Floyd
Floyd County SD
Supt. — See Rome
Midway PS 400/PK-3
5 Midway School Rd SE 30173 706-236-1880
Jeanie Hubbard, prin. Fax 236-1879

Smyrna, Cobb, Pop. 47,643
Cobb County SD
Supt. — See Marietta
Argyle ES 800/PK-5
2420 Spring Rd SE 30080 678-842-6800
Robert Babay, prin. Fax 842-6802
Belmont Hills ES 700/PK-5
605 Glendale Pl SE 30080 678-842-6810
Terry Floyd, prin. Fax 842-6812
Brown ES 200/K-5
3265 Brown Rd SE 30080 678-842-6838
Brett Ward, prin. Fax 842-6840
Campbell MS 1,100/6-8
3295 Atlanta Rd SE 30080 678-842-6873
Denise Magee, prin. Fax 842-6875
Griffin MS 1,100/6-8
4010 King Springs Rd SE 30082 678-842-6917
Darryl York, prin. Fax 842-6919
King Springs ES 600/PK-5
1041 Reed Rd SE 30082 678-842-6944
Linda Keeney, prin. Fax 842-6946
Nickajack ES 800/K-5
4555 Mavell Rd SE 30082 678-842-5814
Beverly Parks, prin. Fax 842-5832
Norton Park ES 800/PK-5
3041 Gray Rd SE 30082 678-842-5833
Douglas Daugherty, prin. Fax 842-5835
Russell ES 700/PK-5
3920 S Hurt Rd SW 30082 770-437-5937
Nancy Dipetrillo, prin. Fax 437-5939
Teasley ES 500/PK-5
3640 Spring Hill Rd SE 30080 770-437-5945
Joanne Robblee, prin. Fax 437-5947

Covenant Christian S 200/PK-8
3130 Atlanta Rd SE 30080 770-435-1596
Barbara Hines, prin. Fax 435-2256
Covered Bridge Academy 100/PK-4
488 Hurt Rd SW 30082 770-801-8292
Kate Walpert, dir. Fax 435-5080

Snellville, Gwinnett, Pop. 19,238
Gwinnett County SD
Supt. — See Suwanee
Annistown ES 600/K-5
3150 Spain Rd 30039 770-979-2950
Lorraine Molock-Sparks, prin. Fax 736-4491
Britt ES 1,000/K-5
2503 Skyland Dr 30078 770-972-4500
Doris Jones, prin. Fax 736-4426
Brookwood ES 1,100/K-5
1330 Holly Brook Rd 30078 770-736-4360
Karen Head, prin. Fax 736-4410
Centerville ES 800/K-5
3115 Centerville Hwy 30039 770-972-2220
Allan Gee, prin. Fax 982-6973
Norton ES 1,900/K-5
3050 Xavier Ray Ct 30039 770-985-1933
Dr. Robert Peterson, prin. Fax 736-2005
Partee ES 700/PK-5
4350 Campbell Rd 30039 770-982-6920
Audrey Baptiste, prin. Fax 982-6923
Pharr ES 1,400/K-5
1500 North Rd 30078 770-985-0244
Gerald Raymond, prin. Fax 736-4516
Shiloh ES 800/K-5
2400 Ross Rd 30039 770-985-6883
Betty Ann Schoeneck, prin. Fax 736-2061
Shiloh MS 1,700/6-8
4285 Shiloh Rd 30039 770-972-3224
Devon Williams, prin. Fax 736-4563
Snellville MS 2,200/6-8
3155 Pate Rd 30078 770-972-1530
Linda Boyd, prin. Fax 736-4444

Gwinnett Christian Academy 100/PK-12
2925 Main St W 30078 770-982-3773
Dr. Daniel Hodges, hdmstr. Fax 344-6687

Social Circle, Walton, Pop. 4,053
Social Circle CSD 1,700/PK-12
240B W Hightower Trl 30025 770-464-2731
Dr. Bettye Ray, supt. Fax 464-0403
www.scboe.org/
Social Circle ES 400/3-5
240A W Hightower Trl 30025 770-464-2664
Jodi Weber, prin. Fax 464-2665
Social Circle MS 400/6-8
154 Alcova Dr 30025 770-464-1932
Theodoris Gibbs, prin. Fax 464-2612
Social Circle PS 500/PK-2
439 Annie P Henderson Dr 30025 770-464-1411
Ronda Estes, prin. Fax 464-9233

Social Circle Christian S 100/PK-6
PO Box 357 30025 770-464-4039
Kay McLendon, prin. Fax 464-2628

Soperton, Treutlen, Pop. 2,747
Treutlen County SD 1,200/K-12
5040 S Third St 30457 912-529-4228
Charles Ellington, supt. Fax 529-4226
www.treutlen.net
Treutlen ES 600/K-5
2166 College St 30457 912-529-4911
Christopher Watkins, prin. Fax 529-6831

Sparks, Cook, Pop. 1,781
Cook County SD
Supt. — See Adel
Cook ES 800/3-5
1512 N Elm St 31647 229-549-6250
Dr. Barbara Pettiford, prin. Fax 549-8568
Cook MS 700/6-8
1601 N Elm St 31647 229-549-5999
Dr. Jeff Shealey, prin. Fax 549-5986

Sparta, Hancock, Pop. 1,374
Hancock County SD 1,400/PK-12
PO Box 488 31087 706-444-5775
Dr. Awana Leslie, supt. Fax 444-7026
www.hancock.k12.ga.us
Hancock Central MS 400/6-8
11311 GA Highway 15 31087 706-444-6652
Willie Gibson, prin. Fax 444-4344
Lewis ES 600/PK-5
11145 GA Highway 15 31087 706-444-7028
Stephanie Birdsong, prin. Fax 444-0380

Springfield, Effingham, Pop. 2,034
Effingham County SD 10,800/PK-12
405 N Ash St 31329 912-754-1537
Randy Shearouse, supt. Fax 754-8899
www.effinghamschools.com/
Central Learning Center PK-PK
434 Wallace Dr 31329 912-754-6417
Fax 754-6427
Effingham County MS 700/6-8
1290 GA Highway 119 S 31329 912-754-3332
Rob Porterfield, prin. Fax 754-7497
Springfield ES 700/PK-5
300 Old Dixie Hwy S 31329 912-754-3326
Terri Johnson, prin. Fax 754-7172
Other Schools – See Guyton, Rincon

Statenville, Echols
Echols County SD 700/PK-12
PO Box 207 31648 229-559-5734
Dr. Larry Allen, supt. Fax 559-0484
www.echols.k12.ga.us/
Echols County S 700/PK-12
PO Box 40 31648 229-559-5413
Tim Ragan, prin. Fax 559-0423

Statesboro, Bulloch, Pop. 24,612
Bulloch County SD 8,900/PK-12
150 Williams Rd Ste A 30458 912-764-6201
Dr. Lewis Holloway, supt. Fax 764-8436
www.bulloch.k12.ga.us
Bryant ES 600/PK-5
400 Donnie Simmons Way 30458 912-764-7585
Shawn Heralson, prin. Fax 489-5867
James MS 500/6-8
18809 US Highway 80 W 30458 912-764-2752
Mike Yawn, prin. Fax 489-5916
Langston Chapel ES 600/PK-5
150 Langston Chapel Rd 30458 912-681-3637
Dr. Karen Doty, prin. Fax 681-7802
Langston Chapel MS 600/6-8
156 Langston Chapel Rd 30458 912-681-8779
Elizabeth Williams, prin. Fax 681-6416
Lively ES 400/PK-5
204 Debbie Dr 30458 912-764-6271
Jennifer Herrington, prin. Fax 489-5891
Mill Creek ES 700/PK-5
239 Beasley Rd 30461 912-764-5979
Patrick Hill, prin. Fax 764-3842
Nevils ES 400/PK-5
8438 Nevils Groveland Rd 30458 912-839-3405
Julie Blackmar, prin. Fax 839-2357
Zetterower ES 400/K-5
900 E Jones Ave 30458 912-764-6392
Todd Williford, prin. Fax 489-5941
Other Schools – See Brooklet, Portal

Bulloch Academy 500/PK-12
873 Westside Rd 30458 912-764-6297
Dr. Brenda Riley, hdmstr. Fax 764-3165
Trinity Christian S 200/K-12
571 E Main St 30461 912-489-1375
David Lattner, hdmstr. Fax 764-3136

Statham, Barrow, Pop. 2,555
Barrow County SD
Supt. — See Winder
Statham ES 800/K-5
1970 Broad St 30666 770-725-7112
Robert Almond, prin. Fax 725-1550

Stillmore, Emanuel, Pop. 755

Emanuel Academy 200/K-12
PO Box 400 30464 912-562-4405
Fax 562-3465

Stockbridge, Henry, Pop. 13,140
Henry County SD
Supt. — See Mc Donough
Austin Road ES 600/PK-5
50 Austin Rd 30281 770-389-6556
James McNealey, prin. Fax 389-5909
Austin Road MS 800/6-8
100 Austin Rd 30281 770-507-5407
Janet Brown-Clayton, prin. Fax 507-5413
Cotton Indian ES 600/PK-5
1201 Old Conyers Rd 30281 770-474-9983
Natalie Metcalf, prin. Fax 474-6959
Fairview ES 700/PK-5
458 Fairview Rd 30281 770-474-8265
Cheryl Carter, prin. Fax 474-5528
Pate's Creek ES 700/PK-5
1309 Jodeco Rd 30281 770-389-8819
Carolyn Flournoy, prin. Fax 507-3558
Pleasant Grove ES 600/PK-5
150 Reagan Rd 30281 770-898-0176
Tracie Copper, prin. Fax 898-0185
Red Oak ES 800/K-5
175 Monarch Village Way 30281 770-389-1464
Tracy Neal-Bulls, prin. Fax 389-1737
Smith-Barnes ES 400/4-5
147 Tye St 30281 770-474-4066
Michael Eddy, prin. Fax 474-0039
Stockbridge ES 800/PK-3
4617 N Henry Blvd 30281 770-474-8743
Dr. LaVern Lynch, prin. Fax 474-2357
Stockbridge MS 700/6-8
533 Old Conyers Rd 30281 770-474-5710
Vicki Davis, prin. Fax 507-8406
Woodland ES 600/K-5
830 Moseley Dr 30281 770-506-6391
Christine Anderson, prin. Fax 506-6396
Woodland MS 700/6-8
820 Moseley Dr 30281 770-389-2774
Dr. Terry Oatts, prin. Fax 389-2780

Rockdale County SD
Supt. — See Conyers
Davis MS 800/6-8
3375 E Fairview Rd SW 30281 770-388-5675
Dr. Wayne Watts, prin. Fax 388-5676
Lorraine ES 700/K-5
3343 E Fairview Rd SW 30281 770-483-0657
Dr. David Ray, prin. Fax 483-5858

Community Christian S 800/PK-12
2001 Jodeco Rd 30281 678-432-0191
Frederick Banke, hdmstr. Fax 914-1217
Mt. Vernon Christian S 200/PK-12
2178 Highway 138 E 30281 770-474-1313
Ricky White, hdmstr. Fax 474-3010

Stone Mountain, DeKalb, Pop. 7,080
DeKalb County SD
Supt. — See Decatur
Allgood ES 600/PK-5
659 Allgood Rd 30083 678-676-5100
Shenandra Price, prin. Fax 676-5110
Champion MS 700/6-8
5265 Mimosa Dr 30083 678-875-1500
Angelique Smith-Hunt, prin. Fax 875-1510
Dunaire ES 700/PK-5
651 S Indian Creek Dr 30083 678-676-5500
Dr. Carolyn Thompson, prin. Fax 676-5510
Freedom MS 900/6-8
505 S Hairston Rd 30088 678-874-8700
Jill Dorsett, prin. Fax 874-8710
Hambrick ES 800/PK-5
1101 Hambrick Rd 30083 678-676-5600
Dr. Linda Priester, prin. Fax 676-5610
Miller ES 600/PK-5
919 Martin Rd 30088 678-676-3300
Anneice Speer, prin. Fax 676-3310
Pine Ridge ES 900/PK-5
750 Pine Ridge Dr 30087 678-676-3400
Debra Phillips, prin. Fax 676-3410
Rockbridge ES 600/PK-5
445 Halwick Way 30083 678-676-6100
Sadie Scott, prin. Fax 676-6110
Rowland ES 500/PK-5
1317 S Indian Creek Dr 30083 678-676-6200
Roberta Walker, prin. Fax 676-6210
Smoke Rise ES 500/PK-5
1991 Silver Hill Rd 30087 678-874-3600
Aaron Moore, prin. Fax 874-3610
Stephenson MS 1,400/6-8
922 Stephenson Rd 30087 678-676-4400
Obelia Hall, prin. Fax 676-4410
Stone Mill ES 600/PK-5
4900 Sheila Ln 30083 678-676-4602
Rita Hastings-Harper, prin. Fax 676-4610
Stone Mountain ES 700/PK-5
6720 James B Rivers Dr 30083 678-676-4700
Jessica Warren, prin. Fax 676-4710
Stone Mountain MS 1,000/6-8
4301 Sarr Pkwy 30083 678-676-4800
Dr. Gloria Dodson, prin. Fax 676-4810
Woodridge ES 600/PK-5
4120 Cedar Ridge Trl 30083 678-874-0200
Dr. Angelique Conner, prin. Fax 874-0210
Wynbrooke ES 1,000/PK-5
440 Wicksbury Way 30087 678-676-5000
Myisha Warren, prin. Fax 676-5010

Action Montessori Academy 100/PK-6
5580 Rockbridge Rd 30088 770-879-8331
Marilyn Bassett, dir. Fax 879-8909
Decatur Adventist Jr. Academy 200/K-8
2584 Young Rd 30088 770-808-2188
Yvonne Brown, prin. Fax 808-2181
Mount Carmel Christian S 200/PK-8
6015 Old Stone Mountain Rd 30087 770-279-8443
Fred Haselden M.Ed., prin. Fax 935-8620
St. Timothy UMC S 200/PK-5
5365 Memorial Dr 30083 404-297-8913
Rev. Rindy Trouteaud, prin. Fax 292-3396
Voices of Faith Academy 100/PK-5
2125 Rockbridge Rd 30087 678-740-0215
Ann Gaines, dir. Fax 740-0217

Suches, Union
Union County SD
Supt. — See Blairsville
Woody Gap S 100/K-12
3736 State Highway 60 30572 706-747-2401
Jinjer Taylor, prin. Fax 747-1419

Sugar Hill, Gwinnett, Pop. 15,696
Gwinnett County SD
Supt. — See Suwanee
Sycamore ES 1,200/K-5
5695 Sycamore Rd 30518 678-714-5770
Wanda Law, prin.

Sugar Hill Christian Academy 200/K-7
4600 Nelson Brogdon Blvd 30518 678-745-4121
Beth Compton, supt. Fax 745-4205

Summerville, Chattooga, Pop. 4,853
Chattooga County SD 2,800/PK-12
33 Middle School Rd 30747 706-857-3447
Dwight Pullen, supt. Fax 857-3440
www.chattooga.k12.ga.us
Massey ES 300/3-5
403 Dot Johnson Way 30747 706-857-6660
Judy England, prin. Fax 857-5898
Summerville ES 400/PK-2
206 Penn St 30747 706-857-2454
Ila King, prin. Fax 857-5767
Summerville MS 400/6-8
200 Middle School Rd 30747 706-857-2444
Kevin Muskett, prin. Fax 857-7769
Other Schools – See Lyerly, Menlo

Surrency, Appling, Pop. 245
Appling County SD
Supt. — See Baxley
Fourth District ES 200/PK-5
13396 Blackshear Hwy 31563 912-367-3250
Curtis Overstreet Ed.D., prin. Fax 367-0992

Suwanee, Gwinnett, Pop. 12,553
Forsyth County SD
Supt. — See Cumming
Johns Creek ES 1,000/K-5
6205 Old Atlanta Rd 30024 678-965-5041
Debbie Smith, prin. Fax 475-1725

Riverwatch MS 1,100/6-8
610 James Burgess Rd 30024 678-455-7311
Kathy Carpenter, prin. Fax 455-7316
Settles Bridge ES 1,000/K-5
600 James Burgess Rd 30024 770-887-1883
Donna Morris, prin. Fax 887-7383
Sharon ES 1,500/K-5
3595 Old Atlanta Rd 30024 770-888-7511
Amy Bartlett, prin. Fax 888-7510

Gwinnett County SD 155,000/PK-12
437 Old Peachtree Rd NW 30024 678-301-6000
J. Alvin Wilbanks, supt. Fax 301-6030
www.gwinnett.k12.ga.us/
Level Creek ES 1,100/K-5
4488 Tench Rd 30024 770-904-7950
Dr. Nancy Kiel, prin. Fax 904-7952
Parsons ES 1,000/K-5
1615 Old Peachtree Rd NW 30024 678-957-3050
Dr. Charlotte Sadler, prin. Fax 957-3055
Riverside ES 1,400/K-5
5445 Settles Bridge Rd 30024 678-482-1000
Dr. Craig Barlow, prin. Fax 482-1018
Suwanee ES 900/K-5
3875 Smithtown Rd 30024 770-945-5763
Kimberly Smith, prin. Fax 932-7433
Walnut Grove ES 900/K-5
75 Taylor Rd 30024 770-513-6892
Nancy Morrison, prin. Fax 682-4219
Other Schools – See Auburn, Berkeley Lake, Buford, Dacula, Duluth, Grayson, Hoschton, Lawrenceville, Lilburn, Loganville, Norcross, Snellville, Sugar Hill, Tucker

Friendship Christian S 100/K-12
3149 Old Atlanta Rd 30024 678-845-0418
Martin Cochran, hdmstr. Fax 845-0417
Horizon Christian S 200/PK-K
2172 Lawrenceville Suwanee 30024 770-962-2897
Judy Wintemute, prin. Fax 806-4860

Swainsboro, Emanuel, Pop. 7,162
Emanuel County SD 4,300/PK-12
PO Box 130 30401 478-237-6674
Dr. Tommy Craft, supt. Fax 237-3404
www.emanuel.k12.ga.us
Emanuel County Preschool Center PK-PK
220 Jefferson St 30401 478-237-9593
Gail McRae, dir. Fax 237-6374
Swainsboro ES 700/3-5
258 Tiger Trl 30401 478-237-7266
Stacey Barber, prin. Fax 237-4203
Swainsboro MS 700/6-8
200 Tiger Trl 30401 478-237-8047
Dr. Eric Carlyle, prin. Fax 237-4295
Swainsboro PS 700/K-2
308 Tiger Trl 30401 478-237-8302
Valorie Watkins, prin. Fax 237-3975
Other Schools – See Adrian, Twin City

Sylvania, Screven, Pop. 2,591
Screven County SD 2,900/PK-12
PO Box 1668 30467 912-564-7114
Dr. Whitney Myers, supt. Fax 564-7104
www.screven.k12.ga.us
Screven County ES 1,300/PK-5
1333 Frontage Rd E 30467 912-564-2081
Rebecca Martin, prin. Fax 564-5511
Screven County MS 700/6-8
126 Friendship Rd 30467 912-564-7468
Jim Thompson, prin. Fax 564-5505

Sylvester, Worth, Pop. 5,924
Worth County SD 3,400/PK-12
504 E Price St 31791 229-776-8600
Jim McMickin, supt. Fax 776-8603
www.worth.k12.ga.us/
Sylvester ES 400/3-5
103 Eldridge St 31791 229-776-8605
Todd Deariso, prin. Fax 776-8607
Worth County MS 900/6-8
1305 N Isabella St 31791 229-776-8620
Paul Zimmer, prin. Fax 776-8624
Worth County PS 900/PK-2
1304 N Isabella St 31791 229-776-8660
Tiffany Sevier, prin. Fax 776-8665

Talbotton, Talbot, Pop. 1,022
Talbot County SD 700/PK-12
PO Box 308 31827 706-665-8528
Robert Patrick, supt. Fax 665-3620
www.talbot.k12.ga.us/
Central ES 300/PK-5
PO Box 308 31827 706-665-8579
Edward Tymes, prin. Fax 665-2732
Central MS 200/6-8
PO Box 308 31827 706-665-8578
Rodney Hester, prin. Fax 665-2733

Tallapoosa, Haralson, Pop. 3,031
Haralson County SD
Supt. — See Buchanan
Haralson County MS 800/6-8
2633 Georgia Highway 120 30176 770-646-8600
Brian Ridley, prin. Fax 646-0108
Tallapoosa PS 500/PK-2
581 Georgia Highway 120 30176 770-574-7444
Jenstie Johns, prin. Fax 574-8932
West Haralson ES 400/3-5
PO Box 246 30176 770-574-7060
Vanessa Thomas, prin. Fax 574-7086

Talmo, Jackson, Pop. 563
Jackson County SD
Supt. — See Jefferson
North Jackson ES 400/PK-5
1880 Old Gainesville Hwy 30575 706-693-2246
Kathy Elrod, prin. Fax 693-4389

Tate, Pickens
Pickens County SD
Supt. — See Jasper
Tate ES 300/K-5
PO Box 268 30177 706-253-5010
Deborah Longshore, prin. Fax 253-1865

Taylorsville, Bartow, Pop. 225
Bartow County SD
Supt. — See Cartersville
Taylorsville ES 500/K-5
1502 Old Alabama Rd 30178 770-606-5867
Bernadette Dipetta, prin. Fax 606-2056

Temple, Paulding, Pop. 3,910
Carroll County SD
Supt. — See Carrollton
Temple ES 900/PK-5
95 Otis St 30179 770-562-3076
Dr. Terie Smith Phillips, prin. Fax 562-0135
Temple MS 500/6-8
275 Rainey Rd 30179 770-562-6001
Charles Johnson, prin. Fax 562-6002
Villa Rica MS 600/6-8
614 Tumlin Lake Rd 30179 770-459-0407
Demarcos Holland, prin. Fax 459-5496

Paulding County SD
Supt. — See Dallas
Union ES 500/K-5
206 Highway 101 S 30179 770-443-4191
Teresa Benefield, prin. Fax 459-5436

Tennille, Washington, Pop. 1,480
Washington County SD
Supt. — See Sandersville
Crawford PS 300/PK-2
PO Box 127 31089 478-552-7858
Roy Wilcher, prin. Fax 552-8135

Thomaston, Upson, Pop. 9,265
Thomaston-Upson County SD 4,800/PK-12
205 Civic Center Dr 30286 706-647-9621
Dr. Maggie Shook, supt. Fax 646-9398
www.upson.k12.ga.us
Upson-Lee MS 1,200/6-8
101 Holston Dr 30286 706-647-6256
Patsy Dean, prin. Fax 647-3631
Upson-Lee North ES 700/4-5
334 Knight Trl 30286 706-647-3632
Tracy Caldwell, prin. Fax 647-0636
Upson-Lee Preschool PK-PK
216 E Lee St 30286 706-646-4729
Jana Marks, dir. Fax 646-9456
Upson-Lee South ES 1,500/K-3
174 Knight Trl 30286 706-647-7540
Alicia Elder, prin. Fax 646-7806

Westwood Academy 100/PK-8
96 Pickard Rd 30286 706-647-8131
Shane Phillips, prin. Fax 647-4476

Thomasville, Thomas, Pop. 18,725
Thomas County SD 5,700/PK-12
200 N Pinetree Blvd 31792 229-225-4380
Dr. Jean Quigg, supt. Fax 225-5012
www.thomas.k12.ga.us
Cross Creek ES 800/3-4
324 Clark Rd 31757 229-225-3900
Bernice Mitchell, prin. Fax 225-3904
Garrison-Pilcher ES 800/1-2
277 Hall Rd 31757 229-225-4387
Sharonda Wilson, prin. Fax 227-2428
Hand-in-Hand PS 700/PK-K
4687 US Highway 84 Byp W 31792 229-225-3908
Jeanna Mayhall, prin. Fax 225-3982
Thomas County MS 1,700/5-8
4681 US Highway 84 Byp W 31792 229-225-4394
Debra Knight, prin. Fax 225-4378

Thomasville CSD 2,700/PK-12
915 E Jackson St 31792 229-225-2600
Sabrina Boykins-Everett, supt. Fax 226-6997
www.tcitys.org
Harper ES 300/PK-5
110 Bartow St 31792 229-225-2622
Allan Rodemoyer, prin. Fax 225-2692
Jerger ES 500/PK-5
1006 S Broad St 31792 229-225-2625
Melanie Chavaux, prin. Fax 225-2676
MacIntyre Park MS 600/6-8
117 Glenwood Dr 31792 229-225-2628
Dr. Jackie Scott, prin. Fax 225-3502
Scott ES 400/PK-5
100 N Hansell St 31792 229-225-2631
Tret Witherspoon, prin. Fax 225-2672

Brookwood S 500/PK-12
301 Cardinal Ridge Rd 31792 229-226-8070
Mike Notaro Ed.D., hdmstr. Fax 227-0326
Thomasville Christian S 100/K-8
1040 Glenwood Dr 31792 229-227-1515
Gail Danner, admin. Fax 226-7744

Thomson, McDuffie, Pop. 6,866
McDuffie County SD 3,700/PK-12
PO Box 957 30824 706-986-4000
Dr. Mark Petersen, supt. Fax 986-4001
www.mcduffie.k12.ga.us
Maxwell ES 400/PK-1
520 Mount Pleasant Rd 30824 706-986-4800
Donna Bennett, prin. Fax 986-4801
Norris ES 400/4-5
PO Box 1075 30824 706-986-4600
Nancy Lovelady, prin. Fax 986-4601
Thomson ES 200/2-5
409 Guill St 30824 706-986-4700
Anita Cummings, prin. Fax 986-4701
Thomson MS 1,000/6-8
PO Box 1140 30824 706-986-4400
Claude Powell, prin. Fax 986-4401
Other Schools – See Dearing

Thunderbolt, Chatham, Pop. 2,467
Savannah-Chatham County SD
Supt. — See Savannah

Thunderbolt ES 600/PK-5
3313 Louis St 31404 912-303-6655
Fax 303-6663

Tifton, Tift, Pop. 16,327
Tift County SD 7,300/PK-12
PO Box 389 31793 229-387-2400
Patrick Atwater, supt. Fax 386-1020
www.tiftschools.com
Bailey PS 500/K-3
1430 Newton Dr 31794 229-387-2415
Diane Lane, prin. Fax 386-1046
Clark PS 800/K-3
1464 Carpenter Rd S 31793 229-387-2410
Dr. Alan Smith, prin. Fax 386-1044
Eighth Street MS 1,200/7-8
700 8th St W 31794 229-387-2445
Dr. Ryan Gravitt, prin. Fax 386-1036
Lastinger PS 500/K-3
1210 Lake Dr 31794 229-387-2420
Dr. Kim Ezekiel, prin. Fax 386-1048
Northside PS 400/K-3
1815 Chestnut Ave 31794 229-387-2425
Stephanie Morrow, prin. Fax 386-1049
Reddick ES 500/4-6
404 Martin Luther King Dr 31794 229-387-2435
Mickey Weldon, prin. Fax 386-1041
Spencer ES 600/4-6
65 Tifton Eldorado Rd 31794 229-387-2430
Beverly Harrison, prin. Fax 386-1040
Tift County Pre-K Center PK-PK
506 12th St W 31794 229-387-2455
Wanda Veazey, prin. Fax 386-1055
Wilson ES 500/4-6
510 17th St W 31794 229-387-2440
Jan Wise, prin. Fax 386-1043
Other Schools – See Omega

Tiger, Rabun, Pop. 319
Rabun County SD
Supt. — See Clayton
Rabun County ES 800/3-6
1115 E Boggs Mountain Rd 30576 706-782-3116
Kent Woerner, prin. Fax 782-2828
Rabun County MS 300/7-8
108 Wildcat Hill Dr 30576 706-782-5470
Charles Wright, prin. Fax 782-4520
South Rabun ES 300/PK-2
PO Box 68 30576 706-782-3831
Penni Jones, prin. Fax 782-7957

Toccoa, Stephens, Pop. 9,103
Stephens County SD 4,200/PK-12
2332 Mize Rd 30577 706-886-9415
Sherrie Whiten, supt. Fax 886-3882
www.stephens.k12.ga.us/
Liberty ES 500/PK-5
222 Old Liberty Hill Rd 30577 706-886-3934
Terri Bridges, prin. Fax 886-9983
Stephens County MS 900/6-8
1315 Rose Ln 30577 706-886-2880
Tony Crunkleton, prin. Fax 886-2882
Toccoa ES 500/K-5
304 N Pond St 30577 706-886-3194
David Jacobsen, prin. Fax 282-0559
Other Schools – See Eastanollee

Trenton, Dade, Pop. 2,155
Dade County SD 2,600/PK-12
PO Box 188 30752 706-657-4361
Patty Priest, supt. Fax 657-4572
www.dadecountyschools.org/
Dade ES 900/PK-5
306 Wolverine Dr 30752 706-657-8253
Cherie Swader, prin. Fax 657-8433
Dade MS 600/6-8
250 Pace Dr 30752 706-657-6491
Karen deMarche, prin. Fax 657-3055
Davis ES 300/PK-5
5491 Highway 301 30752 706-657-6300
Mike Rich, prin. Fax 657-7932

Trion, Chattooga, Pop. 2,048
Trion CSD 1,300/PK-12
1255 Pine St 30753 706-734-2363
Richard Lindsay, supt. Fax 734-3397
www.trionschools.org/
Trion ES 700/PK-5
919 Allgood St 30753 706-734-2991
Cindy Anderson, prin. Fax 734-7549
Trion MS 300/6-8
919 Allgood St 30753 706-734-7433
Doug Wilson, prin. Fax 734-7517

Tucker, DeKalb, Pop. 26,700
DeKalb County SD
Supt. — See Decatur
Brockett ES 400/PK-5
1855 Brockett Rd 30084 678-874-2600
Dr. Tricia Sumpter, prin. Fax 874-2610
Idlewood ES 700/PK-5
1484 Idlewood Rd 30084 678-874-3200
Pat Carter, prin. Fax 874-3210
Livsey ES 300/PK-5
4137 Livsey Rd 30084 678-874-3300
Dr. Melanie Castelle, prin. Fax 874-3310
Midvale ES 400/PK-5
3836 Midvale Rd 30084 678-874-3400
Susan Wilson, prin. Fax 874-3410
Tucker MS 1,300/6-8
2160 Idlewood Rd 30084 678-875-0902
Dr. Kathy Cunningham, prin. Fax 875-0910

Gwinnett County SD
Supt. — See Suwanee
Nesbit ES 1,400/K-5
6575 Cherokee Dr 30084 770-414-2740
James Rayford, prin. Fax 414-2757

Tunnel Hill, Whitfield, Pop. 1,072
Catoosa County SD
Supt. — See Ringgold

Tiger Creek ES 600/PK-5
134 Rhea Mcclanahan Dr 30755 706-935-9890
Rodney Thompson, prin. Fax 965-8906

Whitfield County SD
Supt. — See Dalton
Tunnel Hill ES 300/K-5
203 E School St 30755 706-673-4550
Bert Coker, prin. Fax 673-4956

Twin City, Emanuel, Pop. 1,752
Emanuel County SD
Supt. — See Swainsboro
Twin City ES 500/PK-5
PO Box 280 30471 478-763-2253
Huddie Culbreth, prin. Fax 237-3831

Tybee Island, Chatham, Pop. 3,614

St. Michael S 100/PK-8
714 Lovell Ave 31328 912-786-4507
Holly Lansford, prin. Fax 786-4551

Tyrone, Fayette, Pop. 5,789
Fayette County SD
Supt. — See Fayetteville
Burch ES 700/PK-5
330 Jenkins Rd 30290 770-969-2820
Sharon Walters, prin. Fax 969-2824
Flat Rock MS 900/6-8
325 Jenkins Rd 30290 770-969-2830
Oatha Mann, prin. Fax 969-2835
Tyrone ES 400/PK-5
876 Senoia Rd 30290 770-631-3265
Eddie Pollard, prin. Fax 631-3270

Our Lady of Victory S 300/PK-8
211 Kirkley Rd 30290 770-306-9026
Linda Grace, prin. Fax 306-0323

Union City, Fulton, Pop. 15,382
Fulton County SD
Supt. — See Atlanta
Gullatt ES 600/PK-5
6110 Dodson Rd 30291 770-969-3425
Telana Hicks, prin. Fax 306-3582
Liberty Point ES 1,000/PK-5
9000 Highpoint Rd 30291 770-306-3510
Dr. Vanessa Johnson, prin. Fax 306-3516
Oakley ES 800/K-5
7220 Oakley Ter 30291 770-774-4050
Vonnie Thompson, prin. Fax 774-4057

Union Point, Greene, Pop. 1,645
Greene County SD
Supt. — See Greensboro
Greene County Preschool PK-PK
210 Witcher St 30669 706-486-4131
Barbara Johnson, dir. Fax 486-4556
Union Point ES 400/K-5
1401 Highway 77 N 30669 706-486-4117
Lex Brown, prin. Fax 486-4974

Valdosta, Lowndes, Pop. 45,205
Lowndes County SD 9,500/PK-12
PO Box 1227 31603 229-245-2250
Steve Smith, supt. Fax 245-2255
www.lowndes.k12.ga.us
Clyattville ES 700/PK-5
5386 Madison Hwy 31601 229-559-7062
Dr. Debra Brantley, prin. Fax 559-0396
Dewar ES 800/PK-5
3539 Mount Zion Church Rd 31605 229-219-1370
Beth Lind, prin. Fax 219-1376
Lowndes MS 1,000/6-8
2379 Copeland Rd 31601 229-245-2280
Dr. Samuel Clemons, prin. Fax 245-2470
Moulton-Branch ES 600/PK-5
5725 Inner Perimeter Rd 31601 229-245-2294
Dr. Robin Bennett, prin. Fax 259-5072
Pine Grove ES 700/PK-5
4023 Pine Grove Rd 31605 229-245-2298
Mickie Fisher, prin. Fax 259-5070
Pine Grove MS 6-8
4159 River Rd 31605 229-219-3234
Sol Summerlin, prin. Fax 219-3233
Westside ES, 2470 James Rd 31601 PK-5
Creacy Sermons, prin. 229-245-2289
Other Schools – See Hahira, Lake Park

Valdosta CSD 6,500/K-12
PO Box 5407 31603 229-333-8500
Bill Cason, supt. Fax 247-7757
www.gocats.org
Lomax ES 500/K-5
1450 Howell Rd 31601 229-333-8520
Sandra Allen, prin. Fax 245-5654
Mahone ES 600/K-5
3686 Lake Laurie Dr 31605 229-333-8530
Gary Glover, prin. Fax 245-5652
Mason ES 600/K-5
821 W Gordon St 31601 229-333-8525
John Davis, prin. Fax 245-5650
Newbern MS 600/6-8
2015 E Park Ave 31602 229-333-8566
Dr. Janice Richardson, prin. Fax 245-5655
Nunn ES 700/K-5
1610 Lakeland Ave 31602 229-333-8575
Gary Mims, prin. Fax 245-5653
Southeast ES 500/K-5
930 Old Statenville Rd 31601 229-333-8535
Alvin Hudson, prin. Fax 245-5651
Valdosta Early College Academy 6-7
PO Box 5407 31603 229-333-7594
Ingrid Hall, prin.
Valdosta MS 1,000/6-8
110 Burton St 31602 229-333-8555
Dr. David Cole, prin. Fax 245-5656

Crossroads Baptist S 100/PK-5
3001 Country Club Dr 31602 229-241-1430
Kay Hiers, dir. Fax 242-7627

Georgia Christian S 300/PK-12
4359 Dasher Rd 31601 229-559-5131
Brad Lawson, prin. Fax 559-7401
Open Bible Christian S 300/PK-12
3992 N Oak Street Ext 31605 229-244-6694
Perimeter Christian S 100/PK-3
4091 Inner Perimeter Rd 31602 229-316-2880
Trina Pattullo, dir. Fax 333-9734
St. John the Evangelist S 200/K-8
800 Gornto Rd 31602 229-244-2556
Melanie Lassiter, prin. Fax 244-0865
Southland Christian S 200/K-12
2206 E Hill Ave 31601 229-245-8111
Jackie Noble, prin. Fax 245-8189

Vidalia, Toombs, Pop. 11,037
Vidalia CSD 2,600/PK-12
301 Adams St 30474 912-537-3088
Tim Smith, supt. Fax 538-0938
www.vidalia-city.k12.ga.us
Dickerson PS 800/PK-2
800 North St E 30474 912-537-3421
Carol Welch, prin. Fax 537-6282
Meadows ES 600/3-5
205 Waters Dr 30474 912-537-4755
Cheryl McGowan, prin. Fax 537-1160
Trippe MS 600/6-8
2200 McIntosh St 30474 912-537-3813
Gwen Warren, prin. Fax 537-3223

Vidalia Heritage Academy 100/K-8
PO Box 2005 30475 912-537-6679
Jeff McCormick, admin. Fax 537-2998

Vienna, Dooly, Pop. 2,952
Dooly County SD 1,200/PK-8
202 E Cotton St 31092 229-268-4761
Dr. John Bembry, supt. Fax 268-6148
doolyschools.com/
Other Schools – See Pinehurst

Villa Rica, Carroll, Pop. 9,897
Carroll County SD
Supt. — See Carrollton
Bay Springs MS 700/6-8
122 Bay Springs Rd 30180 770-459-2098
Bruce Tidaback, prin. Fax 459-2097
Glanton-Hindsman ES 700/PK-5
118 Glanton St 30180 770-459-4491
Carla Meigs, prin. Fax 459-9716
Ithica ES 600/PK-5
75 Whitworth Rd 30180 678-840-5101
Mike Roberts, prin. Fax 840-5105
Villa Rica ES 600/PK-5
314 Peachtree St 30180 770-459-5762
Joseph Salley, prin. Fax 459-2041

Douglas County SD
Supt. — See Douglasville
Mirror Lake ES 800/K-5
2613 Tyson Rd 30180 770-651-4300
Cathy Swanger, prin. Fax 947-3842

Paulding County SD
Supt. — See Dallas
New Georgia ES 500/PK-5
5800 Mulberry Rock Rd 30180 770-445-3597
Jody Jordan, prin. Fax 443-2044

Wadley, Jefferson, Pop. 2,016
Jefferson County SD
Supt. — See Louisville
Carver ES 300/PK-5
PO Box 939 30477 478-252-5762
Dr. Shawn Johnson, prin. Fax 252-0577

Waleska, Cherokee, Pop. 816
Cherokee County SD
Supt. — See Canton
Moore ES 600/PK-6
1375 Puckett Rd 30183 770-479-3978
Keith Bryant, prin. Fax 479-4383

Warner Robins, Houston, Pop. 57,907
Houston County SD
Supt. — See Perry
Feagin Mill MS 1,000/6-8
1200 Feagin Mill Rd 31088 478-953-0430
Dr. Jesse Davis, prin. Fax 953-0438
Huntington MS 800/6-8
206 Wellborn Rd 31088 478-988-7200
Dr. Gwen Taylor, prin. Fax 542-2247
Lake Joy ES 200/3-5
985 Lake Joy Rd 31088 478-971-2712
Dr. Doug Rizer, prin. Fax 971-2710
Lake Joy PS 600/PK-2
995 Lake Joy Rd 31088 478-953-0465
April Strevig, prin. Fax 953-0473
Lindsey ES 300/PK-5
81 Tabor Dr 31093 478-929-7818
Anthony Lunceford, prin. Fax 542-2296
Linwood ES 400/PK-5
420 Education Way 31098 478-929-6360
Lazunia Frierson, prin. Fax 929-6366
Miller ES 500/PK-5
101 Pine Valley Dr 31088 478-929-7814
Gwen Pearson-Kilgore, prin. Fax 929-7762
Northside ES 500/PK-5
305 Sullivan Rd 31093 478-929-7816
Jodi Clark, prin. Fax 329-2233
Northside MS 800/6-8
500 Johnson Rd 31093 478-929-7845
Jan Melnick, prin. Fax 929-7124
Parkwood ES 500/PK-5
503 Parkwood Dr 31093 478-929-7822
Lisa Casilli, prin. Fax 542-2273
Perdue ES 500/3-5
115 Sutherlin Dr 31088 478-988-6350
Ed Weeks, prin. Fax 988-6109
Perdue PS 600/PK-2
150 Bear Country Blvd 31088 478-218-7500
Leslie Shultz, prin. Fax 218-7508

Quail Run ES 700/PK-5
250 Smithville Church Rd 31088 478-953-0415
Cheryl Thomas, prin. Fax 953-0425
Russell ES 600/PK-5
101 Patriot Way 31088 478-929-7830
Keith Lauritsen, prin. Fax 542-2272
Shirley Hills ES 500/PK-5
300 Mary Ln 31088 478-929-7824
Traci Jackson, prin. Fax 929-7121
Stephens S 400/PK-8
215 Scott Blvd 31088 478-929-7895
Dr. Marion Ford, prin. Fax 929-7109
Warner Robins MS 800/6-8
425 Mary Ln 31088 478-929-7832
Dr. Donald Warren, prin. Fax 929-7834
Westside ES 500/PK-5
301 N Pleasant Hill Rd 31093 478-929-7820
Cynthia Hammond, prin. Fax 929-7122

Sacred Heart S 200/K-8
250 S Davis Dr 31088 478-923-9668
Staci Erwin, prin. Fax 923-5822
Westside Baptist Academy 200/PK-12
1101 Dunbar Rd 31093 478-784-9153
Thelma Fossum, prin. Fax 785-1099

Warrenton, Warren, Pop. 2,012
Warren County SD 800/PK-12
PO Box 228 30828 706-465-3383
Carole Carey, supt. Fax 465-9141
www.warrenschools.com/
Freeman ES 400/PK-5
93 Hopgood St 30828 706-465-3342
Antonio Hill, prin. Fax 465-9246
Warren County MS 200/6-8
1253 Atlanta Hwy 30828 706-465-3742
Truett Abbott, prin. Fax 465-0901

Briarwood Academy 400/PK-12
4859 Thomson Hwy 30828 706-595-5641
John Hammond, hdmstr. Fax 595-0097

Washington, Wilkes, Pop. 4,150
Wilkes County SD 1,700/PK-12
313 N Alexander Ave Ste A 30673 706-678-2718
Joyce Williams, supt. Fax 678-3799
www.wilkes.k12.ga.us
Washington-Wilkes ES 400/PK-PK, 4-
109 East St 30673 706-678-7124
Wanda Jenkins, prin. Fax 678-7826
Washington-Wilkes MS 400/6-8
304A Gordon St 30673 706-678-7131
Bill Pendrey, prin. Fax 678-3546
Washington-Wilkes PS 500/K-3
910 E Robert Toombs Ave 30673 706-678-2633
Florence Sandifer, prin. Fax 678-2666

Emmanuel Christian Academy 50/PK-8
PO Box 1062 30673 706-678-4270
Vickie Turman, prin. Fax 678-3999

Watkinsville, Oconee, Pop. 2,535
Oconee County SD 6,300/K-12
PO Box 146 30677 706-769-5130
Dr. John Jackson, supt. Fax 769-3500
www.oconee.k12.ga.us
Colham Ferry ES 600/K-5
PO Box 186 30677 706-769-7764
Jackie Carson, prin. Fax 769-3538
Oconee County ES 600/3-5
PO Box 245 30677 706-769-7791
Nannette Varela, prin. Fax 769-3541
Oconee County MS 900/6-8
1101 Mars Hill Rd 30677 706-769-3575
Philip Brown, prin. Fax 769-3572
Oconee County PS 500/K-2
2290 Hog Mountain Rd 30677 706-769-7941
Pat Points, prin. Fax 769-3553
Rocky Branch ES 500/K-5
5250 Hog Mountain Rd 30677 706-769-3235
Evelyn Wages, prin. Fax 769-3778
Other Schools – See Bishop, Bogart

Westminster Christian Academy 300/PK-12
PO Box 388 30677 706-769-9372
Dana James, hdmstr. Fax 769-2050

Waycross, Ware, Pop. 15,112
Ware County SD 6,000/PK-12
1301 Bailey St 31501 912-283-8656
Dr. Joseph Barrow, supt. Fax 283-8698
www.ware.k12.ga.us
Center ES 500/K-5
2114 Dorothy St 31501 912-287-2366
Dr. Sonya Bennett, prin. Fax 287-2361
DAFFODIL Preschool PK-PK
701 Morton Ave 31501 912-287-2311
Mary Thomas, prin. Fax 287-2301
Memorial Drive ES 300/K-5
2580 Ambrose St 31503 912-287-2327
Dr. Maurie DeVane, prin. Fax 287-2326
Ruskin ES 400/K-5
3550 Valdosta Hwy 31503 912-287-2325
Kathy Stevens, prin. Fax 287-2356
Wacona ES 600/K-5
3101 State St 31503 912-287-2362
Dr. Jacki Turner, prin. Fax 284-2057
Ware County MS 700/6-8
2301 Cherokee St 31503 912-287-2341
Lee Robertson, prin. Fax 287-2353
Waresboro ES 400/K-5
3379 W Church St 31503 912-287-2393
Denton Dial, prin. Fax 287-2395
Waycross MS 600/6-8
700 Central Ave 31501 912-287-2333
Tim Dixon, prin. Fax 287-2352
Williams Heights ES 400/K-5
705 Dewey St 31501 912-287-2399
Dr. Lance Brantley, prin. Fax 287-2350

Other Schools – See Manor

Waynesboro, Burke, Pop. 5,999
Burke County SD 4,800/PK-12
789 Burke Veterans Pkwy 30830 706-554-5101
Linda Bailey, supt. Fax 554-8051
www.burke.k12.ga.us
Blakeney ES 800/3-5
100 Olympic Dr 30830 706-554-2265
Renee Sasser, prin. Fax 554-8075
Burke County MS 1,100/6-8
356 Southside Dr 30830 706-554-3532
Dr. Daphney Ivery, prin. Fax 554-8063
Waynesboro PS 1,100/PK-2
352 Southside Dr 30830 706-554-5125
Tommy Mitchell, prin. Fax 554-8064
Other Schools – See Sardis

Burke Academy 400/K-12
403 GA Highway 56 S 30830 706-554-4479
Brent Cribb, hdmstr. Fax 554-7582
Lord's House of Praise Christian S 50/PK-12
PO Box 1070 30830 706-437-1904
Thomas McKinney, admin. Fax 437-1924

Waynesville, Brantley
Brantley County SD
Supt. — See Nahunta
Atkinson ES PK-6
4327 Highway 110 E 31566 912-778-6098
Brandon Carter, prin. Fax 778-6099
Waynesville ES 800/PK-6
5726 Old Waynesville Rd 31566 912-778-3068
Tonya Johnson, prin. Fax 778-3071

West Green, Coffee
Coffee County SD
Supt. — See Douglas
West Green ES 400/PK-5
106 School Circle Rd 31567 912-384-2032
Kim Miller, prin. Fax 383-4166

West Point, Troup, Pop. 3,360
Troup County SD
Supt. — See La Grange
West Point ES 400/PK-5
1701 E 12th St 31833 706-812-7973
Karen Cagle, prin. Fax 812-1250

Whigham, Grady, Pop. 612
Grady County SD
Supt. — See Cairo
Whigham S 500/PK-8
211 W Broad Ave, 229-762-4167
Demetris Cox, prin. Fax 762-4477

White, Bartow, Pop. 716
Bartow County SD
Supt. — See Cartersville
White ES 500/K-5
1395 Cass White Rd NE 30184 770-606-5869
Evie Barge, prin. Fax 606-3876

Whitesburg, Carroll, Pop. 583
Carroll County SD
Supt. — See Carrollton
Whitesburg ES 400/PK-5
868 Main St 30185 770-832-3875
Joyce Davis, prin. Fax 214-8824

Wildwood, Dade

Wildwood Adventist S 50/1-8
PO Box 129 30757 706-820-1493

Willacoochee, Atkinson, Pop. 1,506
Atkinson County SD
Supt. — See Pearson
Willacoochee ES 400/PK-7
430 Vickers St S 31650 912-534-5302
Robert Brown, prin. Fax 534-5337

Winder, Barrow, Pop. 12,451
Barrow County SD 11,200/PK-12
179 W Athens St 30680 770-867-4527
Dr. Ron Saunders, supt. Fax 867-4540
www.barrow.k12.ga.us
County Line ES 800/K-5
334 Rockwell Church Rd NW 30680 770-867-2902
Chris McMichael, prin. Fax 867-8942
Haymon Morris MS 700/6-8
1008 Haymon Morris Rd 30680 678-963-0602
Dr. Sheila Kahrs, prin. Fax 867-1854
Holsenbeck ES 700/K-5
445 Holsenbeck School Rd 30680 770-307-1540
Jackie Robinson, prin. Fax 307-1255
Kennedy ES 500/K-5
200 Matthews School Rd 30680 770-867-3182
Ryan Butcher, prin. Fax 307-4532
Russell MS 700/6-8
84 W Midland Ave 30680 770-867-8181
Dr. Russell Claxton, prin. Fax 868-1215
Westside MS 500/6-8
240 Matthews School Rd 30680 770-307-2972
Dr. Eli Welch, prin. Fax 307-2976
Winder-Barrow MS 700/6-8
163 King St 30680 770-867-2116
Mary Beth Bennett, prin. Fax 868-1421
Yargo ES 700/K-5
1000 Haymon Morris Rd 30680 770-867-1147
Mike Carnathan, prin. Fax 867-1214
Other Schools – See Auburn, Bethlehem, Statham

Hope Christian Academy 200/PK-12
8 Pleasant Hill Church SE 30680 770-725-2521
Fax 725-2530

Winston, Douglas
Douglas County SD
Supt. — See Douglasville

Mason Creek ES 100/K-5
3400 Johnston Rd 30187 770-651-4900
Kathleen French, prin. Fax 920-4282
Mason Creek MS 100/6-8
7777 Mason Creek Rd 30187 770-651-2500
Kay Davis, prin. Fax 920-4278
Winston ES 500/K-5
7465 Highway 78 30187 770-651-4700
Wiley Dailey, prin. Fax 920-4177

Winterville, Clarke, Pop. 1,059
Clarke County SD
Supt. — See Athens
Winterville ES 500/PK-5
305 Cherokee Rd 30683 706-742-8278
Deborah Haney, prin. Fax 742-5660

Woodbine, Camden, Pop. 1,353
Camden County SD
Supt. — See Kingsland
Gross ES 300/K-5
277 Roberts Path 31569 912-576-4800
Dr. Darlene Bruce, prin. Fax 510-6538
Woodbine ES 300/PK-5
495 Broadwood Dr 31569 912-576-5245
Mike Blackerby, prin. Fax 576-3778

Woodbury, Meriwether, Pop. 1,091
Meriwether County SD
Supt. — See Greenville
Washington ES 500/PK-5
18425 Main St 30293 706-553-3951
Janice Owens, prin. Fax 553-2877

Flint River Academy 400/PK-12
PO Box 247 30293 706-553-2541
Marlowe Hinson, hdmstr. Fax 553-9777

Woodstock, Cherokee, Pop. 19,602
Cherokee County SD
Supt. — See Canton
Arnold Mill ES 1,100/PK-6
710 Arnold Mill Rd 30188 770-592-3510
Ann Gazell, prin. Fax 592-3514
Bascomb ES 1,300/PK-4
1335 Wyngate Pkwy 30189 770-592-1091
Ruth Flowers, prin. Fax 592-0907
Booth MS 1,200/7-8
6550 Putnam Ford Dr 30189 770-926-5707
Darrell Herring, prin. Fax 928-2908
Boston ES 900/K-4
105 Othello Dr 30189 770-924-6260
Letitia Cline, prin. Fax 924-0392
Carmel ES 1,600/K-6
2275 Bascomb Carmel Rd 30189 770-926-1237
Dr. Sharron Hunt, prin. Fax 926-5681
Chapman IS 1,200/5-6
6500 Putnam Ford Dr 30189 770-926-6424
Dawn Weinbaum, prin. Fax 926-1382
Johnston ES 1,000/K-6
2031 E Cherokee Dr 30188 770-928-2910
Gena Hood, prin. Fax 591-0109
Little River ES 800/PK-6
3170 Trickum Rd 30188 770-926-7566
Val Bahun, prin. Fax 928-7180
Mill Creek MS 7-8
3170 Trickum Rd 30188 770-924-5489
Elaine Daniel, prin.
Mountain Road ES 600/PK-6
615 Mountain Rd 30188 770-664-9708
Tammy Sandell, prin. Fax 664-8908
Woodstock ES 1,000/K-6
230 Rope Mill Rd 30188 770-926-6969
Christy Bowling, prin. Fax 924-6332
Woodstock MS 1,000/7-8
2000 Twn Lake Hlls South Dr 30189 770-592-3516
Keith Ball, prin. Fax 591-8054

Cherokee Christian S 400/K-12
3075 Trickum Rd 30188 678-494-5464
Michael Lee, hdmstr. Fax 592-4881
Messiah Montessori S 100/PK-6
9626 Hickory Flat Hwy 30188 678-977-6501
Andi Hardy Jory, dir. Fax 867-7189

Wrens, Jefferson, Pop. 2,261
Jefferson County SD
Supt. — See Louisville
Wrens ES 600/PK-5
PO Box 308 30833 706-547-2063
Sharon Dye, prin. Fax 547-0209
Wrens MS 300/6-8
101 Griffin St 30833 706-547-6580
Julia Wells, prin. Fax 547-6224

Wrightsville, Johnson, Pop. 3,183
Johnson County SD 1,200/PK-12
PO Box 110 31096 478-864-3302
Hayward Cordy, supt. Fax 864-4053
www.johnson.k12.ga.us/
Johnson County ES 600/PK-5
601 W Elm St 31096 478-864-3446
Rebecca Thomas, prin. Fax 864-4056
Johnson County MS 300/6-8
210 Trojan Way 31096 478-864-2222
Curtis Dixon, prin. Fax 864-4054

Zebulon, Pike, Pop. 1,194
Pike County SD 3,200/PK-12
PO Box 386 30295 770-567-8489
Dr. Michael Duncan, supt. Fax 567-8349
www.pike.k12.ga.us/
Pike County ES 800/3-5
607 Pirate Dr 30295 770-567-4444
Tammy Bell, prin. Fax 567-0544
Pike County MS 800/6-8
406 Hughley Rd 30295 770-567-3353
Mike Maddox, prin. Fax 567-5054
Pike County PS 800/PK-2
7218 Highway 19 S 30295 770-567-8443
Bonita Fluker, prin. Fax 567-1636

HAWAII

HAWAII DEPARTMENT OF EDUCATION
PO Box 2360, Honolulu 96804-2360
Telephone 808-586-3230
Fax 808-586-3234
Website doe.k12.hi.us

Superintendent of Education   Patricia Hamamoto

HAWAII BOARD OF EDUCATION
PO Box 2360, Honolulu 96804-2360

Chairperson   Garrett Toguchi

PUBLIC, PRIVATE AND CATHOLIC ELEMENTARY SCHOOLS

Aiea, Honolulu, Pop. 8,906
Hawaii SD
Supt. — See Honolulu
Aiea ES — 400/PK-6
99-370 Moanalua Rd 96701 — 808-483-7200
John Erickson, prin. — Fax 483-7201
Aiea IS — 700/7-8
99-600 Kulawea St 96701 — 808-483-7230
Tom Kurashige, prin. — Fax 483-7235
Pearl Ridge ES — 600/K-6
98-940 Moanalua Rd 96701 — 808-483-7250
Laureen Dunn, prin. — Fax 483-7255
Scott ES — 500/PK-6
98-1230 Moanalua Rd 96701 — 808-483-7220
Sandra Watanabe, prin. — Fax 483-7223
Waimalu ES — 600/PK-6
98-825 Moanalua Rd 96701 — 808-483-7210
Sheldon Oshio, prin. — Fax 483-7213
Webling ES — 500/PK-6
99-370 Paihi St 96701 — 808-483-7240
Sherryln Yamada, prin. — Fax 483-7242

Our Savior Lutheran S — 200/PK-8
98-1098 Moanalua Rd 96701 — 808-488-0000
George Evensen, prin. — Fax 488-4515
St. Elizabeth S — 200/K-8
99-310 Moanalua Rd 96701 — 808-488-5322
Sr. Bernarda Sindol, prin. — Fax 486-0856

Captain Cook, Hawaii, Pop. 2,595
Hawaii SD
Supt. — See Honolulu
Honaunau ES — 100/K-5
83-5360 Mamalahoa Hwy 96704 — 808-328-2727
Faye Ogilvie, prin. — Fax 328-2729
Ho'okena ES — 200/PK-5
86-4355 Mamalahoa Hwy 96704 — 808-328-2710
Lyndia Uchimura, prin. — Fax 328-2712

Kona Adventist S — 50/K-8
PO Box 739 96704 — 808-323-2788
Joey Freitas, prin. — Fax 323-2788

Eleele, Kauai, Pop. 1,489
Hawaii SD
Supt. — See Honolulu
Eleele ES — 400/PK-5
PO Box 38 96705 — 808-335-2111
Leila Nitta, prin. — Fax 335-8415

Ewa Beach, Honolulu, Pop. 14,315
Hawaii SD
Supt. — See Honolulu
Ewa Beach ES — 400/PK-6
91-740 Papipi Rd 96706 — 808-689-1271
Sherry Kobayashi, prin. — Fax 689-1275
Ewa ES — 900/PK-6
91-1280 Renton Rd 96706 — 808-681-8202
Stanley Tamashiro, prin. — Fax 681-8206
Holomua ES — 1,500/PK-6
91-1561 Keaunui Dr 96706 — 808-685-2000
Norman Pang, prin. — Fax 685-2003
Ilima IS — 1,200/7-8
91-884 Fort Weaver Rd 96706 — 808-689-1250
Jon Kitabayashi, prin. — Fax 689-1258
Iroquois Point ES — 700/K-6
5553 Cormorant Ave 96706 — 808-499-6500
Heidi Armstrong, prin. — Fax 499-6508
Kaimiloa ES — 700/PK-6
91-1028 Kaunolu St 96706 — 808-689-1280
Deborah Hatada, prin. — Fax 689-1284
Keone'ula ES — K-6
91-970 Kaileolea Dr 96706 — 808-689-1380
Eileen Hirota, prin. — Fax 689-1395
Pohakea ES — 500/PK-6
91-750 Fort Weaver Rd 96706 — 808-689-1290
Stephen Schatz, prin. — Fax 689-1293

Friendship Christian S — 300/PK-12
91-1130 Renton Rd 96706 — 808-687-3638
James Reid, prin. — Fax 681-0904
Our Lady of Perpetual Help S — 200/K-8
91-1010 North Rd 96706 — 808-689-0474
Sr. Davilyn AhChick, prin. — Fax 689-4847

Haiku, Maui, Pop. 4,509
Hawaii SD
Supt. — See Honolulu
Haiku ES — 400/K-5
105 Pauwela Rd 96708 — 808-575-3000
Bernice Takahata, prin. — Fax 575-3003

Haleiwa, Honolulu, Pop. 2,442
Hawaii SD
Supt. — See Honolulu
Haleiwa ES — 200/PK-6
66-505 Haleiwa Rd 96712 — 808-637-8237
Diane Matsukawa, prin. — Fax 637-8240
Sunset Beach ES — 400/K-6
59-360 Kamehameha Hwy 96712 — 808-638-8777
Ruth Holmberg, prin. — Fax 638-8789

Sunset Beach Christian S — 100/K-8
59-578 Kamehameha Hwy 96712 — 808-638-8274
Robert Prasser, prin. — Fax 638-0142

Hana, Maui, Pop. 683
Hawaii SD
Supt. — See Honolulu
Hana S — 400/K-12
PO Box 128 96713 — 808-248-4815
Richard Paul, prin. — Fax 248-4819

Hanalei, Kauai, Pop. 461
Hawaii SD
Supt. — See Honolulu
Hanalei ES — 200/PK-6
PO Box 46 96714 — 808-826-4300
Corey Nakamura, prin. — Fax 826-4302

Hauula, Honolulu, Pop. 3,479
Hawaii SD
Supt. — See Honolulu
Hau'ula ES — 300/K-6
54-046 Kamehameha Hwy 96717 — 808-293-8925
Bradley Odagiri, prin. — Fax 293-8927

Hawi, Hawaii, Pop. 924

Kohala Mission S — 100/K-8
PO Box 99 96719 — 808-889-5646
Beverly Church, prin. — Fax 889-0652

Hilo, Hawaii, Pop. 40,759
Hawaii SD
Supt. — See Honolulu
DeSilva ES — 400/PK-6
278 Ainako Ave 96720 — 808-974-4855
Dennis O'Brien, prin. — Fax 974-4858
Ha'aheo ES — 200/K-6
121 Haaheo Rd 96720 — 808-974-4111
Esther Kanehailua, prin. — Fax 974-4112
Hilo IS — 600/7-8
587 Waianuenue Ave 96720 — 808-974-4955
Elaine Christian, prin. — Fax 974-6184
Hilo Union ES — 500/PK-6
506 Waianuenue Ave 96720 — 808-933-0900
Jasmine Urasaki, prin. — Fax 933-0905
Kapi'olani ES — 400/PK-6
966 Kilauea Ave 96720 — 808-974-4160
Lucia Stewart, prin. — Fax 974-4161
Kaumana ES — 200/K-6
1710 Kaumana Dr 96720 — 808-974-4190
Lloyd Matsunami, prin. — Fax 974-4197
Keaukaha ES — 300/K-6
240 Desha Ave 96720 — 808-974-4181
Lehua Veincent, prin. — Fax 974-4868
Waiakea ES — 900/PK-5
180 W Puainako St 96720 — 808-981-7215
Clifton Iwamoto, prin. — Fax 981-7218
Waiakea IS — 900/6-8
200 W Puainako St 96720 — 808-981-7231
Lloyd Matsunami, prin. — Fax 981-7237
Waiakeawaena ES — 700/K-5
2420 Kilauea Ave 96720 — 808-981-7200
Beverly McCall, prin. — Fax 981-7205

Haili Christian S — 200/PK-8
190 Ululani St 96720 — 808-961-5026
Kim McCarty, admin. — Fax 933-1981
Hale Aloha Nazarene S — 100/PK-PK
595 Kupulau Rd 96720 — 808-959-4949
Gale Ragle, prin. — Fax 959-7020
Mauna Loa S — 50/PK-8
172 Kapiolani St 96720 — 808-935-1545
Vicky Perry, prin. — Fax 935-1545
St. Joseph S - Hilo — 200/PK-6
999 Ululani St 96720 — 808-935-4935
Victoria Torcolini, prin. — Fax 935-6894

Holualoa, Hawaii, Pop. 3,834
Hawaii SD
Supt. — See Honolulu
Holualoa ES — 400/K-5
76-5957 Mamalahoa Hwy 96725 — 808-322-4800
Lauren O'Leary, prin. — Fax 322-4801

Honokaa, Hawaii, Pop. 2,186
Hawaii SD
Supt. — See Honolulu
Honoka'a ES — 400/K-6
45-534 Pakalana St 96727 — 808-775-8820
Katherine Tolentino, prin. — Fax 775-8828

Honolulu, Honolulu, Pop. 378,155
Hawaii SD — 171,900/PK-12
PO Box 2360 96804 — 808-586-3230
Patricia Hamamoto, supt. — Fax 586-3234
doe.k12.hi.us/
Aina Haina ES — 400/PK-6
801 W Hind Dr 96821 — 808-377-2419
Susan Okano, prin. — Fax 377-2426
Ala Wai ES — 500/PK-5
503 Kamoku St 96826 — 808-973-0070
Charlotte Unni, prin. — Fax 973-0081
Aliamanu ES — 700/PK-6
3265 Salt Lake Blvd 96818 — 808-421-4280
Jane Sugimoto, prin. — Fax 421-4283
Aliamanu MS — 800/7-8
3271 Salt Lake Blvd 96818 — 808-421-4100
Robert Eggleston, prin. — Fax 421-4103
Ali'iolani ES — 300/K-5
1240 7th Ave 96816 — 808-733-4750
Len Miyamoto, prin. — Fax 733-4758
Anuenue S — 400/K-12
2528 10th Ave 96816 — 808-733-8465
Charles Naumu, prin. — Fax 733-8467
Central MS — 500/6-8
1302 Queen Emma St 96813 — 808-587-4400
Brian Mizuguchi, prin. — Fax 587-4409
Dole MS — 800/6-8
1803 Kamehameha IV Rd 96819 — 808-832-3340
Myron Monte, prin. — Fax 832-3349
Fern ES — 500/K-6
1121 Middle St 96819 — 808-832-3040
Martina Kapololu, prin. — Fax 832-3043
Haha'ione ES — 400/K-6
595 Pepeekeo St 96825 — 808-397-5822
Lucinda Giorgis, prin. — Fax 397-5827
Hickam ES — 800/PK-6
825 Manzelman Cir 96818 — 808-421-4148
George Okino, prin. — Fax 421-4157
Hokulani ES — 400/PK-6
2940 Kamakini St 96816 — 808-733-4789
Alfredo Carganilla, prin. — Fax 733-4792
Jarrett MS — 300/6-8
1903 Palolo Ave 96816 — 808-733-4888
Donna Lum, prin. — Fax 733-4894
Jefferson ES — 400/PK-6
324 Kapahulu Ave 96815 — 808-971-6922
Vivian Hee, prin. — Fax 971-6933
Ka'ahumanu ES — 600/K-5
1141 Kinau St 96814 — 808-587-4414
Holly Kiyonaga, prin. — Fax 587-4415
Ka'ewai ES — 300/K-5
1929 Kamehameha IV Rd 96819 — 808-832-3500
Bert Carter, prin. — Fax 832-3509
Kahala ES — 500/PK-6
4559 Kilauea Ave 96816 — 808-733-8455
Peter Chun, prin. — Fax 733-4669
Kaimuki MS — 700/6-8
631 18th Ave 96816 — 808-733-4800
Frank Fernandes, prin. — Fax 733-4810

Kaiulani ES 400/K-5
783 N King St 96817 808-832-3160
Thomas Moon, prin. Fax 832-3164
Kalakaua MS 1,100/6-8
821 Kalihi St 96819 808-832-3130
Robert Ginlack, prin. Fax 832-3140
Kalihi ES 200/K-5
2471 Kula Kolea Dr 96819 808-832-3177
Natalie Mun-Takata, prin. Fax 832-3179
Kalihi Kai ES 700/PK-5
626 McNeill St 96817 808-832-3322
Stanley Kayatani, prin. Fax 832-3327
Kalihi Uka ES 200/K-5
2411 Kalihi St 96819 808-832-3310
Kathryn Yoshida, prin. Fax 832-3313
Kalihi Waena ES 600/PK-5
1240 Gulick Ave 96819 808-832-3210
Laura Vines, prin. Fax 832-3213
Kamiloiki ES 300/K-6
7788 Hawaii Kai Dr 96825 808-397-5800
Loretta Yee, prin. Fax 397-5806
Kapalama ES 600/K-6
1601 N School St 96817 808-832-3290
Patricia Dang, prin. Fax 832-3302
Kauluwela ES 400/K-5
1486 Aala St 96817 808-587-4447
Gwendolyn Lee, prin. Fax 587-4453
Kawananakoa MS 800/6-8
49 Funchal St 96813 808-587-4430
Sandra Ishihara-Shibata, prin. Fax 587-4443
Koko Head ES 300/PK-6
189 Lunalilo Home Rd 96825 808-397-5811
Cecilia Lum, prin. Fax 397-5816
Kuhio ES 300/K-5
2759 S King St 96826 808-973-0085
Evelyn Hao, prin. Fax 973-0088
Lanakila ES 300/PK-5
717 N Kuakini St 96817 808-587-4466
Michael Ono, prin. Fax 587-4468
Liholiho ES 300/PK-6
3430 Maunaloa Ave 96816 808-733-4850
Christina Small, prin. Fax 733-4856
Likelike ES 400/PK-5
1618 Palama St 96817 808-832-3370
Stacey Oshio, prin. Fax 832-3374
Lili'uokalani ES 100/PK-6
3633 Waialae Ave 96816 808-733-4680
Kevin Yuen, prin. Fax 733-4685
Linapuni ES 200/K-2
1434 Linapuni St 96819 808-832-3303
Cindy Sunahara, prin. Fax 832-3305
Lincoln ES 400/PK-5
615 Auwaiolimu St 96813 808-587-4480
Irving Emoto, prin. Fax 587-4487
Lunalilo ES 600/K-5
810 Pumehana St 96826 808-973-0270
Dean Nakamoto, prin. Fax 973-0276
Ma'ema'e ES 700/K-6
319 Wyllie St 96817 808-595-5400
Pearline Blaisdell, prin. Fax 595-5405
Makalapa ES 600/PK-6
4435 Salt Lake Blvd 96818 808-421-4110
Raymond Fujii, prin. Fax 421-4112
Manoa ES 600/PK-6
3155 Manoa Rd 96822 808-988-1868
Jeanette Uyeda, prin. Fax 988-1860
Moanalua ES 700/PK-6
1337 Mahiole St 96819 808-831-7878
Denise Arai, prin. Fax 831-7877
Moanalua MS 900/7-8
1289 Mahiole St 96819 808-831-7850
Caroline Wong, prin. Fax 831-7859
Mokulele ES 500/PK-6
250 Aupaka St 96818 808-421-4180
Bart Nakamoto, prin. Fax 421-4182
Nimitz ES 500/PK-6
520 Main St 96818 808-421-4165
Kenneth Lee, prin. Fax 421-4170
Niu Valley MS 500/7-8
310 Halemaumau St 96821 808-377-2440
Justin Mew, prin. Fax 377-2444
Noelani ES 500/K-6
2655 Woodlawn Dr 96822 808-988-1858
Rochelle Mahoe, prin. Fax 988-1855
Nu'uanu ES 400/K-6
3055 Puiwa Ln 96817 808-595-5422
James Toyooka, prin. Fax 595-5425
Palolo ES 300/PK-5
2106 10th Ave 96816 808-733-4700
Ruth Silberstein, prin. Fax 733-4708
Pauoa ES 400/PK-6
2301 Pauoa Rd 96813 808-587-4500
Roberta Richards, prin. Fax 587-4506
Pearl Harbor ES 600/PK-6
1 Moanalua Rdg 96818 808-421-4125
Ellamarie Savidge, prin. Fax 421-4128
Pearl Harbor Kai ES 500/PK-6
1 C Ave 96818 808-421-4245
Elynne Chung, prin. Fax 421-4248
Pu'uhale ES 300/K-6
345 Puuhale Rd 96819 808-832-3190
Calvin Nomiyama, prin. Fax 832-3195
Red Hill ES 300/K-6
1265 Ala Kula Pl 96819 808-831-7866
Mona Smoot, prin. Fax 831-7861
Royal ES 400/K-5
1519 Queen Emma St 96813 808-587-4510
Ann Sugabayashi, prin. Fax 587-4518
Salt Lake ES 800/PK-6
1131 Ala Lilikoi St 96818 808-831-7870
Duwayne Abe, prin. Fax 831-7873
Shafter ES 200/PK-6
2 Fort Shafter 96819 808-832-3560
Sam Ko, prin. Fax 832-3562
Stevenson MS 600/6-8
1202 Prospect St 96822 808-587-4520
Gregg Lee, prin. Fax 587-4523

Waikiki ES 400/K-6
3710 Leahi Ave 96815 808-971-6900
Bonnie Tabor, prin. Fax 971-6902
Wailupe Valley ES 100/K-6
939 Hind Iuka Dr 96821 808-377-2414
Jean Hartmann, prin. Fax 377-2413
Washington MS 1,000/6-8
1633 S King St 96826 808-973-0177
Michael Harano, prin. Fax 973-0181
Wilson ES 600/K-6
4945 Kilauea Ave 96816 808-733-4740
Richard Kiyonaga, prin. Fax 733-4746
Other Schools – See Aiea, Captain Cook, Eleele, Ewa Beach, Haiku, Haleiwa, Hana, Hanalei, Hauula, Hilo, Holualoa, Honokaa, Hoolehua, Kaaawa, Kahuku, Kahului, Kailua, Kailua Kona, Kalaheo, Kamuela, Kaneohe, Kapaa, Kapaau, Kapolei, Kaunakakai, Keaau, Kealakekua, Kekaha, Kihei, Kilauea, Koloa, Kula, Lahaina, Laie, Lanai City, Laupahoehoe, Lihue, Makawao, Maunaloa, Mililani, Mountain View, Naalehu, Paauilo, Pahala, Pahoa, Paia, Papaikou, Pearl City, Wahiawa, Waialua, Waianae, Waikoloa, Wailuku, Waimanalo, Waimea, Waipahu

---

ASSETS S 400/K-12
1 Ohana Nui Way 96818 808-423-1356
Paul Singer, hdmstr. Fax 422-1920
Blessed Marianne Cope Preschool PK-PK
2707 Pamoa Rd 96822 808-988-6528
Sr. Joan of Arc Souza, prin. Fax 988-5497
Calvary by the Sea S 100/PK-K
5339 Kalanianaole Hwy 96821 808-377-5104
Kay Burgoyne, dir.
Cathedral Catholic Academy 100/K-8
1728 Nuuanu Ave 96817 808-533-2069
Jaydee Wagner, prin. Fax 533-3040
Central Union Preschool & K 200/PK-K
1660 S Beretania St 96826 808-946-4025
Marie Hook, prin. Fax 942-5400
Chaminade/Allen Montessori S 50/PK-K
3140 Waialae Ave 96816 808-735-4875
Francesca DeMattos, prin. Fax 735-4876
Christian Academy 300/PK-12
3400 Moanalua Rd 96819 808-836-0233
Klayton Ko, supt. Fax 836-4415
Hanahau'oli S 200/PK-6
1922 Makiki St 96822 808-949-6461
Dr. Robert Peters, hdmstr. Fax 941-2216
Hawaiian Mission S 100/K-8
1415 Makiki St 96814 808-949-2033
John Mooy, prin. Fax 955-2509
Hawaii Baptist Academy 400/K-6
21 Bates St 96817 808-524-5477
Rebecca Sanchez-Ovitt, hdmstr. Fax 524-8193
Holy Family Catholic Academy 500/K-8
830 Main St 96818 808-423-9611
Christina Malins, prin. Fax 422-5030
Holy Family Early Learning Center 100/PK-PK
830 Main St 96818 808-421-1265
Kalei Demello, dir. Fax 422-5030
Holy Nativity S 200/PK-6
5286 Kalanianaole Hwy 96821 808-373-3232
Robert Whiting Ph.D., hdmstr. Fax 377-9618
Holy Trinity S 100/K-8
5919 Kalanianaole Hwy 96821 808-396-8466
Sr. Rose Miriam Schillinger, prin. Fax 396-3310
Hongwanji Mission S 300/PK-8
1728 Pali Hwy 96813 808-532-0522
Dr. Carol Riley, hdmstr. Fax 532-0537
Honolulu Waldorf S 200/PK-8
350 Ulua St 96821 808-377-5471
Connie Starzynski, admin. Fax 373-2040
Iolani S 1,800/K-12
563 Kamoku St 96826 808-949-5355
Dr. Val Iwashita, hdmstr. Fax 943-2297
Kaimuki Christian S 300/PK-8
1117 Koko Head Ave 96816 808-732-1781
Dr. Mark Gallagher, prin. Fax 735-1354
Kamehameha S - Kapalama Campus 3,200/K-12
1887 Makuakane St 96817 808-842-8211
Michael Chun Ph.D., hdmstr. Fax 842-8411
Kawaiaha'o Church S 100/PK-5
872 Mission Ln 96813 808-585-0622
Shari Martin, prin. Fax 585-0831
Lokahi Montessori S 50/PK-6
1506 Piikoi St 96822 808-524-4243
Dr. Patricia Dukes, prin. Fax 524-7924
Maryknoll S 800/PK-8
1526 Alexander St 96822 808-952-7100
Shana Tong, prin. Fax 952-7101
Mid-Pacific Institute 1,500/PK-12
2445 Kaala St 96822 808-973-5000
Joe Rice, pres. Fax 973-5099
Montessori Community S 200/PK-6
1239 Nehoa St 96822 808-522-0244
Patsy Tom, prin. Fax 522-0250
Navy Hale Keiki S 200/PK-3
153 Bougainville Dr 96818 808-423-1727
Shari Gulledge, prin. Fax 423-1778
Our Redeemer Lutheran S 200/PK-8
2428 Wilder Ave 96822 808-945-7765
Bonnie Jo Alle, prin. Fax 944-1414
Punahou S 3,700/K-12
1601 Punahou St 96822 808-944-5711
Dr. James K. Scott, pres. Fax 944-5762
Sacred Hearts Academy 1,100/PK-12
3253 Waialae Ave 96816 808-734-5058
Betty White, prin. Fax 737-7867
St. Andrew's Priory S 500/K-12
224 Queen Emma Sq 96813 808-536-6102
Sandra Theunick, hdmstr. Fax 532-2462
St. Anthony S - Honolulu 100/K-8
640 Puuhale Rd 96819 808-845-2769
Sr. Eleanor Amante, prin. Fax 853-2234
St. Clement's S 100/PK-K
1515 Wilder Ave 96822 808-949-2082
Dr. Patsy Izumo, dir. Fax 943-1049

St. Francis S 400/PK-12
2707 Pamoa Rd 96822 808-988-4111
Sr. Joan of Arc Souza, prin. Fax 988-5497
St. John the Baptist S 200/PK-8
2340 Omilo Ln 96819 808-841-5551
Sr. Laurencia Camayudo, prin. Fax 842-6104
St. Patrick S 400/K-8
3320 Harding Ave 96816 808-734-8979
Sr. Anne Clare DeCosta, prin. Fax 732-2851
St. Philomena Early Learning Center 200/PK-PK
3300 Ala Laulani St 96818 808-833-8080
Angeline Thomas, prin. Fax 834-3438
St. Theresa S 500/K-8
712 N School St 96817 808-536-4703
Robert Gallagher, prin. Fax 524-6861
Soto Academy 100/K-6
1708 Nuuanu Ave 96817 808-533-0452
Rose Ann Nakamoto, prin. Fax 533-0344
Star of the Sea Early Learning Center 200/PK-K
4470 Aliikoa St Rm 100 96821 808-734-3840
Dr. Lisa Foster, prin. Fax 732-1738
Star of the Sea S 300/1-8
4469 Malia St 96821 808-734-0208
Carola Souza, prin. Fax 735-9790
Waolani-Judd Nazarene S 200/PK-6
408 N Judd St 96817 808-531-5251
Florence Teruya, prin. Fax 531-2282
Word of Life Academy 500/PK-12
550 Queen St 96813 808-447-1110
Royce Tanouye, hdmstr. Fax 550-0253

Hoolehua, Maui
Hawaii SD
Supt. — See Honolulu
Moloka'i MS 200/7-8
PO Box 443 96729 808-567-6940
Gary Zukeran, prin. Fax 567-6939

Kaaawa, Honolulu, Pop. 1,138
Hawaii SD
Supt. — See Honolulu
Ka'a'awa ES 200/K-6
51-296 Kamehameha Hwy 96730 808-237-7751
Todd Watanabe, prin. Fax 237-7755

Kahuku, Honolulu, Pop. 2,063
Hawaii SD
Supt. — See Honolulu
Kahuku ES 600/PK-6
56-170 Pualalea St 96731 808-293-8980
Pauline Masaniai, prin. Fax 293-8985

Kahului, Maui, Pop. 16,889
Hawaii SD
Supt. — See Honolulu
Kahului ES 900/PK-5
410 Hina Ave 96732 808-873-3055
Fern Markgraf, prin. Fax 873-3089
Lihikai ES 1,100/K-5
335 S Papa Ave 96732 808-873-3033
Michael Pollock, prin. Fax 873-3570
Maui Waena IS 1,000/6-8
795 Onehee Ave 96732 808-873-3070
Jamie Yap, prin. Fax 873-3066
Pomikai ES K-5
4650 S Kamehameha Ave 96732 808-873-3410
Rene Yamafuji, prin. Fax 873-3414

Christ the King S 100/PK-6
211 Kaulawahine St 96732 808-877-6618
Bernadette Lopez, prin. Fax 871-8101
Emmanuel Lutheran S 200/K-8
520 One St 96732 808-873-6334
Ann Bergman, admin. Fax 877-6819
Ka'ahumanu Hou Christian Schools of Maui 100/PK-12
777 Mokulele Hwy 96732 808-871-2477
Ted Bass, prin. Fax 871-5668
Maui Adventist S 50/K-9
261 S Puunene Ave 96732 808-877-7813
Rhonda Nelson, prin. Fax 893-0219

Kailua, Honolulu
Hawaii SD
Supt. — See Honolulu
Aikahi ES 600/PK-6
281 Ilihau St 96734 808-254-7944
Gay Kong, prin. Fax 254-7962
Enchanted Lake ES 300/PK-6
770 Keolu Dr 96734 808-266-7800
Pua'ala McElhaney, prin. Fax 266-7804
Ka'elepulu ES 200/K-6
530 Keolu Dr 96734 808-266-7811
Sue Stock, prin. Fax 266-7813
Kailua ES 400/PK-6
315 Kuulei Rd 96734 808-266-7878
Lanelle Hibbs, prin. Fax 266-7882
Kailua IS 700/7-8
145 S Kainalu Dr 96734 808-263-1500
Suzanne Mulcahy, prin. Fax 266-7984
Kainalu ES 500/PK-6
165 Kaiholu St 96734 808-266-7835
Sheri Sunabe, prin. Fax 266-7837
Keolu ES 200/PK-6
1416 Keolu Dr 96734 808-266-7818
Alma Souki, prin. Fax 266-7892
Maunawili ES 400/PK-6
1465 Ulupii St 96734 808-266-7822
Ryan Amine, prin. Fax 266-7834
Mokapu ES 800/PK-6
1193 Mokapu Rd 96734 808-254-7964
Annette Ostrem, prin. Fax 254-7969

Le Jardin Academy 800/PK-12
917 Kalanianaole Hwy 96734 808-261-0707
Adrian Allan, hdmstr. Fax 262-9339
Redemption Academy 100/PK-12
361 N Kainalu Dr 96734 808-266-2341
Adrian Yuen Ph.D., dean Fax 266-2342

St. Anthony S - Kailua 400/PK-8
148 Makawao St 96734 808-261-3331
Bridget Olsen, prin. Fax 263-3518
St. John Vianney S 300/PK-8
940 Keolu Dr 96734 808-261-4651
Michael Busekrus, prin. Fax 263-0505
Trinity Christian S 200/PK-9
875 Auloa Rd 96734 808-262-8501
Nancy Shaw, prin. Fax 261-3916
Windward Adventist S 100/K-8
160 Mookua St 96734 808-261-0565
Bruce Lane, prin. Fax 262-0915

Kailua Kona, Hawaii, Pop. 45,944
Hawaii SD
Supt. — See Honolulu
Kahakai ES 600/PK-5
76-147 Royal Poinciana Dr 96740 808-327-4313
Jessica Yamasawa, prin. Fax 327-4333
Kealakehe ES 1,000/PK-5
74-5118 Kealakaa St 96740 808-327-4308
Nancy Matsukawa, prin. Fax 327-4347
Kealakehe IS 900/6-8
74-5062 Onipaa St 96740 808-327-4314
Donald Merwin, prin. Fax 327-4315

Hualalai Academy 200/K-12
74-4966 Kealakaa St 96740 808-326-9866
Kate Mulligan, prin. Fax 329-9542
Kona Christian Academy 200/K-7
PO Box 1179 96745 808-329-3093
Nancy Begley, prin. Fax 329-5449

Kalaheo, Kauai, Pop. 3,592
Hawaii SD
Supt. — See Honolulu
Kalaheo ES 500/K-5
4400 Maka Rd 96741 808-332-6801
Erik Burkman, prin. Fax 332-6804

Kamuela, Hawaii, Pop. 5,972
Hawaii SD
Supt. — See Honolulu
Waimea ES 700/PK-5
67-1225 Mamalahoa Hwy 96743 808-887-7636
Marcella McLelland, prin. Fax 887-7640

Hawaii Prep Academy 600/PK-12
65-1692 Kohala Mountain Rd 96743 808-885-7321
Lindsay Barnes, hdmstr. Fax 881-4003
Parker S 300/K-12
65-1224 Lindsey Rd 96743 808-885-7933
Dr. Carl Sturges, prin. Fax 885-6233
Waimea Christian Academy 50/K-8
65-1078 Mamalahoa Hwy 96743 808-885-8501
Bella Edwards, dir. Fax 885-8502

Kaneohe, Honolulu, Pop. 34,970
Hawaii SD
Supt. — See Honolulu
Ahuimanu ES 400/K-6
47-470 Hui Aeko Pl 96744 808-239-3125
Randolph Scoville, prin. Fax 239-3127
Heeia ES 500/PK-6
46-202 Haiku Rd 96744 808-233-5677
Sheena Alaiasa, prin. Fax 233-5679
Kahaluu ES 200/K-6
47-280 Waihee Rd 96744 808-239-3101
Naomi Matsuzaki, prin. Fax 239-3102
Kane'ohe ES 600/PK-6
45-495 Kamehameha Hwy 96744 808-233-5633
Mitchell Otani, prin. Fax 233-5637
Kapunahala ES 600/K-6
45-828 Anoi Rd 96744 808-233-5650
Joyce Bellino, prin. Fax 233-5651
King IS 700/7-8
46-155 Kamehameha Hwy 96744 808-233-5727
Sheena Alaiasa, prin. Fax 233-5747
Parker ES 300/PK-6
45-259 Waikalua Rd 96744 808-233-5686
Wade Araki, prin. Fax 233-5689
Pu'ohala ES 300/PK-6
45-233 Kulauli St 96744 808-233-5660
Alexis Kane, prin. Fax 233-5663
Waiahole ES 100/PK-6
48-215 Waiahole Valley Rd 96744 808-239-3111
Jean Davidson, prin. Fax 239-3113

Christian Education Institute 50/K-12
45-416 Kamehameha Hwy 96744 808-235-1044
Robin Spencer, admin. Fax 234-5753
Koolau Baptist Academy 200/PK-12
PO Box 1642 96744 808-233-2900
John Goodale, prin. Fax 233-2903
St. Ann's Early Learning Center 200/PK-K
46-125 Haiku Rd 96744 808-247-3092
Clarie Thompson, prin. Fax 235-0717
St. Ann's Model S 300/1-8
46-125 Haiku Rd 96744 808-247-3092
Victoria DeSilva, prin. Fax 235-0717
St. Mark Lutheran S 200/K-8
45-725 Kamehameha Hwy 96744 808-247-5589
R. David Gaudi, prin. Fax 235-6155
Windward Nazarene Academy 200/PK-8
PO Box 1633 96744 808-235-8787
Kay Hishinuma, admin. Fax 236-0174

Kapaa, Kauai, Pop. 8,149
Hawaii SD
Supt. — See Honolulu
Kapaa ES 900/PK-5
4886 Kawaihau Rd 96746 808-821-4424
Jason Kuloloia, prin. Fax 821-4431
Kapaa MS 700/6-8
4867 Olohena Rd 96746 808-821-4460
Nathan Aiwohi, prin. Fax 821-6967

St. Catherine S 100/PK-8
5021 Kawaihau Rd 96746 808-822-4212
Celina Haigh, prin. Fax 823-0991

Kapaau, Hawaii, Pop. 1,083
Hawaii SD
Supt. — See Honolulu
Kohala ES 400/PK-5
PO Box 819 96755 808-889-7100
Eleanor Laszlo, prin. Fax 889-7103
Kohala MS 200/6-8
PO Box 777 96755 808-889-7119
Janette Snelling, prin. Fax 889-7121

Kapolei, Honolulu, Pop. 1,000
Hawaii SD
Supt. — See Honolulu
Barbers Point ES 500/PK-5
3001 Boxer Rd 96707 808-673-7400
Claudia Nakachi, prin. Fax 673-7403
Kapolei ES 1,100/K-5
91-1119 Kamaaha Loop 96707 808-693-7000
Michael Miyamura, prin. Fax 693-7011
Kapolei MS 1,600/6-8
91-5335 Kapolei Pkwy 96707 808-693-7025
Annette Nishikawa, prin. Fax 693-7030
Makakilo ES 500/K-5
92-675 Anipeahi St 96707 808-672-1122
Sean Tajima, prin. Fax 672-1128
Mauka Lani ES 600/PK-5
92-1300 Panana St 96707 808-672-1100
Shelley Ferrara, prin. Fax 672-1114

Island Pacific Academy 700/PK-12
909 Haumea St 96707 808-674-3523
Dr. Daniel White, hdmstr. Fax 674-3575

Kaunakakai, Maui, Pop. 2,658
Hawaii SD
Supt. — See Honolulu
Kaunakakai ES 200/PK-6
PO Box 1950 96748 808-553-1730
Janice Espiritu, prin. Fax 553-1737
Kilohana ES 100/K-6
HC 1 Box 334 96748 808-558-2200
Leighton Kawai, prin. Fax 558-2203

Molokai Mission S, PO Box 248 96748 50/K-8
Krista Hightower, prin. 808-553-4441

Keaau, Hawaii, Pop. 1,584
Hawaii SD
Supt. — See Honolulu
Kea'au ES 800/K-5
16-680 Keaau Pahoa Rd 96749 808-982-4210
Chad Farias, prin. Fax 982-4217
Kea'au MS 600/6-8
16-565 Keaau Pahoa Rd 96749 808-982-4200
Jamil Ahmadia, prin. Fax 982-4219

Christian Liberty S 300/PK-12
16-675 Milo St 96749 808-966-8445
Troy Rimel, prin. Fax 966-8446
Kamehameha S - Hawaii Campus 1,100/K-12
16-716 Volcano Rd 96749 808-982-0000
Dr. Stan Fortuna, hdmstr. Fax 982-0010
Malamalama Waldorf S 100/PK-8
HC 3 Box 13068 96749 808-982-7701
Kehaulani Costa, admin. Fax 982-7806

Kealakekua, Hawaii, Pop. 1,453
Hawaii SD
Supt. — See Honolulu
Konawaena ES 600/PK-5
81-901 Onouli Rd 96750 808-323-4555
Claire Yoshida, prin. Fax 323-4551
Konawaena MS 400/6-8
81-1045 Konawaena School Rd 96750
808-323-4566
Nancy Soderberg, prin. Fax 323-4574

Kekaha, Kauai, Pop. 3,506
Hawaii SD
Supt. — See Honolulu
Kekaha ES 200/K-6
PO Box 580 96752 808-337-7655
Carolyn Shikada, prin. Fax 337-7657

St. Theresa S 100/PK-8
PO Box 277 96752 808-337-1351
Mary Jean Buza-Sims, prin. Fax 337-1714

Kihei, Maui, Pop. 11,107
Hawaii SD
Supt. — See Honolulu
Kamali'i ES 700/K-5
180 Alanui Kealii Dr 96753 808-875-6840
Mary Auvil, prin. Fax 875-6843
Kihei ES 800/PK-5
250 E Lipoa St 96753 808-875-6818
Alvin Shima, prin. Fax 875-6825
Lokelani IS 700/6-8
1401 Liloa Dr 96753 808-875-6800
Donna Whitford, prin. Fax 875-6835

Montessori Hale O Keiki 100/PK-8
PO Box 2348 96753 808-874-7441
Elaine Blasi, dir. Fax 874-2573

Kilauea, Kauai, Pop. 1,685
Hawaii SD
Supt. — See Honolulu
Kilauea ES 300/PK-6
2440 Kolo Rd 96754 808-828-1212
Fred Rose, prin. Fax 828-2034

Koloa, Kauai, Pop. 1,791
Hawaii SD
Supt. — See Honolulu
Koloa ES 200/K-5
3223 Poipu Rd 96756 808-742-8460
Debra Lindsey, prin. Fax 742-8466

Kahili Adventist S 100/K-12
2-4035 Kaumualii Hwy 96756 808-742-9294
Wanda Lee, prin. Fax 742-6628

Kula, Maui
Hawaii SD
Supt. — See Honolulu
Kula ES 400/K-5
5000 Kula Hwy 96790 808-876-7610
Barbara Oura, prin. Fax 876-7616

Haleakala Waldorf S 200/PK-8
4160 Lower Kula Rd 96790 808-878-2511
Jocelyn Demirbag, chrpsn. Fax 878-3341

Lahaina, Maui, Pop. 9,073
Hawaii SD
Supt. — See Honolulu
Kamehameha III ES 700/K-5
611 Front St 96761 808-662-3955
Steve Franz, prin. Fax 662-3958
Lahaina IS 600/6-8
871 Lahainaluna Rd 96761 808-662-3965
Marsha Nakamura, prin. Fax 662-3968
Nahienaena ES 600/PK-5
816 Niheu St 96761 808-662-4020
James Kaipo Miller, prin. Fax 662-4023

Maui Preparatory Academy 200/PK-12
PO Box 186 96767 808-665-9966
George Baker, prin. Fax 665-1075
Sacred Hearts S 200/PK-8
239 Dickenson St 96761 808-661-4720
Susan Hendricks, prin. Fax 667-5363

Laie, Honolulu, Pop. 5,577
Hawaii SD
Supt. — See Honolulu
La'ie ES 600/PK-6
55-109 Kulanui St 96762 808-293-8965
Deborah Voorhies, prin. Fax 293-8968

Lanai City, Maui, Pop. 2,400
Hawaii SD
Supt. — See Honolulu
Lanai S 600/K-12
PO Box 630630 96763 808-565-7900
Pierce Myers, prin. Fax 565-7904

Laupahoehoe, Hawaii, Pop. 508
Hawaii SD
Supt. — See Honolulu
Laupahoehoe S 200/K-12
PO Box 189 96764 808-962-2200
Paul McCarty, prin. Fax 962-2202

Lihue, Kauai, Pop. 5,536
Hawaii SD
Supt. — See Honolulu
Kamakahelei MS 1,000/6-8
4431 Nuhou St 96766 808-241-3200
Debra Badua, prin. Fax 241-3210
Kaumualii ES 500/PK-5
4380 Hanamaulu Rd 96766 808-241-3150
Karen Liu, prin. Fax 241-3159
Wilcox ES 900/K-5
4319 Hardy St 96766 808-274-3150
Terry Proctor, prin. Fax 274-3152

Island S 300/PK-12
3-1875 Kaumualii Hwy 96766 808-246-0233
Robert Springer, prin. Fax 245-6053

Makawao, Maui, Pop. 5,405
Hawaii SD
Supt. — See Honolulu
Kalama IS 900/6-8
120 Makani Rd 96768 808-573-8735
John Costales, prin. Fax 573-8748
Makawao ES 500/PK-5
3542 Baldwin Ave 96768 808-573-8770
Emily De Costa, prin. Fax 573-8774
Pukalani ES 500/K-5
2945 Iolani St 96768 808-572-8760
Chad Okamoto, prin. Fax 572-8766

Kamehameha S Maui 1,100/K-12
270 Aapueo Pkwy 96768 808-572-3100
Lee Ann DeLima, hdmstr. Fax 573-7062
Montessori S of Maui 200/PK-8
2933 Baldwin Ave 96768 808-573-0374
Cynthia Winans-Burns, prin. Fax 573-0389
St. Joseph S - Makawao 100/PK-5
1294 Makawao Ave 96768 808-572-8675
Beth Fobbe-Wills, prin. Fax 572-0748

Maunaloa, Maui, Pop. 405
Hawaii SD
Supt. — See Honolulu
Maunaloa ES 100/K-6
PO Box 128 96770 808-552-2000
Joe Yamamoto, prin. Fax 552-2004

Mililani, Honolulu, Pop. 28,608
Hawaii SD
Supt. — See Honolulu
Kipapa ES 600/PK-5
95-076 Kipapa Dr 96789 808-627-7322
Bruce Naguwa, prin. Fax 627-7326
Mililani 'Ike ES 1,000/K-5
95-1330 Lehiwa Dr 96789 808-626-2980
Steven Nakasoto, prin. Fax 626-2958

Mililani Mauka ES 700/PK-5
95-1111 Makaikai St 96789 808-626-3350
Carol Petersen, prin. Fax 626-3360
Mililani MS 1,800/6-8
95-1140 Lehiwa Dr 96789 808-626-7355
Valarie Kardash, prin. Fax 626-7358
Mililani-Uka ES 700/PK-5
94-380 Kuahelani Ave 96789 808-627-7303
Heather Wilhelm, prin. Fax 627-7387
Mililani-Waena ES 600/PK-5
95-502 Kipapa Dr 96789 808-627-7300
Dale Castro, prin. Fax 627-7455

Hanalani S 800/PK-12
94-294 Anania Dr 96789 808-625-0737
Mark Sugimoto, supt. Fax 625-0691
St. Johns Preschool 100/PK-PK
95-370 Kuahelani Ave 96789 808-623-3332
Catherine Awong, dir. Fax 623-6496

Mountain View, Hawaii, Pop. 3,075
Hawaii SD
Supt. — See Honolulu
Mountain View ES 400/K-6
PO Box 9 96771 808-968-2300
Sylvia Lee, prin. Fax 968-2305

Naalehu, Hawaii, Pop. 1,027
Hawaii SD
Supt. — See Honolulu
Na'alehu S 400/PK-8
PO Box 170 96772 808-939-2413
Teddy Burgess, prin. Fax 939-2419

Paauilo, Hawaii, Pop. 620
Hawaii SD
Supt. — See Honolulu
Paauilo S 200/K-9
PO Box 329 96776 808-776-7710
Stanley Oka, prin. Fax 776-7714

Pahala, Hawaii, Pop. 1,520
Hawaii SD
Supt. — See Honolulu
Ka'u HS & Pahala ES 500/K-12
PO Box 100 96777 808-928-2088
Sharon Beck, prin. Fax 928-2092

Pahoa, Hawaii, Pop. 1,027
Hawaii SD
Supt. — See Honolulu
Keonepoko ES 600/K-6
15-890 Kahakai Blvd 96778 808-965-2131
Kathleen Romero, prin. Fax 965-2138
Pahoa ES 400/PK-6
15-3030 Pahoa Village Rd 96778 808-965-2141
Marilyn Quaccia, prin. Fax 965-2180

Paia, Maui, Pop. 2,091
Hawaii SD
Supt. — See Honolulu
Pa'ia ES 200/K-5
955 Baldwin Ave 96779 808-579-2100
Susan Alivado, prin. Fax 579-2103

Todd Memorial Christian S 100/PK-8
519 Baldwin Ave 96779 808-579-9237
Carolyn Moore, prin. Fax 579-9449

Papaikou, Hawaii, Pop. 1,634
Hawaii SD
Supt. — See Honolulu
Kalanianaole S 400/K-8
27-330 Old Mamalahoa Hwy 96781 808-964-9700
Joyce Iwashita, prin. Fax 964-9703

Pearl City, Honolulu, Pop. 30,976
Hawaii SD
Supt. — See Honolulu
Highlands IS 1,000/7-8
1460 Hoolaulea St 96782 808-453-6480
Amy Martinson, prin. Fax 453-6484
Lehua ES 400/PK-6
791 Lehua Ave 96782 808-453-6490
Fay Toyama, prin. Fax 453-6497
Manana ES 400/K-6
1147 Kumano St 96782 808-453-6430
Brian Loo, prin. Fax 453-6437
Momilani ES 400/K-6
2130 Hookiekie St 96782 808-453-6444
Doreen Higa, prin. Fax 453-6448
Palisades ES 300/K-6
2306 Auhuhu St 96782 808-453-6550
Suzanne Yamada, prin. Fax 453-5910
Pearl City ES 500/PK-6
1090 Waimano Home Rd 96782 808-453-6455
Susan Hirokane, prin. Fax 453-6467
Pearl City Highlands ES 300/PK-6
1419 Waimano Home Rd 96782 808-453-6470
Leroy Ching, prin. Fax 453-6472
Waiau ES 600/PK-6
98-450 Hookanike St 96782 808-453-6530
Troy Takazono, prin. Fax 453-6541

Children's House 400/PK-6
1840 Komo Mai Dr 96782 808-455-4131
Mary Los Banos, prin. Fax 455-2748
Our Lady of Good Counsel S 300/PK-8
1530 Hoolana St 96782 808-455-4533
Cindy Olaso, prin. Fax 455-5587

Wahiawa, Honolulu, Pop. 17,386
Hawaii SD
Supt. — See Honolulu
Hale Kula ES 500/K-5
1 Ayres Ave 96786 808-622-6380
Jan Iwase, prin. Fax 622-6382
Helemano ES 600/K-5
1001 Ihiihi Ave 96786 808-622-6336
Ernest Muh, prin. Fax 622-6340
Iliahi ES 400/K-5
2035 California Ave 96786 808-622-6411
James Albano, prin. Fax 622-6413
Ka'ala ES 400/K-5
130 California Ave 96786 808-622-6366
Theodore Fisher, prin. Fax 622-6368
Solomon ES 800/PK-5
1 Schofield Bks 96786 808-624-9500
Linda Yoshikami, prin. Fax 624-9505
Wahiawa ES 500/PK-5
1402 Glen Ave 96786 808-622-6393
Troy Tamura, prin. Fax 622-6394
Wahiawa MS 900/6-8
275 Rose St 96786 808-622-6500
Dr. Carol Price, prin. Fax 622-6506
Wheeler ES 700/PK-5
1 Wheeler Army Airfield 96786 808-622-6400
Joe Lee, prin. Fax 622-6403
Wheeler MS 600/6-8
2 Wheeler Army Airfield 96786 808-622-6525
Brenda Vierra-Chun, prin. Fax 622-6529

Abundant Life S 100/PK-6
650 Kilani Ave 96786 808-621-5433
Judie Wasson, prin. Fax 621-9388
Ho'ala S 100/PK-12
1067 California Ave Ste A 96786 808-621-1898
Linda Turnbull, hdmstr. Fax 622-3615
Leeward Adventist Mission S 50/K-4
1313 California Ave 96786 808-792-0381
Tricia Koh, prin. Fax 792-0381
Trinity Lutheran S 200/PK-8
1611 California Ave 96786 808-621-6033
Chris Anderson, prin. Fax 621-6029

Waialua, Honolulu, Pop. 3,943
Hawaii SD
Supt. — See Honolulu
Waialua ES 500/PK-6
67-020 Waialua Beach Rd 96791 808-637-8228
Scott Moore, prin. Fax 637-8225

St. Michael S 200/K-8
67-340 Haona St 96791 808-637-7772
Deanna Arecchi, prin. Fax 637-7722

Waianae, Honolulu, Pop. 8,758
Hawaii SD
Supt. — See Honolulu
Leihoku ES 800/PK-6
86-285 Leihoku St 96792 808-697-7100
Randal Miura, prin. Fax 697-7142
Ma'ili ES 800/PK-6
87-360 Kulaaupuni St 96792 808-697-7150
Disa Hauge, prin. Fax 697-7151
Makaha ES 600/K-6
84-200 Ala Naauao Pl 96792 808-695-7900
Nelson Shigeta, prin. Fax 695-7905
Nanaikapono ES 900/PK-6
89-153 Mano Ave 96792 808-668-5800
Elden Esmeralda, prin. Fax 668-5890
Nanakuli ES 500/PK-6
89-778 Haleakala Ave 96792 808-668-5813
Wendy Takahashi, prin. Fax 668-5817
Waianae ES 600/PK-6
85-220 Mcarthur St 96792 808-697-7083
John Wataoka, prin. Fax 697-7090

Adventist Malama S 50/PK-8
86-072 Farrington Hwy 96792 808-696-3988
Alio Santos, prin. Fax 696-7790
Maili Bible S 100/K-12
87-138 Gilipake St 96792 808-696-3038
Larry Estrella, prin. Fax 696-3060

Waikoloa, Hawaii, Pop. 2,248
Hawaii SD
Supt. — See Honolulu
Waikoloa ES 500/PK-5
68-1730 Hooko St 96738 808-883-6808
Kris Kosa-Correia, prin. Fax 883-6811

Wailuku, Maui, Pop. 10,688
Hawaii SD
Supt. — See Honolulu
Iao IS 800/6-8
260 S Market St 96793 808-984-5610
Catherine Kilborn, prin. Fax 984-5617
Waihe'e ES 800/K-5
2125 Kahekili Hwy 96793 808-984-5644
Leila Hayashida, prin. Fax 984-5648
Wailuku ES 1,000/K-5
355 S High St 96793 808-984-5622
Beverly Stanich, prin. Fax 984-5627

St. Anthony Preschool 50/PK-PK
1627 Mill St 96793 808-242-9024
Carlene Santos, dir. Fax 986-0654
St. Anthony S 200/K-6
1627 Mill St 96793 808-244-4976
Winona Martinez, prin. Fax 244-7950

Waimanalo, Honolulu, Pop. 3,508
Hawaii SD
Supt. — See Honolulu
Pope ES 300/PK-6
41-133 Huli St 96795 808-259-0450
Ofelia Carag, prin. Fax 259-0452
Waimanalo S 500/K-8
41-1330 Kalanianaole Hwy 96795 808-259-0460
Susan Hummel, prin. Fax 259-0463

Waimea, Kauai, Pop. 7,812
Hawaii SD
Supt. — See Honolulu
Niihau S 50/K-12
PO Box 339 96796 808-338-6800
Larry Kaliloa, prin. Fax 338-6807
Waimea Canyon S 500/K-8
PO Box 518 96796 808-338-6830
Glenda Miyazaki, prin. Fax 338-6832

Waipahu, Honolulu, Pop. 33,108
Hawaii SD
Supt. — See Honolulu
Ahrens ES 1,300/PK-6
94-1170 Waipahu St 96797 808-675-0202
Dr. Florentina Smith, prin. Fax 675-0216
Honowai ES 800/PK-6
94-600 Honowai St 96797 808-675-0165
Curtis Young, prin. Fax 675-0167
Kaleiopuu ES 1,000/PK-6
94-665 Kaaholo St 96797 808-675-0266
Carolyn Alexander, prin. Fax 675-0269
Kanoelani ES 800/PK-6
94-1091 Oli Loop 96797 808-675-0195
Sandy Ahu, prin. Fax 675-0135
Waikele ES 700/K-6
94-1035 Kukula St 96797 808-677-6100
Carm Minami, prin. Fax 677-6106
Waipahu ES 1,000/K-6
94-465 Waipahu St 96797 808-675-0150
Paul Taga, prin. Fax 675-0121
Waipahu IS 1,300/7-8
94-455 Farrington Hwy 96797 808-675-0177
Randell Dunn, prin. Fax 675-0181

Lanakila Baptist ES 100/K-6
94-1250 Waipahu St 96797 808-677-0731
Cynthia Shirota, prin. Fax 677-0733
Pearl Harbor Christian Academy 200/PK-8
94-1044 Waipio Uka St 96797 808-678-3997
Phebe Sumida, admin. Fax 678-3998
Rosary Preschool 50/PK-K
94-1249A Lumikula St 96797 808-676-1452
Sr. Aurelia Sanchez, dir. Fax 677-1202
St. Joseph S - Waipahu 400/PK-8
94-651 Farrington Hwy 96797 808-677-4475
Beverly Sandobal, prin. Fax 677-8937

IDAHO

IDAHO DEPARTMENT OF EDUCATION
PO Box 83720, Boise 83720-0003
Telephone 208-332-6800
Fax 208-334-2228
Website http://www.sde.idaho.gov

Superintendent of Public Instruction Tom Luna

IDAHO BOARD OF EDUCATION
PO Box 83720, Boise 83720-0003

President Paul Agidius

PUBLIC, PRIVATE AND CATHOLIC ELEMENTARY SCHOOLS

Aberdeen, Bingham, Pop. 1,828
Aberdeen SD 58 800/PK-12
PO Box 610 83210 208-397-4113
Joel Wilson, supt. Fax 397-4114
aberdeen58.org/
Aberdeen ES 400/PK-5
PO Box 610 83210 208-397-4115
Jane Ward, prin. Fax 397-4117
Aberdeen MS 200/6-8
PO Box 610 83210 208-397-3280
Ann Mennear, prin. Fax 397-3281

Albion, Cassia, Pop. 258
Cassia County JSD 151
Supt. — See Burley
Albion ES 50/K-5
PO Box 38 83311 208-673-6653
Becky Hunsaker, prin. Fax 673-6653

Almo, Cassia
Cassia County JSD 151
Supt. — See Burley
Almo ES 50/K-3
PO Box 168 83312 208-824-5526
Eric Boden, prin. Fax 824-5522

American Falls, Power, Pop. 4,162
American Falls JSD 381 1,600/PK-12
827 Fort Hall Ave 83211 208-226-5173
Dr. Ron Bolinger, supt. Fax 226-5754
www.sd381.k12.id.us
American Falls IS 200/4-5
254 Taylor St 83211 208-226-5733
Chris Torgesen, prin. Fax 226-5766
Hillcrest ES 400/PK-3
1045 Bennett Ave 83211 208-226-2391
Tina Fehringer, prin. Fax 226-2677
Thomas MS 400/6-8
355 Bannock Ave 83211 208-226-5203
Randy Jensen, prin. Fax 226-5274

Ammon, Bonneville, Pop. 10,925
Bonneville JSD 93
Supt. — See Idaho Falls
Ammon ES 400/K-6
2900 Central Ave 83406 208-525-4465
Lanie Keller, prin. Fax 525-4467
Bridgewater ES K-6
1499 Indian Hollow Dr 83401 208-552-5577
Brian Armes, prin. Fax 552-5578
Hillview ES 500/PK-6
3075 Teton St 83406 208-525-4460
Gordon Howard, prin. Fax 525-4461
Woodland Hills ES K-6
4700 Sweetwater 83406 208-552-4850
Terri Beseris, prin. Fax 552-4772

Arbon, Power, Pop. 613
Arbon ESD 383 50/K-6
4405 Arbon Valley Hwy 83212 208-335-2197
Fax 335-2195
Arbon ES 50/K-6
4405 Arbon Valley Hwy 83212 208-335-2197
Robin Claunch, lead tchr. Fax 335-2195

Arco, Butte, Pop. 989
Butte County JSD 111 500/PK-12
PO Box 89 83213 208-527-8235
Dr. Amy Pancheri, supt. Fax 527-8950
www.butteschooldistrict.org/
Arco ES 200/PK-5
PO Box 675 83213 208-527-8503
Karen Pyron, prin. Fax 527-3420
Butte County MS 100/6-8
PO Box 695 83213 208-527-3077
Robert Chambers, prin. Fax 527-4950
Other Schools – See Howe

Arimo, Bannock, Pop. 319
Marsh Valley JSD 21 1,300/PK-12
PO Box 180 83214 208-254-3306
Marvin Hansen, supt. Fax 254-9243
www.mvsd21.org
Marsh Valley MS 200/7-8
12805 S Old Highway 91 83214 208-254-3260
Linda Reichardt, prin. Fax 254-3631

Other Schools – See Downey, Inkom, Lava Hot Springs, Mc Cammon

Ashton, Fremont, Pop. 1,105
Fremont County JSD 215
Supt. — See Saint Anthony
Ashton ES 300/PK-5
168 S 1st St 83420 208-652-7601
Jaci Hill, prin. Fax 652-7602

Athol, Kootenai, Pop. 707
Lakeland JSD 272
Supt. — See Rathdrum
Athol ES 400/PK-6
6333 E Menser Ave 83801 208-683-2231
Kathy Thomas, prin. Fax 683-7064

Avery, Shoshone
Avery SD 394 50/K-8
PO Box 7 83802 208-245-2479
Carl Morgan, supt. Fax 245-2760
www.sd394.com/
Avery S 50/K-8
PO Box 7 83802 208-245-2479
Carl Morgan, lead tchr. Fax 245-2760

Bancroft, Caribou, Pop. 363
North Gem SD 149 200/PK-12
PO Box 70 83217 208-648-7848
Kent Stokes, supt. Fax 648-7895
www.sd149.com
North Gem ES 100/PK-6
PO Box 70 83217 208-648-7848
Kent Stokes, prin. Fax 648-7895

Bellevue, Blaine, Pop. 2,203
Blaine County SD 61
Supt. — See Hailey
Bellevue ES 300/K-5
305 N 5th St 83313 208-788-4012
Angie Martinez, prin. Fax 788-5156

Blackfoot, Bingham, Pop. 10,828
Blackfoot SD 55 4,100/K-12
270 E Bridge St 83221 208-785-8800
Dr. Scott Crane, supt. Fax 785-8809
www.d55.k12.id.us
Blackfoot 6th Grade S 300/6-6
50 S Shilling Ave 83221 208-785-8838
Brandon Farris, prin. Fax 785-8840
Groveland ES 300/1-5
375 W 170 N 83221 208-785-8829
Jay Thayne, prin. Fax 785-8859
Irving K 300/K-K
440 W Judicial St 83221 208-785-8835
Christine Silzly, prin. Fax 785-8816
Mountain View MS 600/7-8
645 Mitchell Ln 83221 208-785-8820
Rex Jacobson, prin. Fax 785-8823
Ridge Crest ES 400/1-5
800 Airport Rd 83221 208-785-8894
Colin Folsom, prin. Fax 785-8897
Stalker ES 300/1-5
991 W Center St 83221 208-785-8841
Hal Silzly, prin. Fax 785-8855
Stoddard ES 400/1-5
460 York Dr 83221 208-785-8832
Ryan Wilson, prin. Fax 785-8834
Wapello ES 200/1-5
195 E 350 N 83221 208-785-8844
Brandee Hewatt, prin. Fax 785-8815
Other Schools – See Pocatello

Snake River SD 52 1,600/PK-12
103 S 900 W 83221 208-684-3001
Russell Hammond, supt. Fax 684-3003
www.snakeriver.org
Riverside ES 100/3-3
16 S 700 W 83221 208-684-5102
Wayne Kroll, prin. Fax 684-5193
Rockford ES 50/4-4
1152 W Highway 39 83221 208-684-4451
Wayne Kroll, prin. Fax 684-5190
Snake River JHS 300/7-8
918 W Highway 39 83221 208-684-3018
L.T. Erickson, prin. Fax 684-3047
Snake River MS 300/5-6
1060 W 110 S 83221 208-684-5171
Ed Jackson, prin. Fax 684-5199
Other Schools – See Moreland

Bliss, Gooding, Pop. 260
Bliss JSD 234 200/K-12
PO Box 115 83314 208-352-4447
Kevin Lancaster, supt. Fax 352-4649
www.bliss.k12.id.us
Bliss S 200/K-12
601 E Highway 30 83314 208-352-4445
Jeff LaCroix, prin. Fax 352-4649

Boise, Ada, Pop. 189,847
ISD of Boise City 23,200/PK-12
8169 W Victory Rd 83709 208-854-4000
Dr. Stan Olson, supt. Fax 854-4003
www.boiseschools.org
Adams ES 300/PK-6
1725 Warm Springs Ave 83712 208-854-4190
Dr. Kelly Cross, prin. Fax 854-4191
Amity ES 700/K-6
10000 W Amity Rd 83709 208-854-4220
Darryl Gerber, prin. Fax 854-4221
Collister ES 200/K-6
4426 W Catalpa Dr 83703 208-854-4650
Christine Haggerty, prin. Fax 854-4651
Garfield ES 500/PK-6
1914 S Broadway Ave 83706 208-854-4950
Greg Oram, prin. Fax 854-4951
Hawthorne ES 400/PK-6
2401 W Targee St 83705 208-854-5000
Tedd Hettinga, prin. Fax 854-5001
Highlands ES 300/K-6
3434 N Bogus Basin Rd 83702 208-854-5050
Sally Skinner, prin. Fax 854-5051
Hillcrest ES 300/K-6
2045 S Pond St 83705 208-854-5080
Kurt Thaemert, prin. Fax 854-5081
Horizon ES 700/PK-6
730 N Mitchell St 83704 208-854-5170
Gale Zickefoose, prin. Fax 854-5171
Jefferson ES 300/K-6
200 S Latah St 83705 208-854-5260
Kay Hansen, prin. Fax 854-5261
Jordan ES PK-6
6411 Fairfield Ave 83709 208-854-5080
Tim Lowe, prin. Fax 854-5081
Koelsch ES 300/PK-6
2015 N Curtis Rd 83706 208-854-5300
Rose Beebe, prin. Fax 854-5301
Liberty ES 400/K-6
1740 E Bergeson St 83706 208-854-5410
Betty Hoogland, prin. Fax 854-5411
Longfellow ES 200/K-6
1511 N 9th St 83702 208-854-5450
Deb Watts, prin. Fax 854-5451
Lowell ES 300/K-6
1507 N 28th St 83703 208-854-5480
Paula Bell, prin. Fax 854-5481
Madison ECC 50/PK-PK
2215 W Madison Ave 83702 208-854-5520
Dedra Swanstrom, lead tchr. Fax 854-5521
Mann ES 600/PK-6
5401 W Castle Dr 83703 208-854-4680
Rick Bollman, prin. Fax 854-4681
Maple Grove ES 600/K-6
2800 S Maple Grove Rd 83709 208-854-5540
Mark Jones, prin. Fax 854-5541
Monroe ES 300/K-6
3615 Cassia St 83705 208-854-5620
Beverly Boyd, prin. Fax 854-5621
Mountain View ES 400/K-6
3500 N Cabarton Ln 83704 208-854-5700
Debbie Donovan, prin. Fax 854-5701
Nelson ES PK-6
7701 Northview St 83704 208-854-4610
Lisa Roberts, prin. Fax 854-4611
Owyhee ES 300/K-6
3434 Pasadena Dr 83705 208-854-5850
Nolene Weaver, prin. Fax 854-5851

Pierce Park ES 200/K-6
5015 N Pierce Park Ln 83714 208-854-5880
Kathy Hutchison, prin. Fax 854-5881
Riverside ES 600/PK-6
2100 E Victory Rd 83706 208-854-5980
Larry Bond, prin. Fax 854-5981
Roosevelt ES 300/K-6
908 E Jefferson St 83712 208-854-6030
Julianne Bronner, prin. Fax 854-6031
Shadow Hills ES 700/K-6
8301 W Sloan St 83714 208-854-6060
Leslie Bigham, prin. Fax 854-6061
Taft ES 300/K-6
3722 W Anderson St 83703 208-854-6180
Dr. Susan Williamson, prin. Fax 854-6181
Trail Wind ES 700/K-6
3701 E Lake Forest Dr 83716 208-854-6320
Glen Aguiar, prin. Fax 854-6321
Valley View ES 500/K-6
3555 N Milwaukee St 83704 208-854-6370
Jerry Sloan, prin. Fax 854-6371
Washington ES 300/K-6
1607 N 15th St 83702 208-854-6420
Bob Amburn, prin. Fax 854-6421
White Pine ES 500/PK-6
401 E Linden St 83706 208-854-6530
Sandy Hadden, prin. Fax 854-6531
Whitney ES 400/K-6
1609 S Owyhee St 83705 208-854-6580
Jean Lovelace, prin. Fax 854-6581
Whittier ES 300/K-6
301 N 29th St 83702 208-854-6630
Debby Bailey, prin. Fax 854-6631
Other Schools – See Hidden Springs

Meridian JSD 2
Supt. — See Meridian
Andrus ES 700/K-5
6100 N Park Meadow Way 83713 208-350-4210
Jackie Meyer, prin. Fax 350-4219
Desert Sage ES K-5
9325 W Mossywood Dr 83709 208-350-4020
Joann Grether, prin. Fax 350-4039
Donnell S of the Arts 400/K-8
7075 S Five Mile Rd 83709 208-855-4355
Tina Perry, prin. Fax 855-4364
Frontier ES 500/PK-5
11851 Musket Dr 83713 208-350-4190
Byron Yankey, prin. Fax 350-4199
Joplin ES 400/K-5
12081 W De Meyer St 83713 208-855-4345
Debbie Gourley, prin. Fax 855-4354
Lake Hazel ES 600/K-5
11711 W Lake Hazel Rd 83709 208-350-4075
Jennifer Logan, prin. Fax 350-4084
Lake Hazel MS 1,000/6-8
11625 W La Grange St 83709 208-855-4375
Kenton Travis, prin. Fax 362-0258
McMillan ES 400/K-5
10901 McMillan Rd 83713 208-855-4475
Craig Ayala-Marshall, prin. Fax 855-4484
Pepper Ridge ES 600/PK-5
2252 S Sumpter Way 83709 208-855-4130
Joyce Johnson, prin. Fax 855-4139
Pioneer S of the Arts 700/K-5
13255 W Mcmillan Rd 83713 208-855-4100
Todd Phillips, prin. Fax 855-4109
Scott MS 1,200/6-8
13600 W Mcmillan Rd 83713 208-350-4060
Linda Ventura, prin. Fax 939-1424
Silver Sage ES 300/PK-5
7700 Snohomish St 83709 208-855-4485
Jamie Dobson, prin. Fax 855-4494
Spalding ES 700/PK-5
12311 W Braddock Dr 83709 208-321-2150
Scott Johnstone, prin. Fax 350-4314
Summerwind ES 400/K-5
3675 N Jullion St 83704 208-375-0210
Julie Robideaux-Prince, prin. Fax 350-4323
Ustick ES 500/K-5
12435 W Ustick Rd 83713 208-855-4120
Jack Boggetti, prin. Fax 855-4129

Boise Christian S 100/PK-12
219 N Roosevelt St 83706 208-342-4529
Philip Knisley, admin. Fax 342-4520
Boise Valley Adventist S 100/PK-8
925 N Cloverdale Rd 83713 208-376-7141
Don Krpalek, prin. Fax 376-0120
Calvary Christian S of Boise 100/PK-6
111 Auto Dr 83709 208-376-0260
John Mikkelson, prin. Fax 321-7434
Cole Valley Christian S 400/K-6
8775 Ustick Rd 83704 208-375-3571
Barbara Hemmer, prin. Fax 375-2862
Covenant Academy 50/K-12
PO Box 532 83701 208-377-2385
David Barrett, admin. Fax 362-8061
Foothills S of Arts & Sciences 200/PK-8
618 S 8th St 83702 208-331-9260
Shawn Shepherd, hdmstr. Fax 331-3082
Maranatha Christian S 200/PK-8
12000 W Fairview Ave 83713 208-376-7272
Vern Anderson, prin. Fax 375-0586
Parkcenter Montessori S 200/PK-K
649 E Parkcenter Blvd 83706 208-344-0004
Mike Malterre, prin. Fax 344-0002
Riverstone International School 300/K-12
5493 Warm Springs Ave 83716 208-424-5000
Andrew Derry, hdmstr. Fax 424-0033
Sacred Heart S 200/PK-8
3901 Cassia St 83705 208-344-9738
Anthony Carpenter, prin. Fax 343-1939
St. Joseph's S 300/K-8
825 W Fort St 83702 208-342-4909
Toni Bicandi, prin. Fax 342-0997
St. Mark's S 300/K-8
7503 W Northview St 83704 208-375-6654
Dan Maloney, prin. Fax 375-9471
St. Marys S 200/K-8
2620 W State St 83702 208-342-7476
Marianne White, prin. Fax 345-5154
Shepherd of the Valley Preschool 100/PK-PK
3100 S Five Mile Rd 83709 208-362-5919
Jan Vanderbush, dir.

Bonners Ferry, Boundary, Pop. 2,725
Boundary County SD 101 1,600/PK-12
6577 Main St Ste 101 83805 208-267-3146
Dr. Don Bartling, supt. Fax 267-7217
www.bcsd101.com
Boundary County JHS 400/6-8
6577 Main St Ste 100 83805 208-267-5852
Dick Behrens, prin. Fax 267-8099
Mt. Hall ES 100/K-5
1275 Highway 1 83805 208-267-5276
Angela Armstrong, prin. Fax 267-2957
Valley View ES 400/PK-5
6750 Augusta St 83805 208-267-5519
Cindy Orr, prin. Fax 267-3388
Other Schools – See Moyie Springs, Naples

Cornerstone Christian S 50/K-8
PO Box 1877 83805 208-267-1644
Dennis Shelton, lead tchr. Fax 267-1624

Bovill, Latah, Pop. 285
Whitepine JSD 288
Supt. — See Troy
Bovill ES 100/K-3
PO Box 310 83806 208-826-3314
Tera Reeves, prin. Fax 826-3614

Bruneau, Owyhee
Bruneau-Grand View JSD 365
Supt. — See Grand View
Bruneau ES 100/K-6
PO Box 158 83604 208-845-2492
Gerald Chouinard, prin. Fax 845-2492

Buhl, Twin Falls, Pop. 4,015
Buhl JSD 412 1,300/PK-12
920 Main St 83316 208-543-6436
Margaret Cox, supt. Fax 543-6360
www.d412.k12.id.us
Buhl MS 400/6-8
525 Sawtooth Ave 83316 208-543-8292
Byron Stutzman, prin. Fax 543-5137
Popplewell ES 600/PK-5
200 6th Ave N 83316 208-543-8225
Ronald Anthony, prin. Fax 543-2133

Clover Trinity Lutheran S 100/PK-8
3552 N 1825 E 83316 208-326-5198
Marcus Lutz, admin. Fax 326-5105

Burley, Cassia, Pop. 9,131
Cassia County JSD 151 5,000/PK-12
237 E 19th St 83318 208-878-6600
Gaylen Smyer, supt. Fax 878-4231
www.sd151.k12.id.us
Burley JHS 500/7-8
700 W 16th St 83318 208-878-6613
Steve Copmann, prin. Fax 878-6624
Dworshak ES 500/K-3
102 E 19th St 83318 208-878-6615
Irma Bushman, prin. Fax 878-6342
Mountain View ES 500/PK-3
333 W 27th St 83318 208-878-6615
Delia Valdez, prin. Fax 878-6609
Whitepine ES 700/4-6
1900 Hiland Ave 83318 208-878-6632
Matt Seely, prin. Fax 878-6635
Other Schools – See Albion, Almo, Declo, Malta, Oakley

Zion Lutheran S 50/PK-K
2410 Miller Ave 83318 208-677-2273
Marie E. Veneman, dir.

Caldwell, Canyon, Pop. 34,433
Caldwell SD 132 6,300/K-12
1101 Cleveland Blvd 83605 208-455-3300
Roger Quarles, supt. Fax 455-3302
www.caldwellschools.org/
Jefferson MS 700/6-8
3311 S 10th Ave 83605 208-455-3309
Carol McCloy, prin. Fax 459-6773
Lewis and Clark ES 500/K-5
1102 Laster St 83607 208-455-3345
Dustin Salisbury, prin. Fax 455-3324
Lincoln ES 500/K-5
1200 Grant St 83605 208-455-3321
Tricia Stone, prin. Fax 455-3324
Sacajawea ES 600/K-5
1710 N Illinois Ave 83605 208-455-3333
Gregory Alexander, prin. Fax 455-4462
Syringa MS 700/6-8
1100 Willow St 83605 208-455-3305
Louise Daniels, prin. Fax 455-3353
Van Buren ES 500/K-5
516 N 11th Ave 83605 208-455-3326
LaVaun Dennett, prin. Fax 455-3329
Washington ES 600/K-5
1500 Fillmore St 83605 208-455-3317
Dr. Sherawn Reberry, prin. Fax 455-3338
Wilson ES 500/K-5
400 E Linden St 83605 208-455-3313
Lyla Folkins, prin. Fax 454-0050

Middleton SD 134
Supt. — See Middleton
Middleton Purple Sage ES 400/PK-5
25709 El Paso Rd 83607 208-455-1148
Jerry OldenKamp, prin. Fax 459-2416
Vallivue SD 139 5,500/PK-12
5207 S Montana Ave 83607 208-454-0445
George Grant, supt. Fax 454-0293
www.vallivue.org
Central Canyon ES 700/PK-5
16437 S Florida Ave 83607 208-459-3367
Lisa Colon, prin. Fax 459-3009
Vallivue MS 900/6-8
16412 S 10th Ave 83607 208-454-1426
Rod Lowe, prin. Fax 454-7846
West Canyon ES 700/PK-5
19548 Ustick Rd 83607 208-459-6938
Cindy Dodd, prin. Fax 454-9572
Other Schools – See Nampa

Caldwell Adventist S 100/PK-8
2317 Wisconsin Ave 83605 208-459-4313
Judy Shaner, admin. Fax 459-0357

Cambridge, Washington, Pop. 354
Cambridge JSD 432 200/PK-12
PO Box 39 83610 208-257-3321
Ed Schumacher, supt. Fax 257-3323
www.cambridge432.org/
Cambridge ES 100/PK-6
PO Box 39 83610 208-257-3312
Ed Schumacher, prin. Fax 257-3323

Canyon View SDA S 50/1-8
PO Box 70 83610 208-257-3374
Dianne Eslinger, lead tchr. Fax 257-3624

Carey, Blaine, Pop. 511
Blaine County SD 61
Supt. — See Hailey
Carey S 200/K-12
PO Box 266 83320 208-823-4391
John Peck, prin. Fax 823-4310

Cascade, Valley, Pop. 1,005
Cascade SD 422 400/PK-12
PO Box 291 83611 208-382-4227
Vic Koshuta, supt. Fax 382-3797
www.cascadeschools.org
Cascade ES 200/PK-6
PO Box 291 83611 208-382-4227
Anne Stilwill, dean Fax 382-3797

Castleford, Twin Falls, Pop. 274
Castleford JSD 417 300/PK-12
500 Main St 83321 208-537-6511
Andy Wiseman, supt. Fax 537-6855
www.castlefordschools.com
Castleford S 300/PK-12
500 Main St 83321 208-537-6511
Andy Wiseman, prin. Fax 537-6855

Cataldo, Kootenai
Kellogg JSD 391
Supt. — See Kellogg
Canyon ES 100/1-5
27491 E Schoolhouse Loop Rd 83810 208-682-2749
Susan Hansen-Barber, prin. Fax 682-3047

Challis, Custer, Pop. 844
Challis JSD 181 500/K-12
PO Box 304 83226 208-879-4231
Colby Gull, supt. Fax 879-5473
www.d181.k12.id.us/
Challis ES 200/K-6
PO Box 304 83226 208-879-2439
Mike Olson, prin. Fax 879-5525
Other Schools – See Clayton, May, Stanley

Clayton, Custer, Pop. 26
Challis JSD 181
Supt. — See Challis
Clayton ES 50/K-6
HC 67 Box 586 83227 208-838-2244
Theresa Briggs, lead tchr. Fax 838-2244

Cocolalla, Bonner
Lake Pend Oreille SD 84
Supt. — See Ponderay
Southside ES 200/K-6
PO Box 159 83813 208-263-3020
Pat Valliant, prin. Fax 265-4836

Coeur d Alene, Kootenai, Pop. 36,259
Coeur D'Alene SD 271 9,400/PK-12
311 N 10th St 83814 208-664-8241
Hazel Bauman, supt. Fax 664-1748
www.cdaschools.org
Borah ES 400/K-5
632 E Borah Ave 83814 208-664-5844
Bob Shamberg, prin. Fax 664-4416
Bryan ES 400/K-5
802 E Harrison Ave 83814 208-664-3237
Joel Palmer, prin. Fax 769-2975
Canfield MS 800/6-8
1800 E Dalton Ave 83815 208-664-9188
Jeff Bengtson, prin. Fax 769-2951
Fernan ES 500/PK-5
520 N 21st St 83814 208-664-2659
Warren Olson, prin. Fax 769-2923
Lakes MS 600/6-8
930 N 15th St 83814 208-667-4544
Chris Hammons, prin. Fax 769-2982
Ramsey ES 500/1-5
1351 W Kathleen Ave 83815 208-765-2010
Anna Wilson, prin. Fax 769-0747
Skyway ES 500/1-5
6621 N Courcelles Pkwy 83815 208-664-8998
Kathy Liverman, prin. Fax 664-4658
Sorensen Magnet S for Arts & Humanities 200/K-5
311 N 9th St 83814 208-664-2822
Jim Gray, prin. Fax 664-8241
Winton ES 300/K-5
920 W Lacrosse Ave 83814 208-664-3440
Kristen Gorringe, prin. Fax 769-2984

Woodland MS 800/6-8
2101 W Saint Michelle 83815 208-667-5996
James Lien, prin. Fax 667-5997
Other Schools – See Dalton Gardens, Hayden Lake

Christ the King Lutheran S 100/PK-K
1700 E Pennsylvania Ave 83814 208-765-6736
Fax 664-9233

Coeur D'Alene Christian S 50/K-8
6439 N 4th St 83815 208-772-7118
Dan Dupey, admin. Fax 772-8183
Holy Family S 200/K-8
3005 W Kathleen Ave 83815 208-765-4327
Karen Durgin, prin. Fax 664-2903
Lake City Junior Academy 100/PK-10
111 E Locust Ave 83814 208-667-0877
Allan Sather, prin. Fax 665-1462
Lutheran Academy of the Master 100/PK-5
4800 N Ramsey Rd 83815 208-765-8238
Shelly Matthews, prin. Fax 765-6392

Cottonwood, Idaho, Pop. 1,070
Cottonwood JSD 242 400/K-12
PO Box 158 83522 208-962-3971
Gary Blaz, supt. Fax 962-7780
www.sd242.k12.id.us/District/
Prairie ES 100/K-4
PO Box 570 83522 208-962-3122
Gary Blaz, prin. Fax 962-7006
Prairie MS 100/5-8
PO Box 580 83522 208-962-3521
Rene Forsmann, prin. Fax 962-3319

Council, Adams, Pop. 742
Council SD 13 300/PK-12
PO Box 68 83612 208-253-4217
Murray Dalgleish, supt. Fax 253-4297
www.sd013.k12.id.us
Council ES 100/PK-6
PO Box 68 83612 208-253-4223
Bonnie Thompson, prin. Fax 253-4577

Craigmont, Lewis, Pop. 548
Highland JSD 305 200/PK-12
PO Box 130 83523 208-924-5211
Clair Garrick, supt. Fax 924-5614
www.sd305.k12.id.us/
Highland S 200/PK-12
PO Box 130 83523 208-924-5211
Bill Gehring, prin. Fax 924-5614

Culdesac, Nez Perce, Pop. 375
Culdesac JSD 342 200/PK-12
600 Culdesac Ave 83524 208-843-5413
Darrell Olson, supt. Fax 843-2719
pass.culsch.org/
Culdesac S 200/PK-12
600 Culdesac Ave 83524 208-843-5413
Darrell Olson, prin. Fax 843-2719

Dalton Gardens, Kootenai, Pop. 2,400
Coeur D'Alene SD 271
Supt. — See Coeur d Alene
Dalton Gardens ES 400/K-5
6336 N Mount Carrol St 83815 208-772-5364
Glenda Armstrong, prin. Fax 762-2360

Dayton, Franklin, Pop. 463
West Side JSD 202 600/PK-12
PO Box 39 83232 208-747-3502
Melvin Beutler, supt. Fax 747-3705
www.wssd.k12.id.us
Lee ES 300/PK-5
PO Box 140 83232 208-747-3303
Spencer Barzee, prin. Fax 747-3637
Lee MS 100/6-8
PO Box 140 83232 208-747-3303
Kathy Bright, prin. Fax 747-3637

Declo, Cassia, Pop. 332
Cassia County JSD 151
Supt. — See Burley
Declo ES 400/PK-5
120 E Main St 83323 208-654-2391
Becky Hunsaker, prin. Fax 654-2342
Declo JHS 200/6-8
205 E Main St 83323 208-654-9960
Carl Voigt, prin. Fax 654-2070

Dietrich, Lincoln, Pop. 164
Dietrich SD 314 200/PK-12
406 N Park St 83324 208-544-2158
Neal Hollingshead, supt. Fax 544-2832
www.sd314.k12.id.us/
Dietrich S 200/PK-12
406 N Park St 83324 208-544-2158
Thad Biggers, prin. Fax 544-2832

Donnelly, Valley, Pop. 149
Mc Call-Donnelly JSD 421
Supt. — See Mc Call
Donnelly ES 100/K-5
PO Box 369 83615 208-325-4433
Mary Kuskie, prin. Fax 325-5030

Downey, Bannock, Pop. 577
Marsh Valley JSD 21
Supt. — See Arimo
Downey ES 100/PK-6
88 S 4th St E 83234 208-897-5220
Gary Yearsley, prin. Fax 897-5221

Driggs, Teton, Pop. 1,197
Teton County SD 401 1,400/PK-12
PO Box 775 83422 208-354-2207
Monte Woolstenhulme, supt. Fax 354-2250
www.d401.k12.id.us
Driggs ES 300/K-5
211 E Howard Ave 83422 208-354-2335
Richard Coburn, prin. Fax 354-2336

Teton K 100/PK-K
PO Box 775 83422 208-354-8280
Richard Coburn, prin. Fax 354-2250
Teton MS 300/6-8
935 N 5th E 83422 208-354-2971
Steve Burch, prin. Fax 354-8685
Other Schools – See Tetonia, Victor

Dubois, Clark, Pop. 642
Clark County SD 161 200/PK-12
PO Box 237 83423 208-374-4175
David Kerns, supt. Fax 374-5234
Ross ES 100/PK-6
PO Box 237 83423 208-374-5206
Thomas Monroe, prin. Fax 374-5234

Eagle, Ada, Pop. 17,338
Meridian JSD 2
Supt. — See Meridian
Eagle ES 500/PK-5
475 N Eagle Rd 83616 208-855-4365
Gary Kohlmeier, prin. Fax 855-4374
Eagle Hills ES 500/PK-5
650 Ranch Dr 83616 208-350-4085
Jason Leforgee, prin. Fax 350-4094
Eagle MS 1,300/6-8
1000 W Floating Feather Rd 83616 208-350-4255
Tony Nelson, prin. Fax 350-4269
Galileo Math and Science S K-8
4735 W Saguaro Dr 83616 208-350-4105
Suanne McCullough, prin. Fax 350-4119
Seven Oaks ES 700/PK-5
1441 N Sevenoaks Way 83616 208-350-4095
Kathleen Cornelson-Smith, prin. Fax 350-4104

Eagle Montessori S 100/K-6
533 S Rivershore Ln 83616 208-938-0100
Jody Malterre, prin. Fax 938-0101
Eagle SDA S 50/K-8
PO Box 1148 83616 208-938-0093
David Pitcher, lead tchr. Fax 938-0093

Elk City, Idaho
Mountain View SD 244
Supt. — See Grangeville
Elk City S 50/PK-8
PO Box 419 83525 208-842-2218
Debbie Laymon, lead tchr. Fax 842-2225

Emmett, Gem, Pop. 6,124
Emmett ISD 221 2,900/PK-12
601 E 3rd St 83617 208-365-6301
Sue Beitia, supt. Fax 365-2961
www.isd221.net
Butte View ES 600/PK-3
400 S Pine St 83617 208-365-4691
Jolene Montoya, prin. Fax 398-8282
Carberry IS 400/4-6
1950 E 12th St 83617 208-365-0839
Larry Parks, prin. Fax 365-0871
Shadow Butte ES 400/K-6
3900 W Idaho Blvd 83617 208-365-0877
Cindy Roberts, prin. Fax 365-0887
Other Schools – See Ola, Sweet

Fairfield, Camas, Pop. 392
Camas County SD 121 200/K-12
PO Box 370 83327 208-764-2625
J.T. Stroder, supt. Fax 764-9218
www.camascountyschools.org/
Camas County S 100/K-8
PO Box 99 83327 208-764-2472
Jeff Rast, prin. Fax 764-2018

Fernwood, Benewah
Saint Maries JSD 41
Supt. — See Saint Maries
UpRiver S 100/K-8
PO Box 249 83830 208-245-3650
Jeff Andersen, prin. Fax 245-3066

Filer, Twin Falls, Pop. 1,768
Filer SD 413 1,400/PK-12
700B Stevens St 83328 208-326-5981
John Graham, supt. Fax 326-3350
www.filer.k12.id.us/
Filer ES 600/PK-5
700 Stevens St 83328 208-326-4369
Matt Mahannah, prin. Fax 326-5960
Filer MS 300/6-8
299 Highway 30 83328 208-326-5906
Gregory Lanting, prin. Fax 326-3385
Other Schools – See Twin Falls

Firth, Bingham, Pop. 417
Firth SD 59 800/PK-12
PO Box 69 83236 208-346-6815
Sid Tubbs, supt. Fax 346-6814
www.firthschools.org
Firth MS 200/5-8
410 Roosevelt St 83236 208-346-6240
Deanne Dye, prin. Fax 346-4306
Johnson ES 300/PK-4
735 N 600 E 83236 208-346-6848
David Mecham, prin. Fax 346-4320

Fruitland, Payette, Pop. 4,406
Fruitland SD 373 1,500/PK-12
PO Box A 83619 208-452-3595
Alan Felgenhauer, supt. Fax 452-6430
www.fsd.k12.id.us/
Fruitland ES 600/PK-3
PO Box A 83619 208-452-3999
Joseph Wozniak, prin. Fax 452-3363
Fruitland IS, PO Box A 83619 4-5
Kimi Fitch, prin. 208-452-3360
Fruitland MS 400/6-8
PO Box A 83619 208-452-3350
Geno Bates, prin. Fax 452-4063

Garden City, Ada, Pop. 11,424

Foundations Academy 300/K-12
202 E 42nd St 83714 208-323-3888
David Goodwin, hdmstr. Fax 672-0522

Garden Valley, Boise
Garden Valley SD 71 200/K-12
PO Box 710 83622 208-462-3756
Dr. Michael Tomlin, supt. Fax 462-3570
www.gvsd.net
Garden Valley S 200/K-12
PO Box 710 83622 208-462-3756
Cody Fisher, prin. Fax 462-3570
Lowman ES 50/K-6
PO Box 710 83622 208-259-3333
Cody Fisher, lead tchr. Fax 259-3333

Genesee, Latah, Pop. 879
Genesee JSD 282 300/K-12
PO Box 98 83832 208-285-1161
David Neumann, supt. Fax 285-1495
www.genesee.k12.id.us/
Genesee S 300/K-12
PO Box 98 83832 208-285-1162
Loretta Stowers, prin. Fax 285-1495

Georgetown, Bear Lake, Pop. 494
Bear Lake County SD 33
Supt. — See Paris
Georgetown ES 100/K-5
PO Box 100 83239 208-847-0583
Mary Ann Evans, prin. Fax 847-0588

Glenns Ferry, Elmore, Pop. 1,451
Glenns Ferry JSD 192 500/PK-12
800 Highway 30 83623 208-366-7436
Wayne Rush, supt. Fax 366-7455
www.gfpilots.net/
Glenns Ferry ES 200/PK-5
639 N Bannock St 83623 208-366-7435
Laron Billingsley, prin. Fax 366-2056
Glenns Ferry MS 100/6-8
639 N Bannock St 83623 208-366-7438
Laron Billingsley, prin. Fax 366-2056

Gooding, Gooding, Pop. 3,320
Gooding JSD 231 1,300/PK-12
507 Idaho St 83330 208-934-4321
Dr. Heather Williams, supt. Fax 934-4403
www.goodingschools.org/
Gooding ES 600/PK-5
1045 7th Ave W 83330 208-934-4941
Cheri Vitek, prin. Fax 934-4898
Gooding MS 300/6-8
1045 7th Ave W 83330 208-934-8443
Cheri Vitek, prin. Fax 934-4898

Grace, Caribou, Pop. 972
Grace JSD 148 500/PK-12
PO Box 347 83241 208-425-3984
Gary Brogan, supt. Fax 425-3809
www.sd148.org/
Grace ES 200/PK-6
PO Box 328 83241 208-425-9161
Gary Brogan, prin. Fax 425-3984
Other Schools – See Thatcher

Grand View, Owyhee, Pop. 477
Bruneau-Grand View JSD 365 400/PK-12
PO Box 310 83624 208-834-2253
Vickie Chandler, supt. Fax 834-2293
www.sd365.us
Grand View ES 200/PK-6
PO Box 39 83624 208-834-2775
Gerald Chouinard, prin. Fax 834-2529
Other Schools – See Bruneau

Grangeville, Idaho, Pop. 3,151
Mountain View SD 244 1,100/PK-12
714 Jefferson St 83530 208-983-0990
Greg Bailey, supt. Fax 983-1245
www.sd244.org/
Grangeville S 500/PK-8
400 S Idaho Ave 83530 208-983-0400
Mike Auton, prin. Fax 983-3407
Other Schools – See Elk City, Kooskia

SS. Peter & Paul S 100/1-8
330 S B St 83530 208-983-2182
Teresa Groom, prin. Fax 983-0115

Greenleaf, Canyon, Pop. 890

Greenleaf Friends Academy 300/PK-12
PO Box 368 83626 208-459-6346
Kenneth Sheldon, supt. Fax 459-7700

Hagerman, Gooding, Pop. 838
Hagerman JSD 233 400/K-12
324 N 2nd Ave 83332 208-837-4777
Ron Echols, supt. Fax 837-4737
www.hagerman.k12.id.us
Hagerman ES 200/K-6
324 N 2nd Ave 83332 208-837-4737
Lee Mitchell, prin. Fax 837-6502

Hailey, Blaine, Pop. 7,583
Blaine County SD 61 2,800/K-12
118 W Bullion St 83333 208-578-5000
Jim Lewis, supt. Fax 578-5110
www.blaineschools.org/
Hailey ES 400/K-5
520 S 1st Ave 83333 208-788-3091
Tom Bailey, prin. Fax 788-2183
Wood River MS 700/6-8
900 N 2nd Ave 83333 208-578-5030
Fritz Peters, prin. Fax 578-5130

Woodside ES K-5
1111 Woodside Elementary Bl 83333 208-578-5090
Gary St. George, prin. Fax 578-5190
Other Schools – See Bellevue, Carey, Ketchum

Hamer, Jefferson, Pop. 12
West Jefferson SD 253
Supt. — See Terreton
Hamer ES 100/K-5
2450 E 2100 N 83425 208-662-5238
Steve Riding, prin. Fax 662-5473

Hansen, Twin Falls, Pop. 961
Hansen SD 415 400/PK-12
550 Main St S 83334 208-423-6387
Dennis Coulter, supt. Fax 423-6808
www.hansen.k12.id.us/
Hansen ES 200/PK-6
219 Walnut Ave W 83334 208-423-5475
Tom Standley, prin. Fax 423-6808

Harrison, Kootenai, Pop. 282
Kootenai JSD 274 300/K-12
13030 E Ogara Rd 83833 208-689-3631
Ron Hill, supt. Fax 689-3641
www.sd274.k12.id.us/
Harrison ES 100/K-6
13030 E Ogara Rd 83833 208-689-3511
Kevin Hoyer, prin. Fax 689-3641

Hayden, Kootenai, Pop. 11,906

North Idaho Christian S 300/1-12
251 W Miles Ave 83835 208-772-7546
Larry Kay, supt. Fax 762-2749

Hayden Lake, Kootenai, Pop. 540
Coeur D'Alene SD 271
Supt. — See Coeur d Alene
Atlas ES 1-5
3000 W Honeysuckle Ave 83835 208-762-0626
Scott Freeby, prin. Fax 762-2596
Hayden Meadows ES 600/K-5
900 E Hayden Ave 83835 208-772-5006
Lisa Pica, prin. Fax 772-0703
Kindercenter K-K
9650 N Government Way 83835 208-772-3851
Sharon Hanson, prin.

Hazelton, Jerome, Pop. 720
Valley SD 262 700/PK-12
882 Valley Rd 83335 208-829-5333
Arlyn Bodily, supt. Fax 829-5548
valley.sd262.k12.id.us
Valley S 700/PK-12
882 Valley Rd 83335 208-829-5961
Ruann Meade, prin. Fax 829-5548

Heyburn, Minidoka, Pop. 2,755
Minidoka County JSD 331
Supt. — See Rupert
Heyburn ES 400/PK-5
1151 7th St 83336 208-679-2400
Terry Garner, prin. Fax 679-5877

Hidden Springs, Ada
ISD of Boise City
Supt. — See Boise
Hidden Springs ES 400/K-6
5480 W Hidden Springs Dr, 208-229-4727
Brett Forrey, prin. Fax 229-4747

Homedale, Owyhee, Pop. 2,577
Homedale JSD 370 1,300/K-12
116 E Owyhee Ave 83628 208-337-4611
Tim Rosandick, supt. Fax 337-4911
www.homedaleschools.org
Homedale ES 500/K-4
420 W Washington Ave 83628 208-337-4033
Yvonne Ihli, prin. Fax 337-4703
Homedale MS 400/5-8
3437 Johnstone Rd 83628 208-337-5780
Luci Mereness, prin. Fax 337-5782

Hope, Bonner, Pop. 86
Lake Pend Oreille SD 84
Supt. — See Ponderay
Hope ES 100/K-6
255 Hope School Rd 83836 208-264-5680
Sherri Hatley, prin. Fax 264-5681

Horseshoe Bend, Boise, Pop. 834
Horseshoe Bend SD 73 300/K-12
398 School Dr 83629 208-793-2225
Michael Sessions, supt. Fax 793-2449
www.hsb-73k12.org
Horseshoe Bend ES 200/K-5
398 School Dr 83629 208-793-2225
Michael Sessions, prin. Fax 793-2449

Howe, Butte
Butte County JSD 111
Supt. — See Arco
Howe ES 50/K-5
PO Box 60 83244 208-767-3422
Dr. Amy Pancheri, prin. Fax 767-3432

Idaho City, Boise, Pop. 488
Basin SD 72 500/PK-12
PO Box 227 83631 208-392-4183
John McFarlane, supt. Fax 392-9954
www.idahocityschools.net/
Basin ES 300/PK-6
PO Box 227 83631 208-392-6631
Jamie Pilkerton, prin. Fax 392-4198

Idaho Falls, Bonneville, Pop. 52,338
Bonneville JSD 93 7,600/PK-12
3497 N Ammon Rd 83401 208-525-4400
Dr. Charles Shackett, supt. Fax 529-0104
www3.d93.k12.id.us/
Cloverdale ES 500/K-6
3999 Greenwillow Ln 83401 208-525-4450
Tom Hughes, prin. Fax 524-0171
Discovery ES K-6
2935 N Golden Rod Dr 83401 208-552-7711
Kenneth Marlowe, prin. Fax 552-7712
Fairview ES 300/PK-6
979 E 97th N 83401 208-525-4425
Rex Miller, prin. Fax 525-4426
Falls Valley ES 500/PK-6
2455 Virlow St 83401 208-525-4455
Tom Gauchay, prin. Fax 525-4459
Rimrock ES K-6
4855 Brennan Bnd 83401 208-552-4400
Dan Page, prin. Fax 552-4694
Rocky Mountain MS 600/7-8
3443 N Ammon Rd 83401 208-525-4403
Shalene French, prin. Fax 525-4469
Sandcreek MS 600/7-8
2955 Owen St 83406 208-525-4416
Lyndon Oswald, prin. Fax 525-4438
Tiebreaker ES 600/K-6
3100 1st St 83401 208-525-4480
Kent Patterson, prin. Fax 525-4482
Ucon ES 500/PK-6
10841 N 41st E 83401 208-525-4430
Jill Starnes, prin. Fax 525-4477
Other Schools – See Ammon, Iona

Idaho Falls SD 91 10,100/PK-12
690 John Adams Pkwy 83401 208-525-7500
George Boland, supt. Fax 525-7596
www.d91.k12.id.us
Boyes ES 400/K-6
1875 Brentwood Dr 83402 208-525-7630
Diana Molino, prin. Fax 525-7631
Bunker ES 300/K-6
1385 E 16th St 83404 208-525-7606
Rodger Barlow, prin. Fax 525-7610
Bush ES 400/K-6
380 W Anderson St 83402 208-525-7602
Jeanne Johnson, prin. Fax 525-7605
Edgemont Gardens ES 500/K-6
1240 Azalea Dr 83404 208-525-7618
Mike Marshall, prin. Fax 525-7619
Erickson ES 400/K-6
850 Cleveland St 83401 208-525-7612
Bruce Cook, prin. Fax 525-7616
Foxhollow ES 500/PK-6
2365 Genevieve Way 83402 208-524-7890
Lance Lindley, prin. Fax 524-7891
Hawthorne ES 300/K-6
1520 S Boulevard 83402 208-525-7636
Kelly Coughenour, prin. Fax 525-7637
Linden Park ES 500/K-6
1305 9th St 83404 208-525-7642
Tammi Utter, prin. Fax 525-7643
Longfellow ES 500/K-6
2500 S Higbee Ave 83404 208-525-7648
Kristopher Smith, prin. Fax 525-7649
Sunnyside ES 500/K-6
165 Cobblestone Ln 83404 208-524-7880
Kay Moor, prin. Fax 524-7889
Temple View ES 500/K-6
1500 Scorpius Dr 83402 208-525-7660
Natalie Peters, prin. Fax 525-7661
Westside ES 500/K-6
2680 Newman Dr 83402 208-525-7666
Terry Miller, prin. Fax 525-7667

Adventist Christian S 50/1-8
PO Box 50156 83405 208-528-8582
Carrie Tow, prin.
Calvary Chapel Christian S 200/PK-8
4250 S 25th E 83404 208-524-4747
Bob Peck, prin. Fax 524-0697
Holy Rosary S 200/PK-8
161 9th St 83404 208-522-7781
Marilyn Reilly, prin. Fax 522-7782
Hope Lutheran S 100/PK-6
2071 12th St 83404 208-529-8080
Tanya Johnson, prin. Fax 529-8880
Snake River Montessori S 100/PK-6
2970 1st St 83401 208-524-4730
Margaret Hanson, dir.

Inkom, Bannock, Pop. 686
Marsh Valley JSD 21
Supt. — See Arimo
Inkom ES 200/PK-6
PO Box 430 83245 208-775-3361
Greg Hunsaker, prin. Fax 775-4436

Iona, Bonneville, Pop. 1,256
Bonneville JSD 93
Supt. — See Idaho Falls
Iona ES 600/K-6
PO Box 310 83427 208-525-4440
Brent Bird, prin. Fax 524-4240

Irwin, Bonneville, Pop. 155
Swan Valley ESD 92 50/K-8
PO Box 220 83428 208-483-2405
Monte Woolstenhulme, supt. Fax 483-2415
www.sd92.k12.id.us
Swan Valley S 50/K-8
PO Box 220 83428 208-483-2405
Monte Woolstenhulme, prin. Fax 483-2415

Jerome, Jerome, Pop. 8,503
Jerome JSD 261 3,300/PK-12
125 4th Ave W 83338 208-324-2392
Jim Cobble, supt. Fax 324-7609
www.d261.k12.id.us
Horizon ES 600/PK-3
934 10th Ave E 83338 208-324-4841
Teresa Jones, prin. Fax 324-2015
Jefferson ES 500/K-3
600 N Fillmore St 83338 208-324-8896
Dale Layne, prin. Fax 324-8897
Jerome MS 500/6-8
520 10th Ave W 83338 208-324-8134
Janet Avery, prin. Fax 324-7458
Summit ES 700/4-6
200 10th Ave W 83338 208-324-3396
Alice Hocklander, prin. Fax 324-3399

Juliaetta, Latah, Pop. 561
Kendrick JSD 283
Supt. — See Kendrick
Juliaetta ES 100/PK-6
305 4th St 83535 208-276-3422
Mary Kren, prin. Fax 276-3424

Kamiah, Lewis, Pop. 1,148
Kamiah JSD 304 500/PK-12
1102 Hill St 83536 208-935-2991
Dr. Mike Bundy, supt. Fax 935-4005
www.kamiah.org/
Kamiah ES 200/PK-4
1102 Hill St 83536 208-935-4012
Carrie Nygaard, prin. Fax 935-4014
Kamiah MS 200/5-8
1102 Hill St 83536 208-935-4040
Carrie Nygaard, prin. Fax 935-4041

Kellogg, Shoshone, Pop. 2,298
Kellogg JSD 391 1,400/K-12
800 Bunker Ave 83837 208-784-1348
Sandra Pommerening, supt. Fax 786-3331
www.ksd391.org/
Kellogg MS 300/6-8
810 Bunker Ave 83837 208-784-1311
Cal Ketchum, prin. Fax 784-0134
Sunnyside ES 300/K-5
790 Bunker Ave 83837 208-784-1249
Tracy Ketchum, prin. Fax 784-1240
Other Schools – See Cataldo, Pinehurst

Silver Valley Christian Academy 50/K-12
514 W Brown Ave 83837 208-783-3791
David Gabrielsen, pres. Fax 783-3791

Kendrick, Latah, Pop. 344
Kendrick JSD 283 300/PK-12
PO Box 283 83537 208-289-4211
Calvin Spangler, supt. Fax 289-4201
Other Schools – See Juliaetta

Ketchum, Blaine, Pop. 3,145
Blaine County SD 61
Supt. — See Hailey
Hemingway ES 400/K-5
PO Box 298 83340 208-726-3348
Don Haisley, prin. Fax 726-2537

Kimberly, Twin Falls, Pop. 2,686
Kimberly SD 414 1,400/K-12
141 Center St W 83341 208-423-4170
Kathleen Noh, supt. Fax 423-6155
www.kimberly.edu/
Kimberly ES 600/K-5
141 Center St W 83341 208-423-4170
Craig Maki, prin. Fax 423-6155
Kimberly MS 300/6-8
141 Center St W 83341 208-423-4170
Letha Blick, prin. Fax 423-6155

Kooskia, Idaho, Pop. 665
Mountain View SD 244
Supt. — See Grangeville
Clearwater Valley ES 200/PK-6
PO Box 100 83539 208-926-4311
Alisa Holthaus, prin. Fax 926-7883

Kootenai, Bonner, Pop. 480
Lake Pend Oreille SD 84
Supt. — See Ponderay
Kootenai ES 200/K-6
PO Box 135 83840 208-255-4076
Betsy Walker, prin. Fax 263-4699

Kuna, Ada, Pop. 10,153
Kuna JSD 3 3,600/PK-12
1450 Boise St 83634 208-922-1000
Jay Hummel, supt. Fax 922-5646
www.kunaschools.org
Crimson Point ES PK-6
1941 N Shayla Ave 83634 208-955-0230
Kim Cammack, prin. Fax 955-0239
Hubbard ES 700/PK-3
311 E Porter St 83634 208-922-1007
Jill Cox, prin. Fax 922-1021
Indian Creek ES 300/PK-3
911 W 4th St 83634 208-922-1009
Greta Ankeny, prin. Fax 922-1029
Kuna MS 600/7-8
1360 Boise St 83634 208-922-1002
Deb McGrath, prin. Fax 922-1030
Reed ES PK-6
1670 N Linder Rd 83634 208-955-0275
Chuck Silzly, prin. Fax 955-0279
Ross ES 400/4-6
610 N School Ave 83634 208-922-1011
Karla Reynolds, prin. Fax 922-1018
Teed ES 500/4-6
441 E Porter St 83634 208-922-1005
Ken Lilienkamp, prin. Fax 922-1024

Lapwai, Nez Perce, Pop. 1,116
Lapwai SD 341 400/PK-12
PO Box 247 83540 208-843-2622
Terry Smith, supt. Fax 843-2910
www.lapwaischooldistrict.org/
Lapwai ES 300/PK-5
PO Box 247 83540 208-843-2952
Teri Wagner, prin. Fax 843-2978

Lava Hot Springs, Bannock, Pop. 504
Marsh Valley JSD 21
Supt. — See Arimo
Lava ES 100/PK-6
PO Box 660 83246 208-776-5281
Richard Nielsen, prin. Fax 776-5204

Leadore, Lemhi, Pop. 89
South Lemhi SD 292 100/K-12
PO Box 119 83464 208-768-2441
Dr. Sandra Noland, supt. Fax 768-2797
www.leadoreschool.org
Leadore S 100/K-12
PO Box 119 83464 208-768-2441
Dr. Sandra Noland, prin. Fax 768-2797
Other Schools – See Tendoy

Lenore, Nez Perce
Orofino JSD 171
Supt. — See Orofino
Cavendish Teakean ES 50/K-6
455 Middle Rd 83541 208-476-5393
Jenine Nord, lead tchr. Fax 476-7723

Lewiston, Nez Perce, Pop. 31,081
Lewiston ISD 1 4,900/PK-12
3317 12th St 83501 208-748-3000
Dr. Joy Rapp, supt. Fax 748-3059
www.lewiston.k12.id.us
Camelot ES 500/K-6
1903 Grelle Ave 83501 208-784-3500
Dana Stedman, prin. Fax 784-3519
Centennial ES 400/K-6
815 Burrell Ave 83501 208-748-3550
Ron Rees, prin. Fax 748-3599
McGhee ES 300/K-6
636 Warner Ave 83501 208-748-3600
Greg Kramasz, prin. Fax 748-3649
McSorley ES 300/K-6
2020 15th St 83501 208-748-3650
Kevin Graffis, prin. Fax 748-3669
Orchards ES 300/PK-6
3429 12th St 83501 208-748-3700
Kristina Brinkerhoff, prin. Fax 748-3729
Webster ES 300/K-6
1409 8th St 83501 208-748-3800
Craig Lenzmeier, prin. Fax 748-3849
Whitman ES 300/PK-6
1840 9th Ave 83501 208-748-3850
Brett Clevenger, prin. Fax 748-3899

Beacon Christian S 50/K-9
615 Stewart Ave 83501 208-743-8361
Richard Rasmussen, prin. Fax 743-3787
Cornerstone Christian S 100/K-8
4073 Fairway Dr 83501 208-798-7149
Cynthia Kym, admin. Fax 746-2158
St. Stanislaus Tri-Parish Catholic S 100/K-6
641 5th Ave 83501 208-743-4411
Denise Hammrich, prin. Fax 743-9563

Mc Call, Valley, Pop. 2,876
Mc Call-Donnelly JSD 421 1,100/PK-12
120 Idaho St 83638 208-634-2161
Glen Szymoniak, supt. Fax 634-4075
www.mdsd.org
Morgan ES 300/PK-5
125 N Samson Trl, 208-634-2219
Jim Foudy, prin. Fax 634-4695
Payette Lakes MS 200/6-8
111 N Samson Trl, 208-634-5994
Susan Buescher, prin. Fax 634-5231
Other Schools – See Donnelly

McCall Adventist Christian S 50/1-8
3592 Long View Rd, 208-634-0053
Harold Appel, prin.

Mc Cammon, Bannock, Pop. 800
Marsh Valley JSD 21
Supt. — See Arimo
Mountain View ES 200/PK-6
PO Box 69, 208-254-3223
Dave Wheat, prin. Fax 254-3224

Mackay, Custer, Pop. 529
Mackay JSD 182 200/PK-12
PO Box 390 83251 208-588-2896
Troy Thayne, supt. Fax 588-2269
www.mackayschools.org/
Mackay ES 100/PK-6
PO Box 390 83251 208-588-2834
Troy Thayne, prin. Fax 588-2269

Malad City, Oneida, Pop. 2,124
Oneida County SD 351 900/PK-12
25 E 50 S Ste A 83252 208-766-4701
Lynn Schow, supt. Fax 766-2930
www.oneidaschooldistrict.org
Malad ES 400/PK-5
250 W 400 N 83252 208-766-2255
Robert Hannah, prin. Fax 766-4998
Malad MS 200/6-8
175 Jenkins Ave 83252 208-766-9235
Sheldon Vaughan, prin. Fax 766-9236
Other Schools – See Stone

Malta, Cassia, Pop. 174
Cassia County JSD 151
Supt. — See Burley
Raft River ES 100/PK-6
PO Box 615 83342 208-645-2561
Eric Boden, prin. Fax 645-2564

Marsing, Owyhee, Pop. 976
Marsing JSD 363 800/K-12
PO Box 340 83639 208-896-4111
Harold Schockley, supt. Fax 896-4790
www.marsingschools.org/
Marsing ES 400/K-5
PO Box 340 83639 208-896-4111
Lillian Stewart, prin. Fax 896-4991
Marsing MS 200/6-8
PO Box 340 83639 208-896-4111
Paul Webster, prin. Fax 896-5128

May, Lemhi
Challis JSD 181
Supt. — See Challis
Patterson ES 50/K-6
13 Patterson Rd 83253 208-876-4277
Fax 876-4277

Melba, Canyon, Pop. 544
Melba JSD 136 700/PK-12
PO Box 185 83641 208-495-1141
Robert Larson, supt. Fax 495-1142
www.melbaschools.org
Melba ES 300/PK-5
PO Box 185 83641 208-495-2508
Sherry Adams, prin. Fax 495-2367
Melba MS 100/6-8
PO Box 185 83641 208-495-2221
Kelsey Williams, prin. Fax 495-2188

Menan, Jefferson, Pop. 726
Jefferson County JSD 251
Supt. — See Rigby
Midway ES 500/PK-5
623 N 3500 E 83434 208-754-8604
Jeryl Fluckiger, prin. Fax 754-4847

Meridian, Ada, Pop. 52,240
Meridian JSD 2 31,100/PK-12
1303 E Central Dr 83642 208-855-4500
Dr. Linda Clark, supt. Fax 350-5962
www.meridianschools.org
Chaparral ES 700/K-5
1155 N Deer Creek Ln 83642 208-350-4180
Doni Davis, prin. Fax 350-4189
Chief Joseph ES 600/K-5
1100 E Chateau Dr, 208-350-4200
Brett Nordquist, prin. Fax 350-4209
Discovery ES 600/K-5
2100 E Leighfield Dr, 208-855-4090
Mike Dudley, prin. Fax 855-4096
Heritage MS 6-8
4990 N Meridian Rd, 208-350-4130
Susan McInerney, prin. Fax 350-4139
Hunter ES 800/PK-5
2051 W McMillan Rd, 208-855-4285
Cynthia Clark, prin. Fax 855-4286
Lewis & Clark MS 1,000/6-8
4141 E Pine Ave 83642 208-377-1353
Kelly Davies, prin. Fax 377-3718
Linder ES 500/K-5
1825 W Chateau Dr, 208-855-4430
Jose Melendez, prin. Fax 855-4439
McPherson ES 600/K-5
1050 E Amity Rd 83642 208-855-4300
Khristie Bair, prin. Fax 855-4309
Meridian ES 400/PK-5
1035 W 1st St 83642 208-855-4335
Cathy Alberda, prin. Fax 855-4344
Meridian MS 1,100/6-8
1507 W 8th St 83642 208-855-4225
Lisa Austin, prin. Fax 888-3038
Paramount ES 800/K-5
550 W Producer Dr, 208-350-4120
Dean Brigham, prin. Fax 350-4129
Peregrine ES 600/K-5
1860 Waltman St 83642 208-888-1384
Sandi Scheele, prin. Fax 888-7328
Ponderosa ES 700/K-5
2950 N Naomi Ave, 208-855-4040
Kathy Crowley, prin. Fax 855-4048
Prospect ES K-5
4300 N Red Horse Way, 208-350-4000
Priscilla Anderson, prin. Fax 350-4019
River Valley ES 500/K-5
2900 E River Valley St, 208-884-1741
Jason Robarge, prin. Fax 350-4304
Sawtooth MS 1,400/6-8
3730 N Linder Rd, 208-855-4200
David Moser, prin. Fax 855-4224
Siena K8 Magnet S K-8
2870 E Rome Dr 83642 208-340-4370
Kacey Schneidt, prin. Fax 350-4379
Other Schools – See Boise, Eagle, Star

Middleton, Canyon, Pop. 4,409
Middleton SD 134 2,900/PK-12
5 S 3rd Ave W 83644 208-585-3027
Dr. Rich Bauscher, supt. Fax 585-3028
www.msd134.org
Middleton Heights ES 400/K-5
611 Cemetery Rd 83644 208-585-3021
Robin Gilbert, prin. Fax 585-3080
Middleton MS 700/6-8
200 S 4th Ave W 83644 208-585-3251
Molly Burger, prin. Fax 585-2098
Middleton Mill Creek ES 600/K-5
500 N Middleton Rd 83644 208-585-3065
Valerie Berg, prin. Fax 585-6697
Other Schools – See Caldwell

Midvale, Washington, Pop. 185
Midvale SD 433 100/K-12
PO Box 130 83645 208-355-2234
James Warren, supt. Fax 355-2347
www.midvalerangers.org
Midvale S 100/K-12
PO Box 130 83645 208-355-2234
James Warren, prin. Fax 355-2347

Montpelier, Bear Lake, Pop. 2,507
Bear Lake County SD 33
Supt. — See Paris
Bear Lake MS 300/6-8
633 Washington St 83254 208-847-2255
Bruce Belnap, prin. Fax 847-3626
Winters ES 300/K-5
535 Clay St 83254 208-847-0477
Mary Ann Evans, prin. Fax 847-3959

Moreland, Bingham
Snake River SD 52
Supt. — See Blackfoot
Moreland ES 300/PK-2
PO Box B 83256 208-684-5115
Jane Lofgreen, prin. Fax 684-3094

Moscow, Latah, Pop. 21,862
Moscow SD 281 2,400/PK-12
650 N Cleveland St 83843 208-882-1120
Dr. Candis Donicht, supt. Fax 883-4440
www.sd281.k12.id.us
McDonald ES 400/K-6
2323 E D St 83843 208-882-0228
Laurie Austin, prin. Fax 892-1216
Russell ES 200/4-6
119 N Adams St 83843 208-882-2715
Carole Jones, prin. Fax 892-1241
West Park ES 300/K-3
510 S Home St 83843 208-882-2714
William Marineau, prin. Fax 892-1259
Whitmore ES 300/K-6
110 S Blaine St 83843 208-882-2621
Tony McDonnell, prin. Fax 892-1202

Palouse Hills Christian S 50/K-8
3148 Tomer Rd 83843 208-882-0850
Dan Tyler, prin. Fax 882-0350
St. Mary's S 100/PK-6
412 N Monroe St 83843 208-882-2121
Sr. Margaret Johnson, prin. Fax 882-0970

Mountain Home, Elmore, Pop. 11,565
Mountain Home SD 193 4,100/PK-12
PO Box 1390 83647 208-587-2580
Tim McMurtrey, supt. Fax 587-9896
www.mtnhomesd.org
East ES 400/PK-4
775 N 10th E 83647 208-587-2575
Jackie Harper, prin. Fax 587-2576
Hacker MS 900/5-7
550 E Jackson St 83647 208-587-2500
Nicole Cruser, prin. Fax 587-2564
North ES 500/PK-4
290 E 12th N 83647 208-587-2585
Polly Sanders, prin. Fax 587-2565
Pine S 50/K-8
160 S Lester Creek Rd 83647 208-653-2311
James Gilbert, prin. Fax 587-9896
West ES 500/K-4
415 W 2nd N 83647 208-587-2595
Nancy Brletic, prin. Fax 587-2693
Other Schools – See Mountain Home AFB

Desert View Christian S 50/1-8
PO Box 124 83647 208-580-0512
Dannia Birth, lead tchr. Fax 580-0513

Mountain Home AFB, Elmore, Pop. 5,936
Mountain Home SD 193
Supt. — See Mountain Home
Mountain Home AFB PS 400/K-4
100 Gunfighter Ave 83648 208-832-4651
Ernest Elliot, prin. Fax 832-1120

Moyie Springs, Boundary, Pop. 722
Boundary County SD 101
Supt. — See Bonners Ferry
Evergreen ES 100/K-5
26 Tall Timber Rd 83845 208-267-3489
Jim Nash, prin. Fax 267-9507

Mullan, Shoshone, Pop. 788
Mullan SD 392 100/K-12
PO Box 71 83846 208-744-1118
Robin Stanley, supt. Fax 744-1119
www.mullanschools.com
Mullan ES 100/K-6
PO Box 71 83846 208-744-1118
Robin Stanley, prin. Fax 744-1119

Murtaugh, Twin Falls, Pop. 138
Murtaugh JSD 418 200/PK-12
PO Box 117 83344 208-432-5451
Michelle Capps, supt. Fax 432-5477
www.murtaugh.k12.id.us/
Murtaugh ES 100/PK-5
PO Box 117 83344 208-432-5233
Michelle Capps, prin. Fax 432-5551
Murtaugh MS 50/6-8
PO Box 117 83344 208-432-5451
Heidi Ainsworth, prin. Fax 432-5477

Nampa, Canyon, Pop. 71,713
Nampa SD 131 12,700/PK-12
619 S Canyon St 83686 208-468-4600
Gary Larsen, supt. Fax 468-4638
www.nsd131.org/
Centennial ES 400/K-5
522 Mason Ln 83686 208-468-4627
Paul Harman, prin. Fax 467-9462
Central ES 400/K-5
1415 5th St S 83651 208-468-4611
Cindy Thomas, prin. Fax 465-6363
East Valley MS 1,100/6-8
4085 E Greenhurst Rd 83686 208-468-4760
Terry Adolfson, prin. Fax 461-4069
Endeavor ES K-5
2824 E Victory Rd 83687 208-468-4629
Bill Deakins, prin. Fax 466-1412

Greenhurst ES 600/K-5
1701 Discovery Pl 83686 208-468-4612
Brenda Allen, prin. Fax 465-2771
Iowa ES 600/K-5
626 W Iowa Ave 83686 208-468-4621
Lynnie Hagemeier, prin. Fax 465-2733
Lake Ridge ES K-5
615 Burk Ln 83686 208-468-4626
Nancy Chopko, prin. Fax 461-1880
Lone Star MS 6-8
11055 Lone Star Rd 83651 208-468-4745
Greg Wiles, prin. Fax 442-4763
Owyhee ES 700/K-5
2300 W Iowa Ave 83686 208-468-4616
Greg Carpenter, prin. Fax 442-6469
Park Ridge ES 700/K-5
3313 E Park Ridge Dr 83687 208-468-4622
Keith Field, prin. Fax 465-2722
Parkview Preschool 100/PK-PK
609 15th Ave N 83687 208-465-2728
Ludee Vermaas, prin. Fax 465-6777
Reagan ES 800/K-5
3400 Southside Blvd 83686 208-468-4619
Phil Cano, prin. Fax 461-7618
Roosevelt ES 500/K-5
1901 W Roosevelt Ave 83686 208-468-4620
Korey Mereness, prin. Fax 442-6448
Sherman ES 600/K-5
1521 E Sherman Ave 83686 208-468-4628
John Emerson, prin. Fax 465-2735
Snake River ES 500/K-5
500 Stampede Dr 83687 208-468-4614
Cory Woolstenhulme, prin. Fax 465-6530
South MS 1,000/6-8
229 W Greenhurst Rd 83686 208-468-4740
Stuart Vickers, prin. Fax 465-2779
Sunny Ridge ES 500/K-5
506 Fletcher Dr 83686 208-468-4613
Vicki McNeal, prin. Fax 465-6766
West MS 1,000/6-8
28 S Midland Blvd 83651 208-468-4750
Stefanie Duby, prin. Fax 465-2776
Willow Creek ES 700/K-5
1580 Smith Ave 83651 208-468-4618
Marie Clark, prin. Fax 468-1749

Vallivue SD 139
Supt. — See Caldwell
Birch ES 600/PK-5
6900 Birch Ln 83687 208-461-5960
Greg Scheele, prin. Fax 461-5957
Desert Springs ES PK-5
18178 Santa Anna Ave 83687 208-466-1555
Lisa Boyd, prin. Fax 466-1497
East Canyon ES 800/PK-5
18408 Northside Blvd 83687 208-466-6929
Marlene Parker, prin. Fax 466-6232
Lakevue ES K-5
12843 Cirrus Dr 83651 208-467-1478
Leeta Hobbs, prin. Fax 467-4327
Sage Valley MS 400/6-8
18070 Santa Ana Ave 83687 208-468-4919
RaNae Jones, prin. Fax 468-4904

Nampa Christian S 700/PK-12
439 W Orchard Ave 83651 208-466-8451
David Claar, supt. Fax 466-8452
St. Paul's S 200/PK-8
1515 8th St S 83651 208-467-3601
Bill Graham, prin. Fax 467-6485
Zion Lutheran S 100/PK-6
1012 12th Ave Rd 83686 208-466-9141
Peter Anderson, prin. Fax 463-4420

Naples, Boundary
Boundary County SD 101
Supt. — See Bonners Ferry
Naples ES 100/K-5
145 Schoolhouse Rd 83847 208-267-2956
Jim Nash, prin. Fax 267-2906

New Meadows, Adams, Pop. 492
Meadows Valley SD 11 200/PK-12
PO Box F 83654 208-347-2118
Glen Szymoniak, supt. Fax 347-2624
web.mac.com/meadowsvalleyschool/
Meadows Valley S 200/PK-12
PO Box F 83654 208-347-2118
Rick Tousley, prin. Fax 347-2624

New Plymouth, Payette, Pop. 1,403
New Plymouth SD 372 900/PK-12
103 SE Avenue 83655 208-278-5740
Ryan Kerby, supt. Fax 278-3069
www.sd372.k12.id.us
New Plymouth ES 400/PK-5
704 S Plymouth Ave 83655 208-278-5333
Carrie Aguas, prin. Fax 278-3257
New Plymouth MS 200/6-8
4400 SW 2nd Ave 83655 208-278-5788
Darrell Brown, prin. Fax 278-3773

Nezperce, Lewis, Pop. 514
Nezperce JSD 302 200/K-12
PO Box 279 83543 208-937-2551
Doug Flaming, supt. Fax 937-2136
www.nezpercesd.us/
Nezperce S 200/K-12
PO Box 279 83543 208-937-2551
Dave Snodgrass, prin. Fax 937-2136

Notus, Canyon, Pop. 540
Notus SD 135 300/K-12
PO Box 256 83656 208-459-7442
Jim Doramus, supt. Fax 455-2439
www.nsd135.org
Notus ES 200/K-6
PO Box 256 83656 208-459-7442
Tyson Carter, prin. Fax 455-2439

Oakley, Cassia, Pop. 663
Cassia County JSD 151
Supt. — See Burley
Oakley ES 200/PK-6
PO Box 72 83346 208-862-3203
Dr. Rena Bovee, prin. Fax 862-3380

Ola, Gem
Emmett ISD 221
Supt. — See Emmett
Ola S 50/K-6
PO Box 29 83657 208-584-3589
Amy McBryde, lead tchr. Fax 584-3589

Old Town, Bonner, Pop. 204
West Bonner County SD 83
Supt. — See Priest River
Idaho Hill ES 200/K-6
402 E 3rd St S, 208-437-4227
Susie Luckey, prin. Fax 437-2290

House of the Lord Christian Academy 200/PK-12
754 Silver Birch Ln, 208-437-2184
Michael Croston, admin. Fax 437-0441
Pend Oreille Valley SDA S 50/K-9
33820 Highway 41, 208-437-2638
Jeffrey Wallen, prin.

Orofino, Clearwater, Pop. 3,145
Orofino JSD 171 1,200/PK-12
PO Box 2259 83544 208-476-5593
Dale Durkee, supt. Fax 476-7293
www.sd171.k12.id.us
Orofino ES 500/PK-6
PO Box 2507 83544 208-476-4212
Angie Baldus, prin. Fax 476-0145
Orofino JHS 200/7-8
PO Box 706 83544 208-476-4613
Jerry Uhling, prin. Fax 476-3327
Other Schools – See Lenore, Peck, Weippe

Osburn, Shoshone, Pop. 1,458
Wallace SD 393
Supt. — See Wallace
Silver Hills ES 300/PK-6
PO Box 2160 83849 208-556-1556
Todd Howard, prin. Fax 556-1557

Paris, Bear Lake, Pop. 518
Bear Lake County SD 33 1,200/PK-12
PO Box 300 83261 208-945-2891
Cliff Walters, supt. Fax 945-2893
blsd.net
Paris ES 100/PK-5
PO Box 400 83261 208-945-2113
Mary Ann Evans, prin. Fax 945-2893
Other Schools – See Georgetown, Montpelier

Parma, Canyon, Pop. 1,799
Parma SD 137 1,100/K-12
805 E McConnell Ave 83660 208-722-5115
Jim Norton, supt. Fax 722-7937
www.parmaschools.org
Johnson ES 400/K-4
607 E McConnell Ave 83660 208-722-5115
Diane Hardin, prin. Fax 722-5168
Parma MS 400/5-8
905 E McConnell Ave 83660 208-722-5115
Peggy Sharkey, prin. Fax 722-6913

Paul, Minidoka, Pop. 947
Minidoka County JSD 331
Supt. — See Rupert
Paul ES 400/PK-5
201 N 1st St W 83347 208-438-2211
Colleen Johnson, prin. Fax 438-8767
West Minico MS 500/6-8
155 S 600 W 83347 208-438-5018
Sandra Miller, prin. Fax 438-8513

Payette, Payette, Pop. 7,560
Payette JSD 371 1,800/PK-12
20 N 12th St 83661 208-642-9366
Pauline King, supt. Fax 642-9006
www.payetteschools.org/
McCain MS 400/6-8
400 N Iowa Ave 83661 208-642-4122
Sandy Holloway, prin. Fax 642-2171
Payette PS 600/PK-3
1320 3rd Ave N 83661 208-642-3379
Kipp McKenzie, prin. Fax 642-2169
Westside ES 200/4-5
609 N 5th St 83661 208-642-3241
Mary Beth Bennett, prin. Fax 642-3307

Treasure Valley SDA S 50/1-8
PO Box 396 83661 208-642-2410
Valerie Iwasa, prin. Fax 642-7332

Peck, Nez Perce, Pop. 184
Orofino JSD 171
Supt. — See Orofino
Peck ES 50/K-6
PO Box 48 83545 208-486-7331
Mindy Pollock, lead tchr. Fax 486-7331

Pinehurst, Shoshone, Pop. 1,588
Kellogg JSD 391
Supt. — See Kellogg
Pinehurst ES 300/K-5
201 3rd St 83850 208-682-2193
Paul Currie, prin. Fax 682-2145

Plummer, Benewah, Pop. 985
Plummer/Worley JSD 44 500/PK-12
PO Box 130 83851 208-686-1621
George Olsen, supt. Fax 686-2108
www.pwsd44.com
Lakeside MS 100/6-8
PO Box 130 83851 208-686-1627
Bill Burns, prin. Fax 686-2207
Other Schools – See Worley

Pocatello, Bannock, Pop. 53,372
Blackfoot SD 55
Supt. — See Blackfoot
Fort Hall ES 100/K-5
RR 6 Box 430 83202 208-237-2207
Garth Hansen, prin. Fax 237-9402

Pocatello/Chubbuck SD 25 11,700/PK-12
3115 Pole Line Rd 83201 208-232-3563
Mary Vagner, supt. Fax 235-3280
www.d25.k12.id.us
Chubbuck ES 600/K-6
600 Chastain Dr 83202 208-237-2271
Janna Herdt, prin. Fax 237-2292
Edahow ES 400/K-6
2020 Pocatello Creek Rd 83201 208-233-1844
Tina Orme, prin. Fax 239-7119
Ellis ES 600/K-6
11888 N Whitaker Rd 83202 208-237-4742
Betsy Goeltz Ed.D., prin. Fax 237-4748
Franklin MS 600/7-8
2271 E Terry St 83201 208-233-5590
Howard Peck, prin. Fax 233-1024
Gate City ES 500/K-6
2288 Hiskey St 83201 208-237-2503
Janice Green, prin. Fax 237-2239
Greenacres ES 300/K-6
1250 E Oak St 83201 208-233-2575
Amy Brinkerhoff, prin. Fax 234-5936
Hawthorne MS 500/7-8
1025 W Eldredge Rd 83201 208-237-1680
Christine Stevens, prin. Fax 237-1682
Indian Hills ES 600/K-6
666 Cheyenne Ave 83204 208-232-4086
Lori Craney, prin. Fax 232-8986
Irving MS 500/7-8
911 N Grant Ave 83204 208-232-3039
Susan Pettit, prin. Fax 232-0379
Jefferson ES 600/K-6
1455 Gwen Dr 83204 208-232-2914
Jan Harwood, prin. Fax 232-0440
Lewis & Clark ES 500/K-6
800 Grace Dr 83201 208-233-2552
Evelyn Robinson, prin. Fax 233-9672
Lincoln Preschool Center 100/PK-PK
330 Oakwood Dr 83204 208-233-6606
Kent Hobbs, admin. Fax 232-4906
Syringa ES 500/K-6
388 E Griffith Rd 83201 208-237-4040
Pauline Alessi, prin. Fax 237-4104
Tendoy ES 400/K-6
957 E Alameda Rd 83201 208-233-2921
Dona Applonie, prin. Fax 233-2952
Tyhee ES 500/K-6
12743 W Tyhee Rd 83202 208-237-0551
Janice Nelson, prin. Fax 237-0565
Washington ES 300/K-6
226 S 10th Ave 83201 208-232-2976
Steve Morton, prin. Fax 232-6663
Wilcox ES 600/K-6
427 Lark Ln 83201 208-237-6050
Russ Sion, prin. Fax 237-6073

Grace Lutheran S 400/PK-8
1350 Baldy Ave 83201 208-237-4142
Gaylord Flicker, dir. Fax 237-0931
Holy Spirit Catholic S 200/PK-6
540 N 7th Ave 83201 208-232-5763
Nancy Corgiat, prin. Fax 232-7142

Ponderay, Bonner, Pop. 697
Lake Pend Oreille SD 84 3,900/PK-12
901 N Triangle Dr 83852 208-263-2184
Dick Cvitanich, supt. Fax 263-5053
www.sd84.k12.id.us
Other Schools – See Cocolalla, Hope, Kootenai, Sagle, Sandpoint

---

Sandpoint Community Christian S 100/K-8
477954 Highway 95 83852 208-265-8624
Katrina Arbuckle, prin. Fax 263-6504

Post Falls, Kootenai, Pop. 23,162
Post Falls SD 273 5,200/PK-12
PO Box 40 83877 208-773-1658
Jerry Keane, supt. Fax 773-3218
www.pfsd.com
Mullan Trail ES 400/1-5
PO Box 40 83877 208-457-0772
Katrina Kelly, prin. Fax 773-8312
Ponderosa ES 500/1-5
PO Box 40 83877 208-773-1508
Kathy Baker, prin. Fax 773-0789
Post Falls MS 700/6-8
PO Box 40 83877 208-773-7554
Debbi Davis, prin. Fax 773-0884
Post K 400/PK-K
PO Box 40 83877 208-777-0479
Julie Billetz, prin. Fax 773-2553
Prairie View ES 600/1-5
PO Box 40 83877 208-773-8327
Colleen Kelsey, prin. Fax 777-9665
River City MS 500/6-8
PO Box 40 83877 208-457-0993
Mike Yovetich, prin. Fax 457-1673
Seltice ES 600/1-5
PO Box 40 83877 208-773-1681
Mike Uphus, prin. Fax 777-2572
West Ridge ES 1-5
PO Box 40 83877 208-773-7291
Mandy Surratt-Florin, prin. Fax 773-7327

Classical Christian Academy 200/K-12
2289 W Seltice Way 83854 208-777-4400
Dirk Darrow, hdmstr. Fax 777-2544

Lakes Bible Academy — 50/PK-12
12055 N Hauser Lake Rd 83854 — 208-687-2101
Kelli Uzzi, prin.

Potlatch, Latah, Pop. 735
Potlatch SD 285 — 500/PK-12
130 6th St 83855 — 208-875-0327
Joseph Kren, supt. — Fax 875-1028
www.potlatchschools.org
Potlatch ES — 200/PK-6
130 6th St 83855 — 208-875-1331
Hugh Maxwell, prin. — Fax 875-0599

Prairie, Elmore
Prairie ESD 191 — 50/K-8
73 Smith Creek Rd 83647 — 208-868-3243
Fax 868-3264
Prairie S — 50/K-8
73 Smith Creek Rd 83647 — 208-868-3229
Joseph Burch, lead tchr. — Fax 868-3229

Preston, Franklin, Pop. 5,019
Preston JSD 201 — 2,500/PK-12
120 E 2nd S 83263 — 208-852-0283
Dr. Barbara Taylor, supt. — Fax 852-3976
www.preston.k12.id.us
Oakwood ES — 600/3-5
525 S 4th E 83263 — 208-852-2233
Kalynn Hamblin, prin. — Fax 852-3976
Pioneer ES — 600/PK-2
515 S 4th E 83263 — 208-852-2050
Stan Butler, prin. — Fax 852-3976
Preston JHS — 600/6-8
450 E Valley View Dr 83263 — 208-852-0751
Lance Harrison, prin. — Fax 852-3510

Priest Lake, Bonner
West Bonner County SD 83
Supt. — See Priest River
Priest Lake ES — 100/K-6
27732 Highway 57 83856 — 208-443-2555
Susie Luckey, prin. — Fax 443-3845

Priest River, Bonner, Pop. 1,909
West Bonner County SD 83 — 1,600/PK-12
221 Main St 83856 — 208-448-4439
Michael McGuire, supt. — Fax 448-4629
www.westbonnerschools.org/
Priest River ES — 600/PK-6
418 Harriet St 83856 — 208-448-1181
Kendra McMillan, prin. — Fax 448-1328
Priest River JHS — 200/7-8
1020 Highway 2 83856 — 208-448-1118
Gary Go, prin. — Fax 448-1119
Other Schools – See Old Town, Priest Lake

Rathdrum, Kootenai, Pop. 5,740
Lakeland JSD 272 — 4,300/PK-12
PO Box 39 83858 — 208-687-0431
Dr. Mary Ann Rannells, supt. — Fax 687-1884
www.lakeland272.org/
Brown ES — 500/PK-6
PO Box 10 83858 — 208-687-0551
John Asher, prin. — Fax 687-1083
Garwood ES — 500/K-6
PO Box 990 83858 — 208-687-1265
B.J. DeAustin, prin. — Fax 687-4310
Kiefer ES — 500/K-6
PO Box 130 83858 — 208-687-5206
Lisa Sexton, prin. — Fax 687-3692
Lakeland JHS — 500/7-8
PO Box 98 83858 — 208-687-0661
Todd Spear, prin. — Fax 687-1510
Twin Lakes ES, PO Box 159 83858 — K-6
Mary Havercroft, prin. — 208-687-5870
Other Schools – See Athol, Spirit Lake

Rexburg, Madison, Pop. 26,265
Madison SD 321 — 4,500/K-12
PO Box 830 83440 — 208-359-3300
Dr. Geoffrey Thomas, supt. — Fax 359-3345
www.d321.k12.id.us
Adams ES — 300/K-4
110 N 2nd E 83440 — 208-359-3335
Jeff Hawkes, prin. — Fax 359-3272
Archer ES — 100/K-4
7833 S 200 W 83440 — 208-359-3322
Marche Young, prin. — Fax 359-3368
Burton ES — 200/K-4
2211 W 1000 S 83440 — 208-359-3332
Jordan Busby, prin. — Fax 359-3345
Hibbard ES — 200/K-4
2413 N 3000 W 83440 — 208-359-3333
Scott Shirley, prin. — Fax 359-3269
Kennedy ES — 400/K-4
60 S 5th W 83440 — 208-359-3325
Lyle Jeppesen, prin. — Fax 359-3326
Lincoln ES — 400/K-4
358 E 2nd S 83440 — 208-359-3330
Michael Bone, prin. — Fax 359-3366
Madison MS — 1,000/5-7
575 W 7th S 83440 — 208-359-3320
Mike Bennett, prin. — Fax 359-3348
Union-Lyman ES — 200/K-4
2786 W 5200 S 83440 — 208-359-3334
Marche Young, prin. — Fax 359-3345

Richfield, Lincoln, Pop. 437
Richfield SD 316 — 200/PK-12
555 N Tiger Dr 83349 — 208-487-2241
Barbara Thronson, supt. — Fax 487-2240
Richfield S — 200/PK-12
555 N Tiger Dr 83349 — 208-487-2790
Mike Smith, prin. — Fax 487-2055

Rigby, Jefferson, Pop. 3,245
Jefferson County JSD 251 — 4,200/PK-12
201 Idaho Ave 83442 — 208-745-6693
Ron Tolman, supt. — Fax 745-0848
www.sd251.org/
Harwood ES — 500/K-4
200 W 3rd N 83442 — 208-745-7613
David England, prin. — Fax 745-7995
Jefferson ES — 800/K-5
306 N 3700 E 83442 — 208-745-0758
Ben Lemons, prin. — Fax 745-0762
Midway MS — 600/6-7
305 N 3700 E 83442 — 208-745-8347
Ken Meacham, prin. — Fax 745-0144
Other Schools – See Menan, Roberts

Riggins, Idaho, Pop. 404
Salmon River JSD 243 — 200/PK-12
PO Box 50 83549 — 208-628-3431
Marcus Scheibe, supt. — Fax 628-3840
www.jsd243.org
Riggins ES — 100/PK-6
PO Box 290 83549 — 208-628-3361
Marcus Scheibe, prin. — Fax 628-3265

Ririe, Jefferson, Pop. 531
Ririe JSD 252 — 700/PK-12
PO Box 508 83443 — 208-538-7482
Ron Perrenoud, supt. — Fax 538-7363
www.ririeschools.org
Ririe ES — 200/PK-4
PO Box 528 83443 — 208-538-7778
Reed Williams, prin. — Fax 538-9803
Ririe MS — 200/5-8
PO Box 548 83443 — 208-538-5175
Ron Perrenoud, prin. — Fax 538-7748

Roberts, Jefferson, Pop. 665
Jefferson County JSD 251
Supt. — See Rigby
Roberts ES — 200/K-5
682 N 2858 E 83444 — 208-228-3111
Eric Jensen, prin. — Fax 228-2520

Rockland, Power, Pop. 330
Rockland SD 382 — 100/K-12
PO Box 119 83271 — 208-548-2221
James Woodworth, supt. — Fax 548-2224
www.rbulldogs.org
Rockland S — 100/K-12
PO Box 119 83271 — 208-548-2221
Dan Ralphs, prin. — Fax 548-2224

Rogerson, Twin Falls
Three Creek JESD 416 — 50/K-8
49909 Three Creek Rd 83302 — 208-857-2281
Fax 857-2281
Three Creek S — 50/K-8
49909 Three Creek Rd 83302 — 208-857-2281
Fax 857-2281

Rupert, Minidoka, Pop. 5,225
Minidoka County JSD 331 — 3,800/PK-12
633 Fremont St 83350 — 208-436-4727
Dr. Scott Rogers, supt. — Fax 436-6593
www.minidokaschools.org
Acequia ES — 300/PK-5
360 N 350 E 83350 — 208-436-6985
Suzette Miller, prin. — Fax 436-4359
East Minico MS — 500/6-8
1805 H St 83350 — 208-436-3178
Kevan Vogt, prin. — Fax 436-3235
Rupert ES — 600/K-5
202 18th St 83350 — 208-436-9707
Laurie Copmann, prin. — Fax 436-1726
Other Schools – See Heyburn, Paul

St. Nicholas S — 100/PK-6
PO Box 26 83350 — 208-436-6320
Diane Brumley, prin. — Fax 436-0628

Sagle, Bonner
Lake Pend Oreille SD 84
Supt. — See Ponderay
Sagle ES — 400/K-6
550 Sagle Rd 83860 — 208-263-2757
Donald Moore, prin. — Fax 263-6732

Saint Anthony, Fremont, Pop. 3,375
Fremont County JSD 215 — 2,300/PK-12
945 W 1st N 83445 — 208-624-7542
Dr. Garry Parker, supt. — Fax 624-3385
www.sd215.net
Central ES — 400/PK-3
425 N 3rd W 83445 — 208-624-7422
DelRay Davenport, prin. — Fax 624-7438
Lincoln ES — 200/4-5
825 S 4th W 83445 — 208-624-3372
Neil Hirschi, prin. — Fax 624-7691
Parker-Egin ES — 100/K-5
221 N Center St 83445 — 208-624-7472
Neil Williams, prin. — Fax 624-7472
South Fremont JHS — 400/6-8
550 N 1st W 83445 — 208-624-7880
Chester Peterson, prin. — Fax 624-4386
Other Schools – See Ashton, Teton

Saint Maries, Benewah, Pop. 2,589
Saint Maries JSD 41 — 1,100/PK-12
PO Box 384 83861 — 208-245-2579
Dave Cox, supt. — Fax 245-3970
www.sd41.k12.id.us/
Heyburn ES — 400/PK-5
1405 Main Ave 83861 — 208-245-2025
Connie Mavity, prin. — Fax 245-5418
Saint Maries MS — 200/6-8
1315 W Jefferson Ave 83861 — 208-245-3495
Dennis Kachelmier, prin. — Fax 245-0506
Other Schools – See Fernwood

Saint Maries Christian S — 50/1-8
216 N 9th St 83861 — 208-245-2274
Aleida Quick, prin.

Salmon, Lemhi, Pop. 3,072
Salmon SD 291 — 1,000/PK-12
907 Sharkey St 83467 — 208-756-4271
Tana Kellogg, supt. — Fax 756-6695
www.salmon.k12.id.us/
Salmon MS — 300/5-8
310 S Daisy St 83467 — 208-756-2207
Sue Rodgers, prin. — Fax 756-2099
Salmon Pioneer PS — 300/PK-4
900 Sharkey St 83467 — 208-756-3663
Sue Ann Rodgers, prin. — Fax 756-6695

Salmon SDA S, 400 Fairmont St 83467 — 50/1-8
Mark Law, lead tchr. — 208-756-4439

Sandpoint, Bonner, Pop. 8,105
Lake Pend Oreille SD 84
Supt. — See Ponderay
Farmin Stidwell ES — 700/PK-6
1626 Spruce St 83864 — 208-265-2417
Anne Bagby, prin. — Fax 265-4610
Northside ES — 200/K-6
7881 Colburn Culver Rd 83864 — 208-263-2734
Don Moore, prin. — Fax 255-2944
Sandpoint MS — 500/7-8
310 S Division Ave 83864 — 208-265-4169
Kim Keaton, prin. — Fax 263-5525
Washington ES — 300/K-6
420 S Boyer Ave 83864 — 208-263-4759
Betsy Walker, prin. — Fax 263-1453

Little Lambs Preschool — 50/PK-PK
1900 Pine St 83864 — 208-255-1514
Claudia Vogler, admin. — Fax 255-1326
Sandpoint Jr. Academy — 100/1-9
2255 Pine St 83864 — 208-263-3584
Charla Suppe, prin. — Fax 263-8683
Sandpoint Waldorf S — 100/PK-8
PO Box 95 83864 — 208-265-2683
Susan Prez, prin. — Fax 265-2683

Shelley, Bingham, Pop. 4,131
Shelley JSD 60 — 2,000/PK-12
545 Seminary Ave 83274 — 208-357-3411
Bryan Jolley, supt. — Fax 357-5741
www.shelleyschools.org/
Goodsell PS — PK-K
185 W Center St 83274 — 208-357-5625
Laron Shumway, prin. — Fax 357-3040
Hobbs MS — 500/6-8
350 E Pine St 83274 — 208-357-7667
Joann Montgomery, prin. — Fax 357-3003
Stuart ES — 400/3-5
475 W Center St 83274 — 208-357-5580
Greg Kiester, prin. — Fax 357-7631
Sunrise ES — 400/1-3
200 E Fir St 83274 — 208-357-7688
Laron Shumway, prin. — Fax 357-2536

Shoshone, Lincoln, Pop. 1,574
Shoshone JSD 312 — 400/PK-12
61 E Highway 24 83352 — 208-886-2381
Mel Wiseman, supt. — Fax 886-2038
www.shoshone.k12.id.us
Shoshone ES — 300/PK-5
61 E Highway 24 83352 — 208-886-2381
Emily Nelsen, prin. — Fax 886-2742

Soda Springs, Caribou, Pop. 3,256
Soda Springs JSD 150 — 900/K-12
250 E 2nd S 83276 — 208-547-3371
Dr. Molly Stein, supt. — Fax 547-4878
www.sodaschools.org
Thirkill ES — 300/K-4
60 E 4th S 83276 — 208-547-4426
Robert Daniel, prin. — Fax 547-2617
Tigert MS — 300/5-8
250 E 2nd S 83276 — 208-547-4922
Dr. Molly Stein, prin. — Fax 547-2619

Spirit Lake, Kootenai, Pop. 1,500
Lakeland JSD 272
Supt. — See Rathdrum
Spirit Lake ES — 400/K-6
PO Box 189 83869 — 208-623-2501
Steve Rasor, prin. — Fax 623-5175
Timberlake JHS — 300/7-8
PO Box 1080 83869 — 208-623-2582
Georgeanne Griffith, prin. — Fax 623-2750

Stanley, Custer, Pop. 96
Challis JSD 181
Supt. — See Challis
Stanley S — 50/K-8
PO Box 77 83278 — 208-774-3503
Mary Easom, lead tchr. — Fax 774-3643

Star, Ada, Pop. 2,767
Meridian JSD 2
Supt. — See Meridian
Star ES — 500/K-5
700 N Star Rd 83669 — 208-855-4110
Carla Karnes, prin. — Fax 855-4119

Stone, Oneida
Oneida County SD 351
Supt. — See Malad City
Stone ES — 50/K-3
10808 S 23000 W 83252 — 208-698-3585
Lynn Schow, prin. — Fax 698-3585

Sugar City, Madison, Pop. 1,479
Sugar-Salem JSD 322 — 1,300/PK-12
PO Box 150 83448 — 208-356-8802
Alan Dunn, supt. — Fax 356-7237
www.sd322.k12.id.us/
Central ES — 400/PK-3
PO Box 239 83448 — 208-356-9351
Robert Potter, prin. — Fax 356-0895

Kershaw IS 300/4-6
610 E 3rd N 83448 208-356-0241
Gwen Kerbs, prin. Fax 656-0538
Sugar-Salem JHS 200/7-8
PO Box 180 83448 208-356-4437
Kevin Schultz, prin. Fax 358-9717

Sun Valley, Blaine, Pop. 1,444

Community S 300/PK-12
PO Box 2118 83353 208-622-3955
Andy Jones-Wilkins, hdmstr. Fax 622-3962

Sweet, Gem
Emmett ISD 221
Supt. — See Emmett
Sweet-Montour S 100/K-6
6600 Sweet Ola Hwy 83670 208-584-3378
Kristine Donaldson, lead tchr. Fax 584-3323

Tendoy, Lemhi
South Lemhi SD 292
Supt. — See Leadore
Tendoy ES 50/K-6
PO Box 13 83468 208-756-3524
Dr. Sandra Noland, prin. Fax 768-2797

Terreton, Jefferson
West Jefferson SD 253 700/PK-12
1256 E 1500 N 83450 208-663-4542
Steven Lambertsen, supt. Fax 663-4543
wjsd.org
Terreton S 400/PK-8
1252 E 1500 N 83450 208-663-4393
Richard Hanson, prin. Fax 663-4394
Other Schools – See Hamer

Teton, Fremont, Pop. 573
Fremont County JSD 215
Supt. — See Saint Anthony
Teton ES 100/K-5
126 W Main 83451 208-458-4931
Neil Hirschi, prin. Fax 624-3385

Tetonia, Teton, Pop. 243
Teton County SD 401
Supt. — See Driggs
Tetonia ES 100/1-5
PO Box 129 83452 208-456-2288
Jannifer Cooke, prin. Fax 456-2288

Thatcher, Franklin
Grace JSD 148
Supt. — See Grace
Thatcher ES 100/1-5
PO Box 14 83283 208-427-6346
Diane Elsmore, prin. Fax 427-0008

Troy, Latah, Pop. 744
Troy SD 287 300/K-12
PO Box 280 83871 208-835-3791
Bruce Bradberry Ed.D., supt. Fax 835-3790
www.sd287.k12.id.us
Troy ES 200/K-6
PO Box 280 83871 208-835-4261
Merle Jaques, prin. Fax 835-4250

Whitepine JSD 288 300/K-12
502 First Ave 83871 208-877-1408
Dan Rask, supt. Fax 877-1570
www.sd288.k12.id.us/
Other Schools – See Bovill

Twin Falls, Twin Falls, Pop. 38,630
Filer SD 413
Supt. — See Filer
Hollister ES 100/K-5
2463 Contact Ave 83301 208-655-4215
Teri Peters, prin. Fax 655-4214

Twin Falls SD 411 6,200/PK-12
201 Main Ave W 83301 208-733-6900
Wiley Dobbs, supt. Fax 733-6987
www.tfsd.k12.id.us
Bickel ES 300/K-5
607 2nd Ave E 83301 208-733-4116
Kelli Schroeder, prin. Fax 733-8926
Harrison ES 500/PK-5
600 Harrison St 83301 208-733-4229
Christine Gillette, prin. Fax 733-4256
Lincoln ES 500/K-5
238 Buhl St N 83301 208-733-1321
Beth Olmstead, prin. Fax 733-4243
Morningside ES 500/K-5
701 Morningside Dr 83301 208-733-6507
Steve Hoy, prin. Fax 733-5407
O'Leary JHS 600/6-8
2350 Elizabeth Blvd 83301 208-733-2155
John Hyatt, prin. Fax 733-8666
Oregon Trail ES 500/K-5
660 Park Ave 83301 208-733-8480
Kasey Teske, prin. Fax 733-8686
Perrine ES 600/K-5
452 Caswell Ave W 83301 208-733-4288
Bill Brulotte, prin. Fax 733-7881
Sawtooth ES 600/K-5
1771 Stadium Blvd 83301 208-733-8454
Randy Rutledge, prin. Fax 733-5729
Stuart JHS 500/6-8
644 Caswell Ave W 83301 208-733-4875
Steve Smith, prin. Fax 733-4949

Agape Christian S 100/PK-3
181 Morrison St 83301 208-734-3693
Mindy Sauer, dir. Fax 736-4978
Hilltop SDA S 50/K-8
131 Grandview Dr 83301 208-733-0799
Thomas Sherwood, lead tchr.
Immanuel Lutheran S 200/PK-6
2055 Filer Ave E 83301 208-733-7820
Michelle Jund, prin. Fax 735-9970
Lighthouse Christian S 300/PK-12
960 Eastland Dr 83301 208-737-1425
Kevin Newbry, supt. Fax 737-4671
St. Edwards Community S 200/PK-6
139 6th Ave E 83301 208-734-3872
Kevin Bushman, prin. Fax 734-1214
Twin Falls Christian Academy 100/PK-12
798 Eastland Dr N 83301 208-733-1452
Brent Walker, prin. Fax 734-1417

Victor, Teton, Pop. 1,365
Teton County SD 401
Supt. — See Driggs
Victor ES 200/1-5
PO Box 169 83455 208-787-2245
Jannifer Cooke, prin. Fax 787-2245

Wallace, Shoshone, Pop. 907
Wallace SD 393 600/PK-12
405 7th St 83873 208-753-4515
Dr. Robert Ranells, supt. Fax 753-4151
www.sd393.k12.id.us
Other Schools – See Osburn

Weippe, Clearwater, Pop. 390
Orofino JSD 171
Supt. — See Orofino
Timberline S 200/PK-12
1150 Highway 11 83553 208-435-4411
Christopher Bennett, prin. Fax 435-4846

Weiser, Washington, Pop. 5,420
Weiser SD 431 1,700/PK-12
925 Pioneer Rd 83672 208-414-0616
James Reed, supt. Fax 414-1265
www.sd431.k12.id.us/
Park IS 300/4-5
758 E Park St 83672 208-414-2861
Dave Kerby, prin. Fax 414-0851
Pioneer PS 500/PK-3
624 Pioneer Rd 83672 208-414-3131
Wade Wilson, prin. Fax 414-3198
Weiser MS 400/6-8
320 E Galloway Ave 83672 208-414-2620
Larry Goto, prin. Fax 414-2094

Wendell, Gooding, Pop. 2,396
Wendell SD 232 1,100/PK-12
PO Box 300 83355 208-536-2418
Greg Lowe, supt. Fax 536-2629
www.sd232.k12.id.us
Wendell ES 500/PK-4
150 3rd Ave E 83355 208-536-6611
Kevin Rogers, prin. Fax 536-6602
Wendell MS 300/5-8
800 E Main St 83355 208-536-5531
Luke Kelsey, prin. Fax 536-5957

Wilder, Canyon, Pop. 1,451
Wilder SD 133 400/K-12
PO Box 488 83676 208-482-6228
Daniel Arriola, supt. Fax 482-7019
www.sd133.k12.id.us/
Holmes ES 200/K-5
PO Box 488 83676 208-482-6220
Jeff Dillon, prin. Fax 482-6980

Worley, Kootenai, Pop. 224
Plummer/Worley JSD 44
Supt. — See Plummer
Lakeside ES 200/PK-5
PO Box 99 83876 208-686-1651
Judi Sharrett, prin. Fax 686-2172

ILLINOIS

ILLINOIS DEPARTMENT OF EDUCATION
100 N 1st St, Springfield 62777-0002
Telephone 866-262-6663
Fax 217-524-8585
Website http://www.isbe.state.il.us

Superintendent of Education   Christopher Koch

ILLINOIS BOARD OF EDUCATION
100 N 1st St, Springfield 62777-0002

Chairperson   Jesse Ruiz

REGIONAL OFFICES OF EDUCATION (ROE)

Adams/Pike ROE
Raymond Scheiter, supt. 217-277-2080
507 Vermont St, Quincy 62301 Fax 277-2092
www.wc4.org
Alxndr/Jhnsn/Massac/Pulaski/Union ROE
Janet Ulrich, supt. 618-634-2292
17 Rustic Campus Dr, Ullin 62992 Fax 634-2294
www.roe02.k12.il.us/
Bond/Effingham/Fayette ROE
Mark Drone, supt. 618-283-5011
300 S 7th St, Vandalia 62471 Fax 283-5013
www.fayette.k12.il.us/roeweb/
Boone/Winnebago ROE
Richard Fairgrieves, supt. 815-636-3060
300 Heart Blvd, Loves Park 61111 Fax 636-3069
www.4roe.org/
Brown/Cass/Morgan/Scott ROE
Stephen Breese, supt. 217-243-1804
110 N West St, Jacksonville 62650 Fax 243-5354
www.roe46.net/
Bureau/Henry/Stark ROE
Bruce Dennison, supt. 309-936-7890
107 S State St, Atkinson 61235 Fax 935-6784
www.bhsroe.k12.il.us
Calhoun/Greene/Jersey/Macoupin ROE
Larry Pfeiffer, supt. 217-854-4016
220 N Broad St, Carlinville 62626 Fax 854-2032
www.roe40.k12.il.us/
Carroll/Jo Daviess/Stephenson ROE
Marie Stiefel, supt. 815-947-3810
500 N Rush St, Stockton 61085 Fax 947-2717
roe8.lth2.k12.il.us/
Champaign/Ford ROE
Jane Quinlan, supt. 217-893-3219
200 S Fredrick St, Rantoul 61866 Fax 893-0024
www.roe9.k12.il.us/
Christian/Montgomery ROE
Greg Springer, supt. 217-532-9591
1 Courthouse Sq Rm 202 Fax 824-2464
Hillsboro 62049
www.montgomery.k12.il.us
Clay/Crawford/Jspr/Lwrnce/Rchlnd ROE
Carol S. Steinman, supt. 618-392-4631
103 W Main St Ste 23, Olney 62450 Fax 392-3993
Clinton/Marion/Washington ROE
Keri Jo Garrett, supt. 618-594-2432
930 Fairfax St Ste B, Carlyle 62231 Fax 594-7192
www.roe13.k12.il.us
Clk/Cls/Cumb/Dglas/Edg/Mlt/Shlb ROE
John McNary, supt. 217-348-0151
730 7th St, Charleston 61920 Fax 348-0171
www.roe11.k12.il.us/
DeKalb ROE
Gil Morrison, supt. 815-895-3096
245 W Exchange St Ste 2 Fax 895-4847
Sycamore 60178
DeWitt/Livingston/McLean ROE
Mark Jontry, supt. 309-888-5120
905 N Main St Ste 1, Normal 61761 Fax 862-0420
www.roe17.k12.il.us/

Dupage ROE
Darlene Ruscitti, supt. 630-407-5800
421 N County Farm Rd Fax 682-7773
Wheaton 60187
www.dupage.k12.il.us/
Edwds/Gtn/Hdn/Pope/Sln/Wbsh/Wyn/Wt ROE
Lawrence Fillingim, supt. 618-253-5581
512 N Main St, Harrisburg 62946 Fax 252-8472
www.roe20.k12.il.us/
Franklin/Williamson ROE
Matt Donkin, supt. 618-438-9711
206 Rushing Dr Ste 1, Herrin 62948 Fax 435-2861
www.roe21.k12.il.us/
Fulton/Schuyler ROE
Louise Bassett, supt. 309-547-3041
PO Box 307, Lewistown 61542 Fax 547-3326
www.fulton.k12.il.us/
Grundy/Kendall ROE
Paul Nordstrom, supt. 815-941-3247
1320 Union St, Morris 60450 Fax 942-5384
www.grundy.k12.il.us/
Hamilton/Jefferson ROE
Bryan Cross, supt. 618-244-8040
1714 Broadway St Fax 244-8073
Mount Vernon 62864
www.roe25.com
Hancock/McDonough ROE
Gary Eddington, supt. 309-837-4821
130 S Lafayette St Ste 200 Fax 837-2887
Macomb 61455
mcdonough.k12.il.us/roe26/
Henderson/Mercer/Warren ROE
Jodi Scott, supt. 309-734-6822
200 W Broadway, Monmouth 61462 Fax 734-2452
www.hmwroe27.com
Iroquois/Kankakee ROE
Kathleen Pangle, supt. 815-937-2950
189 E Court St Ste 600 Fax 937-2921
Kankakee 60901
www.i-kan.org
Jackson/Perry ROE
Robert L. Koehn, supt. 618-687-7290
1001 Walnut St Fax 687-7296
Murphysboro 62966
www.roe30.k12.il.us/
Kane ROE
Douglas Johnson, supt. 630-232-5955
210 S 6th St, Geneva 60134 Fax 208-5115
www.kaneroe.org/
Knox ROE
Bonnie Harris, supt. 309-345-3828
PO Box 430, Galesburg 61402 Fax 343-2677
www.knox.k12.il.us/knoxcountyroe33/
Lake ROE
Roycealee Wood, supt. 847-543-7833
800 Lancer Ln Ste E128 Fax 543-7832
Grayslake 60030
www.lake.k12.il.us
LaSalle ROE
Richard Myers, supt. 815-434-0780
119 W Madison St, Ottawa 61350 Fax 434-2453
www.roe35.k12.il.us

Lee/Ogle ROE
Amy Jo Clemens, supt. 815-652-2054
7772 Clinton St, Dixon 61021 Fax 652-2053
Logan/Mason/Menard ROE
Jean Anderson, supt. 217-732-8388
122 N McLean St, Lincoln 62656 Fax 735-1569
logan.k12.il.us/quickanswers38
Macon/Piatt ROE 39
Richard Shelby, supt. 217-872-3721
1690 Huston Dr, Decatur 62526 Fax 872-0239
Madison County ROE
Dr. Robert Daiber, supt. 618-692-6200
PO Box 600, Edwardsville 62025 Fax 692-7018
www.madison.k12.il.us/
Marshall/Putnam/Woodford ROE
Ronda Bangert, supt. 309-248-8212
PO Box 340, Washburn 61570 Fax 248-7983
www.roe43.k12.il.us/
McHenry ROE
Gene Goeglein, supt. 815-334-4475
2200 N Seminary Ave Fax 338-0475
Woodstock 60098
www.mchenry.k12.il.us/
Monroe-Randolph ROE
Marc Kiehna, supt. 618-939-5650
107 E Mill St, Waterloo 62298 Fax 939-5332
www.monroe.k12.il.us/roe45/
Peoria ROE
Gerald Brookhart, supt. 309-672-6906
324 Main St Ste 401, Peoria 61602 Fax 672-6053
www.peoria.k12.il.us/roe48/
Rock Island ROE
Joseph Vermeire, supt. 309-736-1111
3430 Avenue of the Cities Fax 736-1127
Moline 61265
www.riroe.com/
Saint Clair ROE
Brad Harriman, supt. 618-825-3900
1000 S Illinois St, Belleville 62220
www.stclair.k12.il.us/
Sangamon ROE
Helen Tolan, supt. 217-753-6620
200 S 9th St Ste 303 Fax 535-3166
Springfield 62701
www.roe51.org
Suburban Cook ROE
Charles Flowers, supt. 708-865-9330
10110 Gladstone St Fax 865-9338
Westchester 60154
www.cook.k12.il.us/
Tazewell ROE
Robin Houchin, supt. 309-477-2290
414 Court St Ste 104, Pekin 61554 Fax 347-3735
www.tazewell.k12.il.us/quickanswers53
Vermilion ROE
Michael Metzen, supt. 217-431-2668
200 S College St Ste B Fax 431-2671
Danville 61832
www.roe54.k12.il.us/
Whiteside ROE
Gary Steinert, supt. 815-625-1495
1001 W 23rd St, Sterling 61081 Fax 625-1625
www.wside.k12.il.us/
Will ROE
Jennifer Bertino-Tarrant, supt. 815-740-8360
702 W Maple St, New Lenox 60451 Fax 740-4788
www.will.k12.il.us/

PUBLIC, PRIVATE AND CATHOLIC ELEMENTARY SCHOOLS

Abingdon, Knox, Pop. 3,379
Abingdon CUSD 217 600/PK-12
401 W Latimer St 61410 309-462-2301
Tami Roskamp, supt. Fax 462-3870
www.abingdon.k12.il.us/
Hedding ES 300/PK-5
401 W Latimer St 61410 309-462-2363
Michelle Andrews, prin. Fax 462-2105

Addison, DuPage, Pop. 36,811
Addison SD 4 4,100/PK-8
222 N JF Kennedy Dr Rear 2 60101 630-628-2500
Dr. Donald Hendricks, supt. Fax 628-8829
www.asd4.org
Ardmore S 500/PK-K
644 S Ardmore Ave 60101 630-458-2900
Michele Ramsey, prin. Fax 628-2736
Army Trail ES 400/1-5
346 W Army Trail Blvd 60101 630-458-2502
Robert Pape, prin. Fax 628-2516

Fullerton ES 500/1-5
400 S Michigan Ave 60101 630-458-2950
Mary Ellen Reeves, prin. Fax 628-2519
Indian Trail JHS 1,300/6-8
222 N JF Kennedy Dr Frnt 1 60101 630-458-2600
Terry Sliva, prin. Fax 628-2841
Lake Park ES 300/1-5
330 W Lake Park Dr 60101 630-458-3010
Debra Martello, prin. Fax 628-2526
Lincoln ES 300/1-5
720 N Lincoln Ave 60101 630-458-3040
Daniel Johnson, prin. Fax 628-2524

Stone ES 400/K-5
1404 W Stone Ave 60101 630-628-4020
Christine Pfaff, prin. Fax 628-2546
Wesley ES 300/K-5
1111 W Westwood Trl 60101 630-628-4060
Charles Wartman, prin. Fax 628-2536

St. Joseph S 100/PK-8
330 E Fullerton Ave Bldg 2 60101 630-279-4211
Dr. Patricia Schroeder, prin. Fax 279-4032
St. Philip the Apostle S 300/PK-8
1233 W Holtz Ave 60101 630-543-4130
Denise Sedlak, prin. Fax 458-8750

Akin, Franklin
Akin CCSD 91 100/PK-8
PO Box 1 62805 618-627-2180
Brian Hodge, supt. Fax 627-2119
Akin Community Consolidated S 100/PK-8
PO Box 1 62805 618-627-2180
Brian Hodge, prin. Fax 627-2119

Albers, Clinton, Pop. 994
Albers SD 63 200/K-8
PO Box 104 62215 618-248-5146
Sharon Harms, supt. Fax 248-5659
Albers S 200/K-8
PO Box 104 62215 618-248-5146
Sharon Harms, prin. Fax 248-5659

Albion, Edwards, Pop. 1,892
Edwards County CUSD 1 1,000/PK-12
37 W Main St 62806 618-445-2814
David Cowger, supt. Fax 445-2272
www.echs.edwrds.k12.il.us/
Albion S 500/PK-8
361 W Main St 62806 618-445-2327
Marilyn Turner, prin. Fax 445-2672
Other Schools – See West Salem

Aledo, Mercer, Pop. 3,535
Aledo CUSD 201 900/PK-12
402 E Main St 61231 309-582-2238
Alan Boucher, supt. Fax 582-7428
www.aledoschools.org
Aledo JHS 200/6-8
1002 SW 6th St 61231 309-582-2441
Douglas Nelson, prin. Fax 582-2440
Apollo ES 400/PK-5
801 SW 9th St 61231 309-582-5350
Bill Fleuette, prin. Fax 582-3457

Alexander, Morgan
Franklin CUSD 1 400/PK-12
PO Box 140 62601 217-478-3011
Fred Roberts, supt. Fax 478-4921
www.franklinhigh.com
Alexander ES 100/2-5
PO Box 140 62601 217-478-3011
Fred Roberts, prin. Fax 478-4921
Other Schools – See Franklin

Alexis, Mercer, Pop. 823
United CUSD 304 700/PK-12
101 N Holloway St Ofc 2 61412 309-482-3344
Jeffrey Whitsitt, supt. Fax 482-3236
united.k12.il.us/
United ES - North 300/PK-5
411 W Hunt Ave 61412 309-482-3332
Tom Gilliland, prin.
Other Schools – See Monmouth

Algonquin, McHenry, Pop. 29,022
CUSD 300
Supt. — See Carpentersville
Algonquin Lakes ES 500/K-5
1401 Compton Dr 60102 847-854-3900
Ruthann Ryan, prin. Fax 854-3909
Algonquin MS 600/6-8
520 Longwood Dr 60102 847-658-2545
Peggy Thurow, prin. Fax 658-2547
Eastview ES 500/K-5
540 Longwood Dr 60102 847-458-5501
James Zursin, prin. Fax 458-5509
Neubert ES 600/K-5
1100 Huntington Dr 60102 847-658-2540
Darlene Warner, prin. Fax 658-9809
Westfield Community S 1,800/K-8
2100 Sleepy Hollow Rd 60102 847-458-1900
Bill Doran, prin. Fax 458-1909

Consolidated SD 158 7,400/PK-12
650 Academic Dr 60102 847-659-6158
Dr. John Burkey, supt. Fax 659-6122
www.district158.org/
Conley ES 600/3-5
750 Academic Dr 60102 847-659-3700
Alice Stech, prin. Fax 659-3720
Heineman MS 800/6-8
725 Academic Dr 60102 847-659-4300
Jim Stotz, prin. Fax 659-4320
Mackeben ES 700/PK-2
800 Academic Dr 60102 847-659-3400
Jennifer Zayas, prin. Fax 659-3420
Other Schools – See Huntley, Lake in the Hills

Foundations Montessori S 200/PK-6
2651 W Algonquin Rd 60102 847-458-3220
Susan Baroni, prin.
St. John Lutheran S 200/PK-8
300 Jefferson St 60102 847-658-9311
Ralph Peterson, prin. Fax 658-5766
St. Margaret Mary S 400/PK-8
119 S Hubbard St 60102 847-658-5313
Susan Snyder, prin. Fax 854-0501

Alhambra, Madison, Pop. 641
Highland CUSD 5
Supt. — See Highland
Alhambra PS 100/K-2
302 W Main St 62001 618-488-2200
Erick Baer, prin. Fax 488-2201

Allendale, Wabash, Pop. 505
Allendale CCSD 17 100/PK-8
PO Box 130 62410 618-299-3161
Sarah Emery, supt. Fax 299-2015
Allendale S 100/PK-8
PO Box 130 62410 618-299-3161
Sarah Emery, prin. Fax 299-2015

Alpha, Henry, Pop. 704
Alwood CUSD 225
Supt. — See Woodhull
Alwood ES 200/PK-5
101 E A St 61413 309-629-5011
Shannon Bumann, prin. Fax 629-4023

Alsip, Cook, Pop. 19,072
Alsip-Hazelgreen-Oaklawn SD 126 1,600/PK-8
11900 S Kostner Ave 60803 708-389-1900
Robert Berger, supt. Fax 396-3793
www.dist126.k12.il.us
Hazelgreen ES 300/K-6
11751 S Lawler Ave 60803 708-371-5351
Carin Novak, prin. Fax 396-3754
Lane ES 300/K-6
4600 W 123rd St 60803 708-371-0720
Patti Egan, prin. Fax 396-3753
Prairie JHS 400/7-8
11910 S Kostner Ave 60803 708-371-3080
Craig Gwaltney, prin. Fax 396-3798
Stony Creek ES 600/PK-6
11700 S Kolin Ave 60803 708-371-0220
Deborah Otto, prin. Fax 396-3755

Atwood Heights SD 125 700/PK-8
12150 S Hamlin Ave 60803 708-371-0080
Dr. Thomas Livingston, supt. Fax 371-7847
Hamlin Upper Grade Center 200/6-8
12150 S Hamlin Ave 60803 708-597-1550
Lisa West, prin. Fax 396-0515
Other Schools – See Merrionette Park, Oak Lawn

Cook County SD 130
Supt. — See Blue Island
Washington ES 200/K-5
12545 S Homan Ave 60803 708-489-3523
Phyllis Graham, prin. Fax 385-8467

Altamont, Effingham, Pop. 2,259
Altamont CUSD 10 800/PK-12
7 S Ewing St 62411 618-483-6195
Jeff Fritchtnitch, supt. Fax 483-6303
www.altamont.k12.il.us/
Altamont S 500/PK-8
407 S Edwards St 62411 618-483-5171
Michael Gill, prin. Fax 483-6793

Altamont Lutheran S 100/K-8
7 S Edwards St 62411 618-483-6428
Gail Traub, prin. Fax 483-6296

Alton, Madison, Pop. 29,433
Alton CUSD 11 6,100/PK-12
PO Box 9028 62002 618-474-2600
David Elson, supt. Fax 463-2126
www.altonschools.org
Alton MS 600/6-8
2200 College Ave 62002 618-474-2700
David Schwartz, prin. Fax 463-2127
Brown ES 300/K-5
1613 W Delmar 62002 618-463-2175
Mary Venardos, prin. Fax 467-0401
East ES 600/K-5
1035 Washington Ave 62002 618-463-2130
Henrietta Young, prin. Fax 463-2132
Lovejoy ES 300/K-5
2708 Edwards St 62002 618-463-2157
Debra Sheary, prin. Fax 463-2138
Smith ES 300/K-5
2400 Henry St 62002 618-463-2077
Laura Munson-Dewein, prin. Fax 462-3810
West ES 600/K-5
1513 State St 62002 618-463-2134
Cara Lytle, prin. Fax 463-2144
Other Schools – See Godfrey

Mississippi Valley Christian S 100/PK-12
2009 Seminary St 62002 618-462-1071
St. Mary S 400/PK-8
536 E 3rd St 62002 618-465-8523
Peggy Oungst, prin. Fax 465-4725
SS. Peter & Paul S 100/K-8
801 State St 62002 618-465-8711
Melinda Fischer, prin. Fax 465-6405

Altona, Knox, Pop. 544
ROWVA CUSD 208
Supt. — See Oneida
ROWVA East ES, PO Box 238 61414 100/5-6
Ann Grimm, prin. 309-484-2271

Amboy, Lee, Pop. 2,570
Amboy CUSD 272 1,000/PK-12
11 E Hawley St 61310 815-857-2164
Quintin Shepherd, supt. Fax 857-4434
www.amboy.net/
Amboy Central ES 400/PK-4
30 E Provost St 61310 815-857-3619
Jessica McCormick, prin. Fax 857-9024
Amboy JHS 300/5-8
140 S Appleton Ave 61310 815-857-3528
Joyce Schamberger, prin. Fax 857-4603

Andalusia, Rock Island, Pop. 1,059
Rockridge CUSD 300
Supt. — See Taylor Ridge
Andalusia ES 200/PK-6
PO Box 770 61232 309-798-2424
Patrick Helling, prin. Fax 798-9651

Anna, Union, Pop. 5,070
Anna CCSD 37 700/PK-8
301 S Green St 62906 618-833-6812
Linda Craske, supt. Fax 833-3205
Anna JHS 300/5-8
301 S Green St 62906 618-833-6812
Mark Laster, prin. Fax 833-6535
Davie ES 100/3-4
301 S Green St 62906 618-833-8022
Mark Laster, prin. Fax 833-6535
Lincoln ES 200/PK-2
108 Warren St 62906 618-833-6851
Mark Laster, prin. Fax 833-3262

Annawan, Henry, Pop. 919
Annawan CUSD 226 400/PK-12
501 W South St 61234 309-935-6781
Joe Buresh, supt. Fax 935-6065
Annawan S 300/PK-8
501 W South St 61234 309-935-6623
Wayne Brau, prin. Fax 935-6065

Antioch, Lake, Pop. 12,353
Antioch CCSD 34 3,000/PK-8
800 Main St 60002 847-838-8400
Scott Thompson, supt. Fax 838-8404
www.dist34.lake.k12.il.us
Antioch ES 400/2-5
817 Main St 60002 847-838-8901
Judy Hamilton, prin. Fax 395-2358
Antioch MS 1,000/6-8
800 Highview Dr 60002 847-838-8310
Jim Kallieris, prin. Fax 838-8304
Hillcrest ES 700/PK-1
433 E Depot St 60002 847-838-8000
Dawn Benaitis, prin. Fax 838-8004
Oakland ES 500/2-5
22018 W Grass Lake Rd 60002 847-838-8600
Kerstin Santarelli, prin. Fax 838-8604
Petty ES 400/2-5
850 Highview Dr 60002 847-838-8100
Mary Kay McNeill, prin. Fax 838-8104

Emmons SD 33 400/K-8
24226 W Beach Grove Rd 60002 847-395-1105
Dr. Robert Machak, supt. Fax 395-1223
www.emmons-school.com/
Emmons S 400/K-8
24226 W Beach Grove Rd 60002 847-395-1105
Dr. Cynthia Vandrush, prin. Fax 395-1223

Grass Lake SD 36 200/PK-8
26177 W Grass Lake Rd 60002 847-395-1550
Dr. Terry O'Brien, supt. Fax 395-8632
www.gls36.org/
Grass Lake S 200/PK-8
26177 W Grass Lake Rd 60002 847-395-1550
Dr. Terry O'Brien, prin. Fax 395-8632

Faith Evangelical Lutheran S 200/PK-8
1275 Main St 60002 847-395-1660
Stephen Schultz, dir. Fax 589-0519
St. Peter S 200/PK-8
900 Saint Peter St 60002 847-395-0037
Christine Mors, prin. Fax 395-2532

Apple River, Jo Daviess, Pop. 373
Warren CUSD 205
Supt. — See Warren
Apple River MS 100/4-6
301 W Hickory St 61001 815-594-2210
Dee Dee Calow, prin. Fax 594-2215

Arcola, Douglas, Pop. 2,662
Arcola CUSD 306 700/PK-12
351 W Washington St 61910 217-268-4963
Jean Chrostosko, supt. Fax 268-3809
www.arcola.k12.il.us
Arcola ES 400/PK-6
351 W Washington St 61910 217-268-4961
Gary Philippi, prin. Fax 268-4719

Arenzville, Cass, Pop. 418

Trinity Lutheran S 100/PK-6
PO Box 118 62611 217-997-5535

Argenta, Macon, Pop. 852
Argenta-Oreana CUSD 1 1,100/PK-12
PO Box 440 62501 217-795-2313
Damian Jones, supt. Fax 795-2174
www.argenta-oreana.org/
Argenta-Oreana MS 300/6-8
PO Box 439 62501 217-795-2163
Steve Johnson, prin. Fax 795-4502
Other Schools – See Oreana

Arlington Heights, Cook, Pop. 74,620
Arlington Heights SD 25 4,900/PK-8
1200 S Dunton Ave 60005 847-758-4900
Dr. Sarah Jerome, supt. Fax 758-4907
www.sd25.org
Dryden ES 400/K-5
722 S Dryden Pl 60005 847-398-4280
Robert Jares, prin. Fax 394-6946
Greenbrier ES 300/K-5
2330 N Verde Dr 60004 847-398-4272
Shelley Fabrizio, prin. Fax 394-6291
Ivy Hill ES 400/K-5
2211 N Burke Dr 60004 847-398-4275
Kristy Csensich, prin. Fax 394-6556
Olive-Mary Stitt ES 500/K-5
303 E Olive St 60004 847-398-4282
Marybeth Anderson, prin. Fax 394-6935
Patton ES 500/K-5
1616 N Patton Ave 60004 847-398-4288
Donna Devine, prin. Fax 394-6681
South MS 900/6-8
400 S Highland Ave 60005 847-398-4250
Linda Klobucher, prin. Fax 394-6260
Thomas MS 800/6-8
1430 N Belmont Ave 60004 847-398-4260
Thomas O'Rourke, prin. Fax 394-6843
Westgate ES 600/PK-5
500 S Dwyer Ave 60005 847-398-4292
Casimer Badynee, prin. Fax 394-6191

Windsor ES 600/K-5
1315 E Miner St 60004 847-398-4297
Brian Kaye, prin. Fax 394-6611

CCSD 59 6,100/PK-8
2123 S Arlington Heights Rd 60005 847-593-4300
Dr. Dan Schweers, supt. Fax 593-4409
www.ccsd59.org
Low ES 400/PK-5
1530 S Highland Ave 60005 847-593-4383
Brian Ganan, prin. Fax 593-7291
Other Schools – See Des Plaines, Elk Grove Village, Mount Prospect

Wheeling CCSD 21
Supt. — See Wheeling
Poe ES 400/K-5
2800 N Highland Ave 60004 847-670-3200
Pam Lindberg, prin. Fax 670-3216
Riley ES 300/PK-5
1209 E Burr Oak Dr 60004 847-670-3400
Carrie McCulley, prin. Fax 670-3418

Chicago Futabakai Japanese S 200/K-12
2550 N Arlington Heights Rd 60004 847-590-5700
Fax 590-9759
Christian Liberty Academy 900/PK-12
502 W Euclid Ave 60004 847-259-4444
Dr. Philip Bennett, prin. Fax 259-9972
Our Lady of the Wayside S 700/PK-8
432 S Mitchell Ave 60005 847-255-0050
Alan Musial, prin. Fax 253-0543
St. James S 500/PK-8
821 N Arlington Heights Rd 60004 847-255-6746
Judith Pappas, prin. Fax 259-4223
St. Peter Lutheran S 500/PK-8
111 W Olive St 60004 847-253-6638
Bruce Rudi, prin. Fax 259-4185

Armstrong, Vermilion
Armstrong-Ellis Consolidated SD 61 100/K-8
PO Box 7 61812 217-569-2115
William Mulvaney, supt. Fax 569-2116
Armstrong-Ellis S 100/K-8
PO Box 7 61812 217-569-2115
Kurt Thornsbrough, prin. Fax 519-2116

Aroma Park, Kankakee, Pop. 802
Kankakee SD 111
Supt. — See Kankakee
Aroma Park PS 200/K-3
PO Box 239 60910 815-937-1162
Kathleen O'Connor, prin. Fax 933-0765

Arthur, Douglas, Pop. 2,180
Arthur CUSD 305 500/PK-12
301 E Columbia St 61911 217-543-2511
Travis Wilson, supt. Fax 543-2210
www.arthur.k12.il.us
Arthur ES 300/PK-6
126 E Lincoln St 61911 217-543-2109
Gary Alexander, prin. Fax 543-2308
Arthur JHS 100/7-8
301 E Columbia St 61911 217-543-2146
Philip Hise, prin. Fax 543-2174

Ashkum, Iroquois, Pop. 703
Central CUSD 4
Supt. — See Clifton
Ashkum ECC 100/PK-PK
PO Box 158 60911 815-698-2212
Lori Morelock, prin. Fax 698-2635

Ashland, Cass, Pop. 1,376
A-C Central CUSD 262 500/PK-12
PO Box 260 62612 217-476-8112
Rebecca Canty, supt. Fax 476-8100
cass.k12.il.us/ac-central
A-C Central ES 200/PK-5
PO Box 260 62612 217-476-3313
Dan Williams, prin. Fax 476-3730
Other Schools – See Chandlerville

Ashley, Washington, Pop. 581
Ashley CCSD 15 200/K-8
450 N Third St 62808 618-485-6611
Dr. Kay Bennett, supt. Fax 485-2124
Ashley Community Consolidated S 200/K-8
450 N Third St 62808 618-485-6611
Dr. Kay Bennett, prin. Fax 485-2124

Ashmore, Coles, Pop. 767
Charleston CUSD 1
Supt. — See Charleston
Ashmore ES 200/PK-4
PO Box 219 61912 217-349-3000
Terry Diss, prin. Fax 349-3005

Ashton, Lee, Pop. 1,195
Ashton-Franklin Center CUSD 275 600/K-12
611 Western Ave 61006 815-453-7461
John Zick, supt. Fax 453-7462
www.afcschools.net/index.htm
Other Schools – See Franklin Grove

Assumption, Christian, Pop. 1,231
Central A & M CUSD 21 1,000/PK-12
105 N College St 62510 217-226-4042
Randall Grigg, supt. Fax 226-4133
www.cam.k12.il.us
Bond ES 200/PK-5
105 N College St 62510 217-226-4022
David Fitzgerald, prin. Fax 226-4133
Central A & M MS 200/6-8
404 Colegrove St 62510 217-226-4241
Kent Stauder, prin. Fax 226-4442
Other Schools – See Moweaqua

Astoria, Fulton, Pop. 1,160
Astoria CUSD 1 400/PK-12
PO Box 620 61501 309-329-2111
Chester Lien, supt. Fax 329-2214
www.astoria.fulton.k12.il.us
Astoria ES 200/PK-5
402 N Jefferson St 61501 309-329-2158
Jeannie Goodman, prin. Fax 329-2903
Astoria JHS 100/6-8
402 N Jefferson St 61501 309-329-2158
Jeannie Goodman, prin. Fax 329-2963

Athens, Menard, Pop. 1,800
Athens CUSD 213 1,100/PK-12
1 Warrior Way 62613 217-636-8761
Scott Laird, supt. Fax 636-8851
www.athens-213.org
Athens JHS 200/7-8
1 Warrior Way 62613 217-636-8380
Clay Shoufler, prin. Fax 636-8851
Other Schools – See Cantrall

Atlanta, Logan, Pop. 1,671
Olympia CUSD 16
Supt. — See Stanford
Olympia South ES 300/PK-5
103 NE 5th St 61723 217-648-2302
Laura O'Donnell, prin. Fax 648-5248

Atwood, Douglas, Pop. 1,250
Atwood-Hammond CUSD 39 400/K-12
PO Box 890 61913 217-578-3111
Kenneth Schwengel, supt. Fax 578-3531
www.ah.k12.il.us
Atwood-Hammond S 300/K-8
PO Box 860 61913 217-578-2220
Lance Landeck, prin. Fax 578-3314

Auburn, Sangamon, Pop. 4,274
Auburn CUSD 10 1,500/PK-12
606 W North St 62615 217-438-6164
Kathryn Garrett, supt. Fax 438-6483
auburn.k12.il.us
Auburn ES 500/PK-3
445 N 5th St 62615 217-438-6916
Amy Donaldson, prin. Fax 438-3912
Auburn MS 200/4-6
601 N 7th St 62615 217-438-6919
Matt Grimm, prin. Fax 438-3700
Other Schools – See Divernon

Augusta, Hancock, Pop. 625
Southeastern CUSD 337 300/PK-12
PO Box 215 62311 217-392-2172
Don Daily, supt. Fax 392-2174
www.southeastern337.com/
Other Schools – See Bowen

Aurora, Kane, Pop. 168,181
Aurora East Unit SD 131 12,700/PK-12
417 5th St 60505 630-299-5550
Jerome Roberts Ed.D., supt. Fax 299-5500
www.d131.kane.k12.il.us/
Allen ES 800/PK-5
700 S Farnsworth Ave 60505 630-299-5200
Michael Szopinski, prin. Fax 299-5201
Bardwell ES 1,000/PK-5
550 S Lincoln Ave 60505 630-299-5300
Thomas Hartman, prin. Fax 299-5302
Beaupre ES 300/PK-5
954 E Benton St 60505 630-299-5390
Michael Smith, prin. Fax 299-5399
Brady ES 500/PK-5
600 Columbia St 60505 630-299-5425
Francisco Delos Santos, prin. Fax 299-5474
Cowherd MS 900/6-8
441 N Farnsworth Ave 60505 630-299-5900
Crystal England, prin. Fax 299-5901
Dieterich ES 600/K-5
1141 Jackson St 60505 630-299-8280
Gwendolyn Miller, prin. Fax 299-8281
East Aurora ECC 200/PK-PK
278 E Indian Trl 60505 630-844-5102
Donna Scarpino, prin. Fax 844-5236
Gates ES 700/PK-5
800 7th Ave 60505 630-299-5600
Philip Hickman, prin. Fax 299-5601
Hermes ES 800/PK-5
1000 Jungles Ave 60505 630-299-8200
Mavis DeMar, prin. Fax 299-8201
Johnson ES 400/PK-5
1934 Liberty St, 630-299-5400
Kelly McCleary, prin. Fax 299-5401
Krug ES 300/PK-5
240 Melrose Ave 60505 630-299-5280
Twila Garza, prin. Fax 299-5299
Oak Park ES 600/PK-5
1200 Front St 60505 630-299-8250
Robin Hedrich, prin. Fax 299-8251
O'Donnell ES 500/PK-5
1640 Reckinger Rd 60505 630-299-8300
Edward Brouch, prin. Fax 299-8301
Rollins ES 400/PK-5
950 Kane St 60505 630-299-5480
Karen Hart, prin. Fax 299-5481
Simmons MS 900/6-8
1130 Sheffer Rd 60505 630-299-4150
Mechelle Patterson, prin. Fax 299-4151
Waldo MS 900/6-8
56 Jackson St 60505 630-299-8400
Earline Barnes, prin. Fax 299-8401

Aurora West Unit SD 129 12,300/PK-12
80 S River St 60506 630-301-5000
Dr. James Rydland, supt. Fax 844-5710
www.sd129.org/
Freeman ES 600/K-5
153 S Randall Rd 60506 630-301-5002
Michael Smith, prin. Fax 844-4499
Greenman ES 700/K-5
729 W Galena Blvd 60506 630-301-5004
Nick Baughman, prin. Fax 844-4618
Hall ES 600/K-5
2001 Heather Dr 60506 630-301-5005
Lisa Polomsky, prin. Fax 844-4617
Herget MS 700/6-8
1550 Deerpath Rd 60506 630-301-5006
Scott Woods, prin. Fax 301-5222
Hill ES 500/K-5
724 Pennsylvania Ave 60506 630-301-5007
Cynthia Larry, prin. Fax 897-4289
Jefferson MS 800/6-8
1151 Plum St 60506 630-301-5009
Patricia Cross, prin. Fax 844-5711
McCleery ES 600/K-5
1002 W Illinois Ave 60506 630-301-5012
Cherie Esposito, prin. Fax 844-9491
Smith ES 500/K-5
1332 Robinwood Dr 60506 630-301-5015
Pete Clabough, prin. Fax 844-6968
Todd ECC 500/PK-K
100 Oak Ave 60506 630-301-5016
Michelle Shabaker, prin. Fax 844-4522
Washington MS 700/6-8
231 S Constitution Dr 60506 630-301-5017
Deborah Meyer, prin. Fax 844-5712
Other Schools – See Montgomery, North Aurora

Indian Prairie CUSD 204 26,300/PK-12
780 Shoreline Dr 60504 630-375-3000
Dr. Stephen Daeschner, supt. Fax 375-3009
www.ipsd.org
Brooks ES 700/K-5
2700 Stonebridge Blvd, 630-375-3200
Dave Younce, prin. Fax 375-3201
Georgetown ES 600/K-5
995 Long Grove Dr 60504 630-375-3456
Stephen Selle, prin. Fax 375-3461
Gombert ES 500/K-5
2707 Ridge Rd 60504 630-375-3700
David Worst, prin. Fax 375-3701
Granger MS 1,100/6-8
2721 Stonebridge Blvd, 630-375-1010
Mary Kelly, prin. Fax 375-1110
McCarty ES 700/K-5
3000 Village Green Dr 60504 630-375-3400
Kim Earlenbaugh, prin. Fax 375-3401
Prairie Children Preschool 600/PK-PK
780 Shoreline Dr 60504 630-375-3030
LuAnn Shields, prin. Fax 375-3029
Steck ES 700/K-5
460 Inverness Dr 60504 630-375-3500
Kerry Merrill, prin. Fax 375-3501
Still MS 1,100/6-8
787 Meadowridge Dr 60504 630-375-3900
Jennifer Nonnemacher, prin. Fax 375-3901
Young ES 700/K-5
800 Asbury Dr, 630-375-3800
Adrienne Morgan, prin. Fax 375-3801
Other Schools – See Bolingbrook, Naperville

Oswego CUSD 308
Supt. — See Oswego
Bednarcick JHS 700/6-8
3025 Heggs Rd, 630-636-2500
Janet Stutz, prin. Fax 922-3278
Homestead ES 500/K-5
2830 Hillsboro Blvd, 630-636-3100
Patti Decker, prin. Fax 236-7036
Wheatlands ES 600/K-5
2290 Barrington Dr, 630-636-3500
Janet DeMont, prin. Fax 499-1193
Wolfs Crossing ES 600/K-5
3015 Heggs Rd, 630-636-3700
Allison Sulkson, prin. Fax 357-2865

Annunciation S 300/PK-8
1840 Church Rd 60505 630-851-4300
Karen Wollwert, prin. Fax 851-4316
Archbishop Romero Catholic S 100/PK-8
312 High St 60505 630-898-8690
William O'Dea, prin. Fax 898-8866
Aurora Christian S 400/PK-5
801 W Illinois Ave 60506 630-892-5585
Scott Etchison, prin. Fax 892-9717
Aurora Montessori S 200/PK-K
3180 N Aurora Rd, 630-898-4346
Karen Zehnal, prin. Fax 898-7048
Covenant Christian S 100/PK-8
550 Redwood Dr 60506 630-859-8010
Nina Bissett, prin. Fax 859-8085
Fox Valley Montessori S 100/PK-6
850 N Commonwealth Ave 60506 630-896-7557
Judy Hansen, prin. Fax 896-8104
Holy Angels S 600/PK-8
720 Kensington Pl 60506 630-897-3613
Norbert Rozanski, prin. Fax 897-8233
Montessori Childrens Garden 100/PK-5
2300 Montgomery Rd 60504 630-820-1010
Teresa Heinen, prin. Fax 820-1010
Our Lady of Good Counsel S 200/PK-8
601 Talma St 60505 630-851-4400
Elden Stockey, prin. Fax 851-8220
St. Joseph S 200/PK-8
706 High St 60505 630-844-3781
Marie Bockhaus, prin. Fax 844-3656
St. Marks Child Development Center 100/PK-K
1995 W Downer Pl 60506 630-897-6063
St. Pauls Lutheran S 200/PK-8
85 S Constitution Dr 60506 630-896-3250
Melvin Wille, prin. Fax 896-1329
St. Peter S 100/K-8
915 Sard Ave 60506 630-892-1283
Sr. Ann Brummel, prin. Fax 892-4836
St. Rita of Cascia S 300/PK-8
770 Old Indian Trl 60506 630-892-0200
Elizabeth Faxon, prin. Fax 892-4236
St. Therese of Jesus S 100/PK-8
255 N Farnsworth Ave 60505 630-898-0620
Charlotte Traversa, prin. Fax 898-3087

Aviston, Clinton, Pop. 1,540
Aviston SD 21 400/PK-8
350 S Hull St 62216 618-228-7245
Tami Kampwerth, supt. Fax 228-7121
www.avistonk-8.org/
Aviston S 400/PK-8
350 S Hull St 62216 618-228-7245
Tami Kampwerth, prin. Fax 228-7121

Avon, Fulton, Pop. 881
Avon CUSD 176 300/PK-12
320 E Woods St 61415 309-465-3708
Dan Oakley, supt. Fax 465-9030
www.avonschools.us
Avon ES 100/PK-5
320 E Woods St 61415 309-465-3851
Alice King, prin. Fax 465-9055
Avon JHS 100/6-8
320 E Woods St 61415 309-465-3621
Alice King, prin. Fax 465-7194

Bannockburn, Lake, Pop. 1,609
Bannockburn SD 106 200/K-8
2165 Telegraph Rd 60015 847-945-5900
Dr. JoAnn Desmond, supt. Fax 945-5909
www.bannockburnschool.org
Bannockburn S 200/K-8
2165 Telegraph Rd 60015 847-945-5900
Debbie Barnes, prin. Fax 945-5909

Barrington, Cook, Pop. 10,179
Barrington CUSD 220 9,100/PK-12
310 James St 60010 847-381-6300
Tom Leonard, supt. Fax 381-6337
www.cusd220.org
Barrington MS Prairie Campus 1,200/6-8
40 E Dundee Rd 60010 847-304-3990
Art Fessler, prin. Fax 304-3986
Barrington MS Station Campus 1,000/6-8
215 Eastern Ave 60010 847-381-0464
Craig Winkelman, prin. Fax 842-1343
Countryside ES 500/K-5
205 W County Line Rd 60010 847-381-1162
Christy Newhouse, prin. Fax 304-3927
Grove Avenue ES 500/K-5
900 S Grove Ave 60010 847-381-1888
Cynthia Kalogeropoulos, prin. Fax 304-3922
Hough Street ES 300/PK-5
310 S Hough St 60010 847-381-1108
Lori Wilcox, prin. Fax 304-3919
Lines ES 600/K-5
217 Eastern Ave 60010 847-381-7850
Jill Schweiger, prin. Fax 304-3918
North Barrington ES 500/K-5
310 N IL Route 59 60010 847-381-4340
Diane Wood, prin. Fax 304-3924
Rose ES 600/K-5
61 W Penny Rd 60010 847-844-1200
Scott Carlson, prin. Fax 844-1443
Roslyn Road ES 500/K-5
224 Roslyn Rd 60010 847-381-4148
Paul Kirk, prin. Fax 304-3923
Other Schools – See Carpentersville

Atonement Christian Day S 100/PK-K
909 E Main St 60010 847-382-6360
Cynthia Clanton, dir. Fax 381-2427
Creative Care Children's Center 50/PK-6
1410 S Barrington Rd 60010 847-382-2812
Marla Thoma, dir. Fax 382-3423
St. Anne S 500/PK-8
319 Franklin St 60010 847-381-0311
Sr. Ann Busch, prin. Fax 381-0384
St. Mark's Day S 200/PK-K
337 Ridge Rd 60010 847-381-9172
Fax 381-3564

Barry, Pike, Pop. 1,330
Western CUSD 12 500/PK-12
401 McDonough St 62312 217-335-2323
Rodger Hannel, supt. Fax 335-2211
www.westerncusd12.org/
Western Barry ES 200/PK-5
401 McDonough St 62312 217-335-2323
Greg Lesan, prin. Fax 335-2211
Other Schools – See Hull, Kinderhook

Bartelso, Clinton, Pop. 590
Bartelso ESD 57 200/K-8
PO Box 267 62218 618-765-2164
Dr. Karen Zellmer, supt. Fax 765-2712
www.schools.lth5.k12.il.us/bartelso
Bartelso S 200/K-8
PO Box 267 62218 618-765-2164
Dr. Karen Zellmer, prin. Fax 765-2712

Bartlett, Cook, Pop. 38,479
SD U-46
Supt. — See Elgin
Bartlett ES 600/K-6
111 E North Ave 60103 630-213-5545
Merle Erlich, prin. Fax 213-5544
Centennial ES 600/K-6
234 E Stearns Rd 60103 630-213-5632
Dr. Thomas Stiglic, prin. Fax 213-5630
Eastview MS 1,100/7-8
321 N Oak Ave 60103 630-213-5550
Donald Donner, prin. Fax 213-5563
Hawk Hollow ES 500/K-6
235 Jacaranda Dr 60103 630-540-7676
Pamela Snoeck, prin. Fax 372-3365
Independence Early Learning S 300/PK-PK
200 Taylor Ave 60103 630-213-5629
Lynn Reuter, prin. Fax 213-5584
Liberty ES 500/K-6
121 Naperville Rd 60103 630-540-7680
Steve Burger, prin. Fax 540-7666
Nature Ridge ES 700/PK-6
1899 Westridge Blvd 60103 630-372-4647
Terri Lozier, prin. Fax 372-4654
Prairieview ES 600/K-6
285 Mayflower Ln 60103 630-213-5603
Paul Flatley, prin. Fax 213-5588
Sycamore Trails ES 600/PK-6
1025 Sycamore Ln 60103 630-213-5641
Melody Huisinga, prin. Fax 213-5599

Bartlett Christian Academy 100/K-6
1500 W Stearns Rd 60103 630-504-0013
Jerry Gleason, hdmstr. Fax 830-9877

Bartonville, Peoria, Pop. 6,146
Bartonville SD 66 300/PK-8
6000 S Adams St 61607 309-697-3253
Shannon Duling, supt. Fax 697-3254
www.bartonville66.com/
Bartonville S 300/PK-8
6000 S Adams St 61607 309-697-3253
Shannon Duling, prin. Fax 697-3254

Monroe SD 70 300/K-8
5137 W Cisna Rd 61607 309-697-3120
Byron Sondgeroth, supt. Fax 697-3185
peoria.k12.il.us/monroe/
Monroe S, 5137 W Cisna Rd 61607 300/K-8
Byron Sondgeroth, prin. 309-697-3120

Oak Grove SD 68 500/K-8
4812 Pfeiffer Rd 61607 309-697-3367
Marc Devore, supt. Fax 633-2381
www.oakgrove.peoria.k12.il.us/
Oak Grove East ES 300/K-5
4812 Pfeiffer Rd 61607 309-697-3367
Marc Devore, prin. Fax 633-2381
Oak Grove West JHS 200/6-8
6018 W Lancaster Rd 61607 309-697-0621
Chad Wagner, prin. Fax 697-0721

Batavia, Kane, Pop. 27,172
Batavia Unit SD 101 6,300/PK-12
335 W Wilson St 60510 630-937-8800
Dr. Jack Barshinger, supt. Fax 937-8801
www.bps101.net
Gustafson ES 500/K-5
905 Carlisle Rd 60510 630-937-8000
Sandy Miller, prin. Fax 937-8001
Hoover - Wood ES 500/K-5
1640 Wagner Rd 60510 630-937-8300
Lew Girmscheid, prin. Fax 937-8301
McWayne ES 500/PK-5
3501 Hapner Way 60510 630-937-8100
Kevin Skomer, prin. Fax 937-8101
Nelson ES 400/K-5
334 William Wood Ln 60510 630-937-8400
Melissa Kaczkowski, prin. Fax 937-8401
Rotolo MS 1,400/6-8
1501 S Raddant Rd 60510 630-937-8700
Stephen Maciejewski, prin. Fax 937-8701
Storm ES 500/K-5
305 N Van Nortwick Ave 60510 630-937-8200
Cynthia Sikorski, prin. Fax 937-8201
White ES 500/K-5
800 N Prairie St 60510 630-937-8500
Sherry Whyte, prin. Fax 937-8501

Immanuel Lutheran S 300/PK-8
950 Hart Rd 60510 630-406-0157
Glenn Steinbrenner, prin. Fax 879-7614
Montessori Academy 100/PK-8
595 S River St 60510 630-879-2586
Stacie Benjamin, prin. Fax 761-1768

Beach Park, Lake, Pop. 12,486
Beach Park CCSD 3 2,500/PK-8
11315 W Wadsworth Rd 60099 847-599-5070
Dr. Robert Di Virgilio, supt. Fax 263-2133
www.bpd3.org/
Beach Park MS 900/PK-PK, 6-
40667 N Green Bay Rd 60099 847-731-6330
Rene Santiago, prin. Fax 731-2402
Howe ES 400/K-5
10271 W Beach Rd 60087 847-599-5362
Helene Delman, prin. Fax 623-5286
Murphy ES 500/PK-5
11315 W Wadsworth Rd 60099 847-599-5052
Paula Bieneman, prin. Fax 360-8635
Other Schools – See Wadsworth, Zion

Our Lady of Humility S 300/PK-8
10601 W Wadsworth Rd 60099 847-746-3722
Patrick Browne, prin. Fax 731-2870

Beardstown, Cass, Pop. 5,876
Beardstown CUSD 15 1,500/PK-12
500 E 15th St 62618 217-323-3099
Robert Bagby, supt. Fax 323-5190
www.beardstown.com/
Brick ES 100/1-4
10143 N Bluff Springs Rd 62618 217-323-1805
Robert Bagby, prin. Fax 323-1805
Gard ES 500/K-5
400 E 15th St 62618 217-323-1364
Cheryl Summers, prin. Fax 323-1364
Grand Avenue S 100/PK-PK
1301 Grand Ave 62618 217-323-1510
Pam Desollar, prin. Fax 323-5984

Beardstown Christian Academy 100/PK-8
1421 Beard St 62618 217-323-1685
Karen Underwood, admin. Fax 323-1421

Beckemeyer, Clinton, Pop. 1,071
Breese SD 12
Supt. — See Breese
Beckemeyer ES 200/2-4
PO Box 307 62219 618-227-8242
Melanie Becker, prin. Fax 227-8587

Bedford Park, Cook, Pop. 546
Summit SD 104
Supt. — See Summit
Walker ES 200/K-4
7735 W 66th Pl 60501 708-458-7150
Angel Gronkowski, prin. Fax 458-8466

Beecher, Will, Pop. 2,769
Beecher CUSD 200U 1,100/K-12
PO Box 338 60401 708-946-2266
George Obradovich, supt. Fax 946-3404
www.beecher.will.k12.il.us
Beecher ES 500/K-5
PO Box 308 60401 708-946-2202
Linda Goedke, prin. Fax 946-6075
Beecher JHS 300/6-8
101 E Church Rd 60401 708-946-3412
John Jennings, prin. Fax 946-2763

Zion Lutheran S 100/PK-8
PO Box 369 60401 708-946-2272
Fax 946-2611

Beecher City, Effingham, Pop. 498
Beecher City CUSD 20 400/PK-12
PO Box 98 62414 618-487-5100
Dr. Steve Launius, supt. Fax 487-5242
www.bcity.effingham.k12.il.us/
Beecher City ES 200/PK-PK, 3-
PO Box 98 62414 618-487-5108
Other Schools – See Shumway

Belle Rive, Jefferson, Pop. 378
Opdyke-Belle-Rive CCSD 5
Supt. — See Opdyke
Belle Rive ES 100/K-3
601 S Gum St 62810 618-756-2486
Elaine Hemker, prin. Fax 756-2481

Belleville, Saint Clair, Pop. 41,143
Belle Valley SD 119 900/PK-8
1901 Mascoutah Ave 62220 618-234-3445
Dr. Kenneth Hill, supt. Fax 234-7730
www.bellevalley.stclair.k12.il.us
Belle Valley ES North 500/PK-4
100 Andora Dr 62221 618-234-7750
Kathy Goetter, prin. Fax 234-5938
Belle Valley MS South 400/5-8
1901 Mascoutah Ave 62220 618-234-7723
Dr. Tamara Leib, prin. Fax 234-7980

Belleville SD 118 3,600/PK-8
105 W A St 62220 618-233-2830
Matt Klosterman, supt. Fax 233-8355
www.belleville118.org
Central JHS 400/7-8
1801 Central School Rd 62220 618-233-5377
Rocky Horrighs, prin. Fax 233-5440
Douglas ES 300/PK-PK, 1-
125 Carlyle Ave 62220 618-233-2417
Teresa Blomenkamp, prin. Fax 236-0593
Franklin ES 200/PK-PK, 1-
301 N 2nd St 62220 618-233-2413
Brian Mentzer, prin. Fax 236-2704
Jefferson ES 300/PK-PK, 1-
1400 N Charles St 62221 618-233-3798
Jamerson McCloskey, prin. Fax 236-2873
Lincoln ES 400/PK-PK, 1-
820 Royal Heights Rd 62226 618-233-2414
Edmund Langen, prin. Fax 236-2597
Raab ES 200/K-6
1120 Union Ave 62220 618-234-4330
Kim Enriquez, prin. Fax 236-2768
Roosevelt ES 400/K-6
700 W Cleveland Ave 62220 618-233-1608
Craig Hayes, prin. Fax 233-1757
Union ES 400/K-6
20 S 27th St 62226 618-233-4132
Lori Taylor, prin. Fax 236-2548
Washington K 100/PK-K
400 S Charles St 62220 618-277-2018
Kim Enriquez, prin. Fax 277-2504
Westhaven ES 500/PK-6
118 Westhaven School Rd 62220 618-257-9201
Jim Slater, prin. Fax 257-9310
West JHS 400/7-8
840 Royal Heights Rd 62226 618-234-8200
Pam Knobeloch, prin. Fax 234-8220

Harmony Emge SD 175 900/PK-8
7401 Westchester Dr 62223 618-397-8444
Dr. Gina Segobiano, supt. Fax 397-8446
www.harmony175.org/
Ellis ES 500/PK-4
250 Illini Dr 62223 618-397-5512
Pam Leonard, prin. Fax 397-4348
Emge JHS 400/5-8
7401 Westchester Dr 62223 618-397-6557
Brian Karraker, prin. Fax 397-3011

Signal Hill SD 181 400/PK-8
40 Signal Hill Pl 62223 618-397-0325
Suzette Lambert, supt. Fax 397-2828
Signal Hill S 400/PK-8
40 Signal Hill Pl 62223 618-397-0325
R. Dane Gale, prin. Fax 397-2828

Whiteside SD 115 1,300/PK-8
111 Warrior Way 62221 618-239-0000
Peggy Burke, supt. Fax 239-9240
www.whiteside.stclair.k12.il.us/
Whiteside ES 800/PK-4
2028 Lebanon Ave 62221 618-239-0000
Nathan Rakers, prin. Fax 233-7931
Whiteside MS 600/5-8
111 Warrior Way 62221 618-239-0000
Ron Trelow, prin. Fax 239-9240

Blessed Sacrament S 200/PK-8
8809 W Main St 62223 618-397-1111
Claire Hatch, prin. Fax 397-9114
Cathedral Grade S 200/PK-8
200 S 2nd St 62220 618-233-6414
Catherine Bennett, prin. Fax 233-3587
French Academy 200/PK-12
219 W Main St 62220 618-233-7542
Phillip Paeltz, hdmstr. Fax 233-0541
Our Lady Queen of Peace S 200/PK-8
5915 N Belt W 62223 618-234-1206
Sharon Needham, prin. Fax 234-6123
St. Mary/St. Augustine of Canterbury S 100/PK-8
1900 W Belle St 62226 618-234-4958
Linda Putz, prin. Fax 234-3360
St. Teresa S 300/PK-8
1108 Lebanon Ave 62221 618-235-4066
Dennis Grimmer, prin. Fax 235-7930

Zion Lutheran S 300/PK-8
1810 Mcclintock Ave 62221 618-234-0275
Gary Spieler, prin. Fax 233-2972

Bellwood, Cook, Pop. 19,517
Bellwood SD 88 2,500/PK-8
640 Eastern Ave 60104 708-344-9344
Kyle Hastings, supt. Fax 344-9416
www.sd88.org
ECC, 3519 Wilcox Ave 60104 200/PK-PK
Karen Mitchell, prin. 708-544-2815
Lincoln ES 400/K-6
3420 Jackson St 60104 708-544-3373
Carol Taylor, prin. Fax 544-0112
Marshall ES 300/PK-6
2501 Oak St 60104 708-544-6995
Joann Scott, prin. Fax 544-3338
McKinley ES 300/K-6
3317 Butterfield Rd 60104 708-544-5230
Paul Glover, prin. Fax 544-0134
Roosevelt MS 700/7-8
2500 Oak St 60104 708-544-3318
Mark Holder, prin. Fax 544-0192
Other Schools – See Melrose Park, Stone Park

Berkeley SD 87
Supt. — See Berkeley
Jefferson ES 400/PK-5
225 46th Ave 60104 708-449-3165
LaTesh Travis, prin. Fax 649-3046

Living Word Christian Academy 200/PK-8
501 Bellwood Ave 60104 708-697-6100
Theresa Byrd-Smith, prin. Fax 544-8618
Meca Christian S 200/PK-8
425 Bohland Ave 60104 708-547-9980
Pam Lawrence, dir. Fax 547-8715

Belvidere, Boone, Pop. 24,593
Belvidere CUSD 100 8,700/PK-12
1201 5th Ave 61008 815-544-0301
Michael Houselog, supt. Fax 544-4260
www.district100.com
Belvidere Central MS 1,100/6-8
8787 Beloit Rd 61008 815-544-0190
Harry Gries, prin. Fax 544-1128
Belvidere South MS 900/6-8
919 E 6th St 61008 815-544-3175
Peter Sloan, prin. Fax 544-2780
Lincoln ES 700/K-5
1011 Bonus Ave 61008 815-544-2671
Elizabeth Marchini, prin. Fax 547-4222
Meehan ES 600/K-5
1401 E 6th St 61008 815-547-3546
Jody Dahlseng, prin. Fax 547-3946
Perry ES 300/K-5
633 W Perry St 61008 815-544-9274
Sandra LaMendola, prin. Fax 544-1459
Washington ES 1,000/PK-5
1031 5th Ave 61008 815-544-3124
Jack Neil, prin. Fax 544-4182
Whitman ES 700/K-5
8989 Beloit Rd 61008 815-544-3357
Cynthia Connor, prin. Fax 547-7258
Other Schools – See Caledonia, Garden Prairie

Immanuel Lutheran S 300/PK-8
1225 E 2nd St 61008 815-547-5346
Judy Schaefer, prin. Fax 544-5704
Open Bible Academy 100/PK-5
8567 Town Hall Rd 61008 815-544-4499
St. James S 200/PK-8
320 Logan Ave 61008 815-547-7633
Gregory Wilhelm, prin. Fax 544-2294

Bement, Piatt, Pop. 1,739
Bement CUSD 5 400/PK-12
201 S Champaign St 61813 217-678-4200
Dr. Darrell Stevens, supt. Fax 678-4251
www.bement.k12.il.us
Bement ES 200/PK-5
201 S Champaign St 61813 217-678-4200
Matthew Jokisch, prin. Fax 678-4251
Bement MS 100/6-8
201 S Champaign St 61813 217-678-4200
Matthew Jokisch, prin. Fax 678-4251

Benld, Macoupin, Pop. 1,491
Gillespie CUSD 7
Supt. — See Gillespie
Benld ES 600/PK-5
100 E Dorsey St 62009 217-835-6611
Angela Turcol, prin. Fax 835-2119

Bensenville, DuPage, Pop. 20,514
Bensenville SD 2 2,300/PK-8
210 S Church Rd 60106 630-766-5940
Dr. William Jordan, supt. Fax 766-6099
www.bsd2.org
Blackhawk MS 800/6-8
250 S Church Rd 60106 630-766-2601
Gina Piraino, prin. Fax 766-7612
Chippewa ES 400/3-5
322 S York Rd 60106 630-766-7611
Lilith Werner, prin. Fax 766-4489
Johnson ES 300/K-5
252 Ridgewood Ave 60106 630-766-2605
Jennifer Ban, prin. Fax 616-5412
Mohawk ES 300/K-5
917 W Hillside Dr 60106 630-766-2604
Madelyn DiRienzo-Devers, prin. Fax 616-4138
Tioga ES 500/PK-2
212 W Memorial Rd 60106 630-766-2602
Amy Prester, prin. Fax 616-5408

Concord Lutheran S 100/PK-8
865 S Church St 60106 630-766-0228
Paul Kirk, prin. Fax 766-3902
St. Charles Borromeo S 100/PK-8
145 E Grand Ave 60106 630-766-0116
Sr. Mary Evans, prin. Fax 766-0181

Benson, Woodford, Pop. 407
Roanoke-Benson CUSD 60
Supt. — See Roanoke
Roanoke-Benson JHS 200/5-8
PO Box 137 61516 309-394-2233
Kris Kahler, prin. Fax 394-2612

Benton, Franklin, Pop. 6,930
Benton CCSD 47 1,100/PK-8
308 E Church St 62812 618-439-3136
Richard Cook, supt. Fax 435-4840
www.benton47.org/
Benton ES 600/PK-4
1000 E McKenzie St 62812 618-438-7181
Susan Krapf, prin. Fax 439-6112
Benton MS 500/5-8
1000 Forrest St 62812 618-438-4011
Jamie Neal, prin. Fax 435-2152

Berkeley, Cook, Pop. 5,006
Berkeley SD 87 2,900/PK-8
1200 N Wolf Rd 60163 708-449-3350
Eva Smith, supt. Fax 547-3341
www.berkeley87.org
MacArthur MS 500/6-8
1310 N Wolf Rd 60163 708-449-3185
Dr. Keith Wood, prin. Fax 649-3780
Sunnyside ES 500/PK-5
5412 Saint Charles Rd 60163 708-449-3170
Vickie Trotter, prin. Fax 649-3770
Other Schools – See Bellwood, Northlake

Berwyn, Cook, Pop. 51,409
Berwyn North SD 98 3,300/K-8
6633 16th St 60402 708-484-6200
John Belmont, supt. Fax 795-2482
Havlicek ES 700/K-5
6401 15th St 60402 708-795-2451
Nancy Akin, prin. Fax 795-0386
Jefferson ES 600/K-5
7035 16th St 60402 708-795-2454
Violet Tantillo, prin. Fax 795-2465
Lincoln MS 1,100/6-8
6432 16th St 60402 708-795-2475
Gail Quilty-Fejt, prin. Fax 795-2880
Prairie Oak ES 900/K-5
1427 Oak Park Ave 60402 708-795-2442
Evonne Waugh, prin. Fax 795-2443

Berwyn South SD 100 3,500/K-8
3401 Gunderson Ave Ste 1 60402 708-795-2300
Dr. Stanley Fields, supt. Fax 795-2317
www.bsd100.org/
Emerson ES 300/K-5
3105 Clinton Ave 60402 708-795-2322
Laura Massarella, prin. Fax 795-0821
Freedom MS 600/6-8
3016 Ridgeland Ave 60402 708-795-5800
James Calabrese, prin. Fax 795-5806
Heritage MS 600/6-8
6850 31st St 60402 708-749-6110
Leslie Hodes, prin. Fax 749-6124
Hiawatha ES 400/K-5
6539 26th St 60402 708-795-2327
Marilyn Williams, prin. Fax 795-1270
Irving ES 500/K-5
3501 Clinton Ave 60402 708-795-2334
Mary Havis, prin. Fax 795-2336
Komensky ES 400/K-5
2515 Cuyler Ave 60402 708-795-2342
Laura LaSalle, prin. Fax 795-1254
Pershing ES 400/K-5
6537 37th St 60402 708-795-2349
Karen Grindle, prin. Fax 795-1277
Piper ES 300/K-5
2435 Kenilworth Ave 60402 708-795-2364
John Fontanetta, prin. Fax 795-0140

St. Leonard S 300/PK-8
3322 Clarence Ave 60402 708-749-3666
Larry White, prin. Fax 749-7981
St. Odilo S 200/PK-8
6617 23rd St 60402 708-484-0755
William Donegan, prin. Fax 484-3088

Bethalto, Madison, Pop. 9,660
Bethalto CUSD 8 2,700/PK-12
610 Texas Blvd 62010 618-377-7200
Dr. Sandra Wilson, supt. Fax 377-2845
www.bethalto.org
Bethalto East PS 400/PK-3
309 Albers Pl 62010 618-377-7250
Karen Harris, prin. Fax 377-4107
Bethalto West IS 200/4-5
101 School St 62010 618-377-7260
Todd Hannaford, prin. Fax 377-7254
Parkside PS 500/PK-3
600 E Central St 62010 618-377-4100
Kim Heinz, prin. Fax 377-4105
Trimpe MS 600/6-8
910 2nd St 62010 618-377-7240
Kimberly Wilks, prin. Fax 377-7218
Other Schools – See Moro

Our Lady Queen of Peace S 200/PK-8
618 N Prairie St 62010 618-377-6401
Eve Remiszewski, prin. Fax 377-6146
Zion Lutheran S 300/PK-8
625 Church Dr 62010 618-377-5507
Sandra Balsters, prin. Fax 377-3630

Bethany, Moultrie, Pop. 1,261
Okaw Valley CUSD 302 500/PK-12
PO Box 97 61914 217-665-3232
Joel Hackney, supt. Fax 665-3601
www.okawvalley.org
Okaw Valley ES 200/PK-3
PO Box 98 61914 217-665-3541
Paula Duis, prin. Fax 665-3511
Other Schools – See Findlay

Biggsville, Henderson, Pop. 330
West Central CUSD 235 1,100/PK-12
RR 1 Box 72 61418 309-627-2371
Ralph Grimm, supt. Fax 627-2453
www.wc235.k12.il.us/
West Central ES 400/K-5
RR 1 Box 72 61418 309-627-2339
Dale Buss, prin. Fax 627-9919
Other Schools – See Media, Stronghurst

Big Rock, Kane, Pop. 710
Hinckley-Big Rock CUSD 429
Supt. — See Hinckley
Hinckley-Big Rock MS 100/6-8
47W984 US Highway 30 60511 630-556-4180
Jeff Strouss, prin. Fax 556-4181

Bismarck, Vermilion, Pop. 551
Bismarck-Henning CUSD 1 1,000/K-12
PO Box 350 61814 217-759-7261
Randy Hird, supt. Fax 759-7942
www.bismarck.k12.il.us
Bismarck-Henning ES 300/K-4
PO Box 50 61814 217-759-7251
Laura Girton, prin. Fax 759-7263
Bismarck-Henning JHS 300/5-8
PO Box 350 61814 217-759-7301
Rusty Campbell, prin. Fax 759-7313

Bloomingdale, DuPage, Pop. 21,924
Bloomingdale SD 13 1,400/K-8
164 Euclid Ave 60108 630-893-9590
Kim Perkins, supt. Fax 893-1818
www.sd13.org
Du Jardin ES 400/K-5
166 Euclid Ave 60108 630-894-9200
Mark Dwyer, prin. Fax 893-9545
Erickson ES 500/K-5
277 Springfield Dr 60108 630-529-2223
John Markgraf, prin. Fax 893-9849
Westfield MS 500/6-8
149 Fairfield Way 60108 630-529-6211
Debbie Kling, prin. Fax 893-9336

CCSD 93 4,300/PK-8
230 Covington Dr 60108 630-893-9393
William Shields Ed.D., supt. Fax 539-3450
www.ccsd93.com
Stratford MS 800/6-8
251 Butterfield Dr 60108 630-980-9898
Tom Doyle, prin. Fax 980-9914
Other Schools – See Carol Stream, Hanover Park

Marquardt SD 15
Supt. — See Glendale Heights
Winnebago ES 400/K-5
195 Greenway Dr 60108 630-893-1880
Mary Brandt, prin. Fax 307-6524

St. Isidore S 300/PK-8
431 W Army Trail Rd 60108 630-529-9323
Cyndi Collins, prin. Fax 529-8882

Bloomington, McLean, Pop. 69,749
Bloomington SD 87 5,200/K-12
300 E Monroe St 61701 309-827-6031
Robert Nielsen, supt. Fax 827-5717
www.district87.org
Bent ES 300/K-5
904 N Roosevelt Ave 61701 309-828-4315
Vickie Slagell, prin. Fax 828-3587
Bloomington JHS 1,300/6-8
901 Colton Ave 61701 309-827-0086
Dr. Susan Silvey, prin. Fax 829-0084
Irving ES 400/K-5
602 W Jackson St 61701 309-827-8091
Christina Brock-Lammers, prin. Fax 829-2295
Oakland ES 500/K-5
1605 E Oakland Ave 61701 309-662-4302
Dr. Mary Kay Scharf, prin. Fax 663-4385
Sheridan ES 400/K-5
1403 W Walnut St 61701 309-828-2359
Jim Cooper, prin. Fax 829-3209
Stevenson ES 400/K-5
2106 Arrowhead Dr 61704 309-663-2351
Tina Fogal, prin. Fax 827-3613
Washington ES 400/K-5
1201 E Washington St 61701 309-829-7034
Jeffrey Lockenvitz, prin. Fax 829-1207

McLean County Unit SD 5
Supt. — See Normal
Brigham ES 400/PK-5
201 Brigham School Rd 61704 309-862-5036
Geoff Schoonover, prin. Fax 828-4456
Fox Creek ES 300/K-5
3910 Timberwolf Trl, 309-452-1143
Mark Robinson, prin. Fax 827-0768
Northpoint ES 700/K-5
2602 E College Ave 61704 309-663-4669
Bruce Weldy, prin. Fax 452-4267
Pepper Ridge ES 500/K-5
2602 Danbury Dr, 309-452-1042
Sarah Edwards, prin. Fax 821-9122

Blooming Grove Academy 100/PK-8
510 E Washington St Ste 115 61701 309-827-2932
Vicki Kennedy, dir. Fax 827-2932
Cornerstone Christian Acad of McLean Co. 400/PK-12
PO Box 1608 61702 309-662-9900
Becky Shamess, admin. Fax 662-9904
Holy Trinity S 600/PK-8
705 N Roosevelt Ave 61701 309-828-7151
Kay O'Brien, prin. Fax 827-8131
St. Mary S 200/PK-8
603 W Jackson St 61701 309-828-5954
Mark Csanda, prin. Fax 829-3061
Trinity Lutheran S 400/PK-8
1102 W Hamilton Rd 61704 309-829-7513
Shawn Hoffmann, prin. Fax 834-3237

Blue Island, Cook, Pop. 22,788
Cook County SD 130 — 3,900/PK-8
12300 Greenwood Ave 60406 — 708-385-6800
Dr. Michael Korsak, supt. — Fax 385-8467
www.district130.org/
Greenbriar S — PK-PK
12015 Maple Ave 60406 — 708-385-2915
Dr. Carol Crum, prin. — Fax 385-8467
Greenwood K — K-K
12418 Highland Ave 60406 — 708-385-3399
Marlene Talaski, prin.
Kerr MS — 400/6-8
12915 Maple Ave 60406 — 708-385-5959
Carl Gmazel, prin. — Fax 371-6812
Lincoln ES — 600/K-3
2140 Broadway St 60406 — 708-385-5370
Hope Forberg, prin. — Fax 385-8467
Revere IS — 300/4-5
12331 Gregory St 60406 — 708-385-4450
Wendy Bumphis, prin. — Fax 385-8467
Revere PS — 500/K-3
2300 123rd Pl 60406 — 708-489-3533
Theresa Gonzalez-Silva, prin. — Fax 385-8467
Veterans Memorial MS — 400/6-8
12320 Greenwood Ave 60406 — 708-489-6630
Michael McLaughlin, prin. — Fax 489-3522
Whittier ES — 300/4-5
13043 Maple Ave 60406 — 708-385-6170
Joseph Talluto, prin. — Fax 371-2354
Other Schools – See Alsip, Crestwood

St. Benedict S — 200/PK-8
2324 New St 60406 — 708-385-2016
Susan Rys, prin. — Fax 385-4490

Blue Mound, Macon, Pop. 1,056
Meridian CUSD 15
Supt. — See Macon
Meridian IS — 300/PK-PK, 3-
PO Box 350 62513 — 217-692-2535
Paul Carlton, prin. — Fax 692-2013
Meridian MS — 200/6-8
PO Box 320 62513 — 217-692-2148
Andrew Pygott, prin. — Fax 692-2039

Bluffs, Scott, Pop. 729
Scott-Morgan CUSD 2 — 300/PK-12
PO Box 230 62621 — 217-754-3351
Donna Emrick, supt. — Fax 754-3908
www.bluffs-school.com/
Bluffs ES — 100/PK-5
PO Box 230 62621 — 217-754-3714
Roxanne Filson, prin. — Fax 754-3908
Bluffs JHS — 100/6-8
PO Box 230 62621 — 217-754-3815
Roxanne Filson, prin. — Fax 754-3908

Bluford, Jefferson, Pop. 773
Bluford CCSD 114 — 300/PK-8
PO Box 19 62814 — 618-732-8242
Scott Porter, supt. — Fax 732-6114
www.blufordschools.org/default.htm
Bluford S — 300/PK-8
PO Box 19 62814 — 618-732-8242
Scott Porter, prin. — Fax 732-6114

Farrington CCSD 99 — 100/K-8
20941 E Divide Rd 62814 — 618-755-4414
Monte Jo Clark, supt. — Fax 755-4461
209.175.207.86/
Farrington S — 100/K-8
20941 E Divide Rd 62814 — 618-755-4414
Monte Jo Clark, prin. — Fax 755-4461

Bolingbrook, Will, Pop. 68,365
Indian Prairie CUSD 204
Supt. — See Aurora
Builta ES — 700/K-5
1835 Apple Valley Rd 60490 — 630-226-4400
Maranda VanWaning, prin. — Fax 226-4401

Plainfield CCSD 202
Supt. — See Plainfield
Liberty ES — 1,100/K-5
1401 Essington Rd 60490 — 815-609-3037
Raymond Epperson, prin. — Fax 609-5963

Valley View CUSD 365U
Supt. — See Romeoville
Addams MS — 700/6-8
905 Lily Cache Ln 60440 — 630-759-7200
Chris Schaeflein, prin. — Fax 759-6362
Brooks MS — 1,300/6-8
350 Blair Ln 60440 — 630-759-6340
Ronald Krause, prin. — Fax 759-6360
Humphrey MS — 800/6-8
777 Falconridge Way 60440 — 630-972-9240
Angelo Armistead, prin. — Fax 739-8521
Independence ES — 600/PK-5
230 S Orchard Dr 60440 — 630-759-7282
Kim Mulcahy, prin. — Fax 759-6366
McGee ES — 600/K-5
179 Commonwealth Dr 60440 — 630-759-4300
Michael Zolecki, prin. — Fax 759-6363
Oak View ES — 800/K-5
150 N Schmidt Rd 60440 — 630-759-9300
Anitra McGlothin, prin. — Fax 759-6359
Pioneer ES — 900/K-5
1470 Raven Dr 60490 — 630-771-2420
Sandra Robertson, prin. — Fax 771-0199
Salk ES — 500/PK-5
500 King Arthur Way 60440 — 630-739-3603
Michele Romolt, prin. — Fax 739-8518
Tibbott ES — 700/K-5
520 Gary Dr 60440 — 630-739-7155
Ana Wilson, prin. — Fax 739-8522
Ward ES — 600/K-5
200 Recreation Dr 60440 — 630-972-9200
Ted Warpinski, prin. — Fax 972-9420
Wood View ES — 500/K-5
197 Winston Dr 60440 — 630-739-0185
Mark Stange, prin. — Fax 739-8517

New Beginnings Christian Montessori S — 100/PK-8
151 E Briarcliff Rd 60440 — 630-783-9174
St. Dominic S — 300/PK-8
420 E Briarcliff Rd 60440 — 630-739-1633
Bill Eggebrecht, prin. — Fax 739-5989

Bonfield, Kankakee, Pop. 373
Herscher CUSD 2
Supt. — See Herscher
Bonfield ES — 200/4-5
522 E Smith St 60913 — 815-933-6995
Dennis Pankey, prin. — Fax 936-4125

Bourbonnais, Kankakee, Pop. 16,875
Bourbonnais ESD 53 — 2,600/PK-8
281 W John Casey Rd 60914 — 815-929-5100
Myron Palomba Ph.D., supt. — Fax 939-0481
www.besd53.k12.il.us
Bourbonnais Upper Grade Center — 600/7-8
200 W John Casey Rd 60914 — 815-929-5200
Jon Hodge, prin. — Fax 935-7849
Frost S — 400/PK-K
160 W River St 60914 — 815-929-5300
Dan Chamernik, prin. — Fax 935-7847
Levasseur ES — 300/1-4
601 W Bethel Dr 60914 — 815-929-4500
Jeff Gindy, prin. — Fax 935-7856
Liberty IS — 600/5-6
1690 Career Center Rd 60914 — 815-929-5000
Mary Ann Bicknell, prin. — Fax 929-2467
Shabbona ES — 300/1-4
321 N Convent St 60914 — 815-929-4700
Abby Saldivar, prin. — Fax 935-7846
Shepard ES — 500/K-4
325 N Convent St 60914 — 815-929-4600
Shirley Padera, prin. — Fax 935-7834

Saint George CCSD 258 — 300/K-8
5200 E Center St 60914 — 815-933-1503
Dr. Richard Angel, supt. — Fax 802-3102
www.stgeorge.k12.il.us
Saint George S — 300/K-8
5200 E Center St 60914 — 815-933-1503
John Snipes, prin. — Fax 933-1562

Maternity of the B V M S — 300/PK-8
324 E Marsile St 60914 — 815-933-7758
Terry Granger, prin. — Fax 933-1884
St. Paul Lutheran S — 200/PK-8
1780 Career Center Rd 60914 — 815-932-0312
Robert Freymark, prin. — Fax 932-7588

Bowen, Hancock, Pop. 508
Southeastern CUSD 337
Supt. — See Augusta
Southeastern ES — 100/PK-6
PO Box 247 62316 — 217-842-5236
Nancy Akers, prin. — Fax 842-5248

Braceville, Grundy, Pop. 815
Braceville SD 75 — 200/K-8
209 N Mitchell St 60407 — 815-237-8040
James Monfredini, supt. — Fax 237-8044
Braceville S — 200/K-8
209 N Mitchell St 60407 — 815-237-8040
James Monfredini, prin. — Fax 237-8044

Bradford, Stark, Pop. 765
Bradford CUSD 1 — 200/PK-8
PO Box 400 61421 — 309-897-2801
Ellin Lotspeich, supt. — Fax 897-4451
Bradford ES — 200/PK-5
PO Box 400 61421 — 309-897-4441
Ellin Lotspeich, prin. — Fax 897-8361
Bradford JHS, PO Box 400 61421 — 100/6-8
Ellin Lotspeich, prin. — 309-897-4441

Bradley, Kankakee, Pop. 13,812
Bradley SD 61 — 1,500/PK-8
111 N Crosswell Ave 60915 — 815-933-3371
Scott Goselin, supt. — Fax 939-6601
www.bradleyschools.com/
Bradley Central MS — 500/6-8
260 N Wabash Ave 60915 — 815-939-3564
Todd Schweizer, prin. — Fax 939-6603
Bradley East ES — 500/PK-2
610 Liberty St 60915 — 815-933-2233
Michael Hahs, prin. — Fax 933-3810
Bradley West ES — 500/3-5
200 State St 60915 — 815-933-2216
Dave Andriano, prin. — Fax 933-2071

St. Joseph S — 300/PK-8
247 N Center Ave 60915 — 815-933-8013
Sr. Mary Hettel, prin. — Fax 933-2775

Braidwood, Will, Pop. 6,320
Reed-Custer CUSD 255U — 1,900/PK-12
255 Comet Dr 60408 — 815-458-2307
John Asplund, supt. — Fax 458-4106
www.rc255.will.k12.il.us/
Reed-Custer IS — 400/PK-PK, 3-
162 S School St 60408 — 815-458-2145
Robin Bauer, prin. — Fax 458-4106
Reed-Custer MS — 400/6-8
407 Comet Dr 60408 — 815-458-2868
Michael Grace, prin. — Fax 458-4118
Other Schools – See Custer Park

Breese, Clinton, Pop. 4,202
Breese SD 12 — 700/PK-8
777 Memorial Dr 62230 — 618-526-7128
Michael Gauch, supt. — Fax 526-2787
www.bobcatslair.com
Breese S — 500/PK-8
777 Memorial Dr 62230 — 618-526-7128
Jered Weh, prin. — Fax 526-2787
Other Schools – See Beckemeyer

Saint Rose SD 14-15 — 200/PK-8
18004 Saint Rose Rd 62230 — 618-526-7484
Dr. Patricia Cornell, supt. — Fax 526-7168
www.strosedistrict14-15.com/
Saint Rose S — 200/PK-8
18004 Saint Rose Rd 62230 — 618-526-7484
Dr. Patricia Cornell, prin. — Fax 526-7168

All Saints Academy — 400/PK-8
295 N Clinton St 62230 — 618-526-4323
Robin Booth, prin. — Fax 526-2547

Bridgeport, Lawrence, Pop. 2,148
Red Hill CUSD 10 — 1,100/PK-12
1250 Judy Ave 62417 — 618-945-2061
Dennis Kimmel, supt. — Fax 945-7607
www.red.lawrnc.k12.il.us
Bridgeport Grade S — 400/PK-6
1300 N Main St 62417 — 618-945-5721
Deana Brashear, prin. — Fax 945-7111
Other Schools – See Sumner

Bridgeview, Cook, Pop. 14,933
Indian Springs SD 109
Supt. — See Justice
Bridgeview ES — 400/K-6
7800 Thomas Ave 60455 — 708-496-8713
Crystal Skoczylas, prin. — Fax 496-1142
Lyle ES & ECC — 600/PK-6
7801 W 75th St 60455 — 708-496-8722
Christine Baldwin, prin. — Fax 728-3120

Ridgeland SD 122
Supt. — See Oak Lawn
Lieb ES — 400/K-5
9101 Pembroke Ln 60455 — 708-599-1050
Gregory Porod, prin. — Fax 599-8189

Universal S — 700/PK-12
7350 W 93rd St 60455 — 708-599-4100
Farhat Siddiqui, prin. — Fax 599-1588

Brighton, Macoupin, Pop. 2,324
Southwestern CUSD 9
Supt. — See Piasa
Brighton North ES — 500/2-6
PO Box 757 62012 — 618-372-3162
Scott Hopkins, prin. — Fax 372-4915
Brighton West ES — 200/PK-1
PO Box 728 62012 — 618-372-3813
Christy Willman, prin. — Fax 372-4681

Brimfield, Peoria, Pop. 900
Brimfield CUSD 309 — 700/PK-12
216 E Clinton St 61517 — 309-446-3378
Dennis McNamara, supt. — Fax 446-3716
peoria.k12.il.us/brimfield309/
Brimfield Grade S — 500/PK-8
216 E Clinton St 61517 — 309-446-3366
Dennis McNamara, prin. — Fax 446-9500

Bristol, Kendall
Yorkville CUSD 115
Supt. — See Yorkville
Bristol ES — 300/K-3
PO Box 177 60512 — 630-553-4383
Chris Silagi, prin. — Fax 553-4459

Broadlands, Champaign, Pop. 308
Heritage CUSD 8 — 600/PK-12
PO Box 260 61816 — 217-834-3393
Andrew Larson, supt. — Fax 834-3016
www.heritage.k12.il.us
Other Schools – See Homer

Broadview, Cook, Pop. 7,856
Lindop SD 92 — 500/PK-8
2400 S 18th Ave 60155 — 708-345-8834
Karen Carlson Ph.D., supt. — Fax 345-8950
www.lindop92.net/
Lindop S — 500/PK-8
2400 S 18th Ave 60155 — 708-345-3110
DarLynn Terry, prin. — Fax 345-8569

Maywood-Melrose Park-Broadview SD 89
Supt. — See Melrose Park
Roosevelt S — 400/PK-8
1927 S 15th Ave 60155 — 708-450-2047
Dr. Cynthia Hines-Butler, prin. — Fax 344-1179

Brookfield, Cook, Pop. 18,462
Brookfield Lagrange Park SD 95 — 900/K-8
3524 Maple Ave 60513 — 708-485-0606
Thomas Hurlburt, supt. — Fax 485-8066
www.district95.org
Gross MS — 400/5-8
3524 Maple Ave 60513 — 708-485-0600
Todd Fitzgerald, prin. — Fax 485-0638
Other Schools – See La Grange Park

La Grange SD 102
Supt. — See La Grange Park
Congress Park ES — 500/PK-6
9311 Shields Ave 60513 — 708-482-2430
M. Maura Stockmann, prin. — Fax 482-2437

Lyons SD 103
Supt. — See Lyons
Lincoln ES — 400/K-5
4300 Grove Ave 60513 — 708-783-4600
Kathrine McCarthy, prin. — Fax 780-2485

Riverside SD 96
Supt. — See Riverside
Hollywood ES — 100/K-5
3423 Hollywood Ave 60513 — 708-485-7630
Victoria DeVylder, prin. — Fax 485-7925

St. Barbara S — 200/PK-8
8900 Windemere Ave 60513 — 708-485-0806
Janet Erazmus, prin. — Fax 485-2343

St. Paul Lutheran S 100/K-8
9035 Grant Ave 60513 708-485-0650
Fax 485-7448

Brookport, Massac, Pop. 1,061
Massac Unit SD 1
Supt. — See Metropolis
Brookport ES 200/PK-6
PO Box 278 62910 618-564-2482
Debbie Christiansen, prin. Fax 564-3509
Unity S 200/K-8
6846 Unity School Rd 62910 618-564-2582
Randy McDearmon, prin. Fax 564-2014

Brownstown, Fayette, Pop. 708
Brownstown CUSD 201 400/PK-12
421 S College Ave 62418 618-427-3355
Doug Slover, supt. Fax 427-3704
www.bhs.fayette.k12.il.us/Html/Unit/bhsunit1.htm
Brownstown ES 200/PK-6
460 W South St 62418 618-427-3368
Jeanine Wendling, prin. Fax 427-5247
Brownstown JHS 100/7-8
421 S College Ave 62418 618-427-3839
Steve Wilson, prin. Fax 427-3704

Brussels, Calhoun, Pop. 145
Brussels CUSD 42 100/K-12
128 School St 62013 618-883-2131
Tom Knuckles, supt. Fax 883-2514
www.schools.lth5.k12.il.us/brussels/
Brussels ES 100/K-6
128 School St 62013 618-883-2131
Tom Knuckles, prin. Fax 883-2514

St. Mary S 50/K-8
PO Box 39 62013 618-883-2124
Brenda Paynic, prin. Fax 883-2511

Buckley, Iroquois, Pop. 576

St. John Lutheran S 100/PK-8
PO Box 148 60918 217-394-2422
Danny Sandmann, prin. Fax 394-2422

Buda, Bureau, Pop. 581
Bureau Valley CUSD 340
Supt. — See Manlius
Bureau Valley South S 200/3-8
PO Box 277 61314 309-895-2037
Denise Bolin, prin. Fax 895-2200

Buffalo, Sangamon, Pop. 463
Tri-City CUSD 1 600/PK-12
PO Box 290 62515 217-364-4811
David Bruno, supt. Fax 364-4812
www.tc.sangamon.k12.il.us
Tri-City ES 300/PK-5
PO Box 290 62515 217-364-4035
Kara Cummins, prin. Fax 364-4812
Tri-City JHS 200/6-8
PO Box 290 62515 217-364-4530
Duane Schupp, prin. Fax 364-4812

Buffalo Grove, Cook, Pop. 43,115
Aptakisic-Tripp CCSD 102 2,100/PK-8
1231 Weiland Rd 60089 847-353-5660
Dr. John Mink, supt. Fax 634-5334
www.d102.org
Aptakisic JHS 600/7-8
1231 Weiland Rd 60089 847-353-5500
Mark Kuzniewski, prin. Fax 634-5347
Meridian MS 500/5-6
2195 Brandywyn Ln 60089 847-955-3500
Rebecca Jenkins, prin. Fax 634-4229
Pritchett ES 500/PK-4
200 Horatio Blvd 60089 847-353-5700
Dr. Matt Moreland, prin. Fax 215-3259
Tripp ES 600/PK-4
850 Highland Grove Dr 60089 847-955-3600
Julie Brua, prin. Fax 215-3268

Kildeer Countryside CCSD 96 3,400/PK-8
1050 Ivy Hall Ln 60089 847-459-4260
Dr. Thomas Many, supt. Fax 459-2344
www.district96.k12.il.us
Ivy Hall ES 500/1-5
1072 Ivy Hall Ln 60089 847-459-0022
Jennifer Brown, prin. Fax 229-9650
Prairie ES 400/1-5
1530 Brandywyn Ln 60089 847-634-3144
Greg Kleckner, prin. Fax 821-7571
Twin Groves MS 600/6-8
2600 N Buffalo Grove Rd 60089 847-821-8946
Marie Schalke, prin. Fax 821-8949
Willow Grove K 300/PK-K
777 Checker Dr 60089 847-541-3660
Barbara Cirigliano, prin. Fax 821-7572
Other Schools – See Long Grove

Wheeling CCSD 21
Supt. — See Wheeling
Cooper MS 800/6-8
1050 Plum Grove Cir 60089 847-520-2750
Dr. Pamela Kibbons, prin. Fax 419-3071
Kilmer ES 400/K-5
655 Golfview Ter 60089 847-520-2760
Kim Zinman, prin. Fax 520-2601
Longfellow ES 500/K-5
501 Arlington Heights Rd 60089 847-520-2755
Debra Serbin, prin. Fax 419-3078

Buffalo Grove Montessori S 100/PK-K
950 Ellen Dr 60089 847-541-8111
Deborah LaPorte, prin. Fax 541-8169
St. Mary S 500/PK-8
50 N Buffalo Grove Rd 60089 847-459-6270
Gary Campione, prin. Fax 537-2810

Buncombe, Johnson, Pop. 209
Buncombe Consolidated SD 43 100/K-8
PO Box 40 62912 618-658-8830
Steve Karraker, supt. Fax 658-8830
www.buncombegradeschool.com/
Buncombe Consolidated S 100/K-8
PO Box 40 62912 618-658-8830
Steve Karraker, prin. Fax 658-8830

Lick Creek CCSD 16 100/PK-8
7355 Lick Creek Rd 62912 618-833-2545
Rob Wright, supt. Fax 833-3201
www.lcschool.union.k12.il.us/
Lick Creek S 100/PK-8
7355 Lick Creek Rd 62912 618-833-2545
Rob Wright, prin. Fax 833-3201

Bunker Hill, Macoupin, Pop. 1,795
Bunker Hill CUSD 8 800/PK-12
504 E Warren St 62014 618-585-3116
Marg Rogers, supt. Fax 585-3212
bhschools.org
Meissner JHS 200/PK-PK, 6-
504 E Warren St 62014 618-585-4464
Brad Skertich, prin. Fax 585-3222
Wolf Ridge Education Center 300/K-5
700 W Orange St 62014 618-585-4831
Brad Skertich, prin. Fax 585-3123

Burbank, Cook, Pop. 27,634
Burbank SD 111 3,700/PK-8
7600 Central Ave 60459 708-496-0500
Dr. Thomas Long, supt. Fax 496-0510
www.burbank.k12.il.us
Burbank ES 500/K-6
8235 Linder Ave 60459 708-499-0838
Dr. Robert Mocek, prin. Fax 499-0502
Byrd ES 300/K-6
8259 Lavergne Ave 60459 708-499-3049
Dr. Marian Stockhausen, prin. Fax 499-1002
Fry ES 500/K-6
7805 Mobile Ave 60459 708-599-5554
Mary Rein, prin. Fax 599-1348
Kennedy ES 400/K-6
7644 Central Ave 60459 708-496-0563
Charles Roza, prin. Fax 496-8365
Liberty JHS 800/7-8
5900 W 81st St 60459 708-952-3255
James Martin, prin. Fax 229-0659
Maddock ES 400/K-6
8258 Sayre Ave 60459 708-598-0515
Sharon Walker-Hood, prin. Fax 233-6401
McCord ES 400/PK-6
8450 Nashville Ave 60459 708-599-4411
Patricia Donoghue, prin. Fax 233-9104
Tobin ES 400/K-6
8501 Narragansett Ave 60459 708-599-6655
Dr. Mary Sheehan, prin. Fax 233-9014

St. Albert the Great S 200/PK-8
5535 State Rd 60459 708-424-7757
Marilyn Kurowski, prin. Fax 636-6477

Bureau, Bureau, Pop. 370
Leepertown CCSD 175 50/K-8
PO Box 170 61315 815-659-3191
Amber Harper, supt. Fax 659-3073
Leepertown S 50/K-8
PO Box 170 61315 815-659-3191
Amber Harper, prin. Fax 659-3073

Burlington, Kane, Pop. 487
Central CUSD 301 2,900/PK-12
PO Box 396 60109 847-464-6005
Todd Stirn, supt. Fax 464-6021
www.burlington.k12.il.us/
Central MS 700/6-8
PO Box 397 60109 847-464-6000
Lloyd Stover, prin. Fax 464-1709
Thomas ES 500/PK-5
PO Box 395 60109 847-464-6008
Jan Harnish, prin. Fax 464-6022
Other Schools – See Elgin, Maple Park

Burnham, Cook, Pop. 4,080
Burnham SD 154-5 200/PK-8
13945 S Green Bay Ave 60633 708-862-8636
Al Vega, supt. Fax 862-8638
Burnham S 200/PK-8
13945 S Green Bay Ave 60633 708-862-8636
Wendy Whited, prin. Fax 862-8638

Burr Ridge, DuPage, Pop. 10,949
CCSD 180 800/PK-8
15W451 91st St 60527 630-734-6600
Dr. Thomas Schneider, supt. Fax 325-6450
www.ccsd180.org
Burr Ridge MS 300/5-8
15W451 91st St 60527 630-325-5454
Julie Bartell, prin. Fax 325-6450
Other Schools – See Willowbrook

CCSD 181
Supt. — See Westmont
Elm ES 300/K-5
15W201 60th St 60527 630-887-1380
Jeana Considine, prin. Fax 655-9734

Gower SD 62
Supt. — See Willowbrook
Gower MS 500/5-8
7941 S Madison St 60527 630-323-8275
Rebecca Laratta, prin. Fax 323-2055

Pleasantdale SD 107 800/PK-8
7450 Wolf Rd 60527 708-784-2013
Dr. Mark Fredisdorf, supt. Fax 246-0161
www.d107.org/
Pleasantdale MS 300/5-8
7450 Wolf Rd 60527 708-246-3210
Meg Pokorny, prin. Fax 352-0092
Other Schools – See La Grange

Trinity Lutheran S 100/PK-8
11503 German Church Rd 60527 708-839-1444
Neil Hammes, prin. Fax 839-8503

Bushnell, McDonough, Pop. 3,022
Bushnell-Prairie City CUSD 170 800/PK-12
845 Walnut St 61422 309-772-9461
David Messersmith, supt. Fax 772-9462
www.bushnell-pc.k12.il.us/
Bushnell-Prairie City ES 400/PK-5
345 E Hess St 61422 309-772-9464
JoEllen Pensinger, prin. Fax 772-9466
Bushnell-Prairie City JHS 200/6-8
847 Walnut St 61422 309-772-3123
Mike Snowden, prin. Fax 772-2666

Byron, Ogle, Pop. 3,582
Byron CUSD 226 1,700/PK-12
696 N Colfax St 61010 815-234-5491
Dr. Margaret Fostiak, supt. Fax 234-4106
leeogle.org/byron/
Byron MS 400/6-8
325 N Colfax St 61010 815-234-5491
Steve Herkert, prin. Fax 234-4225
Morgan ES 700/PK-5
420 N Colfax St 61010 815-234-5491
Buster Barton, prin. Fax 234-4094

Cahokia, Saint Clair, Pop. 15,608
Cahokia CUSD 187 4,600/PK-12
1700 Jerome Ln 62206 618-332-3700
Jana Bechtoldt, supt. Fax 332-3706
www.cahokia.stclair.k12.il.us
Centerville S 400/K-8
3429 Camp Jackson Rd 62206 618-332-3727
Lela Prince, prin. Fax 332-3788
Cohokia S of Choice K-12
1820 Jerome Ln 62206 618-332-1915
Gustavo Cotto-Rodriguez, prin. Fax 332-1918
Huffman S 300/K-8
600 Saint Robert Dr 62206 618-332-3720
Mary Johnson, prin. Fax 332-3782
Jerome ECC 200/PK-PK
1825 Jerome Ln 62206 618-332-3716
Karen Thompson, prin. Fax 332-3786
Maplewood S 300/K-8
600 Jerome Ln 62206 618-332-3709
Victoria White, prin. Fax 332-3787
Morris S 300/K-8
1500 Andrews Dr 62206 618-332-3718
Gloria Perry, prin. Fax 332-3785
Penniman S 400/K-8
300 Annunciation Ct 62206 618-332-3716
Kevin Bement, prin. Fax 337-6697
Wirth School of Choice 1,000/K-8
1900 Mousette Ln 62206 618-332-3722
Tony Brooks, prin. Fax 332-3741
Other Schools – See East Saint Louis

Holy Family Catholic S 100/K-8
116 E 1st St 62206 618-337-2880
Lindy Graves, prin. Fax 337-7898

Cairo, Alexander, Pop. 3,342
Cairo Unit SD 1 700/PK-12
2403 Dr Martin Luther King 62914 618-734-4102
Dr. Leotis Swopes, supt. Fax 734-4047
Bennett ES 200/3-6
434 18th St 62914 618-734-0344
Rose Gayle Pickett, prin. Fax 734-1447
Emerson ES 200/PK-2
3101 Elm St 62914 618-734-1027
Allene Houston, prin. Fax 734-1806

Caledonia, Boone, Pop. 221
Belvidere CUSD 100
Supt. — See Belvidere
Caledonia ES 600/K-5
2311 Randolph St 61011 815-765-2081
Sara Kirchner, prin. Fax 765-1803

Calumet City, Cook, Pop. 37,795
Calumet City SD 155 1,200/K-8
540 Superior Ave 60409 708-862-7665
Dr. Troy Paraday, supt. Fax 868-7555
www.calumetcity155.org/
Wentworth IS 400/3-5
530 Superior Ave 60409 708-868-7926
Linda Drake, prin. Fax 868-7671
Wentworth JHS 500/6-8
560 Superior Ave 60409 708-862-0750
Ermetra Olawumi, prin. Fax 862-1194
Wilson ES 400/K-2
560 Wentworth Ave 60409 708-862-5166
Delores Lyke, prin. Fax 868-7086

Dolton SD 149 3,600/PK-8
292 Torrence Ave 60409 708-868-7861
Traci Brown, supt. Fax 868-7850
www.schooldistrict149.org
Braun ES 300/1-5
1655 153rd St 60409 708-868-9470
Jamie Hayes, prin. Fax 868-9466
Dirksen MS 1,100/6-8
1650 Pulaski Rd 60409 708-868-2340
Brigitte Garth-Young, prin. Fax 868-7589
Sibley ES 900/K-6
1550 Sibley Blvd 60409 708-868-1870
Gabrielle Herndon, prin. Fax 868-7591
Other Schools – See Dolton, South Holland

Hoover-Schrum Memorial SD 157 900/PK-8
1255 Superior Ave 60409 708-868-7500
Dr. Michele Morris, supt. Fax 868-7511
www.hsdist157.org
Hoover ES 600/PK-5
1260 Superior Ave 60409 708-862-6530
Kathy Bearden-Colbert, prin. Fax 832-3713
Schrum Memorial MS 300/6-8
485 165th St 60409 708-862-4236
Dr. Bennie Knott, prin. Fax 862-4580

Lincoln ESD 156 1,100/PK-8
410 157th St 60409 708-862-6625
Darryl Taylor, supt. Fax 862-1227
www.l156.org
Lincoln S 1,100/PK-8
410 157th St 60409 708-862-6620
Douglas Higgins, prin. Fax 862-1510

Christ Our Savior S East Campus 200/PK-8
320 156th St 60409 708-862-4143
Cynthia Rogers, prin.

Calumet Park, Cook, Pop. 8,124
Calumet Public SD 132 1,200/PK-8
1440 W Vermont Ave 60827 708-388-8920
Dr. Elizabeth Reynolds, supt. Fax 388-2138
www.sd132.org/
Burr Oak Academy 400/PK-2
1441 W 124th St 60827 708-824-3090
Darlett Lawrence, prin. Fax 388-1211
Burr Oak S 400/3-5
1440 W 125th St 60827 708-388-8010
Carole Willis-Ayanlaja, prin. Fax 389-5835
Calumet MS 400/6-8
1440 W Vermont Ave 60827 708-388-8820
Reginald Miller, prin. Fax 388-8557

Cambridge, Henry, Pop. 2,121
Cambridge CUSD 227 500/PK-12
300 S West St 61238 309-937-2144
Thomas Akers, supt. Fax 937-5128
cambridge.il.schoolwebpages.com/
Cambridge Community ES 300/PK-6
312 S West St 61238 309-937-2028
Shelly Logston, prin. Fax 937-5219
Cambridge JHS 100/7-8
300 S West St 61238 309-937-2051
Robert Reagan, prin. Fax 937-5128

Campbell Hill, Jackson, Pop. 314
Trico CUSD 176 900/K-12
PO Box 220 62916 618-426-1111
John DeNosky, supt. Fax 426-3625
www.trico176.org
Trico ES 400/K-5
PO Box 305 62916 618-426-1111
Jerry Ohlau, prin. Fax 426-3988
Trico JHS 200/6-8
PO Box 335 62916 618-426-1111
Jack Smith, prin. Fax 426-3712

Camp Point, Adams, Pop. 1,191
Central CUSD 3 1,000/K-12
2110 Highway 94 N 62320 217-593-7116
Martin Cook, supt. Fax 593-7026
www.cusd3.com/
Central ES 200/K-2
PO Box 379 62320 217-593-7795
Eric Stotts, prin. Fax 593-6514
Central JHS 300/5-8
2110 Highway 94 N 62320 217-593-7741
Donna Veile, prin. Fax 593-7028
Other Schools – See Golden

Canton, Fulton, Pop. 14,938
Canton Union SD 66 2,700/PK-12
20 W Walnut St 61520 309-647-9411
Roy Webb, supt. Fax 649-5036
www.cantonusd.org
Eastview ES 500/K-4
1490 E Myrtle St 61520 309-647-0136
Martha Davis, prin. Fax 647-3430
Ingersoll MS 800/5-8
1605 E Ash St 61520 309-647-6951
Lan Eberle, prin. Fax 647-6959
Lincoln ES 200/K-4
20 Lincoln Rd 61520 309-647-7594
SueEllen Stephenson, prin. Fax 647-2043
Westview ES 400/PK-4
700 Old West Vine St 61520 309-647-2111
Joan Hoschek, prin. Fax 647-2047

Cantrall, Sangamon, Pop. 136
Athens CUSD 213
Supt. — See Athens
Cantrall ES 400/PK-3
1 Braves Ln 62625 217-487-7312
Eric Szoke, prin. Fax 487-7187
Cantrall IS 200/4-6
155 Claypool St 62625 217-487-9082
Jacie Shoufler, prin. Fax 487-9104

Capron, Boone, Pop. 1,326
North Boone CUSD 200
Supt. — See Poplar Grove
Capron ES 200/PK-4
200 N Wooster St 61012 815-569-2314
Matt Klett, prin. Fax 569-2633

Carbondale, Jackson, Pop. 24,806
Carbondale ESD 95 1,300/PK-8
PO Box 2048 62902 618-457-3591
Linda Meredith, supt. Fax 457-2043
www.ces95.org/
Carbondale MS 400/6-8
1150 E Grand Ave 62901 618-457-2174
Charles Goforth, prin. Fax 457-2176
Lewis ES 200/4-5
801 S Lewis Ln 62901 618-457-2632
Stephen Douglas, prin. Fax 351-9816
Parrish ES 500/PK-1
121 N Parrish Ln 62901 618-457-5781
Candy Myers, prin. Fax 457-6661
Thomas ES 200/2-3
1025 N Wall St 62901 618-457-6226
Linda Flowers, prin. Fax 457-5636

Giant City CCSD 130 300/K-8
1062 Boskydell Rd 62902 618-457-5391
Sharon Mayes, supt. Fax 549-5060
www2.giants.jacksn.k12.il.us
Giant City S 300/K-8
1062 Boskydell Rd 62902 618-457-5391
Sharon Mayes, prin. Fax 549-5060

Unity Point CCSD 140 700/PK-8
4033 S Illinois Ave 62903 618-529-4151
Dr. Lori James-Gross, supt. Fax 529-4154
www.up140.jacksn.k12.il.us
Unity Point S 700/PK-8
4033 S Illinois Ave 62903 618-529-4151
Jim Berezow, prin. Fax 529-4154

Trinity Christian S 100/PK-12
1218 W Freeman St 62901 618-529-3733
Paul Plunkett, prin. Fax 549-8252

Carlinville, Macoupin, Pop. 5,768
Carlinville CUSD 1 1,500/PK-12
18456 Shipman Rd 62626 217-854-9823
Mike Kelly, supt. Fax 854-2777
www.carlinvilleschools.net/
Carlinville ECC 200/PK-K
506 N High St 62626 217-854-5071
Elise Schwartz, prin. Fax 854-4708
Carlinville IS 200/4-5
450 W Buchanan St 62626 217-854-9523
Becky Schuchman, prin. Fax 854-3417
Carlinville MS 300/6-8
110 Illinois Ave 62626 217-854-3106
Roy Kulenkamp, prin. Fax 854-4503
Carlinville PS 300/1-3
18456 Shipman Rd 62626 217-854-9849
Elise Schwartz, prin. Fax 854-7867

Carlock, McLean, Pop. 434
McLean County Unit SD 5
Supt. — See Normal
Carlock ES 100/K-5
301 W Washington Rd 61725 309-376-3261
Alison Hampton, prin. Fax 376-2014

Carlyle, Clinton, Pop. 3,377
Carlyle CUSD 1 1,300/PK-12
1400 13th St 62231 618-594-8283
Joe Novsek, supt. Fax 594-8285
www.carlyle.k12.il.us
Carlyle ES 500/PK-4
951 6th St 62231 618-594-3766
Bob Wilson, prin. Fax 594-8110
Carlyle JHS 400/5-8
1631 12th St 62231 618-594-8292
Jay Smith, prin. Fax 594-8294

Carmi, White, Pop. 5,414
Carmi-White County CUSD 5 1,500/PK-12
301 W Main St 62821 618-382-2341
Dr. Keith Talley, supt. Fax 384-3207
www.carmi.white.k12.il.us
Carmi-White County MS 300/6-8
205 W Main St 62821 618-382-4631
Terry Gholson, prin. Fax 384-2076
Jefferson Attendance Center 200/2-3
713 4th St 62821 618-382-7016
Dr. Amy Dixon, prin. Fax 382-7512
Lincoln Attendance Center 200/PK-1
113 10th St 62821 618-384-3421
Maryann Stocke, prin. Fax 382-5138
Prekindergarten Center 100/PK-PK
213 7th St 62821 618-384-3515
Maryann Stocke, prin.
Other Schools – See Crossville

Carol Stream, DuPage, Pop. 40,040
Benjamin SD 25
Supt. — See West Chicago
Evergreen ES 500/K-4
1041 Evergreen Dr 60188 630-876-7810
Jean Peterson, prin. Fax 231-4292

CCSD 93
Supt. — See Bloomingdale
Carol Stream ES 300/K-5
422 Sioux Ln 60188 630-462-8920
Susan Grady, prin. Fax 462-9104
Cloverdale ES 600/PK-5
1182 Merbach Dr 60188 630-784-3600
Terry Dutton, prin. Fax 784-1427
De Shane ES 400/PK-5
475 Chippewa Trl 60188 630-462-8925
Geri Serwach, prin. Fax 462-9192
Heritage Lakes ES 500/K-5
925 Woodhill Dr 60188 630-830-3500
Marie Hoffman Ed.D., prin. Fax 830-3281
Stream MS 800/6-8
283 El Paso Ln 60188 630-462-8940
Peter LaChance, prin. Fax 462-9224
Western Trails ES 500/K-5
860 Idaho St 60188 630-462-8935
James Doyle, prin. Fax 462-9354

SD U-46
Supt. — See Elgin
Spring Trail ES 500/K-6
1384 Spring Valley Dr 60188 630-213-6230
Richard Schroeder, prin. Fax 213-6236

Carol Stream Christian Academy 50/PK-3
610 E North Ave 60188 630-653-1044
Tim Krahenbuhl, prin. Fax 653-1142

Carpentersville, Kane, Pop. 37,204
Barrington CUSD 220
Supt. — See Barrington
Sunny Hill ES 500/K-5
2500 Helm Rd 60110 847-426-4232
Irma Bates, prin. Fax 426-0896
Woodland ES 200/PK-PK
770 Navajo Dr 60110 847-426-7232
Barbara Romano, coord. Fax 426-0829

CUSD 300 18,600/PK-12
300 Cleveland Ave 60110 847-426-1300
Dr. Kenneth Arndt, supt. Fax 551-8356
www.d300.org
Carpentersville MS 700/7-8
100 Cleveland Ave 60110 847-426-1380
Stephanie Ramstad, prin. Fax 426-1404
deLacey Family Educ Center 500/PK-PK
50 Cleveland Ave 60110 847-426-1450
Therese Cronin, prin. Fax 426-1453
Golfview ES 600/K-4
124 Golfview Ln 60110 847-426-1250
Trish Whitecotton, prin. Fax 426-1339
Lakewood IS 800/5-6
1651 Ravine Ln 60110 847-428-1191
Timothy Loversky, prin. Fax 426-1126
Liberty ES 1,000/K-5
6500 Miller Rd 60110 847-851-8300
Kristin Corriveau, prin. Fax 851-8309
Meadowdale ES 500/K-4
14 Ash St 60110 847-426-1475
Rita Janus, prin. Fax 426-1244
Parkview ES 300/K-4
122 Carpenter Blvd 60110 847-426-1260
Ellen Bruning, prin. Fax 426-2962
Perry ES 900/K-4
251 Amarillo Dr 60110 847-426-1440
Craig Zieleniewski, prin. Fax 426-5903
Other Schools – See Algonquin, Gilberts, Hampshire, Lake in the Hills, Sleepy Hollow, West Dundee

Carrier Mills, Saline, Pop. 1,841
Carrier Mills-Stonefort CUSD 2 500/PK-12
PO Box 217 62917 618-994-2392
Richard Morgan, supt. Fax 994-2929
Carrier Mills S 300/PK-8
PO Box 218 62917 618-994-2413
Charles Parks, prin. Fax 994-4141

Carrollton, Greene, Pop. 2,519
Carrollton CUSD 1 500/PK-12
702 5th St 62016 217-942-5314
Dr. Elizabeth Pressler, supt. Fax 942-9259
www.c-hawks.net/
Carrollton S 300/PK-5
721 4th St 62016 217-942-6831
Ann Williamson, prin. Fax 942-6053

St. John the Evangelist S 100/PK-8
426 3rd St 62016 217-942-6814
Lori Loveless, prin. Fax 942-6767

Carterville, Williamson, Pop. 5,099
Carterville CUSD 5 1,800/PK-12
306 Virginia Ave 62918 618-985-4826
Tim Bleyer, supt. Fax 985-2041
www.c-ville.wilmsn.k12.il.us/
Carterville IS 500/5-8
300 School St 62918 618-985-6411
Jeff Hartford, prin. Fax 985-2492
Tri-C ES, 1405 W Grand Ave 62918 800/PK-4
Sarah Barnstable, prin. 618-985-8742

Carthage, Hancock, Pop. 2,548
Carthage ESD 317 500/PK-8
210 S Adams St 62321 217-357-3922
Vicki Hardy, supt. Fax 357-6793
carthageschools.k12.il.us
Carthage MS 200/5-8
210 S Adams St 62321 217-357-3914
Elizabeth Wujek, prin. Fax 357-3755
Carthage PS 300/PK-4
210 S Adams St 62321 217-357-9202
Elizabeth Wujek, prin. Fax 357-0585

Cary, McHenry, Pop. 19,115
Cary CCSD 26 3,500/PK-8
2115 Crystal Lake Rd 60013 847-639-7788
Brian Coleman, supt. Fax 639-3898
www.cary26.k12.il.us/
Briargate ES 400/PK-4
100 S Wulff St 60013 847-639-2348
Chad Nass, prin. Fax 516-5516
Cary JHS 800/7-8
2109 Crystal Lake Rd 60013 847-639-2148
Linda Goeglein, prin. Fax 516-5507
Deer Path ES 600/PK-4
2211 Crystal Lake Rd 60013 847-516-6350
Matthew Bohrer, prin. Fax 516-6355
Maplewood ES 400/K-4
422 Krenz Ave 60013 847-639-2152
Thom Gippert, prin. Fax 516-5523
Prairie Hill IS 800/5-6
233 E Oriole Trl 60013 847-516-5513
Ann Baker, prin. Fax 516-5538
Three Oaks ES 500/K-4
1514 3 Oaks Rd 60013 847-516-5533
Natalie Wishne, prin. Fax 516-5514

Holy Cross Lutheran S 100/PK-K
2107 3 Oaks Rd 60013 847-639-6533
Jean Hoger, dir. Fax 639-6702
SS. Peter & Paul S 500/K-8
416 1st St 60013 847-639-3041
Sr. Katrina Lamkin, prin. Fax 639-5329
Trinity Oaks Christian Academy 200/PK-8
409 1st St 60013 847-462-5971
Paul Wrobbel, hdmstr. Fax 462-5972

Casey, Clark, Pop. 2,948
Casey-Westfield CUSD C4 1,200/PK-12
PO Box 100 62420 217-932-2184
Robert Ehlke, supt. Fax 932-5553
Casey-Westfield JHS 200/7-8
401 E Main St 62420 217-932-2177
Jo Beard, prin. Fax 932-2753
Monroe ES, 301 E Monroe Ave 62420 600/PK-6
Dee Scott, prin. 217-932-2178

Caseyville, Saint Clair, Pop. 4,297
Collinsville CUSD 10
Supt. — See Collinsville

Caseyville ES 200/PK-4
433 S 2nd St 62232 618-346-6205
Dr. Jean Dayton, prin. Fax 343-2743

Cornerstone Christian S 100/K-8
111 S 2nd St 62232 618-345-9571
Anita Gajewski, admin. Fax 345-9756

Catlin, Vermilion, Pop. 2,051
Catlin CUSD 5 500/PK-12
701 1/2 W Vermilion St 61817 217-427-2116
Dr. Guy Banicki, supt. Fax 427-2117
www.catlin.k12.il.us
Catlin S 400/PK-8
216 N Webster St 61817 217-427-5421
Dennis Buesking, prin. Fax 427-9866

Centralia, Marion, Pop. 13,600
Central City SD 133 200/PK-8
129 Douglas St 62801 618-532-9521
Tim Branon, supt. Fax 533-2219
centralcity.il.schoolwebpages.com
Central City S 200/PK-8
129 Douglas St 62801 618-532-9521
Tim Branon, prin. Fax 533-2219

Centralia SD 135 1,400/PK-8
400 S Elm St 62801 618-532-1907
David Rademacher, supt. Fax 532-4986
www.ccs135.com
Centralia JHS 500/6-8
900 S Pine St 62801 618-533-7130
Dustin Foutch, prin. Fax 533-7123
Centralia Pre-Kindergarten Center 100/PK-PK
422 S Elm St 62801 618-533-7122
David Rademacher, prin.
Field Kindergarten Center 200/PK-K
1101 S Locust St 62801 618-533-7133
Victoria Sayles, prin. Fax 533-7134
Irving Fourth Grade Center 200/4-4
200 S Pine St 62801 618-533-7120
Van Brentlinger, prin. Fax 533-7121
Jordan ES 200/1-3
311 Airport Rd 62801 618-533-7145
Craig Bland, prin. Fax 533-7146
Lincoln Fifth Grade Center 100/5-5
501 N Elm St 62801 618-533-7135
Van Brentlinger, prin. Fax 533-7136
Schiller ES 200/1-3
800 W 4th St 62801 618-533-7140
Victoria Sayles, prin. Fax 533-7141

Grand Prairie CCSD 6 100/K-8
21462 N Richview Ln 62801 618-249-6289
Sally Epperson Cherry, supt. Fax 249-8477
209.175.207.90/
Grand Prairie S 100/K-8
21462 N Richview Ln 62801 618-249-6289
Sally Epperson Cherry, prin. Fax 249-8477

North Wamac SD 186 100/K-8
1500 Case St 62801 618-532-1826
Brad Morris, supt. Fax 532-8250
www.schools.lth5.k12.il.us/nwamac/NorthwamacHome.html
North Wamac S 100/K-8
1500 Case St 62801 618-532-1826
Brad Morris, prin. Fax 532-8250

Raccoon Consolidated SD 1 300/K-8
3601 State Route 161 62801 618-532-7329
Tammie Henry, supt. Fax 532-7336
www.raccoonschool.org
Raccoon Grade S 300/K-8
3601 State Route 161 62801 618-532-7329
Darin Loepker, prin. Fax 532-7336

Willow Grove SD 46 200/PK-8
815 W 7th St 62801 618-532-3313
Kim Wiley, supt. Fax 532-5638
Willow Grove S 200/PK-8
815 W 7th St 62801 618-532-3313
Kim Wiley, prin. Fax 532-5638

New Horizon Christian S 100/K-8
12 Greenview Church Rd 62801 618-533-6910
St. Mary S 100/PK-8
424 E Broadway 62801 618-532-3473
Helen Donsbach, prin. Fax 532-5180
Trinity Lutheran S 200/K-8
203 S Pleasant Ave 62801 618-532-5434
Dave Klein, prin. Fax 532-4277

Cerro Gordo, Piatt, Pop. 1,385
Cerro Gordo CUSD 100 600/K-12
PO Box 79 61818 217-763-5221
Brett Robinson, supt. Fax 763-6562
www.cerrogordo.k12.il.us
Cerro Gordo ES 300/K-5
PO Box 66 61818 217-763-2551
Linda McCabe, prin. Fax 763-6562
Cerro Gordo MS 100/6-8
PO Box 79 61818 217-763-6411
Paul Workman, prin. Fax 763-6562

Chadwick, Carroll, Pop. 486
Chadwick-Milledgeville CUSD 399 500/PK-12
15 School St 61014 815-684-5191
Roy Webb, supt. Fax 684-5241
www.dist399.net/
Chadwick ES 100/PK-5
15 School St 61014 815-684-5191
Roy Webb, prin. Fax 684-5241
Chadwick JHS 100/6-8
15 School St 61014 815-684-5191
Roy Webb, prin. Fax 684-5241
Other Schools – See Milledgeville

Champaign, Champaign, Pop. 71,568
Champaign CUSD 4 9,200/PK-12
703 S New St 61820 217-351-3800
Arthur Culver, supt. Fax 352-3590
www.champaignschools.org/
Barkstall ES 400/K-5
2201 Hallbeck Dr 61822 217-373-5580
Trudy Walters, prin. Fax 373-5587
Bottenfield ES 400/K-5
1801 S Prospect Ave 61820 217-351-3807
Foster Matthew, prin. Fax 355-2582
Busey ES 400/K-5
1605 W Kirby Ave 61821 217-351-3811
Zanita Willis, prin. Fax 351-3723
Champaign ECC 300/PK-PK
809 N Neil St 61820 217-351-3881
Amy Hayden, prin. Fax 351-3883
Edison MS 700/6-8
306 W Green St 61820 217-351-3771
Carmella Levy, prin. Fax 355-2564
Franklin MS 600/6-8
817 N Harris Ave 61820 217-351-3819
Angela Smith, prin. Fax 351-3729
Garden Hills ES 300/K-5
2001 Garden Hills Dr 61821 217-351-3872
Cheryl O'Leary, prin. Fax 355-8180
Howard ES 400/K-5
1117 W Park Ave 61821 217-351-3866
Jill VanWaus, prin. Fax 359-7036
Jefferson MS 700/6-8
1115 Crescent Dr 61821 217-351-3790
Dr. Susan Zola, prin. Fax 351-3754
Kenwood ES 400/K-5
1001 Stratford Dr 61821 217-351-3815
Lisa Geren, prin. Fax 355-4944
Robeson ES 500/K-5
2501 Southmoor Dr 61821 217-351-3884
Heather Livengood, prin. Fax 351-3751
South Side ES 300/K-5
712 S Pine St 61820 217-351-3890
William Taylor, prin. Fax 373-7318
Stratton ES 400/K-5
902 N Randolph St 61820 217-373-7330
Orlando Thomas, prin. Fax 373-7337
Washington ES 300/K-5
606 E Grove St 61820 217-351-3901
Sarah Clyne, prin. Fax 373-7350
Westview ES 400/K-5
703 S Russell St 61821 217-351-3905
Trevor Nadrozny, prin. Fax 351-3960

Countryside S 100/K-8
4301 W Kirby Ave 61822 217-355-1253
Catherine Webber, hdmstr. Fax 355-7492
Holy Cross S 400/K-8
410 W White St 61820 217-356-9521
Rose Costello, prin. Fax 356-1745
Judah Christian S 600/PK-12
908 N Prospect Ave 61820 217-359-1701
Daniel Cole, admin. Fax 359-0214
Montessori Habitat S 100/PK-6
PO Box 172 61824 217-366-3260
Julie McGavran, prin.
Next Generation S 200/PK-8
2521 Galen Dr 61821 217-356-6995
Fax 356-6345
St. John Lutheran S 200/PK-8
509 S Mattis Ave 61821 217-359-1714
Ralph Leffler, prin. Fax 359-7972
St. Matthew S 500/K-8
1307 Lincolnshire Dr 61821 217-359-4114
Kathleen Scherer, prin. Fax 359-8319

Chandlerville, Cass, Pop. 716
A-C Central CUSD 262
Supt. — See Ashland
A-C Central JHS 100/6-8
191 S Bluff St 62627 217-458-2224
Deb Rogers, prin. Fax 458-2223

Channahon, Will, Pop. 12,218
Channahon SD 17 1,600/K-8
24920 S Sage St 60410 815-467-4315
Dr. Karin Evans, supt. Fax 467-4343
www.channahon.will.k12.il.us
Channahon JHS 300/7-8
24917 W Sioux Dr 60410 815-467-4314
Chad Uphoff, prin. Fax 467-2188
Galloway ES 500/2-4
24805 W Roberts Rd 60410 815-467-4311
Lorraine Halbesma, prin. Fax 467-3093
Pioneer Path S 300/K-1
24920 S Sage St 60410 815-467-4312
Angela Stallion, prin. Fax 467-8851
Three Rivers S 400/5-6
24150 Minooka Rd 60410 815-467-4313
Susan Kavich, prin. Fax 467-3089

Charleston, Coles, Pop. 20,189
Charleston CUSD 1 2,900/PK-12
410 W Polk Ave 61920 217-639-1000
Jim Littleford, supt. Fax 639-1005
www.charleston.k12.il.us
Charleston MS 400/7-8
920 Smith Dr 61920 217-639-6000
Michael Schmitz, prin. Fax 639-6005
Jefferson ES 600/4-6
801 Jefferson Ave 61920 217-639-7000
Debbie Poffinbarger, prin. Fax 639-7005
Sandburg ES 500/1-3
1924 Reynolds Dr 61920 217-639-4000
Chad Burgett, prin. Fax 639-4005
Twain ES 200/PK-K
1021 13th St 61920 217-639-8000
Terry Diss, prin. Fax 639-8005
Other Schools – See Ashmore

Charleston Christian Academy 50/K-12
2605 University Dr 61920 217-345-4479
John Best, admin.

Chatham, Sangamon, Pop. 9,787
Ball Chatham CUSD 5 4,200/PK-12
201 W Mulberry St 62629 217-483-2416
Robert Gillum, supt. Fax 483-2940
www.chathamschools.org
Ball ES 700/PK-3
1015 New City Rd 62629 217-483-2414
Cathy Rogers, prin. Fax 483-3968
Chatham ES 600/K-3
525 S College St 62629 217-483-2411
Kim Sepich, prin. Fax 483-5270
Glenwood IS 600/4-5
465 Chatham Rd 62629 217-483-1183
Kerry Cox, prin. Fax 483-1254
Glenwood MS 900/6-8
595 Chatham Rd 62629 217-483-2481
Jill Larson, prin. Fax 483-4940

St. Joseph Preschool 50/PK-PK
700 E Spruce St 62629 217-483-3772
Andrea Conlon, dir. Fax 483-4581

Chatsworth, Livingston, Pop. 1,221
Prairie Central CUSD 8
Supt. — See Fairbury
Chatsworth ES 100/PK-4
PO Box 816 60921 815-635-3555
Karen Hazelrigg, prin. Fax 635-3429

Chebanse, Iroquois, Pop. 1,101
Central CUSD 4
Supt. — See Clifton
Chebanse ES 400/K-4
PO Box 8 60922 815-697-2642
Lori Morelock, prin. Fax 697-2448

Zion Lutheran S 100/PK-8
160 Concordia Dr 60922 815-697-2212
Elisa Schendel, prin. Fax 697-3302

Chenoa, McLean, Pop. 1,805
Prairie Central CUSD 8
Supt. — See Fairbury
Chenoa ES 200/PK-4
700 S Division St 61726 815-945-2971
Dan Groce, prin. Fax 945-2068

Cherry, Bureau, Pop. 499
Cherry SD 92 100/K-8
PO Box 219 61317 815-894-2777
Stephen Westrick, supt. Fax 894-2441
Cherry S 100/K-8
PO Box 219 61317 815-894-2777
Stephen Westrick, prin. Fax 894-2441

Cherry Valley, Winnebago, Pop. 2,228
Rockford SD 205
Supt. — See Rockford
Cherry Valley ES 200/3-5
619 E State St 61016 815-332-4938
Rori Regan-Buckner, prin. Fax 332-9661

Chester, Randolph, Pop. 7,872
Chester CUSD 139 1,000/PK-12
1940 Swanwick St 62233 618-826-4509
Rebecca Keim, supt. Fax 826-4500
www.chester139.com
Chester Community S 700/PK-8
650 Opdyke St 62233 618-826-2354
Tim Lochhead, prin. Fax 826-2805

St. John Lutheran S 200/PK-8
302 W Holmes St 62233 618-826-4345
Christopher Urquhart, prin. Fax 826-4804
St. Mary S 100/PK-8
835 Swanwick St 62233 618-826-3120
Janelle Robinson, prin. Fax 826-3486

Chicago, Cook, Pop. 2,842,518
Central Stickney SD 110 500/PK-8
5001 S Long Ave 60638 708-458-1152
Richard Schmitz, supt. Fax 458-1168
www.sahs.k12.il.us/
Sahs S 500/PK-8
5001 S Long Ave 60638 708-458-1152
Jennifer Toschi, prin. Fax 458-1168

City of Chicago SD 299 396,900/PK-12
125 S Clark St 60603 773-553-1000
Ron Huberman, supt. Fax 535-1502
www.cps.edu/
Abbott S 100/K-8
3630 S Wells St 60609 773-535-1660
Carol Hardin, prin. Fax 535-1469
Academia Bilingue 200/K-8
9000 S Exchange Ave 60617 773-535-6360
Luis Ramirez, prin. Fax 535-6303
Academy for Global Citizenship 100/K-1
5101 S Keeler Ave 60632 773-582-1100
Anne Gillespie, prin. Fax 582-1101
Addams S 900/PK-8
10810 S Avenue H 60617 773-535-6210
Noemi Esquivel, prin. Fax 535-6292
Agassiz S 400/PK-8
2851 N Seminary Ave Ste 1 60657 773-534-5725
Mira Weber, prin. Fax 534-5784
Albany Park Multicultural Academy 300/7-8
4929 N Sawyer Ave 60625 773-534-5108
Eileen O'Toole, prin. Fax 534-5178
Alcott S 500/PK-8
2625 N Orchard St 60614 773-534-5460
David Domovic, prin. Fax 534-5789
Aldridge S 200/PK-8
630 E 131st St 60827 773-535-5614
Vincent Payne, prin. Fax 535-5613
Altgeld S 700/PK-8
1340 W 71st St 60636 773-535-3250
Vera Williams-Willis, prin. Fax 535-3639
Ames MS 800/7-8
1920 N Hamlin Ave 60647 773-534-4970
Lorraine Cruz, prin. Fax 534-4975
Andersen S 400/3-8
1148 N Honore St 60622 773-534-4276
Doris Collins-Harmon, prin. Fax 534-4275
Apple S 200/K-8
9000 S Exchange Ave 60617 773-535-6360
Carline Holliman, prin. Fax 535-6303

Ariel Community Academy 400/PK-8
1119 E 46th St 60653 773-535-1996
Lennette Coleman, prin. Fax 535-1931
Armour S 400/PK-8
950 W 33rd Pl 60608 773-535-4530
Shelley Cordova, prin. Fax 535-4501
Armstrong ES 200/3-6
5345 W Congress Pkwy 60644 773-534-6365
Ms. Demetrius Bunch, prin. Fax 534-6027
Armstrong International Studies S 1,300/PK-8
2110 W Greenleaf Ave 60645 773-534-2150
Dr. Arline Hersh, prin. Fax 534-2192
Ashburn Community S 500/K-8
8300 S Saint Louis Ave 60652 773-535-7860
Jewel Diaz, prin. Fax 535-7867
Ashe S 700/K-8
8505 S Ingleside Ave 60619 773-535-3550
Dr. Richadine Murray-Heard, prin. Fax 535-3362
Attucks S 400/PK-8
5055 S State St 60609 773-535-1270
Dr. Carol Perry, prin. Fax 535-1367
Audubon S 400/PK-8
3500 N Hoyne Ave 60618 773-534-5470
John Price, prin. Fax 534-5785
Avalon Park S 700/PK-8
8045 S Kenwood Ave 60619 773-535-6615
S. Allen-Higginbottom, prin. Fax 535-6660
Avondale ES 700/PK-5
2945 N Sawyer Ave 60618 773-534-5244
Ana Martinez-Estka, prin. Fax 534-5069
Banneker S 400/PK-8
6656 S Normal Blvd 60621 773-535-3020
Verona Portis, prin. Fax 535-3272
Barnard S 300/PK-8
10354 S Charles St 60643 773-535-2625
Doris Jordan, prin. Fax 535-2629
Barry ES 800/PK-6
2828 N Kilbourn Ave 60641 773-534-3455
Odette Langer, prin. Fax 534-3489
Barton S 700/PK-8
7650 S Wolcott Ave 60620 773-535-3260
Terrence Carter, prin. Fax 535-3271
Bass S 700/PK-8
1140 W 66th St 60621 773-535-3275
Granzlee Banks, prin. Fax 535-3330
Bateman S 1,000/PK-8
4220 N Richmond St 60618 773-534-5055
Carl Dasko, prin. Fax 534-5052
Beasley Academic Magnet S 1,400/PK-8
5255 S State St 60609 773-535-1230
Dr. Philistine Tweedle, prin. Fax 535-1248
Beaubien S 1,000/PK-8
5025 N Laramie Ave 60630 773-534-3500
Chris Kotis, prin. Fax 534-3517
Beethoven S 500/PK-8
25 W 47th St 60609 773-535-1480
Dyrice Garner, prin. Fax 535-1478
Beidler S 500/K-8
3151 W Walnut St 60612 773-534-6811
Dr. Shirley Ewings, prin. Fax 534-6817
Belding S 500/PK-8
4257 N Tripp Ave 60641 773-534-3590
July Cyrwus, prin. Fax 534-3598
Bell S 900/K-8
3730 N Oakley Ave 60618 773-534-5150
Robert Guercio, prin. Fax 534-5163
Belmont-Cragin Community S 600/PK-8
2456 N Mango Ave 60639 773-534-2900
Maria Cabrera, prin. Fax 534-2907
Bennett S 600/PK-8
10115 S Prairie Ave 60628 773-535-5460
Barbara Ellis, prin. Fax 535-5577
Bethune S 400/PK-8
3030 W Arthington St 60612 773-534-6890
Dr. Dianne Jackson, prin. Fax 534-6889
Black Magnet S 500/K-8
9101 S Euclid Ave 60617 773-535-6390
Thomas Little, prin. Fax 535-6047
Blaine S 800/PK-8
1420 W Grace St 60613 773-534-5750
Gladys Vaccarezza, prin. Fax 534-5748
Bond S 600/PK-8
7050 S May St 60621 773-535-3480
Valesta Cobbs, prin. Fax 535-3433
Bontemps S 400/PK-8
1241 W 58th St 60636 773-535-9175
Allen Moseley, prin. Fax 535-9569
Boone S 1,100/PK-8
6710 N Washtenaw Ave 60645 773-534-2160
Maria Santiago-Pfeifer, prin. Fax 534-2190
Bouchet S 1,000/PK-8
7355 S Jeffery Blvd 60649 773-535-0501
Kim Sims, prin. Fax 535-0559
Bradwell Community Arts Sciences S 900/PK-8
7736 S Burnham Ave 60649 773-535-6600
Yvonne James, prin. Fax 535-6612
Brenneman S 300/PK-8
4251 N Clarendon Ave 60613 773-534-5766
Otis Dunson, prin. Fax 534-5787
Brentano Math & Science Academy 500/K-8
2723 N Fairfield Ave 60647 773-534-4100
Martha Rosa-Salgado, prin. Fax 534-4183
Bridge S 700/K-8
3800 N New England Ave 60634 773-534-3718
Dr. Christopher Brake, prin. Fax 534-3612
Brighton Park S 900/K-8
3825 S Washtenaw Ave 60632 773-535-7237
Dr. Glenda Johnson, prin. Fax 535-7198
Bright S 300/PK-8
10740 S Calhoun Ave 60617 773-535-6215
Millicent Robersone, prin. Fax 535-6373
Brown Academy 300/PK-8
12607 S Union Ave 60628 773-535-5385
Gale Baker, prin. Fax 535-5359
Brownell ES 300/PK-6
6741 S Michigan Ave 60637 773-535-3030
Richard Morgan, prin. Fax 535-3413
Brown S 200/K-8
54 N Hermitage Ave 60612 773-534-7250
Paulette Boston, prin. Fax 534-7323

Brunson Math & Science S 900/PK-8
932 N Central Ave 60651 773-534-6025
Carol Wilson, prin. Fax 534-6031
Budlong S 800/PK-8
2701 W Foster Ave 60625 773-534-2591
Alvin Solomon, prin. Fax 534-2544
Burbank S 1,300/PK-8
2035 N Mobile Ave 60639 773-534-3000
Dr. Hiram Broyls, prin. Fax 534-3338
Burke ES 200/K-8
5356 S King Dr 60615 773-535-1325
Kimberly Ellison, prin. Fax 535-1913
Burley S 500/PK-8
1630 W Barry Ave 60657 773-534-5475
Barbara Kent, prin. Fax 534-5786
Burnham Academy 300/K-8
1903 E 96th St 60617 773-535-6530
Dr. Linda Moore, prin. Fax 535-6515
Burnham S Goldsmith Branch K-8
10211 S Crandon Ave 60617 773-535-6524
Charles Davis, prin. Fax 535-6500
Burnside Scholastic Academy 700/PK-8
650 E 91st Pl 60619 773-535-3300
Anthony Biegler, prin. Fax 535-3230
Burroughs S 500/PK-8
3542 S Washtenaw Ave 60632 773-535-7226
Donald Morris, prin. Fax 535-7126
Burr S 300/PK-8
1621 W Wabansia Ave 60622 773-534-4090
Vinita Scott, prin. Fax 534-4718
Byrne S 700/K-8
5329 S Oak Park Ave 60638 773-535-2170
Robert Deckinga, prin. Fax 535-2227
Caldwell S 400/PK-8
8546 S Cregier Ave 60617 773-535-6300
Charles Slaughter, prin. Fax 535-6611
Calhoun North S 500/PK-8
2833 W Adams St 60612 773-534-6940
Cynthia Hughes-Hannah, prin. Fax 534-6952
Cameron S 1,100/PK-8
1234 N Monticello Ave Ste 1 60651 773-534-4290
David Kovach, prin. Fax 534-0405
Canter MS 300/7-8
4959 S Blackstone Ave 60615 773-535-1410
Dr. Colleen Conlan, prin. Fax 535-1047
Canty S 600/PK-8
3740 N Panama Ave 60634 773-534-1238
Lucja Mirowska-Kopec, prin. Fax 534-1236
Cardenas ES 700/PK-3
2345 S Millard Ave 60623 773-534-1465
Dr. Jeremy Feiwell, prin. Fax 534-1512
Cardenas Modular ES 600/PK-3
2406 S Central Park Ave 60623 773-534-1465
Dr. Jeremy Feiwell, prin. Fax 534-1512
Carnegie S 700/PK-8
1414 E 61st Pl 60637 773-535-0530
Darlene Pollard, prin. Fax 535-0525
Carpenter S 400/PK-8
1250 W Erie St, 773-534-7385
Aida Munoz, prin. Fax 534-7373
Carroll-Rosenwald S 700/PK-8
2929 W 83rd St 60652 773-535-9414
Adell Brock, prin. Fax 535-9568
Carson S 1,300/PK-8
5516 S Maplewood Ave 60629 773-535-9222
Javier Arriola-Lopez, prin. Fax 535-9552
Carter S 400/PK-8
5740 S Michigan Ave 60637 773-535-0860
Anita Harmon, prin. Fax 535-0698
Carver S 400/PK-8
901 E 133rd Pl 60827 773-535-5674
Katherine Tobias, prin. Fax 535-5455
Casals S 600/PK-8
3501 W Potomac Ave 60651 773-534-4444
Paula Jeske, prin. Fax 534-4559
Cassell S 300/PK-8
11314 S Spaulding Ave 60655 773-535-2640
Denise Esposito, prin. Fax 535-2667
Castellanos MS 600/4-8
2524 S Central Park Ave 60623 773-534-1620
Myriam Romero, prin. Fax 534-1611
Catalyst S K-8
5608 W Washington Blvd 60644 773-854-1633
Sala Sims, prin. Fax 854-1635
Chalmers S 300/PK-8
2745 W Roosevelt Rd 60608 773-534-1720
Patricia Vaughn-Dossiea, prin. Fax 534-1718
Chappell S 400/PK-8
2135 W Foster Ave 60625 773-534-2390
Joseph Peila, prin. Fax 534-2638
Chase S 600/PK-8
2021 N Point St 60647 773-534-4185
Elizabeth Gonzalez, prin. Fax 534-4727
Chavez S 1,000/PK-8
4747 S Marshfield Ave 60609 773-535-4600
Ariel Correa, prin. Fax 535-4603
Chicago Academy 600/PK-8
3400 N Austin Ave 60634 773-534-3885
Victor Iturralde, prin. Fax 534-0109
Chopin S 300/PK-8
2450 W Rice St 60622 773-534-4080
Antuanette Mester, prin. Fax 534-4163
Christopher S 200/K-8
5042 S Artesian Ave 60632 773-535-9375
Mary McAloon, prin. Fax 535-9567
Claremont Academy 700/PK-8
2300 W 64th St 60636 773-535-8110
Rebecca Stinson, prin. Fax 535-8108
Clark S 400/PK-8
1045 S Monitor Ave 60644 773-534-6225
Dr. Felicia Stewart, prin. Fax 534-6278
Clay S 800/PK-8
13231 S Burley Ave 60633 773-535-5600
Chris Pagnucco, prin. Fax 535-5606
Cleveland S 600/PK-8
3121 W Byron St 60618 773-534-5130
Debora Ward, prin. Fax 534-5266
Clinton S 1,300/K-8
6110 N Fairfield Ave Ste 1 60659 773-534-2025
Teresa Moy, prin. Fax 534-2069

Clissold S 300/K-8
2350 W 110th Pl 60643 773-535-2560
Edward Podsiadik, prin. Fax 535-2556
Colemon Academy 300/PK-8
1441 W 119th St 60643 773-535-3975
Paulette Williams, prin. Fax 535-3979
Coles Model for Excellence 700/PK-8
8441 S Yates Blvd 60617 773-535-6550
Jeff Dase, prin. Fax 535-6570
Columbia Explorers Academy 1,000/PK-8
4520 S Kedzie Ave 60632 773-535-4050
Jose Barrera, prin. Fax 535-4083
Columbus S 300/PK-8
1003 N Leavitt St 60622 773-534-4350
Joseph Edmonds, prin. Fax 534-4362
Cook S 800/PK-8
8150 S Bishop St 60620 773-535-3315
Rebecca McDaniel, prin. Fax 535-3383
Coonley S 300/PK-8
4046 N Leavitt St 60618 773-534-5140
Katherine Kartheiser, prin. Fax 534-5213
Cooper Dual Language Academy 800/PK-5
1624 W 19th St 60608 773-534-7205
Martha Monrroy, prin. Fax 534-7245
Copernicus S 400/K-8
6010 S Throop St 60636 773-535-9180
Lynn McGinnis-Garner, prin. Fax 535-9428
Corkery S 700/PK-8
2510 S Kildare Ave 60623 773-534-1650
Bertha Arredondo, prin. Fax 534-1674
Courtenay Language Arts S 200/PK-8
1726 W Berteau Ave 60613 773-534-5790
Dr. Patricia Zemba, prin. Fax 534-5799
Crown Community Academy 400/PK-8
2128 S Saint Louis Ave 60623 773-534-1680
Dr. Lee Jackson, prin. Fax 534-1677
Cuffe Math-Science-Tech Academy 800/PK-8
8324 S Racine Ave 60620 773-535-8250
John Jones, prin. Fax 535-3497
Cullen S 400/K-8
10650 S Eberhart Ave 60628 773-535-5375
Carolyn Draper, prin. Fax 535-5366
Curtis S 600/PK-8
32 E 115th St 60628 773-535-5050
Charles Davis, prin. Fax 535-5044
Daley Academy 900/PK-8
5024 S Wolcott Ave 60609 773-535-9091
Rhonda Hoskins, prin. Fax 535-0407
Darwin S 800/PK-8
3116 W Belden Ave 60647 773-534-4110
Graciela Shelley, prin. Fax 534-4323
Davis Academy 400/PK-3
6740 S Paulina St 60636 773-535-9120
Dr. Maxine Toliver, prin. Fax 535-9129
Davis S 1,700/PK-8
3014 W 39th Pl 60632 773-535-4540
Dr. Santos Gomez, prin. Fax 535-4510
Dawes S 1,100/PK-8
3810 W 81st Pl 60652 773-535-2350
Mary Dixon, prin. Fax 535-2367
Decatur Classical ES 300/K-6
7030 N Sacramento Ave 60645 773-534-2200
Susan Kukielka, prin. Fax 534-2191
De Diego Community Academy 1,100/PK-8
1313 N Claremont Ave 60622 773-534-4451
Alice Vera, prin. Fax 534-4696
De La Cruz MS 100/6-8
2317 W 23rd Pl 60608 773-535-4585
Katherine Konopasek, prin. Fax 535-4534
Delano S 500/PK-8
3937 W Wilcox St 60624 773-534-6620
Dr. Sakinah Abdal-Saboor, prin. Fax 534-6614
Deneen S 500/K-8
7240 S Wabash Ave 60619 773-535-3035
Joyce Lockhart-Fisher, prin. Fax 535-3247
De Priest S 800/PK-8
139 S Parkside Ave 60644 773-534-6800
Minnie Watson, prin. Fax 534-6799
Dett S 400/PK-8
2306 W Maypole Ave 60612 773-534-7160
Deborah Bonner, prin. Fax 534-7291
Dever S 800/PK-8
3436 N Osceola Ave 60634 773-534-3090
Rita Ortiz, prin. Fax 534-3337
Dewey Academy of Fine Arts 500/PK-8
5415 S Union Ave 60609 773-535-1666
Dr. Janice Buckley, prin. Fax 535-1802
Dirksen S 600/PK-8
8601 W Foster Ave 60656 773-534-1090
Dr. Patrick Keating, prin. Fax 534-1065
Disney Magnet II ES PK-2
3815 N Kedvale Ave 60641 773-534-3750
Bogdana Chkoumbova, prin.
Disney Magnet S 1,500/PK-8
4140 N Marine Dr 60613 773-534-5840
Dr. Kathleen Hagstrom, prin. Fax 534-5714
Dixon S 700/PK-8
8306 S Saint Lawrence Ave 60619 773-535-3831
Sharon Dale, prin. Fax 535-3811
Doolittle S 600/PK-8
535 E 35th St 60616 773-535-1040
Lori Lennix, prin. Fax 535-1034
Dore S 600/PK-8
6108 S Natoma Ave 60638 773-535-2080
Victor Simon, prin. Fax 535-2084
Drake S 400/PK-8
2722 S King Dr 60616 773-534-9129
Yvonne Jones, prin. Fax 534-9133
Drummond S 300/PK-8
1845 W Cortland St 60622 773-534-4120
J. Espada De Velazquez, prin. Fax 534-4199
Dubois S 300/PK-8
330 E 133rd St 60827 773-535-5582
Vanessa Williams-Johnson, prin. Fax 535-5587
Dulles S 500/PK-8
6311 S Calumet Ave 60637 773-535-0690
Linda Everhart-Lyke, prin. Fax 535-0689
Dumas S 400/PK-8
6650 S Ellis Ave 60637 773-535-0750
Macquline King, prin. Fax 535-0767

Dunne S 500/PK-8
10845 S Union Ave 60628 773-535-5517
Chandra Byrd-Wright, prin. Fax 535-5018
Duprey ES 300/1-8
2620 W Hirsch St 60622 773-534-4230
Gloria Roman Ed.D., prin. Fax 534-4239
Durkin Park S 500/K-8
8445 S Kolin Ave 60652 773-535-2322
Daniel Redmond, prin. Fax 535-2299
Dvorak Math Science Technology Academy 600/K-8
3615 W 16th St 60623 773-534-1690
Alma Thompson, prin. Fax 534-1676
Earhart S 300/K-8
1710 E 93rd St 60617 773-535-6416
Dr. B. DeMar-Williams, prin. Fax 535-6077
Earle S 500/PK-8
6121 S Hermitage Ave 60636 773-535-9130
Lori Campbell, prin. Fax 535-9140
Early Literacy Academy 300/PK-2
9000 S Exchange Ave 60617 773-535-6360
Mary Nolan, prin. Fax 535-6303
Eberhart S 1,800/K-8
3400 W 65th Pl 60629 773-535-9190
Nneka Gunn, prin. Fax 535-9494
Ebinger S 600/PK-8
7350 W Pratt Ave 60631 773-534-1070
Marilyn LeBoy, prin. Fax 534-1088
Edgebrook S 400/K-8
6525 N Hiawatha Ave 60646 773-534-1194
Janice Kepka, prin. Fax 534-1170
Edison Park S 300/PK-8
6220 N Olcott Ave 60631 773-534-0960
Pete Zimmerman, prin. Fax 534-0969
Edison S Regional Gifted Center 300/K-8
4929 N Sawyer Ave 60625 773-534-0540
Saundra Gray, prin. Fax 534-0539
Edwards S 1,200/K-8
4815 S Karlov Ave 60632 773-535-4875
Judith Sauri, prin. Fax 535-4470
Ellington ES 600/PK-8
243 N Parkside Ave 60644 773-534-6361
Shirley Scott, prin. Fax 534-6374
Emmet Math/Science/Tech Academy 600/PK-8
5500 W Madison St 60644 773-534-6050
Dr. Jacqueline Robinson, prin. Fax 534-6036
Ericson Scholastic Academy 600/PK-8
3600 W 5th Ave 60624 773-534-6660
Gloria Fullilove, prin. Fax 534-6636
Esmond S 400/K-8
1865 W Montvale Ave 60643 773-535-2650
Dr. Angela Tucker, prin. Fax 535-2676
Everett ES 400/PK-5
3419 S Bell Ave 60608 773-535-4550
Mary Gutierrez, prin. Fax 535-4615
Evergreen Middle Academy 500/6-8
3537 S Paulina St 60609 773-535-4836
Marian Strok, prin. Fax 535-4853
Evers S 400/PK-8
9811 S Lowe Ave 60628 773-535-2565
Kathleen Singleton, prin. Fax 535-2570
Fairfield Academy 700/K-8
6201 S Fairfield Ave 60629 773-535-9500
Elsa Rubio, prin. Fax 535-0438
Falconer ES 1,500/PK-6
3020 N Lamon Ave 60641 773-534-3560
Michael Perez, prin. Fax 534-3636
Faraday S 300/PK-8
3250 W Monroe St 60624 773-534-6670
Dr. Shirley Scott, prin. Fax 534-6659
Farnsworth S 600/PK-8
5414 N Linder Ave 60630 773-534-3535
Dr. Catherine Wells, prin. Fax 534-3515
Fermi S 300/PK-8
1415 E 70th St 60637 773-535-0540
Dr. Pamela Sanders, prin. Fax 535-0548
Fernwood S 400/PK-8
10041 S Union Ave 60628 773-535-2700
Dr. Deborah Heath, prin. Fax 535-2711
Fine Arts Academy 100/4-6
9000 S Exchange Ave 60617 773-535-6360
Lena Linnear, prin. Fax 535-6303
Finkl S 500/PK-8
2332 S Western Ave 60608 773-535-5850
Abelino Quintero, prin. Fax 535-4409
Fiske S 400/PK-8
6145 S Ingleside Ave 60637 773-535-0990
Cynthia Miller, prin. Fax 535-0580
Fort Dearborn S 700/PK-8
9025 S Throop St 60620 773-535-2680
Arey DeSadier, prin. Fax 535-2891
Foster Park S 600/PK-8
8530 S Wood St 60620 773-535-2725
Dr. Joronda Crawford, prin. Fax 535-2740
Foundations ES 100/K-5
2040 W Adams St 60612 773-534-7605
Dawn Scarlett, prin. Fax 534-7604
Franklin Fine Arts S 400/K-8
225 W Evergreen Ave 60610 773-534-8510
Carol Friedman, prin. Fax 534-8022
Frazier International Magnet S 50/K-6
4027 W Grenshaw St 60624 773-534-6880
Colette Unger-Teasley, prin. Fax 534-6616
Fuller S 300/PK-8
4214 S Saint Lawrence Ave 60653 773-535-1687
Dr. Patricia Kennedy, prin. Fax 535-1689
Fulton S 700/PK-8
5300 S Hermitage Ave 60609 773-535-9000
Rolland Jasper, prin. Fax 535-9464
Funston S 600/PK-6
2010 N Central Park Ave 60647 773-534-4125
Nilma Osiecki, prin. Fax 534-4551
Gale Community Academy 600/PK-8
1631 W Jonquil Ter 60626 773-534-2100
Richard Glass, prin. Fax 534-2188
Galileo Scholastic Academy 600/PK-8
820 S Carpenter St 60607 773-534-7070
Alfonso Valtierra, prin. Fax 534-7109
Gallistel Language Academy 1,300/PK-8
10347 S Ewing Ave Ste 1 60617 773-535-6540
Patrick MacMahon, prin. Fax 535-6569

Ganas/Yearn to Learn 200/2-4
9000 S Exchange Ave 60617 773-535-6360
Margarite Ortega, prin. Fax 535-6303
Garvey S 500/PK-8
10309 S Morgan St 60643 773-535-2763
Michelle Miller, prin. Fax 535-2761
Garvy S 600/K-8
5225 N Oak Park Ave 60656 773-534-1185
Julie McGlade, prin. Fax 534-1124
Gary S 1,300/PK-K, 3-8
3740 W 31st St 60623 773-534-1455
Alberto Juarez, prin. Fax 534-1435
Gillespie S 700/K-8
9301 S State St 60619 773-535-5065
Dr. Michelle Willis, prin. Fax 535-5048
Goethe S 700/PK-8
2236 N Rockwell St 60647 773-534-4135
Barbara Kargas, prin. Fax 534-4138
Goldblatt S 400/PK-8
4257 W Adams St 60624 773-534-6860
Yvette Curington, prin. Fax 534-6847
Gompers Fine Arts Option MS 400/4-8
12302 S State St 60628 773-535-5475
Melody Seaton, prin. Fax 535-5483
Goodlow Magnet S 500/PK-8
2040 W 62nd St 60636 773-535-9365
Patricia Lewis, prin. Fax 535-9111
Goudy S 700/PK-8
5120 N Winthrop Ave 60640 773-534-2480
Pamela Brandt, prin. Fax 534-2588
Graham S 600/PK-8
4436 S Union Ave 60609 773-535-1308
John Nichols, prin. Fax 535-1424
Gray S 1,300/K-8
3730 N Laramie Ave 60641 773-534-3520
Sandra Carlson, prin. Fax 534-3613
Greeley S 500/PK-8
832 W Sheridan Rd 60613 773-534-5800
Carlos Azcoitia, prin. Fax 534-5783
Greene ES 600/K-5
3525 S Honore St 60609 773-535-4560
Gloria Espinosa, prin. Fax 535-4617
Green S 300/K-8
1150 W 96th St 60643 773-535-2575
Tyrone Dowdell, prin. Fax 535-2742
Gregory S 400/PK-8
3715 W Polk St 60624 773-534-6820
Donella Carter, prin. Fax 534-6484
Gresham S 500/PK-8
8524 S Green St 60620 773-535-3350
Diedrus Brown, prin. Fax 535-3563
Grimes S 500/PK-8
5450 W 64th Pl 60638 773-535-2364
Judith Carlson, prin. Fax 535-2366
Grissom S 300/PK-8
12810 S Escanaba Ave 60633 773-535-5380
Kathlene Orr, prin. Fax 535-5362
Guggenheim S 300/K-8
7141 S Morgan St 60621 773-535-3587
Mary McNair, prin. Fax 535-3466
Gunsaulus Scholastic Academy 700/K-8
4420 S Sacramento Ave 60632 773-535-7215
Amy Kotz, prin. Fax 535-7222
Haines S 800/PK-8
247 W 23rd Pl 60616 773-534-9200
Diann Wright, prin. Fax 534-9209
Hale S 900/PK-8
6140 S Melvina Ave 60638 773-535-2265
Therese Connell, prin. Fax 535-2275
Haley S 800/PK-8
11411 S Eggleston Ave 60628 773-535-5340
Vaida Williams, prin. Fax 535-5351
Hamilton S 200/K-8
1650 W Cornelia Ave 60657 773-534-5484
Dr. Mila Strasburg, prin. Fax 534-5782
Hamline S 900/PK-8
4747 S Bishop St 60609 773-535-4565
Valerie Brown, prin. Fax 535-4546
Hammond ES 500/PK-8
2819 W 21st Pl 60623 773-535-4580
Linda Salinas, prin. Fax 535-4579
Hampton Fine & Performing Arts S 700/PK-8
3434 W 77th St 60652 773-535-4030
Dorothy Armour, prin. Fax 535-4031
Hanson Park S 1,500/PK-8
5411 W Fullerton Ave 60639 773-534-3100
Susan Stoll, prin. Fax 534-3374
Harte ES 400/PK-6
1556 E 56th St 60637 773-535-0870
Shenethe Parks, prin. Fax 535-0666
Harvard S 500/PK-8
7525 S Harvard Ave 60620 773-535-3045
Andre Cowling, prin. Fax 535-3332
Haugan ES 1,100/PK-5
4540 N Hamlin Ave 60625 773-534-5040
Rosa Valdez, prin. Fax 534-5045
Hawthorne Scholastic Academy 600/K-8
3319 N Clifton Ave 60657 773-534-5550
Anna Alvarado, prin. Fax 534-5781
Hay Community Academy 700/PK-8
1018 N Laramie Ave Ste 1 60651 773-534-6000
Wayne Williams, prin. Fax 534-6035
Hayt S 900/PK-8
1518 W Granville Ave 60660 773-534-2040
Daniel Gomez, prin. Fax 534-2187
Healy S 1,300/PK-8
3010 S Parnell Ave 60616 773-534-9190
Mary Ellen Ratkovich, prin. Fax 534-9182
Hearst S 700/PK-8
4640 S Lamon Ave 60638 773-535-2376
Eleanora Nickerson, prin. Fax 535-2341
Hedges S 1,000/PK-8
4747 S Winchester Ave 60609 773-535-7360
Adelfio Garcia, prin. Fax 535-4178
Hefferan S 400/PK-8
4409 W Wilcox St 60624 773-534-6192
Jacqueline Hearns, prin. Fax 534-6190
Henderson S 600/PK-8
5650 S Wolcott Ave 60636 773-535-9080
Richard Richardson, prin. Fax 535-9115

Hendricks S 300/PK-8
4316 S Princeton Ave 60609 773-535-1696
Mary Jean Smith, prin. Fax 535-1700
Henry ES 700/PK-6
4250 N Saint Louis Ave 60618 773-534-5060
James Burns, prin. Fax 534-5042
Henson S 400/PK-8
1326 S Avers Ave 60623 773-534-1804
Robert Pales, prin. Fax 534-1819
Herbert S 400/PK-8
2131 W Monroe St 60612 773-534-7806
Denise Gillespie, prin. Fax 534-7884
Herzl S 800/PK-8
3711 W Douglas Blvd 60623 773-534-1480
Patricia Surgeon, prin. Fax 534-1486
Hibbard ES 1,200/PK-6
3244 W Ainslie St 60625 773-534-5191
Scott Ahlman, prin. Fax 534-5208
Higgins Community S 400/PK-8
11710 S Morgan St 60643 773-535-5625
Dr. Mabel Alfred, prin. Fax 535-5623
Hinton S 600/PK-8
644 W 71st St 60621 773-535-3875
Pamela Brunson-Allen, prin. Fax 535-3885
Hitch S 400/K-8
5625 N McVicker Ave 60646 773-534-1189
Deborah Reese, prin. Fax 534-1176
Holden S 600/K-8
1104 W 31st St 60608 773-535-7200
Andrew Wawrzyniak, prin. Fax 535-7113
Holmes S 600/PK-8
955 W Garfield Blvd 60621 773-535-9025
Dorothy Naughton, prin. Fax 535-9127
Howe S 700/PK-8
720 N Lorel Ave 60644 773-534-6060
Keisha Campbell, prin. Fax 534-6080
Hoyne S 400/K-8
8905 S Crandon Ave 60617 773-535-6425
Yvonne Calhoun, prin. Fax 535-6444
Hughes S 400/PK-8
4247 W 15th St 60623 773-534-1762
Lucille Howard, prin. Fax 534-1715
Hughes S 400/PK-8
10211 S Crandon Ave 60617 773-535-6510
Earl Ware, prin. Fax 535-6520
Hurley S 900/K-8
3849 W 69th Pl 60629 773-535-2068
Dolores Cupp, prin. Fax 535-2059
Inter-American Magnet S 600/PK-8
851 W Waveland Ave 60613 773-534-5490
Susan Kilbane, prin. Fax 534-5483
Irving S 500/PK-8
749 S Oakley Blvd 60612 773-534-7295
Valeria Newell, prin. Fax 534-7289
Jackson Language Academy 500/K-8
1340 W Harrison St 60607 773-534-7000
Mathew Ditto, prin. Fax 534-9338
Jackson S 400/PK-8
917 W 88th St 60620 773-535-3341
Dr. Kimberly McNeal, prin. Fax 535-3453
Jahn S 400/K-8
3149 N Wolcott Ave 60657 773-534-5500
Sulma Grigalunas, prin. Fax 534-5533
Jamieson S 800/PK-8
5650 N Mozart St 60659 773-534-2395
Robert Baughman, prin. Fax 534-2579
Jenner Academy of the Arts 500/PK-8
1119 N Cleveland Ave 60610 773-534-8440
Zelma Woodson, prin. Fax 534-8188
Jensen Scholastic Academy 500/PK-8
3030 W Harrison St 60612 773-534-6840
Catherine Jernigan, prin. Fax 534-6722
Johnson S 400/PK-8
1420 S Albany Ave 60623 773-534-1829
Sallie Pinkston, prin. Fax 534-1355
Joplin S 600/K-8
7931 S Honore St 60620 773-535-3425
Alene Mason, prin. Fax 535-3442
Jordan Community S 700/PK-8
7414 N Wolcott Ave 60626 773-534-2220
Willie White, prin. Fax 534-2231
Jungman S 400/PK-8
1746 S Miller St 60608 773-534-7375
Zaida Hernandez, prin. Fax 534-7383
Kanoon Magnet S 700/PK-8
2233 S Kedzie Ave 60623 773-534-1736
Juanita Saucedo, prin. Fax 534-1740
Keller Regional Gifted Center 200/1-8
3020 W 108th St 60655 773-535-2636
LaTanya McDade, prin. Fax 535-2635
Kellman Corporate Community S 300/PK-8
751 S Sacramento Blvd 60612 773-534-6602
Brenda Browder, prin. Fax 534-6601
Kellogg S 300/K-8
9241 S Leavitt St 60643 773-535-2590
Zipporah Hightower, prin. Fax 535-2596
Kershaw S 300/PK-8
6450 S Lowe Ave 60621 773-535-3050
Patricia Johnson, prin. Fax 535-3677
Key S 500/K-8
517 N Parkside Ave 60644 773-534-6230
Sandra Banger, prin. Fax 534-6238
Kilmer S 900/PK-8
6700 N Greenview Ave 60626 773-534-2115
Miguel Trujillo, prin. Fax 534-2186
King S 300/K-8
740 S Campbell Ave 60612 773-534-7898
Shelton Flowers, prin. Fax 534-7881
Kinzie S 700/PK-8
5625 S Mobile Ave 60638 773-535-2425
Dr. Sean Egan, prin. Fax 535-2086
Kipling S 500/PK-8
9351 S Lowe Ave 60620 773-535-3151
LaWanda Bishop, prin. Fax 535-3187
Kohn S 600/PK-8
10414 S State St 60628 773-535-5489
Carol Briggs, prin. Fax 535-5484
Kozminski Community S 500/PK-8
936 E 54th St 60615 773-535-0980
Lionel Bordelon, prin. Fax 535-0982

LaFayette S 700/PK-8
2714 W Augusta Blvd 60622 773-534-4326
Trisha Shrode, prin. Fax 534-4022

Lara Academy 600/PK-8
4619 S Wolcott Ave 60609 773-535-4389
Mary Cavey, prin. Fax 535-4471

LaSalle II Magnet ES PK-6
1148 N Honore St 60622 773-534-0490
Suzanne Velasquez-Sheehy, prin. Fax 534-0491

La Salle Language Academy 600/K-8
1734 N Orleans St 60614 773-534-8470
Elisabeth Heurtefeu, prin. Fax 534-8021

Lathrop S 400/PK-8
1440 S Christiana Ave 60623 773-534-1812
Rhonda Larkin, prin. Fax 534-1814

Lavizzo S 700/PK-8
138 W 109th St 60628 773-535-5300
Arnold Bickham, prin. Fax 535-5313

Lawndale Community Academy 500/PK-8
3500 W Douglas Blvd 60623 773-534-1635
Jeannine Wolf, prin. Fax 534-1644

Lawrence S 700/PK-8
9928 S Crandon Ave 60617 773-535-6320
Jewel McClinton, prin. Fax 535-6318

Lee S 1,100/K-8
6448 S Tripp Ave 60629 773-535-2255
Christiana Arroyo, prin. Fax 535-2287

Leland ES 200/PK-3
5221 W Congress Pkwy 60644 773-534-6340
Dr. Loretta Brown-Lawrence, prin. Fax 534-6040

Lenart Regional Gifted Center 300/K-8
8101 S LaSalle St 60620 773-535-0040
Joanna Theodore, prin. Fax 535-0048

Lewis S 1,000/PK-8
1431 N Leamington Ave Ste 1 60651 773-534-3060
Sharon Brown-Haynes, prin. Fax 534-3010

Libby S 700/PK-8
5300 S Loomis Blvd 60609 773-535-9050
Kurt Jones, prin. Fax 535-9383

Lincoln S 700/K-8
615 W Kemper Pl 60614 773-534-5720
Mark Armendariz, prin. Fax 534-5778

Linne S 700/PK-8
3221 N Sacramento Ave 60618 773-534-5262
Daniel Rohan, prin. Fax 534-5287

Little Village Academy 800/PK-8
2620 S Lawndale Ave 60623 773-534-1880
Elsa Carmona, prin. Fax 534-1893

Lloyd S 1,400/PK-5
2103 N Lamon Ave 60639 773-534-3070
Fernando Kim, prin. Fax 534-3388

Locke S 1,200/K-8
2828 N Oak Park Ave 60634 773-534-3300
Graciano Ortega, prin. Fax 534-3168

Logandale MS 300/6-8
3212 W George St 60618 773-534-5350
Dr. Dennis Sweeney, prin. Fax 534-5349

Lovett S 600/PK-8
6333 W Bloomingdale Ave 60639 773-534-3130
Donna Newton-Holland, prin. Fax 534-3384

Lowell S 800/PK-8
3320 W Hirsch St Ste 1 60651 773-534-4300
Gladys Rivera, prin. Fax 534-4306

Lozano S 500/PK-8
1424 N Cleaver St, 773-534-4150
Dr. Aurelio Acevedo, prin. Fax 534-4260

Lyon S 1,200/K-8
2941 N McVicker Ave 60634 773-534-3120
Ivette Robles, prin. Fax 534-3375

Madero MS 300/6-8
3202 W 28th St 60623 773-535-4466
Jose Illanes, prin. Fax 535-4469

Madison S 500/PK-8
7433 S Dorchester Ave 60619 773-535-0551
Dr. Beverly Greene, prin. Fax 535-0582

Manierre S 600/PK-8
1420 N Hudson Ave 60610 773-534-8456
Shirley Roach, prin. Fax 534-8020

Mann S 800/K-8
8050 S Chappel Ave Ste 1 60617 773-535-6640
Patricia McPherson-Davis, prin. Fax 535-6664

Marconi Community Academy 400/PK-8
230 N Kolmar Ave 60624 773-534-6210
Sean Clayton, prin. Fax 534-6093

Marquette S 1,700/PK-8
6550 S Richmond St 60629 773-535-9260
Paul O'Toole, prin. Fax 535-9266

Marshall MS 400/7-8
3900 N Lawndale Ave 60618 773-534-5200
Jose Barillas, prin. Fax 534-5292

Marsh S 700/PK-8
9822 S Exchange Ave 60617 773-535-6430
Gerald Dugan, prin. Fax 535-6446

Mason S 700/PK-8
4217 W 18th St 60623 773-534-1530
Tonya Tolbert, prin. Fax 534-1544

May Community Academy 700/PK-8
512 S Lavergne Ave 60644 773-534-6140
Roger Lewis, prin. Fax 534-6174

Mayer S 500/PK-8
2250 N Clifton Ave 60614 773-534-5535
Katie Konieczny, prin. Fax 534-5777

Mayo S 500/K-8
249 E 37th St 60653 773-535-1260
Nadine Dillanado, prin. Fax 535-1267

Mays Academy S 400/PK-8
838 W Marquette Rd 60621 773-535-3892
Dr. Patricia McCann, prin. Fax 535-3895

McAuliffe ES 800/PK-6
1841 N Springfield Ave 60647 773-534-4400
David Pino, prin. Fax 534-4744

McClellan S 200/K-8
3527 S Wallace St 60609 773-535-1732
Mary Garcia-Humphreys, prin. Fax 535-1940

McCorkle S 300/PK-8
4421 S State St 60609 773-535-1793
Janet House, prin. Fax 535-1753

McCormick ES 900/PK-5
2712 S Sawyer Ave 60623 773-535-7252
Virginia Rivera, prin. Fax 535-7347

McCutcheon S 400/PK-8
4865 N Sheridan Rd 60640 773-534-2680
Carol Ann Lang, prin. Fax 534-2578

McDade Classical ES 200/K-6
8801 S Indiana Ave 60619 773-535-3669
Rufus Coleman, prin. Fax 535-3667

McDowell ES 200/K-5
1419 E 89th St 60619 773-535-6404
Dr. Jo Easterling-Hood, prin. Fax 535-6434

McKay ES 1,400/PK-8
6901 S Fairfield Ave 60629 773-535-9340
Dawn Prather-Hawk, prin. Fax 535-9443

McKinley Park S 300/K-8
2744 W Pershing Rd 60632 773-535-4180
Frances Garcia, prin. Fax 535-4179

McNair Community Academy 600/PK-8
4820 W Walton St 60651 773-534-8980
Dr. Shirley Dillard, prin. Fax 534-0668

McPherson S 700/PK-8
4728 N Wolcott Ave 60640 773-534-2625
Carmen Mendoza, prin. Fax 534-2637

Medill ES 200/PK-8
1301 W 14th St 60608 773-534-7750
Denise Gamble, prin. Fax 534-7757

Melody S 500/PK-8
412 S Keeler Ave 60624 773-534-6850
Dorothea Lattyak, prin. Fax 534-6839

Metcalfe Community Academy 800/PK-8
12339 S Normal Ave 60628 773-535-5590
Michele Barton, prin. Fax 535-5570

Mireles Academy 1,200/PK-8
9000 S Exchange Ave 60617 773-535-6360
Rosalydia Diaz, prin. Fax 535-6303

Mitchell S 200/PK-8
2233 W Ohio St 60612 773-534-7655
Louis Soria, prin. Fax 534-7633

Mollison S 300/PK-8
4415 S King Dr 60653 773-535-1804
Wilhelmina Kenan, prin. Fax 535-1803

Monroe S 1,300/PK-8
3651 W Schubert Ave 60647 773-534-4155
Edwin Rivera, prin. Fax 534-4593

Moos S 700/PK-8
1711 N California Ave 60647 773-534-4340
Maria Cruz, prin. Fax 534-4535

Morgan S 400/PK-8
8407 S Kerfoot Ave 60620 773-535-3366
Linda Walker, prin. Fax 535-3675

Morrill Math & Science S 1,000/PK-8
6011 S Rockwell St 60629 773-535-9288
Patricia Costello, prin. Fax 535-9214

Morton Career Academy 400/PK-8
431 N Troy St 60612 773-534-6791
Phyllis McCune, prin. Fax 534-6711

Mt. Greenwood S 600/PK-8
10841 S Homan Ave 60655 773-535-2786
Catherine Reidy, prin. Fax 535-2743

Mt. Vernon S 400/PK-8
10540 S Morgan St 60643 773-535-2825
Daphne Strahan, prin. Fax 535-2827

Mozart ES 900/PK-6
2200 N Hamlin Ave 60647 773-534-4160
Sonia Caban, prin. Fax 534-4588

Murphy ES 600/PK-6
3539 W Grace St 60618 773-534-5223
Christine Zelenka, prin. Fax 534-5212

Murray Language Academy 400/K-6
5335 S Kenwood Ave 60615 773-535-0585
Greg Mason, prin. Fax 535-0590

Nash S 600/PK-8
4837 W Erie St 60644 773-534-6125
Dr. Tresa Dunbar, prin. Fax 534-6105

National Teachers Academy 500/PK-8
55 W Cermak Rd 60616 773-534-9970
Amy Rome, prin. Fax 534-9971

Neil S 400/PK-8
8555 S Michigan Ave 60619 773-535-3000
Helen Wells, prin. Fax 535-3010

Nettelhorst S 500/PK-8
3252 N Broadway St 60657 773-534-5810
Cindy Wulbert, prin. Fax 534-5776

Newberry Math Science Academy 600/K-8
700 W Willow St 60614 773-534-8000
Renaud Beaudoin, prin. Fax 534-8018

New Field PS 600/PK-3
1707 W Morse Ave 60626 773-534-2760
Blanca Trevino, prin. Fax 534-2773

Nia MS 50/6-8
2040 W Adams St 60612 773-534-7494
Dawn Scarlett, prin. Fax 534-7497

Nicholson S for Math/Science 500/PK-8
6006 S Peoria St 60621 773-535-3285
Rodney Hull, prin. Fax 535-3443

Nightingale S 1,400/PK-8
5250 S Rockwell St 60632 773-535-9270
Dr. Roy Pletsch, prin. Fax 535-0430

Ninos Heroes Academic Center 700/K-8
8344 S Commercial Ave 60617 773-535-6694
Jeannine Jones, prin. Fax 535-6673

Nixon ES 1,100/PK-6
2121 N Keeler Ave 60639 773-534-4375
Herman Escobar, prin. Fax 534-4539

Nkrumah Academy K-1
901 E 95th St 60619 773-535-8664
Dr. Nadine Headen, prin. Fax 535-8096

Nobel S 900/PK-8
4127 W Hirsch St 60651 773-534-4365
Manuel Adrianzen, prin. Fax 534-4369

North River S 300/K-8
4416 N Troy St 60625 773-534-0590
Dr. Gilberto Sanchez, prin. Fax 534-0597

Northwest MS 1,000/6-8
5252 W Palmer St 60639 773-534-3250
Marilyn Strojny, prin. Fax 534-3251

Norwood Park S 400/PK-8
5900 N Nina Ave 60631 773-534-1198
Dr. William Meuer, prin. Fax 534-1178

Ogden S 600/K-8
24 W Walton St 60610 773-534-8110
Kenneth Staral, prin. Fax 534-8017

Oglesby S 700/PK-8
7646 S Green St 60620 773-535-3060
Clifton Hunt, prin. Fax 535-3390

O'Keefe S 700/K-8
6940 S Merrill Ave 60649 773-535-0600
Linda Martin, prin. Fax 535-0611

Onahan S 600/PK-8
6634 W Raven St 60631 773-534-1180
Karen Koegler, prin. Fax 534-1163

Oriole Park S 600/PK-8
5424 N Oketo Ave 60656 773-534-1201
Elias Estrada, prin. Fax 534-1066

Orozco S 700/1-8
1940 W 18th St 60608 773-534-7215
Coralia Barraza, prin. Fax 534-7329

Ortiz de Dominguez ES 800/PK-2
3000 S Lawndale Ave 60623 773-534-1600
Angelica Herrera-Vest, prin. Fax 534-1415

Otis S 500/PK-8
525 N Armour St, 773-534-7665
Jaime Sanchez, prin. Fax 534-7672

O'Toole S 800/PK-8
6550 S Seeley Ave 60636 773-535-9040
Erick Pruitt, prin. Fax 535-9093

Overton ES 400/PK-8
221 E 49th St 60615 773-535-1430
Barbara Luster, prin. Fax 535-1007

Owen Scholastic Academy 300/K-8
8247 S Christiana Ave 60652 773-535-9330
Dr. Stanley Griggs, prin. Fax 535-9496

Owens Community Academy 400/K-3
12450 S State St 60628 773-535-5661
Sam Jordan, prin. Fax 535-5648

Paderewski Learning Academy 300/PK-8
2221 S Lawndale Ave 60623 773-534-1821
Dr. Jo Anne Roberts, prin. Fax 534-1974

Palmer S 900/K-8
5051 N Kenneth Ave 60630 773-534-3704
Patricia Bowman, prin. Fax 534-3771

Parker Community Academy 700/PK-8
6800 S Stewart Ave 60621 773-535-3375
Bernadette Giles, prin. Fax 535-3336

Park Manor S 400/PK-8
7037 S Rhodes Ave 60637 773-535-3070
Amirita Rodgers, prin. Fax 535-3273

Parkman S 300/PK-8
245 W 51st St 60609 773-535-1739
Sonja James, prin. Fax 535-1742

Parkside Community Academy 400/PK-8
6938 S East End Ave 60649 773-535-0940
Dorothy Thompson, prin. Fax 535-0966

Pasteur S 1,300/K-8
5825 S Kostner Ave 60629 773-535-2270
James Gilliat, prin. Fax 535-2235

Pathways S 200/PK-6
3010 S Parnell Ave 60616 773-534-9190
Rebecca Katsulis, prin. Fax 534-9110

Peabody S 300/PK-8
1444 W Augusta Blvd, 773-534-4170
Federico Flores, prin. Fax 534-4172

Peck S 1,500/PK-8
3826 W 58th St 60629 773-535-2450
Okab Hassan, prin. Fax 535-2228

Peirce S of International Studies 900/PK-8
1423 W Bryn Mawr Ave 60660 773-534-2440
Nancy Mendez, prin. Fax 534-2577

Penn S 400/PK-8
1616 S Avers Ave 60623 773-534-1665
Sherryl Moore-Ollie, prin. Fax 534-1673

Perez S 500/PK-8
1241 W 19th St 60608 773-534-7650
Sylvia Stamatoglou, prin. Fax 534-7621

Performing Arts Academy 200/K-8
9000 S Exchange Ave 60617 773-535-6360
Joyce Carter, prin. Fax 535-6303

Pershing East Magnet S 200/PK-3
3113 S Rhodes Ave 60616 773-534-9272
Antonia Hill, prin. Fax 534-9277

Pershing West MS 300/4-8
3200 S Calumet Ave 60616 773-534-9240
Cheryl Watkins, prin. Fax 534-9249

Peterson S 1,000/PK-8
5510 N Christiana Ave 60625 773-534-5070
Daniel Lucas, prin. Fax 534-5077

Piccolo - Connections S 200/4-6
1040 N Keeler Ave 60651 773-534-4425
Ken Vorhees, prin. Fax 534-4248

Piccolo - Great Expectations S 200/K-5
1040 N Keeler Ave 60651 773-534-4425
Shannon Gahart, prin. Fax 534-4248

Piccolo S 800/PK-8
1040 N Keeler Ave Ste 1 60651 773-534-4425
Althea Hammond, prin. Fax 534-4248

Pickard S 600/PK-8
2301 W 21st Pl 60608 773-535-7280
Rigo Hernandez, prin. Fax 535-7199

Pilsen Community Academy ES 500/PK-6
1420 W 17th St 60608 773-534-7675
Dr. Adel Ali, prin. Fax 534-7797

Pirie Fine Arts & Academic Center 600/PK-6
650 E 85th St 60619 773-535-3435
Senalda Grady, prin. Fax 535-3405

Plamondon S 200/K-8
2642 W 15th Pl 60608 773-534-1789
Dr. Yvonne Austin, prin. Fax 534-1858

Poe Classical ES 200/K-6
10538 S Langley Ave 60628 773-535-5525
Rae Smith, prin. Fax 535-5213

Pope S 200/K-8
1852 S Albany Ave 60623 773-534-1795
Beverly Jordan, prin. Fax 534-1719

Portage Park S 1,100/PK-8
5330 W Berteau Ave 60641 773-534-3576
Mark Berman, prin. Fax 534-3558

Powell S 600/K-8
7530 S South Shore Dr 60649 773-535-6650
Derek Jordan, prin. Fax 535-6602

Prescott S 200/PK-8
1632 W Wrightwood Ave 60614 773-534-5505
Erin Roche, prin. Fax 534-5542

Price S 300/4-8
4351 S Drexel Blvd 60653 773-535-1300
Kimberly Moore, prin. Fax 535-1324
Pritzker S 600/PK-8
2009 W Schiller St 60622 773-534-4415
Joenile Reese, prin. Fax 534-4634
Prussing S 700/PK-8
4650 N Menard Ave 60630 773-534-3460
Dr. Lloyd Ehrenberg, prin. Fax 534-3530
Pulaski Fine Arts Academy 900/PK-8
2230 W McLean Ave 60647 773-534-4391
Leonor Karl, prin. Fax 534-4392
Pullman S 400/PK-8
11311 S Forrestville Ave 60628 773-535-5395
Felicia Hooker, prin. Fax 535-5393
Randolph Magnet S 700/PK-8
7316 S Hoyne Ave 60636 773-535-9015
Michelle Smith, prin. Fax 535-9455
Ravenswood S 500/PK-8
4332 N Paulina St 60613 773-534-5525
Heather Connolly, prin. Fax 534-5775
Ray ES 700/PK-6
5631 S Kimbark Ave 60637 773-535-0970
Bernadette Butler, prin. Fax 535-0842
Reavis S 400/K-8
834 E 50th St 60615 773-535-1060
Michael Johnson, prin. Fax 535-1032
Reed S 300/PK-8
6350 S Stewart Ave 60621 773-535-3075
Rebecca Watson, prin. Fax 535-3232
Reilly S 1,600/PK-8
3650 W School St 60618 773-534-5250
Maria Rodriguez-O'Keefe, prin. Fax 534-5169
Reinberg S 1,300/PK-8
3425 N Major Ave 60634 773-534-3465
Edwin Loch, prin. Fax 534-3798
Revere S 500/PK-8
1010 E 72nd St 60619 773-535-0618
Veronica Thompson, prin. Fax 535-0614
Rising Stars Academy 100/5-8
9000 S Exchange Ave 60617 773-535-6360
Ben Perez, prin. Fax 535-6303
Robinson ES 300/PK-3
4225 S Lake Park Ave 60653 773-535-1777
Jacqueline Wilson-Thomas, prin. Fax 535-1727
Rogers S 600/PK-8
7345 N Washtenaw Ave Ste 1 60645 773-534-2125
Christine Jabbari, prin. Fax 534-2193
Roque De Duprey S 300/K-8
1405 N Washtenaw Ave 60622 773-534-4230
Gloria Roman, prin. Fax 534-4239
Ross S 500/PK-8
6059 S Wabash Ave 60637 773-535-0650
Dr. Joy Pilcher, prin. Fax 535-0649
Ruggles S 400/PK-8
7831 S Prairie Ave 60619 773-535-3085
Ida Patterson, prin. Fax 535-3129
Ruiz S 1,000/PK-8
2410 S Leavitt St 60608 773-535-4825
Dana Andre Butler, prin. Fax 535-7148
Ryder Math & Science S 500/PK-8
8716 S Wallace St 60620 773-535-3843
Janice Preston, prin. Fax 535-3883
Ryerson S 500/PK-8
646 N Lawndale Ave 60624 773-534-6700
Lorenzo Russell, prin. Fax 534-6708
Sabin Magnet S 600/K-8
2216 W Hirsch St 60622 773-534-4491
Barton Dassinger, prin. Fax 534-4511
Salazar Bilingual Center 400/PK-8
160 W Wendell St 60610 773-534-8310
Martha Miranda, prin. Fax 534-8313
Sandoval S 1,300/K-8
5534 S Saint Louis Ave 60629 773-535-0457
Dr. Ana Espinoza, prin. Fax 535-0467
Saucedo Scholastic Academy 1,200/PK-8
2850 W 24th Blvd 60623 773-534-1770
Leticia Gonzalez, prin. Fax 534-1356
Sauganash S 400/K-8
6040 N Kilpatrick Ave 60646 773-534-3470
Christine Munns, prin. Fax 534-3707
Sawyer S 2,000/K-8
5248 S Sawyer Ave 60632 773-535-9275
Nelly Robles-Vazquez, prin. Fax 535-9216
Sayre Language Academy 500/PK-8
1850 N Newland Ave 60707 773-534-3351
Gail Funk, prin. Fax 534-3394
Scammon S 1,100/PK-8
4201 W Henderson St 60641 773-534-3475
Mary Weaver, prin. Fax 534-3516
Schiller S 300/PK-8
640 W Scott St Ste 1 60610 773-534-8490
Sonja James, prin. Fax 534-8016
Schmid S 300/PK-8
9755 S Greenwood Ave 60628 773-535-6235
Deborah Williams, prin. Fax 535-6092
Schneider S 200/PK-8
2957 N Hoyne Ave 60618 773-534-5510
Vivian Edwards, prin. Fax 534-5587
S.M.A.R.T. S 300/1-5
9000 S Exchange Ave 60617 773-535-6360
Yolanda Rangel, prin. Fax 535-6303
Schubert ES 1,400/PK-5
2727 N Long Ave 60639 773-534-3080
Elba Maisonet, prin. Fax 534-3079
Seward S 900/PK-8
4600 S Hermitage Ave 60609 773-535-4890
Marcey Reyes, prin. Fax 535-4884
Sexton S 500/K-8
6020 S Langley Ave 60637 773-535-0640
Ginger Bryant, prin. Fax 535-0712
Sheridan Math & Science Academy 500/K-8
533 W 27th St 60616 773-534-9120
John O'Connell, prin. Fax 534-9124
Sherman S 600/PK-8
1000 W 52nd St 60609 773-535-1757
Lionel Allen, prin. Fax 535-0343
Sherwood S 400/PK-8
245 W 57th St 60621 773-535-0829
Alice Buzanis, prin. Fax 535-0872
Shields S 1,800/PK-8
4250 S Rockwell St 60632 773-535-7285
Phillip Salemi, prin. Fax 535-7129
Shoesmith ES 400/PK-6
1330 E 50th St 60615 773-535-1764
Patricia Watson, prin. Fax 535-1877
Shoop Academy of Math-Science Tech 900/PK-8
1460 W 112th St 60643 773-535-2715
Lisa Moreno, prin. Fax 535-2714
Skinner Classical S 600/K-8
1443 N Ogden Ave 60610 773-534-7790
Deborah Clark, prin. Fax 534-7879
Smith S 500/PK-8
744 E 103rd St 60628 773-535-5689
John Banks, prin. Fax 535-5101
Smyser S 900/PK-8
4310 N Melvina Ave 60634 773-534-3711
Jerry Travlos, prin. Fax 534-3555
Smyth S 600/PK-8
1059 W 13th St 60608 773-534-7180
Ronald Whitmore, prin. Fax 534-7127
Solomon S 300/K-8
6206 N Hamlin Ave 60659 773-534-5226
Susan Moy, prin. Fax 534-5167
Songhai Learning Institute 600/PK-8
11725 S Perry Ave 60628 773-535-5547
Taliva Tillman, prin. Fax 535-5519
South Chicago Community Area S 200/K-8
8255 S Houston Ave 60617 773-535-7930
Marcos Ayala, prin. Fax 535-7934
South Loop S 500/PK-8
1212 S Plymouth Ct 60605 773-534-8690
Tara Shelton, prin. Fax 534-8689
Spencer Math & Science Academy 1,000/PK-8
214 N Lavergne Ave 60644 773-534-6150
Shawn Jackson, prin. Fax 534-6239
Spry Community S 800/PK-8
2400 S Marshall Blvd 60623 773-534-1700
Nilda Medina, prin. Fax 534-1688
Spry - Peace S 300/PK-5
2400 S Marshall Blvd 60623 773-534-1700
Jean Laurence, prin. Fax 534-1688
Stagg S 600/PK-8
7424 S Morgan St 60621 773-535-3565
Ruth Miller, prin. Fax 535-3564
Stevenson S 1,200/PK-8
8010 S Kostner Ave 60652 773-535-2280
Karen Sagodic-Kowalski, prin. Fax 535-2339
Stewart S 400/PK-8
4525 N Kenmore Ave 60640 773-534-2640
Juliet Rempa, prin. Fax 534-2576
Stockton S 600/PK-8
4420 N Beacon St 60640 773-534-2450
Jill Besenjak, prin. Fax 534-2458
Stone Scholastic Academy 600/K-8
6239 N Leavitt St 60659 773-534-2045
Joyce Nakamura, prin. Fax 534-2092
Stowe S 1,100/PK-8
3444 W Wabansia Ave 60647 773-534-4175
Dr. Charles Kyle, prin. Fax 534-4167
Suder Campus Montessori S 100/PK-4
2022 W Washington Blvd 60612 773-534-7685
Stephanie Bloom, prin. Fax 534-7933
Sullivan S 800/PK-8
8331 S Mackinaw Ave 60617 773-535-6585
Dr. Joyce Nelson, prin. Fax 535-6561
Sumner Community Academy 600/PK-8
4320 W 5th Ave 60624 773-534-6730
Delores Robinson, prin. Fax 534-6736
Sutherland S 800/K-8
10015 S Leavitt St 60643 773-535-2580
Catherine Gannon, prin. Fax 535-2621
Swift S 600/PK-8
5900 N Winthrop Ave 60660 773-534-2695
Harlee Till, prin. Fax 534-2575
Talcott Fine Arts & Museum Academy 500/PK-8
1840 W Ohio St 60622 773-534-7130
Craig Benes, prin. Fax 534-7126
Talman Community S 300/K-8
5450 S Talman Ave 60632 773-535-7850
Jacqueline Medina, prin. Fax 535-7857
Tanner S 600/K-8
7350 S Evans Ave 60619 773-535-3870
Mona Miller, prin. Fax 535-3874
Tarkington S of Excellence 900/PK-6
3330 W 71st St 60629 773-535-4700
Vincent Iturralde, prin. Fax 535-4713
Taylor S 700/PK-8
9912 S Avenue H 60617 773-535-6240
Dr. William Truesdale, prin. Fax 535-6232
Telpochcalli S 300/K-8
2832 W 24th Blvd 60623 773-534-1402
Tamara Witzl, prin. Fax 534-1404
Thomas ECC PK-PK
3625 S Hoyne Ave 60609 773-535-4088
Elizabeth Najera, prin. Fax 535-4085
Thorp Scholastic Academy 800/K-8
6024 W Warwick Ave 60634 773-534-3640
Kathleen Bandolik, prin. Fax 534-3639
Thorp S 600/PK-8
8914 S Buffalo Ave 60617 773-535-6250
Tony Fisher, prin. Fax 535-6582
Till S 900/PK-8
6543 S Champlain Ave 60637 773-535-0570
Mary Rogers, prin. Fax 535-0598
Tilton S 500/PK-8
223 N Keeler Ave 60624 773-534-6746
Leatrice Satterwhite, prin. Fax 826-1915
Tonti S 1,100/PK-8
5815 S Homan Ave 60629 773-535-9280
Maria Vallejos-Howell, prin. Fax 535-0470
Trumbull S 500/PK-8
5200 N Ashland Ave 60640 773-534-2430
Robert Wilkin, prin. Fax 534-2401
Turner-Drew Language Academy 400/K-8
9300 S Princeton Ave 60620 773-535-5720
Dr. Sabrina Jackson, prin. Fax 535-5203
Twain S 1,000/K-8
5134 S Lotus Ave 60638 773-535-2290
Sandra James, prin. Fax 535-2248
Vanderpoel Humanities Academy 300/K-8
9510 S Prospect Ave 60643 773-535-2690
A. McClellan-Brown, prin. Fax 535-2677
Volta S 900/PK-8
4950 N Avers Ave 60625 773-534-5080
Roger Johnson, prin. Fax 534-5280
Von Humboldt S 700/PK-8
2620 W Hirsch St 60622 773-534-4480
Christ Kalamatas, prin. Fax 534-4476
Wacker S 300/PK-8
9746 S Morgan St 60643 773-535-2821
Valerie Bratton, prin. Fax 535-2829
Wadsworth S 400/PK-8
6420 S University Ave 60637 773-535-0730
Velma Cooksey, prin. Fax 535-0743
Walsh S 600/PK-8
2015 S Peoria St 60608 773-534-7950
Krish Mohip, prin. Fax 534-7168
Ward S 500/PK-8
2701 S Shields Ave 60616 773-534-9050
Sharon Wilcher, prin. Fax 534-9044
Ward S 500/PK-8
410 N Monticello Ave 60624 773-534-6440
Relanda Hobbs, prin. Fax 534-6718
Warren S 400/PK-8
9239 S Jeffery Ave Ste 1 60617 773-535-6625
Margaret Snyder, prin. Fax 535-6698
Washington S 700/PK-8
3611 E 114th St 60617 773-535-5010
Armando Rodriguez, prin. Fax 535-5124
Washington S 700/PK-8
9130 S University Ave 60619 773-535-6225
Sandra Lewis, prin. Fax 535-6277
Waters S of Fine Arts 300/K-8
4540 N Campbell Ave 60625 773-534-5090
Titia Kipp, prin. Fax 534-5087
Webster S 600/PK-8
4055 W Arthington St 60624 773-534-6925
Princetta Preston-Scott, prin. Fax 534-6949
Wells Preparatory S 100/K-8
244 E Pershing Rd 60653 773-535-1204
Euel Bunton, prin. Fax 535-1009
Wentworth S 500/PK-8
6950 S Sangamon St 60621 773-535-3394
Paula Powers, prin. Fax 535-3434
Wescott S 600/PK-8
409 W 80th St 60620 773-535-3090
Monique Dockery, prin. Fax 535-3099
West Park Academy 800/PK-8
1425 N Tripp Ave 60651 773-534-4940
Saundra Jones, prin. Fax 534-4945
West Pullman S 500/PK-8
11941 S Parnell Ave 60628 773-535-5500
Darlene Reynolds, prin. Fax 535-5781
Whistler S 500/PK-8
11533 S Ada St 60643 773-535-5560
Cara Diggs, prin. Fax 535-5589
White Career Academy 200/K-8
1136 W 122nd St 60643 773-535-5672
Sharon Jenkins, prin. Fax 535-5644
Whitney S 1,100/PK-8
2815 S Komensky Ave 60623 773-534-1560
Jorge Ruiz, prin. Fax 534-1567
Whittier ES 400/PK-7
1900 W 23rd St 60608 773-535-4590
Zoila Garcia, prin. Fax 535-4818
Wildwood World Magnet S 300/K-8
6950 N Hiawatha Ave 60646 773-534-1188
Elena Savoy, prin. Fax 534-1144
Williams Multiplex ES 300/PK-5
2710 S Dearborn St 60616 773-534-9226
Marlene Heath, prin. Fax 534-9236
Williams Preparatory Academy 100/6-8
2710 S Dearborn St 60616 773-534-9235
Theresa Rhea, prin. Fax 534-9236
Woodlawn Community ES 200/K-6
6657 S Kimbark Ave Ste 1 60637 773-535-0801
Frank Embil, prin. Fax 535-0583
Woods Math/Science Academy 600/PK-8
6206 S Racine Ave 60636 773-535-9250
Roslyn Armour, prin. Fax 535-9208
Woodson South S 500/PK-8
4414 S Evans Ave 60653 773-535-1280
Renee Thomas, prin. Fax 535-1390
Yale S 300/K-8
7025 S Princeton Ave 60621 773-535-3190
Mamie Harris, prin. Fax 535-3181
Yates S 800/PK-8
1839 N Richmond St 60647 773-534-4550
Harry Randell, prin. Fax 534-4517
Young S 1,500/PK-8
1434 N Parkside Ave Ste 1 60651 773-534-6200
Crystal Bell, prin. Fax 534-6203
Zapata Academy 900/PK-8
2728 S Kostner Ave 60623 773-534-1390
Ruth Garcia, prin. Fax 534-1398

Academy of St. Benedict the African 100/PK-8
6547 S Stewart Ave 60621 773-994-6100
Ruth Douglas, prin. Fax 994-1433
Academy of St. Benedict the African 200/PK-8
6020 S Laflin St 60636 773-776-3316
Patricia Murphy, prin. Fax 776-3715
Akiba Schechter Jewish Day S 300/PK-8
5235 S Cornell Ave 60615 773-493-8880
Miriam Schiller, prin. Fax 493-9377
Alphonsus Academy 300/PK-8
1439 W Wellington Ave 60657 773-348-4629
Dr. Megan Stanton-Anderson, admin. Fax 348-4829
Ancona S 300/PK-8
4770 S Dorchester Ave 60615 773-924-2356
Bonnie Wishne, dir. Fax 924-8905
Annunciata S 200/PK-8
3750 E 112th St 60617 773-375-5711
Carol Miceli, prin. Fax 375-5704
Ashburn Lutheran S 100/K-8
3345 W 83rd St 60652 773-737-2156
Thelma Sylvester, prin. Fax 737-0994
Bethel Christian S 100/PK-8
4215 W West End Ave 60624 773-533-3636
Tonia Taylor, prin. Fax 533-3635

Bethesda Lutheran S 100/PK-8
6803 N Campbell Ave Ste 1 60645 773-743-0800
Jason Honig, prin. Fax 743-4415
Bethlehem Lutheran S 50/PK-8
3715 E 103rd St 60617 773-768-0441
Pauline Gehrs, prin. Fax 768-0390
Beverly Hills Adventist S 50/PK-8
9356 S Justine St 60620 773-779-5158
Brickton Montessori S 200/PK-8
8622 W Catalpa Ave 60656 773-714-0646
Deborah Kelley, prin. Fax 714-9361
Bridgeport Catholic Academy 300/PK-8
3700 S Lowe Ave 60609 773-376-6223
Lillian Buckley, prin. Fax 376-3864
Cambridge S 100/PK-5
4611 S Ellis Ave 60653 773-924-1200
Derek Barber, admin. Fax 799-1200
Cardinal Bernardin ECC 200/PK-PK
1651 W Diversey Pkwy 60614 773-975-6330
Sr. Barbara Jean Ciszek, prin. Fax 975-6339
Cardinal Bernardin ECC 100/K-3
1940 N Kenmore Ave 60614 773-975-6330
Sr. Barbara Jean Ciszek, prin. Fax 975-6339
Catalyst School Circle-Rock 300/PK-8
118 N Central Ave 60644 773-854-1615
Fax 854-1646
Catherine Cook S 400/PK-8
226 W Schiller St 60610 312-266-3381
Dr. Michael Roberts, hdmstr. Fax 266-3616
Cheder Lubavitch Hebrew Girls S 200/1-8
2809 W Jarvis Ave 60645 773-465-0863
Chicago Christian Academy 200/PK-8
5110 W Diversey Ave 60639 773-205-5102
Robin Berryhill, prin.
Chicago Christian Montessori Academy 50/K-6
5700 N Pulaski Rd 60646 773-509-1296
Gwen Ku, prin. Fax 509-1392
Chicago City Day S 300/PK-8
541 W Hawthorne Pl 60657 773-327-0900
Galeta Kaar Clayton, prin. Fax 327-6381
Chicago International Academy 100/2-12
2451 N Kedzie Blvd 60647 773-489-7271
Rod Post, admin. Fax 384-6057
Chicago Jesuit Academy 100/5-8
5058 W Jackson Blvd 60644 773-638-6103
Dr. Kevin Zajdel, prin. Fax 638-6107
Chicago SDA Academy 100/PK-8
7008 S Michigan Ave 60637 773-873-3005
Fax 873-6953
Chicago Waldorf S 400/PK-12
1300 W Loyola Ave 60626 773-465-2662
Flora Calabrese, admin. Fax 465-6648
Chicago West Side Christian S 200/PK-8
1240 S Pulaski Rd 60623 773-542-0663
Jeralyn Harris, admin. Fax 542-0664
Children of Peace\Holy Trinity S 200/PK-8
1900 W Taylor St Ste 1 60612 312-243-8186
Arlene Redmond, prin. Fax 243-8479
Christ the King Lutheran S 100/PK-8
3701 S Lake Park Ave 60653 773-536-1984
Geraldine Brazeal, prin. Fax 536-2387
Christ the King S 300/PK-8
9240 S Hoyne Ave 60643 773-779-3329
Maureen Aspell, prin. Fax 779-3390
Council Oak Montessori S 100/PK-8
11030 S Longwood Dr 60643 773-779-7606
Patti O'Donoghue, dir. Fax 779-1290
Covenant Christian Academy of Chicago 50/K-8
9905 S Winston Ave 60643 773-881-3235
Linda Culver, prin. Fax 881-1822
Dachs Bais Yaakov S 500/PK-8
3200 W Peterson Ave 60659 773-583-5329
Ahuva Wainhaus, prin. Fax 583-6530
Daystar S 100/K-8
1550 S State St 60605 312-791-0001
Harriet Potoka, prin. Fax 791-0002
Eagles' Wings Urban Academy 100/PK-12
3919 N Monticello Ave 60618 773-297-6326
Cynthia Peterson, admin. Fax 202-8193
Emmanuel Christian S 200/PK-8
8301 S Damen Ave 60620 773-239-6829
Sr. Carolyn Linder, prin. Fax 239-9709
Epiphany S, 4223 W 25th St 60623 200/PK-8
David Burke, prin. 773-762-1542
Evangelical Christian S 700/PK-8
9130 S Vincennes Ave 60620 773-881-8008
Vonita Relf, admin. Fax 881-8474
Ezzard Charles S 100/PK-2
7946 S Ashland Ave 60620 773-487-0227
Gloria Dei Lutheran S 100/PK-8
5259 S Major Ave 60638 773-581-5259
Scott Schilling, prin. Fax 767-4670
Good Shepherd Lutheran S 50/PK-K
4200 W 62nd St 60629 773-581-0096
Grace English Lutheran S 50/PK-8
2725 N Laramie Ave 60639 773-637-2250
Charles Novak, prin. Fax 637-1188
Grace Lutheran S 100/PK-8
4106 W 28th St 60623 773-762-1234
Carlo Giannotta, prin. Fax 762-4476
Holy Angels S 200/PK-8
750 E 40th St 60653 773-624-0727
Shirley DeSadier, prin. Fax 538-9683
Holy Family Lutheran S 100/K-8
3415 W Arthington St 60624 773-265-0550
Cheryl Collins, prin. Fax 265-0508
Humboldt Community Christian S 100/PK-8
1847 N Humboldt Blvd 60647 773-278-6330
Debra Flores, prin. Fax 278-6362
Immaculate Conception S 200/PK-5
1431 N North Park Ave 60610 773-944-0304
C. Sullivan-Wallenfang, prin. Fax 944-0695
Immaculate Conception S 200/K-8
8739 S Exchange Ave 60617 773-375-4674
Sr. Claudia Carrillo, prin. Fax 221-9121
Immaculate Conception S 400/PK-8
7263 W Talcott Ave 60631 773-775-0545
Bernadette Felicione, prin. Fax 775-3822
Jehovah Lutheran S 100/PK-8
3740 W Belden Ave 60647 773-342-5854
JoEllen Hoffman, prin. Fax 342-6048

Lake Shore S 200/PK-PK, 1-
5611 N Clark St 60660 773-561-6707
Fax 271-4564
Latin S of Chicago 1,100/PK-12
59 W North Blvd 60610 312-582-6000
Donald Firke, hdmstr. Fax 582-6011
Lycee Francais de Chicago 400/PK-12
613 W Bittersweet Pl 60613 773-665-0066
Fax 665-1725
Maranatha Christian Academy 300/PK-12
115 W 108th St 60628 773-840-3088
Masters Academy 50/K-6
PO Box 378454 60637 773-363-6448
Delilah Brooks, dir.
Maternity BVM S 200/K-8
1537 N Lawndale Ave 60651 773-227-1140
Paula Calvert, prin.
Messiah Lutheran S 100/PK-8
6200 W Patterson Ave 60634 773-736-6600
Fax 736-6611
Midwestern Christian Academy 200/PK-8
3465 N Cicero Ave 60641 773-685-1106
Vernon Lee, prin. Fax 685-6541
Montessori Academy of Chicago 200/PK-4
1335 W Randolph St 60607 312-243-0977
Fosca White, dir. Fax 243-0997
Morgan Park Academy 500/PK-12
2153 W 111th St 60643 773-881-6700
J. William Adams, hdmstr. Fax 881-8409
Mt. Carmel Academy 200/PK-8
720 W Belmont Ave 60657 773-525-8779
Shane Staszcuk, prin. Fax 525-7810
Muhammad University of Islam 200/PK-8
7351 S Stony Island Ave 60649 773-643-0700
Nativity B V M S 200/PK-8
6820 S Washtenaw Ave 60629 773-476-0571
Donna Christian, prin. Fax 476-0065
Near North Montessorri S 500/PK-8
1434 W Division St, 773-384-1434
Jacqueline Bergen, prin. Fax 384-2711
New Hope Lutheran S 200/PK-PK
6416 S Washtenaw Ave 60629 773-776-2512
Fax 776-7832
New Way Learning Center 50/PK-8
2300 N Narragansett Ave 60639 773-622-1551
Jeff Davis, prin. Fax 622-1771
North Park S 200/K-8
2017 W Montrose Ave 60618 773-327-3144
Lynn Lawrence, prin. Fax 327-0331
North Shore SDA Jr. Academy 100/PK-10
5220 N California Ave 60625 773-769-0733
Fax 769-0928
Northside Catholic Academy- St. Gertrude 300/PK-5
6216 N Glenwood Ave 60660 773-743-6277
Debra Sullivan, prin. Fax 743-6174
Northside Catholic Academy - St. Ita 100/6-8
5525 N Magnolia Ave 60640 773-271-2008
Debra Sullivan, prin. Fax 271-3101
Northwest Inst for Contemp Academy 300/PK-8
5108 W Division St 60651 773-921-2800
Oakdale Christian Academy 300/PK-8
9440 S Vincennes Ave 60620 773-779-9440
Delores Humphries, prin. Fax 779-9531
Old St. Mary's S 100/PK-2
1532 S Michigan Ave 60605 312-386-1560
Dr. Mary Calihan, prin.
Our Lady of Grace S 200/PK-8
2446 N Ridgeway Ave 60647 773-342-0170
Sr. Rita Range, prin. Fax 342-5305
Our Lady of Guadalupe S 200/PK-8
9050 S Burley Ave 60617 773-768-0999
Michael Hughes, prin. Fax 768-0529
Our Lady of Tepayac S 200/PK-8
2235 S Albany Ave 60623 773-522-0024
Marylouise Young, prin. Fax 522-4577
Our Lady of the Gardens S 200/PK-8
13300 S Langley Ave 60827 773-568-4099
Nakia Garcia, admin. Fax 568-4718
Our Lady of the Snows S 200/PK-8
4810 S Leamington Ave Ste 1 60638 773-735-4810
Demetria Castro, prin. Fax 582-3363
Our Lady of Victory S 200/PK-8
4434 N Laramie Ave 60630 773-283-2229
John Kasel, admin. Fax 283-0842
Our Saviour Lutheran S 100/PK-8
7151 W Cornelia Ave 60634 773-736-1157
LaDonna Hoffman, prin. Fax 736-4851
Parker S 900/PK-12
330 W Webster Ave 60614 773-353-3000
Daniel Frank Ph.D., prin. Fax 549-4669
Park View Lutheran S 50/PK-8
3919 N Monticello Ave 60618 773-267-0072
Fax 267-7873
Pilgrim Lutheran S 200/PK-8
4300 N Winchester Ave 60613 773-477-4824
David Maring, prin. Fax 477-8996
Pope John Paul II Catholic S 200/PK-8
4325 S Richmond St 60632 773-523-6161
Cynthia Fogarty, dir. Fax 254-9194
Providence-St. Mel S 600/K-12
119 S Central Park Blvd 60624 773-722-4600
Jeanette DiBella, prin. Fax 722-6032
Pui Tak Christian S 100/PK-6
2301 S Wentworth Ave 60616 312-842-8546
Sylvia Wu, prin. Fax 842-4304
Queen of All Saints S 600/PK-8
6230 N Lemont Ave 60646 773-736-0567
Stephanie M. Di Prima, prin. Fax 736-7142
Queen of Angels S 400/PK-8
4520 N Western Ave 60625 773-769-4211
Julia Kelly, prin. Fax 769-4289
Queen of Martyrs S 500/PK-8
3550 W 103rd St 60655 708-422-1540
Michael Krsek, prin. Fax 422-1811
Queen of the Universe S 300/PK-8
7130 S Hamlin Ave 60629 773-582-4266
Deborah Poturalski, prin. Fax 585-7254
Ravenswood Baptist Christian S 100/K-12
4437 N Seeley Ave 60625 773-561-6576

Resurrection Lutheran S 100/PK-6
9349 S Wentworth Ave 60620 773-928-6312
Shirley Johnson, prin. Fax 928-6311
Rogers Park Montessori S 300/PK-8
1800 W Balmoral Ave 60640 773-271-1700
Debra Langford, prin. Fax 271-0771
Roseland Christian S 300/PK-8
314 W 108th St 60628 773-264-2174
Wendi Waddy, prin. Fax 264-7445
Sacred Heart Academy/Hardey Prep 700/K-8
6250 N Sheridan Rd 60660 773-262-4446
Nat Wilburn, admin. Fax 262-6178
Sacred Heart S 200/K-8
2906 E 96th St 60617 773-768-3728
Thomas Feltz, prin. Fax 768-5034
St. Agatha Catholic Academy 100/PK-3
3151 W Douglas Blvd 60623 773-762-1809
Charlemeine Zemelko, prin. Fax 762-9781
St. Agatha Catholic Academy 100/4-8
3900 W Lexington St 60624 773-638-6555
Charlemeine Zemelko, prin. Fax 638-0070
St. Agnes of Bohemia S 500/PK-8
2643 S Central Park Ave 60623 773-522-0143
Matthew Banach, admin. Fax 522-0132
St. Ailbe S 200/PK-8
9037 S Harper Ave 60619 773-734-1386
Stephani Clausell, prin. Fax 734-1440
St. Andrew Lutheran S 100/PK-8
3659 S Honore St 60609 773-376-5370
Michael DeRuiter, prin. Fax 376-9184
St. Andrew S 400/PK-8
1710 W Addison St 60613 773-248-2500
Jack Percival, prin. Fax 248-2709
St. Angela S 200/PK-8
1332 N Massasoit Ave Ste 1 60651 773-626-2655
Sr. Mary Finnegan, prin. Fax 626-8156
St. Ann S 200/K-8
2211 W 18th Pl 60608 312-829-4153
Brian Morten, prin. Fax 829-4155
St. Barbara S 200/PK-8
2867 S Throop St 60608 312-326-6243
Dorene Hurckes, prin. Fax 842-7960
St. Barnabas S 400/PK-8
10121 S Longwood Dr 60643 773-445-7711
Lenore Barnes, prin. Fax 445-9815
St. Bartholomew S 300/PK-8
4941 W Patterson Ave 60641 773-282-9373
Martin Graham-McHugh, prin. Fax 282-4757
St. Bede the Venerable S 600/PK-8
4440 W 83rd St 60652 773-884-2020
Richard Guerin, prin.
St. Benedict S 300/K-8
3920 N Leavitt St 60618 773-463-6797
Rachel Gemo, prin. Fax 463-0782
St. Bruno S 200/PK-8
4839 S Harding Ave 60632 773-847-0697
Daniel Fleming, prin. Fax 847-1620
St. Cajetan S 300/PK-8
2447 W 112th St 60655 773-233-8844
Terry Reger, prin. Fax 474-7821
St. Christina S 700/PK-8
3333 W 110th St 60655 773-445-2969
Mary Stokes, prin. Fax 445-0444
St. Clement S 400/PK-8
2524 N Orchard St 60614 773-348-8212
Anne Rog, prin. Fax 348-4712
St. Columbanus S 300/PK-8
7120 S Calumet Ave 60619 773-224-3811
Sandra Wilson, prin. Fax 224-3810
St. Constance S 200/K-8
5841 W Strong St 60630 773-283-2311
Eva Panczyk, prin. Fax 283-3515
St. Cornelius S 200/PK-8
5252 N Long Ave 60630 773-283-2192
Margaret Campbell, prin. Fax 283-1377
St. Daniel the Prophet S 700/PK-8
5337 S Natoma Ave 60638 773-586-1225
Kenneth Ucho, prin. Fax 586-1232
St. Dorothy S 300/PK-8
7740 S Eberhart Ave 60619 773-783-0555
Robert Zeegers, prin. Fax 783-3736
St. Edward S 400/PK-8
4343 W Sunnyside Ave 60630 773-736-9133
Sr. Marie Michelle Hackett, prin. Fax 736-9280
St. Elizabeth S 300/PK-8
4052 S Wabash Ave 60653 773-548-4100
Danielle Graham-Harris, prin. Fax 373-8642
St. Ethelreda S 200/PK-8
8734 S Paulina St 60620 773-238-1757
Denise Spells, prin. Fax 238-6059
St. Eugene S 400/PK-8
7930 W Foster Ave 60656 773-763-2235
Dr. Patricia Brown, prin. Fax 763-2775
St. Ferdinand S 300/PK-8
3131 N Mason Ave 60634 773-622-3022
Dr. Lucine Mastalerz, prin. Fax 622-2807
St. Florian S 200/PK-8
13110 S Baltimore Ave 60633 773-646-2868
Phillip McKenna, prin. Fax 646-2891
St. Francis Borgia S 400/K-8
3535 N Panama Ave 60634 773-589-1000
Connie Kohler, prin. Fax 589-0781
St. Gabriel S 200/PK-8
607 W 45th St 60609 773-268-6636
Christine Gresk, prin. Fax 268-2501
St. Gall S 300/PK-8
5515 S Sawyer Ave 60629 773-737-3454
Marilyn Baran, prin. Fax 737-5592
St. Genevieve S 200/PK-8
4854 W Montana St 60639 773-237-7131
Marie Neis, prin. Fax 237-7265
St. Gregory Episcopal S for Boys 100/K-8
2130 S Central Park Ave 60623 773-277-4447
Fr. Kenneth Erickson, prin. Fax 277-4445
St. Helena of the Cross S 200/PK-8
10115 S Parnell Ave 60628 773-238-5432
Patricia Durkin, prin. Fax 238-6026
St. Helen S 300/PK-8
2347 W Augusta Blvd 60622 773-486-1055
Marianne Johnson, prin. Fax 235-3810

St. Hilary S 400/PK-8
5614 N Fairfield Ave 60659 773-561-5885
Michael Neis, admin. Fax 561-6409
St. Hyacinth S 100/PK-8
3640 W Wolfram St 60618 773-342-7550
Sr. Theresa Czarny, prin. Fax 384-0581
St. James Lutheran S 100/PK-8
2101 N Fremont St 60614 773-525-4990
Warren Gast, prin. Fax 525-0518
St. Jane De Chantal S 300/PK-8
5201 S McVicker Ave 60638 773-767-1130
Nancy Andrasco, prin. Fax 767-1387
St. Jerome S 200/PK-8
2801 S Princeton Ave 60616 312-842-7668
Peter Trumblay, prin. Fax 842-3506
St. John Berchmans S 200/PK-8
2511 W Logan Blvd 60647 773-486-1334
Margaret Roketenetz, prin. Fax 486-1782
St. John De La Salle Academy of Fine Art 300/PK-8
10212 S Vernon Ave 60628 773-785-2331
Charles Carroll, prin. Fax 785-0112
St. John Fisher S 800/PK-8
10200 S Washtenaw Ave 60655 773-445-4737
Sr. Jean McGrath, prin. Fax 233-3012
St. John's Lutheran S 100/PK-8
4939 W Montrose Ave 60641 773-736-1196
Douglas Markworth, prin. Fax 736-3614
St. Josaphat S 300/PK-8
2245 N Southport Ave Ste 1 60614 773-549-0909
Colleen Cannon, prin. Fax 549-3127
St. Juliana S 600/PK-8
7400 W Touhy Ave 60631 773-631-2256
Kathleen Barton, prin. Fax 631-1125
St. Ladislaus S 200/PK-8
3330 N Lockwood Ave 60641 773-545-5600
Joe Accardi, prin. Fax 545-5676
St. Luke Academy 100/PK-8
1500 W Belmont Ave 60657 773-472-3837
Donna Beck, prin. Fax 929-3910
St. Malachy S 200/PK-8
2252 W Washington Blvd 60612 312-733-2252
Mary Miller, prin. Fax 733-5703
St. Margaret Mary S 200/PK-8
7318 N Oakley Ave 60645 773-764-0641
Margaret Finnegan, prin. Fax 764-1095
St. Margaret of Scotland S 300/PK-8
9833 S Throop St 60643 773-238-1088
Earl McKay, admin. Fax 238-1049
St. Mary of the Angels S 200/PK-8
1810 N Hermitage Ave 60622 773-486-0119
Meghan Hurley, prin. Fax 486-0996
St. Mary of the Lake S 300/PK-8
1026 W Buena Ave 60613 773-281-0018
Christine Boyd, prin. Fax 281-0112
St. Mary of the Woods S 500/PK-8
7033 N Moselle Ave 60646 773-763-7577
Patrick Kelly, prin. Fax 763-4293
St. Mary Star of the Sea S 400/PK-8
6424 S Kenneth Ave 60629 773-767-6160
Evelyn Califfe, prin. Fax 767-7077
St. Matthias/Transfiguration S 200/PK-8
4910 N Claremont Ave Ste 1 60625 773-784-0999
Sandria Desapio, prin. Fax 784-3601
St. Michael S 300/PK-8
8231 S South Shore Dr 60617 773-221-0212
Barbara Lee, prin. Fax 734-8723
St. Monica Academy 300/PK-8
5115 N Mont Clare Ave 60656 773-631-7880
Raymond Coleman, prin. Fax 631-3266
St. Nicholas of Tolentine S 200/PK-8
3741 W 62nd St 60629 773-735-0772
Carolyn Majorowski, prin. Fax 735-5414
St. Nicholas Ukrainian Cathedral S 100/PK-8
2200 W Rice St 60622 773-384-7243
Maria Finiak, prin. Fax 384-7283
St. Pascal S 300/PK-8
6143 W Irving Park Rd 60634 773-736-8806
Denise Akana, admin. Fax 725-3461
St. Paul Lutheran S 100/PK-8
7621 S Dorchester Ave 60619 773-721-1438
Jeffrey Howell, prin. Fax 721-1749
St. Paul Lutheran S 200/PK-8
5650 N Canfield Ave 60631 708-867-5044
Michael Heinze, prin. Fax 867-0083
St. Paul Lutheran S 100/K-8
846 N Menard Ave 60651 773-378-6644
Glen Kuck, prin. Fax 378-7442
St. Paul-Our Lady of Vilna S 200/K-8
2114 W 22nd Pl 60608 773-847-6078
Sr. Susan Dzikas, prin. Fax 847-2118
St. Philip Lutheran S 200/K-8
2500 W Bryn Mawr Ave 60659 773-561-9830
Nick Hopfensperger, prin. Fax 561-9831
St. Philip Neri S 100/PK-8
2110 E 72nd St 60649 773-288-1138
Mary Lou Piazza, prin. Fax 288-8252
St. Pius V S 400/PK-8
1919 S Ashland Ave 60608 312-226-1590
Nancy Nasko, prin. Fax 226-7265
St. Priscilla S 200/PK-8
7001 W Addison St 60634 773-685-3581
Linda L. Noonan, prin. Fax 685-2127
St. Procopius S 200/PK-8
1625 S Allport St 60608 312-421-5135
Adam Dufault, prin. Fax 492-8368
St. Rene Goupil S 200/PK-8
6340 S New England Ave 60638 773-586-4414
Marlene DeSantis, prin. Fax 586-3747
St. Richard S 300/PK-8
5025 S Kenneth Ave 60632 773-582-8083
Sr. Mary Francine Lagocki, prin. Fax 582-8330
St. Robert Bellarmine S 200/K-8
6036 W Eastwood Ave 60630 773-725-5133
Carrie Mijal, prin. Fax 725-7611
St. Sabina Academy 500/PK-8
7801 S Throop St 60620 773-483-5000
Helen Dumas, prin. Fax 483-0305
St. Stanislaus Kostka S 400/PK-8
1255 N Noble St, 773-278-4560
Marjorie Hill, prin. Fax 278-9097

St. Sylvester S 200/PK-8
3027 W Palmer Blvd 60647 773-772-5222
Daniel Bennett, prin. Fax 772-0352
St. Symphorosa S 300/PK-8
6125 S Austin Ave 60638 773-585-6888
Sr. Margaret Mary Kowalczyk, prin. Fax 585-8411
St. Tarcissus S 400/PK-8
6040 W Ardmore Ave 60646 773-763-7080
Roy Hecker, prin. Fax 775-3893
St. Thecla S 300/PK-8
6323 N Newcastle Ave 60631 773-763-3380
Carol Styka, prin. Fax 763-6151
St. Therese S 300/PK-8
247 W 23rd St 60616 312-326-2837
Phyllis Cavallone-Jurek, prin. Fax 326-6068
St. Thomas of Canterbury S 300/PK-8
4827 N Kenmore Ave 60640 773-271-8655
Christine Boyd, prin. Fax 271-1624
St. Thomas the Apostle S 200/PK-8
5467 S Woodlawn Ave 60615 773-667-1142
Dorothy Murphy, prin. Fax 753-7434
St. Turibius S 200/PK-8
4120 W 57th Pl 60629 773-585-5150
Sharon Dulewski, prin. Fax 585-5328
St. Viator S 200/PK-8
4140 W Addison St 60641 773-545-2173
Kathleen Kowalski, prin. Fax 794-1697
St. Walter S 200/PK-8
11741 S Western Ave 60643 773-445-8850
Daniel Smith, prin. Fax 445-0277
St. William S 200/PK-8
2559 N Sayre Ave 60707 773-637-5130
Mary Bauer, prin. Fax 745-4208
Salem Christian Academy 500/PK-8
11816 S Indiana Ave 60628 773-928-0145
Debra Miller, prin. Fax 928-0208
Salem Christian S 100/PK-8
2845 W McLean Ave 60647 773-227-5580
Cindy Diiorio, prin. Fax 227-8592
San Miguel MS 100/6-8
1949 W 48th St 60609 773-890-1481
Michael McClelland, prin. Fax 254-3382
San Miguel S Gary Comer Campus 100/5-8
819 N Leamington Ave Ste 1 60651 773-261-8851
Caprice Smalley, prin. Fax 261-8854
Santa Lucia S 200/PK-8
3017 S Wells St 60616 312-326-1839
Geraldine Maratea, prin. Fax 326-1945
Socrates S 100/PK-8
5701 N Redwood Dr 60631 773-693-3367
Tabernacle Christian Academy 100/PK-8
1233 W 109th Pl 60643 773-445-3007
Timothy Lutheran S 100/PK-8
1700 W 83rd St 60620 773-874-7333
Karen Fitzpatrick, prin. Fax 874-7032
Tzemach Tzedek S 50/PK-8
432 N Clark St Ste 305 60654 312-644-1000
University of Chicago Lab S 1,700/PK-12
1362 E 59th St Ste 1 60637 773-702-9450
Dr. David Magill, dir. Fax 702-7455
Visitation S 200/PK-8
900 W Garfield Blvd 60609 773-373-5200
Sr. Jean Matijosaitis, prin. Fax 373-5201
Warde-Old St. Patrick's 500/PK-4
120 S Desplaines St 60661 312-466-0700
Mary Reiling, hdmstr. Fax 466-0711
Warde S - Holy Name Cathedral 300/5-8
751 N State St 60654 312-466-0700
Mary Reiling, hdmstr. Fax 337-7180
Wonder Montessori S 50/PK-6
5644 N Pulaski Rd 60646 773-509-1296
Gwen Ku, prin. Fax 509-1392
Yeshiva Shearis Yisroel 100/PK-8
2620 W Touhy Ave 60645 773-262-0885
Yeshivas Tiferes Tzvi 300/K-8
6122 N California Ave 60659 773-973-6150
Fax 973-0830
Zell Anshe Emet Day S 500/PK-8
3751 N Broadway St 60613 773-281-1858
Alyson Horwitz Ed.D., hdmstr. Fax 281-4709

Chicago Heights, Cook, Pop. 31,373
Chicago Heights SD 170 3,300/PK-8
30 W 16th St 60411 708-756-4165
Thomas Amadio, supt. Fax 756-4164
www.sd170.com/
Garfield S 400/K-8
140 E 23rd St 60411 708-756-4150
Josie Rodriguez, prin. Fax 756-4643
Greenbriar S 300/K-8
101 W Greenbriar Ave 60411 708-756-4159
Patricia Leoni, prin. Fax 756-4645
Highland Preschool 200/PK-PK
828 Willow Dr 60411 708-756-0008
Jill Raymond, prin. Fax 756-1730
Jefferson S 300/K-8
176 E 11th St 60411 708-756-4162
Theresa Brink, prin. Fax 756-0132
Kennedy S 200/K-8
1013 Division St 60411 708-756-4830
Michele Kahney, prin. Fax 481-0615
Lincoln S 100/K-8
1520 Center Ave 60411 708-756-4833
Cara Pastere, prin. Fax 758-5879
McKinley ES 300/PK-4
25 W 16th Pl 60411 708-756-4843
Mary Kay Entsminger, prin. Fax 756-1008
Roosevelt S 500/K-8
1345 Sunnyside Ave 60411 708-756-4836
Charles Lofrano, prin. Fax 756-4646
Washington JHS 300/5-8
25 W 16th Pl 60411 708-756-4841
Mary Kay Entsminger, prin. Fax 756-1008
Wilson S 300/K-8
422 W 16th Pl 60411 708-756-4839
Tony Banks, prin. Fax 748-4413
Other Schools – See South Chicago Heights

Flossmoor SD 161 2,600/PK-8
41 E Elmwood Dr 60411 708-647-7000
Dr. Donna Joy, supt. Fax 754-2153
www.sd161.org
Serena Hills ES 400/PK-5
255 Pleasant Dr 60411 708-647-7300
Lynn Westerlund, prin. Fax 756-4465
Other Schools – See Flossmoor

Park Forest SD 163
Supt. — See Park Forest
Beacon Hill Primary Center 400/PK-3
401 Concord Dr 60411 708-668-9100
Ericka Patterson, prin. Fax 283-2358

Sandridge SD 172 400/PK-8
2950 Glenwood Dyer Rd 60411 708-895-2450
Dr. John Sawyer, supt. Fax 895-2451
www.sandridgesd172.org/
Sandridge S 400/PK-8
2950 Glenwood Dyer Rd 60411 708-895-2450
Jay Hollingsworth, prin. Fax 895-2451

Cornerstone Christian S 300/PK-8
PO Box 9 60412 708-756-3566
Fax 756-3678
St. Agnes S 300/PK-8
1501 Chicago Rd 60411 708-756-2333
Matthew Lungaro, prin. Fax 709-2693
St. Kieran S 200/PK-8
700 195th St 60411 708-754-8999
Anthony Simone, prin. Fax 754-9007
St. Paul Lutheran S 100/PK-8
330 W Highland Dr 60411 708-754-4492
David Masengarb, prin. Fax 754-2033

Chicago Ridge, Cook, Pop. 13,668
Chicago Ridge SD 127-5 1,200/PK-8
6135 W 108th St 60415 708-636-2000
Joyce Kleinaitis, supt. Fax 636-0916
www.crsd1275.org
Finley JHS 400/6-8
10835 Lombard Ave 60415 708-636-2005
Laura Hamacher, prin. Fax 636-0045
Ridge Central ES 500/PK-5
10800 Lyman Ave 60415 708-636-2001
Theresa Bollinger, prin. Fax 636-0361
Ridge Lawn ES 400/PK-5
5757 105th St 60415 708-636-2002
Fran Setaro, prin. Fax 636-1062

Our Lady of the Ridge S 200/K-8
10859 Ridgeland Ave 60415 708-424-4409
Sr. Stephanie Kondik, prin. Fax 425-2792

Chillicothe, Peoria, Pop. 5,781
Illinois Valley Central Unit SD 321 2,200/PK-12
1300 W Sycamore St 61523 309-274-5418
Dr. David Kinney, supt. Fax 274-5046
www.ivcschools.com/
Chillicothe Elementary Center 500/3-8
914 W Truitt Ave 61523 309-274-6266
Dianne Pointer, prin. Fax 274-2010
South Grade S 300/PK-2
616 W Hickory St 61523 309-274-4841
Mike Bethel, prin. Fax 274-9715
Other Schools – See Mossville

Richland Christian S 50/K-8
5114 E Richland Ave 61523 309-274-3541
St. Edwards S 200/PK-8
1221 N 5th St 61523 309-274-2994
Jeannine McAllister, prin. Fax 274-4141

Chrisman, Edgar, Pop. 1,259
Edgar County CUSD 6 400/K-12
23231 IL Highway 1 61924 217-269-2513
Norman Tracy, supt. Fax 269-3231
www.chrisman.k12.il.us
Chrisman ES 100/K-4
111 N Pennsylvania St 61924 217-269-2022
Vicki Riggen, prin. Fax 269-3222
Chrisman-Scottland JHS 100/5-8
23231 IL Highway 1 61924 217-269-3980
Terry Furnish, prin. Fax 269-3231

Christopher, Franklin, Pop. 2,833
Christopher Unit SD 99 800/PK-12
1 Bearcat Dr 62822 618-724-9461
Richard Towers, supt. Fax 724-9400
www.cpher.frnkln.k12.il.us
Christopher S, 501 S Snider St 62822 600/PK-8
Karen Cabaness, prin. 618-724-7604

Cicero, Cook, Pop. 82,741
Cicero SD 99 11,700/K-8
5110 W 24th St 60804 708-863-4856
Donna Adamic, supt. Fax 652-8105
cicd99.edu/
Burnham ES 1,200/K-5
1630 S 59th Ave 60804 708-652-9577
Carol Anderson, prin. Fax 780-4441
Cicero East S 900/4-6
2324 S 49th Ave 60804 708-652-9440
Linda Budrik, prin. Fax 780-4444
Cicero West ES 1,000/K-3
4937 W 23rd St 60804 708-780-4487
Kimberly Pros, prin. Fax 656-2937
Columbus East S 700/4-6
3100 S 54th Ave 60804 708-652-6085
Joyce Hodan, prin. Fax 780-4446
Columbus West ES 1,000/K-6
5425 W 31st St 60804 708-780-4482
Suzanne Frost, prin. Fax 780-0735
Drexel ES 700/K-6
5407 W 36th St 60804 708-652-5532
Nancy Cummings, prin. Fax 780-4449
Goodwin ES 800/K-6
2625 S Austin Blvd 60804 708-652-5500
Mary Wygonik, prin. Fax 780-4452

Liberty ES 700/K-3
4946 W 13th St 60804 708-780-4475
Sheila Harris, prin. Fax 780-7062
Lincoln ES 800/K-6
3545 S 61st Ave 60804 708-652-8889
Susan Kleinmeyer, prin. Fax 780-4454
McKinley ES 200/K-3
5900 W 14th St 60804 708-652-8890
Debbie Harris, prin. Fax 780-4458
Roosevelt S 700/3-6
1500 S 50th Ave 60804 708-652-7833
Claudia Jimenez, prin. Fax 780-4461
Sherlock ES 300/K-3
5347 W 22nd Pl 60804 708-652-8885
Mirjana Dukic, prin. Fax 780-4463
Unity JHS 1,300/7-8
2115 S 54th Ave 60804 708-863-8268
Donata Heppner, prin. Fax 656-5652
Warren Park ES 300/K-3
1225 S 60th Ct 60804 708-863-2220
Mary Ellen Patterson, prin. Fax 780-4466
Wilson ES 800/K-6
2310 S 57th Ave 60804 708-652-2552
Gloria Lopez, prin. Fax 780-4468
Woodbine ES 300/K-3
3003 S 50th Ct 60804 708-652-8884
Ruth Grunewald, prin. Fax 780-4470

Our Lady of Charity S 200/PK-8
3620 S 57th Ct 60804 708-652-0262
Linda L. Brusky, prin. Fax 652-0601
St. Frances of Rome S 200/PK-8
1401 S Austin Blvd 60804 708-652-2277
Clement Martin, prin. Fax 780-6360
St. Mary of Czestochowa S 200/PK-8
3001 S 49th Ave 60804 708-656-5010
Al Theis, prin. Fax 656-4043

Cisne, Wayne, Pop. 662
North Wayne CUSD 200 400/PK-12
PO Box 235 62823 618-673-2151
Joyce Carson, supt. Fax 673-2152
Cisne MS 100/5-8
PO Box 69 62823 618-673-2156
Joyce Carson, prin. Fax 673-2152
Other Schools – See Johnsonville, Mount Erie

Wayne City CUSD 100
Supt. — See Wayne City
Berry ES 100/1-2
RR 2 62823 618-898-1125
Tawana Wilson, prin. Fax 898-1285

Cissna Park, Iroquois, Pop. 774
Cissna Park CUSD 6 300/K-12
511 N 2nd St 60924 815-457-2171
Dr. Daniel Hylbert, supt. Fax 457-3033
www.cissnapark.k12.il.us
Cissna Park ES 100/K-5
511 N 2nd St 60924 815-457-2171
Bethanie Marshall, prin. Fax 457-3033
Cissna Park JHS 100/6-8
511 N 2nd St 60924 815-457-2171
Jeffrey Maurer, prin. Fax 457-3033

Clarendon Hills, DuPage, Pop. 8,397
CCSD 181
Supt. — See Westmont
Clarendon Hills MS 800/6-8
301 Chicago Ave 60514 630-887-4260
Griffin Sonntag, prin. Fax 887-4267
Prospect ES 400/PK-5
130 N Prospect Ave 60514 630-887-1420
Anne Kryger, prin. Fax 655-9721
Walker ES 300/PK-5
120 Walker Ave 60514 630-887-1440
Kevin Russell, prin. Fax 887-0387

Maercker SD 60 1,400/PK-8
5800 Holmes Ave 60514 630-323-2086
Dr. Catherine Berning, supt. Fax 323-5541
www.maercker.org
Holmes ES 400/PK-2
5800 Holmes Ave 60514 630-323-2086
Sherri Massa, prin. Fax 323-5541
Other Schools – See Westmont, Willowbrook

Notre Dame S 300/PK-8
66 Norfolk Ave 60514 630-323-1642
Mary Ann Feeney, prin. Fax 654-3255
Seton Montessori S 200/PK-K
5728 Virginia Ave 60514 630-655-1066
Anna Perry, prin. Fax 654-0182

Clay City, Clay, Pop. 961
Clay City CUSD 10 400/PK-12
PO Box 542 62824 618-676-1431
James Jones, supt. Fax 676-1430
www.claycityschools.org
Clay City ES 200/PK-5
PO Box 545 62824 618-676-1521
James Jones, prin. Fax 676-1537
Clay City JHS 100/6-8
PO Box 545 62824 618-676-1521
Michelle Kachmar, prin. Fax 676-1537

Clifton, Iroquois, Pop. 1,279
Central CUSD 4 1,200/PK-12
PO Box 637 60927 815-694-2231
Tonya Evans, supt. Fax 694-2844
www.clifton-u4.k12.il.us/
Nash MS 300/5-8
1134 E 3100 North Rd 60927 815-694-2323
Victoria Marquis, prin. Fax 694-2830
Other Schools – See Ashkum, Chebanse

Clinton, DeWitt, Pop. 7,261
Clinton CUSD 15 2,200/PK-12
1210 State Route 54 W 61727 217-935-8321
Dr. Jeff Holmes, supt. Fax 935-2300
www.cusd15.k12.il.us/
Clinton JHS 500/6-8
701 Illini Dr 61727 217-935-2103
John Pine, prin. Fax 937-1918
Douglas ES 200/PK-1
905 E Main St 61727 217-935-2987
Linda Ruhl, prin. Fax 935-2525
Lincoln ES 300/2-3
407 S Jackson St 61727 217-935-6772
Gary Gullone, prin. Fax 935-8215
Washington ES 300/PK-1
411 N Mulberry St 61727 217-935-6383
Linda Ruhl, prin. Fax 935-3713
Webster ES 300/4-5
612 N George St 61727 217-935-6218
John Smith, prin. Fax 935-3525

Coal City, Grundy, Pop. 5,170
Coal City CUSD 1 2,000/PK-12
100 S Baima St 60416 815-634-2287
Dr. Kent Bugg, supt. Fax 634-8775
www.coalcity.k12.il.us
Coal City ECC 300/PK-1
755 S Carbon Hill Rd 60416 815-634-5042
Patricia Monk, prin. Fax 634-0669
Coal City ES 300/2-3
300 N Broadway St 60416 815-634-2334
Travis Johnson, prin. Fax 634-5036
Coal City IS 300/4-5
305 E Division St 60416 815-634-2182
Robert Brovont, prin. Fax 634-4303
Coal City MS 500/6-8
500 S Carbon Hill Rd 60416 815-634-5039
Frank Perucca, prin. Fax 634-5049

Coal Valley, Rock Island, Pop. 3,904
Moline Unit SD 40
Supt. — See Moline
Bicentennial ES 200/K-6
1004 1st St 61240 309-743-1602
Scott Turnipseed, prin. Fax 799-7789

Cobden, Union, Pop. 1,102
Cobden Unit SD 17 700/PK-12
413 N Appleknocker St 62920 618-893-2313
Karl Sweitzer, supt. Fax 893-4772
www.cobdenappleknockers.com/
Cobden ES 300/PK-6
413 N Appleknocker St 62920 618-893-2311
Terri Waddell, prin. Fax 893-4742
Cobden JHS 100/7-8
413 N Appleknocker St 62920 618-893-4031
Karl Sweitzer, prin. Fax 893-2138

Coffeen, Montgomery, Pop. 708
Hillsboro CUSD 3
Supt. — See Hillsboro
Coffeen ES 200/PK-5
200 School St 62017 217-534-2314
Francine Luckett, prin. Fax 534-6088

Colchester, McDonough, Pop. 1,394
West Prairie CUSD 103 700/PK-12
204 S Hun St 62326 309-776-3180
Dr. Jonathan Heerboth, supt. Fax 776-3194
www.westprairie.org/
West Prairie MS 200/5-8
600 S Hun St 62326 309-776-3220
Eunice Lutz, prin. Fax 776-3194
West Prairie South ES 200/PK-4
310 S Coal St 62326 309-776-3790
Paula Markey, prin. Fax 776-3194
Other Schools – See Good Hope

Colfax, McLean, Pop. 991
Ridgeview CUSD 19 500/PK-12
309 N Harrison St 61728 309-723-5111
Dr. Larry Dodds, supt. Fax 723-6395
www.ridgeview19.org
Ridgeview ES 300/PK-5
300 S Harrison St 61728 309-723-6531
Andy Jones, prin. Fax 723-4851

Collinsville, Madison, Pop. 25,487
Collinsville CUSD 10 6,300/PK-12
201 W Clay St 62234 618-346-6350
Dr. Dennis Craft, supt. Fax 343-3673
www.kahoks.org
Collinsville MS 1,000/7-8
9801 Collinsville Rd 62234 618-343-2100
Perry Hill, prin. Fax 343-2102
Dorris IS 900/5-6
1841 Vandalia St 62234 618-346-6311
Dr. Allen Ellington, prin. Fax 343-2787
Jefferson ES 100/K-4
152 Boskydells Dr 62234 618-346-6212
Dave Stroot, prin. Fax 343-2747
Kreitner ES 300/PK-4
9000 College St 62234 618-346-6213
Vicki Reulecke, prin. Fax 346-6375
Renfro ES 600/PK-4
311 Camelot Dr 62234 618-346-6266
John Griffith, prin. Fax 346-6379
Summit ES 100/K-4
408 Willoughby Ln 62234 618-346-6221
Dave Stroot, prin. Fax 343-2755
Twin Echo ES 200/PK-4
1937 S Morrison Ave 62234 618-346-6228
Julie Haake, prin. Fax 343-2760
Webster ES 400/PK-4
108 W Church St 62234 618-346-6301
Carmen Loemker, prin. Fax 346-6368
Other Schools – See Caseyville, Maryville

Collinsville Chrisitian Academy 100/K-12
1203 Vandalia St 62234 618-345-4224
Debora Legters, prin. Fax 345-4470
Good Shepherd Lutheran S 500/PK-8
1300 Belt Line Rd 62234 618-344-3153
Robert Mayhew, prin. Fax 344-3156
Holy Cross Lutheran S 200/PK-8
304 South St 62234 618-344-3145
Robert Kellar, prin. Fax 344-1222
SS. Peter & Paul S 200/K-8
210 N Morrison Ave 62234 618-344-5450
Mike Palmer, prin. Fax 344-5536

Colona, Henry, Pop. 5,275
Colona SD 190 500/PK-8
700 1st St 61241 309-792-1232
Kyle Ganson, supt. Fax 792-2249
www.colonaschooldistrict190.com
Colona S 500/PK-8
700 1st St 61241 309-792-1232

Columbia, Monroe, Pop. 8,902
Columbia CUSD 4 1,800/K-12
113 S Rapp Ave Ste 1 62236 618-281-4772
Ed Settles, supt. Fax 281-4570
www.chseagles.com
Columbia MS 500/5-8
100 Eagle Dr 62236 618-281-4993
Dr. Roger Chamberlain, prin. Fax 281-4964
Parkview ES 700/K-4
1 Parkview Dr 62236 618-281-4997
Dr. Michael Beczkala, prin. Fax 281-3605

Immaculate Conception S 300/K-8
321 S Metter Ave 62236 618-281-5353
Michael Kish, prin. Fax 281-6044

Concord, Morgan, Pop. 174
Triopia CUSD 27 400/PK-12
2206 Concord Arenzville Rd 62631 217-457-2283
Ron Brumley, supt. Fax 457-2277
www.triopiacusd27.org/
Triopia ES 200/PK-6
2206 Concord Arenzville Rd 62631 217-457-2284
Steve Eisenhauer, prin. Fax 457-2277

Congerville, Woodford, Pop. 493
Eureka CUSD 140
Supt. — See Eureka
Congerville ES 100/K-4
310 E Kauffman St 61729 309-448-2347
Randy Berardi, prin. Fax 448-5122

Cornell, Livingston, Pop. 505
Cornell CCSD 426 100/K-8
300 N 7th St 61319 815-358-2214
James Davis, supt. Fax 358-2217
Cornell S 100/K-8
300 N 7th St 61319 815-358-2214
James Davis, prin. Fax 358-2217

Cortland, DeKalb, Pop. 3,135
De Kalb CUSD 428
Supt. — See DeKalb
Cortland ES 300/K-5
370 E Lexington Ave 60112 815-754-2360
Kim Lyle, prin. Fax 756-9511

Coulterville, Randolph, Pop. 1,189
Coulterville Unit SD 1 200/K-12
PO Box 396 62237 618-758-2881
Louis Obernuefemann, supt. Fax 758-2330
www.coulterville1.org/
Coulterville ES 100/K-5
PO Box 396 62237 618-758-2881
Karyn Albers, prin. Fax 758-2330
Coulterville JHS 100/6-8
PO Box 396 62237 618-758-2881
Karyn Albers, prin. Fax 758-2330

Country Club Hills, Cook, Pop. 16,534
Country Club Hills SD 160 1,600/PK-8
4411 185th St 60478 708-957-6200
Dr. Earline Scott, supt. Fax 957-8686
www.cch160.org
Meadowview ES 600/3-5
4701 179th St 60478 708-957-6220
Adrienne Merritt, prin. Fax 922-2673
Southwood MS 600/6-8
18635 Lee St 60478 708-957-6230
John Macon, prin. Fax 799-4033
Sykuta ES 400/PK-2
4301 180th St 60478 708-957-6210
Dr. Millicent Borishade, prin. Fax 799-2053

Prairie-Hills ESD 144
Supt. — See Markham
Nob Hill ES 300/PK-6
3701 168th St 60478 708-335-9770
Alesa Grove, prin. Fax 335-4879

St. John Lutheran S 200/K-8
4231 183rd St 60478 708-799-7491
Douglas Rebeck, prin. Fax 798-4193

Countryside, Cook, Pop. 5,831
La Grange SD 105
Supt. — See La Grange
Ideal ES 200/K-6
9901 W 58th St 60525 708-482-2750
Steven Bahn, prin. Fax 482-2729

Cowden, Shelby, Pop. 593
Cowden-Herrick Community USD 3A 500/K-12
PO Box 188 62422 217-783-2126
Gary Cadwell, supt. Fax 783-2126
www.cowden-herrick.k12.il.us/
Cowden ES 100/K-6
PO Box 188 62422 217-783-2137
Gary Cadwell, prin. Fax 783-2137
Other Schools – See Herrick

Creal Springs, Williamson, Pop. 718
Marion CUSD 2
Supt. — See Marion
Creal Springs S 200/PK-8
PO Box 408 62922 618-996-2181
Andrew Shelby, prin. Fax 996-3339

Crescent City, Iroquois, Pop. 603
Crescent Iroquois CUSD 249 200/K-12
PO Box 190 60928 815-683-2141
James Mann, supt. Fax 683-2219
www.crescent.k12.il.us
Crescent City S 100/K-8
PO Box 190 60928 815-683-2141
Rodney Miller, prin. Fax 683-2219

Crest Hill, Will, Pop. 19,438
Chaney-Monge SD 88 500/PK-8
400 Elsie Ave, 815-722-6673
August Tomac, supt. Fax 722-7814
Chaney ES 300/PK-5
400 Elsie Ave, 815-722-6673
Cathleen Davis, prin. Fax 722-7814
Monge JHS 200/6-8
400 Elsie Ave, 815-722-6673
Cathleen Davis, prin. Fax 722-7814

Richland SD 88A 800/K-8
1919 Caton Farm Rd, 815-744-7288
Dr. Michael Early, supt. Fax 744-6196
www.d88a.org
Richland S 800/K-8
1919 Caton Farm Rd, 815-744-6166
Brad Buzenski, prin. Fax 745-8491

Joliet Montessori S 200/PK-8
1600 Root St, 815-741-4180
Janet Novotny, admin. Fax 741-9753

Creston, Ogle, Pop. 583
Creston CCSD 161 100/K-8
PO Box 37 60113 815-384-3920
Dr. George Kokaska, supt. Fax 384-3410
www.leeogle.org/creston/
Creston S 100/K-8
PO Box 37 60113 815-384-3920
Dr. George Kokaska, prin. Fax 384-3410

Crestwood, Cook, Pop. 11,207
Cook County SD 130
Supt. — See Blue Island
Hale IS 200/4-5
5312 135th St 60445 708-385-6110
James Duggan, prin. Fax 293-4088
Hale MS 400/6-8
5220 135th St 60445 708-385-6690
Linda Battles, prin. Fax 385-2417
Hale PS 300/PK-3
5324 135th St 60445 708-385-4690
James Duggan, prin. Fax 293-4087

Midlothian SD 143
Supt. — See Midlothian
Kolmar S 700/K-8
4500 143rd St 60445 708-385-6747
Cathy Thompson, prin. Fax 385-8243

Crete, Will, Pop. 8,772
Crete-Monee CUSD 201U 4,600/PK-12
1500 S Sangamon St 60417 708-367-8300
John Rodgers, supt. Fax 672-2698
www.cm201u.org
Balmoral ES 500/K-5
1124 W New Monee Rd 60417 708-672-2643
RaShone Franklin, prin. Fax 672-2613
Crete ES 500/K-5
435 North St 60417 708-672-2647
Josephine Blackmon, prin. Fax 672-2645
Crete-Monee Early Learning Center PK-PK
1500 S Sangamon St 60417 708-367-2770
Paul Kovacevich, dir. Fax 672-2762
Crete-Monee Sixth Grade Center 300/6-6
760 W Exchange St 60417 708-367-2400
Mary Ann Hurley, prin. Fax 672-2763
Other Schools – See Monee, Park Forest, University Park

Illinois Lutheran S 200/PK-6
448 Cass St 60417 708-672-5969
Scott Sievert, prin. Fax 672-0353

Creve Coeur, Tazewell, Pop. 5,261
Creve Coeur SD 76 700/PK-8
400 N Highland St 61610 309-698-3600
Jeanne Davis, supt. Fax 698-9827
www.cc76.k12.il.us/
Lasalle ES 400/PK-4
300 N Highland St 61610 309-698-3605
Brad Bennett, prin. Fax 698-1499
Parkview JHS 300/5-8
800 Groveland St 61610 309-698-3610
Jeremiah Auble, prin. Fax 698-3902

Crossville, White, Pop. 746
Carmi-White County CUSD 5
Supt. — See Carmi
Crossville Attendance Center 200/4-5
700 N State St 62827 618-966-2186
Debra Haley, prin. Fax 966-2184

Crystal Lake, McHenry, Pop. 40,922
Crystal Lake CCSD 47 9,100/K-8
300 Commerce Dr 60014 815-459-6070
Dr. Donn Mendoza, supt. Fax 459-0263
www.d47schools.org
Beardsley MS 1,100/6-8
515 E Crystal Lake Ave 60014 815-477-5897
Ron Ludwig, prin. Fax 479-5119
Bernotas MS 1,100/6-8
170 N Oak St 60014 815-459-9210
Lori Sorensen, prin. Fax 479-5116
Canterbury ES 500/K-5
875 Canterbury Dr 60014 815-459-8180
Rachael Alt, prin. Fax 479-5117
Coventry ES 600/K-5
820 Darlington Ln 60014 815-459-4231
Karen Cragg, prin. Fax 479-5114
Glacier Ridge ES 700/K-5
1120 Village Rd 60014 815-477-5518
John Jacobsen, prin. Fax 477-5547
Husmann ES 600/K-5
131 W Paddock St 60014 815-459-7114
Linda Corteen, prin. Fax 479-5110
Indian Prairie ES 700/K-5
651 Village Rd 60014 815-459-2124
Jim Kelley, prin. Fax 479-5118
Lundahl MS 1,000/6-8
560 Nash Rd 60014 815-459-5971
Matt Grubbs, prin. Fax 479-5113
North ES 900/K-5
500 W Woodstock St 60014 815-459-0122
Kimberly Hornberg, prin. Fax 479-5111
South ES 500/K-5
601 Golf Rd 60014 815-459-1143
Mary Katzler, prin. Fax 479-5112
West ES 800/K-5
100 Briarwood Dr 60014 815-459-2749
Jean Bevevino, prin. Fax 479-5115
Woods Creek ES 800/K-5
1100 Alexandra Blvd 60014 815-356-2720
Betsy Les, prin. Fax 356-2729

Prairie Grove Consolidated SD 46 1,100/K-8
3223 IL Route 176 60014 815-459-3023
Dr. Mary Fasbender, supt. Fax 356-0519
www.dist46.org/
Prairie Grove ES 700/K-5
3223 IL Route 176 60014 815-459-3023
Victor Wight, prin. Fax 356-0519
Prairie Grove JHS 400/6-8
3225 IL Route 176 60014 815-459-3557
Gregory Urbaniak, prin. Fax 459-3785

Immanuel Lutheran S 200/PK-8
178 S McHenry Ave 60014 815-459-1444
David Ingwersen, prin. Fax 459-8487
Lord and Savior Lutheran S 50/PK-8
9300 Ridgefield Rd 60012 815-455-4175
Timothy Schuh, prin. Fax 455-9725
St. Thomas the Apostle S 400/K-8
265 King St 60014 815-459-0496
Deanne Roy, prin. Fax 459-0591

Cuba, Fulton, Pop. 1,382
Fulton County CUSD 3 500/PK-12
PO Box 79 61427 309-785-5021
Brad Kenser, supt. Fax 785-5432
Cuba ES 300/PK-6
PO Box 80 61427 309-785-8054
Angela Simmons, prin. Fax 785-5238
Cuba MS 100/7-8
20325 N State Route 97 61427 309-785-5023
Chad Willis, prin. Fax 785-5102

Custer Park, Will
Reed-Custer CUSD 255U
Supt. — See Braidwood
Reed-Custer PS 400/K-2
35445 Washington St 60481 815-458-6340
Janice Kunz Ph.D., prin. Fax 458-4147

Cypress, Johnson, Pop. 287
Cypress SD 64 200/PK-8
PO Box 109 62923 618-657-2525
Dennis Holland, supt. Fax 657-2570
Cypress S 200/PK-8
PO Box 109 62923 618-657-2525
Dennis Holland, prin. Fax 657-2570

Dahlgren, Hamilton, Pop. 498
Hamilton County CUSD 10
Supt. — See Mc Leansboro
Dahlgren ES 200/K-6
PO Box 70 62828 618-736-2316
Joy Battagliotti, prin. Fax 736-2057

Dakota, Stephenson, Pop. 489
Dakota CUSD 201 900/PK-12
400 Campus Dr 61018 815-449-2832
Wanda Herrmann, supt. Fax 449-2459
www.dakota201.com/
Dakota ES 400/PK-6
400 Campus Dr 61018 815-449-2852
Janet Huene, prin. Fax 449-2459

Dallas City, Hancock, Pop. 1,011
Dallas ESD 327 200/PK-8
921 Creamery Hill Rd 62330 217-852-3204
Jo Campbell, supt. Fax 852-3203
www.dcbulldogs.com
Dallas City S 200/PK-8
921 Creamery Hill Rd 62330 217-852-3201
Gary Miller, prin. Fax 852-3203

Dalzell, Bureau, Pop. 731
Dalzell SD 98 100/K-8
307 Chestnut St 61320 815-663-8821
Dr. Bruce Bauer, supt. Fax 664-4515
Dalzell S 100/K-8
307 Chestnut St 61320 815-663-8821
Steve Parker, prin. Fax 664-4515

Damiansville, Clinton, Pop. 371
Damiansville SD 62 100/PK-8
101 E Main St 62215 618-248-5188
Michael Toeben, supt. Fax 248-5910
www.damiansvilleelem.com
Damiansville S 100/PK-8
101 E Main St 62215 618-248-5188
Michael Toeben, prin. Fax 248-5910

Danforth, Iroquois, Pop. 566
Iroquois West CUSD 10
Supt. — See Gilman
Iroquois West ES - Danforth 100/PK-K
PO Box 185 60930 815-269-2230
Don Keigher, prin. Fax 269-2521

Danvers, McLean, Pop. 1,132
Olympia CUSD 16
Supt. — See Stanford
Olympia North ES 300/PK-5
205 N State St 61732 309-963-4514
Fred Shears, prin. Fax 963-3969

Danville, Vermilion, Pop. 32,920
Danville CCSD 118 6,500/PK-12
516 N Jackson St 61832 217-444-1004
Nanette Mellen, supt. Fax 444-1006
www.danville.k12.il.us
Cannon ES 300/K-5
1202 E Main St 61832 217-444-2600
Johnnie Carey, prin. Fax 444-2632
East Park ES 900/PK-5
930 Colfax Dr 61832 217-444-3200
Valerie Gilbert, prin. Fax 444-3204
Edison ES 300/K-5
2101 N Vermilion St 61832 217-444-3350
Mark Lindvahl, prin. Fax 444-3354
Garfield ES 300/PK-5
1101 N Gilbert St 61832 217-444-1750
DeMarko Wright, prin. Fax 444-1791
Liberty ES 400/PK-5
20 E Liberty Ln 61832 217-444-3000
Diane Hampel, prin. Fax 444-3006
Meade Park ES 500/K-5
200 S Kansas Ave 61834 217-444-1925
Alice Payne, prin. Fax 444-1928
Northeast ES 300/PK-5
1330 E English St 61832 217-444-3050
Cheryl McIntire, prin. Fax 444-3080
North Ridge MS 800/6-8
1619 N Jackson St 61832 217-444-3400
Mark Goodwin, prin. Fax 444-3488
South View MS 700/6-8
133 E 9th St 61832 217-444-1800
Brenda Yoho, prin. Fax 444-1882
Southwest ES 400/PK-5
14794 Catlin Tilton Rd 61834 217-444-3500
John Hart, prin. Fax 444-3507

Oakwood CUSD 76
Supt. — See Fithian
Oakwood JHS 200/7-8
21600 N 900 East Rd 61834 217-443-2883
Jason Bletzinger, prin. Fax 776-2228

Danville Lutheran S 100/PK-8
1930 N Bowman Avenue Rd 61832 217-442-5036
Betty Schneider, prin. Fax 442-1159
First Baptist Christian S 200/PK-12
1211 N Vermilion St 61832 217-442-2434
Holy Family S 200/PK-8
502 E Main St 61832 217-431-5108
Peggy Croy, prin. Fax 442-0732
St. Paul S 300/PK-8
1307 N Walnut St 61832 217-442-3880
Mary Shepherd, prin. Fax 442-5852

Darien, DuPage, Pop. 22,730
Cass SD 63 900/PK-8
8502 Bailey Rd 60561 630-985-2000
Dr. Kerry Foderaro, supt. Fax 985-0225
www.cassd63.org
Cass JHS 400/5-8
8502 Bailey Rd 60561 630-985-1900
Paul Bleuher, prin. Fax 985-2881
Concord ES 500/PK-4
1019 Concord Pl 60561 630-968-3026
Laura Anderson, prin. Fax 968-0826

Center Cass SD 66
Supt. — See Downers Grove
Ide ES 400/PK-2
2000 Manning Rd 60561 630-783-5200
Jill Hansen, prin. Fax 971-3367

Darien SD 61 900/PK-8
7414 S Cass Ave 60561 630-968-7505
Warren Johnson, supt. Fax 968-0872
www.darien61.org
Delay ES 100/PK-2
6801 Wilmette Ave 60561 630-852-0200
Maureen Kelly, prin. Fax 968-7506
Eisenhower JHS 600/6-8
1410 75th St 60561 630-964-5200
Mike Fitzgerald, prin. Fax 968-8002
Lace ES 200/3-5
7414 S Cass Ave 60561 630-968-2589
Martin Casey, prin. Fax 968-5920

Kingswood Academy 100/PK-8
133 Plainfield Rd 60561 630-887-1411
Lisa Grundon, prin. Fax 810-1424
Our Lady of Peace S 400/K-8
709 Plainfield Rd 60561 630-325-9220
Mickey Tovey, prin. Fax 325-1995

Decatur, Macon, Pop. 77,836
Decatur SD 61 9,200/PK-12
101 W Cerro Gordo St 62523 217-424-3011
Gloria Davis, supt. Fax 424-3009
www.dps61.org/
Baum ES 400/K-6
801 S Lake Ridge Ave 62521 217-424-3259
Debbie Bandy, prin. Fax 424-3024
Brush College ES 200/K-6
575 N Brush College Rd 62521 217-424-3185
Joe Smith, prin. Fax 424-3038
Decatur MS 500/7-8
1 Educational Park 62526 217-876-8017
Howard Edwards, prin. Fax 876-8003
Dennis ES 300/K-6
1499 W Main St 62522 217-424-3236
Daniel Fuentes, prin. Fax 424-3067
Durfee ES 300/K-6
1000 W Grand Ave 62522 217-424-3255
Stephanie Strang, prin. Fax 424-3135
Enterprise ES 300/K-6
2115 S Taylor Rd 62521 217-424-3245
Melissa Norfleet, prin. Fax 424-3132
Franklin ES 300/K-6
2440 N Summit Ave 62526 217-424-3220
Rebecca Johnston, prin. Fax 424-3133
French ES 400/K-6
520 W Wood St 62522 217-424-3240
Matt Andrews, prin. Fax 424-3134

Garfield Montessori S 400/PK-8
300 Meadow Terrace Pl 62521 217-424-3244
Mary Anderson, prin. Fax 424-3148
Harris ES 200/K-6
620 E Garfield Ave 62526 217-424-3230
Kathy Thompson, prin. Fax 424-3136
Hope Academy 400/K-8
955 N Illinois St 62521 217-424-3333
Cynthia Houston, prin. Fax 424-3343
Jefferson MS 500/7-8
4735 E Cantrell St 62521 217-424-3190
Shannen Ray, prin. Fax 424-3189
Johns Hill Magnet S 500/K-8
1025 E Johns Ave 62521 217-424-3196
Amanda Reck, prin. Fax 424-3192
Muffley ES 300/K-6
88 S Country Club Rd 62521 217-424-3194
Theresa Bowser, prin. Fax 424-3137
Oak Grove ES 300/K-6
2160 W Center St 62526 217-424-3217
Corrine Holder, prin. Fax 424-3138
Parsons Accelerated ES 300/K-6
3591 N MacArthur Rd 62526 217-424-3252
Jean Reid, prin. Fax 424-3139
Pershing Early Learning Center 400/PK-PK
2912 N University Ave 62526 217-876-8327
Aissa Norris, prin. Fax 424-3253
South Shores ES 400/K-6
2500 S Franklin Street Rd 62521 217-424-3243
Daniel Carie, prin. Fax 424-3176
Stevenson Accelerated ES 300/K-6
3900 N Neely Ave 62526 217-876-8749
Renee Burdick, prin. Fax 876-8753

Antioch Christian Academy 50/K-6
530 W Mound Rd 62526 217-875-0529
Shirley Shaw, prin. Fax 875-1723
Decatur Christian S 300/PK-12
3475 N Maple Ave 62526 217-877-5636
Stephanie Bostick, supt. Fax 877-7627
Holy Family S 200/PK-8
2400 S Franklin Street Rd 62521 217-423-7049
Sr. Mary Kemper, prin. Fax 423-7098
Lutheran School Association 500/K-12
2001 E Mound Rd 62526 217-233-2001
Brian Ryherd, supt. Fax 233-2002
Northwest Christian Campus S 100/PK-12
1306 N Stanley Ave 62526 217-429-0563
Ryan Hubner, admin. Fax 429-0612
Our Lady of Lourdes S 300/PK-8
3950 Lourdes Dr 62526 217-877-4408
Maryrose Hagenbach, prin. Fax 872-3655
St. Patrick S 200/PK-8
412 N Jackson St 62523 217-423-4351
Jan Sweet, prin. Fax 423-7288

Deer Creek, Tazewell, Pop. 700
Deer Creek-Mackinaw CUSD 701
Supt. — See Mackinaw
Deer Creek Mackinaw IS 200/4-6
506 N Logan St 61733 309-447-6226
Frank Relliford, prin. Fax 447-5201

Deerfield, Lake, Pop. 19,471
Deerfield SD 109 3,100/K-8
517 Deerfield Rd 60015 847-945-1844
Dr. Renee Goier, supt. Fax 945-1853
www.dps109.org
Caruso MS 500/6-8
1801 Montgomery Rd 60015 847-945-8430
Dale Fisher, prin. Fax 945-1963
Kipling ES 500/K-5
700 Kipling Pl 60015 847-948-5151
Judith Lindgren, prin. Fax 948-8264
Shepard MS 500/6-8
440 Grove Ave 60015 847-948-0620
Michael Shapiro, prin. Fax 948-8589
South Park ES 500/K-5
1421 Hackberry Rd 60015 847-945-5895
David Sherman, prin. Fax 945-5291
Walden ES 500/K-5
630 Essex Ct 60015 847-945-9660
Kevin Karcz, prin. Fax 945-0035
Wilmot ES 600/K-5
795 Wilmot Rd 60015 847-945-1075
Eileen Brett, prin. Fax 405-9736

Deerfield Montessori S 100/PK-K
760 North Ave 60015 847-945-7580
Carolyn Kambich, prin. Fax 945-8920
Holy Cross S 400/PK-8
720 Elder Ln 60015 847-945-0135
Dr. John Sloan, prin. Fax 945-0705

DeKalb, DeKalb, Pop. 42,085
De Kalb CUSD 428 5,800/PK-12
901 S 4th St 60115 815-754-2350
Dr. James Briscoe, supt. Fax 758-6933
dist428.org
Brooks ES 400/PK-5
3225 Sangamon Dr 60115 815-754-9936
Shahron Spears, prin. Fax 754-1345
Chesebro ES 300/PK-5
900 E Garden St 60115 815-754-2208
Jay Redmond, prin. Fax 758-1185
Huntley MS 600/6-8
821 S 7th St 60115 815-754-2241
Rocky May, prin. Fax 758-6062
Jefferson ES 400/K-5
211 Mccormick Dr 60115 815-754-2263
Karen Mink, prin. Fax 758-1206
Lincoln ES 300/K-5
220 E Sunset Pl 60115 815-754-2212
Cristy Meyer, prin. Fax 758-1279
Littlejohn ES 500/PK-5
1121 School St 60115 815-754-2258
Charlotte Messmore, prin. Fax 758-1065
Rosette MS 700/6-8
650 N 1st St 60115 815-754-2226
Jason Mix, prin. Fax 758-1097

Tyler ES 200/K-5
1021 Alden Circle 60115 815-754-2389
Andria Mitchell, prin. Fax 758-1244
Other Schools – See Cortland, Malta

St. Mary S 200/PK-8
210 Gurler Rd 60115 815-756-7905
Patricia Weis, prin. Fax 758-1459

De Land, Piatt, Pop. 473
Deland-Weldon CUSD 57 200/PK-12
304 E IL Route 10 61839 217-736-2311
Gary Brashear, supt. Fax 736-2654
www.delwel.k12.il.us/
Other Schools – See Weldon

Delavan, Tazewell, Pop. 1,777
Delavan CUSD 703 500/PK-12
907 Locust St 61734 309-244-8283
Mary Parker, supt. Fax 244-7696
www.delavanschools.com/
Delavan ES 300/PK-6
907 Locust St 61734 309-244-8283
Paul Lewis, prin. Fax 244-7301
Delavan JHS 100/7-8
907 Locust St 61734 309-244-8285
Matt Gordon, prin. Fax 244-8694

De Pue, Bureau, Pop. 1,791
De Pue Unit SD 103 500/PK-12
PO Box 800 61322 815-447-2121
Ann Chandler, supt. Fax 447-2067
www.bhsroe.k12.il.us/depue/
De Pue S 400/PK-8
PO Box 800 61322 815-447-2121
E. Robin Staudenmeier, prin. Fax 447-2067

De Soto, Jackson, Pop. 1,583
De Soto CCSD 86 200/PK-8
311 Hurst Rd 62924 618-867-2317
Brad Hall, supt. Fax 867-3233
www.desoto.jacksn.k12.il.us/
De Soto S 200/PK-8
311 Hurst Rd 62924 618-867-2317
Brad Hall, prin. Fax 867-3233

Des Plaines, Cook, Pop. 56,551
CCSD 59
Supt. — See Arlington Heights
Brentwood ES 400/PK-5
260 Dulles Rd 60016 847-593-4401
Wendy Allen, prin. Fax 593-7184
Devonshire ES 300/K-5
1401 Pennsylvania Ave 60018 847-593-4398
Randy Steinkamp, prin. Fax 593-7183
Friendship JHS 700/6-8
550 Elizabeth Ln 60018 847-593-4350
Jane Paterala, prin. Fax 593-7182

CCSD 62 4,700/PK-8
777 E Algonquin Rd 60016 847-824-1136
Jane Westerhold, supt. Fax 824-0612
www.d62.org
Algonquin MS 700/6-8
767 E Algonquin Rd 60016 847-824-1205
John Swanson, prin. Fax 824-1270
Central ES 300/K-5
1526 E Thacker St 60016 847-824-1575
Janice Rashid, prin. Fax 824-1656
Chippewa MS 800/6-8
123 N 8th Ave 60016 847-824-1503
Lillian Mosier, prin. Fax 824-1514
Cumberland ES 400/PK-5
700 E Golf Rd 60016 847-824-1451
Leah Kimmelman, prin. Fax 824-0724
Forest ES 400/PK-5
1375 S 5th Ave 60018 847-824-1380
Julie Fogarty, prin. Fax 824-1732
Iroquois Community S 400/K-8
1836 E Touhy Ave 60018 847-824-1308
Michael Amadei, prin. Fax 824-1310
North ES 500/K-5
1789 Rand Rd 60016 847-824-1399
Carol Gibbs, prin. Fax 824-1768
Orchard Place ES 300/K-5
2727 Maple St 60018 847-824-1255
Lauren Leitao, prin. Fax 824-1752
Plainfield ES 300/K-5
1850 Plainfield Dr 60018 847-824-1301
Rene Carranza, prin. Fax 824-1547
South ES 300/K-5
1535 Everett Ave 60018 847-824-1566
Lori Poelking, prin. Fax 824-1759
Terrace ES 200/K-5
735 S Westgate Rd 60016 847-824-1501
Nancy Bang, prin. Fax 824-1764

East Maine SD 63 3,500/PK-8
10150 Dee Rd 60016 847-299-1900
Dr. Scott Clay, supt. Fax 299-9963
www.emsd63.org
Apollo ES 600/PK-6
10100 Dee Rd 60016 847-827-6231
Fax 827-1785
Stevenson ES 400/K-6
9000 Capitol Dr 60016 847-298-1622
Howard Sussman, prin. Fax 298-1621
Other Schools – See Glenview, Morton Grove, Niles

Immanuel Lutheran S 100/PK-8
832 Lee St 60016 847-390-0990
Gail Spero, prin. Fax 294-9640
Our Lady of Destiny S South Campus S 200/PK-8
1880 Ash St 60018 847-827-2900
Linda Chorazy, prin.
Park Ridge Intercultural Montessori S 50/PK-6
8800 W Ballard Rd 60016 847-298-7740
Charlene Alderete, prin. Fax 298-6293
St. Zachary S 200/PK-8
567 W Algonquin Rd 60016 847-437-4022
Catherine Determann, prin. Fax 758-1064

Science and Arts Academy 100/PK-8
1825 Miner St 60016 847-827-7880
Dr. Marsha Hestad, hdmstr. Fax 827-7716

Dieterich, Effingham, Pop. 597
Dieterich CUSD 30 500/K-12
PO Box 187 62424 217-925-5249
Bruce Owen, supt. Fax 925-5447
www.dieterich.k12.il.us/
Dieterich ES 200/K-6
PO Box 187 62424 217-925-5248
Kathy Pattenaude, prin. Fax 925-5447

Divernon, Sangamon, Pop. 1,145
Auburn CUSD 10
Supt. — See Auburn
Auburn JHS 400/7-8
303 E Kenney St 62530 217-628-3414
Mark Dudley, prin. Fax 628-3814
Divernon ES 100/PK-3
303 E Kenney St 62530 217-628-3611
Mark Dudley, prin. Fax 628-3814

Dix, Jefferson, Pop. 504
Rome CCSD 2 300/K-8
233 W South St 62830 618-266-7214
Dwain Baldridge, supt. Fax 266-7902
rome.roe25.com/
Rome Community Consolidated S 300/K-8
233 W South St 62830 618-266-7214
Peggy Quick, prin. Fax 266-7902

Dixmoor, Cook, Pop. 3,813
West Harvey-Dixmoor SD 147
Supt. — See Harvey
King ES 400/PK-5
14600 Seeley Ave 60426 708-385-5400
Sandra Walls, prin. Fax 385-5436
Lincoln ES 400/PK-5
14100 Honore Ave 60426 708-597-4160
Dr. Gregory Jackson, prin. Fax 597-4173
Parks MS 400/6-8
14700 Robey Ave 60426 708-371-9575
Abigail Phillips, prin. Fax 371-1412

Dixon, Lee, Pop. 15,372
Dixon Unit SD 170 2,900/PK-12
1335 Franklin Grove Rd 61021 815-284-7722
Douglas Creason, supt. Fax 284-8576
www.dps.k12.il.us
Jefferson ES 200/4-4
800 4th Ave 61021 815-284-7724
Jeff Gould, prin. Fax 284-0435
Lincoln ES 400/2-3
501 S Lincoln Ave 61021 815-284-7726
David Suarez, prin. Fax 284-1305
Reagan MS 800/5-8
620 Division St 61021 815-284-7725
Andrew Bullock, prin. Fax 284-1711
Washington ES 400/PK-1
703 E Morgan St 61021 815-284-7727
Dan Rick, prin. Fax 284-0440

Faith Christian S 100/K-12
7571 S Ridge Rd 61021 815-652-4806
Liandro Arellano, supt. Fax 652-4871
St. Anne S 100/PK-8
1112 N Brinton Ave 61021 815-288-5619
Sr. Marcianne Bzdon, prin. Fax 288-5820
St. Mary S 200/PK-8
704 S Peoria Ave 61021 815-284-6986
Jean Spohn, prin. Fax 284-6905

Dolton, Cook, Pop. 24,504
Dolton SD 148
Supt. — See Riverdale
Franklin ES 300/K-6
14701 Chicago Rd 60419 708-201-2083
Lisa Davis-Smith, prin. Fax 201-2083
Lincoln S 300/K-8
14151 Lincoln Ave 60419 708-201-2075
Michael Winston, prin. Fax 849-3758
Roosevelt ES 300/K-6
111 W 146th St 60419 708-201-2070
Dot Weathersby, prin. Fax 849-7880
Roosevelt JHS 500/7-8
111 W 146th St 60419 708-201-2071
Shalonda Randle, prin. Fax 849-1285
Tubman ES 500/K-6
333 E 142nd St 60419 708-849-9848
Kathie McHenry, prin. Fax 201-9122

Dolton SD 149
Supt. — See Calumet City
Berger-Vandenberg ES 400/K-5
14833 Avalon Ave 60419 708-841-3606
Dellnora Winters, prin. Fax 201-4725
Diekman ES 400/PK-5
15121 Dorchester Ave 60419 708-841-3838
April Davis, prin. Fax 201-4719

Dongola, Union, Pop. 803
Dongola Unit SD 66 300/PK-12
PO Box 190 62926 618-827-3841
Brett Gayer, supt. Fax 827-4641
www.dongolaschool.com/
Dongola ES 200/PK-6
PO Box 190 62926 618-827-3524
Brett Gayer, prin. Fax 827-4422
Dongola JHS 50/7-8
PO Box 190 62926 618-827-3524
Brett Gayer, prin. Fax 827-4422

Donovan, Iroquois, Pop. 333
Donovan CUSD 3 500/K-12
PO Box 186 60931 815-486-7397
Jerome Pankey, supt. Fax 486-7060
www.donovan.k12.il.us/
Donovan ES 200/K-6
2561 E US Highway 52 60931 815-486-7321
Tricia Bianchetta, prin. Fax 486-7445

Donovan JHS 100/7-8
PO Box 186 60931 815-486-7395
Robert Abney, prin. Fax 486-7060

Dorsey, Madison

St. Peter Lutheran S 50/K-8
7182 Renken Rd 62021 618-888-2252
Keith Schelp, prin. Fax 888-2353

Dow, Jersey
Jersey CUSD 100
Supt. — See Jerseyville
Dow ES 100/K-6
24621 Elm St 62022 618-885-5422
Michelle Bidlack, prin. Fax 885-5915

Downers Grove, DuPage, Pop. 49,094
Center Cass SD 66 1,300/PK-8
699 Plainfield Rd 60516 630-783-5000
Dr. Jay Tiede, supt. Fax 910-0980
www.ccsd66.org/
Lakeview JHS 500/6-8
701 Plainfield Rd 60516 630-985-2700
Paul Windsor, prin. Fax 985-1545
Prairieview ES 400/3-5
699 Plainfield Rd 60516 630-783-5100
Janeise Schultz, prin. Fax 910-0803
Other Schools – See Darien

Downers Grove SD 58 4,900/PK-8
1860 63rd St 60516 630-719-5800
Paul Zaander, supt. Fax 719-9857
www.dg58.org
Belle Aire ES 300/K-6
3935 Belleaire Ln 60515 630-719-5820
Michael Mitchinson, prin. Fax 719-9311
El Sierra ES 300/K-6
6835 Fairmount Ave 60516 630-719-5825
Lucille Carney, prin. Fax 719-9281
Fairmount ES 300/K-6
6036 Blodgett Ave 60516 630-719-5830
Anthony Coglianese, prin. Fax 719-1161
Herrick MS 600/7-8
4435 Middaugh Ave 60515 630-719-5810
Jason Lynde, prin. Fax 719-1628
Highland ES 300/K-6
3935 Highland Ave 60515 630-719-5835
Judy Kmak, prin. Fax 719-0150
Hillcrest ES 400/K-6
1435 Jefferson Ave 60516 630-719-5840
Paula Thomas, prin. Fax 719-0122
Indian Trail ES 400/PK-6
6235 Stonewall Ave 60516 630-719-5845
Robin Bruebach, prin. Fax 719-1275
Kingsley ES 400/K-6
6509 Powell St 60516 630-719-5850
Charles Purdom, prin. Fax 719-0982
Lester ES 500/K-6
236 Indianapolis Ave 60515 630-719-5855
Carin Novak, prin. Fax 719-0053
O'Neill MS 600/7-8
635 59th St 60516 630-719-5815
Matthew Durbala, prin. Fax 719-1436
Pierce Downer ES 400/K-6
1436 Grant St 60515 630-719-5860
Dr. Lisa Mondale, prin. Fax 719-1176
Puffer ES 300/K-6
2220 Haddow Ave 60515 630-968-0294
Todd McDaniel, prin. Fax 968-4061
Whittier ES 300/K-6
536 Hill St 60515 630-719-5865
Linda Welch, prin. Fax 719-1105

Avery Coonley S 400/PK-8
1400 Maple Ave 60515 630-969-0800
Paul Barton, hdmstr. Fax 969-0131
Downers Grove Adventist S 50/PK-8
5524 Lee Ave 60515 630-968-8848
Patricia Williams, prin.
Downers Grove Christian S 200/PK-8
929 Maple Ave 60515 630-852-0832
Fred Versluys, prin. Fax 852-0880
Good Shepherd Lutheran S 100/K-8
525 63rd St 60516 630-852-5081
Scott Schmudlach, prin. Fax 852-1532
Marquette Manor Baptist Academy 300/PK-12
333 75th St 60516 630-964-5363
Richard Adams, prin. Fax 964-5385
St. Joseph S 400/K-8
4832 Highland Ave 60515 630-969-4306
Rita Stasi, pres. Fax 969-3946
St. Mary of Gostyn S 600/PK-8
440 Prairie Ave 60515 630-968-6155
Dolores Mielzynski, prin. Fax 968-6208

Downs, McLean, Pop. 745
Tri-Valley CUSD 3 1,100/PK-12
410 E Washington St 61736 309-378-2351
Curt Simonson, supt. Fax 378-2223
tri-valley.k12.il.us
Tri-Valley ES 300/PK-3
409 E Washington St 61736 309-378-2031
Sara Burnett, prin. Fax 378-4578
Tri-Valley MS 400/4-8
505 E Washington St 61736 309-378-3414
Jill Lanier, prin. Fax 378-3214

Dunlap, Peoria, Pop. 904
Dunlap CUSD 323 3,000/PK-12
PO Box 395 61525 309-243-7716
Dr. Jay Marino, supt. Fax 243-7720
www.dunlapcusd.net
Banner ES 400/K-5
12610 N Allen Rd 61525 309-243-7774
Greg Fairchild, prin. Fax 243-7775
Dunlap ES 300/PK-5
PO Box 367 61525 309-243-7772
Jeremy Etnyre, prin. Fax 243-9116
Dunlap MS 700/6-8
5200 W Cedar Hills Dr 61525 309-243-7778
Zac Chatterton, prin. Fax 243-1136
Dunlap Valley MS 6-8
13120 N State Route 91 61525 309-243-1034
Jason Holmes, prin. Fax 243-9829
Other Schools – See Peoria

Dupo, Saint Clair, Pop. 3,957
Dupo CUSD 196 1,300/PK-12
600 Louisa Ave 62239 618-286-3812
Dr. Michael Koebel, supt. Fax 286-5554
www.dupo196.org/
Bluffview ES, 905 Bluffview Dr 62239 700/PK-6
John Bione, prin. 618-286-3311
Dupo JHS, 600 Louisa Ave 62239 200/7-8
William Harris, prin. 618-286-3214

Du Quoin, Perry, Pop. 6,412
Du Quoin CUSD 300 1,400/PK-12
845 E Jackson St 62832 618-542-3856
Gary Kelly, supt. Fax 542-6614
dqud300.perry.k12.il.us/
Du Quoin ES 500/PK-4
845 E Jackson St 62832 618-542-3295
Peg Pursell, prin. Fax 542-6291
Du Quoin MS 400/5-8
845 E Jackson St 62832 618-542-2646
Aaron Hill, prin. Fax 542-4373

Christian Fellowship S 100/PK-12
PO Box 227 62832 618-542-6800
Larry Bullock, admin. Fax 542-6806

Durand, Winnebago, Pop. 1,077
Durand CUSD 322 700/K-12
200 W South St 61024 815-248-2171
Douglas DeSchepper Ed.D., supt. Fax 248-2599
www.durandbulldogs.com
Durand ES 300/K-6
200 W South St 61024 815-248-2171
Kurt Alberstett, prin. Fax 248-9968
Durand JHS 100/7-8
200 W South St 61024 815-248-2171
Jeff Pinker, prin. Fax 248-2599

Dwight, Livingston, Pop. 4,360
Dwight Common SD 232 700/PK-8
801 S Columbia St 60420 815-584-6216
Dale Adams, supt. Fax 584-2950
www.dgs.k12.il.us
Dwight Common ES 500/PK-5
801 S Columbia St 60420 815-584-6220
Patricia Marshall, prin. Fax 584-3771
Dwight Common MS 200/6-8
801 S Columbia St 60420 815-584-6220
Mark Pagel, prin. Fax 584-3771

Earlville, LaSalle, Pop. 1,821
Earlville CUSD 9 500/PK-12
PO Box 539 60518 815-246-8361
Patricia Hahto, supt. Fax 246-8672
Earlville S 300/PK-8
PO Box 539 60518 815-246-8361
Denise Helmers, prin. Fax 246-8672

Serena CUSD 2
Supt. — See Serena
Harding S 200/K-8
1643 N 40th Rd 60518 815-792-8216
Rich Faivre, prin. Fax 792-8003

East Alton, Madison, Pop. 6,609
East Alton SD 13 1,000/PK-8
210 E Saint Louis Ave 62024 618-433-2150
Virgil Moore, supt. Fax 254-5048
www.easd13.org/
East Alton MS 300/6-8
1000 3rd St 62024 618-433-2201
Eric Frankford, prin. Fax 433-2203
Eastwood ES 500/K-5
1030 3rd St 62024 618-433-2103
Jill Miller, prin. Fax 433-2181
Washington ES 100/PK-PK
210 E Saint Louis Ave 62024 618-433-2001
Debbie Sims, prin. Fax 254-5048

East Dubuque, Jo Daviess, Pop. 1,985
East Dubuque Unit SD 119 700/PK-12
200 Parklane Dr 61025 815-747-2111
Katherine Kelly, supt. Fax 747-3516
www.edbqhs.org
East Dubuque S 500/PK-8
100 N School Rd 61025 815-747-3117
John Vesely, prin. Fax 747-3827

Nativity of BVM S 100/1-8
15390 W Creek Valley Rd 61025 815-747-3670
Diane Makovec, prin. Fax 747-2050
St. Mary S 100/PK-8
701 IL Route 35 N 61025 815-747-3010
Wendi Kletecka, prin. Fax 747-6188

East Dundee, Kane, Pop. 3,138

Immanuel Lutheran S 300/PK-8
5 S Van Buren St 60118 847-428-1010
Kenneth Becker, prin. Fax 836-6217

East Hazel Crest, Cook, Pop. 1,570
Hazel Crest SD 152-5
Supt. — See Hazel Crest
Lincoln S PK-K
1223 173rd St, 708-798-0945
Alta Lott-Flowers, prin. Fax 798-4517

East Moline, Rock Island, Pop. 21,250
East Moline SD 37 2,500/PK-8
3555 19th St 61244 309-792-2887
Barry Green, supt. Fax 792-6010
www.emsd37.org
Glenview MS 1,000/5-8
3100 7th St 61244 309-755-1919
Jeff Fairweather, prin. Fax 752-2551
Hillcrest ES 400/K-4
451 22nd Ave 61244 309-755-7621
James O'Brien, prin. Fax 752-2569
Ridgewood ES 400/K-4
814 30th Ave 61244 309-755-1585
Sheri Coder, prin. Fax 752-2570
Wells ES 400/PK-4
490 Avenue of the Cities 61244 309-796-1251
Kristin Humphries, prin. Fax 796-1751
Other Schools – See Silvis

East Moline Christian S 300/PK-12
900 46th Ave 61244 309-796-1485
Fax 796-1152

Our Lady of Grace Academy 200/PK-8
602 17th Ave 61244 309-755-9771
Fax 755-7407

St. Johns Center for Early Learning 100/PK-PK
1450 30th Ave 61244 309-792-0755
Shannon Buth, dir. Fax 792-0776

East Peoria, Tazewell, Pop. 22,536
East Peoria SD 86 1,800/PK-8
601 Taylor St 61611 309-427-5100
Tony Ingold, supt. Fax 698-1364
www.epd86.org
Armstrong-Oakview ES 200/PK-2
1848 Highview Rd 61611 309-427-5300
Pat Minasian, prin. Fax 694-0829
Bolin ES 200/3-5
428 Arnold Rd 61611 309-427-5350
Daren Lowery, prin. Fax 698-1365
Central JHS 600/6-8
601 Taylor St Ste 1 61611 309-427-5200
Joe Sander, prin. Fax 699-2595
Glendale ES 200/3-5
1000 Bloomington Rd 61611 309-427-5400
Scott Estes, prin. Fax 698-2949
Lincoln ES 200/3-5
801 Springfield Rd 61611 309-427-5450
Liz Ozog, prin. Fax 698-2969
Shute ES 200/PK-2
300 Briarbrook Dr 61611 309-427-5500
Brad Wood, prin. Fax 698-1362
Wilson ES 200/K-2
300 Oakwood Ave 61611 309-427-5550
Susie Beyer, prin. Fax 698-1369

Riverview CCSD 2 300/PK-8
1421 Spring Bay Rd 61611 309-822-8550
Joe Blessman, supt. Fax 822-8414
www.rgschool.com
Riverview S 300/PK-8
1421 Spring Bay Rd 61611 309-822-8550
Joe Blessman, prin. Fax 822-8414

Robein SD 85 200/K-8
200 Campus Ave 61611 309-694-1409
Dr. Kathryn Marx, supt. Fax 694-1450
www.robein.org/
Robein S 200/K-8
200 Campus Ave 61611 309-694-1409
Dr. Kathryn Marx, prin. Fax 694-1450

East Saint Louis, Saint Clair, Pop. 30,995
Cahokia CUSD 187
Supt. — See Cahokia
Lalumier S 400/K-8
6702 Bond Ave 62207 618-332-3713
John Dozier, prin. Fax 332-3811

East St. Louis SD 189 8,200/PK-12
1005 State St 62201 618-646-3000
Theresa Saunders Ed.D., supt. Fax 583-7186
www.estlps189.net/
Adams ECC 400/PK-PK
501 Katherine Dunham Pl 62201 618-646-3290
Christine Smith, prin. Fax 646-3298
Alta Sita ES 300/PK-5
2601 Bond Ave 62207 618-646-3800
Carolyn Granberry, prin. Fax 646-3808
Avant ES PK-5
1915 N 55th St 62204 618-646-3870
Mary Davis, prin. Fax 646-3878
Brown ES 200/PK-3
4850 Market St 62207 618-646-3820
Theopal Morgan, prin. Fax 646-3828
Bush ES 400/PK-5
1516 Gross Ave 62205 618-646-3930
Elitor Wallace, prin. Fax 397-3938
Davis ES 300/PK-5
725 N 15th St 62205 618-646-3830
Staci Claiborne, prin. Fax 646-3838
Dunbar ES 400/PK-5
1835 Tudor Ave 62207 618-646-3840
Barbara Humphrey, prin. Fax 646-3848
Edgemont ES 200/K-5
8601 Washington St 62203 618-646-3850
Gloria Little, prin. Fax 646-3858
Harper-Wright ES 500/PK-5
7710 State St 62203 618-646-3860
Judith Fernando, prin. Fax 646-3868
Jackson S 300/PK-8
1798 College Ave 62205 618-646-3880
Kimberly Riley, prin. Fax 646-3888
Lily-Freeman ES 300/PK-5
1236 E Broadway 62201 618-646-3900
Katrina Thomas, prin. Fax 646-3908
Lincoln MS 700/6-8
12 S 10th St 62201 618-646-3770
Terrence Curry, prin. Fax 646-3778
Mandella ES 300/PK-5
1800 N 25th St 62204 618-646-3920
Tina Frye, prin. Fax 646-3928
Mason-Clark MS 500/6-8
5510 State St 62203 618-646-3750
Lelon Seaberry, prin. Fax 646-3758
McHenry ES 300/PK-5
2700 Summit Ave 62205 618-646-3950
Lena Dye, prin. Fax 646-3958

Officer ES 300/PK-5
558 N 27th St 62205 618-646-3970
Rowena Lewis, prin. Fax 646-3978
Younge MS 600/6-8
3939 Caseyville Ave 62204 618-646-3760
Vivian Cockrell, prin. Fax 646-3768

Sister Thea Bowman S 100/K-8
8213 Church Ln 62203 618-397-0316
Sr. Janet McCann, prin. Fax 397-0337
Unity Lutheran S 50/K-3
4200 Caseyville Ave 62204 618-874-6605
Paul Miller, prin. Fax 874-7546

Edgewood, Effingham, Pop. 533
Effingham CUSD 40
Supt. — See Effingham
Edgewood ES 100/PK-4
PO Box 207 62426 217-540-1270
Wanda Brooks, prin. Fax 238-9042

Edinburg, Christian, Pop. 1,140
Edinburg CUSD 4 400/PK-12
100 E Martin St 62531 217-623-5603
Lynda Irvin, supt. Fax 623-5604
www.edinburgschools.net
Edinburg ES 200/PK-5
100 E Martin St 62531 217-623-5733
Lynda Irvin, prin. Fax 623-5604
Edinburg JHS 100/6-8
100 E Martin St 62531 217-623-5733
Matt Graham, prin. Fax 623-5604

Edwards, Peoria

St. Marys of Kickapoo S 200/PK-8
9910 W Knox St 61528 309-691-3015
Ron Dwyer, prin. Fax 691-2898

Edwardsville, Madison, Pop. 24,047
Edwardsville CUSD 7 7,300/PK-12
708 Saint Louis St 62025 618-656-1182
Dr. Ed Hightower, supt. Fax 692-7423
www.ecusd7.org
Columbus ES 600/3-5
315 N Kansas St 62025 618-656-5167
Vince Schlueter, prin. Fax 655-1099
Goshen ES, 101 District Dr 62025 PK-2
Tara Wells, prin. 618-655-6250
LeClaire ES 600/PK-2
801 Franklin Ave 62025 618-656-3825
Cornelia Smith, prin. Fax 655-1038
Liberty MS 900/6-8
1 District Dr 62025 618-655-6800
Dennis Cramsey, prin. Fax 655-6801
Lincoln MS 800/6-8
145 West St 62025 618-656-0485
Steve Stuart, prin. Fax 659-1268
Nelson ES 500/PK-2
1225 W High St 62025 618-656-8480
Tanya Patton, prin. Fax 655-1063
Woodland ES 700/3-5
59 S State Route 157 62025 618-692-8791
Tara Fox, prin. Fax 692-7467
Other Schools – See Glen Carbon, Hamel, Moro, Worden

St. Boniface S 300/PK-8
128 N Buchanan St 62025 618-656-6917
Sr. Anna Flanigan, prin. Fax 656-7669
St. Mary S 300/PK-8
1802 Madison Ave 62025 618-656-1230
Peg Bodinet, prin. Fax 656-1715
Trinity Lutheran S 200/PK-8
600 Water St 62025 618-656-7002
Paula Nelson, prin. Fax 656-5941
Westminster Christian Academy 100/K-12
6279 Center Grove Rd 62025 618-659-4810
Greg Myers, hdmstr. Fax 659-4812

Effingham, Effingham, Pop. 12,440
Effingham CUSD 40 3,000/PK-12
PO Box 130 62401 217-540-1500
Daniel Clasby Ph.D., supt. Fax 540-1510
www.effingham.k12.il.us
Central Grade S 600/3-5
10421 N US Highway 45 62401 217-540-1400
Dean Manuel, prin. Fax 540-1454
Early Learning Center 200/PK-K
3224 S Banker St 62401 217-540-1460
Kay Halford, prin. Fax 540-1484
East Side Preschool 100/PK-PK
215 N 1st St 62401 217-540-1380
Kay Halford, prin. Fax 540-1393
Effingham JHS 700/6-8
600 S Henrietta St 62401 217-540-1300
Scott Holst, prin. Fax 540-1362
South Side ES 300/1-2
211 W Douglas Ave 62401 217-540-1530
Amy Niebrugge, prin. Fax 540-1559
West Side ES 100/1-2
900 W Edgar Ave 62401 217-540-1570
Amy Niebrugge, prin. Fax 540-1585
Other Schools – See Edgewood

Sacred Heart S 200/PK-8
407 S Henrietta St 62401 217-342-4060
Judy Luchtefeld, prin. Fax 342-9251
St. Anthony of Padua S 300/1-8
405 N 2nd St 62401 217-347-0419
Mary Byers, prin. Fax 347-2749

Elburn, Kane, Pop. 4,236
Kaneland CUSD 302
Supt. — See Maple Park
Blackberry Creek ES 400/PK-5
1122 Anderson Rd 60119 630-365-1122
Kyle Kuhns, prin. Fax 365-3905
Stewart ES 600/PK-5
817 Prairie Valley St 60119 630-365-8170
Brian Graber, prin. Fax 365-0651

Eldorado, Saline, Pop. 4,416
Eldorado CUSD 4 1,200/PK-12
2200A Illinois Ave 62930 618-273-6394
Gary Siebert, supt. Fax 273-9311
www.eldorado.k12.il.us/
Eldorado ES 600/PK-5
1100 Alexander St 62930 618-273-9324
Steven Nelson, prin. Fax 273-9661
Eldorado MS 300/6-8
1907 1st St 62930 618-273-8056
Chris Morris, prin. Fax 273-2943

Elgin, Kane, Pop. 98,645
Central CUSD 301
Supt. — See Burlington
Country Trails ES K-5
3701 Highland Woods Blvd, 847-717-8000
Carie Walter, prin. Fax 717-8006
Prairie Knolls MS 6-8
225 Nesler Rd, 847-717-8100
Theresa Kolkebeck, prin. Fax 717-8105
Prairie View ES 600/K-5
10n630 Nesler Rd, 847-464-6014
Daniel Schuth, prin. Fax 464-6024

SD U-46 39,900/PK-12
355 E Chicago St 60120 847-888-5000
Jose Torres Ph.D., supt. Fax 608-4173
www.u-46.org/
Abbott MS 600/7-8
949 Van St 60123 847-888-5160
Shelly Hertzog, prin. Fax 608-2740
Century Oaks ES 400/K-6
1235 Braeburn Dr 60123 847-888-5181
Kathleen Marden, prin. Fax 608-2741
Channing Memorial ES 500/K-6
63 S Channing St 60120 847-888-5185
Dr. Ernest Gonzalez, prin. Fax 888-7016
Coleman ES 600/K-6
1220 Dundee Ave 60120 847-888-5190
Brian Stark, prin. Fax 608-2743
Creekside ES 500/K-6
655 N Airlite St 60123 847-289-6270
Randall Verticchio, prin. Fax 289-6040
Ellis MS 500/7-8
225 S Liberty St 60120 847-888-5151
Perry Hayes, prin. Fax 608-2744
Garfield ES 400/K-6
420 May St 60120 847-888-5192
Kimberly Thomas, prin. Fax 608-2745
Gifford ES 500/K-6
240 S Clifton Ave 60123 847-888-5195
Joseph Corcoran, prin. Fax 608-2763
Highland ES 600/K-6
190 N Melrose Ave 60123 847-888-5280
Dr. Steve Johnson, prin. Fax 608-2746
Hillcrest ES 600/K-6
80 N Airlite St 60123 847-888-5282
Dr. Duane Meighan, prin. Fax 742-3297
Hilltop ES 700/PK-6
1855 Rohrson Rd 60120 847-289-6655
Dena Farrell, prin. Fax 888-7199
Huff ES 700/PK-6
801 Hastings St 60120 847-888-5285
Angelica Ernst, prin. Fax 608-2747
Illinois Park Early Learning S 300/PK-PK
1350 Wing St 60123 847-289-6041
Peggy Ondera, prin. Fax 888-5332
Kimball MS 800/7-8
451 N Mclean Blvd 60123 847-888-5290
Alan Tamburrino, prin. Fax 608-2749
Larsen MS 600/7-8
665 Dundee Ave 60120 847-888-5250
Dr. Randy Hodges, prin. Fax 888-7172
Lords Park ES 800/K-6
323 Waverly Dr 60120 847-888-5360
Jeffrey Schleff, prin. Fax 608-2750
Lowrie ES 400/K-6
264 Oak St 60123 847-888-5260
Kelly O'Brien, prin. Fax 608-2751
McKinley ES 500/K-6
258 Lovell St 60120 847-888-5262
Lois Sands, prin. Fax 608-2752
Otter Creek ES 500/K-6
2701 Hopps Rd, 847-888-6995
Jeff Bragg, prin. Fax 888-7607
Sheridan ES 500/K-6
510 Franklin Blvd 60120 847-888-5266
Myrna Burgos, prin. Fax 608-2753
Washington ES 500/K-6
819 W Chicago St 60123 847-888-5270
Colleen White, prin. Fax 608-2754
Other Schools – See Bartlett, Carol Stream, Hanover Park, Hoffman Estates, South Elgin, Streamwood, Wayne

---

Da Vinci Academy 100/PK-8
37W080 Hopps Rd, 847-841-7532
Jeffrey Stroebel, hdmstr. Fax 841-7546
Einstein Academy 100/PK-12
747 Davis Rd 60123 847-697-3836
Fax 697-6084
Elgin Academy 400/PK-12
350 Park St 60120 847-695-0300
John Cooper, hdmstr. Fax 695-5017
Fox River Country Day S 200/PK-8
1600 Dundee Ave 60120 847-888-7910
Karen Morse, hdmstr. Fax 888-7947
Good Shepherd Lutheran S 200/PK-8
1111 Van St 60123 847-741-7795
Fax 741-6904
Harvest Christian Academy 600/PK-11
1000 N Randall Rd 60123 847-214-3500
Dr. Jeff Mattner, supt. Fax 214-3501
Highland Christian Academy 100/PK-8
2250 W Highland Ave 60123 847-741-5530
Jeorge Holmes, hdmstr. Fax 741-6397
St. John's Lutheran S 200/PK-8
109 N Spring St 60120 847-741-7633
Michael Rottmann, prin. Fax 741-0859

St. Joseph S 200/PK-8
274 Division St 60120 847-931-2804
Janine Bolchazy, prin. Fax 931-2810
St. Laurence S 200/PK-8
572 Standish St 60123 847-468-6100
Phyllis Jensen, prin. Fax 468-6104
St. Mary S 200/K-8
103 S Gifford St 60120 847-695-6609
Mary Beth Mitchell, prin. Fax 695-6623
St. Thomas More S 300/PK-8
1625 W Highland Ave 60123 847-742-3959
Margaret Fabrizius, prin. Fax 931-1066
Westminster Christian S 500/PK-12
2700 W Highland Ave, 847-695-0310
Chad Dirkse, admin. Fax 695-0135

Elizabethtown, Hardin, Pop. 335
Hardin County CUSD 1 700/PK-12
PO Box 218 62931 618-287-2411
Dr. Carroll Phelps, supt. Fax 287-2421
www.hardin.k12.il.us/
Hardin County ES, RR 2 62931 400/PK-6
Charles Little, prin. 618-287-7601
Hardin County JHS 100/7-8
RR 2 62931 618-287-2141
Jimmy Swasm, prin. Fax 287-8381

Elk Grove Village, Cook, Pop. 34,025
CCSD 59
Supt. — See Arlington Heights
Byrd ES 400/K-5
265 Wellington Ave 60007 847-593-4388
Maryellen Esser, prin. Fax 472-7188
Clearmont ES 300/K-5
280 Clearmont Dr 60007 847-593-4372
Ross Vittore, prin. Fax 593-7194
Grove JHS 900/6-8
777 W Elk Grove Blvd 60007 847-593-4367
Enza Papeck, prin. Fax 472-3001
Ridge Family Center for Learning 300/PK-5
650 Ridge Ave 60007 847-593-4070
Barbara Zabroske, prin. Fax 593-4075
Rupley ES 300/K-5
305 Oakton St 60007 847-593-4353
Karen Osmanski, prin. Fax 593-4405
Salt Creek ES 600/K-5
65 JF Kennedy Blvd 60007 847-593-4375
Maureen McAbee, prin. Fax 593-7390

Schaumburg CCSD 54
Supt. — See Schaumburg
Link ES 500/K-6
900 W Glenn Trl 60007 847-357-5300
John Schmelzer, prin. Fax 357-5301
Mead JHS 600/7-8
1765 Biesterfield Rd 60007 847-357-6000
Amy Read, prin. Fax 357-6001
Stevenson ES 400/PK-6
1414 Armstrong Ln 60007 847-357-5200
Leslie Eskildsen, prin. Fax 357-5201

Queen of the Rosary S 300/PK-8
690 W Elk Grove Blvd 60007 847-437-3322
Claudia Molick, prin. Fax 437-8961

Elkville, Jackson, Pop. 939
Elverado CUSD 196 400/PK-12
PO Box 130 62932 618-568-1321
John Hostert, supt. Fax 568-1152
www.elv196.com/
Elverado PS 100/PK-2
PO Box 130 62932 618-568-1321
John Hostert, prin. Fax 568-1152
Other Schools – See Vergennes

Elmhurst, DuPage, Pop. 44,976
Elmhurst SD 205 7,700/PK-12
162 S York St 60126 630-834-4530
Dr. Lynn Krizic, supt. Fax 617-2345
www.elmhurst.k12.il.us
Bryan MS 500/6-8
111 W Butterfield Rd 60126 630-617-2350
Brad Hillman, prin. Fax 617-2232
Churchville MS 400/6-8
155 E Victory Pkwy 60126 630-832-8682
Michelle Brown, prin. Fax 617-2387
Edison ES 300/K-5
246 S Fair Ave 60126 630-834-4272
James Pluskota, prin. Fax 617-8333
Emerson ES 400/K-5
400 N West Ave 60126 630-834-5562
Beth Gregor, prin. Fax 993-8883
Field ES 400/K-5
295 N Emroy Ave 60126 630-834-5313
Cynthia Gotha, prin. Fax 993-8896
Fischer ES 400/K-5
888 N Wilson St 60126 630-832-8601
Jane Bailey, prin. Fax 993-8890
Hawthorne ES 600/K-5
145 W Arthur St 60126 630-834-4541
Steven Smith, prin. Fax 993-8886
Jackson ES 400/K-5
925 S Swain Ave 60126 630-834-4544
Karen Beck, prin. Fax 993-8897
Jefferson ES 300/K-5
360 E Crescent Ave 60126 630-834-6261
Laura Pfanenstiel, prin. Fax 993-8888
Lincoln ES 500/K-5
565 S Fairfield Ave 60126 630-834-4548
Mary Ann Kalis, prin. Fax 993-6675
Madison ECC 100/PK-PK
130 W Madison St 60126 630-617-2385
Susan Kondrat, prin. Fax 617-2482
Sandburg MS 700/6-8
345 E Saint Charles Rd 60126 630-834-4534
Ryan Anderson, prin. Fax 617-2380

Salt Creek SD 48
Supt. — See Villa Park
Salt Creek ES 100/PK-1
980 S Riverside Dr 60126 630-832-6122
Nancy Fryzlewicz, prin. Fax 617-2658

Immaculate Conception S 600/PK-8
132 W Arthur St 60126 630-530-3490
Cathy Linley, prin. Fax 530-9787
Immanuel Lutheran S 300/PK-8
148 E 3rd St 60126 630-832-9302
Paul Trettin, prin. Fax 832-8307
Mary Queen of Heaven S PK-PK
426 N West Ave 60126 815-838-2187
Elizabeth Lowery, prin.
Timothy Christian S 700/PK-8
188 W Butterfield Rd 60126 630-833-4717
Timothy Hoeksema, prin. Fax 833-9828
Visitation S 500/PK-8
851 S York St 60126 630-834-3787
Sr. Thomas Monahan, prin. Fax 834-4936

Elmwood, Peoria, Pop. 1,893
Elmwood CUSD 322 700/PK-12
301 W Butternut St 61529 309-742-8464
Dr. Roger Alvey, supt. Fax 742-8812
www.elmwood.peoria.k12.il.us
Elmwood ES 400/PK-6
501 N Morgan St 61529 309-742-4261
Anthony Frost, prin. Fax 742-8833
Elmwood JHS 100/7-8
301 W Butternut St 61529 309-742-2851
Stan Matheny, prin. Fax 742-8350

Elmwood Park, Cook, Pop. 24,499
Elmwood Park CUSD 401 2,800/PK-12
8201 W Fullerton Ave 60707 708-452-7292
Dr. Douglas Rudig, supt. Fax 452-9504
www.sd401.k12.il.us
ECC 200/PK-K
4 W Conti Pkwy 60707 708-583-5860
Joanne Mourikes, prin. Fax 583-5899
Elm MS 500/7-8
7607 W Cortland St 60707 708-452-3550
Kathleen Patton, prin. Fax 452-0662
Elmwood ES 500/1-6
2319 N 76th Ave 60707 708-452-3558
Sue Ponzio, prin. Fax 452-5567
Mills ES 600/1-6
2824 N 76th Ave 60707 708-452-3560
Peter Herbert, prin. Fax 452-0349

St. Celestine S 400/PK-8
3017 N 77th Ave 60707 708-453-8234
Jeanine Rocchi, prin. Fax 452-0237

El Paso, Woodford, Pop. 2,748
El Paso-Gridley CUSD 11 1,100/PK-12
97 W 5th St 61738 309-527-4410
Rick Johnston, supt. Fax 527-4040
www.unit11.org/
Centennial S 200/PK-PK, 4-
135 W 5th St 61738 309-527-4435
Kelly Throneburg, prin. Fax 527-4438
Jefferson Park S 300/K-3
250 W 3rd St 61738 309-527-4405
Kelly Throneburg, prin. Fax 527-4407
Other Schools – See Gridley

Elwood, Will, Pop. 2,237
Elwood CCSD 203 400/K-8
409 N Chicago St 60421 815-423-5588
Dr. Ronald Kanzulak, supt. Fax 423-5184
www.elwood.k12.il.us/
Elwood Community Consolidated S 400/K-8
409 N Chicago St 60421 815-423-5588
Lyell Stark, prin. Fax 423-5808

Emden, Logan, Pop. 494
Hartsburg-Emden CUSD 21
Supt. — See Hartsburg
Emden ES, PO Box 259 62635 100/PK-4
Donald Helm, prin. 217-376-3151

Energy, Williamson, Pop. 1,177

Unity Christian S 200/PK-8
100 E College St 62933 618-942-3802
Debi Barnett, admin. Fax 942-7228

Enfield, White, Pop. 625
Norris City-Omaha-Enfield CUSD 3
Supt. — See Norris City
Booth S 200/PK-8
PO Box 39 62835 618-963-2521
Matthew Vollman, prin. Fax 963-2716

Erie, Whiteside, Pop. 1,573
Erie CUSD 1 700/PK-12
520 5th Ave 61250 309-659-2239
Bradley Cox, supt. Fax 659-2230
www.erie1.net
Erie ES 300/PK-4
605 6th Ave 61250 309-659-2239
Margaret Carey, prin. Fax 659-2588
Erie MS, 500 5th Ave 61250 200/5-8
Keith Morgan, prin. 309-659-2239

Eureka, Woodford, Pop. 5,084
Eureka CUSD 140 1,600/PK-12
109 W Cruger Ave 61530 309-467-3737
Dr. Randy Crump, supt. Fax 467-2377
www.district140.org
Davenport ES 400/PK-4
301 S Main St 61530 309-467-2524
Jerry Babbs, prin. Fax 467-5265
Eureka MS 500/5-8
2005 S Main St 61530 309-467-3771
Robert Gold, prin. Fax 467-2052
Other Schools – See Congerville, Goodfield

Evanston, Cook, Pop. 75,236
Evanston CCSD 65 6,400/PK-8
1500 McDaniel Ave 60201 847-859-8000
Dr. Hardy Murphy, supt. Fax 859-8707
www.district65.net/
Chute MS 500/6-8
1400 Oakton St 60202 847-859-8600
James McHolland, prin. Fax 492-7956
Dawes ES 300/K-5
440 Dodge Ave 60202 847-859-8990
Karen Bradley, prin. Fax 492-9841
Dewey ES 300/K-5
1551 Wesley Ave 60201 847-859-8140
Andrew Krugly, prin. Fax 492-7994
Haven MS 600/6-8
2417 Prairie Ave 60201 847-859-8200
Kathleen Roberson, prin. Fax 492-9983
Hill ECC 300/PK-PK
1500 McDaniel Ave 60201 847-859-8300
Amy Small, prin. Fax 859-8003
King Jr. Lab Experimental S 600/K-8
2424 Lake St 60201 847-859-8500
Jeffrey Brown, prin. Fax 492-1413
Kingsley ES 300/K-5
2300 Green Bay Rd 60201 847-859-8400
Beatrice Davis, prin. Fax 492-5868
Lincoln ES 300/PK-5
910 Forest Ave 60202 847-859-8970
Chris McDermott, prin. Fax 492-1870
Lincolnwood ES 400/K-5
2600 Colfax St 60201 847-859-8880
Fred Hunter, prin. Fax 492-7958
Nichols MS 500/6-8
800 Greenleaf St 60202 847-859-8660
Gordon Hood, prin. Fax 492-7880
Oakton ES 400/K-5
436 Ridge Ave 60202 847-859-8800
Churchill Daniels, prin. Fax 492-7960
Orrington ES 300/K-5
2636 Orrington Ave 60201 847-859-8780
Michael Dougherty, prin. Fax 492-9003
Walker ES 300/K-5
3601 Church St 60203 847-859-8330
Karen Evans, prin. Fax 674-7004
Washington ES 500/PK-5
914 Ashland Ave 60202 847-859-8180
Susan Lewis, prin. Fax 492-8433
Willard ES 300/PK-5
2700 Hurd Ave 60201 847-859-8110
Dr. Shelley Carey, prin. Fax 733-2100
Other Schools – See Skokie

Chiaravalle Montessori S 300/PK-8
425 Dempster St 60201 847-864-2190
Brenda Mizel, hdmstr. Fax 864-2206
Midwest Montessori S 50/PK-K
926 Noyes St 60201 847-328-6630
Mary Strezewski, prin. Fax 328-6630
Pope John XXIII S 300/PK-8
1120 Washington St 60202 847-475-5678
Rosalie Musiala, prin. Fax 475-5683
Roycemore S 300/PK-12
640 Lincoln St 60201 847-866-6055
Joseph Becker, hdmstr. Fax 866-6545
St. Athanasius S 300/K-8
2510 Ashland Ave 60201 847-864-2650
Susan Castagna, prin. Fax 475-7385
St. Joan of Arc S 200/PK-8
9245 Lawndale Ave 60203 847-679-0660
Gail Hulse, prin. Fax 679-0689

Evansville, Randolph, Pop. 697
Sparta CUSD 140
Supt. — See Sparta
Evansville Attendance Center 100/K-8
701 Oak St 62242 618-853-4411
Denise Ebers, prin. Fax 853-2243

Evergreen Park, Cook, Pop. 19,876
Evergreen Park ESD 124 1,900/PK-8
9400 S Sawyer Ave 60805 708-423-0950
Dr. Diane Cody, supt. Fax 423-4292
www.d124.org
Central JHS 500/7-8
9400 S Sawyer Ave 60805 708-424-0148
Rita Sparks, prin. Fax 229-8406
Northeast ES 400/PK-6
9058 S California Ave 60805 708-422-6501
Jeffrey Nightingale, prin. Fax 229-8410
Northwest ES 300/K-6
3630 W 92nd St 60805 708-425-9473
John Stanton, prin. Fax 229-8407
Southeast ES 400/K-6
9800 S Francisco Ave 60805 708-422-1021
Shaton Wolverton, prin. Fax 229-8413
Southwest ES 400/K-6
9900 S Central Park Ave 60805 708-424-2444
Denise Thomas, prin. Fax 229-8416

Most Holy Redeemer S 500/PK-8
9536 S Millard Ave 60805 708-422-8280
Loretta Conroy, prin. Fax 422-4193
St. Bernadette S 200/PK-8
9311 S Francisco Ave 60805 708-422-6429
Arlene Baumann, prin. Fax 422-6484

Ewing, Franklin, Pop. 323
Ewing Northern CCSD 115 200/PK-8
51 N Main St 62836 618-629-2181
Marian Nipper, supt. Fax 629-2510
www.ewinggradeschool.org/
Ewing Northern S 200/PK-8
51 N Main St 62836 618-629-2181
Marian Nipper, prin. Fax 629-2510

Fairbury, Livingston, Pop. 3,919
Prairie Central CUSD 8 2,200/PK-12
605 N 7th St 61739 815-692-2504
Dr. John Capasso, supt. Fax 692-3195
www.prairiecentral.org
Westview ES 400/PK-4
600 S 1st St 61739 815-692-2623
Ron Schramm, prin. Fax 692-3726
Other Schools – See Chatsworth, Chenoa, Forrest

Fairfield, Wayne, Pop. 5,230
Fairfield SD 112 700/PK-8
806 N 1st St 62837 618-842-6501
Rena Talbert, supt. Fax 842-2932
Center Street S 400/PK-PK, 4-
200 W Center St 62837 618-842-2679
David Mills, prin. Fax 842-4719
North Side ES 300/K-3
806 N 1st St 62837 618-847-4341
Rena Talbert, prin. Fax 842-2932

Jasper CCSD 17 200/K-8
RR 3 Box 473 62837 618-842-3048
Jeffrey Mitchell, supt. Fax 842-3289
www.jasper17.wayne.k12.il.us
Jasper S 200/K-8
RR 3 Box 473 62837 618-842-3048
Jeffrey Mitchell, prin. Fax 842-3289

New Hope CCSD 6 200/K-8
RR 4 Box 243 62837 618-842-3296
Donald Haile, supt. Fax 847-7000
New Hope S 200/K-8
RR 4 Box 243 62837 618-842-3296
Donald Haile, prin. Fax 847-7000

Fairview Heights, Saint Clair, Pop. 16,471
Grant CCSD 110 800/PK-8
10110 Old Lincoln Trl 62208 618-398-5577
Dr. Darrel Hardt, supt. Fax 398-5578
www.dist110.com
Grant MS 400/4-8
10110 Old Lincoln Trl 62208 618-397-2764
Matt Stines, prin. Fax 397-7809
Illini ES 400/PK-3
21 Circle Dr 62208 618-398-5552
Linda Kahley, prin. Fax 394-9801

Pontiac-William Holliday SD 105 700/PK-8
400 Ashland Dr 62208 618-233-2320
Michael Loftus, supt. Fax 233-0918
www.pontiac.stclair.k12.il.us
Holliday ES 600/PK-6
400 Joseph Dr 62208 618-233-7588
Bill Fulk, prin. Fax 233-1619
Pontiac JHS 200/7-8
400 Ashland Dr 62208 618-233-6004
Paul Holland, prin. Fax 233-0918

Holy Trinity Catholic S East 200/PK-8
504 Fountains Pkwy 62208 618-632-4937
Michael Oslance, prin. Fax 628-1570

Farmer City, DeWitt, Pop. 2,005
Blue Ridge CUSD 18 900/PK-12
411 N John St 61842 309-928-9141
Jay Harnack, supt. Fax 928-5478
www.blueridge18.org
Schneider ES 300/PK-3
309 N John St 61842 309-928-2611
Susan Wilson, prin. Fax 928-2195
Other Schools – See Mansfield

Farmersville, Montgomery, Pop. 766
Panhandle CUSD 2
Supt. — See Raymond
Farmersville ES 100/K-5
PO Box 170 62533 217-227-3306
Aaron Hopper, prin. Fax 227-3246

Farmington, Fulton, Pop. 2,514
Farmington Central CUSD 265 1,500/PK-12
212 N Lightfoot Rd 61531 309-245-1000
Mark Doan, supt. Fax 245-9161
www.dist265.com/
Farmington Central ES 700/PK-5
108 N Lightfoot Rd 61531 309-245-1000
Jack Small, prin. Fax 245-9165
Farmington Central JHS 300/6-8
300 N Lightfoot Rd 61531 309-245-1000
Perry Miller, prin. Fax 245-9162

Fieldon, Jersey, Pop. 272
Jersey CUSD 100
Supt. — See Jerseyville
Fieldon ES 100/K-6
104 N Public Rd 62031 618-376-4771
Mary Schell, prin. Fax 376-8801

Findlay, Shelby, Pop. 685
Okaw Valley CUSD 302
Supt. — See Bethany
Okaw Valley IS 100/4-5
501 W Division St 62534 217-756-8522
Mike Cummins, prin. Fax 756-8501
Okaw Valley MS 100/6-8
501 W Division St 62534 217-756-8521
Mike Cummins, prin. Fax 756-8599

Fisher, Champaign, Pop. 1,654
Fisher CUSD 1 600/K-12
PO Box 700 61843 217-897-6125
Barbara Thompson, supt. Fax 897-6676
www.fisher.k12.il.us
Fisher ES 300/K-6
PO Box 700 61843 217-897-1133
James Moxley, prin. Fax 897-6676

Fithian, Vermilion, Pop. 552
Oakwood CUSD 76 1,100/PK-12
5834 US Route 150 61844 217-354-4355
Keven Forney, supt. Fax 354-2030
www.oakwood.k12.il.us/
Other Schools – See Danville, Oakwood

Flanagan, Livingston, Pop. 1,061
Flanagan-Cornell Unit SD 74 400/PK-12
202 E Falcon Hwy 61740 815-796-2233
Jerry Farris, supt. Fax 796-2856
www.flanagan.k12.il.us/
Flanagan S 200/PK-8
202 E Falcon Hwy 61740 815-796-2261
Richard Trachsel, prin. Fax 796-2856

Flora, Clay, Pop. 4,855
Flora CUSD 35 — 1,500/PK-12
444 S Locust St 62839 — 618-662-2412
Gary May, supt. — Fax 662-4587
floraschools.com/
Henson JHS — 300/6-8
609 N Stanford Rd 62839 — 618-662-8394
Janette Schade, prin. — Fax 662-8395
Lincoln ES — 200/4-5
7215 Old Highway 50 62839 — 618-662-2226
Leslie Carder, prin.
McEndree ES, 200 N Olive Rd 62839 — 300/PK-3
Julie Pearce, prin. — 618-662-2014
Washington S — 200/PK-K
114 E Washington St 62839 — 618-662-8118
Julie Pearce, prin.
Other Schools – See Xenia

Flossmoor, Cook, Pop. 9,390
Flossmoor SD 161
Supt. — See Chicago Heights
Flossmoor Hills ES — 400/K-5
3721 Beech St 60422 — 708-647-7100
Karen Brown, prin. — Fax 798-8324
Heather Hill ES — 400/K-5
1439 Lawrence Cres 60422 — 708-647-7200
Venus Smith, prin. — Fax 206-2749
Parker JHS — 1,000/6-8
2810 School St 60422 — 708-647-5400
Dr. Vanessa Atkins, prin. — Fax 799-9207
Western Avenue ES — 500/K-5
940 Western Ave 60422 — 708-647-7400
Jennifer Okleshen, prin. — Fax 206-2350

Flossmoor Montessori S — 100/PK-3
740 Western Ave 60422 — 708-798-4600
Lawrence Lewis, admin. — Fax 798-4021
Infant Jesus of Prague S — 600/PK-8
1101 Douglas Ave 60422 — 708-799-5200
Thomas Sedor, prin. — Fax 799-5293

Ford Heights, Cook, Pop. 3,294
Ford Heights SD 169 — 700/PK-8
910 Woodlawn Ave 60411 — 708-758-1370
Gregory Jackson, supt. — Fax 758-1372
www.fordheights169.org
Cottage Grove Upper Grade Center — 300/5-8
800 E 14th St 60411 — 708-758-1400
Stephanie Stephens, prin. — Fax 758-0711
Evers ES — 400/PK-4
1101 E 10th St 60411 — 708-758-2520
Marilyn Powell-Barnes, prin. — Fax 758-2521

Forest Park, Cook, Pop. 15,197
Forest Park SD 91 — 1,000/PK-8
424 Des Plaines Ave 60130 — 708-366-5700
Dr. Louis Cavallo, supt. — Fax 366-5761
www.forestparkschools.org
Field-Stevenson ES — 200/K-5
925 Beloit Ave 60130 — 708-366-5703
Robert Giovannoni, prin. — Fax 366-2091
Forest Park MS — 300/6-8
925 Beloit Ave 60130 — 708-366-5703
Karen Bukowski, prin. — Fax 366-2091
Garfield ES — 200/PK-5
543 Hannah Ave 60130 — 708-366-6945
M. Jamie Stauder, prin. — Fax 366-8044
Grant-White ES — 100/K-5
147 Circle Ave 60130 — 708-366-5704
Wendy Trotter, prin. — Fax 771-1649
Ross ES — 100/K-5
1315 Marengo Ave 60130 — 708-366-7498
William Milnamow, prin. — Fax 771-4232

St. Bernardine S — 100/PK-8
815 Elgin Ave 60130 — 708-366-6890
Zenza Laws, prin. — Fax 366-8015

Forrest, Livingston, Pop. 1,202
Prairie Central CUSD 8
Supt. — See Fairbury
Meadowbrook ES — 200/PK-4
450 N Bach St 61741 — 815-657-8461
Karen Hazelrigg, prin. — Fax 657-8535
Prairie Central JHS — 300/7-8
800 N Wood St 61741 — 815-657-8660
Dan Vaughan, prin. — Fax 657-8677
Prairie Central Upper ES — 300/5-6
PO Box 496 61741 — 815-657-8238
Paula Crane, prin. — Fax 657-8821

Forreston, Ogle, Pop. 1,515
Forrestville Valley CUSD 221 — 1,000/PK-12
PO Box 665 61030 — 815-938-2036
Lowell Taylor, supt. — Fax 938-9028
www.fvdistrict221.org
Forreston ES — 300/PK-5
PO Box 665 61030 — 815-938-2301
Christopher Shockey, prin. — Fax 938-2471
Forreston MS — 200/6-8
PO Box 665 61030 — 815-938-2195
Travis Heinz, prin. — Fax 938-9028
Other Schools – See German Valley

Forsyth, Macon, Pop. 2,762
Maroa-Forsyth CUSD 2
Supt. — See Maroa
Maroa-Forsyth Grade S — 400/K-3
137 S Grant St 62535 — 217-877-2023
Rennie Cluver, prin. — Fax 877-6216

Fox Lake, Lake, Pop. 10,736
Fox Lake Grade SD 114
Supt. — See Spring Grove
Stanton MS — 300/6-8
101 Hawthorne Ln 60020 — 847-973-4200
William Lomas, prin. — Fax 973-4210

Fox River Grove, McHenry, Pop. 5,084
Fox River Grove SD 3 — 500/K-8
403 Orchard St 60021 — 847-516-5100
Tim Mahaffy, supt. — Fax 516-9169
www.dist3.org
Algonquin Road ES — 300/K-4
975 Algonquin Rd 60021 — 847-516-5101
Karen Machroli, prin. — Fax 516-9058
Fox River Grove MS — 200/5-8
401 Orchard St 60021 — 847-516-5105
Eric Runcke, prin. — Fax 516-5104

Frankfort, Will, Pop. 15,819
Frankfort CCSD 157C — 2,300/PK-8
10482 Nebraska St 60423 — 815-469-5922
Dr. Robert Madonia, supt. — Fax 469-8988
www.fsd157c.org
Chelsea ES — 700/3-5
22265 S 80th Ave 60423 — 815-469-2309
Kristin Fuqua, prin. — Fax 464-2043
Grand Prairie ES — 800/PK-2
10480 Nebraska St 60423 — 815-469-3366
Luke Lambatos, prin. — Fax 469-2899
Hickory Creek MS — 800/6-8
22150 S Owens Rd 60423 — 815-469-4474
Kevin Suchinski, prin. — Fax 469-7930

Peotone CUSD 207U
Supt. — See Peotone
Green Garden ES — 200/K-4
9526 E 255th St 60423 — 815-469-5744
Tracy Hiller, prin. — Fax 469-5744

Summit Hill SD 161 — 3,200/PK-8
20100 S Spruce Dr 60423 — 815-469-9103
Keith Pain, supt. — Fax 469-0566
www.summithill.org/
Drew ES — 1-4
20130 S Rosewood Dr 60423 — 815-469-3950
Kathy Klein, prin. — Fax 469-0540
Frankfort Square ES — 200/1-4
7710 W Kingston Dr 60423 — 815-469-3176
Christine Carey, prin. — Fax 464-2068
Full Day K — PK-K
20027 S 88th Ave 60423 — 815-464-2230
Nan Clinton, prin. — Fax 464-2250
Indian Trail ES — 500/1-4
20912 S Frankfort Square Rd 60423 — 815-469-6993
Dan Pierson, prin. — Fax 806-8352
Rogus ES — 500/1-4
20027 S 88th Ave 60423 — 815-464-2034
Michael Ruffalo, prin. — Fax 464-2250
Summit Hill JHS — 800/7-8
7260 W North Ave 60423 — 815-469-4330
Beth Lind, prin. — Fax 464-1596
Other Schools – See Mokena, Tinley Park

St. Anthony Preschool — 100/PK-PK
7661 W Sauk Trl 60423 — 815-469-5417
Christina Breitbarth, dir. — Fax 469-6514

Franklin, Morgan, Pop. 580
Franklin CUSD 1
Supt. — See Alexander
Franklin East ES — 100/PK-1
PO Box 199 62638 — 217-675-2334
Adam Ehrman, prin. — Fax 675-2396

Franklin Grove, Lee, Pop. 1,019
Ashton-Franklin Center CUSD 275
Supt. — See Ashton
Ashton-Franklin Center ES — 200/K-4
PO Box 278 61031 — 815-456-2325
Ann Tilton, prin. — Fax 456-2713
Ashton-Franklin Center MS — 200/5-8
PO Box 188 61031 — 815-456-2323
Ann Tilton, prin. — Fax 456-3211

Franklin Park, Cook, Pop. 18,490
Franklin Park SD 84 — 1,300/PK-8
2915 Maple St 60131 — 847-455-4230
David Nemec, supt. — Fax 455-9094
www.d84.org/
Hester JHS — 400/6-8
2836 Gustav St 60131 — 847-455-2150
John Kosirog, prin. — Fax 455-0945
North ES — 200/K-5
9500 Gage Ave 60131 — 847-678-7962
Judith Martin, prin. — Fax 678-3616
Passow ES — 400/K-5
2838 Calwagner St 60131 — 847-455-6781
Jacqueline Fricke, prin. — Fax 455-1465
Pietrini ES — 300/PK-5
9750 Fullerton Ave 60131 — 847-455-7960
Lois Fronczke, prin. — Fax 455-1809

Mannheim SD 83 — 2,700/K-8
10401 Grand Ave 60131 — 847-455-4413
Bruce Lane Ed.D., supt. — Fax 451-8290
www.d83.org/
Other Schools – See Melrose Park, Northlake

Freeburg, Saint Clair, Pop. 4,092
Freeburg CCSD 70 — 700/PK-8
408 S Belleville St 62243 — 618-539-3188
Dr. Rob Hawkins, supt. — Fax 539-5795
www.frg70.stclair.k12.il.us
Freeburg ES — 500/3-8
408 S Belleville St 62243 — 618-539-3188
Tomi Diefenbach, prin. — Fax 539-6008
Freeburg Primary Center — 200/PK-2
650 S State St 62243 — 618-539-3188
Tomi Diefenbach, prin.

St. Joseph S — 100/K-8
2 N Alton St 62243 — 618-539-3930
Fax 539-3930

Freeport, Stephenson, Pop. 25,612
Freeport SD 145 — 4,300/PK-12
501 E South St 61032 — 815-232-0300
Dr. Peter Flynn, supt. — Fax 232-6717
www.freeport.k12.il.us
Blackhawk ES — 300/1-4
1401 S Blackhawk Ave 61032 — 815-232-0490
Donna Benton, prin. — Fax 232-0578
Center ES — 300/1-4
718 E Illinois St 61032 — 815-232-0480
Danielle Summers, prin. — Fax 232-3247
Empire ES — 300/1-4
1401 W Empire St 61032 — 815-232-0380
Michele Barnes, prin. — Fax 232-0577
Freeport JHS — 700/7-8
701 W Empire St 61032 — 815-232-0500
Scott Wiley, prin. — Fax 232-0536
Jones-Farrar Early Learning Center — 400/PK-K
1386 Kiwanis Dr 61032 — 815-232-0610
Cathy Arnold, prin. — Fax 235-9220
Lincoln-Douglas ES — 200/1-4
1802 W Laurel St 61032 — 815-232-0370
Dr. Debra Kleckner, prin. — Fax 232-0379
Sandburg MS — 600/5-6
1717 W Eby St 61032 — 815-232-0340
Stacey Kleindl, prin. — Fax 232-1241
Taylor Park ES — 200/1-4
806 E Stephenson St 61032 — 815-232-0390
Fax 232-0399

Aquin Catholic ES — 200/PK-6
202 W Pleasant St 61032 — 815-232-6416
David Hawkinson, prin. — Fax 599-8526
Immanuel Lutheran S — 200/PK-8
1993 W Church St 61032 — 815-232-3511
Michael Welton, prin. — Fax 233-9158
Open Bible Learning Center — 50/K-5
3800 W Stephenson St 61032 — 815-235-7216
Dr. Burliss Parker, admin. — Fax 235-9232
Tri-County Christian S — 100/PK-8
2900 Loras Dr 61032 — 815-233-1876
Reginald McGee, admin. — Fax 233-4862

Fulton, Whiteside, Pop. 3,853
River Bend CUSD 2 — 1,000/K-12
1110 3rd St 61252 — 815-589-2711
Jane Bauer, supt. — Fax 589-4630
www.riverbendschools.org
Fulton ES — 400/K-5
1301 7th Ave 61252 — 815-589-2911
Mindy Dunlap, prin. — Fax 589-4614
River Bend MS — 200/6-8
415 12th St 61252 — 815-589-2611
James Spielman, prin. — Fax 589-3130

Unity Christian ES — 100/PK-6
1000 11th Ave 61252 — 815-589-4196
Dick Ritzema, supt. — Fax 589-3746

Gages Lake, Lake, Pop. 8,349
Woodland CCSD 50
Supt. — See Gurnee
Woodland ES East — 2,300/1-3
17261 W Gages Lake Rd 60030 — 847-984-8800
Ken Hyllberg, prin. — Fax 549-9806
Woodland ES West — 1-3
17261 W Gages Lake Rd 60030 — 847-984-8900
David Brown, prin. — Fax 816-0708
Woodland PS — 700/PK-K
17366 W Gages Lake Rd 60030 — 847-984-8700
Lori Casey, prin. — Fax 816-4511

Galatia, Saline, Pop. 988
Galatia CUSD 1 — 400/PK-12
200 N McKinley St 62935 — 618-268-4194
Kirk Abernathy, supt. — Fax 268-4196
Galatia ES — 200/PK-6
200 N Hickory St 62935 — 618-268-6371
Beth Rister, prin. — Fax 268-4949
Galatia JHS — 100/7-8
200 N McKinley St 62935 — 618-268-4194
Kirk Abernathy, prin. — Fax 268-4196

Galena, Jo Daviess, Pop. 3,405
Galena Unit SD 120 — 800/PK-12
1206 Franklin St 61036 — 815-777-3086
Dr. Dale Greimann, supt. — Fax 777-0303
Galena MS — 200/5-8
1230 Franklin St 61036 — 815-777-2413
Ben Soat, prin. — Fax 777-4259
Galena PS — 300/PK-4
219 Kelly Ln 61036 — 815-777-2200
Chad Steckel, prin. — Fax 777-4842

Tri-State Christian S — 200/PK-12
11084 W US Highway 20 61036 — 815-777-3800
Mary Jane Thorne, prin. — Fax 777-2991

Galesburg, Knox, Pop. 32,017
Galesburg CUSD 205 — 4,800/PK-12
PO Box 1206 61402 — 309-343-1151
Dr. S. Gene Denisar, supt. — Fax 343-7757
www.galesburg205.org/
Bright Futures S — PK-PK
932 Harrison St 61401 — 309-343-9848
Maury Lyon, admin.
Churchill JHS — 600/6-8
905 Maple Ave 61401 — 309-342-3129
Bart Arthur, prin. — Fax 342-6384
Cooke ES — 100/K-5
849 S Henderson St 61401 — 309-343-3525
Elnora Brown, prin. — Fax 343-3508
Gale ES — 400/K-5
1131 W Dayton St 61401 — 309-343-0217
Ellen Spittell, prin. — Fax 343-2635
King ES — 400/K-5
1018 S Farnham St 61401 — 309-343-0409
Renee Wallace, prin. — Fax 343-2161
Lombard JHS — 400/6-8
1220 E Knox St 61401 — 309-342-9171
Kim Hanks, prin. — Fax 342-7135
Nielson ES — 400/K-5
547 N Farnham St 61401 — 309-343-0614
Matthew Leclere, prin. — Fax 343-4574
Steele ES — 300/K-5
1480 W Main St 61401 — 309-343-0516
Cary Jacobson, prin. — Fax 343-1259

Willard ES — 400/K-5
495 E Fremont St 61401 — 309-343-3917
John Shelly, prin. — Fax 343-1712

Costa Catholic S — 300/PK-8
2726 Costa Dr 61401 — 309-344-3151
James Kovac, prin. — Fax 344-1594
Galesburg Christian S — 100/PK-9
1881 E Fremont St 61401 — 309-343-8008
Rhonda Flack, admin. — Fax 343-8006

Galt, Whiteside, Pop. 230

Sterling Christian S — 100/PK-12
PO Box 40 61037 — 815-625-0309
Mick Welding, prin. — Fax 625-2658

Galva, Henry, Pop. 2,705
Galva CUSD 224 — 700/PK-12
224 Morgan Rd 61434 — 309-932-2108
Dr. James Minick, supt. — Fax 932-8326
cats.k12.il.us
Galva ES — 400/PK-6
224 Morgan Rd 61434 — 309-932-2420
Doug O'Riley, prin. — Fax 932-8716

Garden Prairie, Boone
Belvidere CUSD 100
Supt. — See Belvidere
Kishwaukee ES — 200/K-5
7133 Garden Prairie Rd 61038 — 815-597-1501
Debbie Anderson, prin. — Fax 597-1421

Gardner, Grundy, Pop. 1,436
Gardner CCSD 72C — 200/K-8
PO Box 347 60424 — 815-237-2313
Dr. Linda Dvorak, supt. — Fax 237-2114
www.ggs.grundy.k12.il.us/
Gardner S — 200/K-8
PO Box 347 60424 — 815-237-2313
Linda Dvorak, prin. — Fax 237-2114

Geff, Wayne
Geff CCSD 14 — 100/K-8
201 E Lafayette St 62842 — 618-897-2465
Anita Pond, supt. — Fax 897-2565
Geff S — 100/K-8
201 E Lafayette St 62842 — 618-897-2465
Anita Pond, prin. — Fax 897-2565

Geneseo, Henry, Pop. 6,524
Geneseo CUSD 228 — 2,600/PK-12
209 S College Ave 61254 — 309-945-0450
Scott Kuffel, supt. — Fax 945-0445
www.dist228.org
Geneseo MS — 700/6-8
333 E Ogden Ave 61254 — 309-945-0599
Matt DeBaene, prin. — Fax 945-0580
Millikin ES — 300/K-5
920 S Congress St 61254 — 309-945-0475
William Menendez, prin. — Fax 945-0480
Northside ES — 300/PK-5
415 N Russell Ave 61254 — 309-945-0625
Jack Selindwein, prin. — Fax 945-0620
Southwest ES — 400/K-5
715 S Center St 61254 — 309-945-0652
Nancy Wiese, prin. — Fax 945-0670

St. Malachy S — 100/PK-6
595 E Ogden Ave 61254 — 309-944-3230
Stan Griffin, prin. — Fax 944-5319

Geneva, Kane, Pop. 23,424
Geneva CUSD 304 — 5,400/PK-12
227 N 4th St 60134 — 630-463-3000
Dr. Kent Mutchler, supt. — Fax 463-3009
www.geneva304.org/
Friendship Station S — 50/PK-PK
227 N 4th St 60134 — 630-463-3060
Dawn George, prin.
Geneva MS North — 700/6-8
1357 Viking Dr 60134 — 630-463-3700
Lawrence Bidlack, prin. — Fax 463-3709
Geneva MS South — 700/6-8
1415 Viking Dr 60134 — 630-463-3600
Terry Bleau, prin. — Fax 208-7172
Harrison Street ES — 500/PK-5
201 N Harrison St 60134 — 630-463-3300
Dan Killeen, prin. — Fax 208-3525
Heartland ES — 500/K-5
3300 Heartland Dr 60134 — 630-463-3200
Dr. Margaret Pennington, prin.
Mill Creek ES — 400/K-5
0n900 Brundige Dr 60134 — 630-463-3400
Andrew Barret, prin. — Fax 208-7595
Western Avenue ES — 600/K-5
1500 Western Ave 60134 — 630-463-3500
Ron Zeman, prin. — Fax 232-4552
Williamsburg ES — K-5
1812 Williamsburg Ave 60134 — 630-463-3100
Julie Dye, prin. — Fax 463-3109

Faith Christian Academy — 50/1-8
1745 Kaneville Rd 60134 — 630-232-7779
DeAnne Appleton, hdmstr. — Fax 232-7344
Mansio Mens Montessori S — 100/PK-K
102 Howard St 60134 — 630-232-6750
Janet Shanahan, prin. — Fax 232-6255
St. Peter S — 500/PK-8
1881 Kaneville Rd 60134 — 630-232-0476
Rosann Feldmann, prin. — Fax 208-5681

Genoa, DeKalb, Pop. 4,671
Genoa-Kingston CUSD 424 — 2,000/PK-12
980 Park Ave 60135 — 815-784-6222
Scott Wakeley, supt. — Fax 784-6059
www.gkschools.org
Davenport ES — 300/PK-1
123 W 1st St 60135 — 815-784-2448
Trevor Steinbach, prin. — Fax 784-3175

Genoa ES — 300/4-5
602 E Hill St 60135 — 815-784-3742
John Francis, prin. — Fax 784-3731
Genoa-Kingston MS — 500/6-8
941 W Main St 60135 — 815-784-5222
Angelo Lekkas, prin. — Fax 784-4323
Other Schools – See Kingston

Georgetown, Vermilion, Pop. 3,516
Georgetown-Ridge Farm CUSD 4 — 1,300/PK-12
400 W West St 61846 — 217-662-8488
Kevin Tate, supt. — Fax 662-3402
www.grf.k12.il.us
Miller JHS — 300/6-8
414 W West St 61846 — 217-662-6606
Lisa Gocken, prin. — Fax 662-6345
Pine Crest ES — 500/PK-3
505 S Kennedy Dr 61846 — 217-662-6981
Cindy Gilliland, prin. — Fax 662-3413
Other Schools – See Ridge Farm

Germantown, Clinton, Pop. 1,105
Germantown SD 60 — 300/PK-8
PO Box 400 62245 — 618-523-4253
Larry Weber, supt. — Fax 523-7879
www.germantownbulldogs.org
Germantown S — 300/PK-8
PO Box 400 62245 — 618-523-4253
Larry Weber, prin. — Fax 523-7879

Germantown Hills, Woodford, Pop. 2,943
Germantown Hills SD 69 — 600/PK-8
110 Fandel Rd, — 309-383-2121
James Dansart, supt. — Fax 383-2123
ghills.metamora.k12.il.us
Germantown Hills ES — 300/PK-5
110 Fandel Rd, — 309-383-2121
Dr. Shelli Nafziger, prin. — Fax 383-2123
Germantown Hills MS — 300/6-8
103 Warrior Way, — 309-383-2121
Rick Simkins, prin. — Fax 383-4739

German Valley, Stephenson, Pop. 465
Forrestville Valley CUSD 221
Supt. — See Forreston
German Valley ES — 100/K-5
PO Box 74 61039 — 815-362-2279
Christopher Shockey, prin. — Fax 362-2235

Gibson City, Ford, Pop. 3,394
Gibson City-Melvin-Sibley CUSD 5 — 1,100/PK-12
217 E 17th St 60936 — 217-784-8296
Charles Aubry, supt. — Fax 784-8558
www.gcms.k12.il.us
GCMS ES — 500/PK-5
902 N Church St 60936 — 217-784-4278
Shelley Overman, prin. — Fax 784-4782
GCMS MS — 300/6-8
316 E 19th St 60936 — 217-784-8731
Michael Bleich, prin. — Fax 784-8726

Gifford, Champaign, Pop. 999
Gifford CCSD 188 — 200/K-8
PO Box 70 61847 — 217-568-7733
Arthur Shaw, supt. — Fax 568-7228
www.gifford.k12.il.us
Gifford Grade S — 200/K-8
PO Box 70 61847 — 217-568-7733
Arthur Shaw, prin. — Fax 568-7228

Gilberts, Kane, Pop. 4,869
CUSD 300
Supt. — See Carpentersville
Gilberts ES — PK-5
729 Paperback Ln 60136 — 847-551-5000
Jeffrey King, prin. — Fax 551-5015

Gillespie, Macoupin, Pop. 3,278
Gillespie CUSD 7 — 1,300/PK-12
510 W Elm St 62033 — 217-839-2464
Paul Skeans, supt. — Fax 839-3353
www.gillespie.macoupin.k12.il.us/
Gillespie MS, 412 Oregon St 62033 — 300/6-8
Lori Emmons, prin. — 217-839-2116
Other Schools – See Benld

Gilman, Iroquois, Pop. 1,788
Iroquois West CUSD 10 — 900/PK-12
PO Box 67 60938 — 815-265-4642
Larry Eyre, supt. — Fax 265-7008
www.iwest.k12.il.us/
Iroquois West ES - Gilman — 200/1-3
PO Box 67 60938 — 815-265-7631
Don Keigher, prin. — Fax 265-7693
Other Schools – See Danforth, Onarga, Thawville

Girard, Macoupin, Pop. 2,237
Girard CUSD 3 — 700/PK-12
525 N 3rd St 62640 — 217-627-2915
Marlene Brady, supt. — Fax 627-3519
www.girardschools.org/
Girard ES — 300/PK-5
525 N 3rd St 62640 — 217-627-2419
Sarah Raynor, prin. — Fax 627-3519
Girard MS — 100/6-8
525 N 3rd St 62640 — 217-627-2136
Rob Horn, prin. — Fax 627-3519

Glasford, Peoria, Pop. 1,038
Illini Bluffs CUSD 327 — 1,000/PK-12
9611 S Hanna City Glsfrd Rd 61533 — 309-389-2231
Samuel Light, supt. — Fax 389-2251
www.illinibluffs.com
Illini Bluffs ES — 500/PK-5
9611 S Hanna City Glsfrd Rd 61533 — 309-389-5025
Karen Peterson, prin. — Fax 389-5027
Illini Bluffs MS — 200/6-8
212 N Saylor St 61533 — 309-389-3451
Joe Stoner, prin. — Fax 389-3454

Glen Carbon, Madison, Pop. 11,932
Edwardsville CUSD 7
Supt. — See Edwardsville

Cassens ES — 3-5
1014 Glen Crossing Rd 62034 — 618-655-6150
Martha Richey, prin.
Glen Carbon ES — 300/PK-2
141 Birger Ave 62034 — 618-692-7460
Curt Schumacher, prin. — Fax 288-1356

Glencoe, Cook, Pop. 8,979
Glencoe SD 35 — 1,400/K-8
620 Greenwood Ave 60022 — 847-835-7800
Cathlene Crawford, supt. — Fax 835-7805
www.glencoeschools.org/
Central S — 600/5-8
620 Greenwood Ave 60022 — 847-835-7600
Ryan Mollet, prin. — Fax 835-7605
South ES — 400/K-2
266 Linden Ave 60022 — 847-835-6400
Catherine Wang, prin. — Fax 835-6405
West ES — 300/3-4
1010 Forestway Dr 60022 — 847-835-6600
David Rongey, prin. — Fax 835-6605

Glendale Heights, DuPage, Pop. 32,465
Marquardt SD 15 — 2,600/PK-8
1860 Glen Ellyn Rd 60139 — 630-469-7615
Dr. Loren May, supt. — Fax 790-1650
www.d15.us/
Black Hawk ES — 500/PK-5
2101 Gladstone Dr 60139 — 630-893-5750
Cynthia Church, prin. — Fax 307-6525
Hall ES — 400/K-5
1447 Wayne Ave 60139 — 630-469-7720
Samia Hefferan, prin. — Fax 790-5040
Marquardt MS — 800/6-8
1912 Glen Ellyn Rd 60139 — 630-858-3850
Marie Cimaglia, prin. — Fax 790-5042
Reskin ES — 500/K-5
1555 Ardmore Ave 60139 — 630-469-0612
Jacob Engler, prin. — Fax 790-5041
Other Schools – See Bloomingdale

Queen Bee SD 16 — 2,100/PK-8
1560 Bloomingdale Rd 60139 — 630-260-6100
Victoria Tabbert, supt. — Fax 260-6103
www.queenbee16.org
Americana IS — 500/4-5
1629 President St 60139 — 630-260-6135
Kevin Wojtkiewicz, prin. — Fax 510-8570
Glen Hill/Pheasant Ridge ES — 1,000/PK-3
43 E Stevenson Dr 60139 — 630-260-6147
Diane Cantalupo, prin. — Fax 510-8566
Glenside MS — 700/6-8
1560 Bloomingdale Rd 60139 — 630-260-6112
Christopher Collins, prin. — Fax 510-8568

St. Matthew S — 400/PK-8
1555 Glen Ellyn Rd Ste 1 60139 — 630-858-3112
Neoma Mastruzzo, prin. — Fax 858-0623

Glen Ellyn, DuPage, Pop. 27,193
Glen Ellyn CCSD 89 — 2,200/PK-8
22W600 Butterfield Rd 60137 — 630-469-8900
Dr. John Perdue, supt. — Fax 469-8936
www.ccsd89.org
Arbor View ES — 300/PK-5
22W430 Ironwood Dr 60137 — 630-469-5505
David Bruno, prin. — Fax 790-6073
Glen Crest MS — 800/6-8
725 Sheehan Ave 60137 — 630-469-5220
Todd Schrage, prin. — Fax 469-5250
Park View ES — 400/K-5
250 S Park Blvd 60137 — 630-858-1600
Amy Warke, prin. — Fax 858-1634
Westfield ES — 300/K-5
2S125 Mayfield Ln 60137 — 630-858-2770
Peggy Marhoefer, prin. — Fax 858-3618
Other Schools – See Wheaton

Glen Ellyn SD 41 — 3,600/PK-8
793 N Main St 60137 — 630-790-6400
Ann Riebock Ed.D., supt. — Fax 790-1867
www.d41.org
Churchill ES — 600/K-5
240 Geneva Rd 60137 — 630-790-6485
Scott Klespitz, prin. — Fax 790-6498
Forest Glen ES — 500/K-5
561 Elm St 60137 — 630-790-6490
Mary Hornacek, prin. — Fax 790-6468
Franklin ES — 600/PK-5
350 Bryant Ave 60137 — 630-790-6480
Kirk Samples, prin. — Fax 790-6403
Hadley JHS — 1,200/6-8
240 Hawthorne St 60137 — 630-790-6450
Dr. Christopher Dransoff, prin. — Fax 790-6469
Lincoln ES — 700/PK-5
380 Greenfield Ave 60137 — 630-790-6475
Shannon Cross, prin. — Fax 790-6404

Montessori Academy of Glen Ellen — 100/PK-6
927 N Main St 60137 — 630-469-4727
Anne Carlson, hdmstr. — Fax 469-2761
St. James the Apostle S — 200/K-8
490 S Park Blvd 60137 — 630-469-8060
Constance Schwab, prin. — Fax 469-1107
St. Petronille S — 500/K-8
425 Prospect Ave Ste 100 60137 — 630-469-5041
Dr. Mary Kelly, prin. — Fax 469-5071

Glenview, Cook, Pop. 45,989
Avoca SD 37
Supt. — See Wilmette
Avoca West ES — 400/K-5
235 Beech Dr 60025 — 847-724-6800
Kevin Jauch, prin. — Fax 724-7323

East Maine SD 63
Supt. — See Des Plaines
Washington ES — 300/K-6
2710 Golf Rd 60025 — 847-965-4780
Terrance Baranowski, prin. — Fax 965-4807

Glenview CCSD 34 — 4,100/K-8
1401 Greenwood Rd 60026 — 847-998-5000
Dr. Gerald Hill, supt. — Fax 998-1629
www.glenview34.org
Attea MS — 700/6-8
2500 Chestnut Ave 60026 — 847-486-7700
James Woell, prin. — Fax 729-6251
Glen Grove ES — 400/3-5
3900 Glenview Rd 60025 — 847-998-5030
Helena Vena, prin. — Fax 998-5101
Henking ES — 500/K-2
2941 Linneman St 60025 — 847-998-5035
Ivy Sukenik, prin. — Fax 998-9938
Hoffman ES — 500/3-5
2000 Harrison St 60025 — 847-998-5040
Mark Walther, prin. — Fax 998-6840
Lyon ES — 400/K-2
1335 Waukegan Rd 60025 — 847-998-5045
Kevin Dorken, prin. — Fax 998-9701
Pleasant Ridge ES — 400/3-5
1730 Sunset Ridge Rd 60025 — 847-998-5050
Dr. Matthew Rich, prin. — Fax 998-5532
Springman MS — 700/6-8
2701 Central Rd 60025 — 847-998-5020
Dr. Heather Hopkins, prin. — Fax 998-4032
Westbrook ES — 500/K-2
1333 Greenwood Rd 60026 — 847-998-5055
Dr. Lori Hinton, prin. — Fax 998-1872

Northbrook/Glenview SD 30
Supt. — See Northbrook
Willowbrook ES — 300/K-5
2500 Happy Hollow Rd 60026 — 847-498-1090
Melissa Hirsch, prin. — Fax 272-0893

West Northfield SD 31
Supt. — See Northbrook
Winkelman ES — 600/K-5
1919 Landwehr Rd 60026 — 847-729-5650
Maria Kalant, prin. — Fax 729-5654

Glenview New Church S — 100/PK-10
74 Park Dr 60025 — 847-724-0057
Our Lady of Perpetual Help S — 1,000/PK-8
1123 Church St 60025 — 847-724-6990
Amy Mills, prin. — Fax 724-7025
St. Catherine Laboure S — 300/PK-8
3425 Thornwood Ave 60026 — 847-724-2240
Laurie Konicek, prin. — Fax 724-5805

Glenwood, Cook, Pop. 8,663
Brookwood SD 167 — 1,300/PK-8
201 E Glenwood Dyer Rd 60425 — 708-758-5190
Pamela Hollich, supt. — Fax 757-2104
www.brookwood167.org
Brookwood JHS — 300/7-8
201 E Glenwood Lansing Rd 60425 — 708-758-5252
Bethany Lindsay, prin. — Fax 758-3954
Brookwood MS — 300/5-6
200 E Glenwood Lansing Rd 60425 — 708-758-5350
Joan Stoiber, prin. — Fax 757-4528
Hickory Bend ES — 300/K-4
600 E 191st Pl 60425 — 708-758-4520
Shirley Bragg, prin. — Fax 758-0364
Longwood ES — 400/PK-4
441 N Longwood Dr 60425 — 708-757-2100
Reginald Patterson, prin. — Fax 756-2504

Godfrey, Madison, Pop. 16,996
Alton CUSD 11
Supt. — See Alton
Alton ECC — 300/PK-PK
6008 Godfrey Rd 62035 — 618-463-2166
Jill Hardimon, coord. — Fax 467-0504
Lewis & Clark ES — 300/K-5
6800 Humbert Rd 62035 — 618-463-2177
Patricia King, prin. — Fax 467-0604
North ES — 500/K-5
5600 Godfrey Rd 62035 — 618-463-2171
Brenda Vernatti, prin. — Fax 466-5680

Evangelical S — 400/PK-8
1212 W Homer M Adams Pkwy 62035 — 618-466-1599
Barbara Jutting, prin. — Fax 466-9498
Faith Lutheran S — 100/PK-8
6809 Godfrey Rd 62035 — 618-466-9153
Mike Roth, prin. — Fax 466-3839
Montessori Children's House — 100/PK-8
5800 Godfrey Rd 62035 — 618-467-2333
Roderick Connell, dir. — Fax 467-2332
St. Ambrose S — 200/PK-8
820 W Homer M Adams Pkwy 62035 — 618-466-4216
Cathy McGarrahan, prin. — Fax 466-4575

Golconda, Pope, Pop. 668
Pope County CUSD 1 — 600/PK-12
RR 2 Box 22 62938 — 618-683-2301
Joseph Vurko, supt. — Fax 683-5181
www.pcusd.com/
Pope County S — 400/PK-8
RR 2 Box 22 62938 — 618-683-4011
Ed Blankenship, prin. — Fax 683-6022

Golden, Adams, Pop. 622
Central CUSD 3
Supt. — See Camp Point
Central MS — 100/3-4
PO Box 219 62339 — 217-696-4652
Eric Stotts, prin. — Fax 696-4385

Goodfield, Woodford, Pop. 786
Eureka CUSD 140
Supt. — See Eureka
Goodfield ES — 100/K-4
308 W Robinson St 61742 — 309-965-2362
Randy Berardi, prin. — Fax 965-2270

Good Hope, McDonough, Pop. 388
West Prairie CUSD 103
Supt. — See Colchester
West Prairie North ES — 100/PK-4
100 N Washington St 61438 — 309-456-3920
Paula Markey, prin. — Fax 456-3936

Goreville, Johnson, Pop. 970
Goreville CUSD 1 — 600/PK-12
201 S Ferne Clyffe Rd 62939 — 618-995-9831
Dr. Steve Webb, supt. — Fax 995-9831
www.gorevilleschools.com/
Goreville S — 500/PK-8
201 S Ferne Clyffe Rd 62939 — 618-995-2142
Jeri Miller, prin. — Fax 995-1188

Grafton, Jersey, Pop. 692
Jersey CUSD 100
Supt. — See Jerseyville
Grafton ES — 200/PK-6
1200 Grafton Hills Dr 62037 — 618-786-3388
Rose DeCourcey, prin. — Fax 786-2180

Grand Ridge, LaSalle, Pop. 523
Grand Ridge CCSD 95 — 300/PK-8
PO Box 37 61325 — 815-249-6225
David Mathis, supt. — Fax 249-5049
Grand Ridge S — 300/PK-8
PO Box 37 61325 — 815-249-6225
Ted Sanders, prin. — Fax 249-5049

Grand Tower, Jackson, Pop. 589
Shawnee CUSD 84
Supt. — See Wolf Lake
Shawnee ES North — 100/K-5
504 2nd St 62942 — 618-565-2211
Leslie Varble, prin. — Fax 565-2231

Granite City, Madison, Pop. 30,796
Granite City CUSD 9 — 7,000/PK-12
1947 Adams St 62040 — 618-451-5800
Harry Briggs Ph.D., supt. — Fax 451-6135
www.granitecityschools.org
Coolidge MS — 800/6-8
3231 Nameoki Rd 62040 — 618-451-5826
Richard Talley, prin. — Fax 876-5154
Frohardt ES — 400/K-5
2040 Johnson Rd 62040 — 618-451-5821
Lori Silva, prin. — Fax 876-7627
Granite City ECC — PK-PK
3201 E 23rd St 62040 — 618-451-5836
Jill Conoyer, coord. — Fax 451-7905
Grigsby MS — 700/6-8
3801 Cargill Rd 62040 — 618-931-5544
Kristen Novacich, prin. — Fax 931-5689
Maryville ES — 500/K-5
4651 Maryville Rd 62040 — 618-931-2044
Linda Logan, prin. — Fax 931-6042
Mitchell ES — 500/K-5
316 E Chain of Rocks Rd 62040 — 618-931-0057
Dr. Debbie Wilkerson, prin. — Fax 931-0059
Niedringhaus ES — 400/K-5
2901 State St 62040 — 618-451-5813
Barbara Vrabec, prin. — Fax 451-5838
Prather ES — 400/K-5
2300 W 25th St 62040 — 618-451-5823
David Keel, prin. — Fax 876-3843
Wilson ES — 400/K-5
2400 Wilson Ave 62040 — 618-451-5817
John Schooley, prin. — Fax 451-6889
Worthen ES — 400/K-5
3200 Maryville Rd 62040 — 618-931-5700
Dr. Debra Kibort, prin. — Fax 797-1360

Holy Family S — 300/PK-8
1900 Saint Clair Ave 62040 — 618-877-5500
Marge Pennell, prin. — Fax 877-5502
Montessori S — 100/PK-6
4405 State Route 162 62040 — 618-931-2508
Mary Beth McGivern, admin. — Fax 931-5816
St. Elizabeth S — 200/PK-8
2300 Pontoon Rd 62040 — 618-877-3348
Karen Jakich, prin. — Fax 877-3352

Grant Park, Kankakee, Pop. 1,557
Grant Park CUSD 6 — 600/PK-12
PO Box 549 60940 — 815-465-6013
Dr. Michael Nicholson, supt. — Fax 465-2505
www.grantpark.k12.il.us/
Grant Park S — 400/PK-8
PO Box 549 60940 — 815-465-2183
Tracy Pearson, prin. — Fax 465-2381

Granville, Putnam, Pop. 1,388
Putnam County CUSD 535 — 900/K-12
402 E Silverspoon Ave 61326 — 815-339-2238
Jay McCracken, supt. — Fax 339-6739
www.pcschools535.org/
Other Schools – See Hennepin, Mc Nabb

Graymont, Livingston
Rooks Creek CCSD 425 — 50/K-8
PO Box 117 61743 — 815-743-5346
Bill James, supt. — Fax 743-5394
www.rookscreek.k12.il.us/
Graymont S — 50/K-8
PO Box 117 61743 — 815-743-5346
Bill James, prin. — Fax 743-5394

Grayslake, Lake, Pop. 21,099
CCSD 46 — 4,100/PK-8
565 Frederick Rd 60030 — 847-223-3650
Ellen Correll, supt. — Fax 223-3695
www.d46.k12.il.us
Frederick MS — 900/5-6
595 Frederick Rd 60030 — 847-543-5300
Eric Detweiler, prin. — Fax 548-7768
Grayslake MS — 900/7-8
440 Barron Blvd 60030 — 847-223-3680
Marcus Smith, prin. — Fax 223-3526
Meadowview ES — 500/K-4
291 Lexington Ln 60030 — 847-223-3656
Laura Morgan, prin. — Fax 223-3531
Woodview ES — 500/K-4
340 N Alleghany Rd 60030 — 847-223-3668
Jeff Knapp, prin. — Fax 223-3525
Other Schools – See Hainesville, Round Lake, Round Lake Beach

---

Old School Montessori — 200/PK-6
144 Commerce Dr 60030 — 847-223-9606
Marilyn Shattuck, admin. — Fax 223-1450
St. Gilbert S — 600/K-8
231 E Belvidere Rd 60030 — 847-223-8600
Gloria Petraitis, prin. — Fax 223-8626
Westlake Christian Academy — 200/PK-12
275 S Lake St 60030 — 847-548-6209
Jeff Wilcox, prin. — Fax 548-6481

Grayville, White, Pop. 1,638
Grayville CUSD 1 — 300/PK-12
728 W North St 62844 — 618-375-7214
David Scott, supt. — Fax 375-5202
www.grayville.white.k12.il.us/district.htm
Wells ES — 200/PK-5
704 W North St 62844 — 618-375-7214
Gary Barbre, prin. — Fax 375-5202

Great Lakes, Lake
North Chicago SD 187
Supt. — See North Chicago
Forrestal ES — 400/K-5
2833 E Washington Ave 60088 — 847-689-6310
Cassandra Brooks, prin. — Fax 689-3501

Greenfield, Greene, Pop. 1,142
Greenfield CUSD 10 — 600/PK-12
311 Mulberry St 62044 — 217-368-2447
Bill Bishop, supt. — Fax 368-2724
Greenfield S — 400/PK-8
115 Prairie St 62044 — 217-368-2551
Doreen Konneker, prin. — Fax 368-2232

Green Valley, Tazewell, Pop. 702
Midwest Central CUSD 191
Supt. — See Manito
Midwest Central MS — 300/6-8
121 N Church St 61534 — 309-352-2300
J. Douglas Cunningham, prin. — Fax 352-2903

Greenview, Menard, Pop. 823
Greenview CUSD 200 — 300/K-12
PO Box 320 62642 — 217-968-2295
Gary DePatis, supt. — Fax 968-2297
www.menard.k12.il.us/greenviewhs/welcome.htm
Greenview ES — 100/K-6
PO Box 320 62642 — 217-968-2295
Steve Plaeger, prin. — Fax 968-2297

Greenville, Bond, Pop. 7,067
Bond County CUSD 2 — 2,000/PK-12
1008 N Hena St 62246 — 618-664-0170
Jeff Stricker, supt. — Fax 664-5000
www.bccu2.k12.il.us
Greenville ES — 700/PK-5
800 N Dewey St 62246 — 618-664-3117
Scott Pasley, prin. — Fax 664-5014
Greenville JHS — 300/6-8
1200 Junior High Dr 62246 — 618-664-1226
Gary Brauns, prin. — Fax 664-5071
Other Schools – See Pocahontas, Sorento

Gridley, McLean, Pop. 1,398
El Paso-Gridley CUSD 11
Supt. — See El Paso
El Paso-Gridley JHS — 200/6-8
403 McLean St 61744 — 309-747-2156
Brian Kurz, prin. — Fax 747-2938
Gridley S — 100/K-3
309 McLean St 61744 — 309-747-2360
Brian Kurz, prin. — Fax 747-3121

Griggsville, Pike, Pop. 1,215
Griggsville-Perry CUSD 4 — 400/PK-12
PO Box 439 62340 — 217-833-2352
Michael Davies, supt. — Fax 833-2354
griggsvilleperry.com
Griggsville-Perry ES — 200/PK-4
PO Box 439 62340 — 217-833-2352
Andrea Allen, prin. — Fax 833-2354
Other Schools – See Perry

Gurnee, Lake, Pop. 30,772
Gurnee SD 56 — 2,200/PK-8
900 Kilbourne Rd 60031 — 847-336-0800
Dr. John Hutton, supt. — Fax 336-1110
www.d56.lake.k12.il.us/
Gurnee Grade S — 400/K-8
940 Kilbourne Rd 60031 — 847-249-6253
Jennifer Glickley, prin. — Fax 249-4662
O'Plaine ES — 500/3-5
333 N Oplaine Rd 60031 — 847-623-4333
Dennis Harnack, prin. — Fax 623-4456
Spaulding ES — 600/PK-2
2000 Belle Plaine Ave 60031 — 847-662-3701
Dr. Diane Donaldson, prin. — Fax 249-6262
Viking MS — 700/6-8
4460 Old Grand Ave 60031 — 847-336-2108
Patrick Jones, prin. — Fax 249-0719

Woodland CCSD 50 — 7,000/PK-8
1105 N Hunt Club Rd 60031 — 847-856-5600
Joy Swoboda, supt. — Fax 856-0311
www.dist50.net
Woodland IS — 1,500/4-5
1115 N Hunt Club Rd 60031 — 847-596-5900
Kent Ashton, prin. — Fax 855-9828
Woodland MS — 2,400/6-8
7000 Washington St 60031 — 847-856-3400
Scott Snyder, prin. — Fax 856-1306
Other Schools – See Gages Lake

Country Meadows Montessori S — 200/PK-6
6151 Washington St 60031 — 847-244-9352
Mary O'Young, prin. — Fax 244-1068
Gurnee Christian S — 50/PK-8
2190 Fuller Rd 60031 — 847-623-7773
Fax 623-7773

Hainesville, Lake, Pop. 3,765
CCSD 46
Supt. — See Grayslake
Prairieview ES 800/PK-4
103 E Belvidere Rd 60030 847-543-6200
Amanda Schoenberg, prin. Fax 543-4125

Hamel, Madison, Pop. 758
Edwardsville CUSD 7
Supt. — See Edwardsville
Hamel ES 100/K-2
PO Box 157 62046 618-692-7444
Barb Hutton, prin. Fax 633-1702

Hamilton, Hancock, Pop. 2,838
Hamilton CCSD 328 700/PK-12
270 N 10th St 62341 217-847-3315
James Jackson, supt. Fax 847-3915
Hamilton ES 300/PK-6
1830 Broadway St 62341 217-847-3811
David Snowden, prin. Fax 847-2337
Hamilton JHS 100/7-8
270 N 10th St 62341 217-847-3314
Ron Gilbert, prin. Fax 847-3915

Hampshire, Kane, Pop. 4,077
CUSD 300
Supt. — See Carpentersville
Hampshire ES 600/K-5
321 Terwilliger Ave 60140 847-683-2171
Jim Aalfs, prin. Fax 683-4806
Hampshire MS 500/6-8
560 S State St 60140 847-683-2522
Jim Wallis, prin. Fax 683-1030
Wright ES PK-5
1500 Ketchum Rd 60140 847-683-5700
Don Wicker, prin. Fax 683-5715

St. Charles Borromeo S 100/PK-8
288 E Jefferson Ave 60140 847-683-3450
Kel Kissamis, prin. Fax 683-3209

Hampton, Rock Island, Pop. 1,746
Hampton SD 29 200/K-8
206 5th St 61256 309-755-0693
Tom Berg, supt. Fax 755-0694
209.7.176.19/hampton/
Hampton S 200/K-8
206 5th St 61256 309-755-0693
Tom Berg, prin. Fax 755-0694

Hanover, Jo Daviess, Pop. 797
River Ridge CUSD 210 500/K-12
4141 IL Route 84 S 61041 815-858-9005
Bradley Albrecht, supt. Fax 858-9006
www.riverridge210.org
River Ridge ES 200/K-5
4141 IL Route 84 S 61041 815-858-9005
Peter Scarano, prin. Fax 858-9006
River Ridge MS 100/6-8
4141 IL Route 84 S 61041 815-858-9005
Michael Foltz, prin. Fax 858-9006

Hanover Park, Cook, Pop. 37,229
CCSD 93
Supt. — See Bloomingdale
Johnson ES 400/K-5
1380 Nautilus Ln 60133 630-830-8770
David Aleman, prin. Fax 830-0442

Keeneyville SD 20 1,700/PK-8
5540 Arlington Dr E 60133 630-894-2250
Dr. Carol Auer, supt. Fax 894-5187
www.esd20.org
Greenbrook ES 500/K-5
5208 Arlington Cir 60133 630-894-4544
Tod Tecktiel, prin. Fax 289-1063
Spring Wood MS 600/6-8
5540 Arlington Dr E 60133 630-893-8900
Craig Barringer, prin. Fax 894-9658
Other Schools – See Roselle

SD U-46
Supt. — See Elgin
Horizon ES 600/K-6
1701 Greenbrook Blvd 60133 630-213-5570
Dr. Deborah Gehrig, prin. Fax 213-5564
Laurel Hill ES 400/K-6
1750 Laurel Ave 60133 630-213-5580
Patricia Stubbs, prin. Fax 213-5569
Ontarioville ES 500/K-6
2100 Elm Ave 60133 630-213-5590
Dr. Carmen Rodriguez, prin. Fax 213-5574
Parkwood ES 500/K-6
2150 Laurel Ave 60133 630-213-5595
Patricia Martinez, prin. Fax 213-5579

Schaumburg CCSD 54
Supt. — See Schaumburg
Einstein ES 500/PK-6
1100 Laurie Ln 60133 630-736-2500
Robert Kaplan, prin. Fax 736-2501
Fox ES 400/K-6
1035 Parkview Dr 60133 630-736-3500
Cyndie Gordon, prin. Fax 736-3501
Hanover Highlands ES 500/PK-6
1451 Cypress Ave 60133 630-736-4230
David Negron, prin. Fax 736-4231

Hardin, Calhoun, Pop. 952
Calhoun CUSD 40 600/PK-12
PO Box 387 62047 618-576-2722
Carole Crum, supt. Fax 576-2641
www.calhoun.k12.il.us/
Calhoun S 400/PK-8
52 Poor Farm Hollow Rd 62047 618-576-2341
Kathy Schell, prin. Fax 576-2787

St. Norbert S 100/1-8
PO Box 525 62047 618-576-2514
Racheal Friedel, prin. Fax 576-8074

Harrisburg, Saline, Pop. 9,628
Harrisburg CUSD 3 2,100/PK-12
PO Box 725 62946 618-253-7637
Dennis Smith, supt. Fax 252-7584
www.hbg.saline.k12.il.us
East Side IS 500/3-5
315 E Church St 62946 618-253-7637
Cindy Mitchell, prin. Fax 252-8674
Harrisburg MS 500/6-8
312 Bulldog Blvd 62946 618-253-7107
Jim Butler, prin. Fax 253-4114
West Side PS 600/PK-2
411 W Lincoln St 62946 618-253-7637
Scott Dewar, prin. Fax 252-8657

Harristown, Macon, Pop. 1,259
Sangamon Valley CUSD 9
Supt. — See Niantic
Harristown ES 200/PK-4
PO Box 79 62537 217-963-2621
Glenda Weldy, prin. Fax 963-2440

Hartford, Madison, Pop. 1,492
Wood River-Hartford ESD 15
Supt. — See Wood River
Hartford ES 200/PK-5
110 W 2nd St 62048 618-254-9814
Ron Simpson, prin. Fax 254-7602

Hartsburg, Montgomery, Pop. 343
Hartsburg-Emden CUSD 21 200/PK-12
400 W Front St 62643 217-642-5244
Donald Helm, supt. Fax 642-5333
www.logan.k12.il.us/hartem/
Other Schools – See Emden

Harvard, McHenry, Pop. 9,104
Harvard CUSD 50 2,400/PK-12
1101 N Jefferson St 60033 815-943-4022
Dr. Lauri Tobias, supt. Fax 943-4282
www.cusd50.org
Central ES 200/2-2
401 N Division St 60033 815-943-6125
Debbie Holland, prin. Fax 943-0115
Harvard JHS 700/5-8
1301 Garfield St 60033 815-943-6466
Margaret Segersten, prin. Fax 943-8521
Jefferson ES 500/1-4
1200 N Jefferson St 60033 815-943-6464
Judy Floeter, prin. Fax 943-7495
Washington S 300/PK-K
305 S Hutchinson St 60033 815-943-6367
Patricia Jones, prin. Fax 943-0293

St. Joseph S 100/PK-8
201 N Division St 60033 815-943-6933
Michael Shukis, prin. Fax 943-0549

Harvey, Cook, Pop. 28,771
Harvey SD 152 2,700/PK-8
16001 Lincoln Ave 60426 708-333-0300
Dr. Lela Bridges, supt. Fax 333-0349
www.harvey152.org/
Angelou ES 200/K-6
15748 Page Ave 60426 708-333-0740
Samantha McNulty, prin. Fax 333-9216
Brooks MS 600/7-8
14741 Wallace St 60426 708-333-6390
Maryann West, prin. Fax 333-3177
Bryant ES 400/K-6
14730 Main St 60426 708-331-1390
Anna Kreske, prin. Fax 225-9510
Holmes ES 400/K-6
16000 Carse Ave 60426 708-333-0440
Phillip Skubal, prin. Fax 225-9511
Lowell-Longfellow ES 300/K-6
15636 Lexington Ave 60426 708-333-0478
Marlon Conway, prin. Fax 333-9214
Riley Pre-Kindergarten Center 200/PK-PK
16001 Lincoln Ave 60426 708-210-3960
Ankhe Bradley, prin. Fax 210-2218
Sandburg ES 200/K-6
14500 Myrtle Ave 60426 708-333-1351
Lorna Dill, prin. Fax 333-9188
Whittier ES 300/K-6
71 E 152nd St 60426 708-331-1130
Roxie Thomas, prin. Fax 333-9162

South Holland SD 151
Supt. — See South Holland
Taft Primary Center 300/PK-1
393 E 163rd St 60426 708-339-2710
Anthony Palomo, prin. Fax 210-3254

West Harvey-Dixmoor SD 147 1,600/PK-8
191 W 155th Pl 60426 708-339-9500
Dr. Alex Boyd, supt. Fax 339-9533
www.whd147.org
Washington ES 400/PK-5
15248 Lincoln Ave 60426 708-333-0237
Dr. Earnest Taylor, prin. Fax 333-2604
Other Schools – See Dixmoor

Harwood Heights, Cook, Pop. 8,188
Union Ridge SD 86 600/PK-8
4600 N Oak Park Ave 60706 708-867-5822
Dr. Raymond Kuper, supt. Fax 867-5826
www.urs86.k12.il.us
Union Ridge S 600/PK-8
4600 N Oak Park Ave 60706 708-867-5822
Michael Maguire, prin. Fax 867-5826

Havana, Mason, Pop. 3,476
Havana CUSD 126 1,200/PK-12
501 S McKinley St 62644 309-543-3384
Patrick Twomey, supt. Fax 543-3385
mason.k12.il.us/havana126
Havana JHS 300/5-8
801 E Laurel Ave 62644 309-543-6677
Jerry Wilson, prin. Fax 543-6678
New Central ES 500/PK-4
215 N Pearl St 62644 309-543-2241
John Dunker, prin. Fax 543-6259

Hawthorn Woods, Lake, Pop. 7,176
Lake Zurich CUSD 95
Supt. — See Lake Zurich
Lake Zurich MS North Campus 800/6-8
95 Hubbard Ln 60047 847-719-3600
Mark Richter, prin. Fax 719-3620
Loomis ES 400/PK-5
1 Hubbard Ln 60047 847-719-3300
Grant Seaholm, prin. Fax 719-3320

St. Matthew Lutheran S 100/PK-8
24480 N Old McHenry Rd 60047 847-438-6103
Doug Duval, admin. Fax 438-0376

Hazel Crest, Cook, Pop. 14,415
Hazel Crest SD 152-5 900/PK-8
1910 170th St 60429 708-335-0790
Dr. Sheila Harrison-Williams, supt. Fax 335-3520
www.sd1525.org/
Palm ES 5-6
1910 170th St 60429 708-335-0224
Andrew Maisonneuve, prin. Fax 335-7150
Woodland ES 300/PK-4
16900 Western Ave 60429 708-335-1995
Rose Lee, prin. Fax 335-1814
Other Schools – See East Hazel Crest, Markham

Prairie-Hills ESD 144
Supt. — See Markham
Chateaux ES 400/PK-6
3600 Chambord Ln 60429 708-335-9776
Michael Chapman, prin. Fax 335-4808
Highlands ES 400/K-6
3420 Laurel Ln 60429 708-335-9773
Michael Moore, prin. Fax 335-1929
Jemison S 500/K-6
3450 W 177th St 60429 708-225-3636
Janice Barry, prin. Fax 799-8363

Hebron, McHenry, Pop. 1,141
Alden Hebron SD 19 500/PK-12
9604 Illinois St 60034 815-648-2886
Dr. Debbie Ehlenburg, supt. Fax 648-2339
www.alden-hebron.org
Alden-Hebron ES 200/PK-5
11915 Price Rd 60034 815-648-2971
Ryan LaDage, prin. Fax 648-2339
Alden-Hebron MS 100/6-8
9604 Illinois St 60034 815-648-2442
Dr. Bridget Belcastro, prin. Fax 648-2339

Hennepin, Putnam, Pop. 704
Putnam County CUSD 535
Supt. — See Granville
Putnam County ES - Hennepin Building 300/K-4
PO Box 229 61327 815-925-7032
Michael McCann, prin. Fax 925-7435

Henry, Marshall, Pop. 2,530
Henry-Senachwine CUSD 5 600/K-12
1023 College St 61537 309-364-3614
Thomas Urban, supt. Fax 364-2990
www.henrysenachwine.org
Henry-Senachwine S 400/K-8
201 Richard St 61537 309-364-2531
Julie Nelson, prin. Fax 364-2000

Herrick, Shelby, Pop. 521
Cowden-Herrick Community USD 3A
Supt. — See Cowden
Herrick S 200/K-8
301 N Broadway St 62431 618-428-5223
Tina Oldham, prin. Fax 428-5222

Herrin, Williamson, Pop. 11,688
Herrin CUSD 4 2,300/PK-12
500 N 10th St 62948 618-988-8024
Dr. Mark Collins, supt. Fax 942-6998
www.herrinunit.org
Herrin ES 700/2-5
5200 Herrin Rd 62948 618-942-2744
Michael Horn, prin. Fax 942-5817
Herrin MS 500/6-8
700 S 14th St 62948 618-942-7461
Steve Robinson, prin. Fax 988-8821
North Side Primary Center 400/PK-1
601 N 17th St 62948 618-942-5418
Gary Hernbeck, prin. Fax 942-3579

Our Lady of Mt. Carmel S 300/K-8
300 W Monroe St 62948 618-942-4484
Cheryl Dreyer, prin. Fax 942-2864

Herscher, Kankakee, Pop. 1,554
Herscher CUSD 2 2,100/PK-12
PO Box 504 60941 815-426-2162
William Davison, supt. Fax 426-2872
www.hsd2.k12.il.us
Herscher S 400/K-8
PO Box 504 60941 815-426-2242
Michelle Chavers, prin. Fax 426-6862
Other Schools – See Bonfield, Kankakee, Reddick

Heyworth, McLean, Pop. 2,470
Heyworth CUSD 4 900/PK-12
522 E Main St 61745 309-473-3727
Randall Merker, supt. Fax 473-2220
www.husd4.k12.il.us/
Heyworth ES 500/PK-6
100 S Joselyn St 61745 309-473-2822
Brian Bradshaw, prin. Fax 473-9013

Hickory Hills, Cook, Pop. 13,542
North Palos SD 117
Supt. — See Palos Hills
Conrady JHS 900/6-8
7950 W 97th St 60457 708-233-4500
Paula Coughlin, prin. Fax 430-8964
Dorn PS 500/K-1
7840 W 92nd St 60457 708-233-5600
Eileen McCaffrey, prin. Fax 430-6649

Glen Oaks ES 600/2-5
9045 S 88th Ave 60457 708-233-6800
Gaylyn Grimm, prin. Fax 430-6636

St. Patricia S 300/K-8
9000 S 86th Ave 60457 708-598-8200
Dr. Robert Smith, prin. Fax 598-8233

Highland, Madison, Pop. 9,200
Highland CUSD 5 3,200/PK-12
400 Broadway 62249 618-654-2106
Michael Sutton, supt. Fax 654-5424
www.highlandcusd5.org
Grantfork Upper ES 100/5-6
400 Broadway 62249 618-675-2200
Donna Suhre, prin. Fax 675-2204
Highland ES 700/3-6
400 Broadway 62249 618-654-2108
Lori Miscik, prin. Fax 654-1551
Highland MS 500/7-8
400 Broadway 62249 618-651-8800
Jeanie Probst, prin. Fax 654-1551
Highland PS 600/PK-2
400 Broadway 62249 618-654-2107
Julie Korte, prin. Fax 654-1591
Other Schools – See Alhambra, New Douglas

St. Paul S 300/PK-8
1416 Main St 62249 618-654-7525
David Timmermann, prin. Fax 654-8795

Highland Park, Lake, Pop. 31,380
North Shore SD 112 4,400/PK-8
1936 Green Bay Rd 60035 847-681-6700
Dr. David Behlow, supt. Fax 266-2379
www.nssd112.org
Braeside ES 300/K-5
150 Pierce Rd 60035 847-433-0155
Pat Kritzman, prin. Fax 433-9064
Edgewood MS 600/6-8
929 Edgewood Rd 60035 847-432-3858
Dr. Jeffrey Zoul, prin. Fax 432-7326
Elm Place MS 500/6-8
2031 Sheridan Rd 60035 847-432-9217
Eric Olson, prin. Fax 432-9213
Green Bay S PK-PK
1936 Green Bay Rd 60035 847-681-6700
Nita Goodman, prin. Fax 681-6712
Indian Trail ES 400/K-5
2075 Saint Johns Ave 60035 847-432-9257
Matt Eriksen, prin. Fax 432-2821
Lincoln ES 300/K-5
711 Lincoln Ave W 60035 847-432-1720
Bill Fredricksen, prin. Fax 432-9209
Northwood JHS 400/6-8
945 North Ave 60035 847-432-4770
Jennifer Ferrari, prin. Fax 432-4886
Ravinia ES 300/K-5
763 Dean Ave 60035 847-432-4260
Jean Banas, prin. Fax 432-4186
Red Oak ES 400/PK-5
530 Red Oak Ln 60035 847-831-4570
Susan Cahail, prin. Fax 831-4572
Sherwood ES 400/PK-5
1900 Stratford Rd 60035 847-831-9152
Shawn Walker, prin. Fax 831-1719
Thomas ES 300/K-5
2939 Summit Ave 60035 847-433-0090
Maureen Deely, prin. Fax 433-7875
Other Schools – See Highwood

Highwood, Lake, Pop. 5,468
North Shore SD 112
Supt. — See Highland Park
Oak Terrace ES 500/PK-5
240 Prairie Ave 60040 847-433-0930
Sandra Anderson, prin. Fax 433-2710

St. James S 200/PK-8
140 North Ave 60040 847-432-2277
Mary Kay Tschanz, prin. Fax 432-1321

Hillsboro, Montgomery, Pop. 4,272
Hillsboro CUSD 3 2,000/PK-12
1311 Vandalia Rd 62049 217-532-2942
Donald Burton, supt. Fax 532-3137
www.hillsboroschools.net
Beckemeyer ES 600/K-5
1035 Seymour Ave 62049 217-532-6994
Pam Delong, prin. Fax 532-5153
Hillsboro JHS 500/6-8
909 Rountree St 62049 217-532-3742
David Powell, prin. Fax 532-6211
Other Schools – See Coffeen, Witt

Hillside, Cook, Pop. 7,771
Hillside SD 93 500/K-8
4804 Harrison St 60162 708-449-7280
Alan Molby, supt. Fax 449-5056
Hillside S 500/K-8
4804 Harrison St 60162 708-449-6491
Steve Bogren, prin. Fax 449-1644

Immanuel Lutheran S 100/PK-8
2329 S Wolf Rd 60162 708-562-5580
Fax 562-6085
St. Domitilla S 100/PK-8
605 N Hillside Ave 60162 708-449-7420
Maryclaire Sypin, prin. Fax 449-9420

Hinckley, DeKalb, Pop. 2,050
Hinckley-Big Rock CUSD 429 600/K-12
700 E Lincoln Ave 60520 815-286-7575
Jim Hammack, supt. Fax 286-7577
www.hbr429.org
Hinckley-Big Rock ES 200/K-5
600 W Lincoln Hwy 60520 815-286-3400
Dennis Owen, prin. Fax 286-3401
Other Schools – See Big Rock

Hinsdale, DuPage, Pop. 17,898
CCSD 181
Supt. — See Westmont
Hinsdale MS 600/6-8
100 S Garfield Ave 60521 630-887-1370
Ruben Pena, prin. Fax 655-9754
Lane ES 400/K-5
500 N Elm St 60521 630-887-1430
Doug Eccarius, prin. Fax 655-9735
Madison ES 400/K-5
611 S Madison St 60521 630-887-1390
Melinda McMahon, prin. Fax 655-9742
Monroe ES 400/K-5
210 N Madison St 60521 630-887-1320
Heidi Fitch, prin. Fax 655-9716
Oak ES 300/K-5
950 S Oak St 60521 630-887-1330
Sean Walsh, prin. Fax 887-0240

Hinsdale Adventist Academy 200/PK-12
631 E Hickory St 60521 630-323-9211
Randal Reece, prin. Fax 323-9237
St. Isaac Jogues S 600/K-8
421 S Clay St 60521 630-323-3244
Richard Cronquist, prin. Fax 655-6676
Zion Lutheran ECC 100/PK-K
204 S Grant St 60521 630-323-0065
Peggy Farrell, dir. Fax 323-0694

Hodgkins, Cook, Pop. 2,073
La Grange SD 105
Supt. — See La Grange
Hodgkins ES 200/K-6
6516 Kane Ave 60525 708-482-2740
John Signatur Ed.D., prin. Fax 482-2728

Hoffman, Clinton, Pop. 450

Trinity Lutheran S 100/PK-8
8701 Huey Rd 62250 618-495-2246
Mark Belli, prin. Fax 495-2692

Hoffman Estates, Cook, Pop. 52,046
Palatine CCSD 15
Supt. — See Palatine
Jefferson ES 600/K-6
3805 Winston Dr 60192 847-963-5400
Arturo Abrego, prin. Fax 963-5406
Whiteley ES 700/K-6
4335 Haman Ct 60192 847-963-7200
Mary Szuch, prin. Fax 963-7206

SD U-46
Supt. — See Elgin
Lincoln ES 600/K-6
1650 Maureen Dr 60192 847-289-6639
Dr. Mariann Alyea, prin. Fax 888-7195
Timber Trails ES 500/K-6
1675 McDonough Rd 60192 847-289-6640
Tom Flanigan, prin. Fax 888-7011

Schaumburg CCSD 54
Supt. — See Schaumburg
Armstrong ES 500/K-6
1320 Kingsdale Rd, 847-357-6700
Dr. Pat Piech, prin. Fax 357-6701
Churchill ES 400/K-6
1520 Jones Rd 60195 847-357-6300
Lisa Hopkins, prin. Fax 357-6301
Eisenhower JHS 600/7-8
800 Hassell Rd, 847-357-5500
Pamela Samson, prin. Fax 357-5501
Fairview ES 500/K-6
375 Arizona Blvd, 847-357-5700
Beth Erbach, prin. Fax 357-5701
Lakeview ES 600/K-6
615 Lakeview Ln, 847-357-6600
Melissa Ribordy, prin. Fax 357-6601
Lincoln Prairie S 400/PK-8
500 Hillcrest Blvd, 847-357-5955
Amanda Stochl, prin. Fax 357-5956
MacArthur ES 500/K-6
1800 Chippendale Rd, 847-357-6650
Danette Meyer, prin. Fax 357-6651
Muir ES 600/PK-6
1973 Kensington Ln, 847-357-6444
Brad Carter, prin. Fax 357-6445

Montessori Learning Center 50/PK-K
1015 W Golf Rd, 847-882-7727
Rochelle Gutstadt, prin. Fax 882-7727
Montessori S of North Hoffman 200/PK-9
1200 Freeman Rd 60192 847-705-1234
Dr. Molood Naghibzadeh, prin. Fax 705-0506
St. Hubert S 600/PK-8
255 Flagstaff Ln, 847-885-7702
Vito DeFrisco, prin. Fax 885-0604

Homer, Champaign, Pop. 1,157
Heritage CUSD 8
Supt. — See Broadlands
Heritage ES - Homer 300/PK-5
512 W 1st St 61849 217-896-2421
Chris Kerns, prin. Fax 896-2338
Heritage JHS 100/6-8
512 W 1st St 61849 217-896-2421
Chris Kerns, prin. Fax 896-2338

Homer Glen, Will
Homer CCSD 33C 3,500/K-8
15733 S Bell Rd, 708-226-7600
J. Michel Morrow, supt. Fax 226-7616
www.homerschools.org
Goodings Grove ES 500/K-4
12914 W 143rd St, 708-226-7650
Robert Rounsaville, prin. Fax 226-7665
Hadley ES 800/5-6
15731 S Bell Rd, 708-226-7725
Kathy Motykowski, prin. Fax 226-7691
Homer JHS 800/7-8
15711 S Bell Rd, 708-226-7800
Troy Mitchell, prin. Fax 226-7859

Schilling ES North 700/K-4
16025 S Cedar Rd, 708-226-7900
Ann Christie, prin. Fax 226-7929
Other Schools – See Lockport

Hometown, Cook, Pop. 4,241
Oak Lawn-Hometown SD 123
Supt. — See Oak Lawn
Hometown ES 400/K-5
8870 S Duffy Ave 60456 708-423-7360
Sherry Alimi, prin. Fax 499-7679

Homewood, Cook, Pop. 18,917
Homewood SD 153 2,100/PK-8
18205 Aberdeen St 60430 708-799-5661
Dr. Dale Mitchell, supt. Fax 799-1377
www.homewoodsd153.org/
Churchill S 400/3-4
1300 190th St 60430 708-798-3424
Cecelia Coffey, prin. Fax 798-0417
Hart JHS 500/7-8
18220 Morgan St 60430 708-799-5544
Michael Klein, prin. Fax 799-8360
Millennium S 500/5-6
18211 Aberdeen St 60430 708-799-8697
Shirley Watkins, prin. Fax 799-8693
Willow S 600/PK-2
1804 Willow Rd 60430 708-798-3720
Mary Ann Savage, prin. Fax 798-0016

Homewood Community Academy 200/PK-8
18620 Kedzie Ave 60430 708-799-6912
Kristeen Merichko, admin. Fax 957-1864
St. Joseph S 200/PK-8
17949 Dixie Hwy 60430 708-798-0467
Sr. Donna Lamoureux, prin. Fax 957-5659
Salem Lutheran ECC 100/PK-K
18328 Ashland Ave 60430 708-206-0350
Marge Grab, prin. Fax 798-1590

Hoopeston, Vermilion, Pop. 5,753
Hoopeston Area CUSD 11 1,400/PK-12
615 E Orange St 60942 217-283-6668
Hank Hornbeck, supt. Fax 283-5431
www.hoopeston.k12.il.us
Greer ES 200/5-6
609 W Main St 60942 217-283-6667
Dan Walder, prin. Fax 283-7038
Honeywell ES 200/3-4
600 E Honeywell Ave 60942 217-283-6666
Linda Sheppard, prin. Fax 283-7689
Hoopeston Area MS 200/7-8
615 E Orange St 60942 217-283-6664
Anne Burton, prin. Fax 283-7943
Maple ES 300/PK-2
500 S 4th St 60942 217-283-6665
Lori Eells, prin. Fax 283-5438

Hopkins Park, Kankakee, Pop. 791
Pembroke CCSD 259 300/K-8
4120 S Wheeler Rd 60944 815-944-5448
Dr. Barbara Jean Howery, supt. Fax 944-6750
www.pembroke.k12.il.us
Smith S 300/K-8
4120 S Wheeler Rd 60944 815-944-5219
Pamela Powell, prin. Fax 944-9214

Hoyleton, Washington, Pop. 500
Hoyleton CCSD 29 100/PK-8
520 N Main St 62803 618-493-7787
Jeff Humes, supt. Fax 493-7314
www.county.washington.k12.il.us/hoyleton/index.htm
Hoyleton Consolidated S 100/PK-8
520 N Main St 62803 618-493-7787
Jeff Humes, prin. Fax 493-7314

Trinity Lutheran S 50/PK-8
155 N Main St 62803 618-493-7754
Terry Fark, prin. Fax 493-7754

Hudson, McLean, Pop. 1,664
McLean County Unit SD 5
Supt. — See Normal
Hudson ES 200/K-5
205 S Mclean St 61748 309-726-1741
Scott Myers, prin. Fax 726-1503

Hull, Pike, Pop. 454
Western CUSD 12
Supt. — See Barry
Western Hull ES 100/PK-4
PO Box 78 62343 217-432-5714
Heath Kendrick, prin. Fax 432-8326

Hume, Edgar, Pop. 373
Shiloh CUSD 1 500/PK-12
21751N N 575th St 61932 217-887-2364
Gary Lewis, supt. Fax 887-2448
www.shiloh.k12.il.us
Shiloh ES 100/3-6
21751N N 575th St 61932 217-887-2364
Mark Hettmansberger, prin. Fax 887-2209
Other Schools – See Newman

Huntley, McHenry, Pop. 17,674
Consolidated SD 158
Supt. — See Algonquin
Leggee ES 800/K-5
13723 Harmony Rd 60142 847-659-6200
Scott Iddings, prin. Fax 659-6220

TLC Preschool 50/PK-PK
PO Box 186 60142 847-669-5781
Fax 669-5978

Hutsonville, Crawford, Pop. 606
Hutsonville CUSD 1 400/PK-12
PO Box 218 62433 618-563-4912
Roger Eddy, supt. Fax 563-9122
Hutsonville S 300/PK-8
PO Box 218 62433 618-563-4812
Guy Rumler, prin. Fax 563-9122

Illinois City, Rock Island
Rockridge CUSD 300
Supt. — See Taylor Ridge
Illinois City ES 200/K-6
24017 122nd Ave W 61259 309-791-0518
Christel Fowler, prin. Fax 791-0710

Illiopolis, Sangamon, Pop. 867
Sangamon Valley CUSD 9
Supt. — See Niantic
Illiopolis ES 200/PK-5
341 Matilda St 62539 217-486-7521
Debby Hawkins, prin. Fax 486-5601
Sangamon Valley MS 200/6-8
341 Matilda St 62539 217-486-2241
Jill Reedy, prin. Fax 486-6038

Ina, Jefferson, Pop. 2,430
Ina CCSD 8 100/K-8
PO Box 129 62846 618-437-5361
Charles Thierry, supt. Fax 437-5333
Ina Community Consolidated S 100/K-8
PO Box 129 62846 618-437-5361
Sandra Gilliam, prin. Fax 437-5333

Industry, McDonough, Pop. 503
Schuyler-Industry CUSD 5
Supt. — See Rushville
Industry ES 200/PK-5
306 E South St 61440 217-322-4311
Kellee Sullivan, prin. Fax 254-3487

Ingleside, See Fox Lake
Big Hollow SD 38 1,400/K-8
33315 N Fish Lake Rd 60041 847-740-1490
Ron Pazanin, supt. Fax 587-2663
www.bighollow.us
Big Hollow ES 400/3-5
33315 N Fish Lake Rd 60041 847-740-1490
Ronald Pazanin, prin.
Big Hollow MS 400/6-8
26051 W Nippersink Rd 60041 847-740-1490
Margaret Webb, prin. Fax 740-9021
Big Hollow PS 500/K-2
33335 N Fish Lake Rd 60041 847-740-5320
Christine Arndt, prin.

Gavin SD 37 1,000/PK-8
25775 W IL Route 134 60041 847-546-2916
Dr. John Ahlemeyer, supt. Fax 546-9584
www.gavin37.org
Gavin Central ES 500/1-5
36414 N Ridge Rd 60041 847-973-3280
Dr. Jo Amburgey, prin. Fax 973-3285
Gavin South JHS 500/PK-K, 6-8
25775 W IL Route 134 60041 847-546-9336
Ron Banion, prin. Fax 546-9338

St. Bede S 300/PK-8
36399 N Wilson Rd 60041 847-587-5541
Michael Fosnot, prin. Fax 587-2713

Inverness, Cook, Pop. 7,343

Holy Family Catholic Academy 200/PK-8
2515 W Palatine Rd 60067 847-907-3452
Dr. Gretchen Ludwig, prin. Fax 359-0639

Irvington, Washington, Pop. 699
Irvington CCSD 11 100/K-8
PO Box 130 62848 618-249-6761
Dr. Ray Puckett, supt.
Irvington S, PO Box 130 62848 100/K-8
Dr. Ray Puckett, prin. 618-249-6761

Island Lake, McHenry, Pop. 8,419
Wauconda CUSD 118
Supt. — See Wauconda
Cotton Creek ES 600/PK-5
545 Newport Ct 60042 847-526-4700
Darlene Baker, prin. Fax 526-4725
Matthews MS 6-8
PO Box 920 60042 847-526-6210
Dr. David Wilm, prin. Fax 526-8918

Itasca, DuPage, Pop. 8,444
Itasca SD 10 900/PK-8
200 N Maple St 60143 630-773-1232
Dr. Marcia Tornatore, supt. Fax 773-1342
www.itasca.k12.il.us
Benson PS 300/PK-2
301 E Washington St 60143 630-773-0554
Dawn Turner, prin. Fax 285-7474
Franzen IS 300/3-5
730 Catalpa Ave 60143 630-773-0100
Joanna Medwick, prin. Fax 285-7468
Peacock MS 300/6-8
301 E North St 60143 630-773-0335
Reinhard Nickisch, prin. Fax 285-7460

St. Luke Lutheran S 200/PK-8
410 S Rush St 60143 630-773-0396
Fax 773-0786
St. Peter the Apostle S 100/PK-8
500 N Cherry St 60143 630-773-1979
Mary Ellyn Billmeyer, prin. Fax 773-2826

Iuka, Marion, Pop. 584
Iuka CCSD 7 300/PK-8
PO Box 68 62849 618-323-6233
Matthew Renaud, supt. Fax 323-6932
www.iuka.marion.k12.il.us/
Iuka S 300/PK-8
PO Box 68 62849 618-323-6233
John Consolino, prin. Fax 323-6932

Jacksonville, Morgan, Pop. 19,470
Jacksonville SD 117 3,600/PK-12
516 Jordan St 62650 217-243-9411
Les Huddle, supt. Fax 243-6844
www.morgan.k12.il.us/jvsd117/index.html
Early Years Pre-K Program 100/PK-PK
110 Walnut Ct 62650 217-243-2876
Mary English, prin. Fax 243-2876
Eisenhower ES 400/K-6
1901 W Lafayette Ave 62650 217-245-5107
Gary Barlow, prin. Fax 243-2433
Franklin ES 300/K-6
352 Franklin Dr 62650 217-245-7005
Cyndee Hurst, prin. Fax 243-2535
Lincoln ES 200/K-6
320 W Independence Ave 62650 217-245-8720
Matt Fraas, prin. Fax 243-3531
North Jacksonville ES 300/K-6
1626 State Highway 78 N 62650 217-245-4084
Leslie Fuhr, prin. Fax 243-2818
South Jacksonville ES 300/K-6
1700 S West St 62650 217-245-5514
David Miller, prin. Fax 245-2804
Turner JHS 500/7-8
664 Lincoln Ave 62650 217-243-3383
Beth Brockschmidt, prin. Fax 243-3459
Washington ES 300/K-6
524 S Kosciusko St 62650 217-243-6711
Mary Camerer, prin. Fax 243-3055
Other Schools – See Murrayville

Our Savior S 200/K-8
455 E State St 62650 217-243-8621
Rita Carney, prin. Fax 245-6185
Salem Lutheran S 100/PK-8
PO Box 1057 62651 217-243-3419
Craig Busseau, prin. Fax 245-0289
Westfair Christian Academy 100/PK-12
14 Clarke Dr 62650 217-243-7100
Randy Cooper, prin. Fax 243-2386

Jacob, Jackson

Christ Lutheran S 50/K-8
146 W Jacob Rd 62950 618-763-4664
Stephen Rockey, prin. Fax 763-4363

Jerseyville, Jersey, Pop. 8,187
Jersey CUSD 100 2,600/PK-12
100 Lincoln Ave 62052 618-498-5561
James Whiteside, supt. Fax 498-5265
www.jersey100.k12.il.us/
Delhi ES 200/PK-5
28968 Delhi Rd 62052 618-885-5613
Michelle Brown, prin. Fax 885-5237
Illini MS 600/6-8
1101 S Liberty St 62052 618-498-5527
Cory Breden, prin. Fax 498-7079
Jerseyville East ES 200/3-5
201 N Giddings Ave 62052 618-498-3814
Cynthia Barnhart, prin. Fax 498-6805
Jerseyville West ES 200/PK-2
1000 W Carpenter St 62052 618-498-4322
Denise Kallal, prin. Fax 498-9870
Other Schools – See Dow, Fieldon, Grafton

St. Francis/Holy Ghost S 500/PK-8
412 S State St 62052 618-498-4823
Janet Goben, prin. Fax 498-3827

Johnsburg, McHenry, Pop. 6,277
Johnsburg CUSD 12 2,600/PK-12
2222 Church St, 815-385-6916
Dr. Dan Johnson, supt. Fax 385-4715
www.jburgd12.k12.il.us
Bush ES 300/3-4
2117 W Church St, 815-385-3731
Derek Straight, prin. Fax 344-7104
Johnsburg JHS 800/5-8
2220 Church St, 815-385-6210
Travis Lobbins, prin. Fax 578-2649
Other Schools – See Ringwood

St. John the Baptist S 200/PK-8
2304 Church St, 815-385-3959
Pamela Dvonch, prin. Fax 363-3337

Johnsonville, Wayne, Pop. 68
North Wayne CUSD 200
Supt. — See Cisne
Johnsonville ES 100/PK-4
PO Box A 62850 618-673-3044
Janice Brashear, prin. Fax 673-3094

Johnston City, Williamson, Pop. 3,476
Johnston City CUSD 1 1,300/PK-12
1103 Monroe Ave 62951 618-983-8021
Gary Schurz, supt. Fax 983-6034
www.jcindians.org/
Jefferson ES 300/PK-4
1108 Grand Ave 62951 618-983-7561
Andria Murrah, prin. Fax 983-6556
Washington S 500/K-8
100 E 12th St 62951 618-983-7581
Chris Grant, prin. Fax 983-6409
Other Schools – See Pittsburg

Joliet, Will, Pop. 136,208
Joliet SD 86 10,300/PK-8
420 N Raynor Ave 60435 815-740-3196
Phyllis Wilson Ph.D., supt. Fax 740-6520
www.joliet86.org
Culbertson ES 300/K-5
1521 E Washington St 60433 815-723-0035
Ardith Neal, prin. Fax 740-5454
Cunningham ES 600/K-5
500 Moran St 60435 815-723-0169
Ana Kasal, prin. Fax 726-3040
Dirksen JHS 500/6-8
203 S Midland Ave 60436 815-729-1566
Kimberly Pfoutz, prin. Fax 744-2346
Eisenhower Academy 300/K-5
406 Burke Dr 60433 815-723-0233
Sandy Gavin, prin. Fax 740-5455
Farragut ES 600/K-5
701 Glenwood Ave 60435 815-723-0394
E. Wesley Russell, prin. Fax 740-5950
Forest Park Individual Education S 300/K-5
1220 California Ave 60432 815-723-0414
Joy Hopkins, prin. Fax 740-5452
Gompers JHS 800/6-8
1501 Copperfield Ave 60432 815-727-5276
Constance Russell, prin. Fax 726-5341
Hufford JHS 1,000/6-8
1125 N Larkin Ave 60435 815-725-3540
Anna White, prin. Fax 744-5974
Jefferson ES 400/K-5
2651 Glenwood Ave 60435 815-725-0262
Brenda Byrnes, prin. Fax 741-7631
Keith ES 500/K-5
400 4th Ave 60433 815-723-3409
Clarence Williams, prin. Fax 740-5951
Marshall ES 800/PK-5
319 Harwood St 60432 815-727-4919
Tawanda Lawrence, prin. Fax 727-9274
Marycrest ECC 300/PK-K
303 Purdue Ct 60436 815-725-1100
Kimberly Gordon, prin. Fax 741-7632
Parks Cultural Studies Academy 100/PK-5
500 Parks Ave 60432 815-723-1911
Linda Scott, prin. Fax 740-5453
Pershing ES 500/K-5
251 N Midland Ave 60435 815-725-0986
Brenda Reiter-Gorman, prin. Fax 741-7633
Sanchez ES 1,000/K-5
1101 Harrison Ave 60432 815-740-2810
Frank Villela, prin. Fax 740-2816
Sandburg ES 300/1-5
1100 Lilac Ln 60435 815-725-0281
Julie Rice-Zurek, prin. Fax 741-7615
Taft ES 300/K-5
1125 Oregon St 60435 815-725-2700
Kathryn Ireland, prin. Fax 741-7635
Thigpen ES 600/K-5
207 S Midland Ave 60436 815-741-7629
Adrian Harries, prin. Fax 729-6612
Washington JHS & Academy 600/6-8
402 Richards St 60433 815-727-5271
Michael Latting, prin. Fax 740-5451
Woodland ES 400/K-5
701 3rd Ave 60433 815-723-2808
Lawrence Head, prin. Fax 740-2633

Laraway CCSD 70C 400/PK-8
275 W Laraway Rd 60436 815-727-5115
Dr. Douglas Hesbol, supt. Fax 727-5289
Laraway S 300/1-8
275 W Laraway Rd 60436 815-727-5196
Sandy Carter, prin. Fax 727-5289
Oak Valley ES 50/PK-K
1705 Richards St 60433 815-727-2359
Sandy Carter, prin. Fax 727-0927

Minooka CCSD 201
Supt. — See Minooka
Jones ES, 800 Barberry Way 60431 K-4
Rodney Hiser, prin. 815-467-6121

Plainfield CCSD 202
Supt. — See Plainfield
Aux Sable MS 900/6-8
2001 Wildspring Pkwy 60431 815-439-7092
Sharon Alexander, prin. Fax 577-9476
Crystal Lawns ES 500/K-5
2544 Crystal Dr 60435 815-436-9519
Kathleen Baxter, prin. Fax 436-8433
Grand Prairie ES 800/K-5
3300 Caton Farm Rd 60431 815-436-7000
Janan Szurek, prin. Fax 436-1233
Jefferson ES K-5
1900 Oxford Way 60431 815-577-2021
Laurie Boyce, prin. Fax 254-6862

Rockdale SD 84 300/K-8
715 Meadow Ave 60436 815-725-5321
Keith Ashcraft, supt. Fax 725-3099
Rockdale S 300/K-8
715 Meadow Ave 60436 815-725-5321
Ricardo Espinoza, prin. Fax 725-3099

Troy CCSD 30C
Supt. — See Plainfield
Troy Craughwell ES 600/K-4
3333 Black Rd 60431 815-729-2340
Kathy Barker, prin. Fax 729-7435
Troy Heritage Trail ES 500/K-4
3389 Longford Dr 60431 815-773-2390
Michele Gantzert, prin. Fax 773-2398

Union SD 81 100/K-8
1661 Cherry Hill Rd 60433 815-726-5218
Barbara Littlejohn, supt. Fax 726-5056
www.union81.com
Union S 100/K-8
1661 Cherry Hill Rd 60433 815-726-5218
Barbara Littlejohn, prin. Fax 726-5056

Cathedral of St. Raymond S 500/PK-8
608 N Raynor Ave 60435 815-722-6626
Dr. Jennifer Groves, prin. Fax 727-4668
Franciscan Early Learning Center 100/PK-PK
1734 Theodore St 60435 815-744-7634
Sr. Margaret McGuckin, prin. Fax 744-2152
Ridgewood Baptist Academy 200/PK-12
1968 Hillcrest Rd 60433 815-726-2121
Dr. Albert Baker, admin. Fax 726-2344
St. Joseph S 200/K-8
409 N Scott St 60432 815-722-1005
David Spesia, prin. Fax 722-1213
St. Jude S 200/K-8
2204 McDonough St 60436 815-729-0288
Sr. Rita Mandella, prin. Fax 729-0344
St. Mary Magdalene S 100/PK-8
201 S Briggs St 60433 815-727-9079
Rev. Richard McGrath, prin. Fax 727-2059

St. Mary Nativity S 100/PK-8
702 N Broadway St 60435 815-722-8518
Joan Matejka, prin. Fax 726-4071
St. Patrick S 300/PK-8
110 Willow Ave 60436 815-726-2924
Dr. Lonnie Hughes, prin. Fax 726-9289
St. Paul the Apostle S 500/PK-8
130 Woodlawn Ave 60435 815-725-3390
Kimberly Schlegel, prin. Fax 725-3180
St. Peter Lutheran S 50/PK-8
310 N Broadway St 60435 815-722-3567
Claudia Pautz, prin. Fax 722-6544

Jonesboro, Union, Pop. 1,843
Jonesboro CCSD 43 500/PK-8
309 Cook Ave 62952 618-833-6651
Gary Hill, supt. Fax 833-8612
www.jes.union.k12.il.us/
Jonesboro S 500/PK-8
309 Cook Ave 62952 618-833-5148
Wanda Honey, prin. Fax 833-3410

Joppa, Massac, Pop. 419
Joppa-Maple Grove CUSD 38 300/PK-12
PO Box 10 62953 618-543-9023
Catherine Trampe Ph.D., supt. Fax 543-9264
Other Schools – See Metropolis

Joy, Mercer, Pop. 362
Westmer CUSD 203 600/PK-12
PO Box 436 61260 309-584-4173
Tom Avery, supt. Fax 584-4115
mercer.k12.il.us/westmer
Westmer JHS 100/6-8
PO Box 436 61260 309-584-4174
Robert Reed, prin. Fax 584-4257
Other Schools – See New Boston

Junction, Gallatin, Pop. 133
Gallatin CUSD 7 900/PK-12
5175 Highway 13 62954 618-272-3821
Les Oyler, supt. Fax 272-4101
Gallatin ES 300/PK-4
5175 Highway 13 62954 618-272-7008
Les Oyler, prin. Fax 272-4101
Gallatin JHS 300/5-8
5175 Highway 13 62954 618-272-7341
Chris Fromm, prin. Fax 272-4101

Justice, Cook, Pop. 12,692
Indian Springs SD 109 2,900/PK-8
7540 S 86th Ave 60458 708-496-8700
Dr. Jon Nebor, supt. Fax 496-8641
www.isd109.org
Brodnicki ES 700/K-6
8641 W 75th St 60458 708-496-8716
Leah Wakefield, prin. Fax 496-8173
Player Primary Center 100/K-1
8600 S Roberts Rd 60458 708-430-8191
Robert Serdar, prin. Fax 430-8295
Wilkins ES 500/K-6
8001 S 82nd Ave 60458 708-496-8708
Miriam Royer, prin. Fax 728-3114
Wilkins JHS 600/7-8
8001 S 82nd Ave 60458 708-496-8708
William Caron, prin. Fax 728-3114
Other Schools – See Bridgeview

Kankakee, Kankakee, Pop. 26,642
Herscher CUSD 2
Supt. — See Herscher
Limestone S 700/PK-8
963 N 5000W Rd 60901 815-933-2243
Leonard Sokoloff, prin. Fax 936-4123

Kankakee SD 111 5,400/PK-12
240 Warren Ave 60901 815-933-0700
Colleen Legge, supt. Fax 936-8944
www.kankakeeschooldistrict.org
Edison PS 200/K-3
1991 E Maple St 60901 815-932-0621
Kathleen O'Connor, prin. Fax 936-4096
Kankakee JHS 800/7-8
2250 E Crestwood St 60901 815-933-0730
Jason Worden, prin. Fax 935-7272
Kennedy MS 700/4-6
1550 W Calista St 60901 815-933-0764
Betty Peters-Lambert, prin. Fax 928-7390
King MS 500/3-6
1440 E Court St 60901 815-933-0750
George Harris, prin. Fax 933-4548
Lafayette PS 300/K-3
369 N 5th Ave 60901 815-933-8116
Barnetta Harris, prin. Fax 936-4097
Lincoln Cultural Center / Montessori 300/K-8
240 Warren Ave 60901 815-933-0709
Deb Dilks, prin. Fax 933-0710
Steuben ES 300/K-3
520 S Wildwood Ave 60901 815-933-7813
Lisa Cullens, prin. Fax 936-4093
Taft PS 500/K-3
1155 W Hawkins St 60901 815-932-0811
Michele Keiser, prin. Fax 933-0684
Twain PS 400/PK-3
2250 E Court St 60901 815-933-0722
Barnetta Harris, prin. Fax 936-4099
Other Schools – See Aroma Park

Aquinas Catholic Academy 200/PK-8
366 E Hickory St 60901 815-932-8124
Michael Wayer, prin. Fax 932-0485
Grace Baptist Academy 200/K-12
2499 Waldron Rd 60901 815-939-4579
Dwight Ascher, prin. Fax 939-1334
Kankakee Trinity Academy 200/PK-12
410 S Small Ave 60901 815-935-8080
Brad Prairie, prin. Fax 935-0280

Kansas, Edgar, Pop. 826
Kansas CUSD 3 300/PK-12
PO Box 350 61933 217-948-5174
Chris Long, supt. Fax 948-5577
Kansas S 200/PK-8
PO Box 350 61933 217-948-5175
Dwight Stricklin, prin. Fax 948-5577

Kell, Marion, Pop. 225
Kell CCSD 2 100/PK-8
207 N Johnson St 62853 618-822-6234
Sharon White, supt. Fax 822-6733
Kell Grade S 100/PK-8
207 N Johnson St 62853 618-822-6234
Sharon White, prin. Fax 822-6733

Kempton, Ford, Pop. 235
Tri-Point CUSD 6-J 600/PK-12
PO Box 128 60946 815-253-6299
Steve Fink, supt. Fax 253-6298
www.tripointschools.org/
Tri-Point ES 200/PK-3
PO Box 128 60946 815-253-6299
Steve Fink, prin. Fax 253-6298
Other Schools – See Piper City

Kenilworth, Cook, Pop. 2,445
Kenilworth SD 38 600/PK-8
542 Abbotsford Rd 60043 847-256-5006
Dr. Kelley Kalinich, supt. Fax 256-4418
www.kenilworth.k12.il.us
Sears S 600/PK-8
542 Abbotsford Rd 60043 847-256-5006
David Brown, prin. Fax 256-4418

Kewanee, Henry, Pop. 12,655
Kewanee CUSD 229 1,400/PK-12
210 Lyle St 61443 309-853-3341
Christopher Sullens Ed.D., supt. Fax 852-5504
www.kcud229.org/
Alexander S, 1401 Lake St 61443 100/K-1
Elizabeth Blachinsky, prin. 309-852-2449
Central JHS 400/4-8
215 E Central Blvd 61443 309-853-4290
Jason Anderson, prin. Fax 853-3195
Irving ES, 609 W Central Blvd 61443 300/2-3
Tammy Brown, prin. 309-853-3013
Lyle S, 920 N Burr St 61443 100/PK-PK
Kelly Walters, coord. 309-853-2741

Wethersfield CUSD 230 700/PK-12
439 Willard St 61443 309-853-4860
Shane Kazubowski, supt. Fax 856-7976
go-geese.net/
Wethersfield ES 400/PK-6
439 Willard St 61443 309-853-4800
Janean Friedman, prin. Fax 856-7800

Visitation S 100/PK-8
107 S Lexington Ave 61443 309-856-7451
David Hobin, prin. Fax 852-4106

Kincaid, Christian, Pop. 1,468
South Fork SD 14 400/PK-12
PO Box 20 62540 217-237-4333
Charlotte Davis, supt. Fax 237-4370
South Fork ES 200/PK-4
PO Box 20 62540 217-237-4331
Charlotte Davis, prin. Fax 237-2245

Kinderhook, Pike, Pop. 241
Western CUSD 12
Supt. — See Barry
Western JHS 50/5-8
PO Box 189 62345 217-432-8324
Heath Kendrick, prin. Fax 432-8003

Kings, Ogle
Kings Consolidated SD 144 100/K-8
100 1st St 61068 815-562-7191
Greg Stott, supt. Fax 562-5405
www.kings144.org
Kings S 100/K-8
100 1st St 61068 815-562-7191
Greg Stott, prin. Fax 562-5405

Kingston, DeKalb, Pop. 1,050
Genoa-Kingston CUSD 424
Supt. — See Genoa
Kingston ES 300/2-3
PO Box 37 60145 815-784-5246
Debbie Dudley, prin. Fax 784-9049

Kinmundy, Marion, Pop. 871
South Central CUSD 401 700/PK-12
PO Box 189 62854 618-547-3414
Judy Cole, supt. Fax 547-7790
southcentralschools.org/
South Central ES 300/PK-4
810 E 1st St 62854 618-547-7696
Kerry Herdes, prin. Fax 547-3144
South Central MS 200/5-8
PO Box 40 62854 618-547-7734
Greg Grinestaff, prin. Fax 547-7441

Kirkland, DeKalb, Pop. 1,607
Hiawatha CUSD 426 600/K-12
PO Box 428 60146 815-522-6676
Christine Demory, supt. Fax 522-6619
www.hiawatha426.k12.il.us
Hiawatha ES 300/K-5
PO Box 428 60146 815-522-3336
Faye Lynch, prin. Fax 522-3312

Knoxville, Knox, Pop. 3,005
Knoxville CUSD 202 1,100/PK-12
600 E Main St 61448 309-289-2328
Lawrence Carlton, supt. Fax 289-9614
www.bluebullets.org
Knoxville JHS 300/5-8
701 E Mill St 61448 309-289-4126
Chris Lensing, prin. Fax 289-4128
Woolsey ES 400/PK-4
106 Pleasant Ave 61448 309-289-4134
Debra Galbreath, prin. Fax 289-9300

Lacon, Marshall, Pop. 1,923
Midland CUSD 7
Supt. — See Varna
Midland ES 300/PK-4
206 N High St 61540 309-246-7215
Julia Albers, prin. Fax 246-4049

Ladd, Bureau, Pop. 1,305
Ladd CCSD 94 200/K-8
232 E Cleveland St 61329 815-894-2363
Michelle Zeko, supt. Fax 894-2364
Ladd Community Consolidated S 200/K-8
232 E Cleveland St 61329 815-894-2363
Michelle Zeko, prin. Fax 894-2364

La Grange, Cook, Pop. 15,482
La Grange Highlands SD 106 900/K-8
1750 W Plainfield Rd 60525 708-246-3085
Dr. Arleen Armanetti, supt. Fax 246-0220
www.district106.net
Highlands ES 600/K-5
5850 Laurel Ave 60525 708-579-6886
Dr. Vivian Powers-Richard, prin. Fax 485-3611
Highlands MS 300/6-8
1850 W Plainfield Rd 60525 708-579-6890
Michael Papierski, prin. Fax 485-3593

La Grange SD 102
Supt. — See La Grange Park
Cossitt Avenue ES 600/PK-6
115 W Cossitt Ave 60525 708-482-2450
Mary Tavegia, prin. Fax 482-2734
Ogden Avenue ES 600/K-6
501 W Ogden Ave 60525 708-482-2480
Dr. Cynthia Boudreau, prin. Fax 482-2488

La Grange SD 105 1,100/PK-8
1001 S Spring Ave 60525 708-482-2700
Glenn Schlichting Ph.D., supt. Fax 482-2727
www.d105.net
Gurrie MS 200/7-8
1001 S Spring Ave 60525 708-482-2720
Edmond Hood, prin. Fax 482-2724
Seventh Avenue ES 200/PK-6
701 7th Ave 60525 708-482-2730
Sherry Krzyzanski, prin. Fax 482-2726
Spring Avenue ES 300/K-6
1001 S Spring Ave 60525 708-482-2710
Elizabeth Webb Peterman, prin. Fax 482-2725
Other Schools – See Countryside, Hodgkins

Pleasantdale SD 107
Supt. — See Burr Ridge
Pleasantdale ES 500/PK-4
8100 School St 60525 708-246-4700
Matt Vandercar, prin. Fax 246-4625

Acacia Academy 100/K-12
6425 Willow Springs Rd 60525 708-579-9040
St. Cletus S 400/PK-8
700 W 55th St 60525 708-352-4820
Jolene Hillgoth, admin. Fax 352-0788
St. Francis Xavier S 700/PK-8
145 N Waiola Ave 60525 708-352-2175
Debra Rodde, prin. Fax 352-2057
St. John's Lutheran S 200/PK-8
505 S Park Rd 60525 708-354-1690
Dr. Richard Block, prin. Fax 354-4910

La Grange Park, Cook, Pop. 12,726
Brookfield Lagrange Park SD 95
Supt. — See Brookfield
Brook Park ES 500/K-4
1214 Raymond Ave 60526 708-354-3740
Michael Sorensen, prin. Fax 354-3146

La Grange SD 102 2,800/PK-8
333 N Park Rd 60526 708-482-2400
Dr. Mark Van Clay, supt. Fax 482-2402
www.dist102.k12.il.us/
Barnsdale Road S K-K
920 Barnsdale Rd 60526 708-482-3003
Kathryn Boxell, prin.
Forest Road ES 500/PK-6
901 Forest Rd 60526 708-482-2525
Rebecca Russow, prin. Fax 352-4573
Park JHS 600/7-8
325 N Park Rd 60526 708-482-2500
Dr. Laura Schwartz, prin. Fax 352-1170
Other Schools – See Brookfield, La Grange

St. Louise De Marillac S 200/PK-8
1125 Harrison Ave 60526 708-352-2202
Michele Bancroft, prin. Fax 352-6654

La Harpe, Hancock, Pop. 1,323
La Harpe CUSD 347 300/PK-8
404 W Main St 61450 217-659-7739
Jo Campbell, supt. Fax 659-7730
hancock.k12.il.us/laharpe/
La Harpe ES 200/PK-5
404 W Main St 61450 217-659-3713
Lila McKeown, prin. Fax 659-7730
La Harpe JHS 100/6-8
404 W Main St 61450 217-659-3713
Lila McKeown, prin. Fax 659-7730

Lake Bluff, Lake, Pop. 6,251
Lake Bluff ESD 65 1,000/K-8
121 E Sheridan Pl 60044 847-234-9400
Dr. David Vick, supt. Fax 234-6237
www.lbelem.lfc.edu/
Central ES 300/3-5
350 W Washington Ave 60044 847-234-9405
Katie Williams, prin. Fax 234-4819
East ES 300/K-2
121 E Sheridan Pl 60044 847-234-9403
Kathleen Tomei, admin. Fax 295-9927
Lake Bluff MS 400/6-8
31 E Sheridan Pl 60044 847-234-9407
Nathan Blackmer, prin. Fax 615-9144

Forest Bluff S 100/PK-8
8 W Scranton Ave 60044 847-295-8338
Paula Preschlack, hdmstr. Fax 295-2457

Lake Forest, Lake, Pop. 21,123
Lake Forest SD 67 2,200/K-8
300 S Waukegan Rd 60045 847-234-6010
Dr. Harry Griffith, supt. Fax 234-2372
www.lfelem.lfc.edu
Cherokee ES 400/K-4
475 Cherokee Rd 60045 847-234-3805
Carol Krumes, prin. Fax 615-4467
Deer Path MS - East 500/5-6
95 W Deerpath 60045 847-615-4770
John Steinert, prin. Fax 615-4464
Deer Path MS - West 500/7-8
155 W Deerpath 60045 847-604-7400
John Steinert, prin. Fax 234-2389
Everett ES 400/K-4
1111 Everett School Rd 60045 847-234-5713
Ingrid Wiemer, prin. Fax 615-4466
Sheridan ES 300/K-4
1360 N Sheridan Rd 60045 847-234-1160
Dr. Michelle Shinn, prin. Fax 615-4465

Rondout SD 72 100/K-8
28593 N Bradley Rd 60045 847-362-2021
Dr. Jenny Wojcik, supt. Fax 816-2067
www.rondout.org
Rondout S 100/K-8
28593 N Bradley Rd 60045 847-362-2021
Stuart Lassiter, prin. Fax 816-2067

East Lake Academy 100/PK-8
13911 W Laurel Dr 60045 847-247-0035
Noel Dowd, prin. Fax 247-1937
Lake Forest Country Day S 400/PK-8
145 S Green Bay Rd 60045 847-234-2350
Michael Robinson, hdmstr. Fax 234-2352
Montessori S of Lake Forest 100/K-6
13700 W Laurel Dr 60045 847-918-1000
Cathy Swan, dir. Fax 918-1304
School of St. Mary MS 300/4-8
185 E Illinois Rd 60045 847-234-0371
Dr. Venette Biancalana, admin. Fax 234-9593
School of St. Mary PS 300/PK-3
900 W Everett Rd 60045 847-283-9800
Dr. Venette Biancalana, admin. Fax 283-0742

Lake in the Hills, McHenry, Pop. 28,786
CUSD 300
Supt. — See Carpentersville
Lake In The Hills ES 500/K-5
519 Willow St, 847-658-2530
Tammy Poole, prin. Fax 658-2563
Lincoln Prairie ES 600/K-5
500 Harvest Gate, 847-960-7735
Trent Halpin, prin. Fax 960-7743

Consolidated SD 158
Supt. — See Algonquin
Chesak ES 1,100/K-2
10910 Reed Rd, 847-659-5700
Chuck Lamb, prin. Fax 659-5720
Marlowe MS 800/6-8
9625 Haligus Rd, 847-659-4700
Mike Moan, prin. Fax 659-4720
Martin ES 1,000/3-5
10920 Reed Rd, 847-659-5300
Rhonda Maciejewski, prin. Fax 659-5320

Lake Villa, Lake, Pop. 8,492
Lake Villa CCSD 41 3,300/PK-8
131 McKinley Ave 60046 847-356-2385
Dr. John VanPelt, supt. Fax 356-2670
www.district41.org
Martin ES 700/K-6
24750 W Dering Ln 60046 847-245-3400
Paul Santopadre, prin. Fax 245-4521
Palombi MS 700/7-8
133 McKinley Ave 60046 847-356-2118
Mary Jordan, prin. Fax 356-0833
Pleviak ES 600/K-6
304 E Grand Ave 60046 847-356-2381
Scott Klene, prin. Fax 356-0923
Thompson ES 700/K-6
515 Thompson Ln 60046 847-265-2488
Sandy Merrill, prin. Fax 265-2667
Other Schools – See Lindenhurst

Calvary Christian S 100/PK-8
134 Monaville Rd 60046 847-356-6198
Darla Tucker, prin. Fax 356-6524
Prince of Peace S 300/PK-8
135 S Milwaukee Ave 60046 847-356-6111
Mary Lou Cacioppo, prin. Fax 356-6121

Lake Zurich, Lake, Pop. 20,045
Lake Zurich CUSD 95 6,000/PK-12
400 S Old Rand Rd 60047 847-438-2831
Dr. Mike Egan, supt. Fax 438-6702
www.lz95.org
Adams ES 500/K-5
555 Old Mill Grove Rd 60047 847-438-5986
Claudia Mall, prin. Fax 438-7740
Fox ES 500/K-5
395 W Cuba Rd 60047 847-540-7020
Jill Brooks, prin. Fax 540-7032
Lake Zurich MS South Campus 800/6-8
435 W Cuba Rd 60047 847-540-7070
Dave Gardner, prin. Fax 540-9438
Paine ES 400/K-5
50 Miller Rd 60047 847-438-2163
Cameron Shapiro, prin. Fax 438-2528
Whitney ES 400/PK-5
100 Church St 60047 847-438-2351
Deb Bruemmer, prin. Fax 438-2696
Other Schools – See Hawthorn Woods

Quentin Road Christian S 200/PK-12
60 Quentin Rd 60047 847-438-4494

St. Francis De Sales S 500/PK-8
11 S Buesching Rd 60047 847-438-7921
Roy Rash, prin. Fax 438-7114

La Moille, Bureau, Pop. 760
La Moille CUSD 303 300/K-12
PO Box 470 61330 815-638-2018
Colette Sutton, supt. Fax 638-2392
Allen JHS 100/4-8
PO Box 470 61330 815-638-2233
James Brandau, prin. Fax 638-2886
Other Schools – See Van Orin

Lanark, Carroll, Pop. 1,483
Eastland CUSD 308 700/PK-12
200 S School St 61046 815-493-6301
Mark Hansen, supt. Fax 493-6303
www.eastland308.com
Eastland ES 200/PK-2
200 S School St 61046 815-493-6301
Mark Hansen, prin. Fax 493-6303
Other Schools – See Shannon

Lansing, Cook, Pop. 27,324
Lansing SD 158 2,400/PK-8
18300 Greenbay Ave 60438 708-474-6700
Cecilia Heiberger, supt. Fax 474-9976
www.d158.net
Coolidge ES 700/K-5
17845 Henry St 60438 708-474-4320
Linda Blomquist, prin. Fax 474-9976
Crawl PS 100/PK-1
18300 Greenbay Ave 60438 708-474-4868
Debra Faczekas, prin. Fax 474-0194
Memorial JHS 900/6-8
2721 Ridge Rd 60438 708-474-2383
Robert Zimbelman, prin. Fax 474-9976
Oak Glen ES 500/K-5
2101 182nd St 60438 708-474-1714
Kim Morley, prin. Fax 474-9976
Reavis ES 300/K-5
17121 Roy St 60438 708-474-8523
Margaret Williams, prin. Fax 474-9976

Sunnybrook SD 171 1,100/PK-8
19266 Burnham Ave 60438 708-895-0750
Joseph Majchrowicz Ed.D., supt. Fax 895-8580
www.sd171.org
Hale ES 600/PK-4
19055 Burnham Ave 60438 708-895-3030
Cindy Hirschboeck, prin. Fax 895-2290
Heritage MS 500/5-8
19250 Burnham Ave 60438 708-895-0790
Bruce Christensen, prin. Fax 895-8580

Lansing Christian S 400/K-8
3660 Randolph St 60438 708-474-1700
Ronald Holwerda, prin. Fax 474-1746
St. Ann S 400/K-8
3014 Ridge Rd 60438 708-895-1661
Elizabeth Gard, prin. Fax 895-6923
St. John Lutheran S 100/PK-8
18100 Wentworth Ave 60438 708-895-9280
David Swanson, prin. Fax 895-9303
Trinity Lutheran S 200/PK-8
18144 Glen Ter 60438 708-474-8539
Mary Meyer, prin. Fax 474-1481

La Salle, LaSalle, Pop. 9,615
Dimmick CCSD 175 100/K-8
297 N 33rd Rd 61301 815-223-2933
Ryan Linnig, supt. Fax 223-0169
www.dimmick175.com
Dimmick Community Consolidated S 100/K-8
297 N 33rd Rd 61301 815-223-2933
Ryan Linnig, prin. Fax 223-0169

La Salle ESD 122 900/PK-8
1165 Saint Vincents Ave 61301 815-223-0786
Dr. Joan McGuire, supt. Fax 223-8740
www.lasalleschools.net/
Lincoln JHS 300/6-8
1165 Saint Vincents Ave 61301 815-223-0933
Jerald Carls, prin. Fax 223-8740
Northwest ES 700/PK-5
1735 Malcolm Ave 61301 815-223-4006
Egan Colbrese, prin. Fax 224-6961

Trinity Catholic Academy 200/PK-8
650 4th St 61301 815-223-8523
Leroy Pesch, prin. Fax 223-7450

Lawrenceville, Lawrence, Pop. 4,513
Lawrence County CUSD 20 1,300/PK-12
1802 Cedar St 62439 618-943-2326
Charles Stegall, supt. Fax 943-4092
www.cusd20.com
Parkside ES, 1900 Cedar St 62439 700/PK-5
Barbara Large, prin. 618-943-3922
Parkview JHS, 1802 Cedar St 62439 300/6-8
Corrie Ray, prin. 618-943-2327

Lebanon, Saint Clair, Pop. 3,749
Lebanon CUSD 9 700/PK-12
200 W Schuetz St 62254 618-537-4611
Harry Cavanaugh, supt. Fax 537-9588
www.lebanon.stclair.k12.il.us
Lebanon S 400/PK-8
102 W Schuetz St 62254 618-537-4553
Karen Buehler, prin. Fax 537-2746
Other Schools – See Summerfield

Leland, LaSalle, Pop. 942
Leland CUSD 1 300/K-12
370 N Main St 60531 815-495-3821
Ronald Abrell, supt. Fax 495-4611
www.leland.lasall.k12.il.us
Leland S 200/K-8
370 N Main St 60531 815-495-3231
Kim Siemers, prin. Fax 495-4611

Lemont, DuPage, Pop. 15,146
Lemont-Bromberek Combined SD 113A 2,600/PK-8
16100 W 127th St 60439 630-257-2286
Dr. Tim Ricker, supt. Fax 243-3005
www.sd113a.org/
Central ES 300/3-5
410 McCarthy Rd 60439 630-257-2286
Gina Rodewald, prin. Fax 243-3003
Oakwood ES 800/PK-2
1130 Kim Pl 60439 630-257-2286
Catherine Slee, prin. Fax 243-3006
Old Quarry MS 1,000/6-8
16100 W 127th St 60439 630-257-2286
Dawn Pechukas, prin. Fax 243-3004
River Valley ES 500/3-5
15425 E 127th St 60439 630-257-2286
Debby Lynch, prin. Fax 243-3007

Montessori S of SWCC 100/PK-8
16427 135th St 60439 815-834-0607
Norine Colby, prin.
SS. Alphonsus & Patrick S 200/PK-8
20W145 Davey Rd 60439 630-783-2220
Renee Payne, prin. Fax 783-2230
SS. Cyril & Methodius S 500/PK-8
607 Sobieski St 60439 630-257-6488
Shirley Tkachuk, prin. Fax 257-6465
White Pines Academy PK-8
14911 E 127th St 60439 630-243-1995
Miriam Brackett, dean Fax 243-1988

Lena, Stephenson, Pop. 2,854
Lena Winslow CUSD 202 900/PK-12
401 Fremont St 61048 815-369-3100
Jane Michael, supt. Fax 369-3102
www.le-win.net/
Lena ES 300/PK-5
401 Fremont St 61048 815-369-3113
Mary Gerbode, prin. Fax 369-3171
Lena-Winslow JHS 200/6-8
517 Fremont St 61048 815-369-3114
Mark Kuehl, prin. Fax 369-3162

Le Roy, McLean, Pop. 3,391
Le Roy CUSD 2 800/PK-12
600 E Pine St 61752 309-962-4211
Gary Tipsord, supt. Fax 962-9312
www.leroy.k12.il.us/
Le Roy ES 500/PK-6
805 N Barnett St 61752 309-962-4771
Erin Conn, prin. Fax 962-2893
Le Roy JHS 100/7-8
505 E Center St 61752 309-962-2911
Steve Reschke, prin. Fax 962-8421

Lewistown, Fulton, Pop. 2,448
Lewistown SD 97 800/PK-12
15501 E Avenue L 61542 309-547-5826
Bill King, supt. Fax 547-5235
www.cusd97.fulton.k12.il.us/
Central MS, 15501 E Avenue L 61542 300/4-8
Jan Braun, prin. 309-547-2231
Lewistown ES 300/PK-3
15501 E Avenue L 61542 309-547-2240
Jan Braun, prin. Fax 547-5235

Lexington, McLean, Pop. 1,866
Lexington CUSD 7 500/PK-12
PO Box 167 61753 309-365-4141
Curt Nettles, supt. Fax 365-7381
www.lexington.k12.il.us
Lexington ES, PO Box 167 61753 300/PK-6
Dale Heidbreder, prin. 309-365-2741
Lexington JHS, PO Box 167 61753 100/7-8
Sean Berry, prin. 309-365-2711

Liberty, Adams, Pop. 515
Liberty CUSD 2 500/PK-12
505 N Park St 62347 217-645-3433
Matt Runge, supt. Fax 645-3241
liberty.il.schoolwebpages.com/
Liberty ES 400/PK-6
505 N Park St 62347 217-645-3481
Jody Obert, prin. Fax 645-3241

Libertyville, Lake, Pop. 21,760
Libertyville SD 70 2,700/PK-8
1381 Lake St 60048 847-362-9695
Dr. Mark Friedman, supt. Fax 362-3003
www.d70schools.org
Adler Park ES 300/PK-5
1740 N Milwaukee Ave 60048 847-362-7275
Janet Brownlie, prin. Fax 362-8158
Butterfield ES 700/K-5
1441 Lake St 60048 847-362-3120
Guy Schumacher, prin. Fax 816-5613
Copeland Manor ES 400/K-5
801 7th Ave 60048 847-362-0240
Erik Youngman, prin. Fax 247-8617
Highland MS 900/6-8
310 W Rockland Rd 60048 847-362-9020
Sharon Aspinall, prin. Fax 362-0870
Rockland ES 400/K-5
160 W Rockland Rd 60048 847-362-3134
Jean LeBlanc, prin. Fax 247-8618

Oak Grove SD 68 1,100/K-8
1700 Oplaine Rd 60048 847-367-4120
Dr. Janice Matthews, supt. Fax 367-4172
www.ogschool.org
Oak Grove S 1,100/K-8
1700 Oplaine Rd 60048 847-367-4120
Mark Clement, prin. Fax 367-4172

St. John's Lutheran S 100/PK-8
501 W Park Ave 60048 847-367-1441
Paul Kaiser, prin. Fax 367-9858
St. Joseph S 500/PK-8
221 Park Pl 60048 847-362-0730
Charles Lynch, prin. Fax 362-8130

Lincoln, Logan, Pop. 14,971
Chester-East Lincoln CCSD 61 300/PK-8
1300 1500th St 62656 217-732-4136
Victoria Childs, supt. Fax 732-3265
www.logan.k12.il.us/CEL/
Chester-East Lincoln S 300/PK-8
1300 1500th St 62656 217-732-4136
Victoria Childs, prin. Fax 732-3265

Lincoln ESD 27 1,300/PK-8
100 S Maple St 62656 217-732-2522
Mary Ahillen, supt. Fax 732-2198
logan.k12.il.us/les27/
Adams ES 100/PK-2
1311 Nicholson Rd 62656 217-732-3253
Christa Healy, prin. Fax 732-8098
Central ES 200/K-5
100 7th St 62656 217-732-3386
Christa Healy, prin. Fax 732-9256
Jefferson ES 100/K-2
710 5th St 62656 217-732-6898
Nancy Rosenbery, prin. Fax 735-1066
Lincoln JHS 400/6-8
208 Broadway St 62656 217-732-3535
Kent Froebe, prin. Fax 732-2685
Northwest ES 200/K-5
506 11th St 62656 217-732-6819
Nancy Rosenbery, prin. Fax 735-2172
Washington-Monroe ES 300/K-5
1002 Pekin St 62656 217-732-4764
Rebecca Cecil, prin. Fax 732-5913

West Lincoln-Broadwell ESD 92 200/K-8
2695 Woodlawn Rd 62656 217-732-2630
Bailey Climer, supt. Fax 732-3623
West Lincoln-Broadwell S 200/K-8
2695 Woodlawn Rd 62656 217-732-2630
Bailey Climer, prin. Fax 732-3623

Carroll Catholic S 100/PK-8
111 4th St 62656 217-732-7518
John Link, prin. Fax 732-7518
Zion Lutheran S 100/PK-8
1600 Woodlawn Rd 62656 217-732-3977
Steve Schumacher, prin. Fax 732-3398

Lincolnshire, Lake, Pop. 6,841
Lincolnshire-Prairieview SD 103 1,700/K-8
1370 N Riverwoods Rd 60069 847-295-4030
Larry Fleming, supt. Fax 295-9196
www.district103.k12.il.us
Half Day ES 400/3-4
239 Olde Half Day Rd 60069 847-634-6463
Jennifer Able, prin. Fax 634-1968
Sprague ES 500/K-2
2425 Riverwoods Rd 60069 847-945-6665
Christy Adler, prin. Fax 945-6718
Wright JHS 800/5-8
1370 N Riverwoods Rd 60069 847-295-1560
Howard Holbrook, prin. Fax 295-7136

Lincolnwood, Cook, Pop. 12,026
Lincolnwood SD 74 1,200/PK-8
6950 N East Prairie Rd 60712 847-675-8234
Mark Klaisner, supt. Fax 675-8244
www.sd74.org
Hall ES 400/PK-2
3925 W Lunt Ave Ste 1 60712 847-675-8235
Kristen McElligatt, prin. Fax 675-9378
Lincoln Hall MS 400/6-8
6855 N Crawford Ave 60712 847-675-8240
Larry Sasso, prin. Fax 675-8124
Rutledge Hall ES 400/3-5
6850 N East Prairie Rd 60712 847-675-8236
Jean Weiss, prin. Fax 675-9320

Lindenhurst, Lake, Pop. 14,403
Lake Villa CCSD 41
Supt. — See Lake Villa
Hooper ES 600/PK-6
2400 E Sand Lake Rd 60046 847-356-2151
Patricia Planic, prin. Fax 356-0934

Millburn CCSD 24
Supt. — See Wadsworth
Millburn West S 600/K-8
640 Freedom Way 60046 847-245-1600
Jake Jorgenson, prin. Fax 265-8198

Lindenwood, Ogle
Eswood CCSD 269 100/K-8
304 Main St 61049 815-393-4477
Dr. Dwight Mayberry, supt. Fax 393-4478
Eswood S 100/K-8
304 Main St 61049 815-393-4477
Dr. Dwight Mayberry, prin. Fax 393-4478

Lisle, DuPage, Pop. 23,376
Lisle CUSD 202 1,600/PK-12
5211 Center Ave 60532 630-493-8000
Dr. Patricia Wernet, supt. Fax 971-4054
www.lisle.dupage.k12.il.us/
Lisle JHS 400/6-8
5207 Center Ave 60532 630-493-8200
Timothy Pociask, prin. Fax 493-8209
Schiesser ES 400/K-K, 3-5
5205 Kingston Ave 60532 630-493-8100
Dr. Linda Kotalik, prin. Fax 968-5976
Tate Woods ES 200/PK-PK, 1-
1736 Middleton Ave 60532 630-493-8050
Wesley Gosselink, prin. Fax 971-4069

Naperville CUSD 203
Supt. — See Naperville
Kennedy JHS 1,100/6-8
2929 Green Trails Dr 60532 630-420-3220
Donald Perry, prin. Fax 420-6960

St. Joan of Arc S 700/PK-8
4913 Columbia Ave 60532 630-969-1732
Sr. Carolyn Sieg, prin. Fax 353-4590

Litchfield, Montgomery, Pop. 6,771
Litchfield CUSD 12 1,600/PK-12
1702 N State St 62056 217-324-2157
Michael Juenger, supt. Fax 324-2158
www.litchfield.k12.il.us
Colt ES 200/2-3
615 E Tyler Ave 62056 217-324-3565
Susan Bennett, prin. Fax 324-3703
Litchfield MS 400/6-8
1701 N State St 62056 217-324-4668
Andrea Lee, prin. Fax 324-5693
Litchfield Prekindergarten 100/PK-PK
601 S State St 62056 217-324-3514
Adam Favre, prin. Fax 324-2129
Madison Park ES 200/K-1
800 N Chestnut St 62056 217-324-2851
Adam Favre, prin. Fax 324-5562
Russell ES 200/4-5
705 N Jefferson St 62056 217-324-4034
Susan Bennett, prin. Fax 324-3977

Zion Lutheran S 100/PK-8
1301 N State St 62056 217-324-3166
Sharon Cordani, prin. Fax 324-3166

Livingston, Madison, Pop. 797
Staunton CUSD 6
Supt. — See Staunton
Graiff ES 100/PK-4
PO Box 400 62058 618-637-2131
Mark Skertich, prin. Fax 637-2986

Loami, Sangamon, Pop. 779
New Berlin CUSD 16
Supt. — See New Berlin
Loami ES 200/4-6
PO Box 238 62661 217-624-2541
Casey Wills, prin. Fax 624-2571

Lockport, Will, Pop. 22,161
Fairmont SD 89 300/PK-8
735 Green Garden Pl 60441 815-726-6318
Dr. Doris Langon, supt. Fax 726-6157
www.fsd89.org/
Fairmont S 300/PK-8
735 Green Garden Pl 60441 815-726-6156
Dr. Stephanie Long, prin. Fax 726-0079

Homer CCSD 33C
Supt. — See Homer Glen
Butler ES 700/K-4
1900 S Farrell Rd 60441 815-226-5155
Laura Staab, prin. Fax 226-5627

Lockport SD 91 700/K-8
808 Adams St 60441 815-838-0737
Donna Gray, supt. Fax 834-4339
www.d91.net/index1.htm
Kelvin Grove MS 400/4-8
808 Adams St 60441 815-838-0737
Mary Jo Slingerland, prin. Fax 834-4339
Milne Grove ES 300/K-3
565 E 7th St 60441 815-838-0542
Tracy Carlson, prin. Fax 838-6893

Taft SD 90 300/K-8
1605 S Washington St 60441 815-838-0408
David Rogowski, supt. Fax 838-5046
www.taft90.org
Taft S 300/K-8
1605 S Washington St 60441 815-838-0408
Dr. Kim Sekulich, prin. Fax 838-5046

Will County SD 92 2,000/PK-8
708 N State St 60441 815-838-8031
Dr. Gary Peck, supt. Fax 838-8034
www.d92.org
Ludwig ES 400/4-5
710 N State St 60441 815-838-8020
Carol Koch, prin. Fax 838-0834
Oak Prairie JHS 800/6-8
15161 S Gougar Rd, 815-836-2724
Mark Murray, prin.
Reed ES 400/2-3
14939 W 143rd St, 708-301-0692
Mary Jasinski, prin. Fax 838-8034
Walsh ES 400/PK-1
514 MacGregor Rd 60441 815-838-7858
Teresa Martin, prin. Fax 838-8034

Crest Hill Christian S 50/K-9
21514 W Division St 60441 815-730-0664
St. Dennis S 200/PK-8
1201 S Washington St 60441 815-838-4494
Lisa Smith, prin. Fax 838-5435
St. Joseph S 300/PK-8
529 Madison St 60441 815-838-8173
Lynne Scheffler, prin. Fax 838-0504

Lombard, DuPage, Pop. 42,816
DuPage County SD 45
Supt. — See Villa Park
Schafer ES 600/PK-5
700 E Pleasant Ln 60148 630-516-6500
Melissa Ingram, prin. Fax 932-6471
Stevenson ES 200/PK-2
18w331 15th St 60148 630-516-7780
Christine Mazaika-Arado, prin. Fax 889-7923
Westmore ES 500/K-5
340 S School St 60148 630-516-7500
Dominic Sepich, prin. Fax 932-6492
York Center ES 200/3-5
895 E 14th St 60148 630-516-6540
Nancy Munoz, prin. Fax 932-6543

Lombard SD 44 3,100/PK-8
150 W Madison St 60148 630-827-4400
James Blanche, supt. Fax 620-3798
www.sd44.org/
Butterfield ES 300/PK-5
2s500 Gray Ave 60148 630-827-4000
Kristine Walsh, prin. Fax 889-7960
Glenn Westlake MS 1,100/6-8
1514 S Main St 60148 630-827-4500
Philip Wieczorek, prin. Fax 620-3791
Hammerschmidt ES 400/K-5
617 Hammerschmidt Ave 60148 630-827-4200
David Danielski, prin. Fax 620-3733
Madison ES 500/PK-5
150 W Madison St 60148 630-827-4100
Lawrence Piatek, prin. Fax 620-3769
Manor Hill ES 300/K-5
1464 S Main St 60148 630-827-4300
Robert Schulz, prin. Fax 889-7964
Park View ES 300/K-5
341 N Elizabeth St 60148 630-827-4040
Roberta Wallerstedt, prin. Fax 620-3749
Pleasant Lane ES 300/K-5
401 N Main St 60148 630-827-4640
Stephanie Loth, prin. Fax 620-3760

Christ the King S 100/PK-8
115 E 15th St 60148 630-627-0640
Jill Placey, prin. Fax 705-0139
College Preparatory S of America 500/PK-12
331 W Madison St 60148 630-889-8000
Yasmin Jamal, prin. Fax 889-8012
Sacred Heart S 200/PK-8
322 W Maple St 60148 630-629-0536
Joseph Benning, prin. Fax 629-4752
St. John Lutheran S 200/PK-8
215 S Lincoln St 60148 630-932-3196
John Aurich, prin. Fax 932-4016
St. Pius X S 400/PK-8
601 Westmore Meyers Rd 60148 630-627-2353
Daniel Flaherty, prin. Fax 627-1810
Trinity Lutheran S 50/PK-8
1008 E Roosevelt Rd Ste 2 60148 630-627-5601
Kenneth Krohse, prin. Fax 627-5676

London Mills, Fulton, Pop. 440
Spoon River Valley CUSD 4 500/PK-12
35265 N IL Route 97 61544 309-778-2204
K. Scot Reynolds, supt. Fax 778-2655
www.spoon-river.k12.il.us
Spoon River Valley ES 200/PK-6
35265 N IL Route 97 61544 309-778-2207
Julie Deignan, prin. Fax 778-2655
Spoon River Valley JHS 100/7-8
35265 N IL Route 97 61544 309-778-2201
Chris Janssen, prin. Fax 778-2655

Long Grove, Lake, Pop. 7,833
Kildeer Countryside CCSD 96
Supt. — See Buffalo Grove
Country Meadows ES 400/1-5
6360 Gilmer Rd 60047 847-353-8600
Jeffrey Brown, prin. Fax 949-8233
Kildeer Countryside ES 500/1-5
3100 Old McHenry Rd 60047 847-634-3243
Heather Frizellie, prin. Fax 229-7570
Woodlawn MS 700/6-8
6362 Gilmer Rd 60047 847-353-8500
Greg Grana, prin. Fax 949-8237

Montessori S of Long Grove 100/PK-6
1115 RFD 60047 847-634-0430
Lyn Pearson, prin. Fax 726-7928

Loraine, Adams, Pop. 359
CUSD 4
Supt. — See Mendon
Loraine ES 100/PK-K
307 N Main St 62349 217-938-4400
Jim Sohn, prin. Fax 938-4402

Lostant, LaSalle, Pop. 481
Lostant Community Unit SD 425 100/K-8
PO Box 320 61334 815-368-3392
Dr. Susan Smith, supt. Fax 368-3132
www.lostant.k12.il.us
Lostant S 100/K-8
PO Box 320 61334 815-368-3392
Dr. Susan Smith, prin. Fax 368-3132

Louisville, Clay, Pop. 1,256
North Clay CUSD 25 700/PK-12
PO Box C 62858 618-665-3358
Monty Aldrich, supt. Fax 665-3893
North Clay S, PO Box 279 62858 500/PK-8
Julie Healy, prin. 618-665-3393

Love Joy, Saint Clair, Pop. 1,099
Brooklyn Unit SD 188 200/PK-12
PO Box 250, 618-271-1028
Dr. Raelynn Parks, supt. Fax 271-9108
www.lovejoy.stclair.k12.il.us
Lovejoy ES 100/PK-5
PO Box 250, 618-271-1014
Catherine Calvert, prin. Fax 271-9108
Lovejoy MS 50/6-8
PO Box 250, 618-271-1014
Dr. Raelynn Parks, prin. Fax 271-9108

Loves Park, Winnebago, Pop. 22,983
Harlem Unit SD 122
Supt. — See Machesney Park
Harlem MS 1,300/7-8
735 Windsor Rd 61111 815-654-4510
John Cusimano, prin. Fax 654-4540
Loves Park ES 400/1-6
344 Grand Ave 61111 815-654-4501
Lisa Clark, prin. Fax 654-4553
Maple ES 400/1-6
1405 Maple Ave 61111 815-654-4502
Becky Girard, prin. Fax 654-4563
Rock Cut ES 500/1-6
7944 Forest Hills Rd 61111 815-654-4506
Jean Akright, prin. Fax 654-4574
Windsor ES 400/1-6
935 Windsor Rd 61111 815-654-4507
Bob Buck, prin. Fax 654-4585

St. Bridget S 400/K-8
604 Clifford Ave 61111 815-633-8255
Roberta Gille, prin. Fax 633-5847

Lovington, Moultrie, Pop. 1,196
Lovington CUSD 303 300/PK-12
445 E Church St 61937 217-873-4310
Roy Smith, supt. Fax 873-5311
www.lovington.k12.il.us/
Lovington S 200/PK-8
330 S High St 61937 217-873-4318
Kyle VonSchnase, prin. Fax 873-6120

Ludlow, Champaign, Pop. 370
Ludlow CCSD 142 100/K-8
PO Box 130 60949 217-396-5261
Drusilla Lobmaster, supt. Fax 396-8858
ludlowgradeschool.com
Ludlow S 100/K-8
PO Box 130 60949 217-396-5261
Drusilla Lobmaster, prin. Fax 396-8858

Lyons, Cook, Pop. 10,466
Lyons SD 103 2,200/K-8
4100 Joliet Ave 60534 708-783-4100
Dr. Michael Warner, supt. Fax 780-9725
www.sd103.com/
Costello ES 300/K-5
4632 Clyde Ave 60534 708-783-4300
Andrea Maslan, prin. Fax 656-2275
Robinson ES 300/K-5
4431 Gage Ave 60534 708-783-4700
Alberto Molina, prin. Fax 780-0172
Washington MS 700/6-8
8101 Ogden Ave 60534 708-783-4200
Michael Kent, prin. Fax 780-9757
Other Schools – See Brookfield, Stickney

Mc Clure, Union
Shawnee CUSD 84
Supt. — See Wolf Lake
Shawnee ES South 100/K-5
Highway 3 S 62957 618-661-1504
Amy Reynolds, prin. Fax 661-1026

Mc Henry, McHenry, Pop. 19,144
Mc Henry CCSD 15 4,800/PK-8
1011 N Green St, 815-385-7210
R. Alan Hoffman Ed.D., supt. Fax 344-7121
www.d15.org
Duker ES 500/4-5
3711 W Kane Ave, 815-344-7125
Debra Holliday, prin. Fax 363-5024
Edgebrook ES 500/PK-3
701 N Green St, 815-385-3123
Michelle Reinhardt, prin. Fax 363-5025
Hilltop ES 500/K-3
2615 W Lincoln Rd, 815-385-4421
Roseann Basford, prin. Fax 363-5027
Landmark ES 200/K-5
3614 Waukegan Rd, 815-385-8120
Bill Burke, prin. Fax 363-5026
Mc Henry MS 900/6-8
2120 W Lincoln Rd, 815-385-2522
Josh Reitz, prin. Fax 578-2101
Parkland S 800/6-8
1802 N Ringwood Rd, 815-385-8810
Mike Adams, prin. Fax 363-5023
Riverwood ES 800/K-5
300 S Driftwood Trl, 815-344-7130
Kathie Robinson, prin. Fax 363-5021
Valley View ES 600/K-5
6515 W IL Route 120, 815-385-0640
Jon Schleusner, prin. Fax 363-5022

Montini MS 300/4-8
1405 N Richmond Rd, 815-385-1022
Sheila Murphy, prin. Fax 363-7536
Montini Primary Catholic S 300/PK-3
3504 Washington St, 815-385-5380
Sheila Murphy, prin. Fax 385-5017
Zion Lutheran S 100/PK-4
4206 W Elm St, 815-385-4488
Pamela Brackmann, dir. Fax 385-0878

Machesney Park, Winnebago, Pop. 21,846
Harlem Unit SD 122 8,000/PK-12
8605 N 2nd St 61115 815-654-4500
Dr. Julie Morris, supt. Fax 654-4600
www.harlem.winbgo.k12.il.us
Machesney IS 500/4-6
8615 N 2nd St 61115 815-654-4509
Dr. Michael Scorzo, prin. Fax 637-7421
Marquette ES 400/PK-PK, 1-
8500 Victory Ln 61115 815-654-4503
Goldy Brown, prin. Fax 654-4565
Olson Park ES 400/1-6
1414 Minahan Dr 61115 815-654-4504
Jan Johnson, prin. Fax 654-4528
Parker Early Education Center 800/PK-K
808 Harlem Rd 61115 815-654-4559
Gail Lanigan, prin. Fax 654-4613
Ralston ES 500/1-6
710 Ralston Rd 61115 815-654-4505
Lisa Jackson, prin. Fax 654-4572
Other Schools – See Loves Park

Concordia Lutheran S 100/PK-8
7424 N 2nd St 61115 815-633-6450
Doris Holecek, prin. Fax 633-1345

Mackinaw, Tazewell, Pop. 1,614
Deer Creek-Mackinaw CUSD 701 1,000/PK-12
401 E 5th St 61755 309-359-8965
Steve Yarnall, supt. Fax 359-5291
www.deemack.org/
Deer Creek Mackinaw S 500/PK-8
PO Box 80 61755 309-359-4321
Christina Lammers, prin. Fax 359-4015
Other Schools – See Deer Creek

Mc Leansboro, Hamilton, Pop. 2,713
Hamilton County CUSD 10 1,300/PK-12
PO Box 369 62859 618-643-2328
Vince Mitchell, supt. Fax 643-2015
www.unit10.com
East Side ES 500/K-6
501 E Randolph St 62859 618-643-2328
Jackie Frey, prin. Fax 643-2070
Hamilton County Preschool 100/PK-PK
204 W Cherry St 62859 618-643-2328
Christina Epperson, prin. Fax 643-5304
Other Schools – See Dahlgren

Mc Nabb, Putnam, Pop. 296
Putnam County CUSD 535
Supt. — See Granville
Putnam County JHS 300/5-8
13183 N 350th Ave 61335 815-882-2116
Carl Carlson, prin. Fax 882-2118

Macomb, McDonough, Pop. 18,587
Macomb CUSD 185 1,900/PK-12
323 W Washington St 61455 309-833-4161
Dr. Alene Reuschel, supt. Fax 836-2133
district185.macomb.com/
Edison ES 400/4-6
521 S Pearl St 61455 309-837-3993
Maureen Hazell, prin. Fax 837-9992
Lincoln ES 500/K-3
315 N Bonham St 61455 309-833-2095
Rose Platt, prin. Fax 837-7802
MacArthur ECC 100/PK-PK
235 W Grant St 61455 309-833-4273
Kelly Carpenter, prin. Fax 833-5651
Macomb JHS 300/7-8
1525 S Johnson St 61455 309-833-2074
Dana Isackson, prin. Fax 836-1034

St. Paul S 100/K-6
322 W Washington St 61455 309-833-2470
Barbara Shrode, prin. Fax 833-2470

Macon, Macon, Pop. 1,151
Meridian CUSD 15 1,100/PK-12
PO Box 347 62544 217-764-5269
Dr. Frank Meyer, supt. Fax 764-5291
www.meridian.k12.il.us
Meridian PS 200/PK-2
PO Box 198 62544 217-764-3896
Frank Meyer, prin. Fax 764-3605
Other Schools – See Blue Mound

Madison, Madison, Pop. 4,558
Madison CUSD 12 1,000/PK-12
602 Farrish St 62060 618-877-1712
Dr. Sandra Schroeder, supt. Fax 877-2690
www.madisoncusd12.org/
Harris ES 300/K-3
1634 7th St 62060 618-877-6864
Valeska Hill, prin. Fax 451-2627
Long ES 200/4-5
1040 College St 62060 618-876-4818
Terrian Fennoy, prin. Fax 877-2696
Madison MS 300/PK-PK, 6-
1003 Farrish St 62060 618-876-6409
Timothy Miller, prin. Fax 877-2693

Mahomet, Champaign, Pop. 5,714
Mahomet-Seymour CUSD 3 2,800/PK-12
PO Box 229 61853 217-586-4995
Keith Oates, supt. Fax 586-5834
www.ms.k12.il.us
Lincoln Trail ES 600/3-5
PO Box 200 61853 217-586-2811
Mary Weaver, prin. Fax 586-5072
Mahomet-Seymour JHS 700/6-8
PO Box 560 61853 217-586-4415
Jeff Starwalt, prin. Fax 586-5869
Middletown ECC 200/PK-K
PO Box 229 61853 217-586-5833
Carol Shallenberger, prin. Fax 586-5834
Sangamon ES 400/1-2
PO Box 198 61853 217-586-4583
Mark Cabutti, prin. Fax 586-4849

Malden, Bureau, Pop. 339
Malden CCSD 84 100/PK-8
PO Box 216 61337 815-643-2436
Debra Dalton, supt. Fax 643-2132
Malden S 100/PK-8
PO Box 216 61337 815-643-2436
Debra Dalton, prin. Fax 643-2132

Malta, DeKalb, Pop. 963
De Kalb CUSD 428
Supt. — See DeKalb
Malta ES 200/K-5
507 N 3rd St 60150 815-825-2082
Connie Rohlman, prin. Fax 825-2082
Wright ES 300/K-5
5068 IL Route 38 60150 815-825-2061
Gina Greenwald, prin. Fax 825-2830

Manhattan, Will, Pop. 5,169
Manhattan SD 114 1,200/PK-8
25440 S Gougar Rd 60442 815-478-6093
Howard Butters, supt. Fax 478-7660
www.manhattan114.org
Manhattan JHS 400/6-8
15606 W Smith Rd 60442 815-478-6090
Ron Pacheco, prin. Fax 478-6094
McDonald ES 400/3-5
200 2nd St 60442 815-478-3310
Ryan McWilliams, prin. Fax 478-4035
Wilson Creek ES 400/PK-2
25440 S Gougar Rd 60442 815-478-4527
Barbara Hogan, prin. Fax 478-6035

Peotone CUSD 207U
Supt. — See Peotone
Wilton Center ES 100/K-4
29520 S Cedar Rd 60442 815-478-3652
Tracy Hiller, prin. Fax 478-4462

St. Joseph S 200/PK-8
PO Box 70 60442 815-478-3951
John Garvey, prin. Fax 478-7412

Manito, Mason, Pop. 1,702
Midwest Central CUSD 191 1,200/PK-12
1010 S Washington St 61546 309-968-6868
Jerry Meyer, supt. Fax 968-7916
www.midwestcentral.org/
Midwest Central PS 500/PK-5
450 E Southmoor St 61546 309-968-6464
Steve McAdams, prin. Fax 968-7652
Other Schools – See Green Valley

Spring Lake CCSD 606 100/K-6
13650 N Manito Rd 61546 309-545-2241
William Reising, supt. Fax 545-2695
Spring Lake ES 100/K-6
13650 N Manito Rd 61546 309-545-2241
William Reising, prin. Fax 545-2695

Manlius, Bureau, Pop. 348
Bureau Valley CUSD 340 1,300/PK-12
PO Box 289 61338 815-445-3101
Terry Gutshall, supt. Fax 445-2802
www.bhsroe.k12.il.us/bureauvalley
Other Schools – See Buda, Walnut, Wyanet

Mansfield, Piatt, Pop. 939
Blue Ridge CUSD 18
Supt. — See Farmer City
Blue Ridge JHS 100/7-8
247 S McKinley St 61854 217-489-5201
John Weaver, prin. Fax 489-9051
Blue Ridge Mansfield ES 200/4-6
250 S McKinley St 61854 217-489-5291
John Weaver, prin. Fax 489-9396

Manteno, Kankakee, Pop. 7,955
Manteno CUSD 5 2,000/K-12
84 N Oak St 60950 815-928-7000
Dawn Russert, supt. Fax 468-6439
www.manteno5.org/
Manteno ES 500/2-4
555 W Cook St 60950 815-928-7200
Roger Schnitzler, prin. Fax 928-7299
Manteno MS 500/5-8
250 N Poplar St 60950 815-928-7154
David Conrad, prin. Fax 468-8082
Manteno PS 300/K-1
251 N Maple St 60950 815-928-7051
Joe Palicki, prin. Fax 468-3030

Maple Park, Kane, Pop. 1,132
Central CUSD 301
Supt. — See Burlington
Lily Lake ES 200/K-5
5N720 IL Route 47 60151 847-464-6011
Trent Lange, prin. Fax 365-2283

Kaneland CUSD 302 3,200/PK-12
47W326 Keslinger Rd 60151 630-365-5111
Dr. Charles McCormick, supt. Fax 365-9428
www.kaneland.org
Other Schools – See Elburn, Montgomery, Sugar Grove

Marengo, McHenry, Pop. 7,381
Marengo-Union Consolidated ESD 165 1,200/PK-8
816 E Grant Hwy 60152 815-568-8323
Lea Damisch, supt. Fax 568-8367
www.marengo.k12.il.us/
Locust ES 600/K-4
539 Locust St 60152 815-568-7632
Suellen Lopez, prin. Fax 568-1830
Marengo Community MS 600/PK-PK, 5-
816 E Grant Hwy 60152 815-568-5720
Tracy Beam, prin. Fax 568-7572

Riley CCSD 18 300/K-8
9406 Riley Rd 60152 815-568-8637
Jerry Trickett, supt. Fax 568-3709
www.riley18.org/
Riley Community Consolidated S 300/K-8
9406 Riley Rd 60152 815-568-8637
Christine Conkling, prin. Fax 568-3709

Zion Lutheran S 300/PK-8
408 Jackson St 60152 815-568-5156
William Steltenpohl, prin. Fax 568-0547

Marine, Madison, Pop. 940
Triad CUSD 2
Supt. — See Troy
Marine ES 200/PK-5
725 W Division St 62061 618-667-5404
Sandra Padak, prin. Fax 667-0285

Marion, Williamson, Pop. 17,104
Crab Orchard CUSD 3 400/PK-12
19189 Bailey St 62959 618-982-2181
Derek Hutchins, supt. Fax 982-2080
www.cocusd3.org/
Crab Orchard S 300/PK-8
19189 Bailey St 62959 618-982-2181
William McSparin, prin. Fax 982-2080

Marion CUSD 2 4,100/PK-12
1700 W Cherry St 62959 618-993-2321
J. Wade Hudgens, supt. Fax 997-0943
www.marionunit2.org/
Jefferson ES 300/K-5
700 E Boulevard St 62959 618-997-5766
John Fletcher, prin. Fax 993-3287
Lincoln ES 600/PK-5
400 Morningside Dr 62959 618-997-6063
Jane Stiritz, prin. Fax 997-0459
Longfellow ES 300/K-5
1400 W Hendrickson St 62959 618-993-3230
Amy Sanders, prin. Fax 997-8046
Marion JHS 800/6-8
1609 W Main St 62959 618-997-1317
Stuart Parks, prin. Fax 997-0477

Washington ES 700/PK-5
420 E Main St 62959 618-993-8534
Deborah Runion, prin. Fax 997-0460
Other Schools – See Creal Springs

Marion Adventist S 50/1-8
9314 Old Route 13 62959 618-997-4443

Marissa, Saint Clair, Pop. 2,044
Marissa CUSD 40 600/PK-12
215 North St 62257 618-295-2313
Kevin Cogdill, supt. Fax 295-2609
www.marissa40.org/
Marissa ES 400/PK-6
206 E Fulton St 62257 618-295-2339
David Deets, prin. Fax 295-3673

Markham, Cook, Pop. 12,304
Hazel Crest SD 152-5
Supt. — See Hazel Crest
Bunche ES 300/PK-4
16500 Park Ave, 708-333-6625
Julia Veazey, prin. Fax 333-6709
Frost MS 300/7-8
2206 W 167th St, 708-210-9929
Jacqueline Scott, prin. Fax 210-9582

Prairie-Hills ESD 144 3,200/PK-8
3015 W 163rd St 60428 708-210-2888
Dr. I.V. Foster, supt. Fax 210-9925
phsd144.net/
Markham Park ES 300/K-6
16239 Lawndale Ave, 708-210-2869
Claudett Taylor, prin. Fax 210-9201
Prairie-Hills JHS 700/7-8
3035 W 163rd St, 708-210-2860
Tiffany Burnett-Johnson, prin. Fax 210-9208
Primary Academic Center 200/K-3
3055 W 163rd St, 708-210-2866
Tyese Sims, prin. Fax 210-2208
Other Schools – See Country Club Hills, Hazel Crest, Oak Forest

---

Markham Lutheran S 50/PK-K
160th and Clifton Park Ave, 708-331-4885

Maroa, Macon, Pop. 1,563
Maroa-Forsyth CUSD 2 1,200/PK-12
PO Box 738 61756 217-794-3488
Mike Williams, supt. Fax 794-3878
www.mfschools.org/
Maroa-Forsyth IS 200/PK-PK, 4-
PO Box 738 61756 217-794-3882
Kathy Massey, prin. Fax 794-3878
Maroa-Forsyth MS 300/6-8
PO Box 738 61756 217-794-5115
Kathy Massey, prin. Fax 794-3351
Other Schools – See Forsyth

Marquette Heights, Tazewell, Pop. 2,826
North Pekin & Marquette Hts SD 102 700/PK-8
51 Yates Rd 61554 309-382-2172
Mike Dickson, supt. Fax 382-2122
www.tazewell.k12.il.us/dist102
Georgetowne MS 200/6-8
51 Yates Rd 61554 309-382-3456
Meredith Caudill, prin. Fax 382-2122
Marquette ES 300/PK-2
100 Joliet Rd 61554 309-382-3612
Jane Lewis, prin. Fax 382-2122
Rogers ES 200/3-5
109 Rogers Rd 61554 309-382-3401
Jane Lewis, prin. Fax 382-2122

Marseilles, LaSalle, Pop. 4,860
Marseilles ESD 150 600/PK-8
201 Chicago St 61341 815-795-2162
JoEllen Fuller, supt. Fax 795-3415
mes150.org
Marseilles S 600/PK-8
201 Chicago St 61341 815-795-2428
Jeff Owens, prin. Fax 795-3415

Miller Township CCSD 210 200/K-8
3197 E 28th Rd 61341 815-357-8151
Dr. Richard Peters, supt. Fax 357-8159
Pope S 200/K-8
3197 E 28th Rd 61341 815-357-8151
Nathaniel Pinter, prin. Fax 357-8159

Marshall, Clark, Pop. 3,724
Marshall CUSD 2C 1,400/PK-12
503 Pine St 62441 217-826-5912
Rick Manuell, supt. Fax 826-5170
www.marshall.k12.il.us/
Marshall JHS 200/7-8
806 N 6th St 62441 217-826-2812
Arlene Lindsay, prin. Fax 826-6065
North ES 400/3-6
1001 N 6th St 62441 217-826-2355
Clare Beaven, prin. Fax 826-6127
South ES 400/PK-2
805 S 6th St 62441 217-826-5041
Jenny Higginbotham, prin. Fax 826-5822

Martinsville, Clark, Pop. 1,230
Martinsville CUSD 3C 400/PK-12
PO Box K 62442 217-382-4321
Jill Rogers, supt. Fax 382-4183
www.martinsville.k12.il.us/
Martinsville ES 200/PK-6
PO Box 396 62442 217-382-4116
Vickie Norton, prin. Fax 382-5219
Martinsville JHS 50/7-8
PO Box K 62442 217-382-4132
Ray Schollenbruch, prin. Fax 382-4761

Maryville, Madison, Pop. 6,629
Collinsville CUSD 10
Supt. — See Collinsville
Maryville ES 500/PK-4
6900 W Main St 62062 618-346-6261
Joanna Luehmann, prin. Fax 343-2750

Maryville Christian S 100/K-6
7110 State Route 162 62062 618-667-8221
Angela Cox, dir. Fax 667-0650
St. John Neumann S 300/PK-8
142 Wilma Dr 62062 618-345-7230
Jack Holmes, prin. Fax 345-4350

Mascoutah, Saint Clair, Pop. 5,824
Mascoutah CUSD 19 2,800/PK-12
720 W Harnett St 62258 618-566-7414
Dr. Sam McGowen, supt. Fax 566-4507
www.mascoutah19.k12.il.us
Mascoutah ES 800/PK-5
533 N 6th St 62258 618-566-2152
Randy Blakely, prin. Fax 566-8543
Mascoutah MS 600/6-8
846 N 6th St 62258 618-566-2305
Bob Stone, prin. Fax 566-2307
Other Schools – See Scott AFB

Holy Childhood S 200/K-8
215 N John St 62258 618-566-2922
Ronald Karcher, prin. Fax 566-2720

Mason City, Mason, Pop. 2,473
Illini Central CUSD 189 900/PK-12
208 N West St 62664 217-482-5180
Patrick Martin, supt. Fax 482-3121
www.illinicentral.org
Illini Central ES 500/PK-5
208 N West St 62664 217-482-3269
Mark Caggiano, prin. Fax 482-3988
Illini Central MS 200/6-8
208 N West St 62664 217-482-3252
Ed Jodlowski, prin. Fax 482-3323

Matherville, Mercer, Pop. 780
Sherrard CUSD 200
Supt. — See Sherrard
Matherville IS 200/5-6
PO Box 639 61263 309-754-8244
Polly Dahlstrom, prin. Fax 754-8245

Matteson, Cook, Pop. 15,675
ESD 159 1,300/PK-8
6202 Vollmer Rd 60443 708-720-1300
Ronald Wynn, supt. Fax 720-3218
www.dist159.com
Powell MS 6-8
20600 Matteson Ave 60443 708-283-9600
Pamela Woods, prin. Fax 283-1885
Sieden Prairie ES 300/K-5
725 Notre Dame Dr 60443 708-720-2626
LaTonya McCaskill, prin. Fax 720-3209
Woodgate ES 300/PK-5
101 Central Ave 60443 708-720-1107
Nina King, prin. Fax 720-3225
Yates S 400/PK-5
6131 Allemong Dr 60443 708-720-1800
Lisa Woods, prin. Fax 720-0343
Other Schools – See Richton Park

Matteson ESD 162 3,200/PK-8
3625 215th St 60443 708-748-0100
Dr. Blondean Davis, supt. Fax 748-7302
www.sd162.org
Huth MS 700/7-8
3718 213th Pl 60443 708-748-0470
Ronald Jones, prin. Fax 503-1119
Matteson ES 600/K-3
21245 Main St 60443 708-748-0480
Patricia Fears, prin. Fax 503-0812
Other Schools – See Olympia Fields, Park Forest, Richton Park

---

St. Lawrence O'Toole S 300/PK-8
4101 Saint Lawrence Ave 60443 708-747-3322
Patricia Hofkamp, prin. Fax 747-4099
Zion Lutheran S 100/PK-8
3840 216th St 60443 708-747-7490
Virginia Terrell, prin. Fax 747-1194

Mattoon, Coles, Pop. 17,385
Mattoon CUSD 2 3,300/K-12
1701 Charleston Ave 61938 217-238-8850
Larry Lilly, supt. Fax 238-8855
www.mattoon.k12.il.us
Mattoon MS 700/6-8
1200 S 9th St 61938 217-238-5800
Jeremie Smith, prin. Fax 238-5805
Riddle ES 700/K-5
4201 Western Ave 61938 217-238-3800
Bruce Barnard, prin. Fax 238-3805
Williams ES 800/K-5
1709 S 9th St 61938 217-238-2800
Kris Maleske, prin. Fax 238-2805

St. John Lutheran S 300/PK-8
200 Charleston Ave 61938 217-234-4911
Fax 234-4925
St. Mary S 100/PK-8
2000 Richmond Ave 61938 217-235-0431
Michelle Buerster, prin. Fax 235-5447

Maywood, Cook, Pop. 25,777
Maywood-Melrose Park-Broadview SD 89
Supt. — See Melrose Park
Emerson S 400/K-8
311 Washington Blvd 60153 708-450-2002
Karen Petties, prin. Fax 338-3495
Garfield S 500/K-8
1514 S 9th Ave 60153 708-450-2009
Cheli Oswald, prin. Fax 344-0593
Irving S 500/K-8
805 S 17th Ave 60153 708-450-2015
Dr. Bonita Cosby, prin. Fax 343-0762
Lexington S 400/K-8
415 Lexington St 60153 708-450-2030
Louise Farrar, prin. Fax 344-1148

Lincoln S 700/K-8
811 Chicago Ave 60153 708-450-2036
Dr. Diane Weitzman, prin. Fax 344-0986
Washington S 400/K-8
1111 Washington Blvd 60153 708-450-2065
John Boyd, prin. Fax 344-1185

Mazon, Grundy, Pop. 918
Mazon-Verona-Kinsman ESD 2C 300/K-8
1013 North St 60444 815-448-2200
Nancy Dillow, supt. Fax 448-3005
www.mvkmavericks.org
Mazon-Verona-Kinsman ES 200/K-4
513 8th St 60444 815-448-2471
Cynthia Christensen, prin. Fax 448-2056
Mazon-Verona-Kinsman MS 100/5-8
1013 North St 60444 815-448-2127
Debra Paulsen, prin. Fax 448-3005

Media, Henderson, Pop. 122
West Central CUSD 235
Supt. — See Biggsville
West Central ECC 100/PK-PK
PO Box 750 61460 309-924-1826
Ralph Grimm, prin. Fax 924-2549

Medinah, DuPage, Pop. 2,512
Medinah SD 11
Supt. — See Roselle
Medinah IS 300/3-5
7N330 Medinah Rd 60157 630-529-6105
Dr. Kara Egger, prin. Fax 539-3812
Medinah PS 200/K-2
22W300 Sunnyside Rd 60157 630-529-9788
Rita Markgraf, prin. Fax 529-6304

Medinah Christian S 300/PK-8
900 Foster Ave 60157 630-980-9423
Ken Parris, admin. Fax 622-0124

Medora, Jersey, Pop. 498
Southwestern CUSD 9
Supt. — See Piasa
Medora ES 100/K-6
PO Box 178 62063 618-729-3231
Diane Milner, prin. Fax 729-4531

Melrose Park, Cook, Pop. 22,512
Bellwood SD 88
Supt. — See Bellwood
Grant ES 400/1-5
1300 N 34th Ave 60160 708-343-0410
Kim Ontiveros, prin. Fax 544-0021

Mannheim SD 83
Supt. — See Franklin Park
Mannheim JHS 900/6-8
2600 Hyde Park Ave 60164 847-455-5020
Timothy Daley, prin. Fax 455-2038
Scott ES 500/K-5
2250 Scott St 60164 847-455-4818
Carrie Novak, prin. Fax 455-2039

Maywood-Melrose Park-Broadview SD 89 5,500/PK-8
906 Walton St 60160 708-450-2460
Dr. Thea Perkins, supt. Fax 450-2461
www.maywood89.org/
Addams S 400/K-8
910 Division St 60160 708-450-2023
Frank Mikl, prin. Fax 344-0982
Melrose Park S 1,000/K-8
1715 W Lake St 60160 708-450-2042
Wanda Carrasquillo, prin. Fax 344-1162
Stevenson S 800/K-8
1630 N 20th Ave 60160 708-450-2053
Janet Kostelaz, prin. Fax 344-1356
Other Schools – See Broadview, Maywood

Sacred Heart S 100/PK-8
815 N 16th Ave 60160 708-681-0240
Barbara Ciconte, prin. Fax 681-0454
St. Paul Lutheran S 200/PK-8
1025 W Lake St 60160 708-343-5000
Douglas Grebasch, prin. Fax 343-8635

Mendon, Adams, Pop. 875
CUSD 4 700/PK-12
PO Box 200 62351 217-936-2111
Diane Robertson, supt. Fax 936-2643
www.cusd4.com
Mendon ES 100/1-2
PO Box 197 62351 217-936-2512
Theresa Fessler, prin. Fax 936-2124
Unity MS 200/5-8
PO Box 200 62351 217-936-2727
Brad Gooding, prin. Fax 936-2730
Other Schools – See Loraine, Ursa

Mendota, LaSalle, Pop. 7,077
Mendota CCSD 289 1,300/PK-8
1806 Guiles Ave 61342 815-539-7631
Marcia Burress, supt. Fax 538-2927
www.m289.lasall.k12.il.us/
Blackstone S 300/K-1
1309 Jefferson St 61342 815-539-6888
Stacy Kelly, prin. Fax 539-2370
Lincoln ES 300/2-3
805 4th Ave 61342 815-538-6226
Vicki Johnson, prin. Fax 539-5757
Northbrook S 800/PK-PK, 4-
1804 Guiles Ave 61342 815-539-6237
Cindy Pozzi, prin. Fax 538-3090

Holy Cross S 100/PK-8
1008 Jefferson St 61342 815-539-7003
Anita Kobilsek, prin. Fax 539-9082

Meredosia, Morgan, Pop. 996
Meredosia-Chambersburg CUSD 11 300/PK-12
PO Box 440 62665 217-584-1744
Eugene Link, supt. Fax 584-1129

Meredosia-Chambersburg ES 100/PK-5
PO Box 440 62665 217-584-1355
Eugene Link, prin. Fax 584-1129
Meredosia-Chambersburg JHS 100/6-8
PO Box 440 62665 217-584-1291
Janet Gladu, prin. Fax 584-1741

Merrionette Park, Cook, Pop. 2,047
Atwood Heights SD 125
Supt. — See Alsip
Meadow Lane IS 200/3-5
11800 S Meadow Lane Dr 60803 708-388-6958
Mark Flood, prin. Fax 388-6983

Metamora, Woodford, Pop. 3,067
Metamora CCSD 1 800/PK-8
PO Box 552 61548 309-367-2361
Trish Jackson, supt. Fax 367-2364
mgs.metamora.k12.il.us/
Metamora S 800/PK-8
PO Box 552 61548 309-367-2361
Cathy Costello, prin. Fax 367-2364

St. Mary S 100/K-8
PO Box 860 61548 309-367-2528
Ryan Bustle, prin. Fax 367-2169

Metropolis, Massac, Pop. 6,468
Joppa-Maple Grove CUSD 38
Supt. — See Joppa
Maple Grove ES 200/PK-6
1698 Grand Chain Rd 62960 618-543-7434
Vickie Artman, prin. Fax 543-7486

Massac Unit SD 1 2,300/PK-12
PO Box 530 62960 618-524-9376
William Hatfield, supt. Fax 524-4432
www.unit1.massac.k12.il.us/
Franklin ES 200/PK-6
1006 Mount Mission Rd 62960 618-524-2243
Pat Windhorst, prin. Fax 524-2725
Jefferson S 200/K-8
4915 Jefferson School Rd 62960 618-524-4390
Pat Windhorst, prin. Fax 524-3019
Massac JHS 300/7-8
PO Box 331 62960 618-524-2645
J.R. Conkle, prin. Fax 524-2765
Metropolis ES 600/PK-6
1015 Filmore St 62960 618-524-4821
Will Black, prin. Fax 524-2278
Other Schools – See Brookport

Middletown, Logan, Pop. 433
New Holland-Middletown ESD 88 100/PK-8
75 1250th St 62666 217-445-2421
Dr. Terrence Scandrett, supt. Fax 445-2632
newholland.il.schoolwebpages.com/
New Holland-Middletown S 100/PK-8
75 1250th St 62666 217-445-2656
Dr. Terrence Scandrett, prin. Fax 445-2632

Midlothian, Cook, Pop. 13,949
Midlothian SD 143 2,000/PK-8
14959 Pulaski Rd 60445 708-388-6450
Michael Hollingsworth, supt. Fax 388-4793
www.msd143.org
Central Park S 700/PK-8
3621 151st St 60445 708-385-0045
Marsha Amraen, prin. Fax 385-7063
Spaulding ES 100/PK-3
14811 Turner Ave 60445 708-385-4546
Linda McGlynn, prin. Fax 385-7406
Springfield ES 400/PK-6
14620 Springfield Ave 60445 708-388-4121
Colleen Sjostrom, prin. Fax 388-3307
Other Schools – See Crestwood

St. Christopher S 200/PK-8
14611 Keeler Ave 60445 708-385-8776
Michael Johnson, prin. Fax 385-8102

Milan, Rock Island, Pop. 5,237
Rock Island SD 41
Supt. — See Rock Island
Jefferson ES 400/K-6
1307 4th St W 61264 309-793-5985
Michael Nitzel, prin. Fax 793-5986

Sherrard CUSD 200
Supt. — See Sherrard
Coyne Center ES 100/PK-PK
11310 16th St 61264 309-787-1512
Kim Hofmann, prin. Fax 787-1538

Milford, Iroquois, Pop. 1,310
Milford CCSD 280 500/PK-8
PO Box 304 60953 815-889-5176
Dale Hastings, supt. Fax 889-5221
www.milford.k12.il.us/
Milford S 300/PK-8
PO Box 228 60953 815-889-4174
David Caldwell, prin. Fax 889-5503
Other Schools – See Sheldon

St. Paul Lutheran S 100/PK-8
108 W Woodworth Rd 60953 815-889-4209
Karen Borgers, prin. Fax 889-4364

Millbrook, Kendall, Pop. 303
Newark CCSD 66
Supt. — See Newark
Millbrook JHS 100/5-8
PO Box 214 60536 630-553-5435
Richard Sjolund, prin. Fax 553-1027

Milledgeville, Carroll, Pop. 946
Chadwick-Milledgeville CUSD 399
Supt. — See Chadwick
Milledgeville ES 200/PK-3
PO Box 609 61051 815-225-7141
Tim Schurman, prin. Fax 225-7847

Millstadt, Saint Clair, Pop. 3,067
Millstadt CCSD 160 900/PK-8
116 N Monroe St 62260 618-476-1803
Allen Scharf, supt. Fax 476-1893
www.millstadt.stclair.k12.il.us
Millstadt PS 300/PK-2
105 W Parkview Dr 62260 618-476-7100
Kevin Juhas, prin. Fax 476-7182
Millstadt S 600/3-8
211 W Mill St 62260 618-476-1681
Gary Huwer, prin. Fax 476-3401

St. James S 100/PK-8
412 W Washington St 62260 618-476-3510
Rebecca Chell, prin. Fax 476-1281

Minier, Tazewell, Pop. 1,255
Olympia CUSD 16
Supt. — See Stanford
Olympia West ES 300/PK-5
302 N School St 61759 309-392-2671
Nicole Rummel, prin. Fax 392-2497

Minonk, Woodford, Pop. 2,158
Fieldcrest CUSD 6 1,300/PK-12
1 Dornbush Dr 61760 309-432-2177
Randy Vincent, supt. Fax 432-3377
www.fieldcrest.k12.il.us/
Fieldcrest ES South 300/PK-4
523 Johnson St 61760 309-432-2838
Dorrene Sokn, prin. Fax 432-2192
Other Schools – See Toluca, Wenona

Minooka, Grundy, Pop. 8,403
Minooka CCSD 201 2,700/PK-8
PO Box 467 60447 815-467-6121
Al Gegenheimer, supt. Fax 467-9544
www.min201.org/
Aux Sable ES 600/1-4
1004 Misty Creek Dr 60447 815-467-5301
Sam Martin, prin. Fax 467-2166
Minooka ES 500/K-4
400 W Coady Dr 60447 815-467-2261
Natalie Baxter, prin. Fax 467-9544
Minooka IS 100/5-6
321 W McEvilly Rd 60447 815-467-4692
Harold King, prin. Fax 467-3120
Minooka JHS 700/PK-PK, 7-
333 W McEvilly Rd 60447 815-467-2136
D.J. Skogsberg, prin. Fax 467-5087
Other Schools – See Joliet, Shorewood

Mokena, Will, Pop. 17,396
Mokena SD 159 2,300/PK-8
11244 Willow Crest Ln 60448 708-342-4900
Dr. Gary Bradbury, supt. Fax 479-3143
www.mokena159.com
Mokena ES 900/PK-3
11244 Willow Crest Ln 60448 708-342-4850
Steve Stein, prin. Fax 479-3120
Mokena IS 500/4-5
11331 195th St 60448 708-342-4860
Michael Krugman, prin. Fax 479-3103
Mokena JHS 800/6-8
19815 Kirkstone Way 60448 708-342-4870
Julia Wheaton, prin. Fax 479-3122

Summit Hill SD 161
Supt. — See Frankfort
Arbury Hills ES 300/1-4
19651 Beechnut Dr 60448 708-479-2106
Dawn Schiro, prin. Fax 464-2249

Noonan Elementary Academy 500/PK-8
19131 Henry Dr 60448 708-479-8988
Dr. Roberta Noonan, prin. Fax 479-6859
St. Mary S 400/K-8
11409 195th St 60448 708-479-3383
Judy Rozgo, prin. Fax 326-9331

Moline, Rock Island, Pop. 42,892
Moline Unit SD 40 7,400/PK-12
1619 11th Ave 61265 309-743-1600
Dr. Cal Lee, supt. Fax 757-3476
www.molineschools.org
Addams ES 300/K-6
3520 53rd St 61265 309-743-1601
Teresa Landon, prin. Fax 757-3580
Butterworth ES 400/K-6
4205 48th St 61265 309-743-1604
Craig Ghinazzi, prin. Fax 757-3503
Deere MS 600/7-8
2035 11th St 61265 309-743-1622
Carl Johnson, prin. Fax 757-3668
Ericsson ES 200/K-6
335 5th Ave 61265 309-743-1606
Juanita Terronez, prin. Fax 757-3508
Franklin ES 300/K-6
5312 11th Avenue C 61265 309-743-1607
Todd DeTaeye, prin. Fax 736-2231
Garfield ES 300/K-6
1518 25th Ave 61265 309-743-1608
Todd Williams, prin. Fax 757-3589
Hamilton ES 200/K-6
700 32nd Ave 61265 309-743-1610
Victoria Diamond-Bohlman, prin. Fax 757-3669
Jefferson ECC 200/PK-PK
3010 26th Ave 61265 309-757-1894
Rachel Fowler, prin. Fax 757-1895
Lincoln-Irving ES 500/K-6
1015 16th Ave 61265 309-743-1612
Faith Carter, prin. Fax 757-3584
Logan ES 500/K-6
1602 25th St 61265 309-743-1613
Marabeth Robertson, prin. Fax 757-3583
Roosevelt ES 300/PK-6
3530 Avenue of the Cities 61265 309-743-1617
Sandra Malahy, prin. Fax 757-3521
Washington ES 300/K-6
1550 41st St 61265 309-743-1619
Tammy Murphy-Flynn, prin. Fax 757-3665

Willard ES 200/K-6
1616 16th St 61265 309-743-1620
Michael Resler, prin. Fax 736-2230
Wilson MS 600/7-8
1301 48th St 61265 309-743-1623
Robert Benson, prin. Fax 757-3586
Other Schools – See Coal Valley

St. Paul Lutheran S 50/PK-8
153 19th Ave 61265 309-762-4494
Robert Pagel, prin. Fax 762-5927
Seton Catholic S 500/PK-8
1320 16th Ave 61265 309-757-5500
Jane Barrett, prin. Fax 762-0545
Temple Christian Academy 100/PK-8
2305 7th Ave 61265 309-764-1302
Connie Drumm, admin. Fax 764-0931
Villa Montessori S 200/PK-6
2100 48th St 61265 309-764-7047
Renee Detloff, prin. Fax 764-9925

Momence, Kankakee, Pop. 3,066
Momence CUSD 1 1,300/PK-12
415 N Dixie Hwy 60954 815-472-3501
Dr. Phillip Smith, supt. Fax 472-3516
www.momence.k12.il.us
Je-Neir ES 300/1-4
1001 W 2nd St 60954 815-472-6646
David Sikma, prin. Fax 472-9822
Momence JHS 400/5-8
801 W 2nd St 60954 815-472-4184
Sheila Brown, prin. Fax 472-3517
Range K 200/PK-K
415 N Dixie Hwy 60954 815-472-4045
David Sikma, prin. Fax 472-3516

St. Patrick Academy 100/PK-8
404 W 2nd St 60954 815-472-2469
Richard Preston, prin. Fax 472-3043
Unity Christian S 50/PK-8
920 W 2nd St 60954 815-472-3230
Michael Van Someren, prin. Fax 472-0325

Monee, Will, Pop. 4,629
Crete-Monee CUSD 201U
Supt. — See Crete
Monee ES 500/K-5
25425 S Will Center Rd 60449 708-672-2655
JoAnn Jones, prin. Fax 534-3691

Monmouth, Warren, Pop. 9,198
Monmouth-Roseville CUSD 238 1,700/PK-12
401 E 2nd Ave 61462 309-734-4712
Martin Payne, supt. Fax 734-4755
titans.k12.il.us/district/
Central ECC, 401 E 2nd Ave 61462 PK-PK
Martin Payne, prin. 309-734-2213
Harding PS 200/K-3
415 E 9th Ave 61462 309-734-4915
Sue Wilson, prin. Fax 734-5221
Lincoln IS 300/4-6
325 S 11th St 61462 309-734-2222
Mike Owen, prin. Fax 734-6712
Willits PS 200/K-3
105 N E St 61462 309-734-4031
Cynthia Fisher, prin. Fax 734-4495
Other Schools – See Roseville

United CUSD 304
Supt. — See Alexis
United ES - West 200/PK-5
2140 State Highway 135 61462 309-734-8513
Dan Renwick, prin. Fax 734-8515
United JHS 100/6-8
2140 State Highway 135 61462 309-734-8511
Kristen Nelson, prin. Fax 734-6094

Immaculate Conception S 100/K-8
111 N B St 61462 309-734-6037
Kathryn Bennett, prin. Fax 734-6082

Monroe Center, Ogle, Pop. 504
Meridian CUSD 223
Supt. — See Stillman Valley
Monroe Center ES 500/K-K, 3-5
PO Box 360 61052 815-393-4424
Adam Zurko, prin. Fax 393-4530

Montgomery, Kane, Pop. 11,959
Aurora West Unit SD 129
Supt. — See Aurora
Nicholson ES 400/K-5
649 N Main St 60538 630-301-5013
Brett Burton, prin. Fax 844-4616

Kaneland CUSD 302
Supt. — See Maple Park
McDole ES 500/PK-5
2901 Foxmoor Dr 60538 630-897-1961
M. McCoy, prin. Fax 897-3229

Oswego CUSD 308
Supt. — See Oswego
Boulder Hill ES 600/K-5
163 Boulder Hill Pass 60538 630-636-2900
Jeff Schafermeyer, prin. Fax 897-0611
Lakewood Creek ES 700/K-5
2301 Lakewood Crk 60538 630-636-3200
David Brusak, prin. Fax 859-9151
Long Beach ES 600/PK-5
67 Longbeach Rd 60538 630-636-3300
Kevin Lipke, prin. Fax 892-1662

St. Luke's Lutheran S 300/PK-8
63 Fernwood Rd 60538 630-892-0310
Ruth Voss, prin. Fax 892-9320

Monticello, Piatt, Pop. 5,275
Monticello CUSD 25 1,400/PK-12
2 Sage Dr 61856 217-762-8511
Dr. Victor Zimmerman, supt. Fax 762-8534
www.sages.us/

Lincoln ES 200/PK-1
700 N Buchanan St 61856 217-762-8511
Mary Vogt, prin. Fax 762-2733
Monticello MS 400/6-8
2015 E Washington St 61856 217-762-8511
Jeanne Handley, prin. Fax 762-7765
Washington ES 300/4-5
3 Sage Dr 61856 217-762-8511
Brad Auten, prin. Fax 762-8508
Other Schools – See White Heath

Monticello Christian Academy 100/PK-8
PO Box 48 61856 217-762-3544
Randy Hinshaw, admin. Fax 762-9579

Montrose, Jasper, Pop. 263
Jasper County CUSD 1
Supt. — See Newton
Grove ES 100/K-6
5251 E 1800th Ave 62445 217-683-2622
Craig Carr, prin. Fax 683-2304

Mooseheart, Kane

Mooseheart S 200/PK-12
255 W James J Davis Ave 60539 630-906-3646
Scott Hart, dir. Fax 906-3617

Moro, Madison
Bethalto CUSD 8
Supt. — See Bethalto
Meadowbrook IS 200/4-5
111 W Roosevelt Dr 62067 618-377-7270
Jill Griffin, prin. Fax 377-7294

Edwardsville CUSD 7
Supt. — See Edwardsville
Midway ES 200/PK-2
6321 Midway Dr 62067 618-692-7446
Mary Miller, prin. Fax 377-2577

Morris, Grundy, Pop. 12,939
Morris SD 54 1,300/PK-8
54 White Oak Dr 60450 815-942-0056
Dr. Dennis Broniecki, supt. Fax 942-0240
dist54.mornet.org
Shabbona MS 400/6-8
725 School St Ste A 60450 815-942-3605
Sheryl Dzuryak, prin. Fax 941-4531
White Oak ES 800/PK-5
2001 Dupont Ave 60450 815-942-0047
Jim Carter, prin. Fax 318-6900

Nettle Creek CCSD 24 C 100/K-8
8820 Scott School Rd 60450 815-942-0511
Peter Pasteris, supt. Fax 942-9124
Erienna ES 50/K-2
8820 Scott School Rd 60450 815-942-5006
Peter Pasteris, prin.
Nettle Creek MS 100/3-8
8820 Scott School Rd 60450 815-942-0511
Peter Pasteris, prin. Fax 942-9124

Saratoga CCSD 60C 700/PK-8
4040 Division St 60450 815-942-2128
Kathy Perry, supt. Fax 942-0301
saratoga.mornet.org
Saratoga S 700/PK-8
4040 Division St 60450 815-942-2128
Liz Peterson, prin. Fax 942-0301

Immaculate Conception S 300/PK-8
505 E North St 60450 815-942-4111
Kim DesLauriers, prin. Fax 942-5094

Morrison, Whiteside, Pop. 4,318
Morrison CUSD 6 1,200/PK-12
643 Genesee Ave 61270 815-772-2064
Dr. Suellen Girard, supt. Fax 772-4644
www.morrisonschools.org
Morrison JHS 300/6-8
300 Academic Dr 61270 815-772-7264
Darryl Hogue, prin. Fax 772-2531
Northside ES 300/PK-2
520 N Genesee St 61270 815-772-2153
Amy Heusinkveld, prin. Fax 772-4952
Southside ES 200/3-5
100 Academic Dr 61270 815-772-2183
Amy Heusinkveld, prin. Fax 772-2371

Morrisonville, Christian, Pop. 1,050
Morrisonville CUSD 1 400/PK-12
PO Box 13 62546 217-526-4431
Wesley Wells, supt. Fax 526-4433
www.mohawks.net/
Morrisonville ES 200/PK-6
PO Box 13 62546 217-526-4441
Fax 526-4433
Morrisonville JHS 100/7-8
PO Box 13 62546 217-526-4432
Ann Little, prin. Fax 526-4452

Morton, Tazewell, Pop. 15,761
Morton CUSD 709 2,700/PK-12
1050 S 4th Ave Ste 200 61550 309-263-2581
Dr. Roger Kilpatrick, supt. Fax 266-6320
www.morton709.org
Brown ES 300/K-6
2550 N Morton Ave 61550 309-266-5309
Robert Bardwell, prin. Fax 263-7986
Grundy ES 300/K-6
1100 S 4th Ave 61550 309-263-1421
Michael Saunders, prin. Fax 263-8120
Jefferson ES 300/K-6
220 E Jefferson St 61550 309-263-2650
Lorna Sherwood, prin. Fax 284-3031
Lincoln ES 400/PK-6
100 S Nebraska Ave 61550 309-266-6989
Sheila Taylor, prin. Fax 263-7877
Morton JHS 500/7-8
225 E Jackson St 61550 309-266-6522
Greg Crider, prin. Fax 284-5031

Bethel Lutheran S 400/PK-8
325 E Queenwood Rd 61550 309-266-6592
John Jacob, prin. Fax 266-8510
Blessed Sacrament S 200/K-8
233 E Greenwood St 61550 309-263-8442
James Eckhart, prin. Fax 263-8443

Morton Grove, Cook, Pop. 22,202
East Maine SD 63
Supt. — See Des Plaines
Melzer ES 400/PK-6
9400 Oriole Ave 60053 847-965-7474
Scott Paul, prin. Fax 965-0539

Golf ESD 67 500/K-8
9401 Waukegan Rd 60053 847-966-8200
Greg Buchanan, supt. Fax 966-8290
www.golf67.net
Golf MS 300/5-8
9401 Waukegan Rd 60053 847-965-3740
Terry Baranowski, prin. Fax 966-9493
Hynes ES 300/K-4
9000 Belleforte Ave 60053 847-965-4500
Carol Westley, prin. Fax 965-4565

Morton Grove SD 70 800/K-8
6200 Lake St 60053 847-965-6200
Dr. Gary Zabilka, supt. Fax 965-6234
www.parkview70.net
Park View S 800/K-8
6200 Lake St 60053 847-965-6200
Susan Wings, prin. Fax 965-0606

Skokie SD 69
Supt. — See Skokie
Edison S 500/3-5
8200 Gross Point Rd 60053 847-966-6210
Maura Zinni, prin. Fax 966-6236

Jerusalem Lutheran S 100/PK-8
6218 Capulina Ave 60053 847-965-4750
Michael Naumann, prin. Fax 965-4750
MCC Full Time S 300/PK-8
8601 Menard Ave 60053 847-470-8801
Fax 470-8873

Mossville, Peoria
Illinois Valley Central Unit SD 321
Supt. — See Chillicothe
Mossville S 700/PK-8
PO Box 178 61552 309-579-2328
Wendy Clary, prin. Fax 579-2168

Mounds, Pulaski, Pop. 1,008
Meridian CUSD 101 700/PK-12
208 Valley Rd 62964 618-342-6776
Dr. Yvonne Bullock, supt. Fax 342-6401
www.meridian101.com
Meridian S 500/PK-8
208 Valley Rd 62964 618-342-6773
Frank Ellis, prin. Fax 342-6613

Mount Carmel, Wabash, Pop. 7,690
Wabash CUSD 348 1,700/K-12
218 W 13th St 62863 618-262-4181
Tim Buss, supt. Fax 262-7912
Mount Carmel MS 400/6-8
1520 Poplar St 62863 618-262-5699
Rick Johnston, prin. Fax 263-9096
North Intermediate Center of Education 400/3-5
1300 N Walnut St 62863 618-263-3876
Mike Hays, prin. Fax 262-7189
South ES 300/K-2
715 W 9th St 62863 618-263-3851
Darlene Weir, prin. Fax 262-8094

St. Marys S 100/PK-8
417 Chestnut St 62863 618-263-3183
Alice Wirth, prin. Fax 263-3596

Mount Carroll, Carroll, Pop. 1,704
West Carroll CUSD 314
Supt. — See Thomson
West Carroll MS 300/6-8
633 S East St 61053 815-244-2002
Jeanette Ashby, prin. Fax 244-1051

Mount Erie, Wayne, Pop. 103
North Wayne CUSD 200
Supt. — See Cisne
Mount Erie ES 100/K-4
RR 1 Box 1 62446 618-854-2611
Donna Williams, prin. Fax 854-2600

Mount Morris, Ogle, Pop. 3,066
Oregon CUSD 220
Supt. — See Oregon
Rahn JHS 300/7-8
105 W Brayton Rd 61054 815-734-6134
Jeff Fitzpatrick, prin. Fax 734-7129

Mount Olive, Macoupin, Pop. 2,100
Mount Olive CUSD 5 600/PK-12
804 W Main St 62069 217-999-7831
Chad Allison, supt. Fax 999-2150
www.schools.lth5.k12.il.us/mtolive/
Mount Olive S, 804 W Main St 62069 400/PK-8
Doug Smith, prin. 217-999-4241

Mount Prospect, Cook, Pop. 54,482
CCSD 59
Supt. — See Arlington Heights
Forest View ES 400/PK-5
1901 W Estates Dr 60056 847-593-4359
Margaret Weickert, prin. Fax 593-4360
Frost ES 400/K-5
1308 S Cypress Dr 60056 847-593-4378
Thomas Seaton, prin. Fax 593-4365
Holmes JHS 400/6-8
1900 W Lonnquist Blvd 60056 847-593-4390
Robert Bohanek, prin. Fax 593-7386

Jay ES 400/PK-5
1835 W Pheasant Trl 60056 847-593-4385
Megan Hernandez, prin. Fax 593-8656

Mount Prospect SD 57 1,800/PK-8
701 W Gregory St 60056 847-394-7300
Bruce Brown, supt. Fax 394-7311
www.dist57.org
Fairview ES 500/1-5
300 N Fairview St 60056 847-394-7320
April Jordan, prin. Fax 394-7328
Lincoln MS 700/6-8
700 W Lincoln St 60056 847-394-7350
Donald Angelaccio, prin. Fax 394-7358
Lions Park ES 500/1-5
300 E Council Trl 60056 847-394-7330
Kristine Gritzmacher, prin. Fax 394-7338
Westbrook S for Young Learners PK-K
103 S Busse Rd 60056 847-394-7340
Janet Ewing, prin. Fax 394-7349

River Trails SD 26 1,600/PK-8
1900 E Kensington Rd 60056 847-297-4120
Dane Delli Ph.D., supt. Fax 297-4124
www.rtsd26.org
Euclid ES 500/K-5
1211 N Wheeling Rd 60056 847-259-3303
Laura Gammons, prin. Fax 259-3395
Indian Grove ES 500/PK-5
1340 N Burning Bush Ln 60056 847-298-1976
Lynn Fisher, prin. Fax 298-3495
River Trails MS 600/6-8
1000 N Wolf Rd 60056 847-298-1750
Keir Rogers, prin. Fax 298-2639

Wheeling CCSD 21
Supt. — See Wheeling
Frost ES 600/PK-5
1805 N Aspen Dr 60056 847-803-4815
Rick Herrejon, prin. Fax 803-4855

St. Emily S 400/PK-8
1400 E Central Rd 60056 847-296-3490
Mary Hemmelman, prin. Fax 296-1155
St. Paul Lutheran S 300/PK-8
18 S School St 60056 847-255-6733
Jennifer Heinze, prin. Fax 255-6834
St. Raymond S 500/PK-8
300 S Elmhurst Ave 60056 847-253-8555
Dawn Kapka, admin. Fax 253-8939

Mount Pulaski, Logan, Pop. 1,632
Mount Pulaski CUSD 23 500/PK-12
119 N Garden St Ste 2 62548 217-792-7222
Philip Shelton, supt. Fax 792-5551
www.mtpulaski.k12.il.us
Mount Pulaski S 300/PK-8
119 N Garden St Ste 1 62548 217-792-7220
Gene Newton, prin. Fax 792-7221

Zion Lutheran S 100/PK-8
203 S Vine St 62548 217-792-5715
Kathy Maske, prin. Fax 792-5915

Mount Sterling, Brown, Pop. 2,011
Brown County CUSD 1 800/PK-12
503 NW Cross St 62353 217-773-3359
Merle Kenady, supt. Fax 773-2121
www.bchornets.com/
Brown County ES 300/PK-4
501 NW Cross St 62353 217-773-2624
Merle Kenady, prin. Fax 773-4471
Brown County MS 200/5-8
504 E Main St 62353 217-773-9152
Ben Ellefritz, prin. Fax 773-9121

St. Mary S 100/PK-8
408 W Washington St 62353 217-773-2825
Charlotte Kock, prin. Fax 773-2399

Mount Vernon, Jefferson, Pop. 16,344
Bethel SD 82 100/K-8
1201 Bethel Rd 62864 618-244-8095
Craig Kujawa, supt. Fax 244-8096
bethel.roe25.com/
Bethel S 100/K-8
1201 Bethel Rd 62864 618-244-8095
Craig Kujawa, prin. Fax 244-8096

Dodds CCSD 7 200/K-8
14975 E Bakerville Rd 62864 618-244-8070
Craig Clark, supt. Fax 244-8071
Dodds S 200/K-8
14975 E Bakerville Rd 62864 618-244-8070
Craig Clark, prin. Fax 244-8071

McClellan CCSD 12 100/K-8
9475 N IL Highway 148 62864 618-244-8072
Angela Mills, supt. Fax 244-8129
mcclellan.roe25.com/
McClellan S 100/K-8
9475 N IL Highway 148 62864 618-244-8072
Angela Mills, prin. Fax 244-8129

Mount Vernon CSD 80 1,800/PK-8
1722 Oakland Ave 62864 618-244-8080
Kevin Settle, supt. Fax 244-8082
district.mtv80.org
Buford Intermediate Education Ctr 300/4-5
623 S 34th St 62864 618-244-8064
Patrick Rice, prin. Fax 244-8103
Casey MS 500/6-8
1829 Broadway St 62864 618-244-8060
Mike Green, prin. Fax 244-8014
Franklin Early Education Ctr 300/PK-PK
500 Harrison St 62864 618-244-8087
Aletta Lawrence, prin. Fax 244-8088
Mount Vernon Primary Center 600/K-3
401 N 30th St 62864 618-244-8068
Dee Ann Schnautz, prin. Fax 244-8075

Summersville SD 79 300/K-8
1118 Fairfield Rd 62864 618-244-8079
Robert Danner, supt. Fax 244-8078
www.summersvilleschool.com
Summersville S 300/K-8
1118 Fairfield Rd 62864 618-244-8079
Robert Danner, prin. Fax 244-8078

St. Mary's S 200/K-8
1416 Main St 62864 618-242-5353
Brett Heinzman, prin. Fax 242-5365

Mount Zion, Macon, Pop. 5,032
Mount Zion CUSD 3 2,100/PK-12
455 Elm St 62549 217-864-2366
Darbe Brinkoetter, supt. Fax 864-2200
www.mtzion.k12.il.us
McGaughey ES 200/PK-1
1320 W Main St 62549 217-864-2711
Nancy Cooper, prin. Fax 864-4126
Mount Zion ES 100/2-3
725 W Main St 62549 217-864-3631
Gary Gruen, prin. Fax 864-6131
Mount Zion IS 500/4-6
310 S Henderson St 62549 217-864-2921
Randall Thacker, prin. Fax 864-5175
Mount Zion JHS 400/7-8
315 S Henderson St 62549 217-864-2369
Jerry Birkey, prin. Fax 864-6829

Moweaqua, Shelby, Pop. 1,845
Central A & M CUSD 21
Supt. — See Assumption
Gregory ES 200/K-5
221 E Pine St 62550 217-768-3860
David Fitzgerald, prin. Fax 768-3797

Mulberry Grove, Bond, Pop. 675
Mulberry Grove CUSD 1 400/PK-12
801 W Wall St 62262 618-326-8812
Gregory Irwin, supt. Fax 326-8482
www.mgschools.com/
Mulberry Grove ES 200/PK-6
801 W Wall St 62262 618-326-8811
Jim Rice, prin. Fax 326-8482
Mulberry Grove JHS 100/7-8
801 W Wall St 62262 618-326-8221
Ryan Bauer, dean Fax 326-8482

Mundelein, Lake, Pop. 32,774
Diamond Lake SD 76 1,300/PK-8
500 Acorn Ln 60060 847-566-9221
Dr. Roger Prosise, supt. Fax 566-5689
www.d76.lake.k12.il.us/
Diamond Lake ES 400/2-4
25807 N Diamond Lake Rd 60060 847-566-6601
Jodie Benton, prin. Fax 566-9851
Fairhaven ES 400/PK-1
634 Countryside Hwy 60060 847-949-0991
Michele Allen, prin. Fax 949-6720
West Oak MS 500/5-8
500 Acorn Ln 60060 847-566-9220
Christopher Willeford, prin. Fax 970-3534

Fremont SD 79 1,800/PK-8
28855 N Fremont Center Rd 60060 847-566-0169
Dr. Rick Taylor, supt. Fax 566-7280
www.fremont.lake.k12.il.us
Fremont ES 700/PK-2
28908 N Fremont Center Rd 60060 847-837-0437
Carol Bennett, prin. Fax 837-9540
Fremont IS 500/3-5
28754 N Fremont Center Rd 60060 847-388-3700
Patricia Reynolds, prin. Fax 388-6900
Fremont MS 700/6-8
28871 N Fremont Center Rd 60060 847-566-9384
Pam Motsenbocker, prin. Fax 566-7805

Mundelein ESD 75 2,100/PK-8
470 N Lake St 60060 847-949-2700
Cynthia Heidorn Ph.D., supt. Fax 949-2727
www.district75.org
Lincoln ES 400/2-5
200 W Maple Ave 60060 847-949-2720
Dr. Kathleen Miller, prin. Fax 949-2725
Mechanics Grove ES 500/2-5
1200 N Midlothian Rd 60060 847-949-2712
Dana Smith, prin. Fax 949-2711
Sandburg MS 700/6-8
855 W Hawley St 60060 847-949-2707
Mark Pilut, prin. Fax 949-2716
Washington ES 400/PK-1
122 S Garfield Ave 60060 847-949-2714
MaryBeth Licke, prin. Fax 949-2710

Libertyville Montessori S 100/PK-K
450 S Butterfield Rd 60060 847-362-5170
Ratti Singh, admin. Fax 367-5133
Mundelein Montessori S 50/PK-6
1401 S Lake St 60060 847-566-4345
Carol Hofbauer, prin. Fax 566-4343
St. Mary of the Annunciation S 200/K-8
22277 W Erhart Rd 60060 847-223-4021
Deborah Dedeo, prin. Fax 223-3489
Santa Maria Del Popolo S 300/K-8
126 N Lake St 60060 847-949-2335
John Lally, prin. Fax 949-9721

Murphysboro, Jackson, Pop. 8,288
Murphysboro CUSD 186 2,000/PK-12
819 Walnut St 62966 618-684-3781
Christopher Grode, supt. Fax 684-2465
www.mboro.jacksn.k12.il.us
Carruthers ES 400/PK-5
80 Candy Ln 62966 618-687-3231
Carla Bunselmeyer, prin. Fax 687-2811
Logan Attendance Center 400/PK-5
320 Watson Rd 62966 618-684-4471
Jeff Keener, prin. Fax 565-8119
Murphysboro MS 500/6-8
2125 Spruce St 62966 618-684-3041
William Huppert, prin. Fax 687-1042

Immanuel Lutheran S 100/PK-8
1915 Pine St 62966 618-687-3917
David Manning, prin. Fax 684-5115
Murphysboro Christian Academy 100/PK-8
805 N 16th St 62966 618-684-5083
Gina Noble, prin. Fax 687-5614
St. Andrew S 100/K-8
723 Mulberry St 62966 618-687-2013
Nancy Borgsmiller, prin. Fax 684-4969

Murrayville, Morgan, Pop. 637
Jacksonville SD 117
Supt. — See Jacksonville
Murrayville-Woodson ES 200/K-6
PO Box 170 62668 217-882-3121
Matt Rhoades, prin. Fax 882-2141

Naperville, DuPage, Pop. 141,579
Indian Prairie CUSD 204
Supt. — See Aurora
Brookdale ES 500/K-5
1200 Redfield Rd 60563 630-428-6800
Theresa Drendel, prin. Fax 428-6801
Clow ES 500/K-5
1301 Springdale Cir 60564 630-428-6060
Barbara Kaufman, prin. Fax 428-6061
Cowlishaw ES 600/K-5
1212 Sanctuary Ln 60540 630-428-6100
Karen Sullivan, prin. Fax 428-6101
Crone MS 1,200/6-8
4020 111th St 60564 630-428-5600
Stan Gorbatkin, prin. Fax 428-5601
Fry ES 900/K-5
3204 Tallgrass Dr 60564 630-428-7400
Kim Stephens, prin. Fax 428-7401
Graham ES 700/K-5
2315 High Meadow Rd 60564 630-428-6900
Joan Peterson, prin. Fax 428-6901
Gregory MS 1,100/6-8
2621 Springdale Cir 60564 630-428-6300
Stephen Severson, prin. Fax 428-6301
Hill MS 900/6-8
1836 Brookdale Rd 60563 630-428-6200
Allan Davenport, prin. Fax 428-6201
Kendall ES 700/K-5
2408 Meadow Lake Dr 60564 630-428-7100
Martha Baumann, prin. Fax 428-7101
Longwood ES 500/K-5
30W240 Bruce Ln 60563 630-428-6789
Laura Devine Johnston, prin. Fax 428-6761
Owen ES 600/K-5
1560 Westglen Dr 60565 630-428-7300
Jason Bednar, prin. Fax 428-7301
Patterson ES 800/K-5
3731 Lawrence Dr 60564 630-428-6500
Quynh Nguyen, prin. Fax 428-6501
Peterson ES K-5
4008 Chinaberry Ln 60564 630-428-5678
Terri Russell, prin. Fax 428-6181
Scullen MS 1,400/6-8
2815 Mistflower Ln 60564 630-428-7000
Kathleen Kosteck, prin. Fax 428-7001
Spring Brook ES 700/K-5
2700 Seiler Dr 60565 630-428-6600
Cynthia McKesson, prin. Fax 428-6601
Watts ES 500/K-5
800 S Whispering Hills Dr 60540 630-428-6700
Michael Raczak, prin. Fax 428-6701
Welch ES 900/K-5
2620 Leverenz Rd 60564 630-428-7200
Sharon Jennings, prin. Fax 428-7201
White Eagle ES 600/K-5
1585 White Eagle Dr 60564 630-375-3600
Ron Zeman, prin. Fax 375-3601

Naperville CUSD 203 18,300/PK-12
203 W Hillside Rd 60540 630-420-6300
Mark Mitrovich, supt. Fax 420-1066
www.naperville203.org
Beebe ES 700/K-5
110 E 11th Ave 60563 630-420-6332
Elizabeth Martinez, prin. Fax 420-6962
Ellsworth ES 300/K-5
145 N Sleight St 60540 630-420-6338
Dick Allen, prin. Fax 637-7321
Elmwood ES 600/PK-5
1024 Magnolia Ln 60540 630-420-6341
Patrick Gaskin, prin. Fax 637-7348
Highlands ES 600/K-5
525 S Brainard St 60540 630-420-6335
Susan Stuckey, prin. Fax 420-6957
Jefferson JHS 900/6-8
1525 N Loomis St 60563 630-420-6307
Nancy Voise, prin. Fax 420-6930
Kingsley ES 600/K-5
2403 Kingsley Dr 60565 630-420-3208
Dr. Mary Alice Lindvall, prin. Fax 420-3213
Lincoln JHS 900/6-8
1320 Olympus Dr 60565 630-420-6370
Pam George, prin. Fax 637-4582
Madison JHS 800/6-8
1000 River Oak Dr 60565 630-420-4257
Erin Anderson, prin. Fax 420-6402
Maplebrook ES 500/K-5
1630 Warbler Dr 60565 630-420-6381
Dr. Gwen Bockman, prin. Fax 420-6638
Meadow Glens ES 600/K-5
1150 Muirhead Ave 60565 630-420-3200
Chuck Freundt, prin. Fax 420-6897
Mill Street ES 800/K-5
1300 N Mill St 60563 630-420-6353
Mark DeMoulin, prin. Fax 637-4680
Naper ES 300/K-5
39 S Eagle St 60540 630-420-6345
Julie Beehler, prin. Fax 637-7328
Prairie ES 500/K-5
500 S Charles Ave 60540 630-420-6348
Mary Ann Porter, prin. Fax 717-0801
Ranch View ES 500/K-5
1651 Ranchview Dr 60565 630-420-6575
Kathy Duncan, prin. Fax 420-0915

River Woods ES 500/K-5
2607 River Woods Dr 60565 630-420-6630
Robyn Rippel, prin. Fax 420-6961
Scott ES 500/K-5
500 Warwick Dr 60565 630-420-6477
Nick Micensky, prin. Fax 420-6471
Steeple Run ES 600/K-5
6S151 Steeple Run Dr 60540 630-420-6385
Karen Currier, prin. Fax 420-6935
Washington JHS 600/6-8
201 N Washington St 60540 630-420-6390
Bob Ross, prin. Fax 420-6474
Other Schools – See Lisle

All Saints Catholic Academy 500/PK-8
1155 Aurora Ave 60540 630-961-6125
Sandy Renehan, prin. Fax 961-3771
Bethany Lutheran S 300/PK-8
1550 Modaff Rd 60565 630-355-6607
Pamela Mueller, prin. Fax 355-2216
Calvary Christian S 400/K-8
9S200 Route 59 60564 630-375-8600
Emery Risdall, prin. Fax 375-8601
DuPage Montessori S 200/PK-8
24W500 Maple Ave 60540 630-369-6899
Sharon Breen, prin. Fax 369-7306
Naperville Christian Academy 100/K-7
1451 Raymond Dr 60563 630-637-9622
Camie Perrin, prin. Fax 983-6929
Naperville Montessori S 200/PK-K
2936 Artesian Rd 60564 630-904-5399
Denise Plasch, prin. Fax 904-4807
St. Raphael S 300/K-8
1215 Modaff Rd 60540 630-355-1880
Karen Udell, prin. Fax 428-4974
SS. Peter & Paul S 600/K-8
201 E Franklin Ave 60540 630-355-0113
Frank Glowaty, prin. Fax 355-9803

Nashville, Washington, Pop. 3,083
Nashville CCSD 49 600/PK-8
750 E Gorman St 62263 618-327-3055
Brent O'Daniell, supt. Fax 327-4503
www.county.washington.k12.il.us
Nashville S 600/PK-8
750 E Gorman St 62263 618-327-4304
Chuck Fairbanks, prin. Fax 327-4501

St. Ann S 100/K-8
675 S Mill St 62263 618-327-8741
Bonnie Paszkiewicz, prin. Fax 327-4904
Trinity-St. John Lutheran S 50/PK-6
680 W Walnut St 62263 618-327-8561
Doug Aschermann, prin. Fax 327-4540

Nauvoo, Hancock, Pop. 1,155
Nauvoo-Colusa CUSD 325 200/PK-8
PO Box 308 62354 217-453-6639
Kent Young, supt. Fax 453-6395
www.nauvoo-colusa.com/
Nauvoo-Colusa JHS 100/7-8
PO Box 308 62354 217-453-2231
Kent Young, prin. Fax 453-6395
Nauvoo ES 200/PK-6
PO Box 308 62354 217-453-2311
Daniel Ayer, prin. Fax 453-6326

SS. Peter & Paul S 100/PK-6
PO Box 160 62354 217-453-2511
Therese Hayes, prin. Fax 453-2015

Nelson, Lee, Pop. 161
Nelson ESD 8
Supt. — See Rock Falls
Nelson S 50/K-8
207 Pope St, 815-251-4412
Dr. Gregory Lutyens, prin. Fax 251-4413

Neoga, Cumberland, Pop. 1,770
Neoga CUSD 3 800/PK-12
PO Box 280 62447 217-895-2201
Charles Castle, supt. Fax 895-3476
www.neoga.k12.il.us
Neoga ES 300/PK-3
PO Box 580 62447 217-895-2208
Seth James, prin. Fax 895-2757
Neoga JHS 100/7-8
PO Box 280 62447 217-895-2205
Benjamin Johnson, prin. Fax 895-3957
Neoga MS 200/4-6
PO Box 310 62447 217-895-2200
Seth James, prin. Fax 895-2974

Neponset, Bureau, Pop. 504
Neponset CCSD 307 100/PK-8
PO Box 148 61345 309-594-2306
Dr. Chris Sullens, supt. Fax 594-2113
Neponset S 100/PK-8
PO Box 148 61345 309-594-2306
Jason Stabler, prin. Fax 594-2113

Newark, Kendall, Pop. 1,031
Lisbon CCSD 90 100/PK-8
127 S Canal St 60541 815-736-6324
Michael Rustman, supt. Fax 736-6326
Lisbon S 100/PK-8
127 S Canal St 60541 815-736-6324
Michael Rustman, prin. Fax 736-6326

Newark CCSD 66 300/K-8
503 Chicago Rd 60541 815-695-5143
John DeMay, supt. Fax 695-5776
Newark ES 100/K-4
503 Chicago Rd 60541 815-695-5143
John DeMay, prin. Fax 695-5776
Other Schools – See Millbrook

New Athens, Saint Clair, Pop. 2,011
New Athens CUSD 60 600/PK-12
501 Hanft St 62264 618-475-2174
Kyle Freeman, supt. Fax 475-2176

New Athens ES 300/PK-5
501 Hanft St 62264 618-475-2172
Jim Marlow, prin. Fax 475-2176
New Athens JHS 100/6-8
501 Hanft St 62264 618-475-2172
Jim Marlow, prin. Fax 475-2176

St. Agatha S 100/K-8
207 S Market St 62264 618-475-2170
Charlotte Newbold, prin. Fax 475-3177

New Baden, Clinton, Pop. 3,048
Wesclin CUSD 3
Supt. — See Trenton
New Baden ES 300/PK-3
700 Marilyn Dr 62265 618-588-3535
James Rahm, prin. Fax 588-4364
St. George ES 200/4-6
317 E Maple St 62265 618-588-3260
James Rahm, prin. Fax 588-3031

New Berlin, Sangamon, Pop. 1,129
New Berlin CUSD 16 800/PK-12
PO Box 230 62670 217-488-6111
Valerie Carr, supt. Fax 488-6418
cusd16.k12.il.us
New Berlin ES 300/PK-3
PO Box 230 62670 217-488-6011
Sally Koltun, prin. Fax 488-3107
New Berlin JHS 100/7-8
PO Box 230 62670 217-488-6012
Brian Bandy, prin. Fax 488-3207
Other Schools – See Loami

St. John Lutheran S 50/1-8
304 E Gibson St 62670 217-488-3190
Ronald Krohse, prin. Fax 488-3190

New Boston, Mercer, Pop. 643
Westmer CUSD 203
Supt. — See Joy
Westmer ES 300/PK-5
301 Jefferson St 61272 309-587-8141
Nancy Robinson, prin. Fax 587-2194

New Douglas, Madison, Pop. 367
Highland CUSD 5
Supt. — See Highland
New Douglas Mid ES 100/3-4
310 S Main St 62074 217-456-7421
Carla Grapperhaus, prin. Fax 456-6105

New Lenox, Will, Pop. 23,197
New Lenox SD 122 5,500/PK-8
102 S Cedar Rd 60451 815-485-2169
Dr. Michael Sass, supt. Fax 485-2236
www.nlsd122.org
Bentley IS 500/4-6
513 E Illinois Hwy 60451 815-485-4451
Michelle Hall, prin. Fax 485-7599
Cherry Hill K 300/PK-K
205 Kingston Dr 60451 815-462-7831
Marianne Cucci, prin. Fax 722-8536
Haines ES 400/1-3
155 Haines Ave 60451 815-485-2115
Jackie Miller, prin. Fax 462-2571
Liberty JHS 600/7-8
151 Lenox St 60451 815-462-7951
Joel Benton, prin. Fax 462-0672
Martino JHS 600/7-8
731 E Joliet Hwy 60451 815-485-7593
Leslie O'Connor, prin. Fax 485-9578
Nelson Prairie ES 500/1-3
2366 Nelson Rd 60451 815-462-2874
Trisha Anderson, prin. Fax 462-2881
Nelson Ridge IS 500/4-6
2470 Nelson Rd 60451 815-462-2870
Megan Baldermann, prin. Fax 462-2880
Oster-Oakview IS 400/4-6
809 N Cedar Rd 60451 815-485-2125
Mark Fleming, prin. Fax 462-2572
Spencer Crossing IS 500/4-6
1711 Spencer Rd 60451 815-462-7997
Shane Street, prin. Fax 462-0958
Spencer Pointe ES 400/1-3
1721 Spencer Rd 60451 815-462-7988
Kim Gray, prin. Fax 462-3978
Spencer Trail K 300/K-K
1701 Spencer Rd 60451 815-462-7007
Lori Motsch, prin. Fax 462-0670
Tyler ES 400/1-3
511 E Illinois Hwy 60451 815-485-2398
Debbie Moy, prin. Fax 462-2570

Providence Early Education Center 100/PK-PK
1800 W Lincoln Hwy 60451 815-485-7129
Laura McErlean, prin. Fax 485-5165
St. Jude S 300/K-8
241 W 2nd Ave 60451 815-485-2549
Luanne Watson, prin. Fax 485-0234
Sears Childrens Academy 100/PK-1
13245 W Lincoln Hwy 60451 815-485-0055

Newman, Douglas, Pop. 936
Shiloh CUSD 1
Supt. — See Hume
Newman ES 200/PK-2
207 S Coffin St 61942 217-837-2475
Mark Hettmansberger, prin. Fax 837-2331

Newton, Jasper, Pop. 3,038
Jasper County CUSD 1 1,100/K-12
609 S Lafayette St 62448 618-783-8459
Ron Alburtus, supt. Fax 783-3679
www.cusd1.jasper.k12.il.us
Newton / Jasper County S 200/1-8
101 Maxwell St 62448 618-783-8464
Travis Wyatt, prin. Fax 783-4106
Other Schools – See Montrose, Sainte Marie, Willow Hill

St. Thomas the Apostle S 200/K-8
306 W Jourdan St 62448 618-783-3517
Vicki Wenthe, prin. Fax 783-2224

Niantic, Macon, Pop. 690
Sangamon Valley CUSD 9 800/PK-12
PO Box 200 62551 217-668-2338
Ernie Fowler, supt. Fax 668-2406
www.sv.k12.il.us
Other Schools – See Harristown, Illiopolis

Niles, Cook, Pop. 29,330
East Maine SD 63
Supt. — See Des Plaines
Gemini JHS 800/7-8
8955 N Greenwood Ave 60714 847-827-1181
Scott Herrmann, prin. Fax 827-3499
Nelson ES 500/K-6
8901 N Ozanam Ave 60714 847-965-0050
Larry Mishkin, prin. Fax 965-7630
Twain ES 400/K-6
9401 N Hamlin Ave 60714 847-296-5341
Nichole Gross, prin. Fax 296-5345

Niles ESD 71 500/K-8
6901 W Oakton St 60714 847-966-9280
Amy Kruppe, supt. Fax 966-0214
www.culver71.net
Culver S 500/K-8
6901 W Oakton St 60714 847-966-9280
Janice Geisheker, prin. Fax 966-0214

Park Ridge-Niles CCSD 64
Supt. — See Park Ridge
Emerson MS 800/6-8
8101 N Cumberland Ave 60714 847-318-8110
Victoria Mogil, prin. Fax 318-8122
Jefferson S 50/PK-PK
8200 W Greendale Ave 60714 847-318-5360
Kathleen Nelson, prin. Fax 318-5442

Childrens Learning World Montessori S 100/PK-6
8101 W Golf Rd 60714 847-470-0370
Rosemary Fish, prin. Fax 470-0934
Logos Christian Academy 200/PK-12
7280 N Caldwell Ave 60714 847-647-9456
Fax 647-7916
St. John Brebeuf S 500/PK-8
8301 N Harlem Ave 60714 847-966-3266
Margaret Witman, prin. Fax 966-5351

Noble, Richland, Pop. 713
West Richland CUSD 2 400/PK-12
PO Box 157 62868 618-723-2334
Anthony Galindo, supt. Fax 723-2113
www.west.rchlnd.k12.il.us/
West Richland ES 200/PK-6
PO Box 157 62868 618-723-2415
Anthony Galindo, prin. Fax 723-2375
West Richland JHS 50/7-8
PO Box 157 62868 618-723-2335
Kevin Westall, prin. Fax 723-2966

Nokomis, Montgomery, Pop. 2,317
Nokomis CUSD 22 700/PK-12
511 Oberle St 62075 217-563-7311
Charles Stortzum, supt. Fax 563-2549
www.nokomis.k12.il.us
Nokomis South MS 100/5-6
316 E South St 62075 217-563-8611
James Rupert, prin. Fax 563-2309
North ES 300/PK-4
110 W Hamilton St 62075 217-563-8521
James Rupert, prin. Fax 563-2675

St. Louis S 100/K-8
509 E Union St 62075 217-563-7445
Sr. Ruth Chausse, prin. Fax 563-7450

Normal, McLean, Pop. 49,927
ISU Lab SD 1,100/PK-12
Campus Box 5300 61790 309-438-8542
Robert Dean, supt. Fax 438-3813
www.uhigh.ilstu.edu/labschool/
Metcalf S 400/PK-8
Campus Box 7000 61790 309-438-7621
Amy Coffman, prin. Fax 438-2580

McLean County Unit SD 5 12,100/PK-12
1809 Hovey Ave 61761 309-452-4476
Dr. Gary Niehaus, supt. Fax 452-7418
www.unit5.org
Chiddix JHS 900/6-8
300 S Walnut St 61761 309-452-1191
Timothy Green, prin. Fax 888-6845
Fairview ES 400/PK-5
416 Fairview St 61761 309-452-4491
James Shaw, prin. Fax 452-1115
Glenn ES 300/K-5
306 Glenn Ave 61761 309-862-5005
Carmen Bergmann, prin. Fax 454-5490
Grove ES 600/K-5
1101 Airport Rd 61761 309-452-1136
John Lutes, prin. Fax 862-3072
Hoose ES 600/K-5
600 Grandview Dr 61761 309-862-3440
Ed Heineman, prin. Fax 862-3419
Kingsley JHS 1,000/6-8
303 Kingsley St 61761 309-452-4461
Dr. Lynette Mehall, prin. Fax 454-1845
Oakdale ES 500/PK-5
601 S Adelaide St 61761 309-452-4439
Darrin Cooper, prin. Fax 454-2374
Parkside ES 300/K-5
1900 W College Ave 61761 309-862-5014
Shelly Erickson, prin. Fax 862-5047
Parkside JHS 900/6-8
101 N Parkside Rd 61761 309-452-8321
Kenneth Lee, prin. Fax 888-6813
Prairieland ES 600/K-5
1300 E Raab Rd 61761 309-888-6838
Tim Arnold, prin. Fax 862-5068

Sugar Creek ES 200/K-5
200 N Towanda Ave 61761 309-452-0935
Scott Peters, prin. Fax 452-5266
Other Schools – See Bloomington, Carlock, Hudson, Towanda

Calvary Baptist Academy 300/K-12
1017 N School St 61761 309-452-7912
Christel Denault, prin. Fax 451-0033
Epiphany S 400/PK-8
1002 E College Ave 61761 309-452-3268
Richard Morehouse, prin. Fax 454-8087

Norridge, Cook, Pop. 14,054
Norridge SD 80 1,000/K-8
8151 W Lawrence Ave 60706 708-583-2068
Dr. Susan Knight, supt. Fax 456-0798
www.norridge80.org
Giles S 500/K-8
4251 N Oriole Ave 60706 708-453-4847
Kerry Leiby, prin. Fax 456-0798
Leigh S 500/K-8
8151 W Lawrence Ave 60706 708-456-8848
Mary Kay Dunne, prin. Fax 583-2053

Pennoyer SD 79 400/PK-8
5200 N Cumberland Ave 60706 708-456-9094
Dr. Thomas Zafiratos, supt. Fax 456-9098
www.pennoyerschool.org
Pennoyer S 400/PK-8
5200 N Cumberland Ave 60706 708-456-9094
Susan Miceli, prin. Fax 456-9098

Norris City, White, Pop. 1,059
Norris City-Omaha-Enfield CUSD 3 800/PK-12
PO Box 399 62869 618-378-3222
Michael Phelps, supt. Fax 378-3286
Norris City-Omaha S 400/K-8
PO Box 399 62869 618-378-3212
Sandra Burke, prin. Fax 378-3286
Other Schools – See Enfield

North Aurora, Kane, Pop. 14,394
Aurora West Unit SD 129
Supt. — See Aurora
Fearn ES 600/K-5
1600 Hawksley Ln 60542 630-301-5001
Anne Giarranti, prin. Fax 264-5042
Goodwin ES 500/K-5
18 Poplar Pl 60542 630-301-5003
Eric Benson, prin. Fax 897-4826
Jewel MS 600/6-8
1501 Waterford Rd 60542 630-301-5010
Greg Scalia, prin. Fax 907-3161
Schneider ES 500/K-5
304 Banbury Rd 60542 630-301-5014
Michael Smith, prin. Fax 844-4513

North Aurora S 50/K-8
940 W Mooseheart Rd 60542 630-896-5188
Fax 896-5789

Northbrook, Cook, Pop. 34,190
Northbrook ESD 27 1,300/K-8
1250 Sanders Rd 60062 847-498-2610
Dr. David Kroeze, supt. Fax 498-5916
www.northbrook27.k12.il.us/
Grove ES 200/K-3
1000 Pfingsten Rd 60062 847-272-1934
Adrienne Moseley, prin. Fax 480-4835
Hickory Point ES 300/K-3
500 Laburnum Dr 60062 847-498-3830
Corrine Hehn, prin. Fax 480-4837
Shabonee ES 300/4-5
2929 Shabonee Trl 60062 847-498-4970
Laurie Heinz, prin. Fax 480-4836
Wood Oaks JHS 500/6-8
1250 Sanders Rd 60062 847-272-1900
Marc Schaffer, prin. Fax 480-4834

Northbrook SD 28 1,700/PK-8
1475 Maple Ave 60062 847-498-7900
Dr. Larry Hewitt, supt. Fax 498-7970
www.northbrook28.net
Greenbriar ES 300/K-5
1225 Greenbriar Ln 60062 847-498-7950
Jill Weininger, prin. Fax 504-3710
Meadowbrook ES 500/K-5
1600 Walters Ave 60062 847-498-7940
Rosanne Scanlan, prin. Fax 504-3610
Northbrook JHS 600/6-8
1475 Maple Ave 60062 847-498-7920
Scott Meek, prin. Fax 656-1712
Westmoor ES 300/PK-5
2500 Cherry Ln 60062 847-498-7960
Chris Finch, prin. Fax 504-3810

Northbrook/Glenview SD 30 1,100/K-8
2374 Shermer Rd 60062 847-498-4190
Dr. Edward Tivador, supt. Fax 498-8981
www.district30.k12.il.us
Maple JHS 400/6-8
2370 Shermer Rd 60062 847-400-8900
Steven Waitz, prin. Fax 272-0979
Wescott ES 400/K-5
1820 Western Ave 60062 847-272-4660
Dr. Terri Carman, prin. Fax 205-5241
Other Schools – See Glenview

West Northfield SD 31 900/K-8
3131 Techny Rd 60062 847-272-6880
Alexandra Nicholson, supt. Fax 272-4818
www.dist31.k12.il.us
Field MS 300/6-8
2055 Landwehr Rd 60062 847-272-6884
Erin Murphy, prin. Fax 272-1050
Other Schools – See Glenview

Countryside Montessori S 100/PK-6
1985 Pfingsten Rd 60062 847-498-1105
Annette Kulle, prin. Fax 564-1709

Sager Soloman Schechter Day S 300/K-5
3210 Dundee Rd 60062 847-412-5600
Susan Cook, prin. Fax 498-5837
Sager Soloman Schechter MS 300/6-8
3210 Dundee Rd 60062 847-412-5700
Rabbi Sheryl Katzman, prin. Fax 412-5837
St. Norbert S 300/PK-8
1817 Walters Ave 60062 847-272-0051
Maureen Brennen, prin. Fax 272-5274

North Chicago, Lake, Pop. 33,376
North Chicago SD 187 4,100/PK-12
2000 Lewis Ave 60064 847-689-8150
Dr. Lauri Hakanen, supt. Fax 689-6328
www.nchi.lfc.edu/
Green Bay ES 400/K-5
2100 Green Bay Rd 60064 847-689-6303
Chandra Medlin, prin. Fax 578-6016
Hart ES 300/K-5
1110 18th St 60064 847-689-6320
William King, prin. Fax 578-6015
Katzenmaier ES 400/K-5
1829 Kennedy Dr 60064 847-689-6330
Antoinette Weatherspoon, prin. Fax 689-2818
Neal Math Science Academy 600/7-8
1905 Argonne Dr 60064 847-689-6313
Michael Grenda, prin. Fax 689-6332
North ES 400/K-5
1210 Adams St 60064 847-689-7345
Domingo Garcia, prin. Fax 578-6018
Novak-King Sixth Grade Center 300/6-6
1500 Kemble Ave 60064 847-689-6336
John Offner, prin. Fax 473-2981
South ES 300/K-5
1812 Morrow Ave 60064 847-689-6326
Fax 578-4725
Yeager K 200/PK-K
1811 Morrow Ave 60064 847-689-6306
Fax 689-7341
Other Schools – See Great Lakes

Northfield, Cook, Pop. 5,543
Sunset Ridge SD 29 500/K-8
525 Sunset Ridge Rd 60093 847-881-9456
Dr. Linda Vieth, supt.
Middlefork PS, 405 Wagner Rd 60093 200/K-3
Dr. Mary Frances Greene, prin. 847-881-9500
Sunset Ridge MS 300/4-8
525 Sunset Ridge Rd 60093 847-881-9400
Bryan Albro, prin.

Christian Heritage Academy 400/PK-8
315 Waukegan Rd 60093 847-446-5252
Rick Lukianuk, hdmstr. Fax 446-5267

Northlake, Cook, Pop. 11,358
Berkeley SD 87
Supt. — See Berkeley
Northlake MS 500/6-8
202 S Lakewood Ave 60164 708-449-3195
Daniel Sullivan, prin. Fax 547-2548
Riley ES 500/PK-5
123 S Wolf Rd 60164 708-449-3180
Michelle Gambardella, prin. Fax 547-2541
Whittier ES 500/PK-5
338 Whitehall Ave 60164 708-449-3175
Stephen Carnes, prin. Fax 547-3313

Mannheim SD 83
Supt. — See Franklin Park
Roy ES 600/K-5
533 N Roy Ave 60164 708-562-6400
Brian Knox, prin. Fax 562-9819
Westdale ES 500/K-5
99 Diversey Ave 60164 847-455-4060
Tara Kjome, prin. Fax 455-2050

St. John Vianney S 200/PK-8
27 N Lavergne Ave 60164 708-562-1466
Jennifer Haggerty, admin. Fax 562-0142

North Riverside, Cook, Pop. 6,382
Komarek SD 94 500/K-8
8940 W 24th St 60546 708-447-8030
Neil Pellicci, supt. Fax 447-9546
www.komarek94.k12.il.us
Komarek S 500/K-8
8940 W 24th St 60546 708-447-8030
Thomas Crisione, prin. Fax 447-9546

Oak Brook, DuPage, Pop. 8,835
Butler SD 53 500/K-8
2801 York Rd 60523 630-573-2887
Sandra Martin, supt. Fax 573-5374
www.butler53.com
Brook Forest ES 300/K-5
60 Regent Dr 60523 630-325-6888
Nina McCabe, prin. Fax 325-8452
Butler JHS 200/6-8
2801 York Rd 60523 630-573-2760
Edward Condon, prin. Fax 573-1725

Oak Brook Christian S 100/PK-K
3100 Midwest Rd 60523 630-986-9693
Maureen Martinson, dir. Fax 986-9841

Oakbrook Terrace, DuPage, Pop. 2,249
Salt Creek SD 48
Supt. — See Villa Park
Swartz ES 200/2-4
17W160 16th St 60181 630-834-9256
Angie Ross, prin. Fax 617-2643

Oakdale, Washington, Pop. 206
Oakdale CCSD 1 100/K-8
280 E Main St 62268 618-329-5292
Larry Beattie, supt. Fax 329-5545
www.oakdalegs.org/
Oakdale Community Consolidated S 100/K-8
280 E Main St 62268 618-329-5292
Larry Beattie, prin. Fax 329-5545

Oak Forest, Cook, Pop. 28,116
Arbor Park SD 145 1,500/PK-8
17301 Central Ave 60452 708-687-8040
Allen Jebens, supt. Fax 687-9498
www.arbor145.org/
Arbor Park MS 700/5-8
17303 Central Ave 60452 708-687-5330
Mary Beth Sexton, prin. Fax 535-4527
Gingerwood ES 300/1-2
16936 Forest Ave 60452 708-560-0092
Jane Kinshaw, prin. Fax 535-5071
Scarlet Oak ES 300/3-4
5731 Albert Dr 60452 708-687-5822
Andrea Sala, prin. Fax 687-4292
Other Schools – See Tinley Park

Forest Ridge SD 142 1,700/PK-8
15000 Laramie Ave 60452 708-687-3334
Dr. Margaret Longo, supt. Fax 687-2970
www.d142.org
Foster ES 500/1-5
5931 School St 60452 708-687-4763
Curtis Beringer, prin. Fax 687-2659
Hille MS 600/6-8
5800 151st St 60452 708-687-2860
Courtney Orzel, prin. Fax 687-8569
Kerkstra ES 400/1-5
14950 Laramie Ave 60452 708-687-5550
Lori Wazny, prin. Fax 687-0571
Ridge ECC 200/PK-K
5151 149th St 60452 708-687-2964
Anne Berry, prin. Fax 687-8458

Prairie-Hills ESD 144
Supt. — See Markham
Fieldcrest ES 300/K-6
4100 Wagman St 60452 708-210-2872
Lisa Adrianzen, prin. Fax 535-0224

Tinley Park CCSD 146
Supt. — See Tinley Park
Fierke ES 300/PK-5
6535 Victoria Dr 60452 708-614-4520
Mark French, prin. Fax 535-0841

St. Damian S 700/K-8
5300 155th St 60452 708-687-4230
Chad Prosen, prin. Fax 687-8347

Oakland, Coles, Pop. 943
Oakland CUSD 5 300/PK-12
PO Box 200 61943 217-346-2555
Michael Smith, supt. Fax 346-2267
www.oak.k12.il.us/
Lake Crest S 200/PK-8
PO Box 200 61943 217-346-2166
Steve Thompson, prin. Fax 346-2267

Oak Lawn, Cook, Pop. 53,991
Atwood Heights SD 125
Supt. — See Alsip
Lawn Manor ES 200/PK-2
4300 W 108th Pl 60453 708-423-3078
Nicholas Henkle, prin. Fax 423-9331

Oak Lawn-Hometown SD 123 2,900/PK-8
4201 W 93rd St 60453 708-423-0150
Kathleen McCord, supt. Fax 423-0160
www.d123.org/
Brandt S PK-K
8901 S 52nd Ave 60453 708-499-7688
Janice Carr, prin. Fax 499-7689
Covington ES 400/1-5
9130 S 52nd Ave 60453 708-423-1530
Kelly Zimmerman, prin. Fax 499-7674
Hannum ES 300/K-5
9800 S Tripp Ave 60453 708-423-1690
Anne McGovern, prin. Fax 499-7676
Kolmar Avenue ES 400/PK-5
10425 S Kolmar Ave 60453 708-422-1800
Anna Schultz, prin. Fax 499-7681
Oak Lawn-Hometown MS 1,000/6-8
5345 W 99th St 60453 708-499-6400
Paul Enderle, prin. Fax 499-7684
Sward ES 400/K-5
9830 Brandt Ave 60453 708-423-7820
Lori Gloodt, prin. Fax 499-7686
Other Schools – See Hometown

Ridgeland SD 122 2,000/PK-8
6500 W 95th St 60453 708-599-5550
Thomas Smyth, supt. Fax 599-5626
www.ridgeland122.com
Columbus Manor ES 300/K-5
9700 Mayfield Ave 60453 708-424-3481
Meghan Dougherty, prin. Fax 424-9412
Harnew ES 500/PK-5
9101 Meade Ave 60453 708-599-7070
Thomas O'Donnell, prin. Fax 599-9636
Kolb ES 300/K-5
9620 Normandy Ave 60453 708-598-8090
Jeffrey Summers, prin. Fax 598-6445
Simmons MS 500/6-8
6450 W 95th St 60453 708-599-8540
Janelle Raine, prin. Fax 599-8015
Other Schools – See Bridgeview

St. Catherine of Alexandria S 500/PK-8
10621 Kedvale Ave 60453 708-425-5547
Catherine Hudson, prin. Fax 425-3701
St. Gerald S 400/PK-8
9320 S 55th Ct Ste 1 60453 708-422-0121
Susan Whisson, prin. Fax 422-9216
St. Germaine S 400/PK-8
9735 S Kolin Ave 60453 708-425-6063
Kevin Reedy, prin. Fax 425-7463
St. Linus S 400/PK-8
10400 Lawler Ave 60453 708-425-1656
Dr. Michael Stritch, prin. Fax 425-1802
St. Louis De Montfort S 200/K-8
8840 Ridgeland Ave 60453 708-599-5781
Holly Gross, prin. Fax 599-5782

St. Paul Lutheran S 200/PK-8
4660 W 94th St 60453 708-423-1058
Aaron Landgrave, prin. Fax 423-1588
South Side Baptist S 100/K-12
5220 W 105th St 60453 708-425-3435
Southwest Chicago Christian S Oak Lawn 300/PK-8
10110 S Central Ave 60453 708-636-8550
Randy Moes, prin. Fax 636-0175

Oak Park, Cook, Pop. 50,757
Oak Park ESD 97 4,900/PK-8
970 Madison St 60302 708-524-3000
Dr. Constance Collins, supt. Fax 524-3019
www.op97.org
Beye ES 400/K-5
230 N Cuyler 60302 708-524-3070
Jonathan Ellwanger, prin. Fax 524-3069
Brooks MS 800/6-8
325 S Kenilworth Ave 60302 708-524-3050
Tom Sindelar, prin. Fax 524-3036
Hatch ES 200/K-5
1000 N Ridgeland Ave 60302 708-524-3095
Sheila Carter, prin. Fax 524-3139
Holmes ES 400/PK-5
508 N Kenilworth Ave 60302 708-524-3100
Suzie Hackmiller, prin. Fax 524-7622
Irving ES 400/K-5
1125 S Cuyler Ave 60304 708-524-3090
John Hodge, prin. Fax 524-3056
Julian MS 800/6-8
416 S Ridgeland Ave 60302 708-524-3040
Dr. Victoria Sharts, prin. Fax 524-3035
Lincoln ES 500/K-5
1111 S Grove Ave 60304 708-524-3110
Catherine Hamilton, prin. Fax 524-3124
Longfellow ES 500/K-5
715 Highland Ave 60304 708-524-3060
Angela Dolezal, prin. Fax 524-3037
Mann ES 400/K-5
921 N Kenilworth Ave 60302 708-524-3085
Nimisha Kumar, prin. Fax 524-3049
Whittier ES 400/PK-5
715 N Harvey Ave 60302 708-524-3080
Carol Young, prin. Fax 524-3047

Alcuin Montessori S 200/PK-6
324 N Oak Park Ave 60302 708-366-1882
Shawn Edwards, prin. Fax 386-1892
Ascension S 500/PK-8
601 Van Buren St 60304 708-386-7282
Mary Jo Burns, prin. Fax 524-4796
Intercultural Montessori Language S 100/PK-6
301 S Ridgeland Ave 60302 708-848-6626
Edina McGivern, dir. Fax 848-0407
Oak Park Montessori S 50/PK-6
1100 Ontario St 60302 708-358-6000
Luisa Raja, contact Fax 763-8458
St. Edmund S 100/PK-8
200 S Oak Park Ave 60302 708-386-5131
Kerry Lynch, prin. Fax 386-5616
St. Giles S 500/PK-8
1034 Linden Ave 60302 708-383-6279
Susan Poetzel, prin. Fax 383-9952
SS. Catherine Siena & Lucy S 300/PK-8
27 Washington Blvd 60302 708-386-5286
Sr. Marian Cypser, prin. Fax 386-7328

Oakwood, Vermilion, Pop. 1,466
Oakwood CUSD 76
Supt. — See Fithian
Oakwood ES 600/PK-6
PO Box 219 61858 217-354-4221
Jean Henigman, prin. Fax 354-2712

Oblong, Crawford, Pop. 1,554
Oblong CUSD 4 800/PK-12
PO Box 40 62449 618-592-3933
Jeffery Patchett, supt. Fax 592-3427
www.oblongschools.net/
Oblong S 500/PK-8
600 W Main St 62449 618-592-4225
Jeffery Patchett, prin. Fax 592-4299

Odell, Livingston, Pop. 1,022
Odell CCSD 435 200/PK-8
203 N East St 60460 815-998-2272
Ty Wolf, supt. Fax 998-2619
odellschool.org/
Odell S 200/PK-8
203 N East St 60460 815-998-2272
Ty Wolf, prin. Fax 998-2619

St. Paul S 100/PK-8
300 S West St 60460 815-998-2194
Daniel Schmitt, prin. Fax 998-1514

Odin, Marion, Pop. 1,082
Odin SD 122 300/PK-8
PO Box 250 62870 618-775-8266
Mike Conlon, supt. Fax 775-8268
Odin S 300/PK-8
PO Box 250 62870 618-775-8266
Sheri Uchitjil, prin. Fax 775-8268

O Fallon, Saint Clair, Pop. 18,600
Central SD 104 500/PK-8
309 Hartman Ln 62269 618-632-6336
Steve Amizich, supt. Fax 632-0870
www.central104.stclair.k12.il.us
Arthur MS 100/6-8
160 Saint Ellen Mine Rd 62269 618-622-9685
Patrick Anderson, prin.
Central ES 300/PK-5
309 Hartman Ln 62269 618-632-6336
Dawn Elser, prin. Fax 632-0870

O'Fallon CCSD 90 3,300/PK-8
118 E Washington St 62269 618-632-3666
Dr. Nancy Gibson, supt. Fax 632-7864
www.ofallon90.net/
Carriel JHS, 450 N 7 Hills Rd 62269 7-8
Dr. Douglas Wood, prin. 618-632-3666

Evans ES | 400/K-5
802 Dartmouth Dr 62269 | 618-632-3335
Ryan Keller, prin. | Fax 632-1530
Fulton JHS | 800/7-8
307 Kyle Rd 62269 | 618-628-0090
Joi Wills, prin. | Fax 624-9390
Hinchcliffe ES | 400/K-5
1050 Ogle Rd 62269 | 618-632-8406
Kristie Belobrajdic, prin. | Fax 632-1774
Kampmeyer ES | 500/K-5
707 N Smiley St 62269 | 618-632-6391
Mark Dismukes, prin. | Fax 632-7580
Moye ES | 800/K-5
1010 Moye School Rd 62269 | 618-206-2300
Paulette Burns, prin. | Fax 632-7864
Schaefer ES | 400/PK-PK, 6-
505 S Cherry St 62269 | 618-632-3621
Tracy Newton, prin. | Fax 632-9258

Shiloh Village SD 85 | 600/PK-8
125 Diamond Ct 62269 | 618-632-7434
Jennifer Filyaw, supt. | Fax 632-8343
www.shiloh.stclair.k12.il.us
Shiloh MS, 1 Wildcat Xing 62269 | 300/5-8
Mark Heuring, prin. | 618-632-7434
Shiloh Village S | 300/PK-4
125 Diamond Ct 62269 | 618-632-7434
Robin Becker, prin. | Fax 632-8343

First Baptist Academy | 100/K-10
1111 E US Highway 50 62269 | 618-632-6223
Jackye Biehl, admin. | Fax 632-8029
St. Clare S | 500/K-8
214 W 3rd St 62269 | 618-632-6327
Ken Pajares, prin. | Fax 632-5587

Ogden, Champaign, Pop. 737
Prairieview-Ogden CCSD 197
Supt. — See Royal
Prairieview-Ogden South ES | 100/K-6
304 N Market St 61859 | 217-582-2725
Jeffrey Isenhower, prin. | Fax 582-2509

Oglesby, LaSalle, Pop. 3,621
Oglesby ESD 125 | 600/PK-8
755 Bennett Ave 61348 | 815-883-9297
Dr. James Boyle, supt. | Fax 883-3568
www.ops125.net/
Lincoln ES | 400/PK-5
755 Bennett Ave 61348 | 815-883-8932
Dr. James Boyle, prin. | Fax 883-3568
Washington MS | 100/6-8
212 W Walnut St 61348 | 815-883-3517
Michael Pillion, prin. | Fax 883-3568

Holy Family S | 200/PK-8
336 Alice Ave 61348 | 815-883-8916
Jyll Jasiek, prin. | Fax 883-8943

Ohio, Bureau, Pop. 530
Ohio CCSD 17 | 100/K-8
PO Box 478 61349 | 815-376-4414
Sharon Flesher, supt. | Fax 376-2102
Ohio Community Consolidated S | 100/K-8
PO Box 478 61349 | 815-376-2934
Mark Downey, prin. | Fax 376-2102

Okawville, Washington, Pop. 1,333
West Washington County CUSD 10 | 400/K-12
PO Box 27 62271 | 618-243-6454
Scott Fuhrhop, supt. | Fax 243-6454
www.okawville-k12.org
Okawville ES | 100/K-5
301 W Illinois St 62271 | 618-243-6157
Dustin Nail, prin. | Fax 243-9066

Immanuel Lutheran S | 100/PK-8
606 S Hanover St 62271 | 618-243-6142
Lynn Lukomski, prin. | Fax 243-6562

Olney, Richland, Pop. 8,470
East Richland CUSD 1 | 2,100/PK-12
1100 E Laurel St 62450 | 618-395-2324
Marilyn Holt, supt. | Fax 392-4147
www.east.rchlnd.k12.il.us
East Richland ES | 1,000/PK-5
1001 N Holly Rd 62450 | 618-395-8540
Suzanne Hahn, prin. | Fax 395-8672
East Richland MS | 500/6-8
1099 N Van St 62450 | 618-395-4372
Andy Thomann, prin. | Fax 392-3399

St. Joseph S | 100/PK-8
520 E Chestnut St 62450 | 618-395-3081
Carol Potter, prin. | Fax 395-8500

Olympia Fields, Cook, Pop. 4,673
Matteson ESD 162
Supt. — See Matteson
Arcadia ES | 500/K-3
20519 Arcadian Dr 60461 | 708-747-3535
Pat Ransford, prin. | Fax 503-0961

Onarga, Iroquois, Pop. 1,396
Iroquois West CUSD 10
Supt. — See Gilman
Iroquois West MS | 200/6-8
303 N Evergreen St 60955 | 815-268-4355
Vicki Killus, prin. | Fax 268-7608

Oneida, Knox, Pop. 717
ROWVA CUSD 208 | 700/K-12
PO Box 69 61467 | 309-483-3711
T. Lloyd Little, supt. | Fax 483-6123
www.rowva.k12.il.us
ROWVA Central ES | 100/K-2
PO Box 69 61467 | 309-483-6376
Nancy Hroziencik, prin. | Fax 483-6378
ROWVA JHS | 100/7-8
PO Box 69 61467 | 309-483-2803
Nancy Hroziencik, prin. | Fax 483-6378
Other Schools – See Altona, Wataga

Opdyke, Jefferson
Opdyke-Belle-Rive CCSD 5 | 200/K-8
PO Box 189 62872 | 618-756-2492
Dr. John Wheatley, supt. | Fax 756-2792
www.roe25.com/obr/
Opdyke MS | 100/4-8
PO Box 189 62872 | 618-756-2492
Dr. John Wheatley, prin. | Fax 756-2355
Other Schools – See Belle Rive

Orangeville, Stephenson, Pop. 767
Orangeville CUSD 203 | 500/PK-12
310 S East St 61060 | 815-789-4450
Randall Otto, supt. | Fax 789-4607
Orangeville ES | 200/PK-6
310 S East St 61060 | 815-789-4613
Sherry Moyer, prin. | Fax 789-4607
Orangeville JHS | 100/7-8
201 S Orange St 61060 | 815-789-4289
Loren Beswick, prin. | Fax 789-4478

Oreana, Macon, Pop. 951
Argenta-Oreana CUSD 1
Supt. — See Argenta
Argenta-Oreana ES | 500/PK-5
400 W South St 62554 | 217-468-2121
Susan Fustin, prin. | Fax 468-2403

Oregon, Ogle, Pop. 4,163
Oregon CUSD 220 | 1,800/PK-12
206 S 10th St 61061 | 815-732-2186
Dr. William Mattingly, supt. | Fax 732-2187
www.ocusd.net
Etnyre ES | 500/3-6
1200 Jefferson St 61061 | 815-732-2181
Mike Lawton, prin. | Fax 732-6108
Jefferson ES | 400/PK-2
1100 Jefferson St 61061 | 815-732-2911
Susan Johnson, prin. | Fax 732-3893
Other Schools – See Mount Morris

Orion, Henry, Pop. 1,703
Orion CUSD 223 | 1,100/PK-12
PO Box 189 61273 | 309-526-3388
David Deets, supt. | Fax 526-3711
orionschools.us/
Hanna ES | 500/PK-5
PO Box 159 61273 | 309-526-3386
R.C. Lowe, prin. | Fax 526-3864
Orion MS | 300/6-8
PO Box 129 61273 | 309-526-3392
Gary Heard, prin. | Fax 526-3872

Orland Hills, Cook, Pop. 7,273

Cardinal Bernardin S | 800/PK-8
9250 W 167th St, | 708-403-6525
Mary Iannucilli, prin. | Fax 403-8621
Christian Hills S | 200/PK-8
9001 159th St, | 708-349-7166
George Thomas, prin. | Fax 349-9665

Orland Park, Cook, Pop. 55,461
Kirby SD 140
Supt. — See Tinley Park
Fernway Park ES | 500/PK-5
16600 S 88th Ave 60462 | 708-349-3810
Carol Novak, prin. | Fax 349-9463

Orland SD 135 | 5,700/K-8
15100 S 94th Ave 60462 | 708-364-3306
Dennis Soustek, supt. | Fax 873-6479
www.orland135.org
Centennial ES | 500/K-3
14101 Creek Crossing Dr 60467 | 708-364-3444
Lynn Zeder, prin. | Fax 873-6450
Century JHS | 900/6-8
10801 W 159th St 60467 | 708-364-3500
Cindy Finley, prin. | Fax 349-5840
High Point ES | 500/3-5
14825 West Ave 60462 | 708-364-4400
Marianne Byrnes, prin. | Fax 460-5970
Jerling JHS | 800/6-8
8851 W 151st St 60462 | 708-364-3700
Pam Hodgson, prin. | Fax 873-6457
Liberty ES | 500/3-5
8801 W 151st St 60462 | 708-364-3800
Cheryl Foertsch, prin. | Fax 873-1103
Meadow Ridge ES | 700/3-5
10959 W 159th St 60467 | 708-364-3600
Kathy Carroll, prin. | Fax 873-6461
Orland Center ES | 500/K-2
9407 W 151st St 60462 | 708-364-3242
Susan Hofferica, prin. | Fax 873-6453
Orland JHS | 600/6-8
14855 West Ave 60462 | 708-364-4200
Linda Kane, prin. | Fax 349-5843
Orland Park ES | 300/K-3
9960 W 143rd St 60462 | 708-364-3900
Sue Kuligoski, prin. | Fax 460-6139
Prairie ES | 500/K-3
14200 S 82nd Ave 60462 | 708-364-4840
Debra Ciaccio, prin. | Fax 873-6451

Tinley Park CCSD 146
Supt. — See Tinley Park
Kruse ES | 300/PK-5
7617 Hemlock Dr 60462 | 708-614-4530
Carey Radde, prin. | Fax 614-7602

Reformation Christian S | K-8
PO Box 827 60462 | 847-757-6120
Shannon Onnink, prin.
St. Michael S | 600/K-8
14355 Highland Ave 60462 | 708-349-0068
Bernadette Cuttone, prin. | Fax 349-2658
Sears Childrens Academy | 200/PK-2
16807 108th Ave 60467 | 708-460-4414

Oswego, Kendall, Pop. 23,330
Oswego CUSD 308 | 14,100/PK-12
4175 State Route 71 60543 | 630-636-3080
Dr. David Behlow, supt. | Fax 554-2168
www.oswego308.org
Brokaw Early Learning Center | 300/PK-PK
1000 5th St 60543 | 630-551-9600
Joanne Hedemann, prin. | Fax 551-9619
Churchill ES | 600/K-5
520 Secretariat Ln 60543 | 630-636-3800
Christine Laughlin, prin. | Fax 636-3891
East View ES | 700/K-5
4209 State Route 71 60543 | 630-636-2800
Jeremy Ricken, prin. | Fax 554-4943
Fox Chase ES | 800/K-5
260 Fox Chase Dr N 60543 | 630-636-3000
Sue Tiedt, prin. | Fax 554-4299
Old Post ES | 600/K-5
100 Old Post Rd 60543 | 630-636-3400
Jodi Ancel, prin. | Fax 554-0495
Plank JHS | 1,000/6-8
510 Secretariat Ln 60543 | 630-551-9400
Byan Buck, prin. | Fax 551-9691
Prairie Point ES | 700/K-5
3650 Grove Rd 60543 | 630-636-3600
Heidi Podjasek, prin. | Fax 554-6945
Southbury ES | K-5
820 Preston Ln 60543 | 630-551-9800
Philip Chapman, prin. | Fax 551-9819
Thompson JHS | 900/6-8
440 Boulder Hill Pass 60543 | 630-636-2600
Tracy Murphy, prin. | Fax 554-5193
Traughber JHS | 600/6-8
570 Colchester Dr 60543 | 630-636-2700
Ralph Kober, prin. | Fax 554-5197
Other Schools – See Aurora, Montgomery, Plainfield

Ottawa, LaSalle, Pop. 18,824
Deer Park CCSD 82 | 100/PK-8
2350 E 1025th Rd 61350 | 815-434-6930
Carolyn Koos, supt. | Fax 434-6942
Deer Park S | 100/PK-8
2350 E 1025th Rd 61350 | 815-434-6930
Carolyn Koos, prin. | Fax 434-6942

Ottawa ESD 141 | 2,100/PK-8
320 W Main St 61350 | 815-433-1133
Craig Doster, supt. | Fax 433-1888
d141.lasall.k12.il.us
Central ES | 500/5-6
400 Clinton St 61350 | 815-433-3761
Jama Wahl, prin. | Fax 433-9572
Jefferson ES | 300/K-4
1709 Columbus St 61350 | 815-434-0726
Cleve Threadgill, prin. | Fax 434-7451
Lincoln ES | 500/PK-4
1110 W Madison St 61350 | 815-434-1250
Michael Cushing, prin. | Fax 434-2931
McKinley ES | 400/PK-4
1320 State St 61350 | 815-433-1907
Julie Prendergast, prin. | Fax 433-9124
Shepherd MS | 400/7-8
701 E McKinley Rd 61350 | 815-434-7925
Lori Kimes, prin. | Fax 433-9447

Rutland CCSD 230 | 100/K-8
3231 N State Route 71 61350 | 815-433-2949
Michael Matteson, supt. | Fax 433-2322
www.rutlandgradeschool.org
Rutland S | 100/K-8
3231 N State Route 71 61350 | 815-433-2949
Mike Ruff, prin. | Fax 433-2322

Wallace CCSD 195 | 300/K-8
1463 N 33rd Rd 61350 | 815-433-2986
Michael Matteson, supt. | Fax 433-2989
Wallace S | 300/K-8
1463 N 33rd Rd 61350 | 815-433-2986
Christopher Dvorak, prin. | Fax 433-2989

St. Columba S | 200/PK-8
1110 La Salle St 61350 | 815-433-1199
Michael Nadeau, prin. | Fax 433-1219
St. Patrick's S | 100/K-8
801 W Jefferson St 61350 | 815-433-2889
Harold Garner, prin. | Fax 431-9419

Palatine, Cook, Pop. 67,232
Palatine CCSD 15 | 12,000/PK-8
580 N 1st Bank Dr 60067 | 847-963-3000
Daniel Lukich, supt. | Fax 963-3200
www.ccsd15.net
Addams ES | 600/K-6
1020 E Sayles Dr 60074 | 847-963-5000
David Morris, prin. | Fax 963-5006
Hunting Ridge ES | 800/K-6
1105 W Illinois Ave 60067 | 847-963-5300
Diane Murphy, prin. | Fax 963-5306
Jordan ES | 600/K-6
100 N Harrison Ave 60067 | 847-963-5500
Dana Petersen, prin. | Fax 963-5506
Lake Louise ES | 800/K-6
500 N Jonathan Dr 60074 | 847-963-5600
Adam Palmer, prin. | Fax 963-5606
Lincoln ES | 800/K-6
1021 N Ridgewood Ln 60067 | 847-963-5700
Christie Samojedny, prin. | Fax 963-5706
Paddock ES | 700/PK-6
225 W Washington St 60067 | 847-963-5800
Guy Herrmann, prin. | Fax 963-5806
Pleasant Hill ES | 600/K-6
434 W Illinois Ave 60067 | 847-963-5900
Matt Palcer, prin. | Fax 963-5906
Sanborn ES | 600/K-6
101 N Oak St 60067 | 847-963-7000
Michael Carmody, prin. | Fax 963-7006
Sundling JHS | 800/7-8
1100 N Smith St 60067 | 847-963-3700
Yvette Davidson, prin. | Fax 963-3706
Virginia Lake ES | 800/K-6
925 N Glenn Dr 60074 | 847-963-7100
Faith Rivera, prin. | Fax 963-7106

Winston ES 500/K-6
900 E Palatine Rd 60074 847-963-7400
Andy Tieman, prin. Fax 963-7406
Winston JHS 700/7-8
900 E Palatine Rd 60074 847-963-7400
Mary Baum, prin. Fax 963-7406
Other Schools – See Hoffman Estates, Rolling Meadows

Immanuel Lutheran S 400/PK-8
200 N Plum Grove Rd 60067 847-359-1936
Aaron Landgrave, prin. Fax 359-1583
Quest Academy 300/PK-8
500 N Benton St 60067 847-202-8035
Ben Hebebrand, hdmstr. Fax 202-8085
St. Theresa S 700/PK-8
445 N Benton St 60067 847-359-1820
Dorothy Aebersold, prin. Fax 705-2084
St. Thomas of Villanova S 200/PK-8
1141 E Anderson Dr 60074 847-358-2110
John Laroche, prin. Fax 776-1435

Palestine, Crawford, Pop. 1,342
Palestine CUSD 3 400/PK-12
PO Box 217 62451 618-586-2713
John Hasten, supt. Fax 586-2905
www.palestinepioneers.org/
Palestine S 300/PK-8
205 S Washington St 62451 618-586-2711
Sheila Mikeworth, prin. Fax 586-5126

Palmyra, Macoupin, Pop. 730
Northwestern CUSD 2 400/PK-12
30953 Route 111 62674 217-436-2210
Gayle Early, supt. Fax 436-2701
northwestern.k12.il.us
Northwestern ES 200/PK-6
30953 Route 111 62674 217-436-2442
Gayle Early, prin. Fax 436-2701
Northwestern JHS 100/7-8
30889 Route 111 62674 217-436-2011
Brenda Mitchell, prin. Fax 436-9112

Palos Heights, Cook, Pop. 12,561
Palos CCSD 118
Supt. — See Palos Park
Palos East ES 700/K-5
7700 W 127th St 60463 708-448-1084
Karen Mrozek, prin. Fax 923-7077

Palos Heights SD 128 700/PK-8
12809 S McVickers Ave 60463 708-597-9040
Dr. Kathleen Casey, supt. Fax 597-9089
www.d128.k12.il.us
Chippewa ES 300/K-3
12425 S Austin Ave 60463 708-388-7260
Mary Redshaw, prin. Fax 388-2761
Independence JHS 200/6-8
6610 W Highland Dr 60463 708-448-0737
Paul McDermott, prin.
Indian Hill S 100/PK-PK
12800 S Austin Ave 60463 708-597-1285
Cathy Leslie, prin. Fax 597-4230
Navajo Heights ES 100/4-5
12401 S Oak Park Ave 60463 708-385-3269
Sharon Herman, prin.

Incarnation S 200/K-8
5705 W 127th St 60463 708-385-6250
Maria Hawk, prin. Fax 597-0588
Palos Lutheran S 50/PK-8
12436 S 71st Ct 60463 708-448-2260
Kyle Swogger, prin. Fax 448-8620
St. Alexander S 400/PK-8
12559 S 71st Ave 60463 708-448-0408
Patricia Lynch, prin. Fax 448-5947
Stone Church Christian Academy 100/K-8
6330 W 127th St 60463 708-385-7717
Carole Farquhar, admin. Fax 385-7348

Palos Hills, Cook, Pop. 17,258
North Palos SD 117 2,800/PK-8
7825 W 103rd St 60465 708-598-5500
Dr. Ken Sorrick, supt. Fax 598-5539
www.d117.s-cook.k12.il.us/
Oak Ridge ES 500/2-5
8791 W 103rd St 60465 708-233-5300
Melissa Murphy, prin. Fax 430-8648
Quin Early Learning Center 300/PK-PK
7825 W 103rd St 60465 708-599-7760
Beth Reich, prin. Fax 599-7762
Other Schools – See Hickory Hills

Koraes S 200/K-8
11025 S Roberts Rd 60465 708-974-3402
Mary Zaharis, prin. Fax 974-0179

Palos Park, Cook, Pop. 4,757
Palos CCSD 118 2,000/PK-8
8800 W 119th St 60464 708-448-4800
Dr. Joseph Dubec, supt. Fax 448-4880
www.palos118.org
Palos South MS 800/6-8
13100 S 82nd Ave 60464 708-448-5971
Christopher Bingen, prin. Fax 448-0754
Palos West ES 500/PK-5
12700 S 104th Ave 60464 708-448-6888
Ron Cozza, prin. Fax 923-7064
Other Schools – See Palos Heights

Pana, Christian, Pop. 5,529
Pana CUSD 8 1,500/PK-12
PO Box 377 62557 217-562-1500
Dr. David Lett, supt. Fax 562-1501
www.panaschools.com
Lincoln ES 300/2-4
614 E 2nd St 62557 217-562-8500
Richard Nicolas, prin. Fax 562-9259
Pana JHS 200/7-8
203 W 8th St 62557 217-562-6500
Paul Lauff, prin. Fax 562-6712

Washington ES 300/PK-1
200 Sherman St 62557 217-562-7500
Richard Nicolas, prin. Fax 562-9262
Other Schools – See Tower Hill

Sacred Heart S 200/PK-8
3 E 4th St 62557 217-562-2425
Mike Guidish, prin. Fax 562-2942

Paris, Edgar, Pop. 8,834
Paris CUSD 4 600/PK-8
15601 US Highway 150 61944 217-465-5391
Lorraine Bailey, supt. Fax 466-1225
www.crestwood.k12.il.us
Crestwood ES 400/PK-5
15601 US Highway 150 61944 217-465-5391
Alan Zuber, prin. Fax 466-1225
Crestwood JHS 200/6-8
15601 US Highway 150 61944 217-465-5391
Alan Zuber, prin. Fax 466-1225

Paris-Union SD 95 1,700/PK-12
300 S Eads Ave 61944 217-465-8448
Connie Sutton, supt. Fax 463-2243
www.paris95.k12.il.us
Creative Center for Children 100/PK-PK
300 S Eads Ave 61944 217-463-4808
Amy Perry, prin.
Mayo MS 300/6-8
310 E Wood St 61944 217-466-3050
Melanie Ogle, prin. Fax 466-3905
Memorial ES 300/PK-2
509 E Newton St 61944 217-466-6170
Jerry Whitacre, prin. Fax 466-5586
Wenz ES 300/3-5
437 W Washington St 61944 217-466-3140
Carol Jones, prin. Fax 466-6718

St. Mary S 100/PK-8
507 Connelly St 61944 217-463-3005
Barbara Holton-Moy, prin. Fax 465-4703

Park Forest, Cook, Pop. 23,036
Crete-Monee CUSD 201U
Supt. — See Crete
Talala ES 300/K-5
430 Talala St 60466 708-672-2659
Connie Hoffman, prin. Fax 672-2620

Matteson ESD 162
Supt. — See Matteson
Illinois S 500/PK-8
210 Illinois St 60466 708-747-0301
Carolyn Palmer, prin. Fax 503-2241
Indiana ES 500/4-6
165 Indiana St 60466 708-747-5300
Millicent Borishade, prin. Fax 503-1012

Park Forest SD 163 2,100/PK-8
242 S Orchard Dr 60466 708-668-9400
Dr. Joyce Carmine, supt. Fax 748-9359
www.sd163.com
Algonquin Primary Center 200/PK-2
170 Algonquin St 60466 708-668-9200
George McJimpsey, prin. Fax 503-2267
Blackhawk Intermediate Center 300/3-5
130 Blackhawk Dr 60466 708-668-9500
Bessie Boyd, prin. Fax 481-0917
Forest Trail MS 800/6-8
215 Wilson St 60466 708-668-9600
Dr. Carolyn Stroud, prin. Fax 503-2297
Mohawk IS 300/3-5
301 Mohawk St 60466 708-668-9300
Karon Nolen, prin. Fax 503-2281
21st Century Preparatory Center 200/PK-3
240 S Orchard Dr 60466 708-668-9490
Caletha White, prin. Fax 747-0261
Other Schools – See Chicago Heights

St. Mary S 200/PK-8
227 Monee Rd 60466 708-748-6686
John Prevost, prin. Fax 748-6907
South Suburban SDA S 50/1-8
115 Chestnut St 60466 708-481-8909

Park Ridge, Cook, Pop. 36,983
Park Ridge-Niles CCSD 64 4,300/PK-8
164 S Prospect Ave 60068 847-318-4300
Dr. Sally Pryor, supt. Fax 318-4351
www.d64.org
Carpenter ES 300/PK-5
300 N Hamlin Ave 60068 847-318-4370
JoAnn Fletcher, prin. Fax 318-4201
Field ES 600/K-5
707 Wisner St 60068 847-318-4385
Kathleen Creely, prin. Fax 318-4202
Franklin ES 400/K-5
2401 Manor Ln 60068 847-318-4390
Daniel Walsh, prin. Fax 318-4203
Lincoln MS 800/6-8
200 S Lincoln Ave 60068 847-318-4215
Barbara West, prin. Fax 318-4210
Roosevelt ES 700/K-5
1001 S Fairview Ave 60068 847-318-4235
Kevin Dwyer, prin. Fax 318-4205
Washington ES 600/K-5
1500 Stewart Ave 60068 847-318-4360
Kimberly Nasshan, prin. Fax 318-4247
Other Schools – See Niles

Mary Seat of Wisdom S 500/PK-8
1352 S Cumberland Ave 60068 847-825-2500
Judith Schutter, prin. Fax 825-1943
Messiah Lutheran K 200/PK-K
1605 Vernon Ave 60068 847-825-3767
Karen Black, dir. Fax 823-6996
St. Andrews Lutheran S 200/PK-8
260 N Northwest Hwy 60068 847-823-9308
Virginia Terrell, prin. Fax 823-1846

St. Paul of the Cross S 800/PK-8
140 S Northwest Hwy 60068 847-825-6366
Lorelei Bobroff, prin. Fax 825-2466

Patoka, Marion, Pop. 618
Patoka CUSD 100 300/PK-12
1220 Kinoka Rd 62875 618-432-5440
David Rademacher, supt. Fax 432-5306
www.schools.lth5.k12.il.us/patoka/phs.htm
Patoka ES 100/PK-6
1220 Kinoka Rd 62875 618-432-5200
Leslie Venezia, prin. Fax 432-5306
Patoka JHS 50/7-8
1220 Kinoka Rd 62875 618-432-5200
Leslie Venezia, prin. Fax 432-5306

Pawnee, Sangamon, Pop. 2,569
Pawnee CUSD 11 500/PK-12
810 4th St 62558 217-625-2471
Lyle Rigdon, supt. Fax 625-2251
Pawnee S 300/PK-6
810 4th St 62558 217-625-2231
Linda Cline, prin. Fax 625-2251

Paw Paw, Lee, Pop. 857
Paw Paw CUSD 271 300/PK-12
PO Box 508 61353 815-627-2841
Robert Priest, supt. Fax 627-2971
www.2paws.net/
Paw Paw ES 200/PK-6
PO Box 508 61353 815-627-2841
Robert Priest, prin. Fax 627-2971

Paxton, Ford, Pop. 4,534
Paxton-Buckley-Loda CUSD 10 1,500/K-12
PO Box 50 60957 217-379-3314
Clifford McClure, supt. Fax 379-2862
www.pbl.k12.il.us/
Eastlawn S 300/3-5
PO Box 50 60957 217-379-2000
Barry Wright, prin. Fax 379-2055
Paxton-Buckley-Loda JHS 300/6-8
PO Box 50 60957 217-379-9202
Jeff Graham, prin. Fax 379-9169
Peterson ES 400/K-2
PO Box 50 60957 217-379-2531
Trent Eshelman, prin. Fax 379-9781

Payson, Adams, Pop. 1,058
Payson CUSD 1 600/PK-12
406 W State St 62360 217-656-3323
Rodger Hannel, supt. Fax 656-4042
www.cusd1.org
Seymour ES 300/PK-6
404 W State St 62360 217-656-3439
Jeff Zanger, prin. Fax 656-4034

Pearl City, Stephenson, Pop. 784
Pearl City CUSD 200 500/PK-12
PO Box 9 61062 815-443-2715
Timothy Thill, supt. Fax 443-2237
www.pcwolves.net/
Pearl City ES 300/PK-6
PO Box 9 61062 815-443-2715
Chris Wallace, prin. Fax 443-2237
Pearl City JHS 100/7-8
PO Box 9 61062 815-443-2715
Michael Schiffman, prin. Fax 443-2237

Pecatonica, Winnebago, Pop. 2,161
Pecatonica CUSD 321 1,000/K-12
PO Box 419 61063 815-239-1639
William Faller, supt. Fax 239-2125
www.pecschools.com/
Pecatonica Community MS 300/5-8
PO Box 419 61063 815-239-2612
Timothy King, prin. Fax 239-1274
Pecatonica ES 300/K-4
PO Box 419 61063 815-239-2550
Carrie Brockway, prin. Fax 239-1418

Pekin, Tazewell, Pop. 33,331
Pekin SD 108 3,800/PK-8
501 Washington St Ste B 61554 309-477-4740
Bill Link, supt. Fax 477-4701
www.pekin.net/pekin108/
Broadmoor JHS 400/7-8
501 Maywood Ave Ste 1 61554 309-477-4731
Marc Fogal, prin. Fax 477-4739
Dirksen PS 200/K-3
501 Maywood Ave Ste 2 61554 309-477-4710
Linda Seth, prin. Fax 477-4760
Edison JHS 400/7-8
1400 Earl St 61554 309-477-4732
Bill Heisel, prin. Fax 477-4738
Jefferson PS 300/K-3
900 S Capitol St 61554 309-477-4712
Jeffrey Erickson, prin. Fax 477-4761
Preschool Family Education Center 300/PK-PK
1000 Koch St 61554 309-477-4730
Lisa VanNatta, prin. Fax 477-4737
Smith PS 300/K-3
1314 Matilda St 61554 309-477-4713
A.J. Schroff, prin. Fax 477-4762
Starke PS 200/PK-3
1610 Holiday Dr 61554 309-477-4714
Stan Fitzanko, prin. Fax 477-4763
Sunset Hills PS 200/K-3
1730 Highwood Ave 61554 309-477-4715
Cynthia Worner, prin. Fax 477-4764
Washington IS 500/4-6
501 Washington St 61554 309-477-4721
Joe Franklin, prin. Fax 477-4729
Willow PS 300/K-3
1110 Veerman St 61554 309-477-4716
Gloria Ranney, prin. Fax 477-4765
Wilson IS 600/4-6
900 Koch St 61554 309-477-4722
Matt Green, prin. Fax 477-4728

Rankin SD 98 — 200/K-8
13716 5th St 61554 — 309-346-3182
John Prinz, supt. — Fax 346-7928
www.rankin98.org/
Rankin S — 200/K-8
13716 5th St 61554 — 309-346-3182
John Prinz, prin. — Fax 346-7928

Good Shepherd Lutheran S — 200/PK-8
333 State St 61554 — 309-347-2020
Ralph Mickley, prin. — Fax 347-9099
St. Joseph S — 300/PK-8
300 S 6th St 61554 — 309-347-7194
Shannon Rogers, prin. — Fax 347-7198

Peoria, Peoria, Pop. 112,685
Dunlap CUSD 323
Supt. — See Dunlap
Ridgeview ES — 400/K-5
3903 W Ridgeview Dr 61615 — 309-692-8260
Ali Bond, prin. — Fax 692-8357
Wilder-Waite ES — 300/K-5
10021 N Pacific St 61615 — 309-243-7728
Todd Jefferson, prin. — Fax 243-5272

Hollis Consolidated SD 328 — 100/K-8
5613 W Tuscarora Rd 61607 — 309-697-1325
Lee Ann Meinhold, supt. — Fax 697-1334
hollis.peoria.k12.il.us/
Hollis Consolidated S — 100/K-8
5613 W Tuscarora Rd 61607 — 309-697-1325
Lee Ann Meinhold, prin. — Fax 697-1334

Limestone Walters CCSD 316 — 200/K-8
8223 W Smithville Rd 61607 — 309-697-3035
Timothy Dotson, supt. — Fax 697-9466
www.limestonewalters.com
Limestone Walters S — 200/K-8
8223 W Smithville Rd 61607 — 309-697-3035
Chad Bentley, prin. — Fax 697-9466

Norwood ESD 63 — 500/PK-8
6521 W Farmington Rd 61604 — 309-676-3523
Dr. Abby Humbles, supt. — Fax 676-6099
peoria.k12.il.us/norwood/Tornadoes.html
Norwood MS — 200/5-8
6521 W Farmington Rd 61604 — 309-676-3523
Fax 676-6099
Norwood PS — 300/PK-4
200 S Main St 61604 — 309-697-6312
Sandra Linhart, prin. — Fax 697-6315

Peoria SD 150 — 14,500/PK-12
3202 N Wisconsin Ave 61603 — 309-672-6512
Ken Hinton, supt. — Fax 672-6820
www.peoria.psd150.org
Bills MS — 300/5-8
6001 N Frostwood Pkwy 61615 — 309-693-4437
Scott Montgomery, prin. — Fax 693-4438
Charter Oak PS — 400/K-4
5221 W Timberedge Dr 61615 — 309-693-4433
John Wetterauer, prin. — Fax 693-8701
Columbia MS — 200/6-8
2612 N Bootz Ave 61604 — 309-672-6508
Cindy Janovetz, prin. — Fax 685-2238
Coolidge MS — 300/5-8
2708 W Rohmann Ave 61604 — 309-672-6506
Thomas Blumer, prin. — Fax 673-7605
Franklin-Edison PS — 400/PK-5
807 W Columbia Ter 61606 — 309-682-2693
Jane Cushing, prin. — Fax 682-7283
Garfield PS — 300/PK-4
1507 S Lydia Ave 61605 — 309-672-6515
Kevin Curtin, prin. — Fax 672-9794
Glen Oak PS — 500/PK-5
809 E Frye Ave 61603 — 309-672-6518
Valda Shipp, prin. — Fax 686-2459
Harrison PS — 400/PK-5
2702 W Krause Ave 61605 — 309-672-6522
Veralee Smith, prin. — Fax 672-6523
Hines PS — 500/K-4
4603 N Knoxville Ave 61614 — 309-672-6525
Cathy Wiggers, prin. — Fax 672-6526
Hinton ECC — 400/PK-1
800 W Romeo B Garrett Ave 61605 — 309-672-6810
Dr. Beth Bussan, prin. — Fax 676-9831
Irving PS — 400/PK-5
519 NE Glendale Ave 61603 — 309-672-6528
Michael Barber, prin. — Fax 673-7439
Jefferson PS — 400/PK-5
918 W Florence Ave 61604 — 309-672-6531
Patsy Santen, prin. — Fax 672-6535
Kellar East PS — 400/K-4
6414 N Mount Hawley Rd 61614 — 309-693-4441
Kendall Turner, prin. — Fax 693-4440
Keller Central PS — 400/K-4
6413 N Mount Hawley Rd 61614 — 309-693-4439
Kendall Turner, prin.
Kingman PS — 300/PK-5
3129 NE Madison Ave 61603 — 309-672-6538
Annette Johnson, prin. — Fax 672-6539
Lincoln MS — 500/6-8
700 Mary St 61603 — 309-672-6542
Fax 676-6615
Lindbergh MS — 400/5-8
6327 N Sheridan Rd 61614 — 309-693-4427
Julie McCardle, prin. — Fax 693-0499
Northmoor-Edison PS — 500/K-4
1819 W Northmoor Rd 61614 — 309-692-9481
Nicole Wood, prin. — Fax 692-9738
Rolling Acres-Edison MS — 300/5-8
5617 N Merrimac Ave 61614 — 309-689-1100
Deloris Turner, prin. — Fax 693-4423
Roosevelt Magnet S — 600/K-8
1704 W Aiken Ave 61605 — 309-672-6574
Magnolia Branscumb, prin. — Fax 676-7723
Sterling MS — 300/5-8
2315 N Sterling Ave 61604 — 309-672-6557
Tim Delinski, prin. — Fax 681-8286
Trewyn MS — 400/6-8
1419 S Folkers Ave 61605 — 309-672-6500
Cheryl Ellis, prin. — Fax 673-8537
Tyng PS — 500/PK-5
2212 W Ann St 61605 — 309-672-6559
Tim Ryon, prin. — Fax 672-1413
Von Steuben MS — 400/5-8
801 E Forrest Hill Ave 61603 — 309-672-6561
David Obergfel, prin. — Fax 685-7631
Washington Gifted MS — 200/5-8
3706 N Grand Blvd 61614 — 309-672-6563
Joan Wojcikewych, prin. — Fax 672-6564
Whittier PS — 400/K-4
1619 W Fredonia Ave 61606 — 309-672-6569
Renee Andrews, prin. — Fax 673-3349
Wilson PS — 400/K-4
1907 W Forrest Hill Ave 61604 — 309-672-6571
Angela Stockman, prin. — Fax 688-0320

Pleasant Hill SD 69 — 200/PK-8
3717 W Malone St 61605 — 309-637-6829
John Bute, supt. — Fax 637-8612
Pleasant Hill S — 200/PK-8
3717 W Malone St 61605 — 309-637-6829
John Bute, prin. — Fax 637-8612

Pleasant Valley SD 62 — 500/PK-8
4623 W Red Bud Dr 61604 — 309-673-6750
Dr. Allen Johnson, supt. — Fax 674-0165
www.peoria.k12.il.us/pvgs/indexpvgs.htm
Pleasant Valley ES — 200/1-4
4623 W Red Bud Dr 61604 — 309-673-6750
Dr. Allen Johnson, prin. — Fax 674-0165
Pleasant Valley MS — 200/5-8
3314 W Richwoods Blvd 61604 — 309-679-0634
Sandy Somogyi, prin. — Fax 679-0652
Pleasant Valley North S — 100/PK-K
4607 W Elwood Dr 61604 — 309-673-2494
Allen Johnson, prin. — Fax 673-5421

Christ Lutheran S — 200/K-8
1311 S Faraday Ave 61605 — 309-637-1512
Terry Mooney, prin. — Fax 637-7829
Concordia Lutheran S — 200/K-8
2000 W Glen Ave 61614 — 309-691-8921
Dr. Scott Russell, prin. — Fax 691-2913
Holy Family S — 200/K-8
2329 W Reservoir Blvd 61615 — 309-688-2931
Sharon Zogby, prin. — Fax 681-5687
Peoria Academy — 400/PK-8
2711 W Willow Knolls Dr 61614 — 309-692-7570
Karen Calder, prin. — Fax 692-7665
Peoria Adventist S — 50/K-8
4019 N Knoxville Ave 61614 — 309-686-3701
Peoria Christian S — 900/PK-12
3506 N California Ave 61603 — 309-686-4500
Steve Hutton, admin. — Fax 686-2569
St. Mark S — 200/PK-8
711 N Underhill St 61606 — 309-676-7131
Steve Hagenbruch, prin. — Fax 677-8060
St. Philomena S — 400/PK-8
3216 N Emery Ave 61604 — 309-685-1208
Jodi Peine, prin. — Fax 681-5676
St. Vincent De Paul S — 600/PK-8
6001 N University St 61614 — 309-691-5012
Michael Birdoes, prin. — Fax 683-1036

Peoria Heights, Peoria, Pop. 6,298
Peoria Heights CUSD 325 — 800/PK-12
500 E Glen Ave 61616 — 309-686-8800
Roger Bergia, supt. — Fax 686-8801
www.phcusd325.net
Peoria Heights S — 600/PK-8
500 E Glen Ave 61616 — 309-686-8809
Gene Beltz, prin. — Fax 686-7272

Peoria Christian S - Monroe — 300/5-8
3725 N Monroe Ave 61616 — 309-681-0500
Steve Bowers, prin. — Fax 681-9371
St. Thomas the Apostle S — 400/K-8
4229 N Monroe Ave 61616 — 309-685-2533
Maureen Bentley, prin. — Fax 681-7262

Peotone, Will, Pop. 3,981
Peotone CUSD 207U — 2,000/K-12
212 W Wilson St 60468 — 708-258-0991
Kevin Carey, supt. — Fax 258-0994
www.peotoneschools.org
Connor Shaw Center — 200/5-5
212 W Wilson St 60468 — 708-258-0991
Kathrina Davis, prin. — Fax 258-0994
Peotone ES — 400/K-4
426 N Conrad St 60468 — 708-258-6955
Tina Nicks, prin. — Fax 258-0455
Peotone JHS — 500/6-8
1 Blue Devil Dr 60468 — 708-258-3246
Greg Oliver, prin. — Fax 258-6669
Other Schools – See Frankfort, Manhattan

Perry, Pike, Pop. 418
Griggsville-Perry CUSD 4
Supt. — See Griggsville
Griggsville-Perry MS — 100/5-8
PO Box 98 62362 — 217-236-9161
Pollee Craven, prin. — Fax 236-7221

Peru, LaSalle, Pop. 9,815
Peru ESD 124 — 900/PK-8
1325 Park Rd 61354 — 815-223-0486
Mark Cross, supt. — Fax 223-0490
www.perued.net
Northview ES — 300/3-5
1429 Shooting Park Rd 61354 — 815-223-2567
Melissa Bosnich, prin. — Fax 223-0618
Peru-Washington JHS — 300/6-8
1325 Park Rd 61354 — 815-223-0301
Lori Madden, prin. — Fax 223-0732
Roosevelt ES — 300/PK-2
2233 6th St 61354 — 815-223-0284
Sara McDonald, prin. — Fax 223-8936

Peru Catholic S — 200/PK-8
2003 5th St 61354 — 815-224-1914
Steven Brockman, prin. — Fax 223-1354

Petersburg, Menard, Pop. 2,240
PORTA CUSD 202 — 1,300/PK-12
PO Box 202 62675 — 217-632-3803
Matthew Brue, supt. — Fax 632-3221
www.porta202.org
Petersburg ES — 300/PK-2
514 W Monroe St 62675 — 217-632-7731
Eric Kesler, prin. — Fax 632-3551
PORTA Central ES — 300/3-6
1500 Owen Ave 62675 — 217-632-7781
Linda Tusek, prin. — Fax 632-5103
PORTA JHS — 200/7-8
PO Box 202 62675 — 217-632-3219
Jeff Hill, prin. — Fax 632-5448
Other Schools – See Tallula

Philo, Champaign, Pop. 1,532
Tolono CUSD 7
Supt. — See Tolono
Unity East ES — 300/PK-5
1638 County Road 1000 N 61864 — 217-684-5218
Laura Fitzgerald, prin. — Fax 684-5220

St. Thomas S — 100/K-8
311 Madison St 61864 — 217-684-2309
Gwendolyn Roche, prin. — Fax 684-2309

Phoenix, Cook, Pop. 2,069
South Holland SD 151
Supt. — See South Holland
Coolidge MS — 500/6-8
15500 7th Ave 60426 — 708-339-5300
Patricia Payne, prin. — Fax 339-5327

New Covenant Christian Academy — 100/PK-12
PO Box 1358 60426 — 708-331-3661
Dr. Richard McCreary, dir. — Fax 331-2459

Piasa, Macoupin
Southwestern CUSD 9 — 1,800/PK-12
PO Box 99 62079 — 618-729-3221
Larry Elsea, supt. — Fax 729-3764
www.piasabirds.net
Southwestern MS — 200/7-8
PO Box 70 62079 — 618-729-3217
Kevin Bowman, prin. — Fax 729-9231
Other Schools – See Brighton, Medora, Shipman

Pinckneyville, Perry, Pop. 5,452
CCSD 204 — 200/PK-8
6067 State Route 154 62274 — 618-357-2419
Patricia Hilliard-Wood, supt. — Fax 357-3016
www.ccsd204.perry.k12.il.us/
Community Consolidated S — 200/PK-8
6067 State Route 154 62274 — 618-357-2419
Patricia Hilliard-Wood, prin. — Fax 357-3016

Pinckneyville SD 50 — 600/PK-8
301 W Mulberry St 62274 — 618-357-5161
Tim O'Leary, supt. — Fax 357-8731
www.p50.perry.k12.il.us/education
Pinckneyville ES — 300/PK-4
301 W Mulberry St 62274 — 618-357-5161
Scott Wagner, prin.
Pinckneyville MS — 300/5-8
700 E Water St 62274 — 618-357-2724
Ryan Swan, prin.

St. Bruno S — 100/PK-8
210 N Gordon St 62274 — 618-357-8276
Sandra Kabat, prin. — Fax 357-6425

Piper City, Ford, Pop. 749
Tri-Point CUSD 6-J
Supt. — See Kempton
Tri-Point MS — 300/PK-K, 4-8
PO Box 158 60959 — 815-686-2247
Jerry Tkachuk, prin. — Fax 686-2663

Pittsburg, Williamson, Pop. 585
Johnston City CUSD 1
Supt. — See Johnston City
Lincoln ES — 100/K-4
20163 Corinth Rd 62974 — 618-982-2130
Kathy Clark, prin. — Fax 983-2353

Pittsfield, Pike, Pop. 4,599
Pikeland CUSD 10 — 1,400/PK-12
512 S Madison St 62363 — 217-285-2147
Paula Hawley, supt. — Fax 285-5059
Pikeland Community S — 600/3-8
601 Piper Ln 62363 — 217-285-9462
Daniel Brue, prin. — Fax 285-9551
Pittsfield South ES — 400/PK-2
655 Clarksville Rd 62363 — 217-285-2431
Brian Rhoades, prin. — Fax 285-5479

Plainfield, Will, Pop. 28,162
Oswego CUSD 308
Supt. — See Oswego
Grande Park ES — 300/K-5
26933 W Grande Park Blvd, — 630-551-9700
Beth Wulff, prin.

Plainfield CCSD 202 — 26,800/PK-12
15732 S Howard St 60544 — 815-577-4000
Dr. John Harper, supt. — Fax 436-7824
www.learningcommunity202.org
Central ES — 900/K-5
23723 Getson Dr 60544 — 815-436-9278
Linda DiLeo, prin. — Fax 436-8415
Creekside ES — 1,100/K-5
13909 S Budler Rd 60544 — 815-577-4700
Kevin Slattery, prin. — Fax 372-0607
Drauden Point MS — 1,000/6-8
1911 Drauden Rd, — 815-577-4900
Patrick Flynn, prin. — Fax 439-9385
Eagle Pointe ES — 1,000/K-5
24562 Norwood Dr, — 815-577-4800
Scott Fink, prin. — Fax 609-9403
Eichelberger ES — K-5
12450 Essington Rd, — 815-577-3606
Trevor Harris, prin. — Fax 577-6407

Freedom ES | K-5
11600 Heritage Meadow Dr, 815-254-4005
Curtis Hudson, prin. Fax 254-9706
Heritage Grove MS 1,200/6-8
12425 S Van Dyke Rd, 815-439-4810
Stephen Diveley, prin. Fax 436-4661
Indian Trail MS 900/6-8
14723 S Eastern Ave 60544 815-436-6128
Christian Rivara, prin. Fax 436-7536
Jones MS 800/6-8
15320 W Wallin Dr 60544 815-267-3600
Edward Boswell, prin. Fax 439-7201
Kennedy MS 6-8
12350 Essington Rd, 815-439-8024
Nancy Voise, prin. Fax 254-7375
Lakewood Falls ES 1,000/K-5
14050 S Budler Rd 60544 815-439-4560
Dr. Tina Olson, prin. Fax 886-0463
Lincoln ES 1,000/K-5
14740 Meadow Ln 60544 815-577-4500
Kelley Gallt, prin. Fax 609-5853
McBeth Learning Center 700/PK-PK
15730 S Howard St 60544 815-439-4288
Mina Griffith, prin. Fax 254-4315
Meadow View ES 1,000/K-5
2501 Mirage Ave, 815-439-4828
Dr. Donald McKinney, prin. Fax 436-3747
Reed ES 1,000/K-5
2110 Clublands Pkwy, 815-254-2160
Beth Wackerlin, prin. Fax 254-9385
Ridge ES 1,100/K-5
1900 Caton Ridge Dr, 815-577-4630
Eileen Nelson, prin. Fax 609-9387
River View ES 900/K-5
2097 S Bronk Rd, 815-439-4840
Joseph Simpkins, prin. Fax 436-4930
Timber Ridge MS 1,200/6-8
2101 S Bronk Rd, 815-439-3410
David Bendis, prin. Fax 439-3412
Walkers Grove ES 800/K-5
24810 W 135th St 60544 815-439-2885
Kellie Sanders, prin. Fax 439-2883
Wesmere ES 1,100/K-5
2001 Wesmere Pkwy, 815-439-3244
Gene Carlson, prin. Fax 439-3413
Other Schools – See Bolingbrook, Joliet

Troy CCSD 30C 4,000/PK-8
5800 Theodore Dr 60586 815-577-6760
Don White Ph.D., supt. Fax 577-3795
www.troy30c.org/
Orenic IS 800/5-6
5820 Theodore Dr, 815-577-6759
Darrell Echols, prin. Fax 577-1233
Troy MS 800/7-8
5800 Theodore Dr, 815-230-9920
Jeffrey Libowitz, prin. Fax 577-2867
Other Schools – See Joliet, Shorewood

Elite Childrens Academy 200/PK-2
23253 W Renwick Rd 60544 815-254-4911
St. Mary Immaculate S 500/PK-8
15629 S Route 59 60544 815-436-3953
Sr. Nancy Gannon, prin. Fax 439-8045

Plano, Kendall, Pop. 7,338
Plano CUSD 88 1,300/PK-12
800 S Hale St 60545 630-552-8978
Dr. Laurel Walker, supt. Fax 552-8548
www.plano88.org/
Centennial ES 100/2-3
800 S West St 60545 630-552-3234
Lisa Lantvit, prin. Fax 552-0324
Johns ES 4-6
430 Mitchell Ct 60545 630-552-9182
Tony Baker, prin. Fax 552-9208
Miller ES 300/PK-1
904 N Lew St 60545 630-552-8504
Jon Runkle, prin. Fax 552-3089
Plano MS 300/7-8
804 S Hale St 60545 630-552-3608
Wayne Czyz, prin. Fax 552-3802

St. Mary S 200/K-8
817 N Center St 60545 630-552-3345
Ed Condon, prin. Fax 552-4385

Pleasant Hill, Pike, Pop. 1,012
Pleasant Hill CUSD 3 300/PK-12
PO Box 207 62366 217-734-2311
Don Peebles, supt. Fax 734-2629
www.phwolves.com/
Pleasant Hill S 300/PK-8
PO Box 207 62366 217-734-2311
Don Peebles, prin. Fax 734-2629

Pleasant Plains, Sangamon, Pop. 738
Pleasant Plains CUSD 8 1,300/PK-12
PO Box 20 62677 217-626-1041
Maureen Talbert, supt. Fax 626-1082
ppcusd8.org
Farmingdale ES 500/PK-4
2473 N Farmingdale Rd 62677 217-626-1221
Jamie Yates, prin. Fax 626-1839
Pleasant Plains MS 400/5-8
2455 N Farmingdale Rd 62677 217-626-1061
John Marsaglia, prin. Fax 626-2272

Pocahontas, Bond, Pop. 728
Bond County CUSD 2
Supt. — See Greenville
Pocahontas S 200/PK-8
PO Box 189 62275 618-669-2296
Eric Swingler, prin. Fax 669-2627

Polo, Ogle, Pop. 2,507
Polo CUSD 222 800/PK-12
100 S Union Ave 61064 815-946-3815
Christopher Rademacher, supt. Fax 946-2493
www.polo222.org/
Aplington MS 200/6-8
610 E Mason St 61064 815-946-2519
Andrew Faivre, prin. Fax 946-2537
Centennial ES 300/PK-5
308 S Pleasant Ave 61064 815-946-3811
Keri Nitzel, prin. Fax 946-4233

Pontiac, Livingston, Pop. 11,457
Pontiac CCSD 429 1,300/PK-8
117 W Livingston St 61764 815-844-5632
Steve Graham, supt. Fax 844-5773
www.p429.k12.il.us/
Central ES 300/PK-5
117 W Livingston St 61764 815-844-3023
Mike Weaver, prin. Fax 844-5773
Lincoln ES 300/PK-5
514 S Main St 61764 815-844-3924
Maggie Janssen, prin. Fax 844-5773
Pontiac JHS 400/6-8
600 N Morrow St 61764 815-842-4343
Judy Donze, prin. Fax 844-6230
Washington ES 300/K-5
400 N Morrow St 61764 815-844-3687
Kel Krenz, prin. Fax 844-5773

Pontiac Christian S 100/PK-8
18034 N 2100 East Rd 61764 815-842-1322
Dean Ridder, admin. Fax 844-2033
St. Mary's S 200/K-8
414 N Main St 61764 815-844-6585
Sharon Warfield, prin. Fax 844-6987

Poplar Grove, Boone, Pop. 3,077
North Boone CUSD 200 1,700/PK-12
17641 Poplar Grove Rd Ste A 61065 815-765-3322
Dr. Rita Brodnax, supt. Fax 765-2053
www.nbcusd.org
Manchester ES 200/K-4
3501 Blaine Rd 61065 815-765-2826
Kristina Crawford, prin. Fax 765-3334
North Boone MS 300/7-8
17641 Poplar Grove Rd 61065 815-765-9274
Terry Carter, prin. Fax 765-9275
North Boone Upper ES 300/5-6
6200 N Boone School Rd 61065 815-765-9006
Michael Greenlee, prin. Fax 765-2496
Poplar Grove ES 200/K-4
208 N State St 61065 815-765-3113
Sharon Olds, prin. Fax 765-1604
Other Schools – See Capron

Port Byron, Rock Island, Pop. 1,623
Riverdale CUSD 100 1,200/PK-12
9624 256th St N 61275 309-523-3184
Ronald Jacobs, supt. Fax 523-3550
www.riroe.k12.il.us/riroe/riverdale/
Riverdale ES 500/PK-5
9424 256th St N 61275 309-523-3186
Julia Evans, prin. Fax 523-2870
Riverdale MS 300/6-8
9822 256th St N 61275 309-523-3131
James Jennings, prin. Fax 523-3934

Posen, Cook, Pop. 4,929
Posen-Robbins ESD 143-5 1,700/PK-8
14025 S Harrison Ave 60469 708-388-7200
Gregory Wright, supt. Fax 388-3868
Gordon ES 500/K-3
14100 S Harrison Ave 60469 708-388-7202
Andrea McKinney, prin. Fax 388-6891
Posen ES 300/4-5
14545 S California Ave 60469 708-388-7204
Emanuel Williams, prin. Fax 388-0075
Other Schools – See Robbins

Potomac, Vermilion, Pop. 666
Potomac CUSD 10 200/PK-8
7915 US Route 136 61865 217-987-6155
Jamie Dorsey, supt. Fax 987-6663
Potomac S 200/PK-8
7915 US Route 136 61865 217-987-6155
Jamie Dorsey, prin. Fax 987-6663

Prairie du Rocher, Randolph, Pop. 589
Prairie Du Rocher CCSD 134 200/PK-8
714 Middle St 62277 618-284-3530
Danny Steele, supt. Fax 284-3444
www.pdr134.com
Prairie Du Rocher S 200/PK-8
714 Middle St 62277 618-284-3530
Danny Steele, prin. Fax 284-3444

Princeton, Bureau, Pop. 7,554
Princeton ESD 115 1,300/PK-8
506 E Dover Rd 61356 815-875-3162
Tim Smith, supt. Fax 875-3101
www.princeton115schools.org
Douglas Attendance Center 200/PK-PK
220 E Lasalle St 61356 815-872-9741
Eleanor Walker, prin. Fax 872-0756
Jefferson ES 200/K-1
725 W Putnam St 61356 815-875-4417
Eleanor Walker, prin. Fax 872-0620
Lincoln ES 200/2-3
501 S Euclid Ave 61356 815-875-1164
Bill Gregory, prin. Fax 872-0801
Logan JHS 400/6-8
302 W Central Ave 61356 815-875-6415
J.D. Orwig, prin. Fax 872-0034
Other Schools – See Tiskilwa

Princeton Christian Academy 100/PK-8
21890 US Highway 34 61356 815-875-2933
Marty Kiser, prin. Fax 875-8113
St. Louis S 100/K-8
631 Park Ave W 61356 815-872-8521
Mary Schmitt, prin. Fax 879-8010

Princeville, Peoria, Pop. 1,574
Princeville CUSD 326 600/PK-12
302 Cordis Ave 61559 309-385-2213
James Colyott, supt. Fax 385-1823
www.princeville326.org/
Princeville S 400/PK-8
602 N Town Ave 61559 309-385-4994
Becky Michel, prin. Fax 385-2518

Prophetstown, Whiteside, Pop. 1,960
Prophetstown-Lyndon-Tampico CUSD 3 1,000/PK-12
79 Grove St 61277 815-537-5101
Dave Rogers, supt. Fax 537-5102
wside.k12.il.us/
Prophetstown ES 300/PK-5
301 W 3rd St 61277 815-537-2345
Karen Anderson, prin. Fax 537-2417
Other Schools – See Tampico

Prospect Heights, Cook, Pop. 16,387
Prospect Heights SD 23 1,500/PK-8
700 N Schoenbeck Rd 60070 847-870-3850
Dr. Gregory Guarrine, supt. Fax 870-3896
www.d23.org/
Eisenhower ES 300/K-5
700 N Schoenbeck Rd 60070 847-870-3875
Luke Lambatos, prin. Fax 870-3877
MacArthur MS 500/6-8
700 N Schoenbeck Rd 60070 847-870-3879
Steven Lee, prin. Fax 870-3881
Ross ES 300/PK-2
700 N Schoenbeck Rd 60070 847-870-3868
Claire Kowalczyk, prin. Fax 870-3898
Sullivan ES 300/3-5
700 N Schoenbeck Rd 60070 847-870-3865
Debbie Gardiner, prin. Fax 870-8113

St. Alphonsus Ligouri S 300/PK-8
411 N Wheeling Rd Side 2 60070 847-255-5538
Peter Tantillo, prin. Fax 255-0353
Sonshine Nursery S 50/PK-PK
304 W Palatine Rd 60070 847-520-1116
Fax 537-4480

Quincy, Adams, Pop. 39,841
Quincy SD 172 6,600/PK-12
1416 Maine St 62301 217-223-8700
Lonny Lemon, supt. Fax 228-7162
www.qps.org
Adams ES 300/K-3
2001 Jefferson St 62301 217-222-2530
Marcey Wells, prin. Fax 221-3461
Baldwin IS 1,300/4-6
3000 Maine St 62301 217-223-0003
Paul Saunders, prin. Fax 228-7148
Berrian ES 200/K-3
1327 S 8th St 62301 217-228-7691
Jill Reis, prin. Fax 228-7115
Dewey ES 200/K-3
2040 Cherry St 62301 217-228-7117
Jerry Ellerman, prin. Fax 221-3462
Early Childhood and Family Center 400/PK-PK
401 S 8th St 62301 217-228-7121
Julie Schuckman, prin. Fax 221-3476
Ellington ES 300/K-3
3001 Lindell Ave 62301 217-222-5697
Anne Cashman, prin. Fax 221-3463
Madison ES 400/K-3
2435 Maine St 62301 217-223-6096
Kelle Bunch, prin. Fax 228-7388
Monroe ES 300/K-3
3211 Payson Rd 62305 217-223-8871
Julie Stratman, prin. Fax 228-7188
Washington ES 200/K-3
1400 N 8th St 62301 217-222-4059
Sara Cramer, prin. Fax 222-8077

Blessed Sacrament Catholic S PK-PK, 1-
1115 S 7th St 62301 217-228-1477
Christine Reichert, prin. Fax 222-6463
Quincy Area Christian S 50/PK-12
PO Box 3643 62305 217-223-5698
Randy Peterson, admin. Fax 223-5724
St. Dominic S 200/PK-8
4100 Columbus Rd 62305 217-224-0041
Sue Kelley, prin. Fax 224-0042
St. Francis Solanus S 300/PK-8
1720 College Ave 62301 217-222-4077
Lee Hoffman, prin. Fax 222-5049
St. James Lutheran S 100/PK-8
900 S 17th St 62301 217-222-8447
Nathan Landskroener, prin. Fax 222-3415
St. Peter S 400/PK-8
2500 Maine St 62301 217-223-1120
Janet Bick, prin. Fax 223-1173

Radom, Washington, Pop. 388

St. Michael S 50/PK-8
PO Box 15 62876 618-485-6461
Sherri Beckham, prin. Fax 485-2272

Ramsey, Fayette, Pop. 1,063
Ramsey CUSD 204 500/PK-12
716 W 6th St 62080 618-423-2335
Barb Shute, supt. Fax 423-2314
www.ramsey.fayette.k12.il.us/
Ramsey S 400/PK-8
610 W 6th St 62080 618-423-2010
Jennifer Garrison, prin. Fax 423-2314

Ransom, LaSalle, Pop. 390
Allen-Otter Creek CCSD 65 100/K-8
400 S Lane St 60470 815-586-4611
Iner Anderson, supt. Fax 586-4306
Ransom S 100/K-8
400 S Lane St 60470 815-586-4611
Mary Baima, prin. Fax 586-4306

Rantoul, Champaign, Pop. 12,483
Rantoul CSD 137 1,600/PK-8
400 E Wabash Ave 61866 217-893-4171
William Trankina, supt. Fax 892-4313
www.rcs.k12.il.us/
Broadmeadow ES 300/3-5
500 Sunview Rd 61866 217-892-2194
Mark J. McCusker, prin.

Eastlawn ES 300/K-2
650 N Maplewood Dr 61866 217-892-2131
Jason Wallace, prin.
Eater JHS, 400 E Wabash Ave 61866 500/6-8
Mike Penicook, prin. 217-892-2115
Northview ES 200/3-5
400 N Sheldon St 61866 217-892-2119
Carolyn Hinton, prin.
Pleasant Acres ES 300/PK-2
1649 Harper Dr 61866 217-893-4141
Cliff Englishharden, prin.

St. Malachy S 200/K-8
340 E Belle Ave 61866 217-892-2011
James Flaherty, prin. Fax 892-5780

Raymond, Montgomery, Pop. 922
Panhandle CUSD 2 600/PK-12
PO Box 49 62560 217-229-4215
Connie Falconer, supt. Fax 229-4216
www.panhandle.k12.il.us/
Lincolnwood JHS 100/6-8
507 N Prairie St 62560 217-229-4237
Richard Mazzolini, prin. Fax 229-3005
Raymond ES 200/PK-5
PO Box 80 62560 217-229-3124
Aaron Hopper, prin. Fax 229-3037
Other Schools – See Farmersville

Red Bud, Randolph, Pop. 3,522
Red Bud CUSD 132 1,000/PK-12
815 Locust St 62278 618-282-3507
Steve Harsy, supt. Fax 282-6151
www.redbud.randolph.k12.il.us/
Red Bud S 600/PK-8
200 W Field Dr 62278 618-282-3858
Larry Lovel, prin. Fax 282-3965

St. John's Lutheran S 200/PK-8
104 E South 6th St 62278 618-282-3873
Deitt Schneider, prin. Fax 282-4087
St. John the Baptist S 100/PK-8
519 Hazel St 62278 618-282-3215
Kris Hill, prin. Fax 282-6790
Trinity Lutheran S 100/K-8
10247 S Prairie Rd 62278 618-282-2881
Mark Sochowski, prin. Fax 282-4045

Reddick, Kankakee, Pop. 218
Herscher CUSD 2
Supt. — See Herscher
Reddick ES 100/4-5
PO Box 67 60961 815-365-2375
Dennis Pankey, prin. Fax 365-2377

Reynolds, Rock Island, Pop. 493
Rockridge CUSD 300
Supt. — See Taylor Ridge
Reynolds ES 200/K-K, 4-6
705 Edgington St 61279 309-372-8822
Tina Sims, prin. Fax 372-8900

Richmond, McHenry, Pop. 2,215
Nippersink SD 2 1,600/PK-8
PO Box 505 60071 815-678-4242
Dr. Dan Oest, supt. Fax 678-2810
www.nippersinkdistrict2.org
Nippersink MS 600/6-8
10006 N Main St 60071 815-678-7129
Tim Molitor, prin. Fax 678-7210
Richmond Consolidated ES 600/PK-5
5815 Broadway St 60071 815-678-4717
Judi Jones, prin. Fax 678-2279
Other Schools – See Spring Grove

Richton Park, Cook, Pop. 12,998
ESD 159
Supt. — See Matteson
Armstrong ES 300/K-5
5030 Imperial Dr 60471 708-481-7424
Dean Singletary, prin. Fax 481-7476

Matteson ESD 162
Supt. — See Matteson
Richton Square S PK-K
22700 Richton Square Rd 60471 708-283-2706
Janiece Jackson, prin. Fax 283-8594
Sauk ES 500/4-6
4435 S Churchill Dr 60471 708-747-2660
Michael Bauer, prin. Fax 503-1335

Ridge Farm, Vermilion, Pop. 877
Georgetown-Ridge Farm CUSD 4
Supt. — See Georgetown
Ridge Farm ES 200/4-5
305 S State St 61870 217-247-2210
Andy Weathers, prin. Fax 247-2205

Ringwood, McHenry, Pop. 490
Johnsburg CUSD 12
Supt. — See Johnsburg
Ringwood School Primary Center 600/PK-2
4700 School Rd 60072 815-728-0459
Cathy Neiss, prin. Fax 728-0690

Riverdale, Cook, Pop. 14,588
Dolton SD 148 2,700/PK-8
114 W 144th St 60827 708-841-2290
Dr. Jayne Purcell, supt. Fax 841-5048
www.district148.net
ECC 100/PK-PK
560 W 144th St 60827 708-841-2602
Dr. Kathy Conroy, prin. Fax 201-2082
Park ES 300/K-6
14200 S Wentworth Ave 60827 708-849-9440
Dr. Dell McFarlane, prin. Fax 201-2144
Riverdale ES 100/K-4
325 W 142nd St 60827 708-849-7153
Dr. Kathy Conroy, prin. Fax 841-5048
Washington S 300/K-8
13900 S School St 60827 708-201-2078
Joy Chase, prin. Fax 841-4971
Other Schools – See Dolton

General George Patton SD 133 400/PK-8
150 W 137th St 60827 708-841-3955
Dr. Frankie Sutherland, supt. Fax 841-5911
www.district133.org/
Patton S 300/K-8
13700 S Stewart Ave 60827 708-841-2420
Sharon Baskerville, prin. Fax 841-2492
School District 133 Annex 50/PK-PK
150 W 137th St 60827 708-841-3955
Gloria Liddell, coord. Fax 841-5911

River Forest, Cook, Pop. 11,289
River Forest SD 90 1,300/PK-8
7776 Lake St 60305 708-771-8282
Dr. Thomas Hagerman, supt. Fax 771-8291
www.district90.org/
Lincoln ES 400/PK-4
511 Park Ave 60305 708-366-7340
Pamela Hyde, prin. Fax 771-8291
Roosevelt JHS 600/5-8
7560 Oak Ave 60305 708-366-9230
Larry Garski, prin. Fax 771-8291
Willard ES 300/PK-4
1250 Ashland Ave 60305 708-366-6740
Fax 771-8291

Grace Lutheran S 200/PK-8
7300 Division St 60305 708-366-6900
Hugh Kress, prin. Fax 366-0966
Keystone Montessori S 200/PK-8
7415 North Ave 60305 708-366-1080
Fax 366-1083
St. Luke S 200/PK-8
519 Ashland Ave 60305 708-366-8587
Barbara Rasinski, prin. Fax 366-3831
St. Vincent Ferrer S 300/PK-8
1515 Lathrop Ave 60305 708-771-5905
Frances Mazzulla, prin. Fax 771-7114

River Grove, Cook, Pop. 10,216
Rhodes SD 84-5 600/PK-8
8931 Fullerton Ave 60171 708-453-1266
Michael Wierzbicki, supt. Fax 453-0817
www.rhodes.k12.il.us/
Rhodes S 600/PK-8
8931 Fullerton Ave 60171 708-453-6813
Debra Suhajda, prin. Fax 452-6324

River Grove SD 85-5 600/K-8
2650 Thatcher Ave 60171 708-453-6172
Jon Bartelt, supt. Fax 453-6186
www.rivergroveschool.org
River Grove S 600/K-8
2650 Thatcher Ave 60171 708-453-6172
Glenn Grieschaber, prin. Fax 453-6186

Bethlehem Lutheran S 50/PK-8
2624 Oak St 60171 708-456-8786
Laurie Schmeiser, hdmstr.
St. Cyprian S 100/PK-8
2561 Clinton St 60171 708-453-6300
Sr. Kathleen Klingen, prin. Fax 453-6141

Riverside, Cook, Pop. 8,485
Riverside SD 96 1,300/PK-8
63 Woodside Rd 60546 708-447-5007
Dr. Jonathan Lamberson, supt. Fax 447-3252
www.district96.org
Ames ES 300/K-5
86 Southcote Rd 60546 708-447-0759
Colleen Lieggi, prin. Fax 447-6904
Blythe Park ES 200/PK-5
735 Leesley Rd 60546 708-447-2168
Robert Chleboun, prin. Fax 447-1703
Central ES 400/K-5
61 Woodside Rd 60546 708-447-1106
Dr. Janice Limperis, prin. Fax 447-3252
Hauser JHS 400/6-8
65 Woodside Rd 60546 708-447-3896
Leslie Berman, prin. Fax 447-5180
Other Schools – See Brookfield

St. Mary S 500/PK-8
97 Herrick Rd 60546 708-442-5747
Frank Valderrama, prin. Fax 442-0125
Singing Winds S 50/PK-8
82 Woodside Rd 60546 708-447-4050

Riverton, Sangamon, Pop. 3,043
Riverton CUSD 14 1,500/PK-12
PO Box 1010 62561 217-629-6009
Tom Mulligan, supt. Fax 629-6008
sangamon.k12.il.us/riverton/
Riverton ES 600/PK-4
PO Box 470 62561 217-629-6001
Stacey Binegar, prin. Fax 629-6023
Riverton MS 400/5-8
PO Box 530 62561 217-629-6002
Fred Lamkey, prin. Fax 629-6017

Riverwoods, Lake, Pop. 4,100

Riverwoods Montessori S 100/PK-6
3140 Riverwoods Rd 60015 847-945-7582
Carolyn Kambich, prin. Fax 948-5136

Roanoke, Woodford, Pop. 1,988
Roanoke-Benson CUSD 60 600/PK-12
PO Box 320 61561 309-923-8921
Rohn Peterson, supt. Fax 923-7508
www.rb60.com/
Sowers ES 300/PK-4
202 W High St 61561 309-923-6241
Kris Kahler, prin. Fax 923-7638
Other Schools – See Benson

Linn Mennonite Christian S 50/K-12
1594 County Road 1700 N 61561 309-923-5641
Jon Yoder, pres.

Robbins, Cook, Pop. 6,375
Posen-Robbins ESD 143-5
Supt. — See Posen
Childs ES 200/K-3
14123 S Lydia Ave 60472 708-388-7203
Tracy Olawumi, prin. Fax 489-4368
Kellar JHS 500/6-8
14123 S Lydia Ave 60472 708-388-7201
Sheila Warfield, prin. Fax 388-6177
Turner Preschool 200/PK-PK
3847 W 135th St 60472 708-388-7205
Vickie Person, prin. Fax 388-0835

Moody Christian Academy 100/PK-8
PO Box 145 60472 708-489-2249
Dr. Marie Moody-James, supt. Fax 489-2264

Robinson, Crawford, Pop. 6,471
Robinson CUSD 2 1,600/K-12
PO Box 190 62454 618-544-7511
Earl Williams, supt. Fax 544-9284
www.robinsonschools.com/
Lincoln ES 300/3-5
301 E Poplar St 62454 618-544-3315
Kevin McConnell, prin. Fax 544-4136
Nuttall MS 400/6-8
400 W Rustic St 62454 618-544-8618
Sue Catt, prin. Fax 544-5304
Washington ES 300/K-2
507 W Condit St 62454 618-544-2233
Joshua Quick, prin. Fax 544-5502

New Hebron Christian S 100/PK-8
10755 E 700th Ave 62454 618-544-7619

Rochelle, Ogle, Pop. 9,712
Rochelle CCSD 231 1,800/PK-8
444 N 8th St 61068 815-562-6363
Todd Prusator, supt. Fax 562-5500
www.d231.rochelle.net/
Central ES 400/PK-5
444 N 8th St 61068 815-562-8251
Jean Kisner, prin. Fax 562-5993
Lincoln ES 300/K-5
108 S Main St 61068 815-562-4520
Lisa Goddard, prin. Fax 561-1005
May ES 300/K-5
1033 N 2nd St 61068 815-562-6331
Barbara Cantlin, prin. Fax 562-2430
Rochelle MS 600/6-8
111 School Ave 61068 815-562-7997
Joe Schwartz, prin. Fax 562-8527
Tilton ES 300/K-5
1050 N 9th St 61068 815-562-6665
Anthony Doyle, prin. Fax 562-2607

St. Paul Lutheran S 200/PK-8
1415 10th Ave 61068 815-562-6323
Daryl Kruse, prin. Fax 561-8074

Rochester, Sangamon, Pop. 3,004
Rochester CUSD 3A 2,200/PK-12
4 Rocket Dr 62563 217-498-6210
Dr. Thomas Bertrand, supt. Fax 498-8045
www.rochester3a.sangamon.k12.il.us
Rochester ES 700/PK-3
707 W Main St 62563 217-498-9778
Therese Borgsmiller, prin. Fax 498-9160
Rochester JHS 300/7-8
3 Rocket Dr 62563 217-498-9761
Brent Ashbaugh, prin. Fax 498-6204
Rochester MS 500/4-6
456 Education Ave 62563 217-498-6215
Laurie Lundin, prin. Fax 498-6218

Rock Falls, Whiteside, Pop. 9,470
East Coloma SD 12 300/K-8
1602 Dixon Rd 61071 815-625-4400
Kevin Andersen, supt. Fax 625-4624
www.ecoloma.net/
East Coloma S 300/K-8
1602 Dixon Rd 61071 815-625-4400
Kevin Andersen, prin. Fax 625-4624

Montmorency CCSD 145 300/K-8
9415 Hoover Rd 61071 815-625-6616
John Rosenberry, supt. Fax 625-8432
mgs.whitesideroe.org/
Montmorency S 300/K-8
9415 Hoover Rd 61071 815-625-6616
John Rosenberry, prin. Fax 625-8432

Nelson ESD 8 50/K-8
PO Box 880 61071 815-251-4412
Dr. Gregory Lutyens, supt. Fax 251-4413
Other Schools – See Nelson

Riverdale SD 14 100/K-8
3505 Prophet Rd 61071 815-625-5280
Sarah Willey, supt. Fax 625-5316
Riverdale S 100/K-8
3505 Prophet Rd 61071 815-625-5280
Sarah Willey, prin. Fax 625-5316

Rock Falls ESD 13 1,000/PK-8
602 4th Ave 61071 815-626-2604
Jack Etnyre, supt. Fax 626-2627
www.rfsd13.org/
Dillon ES 400/PK-2
1901 8th Ave 61071 815-625-3356
Kyle Ackman, prin. Fax 625-2943
Merrill ES 300/3-5
600 4th Ave 61071 815-625-4634
Dan Arickx, prin. Fax 625-1747
Rock Falls MS 300/6-8
1701 12th Ave 61071 815-626-2626
Jeffrey Brown, prin. Fax 626-3198

St. Andrew S 200/PK-8
701 11th Ave 61071 815-625-1456
Philip Bellini, prin. Fax 625-1724

Rockford, Winnebago, Pop. 152,916
Rockford SD 205 29,700/PK-12
201 S Madison St 61104 815-966-3101
Dr. LaVonne Sheffield, supt. Fax 966-3193
www.rps205.com/
Barbour Language Academy 600/K-8
1506 Clover Ave 61102 815-966-3395
Ivelisse Rosas, prin. Fax 967-8039
Beyer ES 300/K-5
333 15th Ave 61104 815-966-3390
William Sadler, prin. Fax 966-3392
Bloom ES 500/PK-5
2912 Brendenwood Rd 61107 815-229-2170
Dr. Sandra Kuzniewski, prin. Fax 229-2457
Brookview ES 500/PK-5
1750 Madron Rd 61107 815-229-2492
LuAnn Widergren, prin. Fax 229-2112
Carlson ES 300/K-5
4015 Pepper Dr 61114 815-654-4955
Dave Nold, prin. Fax 636-3001
Conklin ES 400/K-5
3003 Halsted Rd 61101 815-654-4860
Jan Johnson, prin. Fax 654-4864
Dennis ECC 500/PK-PK
730 Lincoln Park Blvd 61102 815-966-3750
Carol Nelson, prin. Fax 966-3751
Eisenhower MS 900/6-8
3525 Spring Creek Rd 61107 815-229-2450
Jill Davis, prin. Fax 229-2456
Ellis Arts Academy 600/K-8
222 S Central Ave 61102 815-966-3909
Vicki Kested, prin. Fax 966-5266
Fairview ECC 600/PK-PK
512 Fairview Ave 61108 815-229-4230
Larry Turnquist, prin. Fax 229-2445
Flinn MS 900/6-8
2525 Ohio Pkwy 61108 815-229-2800
Todd France, prin. Fax 229-2894
Froberg ES 400/PK-2
4555 20th St 61109 815-874-2464
Toni Gagliano, prin. Fax 874-6228
Gregory ES 300/K-5
4820 Carol Ct 61108 815-229-2176
Vickie Jacobson, prin. Fax 229-2897
Haskell Academy 200/PK-5
515 Maple St 61103 815-966-3355
Ann Rundall, prin. Fax 967-8040
Hillman ES 400/K-5
3701 Green Dale Dr 61109 815-229-2835
Carolyn Kloss, prin. Fax 229-2807
Jackson ES 300/K-5
315 Summit St 61107 815-966-3385
David Molck, prin. Fax 966-3089
Johnson ES 300/K-5
3805 Rural St 61107 815-229-2485
Carol Jeschke, prin. Fax 229-2418
Kennedy MS 700/6-8
4664 N Rockton Ave 61103 815-654-4880
Theresa Kallstrom, prin. Fax 654-4874
King Gifted S 400/1-5
1306 S Court St 61102 815-966-3370
Renneth Richardson, prin. Fax 966-3347
Kishwaukee ES 300/K-5
526 Catlin St 61104 815-966-3380
Al Gagliano, prin. Fax 967-8023
Lathrop ES 400/PK-5
2603 Clover Ave 61102 815-966-3285
Prudy Court, prin. Fax 966-3713
Lemon Global Studies Academy 400/K-5
1993 Mulberry St 61101 815-967-8000
Theresa Harvey, prin. Fax 967-8027
Lincoln MS 800/6-8
1500 Charles St 61104 815-229-2400
Jason Grey, prin. Fax 229-2420
Maria Montessori ES 300/PK-6
4704 N Rockton Ave 61103 815-654-4906
Sue Bauer, prin. Fax 654-4909
Marsh ES 600/K-5
2021 Hawthorne Dr 61107 815-229-2430
Christina Meyer, prin. Fax 229-2461
McIntosh Magnet ES 400/K-5
525 N Pierpont Ave 61101 815-966-3275
Deb Osborne, prin. Fax 966-8922
Nashold ES 400/3-5
3303 20th St 61109 815-229-2155
Peggy Nolte-Heimann, prin. Fax 229-2421
Nelson ES 400/K-5
623 15th St 61104 815-229-2190
Stephen Francisco, prin. Fax 229-2462
New Milford ES 200/3-5
2128 New Milford School Rd 61109 815-874-2446
Christina Ulferts, prin. Fax 874-5551
Riverdahl ES 400/K-2
3520 Kishwaukee St 61109 815-229-2870
Teresa Schneider, prin. Fax 229-2891
Rockford Environmental Science Academy 1,300/6-8
1800 Ogilby Rd 61102 815-489-5509
Dr. Robert DeLacey, prin. Fax 966-5360
Rolling Green ES 600/PK-5
3615 W Gate Pkwy 61108 815-229-2881
Kenneth Held, prin. Fax 229-2135
Spring Creek ES 500/K-5
5222 Spring Creek Rd 61114 815-654-4960
Thomas Schmitt, prin. Fax 654-4969
Stiles ES 200/K-5
315 La Clede Ave 61102 815-966-3790
George Richardson, prin. Fax 966-5244
Summerdale ES 300/K-5
3320 Glenwood Ave 61101 815-966-3280
Julie West, prin. Fax 967-8016
Thompson ES 300/K-5
4949 Marion Ave 61108 815-229-2830
Emma Gentry, prin. Fax 229-2832
Walker ES 400/K-5
1520 Post Ave 61103 815-966-3795
Ray Owens, prin. Fax 966-3172
Washington ES 400/K-5
1421 West St 61102 815-966-3740
Jill Faber, prin. Fax 966-5291
Welsh ES 400/PK-5
2100 Huffman Blvd 61103 815-966-3260
Diana Alt, prin. Fax 966-3259
West MS 800/6-8
1900 N Rockton Ave 61103 815-966-3200
Penny El-Azhari, prin. Fax 966-3216
West View ES 400/PK-5
1720 Halsted Rd 61103 815-654-4945
Veronica Bazan, prin. Fax 654-4903
Whitehead ES 400/K-5
2325 Ohio Pkwy 61108 815-229-2840
John Ulferts, prin. Fax 229-2419
White Swan ES 300/PK-2
7550 Mill Rd 61108 815-229-2184
Dr. Pamela Nichols, prin. Fax 229-2459
Other Schools – See Cherry Valley

Alpine Christian S 50/PK-8
325 N Alpine Rd 61107 815-399-7492
Berean Baptist Christian S 300/PK-12
5626 Safford Rd 61101 815-962-4841
Douglas Swanson, admin. Fax 962-4851
Cathedral of St. Peter S 300/PK-8
1231 N Court St 61103 815-963-3620
Corine Gendron, prin. Fax 963-0551
Christian Life S 1,000/PK-12
5950 Spring Creek Rd 61114 815-877-5749
Roger Beary, prin. Fax 877-4358
Holy Family S 500/K-8
4407 Highcrest Rd 61107 815-398-5331
Anthony Smerko, prin. Fax 398-5902
Keith S 500/PK-12
1 Jacoby Pl 61107 815-399-8823
Betty Giesen, hdmstr. Fax 399-2470
Luther Academy at Alpine 200/PK-6
5001 Forest View Ave 61108 815-227-8894
Fax 227-8899
Montessori Private Academy 100/PK-6
5925 Darlene Dr 61109 815-226-0111
Mary Dunkel, prin. Fax 226-7180
North Love Christian S 200/PK-12
5301 E Riverside Blvd 61114 815-877-6021
Tom Seeley, admin. Fax 877-6076
Rainbow Academy 200/PK-8
6413 Forest Hills Rd 61114 815-877-1489
Rockford Christian S 1,200/PK-12
1401 N Bell School Rd 61107 815-399-3465
Randy Taylor, supt. Fax 391-8004
Rockford Lutheran Academy 400/PK-6
4700 Augustana Dr 61107 815-226-4947
Bruce Bazsali, prin. Fax 226-4886
St. Bernadette S 200/PK-8
2300 Bell Ave 61103 815-968-2288
Elizabeth Heitkamp, prin. Fax 987-9453
St. Edward S 200/PK-8
3020 11th St 61109 815-398-2631
Margo Shifo, prin. Fax 398-3134
St. James S 300/PK-8
409 N 1st St 61107 815-962-8515
Michael Kagan, prin. Fax 962-8526
St. Paul Lutheran S 100/K-8
811 Locust St 61101 815-965-3335
Richard Keske, prin. Fax 965-3335
St. Rita S 300/PK-8
6284 Valley Knoll Dr 61109 815-398-3466
Patrick Flanagan, prin. Fax 398-6104
Spectrum S 200/PK-12
2909 N Main St 61103 815-877-1600
Christine Klekamp, prin. Fax 877-1685

Rock Island, Rock Island, Pop. 38,702
Rock Island SD 41 6,000/PK-12
2101 6th Ave 61201 309-793-5900
Richard Loy, supt. Fax 793-5905
rockislandschools.org/district/
Audubon ES 300/PK-6
2601 18th Ave 61201 309-793-5925
J. Thomas McKinney, prin. Fax 793-4059
Denkmann ES, 4101 22nd Ave 61201 400/PK-6
John Frieden, prin. 309-793-5922
Edison JHS 400/7-8
4141 9th St 61201 309-793-5920
Gary Flecker, prin. Fax 793-5919
Field ES 300/PK-6
2900 31st Ave 61201 309-793-5935
Dennis Weiss, prin. Fax 793-5936
Hanson ES 400/PK-6
4000 9th St 61201 309-793-5930
Debra Taber, prin. Fax 793-4195
Longfellow ES 200/K-6
4198 7th Ave 61201 309-793-5975
David Knuckey, prin. Fax 793-5977
Mann Choice S 300/K-6
3530 38th Ave 61201 309-793-5928
Ruth Ann Tobey-Brown, prin. Fax 793-5965
Ridgewood ES 300/K-6
9607 14th St W 61201 309-793-5980
Nancy Galbraith, prin. Fax 793-5981
Rock Island Intermediate Academy 300/3-6
2100 6th Ave 61201 309-793-5970
Michael Russell, prin. Fax 793-5990
Rock Island Primary Academy 300/PK-2
930 14th St 61201 309-793-5944
Lucille McCorkle, prin. Fax 793-5909
Washington JHS 500/7-8
3300 18th Ave 61201 309-793-5915
Mark Hepner, prin. Fax 793-5917
Willard ES 300/K-6
2503 9th St 61201 309-793-5940
David Bloom, prin. Fax 793-5941
Other Schools – See Milan

Immanuel Lutheran S 100/PK-6
3300 24th St 61201 309-788-8242
Shelley Moeller, prin. Fax 786-3392
Jordan Catholic S 500/PK-8
PO Box 3490 61204 309-793-7350
Michael Daly, prin. Fax 793-7361

Rockton, Winnebago, Pop. 5,348
Rockton SD 140 1,500/PK-8
1050 E Union St 61072 815-624-7143
Jean Harezlak, supt. Fax 624-4640
rockton140.org
Mack MS 500/6-8
11810 Old River Rd 61072 815-624-2611
Kindyl Etnyre, prin. Fax 624-5900
Rockton ES 500/PK-2
1050 E Union St 61072 815-624-8585
Barbara Browning, prin. Fax 624-4640
Whitman Post ES 500/3-5
1060 E Union St 61072 815-624-4006
Scott Rollinson, prin. Fax 624-2125

Rolling Meadows, Cook, Pop. 23,909
Palatine CCSD 15
Supt. — See Palatine
Kimball Hill ES 600/K-6
2905 Meadow Dr 60008 847-963-5200
Rene Valenciano, prin. Fax 963-5206
Plum Grove JHS 800/7-8
2600 Plum Grove Rd 60008 847-963-7600
Dr. Kerry Swalwell, prin. Fax 963-7606
Sandburg JHS 600/7-8
2600 Martin Ln 60008 847-963-7800
Ed Nelson, prin. Fax 963-7806
Willow Bend ES 500/K-6
4700 Barker Ave 60008 847-963-7300
Barbie Rothbauer, prin. Fax 963-7306

Harvest Christian Academy 100/PK-4
800 Rohlwing Rd 60008 847-214-3200
Christina Greiner, prin. Fax 398-7030
St. Collette S 200/PK-8
3900 Pheasant Dr 60008 847-392-4098
Valerie Zemko, prin. Fax 392-8155

Romeoville, Will, Pop. 36,396
Valley View CUSD 365U 17,400/PK-12
755 Luther Dr 60446 815-886-2700
Dr. Phillip Schoffstall, supt. Fax 886-7294
www.vvsd.org/
Hermansen ES 700/K-5
101 Wesglen Pkwy 60446 815-886-7581
Lauren Rentfro, prin. Fax 886-5593
Hill ES 800/PK-5
616 Dalhart Ave 60446 815-886-4343
Paula Bowling, prin. Fax 886-7299
King ES 700/K-5
301 Eaton Ave 60446 815-886-3380
Walter Jamrose, prin. Fax 886-7840
Lukancic MS 6-8
725 W Normantown Rd 60446 815-886-2216
Omar Castillo, prin. Fax 886-2264
Martinez MS 800/6-8
590 Belmont Dr 60446 815-886-6100
Kelly Gilbert, prin. Fax 886-7264
Skoff ES 800/K-5
775 W Normantown Rd 60446 815-886-8384
Jack Shepherd, prin. Fax 886-8389
Valley View ECC 100/PK-PK
753 Luther Dr 60446 815-886-7827
Donna Nylander, prin. Fax 886-7830
Other Schools – See Bolingbrook

Bible Baptist Christian Academy 200/PK-8
301 W Normantown Rd 60446 815-886-4850
St. Andrew the Apostle S 200/PK-8
505 Kingston Dr 60446 815-886-5953
Joseph Leppert, prin. Fax 293-2016

Roodhouse, Greene, Pop. 2,217
North Greene Unit SD 3
Supt. — See White Hall
North Greene JHS 200/6-8
403 W North St 62082 217-589-4623
Cynthia Rice, prin. Fax 589-4028
Roodhouse S 200/PK-PK, 1-
403 W North St 62082 217-589-4623
Cynthia Rice, prin. Fax 589-4028

Roscoe, Winnebago, Pop. 6,355
Kinnikinnick CCSD 131 2,100/PK-8
5410 Pine Ln 61073 815-623-2837
Robert Lauber, supt. Fax 623-9285
www.kinn131.org
Kinnikinnick ES 500/4-5
5410 Pine Ln 61073 815-623-2166
John Schwuchow, prin. Fax 623-1797
Ledgewood ES 500/PK-3
11685 S Gate Rd 61073 815-623-2118
Keli Freedlund, prin. Fax 623-1410
Roscoe MS 700/6-8
6121 Elevator Rd 61073 815-623-1884
Julie Cropp, prin. Fax 623-7604
Stone Creek S 500/PK-3
11633 S Gate Rd 61073 815-623-2865
John Novota, prin. Fax 623-3646

Roselle, DuPage, Pop. 23,240
Keeneyville SD 20
Supt. — See Hanover Park
Waterbury ES 600/PK-5
355 Rodenburg Rd 60172 630-893-8180
Beth Carow, prin. Fax 893-3797

Medinah SD 11 700/K-8
700 E Granville Ave 60172 630-893-3737
Dr. Joseph Bailey, supt. Fax 893-4947
www.medinah.dupage.k12.il.us
Medinah MS 300/6-8
700 E Granville Ave 60172 630-893-3838
Dr. Kara Egger, prin. Fax 893-5198
Other Schools – See Medinah

Roselle SD 12 700/K-8
100 E Walnut St 60172 630-529-2091
Dr. Lori Bein, supt. Fax 529-2467
www.sd12.k12.il.us/
Roselle MS 300/6-8
500 S Park St 60172 630-529-1600
Kathleen Schneiter, prin. Fax 529-1882
Spring Hills ES 500/K-5
560 Pinecroft Dr 60172 630-529-1883
Mary Solomon, prin. Fax 529-1948

Schaumburg CCSD 54
Supt. — See Schaumburg
Nerge ES 600/K-6
660 N Woodfield Trl 60172 847-357-5777
Christopher Martelli, prin. Fax 357-5778

St. Walter S 700/PK-8
201 W Maple Ave 60172 630-529-1721
Mary Lloyd, prin. Fax 529-9290
Trinity Lutheran S 500/PK-8
405 Rush St 60172 630-894-3263
Ed Bower, prin. Fax 894-1430

Rosemont, Cook, Pop. 4,037
Rosemont ESD 78 300/PK-8
6101 Ruby St 60018 847-825-0144
Kevin Anderson, supt. Fax 825-9704
Rosemont S 300/PK-8
6101 Ruby St 60018 847-825-0144
Kevin Anderson, prin. Fax 825-9704

Roseville, Warren, Pop. 998
Monmouth-Roseville CUSD 238
Supt. — See Monmouth
Monmouth-Roseville JHS 300/7-8
200 E Gossett St 61473 309-426-2682
Don Farr, prin. Fax 426-2303
Roseville ES 200/PK-6
265 W Penn Ave 61473 309-426-2841
Debbra Martin, prin. Fax 426-2038

Rossville, Vermilion, Pop. 1,183
Rossville-Alvin CUSD 7 300/PK-8
350 N Chicago St 60963 217-748-6666
Randy Hird, supt. Fax 748-6144
Rossville-Alvin S 300/PK-8
350 N Chicago St 60963 217-748-6666
Nick Chatterton, prin. Fax 748-6121

Round Lake, Lake, Pop. 14,803
CCSD 46
Supt. — See Grayslake
Park S Campus K-8
400 W Townline Rd 60073 847-223-3650
Craig Keer, prin. Fax 201-1971

Round Lake Area SD 116 6,400/PK-12
316 S Rosedale Ct 60073 847-270-9000
Dr. Ben Martindale, supt. Fax 546-3538
www.rlas-116.org/
Early Education Center 700/PK-1
882 W Nippersink Rd 60073 847-270-9490
Jack Melfi, prin. Fax 740-5183
Ellis ES 700/1-5
720 Central Park Dr 60073 847-270-9900
Bill Pritchard, prin. Fax 546-2463
Indian Hill ES 600/1-5
1920 Lotus Dr 60073 847-270-9970
Dr. Ken Rose, prin. Fax 270-3172
Magee MS 6-8
500 N Cedar Lake Rd 60073 847-270-9001
Eric Gallagher, prin.
Murphy ES 600/1-5
220 Greenwood Dr 60073 847-270-9950
Jeffrey Prickett, prin. Fax 546-2394
Round Lake Beach ES 700/1-6
1421 Ardmore Dr 60073 847-270-9930
Keel Vetere, prin. Fax 270-3153
Round Lake MS, 2000 Lotus Dr 60073 1,000/6-8
Brian Minarcik, prin. 847-270-9400
Village ES 400/K-5
880 W Nippersink Rd 60073 847-270-9470
Elizabeth Sullivan, prin. Fax 546-2848

St. Joseph S 300/PK-8
118 Lincoln Ave 60073 847-546-1720
Jeanne Petkus, prin. Fax 546-1720

Round Lake Beach, Lake, Pop. 28,253
CCSD 46
Supt. — See Grayslake
Avon Center ES 500/K-4
1617 Il Route 83, 847-223-3530
Lynn Barkley, prin. Fax 223-3532

Roxana, Madison, Pop. 1,504
Roxana CUSD 1 2,100/PK-12
401 Chaffer Ave 62084 618-254-7544
Debra Kreutztrager, supt. Fax 254-7547
www.roxanaschools.org
Central ES 500/K-5
601 Chaffer Ave 62084 618-254-7594
James Miller, prin. Fax 254-7530
Roxana JHS 500/6-8
401 Chaffer Ave 62084 618-254-7561
Laura Montgomery, prin. Fax 254-8107
Other Schools – See South Roxana

Royal, Champaign, Pop. 273
Prairieview-Ogden CCSD 197 200/K-8
PO Box 27 61871 217-583-3300
Victor White, supt. Fax 583-3391
www.pvo.k12.il.us/
Prairieview-Ogden North ES 100/K-4
PO Box 27 61871 217-583-3300
Victor White, prin. Fax 583-3391
Other Schools – See Ogden, Thomasboro

Rushville, Schuyler, Pop. 3,162
Schuyler-Industry CUSD 5 1,300/PK-12
740 Maple Ave 62681 217-322-4311
R. Mathew Plater, supt. Fax 322-4398
www.sid5.com/
Schuyler-Industry MS 400/6-8
750 N Congress St 62681 217-322-4311
Jim Shepherd, prin. Fax 322-3938
Washington ES 200/PK-1
100 Buchanan St 62681 217-322-4311
Tony Whiston, prin. Fax 322-3195
Webster ES 200/2-4
310 N Monroe St 62681 217-322-4311
Tony Whiston, prin. Fax 322-2391
Other Schools – See Industry

Saint Anne, Kankakee, Pop. 1,188
Saint Anne CCSD 256 400/PK-8
PO Box 530 60964 815-427-8190
John Palan, supt. Fax 427-6019
www.sags.k12.il.us
Saint Anne S 400/PK-8
PO Box 530 60964 815-427-8153
Dawn Garner, prin. Fax 427-6019

Saint Charles, Kane, Pop. 32,010
Saint Charles CUSD 303 13,600/PK-12
201 S 7th St 60174 630-513-3030
Dr. Donald Schlomann, supt. Fax 513-5392
www.d303.org
Anderson ES 500/K-5
35W071 Villa Maria Rd 60174 847-697-5040
Jeff Hildreth, prin. Fax 697-5091
Bell-Graham ES 600/K-5
4N505 Fox Mill Blvd 60175 630-762-6670
Ruth Ann Dunton, prin. Fax 762-6679
Davis ES 600/K-5
1125 S 7th St 60174 630-377-4822
Michael Backer, prin. Fax 513-3016
Ferson Creek ES 600/PK-5
38W160 Bolcum Rd 60175 630-513-4480
Christopher Adkins, prin. Fax 513-4844
Fox Ridge ES 500/PK-5
1905 E Tyler Rd 60174 630-513-4460
Anne VanZandt, prin. Fax 584-9660
Haines MS 1,100/6-8
305 S 9th St 60174 630-377-4827
Charlie Kyle, prin. Fax 377-4830
Lincoln ES 300/K-5
211 S 6th Ave 60174 630-377-4838
Adam Zbrozek, prin. Fax 513-2400
Munhall ES 500/K-5
1400 S 13th Ave 60174 630-377-4862
Jan Geier, prin. Fax 377-4861
Richmond ES 400/K-5
300 S 12th St 60174 630-377-4866
Guillermo Heredia, prin. Fax 584-2944
Thompson MS 900/6-8
705 W Main St 60174 630-377-4872
Stephen Morrill, prin. Fax 584-9591
Wild Rose ES 500/K-5
36W730 Red Haw Ln 60174 630-377-4890
Donna Clavelli, prin. Fax 513-4473
Wredling MS 1,100/6-8
1200 Dunham Rd 60174 630-443-3360
Melissa Dockum, prin. Fax 443-2770
Other Schools – See South Elgin, Wasco, West Chicago

Bridges Montessori Academy 200/PK-5
716 Oak St 60174 630-513-9742
Jan Dangles, admin. Fax 587-6298
St. Patrick S 500/K-8
118 N 5th St 60174 630-584-6367
Joseph Battisto, prin. Fax 584-9759

Saint Elmo, Fayette, Pop. 1,408
Saint Elmo CUSD 202 500/PK-12
1200 N Walnut St 62458 618-829-3264
Deborah Philpot, supt. Fax 829-5161
www.stelmo.org/
Saint Elmo ES 300/PK-6
519 W 2nd St 62458 618-829-3263
Sean Hannagan, prin. Fax 829-5161
Saint Elmo JHS 100/7-8
300 W 12th St 62458 618-829-3227
Brian Garrard, prin. Fax 829-5161

Sainte Marie, Jasper, Pop. 244
Jasper County CUSD 1
Supt. — See Newton
Sainte Marie ES 100/1-6
PO Box 157 62459 618-455-3219
David Parker, prin. Fax 455-3223

Saint Jacob, Madison, Pop. 897
Triad CUSD 2
Supt. — See Troy
Saint Jacob ES 200/PK-5
PO Box 217 62281 618-644-2541
Jay Simpson, prin. Fax 644-5474
Triad MS 900/6-8
9539 US Highway 40 62281 618-644-5511
Dale Sauer, prin. Fax 644-9435

Saint Joseph, Champaign, Pop. 3,266
Saint Joseph CCSD 169 800/PK-8
PO Box 409 61873 217-469-2291
Todd Pence, supt. Fax 469-8906
www.stjoe.k12.il.us
Saint Joseph ES 500/PK-4
PO Box 409 61873 217-469-2291
Mike Sennert, prin. Fax 469-8906
Saint Joseph MS 400/5-8
PO Box 409 61873 217-469-2334
Chris Graham, prin. Fax 469-2537

Saint Libory, Saint Clair, Pop. 592
Saint Libory Consolidated SD 30 100/PK-8
PO Box 323 62282 618-768-4923
Dr. Carl Buehler, supt. Fax 768-4518
www.stlibory30.org

Saint Libory S 100/PK-8
PO Box 323 62282 618-768-4923
Dr. Carl Buehler, prin. Fax 768-4518

Saint Peter, Fayette, Pop. 382

St. Peter Lutheran S 100/PK-8
RR 1 Box 70 62880 618-349-8888
Lawrence Urban, prin. Fax 349-8888

Salem, Marion, Pop. 7,574
Salem SD 111 900/K-8
1300 Hawthorn Rd 62881 618-548-7702
Mark Cartwright, supt. Fax 548-7714
www.salem111.com
Franklin Park MS 500/4-8
1325 N Franklin St 62881 618-548-7704
David Conklin, prin. Fax 548-7712
Hawthorn ES 400/K-3
1300 Hawthorn Rd 62881 618-548-7702
Marty Adams, prin. Fax 548-7714

Selmaville CCSD 10 200/K-8
3185 Selmaville Rd 62881 618-548-2416
Robin Brooks, supt. Fax 548-6063
Selmaville North S 200/K-8
3185 Selmaville Rd 62881 618-548-2416
Margo Wagner, prin. Fax 548-6063

St. Theresa of Avila S 100/K-8
190 N Ohio Ave 62881 618-548-3492
Sr. Margaret Schmidt, prin. Fax 548-9673

Sandoval, Marion, Pop. 1,362
Sandoval CUSD 501 600/PK-12
859 W Missouri Ave 62882 618-247-3233
Dr. John Raymer, supt. Fax 247-3243
Sandoval ES 300/PK-6
300 E Perry Ave 62882 618-247-3450
Charles Schulte, prin. Fax 247-3450
Sandoval JHS 100/7-8
859 W Missouri Ave 62882 618-247-3361
Jim Maddox, prin. Fax 247-3243

Sandwich, DeKalb, Pop. 7,018
Sandwich CUSD 430 2,600/PK-12
720 S Wells St 60548 815-786-2187
Rick Schmitt, supt. Fax 786-6229
www.sandwich430.org
Dummer S 400/4-5
422 S Wells St 60548 815-786-8498
Tom Sodaro, prin. Fax 786-1920
Haskin ES 300/PK-3
720 S Wells St 60548 815-786-8812
Dawn Greenacre, prin. Fax 786-8986
Prairie View ES 300/PK-3
1201 Castle St 60548 815-786-8811
Sherrie Stricklin, prin. Fax 786-7404
Sandwich MS 600/6-8
600 S Wells St 60548 815-786-2138
B.J. Richardson, prin. Fax 786-6606
Woodbury ES 200/PK-3
322 E 3rd St 60548 815-786-6316
Shirley Decorte, prin. Fax 786-2691

Sauk Village, Cook, Pop. 10,486
CCSD 168 1,800/PK-8
21899 Torrence Ave 60411 708-758-1610
Dr. Rudolph Williams, supt. Fax 758-5929
www.d168.org
Rickover JHS 600/6-8
22151 Torrence Ave 60411 708-758-1900
Julie Iverson, prin. Fax 758-1601
Strassburg ES 500/3-5
2002 223rd St 60411 708-758-4754
Lynda Bozeman, prin. Fax 758-2202
Wagoner ES 700/PK-2
1831 215th Pl 60411 708-758-3322
Kathleen Lemler, prin. Fax 758-0801

Saunemin, Livingston, Pop. 449
Saunemin CCSD 438 100/PK-8
PO Box 290 61769 815-832-4421
Julie Schmitt, supt. Fax 832-4435
Saunemin S 100/PK-8
PO Box 290 61769 815-832-4421
Julie Schmitt, prin. Fax 832-4435

Savanna, Carroll, Pop. 3,288
West Carroll CUSD 314
Supt. — See Thomson
West Carroll PS 500/PK-3
2215 Wacker Rd 61074 815-273-7747
Rex Kreuder, prin. Fax 273-3846

Scales Mound, Jo Daviess, Pop. 387
Scales Mound CUSD 211 200/PK-12
210 Main St 61075 815-845-2215
Laura Nelson, supt. Fax 845-2238
www.scalesmound.net
Scales Mound ES 100/PK-5
210 Main St 61075 815-845-2215
Matthew Wiederholt, prin. Fax 845-2238
Scales Mound JHS 100/6-8
210 Main St 61075 815-845-2215
Matthew Wiederholt, prin. Fax 845-2238

Schaumburg, Cook, Pop. 72,805
Schaumburg CCSD 54 14,200/PK-8
524 E Schaumburg Rd 60194 847-357-5000
Ed Rafferty, supt. Fax 357-5006
www.sd54.org/
Addams JHS 700/7-8
700 S Springinsguth Rd 60193 847-357-5900
Steve Pearce, prin. Fax 357-5901
Aldrin ES 600/PK-6
617 Boxwood Dr 60193 847-357-5400
Mary Botterman, prin. Fax 357-5401
Blackwell ES 400/PK-6
345 N Walnut Ln 60194 847-357-5555
Dr. Maria Clifford, prin. Fax 357-5556

Campanelli ES 500/PK-6
310 S Springinsguth Rd 60193 847-357-5333
Steve Kern, prin. Fax 357-5334
Collins ES 600/PK-6
407 Summit Dr 60193 847-357-6100
Laura Rosenblum, prin. Fax 357-6101
Dirksen ES 500/K-6
116 W Beech Dr 60193 847-357-5600
Peter Hannigan, prin. Fax 357-5601
Dooley ES 500/K-6
622 Norwood Ln 60193 847-357-6250
Marion Flaman, prin. Fax 357-6251
Enders/Salk ES 500/K-6
345 N Salem Dr 60194 847-357-6400
Dr. James Tohme, prin. Fax 357-6401
Frost JHS 600/7-8
320 W Wise Rd 60193 847-357-6800
Paul Goldberg, prin. Fax 357-6801
Hale ES 500/K-6
1300 W Wise Rd 60193 847-357-6200
Michael Henry, prin. Fax 357-6201
Hoover ES 600/K-6
315 N Springinsguth Rd 60194 847-357-5800
Jake Chung, prin. Fax 357-5801
Keller JHS 600/7-8
820 Bode Rd 60194 847-357-6500
Sue Mayernick, prin. Fax 357-6501
Other Schools – See Elk Grove Village, Hanover Park, Hoffman Estates, Roselle

---

St. Peter Lutheran S 300/PK-8
208 E Schaumburg Rd 60194 847-885-7636
Roger Kirsch, prin. Fax 882-9157
Schaumburg Christian S 1,400/PK-12
200 N Roselle Rd 60194 847-885-3230
James White, prin. Fax 885-3354

Schiller Park, Cook, Pop. 11,597
Schiller Park SD 81 1,200/PK-8
4050 Wagner Ave 60176 847-671-1816
Dr. Roberta Taylor, supt. Fax 671-1872
www.sd81.org/
Kennedy ES 600/PK-3
3945 Wehrman Ave 60176 847-671-0250
Kimberly Boryszewski, prin. Fax 671-0256
Lincoln MS 400/6-8
4050 Wagner Ave 60176 847-678-2916
Constance Stavrou, prin. Fax 678-4059
Washington ES 200/4-5
4835 Michigan Ave 60176 847-671-1922
Kristin Kopta, prin. Fax 671-1972

St. Beatrice S 100/PK-8
4141 Atlantic Ave 60176 847-678-1752
Marlene Hionis, prin. Fax 678-1033
St. Maria Goretti S 200/PK-8
10050 Ivanhoe Ave 60176 847-678-2560
Christine Weiner, prin. Fax 678-2919

Scott AFB, Saint Clair, Pop. 7,245
Mascoutah CUSD 19
Supt. — See Mascoutah
Scott ES 600/PK-5
4732 Patriots Dr 62225 618-746-4738
Geri Sullivan, prin. Fax 746-2186

Seneca, LaSalle, Pop. 2,057
Seneca CCSD 170 600/PK-8
174 Oak St 61360 815-357-8744
Eric Misener, supt. Fax 357-1516
www.sgs170.org
Seneca ES North Campus 300/PK-4
174 Oak St 61360 815-357-8744
Lynn McGhee, prin. Fax 357-1516
Seneca MS South Campus 300/5-8
174 Oak St 61360 815-357-8744
Shane Severson, prin. Fax 357-1078

Serena, LaSalle
Serena CUSD 2 900/K-12
2283 N 3812th Rd 60549 815-496-2850
Daniel Joyce, supt. Fax 496-2987
www.unit2.net/
Serena S 200/K-8
2283 N 3812th Rd 60549 815-496-9250
Paul Schrik, prin. Fax 496-2987
Other Schools – See Earlville, Sheridan

Sesser, Franklin, Pop. 2,136
Sesser-Valier CUSD 196 800/PK-12
4626 State Highway 154 62884 618-625-5105
Jason Henry, supt. Fax 625-6696
www.s-v.frnkln.k12.il.us/
Sesser-Valier ES 300/PK-5
4626 State Highway 154 62884 618-625-5105
Judy Logsdon, prin. Fax 625-3040
Sesser-Valier JHS 200/6-8
4626 State Highway 154 62884 618-625-5105
Judy Logsdon, prin. Fax 625-3040

Seward, Winnebago
Winnebago CUSD 323
Supt. — See Winnebago
Seward S 100/PK-K
PO Box 100 61077 815-247-8441
Charlene Remer, prin. Fax 247-8896

Shabbona, DeKalb, Pop. 943
Indian Creek CUSD 425 900/K-12
506 S Shabbona Rd 60550 815-824-2197
Pamela Rockwood, supt. Fax 824-2199
www.indiancreekschools.org
Shabbona ES 200/K-5
301 W Cherokee Ave 60550 815-824-2343
David Mantzke, prin. Fax 824-2343
Other Schools – See Waterman

Shannon, Carroll, Pop. 799
Eastland CUSD 308
Supt. — See Lanark
Eastland MS 300/3-8
601 S Chestnut St 61078 815-864-2300
Darcie Feltmeyer, prin. Fax 864-2281

Shelbyville, Shelby, Pop. 4,739
Shelbyville CUSD 4 1,300/PK-12
720 W Main St 62565 217-774-4626
Robert Verdun, supt. Fax 774-2521
Main Street ES 300/PK-PK, 1-
225 W Main St 62565 217-774-4731
Denise Bence, prin. Fax 774-3016
Moulton MS 500/4-8
1101 W North 6th St 62565 217-774-2169
Jacque Eberspacher, prin. Fax 774-3042
Shelbyville K 100/K-K
1001 W North 6th St 62565 217-774-3926
Denise Bence, prin. Fax 774-5836

Sheldon, Iroquois, Pop. 1,178
Milford CCSD 280
Supt. — See Milford
Sheldon ES 100/PK-5
150 S Randolph St 60966 815-429-3317
David Caldwell, prin. Fax 429-3458

Sheridan, LaSalle, Pop. 2,226
Serena CUSD 2
Supt. — See Serena
Sheridan S 200/K-8
PO Box 328 60551 815-496-2002
Randy Goodbred, prin. Fax 496-9521

Sheridan SDA S 50/1-8
3904 E 2603rd Rd 60551 815-496-2947

Sherman, Sangamon, Pop. 3,465
Williamsville CUSD 15
Supt. — See Williamsville
Sherman ES 700/PK-5
312 South St 62684 217-496-2021
Janis Lindsey, prin. Fax 496-2473

Sherrard, Mercer, Pop. 671
Sherrard CUSD 200 1,800/PK-12
PO Box 369 61281 309-593-4075
Rebecca Rodocker, supt. Fax 593-4078
www.sherrard.us
Sherrard ES 300/K-4
209 1st St 61281 309-593-2917
Fax 593-2409
Sherrard JHS 300/7-8
4701 176th Ave 61281 309-593-2135
Fax 593-2143
Other Schools – See Matherville, Milan, Viola

Shiloh, Saint Clair, Pop. 10,367

True Vine Christian Academy 100/PK-3
2241 Country Rd 62221 618-257-8783
Dr. Sandra Rhodes, dir. Fax 257-1190

Shipman, Macoupin, Pop. 655
Southwestern CUSD 9
Supt. — See Piasa
Shipman ES 100/K-6
PO Box 229 62685 618-836-5535
Jason Ehlers, prin. Fax 836-7014

Shirland, Winnebago
Shirland CCSD 134 100/K-8
PO Box 99 61079 815-629-2000
Don Maxwell, supt. Fax 629-2100
www.shirland134.com/
Shirland S 100/K-8
PO Box 99 61079 815-629-2000
Don Maxwell, prin. Fax 629-2100

Shorewood, Will, Pop. 12,114
Minooka CCSD 201
Supt. — See Minooka
Walnut Trails ES 700/K-5
301 Wynstone Dr, 815-725-9360
Kathleen Cheshareck, prin. Fax 725-9366

Troy CCSD 30C
Supt. — See Plainfield
Troy Crossroads ES 700/PK-4
210 E Black Rd, 815-725-6210
Susan Dowse, prin. Fax 729-7441
Troy Hofer ES, 910 Vertin Blvd, K-4
Robert Baughman, prin. 815-577-6758
Troy Shorewood ES 500/K-4
210 School Rd, 815-725-8912
Daniel Malloy, prin. Fax 729-7447

Holy Family S 300/PK-8
600 Brook Forest Ave, 815-725-8149
Judy Strohschein, prin. Fax 725-8649
Trinity Christian S 500/PK-8
901 Shorewood Dr, 815-577-9310
Joan Onwiler, admin. Fax 577-9695

Shumway, Effingham, Pop. 219
Beecher City CUSD 20
Supt. — See Beecher City
Shumway ES 100/K-2
304 S West St 62461 217-868-2788

Sidell, Vermilion, Pop. 603
Jamaica CUSD 12 500/PK-12
7087 N 600 East Rd 61876 217-288-9306
Mark Janesky, supt. Fax 288-9306
Jamaica ES 200/PK-5
7087 N 600 East Rd 61876 217-288-9394
Mollie Pletch, prin.
Jamaica JHS 100/6-8
7087 N 600 East Rd 61876 217-288-9394
Mollie Pletch, prin.

Sigel, Shelby, Pop. 405

St. Michael the Archangel S 100/1-8
PO Box 8 62462 217-844-2231
Irene Koester, prin. Fax 844-2309

Silvis, Rock Island, Pop. 7,489
Carbon Cliff-Barstow SD 36 300/K-8
2002 Eagle Ridge Dr 61282 309-792-2002
Andy Richmond, supt. Fax 792-2244
www.ccb36.com
Eagle Ridge S 300/K-8
2002 Eagle Ridge Dr 61282 309-792-2002
Andy Richmond, prin. Fax 792-2244

East Moline SD 37
Supt. — See East Moline
Bowlesburg ES 400/K-4
2221 10th St 61282 309-792-2947
Catherine Baumgartner, prin. Fax 792-9658

Silvis SD 34 700/PK-8
1305 5th Ave 61282 309-792-9325
Ray Bergles, supt. Fax 792-8092
www.silvis34.com
Barr ES, 1305 5th Ave 61282 400/PK-5
Michael Hughes, prin. 309-792-0639
Silvis JHS, 1305 5th Ave 61282 200/6-8
Art Byczynski, prin. 309-792-3511

Skokie, Cook, Pop. 64,678
East Prairie SD 73 500/PK-8
7634 E Prairie Rd 60076 847-673-1141
Dr. James Schopp, supt. Fax 324-4367
www.eps.n-cook.k12.il.us
East Prairie S 500/PK-8
3907 Dobson St 60076 847-673-1141
Theresa Madl, prin. Fax 673-1186

Evanston CCSD 65
Supt. — See Evanston
Rhodes Magnet S 300/K-8
3701 Davis St 60076 847-859-8440
Jason Ewing, prin. Fax 674-3926

Fairview SD 72 600/K-8
7040 Laramie Ave 60077 847-929-1050
Dr. Cindy Whittaker, supt. Fax 929-1060
www.fairview.k12.il.us
Fairview South S 600/K-8
7040 Laramie Ave 60077 847-929-1048
David Russo, prin. Fax 929-1058

Skokie SD 68 1,600/K-8
9440 Kenton Ave 60076 847-676-9000
Dr. Frances McTague, supt. Fax 676-9232
www.skokie68.org
Devonshire ES 300/K-5
9040 Kostner Ave 60076 847-676-9280
Randy Needlman, prin. Fax 676-4031
Highland ES 300/K-5
9700 Crawford Ave 60076 847-676-9380
Leslie Gordon, prin. Fax 676-4048
Old Orchard JHS 600/6-8
9310 Kenton Ave 60076 847-676-9010
Luis Illa, prin. Fax 676-3827
Stenson ES 300/K-5
9201 Lockwood Ave 60077 847-676-9480
Susan O'Neil, prin. Fax 967-9386

Skokie SD 69 1,500/PK-8
5050 Madison St 60077 847-675-7666
Kenneth Cull Ed.D., supt. Fax 675-7675
www.skokie69.k12.il.us
Lincoln JHS 500/6-8
7839 Lincoln Ave 60077 847-676-3545
James Morrison, prin. Fax 676-3595
Madison S 600/PK-2
5100 Madison St 60077 847-675-3048
Lisa Halverson, prin. Fax 675-1691
Other Schools – See Morton Grove

Skokie SD 73-5 1,100/PK-8
8000 E Prairie Rd 60076 847-673-1220
Kate Donegan, supt. Fax 673-1565
www.skokie735.k12.il.us/
McCracken MS 400/6-8
8000 E Prairie Rd 60076 847-673-1220
Jason Smith, prin. Fax 673-1282
Meyer S 200/PK-K
8100 Tripp Ave 60076 847-673-1223
Alison Gordon, prin. Fax 933-4382
Middleton ES 500/1-5
8300 Saint Louis Ave 60076 847-673-1222
Dana Otto, prin. Fax 673-1256

Arie Crown Hebrew S 600/PK-8
4600 Main St 60076 847-982-9191
Rabbi Eli Samber, prin. Fax 982-9525
Cheder Lubavitch Boys Hebrew S 200/K-8
5201 Howard St 60077 847-675-6777
Gesher HaTorah Day S K-6
5130 Touhy Ave 60077 847-674-6740
Rabbi Meir Shapiro, prin. Fax 674-6741
Hillel Torah North Suburban S 400/PK-8
7120 Laramie Ave 60077 847-674-6533
St. Paul Lutheran Academy 100/PK-8
5201 Galitz St 60077 847-673-5030
Dale Luksha, prin. Fax 673-9828
St. Peter S 200/PK-8
8140 Niles Center Rd 60077 847-673-0918
Joan McCain, prin. Fax 673-6469
Skokie Solomon Schechter S 300/K-5
9301 Gross Point Rd 60076 847-679-6270
Dr. David Abusch-Magder, prin. Fax 679-9186
Torah Montessori S 50/PK-3
4700 Oakton St 60076 847-232-1520
Rivkah Schack, dir. Fax 232-1521

Sleepy Hollow, Kane, Pop. 3,695
CUSD 300
Supt. — See Carpentersville
Sleepy Hollow ES 800/K-5
898 Glen Oak Dr 60118 847-426-1460
Anastasia Epstein, prin. Fax 426-1290

Smithton, Saint Clair, Pop. 2,870
Smithton CCSD 130 400/PK-8
PO Box 395 62285 618-233-6863
Dr. Steven York, supt. Fax 233-8413
www.smithton.stclair.k12.il.us
Smithton S 400/PK-8
PO Box 395 62285 618-233-6863
Vicki Norton, prin. Fax 233-8413

St. John the Baptist S 100/K-8
10 S Lincoln St 62285 618-233-0581
Kevin Spiller, prin. Fax 937-2287

Somonauk, DeKalb, Pop. 1,492
Somonauk CUSD 432 1,000/PK-12
PO Box 278 60552 815-498-2314
M. Susan Workman, supt. Fax 498-9523
www.somonauk.net/
Somonauk MS 300/5-8
PO Box 278 60552 815-498-1866
Matthew Jeffrey, prin. Fax 498-1647
Wood ES 400/PK-4
PO Box 278 60552 815-498-2338
Christine Pruski, prin. Fax 498-9361

Sorento, Bond, Pop. 588
Bond County CUSD 2
Supt. — See Greenville
Sorento S 200/PK-8
PO Box 68 62086 217-272-4111
Bill Carpenter, prin. Fax 272-4591

South Beloit, Winnebago, Pop. 5,421
Prairie Hill CCSD 133 700/K-8
14714 Willowbrook Rd 61080 815-389-4694
Ted Rehl, supt. Fax 389-8582
www.prairiehill.org
Prairie Hill S 700/K-8
14714 Willowbrook Rd 61080 815-389-2791
Michael Michowski, prin. Fax 389-8582

South Beloit CUSD 320 1,100/PK-12
850 Hayes Ave 61080 815-389-3478
Michael Duffy, supt. Fax 389-3477
www.southbeloitschooldistrict.org
Blackhawk ES 200/5-6
840 Blackhawk Blvd 61080 815-389-4001
Michael McCoy, prin. Fax 389-8811
Clark ES 200/PK-1
464 Oak Grove Ave 61080 815-389-2311
Suzanne Deasey, prin. Fax 389-9002
Riverview ES 200/2-4
306 Miller St 61080 815-389-1231
Scott Fisher, prin. Fax 389-9067
South Beloit JHS 200/7-8
840 Blackhawk Blvd 61080 815-389-1421
Michael McCoy, prin. Fax 389-8811

St. Peter S 100/PK-8
320 Elmwood Ave 61080 815-389-3193
John Fitzsimmons, prin. Fax 389-2274

South Chicago Heights, Cook, Pop. 3,873
Chicago Heights SD 170
Supt. — See Chicago Heights
Grant S 300/K-8
2712 Miller Ave 60411 708-756-4156
Lou Angellotti, prin. Fax 756-4644

Steger SD 194
Supt. — See Steger
Saukview ES 400/PK-5
3341 Miller Ave 60411 708-755-9600
Jeff Nelson, prin. Fax 709-2068

South Elgin, Kane, Pop. 20,758
SD U-46
Supt. — See Elgin
Clinton ES 400/K-6
770 Mill St 60177 847-888-7045
John Oliver, prin. Fax 608-2742
Fox Meadow ES 800/K-6
1275 Jenna Dr 60177 847-888-7182
Jacqueline Hazen, prin. Fax 888-7194
Kenyon Woods MS 900/7-8
1515 Raymond St 60177 847-289-6685
Sue Welu, prin. Fax 628-6166
Willard ES 400/K-6
370 W Spring St 60177 847-888-5275
Shawn Schleizer, prin. Fax 608-2755

Saint Charles CUSD 303
Supt. — See Saint Charles
Corron ES 600/K-5
455 Thornwood Way 60177 847-741-7998
Denise Liechty, prin. Fax 741-5802

South Holland, Cook, Pop. 21,552
Dolton SD 149
Supt. — See Calumet City
New Beginnings Learning Academy 500/K-6
156th and Clyde 60473 708-768-5200
Carolyn Franklin, prin. Fax 768-5209

South Holland SD 150 1,100/PK-8
848 E 170th St 60473 708-339-4240
Dr. Jerry Jordan, supt. Fax 339-4244
www.sd150.org
Greenwood ES 500/PK-3
16800 Greenwood Ave 60473 708-339-4433
William Kolloway, prin. Fax 339-3942
McKinley ES 200/4-5
850 E 170th St 60473 708-339-4748
Michelle Coleman, prin. Fax 331-5806
McKinley JHS 400/6-8
16949 Cottage Grove Ave 60473 708-339-8500
Michelle Coleman, prin. Fax 331-5805

South Holland SD 151 1,600/PK-8
525 E 162nd St 60473 708-339-1516
Dr. Douglas Hamilton, supt. Fax 331-7600
www.shsd151.org
Eisenhower ES 300/2-3
16001 Minerva Ave 60473 708-339-5900
Dr. Rhonda Towner, prin. Fax 210-3252
Madison ES 400/4-5
15700 Orchid Dr 60473 708-339-2117
Regina Bridges, prin. Fax 210-3250
Other Schools – See Harvey, Phoenix

Calvary Academy 300/PK-8
16300 State St 60473 708-333-5471
Karen Pender, admin. Fax 333-5771
Calvin Christian S 300/PK-8
528 E 161st Pl 60473 708-331-5027
Ryan Groen, dir. Fax 331-8728
Christ Our Savior S West Campus 300/K-8
900 E 154th St 60473 708-333-8173
Matthew Lungaro, prin. Fax 339-3336

South Pekin, Tazewell, Pop. 1,213
South Pekin SD 137 300/PK-8
PO Box 430 61564 309-348-3695
Andrew Brooks, supt. Fax 348-3162
www.spgs.net
South Pekin S 300/PK-8
PO Box 430 61564 309-348-3695
Andrew Brooks, prin. Fax 348-3162

South Roxana, Madison, Pop. 1,826
Roxana CUSD 1
Supt. — See Roxana
South Roxana ES 500/PK-5
414 Indiana Ave 62087 618-254-7591
Keri Mueller, prin. Fax 254-7592

Bethel Christian Academy 100/K-12
PO Box 535 62087 618-254-0188
Ricky Ham, supt. Fax 254-2067

South Wilmington, Grundy, Pop. 625
South Wilmington CCSD 74 100/K-8
PO Box 459 60474 815-237-2281
Lynn Schroeder, supt. Fax 237-2713
South Wilmington Consolidated S 100/K-8
PO Box 459 60474 815-237-2281
Lynn Schroeder, prin. Fax 237-2713

Sparland, Marshall, Pop. 499
Midland CUSD 7
Supt. — See Varna
Midland MS 300/5-8
901 Hilltop Dr 61565 309-469-3131
Peg Frey, prin. Fax 469-5701

Sparta, Randolph, Pop. 4,395
Sparta CUSD 140 1,500/PK-12
203B Dean Ave 62286 618-443-5331
Karen Perry, supt. Fax 443-2023
www.sparta.k12.il.us
Sparta-Lincoln MS 400/4-8
203A Dean Ave 62286 618-443-5331
Laura Woodworth, prin. Fax 443-2892
Sparta Primary Attendance Center 400/PK-3
119 Legion Dr 62286 618-443-5331
Dennis Hall, prin. Fax 443-2023
Other Schools – See Evansville, Tilden

Springfield, Sangamon, Pop. 115,668
Springfield SD 186 14,300/PK-12
1900 W Monroe St 62704 217-525-3000
Dr. Walter Milton, supt. Fax 525-3005
www.springfield.k12.il.us/
Addams ES 300/K-5
10 Babiak Ln 62702 217-525-3192
Michelle Robertson, prin. Fax 535-2754
Black Hawk ES 300/K-5
2500 S College St 62704 217-525-3195
Robert Mitchell, prin. Fax 525-3168
Butler ES 300/PK-5
1701 S MacArthur Blvd 62704 217-525-3201
Tracy Gage, prin. Fax 788-6250
Dell ES 200/K-5
850 W Lake Shore Dr, 217-525-3223
Michael Grossen, prin. Fax 525-3216
Dubois ES 400/K-5
120 S Lincoln Ave 62704 217-525-3204
Cindy Baugher, prin. Fax 788-6538
Early Learning Center 500/PK-PK
2501 S 1st St 62704 217-525-3163
Jill Grove, prin. Fax 525-7955
Enos ES 300/PK-5
524 W Elliott Ave 62702 217-525-3208
Karen Vogt, prin. Fax 525-3262
Fairview ES 300/K-5
2200 E Ridgely Ave 62702 217-525-3211
Cheree Morrison, prin. Fax 525-3286
Feitshans Academy 400/PK-5
1101 S 15th St 62703 217-525-3030
Claudia Johnson, prin. Fax 525-3333
Franklin MS 800/6-8
1200 Outer Park Dr 62704 217-525-3164
Kristine Huddleston, prin. Fax 525-7937
Graham ES, 900 W Edwards St 62704 300/PK-5
Kimberly Siltman, prin. 217-525-3220
Grant MS 700/6-8
1800 W Monroe St 62704 217-525-3170
Rick Sanders, prin. Fax 525-3390
Harvard Park ES 300/PK-PK, 1-
2501 S 11th St 62703 217-525-3214
Christopher Hampsey, prin. Fax 525-3280
Iles ES 300/PK-PK, 1-
1700 S 15th St 62703 217-525-3226
Susan Rhodes, prin. Fax 525-4408
Jefferson MS 700/6-8
3001 S Allis St 62703 217-525-3176
Sena Nelson, prin. Fax 525-3293
Laketown ES 200/K-5
1825 Lee St 62703 217-525-3230
Renee Colwell, prin. Fax 525-3231

Lee ES 200/PK-5
1201 Bunn Ave 62703 217-525-3154
Joseph Marrin, prin. Fax 535-2755
Lincoln Magnet MS 300/6-8
300 S 11th St 62703 217-525-3236
Margaret Kruger, prin. Fax 525-3294
Lindsay ES, 3600 Fielding Dr, 500/K-5
Wendy Boatman, prin. 217-747-5770
Marsh ES 300/K-5
1100 Avon Dr 62704 217-525-3242
Kathy Wanless, prin. Fax 525-3360
Matheny-Withrow ES 200/K-5
1200 S Pope Ave 62703 217-525-3245
John Fetter, prin. Fax 525-3137
McClernand ES 200/PK-PK, 1-
801 N 6th St 62702 217-525-3247
Jennifer Gill, prin. Fax 525-7925
Pleasant Hill ES 200/K-5
3040 E Linden Ave 62702 217-525-3256
Diane Motley, prin. Fax 535-2756
Ridgely ES 400/PK-5
2040 N 8th St 62702 217-525-3259
Ken Gilmore, prin. Fax 525-7932
Sandburg ES 200/K-5
2051 Wabash Ave 62704 217-525-3264
Keith Kincaid, prin. Fax 535-2759
Southern View ES 200/K-5
3338 S 5th St 62703 217-525-3267
Jonnell Baskett, prin. Fax 525-3268
Wanless ES 300/PK-5
2120 E Reservoir St 62702 217-525-3272
Karen Stapleton-Crump, prin. Fax 788-6535
Washington MS 600/6-8
2300 E Jackson St 62703 217-525-3182
Susan Palmer, prin. Fax 525-3319
Wilcox ES 300/K-5
2000 Hastings Rd 62702 217-525-3281
Douglas Goss, prin. Fax 525-3308

Blessed Sacrament S 400/K-8
748 W Laurel St 62704 217-522-7534
Kathy Wear, prin. Fax 522-7542
Calvary Academy 300/PK-12
1730 W Jefferson St 62702 217-546-9700
Dr. Jay Hinckley, prin. Fax 546-1926
Cathedral S 200/PK-8
815 S 6th St 62703 217-523-2652
Marian Crosby, prin. Fax 523-2750
Christ the King S 500/PK-8
1920 Barberry Dr 62704 217-546-2159
Jeanine Kolb, prin. Fax 546-0291
Concordia Lutheran S 100/PK-8
2300 E Wilshire Rd 62703 217-529-3307
Daniel Henschen, prin. Fax 529-3096
Little Flower S 200/PK-8
900 Adlai Stevenson Dr 62703 217-529-4511
Carissa Cantrell, prin. Fax 529-0405
Montessori Children's House 100/PK-6
4147 Sand Hill Rd 62702 217-544-7702
Suzanne Harris, prin. Fax 544-5502
Montessori Schoolhouse 50/PK-6
717 Rickard Rd 62704 217-787-5505
Nils Westholm, prin.
Our Savior Lutheran S 200/PK-8
2645 Old Jacksonville Rd 62704 217-546-4531
Franklin Parris, prin. Fax 546-0293
St. Agnes S 500/PK-8
251 N Amos Ave 62702 217-793-1370
Sr. Mary Joan Sorge, prin. Fax 793-1238
St. Aloysius S 200/PK-8
2125 N 21st St 62702 217-544-4553
Jean Kennedy, prin. Fax 544-1680
St. Joseph S 200/K-8
1344 N 5th St 62702 217-523-6597
Jennifer Burke, prin. Fax 544-6434
St. Patrick S 50/K-5
1800 S Grand Ave E 62703 217-523-7670
Dr. Cora Benson, dir. Fax 523-0760
Springfield Adventist S 50/K-8
3300 W Jefferson St 62707 217-726-8636
Springfield Christian S 400/K-8
2850 Cider Mill Ln 62702 217-698-1933
Charles Williams, supt. Fax 698-1931
Trinity Lutheran S 100/PK-8
515 S MacArthur Blvd 62704 217-787-2323
Lewis Rodgers, prin. Fax 787-1145

Spring Grove, McHenry, Pop. 5,303
Fox Lake Grade SD 114 900/PK-8
29067 W Grass Lake Rd 60081 847-973-4100
John Donnellan, supt. Fax 973-4010
www.flgs.lake.k12.il.us
Lotus ES 600/PK-5
29067 W Grass Lake Rd 60081 847-973-4100
Janice Mason, prin. Fax 973-4110
Other Schools – See Fox Lake

Nippersink SD 2
Supt. — See Richmond
Spring Grove ES 400/K-5
2018 Main Street Rd 60081 815-675-2342
Chris Pittman, prin. Fax 675-2700

Spring Valley, Bureau, Pop. 5,380
Spring Valley CCSD 99 700/PK-8
800 N Richards St 61362 815-664-4242
Daniel Marenda, supt. Fax 664-2205
Kennedy S 500/2-8
800 N Richards St 61362 815-664-4601
Jim Hermes, prin. Fax 664-2205
Lincoln ES 200/PK-1
501 E Erie St 61362 815-663-5631
Kimberly Lisanby-Barber, prin. Fax 663-0086

Stanford, McLean, Pop. 644
Olympia CUSD 16 1,900/PK-12
903 E 800 North Rd 61774 309-379-6011
Brad Hutchison, supt. Fax 379-2328
www.olympia.org
Olympia MS 300/6-8
911 E 800 North Rd 61774 309-379-5941
Dan Lamboley, prin. Fax 379-5411

Other Schools – See Atlanta, Danvers, Minier

Staunton, Macoupin, Pop. 5,109
Staunton CUSD 6 1,400/PK-12
801 N Deneen St 62088 618-635-2962
Kyle Hlafka, supt. Fax 635-2994
www.stauntonschools.org/
Staunton ES 500/PK-5
801 N Deneen St 62088 618-635-3831
Mark Skertich, prin. Fax 635-4637
Staunton JHS 300/6-8
801 N Deneen St 62088 618-635-3831
Mark Skertich, prin. Fax 635-4637
Other Schools – See Livingston

St. Michael the Archangel S 100/PK-8
419 E Main St 62088 618-635-3210
Carla Moore, prin. Fax 635-3210
Zion Lutheran S 100/PK-8
220 W Henry St 62088 618-635-3060
Fax 635-3994

Steeleville, Randolph, Pop. 2,058
Steeleville CUSD 138 400/K-12
701 S Sparta St 62288 618-965-3432
Stephanie Mulholland, supt. Fax 965-3433
Steeleville S 200/K-8
609 S Sparta St 62288 618-965-3469
Stephanie Mulholland, prin. Fax 965-3433

St. Mark's Lutheran S 200/PK-8
504 N James St 62288 618-965-3838
Verlin Lorenz, prin. Fax 965-3060

Steger, Will, Pop. 10,409
Steger SD 194 1,700/PK-8
3753 Park Ave 60475 708-755-0022
Jeff Stawick, supt. Fax 755-9512
www.sd194.org/
Columbia Central MS 600/6-8
94 Richton Rd 60475 708-755-0021
Mike Smith, prin. Fax 755-1877
Eastview ES 400/PK-5
3411 Hopkins St 60475 708-754-4033
Janet Inglese, prin. Fax 755-1884
Parkview ES 300/K-5
100 Richton Rd 60475 708-755-0020
Stephanie Winborn, prin. Fax 755-5706
Other Schools – See South Chicago Heights

St. Liborius S 300/PK-8
3440 Halsted Blvd 60475 708-754-0192
Mary Jane Bartley, prin. Fax 755-3982

Sterling, Whiteside, Pop. 15,381
Sterling CUSD 5 3,400/PK-12
410 E Le Fevre Rd 61081 815-626-5050
Dr. Tad Everett, supt. Fax 622-4113
www.sterlingschools.org
Challand MS 700/6-8
1700 6th Ave 61081 815-626-3300
Kathy Howard, prin. Fax 622-4173
Franklin ES 400/K-2
1510 E 25th St 61081 815-625-5755
Suzi Hesser, prin. Fax 622-4187
Jefferson ES 400/PK-2
806 E Le Fevre Rd 61081 815-625-6402
Ron Rick, prin. Fax 622-4191
Lincoln ES 400/3-5
1501 E 6th St 61081 815-625-1449
Andy Edmondson, prin. Fax 622-4196
Wallace ECC PK-PK
506 W 4th St 61081 815-625-3000
Sara Dail, prin. Fax 626-4142
Washington ES 400/3-5
815 W Le Fevre Rd 61081 815-625-2372
Patrick Fortney, prin. Fax 622-4199

Christ Lutheran S 100/PK-8
2000 18th Ave 61081 815-625-3800
Stephen Kurek, prin. Fax 625-3585
St. Mary S 300/PK-8
6 W 6th St 61081 815-625-2253
Rebecca Schmitt, prin. Fax 625-8942

Steward, Lee, Pop. 267
Steward ESD 220 100/K-8
602 Main St 60553 815-396-2413
Angelina Bua, supt. Fax 396-2407
www.leeogle.org/steward/index
Steward S 100/K-8
602 Main St 60553 815-396-2413
Angelina Bua, prin. Fax 396-2407

Stewardson, Shelby, Pop. 730

Trinity Lutheran S 100/PK-8
PO Box 307 62463 217-682-3881
Kent Rincker, prin. Fax 682-3881

Stickney, Cook, Pop. 5,899
Lyons SD 103
Supt. — See Lyons
Edison ES 300/K-5
4100 Scoville Ave 60402 708-783-4400
Janice Bernard, prin. Fax 780-0035
Home ES 200/K-5
4400 Home Ave 60402 708-783-4500
Judy Doyle, prin. Fax 780-0041

Stillman Valley, Ogle, Pop. 1,097
Meridian CUSD 223 2,000/PK-12
207 W Main St 61084 815-645-2606
Robert Prusator, supt. Fax 645-4325
www.meridian223.org
Highland ES 400/PK-2
410 S Hickory St 61084 815-645-8188
Mike Coulahan, prin. Fax 645-8200
Meridian JHS 500/6-8
207 W Main St 61084 815-645-2277
William Davidson, prin. Fax 645-8181

Other Schools – See Monroe Center

Stockton, Jo Daviess, Pop. 1,820
Stockton CUSD 206 600/PK-12
236 N Pearl St 61085 815-947-3391
David Gilliland, supt. Fax 947-3055
www.stocktonschools.com
Stockton ES 200/PK-4
236 N Pearl St 61085 815-947-3321
David Gilliland, prin. Fax 947-3055
Stockton MS 200/5-8
500 N Rush St Ste A 61085 815-947-3702
Brad Fox, prin. Fax 947-2114

Stone Park, Cook, Pop. 4,905
Bellwood SD 88
Supt. — See Bellwood
Grant PS 100/K-K
1801 N 36th Ave 60165 708-345-3625
Francesca McDonald, prin. Fax 544-0062

Stonington, Christian, Pop. 924
Taylorville CUSD 3
Supt. — See Taylorville
Stonington ES 200/PK-5
500 E North 62567 217-325-3216
Anita Brown, prin. Fax 325-3783

Strasburg, Shelby, Pop. 582
Stewardson-Strasburg CUSD 5A 400/PK-12
RR 1 Box 67 62465 217-682-3355
Ruth Schneider, supt. Fax 682-3305
www.sscusd.k12.il.us/
Stewardson-Strasburg S 300/PK-8
RR 1 Box 67 62465 217-682-3621
Jennifer Propst, prin. Fax 682-3305

Streamwood, Cook, Pop. 37,312
SD U-46
Supt. — See Elgin
Canton MS 1,000/7-8
1100 Sunset Cir 60107 630-213-5525
Dr. James Hawkins, prin. Fax 213-5709
Glenbrook ES 400/K-6
315 Garden Cir 60107 630-213-5555
Cheryl DeRoo, prin. Fax 213-5548
Hanover Countryside ES 500/K-6
6 S Bartlett Rd 60107 630-213-5560
Leslie Kleiman, prin. Fax 213-6133
Heritage ES 500/K-6
507 Arnold Ave 60107 630-213-5565
Jennifer Bond, prin. Fax 213-5549
Oakhill ES 600/PK-6
502 S Oltendorf Rd 60107 630-213-5585
Patricia Barrett, prin. Fax 213-5573
Ridge Circle ES 600/K-6
420 Ridge Cir 60107 630-213-5600
Irma Molina-Bates, prin. Fax 213-9407
Sunnydale ES 400/K-6
716 Sunnydale Blvd 60107 630-213-5610
Denise Lockwald, prin. Fax 213-5594
Tefft MS 800/7-8
1100 Shirley Ave 60107 630-213-5535
Lavonne Smiley, prin. Fax 213-5646
Woodland Heights Early Learning PK-PK
900 S Park Blvd 60107 630-213-5615
Sue Smith, prin. Fax 213-5711

Grace Lutheran S 50/PK-K
780 S Bartlett Rd 60107 630-289-3996
St. John the Evangelist S 200/K-8
513 Parkside Cir 60107 630-289-3040
Sr. Mary Sergeena, prin. Fax 289-3026

Streator, LaSalle, Pop. 13,899
Streator ESD 44 1,900/PK-8
1520 N Bloomington St 61364 815-672-2926
Dr. Christine Benson, supt. Fax 673-2032
www.ses44.net/
Centennial ES 400/K-5
614 Oakley Ave 61364 815-672-2747
Anne McDonnell, prin. Fax 672-0594
Kimes ES 400/PK-5
1207 Reading St 61364 815-672-2496
Laura Dawson, prin. Fax 672-1344
Northlawn JHS 600/6-8
202 E 1st St 61364 815-672-4558
Darrick Reiley, prin. Fax 672-8109
Oakland Park ES 300/K-5
701 S Sterling St 61364 815-672-2736
Gail Russell, prin. Fax 672-3680
Sherman ES 300/PK-5
1206 E Elm St 61364 815-672-2720
Carodeane Armstrong, prin. Fax 672-3906

Woodland CUSD 5 500/PK-12
5800 E 3000 North Rd 61364 815-672-5974
Douglas Foster, supt. Fax 673-1630
www.woodland5.org/
Woodland S 300/PK-8
5800 E 3000 North Rd 61364 815-672-2909
Debra Derby, prin.

Rhema Christian Academy 50/1-12
1634 State Route 23 N 61364 815-672-5751
Kathy Hawthorne, prin. Fax 672-3451
St. Anthony S 300/PK-8
410 S Park St 61364 815-672-3847
Sr. Carol Royston, prin. Fax 673-3590

Stronghurst, Henderson, Pop. 846
West Central CUSD 235
Supt. — See Biggsville
West Central MS 200/6-8
PO Box 179 61480 309-924-1681
Jeff Nichols, prin. Fax 924-1122

Sugar Grove, Kane, Pop. 8,416
Kaneland CUSD 302
Supt. — See Maple Park
Harter MS, 1601 Esker Dr 60554 6-8
Richard Burchell, prin. 630-466-8400

Shields ES 600/PK-5
85 S Main St 60554 630-466-8500
Shelley Hueber, prin. Fax 466-5320

Sullivan, Moultrie, Pop. 4,323
Sullivan CUSD 300 1,200/PK-12
725 N Main St 61951 217-728-8341
Terry Pearcy, supt. Fax 728-4139
home.sullivan.k12.il.us/
Sullivan ES 500/PK-5
910 N Graham St 61951 217-728-2321
Rita Florey, prin. Fax 728-4399
Sullivan MS 300/6-8
713 N Main St 61951 217-728-8381
Joe Marks, prin. Fax 728-4139

Summerfield, Saint Clair, Pop. 492
Lebanon CUSD 9
Supt. — See Lebanon
Summerfield ES 100/3-4
PO Box 424 62289 618-934-3441
Christy Johnson, prin. Fax 934-3003

Summit, Cook
Summit SD 104 1,600/PK-8
6021 S 74th Ave 60501 708-458-0505
Thomas Dixey, supt. Fax 458-0532
www.sd104.us
Graves ES 400/PK-4
6021 S 74th Ave 60501 708-458-7260
Hope Durkin, prin. Fax 728-3111
Heritage MS 500/6-8
6021 S 74th Ave 60501 708-458-7590
Dennis Lewis, prin. Fax 728-3111
Walsh ES 400/PK-4
5640 S 75th Ave 60501 708-458-7165
Edward Fee, prin. Fax 458-7532
Wharton Fifth Grade Center 200/PK-PK, 5-
7555 W 64th St 60501 708-458-0640
Rudolfo Olavarri, prin. Fax 458-8467
Other Schools – See Bedford Park

St. Joseph S 200/PK-8
5641 S 73rd Ave 60501 708-458-2927
Lawrence Manetti, prin. Fax 458-9750

Sumner, Lawrence, Pop. 1,820
Red Hill CUSD 10
Supt. — See Bridgeport
Petty ES 100/K-4
RR 2 Box 227 62466 618-947-2204
Todd Tiffany, prin. Fax 947-2204
Sumner Attendence Center 200/K-8
110 W Locust St 62466 618-936-2412
Todd Tiffany, prin. Fax 936-2742

Swansea, Saint Clair, Pop. 12,274
High Mount SD 116 500/PK-8
1721 Boul Ave 62226 618-233-1054
Michael Brink, supt. Fax 233-1136
www.highmountschool.com
High Mount S 500/PK-8
1721 Boul Ave 62226 618-233-1054
Michael Brink, prin. Fax 233-1136

Wolf Branch SD 113 900/K-8
410 Huntwood Rd 62226 618-277-2100
Scott Harres, supt. Fax 277-5461
www.wolfbranchschooldistrict.org/
Wolf Branch ES 500/K-5
125 Huntwood Rd 62226 618-277-2100
Nicole Sanderson, prin. Fax 277-9786
Wolf Branch MS 300/6-8
410 Huntwood Rd 62226 618-277-2100
Jeffrey Burkett, prin. Fax 277-5461

Sycamore, DeKalb, Pop. 14,831
Sycamore CUSD 427 3,500/K-12
245 W Exchange St Ste 1 60178 815-899-8100
Wayne Riesen, supt. Fax 899-8110
www.syc427.org
North ES 400/K-5
1680 Brickville Rd 60178 815-899-8209
K. Spiewak, prin. Fax 899-8213
North Grove ES K-5
850 Republic Ave 60178 815-899-8124
Ryan Janisch, prin.
Southeast ES 400/K-5
718 S Locust St 60178 815-899-8219
Mark Ekstrom, prin. Fax 899-8221
South Prairie ES 400/K-5
820 Borden Ave 60178 815-899-8299
Julie Graves, prin. Fax 899-8292
Sycamore MS 800/6-8
150 Maplewood Dr 60178 815-899-8170
Jim Cleven, prin. Fax 899-8177
West ES 300/K-5
240 Fair St 60178 815-899-8199
Mary Currie, prin. Fax 899-8195

Cornerstone Christian Academy 400/PK-12
355 N Cross St 60178 815-895-8522
Tom Olmstead, admin. Fax 895-8717
St. Mary S 300/PK-8
222 Waterman St 60178 815-895-5215
Ross Bubolz, prin. Fax 895-5295

Table Grove, Fulton, Pop. 389
V I T CUSD 2 400/PK-12
1500 E US Highway 136 61482 309-758-5138
John Marshall, supt. Fax 758-5298
vit.k12.il.us
V I T ES 200/PK-6
1500 E US Highway 136 61482 309-758-5138
John Marshall, prin. Fax 758-5298
V I T JHS 100/7-8
1502 E US Highway 136 61482 309-758-5136
Phil Snowden, prin. Fax 758-5126

Tallula, Menard, Pop. 630
PORTA CUSD 202
Supt. — See Petersburg

Tallula ES 100/PK-4
PO Box 260 62688 217-634-4328
Eric Kesler, prin. Fax 634-4432

Tamaroa, Perry, Pop. 732
Tamaroa SD 5 100/K-8
PO Box 175 62888 618-496-5513
Robert Trover, supt. Fax 496-3911
www.tgs5.perry.k12.il.us/
Tamaroa S 100/K-8
PO Box 175 62888 618-496-5513
Robert Trover, prin. Fax 496-3911

Tamms, Alexander, Pop. 1,150
Egyptian CUSD 5 600/PK-12
20023 Diswood Rd 62988 618-776-5306
Brad Misner, supt. Fax 776-5122
www.egyptianschool.com
Egyptian ES 300/PK-5
20023 Diswood Rd 62988 618-776-5251
Danny McCrite, prin. Fax 776-5122
Egyptian JHS 100/6-8
20023 Diswood Rd 62988 618-776-5251
Chuck Doty, prin. Fax 776-5122

Tampico, Whiteside, Pop. 745
Prophetstown-Lyndon-Tampico CUSD 3
Supt. — See Prophetstown
Tampico ES 200/PK-5
PO Box 637 61283 815-438-2255
Darren Erickson, prin. Fax 438-5010
Tampico MS 200/6-8
PO Box 189 61283 815-438-3085
Chad Colmone, prin. Fax 438-3095

Taylor Ridge, Rock Island
Rockridge CUSD 300 1,400/PK-12
14110 134th Ave W 61284 309-795-1167
Jack Bambrick, supt. Fax 795-1719
www.rockridge.k12.il.us
Rockridge JHS 200/7-8
14110 134th Ave W 61284 309-795-1172
Katherine Hasson, prin. Fax 795-9823
Taylor Ridge ES 200/K-3
13227 Turkey Hollow Rd 61284 309-798-2183
Tina Sims, prin. Fax 798-5523
Other Schools – See Andalusia, Illinois City, Reynolds

Taylorville, Christian, Pop. 11,240
Taylorville CUSD 3 2,700/PK-12
512 W Spresser St 62568 217-824-4951
Dr. Greggory Fuerstenau, supt. Fax 824-5157
www.taylorvilleschools.com
Memorial ES 300/PK-5
101 E Adams St 62568 217-287-7929
Nancy Ganci, prin. Fax 287-7696
North ES 400/PK-5
805 N Cherokee St 62568 217-824-3315
Brandi Bruley, prin. Fax 824-5949
South ES 300/K-5
1004 W Prairie St 62568 217-824-2249
Patrick Haugens, prin. Fax 824-2007
Taylorville JHS 600/6-8
120 E Bidwell St 62568 217-824-4924
Kirk Kettelkamp, prin. Fax 824-7180
Other Schools – See Stonington

St. Mary S 100/PK-6
422 S Washington St 62568 217-824-6501
Cathy Robertson, prin. Fax 824-2803
Vision Way Christian S 100/PK-8
PO Box 86 62568 217-824-6722
Glenna Tolliver, prin. Fax 824-6622

Teutopolis, Effingham, Pop. 1,634
Teutopolis CUSD 50 1,200/PK-12
PO Box 607 62467 217-857-3535
Dan Niemerg, supt. Fax 857-6265
www.teutopolisschools.org/
Teutopolis ES 500/PK-6
309 E Main St 62467 217-857-3232
Norma Fisher, prin. Fax 857-6609
Teutopolis JHS 200/7-8
904 W Water St 62467 217-857-6678
Bill Fritcher, prin. Fax 857-6051

Texico, Jefferson
Field CCSD 3 300/PK-8
21075 N Hails Ln 62889 618-755-4611
Gina Ilbery, supt. Fax 755-9701
Field S 300/PK-8
21075 N Hails Ln 62889 618-755-4611
Steve Austin, prin. Fax 755-9701

Thawville, Iroquois, Pop. 284
Iroquois West CUSD 10
Supt. — See Gilman
Iroquois West Upper ES 100/4-5
PO Box 99 60968 217-387-2291
Carolyn Harvey, prin. Fax 387-2205

Thomasboro, Champaign, Pop. 1,222
Prairieview-Ogden CCSD 197
Supt. — See Royal
Prairieview-Ogden JHS 50/7-8
2499 County Road 2100 E 61878 217-694-4122
Jennifer Armstrong, prin. Fax 694-4123

Thomasboro CCSD 130 200/K-8
201 N Phillips St 61878 217-643-3275
Michelle Ramage, supt. Fax 643-2022
www.thomasboro.k12.il.us/
Thomasboro S 200/K-8
201 N Phillips St 61878 217-643-3275
Bonnie McArthur, prin. Fax 643-2022

Thompsonville, Franklin, Pop. 593
Thompsonville CUSD 174 300/K-12
21191 Shawneetown Rd 62890 618-627-2446
Rick Goodman, supt. Fax 627-2446
thompsonville.il.schoolwebpages.com/
Thompsonville S 200/K-8
21165 Shawneetown Rd 62890 618-627-2511
Kim Kaytor, prin. Fax 627-2446

Thompsonville Christian S 50/K-10
PO Box 53 62890 618-627-2065

Thomson, Carroll, Pop. 536
West Carroll CUSD 314 1,500/PK-12
801 South St 61285 815-259-2735
Craig Mathers, supt. Fax 259-3561
West Carroll IS 200/4-5
801 South St 61285 815-259-2736
Pam Delp, prin. Fax 259-5023
Other Schools – See Mount Carroll, Savanna

Thornton, Cook, Pop. 2,458
Thornton SD 154 300/PK-8
200 N Wolcott St 60476 708-877-5160
Dr. Carol Kunst, supt. Fax 877-2537
www.wolcottschool.com/
Wolcott S 300/PK-8
200 N Wolcott St 60476 708-877-2526
Dr. Carol Kunst, prin. Fax 877-2537

Tilden, Randolph, Pop. 902
Sparta CUSD 140
Supt. — See Sparta
Tilden Attendance Center 100/K-4
PO Box 394 62292 618-587-2401
Karen Perry, prin. Fax 587-6301

Tinley Park, Cook, Pop. 57,477
Arbor Park SD 145
Supt. — See Oak Forest
Kimberly Heights K 200/PK-K
6141 Kimberly Dr 60477 708-532-6434
Jane Foster, prin. Fax 532-4495

Kirby SD 140 4,200/PK-8
16931 Grissom Dr 60477 708-532-6462
Dr. Michael Byrne, supt. Fax 532-1512
www.ksd140.org
Bannes ES 500/K-5
16835 Odell Ave 60477 708-532-6466
Terrance Kowalski, prin. Fax 532-8530
Grissom MS 700/6-8
17000 80th Ave 60477 708-429-3030
Kristine Roth, prin. Fax 532-8529
Keller ES 400/PK-5
7846 163rd St 60477 708-532-2144
Shawn Olson, prin. Fax 532-8531
McAuliffe ES 500/K-5
8944 174th St, 708-429-4565
Margaret Sheehan, prin. Fax 532-8533
Millennium ES 700/PK-5
17830 84th Ave, 708-532-3150
Mary Jo Werbiansky, prin. Fax 614-2375
Prairie View MS 900/6-8
8500 175th St, 708-532-8540
Kristine Roth, prin. Fax 532-8544
Other Schools – See Orland Park

Summit Hill SD 161
Supt. — See Frankfort
Walker IS 900/5-6
19900 80th Ave, 815-464-2285
Jan Zevkovich, prin. Fax 464-2160

Tinley Park CCSD 146 2,100/PK-8
6611 171st St 60477 708-614-4500
Dr. Marion Hoyda, supt. Fax 614-8992
www.district146.org
Central MS 800/6-8
18146 Oak Park Ave 60477 708-614-4510
Debra Brennan, prin. Fax 614-7271
Fulton ES, 6601 171st St 60477 300/PK-5
Susan Mulchrone, prin. 708-614-4525
Memorial ES 300/PK-5
6701 179th St 60477 708-614-4535
Bethany Wilson, prin. Fax 614-7501
Other Schools – See Oak Forest, Orland Park

Landmark Christian Academy 100/K-8
16250 84th Ave, 708-623-0332
Ken Darnell, prin. Fax 623-0934
St. George S 400/PK-8
6700 176th St 60477 708-532-2626
Edward Weston, prin. Fax 532-2025
Southwest Chicago Christian S 400/K-8
17171 84th Ave 60477 708-429-7171
Terry Huizenga, prin. Fax 429-7210
Trinity Lutheran S 300/PK-8
6850 159th St 60477 708-532-3529
Steve Stec, prin. Fax 532-0799
Zion Lutheran ECC 100/PK-K
17100 S 69th Ave 60477 708-532-1656
Fax 532-9876

Tiskilwa, Bureau, Pop. 768
Princeton ESD 115
Supt. — See Princeton
Reagan MS 200/4-5
PO Box 329 61368 815-646-4211
Bob Bima, prin. Fax 646-4444

Toledo, Cumberland, Pop. 1,143
Cumberland CUSD 77 1,000/PK-12
1496 Illinois Route 121 62468 217-923-3132
Russell Ragon, supt. Fax 923-3132
www.cumberland.k12.il.us/
Cumberland ES 400/PK-5
1496 Illinois Route 121 62468 217-923-3135
Todd Butler, prin. Fax 923-5449
Cumberland JHS 200/6-8
1496 Illinois Route 121 62468 217-923-3135
Kevin Maynard, prin. Fax 923-5449

Tolono, Champaign, Pop. 2,776
Tolono CUSD 7 1,500/PK-12
PO Box S 61880 217-485-6510
Michael Shonk, supt. Fax 485-3091
www.unitsevenschools.com/
Unity JHS 300/6-8
1121 County Road 800 N 61880 217-485-6735
Mary Hettinger, prin. Fax 485-3218
Unity West ES 400/PK-5
1035 County Road 600 N 61880 217-485-3918
Janet Ellis-Nelson, prin. Fax 485-3451
Other Schools – See Philo

Toluca, Marshall, Pop. 1,311
Fieldcrest CUSD 6
Supt. — See Minonk
Fieldcrest ES West 300/K-6
PO Box 709 61369 815-452-2318
James Demay, prin. Fax 452-2411

Tonica, LaSalle, Pop. 698
Tonica CCSD 79 200/PK-8
535 N 1981st Rd 61370 815-442-3420
Larry Bequeaith, supt. Fax 442-3111
www.tonicagradeschool.org/
Tonica S 200/PK-8
535 N 1981st Rd 61370 815-442-3420
Larry Bequeaith, prin. Fax 442-3111

Toulon, Stark, Pop. 1,368
Stark County CUSD 100
Supt. — See Wyoming
Stark County JHS, PO Box 659 61483 200/6-8
Michael Domico, prin. 309-286-3451

Towanda, McLean, Pop. 479
McLean County Unit SD 5
Supt. — See Normal
Towanda ES 100/K-5
PO Box 260 61776 309-728-2278
Karrah Jensen, prin. Fax 728-2963

Tower Hill, Shelby, Pop. 602
Pana CUSD 8
Supt. — See Pana
Jefferson MS 200/5-6
PO Box 157 62571 217-567-3321
Deb Zueck, prin. Fax 567-3367

Tremont, Tazewell, Pop. 2,065
Tremont CUSD 702 900/PK-12
400 W Pearl St 61568 309-925-3461
Donald Beard, supt. Fax 925-5817
tremont.il.schoolwebpages.com/
Tremont ES 400/PK-4
PO Box 1208 61568 309-925-4841
Kevin Dill, prin. Fax 925-5817
Tremont JHS 200/5-8
400 W Pearl St 61568 309-925-3823
Jeremy Garrett, prin. Fax 925-5817

Trenton, Clinton, Pop. 2,651
Wesclin CUSD 3 1,400/PK-12
10003 State Route 160 62293 618-224-7583
David Daum, supt. Fax 224-9106
wesclin.k12.il.us
St. Mary's ES 100/4-6
313 S Adams St 62293 618-224-9821
Jay Goble, prin. Fax 224-9895
Trenton ES 200/PK-3
308 N Washington St 62293 618-224-9411
Jay Goble, prin. Fax 224-9417
Wesclin JHS 200/7-8
10003 State Route 160 62293 618-224-7355
John Mullett, prin. Fax 224-9106
Other Schools – See New Baden

Troy, Madison, Pop. 9,374
Triad CUSD 2 3,100/PK-12
203 E Throp St 62294 618-667-5400
Leigh Lewis, supt. Fax 667-8854
www.triadunit2.org
Henning ES 500/PK-5
520 E US Highway 40 62294 618-667-5401
Kay Burrough, prin. Fax 667-0247
Silver Creek ES PK-5
209 N Dewey St 62294 618-667-5403
Jason Henderson, prin. Fax 667-8420
Other Schools – See Marine, Saint Jacob

St. Paul Lutheran S 100/PK-8
112 N Border St 62294 618-667-6314
Ida Doyle, prin. Fax 667-2173

Tunnel Hill, Johnson
New Simpson Hill SD 32 300/PK-8
95 Tunnel Hill Rd, 618-658-8536
Kathy Anderson, supt. Fax 658-5034
New Simpson Hill S 300/PK-8
95 Tunnel Hill Rd, 618-658-8536
Joe Nighswander, prin. Fax 658-5034

Tuscola, Douglas, Pop. 4,583
Tuscola CUSD 301 1,000/PK-12
409 S Prairie St 61953 217-253-4241
Joe Burgess, supt. Fax 253-4522
www.tuscola.k12.il.us/
East Prairie JHS 300/5-8
409 S Prairie St 61953 217-253-2828
Cathy Chaplin, prin. Fax 253-3236
North Ward ES 400/PK-4
1201 N Prairie St 61953 217-253-2712
Ann Lamkey, prin. Fax 253-4851

Ullin, Pulaski, Pop. 723
Century CUSD 100 400/PK-12
4721 Shawnee College Rd 62992 618-845-3447
Sheila Donis, supt. Fax 845-3476
www.centuryschooldistrict100.com/
Century ES 200/PK-6
4819 Shawnee College Rd 62992 618-845-3572
Melinda Duke, prin. Fax 845-3586
Century MS 100/7-8
4721 Shawnee College Rd 62992 618-845-3518
Andre Meadows, prin. Fax 845-3476

University Park, Will, Pop. 8,102
Crete-Monee CUSD 201U
Supt. — See Crete
Crete-Monee MS 700/7-8
635 Olmstead Ln, 708-367-2400
Kokona Chrisos, prin. Fax 672-2777

King Magnet S 400/K-8
1009 Blackhawk Dr, 708-672-2651
Erin DeBartolo, prin. Fax 672-2621

Deer Creek Christian S 200/PK-8
425 University Pkwy, 708-672-6200
Jason Gaunt, admin. Fax 672-6226

Urbana, Champaign, Pop. 38,463
Urbana SD 116 4,300/PK-12
PO Box 3039 61803 217-384-3636
Dr. Preston Williams, supt. Fax 337-4973
www.usd116.org/
King ES 300/K-5
1108 Fairview Ave 61801 217-384-3675
Dr. Jennifer Ivory-Tatum, prin. Fax 344-5610
Leal ES 400/K-5
312 W Oregon St 61801 217-384-3618
Spencer Landsman, prin. Fax 384-3622
Paine ES 300/K-5
1801 James Cherry Dr 61802 217-384-3602
Sandra Cooper, prin. Fax 344-1835
Prairie ES 400/K-5
2102 E Washington St 61802 217-384-3628
Yavonnda Smith, prin. Fax 384-3626
Urbana MS 900/6-8
1201 S Vine St 61801 217-384-3685
Nancy Clinton, prin. Fax 367-3156
Washington ECC 200/PK-PK
1102 N Broadway Ave 61801 217-384-3616
Crystal Vowels, prin. Fax 384-3615
Wiley ES 200/K-5
1602 S Anderson St 61801 217-384-3670
Barbara Sartain, prin. Fax 384-3559
Yankee Ridge ES 300/K-5
2102 S Anderson St 61801 217-384-3608
Mary Beth Norris, prin. Fax 384-3611

Kingswood S 50/K-12
PO Box 834 61803 217-344-5540
Marsh Jones, hdmstr. Fax 344-5535

Ursa, Adams, Pop. 590
CUSD 4
Supt. — See Mendon
Greenfield ES 100/3-4
2397 Highway 96 N 62376 217-964-2200
Theresa Fessler, prin. Fax 964-2253

Utica, LaSalle, Pop. 846
Waltham Community CESD 185 200/K-8
946 N 33rd Rd 61373 815-667-4417
Dr. Kristen School, supt. Fax 667-4462
wesd185.org
Waltham North S 200/3-8
946 N 33rd Rd 61373 815-667-4417
Jason Hamann, prin. Fax 667-4462
Waltham South S K-2
248 W Canal St 61373 815-667-4790
Dr. Kristen School, prin. Fax 667-9889

Valmeyer, Monroe, Pop. 778
Valmeyer CUSD 3 500/PK-12
300 S Cedar Bluff Dr 62295 618-935-2100
Brian Charron, supt. Fax 935-2108
www.valmeyerk12.org/
Valmeyer ES 200/PK-5
300 S Cedar Bluff Dr 62295 618-935-2100
Dawn Ivers, prin. Fax 935-2108
Valmeyer JHS 100/6-8
300 S Cedar Bluff Dr 62295 618-939-2100
Dawn Ivers, prin. Fax 939-2108

Vandalia, Fayette, Pop. 6,811
Vandalia CUSD 203 1,800/PK-12
1109 N 8th St 62471 618-283-4525
Rich Well, supt. Fax 283-4107
www.vcs.fayette.k12.il.us/
Jefferson PS 400/PK-1
1500 W Jefferson St 62471 618-283-5160
Donna Cripe, prin. Fax 283-9403
Vandalia ES 400/2-4
1017 W Fletcher St 62471 618-283-5166
Stacy South, prin. Fax 283-9479
Vandalia JHS 500/5-8
1011 W Fletcher St 62471 618-283-5151
Rod Grimsley, prin. Fax 283-5165

Van Orin, Bureau
La Moille CUSD 303
Supt. — See La Moille
Van Orin ES 100/K-3
PO Box 7 61374 815-638-3141
James Brandau, prin. Fax 638-3242

Varna, Marshall, Pop. 432
Midland CUSD 7 800/PK-12
1830 State Route 17 61375 309-463-2364
Rolf Sivertsen, supt. Fax 463-2467
www.midland-7.org
Other Schools – See Lacon, Sparland

Venice, Madison, Pop. 2,448
Venice CUSD 3 100/K-8
300 4th St 62090 618-274-7953
Cleveland Hammonds, supt. Fax 274-7953
www.venice.k12.il.us/
Venice S 100/K-8
300 4th St 62090 618-274-7953
Shirley Davis, prin. Fax 274-7953

Vergennes, Jackson, Pop. 327
Elverado CUSD 196
Supt. — See Elkville
Elverado IS 100/3-5
PO Box 35 62994 618-684-3527
Belinda Conner, prin. Fax 687-3363
Elverado JHS 100/6-8
PO Box 35 62994 618-684-3527
Belinda Conner, prin. Fax 687-3363

Vernon Hills, Lake, Pop. 23,957
Hawthorn CCSD 73 3,700/PK-8
841 W End Ct 60061 847-990-4200
Dr. Youssef Yomtoob, supt. Fax 367-3290
www.hawthorn73.org
Hawthorn Aspen ES 900/PK-5
500 Aspen Dr 60061 847-990-4300
Tom Springborn, prin. Fax 816-6931
Hawthorn ES North 500/K-5
301 W Hawthorn Pkwy 60061 847-990-4500
Rich Viviano, prin. Fax 367-3297
Hawthorn ES South 600/K-5
430 Aspen Dr 60061 847-990-4800
Jill Martin, prin. Fax 918-9251
Hawthorn MS North 600/6-8
201 W Hawthorn Pkwy 60061 847-990-4400
Anna Groh, prin. Fax 367-8124
Hawthorn MS South 600/6-8
600 Aspen Dr 60061 847-816-8317
Joy Mullaney, prin. Fax 816-9259
Hawthorn Townline ES 400/K-5
810 Aspen Dr 60061 847-990-4900
Karen Cencula, prin. Fax 990-4999

Vienna, Johnson, Pop. 1,304
Vienna SD 55 400/PK-8
PO Box 427 62995 618-658-8638
Teri Coscarelli, supt. Fax 658-9036
www.viennagradeschool.com/
Vienna S 400/PK-8
PO Box 427 62995 618-658-6611
Greg Frehner, prin. Fax 658-9036

Villa Grove, Douglas, Pop. 2,507
Villa Grove CUSD 302 600/PK-12
400 N Sycamore St 61956 217-832-2261
Dr. Steven Poznic, supt. Fax 832-8615
www.vg302.org/education/school/school.php?sectionid=2
Villa Grove ES 300/PK-6
400 N Sycamore St 61956 217-832-2261
Marke Hatfield, prin. Fax 832-8615
Villa Grove JHS 100/7-8
400 N Sycamore St 61956 217-832-2261
Marke Hatfield, prin. Fax 832-8615

Villa Park, DuPage, Pop. 22,616
DuPage County SD 45 3,500/PK-8
255 W Vermont St 60181 630-516-7700
Dr. Janice Rosales, supt. Fax 530-1624
www.d45.dupage.k12.il.us
Ardmore ES 500/K-5
225 S Harvard Ave 60181 630-516-7370
Michele Cummins, prin. Fax 530-3660
Jackson MS 800/6-8
301 W Jackson St 60181 630-516-7600
Tony Palmisano, prin. Fax 530-6271
Jefferson MS 500/6-8
255 W Vermont St 60181 630-516-7800
David Katzin, prin. Fax 993-6348
North ES 400/K-5
150 W Sunset Ave 60181 630-516-7790
Debbie Guzan, prin. Fax 530-1385
Other Schools – See Lombard

Salt Creek SD 48 500/PK-8
1110 S Villa Ave 60181 630-279-8400
Dr. John Correll, supt. Fax 279-6167
www.saltcreek48.com
Albright MS 200/5-8
1110 S Villa Ave 60181 630-279-6160
Linda Stasko, prin. Fax 279-1614
Other Schools – See Elmhurst, Oakbrook Terrace

Islamic Foundation S 700/PK-12
300 W Highridge Rd 60181 630-941-8800
Anwar Siddiqui, prin. Fax 941-8804
St. Alexander S 200/PK-8
136 S Cornell Ave 60181 630-834-3787
Glenn Purpura, prin. Fax 834-1961
St. Paul Christian K 50/PK-K
545 S Ardmore Ave 60181 630-832-0420
Ania Folta, dir. Fax 832-7656

Viola, Mercer, Pop. 966
Sherrard CUSD 200
Supt. — See Sherrard
Winola ES 300/K-4
1804 17th Ave 61486 309-596-2114
Egan Colbrese, prin. Fax 596-2979

Virden, Macoupin, Pop. 3,472
Virden CUSD 4 1,000/PK-12
231 W Fortune St 62690 217-965-4226
Ron Graham, supt. Fax 965-3019
www.virdenschools.com/
Virden ES 500/PK-5
231 W Fortune St 62690 217-965-5424
Deborah Bommarito, prin. Fax 965-4342
Virden MS 200/6-8
231 W Fortune St 62690 217-965-3942
Randy Niles, prin. Fax 965-3124

Virginia, Cass, Pop. 1,730
Virginia CUSD 64 400/PK-12
651 S Morgan St 62691 217-452-3085
Lynn Carter, supt. Fax 452-3088
www.go-redbirds.com
Virginia ES 200/PK-5
651 S Morgan St 62691 217-452-3363
Christine Brinkley, prin. Fax 452-3088
Virginia JHS 100/6-8
651 S Morgan St 62691 217-452-3363
Christine Brinkley, prin. Fax 452-3088

Wadsworth, Lake, Pop. 3,651
Beach Park CCSD 3
Supt. — See Beach Park
Newport ES 400/K-5
15872 W 21st St 60083 847-599-5330
John Coburn, prin. Fax 599-0893

Millburn CCSD 24 1,600/PK-8
18550 W Millburn Rd 60083 847-356-8331
James Menzer, supt. Fax 356-9722
www.millburn24.net/
Millburn S 1,100/PK-8
18550 W Millburn Rd 60083 847-356-8331
Jason Lind, prin. Fax 356-9722
Other Schools – See Lindenhurst

St. Patrick S 700/PK-8
15020 W Wadsworth Rd 60083 847-623-8446
Marcella Bosnak, prin. Fax 623-3119

Walnut, Bureau, Pop. 1,421
Bureau Valley CUSD 340
Supt. — See Manlius
Bureau Valley North S 400/PK-8
PO Box 707 61376 815-379-2900
Gina Hall, prin. Fax 379-9285

Waltonville, Jefferson, Pop. 431
Waltonville CUSD 1 300/PK-12
804 W Knob St 62894 618-279-7211
David Thomas, supt. Fax 279-3291
waltonvilleschools.roe25.com/
Waltonville S, 802 W Knob St 62894 200/PK-8
Shlonda Horton, prin. 618-279-7221

Warren, Jo Daviess, Pop. 1,421
Warren CUSD 205 500/PK-12
311 S Water St 61087 815-745-2653
Karen Sirgany Ed.D., supt. Fax 745-2037
www.205warren.net/
Warren ES 200/PK-3
311 S Water St 61087 815-745-2653
Karen Sirgany Ed.D., prin. Fax 745-2037
Other Schools – See Apple River

Warrensburg, Macon, Pop. 1,209
Warrensburg-Latham CUSD 11 1,100/PK-12
430 W North St 62573 217-672-3514
Emmett Aubry, supt. Fax 672-8468
www.wl.k12.il.us
Warrensburg-Latham S 800/PK-8
100 N West St 62573 217-672-3612
T. Taylor, prin. Fax 672-3321

Warrenville, DuPage, Pop. 13,217
CUSD 200
Supt. — See Wheaton
Bower ES 500/K-5
4S241 River Rd 60555 630-393-9413
Mark Kohlmann, prin. Fax 393-9403
Johnson ES 500/K-5
2S700 Continental Dr 60555 630-393-1787
Tim Callahan, prin. Fax 393-7064

Carmel Montessori Academy 100/PK-12
3S238 State Route 59 60555 630-393-2995
Carmen Lafranzo, prin.
Four Winds Waldorf S 200/PK-8
30W160 Calumet Ave W 60555 630-836-9400
Brian Wolff, admin. Fax 836-1732
St. Irene S 200/PK-8
3S601 Warren Ave 60555 630-393-9303
Maureen White, prin. Fax 393-7009

Warsaw, Hancock, Pop. 1,648
Warsaw CUSD 316 400/PK-12
340 S 11th St 62379 217-256-4282
Kim Schilson, supt. Fax 256-4282
hancock.k12.il.us/whs/
Warsaw ES, 340 S 11th St 62379 200/PK-6
Brad Froman, prin. 217-256-4614

Wasco, Kane
Saint Charles CUSD 303
Supt. — See Saint Charles
Wasco ES 500/K-5
4N782 School St 60183 630-377-4886
Barbara Stokke, prin. Fax 513-2214

Washburn, Marshall, Pop. 1,107
Lowpoint-Washburn CUSD 21 400/PK-12
PO Box 580 61570 309-248-7522
Parker Deitrich, supt. Fax 248-7518
www.washburn.k12.il.us/contact_us.htm
Lowpoint-Washburn ES 200/PK-6
PO Box 580 61570 309-248-7221
Gary Heider, prin.

Washington, Tazewell, Pop. 12,759
Central SD 51 800/PK-8
1301 Eagle Ave 61571 309-444-3943
Chad Allaman, supt. Fax 444-9898
www.tazewell.k12.il.us/cgs
Central S 800/PK-8
1301 Eagle Ave 61571 309-444-3943
Brian Hoelscher, prin. Fax 444-9898

District 50 Schools 800/PK-8
304 E Almond Dr 61571 309-745-8914
Susan Dudley, supt. Fax 745-5417
www.d50schools.com
Hensey ES, 304 E Almond Dr 61571 400/PK-3
James Sharp, prin. 309-745-3625
Manor MS, 1014 School St 61571 400/4-8
Rich Fields, prin. 309-745-3921

Washington SD 52 800/PK-8
303 Jackson St 61571 309-444-4182
John Tignor, supt. Fax 444-8538
tazewell.k12.il.us/district52
Lincoln ES 400/PK-4
303 Jackson St 61571 309-444-3321
Eveline Durham, prin. Fax 444-8538
Washington MS 400/5-8
1100 N Main St 61571 309-444-3361
Diane Orr, prin. Fax 444-3941

IL Central Christian S 100/PK-12
22648 Grosenbach Rd 61571 309-698-2000

St. Patrick S — 300/PK-8
100 Harvey St 61571 — 309-444-4345
Dr. Sharon Weiss, prin. — Fax 444-7100

Wataga, Knox, Pop. 810
ROWVA CUSD 208
Supt. — See Oneida
ROWVA West ES, PO Box 467 61488 — 100/3-4
Kerry Danner, prin. — 309-375-6651

Waterloo, Monroe, Pop. 9,225
Waterloo CUSD 5 — 2,700/PK-12
219 Park St 62298 — 618-939-3453
James Helton, supt. — Fax 939-4578
www.wcusd5.net
Rogers ES — 600/3-5
200 Rogers St 62298 — 618-939-3454
Nicholas Schwartz, prin. — Fax 939-7980
Waterloo JHS — 600/6-8
1 Ed Gardner Pl 62298 — 618-939-3457
John Schmieg, prin. — Fax 939-1383
Zahnow ES — 600/PK-2
301 Hamacher St 62298 — 618-939-3458
Mary Gardner, prin. — Fax 939-1377

SS. Peter & Paul S — 400/PK-8
217 W 3rd St 62298 — 618-939-7217
Lisa Buchheit, prin. — Fax 939-5994

Waterman, DeKalb, Pop. 1,214
Indian Creek CUSD 425
Supt. — See Shabbona
Indian Creek MS — 200/6-8
425 S Elm St 60556 — 815-264-7712
Paula Kennedy, prin. — Fax 264-7826
Waterman ES — 200/K-5
220 N Maple St 60556 — 815-264-3351
Steve Simpson, prin. — Fax 264-3480

Watseka, Iroquois, Pop. 5,547
Iroquois County CUSD 9 — 1,200/K-12
1411 W Lafayette St 60970 — 815-432-4931
Steve Bianchetta, supt. — Fax 432-6889
www.watseka-u9.k12.il.us
Davis ES — 200/K-1
495 N 4th St 60970 — 815-432-2112
Robert Walter, prin. — Fax 432-2112
Kendall ES — 200/2-3
535 E Porter Ave 60970 — 815-432-4581
Roy Johnson, prin. — Fax 432-4581
Raymond MS — 300/6-8
101 W Mulberry St 60970 — 815-432-2115
James Bunting, prin. — Fax 432-6896
Other Schools – See Woodland

Wauconda, Lake, Pop. 10,903
Wauconda CUSD 118 — 3,800/PK-12
555 N Main St 60084 — 847-526-7690
Dr. Daniel Coles, supt. — Fax 526-1019
www.cusd118.lake.k12.il.us
Crown ES — 900/PK-5
620 W Bonner Rd 60084 — 847-526-7100
Terrence Brennan, prin. — Fax 487-3596
Wauconda ES — 300/PK-5
225 Osage St 60084 — 847-526-6671
Debra Monroe, prin. — Fax 487-3598
Wauconda MS — 700/6-8
215 Slocum Lake Rd 60084 — 847-526-2122
Cameron Willis, prin. — Fax 487-3597
Other Schools – See Island Lake

Transfiguration S — 200/PK-8
316 W Mill St 60084 — 847-526-6311
Tina Vakilynejad, prin. — Fax 526-4637
Waters Edge Waldorf S — 100/PK-8
150 W Bonner Rd 60084 — 847-526-1372
Fax 717-7314

Waukegan, Lake, Pop. 91,396
Waukegan CUSD 60 — 17,900/PK-12
1201 N Sheridan Rd 60085 — 847-336-3100
Dr. Donaldo Batiste, supt. — Fax 360-5634
www.wps60.org/
Abbott MS — 800/6-8
1319 Washington St 60085 — 847-360-5487
John Samuelian, prin. — Fax 360-5394
Benny MS — 700/6-8
1401 Montesano Ave 60087 — 847-360-5460
Samuel Taylor, prin. — Fax 360-5395
Carman-Buckner ES — 600/1-5
520 Helmholz Ave 60085 — 847-360-5465
Hector Rodriguez, prin. — Fax 360-5380
Clark ES — 300/K-5
601 Blanchard Rd 60087 — 847-360-5466
Renee Sams, prin. — Fax 360-5381
Clearview ES — 700/1-5
1700 Delaware Rd 60087 — 847-360-5467
Jose Lara, prin. — Fax 360-5382
Cooke Magnet ES — 500/K-5
522 Belvidere Rd 60085 — 847-360-5463
Fax 360-5383
EPIC Early Learning Center — 200/PK-PK
540 S McAlister Ave 60085 — 847-360-7021
EPIC - North Shore — 200/PK-PK
326 Julian St 60085 — 847-599-3903
Verna Wilson, prin. — Fax 753-0356
EPIC - Shiloh — 400/PK-PK
800 S Genesee St 60085 — 847-249-6634
Lynnie Bailey, prin. — Fax 753-0356
Glen Flora ES — 500/1-5
1110 Chestnut St 60085 — 847-360-5468
Zenaida Figueroa, prin. — Fax 360-5384
Glenwood ES — 600/1-5
2500 Northmoor Ave 60085 — 847-360-5469
Tierney Eppinger, prin. — Fax 360-5385
Greenwood ES — 300/1-5
1919 North Ave 60087 — 847-360-5470
Joyce Meyer, prin. — Fax 360-5386
Hyde Park ES — 300/1-5
1525 Hyde Park Ave 60085 — 847-360-5471
Brian Carr, prin. — Fax 360-5387
Jefferson MS — 900/6-8
600 S Lewis Ave 60085 — 847-360-5473
Nicole Fishman, prin. — Fax 360-5396
Juarez MS — 800/6-8
201 N Butrick St 60085 — 847-599-4200
Dr. Cathy Watkins, prin. — Fax 263-4797
Little Fort ES — 600/1-5
1775 Blanchard Rd 60087 — 847-360-5478
Dr. Sharon Laviolette, prin. — Fax 360-5388
Lyon Magnet ES — 500/1-5
800 S Elmwood Ave 60085 — 847-360-5479
Alba Avellino, prin. — Fax 599-4032
McCall ES — 300/1-5
3215 N Mcaree Rd 60087 — 847-360-5480
Arlene Vombrack, prin. — Fax 360-5390
North ES — 600/1-5
410 Franklin St 60085 — 847-360-5481
Angel Figueroa, prin. — Fax 360-5391
Oakdale ES — 500/1-5
2230 N Mcaree Rd 60087 — 847-360-5482
Minerva Vega, prin. — Fax 360-5392
Washington ES — 600/1-5
110 S Orchard Ave 60085 — 847-360-5483
Barbara Steinseifer, prin. — Fax 360-5393
Webster MS — 700/6-8
930 New York St 60085 — 847-360-5484
Dr. Joan Brixey, prin. — Fax 360-5397
Whittier K Ctr — 1,200/K-K
901 N Lewis Ave 60085 — 847-360-5577
Karen Bales, prin. — Fax 360-5362

Academy of Our Lady — 200/PK-8
510 Grand Ave 60085 — 847-623-4110
Sandra Prez, prin. — Fax 599-0477
Daniels Christian Academy — 100/PK-8
2313 Washington St 60085 — 847-263-8147
Deborah Stackhouse, admin. — Fax 263-8377
Immanuel Lutheran S — 50/K-8
1310 N Frolic Ave 60085 — 847-249-0011
David Zank, prin. — Fax 249-0011
Lake County Baptist S — 200/PK-12
1550 W Yorkhouse Rd 60087 — 847-623-7600
Timothy Kowach, prin. — Fax 623-2085
Lions' Math & Science Christian Academy — 100/PK-4
1011 Porter St 60085 — 847-360-1054
Dr. Gloria Jean Swopes, dir. — Fax 782-9362
St. Anastasia S — 300/PK-8
629 W Glen Flora Ave 60085 — 847-623-8320
Lourdes Mon, prin. — Fax 623-0556

Waverly, Morgan, Pop. 1,272
Waverly CUSD 6 — 400/PK-12
201 N Miller St 62692 — 217-435-8121
Debra Rust, supt. — Fax 435-3431
www.waverlyscotties.com/
Waverly S — 300/PK-8
PO Box 108 62692 — 217-435-2331
Steve Cline, prin. — Fax 435-2321

Wayne, DuPage, Pop. 2,355
SD U-46
Supt. — See Elgin
Wayne ES — 600/K-6
5N443 School St 60184 — 630-736-7100
Lori Brandes, prin. — Fax 213-5619

Resurrection Preschool — 100/PK-PK
30W350 Army Trail Rd 60184 — 630-289-5400
Mary Jean Bankmann, dir. — Fax 289-5407

Wayne City, Wayne, Pop. 1,075
Wayne City CUSD 100 — 500/PK-12
PO Box 457 62895 — 618-895-3103
Michael Smith, supt. — Fax 895-2331
Oak Grove Learning Center — 100/PK-K
RR 1 62895 — 618-648-2293
Michael Smith, prin. — Fax 648-2296
Wayne City ES — 200/3-6
PO Box 457 62895 — 618-895-3103
Tawana Wilson, prin. — Fax 895-2331
Other Schools – See Cisne

Weldon, DeWitt, Pop. 430
Deland-Weldon CUSD 57
Supt. — See De Land
Deland-Weldon ES — 100/PK-6
2311 N 300 East Rd 61882 — 217-736-2401
Russell Corey, prin. — Fax 736-2654
Deland-Weldon MS — 50/7-8
2311 N 300 East Rd 61882 — 217-736-2401
Russell Corey, prin. — Fax 736-2654

Wenona, Marshall, Pop. 1,077
Fieldcrest CUSD 6
Supt. — See Minonk
Fieldcrest S East — 300/PK-8
102 W Elm St 61377 — 815-853-4331
Doug Roberts, prin. — Fax 853-4786

Westchester, Cook, Pop. 16,177
Westchester SD 92-5 — 1,100/K-8
9981 Canterbury St 60154 — 708-450-2700
Jean Sophie Ed.D., supt. — Fax 450-2718
www.sd925.org
Westchester IS — 400/3-5
10900 Canterbury St 60154 — 708-562-1011
Donald Mrozik, prin. — Fax 562-0299
Westchester MS — 400/6-8
1620 Norfolk Ave 60154 — 708-450-2735
Mary Leidigh, prin. — Fax 450-2752
Westchester PS — 300/K-2
2400 Downing Ave 60154 — 708-562-1509
Akemi Sessler, prin. — Fax 562-1547

Divine Infant Jesus S — 200/PK-8
1640 Newcastle Ave 60154 — 708-865-0122
Leonard Gramarossa, prin. — Fax 865-9495
Divine Providence S — 200/PK-8
2500 Mayfair Ave 60154 — 708-562-2258
Jerry Spatara, prin. — Fax 562-9171

West Chicago, DuPage, Pop. 26,554
Benjamin SD 25 — 900/K-8
28W250 Saint Charles Rd 60185 — 630-876-7800
Philip Ehrhardt, supt. — Fax 876-3325
www.bendist25.org
Benjamin MS — 400/5-8
28W300 Saint Charles Rd 60185 — 630-876-7820
Joseph Salmieri, prin. — Fax 231-3886
Other Schools – See Carol Stream

Saint Charles CUSD 303
Supt. — See Saint Charles
Norton Creek ES — 500/K-5
2033 Smith Rd 60185 — 630-587-7200
Rachel Overton, prin. — Fax 587-7210

West Chicago ESD 33 — 3,800/PK-8
312 E Forest Ave 60185 — 630-293-6000
Dr. Ed Leman, supt. — Fax 293-6088
www.wegoed33.k12.il.us
Currier ES — 500/K-6
800 Garys Mill Rd 60185 — 630-293-6600
Nancy Cordes, prin. — Fax 562-2579
Early Learning Center — PK-PK
300 E Forest Ave 60185 — 630-293-6000
Sandra Warner, prin. — Fax 231-7605
Gary ES — 500/K-6
130 E Forest Ave 60185 — 630-293-6010
Rocio Fisher, prin. — Fax 562-2583
Indian Knoll ES — 400/K-6
0N645 Indian Knoll Rd 60185 — 630-293-6020
Brad Hevron, prin. — Fax 562-2584
Pioneer ES — 600/K-6
615 Kenwood Ave 60185 — 630-293-6040
Gloria Trejo, prin. — Fax 562-2587
Turner ES — 500/K-6
750 Ingalton Ave 60185 — 630-293-6050
John Rodriguez, prin. — Fax 562-2589
Wegner ES — 500/PK-6
1180 Marcella Ln 60185 — 630-293-6400
James Grothendick, prin. — Fax 562-2590
West Chicago MS — 800/7-8
238 E Hazel St 60185 — 630-293-6060
Pat Roszowski, prin. — Fax 562-2586

St. Mary S — 200/PK-8
147 Garden St 60185 — 630-231-1776
Nancy Coughlin, prin. — Fax 293-2671
Trinity Lutheran Preschool — 50/PK-K
331 George St 60185 — 630-231-5849
Fax 231-6926

West Dundee, Kane
CUSD 300
Supt. — See Carpentersville
Dundee Highlands ES — 500/K-5
407 S 5th St 60118 — 847-426-1480
Patricia Schmidt, prin. — Fax 426-1935
Dundee MS — 1,000/6-8
37W450 IL Route 72 60118 — 847-426-1485
Kara Vicente, prin. — Fax 426-4008

Children's House Montessori S — 50/PK-3
417 W Main St 60118 — 847-426-3570
Donna Butcher, dir. — Fax 426-9063
St. Catherine of Siena S — 300/PK-8
845 W Main St 60118 — 847-426-4808
Margaret Sanders, prin. — Fax 426-0437

Western Springs, Cook, Pop. 12,530
Western Springs SD 101 — 1,400/K-8
4335 Howard Ave 60558 — 708-246-3700
Dr. Brian Barnhart, supt. — Fax 482-2581
www.d101.org
Field Park ES — 300/K-5
4335 Howard Ave 60558 — 708-246-7675
Brad Promisel, prin. — Fax 482-2581
Forest Hills ES — 200/K-5
5020 Central Ave 60558 — 708-246-7678
Debra Farrell, prin. — Fax 482-2589
Laidlaw ES — 400/K-5
4072 Forest Ave 60558 — 708-246-7673
Cathy Powell, prin. — Fax 482-2496
McClure JHS — 500/6-8
4225 Wolf Rd 60558 — 708-246-7590
F. Daniel Chick, prin. — Fax 246-4370

St. John of the Cross S — 800/PK-8
708 51st St 60558 — 708-246-4454
Kathleen Gorman, prin. — Fax 246-9010

West Frankfort, Franklin, Pop. 8,285
Frankfort CUSD 168 — 2,000/PK-12
PO Box 425 62896 — 618-937-2421
Gregory Goins, supt. — Fax 932-2025
www.wf168.frnkln.k12.il.us/index.htm
Central JHS — 300/7-8
1500 E 9th St 62896 — 618-937-2444
Gayle Crawford, prin. — Fax 937-2445
Denning ES — 500/PK-2
1401 W 6th St 62896 — 618-937-2464
LeAnn Miller, prin. — Fax 937-2465
Frankfort IS — 600/3-6
800 N Cherry St 62896 — 618-937-1412
Mark Zahm, prin. — Fax 932-2646

St. John the Baptist S — 100/PK-8
702 E Poplar St 62896 — 618-937-2017
Sr. Brenda Engleman, prin. — Fax 937-2017

Westmont, DuPage, Pop. 24,863
CCSD 181 — 4,000/PK-8
1010 Executive Dr Ste 100 60559 — 630-887-1070
Dr. Robert Sabatino, supt. — Fax 887-1079
www.d181.org/
Other Schools – See Burr Ridge, Clarendon Hills, Hinsdale

CUSD 201 1,500/PK-12
200 N Linden Ave 60559 630-468-8000
Dr. Steven Baule, supt. Fax 969-9022
www.cusd201.org
Manning ES 300/PK-5
200 N Linden Ave 60559 630-468-8050
Diana Molby, prin. Fax 969-2492
Miller ES 200/K-5
125 W Traube Ave 60559 630-468-8300
Kelly Baas, prin. Fax 969-5401
Westmont JHS 400/6-8
944 Oakwood Dr 60559 630-468-8200
Ronald Fiala, prin. Fax 654-2203

Maercker SD 60
Supt. — See Clarendon Hills
Maercker ES 500/3-5
5827 S Cass Ave 60559 630-968-6165
Brenda Babinec, prin. Fax 968-3314

Holy Trinity S 200/PK-8
108 S Linden Ave 60559 630-971-0184
Dr. Charles Terry, prin. Fax 971-1175

West Salem, Edwards, Pop. 977
Edwards County CUSD 1
Supt. — See Albion
West Salem S 200/PK-8
PO Box 367 62476 618-456-8881
Dale Schmittler, prin. Fax 456-3510

Westville, Vermilion, Pop. 3,058
Westville CUSD 2 1,200/K-12
125 W Ellsworth St 61883 217-267-3141
James Owens, supt. Fax 267-3144
www.westville.k12.il.us
Giacoma ES 700/K-6
200 S Walnut 61883 217-267-2154
Melinda Pollock, prin. Fax 267-3484
Westville JHS 200/7-8
412 Moses Ave 61883 217-267-2185
Greg Lewis, prin. Fax 267-3621

St. Mary S 100/PK-8
225 N State St 61883 217-267-7730
David Bibb, prin. Fax 267-3327

Wheaton, DuPage, Pop. 54,700
CUSD 200 13,800/PK-12
130 W Park Ave 60189 630-682-2002
Dr. Richard Drury, supt. Fax 682-2068
www.cusd200.org
Edison MS 800/6-8
1125 S Wheaton Ave 60187 630-682-2050
David Kanne, prin. Fax 682-2337
Emerson ES 300/K-5
119 S Woodlawn St 60187 630-682-2055
Daniel Bostrom, prin. Fax 682-2372
Franklin MS 700/6-8
211 E Franklin St 60187 630-682-2060
Susan Wolfe, prin. Fax 682-2340
Hawthorne ES 300/K-5
334 Wakeman Ave 60187 630-682-2065
John Patterson, prin. Fax 682-2392
Hubble MS 900/6-8
603 S Main St 60187 630-682-2160
Beth Sullivan, prin. Fax 682-2299
Jefferson Preschool Center 200/PK-PK
130 N Hazelton Ave 60187 630-682-2474
Stephanie Farrelly, prin. Fax 462-1914
Lincoln ES 400/K-5
630 Dawes Ave 60189 630-682-2075
Kathy DeMarzo, prin. Fax 682-2367
Longfellow ES 500/K-5
311 W Seminary Ave 60187 630-682-2080
Dianne Thornburg, prin. Fax 682-2342
Lowell ES 500/K-5
312 S President St 60187 630-682-2085
Denise DeSalvo, prin. Fax 682-2245
Madison ES 400/K-5
1620 Mayo Ave 60189 630-682-2095
Gene Sikorski, prin. Fax 682-2435
Monroe MS 900/6-8
1855 Manchester Rd 60187 630-682-2285
Jason Stipp, prin. Fax 682-2331
Sandburg ES 400/K-5
1345 Jewell Rd 60187 630-682-2105
Aaron Bacon, prin. Fax 682-2350
Washington ES 400/K-5
911 Bridle Ln 60187 630-682-2222
Sandra Niemiera, prin. Fax 682-2333
Whittier ES 400/K-5
218 W Park Ave 60189 630-682-2185
Joanne Hall, prin. Fax 682-2409
Wiesbrook ES 500/K-5
2160 Durfee Rd 60189 630-682-2190
Brian Turyna, prin. Fax 682-2339
Other Schools – See Warrenville, Winfield

Glen Ellyn CCSD 89
Supt. — See Glen Ellyn
Briar Glen ES 400/K-5
1800 Briarcliffe Blvd 60189 630-545-3300
Emily Tammaru, prin. Fax 665-2847

Clapham S, PO Box 209 60187 100/PK-5
Doug Reynolds, hdmstr. 630-547-5125
Dupage Montessori S 50/PK-K
300 E Cole Ave 60187 630-653-1221
Sharon Breen, prin. Fax 653-0578
Loretto ECC 50/PK-PK
PO Box 508 60187 630-690-8410
Sr. Julie Stapleton, prin. Fax 868-2764
St. John Lutheran S 200/PK-8
125 E Seminary Ave 60187 630-668-0701
Gayle Galloway, prin. Fax 871-9931
St. Michael S 500/PK-8
314 W Willow Ave 60187 630-665-1454
Marcia Opal, prin. Fax 665-1491

Wheaton Christian Grammar S 500/K-8
530 E Harrison Ave 60187 630-668-1385
Stephen Clum, hdmstr. Fax 668-2475
Wheaton Montessori S 100/PK-6
1970 N Gary Ave 60187 630-653-5100
Rebecca Lingo, admin. Fax 653-5699

Wheeling, Cook, Pop. 36,641
Wheeling CCSD 21 6,900/PK-8
999 W Dundee Rd 60090 847-537-8270
Dr. Gary Mical, supt. Fax 520-2848
www.ccsd21.org
Field ES 500/K-5
51 Saint Armand Ln 60090 847-520-2780
LaVonne Knapstein, prin. Fax 419-3077
Hawthorne ECC PK-PK
200 Glendale St 60090 847-465-7290
Dr. Gwen Gage, prin.
Holmes MS 700/6-8
221 S Wolf Rd 60090 847-520-2790
Martin Hopkins, prin. Fax 419-3073
London MS 700/6-8
1001 W Dundee Rd 60090 847-520-2745
Jim Parker, prin. Fax 520-2842
Tarkington ES 500/K-5
310 Scott St 60090 847-520-2775
Dr. Joe Arduino, prin. Fax 419-3074
Twain ES 600/PK-5
515 E Merle Ln 60090 847-520-2785
Jose Celis, prin. Fax 419-3080
Whitman ES 800/PK-5
133 Wille Ave 60090 847-520-2795
Lori Henkels, prin. Fax 520-2607
Other Schools – See Arlington Heights, Buffalo Grove, Mount Prospect

Bell Montessori S 50/PK-6
9300 Capitol Dr 60090 847-297-4660
Carol Martorano, prin. Fax 297-3208

White Hall, Greene, Pop. 2,609
North Greene Unit SD 3 1,000/PK-12
407 N Main St 62092 217-374-2842
Les Stevens, supt. Fax 374-2849
www.northgreene.com/
White Hall ES 300/K-3
250 E Sherman St 62092 217-374-2616
Chris Waltrip, prin. Fax 374-6464
Other Schools – See Roodhouse

White Heath, Piatt
Monticello CUSD 25
Supt. — See Monticello
White Heath ES 50/2-3
300 W High St 61884 217-762-8511
Emily Weidner, prin. Fax 762-8333

Williamsfield, Knox, Pop. 593
Williamsfield CUSD 210 300/PK-12
PO Box 179 61489 309-639-2219
Mary Bush, supt. Fax 639-2618
www.billtown.org/
Williamsfield ES, PO Box 179 61489 200/PK-5
Mary Bush, prin. 309-639-2216
Williamsfield MS, PO Box 179 61489 100/6-8
Mary Bush, prin. 309-639-2216

Williamsville, Sangamon, Pop. 1,396
Williamsville CUSD 15 1,400/PK-12
800 S Walnut St 62693 217-566-2014
David Root, supt. Fax 566-2183
www.wcusd15.org/
Williamsville JHS 300/6-8
500 S Walnut St 62693 217-566-3600
Rod McQuality, prin. Fax 566-2475
Other Schools – See Sherman

Willowbrook, DuPage, Pop. 8,893
CCSD 180
Supt. — See Burr Ridge
Jeans ES 500/PK-4
16W631 91st St 60527 630-325-8186
Dr. Debra LeBlanc, prin. Fax 325-9576

Gower SD 62 1,000/PK-8
7700 Clarendon Hills Rd 60527 630-986-5383
Steve Griesbach, supt. Fax 323-3074
www.gower62.com
Gower West ES 500/PK-4
7650 Clarendon Hills Rd 60527 630-323-6446
Thomas Thering, prin. Fax 323-6494
Other Schools – See Burr Ridge

Maercker SD 60
Supt. — See Clarendon Hills
Westview Hills MS 500/6-8
630 65th St 60527 630-963-1450
Jed Ramsey, prin. Fax 963-0954

Willow Hill, Jasper, Pop. 241
Jasper County CUSD 1
Supt. — See Newton
Willow Hill K 100/K-K
PO Box 39 62480 618-455-3231
David Parker, prin. Fax 455-3622

Willow Springs, Cook, Pop. 6,011
Willow Springs SD 108 300/K-8
8345 Archer Ave 60480 708-839-6828
Frank Patrick, supt. Fax 839-8399
www.willowspringsschool.org
Willow Springs S 300/K-8
8345 Archer Ave 60480 708-839-6828
Karen Triezenberg, prin. Fax 839-8399

Wilmette, Cook, Pop. 26,922
Avoca SD 37 700/PK-8
2921 Illinois Rd 60091 847-251-3587
Dr. Joseph Porto, supt. Fax 251-7742
avoca37.org/
Murphy MS 200/PK-PK, 6-
2921 Illinois Rd 60091 847-251-3617
Dr. Deanna Reed, prin. Fax 251-4179
Other Schools – See Glenview

Wilmette SD 39 3,700/PK-8
615 Locust Rd 60091 847-256-2450
Ray Lechner, supt. Fax 256-1920
wilmette39.org
Central ES 500/K-4
900 Central Ave 60091 847-251-3252
Melanie Horowitz, prin. Fax 251-4086
Harper ES 400/K-4
1101 Dartmouth St 60091 847-251-6754
Sue Kick, prin. Fax 251-4176
Highcrest MS 900/5-6
569 Hunter Rd 60091 847-853-2900
Luke Pavone, prin. Fax 256-0083
McKenzie ES 500/K-4
649 Prairie Ave 60091 847-251-2295
Denise Welter, prin. Fax 251-4067
Romona ES 500/PK-4
600 Romona Rd 60091 847-256-0211
Heather Glowacki, prin. Fax 251-4153
Wilmette JHS 800/7-8
620 Locust Rd 60091 847-256-7280
David Palzet, prin. Fax 256-0204

Baker Demonstration S 400/PK-8
201 Sheridan Rd 60091 847-425-5800
Dr. Andrew Taylor, prin. Fax 425-5801
St. Francis Xavier S 300/PK-8
808 Linden Ave 60091 847-256-0644
Daniel McKenna, prin. Fax 256-0753
St. Joseph S 300/PK-8
1740 Lake Ave 60091 847-256-7870
Ronald Berger, prin. Fax 256-9514

Wilmington, Will, Pop. 5,957
Wilmington CUSD 209U 1,500/PK-12
209U Wildcat Ct 60481 815-926-1751
Anthony Plese, supt. Fax 926-1692
www.wilmington.will.k12.il.us
Booth Central ES 400/2-5
201 N Kankakee St 60481 815-476-7424
Kevin Feeney, prin. Fax 476-4406
Bruning ES 300/PK-1
1910 Bruning Dr 60481 815-476-6671
Venita Dennis, prin. Fax 476-0130
Stevens MS 300/6-8
221 Ryan St 60481 815-476-2189
Joseph Pacetti, prin. Fax 476-1941

St. Rose S 200/PK-8
626 S Kankakee St 60481 815-476-6220
Linda Bland, prin. Fax 476-6544

Winchester, Scott, Pop. 1,609
Winchester CUSD 1 700/PK-12
149 S Elm St 62694 217-742-3175
David Roberts, supt. Fax 742-3312
Winchester S, 283 S Elm St 62694 500/PK-8
Andrew Stremlau, prin. 217-742-9551

Windsor, Shelby, Pop. 1,802
Windsor CUSD 1 400/PK-12
1424 Minnesota Ave 61957 217-459-2636
Sharon Keck, supt. Fax 459-2661
www.windsor.k12.il.us
Windsor ES 200/PK-6
808 Wisconsin Ave 61957 217-459-2447
Zakry Standerfer, prin. Fax 459-2408

Winfield, DuPage, Pop. 9,844
CUSD 200
Supt. — See Wheaton
Pleasant Hill ES 600/K-5
1N230 Pleasant Hill Rd 60190 630-682-2100
Ken Bonomo, prin. Fax 682-2366

Winfield SD 34 400/PK-8
0S150 Winfield Rd 60190 630-909-4900
Dr. Diane Cody, supt. Fax 260-2382
www.winfield34.org/
Winfield Central S 200/3-8
0S150 Park St 60190 630-909-4960
Patti Palagi, prin. Fax 933-9236
Winfield PS 200/PK-2
0S150 Winfield Rd 60190 630-909-4910
Patti Palagi, prin. Fax 260-2382

St. John the Baptist S 200/PK-8
0S259 Church St 60190 630-668-2625
Julie Tobin, prin. Fax 668-7176

Winnebago, Winnebago, Pop. 3,065
Winnebago CUSD 323 1,700/PK-12
304 E McNair Rd 61088 815-335-2456
Dr. Dennis Harezlak, supt. Fax 335-7574
www.winnebagoschools.org/
McNair ES 300/4-5
304 E Mcnair Rd 61088 815-335-1607
Sean Monahan, prin. Fax 335-7574
Simon ES 300/1-3
309 S Benton St 61088 815-335-2318
Frank Mandera, prin. Fax 335-3127
Winnebago MS 400/6-8
407 N Elida St 61088 815-335-2364
James Burns, prin. Fax 335-1437
Other Schools – See Seward

Winnetka, Cook, Pop. 12,452
Winnetka SD 36 2,100/PK-8
1235 Oak St 60093 847-446-9400
Dr. Mary Herrmann, supt. Fax 446-9408
www.winnetka36.org/
Crow Island ES 400/K-4
1112 Willow Rd 60093 847-446-0353
Deirdre Churchill, prin. Fax 446-9021
Greeley ES 300/PK-4
275 Fairview Ave 60093 847-446-6060
Susan Hugebeck, prin. Fax 501-5737
Hubbard Woods ES 400/K-4
1110 Chatfield Rd 60093 847-446-0920
Dr. Maureen Cheever, prin. Fax 501-6124

Skokie S 500/5-6
520 Glendale Ave 60093 847-441-1750
Thomas Eber, prin. Fax 441-2193
Washburne MS 500/7-8
515 Hibbard Rd 60093 847-446-5892
Daniel Schwartz, prin. Fax 446-1380

North Shore Country Day S 500/PK-12
310 Green Bay Rd 60093 847-446-0674
Thomas Doar, hdmstr. Fax 446-0675
Sacred Heart S 300/PK-8
1095 Gage St 60093 847-446-0005
Sr. Kathleen Donnelly, prin. Fax 446-4961
SS. Faith Hope & Charity S 300/PK-8
180 Ridge Ave 60093 847-446-0031
Mary Rehfield, prin. Fax 446-9064

Winthrop Harbor, Lake, Pop. 7,090
Winthrop Harbor SD 1 600/K-8
500 North Ave 60096 847-731-3085
Dr. Dennis Guiser, supt. Fax 731-3156
www.whsd1.org
North Prairie JHS 300/6-8
500 North Ave 60096 847-731-3089
Theodore Brooks, prin. Fax 731-3152
Spring Bluff ES 100/K-1
628 College Ave 60096 847-872-5414
Carrie Nottingham, prin. Fax 746-1572
Westfield ES 200/2-5
2309 9th St 60096 847-872-5438
Patricia Hodge, prin. Fax 746-1477

Witt, Montgomery, Pop. 986
Hillsboro CUSD 3
Supt. — See Hillsboro
Witt ES 100/PK-5
PO Box 447 62094 217-594-2232
Mark Fenske, prin. Fax 594-2234

Wolf Lake, Union
Shawnee CUSD 84 500/K-12
PO Box 128 62998 618-833-5709
Charles Rosenkoetter, supt. Fax 833-4171
Shawnee JHS 100/6-8
PO Box 128 62998 618-833-5307
Crystal Housman, prin. Fax 833-5468
Other Schools – See Grand Tower, Mc Clure

Wonder Lake, McHenry, Pop. 2,751
Harrison SD 36 500/PK-8
6809 McCullom Lake Rd 60097 815-653-2311
Dr. Jill Gildea, supt. Fax 653-1712
www.harrisonschool.org/
Harrison S 500/PK-8
6809 McCullom Lake Rd 60097 815-653-2311
Anne Huff, prin. Fax 653-1712

Wood Dale, DuPage, Pop. 13,419
Wood Dale SD 7 900/PK-8
543 N Wood Dale Rd 60191 630-595-9510
John Corbett, supt. Fax 595-5625
www.wd7.org
Early Childhood Education Center 100/PK-K
543 N Wood Dale Rd 60191 630-694-1174
Constance Tadel, prin. Fax 238-0387
Oakbrook ES 200/K-2
170 S Wood Dale Rd 60191 630-766-6336
Shelly Skarzynski, prin. Fax 766-2174
Westview ES 200/3-5
200 N Addison Rd 60191 630-766-8040
Alan Buttimer, prin. Fax 766-2094
Wood Dale JHS 400/6-8
655 N Wood Dale Rd 60191 630-766-6210
Anthony Murray, prin. Fax 766-1839

Holy Ghost S 200/PK-8
260 N Wood Dale Rd 60191 630-766-4508
Diana Mendez, prin. Fax 860-7697

Woodhull, Henry, Pop. 810
Alwood CUSD 225 500/PK-12
301 E 5th Ave 61490 309-334-2719
Shannon Bumann, supt. Fax 334-2925
www.alwood.net
Other Schools – See Alpha

Woodland, Iroquois, Pop. 311
Iroquois County CUSD 9
Supt. — See Watseka
Woodland ES 200/4-5
PO Box 267 60974 815-473-4241
Christine Yeoman, prin. Fax 473-4309

Woodlawn, Jefferson, Pop. 644
Woodlawn CCSD 4 300/K-8
301 S Central St 62898 618-735-2661
Jerry Travelstead, supt. Fax 242-2720
woodlawn-grade.roe25.com/
Woodlawn S 300/K-8
301 S Central St 62898 618-735-2661
Jerry Travelstead, prin. Fax 242-2720

Woodridge, DuPage, Pop. 34,058
Woodridge SD 68 2,800/PK-8
7925 Janes Ave 60517 630-985-7925
Jerome Brendel, supt. Fax 910-2060
www.woodridge68.org
Edgewood ES 400/PK-6
7900 Woodridge Dr 60517 630-985-3603
Tanya Hughes, prin. Fax 985-1519
Goodrich ES 300/K-6
3450 Hobson Rd 60517 630-969-7271
Paul Scaletta, prin. Fax 963-4648
Jefferson JHS 600/7-8
7200 Janes Ave 60517 630-852-8010
Ron Freed, prin. Fax 969-7168
Meadowview ES 400/K-6
2525 Mitchell Dr 60517 630-969-2390
Jodi Innes, prin. Fax 969-9941
Murphy ES 300/K-6
7700 Larchwood Ln 60517 630-985-3797
Susan Futterer, prin. Fax 910-0251
Sipley ES 400/K-6
2806 83rd St 60517 630-985-7150
Robyne Lewis, prin. Fax 985-0064
Willow Creek ES 400/PK-6
2901 Jackson Dr 60517 630-852-5055
MaryAnn Sanfilipp, prin. Fax 963-4321

Montessori of Woodridge 50/PK-6
6953 Woodridge Dr 60517 630-964-3533
Patricia Whyte, prin. Fax 964-3533
St. Scholastica S 300/K-8
7720 Janes Ave 60517 630-985-2515
Gail Kueper, prin. Fax 985-2395

Wood River, Madison, Pop. 10,985
Wood River-Hartford ESD 15 800/PK-8
501 E Lorena Ave 62095 618-254-0607
Mark Cappel, supt. Fax 254-9048
www.wrh15.org/
Lewis-Clark ES 400/K-5
501 E Lorena Ave 62095 618-254-4354
Patrick Shelton, prin. Fax 254-7601
Lewis-Clark JHS 200/6-8
501 E Lorena Ave 62095 618-254-4355
Sue Rives, prin. Fax 254-7600
Other Schools – See Hartford

Woodstock, McHenry, Pop. 21,985
Woodstock CUSD 200 6,800/PK-12
227 W Judd St 60098 815-338-8200
Ellyn Wrzeski, supt. Fax 338-2005
www.d200.mchenry.k12.il.us
Clay Academy 100/3-12
112 Grove St 60098 815-337-2529
Dawn Cook, prin. Fax 337-2140
Creekside MS 700/6-8
3201 Hercules Rd 60098 815-337-5200
Robert Hackbart, prin. Fax 206-0476
Dean Street ES 500/1-5
600 Dean St 60098 815-338-1133
Pedro Lara-Oliva, prin. Fax 338-3089
Dierzen Early Learning Center 700/PK-K
2045 N Seminary Ave 60098 815-338-8883
Vicki Larson, prin. Fax 337-5431
Endres ES 500/1-5
2181 N Seminary Ave 60098 815-337-8177
Tom Wollpert, prin. Fax 338-5765
Greenwood ES 400/1-5
4618 Greenwood Rd 60098 815-648-2606
Mark Widmer, prin. Fax 648-4808
Northwood MS 800/6-8
2121 N Seminary Ave 60098 815-338-4900
Jerome Wakitsch, prin. Fax 337-2150
Olson ES 600/1-5
720 W Judd St 60098 815-338-0473
Gail Perkins, prin. Fax 338-8142
Prairiewood ES 1-5
3215 Hercules Rd 60098 815-337-5300
Dan Carter, prin. Fax 206-0479
Westwood ES 500/1-5
14124 W South Street Rd 60098 815-337-8173
Jared Skorburg, prin. Fax 337-8175

Crystal Lake Montessori S 100/PK-8
3013 S Country Club Rd 60098 815-338-0013
Penny Cichucki, prin. Fax 338-8588
St. Mary S 400/PK-8
313 N Tryon St 60098 815-338-3598
Dr. Diane Vida, prin. Fax 338-3408
Woodstock Christian S 100/PK-8
1201 Dean St 60098 815-338-1391
Dee Jones, admin. Fax 338-1330

Worden, Madison, Pop. 997
Edwardsville CUSD 7
Supt. — See Edwardsville
Worden ES 200/4-5
110 N Main St 62097 618-692-7442
Beth Renth, prin. Fax 692-7441

Trinity-St. Paul Lutheran S 100/K-8
6961 W Frontage Rd 62097 618-633-2202
Myra Farrell, prin. Fax 633-1709

Worth, Cook, Pop. 10,652
Worth SD 127 1,000/PK-8
11218 S Ridgeland Ave 60482 708-448-2800
Dr. Rita Wojtylewski, supt. Fax 448-6215
www.worthschools.org
Worth ES 400/K-5
11158 S Oak Park Ave 60482 708-448-2801
Joseph Zampillo, prin. Fax 448-6023
Worth JHS 400/6-8
11151 S New England Ave 60482 708-448-2803
Dr. Peter Yuska, prin. Fax 448-6155
Worthridge S PK-PK
11218 S Ridgeland Ave 60482 708-448-2800
Dr. Rita Wojtylewski, prin. Fax 448-6215
Worthwoods ES 300/PK-5
11000 S Oketo Ave 60482 708-448-2802
Tim Hathhorn, prin. Fax 448-5623

Wyanet, Bureau, Pop. 1,010
Bureau Valley CUSD 340
Supt. — See Manlius
Bureau Valley ES Wyanet 100/PK-2
PO Box 341 61379 815-699-2251
Denise Bolin, prin. Fax 699-7046

Wyoming, Stark, Pop. 1,390
Stark County CUSD 100 800/PK-12
300 W Van Buren St 61491 309-695-6123
Jerry Klooster, supt.
www.stark100.com/
Stark County ES 400/PK-5
300 W Van Buren St 61491 309-695-5181
Renee Wallace, prin. Fax 695-4302
Other Schools – See Toulon

Xenia, Clay, Pop. 401
Flora CUSD 35
Supt. — See Flora
Xenia ES, PO Box 235 62899 100/K-4
Leslie Carder, prin. 618-678-2205

Yorkville, Kendall, Pop. 10,791
Yorkville CUSD 115 3,800/PK-12
PO Box 579 60560 630-553-4382
Thomas Engler, supt. Fax 553-4398
www.yorkville.k12.il.us
Autumn Creek ES K-6
2377 Autumn Creek Blvd 60560 630-553-4048
David Ascolani, prin.
Bristol Bay ES K-6
427 Bristol Bay Dr 60560 630-553-5121
Dave Taylor, prin. Fax 882-6267
Circle Center ES 500/K-3
901 Mill St 60560 630-553-4388
Brenda Donahue, prin. Fax 553-4456
Grande Reserve ES 600/K-6
3142 Grande Trl 60560 630-553-5513
Sylvia Torto, prin. Fax 553-5030
Yorkville ES 300/PK-3
201 W Somonauk St 60560 630-553-4390
Tracy Anderson, prin. Fax 553-4450
Yorkville IS 600/4-6
103 E Schoolhouse Rd 60560 630-553-4594
Steve Bjork, prin. Fax 553-4596
Yorkville MS 600/7-8
920 Prairie Crossing Dr 60560 630-553-4544
Jeff Szymczak, prin. Fax 553-5181
Other Schools – See Bristol

Cross Lutheran S 400/PK-8
8535 State Route 47 60560 630-553-7861
Susan Lopez, prin. Fax 553-2580
Parkview Christian Academy 100/K-8
201 W Center St 60560 630-553-5158
Jim Apker, prin. Fax 553-3370
Peaceful Pathways Montessori S 50/PK-5
8250 State Route 71 60560 630-553-4263
Shawna Watkins, prin.

Zeigler, Franklin, Pop. 1,682
Zeigler-Royalton CUSD 188 700/PK-12
PO Box 38 62999 618-596-5841
George Wilkerson, supt. Fax 596-6789
www.z-r.frnkln.k12.il.us/
Zeigler-Royalton ES 400/PK-6
PO Box 87 62999 618-596-2121
Kevin Blankenship, prin. Fax 596-2075
Zeigler-Royalton JHS 100/7-8
PO Box 87 62999 618-596-2121
Kevin Blankenship, prin. Fax 596-2075

Zion, Lake, Pop. 24,303
Beach Park CCSD 3
Supt. — See Beach Park
Oak Crest ES 400/K-5
38550 N Lewis Ave 60099 847-599-5550
John Frederickson, prin. Fax 623-0560

Zion ESD 6 2,900/PK-8
2200 Bethesda Blvd 60099 847-872-5455
Dr. John Ahlgrim, supt. Fax 746-1280
www.zion6.com
Beulah Park ES 400/K-6
1910 Gilboa Ave 60099 847-746-1429
Lynn Butera, prin. Fax 746-7803
Central JHS 600/7-8
1716 27th St 60099 847-746-1431
Joseph Kent, prin. Fax 746-9750
East ES 300/K-6
2913 Elim Ave 60099 847-872-5425
Yvonne Brown, prin. Fax 872-8130
Elmwood ES 300/K-6
3025 Ezra Ave 60099 847-746-1491
Anthony Comella, prin. Fax 746-0052
Lakeview S 200/PK-PK
2200 Bethesda Blvd 60099 847-872-0255
Dr. Carol Hincker, prin. Fax 731-1389
Shiloh Park ES 500/K-6
2635 Gabriel Ave 60099 847-746-8136
Keely Roberts, prin. Fax 731-8453
West ES 500/K-6
2412 Jethro Ave 60099 847-746-8222
Valerie Lampinen, prin. Fax 731-8490

Our Savior Lutheran S 100/PK-8
1800 23rd St 60099 847-872-5922
Hartley Dus, prin. Fax 872-5539

INDIANA

INDIANA DEPARTMENT OF EDUCATION
151 W Ohio St, Indianapolis 46204-2564
Telephone 317-232-6610
Fax 317-232-8004
Website http://www.doe.state.in.us

Superintendent of Public Instruction Tony Bennett

INDIANA BOARD OF EDUCATION
200 W Washington St Ste 229, Indianapolis 46204-2798

Chairperson Tony Bennett

EDUCATIONAL SERVICE CENTERS (ESC)

Central Indiana ESC
Tom Pagan, dir., 6321 La Pas Trl 317-387-7100
Indianapolis 46268 Fax 328-7298
www.ciesc.k12.in.us/
East Central ESC
Walter Harrison, dir. 765-825-1247
1601 Indiana Ave Fax 825-2532
Connersville 47331
www.ecesc.k12.in.us/
Northern Indiana ESC
Ted Chittum, dir. 574-254-0111
56535 Magnetic Dr Fax 254-0148
Mishawaka 46545
www.niesc.k12.in.us/
Northwest Indiana ESC
Dr. Charles Costa, dir. 219-922-0900
2939 41st St, Highland 46322 Fax 922-1246
www.nwiesc.k12.in.us/
Region 8 ESC
Robert Huffman, dir. 260-244-9000
PO Box 409, Columbia City 46725 Fax 244-9001
www.r8esc.k12.in.us/800/intro.htm
Southern Indiana ESC
J. Scott Turney, dir. 812-482-6641
1102 Tree Lane Dr, Jasper 47546 Fax 482-6652
www.siec.k12.in.us/
Wabash Valley ESC
Larry Rausch, dir., 3061 Benton St 765-463-1589
West Lafayette 47906 Fax 463-1580
www.wvec.k12.in.us/
West Central ESC
David Archer, dir. 765-653-2727
PO Box 21, Greencastle 46135 Fax 653-7897
www.wciesc.k12.in.us/
William E. Wilson ESC
Larry Risk, dir., 2101 Grace Ave 812-256-8000
Charlestown 47111 Fax 256-8012
www.wesc.k12.in.us/

PUBLIC, PRIVATE AND CATHOLIC ELEMENTARY SCHOOLS

Acton, Marion
Franklin Township Community SC
Supt. — See Indianapolis
Acton ES 600/K-4
8010 Acton Rd 46259 317-862-6108
Steve Peters, prin. Fax 862-7251

Akron, Kosciusko, Pop. 1,045
Tippecanoe Valley SC 2,200/K-12
8343 S State Road 19 46910 574-353-7741
Brett Boggs, supt. Fax 353-7743
www.tvsc.k12.in.us
Akron ES 500/K-5
202 E Rural St 46910 574-893-4633
Blaine Conley, prin. Fax 893-4746
Tippecanoe Valley MS 500/6-8
11303 W 800 S 46910 574-353-7353
Earl Richter, prin. Fax 353-7189
Other Schools – See Mentone

Albany, Delaware, Pop. 2,315
Delaware Community SC
Supt. — See Muncie
Albany ES 200/K-5
700 W State St 47320 765-789-6102
Christopher Conley, prin. Fax 789-6349

Albion, Noble, Pop. 2,323
Central Noble Community SC 1,400/K-12
200 E Main St 46701 260-636-2175
Dr. Stacey Hughes, supt. Fax 636-7918
www.centralnoble.k12.in.us/
Albion ES 300/K-5
202 Cougar Ct 46701 260-636-7538
Shannon Gleason, prin. Fax 636-7740
Central Noble MS 400/6-8
401 E Highland St 46701 260-636-2279
Geoff Brose, prin. Fax 636-2461
Other Schools – See Wolflake

Alexandria, Madison, Pop. 5,868
Alexandria Community SC 1,600/K-12
202 E Washington St 46001 765-724-4496
James Willey, supt. Fax 724-5049
www.alex.k12.in.us
Alexandria-Monroe ES 500/K-3
800 N Central Ave 46001 765-724-7788
Scott Deetz, prin. Fax 724-5054
Alexandria-Monroe IS 500/4-7
308 W 11th St 46001 765-724-4166
Chris Schnepp, prin. Fax 724-5045

St. Mary S 100/K-8
820 W Madison St 46001 765-724-4459
Sr. Marilyn Huegerich, prin. Fax 724-9711

Amo, Hendricks, Pop. 455
Mill Creek Community SC
Supt. — See Clayton
Mill Creek West ES 300/K-5
4704 Pearl St 46103 317-539-9255
Jeremy Baugh, prin. Fax 539-9280

Anderson, Madison, Pop. 57,500
Anderson Community SC 10,000/K-12
1229 Lincoln St 46016 765-641-2028
Mikella Lowe, supt. Fax 641-2080
www.acsc.net/
Anderson ES 400/K-5
2035 Raible Ave 46011 765-641-2092
Jennette Harris, prin. Fax 683-3014
Eastside ES 600/K-5
844 N Scatterfield Rd 46012 765-641-2101
Patricia Cox, prin. Fax 641-2118
East Side MS 800/6-8
2300 Lindberg Rd 46012 765-641-2047
Lucinda McCord, prin. Fax 641-2050
Edgewood ES 300/K-5
3525 Winding Way 46011 765-641-2119
Scott Merkel, prin. Fax 683-3002
Erskine ES 600/K-5
811 W 60th St 46013 765-641-2114
Kara Miller, prin. Fax 641-2100
Forest Hills ES 400/K-5
1600 Hillcrest Ave 46011 765-641-2130
Gregory Kalisz, prin. Fax 683-3003
Killbuck ES 300/K-5
3070 E 300 N 46012 765-378-0228
Judi Ketring, prin. Fax 378-1589
North Side MS 700/6-8
1815 Indiana Ave 46012 765-641-2055
Yvonne Ritchey, prin. Fax 641-2057
Robinson ES 500/K-5
630 Nichol Ave 46016 765-641-2086
Elizabeth Clark, prin. Fax 641-2088
South Side MS 800/6-8
101 W 29th St 46016 765-641-2051
Patrick Fassnatcht, prin. Fax 641-2053
Southview ES 400/K-5
4500 Main St 46013 765-641-2107
Rebecca Gomez-Bolanos, prin. Fax 683-3010
Tenth Street ES 600/K-5
3124 E 10th St 46012 765-641-2103
Mark Hodson, prin. Fax 641-2167
Valley Grove ES 600/K-5
2160 S 300 E 46017 765-378-3393
Jan Koeniger, prin. Fax 378-7683

Frankton-Lapel Community SD 2,400/PK-12
7916 W 300 N 46011 765-734-1261
Bobby Fields, supt. Fax 734-1129
www.frankton-lapel.org
Other Schools – See Frankton, Lapel

Anderson Christian S 200/PK-9
2625 Lindberg Rd 46012 765-649-0123
Thomas Snell, prin. Fax 649-3844
Cross Street Christian S 50/PK-8
2318 W Cross St 46011 765-649-4141
Matthew Pacer, prin. Fax 649-5953
Indiana Christian Academy 200/K-12
432 W 300 N 46012 765-643-7884
William Newton, prin. Fax 683-4200
Liberty Christian S 300/PK-6
2025 Hillcrest Dr 46012 765-644-7773
Shannon Dare, supt. Fax 644-7778
St. Ambrose S 100/PK-6
2825 Lincoln St 46016 765-642-8428
Stanley Warner, prin. Fax 642-7348
St. Marys S 200/PK-8
1115 Pearl St 46016 765-642-1848
Elizabeth Richards, prin. Fax 642-1828

Andrews, Huntington, Pop. 1,267
Huntington County Community SC
Supt. — See Huntington
Andrews ES 300/K-5
509 E Jefferson St 46702 260-786-3021
Gary Mast, prin. Fax 786-3537

Angola, Steuben, Pop. 7,890
Metropolitan SD of Steuben County 3,000/K-12
400 S Martha St 46703 260-665-2854
Dr. David Goodwin, supt. Fax 665-9155
www.msdsteuben.k12.in.us
Angola MS 700/6-8
1350 E Maumee St 46703 260-665-9581
Ann Rice, prin. Fax 665-9583
Carlin Park ES 400/K-5
800 Williams St 46703 260-665-2014
Sabrina Fritz, prin. Fax 665-7053
Hendry Park ES 400/K-5
805 S Washington St 46703 260-665-3215
Kris Sine, prin. Fax 665-5584
Ryan Park ES 400/K-5
1000 S John McBride Ave 46703 260-668-8873
Michael Christ, prin. Fax 668-8823
Other Schools – See Pleasant Lake

Arcadia, Hamilton, Pop. 1,794
Hamilton Heights SC 2,200/PK-12
PO Box 469 46030 317-984-3538
Anthony Cook, supt. Fax 984-3042
www.hhsc.k12.in.us
Hamilton Heights ES 500/3-5
PO Box 400 46030 317-984-3547
Heather Gorgas, prin. Fax 984-3540
Hamilton Heights MS 600/6-8
PO Box 609 46030 317-984-3588
Chris Walton, prin. Fax 984-3231
Hamilton Heights PS 500/PK-2
PO Box 419 46030 317-984-1530
Keith Ecker, prin. Fax 984-1544

Arcola, Allen
Northwest Allen County SD
Supt. — See Fort Wayne
Arcola ES 200/K-5
11006 Arcola Rd 46704 260-625-3161
Kathleen Perfect, prin. Fax 625-3975

Argos, Marshall, Pop. 1,833
Argos Community SD 700/K-12
410 N First St 46501 574-892-5139
Barbara Flory, supt. Fax 892-6527
www.argos.k12.in.us/
Argos Community ES 400/K-6
600 Yearick St 46501 574-892-5136
Ronald Leichty, prin. Fax 892-5302

Arlington, Rush
Rush County SD
Supt. — See Rushville

Arlington ES 200/K-6
7178 US Highway 52 46104 765-663-2416
Julie Innis, prin. Fax 663-2723

Ashley, DeKalb, Pop. 999
DeKalb County Central United SC
Supt. — See Waterloo
Country Meadow ES 300/K-5
2410 County Road 10 46705 260-920-1017
Bruce Hamilton, prin. Fax 587-9232

Attica, Fountain, Pop. 3,385
Attica Consolidated SC 1,000/PK-12
205 E Sycamore St 47918 765-762-7000
Dr. Judith Bush, supt. Fax 762-7007
www.attica.k12.in.us
Attica ES 500/PK-6
500 E Washington St 47918 765-762-7000
Dusty Goodwin, prin. Fax 762-7019

Auburn, DeKalb, Pop. 12,687
DeKalb County Central United SC
Supt. — See Waterloo
McKenney-Harrison ES 600/K-5
320 Van Auken St 46706 260-920-1015
Mike Ellinger, prin. Fax 925-4668
Watson ES 700/PK-5
901 Eckhart Ave 46706 260-920-1014
Steve Teders, prin. Fax 925-5612

Lakewood Park Christian S 600/PK-12
5555 County Road 29 46706 260-925-1393
Randy Carman, supt. Fax 925-5010

Aurora, Dearborn, Pop. 4,064
South Dearborn Community SC 3,000/PK-12
6109 Squire Pl 47001 812-926-2090
Thomas Book, supt. Fax 926-4216
www.sdcsc.k12.in.us
Aurora ES 700/PK-6
6098 Squire Pl 47001 812-926-2222
Gary Russell, prin. Fax 926-0863
Manchester ES 300/K-6
9387 State Road 48 47001 812-926-1140
Janet Platt, prin. Fax 926-2513
South Dearborn MS 400/7-8
5850 Squire Pl 47001 812-926-6298
Todd Bowers, prin. Fax 926-2149
Other Schools – See Dillsboro, Moores Hill

St. John Lutheran S 100/PK-8
222 Mechanic St 47001 812-926-2656
Terri Schmeltzer, prin. Fax 926-7603
St. Mary S 100/K-8
211 4th St 47001 812-926-1558
Jim Tush, prin. Fax 926-2590

Austin, Scott, Pop. 4,694
Scott County SD 1 1,500/PK-12
PO Box 9 47102 812-794-8750
Berley Goodin, supt. Fax 794-8765
www.scsd1.com/
Austin ES 700/PK-5
165 S Highway 31 47102 812-794-8743
Robert Anderson, prin. Fax 794-8788
Austin MS 300/6-8
401 S Highway 31 47102 812-794-8740
David Deaton, prin. Fax 794-8739

Avilla, Noble, Pop. 2,359
East Noble SC
Supt. — See Kendallville
Avilla ES 400/K-6
PO Box 9 46710 260-897-2301
David Pine, prin. Fax 897-3729

Oak Farm Montessori S 100/PK-9
502 Lemper Rd 46710 260-897-4270
Judith Cunningham, prin. Fax 897-4212
St. Marys S 100/K-6
PO Box 109 46710 260-897-3481
Kathleen Garlitz, prin. Fax 897-3706

Avon, Hendricks, Pop. 8,918
Avon Community SC 7,700/K-12
7203 E US Highway 36 46123 317-544-6000
Timothy Ogle, supt. Fax 544-6001
www.avon-schools.org
Avon IS East 600/5-6
174 S State Road 267 46123 317-544-5800
Brian Scott, prin. Fax 544-5801
Avon IS West 600/5-6
176 S State Road 267 46123 317-544-5900
Scott Raftery, prin. Fax 544-5901
Avon MS North 7-8
1251 N Dan Jones Rd 46123 317-544-5500
Frank Perkins, prin. Fax 544-5501
Avon MS South 1,200/7-8
7199 E US Highway 36 46123 317-544-5700
Dan Chapin, prin. Fax 544-5701
Cedar ES K-4
685 S State Road 267 46123 317-544-6200
Kevin Gray, prin. Fax 544-6201
Hickory ES 600/K-4
907 S State Road 267 46123 317-544-6300
Scott Collins, prin. Fax 544-6301
Maple ES 600/K-4
7237 E US Highway 36 46123 317-544-6400
Nikki Harrison, prin. Fax 544-6401
Pine Tree ES 800/K-4
7866 E County Road 100 S 46123 317-544-6500
Karie Mize, prin. Fax 544-6501
Sycamore ES 600/K-4
7878 E County Road 100 N 46123 317-544-6600
Mike Springer, prin. Fax 544-6601
White Oak ES 500/K-4
7221 E US Highway 36 46123 317-544-6700
Michael Whitman, prin. Fax 544-6701

Kingsway Christian S 700/PK-8
7979 E County Road 100 N 46123 317-272-2227
Alan Hughes, admin. Fax 272-3412

Bainbridge, Putnam, Pop. 785
North Putnam Community SD 1,900/PK-12
300 N Washington St 46105 765-522-6218
Dr. Mary Sugg-Lovejoy, supt. Fax 522-3562
www.nputnam.k12.in.us
Bainbridge ES 600/PK-5
412 N Washington St 46105 765-522-6233
Dean Cook, prin. Fax 522-2903
Other Schools – See Roachdale

Bargersville, Johnson, Pop. 2,461
Center Grove Community SC
Supt. — See Greenwood
Maple Grove ES 600/K-5
3623 W Whiteland Rd 46106 317-881-0561
Shelley Coover, prin. Fax 885-4523

Franklin Community SC
Supt. — See Franklin
Union ES 200/K-5
3990 W Division Rd 46106 317-422-5223
Cindy Mappes, prin. Fax 422-5068

Batesville, Franklin, Pop. 6,407
Batesville Community SC 2,000/PK-12
PO Box 121 47006 812-934-2194
James Roberts, supt. Fax 933-0833
www.batesville.k12.in.us/
Batesville IS 300/4-5
707 Columbus Ave 47006 812-934-5701
Jere Schoettmer, prin. Fax 933-0734
Batesville MS 400/6-8
201 N Mulberry St 47006 812-934-5175
Melvin Siefert, prin. Fax 933-0834
Batesville PS 600/PK-3
760 State Road 46 W 47006 812-934-4509
Melissa Burton, prin. Fax 933-0936

St. Louis S 400/K-8
17 E Saint Louis Pl 47006 812-934-3310
Chad Moeller, prin. Fax 934-6202

Battle Ground, Tippecanoe, Pop. 1,356
Tippecanoe SC
Supt. — See Lafayette
Battle Ground ES 300/K-5
303 Main St 47920 765-567-2200
John Pearl, prin. Fax 567-2030

Bedford, Lawrence, Pop. 13,551
North Lawrence Community SD 5,400/PK-12
PO Box 729 47421 812-279-3521
Dr. Dennis Turner, supt. Fax 275-1577
www.nlcs.k12.in.us
Bedford MS 600/6-8
1501 N St 47421 812-279-9781
David Schlegel, prin. Fax 277-3218
Fayetteville ES 200/K-5
223 Old Farm Rd 47421 812-279-2376
Rhonda Hackler, prin. Fax 278-7602
Lincoln ES 400/K-5
2014 F St 47421 812-275-6311
Richard Bohling, prin. Fax 277-7722
Needmore ES 300/K-5
278 Trogdon Ln 47421 812-279-2192
Wendy Butterfield, prin. Fax 277-1624
Parkview IS 200/3-5
2024 16th St 47421 812-275-3301
Mark Vice, prin. Fax 277-7721
Parkview PS 200/PK-2
1701 Brian Lane Way 47421 812-275-2333
Stephen Ray, prin. Fax 277-7720
Shawswick ES 400/K-5
71 Shawswick School Rd 47421 812-279-3115
Jim Pentzer, prin. Fax 275-0543
Shawswick MS 200/6-8
71 Shawswick School Rd 47421 812-275-6121
Roger Dean, prin. Fax 275-0543
Stalker ES 200/PK-5
420 W St 47421 812-275-4821
Laura Hagel, prin. Fax 277-7726
Other Schools – See Heltonville, Oolitic, Springville

St. Vincent De Paul S 200/PK-8
923 18th St 47421 812-279-2540
Katherine Sleva, prin. Fax 276-4880

Beech Grove, Marion, Pop. 14,069
Beech Grove CSD 2,400/PK-12
5334 Hornet Ave 46107 317-788-4481
Dr. Paul Kaiser, supt. Fax 782-4065
www.bgcs.k12.in.us
Beech Grove MS 400/7-8
1248 Buffalo St 46107 317-784-6649
Thomas Gearhart, prin. Fax 781-2926
Central ES 300/2-3
1000 Main St 46107 317-784-4565
Craig Buckler, prin. Fax 781-2930
Hornet Park ES 400/PK-1
5249 Hornet Ave 46107 317-780-5050
Matthew Davis, prin. Fax 780-5053
South Grove IS 500/4-6
851 S 9th Ave 46107 317-786-7687
Tonya Reid, prin. Fax 781-2933

Holy Name S 200/PK-8
21 N 17th Ave 46107 317-784-9078
Gina Fleming, prin. Fax 788-3616
Montessori Childrens House 50/PK-3
222 S 4th Ave 46107 317-787-9661
Paula Evans, prin.

Berne, Adams, Pop. 4,157
South Adams SD 1,000/K-12
1027 US Highway 27 S 46711 260-589-3133
Cathy Egolf, supt. Fax 589-2065
www.southadams.k12.in.us/
South Adams ES 400/K-5
1012 Starfire Way 46711 260-589-1101
Scott Litwiller, prin.
South Adams MS 100/6-8
1212 Starfire Way 46711 260-589-1102
Jeff Rich, prin.

Bicknell, Knox, Pop. 3,284
North Knox SC 1,400/K-12
11110 N State Road 159 47512 812-735-4434
Joe Adams, supt. Fax 328-6262
www.nknox.k12.in.us
North Knox Central ES 300/K-6
215 E 4th St 47512 812-735-2547
Roy Sloan, prin. Fax 735-2348
Other Schools – See Bruceville, Edwardsport

Birdseye, Dubois, Pop. 472
Southeast Dubois County SC
Supt. — See Ferdinand
Pine Ridge ES 300/K-4
4613 S Pine Ridge Rd 47513 812-326-2324
Stephen Scott, prin. Fax 326-2016

Bloomfield, Greene, Pop. 2,542
Bloomfield SD 1,100/K-12
PO Box 266 47424 812-384-4507
Daniel Sichting, supt. Fax 384-0172
www.bsd.k12.in.us
Bloomfield ES 600/K-6
PO Box 266 47424 812-384-4271
Mary Jane Vandeventer, prin. Fax 384-2405

Eastern Greene SD 1,000/PK-12
11034 E State Road 54 47424 812-825-5722
Ty Mungle, supt. Fax 825-9413
www.egreene.k12.in.us/
Eastern Greene ES 500/PK-4
10503 E State Road 54 47424 812-825-5623
Sharon Abts, prin. Fax 825-3891
Eastern Greene MS 5-8
10503 E State Road 54 47424 812-825-5010
Doug Lewis, prin. Fax 825-7386

Bloomington, Monroe, Pop. 69,017
Monroe County Community SC 11,000/PK-12
315 E North Dr 47401 812-330-7700
James Harvey, supt. Fax 330-7813
www.mccsc.edu
Arlington Heights ES 400/K-6
700 W Parrish Rd 47404 812-330-7747
Dr. Linda Black, prin. Fax 330-7748
Batchelor MS 600/7-8
900 W Gordon Pike 47403 812-330-7763
Paul White, prin. Fax 330-7766
Binford ES 500/3-6
2300 E 2nd St 47401 812-330-7741
Betsy Walsh, prin. Fax 330-7834
Childs ES 500/K-6
2211 S High St 47401 812-330-7756
Mary Sudbury, prin. Fax 349-4798
Clear Creek ES 500/PK-6
300 W Clear Creek Dr 47403 812-824-2811
Tammy Miller, prin. Fax 824-9265
Fairview ES 200/PK-6
627 W 8th St 47404 812-330-7732
Karen Adams, prin. Fax 330-7818
Grandview ES 500/K-6
2300 S Endwright Rd 47403 812-825-3009
James Rose, prin. Fax 825-3302
Highland Park ES 400/PK-6
900 S Park Square Dr 47403 812-825-7673
Jan Williamson, prin. Fax 825-4907
Jackson Creek MS 600/7-8
3980 S Sare Rd 47401 812-330-2451
Donna Noble, prin. Fax 330-2457
Lakeview ES 400/K-6
9090 S Strain Ridge Rd 47401 812-824-7061
Tommy Richardson, prin. Fax 824-9280
Marlin ES 200/K-6
1655 E Bethel Ln 47408 812-330-7750
Chris Finley, prin. Fax 330-7822
Rogers ES 300/K-2
2200 E 2nd St 47401 812-330-7767
Mark Conrad, prin. Fax 330-7820
Summit ES 500/PK-6
1450 W Countryside Ln 47403 812-330-2011
Doug Waltz, prin. Fax 330-2022
Templeton ES 500/K-6
1400 S Brenda Ln 47401 812-330-7735
Cheryl Smith, prin. Fax 330-7779
Tri-North MS 600/7-8
1000 W 15th St 47404 812-330-7745
Dr. Gale Hill, prin. Fax 330-7799
University ES 600/PK-6
1111 N Russell Rd 47408 812-330-7753
Dr. Janice Bizzari, prin. Fax 330-7770
Other Schools – See Unionville

Richland-Bean Blossom Community SC
Supt. — See Ellettsville
Edgewood IS 500/3-5
7600 W Reeves Rd 47404 812-876-2219
Debra Ferree, prin. Fax 876-2269
Edgewood PS 500/K-2
7700 W Reeves Rd 47404 812-876-9600
Brenda Whitaker, prin. Fax 876-9611

Adventist Christian Academy 50/K-8
2230 N Martha St 47408 812-330-9181
Bloomington Montessori S 200/PK-6
1835 S Highland Ave 47401 812-336-2800
Victoria Thevenow, prin. Fax 336-2183

Clear Creek Christian S 100/K-6
5405 S Rogers St 47403 812-824-2567
Penny Adams, prin. Fax 824-6032
Harmony S 200/K-12
PO Box 1787 47402 812-334-8349
Steve Bonchek, dir. Fax 333-3435
Lighthouse Christian Academy 300/PK-12
1201 W That Rd 47403 812-824-2000
Rayna Amerine, prin. Fax 824-2017
St. Charles S 400/PK-8
2224 E 3rd St 47401 812-336-5853
Alec Mayer, prin. Fax 349-0300

Bluffton, Wells, Pop. 9,460
Metro SD of Bluffton-Harrison 1,500/K-12
805 E Harrison Rd 46714 260-824-2620
Dr. Julie Wood, supt. Fax 824-6011
www.bhmsd.k12.in.us
Bluffton-Harrison ES 600/K-4
1100 E Spring St 46714 260-824-0333
Doug Thieme, prin. Fax 824-6011
Bluffton-Harrison MS 500/5-8
1500 Stogdill Rd 46714 260-824-3536
Tom Gibson, prin. Fax 824-6011

Northern Wells Community SD
Supt. — See Ossian
Lancaster Central ES 500/K-5
275 E Jackson St N 46714 260-565-3135
Steve Darnell, prin. Fax 565-3945

Boone Grove, Porter
Porter Township SC
Supt. — See Valparaiso
Boone Grove ES 300/K-5
325 W 550 S 46302 219-462-1032
Robert Lichtenberger, prin. Fax 476-4376
Boone Grove MS 400/6-8
325 W 550 S 46302 219-464-4828
Paul Schlottman, prin. Fax 465-0999

Boonville, Warrick, Pop. 6,782
Warrick County SC 9,000/K-12
300 E Gum St 47601 812-897-0400
Brad Schneider, supt. Fax 897-6033
www.warrick.k12.in.us/
Boonville MS 500/6-8
555 N Yankeetown Rd 47601 812-897-1420
William Wilder, prin. Fax 897-6584
Loge ES 500/K-5
915 N 4th St 47601 812-897-2230
Marty Watson, prin. Fax 897-6052
Oakdale ES 400/K-5
802 S 8th St 47601 812-897-3710
Tad Powless, prin. Fax 897-6049
Other Schools – See Chandler, Elberfeld, Lynnville, Newburgh, Tennyson

Borden, Clark, Pop. 832
West Clark Community SC
Supt. — See Sellersburg
Borden ES 400/K-6
PO Box 230 47106 812-967-2548
Myra Powell, prin. Fax 967-5824

Boswell, Benton, Pop. 783
Benton Community SC
Supt. — See Fowler
Boswell ES 200/K-6
414 W Main St 47921 765-869-5523
Pam Brooks, prin. Fax 869-4384

Bourbon, Marshall, Pop. 1,788
Triton SC 1,100/K-12
100 Triton Dr 46504 574-342-2255
Carl Hilling, supt. Fax 342-8165
www.triton.k12.in.us/
Triton ES 600/K-6
200 Triton Dr 46504 574-342-2355
Jeremy Riffle, prin. Fax 342-0053

Brazil, Clay, Pop. 8,214
Clay Community SD
Supt. — See Knightsville
East Side ES 300/K-5
936 E National Ave 47834 812-448-8755
Mary Ray, prin. Fax 443-1126
Forest Park ES 200/PK-5
800 S Alabama St 47834 812-443-7621
Connie Cook, prin. Fax 442-0204
Jackson Twp. ES 300/K-5
1860 E County Road 600 N 47834 812-986-2177
Jeff Fritz, prin. Fax 443-1406
Meridian Street ES 300/K-5
410 N Meridian St 47834 812-448-8560
Karen Phillips, prin. Fax 442-0410
North Clay MS 900/6-8
3 W Knight Dr 47834 812-448-1530
Dr. Jeff Allen, prin. Fax 442-0608
Staunton ES 300/K-5
6990 N County Road 425 W 47834 812-448-8270
Sheryl Jordan, prin. Fax 446-1038
Van Buren ES 200/K-5
2075 E County Road 1200 N 47834 812-448-1362
Gail Williams, prin. Fax 448-3602

Cornerstone Christian Academy 100/PK-6
PO Box 185 47834 812-446-4416
Linda Somheil, prin. Fax 448-3878

Bremen, Marshall, Pop. 4,569
Bremen Public SD 1,500/K-12
512 W Grant St 46506 574-546-3929
Russ Mikel, supt. Fax 546-6303
www.bps.k12.in.us
Bremen S 1,000/K-8
700 W South St 46506 574-546-3554
Larry Yelaska, prin. Fax 546-3554

St. Paul's Lutheran S 100/PK-8
605 S Center St 46506 574-546-2790
James Russell, prin. Fax 546-3242

Bristol, Elkhart, Pop. 1,635
Elkhart Community SD
Supt. — See Elkhart
Bristol ES 500/PK-6
705 Indiana St 46507 574-848-7421
Melissa Jennette, prin. Fax 848-7422

Middlebury Community SD
Supt. — See Middlebury
York ES 200/K-3
13549 State Road 120 46507 574-825-5312
Yvonne Buller, prin. Fax 825-0146

Kessington Christian S 50/7-8
19153 County Road 104 46507 574-848-4987
Don Dunithan, prin. Fax 641-2118

Brooklyn, Morgan, Pop. 1,540
Metro SD of Martinsville
Supt. — See Martinsville
Brooklyn ES 200/K-5
251 N Church St 46111 317-831-2150
Debra Wagner, prin. Fax 831-2226

Brookston, White, Pop. 1,632
Frontier SC
Supt. — See Chalmers
Frontier ES 400/K-6
811 S Railroad St 47923 765-563-3901
Todd Reagan, prin. Fax 563-6938

Brookville, Franklin, Pop. 2,933
Franklin County Community SC 3,100/PK-12
225 E 10th St 47012 765-647-4128
Dr. William Glentzer, supt. Fax 647-2417
www.fccsc.k12.in.us
Brookville ES 600/PK-4
10160 Oxford Pike 47012 765-647-3503
Michael Biltz, prin. Fax 647-2659
Brookville MS 500/5-8
9092 Wildcat Ln 47012 765-647-6040
Dr. Gary Frost, prin. Fax 647-4960
Other Schools – See Cedar Grove, Laurel

St. Michael S 200/K-8
PO Box J 47012 765-647-4961
Ken Saxon, prin. Fax 647-6802

Brownsburg, Hendricks, Pop. 18,290
Brownsburg Community SC 6,900/K-12
444 E Tilden Dr 46112 317-852-5726
Kathleen Corbin, supt. Fax 852-1015
www.brownsburg.k12.in.us
Brown ES 700/K-5
340 S Stadium Dr 46112 317-852-1498
Julie VanLiew, prin. Fax 858-2171
Brownsburg East MS 1,000/6-8
1250 Airport Rd 46112 317-852-2386
Marsha Webster, prin. Fax 852-1023
Brownsburg West MS 700/6-8
1555 S Odell St 46112 317-852-3143
Jeffrey Hubble, prin. Fax 858-4100
Cardinal ES 600/K-5
3590 Hornaday Rd 46112 317-852-1036
Carla Schubert, prin. Fax 858-4117
Delaware Trail ES 600/K-5
3680 Hornaday Rd 46112 317-852-1062
Philip Utterback, prin. Fax 858-4118
Eagle ES 700/K-5
555 Sycamore St 46112 317-852-1050
Ryan Hoover, prin. Fax 858-4119
Reagan ES K-5
4845 Bulldog Way 46112 317-852-1060
Dana Hicks, prin. Fax 852-1064
White Lick ES 600/K-5
1400 S Odell St 46112 317-852-3126
Kristine Quandt, prin. Fax 858-4120

Bethesda Christian S 400/K-12
7950 N County Road 650 E 46112 317-852-3101
Dee Tidball, prin. Fax 852-4301
St. Malachy S 400/K-8
330 N Green St 46112 317-852-2242
Mary Sullivan, prin. Fax 852-3604

Brownstown, Jackson, Pop. 3,050
Brownstown Central Community SC 1,800/PK-12
608 W Commerce St 47220 812-358-4271
Roger Bane, supt. Fax 358-5303
www.btownccs.k12.in.us
Brownstown Central MS 400/6-8
520 W Walnut St 47220 812-358-4947
Peggy Cannon, prin. Fax 358-3940
Brownstown ES 700/PK-5
612 S Base Rd 47220 812-358-3680
Tom McCool, prin. Fax 358-9099
Other Schools – See Freetown

Lutheran Central S 200/K-8
415 N Elm St 47220 812-358-2512
Nickie Isaacs, prin. Fax 358-9905

Bruceville, Knox, Pop. 457
North Knox SC
Supt. — See Bicknell
North Knox West ES 200/K-6
7820 N Camp Arthur Rd 47516 812-324-2291
Don Osburn, prin. Fax 324-9002

Bryant, Jay, Pop. 262
Jay SC
Supt. — See Portland
Bloomfield ES 300/K-5
350 E 500 N 47326 260-726-9417
Dan Hoffman, prin. Fax 726-4680

Buffalo, White
North White SC
Supt. — See Monon
Buffalo ES 100/K-5
306 S Bluff St 47925 574-278-7176
Michelle Hay, prin. Fax 278-6186

Bunker Hill, Miami, Pop. 1,017
Maconaquah SC 2,100/PK-12
7932 S Strawtown Pike 46914 765-689-9131
Dr. Debra Jones, supt. Fax 689-0995
www.maconaquah.k12.in.us
Maconaquah ES 600/2-5
7784 S Strawtown Pike 46914 765-689-9131
Kelly McPike, prin. Fax 689-9693
Maconaquah MS 500/6-8
594 E 800 S 46914 765-689-9131
James Callane, prin. Fax 689-9360
Other Schools – See Peru

Burnettsville, White, Pop. 354
Twin Lakes SC
Supt. — See Monticello
Eastlawn ES 200/PK-5
47 S 1300 E 47926 574-943-3637
Karla Cronk, prin. Fax 943-3618

Butler, DeKalb, Pop. 2,714
DeKalb County Eastern Community SD 1,500/K-12
300 E Washington St 46721 260-868-2125
Dr. Jeffrey Stephens, supt. Fax 868-2562
www.eastsideblazers.net
Butler ES 500/K-6
1025 S Broadway St 46721 260-868-2123
Kim Clark, prin. Fax 868-1709
Other Schools – See Saint Joe

Cambridge City, Wayne, Pop. 2,027
Western Wayne SD
Supt. — See Pershing
Lincoln MS 300/6-8
205 E Parkway Dr 47327 765-478-5840
John Engle, prin. Fax 478-3265
Western Wayne ES 500/K-5
801 E Delaware St 47327 765-478-3622
Renee Ahrens, prin. Fax 478-4332

Camby, Morgan
Mooresville Consolidated SC
Supt. — See Mooresville
North Madison ES 700/PK-6
7456 E Hadley Rd 46113 317-831-9214
Larry Schneider, prin. Fax 831-9238

Campbellsburg, Washington, Pop. 585
West Washington SC 1,000/K-12
9699 W Mount Tabor Rd 47108 812-755-4996
Gerald Jackson, supt. Fax 755-4843
www.wwcs.k12.in.us
West Washington ES 500/K-6
8030 W Batts Rd 47108 812-755-4934
Tom Rosenbaum, prin. Fax 755-4788

Canaan, Jefferson
Madison Consolidated SD
Supt. — See Madison
Canaan ES 100/K-5
8775 N Canaan Main St 47224 812-839-3151
Alvin Sonner, prin. Fax 839-3428

Cannelton, Perry, Pop. 1,168
Cannelton CSD 100/PK-12
125 S 6th St 47520 812-547-2637
Marion Chapman, supt. Fax 547-4142
www.cannelton.k12.in.us
Bennett Early Learning Center PK-K
411 Washington St 47520 812-544-8996
Beverly Conrad, prin.
Myers ES 1-5
615 Taylor St 47520 812-547-4126
Beverly Conrad, prin. Fax 547-4142

Carlisle, Sullivan, Pop. 694
Southwest SC
Supt. — See Sullivan
Carlisle S 300/PK-8
PO Box 649 47838 812-398-3851
Ryan Clark, prin. Fax 398-2221

Carmel, Hamilton, Pop. 59,243
Carmel Clay SD 14,500/PK-12
5201 E 131st St 46033 317-844-9961
Dr. Barbara Underwood, supt. Fax 844-9965
www.ccs.k12.in.us
Carmel ES 600/PK-5
101 4th Ave SE 46032 317-844-0168
Megan Klinginsmith, prin. Fax 571-4024
Carmel MS 1,200/6-8
300 S Guilford Rd 46032 317-846-7331
Denise Jacobs, prin. Fax 571-4067
Cherry Tree ES 600/K-5
13989 Hazel Dell Pkwy 46033 317-846-3086
Lori Storer, prin. Fax 571-4053
Clay MS 1,200/6-8
5150 E 126th St 46033 317-844-7251
Gary Huddleston, prin. Fax 571-4020
College Wood ES 600/K-5
12415 Shelborne Rd 46032 317-733-6430
Deanna Pitman, prin. Fax 571-4028
Creekside MS 1,100/6-8
3525 W 126th St 46032 317-733-6420
Tom Harmas, prin. Fax 733-6422
Forest Dale ES 700/K-5
10721 W Lakeshore Dr 46033 317-844-4948
Kathy Olssen, prin. Fax 571-4031

Mohawk Trails ES 600/K-5
4242 E 126th St 46033 317-844-1158
Linda Wilson, prin. Fax 571-4034
Prairie Trace ES 700/K-5
14200 River Rd 46033 317-571-7925
Jennifer Szuhaj, prin. Fax 571-7926
Smoky Row ES 700/K-5
900 W 136th St 46032 317-571-4084
Kim Barrett, prin. Fax 571-4088
Towne Meadow ES 700/K-5
10850 Towne Rd 46032 317-733-2645
Ryan Newman, prin. Fax 733-2655
West Clay ES 600/K-5
3495 W 126th St 46032 317-733-6500
Mary Jo Kinnaman, prin. Fax 733-6501
Woodbrook ES 600/PK-5
4311 E 116th St 46033 317-846-4225
Kelly Davis, prin. Fax 571-4037
Other Schools – See Indianapolis

Kids of the Kingdom Lutheran S 200/PK-K
4850 E 131st St 46033 317-814-4262
Janice Heins, prin. Fax 814-4260
Montessori Learning Center 50/1-3
PO Box 3847 46082 317-846-8182
Elizabeth Williams, dir.
Our Lady of Mt. Carmel S 700/K-8
14596 Oakridge Rd 46032 317-846-1118
Sr. Maryanne Zuberbueler, prin. Fax 582-2375

Carthage, Rush, Pop. 880
C.A. Beard Memorial SC
Supt. — See Knightstown
Carthage ES 100/K-4
511 E 2nd St 46115 765-565-6309
Shirley Heck, prin. Fax 565-6577

Cayuga, Vermillion, Pop. 1,116
North Vermillion Community SC 800/K-12
5551 N Falcon Dr 47928 765-492-4033
Michael Turner, supt. Fax 492-7001
www.nvc.k12.in.us
North Vermillion ES 400/K-6
5585 N Falcon Dr 47928 765-492-7010
Holly Wheaton, prin. Fax 492-7017

Cedar Grove, Franklin, Pop. 184
Franklin County Community SC
Supt. — See Brookville
Mt. Carmel S 500/K-8
6178 Johnson Fork Rd 47016 765-647-4191
Laura Blessing, prin. Fax 647-4009

Cedar Lake, Lake, Pop. 9,901
Crown Point Community SC
Supt. — See Crown Point
MacArthur ES 400/K-5
12900 Fairbanks St 46303 219-374-7866
Marian Buchko, prin. Fax 374-7567

Hanover Community SC 1,800/K-12
PO Box 645 46303 219-374-3500
Carol Kaiser, supt. Fax 374-4411
www.hanover.k12.in.us
Ball ES 500/K-5
13313 Parrish Ave 46303 219-374-3700
Eric Dillon, prin. Fax 374-4430
Hanover Central MS 400/6-8
10120 W 133rd Ave 46303 219-374-3800
William Cope, prin. Fax 374-4408
Lincoln ES 300/K-5
12245 W 109th Ave 46303 219-374-3600
Jodi Attar Gee, prin. Fax 365-1432

Celestine, Dubois
Northeast Dubois County SC
Supt. — See Dubois
Celestine ES 100/K-4
6748 E Main Cross St 47521 812-634-1261
Brenda Wittmann, prin. Fax 634-1266

Centerville, Wayne, Pop. 2,590
Centerville-Abington Community SD 1,200/PK-12
115 W South St 47330 765-855-3475
Philip Stevenson, supt. Fax 855-2524
www.centerville.k12.in.us
Centerville-Abington ES 300/3-6
200 W South St 47330 765-855-5132
Paula Hollenberg, prin. Fax 855-5719
Centerville-Abington JHS 300/7-8
509 Willow Grove Rd 47330 765-855-5113
Rick Schauss, prin. Fax 855-5207
Hamilton ES 100/PK-2
1281 S Round Barn Rd 47330 765-966-3911
Lee Stienbarger, prin. Fax 966-4491

Central, Harrison
South Harrison Community SD
Supt. — See Corydon
Heth-Washington ES 200/K-6
2450 Heth Washington Rd SW 47110 812-732-4766
Nissa Ellett, prin. Fax 738-2158

Chalmers, White, Pop. 485
Frontier SC 800/K-12
PO Box 809 47929 219-984-5009
Bernard Graser, supt. Fax 984-5022
www.frontier.k12.in.us
Other Schools – See Brookston

Chandler, Warrick, Pop. 3,065
Warrick County SC
Supt. — See Boonville
Chandler ES 600/K-5
401 S Jaycee St 47610 812-925-6021
Stephanie Virgin, prin. Fax 925-3273

Charlestown, Clark, Pop. 8,052
Greater Clark County SD
Supt. — See Jeffersonville
Charlestown MS 500/6-8
8804 High Jackson Rd 47111 812-256-6363
Joyce Traub, prin. Fax 256-7282
Jennings ES 400/PK-5
603 Market St 47111 812-256-7284
Mindy Dablow, prin. Fax 256-7291
Pleasant Ridge ES 600/K-5
1250 Monroe St 47111 812-256-7286
Michelle Dyer, prin. Fax 256-7290

Charlottesville, Hancock
Eastern Hancock County Community SC 1,100/PK-12
10370 E County Road 250 N 46117 317-467-0064
Dr. Larry Moore, supt. Fax 936-5516
www.easternhancock.org
Eastern Hancock ES 500/PK-5
10450 E County Road 250 N 46117 317-936-5829
Mark McIntire, prin. Fax 936-5318
Eastern Hancock MS 300/6-8
10380 E County Road 250 N 46117 317-936-5324
David Pfaff, prin. Fax 936-5516

Chesterton, Porter, Pop. 12,032
Duneland SC 5,800/K-12
601 W Morgan Ave 46304 219-983-3600
Dr. Dirk Baer, supt. Fax 983-3614
www.duneland.k12.in.us
Bailly ES 500/K-4
800 S 5th St 46304 219-983-3670
Michael Grubb, prin. Fax 983-3679
Brummit ES 400/K-4
2500 Indian Boundary Rd 46304 219-983-3660
Nino Cammarata, prin. Fax 983-3669
Chesterton MS 900/7-8
651 W Morgan Ave 46304 219-983-3776
James Ton, prin. Fax 983-3798
Liberty ES 400/K-4
50-1 W 900 N 46304 219-983-3650
Christy Jarka, prin. Fax 983-3659
Liberty IS 400/5-6
50 W 900 N 46304 219-983-3690
Greg Guernsey, prin. Fax 983-3709
Westchester IS 500/5-6
1050 S 5th St 46304 219-983-3710
Shawn Longacre, prin. Fax 983-3759
Other Schools – See Porter, Valparaiso

Chesterton Montessori S 100/K-6
270 E Burdick Rd 46304 219-926-2359
Terry Cavallo, prin. Fax 926-2359
Duneland Montessori Academy 50/PK-1
PO Box 797 46304 219-331-6635
Kimberly Ehn, prin.
Fairhaven Baptist Academy 100/K-12
86 E Oak Hill Rd 46304 219-926-6636
St. Patrick S 400/PK-8
640 N Calumet Rd 46304 219-926-1707
Lee Ann Cosh, prin. Fax 921-1922

Chrisney, Spencer, Pop. 539
North Spencer County SC
Supt. — See Lincoln City
Chrisney ES 200/K-6
311 N Church St 47611 812-362-8200
Julie Kemp, prin. Fax 362-8201

Churubusco, Whitley, Pop. 1,773
Smith-Green Community SD 1,300/PK-12
222 W Tulley St 46723 260-693-2007
Carol Kaiser, supt. Fax 693-6434
www.sgcs.k12.in.us/
Churubusco ES 600/PK-5
3 Eagle Dr 46723 260-693-2188
Nicole Singer, prin. Fax 693-2683
Churubusco MS 300/6-8
2 Eagle Dr 46723 260-693-1460
John Davis, prin. Fax 693-1437

Cicero, Hamilton, Pop. 4,368

Cicero Adventist S 100/K-8
24089 State Rd 19 46034 317-984-3252
Stacy Gusky, prin. Fax 984-3252

Clarksville, Clark, Pop. 21,060
Clarksville Community SC 1,400/K-12
200 Ettels Ln 47129 812-282-7753
Kim Knott, supt. Fax 282-7754
www.ccsc.k12.in.us/
Clark ES 200/K-5
435 W Stansifer Ave 47129 812-282-9644
Leon Stocksdale, prin. Fax 280-5033
Clarksville MS 400/6-8
101 Ettels Ln 47129 812-282-8235
Pamela Cooper, prin. Fax 280-5004
Greenacres ES 400/K-5
700 N Randolph Ave 47129 812-282-1447
Donald Maymon, prin. Fax 280-5019

Greater Clark County SD
Supt. — See Jeffersonville
Parkwood ES 500/K-5
748 Spicewood Dr 47129 812-945-2387
Janice Korfhage, prin. Fax 945-4072

St. Anthony S 400/PK-8
320 N Sherwood Ave 47129 812-282-2144
Sheila Noone, prin. Fax 282-2169

Clay City, Clay, Pop. 1,036
Clay Community SD
Supt. — See Knightsville
Clay City ES 400/K-6
681 Lankford St 47841 812-939-3120
Jon Russell, prin. Fax 446-5019

Clayton, Hendricks, Pop. 817
Mill Creek Community SC 1,700/PK-12
6631 S County Road 200 W 46118 317-539-9200
Dr. Patrick Spray, supt. Fax 539-9215
www.mccsc.k12.in.us/
Cascade MS 400/6-8
6423 S County Road 200 W 46118 317-539-9285
Fax 539-9310
Mill Creek East ES 500/PK-5
4740 Iowa St 46118 317-539-9225
Jill Jay, prin. Fax 539-9250
Other Schools – See Amo

Clinton, Vermillion, Pop. 4,906
South Vermillion Community SC 2,000/K-12
PO Box 387 47842 765-832-2426
David Chapman, supt. Fax 832-7391
www.svcs.k12.in.us
Central ES 400/K-5
208 S 9th St 47842 765-832-7731
John Scioldo, prin. Fax 832-5327
Pyle ES 300/K-5
72 E 1100 S 47842 765-832-7718
Ronda Foster, prin. Fax 832-5321
South Vermillion MS 500/6-8
950 Wildcat Dr 47842 765-832-7727
Angela Harris, prin. Fax 832-5316
Van Duyn ES 300/K-5
15095 S Rangeline Rd 47842 765-832-7761
Mike Costello, prin. Fax 832-5324

Cloverdale, Putnam, Pop. 2,262
Cloverdale Community SD 1,500/PK-12
310 E Logan St 46120 765-795-4664
Carrie Milner, supt. Fax 795-5166
www.cloverdale.k12.in.us
Cloverdale ES 600/PK-4
311 E Logan St 46120 765-795-4339
Stacey Baugh, prin. Fax 795-5449
Cloverdale MS 400/5-8
312 E Logan St 46120 765-795-2900
Shelia Anderson, prin. Fax 795-2901

Columbia City, Whitley, Pop. 8,024
Whitley County Consolidated SD 3,600/PK-12
107 N Walnut St 46725 260-244-5772
Dr. Laura Huffman, supt. Fax 244-4099
www.wccs.k12.in.us
Coesse ES 300/K-5
2250 S 500 E 46725 260-244-3351
Tammy Weimer, prin. Fax 244-4086
Indian Springs MS 800/6-8
1692 S State Road 9 46725 260-244-5148
Jan Boylen, prin. Fax 244-4710
Little Turtle ES 500/K-5
1710 S State Road 9 46725 260-244-3343
Dan Curless, prin. Fax 244-3229
Northern Heights ES 500/K-5
5209 N State Road 109 46725 260-691-2371
Robert Hoke, prin. Fax 691-3228
Raber ES 400/PK-5
700 E Jackson St 46725 260-244-5857
Julie Turpin, prin. Fax 244-4059

Faith Christian Academy of Whitley Co. 50/PK-8
1550 E State Road 205 46725 260-248-4872
Larry Schmoekel, admin. Fax 248-4872

Columbus, Bartholomew, Pop. 39,380
Bartholomew Consolidated SC 11,000/PK-12
1200 Central Ave 47201 812-376-4220
Dr. John Quick, supt. Fax 376-4486
www.bcsc.k12.in.us
Central MS 800/7-8
725 7th St 47201 812-376-4287
Randy Gratz, prin. Fax 376-4511
Clifty Creek ES 600/PK-6
4625 E 50 N 47203 812-376-4342
Diane Clancy, prin. Fax 376-4305
Fodrea Community ES 300/K-6
2775 Illinois Ave 47201 812-376-4321
Mary Ann Ransdell, prin. Fax 376-4501
Mt. Healthy ES 400/K-6
12150 S State Road 58 47201 812-342-2463
Jeff Backmeyer, prin. Fax 342-0584
Northside MS 900/7-8
1400 27th St 47201 812-376-4405
Amy Dixon, prin. Fax 376-4479
Parkside ES 700/PK-6
1400 Parkside Dr 47203 812-376-4314
Chris Smith, prin. Fax 376-4324
Richards ES 600/PK-6
3311 Fairlawn Dr 47203 812-376-4311
Cynthia Frost, prin. Fax 376-4505
Rockcreek ES 300/PK-6
13000 E 200 S 47203 812-579-5221
Darin Sprong, prin. Fax 579-6488
Schmitt ES 800/PK-6
2675 California St 47201 812-376-4307
Teresa Heiny, prin. Fax 376-4506
Signature Academy ES 200/K-6
750 5th St 47201 812-376-4447
Chad Phillips, prin. Fax 376-4446
Signature Academy MS 7-8
725 7th St 47201 812-376-4287
Randy Gratz, admin. Fax 376-4511
Smith ES 400/PK-6
4505 Waycross Dr 47203 812-376-4317
Laura Hack, prin. Fax 376-4502
Southside ES 900/K-6
1320 W 200 S 47201 812-376-4423
Joel Metzler, prin. Fax 376-4507
Other Schools – See Taylorsville

Flat Rock-Hawcreek SC
Supt. — See Hope
Cross Cliff PS 200/PK-2
4355 E 600 N 47203 812-372-4849
Michael Wilkerson, prin. Fax 378-0564

Children's Garden of ABC Learning Center 200/PK-6
6691 W State Road 46 47201 812-342-3029
Mike Gorday, dir. Fax 342-0296
Columbus Christian S 200/PK-12
3170 Indiana Ave 47201 812-372-3780
Amy Mathis, admin. Fax 372-3878
St. Bartholomew S 400/PK-8
1306 27th St 47201 812-372-6830
Kathryn Schubel, prin. Fax 376-0377
St. Peter Lutheran S 400/K-8
719 5th St 47201 812-372-5266
Scott Schumacher, prin. Fax 372-7556
White Creek Lutheran S 100/K-8
16270 S 300 W 47201 812-342-6832
Janice Buss, prin. Fax 342-6832

Commiskey, Jennings
Jennings County SC
Supt. — See North Vernon
Graham Creek ES 300/K-6
7910 S County Road 90 W 47227 812-346-4179
Peggy Fear, prin. Fax 346-8482

Connersville, Fayette, Pop. 14,368
Fayette County SC 4,200/PK-12
1401 Spartan Dr 47331 765-825-2178
Dr. Russell Hodges, supt. Fax 825-8060
www.fayette.k12.in.us
Alquina ES 100/K-6
4397 E Alquina Rd 47331 765-825-2995
Debra Williams, prin. Fax 827-5131
Connersville MS 700/7-8
1900 N Grand Ave 47331 765-825-1139
Beth Denham, prin. Fax 827-4346
Eastview ES 300/PK-6
401 S Fountain St 47331 765-825-5541
Will Hurst, prin. Fax 827-1584
Everton ES 200/K-6
2440 E Everton Rd 47331 765-825-5840
Bryan Jennings, prin. Fax 825-4275
Fayette Central ES 400/PK-6
2928 N County Road 225 W 47331 765-825-6261
Kay Rowley, prin. Fax 825-5956
Frazee ES 400/PK-6
600 W 3rd St 47331 765-825-6811
Mia McCreary, prin. Fax 827-4805
Grandview ES 400/PK-6
2620 Iowa Ave 47331 765-825-2981
Kathryn Schlichte, prin. Fax 825-4703
Maplewood ES 400/PK-6
1800 N Eastern Ave 47331 765-825-3941
Kim Corsaro, prin. Fax 825-8583
Other Schools – See Glenwood

St. Gabriel S 100/PK-6
224 W 9th St 47331 765-825-7951
Sue Barth, prin. Fax 827-4347
Victory Christian S 50/K-8
PO Box 221 47331 765-827-5561
Pamela Roschi, admin. Fax 825-8306

Converse, Miami, Pop. 1,116
Oak Hill United SC 1,500/PK-12
PO Box 550 46919 765-395-3341
Joel Martin, supt. Fax 395-3343
www.ohusc.k12.in.us
Converse ES 200/K-2
PO Box 489 46919 765-395-3560
Valree Kinch, prin. Fax 395-7830
Oak Hill JHS 200/7-8
7760 W Delphi Pike Ste 27 46919 765-384-4385
Greg Perkins, prin. Fax 384-4386
Other Schools – See Swayzee, Sweetser

Corydon, Harrison, Pop. 2,787
South Harrison Community SD 3,200/K-12
315 S Harrison Dr 47112 812-738-2168
Dr. Neyland Clark, supt. Fax 738-2158
www.shcsc.k12.in.us/
Corydon Central JHS 400/7-8
377 Country Club Rd 47112 812-738-4184
Mark Black, prin. Fax 738-5752
Corydon ES 500/K-3
125 Beechmont Dr NE 47112 812-738-4183
Tamela Brewer, prin. Fax 738-7963
Corydon IS 400/4-6
100 High School Rd 47112 812-738-6548
Sandra Joseph, prin. Fax 738-2158
Other Schools – See Central, Elizabeth, New Middletown

St. Joseph S 100/PK-6
512 N Mulberry St 47112 812-738-4549
Heidi Imberi, prin. Fax 738-2722

Covington, Fountain, Pop. 2,465
Covington Community SC 1,000/PK-12
601 Market St 47932 765-793-4877
Dennis Cahill Ph.D., supt. Fax 793-5209
www.covington.k12.in.us/
Covington ES 500/PK-5
1110 7th St 47932 765-793-2254
Alison Karrfalt, prin. Fax 793-5214
Covington MS 200/6-8
514 Railroad St 47932 765-793-4451
Steve Reynolds, prin. Fax 793-5200

Crawfordsville, Montgomery, Pop. 15,155
Crawfordsville Community SD 1,800/PK-12
1000 Fairview Ave 47933 765-362-2342
Kathleen Steele, supt. Fax 364-3237
www.cville.k12.in.us
Hoover ES 100/4-5
1301 S Elm St 47933 765-362-2691
Kim Nixon, prin. Fax 362-1149
Hose ES 100/K-1
800 Fairview Ave 47933 765-362-2886
Carol Starlin, prin. Fax 362-3957

Nicholson ES 100/2-3
1010 Lane Ave 47933 765-362-2607
Karen Cushman, prin. Fax 361-0767
Tuttle MS 500/6-8
612 S Elm St 47933 765-362-2992
John Strickland, prin. Fax 364-3219
Willson S 200/PK-PK
500 E Jefferson St 47933 765-364-6174
Carol Carrington, dir. Fax 364-3229

North Montgomery Community SC 2,200/PK-12
480 W 580 N 47933 765-359-2112
Dr. Robert Brower, supt. Fax 359-2111
www.nm.k12.in.us/
Northridge MS 600/6-8
482 W 580 N 47933 765-364-1071
Angela Blessing, prin. Fax 362-7985
Pleasant Hill ES 300/PK-5
6895 N 100 W 47933 765-339-4403
Tara Rinehart, prin. Fax 339-4600
Sommer ES 300/K-5
3794 W US Highway 136 47933 765-362-3979
Robin Mills, prin. Fax 362-5619
Sugar Creek ES 400/K-5
4702 E 300 N 47933 765-794-4855
Thomas Mellish, prin. Fax 794-4578

South Montgomery Community SC
Supt. — See New Market
Southmont JHS 400/7-8
6425 S US Highway 231 47933 765-866-2023
Mike Sowers, prin. Fax 866-2045

Maranatha Christian S 50/K-12
PO Box 29 47933 765-364-0628
Gloria Stevens, prin. Fax 362-0151

Crothersville, Jackson, Pop. 1,544
Crothersville Community SD 600/K-12
201 S Preston St 47229 812-793-2601
Dr. Terry Goodin, supt. Fax 793-3004
www.crothersville.k12.in.us/
Crothersville ES 300/K-5
109 S Preston St 47229 812-793-2622
Chris Marshall, prin. Fax 793-3004

Crown Point, Lake, Pop. 22,697
Crown Point Community SC 6,500/PK-12
200 E North St 46307 219-663-3371
Dr. Teresa Eineman, supt. Fax 662-3414
www.cps.k12.in.us
Ball ES 400/K-5
720 W Summit St 46307 219-663-0047
Arthur Equihua, prin. Fax 662-4320
Colonel John Wheeler MS 6-8
401 W Joliet St 46307 219-663-2173
Timothy Vassar, prin. Fax 662-4378
Eisenhower ES 300/K-5
1450 S Main St 46307 219-663-8800
Mary Ann Chapko, prin. Fax 662-4333
Lake Street ES 500/K-5
475 Lake St 46307 219-663-5683
Melinda Bateman, prin. Fax 662-4329
Robinson ES 500/K-5
601 Pettibone St 46307 219-663-2525
Barbara Merrill, prin. Fax 662-4365
Ross ES 500/3-5
11319 Randolph St 46307 219-663-3010
Jennifer Johansson, prin. Fax 662-3529
Taft MS 1,100/6-8
1000 S Main St 46307 219-663-1507
Michael Hazen, prin. Fax 662-4349
Winfield ES 500/PK-2
13128 Montgomery St 46307 219-663-2287
Patricia Carnahan, prin. Fax 663-1138
Other Schools – See Cedar Lake

Northwest Adventist Christian S 50/1-8
10570 Randolph St 46307 219-663-4472
Rita Wagner, prin.
St. Mary Catholic Community S 600/PK-8
405 E Joliet St 46307 219-663-0676
L. Thomas Ruiz, prin. Fax 663-1347
Trinity Lutheran S 200/PK-8
250 S Indiana Ave 46307 219-663-1586
John Schultz, prin. Fax 663-9606

Culver, Marshall, Pop. 1,526
Culver Community SC 1,100/K-12
PO Box 231 46511 574-842-3364
Brad Schuldt, supt. Fax 842-4615
www.culver.k12.in.us
Culver Community MS 200/7-8
1 Cavalier Dr 46511 574-842-5690
Kelly Pulliam, prin. Fax 842-5691
Culver ES 500/K-6
401 School St 46511 574-842-3389
Charles Kitchell, prin. Fax 842-3380
Other Schools – See Monterey

Dale, Spencer, Pop. 1,539
North Spencer County SC
Supt. — See Lincoln City
Turnham Educational Center 300/K-6
PO Box 432 47523 812-937-4300
Dianne Litkenhus, prin. Fax 937-4317

Daleville, Delaware, Pop. 1,573
Daleville Community SD 700/K-12
14300 W 2nd St 47334 765-378-3329
Paul Garrison, supt. Fax 378-3649
www.daleville.k12.in.us
Daleville ES 400/K-6
8600 S Bronco Dr 47334 765-378-0251
David Stashevsky, prin. Fax 378-4085

Danville, Hendricks, Pop. 7,425
Danville Community SC 2,600/PK-12
200 Warrior Way 46122 317-745-2212
Dr. Denis Ward, supt. Fax 745-3924
www.danville.k12.in.us
Danville MS 400/7-8
1425 W Lincoln St 46122 317-745-5491
Matthew Vandermark, prin. Fax 745-3949
North ES 800/PK-3
398 Urban St 46122 317-745-2610
Kathryn Raasch, prin. Fax 745-3921
South ES 600/4-6
1375 W Lincoln St 46122 317-745-2131
Tina Carlton, prin. Fax 745-3918

Dayton, Tippecanoe, Pop. 1,149
Tippecanoe SC
Supt. — See Lafayette
Dayton ES 500/K-5
PO Box 187 47941 765-447-5004
Barbara Maitland, prin. Fax 448-6212

Decatur, Adams, Pop. 9,547
North Adams Community SD 2,200/K-12
PO Box 670 46733 260-724-7146
Wylie Sirk, supt. Fax 724-4777
www.nadams.k12.in.us
Bellmont MS 500/6-8
1200 E North Adams Dr 46733 260-724-3137
Scott Miller, prin. Fax 724-4495
Monmouth ES 200/K-5
251 W 850 N 46733 260-724-9195
Michael Casper, prin. Fax 724-9565
Northwest ES 300/K-5
1109 Dayton St 46733 260-724-3633
Neal Rich, prin. Fax 724-9247
Southeast ES 300/K-5
901 Everhart Dr 46733 260-724-3118
Rebecca Lamon, prin. Fax 724-3956

St. Joseph S 200/K-8
127 N 4th St 46733 260-724-2765
Karla Hormann, prin. Fax 724-4953
St. Peter Immanuel S 100/K-8
3845 E 1100 N 46733 260-623-6115
Connie Jeffrey, prin. Fax 623-3865
Wyneken Memorial Lutheran S 200/PK-8
11565 N US Highway 27 46733 260-639-6177
Lowell Timm, prin. Fax 639-3050
Zion Lutheran S 100/PK-8
1022 W Monroe St 46733 260-728-9995
Lon Buuck, prin. Fax 724-9440

Delphi, Carroll, Pop. 2,980
Delphi Community SC 1,400/K-12
501 Armory Rd 46923 765-564-2100
Ralph Walker, supt. Fax 564-6919
www.delphi.k12.in.us/
Delphi Community ES 500/K-5
300 W Vine St 46923 765-564-3895
William Shidler, prin. Fax 564-2341
Delphi Community MS 400/6-8
501 Armory Rd 46923 765-564-3411
Robert DeLaRosa, prin. Fax 564-2135

Demotte, Jasper, Pop. 3,738
Kankakee Valley SC
Supt. — See Wheatfield
Demotte ES 600/K-3
1000 S Halleck St 46310 219-987-2789
Joan Kiersma, prin. Fax 987-4789

North Newton SC
Supt. — See Morocco
Lincoln ES 400/K-6
10280 N 450 E 46310 219-345-3458
Denise Thrasher, prin. Fax 345-3488

DeMotte Christian S 300/PK-8
PO Box 430 46310 219-987-3721
James Rozendal, admin. Fax 987-3724

Denver, Miami, Pop. 521
North Miami Community SD 1,100/K-12
PO Box 218 46926 765-985-3891
Brent Kaufman, supt. Fax 985-3904
www.nmcs.k12.in.us/
North Miami ES 600/K-6
632 E 900 N 46926 765-985-2251
Becky Saddlemire, prin. Fax 985-2058

Deputy, Jefferson
Madison Consolidated SD
Supt. — See Madison
Deputy ES 100/K-5
14350 W Mulberry 47230 812-273-8517
Karlyn Lamb, prin. Fax 273-8518

Dillsboro, Dearborn, Pop. 1,455
South Dearborn Community SC
Supt. — See Aurora
Dillsboro ES 300/K-6
13200 North St 47018 812-432-5438
Bill Lakes, prin. Fax 432-5203

Dubois, Dubois
Northeast Dubois County SC 1,000/K-12
5379 E Main St 47527 812-678-2781
Dan Balka, supt. Fax 678-4418
www.nedubois.k12.in.us
Dubois ES 200/K-4
5533 E Saint Raphael St 47527 812-678-3011
Brenda Wittmann, prin. Fax 678-2013
Dubois MS 300/5-8
4550 N 4th St 47527 812-678-2181
Bill Hochgesang, prin. Fax 678-2282
Other Schools – See Celestine

Dugger, Sullivan, Pop. 959
Northeast SC
Supt. — See Hymera
Dugger ES 200/PK-6
7356 E County Road 50 S 47848 812-648-2025
Beth Langel, prin. Fax 648-2025

Dunkirk, Jay, Pop. 2,639
Jay SC
Supt. — See Portland
West Jay MS 300/6-8
140 E Highland Ave 47336 765-768-7648
Mike Crull, prin. Fax 768-6152
Westlawn ES 300/K-5
234 W Pearl St 47336 765-768-6075
Jeff Davis, prin. Fax 768-7984

Dupont, Jefferson, Pop. 393
Madison Consolidated SD
Supt. — See Madison
Dupont ES 100/K-5
7045 W Main St 47231 812-273-8520
Karlyn Lamb, prin. Fax 273-8521

Dyer, Lake, Pop. 15,071
Lake Central SC
Supt. — See Saint John
Bibich ES 700/K-5
14600 81st Ave 46311 219-322-1185
Janice Malchow, prin. Fax 864-2381
Kahler MS 1,300/6-8
600 Joliet St 46311 219-865-3535
Karen Brownell, prin. Fax 865-4428
Protsman ES 800/PK-5
1121 Harrison Ave 46311 219-322-2040
Jack Thomas, prin. Fax 865-4437

St. Joseph S 200/PK-8
430 Joliet St 46311 219-865-2750
Jane Smith, prin. Fax 865-3740

East Chicago, Lake, Pop. 30,946
City of East Chicago SD 5,800/PK-12
210 E Columbus Dr 46312 219-391-4100
Juan Anaya, supt. Fax 391-4126
www.ecps.org
Block JHS 500/7-8
2700 Cardinal Dr 46312 219-391-4084
Leslie Yanders, prin. Fax 391-4282
Franklin ES 600/PK-6
2400 Cardinal Dr 46312 219-391-4077
Lidia Gil, prin. Fax 391-4269
Gosch ES 400/PK-6
455 E 148th St 46312 219-391-4172
Constance El-Amin, prin. Fax 391-4272
Harrison ES 600/K-6
4411 Magoun Ave 46312 219-391-4192
David Muniz, prin. Fax 391-4280
Lincoln ES 500/PK-6
2001 E 135th St 46312 219-391-4096
Nancy Sharp, prin. Fax 391-4274
McKinley ES 800/PK-6
4825 Magoun Ave 46312 219-391-4186
Betty Bullard, prin. Fax 391-4278
Washington ES 500/K-6
1401 E 144th St 46312 219-391-4169
Gloria Velasco, prin. Fax 391-4296
West Side JHS 500/7-8
4001 Indianapolis Blvd 46312 219-391-4068
Michelle Pluchinsky, prin. Fax 391-4284

St. Stanislaus S 200/PK-8
4930 Indianapolis Blvd 46312 219-398-1316
Kathleen Lowry, prin. Fax 398-9080

East Enterprise, Switzerland
Switzerland County SC
Supt. — See Vevay
Switzerland County ES 500/K-5
1390 Highway 250 47019 812-534-3128
Michael Jones, prin. Fax 534-2042

Eaton, Delaware, Pop. 1,515
Delaware Community SC
Supt. — See Muncie
Eaton ES 300/K-5
200 NE Union St 47338 765-396-3301
Kathy Hottinger, prin. Fax 396-3641

Eckerty, Crawford
Crawford County Community SC
Supt. — See Marengo
Patoka ES 200/K-6
5600 W Patoka School Rd 47116 812-338-2916
Nan Dupont, prin. Fax 338-2917

Edinburgh, Johnson, Pop. 4,517
Edinburgh Community SC 900/K-12
202 Keeley St 46124 812-526-2681
Richard Arkanoff, supt. Fax 526-0271
www.edinburgh.k12.in.us
East Side ES 400/K-5
810 E Main Cross St 46124 812-526-9771
Brooke Phillips, prin. Fax 526-3433
Edinburgh Community MS 200/6-8
300 Keeley St 46124 812-526-3418
Josh Edwards, prin. Fax 526-3430

Edwardsport, Knox, Pop. 350
North Knox SC
Supt. — See Bicknell
North Knox East S 500/K-8
PO Box 128 47528 812-735-5780
Rodney Perry, prin. Fax 735-5264

Elberfeld, Warrick, Pop. 648
Warrick County SC
Supt. — See Boonville
Elberfeld ES 200/K-6
45 S 5th St 47613 812-983-4221
Lynn Pierce, prin. Fax 983-4221

Elizabeth, Harrison, Pop. 140
South Harrison Community SD
Supt. — See Corydon
South Central ES 400/K-6
6595 E Highway 11 SE 47117 812-969-2973
Laura McDermott, prin. Fax 969-2236

Elkhart, Elkhart, Pop. 52,270
Baugo Community SD 1,900/K-12
29125 County Road 22 46517 574-293-8583
James DuBois, supt. Fax 294-2171
www.baugo.org/
Jimtown IS 400/4-6
58703 County Road 3 46517 574-294-2158
Scott Kovatch, prin. Fax 522-7649
Jimtown JHS 300/7-8
58903 County Road 3 46517 574-294-6586
Mitchell Mawhorter, prin. Fax 294-8557
Jimtown North ES 300/K-3
30046 County Road 16 46516 574-293-3507
Carol Deak, prin. Fax 293-3299
Jimtown South ES 300/K-3
58901 County Road 3 46517 574-522-0379
Mike Stout, prin. Fax 522-3899

Concord Community SD 4,800/K-12
59040 Minuteman Way 46517 574-875-5161
George Dyer, supt. Fax 875-8762
www.concord.k12.in.us
Concord East Side ES 700/K-6
57156 County Road 13 46516 574-875-8517
Rhett Butler, prin. Fax 875-5985
Concord JHS 700/7-8
57197 County Road 13 46517 574-875-5122
Kevin Caird, prin. Fax 875-1089
Concord Ox-Bow ES 600/K-6
23525 County Road 45 46516 574-875-8538
Elizabeth Hollingsworth, prin. Fax 875-4108
Concord South Side ES 600/K-6
23702 Arlene Ave 46517 574-875-6565
Bryan Waltz, prin. Fax 875-4208
Concord West Side ES 600/K-6
230 W Mishawaka Rd 46517 574-293-2531
Gerard Donlon, prin. Fax 293-9507

Elkhart Community SD 13,400/PK-12
2720 California Rd 46514 574-262-5516
Mark Mow, supt. Fax 262-5733
www.elkhart.k12.in.us
Beardsley ES 500/PK-6
1027 McPherson St 46514 574-262-5575
Jennifer Sager, prin. Fax 262-5576
Beck ES 500/K-6
818 McDonald St 46516 574-295-4830
Richard Mendez, prin. Fax 295-4839
Cleveland ES 700/K-6
53403 County Road 1 46514 574-262-5580
Martha Strickler, prin. Fax 262-5582
Daly ES 500/PK-6
1735 Strong Ave 46514 574-295-4870
Arlene Silba, prin. Fax 295-4877
Eastwood ES 600/K-6
53215 County Road 15 46514 574-262-5583
Kevin Beveridge, prin. Fax 262-5585
Feeser ES 700/K-6
26665 County Road 4 46514 574-262-5586
Kevin Dean, prin. Fax 262-5588
Hawthorne ES 600/3-6
501 W Lusher Ave 46517 574-295-4820
Bruce Klonowski, prin. Fax 295-4828
Monger ES 500/K-6
1100 E Hively Ave 46517 574-295-4860
Donald Kominowski, prin. Fax 295-4865
Moran MS 700/7-8
200 W Lusher Ave 46517 574-295-4805
Levon Johnson, prin. Fax 295-4807
North Side MS 700/7-8
300 Lawrence St 46514 574-262-5570
Sara Jackowiak, prin. Fax 262-5573
Osolo ES 700/K-6
24975 County Road 6 46514 574-262-5590
Jean Creasbaum, prin. Fax 262-5799
Pinewood ES 700/K-6
3420 E Bristol St 46514 574-262-5595
Melinda Shaw, prin. Fax 262-5745
Riverview ES 400/K-6
2509 Wood St 46516 574-295-4850
Susan Edmundson, prin. Fax 295-4901
Roosevelt ES 500/PK-2
201 W Wolf Ave 46516 574-295-4840
Levar Johnson, prin. Fax 295-4845
West Side MS 700/7-8
101 S Nappanee St 46514 574-295-4815
Kristie Stutsman, prin. Fax 295-4812
Woodland ES 400/K-6
1220 County Road 3 46514 574-262-5578
John Payne, prin. Fax 262-5746
Other Schools – See Bristol

Elkhart Adventist Christian S 50/PK-8
3601 E Bristol St 46514 574-266-9018
Elkhart Christian Academy 500/PK-12
25943 County Road 22 46517 574-293-1609
Dr. Brian Dougherty, admin. Fax 293-3238
Montessori S of Elkhart 100/PK-6
1 Montessori Dr 46514 574-264-3037
Christina Miller, dir. Fax 262-1387
St. Thomas the Apostle S 400/PK-8
1331 N Main St 46514 574-264-4855
Fred Stump, prin. Fax 262-8477
St. Vincent De Paul S 100/PK-6
1114 S Main St 46516 574-293-8451
Donna Quinn, prin. Fax 295-9702

Trinity Lutheran S 300/PK-8
30888 County Road 6 46514 574-674-8800
Sandy Price, prin. Fax 674-6410

Ellettsville, Monroe, Pop. 5,294
Richland-Bean Blossom Community SC 2,800/PK-12
600 Edgewood Dr 47429 812-876-7100
Steven Kain, supt. Fax 876-7020
www.rbbcsc.k12.in.us/
Edgewood ECC 100/PK-PK
8045 W State Rd 46 47429 812-876-6325
Kelly Walsh, dir. Fax 876-6591
Edgewood JHS 600/6-8
851 W Edgewood Dr 47429 812-876-2005
Larry Sparks, prin. Fax 876-8985
Other Schools – See Bloomington, Stinesville

Elnora, Daviess, Pop. 743
North Daviess Community SD 1,100/K-12
5494 E State Road 58 47529 812-636-8000
Robert Bell, supt. Fax 636-7546
www.ndaviess.k12.in.us
North Daviess ES 600/K-6
5498 E State Road 58 47529 812-636-8000
Jodi Berry, prin. Fax 636-7444

Elwood, Madison, Pop. 9,167
Elwood Community SC 1,900/K-12
1306 N Anderson St 46036 765-552-9861
Thomas Austin, supt. Fax 552-8088
www.elwood.k12.in.us
Edgewood ES 500/K-5
1803 N J St 46036 765-552-7381
Mary Hamilton, prin. Fax 552-2826
Elwood Community MS 500/6-8
1207 N 19th St 46036 765-552-7378
Amy Rauch, prin. Fax 552-2017
Oakland ES 400/K-5
2100 S P St 46036 765-552-9823
Beverly Groover, prin. Fax 552-9824

Eminence, Morgan
Eminence Community SC 500/K-12
PO Box 135 46125 765-528-2101
Dr. Susan Phillips, supt. Fax 528-2262
www.eminence.k12.in.us
Eminence ES 200/K-5
PO Box 105 46125 765-528-2141
Terry Terhune, prin. Fax 528-2276

English, Crawford, Pop. 695
Crawford County Community SC
Supt. — See Marengo
English ES 200/K-6
PO Box 339 47118 812-338-2855
Deborah Ade, prin. Fax 338-2856

Evansville, Vanderburgh, Pop. 115,918
Evansville-Vanderburgh SC 22,100/PK-12
1 SE 9th St 47708 812-435-8453
Dr. Vincent Bertram, supt. Fax 435-8421
www.evsc.k12.in.us/
Caze ES 500/K-5
2013 S Green River Rd 47715 812-477-5567
Anna Jo Wyman, prin. Fax 474-6901
Cedar Hall ES 400/PK-5
2100 N Fulton Ave 47710 812-435-8223
Jacqueline Kuhn, prin. Fax 435-8225
Culver ES 400/PK-5
1301 Judson St 47713 812-435-8219
Carrie Hillyard, prin. Fax 435-8374
Cynthia Heights ES 500/K-5
7225 Cynthiana Rd 47720 812-435-8740
Lee Ann Shields, prin.
Delaware ES 500/PK-5
700 N Garvin St 47711 812-435-8227
Jennifer Garland, prin. Fax 435-8398
Dexter ES 400/K-5
917 S Dexter Ave 47714 812-476-1321
Stephanie Stewart, prin. Fax 474-6905
Evans MS 500/6-8
2727 N Evans Ave 47711 812-435-8330
Elizabeth Wells, prin. Fax 435-8332
Fairlawn ES 500/K-5
2021 S Alvord Blvd 47714 812-476-4997
Lisa Hale, prin. Fax 464-6908
Glenwood MS 200/6-8
901 Sweetser Ave 47713 812-435-8242
Sheila Huff, prin. Fax 435-8245
Harper ES 400/K-5
21 S Alvord Blvd 47714 812-476-1308
Lana Burton, prin. Fax 474-6911
Harwood MS 300/6-8
3013 N 1st Ave 47710 812-435-8316
Mike Raisor, prin. Fax 435-8517
Hebron ES 700/K-5
4400 Bellemeade Ave 47714 812-477-8915
Jason Woebkenberg, prin. Fax 474-6981
Helfrich Park MS 500/6-8
2603 W Maryland St 47712 812-435-8246
Timothy McIntosh, prin. Fax 435-8249
Highland ES 900/K-5
6701 Darmstadt Rd 47710 812-867-6401
Elizabeth Johns, prin. Fax 867-4756
Lincoln ES 300/PK-5
635 Lincoln Ave 47713 812-435-8235
Kimberly Johnson, prin. Fax 435-8525
Lodge ES 300/PK-5
2000 Lodge Ave 47714 812-477-5319
Patricia Edwards, prin. Fax 474-6915
McGary MS 500/6-8
1535 Joyce Ave 47714 812-476-3035
Don Mosbey, prin. Fax 474-6919
Oak Hill MS 800/6-8
7700 Oak Hill Rd 47725 812-867-6426
Kenneth Wempe, prin. Fax 867-4750
Perry Heights MS 500/6-8
5800 Hogue Rd 47712 812-435-8326
Charles Goodman, prin. Fax 435-8363

Plaza Park MS 700/6-8
7301 Lincoln Ave 47715 812-476-4971
Jo Adams, prin. Fax 474-6922
Roosa ES 400/PK-5
1230 E Illinois St 47711 812-435-8231
Patricia Day-Kohlman, prin. Fax 435-8354
Scott ES 900/K-5
14940 Old State Rd 47725 812-867-2427
Vicki Duncan, prin. Fax 857-1941
Stockwell ES 500/K-5
2501 N Stockwell Rd 47715 812-477-5345
Tijuanna Tolliver, prin. Fax 474-6925
Stringtown ES 600/K-5
4720 Stringtown Rd 47711 812-435-8320
Martin Brown, prin. Fax 435-8558
Tekoppel ES 400/K-5
111 N Tekoppel Ave 47712 812-435-8333
Sally Bagby, prin. Fax 435-8513
Thomkins MS 700/6-8
1300 W Mill Rd 47710 812-435-8323
Terry Yunker, prin. Fax 435-8588
Vogel ES 700/K-5
1500 Oak Hill Rd 47711 812-477-6109
Thomas Bennett, prin. Fax 477-6909
Washington MS 500/6-8
1801 Washington Ave 47714 812-477-8983
Rance Ossenberg, prin. Fax 474-6930
Wertz ES 300/PK-5
1701 S Red Bank Rd 47712 812-435-8312
Michael Taylor, prin. Fax 435-8314
West Terrace ES 500/K-5
8000 W Terrace Dr 47712 812-435-8733
Todd Slagle, prin. Fax 985-7311

Christ the King S 200/PK-8
3101 Bayard Park Dr 47714 812-476-1792
Fax 475-6804
Corpus Christi S 200/PK-8
5530 Hogue Rd 47712 812-422-1208
Martha Craig, prin. Fax 422-1243
Evansville Christian S 600/PK-8
4400 Lincoln Ave 47714 812-477-7777
Paul Bair, dir. Fax 469-0261
Evansville Day S 300/PK-12
3400 N Green River Rd 47715 812-476-3039
Kendall Berry, hdmstr. Fax 476-4061
Evansville Lutheran S 200/K-8
120 E Michigan St 47711 812-424-7252
Tony Shull, prin. Fax 424-7340
Evansville SDA S 50/K-8
41 W Camp Ground Rd 47710 812-425-2455
Good Shepherd S 300/K-8
2301 N Stockwell Rd 47715 812-476-4477
Judy VanHoosier, prin. Fax 476-4495
Holy Redeemer S 400/PK-8
918 W Mill Rd 47710 812-422-3688
Marianne Webster, prin. Fax 424-7166
Holy Rosary S 500/PK-8
1303 S Green River Rd 47715 812-477-2271
Joan Fredrich, prin. Fax 471-7230
Holy Spirit S 200/PK-8
1760 Lodge Ave 47714 812-477-9082
Nancy Mills, prin. Fax 469-6636
Montessori Academy of Evansville 100/PK-3
4611 Adams Ave 47714 812-479-1776
Diane Barron, prin. Fax 479-1776
Resurrection S 400/PK-8
5301 New Harmony Rd 47720 812-963-6148
Angela Johnson, prin. Fax 963-1141
St. Benedict Cathedral S 500/PK-8
530 S Harlan Ave 47714 812-425-4596
Sr. Karlene Sensmeier, prin. Fax 463-5206
St. Joseph S 200/PK-8
6130 W Saint Joseph Rd 47720 812-963-3335
Melba Wilderman, prin. Fax 963-3335
St. Theresa S 200/PK-8
700 Herndon Dr 47711 812-423-1763
Theresa Berendes, prin. Fax 422-5346
Trinity Lutheran S 100/PK-8
1403 W Bnvll New Harmony Rd 47725 812-867-5279
Wes Wrucke, prin. Fax 867-5333
Westside Catholic S Sacred Heart Campus 100/PK-PK
2735 W Franklin St 47712 812-425-0874
Cyndi Schneider, prin. Fax 425-0883
Westside Catholic S St. Agnes Campus 100/K-3
1620 Glendale Ave 47712 812-423-9115
Fax 423-1953
Westside Catholic S St. Boniface Campus 100/4-8
2031 W Michigan St 47712 812-422-1014
Fax 422-1057

Fairland, Shelby, Pop. 1,348
Northwestern Consolidated SC 1,600/PK-12
4920 W 600 N 46126 317-835-7461
Ellen Welk, supt. Fax 835-4441
www.nwshelby.k12.in.us/
Triton ES 600/PK-4
4976 W 600 N 46126 317-835-3003
Linda Warnecke, prin. Fax 835-3005
Triton MS 500/5-8
4740 W 600 N 46126 317-835-3006
Todd Crosby, prin. Fax 835-3008

Fairmount, Grant, Pop. 2,814
Madison-Grant United SC 1,600/PK-12
11580 S E 00 W 46928 765-948-4143
John Trout, supt. Fax 948-4150
www.mgargylls.com
Liberty ES 100/K-6
8720 S 300 W 46928 765-948-5620
Stephen Wilson, prin. Fax 948-3847
Madison-Grant JHS 300/7-8
11640 S E 00 W 46928 765-948-5132
Tom Daniel, prin. Fax 948-3671
Park ES 400/PK-6
500 S Sycamore St 46928 765-948-5232
DeShawn Wert, prin. Fax 948-5240
Other Schools – See Summitville

Farmersburg, Sullivan, Pop. 1,208
Northeast SC
Supt. — See Hymera
Farmersburg ES 200/K-6
PO Box 689 47850 812-696-2176
Ronald Kamman, prin. Fax 696-2433

Ferdinand, Dubois, Pop. 2,299
North Spencer County SC
Supt. — See Lincoln City
Hanks ES 300/PK-6
19260 N State Road 162 47532 812-357-5091
Teresa Boyd, prin. Fax 357-5092

Southeast Dubois County SC 1,500/K-12
432 E 15th St 47532 812-367-1653
Robert Johnson, supt. Fax 367-1075
www.sedubois.k12.in.us
Ferdinand ES 300/K-4
402 E 8th St 47532 812-367-2721
Lee Begle, prin. Fax 367-1194
Other Schools – See Birdseye, Huntingburg

Fillmore, Putnam, Pop. 565
South Putnam Community SD
Supt. — See Greencastle
Fillmore ES 200/K-6
161 S Main St 46128 765-246-6136
Bradley Hayes, prin. Fax 246-6912

Fishers, Hamilton, Pop. 57,220
Hamilton Southeastern SD 14,800/PK-12
13485 Cumberland Rd 46038 317-594-4100
Fax 594-4109
www.hse.k12.in.us/
Brooks ES 700/K-4
12451 Brooks School Rd, 317-915-4250
Tim Harshbarger, prin. Fax 915-4259
Cumberland Road ES 600/K-4
13535 Cumberland Rd 46038 317-594-4170
Stephane Harris, prin. Fax 594-4179
Fall Creek ES 700/K-4
12131 Olio Rd, 317-594-4180
Jerril Staley, prin. Fax 594-4189
Fall Creek IS 1,000/5-6
12011 Olio Rd, 317-915-4220
Randall Schoeff, prin. Fax 915-4229
Fishers ES 500/K-4
11442 Lantern Rd 46038 317-594-4160
Patricia Mansfield, prin. Fax 594-4169
Fishers JHS 900/7-8
13257 Cumberland Rd 46038 317-594-4150
Crystal Thorpe, prin. Fax 594-4159
Hamilton Southeastern JHS 900/7-8
12001 Olio Rd, 317-594-4120
Shari Switzer, prin. Fax 594-4129
Harrison Parkway ES 600/PK-4
14135 Harrison Pkwy 46038 317-915-4210
Andrea Burke, prin. Fax 915-4219
Hoosier Road ES 600/K-6
11300 E 121st St, 317-915-4240
William Hurst, prin. Fax 915-4249
Lantern Road ES 600/K-4
10595 Lantern Rd, 317-594-4140
Danielle Thompson, prin. Fax 594-4149
New Britton ES 600/K-4
8660 E 131st St 46038 317-594-4130
Michael Zahm, prin. Fax 594-4139
Riverside IS 5-6
11014 Eller Rd 46038 317-594-4320
Scott Chambers, prin. Fax 594-4329
Riverside JHS 500/7-8
10910 Eller Rd 46038 317-915-4280
Matt Kegley, prin. Fax 915-4289
Sand Creek ES 800/K-4
11420 E 131st St 46038 317-915-4270
Cindy Miller, prin. Fax 915-4279
Sand Creek IS 1,000/5-6
11550 E 131st St 46038 317-915-4230
Chad Hudson, prin. Fax 915-4239
Thorpe Creek ES K-4
14642 E 126th St, 317-594-4310
Shawn Greiner, prin. Fax 594-4319
Other Schools – See Fortville, Noblesville

Community Montessori S 100/PK-6
9069 E 141st St 46038 317-774-8551
Barbara Stuckwisch, dir. Fax 774-8991
Family of Christ Lutheran S 100/PK-K
11965 Allisonville Rd 46038 317-594-9157
Juliana Hughes, dir. Fax 594-9155
Fishers Montessori S 50/PK-PK
PO Box 615 46038 317-845-4248
Margaret White, prin. Fax 578-8582
St. Louis de Montfort S 400/K-8
11421 Hague Rd 46038 317-842-1125
Annette Jones, prin. Fax 842-1126

Flora, Carroll, Pop. 2,161
Carroll Consolidated SC 1,100/K-12
2 S 3rd St 46929 574-967-4113
John Sayers, supt. Fax 967-3831
www.carroll.k12.in.us/
Carroll ES 600/K-6
105 S 225 E 46929 574-967-4881
Carolyn O'Connell, prin. Fax 967-4882

Floyds Knobs, Floyd
New Albany-Floyd County Consolidated SD
Supt. — See New Albany
Floyds Knobs ES 700/K-5
4484 Scottsville Rd 47119 812-923-8770
Elaine Murphy, prin. Fax 949-4298
Galena ES 400/K-5
6697 Old Vincennes Rd 47119 812-923-5150
Dwight Beall, prin. Fax 949-4299

St. Mary of the Knobs S 200/PK-6
3033 Martin Rd 47119 812-923-1630
Mary Ann Bennett, prin. Fax 923-0310

Fort Branch, Gibson, Pop. 2,342
South Gibson SC 2,000/K-12
1029 W 650 S 47648 812-753-4230
Stacey Humbaugh, supt. Fax 753-4081
www.sgibson.k12.in.us
Fort Branch Community S 500/K-8
7670 S Eastview Ln 47648 812-753-3641
Michael Galvin, prin. Fax 753-4174
Other Schools – See Haubstadt, Owensville

Holy Cross S 100/PK-5
202 S Church St 47648 812-753-3280
Tracey Unfried, prin. Fax 753-3034

Fortville, Hancock, Pop. 3,626
Hamilton Southeastern SD
Supt. — See Fishers
Geist ES 700/K-4
14051 E 104th St 46040 317-915-4260
Kelly Jackson, prin. Fax 915-4269

Mt. Vernon Community SC 3,500/PK-12
1776 W State Road 234 46040 317-485-3100
Dr. William Riggs, supt. Fax 485-3113
www.mvcsc.k12.in.us
Fortville ES 400/PK-4
1806 W State Road 234 46040 317-485-3180
Susan Bennett, prin. Fax 485-3185
Mt. Vernon IS 500/5-6
8414 N 200 W 46040 317-482-0020
Scott Shipley, prin. Fax 482-0027
Mt. Vernon MS 600/7-8
1862 W State Road 234 46040 317-485-3160
John Price, prin. Fax 485-3171
Other Schools – See Greenfield, Mc Cordsville

Fort Wayne, Allen, Pop. 223,341
East Allen County SD
Supt. — See New Haven
Cedarville ES 600/K-3
12225 Hardisty Rd 46845 260-446-0110
Brad Bakie, prin. Fax 446-0113
Prince Chapman Academy 500/6-8
4808 E Paulding Rd 46816 260-446-0270
Thelma Green, prin. Fax 446-0275
Southwick ES 500/K-5
6500 Wayne Trce 46816 260-446-0250
Teresa Gremaux, prin. Fax 446-0253
Village ES 300/PK-5
4625 Werling Dr 46806 260-446-0260
Donna Abbott, prin. Fax 446-0263

Fort Wayne Community SD 31,500/PK-12
1200 S Clinton St 46802 260-467-1000
Dr. Wendy Robinson, supt. Fax 467-1980
www.fwcs.k12.in.us
Abbett ES 300/PK-5
4325 Smith St 46806 260-467-5800
Robin Peterman, prin. Fax 467-5833
Adams ES 300/PK-5
3000 New Haven Ave 46803 260-467-5850
Brenda Edwards-West, prin. Fax 467-5881
Arlington ES 500/K-5
8118 Saint Joe Center Rd 46835 260-467-6000
Jana Ankenbruck, prin. Fax 467-6043
Blackhawk MS 800/6-8
7200 E State Blvd 46815 260-467-4885
Timothy Matthias, prin. Fax 467-4943
Bloomingdale ES 300/K-5
1300 Orchard St 46808 260-467-6700
Lucy Schmidt, prin. Fax 467-6748
Brentwood ES 500/PK-5
3710 Stafford Dr 46805 260-467-6775
Dianna Chadd, prin. Fax 467-6848
Bunche Montessori ES 200/PK-5
1111 Greene St 46803 260-467-4790
Marilyn Horan, prin. Fax 467-4816
Croninger ES 600/K-5
6700 Trier Rd 46815 260-467-6050
Rebecca Dennis, prin. Fax 467-6091
Fairfield ES 600/PK-5
2825 Fairfield Ave 46807 260-467-5900
Jeff Cline, prin. Fax 467-5953
Forest Park ES 600/K-5
2004 Alabama Ave 46805 260-467-6850
Jay Peters, prin. Fax 467-6923
Franke Park ES 600/K-5
828 Mildred Ave 46808 260-467-6925
James Emmerson, prin. Fax 467-6998
Glenwood Park ES 600/K-5
4501 Vance Ave 46815 260-467-6200
David Weber, prin. Fax 467-6237
Haley ES 600/PK-5
2201 Maplecrest Rd 46815 260-467-4510
Nate Spicer, prin. Fax 467-4558
Harris ES 400/K-5
4501 Thorngate Dr 46835 260-467-6300
Carolyn Sleet, prin. Fax 467-6338
Harrison Hill ES 600/K-5
355 S Cornell Cir 46807 260-467-7000
Linda Sneeringer, prin. Fax 467-7073
Holland ES 500/PK-5
7000 Red Haw Dr 46825 260-467-7075
J. Michael Caywood, prin. Fax 467-7148
Indian Village ES 400/PK-5
3835 Wenonah Ln 46809 260-467-5200
Stephany Bourne, prin. Fax 467-5237
Irwin ES 300/K-5
3501 S Anthony Blvd 46806 260-467-5310
Ingrid Laidroo-Martin, prin. Fax 467-5341
Jefferson MS 700/6-8
5303 Wheelock Rd 46835 260-467-4825
Jeff King, prin. Fax 467-4883

Kekionga MS 600/6-8
2929 Engle Rd 46809 260-467-6600
Gary Schafer, prin. Fax 467-6658
Lakeside MS 600/6-8
2100 Lake Ave 46805 260-467-8625
Amy Sivley, prin. Fax 467-8672
Lane MS 700/6-8
4901 Vance Ave 46815 260-467-4400
Jennifer Peckham, prin. Fax 467-4437
Lincoln ES 600/K-5
1001 E Cook Rd 46825 260-467-5400
Mike Shaffer, prin. Fax 467-5441
Lindley ES 400/K-5
2201 Ardmore Ave 46802 260-467-5350
Gerald Arthur, prin. Fax 467-5384
Maplewood ES 400/K-5
2200 Maplewood Rd 46819 260-467-7150
Frank Kline, prin. Fax 467-7223
Memorial Park MS 600/6-8
2200 Maumee Ave 46803 260-467-5300
Tim Rayl, prin. Fax 467-5298
Miami MS 700/6-8
8100 Amherst Dr 46819 260-467-8560
Harold Stevens, prin. Fax 467-8606
Nebraska ES 300/PK-5
1525 Boone St 46808 260-467-8000
Federa Smith, prin. Fax 467-8028
Northcrest ES 500/PK-5
5301 Archwood Ln 46825 260-467-5450
Steven Jones, prin. Fax 467-5486
Northwood MS 800/6-8
1201 E Washington Center Rd 46825 260-467-2930
Eric Lambright, prin. Fax 467-2987
Pleasant Center ES 300/PK-5
2323 W Pleasant Center Rd 46819 260-467-4750
Carolyn Kennedy, prin. Fax 467-4780
Portage MS 700/6-8
3521 Taylor St 46802 260-467-4500
V. Jane Rentschler, prin. Fax 467-4497
Price ES 500/PK-5
1901 W State Blvd 46808 260-467-4950
William Critell, prin. Fax 467-4994
St. Joseph Central ES 500/K-5
6341 Saint Joe Center Rd 46835 260-467-6100
Theodore Davis, prin. Fax 467-6135
Scott Academy 300/PK-5
950 E Fairfax Ave 46806 260-467-8050
Crystal Thomas, prin. Fax 467-8077
Shambaugh ES 500/K-5
5320 Rebecca St 46835 260-467-6150
Shawn Smiley, prin. Fax 467-6187
Shawnee MS 700/6-8
1000 E Cook Rd 46825 260-467-6525
Matt Schiebel, prin. Fax 467-6527
South Wayne ES 400/PK-5
810 Cottage Ave 46807 260-467-8100
Tim Bobay, prin. Fax 467-8134
Study ES 300/K-5
2414 Brooklyn Ave 46802 260-467-8500
Trudy Grafton, prin. Fax 467-8532
Towles IS 100/6-8
420 E Paulding Rd 46816 260-467-4300
Tamara Lake, prin. Fax 467-4364
Washington Center ES 600/K-5
1936 W Wallen Rd 46818 260-467-6250
Richelle Miller, prin. Fax 467-6252
Washington ES 200/PK-5
1015 W Washington Blvd 46802 260-467-8150
Dawn Starks, prin. Fax 467-8178
Waynedale ES 400/K-5
7201 Elzey St 46809 260-467-8820
Kent Martz, prin. Fax 467-8852
Weisser Park ES 600/1-5
902 Colerick St 46806 260-467-8875
John Key, prin. Fax 467-8924
Young ECC 300/PK-K
1026 E Pontiac St 46803 260-467-8950
Sherry Britt, prin. Fax 467-8972

Metro SD of Southwest Allen County 6,600/K-12
4824 Homestead Rd 46814 260-431-2051
Brian Smith, supt. Fax 431-2099
www.sacs.k12.in.us
Aboite ES 500/K-5
5004 Homestead Rd 46814 260-431-2101
Greg Lobdell, prin. Fax 431-2118
Covington ES 700/K-5
2430 W Hamilton Rd S 46814 260-431-0502
Fred Graf, prin. Fax 431-0599
Deer Ridge ES 400/K-5
1515 S Scott Rd 46814 260-431-2151
Kevin Kempton, prin. Fax 431-2158
Haverhill ES 400/K-5
4725 Weatherside Run 46804 260-431-2201
Jeanine Kleber, prin. Fax 431-2228
Summit MS 700/6-8
4509 Homestead Rd 46814 260-431-2552
Jim Leinker, prin. Fax 431-2568
Whispering Meadow ES 400/K-5
415 Mission Hill Dr 46804 260-431-2651
Jackie Wolpert, prin. Fax 431-2668
Woodside MS 900/6-8
2310 W Hamilton Rd S 46814 260-431-2702
Jerry Schillinger, prin. Fax 431-2723
Other Schools – See Roanoke

Northwest Allen County SD 5,300/PK-12
13119 Coldwater Rd 46845 260-338-5300
Dr. Steven Yager, supt. Fax 637-8355
www.nacs.k12.in.us/
Carroll MS 700/6-8
4027 Hathaway Rd 46818 260-637-5159
John Miller, prin. Fax 637-5478
Cedar Canyon ES 400/K-5
15011 Coldwater Rd 46845 260-637-6101
Philip Downs, prin. Fax 637-6120
Hickory Center ES 700/PK-5
3606 Baird Rd 46818 260-338-5375
Richard Vorick, prin. Fax 637-2081
Maple Creek MS 700/6-8
425 Union Chapel Rd 46845 260-338-5350
Mark Seele, prin. Fax 338-0369
Oak View ES 400/K-5
13123 Coldwater Rd 46845 260-338-5385
Pam Kaylor, prin. Fax 637-5055
Perry Hill ES 200/3-5
13121 Coldwater Rd 46845 260-338-5390
Lynn Simmers, prin. Fax 637-8347
Other Schools – See Arcola, Huntertown

Ascension Lutheran S 100/PK-8
8811 Saint Joe Rd 46835 260-486-2226
Ms. Tommy Franke, prin. Fax 486-5793
Bethlehem Lutheran S 100/PK-8
3705 S Anthony Blvd 46806 260-456-3587
Philip Amt, prin. Fax 744-3229
Blackhawk Christian S 700/PK-12
7400 E State Blvd 46815 260-493-7000
Trent Lehman, prin. Fax 749-8527
Canterbury S 500/PK-8
5601 Covington Rd 46804 260-432-7776
Jonathan Hancock, hdmstr. Fax 436-9069
Central Christian S 100/PK-8
5801 Schwartz Rd 46835 260-493-0193
Boyd Leichty, admin. Fax 493-0193
Concordia Evangelical Lutheran S 400/PK-8
4245 Lake Ave 46815 260-426-9922
Robert Boyd, prin. Fax 422-3415
Emmanuel St. Michael Lutheran S 200/K-8
1123 Union St 46802 260-422-6712
Jacob Pennekamp, prin. Fax 422-3553
Emmaus Lutheran S 100/PK-8
8626 Covington Rd 46804 260-459-7722
Keith Martin, prin. Fax 459-7766
Holy Cross Lutheran S 400/PK-8
3425 Crescent Ave 46805 260-483-3173
Cecily Chandler, prin. Fax 484-9115
Keystone S 50/PK-PK
5421 Homestead Rd 46814 260-436-2332
Tammy Henline, dir. Fax 436-2332
Keystone S 200/PK-12
1800 Laverne Ave 46805 260-424-4523
Tammy Henline, dir. Fax 424-4525
Most Precious Blood S 200/PK-8
1529 Barthold St 46808 260-424-4832
Alexandria Bergman, prin. Fax 426-5904
Praise Lutheran S 50/K-K
1115 W DuPont Rd 46825 260-490-9529
Alicia Levitt, dir. Fax 490-7729
Queen of Angels S 300/PK-8
1600 W State Blvd 46808 260-483-8214
Marsha Jordan, prin. Fax 471-0005
St. Charles Borromeo S 700/K-8
4910 Trier Rd 46815 260-484-3392
Rob Sordelet, prin. Fax 482-2006
St. John Lutheran S 100/K-8
725 W Washington Blvd 46802 260-426-4193
Martin Gigler, prin. Fax 420-9158
St. John the Baptist S 300/K-8
4500 Fairfield Ave 46807 260-456-3321
Jane Sandor, prin. Fax 456-3072
St. Joseph Hessen Cassel S 100/PK-8
11521 Old Decatur Rd 46816 260-639-3580
Louise Schultheis, prin. Fax 639-3675
St. Joseph - St. Elizabeth S 500/K-8
2211 Brooklyn Ave 46802 260-432-4000
Lois Widner, prin. Fax 432-8642
St. Jude S 600/PK-8
2110 Pemberton Dr 46805 260-484-4611
Sr. Kathleen Knueven, prin. Fax 969-1607
St. Paul Lutheran S 200/K-8
1125 Barr St 46802 260-424-0049
Mark Muehl, prin. Fax 969-2052
St. Peter Lutheran S 200/K-8
7810 Maysville Rd 46815 260-749-5811
Daniel Bultemeyer, prin. Fax 749-9967
St. Therese S 100/K-8
2222 Lower Huntington Rd 46819 260-747-2343
Charles Grimm, prin. Fax 747-4767
St. Vincent De Paul S 700/1-8
1720 E Wallen Rd 46825 260-489-3537
Sandra Guffey, prin. Fax 489-5318
Suburban Bethlehem Lutheran S 200/K-8
6318 W California Rd 46818 260-483-9371
Richard Brune, prin. Fax 471-2159
Trinity Lutheran ECC 50/PK-PK
1636 Saint Marys Ave 46808 260-422-7931
Larry Hencye, prin. Fax 969-4005
Unity Lutheran S 200/K-8
5401 S Calhoun St 46807 260-744-0459
LuAnn LeBeau, prin. Fax 745-9265
Zion Lutheran Academy 100/PK-8
2313 Hanna St 46803 260-745-2979
Ronald Stephens, hdmstr. Fax 744-2421

Fountain City, Wayne, Pop. 705
Northeastern Wayne SD 1,100/PK-12
PO Box 406 47341 765-847-2821
Stephen Bailey, supt. Fax 847-5355
www.nws.k12.in.us
Northeastern ES 600/PK-6
534 W Wallace Rd 47341 765-847-2595
Katherine Pribble, prin. Fax 847-5355

Fowler, Benton, Pop. 2,271
Benton Community SC 1,500/K-12
PO Box 512 47944 765-884-0850
Ross Sloat, supt. Fax 884-1614
www.benton.k12.in.us
Other Schools – See Boswell, Otterbein, Oxford

Sacred Heart S 100/PK-6
607 N Washington Ave 47944 765-884-0710
Terri Goodman, prin. Fax 884-0710

Francesville, Pulaski, Pop. 869
West Central SC 900/K-12
117 E Montgomery St 47946 219-567-9161
Charles Mellon, supt. Fax 567-9761
www.west-central.k12.in.us
West Central ES 400/K-5
1842 S US Highway 421 47946 219-567-9741
Tony Brose, prin. Fax 567-9445
West Central MS 200/6-8
1850 S US Highway 421 47946 219-567-2534
Kay Beasey, prin. Fax 567-9535

Francisco, Gibson, Pop. 547
East Gibson SC
Supt. — See Oakland City
Francisco ES 100/PK-6
320 E Main St 47649 812-782-3207
Peter Humbaugh, prin. Fax 782-3342

Frankfort, Clinton, Pop. 16,432
Clinton Prairie SC 1,000/K-12
4431 W State Road 28 46041 765-659-1339
Charles Fink, supt. Fax 659-5305
www.clintonprairie.com/
Clinton Prairie ES 500/K-6
2500 S County Road 450 W 46041 765-654-4473
Joe Walker, prin. Fax 659-9560

Frankfort Community SC 2,700/PK-12
50 S Maish Rd 46041 765-654-5585
Dr. Kevin Caress, supt. Fax 659-6220
www.frankfort.k12.in.us
Blue Ridge PS 200/K-2
1910 S Jackson St 46041 765-659-3822
Tami Hicks, prin. Fax 659-2993
Frankfort MS 800/6-8
329 N Maish Rd 46041 765-659-3321
Mike McLaughlin, prin. Fax 659-6260
Green Meadows IS 200/3-5
1900 S Jackson St 46041 765-659-3233
Charles Queen, prin. Fax 659-3889
Suncrest ES 700/PK-5
1608 W Kyger St 46041 765-659-6265
Kim Becker, prin. Fax 659-6244

Franklin, Johnson, Pop. 21,747
Clark-Pleasant Community SC
Supt. — See Whiteland
Clark ES 600/K-4
5764 E 700 N 46131 317-535-8503
Shelley Gies, prin. Fax 535-5521

Franklin Community SC 4,200/K-12
998 Grizzly Cub Dr 46131 317-738-5800
Dr. Victoria Davis, supt. Fax 738-5812
www.fcsc.k12.in.us
Creekside ES 700/K-5
700 E State Road 44 46131 317-738-5750
Sally Jones, prin. Fax 738-5767
Custer Baker IS 400/5-6
101 W State Road 44 46131 317-738-5840
Brenda Crauder, prin. Fax 738-5867
Franklin Community MS 7-8
625 Grizzly Cub Dr 46131 317-346-8400
Pam Millikan, prin. Fax 346-8411
Needham ES 500/K-5
1399 Upper Shelbyville Rd 46131 317-738-5780
Delbert Cragen, prin. Fax 738-5787
Northwood ES 600/K-5
965 Grizzly Cub Dr 46131 317-738-5740
Debra Brown-Nally, prin. Fax 738-5757
Webb ES 400/K-5
1400 Webb Ct 46131 317-738-5790
Sandra Brown, prin. Fax 738-5797
Other Schools – See Bargersville

St. Rose of Lima S 200/PK-8
114 Lancelot Dr 46131 317-738-3451
Kelly England, prin. Fax 738-3583

Frankton, Madison, Pop. 1,864
Frankton-Lapel Community SD
Supt. — See Anderson
Frankton ES 700/PK-6
1303 State Road 128 E 46044 765-754-7545
Ronda Podzielinski, prin. Fax 754-8598

Freetown, Jackson
Brownstown Central Community SC
Supt. — See Brownstown
Freetown ES 100/K-5
4696 W Columbus Pike 47235 812-497-2911
Trent Shelton, prin. Fax 497-3154

Fremont, Steuben, Pop. 1,659
Fremont Community SD 1,200/K-12
PO Box 665 46737 260-495-5005
Loraine Vaughn, supt. Fax 495-9798
www.fremonteagles.org/
Fremont ES 400/K-4
PO Box 625 46737 260-495-4385
Shawn Caldwell, prin. Fax 495-2133
Fremont MS 400/5-8
PO Box E 46737 260-495-6100
Mark Fowerbaugh, prin. Fax 495-7301

French Lick, Orange, Pop. 1,923
Springs Valley Community SC 1,000/K-12
498 S Larry Bird Blvd 47432 812-936-4474
Todd Pritchett, supt. Fax 936-9392
www.svalley.k12.in.us
Springs Valley ES 400/K-5
356 S Larry Bird Blvd 47432 812-936-4820
Anthony Whitaker, prin. Fax 936-9788

Fulton, Fulton, Pop. 328
Caston SC 800/K-12
PO Box 8 46931 574-857-2035
Dan Foster, supt. Fax 857-6795
www.caston.k12.in.us/
Caston ES 400/K-6
PO Box 128 46931 574-857-3025
Lucinda Douglass, prin. Fax 857-6795

Galveston, Cass, Pop. 1,441
Southeastern SC
Supt. — See Walton
Galveston ES 300/K-6
401 S Maple St 46932 574-699-6687
Trudie Hedrick, prin. Fax 699-6693

Garrett, DeKalb, Pop. 5,760
Garrett-Keyser-Butler Community SD 1,700/K-12
801 E Houston St 46738 260-357-3185
Dennis Stockdale, supt. Fax 357-4565
gkb.schoolwires.net/gkb/site/default.asp
Garrett MS 600/5-8
801 E Houston St 46738 260-357-5745
Linda DePew, prin. Fax 357-3575
Ober ES 600/K-4
801 E Houston St 46738 260-357-3112
Greg Myers, prin. Fax 357-3317

St. Joseph S 100/K-6
301 W Houston St 46738 260-357-5137
Kris Call, prin. Fax 357-5138

Gary, Lake, Pop. 98,715
Gary Community SC 13,900/PK-12
620 E 10th Pl 46402 219-881-5401
Dr. Myrtle Campbell, supt. Fax 881-4102
www.garycsc.k12.in.us/
Bailly MS 700/7-8
4621 Georgia St 46409 219-980-6326
Vera Blount, prin. Fax 981-4463
Banneker ES 500/K-6
1912 W 23rd Ave 46404 219-977-2116
Sara Givens, prin. Fax 977-4261
Bethune ECC 600/PK-PK
2367 E 21st Ave 46407 219-886-6542
Ava Ligon, prin. Fax 883-2231
Beveridge ES 500/K-6
1234 Cleveland St 46404 219-977-2123
Stephanie Billups, prin. Fax 977-2449
Brunswick ES 500/K-6
5701 W 7th Ave 46406 219-977-2162
Gloria Terry, prin. Fax 977-2434
Dunbar-Pulaski MS 600/7-8
920 E 19th Ave 46407 219-886-6581
Michael Collins, prin. Fax 881-2057
Glen Park Academy for Learning 700/K-6
5002 Madison St 46408 219-881-3620
Alicia Skinner-Kelley, prin. Fax 980-0161
Ivanhoe ES 400/K-6
5700 W 15th Ave 46406 219-977-2136
Cheryl Pruitt, prin. Fax 944-7725
Jefferson ES 500/K-6
601 Jackson St 46402 219-886-6570
Florine Lacefield, prin. Fax 881-2050
Kuny ES 300/K-3
5050 Vermont St 46409 219-980-6333
Hattie Stallings, prin. Fax 981-6086
Marquette ES 600/K-6
6401 Hemlock Ave 46403 219-938-1191
Dr. Becky Holloway, prin. Fax 939-3966
Pyle ES 400/K-6
2545 W 19th Pl 46404 219-977-2142
Dr. Lucille Washington, prin. Fax 977-2429
Tolleston MS 800/7-8
2700 W 19th Ave 46404 219-977-2145
Cliff Gooden, prin. Fax 977-9359
Vohr ES 400/K-6
1900 W 7th Ave 46404 219-886-6580
Sheila Baker, prin. Fax 881-4104
Webster ES 400/K-6
3720 Pierce St 46408 219-980-6345
Gina Watts, prin. Fax 981-4790
Williams ES 600/K-6
1320 E 19th Ave 46407 219-881-3600
Fax 881-2071

Lake Ridge SC 2,300/K-12
6111 W Ridge Rd 46408 219-838-1819
Dr. Sharon Johnson-Shirley, supt. Fax 989-7802
www.lakeridge.k12.in.us
Grissom ES 400/K-5
7201 W 25th Ave 46406 219-844-2255
Anne Wodetzki, prin. Fax 844-3875
Hosford Park ES 300/K-5
4735 Arthur St 46408 219-980-3390
J. Eric Worthington, prin. Fax 980-3671
Lake Ridge MS 500/6-8
3601 W 41st Ave 46408 219-980-0730
Robert Mastej, prin. Fax 980-0731
Longfellow ES 500/K-5
4500 Calhoun St 46408 219-923-7004
D. Carlson, prin. Fax 923-7103

Ambassador Academy 200/PK-9
900 W Ridge Rd 46408 219-887-4473
Dr. Vercena Stewart, admin. Fax 887-1749
Spirit of God S 100/PK-6
1010 Roosevelt St 46404 219-944-1743
Faith Davis, prin. Fax 944-3890

Gas City, Grant, Pop. 5,819
Mississinewa Community SC 2,200/PK-12
424 E South A St 46933 765-674-8528
Michael Powell, supt. Fax 674-8529
www.olemiss.k12.in.us/
Baskett MS 500/6-8
125 N Broadway St 46933 765-674-8536
J. Eckstein, prin. Fax 677-4452
Northview ES 700/K-5
725 E North H St 46933 765-677-4400
Tab McKenzie, prin. Fax 677-4733
Other Schools – See Jonesboro

Gaston, Delaware, Pop. 963
Wes-Del Community SD 800/K-12
10290 N County Road 600 W 47342 765-358-4006
Steve McColley, supt. Fax 358-4065
www.wes-del.k12.in.us/
Wes-Del ES 300/K-5
PO Box 308 47342 765-358-3079
Tracy Shafer, prin. Fax 358-3573

Georgetown, Floyd, Pop. 2,682
New Albany-Floyd County Consolidated SD
Supt. — See New Albany
Georgetown ES 600/PK-5
8800 High St 47122 812-951-2901
Rhonda Benz, prin. Fax 941-3420
Highland Hills MS 1,200/6-8
3492 Edwardsville Galena Rd 47122 812-923-4014
Steve Griffin, prin. Fax 923-4031

Glenwood, Fayette, Pop. 302
Fayette County SC
Supt. — See Connersville
Orange ES 100/1-6
8318 W Key St 46133 765-827-0180
Debra Williams, prin. Fax 679-1408

Goshen, Elkhart, Pop. 31,269
Fairfield Community SD 2,100/K-12
67240 County Road 31 46528 574-831-2188
Thomas Tumey, supt. Fax 831-5698
www.fairfield.k12.in.us
Benton ES 400/K-6
68350 County Road 31 46526 574-831-2192
Dan Sharp, prin. Fax 831-2200
Other Schools – See Millersburg, New Paris

Goshen Community SD 6,200/K-12
613 E Purl St 46526 574-533-8631
Bruce Stahly, supt. Fax 533-2505
www.goshenschools.org/
Chamberlain ES 400/K-5
428 N 5th St 46528 574-534-2691
Don Jantzi, prin. Fax 534-5918
Chandler ES 500/K-5
419 S 8th St 46526 574-533-5085
Lisa Lederach, prin. Fax 533-1702
Goshen MS 1,400/6-8
1216 S Indiana Ave 46526 574-533-0391
Ann Eaton, prin. Fax 534-3042
Model ES 500/K-5
412 S Greene Rd 46526 574-533-7677
Susan Olinghouse, prin. Fax 534-4220
Parkside ES 400/K-5
1202 S 7th St 46526 574-533-7765
Betts McFarren, prin. Fax 533-1648
Prairie View ES 400/K-5
1730 Regent St 46526 574-534-4710
Ray Helmuth, prin. Fax 534-4862
Waterford ES 400/K-5
65560 State Road 15 46526 574-533-6811
Kim Gallagher, prin. Fax 533-1408
West Goshen ES 500/K-5
215 Dewey Ave 46526 574-533-7855
Alan Metcalfe, prin. Fax 533-1362

Middlebury Community SD
Supt. — See Middlebury
Jefferson ES 500/K-3
18565 County Road 20 46528 574-822-5399
Curt Schwartz, prin.

Clinton Christian S 100/K-12
61763 County Road 35 46528 574-642-3940
Carlin Yoder, admin. Fax 642-3674
Harrison Christian S 200/1-12
64784 County Road 11 46526 574-862-2515
St. John the Evangelist S 100/PK-5
117 W Monroe St 46526 574-533-9480
Amy Weidner, prin. Fax 533-1814

Gosport, Owen, Pop. 748
Spencer-Owen Community SD
Supt. — See Spencer
Gosport ES 200/K-6
PO Box 159 47433 812-879-4694
Carol Watson, prin. Fax 879-4032

Granger, Saint Joseph, Pop. 20,241
Penn-Harris-Madison SC
Supt. — See Mishawaka
Discovery MS 800/6-8
10050 Brummitt Rd 46530 574-674-6010
Sheryll Harper, prin. Fax 679-4214
Frank/Harris ES 400/K-5
13111 Adams Rd 46530 574-272-0340
Deb Hildreth, prin. Fax 272-3806
Horizon ES 600/K-5
10060 Brummitt Rd 46530 574-679-9788
Deb Becraft, prin. Fax 674-8395
Northpoint ES 600/K-5
50800 Cherry Rd 46530 574-271-8598
Chris Stephan, prin. Fax 968-6003
Prairie Vista ES 500/K-5
15400 Brick Rd 46530 574-271-0055
Keely Twibell, prin. Fax 273-1846

Granger Christian S 300/K-12
52025 Gumwood Rd 46530 574-272-5815
Ed Ryan, admin. Fax 968-2664
New Creation Academy 100/K-8
30190 County Road 10 46530 574-264-0469
David Klahr, prin. Fax 262-9016
Peace Lutheran S 50/K-8
16791 Cleveland Rd 46530 574-273-8260
Bradley Pleuss, prin.
St. Pius X S PK-7
52553 Fir Rd 46530 574-272-8462
Elaine Holmes, prin. Fax 855-5400

Greencastle, Putnam, Pop. 10,065
Greencastle Community SC 2,000/K-12
PO Box 480 46135 765-653-9771
Dr. Robert Green, supt. Fax 653-1282
www.greencastle.k12.in.us
Deer Meadow PS 300/K-2
1000 Deer Meadow Dr 46135 765-653-3518
Gwen Morris, prin. Fax 653-1150
Greencastle MS 500/6-8
400 Percy L Julian Dr 46135 765-653-9774
Shawn Gobert, prin. Fax 653-5381
Ridpath PS 200/K-2
711 S Central Ave 46135 765-653-3315
Janice True, prin. Fax 653-9236
Tzouanakis IS 500/3-5
500 Linwood Dr 46135 765-653-4700
Dan TeGrotenhuis, prin. Fax 653-6449

South Putnam Community SD 1,400/K-12
3999 S US Highway 231 46135 765-653-3119
Bruce Bernhardt, supt. Fax 653-7476
www.sputnam.k12.in.us
Central ES 300/K-6
1888 E US Highway 40 46135 765-653-6175
Debbie Steffy, prin. Fax 653-2532
Other Schools – See Fillmore, Reelsville

Peace Lutheran S 100/PK-6
PO Box 778 46135 765-653-6995
Elaine Hoffmann, dir. Fax 653-6995

Greenfield, Hancock, Pop. 16,654
Greenfield-Central Community SD 4,700/PK-12
110 W North St 46140 317-462-4434
Dr. Linda Gellert, supt. Fax 467-4227
www.gcsc.k12.in.us/
Eden ES 400/K-5
8185 N State Road 9 46140 317-326-3117
Jobie Whitaker, prin. Fax 326-2191
Greenfield MS 500/6-8
204 W Park Ave 46140 317-462-6827
James Bever, prin. Fax 467-6730
Harris ES 500/PK-5
200 W Park Ave 46140 317-462-6731
Jan Kehrt, prin. Fax 467-6733
Stephens ES 900/PK-5
1331 N Blue Rd 46140 317-462-4491
Candy Short, prin. Fax 467-6735
Weston ES 500/K-5
140 Polk Ave 46140 317-462-1492
Stephen Burt, prin. Fax 467-6738
Other Schools – See Maxwell

Mt. Vernon Community SC
Supt. — See Fortville
Mt. Comfort ES 600/K-4
5694 W 300 N 46140 317-894-7667
Phillip Davis, prin. Fax 894-7702

Southern Hancock County Community SC
Supt. — See New Palestine
Brandywine ES 300/PK-5
413 E 400 S 46140 317-462-7396
Bruce Miller, prin. Fax 467-0174

St. Michael S 200/PK-8
519 Jefferson Blvd 46140 317-462-6380
Therese Slipher, prin. Fax 462-2571

Greensburg, Decatur, Pop. 10,536
Decatur County Community SD 2,300/PK-12
1645 W State Road 46 47240 812-663-4595
Daniel Roach, supt. Fax 663-4168
www.decaturco.k12.in.us
North Decatur ES 600/PK-6
3300 N State Road 3 47240 812-663-9215
Robert Smith, prin. Fax 663-9782
South Decatur ES 600/K-6
9302 S County Road 420 W 47240 812-591-3115
Teresa Boyd, prin. Fax 591-2203

Greensburg Community SD 2,100/K-12
1312 W Westridge Pkwy 47240 812-663-4774
Tom Hunter, supt. Fax 663-5713
www.greensburg.k12.in.us
Greensburg Community JHS 500/6-8
505 E Central Ave 47240 812-663-7523
Rodney King, prin. Fax 663-9425
Greensburg ES 1,000/K-5
900 Big Blue Ave 47240 812-663-8112
R. D. Linville, prin. Fax 662-6516

Good Shepherd Christian Academy 50/K-4
209 W Washington St 47240 812-663-2410
Janet Hodson, admin. Fax 663-6599
St. Mary S 200/PK-6
210 S East St 47240 812-663-2844
Nancy Buening, prin. Fax 222-6279

Greentown, Howard, Pop. 2,459
Eastern Howard SC 1,300/K-12
221 W Main St Ste 1 46936 765-628-3391
Dr. Tracy Caddell, supt. Fax 628-5017
www.eastern.k12.in.us
Eastern ES 700/K-6
301 S Meridian St 46936 765-628-7866
Linda Stephenson, prin. Fax 628-2405

Greenville, Floyd, Pop. 586
New Albany-Floyd County Consolidated SD
Supt. — See New Albany

Greenville ES 300/K-5
7025 Cross St 47124 812-923-8231
Harlan Uhl, prin. Fax 923-4015

Greenwood, Johnson, Pop. 42,236
Center Grove Community SC 7,300/K-12
4800 W Stones Crossing Rd 46143 317-881-9326
Dr. Steven Stephanoff, supt. Fax 881-0241
www.centergrove.k12.in.us
Center Grove ES 600/K-5
2455 S Morgantown Rd 46143 317-881-1720
Bruce Haddix, prin. Fax 885-4535
Center Grove MS Central 900/6-8
4900 W Stones Crossing Rd 46143 317-882-9391
Jack Parker, prin. Fax 885-4534
Center Grove MS North 800/6-8
202 N Morgantown Rd 46142 317-885-8800
Matt Kaiser, prin. Fax 885-3388
North Grove ES 500/K-5
3280 W Fairview Rd 46142 317-881-5653
Brian Proctor, prin. Fax 885-4547
Pleasant Grove ES 400/K-5
5199 W Fairview Rd 46142 317-887-8525
Trael Kelly, prin. Fax 885-4605
Sugar Grove ES 700/K-5
4135 W Smith Valley Rd 46142 317-887-4707
Patti Duckworth, prin. Fax 885-5249
West Grove ES 600/K-5
5800 W Smith Valley Rd 46142 317-888-0185
Fax 885-4544

Other Schools – See Bargersville

Clark-Pleasant Community SC
Supt. — See Whiteland
Clark Pleasant IS 800/5-6
2111 Sheek Rd 46143 317-535-3980
Kurt Saugstad, prin. Fax 888-8774

Greenwood Community SC 3,800/K-12
605 W Smith Valley Rd 46142 317-889-4060
Dr. David Edds, supt. Fax 889-4068
gws.k12.in.us
Greenwood MS 900/6-8
523 S Madison Ave 46142 317-889-4040
Vicki Noblitt, prin. Fax 889-4044
Greenwood Northeast ES 500/K-5
99 Crestview Dr 46143 317-889-4080
Amy Sander, prin. Fax 889-4087
Greenwood Southwest ES 500/K-5
619 W Smith Valley Rd 46142 317-889-4090
Scott Chambers, prin. Fax 889-4115
Isom Central ES 300/K-5
50 E Broadway St 46143 317-889-4070
Bobby Prewitt, prin. Fax 889-4115
Westwood ES 400/K-5
899 S Honey Creek Rd 46143 317-859-4200
Lisa Harkness, prin. Fax 859-4209

Greenwood Christian Academy 300/PK-12
PO Box 387 46142 317-215-5300
Bruce Peters, hdmstr. Fax 535-1070
Greenwood Christian S 300/PK-5
2045 Averitt Rd 46143 317-881-9970
Ellen Sheets, admin. Fax 859-5234
Our Lady of Greenwood S 500/PK-8
399 S Meridian St 46143 317-881-1300
Kent Clady, prin. Fax 885-5005
SS. Francis & Clare of Assisi ES PK-2
5901 Olive Branch Rd 46143 317-215-2826
Sandi Patel, prin. Fax 859-4678

Griffith, Lake, Pop. 16,666
Griffith Public SD 2,700/K-12
PO Box 749 46319 219-924-4250
Peter Morikis, supt. Fax 922-5933
www.griffith.k12.in.us
Beiriger ES 300/K-6
601 N Lillian St 46319 219-924-4030
Glenn Brown, prin. Fax 922-6154
Franklin ES 300/K-6
201 N Griffith Blvd 46319 219-924-4975
Edward Skaggs, prin. Fax 924-4934
Griffith MS 500/7-8
600 N Raymond St 46319 219-924-4280
Aron Borowiak, prin. Fax 922-5927
Ready ES 400/K-6
1345 N Broad St 46319 219-838-4214
Kathleen Sapyta, prin. Fax 838-4237
Wadsworth ES 300/K-6
600 N Jay St 46319 219-923-4488
Theresa Schoon, prin. Fax 838-6770

St. Mary S 300/PK-8
525 N Broad St 46319 219-924-8633
Rebecca Maskovich, prin. Fax 922-2279

Guilford, Dearborn
Sunman-Dearborn Community SC
Supt. — See Sunman
North Dearborn ES 600/K-4
5687 N Dearborn Rd 47022 812-656-8383
Jeffrey Bond, prin. Fax 656-8321

St. Paul S 100/PK-6
9788 N Dearborn Rd 47022 812-623-2631
Michael Monnig, prin. Fax 623-4758

Hagerstown, Wayne, Pop. 1,673
Nettle Creek SC 1,300/PK-12
297 E Northmarket St 47346 765-489-4543
Joseph Backmeyer, supt. Fax 489-4914
www.nettlecreek.k12.in.us
Hagerstown ES 700/PK-6
299 N Sycamore St 47346 765-489-4555
Lora Wilson, prin. Fax 489-6275

Hamilton, DeKalb, Pop. 1,504
Hamilton Community SD 600/K-12
903 S Wayne St 46742 260-488-2513
Mark Gould, supt. Fax 488-2348
www.hamiltoncomm.com/
Hamilton Community ES 300/K-6
903 S Wayne St 46742 260-488-2101
Kimberly Fifer, prin. Fax 488-3634

Hamlet, Starke, Pop. 768
Oregon-Davis SC 700/K-12
5998 N 750 E 46532 574-867-2111
Dr. Steven Disney, supt. Fax 867-8191
www.od.k12.in.us
Oregon-Davis ES 400/K-6
5860 N 750 E 46532 574-867-2711
George Gordon, prin. Fax 867-2721

Hammond, Lake, Pop. 79,217
Hammond CSD 14,000/PK-12
41 Williams St 46320 219-933-2400
Dr. Walter Watkins, supt. Fax 933-2495
www.hammond.k12.in.us
Columbia ES 400/K-5
1238 Michigan St 46320 219-933-2461
Anthony Salinas, prin. Fax 933-2448
Edison ES 700/K-5
7025 Madison Ave 46324 219-933-2464
Marsha Frey, prin. Fax 933-1544
Eggers MS 700/6-8
5825 Blaine Ave 46320 219-933-2449
Barbara Fleming, prin. Fax 933-1675
Harding ES 600/K-5
3211 165th St 46323 219-989-7351
Anne Davis, prin. Fax 989-7350
Hess ES 300/K-5
3640 Orchard Dr 46323 219-989-7355
Nancy Snider, prin. Fax 989-7367
Irving ES 600/K-5
4727 Pine Ave 46327 219-933-2467
Dusty Rhodes, prin. Fax 933-1676
Jefferson ES 400/K-5
6940 Northcote Ave 46324 219-989-7353
Denise Hughes, prin. Fax 989-7364
Kenwood ES 300/K-5
6416 Hohman Ave 46324 219-933-2469
Mary Beth Nickolaou, prin. Fax 933-1527
Lafayette ES 400/PK-5
856 Sibley St 46320 219-933-2472
Colette Weitcknecht, prin. Fax 933-2485
Lincoln ES 600/K-5
4221 Towle Ave 46327 219-933-2475
Steve Disney, prin. Fax 933-1681
Maywood ES 400/K-5
1001 165th St 46324 219-933-2477
Michael Nance, prin. Fax 933-1668
Morton ES 600/PK-5
7006 Marshall Ave 46323 219-989-7336
Janette Whelan, prin. Fax 989-7337
O'Bannon ES 700/K-5
1317 173rd St 46324 219-989-7360
Catherine Danko, prin. Fax 989-7571
Scott MS 1,000/6-8
3635 173rd St 46323 219-989-7340
Bobbie Escalante, prin. Fax 989-7342
Wallace ES 500/PK-5
6235 Jefferson Ave 46324 219-933-2479
Tom Wisch, prin. Fax 933-2418
Other Schools – See Whiting

Montessori Childrens Schoolhouse 200/PK-6
5935 Hohman Ave 46320 219-932-5666
Kathleen Hill, prin.
St. Casimir S 200/PK-8
4329 Cameron Ave 46327 219-932-2686
Daniel McCabe, prin. Fax 932-4458
St. John Bosco S 300/PK-8
1231 171st Pl 46324 219-845-6226
Mark Kielbania, prin. Fax 989-7946

Hanover, Jefferson, Pop. 3,768
Southwestern-Jefferson County Cons SC 1,100/K-12
239 S Main Cross St 47243 812-866-6250
Stephen Telfer, supt. Fax 866-6256
www.swjcs.k12.in.us/
Southwestern ES 600/K-5
273 S Main Cross St 47243 812-866-6200
Steven Fleenor, prin. Fax 866-6205
Southwestern MS 6-8
206 S Main Cross St 47243 812-866-6250
Trevor Jones, prin.

Harlan, Allen
East Allen County SD
Supt. — See New Haven
Harlan ES 400/K-6
12616 Spencerville Rd 46743 260-446-0130
Dr. Ed Yoder, prin. Fax 446-0133

Hartford City, Blackford, Pop. 6,684
Blackford County SD 2,300/PK-12
668 W 200 S 47348 765-348-7550
Ken Kline, supt. Fax 348-7552
www.bcs.k12.in.us
Hartford City MS 400/6-8
800 W Van Cleve St 47348 765-348-7590
Andrew Glentzer, prin. Fax 348-7593
North Side ES 400/3-5
400 E McDonald St 47348 765-348-7595
Judy Clamme, prin. Fax 348-7552
Southside ES 300/PK-2
1515 S Monroe St 47348 765-348-7584
Ryan Glaze, prin. Fax 348-7580
Other Schools – See Montpelier

Haubstadt, Gibson, Pop. 1,537
South Gibson SC
Supt. — See Fort Branch
Haubstadt Community S 400/K-8
158 E 1025 S 47639 812-768-6487
John Obermeier, prin. Fax 768-5020

St. James S 100/PK-8
12394 S 40 W 47639 812-867-2661
Michelle Priar, prin. Fax 867-2696
SS. Peter & Paul S 100/PK-5
210 N Vine St 47639 812-768-6775
Kalyn Herrmann, prin. Fax 768-5039

Hayden, Jennings
Jennings County SC
Supt. — See North Vernon
Hayden ES 300/K-6
55 S County Road 685 W 47245 812-346-2813
Vickie McGuire, prin. Fax 346-6295

Hebron, Porter, Pop. 3,570
Metro SD of Boone Township 1,100/K-12
307 S Main St 46341 219-996-4771
George Letz, supt. Fax 996-5777
www.hebronschools.k12.in.us/
Hebron ES 500/K-5
307 S Main St 46341 219-996-4771
James Martin, prin. Fax 996-5777
Hebron MS 300/6-8
307 S Main St 46341 219-996-4771
Rick Ankney, prin. Fax 996-5777

Porter Township SC
Supt. — See Valparaiso
Porter Lakes ES 400/K-5
208 S 725 W 46341 219-988-2727
Kevin Donnell, prin. Fax 988-2728

Heltonville, Lawrence
North Lawrence Community SD
Supt. — See Bedford
Heltonville ES 100/K-5
580 Diamond Rd 47436 812-834-6632
Douglas Martin, prin. Fax 834-0704

Henryville, Clark
West Clark Community SC
Supt. — See Sellersburg
Henryville ES 600/PK-6
213 N Ferguson St 47126 812-294-4806
Dr. Glenn Riggs, prin. Fax 294-4940

Highland, Lake, Pop. 23,172
Town of Highland SD 3,400/K-12
9145 Kennedy Ave 46322 219-924-7400
Michael Boskovich, supt. Fax 922-5637
www.highland.k12.in.us
Highland MS 600/7-8
2941 41st St 46322 219-922-5620
Terry Mucha, prin. Fax 922-2270
Johnston ES 400/K-6
8220 5th St 46322 219-923-2428
Kevin Trezak, prin. Fax 838-9866
Merkley ES 400/K-6
9340 5th St 46322 219-922-5640
Rose Alexander, prin. Fax 922-5638
Southridge ES 500/K-6
9221 Johnston St 46322 219-922-5650
John McCormick, prin. Fax 922-5639
Warren ES 400/K-6
2901 100th St 46322 219-922-5660
James Boylan, prin. Fax 922-5674

Highland Christian S 400/PK-8
3040 Ridge Rd 46322 219-838-0356
Richard VandenBerg, prin. Fax 838-7817
Our Lady of Grace S 200/PK-8
3025 Highway Ave 46322 219-838-2901
Marilyn Tomko, prin. Fax 972-6389

Hoagland, Allen
East Allen County SD
Supt. — See New Haven
Hoagland ES 400/K-6
12009 Hoagland Rd 46745 260-446-0160
Marilyn Hissong, prin. Fax 446-0163

Hobart, Lake, Pop. 27,768
Hobart CSD 3,800/K-12
32 E 7th St 46342 219-942-8885
Dr. Peggy Buffington, supt. Fax 942-0081
www.hobart.k12.in.us
Earle ES 300/K-5
400 N Wilson St 46342 219-942-7263
Kacey Allen, prin. Fax 942-0249
Hobart MS 900/6-8
705 E 4th St 46342 219-942-8541
Denise Galovic, prin. Fax 947-7194
Liberty ES 400/K-5
130 E 4th St 46342 219-942-4251
Sara Gutierrez, prin. Fax 942-0346
Martin ES 800/K-5
301 E 10th St 46342 219-947-7869
Debra Misecko, prin. Fax 942-0411
Ridge View ES 300/K-5
3333 W Old Ridge Rd 46342 219-942-5614
Mary Beth Ginalski, prin. Fax 942-0600

River Forest Community SC 1,200/PK-12
3250 Michigan St 46342 219-962-2909
Dr. James Rice, supt. Fax 962-4951
www.rfcsc.k12.in.us
Meister ES 200/PK-5
3300 Jay St 46342 219-962-1103
Nancy Wojcik, prin. Fax 962-1459
River Forest ES 200/K-6
3350 Indiana St 46342 219-962-7716
Ray Satterblom, prin. Fax 962-2341
Other Schools – See Lake Station

Hobart Baptist S 100/PK-8
PO Box 156 46342 219-942-0502
Richard Brown, prin. Fax 940-3092
Montessori Academy in the Oaks 100/PK-6
2109 57th St 46342 219-942-9410
Carol Sistanich, prin. Fax 942-3314
St. Bridget S 200/PK-8
107 Main St 46342 219-942-1894
Douglas Pearson, prin. Fax 942-0939
Trinity Lutheran S 100/PK-8
891 S Linda St 46342 219-942-3147
Keith Boehlke, prin. Fax 942-6637

Holland, Dubois, Pop. 699
Southwest Dubois County SC
Supt. — See Huntingburg
Holland ES 100/PK-5
408 S Meridian St 47541 812-536-2441
Sarah Bardwell, prin. Fax 536-2282

Hope, Bartholomew, Pop. 2,185
Flat Rock-Hawcreek SC 1,100/PK-12
PO Box 34 47246 812-546-2000
Dr. Phillip Deardorff, supt. Fax 546-5617
www.flatrock.k12.in.us
Hope IS 300/3-6
9575 N State Road 9 47246 812-546-5001
Lisa Smith, prin. Fax 546-5617
Other Schools – See Columbus

Howe, Lagrange
Lakeland SC
Supt. — See Lagrange
Lima-Brighton ES 300/K-5
PO Box 158 46746 260-499-2440
Marty Burns, prin. Fax 562-2840

Huntertown, Allen, Pop. 2,136
Northwest Allen County SD
Supt. — See Fort Wayne
Huntertown ES 700/K-5
15330 Lima Rd 46748 260-637-3181
John MacLeod, prin. Fax 637-8348

Our Hope Lutheran S 100/PK-6
PO Box 365 46748 260-338-1121
Joshua Swartz, admin. Fax 637-4673

Huntingburg, Dubois, Pop. 5,929
Southeast Dubois County SC
Supt. — See Ferdinand
Cedar Crest IS 200/5-6
4770 S State Road 162 47542 812-634-2006
Mark Jahn, prin. Fax 481-2963

Southwest Dubois County SC 1,800/PK-12
113 N Jackson St 47542 812-683-3971
Terry Enlow, supt. Fax 683-2752
www.swdubois.k12.in.us
Huntingburg ES 700/K-5
501 W Sunset Dr 47542 812-683-1172
John Seger, prin. Fax 683-5605
Southridge MS 400/6-8
1112 S Main St 47542 812-683-3372
Al Mihajlovits, prin. Fax 683-2817
Other Schools – See Holland

Huntington, Huntington, Pop. 17,011
Huntington County Community SC 6,200/PK-12
1360 N Warren Rd 46750 260-356-7812
Tracey Shafer, supt. Fax 358-2216
www.hccsc.k12.in.us
Crestview MS 700/6-8
1151 W 500 N 46750 260-356-6210
Charles Daugherty, prin. Fax 358-2232
Flint Springs ES 500/K-5
1360 E Tipton St 46750 260-356-7612
Cindy Kiefer, prin. Fax 358-2228
Lancaster ES 200/K-5
2932 W 300 S 46750 260-468-2816
John Purcell, prin. Fax 468-4273
Lincoln ES 400/PK-5
2037 E Taylor St 46750 260-356-2914
Adam Drummond, prin. Fax 358-2234
Mann ES 400/PK-5
2485 Waterworks Rd 46750 260-356-8312
Amy Ashcraft, prin. Fax 358-2222
Northwest ES 400/K-5
4524 W 800 N 46750 260-344-1455
Terry Pierce, prin. Fax 344-1035
Riverview MS 600/6-8
2465 Waterworks Rd 46750 260-356-0910
Curt Crago, prin. Fax 358-2243
Other Schools – See Andrews, Roanoke, Warren

Huntington Catholic S 200/PK-8
960 Warren St 46750 260-356-1926
Jason Woolard, prin. Fax 359-8419

Hymera, Sullivan, Pop. 823
Northeast SC 1,500/PK-12
PO Box 493 47855 812-383-5761
Dr. Mark Baker, supt. Fax 383-4591
www.nesc.k12.in.us/
Hymera ES 200/K-6
PO Box 494 47855 812-383-4671
Tara Jenkins, prin. Fax 383-7213
Other Schools – See Dugger, Farmersburg, Shelburn

Indianapolis, Marion, Pop. 783,612
Carmel Clay SD
Supt. — See Carmel
Orchard Park ES 600/PK-5
10404 Orchard Park Dr S 46280 317-848-1918
Tim Phares, prin. Fax 571-4043

Franklin Township Community SC 8,300/PK-12
6141 S Franklin Rd 46259 317-862-2411
Walter Bourke, supt. Fax 862-7238
www.ftcsc.k12.in.us
Adams ES 500/K-4
7341 E Stop 11 Rd 46259 317-862-2065
Karen Schuldt, prin. Fax 862-7255
Arlington ES 500/K-4
5814 S Arlington Ave 46237 317-782-4274
David Henriott, prin. Fax 784-6698
Bunker Hill ES 500/PK-4
6620 Shelbyville Rd 46237 317-787-3421
Brooke Wessel-Burke, prin. Fax 781-9163
Edgewood IS 5-6
7620 E Edgewood Ave 46239 317-803-8200
Toni Stevenson, prin. Fax 803-8299
Franklin Township MS East 7-8
10440 Indian Creek Rd S 46259 317-803-8100
Charlie McCoy, prin. Fax 803-8199
Franklin Township MS West 1,300/7-8
6019 S Franklin Rd 46259 317-862-2446
Leland Thompson, prin. Fax 862-7271
Kitley IS 1,400/5-6
8735 Indian Creek Rd S 46259 317-803-5900
Jeff Eaton, prin. Fax 803-5970
South Creek ES K-4
9010 E Southport Rd 46259 317-860-4700
Davin Harpe, prin. Fax 860-4770
Thompson Crossing ES 700/K-4
7525 E Thompson Rd 46239 317-860-4600
Teresa Brown, prin. Fax 860-4610
Wanamaker ES 600/K-4
4150 S Bazil Ave 46239 317-862-4100
Russell Wright, prin. Fax 862-7269
Other Schools – See Acton

Indianapolis SD 34,300/PK-12
120 E Walnut St 46204 317-226-4000
Eugene White Ed.D., supt. Fax 226-4936
www.ips.k12.in.us
Arlington Woods ES 400/K-6
5801 E 30th St 46218 317-226-4299
Marcia Johnson, prin. Fax 226-3711
Bellamy ES 300/K-6
9501 E 36th Pl 46235 317-226-4102
Joyce Buntin, prin. Fax 226-3719
Bell ES 400/K-6
3330 N Pennsylvania St 46205 317-226-4260
Melissa Richards, prin. Fax 226-4201
Blaker ES 300/K-6
1349 E 54th St 46220 317-226-4255
Stephanie West, prin. Fax 226-4811
Brandes ES 300/K-6
4065 Asbury St 46227 317-226-4265
Janet Troutman, prin. Fax 226-3392
Brochhausen ES 400/K-6
5801 E 16th St 46218 317-226-4288
Emilee Matthews, prin. Fax 226-3637
Brookside ES 400/K-6
3150 E 10th St 46201 317-226-4254
Julie Bakehorn, prin. Fax 226-3368
Brown ES 300/K-6
1849 Pleasant Run Pkwy S Dr 46203 317-226-4220
DaJuan Major, prin. Fax 226-3188
Buck ES 300/K-6
2701 N Devon Ave 46219 317-226-4294
Jennifer Sweeney, prin. Fax 226-3687
Center for Inquiry @ School 2 300/K-8
725 N New Jersey St 46202 317-226-4202
Christine Collier, prin. Fax 226-3740
Center for Inquiry @ School 84 200/K-8
440 E 57th St 46220 317-226-4284
Christine Collier, prin. Fax 226-3460
Christian Park ES 400/K-6
4700 English Ave 46201 317-226-4282
Margo Myers, prin. Fax 226-3435
Cold Spring S 300/K-8
3650 Cold Spring Rd 46222 317-226-4155
Cathleen Darragh, prin. Fax 226-4157
Diggs ES 500/K-6
1002 W 25th St 46208 317-226-4242
Teresa James, prin. Fax 226-3315
Donnan MS 600/7-8
1202 E Troy Ave 46203 317-226-4272
Viveca Carter, prin. Fax 226-4355
Douglass ES 400/K-6
2020 Dawson St 46203 317-226-4219
Theresa Garner, prin. Fax 226-4762
Dye ES 300/K-6
545 E 19th St 46202 317-226-4227
Jamie Brady, prin. Fax 226-4808
Emerson ES 300/K-6
321 N Linwood Ave 46201 317-226-4258
Vicky Kelley, prin. Fax 226-3375
Evans ES 200/K-6
3202 E 42nd St 46205 317-226-4211
Betty Beene, prin. Fax 226-4955
Fairbanks ES 400/K-6
8620 Montery Rd 46226 317-226-4105
Lynn Henderson, prin. Fax 226-2018
Farrington ES 400/K-6
4326 Patricia St 46222 317-226-4261
Lisa Sackman, prin. Fax 226-4078
Fisher ES 400/K-6
7151 E 35th St 46226 317-226-4293
Maria Manzola, prin. Fax 226-3663
Foster S 800/K-8
653 N Somerset Ave 46222 317-226-4267
Sharon Heathcock, prin. Fax 226-3393
Frost ES 400/K-6
5301 Roxbury Rd 46226 317-226-4106
Tina Foster, prin. Fax 226-4551
Gambold MS 500/7-8
3725 N Kiel Ave 46224 317-226-4108
Yvonne Rambo, prin. Fax 226-3750
Garfield ES 400/K-6
307 Lincoln St 46225 317-226-4231
George Ginder, prin. Fax 226-3336

Gregg ES 600/K-6
2302 E Michigan St 46201 317-226-4215
Justin Hunter, prin. Fax 226-4600
Harshman MS 500/7-8
1501 E 10th St 46201 317-226-4101
Mattie Solomon, prin. Fax 226-3444
Hartmann ES 400/K-6
3734 E Vermont St 46201 317-226-4278
Paula Bias, prin. Fax 226-4877
Irving ES 600/K-6
1250 E Market St 46202 317-226-4214
Elizabeth Odle, prin. Fax 226-4430
Jennings ES 300/K-6
6150 Gateway Dr 46254 317-226-4109
Kevin McMahan, prin. Fax 226-3734
Julian ES 200/K-6
5435 E Washington St 46219 317-226-4257
Debra Brown, prin. Fax 226-3371
Key ES 300/K-6
3920 Baker Dr 46235 317-226-4103
Elizabeth Gehm, prin. Fax 226-3730
Key Learning Community S - North 200/K-5
2411 Indianapolis Ave 46208 317-226-4287
Chris Kunkel, prin. Fax 226-3636
Key Learning Community S - River 400/K-12
777 S White River Pkwy W Dr 46221 317-226-4992
Chris Kunkel, prin. Fax 226-3049
Kilmer Academy 300/K-6
3421 N Keystone Ave 46218 317-226-4269
Charles Gray, prin. Fax 226-3338
Lowell ES 300/K-6
3426 Roosevelt Ave 46218 317-226-4251
Toni Trice, prin. Fax 226-3312
McClellan S 500/K-8
5111 Evanston Ave 46205 317-226-4291
Margaret Higgs, prin. Fax 226-4544
McKinley ES 500/K-6
1733 Spann Ave 46203 317-226-4239
Linda Burchfield, prin. Fax 226-4400
Miller ES 400/K-6
2251 Sloan Ave 46203 317-226-4114
Marjorie Lindeman, prin. Fax 226-3511
Nicholson ES 400/K-6
3651 N Kiel Ave 46224 317-226-4296
Linda Ededuwa, prin. Fax 226-4543
Nicholson Performing Arts Academy 300/K-6
510 E 46th St 46205 317-226-4270
David Newman, prin. Fax 226-4813
Parker S 300/K-8
2353 Columbia Ave 46205 317-226-4256
Mark Nardo, prin. Fax 226-3370
Parkview ES 300/K-6
3092 Brookside Parkway N Dr 46218 317-226-4281
Montinia Donald, prin. Fax 226-4890
Penn ES 700/K-6
1720 W Wilkins St 46221 317-226-4249
Rhonda Akers, prin. Fax 226-3683
Phillips ES 500/K-6
1163 N Belmont Ave 46222 317-226-4263
Evelyn Bushrod, prin. Fax 226-3303
Potter ES 300/K-6
1601 E 10th St 46201 317-226-4274
Tim Clevenger, prin. Fax 226-3421
Pyle ES 300/K-6
3351 W 18th St 46222 317-226-4290
Mark Pugh, prin. Fax 226-4539
Riley ES 500/K-6
150 W 40th St 46208 317-226-4243
Kamona McDowell, prin. Fax 226-3352
Riverside ES 400/PK-6
2033 Sugar Grove Ave 46202 317-226-4244
Alexis Johnson, prin. Fax 226-3469
Russell ES 400/K-6
3445 Central Ave 46205 317-226-4248
Deloris Sangster, prin. Fax 226-2027
Shortridge MS 800/7-8
3401 N Meridian St 46208 317-226-2810
Brandon Cosby, prin. Fax 226-3725
Sidener Gifted Academy 400/2-5
2424 Kessler Boulevard E Dr 46220 317-226-4259
James Whisler, prin. Fax 226-3059
Skillen ES 500/K-6
1410 Wade St 46203 317-226-4234
Deborah Vawter, prin. Fax 226-4876
Steele ES 400/K-6
3698 Dubarry Rd 46226 317-226-4298
Carmen Sharp, prin. Fax 226-4547
Torrence ES 400/K-6
5050 E 42nd St 46226 317-226-4283
Samra Rogers, prin. Fax 226-4994
Wallace ES 500/K-6
3307 Ashway Dr 46224 317-226-4107
Jennifer Botts, prin. Fax 226-3733
Webster S 300/K-8
1450 S Reisner St 46221 317-226-4246
Kathryn Rowe, prin. Fax 226-4377
Wilde ES 500/K-6
5002 W 34th St 46224 317-226-4279
Joyce Akridge, prin. Fax 226-2007

Metro SD of Decatur Township 6,000/K-12
5275 Kentucky Ave 46221 317-856-5265
Donald Stinson, supt. Fax 856-2156
www.msddecatur.k12.in.us
Decatur ECC 500/K-K
5106 S High School Rd 46221 317-856-2200
Susan Bryant, prin. Fax 856-2202
Decatur ES 400/1-4
3425 Foltz St 46221 317-241-0183
Robert Kehrein, prin. Fax 241-7580
Decatur IS Blue Academy 500/5-6
5650 Mann Rd 46221 317-856-5265
Matt Prusiecki, prin. Fax 856-2183
Decatur IS Gold Academy 500/5-6
5650 Mann Rd 46221 317-856-5265
Jeff Harvey, prin. Fax 856-2197

Decatur MS 1,000/7-8
5108 S High School Rd 46221 317-856-5274
Mark Anderson, prin. Fax 856-2163
Lynwood ES 400/1-4
4640 Santa Fe Dr 46241 317-243-7559
Nan Wiseman, prin. Fax 486-4208
Valley Mills ES 500/1-4
5101 S High School Rd 46221 317-856-6363
Nan Wiseman, prin. Fax 856-2142
Other Schools – See West Newton

Metro SD of Lawrence Township 16,100/PK-12
7601 E 56th St 46226 317-423-8200
Dr. Concetta Raimondi, supt. Fax 543-3534
www.ltschools.org/
Belzer MS 1,300/6-8
7555 E 56th St 46226 317-964-6200
Ronald Davie, prin. Fax 543-3355
Beverland Early Learning Center PK-K
11660 Fox Rd 46236 317-423-8214
Denna Renbarger, prin.
Beverland ES 400/1-5
11650 Fox Rd 46236 317-964-4000
M. Susan Jordan, prin. Fax 823-5230
Brook Park Early Learning Center PK-K
5249 David St 46226 317-423-8215
Denna Renbarger, prin.
Brook Park ES 600/1-5
5259 David St 46226 317-964-4100
Barbara Stryker, prin. Fax 543-3525
Castle Early Learning Center 1,000/PK-K
8510 E 82nd St 46256 317-423-8216
Denna Renbarger, prin.
Castle ES 500/1-5
8502 E 82nd St 46256 317-964-4600
Dorothea Irwin, prin. Fax 570-4301
Craig MS 1,200/6-8
6501 Sunnyside Rd 46236 317-964-6400
Troy Knoderer, prin. Fax 823-5223
Crestview ES 500/1-5
7600 E 71st St 46256 317-964-4200
Tom Linkmeyer, prin. Fax 576-6172
Fall Creek Valley MS 1,500/6-8
9701 E 63rd St 46236 317-964-6600
Kathy Luessow, prin. Fax 823-5497
Forest Glen ES 600/1-5
6333 Lee Rd 46236 317-964-4900
Danielle Shockey, prin. Fax 823-5455
Harrison Hill ES 500/1-5
7510 E 53rd St 46226 317-964-4300
Sharon Smith, prin. Fax 543-3315
Indian Creek ES 700/1-5
10833 E 56th St 46235 317-964-4400
Dennis Brooks, prin. Fax 823-3400
Oaklandon ES 500/1-5
6702 Oaklandon Rd 46236 317-964-4800
Doris Downing, prin. Fax 823-5227
Skiles Test ES 500/1-5
7001 Johnson Rd 46220 317-964-4700
Carla Johnson, prin. Fax 576-6171
Sunnyside ES 500/1-5
6345 Sunnyside Rd 46236 317-964-4500
Connie Thomas, prin. Fax 823-3418
Winding Ridge Early Learning Center PK-K
11845 E 46th St 46235 317-423-8217
Denna Renbarger, prin.
Winding Ridge ES 700/PK-5
11825 E 46th St 46235 317-964-6800
Patrick Horan, prin. Fax 964-6809

Metro SD of Perry Township 14,200/PK-12
6548 Orinoco Ave 46227 317-789-3700
Thomas Little, supt. Fax 789-3709
www.msdpt.k12.in.us
Bryan ES 700/PK-5
4355 E Stop 11 Rd 46237 317-789-2600
Andrea Korreck, prin. Fax 865-2693
Burkhart ES 400/K-5
5701 Brill Rd 46227 317-789-3600
John Happersberger, prin. Fax 780-4285
Glenns Valley ES 500/PK-5
8239 Morgantown Rd 46217 317-789-2800
Amanda Osborne, prin. Fax 865-2685
Gray-Edison ES 700/K-5
5225 Gray Rd 46237 317-789-4300
Elizabeth Fox, prin. Fax 789-4309
Homecroft ES 400/K-5
1551 Southview Dr 46227 317-789-3500
Thomas Wade, prin. Fax 780-4292
Lincoln ES 800/K-5
5241 Brehob Rd 46217 317-789-3800
Whitney Wilkowski, prin. Fax 780-4345
MacArthur ES 600/K-5
454 E Stop 11 Rd 46227 317-789-2500
Stephen Craig, prin. Fax 865-2679
Parks-Edison ES 700/K-5
7525 Wellingshire Blvd 46217 317-789-2900
Gary Robinson, prin. Fax 859-5750
Perry Meridian 6th Grade Academy 600/6-6
202 W Meridian School Rd 46217 317-789-1300
John Ralston, prin. Fax 859-5752
Perry Meridian MS 1,200/7-8
202 W Meridian School Rd 46217 317-789-4100
Scott Johnson, prin. Fax 865-2710
Southport 6th Grade Academy 500/6-6
5715 S Keystone Ave 46227 317-789-1400
Kim Campbell, prin. Fax 780-4401
Southport ES 500/K-5
261 Anniston Dr 46227 317-789-3300
Daniel Mendez, prin. Fax 780-4299
Southport MS 1,100/7-8
5715 S Keystone Ave 46227 317-789-4600
Robert Bohannon, prin. Fax 780-4302
Young ES 700/K-5
5740 McFarland Rd 46227 317-789-3400
Fax 780-4338
Other Schools – See Southport

Metro SD of Pike Township 10,700/PK-12
6901 Zionsville Rd 46268 317-293-0393
Nathaniel Jones, supt. Fax 297-7896
www.pike.k12.in.us
Central ES 800/PK-5
7001 Zionsville Rd 46268 317-298-2778
Pat Burton, prin. Fax 299-1261
College Park ES 400/K-5
2811 Barnard St 46268 317-298-2788
Twyla Pitman, prin. Fax 299-1262
Deer Run ES 700/K-5
5401 N High School Rd 46254 317-299-1266
David Holly, prin. Fax 328-7231
Eagle Creek ES 500/PK-5
6905 W 46th St 46254 317-291-1311
Cynthia Huffman, prin. Fax 328-7234
Eastbrook ES 500/K-5
7839 New Augusta Rd 46268 317-802-5900
J. Glenn, prin. Fax 872-0562
Fishback Creek Public Academy 500/PK-5
8301 W 86th St 46278 317-347-8470
Larry Young, prin. Fax 347-8471
Guion Creek ES 500/K-5
4301 W 52nd St 46254 317-298-2780
Pam Conley, prin. Fax 290-0406
Guion Creek MS 900/6-8
4401 W 52nd St 46254 317-293-4549
K. Benjamin, prin. Fax 298-2794
Lincoln MS 900/6-8
5353 W 71st St 46268 317-291-9499
Shelly Haley, prin. Fax 297-1673
New Augusta Public Academy North 900/6-8
6450 Rodebaugh Rd 46268 317-387-4328
Kenneth Coudret, prin. Fax 388-7786
New Augusta Public Academy South 500/K-5
6250 Rodebaugh Rd 46268 317-388-7800
Shari Adams, prin. Fax 388-7838
Snacks Crossing ES 700/PK-5
5455 W 56th St 46254 317-295-7200
Patricia S. Brooks, prin. Fax 298-0686

Metro SD of Warren Township 12,500/PK-12
975 N Post Rd 46219 317-869-4300
Dr. Peggy Hinckley, supt. Fax 869-4348
www.warren.k12.in.us
Brookview ES 600/K-5
1550 Cumberland Rd 46229 317-532-3050
Tim Hanson, prin. Fax 532-3089
Creston MS 1,000/6-8
10925 Prospect St 46239 317-532-6800
Tim Mankin, prin. Fax 532-6899
Eastridge ES 400/K-5
10930 E 10th St 46229 317-532-3150
Paulette Conner, prin. Fax 532-3189
Grassy Creek ES 400/K-5
10330 Prospect St 46239 317-532-3100
Leon Carter, prin. Fax 532-3139
Hawthorne ES 400/K-5
8301 Rawles Ave 46219 317-532-3950
Phil Talbert, prin. Fax 532-3989
Heather Hills ES 400/K-5
10502 E 21st St 46229 317-532-3000
Richard Hunt, prin. Fax 532-3049
Lakeside ES 500/K-5
9601 E 21st St 46229 317-532-2850
Stephen Foster, prin. Fax 532-2889
Liberty Park ES 400/K-5
8425 E Raymond St 46239 317-532-1850
Rob Lugo, prin. Fax 532-1895
Lowell ES 600/K-5
2150 S Hunter Rd 46239 317-532-3900
Susan Howard, prin. Fax 532-3939
Moorhead ES 500/K-5
8400 E 10th St 46219 317-532-3850
Judith Miller, prin. Fax 532-3889
Pleasant Run ES 500/K-5
1800 N Franklin Rd 46219 317-532-3800
Patrick Anderson, prin. Fax 532-3839
Raymond Park MS 900/6-8
8575 E Raymond St 46239 317-532-8900
John Kleine, prin. Fax 532-8999
Stonybrook MS 1,100/6-8
11300 Stonybrook Dr 46229 317-532-8800
Jimmy Meadows, prin. Fax 532-8899
Sunny Heights ES 500/K-5
11149 Stonybrook Dr 46229 317-532-2900
Kathy Handy, prin. Fax 532-2938
Warren ECC 400/PK-K
1401 N Mitthoeffer Rd 46229 317-869-4750
Ron Smith, prin. Fax 869-4752

Metro SD of Washington Township 9,600/K-12
8550 Woodfield Crossing Blv 46240 317-845-9400
Dr. James Mervilde, supt. Fax 205-3362
www.msdwt.k12.in.us
Allisonville ES 700/1-5
4900 E 79th St 46250 317-845-9441
Mike Pomerenke, prin. Fax 576-5255
Crooked Creek ES 500/K-5
2150 Kessler Boulevard West 46228 317-259-5478
Mary Beth Reffett, prin. Fax 259-5453
Eastwood MS 700/6-8
4401 E 62nd St 46220 317-259-5401
Sylvia Lane, prin. Fax 259-5407
Fox Hill ES 600/K-5
802 Fox Hill Dr 46228 317-259-5371
Kathy Levine, prin. Fax 259-5383
Greenbriar ES 500/K-5
8201 Ditch Rd 46260 317-259-5445
Dana Kaminski, prin. Fax 259-5494
Nora ES 700/K-5
1000 E 91st St 46240 317-844-5436
Suzanne Zybert, prin. Fax 571-7172
Northview MS 800/6-8
8401 Westfield Rd 46240 317-259-5421
Tina Merriweather, prin. Fax 259-5431

Spring Mill ES 600/K-5
8250 Spring Mill Rd 46260 317-259-5462
Subahashini Balagopal, prin. Fax 259-5484
Strange ES 400/1-5
3660 E 62nd St 46220 317-259-5465
Maravene Beas, prin. Fax 259-5469
Westlane MS 900/6-8
1301 W 73rd St 46260 317-259-5412
Linda Lawrence, prin. Fax 259-5409

Metro SD of Wayne Township 14,700/PK-12
1220 S High School Rd 46241 317-243-8251
Terry Thompson Ed.D., supt. Fax 243-5744
www.wayne.k12.in.us
Bridgeport ES 800/PK-6
9035 W Morris St 46231 317-227-1200
Angela Lewis, prin. Fax 390-0351
Chapel Glen ES 600/PK-6
701 Lansdowne Rd 46234 317-243-5673
Marc Coapstick, prin. Fax 243-5676
Chapel Hill 7th & 8th Grade Center 1,100/7-8
7320 W 10th St 46214 317-277-2100
Sheri Marcotte, prin. Fax 243-5535
Chapelwood ES 700/K-6
1129 N Girls School Rd 46214 317-241-3507
Heather Pierce, prin. Fax 243-5681
Garden City ES 800/PK-6
4901 Rockville Rd 46224 317-241-3940
Pam Hardy, prin. Fax 484-3127
Lynhurst 7th & 8th Grade Center 1,300/7-8
2805 S Lynhurst Dr 46241 317-247-6265
Dan Wilson, prin. Fax 243-5532
Maplewood ES 700/PK-6
1643 Dunlap Ave 46241 317-243-6733
Moira Clark, prin. Fax 243-5724
McClelland ES 600/PK-6
6740 W Morris St 46241 317-241-2569
Trevor Ewing, prin. Fax 484-3123
North Wayne ES 700/PK-6
6950 W 34th St 46214 317-387-7500
Aretha Britton, prin. Fax 387-7505
Rhoades ES 800/PK-6
502 S Auburn St 46241 317-241-4488
Karen Boatright, prin. Fax 243-5718
Robey ES 800/PK-6
8700 W 30th St 46234 317-243-5712
Kyle Fessler, prin. Fax 243-5714
Stout Field ES 600/PK-6
3820 W Bradbury Ave 46241 317-247-4677
Judy Stegemann, prin. Fax 243-5698
Westlake ES 700/PK-6
271 N Sigsbee St 46214 317-244-9759
Dennisha Murff, prin. Fax 484-3122

Baptist Academy 300/PK-12
2565 Villa Ave 46203 317-788-1587
Tracy Brown, prin. Fax 781-4759
Calvary Christian S 200/PK-12
3939 S Keystone Ave 46227 317-789-8710
Charles Barcus, prin. Fax 789-8718
Calvary Lutheran S 200/PK-12
6111 Shelby St 46227 317-783-2305
Stephen Rensner, prin.
Capitol City S 100/1-8
2143 Boulevard Pl 46202 317-602-3524
Marjorie Morgan-McField, prin. Fax 602-3529
Central Catholic S 200/K-8
1155 Cameron St 46203 317-783-7759
Sara Browning, prin. Fax 781-5964
Christ the King S 400/K-8
5858 Crittenden Ave 46220 317-257-9366
Scott Stewart, prin. Fax 475-6581
Colonial Christian S 200/PK-12
8140 Union Chapel Rd 46240 317-253-0649
Daniel Nelson, prin. Fax 254-2840
Crosspointe Christian Academy 200/K-12
220 Country Club Rd 46234 317-271-1600
Brent Floyd, prin. Fax 209-8227
Emmaus Lutheran S 100/PK-8
1224 Laurel St 46203 317-632-1486
Robert Groth, prin. Fax 632-2620
God's Kids Preschool & K 200/PK-K
6049 E 91st St 46250 317-849-1261
Cynthia Hall, dir. Fax 576-6124
Gray Road Christian S 200/PK-6
5500 Gray Rd 46237 317-786-3559
Ann Wall, prin. Fax 789-4046
Hasten Hebrew Academy of Indianapolis 200/PK-8
6602 Hoover Rd 46260 317-251-1261
Miriam Gettinger, prin. Fax 479-3123
Heritage Christian S 1,600/K-12
6401 E 75th St 46250 317-849-3441
Ray Casey, supt. Fax 594-5863
Holy Angels S 100/PK-6
2822 Dr Mrtn Lthr Kng Jr St 46208 317-926-5211
Cindy Greer, prin. Fax 926-5219
Holy Cross Central S 100/PK-8
125 N Oriental St 46202 317-638-9068
Ruth Tinsley, prin. Fax 638-0116
Holy Cross Lutheran S 300/PK-4
8115 Oaklandon Rd 46236 317-826-1234
Michelle Searcy, prin. Fax 826-0622
Holy Spirit S 400/PK-8
7241 E 10th St 46219 317-352-1243
Rita Parsons, prin. Fax 351-1822
Horizon Christian S 300/PK-12
7702 Indian Lake Rd 46236 317-823-4538
Frank Onorio, prin. Fax 826-2438
Immaculate Heart of Mary S 400/K-8
317 E 57th St 46220 317-255-5468
Jeanne Vesper, prin. Fax 475-7379
Indianapolis Christian S 50/K-12
620 E 10th St 46202 317-636-4560
Indianapolis Junior Academy 50/PK-8
2910 E 62nd St 46220 317-251-0560
Carol Hughey, prin. Fax 251-6486

Indianapolis Southside Christian Academy K-8
4801 Shelbyville Rd 46237 317-786-7002
International S of Indiana 500/PK-12
4330 Michigan Rd 46208 317-923-1951
David Garner, hdmstr. Fax 923-1910
JEWEL Christian Academy 200/K-5
5750 E 30th St 46218 317-591-7200
Michael Bryant, prin. Fax 591-5093
Nativity S 400/PK-8
3310 S Meadow Dr 46239 317-357-1459
Terri Rodriguez, prin. Fax 357-9175
Orchard S 600/PK-8
615 W 64th St 46260 317-251-9253
Joseph Marshall, hdmstr. Fax 254-8454
Our Lady of Lourdes S 300/PK-8
30 S Downey Ave 46219 317-357-3316
Cara Swinefurth, prin. Fax 357-0980
Our Shepherd Lutheran S 200/PK-8
9101 W 10th St 46234 317-271-9100
Nancy Hebel, prin. Fax 271-3084
Park Tudor S 1,000/PK-12
7200 N College Ave 46240 317-415-2700
Douglas S. Jennings, prin. Fax 254-2714
St. Andrew / St. Rita Catholic Academy 200/PK-8
4050 E 38th St 46218 317-549-6305
Yo McCormick, prin. Fax 549-6306
St. Anthony S 100/PK-6
349 N Warman Ave 46222 317-636-3739
Cindy Greer, prin. Fax 636-3740
St. Barnabas S 600/K-8
8300 Rahke Rd 46217 317-881-7422
Debra Perkins, prin. Fax 887-8933
St. Christopher S 200/PK-6
5335 W 16th St 46224 317-241-6314
Vincent Schurger, prin. Fax 244-6678
St. Gabriel S 100/PK-8
6000 W 34th St 46224 317-297-1414
Sarah Watson, prin. Fax 297-6453
St. Joan of Arc S 200/PK-8
500 E 42nd St 46205 317-283-1518
Mary Pat Sharpe, prin. Fax 931-3380
St. John Lutheran S 200/PK-8
6630 Southeastern Ave 46203 317-352-9196
Rick Kerr, prin. Fax 352-9740
St. Jude S 500/K-8
5375 Mcfarland Rd 46227 317-784-6828
Sr. James Kesterson, prin. Fax 780-7594
St. Lawrence S 400/PK-8
6950 E 46th St 46226 317-543-4923
Betty Popp, prin. Fax 543-4929
St. Luke S 600/K-8
7650 N Illinois St 46260 317-255-3912
Stephen Weber, prin. Fax 254-3210
St. Mark S 200/K-8
541 E Edgewood Ave 46227 317-786-4013
Kent Schwartz, prin. Fax 783-9574
St. Matthew S 400/PK-8
4100 E 56th St 46220 317-251-3997
Martin Erlenbaugh, prin. Fax 251-3997
St. Michael the Archangel S 200/K-8
3352 W 30th St 46222 317-926-0516
Steve Padgett, prin. Fax 921-3282
St. Monica S 500/K-8
6131 Michigan Rd 46228 317-255-7153
Timothy Weaver, prin. Fax 259-5570
St. Paul's S 100/PK-PK
3932 Mi Casa Ave 46237 317-787-4464
Beth Larimore, dir. Fax 787-0838
St. Philip Neri S 200/PK-8
545 Eastern Ave 46201 317-636-0134
Mary McCoy, prin. Fax 636-3231
St. Pius X S 400/K-8
7200 Sarto Dr 46240 317-466-3361
Ted Caron, prin. Fax 466-3354
St. Richard's S 400/PK-8
33 E 33rd St 46205 317-926-0425
Patricia Swenson, hdmstr. Fax 921-3367
St. Roch S 300/PK-8
3603 S Meridian St 46217 317-784-9144
Joe Hansen, prin. Fax 784-7051
St. Simon the Apostle S 800/PK-8
8155 Oaklandon Rd 46236 317-826-6000
Kathy Wright, prin. Fax 826-6020
St. Therese Little Flower S 200/PK-8
1401 N Bosart Ave 46201 317-353-2282
Kevin Gawrys, prin. Fax 322-7702
St. Thomas Aquinas S 200/K-8
4600 N Illinois St 46208 317-255-6244
Jerry Flynn, prin. Fax 255-6106
Southport Presbyterian Christian S 400/PK-8
7525 McFarland Blvd 46237 317-534-2929
Susie Manning, prin. Fax 534-2921
Suburban Christian S 100/PK-12
722 E County Line Rd 46227 317-888-3366
Jeremy Wilhelm, prin. Fax 884-4025
Sycamore S 400/PK-8
1750 W 64th St 46260 317-202-2500
Dianne Borgmann, hdmstr. Fax 202-2501
Trinity Christian S 100/K-12
440 Saint Peter St 46201 317-631-3194
Deanna Kitchens, prin. Fax 631-7230
Trinity Lutheran S 200/PK-8
8540 E 16th St 46219 317-897-0243
Joel Rolf, prin. Fax 897-5277
Westside Christian S 200/K-8
8610 W 10th St 46234 317-271-7609
Thomas Williams, prin. Fax 273-1071

Ireland, Dubois
Greater Jasper Consolidated SD
Supt. — See Jasper
Ireland ES 400/PK-5
2386 N 500 W 47545 812-482-7751
Ray Mehling, prin. Fax 482-7765

Jamestown, Boone, Pop. 957
Western Boone County Community SD
Supt. — See Thorntown
Wells ES 600/PK-6
5046 S State Road 75 46147 765-485-6311
John Waymire, prin. Fax 676-5012

Trinity Christian S 50/K-7
6461 S State Road 75 46147 765-676-9118
Carolyn Taylor, admin. Fax 676-9118

Jasonville, Greene, Pop. 2,508
Metro SD Shakamak 900/K-12
RR 2 Box 42 47438 812-665-3550
Mike Mogan, supt. Fax 665-5001
www.shakamak.k12.in.us/
Shakamak ES 500/K-6
RR 2 Box 42 47438 812-665-3550
Chris Ross, prin. Fax 665-5001

Jasper, Dubois, Pop. 13,767
Greater Jasper Consolidated SD 3,200/PK-12
1520 Saint Charles St 47546 812-482-1801
Dr. Jerrill Vandeventer, supt. Fax 482-3388
www.gjcs.k12.in.us
Fifth Street ES 500/PK-2
500 W 5th St 47546 812-482-1406
Becky Ewin, prin. Fax 482-1413
Jasper MS 700/6-8
3600 N Portersville Rd 47546 812-482-6454
Matt Day, prin. Fax 482-6457
Tenth Street ES 500/3-5
328 W 10th St 47546 812-482-2529
Kent Taylor, prin. Fax 482-2043
Other Schools – See Ireland

Holy Family S 300/PK-8
990 Church Ave 47546 812-482-5050
Jeanne Heltzel, prin. Fax 481-9909
Precious Blood S 300/PK-5
1385 W 6th St 47546 812-482-4461
Fax 482-7762

Jeffersonville, Clark, Pop. 28,621
Greater Clark County SD 10,800/PK-12
2112 Utica Sellersburg Rd 47130 812-283-0701
Dr. Tony Bennett, supt. Fax 288-4804
www.gcs.k12.in.us
Bridgepoint ES 400/K-5
420 Ewing Ln 47130 812-288-4858
Tim Whitaker, prin. Fax 288-2852
Jefferson ES 400/K-5
2710 Hamburg Pike 47130 812-288-4855
Charles King, prin. Fax 288-4870
Maple ES 300/PK-5
429 Division St 47130 812-288-4860
Lauraetta Starks, prin. Fax 288-4899
Northaven ES 400/K-5
1907 Oakridge Dr 47130 812-288-4865
Ronda Hostetler, prin. Fax 288-4862
Parkview MS 800/6-8
1600 Brigman Ave 47130 812-288-4844
Mark Laughner, prin. Fax 288-2849
Riverside ES 400/K-5
17 Laurel Dr 47130 812-288-4868
Beth Kimmel, prin. Fax 288-4894
River Valley MS 900/6-8
2220 Veterans Pkwy 47130 812-288-4848
Vicki Lete, prin. Fax 288-4851
Spring Hill ES 200/PK-5
201 E 15th St 47130 812-288-4874
Virenda Cunningham, prin. Fax 288-4876
Utica ES 500/PK-5
210 Maplehurst Dr 47130 812-288-4878
Doug Chinn, prin. Fax 288-2846
Wilson ES 600/PK-5
2915 Charlestown Pike 47130 812-288-4888
Rebecca Kischnick, prin. Fax 288-4895
Other Schools – See Charlestown, Clarksville, New Washington

Sacred Heart S 200/PK-8
1842 E 8th St 47130 812-283-3123
Becky Spitznagel, prin. Fax 284-6678

Jonesboro, Grant, Pop. 1,759
Mississinewa Community SC
Supt. — See Gas City
Westview ES 400/PK-5
709 W 6th St 46938 765-677-4437
Parr Reed, prin. Fax 677-4449

King's Academy 100/K-12
1201 S Water St 46938 765-674-1722
Tony Miner, dean Fax 674-1722

Kendallville, Noble, Pop. 10,018
East Noble SC 3,300/K-12
126 W Rush St 46755 260-347-2502
Dr. H. Steve Sprunger, supt. Fax 347-0111
www.eastnoble.net
East Noble MS 300/7-8
401 E Diamond St 46755 260-347-0100
Travis Heavin, prin. Fax 347-7168
North Side ES 300/K-6
302 Harding St 46755 260-347-1354
Susan Avery, prin. Fax 347-3319
South Side ES 400/K-6
1350 Sherman St 46755 260-349-2200
James Nixon, prin. Fax 349-2210
Wayne Center ES 300/K-6
1231 E Appleman Rd 46755 260-347-2548
Karen Gandy, prin. Fax 347-7172
Other Schools – See Avilla, Rome City

St. John Lutheran S 200/PK-8
301 S Oak St 46755 260-347-2444
Fax 349-2854

Kennard, Henry, Pop. 433
C.A. Beard Memorial SC
Supt. — See Knightstown
Kennard ES 100/K-4
232 Vine St 47351 765-785-2221
Shirley Heck, prin. Fax 785-2612

Kentland, Newton, Pop. 1,747
South Newton SC 900/PK-12
110 N 3rd St 47951 219-474-5184
Todd Rudnick, supt. Fax 474-6966
www.newton.k12.in.us/
South Newton ES 400/PK-5
13188 S 50 E 47951 219-474-5167
Sandra Arini, prin. Fax 474-3621
South Newton MS 200/6-8
13100 S 50 E 47951 219-474-5167
Fax 474-3624

Kingsford Heights, LaPorte, Pop. 1,407
La Porte Community SC
Supt. — See La Porte
Kingsford Heights ES 200/K-5
460 Evanston Rd 46346 219-393-3116
Marcia Alexander, prin. Fax 393-5082

Knightstown, Henry, Pop. 2,026
C.A. Beard Memorial SC 1,400/K-12
345 N Adams St 46148 765-345-5101
Gary Storie, supt. Fax 345-5103
www.cabeard.k12.in.us
Knightstown ES 300/K-4
8632 S State Road 109 46148 765-345-2151
Christine Brokamp, prin. Fax 345-7134
Knightstown IS 400/5-8
1 Panther Trl 46148 765-345-5455
Don Scheumann, prin. Fax 345-5523
Other Schools – See Carthage, Kennard

Morton Memorial S 100/1-12
10892 N State Road 140 46148 765-345-5141
P. Kevin Porter, prin. Fax 345-2063

Knightsville, Clay, Pop. 635
Clay Community SD 4,700/PK-12
PO Box 169 47857 812-443-4461
Dr. Dan Schroeder, supt. Fax 442-0849
www.clay.k12.in.us
Other Schools – See Brazil, Clay City

Knox, Starke, Pop. 3,667
Knox Community SC 2,000/K-12
2 Redskin Trl 46534 574-772-1600
A.J. Gappa, supt. Fax 772-1608
www.knox.k12.in.us
Knox Community ES 900/K-5
210 W Culver Rd 46534 574-772-1633
Glenn Barnes, prin. Fax 772-1646
Knox Community MS 500/6-8
901 S Main St 46534 574-772-1654
Steve Cronk, prin. Fax 772-1664

Kokomo, Howard, Pop. 46,178
Kokomo-Center Twp Consolidated SC 7,000/PK-12
PO Box 2188 46904 765-455-8000
Chris Himsel, supt. Fax 455-8018
www.kokomo.k12.in.us
Bon Air ES 300/K-5
2800 N Apperson Way 46901 765-454-7030
Marilyn Ritchie, prin. Fax 454-7034
Bon Air MS 300/6-8
2796 N Apperson Way 46901 765-454-7035
Michael Sargent, prin. Fax 454-7039
Boulevard ES 300/K-5
1901 W Boulevard 46902 765-455-8070
Jacquelyn Thomas-Miller, prin. Fax 455-8079
Central MS 500/6-8
303 E Superior St 46901 765-454-7000
Brian Van Buskirk, prin. Fax 454-7007
Columbian ES 200/K-5
1234 N Courtland Ave 46901 765-454-7040
Sharon Hahn, prin. Fax 454-7041
Darrough Chapel ES 300/K-5
900 S Goyer Rd 46901 765-454-7045
Paula Concus, prin. Fax 454-7048
Haynes ES 400/K-5
910 S Cooper St 46901 765-454-7050
Linda Campbell, prin. Fax 454-7052
Lafayette Park ES 400/K-5
919 Korby St 46901 765-454-7060
Patrick Quillen, prin. Fax 454-7062
Lafayette Park MS 400/6-8
923 Korby St 46901 765-454-7065
Debbie Glass, prin. Fax 454-7067
Maple Crest ES 300/K-5
300 W Lincoln Rd 46902 765-455-8080
David Buckalew, prin. Fax 455-8082
Maple Crest MS 400/6-8
2727 S Washington St 46902 765-455-8085
Jonathan Schuck, prin. Fax 455-8062
Pettit Park ES 300/K-5
901 W Havens St 46901 765-454-7075
Claudette Renfro, prin. Fax 454-7078
Sycamore ES 400/PK-5
1600 E Sycamore St 46901 765-454-7090
Charley Hinkle, prin. Fax 454-7093
Wallace ES 300/K-5
2326 W Jefferson St 46901 765-454-7095
Sharon Hahn, prin. Fax 454-7096
Washington ES 200/K-5
1500 S Washington St 46902 765-454-7100
Anne Wiles, prin. Fax 454-7101

Northwestern SC 1,700/K-12
3075 N Washington St 46901 765-452-3060
Ryan Snoddy, supt. Fax 452-3065
nwsc.k12.in.us
Howard ES 200/K-6
3526 N 300 E 46901 765-454-2326
Jon Willman, prin. Fax 868-8395

Northwestern ES 600/K-6
4223 W 350 N 46901 765-454-2335
Ron Owings, prin. Fax 454-2334
Northwestern MS 300/7-8
3431 N 400 W 46901 765-454-2323
Brett Davis, prin. Fax 457-2324

Taylor Community SC 1,500/PK-12
3750 E 300 S 46902 765-453-3035
Dr. John Magers, supt. Fax 455-8531
www.taylor.k12.in.us
Taylor IS 200/4-5
3700 E 300 S 46902 765-453-1500
Stan Williams, prin. Fax 455-5165
Taylor MS 400/6-8
3794 E 300 S 46902 765-455-5186
Heather Hord, prin. Fax 455-5157
Taylor PS 400/PK-3
5500 Wea Dr 46902 765-453-3800
Erin Casper, prin. Fax 455-5173

Acacia Academy K-8
1820 Timber Ct 46902 765-864-0951
Rob Hoshaw, admin.
Kokomo Christian S 100/K-5
2635 S Dixon Rd 46902 765-455-1447
Suzette Randall, admin. Fax 864-0944
Redeemer Lutheran S 200/PK-8
705 E Southway Blvd 46902 765-864-6466
Ruth Lavrenz, prin. Fax 864-6465
SS. Joan of Arc & Patrick S 300/PK-8
3155 S 200 W 46902 765-865-9960
JoAnne Werling, prin. Fax 865-9962

Kouts, Porter, Pop. 1,766
East Porter County SC 2,200/K-12
PO Box 370 46347 219-766-2214
Dr. Rod Gardin, supt. Fax 766-2885
www.epcsc.k12.in.us
Kouts ES 400/K-5
PO Box 699 46347 219-766-2232
Patti Eich, prin. Fax 766-3763
Other Schools – See Valparaiso

La Crosse, LaPorte, Pop. 561
Dewey Township SD
Supt. — See La Porte
La Crosse S 200/K-12
PO Box 360 46348 219-754-2461
Timothy Somers, prin. Fax 754-2511

Ladoga, Montgomery, Pop. 1,038
South Montgomery Community SC
Supt. — See New Market
Ladoga ES 200/K-6
418 E Taylor St 47954 765-942-2203
Brett Higgins, prin. Fax 942-2204

Lafayette, Tippecanoe, Pop. 60,459
Lafayette SC 7,400/K-12
2300 Cason St 47904 765-771-6000
Edward Eiler, supt. Fax 771-6049
www.lsc.k12.in.us
Earhart ES 500/K-5
3280 S 9th St 47909 765-772-4740
Pat Miller, prin. Fax 772-4744
Edgelea ES 600/K-5
2910 S 18th St 47909 765-772-4780
Vicki Vaughn, prin. Fax 772-4786
Glen Acres ES 500/K-5
3767 Kimberly Dr 47905 765-771-6150
Karen Combs, prin. Fax 771-6154
Miami ES 500/K-5
2401 Beck Ln 47909 765-772-4800
Matt Rhoda, prin. Fax 772-4804
Miller ES 400/K-5
700 S 4th St 47905 765-476-2930
Brandon Hawkins, prin. Fax 476-2934
Murdock ES 200/K-5
2100 Cason St 47904 765-771-6120
Janell Uerkwitz, prin. Fax 771-6126
Oakland ES 200/K-5
611 S 21st St 47905 765-771-6130
Kelly Coleman, prin. Fax 771-6134
Sunnyside MS 500/6-6
2500 Cason St 47904 765-771-6100
Greg Louk, prin. Fax 771-6113
Tecumseh JHS 1,200/7-8
2101 S 18th St 47905 765-772-4750
Brett Gruetzmacher, prin. Fax 772-4763
Vinton ES 500/K-5
3101 Elmwood Ave 47904 765-771-6140
Rick Hobbs, prin. Fax 771-6144

Tippecanoe SC 11,300/K-12
21 Elston Rd 47909 765-474-2481
Scott Hanback, supt. Fax 474-0533
www.tsc.k12.in.us
Cole ES 300/K-5
6418 E 900 S 47909 765-523-2141
Michael Pinto, prin. Fax 523-2864
East Tipp MS 400/6-8
7501 E 300 N 47905 765-589-3566
Linda McTaggart, prin. Fax 589-3129
Hershey ES 800/K-5
7521 E 300 N 47905 765-589-3907
Samuel Perdue, prin. Fax 589-8628
Mayflower Mill ES 700/K-5
200 E 500 S 47909 765-538-3875
Mary Beth Fitzgerald, prin. Fax 538-2014
Mintonye ES 400/K-5
2000 W 800 S 47909 765-538-2780
Robert Skaggs, prin. Fax 538-2988
Southwestern MS 300/6-8
2100 W 800 S 47909 765-538-3025
Marilyn Ferguson, prin. Fax 538-2877
Wainwright MS 400/6-8
7501 E 700 S 47905 765-523-2151
Neal McCutcheon, prin. Fax 523-2709
Wea Ridge ES 900/K-5
1333 E 430 S 47909 765-471-9321
Timothy Schirack, prin. Fax 471-9329
Wea Ridge MS 600/6-8
4410 S 150 E 47909 765-471-2164
Cory Marshall, prin. Fax 474-5347
Other Schools – See Battle Ground, Dayton, West Lafayette

First Assembly Christian Academy 100/PK-12
108 Beck Ln 47909 765-477-5803
Lafayette Christian S 200/PK-8
525 N 26th St 47904 765-447-3052
Abe Vreeke, prin. Fax 448-1850
St. Boniface S 100/4-6
813 North St 47901 765-742-7913
Sr. Lenore Schwartz, prin. Fax 423-4988
St. James Lutheran S 100/K-8
615 N 8th St 47901 765-742-6464
Randall Strakis, prin. Fax 742-4642
St. Lawrence S 300/PK-6
1902 Meharry St 47904 765-742-4450
Jodi Williams, prin. Fax 742-4450
St. Mary Cathedral S 300/PK-3
1200 South St 47901 765-742-6302
Judith Brewer, prin. Fax 742-8933

La Fontaine, Wabash, Pop. 859
Metro SD of Wabash County
Supt. — See Wabash
La Fontaine ES 200/K-6
207 N Wabash Ave 46940 260-563-8050
Douglas Ballinger, prin. Fax 569-6837

Lagrange, Lagrange, Pop. 2,972
Lakeland SC 2,300/K-12
200 S Cherry St 46761 260-499-2400
Risa Herber, supt. Fax 463-4800
www.lakeland.k12.in.us
Lakeland MS 500/6-8
1055 E 075 N 46761 260-499-2480
Karen Lake, prin. Fax 463-2648
Parkside ES 500/K-5
1 Lemaster Cir 46761 260-499-2430
Galen Mast, prin. Fax 463-3730
Other Schools – See Howe, Wolcottville

Prairie Heights Community SC 1,700/K-12
305 S 1150 E 46761 260-351-3214
Dr. Paul Thomas, supt. Fax 351-3614
www.ph.k12.in.us/
Prairie Heights ES 400/K-4
455 S 1150 E 46761 260-351-3214
Patricia Long, prin. Fax 351-2182
Prairie Heights MS 600/5-8
395 S 1150 E 46761 260-351-3214
Brenda Rummel, prin. Fax 351-2182
Other Schools – See Wolcottville

Lake Station, Lake, Pop. 13,565
Lake Station Community SD 1,500/K-12
2500 Pike St 46405 219-962-1159
Dan DeHaven, supt. Fax 962-4011
www.lakes.k12.in.us
Bailey ES 300/K-5
2100 Union St 46405 219-962-1302
Terry Kolopanis, prin. Fax 962-5222
Central S 100/6-6
2540 Pike St 46405 219-962-1656
Juan Hernandez, prin. Fax 962-4994
Hamilton ES 300/K-5
2900 Lake St 46405 219-962-1824
Tara Gordon, prin. Fax 962-4559
Polk ES 200/K-5
2460 Vermillion St 46405 219-962-1360
Linda Halas, prin. Fax 962-4603

River Forest Community SC
Supt. — See Hobart
Evans ES 300/K-5
2915 E 35th Ave 46405 219-962-1608
Robert Koval, prin. Fax 962-1643

Laketon, Wabash
Manchester Community SD
Supt. — See North Manchester
Manchester IS 200/5-6
PO Box 234 46943 260-982-8685
Bill Reichhart, prin. Fax 982-8085

Lake Village, Newton
North Newton SC
Supt. — See Morocco
Lake Village ES 200/K-6
3281 W 950 N 46349 219-992-3311
Carolyn Bucko, prin. Fax 992-2404

Lakeville, Saint Joseph, Pop. 557
Union-North United SC 1,300/K-12
22601 Tyler Rd 46536 574-784-8141
Larry Phillips, supt. Fax 784-2181
www.unorth.k12.in.us
Laville ES 700/K-6
12645 Tyler Rd 46536 574-784-2311
John Farthing, prin. Fax 784-8051

Lamar, Spencer
North Spencer County SC
Supt. — See Lincoln City
Lincoln Trail ES 300/K-6
13726 N State Road 245 47550 812-544-2929
Patricia Gilliland, prin. Fax 544-2930

Lanesville, Harrison, Pop. 630
Lanesville Community SC 600/K-12
2725 Crestview Ave NE 47136 812-952-2555
Samuel Gardner, supt. Fax 952-3762
www.lanesville.k12.in.us/
Lanesville ES 300/K-6
2725 Crestview Ave NE 47136 812-952-3000
Marsha Himmelhaver, prin. Fax 952-3762

St. John's Lutheran S 100/PK-8
1507 St Johns Church Rd NE 47136 812-952-2737
Pam Eisert, prin. Fax 952-3269

Lapel, Madison, Pop. 1,846
Frankton-Lapel Community SD
Supt. — See Anderson
Lapel ES 500/PK-6
2865 S State Road 13 46051 765-534-3101
Woody Fields, prin. Fax 534-4426
Lapel MS 200/7-8
2883 S State Road 13 46051 765-534-3137
Bill Chase, prin. Fax 534-3883

La Porte, LaPorte, Pop. 21,092
Cass Township SD 200/K-8
555 Michigan Ave Ste 203 46350 219-326-6808
Norm Kleist, supt. Fax 362-3313
Other Schools – See Wanatah

Dewey Township SD 200/K-12
555 Michigan Ave Ste 203 46350 219-326-6808
Norm Kleist, supt. Fax 362-3313
www.lacrosse.k12.in.us/
Other Schools – See La Crosse

La Porte Community SC 6,500/K-12
1921 A St 46350 219-362-7056
Dr. Judith DeMuth, supt. Fax 324-9347
www.lpcsc.k12.in.us
Boston MS 700/6-8
1000 Harrison St 46350 219-326-6930
Dave Birkholz, prin. Fax 324-7108
Crichfield ES 600/K-5
336 W Johnson Rd 46350 219-362-2020
Linda Wiltfong, prin. Fax 324-1399
Hailmann ES 400/K-5
1001 Ohio St 46350 219-362-2080
Denise Sanders, prin. Fax 362-8102
Handley ES 400/K-5
408 W 10th St 46350 219-362-2561
Dorothy Davis, prin. Fax 362-1428
Indian Trail ES 400/K-5
3214 S State Road 104 46350 219-369-9016
Kimberly Rehlander, prin. Fax 369-1290
Kesling MS 800/6-8
306 E 18th St 46350 219-362-7507
Bill Wilmsen, prin. Fax 324-5712
Kingsbury ES 400/K-5
802 W 400 S 46350 219-362-1823
Greg Hunt, prin. Fax 324-6727
Lincoln ES 300/K-5
402 Harrison St 46350 219-362-3755
Diane Szynal, prin. Fax 324-6297
Riley ES 300/K-5
516 Weller Ave 46350 219-362-3235
Steve Manering, prin. Fax 362-4903
Other Schools – See Kingsford Heights

Door Prairie Adventist S 100/PK-8
1480 Boyd Blvd 46350 219-362-6959
Lori Thordarson, prin. Fax 362-2269
St. John Lutheran S 100/PK-8
111 Kingsbury Ave 46350 219-362-6692
David Wippich, prin. Fax 362-4742
St. Joseph S 200/PK-8
101 C St 46350 219-362-6472
Fonda Mauch, prin. Fax 362-2707

Larwill, Whitley, Pop. 282
Whitko Community SC
Supt. — See Pierceton
Whitko MS 400/6-8
710 N State Road 5 46764 260-327-3603
Jerry Klausing, prin. Fax 327-3805

Laurel, Franklin, Pop. 580
Franklin County Community SC
Supt. — See Brookville
Laurel S 600/PK-8
PO Box 322 47024 765-698-3851
Jill Brack, prin. Fax 698-2611

Lawrenceburg, Dearborn, Pop. 4,750
Lawrenceburg Community SC 1,600/K-12
300 Tiger Blvd 47025 812-537-7200
Stephen Gookins, supt. Fax 537-0759
www.lburg.k12.in.us
Central ES 300/3-5
500 Short St 47025 812-537-7288
Ralph Haynes, prin. Fax 537-7063
Greendale MS 300/6-8
200 Tiger Blvd 47025 812-537-7260
Karl Galey, prin. Fax 537-6385
Lawrenceburg PS 400/K-2
400 Tiger Blvd 47025 812-537-7272
Tammy Gregory, prin. Fax 537-5746

Sunman-Dearborn Community SC
Supt. — See Sunman
Bright ES 500/K-4
22593 State Line Rd 47025 812-637-4600
Norb Goessling, prin. Fax 637-4606

St. Lawrence S 300/K-8
524 Walnut St 47025 812-537-3690
Dena Steiner, prin. Fax 537-9685

Leavenworth, Crawford, Pop. 353
Crawford County Community SC
Supt. — See Marengo
Leavenworth ES 200/K-6
346 E State Road 62 47137 812-739-2210
Mike Key, prin. Fax 739-2211

Lebanon, Boone, Pop. 14,633
Lebanon Community SC 3,500/K-12
1810 N Grant St 46052 765-482-0380
Dr. Robert Taylor, supt. Fax 483-3053
www.leb.k12.in.us/
Central ES 300/K-5
515 E Williams St 46052 765-482-2000
Marie Roth, prin. Fax 483-3059
Harney ES 500/K-5
1500 Garfield St 46052 765-482-5940
Janet Yonts, prin. Fax 483-3062
Lebanon MS 800/6-8
1800 N Grant St 46052 765-482-3400
Brad Allen, prin. Fax 483-3049
Stokes ES 500/K-5
1005 Hendricks Dr 46052 765-482-5950
Kelly Sollman, prin. Fax 483-3056
Worth ES 300/K-5
3900 E 300 S 46052 317-769-3286
Ambert Targgart, prin. Fax 769-5236

Leesburg, Kosciusko, Pop. 613
Warsaw Community SC
Supt. — See Warsaw
Leesburg ES 600/K-6
PO Box 247 46538 574-453-4121
Randy Dahms, prin. Fax 371-5004

Leo, Allen
East Allen County SD
Supt. — See New Haven
Leo ES 500/4-6
14811 Wayne St 46765 260-446-0170
William Diehl, prin. Fax 446-0173

Leopold, Perry
Perry Central Community SC 1,200/PK-12
18677 Old State Road 37 47551 812-843-5576
Mary Roberson, supt. Fax 843-4746
www.pccs.k12.in.us/
Perry Central ES 600/PK-6
18677 Old State Road 37 47551 812-843-5122
Ray James, prin. Fax 843-5242

Lexington, Scott, Pop. 350
Scott County SD 2
Supt. — See Scottsburg
Lexington ES 200/K-5
7980 E Walnut St 47138 812-752-8924
Charles Rose, prin. Fax 889-2094

Liberty, Union, Pop. 1,940
Union County/College Corner JSD 1,600/K-12
107 S Layman St 47353 765-458-7471
Lynn Sheets, supt. Fax 458-5647
www.uc.k12.in.us/
Liberty ES 500/K-5
501 Eaton St 47353 765-458-5521
Kathy Sourbeer, prin. Fax 458-6223
Union County MS 400/6-8
488 E State Road 44 47353 765-458-7438
Vicky Snyder, prin. Fax 458-6041

Ligonier, Noble, Pop. 4,423
West Noble SC 2,600/K-12
5050 N US Highway 33 46767 260-894-3191
Dave Speakman, supt. Fax 894-3260
westnoble.k12.in.us/
Ligonier ES 500/K-4
601 Grand St 46767 260-894-3191
Brian Shepherd, prin. Fax 894-3189
West Noble ES 700/K-4
5294 N US Highway 33 46767 260-894-3191
Mark Yoder, prin. Fax 894-3199
West Noble MS 800/5-8
5194 N US Highway 33 46767 260-894-3191
C. Bill Anders, prin. Fax 894-4703

Lincoln City, Spencer
North Spencer County SC 2,300/PK-12
3720 E State Road 162 47552 812-937-2400
Joan Keller, supt. Fax 937-7187
www.nspencer.k12.in.us
Heritage Hills MS 400/7-8
PO Box 1777 47552 812-937-4472
Susan Grundhoefer, prin. Fax 937-4327
Other Schools – See Chrisney, Dale, Ferdinand, Lamar

Linton, Greene, Pop. 5,808
Linton-Stockton SC 1,300/PK-12
801 1st St NE 47441 812-847-6020
Ronald Bush, supt. Fax 847-8659
www.lssc.k12.in.us/
Linton-Stockton ES 700/PK-6
900 NE 4th St 47441 812-847-6039
Kent Brewer, prin. Fax 847-6030
Linton-Stockton JHS 200/7-8
109 I St NE 47441 812-847-6022
Jeff Sparks, prin. Fax 847-6032

Lizton, Hendricks, Pop. 358
North West Hendricks SD 1,800/K-12
PO Box 70 46149 317-994-4100
Dr. Leo Philbin, supt. Fax 994-5963
www.hendricks.k12.in.us/
Tri-West MS 400/6-8
555 W US Highway 136 46149 317-994-4100
Ronald Ward, prin. Fax 994-4230
Other Schools – See North Salem, Pittsboro

Logansport, Cass, Pop. 19,211
Logansport Community SC 4,300/PK-12
2829 George St 46947 574-722-2911
Julie Lauck, supt. Fax 753-0143
www.lcsc.k12.in.us
Columbia ES 400/K-5
20 E Columbia St 46947 574-753-3432
Elizabeth Loposser, prin. Fax 753-6072
Columbia MS 400/6-8
1300 N 3rd St 46947 574-753-3797
Greg Grostefon, prin. Fax 753-6159
Fairview ES 500/PK-5
846 S Cicott St 46947 574-722-5288
Christine Hess, prin. Fax 753-6318
Franklin ES 400/K-5
410 W Miami Ave 46947 574-722-3200
Hayley LaDow, prin. Fax 722-1172
Landis ES 700/K-5
1 Landis Ln 46947 574-722-5466
Rita McLochlin, prin. Fax 753-5513
Lincoln MS 600/6-8
2901 Usher St 46947 574-753-7115
Jeff Canady, prin. Fax 753-5826

All Saints S 100/PK-5
121 Eel River Ave 46947 574-753-3410
James McNeany, prin. Fax 753-1608

Loogootee, Martin, Pop. 2,680
Loogootee Community SC 1,100/K-12
PO Box 282 47553 812-295-2595
Larry Weitkamp, supt. Fax 295-5595
www.loogootee.k12.in.us/
Loogootee East ES 200/4-6
510 Church St 47553 812-295-2924
Bill Powell, prin. Fax 295-5595
Loogootee West ES 300/K-3
101 Costello Dr 47553 812-295-2833
Laura Mattingly, prin. Fax 295-5595

Lowell, Lake, Pop. 8,039
Tri-Creek SC 3,700/K-12
195 W Oakley Ave 46356 219-696-6661
Dr. Alice Neal, supt. Fax 696-2150
www.tricreek.k12.in.us
Lake Prairie ES 500/K-5
11601 W 181st Ave 46356 219-696-7541
Lisa Patton, prin. Fax 690-2616
Lowell MS 900/6-8
200 W Oakley Ave 46356 219-696-7701
John Alessia, prin. Fax 690-2620
Oak Hill ES 600/K-5
425 S Nichols St 46356 219-696-9285
Lynne Haberlin, prin. Fax 690-2621
Three Creeks ES 500/K-5
670 S Burr St 46356 219-696-5740
Connie Bales, prin. Fax 696-3051

St. Edward S 100/PK-6
210 S Nichols St 46356 219-696-9876
Colleen Kennedy, prin. Fax 696-2524

Lynn, Randolph, Pop. 1,095
Randolph Southern SC 600/K-12
1 Rebel Dr 47355 765-874-1181
Michael Necessary, supt. Fax 874-1298
www.rssc.k12.in.us
Randolph Southern ES 300/K-6
3 Rebel Dr 47355 765-874-1141
Donnie Bowsman, prin. Fax 874-1298

Lynnville, Warrick, Pop. 819
Warrick County SC
Supt. — See Boonville
Lynnville ES 200/K-6
320 E 4th St 47619 812-922-3828
Gene Raber, prin. Fax 922-5646

Lyons, Greene, Pop. 753
White River Valley SD
Supt. — See Switz City
Lyons ES 200/K-6
8261 W 250 S 47443 812-659-3915
Kurt Lentz, prin. Fax 659-2599

Mc Cordsville, Hancock, Pop. 790
Mt. Vernon Community SC
Supt. — See Fortville
Mc Cordsville ES 300/K-4
7177 N 600 W 46055 317-336-7760
Dan Denbo, prin. Fax 336-7765

Mackey, Gibson, Pop. 142
East Gibson SC
Supt. — See Oakland City
Barton Township ES 100/K-6
PO Box 48 47654 812-795-2292
Peter Humbaugh, prin. Fax 795-2254

Madison, Jefferson, Pop. 12,443
Madison Consolidated SD 3,500/K-12
2421 Wilson Ave 47250 812-273-8511
Dr. Thomas Patterson, supt. Fax 273-8516
www.madison.k12.in.us/
Anderson ES 200/K-5
2325 Cherry Dr 47250 812-273-8528
Jill Deputy, prin. Fax 273-6622
Madison Consolidated JHS 800/6-8
701 8th St 47250 812-265-6756
Karen Sinders, prin. Fax 265-5685
Middleton ES 200/K-5
714 W Main St 47250 812-273-8524
Karla Gauger, prin. Fax 273-8525
Muncie ES 500/K-5
800 Lanier Dr 47250 812-273-8536
Joyce Imel, prin. Fax 273-3805
Rykers Ridge ES 200/K-5
2485 N Rykers Ridge Rd 47250 812-273-8543
James Hough, prin. Fax 273-8544
Other Schools – See Canaan, Deputy, Dupont

Christian Academy at Madison 100/PK-8
477 W Hutchinson Ln 47250 812-273-5000
Anna Gosman, admin. Fax 265-0700
Kent Christian Academy 50/PK-12
8082 W Kent SR 256 47250 812-866-3313
Dr. Danny Gabbard, admin.
Pope John XXIII S 300/PK-6
221 W State St 47250 812-273-3957
Jill Mires, prin. Fax 265-4566

Marengo, Crawford, Pop. 862
Crawford County Community SC 1,800/PK-12
5805 E Administration Rd 47140 812-365-2135
Dr. Mark Eastridge, supt. Fax 365-2783
www.cccs.k12.in.us/
Marengo ES 200/PK-6
177 S 2nd St 47140 812-365-2116
Judy Bueckert, prin. Fax 365-2814
Other Schools – See Eckerty, English, Leavenworth, Milltown

Marion, Grant, Pop. 30,644
Eastbrook Community SC 1,800/K-12
560 S 900 E 46953 765-664-0624
Jerry Harshman, supt. Fax 664-0626
www.eastbrookschools.net/index.php
Eastbrook JHS 300/7-8
560 S 900 E 46953 765-668-7136
Elizabeth Duckwall, prin. Fax 668-7137
Washington ES 100/K-6
3031 E 450 N 46952 765-664-8620
Sheila Weiland, prin. Fax 664-8138
Other Schools – See Matthews, Upland, Van Buren

Marion Community SD 4,600/PK-12
1240 S Adams St 46953 765-662-2546
Fax 651-2043
www.marion.k12.in.us/
Allen ES 400/PK-5
1115 E Bradford St 46952 765-664-7355
Kevin Biddle, prin. Fax 651-2059
Kendall ES 500/K-5
2009 W Kem Rd 46952 765-662-7364
David Khalouf, prin. Fax 651-2093
Lincoln ES 300/K-5
759 S Lenfesty Ave 46953 765-662-3941
Scott Simpson, prin. Fax 651-4677
Marshall MS 700/6-8
720 N Miller Ave 46952 765-664-0507
James Fox, prin. Fax 651-2086
McCulloch MS 600/6-8
3528 S Washington St 46953 765-674-6917
Kelley Bowyer, prin. Fax 674-8943
Riverview ES 400/K-5
513 W Buckingham Dr 46952 765-662-2427
Michelle Lochner, prin. Fax 651-4665
Slocum ES 400/PK-5
2909 S Torrence St 46953 765-664-0589
Yvonne Stokes, prin. Fax 651-2061

Lakeview Christian S 300/PK-12
5318 S Western Ave 46953 765-677-4266
Kenneth Kitchen, admin. Fax 677-4269
St. Paul S 100/PK-5
1009 W Kem Rd 46952 765-662-2883
Jackie Certain, prin. Fax 664-5953

Marshall, Parke, Pop. 365
Turkey Run Community SC 600/PK-12
1497 E State Road 47 47859 765-597-2750
Dr. Thomas Rohr, supt. Fax 597-2755
www.tr.k12.in.us
Turkey Run ES 300/PK-6
1551 E State Road 47 47859 765-597-2760
Aaron Hart, prin. Fax 597-2813

Martinsville, Morgan, Pop. 11,657
Metro SD of Martinsville 5,700/PK-12
460 S Main St 46151 765-342-6641
Ron Furniss, supt. Fax 342-6877
msdadmin.scican.net
Centerton ES 200/K-5
6075 High St 46151 317-831-3410
Debbie Lipps, prin. Fax 831-3439
Central ES 300/K-5
389 E Jackson St 46151 765-342-6611
Peter Jochim, prin. Fax 349-5250
Green Township ES 300/K-5
6275 Maple Grove Rd 46151 765-342-0505
Roger Cazee, prin. Fax 349-7428
Martinsville East MS 700/6-8
1459 E Columbus St 46151 765-342-6675
Eric Bowlen, prin. Fax 349-5236
Martinsville West MS 600/6-8
109 E Garfield Ave 46151 765-342-6628
Suzie Lipps, prin. Fax 349-5232
Poston Road ES 400/K-5
139 E Poston Rd 46151 765-342-8408
Jill Vlcan, prin. Fax 349-5240
Smith ES 300/PK-5
1359 E Columbus St 46151 765-342-8488
Jan Gearhart, prin. Fax 349-5255
South ES 500/K-5
500 E Mahalasville Rd 46151 765-349-1486
Michael Bodine, prin. Fax 349-5247
Other Schools – See Brooklyn, Paragon

Mooresville Consolidated SC
Supt. — See Mooresville
Waverly ES 300/K-6
8525 Waverly Rd 46151 317-831-9218
Warren DuBois, prin. Fax 831-9235

Prince of Peace Lutheran S 100/PK-5
3496 E Morgan St 46151 765-349-8873
Dr. Merlin Petersen, prin. Fax 813-0036
Tabernacle Christian S 200/K-12
2189 Burton Ln 46151 765-342-0501

Matthews, Grant, Pop. 558
Eastbrook Community SC
Supt. — See Marion
Matthews ES 100/K-6
PO Box 7 46957 765-998-2208
Laura Ramsey, prin. Fax 998-0519

Maxwell, Hancock
Greenfield-Central Community SD
Supt. — See Greenfield

Maxwell MS 600/6-8
102 N Main St 46154 317-326-3121
Harold Olin, prin. Fax 326-4711

Mays, Rush
Rush County SD
Supt. — See Rushville
Mays ES 200/K-6
929 E South St 46155 765-645-5035
Nancy Schroeder, prin. Fax 645-5183

Medora, Jackson, Pop. 553
Medora Community SC 300/K-12
PO Box 369 47260 812-966-2210
Dr. John Reed, supt. Fax 966-2217
www.medorahornets.org/
Medora ES 100/K-6
PO Box 369 47260 812-966-2201
Dr. John Reed, prin. Fax 966-2217

Mentone, Kosciusko, Pop. 891
Tippecanoe Valley SC
Supt. — See Akron
Mentone ES 600/K-5
PO Box 457 46539 574-353-7465
Catherine Miller, prin. Fax 353-7454

Merrillville, Lake, Pop. 31,525
Merrillville Community SC 7,100/K-12
6701 Delaware St 46410 219-650-5300
Dr. Anthony Lux, supt. Fax 650-5320
www.mvsc.k12.in.us
Fieler ES 400/K-4
407 W 61st Ave 46410 219-650-5301
Lisa Patrick, prin. Fax 650-5411
Iddings ES 800/K-4
7249 Van Buren St 46410 219-650-5302
Chris Foltz, prin. Fax 650-5422
Merrillville IS 1,100/5-6
1400 W 61st Ave 46410 219-650-5306
Shirley Renner, prin. Fax 650-5463
Miller ES 500/K-4
5901 Waite St 46410 219-650-5303
Kathy Martin, prin. Fax 650-5431
Pierce MS 1,100/7-8
199 E 70th Ave 46410 219-650-5308
Paul McKinney, prin. Fax 650-5483
Salk ES 500/K-4
3001 W 77th Ave 46410 219-650-5304
Kara Bonin, prin. Fax 650-5442
Wood ES 300/K-4
6100 E 73rd Ave 46410 219-650-5305
Mary Hoffman, prin. Fax 650-5451

Aquinas Catholic Community S 100/K-8
801 W 73rd Ave 46410 219-769-2049
W. Bruce Schooler, prin. Fax 769-8543
Laurel Preparatory Academy 100/PK-8
7525 Taft St 46410 219-738-1991
Linda Romo, prin. Fax 794-7293

Michigan City, LaPorte, Pop. 32,205
Michigan City Area SD 6,600/PK-12
408 S Carroll Ave 46360 219-873-2000
Michael Harding, supt. Fax 873-2072
www.mcas.k12.in.us
Barker MS 400/6-8
319 Barker Rd 46360 219-873-2057
Peggy Scope, prin. Fax 873-3099
Coolspring ES 400/K-5
9121 W 300 N 46360 219-873-2073
Lisa Suter, prin. Fax 873-2074
Eastport Early Learning Center 300/PK-PK
1201 E Michigan Blvd 46360 219-873-2149
Kent Davis, prin. Fax 873-2134
Edgewood ES 400/K-5
502 Boyd Cir 46360 219-873-2079
Gloria Dombkowski, prin. Fax 873-2019
Elston MS 700/6-8
317 Detroit St 46360 219-873-2035
Kelly Fargo, prin. Fax 873-2157
Joy ES 400/PK-5
1600 E Coolspring Ave 46360 219-873-2090
Karen Williams, prin. Fax 873-2170
Knapp ES 400/K-5
321 Bolka Ave 46360 219-873-2096
Toni Mitchell, prin. Fax 873-2097
Krueger MS 400/6-8
2001 Springland Ave 46360 219-873-2061
Martha Birkholtz, prin. Fax 873-2063
Lake Hills ES PK-5
201 Ferguson Rd 46360 219-873-2105
Connie Bachmann, prin. Fax 873-2106
Marsh ES 300/K-5
401 E Homer St 46360 219-873-2102
Kim Palmer, prin. Fax 873-2103
Niemann ES 300/PK-5
811 Royal Rd 46360 219-873-2108
Marsha Tappan, prin. Fax 873-2183
Pine ES 300/PK-5
1594 N 500 E 46360 219-873-2114
Sally Roberts, prin. Fax 873-2115
Springfield ES 400/K-5
3054 W 800 N 46360 219-873-2117
Lisa Emshwiller, prin. Fax 362-4631

Notre Dame S 200/PK-8
1000 Moore Rd 46360 219-872-6216
Karen Breen, prin. Fax 872-6216
Queen of All Saints S 400/PK-8
1715 E Barker Ave 46360 219-872-4420
Anita Peters, prin. Fax 872-1943
St. Paul Lutheran S 200/K-8
818 Franklin St 46360 219-874-7409
R. Allen Boone, prin. Fax 874-6462
St. Stanislaus Kostka S 100/PK-8
1506 Washington St 46360 219-872-2258
Susan Bryant Ph.D., prin. Fax 872-2295

Michigantown, Clinton, Pop. 407
Clinton Central SC 1,100/K-12
PO Box 118 46057 765-249-2515
Philip Boley, supt. Fax 249-2504
www.clinton.k12.in.us/
Clinton Central ES 600/K-6
PO Box 238 46057 765-249-2244
John Sloggett, prin. Fax 249-2504

Middlebury, Elkhart, Pop. 3,150
Middlebury Community SD 3,500/K-12
56853 Northridge Dr 46540 574-825-9425
Jim Conner, supt. Fax 825-9426
www.mcsin-k12.org/
Heritage IS 4-5
56647 Northridge Dr 46540 574-822-5396
Chad Stamm, prin. Fax 825-2038
Middlebury ES 300/K-3
432 S Main St 46540 574-825-2158
Jeremy Miller, prin. Fax 825-7959
Northridge MS 1,000/6-8
56691 Northridge Dr 46540 574-825-9531
Robby Goodman, prin. Fax 825-9154
Orchard View ES 300/K-3
56734 Northridge Dr 46540 574-825-5405
Brian Sloan, prin. Fax 825-5479
Other Schools – See Bristol, Goshen

Middletown, Henry, Pop. 2,384
Shenandoah SC 1,400/K-12
5100 N Raider Rd 47356 765-354-2266
Ronald Green, supt. Fax 354-2274
www.shenandoah.k12.in.us/
Shenandoah ES 600/K-5
5256 N Raider Rd 47356 765-354-6636
Linda McGalliard, prin. Fax 354-3130
Shenandoah MS 300/6-8
5156 N Raider Rd 47356 765-354-6638
Greg Allen, prin. Fax 354-3120

Milan, Ripley, Pop. 1,806
Milan Community SC 1,300/K-12
412 E Carr St 47031 812-654-2365
O. Eugene Pitts, supt. Fax 654-2441
www.milan.k12.in.us
Milan ES 500/K-4
418 E Carr St 47031 812-654-2922
Jane Rogers, prin. Fax 654-2796
Milan MS 400/5-8
609 N Warpath Dr 47031 812-654-1616
J. Martin Layden, prin. Fax 654-2368

Milford, Kosciusko, Pop. 1,667
Wawasee Community SC
Supt. — See Syracuse
Milford S 600/K-8
PO Box 548 46542 574-658-9444
Cynthia Kaiser, prin. Fax 658-3429

Millersburg, Elkhart, Pop. 909
Fairfield Community SD
Supt. — See Goshen
Millersburg ES 400/K-6
PO Box 238 46543 574-642-3074
Christine Ralston, prin. Fax 642-3918

Milltown, Crawford, Pop. 931
Crawford County Community SC
Supt. — See Marengo
Milltown ES 200/K-6
518 Speed Rd 47145 812-633-4335
Tami Geltmaker, prin. Fax 633-4336

Milroy, Rush
Rush County SD
Supt. — See Rushville
Milroy ES 300/K-6
215 N Pleasant St 46156 765-629-2323
Sue Lebo, prin. Fax 629-2250

Mishawaka, Saint Joseph, Pop. 48,497
Mishawaka CSD 5,400/K-12
1402 S Main St 46544 574-254-4500
R. Steven Mills, supt. Fax 254-4585
www.mishawaka.k12.in.us
Battell ES 300/K-6
715 E Broadway St 46545 574-254-3900
John Hess, prin. Fax 254-3982
Beiger ES 400/K-6
1600 E 3rd St 46544 574-254-4700
Steven VanBruaene, prin. Fax 254-4781
Emmons ES 400/K-6
1306 S Main St 46544 574-254-4600
Jeffrey Sherrill, prin. Fax 254-4680
Hums ES 400/K-6
3208 Harrison Rd 46544 574-254-3800
Judith Welling, prin. Fax 254-3882
LaSalle ES 500/K-6
1511 Milburn Blvd 46544 574-254-4800
Rhonda Myers, prin. Fax 254-4882
Liberty ES 400/K-6
600 Pregel Dr 46545 574-254-3700
Dean Fecher, prin. Fax 258-3089
Twin Branch Model S 300/K-6
3810 Lincoln Way E 46544 574-254-3500
Mickey Roelandts, prin. Fax 254-3582
Young MS 800/7-8
1801 N Main St 46545 574-254-3600
Dave Troyer, prin. Fax 258-3021

Penn-Harris-Madison SC 10,600/K-12
55900 Bittersweet Rd 46545 574-259-7941
Dr. Jerry Thacker, supt. Fax 258-9547
www.phm.k12.in.us
Bittersweet ES 400/K-5
55860 Bittersweet Rd 46545 574-259-6341
Cathy Stone, prin. Fax 254-2866
Disney ES 500/K-5
4015 Filbert Rd 46545 574-259-2486
Diane Wirth, prin. Fax 257-8468
Elm Road ES 500/K-5
59400 Elm Rd 46544 574-259-3743
Lynn Johnson, prin. Fax 254-9384
Grissom MS 600/6-8
13881 Kern Rd 46544 574-633-4061
Tammy Matz, prin. Fax 633-2134
Meadows Edge ES 400/K-5
16333 Kern Rd 46544 574-255-9347
Becky Bartlett, prin. Fax 968-6005
Rogers ES 300/K-5
56219 Currant Rd 46545 574-259-5231
Janet Birch, prin. Fax 254-9087
Schmucker MS 1,100/6-8
56045 Bittersweet Rd 46545 574-259-5661
Janet Scott, prin. Fax 259-0807
Other Schools – See Granger, Osceola, Wakarusa

Covenant Christian S 100/PK-8
54790 Fir Rd 46545 574-255-5972
Barb Hesselink, prin. Fax 255-5196
First Baptist Christian S 100/PK-12
724 N Main St 46545 574-255-3242
Douglas Culp, prin. Fax 258-0397
Montessori Academy at Edison Lakes 200/PK-8
530 E Day Rd 46545 574-256-5313
Mary MacIntosh, prin. Fax 256-5493
Queen of Peace S 200/PK-3
4508 Vistula Rd 46544 574-255-0392
Chad Berndt, prin. Fax 255-1029
St. Bavo S 200/PK-8
524 W 8th St 46544 574-259-4214
Linda Hixon, prin. Fax 258-0403
St. Joseph S 200/K-8
230 S Spring St 46544 574-255-5554
Mary Giest, prin. Fax 255-6381
St. Monica S 200/K-8
223 W Grove St 46545 574-255-0709
Sr. Pat Gavin, prin. Fax 255-0311
South Bend Hebrew S 100/PK-8
206 W 8th St 46544 574-255-3351
Rabbi Reuven Pelberg, prin. Fax 255-7553

Mitchell, Lawrence, Pop. 4,626
Mitchell Community SD 2,100/PK-12
441 N 8th St 47446 812-849-4481
John Lantis, supt. Fax 849-2133
www.mitchell.k12.in.us
Burris ES 500/3-5
1755 Hancock Ave 47446 812-849-2509
Steve Dorsett, prin. Fax 849-5638
Hatfield ES 500/PK-2
1081 Teke Burton Dr 47446 812-849-3834
Rex Meyer, prin. Fax 849-5722
Mitchell JHS 500/6-8
1010 W Bishop Blvd 47446 812-849-3747
Troy Pritchett, prin. Fax 849-5841

Modoc, Randolph, Pop. 216
Union SC 500/K-12
8707 W US Highway 36 47358 765-853-5464
Philip Wray, supt. Fax 853-5070
www.usc.k12.in.us
Union ES 300/K-6
8707 W US Highway 36 47358 765-853-5481
Shane Bryant, prin. Fax 853-5070

Monon, White, Pop. 1,654
North White SC 1,000/K-12
121 W State Road 16 47959 219-253-6618
Steven Wittenauer, supt. Fax 253-6488
www.nwhite.k12.in.us/
Monon ES 200/K-5
167 W State Road 16 47959 219-253-6663
Theresa Diener, prin. Fax 253-8178
North White MS 300/6-8
310 E Broadway St 47959 219-253-7701
Curt Craig, prin. Fax 253-8462
Other Schools – See Buffalo, Reynolds

Monroe, Adams, Pop. 778
Adams Central Community SD 1,200/K-12
222 W Washington St 46772 260-692-6193
Michael Pettibone, supt. Fax 692-6198
www.accs.k12.in.us/
Adams Central ES 500/K-5
222 W Washington St 46772 260-692-6629
Terri Laurent, prin. Fax 692-6198
Adams Central MS 300/6-8
222 W Washington St 46772 260-692-6151
Aaron McClure, prin. Fax 692-6192

Monroeville, Allen, Pop. 1,277
East Allen County SD
Supt. — See New Haven
Monroeville ES 200/K-6
401 Monroe St 46773 260-446-0200
Karen Charters, prin. Fax 446-0203

St. John Emmanuel Lutheran S 100/PK-8
12912 Franke Rd 46773 260-639-0123
Fax 639-7383
St. Joseph S 50/K-8
209 Mulberry St 46773 260-623-3447
Carolyn Kirkendall, prin. Fax 623-3447

Monrovia, Morgan, Pop. 624
Monroe-Gregg SD 1,400/PK-12
135 S Chestnut St 46157 317-996-3720
Dr. Julie Wood, supt. Fax 996-2977
www.scican.net/mgsd
Monrovia ES 600/PK-5
135 S Chestnut St 46157 317-996-2246
Chris Sampson, prin. Fax 996-4199
Monrovia MS 300/6-8
135 S Chestnut St 46157 317-996-2352
Bobbie Jo Monahan, prin. Fax 996-3429

Monterey, Pulaski, Pop. 226
Culver Community SC
Supt. — See Culver
Monterey ES 100/K-6
5973 E 700 N 46960 574-542-2601
Julie Berndt, prin. Fax 542-2601

Montezuma, Parke, Pop. 1,151
Southwest Parke Community SC 1,000/K-12
4851 S Coxville Rd 47862 765-569-2073
Leonard Orr, supt. Fax 569-0309
www.swparke.k12.in.us
Montezuma ES 200/K-6
PO Box 400 47862 765-245-2303
Jami Britton, prin. Fax 245-2354
Other Schools – See Rosedale

Montgomery, Daviess, Pop. 381
Barr-Reeve Community SD 700/K-12
PO Box 97 47558 812-486-3220
Brian Harmon, supt. Fax 486-3509
www.barr.k12.in.us/
Barr-Reeve IS 300/2-6
PO Box 129 47558 812-486-3224
Linda Parsons, prin. Fax 486-3224
Barr-Reeve PS 100/K-1
PO Box 127 47558 812-486-3235
Linda Parsons, prin. Fax 486-3216

Monticello, White, Pop. 5,462
Twin Lakes SC 2,600/PK-12
565 S Main St 47960 574-583-7211
Dr. Thomas Fletcher, supt. Fax 583-8963
www.twinlakes.k12.in.us/
Meadowlawn ES 400/K-5
715 W Ohio St 47960 574-583-7720
Margaret Xioufaridou, prin. Fax 583-7791
Oaklawn ES 300/K-5
402 E South St 47960 574-583-5651
Jennifer Lingenfelter, prin. Fax 583-5360
Roosevelt MS 600/6-8
721 W Broadway St 47960 574-583-5552
Scott Clifford, prin. Fax 583-3675
Woodlawn ES 200/K-5
300 S Beach Dr 47960 574-583-7005
Gloria Kinnard, prin. Fax 583-6475
Other Schools – See Burnettsville

Montpelier, Blackford, Pop. 1,857
Blackford County SD
Supt. — See Hartford City
Montpelier S 500/K-8
107 E Monroe St 47359 765-728-2402
Ross Elwood, prin. Fax 728-2403

Moores Hill, Dearborn, Pop. 652
South Dearborn Community SC
Supt. — See Aurora
Moores Hill ES 300/K-6
14733 Main St 47032 812-744-3184
Beverly Moore, prin. Fax 744-5660

Mooresville, Morgan, Pop. 11,111
Mooresville Consolidated SC 4,500/PK-12
11 W Carlisle St 46158 317-831-0950
Curtis Freeman, supt. Fax 831-9202
www.mcsc.k12.in.us
Armstrong ES 600/K-6
1000 State Road 144 46158 317-831-9210
L. Paul Spencer, prin. Fax 831-9230
Hadley MS 700/7-8
200 W Carlisle St 46158 317-831-9208
Larry Goldsberry, prin. Fax 831-9249
Newby Memorial ES 300/PK-6
240 N Monroe St 46158 317-831-9212
Mitchell Fortune, prin. Fax 831-9234
Northwood ES 500/K-6
630 N Indiana St 46158 317-831-9216
Holly Cooney, prin. Fax 831-9233
Other Schools – See Camby, Martinsville

Mooresville Christian Academy 300/PK-8
4271 E State Road 144 46158 317-831-0799
Michael Osborn, prin. Fax 831-5364

Morgantown, Brown, Pop. 966
Brown County SC
Supt. — See Nashville
Helmsburg ES 300/K-6
5378 Helmsburg School Rd 46160 812-988-6651
Kelli Bruner, prin. Fax 988-0852

Morocco, Newton, Pop. 1,159
North Newton SC 1,600/K-12
PO Box 8 47963 219-285-2228
Brian Smith, supt. Fax 285-2708
www.nn.k12.in.us/
Morocco ES 200/K-6
PO Box 50 47963 219-285-2258
Karen Spencer, prin. Fax 285-6429
Other Schools – See Demotte, Lake Village

Morristown, Shelby, Pop. 1,218
Shelby Eastern SD
Supt. — See Shelbyville
Morristown ES 300/K-5
PO Box 910 46161 765-763-6648
Stephanie Miller, prin. Fax 763-6969

Mount Summit, Henry, Pop. 297
Blue River Valley SD 800/PK-12
PO Box 217 47361 765-836-4816
Stephen Welsh, supt. Fax 836-4817
www.brv.k12.in.us
Other Schools – See New Castle

Mount Vernon, Posey, Pop. 7,238
Metro SD of Mt. Vernon 2,500/PK-12
1000 W 4th St 47620 812-838-4471
Dr. Keith Spurgeon, supt. Fax 833-2078
www.msdmv.k12.in.us
Farmersville ES 200/K-5
4065 Highway 69 S 47620 812-838-6593
Gary Wilsey, prin. Fax 838-4826
Hedges Central ES 300/PK-5
716 Locust St 47620 812-833-2069
Paul Swanson, prin. Fax 833-2071
Marrs ES 300/K-5
9201 Highway 62 E 47620 812-985-2082
Gregory DeWeese, prin. Fax 985-9453
Mount Vernon JHS 600/6-8
701 Tile Factory Rd 47620 812-833-2077
Jerry Funkhouser, prin. Fax 833-2083
West ES 300/K-5
1105 W 4th St 47620 812-833-2072
Jody Pfister, prin. Fax 833-2095

St. Matthew S 100/PK-5
401 Mulberry St 47620 812-838-3621
Vickie Wannemuehler, prin. Fax 838-6971
St. Philip S 200/PK-8
3420 Saint Phillips Rd S 47620 812-985-2447
Andrea Lodato, prin. Fax 985-2457

Muncie, Delaware, Pop. 66,164
Cowan Community SC 700/K-12
1000 W County Road 600 S 47302 765-289-4866
Larry John, supt. Fax 284-0315
www.cowan.k12.in.us
Cowan ES 400/K-6
1000 W County Road 600 S 47302 765-289-7129
Michael Garringer, prin. Fax 741-5958

Delaware Community SC 2,800/K-12
7821 N State Road 3 47303 765-284-5074
Patrick Mapes, supt. Fax 284-5259
www.delcomschools.org
Delta MS 700/6-8
9800 N County Road 200 E 47303 765-747-0869
Don Harman, prin. Fax 213-2131
Desoto ES 200/K-5
8400 E County Road 400 N 47303 765-289-3544
Joe Schmaltz, prin. Fax 213-2146
Royerton ES 500/K-5
1401 E Royerton Rd 47303 765-282-2044
Doug Marshall, prin. Fax 288-3584
Other Schools – See Albany, Eaton

Muncie Community SD 7,500/K-12
2501 N Oakwood Ave 47304 765-747-5205
Dr. Eric King, supt. Fax 747-5341
www.muncie.k12.in.us
Garfield ES 300/K-5
1600 S Madison St 47302 765-747-5398
Shawn Davis, prin. Fax 747-5405
Grissom Memorial ES 500/K-5
3201 S Macedonia Ave 47302 765-747-5401
Pam Necessary, prin. Fax 747-5403
Longfellow ES 300/K-5
1900 E Centennial Ave 47303 765-747-5410
Derrick Jamerson, prin. Fax 751-0661
Mitchell ES 200/K-5
2809 W Purdue Ave 47304 765-747-5413
Cynthia Iavagnilio, prin. Fax 747-5414
Northside MS 800/6-8
2400 W Bethel Ave 47304 765-747-5290
Todd Terrill, prin. Fax 751-0616
North View ES 300/K-5
807 W Yale Ave 47304 765-747-5422
Scott Blakely, prin. Fax 751-0615
South View ES 500/K-5
2100 S Franklin St 47302 765-747-5226
Bill Hall, prin. Fax 751-0671
Storer ES 400/K-5
3211 W Mansfield Dr 47304 765-747-5360
Ingrid Grubb, prin. Fax 747-5363
Sutton ES 500/K-5
3100 E Memorial Dr 47302 765-747-5431
Dea Moore-Young, prin. Fax 747-5404
Washington-Carver Community ES 300/K-5
1000 E Washington St 47305 765-747-5434
Fax 281-6740
West View ES 300/K-5
3401 W Gilbert St 47304 765-747-5437
Kathy Ray, prin. Fax 747-5406
Wilson MS 800/6-8
3100 S Tillotson Ave 47302 765-747-5370
Gary Brown, prin. Fax 751-0666

University Schools 800/K-12
2000 W University Ave 47306 765-285-8488
Fax 285-2166
www.bsu.edu
Burris Laboratory S 500/K-12
2201 W University Ave 47306 765-285-1131
Fax 285-8620

Heritage Hall Christian S 300/PK-12
6401 W River Rd 47304 765-289-6371
Dennis Ice, prin. Fax 288-9584
St. Lawrence S 100/PK-8
2801 E 16th St 47302 765-282-9353
Lynn Ranieri, prin. Fax 282-0475
St. Mary S 200/PK-8
2301 W Gilbert St 47303 765-288-5878
Fax 284-3685

Munster, Lake, Pop. 22,347
Town of Munster SD 4,200/K-12
8616 Columbia Ave 46321 219-836-9111
William Pfister, supt. Fax 836-3215
www.munster.k12.in.us
Eads ES 500/K-5
8001 Harrison Ave 46321 219-836-8635
Linda Bevil, prin. Fax 836-3217
Elliott ES 400/K-5
8718 White Oak Ave 46321 219-838-5250
Nicole Guernsey, prin. Fax 838-7867
Hammond ES 700/K-5
1301 Fran Lin Pkwy 46321 219-838-2060
Nancy Ellis, prin. Fax 838-7964
Wright MS 1,000/6-8
8650 Columbia Ave 46321 219-836-6260
David Knish, prin. Fax 836-0501

St. Paul's Lutheran S 300/PK-8
8601 Harrison Ave 46321 219-836-6270
Martin Zimmer, prin. Fax 836-3724
St. Thomas More S 600/PK-8
8435 Calumet Ave 46321 219-836-9151
Chet Nordyke, prin. Fax 836-0982

Nappanee, Elkhart, Pop. 6,955
Wa-Nee Community SD 3,300/K-12
1300 N Main St 46550 574-773-3131
Joe Sabo, supt. Fax 773-5593
www.wanee.org
Nappannee ES 500/K-5
755 E Van Buren St 46550 574-773-7421
Randy Cripe, prin. Fax 773-2199
Woodview ES 500/K-5
800 E Woodview Dr 46550 574-773-3117
Alan Thompson, prin. Fax 773-3011
Other Schools – See Wakarusa

United Christian S 100/1-12
29522 County Road 52 46550 574-773-7505
Terrill Yoder, admin. Fax 773-7513

Nashville, Brown, Pop. 804
Brown County SC 2,300/PK-12
PO Box 38 47448 812-988-6601
David Shaffer, supt. Fax 988-5403
www.brownco.k12.in.us
Brown County JHS 400/7-8
PO Box 578 47448 812-988-6605
Michael Roane, prin. Fax 988-5415
Nashville ES 300/PK-6
PO Box 157 47448 812-988-6607
Shane Killinger, prin. Fax 988-5417
Van Buren ES 300/K-6
4045 State Road 135 S 47448 812-988-6658
Lucy McGrayel, prin. Fax 988-5418
Other Schools – See Morgantown, Nineveh

New Albany, Floyd, Pop. 36,772
New Albany-Floyd County Consolidated SD 11,900/PK-12
PO Box 1087 47151 812-949-4200
Dr. Bruce Hibbard, supt. Fax 949-6900
www.nafcs.k12.in.us
Children's Academy of New Albany 300/PK-3
1111 Pearl St 47150 812-949-4295
Terri Boutin, prin. Fax 949-6958
Fairmont ES 300/K-5
1725 Abbeydell Ave 47150 812-949-4286
Susanne Gahan, prin. Fax 949-6924
Grant Line ES 600/K-5
4811 Grant Line Rd 47150 812-949-4290
Leland Lang, prin. Fax 949-4261
Green Valley ES 400/K-5
2230 Green Valley Rd 47150 812-949-4292
Rebecka Banet, prin. Fax 949-6947
Hazelwood JHS 800/6-8
1021 Hazelwood Ave 47150 812-949-4280
Terry Weilbaker, prin. Fax 949-6962
Jones ES 200/K-5
600 E 11th St 47150 812-949-4306
Susie Reis, prin. Fax 949-6954
Mt. Tabor ES 600/PK-5
800 Mount Tabor Rd 47150 812-949-4301
Tony Duffy, prin. Fax 949-6993
Pine View ES 400/K-5
2524 Corydon Pike 47150 812-949-4304
Kyle Lanoue, prin. Fax 949-6917
Scribner JHS 800/6-8
910 Old Vincennes Rd 47150 812-949-4283
Rhonda Mull, prin. Fax 949-6974
Silver Street ES 300/K-5
2023 Ekin Ave 47150 812-949-4309
Theresa Duke, prin. Fax 949-6944
Slate Run ES 300/PK-5
1452 Slate Run Rd 47150 812-949-4311
Sharon Jones, prin. Fax 949-6963
Other Schools – See Floyds Knobs, Georgetown, Greenville

Christian Academy of Indiana 800/PK-12
1000 Academy Dr 47150 812-944-6200
Timothy Greener, supt. Fax 944-6903
Grace Lutheran S 100/PK-K
1787 Klerner Ln 47150 812-941-1912
Georgianne Weathers, prin. Fax 941-9884
Holy Family S 400/PK-8
217 W Daisy Ln 47150 812-944-6090
Gerald Ernstberger, prin. Fax 944-7299
Our Lady of Perpetual Help S 400/PK-8
1752 Scheller Ln 47150 812-944-7676
Terry Horton, prin. Fax 948-2944
St. Mary S 200/PK-8
420 E 8th St 47150 812-944-0888
Kim Hartlage, prin. Fax 945-4770

Newburgh, Warrick, Pop. 3,298
Warrick County SC
Supt. — See Boonville
Castle ES 800/K-5
3077 Highway 261 47630 812-853-8878
Debbie Scales, prin. Fax 853-6061
Castle North MS 900/6-8
2800 State Route 261 47630 812-853-7347
John Bertram, prin. Fax 858-1089
Castle South MS 6-8
3711 Casey Rd 47630 812-490-7930
Walter Lambert, prin.

Newburgh ES 500/K-5
306 State St 47630 812-853-8921
Kurt Krodel, prin. Fax 853-6866
Sharon ES 700/K-5
7300 Sharon Rd 47630 812-853-3349
Ashlee Bruggenschmidt, prin. Fax 853-6955
Yankeetown ES 300/K-5
7422 Yankeetown Rd 47630 812-853-8500
Jamie Pryor, prin. Fax 858-1296

Newburgh Christian S 100/PK-12
PO Box 644 47629 812-842-0455
Sharon Dunsworth, admin. Fax 853-3511
St. John the Baptist S 500/PK-8
725 Frame Rd 47630 812-853-8511
Charlotte Bennett, prin. Fax 853-8006

New Carlisle, Saint Joseph, Pop. 1,629
New Prairie United SC 2,600/K-12
5327 N Cougar Rd 46552 574-654-7273
Philip Bender, supt. Fax 654-7274
www.npusc.k12.in.us
New Prairie MS 500/6-8
5325 N Cougar Rd 46552 574-654-3070
Jim Holifield, prin. Fax 654-7009
Olive Township ES 400/K-5
300 W Ben St 46552 574-654-7531
Sherry Bailey, prin. Fax 654-7964
Other Schools – See Rolling Prairie

New Castle, Henry, Pop. 18,718
Blue River Valley SD
Supt. — See Mount Summit
Blue River Valley ES 400/PK-6
4713 N Hillsboro Rd 47362 765-836-4851
Kevin Lester, prin. Fax 836-3258

New Castle Community SC 3,900/PK-12
322 Elliott Ave 47362 765-521-7201
Dr. John Newby, supt. Fax 521-7268
www.nccsc.k12.in.us
Eastwood ES 300/K-6
806 S 22nd St 47362 765-521-7205
Chris Tillett, prin. Fax 593-6643
Greenstreet ES 200/PK-6
329 S 5th St 47362 765-521-7207
Deborah Hartzler, prin. Fax 593-6644
New Castle MS 600/7-8
601 Parkview Dr 47362 765-521-7230
Jaci Hadsell, prin. Fax 521-7269
Parker ES 400/K-6
1819 Roosevelt Ave 47362 765-521-7209
Robert Malloy, prin. Fax 593-6645
Riley ES 400/K-6
1201 Riley Rd 47362 765-521-7211
Richard Bouslog, prin. Fax 593-6646
Sunnyside ES 200/K-6
2601 S 14th St 47362 765-521-7213
Linda Kinnett, prin. Fax 593-6647
Westwood ES 300/K-6
1015 S Greensboro Pike 47362 765-521-7215
E. Carter, prin. Fax 593-6648
Wright ES 300/K-6
1950 Washington St 47362 765-521-7217
Tony Personett, prin. Fax 593-6649

New Harmony, Posey, Pop. 885
New Harmony Town & Twp Cons SD 200/PK-12
1000 East St 47631 812-682-4401
Fran Thoele, supt. Fax 682-3659
www.harmoniehundred.net/index.html
New Harmony S 200/PK-12
1000 East St 47631 812-682-4401
Douglas Mills, prin. Fax 682-3659

New Haven, Allen, Pop. 13,676
East Allen County SD 10,200/PK-12
1240 State Road 930 E 46774 260-446-0100
Karyle Green, supt. Fax 446-0107
www.eacs.k12.in.us
Highland Terrace ES 500/K-5
1445 Berwick Ln 46774 260-446-0150
Teresa Knoblauch, prin. Fax 446-0153
Meadowbrook ES 300/PK-5
1065 Woodmere Dr 46774 260-446-0190
Matt Widenhoefer, prin. Fax 446-0193
New Haven ES 400/K-5
800 Homestead Dr 46774 260-446-0210
William Hoppus, prin. Fax 446-0213
New Haven MS 600/6-8
900 Prospect Ave 46774 260-446-0230
Pete Downey, prin. Fax 446-0236
Other Schools – See Fort Wayne, Harlan, Hoagland, Leo, Monroeville, Woodburn

---

Central Lutheran S 300/K-8
1400 Elm St 46774 260-493-2502
Greg Rehberg, prin. Fax 493-2503
St. John the Baptist S 300/PK-8
204 S Rufus St 46774 260-749-9903
Jan Comito, prin. Fax 749-6047
St. Louis S 100/PK-8
15529 Lincoln Hwy E 46774 260-749-5815
Cheryl Layton, prin. Fax 749-5815
Three Rivers Montessori S 100/PK-3
2315 Long Rd 46774 260-493-3114
Vyju Kadambi, dir. Fax 493-9089

New Market, Montgomery, Pop. 654
South Montgomery Community SC 2,000/K-12
PO Box 8 47965 765-866-0203
Dr. J. Bret Lewis, supt. Fax 866-0736
www.southmont.k12.in.us
New Market ES 500/K-6
PO Box 128 47965 765-866-0740
Cathy Rowe, prin. Fax 866-2031
Other Schools – See Crawfordsville, Ladoga, New Ross, Waveland

New Middletown, Harrison, Pop. 79
South Harrison Community SD
Supt. — See Corydon
New Middletown ES 100/K-6
2460 New Middletown Rd SE 47160 812-968-3225
Sharon Mathes, prin. Fax 968-3017

New Palestine, Hancock, Pop. 1,826
Southern Hancock County Community SC 3,400/PK-12
PO Box 508 46163 317-861-4463
James Halik, supt. Fax 861-2142
shancock.newpal.k12.in.us/
Doe Creek MS 800/6-8
PO Box 478 46163 317-861-4487
James Voelz, prin. Fax 861-2136
New Palestine ES 500/K-5
PO Box 538 46163 317-861-5287
Mark Kern, prin. Fax 861-2146
Sugar Creek ES 700/PK-5
PO Box 558 46163 317-861-6747
Tony Strangeway, prin. Fax 861-8656
Other Schools – See Greenfield

Zion Lutheran S 200/PK-8
6513 W 300 S 46163 317-861-4210
Mark Boerger, prin. Fax 861-8153

New Paris, Elkhart, Pop. 1,007
Fairfield Community SD
Supt. — See Goshen
New Paris ES 300/K-6
18665 County Road 46 46553 574-831-2196
Lisa Litwiller, prin. Fax 831-3160

New Ross, Montgomery, Pop. 331
South Montgomery Community SC
Supt. — See New Market
Walnut ES 200/K-6
3548 S 775 E 47968 765-362-0542
Richard Carty, prin. Fax 362-0545

New Washington, Clark
Greater Clark County SD
Supt. — See Jeffersonville
New Washington ES 400/K-5
PO Box 130 47162 812-293-3331
Elizabeth Bennett, prin. Fax 293-5808

New Whiteland, Johnson, Pop. 4,431
Clark-Pleasant Community SC
Supt. — See Whiteland
Break-O-Day ES 500/2-4
900 Sawmill Rd 46184 317-535-7536
Cindy Conner, prin. Fax 535-0817
Sawmill Woods ES 500/K-1
700 Sawmill Rd 46184 317-535-2069
Jenni Baker, prin. Fax 535-5530

Nineveh, Brown
Brown County SC
Supt. — See Nashville
Sprunica ES 300/K-6
3611 Sprunica Rd 46164 812-988-6625
Abbie Nichols, prin. Fax 988-0940

Noblesville, Hamilton, Pop. 38,825
Hamilton Southeastern SD
Supt. — See Fishers
Durbin ES 400/K-4
18000 Durbin Rd 46060 765-534-3188
Kelly Treinen, prin. Fax 534-4238

Noblesville SD 8,300/PK-12
1775 Field Dr 46060 317-773-3171
Libbie Conner, supt. Fax 773-7845
www.noblesvilleschools.org
Dell ES 800/PK-4
3025 Westfield Rd, 317-867-0021
John Land, prin. Fax 867-4032
Forest Hill ES 500/PK-4
470 Lakeview Dr 46060 317-773-3586
Jack Lawrence, prin. Fax 776-6272
Hinkle Creek ES 600/K-4
595 S Harbour Dr, 317-776-0840
Phillip Harrold, prin. Fax 776-6267
Noble Crossing ES PK-4
5670 Noble Crossing Pkwy E, 317-817-0808
Pat Haney, prin. Fax 817-0810
Noblesville IS 1,300/5-6
19900 Hague Rd, 317-776-7792
Jeff Bragg, prin. Fax 776-7797
Noblesville MS 1,200/7-8
300 N 17th St 46060 317-773-0782
Kyle Barrentine, prin. Fax 776-6261
North ES 400/PK-4
440 N 10th St 46060 317-773-0482
Vince Barnes, prin. Fax 776-6274
Stony Creek ES 600/PK-4
1350 Greenfield Ave 46060 317-773-0582
Heidi Karst, prin. Fax 776-6270
White River ES 700/PK-4
19000 Cumberland Rd 46060 317-770-2080
Robert Harvey, prin. Fax 770-2081

Noblesville Christian S 300/PK-8
1687 N 10th St 46060 317-776-4186
Rolland Abraham, hdmstr. Fax 776-0356
Our Lady of Grace S 400/PK-8
9900 E 191st St 46060 317-770-5660
Maureen Clerkin, prin. Fax 770-5663

North Judson, Starke, Pop. 1,867
North Judson-San Pierre SC 1,300/K-12
801 Campbell Dr 46366 574-896-2155
Iran Floyd, supt. Fax 896-2156
njsp.schoolwires.com/
Liberty ES 500/1-5
809 W Talmer Ave 46366 574-896-2128
Michael McBride, prin. Fax 896-2129
North Judson JHS 400/6-8
950 Campbell Dr 46366 574-896-2167
Annette Zupin, prin. Fax 896-3036
Other Schools – See San Pierre

St. Peter Lutheran S 100/PK-8
810 W Talmer Ave 46366 574-896-5933
Rhonda Reimers, prin. Fax 896-2082

North Liberty, Saint Joseph, Pop. 1,362
John Glenn SC
Supt. — See Walkerton
North Liberty ES 500/K-6
400 School Dr 46554 574-656-8123
Robert Lichtenberger, prin. Fax 656-8345

North Liberty Christian S 50/K-5
65225 State Road 23 46554 574-656-8488
Stephanie Reynolds, admin. Fax 656-3374

North Manchester, Wabash, Pop. 5,980
Manchester Community SD 1,500/K-12
107 S Buffalo St 46962 260-982-7518
Dr. Diana Showalter, supt. Fax 982-4583
www.mcs.k12.in.us
Manchester ES 600/K-4
301 S River Rd 46962 260-982-7541
Bonnie Ingraham, prin. Fax 982-8020
Manchester JHS 200/7-8
404 W 9th St 46962 260-982-8602
Nancy Alspaugh, prin. Fax 982-1162
Other Schools – See Laketon

North Salem, Hendricks, Pop. 636
North West Hendricks SD
Supt. — See Lizton
North Salem ES 200/K-5
PO Box 69 46165 317-994-3000
Brenda Coley, prin. Fax 994-3030

North Vernon, Jennings, Pop. 6,433
Jennings County SC 5,300/K-12
34 W Main St 47265 812-346-4483
Dr. Michael Bushong, supt. Fax 346-4490
www.jcsc.org
Brush Creek ES 300/K-6
4275 E US Highway 50 47265 812-458-6582
Jeanie Koelmel, prin. Fax 458-6357
Early Learning Center 100/K-K
100 S Webster St 47265 812-346-7830
Patricia Robinson, prin. Fax 346-4193
Jennings County MS 900/7-8
820 W Walnut St 47265 812-346-4940
Floyd Bowman, prin. Fax 346-4497
North Vernon ES 800/1-6
810 W Walnut St 47265 812-346-4903
Donna Eaton, prin. Fax 346-4863
Sand Creek ES 500/K-6
1450 W County Road 500 N 47265 812-352-9343
Patricia Ertel, prin. Fax 352-0674
Other Schools – See Commiskey, Hayden, Scipio

St. Mary S 200/K-8
209 Washington St 47265 812-346-3445
Sr. Joanita Koors, prin. Fax 346-5930

North Webster, Kosciusko, Pop. 1,057
Wawasee Community SC
Supt. — See Syracuse
North Webster ES 600/PK-5
5475 N 750 E 46555 574-834-7644
Kristine Woodard, prin. Fax 834-1046

Oakland City, Gibson, Pop. 2,596
East Gibson SC 1,000/PK-12
133 E Morton St 47660 812-749-4755
Dr. Franzy Fleck, supt. Fax 749-3343
www.egsc.k12.in.us
Oakland City ES 300/K-6
945B S Franklin St 47660 812-749-6133
David Chamness, prin. Fax 749-4633
Wood Memorial JHS 200/7-8
945A S Franklin St 47660 812-749-4715
Dr. Mike Brewster, prin. Fax 749-4988
Other Schools – See Francisco, Mackey

Oolitic, Lawrence, Pop. 1,123
North Lawrence Community SD
Supt. — See Bedford
Dollens ES 300/K-5
903 Hoosier Ave 47451 812-275-3885
Daniel Dyke, prin. Fax 277-3219
Oolitic MS 400/6-8
903 Hoosier Ave 47451 812-275-7551
Larry Lafferty, prin. Fax 277-3219

Orleans, Orange, Pop. 2,294
Orleans Community SD 900/K-12
173 Marley St 47452 812-865-2688
James Terrell, supt. Fax 865-3428
www.orleans.k12.in.us/
Orleans ES 500/K-6
637 E Washington St 47452 812-865-2688
Roy Kline, prin. Fax 865-3844

Osceola, Saint Joseph, Pop. 1,811
Penn-Harris-Madison SC
Supt. — See Mishawaka
Moran ES 400/K-5
305 N Beech Rd 46561 574-674-8504
Frank Anglin, prin. Fax 674-4375

Osgood, Ripley, Pop. 1,655
Jac-Cen-Del Community SC 1,000/K-12
723 N Buckeye St 47037 812-689-4114
Bill Narwold, supt. Fax 689-7423
www.jaccendel.k12.in.us/
Jac-Cen-Del ES 500/K-6
4544 N US Highway 421 47037 812-689-4144
Leanna Phillippe, prin. Fax 689-6512

Ossian, Wells, Pop. 2,908
Northern Wells Community SD 2,600/PK-12
PO Box 386 46777 260-622-4125
Dr. Scott Mills, supt. Fax 622-7893
www.nwcs.k12.in.us
Norwell MS 600/6-8
1100 E US Highway 224 46777 260-543-2218
Robert Hansbarger, prin. Fax 543-2510
Ossian ES 600/PK-5
213 S Jefferson St 46777 260-622-4179
Shellie Miller, prin. Fax 622-7161
Other Schools – See Bluffton

Bethlehem Lutheran S 100/K-8
7545 N 650 E 46777 260-597-7366
Dan Buchinger, prin. Fax 597-7366

Otterbein, Benton, Pop. 1,242
Benton Community SC
Supt. — See Fowler
Otterbein ES 300/K-6
PO Box 368 47970 765-583-4401
Gary Schneck, prin. Fax 583-2428

Otwell, Pike
Pike County SC
Supt. — See Petersburg
Otwell ES 200/PK-5
1869 N State Road 257 47564 812-354-2600
Rick Fears, prin. Fax 354-2655

Owensville, Gibson, Pop. 1,339
South Gibson SC
Supt. — See Fort Branch
Owensville Community S 500/K-8
6569 S State Road 65 47665 812-724-3705
Michael Woods, prin. Fax 724-4201

Oxford, Benton, Pop. 1,208
Benton Community SC
Supt. — See Fowler
Prairie Crossing ES K-6
2758 S 400 E 47971 765-884-3000
Jae Ann Brier, prin. Fax 884-3030

Palmyra, Harrison, Pop. 716
North Harrison Community SC
Supt. — See Ramsey
Morgan ES 500/K-5
12225 Highway 135 NE 47164 812-364-6138
Lance Richards, prin. Fax 364-4085

Paoli, Orange, Pop. 3,947
Paoli Community SC 1,600/K-12
501 Elm St 47454 812-723-4717
Dr. Alva Sibbitt, supt. Fax 723-5100
www.paoli.k12.in.us
Throop ES 900/K-6
301 Elm St 47454 812-723-3537
Sharon Tucker, prin. Fax 723-0384

Paragon, Morgan, Pop. 642
Metro SD of Martinsville
Supt. — See Martinsville
Paragon ES 300/K-5
PO Box 27 46166 765-537-2276
Druscilla Voiles, prin. Fax 537-2105

Parker City, Randolph, Pop. 1,359
Monroe Central SC 1,000/K-12
1918 N 1000 W 47368 765-468-6868
Shane Robbins, supt. Fax 468-6578
www.monroec.k12.in.us
Monroe Central ES 500/K-6
10421 W State Rd 32 47368 765-468-7725
Doug Jacobs, prin. Fax 468-8409

Patricksburg, Owen
Spencer-Owen Community SD
Supt. — See Spencer
Patricksburg ES 300/K-6
PO Box 212 47455 812-859-4525
Caleb Petree, prin. Fax 859-4535

Pekin, Washington, Pop. 1,236
East Washington SC 1,700/K-12
1050 N Eastern School Rd 47165 812-967-3926
Dr. Phyllis Amick, supt. Fax 967-3926
www.ewsc.k12.in.us
East Washington ES 700/K-4
1020 N Eastern School Rd 47165 812-967-2929
Deborah Esarey, prin. Fax 967-2929
East Washington MS 500/5-8
1100 N Eastern School Rd 47165 812-967-5000
Linda Luedeman, prin. Fax 967-5000

Pendleton, Madison, Pop. 3,859
South Madison Community SC 3,800/K-12
203 S Heritage Way 46064 765-778-2152
Dr. Thomas Warmke, supt. Fax 778-8207
www.smadison.k12.in.us
East ES 600/K-6
893 E US Highway 36 46064 765-779-4445
Gayle Gernand, prin. Fax 779-4594
Maple Ridge ES 800/K-6
8537 S 650 W 46064 765-778-3818
John Lord, prin. Fax 778-8677
Pendleton Heights MS 600/7-8
7450 S 300 W 46064 765-778-2139
Daniel Joyce, prin. Fax 778-0557
Pendleton IS, 301 S East St 46064 5-6
Arlene Dawson, prin. 765-221-0004
Pendleton PS 500/K-4
327 S East St 46064 765-778-2117
William Hutton, prin. Fax 778-1712

Pennville, Jay, Pop. 740
Jay SC
Supt. — See Portland
Pennville ES 100/K-5
PO Box 245 47369 260-731-2551
Larry Wilson, prin. Fax 731-2541

Pershing, Wayne, Pop. 1,531
Western Wayne SD 1,200/K-12
PO Box 217 47370 765-478-5375
Robert Mahon, supt. Fax 478-4577
www.wwayne.k12.in.us
Other Schools – See Cambridge City

Peru, Miami, Pop. 12,732
Maconaquah SC
Supt. — See Bunker Hill
Pipe Creek ES 200/PK-1
3036 W 400 S 46970 765-473-3121
Laura Fulton, prin. Fax 473-7074

Peru Community SC 2,300/PK-12
35 W 3rd St 46970 765-473-3081
Andrew Melin, supt. Fax 472-5129
www.peru.k12.in.us
Blair Pointe Upper ES 500/4-6
300 Blair Pike 46970 765-473-4741
David Hahn, prin. Fax 472-5155
Elmwood Learning Center 500/1-3
515 N Wayne St 46970 765-473-7335
Ron Mullett, prin. Fax 472-5158
Peru JHS 400/7-8
30 Daniel St 46970 765-473-3084
Sam Watkins, prin. Fax 473-4007
South Peru Learning Center 200/PK-K
19 Park Dr 46970 765-472-2961
Sheryl West, prin. Fax 472-5161

Petersburg, Pike, Pop. 2,501
Pike County SC 2,100/PK-12
907 E Walnut St 47567 812-354-8731
D. Thomas, supt. Fax 354-8733
www.pcsc.k12.in.us
Petersburg ES 500/PK-5
1415 E Alford St 47567 812-354-6876
Rick King, prin. Fax 354-8718
Pike Central MS 500/6-8
1814 E State Road 56 47567 812-354-8478
Phil Ludington, prin. Fax 354-9559
Other Schools – See Otwell, Winslow

Pierceton, Kosciusko, Pop. 686
Whitko Community SC 1,900/K-12
PO Box 114 46562 574-594-2658
Steven Clason, supt. Fax 594-2326
whitko.org
Pierceton ES 500/K-5
PO Box 94 46562 574-594-2210
Barb Ihnen, prin. Fax 594-3523
Other Schools – See Larwill, South Whitley

Pine Village, Warren, Pop. 252
Metro SD of Warren County
Supt. — See Williamsport
Pine Village ES 100/K-6
3756 E State Road 26 47975 765-385-2651
Gail Anderson, prin. Fax 385-0124

Pittsboro, Hendricks, Pop. 2,245
North West Hendricks SD
Supt. — See Lizton
Pittsboro ES 500/K-5
206 N Meridian St 46167 317-994-2000
Gwen Taylor, prin. Fax 892-2010

Plainfield, Hendricks, Pop. 23,532
Plainfield Community SC 3,200/K-12
985 Longfellow Ln 46168 317-839-2578
Scott Olinger, supt. Fax 838-3664
www.plainfield.k12.in.us
Brentwood ES 300/K-3
1630 Oliver Ave 46168 317-839-4802
Patrick Cooney, prin. Fax 838-3651
Central ES 400/K-3
110 Wabash St 46168 317-839-7707
Laura Penman, prin. Fax 838-3646
Clarks Creek ES 4-5
401 Elm Dr 46168 317-839-0120
Mike Underwood, prin. Fax 838-7316
Plainfield Community MS 1,000/6-8
709 Stafford Rd 46168 317-838-3966
Jerry Goldsberry, prin. Fax 838-3965
Van Buren ES 300/K-3
233 Shaw St 46168 317-839-2575
Diana Van Middlesworth, prin. Fax 838-3993

St. Susanna S 300/PK-8
1212 E Main St 46168 317-839-3713
Tina Albin Davis, prin. Fax 838-7718

Pleasant Lake, Steuben
Metropolitan SD of Steuben County
Supt. — See Angola
Pleasant Lake ES 200/K-5
PO Box 69 46779 260-475-5055
Sue San Giacomo, prin. Fax 475-5673

Plymouth, Marshall, Pop. 10,876
Plymouth Community SC 3,500/PK-12
611 Berkley St 46563 574-936-3115
Daniel Tyree, supt. Fax 936-3160
www.plymouth.k12.in.us/
Jefferson ES 300/K-4
401 Klinger St 46563 574-936-2443
Bob Remenih, prin. Fax 936-3532
Lincoln JHS 500/7-8
220 N Liberty St 46563 574-936-3113
Dan Funston, prin. Fax 936-3574
Menominee ES 400/K-4
815 Discovery Ln 46563 574-936-2001
Michael Dunn, prin. Fax 936-2822
Riverside IS 500/5-6
905 Baker St 46563 574-936-3787
Donna Burroughs, prin. Fax 936-2822
Washington ES 400/K-4
1500 Lake Ave 46563 574-936-4072
Michele Riise, prin. Fax 936-4073
Webster ES 400/PK-4
1101 S Michigan St 46563 574-936-2520
Carrie McGuire, prin. Fax 935-4976

St. Michael S 200/PK-6
612 N Center St 46563 574-936-4329
Gertrude Nawara, prin. Fax 936-1151

Poneto, Wells, Pop. 235
Southern Wells Community SD 800/K-12
9120 S 300 W 46781 765-728-5537
James Craig, supt. Fax 728-8124
www.swraiders.com
Southern Wells ES 400/K-6
9120 S 300 W 46781 765-728-2121
Brett Garrett, prin. Fax 728-8124

Portage, Porter, Pop. 35,687
Portage Township SD 8,400/PK-12
6240 US Highway 6 46368 219-762-6511
Michael Berta, supt. Fax 762-3263
www.portage.k12.in.us
Aylesworth ES 600/K-5
5910 Central Ave 46368 219-763-8010
Mary Tracy, prin. Fax 763-8034
Central ES 600/K-5
2825 Russell St 46368 219-763-8015
Gaye Lindsley, prin. Fax 763-8029
Crisman ES 500/K-5
6161 Old Porter Rd 46368 219-763-8020
Linda Kuss, prin. Fax 763-8042
Fegely MS 700/6-8
5384 Stone Ave 46368 219-763-8150
Rebecca Lyons, prin. Fax 763-8157
Jones ES 400/K-5
2374 McCool Rd 46368 219-763-8025
Mitchell Miller, prin. Fax 763-8044
Kyle ES 500/K-5
2701 Hamstrom Rd 46368 219-763-8030
Aris Psimos, prin. Fax 763-8046
Myers ES 500/K-5
3100 Willowdale Rd 46368 219-763-8035
Jeff King, prin. Fax 763-8047
Willowcreek MS 1,300/6-8
5962 Central Ave 46368 219-763-8090
Michelle Stewart, prin. Fax 763-8069
Other Schools – See Valparaiso

Nativity of Our Savior S 200/K-8
2929 Willowcreek Rd 46368 219-763-2400
Kemberly Markham, prin. Fax 764-3225
Portage Christian S 200/PK-12
3040 Arlene St 46368 219-762-8962
Tim Rumley, admin. Fax 763-9931

Porter, Porter, Pop. 5,217
Duneland SC
Supt. — See Chesterton
Yost ES 400/K-4
100 W Beam St 46304 219-983-3640
Anne Stillman, prin. Fax 983-3649

Portland, Jay, Pop. 6,191
Jay SC 3,900/PK-12
PO Box 1239 47371 260-726-9341
Dr. Timothy Long, supt. Fax 726-4959
www.jayschools.k12.in.us
East ES 300/K-5
705 E Tallman St 47371 260-726-9418
Andy Schemenaur, prin. Fax 726-9836
East Jay MS 600/6-8
225 E Water St 47371 260-726-9371
Lee Newman, prin. Fax 726-2383
Haynes ES 300/K-5
800 W High St 47371 260-726-8890
Trent Paxson, prin. Fax 726-3587
Shanks ES 300/K-5
414 E Floral Ave 47371 260-726-8868
Michael Eads, prin. Fax 729-5111
Other Schools – See Bryant, Dunkirk, Pennville, Redkey

Poseyville, Posey, Pop. 1,151
Metro SD of North Posey County 1,500/PK-12
101 N Church St 47633 812-874-2243
John Wood, supt. Fax 874-8806
www.northposey.k12.in.us/
North ES 400/PK-6
63 W Fletchall St 47633 812-874-2710
Timothy Teel, prin. Fax 874-8811
North Posey JHS 200/7-8
5800 High School Rd 47633 812-673-4244
Linda Crick, prin. Fax 673-6622
Other Schools – See Wadesville

Princeton, Gibson, Pop. 8,652
North Gibson SC 2,100/K-12
1108 N Embree St 47670 812-385-4851
Dale McCuiston, supt. Fax 386-1531
www.ngsc.k12.in.us
Brumfield ES 500/3-5
813 W Archer Rd 47670 812-386-1221
Mary O'Neal, prin. Fax 386-1577
Lowell ES 400/K-2
215 W Water St 47670 812-385-4772
Lisa Feldman, prin. Fax 385-4682
Princeton Community MS 600/6-8
410 E State St 47670 812-385-2020
Kevin Spitler, prin. Fax 386-6746

St. Joseph S 200/PK-5
427 S Stormont St 47670 812-385-2228
Dan Gilbert, prin. Fax 385-2590

Ramsey, Harrison
North Harrison Community SC 2,300/K-12
1260 Highway 64 NW 47166 812-347-2407
Phil Partenheimer, supt. Fax 347-2870
www.nhcs.k12.in.us
North Harrison ES 600/K-5
1115 W Whiskey Run Rd NW 47166 812-347-2419
Lisa Jones, prin. Fax 347-2489
North Harrison MS 500/6-8
1180 Highway 64 NW 47166 812-347-2421
Karen Lambertus, prin. Fax 347-2835
Other Schools – See Palmyra

Redkey, Jay, Pop. 1,418
Jay SC
Supt. — See Portland
Redkey ES 200/PK-5
PO Box 6 47373 765-369-2571
Tomas Jerles, prin. Fax 369-2089

Reelsville, Putnam
South Putnam Community SD
Supt. — See Greencastle
Reelsville ES 200/K-6
7840 S County Road 625 W 46171 765-672-4248
Teresa Vapor, prin. Fax 672-4248

Remington, Jasper, Pop. 1,262
Tri-County SC
Supt. — See Wolcott
Tri-County PS 200/K-2
PO Box 95 47977 219-261-2214
Steve Ulrich, prin. Fax 261-2221

Rensselaer, Jasper, Pop. 6,234
Rensselaer Central SC 1,800/PK-12
605 W Grove St 47978 219-866-7822
Ned Speicher, supt. Fax 866-8360
www.rcsc.k12.in.us/
Monnett ES 300/PK-1
615 W Grove St 47978 219-866-5441
Barbara Lucas, prin. Fax 866-8135
Rensselaer Central MS 400/6-8
1106 E Bomber Dr 47978 219-866-4661
Kelly Berenda, prin. Fax 866-2103
Van Rensselaer ES 500/2-5
902 E Washington St 47978 219-866-8212
Barbara Lucas, prin. Fax 866-8215

St. Augustine S 100/PK-5
328 N McKinley Ave 47978 219-866-5480
Anne Dumas, prin. Fax 866-5663

Reynolds, White, Pop. 524
North White SC
Supt. — See Monon
Reynolds ES 100/K-5
401 W 2nd St 47980 219-984-5191
Michelle Hay, prin. Fax 984-6105

Richland, Spencer, Pop. 500
South Spencer County SC
Supt. — See Rockport
Luce ES 300/K-5
1057 N County Road 700 W 47634 812-359-4401
Susan Reagan, prin. Fax 359-4402

Richmond, Wayne, Pop. 37,560
Richmond Community SC 5,400/K-12
300 Hub Etchison Pkwy 47374 765-973-3300
Allen Bourff, supt. Fax 973-3417
www.rcs.k12.in.us
Charles ES 400/K-6
2400 Reeveston Rd 47374 765-973-3441
Terri Lane, prin. Fax 973-3701
Crestdale ES 300/K-6
701 Crestdale Dr 47374 765-973-3415
Connie Miller, prin. Fax 973-3702
Fairview ES 300/K-6
60 NW L St 47374 765-973-3442
Jennifer O'Brien, prin. Fax 973-3704
Garrison ES 400/K-6
4138 Niewoehner Rd 47374 765-973-3431
Kelly Andrews, prin. Fax 973-3705
Highland Heights ES 300/K-6
1751 E Chester Rd 47374 765-973-3408
Amy Dishman, prin. Fax 973-3707
Richardson ES 300/K-6
1215 S J St 47374 765-973-3429
William Doering, prin. Fax 973-3710
Starr Academy 200/K-6
301 N 19th St 47374 765-973-3426
Stephanie Quinn, prin. Fax 973-3711
Test MS 400/7-8
33 S 22nd St 47374 765-973-3412
Luann Spicer, prin. Fax 973-3712
Vaile ES 300/K-6
300 S 14th St 47374 765-973-3433
Tammy Rhoades, prin. Fax 973-3713
Westview ES 400/K-6
1707 SW A St 47374 765-973-3445
Shelia Hobbs, prin. Fax 973-3714
Worth MS 300/7-8
222 NW 7th St 47374 765-973-3495
Kathy McCarty, prin. Fax 973-3703

Community Christian S 200/PK-8
PO Box 1393 47375 765-935-3215
Kim Soots, admin. Fax 535-5152
New Creations Christian S 100/K-12
6400 National Rd E 47374 765-935-2790
Greg Paxson, prin. Fax 935-3961
Richmond Friends S 50/K-6
607 W Main St 47374 765-966-5767
Marcie Roberts, admin.
Seton Catholic S 300/PK-6
801 W Main St 47374 765-962-5010
Cynthia Johnson, prin. Fax 962-3399

Ridgeville, Randolph, Pop. 818
Randolph Central SC
Supt. — See Winchester
Deerfield ES 300/K-5
213 W State Road 28 47380 765-857-2554
Greg Kile, prin. Fax 857-2606

Riley, Vigo, Pop. 155
Vigo County SC
Supt. — See Terre Haute
Riley ES 500/PK-5
PO Box 127 47871 812-462-4449
David Lotter, prin. Fax 462-4503

Rising Sun, Ohio, Pop. 2,405
Rising Sun-Ohio County Community SD 1,000/K-12
110 S Henrietta St 47040 812-438-2655
Stephen Patz, supt. Fax 438-4636
www.risingsunschools.com/
Rising Sun-Ohio County S 600/K-8
436 S Mulberry St 47040 812-438-2626
Gloria Holland, prin. Fax 438-2456

Roachdale, Putnam, Pop. 976
North Putnam Community SD
Supt. — See Bainbridge
North Putnam MS 500/6-8
8905 N County Road 250 E 46172 765-522-2900
Terry Tippin, prin. Fax 522-2863
Roachdale ES 300/PK-5
305 S Indiana St 46172 765-522-1732
Scott Spencer, prin. Fax 522-2094

Roanoke, Huntington, Pop. 1,468
Huntington County Community SC
Supt. — See Huntington
Roanoke ES 300/K-5
423 W Vine St 46783 260-672-2806
Paul Roth, prin. Fax 672-3391

Metro SD of Southwest Allen County
Supt. — See Fort Wayne
Lafayette Meadows ES 400/K-5
11420 Ernst Rd 46783 260-431-0602
Lauvonnia Conrad, prin. Fax 431-0699

Aboite Christian S 50/PK-8
14615 Winters Rd 46783 260-672-8544
Sheldon Schultz, prin. Fax 672-8544

Rochester, Fulton, Pop. 6,451
Rochester Community SC 1,900/PK-12
PO Box 108 46975 574-223-2159
Dr. Debra Howe, supt. Fax 223-4909
www.rochester.k12.in.us
Columbia ES 500/PK-2
PO Box 108 46975 574-223-2501
Mary Bohr, prin. Fax 223-0530
Riddle ES 400/3-5
PO Box 108 46975 574-223-2880
Tracy Tredway, prin. Fax 223-4909
Rochester Community MS 500/6-8
PO Box 108 46975 574-223-2280
Deborah Carter, prin. Fax 223-1531

Rockport, Spencer, Pop. 2,091
South Spencer County SC 1,500/PK-12
PO Box 26 47635 812-649-2591
H. Mike Robinson, supt. Fax 649-4249
www.sspencer.k12.in.us
Rockport-Ohio ES 400/PK-5
201 S 6th St 47635 812-649-2201
Scot French, prin. Fax 649-2202
South Spencer MS 400/6-8
1298 N Orchard Rd 47635 812-649-2203
J. Wilson, prin. Fax 649-9630
Other Schools – See Richland

St. Bernard S 100/K-8
547 Elm St 47635 812-649-2501
Sara Guth, prin. Fax 649-4176

Rockville, Parke, Pop. 2,701
Rockville Community SC 900/K-12
602 Howard Ave 47872 765-569-5582
Dr. Randall Kerkhoff, supt. Fax 569-6650
www.rockville.k12.in.us
Rockville ES 400/K-6
406 Elm St 47872 765-569-5363
Sheila Rohr, prin. Fax 569-5181

Rolling Prairie, LaPorte
New Prairie United SC
Supt. — See New Carlisle
Prairie View ES 400/K-5
6434 E 700 N 46371 574-654-7258
Marcia Kelly, prin. Fax 654-3871
Rolling Prairie ES 500/K-5
605 E Michigan St 46371 219-778-2018
Angela Hambling, prin. Fax 778-4911

Rome City, Noble, Pop. 1,645
East Noble SC
Supt. — See Kendallville
Rome City ES 300/K-6
PO Box 218 46784 260-854-3241
James Taylor, prin. Fax 854-9404

Rosedale, Parke, Pop. 759
Southwest Parke Community SC
Supt. — See Montezuma
Rosedale ES 300/K-6
613 E Central St 47874 765-548-2454
Adrienne Gideon, prin. Fax 548-2608

Rossville, Clinton, Pop. 1,540
Rossville Consolidated SD 1,000/K-12
PO Box 11 46065 765-379-2990
Dr. James Hanna, supt. Fax 379-3014
www.rossville.k12.in.us/
Rossville ES 500/K-5
PO Box 530 46065 765-379-2119
Chad Dennison, prin. Fax 379-9236
Rossville MS 200/6-8
PO Box 530 46065 765-379-2551
Shawn McCracken, prin. Fax 379-2556

Royal Center, Cass, Pop. 817
Pioneer Regional SC 1,000/K-12
PO Box 577 46978 574-643-2605
Dr. David Bess, supt. Fax 643-9977
www.pioneer.k12.in.us/
Pioneer ES 500/K-6
PO Box 517 46978 574-643-2255
Dennis Ide, prin. Fax 643-9977

Rushville, Rush, Pop. 5,679
Rush County SD 2,700/PK-12
330 W 8th St 46173 765-932-4186
Dr. John Williams, supt. Fax 938-1608
rcs.rushville.k12.in.us/
Rush MS 400/7-8
1601 N Sexton St 46173 765-932-2968
Marla Stevens, prin. Fax 938-2011
Rushville ES 800/PK-6
400 W 16th St 46173 765-932-2961
Dr. Scott Stevens, prin. Fax 938-2417
Other Schools – See Arlington, Mays, Milroy

St. Mary S 100/PK-6
226 E 5th St 46173 765-932-3639
Jann Metelko, prin. Fax 938-1322

Russiaville, Howard, Pop. 1,186
Western SC 2,500/K-12
2600 S 600 W 46979 765-883-5576
Dr. Peter O'Rourke, supt. Fax 883-7946
www.western.k12.in.us
Western IS 600/3-5
2607 S 600 W 46979 765-883-5554
Heather Hendrich, prin. Fax 883-7946
Western MS 600/6-8
2600 S 600 W 46979 765-883-5566
Julie Pownall, prin. Fax 883-4531
Western PS 600/K-2
2671 S 600 W 46979 765-883-5528
Steve Arthur, prin. Fax 883-7946

Saint Joe, DeKalb, Pop. 475
DeKalb County Eastern Community SD
Supt. — See Butler
Riverdale ES 300/K-6
6127 State Road 1 46785 260-337-5464
Brennen Kitchen, prin. Fax 337-5114

Saint John, Lake, Pop. 9,545
Lake Central SC 9,700/PK-12
8260 Wicker Ave 46373 219-365-8507
Dr. Gerald Chabot, supt. Fax 365-6406
www.lcsc.us
Clark MS 6-8
8915 W 93rd Ave 46373 219-365-9203
Scott Graber, prin. Fax 365-9348
Kolling ES 800/K-5
8801 Wicker Ave 46373 219-365-8577
Janice Hines, prin. Fax 365-6402
Other Schools – See Dyer, Schererville

Crown Point Christian S 300/PK-8
10550 Park Pl 46373 219-365-5694
Dr. Harley VerBeek, admin. Fax 365-5729
St. John Evangelist S 300/PK-8
9400 Wicker Ave 46373 219-365-5451
Candace Scheidt, prin. Fax 365-6173

Saint Leon, Franklin, Pop. 496
Sunman-Dearborn Community SC
Supt. — See Sunman
Sunman-Dearborn MS 700/7-8
8356 Schuman Rd, Brookville IN 47012
812-576-3500
Mark Watkins, prin. Fax 576-3506

Salem, Washington, Pop. 6,453
Salem Community SD 2,200/K-12
500 N Harrison St 47167 812-883-4437
Dr. D. Lynn Reed, supt. Fax 883-1031
www.salemschools.com/
Salem MS 500/6-8
1001 N Harrison St 47167 812-883-3808
Ray Oppel, prin. Fax 883-8049
Shrum Lower ES 500/K-2
1103 N Shelby St 47167 812-883-3700
Gene Sutton, prin. Fax 883-6892
Shrum Upper ES 500/3-5
1101 N Shelby St 47167 812-883-4376
Tony Stone, prin. Fax 883-9118

San Pierre, Starke
North Judson-San Pierre SC
Supt. — See North Judson
San Pierre K K-K
205 N Jackson 46374 219-828-4254
Michael McBride, prin. Fax 828-4314

Schererville, Lake, Pop. 28,394
Lake Central SC
Supt. — See Saint John
Grimmer MS 1,100/6-8
225 W 77th Ave 46375 219-865-6985
Janet Zeck, prin. Fax 865-4423
Homan ES 700/K-5
210 E Joliet St 46375 219-322-4451
Kathi Tucker, prin. Fax 865-4442
Peifer ES 600/K-5
1824 Cline Ave 46375 219-322-5335
Douglas DeLaughter, prin. Fax 865-4426
Watson ES 700/K-5
333 W 77th Ave 46375 219-322-1365
Michael Buckner, prin. Fax 865-4431

Forest Ridge Academy 100/K-8
7300 Forest Ridge Dr 46375 219-756-7300
St. Michael S 300/PK-8
16 W Wilhelm St 46375 219-322-4531
Margaret Harangody, prin. Fax 322-1710

Scipio, Jennings
Jennings County SC
Supt. — See North Vernon
Scipio ES 400/K-6
6320 N State Highway 7 47273 812-392-2055
Teresa Helton, prin. Fax 392-2564

Scottsburg, Scott, Pop. 6,060
Scott County SD 2 2,900/K-12
375 E Mcclain Ave 47170 812-752-8946
Robert Hooker, supt. Fax 752-8951
www.scsd2.k12.in.us/
Johnson ES 200/K-5
4235 E State Road 256 47170 812-752-8923
Doris Marcum, prin. Fax 794-4979
Scottsburg ES 600/K-5
49 N Hyland St 47170 812-752-8922
Michelle Neibert-Levine, prin. Fax 752-9620
Scottsburg MS 700/6-8
425 S 3rd St 47170 812-752-8926
Kristin Nass, prin. Fax 752-8864
Vienna-Finley ES 300/K-5
445 E Ivan Rogers Dr 47170 812-752-8925
Brent Comer, prin. Fax 752-5379
Other Schools – See Lexington

Sellersburg, Clark, Pop. 6,028
West Clark Community SC 3,800/PK-12
601 Renz Ave 47172 812-246-3375
Monty Schneider, supt. Fax 246-9731
www.wclark.k12.in.us
Silver Creek ES 900/K-5
503 N Indiana Ave 47172 812-246-3312
Dr. David Losey, prin. Fax 246-7435
Silver Creek MS 500/6-8
495 N Indiana Ave 47172 812-246-4421
Reid Bailey, prin. Fax 246-7430
Other Schools – See Borden, Henryville

Rock Creek Christian Academy 300/PK-12
11515 Highway 31 47172 812-246-9271
Sara Hauselman, prin. Fax 246-0722
St. Paul S 300/PK-6
105 Saint Paul St 47172 812-246-3266
Fran Matusky, prin. Fax 246-7632

Selma, Delaware, Pop. 830
Liberty-Perry Community SC 1,100/K-12
PO Box 337 47383 765-282-5615
Bryan Rausch, supt. Fax 281-3733
www.selma.bsu.edu/
Perry ES 200/K-1
9400 E Windsor Rd 47383 765-289-2031
Joel Mahaffey, prin. Fax 281-3731
Selma ES 300/2-5
PO Box 336 47383 765-282-2455
Joel Mahaffey, prin. Fax 281-3730
Selma MS 300/6-8
10501 E County Road 167 S 47383 765-288-7242
Dennis Thompson, prin. Fax 281-3727

Seymour, Jackson, Pop. 18,890
Seymour Community SD 4,000/PK-12
1638 S Walnut St 47274 812-522-3340
Teran Armstrong Ph.D., supt. Fax 522-8031
www.scsc.k12.in.us
Brown ES 300/K-5
550 Miller Ln 47274 812-522-5539
Kathy Ross, prin. Fax 522-4544
Cortland ES 100/K-5
6687 N County Road 400 E 47274 812-522-7483
Jeff Klakamp, prin. Fax 522-6164
Emerson ES 300/K-5
500 Emerson Dr 47274 812-522-2596
Talmadge Reasoner, prin. Fax 523-3338
Seymour-Jackson ES 600/PK-5
508 B Ave E 47274 812-522-5709
Marti Colglazier, prin. Fax 522-7095
Seymour MS 900/6-8
920 N Obrien St 47274 812-522-5453
Dennis Howland, prin. Fax 523-8134
Seymour-Redding ES 600/K-5
1700 N Ewing St 47274 812-522-5621
Julia Kelly, prin. Fax 522-1593

Immanuel Lutheran S 400/1-8
520 S Chestnut St 47274 812-522-1301
Todd Behmlander, prin. Fax 523-2186
St. Ambrose S 100/PK-8
301 S Chestnut St 47274 812-522-3522
Sr. Anna Lueken, prin. Fax 522-3545
St. John Lutheran S 100/PK-8
1058 S County Road 460 E 47274 812-523-3131
Sharon Rohr, prin. Fax 523-3131
Zion Lutheran S 200/PK-K
1501 Gaiser Dr 47274 812-552-5911
Roy Stuckwisch, prin. Fax 523-7526

Sharpsville, Tipton, Pop. 620
Northern Comm Tipton County SD 1,000/K-12
4774 N 200 W 46068 765-963-2585
Dr. Lee Williford, supt. Fax 963-3042
www.ncstc.k12.in.us/
Tri Central ES 400/K-5
2115 W 500 N 46068 765-963-5885
Tim Henderson, prin. Fax 963-3072

Shelburn, Sullivan, Pop. 1,279
Northeast SC
Supt. — See Hymera
Shelburn ES 200/K-6
620 N Washington St 47879 812-397-5390
Lisa Hollingsworth, prin. Fax 397-2886

Shelbyville, Shelby, Pop. 18,063
Shelby Eastern SD 1,500/K-12
2451 N 600 E 46176 765-544-2246
Don Swisher, supt. Fax 544-2247
www.ses.k12.in.us/
Other Schools – See Morristown, Waldron

Shelbyville Central SD 3,900/K-12
803 Saint Joseph St 46176 317-392-2505
David Adams, supt. Fax 392-5737
www.shelbycs.org
Coulston ES 500/K-5
121 N Knightstown Rd 46176 317-398-3185
James Conner, prin. Fax 392-5721
Hendricks ES 700/K-5
1111 Saint Joseph St 46176 317-398-7432
Pat Lumbley, prin. Fax 392-5725
Loper ES 700/K-5
901 Loper Dr 46176 317-398-9725
Sally Vaught, prin. Fax 392-5732
Shelbyville MS 900/6-8
1200 W McKay Rd 46176 317-392-2551
Denny Ramsey, prin. Fax 392-5713

Southwestern Cons Shelby County SC 800/K-12
3406 W 600 S 46176 317-729-5746
Dr. Terry Sargent, supt. Fax 729-5330
www.swshelby.k12.in.us
Southwestern ES 400/K-6
3406 W 600 S 46176 317-729-5320
Paula Maurer, prin. Fax 729-5370

St. Joseph S 200/PK-5
127 E Broadway St 46176 317-398-4202
Joan Livingston, prin. Fax 398-0270

Sheridan, Hamilton, Pop. 2,661
Sheridan Community SD 1,200/PK-12
509 E 4th St 46069 317-758-4172
Derek Arrowood, supt. Fax 758-6248
www.sheridan.org/school/
Adams ES 500/PK-5
509 E 4th St 46069 317-758-4491
Dean Welbaum, prin. Fax 758-2409
Sheridan MS 300/6-8
3030 W 246th St 46069 317-758-6780
Ed Baker, prin. Fax 758-2435

Shipshewana, Lagrange, Pop. 530
Westview SC
Supt. — See Topeka
Meadowview ES 400/K-4
7950 W 050 S 46565 260-768-7702
Toni Whitney, prin. Fax 768-7906
Shipshewana-Scott ES 400/K-4
PO Box 217 46565 260-768-4158
Ian Zuercher, prin. Fax 768-4159

Shoals, Martin, Pop. 817
Shoals Community SC 700/PK-12
11741 Ironton Rd 47581 812-247-2060
Dr. Anthony Nonte, supt. Fax 247-2278
shoals.k12.in.us/
Shoals Community ES 300/PK-6
11741 Ironton Rd 47581 812-247-2085
Carolyn Eubank, prin. Fax 247-9913

South Bend, Saint Joseph, Pop. 105,262
South Bend Community SC 21,300/PK-12
215 S Saint Joseph St 46601 574-283-8000
James Kapsa, supt. Fax 283-8143
www.sbcsc.k12.in.us
Brown Intermediate Center 700/5-8
737 Beale St 46616 574-287-9680
Fax 283-5581
Clay Intermediate Center 600/5-8
52900 Lily Rd 46637 574-243-7145
James Knight, prin. Fax 243-7151
Coquilliard PS 500/K-4
1245 N Sheridan St 46628 574-283-8610
William Soderberg, prin. Fax 283-8613
Darden PS 600/K-4
18645 Janet Dr 46637 574-243-7335
James Bankowski, prin. Fax 243-7338
Dickinson Fine Arts Academy 600/5-8
4404 Elwood Ave 46628 574-283-7625
Dwight Fulce, prin. Fax 283-7633
Edison Intermediate Center 600/5-8
2701 Eisenhower Ave 46615 574-283-8900
Karla Lee, prin. Fax 283-8903
Greene Intermediate Center 500/5-8
24702 Roosevelt Rd 46614 574-283-7900
Sherry Bolden-Simpson, prin. Fax 283-7903
Hamilton PS 300/K-4
1530 E Jackson Rd 46614 574-231-5672
Dennis Giden, prin. Fax 231-5675
Harrison PS 700/PK-4
3302 W Western Ave 46619 574-283-7300
Delba Smith, prin. Fax 283-7303
Hay PS 400/K-4
19685 Johnson Rd 46614 574-231-5735
Craig Haenes, prin. Fax 231-5738
Jackson IS 600/5-8
5001 Miami St 46614 574-231-5600
Margaret Schaller, prin. Fax 231-5605
Jefferson IS 500/5-8
528 S Eddy St 46617 574-283-8700
Byron Sanders, prin. Fax 283-8703
Kennedy Academy 600/PK-4
609 N Olive St 46628 574-283-7435
Kris Torok, prin. Fax 283-7441
Lafayette Traditional S 500/K-4
245 N Lombardy Dr 46619 574-283-8650
Sharon Jones, prin. Fax 283-8653
LaSalle Academy 800/5-8
2701 Elwood Ave 46628 574-283-7500
Cynthia Oudghiri, prin. Fax 283-7513
Lincoln PS 700/K-4
1425 E Calvert St 46613 574-283-8960
Jim Kowalski, prin. Fax 283-8963
Madison PS 600/K-4
832 N Lafayette Blvd 46601 574-283-8325
Angela Buysse, prin. Fax 283-8328
Marquette Montessori Primary Academy 300/K-4
1905 College St 46628 574-283-8370
Cheryl Batteast, prin. Fax 283-8373
Marshall Intermediate Center 500/5-8
1433 Byron Dr 46614 574-231-5801
Thomas Sims, prin. Fax 231-5804
McKinley PS 400/K-4
228 N Greenlawn Ave 46617 574-283-8570
Deb Martin, prin. Fax 283-8573
Monroe PS 500/K-4
724 E Dubail Ave 46613 574-231-5831
Jill Vandriessche, prin. Fax 231-5834
Muessel PS 500/PK-4
1021 Blaine Ave 46616 574-283-7800
Margaret Lewis, prin. Fax 283-7803
Navarre Intermediate Center 700/5-8
4702 Ford St 46619 574-283-7345
Derrick White, prin. Fax 283-7351
Nuner PS 400/K-4
2716 Pleasant St 46615 574-283-7850
Deb Herring, prin. Fax 283-7853
Perley Fine Arts Academy 300/K-4
740 N Eddy St 46617 574-283-8735
Darice Austin-Phillips, prin. Fax 283-8738
Swanson Highlands PS 400/K-4
17677 Parker Dr 46635 574-243-7250
Wendy Folk, prin. Fax 243-7253
Tarkington Traditional S 300/K-4
3414 Hepler St 46635 574-243-7210
Melinda Ehmer, prin. Fax 243-7213
Warren PS 300/K-4
55400 Quince Rd 46619 574-283-7950
Carla Killelea, prin. Fax 283-7953
Wilson PS 600/K-4
56660 Oak Rd 46619 574-283-7400
Mary Jo Costello, prin. Fax 283-7407

Christ the King S 500/K-8
52473 IN State Route 933 46637 574-272-3922
Stephen Hoffman, prin. Fax 273-6707
Clark S 400/PK-8
3123 Miami St 46614 574-291-4200
Robert Douglass, prin. Fax 299-4170
Community Baptist Christian S 200/K-12
5715 Miami St 46614 574-291-3620
Jay Bradford, prin. Fax 291-3648
Corpus Christi S 400/PK-8
2817 Corpus Christi Dr 46628 574-272-9868
Maggie Mackowiak, prin. Fax 272-9894
Good Shepherd Montessori S 100/1-8
1101 E Jefferson Blvd 46617 574-288-0098
Daniel Driscoll, hdmstr. Fax 288-0077
Holy Cross S 400/PK-8
1020 Wilber St 46628 574-234-3422
Angela Budzinski, prin. Fax 237-6725
Holy Family S 400/PK-8
56407 Mayflower Rd 46619 574-289-7375
Sr. Joan Shillinger, prin. Fax 289-7386
Michiana Christian S 100/K-4
2730 S Ironwood Dr 46614 574-288-0234
Don Lorah, prin. Fax 472-2917
Our Lady of Hungary S 100/PK-8
735 W Calvert St 46613 574-289-3272
Clem Wroblewski, prin. Fax 289-3272
Resurrection Lutheran Academy 100/PK-7
6840 Nimtz Pkwy 46628 574-272-2200
Walter Mischnick, prin. Fax 968-0345
St. Adalbert S 200/PK-8
519 S Olive St 46619 574-288-6645
MaryAnn Bachman, prin. Fax 251-2788
St. Anthony De Padua S 400/K-8
2310 E Jefferson Blvd 46615 574-233-7169
Chad Barwick, prin. Fax 233-7290
St. John the Baptist S 200/PK-8
3616 Saint Johns Way 46628 574-232-9849
Janet Wroblewski, prin. Fax 232-9855
St. Joseph S 400/K-8
216 N Hill St 46617 574-234-0451
Suzanne Wiwi, prin. Fax 234-0524
St. Jude S 200/K-8
19657 Hildebrand St 46614 574-291-3820
Stephen Donndelinger, prin. Fax 299-3053
St. Matthew Cathedral S 400/K-8
1015 E Dayton St 46613 574-289-4535
Mary Retseck, prin. Fax 289-4539
South Bend Jr. Academy 50/K-8
1910 Altgeld St 46614 574-287-3713
Carol Grannan, prin. Fax 287-3713

Southport, Marion, Pop. 1,729
Metro SD of Perry Township
Supt. — See Indianapolis
Winchester Village ES 500/K-5
1900 E Stop 12 Rd 46227 317-789-2700
David Rohl, prin. Fax 865-2703

South Whitley, Whitley, Pop. 1,847
Whitko Community SC
Supt. — See Pierceton
South Whitley ES 400/K-5
406 W Wayne St 46787 260-723-6342
George Roth, prin. Fax 723-5165

Speedway, Marion, Pop. 12,408
Town of Speedway SD 1,600/K-12
5335 W 25th St 46224 317-244-0236
Kenneth Hull, supt. Fax 486-4843
www.speedway.k12.in.us

Allison ES 200/K-6
5240 W 22nd St 46224 317-244-9836
Jay Bedwell, prin. Fax 486-4847
Fisher ES 200/K-6
5151 W 14th St 46224 317-241-6543
Kathryn Richards, prin. Fax 486-4845
Newby ES 200/K-6
1849 N Whitcomb Ave 46224 317-241-0572
Anthony Gagliano, prin. Fax 486-4848
Speedway JHS 300/7-8
5151 W 14th St 46224 317-244-3359
John Dizney, prin. Fax 486-4845
Wheeler ES 300/K-6
5700 Meadowood Dr 46224 317-291-4274
Brenda Wolfe, prin. Fax 291-4515

Spencer, Owen, Pop. 2,549
Spencer-Owen Community SD 3,100/PK-12
205 E Hillside Ave 47460 812-829-2233
Greg Linton, supt. Fax 829-6614
www.socs.k12.in.us
McCormick's Creek ES 500/K-6
1601 Flatwoods Rd 47460 812-828-6000
Linda Epeards, prin. Fax 828-6010
Owen Valley MS 500/7-8
626 W State Highway 46 47460 812-829-2249
Amy Elkins, prin. Fax 829-6635
Spencer ES 700/PK-6
151 E Hillside Ave 47460 812-829-2253
Donnie Carver, prin. Fax 829-6629
Other Schools – See Gosport, Patricksburg

Spencer Adventist Christian S 50/1-8
1674 Timber Ridge Rd 47460 812-829-2485
Lutricia Whitlow, prin.

Spiceland, Henry, Pop. 900
South Henry SC 700/K-12
6449 S Cemetery Dr 47385 765-987-7882
Dr. William Roberson, supt. Fax 987-7589
www.shenry.k12.in.us/
Other Schools – See Straughn

Springville, Lawrence
North Lawrence Community SD
Supt. — See Bedford
Springville ES 200/K-5
PO Box 61 47462 812-279-1388
Robert Stipp, prin. Fax 278-7703

Stinesville, Monroe, Pop. 188
Richland-Bean Blossom Community SC
Supt. — See Ellettsville
Stinesville ES 200/K-5
7973 W Main St 47464 812-876-2474
William Buxton, prin. Fax 876-2475

Straughn, Henry, Pop. 249
South Henry SC
Supt. — See Spiceland
Tri ES 400/K-6
6972 S State Road 103 47387 765-987-7090
Jean McAllister, prin. Fax 987-7788

Sullivan, Sullivan, Pop. 4,537
Southwest SC 1,800/PK-12
110 N Main St 47882 812-268-6311
Walter Hoke, supt. Fax 268-6312
www.swest.k12.in.us/
Sullivan ES 700/PK-5
351 W Frakes St 47882 812-268-3341
Ross Martin, prin. Fax 268-5624
Sullivan MS 200/6-8
415 W Frakes St 47882 812-268-4000
Dustin Hitt, prin. Fax 268-5368
Other Schools – See Carlisle

Summitville, Madison, Pop. 1,052
Madison-Grant United SC
Supt. — See Fairmount
Summitville ES 200/K-6
405 E Mill St 46070 765-536-2875
Wendy Barr, prin. Fax 536-2636

Sunman, Ripley, Pop. 803
Sunman-Dearborn Community SC 4,400/K-12
PO Box 210 47041 812-576-1900
Jeffrey Hendrix, supt. Fax 623-3341
sunmandearborn.k12.in.us
Sunman ES 400/K-4
925 N Meridian St 47041 812-623-2235
Cynthia Morton, prin. Fax 623-4330
Other Schools – See Guilford, Lawrenceburg, Saint Leon, West Harrison

---

St. Nicholas S 200/PK-8
6459 E Saint Nicholas Dr 47041 812-623-2348
Maggie Jackson, prin. Fax 623-2964

Swayzee, Grant, Pop. 935
Oak Hill United SC
Supt. — See Converse
Swayzee ES 300/PK-K, 5-6
PO Box 217 46986 765-922-7926
Terry Renbarger, prin. Fax 922-7927

Sweetser, Grant, Pop. 842
Oak Hill United SC
Supt. — See Converse
Sweetser ES 200/K-K, 3-4
PO Box 230 46987 765-384-4371
Nijaul Drollinger, prin. Fax 384-7217

Switz City, Greene, Pop. 311
White River Valley SD 900/K-12
PO Box 1470 47465 812-659-1424
Layton Wall, supt. Fax 659-2278
www.wrv.k12.in.us
Other Schools – See Lyons, Worthington

Syracuse, Kosciusko, Pop. 3,030
Wawasee Community SC 3,500/PK-12
1 Warrior Path Bldg 2 46567 574-457-3188
Thomas Edington, supt. Fax 457-4962
www.wawasee.k12.in.us/
Syracuse ES 600/K-5
502 W Brooklyn St 46567 574-457-4484
Jim Garner, prin. Fax 457-4486
Wawasee MS 600/6-8
9850 N State Rd 13 46567 574-457-8839
Anthony Cassel, prin. Fax 457-3575
Other Schools – See Milford, North Webster

Taylorsville, Bartholomew, Pop. 1,044
Bartholomew Consolidated SC
Supt. — See Columbus
Taylorsville ES 600/PK-6
PO Box 277 47280 812-526-5448
Karen Turner, prin. Fax 526-2233

Tell City, Perry, Pop. 7,690
Tell City-Troy Township SC 1,600/PK-12
837 17th St 47586 812-547-3300
Ronald Etienne, supt. Fax 547-9704
www.tellcity.k12.in.us
Tell City JHS 400/6-8
3515 Mozart St 47586 812-547-3748
Brad Ramsey, prin. Fax 547-9737
Tell ES 700/PK-5
1235 31st St 47586 812-547-9727
Laura Noble, prin. Fax 547-9746

Tennyson, Warrick, Pop. 302
Warrick County SC
Supt. — See Boonville
Tennyson ES 100/K-5
323 N Main St 47637 812-567-4715
Gerry Howard, prin. Fax 567-4715

Terre Haute, Vigo, Pop. 56,893
Vigo County SC 16,400/PK-12
PO Box 3703 47803 812-462-4216
Daniel Tanoos, supt. Fax 462-4115
www.vigoco.k12.in.us
Davis Park ES 400/K-5
310 S 18th St 47807 812-462-4425
Dr. Tammy Roeschlein, prin. Fax 462-4400
Deming ES 300/K-5
1750 8th Ave 47804 812-462-4431
Susan Mardis, prin. Fax 462-4285
De Vaney ES 400/K-5
1011 S Brown Ave 47803 812-462-4497
Paul Utterback, prin. Fax 462-4317
Dixie Bee ES 600/K-5
1655 E Jessica Dr 47802 812-462-4445
Mika Cassell, prin. Fax 462-4447
Farrington Grove ES 400/K-5
1826 S 6th St 47802 812-462-4423
William Smith, prin. Fax 462-4424
Franklin ES 300/PK-5
1600 Dr Iverson C Bell Ln 47807 812-462-4441
Annette Engle, prin. Fax 462-4438
Fuqua ES 300/PK-5
1111 E Wheeler Ave 47802 812-462-4304
Mary Beth Harris, prin. Fax 462-4306
Honey Creek MS 800/6-8
6601 S Carlisle St 47802 812-462-4372
Patrick Sheehan, prin. Fax 462-4367
Hoosier Prairie ES 400/K-5
2800 W Harlan Dr 47802 812-462-4236
Dallas Kelsey, prin. Fax 462-4233
Lost Creek ES 600/PK-5
6701 Wabash Ave 47803 812-462-4456
Madonna Johnson, prin. Fax 877-4815
Meadows ES 300/K-5
55 S Brown Ave 47803 812-462-4301
Susan Newton, prin. Fax 462-4303
Otter Creek MS 700/6-8
4801 N Lafayette St 47805 812-462-4391
Scott Moore, prin. Fax 462-4388
Ouabache ES 400/PK-5
501 Maple Ave 47804 812-462-4493
Joyce Schopmeyer, prin. Fax 462-4214
Rio Grande ES 600/PK-5
5555 E Rio Grande Ave 47805 812-462-4307
Dr. Diane Cargile, prin. Fax 462-4309
Rose MS 500/6-8
1275 3rd Ave 47807 812-462-4474
Claire Marchese, prin. Fax 462-4473
Scott MS 500/6-8
1000 Grant St 47802 812-462-4381
Mark Miller, prin. Fax 462-4370
Sugar Grove ES 500/PK-5
2800 Wallace Ave 47802 812-462-4416
Alice Fuller, prin. Fax 462-4471
Terre Town ES 700/PK-5
2121 Boston Ave 47805 812-462-4385
Cinda Taylor, prin. Fax 462-4413
Wilson MS 800/6-8
301 S 25th St 47803 812-462-4396
Dr. Sharon Pitts, prin. Fax 232-2217
Other Schools – See Riley, West Terre Haute

Community Christian S 100/PK-5
2000 N 13th St 47804 812-235-7017
Cathi Myers, admin. Fax 235-7017
St. Patrick S 300/PK-8
449 S 19th St 47803 812-232-2157
Kathy Sternal, prin. Fax 478-9384
Terre Haute Adventist S 50/K-10
900 S 29th St 47803 812-232-1339
Terre Haute Christian S 100/K-12
2500 Margaret Ave 47802 812-238-2541

Thorntown, Boone, Pop. 1,573
Western Boone County Community SD 1,900/PK-12
1201 N State Road 75 46071 765-482-6333
Dr. Judi Hendrix, supt. Fax 482-0890
www.weboschools.org/
Thorntown ES 500/PK-6
200 W Mill St 46071 765-485-2447
Gary Lanpher, prin. Fax 436-2630
Other Schools – See Jamestown

Tipton, Tipton, Pop. 5,254
Tipton Community SC 1,800/K-12
221 N Main St 46072 765-675-2147
Robert Schultz, supt. Fax 675-3857
www.tcsc.k12.in.us
Tipton ES 800/K-5
1099 S Main St 46072 765-675-7397
Kathryn Heaston, prin. Fax 675-6211
Tipton MS 400/6-8
817 S Main St 46072 765-675-7521
Shayne Clark, prin. Fax 675-9027

St. John the Baptist S 100/PK-5
323 Mill St 46072 765-675-4741
Tina McCullough, prin. Fax 675-2163

Topeka, Lagrange, Pop. 1,194
Westview SC 2,300/K-12
1545 S 600 W 46571 260-768-4404
Dr. Randall Zimmerly, supt. Fax 768-7368
www.westview.k12.in.us
Topeka ES 300/K-4
PO Box 39 46571 260-593-2897
Becky Siegel, prin. Fax 593-2899
Westview ES 400/5-6
1715 S 600 W 46571 260-768-7717
Juli Leeper, prin. Fax 768-7737
Other Schools – See Shipshewana

Trafalgar, Johnson, Pop. 936
Nineveh-Hensley-Jackson United SD 1,800/K-12
802 S Indian Creek Dr 46181 317-878-2100
Mark Millis, supt. Fax 878-5765
www.nhj.k12.in.us
Indian Creek ES 400/K-2
PO Box 68 46181 317-878-2150
Keith Grant, prin. Fax 878-5486
Indian Creek IS 400/3-5
1000 S Indian Creek Dr 46181 317-878-2160
Dave Ennis, prin. Fax 878-2165
Indian Creek MS 500/6-8
801 W Indian Creek Dr 46181 317-878-2130
Connie Richhart, prin. Fax 878-2149

Union City, Randolph, Pop. 3,471
Randolph Eastern SC 1,000/K-12
907 N Plum St 47390 765-964-4994
Cathy Stephen, supt. Fax 964-6590
www.resc.k12.in.us/
North Side ES 500/K-5
905 N Plum St 47390 765-964-6430
Mark Winkle, prin. Fax 964-3445
West Side MS 200/6-8
731 N Plum St 47390 765-964-4830
Janet Caudle, prin. Fax 964-7344

Union Mills, LaPorte
South Central Community SC 900/K-12
9808 S 600 W 46382 219-767-2263
Christopher Smith, supt. Fax 767-2260
www.scentral.k12.in.us/
South Central ES 400/K-6
9808 S 600 W 46382 219-767-2269
Allisa Schnick, prin. Fax 767-2260

Unionville, Monroe
Monroe County Community SC
Supt. — See Bloomington
Unionville ES 300/K-6
8144 E State Rd 45 47468 812-332-0175
David Marshall, prin. Fax 339-2717

Upland, Grant, Pop. 3,735
Eastbrook Community SC
Supt. — See Marion
Upland ES 400/K-6
694 S Second St 46989 765-998-2550
Mickey Lazard, prin. Fax 998-2740

Valparaiso, Porter, Pop. 29,102
Duneland SC
Supt. — See Chesterton
Jackson ES 400/K-4
811 N 400 E 46383 219-983-3680
Linda Rugg, prin. Fax 983-3689

East Porter County SC
Supt. — See Kouts
Morgan Township ES 300/K-5
299 S State Road 49 46383 219-462-8373
Michelle Friesen-Carper, prin. Fax 462-4014
Washington Township ES 300/K-5
383 E State Road 2 46383 219-464-3597
Rik Ihssen, prin. Fax 465-1753

Portage Township SD
Supt. — See Portage
Saylor ES 400/K-5
331 Midway Dr 46385 219-763-8040
Ken Galik, prin. Fax 764-6792
South Haven ES 400/PK-5
395 Midway Dr 46385 219-763-8045
Christopher Evans, prin. Fax 759-6985

Porter Township SC 1,600/K-12
248 S 500 W 46385 219-477-4933
Nicholas Brown, supt. Fax 477-4834
www.ptsc.k12.in.us/
Other Schools – See Boone Grove, Hebron

Union Township SC 1,700/K-12
599 W 300 N Ste A 46385 219-759-2531
John Hunter, supt. Fax 759-3250
www.union.k12.in.us
Simatovich ES 300/K-5
424 W 500 N 46385 219-759-2508
Phyllis Allison, prin. Fax 759-6634
Union Center ES 400/K-5
272 N 600 W 46385 219-759-2544
Cathy Polichronopoulos, prin. Fax 759-6360
Union Township MS 400/6-8
599 W 300 N 46385 219-759-2562
Jerry Lasky, prin. Fax 759-4359

Valparaiso Community SD 6,200/K-12
3801 Campbell St 46385 219-531-3000
Dr. Michael Benway, supt. Fax 531-3009
www.valpo.k12.in.us
Central ES 300/K-5
305 Franklin St 46383 219-531-3030
Elizabeth Krutz, prin. Fax 531-1251
Cooks Corner ES 300/K-5
358 Bullseye Lake Rd 46383 219-531-3040
Thomas Wisch, prin. Fax 531-3041
Flint Lake ES 500/K-5
4106 Calumet Ave 46383 219-531-3160
Candace Swanson, prin. Fax 531-3164
Franklin MS 700/6-8
605 Campbell St 46385 219-531-3020
Christopher Fields, prin. Fax 531-3026
Hayes-Leonard ES 300/K-5
653 Hayes Leonard Rd 46385 219-531-3060
William Eichelberg, prin. Fax 531-3068
Jefferson ES 300/K-5
1700 Roosevelt Rd 46383 219-531-3130
Dr. Bonnie Stephens, prin. Fax 531-3131
Jefferson MS 700/6-8
1600 Roosevelt Rd 46383 219-531-3140
Paul Knauff, prin. Fax 531-3146
Memorial ES 300/K-5
1052 Park Ave 46385 219-531-3090
Aaron Case, prin. Fax 531-3009
Northview ES 300/K-5
257 Northview Dr 46383 219-531-3100
Loren Hershberger, prin. Fax 531-3108
Parkview ES 300/K-5
1405 Wood St 46383 219-531-3110
Anne Wodetzki, prin. Fax 531-3112

Immanuel Lutheran S 200/PK-8
1700 Monticello Park Dr 46383 219-462-8207
Lynn Bremer, prin. Fax 531-2238
St. Paul S 400/K-8
1755 Harrison Blvd 46385 219-462-3374
Jane Scupham, prin. Fax 477-1763
South Haven Christian S 100/PK-8
786 Juniper Rd 46385 219-759-5313
Vivian Szostek, admin. Fax 759-1577
Tall Oaks Christian S 50/K-8
1901 Evans Ave 46383 219-464-9862
Sarah Floyd, admin.
Victory Christian Academy 200/PK-12
3805 LaPorte Ave 46383 219-548-8803
Joyce Folk, admin. Fax 548-8803

Van Buren, Grant, Pop. 870
Eastbrook Community SC
Supt. — See Marion
Van Buren ES 200/K-6
504 S 1st St 46991 765-934-3551
Randy Atkins, prin. Fax 934-3552

Veedersburg, Fountain, Pop. 2,228
Southeast Fountain SC 1,400/K-12
744 E US Highway 136 47987 765-294-2254
Corey Austin, supt. Fax 294-3200
www.sefschools.org/
Southeast Fountain ES 700/K-6
780 E US Highway 136 47987 765-294-2216
Tony Coleman, prin. Fax 294-3206

Versailles, Ripley, Pop. 1,766
South Ripley Community SC 1,300/K-12
207 W Tyson St 47042 812-689-6282
Ted Ahaus, supt. Fax 689-6760
www.sripley.k12.in.us/
South Ripley ES 700/K-6
1568 S Benham Rd 47042 812-689-5383
Mark Collier, prin. Fax 689-6415

Vevay, Switzerland, Pop. 1,655
Switzerland County SC 1,600/PK-12
305 W Seminary St 47043 812-427-2611
Elizabeth Jones, supt. Fax 427-3695
www.switzerland.k12.in.us
Jefferson-Craig ES 300/PK-5
1002 W Main St 47043 812-427-2170
Darin Gullion, prin. Fax 427-3260
Switzerland County MS 300/6-8
1004 W Main St 47043 812-427-3809
Nancy Stearns, prin. Fax 427-3807
Other Schools – See East Enterprise

Vincennes, Knox, Pop. 18,077
South Knox SC 1,200/K-12
6116 E State Road 61 47591 812-726-4440
Bradley Case, supt. Fax 743-2110
www.sknox.k12.in.us
South Knox ES 600/K-6
6078 E State Road 61 47591 812-743-2591
Alan Drew, prin. Fax 726-4585

Vincennes Community SC 2,800/K-12
1712 S Hart Street Rd 47591 812-882-4844
Douglas Rose, supt. Fax 885-1427
www.vcsc.k12.in.us
Clark MS 600/6-8
500 Buntin St 47591 812-882-5172
Brian Wilson, prin. Fax 885-1419
Franklin ES 400/K-5
2600 Wabash Ave 47591 812-882-8176
Richard Rutherford, prin. Fax 885-1440
Riley ES 100/K-5
1008 Upper 11th St 47591 812-882-7953
Susan Marchino, prin. Fax 885-1451
Tecumseh-Harrison ES 300/K-5
2116 N 2nd St 47591 812-882-8458
Melissa Gurchiek, prin. Fax 885-1422
Vigo ES 400/K-5
1513 Main St 47591 812-882-5817
Kelley Crowley, prin. Fax 885-1454
Washington ES 100/K-5
2134 Washington Ave 47591 812-882-5167
Eric Goggins, prin. Fax 885-1457

Flaget S 300/PK-5
800 Vigo St 47591 812-882-5460
Anne Pratt, prin. Fax 882-5596

Wabash, Wabash, Pop. 11,209
Metro SD of Wabash County 2,600/K-12
204 N 300 W 46992 260-563-8050
Dr. Sandra Weaver, supt. Fax 569-6836
www.msdwc.k12.in.us
Metro North ES 200/K-6
3844 W 200 N 46992 260-563-8050
Mark Coppler, prin. Fax 569-6838
Sharp Creek ES 300/K-6
264 W 200 N 46992 260-563-8050
Oren Guenin, prin. Fax 569-6841
Southwood ES 500/K-6
840 E State Road 124 46992 260-563-8050
Janet Shoemaker, prin. Fax 569-6842
Other Schools – See La Fontaine

Wabash CSD 1,500/K-12
PO Box 744 46992 260-563-2151
Celia Briggs, supt. Fax 563-2066
www.apaches.k12.in.us
Mills ES 200/4-5
1721 Vernon St 46992 260-563-2645
Mike Mattern, prin. Fax 563-8497
Neighbours ES 500/K-3
1545 N Wabash St 46992 260-563-2345
Melissa Jessup, prin. Fax 563-8883
Wabash MS 300/6-8
150 Colerain St 46992 260-563-4137
Jason Callahan, prin. Fax 569-9805

St. Bernard S 100/PK-6
191 N Cass St 46992 260-563-5746
Theresa Carroll, prin. Fax 563-4898

Wadesville, Posey
Metro SD of North Posey County
Supt. — See Poseyville
South Terrace ES 300/K-6
8427 Haines Rd 47638 812-985-3180
Kelly Carlton, prin. Fax 985-3146

St. Wendel S 100/K-8
4725 St Wendel Cynthiana Rd 47638 812-963-3958
Ron Pittman, prin. Fax 963-3061

Wakarusa, Elkhart, Pop. 1,666
Penn-Harris-Madison SC
Supt. — See Mishawaka
Madison ES 200/K-5
66030 Dogwood Rd 46573 574-633-4531
Lisa Soto-Kile, prin. Fax 633-4987

Wa-Nee Community SD
Supt. — See Nappanee
Northwood MS 800/6-8
301 N Elkhart St 46573 574-862-2710
George Roelandts, prin. Fax 862-2327
Wakarusa ES 600/K-5
400 N Washington St 46573 574-862-2000
Larry Nafziger, prin. Fax 862-2095

Waldron, Shelby
Shelby Eastern SD
Supt. — See Shelbyville
Waldron ES 300/K-5
PO Box 38 46182 765-525-6505
Gina Pleak, prin. Fax 525-4591

Walkerton, Saint Joseph, Pop. 2,200
John Glenn SC 1,800/K-12
101 John Glenn Dr 46574 574-586-3129
Richard Reese, supt. Fax 586-2660
www.jgsc.k12.in.us
Urey MS 300/7-8
407 Washington St 46574 574-586-3184
Janet Carey, prin. Fax 586-3714
Walkerton ES 400/K-6
805 Washington St 46574 574-586-3186
Tim Davis, prin. Fax 586-3280
Other Schools – See North Liberty

Walton, Cass, Pop. 1,028
Southeastern SC 1,600/K-12
6422 E State Road 218 46994 574-626-2525
Dr. John Bevan, supt. Fax 626-2751
www.sesc.k12.in.us
Thompson ES 500/K-6
6540 E State Road 218 46994 574-626-2504
Elizabeth Billman, prin. Fax 626-3483
Other Schools – See Galveston

Wanatah, LaPorte, Pop. 990
Cass Township SD
Supt. — See La Porte
Wanatah Public S 200/K-8
PO Box 249 46390 219-733-2815
Victorine DePrey, prin. Fax 733-9974

Warren, Huntington, Pop. 1,248
Huntington County Community SC
Supt. — See Huntington
Salamonie S 500/K-8
1063 E 900 S 46792 260-375-3434
Rick Reed, prin. Fax 375-3435

Warsaw, Kosciusko, Pop. 12,735
Warsaw Community SC 6,900/K-12
PO Box 288 46581 574-371-5098
Craig Hintz Ed.D., supt. Fax 371-5046
www.warsaw.k12.in.us
Edgewood MS 500/7-8
900 S Union St 46580 574-371-5096
JoElla Smyth, prin. Fax 371-5010
Eisenhower ES 600/K-6
1900 S County Farm Rd 46580 574-269-7440
Melissa Rees, prin. Fax 371-5011
Harrison ES 700/K-6
1300 Husky Trl 46582 574-269-7533
Randy Polston, prin. Fax 371-5007
Lakeview MS 500/7-8
848 E Smith St 46580 574-269-7211
Jon Lippe, prin. Fax 371-5013
Lincoln ES 500/K-6
203 N Lincoln St 46580 574-267-7474
Cathy Snyder, prin. Fax 371-5005
Madison ES 600/K-6
201 N Union St 46580 574-267-6231
Jacob Hoag, prin. Fax 371-5006
Washington ES 600/K-6
423 Kincaide St 46580 574-371-5097
Tom Ray, prin. Fax 371-5009
Other Schools – See Leesburg, Winona Lake

Sacred Heart S 200/PK-6
135 N Harrison St 46580 574-267-5874
Jim Faroh, prin. Fax 267-5136
Warsaw Christian S 200/PK-6
909 S Buffalo St 46580 574-267-5788
Doug Buller, prin. Fax 267-1486

Washington, Daviess, Pop. 11,357
Washington Community SD 2,400/K-12
301 E South St 47501 812-254-5536
Dr. Bruce Hatton, supt. Fax 254-8346
www.wcs.k12.in.us
Dunn ES 400/K-6
801 NW 11th St 47501 812-254-8366
Brenda Butcher, prin. Fax 254-9420
Griffith ES 400/K-6
803 E National Hwy 47501 812-254-8360
Richard Lloyd, prin. Fax 253-8362
North ES 300/K-6
600 NE 6th St 47501 812-254-8363
Jay Wildman, prin. Fax 254-6955
Veale ES 200/K-6
326 E 450 S 47501 812-254-3968
Rob McCormick, prin. Fax 254-4273
Washington JHS 400/7-8
210 NE 6th St 47501 812-254-2682
Mark Arnold, prin. Fax 254-8381

Washington Catholic S 300/PK-5
310 NE 2nd St 47501 812-254-3845
David Memmer, prin. Fax 254-8741

Waterloo, DeKalb, Pop. 2,198
DeKalb County Central United SC 4,200/PK-12
3326 County Road 427 46793 260-920-1011
Sherry Grate Ed.D., supt. Fax 837-7767
www.dekalb.k12.in.us
DeKalb MS 1,000/6-8
3338 County Road 427 46793 260-920-1013
Thomas Sanborn, prin. Fax 837-7812
Waterloo ES 300/K-5
300 E Douglas St 46793 260-920-1016
Mark Benbow, prin. Fax 837-7051
Other Schools – See Ashley, Auburn

Waveland, Montgomery, Pop. 412
South Montgomery Community SC
Supt. — See New Market
Waveland ES 200/K-6
506 E Green St 47989 765-435-2465
Rodney Simpson, prin. Fax 435-2026

Westfield, Hamilton, Pop. 12,322
Westfield Washington SD 5,400/PK-12
322 W Main St 46074 317-867-8000
Mark Keen, supt. Fax 867-0929
www.wws.k12.in.us
Carey Ridge ES 600/PK-4
16231 Carey Rd 46074 317-867-6200
Susan Hobson, prin. Fax 867-2363
Maple Glen ES 300/PK-4
17171 Ditch Rd 46074 317-896-4700
Joe Montalone, prin. Fax 867-2952
Monon Trail ES PK-4
19400 Tomlinson Rd 46074 317-867-8600
Randy Miller, prin.
Oak Trace ES 400/PK-4
16504 Oak Ridge Rd 46074 317-867-6400
Robin Lynch, prin. Fax 867-4361
Shamrock Springs ES 500/K-4
747 W 161st St 46074 317-867-7400
Corey Hartley, prin. Fax 867-1724
Washington Woods ES 500/K-4
17950 Grassy Branch Rd 46074 317-867-7900
Scott Williams, prin. Fax 867-1501
Westfield IS 900/5-6
326 W Main St 46074 317-867-6500
Dave Mundy, prin. Fax 896-1987
Westfield MS 800/7-8
345 W Hoover St 46074 317-867-6600
Linda Konkle, prin. Fax 867-1407

St. Maria Goretti S 400/K-8
17104 Springmill Rd 46074 317-896-5582
Rebecca Hammel, prin. Fax 867-0783

West Harrison, Dearborn, Pop. 317
Sunman-Dearborn Community SC
Supt. — See Sunman
Sunman-Dearborn IS 700/5-6
27650 Old State Route 1 47060 812-576-1900
Chris Vennemeir, prin. Fax 576-1901

West Lafayette, Tippecanoe, Pop. 28,599
Tippecanoe SC
Supt. — See Lafayette
Battle Ground MS 400/6-8
6100 N 50 W 47906 765-567-2122
BeAnn Younker, prin. Fax 567-2325
Burnett Creek ES 500/K-5
5700 N 50 W 47906 765-463-2237
Mark Pearl, prin. Fax 463-2691
Klondike ES 900/K-5
3311 Klondike Rd 47906 765-463-5505
Scott Peters, prin. Fax 497-0023
Klondike MS 400/6-8
3307 Klondike Rd 47906 765-463-2544
Christine Cannon, prin. Fax 497-9413

West Lafayette Community SC 2,000/K-12
1130 N Salisbury St 47906 765-746-1641
Rocky Killion, supt. Fax 746-1644
www.wl.k12.in.us/
Cumberland ES 500/K-3
600 Cumberland Ave 47906 765-464-3212
Kimberly Bowers, prin. Fax 464-3210
Happy Hollow ES 500/4-6
1200 N Salisbury St 47906 765-746-0500
Sally Downham Miller, prin. Fax 746-0507
West Lafayette JHS 300/7-8
1105 N Grant St 47906 765-746-0404
Ronald Shriner, prin. Fax 746-0420

Montessori S of Greater Lafayette 200/PK-3
PO Box 2311 47996 765-464-1133
Suman Harshvardhan, prin. Fax 464-8363
Pleasantview SDA S 50/PK-6
3509 Soldiers Home Rd 47906 765-497-7978
Michelle McCaw, prin. Fax 463-1221

West Lebanon, Warren, Pop. 789
Metro SD of Warren County
Supt. — See Williamsport
Warren Central ES 300/K-6
1224 S State Road 263 47991 765-893-4525
Douglas Allison, prin. Fax 893-8355

West Newton, Marion
Metro SD of Decatur Township
Supt. — See Indianapolis
West Newton ES 600/1-4
7529 Mooresville Rd 46183 317-856-5237
Dr. Janet Larch, prin. Fax 856-2148

West Terre Haute, Vigo, Pop. 2,255
Vigo County SC
Supt. — See Terre Haute
Fayette ES 300/K-5
9400 N Beech Pl 47885 812-462-4451
Susan Hudson, prin. Fax 462-4453
Sugar Creek Consolidated ES 300/K-5
4226 W Old US Highway 40 47885 812-462-4443
Marsha Jones, prin. Fax 462-4444
West Vigo ES 400/PK-5
501 W Olive St 47885 812-462-4418
Peggy Pfrank, prin. Fax 462-4410
West Vigo MS 500/6-8
4750 W Sarah Myers Dr 47885 812-462-4361
Tim Vislosky, prin. Fax 462-4358

Westville, LaPorte, Pop. 5,219
Metro SD of New Durham Township 900/K-12
207 E Valparaiso St 46391 219-785-2239
Robert Harbart, supt. Fax 785-4584
www.westville.k12.in.us/
Westville ES 500/K-6
207 E Valparaiso St 46391 219-785-2532
Larry Cook, prin. Fax 785-6135

Wheatfield, Jasper, Pop. 865
Kankakee Valley SC 3,500/K-12
PO Box 278 46392 219-987-4711
Dr. Glenn Krueger, supt. Fax 987-4710
www.kv.k12.in.us
Kankakee Valley IS 800/4-6
12345 N 550 W 46392 219-987-2027
John Shank, prin. Fax 987-3207
Kankakee Valley MS 500/7-8
3923 W State Road 10 46392 219-956-3143
William Auker, prin. Fax 956-3143
Wheatfield ES 400/K-3
PO Box 158 46392 219-956-3221
Richard Bolinger, prin. Fax 987-4710
Other Schools – See Demotte

Whiteland, Johnson, Pop. 4,271
Clark-Pleasant Community SC 5,200/K-12
50 Center St 46184 317-535-7579
Dr. J.T. Coopman, supt. Fax 535-4931
www.cpcsc.k12.in.us
Clark Pleasant MS 800/7-8
222 Tracy St 46184 317-535-7121
Sondra Wooton, prin. Fax 535-2064
Pleasant Crossing ES K-4
3030 N 125 W 46184 317-535-3244
Terry Magnuson, prin. Fax 535-0706
Whiteland ES 600/K-4
120 Center St 46184 317-535-4211
Dr. Courtney Knight, prin. Fax 535-2091
Other Schools – See Franklin, Greenwood, New Whiteland

Whitestown, Boone, Pop. 688
Zionsville Community SC
Supt. — See Zionsville
Zionsville West MS 400/5-6
5565 S 700 E 46075 317-873-1240
Tim East, prin. Fax 769-6909

Traders Point Christian Academy 400/PK-10
6600 S Indianapolis Rd 46075 317-769-2450
Dr. Jack Powell, supt. Fax 769-2456

Whiting, Lake, Pop. 4,893
Hammond CSD
Supt. — See Hammond
Franklin ES 300/K-5
1000 116th St 46394 219-659-1241
Perry Palmer, prin. Fax 659-1242

Whiting CSD 900/PK-12
1500 Center St 46394 219-659-0656
Dr. Sandra Martinez, supt. Fax 473-4008
www.whiting.k12.in.us
Hale ES 400/PK-5
1831 Oliver St 46394 219-659-0738
Penny Banfield, prin. Fax 473-1343
Whiting MS 200/6-8
1800 New York Ave 46394 219-473-1344
Cindy Scroggins, prin. Fax 473-1341

St. John the Baptist S 500/PK-8
1844 Lincoln Ave 46394 219-659-3042
Mark Topp, prin. Fax 473-7553

Williamsport, Warren, Pop. 1,928
Metro SD of Warren County 1,300/K-12
101 N Monroe St 47993 765-762-3364
Ralph Shrader, supt. Fax 762-6623
www.msdwarco.k12.in.us/
Williamsport ES 200/K-6
206 E Monroe St 47993 765-762-2500
Moira Clark, prin. Fax 762-0371
Other Schools – See Pine Village, West Lebanon

Winamac, Pulaski, Pop. 2,436
Eastern Pulaski Community SC 1,400/K-12
711 School Dr 46996 574-946-4010
Robert Klitzman, supt. Fax 946-4510
www.epulaski.k12.in.us/
Eastern Pulaski ES 600/K-5
815 School Dr 46996 574-946-3955
Jill Collins, prin. Fax 946-4510
Winamac Community MS 300/6-8
715 School Dr 46996 574-946-6525
Stan Good, prin. Fax 946-4219

Winchester, Randolph, Pop. 4,845
Randolph Central SC 1,700/K-12
103 N East St 47394 765-584-1401
Dr. Gregory Hinshaw, supt. Fax 584-1403
www.rc.k12.in.us
Baker ES 300/K-2
600 S Oak St 47394 765-584-5581
Cynthia Winkle, prin. Fax 584-7900
Driver MS 400/6-8
130 S 100 E 47394 765-584-4671
Tim Passmore, prin. Fax 584-6271
Willard ES 300/3-5
615 W South St 47394 765-584-9171
Randy Rains, prin. Fax 584-1961
Other Schools – See Ridgeville

Winona Lake, Kosciusko, Pop. 4,235
Warsaw Community SC
Supt. — See Warsaw
Jefferson ES 400/K-6
1 Jefferson Dr 46590 574-267-7361
Dennis Duncan, prin. Fax 371-5003

Winslow, Pike, Pop. 856
Pike County SC
Supt. — See Petersburg
Winslow ES 300/PK-5
301 E Porter St 47598 812-789-2209
Ritchie Luker, prin. Fax 789-2795

Wolcott, White, Pop. 939
Tri-County SC 700/K-12
105 N 2nd St 47995 219-279-2418
Dr. Gib Crimmins, supt. Fax 279-2242
www.trico.k12.in.us
Tri-County IS 200/3-6
200 W North St 47995 219-279-2138
Steve Ulrich, prin. Fax 279-2026
Other Schools – See Remington

Wolcottville, Lagrange, Pop. 953
Lakeland SC
Supt. — See Lagrange
Wolcott Mills ES 300/K-5
PO Box 308 46795 260-499-2450
Brad Targgart, prin. Fax 854-3089

Prairie Heights Community SC
Supt. — See Lagrange
Milford ES 200/K-4
9245 E 500 S 46795 260-351-3083
Dr. Gayle Green, prin. Fax 351-2036

Wolflake, Noble
Central Noble Community SC
Supt. — See Albion
Wolf Lake ES 300/K-5
PO Box 67 46796 260-635-2432
Lonnie Ladig, prin. Fax 635-2372

Woodburn, Allen, Pop. 1,635
East Allen County SD
Supt. — See New Haven
Woodburn ES 400/K-6
23005 Woodburn Rd 46797 260-446-0280
Jodie Clark, prin. Fax 446-0283

Woodburn Lutheran S 100/PK-8
PO Box 159 46797 260-632-5493
Dexter Hoyer, prin. Fax 632-0005

Worthington, Greene, Pop. 1,488
White River Valley SD
Supt. — See Switz City
Worthington ES 200/K-6
484 W Main St 47471 812-875-3839
Kevin Keller, prin. Fax 875-2199

Yoder, Allen

St. Aloysius S 100/K-8
14607 Bluffton Rd 46798 260-622-7151
Chuck Grimm, prin. Fax 622-7961

Yorktown, Delaware, Pop. 4,966
Mt. Pleasant Township Community SC 2,300/K-12
8800 W Smith St 47396 765-759-2720
Dr. Zach Rozelle, supt. Fax 759-7894
www.yorktown.k12.in.us
Pleasant View ES 500/K-2
9101 W River Rd 47396 765-759-2800
Dennis Bigler, prin. Fax 759-3258
Yorktown ES 600/3-5
8810 W Smith St 47396 765-759-2770
Amanda Eller, prin. Fax 759-4038
Yorktown MS 500/6-8
8820 W Smith St 47396 765-759-2660
Heath Dudley, prin. Fax 759-3243

Zionsville, Boone, Pop. 11,853
Zionsville Community SC 4,600/PK-12
900 Mulberry St 46077 317-873-2858
Scott Robison, supt. Fax 873-8003
www.zcs.k12.in.us
Eagle ES 400/K-4
350 N 6th St 46077 317-873-1234
Deb P'Pool, prin. Fax 873-5868
Pleasant View ES 500/PK-4
4700 S 975 E 46077 317-873-2376
Chad Smith, prin. Fax 873-1250
Stonegate ES 500/K-4
7312 W Stonegate Dr 46077 317-873-8050
Kristin Cavolick, prin. Fax 769-4975
Union ES 100/K-4
11750 E 300 S 46077 317-733-4007
Jenny Bivans, prin. Fax 733-4008
Zionsville MS 1,200/5-8
900 N Ford Rd 46077 317-873-2426
Sean Conner, prin. Fax 733-4001
Other Schools – See Whitestown

IOWA

IOWA DEPARTMENT OF EDUCATION
400 E 14th St, Des Moines 50319-0146
Telephone 515-281-5294
Fax 515-242-5988
Website http://www.state.ia.us/educate

Director of Education Judy Jeffrey

IOWA BOARD OF EDUCATION
400 E 14th St, Des Moines 50319-9000

President Rosie Hussey

AREA EDUCATION AGENCIES (AEA)

AEA 267
Dean Meier, admin. 319-273-8200
3712 Cedar Heights Dr Fax 273-8229
Cedar Falls 50613
www.aea267.k12.ia.us

Grant Wood AEA 10
Ron Fielder, admin., 4401 6th St SW 319-399-6700
Cedar Rapids 52404 Fax 399-6457
www.aea10.k12.ia.us/

Great Prairie AEA
Joe Crozier, admin. 641-682-8591
2814 N Court St, Ottumwa 52501 Fax 682-9083
www.gpaea.k12.ia.us

Green Valley AEA 14
Connie Maxson, admin. 641-782-8443
1405 N Lincoln St, Creston 50801 Fax 782-4298
www.aea14.k12.ia.us/

Heartland AEA 11
Maxine Kilcrease, admin. 515-270-9030
6500 Corporate Dr Fax 270-5383
Johnston 50131
www.aea11.k12.ia.us/

Keystone AEA 1
Robert Vittengl, admin. 563-245-1480
1400 2nd St NW, Elkader 52043 Fax 245-1484
www.aea1.k12.ia.us

Loess Hills AEA 13
Glenn Grove, admin. 712-366-0503
PO Box 1109, Council Bluffs 51502 Fax 366-3431
www.aea13.org/

Mississippi Bend AEA 9
Glen Pelecky, admin. 563-359-1371
729 21st St, Bettendorf 52722 Fax 359-5967
www.aea9.k12.ia.us/

Northwest AEA
Tim Grieves, admin. 712-222-6000
1520 Morningside Ave Fax 222-6123
Sioux City 51106
www.aea12.k12.ia.us

Prairie Lakes AEA 8
Kay Forsythe, admin. 712-335-3588
PO Box 802, Pocahontas 50574 Fax 335-4600
www.aea8.k12.ia.us/

PUBLIC, PRIVATE AND CATHOLIC ELEMENTARY SCHOOLS

Ackley, Hardin, Pop. 1,738
AGWSR Community SD 600/PK-12
511 State St 50601 641-847-2611
Robert Weber, supt. Fax 847-2612
www.agwsr.k12.ia.us
Ackley ES 200/K-3
511 State St 50601 641-847-2611
Teresa Keninger, prin. Fax 847-2612
Cougars Den Preschool Center PK-PK
413 State St 50601 – Amy Sill, dir. 641-847-2699
Other Schools – See Wellsburg

Adair, Guthrie, Pop. 773
Adair-Casey Community SD 400/PK-12
3384 Indigo Ave 50002 641-746-2241
Steve Smith, supt. Fax 746-2243
accs.k12.ia.us
Adair-Casey ES 200/PK-6
3384 Indigo Ave 50002 641-746-2242
Cynthia Jensen, prin. Fax 746-2243

Adel, Dallas, Pop. 4,046
Adel-De Soto-Minburn Community SD 1,300/PK-12
801 Nile Kinnick Dr S 50003 515-993-4283
Greg Dufoe, supt. Fax 993-4866
www.adel.k12.ia.us
Adel-De Soto-Minburn ES 300/PK-2
1608 Grove St 50003 515-993-4285
Carol Erickson, prin. Fax 993-4403
Adel-De Soto-Minburn MS 200/6-7
215 N 11th St 50003 515-993-4778
Kim Timmerman, prin. Fax 993-4839
Other Schools – See De Soto, Minburn

Afton, Union, Pop. 886
East Union Community SD 500/K-12
1916 High School Dr 50830 641-347-5215
Dr. Pam Vogel, supt. Fax 347-5514
www.east-union.k12.ia.us
East Union IS 100/2-5
1916 High School Dr 50830 641-347-8774
Joan Gordon, prin. Fax 347-5514
East Union PS 100/K-1
103 S Douglas St 50830 641-347-5411
Joan Gordon, prin. Fax 347-5514

Ainsworth, Washington, Pop. 546
Highland Community SD
Supt. — See Riverside
Ainsworth ES 100/PK-5
PO Box 220 52201 319-657-3151
Shawn Donovan, prin. Fax 657-2203

Akron, Plymouth, Pop. 1,467
Akron Westfield Community SD 600/PK-12
PO Box 950 51001 712-568-2616
Ron Flynn, supt. Fax 568-2997
www.akron-westfield.k12.ia.us
Akron Westfield ES 200/PK-5
PO Box 950 51001 712-568-3322
Cathy Bobier, prin. Fax 568-2997
Akron Westfield MS 100/6-8
PO Box 950 51001 712-568-2020
Cathy Bobier, prin. Fax 568-2997

Albert City, Buena Vista, Pop. 696
Albert City-Truesdale Community SD 100/PK-6
PO Box 98 50510 712-843-5496
Marlin Lode, supt. Fax 843-2195
www.albertct.k12.ia.us
Albert City-Truesdale ES 100/PK-6
PO Box 98 50510 712-843-5416
Barbara Kady, prin. Fax 843-5551

Albia, Monroe, Pop. 3,679
Albia Community SD 1,200/K-12
120 Benton Ave E 52531 641-932-5165
Kevin Crall, supt. Fax 932-5192
www.albia.k12.ia.us
Albia JHS 200/7-8
505 C Ave E 52531 641-932-2161
Alan Schwarte, prin. Fax 932-7069
Grant Center ES 200/1-2
520 S Clinton St 52531 641-932-2161
Nancy Foust, prin. Fax 932-5192
Kendall Center K 100/K-K
701 Washington Ave E 52531 641-932-2161
Nancy Foust, prin. Fax 932-5192
Lincoln Center ES 300/3-6
222 N 3rd St 52531 641-932-2161
Larry Achenbach, prin. Fax 932-5192

Alburnett, Linn, Pop. 539
Alburnett Community SD 600/K-12
PO Box 400 52202 319-842-2261
Mike Harrold, supt. Fax 842-2398
www.alburnett.k12.ia.us
Alburnett ES 300/K-6
PO Box 400 52202 319-842-2261
Julie Lines, prin. Fax 842-2398

Alden, Hardin, Pop. 854
Alden Community SD 200/K-6
PO Box 48 50006 515-859-3393
John Robbins, supt. Fax 859-3395
www.alden.k12.ia.us
Alden ES 200/K-6
PO Box 48 50006 515-859-3394
Kim Nelson, prin. Fax 859-3395

Algona, Kossuth, Pop. 5,505
Algona Community SD 1,200/PK-12
PO Box 717 50511 515-295-3528
Marty Fonley, supt. Fax 295-5166
www.algona.k12.ia.us
Bryant ES 100/2-3
120 E North St 50511 515-295-7773
Dave Kerkove, prin. Fax 295-5824
Godfrey ES 200/PK-1
124 N Main St 50511 515-295-3586
Dave Kerkove, prin. Fax 295-5328
Laing MS 300/6-8
213 S Harlan St 50511 515-295-9447
Gregory Stewart, prin. Fax 295-9448
Wallace IS 200/4-5
729 E Kennedy St 50511 515-295-7296
Greg Stewart, prin. Fax 295-6068

Seton S 400/PK-8
808 E Lucas St 50511 515-295-3509
Kathee Froehlich, prin. Fax 295-5688

Alleman, Polk, Pop. 430
North Polk Community SD 1,100/PK-12
313 NE 141st Ave 50007 515-685-3014
Dr. Ann Curphey, supt. Fax 685-2002
www.n-polk.k12.ia.us
North Polk Central ES 300/K-6
311 NE 141st Ave 50007 515-685-3330
Terry Anselme, prin. Fax 685-2304
Other Schools – See Polk City

Allison, Butler, Pop. 981
Allison-Bristow Community SD 300/K-8
PO Box 428 50602 319-267-2205
Warren Davison, supt. Fax 267-2926
www.alli-bris.k12.ia.us/
Allison ES, PO Box 428 50602 100/K-4
Ann Chinander, prin. 319-267-2212
North Butler MS 200/5-8
PO Box 428 50602 319-267-2552
Dan Huff, prin. Fax 267-2926

Alta, Buena Vista, Pop. 1,874
Alta Community SD 600/PK-12
101 W 5th St 51002 712-200-1010
Dr. Fred Maharry, supt. Fax 200-1602
www.alta.k12.ia.us
Alta ES 200/PK-4
1009 S Main St 51002 712-200-1400
Maxine Lampe, prin. Fax 200-2459
Alta MS 200/5-8
1009 S Main St 51002 712-200-1401
Maxine Lampe, prin. Fax 200-2459

Alton, Sioux, Pop. 1,117
MOC-Floyd Valley Community SD
Supt. — See Orange City
MOC-Floyd Valley MS 300/6-8
1104 5th Ave 51003 712-756-4128
John VandeWeerd, prin. Fax 756-4100

Spalding Catholic S 100/PK-6
PO Box 436 51003 712-756-4532
Kathy Alons, prin. Fax 756-4532

Altoona, Polk, Pop. 12,938
Southeast Polk Community SD
Supt. — See Pleasant Hill
Altoona ES 400/K-6
301 6th St SW 50009 515-967-3771
Dennis O'Lear, prin. Fax 967-2079
Centennial ES 600/K-6
910 7th Ave SE 50009 515-967-2109
Steve Stotts, prin. Fax 967-7076

Clay ES PK-6
3200 1st Ave S 50009 515-967-4198
Lea Morris, prin. Fax 967-2018
Willowbrook ES 500/PK-6
300 17th Ave SW 50009 515-967-7512
Robin Norris, prin. Fax 967-1620

Ames, Story, Pop. 52,263
Ames Community SD 4,400/PK-12
415 Stanton Ave 50014 515-268-6600
Dr. Linda Beyea, supt. Fax 268-6633
www.ames.k12.ia.us
Ames MS 1,000/6-8
3915 Mortensen Rd 50014 515-268-2400
Jeff Anderson, prin. Fax 268-2419
Edwards ES 200/K-5
3622 Woodland St 50014 515-239-3760
Dave Peterson, prin. Fax 239-3814
Fellows ES 500/K-5
1400 Mckinley Dr 50010 515-239-3765
Carol Page, prin. Fax 239-3837
Meeker ES 400/K-5
300 20th St 50010 515-239-3770
Steve Flynn, prin. Fax 239-3812
Mitchell ES 200/K-5
3521 Jewel Dr 50010 515-239-3775
Pam Stangeland, prin. Fax 239-3823
Northwood ECC 200/PK-K
601 28th St 50010 515-268-2470
Jody Klaver, prin. Fax 268-2471
Sawyer ES 400/K-5
4316 Ontario St 50014 515-239-3790
Dr. Randy Podhaski, prin. Fax 239-3815

Ames Christian S 100/PK-8
925 S 16th St 50010 515-233-0772
Peggy Smith, admin. Fax 232-0005
St. Cecilia S 200/PK-5
2900 Hoover Ave 50010 515-232-5290
Thomas Budnik, prin. Fax 233-6423

Anamosa, Jones, Pop. 5,616
Anamosa Community SD 1,300/PK-12
200 S Garnavillo St 52205 319-462-4321
Dr. Dale Monroe, supt. Fax 462-4322
www.anamosa.k12.ia.us
Strawberry Hill ES 500/PK-5
203 Hamilton St 52205 319-462-3549
Josh Lyons, prin. Fax 462-5317
West MS 300/6-8
200 S Garnavillo St 52205 319-462-3553
Linda Vaughn, prin. Fax 462-4322

St. Patrick S 100/PK-6
216 N Garnavillo St 52205 319-462-2688
Charlotte Scheckel, prin. Fax 462-3239

Andrew, Jackson, Pop. 452
Andrew Community SD 300/PK-12
PO Box 230 52030 563-672-3221
Kent Hammer, supt. Fax 672-9750
www.andrew.k12.ia.us
Andrew ES 200/PK-6
PO Box 230 52030 563-672-3221
William Hamilton, prin. Fax 672-9750

Anita, Cass, Pop. 1,166
Anita Community SD 200/K-12
1000 Victory Park Rd 50020 712-762-3231
John Brazell, supt. Fax 762-3713
www.anita.k12.ia.us
Anita ES 100/K-5
709 McIntyre Dr 50020 712-762-3343
John Brazell, prin. Fax 762-3249

Ankeny, Polk, Pop. 36,681
Ankeny Community SD 7,200/PK-12
PO Box 189 50021 515-965-9600
Dr. Matthew Wendt, supt. Fax 965-4234
www.ankenyschools.org/
Ashland Ridge ES K-5
2600 NW Ash Dr, 515-965-9594
Mark Moss, prin. Fax 965-9593
Crocker ES 600/K-5
2910 SW Applewood St, 515-965-9710
Dr. Tom Muhlenbruck, prin. Fax 965-9714
East ES 300/PK-5
710 SE 3rd St 50021 515-965-9660
Julianne Steven, prin. Fax 965-9663
Northeast ES 700/K-5
1705 NE Trilein Dr 50021 515-965-9620
Al Neppl, prin. Fax 965-9621
Northwest ES 400/K-5
1202 W 1st St, 515-965-9680
Jason Albrecht, prin. Fax 965-9683
Parkview MS 1,100/6-7
105 NW Pleasant St, 515-965-9640
Jeff Schumacher, prin. Fax 965-9648
Southeast ES 500/K-5
1005 SE Trilein Dr 50021 515-965-9650
Matt Adams, prin. Fax 965-9653
Terrace ES 500/K-5
310 NW School St, 515-965-9670
Tiffany O'hara, prin. Fax 965-9672
Westwood ES 600/K-5
2920 NW 9th St, 515-965-9690
Jim Ford, prin. Fax 965-9693

Ankeny Christian Academy 200/PK-12
1604 W 1st St, 515-965-8114
Joyce Hansen, admin. Fax 965-8210

Anthon, Woodbury, Pop. 634
Anthon-Oto Community SD 300/K-8
PO Box E 51004 712-373-5246
Steve Oberg, supt. Fax 373-5326
www.maple-valley.k12.ia.us/
Anthon-Oto ES 100/K-5
PO Box E 51004 712-373-5244
Jane Ellis, prin. Fax 373-5326
Anthon-Oto-Maple Valley MS 200/6-8
PO Box E 51004 712-373-5244
Jane Ellis, prin. Fax 373-5326

Aplington, Butler, Pop. 1,023
Aplington-Parkersburg Community SD 800/PK-12
215 10th St 50604 319-347-2394
Jon Thompson, supt. Fax 347-2395
www.apl-park.k12.ia.us
Aplington ES 200/PK-5
215 10th St 50604 319-347-6621
Amy May, prin. Fax 347-2395
Aplington-Parkersburg MS 200/6-8
215 10th St 50604 319-347-6621
Jon Thompson, prin. Fax 347-2395
Other Schools – See Parkersburg

Arcadia, Carroll, Pop. 429
Ar-We-Va Community SD
Supt. — See Westside
Arcadia ES, 421 W Center St 51430 100/3-5
Rosemary Cameron, prin. 712-689-2227

Arlington, Fayette, Pop. 481
Starmont Community SD 700/PK-12
3202 40th St 50606 563-933-4598
Matt O'Loughlin, supt. Fax 933-2134
www.starmont.k12.ia.us
Starmont ES 300/PK-4
3202 40th St 50606 563-933-2238
Sandy Klaus, prin. Fax 933-2134
Starmont MS 200/5-8
3202 40th St 50606 563-933-4902
Sandy Klaus, prin. Fax 933-2134

Armstrong, Emmet, Pop. 902
Armstrong-Ringsted Community SD 300/PK-12
PO Box 75 50514 712-868-3550
Randy Collins, supt. Fax 868-3550
www.armstrong.k12.ia.us
Other Schools – See Ringsted

Arnolds Park, Dickinson, Pop. 1,211
Okoboji Community SD
Supt. — See Milford
Okoboji MS 300/5-8
10 W Broadway St 51331 712-332-5641
Ryan Cunningham, prin. Fax 332-7180

Atkins, Benton, Pop. 1,330
Benton Community SD
Supt. — See Van Horne
Atkins ES 200/PK-4
217 4th Ave 52206 319-446-7525
Jason West, prin. Fax 446-7966

Atlantic, Cass, Pop. 6,959
Atlantic Community SD 1,500/K-12
1100 Linn St 50022 712-243-4252
Dan Crozier, supt. Fax 243-8023
www.atlantic.k12.ia.us/
Atlantic MS 300/6-8
1100 Linn St 50022 712-243-1330
Todd Roecker, prin. Fax 243-7732
Schuler ES 200/4-5
1100 Linn St 50022 712-243-1370
Matt Alexander, prin. Fax 243-2120
Washington ES 400/K-3
500 E 14th St 50022 712-243-5234
Stacey Hornung, prin. Fax 243-5275

Audubon, Audubon, Pop. 2,257
Audubon Community SD 600/PK-12
800 3rd Ave 50025 712-563-2607
Brett Gibbs, supt. Fax 563-3607
www.audubon.k12.ia.us/
Audubon ES 200/PK-4
600 Tracy St 50025 712-563-3751
Sam Graeve, prin. Fax 563-3607
Audubon MS 100/5-8
800 3rd Ave 50025 712-563-3779
Bonnie Lynam, prin. Fax 563-3607

Aurelia, Cherokee, Pop. 973
Aurelia Community SD 300/PK-12
300 Ash St 51005 712-434-2284
Lynn Evans, supt. Fax 434-2053
www.aurelia.k12.ia.us
Aurelia ES 100/PK-4
300 Ash St 51005 712-434-5682
Ann Sandine, prin. Fax 434-2053
Aurelia MS 100/5-8
300 Ash St 51005 712-434-5682
Tom Vint, prin. Fax 434-2053

Avoca, Pottawattamie, Pop. 1,562
A-H-S-T Community SD 600/PK-12
PO Box 158 51521 712-343-6304
Michael Alexander, supt. Fax 343-6915
www.ahst.k12.ia.us
A-H-S-T ES 300/PK-5
PO Box 398 51521 712-343-6364
Staci Edwards, prin. Fax 343-2170

Bancroft, Kossuth, Pop. 752

St. John the Baptist S 50/K-5
PO Box 258 50517 515-885-2580
Lynn Miller, prin. Fax 885-2462

Barnum, Webster, Pop. 196
Manson NW Webster Community SD
Supt. — See Manson
Manson Northwest Webster ES 100/PK-6
303 Pierce St 50518 515-542-3211
Rose Davis, prin. Fax 542-3214

Battle Creek, Ida, Pop. 716
Battle Creek-Ida Grove Community SD
Supt. — See Ida Grove
Battle Creek-Ida Grove MS 200/5-8
600 Chestnut St 51006 712-365-4354
Russ Freeman, prin. Fax 365-4357

Baxter, Jasper, Pop. 1,063
Baxter Community SD 400/K-12
PO Box 189 50028 641-227-3102
Neil Seales, supt. Fax 227-3217
www.baxter.k12.ia.us
Baxter ES 200/K-6
PO Box 189 50028 641-227-3102
Joseph Engel, prin. Fax 227-3217

Bedford, Taylor, Pop. 1,525
Bedford Community SD 500/PK-12
PO Box 234 50833 712-523-2656
Joe Drake, supt. Fax 523-3166
www.bedford.k12.ia.us
Bedford ES 200/PK-5
PO Box 234 50833 712-523-2116
Dana Nally, prin. Fax 523-2308

Belle Plaine, Benton, Pop. 2,919
Belle Plaine Community SD 600/PK-12
707 7th St 52208 319-444-3611
William Lynch, supt. Fax 444-3617
www.belle-plaine.k12.ia.us
Central ES 200/2-6
807 16th St 52208 319-444-3137
Dennis Phelps, prin. Fax 444-3180
Lincoln JHS 100/7-8
1511 9th Ave 52208 319-444-3631
Dennis Phelps, prin. Fax 444-3671
Longfellow ES 100/PK-1
707 7th St 52208 319-444-3002
Dennis Phelps, prin. Fax 444-3064

Bellevue, Jackson, Pop. 2,358
Bellevue Community SD 700/PK-12
1601 State St 52031 563-872-4913
Dr. Mike Healy, supt. Fax 872-3216
www.bellevue.k12.ia.us
Bellevue ES 300/PK-5
100 S 3rd St 52031 563-872-4003
Linda Nudd, prin. Fax 872-5049

St. Joseph S 200/PK-8
403 Park St 52031 563-872-3284
James Squiers, prin. Fax 872-3285

Belmond, Wright, Pop. 2,451
Belmond-Klemme Community SD 300/PK-12
411 10th Ave NE 50421 641-444-4300
Larry Frakes, supt. Fax 444-4524
www.belmond-klemme.k12.ia.us
Jacobson ES, 1004 7th St NE 50421 PK-6
Larry Frakes, prin. 641-444-4300

Bennett, Cedar, Pop. 386
Bennett Community SD 100/K-6
PO Box D 52721 563-890-2226
John Sauer, supt. Fax 890-2937
Bennett ES 100/K-6
PO Box D 52721 563-890-2226
Gene Schroeder, prin. Fax 890-2937

Bernard, Dubuque, Pop. 95
Western Dubuque Community SD
Supt. — See Farley
Bernard ES 100/PK-6
867 Bernard Rd 52032 563-879-3190
Janelle Brouwer, prin. Fax 879-3190

Bettendorf, Scott, Pop. 31,890
Bettendorf Community SD 4,300/K-12
PO Box 1150 52722 563-359-3681
Harrison Cass, supt. Fax 359-3685
www.bettendorf.k12.ia.us
Armstrong ES 300/K-5
3311 Central Ave 52722 563-359-8275
Kevin Hatfield, prin. Fax 359-5228
Bettendorf MS 1,000/6-8
2030 Middle Rd 52722 563-359-3686
Linda Goff, prin. Fax 359-3855
Hoover ES 300/K-5
3223 S Hampton Dr 52722 563-332-8636
Jeffrey Johannsen, prin. Fax 332-5148
Jefferson ES 100/K-5
610 Holmes St 52722 563-359-8261
Bonnie Fisher, prin. Fax 359-6641
Norton ES 500/K-5
4485 Greenbrier Dr 52722 563-332-8936
Julie Trepa, prin. Fax 332-9619
Twain ES 300/K-5
1620 Lincoln Rd 52722 563-359-8263
Caroline Olson, prin. Fax 355-2735
Wood ES 400/K-5
1423 Hillside Dr 52722 563-359-8277
Jerry Fagle, prin. Fax 359-5254

Pleasant Valley Community SD 3,400/PK-12
525 Belmont Rd 52722 563-332-5550
Jim Spelhaug, supt. Fax 332-4372
www.pleasval.k12.ia.us
Pleasant View ES 600/K-6
6333 Crow Creek Rd 52722 563-332-5575
Don Dehner, prin. Fax 332-0223
Riverdale Heights ES 600/K-6
2125 Devils Glen Rd 52722 563-332-0525
Jim Wichman, prin. Fax 332-0525
Other Schools – See Le Claire

Lourdes Catholic S 400/PK-8
1453 Mississippi Blvd 52722 563-359-3466
Katie Selden, prin. Fax 823-1595

Morning Star Academy 300/PK-12
1426 Tanglefoot Ln 52722 563-359-5700
Homar Ramirez, hdmstr. Fax 359-5737
Rivermont Collegiate 200/PK-12
1821 Sunset Dr 52722 563-359-1366
Rick St. Laurent, hdmstr. Fax 359-7576

Birmingham, Van Buren, Pop. 427
Van Buren Community SD
Supt. — See Keosauqua
Birmingham ECC 50/PK-PK
PO Box 125 52535 319-498-4232
Shelly Huffman, dir. Fax 498-4234

Blairsburg, Hamilton, Pop. 227
Northeast Hamilton Community SD 300/K-12
606 Illinois St 50034 515-325-6234
Andrew Woiwood, supt. Fax 325-6235
www.ne-hamilton.k12.ia.us
Northeast Hamilton ES 100/K-5
606 Illinois St 50034 515-325-6234
Patrick Hocking, prin. Fax 325-6235
Northeast Hamilton MS 100/6-8
606 Illinois St 50034 515-325-6234
Patrick Hocking, prin. Fax 325-6235

Blakesburg, Wapello, Pop. 364
Eddyville-Blakesburg Community SD
Supt. — See Eddyville
Blakesburg ES 100/PK-6
407 Wilson St 52536 641-938-2202
Dennis Rutledge, prin. Fax 938-2613
Eddyville-Blakesburg MS 100/7-8
407 Wilson St 52536 641-938-2202
Dennis Rutledge, prin. Fax 938-2613

Bloomfield, Davis, Pop. 2,597
Davis County Community SD 1,200/PK-12
608 S Washington St 52537 641-664-2200
Sam Miller, supt. Fax 664-2221
www.dcmustangs.com/
Davis County ES 500/PK-4
500 E North St 52537 641-664-2200
Linda Perry, prin.
Davis County MS 400/5-8
500 E North St 52537 641-664-2200
Joel Pedersen, prin.

Blue Grass, Scott, Pop. 1,285
Davenport Community SD
Supt. — See Davenport
Blue Grass ES 300/K-5
226 W Sycamore St 52726 563-381-1712
Jeanne Wolf, prin. Fax 381-9024

Bode, Humboldt, Pop. 315
Twin Rivers Community SD 200/PK-12
PO Box 153 50519 515-379-1526
James Kenton, supt. Fax 379-1645
www.trv.k12.ia.us
Twin Rivers ES 50/PK-3
PO Box 121 50519 515-379-1309
Tamela Johnson, prin. Fax 379-1645

Bonaparte, Van Buren, Pop. 455
Harmony Community SD
Supt. — See Farmington
Harmony ES 200/PK-6
602 8th St 52620 319-592-3235
Kim Johnson, prin. Fax 592-3234

Bondurant, Polk, Pop. 2,203
Bondurant-Farrar Community SD 1,200/PK-12
300 Garfield St SW 50035 515-967-7819
Peggy Vint, supt. Fax 967-7847
www.bondurant.k12.ia.us/
Anderson ES 600/PK-6
400 Garfield St SW 50035 515-967-7494
Paul Mills, prin. Fax 957-9099

Boone, Boone, Pop. 12,831
Boone Community SD 1,900/PK-12
500 7th St 50036 515-433-0750
Dr. Bradley Manard, supt. Fax 433-0753
boone.k12.ia.us/
Boone MS 400/6-8
1640 1st St 50036 515-433-0020
Carolyn Clark, prin. Fax 433-0026
Bryant ES 100/5-5
511 Cedar St 50036 515-433-0760
Dr. Pam Nystrom, prin. Fax 433-0762
Franklin ES 300/2-4
1903 Crawford St 50036 515-433-0860
Daniel Gould, prin. Fax 433-0950
Lincoln ES 100/PK-1
711 W Mamie Eisenhower Ave 50036
Christopher Myers, prin. 515-433-0800
Page ES 200/PK-1
102 S Boone St 50036 515-433-0840
Christopher Myers, prin. Fax 433-0762

United Community SD 300/PK-6
1284 U Ave 50036 515-432-5319
Dr. Michele Schleuning, supt. Fax 432-8930
www.united.k12.ia.us
United Community ES 300/PK-6
1284 U Ave 50036 515-432-5393
Robert Thompson, prin. Fax 432-8930

Sacred Heart S 200/PK-8
1111 Marshall St 50036 515-432-4124
Duane Siepker, prin. Fax 433-9927
Trinity Lutheran S 100/PK-8
712 12th St 50036 515-432-6912
Jeffrey Fick, prin. Fax 432-1059

Boxholm, Boone, Pop. 208
Southeast Webster-Grand Community SD
Supt. — See Burnside
Southeast Webster-Grand ES 100/PK-6
PO Box 79 50040 515-846-6214
Richard Wagner, prin. Fax 846-6212

Boyden, Sioux, Pop. 669
Boyden-Hull Community SD
Supt. — See Hull
Boyden ES 300/K-6
PO Box 129 51234 712-725-2381
Tom Kerr, prin. Fax 725-2082

Bridgewater, Adair, Pop. 170
Nodaway Valley Community SD
Supt. — See Greenfield
Nodaway Valley West ES 100/4-5
502 N Main St 50837 641-369-2571
Connie Lundy, prin. Fax 369-4005

Britt, Hancock, Pop. 2,011
West Hancock Community SD 600/PK-12
PO Box 128 50423 641-843-3833
Richard Keith, supt. Fax 843-4717
www.whancock.org/
Britt ES 300/PK-4
PO Box 128 50423 641-843-3833
Richard Keith, prin. Fax 843-4717
Other Schools – See Kanawha

Bronson, Woodbury, Pop. 280
Lawton-Bronson Community SD
Supt. — See Lawton
Bronson ES 300/PK-5
115 W 1st St 51007 712-948-3361
Chad Shook, prin. Fax 948-3211

Brooklyn, Poweshiek, Pop. 1,389
Brooklyn-Guernsey-Malcom Community SD 700/PK-12
1090 Jackson St 52211 641-522-7058
Brad Hohensee, supt. Fax 522-7211
www.brooklyn.k12.ia.us
Brooklyn-Guernsey-Malcom ES 300/PK-6
1090 Jackson St 52211 641-522-9268
Brad Hohensee, prin. Fax 522-7009

Buffalo, Scott, Pop. 1,275
Davenport Community SD
Supt. — See Davenport
Buffalo ES 300/K-5
329 Dodge St 52728 563-381-2232
Jodi Hoogland, prin. Fax 381-1048

Buffalo Center, Winnebago, Pop. 897
North Iowa Community SD 600/PK-12
111 3rd Ave NW 50424 641-562-2525
Larry Hill, supt. Fax 562-2921
www.northiowa.org
North Iowa ES 200/PK-4
111 3rd Ave NW 50424 641-562-2525
Larry Hill, prin. Fax 562-2921
Other Schools – See Thompson

Burlington, Des Moines, Pop. 25,436
Burlington Community SD 4,200/K-12
1429 West Ave 52601 319-753-6791
Dr. Lee Morrison, supt. Fax 753-6796
www.burlington.k12.ia.us
Black Hawk ES 400/K-5
2804 S 14th St 52601 319-753-5300
Shawn Stringer, prin. Fax 753-5097
Corse ES 400/K-5
700 S Starr Ave 52601 319-753-2707
Dave Van Ness, prin. Fax 753-9862
Grimes ES 300/K-5
800 South St 52601 319-753-0420
Joe Rector, prin. Fax 753-6039
Leopold MS 6-8
3075 Sunnyside Ave 52601 319-753-6791
Madison MS 500/6-8
2132 Madison Ave 52601 319-753-6253
Tim Bolander, prin. Fax 753-6514
North Hill ES 300/K-5
825 N 9th St 52601 319-753-6363
Phillip Noonan, prin. Fax 753-6901
Oak Street MS 500/6-8
903 Oak St 52601 319-753-6773
Geane Cleland, prin. Fax 753-0554
Sunnyside ES 500/K-5
2040 Sunnyside Ave 52601 319-753-5244
Terri Rauhaus, prin. Fax 753-1856

Great River Christian S 100/PK-12
426 Harrison Ave 52601 319-753-2255
Jon Frischkorn, admin. Fax 753-2030
Notre Dame ES 300/PK-6
700 S Roosevelt Ave 52601 319-752-3776
Robert Carr, prin. Fax 752-8690

Burnside, Webster
Southeast Webster-Grand Community SD 600/PK-12
PO Box 49 50521 515-359-2235
Mike Jorgensen, supt. Fax 359-2236
www.se-webster.k12.ia.us
Other Schools – See Boxholm, Dayton

Bussey, Marion, Pop. 456
Twin Cedars Community SD 600/PK-12
2204 Highway G71 50044 641-944-5241
Brian VanderSluis, supt. Fax 944-5824
www.twincedars.k12.ia.us
Twin Cedars ES 300/PK-6
2204 Highway G71 50044 641-944-5245
Brian VanderSluis, prin. Fax 944-5824

Calamus, Clinton, Pop. 404
Calamus-Wheatland Community SD
Supt. — See Wheatland
Calamus-Wheatland ES 300/K-6
PO Box 158 52729 563-246-2221
John Cain, prin. Fax 246-2680

Callender, Webster, Pop. 431
Prairie Valley Community SD
Supt. — See Gowrie
Prairie Valley ES 300/PK-4
PO Box 128 50523 515-548-3265
James Duncan, prin. Fax 548-3806

Calmar, Winneshiek, Pop. 1,062
South Winneshiek Community SD 600/PK-12
PO Box 430 52132 563-562-3269
Richard Janson, supt. Fax 562-3260
www.s-winneshiek.k12.ia.us
Other Schools – See Ossian

C F S Consolidated S 50/6-8
PO Box 815 52132 563-562-3291
Kathryn Schmitt, prin. Fax 562-3292

Camanche, Clinton, Pop. 4,260
Camanche Community SD 1,100/K-12
702 13th Ave 52730 563-259-3000
Thomas Parker, supt. Fax 259-3005
www.camanche.k12.ia.us
Camanche ES 400/K-4
508 11th Pl 52730 563-259-3016
Micah Gearhart, prin. Fax 259-3053
Camanche MS 300/5-8
1400 9th St 52730 563-259-3014
Phil Cochran, prin. Fax 259-3031

Cambridge, Story, Pop. 756
Ballard Community SD
Supt. — See Huxley
Ballard East ES 300/4-6
PO Box 110 50046 515-220-4306
Jamie Coquyt, prin. Fax 220-4310

Carlisle, Warren, Pop. 3,544
Carlisle Community SD 1,200/PK-12
430 School St 50047 515-989-3589
Tom Lane, supt. Fax 989-3075
www.carlisle.k12.ia.us/
Carlisle ES 600/PK-3
430 School St 50047 515-989-0339
Barb Niemeyer, prin. Fax 989-3075
Carlisle JHS 6-8
430 School St 50047 515-989-0833
Keri Schlueter, prin. Fax 989-3075
Other Schools – See Hartford

Carroll, Carroll, Pop. 10,047
Carroll Community SD 1,800/PK-12
1026 N Adams St 51401 712-792-8001
Robert Cordes, supt. Fax 792-8008
www.carroll.k12.ia.us
Adams ES 200/4-5
1026 N Adams St 51401 712-792-8040
Sue Ruch, prin. Fax 792-8008
Carroll MS 500/6-8
3203 N Grant Rd 51401 712-792-8020
Jerry Raymond, prin. Fax 792-8024
Fairview ES 500/PK-3
525 E 18th St 51401 712-792-8030
Sue Ruch, prin. Fax 792-8074

Kuemper Catholic Grade S 400/PK-3
201 S Clark St 51401 712-792-3610
Mary Dobson, prin. Fax 792-8072
Kuemper Catholic Grade S 100/4-5
116 S East St 51401 712-792-8071
Mary Dobson, prin. Fax 792-8072
Kuemper Catholic MS 200/6-8
1519 N West St 51401 712-792-2123
Earl Schiltz, prin. Fax 792-3365

Carson, Pottawattamie, Pop. 706
Riverside Community SD 700/PK-12
PO Box 218 51525 712-484-2212
James Sutton Ed.D., supt. Fax 484-3957
Riverside Community MS 200/5-8
PO Box 218 51525 712-484-2291
Nathan Perrien, prin. Fax 484-3957
Other Schools – See Oakland

Carter Lake, Pottawattamie, Pop. 3,404
Council Bluffs Community SD
Supt. — See Council Bluffs
Carter Lake ES 400/PK-5
1105 Redick Blvd 51510 712-347-5876
Kim Kazmierczak, prin. Fax 347-5273

Cascade, Dubuque, Pop. 2,030
Western Dubuque Community SD
Supt. — See Farley
Cascade ES 200/PK-6
110 Harrison St SE 52033 563-852-3335
Janelle Brouwer, prin. Fax 852-7322

Aquin Catholic S 200/K-8
PO Box 460 52033 563-852-3331
Mary Yamoah, prin. Fax 852-5269

Cedar Falls, Black Hawk, Pop. 36,471
Cedar Falls Community SD 4,500/K-12
1002 W 1st St 50613 319-553-3000
David Stoakes, supt. Fax 277-0614
www.cedar-falls.k12.ia.us
Cedar Heights ES 500/K-6
2417 Rainbow Dr 50613 319-553-2855
Jon Wiebers, prin. Fax 268-2355
Hansen ES 500/K-6
616 Holmes Dr 50613 319-553-2775
Dr. Tony Reid, prin. Fax 268-2347
Lincoln ES 500/K-6
321 W 8th St 50613 319-553-2950
Deb Beving, prin. Fax 266-2827
North Cedar ES 200/K-6
2419 Fern Ave 50613 319-553-2810
Jennifer Hartman, prin. Fax 268-2336

Orchard Hill ES 300/K-6
3909 Rownd St 50613 319-553-2465
Kim Cross, prin. Fax 268-2353
Southdale ES 400/K-6
627 Orchard Dr 50613 319-553-2900
Matt Brummond, prin. Fax 266-3448

St. Patrick S 300/PK-8
615 Washington St 50613 319-277-6781
Sr. Marilou Irons, prin. Fax 266-5806

Cedar Rapids, Linn, Pop. 123,119
Cedar Rapids Community SD 17,000/PK-12
907 15th St SW 52404 319-558-2000
Fax 558-2224
www.cr.k12.ia.us
Arthur ES 300/PK-5
2630 B Ave NE 52402 319-558-2264
William Utterback, prin. Fax 398-2266
Cleveland ES 400/K-5
2200 1st Ave NW 52405 319-558-2463
Denise Pape, prin. Fax 398-2133
Coolidge ES 400/PK-5
6225 1st Ave SW 52405 319-558-2167
Laurinda Fitzgerald, prin. Fax 390-0470
Erskine ES 400/1-5
600 36th St SE 52403 319-558-2364
Annette Zimmerman, prin. Fax 398-2050
Franklin MS 600/6-8
300 20th St NE 52402 319-558-2452
Shannon Bucknell, prin. Fax 398-2454
Garfield ES 300/PK-5
1201 Maplewood Dr NE 52402 319-558-2169
Christopher Myers, prin. Fax 398-2160
Gibson ES 500/PK-5
6101 Gibson Dr NE 52411 319-558-2920
Kevin Uhde, prin. Fax 393-0412
Grant ES 200/PK-1
254 Outlook Dr SW 52404 319-558-2020
Val Dolezal, prin. Fax 398-2022
Harding MS 1,000/6-8
4801 Golf St NE 52402 319-558-2254
Randy Krejci, prin. Fax 378-0671
Harrison ES 400/PK-5
1310 11th St NW 52405 319-558-2269
Joyce Fowler, prin. Fax 398-2268
Hoover ES 300/K-5
4141 Johnson Ave NW 52405 319-558-2369
Brian Krob, prin. Fax 390-0530
Jackson ES 300/K-5
1300 38th St NW 52405 319-558-2471
Carla Davidson, prin. Fax 390-3865
Johnson ES 300/1-5
355 18th St SE 52403 319-558-2174
Craig Saddler, prin. Fax 398-2185
Kenwood ES 300/K-5
3700 E Ave NE 52402 319-558-2273
Tim Cronin, prin. Fax 398-2275
Madison ES 300/K-5
1341 Woodside Dr NW 52405 319-558-2473
Jim Girdner, prin. Fax 390-0534
McKinley MS 600/6-8
620 10th St SE 52403 319-558-2348
Kristen Rickey, prin. Fax 398-2347
Monroe S 300/PK-K
3200 Pioneer Ave SE 52403 319-558-2176
Lisa Quinby, prin. Fax 398-2179
Pierce ES 400/K-5
4343 Marilyn Dr NE 52402 319-558-2373
Becky DeWald, prin. Fax 378-0699
Polk ES 200/PK-5
1500 B Ave NE 52402 319-558-2475
Eric Christenson, prin. Fax 398-2282
Roosevelt MS 600/6-8
300 13th St NW 52405 319-558-2153
Steve Hilby, prin. Fax 398-2424
Taft MS 700/6-8
5200 E Ave NW 52405 319-558-2243
Gary Hatfield, prin. Fax 654-8619
Taylor ES 200/PK-5
720 7th Ave SW 52404 319-558-2477
Brian Christoffersen, prin. Fax 398-2209
Truman ES 300/PK-5
441 W Post Rd NW 52405 319-558-2375
Tammi Kuba, prin. Fax 654-8637
Van Buren ES 400/PK-5
2525 29th St SW 52404 319-558-2377
Cindy Stock, prin. Fax 654-8647
Wilson S 300/2-8
2301 J St SW 52404 319-558-2156
Kathleen Conley, prin. Fax 398-2368
Wood ES 300/1-5
645 26th St SE 52403 319-558-2467
Ellen Daye-Williams, prin. Fax 398-2469
Wright ES 200/PK-5
1524 Hollywood Blvd NE 52402 319-558-2278
Greg O'Connell, prin. Fax 294-9350
Other Schools – See Hiawatha

College Community SD 3,200/K-12
401 76th Ave SW 52404 319-848-5201
Richard Whitehead, supt. Fax 848-4019
www.prairiepride.org
Prairie Creek IS 5-6
401 76th Ave SW 52404 319-848-5310
Sue Skala, prin. Fax 848-5323
Prairie Crest ES 300/K-4
401 76th Ave SW 52404 319-848-5280
Laura Medberry, prin. Fax 848-5283
Prairie Heights ES 400/K-4
401 76th Ave SW 52404 319-848-5230
Scott Schipper, prin. Fax 848-5254
Prairie Ridge ES 400/K-4
401 76th Ave SW 52404 319-848-5100
Tracy Laue, prin. Fax 848-5103
Prairie View ES 400/K-4
401 76th Ave SW 52404 319-848-5260
Ann Wooldridge, prin. Fax 848-5255

Linn-Mar Community SD
Supt. — See Marion
Bowman Woods ES 500/K-5
151 Boyson Rd NE 52402 319-447-3240
John Zimmerman, prin. Fax 373-2592

All Saints S 300/PK-5
720 29th St SE 52403 319-363-4110
Marlene Bartlett, prin. Fax 363-9547
Andrews Christian Academy 50/K-8
2773 Loggerhead Rd 52411 319-393-1664
Fax 294-3036
Cedar Valley Christian S 300/PK-12
3636 Cottage Grove Ave SE 52403 319-366-7462
Joel DeSousa, prin. Fax 247-0037
Good Shepherd Lutheran S 50/K-8
2900 42nd St NE 52402 319-393-5656
Timothy Vogel, prin.
Holy Family - LaSalle MS 200/6-8
3700 1st Ave NW 52405 319-396-7792
Rick Louk, prin. Fax 390-6527
Holy Family - St. Jude Center 200/3-5
3700 1st Ave NW 52405 319-396-7818
Ronda Krystofiak, prin. Fax 362-0952
Holy Family - St. Ludmila S 50/PK-2
215 21st Ave SW 52404 319-362-1943
Janet Whitney, prin. Fax 364-4149
Newton Christian Academy 200/PK-8
1635 Linmar Dr NE 52402 319-362-9512
Ned Jondle, admin. Fax 362-5610
Regis MS 500/6-8
735 Prairie Dr NE 52402 319-378-0547
Rick Blackwell, prin. Fax 247-6099
St. Matthew S 300/PK-5
125 24th St NE 52402 319-362-3021
Joseph Wolf, prin. Fax 362-7946
St. Pius X/St. Elizabeth Ann Seton S 500/K-5
4901 Council St NE 52402 319-393-4507
Candace Hurley, prin. Fax 393-9424
Summit S 100/PK-5
1010 Regent St NE 52402 319-294-2036
Erikka Benhart, admin. Fax 294-2039
Trinity Lutheran S 200/PK-8
1361 7th Ave SW 52404 319-362-6952
Vern Piering, prin. Fax 366-1569

Center Point, Linn, Pop. 2,214
Center Point-Urbana Community SD 1,300/PK-12
PO Box 296 52213 319-849-1102
Alan Marshall, supt. Fax 849-2312
www.cpuschools.org/
Center Point-Urbana ES 500/PK-4
PO Box 296 52213 319-849-1102
Jon Hasleiet, prin. Fax 849-1134
Other Schools – See Urbana

Centerville, Appanoose, Pop. 5,788
Centerville Community SD 1,500/PK-12
PO Box 370 52544 641-856-0601
Richard Turner, supt. Fax 856-0656
www.centerville.k12.ia.us
Centerville Community Preschool 50/PK-PK
838 S 18th St 52544 641-437-7014
Kathy Cossolotto, prin.
Central ES 100/K-3
320 Drake Ave 52544 641-856-0709
Scott Clark, prin. Fax 856-0881
Garfield ES 100/K-3
505 E Walsh St 52544 641-856-0759
Scott Clark, prin. Fax 856-0885
Howar JHS 200/7-8
850 S Park Ave 52544 641-856-0760
Bruce Karpen, prin. Fax 856-0761
Lakeview ES 300/4-6
1800 S 11th St 52544 641-856-0637
Mike Halupnick, prin. Fax 856-0641
Lincoln ES 100/K-3
603 N 10th St 52544 641-856-0749
Scott Clark, prin. Fax 856-0884
Other Schools – See Cincinnati, Mystic

Central City, Linn, Pop. 1,142
Central City Community SD 400/K-12
400 Barber St 52214 319-438-6183
John Dotson, supt. Fax 438-6110
www.central-city.k12.ia.us
Central City ES 200/K-6
400 Barber St 52214 319-438-6181
Gretchen DeVore, prin. Fax 438-6110
Central City MS 100/7-8
400 Barber St 52214 319-438-6181
Jay Meier, prin. Fax 438-6110

Chariton, Lucas, Pop. 4,609
Chariton Community SD 1,500/PK-12
PO Box 738 50049 641-774-5967
Paula Wright, supt. Fax 774-8511
www.chariton.k12.ia.us/
Chariton MS 300/6-8
1300 N 16th St 50049 641-774-5114
Beth Scott-Thomas, prin. Fax 774-8511
Columbus ES 300/PK-2
1215 Linden Ave 50049 641-774-4712
Tracy Hall, prin. Fax 774-0988
Van Allen ES 300/3-5
1129 Ashland Ave 50049 641-774-5047
Michael Nicodemus, prin. Fax 774-8511

Charles City, Floyd, Pop. 7,606
Charles City Community SD 1,600/K-12
500 N Grand Ave 50616 641-257-6500
Andey Pattee, supt. Fax 257-6509
www.charlescityschools.org
Charles City MS 400/6-8
500 N Grand Ave 50616 641-257-6530
Ron Hoffman, prin. Fax 228-9842
Lincoln ES 300/K-5
600 5th Ave 50616 641-257-6560
Doug Bengtson, prin. Fax 257-6562

Washington ES 400/K-5
1406 N Grand Ave 50616 641-257-6570
Wendy Cruse, prin. Fax 257-6573

Immaculate Conception S 200/PK-6
1203 Clark St 50616 641-228-1225
Mindy Hart, prin. Fax 228-7692

Charter Oak, Crawford, Pop. 525
Charter Oak-Ute Community SD 300/PK-12
321 Main St 51439 712-678-3325
Rollie Wiebers, supt. Fax 678-3626
Charter Oak-Ute JHS 100/7-8
321 Main St 51439 712-678-3325
Rollie Wiebers, prin. Fax 678-3626
Other Schools – See Ute

Cherokee, Cherokee, Pop. 5,027
Cherokee Community SD 1,000/PK-12
PO Box 801 51012 712-225-6767
John Chalstrom, supt. Fax 225-6769
www.cherokee.k12.ia.us/
Cherokee MS 300/5-8
PO Box 801 51012 712-225-6750
Larry Weede, prin. Fax 225-4841
Early Childhood Learning Center 50/PK-PK
PO Box 801 51012 712-225-6760
Barb Radke, prin. Fax 225-6769
Roosevelt ES 400/K-4
PO Box 801 51012 712-225-6760
Barb Radke, prin. Fax 225-4202

Churdan, Greene, Pop. 392
Paton-Churdan Community SD 200/PK-12
PO Box 157 50050 515-389-3111
Jess Toliver, supt. Fax 389-3113
www.paton-churdan.k12.ia.us
Paton-Churdan ES 100/PK-5
PO Box 157 50050 515-389-3111
Jess Toliver, prin. Fax 389-3113

Cincinnati, Appanoose, Pop. 425
Centerville Community SD
Supt. — See Centerville
Cincinnati ES 50/K-3
PO Box 158 52549 641-856-0739
Scott Clark, prin. Fax 658-2730

Clarence, Cedar, Pop. 993
North Cedar Community SD
Supt. — See Stanwood
North Cedar MS 200/5-8
PO Box 310 52216 563-452-3179
Mark Glover, prin. Fax 452-3972

Clarinda, Page, Pop. 5,523
Clarinda Community SD 1,200/PK-12
PO Box 59 51632 712-542-5165
Paul Honnold, supt. Fax 542-3802
www.clarinda.k12.ia.us
Clarinda MS 300/5-8
PO Box 59 51632 712-542-2132
Gary McNeal, prin. Fax 542-5949
Garfield ES 300/PK-4
PO Box 59 51632 712-542-4510
Margaret Nordland, prin. Fax 542-5949

Clarinda Lutheran S 100/K-8
707 W Scidmore St 51632 712-542-3657
Merrilee Sump, prin. Fax 542-3657
St. John Lutheran S 50/PK-PK
301 N 13th St 51632 712-542-3708

Clarion, Wright, Pop. 2,873
Clarion-Goldfield Community SD 800/PK-12
319 3rd Ave NE 50525 515-532-3423
Robert Olson, supt. Fax 532-2628
www.clargold.k12.ia.us
Clarion ES 200/PK-5
319 3rd Ave NE 50525 515-532-2873
Tricia Rosendahl, prin. Fax 532-2628
Clarion-Goldfield MS 200/6-8
300 3rd Ave NE 50525 515-532-2412
Steve Haberman, prin. Fax 532-2741

Clarksville, Butler, Pop. 1,403
Clarksville Community SD 400/PK-12
PO Box 689 50619 319-278-4008
Robert Longmuir, supt. Fax 278-4618
www.clarksville.k12.ia.us/
Clarksville ES 200/PK-6
PO Box 689 50619 319-278-4560
Linda Johnson, prin. Fax 278-4618

Clearfield, Taylor, Pop. 362
Clearfield Community SD 100/PK-6
PO Box 99 50840 641-336-2353
Joe Drake, supt. Fax 336-2267
Clearfield ES 100/PK-6
PO Box 99 50840 641-336-2353
Amy Whittington, prin. Fax 336-2267

Clear Lake, Cerro Gordo, Pop. 7,913
Clear Lake Community SD 1,300/PK-12
1529 3rd Ave N 50428 641-357-2181
Dwight Pierson, supt. Fax 357-2182
www.clearlakeschools.org
Clear Creek ES 300/1-5
901 S 14th St 50428 641-357-5288
Mike Barkley, prin. Fax 357-5701
Clear Lake MS 400/6-8
1601 3rd Ave N 50428 641-357-6114
Tracy Thomsen, prin. Fax 357-8353
Sunset View S 200/PK-K
408 Mars Hill Dr 50428 641-357-6171
Michael Barkley, prin. Fax 357-8338

Cleghorn, Cherokee, Pop. 240
Marcus-Meriden-Cleghorn Community SD
Supt. — See Marcus

Marcus-Meriden-Cleghorn MS 100/4-6
PO Box 97 51014 712-436-2244
Kathy Tritz-Rhodes, prin. Fax 436-2695

Clemons, Marshall, Pop. 148

Clemons Lutheran S 50/PK-8
PO Box 120 50051 641-477-8263
Jeff Fick, prin. Fax 477-8262

Clinton, Clinton, Pop. 27,086
Clinton Community SD 4,000/PK-12
600 S 4th St 52732 563-243-9600
Richard Basden, supt. Fax 243-2415
www.clinton.k12.ia.us
Bluff ES 600/PK-5
1421 S Bluff Blvd 52732 563-242-1606
John Jorgensen, prin. Fax 243-0488
Eagle Heights ES 300/K-5
1350 Main Ave 52732 563-243-4288
Roger Winterlin, prin. Fax 243-4289
Jefferson ES 400/PK-5
720 4th Ave S 52732 563-243-0479
Bonnie Freitag, prin. Fax 243-0462
Lyons MS 300/6-8
2810 N 4th St 52732 563-242-7858
Dan Boyd, prin. Fax 242-6168
Washington MS 600/6-8
751 2nd Ave S 52732 563-243-0466
Brian Kenney, prin. Fax 242-3735
Whittier ES 400/PK-5
1310 2nd Ave S 52732 563-243-3230
Bev Goerdt, prin. Fax 243-0461

Prince of Peace Academy College Prep S 300/K-12
312 S 4th St 52732 563-242-1663
Nancy Peart, prin. Fax 243-8272
Prince of Peace Early Learning Center 50/PK-PK
245 26th Ave N 52732 563-242-9258
Nancy Peart, prin. Fax 242-9258

Clive, Polk, Pop. 13,851
West Des Moines Community SD
Supt. — See West Des Moines
Crestview ES 500/K-6
8355 Franklin Ave 50325 515-633-5700
John Villotti, prin. Fax 633-5799
Indian Hills JHS 600/7-8
9401 Indian Hills Dr 50325 515-633-4700
Shane Christensen, prin. Fax 633-4799

Coggon, Linn, Pop. 701
North Linn Community SD
Supt. — See Troy Mills
Coggon ES 100/K-5
PO Box 227 52218 319-435-2396
Steve McPherson, prin. Fax 435-2208

Colesburg, Delaware, Pop. 394
Edgewood-Colesburg Community SD
Supt. — See Edgewood
Edgewood-Colesburg ES 300/PK-6
PO Box 125 52035 563-856-2415
Paul Wenger, prin. Fax 856-2113

Colfax, Jasper, Pop. 2,228
Colfax-Mingo Community SD 800/K-12
1000 N Walnut St 50054 515-674-3646
Ed Ackerman, supt. Fax 674-3921
www.colfax-mingo.k12.ia.us
Colfax-Mingo ES 300/K-5
20 W Broadway St 50054 515-674-3465
Brian Summy, prin. Fax 674-4396
Other Schools – See Mingo

College Springs, Page, Pop. 241
South Page Community SD 200/PK-12
PO Box 98 51637 712-582-3212
Joy Jones, supt. Fax 582-3217
www.southpageschools.com
South Page ES 100/PK-5
PO Box 98 51637 712-582-3212
Denise Green, prin. Fax 582-3217

Collins, Story, Pop. 450
Collins-Maxwell Community SD
Supt. — See Maxwell
Collins-Maxwell ES 300/K-5
416 4th Ave 50055 641-385-2446
Scott Cakerice, prin. Fax 385-2447

Colo, Story, Pop. 808
Colo-Nesco Comm SD
Supt. — See Mc Callsburg
Colo ES 100/K-4
PO Box 215 50056 641-377-2282
Gary Pillman, prin. Fax 377-2283

Columbus Junction, Louisa, Pop. 1,835
Columbus Community SD 1,000/PK-12
1210 Colton St 52738 319-728-2911
Richard Bridenstine, supt. Fax 728-8750
www.columbus.k12.ia.us
Columbus Community MS 300/6-8
1004 Colton St 52738 319-728-2233
Jeff Maeder, prin. Fax 728-2205
Roundy ES 500/PK-5
1212 Colton St 52738 319-728-6218
Daniel Vogeler, prin. Fax 728-2134

Conrad, Grundy, Pop. 1,009
BCLUW Community SD 700/K-12
PO Box 670 50621 641-366-2819
Mike Ashton, supt. Fax 366-2175
www.bcluw.k12.ia.us
BCLUW ES 200/K-4
PO Box 670 50621 641-366-2811
Mary Petty, prin. Fax 366-2177
Other Schools – See Union

Coon Rapids, Carroll, Pop. 1,263
Coon Rapids-Bayard Community SD 500/PK-12
PO Box 297 50058 712-999-2207
Rich Stoffers, supt. Fax 999-7740
www.crbcrusaders.org
Deal ES 100/PK-3
PO Box 297 50058 712-999-2845
Rich Stoffers, prin. Fax 999-2913

Coralville, Johnson, Pop. 17,811
Iowa City Community SD
Supt. — See Iowa City
Coralville Central ES 400/K-6
501 6th St 52241 319-688-1100
Barb Mueller-Jenkins, prin. Fax 339-5707
Kirkwood ES 400/K-6
1401 9th St 52241 319-688-1120
Bart Mason, prin. Fax 339-5716
Northwest JHS 600/7-8
1507 8th St 52241 319-688-1060
Gregg Shoultz, prin. Fax 339-5728
Wickham ES 500/PK-6
601 Oakdale Blvd 52241 319-688-1175
Lora Daily, prin. Fax 339-5792

Corning, Adams, Pop. 1,688
Corning Community SD 500/K-12
904 8th St 50841 641-322-4242
Mike Wells, supt. Fax 322-5149
www.corning.k12.ia.us
Corning ES 200/K-6
1012 10th St 50841 641-322-4020
Myrna Rummer, prin. Fax 322-5149
Corning JHS 100/7-8
902 9th St 50841 641-322-3213
Patty Morris, prin. Fax 322-4884

Correctionville, Woodbury, Pop. 859
River Valley Community SD 500/PK-12
PO Box 8 51016 712-372-4420
Julie Destiger, supt. Fax 372-4677
www.river-valley.k12.ia.us/
Other Schools – See Washta

Corwith, Hancock, Pop. 330
Corwith-Wesley Community SD 200/PK-12
PO Box 220 50430 515-583-2304
Willie Stone, supt. Fax 583-2030
www.corwith-wesley.k12.ia.us
Other Schools – See Wesley

Corydon, Wayne, Pop. 1,521
Wayne Community SD 600/K-12
102 N Dekalb St 50060 641-872-1220
Robert Busch, supt. Fax 872-2091
www.wayne.k12.ia.us
Wayne Community JHS 100/7-8
102 N Dekalb St 50060 641-872-2184
Shane Brown, prin. Fax 872-2091
Wayne ES 300/K-6
102 N Dekalb St 50060 641-872-1034
Denise Becker, prin. Fax 872-2543

Council Bluffs, Pottawattamie, Pop. 59,568
Council Bluffs Community SD 9,000/PK-12
12 Scott St 51503 712-328-6446
Martha Bruckner, supt. Fax 328-6548
www.cb-schools.org
Bloomer ES 500/PK-5
210 S 7th St 51501 712-328-6519
Doreen Knuth, prin. Fax 328-6545
Edison ES 400/PK-5
2218 3rd Ave 51501 712-328-6516
Darrin Praska, prin. Fax 328-6507
Franklin ES 500/PK-5
3130 Avenue C 51501 712-328-6469
Lori Swanson, prin. Fax 328-6468
Gunn ES 200/K-5
1735 N Broadway 51503 712-328-6452
Sue Rice, prin. Fax 328-6465
Hoover ES 400/K-5
1205 N Broadway 51503 712-328-6537
Joy Stein, prin. Fax 328-6538
Kirn JHS 700/6-8
100 North Ave 51503 712-328-6454
Dave Schweitzer, prin. Fax 328-6554
Lewis & Clark ES 200/PK-5
1603 Grand Ave 51503 712-328-6471
Garry Milbourn, prin. Fax 328-6563
Longfellow ES 400/PK-5
2011 S 10th St 51501 712-328-6522
Peg Shea, prin. Fax 328-6524
Pusey ES 100/PK-5
147 15th Ave 51503 712-328-6463
Melissa Chalupnik, prin. Fax 328-6542
Roosevelt ES 300/PK-5
517 N 17th St 51501 712-328-6528
Mark Schuldt, prin. Fax 328-6566
Rue ES 400/PK-5
3326 6th Ave 51501 712-328-6540
Trudy Evans, prin. Fax 328-6556
Walnut Grove ES 400/PK-5
2920 Avenue J 51501 712-328-6525
Jerri Larson, prin. Fax 328-6527
Washington ES 300/PK-5
207 Scott St 51503 712-328-6403
Jason Plourde, prin. Fax 328-6503
Wilson JHS 700/6-8
715 N 21st St 51501 712-328-6476
Joel Beyenhof, prin. Fax 328-6479
Other Schools – See Carter Lake, Crescent

Lewis Central Community SD 2,700/PK-12
1600 E South Omaha Brdge Rd 51503
712-366-8202
Mark Schweer, supt. Fax 366-8315
www.lewiscentral.k12.ia.us
Kreft PS 500/PK-1
3206 Renner Dr 51501 712-366-8290
Barb Grell, prin. Fax 366-8294
Lewis Central MS 700/6-8
3820 Harry Langdon Blvd 51503 712-366-8251
Sean Dunphy, prin. Fax 366-8324
Titan Hill IS 600/2-5
4125 Harry Langdon Blvd 51503 712-366-8380
Kent Stopak, prin. Fax 366-8302

Heartland Christian S 100/PK-12
400 Wright Rd 51501 712-322-5817
Gary Wilson, dir. Fax 322-4287
St. Albert's IS 200/4-6
400 Gleason Ave 51503 712-322-7004
Anne Jensen, prin. Fax 322-0399
St. Albert's S 300/PK-3
2912 9th Ave 51501 712-323-3703
Anne Jensen, prin. Fax 323-6132

Crawfordsville, Washington, Pop. 306
Waco Community SD
Supt. — See Wayland
Waco ES 300/PK-6
200 S Main St 52621 319-658-2931
Vicki Reynolds, prin. Fax 658-3104

Crescent, Pottawattamie, Pop. 603
Council Bluffs Community SD
Supt. — See Council Bluffs
Crescent ES 100/K-5
401 E Welch St 51526 712-545-3566
Melissa Chalupnik, prin. Fax 545-4492

Cresco, Howard, Pop. 3,774
Howard-Winneshiek Community SD 1,300/K-12
1000 Schroder Dr 52136 563-547-2762
Brian Ney, supt. Fax 547-5973
www.howard-winn.k12.ia.us
Cresco JHS 200/7-8
1000 4th Ave E 52136 563-547-2300
Todd Knobloch, prin. Fax 547-2679
Crestwood ES 300/K-6
1000 4th Ave E 52136 563-547-2340
Shirley Sovereign, prin. Fax 547-2679
Other Schools – See Lime Springs, Ridgeway

Notre Dame S 200/PK-6
221 2nd Ave E 52136 563-547-4513
Wendy Schatz, prin. Fax 547-3835

Creston, Union, Pop. 7,359
Creston Community SD 1,500/PK-12
619 N Maple St 50801 641-782-7028
Tim Hood, supt. Fax 782-7020
www.creston.k12.ia.us/
Creston ECC 100/PK-K
901 N Elm St 50801 641-782-2724
Sharon Snodgrass, prin. Fax 782-5852
Creston ES 500/1-5
805 Academic Ave 50801 641-782-1155
Brad Baker, prin. Fax 782-6983
Creston MS 300/6-8
805 Academic Ave 50801 641-782-2129
Larry Otten, prin.

St. Malachy S 100/PK-8
403 W Clark St 50801 641-782-7125
John Walsh, prin. Fax 782-5924

Crystal Lake, Hancock, Pop. 271
Woden-Crystal Lake Community SD 100/PK-12
PO Box 130 50432 641-926-5311
Dwight Widen, supt. Fax 926-3320
www.w-cl-t.org
Woden ES 50/PK-1
PO Box 130 50432 641-565-3211
Susan Lewerke, prin. Fax 656-3320

Dakota City, Humboldt, Pop. 852
Humboldt Community SD
Supt. — See Humboldt
Mease ES 200/PK-1
23 3rd St N 50529 515-332-3578
George Bruder, prin. Fax 332-7151

Dallas, See Melcher
Melcher-Dallas Community SD
Supt. — See Melcher
Melcher-Dallas ES 200/PK-6
PO Box C 50062 641-947-3151
Greg Horstmann, prin. Fax 947-4032

Dallas Center, Dallas, Pop. 1,828
Dallas Center-Grimes Community SD 1,900/K-12
PO Box 512 50063 515-992-3866
Gary Sinclair, supt. Fax 992-3079
www.dc-grimes.k12.ia.us
Dallas Center ES 400/K-5
PO Box 400 50063 515-992-3838
Fax 992-3467
Dallas Center-Grimes MS 400/6-8
PO Box 608 50063 515-992-4343
Lori Phillips, prin. Fax 992-4076
Other Schools – See Grimes

Danbury, Woodbury, Pop. 326

Danbury Catholic S 50/K-6
602 Peach St 51019 712-883-2244
Kristy Liechti, prin. Fax 883-2458

Danville, Des Moines, Pop. 859
Danville Community SD 600/PK-12
419 S Main St 52623 319-392-4223
Stephen McAllister, supt. Fax 392-8390
www.danville.k12.ia.us/
Danville ES 300/PK-6
419 S Main St 52623 319-392-4221
Steve Ita, prin. Fax 392-8390

Davenport, Scott, Pop. 98,845
Davenport Community SD 15,400/PK-12
1606 Brady St 52803 563-336-5000
Julio Almanza, supt. Fax 336-5080
www.davenport.k12.ia.us
Adams ES 600/K-5
3029 N Division St 52804 563-391-6563
John Maaske, prin. Fax 391-6564
Buchanan ES 300/PK-5
4515 N Fairmount St 52806 563-391-1463
Diane Simmons, prin. Fax 388-9064
Childrens Village S at Hoover 100/PK-PK
1002 Spring St 52803 563-322-7649
Kathy Schulte, admin. Fax 322-6608
Eisenhower ES 400/K-5
2827 Jersey Ridge Rd 52803 563-355-2604
Steve Mielenhausen, prin. Fax 355-9770
Fillmore ES 400/K-5
7307 Pacific St 52806 563-391-1740
Kent Ryan, prin. Fax 388-6397
Garfield ES 400/K-5
902 E 29th St 52803 563-322-1922
Deb Miller, prin. Fax 322-7220
Harrison ES 500/K-5
1032 W 53rd St 52806 563-391-3113
Tom Green, prin. Fax 391-3881
Hayes ES 300/PK-5
622 S Concord St 52802 563-322-2601
Sheri Day, prin. Fax 324-4518
Jackson ES 400/PK-5
1307 Wisconsin Ave 52804 563-322-1787
Tonya Wilkins, prin. Fax 322-2804
Jefferson ES 500/PK-5
1027 N Marquette St 52804 563-322-3557
Robert McGarry, prin. Fax 322-7562
Madison ES 400/PK-5
116 E Locust St 52803 563-326-5391
Sheri Womack, prin. Fax 326-0783
McKinley ES 400/PK-5
1716 Kenwood Ave 52803 563-324-0403
Teresa Bechen, prin. Fax 324-0038
Monroe ES 400/PK-5
1926 W 4th St 52802 563-322-3559
Linda Reysack, prin. Fax 322-7447
Smart IS 500/6-8
1934 W 5th St 52802 563-323-1837
Linda Heiden, prin. Fax 323-3093
Sudlow IS 600/6-8
1414 E Locust St 52803 563-326-3502
Bruce Potts, prin. Fax 326-2248
Truman ES 400/PK-5
5506 N Pine St 52806 563-386-6450
Lisa Baxter, prin. Fax 386-6452
Washington ES 300/K-5
1608 E Locust St 52803 563-322-0905
Diana Allen, prin. Fax 322-2114
Williams IS 700/6-8
3040 N Division St 52804 563-391-6550
Scott McKissick, prin. Fax 391-0149
Wilson ES 500/PK-5
2002 N Clark St 52804 563-391-0903
William Schneden, prin. Fax 391-5120
Wood IS 700/6-8
5701 N Division St 52806 563-391-6350
Sheri Simpson-Schultz, prin. Fax 391-4416
Young IS 300/6-8
1702 N Main St 52803 563-326-4432
Marianne Corbin, prin. Fax 326-1165
Other Schools – See Blue Grass, Buffalo, Walcott

All Saints S 400/PK-8
1926 N Marquette St 52804 563-324-3205
Tammy Conrad, prin. Fax 324-9331
Kennedy Catholic S 400/PK-8
1627 W 42nd St 52806 563-391-3030
Chad Steimle, prin. Fax 388-5206
Quad City Montessori S 100/PK-6
2400 E 46th St 52807 563-355-1289
Lynn Wicklund, admin. Fax 355-7798
Quad City SDA Christian S 50/PK-8
4444 W Kimberly Rd 52806 563-391-9499
St. Paul the Apostle S 500/PK-8
1007 E Rusholme St 52803 563-322-2923
Julie Delaney, prin. Fax 322-2530
Trinity Lutheran S 300/PK-8
1122 W Central Park Ave 52804 563-322-5224
Bill Meyer, prin. Fax 324-9153

Dayton, Webster, Pop. 837
Southeast Webster-Grand Community SD
Supt. — See Burnside
Dayton ES 200/PK-3
PO Box 26 50530 515-547-2314
Sharron Heggen, prin. Fax 547-2213
Southeast Webster-Grand JHS 100/7-8
30850 Paragon Ave 50530 515-359-2235
Daniel Grandfield, prin. Fax 359-2236

Decorah, Winneshiek, Pop. 8,084
Decorah Community SD 1,600/PK-12
510 Winnebago St 52101 563-382-4208
Michael Haluska, supt. Fax 387-0753
decorah.k12.ia.us/
Cline ES 400/PK-2
101 E Claiborne Dr 52101 563-382-3125
Rick Varney, prin. Fax 387-4059
Decorah MS 500/5-8
210 Vernon St 52101 563-382-8427
Leona Hoth, prin. Fax 387-4052
Lee ES 3-4
210 Vernon St 52101 563-382-3771
Cheryl Sommers, prin. Fax 382-8171
West Side ES 200/3-4
301 Center St 52101 563-382-4451
Rick Varney, prin. Fax 387-0716

North Wineshiek Community SD 200/PK-8
3495 N Winn Rd 52101 563-735-5411
Tim Dugger, supt. Fax 735-5430
www.n-winn.k12.ia.us/
North Winneshiek ES 100/PK-5
3495 N Winn Rd 52101 563-735-5411
Tim Dugger, prin. Fax 735-5430
North Winneshiek MS 100/6-8
3495 N Winn Rd 52101 563-735-5411
Tim Dugger, prin. Fax 735-5430

St. Benedict S 100/K-8
402 Rural Ave 52101 563-382-4668
Ruth Palmer, prin. Fax 382-3193

Delhi, Delaware, Pop. 511
Maquoketa Valley Community SD 800/PK-12
PO Box 186 52223 563-922-9422
Doug Tuetken, supt. Fax 922-2160
www.maquoketa-v.k12.ia.us
Delhi ES 100/K-5
PO Box 186 52223 563-922-9411
Thomas Gatto, prin. Fax 922-9502
Maquoketa Valley MS 200/6-8
PO Box 186 52223 563-922-9411
Thomas Gatto, prin. Fax 922-9502
Other Schools – See Earlville, Hopkinton

Delmar, Clinton, Pop. 505
Delwood Community SD 100/PK-6
PO Box 292 52037 563-674-4164
Sue Goodall, supt. Fax 674-4134
delwood.iowapages.org
Delwood ES 100/PK-6
PO Box 292 52037 563-674-4164
Sue Goodall, prin. Fax 674-4134

Denison, Crawford, Pop. 7,374
Denison Community SD 1,700/K-12
819 N 16th St 51442 712-263-2176
Michael Pardun, supt. Fax 263-5233
www.denison.k12.ia.us
Denison Broadway ES 4-5
1515 Broadway 51442 712-263-3103
Stephen Meinen, prin. Fax 263-3187
Denison ES 500/K-3
38 N 20th St 51442 712-263-3104
Christopher Schulz, prin. Fax 263-8360
Denison MS 400/6-8
1201 N 16th St 51442 712-263-9393
Patricia Roush, prin. Fax 263-5418

St. Rose of Lima S 100/K-6
1012 2nd Ave S 51442 712-263-5408
Susan King, prin. Fax 263-9370
Zion Lutheran S 200/PK-8
1004 1st Ave S 51442 712-263-4766
Brian L'Heureux, prin. Fax 263-6010

Denmark, Lee
Fort Madison Community SD
Supt. — See Fort Madison
Denmark ES 300/K-5
502 Academy Ave 52624 319-528-4337
Kent Bailey, prin. Fax 528-4313

Denver, Bremer, Pop. 1,642
Denver Community SD 700/PK-12
PO Box 384 50622 319-984-6323
Kathryny Gilbert, supt. Fax 984-5345
www.denver.k12.ia.us
Denver 3-5 ES 100/3-5
PO Box 384 50622 319-984-5611
Kim Tierney, prin. Fax 984-5345
Denver Early ES 200/PK-2
PO Box 384 50622 319-984-5611
Kim Tierney, prin. Fax 984-5345
Denver MS 200/6-8
PO Box 384 50622 319-984-6041
Paul Gebel, prin. Fax 984-5630

Des Moines, Polk, Pop. 194,163
Des Moines Independent Community SD 28,000/PK-12
901 Walnut St 50309 515-242-7911
Dr. Nancy Sebring, supt. Fax 242-7579
www.dmps.k12.ia.us
Brody MS 700/6-8
2501 Park Ave 50321 515-242-8443
Randy Gordon, prin. Fax 244-0927
Brubaker ES 700/K-5
2900 E 42nd St 50317 515-242-8405
Mike Lord, prin. Fax 265-5690
Callanan MS 600/6-8
3010 Center St 50312 515-242-8101
Doug Calaway, prin. Fax 242-8103
Capitol View ES 600/K-5
320 E 16th St 50316 515-242-8402
Marcia Johnson, prin. Fax 262-3471
Carver Community ES K-5
700 E University Ave 50316 515-242-8418
Cecil Brewton, prin. Fax 262-1095
Cattell ES 300/K-5
3101 E 12th St 50316 515-242-8403
Deb Gregor, prin. Fax 266-1605
Downtown S 300/K-5
500 Grand Ave 50309 515-284-5848
John Johnson, prin. Fax 284-0890
Edmunds Academy of Fine Arts ES 100/K-5
1601 Crocker St 50314 515-243-1174
Jack Cavanaugh, prin. Fax 244-1568
Findley ES 300/PK-5
3000 Cambridge St 50313 515-242-8407
Lois Brass, prin. Fax 244-7410
Garton ES 400/PK-5
2820 E 24th St 50317 515-242-8408
Jaynette Rittman, prin. Fax 263-0046
Goodrell MS 600/6-8
3300 E 29th St 50317 515-242-8444
Dawn Stahly, prin. Fax 242-7365
Greenwood ES 400/K-5
316 37th St 50312 515-242-8410
Rhonda McFadden, prin. Fax 277-5673
Hanawalt ES 400/K-5
225 56th St 50312 515-242-8411
Julia Burton, prin. Fax 255-1792
Harding MS 600/6-8
203 E Euclid Ave 50313 515-242-8445
Thomas Ahart, prin. Fax 244-3566
Hiatt MS 500/6-8
1214 E 15th St 50316 515-242-7774
Spence Evans, prin. Fax 242-7789
Hillis ES 300/K-5
2401 56th St 50310 515-242-8412
Beth Sloan, prin. Fax 279-5003
Howe ES 200/K-5
2900 Indianola Ave 50315 515-242-8413
Dianne Anderson, prin. Fax 288-4128
Hoyt MS 600/6-8
2700 E 42nd St 50317 515-242-8446
Laura Kacer, prin. Fax 265-5059
Hubbell ES 400/K-5
800 42nd St 50312 515-242-8414
Tim Schott, prin. Fax 242-8290
Jackson ES 400/K-5
3825 Indianola Ave 50320 515-288-0157
Deanna Culp, prin. Fax 288-1228
Jefferson ES 400/K-5
2425 Watrous Ave 50321 515-242-8416
David Lingwall, prin. Fax 287-8601
King ES 200/PK-2
1849 Forest Ave 50314 515-242-8417
Thomas Simmons, prin. Fax 243-1298
Lovejoy ES 300/K-5
801 E Kenyon Ave 50315 515-242-8419
Dr. Bill Szakacs, prin. Fax 285-0279
Madison ES 300/K-5
806 Hoffman Ave 50316 515-265-5609
Marsha Kerper, prin. Fax 265-6080
McCombs MS 600/6-8
201 County Line Rd 50320 515-242-8447
Barb Mullahey, prin. Fax 287-2644
McKinley ES 400/PK-5
1610 SE 6th St 50315 515-242-8423
Lorenzo Jasso, prin. Fax 282-1327
Meredith MS 700/6-8
4827 Madison Ave 50310 515-242-7250
Cindy Flesch, prin. Fax 242-8291
Merrill MS 600/6-8
5301 Grand Ave 50312 515-242-8448
Alex Hanna, prin. Fax 274-1844
Monroe ES 500/PK-5
2250 30th St 50310 515-242-8425
Cindy Wissler, prin. Fax 279-4331
Morris ES 600/K-5
1401 Geil Ave 50315 515-242-8421
Todd Martin, prin. Fax 285-1868
Moulton Extended Learning Center 500/PK-8
1541 8th St 50314 515-242-8427
Craig Saddler, prin. Fax 288-1346
Oak Park ES 400/K-5
3928 6th Ave 50313 515-242-8428
Holly Crandell, prin. Fax 244-0302
Park Avenue ES 400/K-5
3141 SW 9th St 50315 515-242-8429
Wayne Knutsen, prin. Fax 244-8238
Perkins Academy 200/3-5
4301 College Ave 50311 515-242-8430
Penny Rittgers, prin. Fax 274-1367
Phillips ES 300/K-5
1701 Lay St 50317 515-242-8431
Laurel Prior-Sweet, prin. Fax 265-3406
River Woods ES 500/K-5
2929 SE 22nd St 50320 515-242-8433
Jill Burnett, prin. Fax 244-2386
Samuelson ES 400/K-5
3929 Bel Aire Rd 50310 515-242-8441
Cindy Roerig, prin. Fax 279-8545
South Union ES K-5
4201 S Union St 50315 515-242-8409
Constance VanderKrol, prin. Fax 953-0486
Stowe ES 300/K-5
1411 E 33rd St 50317 515-242-8435
Dawn Vetter, prin. Fax 262-3755
Studebaker ES 500/K-5
300 E County Line Rd 50320 515-287-2330
Gene Fracek, prin. Fax 287-1740
Walnut Street ES K-5
901 Walnut St 50309 515-242-8438
Craig Laeger, prin. Fax 242-8372
Weeks MS 700/6-8
901 E Park Ave 50315 515-242-8449
James Mollison, prin. Fax 288-8740
Willard ES 400/PK-5
2941 Dean Ave 50317 515-242-8439
Raul DeAnda, prin. Fax 262-7884
Windsor ES 300/K-5
5912 University Ave 50311 515-242-8440
Barry Jones, prin. Fax 279-5372
Wright ES 300/K-5
5001 SW 14th St 50315 515-242-8442
Lindsey Cornwell, prin. Fax 285-6247
Other Schools – See Pleasant Hill, Windsor Heights

Saydel Community SD 1,400/PK-12
5740 NE 14th St 50313 515-264-0866
Dr. Debra VanGorp, supt. Fax 264-0869
www.saydel.k12.ia.us
Cornell ES 400/PK-3
5817 NE 3rd St 50313 515-244-8173
Debra Chiodo, prin. Fax 244-0084
Norwoodville ES 200/4-5
2905 NE 46th Ave 50317 515-266-3109
Teri Burnett, prin. Fax 266-3100
Woodside MS 300/6-8
5810 NE 14th St 50313 515-265-3451
Steve Seid, prin. Fax 265-0950

Southeast Polk Community SD
Supt. — See Pleasant Hill
Delaware ES 500/K-6
4401 NE 46th St 50317 515-262-3197
Kevin Walker, prin. Fax 264-8239

Academy 100/PK-8
100 45th St 50312 515-274-0453
Kathleen Ricker, prin. Fax 277-6907
Christ the King S 200/K-8
701 Wall Ave 50315 515-285-3349
Becky Johnson, prin. Fax 285-0381
Des Moines Adventist S 50/K-9
2317 Watrous Ave 50321 515-285-7729
Grandview Park Baptist S 400/PK-12
1701 E 33rd St 50317 515-265-7579
Dick McWilliams, prin. Fax 266-9834
Holy Family S 200/PK-8
1265 E 9th St 50316 515-262-8025
Martin Flaherty, prin. Fax 262-9665
Holy Trinity S 400/PK-8
2922 Beaver Ave 50310 515-255-3162
Audra Meyer, prin. Fax 255-1381
Mt. Olive Lutheran S 100/K-8
5625 Franklin Ave 50310 515-277-0247
Orval Spence, prin. Fax 274-2723
St. Anthony S 300/K-8
16 Columbus Ave 50315 515-243-1874
Dr. Joseph Cordaro, prin. Fax 243-4467
St. Augustin S 300/PK-8
4320 Grand Ave 50312 515-279-5947
Dr. Nancy Dowdle, prin. Fax 279-8049
St. Joseph S 200/K-8
2107 E 33rd St 50317 515-266-3433
Phyllis Konchar, prin. Fax 266-2860
St. Theresa S 300/PK-8
5810 Cara Carpenter Ave 50311 515-277-0178
Ellen Stemler, prin. Fax 255-2415

De Soto, Dallas, Pop. 1,164
Adel-De Soto-Minburn Community SD
Supt. — See Adel
De Soto IS 300/3-5
317 W Spruce St 50069 515-834-2424
Jodi Banse, prin. Fax 834-2056

De Witt, Clinton, Pop. 5,204
Central Clinton Community SD 1,500/K-12
PO Box 110 52742 563-659-0700
Dan Peterson, supt. Fax 659-0707
www.central-clinton.k12.ia.us
Central MS 300/6-8
PO Box 110 52742 563-659-0735
Dan Ziesmer, prin. Fax 659-0766
Ekstrand ES 600/K-5
PO Box 110 52742 563-659-0750
Terri Selzer, prin. Fax 659-0751

St. Joseph S 200/K-8
417 6th Ave 52742 563-659-3812
Chris Meyer, prin. Fax 659-1565

Dexter, Dallas, Pop. 803
West Central Valley Community SD
Supt. — See Stuart
Dexter ES 200/PK-5
PO Box 157 50070 515-789-4480
David Arnold, prin. Fax 789-4613

Diagonal, Ringgold, Pop. 297
Diagonal Community SD 100/PK-12
403 W 2nd St 50845 641-734-5331
Karlene Stephens, supt. Fax 734-5729
www.diagonal.k12.ia.us
Diagonal ES 100/PK-5
403 W 2nd St 50845 641-734-5331
Karleen Stephens, prin. Fax 734-5729

Dike, Grundy, Pop. 1,157
Dike-New Hartford Community SD 800/PK-12
PO Box D 50624 319-989-2552
Lindsey Beecher, supt. Fax 989-2735
www.dikenh.k12.ia.us
Dike ES 200/PK-6
PO Box D 50624 319-989-2487
Thomas Textor, prin. Fax 989-2723
Other Schools – See New Hartford

Donahue, Scott, Pop. 289
North Scott Community SD
Supt. — See Eldridge
Glenn ES 300/K-6
PO Box 168 52746 563-282-9627
C.J. Albertson, prin. Fax 282-9720

Donnellson, Lee, Pop. 923
Central Lee Community SD 1,100/K-12
2642 Highway 218 52625 319-835-9510
John Henriksen, supt. Fax 835-3910
www.central-lee.k12.ia.us
Central Lee ES 400/K-5
2642 Highway 218 52625 319-835-9510
Nicole Herdrich, prin. Fax 835-5020
Central Lee MS 200/6-8
2642 Highway 218 52625 319-835-9510
Kim Ensminger, prin. Fax 835-5020

Doon, Lyon, Pop. 537

Doon Christian S 50/K-8
PO Box 8 51235 712-726-3404
Sharla Tubergen, prin. Fax 726-3404

Douds, Van Buren
Van Buren Community SD
Supt. — See Keosauqua
Van Buren ES - Douds Attendance Center 200/K-6
14574 Jefferson St 52551 641-936-4321
Charles Russell, prin. Fax 936-4619

Dow City, Crawford, Pop. 470
Boyer Valley Community SD
Supt. — See Dunlap
Boyer Valley ES 200/K-5
212 S School St 51528 712-674-3248
Mike Weber, prin. Fax 674-3792

Dows, Wright, Pop. 604
Dows Community SD 100/K-6
404 Park Ave 50071 515-852-4164
Robert Olson, supt. Fax 852-4165
Dows ES 100/K-6
404 Park Ave 50071 515-852-4162
Sara Pralle, prin. Fax 852-4165

Dubuque, Dubuque, Pop. 57,798
Dubuque Community SD 10,300/PK-12
2300 Chaney Rd 52001 563-552-3012
Dr. Larie Godinez, supt. Fax 552-3014
www.dubuque.k12.ia.us
Audubon ES 300/K-5
605 Lincoln Ave 52001 563-552-3300
Andrew Ferguson, prin. Fax 552-3301
Bryant ES 300/K-5
1280 Rush St 52003 563-552-3400
Vicki Sullivan, prin. Fax 552-3401
Carver ES K-5
2007 Radford Rd 52002 563-552-4500
Cynthia Steffens, prin. Fax 552-4501
Eisenhower ES 600/PK-5
3170 Spring Valley Rd 52001 563-552-3500
Nan Welch, prin. Fax 552-3501
Fulton ES 300/K-5
2540 Central Ave 52001 563-552-3650
Jean McDonald, prin. Fax 552-3651
Hand-in-Hand ECC PK-PK
1090 Alta Vista St 52001 563-552-5850
Susan Meehan, prin. Fax 552-5851
Hoover ES 300/K-5
3259 Saint Anne Dr 52001 563-552-3700
Kathleen Walech-Haas, prin. Fax 552-3701
Irving ES 500/K-5
2520 Pennsylvania Ave 52001 563-552-3800
Joe Maloney, prin. Fax 552-3801
Jefferson MS 700/6-8
1105 Althauser Ave 52001 563-552-4700
Phillip Kramer, prin. Fax 552-4701
Kennedy ES 700/K-5
2135 Woodland Dr 52002 563-552-3900
T. J. Potts, prin. Fax 552-3901
Lincoln ES 300/K-5
555 Nevada St 52001 563-552-4050
Donna Loewen, prin. Fax 552-4051
Marshall ES 300/K-5
1450 Rhomberg Ave 52001 563-552-4100
Brenda Mitchell, prin. Fax 552-4101
Roosevelt MS 1,100/6-8
2001 Radford Rd 52002 563-552-5000
Dale Lass, prin. Fax 552-5001
Sageville ES 300/K-5
12015 Sherrill Rd 52002 563-552-4300
Robert Burke, prin. Fax 552-4301
Table Mound ES 400/K-5
100 Tower Dr 52003 563-552-4400
Roy Hansen, prin. Fax 552-4401
Washington MS 700/6-8
51 N Grandview Ave 52001 563-552-4800
Mark Burns, prin. Fax 552-4801

Dubuque Lutheran S 50/K-5
2145 John F Kennedy Rd 52002 563-588-0614
Barbara Schubert, prin. Fax 588-3475
Holy Ghost S 100/PK-8
2981 Central Ave 52001 563-556-1511
Denise Grant, prin. Fax 556-4768
Mazzuchelli MS 400/6-8
2005 Kane St 52001 563-582-7236
Kim Hermsen, prin. Fax 582-7857
Resurrection S 300/PK-8
4300 Asbury Rd 52002 563-583-9488
Dave Gross, prin. Fax 557-7995
St. Anthony OLG S PK-5
2175 Rosedale Ave 52001 563-556-4194
Lori Apel, prin. Fax 585-1987
St. Anthony S 200/PK-5
2175 Rosedale Ave 52001 563-556-2820
Denise Grant, prin. Fax 556-2131
St. Columbkille S 300/PK-8
1198 Rush St 52003 563-582-3532
Barb Roling, prin. Fax 583-4884

Dumont, Butler, Pop. 658
Hampton-Dumont Community SD
Supt. — See Hampton
Hampton-Dumont IS 100/3-4
512 2nd St 50625 641-857-3201
Jerry Buseman, prin. Fax 857-3302

Dunkerton, Black Hawk, Pop. 768
Dunkerton Community SD 500/PK-12
509 S Canfield St 50626 319-822-4295
Jim Stanton, supt. Fax 822-9456
www.dunkerton.k12.ia.us
Dunkerton ES 300/PK-6
509 S Canfield St 50626 319-822-4295
Julie Woods, prin. Fax 822-9456

Dunlap, Harrison, Pop. 1,117
Boyer Valley Community SD 500/K-12
1102 Iowa Ave 51529 712-643-2251
Thomas Vint, supt. Fax 643-2279
www.boyer-valley.k12.ia.us
Other Schools – See Dow City

Durant, Cedar, Pop. 1,677
Durant Community SD 700/K-12
PO Box 607 52747 563-785-4432
Duane Bark, supt. Fax 785-4611
www.durant.k12.ia.us
Durant ES 200/K-4
PO Box 607 52747 563-785-4433
Rebecca Stineman, prin. Fax 785-6558
Durant MS 200/5-8
PO Box 607 52747 563-785-4433
Rebecca Stineman, prin. Fax 785-6558

Dyersville, Dubuque, Pop. 4,043
Western Dubuque Community SD
Supt. — See Farley
Dyersville K 50/PK-K
625 3rd Ave SE 52040 563-875-8484
Linda Martin, prin. Fax 875-8265

Hennessy Catholic IS 50/4-6
PO Box 116 52040 563-875-7572
Vicki Palmer, prin. Fax 875-6140
St. Francis Xavier S 400/K-6
203 2nd St SW 52040 563-875-7376
Peter Smith, prin. Fax 875-7037

Dysart, Tama, Pop. 1,289
Union Community SD
Supt. — See La Porte City
Dysart-Geneseo ES 200/K-5
PO Box 159 52224 319-476-7110
David Hill, prin. Fax 476-2260
Union MS 300/6-8
PO Box 159 52224 319-476-5100
Mark Albertsen, prin. Fax 476-2385

Eagle Grove, Wright, Pop. 3,515
Eagle Grove Community SD 800/PK-12
325 N Commercial Ave 50533 515-448-4749
Jess Toliver, supt. Fax 448-3156
www.eagle-grove.k12.ia.us
Blue MS 200/5-8
1015 NW 2nd St 50533 515-448-4767
Scott Jeske, prin. Fax 448-5527
Eagle Grove ES 200/PK-4
425 N Fort Ave 50533 515-448-3126
Michael Kruger, prin. Fax 603-6571

Earlham, Madison, Pop. 1,332
Earlham Community SD 700/PK-12
PO Box 430 50072 515-758-2235
Michael Wright, supt. Fax 758-2215
earlham.k12.ia.us/
Earlham ES 400/PK-6
PO Box 430 50072 515-758-2213
Jason Hammen, prin. Fax 758-2215
Earlham MS 100/7-8
PO Box 430 50072 515-758-2213
Jan Fletcher, prin. Fax 758-2215

Earlville, Delaware, Pop. 863
Maquoketa Valley Community SD
Supt. — See Delhi
Earlville ES 100/PK-5
PO Box 218 52041 563-923-3225
Joann Swinton, prin. Fax 923-3305

Eddyville, Wapello, Pop. 1,072
Eddyville-Blakesburg Community SD 800/PK-12
1301 Berdan Ext 52553 641-969-4226
Dean Cook, supt. Fax 969-4547
www.ebcsd.com/
Eddyville ES 300/PK-6
702 Vance St 52553 641-969-4281
Lonna McGrath, prin. Fax 969-5318
Other Schools – See Blakesburg

Edgewood, Clayton, Pop. 898
Edgewood-Colesburg Community SD 600/PK-12
PO Box 315 52042 563-928-6411
Ed Klamfoth, supt. Fax 928-6414
www.edge-cole.k12.ia.us
Other Schools – See Colesburg

Eldon, Wapello, Pop. 974
Cardinal Community SD 700/PK-12
4045 Ashland Rd 52554 641-652-7531
Arnie Snook, supt. Fax 652-3143
Cardinal ES 300/PK-5
5414 Highway 16 52554 641-652-3591
Kerry Phillips, prin. Fax 652-3173

Eldora, Hardin, Pop. 2,847
Eldora-New Providence Community SD 500/PK-12
1010 Edgington Ave 50627 641-939-5631
Randall Nichols, supt. Fax 939-3667
www.eldora-np.k12.ia.us
Eldora-New Providence ES 300/PK-5
1101 10th Ave 50627 641-939-9350
Paul Henely, prin. Fax 939-5664

Eldridge, Scott, Pop. 4,484
North Scott Community SD 3,100/K-12
251 E Iowa St 52748 563-285-4819
Jeff Schwiebert, supt. Fax 285-6075
www.north-scott.k12.ia.us
Armstrong ES 300/K-6
212 S Parkview Dr 52748 563-285-8223
Curt Rheingans, prin. Fax 285-6169
North Scott JHS 500/7-8
502 S 5th St 52748 563-285-8272
David Griffin, prin. Fax 285-6045
White ES 400/K-6
121 S 5th St 52748 563-285-4544
John Langenhan, prin. Fax 285-6173
Other Schools – See Donahue, Long Grove, Princeton

Heritage Christian S 100/K-12
507 Parkview Dr 52748 563-285-9382
Cindy Nees, admin. Fax 285-9343

Elgin, Fayette, Pop. 656
Valley Community SD 500/K-12
23493 Canoe Rd 52141 563-426-5501
Cathleen Molumby, supt. Fax 426-5502
www.valley.k12.ia.us

Valley ES 300/K-6
23493 Canoe Rd 52141 563-426-5891
Betsy Netzger, prin. Fax 426-5502

Elkader, Clayton, Pop. 1,383
Central Community SD 600/K-12
400 1st St NW 52043 563-245-1751
Brian Rodenberg, supt. Fax 245-1763
www.central.k12.ia.us/
Elkader ES 300/K-6
400 1st St NW 52043 563-245-1472
Troy Lentell, prin. Fax 245-1763

Elk Horn, Shelby, Pop. 613
Elk Horn-Kimballton Community SD 200/PK-12
PO Box 388a 51531 712-764-4616
Casey Berlau, supt. Fax 764-4626
www.elk-horn.k12.ia.us
Elk Horn-Kimballton ES 100/PK-4
PO Box 388a 51531 712-764-4616
Casey Berlau, prin. Fax 764-4626

Elliott, Montgomery, Pop. 381
Griswold Community SD
Supt. — See Griswold
Elliott ES 100/K-5
PO Box 140A 51532 712-767-2221
Betty Johnston, prin. Fax 767-2211

Emmetsburg, Palo Alto, Pop. 3,706
Emmetsburg Community SD 700/PK-12
205 King St 50536 712-852-3201
John Joynt, supt. Fax 852-3338
www.emmetsburg.k12.ia.us
Emmetsburg MS 200/5-8
1001 Palmer St 50536 712-852-2892
Jay Jurrens, prin. Fax 852-3811
West ES 300/PK-4
602 Call St 50536 712-852-4485
Matt Pugh, prin. Fax 852-3420

Emmetsburg Catholic S 100/K-8
1903 Broadway St 50536 712-852-3464
Jean Hyslop, prin. Fax 852-3464

Epworth, Dubuque, Pop. 1,580
Western Dubuque Community SD
Supt. — See Farley
Epworth ES 300/PK-5
PO Box 270 52045 563-876-5514
Shari Steward, prin. Fax 876-3208

Seton Catholic St. Patrick S 100/K-2
106 1st St SE 52045 563-876-5586
Mary Smock, prin. Fax 876-3055

Essex, Page, Pop. 840
Essex Community SD 300/K-12
111 Forbes St 51638 712-379-3117
Ron Flynn, supt. Fax 379-3200
www.ehs-ees.com/
Essex ES 200/K-6
111 Forbes St 51638 712-379-3114
Allen Stuart, prin. Fax 379-3200

Estherville, Emmet, Pop. 6,347
Estherville Lincoln Central Comm SD 1,200/PK-12
301 N 6th St 51334 712-362-2692
Richard Magnuson, supt. Fax 362-2410
www.estherville.k12.ia.us
DeMoney ES 300/PK-2
109 S 17th St 51334 712-362-2181
Kristine Schlievert, prin. Fax 362-7842
Estherville Lincoln Central MS 600/3-8
315 N 6th St 51334 712-362-2335
Michael Peterson, prin. Fax 362-7822

Evansdale, Black Hawk, Pop. 4,585
Waterloo Community SD
Supt. — See Waterloo
Bunger MS 500/6-8
157 S Roosevelt Rd 50707 319-433-2550
Andrew Miehe, prin. Fax 433-2564
Poyner ES K-5
1138 Central Ave 50707 319-433-1534
Pam Zeigler, prin. Fax 433-1534

Exira, Audubon, Pop. 775
Exira Community SD 300/PK-12
PO Box 335 50076 712-268-5555
Rodney Montang, supt. Fax 268-2188
www.exira.k12.ia.us
Exira ES 100/PK-6
PO Box 335 50076 712-268-5337
Rodney Montang, prin. Fax 268-2188

Fairbank, Buchanan, Pop. 1,034
Wapsie Valley Community SD 700/K-12
2535 Viking Ave 50629 319-638-6711
Chad Garber, supt. Fax 638-7061
www.wapsievalleyschools.com/
Fairbank ES 200/K-6
505 Forest St 50629 319-635-2071
Laura Medberry, prin. Fax 635-2501
Rural S 1 50/K-8
1099 Amish Blvd 50629 319-635-2071
Laura Medberry, prin. Fax 635-2501
Rural S 2 50/K-8
CR C57 and Amish Blvd 50629 319-635-2071
Laura Medberry, prin. Fax 635-2501
Rural S 3 50/K-8
1503 130th St 50629 319-635-2071
Laura Medberry, prin. Fax 635-2501
Rural S 4 50/K-8
1153 Denison Ave 50629 319-635-2071
Laura Medberry, prin. Fax 635-2501
Other Schools – See Readlyn

Fairfield, Jefferson, Pop. 9,404
Fairfield Community SD 1,900/K-12
403 S 20th St 52556 641-472-2655
Donald Achelpohl, supt. Fax 472-0269
www.fairfieldsfuture.org/
Fairfield MS 400/6-8
404 W Fillmore Ave 52556 641-472-5019
Mike Dailey, prin. Fax 472-5301
Lincoln ES 100/K-5
401 W Stone Ave 52556 641-472-2114
Susan McCracken, prin. Fax 472-4630
Pence ES 300/K-5
1000 S 6th St 52556 641-472-2957
Nathan Wear, prin. Fax 472-6506
Washington ES 300/K-5
406 E Madison Ave 52556 641-472-2110
Joe Carr, prin. Fax 469-5774
Other Schools – See Libertyville

Immanuel Lutheran S 100/PK-PK
1601 S Main St 52556 641-469-6634
Victoria Eastburn, dir.
Maharishi S of the Age of Enlightenment 200/PK-12
804 Dr Robert Keith Wallace 52556 641-472-9400
Ashley Deans Ph.D., hdmstr. Fax 472-1211

Farley, Dubuque, Pop. 1,363
Western Dubuque Community SD 2,500/PK-12
PO Box 279 52046 563-744-3885
Jeffory Corkery, supt. Fax 744-3093
www.w-dubuque.k12.ia.us
Drexler ES 400/PK-5
PO Box 279 52046 563-744-3308
Linda Martin, prin. Fax 744-9190
Drexler MS 400/6-8
PO Box 279 52046 563-744-3371
Tim Showalter, prin. Fax 744-3711
Other Schools – See Bernard, Cascade, Dyersville, Epworth, Peosta

---

Seton Catholic St. Joseph S 400/PK-8
PO Box 249 52046 563-744-3290
Mary Smock, prin. Fax 744-3450

Farmington, Van Buren, Pop. 731
Harmony Community SD 400/PK-12
33727 Route J40 52626 319-592-3600
Joseph Hundeby, supt. Fax 592-3690
www.harmony.k12.ia.us/
Other Schools – See Bonaparte

Farnhamville, Calhoun, Pop. 399
Prairie Valley Community SD
Supt. — See Gowrie
Prairie Valley MS 200/5-8
3116 Zearing Ave 50538 515-467-5700
Dennis Hammen, prin. Fax 467-5646

Farragut, Fremont, Pop. 480
Farragut Community SD 300/PK-12
PO Box 36 51639 712-385-8131
Jay Lutt, supt. Fax 385-8135
www.farragutschools.org
Farragut ES 100/PK-6
PO Box 36 51639 712-385-8131
Penny Bredensteiner, prin. Fax 385-8135

Fayette, Fayette, Pop. 1,341
North Fayette Community SD
Supt. — See West Union
Fayette ES 100/K-5
PO Box 10 52142 563-425-3303
Kathleen Bauer, prin. Fax 425-3304

Fenton, Kossuth, Pop. 288
Sentral Community SD 100/PK-8
PO Box 109 50539 515-889-2261
Arthur Pixler, supt. Fax 889-2264
www.sentralschools.org
North Sentral Kossuth MS 50/6-8
PO Box 109 50539 515-889-2261
Arthur Pixler, prin. Fax 889-2264
Sentral ES 100/PK-5
PO Box 109 50539 515-889-2261
Art Pixler, prin. Fax 889-2264

Fonda, Pocahontas, Pop. 588
Newell-Fonda Community SD
Supt. — See Newell
Newell-Fonda MS 100/6-8
PO Box 503 50540 712-288-4445
Randall Nielsen, prin. Fax 288-5710
Newell-Fonda Upper ES 100/4-5
PO Box 503 50540 712-288-4445
Randall Nielsen, prin. Fax 288-5710

Fontanelle, Adair, Pop. 679
Nodaway Valley Community SD
Supt. — See Greenfield
Nodaway Valley MS 200/6-8
112 S 1st St 50846 641-745-2291
Chris Hoover, prin. Fax 745-3501

Forest City, Winnebago, Pop. 4,250
Forest City Community SD 1,300/PK-12
810 W K St 50436 641-585-2323
Darwin Lehmann, supt. Fax 585-5218
www.forestcity.k12.ia.us
Forest City ES 600/PK-5
1405 W I St 50436 641-585-2670
Steven Putz, prin. Fax 585-5903
Forest City MS 300/6-8
216 W School St 50436 641-585-4772
Zach Dillavou, prin. Fax 585-3432

Forest City Christian S 50/PK-12
305 Walnut St 50436 641-585-3233
Ivon Tokheim, admin. Fax 585-1390

Fort Dodge, Webster, Pop. 25,493
Fort Dodge Community SD 3,900/K-12
104 S 17th St 50501 515-576-1161
Linda Brock, supt. Fax 576-1988
www.fort-dodge.k12.ia.us
Butler ES 300/K-4
945 S 18th St 50501 515-574-5882
Mike Woodall, prin. Fax 574-5813
Cooper ES 300/K-4
2420 14th Ave N 50501 515-574-5602
Marlene Johnson, prin. Fax 574-5518
Duncombe ES 300/K-4
615 N 16th St 50501 515-576-5623
Patrick Reding, prin. Fax 576-8774
Fair Oaks MS 600/5-6
416 S 10th St 50501 515-574-5691
Jess Matsen, prin. Fax 576-0501
Feelhaver ES 200/K-4
1300 14th Ave N 50501 515-574-5680
Bruce Hartley, prin. Fax 574-5513
Hillcrest ES 200/K-4
712 3rd St NW 50501 515-574-5613
Lis Ristau, prin. Fax 574-5519
Phillips MS 600/7-8
1015 5th Ave N 50501 515-574-5711
Mark Johnson, prin. Fax 576-3160
Riverside ES 100/K-4
733 F St 50501 515-574-5740
Bruce Hartley, prin. Fax 955-8818

Community Christian S 100/PK-8
3058 10th Ave N 50501 515-573-3011
Roger Everett, admin. Fax 576-7698
St. Edmond S 400/PK-5
2321 6th Ave N 50501 515-576-5182
Linda Mitchell, prin. Fax 573-3601
St. Paul Lutheran S 200/PK-8
1217 4th Ave S 50501 515-955-7208
Gene Sommerfeld, prin. Fax 573-7839

Fort Madison, Lee, Pop. 11,048
Fort Madison Community SD 2,200/PK-12
PO Box 1423 52627 319-372-7252
Kenneth Marang, supt. Fax 372-7255
www.ft-madison.k12.ia.us
Fort Madison MS 500/6-8
1801 Avenue G 52627 319-372-4687
Todd Dirth, prin. Fax 372-0378
Lincoln ES 300/K-5
1326 Avenue E 52627 319-372-2896
Janice Burch, prin. Fax 372-8927
Richardson ES 400/PK-5
3301 Avenue L 52627 319-372-2765
Michelle Earhart, prin. Fax 376-2284
Other Schools – See Denmark

Holy Trinity ECC 100/PK-K
2213 Avenue J 52627 319-372-6428
Kathy Osipowicz, dir. Fax 372-6443

Fredericksburg, Chickasaw, Pop. 903
Fredericksburg Community SD 300/K-8
PO Box 337 50630 563-237-5364
Rick Pederson, supt. Fax 237-5888
www.aea1.k12.ia.us/districts/fredericksburg.html
Fredericksburg ES 100/K-5
PO Box 337 50630 563-237-5364
Amy Moine, prin. Fax 237-5888
Sumner-Fredericksburg MS 200/6-8
PO Box 337 50630 563-237-5334
Jill Glenn, prin. Fax 237-6329

Fremont, Mahaska, Pop. 690
Fremont Community SD 200/PK-8
525 E Main St 52561 641-933-4211
J. Dotson, supt. Fax 933-4123
fremontcsd.com
Fremont ES 100/PK-5
525 E Main St 52561 641-933-4211
Brandt Snakenburg, prin. Fax 933-4123
Fremont MS 50/6-8
525 E Main St 52561 641-933-4211
Brandt Snakenburg, prin. Fax 933-4123

Galva, Ida, Pop. 340
Galva-Holstein Community SD
Supt. — See Holstein
Galva-Holstein MS 100/5-8
207 Noll St 51020 712-282-4213
Mike Richard, prin. Fax 282-4210

Garnavillo, Clayton, Pop. 744
Clayton Ridge Community SD
Supt. — See Guttenberg
Clayton Ridge MS 200/5-8
PO Box 9 52049 563-964-2321
Michael Siebersma, prin. Fax 964-2756

Garner, Hancock, Pop. 2,975
Garner-Hayfield Community SD 800/PK-12
PO Box 449 50438 641-923-2718
Tyler Williams, supt. Fax 923-3825
www.garner.k12.ia.us
Garner ES 400/PK-6
PO Box 449 50438 641-923-2831
Cheryl Toppin, prin. Fax 923-2031
Garner-Hayfield MS 100/7-8
PO Box 449 50438 641-923-2809
Paul Schoneman, prin. Fax 923-2031

Garwin, Tama, Pop. 549
GMG Community SD 500/K-12
306 Park St 50632 641-499-2239
Michael Ashton, supt. Fax 499-2159
www.garwin.k12.ia.us
Other Schools – See Green Mountain

George, Lyon, Pop. 1,025
George-Little Rock Community SD 500/PK-12
PO Box 6 51237 712-475-3311
David Ackerman, supt. Fax 475-3574
www.george-lr.k12.ia.us
George ES 100/K-5
PO Box 6 51237 712-475-3675
Mike Munson, prin. Fax 475-3594
Other Schools – See Little Rock

Gilbert, Story, Pop. 973
Gilbert Community SD 700/K-12
103 Mathews Dr 50105 515-232-3740
John Kinley, supt. Fax 232-0099
www.gilbert.k12.ia.us
Gilbert ES 400/K-4
109 Rothmoor St 50105 515-232-3744
Staci Edwards, prin. Fax 233-4271
Gilbert MS 5-8
201 E Mathews Dr 50105 515-232-0540
Chris Billings, prin. Fax 232-0541

Gilbertville, Black Hawk, Pop. 779

Immaculate Conception S 300/K-8
311 16th Ave 50634 319-296-1089
Julie Niemeyer, prin. Fax 296-3847

Gillett Grove, Clay, Pop. 59
South Clay Community SD 100/PK-6
PO Box 68 51341 712-835-2270
David Schulz, supt. Fax 835-2277
www.s-clay.k12.ia.us
South Clay ES 100/PK-6
PO Box 68 51341 712-835-2270
David Schulz, prin. Fax 835-2277

Gilman, Marshall, Pop. 575
East Marshall Community SD 700/PK-12
PO Box 159 50106 641-498-7481
Alan Meyer, supt. Fax 498-2035
www.e-marshall.k12.ia.us
East Marshall MS 300/5-8
PO Box 159 50106 641-498-7483
Robert Schelp, prin. Fax 498-2180
Other Schools – See Laurel

Gilmore City, Humboldt, Pop. 515
Gilmore City-Bradgate Community SD 100/PK-8
402 SE E Ave 50541 515-373-6619
Ron Bollmeyer, supt. Fax 373-6092
www.trv.k12.ia.us
Gilmore City ES 100/PK-5
402 SE E Ave 50541 515-373-6124
Tamela Johnson, prin. Fax 373-6092
Twin River Valley MS 100/6-8
402 SE E Ave 50541 515-373-6124
Ronald Bollmeyer, prin. Fax 373-6092

Gladbrook, Tama, Pop. 1,021
Gladbrook-Reinbeck Community SD
Supt. — See Reinbeck
Gladbrook ES 100/K-4
PO Box 370 50635 641-473-2875
Bill Parker, prin. Fax 473-2913
Gladbrook-Reinbeck MS 200/5-8
PO Box 370 50635 641-473-2842
Doran Dahms, prin. Fax 473-2913

Glenwood, Mills, Pop. 5,650
Glenwood Community SD 2,000/K-12
103 Central St Ste 300 51534 712-527-9034
Dr. Stan Sibley, supt. Fax 527-4287
www.glenwood.k12.ia.us
Glenwood MS 300/7-8
400 Sivers Rd 51534 712-527-4887
Heidi Stanley, prin. Fax 527-3411
Northeast ES 600/K-3
901 N Vine St 51534 712-527-4875
Joan Crowl, prin. Fax 527-4054
West ES 400/4-6
707 Sharp St 51534 712-527-4886
Kevin Farmer, prin. Fax 527-5486

Glidden, Carroll, Pop. 1,228
Glidden-Ralston Community SD 400/PK-12
PO Box 488 51443 712-659-3411
Vicki Lowe, supt. Fax 659-2248
www.glidden-ralston.k12.ia.us
Glidden-Ralston ES 200/PK-6
PO Box 488 51443 712-659-3863
Vicki Lowe, prin. Fax 659-2248

Goose Lake, Clinton, Pop. 234
Northeast Community SD 700/K-12
PO Box 66 52750 563-577-2249
James Cox, supt. Fax 577-2450
www.northeast.k12.ia.us
Northeast ES 300/K-6
PO Box 130 52750 563-577-2249
Diane Schumacher, prin. Fax 577-2450

Gowrie, Webster, Pop. 1,045
Prairie Valley Community SD 700/PK-12
PO Box 49 50543 515-352-3173
James Dick, supt. Fax 352-5573
www.gowrie.k12.ia.us
Other Schools – See Callender, Farnhamville

Graettinger, Palo Alto, Pop. 866
Graettinger Community SD 100/PK-12
PO Box 58 51342 712-859-3286
Randy Collins, supt. Fax 859-3509
www.graettinger.k12.ia.us
Graettinger/Terril S 100/PK-12
PO Box 58 51342 712-859-3286
Chris Richards, prin. Fax 859-3509

Grand Junction, Greene, Pop. 927
East Greene Community SD 300/PK-12
PO Box 377 50107 515-738-5741
G. Mike Harter, supt. Fax 738-5719
www.east-greene.k12.ia.us
Other Schools – See Rippey

Granger, Dallas, Pop. 943
Woodward-Granger Community SD
Supt. — See Woodward
Woodward-Granger ES 300/PK-5
2200 State St 50109 515-999-2357
Brad Andersen, prin. Fax 999-9299

Assumption S 100/PK-8
PO Box 100 50109 515-999-2211
Herb Hartman, prin. Fax 999-2208

Greene, Butler, Pop. 1,015
Greene Community SD 400/PK-12
PO Box 190 50636 641-816-5523
Terry Kenealy, supt. Fax 816-5921
www.greene.k12.ia.us
Greene ES 100/PK-4
PO Box 190 50636 641-816-5629
Mary Oelmann, prin. Fax 816-3629

Greenfield, Adair, Pop. 1,984
Nodaway Valley Community SD 800/K-12
410 NW 2nd St 50849 641-743-6127
John Dayton, supt. Fax 343-7173
www.nod-valley.k12.ia.us
Nodaway Valley East ES 200/K-3
324 NW 2nd St 50849 641-743-6136
Connie Lundy, prin. Fax 743-8458
Other Schools – See Bridgewater, Fontanelle

Green Mountain, Marshall
GMG Community SD
Supt. — See Garwin
GMG ES 200/K-6
1710 Wallace Ave 50632 641-474-2251
Patricia Smith, prin. Fax 474-2253

Grimes, Polk, Pop. 6,037
Dallas Center-Grimes Community SD
Supt. — See Dallas Center
North Ridge ES 300/3-4
PO Box 770 50111 515-986-5674
Lea Davidson, prin. Fax 986-5376
South Prairie ES 400/K-2
PO Box 650 50111 515-986-4057
Ann Bass, prin. Fax 986-4532

Grinnell, Poweshiek, Pop. 9,332
Grinnell-Newburg Community SD 1,800/PK-12
927 4th Ave 50112 641-236-2700
Edith Eckles, supt. Fax 236-2699
www.grinnell.k12.ia.us
Bailey Park ES 200/K-2
210 8th Ave 50112 641-236-2770
Nancy Beck, prin. Fax 236-2682
Davis ES 300/3-4
818 Hamilton Ave 50112 641-236-2790
Nancy Beck, prin. Fax 236-2785
Fairview ES 200/PK-2
1310 Hobart St 50112 641-236-2780
Nancy Beck, prin. Fax 236-2674
Grinnell Community MS 500/5-8
132 East St S 50112 641-236-2750
Sara Hegg-Dunne, prin. Fax 236-2732

Central Iowa Christian S 100/PK-8
201 380th Ave 50112 641-236-3000
Gary Larsson, admin. Fax 236-1433

Griswold, Cass, Pop. 983
Griswold Community SD 600/PK-12
PO Box 280 51535 712-778-2152
Dana Kunze, supt. Fax 778-4145
www.griswold.k12.ia.us
Other Schools – See Elliott, Lewis

Grundy Center, Grundy, Pop. 2,583
Grundy Center Community SD 700/PK-12
1301 12th St 50638 319-825-5418
John Stevens, supt. Fax 825-5419
www.grundy-center.k12.ia.us
Grundy Center ES 300/PK-5
903 9th St 50638 319-825-5461
Lisa Miller, prin. Fax 825-6817
Grundy Center MS 100/6-8
1006 M Ave 50638 319-825-5464
Cassandra Murra, prin. Fax 825-6415

Guthrie Center, Guthrie, Pop. 1,617
Guthrie Center Community SD 600/PK-12
906 School St 50115 641-332-2972
Steve Smith, supt. Fax 332-2973
www.guthrie.k12.ia.us
Guthrie Center ES 300/PK-6
900 N 4th St 50115 641-332-2720
Randy Mohning, prin. Fax 332-2721
Guthrie Center JHS 100/7-8
906 School St 50115 641-332-2974
Brent Meier, prin. Fax 332-2973

Guttenberg, Clayton, Pop. 1,943
Clayton Ridge Community SD 600/K-12
PO Box 520 52052 563-252-2341
Allen Nelson, supt. Fax 252-2656
www.guttenberg.k12.ia.us
Clayton Ridge ES 200/K-4
PO Box 520 52052 563-252-1747
Sherry Oliver, prin. Fax 252-2656
Other Schools – See Garnavillo

St. Marys S 100/K-8
PO Box 100 52052 563-252-1577
Sr. Suzanne Gallagher, prin. Fax 252-4065

Hamburg, Fremont, Pop. 1,221
Hamburg Community SD 300/PK-12
105 E St 51640 712-382-1063
Dr. Paul Sellon, supt. Fax 382-1211
www.hamburg.k12.ia.us
Simons ES 200/PK-6
309 S St 51640 712-382-2017
Ken Wathen, prin. Fax 382-1922

Hampton, Franklin, Pop. 4,224
Hampton-Dumont Community SD 900/PK-12
601 12th Ave NE 50441 641-456-2175
Todd Lettow, supt. Fax 456-5750
www.hdcsd.org/
Hampton-Dumont MS 300/5-8
601 12th Ave NE 50441 641-456-4735
Dave Wempen, prin. Fax 456-2023
North Side S 50/PK-PK
114 11th Pl NE 50441 641-456-4481
Charlane Pralle-Janssen, prin. Fax 456-4173
South Side ES 200/K-2
507 4th Ave SE 50441 641-456-2261
Jerry Buseman, prin. Fax 456-5753
Other Schools – See Dumont

Harlan, Shelby, Pop. 5,170
Harlan Community SD 1,700/PK-12
2102 Durant St 51537 712-755-2152
Bob Broomfield, supt. Fax 755-7312
www.harlan.k12.ia.us
Harlan Community MS 400/6-8
2108 Durant St 51537 712-755-3196
Bill Mueller, prin. Fax 755-3699
New Park ES 300/PK-3
1003 Tarkington St 51537 712-755-5903
Scott Frohlich, prin. Fax 755-3661
West Ridge ES 400/K-5
1401 19th St 51537 712-755-2725
Jeff Moser, prin. Fax 755-7880

Shelby County Catholic S 100/K-8
2005 College Pl 51537 712-755-5634
Ann Andersen, prin. Fax 755-3332

Hartford, Warren, Pop. 754
Carlisle Community SD
Supt. — See Carlisle
Hartford MS 100/4-5
500 N Vine St 50118 515-989-0316
Julie Halbur, prin. Fax 989-3897

Hartley, O'Brien, Pop. 1,565
Hartley-Melvin-Sanborn Community SD 700/PK-12
240 1st St SE 51346 712-928-2022
Lynn Evans, supt. Fax 928-3607
www.hartley-ms.k12.ia.us
Hartley-Melvin-Sanborn ES 200/PK-4
240 1st St SE 51346 712-928-2020
Lynn Evans, prin. Fax 928-3536
Other Schools – See Sanborn

Hastings, Mills, Pop. 191
Nishna Valley Community SD 100/PK-8
58962 380th St 51540 712-624-8696
William Crilly, supt. Fax 624-9131
www.nishna-valley.k12.ia.us/
East Mills MS 50/5-8
58962 380th St 51540 712-624-8696
Deborah Taylor, prin. Fax 624-9131
Nishna Valley ES 100/PK-4
58962 380th St 51540 712-624-8696
William Crilly, prin. Fax 624-9131

Hawarden, Sioux, Pop. 2,440
West Sioux Community SD 700/K-12
1300 Falcon Dr 51023 712-551-1461
Paul Olson, supt. Fax 551-1367
www.westsiouxschools.org/
Hawarden ES 200/2-5
806 13th St 51023 712-551-1454
Ryan Kramer, prin. Fax 551-2829
West Sioux MS 100/6-8
1300 Falcon Dr 51023 712-551-1022
Kim Buryanek, prin. Fax 551-1367
Other Schools – See Ireton

Hawkeye, Fayette, Pop. 464
North Fayette Community SD
Supt. — See West Union
Hawkeye ES 100/K-2
PO Box 9 52147 563-427-3216
Kathleen Bauer, prin. Fax 427-3224

Hiawatha, Linn, Pop. 6,596
Cedar Rapids Community SD
Supt. — See Cedar Rapids
Hiawatha ES 400/PK-5
603 Emmons St 52233 319-558-2172
Michelle Elam, prin. Fax 378-1912
Nixon ES 300/K-5
200 Nixon Dr 52233 319-558-2188
Kay Coe, prin. Fax 294-9242

Hills, Johnson, Pop. 617
Iowa City Community SD
Supt. — See Iowa City
Hills ES 200/PK-6
PO Box 218 52235 319-688-1105
Perry Ross, prin. Fax 679-2223

Hinton, Plymouth, Pop. 847
Hinton Community SD 700/PK-12
PO Box 128 51024 712-947-4329
Allen Steen, supt. Fax 947-4427
www.hintonschool.com/
Hinton ES, PO Box 128 51024 300/PK-5
Jane Krehbiel, prin. 712-947-4428
Hinton MS 100/6-8
PO Box 128 51024 712-947-4328
Peter Stuerman, prin. Fax 947-4947

Holstein, Ida, Pop. 1,415
Galva-Holstein Community SD 500/PK-12
PO Box 320 51025 712-368-4353
Harold Post, supt. Fax 368-4843
www.galva-holstein.k12.ia.us
Galva-Holstein ES 200/PK-4
PO Box 320 51025 712-368-4353
Mike Richard, prin. Fax 368-4843
Other Schools – See Galva

Holy Cross, Dubuque, Pop. 339

LaSalle S - Holy Cross Center 100/4-8
PO Box 368 52053 563-870-2405
John Pesetski, prin. Fax 870-4101

Hopkinton, Delaware, Pop. 656
Maquoketa Valley Community SD
Supt. — See Delhi
Johnston ES 100/PK-5
PO Box 390 52237 563-926-2701
Joann Swinton, prin. Fax 926-2093

Hospers, Sioux, Pop. 674
MOC-Floyd Valley Community SD
Supt. — See Orange City
Hospers ES 200/K-5
201 4th Ave S 51238 712-752-8480
Marcia DeGraaf, prin. Fax 752-8498

Hubbard, Hardin, Pop. 845
Hubbard-Radcliffe Community SD 200/PK-8
PO Box 129 50122 641-864-2211
Joel Semprini, supt. Fax 864-2422
www.hubbard.k12.ia.us
South Hardin MS 50/6-8
PO Box 129 50122 641-864-2211
Patricia Heinz, prin. Fax 864-2422
Other Schools – See Radcliffe

Hudson, Black Hawk, Pop. 2,127
Hudson Community SD 800/K-12
PO Box 240 50643 319-988-3233
Roark Horn, supt. Fax 988-3235
www.hudson.k12.ia.us
Hudson ES, PO Box 240 50643 200/K-4
Mark Schlatter, prin. 319-988-3239
Hudson MS 300/5-8
PO Box 240 50643 319-988-4137
Melissa Reimer, prin. Fax 988-4137

Hull, Sioux, Pop. 2,039
Boyden-Hull Community SD 600/K-12
PO Box 678 51239 712-439-2711
Steve Grond, supt. Fax 439-1419
www.boyden-hull.k12.ia.us
Other Schools – See Boyden

Hull Christian S 100/K-8
PO Box 550 51239 712-439-2273
Randel Ten Pas, prin. Fax 439-1713
Hull Protestant Reformed Christian S 100/K-8
218 2nd St 51239 712-439-2490
Peter Brummel, prin. Fax 439-2490

Humboldt, Humboldt, Pop. 4,366
Humboldt Community SD 1,300/PK-12
1408 9th Ave N 50548 515-332-1330
Greg Darling, supt. Fax 332-4478
www.humboldt.k12.ia.us
Humboldt MS 300/6-8
210 Taft St N 50548 515-332-2812
Bob Pattee, prin. Fax 332-2023
Taft ES 300/2-5
612 2nd Ave N 50548 515-332-3216
George Bruder, prin. Fax 332-7102
Other Schools – See Dakota City

St. Mary S 200/PK-6
303 3rd St N 50548 515-332-2134
Sr. Louise Scieszinski, prin. Fax 332-1487

Humeston, Wayne, Pop. 545
Mormon Trail Community SD 300/PK-12
PO Box 156 50123 641-877-2521
Tucker Lillis, supt. Fax 877-3400
www.mormontrail.k12.ia.us
Mormon Trail ES 100/PK-6
PO Box 156 50123 641-877-2521
Denise Dent, prin. Fax 877-3400

Huxley, Story, Pop. 2,347
Ballard Community SD 1,500/PK-12
PO Box 307 50124 515-597-2811
John Speer, supt. Fax 597-2965
www.ballard.k12.ia.us/
Ballard Community JHS 200/7-8
PO Box 307 50124 515-597-2971
John Ronca, prin. Fax 597-2764
Other Schools – See Cambridge, Slater

Ida Grove, Ida, Pop. 2,218
Battle Creek-Ida Grove Community SD 700/PK-12
301 Moorehead St 51445 712-364-3687
Russ Freeman, supt. Fax 364-3609
www.bc-ig.k12.ia.us
Ida Grove ES 200/PK-4
403 Barnes St 51445 712-364-2360
Alan Henderson, prin. Fax 364-3103
Other Schools – See Battle Creek

Independence, Buchanan, Pop. 6,054
Independence Community SD 1,400/K-12
1207 1st St W 50644 319-334-7400
Devin Embray, supt. Fax 334-7404
www.independence.k12.ia.us/
East ES 300/K-2
211 9th Ave SE 50644 319-334-7425
Mary Blaisdell, prin. Fax 334-7427
Independence MS 300/6-8
1301 1st St W 50644 319-334-7415
Dave Jacobson, prin. Fax 334-7418
West ES 300/3-5
1103 1st St W 50644 319-334-7430
Rudi Hameister, prin. Fax 334-7433

St. John S 100/K-8
314 3rd St NE 50644 319-334-7173
Peter Bellaver, prin. Fax 334-9088

Indianola, Warren, Pop. 13,944
Indianola Community SD 3,300/K-12
1304 E 2nd Ave 50125 515-961-9500
Michael Teigland, supt. Fax 961-9505
www.indianola.k12.ia.us
Emerson ES 500/K-5
1109 E Euclid Ave 50125 515-961-9550
Mark Timmerman, prin. Fax 961-9555
Indianola MS 700/6-8
403 S 15th St 50125 515-961-9530
Annette Jauron, prin. Fax 961-9535
Irving ES 600/K-5
500 W Clinton Ave 50125 515-961-9560
AmyJo Naughton, prin. Fax 961-9566
Whittier ES 400/K-5
1306 W Salem Ave 50125 515-961-9570
Ed Johnson, prin. Fax 961-9575
Wilder ES K-5
2303 W Euclid Ave 50125 515-961-9540
Craig Sexton, prin. Fax 961-9544

Inwood, Lyon, Pop. 874
West Lyon Community SD 700/PK-12
1787 182nd St 51240 712-753-4917
Jim Hargens, supt. Fax 753-4928
www.west-lyon.k12.ia.us/
West Lyon ES 400/PK-6
1787 182nd St 51240 712-753-4917
Tim Snyder, prin. Fax 753-4928
West Lyon JHS 100/7-8
1787 182nd St 51240 712-753-4917
Doug Jiskoot, prin. Fax 753-4928

Inwood Christian S 100/PK-8
PO Box C 51240 712-753-4541
William Wolfswinkel, prin. Fax 753-2434

Iowa City, Johnson, Pop. 62,887
Iowa City Community SD 10,800/PK-12
509 S Dubuque St 52240 319-688-1000
Dr. Lane Plugge, supt. Fax 688-1009
www.iccsd.k12.ia.us/
Hoover ES 300/K-6
2200 E Court St 52245 319-688-1110
Shannon Kehoe, prin. Fax 339-5711
Horn ES 300/K-6
600 Koser Ave 52246 319-688-1115
Kristin Cannon, prin. Fax 339-5713
Lemme ES 300/K-6
3100 E Washington St 52245 319-688-1125
John Bacon, prin. Fax 339-5709
Lincoln ES 300/K-6
300 Teeters Ct 52246 319-688-1130
Christine Kolarik, prin. Fax 339-5718
Longfellow ES 300/K-6
1130 Seymour Ave 52240 319-688-1135
Chris Pisarik, prin. Fax 339-5720
Lucas ES 400/PK-6
830 Southlawn Dr 52245 319-688-1140
Brian Lehmann, prin. Fax 339-5722
Mann ES 300/PK-6
521 N Dodge St 52245 319-688-1145
Kris Quinn, prin. Fax 339-5724
Roosevelt ES 300/K-6
611 Greenwood Dr 52246 319-688-1155
Mindy Paulsen, prin. Fax 339-5729
Shimek ES 200/PK-6
1400 Grissell Pl 52245 319-688-1160
Charles Towers, prin. Fax 339-5731
Southeast JHS 700/7-8
2501 Bradford Dr 52240 319-688-1070
Deb Wretman, prin. Fax 339-5735
Twain ES 200/PK-6
1355 Deforest Ave 52240 319-688-1165
Mary Bontrager, prin. Fax 339-5725
Weber ES 500/K-6
3850 Rohret Rd 52246 319-688-1170
Chris Gibson, prin. Fax 339-5763
Wood ES 500/K-6
1930 Lakeside Dr 52240 319-688-1180
Kate Callahan, prin. Fax 339-5740
Other Schools – See Coralville, Hills, North Liberty

Regina ES 600/PK-6
2120 Rochester Ave 52245 319-337-5739
Celeste Vincent, prin. Fax 337-4109

Iowa Falls, Hardin, Pop. 5,112
Iowa Falls Community SD 1,100/PK-12
710 North St 50126 641-648-6400
John Robbins, supt. Fax 648-6401
www.iowa-falls.k12.ia.us
Pineview ES 300/PK-2
1510 Washington Ave 50126 641-648-6410
Ryan Robison, prin. Fax 648-6411
Riverbend MS 200/7-8
1124 Union St 50126 641-648-6430
Jeff Burchfield, prin. Fax 648-6432
Rock Run ES 300/3-5
710 North St 50126 641-648-6420
Mike Swartzendruber, prin. Fax 648-6422

Ireton, Sioux, Pop. 592
West Sioux Community SD
Supt. — See Hawarden
Ireton ES 100/K-1
PO Box 248 51027 712-278-2374
Ryan Kramer, prin. Fax 278-2383

Ireton Christian S 100/PK-8
104 5th St 51027 712-278-2245
Marlin Schoonhoven, prin. Fax 278-2245

Irwin, Shelby, Pop. 369
IKM Community SD
Supt. — See Manilla
IKM Community ES 100/PK-4
PO Box 217 51446 712-782-3126
Wendy Hammrich, prin. Fax 782-3128

Janesville, Bremer, Pop. 875
Janesville Consolidated SD 300/PK-12
PO Box 478 50647 319-987-2581
Steve Gray, supt. Fax 987-2824
www.janesville.k12.ia.us
Janesville ES 100/PK-5
PO Box 478 50647 319-987-2581
Christine Thompson, prin. Fax 987-2824

Jefferson, Greene, Pop. 4,407
Jefferson-Scranton Community SD 900/PK-12
204 W Madison St 50129 515-386-4168
Tim Christensen, supt. Fax 386-3591
www.jefferson-scranton.k12.ia.us
Jefferson-Scranton ES 200/K-5
401 E Russell St 50129 515-386-3178
Tom Yepsen, prin. Fax 386-3483
Jefferson-Scranton MS 200/6-8
203 W Harrison St 50129 515-386-8126
Scott Johnson, prin. Fax 386-2142
South K 100/PK-K
204 W Madison St 50129 515-386-4168
Tom Yepsen, prin. Fax 386-3591

Jesup, Buchanan, Pop. 2,413
Jesup Community SD 800/PK-12
PO Box 287 50648 319-827-1700
Sarah Pinion, supt. Fax 827-3905
www.jesup.k12.ia.us
Jesup ES 300/PK-4
PO Box 287 50648 319-827-1700
Brian Pottebaum, prin. Fax 827-3905
Jesup MS 200/5-8
PO Box 287 50648 319-827-1700
Lisa Loecher, prin. Fax 827-3905
Perry #1 S 50/K-8
PO Box 287 50648 319-827-1700
Brian Pottebaum, prin. Fax 827-3905
Prairie Grove S 50/K-8
PO Box 287 50648 319-827-1700
Brian Pottebaum, prin. Fax 827-3905
Triumph S 50/K-8
PO Box 287 50648 319-827-1700
Brian Pottebaum, prin. Fax 827-3905

St. Anthanasius S 100/K-8
PO Box 288 50648 319-827-1314
Julie Niemeyer, prin. Fax 827-1124

Jewell, Hamilton, Pop. 1,090
South Hamilton Community SD 800/PK-12
315 Division St 50130 515-827-5479
Lyle Schwartz, supt. Fax 827-5368
www.s-hamilton.k12.ia.us
South Hamilton ES 400/PK-6
404 Blaine St 50130 515-827-5096
Paul Hemphill, prin. Fax 827-5868

Johnston, Polk, Pop. 12,931
Johnston Community SD 5,400/PK-12
PO Box 10 50131 515-278-0470
Clay Guthmiller, supt. Fax 278-5884
www.johnston.k12.ia.us
Beaver Creek ES 900/PK-5
PO Box 10 50131 515-278-6228
Eric Toot, prin. Fax 278-1049
Horizon ES 600/K-5
PO Box 10 50131 515-986-1121
Timothy Salmon, prin. Fax 986-1131
Lawson ES 500/K-5
PO Box 10 50131 515-278-0478
Trisha Lenarz-Garmoe, prin. Fax 278-4851
Summit MS 800/6-7
PO Box 10 50131 515-986-0318
Linda Hansen, prin. Fax 986-0952
Timber Ridge ES PK-5
PO Box 10 50131 515-331-4379
Cheryl Henkenius, prin. Fax 331-9093
Wallace ES 600/K-5
PO Box 10 50131 515-278-6977
Suzie Pearson, prin. Fax 278-9894

Kalona, Washington, Pop. 2,486
Mid-Prairie Community SD
Supt. — See Wellman
Kalona ES 200/PK-5
204 6th St 52247 319-656-2243
Jim Cayton, prin. Fax 656-2238
Mid-Prairie MS 300/6-8
713 F Ave 52247 319-656-2241
Nancy Hurd, prin. Fax 656-2207
Washington Township ES 100/K-5
1592 Angle Rd SW 52247 319-683-2770
Evan Parrott, prin. Fax 683-2286

Kanawha, Hancock, Pop. 691
West Hancock Community SD
Supt. — See Britt
West Hancock MS 200/5-8
PO Box 130 50447 641-762-3261
Wayne Kronemann, prin. Fax 762-3263

Kanawha Christian S — 50/PK-8
470 E 5th St 50447 — 641-762-3322
Ryan Zonnefeld, prin. — Fax 762-8362

Keokuk, Lee, Pop. 10,762
Keokuk Community SD — 2,000/K-12
727 Washington St 52632 — 319-524-1402
Lora Wolff, supt. — Fax 524-1114
www.keokuk.k12.ia.us
Hawthorne ES — 400/K-5
2940 Decatur St 52632 — 319-524-3503
Rudi Hameister, prin. — Fax 526-5946
Keokuk MS — 500/6-8
2002 Orleans Ave 52632 — 319-524-3737
Steven Carman, prin. — Fax 524-1511
Torrence ES — 100/1-5
1721 Fulton St 52632 — 319-524-2263
Russ Derr, prin. — Fax 524-2014
Washington ES — 200/1-5
116 N 8th St 52632 — 319-524-1953
Kim Hartweg, prin. — Fax 526-3081
Wells-Carey ES — 200/1-5
918 Timea St 52632 — 319-524-2581
Russ Derr, prin. — Fax 524-8006

Keokuk Catholic S — 100/K-8
2981 Plank Rd 52632 — 319-524-5450
Laurie Mendenhall, prin. — Fax 524-5458

Keosauqua, Van Buren, Pop. 1,076
Van Buren Community SD — 700/PK-12
503 Henry Dr 52565 — 319-293-3334
Karen Stinson, supt. — Fax 293-3301
www.van-buren.k12.ia.us
Other Schools – See Birmingham, Douds, Stockport

Keota, Keokuk, Pop. 939
Keota Community SD — 400/PK-12
PO Box 88 52248 — 641-636-2189
Todd Abrahamson, supt. — Fax 636-3009
www.keota.k12.ia.us/
Keota ES, PO Box 88 52248 — 200/PK-6
Margaret Jarrard, prin. — 641-636-2323

Keystone, Benton, Pop. 690
Benton Community SD
Supt. — See Van Horne
Keystone ES — 200/3-6
280 4th Ave 52249 — 319-442-3221
Tanya Langholdt, prin. — Fax 442-3702

Kingsley, Plymouth, Pop. 1,248
Kingsley-Pierson Community SD — 500/K-12
PO Box 520 51028 — 712-378-2861
Scott Bailey, supt. — Fax 378-3729
www.kingsley-pierson.k12.ia.us
Kingsley ES — 200/K-4
322 Quest Ave 51028 — 712-378-2861
Robert Wiese, prin. — Fax 378-3729
Other Schools – See Pierson

Knoxville, Marion, Pop. 7,512
Knoxville Community SD — 2,000/PK-12
309 W Main St 50138 — 641-842-6552
Randy Flack, supt. — Fax 842-2109
www.knoxville.k12.ia.us
East ES — 300/K-5
614 E Washington St 50138 — 641-842-6541
Michael Montgomery, prin. — Fax 842-4572
Knoxville MS — 500/6-8
102 N Lincoln St 50138 — 641-842-3315
Annette Jauron, prin. — Fax 842-5754
Northstar ES — 300/PK-5
407 W Larson St 50138 — 641-842-6527
Linda Abbott, prin. — Fax 828-8052
West ES — 300/PK-5
306 S Park Lane Dr 50138 — 641-842-2185
John Keitges, prin. — Fax 842-6029

Lacona, Warren, Pop. 354
Southeast Warren Community SD
Supt. — See Liberty Center
Lacona ES — 100/4-6
PO Box 67 50139 — 641-534-4701
Charlotte Weaklend, prin. — Fax 534-1300

Lake City, Calhoun, Pop. 1,693
Southern Cal Community SD — 400/PK-12
709 W Main St 51449 — 712-464-7210
Eric Wood, supt. — Fax 464-3724
www.southern-cal.k12.ia.us
Other Schools – See Lohrville

Lake Mills, Winnebago, Pop. 2,060
Lake Mills Community SD — 700/PK-12
102 S 4th Ave E 50450 — 641-592-0881
Daryl Sherman, supt. — Fax 592-0883
www.lake-mills.k12.ia.us
Lake Mills ES — 300/PK-5
102 S 4th Ave E 50450 — 641-592-1882
Cynthia Witt, prin. — Fax 592-0883
Lake Mills MS — 200/6-8
102 S 4th Ave E 50450 — 641-592-0894
James Scholbrock, prin. — Fax 592-0883

Lake Park, Dickinson, Pop. 993
Harris-Lake Park Community SD — 300/PK-12
PO Box 8 51347 — 712-832-3809
Dennis Peters, supt. — Fax 832-3812
www.harris-lp.k12.ia.us
Harris-Lake Park ES — 100/PK-5
PO Box 277 51347 — 712-832-3437
Judith Brueggman, prin. — Fax 832-3640

Lake View, Sac, Pop. 1,221
East Sac County SD — 400/PK-12
PO Box 110 51450 — 712-664-5000
Barb Kruthoff, supt. — Fax 664-5021
www.eastsac.k12.ia.us/
Other Schools – See Sac City, Wall Lake

Lamoni, Decatur, Pop. 2,470
Lamoni Community SD — 400/PK-12
202 N Walnut St 50140 — 641-784-3342
Diane Fine, supt. — Fax 784-6602
lamoni.k12.ia.us
Lamoni ES — 200/PK-5
202 N Walnut St 50140 — 641-784-3422
Diane Fine, prin. — Fax 784-6602
Lamoni MS — 100/6-8
202 N Walnut St 50140 — 641-784-7299
E.B. Sherman, prin. — Fax 784-6602

Lansing, Allamakee, Pop. 987
Eastern Allamakee Community SD — 400/K-12
569 Center St 52151 — 563-538-4201
Patrick Heiderscheit, supt. — Fax 538-4969
www.e-allamakee.k12.ia.us/
Lansing MS — 100/6-8
569 Center St 52151 — 563-538-4201
Marcia Kruse, prin. — Fax 538-4969
Other Schools – See New Albin

La Porte City, Black Hawk, Pop. 2,301
Union Community SD — 1,300/K-12
200 Adams St 50651 — 319-342-2674
Neil Mullen, supt. — Fax 342-2393
www.union.k12.ia.us/
La Porte City ES — 300/K-5
515 Fillmore St 50651 — 319-342-3033
Todd Parker, prin. — Fax 342-3816
Other Schools – See Dysart

Latimer, Franklin, Pop. 550
CAL Community SD — 300/PK-12
PO Box 459 50452 — 641-579-6087
Steven Lane, supt. — Fax 579-6408
www.cal.k12.ia.us
CAL Community ES — 100/PK-6
PO Box 459 50452 — 641-579-6087
Steven Lane, prin. — Fax 579-6408

St. Paul's Lutheran S — 50/K-8
PO Box 609 50452 — 641-579-6046
Barb Buscher, prin. — Fax 579-6285

Laurel, Marshall, Pop. 268
East Marshall Community SD
Supt. — See Gilman
East Marshall ES — 100/PK-4
PO Box 10 50141 — 641-476-3342
Darlys Baker, prin. — Fax 476-3904

Laurens, Pocahontas, Pop. 1,326
Laurens-Marathon Community SD — 400/K-12
300 W Garfield St 50554 — 712-841-5000
Iner Joelson, supt. — Fax 841-5010
www.laurens-marathon.k12.ia.us
Laurens-Marathon ES — 100/K-5
300 W Garfield St 50554 — 712-841-5000
Iner Joelson, prin. — Fax 841-5010
Laurens-Marathon MS — 100/6-8
300 W Garfield St 50554 — 712-841-5000
David Ross, prin. — Fax 841-5010

Lawton, Woodbury, Pop. 729
Lawton-Bronson Community SD — 600/PK-12
100 Tara Way 51030 — 712-944-5183
Jeff Thelander, supt. — Fax 944-5568
www.lawton-bronson.k12.ia.us
Other Schools – See Bronson

Le Claire, Scott, Pop. 3,123
Pleasant Valley Community SD
Supt. — See Bettendorf
Bridgeview ES — 300/PK-6
316 S 12th St 52753 — 563-289-4781
Tony Hiatt, prin. — Fax 332-0218
Cody ES — 300/K-6
2100 Territorial Rd 52753 — 563-289-5131
Tim Bradley, prin. — Fax 332-0213
Pleasant Valley JHS — 500/7-8
3501 Wisconsin St 52753 — 563-289-4507
Brian Strusz, prin. — Fax 289-4666

Le Mars, Plymouth, Pop. 9,349
Le Mars Community SD — 2,200/K-12
940 Lincoln St SW 51031 — 712-546-4155
Dr. Todd Wendt, supt. — Fax 546-4157
www.lemars.k12.ia.us
Clark ES — 200/K-5
940 Lincoln St SW 51031 — 712-546-8121
Dave Horken, prin. — Fax 546-8122
Franklin ES — 200/K-5
940 Lincoln St SW 51031 — 712-546-4185
Dave Horken, prin. — Fax 546-4186
Kluckhohn ES — 400/K-5
940 Lincoln St SW 51031 — 712-546-7064
Scott Parry, prin. — Fax 546-7069
Le Mars MS — 500/6-8
940 Lincoln St SW 51031 — 712-546-7022
Steve Webner, prin. — Fax 546-7024
Other Schools – See Merrill

Gehlen S — 200/K-6
709 Plymouth St NE 51031 — 712-546-4181
Lorie Nussbaum, prin. — Fax 546-9384

Lenox, Taylor, Pop. 1,310
Lenox Community SD — 400/K-12
600 S Locust St 50851 — 641-333-2244
David Henrichs, supt. — Fax 333-2247
www.lenox.k12.ia.us
Lenox ES — 200/K-6
600 S Locust St 50851 — 641-333-2244
Derek Morris, prin. — Fax 333-2247

Leon, Decatur, Pop. 1,924
Central Decatur Community SD — 700/PK-12
1201 NE Poplar St 50144 — 641-446-4818
Dr. Tucker Lillis, supt. — Fax 446-7990
www.central-decatur.k12.ia.us/
North ES — 100/4-5
1203 NE Poplar St 50144 — 641-446-4452
Chris Coffelt, prin. — Fax 446-8729
South ES — 200/PK-3
201 SE 6th St 50144 — 641-446-6521
Chris Coffelt, prin. — Fax 446-3856

Letts, Louisa, Pop. 390
Louisa-Muscatine Community SD — 900/PK-12
14478 170th St 52754 — 319-726-3541
Scott Grimes, supt. — Fax 726-3334
www.louisa-muscatine.k12.ia.us
Louisa-Muscatine ES — 500/PK-6
14506 170th St 52754 — 319-726-3634
Doug McBride, prin. — Fax 726-4600
Louisa-Muscatine JHS — 200/7-8
14354 170th St 52754 — 319-726-3421
Stacy Beatty, prin. — Fax 726-3649

Lewis, Cass, Pop. 441
Griswold Community SD
Supt. — See Griswold
Lewis ES — 100/PK-5
PO Box E 51544 — 712-769-2221
Betty Johnston, prin. — Fax 769-2211

Liberty Center, Warren
Southeast Warren Community SD — 600/PK-12
PO Box 19 50145 — 641-466-3510
Delane Galvin, supt. — Fax 466-3525
www.se-warren.k12.ia.us
Other Schools – See Lacona, Milo

Libertyville, Jefferson, Pop. 323
Fairfield Community SD
Supt. — See Fairfield
Libertyville ES — 100/K-5
PO Box 160 52567 — 641-693-3971
Susan McCracken, prin. — Fax 693-8300

Lime Springs, Howard, Pop. 482
Howard-Winneshiek Community SD
Supt. — See Cresco
Lime Springs ES — 100/K-6
PO Box 56 52155 — 563-566-2221
Robert Hughes, prin. — Fax 547-5973

Lineville, Wayne, Pop. 238
Lineville-Clio Community SD — 100/PK-12
PO Box 98 50147 — 641-876-5345
Robert Busch, supt. — Fax 876-2805
www.lineville-clio.k12.ia.us
Lineville ES — 50/PK-6
PO Box 98 50147 — 641-876-5345
Mike Snyder, prin. — Fax 876-2805

Lisbon, Linn, Pop. 1,944
Lisbon Community SD — 600/PK-12
PO Box 839 52253 — 319-455-2075
Vincent Smith, supt. — Fax 455-2733
www.lisbon.k12.ia.us
Lisbon ES — 300/PK-5
PO Box 839 52253 — 319-455-2659
Roger Teeling, prin. — Fax 455-3303
Lisbon MS — 100/6-8
PO Box 839 52253 — 319-455-2659
Roger Teeling, prin. — Fax 455-3303

Little Rock, Lyon, Pop. 482
George-Little Rock Community SD
Supt. — See George
George-Little Rock MS — 100/6-8
PO Box 247 51243 — 712-479-2771
Janel Guse, prin. — Fax 479-2770
Little Rock ES — 100/PK-5
PO Box 247 51243 — 712-479-2771
Janel Guse, prin. — Fax 479-2770

Logan, Harrison, Pop. 1,319
Logan-Magnolia Community SD — 700/PK-12
1200 N 2nd Ave 51546 — 712-644-2250
James Hammrich, supt. — Fax 644-2934
www.logan.k12.ia.us
Logan-Magnolia ES — 400/PK-6
1200 N 2nd Ave 51546 — 712-644-2168
James Makey, prin. — Fax 644-2501

Lohrville, Calhoun, Pop. 373
Southern Cal Community SD
Supt. — See Lake City
Lohrville ES — 100/PK-6
305 3rd St 51453 — 712-465-3425
Barb Mortensen, prin. — Fax 465-3605

Lone Tree, Johnson, Pop. 1,081
Lone Tree Community SD — 500/PK-12
PO Box 520 52755 — 319-629-4212
Michael Reeves, supt. — Fax 629-4324
www.lone-tree.k12.ia.us
Lone Tree ES — 300/PK-5
PO Box 520 52755 — 319-629-4213
Amber Jacque, prin. — Fax 629-4324

Long Grove, Scott, Pop. 737
North Scott Community SD
Supt. — See Eldridge
Shepard ES — 300/K-6
220 W Grove St 52756 — 563-285-8041
Sherri Marceau, prin. — Fax 285-6172

Lost Nation, Clinton, Pop. 475
Midland Community SD
Supt. — See Wyoming
Midland ES — 50/2-5
PO Box 217 52254 — 563-678-2142
Marilyn Jackson, prin. — Fax 678-2135

Lowden, Cedar, Pop. 818
North Cedar Community SD
Supt. — See Stanwood
North Cedar Lowden ES — 200/PK-4
PO Box 250 52255 — 563-941-5383
Jerry Johnson, prin. — Fax 941-7533

Lu Verne, Kossuth, Pop. 289
Lu Verne Community SD — 100/5-8
PO Box 69 50560 — 515-882-3357
William Stone, supt. — Fax 882-3417
www.luverne.k12.ia.us/
Lu Verne S — 100/5-8
PO Box 69 50560 — 515-882-3357
Willie Stone, prin. — Fax 882-3417

Luxemburg, Dubuque, Pop. 241

LaSalle S - Holy Trinity Center — 100/PK-3
PO Box 13 52056 — 563-853-2325
John Pesetski, prin. — Fax 870-4101

Lytton, Calhoun, Pop. 273
Rockwell City-Lytton Community SD
Supt. — See Rockwell City
Rockwell City-Lytton MS — 100/5-8
PO Box 49 50561 — 712-466-2224
Marc DeMoss, prin. — Fax 466-2658

Mc Callsburg, Story, Pop. 269
Colo-Nesco Comm SD — 500/PK-12
400 Latrobe Ave 50154 — 515-434-2302
Gary Pillman, supt. — Fax 434-2104
www.colo-nesco.k12.ia.us
Mc Callsburg ES — 100/PK-4
400 Latrobe Ave 50154 — 515-434-2302
Gary Pillman, prin. — Fax 434-2104
Other Schools – See Colo, Zearing

Mc Gregor, Clayton, Pop. 789
MFL MarMac Community SD
Supt. — See Monona
MFL MarMac MS — 200/4-8
PO Box D 52157 — 563-873-3463
Josh Mallicoat, prin. — Fax 873-2371

Madrid, Boone, Pop. 2,420
Madrid Community SD — 600/K-12
201 N Main St 50156 — 515-795-3241
Brian Horn, supt. — Fax 795-2121
madrid.k12.ia.us
Madrid ES — 400/K-6
213 W 1st St 50156 — 515-795-2359
Gayle Strickland, prin. — Fax 795-2121
Madrid JHS — 100/7-8
599 N Kennedy Ave 50156 — 515-795-3240
Kevin Williams, prin. — Fax 795-4408

Mallard, Palo Alto, Pop. 284
West Bend - Mallard Community SD
Supt. — See West Bend
Mallard S — 100/PK-12
PO Box 326 50562 — 712-425-3452
Amanda Schmidt, prin. — Fax 425-3413
West Bend - Mallard MS — 100/6-8
PO Box 326 50562 — 712-425-3452
Amanda Schmidt, prin. — Fax 425-3413

Malvern, Mills, Pop. 1,342
Malvern Community SD — 200/K-12
422 Main St 51551 — 712-624-8700
Curtis Barclay, supt. — Fax 624-8279
www.malvernschools.org/
Chantry ES — 100/K-4
409 E 9th St 51551 — 712-624-8681
Lynn Kilpatrick, prin. — Fax 624-8440

Manchester, Delaware, Pop. 5,074
West Delaware County Community SD — 1,600/PK-12
601 New St 52057 — 563-927-3515
Robert Cue, supt. — Fax 927-2785
www.w-delaware.k12.ia.us
Kindergarten — 100/PK-K
300 E Howard St 52057 — 563-927-3515
Carol Tjaden, prin. — Fax 927-9235
Lambert ES — 500/K-4
1001 Doctor St 52057 — 563-927-3515
Carol Tjaden, prin. — Fax 927-9235
West Delaware MS — 500/5-8
1101 Doctor St 52057 — 563-927-3515
Randy Stanek, prin. — Fax 927-9115

St. Mary S — 200/K-6
132 W Butler St 52057 — 563-927-3689
Justin Nosbisch, prin. — Fax 927-9949

Manilla, Crawford, Pop. 833
IKM Community SD — 200/PK-8
PO Box 580 51454 — 712-654-2852
Jeff Kruse, supt. — Fax 654-9280
www.ikm-manning.k12.ia.us/
IKM-Manning MS — 100/5-8
PO Box 580 51454 — 712-654-9385
Denise Philipp, prin. — Fax 654-9282
Other Schools – See Irwin

Manly, Worth, Pop. 1,336
North Central Community SD — 400/K-12
PO Box 190 50456 — 641-454-2211
Bruce Burton, supt. — Fax 454-2212
www.northcentral.k12.ia.us
North Central ES — 200/K-4
PO Box 130 50456 — 641-454-3283
Casey Christenson, prin. — Fax 454-3289

Manning, Carroll, Pop. 1,447
Manning Community SD — 300/PK-12
209 10th St 51455 — 712-655-3771
Roger Schmiedeskamp, supt. — Fax 655-3311
www.ikm-manning.k12.ia.us/
Manning ES — 200/PK-4
209 10th St 51455 — 712-655-3761
Sharon Whitson, prin. — Fax 655-3311

Manson, Calhoun, Pop. 1,760
Manson NW Webster Community SD — 400/PK-12
1227 16th St 50563 — 712-469-2202
Mark Egli, supt. — Fax 469-2298
www.manson-nw.k12.ia.us
Other Schools – See Barnum

Mapleton, Monona, Pop. 1,230
Maple Valley Community SD — 500/PK-12
501 S 7th St 51034 — 712-881-1315
Steve Oberg, supt. — Fax 881-1316
www.maple-valley.k12.ia.us
Mapleton ES — 200/PK-5
501 S 7th St 51034 — 712-881-1319
Mahlon Carothers, prin. — Fax 881-1320

Maquoketa, Jackson, Pop. 6,054
Maquoketa Community SD — 1,600/PK-12
612 S Vermont St 52060 — 563-652-4984
Kim Huckstadt, supt. — Fax 652-6958
www.maquoketa.k12.ia.us
Briggs ES — 300/3-5
400 W Quarry St 52060 — 563-652-4996
Patrick Bollman, prin. — Fax 652-0231
Cardinal ES — 300/PK-2
1003 Pershing Rd 52060 — 563-652-5157
Joan Bollman, prin. — Fax 652-6507
Maquoketa MS — 400/6-8
200 E Locust St 52060 — 563-652-4956
Autumn Pino, prin. — Fax 652-6885

Sacred Heart S — 100/K-6
806 Eddy St 52060 — 563-652-3743
Sr. Shirley Steines, prin. — Fax 652-2698

Marcus, Cherokee, Pop. 1,064
Marcus-Meriden-Cleghorn Community SD — 400/PK-12
PO Box 667 51035 — 712-376-4171
Jan Brandhorst, supt. — Fax 376-4302
www.marcus-mer-cleg.k12.ia.us
Marcus-Meriden-Cleghorn ES — 100/PK-3
PO Box 667 51035 — 712-376-2615
Kathy Tritz-Rhodes, prin. — Fax 376-2819
Other Schools – See Cleghorn

Marengo, Iowa, Pop. 2,539
Iowa Valley Community SD — 600/PK-12
359 E Hilton St 52301 — 319-642-7714
Alan Jensen, supt. — Fax 642-3023
www.iowa-valley.k12.ia.us
Iowa Valley ES — 300/PK-6
151 E May St 52301 — 319-642-3812
Cynthia Miller, prin. — Fax 642-3023

Marion, Linn, Pop. 30,233
Linn-Mar Community SD — 5,300/PK-12
3333 10th St 52302 — 319-447-3000
Dr. Kathleen Mulholland, supt. — Fax 377-9252
www.linnmar.k12.ia.us/
Echo Hill ES — K-5
400 Echo Hill Rd 52302 — 319-730-3560
Dan Ludwig, prin. — Fax 447-0481
Excelsior MS — 800/6-8
3555 10th St 52302 — 319-447-3130
John Christian, prin. — Fax 373-4930
Indian Creek ES — 500/K-5
2900 Indian Creek Rd 52302 — 319-447-3270
Tina Monroe, prin. — Fax 373-9233
Linn Grove ES — PK-5
2301 50th St 52302 — 319-730-3500
Shannon Bisgard, prin. — Fax 447-0950
Novak ES — 400/K-5
2999 10th St 52302 — 319-447-3300
Joseph North, prin. — Fax 373-9144
Oak Ridge MS — 400/6-8
4901 Alburnett Rd 52302 — 319-447-3410
Erica Rausch, prin. — Fax 373-3222
Wilkins ES — 500/K-5
2127 27th St 52302 — 319-447-3380
Marilee McConnell, prin. — Fax 373-9195
Other Schools – See Cedar Rapids, Robins

Marion ISD — 2,000/PK-12
PO Box 606 52302 — 319-377-4691
Sarah Pinion, supt. — Fax 377-4692
www.marion.k12.ia.us/
Bright Beginnings Preschool — PK-PK
1080 E Post Rd Ste 2 52302 — 319-389-7729
Jennifer Ringwald, dir. — Fax 389-7730
Emerson ES — 200/PK-3
1400 10th Ave 52302 — 319-377-0183
Cheryl Toppin, prin. — Fax 377-8404
Marion IS — 300/4-5
2301 3rd Ave 52302 — 319-373-4766
Mike Murphy, prin. — Fax 373-4767
Starry ES — 400/K-3
700 15th St 52302 — 319-377-4698
Karen Asa, prin. — Fax 377-9492
Vernon MS — 400/6-8
1301 5th Ave 52302 — 319-377-9401
Amy Johnson, prin. — Fax 377-7670

St. Joseph S — 300/PK-8
1430 14th St 52302 — 319-377-6348
Tony Voss, prin. — Fax 377-9358

Marshalltown, Marshall, Pop. 25,977
Marshalltown Community SD — 4,300/PK-12
317 Columbus Dr 50158 — 641-754-1000
Marvin Wade, supt. — Fax 754-1003
www.marshalltown.k12.ia.us
Anson ES — 300/K-4
1016 S 3rd Ave 50158 — 641-754-1020
Beatrice Niblock, prin. — Fax 754-1027
Fisher ES — 300/K-4
2001 S 4th St 50158 — 641-754-1030
Vicki Vopava, prin. — Fax 754-1037
Franklin ES — 400/PK-4
1315 W Main St 50158 — 641-754-1041
Tim Holmgren, prin. — Fax 754-1043
Hoglan ES — 300/PK-4
2306 S 3rd Ave 50158 — 641-754-1060
Amy Williams, prin. — Fax 754-1062
Lenihan IS — 5-6
212 W Ingledue St 50158 — 641-754-1160
Ralph Bryant, prin. — Fax 754-1190
Miller MS — 800/7-8
125 S 11th St 50158 — 641-754-1110
Burton Clement, prin. — Fax 754-1115
Rogers ES — 200/K-4
406 Summit St 50158 — 641-754-1070
Michael Jurgensen, prin. — Fax 754-1072
Woodbury ES — 300/K-4
8 N 7th Ave 50158 — 641-754-1080
Jack Shepherd, prin. — Fax 754-1083

Marshalltown Catholic S — 300/PK-6
10 W Linn St 50158 — 641-753-7977
James Wessling, prin. — Fax 753-0337
Marshalltown Christian S — 50/K-5
PO Box 1514 50158 — 641-753-8824
Alice Hagar, dir.

Martensdale, Warren, Pop. 459
Martensdale-St. Mary's Community SD — 500/PK-12
PO Box 350 50160 — 641-764-2466
Jean Peterson, supt. — Fax 764-2100
www.m-stmarys.k12.ia.us/
Martensdale-St. Marys ES — 300/PK-6
PO Box 350 50160 — 641-764-2621
Tom Wood, prin. — Fax 764-2100

Mason City, Cerro Gordo, Pop. 27,909
Mason City Community SD — 3,800/PK-12
1515 S Pennsylvania Ave 50401 — 641-421-4400
Anita Micich, supt. — Fax 421-4448
www.masoncityschools.org
Adams MS — 500/6-8
29 S Illinois Ave 50401 — 641-421-4420
T.J. Jumper, prin. — Fax 421-4476
Harding ES — 400/K-5
1239 N Rhode Island Ave 50401 — 641-421-4406
Michael Penca, prin. — Fax 421-3365
Hoover ES — 400/K-5
1123 8th St NW 50401 — 641-421-4408
Allison Pattee, prin. — Fax 421-4530
Jefferson ES — 400/K-5
1421 4th St SE 50401 — 641-421-4411
Dudley Humphrey, prin. — Fax 421-3367
Madison ECC — 50/PK-PK
2620 S Jefferson Ave 50401 — 641-421-4413
Gary VanHemert, prin. — Fax 421-3361
Roosevelt ES — 300/K-5
313 15th St SE 50401 — 641-421-4415
Allison Stevenson, prin. — Fax 423-5731
Roosevelt MS — 400/6-8
1625 S Pennsylvania Ave 50401 — 641-421-4423
Jason Wedgbury, prin. — Fax 423-3387
Washington ECC — 50/PK-PK
700 N Washington Ave 50401 — 641-421-4418
Gary VanHemert, prin. — Fax 421-4534

Newman Catholic S — 400/K-8
2000 S McKinley Ave 50401 — 641-423-3101
Jan Avery, prin. — Fax 422-1181
North Iowa Christian S — 50/K-12
811 N Kentucky Ave 50401 — 641-423-6440
Janna Voss, admin. — Fax 423-6440

Massena, Cass, Pop. 407
C and M Community SD — 200/K-8
PO Box 7 50853 — 712-779-2211
Steve Pelzer, supt. — Fax 779-3365
www.camcougars.org/
CAM MS — 100/6-8
PO Box 7 50853 — 712-779-2212
Steve Pelzer, prin. — Fax 779-3365
C and M ES — 100/K-5
PO Box 7 50853 — 712-779-2211
Steve Pelzer, prin. — Fax 779-3365

Maxwell, Story, Pop. 764
Collins-Maxwell Community SD — 500/K-12
400 Metcalf St 50161 — 515-387-1115
Doug Miller, supt. — Fax 387-8842
www.collins-maxwell.k12.ia.us
Other Schools – See Collins

Maynard, Fayette, Pop. 464
West Central Community SD — 300/K-12
PO Box 54 50655 — 563-637-2283
John Johnson, supt. — Fax 637-2294
www.w-central.k12.ia.us/
West Central ES — 200/K-6
PO Box 54 50655 — 563-637-2283
Cathy Timmerman, prin. — Fax 637-2294

Mechanicsville, Cedar, Pop. 1,177
North Cedar Community SD
Supt. — See Stanwood
North Cedar Mechanicsville ES — 200/PK-4
609 125th St 52306 — 563-432-6933
Jerry Johnson, prin. — Fax 432-6666

Mediapolis, Des Moines, Pop. 1,587
Mediapolis Community SD — 900/K-12
PO Box 358 52637 — 319-394-3237
Fred Whipple, supt. — Fax 394-3021
www.meposchools.org/
Mediapolis ES — 400/K-5
725 N Northfield St 52637 — 319-394-3101
Tanya Langholdt, prin. — Fax 394-9753

Mediapolis MS 200/6-8
725 N Northfield St 52637 319-394-3101
Dennis Heiman, prin. Fax 394-9198

Melcher, Marion, Pop. 1,310
Melcher-Dallas Community SD 400/PK-12
PO Box 489 50163 641-947-2321
Steve Mitchell, supt. Fax 947-2203
www.melcher-dallas.k12.ia.us
Melcher-Dallas JHS 100/7-8
PO Box 158 50163 641-947-3731
Greg Horstmann, prin. Fax 947-2203
Other Schools – See Dallas

Menlo, Guthrie, Pop. 373
West Central Valley Community SD
Supt. — See Stuart
Menlo ES 300/PK-5
410 Sheridan St 50164 641-524-2661
Sharon Sloss, prin. Fax 524-4951

Merrill, Plymouth, Pop. 772
Le Mars Community SD
Supt. — See Le Mars
Kissinger ES 100/K-5
608 Main St 51038 712-938-2562
Scott Parry, prin. Fax 938-2563

Middle Amana, Iowa, Pop. 350
Clear Creek Amana Community SD
Supt. — See Oxford
Amana ES 100/K-5
PO Box 70 52307 319-622-3255
Brad Fox, prin. Fax 622-3108
Clear Creek Amana MS 300/6-8
PO Box 70 52307 319-622-3255
Brad Fox, prin. Fax 622-3108

Miles, Jackson, Pop. 457
East Central Community SD 300/PK-12
PO Box 367 52064 563-682-7510
James House, supt. Fax 682-7194
www.east-central.k12.ia.us
Miles ES 50/PK-2
PO Box 367 52064 563-682-7131
Neil Gray, prin. Fax 682-7194
Other Schools – See Sabula

Milford, Dickinson, Pop. 2,441
Okoboji Community SD 900/PK-12
PO Box 147 51351 712-338-4757
Robert Miller, supt. Fax 338-4758
www.okoboji.k12.ia.us
Okoboji ES 400/PK-4
PO Box 147 51351 712-338-2458
Rob Olsen, prin. Fax 338-4758
Other Schools – See Arnolds Park

Milo, Warren, Pop. 828
Southeast Warren Community SD
Supt. — See Liberty Center
Milo Primary Center 200/PK-3
PO Box 135 50166 641-942-6216
Charlotte Weaklend, prin. Fax 942-6308

Minburn, Dallas, Pop. 434
Adel-De Soto-Minburn Community SD
Supt. — See Adel
Minburn ES 100/K-5
PO Box 186 50167 515-677-2222
Jim DePue, prin. Fax 677-2704

Mingo, Jasper, Pop. 275
Colfax-Mingo Community SD
Supt. — See Colfax
Colfax-Mingo MS 200/6-8
307 W Mohawk Dr 50168 641-363-4282
Rebecca Maher, prin. Fax 363-3256

Missouri Valley, Harrison, Pop. 2,932
Missouri Valley Community SD 900/PK-12
109 E Michigan St 51555 712-642-2706
Dr. Tom Micek, supt. Fax 642-2456
www.movalley.k12.ia.us
Missouri Valley ES 400/PK-5
602 N 9th St 51555 712-642-2279
Bill Huggett, prin. Fax 642-2656
Missouri Valley MS 200/6-8
607 Lincoln Hwy 51555 712-642-2707
Justin Gross, prin. Fax 642-3738

Mitchellville, Polk, Pop. 2,092
Southeast Polk Community SD
Supt. — See Pleasant Hill
Mitchellville ES 200/K-6
308 Elm Ave NW 50169 515-967-4274
Joseph Nelson, prin. Fax 967-4934

Mondamin, Harrison, Pop. 419
West Harrison Community SD 500/PK-12
410 Pine St 51557 712-646-2231
Richard Gerking, supt. Fax 646-2891
www.w-harrison.k12.ia.us/
West Harrison ES 200/PK-5
410 Pine St 51557 712-646-2016
Michael Bunde, prin. Fax 646-2891

Monona, Clayton, Pop. 1,445
MFL MarMac Community SD 800/PK-12
PO Box D 52159 563-539-4795
Dale Crozier, supt. Fax 539-4913
www.mflmarmac.k12.ia.us
MFL MarMac ES 300/PK-3
PO Box D 52159 563-539-2032
Kathy Koether, prin. Fax 539-4913
Other Schools – See Mc Gregor

Monroe, Jasper, Pop. 1,838
PCM Community SD
Supt. — See Prairie City
Monroe ES 200/PK-5
PO Box 610 50170 641-259-2314
Jane Babcock, prin. Fax 259-2944

Montezuma, Poweshiek, Pop. 1,419
Montezuma Community SD 500/K-12
PO Box 580 50171 641-623-5185
Dave Versteeg, supt. Fax 623-5733
www.montezuma.k12.ia.us
Montezuma ES 300/K-6
PO Box 580 50171 641-623-5129
Darin Jones, prin. Fax 623-5733
Montezuma JHS 100/7-8
PO Box 580 50171 641-623-5121
Dave Schroeder, prin. Fax 623-5733

Monticello, Jones, Pop. 3,701
Monticello Community SD 1,100/PK-12
711 N Maple St 52310 319-465-5963
Chris Anderson, supt. Fax 465-4092
www.monticello.k12.ia.us/
Carpenter ES, 615 N Gill St 52310 200/2-4
Dennis Folken, prin. 319-465-3551
Monticello MS 300/5-8
217 S Maple St 52310 319-465-3575
William Gilkerson, prin. Fax 465-6959
Shannon ES 100/PK-1
321 W South St 52310 319-465-5425
Dennis Folken, prin. Fax 465-3370

Sacred Heart S 200/PK-6
234 N Sycamore St 52310 319-465-4605
Carrie Manternach, prin. Fax 465-6183

Moravia, Appanoose, Pop. 731
Moravia Community SD 300/PK-12
505 N Trussell Ave 52571 641-724-3240
Brad Breon, supt. Fax 724-0629
www.moravia.k12.ia.us
Moravia ES 200/PK-6
507 N Trussell Ave 52571 641-724-3311
Brad Breon, prin. Fax 724-3591

Morning Sun, Louisa, Pop. 857
Morning Sun Community SD 200/PK-6
PO Box 129 52640 319-868-7701
Douglas Graber, supt. Fax 868-7703
Morning Sun ES 100/PK-6
PO Box 129 52640 319-868-7701
Douglas Graber, prin. Fax 868-7703

Moulton, Appanoose, Pop. 683
Moulton-Udell Community SD 300/PK-12
305 E 8th St 52572 641-642-3665
Richard Turner, supt. Fax 642-3845
www.moulton-udell.k12.ia.us
Moulton ES 100/PK-6
305 E 8th St 52572 641-642-3665
Margie Tippett, prin. Fax 642-8351

Mount Ayr, Ringgold, Pop. 1,764
Mount Ayr Community SD 700/PK-12
1001 E Columbus St 50854 641-464-0500
Russ Reiter, supt. Fax 464-2325
www.mtayr.k12.ia.us
Mount Ayr ES 300/PK-6
607 E Jefferson St 50854 641-464-0537
Lynne Wallace, prin. Fax 464-2325

Mount Pleasant, Henry, Pop. 8,767
Mount Pleasant Community SD 2,200/PK-12
400 E Madison St 52641 319-385-7750
John Roederer, supt. Fax 385-7788
www.mt-pleasant.k12.ia.us
Harlan ES 200/K-5
400 E Madison St 52641 319-385-7762
Tom Perry, prin. Fax 385-7759
Lincoln ES 200/K-5
501 S Corkhill St 52641 319-385-7765
Tom Perry, prin. Fax 385-7331
Mount Pleasant MS 500/6-8
400 E Madison St 52641 319-385-7730
Darren Hanna, prin. Fax 385-7735
Van Allen ES 400/PK-5
801 E Henry St 52641 319-385-7771
Linda Wilkerson, prin. Fax 385-1167
Other Schools – See Salem

Mount Pleasant Christian S 100/PK-12
1505 E Washington St 52641 319-385-8613
Gary Shankles, admin. Fax 385-8415

Mount Vernon, Linn, Pop. 4,051
Mount Vernon Community SD 1,100/PK-12
525 Palisades Rd SW 52314 319-895-8845
Jeff Schwiebert, supt. Fax 895-8875
www.mountvernon.k12.ia.us/
Mount Vernon MS 300/5-8
525 Palisades Rd SW 52314 319-895-6254
John Krumbholz, prin. Fax 895-8134
Washington ES 500/PK-4
615 5th Ave SW 52314 319-895-6251
Gary Nelson, prin. Fax 895-0348

Moville, Woodbury, Pop. 1,480
Woodbury Central Community SD 600/PK-12
PO Box 586 51039 712-873-3128
Thomas Cooper, supt. Fax 873-3162
www.woodbury-central.k12.ia.us
Moville ES 300/PK-5
PO Box 586 51039 712-873-3128
Dyane Mathers, prin. Fax 873-3162
Woodbury Central MS 100/6-8
PO Box 586 51039 712-873-3128
Steve Shanks, prin. Fax 873-3162

Murray, Clarke, Pop. 786
Murray Community SD 300/PK-12
PO Box 187 50174 641-447-2517
Dr. Dennis Bishop, supt. Fax 447-2313
www.murray.k12.ia.us/
Murray ES 200/PK-6
PO Box 187 50174 641-447-2517
Danny Jensen, prin. Fax 447-2313

Muscatine, Muscatine, Pop. 22,757
Muscatine Community SD 5,300/PK-12
2900 Mulberry Ave 52761 563-263-7223
Thomas Williams, supt. Fax 263-7729
www.muscatine.k12.ia.us
Central MS 600/6-8
901 Cedar St 52761 563-263-7784
Terry Hogenson, prin. Fax 263-0145
Colorado ES 200/K-5
149 Colorado St 52761 563-263-4998
Joe Prosek, prin. Fax 263-0273
Franklin ES 200/2-5
210 Taylor St 52761 563-263-5040
Victoria Connelly, prin. Fax 262-3923
Garfield ES 100/PK-1
1409 Wisconsin St 52761 563-263-6079
Victoria Connelly, prin. Fax 263-0664
Grant ES 300/PK-5
705 Barry Ave 52761 563-263-7005
Becky Wichers, prin. Fax 263-1030
Jefferson ES 300/PK-5
1000 Mulberry Ave 52761 563-263-8800
Shane Williams, prin. Fax 264-0757
Madison ES 300/K-5
1820 1st Ave 52761 563-263-6062
Dana Ford, prin. Fax 263-0212
McKinley ES 300/PK-5
621 Kindler Ave 52761 563-263-9049
Perry Rodocker, prin. Fax 264-1271
Mulberry ES 200/PK-5
3211 Mulberry Ave 52761 563-263-8143
Ann Goodman, prin. Fax 263-8487
Washington ES 400/K-5
610 Maiden Ln 52761 563-263-9135
Joelle McConnaha, prin. Fax 263-9927
West MS 600/6-8
600 Kindler Ave 52761 563-263-0411
John Lawrence, prin. Fax 263-6645

Bishop Hayes Catholic S 200/PK-5
2407 Cedar St 52761 563-263-3264
Ann Gomez, prin. Fax 263-6700

Mystic, Appanoose, Pop. 618
Centerville Community SD
Supt. — See Centerville
Mystic ES 50/K-3
500 Clarkdale Rd 52574 641-856-0729
Scott Clark, prin. Fax 647-2726

Nashua, Chickasaw, Pop. 1,574
Nashua-Plainfield Community SD 700/PK-12
PO Box 569 50658 641-435-4835
Randall Strabala, supt. Fax 435-4835
www.nashua-plainfield.k12.ia.us
Nashua-Plainfield ES 200/PK-4
PO Box 569 50658 641-435-4114
Edwin Anderson, prin. Fax 435-4886
Other Schools – See Plainfield

Neola, Pottawattamie, Pop. 840
Tri-Center Community SD 800/PK-12
33980 310th St 51559 712-485-2257
Brett Nanninga, supt. Fax 485-2411
www.tri-center.k12.ia.us
Tri-Center ES 400/PK-5
33980 310th St 51559 712-485-2271
Diane White, prin. Fax 485-2027
Tri-Center MS 200/6-8
33980 310th St 51559 712-485-2211
Brian Wedemeyer, prin. Fax 485-2402

Nevada, Story, Pop. 6,129
Nevada Community SD 1,500/PK-12
1035 15th St 50201 515-382-2783
James Walker, supt. Fax 382-2836
www.nevada.k12.ia.us
Central ES 600/PK-4
925 H Ave 50201 515-382-2383
Kathy Goecke, prin. Fax 382-5345
Nevada MS 400/5-8
1035 15th St 50201 515-382-2751
Chris Schmidt, prin. Fax 382-2836

Nevada SDA S 50/K-8
224 6th St 50201 515-382-4932

New Albin, Allamakee, Pop. 529
Eastern Allamakee Community SD
Supt. — See Lansing
New Albin ES 100/K-5
PO Box 28 52160 563-544-4246
Cynthia Lapel, prin. Fax 544-4247

Newell, Buena Vista, Pop. 869
Newell-Fonda Community SD 400/PK-12
PO Box 297 50568 712-272-3324
Jeff Dicks, supt. Fax 272-4276
www.newell-fonda.k12.ia.us
Newell-Fonda Lower ES 100/PK-3
PO Box 297 50568 712-272-3324
Randall Nielsen, prin. Fax 272-4276
Other Schools – See Fonda

Newhall, Benton, Pop. 989

Central Lutheran S 200/PK-8
PO Box 190 52315 319-223-5271
Janet Doellinger, prin. Fax 223-5257

New Hampton, Chickasaw, Pop. 3,528
New Hampton Community SD 1,200/PK-12
710 W Main St 50659 641-394-2134
Stephen Nicholson, supt. Fax 394-2921
www.new-hampton.k12.ia.us
New Hampton ES 400/PK-4
206 W Main St 50659 641-394-5858
Barb Blake, prin. Fax 394-2662
New Hampton MS 300/5-8
206 W Main St 50659 641-394-2259
Donita Landers, prin. Fax 394-2662

St. Joseph Community S 200/PK-8
216 N Broadway Ave 50659 641-394-2865
Beth Wright, prin. Fax 394-5154

New Hartford, Butler, Pop. 640
Dike-New Hartford Community SD
Supt. — See Dike
Dike-New Hartford JHS 100/7-8
508 Beaver St 50660 319-983-2206
Jerold Martinek, prin. Fax 983-2207
New Hartford ES 200/PK-6
508 Beaver St 50660 319-983-2206
Jerold Martinek, prin. Fax 983-2207

New London, Henry, Pop. 1,871
New London Community SD 500/K-12
PO Box 97 52645 319-367-0512
Charles Reighard, supt. Fax 367-0513
www.new-london.k12.ia.us
Clark ES 200/K-5
PO Box 97 52645 319-367-0507
Todd Palmatier, prin. Fax 367-0506

New Sharon, Mahaska, Pop. 1,307
North Mahaska Community SD 600/PK-12
PO Box 89 50207 641-637-2295
Randy Moffit, supt. Fax 637-4559
www.n-mahaska.k12.ia.us
North Mahaska ES 300/PK-6
PO Box 89 50207 641-637-4041
Angela Livezey, prin. Fax 637-4042

Newton, Jasper, Pop. 15,607
Newton Community SD 3,200/PK-12
807 S 6th Ave W 50208 641-792-5809
Steven McDermott, supt. Fax 792-9159
www.newton.k12.ia.us
Aurora Heights ES 300/K-6
310 E 23rd St S 50208 641-792-7324
Carol Farver, prin. Fax 792-7701
Berg ES 500/K-6
1900 N 5th Ave E 50208 641-792-7742
Todd Schuster, prin. Fax 792-7779
Berg MS 500/7-8
1900 N 5th Ave E 50208 641-792-7741
Dave Gallaher, prin. Fax 792-7779
Hough ES 300/PK-6
700 N 4th Ave E 50208 641-792-3982
Jolene Comer, prin. Fax 792-1504
Jefferson ES 300/K-6
112 Thomas Jefferson Dr 50208 641-792-2498
Nancy Van Wyk, prin. Fax 792-2716
Wilson ES 300/K-6
801 S 8th Ave W 50208 641-792-7311
Lisa Sharp, prin. Fax 792-0186

Newton Christian S 100/K-8
1710 N 11th Ave E 50208 641-792-1924
Ginny Tull, admin. Fax 792-1924

New Vienna, Dubuque, Pop. 401

Hennessy Catholic S 50/K-3
PO Box 170 52065 563-921-2635
Vicki Palmer, prin. Fax 921-3003

Nora Springs, Floyd, Pop. 1,466
Nora Springs-Rock Falls Community SD 300/PK-8
PO Box 367 50458 641-749-5306
Eldon Pyle, supt. Fax 749-5334
www.ns-rf.com
Nora Springs ES 100/PK-4
PO Box 367 50458 641-749-5302
Ronald Billings, prin. Fax 749-5898
Nora Springs-Rock Falls MS 100/5-8
PO Box 367 50458 641-749-5301
Lynn Baldus, prin. Fax 749-5898

North English, Iowa, Pop. 1,004
English Valleys Community SD 500/PK-12
PO Box 490 52316 319-664-3634
Alan Jensen, supt. Fax 664-3636
www.english-valleys.k12.ia.us
English Valleys ES 200/PK-6
PO Box 490 52316 319-664-3638
Amy Andreassen, prin. Fax 664-3636

North Liberty, Johnson, Pop. 8,808
Clear Creek Amana Community SD
Supt. — See Oxford
North Bend ES PK-5
2230 Saint Andrews Dr 52317 319-828-4510
Brenda Parker, prin.

Iowa City Community SD
Supt. — See Iowa City
North Central JHS 7-8
180 Forevergreen Rd E 52317 319-688-1210
Jane Fry, prin. Fax 688-1219
Penn ES 400/K-6
230 N Dubuque St 52317 319-688-1150
Julie Robinson, prin. Fax 626-2486
Van Allen ES 500/PK-6
170 Abigail Rd 52317 319-688-1185
Carmen Dixon, prin. Fax 688-1186

Heritage Christian S 100/PK-8
2709 Dubuque St NE 52317 319-626-4777
Michael Annis, admin. Fax 626-4778

Northwood, Worth, Pop. 2,036
Northwood-Kensett Community SD 500/K-12
PO Box 289 50459 641-324-2021
Thomas Nugent, supt. Fax 324-2092
www.nwood-kensett.k12.ia.us
Northwood-Kensett ES 300/K-6
PO Box 289 50459 641-324-1127
Brian Costello, prin. Fax 324-1353

Norwalk, Warren, Pop. 7,877
Norwalk Community SD 2,000/PK-12
906 School Ave 50211 515-981-0676
Dennis Wulf, supt. Fax 981-0559
www.norwalk.k12.ia.us/
Lakewood ES 400/4-5
9210 Happy Hollow Dr 50211 515-285-2948
Jill Anderson, prin. Fax 256-7823
Norwalk MS 400/6-7
200 Cherry Pkwy 50211 515-981-0435
Ken Foster, prin. Fax 981-0771
Oviatt ES 700/PK-3
713 School Ave 50211 515-981-0907
Rodney Martinez, prin. Fax 981-5760

Norway, Benton, Pop. 618
Benton Community SD
Supt. — See Van Horne
Norway ES 300/PK-6
100 School Dr 52318 319-227-7142
Elizabeth Strempke, prin. Fax 227-7969

Oakland, Pottawattamie, Pop. 1,460
Riverside Community SD
Supt. — See Carson
Riverside Community ES 300/PK-4
708 Glass St 51560 712-482-6296
James Sutton Ed.D., prin. Fax 482-6646

Ocheyedan, Osceola, Pop. 512
Sibley-Ocheyedan Community SD
Supt. — See Sibley
Ocheyedan ES 100/4-4
896 Main St 51354 712-758-3202
Cory Jeness, prin. Fax 758-3221

Ocheyedan Christian S 50/K-8
1155 Oak St 51354 712-758-3210
Stan VandenBerg, admin. Fax 758-3210

Odebolt, Sac, Pop. 1,045
OA-BCIG SD 400/PK-12
PO Box 475 51458 712-668-2289
Danielle Trimble, supt. Fax 668-2631
www.odebolt-arthur.net
Odebolt-Arthur S 100/K-8
PO Box 475 51458 712-668-2767
Tony Spradlin, prin. Fax 668-2631

Oelwein, Fayette, Pop. 6,371
Oelwein Community SD 1,400/PK-12
307 8th Ave SE 50662 319-283-3536
Jim Patera, supt. Fax 283-4497
www.oelwein.k12.ia.us
Harlan ES 100/2-2
412 2nd Ave NW 50662 319-283-2726
Dan Ratcliff, prin. Fax 283-4497
Little Husky Learning Center 100/PK-K
317 8th Ave SE Ste D 50662 319-283-2302
Mary Beth Steggall, prin. Fax 283-4497
Oelwein MS 300/6-8
300 12th Ave SE 50662 319-283-3015
John Amick, prin. Fax 283-4497
Parkside ES 100/1-1
301 6th Ave SW 50662 319-283-1245
Mary Beth Steggall, prin. Fax 283-4497
Wings Park ES 300/3-5
111 8th Ave NE 50662 319-283-1982
Dan Ratcliff, prin. Fax 283-5508

Sacred Heart S 100/PK-6
601 1st Ave SW 50662 319-283-1366
Nicholas Trenkamp, prin. Fax 283-5279

Ogden, Boone, Pop. 2,019
Ogden Community SD 800/PK-12
PO Box 250 50212 515-275-2894
Bill Roederer, supt. Fax 275-4537
www.ogdenschools.org/
Howe ES 200/PK-4
PO Box 250 50212 515-275-2795
Rickey Gustafson, prin. Fax 275-4914
Ogden MS 200/5-8
PO Box 250 50212 515-275-2912
Mike Van Sickle, prin. Fax 275-2908

Olin, Jones, Pop. 714
Olin Consolidated SD 200/K-12
212 Trilby St 52320 319-484-2155
Charles Liston, supt. Fax 484-2258
www.olin.k12.ia.us
Olin ES 100/K-6
212 Trilby St 52320 319-484-2170
Megan Brunscheen, prin. Fax 484-2258

Onawa, Monona, Pop. 2,921
West Monona Community SD 700/PK-12
1314 15th St 51040 712-433-2043
James Simmelink, supt. Fax 433-3803
www.west-monona.k12.ia.us/
Central ES, 1100 10th St 51040 200/3-5
Mary Black, prin. 712-433-1056
Lark ES 200/PK-2
611 4th St 51040 712-433-1393
Mary Black, prin. Fax 433-3379
West Monona MS 200/6-8
1314 15th St 51040 712-433-9098
Steve Peiffer, prin. Fax 433-1142

Orange City, Sioux, Pop. 5,775
MOC-Floyd Valley Community SD 1,300/PK-12
PO Box 257 51041 712-737-4873
Gary Richardson, supt. Fax 737-8789
www.moc-fv.k12.ia.us/
Orange City ES 400/PK-5
312 1st St SW 51041 712-737-4606
Mike Landhuis, prin. Fax 737-8006
Other Schools – See Alton, Hospers

Orange City Christian S 300/PK-8
604 3rd St SW 51041 712-737-2274
Arlyn Schaap, prin. Fax 737-8608

Orient, Adair, Pop. 394
Orient-Macksburg Community SD 200/K-12
PO Box 129 50858 641-337-5061
Douglas Latham, supt. Fax 337-5013
www.orient-macks.k12.ia.us
Orient-Macksburg S 200/K-12
PO Box 129 50858 641-337-5061
Teresa Thompson, prin. Fax 337-5591

Osage, Mitchell, Pop. 3,462
Osage Community SD 1,000/PK-12
820 Sawyer Dr 50461 641-732-5381
Stephen Williams, supt. Fax 732-5381
www.osage.k12.ia.us
Lincoln ES 300/PK-3
515 Chase St 50461 641-732-5856
Mark Knudtson, prin. Fax 732-5857
Osage MS 200/6-8
820 Sawyer Dr 50461 641-732-3127
Ross Grafft, prin. Fax 732-5450
Washington ES 100/4-5
314 S 7th St 50461 641-732-5492
Mark Knudtson, prin. Fax 732-1113

Sacred Heart S 100/PK-6
218 S 12th St 50461 641-732-5221
Kim Weigle, prin. Fax 732-5221

Osceola, Clarke, Pop. 4,783
Clarke Community SD 1,300/K-12
PO Box 535 50213 641-342-4969
Ned Cox, supt. Fax 342-6101
www.clarke.k12.ia.us
Clarke Community ES 600/K-6
420 E Jefferson St 50213 641-342-6320
Dan Thomas, prin. Fax 342-4861
Clarke MS 200/7-8
800 N Jackson St 50213 641-342-4221
Jeff Sogard, prin. Fax 342-2213

Oskaloosa, Mahaska, Pop. 11,026
Oskaloosa Community SD 2,300/K-12
PO Box 710 52577 641-673-8345
Dr. Carolyn McGaughey, supt. Fax 673-8370
www.oskaloosa.k12.ia.us
Oskaloosa ES 1,100/K-5
1801 Orchard Ave 52577 641-673-8092
Neal Hadden, prin. Fax 672-3776
Oskaloosa MS 500/6-8
1704 N 3rd St 52577 641-673-8308
Andy Hotek, prin. Fax 673-8308

Oskaloosa Christian S 200/K-8
726 N E St 52577 641-672-2174
Jason Alons, prin. Fax 672-1451

Ossian, Winneshiek, Pop. 836
South Winneshiek Community SD
Supt. — See Calmar
South Winneshiek ES 200/PK-5
PO Box 298 52161 563-532-9365
Barb Schwamman, prin. Fax 532-9855
South Winneshiek MS 100/6-8
PO Box 298 52161 563-532-9365
Barb Schwamman, prin. Fax 532-9855

St. Francis Desales S 100/PK-8
414 E Main St 52161 563-532-9352
Mae Becker, prin. Fax 532-9353

Ottumwa, Wapello, Pop. 24,798
Ottumwa Community SD 4,900/PK-12
422 McCarroll Dr 52501 641-684-6596
Jon Sheldahl, supt. Fax 684-6522
www.ottumwa.k12.ia.us
Agassiz ES 200/K-6
608 E Williams St 52501 641-684-7179
Dana Warnecke, prin. Fax 683-2650
Douma ES 400/K-6
307 W Mary St 52501 641-684-4668
Jeff Hendred, prin. Fax 683-9521
ECC 100/PK-PK
422 Mccarroll Dr 52501 641-682-1151
Deb Cook, prin. Fax 684-6522
Eisenhower ES 200/K-6
2624 Marilyn Rd 52501 641-684-5617
Gary Gullion, prin. Fax 684-4534
Evans JHS 700/7-8
812 Chester Ave 52501 641-684-6511
Dan Maeder, prin. Fax 684-7386
James ES 300/K-6
1001 N Benton St 52501 641-684-5411
Jay Green, prin. Fax 682-6539
Mann ES 300/K-6
1523 N Court St 52501 641-684-4661
Missy Carson-Roark, prin. Fax 684-6419
Pickwick ES 300/PK-6
1306 W Williams St 52501 641-682-4502
Dawn Sievertsen, prin. Fax 682-9251

Wildwood ES 400/K-6
438 McKinley Ave 52501 641-683-1843
Greg Pixley, prin. Fax 683-5632
Wilson ES 400/K-6
1102 E 4th St 52501 641-684-5441
Jody Williams, prin. Fax 684-4934

Seton Catholic S 100/PK-5
117 E 4th St 52501 641-682-8826
Terri Schofield, prin. Fax 682-6202

Oxford, Johnson, Pop. 645
Clear Creek Amana Community SD 1,400/PK-12
PO Box 487 52322 319-828-4510
Paula Vincent, supt. Fax 828-4743
www.cca.k12.ia.us
Clear Creek ES 500/PK-5
PO Box 488 52322 319-828-4505
Dan Dvorak, prin. Fax 828-8140
Other Schools – See Middle Amana, North Liberty

Oxford Junction, Jones, Pop. 561
Midland Community SD
Supt. — See Wyoming
Midland ES 100/PK-1
PO Box F 52323 563-826-2091
Marilyn Jackson, prin. Fax 486-2681

Packwood, Jefferson, Pop. 221
Pekin Community SD 600/PK-12
1062 Birch Ave 52580 319-695-3707
Dr. Roger Macklem, supt. Fax 695-5130
www.pekincsd.org
Pekin ES 300/PK-5
1062 Birch Ave 52580 641-661-2351
Jeff Eeling, prin. Fax 695-5130

Panora, Guthrie, Pop. 1,214
Panorama Community SD 800/PK-12
PO Box 39 50216 641-755-2317
John Millhollin, supt. Fax 755-3008
www.panorama.k12.ia.us/
Panorama ES 400/PK-5
401 Panther Dr 50216 641-755-2021
Cory Heiman, prin. Fax 755-3715
Panorama MS 200/6-8
PO Box 39 50216 641-755-2317
Mark Johnston, prin. Fax 755-3008

Parkersburg, Butler, Pop. 1,881
Aplington-Parkersburg Community SD
Supt. — See Aplington
Parkersburg ES 200/PK-5
602 Lincoln St 50665 319-346-2446
Amy May, prin. Fax 346-2255

Paullina, O'Brien, Pop. 1,041
South O'Brien Community SD 700/K-12
PO Box 638 51046 712-949-2115
Dick Nervig, supt. Fax 949-2149
www.s-obrien.k12.ia.us
Other Schools – See Primghar

Zion-St. John Lutheran S 100/K-8
PO Box 249 51046 712-949-3915
Jon Baumgartel, prin. Fax 949-3657

Pella, Marion, Pop. 10,291
Pella Community SD 1,700/PK-12
PO Box 468 50219 641-628-1111
Mark Wittmer, supt. Fax 628-1116
www.pella.k12.ia.us
Jefferson IS 300/4-6
801 E 13th St 50219 641-628-8267
Brian Miller, prin. Fax 628-8241
Lincoln ES 400/PK-3
1102 Broadway St 50219 641-628-3970
Rich Schulte, prin. Fax 628-8712
Madison ES PK-3
950 E University St 50219 641-628-4638
Donna Hancock, prin. Fax 628-9183
Pella MS 300/7-8
613 E 13th St 50219 641-628-4784
Matt Patton, prin. Fax 628-6804

Pella Christian Grade S 500/PK-8
216 Liberty St 50219 641-628-2414
David DeJong, prin. Fax 628-9506
Peoria Christian S 50/K-8
110 Peoria West St 50219 641-625-4131
James Warden, prin. Fax 625-4131

Peosta, Dubuque, Pop. 933
Western Dubuque Community SD
Supt. — See Farley
Peosta ES PK-5
8522 Burds Rd 52068 563-588-9010
Shari Steward, prin. Fax 588-9013

Seton Catholic S St. John 300/PK-5
10801 Sundown Rd 52068 563-556-5967
Mary Smock, prin. Fax 556-7579

Perry, Dallas, Pop. 8,865
Perry Community SD 1,800/PK-12
1219 Warford St 50220 515-465-4656
Randall McCaulley Ed.D., supt. Fax 465-2426
www.perry.k12.ia.us/
Perry ES 800/PK-5
1600 8th St 50220 515-465-5656
Clark Wicks, prin. Fax 465-7769
Perry MS 400/6-8
1200 18th St 50220 515-465-3531
Shaun Kruger, prin. Fax 465-8555

St. Patrick S 100/PK-8
1302 5th St 50220 515-465-4186
Cory Wenthe, prin. Fax 465-9808

Pierson, Woodbury, Pop. 361
Kingsley-Pierson Community SD
Supt. — See Kingsley
Pierson ES 50/5-5
321 4th St 51048 712-375-5939
Robert Wiese, prin. Fax 375-5771
Pierson MS 100/6-8
321 4th St 51048 712-375-5939
Robert Wiese, prin. Fax 375-5771

Plainfield, Bremer, Pop. 432
Nashua-Plainfield Community SD
Supt. — See Nashua
Nashua-Plainfield MS 200/5-8
PO Box 38 50666 319-276-4451
Edwin Anderson, prin. Fax 276-3541

Pleasant Hill, Polk, Pop. 6,229
Des Moines Independent Community SD
Supt. — See Des Moines
Pleasant Hill ES 300/K-5
4801 E Oakwood Dr 50327 515-242-8432
Terrie Price, prin. Fax 265-8344

Southeast Polk Community SD 5,500/PK-12
8379 NE University Ave 50327 515-967-4294
Thomas Downs, supt. Fax 967-4257
www.se-polk.k12.ia.us/
Four Mile ES 600/K-6
670 SE 68th St 50327 515-265-1972
Randy Mohning, prin. Fax 262-1933
Southeast Polk JHS 900/7-8
8031 NE University Ave 50327 515-967-5509
Glenn Dietzenbach, prin. Fax 967-1676
Other Schools – See Altoona, Des Moines, Mitchellville, Runnells

Pleasantville, Marion, Pop. 1,607
Pleasantville Community SD 700/PK-12
415 Jones St 50225 515-848-0555
Dave Isgrig, supt. Fax 848-0561
www.pleasantville.k12.ia.us
Pleasantville ES 300/PK-5
415 Jones St 50225 515-848-0566
Jan Haugen, prin. Fax 848-0561
Pleasantville MS 200/6-8
415 Jones St 50225 515-848-0528
Susan Phillips, prin. Fax 848-0561

Pocahontas, Pocahontas, Pop. 1,876
Pocahontas Area Community SD 500/PK-12
202 1st Ave SW 50574 712-335-4311
Joseph Kramer, supt. Fax 335-4206
www.pocahontas.k12.ia.us/
Pocahontas Area All Start PK 50/PK-PK
205 2nd Ave NW 50574 712-335-4025
Lynn Moody, prin. Fax 335-4206
Pocahontas Area ES 200/K-5
208 1st Ave SW 50574 712-335-4642
Lynn Moody, prin. Fax 335-3627

Pocahontas Catholic S 100/K-6
305 SW 3rd St 50574 712-335-3603
Ron Olberding, prin. Fax 335-3603

Polk City, Polk, Pop. 2,940
North Polk Community SD
Supt. — See Alleman
North Polk West ES 300/PK-5
1400 W Broadway St 50226 515-984-6344
Ann Stadtmueller, prin. Fax 984-9414

Pomeroy, Calhoun, Pop. 658
Pomeroy-Palmer Community SD 200/PK-12
202 E Harrison St 50575 712-468-2268
Vicki Caldwell, supt. Fax 468-2453
www.pom-palm.k12.ia.us
Pomeroy-Palmer ES 100/PK-8
202 E Harrison St 50575 712-468-2268
Joel Foster, prin. Fax 468-2453

Postville, Allamakee, Pop. 2,322
Postville Community SD 600/K-12
PO Box 717 52162 563-864-7651
Ottie Maxey, supt. Fax 864-7659
www.postville.k12.ia.us
Darling S 400/K-8
PO Box 717 52162 563-864-7651
Chad Wahls, prin. Fax 864-7659

Bais Chaya Mushka/Oholei Menachem 200/PK-8
PO Box 1025 52162 563-864-3632

Prairie City, Jasper, Pop. 1,424
PCM Community SD 1,000/PK-12
PO Box 490 50228 515-994-2685
Jane Babcock, supt. Fax 994-2699
www.pcmonroe.k12.ia.us
PCM MS 200/6-8
PO Box 490 50228 515-994-2686
Gary Friday, prin. Fax 994-2686
Prairie City ES 200/PK-5
PO Box 490 50228 515-994-2377
Mary Poulter, prin. Fax 994-3280
Other Schools – See Monroe

Prescott, Adams, Pop. 260
Prescott Community SD 50/PK-6
PO Box 1 50859 641-335-2212
Douglas Latham, supt. Fax 335-2400
www.prescott.k12.ia.us/
Prescott ES 50/PK-6
PO Box 1 50859 641-335-2211
Lynne Rasmussen, lead tchr. Fax 335-2400

Preston, Jackson, Pop. 946
Preston Community SD 300/K-12
121 S Mitchell St 52069 563-689-3431
Dianne Anderson, supt. Fax 689-5823
www.prestonschools.com/
Preston ES 200/K-6
121 S Mitchell St 52069 563-689-3431
David Miller, prin. Fax 689-5823

Primghar, O'Brien, Pop. 841
South O'Brien Community SD
Supt. — See Paullina
South O'Brien ES 300/K-6
PO Box P 51245 712-957-3755
Lisa Wiese, prin. Fax 957-0205

Princeton, Scott, Pop. 931
North Scott Community SD
Supt. — See Eldridge
Grissom ES 200/K-6
500 Lost Grove Rd 52768 563-289-4404
Kelly Rohlf, prin. Fax 289-9016

Protivin, Howard, Pop. 313

Trinity Catholic S 100/PK-6
PO Box 246 52163 563-569-8556
Dana Spry, prin. Fax 569-8477

Radcliffe, Hardin, Pop. 575
Hubbard-Radcliffe Community SD
Supt. — See Hubbard
Hubbard-Radcliffe ES 200/PK-5
PO Box 410 50230 515-899-2111
Joel Semprini, prin. Fax 899-2116

Readlyn, Bremer, Pop. 767
Wapsie Valley Community SD
Supt. — See Fairbank
Readlyn ES 100/K-6
PO Box 280 50668 319-279-3323
Debra Rich, prin. Fax 279-3187

Community Lutheran S 100/PK-8
2681 Quail Ave 50668 319-279-3968
Chris Jesse, prin. Fax 279-3168

Redfield, Dallas, Pop. 965
West Central Valley Community SD
Supt. — See Stuart
West Central Valley MS 200/6-8
PO Box B 50233 515-833-2331
Anthony Lohse, prin. Fax 833-2629

Red Oak, Montgomery, Pop. 5,919
Red Oak Community SD 1,200/PK-12
904 N Broad St 51566 712-623-6600
Terry Schmidt, supt. Fax 623-6603
www.redoakschooldistrict.com
Inman PS 400/PK-3
900 Inman Dr 51566 712-623-6635
Fred Laughlin, prin. Fax 623-6638
Red Oak MS 300/6-8
308 E Corning St 51566 712-623-6620
Barbara Sims, prin. Fax 623-6626
Right Start Preschool 50/PK-PK
904 N Broad St 51566 712-623-6635
Fred Laughlin, prin. Fax 623-6603
Washington IS 200/4-5
400 2nd Ave 51566 712-623-6630
Doug Barry, prin. Fax 623-6634

Reinbeck, Grundy, Pop. 1,687
Gladbrook-Reinbeck Community SD 700/K-12
300 Cedar St 50669 319-345-2712
Tim Kuehl, supt. Fax 345-2242
www.gladbrook-reinbeck.k12.ia.us
Reinbeck ES 100/K-4
300 Cedar St 50669 319-345-2822
Bill Parker, prin. Fax 345-2242
Other Schools – See Gladbrook

Remsen, Plymouth, Pop. 1,735
Remsen-Union Community SD 400/PK-12
511 Roosevelt Ave 51050 712-786-1101
Kenneth Howard, supt. Fax 786-1104
www.remsen-union.k12.ia.us/
Remsen-Union ES 200/PK-5
511 Roosevelt Ave 51050 712-786-1192
Ken Howard, prin. Fax 786-1104
Remsen-Union MS 100/6-8
511 Roosevelt Ave 51050 712-786-1101
Steve Harmon, prin. Fax 786-1104

St. Catherine & St. Mary S 100/PK-8
321 Fulton St 51050 712-786-1160
Elizabeth Gibney, prin. Fax 786-1167

Riceville, Howard, Pop. 834
Riceville Community SD 300/K-12
912 Woodland Ave 50466 641-985-2288
Tom Hamrick, supt. Fax 985-4171
www.riceville.k12.ia.us
Riceville ES 100/K-4
912 Woodland Ave 50466 641-985-2288
Tom Hamrick, prin. Fax 985-4171

Ridgeway, Winneshiek, Pop. 291
Howard-Winneshiek Community SD
Supt. — See Cresco
Ridgeway ES 100/K-6
PO Box 18 52165 563-737-2211
Jerry Brown, prin. Fax 547-5973

Ringsted, Emmet, Pop. 427
Armstrong-Ringsted Community SD
Supt. — See Armstrong
Armstrong-Ringsted ES 100/PK-3
PO Box 218 50578 712-866-0191
Randy Collins, prin. Fax 866-0019

Rippey, Greene, Pop. 302
East Greene Community SD
Supt. — See Grand Junction

Rippey ES 200/PK-6
PO Box 290 50235 515-436-7721
G. Mike Harter, prin. Fax 436-7722

Riverside, Washington, Pop. 961
Highland Community SD 700/PK-12
1715 Vine Ave 52327 319-648-3822
Chris Armstrong, supt. Fax 648-4055
www.highland.k12.ia.us
Highland MS 100/6-8
1715 Vine Ave 52327 319-648-5018
Joel Diederichs, prin. Fax 648-4055
Riverside ES 200/PK-5
220 Schnoebelen St 52327 319-648-2821
Shawn Donovan, prin. Fax 648-5503
Other Schools – See Ainsworth

Robins, Linn, Pop. 2,270
Linn-Mar Community SD
Supt. — See Marion
Westfield ES 400/K-5
901 E Main St NE 52328 319-447-3350
Ed Rodgers, prin. Fax 832-1581

Rockford, Floyd, Pop. 899
Rudd-Rockford-Marble Rock Community SD 600/PK-12
PO Box 218 50468 641-756-3610
Steve Ward, supt. Fax 756-2369
www.rockford.k12.ia.us
Rudd-Rockford-Marble Rock ES 300/PK-6
PO Box 218 50468 641-756-3508
Makaela Hoffman, prin. Fax 756-2369

Rock Rapids, Lyon, Pop. 2,598
Central Lyon Community SD 600/K-12
PO Box 471 51246 712-472-2664
Dave Ackerman, supt. Fax 472-3543
Central Lyon ES 300/K-5
PO Box 471 51246 712-472-4041
Dan Kruse, prin. Fax 472-2346
Central Lyon MS 200/6-8
PO Box 471 51246 712-472-4041
Dan Kruse, prin. Fax 472-2346

Rock Valley, Sioux, Pop. 2,852
Rock Valley Community SD 600/PK-12
1712 20th Ave 51247 712-476-2701
Dennis Mozer, supt. Fax 476-2125
www.rvcsd.org
Rock Valley ES 300/PK-5
1910 15th St 51247 712-476-2769
Donald Ortman, prin. Fax 476-2760

Netherlands Reformed Christian S 300/K-12
712 20th Ave SE 51247 712-476-2821
Harold Schelling, prin. Fax 476-5438
Rock Valley Christian S 200/PK-8
1405 17th St 51247 712-476-2615
Brad Vis, prin. Fax 476-2777

Rockwell, Cerro Gordo, Pop. 973
Rockwell-Swaledale Community SD 200/PK-8
PO Box 60 50469 641-822-3236
Tom Fey, supt. Fax 822-4882
www.westforkschool.org/
West Fork ES - Rockwell 100/PK-3
PO Box 60 50469 641-822-3233
Abe Maske, prin. Fax 822-3273
West Fork MS 100/4-8
PO Box 60 50469 641-822-3234
Abe Maske, prin. Fax 822-3273

Rockwell City, Calhoun, Pop. 2,096
Rockwell City-Lytton Community SD 500/PK-12
1000 Tonawanda St 50579 712-297-7341
Jeff Kruse, supt. Fax 297-7320
www.rockwell-city-lytton.k12.ia.us
Rockwell City ES 200/PK-4
330 Brower St 50579 712-297-8621
Nicole McChesney, prin. Fax 297-7181
Other Schools – See Lytton

Roland, Story, Pop. 1,242
Roland-Story Community SD
Supt. — See Story City
Roland-Story MS 300/5-8
206 S Main St 50236 515-388-4348
John Sheahan, prin. Fax 388-4435

Royal, Clay, Pop. 432
Clay Central/Everly Community SD 400/PK-12
PO Box 110 51357 712-933-2242
Monte Montgomery, supt. Fax 933-2243
www.claycentraleverly.com
Clay Central/Everly ES 100/PK-4
PO Box 110 51357 712-933-2241
Monte Montgomery, prin. Fax 933-2243
Clay Central/Everly MS 100/5-8
PO Box 110 51357 712-933-2241
Monte Montgomery, prin. Fax 933-2243

Runnells, Polk, Pop. 363
Southeast Polk Community SD
Supt. — See Pleasant Hill
Runnells ES 200/K-6
6575 SE 116th St 50237 515-966-2068
Lori Waddell, prin. Fax 966-2396

Ruthven, Palo Alto, Pop. 716
Ruthven-Ayrshire Community SD 300/PK-12
PO Box 159 51358 712-837-5211
Ervin Rowlands, supt. Fax 837-5210
www.ruthven.k12.ia.us
Ruthven-Ayrshire ES 100/PK-6
PO Box 159 51358 712-837-5211
Ervin Rowlands, prin. Fax 837-5210

Sabula, Jackson, Pop. 667
East Central Community SD
Supt. — See Miles
Sabula ES 50/3-5
PO Box 307 52070 563-687-2427
Neil Gray, prin. Fax 687-2473
Sabula MS 100/6-8
PO Box 307 52070 563-687-2427
Neil Gray, prin. Fax 687-2473

Sac City, Sac, Pop. 2,157
East Sac County SD
Supt. — See Lake View
East Sac County MS 100/5-8
300 S 11th St 50583 712-662-3259
Denny Olhausen, prin. Fax 662-4323

Sac Community SD 200/PK-4
400 S 16th St 50583 712-662-7030
Barb Kruthoff, supt. Fax 662-6245
www.eastsac.k12.ia.us
East Sac County ES 200/PK-4
400 S 16th St 50583 712-662-7200
Mike Fischer, prin. Fax 662-6245

Saint Ansgar, Mitchell, Pop. 1,022
St. Ansgar Community SD 700/K-12
PO Box 398 50472 641-713-4681
James Woodward, supt. Fax 713-4042
www.st-ansgar.k12.ia.us
Saint Ansgar ES 200/K-5
PO Box 369 50472 641-713-2331
Bill Carlson, prin. Fax 713-2037
Saint Ansgar MS 200/6-8
PO Box 398 50472 641-713-4040
Scott Dryer, prin. Fax 713-4042

Saint Paul, Lee, Pop. 119

Holy Trinity ECC 50/PK-K
2040 Locust St 52657 319-469-3881
Doris Turner, prin. Fax 469-2070

Salem, Henry, Pop. 460
Mount Pleasant Community SD
Supt. — See Mount Pleasant
Salem ES 100/K-5
412 E Jackson St 52649 319-258-7799
Linda Wilkerson, prin. Fax 258-4050

Sanborn, O'Brien, Pop. 1,309
Hartley-Melvin-Sanborn Community SD
Supt. — See Hartley
Hartley-Melvin-Sanborn MS 200/5-8
PO Box 557 51248 712-930-3281
Dorhout Mark, prin. Fax 930-5414

Sanborn Christian S 100/PK-8
405 W 2nd St 51248 712-729-3288
Anthony Minderhoud, admin. Fax 729-3289

Schaller, Sac, Pop. 728
Schaller-Crestland Community SD 400/PK-12
PO Box 249 51053 712-275-4267
Dave Kwikkel, supt. Fax 275-4269
www.schaller-crest.k12.ia.us/
Schaller-Crestland S 200/PK-8
PO Box 249 51053 712-275-4267
Ellen Pickhinke, prin. Fax 275-4269

Schleswig, Crawford, Pop. 828
Schleswig Community SD 200/PK-8
PO Box 250 51461 712-676-3313
Brian Johnson, supt. Fax 676-3539
www.schleswig.k12.ia.us
Schleswig ES 100/PK-4
PO Box 250 51461 712-676-3314
Brian Johnson, prin. Fax 676-3539
Schleswig MS 100/5-8
PO Box 250 51461 712-676-3313
Brian Johnson, prin. Fax 676-3539

Sergeant Bluff, Woodbury, Pop. 3,819
Sergeant Bluff-Luton Community SD 1,500/PK-12
PO Box 97 51054 712-943-4338
Rod Earleywine, supt. Fax 943-1131
www.sergeant-bluff.k12.ia.us
Sergeant Bluff-Luton ES 300/3-5
PO Box 97 51054 712-943-5563
Carolyn Pint, prin. Fax 943-1131
Sergeant Bluff-Luton MS 300/6-8
PO Box 97 51054 712-943-4235
Joe Trotzig, prin. Fax 943-8780
Sergeant Bluff-Luton PS 400/PK-2
PO Box 97 51054 712-943-5563
Kelly Adams, prin. Fax 943-1161

Seymour, Wayne, Pop. 787
Seymour Community SD 300/PK-12
100 S Park Ave 52590 641-898-2291
Gary Drummond, supt. Fax 898-7500
www.seymour.k12.ia.us/
Seymour ES 100/PK-6
100 S Park Ave 52590 641-898-2291
Gary Drummond, prin. Fax 898-7500

Sheffield, Franklin, Pop. 1,002
Sheffield Chapin Meservey Thorntn Comm SD 300/PK-12
PO Box 617 50475 641-892-4160
Darrin Strike, supt. Fax 892-4379
www.sheffield-chapin.k12.ia.us
West Fork ES - Sheffield 100/PK-3
PO Box 617 50475 641-892-4159
Darrin Strike, prin. Fax 892-4379

Sheldon, O'Brien, Pop. 4,807
Sheldon Community SD 1,000/PK-12
1700 E 4th St 51201 712-324-2504
Robin Spears, supt. Fax 324-5607
www.sheldon.k12.ia.us
East ES 400/PK-4
501 Normal College Ave 51201 712-324-4337
Jenni McCrory, prin. Fax 324-4338
Sheldon MS 300/5-8
310 23rd Ave 51201 712-324-4346
Cindy Barwick, prin. Fax 324-4347

St. Patrick S 100/PK-8
1020 4th Ave 51201 712-324-3181
Virginia Huss, prin. Fax 324-3559
Sheldon Christian S 100/PK-8
1425 E 9th St 51201 712-324-2429
Peter Vanvelzen, prin. Fax 324-8444

Shell Rock, Butler, Pop. 1,266
Waverly-Shell Rock Community SD
Supt. — See Waverly
Shell Rock ES 100/PK-4
214 N Cherry St 50670 319-885-4311
Micky Bahlmann, prin. Fax 885-6111

Shellsburg, Benton, Pop. 1,028
Vinton-Shellsburg Community SD
Supt. — See Vinton
Shellsburg ES 300/K-5
PO Box C 52332 319-436-4728
Shelly Petersen, prin. Fax 436-2294

Shenandoah, Page, Pop. 5,239
Shenandoah Community SD 1,100/PK-12
304 W Nishna Rd 51601 712-246-1581
Dick Profit, supt. Fax 246-3722
www.shenandoah.k12.ia.us
Shenandoah ES 400/PK-4
601 Dr Creighton Cir 51601 712-246-2520
Becky Pringle, prin. Fax 246-6390
Shenandoah MS 300/5-8
601 Dr Creighton Cir 51601 712-246-2520
Monte Munsinger, prin. Fax 246-6390

Sibley, Osceola, Pop. 2,690
Sibley-Ocheyedan Community SD 900/PK-12
120 11th Ave NE 51249 712-754-2533
Jeff Herzberg, supt. Fax 754-2534
www.sibley-ocheyedan.k12.ia.us/
Sibley-Ocheyedan ES 200/PK-3
416 9th Ave 51249 712-754-3636
Corey Jeness, prin. Fax 754-3994
Sibley-Ocheyedan MS 300/5-8
120 11th Ave NE 51249 712-754-2542
Bill Mueller, prin. Fax 754-3651
Other Schools – See Ocheyedan

Sidney, Fremont, Pop. 1,190
Sidney Community SD 400/PK-12
PO Box 609 51652 712-374-2141
Gregg Cruickshank, supt. Fax 374-2013
www.sidney.k12.ia.us
Sidney ES 200/PK-6
PO Box 609 51652 712-374-2647
Carolyn Maher, prin. Fax 374-2648

Sigourney, Keokuk, Pop. 2,168
Sigourney Community SD 700/PK-12
107 W Marion St 52591 641-622-2025
Todd Abrahamson, supt. Fax 622-2319
www.sigourneyschools.com
Sigourney ES 300/PK-6
509 S Jefferson St 52591 641-622-2350
Barb Tomow, prin. Fax 622-3604
Sigourney Preschool PK-PK
300 W Kelley St 52591 641-622-2566
Barb Tornow, prin. Fax 622-3604

Sioux Center, Sioux, Pop. 6,513
Sioux Center Community SD 1,000/PK-12
550 9th St NE 51250 712-722-2985
Patrick O'Donnell, supt. Fax 722-2986
www.sioux-center.k12.ia.us
Kinsey ES 400/PK-4
550 9th St NE 51250 712-722-1541
Robert Mars, prin. Fax 722-0583
Sioux Center MS 300/5-8
550 9th St NE 51250 712-722-3783
Julie Schley, prin. Fax 722-2986

Sioux Center Christian S 400/K-8
PO Box 165 51250 712-722-0777
Joe Dirksen, prin. Fax 722-0782

Sioux City, Woodbury, Pop. 83,148
Sioux City Community SD 13,000/PK-12
1221 Pierce St 51105 712-279-6667
Larry Williams, supt. Fax 279-6690
www.siouxcityschools.org/
Bryant ES 500/PK-5
821 30th St 51104 712-279-6819
Mary Kay Kollars, prin. Fax 279-6748
Clark ES 300/PK-5
4315 Hamilton Blvd 51104 712-239-7030
Angela Banks, prin. Fax 239-7030
Crescent Park ES 200/PK-5
1114 W 27th St 51103 712-279-6825
Mike Bartek, prin. Fax 239-6065
East MS 1,000/6-8
5401 Lorraine Ave 51106 712-274-4030
Thomas Peterson, prin. Fax 274-4668
Emerson ES 200/K-5
2410 W 1st St 51103 712-279-6826
Jean Carlson, prin. Fax 279-6846
Everett ES 300/K-5
1314 W 3rd St 51103 712-279-6827
Mette Malek, prin. Fax 279-6808
Hunt ES 200/K-5
615 20th St 51104 712-279-6833
Amy Denney, prin. Fax 279-6052
Irving ES 600/K-5
901 Floyd Blvd 51105 712-279-6834
Rich McGrath, prin. Fax 279-6092
Joy ES 300/K-5
3409 Indiana Ave 51106 712-274-4039
Mary Motz, prin. Fax 274-4681

Leeds ES 200/3-5
3919 Jefferson St 51108 712-239-7034
Rita Vannatta, prin. Fax 239-7036
Lincoln ES 300/K-5
115 Midvale Ave 51104 712-279-6836
Dr. Angela Banks, prin. Fax 279-6837
Longfellow ES 300/K-5
1800 Sioux Trl 51106 712-274-4043
Mary Motz, prin. Fax 274-4036
Nodland ES 200/K-2
5000 Mayhew Ave 51106 712-274-4044
Karen Hess, prin. Fax 266-8934
North MS 1,200/6-8
2101 Outer Dr N 51108 712-279-6667
Jeanene Sampson, prin. Fax 277-5941
Riverside ES 400/PK-5
2303 Riverside Blvd 51109 712-279-6811
J. Douglas Robbins, prin. Fax 277-6139
Roosevelt ES 200/K-5
2015 W 6th St 51103 712-279-6843
Lennard Hansen, prin. Fax 279-6844
Smith ES 400/PK-5
1623 Rebecca St 51103 712-279-6845
Mette Malek, prin. Fax 279-6727
Sunnyside ES 200/3-5
2700 S Maple St 51106 712-274-4047
Karen Hess, prin. Fax 274-4680
Unity ES, 1901 Unity Ave 51105 K-5
Dr. Michael Rogers, prin. 712-279-6839
Washington ES 400/K-5
2550 S Martha St 51106 712-274-4048
Dawn Stansbury, prin. Fax 279-4049
West MS 1,000/6-8
3301 W 19th St 51103 712-279-6813
Cynthia Washinowski, prin. Fax 277-6138
Whittier ES 400/K-5
4820 4th Ave 51106 712-274-4050
Linda Waugh, prin. Fax 274-4054

Holy Cross S / Blessed Sacrament Ctr 300/3-8
3030 Jackson St 51104 712-277-4739
Michael Sweeney, prin. Fax 258-3698
Holy Cross S - St. Michael Ctr 100/K-2
4105 Harrison St 51108 712-239-1090
Michael Sweeney, prin. Fax 239-8546
Mater Dei S - Immaculate Conception Ctr 200/K-5
3719 Ridge Ave 51106 712-276-6216
Mary Fischer, prin. Fax 274-1221
Mater Dei S - Nativity Center 100/6-8
4243 Natalia Way 51106 712-274-0268
Mary Fischer, prin. Fax 274-0377
Peace Makers Academy 100/PK-12
6000 Gordon Dr 51106 712-274-2450
Douglas Daniels, admin. Fax 276-8049
Sacred Heart S 300/K-8
5010 Military Rd 51103 712-233-1624
Brenda Ferrie, prin. Fax 233-1469
St. Paul Lutheran S 100/K-6
614 Jennings St 51101 712-258-6325
Lon Stuhr, prin. Fax 252-1141
Siouxland Community Christian S 200/PK-12
6100 Morningside Ave 51106 712-276-4732
Steve Clark, supt. Fax 276-4752

Sioux Rapids, Buena Vista, Pop. 700
Sioux Central Community SD 600/PK-12
4440 US Highway 71 50585 712-283-2571
Dan Frazier, supt. Fax 283-2989
www.sioux-central.k12.ia.us
Sioux Central ES 200/PK-6
4440 US Highway 71 50585 712-283-2571
Kevin Teno, prin. Fax 283-2285
Sioux Central MS 100/7-8
4440 US Highway 71 50585 712-283-2571
Jeff Scharn, prin. Fax 283-2285

Slater, Story, Pop. 1,421
Ballard Community SD
Supt. — See Huxley
Ballard West ES 500/PK-3
PO Box 267 50244 515-228-3890
Marty Jimmerson, prin. Fax 228-3892

Sloan, Woodbury, Pop. 1,022
Westwood Community SD 700/PK-12
1000 Rebel Way 51055 712-428-3355
Kirk Ahrends, supt. Fax 428-3246
www.westwood.k12.ia.us/
Westwood ES 300/PK-6
1000 Rebel Way 51055 712-428-3200
Diana Nordstrom, prin. Fax 428-3246

Solon, Johnson, Pop. 1,352
Solon Community SD 1,300/PK-12
301 S Iowa St 52333 319-624-3401
Brad Manard, supt. Fax 624-2518
www.solon.k12.ia.us
Solon ES 500/PK-4
111 N Chabal St 52333 319-624-3401
Jodi Rickels, prin. Fax 624-4091
Solon MS 400/5-8
313 S Iowa St 52333 319-624-3401
Mike Herdliska, prin. Fax 624-2518

Spencer, Clay, Pop. 11,117
Spencer Community SD 2,100/PK-12
PO Box 200 51301 712-262-8950
Greg Ebeling, supt. Fax 262-1116
Fairview Park ES, PO Box 200 51301 300/K-6
Lucas Dewitt, prin. 712-262-4842
Johnson ES, PO Box 200 51301 300/PK-6
Stephanie Anderson, prin. 712-262-2710
Lincoln ES, PO Box 200 51301 300/K-6
Bob Kirschbaum, lead tchr. 712-262-3752
Spencer MS 300/7-8
PO Box 200 51301 712-262-3345
Steve Barber, prin. Fax 264-3444

Iowa Great Lakes Lutheran S 50/K-6
500 4th Ave SW 51301 712-262-8237
Donald Pipho, prin. Fax 262-8237
Sacred Heart S, PO Box 817 51301 200/K-6
Ronald Olberding, prin. 712-262-6428

Spillville, Winneshiek, Pop. 381

C F S Consolidated S 100/1-4
PO Box 68 52168 563-562-3617
Kathryn Schmitt, prin. Fax 562-3292

Spirit Lake, Dickinson, Pop. 4,590
Spirit Lake Community SD 1,300/PK-12
711 23rd St 51360 712-336-2820
Doug Latham, supt. Fax 336-4641
www.spirit-lake.k12.ia.us/
Spirit Lake ES 500/PK-4
711 23rd St 51360 712-336-2822
Nick Sauers, prin. Fax 336-8966
Spirit Lake MS 400/5-8
711 23rd St 51360 712-336-1370
Nick Sauers, prin. Fax 336-4758

Springville, Linn, Pop. 1,001
Springville Community SD 500/K-12
400 Academy St 52336 319-854-6197
Terry Rhinehart, supt. Fax 854-6199
www.springville.k12.ia.us
Springville ES 200/K-5
602 Mill Ave 52336 319-854-6195
Shauna Dennison, prin. Fax 854-9957

Stanton, Montgomery, Pop. 710
Stanton Community SD 300/K-12
605 Elliott St 51573 712-829-2162
Judson Ashley, supt. Fax 829-2164
www.stantonschools.com
Stanton ES 100/K-6
605 Elliott St 51573 712-829-2171
Dennis McClain, prin. Fax 829-2717

Stanwood, Cedar, Pop. 651
North Cedar Community SD 800/PK-12
PO Box 247 52337 563-942-3358
Mary Jo Hainstock, supt. Fax 942-3596
www.north-cedar.k12.ia.us
Other Schools – See Clarence, Lowden, Mechanicsville

State Center, Marshall, Pop. 1,337
West Marshall Community SD 900/PK-12
PO Box 670 50247 641-483-2660
Ned Sellers, supt. Fax 483-2665
www.w-marshall.k12.ia.us
West Marshall ES 300/PK-4
PO Box 370 50247 641-483-2671
Christina deNeui, prin. Fax 483-9951
West Marshall MS 300/5-8
PO Box 340 50247 641-483-2165
Jeff Barry, prin. Fax 483-9951

Stockport, Van Buren, Pop. 286
Van Buren Community SD
Supt. — See Keosauqua
Van Buren ES - Stockport Attendance Ctr 100/K-6
PO Box 120 52651 319-796-4414
Charles Russell, prin. Fax 796-4480

Storm Lake, Buena Vista, Pop. 9,963
Storm Lake Community SD 1,300/PK-12
PO Box 638 50588 712-732-8060
Paul Tedesco, supt. Fax 732-8063
www.storm-lake.k12.ia.us
East ECC 50/PK-PK
PO Box 638 50588 712-732-8076
Julie Kwikkel, prin. Fax 732-8108
Storm Lake ES K-4
PO Box 638 50588 712-732-8074
Julie Kwikkel, prin. Fax 732-8111
Storm Lake MS 600/5-8
PO Box 638 50588 712-732-8080
Diane Jones, prin. Fax 732-8084

Concordia Lutheran S 50/K-8
PO Box 1383 50588 712-732-8356
Sherrie Grieme, coord. Fax 732-8357
St. Marys S 100/PK-4
312 Seneca St 50588 712-732-1856
Beverly Mach, prin. Fax 732-4590

Story City, Story, Pop. 3,141
Roland-Story Community SD 1,000/PK-12
1009 Story St 50248 515-733-4301
Mike Billings, supt. Fax 733-2131
www.roland-story.k12.ia.us
Roland-Story ES 400/PK-4
900 Hillcrest Ave 50248 515-733-4386
Kate Hartzler, prin. Fax 733-5357
Other Schools – See Roland

Stratford, Hamilton, Pop. 737
Stratford Community SD 100/PK-6
PO Box 190 50249 515-838-2208
Sarah Binder, supt. Fax 838-1938
www.stratford.k12.ia.us
Stratford ES 100/PK-6
PO Box 190 50249 515-838-2208
Sarah Binder, prin. Fax 838-1938

Stuart, Guthrie, Pop. 1,750
West Central Valley Community SD 900/PK-12
PO Box 550 50250 515-523-1165
David Arnold, supt. Fax 523-1166
www.wcv.k12.ia.us
Other Schools – See Dexter, Menlo, Redfield

Sully, Jasper, Pop. 888
Lynnville-Sully Community SD 500/K-12
PO Box 210 50251 641-594-4445
Duane Willhite, supt. Fax 594-2770
www.lynnville-sully.k12.ia.us
Lynnville-Sully ES 200/K-5
PO Box 310 50251 641-594-4445
Teri Bowlin, prin. Fax 594-2770
Lynnville-Sully MS 100/6-8
PO Box 310 50251 641-594-4445
Teri Bowlin, prin. Fax 594-2770

Sully Christian S 100/K-8
12629 S 92nd Ave E 50251 641-594-4180
Ginny Tull, prin. Fax 594-3799

Sumner, Bremer, Pop. 2,042
Sumner Community SD 600/K-12
PO Box 178 50674 563-578-3425
Rick Pederson, supt. Fax 578-3424
www.sumner.k12.ia.us/
Durant ES 200/K-5
PO Box 178 50674 563-578-3354
Amy Moine, prin. Fax 578-5400

Swea City, Kossuth, Pop. 596
North Kossuth Community SD 200/K-12
PO Box 567 50590 515-272-4361
Mike Landstrum, supt. Fax 272-4391
www.nsk.k12.ia.us
North Kossuth ES 100/K-5
PO Box 567 50590 515-272-4361
Julie Runksmeier, prin. Fax 272-4391

Tabor, Fremont, Pop. 975
Fremont-Mills Community SD 500/PK-12
PO Box 310 51653 712-629-2325
Christopher Herrick, supt. Fax 629-5155
www.fmtabor.k12.ia.us/fm/index.htm
Fremont-Mills ES 200/PK-6
PO Box 310 51653 712-629-6555
Allyson Forney, prin. Fax 629-5155

Tama, Tama, Pop. 2,603
South Tama County Community SD 1,200/PK-12
1702 Harding St 52339 641-484-4811
Kerri Nelson, supt. Fax 484-4861
www.s-tama.k12.ia.us/
South Tama County ES 300/PK-5
1611 Country Club Dr 52339 641-484-3999
Jim Bugge, prin. Fax 484-3744
Other Schools – See Toledo

Terril, Dickinson, Pop. 375
Terril Community SD 100/3-8
PO Box 128 51364 712-853-6111
Randy Collins, supt. Fax 853-6199
www.terril.k12.ia.us
Terril/Graettinger MS 100/3-8
PO Box 128 51364 712-853-6111
Jesse Ulrich, prin. Fax 853-6199

Thompson, Winnebago, Pop. 567
North Iowa Community SD
Supt. — See Buffalo Center
North Iowa MS 200/5-8
PO Box 27 50478 641-584-2231
Mike Evans, prin. Fax 584-2230

Thornburg, Keokuk, Pop. 68
Tri-County Community SD 300/PK-12
PO Box 17 50255 641-634-2408
Bill Cox, supt. Fax 634-2145
www.tri-county.k12.ia.us/
Tri-County S 200/PK-8
PO Box 17 50255 641-634-2632
Sandy O'Rourke, prin. Fax 634-2145

Tipton, Cedar, Pop. 3,132
Tipton Community SD 900/PK-12
400 E 6th St 52772 563-886-6121
Richard Grimoskas, supt. Fax 886-2341
www.tipton.k12.ia.us
Tipton ES 400/PK-5
400 E 6th St 52772 563-886-6131
Lori Foley, prin. Fax 886-2555
Tipton MS 200/6-8
400 E 6th St 52772 563-886-6025
Lori Foley, prin. Fax 886-2555

Titonka, Kossuth, Pop. 543
Titonka Consolidated SD 100/PK-8
PO Box 287 50480 515-928-2717
Ron Sadler, supt. Fax 928-2718
www.titonka.k12.ia.us
Titonka ES 100/PK-5
PO Box 287 50480 515-928-2717
Keith Buckridge, prin. Fax 928-2718
Titonka MS 100/6-8
PO Box 287 50480 515-928-2720
Keith Buckridge, prin. Fax 928-2718

Toledo, Tama, Pop. 2,687
South Tama County Community SD
Supt. — See Tama
South Tama County MS 400/6-8
201 S Green St 52342 641-484-4121
Steve Cose, prin. Fax 484-2699

Traer, Tama, Pop. 1,586
North Tama County Community SD 500/K-12
605 Walnut St 50675 319-478-2265
Gary Janssen, supt. Fax 478-2917
Traer ES 300/K-6
605 Walnut St 50675 319-478-8444
Stephen Foster, prin. Fax 478-2917

Treynor, Pottawattamie, Pop. 914
Treynor Community SD 700/K-12
PO Box 369 51575 712-487-3414
Kevin Elwood, supt. Fax 487-3332
www.treynor.k12.ia.us
Treynor ES 400/K-6
PO Box 369 51575 712-487-3422
Tim Larsen, prin. Fax 487-3625

Tripoli, Bremer, Pop. 1,269
Tripoli Community SD 500/PK-12
209 8th Ave SW 50676 319-882-4201
Troy Heller, supt. Fax 882-3103
www.tripoli.k12.ia.us
Tripoli ES 200/PK-5
309 9th Ave SW 50676 319-882-4203
Sara Figanbaum, prin. Fax 882-3649

Troy Mills, Linn
North Linn Community SD 700/PK-12
PO Box 200 52344 319-224-3291
Larry G. Boer, supt. Fax 224-3727
www.northlinn.k12.ia.us
North Linn MS 200/6-8
PO Box 200 52344 319-224-3291
Scott Beaty, prin. Fax 224-3232
Other Schools – See Coggon, Walker

Truro, Madison, Pop. 480
Interstate 35 Community SD 900/PK-12
PO Box 79 50257 641-765-4291
Bill Maske, supt. Fax 765-4593
www.i-35.k12.ia.us/
ADAPT Preschool 100/PK-PK
PO Box 170 50257 641-765-4901
Chris Fenster, prin. Fax 765-4593
Interstate 35 ES 300/PK-4
PO Box 170 50257 641-765-4901
Chris Fenster, prin. Fax 765-4905
Interstate 35 MS 300/5-8
PO Box 200 50257 641-765-4908
Sharon McKimpson, prin. Fax 765-4905

Underwood, Pottawattamie, Pop. 818
Underwood Community SD 800/PK-12
PO Box 130 51576 712-566-2332
Ed Hawks, supt. Fax 566-2070
www.underwoodeagles.org/
Underwood ES 400/PK-5
PO Box 160 51576 712-566-2326
Jeffrey Privia, prin. Fax 566-2963
Underwood MS 200/6-8
PO Box 130 51576 712-566-2332
J. Lewis Curtis, prin. Fax 566-2070

Union, Hardin, Pop. 402
BCLUW Community SD
Supt. — See Conrad
BCLUW MS 200/5-8
704 Commercial St 50258 641-486-5371
Dirk Borgman, prin. Fax 486-5372

Urbana, Benton, Pop. 1,344
Center Point-Urbana Community SD
Supt. — See Center Point
Urbana-Center Point MS 400/5-8
202 W Main St 52345 319-443-2426
Brent Winterhof, prin. Fax 443-2764

Urbandale, Polk, Pop. 34,696
Urbandale Community SD 3,300/PK-12
11152 Aurora Ave 50322 515-457-5000
Dr. Greg Robinson, supt. Fax 457-5018
www.urbandaleschools.com/
Jensen ES 200/1-5
6301 Aurora Ave 50322 515-457-5100
Greg Cavenza, prin. Fax 457-5104
Karen Acres ES 200/1-5
3500 74th St 50322 515-457-5700
Patty Schlotterbeck, prin. Fax 457-5704
Olmsted ES 400/PK-5
7110 Prairie Ave 50322 515-457-5800
Mark Lane, prin. Fax 457-5804
Rolling Green ES 200/K-5
8100 Airline Ave 50322 515-457-5900
Julia Taylor, prin. Fax 457-5904
Urbandale MS 800/6-8
7701 Aurora Ave 50322 515-457-6600
Daniel Meyer, prin. Fax 457-6610
Valerius ES 300/1-5
3305 92nd St 50322 515-457-6500
Jill Karch, prin. Fax 457-6504
Webster ES K-5
12955 Aurora Ave 50323 515-331-8600
Connie Toenjes, prin. Fax 331-8604

Waukee Community SD
Supt. — See Waukee
Walnut Hills ES 800/PK-5
4240 156th St 50323 515-987-3585
Chris Smith, prin. Fax 987-9784

Des Moines Christian S 900/PK-12
13007 Douglas Pkwy Ste 100 50323 515-252-2480
Dr. Robert Stouffer, supt. Fax 251-6911
St. Pius X S 400/K-8
3601 66th St 50322 515-276-1061
Larry Zahm, prin. Fax 276-0350

Ute, Monona, Pop. 348
Charter Oak-Ute Community SD
Supt. — See Charter Oak
Charter Oak-Ute ES 200/PK-6
329 E Main St 51060 712-885-2261
Tina Gress, prin. Fax 885-1707

Vail, Crawford, Pop. 453
Ar-We-Va Community SD
Supt. — See Westside
Vail ES 100/PK-2
509 1st Ave 51465 712-677-2236
Rosemary Cameron, prin. Fax 677-5525

Van Horne, Benton, Pop. 750
Benton Community SD 1,600/PK-12
PO Box 70 52346 319-228-8701
Gary Zittergruen, supt. Fax 228-8254
www.benton.k12.ia.us
Benton Community MS 300/7-8
PO Box 70 52346 319-228-8701
Jo Prusha, prin. Fax 228-8747
Van Horne ES 100/PK-2
PO Box 70 52346 319-228-8701
Tanya Langholdt, prin. Fax 228-8305
Other Schools – See Atkins, Keystone, Norway

Van Meter, Dallas, Pop. 1,088
Van Meter Community SD 600/K-12
PO Box 257 50261 515-996-9960
Greg DeTimmerman, supt. Fax 996-9954
www.vanmeter.k12.ia.us
Van Meter ES 300/K-6
PO Box 257 50261 515-996-2221
Mary Beth Arentsen, prin. Fax 996-2488

Ventura, Cerro Gordo, Pop. 676
Ventura Community SD 300/K-12
PO Box 18 50482 641-829-4482
Brian Rodemeyer, supt. Fax 829-3906
www.venturaschools.org
Ventura ES 200/K-6
PO Box 18 50482 641-829-4482
Brian Rodemeyer, prin. Fax 829-3906

Victor, Iowa, Pop. 1,004
H-L-V Community SD 400/PK-12
PO Box B 52347 319-647-2161
William Lynch, supt. Fax 647-2164
www.hlv.k12.ia.us
H-L-V ES 200/PK-6
PO Box B 52347 319-647-2161
John Long, prin. Fax 647-2164

Villisca, Montgomery, Pop. 1,300
Villisca Community SD 400/K-12
406 E 3rd St 50864 712-826-2552
William Stone, supt. Fax 826-4072
www.villisca.k12.ia.us
Enarson ES 100/K-5
219 Central Ave 50864 712-826-5982
JoAnne Morenz, prin. Fax 826-4072

Vinton, Benton, Pop. 5,219
Vinton-Shellsburg Community SD 1,600/K-12
1502 C Ave 52349 319-436-4728
Mary Jo Hainstock, supt. Fax 472-3889
www.vinton-shellsburg.k12.ia.us
Tilford ES 300/K-4
308 E 13th St 52349 319-436-4728
Jim Murray, prin. Fax 472-5293
Vinton-Shellsburg MS 400/6-8
212 W 15th St 52349 319-436-4728
Mike Timmermans, prin. Fax 472-4014
Other Schools – See Shellsburg

Walcott, Scott, Pop. 1,530
Davenport Community SD
Supt. — See Davenport
Walcott ES 200/K-5
545 E James St 52773 563-284-6253
Erica Goldstone, prin. Fax 284-5081
Walcott IS 400/6-8
545 E James St 52773 563-284-6253
Erica Goldstone, prin. Fax 284-5081

Walker, Linn, Pop. 727
North Linn Community SD
Supt. — See Troy Mills
Walker ES 200/PK-5
PO Box 8 52352 319-448-4325
Steve McPherson, prin. Fax 448-4603

Cono Christian S 100/PK-12
3269 Quasqueton Ave 52352 319-448-4395
Thomas Bingham, hdmstr. Fax 448-4397

Wall Lake, Sac, Pop. 766
East Sac County SD
Supt. — See Lake View
East Sac County ES 200/PK-4
PO Box 40 51466 712-664-2627
Mike Fischer, prin. Fax 664-2607

Walnut, Pottawattamie, Pop. 750
Walnut Community SD 300/PK-12
PO Box 528 51577 712-784-2251
Dr. Tim Peterson, supt. Fax 784-2177
www.walnutcs.walnut.iowapages.org
Walnut ES 100/PK-5
PO Box 528 51577 712-784-3615
Tim Peterson, prin. Fax 784-2177
Walnut MS 100/6-8
PO Box 528 51577 712-784-3615
Chris Binns, prin. Fax 784-2177

Wapello, Louisa, Pop. 2,042
Wapello Community SD 800/PK-12
445 N Cedar St 52653 319-523-3641
John Weidner, supt. Fax 523-8151
www.wapello.k12.ia.us
Wapello ES 400/PK-6
505 N Cedar St 52653 319-523-5571
John Kerr, prin. Fax 523-8125
Wapello JHS 100/7-8
501 Buchanan Ave 52653 319-523-8131
Gwen Schaeffer, prin. Fax 523-4408

Washington, Washington, Pop. 7,207
Washington Community SD 1,700/K-12
PO Box 926 52353 319-653-6543
Dave Sextro, supt. Fax 653-5685
www.washington.k12.ia.us/
Lincoln ES 400/4-6
606 S 4th Ave 52353 319-653-3691
David Hoffman, prin. Fax 653-6800
Stewart ES 500/K-3
821 N 4th Ave 52353 319-653-3244
Rhoda Harris, prin. Fax 653-5313

St. James S 100/K-6
616 W 2nd St 52353 319-653-3631
Brad Thiel, prin. Fax 653-4019

Washta, Cherokee, Pop. 247
River Valley Community SD
Supt. — See Correctionville
River Valley ES 200/PK-6
PO Box 151 51061 712-447-6318
Debra Bagenstos, prin. Fax 447-6168

Waterloo, Black Hawk, Pop. 66,483
Waterloo Community SD 9,200/PK-12
1516 Washington St 50702 319-433-1800
Dr. Gary Norris, supt. Fax 433-1886
www.waterloo.k12.ia.us
Black Hawk ES 200/K-5
1700 Downing Ave 50701 319-433-2150
Melinda Ostergren, prin. Fax 433-2178
Central MS 600/6-8
1350 Katoski Dr 50701 319-433-2100
Marla Padget, prin. Fax 433-2149
Edison ES 400/PK-5
740 Magnolia Pkwy 50701 319-433-2180
Melissa Steggall, prin. Fax 433-2187
Henry ES 500/K-5
312 Rachael St 50701 319-433-2860
Brian Ortman, prin. Fax 433-3040
Hoover MS 700/6-8
630 Hillcrest Rd 50701 319-433-2830
Don Blau, prin. Fax 433-2843
Irving ES 400/K-5
1115 W 5th St 50702 319-433-2800
Sharrie Phillips, prin. Fax 433-2829
Kingsley ES K-5
201 Sunset Rd 50701 319-433-2210
Linda Garlinghouse, prin. Fax 433-2216
Kittrell ES 400/K-5
1520 Easton Ave 50702 319-433-2910
Audrey Wallican-Green, prin. Fax 433-2916
Lincoln ES 400/K-5
302 Cedar Bend St 50703 319-433-1990
Lucy Evans, prin. Fax 433-1997
Logan MS 400/6-8
1515 Logan Ave 50703 319-433-2500
Brad Schweppe, prin. Fax 433-2548
Lowell ES 300/K-5
1628 Washington St 50702 319-433-1900
Stephanie Mohorne, prin. Fax 433-1905
McKinstry ES 500/PK-5
1410 Independence Ave 50703 319-433-2630
Mary Jo Wagner, prin. Fax 433-2633
Orange ES 300/K-5
6028 Kimball Ave 50701 319-433-2880
Kenneth Erpelding, prin. Fax 433-2888
Other Schools – See Evansdale

Blessed Sacrament S 300/PK-8
600 Stephan Ave 50701 319-233-7863
Nancy Stirm, prin. Fax 233-8237
Immanuel Lutheran S 200/PK-8
207 Franklin St 50703 319-233-3967
Barb Buescher, prin. Fax 232-6184
Sacred Heart S 200/PK-8
620 W 5th St 50702 319-234-6593
Amy Sandvold, prin. Fax 235-7987
St. Edward S 500/PK-8
139 E Mitchell Ave 50702 319-233-6202
Pamela Schowalter, prin. Fax 235-2898
Walnut Ridge Baptist Academy 200/K-12
1307 W Ridgeway Ave 50701 319-235-9309
Lisa Goedken, prin. Fax 833-4780

Waterville, Allamakee, Pop. 142
Allamakee Community SD
Supt. — See Waukon
Waterville ES 100/K-6
115 Main St 52170 563-535-7245
Joe Griffith, prin. Fax 535-7110

Waucoma, Fayette, Pop. 252
Turkey Valley Community SD 500/PK-12
3219 Highway 24 52171 563-776-6011
John Rothlisberger, supt. Fax 776-4271
www.turkey-v.k12.ia.us
Turkey Valley ES 200/PK-6
3219 Highway 24 52171 563-776-6011
John Rothlisberger, prin. Fax 776-4271

Waukee, Dallas, Pop. 9,213
Waukee Community SD 5,100/PK-12
560 SE University Ave 50263 515-987-5161
Dr. David Wilkerson, supt. Fax 987-2701
www.waukee.k12.ia.us
Eason ES 600/K-5
605 Boone Dr 50263 515-987-5200
Peg Erke, prin. Fax 987-2707
Waukee ES 800/PK-5
400 Locust St 50263 515-987-5193
Nicole Tjaden, prin. Fax 987-2731
Waukee MS 700/6-7
905 Warrior Ln 50263 515-987-5177
Jill Urich, prin. Fax 987-2741
Other Schools – See Urbandale, West Des Moines

Waukon, Allamakee, Pop. 4,013
Allamakee Community SD 1,200/K-12
1059 3rd Ave NW 52172 563-568-3409
Dave Herold, supt. Fax 568-2677
www.allamakee.k12.ia.us/
Allamakee JHS 300/7-8
1059 3rd Ave NW 52172 563-568-6321
Joe Griffith, prin. Fax 568-2677
East Campus ES 300/3-6
107 6th St NW 52172 563-568-6304
Ann Hart, prin. Fax 568-6410
West Campus ES 200/K-2
953 3rd Ave NW 52172 563-568-6375
Ann Hart, prin. Fax 568-2677
Other Schools – See Waterville

St. Patrick S 100/PK-8
200 2nd St SW 52172 563-568-2415
Richard Wede, prin. Fax 568-2170

Waverly, Bremer, Pop. 9,298
Waverly-Shell Rock Community SD 1,900/PK-12
1415 4th Ave SW 50677 319-352-3630
Jere Vyverberg, supt. Fax 352-5676
www.waverly-shellrock.k12.ia.us
Carey ES, 220 9th Ave NW 50677 200/K-4
Micky Bahlmann, prin. 319-352-2855
Irving ES 200/5-6
195 20th St NW 50677 319-352-2658
Roger Wilcox, prin. Fax 352-5676
Southeast ES, 809 4th St SE 50677 100/K-4
Christi Lines, prin. 319-352-3582
Waverly-Shell Rock JHS 300/7-8
215 3rd St NW 50677 319-352-3632
Steve Kwikkel, prin. Fax 352-5199
West Cedar ES 200/K-4
221 15th St NW 50677 319-352-2754
Roger Wilcox, prin.
Other Schools – See Shell Rock

St. Paul's Lutheran S 200/PK-6
212 2nd Ave NW 50677 319-352-1484
Christi Lines, prin. Fax 352-3999

Wayland, Henry, Pop. 944
Waco Community SD 500/PK-12
PO Box 158 52654 319-256-6200
Greg Ray, supt. Fax 256-6213
www.wacohs.com
Other Schools – See Crawfordsville

Webster City, Hamilton, Pop. 8,077
Webster City Community SD 1,400/PK-12
825 Beach St 50595 515-832-9200
Mike Sherwood, supt. Fax 832-9204
www.webster-city.k12.ia.us
Pleasant View ES 100/PK-1
1901 Willson Ave 50595 515-832-9241
Mindy Mossman, prin. Fax 832-9244
Sunset Heights ES 200/2-4
1101 Boone St 50595 515-832-9245
Chuck Bonjour, prin. Fax 832-9248
Webster City MS 500/5-8
1101 Des Moines St 50595 515-832-9220
Becky Hacker-Kluver, prin. Fax 832-9225

St. Thomas Aquinas S 100/K-6
624 Dubuque St 50595 515-832-1346
Michael Pavik, prin. Fax 832-1212

Wellman, Washington, Pop. 1,470
Mid-Prairie Community SD 1,200/PK-12
PO Box 150 52356 319-646-6093
Mark Schneider, supt. Fax 646-2093
www.mid-prairie.k12.ia.us
Wellman ES 200/K-5
PO Box H 52356 319-646-2984
Evan Parrott, prin. Fax 646-2987
Other Schools – See Kalona

Wellsburg, Grundy, Pop. 681
AGWSR Community SD
Supt. — See Ackley
AGWSR MS 200/4-8
PO Box 188 50680 641-869-5121
Sheryl Arends, prin. Fax 869-3426

Timothy Christian S 100/K-8
PO Box 70 50680 641-869-3679
Janna Voss, prin. Fax 869-3510

Wesley, Kossuth, Pop. 435
Corwith-Wesley Community SD
Supt. — See Corwith
Wesley ES 100/PK-4
PO Box 296 50483 515-679-4450
Cory Myer, prin. Fax 679-9440

West Bend, Palo Alto, Pop. 817
West Bend - Mallard Community SD 300/PK-12
PO Box 247 50597 515-887-7821
Darrell Smith, supt. Fax 887-7785
www.west-bend.k12.ia.us
West Bend ES 100/PK-2
PO Box 247 50597 515-887-7821
Amanda Schmidt, prin. Fax 887-7853
Other Schools – See Mallard

West Branch, Cedar, Pop. 2,269
West Branch Community SD 800/PK-12
PO Box 637 52358 319-643-7213
Craig Artist, supt. Fax 643-7122
www.west-branch.k12.ia.us
Hoover ES 300/PK-5
PO Box 637 52358 319-643-7211
Jessica Burger, prin. Fax 643-7122
West Branch MS 200/6-8
PO Box 637 52358 319-643-5324
Sara Oswald, prin. Fax 643-5447

West Burlington, Des Moines, Pop. 3,231
West Burlington ISD 700/PK-12
211 Ramsey St 52655 319-752-8747
James Sleister, supt. Fax 754-9382
www.wbschools.us
West Burlington ES 400/PK-6
545 Ramsey St 52655 319-754-5726
Dee Crozier, prin. Fax 758-6768
West Burlington JHS 100/7-8
408 W Van Weiss Blvd 52655 319-752-7138
Dan Reid, prin. Fax 754-0075

West Des Moines, Polk, Pop. 52,768
Waukee Community SD
Supt. — See Waukee
Brookview ES 600/K-5
8000 EP True Pkwy 50266 515-987-5166
Terry Hurlburt, prin. Fax 987-5168
Maple Grove ES PK-5
1455 98th St 50266 515-987-3363
Michelle Lettington, prin. Fax 987-3903

West Des Moines Community SD 8,600/PK-12
3550 Mills Civic Pkwy 50265 515-633-5000
Thomas Narak, supt. Fax 633-5099
www.wdmcs.org
Crossroads Park ES 500/K-6
1050 50th St 50266 515-633-5600
Britt Cameron, prin. Fax 633-5699
Fairmeadows ES 500/K-6
807 23rd St 50265 515-633-6500
Carol Seid, prin. Fax 633-6599
Hillside ES 600/K-6
713 8th St 50265 515-633-6200
Robert Davis, prin. Fax 633-6299
Jordan Creek ES 800/PK-6
4105 Fuller Rd 50265 515-633-5200
Nancy Moorhead, prin. Fax 633-5299
Phenix ES 200/K-3
415 7th St 50265 515-633-6600
Andrea Boyd, prin. Fax 633-6699
Stilwell JHS 700/7-8
1601 Vine St 50265 515-633-6000
Tim Miller, prin. Fax 633-6099
Western Hills ES 400/K-6
600 39th St 50265 515-633-5900
Beth Thornton, prin. Fax 633-5999
Westridge ES 700/K-6
5500 EP True Pkwy 50266 515-633-5400
Mary Jane Stites, prin. Fax 633-5499
Other Schools – See Clive, Windsor Heights

Iowa Christian Academy 200/PK-12
2501 Vine St 50265 515-221-3999
Dr. Aaron Gonzalez, supt. Fax 225-2387
Sacred Heart S 500/K-8
1601 Grand Ave 50265 515-223-1284
Frank Vito, prin. Fax 223-9413
St. Francis of Assisi S 700/K-8
7075 Ashworth Rd 50266 515-457-7167
Misty Hade, prin. Fax 440-1042
Shepherds Flock Lutheran S 50/PK-K
3900 Ashworth Rd 50265 515-225-1952
Fax 225-0871

West Liberty, Muscatine, Pop. 3,603
West Liberty Community SD 1,200/PK-12
203 E 7th St 52776 319-627-2116
Robert Mata, supt. Fax 627-2963
www.wl.k12.ia.us
ECC 100/PK-PK
203 E 7th St 52776 319-627-2116
West Liberty ES 300/K-2
111 W 7th St 52776 319-627-4243
Nancy Gardner, prin. Fax 627-2099
West Liberty MS 500/3-8
806 N Miller St 52776 319-627-2118
Vicki Vernon, prin. Fax 627-2092

West Point, Lee, Pop. 961

Holy Trinity S 200/K-6
413 Avenue C 52656 319-837-6131
Doris Turner, prin. Fax 837-8112

Westside, Crawford, Pop. 331
Ar-We-Va Community SD 400/PK-12
PO Box 108 51467 712-663-4311
Kurt Brosamle, supt. Fax 663-4313
www.ar-we-va.k12.ia.us
Other Schools – See Arcadia, Vail

West Union, Fayette, Pop. 2,485
North Fayette Community SD 1,000/PK-12
PO Box 73 52175 563-422-3851
John Rothlisberger, supt. Fax 422-3854
www.n-fayette.k12.ia.us/
North Fayette MS 200/6-8
PO Box 73 52175 563-422-3853
Kenneth Haught, prin. Fax 422-3854
West Union ES 200/PK-4
PO Box 73 52175 563-422-5514
Kathleen Bauer, prin. Fax 422-3085
Other Schools – See Fayette, Hawkeye

Wheatland, Clinton, Pop. 760
Calamus-Wheatland Community SD 600/K-12
PO Box 279 52777 563-374-1292
Charles Freese, supt. Fax 374-1080
www.cal-wheat.k12.ia.us
Other Schools – See Calamus

Whiting, Monona, Pop. 772
Whiting Community SD 200/K-12
PO Box 295 51063 712-455-2468
Myron Ballain, supt. Fax 455-2601
www.whiting.k12.ia.us/
Whiting ES 100/K-5
PO Box 295 51063 712-455-2468
Myron Ballain, prin. Fax 455-2601

Williamsburg, Iowa, Pop. 2,751
Williamsburg Community SD 1,200/PK-12
PO Box 120 52361 319-668-1059
Carol Montz, supt. Fax 668-9311
www.williamsburg.k12.ia.us
Welsh ES 400/2-6
PO Box 270 52361 319-668-2301
David Widmer, prin. Fax 668-9552
Williamsburg ES 200/PK-1
PO Box 49 52361 319-668-1864
David Widmer, prin. Fax 668-9311

Lutheran Interparish S 200/PK-8
PO Box 750 52361 319-668-1711
William Sitas, prin. Fax 668-9054

Wilton, Muscatine, Pop. 2,866
Wilton Community SD 900/PK-12
1002 Cypress St 52778 563-732-2035
Joe Burnett, supt. Fax 732-4121
www.wiltoncsd.org/
Wilton ES 400/PK-6
1002 Cypress St 52778 563-732-2880
Jamie Meyer, prin. Fax 732-4181

Zion Lutheran S 50/K-5
PO Box 429 52778 563-732-2912
Jan Doellinger, prin. Fax 732-2106

Windsor Heights, Polk, Pop. 4,607
Des Moines Independent Community SD
Supt. — See Des Moines
Cowles ES 200/K-5
6401 College Ave, 515-242-7818
Amy Moore, prin. Fax 242-7358

West Des Moines Community SD
Supt. — See West Des Moines
Clive ES 400/K-6
1600 73rd St, 515-633-5800
Brandon Pierce, prin. Fax 633-5899

Winfield, Henry, Pop. 1,105
Winfield-Mt. Union Community SD 400/K-12
PO Box E 52659 319-257-7700
M. Lynn Ubben, supt. Fax 257-7714
www.wmu.k12.ia.us/
Winfield ES 200/K-6
PO Box E 52659 319-257-7702
M. Lynn Ubben, prin. Fax 257-7703

Winterset, Madison, Pop. 4,877
Winterset Community SD 1,700/PK-12
PO Box 30 50273 515-462-2718
Doyle Scott Ph.D., supt. Fax 462-2732
www.winterset.k12.ia.us
Winterset ES 700/PK-4
404 S 2nd Ave 50273 515-462-1551
Gary Anker, prin. Fax 462-5025
Winterset JHS 300/7-8
720 Husky Dr 50273 515-462-3336
Molly Clark, prin. Fax 462-2178
Winterset MS 200/5-6
110 W Washington St 50273 515-462-3010
Molly Clark, prin. Fax 462-4149

Winthrop, Buchanan, Pop. 769
East Buchanan Community SD 600/PK-12
414 5th St N 50682 319-935-3767
Daniel Fox, supt. Fax 935-3749
www.east-buc.k12.ia.us
East Buchanan ES 200/PK-5
414 5th St N 50682 319-935-3660
Daniel Fox, prin. Fax 935-3614
East Buchanan MS 100/6-8
414 5th St N 50682 319-935-3367
Tom Mossman, prin. Fax 935-3615

Woodbine, Harrison, Pop. 1,624
Woodbine Community SD 500/PK-12
501 Weare St 51579 712-647-2411
Thomas Vint, supt. Fax 647-2526
www.woodbineschools.com
Woodbine ES 300/PK-6
501 Weare St 51579 712-647-2440
Kathy Waite, prin. Fax 647-2428

Woodward, Dallas, Pop. 1,305
Woodward-Granger Community SD 700/PK-12
306 W 3rd St 50276 515-438-4333
Jody Gray, supt. Fax 438-2497
www.woodward-granger.k12.ia.us
Woodward-Granger MS 100/6-8
306 W 3rd St 50276 515-438-4653
Linda Carroll, prin. Fax 438-4329
Other Schools – See Granger

Worthington, Dubuque, Pop. 371

St. Paul S 50/PK-6
PO Box 68 52078 563-855-2125
Jayne Intlekofer, prin. Fax 855-2125

Wyoming, Jones, Pop. 623
Midland Community SD 300/PK-12
PO Box 109 52362 563-488-2292
Brian Rodenberg, supt. Fax 488-2253
www.midland.k12.ia.us
Other Schools – See Lost Nation, Oxford Junction

Zearing, Story, Pop. 536
Colo-Nesco Comm SD
Supt. — See Mc Callsburg
Colo-Nesco MS 100/5-8
407 N Center St 50278 641-487-7411
Andrew Ward, prin. Fax 487-7414

KANSAS

KANSAS DEPARTMENT OF EDUCATION
120 SE 10th Ave, Topeka 66612-1182
Telephone 785-296-3202
Fax 785-296-7933
Website http://www.ksde.org

Commissioner of Education Dr. Alexa Posny

KANSAS BOARD OF EDUCATION
120 SE 10th Ave, Topeka 66612-1103

Chairperson Janet Waugh

PUBLIC, PRIVATE AND CATHOLIC ELEMENTARY SCHOOLS

Abilene, Dickinson, Pop. 6,409
Abilene USD 435 1,600/PK-12
PO Box 639 67410 785-263-2630
Larry Schmidt, supt. Fax 263-7610
www.abileneschools.org/
Abilene MS 400/6-8
500 NW 14th St 67410 785-263-1471
Ron Wilson, prin. Fax 263-4443
Garfield IS 200/4-5
300 NW 7th St 67410 785-263-1643
Chris Cooper, prin. Fax 263-9825
Kennedy ES 200/PK-1
1501 N Kuney St 67410 785-263-1088
Debbie Elliott, prin. Fax 263-3078
McKinley ES 200/2-3
112 N Rogers St 67410 785-263-2311
Tom Schwartz, prin. Fax 263-9923

Chapman USD 473
Supt. — See Chapman
Blue Ridge ES 100/K-5
1539 Highway 18 67410 785-598-2226
Luan Sparks, prin. Fax 598-2287
Rural Center ES 50/K-4
902 1400 Ave 67410 785-479-2213
Cecil Cromwell, prin. Fax 479-2213

St. Andrews S 100/PK-5
301 S Buckeye Ave 67410 785-263-2453
Christina Bacon, prin. Fax 263-3884

Admire, Lyon, Pop. 178
North Lyon County USD 251
Supt. — See Americus
Admire S 100/PK-8
100 E 3rd St 66830 620-528-3431
Craig Idacavage, prin. Fax 528-3389

Agra, Phillips, Pop. 278
Thunder Ridge SD
Supt. — See Kensington
Thunder Ridge MS 50/3-8
941 Kansas Ave 67621 785-638-2244
Roger Antle, prin. Fax 638-2254

Alma, Wabaunsee, Pop. 764
Mill Creek Valley USD 329 500/PK-12
PO Box 157 66401 785-765-3394
Dr. Phil Mahan, supt. Fax 765-3624
www.usd329.com/
Alma ES 100/PK-4
215 E 9th St 66401 785-765-3349
Robin Schuckman, prin. Fax 765-3956
Other Schools – See Maple Hill, Paxico

St. John Lutheran S 50/K-8
PO Box 368 66401 785-765-3914
Orville Altevogt, prin. Fax 765-7777

Almena, Norton, Pop. 454
Northern Valley USD 212 200/PK-12
PO Box 217 67622 785-669-2445
George Griffith, supt. Fax 669-2263
www.nvhuskies.org
Almena ES 100/PK-4
PO Box 217 67622 785-664-2446
Chris Robertson, prin. Fax 664-4060
Other Schools – See Long Island

Altamont, Labette, Pop. 1,065
Labette County USD 506 1,600/K-12
PO Box 189 67330 620-784-5326
Chuck Stockton, supt. Fax 784-5879
www.506.k12.ks.us
Altamont S 200/K-8
PO Box 306 67330 620-784-5511
Glenda Aikins, prin. Fax 784-2675
Other Schools – See Bartlett, Edna, Mound Valley, Parsons

Alta Vista, Wabaunsee, Pop. 425
Morris County USD 417
Supt. — See Council Grove
Prairie Heights MS 100/5-8
801 Center St 66834 785-499-6313
Cynthia Schrader, prin. Fax 499-5342

Altoona, Wilson, Pop. 472
Altoona-Midway USD 387 200/K-12
PO Box 128 66710 620-568-5725
Bill Orth, supt. Fax 568-5755
www.altoonamidway.org/
Altoona-Midway ES 100/K-5
PO Box 128 66710 620-568-5725
Bill Orth, prin. Fax 568-5755

Americus, Lyon, Pop. 932
North Lyon County USD 251 600/PK-12
PO Box 527 66835 620-443-5116
Steven Mollach, supt. Fax 443-5659
www.usd251.org/
Americus S 200/PK-8
PO Box 497 66835 620-443-5165
Aron Dody, prin. Fax 443-5840
Other Schools – See Admire, Reading

Andale, Sedgwick, Pop. 808
Renwick USD 267 1,700/K-12
PO Box 68 67001 316-444-2165
Dr. Dan Peters, supt. Fax 445-2241
www.usd267.com
Andale S 300/K-8
500 Rush Ave 67001 316-444-2628
Kelly Bielefeld, prin. Fax 445-2252
Other Schools – See Colwich, Garden Plain

Andover, Butler, Pop. 9,114
Andover USD 385 4,100/K-12
1432 N Andover Rd 67002 316-218-4660
Mark Evans, supt. Fax 733-3604
www.usd385.org
Andover Central MS 500/6-8
903 E Central Ave 67002 316-218-4710
Doug Baber, prin. Fax 266-8878
Andover MS 500/6-8
1628 N Andover Rd 67002 316-218-4610
Brett White, prin. Fax 733-3666
Cottonwood ES 500/K-5
1747 N Andover Rd 67002 316-218-4620
Shari Rooks, prin. Fax 733-3648
Meadowlark ES 300/K-5
654 S YMCA Dr 67002 316-218-4630
Jody Baker, prin. Fax 733-3651
Sunflower ES 500/K-5
616 E Douglas Ave 67002 316-218-4730
Rita Decker, prin. Fax 266-8890
Other Schools – See Wichita

Anthony, Harper, Pop. 2,302
Anthony-Harper USD 361 800/PK-12
PO Box 486 67003 620-842-5183
Keith Custer, supt. Fax 842-5307
www.usd361.org/
Anthony S 300/PK-8
215 S Springfield Ave 67003 620-842-3743
Robert Reed, prin. Fax 842-5236
Other Schools – See Harper

Argonia, Sumner, Pop. 500
Argonia USD 359 200/PK-12
504 N Pine St 67004 620-435-6311
Dr. Julie Dolley, supt. Fax 435-6623
www.usd359.k12.ks.us/
Argonia ES 100/PK-6
202 E Allen St 67004 620-435-6716
Dennis Murray, prin. Fax 435-6623

Arkansas City, Cowley, Pop. 11,581
Arkansas City USD 470 2,800/PK-12
PO Box 1028 67005 620-441-2000
Ron Ballard, supt. Fax 441-2009
www.arkcity.com
Adams ES 200/PK-5
1201 N 10th St 67005 620-441-2040
Nancy Haas, prin. Fax 441-2042
Arkansas City MS 700/6-8
400 E Kansas Ave 67005 620-441-2030
Mark Whitener, prin. Fax 441-2036
C-4 ES 100/K-5
11945 292nd Rd 67005 620-441-2045
Cheryl Carter, prin. Fax 441-2009
I X L ES 200/K-5
6758 322nd Rd 67005 620-441-2055
Marjorie Schuckman, prin. Fax 441-2009
Jefferson ES 200/PK-5
131 E Osage Ave 67005 620-441-2060
Sheryl Leeds, prin. Fax 441-2063
Roosevelt ES 200/PK-5
300 N B St 67005 620-441-2070
Jeri Crumbliss, prin. Fax 441-2009
Willard ES 200/PK-5
201 N 4th St 67005 620-441-2050
Amy Jones, prin. Fax 441-2009

Ark City Christian Academy 100/PK-12
PO Box 1181 67005 620-442-0022
Cynde Feste, prin. Fax 442-0022
Sacred Heart Catholic S 100/PK-5
312 S B St 67005 620-442-6550
Richard Sleefe, prin. Fax 441-0935

Arlington, Reno, Pop. 440
Fairfield USD 310
Supt. — See Langdon
Fairfield East ES 100/K-4
900 W Main St 67514 620-538-3621
Shawn Koehn, prin. Fax 538-2232

Arma, Crawford, Pop. 1,495
Northeast USD 246 500/K-12
PO Box 669 66712 620-347-4116
Mike Philpot, supt. Fax 347-4087
www.usd246.net
Northeast ES 300/K-5
PO Box 669 66712 620-347-8461
Ronda Fincher, prin. Fax 347-4140
Northeast MS 6-8
PO Box 669 66712 620-347-8461
Lawrence Hill, prin. Fax 347-4140

Ashland, Clark, Pop. 943
Ashland USD 220 200/PK-12
PO Box 187 67831 620-635-2220
Bill Day, supt. Fax 635-2637
www.ashland.k12.ks.us
Ashland ES 100/PK-6
PO Box 187 67831 620-635-2722
Jason Endicott, prin. Fax 635-2851
Ashland Upper MS 50/7-8
PO Box 187 67831 620-635-2814
Bill Day, prin. Fax 635-2637

Atchison, Atchison, Pop. 10,169
Atchison USD 409 1,700/PK-12
626 Commercial St 66002 913-367-4384
Susan Myers, supt. Fax 367-2246
www.usd409.net/
Atchison ES 800/PK-5
825 N 17th St 66002 913-367-1161
Tom Sack, prin. Fax 367-1602
Atchison MS 300/6-8
301 N 5th St 66002 913-367-5363
James Krone, prin. Fax 367-1302

Atchison Catholic S 200/PK-8
201 Division St 66002 913-367-3503
Rick Weber, prin. Fax 367-9324
Trinity Lutheran S 100/PK-8
611 N 8th St 66002 913-367-4763
Lottie Lee, prin. Fax 367-4823

Attica, Harper, Pop. 604
Attica USD 511 100/K-12
PO Box 415 67009 620-254-7661
Troy Piper, supt. Fax 254-7872
www.usd511.net
Puls ES 100/K-6
PO Box 415 67009 620-254-7915
Troy Piper, prin. Fax 254-7872

Atwood, Rawlins, Pop. 1,139
Rawlins County USD 105 300/PK-12
205 N 4th St Ste 1 67730 785-626-3236
Mark Wolters, supt. Fax 626-3083
www.usd105.org

Rawlins County ES 100/PK-6
205 N 4th St 67730 785-626-3217
Mark Wolters, prin. Fax 626-1011

Auburn, Shawnee, Pop. 1,131
Auburn Washburn USD 437
Supt. — See Topeka
Auburn ES 400/PK-6
PO Box 9 66402 785-339-4400
Mark Koepsel, prin. Fax 339-4425

Augusta, Butler, Pop. 8,608
Augusta USD 402 2,300/PK-12
2345 Greyhound Dr 67010 316-775-5484
Jim Lentz, supt. Fax 775-5035
www.usd402.com
Augusta MS 500/6-8
1001 State St 67010 316-775-6383
Eileen Dreiling, prin. Fax 775-3853
Ewalt ES 400/PK-5
2340 Greyhound Dr 67010 316-775-0056
Greg Clark, prin. Fax 775-1556
Garfield ES 200/PK-5
135 High St 67010 316-775-6601
Kim Christner, prin. Fax 775-1669
Lincoln ES 200/K-5
1801 Dearborn St 67010 316-775-5415
Pam Karslake, prin. Fax 775-5355
Robinson ES 200/K-5
1301 Helen St 67010 316-775-7561
Greg Taylor, prin. Fax 775-0867

St. James Catholic S 100/PK-5
1010 Belmont Ave 67010 316-775-5721
Richard Guy, prin. Fax 775-7160

Axtell, Marshall, Pop. 433
Axtell USD 488 300/K-12
PO Box N 66403 785-736-2304
Bob Bartkoski, supt. Fax 736-2864
www.usd488.org/
Other Schools – See Bern, Summerfield

St. Michael S 50/1-6
605 Elm St 66403 785-736-2257
Todd Leonard, prin. Fax 736-2257

Baileyville, Nemaha
B & B USD 451 200/K-12
PO Box 69 66404 785-336-2326
Jerry Turner, supt. Fax 336-2326
bbh.usd451.k12.ks.us/
Other Schools – See St Benedict

Baldwin City, Douglas, Pop. 3,746
Baldwin City USD 348 1,400/PK-12
PO Box 67 66006 785-594-2721
Paul Dorathy, supt. Fax 594-3408
www.usd348.com/
Baldwin ES - Intermediate Center 200/3-5
PO Box 67 66006 785-594-2446
Tom Mundinger, prin. Fax 594-2447
Baldwin ES - Primary Center 200/PK-2
PO Box 67 66006 785-594-2444
Dr. Deb Ehling-Gwin, prin. Fax 594-2445
Baldwin JHS 300/6-8
PO Box 67 66006 785-594-2448
Connie Wright, prin. Fax 594-2449
Marion Springs ES 100/K-5
PO Box 67 66006 785-594-3081
Dr. Gus Wegner, prin. Fax 594-4111
Vinland ES 100/K-5
PO Box 67 66006 785-594-3912
Dr. Gus Wegner, prin. Fax 594-4128

Barnes, Washington, Pop. 142
Barnes USD 223 400/PK-12
PO Box 188 66933 785-763-4231
Steve Joonas, supt. Fax 763-4461
www.usd223.org
Other Schools – See Hanover, Linn

Bartlett, Labette, Pop. 124
Labette County USD 506
Supt. — See Altamont
Bartlett S 100/K-8
PO Box 4676 67332 620-226-3414
Bob Homer, prin. Fax 226-3340

Basehor, Leavenworth, Pop. 3,287
Basehor-Linwood USD 458 2,000/PK-12
PO Box 282 66007 913-724-1396
David Howard, supt. Fax 724-2709
www.usd458.org
Basehor ES 400/PK-5
15602 Leavenworth Rd 66007 913-724-1038
Teri Boyd, prin. Fax 724-1492
Basehor-Linwood Sixth Grade Center 6-6
3102 N 155th St 66007 913-724-2348
Teri Boyd, prin. Fax 723-3724
Other Schools – See Bonner Springs, Linwood

Baxter Springs, Cherokee, Pop. 4,246
Baxter Springs USD 508 900/PK-12
1520 Cleveland Ave 66713 620-856-2375
Dennis Burke, supt. Fax 856-3943
www.usd508.org
Baxter Springs MS 200/6-8
1520 Cleveland Ave 66713 620-856-3355
David Jackson, prin. Fax 856-3943
Central ES 200/3-5
1501 Park Ave 66713 620-856-3311
Robert Womack, prin. Fax 856-3792
Lincoln ES 300/PK-2
801 Lincoln Ave 66713 620-856-3322
Steven Taylor, prin. Fax 856-4173

Bazine, Ness, Pop. 263
Western Plains USD 106
Supt. — See Ransom
Western Plains South S 100/PK-8
PO Box 218 67516 785-398-2535
Teresa Lacock, prin. Fax 398-2492

Belle Plaine, Sumner, Pop. 1,618
Belle Plaine USD 357 800/PK-12
PO Box 760 67013 620-488-2288
Lonn Poage, supt. Fax 488-3517
www.usd357.k12.ks.us
Belle Plaine ES 300/PK-5
PO Box 338 67013 620-488-2617
Sherra Taylor, prin. Fax 488-3976
Belle Plaine MS 200/6-8
PO Box 457 67013 620-488-2222
Morey Balzer, prin. Fax 488-3391

Belleville, Republic, Pop. 1,956
Republic County USD 109 400/K-12
PO Box 469 66935 785-527-5621
Troy Damman, supt. Fax 527-5375
www.usd109.org/
East ES 100/K-4
PO Box 469 66935 785-527-2330
Donald Westphal, prin. Fax 527-2121
Republic County MS 100/5-8
PO Box 469 66935 785-527-5669
Mabel Woodman, prin. Fax 527-5375

Beloit, Mitchell, Pop. 3,703
Beloit USD 273 700/PK-12
PO Box 547 67420 785-738-3261
Dr. Joe Harrison, supt. Fax 738-4103
usd273.org
Beloit ES 400/PK-6
PO Box 586 67420 785-738-3581
Byron Marshall, prin. Fax 738-3357

St. Johns S 100/K-6
712 E Main St 67420 785-738-3941
Martin Hesting, prin. Fax 460-9688

Bennington, Ottawa, Pop. 614
Twin Valley USD 240 600/PK-12
PO Box 38 67422 785-488-3325
Richard Harlan, supt. Fax 488-3326
www.usd240.org
Bennington S 300/PK-8
PO Box 8 67422 785-488-3323
Craig Gantenbein, prin. Fax 488-2939
Other Schools – See Tescott

Bentley, Sedgwick, Pop. 442
Halstead USD 440
Supt. — See Halstead
Bentley PS 200/K-3
PO Box 65 67016 316-796-0210
Larry Hobbs, prin. Fax 796-9958

Benton, Butler, Pop. 817
Circle USD 375
Supt. — See Towanda
Benton ES 300/K-6
PO Box 39 67017 316-778-1151
Dorsey Burgess, prin. Fax 778-1789
Circle MS 300/7-8
14697 SW 20th St 67017 316-778-1470
Doug Bacon, prin. Fax 778-1749

Bern, Nemaha, Pop. 200
Axtell USD 488
Supt. — See Axtell
Bern ES 100/K-6
PO Box 144 66408 785-336-2293
Rick Schnacker, prin. Fax 336-2507

Berryton, Shawnee
Shawnee Heights USD 450
Supt. — See Tecumseh
Berryton ES 400/PK-6
2921 SE 69th St 66409 785-861-1300
Stacey Giebler, prin. Fax 861-1315

Bird City, Cheyenne, Pop. 438
Cheylin USD 103 100/K-12
PO Box 28 67731 785-734-2341
William Porter, supt. Fax 734-2489
www.cheylin.com/
Cheylin West ES 100/K-6
PO Box 28 67731 785-734-2351
William Porter, prin. Fax 734-2489

Blue Rapids, Marshall, Pop. 1,048
Valley Heights USD 498
Supt. — See Waterville
Valley Heights ES 100/4-6
508 Chestnut St 66411 785-363-7693
Rhonda Trimble, prin. Fax 363-7713

Bonner Springs, Wyandotte, Pop. 6,942
Basehor-Linwood USD 458
Supt. — See Basehor
Glenwood Ridge ES 300/K-5
17550 157th Ter 66012 913-724-3536
Jan Hancock, prin. Fax 724-3539

Bonner Springs USD 204 2,400/PK-12
PO Box 435 66012 913-422-5600
Dr. Robert Van Maren, supt. Fax 422-4193
www.usd204.net
Bonner Springs ES 600/K-5
212 S Neconi Ave 66012 913-441-1777
Kim Mitchell, prin. Fax 441-3447
Clark MS 500/6-8
PO Box 336 66012 913-422-5115
Steve Cook, prin. Fax 422-1644
Other Schools – See Edwardsville, Kansas City

Brewster, Thomas, Pop. 262
Brewster USD 314 100/PK-12
PO Box 220 67732 785-694-2236
Sherri Edmundson, supt. Fax 694-2746
www.usd314.k12.ks.us
Brewster ES 100/PK-6
PO Box 220 67732 785-694-2236
Sherri Edmundson, prin. Fax 694-2746

Brookville, Saline, Pop. 253
Ell-Saline USD 307 500/K-12
PO Box 157 67425 785-225-6813
Jerry Minneman, supt. Fax 225-6815
www.ellsaline.org
Other Schools – See Salina

Bucklin, Ford, Pop. 734
Bucklin USD 459 200/PK-12
PO Box 8 67834 620-826-3828
W.S. Landis, supt. Fax 826-3377
www.usd459.k12.ks.us/
Bucklin ES 100/PK-4
PO Box 8 67834 620-826-3241
Sandy Schadegg, prin. Fax 826-9966

Bucyrus, Miami

Holy Rosary Wea S 200/PK-8
22705 Metcalf Ave 66013 913-533-2462
Rebecca Sachen, prin. Fax 533-2460

Buhler, Reno, Pop. 1,335
Buhler USD 313 2,100/PK-12
PO Box 320 67522 620-543-2258
David Brax, supt. Fax 543-2510
www.buhlerschools.org
Buhler ES 300/PK-6
PO Box 377 67522 620-543-2240
Nancy Bether, prin. Fax 543-2154
Other Schools – See Hutchinson

Burden, Cowley, Pop. 553
Central USD 462 300/PK-12
PO Box 128 67019 620-438-2218
Marian Hedges, supt. Fax 438-2217
www.usd462.org
Central ES 200/PK-6
1045 N Oak St 67019 620-438-3195
Marian Hedges, prin. Fax 438-3198

Burdett, Pawnee, Pop. 241
Pawnee Heights USD 496 100/K-12
PO Box 45 67523 620-525-6771
Dan Binder, supt. Fax 525-6788
www.phtigers.net
Pawnee Heights ES 50/K-5
PO Box 5 67523 620-525-6291
Dan Binder, prin. Fax 525-6246
Other Schools – See Hanston

Burlingame, Osage, Pop. 1,015
Burlingame USD 454 300/PK-12
100 Bloomquist Dr Ste A 66413 785-654-3328
Allen Konicek, supt. Fax 654-3570
www.usd454.net
Burlingame ES 200/PK-6
100 Bloomquist Dr Ste A 66413 785-654-3713
Tamara Buche, prin. Fax 654-3119

Burlington, Coffey, Pop. 2,707
Burlington USD 244 800/PK-12
200 S 6th St 66839 620-364-8478
Dr. Dale Rawson, supt. Fax 364-8548
www.usd244ks.org
Burlington ES 400/PK-5
706 Niagara St 66839 620-364-8882
Jane Nuessen, prin. Fax 364-2999
Burlington MS 200/6-8
720 Cross St 66839 620-364-2156
Tim Martin, prin. Fax 364-8560

Burr Oak, Jewell, Pop. 226
Rock Hills USD 107
Supt. — See Mankato
Rock Hills MS 5-8
221 N Main St 66936 785-647-6361
Beverly Roemer, prin. Fax 647-5391

Burrton, Harvey, Pop. 913
Burrton USD 369 200/K-12
PO Box 369 67020 620-463-3840
Dale Herl, supt. Fax 463-2636
www.burrton.k12.ks.us/
Burrton ES 100/K-5
PO Box 369 67020 620-463-3860
Dale Herl, prin. Fax 463-2636

Caldwell, Sumner, Pop. 1,215
Caldwell USD 360 200/PK-12
22 N Webb St 67022 620-845-2585
Alan Jamison, supt. Fax 845-2610
www.usd360.com
Caldwell ES 100/PK-5
1 N Osage St 67022 620-845-2585
Jim Bolden, prin. Fax 845-2332

Caney, Montgomery, Pop. 1,975
Caney Valley USD 436 800/PK-12
700 E Bullpup Blvd 67333 620-879-9200
Danny Fulton, supt. Fax 879-9209
www.caney.com
Lincoln Memorial ES 400/PK-6
201 E 1st Ave 67333 620-879-9240
Sherman Jones, prin. Fax 879-9247

Canton, McPherson, Pop. 812
Canton-Galva USD 419 400/PK-12
PO Box 317 67428 620-628-4901
Bill Seidl, supt. Fax 628-4380
www.canton-galva.k12.ks.us
Canton-Galva ES 200/PK-3
PO Box 297 67428 620-628-4451
Darren Ballantyne, prin. Fax 628-4702
Other Schools – See Galva

Carbondale, Osage, Pop. 1,451
Santa Fe Trail USD 434 — 1,200/PK-12
PO Box 310 66414 — 785-665-7168
Dr. Steve Pegram, supt. — Fax 665-7164
www.usd434.org
Carbondale Attendance Center — 400/PK-8
PO Box 160 66414 — 785-836-7188
Michael Flax, prin. — Fax 836-7696
Other Schools – See Overbrook, Scranton

Cassoday, Butler, Pop. 128
Flinthills USD 492
Supt. — See Rosalia
Flinthills PS — 100/K-2
200 N Washington 66842 — 620-735-4428
Larry Gawith, prin. — Fax 735-4429

Cawker City, Mitchell, Pop. 474
Waconda USD 272 — 400/K-12
PO Box 326 67430 — 785-781-4328
Jeff Teavis, supt. — Fax 781-4318
www.usd272.org
Lakeside IS — 100/4-6
PO Box 46 67430 — 785-781-4911
Robert Green, prin. — Fax 781-4861
Lakeside JHS — 100/7-8
PO Box 46 67430 — 785-781-4911
Robert Green, prin. — Fax 781-4861
Other Schools – See Downs, Glen Elder

Cedar Vale, Chautauqua, Pop. 669
Cedar Vale USD 285 — 100/PK-12
PO Box 458 67024 — 620-758-2265
Kenneth Tarrant, supt. — Fax 758-2647
www.cvs285.net
Cedar Vale ES — 100/PK-5
PO Box 458 67024 — 620-758-2265
Jackie Burdette, prin. — Fax 758-2647

Centralia, Nemaha, Pop. 504
Vermillion USD 380
Supt. — See Vermillion
Centralia ES — 200/PK-6
PO Box 367 66415 — 785-857-3324
John Whetzal, prin. — Fax 857-3847

Chanute, Neosho, Pop. 9,006
Chanute USD 413 — 1,200/PK-12
315 Chanute 35 Pkwy 66720 — 620-432-2500
Stephen Parsons, supt. — Fax 431-6810
www.usd413.org/
Chanute ES — K-5
500 Osa Martin Blvd 66720 — 620-432-2530
Jim Gorake, prin. — Fax 432-2542
Lincoln K — 200/PK-PK
1000 W Main St 66720 — 620-432-2550
Sandy Roecker, prin. — Fax 432-2552
Royster MS — 500/6-8
400 W Main St 66720 — 620-432-2520
Brad Miner, prin. — Fax 431-7841

St. Patrick Catholic S — 100/PK-5
424 S Malcolm Ave 66720 — 620-431-4020
Jeff Brownfield, prin. — Fax 431-6587

Chapman, Dickinson, Pop. 1,243
Chapman USD 473 — 900/K-12
PO Box 249 67431 — 785-922-6521
Tony Frieze, supt. — Fax 922-6446
usd473.net
Chapman ES — 200/K-5
PO Box 249 67431 — 785-922-7171
Kayla Wiedeman, prin. — Fax 922-7079
Chapman MS — 200/6-8
PO Box 249 67431 — 785-922-6555
Bruce Hurford, prin. — Fax 922-6601
Other Schools – See Abilene, Enterprise

Chase, Rice, Pop. 467
Chase-Raymond USD 401 — 100/K-12
PO Box 366 67524 — 620-938-2913
Carl Helm, supt. — Fax 938-2622
www.usd401.com/
Chase ES — 100/K-6
PO Box 366 67524 — 620-938-2996
Gene Short, prin. — Fax 938-1107
Raymond JHS — 50/7-8
PO Box 366 67524 — 620-938-2923
Carl Helm, prin. — Fax 938-2456

Cheney, Sedgwick, Pop. 1,843
Cheney USD 268 — 800/PK-12
100 W 6th Ave 67025 — 316-542-3512
Thomas Alstrom, supt. — Fax 542-0326
www.cheney268.com
Cheney ES — 300/PK-5
100 W 6th Ave 67025 — 316-542-3137
Jamie Rumford, prin. — Fax 542-3520
Cheney MS — 200/6-8
100 W 6th Ave 67025 — 316-542-0060
Amy Wallace, prin. — Fax 542-3789

St. Paul Lutheran S — 100/PK-8
PO Box 278 67025 — 316-542-3584
Jonathan Kamin, prin. — Fax 542-3584

Cherokee, Crawford, Pop. 718
Cherokee USD 247 — 800/K-12
PO Box 270 66724 — 620-457-8350
Tim Burns, supt. — Fax 457-8428
www.usd247.com
Cherokee S — 200/K-8
PO Box 280 66724 — 620-457-8315
Curtis Squire, prin. — Fax 457-8380
Other Schools – See Mc Cune, Weir

Cherryvale, Montgomery, Pop. 2,266
Cherryvale USD 447 — 800/PK-12
618 E 4th St 67335 — 620-336-8130
Randy Wagoner, supt. — Fax 336-8133
www.usd447.org
Lincoln Central ES — 300/PK-6
401 E Main St 67335 — 620-336-8140
Steve Pefley, prin. — Fax 336-8159
Other Schools – See Thayer

Chetopa, Labette, Pop. 1,231
Chetopa - St. Paul USD 505 — 600/PK-12
430 Elm St 67336 — 620-236-7959
Kim Juenemann, supt. — Fax 236-4271
www.usd505.org
Chetopa ES — 100/PK-6
430 Elm St 67336 — 620-236-7959
George Staten, prin. — Fax 236-4271
Other Schools – See Saint Paul

Cimarron, Gray, Pop. 2,029
Cimarron-Ensign USD 102 — 600/K-12
PO Box 489 67835 — 620-855-7743
William Stattelman, supt. — Fax 855-7745
www.cimarronschools.net
Cimarron ES — 400/K-6
PO Box 489 67835 — 620-855-3343
Rocky Stewart, prin. — Fax 855-3765

Claflin, Barton, Pop. 688
Claflin USD 354 — 300/K-12
PO Box 346 67525 — 620-587-3878
Jane Oeser, supt. — Fax 587-2389
www.claflinschools.org
Claflin ES — 100/K-6
PO Box 287 67525 — 620-587-3896
Jane Oeser, prin. — Fax 587-3642

Clay Center, Clay, Pop. 4,378
Clay Center USD 379 — 1,300/K-12
PO Box 97 67432 — 785-632-3176
Michael Folks, supt. — Fax 632-5020
www.usd379.org/
Clay Center Community MS — 200/6-8
935 Prospect St 67432 — 785-632-3232
Keith Hoffman, prin. — Fax 632-6013
Garfield ES — 100/4-5
815 4th St 67432 — 785-632-2125
Jaclyn Pfizenmaier, prin. — Fax 632-5912
Lincoln ES — 300/K-3
1020 Grant Ave 67432 — 785-632-2156
Jill Sanneman, prin. — Fax 632-2158
Other Schools – See Longford, Wakefield

Clearwater, Sedgwick, Pop. 2,214
Clearwater USD 264 — 1,300/PK-12
PO Box 248 67026 — 620-584-5188
Mike Roth, supt. — Fax 584-6113
www.usd264.org
Clearwater East ES — 100/PK-K
615 E Ross St 67026 — 620-584-6317
Diane Nickelson, prin. — Fax 584-6244
Clearwater Intermediate Center — 300/4-6
801 E Ross St 67026 — 620-584-8188
Sterrette Coffman, prin. — Fax 584-5188
Clearwater MS — 200/7-8
140 S 4th St 67026 — 620-584-2036
Keith Pauly, prin. — Fax 584-2199
Clearwater West ES — 200/1-3
100 S Prospect St 67026 — 620-584-2081
Diane Nickelson, prin. — Fax 584-3523

Clifton, Washington, Pop. 508
Clifton-Clyde USD 224 — 300/PK-12
PO Box A 66937 — 785-455-3313
David Roberts, supt. — Fax 455-3314
www.usd224.com/
Clifton-Clyde ES — 100/PK-3
120 Cloud St 66937 — 785-455-3319
David Roberts, prin. — Fax 455-3572
Clifton-Clyde MS — 100/4-8
PO Box B 66937 — 785-455-3323
David Roberts, prin. — Fax 455-3524

Coffeyville, Montgomery, Pop. 10,359
Coffeyville USD 445 — 1,800/PK-12
615 Ellis St 67337 — 620-252-6400
Robert Morten, supt. — Fax 252-6807
cvilleschools.com
Community ES — 1,000/PK-6
102 Cline Rd 67337 — 620-252-6430
Jennifer Bright, prin. — Fax 251-3691
Roosevelt MS — 300/7-8
1000 W 8th St 67337 — 620-252-6420
Alice Morris, prin. — Fax 252-6844

Holy Name Catholic S — 100/PK-6
406 Willow St 67337 — 620-251-0480
Lisa Payne, prin. — Fax 251-1651

Colby, Thomas, Pop. 5,030
Colby USD 315 — 900/K-12
600 W 3rd St 67701 — 785-460-5000
Terrel Harrison, supt. — Fax 460-5050
www.colbyeagles.org/
Colby ES — 400/K-5
210 N Grant Ave 67701 — 785-460-5100
Lance Krannawitter, prin. — Fax 460-5150
Colby MS — 200/6-8
750 W 3rd St 67701 — 785-460-5200
Robb Ross, prin. — Fax 460-5250

Heartland Christian S — 100/PK-12
1995 W 4th St 67701 — 785-460-6419
Jesse Vincent, admin. — Fax 460-8337
Sacred Heart S — 100/PK-5
1150 W 6th St 67701 — 785-460-2813
David Evert, prin. — Fax 460-9688

Coldwater, Comanche, Pop. 774
Comanche County USD 300 — 300/K-12
PO Box 721 67029 — 620-582-2181
Michael Baldwin, supt. — Fax 582-2540
www.southcentralusd300ks.com
Other Schools – See Protection

Colony, Anderson, Pop. 390
Crest USD 479 — 200/K-12
PO Box 305 66015 — 620-852-3540
Duane Thomas, supt. — Fax 852-3542
Crest S — 100/K-8
PO Box 325 66015 — 620-852-3521
Duane Thomas, prin. — Fax 852-3357

Columbus, Cherokee, Pop. 3,259
Columbus USD 493 — 1,100/PK-12
802 S Highschool Ave 66725 — 620-429-3661
Ken Jones, supt. — Fax 429-2673
www.usd493.com
Central S — 400/4-8
810 S Highschool Ave 66725 — 620-429-3943
Bobbi Williams, prin. — Fax 429-2882
Highland ES — 100/2-3
319 N Highschool Ave 66725 — 620-429-3032
Terry North, prin. — Fax 429-1445
Park ES — 200/PK-1
724 Garfield St 66725 — 620-429-3905
Jack Redden, prin. — Fax 429-1094
Other Schools – See Scammon

Colwich, Sedgwick, Pop. 1,328
Renwick USD 267
Supt. — See Andale
Colwich S — 300/K-8
PO Box 248 67030 — 316-796-1331
Dennis McCall, prin. — Fax 796-0665

Concordia, Cloud, Pop. 5,371
Concordia USD 333 — 1,100/K-12
217 W 7th St 66901 — 785-243-3518
Beverly Mortimer, supt. — Fax 243-8883
www.usd333.com
Concordia ES — 400/K-4
1500 E 9th St 66901 — 785-243-8853
Chris Fall, prin. — Fax 243-8856
Concordia MS — 200/5-6
1001 E 7th St 66901 — 785-243-2114
Karl Stricker, prin. — Fax 243-8844

Conway Springs, Sumner, Pop. 1,253
Conway Springs USD 356 — 700/K-12
110 N Monnett St 67031 — 620-456-2961
Clay Murphy, supt. — Fax 456-3173
www.usd356.org
Conway Springs MS — 200/6-8
112 N Cranmer St 67031 — 620-456-2965
Vance Williams, prin. — Fax 456-3313
Trueblood ES — 300/K-5
111 N Highland St 67031 — 620-456-2966
Ronald Ronnau, prin. — Fax 456-3312

St. Joseph Catholic S — 100/K-6
218 N 5th St 67031 — 620-456-2270
Patrick Carl, prin. — Fax 456-2272

Copeland, Gray, Pop. 321
Copeland USD 476 — 100/PK-8
PO Box 156 67837 — 620-668-5565
Jay Zehr, supt. — Fax 668-5568
www1.usd476.org:81/
Copeland ES — 100/PK-5
PO Box 156 67837 — 620-668-5565
Jim Howard, prin. — Fax 668-5568
South Gray JHS — 50/6-8
PO Box 156 67837 — 620-668-5565
Jim Howard, prin. — Fax 668-5568

Cottonwood Falls, Chase, Pop. 959
Chase County USD 284 — 500/K-12
PO Box 569 66845 — 620-273-6303
Greg Markowitz, supt. — Fax 273-6717
www.usd284.org/
Chase County ES — 200/K-4
PO Box 370 66845 — 620-273-6396
Cammy Onek, prin. — Fax 273-8923
Other Schools – See Strong City

Council Grove, Morris, Pop. 2,275
Morris County USD 417 — 800/PK-12
17 Wood St 66846 — 620-767-5192
Diane Miller, supt. — Fax 767-5444
www.usd417.net
Council Grove ES — 300/PK-5
706 E Main St 66846 — 620-767-6851
Judy Parks, prin. — Fax 767-5260
Council Grove MS — 100/6-8
706 E Main St 66846 — 620-767-6852
Sherry Edmiston, prin. — Fax 767-5260
Other Schools – See Alta Vista, Dwight

Courtland, Republic, Pop. 291
Pike Valley USD 426
Supt. — See Scandia
Pike Valley ES — 100/PK-5
PO Box 320 66939 — 785-374-4221
Mike Gritten, prin. — Fax 374-4268
Pike Valley JHS — 100/6-8
PO Box 320 66939 — 785-374-4221
Mike Gritten, prin. — Fax 374-4268

Cunningham, Kingman, Pop. 477
Cunningham USD 332 — 200/K-12
PO Box 67 67035 — 620-298-3271
Glenn Fortmayer, supt. — Fax 298-2562
www.usd332.org/
Cunningham S — 100/K-8
PO Box 98 67035 — 620-298-2462
Bob Stackhouse, prin. — Fax 298-2320

Damar, Rooks, Pop. 150
Palco USD 269
Supt. — See Palco
Damar JHS — 50/6-8
PO Box 38 67632 — 785-839-4265
Lisa Gehring, prin. — Fax 839-4278

Deerfield, Kearny, Pop. 892
Deerfield USD 216 300/PK-12
PO Box 274 67838 620-426-8516
Jon Ansley, supt. Fax 426-7890
www.usd216.org/
Deerfield ES 200/PK-5
PO Box 274 67838 620-426-8301
Amy DeLarosa, prin. Fax 426-8207
Deerfield MS 100/6-8
PO Box 274 67838 620-426-8401
Jon Ansley, prin. Fax 426-6903

Denton, Doniphan, Pop. 178
Midway USD 433 100/K-8
642 Highway 20 E 66017 785-359-6525
Rex Bollinger, supt. Fax 359-6522
www.doniphanwest.org
Doniphan West MS 100/6-8
642 Highway 20 E 66017 785-359-6526
Deanna Scherer, prin. Fax 359-6522
Midway ES 100/K-5
642 Highway 20 E 66017 785-359-6526
Deanna Scherer, prin. Fax 359-6522

Derby, Sedgwick, Pop. 20,543
Derby USD 260 6,500/PK-12
120 E Washington St 67037 316-788-8400
Craig Wilford, supt. Fax 788-8449
www.derbyschools.com
Derby Hills ES 400/PK-5
2230 N Woodlawn Blvd 67037 316-788-8540
Debbie Sanders, prin. Fax 788-8536
Derby MS 1,000/7-8
801 E Madison Ave 67037 316-788-8580
Rod Coykendall, prin. Fax 788-8062
Derby Sixth Grade Center 500/6-6
715 E Madison Ave 67037 316-788-8408
Jeff Smith, prin. Fax 788-8497
El Paso ES 400/K-5
900 E Crestway St 67037 316-788-8545
Melissa Turner, prin. Fax 788-8495
Park Hill ES 300/K-5
1500 E Woodbrook Ln 67037 316-788-8095
Jason Watkins, prin. Fax 788-8098
Pleasantview ES 300/K-5
1101 N Georgie Ave 67037 316-788-8555
Yvonne Rothe, prin. Fax 788-8496
Swaney ES 300/PK-5
501 English St 67037 316-788-8560
Scott May, prin. Fax 788-8494
Tanglewood ES 300/PK-5
830 Ridgecrest Rd 67037 316-788-8565
Mary Sites, prin. Fax 788-8493
Other Schools – See Wichita

Faith Lutheran S 200/PK-6
208 S Derby Ave 67037 316-788-1715
Paul Mieger, prin. Fax 789-0043
St. Mary's Parish Catholic S 300/PK-8
618 N Derby Ave 67037 316-788-3151
Richard Montgomery, prin. Fax 788-6895

De Soto, Johnson, Pop. 5,170
De Soto USD 232 5,600/K-12
35200 W 91st St 66018 913-667-6200
Dr. Ron Wimmer, supt. Fax 667-6201
www.usd232.org
Lexington Trails MS 500/6-8
8800 Penner Ave 66018 913-667-6260
Steve Ludwig, prin. Fax 667-6261
Starside ES 500/K-5
35400 W 91st St 66018 913-667-6270
Dr. Jessica Dain, prin. Fax 667-6271
Other Schools – See Lenexa, Shawnee

Dexter, Cowley, Pop. 350
Dexter USD 471 200/PK-12
PO Box 97 67038 620-876-5415
Ken Tarrant, supt. Fax 876-5548
www.usd471.org
Dexter ES 100/PK-6
PO Box 97 67038 620-876-5415
Robert Holmes, prin. Fax 876-5548

Dighton, Lane, Pop. 1,106
Dighton USD 482 300/PK-12
PO Box 878 67839 620-397-2835
Angela Lawrence, supt. Fax 397-5932
www.usd482.k12.ks.us/
Dighton ES 200/PK-6
PO Box 1029 67839 620-397-5319
Roger Timken, prin. Fax 397-5932

Dodge City, Ford, Pop. 26,104
Dodge City USD 443 5,700/K-12
PO Box 460 67801 620-227-1700
Alan Cunningham, supt. Fax 227-1695
www.usd443.org
Beeson ES 300/K-4
1700 W Beeson Rd 67801 620-227-1605
Annette Aldape, prin. Fax 227-1745
Central ES 300/K-4
1100 Central Ave 67801 620-227-1601
Kelly Bolin, prin. Fax 227-1721
Comanche Intermediate Center 600/5-6
1601 1st Ave 67801 620-227-1609
Marc Woofter, prin. Fax 339-4802
Dodge City MS 800/7-8
2000 6th Ave 67801 620-227-1610
Mike King, prin. Fax 227-1731
Linn ES 500/K-4
1900 Linn St 67801 620-227-1602
Chris Pyle, prin. Fax 227-1722
Miller ES 300/K-4
1100 Avenue G 67801 620-227-1603
Joyce Warshaw, prin. Fax 227-1723
Northwest ES 500/K-4
2100 6th Ave 67801 620-227-1604
Kathy Ramsour, prin. Fax 227-1724
Ross ES K-4
3001 6th Ave 67801 620-227-1780
Teri Merrifield, prin. Fax 227-1781
Soule Intermediate Center 300/5-6
401 Soule St 67801 620-227-1606
Greg Preston, prin. Fax 227-1719
Sunnyside ES 400/K-4
511 Sunnyside Ave 67801 620-227-1607
Patti Ansley, prin. Fax 227-1727
Wilroads Gardens ES 100/K-4
11558 E Main Rd 67801 620-227-1608
Bennie Bethea, prin. Fax 227-1728

Sacred Heart Cathedral S 300/K-8
905 Central Ave 67801 620-227-6532
Bonnie Schuette, lead tchr. Fax 227-3221

Douglass, Butler, Pop. 1,799
Douglass USD 396 800/PK-12
921 E 1st St 67039 316-747-3300
Robert Reynolds, supt. Fax 747-3305
www.usd396.net/
Seal ES 300/PK-5
320 S Chestnut St 67039 316-747-3350
Sandy Rusher, prin. Fax 747-3359
Sisk MS 200/6-8
950 E 1st St 67039 316-747-3340
Robert Swigart, prin. Fax 747-3346

Downs, Osborne, Pop. 938
Waconda USD 272
Supt. — See Cawker City
Lakeside ES @ Downs 50/K-3
817 College St 67437 785-454-3344
Jim Gierbrecht, prin. Fax 454-3747

Dwight, Morris, Pop. 332
Morris County USD 417
Supt. — See Council Grove
Prairie Heights ES 100/PK-4
PO Box 128 66849 785-482-3224
Cynthia Schrader, prin. Fax 499-5342

Easton, Leavenworth, Pop. 357
Easton USD 449 700/K-12
32502 Easton Rd 66020 913-651-9740
Charles Coblentz, supt. Fax 651-6740
www.easton449.org
Pleasant Ridge ES 200/K-3
20753 Easton Rd 66020 913-651-5595
Tim Beying, prin. Fax 758-1760
Pleasant Ridge MS 200/6-8
32504 Easton Rd 66020 913-651-5522
Lisa Powers, prin. Fax 651-0049
Other Schools – See Leavenworth

Edgerton, Johnson, Pop. 1,692
Gardner Edgerton USD 231
Supt. — See Gardner
Edgerton ES 200/PK-4
PO Box 256 66021 913-856-3500
Sharon Buffington, prin. Fax 856-3577

Edna, Labette, Pop. 422
Labette County USD 506
Supt. — See Altamont
Edna S 200/K-8
PO Box 220 67342 620-922-7210
Tim Traxson, prin. Fax 922-3417

Edwardsville, Wyandotte, Pop. 4,503
Bonner Springs USD 204
Supt. — See Bonner Springs
Edwardsville ES 500/K-5
1700 S 104th St 66111 913-422-4036
Aaron Miller, prin. Fax 422-7165

Effingham, Atchison, Pop. 582
Atchison County Community USD 377 400/PK-12
PO Box 289 66023 913-833-5050
Stephen Wiseman, supt. Fax 833-5210
www.usd377.org/
Atchison County Community IS 100/2-6
PO Box 289 66023 913-833-4420
Jamie Wetig, prin. Fax 833-4281
Atchison County Community PS 50/PK-1
PO Box 289 66023 913-833-2200
Tom Hinrichs, prin. Fax 833-5411

Elbing, Butler, Pop. 208

Berean Academy 300/K-12
201 S Elbing Rd 67041 316-799-2211
Terry Tilson, supt. Fax 799-2601

El Dorado, Butler, Pop. 12,659
Circle USD 375
Supt. — See Towanda
Oil Hill ES 200/K-6
2700 W 6th Ave 67042 316-320-9515
Michael Janzen, prin. Fax 321-2342

El Dorado USD 490 2,000/PK-12
124 W Central Ave 67042 316-322-4800
Sue Givens, supt. Fax 322-4801
www.eldoradoschools.org
El Dorado MS 500/6-8
500 W Central Ave 67042 316-322-4820
Mike Browne, prin. Fax 322-4821
Grandview ES 200/K-5
1300 Lawndale Ave 67042 316-322-4830
Kim McCune, prin. Fax 322-4831
Jefferson ES 200/K-2
1216 W 3rd Ave 67042 316-322-4840
Miles Harvey, prin. Fax 322-4841
Lincoln ES 200/3-5
522 W 5th Ave 67042 316-322-4850
Amy Clites, prin. Fax 322-4851
Skelly ES 200/PK-2
1421 W Towanda Ave 67042 316-322-4860
Linda Johnson, prin. Fax 322-4861
Washington ES 200/3-5
701 S Atchison St 67042 316-322-4870
Stan Ruff, prin. Fax 322-4871

Elkhart, Morton, Pop. 2,036
Elkhart USD 218 700/PK-12
PO Box 999 67950 620-697-2195
Nancy Crowell, supt. Fax 697-2607
www.usd218.org
Elkhart ES 300/PK-4
PO Box 778 67950 620-697-2133
Lynn Thrall, prin. Fax 697-2768
Elkhart MS 200/5-8
PO Box 999 67950 620-697-2197
Mark Lackey, prin. Fax 697-4828

Ellinwood, Barton, Pop. 2,119
Ellinwood USD 355 500/K-12
300 N Schiller Ave 67526 620-564-3226
Richard Goodschmidt, supt. Fax 564-2206
www.usd355.org/
Ellinwood ES 200/K-6
310 E 6th St 67526 620-564-2750
Eric Sjogren, prin. Fax 564-2667
Ellinwood MS 100/7-8
210 E 2nd St 67526 620-564-3136
Brian Rowley, prin. Fax 564-2816

St. Josephs S 100/K-8
111 W 3rd St 67526 620-564-2721
Marlene Clayton, lead tchr. Fax 564-2714

Ellis, Ellis, Pop. 1,812
Ellis USD 388 400/K-12
PO Box 256 67637 785-726-4281
Steve Taylor, supt. Fax 726-4677
www.usd388.k12.ks.us
Washington S 300/K-8
100 E 13th St 67637 785-726-3136
Larry Campbell, prin. Fax 726-3137

St. Marys S 100/K-6
605 Monroe St 67637 785-726-3185
James Moeder, prin. Fax 726-3166

Ellsworth, Ellsworth, Pop. 2,887
Ellsworth USD 327 600/K-12
PO Box 306 67439 785-472-5561
Ken Arnhold, supt. Fax 472-5563
www.usd327.org
Ellsworth ES 300/K-5
110 E 3rd St 67439 785-472-5554
Eric Reid, prin. Fax 472-8118
Other Schools – See Kanopolis

Elwood, Doniphan, Pop. 1,153
Elwood USD 486 300/PK-12
PO Box 368 66024 913-365-6735
Michael Newman, supt. Fax 365-3503
www.usd486.org/
Elwood S 200/PK-8
PO Box 368 66024 913-365-6735
Steve Taylor, prin. Fax 365-0012

Emmett, Pottawatomie, Pop. 270
Kaw Valley USD 321
Supt. — See Saint Marys
Emmett S 100/PK-8
PO Box 8 66422 785-535-2510
David Steele, prin. Fax 535-2161

Emporia, Lyon, Pop. 26,456
Emporia USD 253 4,500/PK-12
PO Box 1008 66801 620-341-2200
John Heim, supt. Fax 341-2205
www.usd253.org
Emporia MS 700/7-8
2300 Graphic Arts Rd 66801 620-341-2335
Steve Ternes, prin. Fax 341-2341
Logan Avenue ES 200/K-4
521 S East St 66801 620-341-2264
Jared Giffin, prin. Fax 341-2267
Lowther North IS 300/6-6
216 W 6th Ave 66801 620-341-2350
Wade Redeker, prin. Fax 341-2357
Lowther South IS 300/5-5
215 W 6th Ave 66801 620-341-2400
Jessica Griffin, prin. Fax 341-2444
Maynard ECC PK-PK
19 Constitution St 66801 620-341-2260
Allison Anderson, dir. Fax 341-2261
Riverside ES 300/K-4
327 S West St 66801 620-341-2276
John Wyrick, prin. Fax 341-2279
Timmerman ES 400/K-4
2901 Timmerman Dr 66801 620-341-2270
Kim Kirk, prin. Fax 341-2272
Village ES 400/K-4
2302 W 15th Ave 66801 620-341-2282
Wendy Moore, prin. Fax 341-2285
Walnut ES 200/K-4
801 Grove Ave 66801 620-341-2288
Ben Coltrane, prin. Fax 341-2291
White ES 200/K-4
902 Exchange St 66801 620-341-2294
Alberto Carrillo, prin. Fax 341-2296

Emporia Christian S 100/PK-8
1325 C of E Dr 66801 620-342-5353
James Sanborn, admin. Fax 342-8686
Sacred Heart S 100/PK-6
102 Cottonwood St 66801 620-343-7394
Theresa Lein, prin. Fax 343-7395

Enterprise, Dickinson, Pop. 811
Chapman USD 473
Supt. — See Chapman
Enterprise ES 100/K-5
PO Box 247 67441 785-263-8248
Luan Sparks, prin. Fax 263-8281

Enterprise Adventist S 50/1-8
PO Box 367 67441 785-263-8936
Joy Burton, lead tchr.

Erie, Neosho, Pop. 1,167
Erie-Galesburg USD 101 300/K-8
PO Box 137 66733 620-244-3264
Mike Carson, supt. Fax 244-3664
www.cusd101.org/
Erie S 300/K-8
PO Box 18 66733 620-244-5191
John Cole, prin. Fax 244-3560

Eskridge, Wabaunsee, Pop. 571
Mission Valley USD 330 500/K-12
PO Box 158 66423 785-449-2282
Jim Markos, supt. Fax 449-2669
www.mv330.org
Mission Valley S 300/K-8
12685 Mission Valley Rd 66423 785-449-2281
Braden Anshutz, prin. Fax 449-2436

Eudora, Douglas, Pop. 5,284
Eudora USD 491 1,300/PK-12
PO Box 500 66025 785-542-4910
Don Grosdidier, supt. Fax 542-4909
www.eudoraschools.org/
Eudora MS 300/6-8
PO Box 701 66025 785-542-4960
Richard Proffitt, prin. Fax 542-4970
Eudora West ES 300/3-5
PO Box 602 66025 785-542-4940
Jan Irby, prin. Fax 542-4950
Nottingham ES 300/PK-2
PO Box 711 66025 785-542-4920
Jim Lauer, prin. Fax 542-4930

Eureka, Greenwood, Pop. 2,739
Eureka USD 389 700/PK-12
216 N Main St 67045 620-583-5588
Randy Corns, supt. Fax 583-8200
www.389ks.org
Marshall ES 300/PK-6
1015 N Jefferson St 67045 620-583-5537
Robert Leis, prin. Fax 583-8206

Yates Memorial SDA S 50/K-8
PO Box 307 67045 620-583-7529
Marva Lee Purkypile, lead tchr.

Everest, Brown, Pop. 304
South Brown County USD 430
Supt. — See Horton
Everest MS 200/5-8
713 S 7th St 66424 785-548-7536
Jackie Wenger, prin. Fax 548-7538

Fontana, Miami, Pop. 169
Prairie View USD 362
Supt. — See La Cygne
Fontana ES 100/K-5
PO Box 109 66026 913-849-3141
Mark Staab, prin. Fax 849-3289

Fort Leavenworth, Leavenworth, Pop. 1,300
Ft. Leavenworth USD 207 1,700/K-9
207 Education Way 66027 913-651-7373
Deborah Baeuchle, supt. Fax 758-6010
www.ftlvn.com
Bradley ES 400/K-6
1 Bradley Cir 66027 913-651-6915
Brian Schwanz, prin. Fax 758-6090
Eisenhower ES 500/K-6
1 Eisenhower Cir 66027 913-651-6663
Marlene Black, prin. Fax 758-6077
MacArthur ES 400/K-6
1 McArthur Cir 66027 913-651-6517
Dr. Jeanne Berg, prin. Fax 758-6028

Fort Riley, Geary, Pop. 112
Geary County USD 475
Supt. — See Junction City
Custer Hill ES 300/K-5
6344 Hampton Pl 66442 785-717-4320
Melanie Laster, prin. Fax 717-4321
Fort Riley ES 300/K-5
104 Morris Ave 66442 785-717-4450
Becky Lay, prin. Fax 717-4451
Fort Riley MS 600/6-8
4020 1st Division Rd 66442 785-717-4500
Joseph Handlos, prin. Fax 717-4501
Jefferson ES 300/PK-5
4720 Jackson Ave 66442 785-717-4550
Vern Steffens, prin. Fax 717-4551
Morris Hill ES 200/K-5
4400 1st Division Rd 66442 785-717-4650
Greg Lumb, prin. Fax 717-4651
Ware ES 500/PK-5
6795 Thomas Ave 66442 785-717-4600
Deb Gustafson, prin. Fax 717-4601

Fort Scott, Bourbon, Pop. 7,990
Ft. Scott USD 234 1,900/PK-12
424 S Main St 66701 620-223-0800
Dr. Rick Werling, supt. Fax 223-2760
www.usd234.org
Fort Scott MS 400/6-8
1105 E 12th St 66701 620-223-3262
Barbara Albright, prin. Fax 223-8946
Scott ES 400/PK-5
316 W 10th St 66701 620-223-0450
David Elliott, prin. Fax 223-6420
Ware ES 500/PK-5
900 E 3rd St 66701 620-223-3380
Billie Jo Drake, prin. Fax 223-1531

Fort Scott Christian Heights S 100/K-12
1101 S Barbee St 66701 620-223-4330
Terry Chance, prin. Fax 223-2721
St. Mary's Catholic S 50/PK-5
702 S Eddy St 66701 620-223-6060
Krista Gorman, prin. Fax 223-6060

Fowler, Meade, Pop. 578
Fowler USD 225 200/PK-12
PO Box 170 67844 620-646-5661
Sam Seybold, supt. Fax 646-5713
www.usd225.org/
Fowler ES 100/PK-6
PO Box 170 67844 620-646-5234
Sam Seybold, prin. Fax 646-5862

Frankfort, Marshall, Pop. 795
Vermillion USD 380
Supt. — See Vermillion
Frankfort ES 100/PK-6
PO Box 203 66427 785-292-4486
Dean Dalinghaus, prin. Fax 292-4636

Fredonia, Wilson, Pop. 2,455
Fredonia USD 484 800/PK-12
PO Box 539 66736 620-378-4177
Jim Porter, supt. Fax 378-4345
www.fredoniaks.com
Fredonia MS 200/6-8
203 N 8th St 66736 620-378-4167
Laura Fitzmorris, prin. Fax 378-3635
Lincoln ES 300/PK-5
713 N 9th St 66736 620-378-4138
Aaron Chard, prin. Fax 378-3707

Frontenac, Crawford, Pop. 3,101
Frontenac USD 249 800/PK-12
208 S Cayuga St 66763 620-231-7551
Destry Brown, supt. Fax 231-1312
www.frontenac249.org
Frontenac JHS 100/7-8
208 S Cayuga St 66763 620-231-7550
Ted Hessong, prin. Fax 231-2043
Layden ES 500/PK-6
200 E Lanyon St 66763 620-231-7790
Mark Allai, prin. Fax 231-3727

Galena, Cherokee, Pop. 3,163
Galena USD 499 700/PK-12
702 E 7th St 66739 620-783-4499
Brian Smith, supt. Fax 783-5547
www.usd499.org
Galena MS 200/6-8
702 E 7th St 66739 620-783-4499
Danny Albright, prin. Fax 783-5214
Liberty ES 200/3-5
702 E 7th St 66739 620-783-4499
Susan New, prin. Fax 783-5433
Spring Grove ES 200/PK-2
702 E 7th St 66739 620-783-2555
Toby VanCleave, prin. Fax 783-2804

Galva, McPherson, Pop. 773
Canton-Galva USD 419
Supt. — See Canton
Canton-Galva MS 200/4-8
PO Box 96 67443 620-654-3321
Jim Struber, prin. Fax 654-3335

Garden City, Finney, Pop. 27,098
Garden City USD 457 7,100/PK-12
1205 Fleming St 67846 620-805-7000
Dr. Richard Atha, supt. Fax 805-7190
www.gckschools.com
Barker ES 100/K-6
5585 N Jennie Barker Rd 67846 620-805-7700
Melinda Stewart, prin. Fax 805-7748
Brown ES 300/PK-4
1110 E Pine St 67846 620-805-7200
Julie Koerperich, prin. Fax 805-7298
Buffalo Jones ES 300/PK-4
708 N Taylor Ave 67846 620-805-7300
Rafaela Solis, prin. Fax 805-7348
Garfield ES 300/PK-4
121 W Walnut St 67846 620-805-7500
Willis Pracht, prin. Fax 805-7548
Henderson MS 500/7-8
2406 Fleming St 67846 620-805-8500
Jessica Bird, prin. Fax 805-8598
Hubert MS 500/7-8
1205 A St 67846 620-805-8400
Brad Springston, prin. Fax 805-8497
Matthews ES 200/PK-4
111 E Johnson St 67846 620-805-7550
Carma Harman, prin. Fax 805-7598
Ornelas ES 500/PK-4
3401 E Spruce St 67846 620-805-7900
Heath Hogan, prin. Fax 805-7998
Plymell ES 100/K-6
20 W Plymell Rd 67846 620-805-7800
Martha Darter, prin. Fax 805-7848
Russell Child Development Center PK-PK
714 Ballinger St 67846 620-275-0291
Deanna Berry, prin. Fax 275-0364
Scheuerman ES 300/K-4
1901 W Wilcox St 67846 620-805-7350
Sandra Almos, prin. Fax 805-7398
Sitts Intermediate Center 500/5-6
3101 N Belmont Pl 67846 620-805-8200
Barbara Hauschild, prin. Fax 805-8298
Stones Intermediate Center 500/5-6
401 N Jennie Barker Rd 67846 620-805-8300
Janet Smith, prin. Fax 805-8398
Walker ES 300/PK-4
805 W Fair St 67846 620-805-7600
Suzanne Smith, prin. Fax 805-7698
Wilson ES 500/PK-4
1709 E Labrador Blvd 67846 620-805-7400
Connie Pracht, prin. Fax 805-7498
Wilson ES 200/PK-4
1401 Harding Ave 67846 620-805-7750
Bonita Green, prin. Fax 805-7798

Bible Christian Academy 100/PK-6
1404 E Mary St 67846 620-275-2816
Vestal Teeter, dir. Fax 276-2660
High Plains Christian S 50/1-8
2710 N Fleming St 67846 620-275-9356
Harold Reynolds, prin.
St. Dominic S 200/PK-6
617 J C St 67846 620-276-8981
Trina Delgado, prin. Fax 276-2086
St. Mary S 200/K-6
503 Saint John St 67846 620-276-2241
Trina Delgado, prin. Fax 272-7067

Garden Plain, Sedgwick, Pop. 823
Renwick USD 267
Supt. — See Andale
Garden Plain S 400/K-8
PO Box 375 67050 316-531-2261
J. Michael Kimberlin, prin. Fax 535-8868

Gardner, Johnson, Pop. 14,317
Gardner Edgerton USD 231 3,400/PK-12
PO Box 97 66030 913-856-2000
Dr. Bill Gilhaus, supt. Fax 856-7330
www.usd231.com
Gardner ES 400/K-4
218 E Shawnee St 66030 913-856-3300
Pam Tate, prin. Fax 856-3385
Madison ES 400/K-4
800 W Madison St 66030 913-856-0400
Christy Whitter, prin. Fax 856-0490
Moonlight ES 400/K-4
17960 S Moonlight Rd 66030 913-856-3100
Ryan Horne, prin. Fax 856-3136
Nike ES K-4
19500 S Gardner Rd 66030 913-856-3000
Lana Gerber, prin. Fax 856-3085
Pioneer Ridge MS 5-8
16200 S Kill Creek Rd 66030 913-856-3850
Lachelle Sigg, prin. Fax 856-3694
Sunflower ES 400/K-4
775 N Center St 66030 913-856-3700
Dustin Mortenson, prin. Fax 856-3790
Wheatridge MS 600/5-8
318 E Washington St 66030 913-856-2900
G. A. Buie, prin. Fax 856-2980
Other Schools – See Edgerton

Garnett, Anderson, Pop. 3,338
Garnett USD 365 1,200/K-12
PO Box 328 66032 785-448-6155
Donald Blome, supt. Fax 448-6157
www.usd365.org
Garnett Elementary Center 300/2-6
305 N Oak St 66032 785-448-3177
Debbie Alford, prin. Fax 448-6861
Irving Primary Center 100/K-1
212 S Pine St 66032 785-448-5434
Krista Hedrick, prin. Fax 448-3902
Other Schools – See Greeley, Welda, Westphalia

St. Rose Duschene S 100/1-8
530 E 4th Ave 66032 785-448-3423
Nancy Butters, prin. Fax 448-3164

Girard, Crawford, Pop. 2,686
Girard USD 248 1,000/PK-12
415 N Summit St 66743 620-724-4325
Gary Snawder, supt. Fax 724-8446
www.girard248.org/
Girard MS 300/6-8
415 N Summit St 66743 620-724-4114
Randy Heatherly, prin. Fax 724-4610
Haderlein ES 500/PK-5
415 N Summit St 66743 620-724-4327
Dan Duling, prin. Fax 724-6266

Glasco, Cloud, Pop. 504
Southern Cloud USD 334 200/K-12
PO Box 427 67445 785-568-2247
Roger Perkins, supt. Fax 568-2298
www.usd334.org/miltonvale/
Glasco S 100/K-8
PO Box 158 67445 785-568-2291
David Blochlinger, prin. Fax 568-2298
Other Schools – See Miltonvale

Glen Elder, Mitchell, Pop. 399
Waconda USD 272
Supt. — See Cawker City
Lakeside ES @ Glen Elder 50/K-3
PO Box 238 67446 785-545-3522
Robert Green, prin. Fax 545-3542

Goddard, Sedgwick, Pop. 3,337
Goddard USD 265 4,200/K-12
PO Box 249 67052 316-794-4000
Charles Edmonds, supt. Fax 794-2222
www.goddardusd.com
Challenger IS 400/5-6
PO Box 277 67052 316-794-4040
Jeff Hersh, prin. Fax 794-4266
Davidson ES 400/K-4
PO Box 278 67052 316-794-4260
Ruth Wood, prin. Fax 794-4280
Discovery IS 400/5-6
PO Box 248 67052 316-794-4030
Kevin Mckay, prin. Fax 794-4266
Earhart ES 500/K-4
PO Box 319 67052 316-794-4080
Natalie Rust, prin. Fax 794-4062
Eisenhower MS 300/7-8
PO Box 349 67052 316-794-4150
Jerold Longabaugh, prin. Fax 794-4063
Explorer ES K-4
PO Box 217 67052 316-794-4181
Don Howell, prin. Fax 794-4182
Goddard MS 400/7-8
PO Box 279 67052 316-794-4230
Lisa Hogarth, prin. Fax 794-4254

Oak Street ES 400/K-4
PO Box 188 67052 316-794-4200
Ashley Miller, prin. Fax 794-4220

Holy Spirit Catholic S 100/K-8
18218 W US Highway 54 67052 316-794-8139
Kelly Bright, prin. Fax 794-2055

Goessel, Marion, Pop. 547
Goessel USD 411 300/K-12
PO Box 68 67053 620-367-4601
John Fast, supt. Fax 367-4603
www.usd411.org
Goessel ES 100/K-5
PO Box 68 67053 620-367-8118
John Fast, prin. Fax 367-8156

Goodland, Sherman, Pop. 4,485
Goodland USD 352 800/PK-12
PO Box 509 67735 785-890-2397
Shelly Angelos, supt. Fax 890-8504
www.usd352.k12.ks.us
Central ES 100/3-4
PO Box 509 67735 785-890-6558
Harvey Swager, prin. Fax 890-8536
Grant JHS 100/7-8
PO Box 509 67735 785-890-7561
Steve Raymer, prin. Fax 890-8525
North ES 100/5-6
PO Box 509 67735 785-890-3912
James Mull, prin. Fax 890-8543
West ES 200/PK-2
PO Box 509 67735 785-890-6163
Verna Milnes, prin. Fax 890-8526

Grainfield, Gove, Pop. 298
Wheatland USD 292 100/PK-12
PO Box 165 67737 785-673-4213
Darrin Herl, supt. Fax 673-4234
www.usd292.org
Wheatland ES K-6
PO Box 174 67737 785-673-4365
Darrin Herl, prin. Fax 673-4371
Wheatland Preschool 50/PK-PK
PO Box 174 67737 785-673-4204
Darrin Herl, prin. Fax 673-4371

Great Bend, Barton, Pop. 15,440
Great Bend USD 428 3,000/PK-12
201 S Patton Rd 67530 620-793-1500
Dr. Thomas Vernon, supt. Fax 793-1585
www.usd428.net
Eisenhower ES 300/K-6
1212 Garfield St 67530 620-793-1501
Tricia Reiser, prin. Fax 793-1644
Great Bend MS 500/7-8
1919 Harrison St 67530 620-793-1510
David Reiser, prin. Fax 793-1549
Jefferson ES 300/K-6
2716 24th St 67530 620-793-1502
Art Baker, prin. Fax 793-1588
Lincoln ES 300/K-6
5630 Broadway Ave 67530 620-793-1503
Alvena Spangenberg, prin. Fax 793-1612
Park ES 200/K-6
1801 Williams St 67530 620-793-1505
Mike Young, prin. Fax 793-1545
Riley ES 400/PK-6
1515 10th St 67530 620-793-1506
Laura Blevins, prin. Fax 793-1544

Central Kansas Christian Academy 100/K-8
215 McKinley St 67530 620-792-3477
Jane Thier, admin. Fax 793-3438
Great Bend SDA S 50/K-8
7 SW 30 Ave 67530 620-793-9247
Holy Family S 200/K-6
4200 Broadway Ave 67530 620-793-3265
Karen Moeder, prin. Fax 792-1397

Greeley, Anderson, Pop. 333
Garnett USD 365
Supt. — See Garnett
Greeley ES 100/K-6
101 S Mary 66033 785-867-3460
Alan Quaintance, prin. Fax 867-2420

Greensburg, Kiowa, Pop. 1,398
Greensburg USD 422 300/PK-12
600 S Main St 67054 620-723-2145
Darin Headrick, supt. Fax 723-2705
www.usd422.org
Day S 200/PK-8
600 S Main St 67054 620-723-2332
Staci Derstein, prin. Fax 723-7082

Gridley, Coffey, Pop. 365
Le Roy-Gridley USD 245
Supt. — See Le Roy
Gridley ES 50/PK-4
PO Box 426 66852 620-836-2182
Gary Haehn, prin. Fax 836-4041
Southern Coffey County JHS 100/5-8
PO Box 426 66852 620-836-2151
Gary Haehn, prin. Fax 836-4041

Grinnell, Gove, Pop. 299
Grinnell USD 291 100/K-8
PO Box 68 67738 785-824-3277
Rose Kane, supt. Fax 824-3215
skyways.lib.ks.us/kansas/schools/grinnell/
Grinnell ES 50/K-4
PO Box 129 67738 785-824-3296
Rose Kane, prin. Fax 824-3215
Grinnell MS 50/5-8
PO Box 68 67738 785-824-3277
Rose Kane, prin. Fax 824-3215

Gypsum, Saline, Pop. 399
Southeast of Saline USD 306 700/K-12
5056 E Highway K4 67448 785-536-4291
Justin Henry, supt. Fax 536-4247
www.usd306.k12.ks.us
Southeast Saline ES 300/K-6
5056 E Highway K4 67448 785-536-4215
Sharlene Ramsey, prin. Fax 536-4292

Halstead, Harvey, Pop. 1,912
Halstead USD 440 800/K-12
521 W 6th St 67056 316-835-2641
Dr. Tom Bishard, supt. Fax 835-2305
www.usd440.com
Halstead MS 300/4-8
221 W 6th St 67056 316-835-2694
Matt McKee, prin. Fax 835-2469
Other Schools – See Bentley

Hamilton, Greenwood, Pop. 325
Hamilton USD 390 100/K-12
2596 W Rd N 66853 620-678-3244
Richard Stapp, supt. Fax 678-3321
www.hamilton390.net
Hamilton ES 50/K-6
2596 W Rd N 66853 620-678-3410
Richard Stapp, prin. Fax 678-3321

Hanover, Washington, Pop. 593
Barnes USD 223
Supt. — See Barnes
Hanover S 200/PK-8
209 E North St 66945 785-337-2281
Val Converse, prin. Fax 337-2307

St. Johns S 100/1-8
100 S Church St 66945 785-337-2368
Timothy Rundle, prin. Fax 337-8950

Hanston, Hodgeman, Pop. 262
Pawnee Heights USD 496
Supt. — See Burdett
Hanston JHS 50/6-8
PO Box 219 67849 620-623-2611
Fax 623-4488

Harper, Harper, Pop. 1,478
Anthony-Harper USD 361
Supt. — See Anthony
Harper S 300/K-8
1317 Walnut St 67058 620-896-7614
Bill Giesen, prin. Fax 896-7983

Hartford, Lyon, Pop. 505
Southern Lyon County USD 252 600/PK-12
PO Box 278 66854 620-392-5519
Michael Argabright, supt. Fax 392-5841
www.usd252.org/
Other Schools – See Neosho Rapids, Olpe

Haven, Reno, Pop. 1,170
Haven USD 312 900/K-12
PO Box 130 67543 620-465-7727
Dr. Patrick Call, supt. Fax 465-3595
www.havenschools.com
Haven ES 300/K-6
PO Box 489 67543 620-465-2501
Brad Miller, prin. Fax 465-2775
Haven MS 100/7-8
PO Box B 67543 620-465-2587
Tracy Giddens, prin. Fax 465-2588
Other Schools – See Mount Hope, Partridge

St. Paul Lutheran S 50/PK-PK
8403 E Arlington Rd 67543 620-465-3425
Hollie Judd, prin. Fax 465-3425

Haviland, Kiowa, Pop. 574
Haviland USD 474 100/K-12
PO Box 243 67059 620-862-5256
John Wyrick, supt. Fax 862-5257
www.usd474.org/
Haviland S 100/K-8
PO Box 243 67059 620-862-5277
Clint Corby, prin. Fax 862-5260

Hays, Ellis, Pop. 19,632
Hays USD 489 2,800/K-12
323 W 12th St 67601 785-623-2400
Fred Kaufman, supt. Fax 623-2409
www.usd489.com/
Felten MS 500/6-8
201 E 29th St 67601 785-623-2450
Craig Pallister, prin. Fax 623-2456
Kennedy MS 200/6-8
1309 Fort St 67601 785-623-2470
Lee Keffer, prin. Fax 623-2476
Lincoln ES 200/K-5
1906 Ash St 67601 785-623-2500
Elaine Rohleder, prin. Fax 623-2507
McCarthy ES 300/K-5
1401 Hall St 67601 785-623-2510
Nancy Harman, prin. Fax 623-2518
Roosevelt ES 300/K-5
2000 MacArthur Rd 67601 785-623-2520
Janci Kugler, prin. Fax 623-2526
Washington ES 100/K-5
305 Main St 67601 785-623-2540
Allen Park, prin. Fax 623-2544
Wilson ES 300/K-5
101 E 28th St 67601 785-623-2550
Tom Meagher, prin. Fax 623-2556
Other Schools – See Munjor

Holy Family S 300/PK-6
1800 Milner St 67601 785-625-3131
Jana Simon, prin. Fax 625-2098
Maranatha Christian S 50/K-8
1410 Toulon Ave 67601 785-625-3975
Rita Spears, prin.

Haysville, Sedgwick, Pop. 9,817
Haysville USD 261 4,700/PK-12
1745 W Grand Ave 67060 316-554-2200
Dr. John Burke, supt. Fax 554-2230
www.usd261.com
Freeman ES 500/PK-5
7303 S Meridian St 67060 316-554-2265
Andria Williams, prin. Fax 554-2295
Haysville ECC PK-PK
7101 S Meridian St 67060 316-554-2233
Becky Cezar, prin. Fax 529-3520
Haysville MS 1,100/6-8
900 W Grand Ave 67060 316-554-2251
Dr. Mike Maurer, prin. Fax 554-2258
Haysville West MS 6-8
1956 W Grand Ave 67060 316-554-2370
Ildo Martins, prin. Fax 554-2377
Nelson ES 500/PK-5
245 N Delos Ave 67060 316-554-2273
Mike Mitchener, prin. Fax 554-2275
Prairie ES PK-5
7101 S Meridian St 67060 316-554-2350
Dr. Marcy Aycock, prin. Fax 554-2357
Rex ES 500/PK-5
1100 W Grand Ave 67060 316-554-2281
Brian Howard, prin. Fax 554-2043
Other Schools – See Wichita

St. Cecilia Catholic S 100/PK-8
1912 W Grand Ave 67060 316-522-0461
Winston Kenton, prin. Fax 524-6183

Healy, Lane
Healy USD 468 100/K-12
5006 N Dodge Rd 67850 620-398-2248
John LaFave, supt. Fax 398-2435
Healy ES 50/K-6
5006 N Dodge Rd 67850 620-398-2248
John LaFave, prin. Fax 398-2435

Herington, Dickinson, Pop. 2,468
Herington USD 487 500/PK-12
19 N Broadway 67449 785-258-2263
John Thissen, supt. Fax 258-2982
www.heringtonschools.org
Herington ES 200/PK-5
201 E Hawley St 67449 785-258-3234
Rich DeMont, prin. Fax 258-2915
Herington MS 100/6-8
1317 N D St 67449 785-258-2448
Steve Mies, prin. Fax 258-3976

Hesston, Harvey, Pop. 3,631
Hesston USD 460 800/K-12
PO Box 2000 67062 620-327-4931
Steve Woolf, supt. Fax 327-7157
www.hesstonschools.org
Hesston ES 300/K-4
PO Box 2000 67062 620-327-7102
Patrick Duffy, prin. Fax 327-7153
Hesston MS 300/5-8
PO Box 2000 67062 620-327-7111
Randy Linton, prin. Fax 327-7115

Hiawatha, Brown, Pop. 3,236
Hiawatha USD 415 900/K-12
PO Box 398 66434 785-742-2266
John Severin, supt. Fax 742-2301
www.hiawathaschools.org/
Hiawatha ES 300/K-4
600 Miami St 66434 785-742-7181
Tom Schmitz, prin. Fax 742-2545
Hiawatha MS 300/5-8
307 S Morrill Ave 66434 785-742-4172
David Coufal, prin. Fax 742-1744

Highland, Doniphan, Pop. 941
Highland USD 425 200/K-12
PO Box 8 66035 785-442-3286
Rex Bollinger, supt. Fax 442-3289
www.doniphanwest.org/
Highland ES 100/K-5
PO Box 308 66035 785-442-3671
Cathy Gunderson, prin. Fax 442-3663

Hill City, Graham, Pop. 1,451
Graham County USD 281 400/PK-12
PO Box 309 67642 785-421-2135
Jim Hickel, supt. Fax 421-5657
www.usd281.com/
Hill City ES 200/PK-4
216 N 4th Ave 67642 785-421-3425
Bill Goodwin, prin. Fax 421-4144
Longfellow MS 100/5-8
203 N 2nd Ave 67642 785-421-3451
Bill Goodwin, prin. Fax 421-6395

Hillsboro, Marion, Pop. 2,731
Durham-Hillsboro-Lehigh USD 410 700/K-12
812 E A St 67063 620-947-3184
Doug Huxman, supt. Fax 947-3475
www.usd410.net
Hillsboro ES 300/K-5
812 E A St 67063 620-947-3981
Evan Yoder, prin. Fax 947-3263
Hillsboro MS 200/6-8
400 E Grand Ave 67063 620-947-3297
Greg Brown, prin. Fax 947-5565

Hillsdale, Miami
Paola USD 368
Supt. — See Paola
Hillsdale ES 200/PK-5
PO Box 98 66036 913-294-8060
Amy Hastert, prin. Fax 294-8061

Hoisington, Barton, Pop. 2,996
Hoisington USD 431 500/PK-12
165 W 3rd St 67544 620-653-4134
Bill Lowry, supt. Fax 653-4073
www.usd431.net/

Hoisington MS 100/5-8
360 W 11th St 67544 620-653-4951
Patricia Reinhardt, prin. Fax 653-4483
Lincoln ES 50/3-4
516 N Pine St 67544 620-653-4549
Alan Charles, prin. Fax 653-4384
Roosevelt ES 100/PK-2
315 N Vine St 67544 620-653-4470
Alan Charles, prin. Fax 653-4394

Holcomb, Finney, Pop. 1,888
Holcomb USD 363 900/PK-12
PO Box 8 67851 620-277-2629
Robert O'Connor, supt. Fax 277-2010
users.pld.com/holcomb
Holcomb ES 100/4-5
PO Box 1025 67851 620-277-2257
Phil Keidel, prin. Fax 277-0239
Holcomb MS 200/6-8
PO Box 89 67851 620-277-2699
Kristin Ellis, prin. Fax 277-0239
Wiley ES 300/PK-3
PO Box 37 67851 620-277-4431
Phil Keidel, prin. Fax 277-4424

Holton, Jackson, Pop. 3,400
Holton USD 336 1,100/PK-12
PO Box 352 66436 785-364-3650
Dr. Jim Karleskint, supt. Fax 364-3975
www.holton.k12.ks.us
Central ES 300/3-5
415 New Jersey Ave 66436 785-364-2051
Kathy Cooney, prin. Fax 364-3529
Colorado ES 200/PK-2
500 Colorado Ave 66436 785-364-3251
Mark Wilson, prin. Fax 364-4844
Holton MS 300/6-8
900 Iowa Ave 66436 785-364-2441
Ralph Blevins, prin. Fax 364-5460

North Jackson USD 335 400/PK-12
12692 266th Rd 66436 785-364-2194
Paul Becker, supt. Fax 364-4346
www.jhcobras.net
Jackson Heights S 300/PK-8
12763 266th Rd 66436 785-364-2244
Adrianne McDaniel, prin. Fax 364-4712

Holyrood, Ellsworth, Pop. 452
Lorraine USD 328
Supt. — See Lorraine
Quivira Heights S 200/PK-8
600 S Main St 67450 785-252-3666
Jeff Potter, prin. Fax 252-3653

Hope, Dickinson, Pop. 367
Rural Vista USD 481 500/PK-12
PO Box 217 67451 785-366-7215
Renae Hickert, supt. Fax 366-7217
www.usd481.org
Hope S 200/PK-8
PO Box 218 67451 785-366-7221
Ethan Gruen, prin. Fax 366-7115
Other Schools – See White City

Horton, Brown, Pop. 1,843
South Brown County USD 430 600/PK-12
522 Central Ave 66439 785-486-2611
Dr. Steven Davies, supt. Fax 486-2496
usd430.k12.ks.us
Horton ES 200/PK-4
300 E 16th St 66439 785-486-2616
Charles Patry, prin. Fax 486-2527
Other Schools – See Everest

Howard, Elk, Pop. 764
West Elk USD 282 400/PK-12
PO Box 607 67349 620-374-2113
Corey Reese, supt. Fax 374-2414
Other Schools – See Moline, Severy

Hoxie, Sheridan, Pop. 1,149
Hoxie USD 412 300/PK-12
PO Box 348 67740 785-675-3258
Scott Hoyt, supt. Fax 675-2126
www.hoxie.org/
Hoxie ES 200/PK-6
PO Box 969 67740 785-675-3254
Scott Hoyt, prin. Fax 675-2126

Hoyt, Jackson, Pop. 600
Royal Valley USD 337
Supt. — See Mayetta
Royal Valley ES 300/PK-4
PO Box 68 66440 785-986-6286
Susan Pfrang, prin. Fax 986-6333

Hugoton, Stevens, Pop. 3,644
Hugoton USD 210 700/PK-12
205 E 6th St 67951 620-544-4397
Mark Crawford, supt. Fax 544-7138
www.usd210.org
Hugoton IS 3-6
304 E 6th St 67951 620-544-4376
Mark Newton, prin. Fax 544-4871
Hugoton MS 100/7-8
115 W 11th St 67951 620-544-4341
Mischel Miller, prin. Fax 544-4856
Hugoton PS 300/PK-2
304 E 6th St 67951 620-544-4376
Tiffany Boxum, prin. Fax 544-4871

Heritage Christian Academy 100/PK-6
PO Box 744 67951 620-544-7005
Debbie Eshbaugh, admin. Fax 544-8748

Humboldt, Allen, Pop. 1,921
Humboldt USD 258 500/K-12
801 New York St 66748 620-473-3121
Robert Heigele, supt. Fax 473-2023
www.usd258.net
Humboldt ES 200/K-5
1100 Central St 66748 620-473-2461
Kay Bolt, prin. Fax 473-2642
Humboldt MS 100/6-8
1105 Bridge St 66748 620-473-3348
K.B. Criss, prin. Fax 473-3141

Hutchinson, Reno, Pop. 40,961
Buhler USD 313
Supt. — See Buhler
Obee ES 200/PK-6
4712 E 4th Ave 67501 620-662-2561
Mike Bryan, prin. Fax 694-1045
Prairie Hills MS 300/7-8
3200 Lucille Dr 67502 620-662-6027
E. Craig Williams, prin. Fax 694-1002
Prosperity ES 200/4-6
4601 N Plum St 67502 620-662-5535
Randy Doerksen, prin. Fax 694-1032
Union Valley ES 400/PK-3
2501 E 30th Ave 67502 620-662-4891
Randy Roberts, prin. Fax 694-1022

Hutchinson USD 308 4,100/K-12
PO Box 1908 67504 620-665-4400
Dr. David Flowers, supt. Fax 665-4497
www.usd308.com/
Avenue A ES 200/K-6
111 S Madison St 67501 620-665-4610
Beth Redinger, prin. Fax 665-4612
Faris ES 200/K-6
300 E 9th Ave 67501 620-665-4620
Denise Neighbors, prin. Fax 665-4625
Graber ES 300/K-6
1600 N Cleveland St 67501 620-665-4630
Jo McFadden, prin. Fax 665-4633
Hutchinson Magnet S at Allen 300/K-6
403 W 10th Ave 67501 620-665-4600
Stan Ploutz, prin. Fax 665-4602
Hutchinson MS 7 7-7
210 E Avenue A 67501 620-665-4800
Mike Ellegood, prin. Fax 665-4806
Hutchinson MS 8 300/8-8
200 W 14th Ave 67501 620-665-4700
Mike Ellegood, prin. Fax 665-4703
Lincoln ES 200/K-6
315 E Bigger St 67501 620-665-4650
Ron Brummett, prin. Fax 665-4656
McCandless ES 400/K-6
700 N Baker St 67501 620-665-4660
Glenn Owen, prin. Fax 665-4669
Morgan ES 500/K-6
100 W 27th Ave 67502 620-665-4670
Rod Rathbun, prin. Fax 665-4673
Wiley ES 300/K-6
900 W 21st Ave 67502 620-665-4685
Cindy Cooprider, prin. Fax 665-4688

Nickerson USD 309 1,200/K-12
4501 W 4th Ave 67501 620-663-7141
Jerry Burch, supt. Fax 663-7148
www.usd309ks.org
Reno Valley MS 200/7-8
1616 Wilshire Dr 67501 620-662-4573
Vince Naccarato, prin. Fax 662-6708
Other Schools – See Nickerson, South Hutchinson

Central Christian S 200/PK-12
1910 E 30th Ave 67502 620-663-2174
Ken Anderson, admin. Fax 663-2176
Holy Cross Catholic S 300/PK-6
2633 Independence Rd 67502 620-665-6168
Kevin Hedrick, prin. Fax 665-0368
St. Teresa Catholic S 200/PK-6
215 E 5th Ave 67501 620-662-5601
Ellen Albert, prin. Fax 662-5601

Independence, Montgomery, Pop. 9,284
Independence USD 446 1,900/K-12
PO Box 487 67301 620-332-1800
Chuck Schmidt, supt. Fax 332-1811
www.indyschools.com
Eisenhower ES 400/K-2
501 Spruce St 67301 620-332-1854
Brad Carroll, prin. Fax 332-1859
Independence MS 400/6-8
300 W Locust St 67301 620-332-1836
Mark Hayward, prin. Fax 332-1841
Lincoln ES 300/3-4
701 W Laurel St 67301 620-332-1847
Rick Boyer, prin. Fax 332-1851
Washington ES 100/5-5
300 E Myrtle St 67301 620-332-1875
Debra Toomey, prin. Fax 332-1878

Independence Bible S 200/PK-12
2246 S 10th St 67301 620-331-3780
Matthew Brewer, prin. Fax 331-3781
St. Andrew Catholic S 200/PK-8
215 N Park Blvd 67301 620-331-2870
Becky Brown, prin. Fax 331-6496
Zion Lutheran S 100/PK-8
301 S 11th St 67301 620-332-3331
Dawn Oldenettel, prin. Fax 332-3330

Ingalls, Gray, Pop. 312
Ingalls USD 477 300/PK-12
PO Box 99 67853 620-335-5136
Dave Novack, supt. Fax 335-5678
www.ingallsusd477.com/
Ingalls ES 100/PK-5
PO Box 99 67853 620-335-5134
Dave Novack, prin. Fax 335-5678

Inman, McPherson, Pop. 1,194
Inman USD 448 400/PK-12
PO Box 129 67546 620-585-6424
Kevin Case, supt. Fax 585-2689
www.usd448.com/
Inman ES 200/PK-6
PO Box 277 67546 620-585-6555
Sharon Brannan, prin. Fax 585-6647

Iola, Allen, Pop. 6,008
Iola USD 257 1,300/K-12
408 N Cottonwood St 66749 620-365-4700
Dr. Craig Neuenswander, supt. Fax 365-4708
www.usd257.org
Iola MS 300/6-8
600 East St 66749 620-365-4785
Jack Stanley, prin. Fax 365-4770
Jefferson ES 200/K-5
300 S Jefferson Ave 66749 620-365-4840
Brad Crusinbery, prin. Fax 365-4845
Lincoln ES 200/K-5
700 N Jefferson Ave 66749 620-365-4820
Larry Hart, prin. Fax 365-4829
McKinley ES 100/K-5
209 S Kentucky St 66749 620-365-4860
Lori Maxwell, prin. Fax 365-5790

Iola Area Community Christian S 50/PK-6
PO Box 652 66749 620-365-2300
Marty Meadows, admin.

Jetmore, Hodgeman, Pop. 914
Jetmore USD 227 300/PK-12
PO Box 398 67854 620-357-8301
Doug Chaney, supt. Fax 357-8437
www.jetmorek12.org/
Jetmore ES 100/PK-6
PO Box 398 67854 620-357-8396
Doug Chaney, prin. Fax 357-8437

Jewell, Jewell, Pop. 439
Jewell USD 279 100/PK-12
PO Box 19 66949 785-428-3311
Bob Tipton, supt. Fax 428-3344
www.usd279.org/
Jewell ES 50/PK-4
PO Box 20 66949 785-428-3233
Eric Burks, prin. Fax 428-3602
Jewell JHS 50/5-8
PO Box 20 66949 785-428-3233
Eric Burks, prin. Fax 428-3602

Johnson, Stanton, Pop. 1,314
Stanton County USD 452 500/PK-12
PO Box C 67855 620-492-6226
Susan Scherling, supt. Fax 492-1326
www.usd452.org
Stanton County ES 200/PK-5
PO Box C 67855 620-492-6216
Gayla Myers, prin. Fax 492-1549
Stanton County MS 100/6-8
PO Box C 67855 620-492-2223
Matt Berens, prin. Fax 492-1375

Junction City, Geary, Pop. 16,402
Geary County USD 475 6,300/PK-12
PO Box 370 66441 785-717-4000
Ronald Walker, supt. Fax 717-4003
www.usd475.org/
Eisenhower ES 300/K-5
1625 Saint Marys Rd 66441 785-717-4340
Susan Kamphaus, prin. Fax 717-4341
Franklin ES 200/K-5
410 W 2nd St 66441 785-717-4380
Phyllis Gibson, prin. Fax 717-4381
Grandview ES 100/K-5
109 E Grandview Dr 66441 785-717-4470
Lynn Inkman, prin. Fax 717-4471
Heim ECC PK-PK
1811 Elmdale Ave 66441 785-717-4730
Carolyn Tate, dir. Fax 717-4731
Junction City MS 700/6-8
700 Wildcat Ln 66441 785-717-4400
Mary Wright, prin. Fax 717-4401
Lincoln ES 200/PK-5
300 Lincoln School Dr 66441 785-717-4570
Samrie Devin, prin. Fax 717-4571
Sheridan ES 200/K-5
429 W Ash St 66441 785-717-4670
Nancy Hubbard, prin. Fax 717-4671
Spring Valley ES K-5
1600 Hickory Ln 66441 785-717-4790
Sierra Jackson, prin. Fax 717-4791
Washington ES 300/PK-5
1500 N Washington St 66441 785-717-4690
Lorraine Walker, prin. Fax 717-4691
Westwood ES 300/K-5
1600 N Eisenhower Dr 66441 785-717-4150
Shelley Kite, prin. Fax 717-4151
Other Schools – See Fort Riley, Milford

Immanuel Lutheran S 50/PK-PK
630 S Eisenhower Dr 66441 785-238-5921
Ann Gardels, prin. Fax 238-6473
St. Xaviers S 100/K-12
200 N Washington St 66441 785-238-2841
Lori Balderrama, prin. Fax 238-5021

Kanopolis, Ellsworth, Pop. 516
Ellsworth USD 327
Supt. — See Ellsworth
Kanopolis MS 100/6-8
PO Box 37 67454 785-472-4477
Mary Brown, prin. Fax 472-4068

Kansas City, Wyandotte, Pop. 144,210
Bonner Springs USD 204
Supt. — See Bonner Springs
Delaware Ridge ES PK-5
1601 N 130th St 66109 913-441-2126
Cindy Lockyear, prin. Fax 721-1369

Kansas City USD 500 18,800/PK-12
625 Minnesota Ave 66101 913-551-3200
Dr. Jill Shackelford, supt. Fax 551-3217
www.kckps.org
Argentine MS 600/6-8
2123 Ruby Ave 66106 913-627-6750
Jereme Brueggeman, prin. Fax 627-6783
Arrowhead MS 500/6-8
1715 N 82nd St 66112 913-627-6600
Laurie Boyd, prin. Fax 627-6654
Banneker ES 400/K-5
2026 N 4th St 66101 913-627-4700
Angela Brockman, prin. Fax 627-4776
Bethel ES 200/K-5
7850 Yecker Ave 66109 913-627-3000
Faye Thicklin, prin. Fax 627-3046
Caruthers ES 300/K-5
1100 Waverly Ave 66104 913-627-4750
Stacia Bradley Brown, prin. Fax 627-4786
Central MS 600/6-8
925 Ivandale St 66101 913-627-6150
Kris Ludwig, prin. Fax 627-6152
Coronado MS 400/6-8
1735 N 64th Ter 66102 913-627-6300
Jewell Ragsdale, prin. Fax 627-6358
Douglass ES 200/K-5
1310 N 9th St 66101 913-627-5100
Marguerite Martinez, prin. Fax 551-3556
Edison ES 200/K-5
1000 Locust St 66103 913-627-4900
Cynthia Cop, prin. Fax 722-7486
Eisenhower MS 600/6-8
2901 N 72nd St 66109 913-627-6450
Freda Ogburn, prin. Fax 627-6455
Emerson ES 300/K-5
1429 S 29th St 66106 913-627-5900
Colleen Dudley, prin. Fax 627-5937
Fiske ES 400/K-5
625 S Valley St 66105 913-627-4850
Josie Herrera, prin. Fax 627-4876
Grant ES 300/K-5
1510 N 4th St 66101 913-627-4300
Janice McConnell-Miller, prin. Fax 627-4303
Hazel Grove ES 400/K-5
2401 N 67th St 66104 913-627-7000
Sue Elliott, prin. Fax 627-7027
Huyck ES 200/K-5
1530 N 83rd St 66112 913-627-4650
Vicki Smothers, prin. Fax 627-4686
Kennedy ES 400/K-5
2600 N 72nd St 66109 913-627-4950
Flora Anderson, prin. Fax 627-4986
Lindbergh ES 200/K-5
641 N 57th St 66102 913-627-5150
DeeDee Hines, prin. Fax 627-5176
Lowell Preschool PK-PK
1030 Orville Ave 66102 913-551-3790
Debi Apple, prin. Fax 342-3948
McKinley ES 200/K-5
611 N 14th St 66102 913-627-7350
Theresa Schneweis, prin. Fax 551-3645
Morse Preschool PK-PK
912 S Baltimore St 66105 913-627-6550
Debi Apple, prin. Fax 627-6566
New Chelsea ES 500/PK-5
2500 Wood Ave 66104 913-627-5000
Janice Turner, prin. Fax 627-5013
New Stanley ES 400/K-5
3604 Metropolitan Ave 66106 913-627-3950
Sharyn Connor, prin. Fax 627-3976
Northwest Magnet MS 400/6-8
2400 N 18th St 66104 913-627-4000
Donnie Mitchell, prin. Fax 627-4052
Pearson ES 600/K-5
310 N 11th St 66102 913-627-3150
Connie Horner, prin. Fax 627-3176
Prentis ES 200/PK-5
2337 S 14th St 66103 913-627-5250
James Poplau, prin. Fax 627-5276
Preschool - Ed Center PK-PK
4601 State Ave Unit 38 66102 913-627-6590
Beverly Manlove, prin. Fax 627-6592
Quindaro ES 300/PK-5
2800 Farrow Ave 66104 913-627-4400
Linnie McClunney, prin. Fax 551-3677
Rosedale MS 400/6-8
3600 Springfield St 66103 913-627-6900
Connie Horner, prin. Fax 627-6957
Rushton ES 400/K-5
2605 W 43rd Ave 66103 913-627-3050
Mary Welsh, prin. Fax 627-3088
Silver City ES 200/K-5
2515 Lawrence Ave 66106 913-627-4550
Mary Gulick, prin. Fax 627-4576
Stony Point North ES 300/PK-5
8200 Elizabeth Ave 66112 913-627-4500
Michael Windes, prin. Fax 627-4537
Stony Point South ES 300/K-5
150 S 78th St 66111 913-627-4600
Lori Cooper, prin. Fax 627-4626
Twain ES 200/K-5
2300 Minnesota Ave 66102 913-627-5200
Sandra Egidy, prin. Fax 627-5246
Ware ES 300/PK-5
4820 Oakland Ave 66102 913-627-5950
Bobbie Beverlin, prin. Fax 627-5986
Welborn ES 500/K-5
5200 Leavenworth Rd 66104 913-627-4450
Cheryl Rainey, prin. Fax 627-4477
West MS 500/6-8
2600 N 44th St 66104 913-627-6000
Shelly Beech, prin. Fax 627-6053
White Church ES 200/K-5
2226 N 85th St 66109 913-627-4250
Bruce Haber, prin. Fax 627-4276
White ES 300/K-5
2600 N 43rd Ter 66104 913-627-6250
Alexis Etier, prin. Fax 627-6276

Whittier ES 600/K-5
295 S 10th St 66102 913-627-6400
Geri Cunningham, prin. Fax 627-6449
Willard ES 400/K-5
3400 Orville Ave 66102 913-627-6100
Brett Bernard, prin. Fax 627-6126

Piper-Kansas City USD 203 1,500/PK-12
12036 Leavenworth Rd 66109 913-721-2088
Steve Adams, supt. Fax 721-3573
www.piperschools.com/
Piper ES East 300/3-5
4410 N 107th St 66109 913-721-5000
Allan Amos, prin. Fax 721-5336
Piper ES West 300/PK-2
3130 N 122nd St 66109 913-721-1243
Kate Schmidt, prin. Fax 721-3656
Piper MS 400/6-8
4420 N 107th St 66109 913-721-1144
Laurence Breedlove, prin. Fax 721-1526

Turner USD 202 3,300/PK-12
800 S 55th St 66106 913-288-4100
Michelle Sedler, supt. Fax 288-3401
www.turnerusd202.org/
Junction ES 300/PK-6
2570 S 42nd St 66106 913-288-3600
Jay Douglas, prin. Fax 288-3601
Midland Trail ES 400/PK-6
3101 S 51st St 66106 913-288-3500
Lynnette Hatfield, prin. Fax 288-3501
Oak Grove ES 400/PK-6
5340 Oak Grove Rd 66106 913-288-3900
Gayle Bertram, prin. Fax 288-3901
Turner Early Learning Center PK-K
6425 Riverview Ave 66102 913-288-3800
Becky Letcher, prin. Fax 288-3801
Turner ES 400/PK-6
1800 S 55th St 66106 913-288-3400
Deb Ayers-Geist, prin. Fax 288-3402
Turner MS 600/7-8
1312 S 55th St 66106 913-288-4000
Michael Koonce, prin. Fax 288-4001

Christ the King S 200/PK-8
3027 N 54th St 66104 913-287-8883
Cathy Fithian, prin. Fax 287-7409
Holy Name S 200/PK-8
1007 Southwest Blvd 66103 913-722-1032
Kathy Rhodes, prin. Fax 722-4175
Kansas City Christian MS 100/7-8
5500 Woodend Ave 66106 913-722-9955
Kathy Hirleman, prin. Fax 236-5996
Lindsay SDA S 50/PK-8
3310 Garfield Ave 66104 913-342-4435
Muncie Christian S 200/PK-12
3650 N 67th St 66104 913-299-9884
Mendy Lietzen, admin. Fax 299-9884
Open Door Christian S 100/K-8
3033 N 103rd Ter 66109 913-334-7777
Anita Sims, prin. Fax 334-0678
Our Lady of Unity S 100/K-8
2646 S 34th St 66106 913-262-7022
Karen Davis, prin. Fax 262-7836
Resurrection S at the Cathedral 300/PK-8
422 N 14th St 66102 913-371-8101
Ann Connor, prin. Fax 371-2151
St. Patrick S 300/PK-8
1066 N 94th St 66112 913-299-8131
Mary Staley, prin. Fax 299-2845

Kensington, Smith, Pop. 490
Thunder Ridge SD 100/K-12
128 S Kansas St 66951 785-476-2218
Jeff Yoxall, supt. Fax 476-2258
Thunder Ridge ES 50/K-2
128 S Kansas St 66951 785-476-3241
Jeff Yoxall, prin. Fax 476-2258
Other Schools – See Agra

Kingman, Kingman, Pop. 3,183
Kingman-Norwich USD 331 1,100/PK-12
PO Box 416 67068 620-532-3134
Scott Carter, supt. Fax 532-3251
www.knusd331.com/
Kingman S 500/PK-8
607 N Spruce St 67068 620-532-3186
Brent Garrison, prin. Fax 532-5137
Other Schools – See Norwich

St. Patrick Catholic S 200/PK-8
630 W D Ave 67068 620-532-2791
Bob Lyall, prin. Fax 532-2392

Kinsley, Edwards, Pop. 1,547
Kinsley-Offerle USD 347 100/K-6
120 W 8th St 67547 620-659-3646
Bob Davies, supt. Fax 659-2669
www.kinsleypublicschools.org/
Other Schools – See Offerle

Kiowa, Barber, Pop. 965
South Barber County USD 255 200/K-12
512 Main St 67070 620-825-4115
Brad Morris, supt. Fax 825-4145
www.southbarber.com/
South Barber S 100/K-8
913 Main St 67070 620-825-4114
Marcia Cantrell, prin. Fax 825-4145

Kismet, Seward, Pop. 521
Kismet-Plains USD 483 700/PK-12
23456 US Highway 54 67859 620-563-7103
Elton Argo, supt. Fax 563-7348
www.usd483.net
Kismet ES 200/K-5
PO Box 336 67859 620-563-7248
John Jones, prin. Fax 563-7035

Southwestern Heights JHS 200/6-8
23456 US Highway 54 67859 620-563-7100
Mark Webb, prin. Fax 563-7342
Other Schools – See Plains

La Crosse, Rush, Pop. 1,305
La Crosse USD 395 300/K-12
PO Box 778 67548 785-222-2505
Bill Keeley, supt. Fax 222-3240
www.usd395.org
La Crosse ES 100/K-6
PO Box 700 67548 785-222-2622
Bill Keeley, prin. Fax 222-3522
La Crosse MS 50/7-8
PO Box 810 67548 785-222-3030
Kathy Keeley, prin. Fax 222-3480

La Cygne, Linn, Pop. 1,146
Prairie View USD 362 1,100/PK-12
13799 KS Highway 152 66040 913-757-2677
Chris Kleidosty, supt. Fax 757-4442
www.pv362.org
LaCygne ES, 710 Walnut St 66040 300/PK-5
Dennis Hargis, prin. 913-757-4417
Prairie View MS 200/6-8
13667 KS Highway 152 66040 913-757-4447
Ken Bolt, prin. Fax 757-4497
Other Schools – See Fontana, Parker

Lakin, Kearny, Pop. 2,292
Lakin USD 215 700/PK-12
1003 W Kingman Ave 67860 620-355-6761
Randall Steinle, supt. Fax 355-7317
www.usd215.org/
Lakin ES 300/PK-4
PO Box 26 67860 620-355-6191
Mindi Brennaman, prin. Fax 355-6491
Lakin MS 200/5-8
1201 W Kingman Ave 67860 620-355-6973
Tammie Huggard, prin. Fax 355-8313

Langdon, Reno, Pop. 72
Fairfield USD 310 300/K-12
16115 S Langdon Rd 67583 620-596-2152
Mary Treaster, supt. Fax 596-2835
www.usd310.org
Fairfield MS 100/5-8
16115 S Langdon Rd 67583 620-596-2615
Letha Warner, prin. Fax 596-2835
Other Schools – See Arlington, Sylvia

Lansing, Leavenworth, Pop. 10,214
Lansing USD 469 1,900/PK-12
401 S 2nd St 66043 913-727-1100
Dr. Randal Bagby, supt. Fax 727-1619
www.usd469.net/
Lansing ES 600/PK-5
450 W Mary St 66043 913-727-1128
Tim Newton, prin. Fax 727-6577
Lansing MS 500/6-8
509 Ida St 66043 913-727-1197
Kerry Brungardt, prin. Fax 727-1349

Larned, Pawnee, Pop. 3,874
Ft. Larned USD 495 900/PK-12
120 E 6th St 67550 620-285-3185
Jon Flint, supt. Fax 285-2973
www.usd495.net
Hillside ES 100/PK-K
502 W 5th St 67550 620-285-2311
Lea Harding, prin. Fax 285-8424
Larned MS 300/5-8
904 Corse Ave 67550 620-285-8430
Derek Reinhardt, prin. Fax 285-8433
Northside ES 100/3-4
1604 State St 67550 620-285-2141
Amy Herter, prin. Fax 285-2584
Phinney ES 100/1-2
523 E 12th St 67550 620-285-3181
Lea Harding, prin. Fax 285-8439

Lawrence, Douglas, Pop. 81,816
Lawrence USD 497 9,700/PK-12
110 McDonald Dr 66044 785-832-5000
Rick Doll, supt. Fax 832-5016
www.usd497.org
Broken Arrow ES 300/K-6
2704 Louisiana St 66046 785-832-5600
Brian McCaffrey, prin. Fax 832-5602
Cordley ES 200/K-6
1837 Vermont St 66044 785-832-5640
Scott Cinnamon, prin. Fax 832-5658
Deerfield ES 500/K-6
101 Lawrence Ave 66049 785-832-5660
Joni Appleman, prin. Fax 832-5663
East Heights ECC PK-PK
1430 Haskell Ave 66044 785-832-5680
Cris Anderson, prin. Fax 832-5682
Hillcrest ES 500/K-6
1045 Hilltop Dr 66044 785-832-5720
Tammy Becker, prin. Fax 832-5722
Hughes ES 400/K-6
1101 George William Way 66049 785-832-5890
Lisa Williams-Thompson, prin. Fax 832-5898
Kennedy ES 300/K-6
1605 Davis Rd 66046 785-832-5760
Felton Avery, prin. Fax 832-5762
New York ES 100/K-6
936 New York St 66044 785-832-5780
Nancy DeGarmo, prin. Fax 832-5784
Pinckney ES 300/K-6
810 W 6th St 66044 785-832-5800
Lesa Frantz, prin. Fax 832-5802
Prairie Park ES 400/K-6
2711 Kensington Rd 66046 785-832-5740
David Williams, prin. Fax 832-5742
Quail Run ES 400/PK-6
1130 Inverness Dr 66049 785-832-5820
Debbie Booher Tann, prin. Fax 832-5823

Schwegler ES 400/K-6
2201 Ousdahl Rd 66046 785-832-5860
Jared Comfort, prin. Fax 832-5863
Sunflower ES 500/K-6
2521 Inverness Dr 66047 785-832-5870
Sue Hosey, prin. Fax 832-5873
Sunset Hill ES 300/K-6
901 Schwarz Rd 66049 785-832-5880
Chris Bay, prin. Fax 832-5882
Wakarusa Valley ES 200/K-6
1105 E 1000 Rd 66047 785-832-5900
Elias Espinoza, prin. Fax 832-5902
Woodlawn ES 200/K-6
508 Elm St 66044 785-832-5920
Jeanne Fridell, prin. Fax 832-5922

Corpus Christi Catholic S 200/PK-6
6001 Bob Billings Pkwy 66049 785-331-3374
Mary Mattern, prin. Fax 865-3933
Prairie Moon S 50/PK-6
PO Box 1266 66044 785-841-8800
Dr. Mary Veerkamp, admin. Fax 841-8800
Raintree Montessori S 300/PK-6
4601 Clinton Pkwy 66047 785-843-6800
Lleanna McReynolds, admin. Fax 843-7003
St. John S 300/PK-6
1208 Kentucky St 66044 785-843-9511
Patricia Newton, prin. Fax 843-7143
Veritas Christian S 100/K-12
256 N Michigan St 66044 785-749-0083
Dr. Jeffrey Barclay, admin. Fax 749-0580

Leavenworth, Leavenworth, Pop. 35,213
Easton USD 449
Supt. — See Easton
Salt Creek Valley IS 100/4-5
32325 167th St 66048 913-682-6032
Nancy Wilson, prin. Fax 682-8110

Leavenworth USD 453 2,600/PK-12
PO Box 969 66048 913-684-1400
Dr. Kelly Harris, supt. Fax 684-1407
www.usd453.org
Day ES 50/K-K, 4-4
1100 3rd Ave 66048 913-684-1440
Kevin Lunsford, prin. Fax 684-1443
Hartnett/Day ES 100/1-3
1000 3rd Ave 66048 913-684-1450
Janine Kempker, prin. Fax 684-1455
Lawson ES 200/PK-4
820 N 5th St 66048 913-684-1570
Pamela Robinson, prin. Fax 684-1572
Leavenworth West MS 100/5-6
1901 Spruce St 66048 913-684-1520
Jennifer Kramer, prin. Fax 684-1523
Muncie ES 200/PK-4
PO Box 354 66048 913-727-6070
Gina Grigaitis, prin. Fax 727-6671
Warren MS 300/7-8
PO Box 7 66048 913-684-1530
J.D. Nelson, prin. Fax 684-1539
Wilson ES 200/PK-4
616 Grand Ave 66048 913-684-1480
Neoma Bates, prin. Fax 684-1483

St. Paul Lutheran S 200/PK-8
320 N 7th St 66048 913-682-5553
Jay Floetke, prin. Fax 682-5553
Trinity Lutheran S 100/PK-K
2101 10th Ave 66048 913-682-4747
Tobye Baeuchle, prin. Fax 682-7767
Xavier ECC 100/PK-PK
727 Pennsylvania Ave 66048 913-682-6348
Scott Hulshoff, prin. Fax 682-5262
Xavier S - 2nd Avenue Campus 100/K-2
1409 2nd Ave 66048 913-682-1943
Scott Hulshoff, prin. Fax 682-5262
Xavier S - Kickapoo Center 100/3-5
522 Kickapoo St 66048 913-682-5527
Scott Hulshoff, prin. Fax 682-5262
Xavier S - Osage Center 100/6-8
721 Osage St 66048 913-682-3135
Scott Hulshoff, prin. Fax 682-5262

Leawood, Johnson, Pop. 30,145
Blue Valley USD 229
Supt. — See Overland Park
Leawood ES 400/K-5
2400 W 123rd St 66209 913-239-6600
Doug Harris, prin. Fax 239-6648
Leawood MS 500/6-8
2410 W 123rd St 66209 913-239-5300
Marcia Wiseman Ed.D., prin. Fax 239-5348
Mission Trail ES 500/K-5
13200 Mission Rd 66209 913-239-6700
Debbie Bond, prin. Fax 239-6748
Prairie Star ES 500/PK-5
3800 W 143rd St 66224 913-239-7100
Amy Farthing, prin. Fax 239-7148
Prairie Star MS 500/6-8
14201 Mission Rd 66224 913-239-5600
Lyn Rantz Ed.D., prin. Fax 239-5648

Cure of Ars S 600/PK-8
9403 Mission Rd 66206 913-648-2620
Marlene Rowe, prin. Fax 648-3810
Nativity S 600/K-8
3700 W 119th St 66209 913-338-4330
Maureen Huppe, prin. Fax 338-2050
St. Michael the Archangel S 600/K-8
14201 Nall Ave, 913-402-3950
Michael Cullinan, prin. Fax 851-8221

Lebo, Coffey, Pop. 950
Lebo-Waverly USD 243
Supt. — See Waverly
Lebo ES 200/K-6
PO Box 45 66856 620-256-6161
Darla Long, prin. Fax 256-6342

Lecompton, Douglas, Pop. 589
Perry USD 343
Supt. — See Perry
Lecompton ES 100/2-4
PO Box 108 66050 785-887-6343
Connie Thornton, prin. Fax 887-6755

Lenexa, Johnson, Pop. 43,434
De Soto USD 232
Supt. — See De Soto
Mill Creek MS 6-8
8001 Mize Blvd 66227 913-667-3512
Tim Drake, prin. Fax 422-9229

Olathe USD 233
Supt. — See Olathe
Manchester Park ES 600/K-6
9810 Prairie Creek Rd 66220 913-780-7540
Susan DeGroot, prin. Fax 780-7549

Shawnee Mission USD 512
Supt. — See Shawnee Mission
Bonjour ES 300/K-6
9400 Pflumm Rd 66215 913-993-2100
Alejandro Schlagel, prin. Fax 993-2199
Rising Star ES 400/K-6
8600 Candlelight Ln 66215 913-993-4500
Chris Lash, prin. Fax 993-4599
Rosehill ES 500/K-6
9801 Rosehill Rd 66215 913-993-4800
Greg Lawrence, prin. Fax 993-4899
Shawanoe ES 300/K-6
11230 W 75th St 66214 913-993-5100
Vickie Zirbel, prin. Fax 993-5199

Holy Trinity S 700/K-8
13600 W 92nd St 66215 913-888-3250
Gary Lammers, prin. Fax 438-2572

Lenora, Norton, Pop. 285
West Solomon Valley USD 213 50/PK-6
PO Box 98 67645 785-567-4350
Garry Baxter, supt. Fax 567-4540
www.usd213.com
Lenora ES 50/PK-6
PO Box 98 67645 785-567-4350
Garry Baxter, prin. Fax 567-4540

Leon, Butler, Pop. 648
Bluestem USD 205 600/PK-12
PO Box 8 67074 316-742-3261
Randy Rivers, supt. Fax 742-9265
www.usd205.com
Bluestem ES 300/PK-6
501 S Mill Rd 67074 316-742-3291
Debbie Webster, prin. Fax 742-9966
Bluestem MS 100/7-8
625 S Mill Rd 67074 316-742-3263
Kevin Hood, prin. Fax 742-3748

Leoti, Wichita, Pop. 1,440
Leoti USD 467 500/PK-12
PO Box 967 67861 620-375-4677
Dr. James Hardy, supt. Fax 375-2304
www.leoti.org/
Stewart ES 300/PK-5
PO Box 807 67861 620-375-2314
Dawn McKinney, prin. Fax 375-2589
Wichita County JHS 100/6-8
PO Box 908 67861 620-375-2219
Dawn McKinney, prin. Fax 375-2352

Le Roy, Coffey, Pop. 579
Le Roy-Gridley USD 245 300/PK-12
PO Box 278 66857 620-964-2212
Mike Kastle, supt. Fax 964-2413
Le Roy ES 100/PK-4
PO Box 188 66857 620-964-2608
Mike Kastle, prin. Fax 964-2410
Other Schools – See Gridley

Lewis, Edwards, Pop. 475
Lewis USD 502 100/PK-6
PO Box 97 67552 620-324-5547
Virgil Ritchie, supt. Fax 324-5297
skyways.lib.ks.us/schools/usd502/index.htm
Lewis ES 100/PK-6
PO Box 97 67552 620-324-5547
Virgil Ritchie, prin. Fax 324-5297

Liberal, Seward, Pop. 20,257
Liberal USD 480 4,600/PK-12
PO Box 949 67905 620-604-1010
Vernon Welch, supt. Fax 604-1011
www.usd480.net/
Cottonwood IS 500/4-6
1100 W 11th St 67901 620-604-2700
Donna Sill, prin. Fax 604-2701
Garfield ES 200/K-3
516 W 1st St 67901 620-604-1500
Brandon Hyde, prin. Fax 604-1501
Liberal South MS 300/7-8
950 S Grant Ave 67901 620-604-1300
Gilberto Rito, prin. Fax 604-1301
Liberal West MS 400/7-8
500 N Western Ave 67901 620-604-1400
Troy McCarter, prin. Fax 604-1501
Lincoln ES 200/K-3
1002 W 11th St 67901 620-604-1600
Melinda Cline, prin. Fax 604-1601
MacArthur ES 200/K-3
925 S Holly Dr 67901 620-604-1700
Shawna Evans, prin. Fax 604-1701
McDermott ES 200/K-3
439 S Pennsylvania Ave 67901 620-604-1800
Kathy Fitzgerald, prin. Fax 604-1801
McKinley ES 200/K-3
615 W 7th St 67901 620-604-1900
Kathaleen Wedel, prin. Fax 604-1901
Southlawn ES 300/K-3
PO Box 949 67905 620-604-2000
Gloria Quattrone, prin. Fax 604-2001
Sunflower IS 500/4-6
310 W Pine St 67901 620-604-2800
Sheri King, prin. Fax 604-2801
Washington ES 300/PK-3
840 N Washington Ave 67901 620-604-2100
John Jones, prin. Fax 604-2101

Lincoln, Lincoln, Pop. 1,289
Lincoln USD 298 300/PK-12
PO Box 289 67455 785-524-4436
Gary Nelson, supt. Fax 524-3080
www.usd298.com
Lincoln ES 200/PK-6
304 S 4th St 67455 785-524-4487
Jackie Combs, prin. Fax 524-5454

Lindsborg, McPherson, Pop. 3,305
Smoky Valley USD 400 1,000/PK-12
126 S Main St 67456 785-227-2981
Glen Suppes, supt. Fax 227-2982
www.smokyvalley.org/
Lindsborg MS 200/5-8
401 N Cedar St 67456 785-227-4249
John Denk, prin. Fax 227-3650
Soderstrom ES 300/PK-4
227 N Washington St 67456 785-227-2945
Debbie Watson, prin. Fax 227-2946
Other Schools – See Marquette

Linn, Washington, Pop. 388
Barnes USD 223
Supt. — See Barnes
Linn S 100/PK-8
300 Parkview St 66953 785-348-5531
Mike Savage, prin. Fax 348-5534

Linn Lutheran S 50/1-8
112 Church St 66953 785-348-5792
Neal Kurtz, prin. Fax 348-5792

Linwood, Leavenworth, Pop. 382
Basehor-Linwood USD 458
Supt. — See Basehor
Basehor-Linwood MS 400/7-8
215 Park St 66052 913-724-2323
Mike Wiley, prin. Fax 724-3132
Linwood ES 100/K-5
215 Park St 66052 913-724-2323
Cindy Hiebert, prin. Fax 724-3132

Little River, Rice, Pop. 528
Little River USD 444 300/PK-12
PO Box 218 67457 620-897-6325
Milt Dougherty, supt. Fax 897-6788
www.usd444.com/
Little River JHS 100/6-8
PO Box 8 67457 620-897-6201
Dawn Johnson, prin. Fax 897-6203
Other Schools – See Windom

Logan, Phillips, Pop. 549
Logan USD 326 200/K-12
PO Box 98 67646 785-689-7595
Robert Jackson, supt. Fax 689-7517
www.usd326.k12.ks.us/
Logan ES 100/K-6
PO Box 98 67646 785-689-4631
Robert Jackson, prin. Fax 689-7517

Longford, Clay, Pop. 89
Clay Center USD 379
Supt. — See Clay Center
Longford ES 50/K-5
PO Box 187 67458 785-388-2322
Jaclyn Pfizenmaier, prin. Fax 388-2362

Long Island, Phillips, Pop. 145
Northern Valley USD 212
Supt. — See Almena
Long Island MS 100/5-8
PO Box 98 67647 785-854-7681
Chris Robertson, prin. Fax 854-7684

Longton, Elk, Pop. 371
Elk Valley USD 283 200/PK-12
PO Box 87 67352 620-642-2811
Art Haibon, supt. Fax 642-6551
www.usd283.org
Elk Valley ES 100/PK-5
PO Box 87 67352 620-642-3021
Art Haibon, prin. Fax 642-2092

Lorraine, Ellsworth, Pop. 133
Lorraine USD 328 400/PK-12
PO Box 109 67459 785-472-5241
Roger Robinson, supt. Fax 472-5229
www.usd328.org
Other Schools – See Holyrood, Wilson

Lost Springs, Marion, Pop. 68
Centre USD 397 300/PK-12
PO Box 38 66859 785-983-4304
Jerri Kemble, supt. Fax 983-4352
www.usd397.com/
Centre ES 100/PK-6
PO Box 38 66859 785-983-4304
Jerri Kemble, prin. Fax 983-4352

Louisburg, Miami, Pop. 3,313
Louisburg USD 416 900/PK-12
PO Box 550 66053 913-837-1700
Dr. Rick Doll, supt. Fax 837-1701
www.usd416.org
Broadmoor ES 3-5
PO Box 367 66053 913-837-1900
Dr. Rick Doll, prin. Fax 837-1919
Louisburg MS 400/6-8
PO Box 308 66053 913-837-1800
Brian Biermann, prin. Fax 837-1801

Rockville ES PK-2
PO Box 129 66053 913-837-1970
Becky Bowes, prin. Fax 837-1978

Luray, Russell, Pop. 186
Russell County USD 407
Supt. — See Russell
Luray-Lucas S 100/K-8
400 N Fairview Ave 67649 785-698-2217
Larry Geist, prin. Fax 698-2218

Lyndon, Osage, Pop. 1,041
Lyndon USD 421 500/PK-12
PO Box 488 66451 785-828-4413
Brian Spencer, supt. Fax 828-3686
Lyndon S 300/PK-8
PO Box 488 66451 785-828-4622
Jeff Kohlman, prin. Fax 828-4110

Lyons, Rice, Pop. 3,554
Lyons USD 405 800/PK-12
800 S Workman St 67554 620-257-5196
Darrel Kellerman, supt. Fax 257-5197
www.usd405.com
Lyons Central ES 200/3-5
501 W Lincoln St 67554 620-257-5612
Bob Turner, prin. Fax 257-7032
Lyons MS 200/6-8
401 S Douglas Ave 67554 620-257-3961
Kevin Logan, prin. Fax 257-3518
Lyons Park ES 300/PK-2
121 S Workman St 67554 620-257-5624
Nancy Barlow, prin. Fax 257-7042

Mc Cune, Crawford, Pop. 492
Cherokee USD 247
Supt. — See Cherokee
Mc Cune S 100/K-8
PO Box 108 66753 620-632-4217
Warren McGown, prin. Fax 632-4500

Macksville, Stafford, Pop. 494
Macksville USD 351 300/PK-12
PO Box 487 67557 620-348-3415
Mike Harvey, supt. Fax 348-3217
www.usd351.com
Macksville S 200/PK-8
PO Box 308 67557 620-348-2835
Laura Davis, prin. Fax 348-3217

Mc Louth, Jefferson, Pop. 785
Mc Louth USD 342 600/PK-12
PO Box 40 66054 913-796-2201
Jean Rush, supt. Fax 796-6440
www.mclouth.org
Mc Louth ES 300/PK-5
PO Box 40 66054 913-796-6152
Robert Batman, prin. Fax 796-6440
Mc Louth MS 100/6-8
PO Box 40 66054 913-796-6122
Mike Bogard, prin. Fax 796-6124

Mc Pherson, McPherson, Pop. 12,746
Mc Pherson USD 418 2,400/PK-12
514 N Main St 67460 620-241-9400
Dr. Randy Watson, supt. Fax 241-9410
www.mcpherson.com/418
ECC PK-PK
128 N Park St 67460 620-241-9590
Penny Stoss, prin. Fax 241-9565
Eisenhower ES 300/K-5
301 Wickersham Dr 67460 620-241-9430
Craig Marshall, prin. Fax 241-9431
Lincoln ES 200/K-5
900 N Ash St 67460 620-241-9540
Jana Koehn, prin. Fax 241-9542
Mc Pherson MS 500/6-8
700 E Elizabeth St 67460 620-241-9450
Brad Plackemeier, prin. Fax 241-9456
Roosevelt ES 300/K-5
800 S Walnut St 67460 620-241-9550
Todd Beam, prin. Fax 241-9552
Washington ES 200/PK-5
128 N Park St 67460 620-241-9560
Jill Beam, prin. Fax 241-9565

Elyria Christian S 200/K-12
1644 Comanche Rd 67460 620-241-2994
Richard Roberts, admin. Fax 241-1238
St. Joseph Catholic S 100/PK-6
520 E Northview Ave 67460 620-241-3913
Peggy Bahr, prin. Fax 245-9677

Madison, Greenwood, Pop. 799
Madison-Virgil USD 386 300/PK-12
PO Box 398 66860 620-437-2910
Darrel Finch, supt. Fax 437-2916
www.usd386.org/
Madison ES 100/PK-6
PO Box 398 66860 620-437-2918
Standiferd Mitchell, prin. Fax 437-2916

Maize, Sedgwick, Pop. 2,117
Maize USD 266 6,200/PK-12
11611 W 49th St N 67101 316-722-0614
Milt Pippenger, supt. Fax 722-8538
www.usd266.com
Maize Central ES 700/K-5
304 W Central St 67101 316-722-0427
David Jennings, prin. Fax 722-8307
Maize ES 700/2-5
305 Jones St 67101 316-722-8230
Tyler Ewert, prin. Fax 722-5456
Maize MS 800/6-8
4600 N Maize Rd 67101 316-729-2464
Jeannine Pfannenstiel, prin. Fax 729-2479
Pray-Woodman ES 700/2-5
11111 W 49th St N 67101 316-721-0902
Shelley Jonas, prin. Fax 721-0486

Vermillion PS 600/PK-1
501 S James Ave 67101 316-722-0266
Mike Mountain, prin. Fax 722-5020
Other Schools – See Wichita

Manhattan, Riley, Pop. 48,668
Manhattan-Ogden USD 383 5,300/PK-12
2031 Poyntz Ave 66502 785-587-2000
Dr. Robert Shannon, supt. Fax 587-2006
www.usd383.org
Anthony MS 400/7-8
2501 Browning Ave 66502 785-587-2890
Vickie Kline, prin. Fax 587-2899
Arnold ES 400/PK-6
1435 Hudson Ave 66503 785-587-2020
Larry Liotta, prin. Fax 587-2023
Bergman ES 500/K-6
3430 Lombard Dr 66503 785-587-2865
Lori Martin, prin. Fax 587-2869
Bluemont ES K-6
714 Bluemont Ave 66502 785-587-2030
Kathy Stitt, prin. Fax 587-2034
Eisenhower MS 300/7-8
800 Walters Dr 66502 785-587-2880
Greg Hoyt, prin. Fax 587-2888
Lee ES 300/K-6
701 Lee St 66502 785-587-2050
Dr. Nancy Kole, prin. Fax 587-2057
Marlatt ES 400/K-6
2715 Hobbs Dr 66502 785-587-2060
Claudia Conner, prin. Fax 587-2064
Northview ES 500/PK-6
300 Griffith Dr 66502 785-587-2070
Shelley Aistrup, prin. Fax 587-2075
Roosevelt ES 300/K-6
1401 Houston St 66502 785-587-2090
Andrea Tiede, prin. Fax 587-2139
Wilson ES 400/K-6
312 N Juliette Ave 66502 785-587-2170
Eric Koppes, prin. Fax 587-2173
Other Schools – See Ogden

Flint Hills Christian S 200/PK-12
3905 Green Valley Rd 66502 785-776-2223
Frank Leone, admin. Fax 776-3016
Manhattan Catholic S 300/K-8
306 S Juliette Ave 66502 785-565-5050
Linda Roggenkamp, prin. Fax 565-5055

Mankato, Jewell, Pop. 843
Rock Hills USD 107 100/PK-12
301 N West St 66956 785-378-3102
William Walker, supt. Fax 378-3438
www.usd107.org/
Rock Hills ES 100/PK-4
301 N West St 66956 785-378-3822
Bill Walker, prin. Fax 378-3467
Other Schools – See Burr Oak

Maple Hill, Wabaunsee, Pop. 492
Mill Creek Valley USD 329
Supt. — See Alma
Maple Hill ES 100/K-4
PO Box 68 66507 785-256-4223
Robin Schuckman, prin. Fax 256-4129

Marion, Marion, Pop. 2,028
Marion-Florence USD 408 600/K-12
101 N Thorp St 66861 620-382-2117
Lee Leiker, supt. Fax 382-2118
www.usd408.com
Marion ES 300/K-6
1400 E Lawrence St 66861 620-382-3771
Rod Garman, prin. Fax 382-6012
Marion MS 100/7-8
125 S Lincoln St 66861 620-382-6070
Tod Gordon, prin. Fax 382-6073

Marquette, McPherson, Pop. 585
Smoky Valley USD 400
Supt. — See Lindsborg
Marquette S 100/K-8
PO Box 309 67464 785-546-2275
Darryl Talbott, prin. Fax 546-2492

Marysville, Marshall, Pop. 3,151
Marysville USD 364 800/PK-12
211 S 10th St 66508 785-562-5308
Doug Powers, supt. Fax 562-5309
www.marysvilleschools.org
Marysville ES 300/PK-6
1010 Carolina St 66508 785-562-3641
Bert Lord, prin. Fax 562-3411
Marysville JHS 100/7-8
1005 Walnut St 66508 785-562-5356
Cindy Scarbrough, prin. Fax 562-5390

Good Shepherd Lutheran S 100/PK-8
206 S 17th St 66508 785-562-3181
John Macy, prin. Fax 562-3679
St. Gregory S 100/PK-6
207 N 14th St 66508 785-562-2831
Barbara Hawkins, prin. Fax 562-4039

Mayetta, Jackson, Pop. 359
Royal Valley USD 337 900/PK-12
PO Box 219 66509 785-966-2246
John Rundle, supt. Fax 966-2490
www.rv337.com/
Royal Valley MS 300/5-8
PO Box 189 66509 785-966-2251
Dr. Don DeKeyser, prin. Fax 966-2833
Other Schools – See Hoyt

Meade, Meade, Pop. 1,629
Meade USD 226 500/PK-12
PO Box 400 67864 620-873-2081
Robert Herbig, supt. Fax 873-2201
meade.ks.schoolwebpages.com/

Meade S 300/PK-8
PO Box 400 67864 620-873-2671
Ken Harshberger, prin. Fax 873-2752

Medicine Lodge, Barber, Pop. 2,028
Barber County North USD 254 600/PK-12
PO Box 288 67104 620-886-3370
Jerry Cullen, supt. Fax 886-3640
www.usd254.org/
Medicine Lodge ES 200/PK-5
320 N Walnut St 67104 620-886-5608
Dennis Blake, prin. Fax 886-5990
Medicine Lodge MS 100/6-8
100 BH Born Blvd 67104 620-886-5644
Mark Buck, prin. Fax 886-3082

Melvern, Osage, Pop. 430
Marais Des Cygnes Valley USD 456 200/K-12
PO Box 158 66510 785-549-3521
Ted Vannocker, supt. Fax 549-3659
www.usd456.org
Other Schools – See Quenemo

Meriden, Jefferson, Pop. 708
Jefferson West USD 340 900/PK-12
PO Box 267 66512 785-484-3444
Scott Myers, supt. Fax 484-3148
www.usd340.org
Jefferson West ES 300/PK-3
PO Box 265 66512 785-484-2455
Patton Happer, prin. Fax 484-3340
Jefferson West MS 200/6-8
PO Box 410 66512 785-484-2900
John Hamon, prin. Fax 484-2904
Other Schools – See Ozawkie

Milford, Geary, Pop. 444
Geary County USD 475
Supt. — See Junction City
Milford ES 100/K-5
402 12th St 66514 785-717-4170
Greg Lumb, prin. Fax 717-4171

Miltonvale, Cloud, Pop. 486
Southern Cloud USD 334
Supt. — See Glasco
Miltonvale ES 50/K-6
PO Box 394 67466 785-427-3365
Roger Perkins, prin. Fax 427-3125

Minneapolis, Ottawa, Pop. 2,015
North Ottawa County USD 239 600/K-12
PO Box 257 67467 785-392-2167
Dr. Larry Combs, supt. Fax 392-3038
www.usd239.org/
Minneapolis ES 300/K-6
PO Box 48 67467 785-392-2111
Pat Anderson, prin. Fax 392-2198

Minneola, Clark, Pop. 681
Minneola USD 219 300/K-12
PO Box 157 67865 620-885-4372
Mark Walker, supt. Fax 885-4509
www.usd219.k12.ks.us/
Minneola S 200/K-8
PO Box 157 67865 620-885-4571
Patrick Schroeder, prin. Fax 885-4509

Mission, Johnson, Pop. 9,751
Shawnee Mission USD 512
Supt. — See Shawnee Mission
Rushton ES 300/K-6
6001 W 52nd St 66202 913-993-4900
Pam Carter, prin. Fax 993-4999

Moline, Elk, Pop. 431
West Elk USD 282
Supt. — See Howard
Moline ES 100/PK-5
PO Box 306 67353 620-647-3289
Shirley Hugill, prin. Fax 374-2414

Montezuma, Gray, Pop. 964
Montezuma USD 371 200/PK-12
PO Box 355 67867 620-846-2293
Jay Zehr, supt. Fax 846-2294
sghs.musd371.k12.ks.us/
Montezuma ES 100/PK-5
PO Box 355 67867 620-846-2283
Tim Skinner, prin. Fax 846-2294

Moran, Allen, Pop. 541
Marmaton Valley USD 256 400/K-12
128 W Oak St 66755 620-237-4250
Nancy Meyer, supt. Fax 237-8872
www.usd256.org
Marmaton Valley ES 200/K-6
128 W Oak St 66755 620-237-4381
Ken McWhirter, prin. Fax 237-8872

Moscow, Stevens, Pop. 251
Moscow USD 209 200/K-12
PO Box 158 67952 620-598-2205
Larry Philippi, supt. Fax 598-2233
moscowschools.us/
Moscow ES 100/K-5
PO Box 130 67952 620-598-2224
Aaron Roop, prin. Fax 598-2233

Mound City, Linn, Pop. 820
Jayhawk USD 346 500/PK-12
PO Box 278 66056 913-795-2247
Royce Powelson, supt. Fax 795-2185
www.usd346.org/
Jayhawk ES 200/PK-6
PO Box 305 66056 913-795-2519
Mark Proffitt, prin. Fax 795-2105

Moundridge, McPherson, Pop. 1,643
Moundridge USD 423 400/K-12
PO Box K 67107 620-345-5500
Rustin Clark, supt. Fax 345-8617
www.usd423.org

Moundridge ES 100/K-4
PO Box F 67107 620-345-5500
JoAnn Browne, prin. Fax 345-5408
Moundridge MS 100/5-8
PO Box 607 67107 620-345-5500
Vance Unrau, prin. Fax 345-5307

Mound Valley, Labette, Pop. 414
Labette County USD 506
Supt. — See Altamont
Mound Valley S 200/K-8
402 Walnut St 67354 620-328-3121
Rod Sprague, prin. Fax 328-2078

Mount Hope, Sedgwick, Pop. 842
Haven USD 312
Supt. — See Haven
Mount Hope S 100/K-8
500 W Main St 67108 316-667-2412
Mike Fast, prin. Fax 667-8977

St. Joseph Catholic S 100/K-8
12917 E Maple Grove Rd 67108 316-444-2548
Eva Harmon, prin. Fax 444-2448

Mullinville, Kiowa, Pop. 258
Mullinville USD 424 50/PK-8
PO Box 6 67109 620-548-2521
Darrel Kohlman, supt. Fax 548-2515
www.mullinville.org
Mullinville ES 50/PK-6
PO Box 6 67109 620-548-2217
Darrel Kohlman, prin. Fax 548-2278
Mullinville JHS 50/7-8
PO Box 6 67109 620-548-2217
Darrel Kohlman, prin. Fax 548-2278

Mulvane, Sedgwick, Pop. 5,628
Mulvane USD 263 1,800/PK-12
PO Box 130 67110 316-777-1102
Donna Augustine-Shaw, supt. Fax 777-1103
www.usd263.com
Mulvane Grade S 400/3-5
411 SE Louis Dr 67110 316-777-1981
Raquel Charbonneau, prin. Fax 777-2799
Mulvane MS 500/6-8
915 Westview Dr 67110 316-777-2022
Traci Becker, prin. Fax 777-4967
Munson PS 400/PK-2
1007 Westview Dr 67110 316-777-0151
Terri Lemos, prin. Fax 777-2798

St. Michael Preschool PK-PK
525 E Main St 67110 316-777-4221
Joyce Abel, prin. Fax 777-9456

Munjor, Ellis, Pop. 400
Hays USD 489
Supt. — See Hays
Munjor ES 50/K-5
892 Munjor Main St, Hays KS 67601 785-623-2630
Dr. Will Roth, prin. Fax 623-2632

Natoma, Osborne, Pop. 329
Paradise USD 399 200/PK-12
PO Box 100 67651 785-885-4843
Aaron Homburg, supt. Fax 885-4523
www.usd399.com/
Natoma ES 100/PK-6
PO Box 10 67651 785-885-4478
Aaron Homburg, prin. Fax 885-4479

Neodesha, Wilson, Pop. 2,652
Neodesha USD 461 800/PK-12
PO Box 88 66757 620-325-2610
Daryl Pruter, supt. Fax 325-2368
www.neodesha.com/neodesha/district.html
Heller ES 300/PK-3
415 N 8th St 66757 620-325-3066
Teresa Evensvold, prin. Fax 325-2933
North Lawn ES 200/4-6
620 W Granby Ave 66757 620-325-3011
Melissa Johnson, prin. Fax 325-8106

Neosho Rapids, Lyon, Pop. 278
Southern Lyon County USD 252
Supt. — See Hartford
Neosho Rapids ES 100/PK-6
PO Box 38 66864 620-342-8105
Bill Warner, prin. Fax 341-9464

Ness City, Ness, Pop. 1,326
Ness City USD 303 300/PK-12
414 E Chestnut St 67560 785-798-2210
Randall Jansonius, supt. Fax 798-3581
www.nesscityschools.org
Ness City ES 100/PK-6
500 E Chestnut St 67560 785-798-2222
Randall Jansonius, prin. Fax 798-3581

Sacred Heart S 100/K-8
510 S School St 67560 785-798-3530
Ann Depperschmidt, prin. Fax 798-3004

Newton, Harvey, Pop. 18,229
Newton USD 373 3,500/PK-12
308 E 1st St 67114 316-284-6200
Dr. John Morton, supt. Fax 284-6207
www.newton.k12.ks.us
Chisholm MS 400/6-8
900 E 1st St 67114 316-284-6260
George Leary, prin. Fax 284-6267
Northridge ES 300/PK-5
1900 Windsor Dr 67114 316-284-6540
Arthur Whillock, prin. Fax 284-6545
Santa Fe MS 400/6-8
130 W Broadway St 67114 316-284-6270
Victoria Adame, prin. Fax 284-6596
Slate Creek ES 500/K-5
901 E 4th St 67114 316-284-6550
Kevin Neuenswander, prin. Fax 284-6556
South Breeze ES 400/PK-5
1020 Old Main St 67114 316-284-6560
Jannan Plummer, prin. Fax 284-6565
Sunset ES 400/K-5
619 Boyd Ave 67114 316-284-6570
Janet Weaver, prin. Fax 284-6575

St. Mary Catholic S 100/PK-8
101 E 9th St 67114 316-282-1974
Philip Stutey, prin. Fax 283-3642

Nickerson, Reno, Pop. 1,164
Nickerson USD 309
Supt. — See Hutchinson
Nickerson ES 300/K-6
400 N Nickerson St 67561 620-422-3215
Terry George, prin. Fax 422-3216

Norton, Norton, Pop. 2,806
Norton USD 211 700/PK-12
105 E Waverly St 67654 785-877-3386
Greg Mann, supt. Fax 877-2030
www.usd211.org/
Eisenhower ES 300/PK-6
1100 Eisenhower Dr 67654 785-877-5113
Corey Roy, prin. Fax 877-6516
Norton JHS 100/7-8
706 Jones Ave 67654 785-877-5851
Jeff Wallingford, prin. Fax 877-3771

Nortonville, Jefferson, Pop. 598
Jefferson County North USD 339
Supt. — See Winchester
Jefferson County North S 300/PK-8
100 Charger Ln 66060 913-886-3870
Denise Jennings, prin. Fax 886-6280

Norwich, Kingman, Pop. 522
Kingman-Norwich USD 331
Supt. — See Kingman
Norwich S 200/PK-8
209 S Parkway St 67118 620-478-2235
Deana Waltrip, prin. Fax 478-2879

Oakley, Logan, Pop. 1,984
Oakley USD 274 400/PK-12
621 Center Ave # 103 67748 785-672-4588
Bill Steiner, supt. Fax 672-3044
www.oakleyschoolsks.com/
Oakley ES 200/PK-5
115 W 6th St 67748 785-672-3842
Robert Sattler, prin. Fax 672-4574
Oakley MS 100/6-8
611 Center Ave 67748 785-672-3820
Robert Sattler, prin. Fax 672-3010

St. Joseph S 100/PK-6
725 Freeman Ave 67748 785-672-4451
Kimberly Shirley, prin. Fax 672-3819

Oberlin, Decatur, Pop. 1,811
Oberlin USD 294 400/PK-12
131 E Commercial St 67749 785-475-3805
Dr. Pat Cullen, supt. Fax 475-3076
www.usd294.org
Oberlin ES 200/PK-6
201 W Ash St 67749 785-475-2122
Duane Dorshorst, prin. Fax 475-2579

Offerle, Edwards, Pop. 214
Kinsley-Offerle USD 347
Supt. — See Kinsley
Kinsley-Offerle ES 100/K-6
325 S Elm St 67563 620-659-2866
Becky Burcher, prin. Fax 659-3468

Ogden, Riley, Pop. 1,432
Manhattan-Ogden USD 383
Supt. — See Manhattan
Ogden ES 200/PK-6
PO Box 851 66517 785-587-2080
Jim Armendariz, prin. Fax 587-2085

Olathe, Johnson, Pop. 111,334
Blue Valley USD 229
Supt. — See Overland Park
Liberty View ES 600/K-5
14800 S Greenwood St 66062 913-239-7700
Susan Lonergan, prin. Fax 239-7748

Olathe USD 233 25,000/PK-12
PO Box 2000 66063 913-780-7000
Dr. Patricia All, supt. Fax 780-8007
www.olatheschools.com/
Arbor Creek ES 600/PK-6
16150 S Brougham Dr 66062 913-780-7300
Dr. Melanie DeMoss, prin. Fax 780-7309
Black Bob ES 400/K-6
14701 S Brougham Dr 66062 913-780-7310
Dr. Barry Cook, prin. Fax 780-7319
Briarwood ES 500/PK-6
14101 S Brougham Dr 66062 913-780-7330
Julie Richards, prin. Fax 780-7339
Brougham ES 500/PK-6
15500 S Brougham Dr 66062 913-780-7350
Brian Lowe, prin. Fax 780-7359
Cedar Creek ES 400/K-6
11150 S Clare Rd 66061 913-780-7360
Stephanie Prichard, prin. Fax 780-7369
Central ES 300/K-6
324 S Water St 66061 913-780-7370
Stephanie Dancso, prin. Fax 780-7379
Clearwater Creek ES 400/K-6
930 S Clearwater Creek Dr 66061 913-780-7380
Randy Smith, prin. Fax 780-7369
Countryside ES 500/PK-6
15800 W 124th Ter 66062 913-780-7390
Amy Hercules, prin. Fax 780-7395
Fairview ES 300/PK-6
600 N Marion St 66061 913-780-7430
Brett Yeager, prin. Fax 780-7439
Forest View ES PK-6
12567 S Canyon Dr 66061 913-780-7440
Dr. Mark Heck, prin. Fax 780-7449
Green Springs ES 400/K-6
14675 S Alden St 66062 913-780-7450
Brenda Traughber, prin. Fax 780-7457
Havencroft ES 300/PK-6
1700 E Sheridan St 66062 913-780-7470
Angela Thrasher, prin. Fax 780-7479
Heatherstone ES 600/K-6
13745 W 123rd St 66062 913-780-7480
Dr. Ruth Waggoner, prin. Fax 780-7489
Heritage ES 400/K-6
1700 E Pawnee Dr 66062 913-780-7490
Tim Reves, prin. Fax 780-7499
Indian Creek ES 400/K-6
15800 Indian Creek Pkwy 66062 913-780-7510
Linda Voyles, prin. Fax 780-7519
Madison Place ES K-6
16651 Warwick St 66062 913-780-7520
Gary Stevenson, prin. Fax 780-7529
Mahaffie ES 500/K-6
1300 N Nelson Rd 66061 913-780-7530
Peggy Head, prin. Fax 780-7537
Meadow Lane ES 500/K-6
21880 College Blvd 66061 913-780-7550
Terry Croskey, prin. Fax 780-7559
Northview ES 300/K-6
905 N Walker Ln 66061 913-780-7570
Todd Wheat, prin. Fax 780-7579
Prairie Center ES 400/K-6
629 N Persimmon Dr 66061 913-780-7610
Natalie Browning, prin. Fax 780-7619
Ravenwood ES 400/K-6
12211 S Clinton St 66061 913-780-7640
Tanya Channell, prin. Fax 780-7649
Regency Place ES 700/K-6
13250 S Greenwood St 66062 913-780-7620
Greg Oborny, prin. Fax 780-7629
Ridgeview ES 300/K-6
1201 E Elm St 66061 913-780-7630
Kelly Ralston, prin. Fax 780-7639
Rolling Ridge ES 400/PK-6
1500 W Elm Ter 66061 913-780-7650
Lori Fielder, prin. Fax 780-7659
Scarborough ES 500/PK-6
2000 S Lindenwood Dr 66062 913-780-7670
Jami Craig, prin. Fax 780-7675
Sunnyside ES 800/K-6
16025 S Lindenwood Dr 66062 913-780-7680
David Kearney, prin. Fax 780-7689
Tomahawk ES 400/K-6
13820 S Brougham Dr 66062 913-780-7690
Linda Armstrong, prin. Fax 780-7699
Walnut Grove ES 500/PK-6
11800 S Pflumm Rd 66062 913-780-7710
Lynne Borchers, prin. Fax 780-7719
Washington ES 500/K-6
1202 N Ridgeview Rd 66061 913-780-7730
Christi Gottschalk, prin. Fax 780-7739
Westview ES 200/K-6
601 S Lee Ave 66061 913-780-7750
John Harriss, prin. Fax 780-7759
Woodland ES K-6
11601 S Woodland St 66061 913-780-7770
Stacy Shipley, prin. Fax 780-7779
Other Schools – See Lenexa, Overland Park

Spring Hill USD 230
Supt. — See Spring Hill
Prairie Creek ES K-5
17077 W 165th St 66062 913-592-7255
Jody Cole, prin. Fax 393-4849

Metro Academy 300/K-12
17550 W 159th St 66062 913-782-0662
Robin Sullivan, admin.
Prince of Peace S 600/K-8
16000 W 143rd St 66062 913-764-0650
Jane Shriver, prin. Fax 393-0819
St. Paul S 200/PK-8
920 W Honeysuckle Dr 66061 913-764-0619
Stephanie Hill, prin. Fax 768-6040

Olpe, Lyon, Pop. 509
Southern Lyon County USD 252
Supt. — See Hartford
Olpe ES 100/PK-6
PO Box 206 66865 620-475-3277
Bill Warner, prin. Fax 475-3951

St. Joseph S, PO Box 147 66865 100/PK-6
Theresa Lein, prin. 620-475-3416

Olsburg, Pottawatomie, Pop. 191
Blue Valley USD 384
Supt. — See Randolph
Olsburg ES 100/K-4
PO Box 68 66520 785-468-3551
Jim McCormick, prin. Fax 468-3669

Onaga, Pottawatomie, Pop. 683
Onaga-Havensville-Wheaton USD 322 400/PK-12
PO Box 60 66521 785-889-4614
Fred Marten, supt. Fax 889-4662
www.usd322.org
Onaga S 200/PK-8
PO Box 70 66521 785-889-7101
Sandra Zahn, prin. Fax 889-7101

Osage City, Osage, Pop. 2,987
Osage City USD 420 500/K-12
520 Main St 66523 785-528-3176
David Carriger, supt. Fax 528-3932
www.usd420.org
Osage City ES 300/K-5
420 S 4th St 66523 785-528-3171
Dwight Stoppel, prin. Fax 528-2986

Osage City MS 6-8
420 S 5th St 66523 785-528-3175
Tony Heward, prin. Fax 528-2980

Osawatomie, Miami, Pop. 4,616
Osawatomie USD 367 1,200/PK-12
1200 Trojan Dr 66064 913-755-4172
Gary French, supt. Fax 755-2031
www.usd367.org/
Osawatomie MS 300/6-8
428 Pacific Ave 66064 913-755-4155
Dan Welch, prin. Fax 755-2197
Swenson Early Childhood Education Center 100/PK-K
608 10th St 66064 913-755-3220
Andrea Manes, prin. Fax 755-3987
Trojan ES 500/1-5
1901 Parker Ave 66064 913-755-4133
Jeff White, prin. Fax 755-4080

Osborne, Osborne, Pop. 1,440
Osborne County USD 392 400/PK-12
234 W Washington St 67473 785-346-2145
Keith Hall, supt. Fax 346-2448
www.usd392.k12.ks.us
Osborne ES 200/PK-6
234 N 3rd St 67473 785-346-5491
Henry Armknecht, prin. Fax 346-2668

Oskaloosa, Jefferson, Pop. 1,149
Oskaloosa USD 341 500/PK-12
404 Park St 66066 785-863-2539
Jon Pfau, supt. Fax 863-3080
www.usd341.org
Oskaloosa ES 300/PK-6
404 Park St 66066 785-863-3237
Darren Shupe, prin. Fax 863-9247

Oswego, Labette, Pop. 1,996
Oswego USD 504 400/PK-12
719 4th St 67356 620-795-2126
Terry Karlin, supt. Fax 795-4871
www.usd504.org
Oswego MS 100/6-8
410 Kansas St 67356 620-795-4724
Mikel Ward, prin. Fax 795-4799
Oswego Neosho Heights ES 200/PK-5
12 Oregon St 67356 620-795-4541
Cynthia Sanders, prin. Fax 795-4591

Otis, Rush, Pop. 319
Otis-Bison USD 403 200/K-12
PO Box 227 67565 620-923-4661
John Vincent, supt. Fax 923-4224
Otis-Bison ES 100/K-6
PO Box 288 67565 785-387-2371
Mark Goodheart, prin. Fax 387-2646

Ottawa, Franklin, Pop. 12,597
Ottawa USD 290 2,200/K-12
416 S Main St 66067 785-229-8010
Dean Katt, supt. Fax 229-8019
www.usd290.org
Eisenhower ES 100/K-5
1404 S Ash St 66067 785-229-8040
Nancy Johnson, prin. Fax 229-8049
Field ES 200/K-5
720 S Tremont Ave 66067 785-229-8050
Josh Robinson, prin. Fax 229-8059
Garfield ES 300/K-5
1213 S College St 66067 785-229-8060
Jeff Green, prin. Fax 229-8149
Lincoln ES 300/K-5
1102 N Milner St 66067 785-229-8080
Vicki Schweinler, prin. Fax 229-8089
Ottawa MS 500/6-8
1230 S Ash St 66067 785-229-8030
Carmen Schaefer, prin. Fax 229-8039

Bethel Christian Academy 50/K-12
3755 Nevada Rd 66067 785-242-1226
Donita Callahan, admin. Fax 242-1226
Sacred Heart ES 100/K-5
426 S Cedar St 66067 785-242-4297
Diane Chapman, prin. Fax 242-0820

Overbrook, Osage, Pop. 971
Santa Fe Trail USD 434
Supt. — See Carbondale
Overbrook Attendance Center 300/PK-8
PO Box 324 66524 785-665-7135
Gary Foulke, prin. Fax 665-7189

Overland Park, Johnson, Pop. 164,811
Blue Valley USD 229 19,800/PK-12
PO Box 23901 66283 913-239-4000
Tom Trigg Ed.D., supt. Fax 239-4150
www.bluevalleyk12.org
Blue River ES 600/PK-5
5101 W 163rd Ter, 913-239-6000
Deborah Kelly, prin. Fax 239-6048
Blue Valley MS 600/6-8
5001 W 163rd Ter, 913-239-5100
Roxana Rogers, prin. Fax 239-5148
Cedar Hills ES 500/PK-5
9100 W 165th St, 913-239-3300
Steve Marsh, prin. Fax 239-3348
Cottonwood Point ES 500/K-5
10521 W 129th St 66213 913-239-6100
Jill Smith Ed.D., prin. Fax 239-6148
Harmony ES 600/PK-5
14140 Grant St 66221 913-239-6200
Cathy Austin Ed.D., prin. Fax 239-6248
Harmony MS 600/6-8
10101 W 141st St 66221 913-239-5200
Sheila Albers, prin. Fax 239-5248
Heartland ES 500/PK-5
12775 Goodman St 66213 913-239-6300
Sherry Sims, prin. Fax 239-6348
Indian Valley ES 300/K-5
11600 Knox St 66210 913-239-6400
Marilyn Shetlar, prin. Fax 239-6448
Lakewood ES 700/K-5
14600 Lamar Ave 66223 913-239-6500
Nancy Layton, prin. Fax 239-6548
Lakewood MS 700/6-8
6601 Edgewater Dr 66223 913-239-5800
Scott Currier, prin. Fax 239-5848
Morse ES 400/PK-5
15201 Monrovia St 66221 913-239-6800
Mark Lange, prin. Fax 239-6848
Oak Hill ES 400/K-5
10200 W 124th St 66213 913-239-6900
David Sanders, prin. Fax 239-6948
Overland Trail ES 600/PK-5
6225 W 133rd St 66209 913-239-7000
Doris Moore, prin. Fax 239-7048
Overland Trail MS 600/6-8
6201 W 133rd St 66209 913-239-5400
Phoebe Lewis, prin. Fax 239-5448
Oxford MS 700/6-8
12500 Switzer Rd 66213 913-239-5500
Linda Crosthwait, prin. Fax 239-5548
Stanley ES 400/K-5
6121 W 158th St 66223 913-239-7200
Stacy Graff, prin. Fax 239-7248
Sunrise Point ES K-5
15800 Roe Blvd 66224 913-239-7500
Jeff McClelland, prin. Fax 239-7548
Sunset Ridge ES 600/K-5
14901 England St 66221 913-239-7400
Mandy Shoemaker, prin. Fax 239-7448
Timber Creek ES 100/K-5
16451 Flint St, 913-239-7800
Pam Bakke Ed.D., prin. Fax 239-7848
Valley Park ES 500/PK-5
12301 Lamar Ave 66209 913-239-7600
Marlene Wedel, prin. Fax 239-7648
Other Schools – See Leawood, Olathe, Stilwell

Olathe USD 233
Supt. — See Olathe
Bentwood ES 500/K-6
13000 Bond St 66213 913-897-8830
Dr. Catherine McDonald, prin. Fax 897-8839
Pleasant Ridge ES 500/PK-6
12235 Rosehill St 66213 913-897-7595
Krystal Actkinson, prin. Fax 897-8807

Shawnee Mission USD 512
Supt. — See Shawnee Mission
Apache ES 300/PK-6
8910 Goddard St 66214 913-993-1600
Jennifer Monroe, prin. Fax 993-1699
Brookridge ES 400/K-6
9920 Lowell Ave 66212 913-993-2400
Dr. Sue Adams, prin. Fax 993-2499
Diemer ES 300/K-6
9600 Lamar Ave 66207 913-993-3100
Jan Turner, prin. Fax 993-3199
East Antioch ES 400/PK-6
7342 Lowell Ave 66204 913-993-3200
Karen Metz, prin. Fax 993-3299
Moody ES 300/K-6
10101 England Dr 66212 913-993-3800
Marilyn Webb, prin. Fax 993-3899
Oak Park - Carpenter ES 300/K-6
10000 Nieman Rd 66214 913-993-4100
Jennifer Gill, prin. Fax 993-4199
Overland Park ES 400/K-6
8150 Santa Fe Dr 66204 913-993-4200
J. Leah Pearl, prin. Fax 993-4299
Pawnee ES 500/K-6
9501 W 91st St 66212 913-993-4300
Justin Green, prin. Fax 993-4399
Santa Fe Trail ES 300/PK-6
7100 Lamar Ave 66204 913-993-5000
Steve Vandemark, prin. Fax 993-5099
Tomahawk ES 300/K-6
6301 W 78th St 66204 913-993-5500
Scott Merfen, prin. Fax 993-5599
Trailwood ES 300/PK-6
5101 W 95th St 66207 913-993-5600
Michael Stouffer, prin. Fax 993-5699

Ascension S 600/K-8
9510 W 127th St 66213 913-851-2531
Margaret Sachs, prin. Fax 851-2518
Bethany Lutheran S 100/K-8
9101 Lamar Ave 66207 913-648-2228
Pam Nummela, prin. Fax 648-2283
Brookridge Day S 200/PK-3
9555 Hadley Dr 66212 913-649-2228
Barbara Brown, prin. Fax 649-6710
Christ Lutheran S 100/K-7
11720 Nieman Rd 66210 913-754-5888
Jon Skilton, prin. Fax 345-9707
First Family Academy 100/PK-K
7700 W 143rd St 66223 913-312-6010
Shelta Collins, prin. Fax 681-7819
Holy Cross S 400/K-8
8101 W 95th St 66212 913-381-7408
Mary Jo Gates, prin. Fax 381-1312
Holy Spirit S 500/PK-8
11300 W 103rd St 66214 913-492-2582
Michele Watson, prin. Fax 492-9613
John Paul II Catholic S 300/PK-8
6915 W 71st St 66204 913-432-6350
Susie English, prin. Fax 432-5081
Mt. Olive Lutheran S 50/K-8
9514 Perry Ln 66212 913-888-6293
Dale Rundgren, prin. Fax 492-2326
Overland Christian S 100/PK-12
7401 Metcalf Ave 66204 913-722-0272
Marla Cook, prin. Fax 403-0595
Small Beginnings Montessori S 200/PK-2
15801 Metcalf Ave 66223 913-851-2223
Robert O'Reilly, admin. Fax 851-2224
Westminster Christian Academy 200/K-12
9333 W 159th St 66221 913-681-7622
Kathleen Sievert, admin. Fax 851-8056

Oxford, Sumner, Pop. 1,117
Oxford USD 358 400/PK-12
PO Box 937 67119 620-455-2227
Dr. Deborah Hamm, supt. Fax 455-3680
www.usd358.com
Oxford ES 200/PK-6
PO Box 1000 67119 620-455-2422
Terri Wiseman, prin. Fax 455-3842

Ozawkie, Jefferson, Pop. 574
Jefferson West USD 340
Supt. — See Meriden
Jefferson West IS 100/4-5
PO Box 10 66070 785-876-2110
Patton Happer, prin. Fax 876-2799

Palco, Rooks, Pop. 228
Palco USD 269 200/PK-12
PO Box B 67657 785-737-4635
David Miller, supt. Fax 737-4646
www.usd269.k12.ks.us/
Palco ES 100/PK-5
PO Box B 67657 785-737-4625
Lisa Gehring, prin. Fax 737-4636
Other Schools – See Damar

Paola, Miami, Pop. 5,292
Paola USD 368 2,000/PK-12
PO Box 268 66071 913-294-8000
Dr. Rod Allen, supt. Fax 294-8001
www.usd368.org/
Cottonwood ES 400/K-2
709 Hedge Ln 66071 913-294-8050
Janis Grandon, prin. Fax 294-8051
Paola MS 500/6-8
405 N Hospital Dr 66071 913-294-8030
Matt Meek, prin. Fax 294-8031
Sunflower ES 400/3-5
1401 E 303rd St 66071 913-294-8040
Staci Wokutch, prin. Fax 294-8041
Other Schools – See Hillsdale

Holy Trinity S 200/K-8
601 E Chippewa St 66071 913-294-3286
Eric White, prin. Fax 294-5286
Trinity Lutheran S 50/1-8
34944 Block Rd 66071 913-849-3343
Ray Diepenbrock, prin. Fax 849-3343

Park City, Sedgwick, Pop. 7,173
Wichita USD 259
Supt. — See Wichita
Chisholm Trail ES 500/PK-5
6015 N Independence St 67219 316-973-9400
Susan Hussey, prin. Fax 973-9410

Parker, Linn, Pop. 306
Prairie View USD 362
Supt. — See La Cygne
Parker ES, 421 N Center Ave 66072 100/PK-5
Mark Staab, prin. 913-898-3160

Parsons, Labette, Pop. 11,212
Labette County USD 506
Supt. — See Altamont
Meadow View S 400/K-8
1377 21000 Rd 67357 620-421-1857
Chris Kastler, prin. Fax 421-0379

Parsons USD 503 1,400/PK-12
PO Box 1056 67357 620-421-5950
Dr. Deborah Perbeck, supt. Fax 421-5954
www.vikingnet.net
Garfield ES 200/K-5
300 S 14th St 67357 620-421-3530
Lori Ray, prin. Fax 423-8838
Guthridge ES 200/PK-5
1020 S 31st St 67357 620-421-6800
Amber Wheeler, prin. Fax 423-8843
Lincoln ES 200/K-5
1800 Dirr Ave 67357 620-421-3510
Lee Ann Hunter, prin. Fax 423-8831
Parsons MS 300/6-8
2719 Main St 67357 620-421-4190
Terry Smith, prin. Fax 423-8822

St. Patrick Catholic S 100/PK-8
1831 Stevens Ave 67357 620-421-0710
Tim Born, prin. Fax 421-2429

Partridge, Reno, Pop. 266
Haven USD 312
Supt. — See Haven
Partridge S 100/K-8
PO Box 98 67566 620-567-2641
Ellis Miller, prin. Fax 567-2816

Paxico, Wabaunsee, Pop. 212
Mill Creek Valley USD 329
Supt. — See Alma
Mill Creek Valley JHS 100/7-8
PO Box 128 66526 785-636-5353
Cleion Morton, prin. Fax 636-5116
Mill Creek Valley MS 100/5-6
PO Box 128 66526 785-636-5343
Cleion Morton, prin. Fax 636-5276

Peabody, Marion, Pop. 1,302
Peabody-Burns USD 398 400/PK-12
506 N Elm St 66866 620-983-2198
Rex Watson, supt. Fax 983-2247
www.usd398.com
Peabody-Burns ES 200/PK-6
506 N Elm St 66866 620-983-2188
Ken Parry, prin. Fax 983-2247

Perry, Jefferson, Pop. 883
Perry USD 343 800/PK-12
PO Box 729 66073 785-597-5138
Dr. Denis Yoder, supt. Fax 597-2254
www.usd343.org/

Perry ES 100/PK-1
PO Box 168 66073 785-597-5156
Connie Thornton, prin. Fax 597-5157
Perry-Lecompton MS 300/5-8
PO Box 31 66073 785-597-5159
Armin Landis, prin. Fax 597-5014
Other Schools – See Lecompton

Phillipsburg, Phillips, Pop. 2,432
Phillipsburg USD 325 600/PK-12
240 S 7th St 67661 785-543-5281
Kent Otte, supt. Fax 543-2271
www.usd325.com
Phillipsburg ES 200/PK-4
300 Nebraska Ave 67661 785-543-2174
Mike Gower, prin. Fax 543-5332
Phillipsburg MS 200/5-8
647 7th St 67661 785-543-5114
Rick Riffel, prin. Fax 543-2934

Pittsburg, Crawford, Pop. 19,214
Pittsburg USD 250 2,500/K-12
PO Box 75 66762 620-235-3100
Destry Brown, supt. Fax 235-3106
www.usd250.org
Lakeside ES 400/K-5
709 S College St 66762 620-235-3140
Courtney McCartney, prin. Fax 235-3145
Meadowlark ES 300/K-5
1602 E 20th St 66762 620-235-3130
Phillis Scorse, prin. Fax 235-3134
Nettels ES 300/K-5
2012 S Homer St 66762 620-235-3160
Andy Gottlob, prin. Fax 235-3163
Pittsburg MS 500/6-8
1310 N Broadway St 66762 620-235-3240
Lonnie Moser, prin. Fax 235-3248
Westside ES 300/K-5
430 W 5th St 66762 620-235-3170
Ruth Miller, prin. Fax 235-3174

St. Mary's S 300/PK-6
301 E 9th St 66762 620-231-6941
Michael Martin, prin. Fax 231-0690

Plains, Meade, Pop. 1,163
Kismet-Plains USD 483
Supt. — See Kismet
Plains ES 200/PK-5
PO Box 337 67869 620-563-7285
Kyle Griffitts, prin. Fax 563-7873

Plainville, Rooks, Pop. 1,889
Plainville USD 270 400/PK-12
111 W Mill St 67663 785-434-4678
Beth Reust, supt. Fax 434-7404
Plainville S 300/PK-8
203 SE Cardinal Ave 67663 785-434-4508
Karen Crowe, prin. Fax 434-2096

Sacred Heart S 100/PK-6
300 N Washington St 67663 785-434-7459
Carol Parker, prin. Fax 434-2480

Pleasanton, Linn, Pop. 1,368
Pleasanton USD 344 400/K-12
PO Box 480 66075 913-352-8534
Greg Gorman, supt. Fax 352-6588
www.usd344.org/
Pleasanton ES 200/K-6
PO Box 480 66075 913-352-8531
Nichola Traul, prin. Fax 352-6588

Pomona, Franklin, Pop. 942
West Franklin USD 287 500/PK-12
510 E Franklin St 66076 785-566-3396
Dotson Bradbury, supt. Fax 566-8325
www.usd287.org
Appanoose ES 100/PK-5
600 Shawnee Rd 66076 785-566-3386
Cathy Brandt, prin. Fax 566-3750
West Franklin MS 100/6-8
331 E D St 66076 785-566-3541
Rick Smith, prin. Fax 566-3634
Other Schools – See Williamsburg

Potwin, Butler, Pop. 438
Remington-Whitewater USD 206
Supt. — See Whitewater
Remington ES at Potwin 200/K-5
PO Box 277 67123 620-752-3239
Jason Marciano, prin. Fax 752-3611

Prairie Village, Johnson, Pop. 21,454
Shawnee Mission USD 512
Supt. — See Shawnee Mission
Belinder ES 400/K-6
7230 Belinder Ave 66208 913-993-1800
Karen Faucher, prin. Fax 993-1899
Briarwood ES 500/K-6
5300 W 86th St 66207 913-993-2200
Steve Frazell, prin. Fax 993-2299
Highlands ES 300/K-6
2700 Somerset Dr 66206 913-993-3300
Jennifer Spencer, prin. Fax 993-3399

Kansas City Christian ES 200/K-6
4801 W 79th St 66208 913-648-5227
Kathy Hirleman, prin. Fax 648-5269
St. Ann S 500/K-8
7241 Mission Rd 66208 913-660-1101
Becky Akright, prin. Fax 660-1132

Pratt, Pratt, Pop. 6,447
Pratt USD 382 1,100/PK-12
401 N Ninnescah St 67124 620-672-4500
Dr. Glen Davis, supt. Fax 672-4509
www.usd382.com

Haskins ES 100/PK-3
900 School St 67124 620-672-4510
Mike Couch, prin. Fax 672-4519
Liberty MS 200/6-8
300 S Iuka St 67124 620-672-4530
Mike McDermeit, prin. Fax 672-4539
Southwest ES 300/PK-5
900 W 8th St 67124 620-672-4520
Jason May, prin. Fax 672-4529

Skyline USD 438 400/K-12
20269 W US Highway 54 67124 620-672-5651
Mike Sanders, supt. Fax 672-9377
www.usd438.k12.ks.us
Skyline S 300/K-8
20269 W US Highway 54 67124 620-672-5651
Richard Thompson, prin. Fax 672-9377

Sacred Heart S 100/PK-5
330 N Oak St 67124 620-672-3687
Linda Conkle, lead tchr. Fax 672-3607

Pretty Prairie, Reno, Pop. 600
Pretty Prairie USD 311 300/K-12
PO Box 218 67570 620-459-6241
Brad Wade, supt. Fax 459-6810
www.usd311.com
Pretty Prairie ES 100/K-4
PO Box 98 67570 620-459-6621
Brad Wade, prin. Fax 459-6616
Pretty Prairie MS 100/5-8
PO Box 307 67570 620-459-6911
Randy Hendrickson, prin. Fax 459-6729

Protection, Comanche, Pop. 541
Comanche County USD 300
Supt. — See Coldwater
South Central ES 200/K-5
PO Box 38 67127 620-622-4545
Matt Jellison, prin. Fax 622-4844
South Central MS 100/6-8
PO Box 38 67127 620-622-4545
Matt Jellison, prin. Fax 622-4844

Quenemo, Osage, Pop. 455
Marais Des Cygnes Valley USD 456
Supt. — See Melvern
Marais Des Cygnes Valley ES 100/K-5
PO Box 139 66528 785-759-3512
Twila Wollenberg, prin. Fax 759-3515

Quinter, Gove, Pop. 846
Quinter USD 293 300/PK-12
PO Box 540 67752 785-754-2470
Allaire Homburg, supt. Fax 754-3365
www.quinterhs.org
Quinter ES 200/PK-6
PO Box 429 67752 785-754-3953
Linda Zeigler, prin. Fax 754-2487

Randolph, Riley, Pop. 135
Blue Valley USD 384 200/K-12
PO Box 98 66554 785-293-5256
Brady Burton, supt. Fax 293-5607
www.usd384.org/
Randolph MS 100/5-8
PO Box 38 66554 785-293-5253
Tim Winter, prin. Fax 293-4405
Other Schools – See Olsburg

Ransom, Ness, Pop. 292
Western Plains USD 106 200/PK-12
311 W Ogden St 67572 785-398-2535
James Frank, supt. Fax 398-2492
www.usd106.k12.ks.us/
Western Plains North S 100/PK-5
311 W Ogden St 67572 785-731-2434
James Frank, prin. Fax 731-2624
Other Schools – See Bazine

Reading, Lyon, Pop. 249
North Lyon County USD 251
Supt. — See Americus
Reading S 100/K-8
424 1st St 66868 620-699-3827
Peggy Fort, prin. Fax 699-3361

Rexford, Thomas, Pop. 151
Golden Plains USD 316
Supt. — See Selden
Golden Plains MS 50/6-8
PO Box 100 67753 785-687-3265
Mary Welshhon, prin. Fax 687-2285

Richmond, Franklin, Pop. 514
Central Heights USD 288 600/K-12
3521 Ellis Rd 66080 785-869-3455
Jim Reece, supt. Fax 869-2675
www.usd288.org/
Central Heights ES 300/K-5
3521 Ellis Rd 66080 785-869-3355
Luis Hinojosa, prin. Fax 869-2675
Central Heights MS 100/6-8
3521 Ellis Rd 66080 785-869-3809
Buddy Welch, prin.

Riley, Riley, Pop. 692
Riley County USD 378 700/PK-12
PO Box 326 66531 785-485-4000
Brad Starnes, supt. Fax 485-2860
www.usd378.org/
Riley County S 400/PK-8
PO Box 248 66531 785-485-4010
Teresa Grant, prin. Fax 485-2929

Riverton, Cherokee
Riverton USD 404 900/K-12
PO Box 290 66770 620-848-3386
Todd Berry, supt. Fax 848-9853
www.usd404.org/

Riverton ES 400/K-5
PO Box 260 66770 620-848-4078
Keith Wilson, prin. Fax 848-4025
Riverton MS 200/6-8
PO Box 260 66770 620-848-3355
Becky Murray, prin. Fax 848-3288

Roeland Park, Johnson, Pop. 6,975

St. Agnes S 400/PK-8
5130 Mission Rd 66205 913-262-1686
Kim Hammers, prin. Fax 384-1567

Rolla, Morton, Pop. 445
Rolla USD 217 200/PK-12
PO Box 167 67954 620-593-4344
Richard Spencer, supt. Fax 593-4250
www.usd217.org
Rolla ES 100/PK-5
PO Box 167 67954 620-593-4731
Sam Eiland, prin. Fax 593-4608

Rosalia, Butler
Flinthills USD 492 300/K-12
PO Box 188 67132 620-476-2237
Bob Diepenbrock, supt. Fax 476-2253
www.usd492.org/
Flinthills IS 100/3-6
PO Box 188 67132 620-476-2218
Larry Gawith, prin. Fax 476-2391
Other Schools – See Cassoday

Rose Hill, Butler, Pop. 3,896
Rose Hill USD 394 1,700/PK-12
104 N Rose Hill Rd 67133 316-776-3300
Randal Chickadonz, supt. Fax 776-3309
www.usd394.com
Rose Hill IS 400/3-5
104 N Rose Hill Rd 67133 316-776-3330
Kevin Collier, prin. Fax 776-3335
Rose Hill MS 400/6-8
104 N Rose Hill Rd 67133 316-776-3320
Kay Walker, prin. Fax 776-3319
Rose Hill PS 300/PK-2
104 N Rose Hill Rd 67133 316-776-3340
Terri Reilly, prin. Fax 776-3379

Rossville, Shawnee, Pop. 996
Kaw Valley USD 321
Supt. — See Saint Marys
Rossville ES 200/K-6
PO Box 248 66533 785-584-6188
Ann McCullough, prin. Fax 584-6695

Russell, Russell, Pop. 4,342
Russell County USD 407 1,000/K-12
802 N Main St 67665 785-483-2173
David Couch, supt. Fax 483-2175
www.usd407.org/
Bickerdyke ES 200/3-5
348 N Maple St 67665 785-483-6066
Kent Michel, prin. Fax 483-5982
Ruppenthal MS 200/6-8
400 N Elm St 67665 785-483-3174
Gaylon Walter, prin. Fax 483-5386
Simpson ES 200/K-2
1323 N Main St 67665 785-483-6180
Kent Michel, prin. Fax 483-5459
Other Schools – See Luray

Sabetha, Nemaha, Pop. 2,523
Sabetha USD 441 900/PK-12
1619 S Old Hwy 75 66534 785-284-2175
Dennis Stones, supt. Fax 284-3739
sabetha441.k12.ks.us
Sabetha ES 300/PK-5
101 Oregon St 66534 785-284-3448
Matthew Garber, prin. Fax 284-2480
Sabetha MS 200/6-8
751 Blue Jay Blvd 66534 785-284-2151
Thomas Palmer, prin. Fax 284-0061
Other Schools – See Wetmore

St Benedict, Nemaha
B & B USD 451
Supt. — See Baileyville
St. Benedict ES 100/K-6
9897 State Highway 178, 785-336-3201
Jerry Turner, prin. Fax 336-3201

Saint Francis, Cheyenne, Pop. 1,390
St. Francis Community USD 297 300/K-12
PO Box 1110 67756 785-332-8182
Robert Schiltz, supt. Fax 332-8177
www.usd297.org/
Saint Francis ES 100/K-6
PO Box 1110 67756 785-332-8143
Scott Carmichael, prin. Fax 332-8144

Saint George, Pottawatomie, Pop. 457
Rock Creek USD 323
Supt. — See Westmoreland
Saint George ES 300/PK-6
PO Box 31 66535 785-494-2482
Debbie Edwards, prin. Fax 494-2481

Saint John, Stafford, Pop. 1,249
St. John-Hudson USD 350 400/K-12
505 N Broadway St 67576 620-549-3564
Dr. James Kenworthy, supt. Fax 549-3964
www.usd350.com/
Saint John ES 200/K-6
505 N Broadway St 67576 620-549-3518
David Losey, prin. Fax 549-3678

Saint Marys, Pottawatomie, Pop. 2,253
Kaw Valley USD 321 1,100/PK-12
411 W Lasley St 66536 785-437-2254
James McDaniel, supt. Fax 437-3155
www.kawvalley.k12.ks.us/

Saint Marys ES 200/K-6
312 S Grand Ave 66536 785-437-6159
Bill Russell, prin. Fax 437-3165
Other Schools – See Emmett, Rossville

Saint Paul, Neosho, Pop. 657
Chetopa - St. Paul USD 505
Supt. — See Chetopa
Saint Paul ES 100/K-6
PO Box 68 66771 620-449-2245
Mark LaTurner, prin. Fax 449-8960

Salina, Saline, Pop. 45,956
Ell-Saline USD 307
Supt. — See Brookville
Ell-Saline ES 300/K-6
1757 N Halstead Rd 67401 785-827-8891
Dana Sprinkle, prin. Fax 825-7355

Salina USD 305 7,200/PK-12
PO Box 797 67402 785-309-4700
Dr. Robert Winter, supt. Fax 309-4737
www.usd305.com
Coronado ES 400/K-5
518 E Neal Ave 67401 785-309-4100
Tina Daniels, prin. Fax 309-4101
Cottonwood ES 400/K-5
215 S Phillips Ave 67401 785-309-4600
Jerry Baxa, prin. Fax 309-4601
Heusner ES 400/K-5
1300 Norton St 67401 785-309-4200
Lori Munsell, prin. Fax 309-4201
Kennedy Early Learning Center PK-PK
700 Jupiter Ave 67401 785-309-5000
Korey Hensley, dir. Fax 309-5001
Lakewood MS 800/6-8
1135 E Lakewood Cir 67401 785-309-4000
Mike Lowers, prin. Fax 309-4001
Meadowlark Ridge ES 400/K-5
2200 Glen Ave 67401 785-309-4300
Deena Hilbig, prin. Fax 309-4301
Oakdale ES 400/K-5
811 E Iron Ave 67401 785-309-4310
Carmen Flax, prin. Fax 309-4311
Salina South MS 900/6-8
2040 S 4th St 67401 785-309-3900
Beth Morrison, prin. Fax 309-3901
Schilling ES 400/K-5
3121 Canterbury Dr 67401 785-309-4400
Leigh Hendrix, prin. Fax 309-4401
Stewart ES 400/K-5
2123 Roach St 67401 785-309-4450
Juanita Erickson, prin. Fax 309-4451
Sunset ES 400/K-5
1510 W Republic Ave 67401 785-309-4520
Lonny Schropp, prin. Fax 309-4521

St. Marys S 400/PK-6
304 E Cloud St 67401 785-827-4200
Nick Compagnone, prin. Fax 827-7765
Salina Christian Academy 100/PK-8
1009 Highland Ave 67401 785-452-9929
Janice Krause, prin. Fax 825-2506

Satanta, Haskell, Pop. 1,179
Satanta USD 507 400/PK-12
PO Box 279 67870 620-649-2234
Ardith Dunn, supt. Fax 649-2668
www.usd507.org
Satanta ES 200/PK-6
PO Box 129 67870 620-649-2612
Leanne Tschanz, prin. Fax 649-2627

Scammon, Cherokee, Pop. 475
Columbus USD 493
Supt. — See Columbus
Scammon ES 100/K-6
400 E Katy St 66773 620-479-3631
Jack Redden, prin. Fax 479-2516

Scandia, Republic, Pop. 374
Pike Valley USD 426 300/PK-12
PO Box 291 66966 785-335-2206
Chris Vignery, supt. Fax 335-2219
www.pikevalley.com
Other Schools – See Courtland

Scott City, Scott, Pop. 3,474
Scott County USD 466 900/PK-12
PO Box 288 67871 620-872-7600
Dr. Don Wells, supt. Fax 872-7609
www.usd466.com/
Scott City ES 400/PK-4
410 E 8th St 67871 620-872-7660
Shawn Roberts, prin. Fax 872-7669
Scott City MS 300/5-8
809 W 9th St 67871 620-872-7640
Neal George, prin. Fax 872-7649

Scranton, Osage, Pop. 712
Santa Fe Trail USD 434
Supt. — See Carbondale
Scranton Attendance Center 100/K-8
104 S Burlingame Ave 66537 785-793-2256
Sheryl Gill, prin. Fax 793-2828

Sedan, Chautauqua, Pop. 1,269
Chautauqua County Community USD 286 400/PK-12
302 Sherman St 67361 620-725-3187
Scott Hills, supt. Fax 725-5642
www.usd286-sedan-ks.org
Sedan ES 200/PK-6
404 Sherman St 67361 620-725-5611
Scott Hills, prin. Fax 725-5614

Sedgwick, Harvey, Pop. 1,644
Sedgwick USD 439 500/K-12
PO Box K 67135 316-772-5783
Michael Hull, supt. Fax 772-0274
www.usd439.k12.ks.us
Wright S 400/K-8
PO Box K 67135 316-772-5604
Pat Breckunitch, prin. Fax 772-5294

Selden, Sheridan, Pop. 185
Golden Plains USD 316 200/PK-12
PO Box 199 67757 785-386-4559
Mary Welshhon, supt. Fax 386-4562
usd316.k12.ks.us/
Golden Plains ES 100/PK-5
PO Box 199 67757 785-386-4560
Mary Welshhon, prin. Fax 386-4562
Other Schools – See Rexford

Seneca, Nemaha, Pop. 2,068
Nemaha Valley USD 442 500/K-12
318 Main St 66538 785-336-6101
Brian Harris, supt. Fax 336-2268
www.usd442.org
Seneca/Nehama Valley S 300/K-8
709 Nemaha St 66538 785-336-2173
Amy Beck, prin. Fax 336-2174

SS. Peter & Paul S 200/PK-8
401 Pioneer St 66538 785-336-2727
Todd Leonard, prin. Fax 336-3817

Severy, Greenwood, Pop. 352
West Elk USD 282
Supt. — See Howard
Severy ES 100/PK-5
PO Box 187 67137 620-736-2301
Pam Leiker, prin. Fax 374-2414

Sharon Springs, Wallace, Pop. 733
Wallace County USD 241 200/PK-12
521 N Main St 67758 785-852-4252
Robert Young, supt. Fax 852-4603
www.usd241.org/
Sharon Springs S 100/PK-8
521 N Main St 67758 785-852-4267
Robert Young, prin. Fax 852-4603

Shawnee, Johnson, Pop. 57,628
De Soto USD 232
Supt. — See De Soto
Clear Creek ES 600/K-5
5815 Monticello Rd 66226 913-422-8700
Mike Stithem, prin. Fax 422-3484
Horizon ES K-5
7210 Chouteau St 66227 913-667-3535
Kim Gracy, prin. Fax 422-9694
Mize ES 600/K-5
7301 Mize Rd 66227 913-441-0880
Pam Hargrove, prin. Fax 441-9452
Monticello Trails MS 800/6-8
6100 Monticello Rd 66226 913-422-1100
Tobie Waldeck, prin. Fax 422-4990
Prairie Ridge ES 500/K-5
22405 Clear Creek Pkwy 66226 913-667-1800
Dr. Jan McKinley, prin. Fax 667-3612
Riverview ES 600/K-5
21550 W 47th St 66226 913-441-0808
Mark Dodge, prin. Fax 441-1179

Shawnee Mission USD 512
Supt. — See Shawnee Mission
Benninghoven ES 600/K-6
6720 Caenen Ave 66216 913-993-1900
Dr. Mike Wilhoit, prin. Fax 993-1999
Broken Arrow ES 500/K-6
5901 Alden St 66216 913-993-2300
Michael Weiler, prin. Fax 993-2399
Marsh ES 500/K-6
5642 Rosehill Rd 66216 913-993-3400
Pam Lewis, prin. Fax 993-3499
Nieman ES 400/K-6
10917 W 67th St 66203 913-993-4000
Stan Anderson, prin. Fax 993-4099

Good Shepherd S 400/K-8
12800 W 75th St 66216 913-631-0400
Ann McGuff, prin. Fax 631-3539
Grace Christian Academy 50/K-6
7230 Quivira Rd 66216 913-268-6363
Phil Ellsworth, dir. Fax 268-6307
Hope Lutheran S 200/K-8
6308 Quivira Rd 66216 913-631-6940
Richard Hanebutt, prin. Fax 268-9525
Maranatha Academy 400/PK-6
15000 W 63rd St 66216 913-631-9286
Laura Burch, prin. Fax 631-2324
Midland Adventist Academy 200/K-12
6915 Maurer Rd 66217 913-268-7400
Gary Kruger, prin. Fax 268-4968
Sacred Heart of Jesus S 400/K-8
21801 Johnson Dr 66218 913-422-5520
Nick Antista, prin. Fax 745-0290
St. Joseph S 600/K-8
11505 Johnson Dr 66203 913-631-7730
Sue Carter, prin. Fax 631-3608

Shawnee Mission, See Merriam
Shawnee Mission USD 512 27,700/PK-12
7235 Antioch Rd 66204 913-993-6200
Gene Johnson Ed.D., supt. Fax 993-6247
www.smsd.org
Antioch MS 500/7-8
8200 W 71st St 66204 913-993-0000
Scott Sherman, prin. Fax 993-0199
Blue Jacket-Flint ES 500/PK-6
11615 W 49th Ter 66203 913-993-2000
Dr. Linda Tinsley, prin. Fax 993-2099
Brookwood ES 300/K-6
3411 W 103rd St 66206 913-993-2500
Teddi Stern, prin. Fax 993-2599
Comanche ES 500/K-6
8200 Grant Ave 66204 913-993-2800
Rob Bell, prin. Fax 993-2899
Corinth ES 500/K-6
8301 Mission Rd 66206 913-993-2900
Dr. Kenneth Emley, prin. Fax 993-2999
Crestview ES 400/K-6
6101 Craig St 66202 913-993-3000
Dr. Rod Smith, prin. Fax 993-3099
Hocker Grove MS 600/7-8
10400 Johnson Dr 66203 913-993-0200
Debbie Pfortmiller, prin. Fax 993-0399
Indian Hills MS 500/7-8
6400 Mission Rd 66208 913-993-0400
Carla Allen, prin. Fax 993-0599
Indian Woods MS 700/7-8
9700 Woodson Dr 66207 913-993-0600
Jim Wink, prin. Fax 993-0799
McAuliffe ES 500/K-6
15600 W 83rd St 66219 913-993-3500
Dr. Kent Peach, prin. Fax 993-3599
Merriam Park ES 200/K-6
6100 Mastin St 66203 913-993-3600
Darla Berry, prin. Fax 993-3699
Mill Creek ES 500/K-6
13951 W 79th St 66215 913-993-3700
John Bartel, prin. Fax 993-3799
Mission Valley MS 600/7-8
8500 Mission Rd 66206 913-993-0800
Dr. Susie Ostmeyer, prin. Fax 993-0999
Prairie ES 400/K-6
6642 Mission Rd 66208 913-993-4400
Tom Tracey, prin. Fax 993-4499
Roesland ES 300/K-6
4900 Parish Dr 66205 913-993-4700
Dr. Mark Kelly, prin. Fax 993-4799
Sunflower ES 600/PK-6
8955 Loiret Blvd 66219 913-993-5400
Dennis Way, prin. Fax 993-5499
Trailridge MS 600/7-8
7500 Quivira Rd 66216 913-993-1000
Dr. Larry King, prin. Fax 993-1199
Westridge MS 900/7-8
9300 Nieman Rd 66214 913-993-1200
Matt Johnson, prin. Fax 993-1399
Other Schools – See Lenexa, Mission, Overland Park, Prairie Village, Shawnee, Westwood

Silver Lake, Shawnee, Pop. 1,352
Silver Lake USD 372 700/PK-12
PO Box 39 66539 785-582-4026
Dr. Randy Freeman, supt. Fax 582-5259
www.silverlakeeagles.org
Silver Lake ES 300/PK-6
PO Box 39 66539 785-582-4081
Ronda Pegram, prin. Fax 582-5259

Smith Center, Smith, Pop. 1,725
Smith Center USD 237 400/PK-12
216 S Jefferson St 66967 785-282-6665
Ron Meitler, supt. Fax 282-6518
www.usd237.com
Smith Center ES 200/PK-6
216 S Jefferson St 66967 785-282-6614
Kelly Burgess, prin. Fax 282-5212

Solomon, Dickinson, Pop. 1,056
Solomon USD 393 400/K-12
113 E 7th St 67480 785-655-2541
Jim Runge, supt. Fax 655-2505
www.solomon393.k12.ks.us
Solomon ES 200/K-5
411 N Pine St 67480 785-655-2521
Kerri Lacy, prin. Fax 655-2505

South Haven, Sumner, Pop. 368
South Haven USD 509 300/PK-12
PO Box 229 67140 620-892-5216
John Showman, supt. Fax 892-5814
www.usd509.org/
South Haven ES 100/PK-5
PO Box 229 67140 620-892-5216
John Showman, prin. Fax 892-5814

South Hutchinson, Reno, Pop. 2,481
Nickerson USD 309
Supt. — See Hutchinson
South Hutchinson ES 400/K-6
405 S Poplar St 67505 620-665-8441
Midge Simmons, prin. Fax 663-7481

Spearville, Ford, Pop. 858
Spearville USD 381 300/K-12
PO Box 338 67876 620-385-2676
Mark Littell, supt. Fax 385-2614
www.usd381.org/
Spearville ES 200/K-5
PO Box 337 67876 620-385-2556
Marvin Hartzler, prin. Fax 385-2566

Spring Hill, Johnson, Pop. 4,494
Spring Hill USD 230 1,300/K-12
101 E South St 66083 913-592-7200
Dr. Barton Goering, supt. Fax 592-7270
www.usd230.org
Spring Hill ES K-2
300 S Webster St 66083 913-592-7277
Michelle Toon, prin. Fax 592-5483
Spring Hill IS 300/3-5
300 E South St 66083 913-592-7244
Dr. Pam Bevan, prin. Fax 592-7225
Spring Hill MS 400/6-8
301 E South St 66083 913-592-7288
Stephen Fleer, prin. Fax 592-5424
Other Schools – See Olathe

Stafford, Stafford, Pop. 1,067
Stafford USD 349 200/PK-12
PO Box 400 67578 620-234-5243
Dr. Mary Jo Taylor, supt. Fax 234-6986
stafford.ks.schoolwebpages.com
Stafford S 100/PK-8
PO Box 400 67578 620-234-5255
Kimberly Woolf, prin. Fax 234-5185

Sterling, Rice, Pop. 2,576
Sterling USD 376 500/PK-12
PO Box 188 67579 620-278-3621
Fred Dierksen, supt. Fax 278-3882
www.usd376.com
Sterling ES 200/PK-6
218 S 5th St 67579 620-278-3112
Brennan Riffel, prin. Fax 278-2913
Sterling JHS 100/7-8
412 N 5th St 67579 620-278-3646
Bill Anderson, prin. Fax 278-3673

Stilwell, Johnson
Blue Valley USD 229
Supt. — See Overland Park
Pleasant Ridge MS 600/6-8
9000 W 165th St 66085 913-239-5700
Diana Tate, prin. Fax 239-5748
Stilwell ES 400/K-5
6410 W 199th St 66085 913-239-7300
Pam DeVuyst, prin. Fax 239-7348

Stockton, Rooks, Pop. 1,453
Stockton USD 271 300/PK-12
421 Main St 67669 785-425-6367
Luis Cass, supt. Fax 425-6923
www.usd271.k12.ks.us/
Stockton S 200/PK-8
201 N Cypress St 67669 785-425-6120
Todd Berry, prin. Fax 425-7407

Strong City, Chase, Pop. 583
Chase County USD 284
Supt. — See Cottonwood Falls
Chase County MS 100/5-8
PO Box 279 66869 620-273-6676
Jay Talkington, prin. Fax 273-6690

Sublette, Haskell, Pop. 1,582
Sublette USD 374 400/PK-12
PO Box 670 67877 620-675-2277
Rex Bruce, supt. Fax 675-2652
www.usd374.org/
Sublette ES 200/PK-6
PO Box 550 67877 620-675-2286
Connie Myers, prin. Fax 675-2296

Summerfield, Marshall, Pop. 204
Axtell USD 488
Supt. — See Axtell
Summerfield ES 100/K-6
PO Box 130 66541 785-244-6221
Bob Bartkoski, prin. Fax 244-6510

Sylvan Grove, Lincoln, Pop. 301
Sylvan USD 299 100/K-12
504 W 4th St 67481 785-526-7175
Jude Stecklein, supt. Fax 526-7182
www.usd299.org/
Sylvan Unified S 100/K-12
504 W 4th St 67481 785-526-7175
Karen Meyer, prin. Fax 526-7182

Sylvia, Reno, Pop. 297
Fairfield USD 310
Supt. — See Langdon
Fairfield West ES 100/K-4
203 Old Highway 50 W 67581 620-486-2233
Shawn Koehn, prin. Fax 486-2165

Syracuse, Hamilton, Pop. 1,788
Syracuse USD 494 500/PK-12
PO Box 1187 67878 620-384-7872
Joan Friend, supt. Fax 384-7692
www.syracuse.k12.ks.us
Syracuse ES 300/PK-6
PO Box 1187 67878 620-384-5203
Rhonda Heim, prin. Fax 384-7660

Tecumseh, Shawnee
Shawnee Heights USD 450 3,400/PK-12
4401 SE Shawnee Heights Rd 66542 785-379-5800
Dr. Martin Stessman, supt. Fax 379-5810
www.usd450.net
Shawnee Heights MS 500/7-8
4335 SE Shawnee Heights Rd 66542 785-379-5830
Tim Hallacy, prin. Fax 379-5848
Tecumseh North ES 300/PK-6
314 SE Stanton Rd 66542 785-379-5910
Christopher Korb, prin. Fax 379-5915
Tecumseh South ES 500/PK-6
3346 SE Tecumseh Rd 66542 785-379-5950
Scott Dial, prin. Fax 379-5965
Other Schools – See Berryton, Topeka

Tescott, Ottawa, Pop. 331
Twin Valley USD 240
Supt. — See Bennington
Tescott S 100/PK-8
PO Box 235 67484 785-283-4774
Dr. Becky Cheney, prin. Fax 283-4347

Thayer, Neosho, Pop. 500
Cherryvale USD 447
Supt. — See Cherryvale
Thayer S 100/K-8
300 W Wilson St 66776 620-839-5203
Craig Bagshaw, prin. Fax 839-5384

Tonganoxie, Leavenworth, Pop. 3,774
Tonganoxie USD 464 1,800/K-12
PO Box 199 66086 913-845-2153
Dr. Richard Erickson, supt. Fax 845-3629
www.tong464.org/
Tonganoxie ES 900/K-6
PO Box 259 66086 913-845-2290
Tammy George, prin. Fax 845-3016

Genesis Christian S 200/PK-8
PO Box 994 66086 913-845-9498
Sharon Beeman, prin.

Topeka, Shawnee, Pop. 121,946
Auburn Washburn USD 437 5,300/PK-12
5928 SW 53rd St 66610 785-339-4000
Dr. Brenda Dietrich, supt. Fax 339-4025
www.usd437.net
Farley ES PK-6
6701 SW 33rd St 66614 785-408-8300
Marcy Cassidy, prin. Fax 408-8325
Indian Hills ES 600/K-6
7445 SW 29th St 66614 785-339-4500
George Huckabee, prin. Fax 339-4525
Pauline Central PS 500/PK-3
6625 SW Westview Rd 66619 785-339-4700
Alan Hageman, prin. Fax 339-4725
Shideler ES 600/PK-6
4948 SW Wanamaker Rd 66610 785-339-4600
Jeff Freeman, prin. Fax 339-4625
Wanamaker ES 500/K-6
6630 SW 10th Ave 66615 785-339-4800
Marc Sonderegger, prin. Fax 339-4825
Washburn Rural MS 900/7-8
5620 SW 61st St 66619 785-339-4300
Gerald Meier, prin. Fax 339-4325
Other Schools – See Auburn, Wakarusa

Seaman USD 345 2,700/PK-12
901 NW Lyman Rd 66608 785-575-8600
Mike Mathes, supt. Fax 575-8620
www.usd345.com/
Elmont ES 200/PK-6
6432 NW Elmont Rd 66618 785-286-8450
Annie Diederich, prin. Fax 286-8453
Logan ES, 1124 NW Lyman Rd 66608 400/K-6
Kim Crooks, prin. 785-575-8700
North Fairview ES 200/PK-6
1941 NE 39th St 66617 785-286-8500
Ed Albert, prin. Fax 286-8503
Pleasant Hill ES 300/K-6
5830 NW Topeka Blvd 66617 785-286-8510
Dedra Raines, prin. Fax 286-8513
Rochester ES 200/K-6
3421 NW Rochester Rd 66617 785-286-8530
Kyle Hicks, prin. Fax 286-8542
Seaman MS 300/7-8
5620 NW Topeka Blvd 66617 785-286-8400
Robert Horton, prin. Fax 286-8403
West Indianola ES 300/K-6
4201 NW Brickyard Rd 66618 785-286-8550
Steve Yeoman, prin.

Shawnee Heights USD 450
Supt. — See Tecumseh
Shawnee Heights ES 400/PK-6
2410 SE Burton St 66605 785-357-5400
Charlotte Hunley, prin. Fax 357-5415

Topeka USD 501 12,600/PK-12
624 SW 24th St 66611 785-295-3000
Kevin Singer, supt. Fax 575-6161
www.topeka.k12.ks.us
Avondale East ES 200/K-5
455 SE Golf Park Blvd 66605 785-274-6230
Duke Palmer, prin. Fax 274-4782
Avondale West ES 200/K-5
3229 SW Westview Ave 66611 785-274-6400
Scott Henson, prin. Fax 274-4781
Bishop ES 300/K-5
3601 SW 31st St 66614 785-438-4390
Amanda Czechanski, prin. Fax 271-3740
Chase MS 500/6-8
2250 NE State St 66616 785-295-3840
Teresa Songs, prin. Fax 575-6632
Eisenhower MS 400/6-8
3305 SE Minnesota Ave 66605 785-274-6160
Steven Roberts, prin. Fax 274-4603
French MS 500/6-8
5257 SW 33rd St 66614 785-438-4150
Kelli Hoffman, prin. Fax 271-3609
Highland Park Central ES 300/K-5
2717 SE Illinois Ave 66605 785-235-7000
Dr. Larita Owens, prin. Fax 575-6649
Jardine MS 500/6-8
2600 SW 33rd St 66611 785-274-6330
Jeanne Vawter, prin. Fax 274-4768
Landon MS 400/6-8
731 SW Fairlawn Rd 66606 785-438-4220
Robert Cronkhite, prin. Fax 271-3737
Linn ES 200/PK-5
200 SE 40th St 66609 785-274-6440
Dr. Jennifer Gordon, prin. Fax 274-4759
Lowman Hill ES 300/PK-5
1101 SW Garfield Ave 66604 785-235-7060
Russ Hutchins, prin. Fax 575-6884
Lundgren ES 200/K-5
1020 NE Forest Ave 66616 785-235-7110
Janetta Araiza, prin. Fax 575-6790
McCarter ES 400/K-5
5512 SW 16th St 66604 785-438-4660
Jackie Mickel, prin. Fax 271-3760
McClure ES 300/K-5
2529 SW Chelsea Dr 66614 785-438-4340
Nancy Hedstrom, prin. Fax 271-3794
McEachron ES 300/K-5
4433 SW 29th Ter 66614 785-438-4430
Victor Williams, prin. Fax 271-3774
Meadows ES 500/PK-5
201 SW Clay St 66606 785-235-7150
Dr. Cathy Kesner, prin. Fax 291-1515
Parkdale Preschool Center PK-PK
1115 SE 10th Ave 66607 785-235-7240
Shara Meyer, coord. Fax 575-6980
Quincy ES 200/K-5
1500 NE Quincy St 66608 785-235-7420
Neely Gower, prin. Fax 575-6820
Quinton Heights ES 200/K-5
2331 SW Topeka Blvd 66611 785-295-3960
Raymond Thomas, prin. Fax 575-6834
Randolph ES 400/PK-5
1400 SW Randolph Ave 66604 785-438-4480
Nicole Dial, prin. Fax 575-6837
Robinson MS 400/6-8
1125 SW 14th St 66604 785-295-3770
Tammy Austin, prin. Fax 575-6720
Ross ES 300/K-5
1400 SE 34th St 66605 785-274-6280
Nick Nichols, prin. Fax 274-4674
Scott Computer Technology Magnet ES 500/K-5
401 SE Market St 66607 785-235-7480
Deborah Sidwell, prin. Fax 291-1615
Shaner ES 200/K-5
1600 SW 34th St 66611 785-438-4620
Robert Gay, prin. Fax 274-4774
State Street ES 300/PK-5
500 NE Sumner St 66616 785-235-7280
Clardy Vinson, prin. Fax 575-6854
Stout ES 200/K-5
2303 SW College Ave 66611 785-438-4710
Cleo Gardner, prin. Fax 575-6864
Whitson ES 400/K-5
1725 SW Arnold Ave 66604 785-438-4570
Rebecca Kramer, prin. Fax 271-3782
Williams Science and Fine Arts Magnet ES 600/K-5
1301 SE Monroe St 66612 785-235-7330
Martin Gies, prin. Fax 291-1710

Cair Paravel Latin S 300/K-12
635 SW Clay St 66606 785-232-3878
James Waldy, dean Fax 232-0047
Christ the King S 400/K-8
5973 SW 25th St 66614 785-272-2220
Relynn Reynoso, prin. Fax 272-9255
Heritage Christian S 200/PK-12
3102 NW Topeka Blvd 66617 785-286-0427
Aletha Rogers, prin. Fax 286-9898
Holy Family S - East Campus 200/K-8
1725 NE Seward Ave 66616 785-234-8980
Lee Schmidt, prin. Fax 234-6778
Holy Family S - West Campus 50/PK-PK
210 NE Branner St 66616 785-233-9171
Lee Schmidt, prin. Fax 232-8800
Mater Dei S 300/K-8
934 SW Clay St 66606 785-233-1727
Andrea Hillebert, prin. Fax 233-1728
Most Pure Heart of Mary S 500/K-8
1750 SW Stone Ave 66604 785-272-4313
William Hund, prin. Fax 272-1138
St. Matthew S 200/K-8
1000 SE 28th St 66605 785-235-2188
Heather Huscher, prin. Fax 232-0028
Topeka Collegiate S 300/PK-8
2200 SW Eveningside Dr 66614 785-228-0490
David Hudspeth, hdmstr. Fax 228-0504
Topeka Lutheran S 200/PK-8
701 SW Roosevelt St 66606 785-357-0382
Forrest Schultz, prin. Fax 357-7338
Topeka SDA S 50/K-8
2431 SW Wanamaker Rd 66614 785-272-9474
David Reynolds, prin.

Towanda, Butler, Pop. 1,355
Circle USD 375 1,400/K-12
PO Box 9 67144 316-541-2577
Jim Keller, supt. Fax 536-2249
www.usd375.org
Towanda IS 100/4-6
501 N 6th St 67144 316-541-2281
Don Coffman, prin. Fax 541-2755
Towanda PS K-3
501 N 6th St 67144 316-541-2755
Don Coffman, prin. Fax 536-2728
Other Schools – See Benton, El Dorado

Tribune, Greeley, Pop. 722
Greeley County USD 200 200/PK-12
400 W Lawrence St 67879 620-376-4211
Bill Wilson, supt. Fax 376-2465
www.tribuneschools.org
Greeley County ES 100/PK-6
400 W Lawrence St 67879 620-376-4274
Bill Wilson, prin. Fax 376-2465

Troy, Doniphan, Pop. 1,017
Troy USD 429 400/PK-12
PO Box 190 66087 785-985-3950
Sue King, supt. Fax 985-3688
www.troyusd.org/
Troy ES 200/PK-6
PO Box 130 66087 785-985-3538
Sue King, prin. Fax 985-3688

Tyro, Montgomery, Pop. 222

Tyro Community Christian S 100/K-12
PO Box 308 67364 620-289-4450
Terry Byrd, prin. Fax 289-4283

Udall, Cowley, Pop. 766
Udall USD 463 400/PK-12
303 S Seymour St 67146 620-782-3355
Kim Stephens, supt. Fax 782-9690
www.usd463.org/
Udall ES 200/PK-5
308 W 3rd St 67146 620-782-3632
Lyle Pfannenstiel, prin. Fax 782-3108
Udall MS 100/6-8
301 W 4th St 67146 620-782-3623
Lyle Pfannenstiel, prin. Fax 782-9689

Ulysses, Grant, Pop. 5,650
Ulysses USD 214 1,600/PK-12
111 S Baughman St 67880 620-356-3655
Bill Hall, supt. Fax 356-5181
www.ulysses.org
Hickok ES 400/K-5
810 N Missouri St 67880 620-356-3919
Kenneth Warner, prin. Fax 424-1075

Kepley MS — 300/6-8
113 N Colorado St 67880 — 620-356-3025
Juan Perez, prin. — Fax 356-3024
Sullivan ES — 400/PK-5
600 W Nebraska Ave 67880 — 620-356-1742
Jodi Pfingsten, prin. — Fax 424-1074

Uniontown, Bourbon, Pop. 278
Uniontown USD 235 — 500/PK-12
601 5th St 66779 — 620-756-4302
Randy Rockhold, supt. — Fax 756-4492
www.uniontown235.org
West Bourbon ES — 300/PK-6
602 5th St 66779 — 620-756-4335
Marianna Daugherty, prin. — Fax 756-4373

Valley Center, Sedgwick, Pop. 5,508
Valley Center USD 262 — 2,500/PK-12
132 S Park Ave 67147 — 316-755-7100
Scott Springston, supt. — Fax 755-7102
www.usd262.net
Abilene ES — 400/K-3
522 N Abilene Ave 67147 — 316-755-7190
Mark Hoy, prin. — Fax 755-7195
Valley Center MS — 600/6-8
737 N Meridian Ave 67147 — 316-755-7160
Tim Hayden, prin. — Fax 755-7164
West ES — 400/PK-3
501 N Sheridan Ave 67147 — 316-755-7200
Peter Bastian, prin. — Fax 755-7205
Wheatland ES — 400/4-5
800 N Meadow Rd 67147 — 316-755-7220
Kathy Bradham, prin. — Fax 755-7225

Valley Falls, Jefferson, Pop. 1,209
Valley Falls USD 338 — 400/K-12
700 Oak St 66088 — 785-945-3214
Loren Feldkamp, supt. — Fax 945-3215
www.usd338.com
Valley Falls S — 300/K-8
700 Oak St 66088 — 785-945-3221
Susan Grey, prin. — Fax 945-3222

Vermillion, Marshall, Pop. 98
Vermillion USD 380 — 600/PK-12
PO Box 107 66544 — 785-382-6216
Patrick Meier, supt. — Fax 382-6213
www.usd380.org
Other Schools – See Centralia, Frankfort

Victoria, Ellis, Pop. 1,164
Victoria USD 432 — 300/K-12
PO Box 139 67671 — 785-735-9212
Linda Kenne, supt. — Fax 735-9229
Victoria S — 200/K-8
602 10th St 67671 — 785-735-2870
David Ottley, prin. — Fax 735-9204

Wakarusa, Shawnee
Auburn Washburn USD 437
Supt. — See Topeka
Pauline South IS — 300/4-6
7035 SW Morrill Rd 66546 — 785-339-4750
Chris Holman, prin. — Fax 339-4775

Wakeeney, Trego, Pop. 1,800
WaKeeney USD 208 — 400/PK-12
527 Russell Ave 67672 — 785-743-2145
Mark Bejot, supt. — Fax 743-2071
www.tregoeagles.com/
Trego Grade S — 300/PK-8
612 Junction Ave 67672 — 785-743-2472
Tavis Desormiers, prin. — Fax 743-5244

Wakefield, Clay, Pop. 874
Clay Center USD 379
Supt. — See Clay Center
Wakefield ES — 100/K-5
PO Box 40 67487 — 785-461-5437
Dan Wagner, prin. — Fax 461-5892

Wamego, Pottawatomie, Pop. 4,243
Wamego USD 320 — 1,300/PK-12
510 E US Highway 24 66547 — 785-456-7643
Doug Conwell, supt. — Fax 456-8125
www.usd320.com
Central ES — 300/PK-2
700 Poplar St 66547 — 785-456-7271
Jeanne Stroh, prin. — Fax 456-7172
Wamego MS — 300/6-8
1701 Kaw Valley Rd 66547 — 785-456-7682
Vici Jennings, prin. — Fax 456-2944
West ES — 300/3-5
1911 6th St 66547 — 785-456-8333
Amy Flinn, prin. — Fax 456-7267

Washington, Washington, Pop. 1,145
Washington County USD 108 — 400/PK-12
PO Box 275 66968 — 785-325-2261
Michael Stegman, supt. — Fax 325-2771
www.usd108.org/
Washington ES — 200/PK-6
PO Box 275 66968 — 785-325-2261
Ronald Scott, prin. — Fax 325-2801

Waterville, Marshall, Pop. 628
Valley Heights USD 498 — 400/K-12
PO Box 89 66548 — 785-363-2398
John Bergkamp, supt. — Fax 363-2269
www.valleyheights.org/
Valley Heights ES — 100/K-3
PO Box 389 66548 — 785-363-2530
Rhonda Trimble, prin. — Fax 363-2758
Other Schools – See Blue Rapids

Wathena, Doniphan, Pop. 1,290
Wathena USD 406 — 400/PK-12
PO Box 38 66090 — 785-989-4427
Mike Newman, supt. — Fax 989-4680
www.wathenaschools.org/
Wathena ES — 200/PK-6
PO Box 38 66090 — 785-989-4425
Cindy Murphy, prin. — Fax 989-4680

Waverly, Coffey, Pop. 556
Lebo-Waverly USD 243 — 600/PK-12
PO Box 457 66871 — 785-733-2651
Allen Pokorny, supt. — Fax 733-2707
www.usd243ks.org/
Waverly ES — 100/PK-6
PO Box 589 66871 — 785-733-2551
Anthony Houchin, prin. — Fax 733-2707
Other Schools – See Lebo

Weir, Cherokee, Pop. 752
Cherokee USD 247
Supt. — See Cherokee
Weir S — 200/K-8
PO Box 308 66781 — 620-396-8211
Randy Turnbull, prin. — Fax 396-8160

Welda, Anderson
Garnett USD 365
Supt. — See Garnett
Mont Ida S — 50/1-8
22077 NW Broomall St 66091 — 785-489-2518
Stephen Smith, prin. — Fax 489-2518

Wellington, Sumner, Pop. 8,098
Wellington USD 353 — 1,700/K-12
PO Box 648 67152 — 620-326-4300
Dr. Rick Weiss, supt. — Fax 326-4304
www.usd353.com/
Eisenhower ES — 200/K-5
924 N Plum St 67152 — 620-326-4340
Kelly Adams, prin. — Fax 326-6322
Kennedy ES — 200/K-5
501 N Woodlawn St 67152 — 620-326-4350
Adam Hatfield, prin. — Fax 326-7813
Lincoln ES — 200/K-5
104 S F St 67152 — 620-326-4360
John Walton, prin. — Fax 326-3273
Washington ES — 100/K-5
1100 N Washington Ave 67152 — 620-326-4370
John Walton, prin. — Fax 326-6480
Wellington MS — 400/6-8
605 N A St 67152 — 620-326-4320
Jerry Hodson, prin. — Fax 326-4390

Wellsville, Franklin, Pop. 1,631
Wellsville USD 289 — 800/PK-12
602 Walnut St 66092 — 785-883-2388
Denise O'Dea, supt. — Fax 883-4453
www.wellsville-usd289.org
Wellsville ES — 400/PK-5
218 Ash St 66092 — 785-883-2996
Randall Renoud, prin. — Fax 883-4850
Wellsville MS — 200/6-8
602 Walnut St 66092 — 785-883-4350
Mitchell Lubin, prin. — Fax 883-2260

Weskan, Wallace
Weskan USD 242 — 100/PK-12
219 Coyote Blvd 67762 — 785-943-5222
Mike Nulton, supt. — Fax 943-5303
www.weskanschools.org/
Weskan ES — 100/PK-6
219 Coyote Blvd 67762 — 785-943-5222
Mike Nulton, prin. — Fax 943-5303

Westmoreland, Pottawatomie, Pop. 655
Rock Creek USD 323 — 800/PK-12
PO Box 70 66549 — 785-457-3732
Darrel Stufflebeam, supt. — Fax 457-3701
www.rockcreekschools.org
Westmoreland ES — 200/PK-6
PO Box 350 66549 — 785-457-3462
Gary Glendening, prin. — Fax 457-3701
Other Schools – See Saint George

Westphalia, Coffey, Pop. 168
Garnett USD 365
Supt. — See Garnett
Westphalia S — 100/K-8
500 Liberty St 66093 — 785-489-2511
Stephen Smith, prin. — Fax 489-2491

Westwood, Johnson, Pop. 1,483
Shawnee Mission USD 512
Supt. — See Shawnee Mission
Westwood View ES — 300/K-6
2511 W 50th St 66205 — 913-993-5800
Susan Knight, prin. — Fax 993-5899

Wetmore, Nemaha, Pop. 356
Sabetha USD 441
Supt. — See Sabetha
Wetmore S — 100/PK-8
PO Box AB 66550 — 785-866-2860
David Schmitz, prin. — Fax 866-5450

White City, Morris, Pop. 499
Rural Vista USD 481
Supt. — See Hope
White City S — 200/PK-8
PO Box 8 66872 — 785-349-2211
Adam McDaniel, prin. — Fax 349-2138

Whitewater, Butler, Pop. 639
Remington-Whitewater USD 206 — 500/K-12
PO Box 243 67154 — 316-799-2115
James Regier, supt. — Fax 799-2307
remington.ks.schoolwebpages.com
Remington MS — 100/6-8
PO Box 99 67154 — 316-799-2131
Bruce Krase, prin. — Fax 799-2581
Other Schools – See Potwin

Wichita, Sedgwick, Pop. 354,865
Andover USD 385
Supt. — See Andover
Martin ES — 400/K-5
2342 N 159th St E 67228 — 316-218-4720
Dr. Crystal Hummel, prin. — Fax 733-3682
Wheatland ES — K-5
15200 E 21st St N 67230 — 316-218-4820
Elton Armbrister, prin. — Fax 218-4821

Derby USD 260
Supt. — See Derby
Cooper ES — 300/PK-5
4625 S Juniper St 67216 — 316-554-0934
Vince Evans, prin. — Fax 524-9407
Oaklawn ES — 200/PK-5
5000 S Clifton Ave 67216 — 316-554-0704
David Engelking, prin. — Fax 524-9411
Wineteer ES — 400/K-5
8801 E Ent Dr 67210 — 316-684-9373
Kathy Raymond, prin. — Fax 687-2418

Haysville USD 261
Supt. — See Haysville
Clark ES — 300/PK-5
1900 W 55th St S 67217 — 316-554-2333
Missy Hollenbeck, prin. — Fax 554-2340
Oatville ES — 400/PK-5
4335 S Hoover Rd 67215 — 316-554-2290
Patricia Yorgensen, prin. — Fax 554-2292

Maize USD 266
Supt. — See Maize
Maize South MS — 700/7-8
3701 N Tyler Rd 67205 — 316-722-0421
Jess Herbig, prin. — Fax 722-4077

Wichita USD 259 — 46,000/PK-12
201 N Water St 67202 — 316-973-4000
Martin Libhart, supt. — Fax 973-4595
www.usd259.com
Adams ES — 300/K-5
1002 N Oliver Ave 67208 — 316-973-2650
Kimberly Jackson, prin. — Fax 973-2660
Allen ES — 400/K-5
1881 Elpyco St 67218 — 316-973-1750
Molly Nespor, prin. — Fax 973-1760
Allison Traditional Magnet MS — 500/6-8
221 S Seneca St 67213 — 316-973-4800
Dr. Deborah Laudermilk, prin. — Fax 973-4810
Anderson ES — 500/K-5
2945 S Victoria Ave 67216 — 316-973-1900
Laura Thompson, prin. — Fax 973-1910
Beech ES — 500/K-5
1830 S Cypress St 67207 — 316-973-9800
Laquita Lugrand, prin. — Fax 973-9810
Benton ES — 400/K-5
338 S Woodchuck St 67209 — 316-973-3300
Ann Welborn, prin. — Fax 973-3305
Black Traditional Magnet ES — 300/PK-5
1045 N High St 67203 — 316-973-3500
Janet Tilton, prin. — Fax 973-3510
Bostic Traditional Magnet ES — 300/K-5
8103 E Gilbert St 67207 — 316-973-1800
Tiffinie Irving, prin. — Fax 973-1810
Brooks Technology & Arts Magnet MS — 600/6-8
3802 E 27th St N 67220 — 316-973-6450
Robert Garner, prin. — Fax 973-6581
Bryant Core Knowledge Magnet ES — 400/PK-5
4702 W 9th St N 67212 — 316-973-9700
Bill Savage, prin. — Fax 973-9716
Buckner Performing Arts ES — 300/K-5
3530 E 27th St N 67220 — 316-973-9350
Lichelle Alford, prin. — Fax 973-9360
Caldwell ES — 500/PK-5
1441 S Edgemoor St 67218 — 316-973-0800
Amanda Kingrey, prin. — Fax 973-0810
Cessna ES — 400/K-5
2101 W 45th St S 67217 — 316-973-6900
Chris Wendt, prin. — Fax 973-6910
Clark ES — 300/K-5
650 S Apache Dr 67207 — 316-973-5850
Judy Wright, prin. — Fax 973-5860
Cleaveland Traditional Magnet ES — 300/K-5
3345 W 33rd St S 67217 — 316-973-8750
Jim Johnson, prin. — Fax 973-8760
Cloud ES — 800/PK-5
1212 W 25th St N 67204 — 316-973-9200
Carla Smith, prin. — Fax 973-9210
Coleman MS — 600/6-8
1544 N Governeour Rd 67206 — 316-973-6600
Gil Alvarez, prin. — Fax 973-6699
College Hill ES — 400/K-5
211 N Clifton Ave 67208 — 316-973-9600
Kathy Stybr, prin. — Fax 973-9610
Colvin ES — 800/PK-5
2820 S Roosevelt St 67210 — 316-973-7600
Karen Whittle, prin. — Fax 973-7610
Curtis MS — 700/6-8
1031 S Edgemoor St 67218 — 316-973-7350
Keith Wilson, prin. — Fax 973-7410
Dodge Literacy Magnet ES — 400/K-5
4801 W 2nd St N 67212 — 316-973-3150
Janet Jump, prin. — Fax 973-3160
Dunbar ECC — PK-PK
923 N Cleveland Ave 67214 — 316-866-8153
Linda Tillman, prin. — Fax 866-8157
Earhart Environmental Magnet ES — 300/K-5
4401 N Arkansas Ave 67204 — 316-973-3250
Chris Waterbury, prin. — Fax 973-3256
Emerson Open Magnet ES — 200/K-5
2330 W 15th St N 67203 — 316-973-9250
LaJuana Bobbitt, prin. — Fax 973-9260
Enterprise ES — 400/PK-5
3605 S Gold St 67217 — 316-973-6800
Pam Stead, prin. — Fax 973-6805
Franklin ES — 300/K-5
214 S Elizabeth St 67213 — 316-973-9850
Heather Vincent, prin. — Fax 973-9860
Gammon ES — 500/K-5
3240 N Rushwood St 67226 — 316-973-4900
Debbie Thompson, prin. — Fax 973-4910

Gardiner ES 500/PK-5
1951 S Laura St 67211 316-973-1700
Craig Bright, prin. Fax 973-1710
Griffith ES 400/K-5
1802 S Bluff St 67218 316-973-8900
Linda Brown, prin. Fax 973-8910
Hadley MS 700/6-8
1101 N Dougherty Ave 67212 316-973-7800
Charles Wakefield, prin. Fax 973-7737
Hamilton MS 600/6-8
1407 S Broadway St 67211 316-973-5350
Amy Hungria, prin. Fax 973-5360
Harry Street ES 300/K-5
1605 S Market St 67211 316-973-0700
Stacie Meyer, prin. Fax 973-0712
Hyde Intl Studies Community Magnet ES 300/K-5
210 N Oliver Ave 67208 316-973-0650
Heather Eubank, prin. Fax 973-0660
Irving ES 300/K-2
1642 N Market St 67214 316-973-0050
Larry Perlman, prin. Fax 973-0070
Isely Traditional Magnet S 200/K-5
2500 E 18th St N 67214 316-973-8200
Jane Walker, prin. Fax 973-8210
Jackson ES 500/K-5
2717 N Woodlawn Blvd 67220 316-973-1200
Kamiel Evans, prin. Fax 973-1210
Jardine MS Magnet 400/6-8
3550 E Ross Pkwy 67210 316-973-4300
Dave Saunders, prin. Fax 973-4310
Jefferson ES 500/PK-5
4615 E Orme St 67218 316-973-3000
Janice Aschenbrenner, prin. Fax 973-3010
Kelly Liberal Arts Academy 600/K-5
3143 S Millwood Ave 67217 316-973-4150
Brian Huffman, prin. Fax 973-4160
Kensler ES 600/PK-5
1030 N Wilbur Ln 67212 316-973-1350
Kim Pruitt, prin. Fax 973-1360
Lawrence ES 400/K-5
3440 W Maple St 67213 316-973-9900
Pam Klos, prin. Fax 973-9910
Lewis Open Magnet ES 200/K-5
3030 S Osage Ave 67217 316-973-6750
Judy Zimbelman, prin. Fax 973-6760
Lincoln ES 200/K-5
1210 S Topeka St 67211 316-973-9300
Dr. Laura McLemore, prin. Fax 973-9310
Linwood ES 400/K-5
1654 S Hydraulic St 67211 316-973-8100
Trina Wynn, prin. Fax 973-8110
Little ECC PK-PK
1613 Piatt St 67214 316-973-5300
Linda Tillman, prin. Fax 973-5310
L'Overture Computer Technology Magnet ES 400/K-5
1539 N Ohio Ave 67214 316-973-5050
Greg Croomes, prin. Fax 973-5060
Mann Dual Language Magnet S 600/K-8
1243 N Market St 67214 316-973-3100
Dr. Ken Jantz, prin. Fax 973-3128
Marshall MS 400/6-8
1510 N Payne Ave 67203 316-973-9000
Mark Jollife, prin. Fax 973-9010
Mayberry Cultural & Fine Arts Magnet MS 600/6-8
207 S Sheridan St 67213 316-973-5800
Tim Seguine, prin. Fax 973-5808
McCollom ES 400/K-5
1201 N Waddington Ave 67212 316-973-0350
Tammy McKean, prin. Fax 973-0360
Mclean Science/Tech Magnet ES 300/K-5
2277 N Marigold Ln 67204 316-973-8250
Keli Gustafson, prin. Fax 973-8260
Mead MS 500/6-8
2601 E Skinner St 67211 316-973-8500
Toby Martin, prin. Fax 973-8503
Midtown ECC PK-PK
1150 N Broadway St 67214 316-866-8050
Linda Tillman, prin. Fax 855-8055
Minneha Core Knowledge ES 600/K-5
701 N Webb Rd 67206 316-973-8800
Dr. Linda Hope, prin. Fax 973-8810
Mueller ES 600/PK-5
2821 E 24th St N 67219 316-973-8300
Anne Clemens, prin. Fax 973-8310
OK ES 200/K-5
1607 N West St 67203 316-973-0600
Stacey Hall, prin. Fax 973-0610
Park ES 200/K-2
1025 N Main St 67203 316-973-5250
Jeanna Hernandez, prin. Fax 973-5260
Parks Academy K-8
2201 E 25th St N 67219 316-973-7500
Stefanie Stovall, prin. Fax 973-7510
Payne ES 300/K-5
1601 S Edwards St 67213 316-973-7850
Donna Welty, prin. Fax 973-7860
Peterson ES 400/PK-5
9710 W Central Ave 67212 316-973-0400
Bruce Shelton, prin. Fax 973-0410

Pleasant Valley ES 400/K-5
2000 W 29th St N 67204 316-973-5200
Cindy Rissell, prin. Fax 973-5210
Pleasant Valley MS 600/6-8
2220 W 29th St N 67204 316-973-8000
Ron VanSickle, prin. Fax 973-8008
Price - Harris Communications Magnet ES 500/K-5
706 N Armour St 67206 316-973-1650
Shawn Springer, prin. Fax 973-1660
Riverside Leadership Magnet ES 200/PK-5
1001 N Porter Ave 67203 316-973-4050
Susan Rosell, prin. Fax 973-4060
Robinson MS 800/6-8
328 N Oliver Ave 67208 316-973-8600
Buddy Dooley, prin. Fax 973-8625
Seltzer ES 600/K-5
11660 E Lincoln St 67207 316-973-4001
Modena Spurlock, prin. Fax 973-4010
Spaght Multimedia Magnet Academy 300/K-5
2316 E 10th St N 67214 316-973-7300
Kim Sherfield, prin. Fax 973-7310
Stanley ES 400/PK-5
1749 S Martinson St 67213 316-973-1300
Kristi Franks, prin. Fax 973-1310
Stucky MS 800/6-8
4545 N Broadview Cir 67220 316-973-8400
Terrell Davis, prin. Fax 973-8410
Truesdell MS 800/6-8
2464 S Glenn Ave 67217 316-973-3900
Jennifer Sinclair, prin. Fax 973-3904
Washington Accelerated Learning ES 500/K-5
424 N Pennsylvania Ave 67214 316-973-1150
Julie Bettis, prin. Fax 973-1160
White ES 600/PK-5
5148 S Kansas St 67216 316-973-1250
Marcia Shepler, prin. Fax 973-1260
Wilbur MS 1,000/6-8
340 N Tyler Rd 67212 316-973-1100
Karen Pickert, prin. Fax 973-1110
Woodland Health & Wellness Magnet ES 200/K-5
1705 N Salina Ave 67203 316-973-0100
Elbert McGhee, prin. Fax 973-0110
Woodman ES 700/PK-5
2500 S Hiram Ave 67217 316-973-0200
Jana Epperly, prin. Fax 973-0210
Other Schools – See Park City

All Saints Catholic S 200/PK-8
3313 Grand St 67218 316-682-6021
Paul Spacil, prin. Fax 682-8734
Bethany Lutheran S 50/PK-8
1000 W 26th St S 67217 316-265-3033
Fax 265-0887
Bethel Life S 200/PK-8
3777 S Meridian Ave 67217 316-522-7148
Jason Soule, admin. Fax 522-0529
Blessed Sacrament Catholic S 400/PK-8
125 N Quentin St 67208 316-684-3752
James Grogan, prin. Fax 687-1082
Calvary Christian S 100/PK-12
3003 E Kellogg Dr 67211 316-652-0773
Greg Dillon, admin. Fax 618-0375
Central Christian Academy 500/K-8
2900 N Rock Rd 67226 316-688-1161
David Funk, hdmstr. Fax 691-8853
Christ the King Catholic S 200/PK-8
4501 W Maple St 67209 316-943-0111
Cindy Chrisman, prin. Fax 943-0147
Holy Cross Lutheran S 200/PK-8
600 N Greenwich Rd 67206 316-684-4431
Bill Dieckhoff, prin. Fax 684-2847
Holy Savior Catholic Academy 200/PK-8
4640 E 15th St N 67208 316-684-2141
Delia Barnett, prin. Fax 682-4318
Independent S 800/K-12
8301 E Douglas Ave 67207 316-686-0152
Ed Walters, hdmstr. Fax 686-3918
Magdalen Catholic S 500/PK-8
2221 N 127th St E 67226 316-634-1572
Janice Palmer, prin. Fax 634-6957
Resurrection Catholic S 200/PK-8
4900 N Woodlawn Blvd 67220 316-744-3576
James Finkeldei, prin. Fax 744-1582
Riverlawn Christian Academy 100/K-5
4243 N Meridian Ave 67204 316-832-0544
Loretta Bouche, admin. Fax 838-5464
St. Anne Catholic S 200/PK-8
1121 W Regal St 67217 316-522-6131
Winston Kenton, prin. Fax 524-2370
St. Elizabeth Ann Seton Catholic S 700/K-8
645 N 119th St W 67235 316-721-5693
David Charles, prin. Fax 721-1723
St. Francis of Assisi Catholic S 700/PK-8
853 N Socora St 67212 316-722-5171
Mary Carter, prin. Fax 722-0492
St. Joseph Catholic S 100/K-8
139 S Millwood St 67213 316-261-5801
Dan McAdam, prin. Fax 261-5804
St. Jude Catholic S 300/PK-8
3030 N Amidon Ave 67204 316-838-0800
Dan Dester, prin. Fax 838-0866

St. Margaret Mary Catholic S 200/PK-8
2635 S Pattie St 67216 316-267-4911
Mary Samms, prin. Fax 267-1707
St. Patrick Catholic S 200/PK-8
2023 N Arkansas Ave 67203 316-262-4071
Theresa Lam, prin. Fax 262-6217
St. Peter Catholic S 400/PK-8
11010 Southwest Blvd 67215 316-524-6585
Brenda Hickok, prin. Fax 524-1656
St. Thomas Aquinas Catholic S 700/PK-8
1215 N Stratford Ln 67206 316-684-9201
Mary Sweet, prin. Fax 684-7421
Sunrise Christian Academy 700/PK-12
5500 E 45th St N 67220 316-744-9262
Dr. Robert Lindsted, supt. Fax 744-7449
Wichita Adventist Christian Academy 50/K-10
2725 S Osage Ave 67217 316-267-9472
Sharon Burton, prin. Fax 267-1065
Wichita Collegiate S 1,000/PK-12
9115 E 13th St N 67206 316-634-0433
Tom Davis, hdmstr. Fax 634-0598
Wichita Friends S 50/PK-6
14700 W US Highway 54 67235 316-729-0303
Shelli Kadel, hdmstr.

Williamsburg, Franklin, Pop. 359
West Franklin USD 287
Supt. — See Pomona
Williamsburg ES 100/PK-5
PO Box 7 66095 785-746-5777
Susan Wildeman, prin. Fax 746-5250

Wilson, Ellsworth, Pop. 767
Lorraine USD 328
Supt. — See Lorraine
Wilson ES 100/PK-6
PO Box K 67490 785-658-3555
Brian Smith, prin. Fax 658-2205

Winchester, Jefferson, Pop. 582
Jefferson County North USD 339 500/PK-12
310 5th St 66097 913-774-2000
Timothy Marshall, supt. Fax 774-2027
www.usd339.net
Other Schools – See Nortonville

Windom, McPherson, Pop. 136
Little River USD 444
Supt. — See Little River
Windom ES 100/PK-5
PO Box 67 67491 620-489-6241
Jon Paden, prin. Fax 489-6434

Winfield, Cowley, Pop. 11,861
Winfield USD 465 2,100/PK-12
1407 Wheat Rd 67156 620-221-5100
Marvin Estes, supt. Fax 221-0508
usd465.com/cms/
Country View ES 100/K-4
16300 151st Rd 67156 620-221-5155
Nancy Burger, prin. Fax 221-5156
Irving ES 200/PK-4
311 Harter St 67156 620-221-5140
Jeff Everett, prin. Fax 221-5142
Lowell ES 200/K-4
1404 Millington St 67156 620-221-5136
Aaron Birkhofer, prin. Fax 221-5191
Webster Preschool 100/PK-PK
900 E 12th Ave 67156 620-221-5170
Shay Pickering, prin. Fax 221-5169
Whittier ES 300/K-4
1400 Mound St 67156 620-221-5150
William Pittman, prin. Fax 221-5154
Winfield IS 400/5-6
400 E 9th Ave 67156 620-221-5180
David Hammer, prin. Fax 221-5183
Winfield MS 7-8
130 Viking Blvd 67156 620-221-5130
Dennis Gerber, prin. Fax 221-5147

Holy Name Catholic S 100/PK-6
700 Fuller St 67156 620-221-0230
Kim Porter, prin. Fax 221-4047
Trinity Lutheran S 100/PK-6
910 Mound St 67156 620-221-1820
Mark Schotte, prin. Fax 221-3779

Winona, Logan, Pop. 205
Triplains USD 275 100/PK-12
PO Box 97 67764 785-846-7869
David Porter, supt. Fax 846-7767
Winona S 100/PK-8
PO Box 97 67764 785-846-7496
David Porter, prin. Fax 846-7767

Yates Center, Woodson, Pop. 1,493
Woodson USD 366 500/PK-12
PO Box 160 66783 620-625-8804
Rusty Arnold, supt. Fax 625-8806
www.usd366.net
Yates Center S 300/PK-8
PO Box 160 66783 620-625-8860
Frank Bettega, prin. Fax 625-8851

KENTUCKY

KENTUCKY DEPARTMENT OF EDUCATION
500 Mero St, Frankfort 40601-1975
Telephone 502-564-4770
Fax 502-564-5680
Website http://www.education.ky.gov

Commissioner of Education Terry Holliday

KENTUCKY BOARD OF EDUCATION
500 Mero St Ste 1, Frankfort 40601-1957

Chairperson Joe Brothers

PUBLIC, PRIVATE AND CATHOLIC ELEMENTARY SCHOOLS

Adairville, Logan, Pop. 930
Logan County SD
Supt. — See Russellville
Adairville S — 400/PK-8
PO Box 277 42202 — 270-539-7711
Paul Sansom, prin. — Fax 539-3121

Albany, Clinton, Pop. 2,288
Clinton County SD — 1,600/PK-12
2353 N Highway 127 42602 — 606-387-6480
Mickey McFall, supt. — Fax 387-5437
www.clinton.k12.ky.us
Albany ES — 700/K-4
819 3rd St 42602 — 606-387-5828
Tim Armstrong, prin. — Fax 387-4930
Clinton County MS — 500/5-8
169 Middle School Rd 42602 — 606-387-6466
Jimmy Brown, prin. — Fax 387-6469
ECC, 204 King Dr 42602 — PK-K
Julie Daniels, prin. — 606-387-4283

Alexandria, Campbell, Pop. 7,996
Campbell County SD — 4,300/K-12
101 Orchard Ln 41001 — 859-635-2173
Anthony Strong, supt. — Fax 448-2439
www.campbellcountyschools.org/
Campbell County MS — 1,000/6-8
8000 Alexandria Pike 41001 — 859-635-6077
Dave Sandlin, prin. — Fax 448-4863
Campbell Ridge ES — 600/K-5
2500 Grandview Rd 41001 — 859-448-4780
Anthony Mazzei, prin. — Fax 448-4788
Grants Lick ES — 200/K-5
944 Clayridge Rd 41001 — 859-635-2129
Amy Razor, prin. — Fax 448-4871
Reiley ES — 500/K-5
10631 Alexandria Pike 41001 — 859-635-2118
Julie Hubbard, prin. — Fax 448-4852
Other Schools – See Cold Spring

St. Mary S — 400/K-8
9 S Jefferson St 41001 — 859-635-9539
Michele Ulrich, prin. — Fax 448-4824

Allen, Floyd, Pop. 149
Floyd County SD
Supt. — See Prestonsburg
Allen S — 500/K-8
112 Eagle Ln 41601 — 606-874-2165
Tony Childers, prin. — Fax 874-5565

Wesley Christian S — 100/PK-8
PO Box 233 41601 — 606-874-8328
Janie Tincher, prin. — Fax 874-6104

Alvaton, Warren
Warren County SD
Supt. — See Bowling Green
Alvaton ES — 500/PK-6
1 Robert Morgan Ln 42122 — 270-843-8067
Mark Rathbun, prin. — Fax 842-1668

Anchorage, Jefferson, Pop. 2,529
Anchorage ISD — 400/PK-8
11400 Ridge Rd 40223 — 502-245-8927
Don Cravens, supt. — Fax 245-2124
www.anchorage-school.org
Anchorage S — 400/PK-8
11400 Ridge Rd 40223 — 502-245-2121
Cathy Barnard, prin. — Fax 245-6249

Argillite, Greenup
Greenup County SD
Supt. — See Greenup
Argillite ES — 300/K-5
4157 State Route 1 41121 — 606-473-7213
Thomas Crump, prin. — Fax 473-1057

Ary, Perry
Perry County SD
Supt. — See Hazard
Robinson S — 300/K-8
3311 Pigeonroost Rd 41712 — 606-378-7761
Thomas Neace, prin. — Fax 378-4350

Ashland, Boyd, Pop. 21,510
Ashland ISD — 3,100/PK-12
PO Box 3000 41105 — 606-327-2706
Stephen Gilmore, supt. — Fax 327-2705
www.ashland.k12.ky.us/
Crabbe ES — 200/K-6
520 17th St 41101 — 606-327-2730
Steve Hall, prin. — Fax 327-2759
Hager ES — 300/K-6
1600 Blackburn Ave 41101 — 606-327-2731
Linda Calhoun, prin. — Fax 327-2788
Hatcher ES — 200/K-6
1820 Hickman St 41101 — 606-327-2732
David Greene, prin. — Fax 327-2768
Oakview ES — 400/K-6
3111 Blackburn Ave 41101 — 606-327-2733
Nancy McHenry, prin. — Fax 327-2756
Poage ES — 200/PK-6
3215 S 29th St 41102 — 606-327-2734
Bob Blankenship, prin. — Fax 327-2770
Russell ES — 300/K-6
1100 Russell St 41101 — 606-327-2735
Steve Salyers, prin. — Fax 327-2763
Verity MS — 500/7-8
2800 Kansas St 41102 — 606-327-2727
Richard Oppenheimer, prin. — Fax 327-2765

Boyd County SD — 3,300/PK-12
1104 Bob McCullough Dr 41102 — 606-928-4141
Howard Osborne, supt. — Fax 928-4771
www.boyd.k12.ky.us
Boyd County MS — 700/6-8
1226 Summitt Rd 41102 — 606-928-9547
Bill Boblett, prin. — Fax 928-2067
Cannonsburg ES — 300/K-5
12219 Midland Trail Rd 41102 — 606-928-7131
Deborah Gould, prin. — Fax 928-2685
Early Childhood Learning Center - North — PK-PK
1104B Bob McCullough Dr 41102 — 606-928-8022
Ginger Clark, dir. — Fax 928-4410
Early Childhood Learning Ctr - South — PK-PK
12862 State Route 180 41102 — 606-929-5500
Ginger Clark, dir. — Fax 929-5568
Summit ES — 500/K-5
830 State Route 716 41102 — 606-928-6533
Tamala Martin, prin. — Fax 928-5234
Other Schools – See Catlettsburg

Fairview ISD — 700/PK-12
2201 Main St W 41102 — 606-324-3877
Bill Musick, supt. — Fax 324-2288
www.fairview.k12.ky.us
Fairview ES — 300/PK-6
258 Mcknight St 41102 — 606-325-1528
Gregory Sallie, prin. — Fax 326-1777

Holy Family S — 200/PK-8
932 Winchester Ave 41101 — 606-324-7040
Mary Chandler, prin. — Fax 324-6888
Rose Hill Christian S — 400/PK-12
1001 Winslow Rd 41102 — 606-324-6105
Jerry Foster, prin. — Fax 324-6420

Auburn, Logan, Pop. 1,489
Logan County SD
Supt. — See Russellville
Auburn S — 700/PK-8
221 College St 42206 — 270-542-4181
David Ward, prin. — Fax 542-7921

Augusta, Bracken, Pop. 1,257
Augusta ISD — 300/K-12
307 Bracken St 41002 — 606-756-2545
John Cordle, supt. — Fax 756-2149
www.augusta.k12.ky.us
Augusta ES — 100/K-5
207 Bracken St 41002 — 606-756-2105
Lisa McCane, prin. — Fax 756-3000

St. Augustine S — 100/PK-8
203 E 4th St 41002 — 606-756-3229
Michael Ruf, prin. — Fax 756-2530

Avawam, Perry
Perry County SD
Supt. — See Hazard

Big Creek S — 200/K-8
PO Box 129 41713 — 606-436-5632
Jeffrey Castle, prin. — Fax 436-5632

Barbourville, Knox, Pop. 3,520
Barbourville ISD — 600/PK-12
PO Box 520 40906 — 606-546-3120
Larry Warren, supt. — Fax 546-3452
www.barbourvilleind.com
Barbourville S — 600/PK-12
PO Box 520 40906 — 606-546-3129
Paul Middleton, prin. — Fax 546-3337

Knox County SD — 4,700/PK-12
200 Daniel Boone Dr 40906 — 606-546-3157
Walter Hulett, supt. — Fax 546-2819
www.knox.k12.ky.us/
Central ES — 300/K-6
1000 KY 3439 40906 — 606-546-3496
Kevin Disney, prin. — Fax 546-3761
Hampton ES — 400/PK-6
60 KY 3441 40906 — 606-546-4169
Scott Broughton, prin. — Fax 546-9202
Knox County MS — 600/7-8
311 N Main St 40906 — 606-545-5267
Kelly Sprinkles, prin. — Fax 546-2161
Lay ES — 400/PK-6
220 N Allison Ave 40906 — 606-546-6524
Jeff Frost, prin. — Fax 546-3993
Other Schools – See Corbin, Dewitt, Flat Lick, Girdler

Bardstown, Nelson, Pop. 10,984
Bardstown ISD — 1,900/PK-12
308 N 5th St 40004 — 502-331-8800
Brent Holsclaw, supt. — Fax 331-8830
www.btown.k12.ky.us
Bardstown ECC — PK-PK
980 Templin Ave 40004 — 502-331-8804
John Jones, prin. — Fax 331-8830
Bardstown ES — 400/3-5
420 N 5th St 40004 — 502-331-8801
Robin Kelly, prin. — Fax 331-8831
Bardstown MS — 500/6-8
410 N 5th St 40004 — 502-331-8803
Bob Blackmon, prin. — Fax 331-8833
Bardstown PS — 500/K-2
1000 Templin Ave 40004 — 502-331-8810
Michelle Ryan, prin. — Fax 331-8834

Nelson County SD — 4,600/PK-12
PO Box 2277 40004 — 502-349-7000
Janice Lantz, supt. — Fax 349-7004
www.nelson.kyschools.us
Foster Heights ES — 400/PK-3
211 E Muir Ave 40004 — 502-349-7030
Gail Kamer, prin. — Fax 349-7031
Old Kentucky Home IS — 200/4-5
221 E Muir Ave 40004 — 502-349-7220
Donna Paulin, prin. — Fax 349-7221
Old Kentucky Home MS — 500/6-8
301 Wildcat Ln 40004 — 502-349-7040
Ryan Clark, prin. — Fax 349-7042
Other Schools – See Bloomfield, Boston, Coxs Creek, New Haven

---

St. Joseph S — 400/PK-8
320 W Stephen Foster Ave 40004 — 502-348-5994
Michael Bickett, prin. — Fax 348-4692

Bardwell, Carlisle, Pop. 793
Carlisle County SD — 800/PK-12
4557 State Route 1377 42023 — 270-628-3800
Dr. Keith Shoulders, supt. — Fax 628-5477
www.carlisle.k12.ky.us/
Carlisle County ES — 300/PK-5
4557 State Route 1377 42023 — 270-628-3800
Jessica Thomas, prin. — Fax 628-0126
Carlisle County MS — 200/6-8
4557 State Route 1377 42023 — 270-628-3800
Jackie Ballard, prin. — Fax 628-3974

Barlow, Ballard, Pop. 713
Ballard County SD — 1,400/PK-12
3465 Paducah Rd 42024 — 270-665-8400
Edward Adami, supt. — Fax 665-9844
www.ballard.k12.ky.us

Ballard County ES 600/K-5
3383 Paducah Rd 42024 270-665-8400
Phillip Harned, prin. Fax 665-9168
Ballard County MS 300/6-8
3565 Paducah Rd 42024 270-665-8400
Casey Allen, prin. Fax 665-5153
Other Schools – See La Center

Battletown, Meade
Meade County SD
Supt. — See Brandenburg
Battletown ES 100/PK-6
8585 Battletown Rd 40104 270-422-7560
Jeff Turner, prin. Fax 497-4499

Baxter, Harlan
Harlan County SD
Supt. — See Harlan
Rosspoint S 400/K-8
132 Highway 522 40806 606-573-4600
Bryan Howard, prin. Fax 573-9596

Beattyville, Lee, Pop. 1,153
Lee County SD 1,200/K-12
PO Box 668 41311 606-464-5000
James Evans, supt. Fax 464-5009
www.lee.kyschools.us
Beattyville ES 300/K-5
PO Box L 41311 606-464-5015
Maureen Patrick, prin. Fax 464-8454
Lee County MS 300/6-8
PO Box N 41311 606-464-5010
Alice Sipple, prin. Fax 464-5011
South Side ES 200/K-5
1700 Highway 11 S 41311 606-464-5020
Steve Carroll, prin. Fax 464-8829

Beaver Dam, Ohio, Pop. 3,113
Ohio County SD
Supt. — See Hartford
Beaver Dam ES 500/PK-6
183 US Highway 62 E 42320 270-274-4478
Jackie Phelps, prin. Fax 274-3886
Southern ES 200/PK-6
3836 US Highway 231 S 42320 270-274-3462
Teresa Byers, prin. Fax 274-4420

Faith Foundation Academy 50/K-6
343 S Main St 42320 270-274-1010
Jerriann Young, admin. Fax 274-1010

Bedford, Trimble, Pop. 740
Trimble County SD 1,600/K-12
PO Box 275 40006 502-255-3201
Marcia Haney-Dunaway, supt. Fax 255-5105
www.trimble.k12.ky.us/
Bedford ES 400/K-5
204 Mount Pleasant Rd 40006 502-255-3217
Deborah Beeles, prin. Fax 255-5109
Trimble County MS 400/6-8
116 Wentworth Ave 40006 502-255-7361
Mike Genton, prin. Fax 255-5102
Other Schools – See Milton

Beechmont, Muhlenberg
Muhlenberg County SD
Supt. — See Powderly
Muhlenberg South ES 600/K-5
2005 US Highway 431 S 42323 270-476-2204
Joe Wells, prin. Fax 476-1411

Belfry, Pike
Pike County SD
Supt. — See Pikeville
Belfry MS 600/6-8
PO Box 850 41514 606-353-9688
James Hurley, prin. Fax 353-9327
Southside ES 500/K-5
PO Box 500 41514 606-353-7296
Ronnie Dotson, prin. Fax 353-7092

Bellevue, Campbell, Pop. 6,022
Bellevue ISD 800/PK-12
219 Center St 41073 859-261-2108
Wayne Starnes, supt. Fax 261-1708
www.bellevue.k12.ky.us/
Grandview ES 400/PK-6
500 Grandview Ave 41073 859-261-4355
Candice Simpkins, prin. Fax 261-1707

Holy Trinity S 100/PK-5
235 Division St 41073 859-291-6937
Jeff Finke, prin. Fax 291-6970

Benton, Marshall, Pop. 4,335
Marshall County SD 4,700/PK-12
86 High School Rd 42025 270-527-8628
Ruth Buchanan, supt. Fax 527-0804
www.marshall.k12.ky.us
Benton ES 500/PK-5
208 W 11th St 42025 270-527-3373
Abby Johnson, prin. Fax 527-5995
Benton MS 200/6-8
906 Joe Creason Dr 42025 270-527-9091
Kem Cothran, prin. Fax 527-9992
Central ES 500/PK-5
115 Jim Goheen Dr 42025 270-527-0796
Shannon Solomon, prin. Fax 527-7713
Jonathan ES 200/PK-5
9207 US Highway 68 E 42025 270-354-6462
Pat Gold, prin. Fax 354-6462
Sharpe ES 300/PK-5
8400 US Highway 68 W 42025 270-898-2852
Angie Kerrick, prin. Fax 898-2972
South Marshall ES 300/PK-5
155 Sid Darnall Rd 42025 270-527-1581
Gavin Thompson, prin. Fax 527-7757
South Marshall MS 300/6-8
85 Sid Darnall Rd 42025 270-527-3828
Russell Buchanan, prin. Fax 527-7616
Other Schools – See Calvert City

Christian Fellowship S 200/PK-12
1343 US Highway 68 E 42025 270-527-8377
Bill Rowley, prin. Fax 527-2872

Berea, Madison, Pop. 13,230
Berea ISD 1,100/PK-12
3 Pirate Pkwy 40403 859-986-8446
Gary Conkin, supt. Fax 986-1839
www.berea.k12.ky.us
Berea Community ES 500/PK-5
2 Pirate Pkwy 40403 859-986-4065
Mike Hogg, prin. Fax 986-0727
Berea Community MS 300/6-8
1 Pirate Pkwy 40403 859-986-4911
John Masters, prin. Fax 986-4640

Madison County SD
Supt. — See Richmond
Foley MS 800/6-8
211 Glades Rd 40403 859-986-8473
Arno Norwell, prin. Fax 986-3362
Johnson ES 400/PK-5
109 Oakwood Dr 40403 859-986-8233
LeeAnne Browder, prin. Fax 986-8405
Kingston ES 500/K-5
2845 Battlefield Memorial 40403 859-986-4668
Fax 986-4653
Silver Creek ES 600/PK-5
75 Old US 25 N 40403 859-986-4991
Dustin Brumbaugh, prin. Fax 986-1932

Bethany, Wolfe

Bethany Christian S 50/K-8
General Delivery 41313 606-668-6355
David Kunze, prin. Fax 668-7315

Betsy Layne, Floyd
Floyd County SD
Supt. — See Prestonsburg
Betsy Layne S 700/K-8
PO Box 128 41605 606-478-9755
John Kidd, prin. Fax 478-9787

Beverly, Bell

Red Bird Mission S 200/K-12
15420 S Highway 66 40913 606-598-2416
Robert Ferguson, prin. Fax 598-7314

Bevinsville, Floyd
Floyd County SD
Supt. — See Prestonsburg
Osborne ES 300/K-5
43 Osborne Br 41606 606-452-2131
Dale Pack, prin. Fax 452-9765

Blaine, Lawrence, Pop. 253
Lawrence County SD
Supt. — See Louisa
Blaine S 300/PK-8
600 Highway 2562 41124 606-652-3624
Steven Hicks, prin. Fax 652-3626

Bledsoe, Harlan
Harlan County SD
Supt. — See Harlan
Green Hills S 200/PK-8
123 W Highway 221 40810 606-558-3533
Darlene Brock, prin. Fax 558-3960

Bloomfield, Nelson, Pop. 873
Nelson County SD
Supt. — See Bardstown
Bloomfield ES 400/PK-5
360 Arnold Ln 40008 502-349-7211
Utona Bieber, prin. Fax 349-7210
Bloomfield MS 400/6-8
96 Arnold Ln 40008 502-349-7201
Glenn Spalding, prin. Fax 349-7203

Bonnieville, Hart, Pop. 365
Hart County SD
Supt. — See Munfordville
Bonnieville S 300/PK-8
7874 N Dixie Hwy 42713 270-531-1111
Lori Chapman, prin. Fax 531-3331

Booneville, Owsley, Pop. 152
Breathitt County SD
Supt. — See Jackson
Highland-Turner ES 200/PK-6
10355 Highway 30 W 41314 606-295-7128
Robert Stewart, prin. Fax 295-2710

Owsley County SD 800/PK-12
RR 3 Box 340 41314 606-593-6363
Melinda Turner, supt. Fax 593-6368
www.owsley.k12.ky.us
Owsley County ES 400/K-6
RR 3 Box 3 41314 606-593-5186
Stephen Gabbard, prin. Fax 593-6758
Owsley County Preschool PK-PK
RR 3 Box 340 41314 606-593-5101
Sheila Thomas, dir. Fax 593-5129

Boston, Nelson
Nelson County SD
Supt. — See Bardstown
Boston S 200/PK-8
130 Wilson Creek Rd 40107 502-833-4644
Kim Whitley, prin. Fax 833-4645

Bowling Green, Warren, Pop. 52,272
Bowling Green ISD 3,600/PK-12
1211 Center St 42101 270-746-2200
Mr. Joseph Tinius, supt. Fax 746-2205
www.b-g.k12.ky.us
Bowling Green JHS 800/6-8
900 Campbell Ln 42104 270-746-2290
Dr. Penny Masden, prin. Fax 746-2295
Cherry ES 300/K-5
1001 Liberty Way 42104 270-746-2230
Judy Whitson, prin. Fax 746-2235
Gray ES 400/K-5
610 Wakefield St 42103 270-746-2280
Jim Tinius, prin. Fax 746-2285
McGinnis ES 300/PK-5
503 Old Morgantown Rd 42101 270-746-2250
Michael Wix, prin. Fax 746-2255
McNeill ES 400/K-5
1800 Creason St 42101 270-746-2260
Marsha Ingram, prin. Fax 746-2265
Parker-Bennett-Curry ES 400/K-5
165 Webb Dr 42101 270-746-2270
Cheri Smith, prin. Fax 746-2275

Warren County SD 12,400/PK-12
PO Box 51810 42102 270-781-5150
Dale Brown, supt. Fax 781-2392
www.warren.k12.ky.us/
Briarwood ES 700/PK-6
265 Lovers Ln 42103 270-782-5554
Debbie Richey, prin. Fax 746-9264
Bristow ES 600/PK-6
6151 Louisville Rd 42101 270-842-1960
Terry Cook, prin. Fax 782-6543
Cumberland Trace ES 500/PK-6
830 Cumberland Trace Rd 42103 270-781-1356
Mary Evans, prin. Fax 781-7036
Drakes Creek MS 800/7-8
704 Cypress Wood Ln 42104 270-843-0165
David Hutchison, prin. Fax 782-6138
Lost River ES 700/PK-6
450 Modern Way 42101 270-746-0334
Jim Goff, prin. Fax 796-2849
Moss MS 500/7-8
2565 Russellville Rd 42101 270-843-0166
Tom Renick, prin. Fax 843-8512
Natcher ES 600/PK-6
1434 Cave Mill Rd 42104 270-842-1364
Stephanie Martin, prin. Fax 842-1563
Plano ES 400/PK-6
2650 Plano Rd 42104 270-467-0411
Melissa Stephanski, prin. Fax 467-0526
Richardsville ES 400/PK-6
1775 Richardsville Rd 42101 270-777-3232
Kory Twyman, prin. Fax 777-3463
Rich Pond ES 800/PK-6
530 Richpond Rd 42104 270-781-9627
Shawn Holland, prin. Fax 846-3041
Rockfield ES 600/PK-6
7597 Russellville Rd 42101 270-843-8437
Monte Cassady, prin. Fax 843-2724
Warren County ES 600/PK-6
1846 Loop St 42101 270-781-2385
Phillip Shelton, prin. Fax 793-0414
Warren East MS 500/7-8
7031 Louisville Rd 42101 270-843-0181
Beverly Dillard, prin. Fax 781-8565
Other Schools – See Alvaton, Oakland, Smiths Grove

Bowling Green Christian Academy 100/PK-8
1730 Destiny Ln 42104 270-782-9552
Mattie Cobb, prin. Fax 782-9585
Holy Trinity Lutheran S 100/PK-6
553 Ashmoor Ave 42101 270-843-1001
Karen Mitchell, dir. Fax 843-7466
St. Joseph S 400/PK-8
416 Church Ave 42101 270-842-1235
Jan Lange, prin. Fax 842-9072

Brandenburg, Meade, Pop. 2,214
Meade County SD 4,800/PK-12
PO Box 337 40108 270-422-7500
Mitch Crump, supt. Fax 422-5494
www.meade.k12.ky.us
Brandenburg PS 600/PK-3
750 Broadway St 40108 270-422-7545
Gloria Bertrand, prin. Fax 422-5235
Pepper MS 800/7-8
1055 Old Ekron Rd 40108 270-422-7530
Chad Butler, prin. Fax 422-5515
Wilson ES 400/PK-PK, 4-
1075 Old Ekron Rd 40108 270-422-7540
Donna Foushee, prin. Fax 422-3434
Other Schools – See Battletown, Ekron, Muldraugh, Payneville

Bremen, Muhlenberg, Pop. 363
Muhlenberg County SD
Supt. — See Powderly
Bremen ES 400/K-5
PO Box 10 42325 270-525-6686
Rick Carver, prin. Fax 525-3380

Brodhead, Rockcastle, Pop. 1,194
Rockcastle County SD
Supt. — See Mount Vernon
Brodhead ES 400/PK-5
PO Box 187 40409 606-758-8512
Caroline Graves, prin. Fax 758-8514

Brooksville, Bracken, Pop. 609
Bracken County SD 1,200/PK-12
348 W Miami St 41004 606-735-2523
Tony Johnson, supt. Fax 735-3640
www.bracken.k12.ky.us
Bracken County MS 400/5-8
167 Parsley Dr 41004 606-735-3425
Leah Jefferson, prin. Fax 735-2057
Taylor ES 500/PK-4
140 Gibson Dr 41004 606-735-2169
Raye Jean Hopper, prin. Fax 735-2058

Brownsville, Edmonson, Pop. 1,039
Edmonson County SD 2,000/K-12
PO Box 129 42210 270-597-2101
Patrick Waddell, supt. Fax 597-2103
www.edmonson.k12.ky.us
Edmonson County 5/6 Center 300/5-6
191 W Center St 42210 270-597-3900
Phil Rich, prin. Fax 597-3903
Edmonson County MS 300/7-8
210 Wild Cat Way 42210 270-597-2932
Kyle Cassady, prin. Fax 597-2182
Other Schools – See Smiths Grove, Sweeden

Buckhorn, Perry, Pop. 149
Perry County SD
Supt. — See Hazard
Buckhorn S 200/K-8
18391 KY Highway 28 41721 606-398-7176
Ronn Turner, prin. Fax 398-7930

Buckner, Oldham
Oldham County SD
Supt. — See Crestwood
Buckner ES 700/K-5
PO Box 277 40010 502-222-3712
Lisa Cheek, prin. Fax 222-3713
Oldham County MS 700/6-8
PO Box 157 40010 502-222-1451
Chris Kraft, prin. Fax 222-5178
Oldham County Preschool PK-PK
PO Box 218 40010 502-222-3700
Carol Hughey, prin. Fax 222-6651

Burdine, See Jenkins
Jenkins ISD
Supt. — See Jenkins
Jenkins ES 300/PK-6
PO Box 300 41517 606-832-2711
Dianne Baker, prin. Fax 832-4191

Burgin, Mercer, Pop. 873
Burgin ISD 400/PK-12
PO Box B 40310 859-748-4000
Richard Webb, supt. Fax 748-4010
www.burgin.k12.ky.us
Burgin ES 200/PK-5
PO Box B 40310 859-748-5282
Martha Collier, prin. Fax 748-4002

Burkesville, Cumberland, Pop. 1,760
Cumberland County SD 1,100/K-12
PO Box 420 42717 270-864-3377
John Hurt, supt. Fax 864-5803
www.cland.k12.ky.us
Cumberland County ES 500/K-5
PO Box 190 42717 270-864-4390
Rodney Schwartz, prin. Fax 864-2756
Cumberland County MS 300/6-8
PO Box 70 42717 270-864-5818
Glen Murphy, prin. Fax 864-2590

Burlington, Boone, Pop. 6,070
Boone County SD
Supt. — See Florence
Burlington ES 800/K-5
5946 N Orient St 41005 859-334-4440
David Sammons, prin. Fax 334-4446
Camp Ernst MS 800/6-8
6515 Camp Ernst Rd 41005 859-534-4000
Eric McArtor, prin. Fax 534-4001
Kelly ES 300/K-5
6775 McVille Rd 41005 859-334-4450
Joe Beil, prin. Fax 334-4454
Stephens ES 1,000/K-5
5687 N Bend Rd 41005 859-334-4460
Karen Lowe, prin. Fax 334-4463

Immaculate Heart of Mary S 700/PK-8
5876 Veterans Way 41005 859-689-4303
Michael Jacks, prin. Fax 689-5636

Burna, Livingston
Livingston County SD
Supt. — See Smithland
Livingston County MS 200/7-8
PO Box 109 42028 270-988-3263
Larry McGregor, prin. Fax 988-2518
North Livingston County ES 200/PK-6
PO Box 107 42028 270-988-4000
Sandra Crowley, prin. Fax 988-4779

Burnside, Pulaski, Pop. 673
Pulaski County SD
Supt. — See Somerset
Burnside ES 500/K-5
435 E Lakeshore Dr 42519 606-561-4250
April Mounce, prin. Fax 561-4562

Busy, Perry
Perry County SD
Supt. — See Hazard
Willard S 300/K-8
625 Big Willard Rd 41723 606-436-6807
Jody Campbell, prin. Fax 436-6677

Butler, Pendleton, Pop. 634
Pendleton County SD
Supt. — See Falmouth
Northern ES 600/PK-5
925 KY Highway 177 E 41006 859-472-7341
Darell Pugh, prin. Fax 472-6548
Sharp MS 700/6-8
35 Wright Rd 41006 859-472-7000
Jeff Aulick, prin. Fax 472-7011

Cadiz, Trigg, Pop. 2,550
Trigg County SD 1,900/K-12
202 Main St 42211 270-522-6075
Tim McGinnis, supt. Fax 522-7782
www.trigg.kyschools.us
Trigg County IS 400/3-5
205 Main St 42211 270-522-2220
Brian Futrell, prin. Fax 522-2234
Trigg County MS 500/6-8
206 Lafayette St 42211 270-522-2210
James Mangels, prin. Fax 522-2203
Trigg County PS 300/K-2
205 Main St 42211 270-522-2220
Ann Taylor, prin. Fax 522-2234

Calhoun, McLean, Pop. 813
McLean County SD 1,600/K-12
PO Box 245 42327 270-273-5257
Tres Settle, supt. Fax 273-5259
www.mclean.k12.ky.us
Calhoun ES 300/K-5
755 Main St 42327 270-273-3264
Ronnie Cartwright, prin. Fax 273-5060
McLean County MS 400/6-8
1901 State Route 136 E 42327 270-273-5191
Jodi Brackett, prin. Fax 273-9876
Other Schools – See Livermore, Sacramento

California, Campbell, Pop. 81

SS. Peter & Paul S 200/PK-8
2160 California Cross Rd 41007 859-635-4382
Harry Luebbers, prin. Fax 635-9184

Calvert City, Marshall, Pop. 2,749
Marshall County SD
Supt. — See Benton
Calvert City ES 300/PK-5
PO Box 215 42029 270-395-4664
Phyllis O'Neal, prin. Fax 395-4027
North Marshall MS 600/6-8
3111 US Highway 95 42029 270-395-7108
Aimee Lepisto, prin. Fax 395-5449

Campbellsburg, Henry, Pop. 714
Henry County SD
Supt. — See New Castle
Campbellsburg ES 300/K-5
270 Cardinal Dr 40011 502-845-8630
Mark Johnson, prin. Fax 845-8631

Campbellsville, Taylor, Pop. 10,906
Campbellsville ISD 1,100/K-12
136 S Columbia Ave 42718 270-465-4162
Diane Woods-Ayers, supt. Fax 465-3918
www.cville.k12.ky.us/
Campbellsville ES 500/K-4
230 W Main St 42718 270-465-4561
David Petett, prin. Fax 789-3827
Campbellsville MS 300/5-8
315 Roberts Rd 42718 270-465-5121
Chris Kidwell, prin. Fax 789-3718

Taylor County SD 2,600/K-12
1209 E Broadway St 42718 270-465-5371
Roger Cook, supt. Fax 789-3954
www.taylor.k12.ky.us
Taylor County ES 1,100/K-5
1100 Lebanon Ave 42718 270-465-5691
Brian Clifford, prin. Fax 465-6219
Taylor County MS 600/6-8
1207 E Broadway St 42718 270-465-2877
Cherry Harvey, prin. Fax 789-1753

Kentucky Christian S 100/PK-5
1190 New Columbia Rd 42718 270-789-2462
Gail Gabehart, dir. Fax 789-4451

Campsprings, Campbell

St. Joseph S 50/K-8
6829 Four Mile Rd 41059 859-635-5652
Ron Christensen, prin. Fax 635-7336

Campton, Wolfe, Pop. 410
Wolfe County SD 1,300/PK-12
PO Box 160 41301 606-668-8002
Stephen Butcher, supt. Fax 668-8050
www.wolfe.k12.ky.us
Campton ES 300/PK-5
PO Box 810 41301 606-668-8102
Russell Halsey, prin. Fax 668-8150
Wolfe County MS 300/6-8
PO Box 460 41301 606-668-8152
Wilma Terrill, prin. Fax 668-8100
Other Schools – See Hazel Green, Rogers

Caneyville, Grayson, Pop. 653
Grayson County SD
Supt. — See Leitchfield
Caneyville ES 400/PK-5
521 E Maple St 42721 270-879-4211
Ronnie Sarver, prin. Fax 879-9022

Carlisle, Nicholas, Pop. 2,030
Nicholas County SD 1,200/PK-12
395 W Main St 40311 859-289-3770
Gregory Reid, supt. Fax 289-3777
www.nicholas.k12.ky.us
Nicholas County S 800/PK-8
105 School Dr 40311 859-289-3785
Shawn Parrish, prin. Fax 289-6240

Carrollton, Carroll, Pop. 3,861
Carroll County SD 1,800/K-12
813 Hawkins St 41008 502-732-7070
Lisa James, supt. Fax 732-7073
www.carroll.kyschools.us
Carroll County MS 400/6-8
408 5th St 41008 502-732-7080
Dana Oak, prin. Fax 732-7107
Cartmell ES 300/4-5
1708 Highland Ave 41008 502-732-7085
Doug Oak, prin. Fax 732-7100
Winn PS 600/K-3
907 Hawkins St 41008 502-732-7090
Sharon Haun, prin. Fax 732-7091

Christian Academy of Carrollton 100/PK-12
1703 Easterday Rd 41008 502-732-4734
Katie Matson, admin. Fax 732-4732

Catlettsburg, Boyd, Pop. 1,927
Boyd County SD
Supt. — See Ashland
Catlettsburg ES 300/PK-5
3348 Court St 41129 606-739-5515
Marci Prater, prin. Fax 739-8625
Ponderosa ES 400/K-5
16701 Ponderosa Dr 41129 606-928-2330
Kathy Rice, prin. Fax 928-2337

Calvary Christian S 100/PK-12
17839 Bear Creek Rd 41129 606-929-5599
Denise Wallace, dir. Fax 928-9219

Cave City, Barren, Pop. 2,054
Caverna ISD 800/PK-12
PO Box 428 42127 270-773-2530
Samuel Dick, supt. Fax 773-2524
www.caverna.k12.ky.us
Caverna ES 300/PK-5
1106 N Dixie Hwy 42127 270-773-3671
Nathan Wyatt, prin. Fax 773-4120
Other Schools – See Horse Cave

Cawood, Harlan
Harlan County SD
Supt. — See Harlan
Cawood S 300/K-8
PO Box 308 40815 606-573-2502
Mike Cox, prin. Fax 573-4779

Cecilia, Hardin
Hardin County SD
Supt. — See Elizabethtown
Howevalley ES 200/PK-5
8450 Hardinsburg Rd 42724 270-862-3287
Beth Handel, prin. Fax 862-3497
Lakewood ES 500/PK-5
265 Learning Place Ln 42724 270-862-4516
Kerry Reeves, prin. Fax 862-3807
West Hardin MS 600/6-8
10471 Leitchfield Rd 42724 270-862-3924
James Roe, prin. Fax 862-3647

Centertown, Ohio, Pop. 427
Ohio County SD
Supt. — See Hartford
Western ES 300/PK-6
4008 State Route 85 E 42328 270-274-7643
Kara Bullock, prin. Fax 274-7271

Central City, Muhlenberg, Pop. 5,785
Muhlenberg County SD
Supt. — See Powderly
Central City ES 400/K-5
1501 N 2nd St 42330 270-754-4474
Mary Ann Payton, prin. Fax 754-9570

Chavies, Perry
Perry County SD
Supt. — See Hazard
Chavies S 300/K-8
PO Box 278 41727 606-436-5101
Charles Browning, prin. Fax 436-3999

Clarkson, Grayson, Pop. 826
Grayson County SD
Supt. — See Leitchfield
Clarkson ES 600/PK-5
301 E Main St 42726 270-242-3061
Edward Chambers, prin. Fax 242-9425

Clay, Webster, Pop. 1,180
Webster County SD
Supt. — See Dixon
Clay S 400/PK-8
210 College St 42404 270-664-2227
Georgiann McCord, prin. Fax 639-0329

Clay City, Powell, Pop. 1,344
Powell County SD
Supt. — See Stanton
Clay City ES 500/K-5
PO Box 670 40312 606-663-3315
Susan Miller, prin. Fax 663-3404

Clearfield, Rowan
Rowan County SD
Supt. — See Morehead
Clearfield ES 300/K-5
460 McBrayer Rd 40313 606-784-5792
Tamela Buttry, prin. Fax 783-0557

Clinton, Hickman, Pop. 1,364
Hickman County SD 700/PK-12
416 N Waterfield Dr 42031 270-653-2341
Steve Bayko, supt. Fax 653-6007
www.hickman.k12.ky.us
Hickman County ES 400/PK-6
416 McMorris St 42031 270-653-4067
Janet Byassee Johnson, prin. Fax 653-4069

Cloverport, Breckinridge, Pop. 1,262
Cloverport ISD 300/PK-12
PO Box 37 40111 270-788-3910
Dr. John Millay, supt. Fax 788-6290
www.cport.k12.ky.us
Fraize MS 100/6-8
101 4th St 40111 270-788-3388
Sheri McKinney, prin. Fax 788-6640
Natcher ES 200/PK-5
101 4th St 40111 270-788-3388
Sheri McKinney, prin. Fax 788-6640

Cold Spring, Campbell, Pop. 5,255
Campbell County SD
Supt. — See Alexandria
Cline ES 500/K-5
5586 E Alexandria Pike 41076 859-781-4544
Lynn Poe, prin. Fax 442-3592
Crossroads ES K-5
475 Cross Roads Blvd 41076 859-441-9174
Kim Visse, prin. Fax 442-3581

St. Joseph S 600/K-8
4011 Alexandria Pike 41076 859-441-2025
Melissa Holzmacher, prin. Fax 441-2057

Columbia, Adair, Pop. 4,174
Adair County SD 2,400/PK-12
1204 Greensburg St 42728 270-384-2476
Darrell Treece, supt. Fax 384-5841
www.adair.k12.ky.us

Adair County ES 500/PK-6
870 Indian Dr 42728 270-384-0077
Robbie Harmon, prin. Fax 384-0079
Adair County MS 400/7-8
322 General John Adair Dr 42728 270-384-5308
Alma Rich, prin. Fax 384-2168
Adair IS 300/3-5
202 General John Adair Dr 42728 270-384-3341
Jane Branham, prin. Fax 384-6693
Casey ES 300/PK-2
220 General John Adair Dr 42728 270-384-3367
Patty Jones, prin. Fax 384-6668

Columbia SDA S, PO Box 597 42728 50/K-8
Nancy Price, prin. 270-384-6798

Combs, Perry
Perry County SD
Supt. — See Hazard
Combs S 500/K-8
PO Box 140 41729 606-436-4932
Anthony Feltner, prin. Fax 439-5194

Corbin, Whitley, Pop. 8,230
Corbin ISD 1,300/K-12
108 Roy Kidd Ave 40701 606-528-1303
Ed McNeel, supt. Fax 523-1747
www.corbinschools.org
Corbin ES 100/3-4
710 W 8th St 40701 606-528-4367
Sharon Ball, prin. Fax 523-3606
Corbin IS 200/5-6
404 17th St 40701 606-528-1651
Bill Jones, prin. Fax 523-3615
Corbin MS 300/7-8
706 S Kentucky Ave 40701 606-523-3619
Ramona Jaynes, prin. Fax 523-3621
Corbin PS K-2
3551 5th Street Rd 40701 606-523-3638
Travis Wilder, prin. Fax 523-3640

Knox County SD
Supt. — See Barbourville
West Knox County ES 600/PK-6
366 N KY 830 40701 606-523-1814
Herman Moore, prin. Fax 523-0872

Laurel County SD
Supt. — See London
Hunter Hills ES 700/K-5
8325 S US Highway 25 40701 606-862-4655
Penny Moore, prin. Fax 862-4658

Whitley County SD
Supt. — See Williamsburg
Oak Grove ES 600/PK-6
4505 Cumberland Falls Hwy 40701 606-549-7867
Regina Paul, prin. Fax 528-0968

St. Camillus Academy 200/PK-8
709 Roy Kidd Ave 40701 606-528-5077
Patricia Beckert, prin. Fax 526-0106

Corydon, Henderson, Pop. 773
Henderson County SD
Supt. — See Henderson
Chandler ES 300/K-5
PO Box 225 42406 270-533-1760
Brian Gardner, prin. Fax 533-9128

Covington, Kenton, Pop. 42,811
Covington ISD 4,000/PK-12
25 E 7th St 41011 859-392-1000
Lynda Jackson, supt. Fax 292-5808
covschools.us/
Biggs ECC 300/PK-PK
1124 Scott St 41011 859-292-5895
Sarina Ball, prin. Fax 292-5956
Carlisle ES 300/K-5
910 Holman Ave 41011 859-292-5812
Joy Collins, prin. Fax 292-5983
Edison ES 300/K-5
1516 Scott St 41011 859-292-5817
Karen Lyon, prin. Fax 292-5809
Latonia ES 400/K-5
3901 Huntington Ave 41015 859-292-5825
Lee Turner, prin. Fax 292-5918
Ninth District ES 400/K-5
2800 Indiana Ave 41015 859-292-5823
Lori Duffy, prin. Fax 655-6933
Sixth District ES 400/K-5
1901 Maryland Ave 41014 859-292-5819
Anthony Ross, prin. Fax 655-6979
Swing ES 400/K-5
501 W 19th St 41014 859-292-5821
Frank Price, prin. Fax 655-6937
Two Rivers MS 500/6-7
525 Scott St 41011 859-392-1100
Eric Neff, prin. Fax 292-5810

Calvary Christian S 500/PK-12
5955 Taylor Mill Rd 41015 859-356-9201
Donald James, admin. Fax 356-8962
Holy Cross S 200/K-8
3615 Church St 41015 859-581-6599
Mary Ellen Matts, prin. Fax 392-3992
Holy Family S 100/K-8
338 E 16th St 41014 859-581-0290
Polly Duplace, prin. Fax 581-0624
Prince of Peace S 100/K-8
625 Pike St 41011 859-431-5153
Sr. Mary Suzanne Rose, prin. Fax 291-8632
St. Augustine S 100/K-8
1840 Jefferson Ave 41014 859-261-5564
Sr. Mary Shelton, prin. Fax 261-5402

Coxs Creek, Nelson
Nelson County SD
Supt. — See Bardstown
Coxs Creek ES 500/PK-5
5635 Louisville Rd 40013 502-349-7050
Jan Lanham, prin. Fax 349-7024

St. Gregory S 100/PK-8
350 Samuels Loop 40013 502-348-9583
Paula Cecil, prin. Fax 348-9597

Crab Orchard, Lincoln, Pop. 866
Lincoln County SD
Supt. — See Stanford
Crab Orchard ES 300/PK-5
137 Lancaster St 40419 606-355-2331
Dreama Tomlison, prin. Fax 355-2331

Crescent Springs, Kenton, Pop. 3,975

St. Joseph S 500/K-8
2474 Lorraine Ct 41017 859-578-2742
Rebecca Brown, prin. Fax 578-2754

Crestwood, Oldham, Pop. 2,250
Oldham County SD 11,200/PK-12
6165 W Highway 146 40014 502-241-3500
Paul Upchurch, supt. Fax 241-3209
www.oldham.k12.ky.us
Camden Station ES 500/K-5
6401 W Highway 146 40014 502-241-1271
Stu Martin, prin. Fax 241-1273
Centerfield ES 500/K-5
4512 Centerfield Dr 40014 502-241-1772
Diane Morgan, prin. Fax 241-5502
Crestwood ES 500/K-5
6500 W Highway 146 40014 502-241-8401
Lori Wright, prin. Fax 241-5501
East Oldham MS 500/6-8
1201 E Highway 22 40014 502-222-8480
Lynda Redmon, prin. Fax 222-8489
Kenwood Station ES 700/K-5
6321 Veterans Memorial Pkwy 40014 502-241-1452
Phillip Moore, prin. Fax 241-1650
Locust Grove ES K-5
1231 E Highway 22 40014 502-222-3521
MariAnn Arnold, prin. Fax 222-3530
South Oldham MS 700/6-8
6403 W Highway 146 40014 502-241-0320
Rob Clayton, prin. Fax 241-1438
Other Schools – See Buckner, Goshen, La Grange, Prospect

Crofton, Christian, Pop. 825
Christian County SD
Supt. — See Hopkinsville
Crofton ES 300/K-5
12145 S Madisonville Rd 42217 270-887-7180
Geoff Bailey, prin. Fax 424-9192

Cub Run, Edmonson
Hart County SD
Supt. — See Munfordville
Cub Run S 200/PK-8
170 Gap Hill Rd 42729 270-524-2925
Nathan Smith, prin. Fax 524-0531

Cumberland, Harlan, Pop. 2,330
Harlan County SD
Supt. — See Harlan
Cumberland S 700/PK-8
322 Golf Course Rd 40823 606-589-2511
Shelia Hall, prin. Fax 589-2610

Custer, Breckinridge
Breckinridge County SD
Supt. — See Hardinsburg
Custer ES 200/K-5
PO Box 9 40115 270-756-3040
Mary Beth Hodge, prin. Fax 756-3041

Cynthiana, Harrison, Pop. 6,311
Harrison County SD 3,100/K-12
324 Webster Ave 41031 859-234-7110
Andy Dotson, supt. Fax 234-8164
www.harrison.kyschools.us
Eastside ES 400/K-5
1226 US Highway 62 E 41031 859-234-7121
Richard Dycus, prin. Fax 234-7189
Harrison County MS 700/6-8
269 Education Dr 41031 859-234-7123
Michael McIntire, prin. Fax 234-8385
Northside ES 400/K-5
2415 US Highway 27 N 41031 859-234-7114
Sharon Hill, prin. Fax 234-7167
Southside ES 300/K-5
106 Education Dr 41031 859-234-7120
Steven Fowler, prin. Fax 234-7176
Westside ES 400/K-5
1585 KY Highway 356 41031 859-234-7115
Jon Hoskins, prin. Fax 234-7199

St. Edward S 50/K-5
107 N Walnut St 41031 859-234-2731
Mary Grable, prin. Fax 234-9823

Danville, Boyle, Pop. 15,409
Boyle County SD 2,700/PK-12
352 N Danville Byp 40422 859-236-6634
Mike LaFavers, supt. Fax 236-8624
www.boyle.kyschools.us
Boyle County MS 700/6-8
1651 Perryville Rd 40422 859-236-4212
Nate Bordeaux, prin. Fax 236-9596
Woodlawn ES 500/K-5
1661 Perryville Rd 40422 859-236-7688
Sharon Jackman, prin. Fax 236-7360
Other Schools – See Junction City, Perryville

Danville ISD 1,800/K-12
152 E Martin L King Blvd 40422 859-238-1300
Dr. Carmen Coleman, supt. Fax 238-1330
www.danville.k12.ky.us
Bate MS 400/6-8
460 Stanford Ave 40422 859-238-1305
Michael Godbey, prin. Fax 238-1343
Hogsett ES 300/K-5
300 Waveland Ave 40422 859-238-1313
Rebecca Goode, prin. Fax 238-1341

Rogers ES 300/K-5
410 E Main St 40422 859-238-1316
Gina Bernard, prin. Fax 238-1342
Toliver ES 300/K-5
209 N Maple Ave 40422 859-238-1319
Judith Spellacy, prin. Fax 238-1334

Danville Christian Academy 200/PK-12
401 Waveland Ave 40422 859-238-9736
Robert Moler, admin. Fax 238-0085
Danville Montessori S 100/PK-6
PO Box 651 40423 859-236-6414
Patricia Critchfield, prin. Fax 236-9677

Dawson Springs, Hopkins, Pop. 2,953
Dawson Springs ISD 400/PK-12
118 E Arcadia Ave 42408 270-797-3811
Alexis Seymore, supt. Fax 797-5201
www.dsprings.k12.ky.us/
Dawson Springs ES 300/PK-6
317 Eli St 42408 270-797-2991
Barbara Barr, prin. Fax 797-5202

Dayton, Campbell, Pop. 5,556
Dayton ISD 1,000/K-12
200 Clay St 41074 859-491-6565
Gary Rye, supt. Fax 292-3995
www.dayton.k12.ky.us
Lincoln ES 500/K-6
701 5th Ave 41074 859-292-7492
Bonnie Sizemore, prin. Fax 292-7481

Denniston, Menifee
Menifee County SD
Supt. — See Frenchburg
Botts ES 200/K-5
PO Box 39 40316 606-768-8052
Dana Thomas, prin. Fax 768-8100

Dewitt, Knox
Knox County SD
Supt. — See Barbourville
Dewitt ES 200/PK-6
PO Box 9 40930 606-542-4274
Marcie Walker, prin. Fax 542-4279

Dixon, Webster, Pop. 611
Webster County SD 2,200/PK-12
28 State Route 1340 42409 270-639-5083
James Kemp, supt. Fax 639-0117
www.webster.k12.ky.us
Dixon S 300/K-8
277 State Route 1340 42409 270-639-9080
Eric Wheatley, prin. Fax 639-0129
Other Schools – See Clay, Providence, Sebree, Slaughters

Dorton, Pike
Pike County SD
Supt. — See Pikeville
Dorton S 300/K-8
PO Box 260 41520 606-639-2832
Randy Burke, prin. Fax 639-4247

Dry Ridge, Grant, Pop. 2,176
Grant County SD
Supt. — See Williamstown
Crittenden Mt. Zion ES 700/K-5
270 Crittenden Mt Zion Rd 41035 859-428-2171
Heather Clay, prin. Fax 428-1890
Dry Ridge ES 700/K-5
275 School Rd 41035 859-824-4484
Ralph Rose, prin. Fax 824-4924
Grant County MS 900/6-8
305 School Rd 41035 859-824-7161
Martha Hall, prin. Fax 824-7163
Sherman ES, 3987 Dixie Hwy 41035 K-5
David Fordyce, prin. 859-428-5500

Earlington, Hopkins, Pop. 1,601
Hopkins County SD
Supt. — See Madisonville
Earlington ES 300/PK-5
1976 Championship Dr 42410 270-825-6154
Lonnie Strader, prin. Fax 825-6029

East Bernstadt, Laurel
East Bernstadt ISD 500/PK-8
PO Box 128 40729 606-843-7373
Homer Radford, supt. Fax 843-6249
www.e-bernstadt.k12.ky.us
East Bernstadt S 500/PK-8
PO Box 128 40729 606-843-6221
James Meding, prin. Fax 843-7671

Laurel County SD
Supt. — See London
Hazel Green ES 300/K-5
2515 Highway 1394 40729 606-862-4647
Danny Hacker, prin. Fax 862-4648

Eastern, Floyd
Floyd County SD
Supt. — See Prestonsburg
Allen Central MS 300/6-8
PO Box 193 41622 606-358-0110
Davida Bickford, prin. Fax 358-0112
Duff ES 300/K-5
PO Box 129 41622 606-358-9420
Tonya Goodman, prin. Fax 358-2414

Eddyville, Lyon, Pop. 2,373
Lyon County SD 1,000/K-12
217 Jenkins Rd 42038 270-388-9715
Quin Sutton, supt. Fax 388-4962
www.lyon.k12.ky.us
Lyon County ES 400/K-5
201 W Fairview Ave 42038 270-388-9715
Kay Lane, prin. Fax 388-9011
Lyon County MS 200/6-8
111 W Fairview Ave 42038 270-388-9715
Victor Zimmerman, prin. Fax 388-0517

Edgewood, Kenton, Pop. 8,913
Kenton County SD
Supt. — See Fort Wright
Caywood ES 500/PK-5
3300 Turkeyfoot Rd 41017 859-341-7062
Dwight Raleigh, prin. Fax 344-3151
Hinsdale ES 600/K-5
440 Dudley Pike 41017 859-341-8226
Connie Ryle, prin. Fax 341-0759
Turkey Foot MS 800/6-8
3230 Turkeyfoot Rd 41017 859-341-0216
Tom Arnzen, prin. Fax 341-7217

St. Pius X S 600/K-8
348 Dudley Pike 41017 859-341-4900
Elizabeth Trenkamp, prin. Fax 341-3440

Edmonton, Metcalfe, Pop. 1,600
Metcalfe County SD 1,500/PK-12
1007 W Stockton St 42129 270-432-3171
Patricia Hurt, supt. Fax 432-3170
www.metcalfe.k12.ky.us
Edmonton ES 500/PK-5
104 Hornet Ave 42129 270-432-2051
Jamie Howard, prin. Fax 432-4678
Metcalfe 6th Grade Center 6-6
102 Hornet Ave 42129 270-432-0045
Rita McMurtrey, prin. Fax 432-0046
Metcalfe County MS 300/7-8
100 Hornet Ave 42129 270-432-3359
Allen Trotter, prin. Fax 432-5828
North Metcalfe ES 100/PK-5
1815 N Metcalf School Rd 42129 270-565-3215
Angela Welsh, prin. Fax 565-3534
Other Schools – See Summer Shade

Ekron, Meade, Pop. 178
Meade County SD
Supt. — See Brandenburg
Ekron ES 400/PK-6
2500 Haysville Rd 40117 270-422-7570
Jon Thomas, prin. Fax 828-5447
Flaherty ES 700/PK-6
2615 Flaherty Rd 40117 270-422-7565
Amanda Richardson, prin. Fax 828-3632

Elizabethtown, Hardin, Pop. 23,450
Elizabethtown ISD 2,300/K-12
219 Helm St 42701 270-765-6146
Fax 765-2158
www.etown.k12.ky.us
Helmwood Heights ES 500/K-5
307 Cardinal Dr 42701 270-769-1328
Michelle Hart, prin. Fax 763-0735
Morningside ES 600/K-5
313 Morningside Dr 42701 270-769-3359
Kelli Bush, prin. Fax 763-0017
Stone MS 500/6-8
323 Morningside Dr 42701 270-769-6343
Beth Mather, prin. Fax 769-6749

Hardin County SD 13,400/PK-12
65 W A Jenkins Rd 42701 270-769-8800
Nannette Johnston, supt. Fax 769-8888
www.hardin.k12.ky.us
Bluegrass MS 700/6-8
170 W A Jenkins Rd 42701 270-765-2658
Brenda Pirtle, prin. Fax 737-0450
Burkhead ES 800/PK-5
521 Charlemagne Blvd 42701 270-769-5983
Bryan Lewis, prin. Fax 737-0989
Heartland ES PK-5
2300 Nelson Dr 42701 270-769-8930
Emily Campbell, prin. Fax 769-8949
Lincoln Trail ES 700/PK-5
3154 Bardstown Rd 42701 270-737-7227
Jennifer Lewis, prin. Fax 769-0246
New Highland ES 600/K-5
110 W A Jenkins Rd 42701 270-737-6612
Connie Goff, prin. Fax 769-0183
Other Schools – See Cecilia, Glendale, Radcliff, Rineyville, Sonora, Vine Grove

Elizabethtown Christian Academy 100/PK-12
PO Box 605 42702 270-234-8174
Linda French, prin. Fax 982-3774
Gloria Dei Lutheran S 100/K-8
1711 Ring Rd 42701 270-769-5910
William Knea, admin. Fax 769-5703
St. James Regional S 400/PK-8
114 N Miles St 42701 270-765-7011
Sr. Michael Marie Friedman, prin. Fax 769-5745

Elkhorn City, Pike, Pop. 1,030
Pike County SD
Supt. — See Pikeville
Elkhorn City S 500/K-8
180 Cougar Dr 41522 606-754-4542
James Mercer, prin. Fax 754-7436

Elkton, Todd, Pop. 1,941
Todd County SD 2,000/PK-12
205 Airport Rd 42220 270-265-2436
Mike Kenner, supt. Fax 265-5414
www.todd.k12.ky.us
North Todd ES 400/PK-5
7300 Greenville Rd 42220 270-277-6800
Contessa Orr, prin. Fax 277-9919
Todd County MS 500/6-8
515 W Main St 42220 270-265-2511
Connie Wofford, prin. Fax 265-9414
Other Schools – See Guthrie

Eminence, Henry, Pop. 2,257
Eminence ISD 600/PK-12
291 W Broadway St 40019 502-845-4788
Don Aldridge, supt. Fax 845-2339
www.eminence.k12.ky.us
Eminence ES 300/PK-4
PO Box 146 40019 502-845-5427
Mike Doran, prin. Fax 845-1310

Emmalena, Knott
Knott County SD
Supt. — See Hindman
Emmalena S 300/PK-8
PO Box 149 41740 606-251-3651
Sharon Johnson, prin. Fax 251-3674

Eolia, Letcher
Letcher County SD
Supt. — See Whitesburg
Boggs S 100/PK-8
PO Box 87 40826 606-633-4654
Christopher Hogue, prin. Fax 633-8102

Erlanger, Kenton, Pop. 16,852
Erlanger-Elsmere ISD 2,300/PK-12
500 Graves Ave 41018 859-727-2009
Dr. Kathlyn Burkhardt, supt. Fax 727-5653
www.erlanger.k12.ky.us
Arnett ES 300/PK-5
3552 Kimberly Dr 41018 859-727-1488
Matt Engel, prin. Fax 342-2481
Howell ES 300/K-5
909 Central Row Rd 41018 859-727-1108
Eric Sayler, prin. Fax 342-2354
Lindeman ES 300/K-5
558 Erlanger Rd 41018 859-727-1188
Michael Shires, prin. Fax 342-2451
Miles ES 300/K-5
208 Sunset Ave 41018 859-727-2231
Bryant Gillis, prin. Fax 342-2371
Tichenor MS 500/6-8
305 Bartlett Ave 41018 859-727-2255
Carl Schwierjohann, prin. Fax 342-2425

Mary Queen of Heaven S 200/PK-8
1130 Donaldson Hwy 41018 859-371-8100
Lynn Mowery, prin. Fax 371-3362
St. Henry S 400/PK-8
3825 Dixie Hwy 41018 859-342-2551
Philip Gessner, prin. Fax 342-2554

Eubank, Pulaski, Pop. 371
Pulaski County SD
Supt. — See Somerset
Eubank ES 300/K-5
285 W Highway 70 42567 606-379-2712
Lisa Black, prin. Fax 379-5304

Evarts, Harlan, Pop. 1,052
Harlan County SD
Supt. — See Harlan
Evarts S 400/K-8
132 Keister St 40828 606-837-2386
Connie Stallard, prin. Fax 837-8535

Ewing, Fleming, Pop. 296
Fleming County SD
Supt. — See Flemingsburg
Ewing ES 200/K-6
PO Box 248 41039 606-267-2601
Greg Emmons, prin. Fax 267-6024

Ezel, Morgan
Morgan County SD
Supt. — See West Liberty
Ezel ES 200/K-5
PO Box 9 41425 606-725-8202
Anna Carol Rose, prin. Fax 725-8250

Fairdale, Jefferson, Pop. 6,563
Jefferson County SD
Supt. — See Louisville
Coral Ridge ES 400/PK-5
10608 National Tpke 40118 502-485-8234
Beverly Goodwin, prin. Fax 485-8369
Fairdale ES 500/K-5
10104 Mitchell Hill Rd 40118 502-485-8247
Carol Baron, prin. Fax 485-8371

Falmouth, Pendleton, Pop. 2,096
Pendleton County SD 2,800/PK-12
2525 US Highway 27 N 41040 859-654-6911
J. Robert Yost, supt. Fax 654-6143
www.pendleton.k12.ky.us
Southern ES 600/PK-5
900 Woodson Rd 41040 859-654-6981
Teresa Wilson, prin. Fax 654-2906
Other Schools – See Butler

Fancy Farm, Graves
Graves County SD
Supt. — See Mayfield
Fancy Farm ES 200/PK-6
PO Box 189 42039 270-674-4820
Susan Higdon, prin. Fax 623-6393

Fedscreek, Pike
Pike County SD
Supt. — See Pikeville
Fedscreek S 300/K-8
221 Fedscreek Rd 41524 606-835-4757
Harold Wallace, prin. Fax 835-1382

Fern Creek, Jefferson, Pop. 16,406
Jefferson County SD
Supt. — See Louisville
Fern Creek ES 800/K-5
8815 Ferndale Rd 40291 502-485-8250
Cheryl Rigsby, prin. Fax 485-8377

St. Gabriel the Archangel S 800/PK-8
5503 Bardstown Rd 40291 502-239-5535
Pam Huelsman, prin. Fax 231-1464

Flatgap, Johnson
Johnson County SD
Supt. — See Paintsville
Flat Gap ES 300/PK-6
1450 KY Route 689 E 41219 606-265-3110
Tracy May, prin. Fax 265-4409

Flat Lick, Knox
Knox County SD
Supt. — See Barbourville
Flat Lick ES 200/K-6
PO Box 379 40935 606-542-4712
Steve Partin, prin. Fax 542-4737

Flatwoods, Greenup, Pop. 7,621
Russell ISD
Supt. — See Russell
Russell-McDowell IS 300/4-5
1900 Long St 41139 606-836-8186
Heather Aldrich, prin. Fax 836-3547

Flemingsburg, Fleming, Pop. 3,104
Fleming County SD 2,400/K-12
211 W Water St 41041 606-845-5851
Kelley Crain, supt. Fax 849-3158
www.fleming.kyschools.us/
Flemingsburg ES 600/K-6
245 W Water St 41041 606-845-9871
Justin Hollingsworth, prin. Fax 845-2404
Simons MS 400/7-8
242 W Water St 41041 606-845-9331
Lesia Eldridge, prin. Fax 849-2309
Other Schools – See Ewing, Hillsboro, Wallingford

Florence, Boone, Pop. 26,349
Boone County SD 17,400/K-12
8330 US Highway 42 41042 859-283-1003
Randy Poe, supt. Fax 282-2376
www.boone.kyschools.us/
Collins ES 600/K-5
9000 Spruce Dr 41042 859-282-2350
Carol Elliott, prin. Fax 282-2356
Erpenbeck ES 800/K-5
9001 Wetherington Blvd 41042 859-384-7200
Becky Brown, prin. Fax 384-5376
Florence ES 500/K-5
103 Center St 41042 859-282-2610
Charles Walton, prin. Fax 282-2615
Jones MS 600/6-8
8000 Spruce Dr 41042 859-282-4610
David Rust, prin. Fax 282-2364
Ockerman ES 700/K-5
8250 US Highway 42 41042 859-282-4620
T.W. Loring, prin. Fax 282-4625
Ockerman MS 700/6-8
8300 US Highway 42 41042 859-282-3240
David Claggett, prin. Fax 282-3242
Yealey ES 700/K-5
10 Yealey Dr 41042 859-282-3333
Nancy Rogers, prin. Fax 282-3337
Other Schools – See Burlington, Hebron, Union

Heritage Academy 200/PK-12
7216 US Highway 42 41042 859-525-0213
Howard Davis, admin. Fax 525-0650
St. Paul S 500/K-8
7303 Dixie Hwy 41042 859-647-4070
David Maher, prin. Fax 647-4073

Fordsville, Ohio, Pop. 546
Ohio County SD
Supt. — See Hartford
Fordsville ES 300/PK-6
PO Box 139 42343 270-276-3601
Jackie McClure, prin. Fax 276-9556

Fort Mitchell, Kenton, Pop. 7,605
Beechwood ISD 1,000/PK-12
50 Beechwood Rd 41017 859-331-3250
Glen Miller, supt. Fax 331-7528
www.beechwood.kyschools.us/
Beechwood ES 500/PK-6
54 Beechwood Rd 41017 859-331-1220
Jamee Flaherty, prin. Fax 426-3743

Blessed Sacrament S 600/K-8
2407 Dixie Hwy 41017 859-331-3062
Maureen Hannon, prin. Fax 344-7323

Fort Thomas, Campbell, Pop. 15,592
Fort Thomas ISD 2,400/PK-12
28 N Fort Thomas Ave 41075 859-781-3333
John Williamson, supt. Fax 442-4016
www.fortthomas.kyschools.us/
Highlands MS 500/6-8
2350 Memorial Pkwy 41075 859-441-5222
Mary Adams, prin. Fax 441-9371
Johnson ES 400/PK-5
1180 N Fort Thomas Ave 41075 859-441-2444
Jon Stratton, prin. Fax 572-4948
Moyer ES 400/K-5
219 Highland Ave 41075 859-441-1180
Jay Brewer, prin. Fax 441-9440
Woodfill ES 300/K-5
1025 Alexandria Pike 41075 859-441-0506
Diana Stratton, prin. Fax 441-2755

St. Catherine of Siena S 200/K-8
23 Rossford Ave 41075 859-572-2680
Doug Lonneman, prin. Fax 572-2699
St. Thomas S 200/PK-8
428 S Fort Thomas Ave 41075 859-572-4641
Sharon Bresler, prin. Fax 572-4644

Fort Wright, Kenton, Pop. 5,438
Kenton County SD 13,200/PK-12
1055 Eaton Dr 41017 859-344-8888
Tim Hanner, supt. Fax 344-1531
www.kenton.kyschools.us/
Fort Wright ES 400/K-5
501 Farrell Dr 41011 859-331-7742
Barb Juengling, prin. Fax 331-7763
Other Schools – See Edgewood, Independence, Morning View, Ryland Heights, Taylor Mill, Villa Hills

St. Agnes S 400/K-8
1322 Sleepy Hollow Rd 41011 859-261-0543
Linda Groh, prin. Fax 261-9778

Fourmile, Bell
Bell County SD
Supt. — See Pineville

Lone Jack Center 300/PK-8
PO Box 98 40939 606-337-9461
Kevin Wilder, prin. Fax 337-8136

Frakes, Bell
Bell County SD
Supt. — See Pineville
Frakes Center 200/PK-8
PO Box 201 40940 606-337-2921
Steve Ely, prin. Fax 337-2928

Frankfort, Franklin, Pop. 27,210
Frankfort ISD 700/PK-12
506 W 2nd St Ste 2 40601 502-875-8661
Rich Crowe, supt. Fax 875-8663
www.frankfort.k12.ky.us
Second Street S 400/PK-6
506 W 2nd St 40601 502-875-8658
Travis Harley, prin. Fax 875-8665

Franklin County SD 6,100/PK-12
916 E Main St 40601 502-695-6700
Harrie Buecker, supt. Fax 695-6708
www.franklin.kyschools.us
Bondurant MS 600/6-8
300 Bondurant Dr 40601 502-875-8440
David Raleigh, prin. Fax 875-8442
Bridgeport ES 400/PK-5
411 Kings Daughters Dr 40601 502-875-8430
Martha Lail, prin. Fax 875-8432
Collins Lane ES 500/PK-5
1 Cougar Ln 40601 502-875-8410
Sharla Six, prin. Fax 875-8412
Early Learning Village - East 500/PK-1
200 Laralan Ave 40601 502-352-2585
Donnie Owens, prin. Fax 352-2586
Elkhorn ES 300/2-5
928 E Main St 40601 502-695-6730
David Scholl, prin. Fax 695-6731
Elkhorn MS 700/6-8
1060 E Main St 40601 502-695-6740
Willie Bartley, prin. Fax 695-6745
Hearn ES 600/PK-5
300 Copperleaf Blvd 40601 502-695-6760
Kyle Sexton, prin. Fax 695-6762
Peaks Mill ES 300/2-5
100 Peaks Mill Rd 40601 502-875-8450
Beth Nickel, prin. Fax 875-8452
Westridge ES 400/PK-5
200 Pebblebrook Way 40601 502-875-8420
Greg Roush, prin. Fax 875-8422

Capital Day S 100/PK-8
120 Deepwood Dr 40601 502-227-7121
Faye McDonough, hdmstr. Fax 227-7558
Christian Enrichment Program 100/K-12
102 Cedar Rdg 40601 502-695-8839
Kim Cornett, contact
Frankfort Christian Academy 300/PK-12
1349A US Highway 421 S 40601 502-695-0744
Robert Roach, hdmstr. Fax 695-8725
Good Shepherd S 200/PK-8
316 Wapping St 40601 502-223-5041
Debra Pack, prin. Fax 223-2755

Franklin, Simpson, Pop. 8,079
Simpson County SD 3,000/PK-12
PO Box 467 42135 270-586-8877
James Flynn, supt. Fax 586-2011
www.simpson.k12.ky.us
Franklin ES 200/PK-K
PO Box 506 42135 270-586-3241
Stacy Raymer, prin. Fax 586-2042
Franklin Simpson MS 700/6-8
PO Box 637 42135 270-586-4401
Shelina Smith, prin. Fax 586-2048
Lincoln ES 500/4-5
PO Box 429 42135 270-586-7133
April McNaughton, prin. Fax 586-2045
Simpson ES 700/1-3
PO Box 409 42135 270-586-4414
Joyce Pais, prin. Fax 598-6059

Frenchburg, Menifee, Pop. 569
Menifee County SD 1,100/K-12
PO Box 110 40322 606-768-8002
Charles Mitchell, supt. Fax 768-8050
www.menifee.k12.ky.us
Menifee County ES 300/K-5
57 Indian Creek Rd 40322 606-768-8351
Phillip Daugherty, prin. Fax 768-8355
Menifee County MS 300/6-8
59 Indian Creek Rd 40322 606-768-8252
Benny Patrick, prin. Fax 768-8300
Other Schools – See Denniston

Fulton, Fulton, Pop. 2,564
Fulton ISD 400/K-12
304 W State Line St 42041 270-472-1553
Dianne Owen, supt. Fax 472-6921
www.fultonind.kyschools.us
Carr ES 200/K-6
400 W State Line St 42041 270-472-1637
Robin Arnzen, prin. Fax 472-2277

Gamaliel, Monroe, Pop. 431
Monroe County SD
Supt. — See Tompkinsville
Gamaliel ES 300/PK-5
320 E Main St 42140 270-457-2341
Tommy Geralds, prin. Fax 457-2702

Garrison, Lewis
Lewis County SD
Supt. — See Vanceburg
Garrison ES 400/PK-6
PO Box 547 41141 606-757-2122
Dale McDowell, prin. Fax 757-2161

Georgetown, Scott, Pop. 19,988
Scott County SD 7,200/PK-12
PO Box 578 40324 502-863-3663
Patricia Putty, supt. Fax 863-5367
www.scott.k12.ky.us
Eastern ES 500/PK-5
3407 Newtown Pike 40324 502-863-0275
Ed Denney, prin. Fax 863-0537
Garth ES 500/PK-5
501 S Hamilton St 40324 502-863-1170
Rusty Andes, prin. Fax 867-0794
Georgetown MS 400/6-8
730 S Hamilton St 40324 502-863-3805
Tommy Hurt, prin. Fax 867-1372
Mason ES 600/PK-5
350 Champion Way 40324 502-570-3050
Leah Riney, prin. Fax 570-0391
Northern ES 300/PK-5
3600 Cincinnati Rd 40324 502-868-5007
Judi Hunter, prin. Fax 863-6654
Royal Spring MS 500/6-8
332 Champion Way 40324 502-570-2390
Shannon Gullett, prin. Fax 863-3621
Scott County MS 800/6-8
1036 Cardinal Dr 40324 502-863-7202
Jennifer Sutton, prin. Fax 863-7452
Southern ES 600/PK-5
1200 Fairfax Way 40324 502-863-0772
Bryan Blankenship, prin. Fax 863-3421
Western ES 600/PK-5
1901 Frankfort Rd 40324 502-863-1393
Deborah Haddad, prin. Fax 867-0840
Other Schools – See Stamping Ground

Providence Christian Academy 200/PK-6
172 Southgate Dr 40324 502-868-9393
Wayne Embry, admin. Fax 867-9927
St. John S 200/PK-8
106 Military St 40324 502-863-2607
Kathleen Boothe, prin. Fax 863-2259

Girdler, Knox
Knox County SD
Supt. — See Barbourville
Girdler ES 400/K-6
PO Box 259 40943 606-546-4859
Charles Hill, prin. Fax 546-4366

Glasgow, Barren, Pop. 14,062
Barren County SD 4,100/PK-12
202 W Washington St 42141 270-651-3787
Jerry Ralston, supt. Fax 651-8836
www.trojan2000.org
Barren County MS 700/7-8
555 Trojan Trl 42141 270-651-4909
Cortni Crews, prin. Fax 651-5137
Eastern ES 400/PK-6
4601 New Salem Rd 42141 270-678-2722
Will Compton, prin. Fax 678-5885
North Jackson ES 100/PK-6
2002 N Jackson Hwy 42141 270-629-2300
Anthony Frazier, prin. Fax 629-2301
Red Cross ES 700/PK-6
215 Parkview Dr 42141 270-659-2400
Jeff Moore, prin. Fax 659-0052
Temple Hill ES 300/PK-6
8788 Tompkinsville Rd 42141 270-427-2611
John Hall, prin. Fax 427-4176
Other Schools – See Hiseville, Lucas, Park City

Glasgow ISD 1,900/PK-12
PO Box 1239 42142 270-651-6757
Kathy Goff, supt. Fax 651-9791
www.glasgow.kyschools.us/
Glasgow MS 500/6-8
105 Scottie Dr 42141 270-651-2256
Mike Vaught, prin. Fax 651-3090
Highland ES 500/PK-5
164 Scottie Dr 42141 270-659-0432
Kelly Oliver, prin. Fax 659-0478
South Green ES 400/K-5
300 James T Rogers Dr 42141 270-651-3806
Bill Philbeck, prin. Fax 651-8957

Glasgow Christian Academy 100/PK-12
600 Old Cavalry Dr 42141 270-651-7729
Tracy Shaw, admin. Fax 651-6811

Glendale, Hardin
Hardin County SD
Supt. — See Elizabethtown
East Hardin MS 700/6-8
129 College St 42740 270-369-7370
Paul Connelly, prin. Fax 369-6380

Goshen, Oldham, Pop. 987
Oldham County SD
Supt. — See Crestwood
Harmony ES 500/K-5
1901 S Highway 1793 40026 502-222-8880
Tracey Harris, prin. Fax 222-8885
Liberty ES 400/K-5
8120 W Highway 42 40026 502-228-1839
Jane Smith, prin. Fax 228-3666
North Oldham MS 700/6-8
1801 S Highway 1793 40026 502-228-9998
Rob Smith, prin. Fax 228-0985

St. Francis S 300/PK-8
11000 W Highway 42 40026 502-228-1197
John Delautre, hdmstr. Fax 228-6723

Grayson, Carter, Pop. 3,986
Carter County SD 4,800/PK-12
228 S Carol Malone Blvd 41143 606-474-6696
Darlene Gee, supt. Fax 474-6125
www.carter.k12.ky.us
East Carter MS 700/6-8
520 Robert and Mary St 41143 606-474-5156
Shannon Wilburn, prin. Fax 474-4027
Heritage ES 500/PK-5
4863 S State Highway 1 41143 606-474-5784
J.C. Perkins, prin. Fax 474-2023
Prichard ES 700/PK-5
401 E Main St 41143 606-474-8815
Jason McGlone, prin. Fax 474-8557
Other Schools – See Olive Hill, Rush

Carter Christian Academy 50/PK-8
PO Box 490 41143 606-475-1919
Elizabeth Stepp, admin. Fax 475-0765

Greensburg, Green, Pop. 2,396
Green County SD 1,300/K-12
PO Box 369 42743 270-932-5231
Marshall Lowe, supt. Fax 932-3624
www.green.k12.ky.us
Green County IS 100/3-5
401 E Hodgenville Ave 42743 270-932-2743
Tony Patterson, prin. Fax 932-2725
Green County MS 400/6-8
PO Box 176 42743 270-932-7773
Timothy Deaton, prin. Fax 932-7617
Green County PS 300/K-2
PO Box 150 42743 270-932-4388
Paul McQueary, prin. Fax 932-6172

Greenup, Greenup, Pop. 1,184
Greenup County SD 3,100/K-12
45 Musketeer Dr 41144 606-473-9819
Randy Hughes, supt. Fax 473-5710
www.greenup.kyschools.us/
Greysbranch ES 300/K-5
1279 Ohio River Rd 41144 606-473-9653
Jeff Wireman, prin. Fax 473-6645
Other Schools – See Argillite, South Shore, Wurtland

Greenville, Muhlenberg, Pop. 4,273
Muhlenberg County SD
Supt. — See Powderly
Greenville ES 500/K-5
201 E Main Cross St 42345 270-338-4830
Lee Freeman, prin. Fax 338-4847
Longest ES 500/K-5
1020 N Main St 42345 270-338-2842
Brent Hardison, prin. Fax 338-3002
Muhlenberg North MS 600/6-8
1000 N Main St 42345 270-338-3550
Robby Davis, prin. Fax 338-2911
Muhlenberg South MS 500/6-8
200 Pritchett Dr 42345 270-338-4650
Ed McCarraher, prin. Fax 338-0151

Grethel, Floyd
Floyd County SD
Supt. — See Prestonsburg
Stumbo S 400/K-8
6945 KY Route 979 41631 606-587-2212
Deresa Ray, prin. Fax 587-2218

Guthrie, Todd, Pop. 1,434
Todd County SD
Supt. — See Elkton
South Todd ES 500/PK-5
4115 Guthrie Rd 42234 270-265-5785
Camille Dillingham, prin. Fax 265-3808

Hagerhill, Johnson
Johnson County SD
Supt. — See Paintsville
Porter ES 400/PK-6
210 US Highway 321 S 41222 606-789-2545
Tom Salyer, prin. Fax 789-6837

Hanson, Hopkins, Pop. 592
Hopkins County SD
Supt. — See Madisonville
Hanson ES 500/K-5
121 Veterans Dr 42413 270-825-6158
Jon Wells, prin. Fax 825-6121

Happy, Perry
Perry County SD
Supt. — See Hazard
Combs S 400/K-8
9165 S KY Highway 15 41746 606-476-2518
Darren Brown, prin. Fax 476-8502

Hardinsburg, Breckinridge, Pop. 2,452
Breckinridge County SD 2,600/PK-12
86 Airport Rd 40143 270-756-3000
Janet Meeks, supt. Fax 756-6888
www.breck.k12.ky.us/
Hardinsburg ES 500/PK-5
419 E 3rd St 40143 270-756-3020
Jayme Knochel, prin. Fax 756-3021
Other Schools – See Custer, Harned, Irvington, Mc Daniels

St. Romuald S 300/PK-8
295 N Main St 40143 270-756-5504
Rob Cox, prin. Fax 756-2099

Hardyville, Hart
Hart County SD
Supt. — See Munfordville
Memorial S 400/PK-8
1400 N Jackson Hwy 42746 270-528-2271
Steven Caven, prin. Fax 528-2273

Harlan, Harlan, Pop. 1,912
Harlan County SD 4,400/PK-12
251 Ball Park Rd 40831 606-573-4330
Timothy Saylor, supt. Fax 573-5767
www.harlan.k12.ky.us/
Cawood ES 300/PK-8
269 Ball Park Rd 40831 606-573-1950
James Clem, prin. Fax 573-1291
Other Schools – See Baxter, Bledsoe, Cawood, Cumberland, Evarts, Kenvir, Wallins Creek

Harlan ISD 800/K-12
420 E Central St 40831 606-573-8700
David Johnson, supt. Fax 573-8711
www.harlan-ind.k12.ky.us
Harlan ES 300/K-4
420 E Central St 40831 606-573-8715
Donna Bushnell, prin. Fax 573-8720

Harned, Breckinridge
Breckinridge County SD
Supt. — See Hardinsburg

Breckinridge County MS 600/6-8
PO Box 39 40144 270-756-3060
Kathy Gedling, prin. Fax 756-3061

Harrodsburg, Mercer, Pop. 8,126
Mercer County SD 2,700/PK-12
371 E Lexington St 40330 859-733-7000
Bruce Johnson, supt.
www.mercer.kyschools.us/
Harlow ES, 530 Perryville St 40330 300/PK-4
Dr. Karen Hatfield, prin. 859-733-7020
King MS 600/6-8
1101 Moberly Rd 40330 859-733-7060
Terry Gordon, prin. Fax 733-7064
Mercer County 5th Grade Academy 200/5-5
443 E Lexington St 40330 859-733-7080
Dana Cobb, prin.
Mercer County ES 800/K-4
741 Tapp Rd 40330 859-733-7040
Jennifer Meadows, prin. Fax 733-7044

Central Kentucky Christian S 100/PK-12
PO Box 207 40330 859-734-9347
Jill Cutler, prin. Fax 734-9348

Hartford, Ohio, Pop. 2,652
Ohio County SD 3,800/PK-12
PO Box 70 42347 270-298-3249
Soretta Ralph, supt. Fax 298-3886
www.ohio.k12.ky.us
Alexander ES 600/PK-6
1250 Oakwood Dr 42347 270-298-3462
Adam Cross, prin. Fax 298-9354
Ohio County MS 600/7-8
1404 S Main St 42347 270-274-7893
Cheston Hoover, prin. Fax 274-7320
Other Schools – See Beaver Dam, Centertown, Fordsville, Horse Branch

Hawesville, Hancock, Pop. 981
Hancock County SD 1,600/K-12
83 State Route 271 N 42348 270-927-6914
Scott Lewis, supt. Fax 927-6916
www.hancock.k12.ky.us/
South Hancock ES 200/K-5
8631 State Route 69 42348 270-927-6762
Barbara Spindel, prin. Fax 927-9400
Other Schools – See Lewisport

Hazard, Perry, Pop. 4,819
Hazard ISD 900/K-12
705 Main St 41701 606-436-3911
Sandra Johnson, supt. Fax 436-2742
www.hazard.k12.ky.us
Eversole MS 300/4-8
601 Broadway St 41701 606-436-4721
Vivian Carter, prin. Fax 439-3726
Walkertown ES 300/K-3
325 School St 41701 606-436-4421
Sondra Combs, prin. Fax 435-0407

Knott County SD
Supt. — See Hindman
Cordia ES 100/PK-6
6050 Lotts Creek Rd 41701 606-785-4457
Dwight Creech, prin. Fax 785-4669

Perry County SD 4,200/K-12
315 Park Ave 41701 606-439-5814
John Paul Amis, supt. Fax 439-2512
www.perry.kyschools.us/
Wooton ES 400/K-6
41 Runway Ave 41701 606-436-3423
Nadine Vannarsdall, prin. Fax 439-3353
Other Schools – See Ary, Avawam, Buckhorn, Busy, Chavies, Combs, Happy, Leatherwood, Viper

Hazel Green, Wolfe
Wolfe County SD
Supt. — See Campton
Red River Valley ES 100/K-5
PO Box 219 41332 606-662-8252
Brian Creech, prin. Fax 662-8200

Hebron, Boone
Boone County SD
Supt. — See Florence
Conner MS 900/6-8
3300 Cougar Path 41048 859-334-4410
Jamie Brewer, prin. Fax 334-4435
Goodridge ES 800/K-5
3330 Cougar Path 41048 859-334-4420
Patricia Breitholle, prin. Fax 334-4422
North Pointe ES 800/K-5
875 N Bend Rd 41048 859-334-7000
Dave Thompson, prin. Fax 334-7010

Henderson, Henderson, Pop. 27,666
Henderson County SD 6,900/K-12
1805 2nd St 42420 270-831-5000
Dr. Thomas Richey, supt. Fax 831-5009
www.hendersonschools.net/
Bend Gate ES 500/K-5
920 Bend Gate Rd 42420 270-831-5040
Steve Steiner, prin. Fax 831-5043
Cairo ES 300/K-5
10694 US Highway 41 S 42420 270-831-5154
Juli Collins, prin. Fax 831-5156
East Heights ES 500/K-5
1776 Adams Ln 42420 270-831-5070
Nancy Gibson, prin. Fax 831-5072
Henderson County North MS 800/6-8
1707 2nd St 42420 270-831-5060
Scottie Long, prin. Fax 831-5064
Henderson County South MS 700/6-8
800 S Alves St 42420 270-831-5050
Leo Peckenpaugh, prin. Fax 831-5058
Jefferson ES 300/K-5
315 Jackson St 42420 270-831-5090
Kasey Farmer, prin. Fax 831-5091
Niagara ES 300/K-5
13043 State Route 136 E 42420 270-831-5142
Patty Sellers, prin. Fax 826-0416

South Heights ES 500/K-5
1200 Wright St 42420 270-831-5081
Rob Carroll, prin. Fax 831-5083
Other Schools – See Corydon, Spottsville

Holy Name S 500/PK-8
628 2nd St 42420 270-827-3425
Daryl Hagan, prin. Fax 827-4027

Herndon, Christian
Christian County SD
Supt. — See Hopkinsville
South Christian ES 600/K-5
12340 Herndon Oak Grove Rd 42236 270-887-7350
Janie Giles, prin. Fax 271-9276

Hickman, Fulton, Pop. 2,371
Fulton County SD 600/PK-12
2780 Moscow Ave 42050 270-236-3923
Dr. Charles Holliday, supt. Fax 236-2184
www.fulton.k12.ky.us
Fulton County S 400/PK-8
2750 Moscow Ave 42050 270-236-2070
Julie Jackson, prin. Fax 236-9523

Highland Heights, Campbell, Pop. 5,791

Cornerstone Montessori S 50/K-6
2048 Alexandria Pike 41076 859-491-9960
Mary Schadler, prin. Fax 491-1887

Hi Hat, Floyd
Floyd County SD
Supt. — See Prestonsburg
South Floyd MS 200/6-8
299 Mt Raider Dr Ste 102 41636 606-452-9607
Carolyn Martin, prin. Fax 452-4810

Hillsboro, Fleming
Fleming County SD
Supt. — See Flemingsburg
Hillsboro ES 200/K-6
PO Box 8 41049 606-876-2251
Carol Thompson, prin. Fax 876-2478

Hindman, Knott, Pop. 772
Knott County SD 2,500/PK-12
PO Box 869 41822 606-785-3153
Kimberly King, supt. Fax 785-0800
www.knott.k12.ky.us
Hindman S 500/PK-8
PO Box 816 41822 606-785-5872
Wes Halbert, admin. Fax 785-5860
Other Schools – See Emmalena, Hazard, Littcarr, Mousie, Topmost

Hiseville, Barren, Pop. 224
Barren County SD
Supt. — See Glasgow
Hiseville ES 400/PK-6
General Delivery 42152 270-453-2611
Steven Murphy, prin. Fax 453-2612

Hodgenville, Larue, Pop. 2,788
LaRue County SD 2,000/K-12
PO Box 39 42748 270-358-4111
Sam Sanders, supt. Fax 358-3053
www.larue.k12.ky.us
Hodgenville ES 500/K-5
33 Eagle Ln 42748 270-358-3506
Penny Cecil, prin. Fax 358-8800
LaRue County MS 400/6-8
911 S Lincoln Blvd 42748 270-358-3196
Corey Keith, prin. Fax 358-9088
Lincoln ES 400/K-5
2101 Lincoln Farm Rd 42748 270-358-4112
Amber Thurman, prin. Fax 358-4113

Hopkinsville, Christian, Pop. 28,821
Christian County SD 8,400/K-12
PO Box 609 42241 270-887-7000
Brady Link, supt. Fax 887-1316
www.christian.k12.ky.us
Belmont ES 400/K-5
814 Belmont St 42240 270-887-7170
Anita Hopson, prin. Fax 887-1175
Christian County MS 800/6-8
210 Glass Ave 42240 270-887-7070
Fax 887-1189
Holiday ES 600/K-5
3910 Nassau Cir 42240 270-887-7210
Karen Shields, prin. Fax 887-1196
Hopkinsville MS 700/6-8
434 Koffman Dr 42240 270-887-7130
Wendy Duvall, prin. Fax 887-1234
Indian Hills ES 500/K-5
313 Blane Dr 42240 270-887-7230
Helena Radford, prin. Fax 887-1199
King ES K-5
14405 Martin Lther King Way 42240 270-887-7310
Sarah Newman, prin. Fax 890-6014
Lacy ES 300/K-5
12015 Greenville Rd 42240 270-887-7250
Chris Bentzel, prin. Fax 269-9556
Millbrooke ES 600/K-5
415 Millbrooke Dr 42240 270-887-7270
Anissa Hendricks, prin. Fax 887-1214
North Drive MS 500/6-8
831 North Dr 42240 270-887-7150
Nathan Howton, prin. Fax 887-1287
Sinking Fork ES 400/K-5
5005 Princeton Rd 42240 270-887-7330
Kathleen Carter, prin. Fax 887-1217
Other Schools – See Crofton, Herndon, Pembroke

Grace Episcopal Church K 50/PK-K
216 E 6th St 42240 270-885-8757
Barbara Kirkham, dir. Fax 885-2697
Heritage Christian Academy 400/PK-12
8349 Eagle Way 42240 270-885-2417
Linda Garris, admin. Fax 885-0094

SS. Peter & Paul S 200/PK-8
902 E 9th St 42240 270-886-0172
Sarah Kranz, prin. Fax 887-9924
University Heights Academy 300/PK-12
1300 Academy Dr 42240 270-886-0254
Pam Nunn, prin. Fax 886-2716

Horse Branch, Ohio
Ohio County SD
Supt. — See Hartford
Horse Branch ES 200/PK-6
11980 US Highway 62 E 42349 270-274-4662
Jeff Martin, prin. Fax 274-7866

Horse Cave, Hart, Pop. 2,314
Caverna ISD
Supt. — See Cave City
Caverna MS 200/6-8
2278 S Dixie St 42749 270-773-4665
Barry Nesbitt, prin. Fax 773-4668

Hart County SD
Supt. — See Munfordville
LeGrande S 200/PK-8
70 Legrande School Rd 42749 270-786-2746
Jerri Lyle, prin. Fax 786-5747

Hoskinston, Leslie
Leslie County SD
Supt. — See Hyden
Stinnett ES 300/PK-6
12975 Highway 421 40844 606-374-3641
Britt Lawson, prin. Fax 374-6655

Howardstown, Nelson

St. Ann S 50/1-8
7500 Howardstown Rd 40051 502-549-7310
Lois Cecil, prin.

Hustonville, Lincoln, Pop. 356
Lincoln County SD
Supt. — See Stanford
Hustonville ES 400/PK-5
93 College St 40437 606-346-3831
Marilyn Hafley, prin. Fax 346-2201

Hyden, Leslie, Pop. 196
Leslie County SD 1,800/PK-12
PO Box 949 41749 606-672-2397
Larry Sparks, supt. Fax 672-4224
www.leslie.k12.ky.us
Hyden ES 300/PK-6
PO Box 926 41749 606-672-2425
Randy Williams, prin. Fax 672-6545
Leslie County MS 300/7-8
PO Box 965 41749 606-672-5580
Dana Coots, prin. Fax 672-5320
Other Schools – See Hoskinston, Wooton, Yeaddiss

Independence, Kenton, Pop. 19,065
Kenton County SD
Supt. — See Fort Wright
Beech Grove ES 600/PK-5
1029 Bristow Rd 41051 859-371-1636
Debbie Howard, prin. Fax 371-7958
Kenton ES 700/K-5
11246 Madison Pike 41051 859-356-3781
Pat Goetz, prin. Fax 356-5397
Summit View ES 700/PK-5
5006 Madison Pike 41051 859-363-4700
Lesley Smith, prin. Fax 363-4703
Summit View MS 800/6-8
5002 Madison Pike 41051 859-363-4800
David Johnstone, prin. Fax 363-4804
Twenhofel MS 800/6-8
11846 Taylor Mill Rd 41051 859-356-5559
Cheryl Jones, prin. Fax 356-1137
White's Tower ES 500/PK-5
2977 Harris Pike 41051 859-356-9668
Angela Spencer, prin. Fax 356-6799

Community Christian Academy 200/PK-12
11875 Taylor Mill Rd 41051 859-356-7990
Tara Bates, prin. Fax 356-7991
St. Cecilia S 300/PK-8
5313 Madison Pike 41051 859-363-4314
Carol Roberts, prin. Fax 363-4315

Inez, Martin, Pop. 457
Martin County SD 2,200/PK-12
PO Box 366 41224 606-298-3572
Mark Blackburn, supt. Fax 298-4427
www.martin.k12.ky.us
Eden ES 300/PK-5
179 Eden Ln 41224 606-298-3471
Wila Preston, prin. Fax 298-0901
Inez ES 300/K-5
5000 Elementary Dr 41224 606-298-3428
Mike Cassady, prin. Fax 298-0386
Inez MS 300/6-8
388 Inez Middle School Rd 41224 606-298-3045
Brent Haney, prin. Fax 298-7314
Martin County Headstart Center PK-PK
PO Box 516 41224 606-298-7990
Lisa Kirk, prin. Fax 298-2472
Other Schools – See Warfield

Irvine, Estill, Pop. 2,714
Estill County SD 2,200/PK-12
PO Box 930 40336 606-723-2181
Bert Hensley, supt. Fax 723-6029
www.estill.k12.ky.us
Estill County MS 600/6-8
2805 Winchester Rd 40336 606-723-5136
Tim Burkhart, prin. Fax 723-2041
Estill Springs ES 400/1-5
314 Main St 40336 606-723-7703
Lorretta Cruse, prin. Fax 723-7683
South Irvine S 100/PK-K
1000 S Irvine Rd 40336 606-723-4700
Lisa Reece, prin. Fax 723-6724

West Irvine ES 400/1-5
155 Riverview Rd 40336 606-723-4800
Tonya Isaacs, prin. Fax 723-5350

Irvington, Breckinridge, Pop. 1,359
Breckinridge County SD
Supt. — See Hardinsburg
Irvington ES 300/K-5
PO Box 90 40146 270-756-3050
Jon Miller, prin. Fax 756-3051

Isonville, Elliott
Elliott County SD
Supt. — See Sandy Hook
Isonville ES 100/K-6
PO Box 199 41149 606-738-8152
Felicia Dickerson, prin. Fax 738-8150

Jackson, Breathitt, Pop. 2,413
Breathitt County SD 2,200/PK-12
PO Box 750 41339 606-666-2491
Arch Turner, supt. Fax 666-2493
www.breathitt.kyschools.us
L.B.J. ES 500/PK-6
90 L B J Rd 41339 606-666-7181
Ron Combs, prin. Fax 666-7778
Sebastian MS 400/7-8
244 L B J Rd 41339 606-666-8894
Tim Bobrowski, prin. Fax 666-5336
Other Schools – See Booneville, Lost Creek, Rousseau

Jackson ISD 400/PK-12
940 Highland Ave 41339 606-666-4979
Timothy Spencer, supt. Fax 666-4350
www.jacksonind.kyschools.us/
Jackson City S 400/PK-12
940 Highland Ave 41339 606-666-5164
James Yount, prin. Fax 666-2555

Jamestown, Russell, Pop. 1,711
Russell County SD 2,900/PK-12
PO Box 440 42629 270-343-3191
Scott Pierce, supt. Fax 343-3072
www.russell.k12.ky.us/
Jamestown ES 500/PK-6
342 S Main St 42629 270-343-3966
Wayne Ackerman, prin. Fax 343-3350
Union Chapel ES 200/PK-6
1085 Highway 1058 42629 270-343-4666
Cynthia Roberts, prin. Fax 343-6153
Other Schools – See Russell Springs

Jeffersontown, Jefferson, Pop. 26,100
Jefferson County SD
Supt. — See Louisville
Tully ES 800/PK-5
3300 College Dr 40299 502-485-8338
John Ansman, prin. Fax 485-8393

Christ Lutheran K 100/PK-K
9212 Taylorsville Rd 40299 502-267-5082

Jenkins, Letcher, Pop. 2,297
Jenkins ISD 600/PK-12
PO Box 74 41537 606-832-2183
Deborah Watts, supt. Fax 832-2181
www.jenkins.k12.ky.us
Other Schools – See Burdine

Junction City, Boyle, Pop. 2,175
Boyle County SD
Supt. — See Danville
Junction City ES 300/PK-5
PO Box 200 40440 859-936-7524
James Young, prin. Fax 854-0250

Keavy, Laurel
Laurel County SD
Supt. — See London
Keavy ES 300/K-5
598 W Highway 312 40737 606-862-4672
Joe Floyd, prin. Fax 862-4673

Kenvir, Harlan
Harlan County SD
Supt. — See Harlan
Black Mountain S 400/PK-8
PO Box 590 40847 606-837-2214
Kenny Watkins, prin. Fax 837-9930

Kimper, Pike
Pike County SD
Supt. — See Pikeville
Kimper S 200/K-8
8151 State Highway 194 E 41539 606-631-1509
Lisa Hess, prin. Fax 631-9197

Knottsville, Daviess

Carrico Memorial S 100/K-8
9546 State Route 144 42366 270-281-5526
P. Mike Clark, prin. Fax 281-9556

Kona, Letcher
Letcher County SD
Supt. — See Whitesburg
Potter S 400/K-8
55 Kona Dr 41858 606-855-7544
Linda Hall, prin. Fax 855-4929

La Center, Ballard, Pop. 1,034
Ballard County SD
Supt. — See Barlow
Ballard County Preschool Headstart PK-PK
PO Box 120 42056 270-665-8400
Fanetta Puckett, prin. Fax 665-9228

La Grange, Oldham, Pop. 6,046
Oldham County SD
Supt. — See Crestwood
La Grange ES 800/K-5
500 W Jefferson St 40031 502-222-9454
John Finch, prin. Fax 222-0685

Lancaster, Garrard, Pop. 4,207
Garrard County SD 2,600/PK-12
322 W Maple Ave 40444 859-792-3018
Donald Aldridge, supt. Fax 792-4733
www.garrard.k12.ky.us/
Camp Robinson ES 500/PK-5
7541 Lexington Rd 40444 859-792-6136
Janet Overstreet, prin. Fax 792-8908
Garrard MS 600/6-8
324 W Maple Ave 40444 859-792-2108
Scotty Merida, prin. Fax 792-9618
Lancaster ES 400/PK-5
205 Lexington St 40444 859-792-3047
Tracie Bottoms, prin. Fax 792-4855
Other Schools – See Paint Lick

Lawrenceburg, Anderson, Pop. 9,403
Anderson County SD 3,900/PK-12
1160 Bypass N 40342 502-839-3406
Kim Shaw, supt. Fax 839-2501
www.anderson.k12.ky.us/
Anderson County ECC 200/PK-K
126 N Main St 40342 502-839-2504
Melissa Lentz, prin. Fax 839-3407
Anderson County MS 900/6-8
200 Mustang Trl 40342 502-839-9261
Steve Karsner, prin. Fax 839-2534
Saffell Street ES 600/1-5
210 Saffell St 40342 502-839-3565
Derek Shouse, prin. Fax 839-2539
Turner ES 500/K-5
1411 Fox Creek Rd 40342 502-839-2500
Wayne Reese, prin. Fax 839-2520
Ward ES 500/1-5
730 W Broadway St 40342 502-839-4236
Amanda Ellis, prin. Fax 839-2506

Christian Academy of Lawrenceburg 100/PK-12
PO Box 498 40342 502-839-9992
Carla Andrade, admin. Fax 839-3728

Leatherwood, Perry
Perry County SD
Supt. — See Hazard
Leatherwood S 200/K-8
7777 KY Highway 699 41731 606-675-4431
Kenny Roark, prin. Fax 675-6888

Lebanon, Marion, Pop. 5,959
Marion County SD 3,100/PK-12
755 E Main St 40033 270-692-3721
Donald Smith, supt. Fax 692-1899
www.marion.k12.ky.us
Calvary ES 300/K-5
3345 Highway 208 40033 270-692-3676
Pamela Marks, prin. Fax 692-0766
Glasscock ES 400/PK-5
773 E Main St 40033 270-692-3223
Lee Ann Divine, prin. Fax 692-1895
Lebanon ES 400/PK-5
420 W Main St 40033 270-692-3883
Donna Royse, prin. Fax 692-6028
Lebanon MS 400/6-8
200 Corporate Dr 40033 270-692-3441
Todd Farmer, prin. Fax 692-0266
St. Charles MS 300/6-8
1155 Highway 327 40033 270-692-4578
John Brady, prin. Fax 692-1176
Other Schools – See Loretto

St. Augustine S 200/PK-8
236 S Spalding Ave 40033 270-692-2063
Alicia Riggs, prin. Fax 692-6597

Lebanon Junction, Bullitt, Pop. 1,934
Bullitt County SD
Supt. — See Shepherdsville
Lebanon Junction ES 300/PK-5
10920 S Preston Hwy 40150 502-833-4618
Staci Goedde, prin. Fax 833-3727

Leitchfield, Grayson, Pop. 6,462
Grayson County SD 4,200/PK-12
PO Box 4009 42755 270-259-4011
Barry Anderson, supt. Fax 259-4756
www.grayson.k12.ky.us
Grayson County MS 1,000/6-8
726 John Hill Taylor Dr 42754 270-259-4175
Jim Blain, prin. Fax 259-5875
Lawler ES 400/PK-5
174 School House Rd 42754 270-259-9322
Marcia Downs, prin. Fax 259-0690
Wilkey ES 500/PK-5
130 Wallace Ave 42754 270-259-4058
Gwen Lucas, prin. Fax 259-6332
Other Schools – See Caneyville, Clarkson

Leitchfield Christian Academy 100/PK-12
106 E Walnut St 42754 270-259-4076
Linda Gentry, prin. Fax 259-3240
St. Paul S, 1812 Saint Paul Rd 42754 50/K-8
Sr. Anne Mudd, prin. 270-242-7483

Letcher, Letcher
Letcher County SD
Supt. — See Whitesburg
Letcher S 300/K-8
School Rd 41832 606-633-2524
Wendy Mullins, prin. Fax 633-8190

Lewisburg, Logan, Pop. 918
Logan County SD
Supt. — See Russellville
Lewisburg S 600/PK-8
750 Stacker St 42256 270-755-4823
Barrett Nelson, prin. Fax 755-4870

Lewisport, Hancock, Pop. 1,655
Hancock County SD
Supt. — See Hawesville
Hancock County MS 400/6-8
100 State Route 271 S 42351 270-927-6712
Gina Biever, prin. Fax 927-6712

North Hancock ES 500/K-5
330 Frank Lutrell Rd 42351 270-295-6330
Martha Warren, prin. Fax 295-6332

Lexington, Fayette, Pop. 263,618
Fayette County SD 35,400/PK-12
701 E Main St 40502 859-381-4000
Stu Silberman, supt. Fax 381-4303
www.fcps.net
Allen ES 500/PK-5
1901 Appomattox Rd 40504 859-381-3456
Greg Williams, prin. Fax 381-3459
Arlington ES 300/PK-5
123 E 6th St 40508 859-381-3030
Robert Wilkirson, prin. Fax 381-3027
Ashland ES 300/K-5
195 N Ashland Ave 40502 859-381-3243
Schuronda Morton, prin. Fax 381-3252
Athens-Chilesburg ES 600/PK-5
930 Jouett Creek Dr 40509 859-381-4955
Peggy Henderson, prin. Fax 381-4965
Beaumont MS 1,000/6-8
2080 Georgian Way 40504 859-381-3094
Kate McAnelly, prin. Fax 381-3109
Breckinridge ES 500/PK-5
2101 Saint Mathilda Dr 40502 859-381-3273
Karen Haskins, prin. Fax 381-3284
Brown ES K-6
555 E 5th St 40508 859-381-4990
Yvonne Peace, prin. Fax 381-3166
Bryan Station Magnet MS 600/6-8
1865 Wickland Dr 40505 859-381-3288
Jim Thomas, prin. Fax 381-3292
Cardinal Valley ES 600/PK-5
218 Mandalay Rd 40504 859-381-3340
Ivonne Beegle, prin. Fax 381-3341
Cassidy ES 500/PK-5
1125 Tates Creek Rd 40502 859-381-3018
Rhonda Fister, prin. Fax 381-3019
Clark MS 900/6-8
3341 Clays Mill Rd 40503 859-381-3036
Lisa Goodin, prin. Fax 381-3037
Clays Mill Magnet ES 600/PK-5
2319 Clays Mill Rd 40503 859-381-3355
Edwina Smith, prin. Fax 381-3359
Crawford MS 500/6-8
1813 Charleston Dr 40505 859-381-3370
Joyce Florence, prin. Fax 381-3378
Deep Springs ES 400/PK-5
1919 Brynell Dr 40505 859-381-3069
Matthew Thompson, prin. Fax 381-3364
Dixie Magnet ES 500/PK-5
1940 Eastland Pkwy 40505 859-381-3116
Loraye Jones, prin. Fax 381-3127
Garden Springs ES 600/K-5
2151 Garden Springs Dr 40504 859-381-3388
Karen Borders, prin. Fax 381-3400
Glendover ES 600/K-5
710 Glendover Rd 40502 859-381-3403
Cathy Fine, prin. Fax 381-3417
Harrison ES 300/PK-5
161 Bruce St 40507 859-381-3418
Tammie Franks, prin. Fax 381-3286
Hayes MS 800/6-8
260 Richardson Pl 40509 859-381-4920
Sherri Heise, prin. Fax 381-4937
Lansdowne ES 700/PK-5
336 Redding Rd 40517 859-381-3500
Leah Winkler, prin. Fax 381-3711
Leestown Math Science & Tech MS 600/6-8
2010 Leestown Rd 40511 859-381-3181
Jennifer Kendall, prin. Fax 381-3180
Lexington Traditional Magnet MS 700/6-8
350 N Limestone 40508 859-381-3192
Clay Goode, prin. Fax 381-3199
Liberty ES 600/PK-5
2585 Liberty Rd 40509 859-381-4979
Vickie Burke, prin. Fax 381-3468
Marks ES 600/PK-5
3277 Pepperhill Rd 40502 859-381-3470
Sandra Adams, prin. Fax 381-3472
Maxwell Spanish Immersion Magnet ES 500/K-5
301 Woodland Ave 40508 859-381-3516
Heather Bell, prin. Fax 381-3517
Meadowthorpe ES 500/PK-5
1710 N Forbes Rd 40511 859-381-3521
Mike Stacy, prin. Fax 381-3525
Millcreek ES 600/PK-5
1212 Reva Ridge Way 40517 859-381-3527
Lorraine Williams, prin. Fax 381-3529
Morton MS 700/6-8
1225 Tates Creek Rd 40502 859-381-3533
Rhonda Runyon, prin. Fax 381-3536
Northern ES 500/PK-5
340 Rookwood Pkwy 40505 859-381-3541
Maribeth Gaines, prin. Fax 381-3966
Parks Language & Communications ES 700/PK-5
1251 Beaumont Centre Ln 40513 859-381-3132
Leslie Thomas, prin. Fax 381-3146
Picadome ES 600/PK-5
1642 Harrodsburg Rd 40504 859-381-3563
Darla Simms, prin. Fax 381-3565
Russell Cave Model Magnet ES 200/PK-5
3375 Russell Cave Rd 40511 859-381-3571
Betsy Rutherford, prin. Fax 381-3575
Sandersville ES 700/PK-5
3025 Sandersville Rd 40511 859-381-4980
Sandy Mefford, prin. Fax 381-3712
School for Creative and Performing Arts 300/4-8
400 Lafayette Pkwy 40503 859-381-3332
M. Cunningham-Amos, prin. Fax 381-3334
Southern ES 700/PK-5
340 Wilson Downing Rd 40517 859-381-3589
Freida Collins, prin. Fax 381-3590
Southern MS 600/6-8
400 Wilson Downing Rd 40517 859-381-3582
Jane Dreidame, prin. Fax 381-3588
Squires ES 500/PK-5
3337 Squire Oak Dr 40515 859-381-3002
Sabrina Adkins, prin. Fax 381-3005

Stonewall ES 700/K-5
3215 Cornwall Dr 40503 859-381-3079
Bill Gatliff, prin. Fax 381-3080
Tates Creek ES 400/PK-5
1113 Centre Pkwy 40517 859-381-3606
Dee Patrick, prin. Fax 381-3772
Tates Creek MS 600/6-8
1105 Centre Pkwy 40517 859-381-3052
Greg Quenon, prin. Fax 381-3053
Todd ES 400/PK-5
551 Parkside Dr 40505 859-381-3512
Margetta McFarland, prin. Fax 381-3720
Veterans Park Math Science & Tech ES 700/PK-5
4351 Clearwater Way 40515 859-381-3161
Amy McVey, prin. Fax 381-3151
Washington Academy 500/PK-5
707 Howard St 40508 859-381-3263
Wendy Brown, prin. Fax 381-3267
Winburn MS 600/6-8
1060 Winburn Dr 40511 859-381-3967
Tina Stevenson, prin. Fax 381-3971
Yates ES 400/PK-5
695 E New Circle Rd 40505 859-381-3613
Ketsy Fields, prin. Fax 381-3615

Blue Grass Baptist S 200/K-12
3743 Red River Dr 40517 859-272-1217
Phillip Ritchey, admin. Fax 273-8658
Christ the King S 500/PK-8
412 Cochran Rd 40502 859-266-5641
Karen Thomas, prin. Fax 266-4547
Community Montessori S 200/PK-6
166 Crestwood Dr 40503 859-277-4805
Janet Ashby, admin. Fax 277-6765
Good Shepherd Day S 100/PK-K
544 Sayre Ave 40508 859-255-9734
Fax 977-3844
Lexington Christian Academy 700/K-3
3100 Tates Creek Rd 40502 859-268-3071
Denny McCardle, prin. Fax 268-3352
Lexington Christian Academy 200/4-6
3100 Tates Creek Rd Ste 50 40502 859-269-5811
Tim McAboy, prin. Fax 269-5695
Lexington Christian Academy-East 200/PK-3
2598 Liberty Rd 40509 859-263-7245
Denny McCardle, prin. Fax 263-5406
Lexington Christian Academy JHS 300/7-8
450 W Reynolds Rd 40503 859-422-5702
John Eckelbarger, prin. Fax 422-5792
Lexington Christian Academy-Rose Campus 600/PK-3
450 W Reynolds Rd 40503 859-422-5703
Sally Myers, prin. Fax 271-0794
Lexington Junior Academy 50/K-8
968 Lane Allen Rd 40504 859-278-0295
Kieth Boyson, prin. Fax 277-0093
Lexington S 500/PK-8
1050 Lane Allen Rd 40504 859-278-0501
Charles Baldecchi, hdmstr. Fax 278-8604
Lutheran S of Lexington PK-8
425 Patchen Dr 40517 859-268-7787
Kimberly Hurley, dir.
Mary Queen of Holy Rosary S 500/PK-8
605 Hill N Dale Rd 40503 859-277-3030
Rebecca Brown, prin. Fax 278-1784
Providence Montessori S 200/PK-6
1209 Texaco Rd 40508 859-255-7330
Kathy Regan, dir. Fax 253-0886
St. Michael's Day S 100/PK-K
2025 Bellefonte Dr 40503 859-277-7541
Barbara Rial, dir. Fax 275-2118
Sayre S 600/PK-12
194 N Limestone 40507 859-254-1361
Clayton Chambliss, hdmstr. Fax 231-0508
Seton Catholic S 500/PK-8
1740 Summerhill Dr 40515 859-273-7827
Lee Coomer, prin. Fax 273-0115
SS. Peter & Paul S 400/PK-8
133 Barr St 40507 859-254-9257
Julie Wright, prin. Fax 254-9050
Summit Christian Academy 100/PK-8
2780 Clays Mill Rd 40503 859-277-0503
Marjorie Johnson, prin. Fax 276-1450

Liberty, Casey, Pop. 1,892
Casey County SD 2,000/PK-12
1922 N US 127 42539 606-787-6941
Linda Hatter, supt. Fax 787-5231
www.casey.k12.ky.us
Casey County MS 400/7-8
1673 E KY 70 42539 606-787-6769
Terry Price, prin. Fax 787-5337
Jones Park ES 500/PK-6
6295 E KY 70 42539 606-787-1217
Joyce Goodlett, prin. Fax 787-0558
Liberty ES 300/K-6
75 College St 42539 606-787-6961
Boyd Harris, prin. Fax 787-2136
Walnut Hill ES, 2834 S US 127 42539 PK-6
Tim Goodlett, prin. 606-787-0045

Lily, Laurel

Cornerstone Christian S 200/PK-8
PO Box 180 40740 606-526-8893
Matthew Webb, prin. Fax 526-8801

Littcarr, Knott
Knott County SD
Supt. — See Hindman
Carr Creek S 400/K-8
8596 Highway 160 S 41834 606-642-3833
Dana Slone, prin. Fax 642-3786

Livermore, McLean, Pop. 1,469
McLean County SD
Supt. — See Calhoun
Livermore ES 300/K-5
PO Box 9 42352 270-278-2522
Carrie Ellis, prin. Fax 278-2363

London, Laurel, Pop. 7,787
Laurel County SD 9,100/K-12
718 N Main St 40741 606-862-4600
David Young, supt. Fax 862-4601
www.laurel.k12.ky.us
Bush ES 400/K-5
1832 E Laurel Rd 40741 606-862-4618
Mary Robbins, prin. Fax 862-4619
Camp Ground ES 300/K-5
6800 Barbourville Rd 40744 606-862-4625
Teressa Gibbs, prin. Fax 862-4626
Cold Hill ES 500/K-5
4012 W Laurel Rd 40741 606-862-4632
Vicki Jones, prin. Fax 862-4633
Colony ES 400/K-5
3656 Somerset Rd 40741 606-862-4639
Sue Botner, prin. Fax 862-4640
Johnson ES 300/K-5
1781 McWhorter Rd 40741 606-862-4664
Tyler McWhorter, prin. Fax 862-4665
London ES 700/K-5
600 N Main St 40741 606-862-4679
Mary Bowling, prin. Fax 862-4681
North Laurel MS 1,000/6-8
101 Johnson Rd 40741 606-862-4715
David Hensley, prin. Fax 862-4717
South Laurel MS 1,100/6-8
223 S Laurel Rd 40744 606-862-4745
Jeff Reed, prin. Fax 862-4746
Sublimity ES 400/K-5
900 Sublimity School Rd 40744 606-862-4692
Betty Hodges, prin. Fax 862-4693
Wyan-Pine Grove ES K-5
2330 Keavy Rd 40744 606-862-5400
Jeff Durham, prin. Fax 862-5401
Other Schools – See Corbin, East Bernstadt, Keavy

Loretto, Marion, Pop. 650
Marion County SD
Supt. — See Lebanon
West Marion ES 500/PK-5
8175 Loretto Rd 40037 270-699-4320
Benji Mattingly, prin. Fax 699-4323

Lost Creek, Breathitt
Breathitt County SD
Supt. — See Jackson
Roberts-Caney ES 300/PK-6
115 Red Skin Run 41348 606-666-7775
Darwin Noble, prin. Fax 666-8307

Riverside Christian S 100/K-12
114 Riverside School Rd 41348 606-666-2359
Beverly Burroughs, prin. Fax 666-5211

Louisa, Lawrence, Pop. 2,051
Lawrence County SD 2,400/PK-12
50 Bulldog Ln 41230 606-638-9671
Jeffery May, supt. Fax 638-0128
www.lawrence.kyschools.us
Fallsburg S 300/PK-8
6869 N Highway 3 41230 606-686-2351
James Lester, prin. Fax 686-2355
Lawrence County Early Learning Center 50/PK-PK
325 W Powhatan St 41230 606-638-4574
Toni Armstrong, dir. Fax 638-9095
Louisa East ES 400/2-5
235 E Powhattan St 41230 606-638-4574
Debra Hixson, prin. Fax 638-9095
Louisa MS 400/6-8
9 Bulldog Ln 41230 606-638-4090
Thomas Castle, prin. Fax 638-4865
Louisa West ES 200/K-1
201 S Boone St 41230 606-638-4726
Joann Hurley, prin. Fax 638-4725
Other Schools – See Blaine

Trinity Christian Academy 100/PK-9
409 W Pike St 41230 606-638-0135
Denise Dillow, prin. Fax 638-0179

Louisville, Jefferson, Pop. 248,762
Bullitt County SD
Supt. — See Shepherdsville
Maryville ES 400/PK-5
4504 Summers Dr 40229 502-955-6553
Sam Cowan, prin. Fax 955-5753
Overdale ES 500/PK-5
651 Overdale Dr 40229 502-869-2800
Pam Robertson, prin. Fax 957-2419

Jefferson County SD 88,600/PK-12
PO Box 34020 40232 502-485-3011
Dr. Sheldon Berman, supt. Fax 485-3991
www.jefferson.k12.ky.us
Atkinson ES 500/PK-5
2800 Alford Ave 40212 502-485-8203
Dewey Hensley, prin. Fax 485-8743
Auburndale ES 400/PK-5
5749 New Cut Rd 40214 502-485-8204
KaTonya Parker, prin. Fax 485-8461
Audubon Traditional ES 600/K-5
1051 Hess Ln 40217 502-485-8205
Angela Coles, prin. Fax 485-8798
Barret MS 600/6-8
2561 Grinstead Dr 40206 502-485-8207
Tom Wortham, prin. Fax 485-8579
Bates ES 600/PK-5
7601 Bardstown Rd 40291 502-485-8208
Julia Gantt, prin. Fax 485-8960
Blake ES 400/PK-5
3801 Bonaventure Blvd 40219 502-485-8210
Timothy Brown, prin. Fax 485-8469
Bloom ES 500/K-5
1627 Lucia Ave 40204 502-485-8211
Janice Bobo, prin. Fax 485-8809
Blue Lick ES 500/PK-5
9801 Blue Lick Rd 40229 502-485-8212
Melody Raymond, prin. Fax 485-8131
Brandeis ES 500/PK-5
2817 W Kentucky St 40211 502-485-8214
Shervita West-Jordan, prin. Fax 778-7354
Breckinridge-Franklin ES 300/K-5
1351 Payne St 40206 502-485-8215
Alicia Averette, prin. Fax 485-8628
Brown S 700/K-12
546 S 1st St 40202 502-485-8216
Timothy Healy, prin. Fax 485-8741
Byck ES 400/PK-5
2328 Cedar St 40212 502-485-8221
Tamara Darden, prin. Fax 485-8805
Camp Taylor ES 400/PK-5
1446 Belmar Dr 40213 502-485-8222
LaRae Whitely, prin. Fax 485-8812
Cane Run ES 400/PK-5
3951 Cane Run Rd 40211 502-485-8223
Gwen Goffner, prin. Fax 485-8659
Carrithers MS 600/6-8
4320 Billtown Rd 40299 502-485-8224
Pat Gausepohl, prin. Fax 485-8394
Carter Traditional ES 600/K-5
3600 Bohne Ave 40211 502-485-8225
Connie Hayes, prin. Fax 485-6584
Chancey ES 700/K-5
4301 Murphy Ln 40241 502-485-8387
Ronda Cosby, prin. Fax 485-8412
Chenoweth ES 500/PK-5
3622 Brownsboro Rd 40207 502-485-8227
Penny Deatrick, prin. Fax 485-8458
Cochrane ES 300/PK-5
2511 Tregaron Ave 40299 502-485-8231
Jacqueline Hinds, prin. Fax 485-8392
Cochran ES 300/PK-5
500 W Gaulbert Ave 40208 502-485-8230
Lorraine Cunningham, prin. Fax 485-8498
Coleridge-Taylor Montessori ES 600/PK-5
1115 W Chestnut St 40203 502-485-8232
Yvette Stockwell, prin. Fax 485-8629
Conway MS 900/6-8
6300 Terry Rd 40258 502-485-8233
Debra Mercer, prin. Fax 485-8076
Crums Lane ES 300/PK-5
3212 Crums Ln 40216 502-485-8236
Julie Buckner, prin. Fax 485-8536
Dixie ES 400/PK-5
10201 Casalanda Dr 40272 502-485-8238
Lori Holland, prin. Fax 485-8448
Dunn ES 600/K-5
2010 Rudy Ln 40207 502-485-8240
Margaret Eckerle, prin. Fax 485-8829
Eisenhower ES 500/PK-5
5300 Jessamine Ln 40258 502-485-8244
Julie Cummings, prin. Fax 485-8552
Engelhard ES 400/PK-5
1004 S 1st St 40203 502-485-8246
Teresa Meyer, prin. Fax 485-8793
Farmer ES PK-5
6405 Gellhaus Ln 40299 502-485-8625
Shannon Conlon, prin. Fax 485-8970
Farnsley MS 1,000/6-8
3400 Lees Ln 40216 502-485-8242
Rob Stephenson, prin. Fax 485-8663
Field ES 400/PK-5
120 Sacred Heart Ln 40206 502-485-8252
Susan French, prin. Fax 485-8576
Foster Academy 600/K-5
1401 S 41st St 40211 502-485-8253
Susan Quinlan, prin. Fax 485-8665
Frayser ES 300/PK-5
1230 Larchmont Ave 40215 502-485-8255
Teresa Durham, prin. Fax 485-8530
Gilmore Lane ES 300/PK-5
1281 Gilmore Ln 40213 502-485-8257
Cindy Butterfield, prin. Fax 485-8989
Goldsmith Lane ES 600/PK-5
3520 Goldsmith Ln 40220 502-485-8258
Cynthia Jones, prin. Fax 485-8977
Greathouse/Shryock Traditional ES 600/K-5
2700 Browns Ln 40220 502-485-8259
Karla Davis, prin. Fax 485-8768
Greenwood ES 500/PK-5
5801 Greenwood Rd 40258 502-485-8260
June Wade, prin. Fax 485-8046
Guthermuth ES 500/PK-5
1500 Sanders Ln 40216 502-485-8261
Donna Wiseman, prin. Fax 485-8379
Hartstern ES 500/PK-5
5200 Morningside Way 40219 502-485-8262
Patricia Cox, prin. Fax 485-8470
Hawthorne ES 300/PK-5
2301 Clarendon Ave 40205 502-485-8263
Emil Salman, prin. Fax 485-8358
Hazelwood ES 300/PK-5
1325 Bluegrass Ave 40215 502-485-8264
Tom Peterson, prin. Fax 485-8965
Highland MS 1,000/6-8
1700 Norris Pl 40205 502-485-8266
Steven Heckman, prin. Fax 485-8831
Indian Trail ES 500/PK-5
3709 E Indian Trl 40213 502-485-8268
Georgia Hampton, prin. Fax 485-8477
Jacob ES 500/PK-5
3701 E Wheatmore Dr 40215 502-485-8271
Cheryl Williams, prin. Fax 485-7157
Jefferson County Traditional MS 900/6-8
1418 Morton Ave 40204 502-485-8272
Mark Rose, prin. Fax 485-8635
Jefferson MS 1,000/6-8
1501 Rangeland Rd 40219 502-485-8273
Kimberly Gregory, prin. Fax 485-8045
Jeffersontown ES 800/PK-5
3610 Cedarwood Way 40299 502-485-8274
Larry Foley, prin. Fax 485-8408
Johnsontown Road ES 400/PK-5
7201 Johnsontown Rd 40272 502-485-8278
Malinda Dutkowski, prin. Fax 485-8156
Johnson Traditional MS 900/6-8
2509 Wilson Ave 40210 502-485-8277
Beverly Johnson, prin. Fax 485-8679
Kammerer MS 800/6-8
7315 Wesboro Rd 40222 502-485-8279
David Armour, prin. Fax 485-8618

Kennedy Metro MS 100/5-8
4515 Taylorsville Rd 40220 502-485-6950
Donald Reid, prin. Fax 491-7290
Kennedy Montessori ES 500/PK-5
3800 Gibson Ln 40211 502-485-8280
Opal Dawson, prin. Fax 485-8709
Kenwood ES 500/PK-5
7420 Justan Ave 40214 502-485-8283
Jill Handley, prin. Fax 485-8535
Kerrick ES 400/PK-5
2210 Upper Hunters Trce 40216 502-485-8284
Maria Clemons, prin. Fax 448-0598
King ES 400/PK-5
4325 Vermont Ave 40211 502-485-8285
Julia Lewis, prin. Fax 485-8668
Klondike Lane ES 600/PK-5
3807 Klondike Ln 40218 502-485-8286
Christine Deely, prin. Fax 485-8146
Knight MS 500/6-8
9803 Blue Lick Rd 40229 502-485-8287
Kenneth Black, prin. Fax 485-8073
Lassiter MS 600/6-8
8200 Candleworth Dr 40214 502-485-8288
Dwayne Roberts, prin. Fax 485-8373
Laukhuf ES 500/PK-5
5100 Capewood Dr 40229 502-485-8289
Fax 485-8478
Lincoln ES 300/PK-5
930 E Main St 40206 502-485-8291
Sonya Unseld, prin. Fax 485-8142
Lowe ES 600/K-5
210 Oxfordshire Ln 40222 502-485-8293
Kris Raitzer, prin. Fax 485-8594
Luhr ES 500/PK-5
6900 Fegenbush Ln 40228 502-485-8295
Lynley Schroering, prin. Fax 485-8426
Maupin ES 500/PK-5
1312 Catalpa St 40211 502-485-8310
Deborah Jones, prin. Fax 485-8752
McFerran Preparatory Academy 600/PK-5
1900 S 7th St 40208 502-485-8297
Carol Miller, prin. Fax 485-8362
Meyzeek MS 1,000/6-8
828 S Jackson St 40203 502-485-8299
Chris Burba, prin. Fax 485-8641
Mill Creek ES 400/PK-5
3816 Dixie Hwy 40216 502-485-8301
Michelle Pennix, prin. Fax 485-8524
Minors Lane ES 300/PK-5
8510 Minor Ln 40219 502-485-8303
Paige Orman, prin. Fax 485-8480
Myers MS 800/6-8
3741 Pulliam Dr 40218 502-485-8305
William Bennett, prin. Fax 485-8157
Newburg MS 1,000/6-8
4901 Exeter Ave 40218 502-485-8306
Dianna Drake-Hicks, prin. Fax 485-8883
Noe MS 1,200/6-8
121 W Lee St 40208 502-485-8307
Janice McDowell, prin. Fax 485-8056
Okolona ES 400/PK-5
7606 Preston Hwy 40219 502-485-8309
Tracy Barber, prin. Fax 485-8482
Olmsted Academy North 700/6-8
4530 Bellevue Ave 40215 502-485-8331
Bill Perkins, prin. Fax 485-8381
Olmsted Academy South 600/6-8
5650 Southern Pkwy 40214 502-485-8270
Betty Graham, prin. Fax 485-8380
Orman ECC PK-PK
900 S Floyd St 40203 502-485-7008
Mark Sauer, prin. Fax 485-6910
Portland ES 300/PK-5
3410 Northwestern Pkwy 40212 502-485-8313
Angela Simmons, prin. Fax 485-8631
Price ES 500/PK-5
5001 Garden Green Way 40218 502-485-8315
Floria Clay, prin. Fax 485-8485
Ramsey MS 6-8
6409 Gellhaus Ln 40299 502-485-8391
Jennifer Colley, prin. Fax 485-8973
Rangeland ES 300/PK-5
1701 Rangeland Rd 40219 502-485-8317
Mashelle Kiggins, prin. Fax 485-8874
Roosevelt/Perry ES 300/PK-5
1606 Magazine St 40203 502-485-8319
Pamela Howell, prin. Fax 585-5239
Rutherford ES 500/PK-5
301 Southland Blvd 40214 502-485-8320
Fax 485-8378
St. Matthew's ES 500/K-5
601 Browns Ln 40207 502-485-8321
Joe Leffert, prin. Fax 485-8582
Sanders ES 500/PK-5
8408 Terry Rd 40258 502-485-8322
Pam Cooper, prin. Fax 485-8555
Schaffner Traditional ES 600/PK-5
2701 Crums Ln 40216 502-485-8217
Phillip Poore, prin. Fax 485-8218
Semple ES 500/PK-5
724 Denmark St 40215 502-485-8324
Tiffeny Gerstner, prin. Fax 485-8144
Shacklette ES 500/PK-5
5310 Mercury Dr 40258 502-485-8325
Mary Keith, prin. Fax 485-8526
Shelby ES 400/K-5
735 Ziegler St 40217 502-485-8327
Patti Cosby, prin. Fax 485-8507
Slaughter ES 300/PK-5
3805 Fern Valley Rd 40219 502-485-8328
Kathy Pendleton, prin. Fax 485-8486
Smyrna ES 600/PK-5
6401 Outer Loop 40228 502-485-8329
Linda Compton, prin. Fax 485-8484
Stopher ES PK-5
14417 Aiken Rd 40245 502-485-8281
Dr. Brigitte Owens, prin. Fax 485-8971
Trunnell ES 600/PK-5
7609 Saint Andrews Church 40214 502-485-8337
Pamela Madeya, prin. Fax 485-8627

Watson Lane ES 500/PK-5
7201 Watson Ln 40272 502-485-8341
Rosemarie Young, prin. Fax 485-8455
Watterson ES 600/PK-5
3900 Breckenridge Ln 40218 502-485-8342
Vickie Talbott, prin. Fax 485-8999
Wellington ES 400/PK-5
4800 Kaufman Ln 40216 502-485-8343
Michael Alexander, prin. Fax 485-8525
Western MS 500/6-8
2201 W Main St 40212 502-485-8345
Beth Johnson, prin. Fax 485-8047
Westport MS and Fine Arts Academy 800/6-8
8100 Westport Rd 40222 502-485-8346
Devon Woodlee, prin. Fax 485-8590
Wheatley ES 400/PK-5
1107 S 17th St 40210 502-485-8348
Robert Wagner, prin. Fax 485-8998
Wheeler ES 700/PK-5
5700 Cynthia Dr 40291 502-485-8349
Julie Barrett, prin. Fax 485-8607
Wilder ES 500/K-5
1913 Herr Ln 40222 502-485-8350
David Bodine, prin. Fax 485-8591
Wilkerson ES 500/PK-5
5601 Johnsontown Rd 40272 502-485-8351
David Cummings, prin. Fax 485-8454
Wilt ES 500/PK-5
6700 Price Lane Rd 40229 502-485-8353
Kimberly Kent, prin. Fax 485-8493
Young ES 400/PK-5
3526 W Muhammad Ali Blvd 40212 502-485-8354
Mary Minyard, prin. Fax 485-8880
Other Schools – See Fairdale, Fern Creek, Jeffersontown, Lyndon, Middletown, Valley Station

---

Ascension S 300/K-8
4600 Lynnbrook Dr 40220 502-451-2535
Mary Jo Ellis, prin. Fax 451-2535
Beth Haven Christian S 400/PK-12
5515 Johnsontown Rd 40272 502-937-3516
Kevin Sample, admin. Fax 937-3364
Chance S 200/PK-5
4200 Lime Kiln Ln 40222 502-425-6904
Gail Lotze, dir. Fax 326-5462
Christian Academy of Louisville 500/PK-5
3110 Rock Creek Dr 40207 502-897-3372
Marilyn James, prin. Fax 897-3207
Christian Academy of Louisville 3,200/PK-12
700 S English Station Rd 40245 502-244-3225
Timothy Greener, supt. Fax 244-1824
Christian Academy of Louisville 200/PK-10
8307 St Andrews Church Rd 40258 502-447-6500
Kevin Schooling, prin. Fax 447-6508
Covenant Classical Academy 50/K-12
13902 Factory Ln 40245 502-243-0404
R. Lance Harris, hdmstr. Fax 243-0404
DePaul S 200/1-8
1925 Duker Ave 40205 502-459-6131
Anthony Kemper, hdmstr. Fax 458-0827
Eastside Christian Academy 100/K-8
3402 Goose Creek Rd 40241 502-339-0041
Tim Caldwell, prin. Fax 339-0041
Evangel Christian S 300/K-12
5400 Minor Ln 40219 502-968-7744
Dr. Roger Hoagland, supt. Fax 968-8414
Holy Family S 300/PK-8
3934 Poplar Level Rd 40213 502-458-4531
Gayle Bauch, prin. Fax 456-9198
Holy Spirit S 400/K-8
322 Cannons Ln 40206 502-893-7700
Doris Swenson, prin. Fax 893-8078
Holy Trinity S 700/K-8
423 Cherrywood Rd 40207 502-897-2785
Jack Richards, prin. Fax 896-0990
John Paul II Academy 300/PK-8
3525 Goldsmith Ln 40220 502-452-1712
Lynn Wilt, prin. Fax 451-2462
Kentucky Country Day S 900/PK-12
4100 Springdale Rd 40241 502-423-0440
Brad Lyman, hdmstr. Fax 423-0445
Louisville Collegiate S 600/K-12
2427 Glenmary Ave 40204 502-479-0340
Junius Prince, hdmstr. Fax 454-8549
Louisville Jr. Academy 100/K-10
2988 Newburg Rd 40205 502-452-2965
Sheila Barnett, prin. Fax 452-2965
Meredith-Dunn S 200/K-8
3023 Melbourne Ave 40220 502-456-5819
Kathy Beam, prin. Fax 456-5953
Minnis SDA S 50/PK-8
1337 Dixie Hwy 40210 502-774-2108
Montessori S of Louisville 100/PK-8
PO Box 6271 40206 502-640-8585
Cynthia Gonzalez, prin. Fax 413-5699
Nativity Academy at St. Boniface 50/6-8
531 E Liberty St 40202 502-562-2190
Sheila Carson, prin. Fax 562-2192
Notre Dame Academy 400/PK-8
1927 Lewiston Dr 40216 502-447-3155
Bernice Scherr, prin. Fax 448-2163
On Fire Christian Academy 100/PK-12
5627 New Cut Rd 40214 502-368-0080
Kristine Salvo, admin. Fax 361-5179
Our Lady of Lourdes S 400/K-8
510 Breckenridge Ln 40207 502-895-5122
Laura Glaser, prin. Fax 893-5051
Our Savior Lutheran S 200/PK-8
8307 Nottingham Pkwy 40222 502-426-0864
Martin Brieschke, prin. Fax 394-0648
Pitt Academy 50/PK-12
6010 Preston Hwy 40219 502-966-6979
Sherry Downey, prin. Fax 962-8878
Portland Christian S 100/K-12
2500 Portland Ave 40212 502-778-6114
Mary Jodell Seay, dir. Fax 772-7027
Portland Christian S East 100/K-7
12610 Taylorsville Rd 40299 502-266-9892
Mary Jodell Seay, dir. Fax 263-5489

Sacred Heart Model S 400/K-8
3107 Lexington Rd 40206 502-896-3931
Dr. Mary Beth Bowling, prin. Fax 896-3932
St. Agnes S 400/K-8
1800 Newburg Rd 40205 502-458-2850
Carol Meirose, prin. Fax 459-5215
St. Albert the Great S 700/K-8
1395 Girard Dr 40222 502-425-1804
Jeanne Flowers, prin. Fax 394-9896
St. Andrew Academy 400/PK-8
7724 Columbine Dr 40258 502-935-4578
Suzanne Miller, prin. Fax 935-2021
St. Athanasius S 500/PK-8
5915 Outer Loop 40219 502-969-2345
Diane Arrow, prin. Fax 966-8974
St. Bernard S 500/PK-8
7501 Tangelo Dr 40228 502-239-5178
Fred Klausing, prin. Fax 239-9025
St. Edward S 500/PK-8
9610 Sue Helen Dr 40299 502-267-6633
Susan Jones, prin. Fax 267-4474
St. Francis Assisi S 200/K-8
1938 Alfresco Pl 40205 502-459-3088
Paula Watkins, prin. Fax 456-9462
St. James S 200/PK-8
1818 Edenside Ave 40204 502-454-0330
Tom Schmitt, prin. Fax 454-0330
St. Leonard S 200/PK-8
440 Zorn Ave 40206 502-897-5265
Linda Kinderman, prin. Fax 896-8259
St. Margaret Mary S 700/K-8
7813 Shelbyville Rd 40222 502-426-2635
John Westerfield, prin. Fax 426-1304
St. Martha S 600/PK-8
2825 Klondike Ln 40218 502-491-3171
Sharon Dutton, prin. Fax 495-6107
St. Michael S 600/PK-8
3705 Stone Lakes Dr 40299 502-267-6155
Sheila Marstiller, prin. Fax 267-4272
St. Nicholas Academy North 200/PK-8
4333 Hazelwood Ave 40215 502-366-2424
Carol Nord, prin. Fax 366-0208
St. Nicholas Academy South 600/K-8
5501 New Cut Rd 40214 502-368-8506
Kitty Schloemer, prin. Fax 368-9972
St. Patrick S 700/K-8
1000 N Beckley Station Rd 40245 502-244-7083
Elaine Wnorowski, prin. Fax 244-7083
St. Raphael the Archangel S 500/PK-8
2131 Lancashire Ave 40205 502-456-1541
Paul DeZarn, prin. Fax 451-3632
St. Rita S 300/PK-8
8709 Preston Hwy 40219 502-969-7067
Dr. Mary Lee Lanning, prin. Fax 969-3679
St. Stephen Martyr S 400/PK-8
2931 Pindell Ave 40217 502-635-7141
Margaret Bowen, prin. Fax 635-1576
Summit Academy 100/K-8
11508 Main St 40243 502-244-7090
Margaret Thornton, dir. Fax 244-3371
Torah Academy 50/PK-7
3700 Dutchmans Ln 40205 502-451-3122
Golda Litvin, prin. Fax 451-3123
Ursuline Montessori S 100/PK-K
3105 Lexington Rd 40206 502-896-3941
Vicki Furlow, dir. Fax 896-3966
Ursuline S for Performing Arts 200/K-12
3105 Lexington Rd 40206 502-897-1816
Lynn Slaughter, dir. Fax 896-3927
Valor Traditional Academy 100/K-12
11501 Schlatter Rd 40291 502-239-3345
JP Fugate, hdmstr. Fax 239-3344
Walden S 300/K-12
4238 Westport Rd 40207 502-893-0433
Linda VanHouten, prin. Fax 895-8668
Waldorf S of Louisville 100/PK-5
8005 New La Grange Rd 40222 502-327-0122
Fax 327-7772
Whitefield Academy 700/K-12
7711 Fegenbush Ln 40228 502-239-2509
Bill McKinley, hdmstr. Fax 239-3144

Lowes, Graves
Graves County SD
Supt. — See Mayfield
Lowes ES 300/PK-6
6775 State Route 440 42061 270-674-4840
Cheryl Goodman, prin. Fax 674-5189

Lucas, Barren
Barren County SD
Supt. — See Glasgow
Tracy ES 300/PK-6
2477 Austin Tracy Rd 42156 270-646-2236
Scott Harper, prin. Fax 646-2292

Ludlow, Kenton, Pop. 4,647
Ludlow ISD 700/PK-12
525 Elm St 41016 859-261-8210
Curtis Hall, supt. Fax 291-6811
www.ludlow.k12.ky.us
Goetz ES 400/PK-6
512 Oak St 41016 859-261-2100
Josh Jackson, prin. Fax 291-6811

Lyndon, Jefferson, Pop. 10,248
Jefferson County SD
Supt. — See Louisville
Bowen ES 800/K-5
1601 Roosevelt Ave 40242 502-485-8213
Steve Tyra, prin. Fax 485-8578
Norton ES 700/K-5
8101 Brownsboro Rd 40241 502-485-8308
Ken Stites, prin. Fax 485-8600
Taylor ES 500/K-5
9620 Westport Rd 40241 502-485-8336
William Patterson, prin. Fax 485-8584

Mc Daniels, Breckinridge
Breckinridge County SD
Supt. — See Hardinsburg

Johnson ES 200/K-5
PO Box 51 40152 270-756-3070
Becky Hook, prin. Fax 756-3071

Mc Dowell, Floyd
Floyd County SD
Supt. — See Prestonsburg
Mc Dowell ES 300/K-5
PO Box 282 41647 606-377-6640
Jerri Turner, prin. Fax 377-6363

Mc Kee, Jackson, Pop. 969
Jackson County SD 2,300/PK-12
PO Box 217 40447 606-287-7181
Ralph Hoskins, supt. Fax 287-8469
www.jackson.k12.ky.us
Jackson County MS 500/6-8
PO Box 1329 40447 606-287-8351
Keith Bingham, prin. Fax 287-8360
Mc Kee ES 400/PK-5
PO Box 429 40447 606-287-7157
David Lunsford, prin. Fax 287-4775
Other Schools – See Sandgap, Tyner

Mc Kinney, Lincoln
Lincoln County SD
Supt. — See Stanford
Mc Kinney ES 200/PK-5
PO Box 67 40448 606-346-4741
Don Leigh, prin. Fax 346-9905

Madisonville, Hopkins, Pop. 19,273
Hopkins County SD 7,000/PK-12
320 S Seminary St 42431 270-825-6000
James Stevens, supt. Fax 825-6072
www.hopkins.k12.ky.us
Browning Springs MS 500/6-8
357 W Arch St 42431 270-825-6006
Rick Larson, prin. Fax 825-6009
Grapevine ES 300/K-5
1150 Hayes Ave 42431 270-825-6012
Joan Radford, prin. Fax 825-6026
Madison MS 500/6-8
510 Brown Rd 42431 270-825-6160
Steve Gilliam, prin. Fax 825-6016
Pride Avenue ES 400/K-5
861 Pride Ave 42431 270-825-6030
Cristy Tomes, prin. Fax 825-6031
Stuart ES 400/K-5
1710 Anton Rd 42431 270-825-6033
Phyllis Sugg, prin. Fax 825-6120
West Broadway ES 400/PK-5
127 W Broadway St 42431 270-825-6036
Fax 825-6025
Other Schools – See Earlington, Hanson, Nebo, Nortonville

Christ the King S 100/K-8
1600 Kingsway Dr 42431 270-821-8271
Larry Bishop, prin. Fax 825-9394

Majestic, Pike
Pike County SD
Supt. — See Pikeville
Majestic Knox Creek ES 200/K-6
PO Box 199 41547 606-456-3982
Mary Beth Stiltner, prin. Fax 456-4041

Manchester, Clay, Pop. 1,968
Clay County SD 3,400/PK-12
128 Richmond Rd 40962 606-598-2168
Douglas Adams, supt. Fax 598-7829
www.clay.k12.ky.us
Burning Springs ES 300/PK-6
9847 N Highway 421 40962 606-598-3138
Geraldine Phillips, prin. Fax 598-0079
Clay County MS 600/7-8
239 Richmond Rd 40962 606-598-1810
Wayne Napier, prin. Fax 598-1230
Goose Rock ES 200/PK-6
364 Highway 1524 40962 606-598-3740
William Sexton, prin. Fax 598-3758
Hacker ES 200/K-6
84 Hooker Rd 40962 606-598-3338
Todd McDaniel, prin. Fax 598-7119
Manchester ES 400/PK-6
1908 N Highway 421 40962 606-598-3444
Jimmy Samples, prin. Fax 598-8786
Paces Creek ES 200/PK-6
1983 S Highway 421 40962 606-598-6333
David Murray, prin. Fax 598-0359
Other Schools – See Oneida

Appalachian Christian Academy 50/1-8
168 SDA School Rd 40962 606-598-5427
Debbie Brock, prin.

Marion, Crittenden, Pop. 3,033
Crittenden County SD 1,300/K-12
601 W Elm St 42064 270-965-3525
Dr. Rachel Yarbrough, supt. Fax 965-9064
www.crittenden.k12.ky.us
Crittenden County ES 600/K-5
120 Autumn Ln 42064 270-965-2244
Melissa Tabor, prin. Fax 965-4113
Crittenden County MS 300/6-8
519 W Gum St 42064 270-965-5221
Teresa Marshall, prin. Fax 965-5082

Martin, Floyd, Pop. 636
Floyd County SD
Supt. — See Prestonsburg
May Valley ES 400/K-5
481 Stephens Branch Rd 41649 606-285-0883
Tonya Horne-Williams, prin. Fax 285-0884

Mayfield, Graves, Pop. 10,288
Graves County SD 4,700/PK-12
2290 State Route 121 N 42066 270-328-2656
Brady Link, supt. Fax 328-1561
www.graves.k12.ky.us
Cuba ES 200/PK-6
92 Cuba School Rd 42066 270-674-4810
Jill McClain, prin. Fax 382-2494
Farmington ES 300/PK-6
7730 State Route 121 S 42066 270-674-4830
Denise Whitaker, prin. Fax 345-2163
Graves Central ES 400/PK-6
2262 State Route 121 N 42066 270-328-4900
Stephanie Sullivan, prin. Fax 247-4626
Graves County MS 700/7-8
625 Jimtown Rd 42066 270-674-4890
Rim Watson, prin. Fax 251-3693
Sedalia ES 300/PK-6
5252 State Route 97 42066 270-674-4850
Robert Braden, prin. Fax 328-8266
Other Schools – See Fancy Farm, Lowes, Symsonia, Wingo

Mayfield ISD 1,500/PK-12
914 E College St 42066 270-247-3868
Lonnie Burgett, supt. Fax 247-3854
www.mayfield.kyschools.us/
Mayfield City Head Start/KERA Preschool PK-K
1004 Backusburg Rd 42066 270-247-8841
Kathy Jackson, prin. Fax 247-4590
Mayfield ES 700/K-5
1004 Backusburg Rd 42066 270-247-8696
Jeff Hill, prin. Fax 247-0017
Mayfield MS 300/6-8
112 W College St 42066 270-247-7521
Ricky Hayes, prin. Fax 247-8297

Northside Baptist Christian S 100/PK-12
711 N 12th St 42066 270-247-0516
Jeannette Lewis, prin. Fax 247-7125
St. Joseph S 100/PK-6
112 S 14th St 42066 270-247-4420
Susan Brinkley, prin. Fax 247-2612

Maysville, Mason, Pop. 9,136
Mason County SD 2,500/PK-12
PO Box 130 41056 606-564-5563
Tim Moore, supt. Fax 564-5392
www.masoncoschools.com
Mason County IS 500/3-5
720 Clarks Run Rd 41056 606-759-2000
Matt Stanfield, prin. Fax 759-2001
Mason County MS 600/6-8
420 Chenault Dr 41056 606-564-6748
Betsy Cook, prin. Fax 564-5958
Straub ES 500/PK-2
387 Chenault Dr 41056 606-564-9047
Robert Moore, prin. Fax 564-3345

Highland Christian S 50/PK-10
PO Box 117 41056 606-563-0444
Fonda Childers, admin. Fax 563-0460
St. Patrick S 300/PK-12
318 Limestone St 41056 606-564-5949
Jennifer Griffith, prin. Fax 564-8795

Melbourne, Campbell, Pop. 453

St. Philip S 100/K-8
1400 Mary Ingles Hwy 41059 859-441-3423
Sr. Dolores Gohs, prin. Fax 441-2611

Middlesboro, Bell, Pop. 10,858
Bell County SD
Supt. — See Pineville
Yellow Creek Center 400/PK-8
RR 1 Box 370 40965 606-248-1794
Jerry Lawson, prin. Fax 248-6399

Middlesboro ISD 1,600/K-12
PO Box 959 40965 606-242-8800
Darryl Wilder, supt. Fax 242-8805
www.mboro.k12.ky.us
Middlesboro IS 200/4-5
502 Ashbury Ave 40965 606-242-8840
Steve Martin, prin. Fax 242-8845
Middlesboro MS 400/6-8
4400 Cumberland Ave 40965 606-242-8880
Steve Spangler, prin. Fax 242-8885
Middlesboro PS 500/K-3
3400 Cumberland Ave 40965 606-242-8860
Janis Barton, prin. Fax 242-8865

St. Julian S 100/PK-6
116 E Chester Ave 40965 606-248-8309
Thomas Kelemen, prin. Fax 248-8309

Middletown, Jefferson, Pop. 6,072
Jefferson County SD
Supt. — See Louisville
Crosby MS 1,200/6-8
303 Gatehouse Ln 40243 502-485-8235
Kirk Lattimore, prin. Fax 485-8424
Hite ES 500/PK-5
12408 Old Shelbyville Rd 40243 502-485-8267
Timothy Hagan, prin. Fax 485-7006
Middletown ES 600/PK-5
218 N Madison Ave 40243 502-485-8300
Patty Holladay, prin. Fax 485-8465

Midway, Woodford, Pop. 1,622
Woodford County SD
Supt. — See Versailles
Northside ES 400/K-5
500 Northside Dr 40347 859-846-4415
Ryan Asher, prin. Fax 846-4716

Milton, Trimble, Pop. 595
Trimble County SD
Supt. — See Bedford
Milton ES 300/K-5
9245 Highway 421 N 40045 502-268-3322
Sharon James, prin. Fax 268-5316

Monticello, Wayne, Pop. 6,062
Monticello ISD 800/PK-12
161 S Main St 42633 606-348-5311
Donnie Robison, supt. Fax 348-3664
www.monticello.k12.ky.us/
Monticello ES 400/PK-5
120 Cave St 42633 606-348-1814
Johnny Chaplin, prin. Fax 348-1974
Monticello MS 200/6-8
160 Cave St 42633 606-348-5312
Johnny Chaplin, prin. Fax 348-3039

Wayne County SD 2,200/PK-12
1025 S Main St 42633 606-348-8484
John Dalton, supt. Fax 348-0734
www.wayne.kyschools.us/
Bell ES 500/2-4
278 Kenny Davis Blvd 42633 606-348-8150
Donna Rice, prin. Fax 348-7871
Turner IS 400/5-6
250 Cardinal Way 42633 606-348-6122
Don Neal, prin. Fax 348-0545
Walker ES 300/K-1
1080 S Main St 42633 606-348-4251
Derrick Harris, prin. Fax 348-0168
Wayne County ECC PK-PK
99 Lloyd St 42633 606-348-1494
Carolyn Davis, dir. Fax 348-6358
Wayne County MS 400/7-8
95 Champion Dr 42633 606-348-6691
Tracy Bale, prin. Fax 348-5495

Immanuel Christian Academy 50/PK-4
130 N Main St 42633 606-348-8220
David Smith, prin. Fax 348-7184

Morehead, Rowan, Pop. 7,592
Rowan County SD 3,100/PK-12
121 E 2nd St 40351 606-784-8928
Marvin Moore, supt. Fax 783-1011
www.rowan.k12.ky.us
Hogge ES 200/K-5
5955 Cranston Rd 40351 606-784-4604
Larry Tapp, prin. Fax 784-2456
McBrayer ES 500/K-5
550 Viking Dr 40351 606-784-1204
Rhonda Banks, prin. Fax 784-3567
Rodburn ES 500/K-5
91 Christy Crk 40351 606-784-3000
Beverly Gilliam, prin. Fax 783-7264
Rowan County MS 700/6-8
415 W Sun St 40351 606-784-8911
Tresia Swain, prin. Fax 784-5579
Rowan County Preschool PK-PK
455 W Sun St 40351 606-784-7721
Shirley Burge, dir. Fax 783-9994
Other Schools – See Clearfield

Lakeside Christian Academy 200/PK-12
2535 US Highway 60 W 40351 606-784-2751
Tammy McKinney, admin. Fax 784-0056
Rowan County Christian Academy 100/PK-8
576 Sunset Ln 40351 606-780-9566
Greta Bennett, admin. Fax 784-2326

Morganfield, Union, Pop. 3,430
Union County SD 2,300/PK-12
510 S Mart St 42437 270-389-1694
Joshua Powell, supt. Fax 389-9806
www.union.k12.ky.us/
Morganfield ES 500/PK-5
511 S Mart St 42437 270-389-2611
Heady Larson, prin. Fax 389-2994
Union County MS 500/6-8
4465 US Highway 60 W 42437 270-389-0224
Rhonda Callaway, prin. Fax 389-0245
Other Schools – See Sturgis, Uniontown

St. Ann S 200/PK-8
320 S Church St 42437 270-389-1898
Fax 389-1834

Morgantown, Butler, Pop. 2,552
Butler County SD 2,100/PK-12
PO Box 339 42261 270-526-5624
Scott Howard, supt. Fax 526-5625
www.butler.k12.ky.us/
Butler County MS 400/6-8
PO Box 10 42261 270-526-5647
Jeff Jennings, prin. Fax 526-3238
Morgantown ES 600/PK-5
PO Box 337 42261 270-526-3361
Gregory Woodcock, prin. Fax 526-2868
North Butler ES 400/PK-5
5512 Brownsville Rd 42261 270-526-8936
Elaine Daugherty, prin. Fax 526-8941

Morning View, Kenton
Kenton County SD
Supt. — See Fort Wright
Piner ES 300/PK-5
2845 Rich Rd 41063 859-356-2155
Jo Craven, prin. Fax 356-6203

Mount Olivet, Robertson, Pop. 287
Robertson County SD 400/K-12
PO Box 108 41064 606-724-5431
Charles Brown, supt. Fax 724-5921
school.robertson.k12.ky.us
Deming ES 200/K-6
PO Box 168 41064 606-724-5421
Jeremy McCloud, prin. Fax 724-5921

Mount Sterling, Montgomery, Pop. 6,317
Montgomery County SD 4,400/PK-12
700 Woodford Dr 40353 859-497-8760
Daniel Freeman, supt. Fax 497-8780
www.montgomery.kyschools.us
Camargo ES 700/PK-5
4307 Camargo Rd 40353 859-497-8776
Sharon Smith, prin. Fax 497-8755

Mapleton ES 700/PK-5
809 Indian Mound Dr 40353 859-497-8752
Melody Claypoole, prin. Fax 497-8756
McNabb MS 1,000/6-8
3570 Indian Mound Dr 40353 859-497-8770
Rick Mattox, prin. Fax 497-9683
Montgomery County Early Learning Center PK-PK
212 N Maysville St 40353 859-497-8724
Tammy McCarty, prin. Fax 497-8760
Mount Sterling ES 700/PK-5
6601 Indian Mound Rd 40353 859-497-8730
Richard DeAngelis, prin. Fax 497-8704

Mount Vernon, Rockcastle, Pop. 2,599
Rockcastle County SD 2,900/PK-12
245 Richmond St 40456 606-256-2125
Larry Hammond, supt. Fax 256-2126
www.rockcastle.kyschools.us/
Mount Vernon ES 600/PK-5
PO Box 1530 40456 606-256-2953
J. Leon Davidson, prin. Fax 256-3948
Rockcastle County MS 700/6-8
PO Box 1730 40456 606-256-5118
Jason Coguer, prin. Fax 256-2622
Roundstone ES 300/PK-5
6701 N Wilderness Rd 40456 606-256-2235
James Ward, prin. Fax 256-2259
Other Schools – See Brodhead

Mount Washington, Bullitt, Pop. 8,624
Bullitt County SD
Supt. — See Shepherdsville
Eastside MS 500/6-8
6925 Highway 44 E 40047 502-538-3767
Bonita Franklin, prin. Fax 538-0659
Mt. Washington ES 600/PK-5
9234 Highway 44 E 40047 502-538-4273
Terri Lewis, prin. Fax 538-2744
Mt. Washington MS 500/6-8
269 Water St 40047 502-538-4227
Denise Allen, prin. Fax 955-9530
Old Mill ES 600/PK-5
11540 Highway 44 E 40047 502-538-7994
Les McIntosh, prin. Fax 538-6641
Pleasant Grove ES 700/PK-5
6415 Highway 44 E 40047 502-538-3129
Joe Reister, prin. Fax 538-8732

Mousie, Knott
Knott County SD
Supt. — See Hindman
Jones Fork S 200/PK-8
PO Box 129 41839 606-946-2132
Kimberly Potter, prin. Fax 946-2629

Muldraugh, Meade, Pop. 1,346
Meade County SD
Supt. — See Brandenburg
Muldraugh ES 100/PK-6
202 Wendell St 40155 270-422-7555
T. Parker, prin. Fax 942-9411

Munfordville, Hart, Pop. 1,603
Hart County SD 2,400/PK-12
511 W Union St 42765 270-524-2631
Ricky Line, supt. Fax 524-2634
www.hart.k12.ky.us/
Munfordville S 500/PK-8
215 N West St 42765 270-524-4651
Vyetta Reynolds, prin. Fax 524-4652
Other Schools – See Bonnieville, Cub Run, Hardyville, Horse Cave

Murray, Calloway, Pop. 15,538
Calloway County SD 3,000/PK-12
PO Box 800 42071 270-762-7300
Steve Hoskins, supt. Fax 762-7310
www.calloway.k12.ky.us
Calloway County MS 800/6-8
2112 College Farm Rd 42071 270-762-7355
Tawnya Hunter, prin. Fax 762-7360
Calloway County Preschool PK-PK
2106A College Farm Rd 42071 270-762-7410
Jason Scarbrough, prin. Fax 762-7412
East ES 300/K-5
1169 Pottertown Rd 42071 270-762-7325
Kathy Crouch, prin. Fax 762-7330
North ES 600/K-5
2928 Brinn Rd 42071 270-762-7335
Margaret Cook, prin. Fax 762-7340
Southwest ES 400/K-5
3426 Wiswell Rd W 42071 270-762-7345
Dennis Fisher, prin. Fax 762-7350

Murray ISD 1,600/K-12
208 S 13th St 42071 270-753-4363
Bob Rogers, supt. Fax 759-4906
www.murray.kyschools.us
Murray ES 500/K-3
111 S Broach St 42071 270-753-5022
Janet Caldwell, prin. Fax 753-3856
Murray MS 600/4-8
801 Main St 42071 270-753-5125
Lou Carter, prin. Fax 753-9039

Nancy, Pulaski
Pulaski County SD
Supt. — See Somerset
Nancy ES 400/K-5
240 Highway 196 42544 606-636-6338
Shane Hansen, prin. Fax 636-6841

Nebo, Hopkins, Pop. 221
Hopkins County SD
Supt. — See Madisonville
West Hopkins Accelerated S 500/K-8
2695 Rabbit Ridge Rd 42441 270-825-6130
Valerie Willis, prin. Fax 249-9454

Neon, Letcher, Pop. 749
Letcher County SD
Supt. — See Whitesburg
Fleming Neon S 200/K-8
PO Box 425 41840 606-855-7864
Sharon Meade, prin. Fax 855-4485

New Castle, Henry, Pop. 929
Henry County SD 2,100/K-12
326 S Main St 40050 502-845-8600
Tim Abrams, supt. Fax 845-8601
www.henry.kyschools.us
Henry County MS 500/6-8
1124 Eminence Rd 40050 502-845-8660
Zach Woods, prin. Fax 845-8661
New Castle ES 400/K-5
182 S Property Rd 40050 502-845-8650
Barbara James, prin. Fax 845-8651
Other Schools – See Campbellsburg, Pleasureville

New Haven, Nelson, Pop. 864
Nelson County SD
Supt. — See Bardstown
New Haven S 400/K-8
489 High St 40051 502-349-7232
Cindy Phelps, prin. Fax 349-7231

St. Catherine S 100/PK-8
PO Box 88 40051 502-549-3680
Jo Renee O'Bryan, prin. Fax 549-5410

Newport, Campbell, Pop. 15,911
Newport ISD 2,000/PK-12
301 E 8th St 41071 859-292-3004
Michael Brandt, supt. Fax 292-3073
www.newportwildcats.org/
Dean ES 200/PK-5
1360 Grand Ave 41071 859-292-3009
Steve McCafferty, prin. Fax 441-0980
Fourth Street ES 300/K-5
101 E 4th St 41071 859-292-3021
Emily Daniels, prin. Fax 292-0222
Newport MS 400/6-8
30 W 8th St 41071 859-292-3017
David Upchurch, prin. Fax 292-3049
Owens ES 400/PK-5
1102 York St 41071 859-292-3011
Gregory Frank, prin. Fax 292-0771

Holy Trinity JHS 50/6-8
840 Washington Ave 41071 859-292-0487
Jeff Finke, prin. Fax 431-8745

Nicholasville, Jessamine, Pop. 23,897
Jessamine County SD 7,300/PK-12
871 Wilmore Rd 40356 859-885-4179
Lu Young, supt. Fax 887-4811
www.jessamine.k12.ky.us
Brookside ES 600/PK-5
199 Brookside Dr 40356 859-887-2012
JonAnn Horn, prin. Fax 885-9934
East Jessamine MS 800/6-8
851 Wilmore Rd 40356 859-885-5561
Donna Givens, prin. Fax 887-1797
Nicholasville ES 500/PK-5
414 W Maple St 40356 859-885-5351
Karen McGuire, prin. Fax 885-1011
Rosenwald Dunbar ES 600/PK-5
1500 Wilmore Rd 40356 859-885-6670
Beth Osborne, prin. Fax 887-2052
Warner ES 600/PK-5
821 Wilmore Rd 40356 859-885-3085
Val Gallutia, prin. Fax 881-5655
West Jessamine MS 800/6-8
1400 Wilmore Rd 40356 859-885-2244
James Freeman, prin. Fax 885-8078
Other Schools – See Wilmore

North Middletown, Bourbon, Pop. 561
Bourbon County SD
Supt. — See Paris
North Middletown ES 200/PK-5
PO Box 67 40357 859-362-4523
Greg Ramey, prin. Fax 362-4047

Nortonville, Hopkins, Pop. 1,252
Hopkins County SD
Supt. — See Madisonville
South Hopkins MS 500/6-8
9140 Hopkinsville Rd 42442 270-825-6125
Stuart Fitch, prin. Fax 825-6085
Southside ES 500/PK-5
9220 Hopkinsville Rd 42442 270-825-6143
C. Steve Eakins, prin. Fax 825-6111

Oakland, Warren, Pop. 255
Warren County SD
Supt. — See Bowling Green
Oakland ES 300/PK-6
PO Box 128 42159 270-563-4719
Mike Johnson, prin. Fax 563-2210

Olive Hill, Carter, Pop. 1,823
Carter County SD
Supt. — See Grayson
Carter ES 100/PK-5
12594 State Highway 2 41164 606-474-6121
Ronald Morgan, prin. Fax 474-2044
Olive Hill ES 600/PK-5
PO Box 540 41164 606-286-5385
Cherri Keaton, prin. Fax 286-5982
Upper Tygart ES 300/PK-5
21039 W US Highway 60 41164 606-286-2110
Tim Johnson, prin. Fax 286-8193
West Carter County MS 500/6-8
PO Box 1510 41164 606-286-5354
Sherry Horsley, prin. Fax 286-8556

Olmstead, Logan
Logan County SD
Supt. — See Russellville
Olmstead S 400/PK-8
1170 Olmstead Rd 42265 270-726-3811
Benjamin Kemplin, prin. Fax 726-1591

Oneida, Clay
Clay County SD
Supt. — See Manchester
Big Creek ES 200/PK-6
523 N Highway 66 40972 606-598-2812
Nadine Couch, prin. Fax 598-2853
Oneida ES 100/PK-6
435 Newfound Rd 40972 606-847-4212
Steve Burchfield, prin. Fax 847-4340

Oneida Baptist Institute 300/K-12
PO Box 67 40972 606-847-4111
Dan Stockton, prin. Fax 847-4496

Owensboro, Daviess, Pop. 55,459
Daviess County SD 10,900/PK-12
PO Box 21510 42304 270-852-7000
Tom Shelton, supt. Fax 852-7010
www.daviess.k12.ky.us/
Audubon ES 500/PK-5
300 Worthington Rd 42301 270-852-7150
Robin Winnecke, prin. Fax 852-7160
Burns ES 600/PK-5
4514 Goetz Dr 42301 270-852-7170
Amy Shutt, prin. Fax 852-7180
Burns MS 800/6-8
4610 Goetz Dr 42301 270-852-7400
Dane Ferguson, prin. Fax 852-7410
College View MS 800/6-8
5061 New Hartford Rd 42303 270-852-7500
Jennifer Crume, prin. Fax 852-7510
Country Heights ES 400/PK-5
4961 State Route 54 42303 270-852-7250
Deborah Crowe, prin. Fax 852-7260
Daviess County MS 700/6-8
1415 E 4th St 42303 270-852-7600
Gates Settle, prin. Fax 852-7610
Deer Park ES 500/PK-5
4959 New Hartford Rd 42303 270-852-7270
Cindy Galloway, prin. Fax 852-7280
East View ES 500/PK-5
6104 State Route 405 42303 270-852-7350
Ann Marie Williams, prin. Fax 852-7360
Highland ES 500/PK-5
2909 Highway 54 42303 270-852-7370
Anita Newman, prin. Fax 852-7380
Meadow Lands ES 400/PK-5
3500 Hayden Rd 42303 270-852-7450
Kevin Lowe, prin. Fax 852-7460
Sorgho ES 400/PK-5
5390 Highway 56 42301 270-852-7470
Beverly Dawson, prin. Fax 852-7480
Tamarack ES 500/PK-5
1733 Tamarack Rd 42301 270-852-7550
Allison Coomes, prin. Fax 852-7560
West Louisville ES 300/PK-5
9661 State Route 56 42301 270-852-7650
Connie Morgan, prin. Fax 852-7660
Other Schools – See Utica, Whitesville

Owensboro ISD 3,900/PK-12
PO Box 249 42302 270-686-1000
Dr. Larry Vick, supt. Fax 684-5756
www.owensboro.k12.ky.us
Cravens ES 300/K-4
2741 Cravens Ave 42301 270-686-1010
Chris Gaddis, prin. Fax 683-9678
Estes ES 400/K-4
1675 Leitchfield Rd 42303 270-686-1030
Shari Flagg, prin. Fax 686-1176
Foust ES 300/K-4
601 Foust Ave 42301 270-686-1060
Janie Moseley, prin. Fax 686-1021
Hager Preschool PK-PK
1701 W 7th St 42301 270-686-1125
Sherry Baber, prin. Fax 686-1161
Newton Parrish ES 400/K-4
510 W Byers Ave 42303 270-686-1100
Steve Bratcher, prin. Fax 926-9637
Owensboro 5-6 Center 500/5-6
2631 S Griffith Ave 42301 270-686-1128
Lynne Beavers, prin. Fax 686-1183
Owensboro MS 600/7-8
1300 Booth Ave 42301 270-686-1130
Janice Eaves, prin. Fax 686-1173
Sutton ES 300/K-4
2060 Lewis Ln 42301 270-686-1140
James Lyddane, prin. Fax 686-1158

Owensboro Catholic MS 200/7-8
2540 Christie Pl 42301 270-683-0480
Ann Flaherty, prin. Fax 683-0495
Owensboro S 4-6 Campus 300/4-6
525 E 23rd St 42303 270-683-6989
Tracy Conkright, prin. Fax 684-5956
Owensboro S K-3 Campus 400/K-3
4017 Frederica St 42301 270-684-7583
Lori Whitehouse, prin. Fax 684-4938

Owenton, Owen, Pop. 1,470
Owen County SD 1,700/K-12
1600 Highway 22 E 40359 502-484-3934
Mark Cleveland, supt. Fax 484-9095
www.owen.k12.ky.us
Bowling MS 500/6-8
1960 Highway 22 E 40359 502-484-5701
Jo Ella Wallace, prin. Fax 484-3044
Owen County ES 300/3-5
1945 Highway 22 E 40359 502-484-3417
Charlotte Elkins, prin. Fax 484-5764
Owen County PS 400/K-2
1925 Highway 22 E 40359 502-484-5499
Sharen Hubbard, prin. Fax 484-0095

Owingsville, Bath, Pop. 1,564
Bath County SD 2,000/PK-12
405 W Main St 40360 606-674-6314
Nancy Hutchinson, supt. Fax 674-2647
www.bath.k12.ky.us
Bath County MS 500/6-8
432 W Main St 40360 606-674-8165
Lloyd Sartin, prin. Fax 674-2676
Owingsville ES 600/PK-5
50 Chenault Dr 40360 606-674-2722
Wesley Vernon, prin. Fax 674-6621
Other Schools – See Salt Lick, Sharpsburg

Paducah, McCracken, Pop. 25,575
McCracken County SD 6,900/PK-12
435 Berger Rd 42003 270-538-4000
M. Tim Heller, supt. Fax 538-4001
www.mccracken.k12.ky.us
Concord ES 400/PK-5
5184 Hinkleville Rd 42001 270-538-4050
Ginger Hollowell, prin. Fax 538-4051
Farley ES 500/PK-5
1250 Husband Rd 42003 270-538-4170
Jimmie Johnson, prin. Fax 538-4171
Hendron Lone Oak ES 700/PK-5
2501 Marshall Ave 42003 270-538-4110
Mark Buchanan, prin. Fax 538-4111
Lone Oak ES 700/PK-5
301 Cumberland Ave 42001 270-538-4120
Dan Pope, prin. Fax 538-4121
Lone Oak MS 700/6-8
300 Cumberland Ave 42001 270-538-4130
Michael White, prin. Fax 538-4131
Reidland ES 400/K-5
5741 Benton Rd 42003 270-538-4180
Linda Hunt, prin. Fax 538-4181
Reidland MS 400/6-8
5347 Benton Rd 42003 270-538-4190
Scott Pullen, prin. Fax 538-4191
Other Schools – See West Paducah

Paducah ISD 2,700/K-12
PO Box 2550 42002 270-444-5600
R.J. Greene, supt. Fax 444-5607
www.paducah.kyschools.us/
Clark ES 600/K-5
3401 Buckner Ln 42001 270-444-5730
Sara West, prin. Fax 444-5737
McNabb ES 400/K-5
2100 Park Ave 42001 270-444-5750
Kim Bryant, prin. Fax 444-5772
Morgan ES 300/K-5
2200 S 28th St 42003 270-444-5760
Stan Lafferty, prin. Fax 444-5763
Paducah MS 700/6-8
342 Lone Oak Rd 42001 270-444-5710
Tim Huddleston, prin. Fax 444-5709

Community Christian Academy 200/K-6
3230 Buckner Ln 42001 270-575-0025
Larry Nichols, admin. Fax 443-2230
St. Mary MS 200/6-8
1243 Elmdale Rd 42003 270-442-1681
Tony Burkeen, prin. Fax 442-7920
St. Mary S 200/K-5
377 Highland Blvd 42003 270-442-1681
Tony Riegling, prin. Fax 442-7920

Paint Lick, Garrard
Garrard County SD
Supt. — See Lancaster
Paint Lick ES 300/PK-5
6798 Richmond Rd 40461 859-792-2122
Larry Sparks, prin. Fax 792-4873

Paintsville, Johnson, Pop. 4,141
Johnson County SD 3,700/PK-12
253 N Mayo Trl 41240 606-789-2530
Steve Trimble, supt. Fax 789-2506
www.johnson.k12.ky.us
Central ES 400/PK-6
1715 Euclid Ave 41240 606-789-2541
Ben Hamilton, prin. Fax 789-2527
Johnson County MS 600/7-8
251 N Mayo Trl 41240 606-789-4133
Tim Adams, prin. Fax 789-4135
Other Schools – See Flatgap, Hagerhill, Staffordsville, Williamsport, Wittensville

Paintsville ISD 800/PK-12
305 2nd St 41240 606-789-2654
Coy Samons, supt. Fax 789-7412
www.paintsville.k12.ky.us
Paintsville ES 400/PK-6
325 2nd St 41240 606-789-2651
Bryan Auxier, prin. Fax 789-2575

Our Lady of the Mountains S 100/PK-8
405 3rd St 41240 606-789-3661
Cathy Cybriwsky, prin. Fax 789-3661

Paris, Bourbon, Pop. 9,334
Bourbon County SD 2,700/PK-12
3343 Lexington Rd 40361 859-987-2180
Lana Fryman, supt. Fax 987-2182
www.bourbon.k12.ky.us/boco/
Bourbon Central ES 600/PK-5
367 Bethlehem Rd 40361 859-987-2195
Ben Rankin, prin. Fax 987-2104
Bourbon County MS 600/6-8
3343 Lexington Rd 40361 859-987-2189
Larry Dixon, prin. Fax 987-5854
Bourbon County Preschool PK-PK
369 Bethlehem Rd 40361 859-987-2183
Ann Stewart, prin.
Cane Ridge ES 400/PK-5
8000 Bypass Rd 40361 859-987-2106
Gerry Brooks, prin. Fax 987-2107
Other Schools – See North Middletown

Paris ISD 700/K-12
310 W 7th St 40361 859-987-2160
Janice Cox-Blackburn, supt. Fax 987-6749
www.paris.k12.ky.us
Paris ES 300/K-5
1481 S Main St 40361 859-987-2166
Rachelle Schjoll, prin. Fax 987-2176
Paris MS 200/6-8
304 W 7th St 40361 859-987-2163
Travis Earlywine, prin. Fax 987-2164

St. Mary S 100/PK-8
1121 Main St 40361 859-987-3815
Richard Martinez, prin. Fax 987-3815

Park City, Barren, Pop. 542
Barren County SD
Supt. — See Glasgow
Park City ES 300/PK-6
PO Box 45 42160 270-749-5665
Anthony Janes, prin. Fax 749-5074

Payneville, Meade
Meade County SD
Supt. — See Brandenburg
Payneville ES 200/K-6
520 Rhodelia Rd 40157 270-422-7550
Marie Barr, prin. Fax 496-4774

Pembroke, Christian, Pop. 778
Christian County SD
Supt. — See Hopkinsville
Pembroke ES 400/K-5
1600 Pembroke Oak Grove Rd 42266 270-887-7290
Laura Morris, prin. Fax 475-9897

Perryville, Boyle, Pop. 755
Boyle County SD
Supt. — See Danville
Perryville ES 200/PK-5
PO Box 8 40468 859-936-7500
Christopher Holderman, prin. Fax 332-2324

Pewee Valley, Oldham, Pop. 1,546

Pewee Valley Junior Academy 50/K-8
PO Box 738 40056 502-241-4354
Chris Juhl, prin. Fax 241-4354
St. Aloysius S 500/PK-8
PO Box 190 40056 502-241-8452
Maryann Hayslip, prin. Fax 243-2241

Phelps, Pike, Pop. 1,298
Pike County SD
Supt. — See Pikeville
Phelps ES 300/K-6
PO Box 529 41553 606-456-7716
Wanda Hurley, prin. Fax 456-8200

Pikeville, Pike, Pop. 6,312
Pike County SD 9,100/K-12
PO Box 3097 41502 606-433-9200
Roger Wagner, supt. Fax 432-3321
www.pike.k12.ky.us
Johns Creek S 800/K-8
8302 Meta Hwy 41501 606-631-1097
Reed Adkins, prin. Fax 631-9604
Millard S 400/K-8
8015 Millard Hwy 41501 606-437-3380
David Slone, prin. Fax 433-9677
Mullins S 500/K-8
101 Tiger Way 41501 606-432-2733
Phillip Birchfield, prin. Fax 432-2393
Other Schools – See Belfry, Dorton, Elkhorn City, Fedscreek, Kimper, Majestic, Phelps, Pinsonfork, Ransom, Robinson Creek, Sidney, Virgie

Pikeville ISD 1,200/K-12
148 2nd St 41501 606-432-8161
Jerry Green, supt. Fax 432-2119
www.pikevilleschools.us
Pikeville ES 700/K-6
105 Bailey Blvd 41501 606-432-4196
Robert Jones, prin. Fax 432-1234

Christ Central S 100/PK-8
PO Box 2154 41502 606-432-9565
Gloria Janet Burnette, admin. Fax 432-6747
St. Francis of Assisi S 100/K-6
147 Bryan St 41501 606-437-6117
Theresa Dawahare, prin. Fax 437-6822

Pine Knot, McCreary, Pop. 1,549
McCreary County SD
Supt. — See Stearns
Pine Knot IS 400/4-6
6519 S Highway 1651 42635 606-354-2511
Mitzi Stephens, prin. Fax 354-9353
Pine Knot Preschool PK-PK
6461 S Highway 1651 42635 606-354-3590
Jenny Worley, dir. Fax 376-5584
Pine Knot PS 600/K-3
119 E Highway 92 42635 606-354-2161
Eugenia Jones, prin. Fax 354-4418

Pineville, Bell, Pop. 2,014
Bell County SD 3,100/PK-12
PO Box 340 40977 606-337-7051
George Thompson, supt. Fax 337-1412
www.bell.kyschools.us/
Bell Central S Center 600/PK-8
RR 1 Box 87C 40977 606-337-3104
Greg Wilson, prin. Fax 337-0808
Page Center 400/PK-8
239 Page School Rd 40977 606-337-5207
Teresa Wilson, prin. Fax 337-9534
Other Schools – See Fourmile, Frakes, Middlesboro, Stoney Fork

Pineville ISD 600/PK-12
401 W Virginia Ave 40977 606-337-5701
Michael White, supt. Fax 337-9983
www.pineville.k12.ky.us
Pineville ES 300/PK-6
401 W Virginia Ave 40977 606-337-3412
Bobby Bennett, prin. Fax 337-4395

Pinsonfork, Pike
Pike County SD
Supt. — See Pikeville
Runyon S 200/K-8
24 Runyon Branch Rd 41555 606-353-7483
Rosa Wolfe, prin. Fax 353-1102

Pippa Passes, Knott, Pop. 448

Buchanan S 200/K-12
100 Purpose Rd 41844 606-368-6108
Yvon Allen, prin. Fax 368-6216

Pleasure Ridge Park, Jefferson, Pop. 25,131

St. Paul S 200/PK-8
6901 Dixie Hwy 40258 502-935-5511
Kevin Brever, prin. Fax 935-5596

Pleasureville, Henry, Pop. 888
Henry County SD
Supt. — See New Castle
Eastern ES 200/K-5
6928 Bethlehem Rd 40057 502-845-8640
Sharon Bright, prin. Fax 845-8641

Powderly, Muhlenberg, Pop. 843
Muhlenberg County SD 4,500/K-12
510 W Main St 42367 270-338-2871
Dale Todd, supt. Fax 338-0529
www.mberg.k12.ky.us
Other Schools – See Beechmont, Bremen, Central City, Greenville

Prestonsburg, Floyd, Pop. 3,706
Floyd County SD 6,100/K-12
106 N Front Ave 41653 606-886-2354
Henry Webb, supt. Fax 886-8862
www.floyd.kyschools.us
Adams MS 400/6-8
2520 S Lake Dr 41653 606-886-2671
Jack Goodman, prin. Fax 886-7026
Prestonsburg ES 600/K-5
140 Clark Dr 41653 606-886-3891
Brent Rose, prin. Fax 886-9081
Other Schools – See Allen, Betsy Layne, Bevinsville, Eastern, Grethel, Hi Hat, Mc Dowell, Martin

Princeton, Caldwell, Pop. 6,447
Caldwell County SD 1,800/PK-12
PO Box 229 42445 270-365-8000
Carrell Boyd, supt. Fax 365-5742
www.caldwell.k12.ky.us/
Caldwell County ES 300/3-5
105 Educational Dr 42445 270-365-8030
Kay Lane, prin. Fax 365-3164
Caldwell County MS 500/6-8
440 Beckner Ln 42445 270-365-8020
Chad Burgett, prin. Fax 365-9573
Caldwell PS 300/PK-2
1000 Marion Rd 42445 270-365-8040
Paulette Gray, prin. Fax 365-7038

Prospect, Oldham, Pop. 4,877
Oldham County SD
Supt. — See Crestwood
Goshen ES 700/K-5
12518 Ridgemoor Dr 40059 502-228-0101
Candace Sellars, prin. Fax 228-3777

St. Mary Academy 300/PK-8
11311 Saint Mary Ln 40059 502-425-2637
Mary Zettel, prin. Fax 425-2699

Providence, Webster, Pop. 3,549
Webster County SD
Supt. — See Dixon
Providence S 300/K-8
470 S Broadway St 42450 270-667-7041
Teresa Marshall, prin. Fax 667-5893

Raceland, Greenup, Pop. 2,477
Raceland-Worthington ISD 1,000/K-12
600 Rams Blvd 41169 606-836-2144
Frank Melvin, supt. Fax 833-5807
www.raceland.k12.ky.us
Campbell ES 300/K-3
550 Rams Blvd 41169 606-836-3844
Jill Imes, prin. Fax 494-2417
Other Schools – See Worthington

Radcliff, Hardin, Pop. 21,471
Hardin County SD
Supt. — See Elizabethtown
Meadow View ES 500/K-5
1255 W Vine St 40160 270-352-0500
Jim Sullivan, prin. Fax 352-0526
Parkway ES 600/K-5
1080 S Logsdon Pkwy 40160 270-351-4491
Joan Jackson-Cooke, prin. Fax 351-6050
Radcliff MS 400/6-8
1145 S Dixie Blvd 40160 270-351-1171
Laura McGray, prin. Fax 352-5193
Woodland ES 500/PK-5
6000 S Woodland Dr 40160 270-352-5828
Teresa Morgan, prin. Fax 352-5835

Christian Heritage Community S 100/PK-K
95 Park Ave 40160 270-352-2352
Richard Johnson, admin. Fax 351-6057
North Hardin Christian S 400/PK-12
1298 Rogersville Rd 40160 270-351-7700
A. Paige Hardin, prin. Fax 351-7757

Ransom, Pike
Pike County SD
Supt. — See Pikeville
Blackberry S 100/K-8
40 Big Blue Springs Rd 41558 606-427-7171
Paul May, prin. Fax 427-8800

Richmond, Madison, Pop. 30,893
Madison County SD 10,200/PK-12
PO Box 768 40476 859-624-4500
Thomas Floyd, supt. Fax 624-4508
www.madison.k12.ky.us/
Boone ES 400/K-5
710 N 2nd St 40475 859-624-4530
Shane Lakes, prin. Fax 624-4589
Carson ES 600/PK-5
450 Tates Creek Rd 40475 859-624-4525
Beth Jones, prin. Fax 624-4526
Caudill MS 6-8
1428 Robert R Martin Bypass 40475 859-625-6172
Ken Bicknell, prin. Fax 625-4494

Kirksville ES 400/K-5
2399 Lancaster Rd 40475 859-624-4582
Fax 624-4595
Madison MS 700/6-8
101 Summit St 40475 859-624-4550
Brad Winkler, prin. Fax 624-4543
Marshall ES 400/PK-5
1442 Dr Robert R Martin Byp 40475 859-624-4481
Penny Begley, prin. Fax 624-4021
Mayfield ES 300/PK-5
300 Bond St 40475 859-624-4540
Richard Lowe, prin. Fax 624-4541
Model Laboratory ES 300/PK-5
521 Lancaster Ave 40475 859-622-3766
Deborah Brown, prin. Fax 622-6658
Model Laboratory MS 200/6-8
521 Lancaster Ave 40475 859-622-3766
James Dantic, prin. Fax 622-6658
Moores MS 600/6-8
1143 Berea Rd 40475 859-624-4545
Kevin Combs, prin. Fax 624-4534
White Hall ES 600/PK-5
2166 Lexington Rd 40475 859-624-4510
Randy Neeley, prin. Fax 624-4512
Other Schools – See Berea, Waco

Blue Grass Christian S 200/PK-12
211 Pin Oak Dr 40475 859-624-3083
Nora Thompson, admin. Fax 624-3099
St. Mark S 200/PK-8
115 Parrish Ave 40475 859-623-2989
Paul Doty, prin. Fax 626-5492

Rineyville, Hardin
Hardin County SD
Supt. — See Elizabethtown
Rineyville ES 400/PK-5
275 Rineyville School Rd 40162 270-737-7371
Billy Coffey, prin. Fax 737-0916

Robinson Creek, Pike
Pike County SD
Supt. — See Pikeville
Robinson Creek ES 200/K-5
PO Box 400 41560 606-639-4415
Patricia Burke, prin. Fax 639-9318

Rockholds, Whitley
Whitley County SD
Supt. — See Williamsburg
Whitley County North ES 400/PK-6
6670 Highway 26 40759 606-549-7869
Larry Brown, prin. Fax 523-5383

Rogers, Wolfe
Wolfe County SD
Supt. — See Campton
Rogers ES 100/K-5
1750 KY 715 41365 606-668-8302
Kim Graham, prin. Fax 668-8350

Rousseau, Breathitt
Breathitt County SD
Supt. — See Jackson
Rousseau ES 100/PK-6
13462 Highway 30 E 41366 606-666-7276
Karen Tharp, lead tchr. Fax 666-7411

Rush, Boyd
Carter County SD
Supt. — See Grayson
Star ES 100/PK-5
8249 E US Highway 60 41168 606-474-5756
Charles Baker, prin. Fax 475-9595

Russell, Greenup, Pop. 3,597
Russell ISD 2,200/PK-12
409 Belfonte St 41169 606-836-9679
Dr. Susan Compton, supt. Fax 836-2865
www.russellind.kyschools.us
Russell MS 500/6-8
707 Red Devil Ln 41169 606-836-8135
Sean Horne, prin. Fax 836-0614
Russell PS 700/PK-3
710 Red Devil Ln 41169 606-836-0007
Debbie Finley, prin. Fax 834-9300
Other Schools – See Flatwoods

Russell Springs, Russell, Pop. 2,537
Russell County SD
Supt. — See Jamestown
Russell County MS 400/7-8
2258 S Highway 127 42642 270-866-2224
Kenneth Pickett, prin. Fax 866-8679
Russell Springs ES 600/PK-6
1554 N Highway 127 42642 270-866-3587
Kathy Hammond, prin. Fax 866-7456
Salem ES 400/PK-6
1409 S Highway 76 42642 270-866-6197
Terry Grider, prin. Fax 866-3687

Russellville, Logan, Pop. 7,271
Logan County SD 3,500/PK-12
PO Box 417 42276 270-726-2436
Marshall Kemp, supt. Fax 726-8892
www.logan.k12.ky.us/
Chandlers S 400/PK-8
6000 Morgantown Rd 42276 270-542-4139
Elisa Brown, prin. Fax 542-4108
Other Schools – See Adairville, Auburn, Lewisburg, Olmstead

Russellville ISD 1,000/PK-12
355 S Summer St 42276 270-726-8405
Roger Cook, supt. Fax 726-4036
www.rville.k12.ky.us/district/
Russellville MS 100/7-8
210 E 7th St 42276 270-726-8428
Kim McDaniel, prin. Fax 726-8888
Stevenson ES 500/PK-6
1000 N Main St 42276 270-726-8425
Tammy Corum, prin. Fax 726-1109

Ryland Heights, Kenton, Pop. 819
Kenton County SD
Supt. — See Fort Wright
Ryland Heights ES 400/PK-5
3845 Stewart Dr 41015 859-356-9270
Cathy Barwell, prin. Fax 356-2846

Sacramento, McLean, Pop. 515
McLean County SD
Supt. — See Calhoun
Gatton ES 100/K-5
PO Box 288 42372 270-736-2343
Judith Walker, prin. Fax 736-5520

Salt Lick, Bath, Pop. 355
Bath County SD
Supt. — See Owingsville
Salt Lick ES 200/K-5
PO Box 229 40371 606-683-3341
Lisa Henderson, prin. Fax 683-6431

Salyersville, Magoffin, Pop. 1,604
Magoffin County SD 1,600/PK-12
PO Box 109 41465 606-349-6117
Joe Hunley, supt. Fax 349-3417
www.magoffin.k12.ky.us/
North Magoffin ES K-6
1991 Highway 460 W 41465 606-349-2847
Jill Howard, prin. Fax 349-6466
Salyersville Grade S 500/PK-6
204 Hornet Dr 41465 606-349-3411
Fax 349-3483
South Magoffin ES K-6
171 Half Mountain Rd 41465 606-884-7325
Bronna Francis, prin. Fax 884-7322
Whitaker MS 300/7-8
221 Hornet Dr 41465 606-349-5190
Johnnie Johnson, prin. Fax 349-5139

Sandgap, Jackson
Jackson County SD
Supt. — See Mc Kee
Sand Gap ES 300/PK-5
PO Box 320 40481 606-965-3171
Robert Williams, prin. Fax 965-2917

Sandy Hook, Elliott, Pop. 687
Elliott County SD 1,100/K-12
PO Box 767 41171 606-738-8002
John Williams, supt. Fax 738-8050
www.elliott.k12.ky.us/
Lakeside ES 200/K-6
PO Box 749 41171 606-738-8202
Marisa Adkins, prin. Fax 738-8249
Sandy Hook ES 300/K-6
PO Box 708 41171 606-738-8402
Vanessa Maggard, prin. Fax 738-8450
Other Schools – See Isonville

Science Hill, Pulaski, Pop. 653
Science Hill ISD 500/PK-8
6007 N Highway 27 42553 606-423-3341
Rick Walker, supt. Fax 423-3313
www.science.k12.ky.us
Science Hill S 500/PK-8
6007 N Highway 27 42553 606-423-3341
Rita Presley, prin. Fax 423-3313

Scottsville, Allen, Pop. 4,525
Allen County SD 3,000/PK-12
570 Oliver St 42164 270-618-3181
Randall Jackson, supt. Fax 618-3185
www.allen.kyschools.us
Allen County IS 700/4-6
720 Oliver St 42164 270-618-8200
Chad Cooper, prin. Fax 618-8205
Allen County PS 900/PK-3
721 New Gallatin Rd 42164 270-618-7200
LaVonna Tarry, prin. Fax 618-7206
Bazzell MS 500/7-8
201 New Gallatin Rd 42164 270-622-7140
Rick Fisher, prin. Fax 622-4649

Sebree, Webster, Pop. 1,569
Webster County SD
Supt. — See Dixon
Sebree S 300/PK-8
PO Box 37 42455 270-835-7891
David Rupsch, prin. Fax 639-0374

Sharpsburg, Bath, Pop. 312
Bath County SD
Supt. — See Owingsville
Bethel ES 100/K-5
4326 N Highway 11 40374 606-247-2621
Lisa Henderson, prin. Fax 247-4701

Shelbyville, Shelby, Pop. 10,730
Shelby County SD 6,100/PK-12
PO Box 159 40066 502-633-2375
James Neihof, supt. Fax 633-1988
www.shelby.kyschools.us
Clear Creek ES 600/K-5
279 Chapel Hl 40065 502-633-3452
Karen Downs, prin. Fax 647-0232
Painted Stone ES 500/K-5
150 Warriors Way 40065 502-647-4505
Michelle Shipley, prin. Fax 647-4508
Shelby County East MS 700/6-8
600 Rocket Ln 40065 502-633-1478
Anthony Sieg, prin. Fax 633-6981
Shelby County Preschool Center PK-PK
150 Warriors Way 40065 502-633-5123
Lisa Waller, prin.
Shelby County West MS 800/6-8
100 Warriors Way 40065 502-633-4869
Lorri Stivers, prin. Fax 647-4525
Southside ES, 728 Ginkgo Dr 40065 300/K-5
Michael Rowe, prin. 502-633-4460
Wright ES 500/K-5
500 Rocket Ln 40065 502-633-5222
Lynn Gottbrath, prin. Fax 647-0243
Other Schools – See Simpsonville, Waddy

Cornerstone Christian Academy 200/PK-12
3850 Frankfort Rd 40065 502-633-4070
Matt Maxwell, prin. Fax 633-4605

Shepherdsville, Bullitt, Pop. 8,874
Bullitt County SD 12,200/PK-12
1040 Highway 44 E 40165 502-869-8000
Keith Davis, supt. Fax 543-3608
www.bullittschools.org
Bernheim MS 500/6-8
700 Audubon Dr 40165 502-543-7614
Bob Bright, prin. Fax 543-8295
Brooks ES 400/PK-5
1800 E Blue Lick Rd 40165 502-957-4795
Leslie Hicks, prin. Fax 957-5498
Bullitt Lick MS 500/6-8
555 W Blue Lick Rd 40165 502-543-6806
Johnda Conley, prin. Fax 543-1685
Cedar Grove ES 500/PK-5
1900 Cedar Grove Rd 40165 502-543-2344
Andy Moberly, prin. Fax 543-3691
Freedom ES 600/PK-5
4682 N Preston Hwy 40165 502-955-9795
Michelle Sharp, prin. Fax 955-8866
Hebron MS 400/6-8
3300 E Hebron Ln 40165 502-957-3540
John Barbagallo, prin. Fax 957-6014
Roby ES 400/PK-5
1148 Highway 44 E 40165 502-869-7200
Gayle Korfhage, prin. Fax 543-2328
Shepherdsville ES 500/PK-5
527 W Blue Lick Rd 40165 502-543-7737
David Pate, prin. Fax 543-7838
Zoneton MS 600/6-8
797 Old Preston Hwy N 40165 502-955-7067
Rita Muratalla, prin. Fax 955-7027
Other Schools – See Lebanon Junction, Louisville, Mount Washington, West Point

---

Little Flock Christian Academy 200/K-8
5500 N Preston Hwy 40165 502-957-7686
Brian Trees, prin. Fax 957-4122
St. Aloysius S 200/K-8
197 S Plum St 40165 502-543-6721
Steve Hart, prin. Fax 955-1490

Sidney, Pike
Pike County SD
Supt. — See Pikeville
Bevins S 200/K-8
17275 E Big Creek Rd 41564 606-353-7078
Coletta Parsley, prin. Fax 353-0884

Siler, Whitley
Whitley County SD
Supt. — See Williamsburg
Whitley County East ES 100/PK-6
PO Box 949 40763 606-549-7097
Otis Reeves, prin. Fax 549-7098

Silver Grove, Campbell, Pop. 1,174
Silver Grove ISD 300/PK-12
PO Box 400 41085 859-441-3894
Danny Montgomery, supt. Fax 441-4299
www.s-g.k12.ky.us
Silver Grove S 300/PK-12
PO Box 400 41085 859-441-3873
Dennis Bledsoe, prin. Fax 441-4299

Simpsonville, Shelby, Pop. 1,369
Shelby County SD
Supt. — See Shelbyville
Simpsonville ES 600/K-5
6725 Shelbyville Rd 40067 502-722-8855
Fax 722-9607

Slaughters, Webster, Pop. 240
Webster County SD
Supt. — See Dixon
Slaughters S 200/K-8
10362 State Route 138 42456 270-884-3215
Kim Saalwaechter, prin. Fax 639-0288

Smithland, Livingston, Pop. 395
Livingston County SD 1,300/PK-12
PO Box 219 42081 270-928-2111
Kennith Bargo, supt. Fax 928-2112
www.livingston.kyschools.us/
South Livingston ES 500/PK-6
850 Cutoff Rd 42081 270-928-3500
Sheri Henson, prin. Fax 928-3530
Other Schools – See Burna

Smiths Grove, Warren, Pop. 752
Edmonson County SD
Supt. — See Brownsville
South Edmonson ES 400/K-4
1050 Chalybeate School Rd 42171 270-597-2379
Greg Tyree, prin. Fax 597-9031

Warren County SD
Supt. — See Bowling Green
North Warren ES 400/PK-6
420 College St 42171 270-563-2041
Amy Ground, prin. Fax 563-3971

Somerset, Pulaski, Pop. 12,136
Pulaski County SD 7,600/K-12
PO Box 1055 42502 606-679-1123
Tim Eaton, supt. Fax 679-1438
www.pulaski.net
Northern MS 800/6-8
650 Oak Leaf Ln 42503 606-678-5230
Angela Murphy, prin. Fax 678-2729
Oak Hill ES 500/K-5
1755 WTLO Rd 42503 606-679-2014
Jane Jones, prin. Fax 677-0044
Pulaski ES 700/K-5
107 W University Dr 42503 606-678-4713
Mike Murphy, prin. Fax 679-9388
Shopville ES 400/K-5
10 Shopville Rd 42503 606-274-4411
Billy Ray Norris, prin. Fax 274-5186

Southern ES 600/K-5
198 Enterprise Dr 42501 606-678-5229
Keith Patrick, prin. Fax 678-8517
Southern MS 900/6-8
200 Enterprise Dr 42501 606-679-6855
Troy Dotson, prin. Fax 679-2270
Woodstock ES 100/K-5
13215 Highway 39 42503 606-379-2151
Julie Cottrell, prin. Fax 379-6743
Other Schools – See Burnside, Eubank, Nancy

Somerset ISD 1,500/PK-12
305 College St 42501 606-679-4451
Dr. Teresa Wallace, supt. Fax 678-0864
www.somerset.k12.ky.us
Hopkins ES 500/PK-4
200 May St 42501 606-678-8707
Fonda Crawford, prin. Fax 678-3062
Meece MS 400/5-8
210 Barnett St 42501 606-678-5821
Nathan Nevels, prin. Fax 678-2934

Somerset Christian S 300/PK-12
815 Grande Central Blvd 42503 606-451-1600
John Hale, prin. Fax 677-9850

Sonora, Hardin, Pop. 336
Hardin County SD
Supt. — See Elizabethtown
Creekside ES 400/PK-5
151 Horseshoe Bend Rd 42776 270-369-8460
Laura Price, prin. Fax 369-8573

Southgate, Campbell, Pop. 3,356
Southgate ISD 200/PK-8
6 William F Blatt St 41071 859-441-0743
James Palm, supt. Fax 441-6735
www.southgate.k12.ky.us
Southgate S 200/PK-8
6 William F Blatt St 41071 859-441-0743
Michele Kells, prin. Fax 441-6735

St. Therese S 400/K-8
2516 Alexandria Pike 41071 859-441-0449
Dorothy O'Leary, prin. Fax 441-0449

S Portsmouth, Greenup

Harvest Christian Academy 100/K-12
PO Box 398 41174 606-932-3007
John Bower, prin. Fax 932-2240

South Shore, Greenup, Pop. 1,243
Greenup County SD
Supt. — See Greenup
McKell ES 500/K-5
28978 US 23 Hwy 41175 606-932-3383
Thomas Kouns, prin. Fax 473-3438
McKell MS 400/6-8
129 Bulldog Ln 41175 606-932-3221
Brenda Box, prin. Fax 932-9844

Spottsville, Henderson
Henderson County SD
Supt. — See Henderson
Spottsville ES 500/K-5
9190 US Highway 60 E 42458 270-831-5136
Terry Adkins, prin. Fax 831-5138

Springfield, Washington, Pop. 2,806
Washington County SD 1,700/PK-12
120 Mackville Hl 40069 859-336-5470
Sonny Fentress, supt. Fax 336-5480
www.washington.k12.ky.us
Washington County ES 400/PK-5
520 Lincoln Park Rd 40069 859-336-5490
Susan Osborne, prin. Fax 336-0446
Washington County MS 200/6-8
603 Lincoln Park Rd 40069 859-336-5475
Christina Sagrecy, prin. Fax 336-5477
Other Schools – See Willisburg

St. Dominic S 200/1-8
309 W Main St 40069 859-336-7165
Pamela Breunig, prin. Fax 336-7169

Staffordsville, Johnson
Johnson County SD
Supt. — See Paintsville
Highland ES 500/PK-6
649 US Highway 23 S 41256 606-297-3674
Thom Cochran, prin. Fax 297-6080

Stamping Ground, Scott, Pop. 631
Scott County SD
Supt. — See Georgetown
Stamping Ground ES 400/PK-5
3233 Main St 40379 502-570-8800
Paul Krueger, prin. Fax 570-8804

Stanford, Lincoln, Pop. 3,452
Lincoln County SD 4,100/PK-12
PO Box 265 40484 606-365-2124
Larry Woods, supt. Fax 365-1660
www.lincoln.kyschools.us
Lincoln County MS 600/7-8
285 Education Way 40484 606-365-8400
Debbie Sims, prin. Fax 365-8600
McGuffey Sixth Grade Center 300/6-6
342 Education Way 40484 606-365-8272
Jimmy Dyehouse, prin. Fax 365-8072
Stanford ES 600/PK-5
101 Old Fort Rd 40484 606-365-2191
Dan Story, prin. Fax 365-1533
Other Schools – See Crab Orchard, Hustonville, Mc Kinney, Waynesburg

Stanton, Powell, Pop. 3,109
Powell County SD 2,500/PK-12
PO Box 430 40380 606-663-3300
Evelyn Neely, supt. Fax 663-3303
www.powell.k12.ky.us/
Bowen ES 300/K-5
5099 Campton Rd 40380 606-663-3313
Golia Simon, prin. Fax 663-3314
Powell County MS 600/6-8
770 W College Ave 40380 606-663-3308
Karen Rose, prin. Fax 663-3307
Stanton ES 400/PK-5
651 Breckenridge St 40380 606-663-3311
Kyle Lively, prin. Fax 663-3305
Other Schools – See Clay City

Stearns, McCreary, Pop. 1,550
McCreary County SD 3,200/PK-12
120 Raider Way 42647 606-376-2591
Arthur Wright, supt. Fax 376-5584
www.mccreary.kyschools.us
McCreary County MS 500/7-8
180 Raider Way 42647 606-376-5081
Jason Creekmore, prin. Fax 376-9580
Other Schools – See Pine Knot, Whitley City

Stoney Fork, Bell
Bell County SD
Supt. — See Pineville
Right Fork Center 300/PK-8
5296 Highway 221 40988 606-337-3271
Pam Collett, prin. Fax 337-5180

Sturgis, Union, Pop. 2,008
Union County SD
Supt. — See Morganfield
Sturgis ES 400/K-5
1101 N Grant St 42459 270-333-4088
Melissa Brantley, prin. Fax 333-4820

Summer Shade, Barren
Metcalfe County SD
Supt. — See Edmonton
Summer Shade ES 100/PK-5
235 E Nobob Rd 42166 270-428-3962
Michele Kells, prin. Fax 428-4244

Sweeden, Edmonson
Edmonson County SD
Supt. — See Brownsville
Kyrock ES 300/K-4
5270 KY Highway 259 42285 270-286-4013
Mary Cole, prin. Fax 286-4603

Symsonia, Graves
Graves County SD
Supt. — See Mayfield
Symsonia ES 300/PK-6
11730 State Route 131 42082 270-674-4860
Lisa Gamble, prin. Fax 851-4386

Taylor Mill, Kenton, Pop. 6,733
Kenton County SD
Supt. — See Fort Wright
Taylor Mill ES 600/K-5
5907 Taylor Mill Rd 41015 859-356-2566
Lois White, prin. Fax 356-5750
Woodland MS 700/6-8
5399 Old Taylor Mill Rd 41015 859-356-7300
Eric Morwessel, prin. Fax 356-7595

St. Anthony S 100/K-8
485 Grand Ave 41015 859-431-5987
Joanne Browarsky, prin. Fax 431-5972

Taylorsville, Spencer, Pop. 1,173
Spencer County SD 2,700/PK-12
207 W Main St 40071 502-477-3250
Charles Adams, supt. Fax 477-3259
www.spencer.k12.ky.us
Spencer County ES 700/PK-5
1265 Mount Washington Rd 40071 502-477-6950
Karen Larimore, prin. Fax 477-6955
Spencer County MS 600/6-8
1263 Mount Washington Rd 40071 502-477-3260
Ed Downs, prin. Fax 477-6796
Spencer County Preschool 100/PK-PK
110 Reasor Ave 40071 502-477-3250
Nina Beck, prin. Fax 477-3259
Taylorsville ES 400/K-5
206 Reasor Ave 40071 502-477-3339
Chuck Abell, prin. Fax 477-3214

Tollesboro, Lewis
Lewis County SD
Supt. — See Vanceburg
Tollesboro ES 300/PK-6
2431 W KY 10 41189 606-798-3231
Tim Douglas, prin. Fax 798-2515

Tompkinsville, Monroe, Pop. 2,633
Monroe County SD 2,000/PK-12
309 Emberton St 42167 270-487-5456
George Wilson, supt. Fax 487-5571
www.monroe.k12.ky.us
Carter ES 200/PK-5
3888 Edmonton Rd 42167 270-487-5621
Mike Gee, prin. Fax 487-9515
Monroe County MS 500/6-8
759 Old Mulkey Rd 42167 270-487-9624
Amy Thompson, prin. Fax 487-9534
Tompkinsville ES 400/PK-5
420 Elementary School Rd 42167 270-487-6472
Kirk Biggerstaff, prin. Fax 487-9203
Other Schools – See Gamaliel

Topmost, Knott
Knott County SD
Supt. — See Hindman
Beaver Creek S 300/K-8
8000 Highway 7 S 41862 606-447-2833
Bill Hall, prin. Fax 447-2366

Tyner, Jackson
Jackson County SD
Supt. — See Mc Kee
Tyner ES 400/PK-5
PO Box 190 40486 606-364-5105
Tim Johnson, prin. Fax 364-2656

Union, Boone, Pop. 3,379
Boone County SD
Supt. — See Florence
Gray MS 900/6-8
10400 US Highway 42 41091 859-384-5333
Tom Hummel, prin. Fax 384-5318
Mann ES 700/K-5
10435 US Highway 42 41091 859-384-5000
Connie Crigger, prin. Fax 384-5007
New Haven ES 700/K-5
10854 US Highway 42 41091 859-384-5325
Nancy Duley, prin. Fax 384-5253

Uniontown, Union, Pop. 1,063
Union County SD
Supt. — See Morganfield
Uniontown ES 200/K-5
PO Box 517 42461 270-822-4462
Dan Whitesides, prin. Fax 822-4286

Utica, Daviess
Daviess County SD
Supt. — See Owensboro
Southern Oaks ES 300/PK-5
7525 US Highway 431 42376 270-852-7570
Pamela Burns, prin. Fax 852-7580

Valley Station, Jefferson, Pop. 22,840
Jefferson County SD
Supt. — See Louisville
Frost MS 300/6-8
13700 Sandray Blvd 40272 502-485-8256
Ursula Wade, prin. Fax 485-8453
Layne ES 500/PK-5
9831 East Ave 40272 502-485-8290
Brenda Michaud, prin. Fax 485-8557
Medora ES 400/PK-5
11801 Deering Rd 40272 502-485-8298
Betsy Pickup, prin. Fax 485-8572
Stonestreet ES 500/PK-5
10007 Stonestreet Rd 40272 502-485-8333
Barbara Harris, prin. Fax 485-8450
Stuart MS 1,100/6-8
4601 Valley Station Rd 40272 502-485-8334
DeLena Alexander, prin. Fax 485-8713

Vanceburg, Lewis, Pop. 1,698
Lewis County SD 2,400/PK-12
PO Box 159 41179 606-796-2811
Maurice Reeder, supt. Fax 796-3081
www.lewis.k12.ky.us
Laurel ES 100/PK-6
116 Laurel School Rd 41179 606-796-2214
Jerry Bloomfield, prin. Fax 796-0805
Lewis County Central ES 500/K-5
PO Box 220 41179 606-796-2831
Richard Anderson, prin. Fax 796-3103
Lewis County MS 500/6-8
PO Box 69 41179 606-796-6228
Chad Kidwell, prin. Fax 796-6255
Other Schools – See Garrison, Tollesboro

Vancleve, Breathitt

Mt. Carmel S 50/K-7
PO Box 2 41385 606-666-8720
Ruby Brown, prin. Fax 666-4612

Verona, Boone
Walton-Verona ISD
Supt. — See Walton
Walton-Verona ES 500/PK-4
15066 Porter Rd 41092 859-485-4432
Rob Hartman, prin. Fax 485-1977

Versailles, Woodford, Pop. 7,728
Woodford County SD 3,900/PK-12
330 Pisgah Rd 40383 859-873-4701
D. Scott Hawkins, supt. Fax 873-1614
www.woodford.k12.ky.us
Huntertown ES 500/K-5
120 Woodburn Hall Dr 40383 859-873-3731
Kimberly Parker-Brown, prin. Fax 873-6292
Simmons ES 400/K-5
830 Tyrone Pike 40383 859-873-4889
Larry Caudill, prin. Fax 873-6914
Southside ES 500/K-5
1300 Troy Pike 40383 859-873-4850
Michelle Cassady, prin. Fax 873-4571
Woodford County MS 900/6-8
100 School House Rd 40383 859-873-4721
Stephanie Koontz, prin. Fax 873-4436
Woodford County Preschool PK-PK
299 S Main St 40383 859-873-2421
Kathy Hogg, prin. Fax 873-1328
Other Schools – See Midway

St. Leo S 200/K-8
239 N Main St 40383 859-873-4591
Catherine Nuno, prin. Fax 873-2244
Versailles Montessori S 50/K-8
480 Pinckard Pike 40383 859-873-1998
Tony Guagliardo, prin. Fax 879-9462
Woodford Christian S 100/K-8
320 Hope Ln 40383 859-873-0288
Cindy Roseberry, admin. Fax 873-0566

Villa Hills, Kenton, Pop. 7,749
Kenton County SD
Supt. — See Fort Wright
River Ridge ES 800/PK-5
2772 Amsterdam Rd 41017 859-341-5260
Shawna Harney, prin. Fax 341-5962

Villa Madonna Academy 400/K-8
2500 Amsterdam Rd 41017 859-331-6333
Soshana Bosley, prin. Fax 331-8615

Vine Grove, Hardin, Pop. 3,983
Hardin County SD
Supt. — See Elizabethtown

Alton MS 600/6-8
100 Country Club Rd 40175 270-877-2135
Jama Bennett, prin. Fax 877-6297
Vine Grove ES 500/PK-5
309 1st St 40175 270-877-5410
Lonnie Dennis, prin. Fax 877-0146

Viper, Perry
Perry County SD
Supt. — See Hazard
Viper S 300/K-8
20 Eddington Ln 41774 606-436-3837
Delilah Brashear, prin. Fax 436-0426

Virgie, Pike
Pike County SD
Supt. — See Pikeville
Johnson ES 300/K-5
2172 Longfork Rd 41572 606-639-4076
Freddie Bowling, prin. Fax 639-4076
Virgie MS 300/6-8
PO Box 310 41572 606-639-2774
Danny Osborne, prin. Fax 639-4086

Valley Christian Academy 50/PK-4
4908 Long Fork Rd 41572 606-639-8921
Gregory White, prin. Fax 639-8921

Waco, Madison
Madison County SD
Supt. — See Richmond
Waco ES 500/PK-5
359 Waco Loop Rd 40385 859-369-5540
Mendy Mills, prin. Fax 369-3819

Waddy, Shelby
Shelby County SD
Supt. — See Shelbyville
Heritage ES 500/PK-5
8300 Frankfort Rd 40076 502-829-5242
Cindy Adkins, prin. Fax 829-9605

Wallingford, Fleming
Fleming County SD
Supt. — See Flemingsburg
Ward ES 200/K-6
12811 Morehead Rd 41093 606-876-2061
Terra Greer, prin. Fax 876-4487

Wallins Creek, Harlan, Pop. 239
Harlan County SD
Supt. — See Harlan
Wallins S 500/PK-8
PO Box 10 40873 606-664-3444
Otis Belcher, prin. Fax 664-3478

Walton, Boone, Pop. 2,856
Walton-Verona ISD 1,100/PK-12
16 School Rd 41094 859-485-4181
Bill Boyle, supt. Fax 485-1810
www.w-v.k12.ky.us
Walton-Verona MS 200/5-8
32 School Rd 41094 859-485-7721
Malina Owens, prin. Fax 485-7739
Other Schools – See Verona

St. Joseph Academy 200/PK-8
48 Needmore St 41094 859-485-6444
Sr. Elizebeth Barkett, prin. Fax 485-4262

Warfield, Martin, Pop. 274
Martin County SD
Supt. — See Inez
Warfield ES 300/K-5
33 Warfield Elementary Loop 41267 606-395-5121
Michael Marcum, prin. Fax 395-5980
Warfield MS 200/6-8
HC 69 Box 812 41267 606-395-5900
Robbie Fletcher, prin. Fax 395-5902

Warsaw, Gallatin, Pop. 1,838
Gallatin County SD 1,500/PK-12
75 Boardwalk 41095 859-567-2828
Dorothy Perkins, supt. Fax 567-4528
www.gallatin.k12.ky.us
Gallatin County ES 500/PK-3
25 Boaz Dr 41095 859-567-4723
Joe Wright, prin. Fax 567-6205
Gallatin County MS 400/6-8
88 Paw Print Path 41095 859-567-5791
Curt Bieger, prin. Fax 567-6107
Gallatin County Upper ES 200/4-5
50 Paw Print Path 41095 859-567-4646
Debra Brown, prin. Fax 567-2715

Waynesburg, Lincoln
Lincoln County SD
Supt. — See Stanford
Highland ES 200/PK-5
75 Tick Ridge Rd 40489 606-365-2768
Darren Yaden, prin. Fax 365-1470
Waynesburg ES 300/PK-5
345 KY Highway 328 W 40489 606-379-6413
Mark Upchurch, prin. Fax 379-6413

West Liberty, Morgan, Pop. 3,349
Morgan County SD 1,900/K-12
PO Box 489 41472 606-743-8002
Joe Dan Gold, supt. Fax 743-8050
www.morgancountyschools.com/
East Valley ES 200/K-5
7585 Highway 172 41472 606-522-8152
C. Thomas Potter, prin. Fax 522-8200
Morgan Central ES K-5
3201 Highway 460 W 41472 606-743-8552
Janea Chaney, prin. Fax 743-8599
Morgan County MS 500/6-8
PO Box 580 41472 606-743-8102
Darren Sparkman, prin. Fax 743-8150
West Liberty ES 400/K-5
717 Liberty Rd 41472 606-743-8302
Vickie Oldfield, prin. Fax 743-8350
Other Schools – See Ezel

Morgan County Christian Academy 50/PK-5
1749 W Main St 41472 606-743-1824
Shirley Evans, admin. Fax 743-2933

West Paducah, McCracken
McCracken County SD
Supt. — See Paducah
Heath ES 500/PK-5
4365 Metropolis Lake Rd 42086 270-538-4060
Donna Owen, prin. Fax 538-4061
Heath MS 500/6-8
4336 Metropolis Lake Rd 42086 270-538-4070
Matthew Blackwell, prin. Fax 538-4071

West Point, Hardin, Pop. 1,032
Bullitt County SD
Supt. — See Shepherdsville
Nichols ES 100/PK-5
10665 Highway 44 W 40177 502-922-4718
Donna Taylor-LaFountain, prin. Fax 922-3372

West Point ISD 200/PK-8
PO Box 367 40177 502-922-4617
Dr. Pamela Stephens, supt. Fax 922-9372
www.westpoint.k12.ky.us
West Point S 200/PK-8
PO Box 367 40177 502-922-4797
Fawnda Cox, prin. Fax 922-9372

Whitesburg, Letcher, Pop. 1,512
Letcher County SD 3,300/PK-12
224 Parks St 41858 606-633-4455
Anna Craft, supt. Fax 633-4724
www.letcher.k12.ky.us/
Bates S 200/K-8
6868 Highway 7 N 41858 606-633-7812
Ricky Warf, prin. Fax 633-5731
Cowan S 300/K-8
PO Box 767 41858 606-633-7195
David Robinson, prin. Fax 633-0763
West Whitesburg ES 400/PK-5
330 Parks St 41858 606-633-9538
Tex Issac, prin. Fax 633-1085
Whitesburg MS 200/6-8
366 Parks St 41858 606-633-2761
Henry Frazier, prin. Fax 633-4137
Other Schools – See Eolia, Kona, Letcher, Neon

Whitesville, Daviess, Pop. 596
Daviess County SD
Supt. — See Owensboro
Whitesville ES 400/PK-5
9656 State Route 54 42378 270-852-7670
Cindy Appleby, prin. Fax 852-7680

St. Mary of the Woods S 200/K-8
10521 Franklin St 42378 270-233-5253
Allison Brant, prin. Fax 233-9360

Whitley City, McCreary, Pop. 1,133
McCreary County SD
Supt. — See Stearns
Whitley City ES 600/K-6
2819 N Highway 27 42653 606-376-2690
Foster Jones, prin. Fax 376-4150

Williamsburg, Whitley, Pop. 5,162
Whitley County SD 4,300/PK-12
300 Main St 40769 606-549-7000
Lonnie Anderson, supt. Fax 549-7006
www.whitley.k12.ky.us/
Boston ES 200/PK-6
3291 Highway 1804 40769 606-549-7872
Robin Head, prin. Fax 786-3302
Pleasant View ES 300/PK-6
85 Stringtown Rd 40769 606-549-7085
Bobby Blakley, prin. Fax 549-7086
Whitley County Central IS 300/3-6
2940 N Highway 25 W 40769 606-549-8011
Alan Sweet, prin. Fax 549-8112
Whitley County Central PS 300/PK-2
520 Boulevard Of Champions 40769 606-549-7060
Lee Hensley, prin. Fax 549-7065
Whitley County MS 700/7-8
351 Boulevard Of Champions 40769 606-549-7050
Rich Prewitt, prin. Fax 549-7055
Other Schools – See Corbin, Rockholds, Siler

Williamsburg ISD 800/PK-12
1000 Main St 40769 606-549-6044
Dennis Byrd, supt. Fax 549-6076
www.wburg.k12.ky.us
Williamsburg S 700/PK-12
1000 Main St 40769 606-549-6044
Gary Peters, prin. Fax 549-6076

Williamsport, Johnson
Johnson County SD
Supt. — See Paintsville
Meade Memorial ES 200/PK-6
8446 KY Route 40 E 41271 606-789-5050
Vanessa Dials, prin. Fax 789-6755

Williamstown, Grant, Pop. 3,423
Grant County SD 3,900/K-12
820 Arnie Risen Blvd 41097 859-824-3323
Michael Hibbett, supt. Fax 824-3508
www.grant.k12.ky.us/
Mason Corinth ES 400/K-5
225 Heekin Rd 41097 859-824-9510
Lisa Hollandsworth, prin. Fax 824-4225
Other Schools – See Dry Ridge

Williamstown ISD 900/PK-12
300 Helton St 41097 859-824-7144
Charles Wilson, supt. Fax 824-3237
www.wtown.k12.ky.us
Williamstown ES 400/PK-5
300 Helton St 41097 859-824-3760
David Poer, prin. Fax 824-3745

Willisburg, Washington, Pop. 316
Washington County SD
Supt. — See Springfield
North Washington S 500/PK-8
5658 Highway 433 40078 859-375-4038
Robin Cochran, prin. Fax 375-0214

Wilmore, Jessamine, Pop. 5,826
Jessamine County SD
Supt. — See Nicholasville
Jessamine Early Learning Village 600/PK-K
210 S Lexington Ave 40390 859-858-0868
Kelly Sampson, prin. Fax 858-0449
Wilmore ES 600/K-5
150 Campground Ln 40390 859-858-3134
Andrea McNeal, prin. Fax 858-3108

Winchester, Clark, Pop. 16,494
Clark County SD 5,500/K-12
1600 W Lexington Ave 40391 859-744-4545
Elaine Farris, supt. Fax 745-3935
www.clarkschools.net
Bush ES 300/K-5
250 N Main St 40391 859-744-4834
Angela Taylor, prin. Fax 745-0109
Central ES 400/K-5
330 Mount Sterling Rd 40391 859-744-2243
Andy Biggers, prin. Fax 737-4842
Clark MS 700/6-8
1 Educational Plz 40391 859-744-0427
Pamela Whitesides, prin. Fax 745-3907
Conkwright MS 600/6-8
360 Mount Sterling Rd 40391 859-744-8433
Luke Wright, prin. Fax 745-2027
McClure ES 300/K-5
30 Beckner St 40391 859-744-6922
Kathy Howard, prin. Fax 745-2147
Pilot View ES 100/K-5
7501 Ironworks Rd 40391 859-842-5231
Steven Jenkins, prin. Fax 842-4238
Providence ES 300/K-5
7076 Old Boonesboro Rd 40391 859-527-3163
Brenda Considine, prin. Fax 527-6392
Shearer ES 400/K-5
244 E Broadway St 40391 859-744-4978
Fax 745-0864
Strode Station ES 600/K-5
2 Educational Plz 40391 859-745-3915
Cynthia Powell, prin. Fax 745-3094
Trapp ES 100/K-5
11400 Irvine Rd 40391 859-744-0027
Steven Jenkins, prin. Fax 745-5801

Calvary Christian S 200/PK-8
15 Redwing Dr 40391 859-737-0205
Ned Hess, prin. Fax 744-9204
Clark County Christian S 100/PK-6
2450 Colby Rd 40391 859-745-6555
Linda Carter, prin. Fax 745-9502
St. Agatha Academy 200/PK-8
244 S Main St 40391 859-744-6484
Christine Rickert, prin. Fax 744-0268

Wingo, Graves, Pop. 595
Graves County SD
Supt. — See Mayfield
Wingo ES 400/PK-6
449 Lebanon St 42088 270-674-4870
Sarah Saylor, prin. Fax 376-2223

Wittensville, Johnson
Johnson County SD
Supt. — See Paintsville
Castle Memorial ES 300/PK-6
3936 N US Highway 23 41274 606-297-3738
Jeff Cochran, prin. Fax 297-7411

Wooton, Leslie
Leslie County SD
Supt. — See Hyden
Muncy ES 200/PK-6
PO Box 140 41776 606-279-4155
Todd Horton, prin. Fax 279-4451

Worthington, Greenup, Pop. 1,679
Raceland-Worthington ISD
Supt. — See Raceland
Worthington ES 200/4-6
800 Center Ave 41183 606-836-8014
Michael Mullins, prin. Fax 836-3449

Wurtland, Greenup, Pop. 1,046
Greenup County SD
Supt. — See Greenup
Wurtland ES 300/K-5
611 East St 41144 606-836-6987
Barbara Cook, prin. Fax 836-5375
Wurtland MS 400/6-8
700 Center St 41144 606-836-1023
Tracy Claxon, prin. Fax 836-3939

Yeaddiss, Leslie
Leslie County SD
Supt. — See Hyden
Hayes Lewis ES 100/PK-6
PO Box 70 41777 606-279-4121
Kevin Gay, prin. Fax 279-4291

LOUISIANA

LOUISIANA DEPARTMENT OF EDUCATION
PO Box 94064, Baton Rouge 70804-9064
Telephone 225-342-3602
Fax 225-342-7316
Website http://www.doe.state.la.us

Superintendent of Education Paul Pastorek

LOUISIANA BOARD OF EDUCATION
PO Box 94064, Baton Rouge 70804-9064

Executive Director Jeanette Vosburg

PUBLIC, PRIVATE AND CATHOLIC ELEMENTARY SCHOOLS

Abbeville, Vermilion, Pop. 11,664
Vermilion Parish SD 9,000/PK-12
PO Box 520 70511 337-893-3973
Randy Schexnayder, supt. Fax 898-0939
www.vrml.k12.la.us
Eaton Park ES 700/PK-5
1502 Sylvester St 70510 337-893-4978
E. Paul Hebert, prin. Fax 898-1274
Forked Island/E Broussard S 300/PK-8
19635 Columbus Rd 70510 337-642-9100
Chris St. Romain, prin. Fax 642-9120
Herod ES 600/PK-5
120 Odea St 70510 337-893-4258
Diane DeJean, prin. Fax 893-4275
Meaux ES 400/PK-6
12419 LA Highway 696 70510 337-893-3901
Charles Robichaux, prin. Fax 893-7112
Seventh Ward ES 300/PK-5
12012 Audubon Rd 70510 337-893-5875
Christine Dubois, prin. Fax 893-8984
Williams MS 600/6-8
1105 Prairie Ave 70510 337-893-3943
Mikal Stall, prin. Fax 893-5190
Other Schools – See Erath, Gueydan, Kaplan, Maurice, Rayne

Mt. Carmel S 400/K-8
405 Park Ave 70510 337-898-0859
Sr. Janet LeBlanc, prin. Fax 893-5968

Abita Springs, Saint Tammany, Pop. 2,211
St. Tammany Parish SD
Supt. — See Covington
Abita Springs ES 600/K-3
22410 Level St 70420 985-892-8184
Rebecca Stogner, prin. Fax 892-2757
Abita Springs MS 400/4-6
PO Box 217 70420 985-892-2070
Donna Forrest, prin. Fax 893-2304

Albany, Livingston, Pop. 1,002
Livingston Parish SD
Supt. — See Livingston
Albany Lower ES 500/PK-2
PO Box 970 70711 225-567-9281
Marsha Sherburne, prin. Fax 567-2972
Albany MS 500/6-8
PO Box 1210 70711 225-567-5231
Melvin Wild, prin. Fax 567-9177
Albany Upper ES 400/3-5
PO Box 1750 70711 225-567-5030
Debbie Tate, prin. Fax 567-5085

Alexandria, Rapides, Pop. 45,693
Rapides Parish SD 22,900/PK-12
PO Box 1230 71309 318-487-0888
Gary Jones, supt. Fax 449-3190
www.rapides.k12.la.us
Acadian ES 300/K-5
310 Richmond Dr 71302 318-487-1202
Jamese Wimbley, prin. Fax 449-1954
Alexandria MS 700/6-8
122 Maryland Ave 71301 318-445-5343
Tim Tharp, prin. Fax 442-8650
Brame MS 800/6-8
4800 Dawn St 71301 318-443-3688
Walter Fall, prin. Fax 442-3966
Brasher ES 300/PK-6
601 Cloverleaf Blvd 71303 318-442-0878
Sidney Cox, prin. Fax 487-8052
Cherokee ES 700/PK-5
5700 Prescott Rd 71301 318-442-1987
Bonnie Lord, prin. Fax 442-4767
Hadnot-Hayes ES 300/PK-5
4020 Aaron St 71302 318-445-0031
Janet Burgess, prin. Fax 484-6174
Hall Magnet ES 300/PK-5
PO Box 121 71309 318-443-9093
Alison Andrews, prin. Fax 442-7104
Horseshoe Drive ES 300/PK-5
2905 Horseshoe Dr 71301 318-443-0579
Denese Carter, prin. Fax 448-4788
Huddle ES 400/PK-6
505 Texas Ave 71301 318-442-7921
Sylvia Adkins, prin. Fax 442-5498
Martin Park ES 300/PK-5
4203 Lisa St 71302 318-448-1695
Wayne Jowers, prin. Fax 448-0511
Nachman ES 600/K-5
4102 Wakefield Blvd 71303 318-445-7725
Rick Tison, prin. Fax 448-3890
North Bayou Rapides ES 300/PK-6
5500 England Dr 71303 318-445-4260
Jackie Trottie, prin. Fax 442-1662
Patrick ES 300/PK-5
1402 Reed Ave 71301 318-443-5443
Faith Washington, prin. Fax 561-2008
Peabody Montessori ES 400/PK-6
PO Box 1747 71309 318-442-5012
Rena Linzay, prin. Fax 487-6704
Phoenix Magnet ES 600/K-6
4500 Lincoln Rd 71302 318-445-6296
John Grimes, prin. Fax 442-2213
Poland S 300/PK-8
3348 Highway 457 71302 318-445-9224
Charles Stevens, prin. Fax 442-7582
Redwine ES 200/PK-6
2121 Mason St 71301 318-442-7977
Deidra Anderson, prin. Fax 442-7940
Rosenthal Montessori ES 300/PK-6
1951 Monroe St 71301 318-442-5791
Debbie Whatley, prin. Fax 443-1667
Rugg ES 300/PK-5
1319 Bush Ave 71301 318-442-4536
Vickie Smith, prin. Fax 445-8476
Smith MS 500/6-8
3100 Jones Ave 71302 318-445-6241
David Brasher, prin. Fax 445-9255
Other Schools – See Ball, Deville, Elmer, Forest Hill, Glenmora, Lecompte, Lena, Pineville

---

Alexandria Country Day S 500/PK-8
5603 Bayou Rapides Rd 71303 318-448-1475
Evelyn Sisco, prin. Fax 442-7924
Grace Christian S 400/PK-12
4900 Jackson Street Ext 71303 318-445-8735
Kay Blackburn, prin. Fax 443-1034
Montessori Education Center 100/PK-6
4209 N Bolton Ave 71303 318-445-0138
Bessie Bannister, hdmstr. Fax 445-0165
Our Lady of Prompt Succor S 500/PK-6
420 21st St 71301 318-487-1862
Johanna Tassin, prin. Fax 473-9321
St. Frances Cabrini S 100/PK-7
2215 E Texas Ave 71301 318-448-3333
Joe Weiderholt, prin. Fax 448-3343
Smyrna Adventist S 50/PK-8
916 Richmond Dr 71302 318-442-3621
Alberta Jefferson, prin.

Amelia, Saint Mary, Pop. 2,447
St. Mary Parish SD
Supt. — See Centerville
Aucoin ES 200/PK-5
PO Box 1040 70340 985-631-2464
Joseph Stadalis, prin. Fax 631-1008

Amite, Tangipahoa, Pop. 4,390
Tangipahoa Parish SD 19,200/PK-12
59656 Puleston Rd 70422 985-748-7153
Mark Kolwe, supt. Fax 748-8587
www.tangischools.org
Amite ES 700/PK-4
301 Vernon Ave 70422 985-748-6953
Kay Christmas, prin. Fax 748-8609
West Side MS 600/5-8
401 W Oak St 70422 985-748-9073
Melissa Ryan, prin. Fax 748-9225
Other Schools – See Hammond, Independence, Kentwood, Loranger, Natalbany, Ponchatoula, Roseland, Tickfaw

---

Oak Forest Academy 600/PK-12
600 Walnut St 70422 985-748-4321
Jason Brabham, prin. Fax 748-4320

Anacoco, Vernon, Pop. 782
Vernon Parish SD
Supt. — See Leesville
Anacoco ES 500/PK-6
4726 Port Arthur Ave 71403 337-239-3040
Kevin Dowdle, prin. Fax 239-6245

Angie, Washington, Pop. 236
Washington Parish SD
Supt. — See Franklinton
Angie JHS 200/6-8
64433 Dixon St 70426 985-986-3105
Randy Branch, prin. Fax 986-5515
Ray ES 200/PK-5
30523 Wesley Ray Rd 70426 985-986-3131
Dorothy Young, prin. Fax 986-3122
Varnado ES 200/PK-5
64139 Jones Creek Rd 70426 985-735-5765
Ginger Champagne, prin. Fax 735-1106

Arcadia, Bienville, Pop. 2,854
Bienville Parish SD 2,400/PK-12
PO Box 418 71001 318-263-9416
William Britt, supt. Fax 263-3100
www.bpsb.us/
Crawford ES 400/PK-6
935 Daniel St 71001 318-263-8757
Oswald Townsend, prin. Fax 263-9010
Other Schools – See Bienville, Castor, Gibsland, Ringgold, Saline

Arnaudville, Saint Landry, Pop. 1,395
St. Landry Parish SD
Supt. — See Opelousas
Arnaudville S 400/K-8
PO Box 770 70512 337-754-5320
Elsie Semien, prin. Fax 754-5326

Athens, Claiborne, Pop. 254
Claiborne Parish SD
Supt. — See Homer
Athens S 200/PK-12
15520 Highway 9 71003 318-258-3241
Craig Roberson, prin. Fax 258-6160

Mount Olive Christian S 100/PK-12
15349 Highway 9 71003 318-258-5661
Linda Gantt, prin. Fax 258-5662

Atlanta, Winn, Pop. 143
Winn Parish SD
Supt. — See Winnfield
Atlanta S 300/PK-12
118 School Rd 71404 318-628-4613
Susan Horne, prin. Fax 628-4247

Avondale, Jefferson, Pop. 5,813
Jefferson Parish SD
Supt. — See Harvey
Ford MS 600/6-8
435 S Jamie Blvd 70094 504-436-2474
Faith Joseph, prin. Fax 436-0604

Baker, East Baton Rouge, Pop. 13,250
City of Baker SD 2,200/PK-12
PO Box 680 70704 225-774-5795
Estes Taplin, supt. Fax 774-5797
www.bakerschools.org
Bakerfield ES 300/2-3
2550 South St 70714 225-775-0550
Samantha Williams, prin. Fax 775-0822
Baker Heights ES 500/PK-1
3750 Harding St 70714 225-775-1496
Dave Carter, prin. Fax 774-4629
Baker MS 500/6-8
5903 Groom Rd 70714 225-775-9750
Charles Johnson, prin. Fax 775-9753
Park Ridge ES 300/4-5
5905 Groom Rd 70714 225-775-5924
Stephanie Simmons, prin. Fax 774-0154

East Baton Rouge Parish SD
Supt. — See Baton Rouge
White Hills ES 400/K-5
5300 Bentley Dr 70714 225-775-5891
Myra Varmall, prin. Fax 775-0557

Bethany Christian S 400/K-12
13855 Plank Rd 70714 225-774-0133
Carolyn DeSalvo, prin. Fax 774-0163
Central Private S 400/PK-12
12801 Centerra Ct 70714 225-261-3341
Ellen Frazier, prin. Fax 261-3490

Baldwin, Saint Mary, Pop. 2,603
St. Mary Parish SD
Supt. — See Centerville
Baldwin ES 100/PK-5
PO Box 60 70514 337-923-7594
Michael Payton, prin. Fax 923-4004
Boudreaux MS 300/6-8
PO Box 120 70514 337-924-7990
Naomi Harding, prin. Fax 924-7999
Hamilton ES 200/PK-5
PO Box 10 70514 337-923-7212
Leroy Willis, prin. Fax 923-7213

Ball, Rapides, Pop. 3,684
Rapides Parish SD
Supt. — See Alexandria
Ball ES 400/PK-6
89 Camp Livingston Rd 71405 318-640-5394
Shirley Ryder, prin. Fax 640-9396
Paradise ES 500/PK-6
5010 Monroe Hwy 71405 318-640-1033
Charles Howard, prin. Fax 641-1315
Tioga ES 500/PK-6
4310 Pardue Rd 71405 318-640-9494
Becky Pippen, prin. Fax 641-8752
Tioga JHS 600/7-8
1150 Tioga Rd 71405 318-640-9412
Jeff Powell, prin. Fax 640-0126

Basile, Evangeline, Pop. 2,382
Evangeline Parish SD
Supt. — See Ville Platte
Stewart ES 300/PK-4
1032 Belton St 70515 337-432-6412
Christine Bacon, prin. Fax 432-6791

Baskin, Franklin, Pop. 180
Franklin Parish SD
Supt. — See Winnsboro
Baskin S 400/PK-8
1926 Highway 857 71219 318-248-2381
James Shirley, prin. Fax 248-2187

Bastrop, Morehouse, Pop. 12,403
Morehouse Parish SD 4,900/PK-12
PO Box 872 71221 318-281-5784
Tom Thrower, supt. Fax 283-3456
www.mpsb.us/
Adams ES 300/PK-6
804 Kammell St 71220 318-281-5244
Marilyn Johnson, prin. Fax 281-7240
Beekman S 300/PK-8
15190 A M Baker Rd 71220 318-281-1743
Roy McCoy, prin. Fax 283-5100
Carver ES 200/4-6
1510 Elm St 71220 318-281-3832
Prince Ella Williams, prin. Fax 281-8386
Cherry Ridge ES 400/PK-6
6281 Cherry Ridge Rd 71220 318-281-2002
Glenda Eppinette, prin. Fax 283-8666
East Side ES 400/K-6
115 Mccreight St 71220 318-281-2634
Shelia Minor, prin. Fax 283-2746
Morehouse JHS 500/7-8
1001 W Madison Ave 71220 318-281-0776
Rene Fonte, prin. Fax 283-1846
Morehouse Magnet S 400/1-8
909 Larche Ln 71220 318-281-3126
Gwen Seay, prin. Fax 281-3181
Oak Hill ES 300/PK-3
630 Collinston Rd 71220 318-281-4495
Georgia White, prin. Fax 281-3138
Pine Grove ES 400/PK-6
7261 Pine Grove Loop Rd 71220 318-281-1289
Heath Murry, prin. Fax 281-5295
South Side ES 400/PK-6
500 S Vine St 71220 318-281-4488
Pat Thompson, prin. Fax 281-4483
Other Schools – See Mer Rouge

Prairie View Academy 300/K-12
9942 Edwin St 71220 318-281-7044
Edward Bain, prin. Fax 281-4113

Batchelor, Pointe Coupee
Pointe Coupee Parish SD
Supt. — See New Roads
Upper Pointe Coupee S 300/PK-8
4739 LA Highway 419 70715 225-492-2555
Marcia Pinsonat, prin. Fax 492-3138

Baton Rouge, East Baton Rouge, Pop. 222,064
Central Community SD 2,500/PK-12
PO Box 78094 70837 225-262-1919
Michael Faulk, supt. Fax 262-1989
www.centralcss.org
Central IS 200/4-5
10510 Joor Rd 70818 225-261-1390
Rhonda Taylor, prin. Fax 261-1080
Central MS 800/6-8
11526 Sullivan Rd 70818 225-261-2237
John Cashio, prin. Fax 261-9973
Tanglewood ES 100/2-3
9352 Rustling Oaks Dr 70818 225-261-3454
Sandy Davis, prin. Fax 261-3535
Other Schools – See Greenwell Springs

East Baton Rouge Parish SD 42,300/PK-12
PO Box 2950 70821 225-922-5400
Charlotte Placide, supt. Fax 922-5499
www.ebrschools.org/
Audubon ES 400/PK-5
10730 Goodwood Blvd 70815 225-272-2620
Susan Kornuta, prin. Fax 272-2581
Banks ES 300/PK-5
2401 72nd Ave 70807 225-357-3371
Lee Coleman, prin. Fax 356-2665
Baton Rouge Visual & Performing Arts ES 400/PK-5
2040 S Acadian Thruway 70808 225-344-0084
Mark Richterman, prin. Fax 343-6227
Belfair Montessori Magnet ES 400/PK-5
4451 Fairfields Ave 70802 225-356-6191
Lauretta Clark, prin. Fax 355-8418
Bernard Terrace ES 500/PK-5
241 Edison St 70806 225-343-5769
Deborah Daniels, prin. Fax 338-0534
Broadmoor ES 700/PK-5
9650 Goodwood Blvd 70815 225-925-0343
Lawrence Harris, prin. Fax 926-4689
Broadmoor MS 800/6-8
1225 Sharp Rd 70815 225-272-0540
Rebel Ellerbee, prin. Fax 272-0195
Brookstown ES 600/PK-5
4375 E Brookstown Dr 70805 225-355-0382
Toni Morgan, prin. Fax 359-9192
Brownfields ES 400/PK-5
11615 Ellen Dr 70811 225-775-3527
Sarah Raines, prin. Fax 774-5437
Buchanan ES 500/PK-5
1222 E Buchanan St 70802 225-343-4585
Josephine Batiste, prin. Fax 343-4673
Capitol ES K-5
4141 Gus Young Ave 70802 225-343-9364
Joni Rolle, prin. Fax 344-5861
Capitol MS 800/6-8
5100 Greenwell Springs Rd 70806 225-231-9292
Lamont Cole, prin. Fax 231-9291
Cedarcrest-Southmoor ES 600/PK-5
10187 Twin Cedars St 70816 225-293-9950
Nancy Hammatt, prin. Fax 293-5028
Claiborne ES 400/PK-5
4700 Denham St 70805 225-357-9712
Sandra Douglas, prin. Fax 357-7141
Crestworth ES 400/PK-5
11200 Avenue F 70807 225-778-1317
Brenda Wilkinson, prin. Fax 778-1114
Crestworth MS 500/7-8
10650 Avenue F 70807 225-775-6845
Angela Thomas, prin. Fax 775-0051
Crestworth Pre-Engineering Academy 800/6-8
2555 DeSoto Dr 70807 225-775-0776
Onetha Albert, prin. Fax 775-2104
Dalton ES 400/PK-5
3605 Ontario St 70805 225-355-2398
James Mullens, prin. Fax 357-1171
Delmont ES 500/PK-5
5300 Douglas Ave 70805 225-355-2106
Antoinette Bienemy, prin. Fax 359-6515
DuFrocq ES 300/PK-5
4501 Winbourne Ave 70805 225-343-6323
Mary Robvais, prin. Fax 346-8780
Forest Heights Academy of Excellence 400/PK-5
7447 Sumrall Dr 70812 225-355-5681
Myra Varmall, prin. Fax 357-0646
Glasgow MS 600/6-8
1676 Glasgow Ave 70808 225-925-2942
Nellwyn East, prin. Fax 928-3565
Glen Oaks Park ES 500/PK-5
5656 Lanier Dr 70812 225-356-4521
Cynthia Lange, prin. Fax 356-8821
Greenbrier ES 400/PK-5
12203 Canterbury Dr 70814 225-275-4260
Andrea Johnson, prin. Fax 275-6570
Greenville ES 500/PK-5
1645 N Foster Dr 70806 225-357-0139
Mona Collins, prin. Fax 356-6358
Highland ES 400/PK-5
280 Sunset Blvd 70808 225-766-1272
Kay Van Sickle, prin. Fax 769-0630
Howell Park ES 600/PK-5
6125 Winbourne Ave 70805 225-356-0104
Mary Lynn Langlois, prin. Fax 357-8134
Jefferson Terrace ES 600/PK-5
9902 Cal Rd 70809 225-293-3210
Ruth McNeiland, prin. Fax 291-6627
Kenilworth MS 600/6-8
7600 Boone Ave 70808 225-766-8111
Viola Jackson, prin. Fax 767-9061
LaBelle Aire ES 700/PK-5
12255 Tams Dr 70815 225-275-7480
Da'Anne Lipscomb, prin. Fax 272-6322
Lanier ES 400/PK-5
4705 Lanier Dr 70812 225-357-5953
Deborah Morrison, prin. Fax 358-1606
LaSalle ES 400/PK-5
8000 Lasalle Ave 70806 225-927-6130
Kim Mims, prin. Fax 923-1247
Magnolia Woods ES 500/PK-5
760 Maxine Dr 70808 225-769-6845
Donna Wallette, prin. Fax 769-3340
McKinley Magnet MS 600/6-8
1550 Eddie Robinson Sr Dr 70802 225-388-0089
Joyce Green-Graham, prin. Fax 387-1434
Melrose ES 400/PK-5
1348 Valcour Dr 70806 225-926-2353
Catherine Greenwood, prin. Fax 927-7808
Merrydale ES 500/PK-5
6700 Rio Dr 70812 225-355-0346
Stephanie Weaver, prin. Fax 355-6217
Park ES 400/PK-5
2700 Fuqua St 70802 225-344-2145
Marva Spears, prin. Fax 336-1616
Park Forest ES 500/PK-5
10717 Elain Dr 70814 225-272-0814
Mary Jane Clark, prin. Fax 275-3194

Park Forest MS 900/6-8
3760 Aletha Dr 70814 225-275-6650
Adam Smith, prin. Fax 275-3058
Parkview ES 500/PK-5
5660 Parkforest Dr 70816 225-753-5615
Norma Church, prin. Fax 751-6546
Polk ES 300/PK-5
408 E Polk St 70802 225-383-2611
Cheryl Matthews, prin. Fax 338-0471
Progress ES 400/PK-5
855 Progress Rd 70807 225-775-4986
Stephanie Tate, prin. Fax 774-2028
Riveroaks ES 500/PK-5
950 Fontainbleau Dr 70819 225-275-4600
Shilonda Shamlin, prin. Fax 272-2447
Ryan ES 400/PK-5
10337 Elmgrove Garden Dr 70807 225-775-2407
Darlene Brister, prin. Fax 778-2709
Scotlandville ES 200/PK-5
9147 Elmgrove Garden Dr 70807 225-774-2510
Monica Boudouin, prin. Fax 775-6441
Sharon Hills ES 400/PK-5
6450 Guynell Dr 70811 225-355-6522
Sandra Williams, prin. Fax 355-4428
Shenandoah ES 600/PK-5
16555 Appomattox Ave 70817 225-753-3560
Carolyn Sauer, prin. Fax 756-0521
Sherwood MS 500/6-8
1020 Marlbrook Dr 70815 225-272-3090
Phyllis Crawford, prin. Fax 273-9459
South Boulevard Foreign Lang Immersion S 200/PK-5
802 Mayflower St 70802 225-343-6630
Cheryl Miller, prin. Fax 344-4962
Southeast MS 800/6-8
15000 S Harrells Ferry Rd 70816 225-753-5930
Hollis Milton, prin. Fax 756-8601
Twin Oaks ES 500/PK-5
819 Trammell Dr 70815 225-275-6620
Christa Bordelon, prin. Fax 275-2828
University Terrace ES 500/PK-5
575 W Roosevelt St 70802 225-387-2328
Linda Daniel, prin. Fax 387-3324
Villa Del Ray ES 600/PK-5
9765 Cuyhanga Pkwy 70815 225-924-1606
Dawn Brewster, prin. Fax 926-6806
Wedgewood ES 600/PK-5
2330 Aspenwood Dr 70816 225-753-7301
Sheridan Harris, prin. Fax 756-8418
Westdale Hts Academic Magnet S 400/PK-5
2000 College Dr 70808 225-926-5421
Cheryl Singer, prin. Fax 926-9885
Westdale MS 900/6-8
5650 Claycut Rd 70806 225-924-1308
Sherry Brock, prin. Fax 926-9929
Westminster ES 400/PK-5
8935 Westminister Dr 70809 225-927-2930
Elizabeth Lay, prin. Fax 927-4009
Wildwood ES 500/PK-5
444 Halfway Tree Rd 70810 225-766-6002
Alyce Kelley, prin. Fax 769-6803
Winbourne ES 300/PK-5
4503 Winbourne Ave 70805 225-355-4446
Brenda Wilkinson, prin. Fax 355-6570
Woodlawn MS 800/6-8
14939 Tiger Bend Rd 70817 225-751-0436
Shelly Colvin, prin. Fax 753-0159
Other Schools – See Baker, Pride

Baton Rouge International S 200/PK-5
5015 Auto Plex Dr 70809 225-293-4338
Nathalie Guyon, prin. Fax 293-4307
Baton Rouge Lutheran S 200/PK-8
10925 Florida Blvd 70815 225-272-1288
Gordon Schamber, prin. Fax 272-8504
Berean SDA S 100/PK-9
5100 Osborne Ave 70805 225-355-4472
J. Julies, prin. Fax 355-4444
Brighton S 200/K-12
12108 Parkmeadow Ave 70816 225-291-2524
Gary Kinchen, prin.
Christian Life Academy 700/PK-12
2037 Quail Dr 70808 225-769-6760
Larry Perdue, prin. Fax 769-8068
Comite Christian Academy 100/K-8
12250 Greenwell Springs Rd 70814 225-273-2699
Paul Miceli, prin. Fax 275-6802
Dunham S 700/PK-12
11111 Roy Emerson Dr 70810 225-767-7097
Dr. Bobby Welch, hdmstr. Fax 767-7056
Elan Vitale Montessori S 50/PK-6
5228 Perkins Rd 70808 225-767-6620
Connie Guiberson, hdmstr. Fax 769-8122
Episcopal S of Baton Rouge 1,000/PK-12
3200 Woodland Ridge Blvd 70816 225-753-3180
Kay Betts, hdmstr. Fax 756-0926
Family Christian Academy 200/K-12
PO Box 262550 70826 225-768-3026
Dave Smith, admin. Fax 768-3213
Hosanna Christian Academy 500/PK-12
8850 Goodwood Blvd 70806 225-926-4885
Dr. James Bentley, admin. Fax 926-8458
Jehovah-Jireh Christian Academy 200/PK-12
1771 N Lobdell Ave 70806 225-932-2357
Glenda Colbert, prin. Fax 932-2360
Jones Creek Adventist Academy 50/PK-8
4363 Jones Creek Rd 70817 225-751-8219
Norman Rangel, prin. Fax 751-3404
King Christian Academy 200/K-8
4295 Prescott Ct 70805 225-356-7407
Lola Miller, prin. Fax 356-7407
Most Blessed Sacrament S 500/K-8
8033 Baringer Rd 70817 225-751-0273
Maria Cloessner, prin. Fax 753-7259
Our Lady of Mercy Catholic S 800/PK-8
400 Marquette Ave 70806 225-924-1054
Tina Villa, prin. Fax 923-2201

Parkview Baptist S 1,400/K-12
5750 Parkview Church Rd 70816 225-291-2500
Dr. Melanie Ezell, supt. Fax 293-4135
Paul's Christian Academy 100/PK-5
4006 Platt Dr 70814 225-924-1914
Debbie Ruckman, prin. Fax 924-5035
Riverdale Christian Academy 200/PK-12
2791 Oneal Ln 70816 225-753-6722
Todd Whirley, prin. Fax 751-4341
Runnels S 800/PK-12
17255 S Harrells Ferry Rd 70816 225-751-5712
Dr. L. K. Runnels, prin. Fax 753-0276
Sacred Heart of Jesus S 500/PK-8
2251 Main St 70802 225-383-7481
Br. Augustine Kozdroj, prin. Fax 383-1810
St. Aloysius S 1,100/PK-8
2025 Stuart Ave 70808 225-383-3871
John Bennett, prin. Fax 383-4500
St. Francis Xavier S 300/PK-8
1150 S 12th St 70802 225-387-6639
Sr. Joseph Charles, prin. Fax 383-1215
St. George S 1,100/K-8
7880 Saint George Dr 70809 225-293-1298
Lizette Leader, prin. Fax 293-4886
St. Gerard Majella S 200/PK-6
3655 Saint Gerard Ave 70805 225-355-1437
Joan Hutson, prin. Fax 355-1879
St. Isidore S 200/PK-6
5667 Thomas Rd 70811 225-775-3336
Linda March, prin. Fax 775-3351
St. James Episcopal Day S 300/PK-5
PO Box 3011 70821 225-344-0805
Linda Chauviere, hdmstr. Fax 343-4873
St. Jean Vianney S 500/K-8
16266 S Harrells Ferry Rd 70816 225-751-1831
Wendy Gilmore, prin. Fax 752-8774
St. Jude the Apostle S 600/PK-8
9150 Highland Rd 70810 225-769-2344
Karen Jakuback, prin. Fax 769-0671
St. Louis King of France S 300/PK-8
2311 N Sherwood Forest Dr 70815 225-273-3932
Mary Polito, prin. Fax 273-3978
St. Lukes Episcopal Day S 300/PK-8
8833 Goodwood Blvd 70806 225-927-8601
Amy Whitley, prin. Fax 928-2542
St. Thomas More S 1,000/K-8
11400 Sherbrook Dr 70815 225-275-2820
Dr. Judy Armstrong, prin. Fax 275-0376
Trinity Episcopal Day S 100/PK-5
3550 Morning Glory Ave 70808 225-387-0398
Kathy Davison, hdmstr. Fax 387-3145
Victory Academy 400/PK-8
3953 N Flannery Rd 70814 225-272-8339
Janet Cashio, prin. Fax 272-0674

Belcher, Caddo, Pop. 270
Caddo Parish SD
Supt. — See Shreveport
Herndon Magnet S 800/PK-8
11845 Gamm Rd 71004 318-221-7676
Brenda McDonald, prin. Fax 296-4554

Bell City, Calcasieu
Calcasieu Parish SD
Supt. — See Lake Charles
Bell City S 500/K-12
PO Box 100 70630 337-622-3210
Reinette Guillory, prin. Fax 622-3595

Belle Chasse, Plaquemines, Pop. 8,512
Plaquemines Parish SD 3,600/PK-12
1484 Woodland Hwy 70037 504-595-6400
Denis Rousselle, supt. Fax 398-9990
www.ppsb.org/
Belle Chasse MS 700/5-8
13476 Highway 23 70037 504-595-6640
Joe Williamson, prin. Fax 656-2399
Belle Chasse PS 1,100/PK-4
539 F Edward Hebert Blvd 70037 504-595-6620
Shelly Ritz, prin. Fax 393-8068
Other Schools – See Boothville, Braithwaite, Port Sulphur

Our Lady of Perpetual Help S 300/PK-8
8970 Highway 23 70037 504-394-0757
Sr. Elizabeth Hebert, prin. Fax 394-1627

Belle Rose, Assumption
Assumption Parish SD
Supt. — See Napoleonville
Belle Rose MS 200/5-8
PO Box 229 70341 225-473-8917
Stacy Garrison, prin. Fax 473-8429
Belle Rose PS 300/PK-4
PO Box 9 70341 225-473-7706
Damian Buggage, prin. Fax 473-8868

Benton, Bossier, Pop. 2,886
Bossier Parish SD 19,100/PK-12
PO Box 2000 71006 318-549-5000
Kenneth Kruithof, supt. Fax 549-5004
www.bossierschools.org
Benton ES 800/K-5
562 Highway 162 71006 318-549-5170
Norma Anderson, prin. Fax 549-5183
Benton MS 500/6-8
6140 Highway 3 71006 318-549-5310
Dwayne Slack, prin. Fax 549-5323
Other Schools – See Bossier City, Elm Grove, Haughton, Plain Dealing, Princeton

Bernice, Union, Pop. 1,727
Union Parish SD
Supt. — See Farmerville
Bernice S 400/K-12
PO Box 570 71222 318-285-7606
Alice Bolton, prin. Fax 285-5006

Berwick, Saint Mary, Pop. 4,286
St. Mary Parish SD
Supt. — See Centerville
Berwick ES 500/K-5
400 Texas St 70342 985-384-8355
Steve Russo, prin. Fax 384-5427
Berwick JHS 400/6-8
3955 Highway 182 70342 985-384-5664
Thomas D. Bourgeois, prin. Fax 384-5663

Bienville, Bienville, Pop. 254
Bienville Parish SD
Supt. — See Arcadia
Bienville S 100/K-12
PO Box 212 71008 318-385-7591
Billy Rogers, prin. Fax 385-7750

Bogalusa, Washington, Pop. 12,964
Bogalusa City SD 2,300/PK-12
1705 Sullivan Dr 70427 985-281-2100
Ruth Horne, supt. Fax 735-1358
www.bogalusaschools.org/
Bogalusa MS 500/5-8
1403 North Ave 70427 985-281-2230
Don McDaniel, prin. Fax 735-6430
Byrd Avenue ES 300/K-4
1600 Byrd Ave 70427 985-281-2188
Tonja Varnado, prin. Fax 735-6258
Denhamtown S 100/PK-PK
1101 Avenue M 70427 985-281-2193
Barbara Greely, prin. Fax 735-0093
Northside Tech MS 200/5-8
517 Mississippi Ave 70427 985-281-2202
April Nobles, prin. Fax 732-3502
Pleasant Hill ES 200/K-4
725 Avenue C 70427 985-281-2208
Shelia Lawrence, prin. Fax 281-2181
Superior Avenue ES 300/K-4
625 Superior Ave 70427 985-281-2169
Melessa Walker, prin. Fax 732-4860

Annunciation S 200/PK-8
511 Avenue C 70427 985-735-6643
Sybil Skansi, prin. Fax 735-6119
Ben's Ford Christian School 300/PK-12
59253 Mount Pleasant Rd 70427 985-735-0387
Debbie Penton, prin. Fax 735-0382

Boothville, Plaquemines, Pop. 2,743
Plaquemines Parish SD
Supt. — See Belle Chasse
Boothville-Venice ES 200/PK-6
1 Oiler Dr 70038 504-595-6455
Maria Prout, prin. Fax 534-1799

Bossier City, Bossier, Pop. 60,505
Bossier Parish SD
Supt. — See Benton
Apollo ES 1,000/K-5
2400 Viking Dr 71111 318-549-6010
Julie Dupree, prin. Fax 549-6023
Bellaire ES 400/K-3
1310 Bellaire Blvd 71112 318-549-6300
Brenda Weaver, prin. Fax 549-6313
Bossier ES 300/PK-5
322 Traffic St 71111 318-549-6350
Cathleen Johnson, prin. Fax 549-6363
Central Park ES 400/PK-5
900 Central Park Dr 71112 318-549-6400
Pat Branton, prin. Fax 549-6413
Cope MS 600/6-8
4814 Shed Rd 71111 318-549-5380
Judy Grooms, prin. Fax 549-5393
Curtis ES 500/4-5
5600 Barksdale Blvd 71112 318-549-6450
Sherri Pool, prin. Fax 549-6463
Greenacres MS 700/6-8
2220 Airline Dr 71111 318-549-6210
Kathy Bouck, prin. Fax 549-6223
Kerr ES 600/K-5
1700 Airline Dr 71112 318-549-6560
Janet Doughty, prin. Fax 549-6573
Legacy ES K-5
4830 Swan Lake Rd 71111 318-759-2000
Pam Williamson, prin. Fax 759-2003
Lewis ES K-5
4701 Modica Lott Rd 71111 318-759-2100
Janiene Batchelor, prin. Fax 759-2103
Meadowview ES 600/PK-5
4312 Shed Rd 71111 318-549-5640
Dr. Shelly Barrett, prin. Fax 549-5653
Plantation Park ES 600/PK-5
2410 Plantation Dr 71111 318-549-5700
Carolyn Moody, prin. Fax 549-5713
Rusheon MS 700/6-8
2401 Old Minden Rd 71112 318-549-6610
Harriet Johnson, prin. Fax 549-6623
Stockwell Place ES 800/K-5
5801 Shed Rd 71111 318-549-5820
Tim Thompson, prin. Fax 549-5833
Sun City ES 600/K-3
4230 Van Deeman St 71112 318-549-7000
Curtis Melancon, prin. Fax 549-7011
Waller ES 600/PK-5
1130 Patricia Dr 71112 318-549-6850
Jan Hollis, prin. Fax 549-6863

Bourg, Terrebonne
Terrebonne Parish SD
Supt. — See Houma
Bourg ES 400/PK-4
4413 St Andrew St 70343 985-594-3663
Mac Sevin, prin. Fax 594-9665

Boutte, Saint Charles, Pop. 2,702

Boutte Christian Academy 400/PK-8
13271 Highway 90 70039 985-785-2447
Linda Davis, admin. Fax 785-6641

Braithwaite, Plaquemines
Plaquemines Parish SD
Supt. — See Belle Chasse
Phoenix S 200/PK-12
13073 Highway 15 70040 504-595-6480
John Barthelemy, prin. Fax 333-7073

Lynn Oaks S 100/PK-8
1 Lynn Oaks Dr 70040 504-682-3171
Troy Dean, prin. Fax 682-3173

Branch, Acadia
Acadia Parish SD
Supt. — See Crowley
Branch S 200/PK-8
PO Box 450 70516 337-334-5708
Keith Cahanin, prin. Fax 334-7352

Breaux Bridge, Saint Martin, Pop. 7,902
St. Martin Parish SD
Supt. — See Saint Martinville
Breaux Bridge ES 500/4-6
702 W Bridge St 70517 337-332-1270
Katrina Williams, prin. Fax 332-1274
Breaux Bridge JHS 300/7-8
100 Martin St 70517 337-332-2844
Denise Frederick, prin. Fax 332-4831
Breaux Bridge PS 800/PK-3
1020 E Bridge St 70517 337-332-1821
Pennye Huval, prin. Fax 332-2547
Teche ES 600/4-6
2439 Main Hwy 70517 337-667-6400
Pattie Guidry, prin. Fax 667-7428

St. Bernard S 500/PK-8
251 E Bridge St 70517 337-332-5350
Robin Couvillon, prin. Fax 332-5894

Bridge City, Jefferson, Pop. 8,327
Jefferson Parish SD
Supt. — See Harvey
Bridge City ES 400/PK-5
1805 Bridge City Ave 70094 504-436-4626
Simone Duhon, prin. Fax 436-6046

Broussard, Lafayette, Pop. 6,754
Lafayette Parish SD
Supt. — See Lafayette
Broussard MS 600/5-8
1325 S Morgan Ave 70518 337-837-9031
Keisha Hawkins, prin. Fax 837-1057
Drexel ES 700/PK-4
409 Saint Deporres St 70518 337-837-9066
Sueline Wiltz, prin. Fax 837-1620

Episcopal S of Acadiana 500/PK-12
1557 Smede Hwy 70518 337-365-1416
Chris Taylor, hdmstr. Fax 367-9841
St. Cecilia S 500/PK-8
302 W Main St 70518 337-837-6363
George Fontenot, prin. Fax 837-3688

Brusly, West Baton Rouge, Pop. 2,028
West Baton Rouge Parish SD
Supt. — See Port Allen
Brusly ES 400/K-2
400 S Labauve Rd 70719 225-749-2125
Hope Supple, prin. Fax 749-0510
Brusly MS 400/6-8
601 N Kirkland St 70719 225-749-3123
Callie Kershaw, prin. Fax 749-8570
Lukeville Upper ES 400/3-5
6123 LA Highway 1 S 70719 225-749-8386
Nakeithia Thomas, prin. Fax 749-9240

Bunkie, Avoyelles, Pop. 4,502
Avoyelles Parish SD
Supt. — See Marksville
Bunkie ES 500/PK-6
311 Pershing Ave 71322 318-346-7292
Fax 346-6164

St. Anthony S 300/PK-8
116 S Knoll Ave 71322 318-346-2739
Martha Coulon, prin. Fax 346-9191

Bush, Saint Tammany
St. Tammany Parish SD
Supt. — See Covington
Fifth Ward S 500/K-8
81419 Highway 21 70431 985-886-3273
James Smith, prin. Fax 886-2228

Calhoun, Ouachita
Ouachita Parish SD
Supt. — See Monroe
Calhoun ES 500/PK-2
237 Calhoun School Rd 71225 318-644-1114
Shirley Buford, prin. Fax 644-7146
Calhoun MS 500/6-8
191 Highway 80 E 71225 318-644-5840
Werner Aswell, prin. Fax 644-5418
Central ES 400/3-5
1163 Highway 151 S 71225 318-644-5842
Carmen Banks, prin. Fax 644-5756

Calvin, Winn, Pop. 226
Winn Parish SD
Supt. — See Winnfield
Calvin S 300/PK-12
PO Box 80 71410 318-727-8784
Rodney Shelton, prin. Fax 727-9224

Cameron, Cameron, Pop. 2,041
Cameron Parish SD
Supt. — See Lake Charles
Johnson Bayou S 100/PK-12
6304 Gulf Beach Hwy 70631 337-569-2138
Gene Reynolds, prin. Fax 569-2673

Campti, Natchitoches, Pop. 1,054
Natchitoches Parish SD
Supt. — See Natchitoches

Fairview-Alpha S 700/PK-8
1439 Highway 71 71411 318-476-4616
Mona Bamburg, prin. Fax 476-4558

Carencro, Lafayette, Pop. 6,097
Lafayette Parish SD
Supt. — See Lafayette
Carencro Heights ES 400/PK-5
601 Teema Rd 70520 337-896-6171
Kathleen Anderson, prin. Fax 896-7541
Carencro MS 700/6-8
4301 N University Ave 70520 337-896-6127
Matthew Harman, prin. Fax 896-7620

Carencro Catholic S 500/PK-8
200 W Saint Peter St 70520 337-896-8973
Blaine Castille, prin. Fax 896-1931

Castor, Bienville, Pop. 212
Bienville Parish SD
Supt. — See Arcadia
Castor S 400/PK-12
PO Box 69 71016 318-544-7271
James Guin, prin. Fax 544-9077

Cecilia, Saint Martin, Pop. 1,374
St. Martin Parish SD
Supt. — See Saint Martinville
Cecilia JHS 400/7-8
PO Box 129 70521 337-667-6226
Dianetta Young, prin. Fax 667-7352
Cecilia PS 900/PK-3
PO Box 97 70521 337-667-6700
Wanda Guidry, prin. Fax 667-7756

Centerville, Saint Mary
St. Mary Parish SD 9,800/PK-12
PO Box 170 70522 337-836-9661
Dr. Donald Aguillard, supt. Fax 836-5461
www.stmary.k12.la.us
Centerville S 600/PK-12
PO Box 59 70522 337-836-5103
Mike Galler, prin. Fax 836-9594
Other Schools – See Amelia, Baldwin, Berwick, Charenton, Franklin, Morgan City, Patterson

Chalmette, Saint Bernard, Pop. 32,100
St. Bernard Parish SD 4,400/PK-12
200 E Saint Bernard Hwy 70043 504-301-2000
Doris Voitier, supt. Fax 301-2010
www.stbernard.k12.la.us
Jackson ES 1,800/PK-5
201 8th St 70043 504-301-1500
Susan Landry, prin. Fax 301-1510
Other Schools – See Meraux, Saint Bernard, Violet

Our Lady of Prompt Succor S 400/PK-8
2305 Fenelon St 70043 504-271-2953
Sharon Coll, prin. Fax 271-1490

Charenton, Saint Mary, Pop. 1,584
St. Mary Parish SD
Supt. — See Centerville
Hines ES 200/PK-5
PO Box 370 70523 337-923-7261
Barbara Lancelin, prin. Fax 923-7228

Chataignier, Evangeline, Pop. 379
Evangeline Parish SD
Supt. — See Ville Platte
Chataignier S 400/PK-8
PO Box 189 70524 337-885-3173
Peggy Edwards, prin. Fax 885-2236

Chauvin, Terrebonne, Pop. 3,375
Terrebonne Parish SD
Supt. — See Houma
Boudreaux Canal ES 100/PK-4
208 Doctor Hugh St Martin 70344 985-594-2570
Monica Breaux, prin. Fax 594-9958
Lacache MS 500/5-8
5266 Highway 56 70344 985-594-3945
Anita Landry, prin. Fax 594-4128
Upper Little Caillou ES 400/PK-4
4824 Highway 56 70344 985-594-4071
Riley Vordick, prin. Fax 594-7504

Choudrant, Lincoln, Pop. 580
Lincoln Parish SD
Supt. — See Ruston
Choudrant ES 400/K-6
PO Box 427 71227 318-768-4106
Charles Hogan, prin. Fax 768-2679

Church Point, Acadia, Pop. 4,682
Acadia Parish SD
Supt. — See Crowley
Church Point ES 600/PK-5
415 E Lougarre St 70525 337-684-5722
Joe Jacobi, prin. Fax 684-3587
Church Point MS 200/6-8
340 W Martin Luther King Dr 70525 337-684-6381
Paul Derousselle, prin. Fax 684-0123
Richard S 300/PK-8
1616 Charlene Hwy 70525 337-684-3339
John LeJeune, prin. Fax 684-6892

Our Mother of Peace S 300/PK-8
218 N Rogers St 70525 337-684-5780
Don Courville, prin. Fax 684-5780

Clarks, Caldwell, Pop. 1,060

Old Bethel Christian Academy 50/1-7
PO Box 95 71415 318-649-0281
Sandra Richmond, prin. Fax 649-0281

Clinton, East Feliciana, Pop. 1,922
East Feliciana Parish SD 2,300/PK-12
PO Box 397 70722 225-683-8277
Douglas Beauchamp, supt. Fax 683-9319
www.efpsb.k12.la.us
Clinton ES 500/PK-5
PO Box 366 70722 225-683-8293
Andrea Jefferson, prin. Fax 683-6197
Clinton MS 300/6-8
12126 Liberty St 70722 225-683-5267
Delsia Marshall, prin. Fax 683-9592
Other Schools – See Jackson, Slaughter

Silliman Institute 500/PK-12
PO Box 946 70722 225-683-5383
Sam Barham, hdmstr. Fax 683-6728

Cloutierville, Natchitoches
Natchitoches Parish SD
Supt. — See Natchitoches
Cloutierville S 400/PK-8
PO Box 100 71416 318-379-2577
Kerry Braden, prin. Fax 379-1117

Colfax, Grant, Pop. 1,676
Grant Parish SD 3,500/PK-12
PO Box 208 71417 318-627-3274
Sheila Jackson, supt. Fax 627-5931
www.gpsb.org
Colfax ES 400/PK-6
250 3rd St 71417 318-627-3254
Stacy Felton, prin. Fax 627-3245
Other Schools – See Dry Prong, Georgetown, Montgomery, Pollock

Columbia, Caldwell, Pop. 467
Caldwell Parish SD 1,700/PK-12
PO Box 1019 71418 318-649-2689
John Sartin, supt. Fax 649-0636
www.caldwelledu.org/
Caldwell Parish JHS 300/7-8
114 Trojan Dr 71418 318-649-2340
Blaine Dauzat, prin. Fax 649-2341
Caldwell Parish PreSchool PK-PK
182 Spartan Dr 71418 318-649-6139
Monica Coates, prin. Fax 649-0508
Columbia ES 300/K-6
PO Box 1679 71418 318-649-2654
Jeff Farrar, prin. Fax 649-7589
Union Central ES 200/K-6
PO Box 1439 71418 318-649-2569
Nicki McCann, prin. Fax 649-2522
Other Schools – See Grayson, Kelly

Convent, Saint James
St. James Parish SD
Supt. — See Lutcher
Romeville ES 200/PK-6
9156 Central School St 70723 225-562-3684
Becky Louque, prin. Fax 562-7723

Converse, Sabine, Pop. 407
Sabine Parish SD
Supt. — See Many
Converse S 500/K-12
PO Box 10 71419 318-567-2673
Cade Brumley, prin. Fax 567-3400

Cottonport, Avoyelles, Pop. 2,266
Avoyelles Parish SD
Supt. — See Marksville
Cottonport ES 500/PK-6
950 Lemoine St 71327 318-876-3404
Celeste Voinche, prin. Fax 876-3762

St. Mary's Assumption S 200/PK-8
PO Box 309 71327 318-876-3651
Gale Jeansonne, prin. Fax 876-2955

Cotton Valley, Webster, Pop. 1,169
Webster Parish SD
Supt. — See Minden
Cotton Valley S 300/PK-12
PO Box 457 71018 318-832-4716
Beatha Brantley, prin. Fax 832-5273

Coushatta, Red River, Pop. 2,205
Red River Parish SD 1,500/PK-12
PO Box 1369 71019 318-932-4081
Kay Easley, supt. Fax 932-4367
www.rrbulldogs.com/
Red River ES 800/PK-5
1001 Ashland Rd 71019 318-932-9290
Jamie Lawrence, prin. Fax 932-9289
Red River JHS 300/6-8
931 E Carrol St 71019 318-932-5265
Jacqueline Daniels, prin. Fax 932-9052

Riverdale Academy 300/PK-12
100 Riverdale Rd 71019 318-932-5876
Susan Taylor, prin. Fax 932-4355

Covington, Saint Tammany, Pop. 9,347
St. Tammany Parish SD 34,000/PK-12
PO Box 940 70434 985-892-2276
Gayle Sloan, supt. Fax 898-3267
www.stpsb.org
Covington ES 400/K-3
325 S Jackson St 70433 985-892-4311
Martha Romo, prin. Fax 871-1480
Lee Road S 700/K-8
79131 Highway 40 70435 985-892-3636
Anna Bowie, prin. Fax 892-3169
Lyon ES 500/K-3
1615 N Florida St 70433 985-892-0869
Jeanine Barnes, prin. Fax 892-7971
Pine View MS 600/4-6
1200 W 27th Ave 70433 985-892-6204
Janis Daviston, prin. Fax 893-3736
Pitcher JHS 300/7-8
415 S Jefferson Ave 70433 985-892-3021
Roslyn Hanson, prin. Fax 892-1188
Other Schools – See Abita Springs, Bush, Folsom, Lacombe, Madisonville, Mandeville, Pearl River, Slidell

---

Christ Episcopal S 100/PK-K
120 S New Hampshire St 70433 985-892-9156
Greg Homer, dir. Fax 871-1626
Christ Episcopal S 400/1-8
80 Christwood Blvd 70433 985-871-9902
Greg Homer, hdmstr. Fax 871-9912
Holy Trinity Lutheran S PK-3
1 N Marigold Dr 70433 985-892-6146
Mimi McKinney, prin. Fax 892-3012
Kehoe-France Northshore S 400/PK-7
25 Patricia Dr 70433 985-892-4415
Mitch Bilbe, prin. Fax 875-7636
Northlake Christian S 900/PK-12
70104 Wolverine Dr 70433 985-635-0400
Dr. Joe Shorter, hdmstr. Fax 893-4363
St. Peter S 700/PK-8
130 E Temperance St 70433 985-892-1831
Lana O'Dwyer, prin. Fax 898-2185

Crowley, Acadia, Pop. 13,861
Acadia Parish SD 9,500/PK-12
PO Box 309 70527 337-783-3664
John Bourque, supt. Fax 783-3761
www.acadia.k12.la.us/
Crowley K 300/PK-K
1119 N Parkerson Ave 70526 337-783-4670
Ida Yeager, prin. Fax 783-4696
Crowley MS 600/6-8
401 W Northern Ave 70526 337-783-5305
Chad Lemelle, prin. Fax 783-5338
North Crowley ES 400/1-5
820 W 15th St 70526 337-783-8755
Pamela Dequeant, prin. Fax 783-5135
Ross ES 400/1-5
1809 W Hutchinson Ave 70526 337-783-0927
T.J. Sonnier, prin. Fax 783-6349
South Crowley ES 400/1-5
1102 S Parkerson Ave 70526 337-783-1300
Robert Gates, prin. Fax 783-8025
Other Schools – See Branch, Church Point, Egan, Estherwood, Evangeline, Iota, Mermentau, Morse, Rayne

---

Northside Christian S 300/K-12
809 E Northern Ave 70526 337-783-3620
Rev. Randy Trahan, prin. Fax 788-3461
Redemptorist S 200/PK-8
606 S Avenue N 70526 337-783-4466
Carl LeJeune, prin. Fax 788-0961
St. Michael S 400/PK-8
805 E Northern Ave 70526 337-783-1410
Myra Broussard, prin. Fax 783-8547

Crowville, Franklin
Franklin Parish SD
Supt. — See Winnsboro
Crowville S 600/PK-8
PO Box 128 71230 318-435-4749
Terri Shirley, prin. Fax 435-4701

Cut Off, Lafourche, Pop. 5,325
Lafourche Parish SD
Supt. — See Thibodaux
Cut Off ES 500/PK-5
177 W 55th St 70345 985-632-3116
Deborah Griffin, prin. Fax 632-3219
Larose-Cut Off MS 600/6-8
13356 W Main St, 985-693-3273
Matthew Hodson, prin. Fax 693-3270

Delcambre, Vermilion, Pop. 2,146
Iberia Parish SD
Supt. — See New Iberia
Delcambre ES 500/PK-5
706 Mrtin Luther King Jr Dr 70528 337-685-2376
Danelle Renard, prin. Fax 685-4811

Delhi, Richland, Pop. 3,055
Richland Parish SD
Supt. — See Rayville
Delhi ES 300/PK-4
509 Main St 71232 318-878-2269
Shelly Crawford, prin. Fax 878-0222
Delhi MS 200/5-8
106 Toombs St 71232 318-878-3748
Shirley McDade, prin. Fax 878-3749

Denham Springs, Livingston, Pop. 10,206
Livingston Parish SD
Supt. — See Livingston
Denham Springs ES 500/K-5
306 N Range Ave 70726 225-665-5855
Ronald Kropog, prin. Fax 664-8672
Denham Springs JHS 900/6-8
401 Hatchell Ln 70726 225-665-8898
Jennifer Barclay, prin. Fax 665-8601
Eastside ES 500/PK-5
9735 Lockhart Rd 70726 225-791-8581
Cindy Riddle, prin. Fax 791-8582
Freshwater ES 500/K-5
1025 Cockerham Rd 70726 225-665-5371
Madeline Miller, prin. Fax 664-6577
Gray's Creek ES 600/PK-5
11400 LA Highway 1033 70726 225-667-1808
Jim Richardson, prin. Fax 667-3597
North Live Oak ES 800/PK-5
36605 Outback Rd 70706 225-667-3135
Michelle Stone, prin. Fax 667-1994
Northside ES 500/PK-5
1090 Robbie St 70726 225-664-4223
Sharon Anderson, prin. Fax 664-5660
Seventh Ward ES 500/PK-5
24495 LA Highway 16 70726 225-665-5815
Belinda Watson, prin. Fax 665-7280

Southside ES 400/PK-5
1129 S Range Ave 70726 225-665-5500
Linda Painter, prin. Fax 667-3171
Southside JHS 900/6-8
26535 LA Highway 16 70726 225-664-4221
Myra Holmes, prin. Fax 664-3307
Vincent ES 600/PK-5
7686 Vincent Rd 70726 225-665-8198
Carol Robertson, prin. Fax 665-9713

Community Christian Academy 100/PK-12
400 N River Rd 70726 225-665-5696
Joyce Wilson, prin. Fax 665-3098

Dequincy, Calcasieu, Pop. 3,310
Calcasieu Parish SD
Supt. — See Lake Charles
DeQuincy ES 700/PK-5
304 McNeese St 70633 337-786-7251
Claude LeCompte, prin. Fax 786-5995
DeQuincy MS 300/6-8
1603 W 4th St 70633 337-786-3000
Billy Kellogg, prin. Fax 786-5778

Deridder, Beauregard, Pop. 11,103
Beauregard Parish SD 5,800/PK-12
PO Box 938 70634 337-463-5551
Rita Mann, supt. Fax 463-6735
www.beau.k12.la.us/
Carver ES 400/2-3
220 Martin Luther King Dr 70634 337-463-7380
Ellis Spikes, prin. Fax 463-2119
DeRidder JHS 600/6-8
415 N Frusha Dr 70634 337-463-9083
Kim Hayes, prin. Fax 463-7696
East Beauregard ES 400/K-5
5368 Highway 113 70634 337-328-8551
Lynne Boggs, prin. Fax 328-8803
Hanchey ES 500/PK-1
611 N Frusha Dr 70634 337-463-4479
Elizabeth Maricle, prin. Fax 463-4482
Pine Wood ES 400/4-5
800 Mel Branch Mem Dr 70634 337-463-8810
Stan Lery, prin. Fax 463-2515
Other Schools – See Longville, Merryville, Singer

Des Allemands, Saint Charles, Pop. 2,504
St. Charles Parish SD
Supt. — See Luling
Allemands ES 300/PK-2
1471 WPA Rd 70030 985-758-7427
Marsha Walters, prin. Fax 758-2221

Destrehan, Saint Charles, Pop. 8,031
St. Charles Parish SD
Supt. — See Luling
Hurst MS 500/7-8
170 Rd Runner Ln 70047 985-764-6367
Margaret Herzog-Flair, prin. Fax 764-2678
New Sarpy ES 500/PK-3
130 Plantation Rd 70047 985-764-1275
Karen Tweedy, prin. Fax 764-6942
Schoeffner ES 400/4-6
140 Plantation Rd 70047 985-725-0123
Mary Schmidt, prin. Fax 725-0131

St. Charles Borromeo S 500/PK-8
13396 River Rd Bldg 3 70047 985-764-9232
Donalyn Hassenboehler Ph.D., prin. Fax 764-3726

Deville, Rapides, Pop. 1,113
Rapides Parish SD
Supt. — See Alexandria
Buckeye ES 500/PK-2
PO Box 529 71328 318-466-3233
Susan Bates, prin. Fax 466-3288
Lawrence MS 300/3-5
PO Box 509 71328 318-466-5858
Dwayne Floyd, prin. Fax 466-9204

Dodson, Winn, Pop. 341
Winn Parish SD
Supt. — See Winnfield
Dodson S 400/PK-12
PO Box 97 71422 318-628-2172
Crystal Stewart, prin. Fax 628-7515

Donaldsonville, Ascension, Pop. 7,535
Ascension Parish SD 17,900/PK-12
PO Box 189 70346 225-473-7981
Donald Songy, supt. Fax 473-8058
www.apsb.org
Donaldsonville PS 600/PK-2
38210 Highway 3089 70346 225-474-2720
Marydine Emery, prin. Fax 474-6920
Lowery ES 300/3-4
2389 Highway 1 S Ste B 70346 225-621-2470
Sheila Savoy, prin.
Lowery IS 300/5-6
2389 Highway 1 S Ste A 70346 225-473-2534
Monica Hills, prin. Fax 473-2514
Other Schools – See Geismar, Gonzales, Prairieville, Saint Amant

---

Ascension Catholic S 400/PK-8
618 Iberville St 70346 225-473-8540
Janice Burns, prin. Fax 473-8559

Downsville, Union, Pop. 114
Union Parish SD
Supt. — See Farmerville
Downsville S 400/K-12
PO Box 8 71234 318-982-5318
Curtis Williams, prin. Fax 982-5737

Doyline, Webster, Pop. 831
Webster Parish SD
Supt. — See Minden
Union ES 300/PK-5
PO Box 627 71023 318-745-2613
Yolanda Palmer, prin. Fax 745-2459

Dry Prong, Grant, Pop. 437
Grant Parish SD
Supt. — See Colfax
Dry Prong JHS 400/7-8
800 Grove St 71423 318-899-5697
Robert Smith, prin. Fax 899-7364
South Grant ES 500/K-6
1000 Highway 1241 71423 318-641-1882
Shana Delrie, prin. Fax 641-1899

Dubach, Lincoln, Pop. 776
Lincoln Parish SD
Supt. — See Ruston
Hico ES 200/PK-5
2253 Highway 545 71235 318-777-3447
Vicki Key, prin. Fax 777-3433

Dubberly, Webster, Pop. 286
Webster Parish SD
Supt. — See Minden
Central ES 600/PK-6
5701 Highway 531 71024 318-377-2591
Marvin Jones, prin. Fax 377-2592

Dulac, Terrebonne, Pop. 3,273
Terrebonne Parish SD
Supt. — See Houma
Grand Caillou ES 400/PK-3
6741 Grand Caillou Rd 70353 985-563-4488
Lois Carter, prin. Fax 563-7838

Duson, Lafayette, Pop. 1,619
Lafayette Parish SD
Supt. — See Lafayette
Burke ES 700/K-5
2845 Ridge Rd 70529 337-873-4669
Loretta Williams-Durand, prin. Fax 873-2432
Duson ES 300/K-5
PO Box 7 70529 337-873-6629
Katherine Rayburn, prin. Fax 873-8168
Judice MS 600/6-8
2645 S Fieldspan Rd 70529 337-984-1250
Samuel Clay, prin. Fax 988-3693
Ridge ES 600/K-5
2901 S Fieldspan Rd 70529 337-981-9144
Cathy Fulcher, prin. Fax 984-0156

Edgard, Saint John the Baptist, Pop. 2,753
St. John The Baptist Parish SD
Supt. — See Reserve
West St. John ES 400/PK-7
PO Box 130 70049 985-497-3347
Gail Creecy, prin. Fax 497-5755

Effie, Avoyelles
Avoyelles Parish SD
Supt. — See Marksville
Lafargue ES 700/PK-6
3366 Highway 107 71331 318-253-9591
Randy Littleton, prin. Fax 253-4545

Egan, Acadia
Acadia Parish SD
Supt. — See Crowley
Egan S 200/PK-8
2166 Egan Hwy 70531 337-783-4148
Julie Myers, prin. Fax 788-3774

Elizabeth, Allen, Pop. 570
Allen Parish SD
Supt. — See Oberlin
Elizabeth S 300/PK-12
PO Box 580 70638 318-634-5341
Michael Stainback, prin. Fax 634-5218

Elmer, Rapides
Rapides Parish SD
Supt. — See Alexandria
Oak Hill ES 500/PK-6
7362 Highway 112 71424 318-793-5177
Emily Weatherford, prin. Fax 793-5138

Elm Grove, Bossier
Bossier Parish SD
Supt. — See Benton
Elm Grove MS 800/6-8
PO Box 108 71051 318-549-6500
Robert Marlow, prin. Fax 549-6513

Elton, Jefferson Davis, Pop. 1,249
Jefferson Davis Parish SD
Supt. — See Jennings
Elton ES 300/PK-5
614 Powell St 70532 337-584-2892
Mike Darbonne, prin. Fax 584-2052

Epps, West Carroll, Pop. 1,120
West Carroll Parish SD
Supt. — See Oak Grove
Epps S 300/K-12
PO Box 277 71237 318-926-3624
Edwin Guchereau, prin. Fax 926-5655

Erath, Vermilion, Pop. 2,177
Vermilion Parish SD
Supt. — See Abbeville
Dozier ES 700/PK-3
12725 North Rd 70533 337-937-6915
Elizabeth Gremillion, prin. Fax 937-0630
Erath MS 700/4-8
800 S Broadway St 70533 337-937-4441
Lynn Moss, prin. Fax 937-5125

Estherwood, Acadia, Pop. 836
Acadia Parish SD
Supt. — See Crowley
Estherwood S 200/PK-7
214 Jefferson Ave 70534 337-783-6788
Johnette LeLeux, prin. Fax 783-9653

Eunice, Saint Landry, Pop. 11,527
St. Landry Parish SD
Supt. — See Opelousas
Central MS 300/5-6
602 S Martin L King Dr 70535 337-457-5895
Horace Pickney, prin. Fax 457-8452
East ES 300/K-4
550 Brother J Rd 70535 337-457-2215
Mary Ellen Donatto, prin. Fax 457-2257
Eunice ES 200/K-4
451 S 9th St 70535 337-457-2380
Irma Trosclair, prin. Fax 457-2389
Eunice JHS 400/7-8
751 W Oak Ave 70535 337-457-7386
Lakesha Miller, prin. Fax 457-1764
Glendale ES 300/PK-4
900 W Dean St 70535 337-457-4121
Phyllis Ortego, prin. Fax 457-0308
Highland ES 300/PK-4
1341 Duck Ave 70535 337-457-5161
Lorie Ledoux, prin. Fax 457-0207

St. Edmund S 400/PK-6
331 N 3rd St 70535 337-457-5988
Beth Christ, prin. Fax 457-5989

Evangeline, Acadia
Acadia Parish SD
Supt. — See Crowley
Evangeline S 200/PK-8
1448 Old Evangeline Hwy 70537 337-824-1368
Marie Janise, prin. Fax 824-7193

Evans, Vernon
Vernon Parish SD
Supt. — See Leesville
Evans S 300/PK-12
PO Box 67 70639 337-286-5289
Jimmy Maricle, prin. Fax 286-9298

Farmerville, Union, Pop. 3,662
Union Parish SD 3,000/PK-12
PO Box 308 71241 318-368-9715
Steve Dozier, supt. Fax 368-1012
www.unionpsd.org/
Farmerville ES 700/PK-5
7195 Highway 33 71241 318-368-9542
Carol Smith, prin. Fax 368-6081
Farmerville JHS 300/6-8
606 Bernice St 71241 318-368-9235
Andy Allred, prin. Fax 368-1989
Other Schools – See Bernice, Downsville, Marion, Spearsville

Union Christian Academy 400/PK-12
PO Box 189 71241 318-368-8890
Paul Murray, pres. Fax 368-2920

Fenton, Jefferson Davis, Pop. 378
Jefferson Davis Parish SD
Supt. — See Jennings
Fenton S 100/PK-8
PO Box 250 70640 337-756-2326
Delmar Bentley, prin. Fax 756-2500

Ferriday, Concordia, Pop. 3,568
Concordia Parish SD
Supt. — See Vidalia
Ferriday JHS 300/6-8
201 Martin Luther King Blvd 71334 318-757-8695
James Davis, prin. Fax 757-8696
Ferriday Lower ES 500/PK-2
110 Bateman Dr 71334 318-757-3293
Sheila Alwood, prin. Fax 757-8947
Ferriday Upper ES 300/3-5
151 Martin Luther King Blvd 71334 318-757-3105
Cindy Smith, prin. Fax 757-1924

Huntington S 200/PK-12
300 Lynwood Dr 71334 318-757-4515
Fax 757-4516

Florien, Sabine, Pop. 701
Sabine Parish SD
Supt. — See Many
Florien S 200/PK-12
500 High School Rd 71429 318-586-3681
Eddie Jones, prin. Fax 586-4818

Folsom, Saint Tammany, Pop. 651
St. Tammany Parish SD
Supt. — See Covington
Folsom ES 400/K-5
82144 Highway 25 70437 985-796-3820
Lesa Bodnar, prin. Fax 796-0165
Folsom JHS 200/6-8
83055 Hay Hollow Rd 70437 985-796-3724
Sharon Garrett, prin. Fax 796-3701

Forest, West Carroll, Pop. 264
West Carroll Parish SD
Supt. — See Oak Grove
Forest S 500/K-12
PO Box 368 71242 318-428-3672
James Harris, prin. Fax 428-8875

Forest Hill, Rapides, Pop. 458
Rapides Parish SD
Supt. — See Alexandria
Forest Hill ES 400/PK-6
PO Box 400 71430 318-748-6844
Nancy Rials, prin. Fax 748-6848

Fort Necessity, Franklin
Franklin Parish SD
Supt. — See Winnsboro
Fort Necessity S 400/PK-8
PO Box 159 71243 318-723-4793
Milton Linder, prin. Fax 723-4343

Fort Polk, Vernon
Vernon Parish SD
Supt. — See Leesville
North Polk ES 700/PK-1
4978 University Pkwy 71459 337-537-5109
James Wesley, prin. Fax 537-8429

Franklin, Saint Mary, Pop. 7,822
St. Mary Parish SD
Supt. — See Centerville
Foster ES 200/PK-5
101 2nd St 70538 337-828-1905
Karen Davison, prin. Fax 828-9063
Franklin JHS 400/6-8
525 Morris St 70538 337-828-0855
Jane Bowles, prin. Fax 828-5095
Gibbs ES 200/PK-5
264 Highway 318 70538 337-923-7722
Charlene Borne, prin. Fax 923-9091
Hernandez ES 300/PK-5
1400 Willow St 70538 337-828-1423
Sylvia Lockett, prin. Fax 828-3930
LaGrange ES 200/K-5
2129 Chatsworth Rd 70538 337-828-1991
Ronald Hawkins, prin. Fax 828-1999

St. John S 200/PK-5
924 Main St 70538 337-828-2648
Sheri Higdon, prin. Fax 828-2112

Franklinton, Washington, Pop. 3,708
Washington Parish SD 5,200/PK-12
PO Box 587 70438 985-839-3436
Darrell Fairburn, supt. Fax 839-5464
www.wpsb.org
Enon ES 400/PK-6
14058 Highway 16 70438 985-839-3976
Jackie Boone, prin. Fax 839-3402
Franklinton ES 500/3-5
345 Jaquar Dr 70438 985-839-3580
Polly Thigpen, prin. Fax 839-5149
Franklinton JHS 600/6-8
617 Main St 70438 985-839-3501
Pauline Bankston, prin. Fax 839-6912
Franklinton PS 500/PK-2
610 T W Barker Dr 70438 985-839-5674
Aylene Crain, prin. Fax 839-9546
Thomas ES 600/PK-5
30341 Highway 424 70438 985-848-2881
Steven Knight, prin. Fax 848-5497
Other Schools – See Angie, Mount Hermon

Bowling Green S 500/PK-12
700 Varnado St 70438 985-839-5317
Bill Murray, admin. Fax 839-5668

French Settlement, Livingston, Pop. 1,053
Livingston Parish SD
Supt. — See Livingston
French Settlement ES 500/PK-6
15810 LA Highway 16 70733 225-698-6848
Cynthia Gill, prin. Fax 698-6849

Galliano, Lafourche, Pop. 4,294
Lafourche Parish SD
Supt. — See Thibodaux
Galliano ES 400/PK-5
PO Box 517 70354 985-632-7211
Regan Lorraine, prin. Fax 632-3577

Garyville, Saint John the Baptist, Pop. 3,181
St. John The Baptist Parish SD
Supt. — See Reserve
St. John Child Development Center 100/PK-PK
117 Stebbins St 70051 985-535-3917
Jacqueline Forest, prin. Fax 535-6406

Geismar, Ascension
Ascension Parish SD
Supt. — See Donaldsonville
Dutchtown ES 1,000/K-5
13046 Highway 73 70734 225-621-2380
Mary McMahan, prin. Fax 621-2383
Dutchtown MS 1,000/6-8
13078 Highway 73 70734 225-621-2355
Doug Walker, prin. Fax 621-2351

Georgetown, Grant, Pop. 313
Grant Parish SD
Supt. — See Colfax
Georgetown S 300/PK-12
PO Box 99 71432 318-827-5306
William Norris Ph.D., prin. Fax 827-9481

Gibsland, Bienville, Pop. 1,082
Bienville Parish SD
Supt. — See Arcadia
Gibsland-Coleman S 300/K-12
PO Box 70 71028 318-843-6247
Kenneth Gipson, prin. Fax 843-9804

Gibson, Terrebonne
Terrebonne Parish SD
Supt. — See Houma
Gibson ES 200/PK-4
6357 S Bayou Black Dr 70356 985-575-3260
Ara Ramagos, prin. Fax 575-3277
Greenwood MS 200/5-7
5001 Bayou Black Dr 70356 985-575-3261
Myra Austin, prin. Fax 575-3477

Gilbert, Franklin, Pop. 527
Franklin Parish SD
Supt. — See Winnsboro
Gilbert S 600/PK-8
PO Box 900 71336 318-435-5961
George Johnson, prin. Fax 435-3739

Glenmora, Rapides, Pop. 1,558
Rapides Parish SD
Supt. — See Alexandria
Glenmora ES 400/PK-6
PO Box 788 71433 318-748-4200
Brian Parmley, prin. Fax 748-4202
Plainview S 300/PK-12
PO Box 698 71433 318-634-5944
Sonia Rasmussen, prin. Fax 634-5389

Golden Meadow, Lafourche, Pop. 2,145
Lafourche Parish SD
Supt. — See Thibodaux
Golden Meadow Lower ES 300/PK-2
118 Alcide St 70357 985-475-7385
Linda Guidry, prin. Fax 475-7865
Golden Meadow MS 500/6-8
630 S Bayou Dr 70357 985-475-7314
Aubrey Argeron, prin. Fax 475-6623
Golden Meadow Upper ES 300/3-5
124 N 3rd St 70357 985-475-7669
Gaye Cheramie, prin. Fax 475-7769

Goldonna, Natchitoches, Pop. 451
Natchitoches Parish SD
Supt. — See Natchitoches
Goldonna S 200/PK-8
PO Box 231 71031 318-727-9449
Randy Warren, prin. Fax 727-9449

Gonzales, Ascension, Pop. 8,499
Ascension Parish SD
Supt. — See Donaldsonville
Carver ES 600/PK-5
518 W Oak St 70737 225-621-2550
Barbara Guthrie, prin. Fax 621-2556
Central S 1,000/K-8
14101 Roddy Rd 70737 225-621-2500
Lynette Lacaze, prin. Fax 621-2682
Duplessis ES 1,000/K-5
38101 Highway 621 70737 225-621-8100
Jevella Williamson, prin. Fax 677-5984
Gonzales ES 700/PK-5
521 N Burnside Ave 70737 225-621-2660
Eleanor Lassiter, prin. Fax 621-2663
Gonzales MS 600/6-8
1502 W Orice Roth Rd 70737 225-621-2505
Lori Charlet, prin. Fax 621-2509
Pecan Grove ES K-5
1712 Pecan Ave 70737 225-391-7450
Marjorie Meyers, prin.

Faith Academy 400/PK-8
10473 Airline Hwy 70737 225-644-3110
Kirby Veron, hdmstr. Fax 647-2368
St. Theresa S 500/2-8
212 E New River St 70737 225-647-2803
Christine Musso, prin. Fax 647-7814

Grambling, Lincoln, Pop. 4,522
Lincoln Parish SD
Supt. — See Ruston
Brown ES 200/K-5
300 RWE Jones St 71245 318-274-3118
Regina Gregory, prin. Fax 274-3824
Grambling State University MS 100/6-8
407 Central Ave 71245 318-274-6531
Ronnie Harrison, prin. Fax 274-3360

Gramercy, Saint James, Pop. 3,178
St. James Parish SD
Supt. — See Lutcher
Gramercy ES 400/PK-6
601 E Second St 70052 225-869-3001
Kay Dornier, prin. Fax 869-3107

Grand Cane, DeSoto, Pop. 197

Central S 200/K-12
PO Box 71 71032 318-858-3319
Dr. Robert Peters, hdmstr. Fax 858-6394

Grand Chenier, Cameron
Cameron Parish SD
Supt. — See Lake Charles
South Cameron S 200/PK-12
753 Oak Grove Hwy 70643 337-542-4401
Zeke Wainwright, prin. Fax 542-4561

Grand Coteau, Saint Landry, Pop. 1,035
St. Landry Parish SD
Supt. — See Opelousas
Grand Coteau S 300/K-8
PO Box K 70541 337-662-5421
Kent Auzenne, prin. Fax 662-5439

St. Ignatius S 400/PK-8
PO Box J 70541 337-662-3325
Cynthia Prather, prin. Fax 662-3349
School of the Sacred Heart 400/PK-12
PO Box 310 70541 337-662-5275
Lynne Lieux, hdmstr. Fax 662-3011

Grand Isle, Jefferson, Pop. 1,594
Jefferson Parish SD
Supt. — See Harvey
Grand Isle S 100/PK-12
PO Box 995 70358 504-522-8015
Richard Augustin, prin. Fax 787-3878

Grant, Allen
Allen Parish SD
Supt. — See Oberlin
Fairview S 400/PK-12
PO Box 216 70644 318-634-5354
Gary Lockhart, prin. Fax 634-5357

Grayson, Caldwell, Pop. 527
Caldwell Parish SD
Supt. — See Columbia
Grayson ES 300/K-6
5237 Highway 126 E 71435 318-649-2703
Cheryl Mullican, prin. Fax 649-2765

Greensburg, Saint Helena, Pop. 615
St. Helena Parish SD 1,300/PK-12
PO Box 540 70441 225-222-4349
Gloristine Tanner, supt. Fax 222-4937
www.sthpk-12.net
St. Helena Central ES 500/PK-4
1798 Highway 1042 70441 225-222-4364
Linda Saucier, prin. Fax 222-4399
St. Helena Central MS 400/5-8
1590 Highway 1042 70441 225-222-6291
Byron Hurst, prin. Fax 222-6780

Greenwell Springs, East Baton Rouge
Central Community SD
Supt. — See Baton Rouge
Bellingrath Hills ES 200/PK-1
6612 Audusson Dr 70739 225-261-4093
Laurie Gehling, prin. Fax 261-4047

St. Alphonsus Liquori S 500/PK-8
13940 Greenwell Springs Rd 70739 225-261-5299
Cynthia Ryals, prin. Fax 261-2795

Gretna, Jefferson, Pop. 17,161
Jefferson Parish SD
Supt. — See Harvey
Boudreaux ES 600/PK-5
950 Behrman Hwy 70056 504-393-8732
Dorothy Bailey, prin. Fax 394-4836
Cox ES 400/PK-5
2630 Belle Chasse Hwy 70056 504-394-5890
Dr. Scott Steckler, prin. Fax 392-3115
Douglass ES 100/1-6
1400 Huey P Long Ave 70053 504-368-5962
Joyce Duncan, prin. Fax 362-1904
Gretna #2 Academy 100/PK-5
701 Amelia St 70053 504-366-3582
Patricia Wilty, prin. Fax 364-1268
Gretna MS 900/6-8
910 Gretna Blvd 70053 504-366-0120
Edith Dozier, prin. Fax 366-8807
Hart ES 300/PK-5
2001 Hancock St 70053 504-366-4346
Christi Rome, prin. Fax 366-2054
Johnson/Gretna Park ES 600/PK-5
1130 Gretna Blvd 70053 504-366-1660
Mary Ellen Hepting, prin. Fax 366-0143
Livaudais MS 600/6-8
925 Lamar Ave 70056 504-393-7544
Billie Gassen, prin. Fax 393-9610
McDonogh #26 ES 400/PK-5
1200 Jefferson St 70053 504-362-9929
Janet Herbez, prin. Fax 368-2114
Middleton ES 300/PK-5
1407 Virgil St 70053 504-366-8164
Aretha Eldridge-Williams, prin. Fax 361-7704
Solis ES 700/K-5
2850 Mount Laurel Dr 70056 504-392-7867
Vicki Esquivel, prin. Fax 392-6047
Terrytown ES 400/PK-5
550 E Forest Lawn Dr 70056 504-376-8928
Cherie Varisco, prin. Fax 376-2389

Cahill Academy 700/PK-8
3101 Wall Blvd 70056 504-392-0902
Mary Cahill, prin. Fax 392-3813
Muslim Academy 200/1-11
460 Realty Dr 70056 504-433-1960
Nabil Abukhader, prin. Fax 433-1959
St. Anthony S 200/PK-8
900 Franklin Ave 70053 504-367-0689
Marie Cannon, prin. Fax 361-0054
St. Cletus S 600/PK-8
3610 Claire Ave 70053 504-366-3538
Mary Hitt, prin. Fax 366-0011
Salem Lutheran S 300/PK-8
418 4th St 70053 504-367-5144
Joseph Althage, prin. Fax 367-5128

Gueydan, Vermilion, Pop. 1,603
Vermilion Parish SD
Supt. — See Abbeville
Owens ES 200/PK-5
203 13th St 70542 337-536-6541
Jonathan Williams, prin. Fax 536-6481

St. Peter S 100/PK-8
513 6th St 70542 337-536-7930
Sr. Ann Arno, prin. Fax 536-7930

Hackberry, Cameron, Pop. 1,664
Cameron Parish SD
Supt. — See Lake Charles
Hackberry S 300/PK-12
1390 School St 70645 337-762-3305
Brenda Sanders, prin. Fax 762-3304

Hammond, Tangipahoa, Pop. 18,096
Tangipahoa Parish SD
Supt. — See Amite
Hammond Eastside PS 400/PK-3
45050 River Rd 70401 985-345-8481
Glenda O'Banion, prin. Fax 345-0641
Hammond Eastside Upper ES 300/4-6
45046 River Rd 70401 985-345-8494
Cheryl Rousseau, prin. Fax 345-2469
Hammond JHS 500/7-8
111 J W Davis Dr 70403 985-345-2654
Janice Williams, prin. Fax 542-4215
Hammond Westside PS 500/1-3
2500 Westpark Ave 70403 985-345-6857
Lisa Raiford, prin. Fax 542-0704
Hammond Westside Upper ES 500/4-6
2600 Westpark Ave 70403 985-345-7233
Alexa Hookfin, prin. Fax 345-4755
Southeastern Louisiana University Lab S 200/K-8
PO Box 832 70404 985-549-2185
Fawn Ukpolo, prin. Fax 549-2771

Woodland Park Early Learning Center 500/PK-K
1000 S Range Rd 70403 985-542-6373
Wanda Davis, prin. Fax 542-9959

Emmanuel SDA S 50/PK-8
702 N Cherry St 70401 985-345-7713
Holy Ghost S 800/PK-8
507 N Oak St 70401 985-345-0977
Tangee Daugereaux, prin. Fax 542-6545
Trafton Academy 200/PK-8
PO Box 2845 70404 985-542-7212
Fax 542-7213

Harahan, Jefferson, Pop. 9,716
Jefferson Parish SD
Supt. — See Harvey
Harahan ES 500/PK-5
6723 Jefferson Hwy 70123 504-737-3918
Gerri Settoon, prin. Fax 737-2028

Faith Lutheran S 100/PK-8
300 Colonial Club Dr 70123 504-737-9554
Diane Oestriecher, prin. Fax 737-9599
St. Rita S 500/PK-8
194 Ravan Ave 70123 504-737-0744
Melanie Verges, prin. Fax 738-2184

Harrisonburg, Catahoula, Pop. 728
Catahoula Parish SD 1,800/PK-12
PO Box 290 71340 318-744-5727
Dr. Gwile Freeman, supt. Fax 744-9221
cpsbla.org/
Harrisonburg S 200/K-8
PO Box 710 71340 318-744-5679
Sandy Floyd, prin. Fax 744-5357
Other Schools – See Jonesville, Sicily Island

Harvey, Jefferson, Pop. 21,222
Jefferson Parish SD 43,000/PK-12
501 Manhattan Blvd 70058 504-349-7600
Dr. Diane Roussel, supt. Fax 349-7960
www.jppss.k12.la.us
Harvey K 100/PK-K
3400 6th St 70058 504-341-2051
Becky Brown, prin. Fax 340-6038
Homedale ES 300/PK-5
500 Maple Ave 70058 504-366-7258
Diane Nowik, prin. Fax 363-4284
Pittman ES 600/1-5
3800 13th St 70058 504-340-4937
Sherry Calcagno, prin. Fax 340-4531
St. Ville Academy for HS Prep 200/5-8
1121 Pailet Ave 70058 504-366-1708
Dominick Palmisano, prin. Fax 362-4907
Woodland West ES 700/PK-5
2143 Mars St 70058 504-366-5308
Peggy Rome, prin. Fax 366-6962
Woodmere ES 700/PK-5
3190 Destrehan Ave 70058 504-371-0476
Suzanne Bordlee, prin. Fax 371-0517
Other Schools – See Avondale, Bridge City, Grand Isle, Gretna, Harahan, Jefferson, Kenner, Lafitte, Marrero, Metairie, River Ridge, Waggaman, Westwego

Learning Unlimited Christian Academy 100/1-8
2074 Paxton St 70058 504-328-4993
Kathy Morgan, prin. Fax 328-4997
St. Rosalie MS 200/6-8
2115 Oakmere Dr 70058 504-348-9330
Mary Wenzel, prin. Fax 348-9331
St. Rosalie S 700/PK-5
617 2nd Ave 70058 504-341-4342
Mary Wenzel, prin. Fax 347-0271

Haughton, Bossier, Pop. 2,791
Bossier Parish SD
Supt. — See Benton
Haughton MS 900/6-8
395 S Elm St 71037 318-549-5560
Susan Salter, prin. Fax 549-5573
Platt ES 600/2-3
4680 Highway 80 71037 318-549-5870
Brenda Estess, prin. Fax 549-5883
Rodes ES 700/K-1
4670 Highway 80 71037 318-549-5940
Roland Champagne, prin. Fax 549-5952

Haynesville, Claiborne, Pop. 2,540
Claiborne Parish SD
Supt. — See Homer
Haynesville ES 300/PK-4
9777 Highway 79 71038 318-624-1084
Robert Bond, prin. Fax 624-0598

Claiborne Academy 200/PK-12
6741 Highway 79 71038 318-927-2747
Chuck Herrington, prin. Fax 927-4519

Holden, Livingston
Livingston Parish SD
Supt. — See Livingston
Holden S 700/K-12
30120 LA 441 Hwy 70744 225-567-9367
Paula Green, prin. Fax 567-5248

Homer, Claiborne, Pop. 3,552
Claiborne Parish SD 2,300/PK-12
PO Box 600 71040 318-927-3502
Janice Williams, supt. Fax 927-9184
www.claibornepsb.org/
Homer ES 500/PK-5
624 Pelican Dr 71040 318-927-2393
Patrice Lee, prin. Fax 927-2302
Homer JHS 300/6-8
621 Pelican Dr 71040 318-927-2826
Twyla Pugh, prin. Fax 927-4376
Other Schools – See Athens, Haynesville, Summerfield

Hornbeck, Vernon, Pop. 403
Vernon Parish SD
Supt. — See Leesville
Hornbeck S 400/PK-12
PO Box 9 71439 318-565-4440
Joey Whiddon, prin. Fax 565-4136

Houma, Terrebonne, Pop. 32,105
Lafourche Parish SD
Supt. — See Thibodaux
Bayou Blue ES 800/PK-5
1916 Bayou Blue Rd 70364 985-879-4378
John Danigole, prin. Fax 879-1787
Bayou Blue MS 6-8
196 Mazerac St 70364 985-851-1952
Sharon Dugas, prin. Fax 851-1849

Terrebonne Parish SD 18,800/PK-12
201 Stadium Dr 70360 985-876-7400
Philip Martin, supt. Fax 872-0054
www.tpsd.org
Acadian ES 700/PK-4
1020 Saadi St 70363 985-876-0612
Arthur Joffrion, prin. Fax 876-0652
Bayou Black ES 100/PK-4
4449 Bayou Black Dr 70360 985-872-2460
Gertrude Begue, prin. Fax 872-3433
Broadmoor ES 700/K-6
1010 Broadmoor Ave 70364 985-879-1042
Pamela McCann, prin. Fax 879-2108
Coteau-Bayou Blue ES 700/PK-6
2550 Coteau Rd 70364 985-868-4267
Tess Daigle, prin. Fax 868-4425
Dularge MS 200/3-7
621 Bayou Dularge Rd 70363 985-876-0176
Cheryl Degruise, prin. Fax 876-0177
East Houma ES 300/PK-2
222 Connely St 70363 985-872-1990
Sylvia Champagne, prin. Fax 879-4900
Elysian Fields MS 400/4-6
700 Hibernia Pl 70363 985-876-2041
Melissa Badeaux, prin. Fax 876-9741
Grand Caillou MS 500/4-8
3933 Grand Caillou Rd 70363 985-879-3001
Sharon Henry, prin. Fax 879-3009
Honduras ES 300/PK-3
530 Grand Caillou Rd 70363 985-872-5695
Dr. Sandra Hebert, prin. Fax 868-4727
Legion Park MS 200/4-6
710 Williams Ave 70364 985-876-2272
Clyde Hamner, prin. Fax 876-2352
Mulberry ES 800/K-6
450 Cougar Dr 70360 985-872-5328
Mary Aucoin, prin. Fax 872-5445
Oaklawn JHS 600/7-8
2215 Acadian Dr 70363 985-872-3904
Demetria Maryland, prin. Fax 917-1917
Oakshire ES 600/PK-6
5459 Vicari St 70364 985-876-1007
Cathy Kosior, prin. Fax 851-4710
Park ES 600/K-7
6639 Lisa Park Ave 70364 985-876-1055
Stacy Solet, prin. Fax 868-6373
Southdown ES 500/PK-6
1124 Saint Charles St 70360 985-872-9429
William Simmons, prin. Fax 879-1841
Village East ES 400/3-6
315 Lafayette Woods Blvd 70363 985-868-4900
Rosa Pitre, prin. Fax 851-5059
West Park ES 300/PK-3
7573 Park Ave 70364 985-873-7434
Glenn Sikes, prin. Fax 873-7441
Other Schools – See Bourg, Chauvin, Dulac, Gibson, Montegut, Schriever, Theriot

Covenant Christian Academy 100/K-8
7382 Main St 70360 985-851-7567
Brent Johns, prin.
Houma Christian S 300/K-12
109 Valhi Blvd 70360 985-851-7423
Rev. John Foster, prin. Fax 872-4958
Maria Immacolata S 200/PK-7
324 Estate Dr 70364 985-876-1631
Sr. Theresa Gossen, prin. Fax 876-1608
Messiah Montessori S 100/PK-4
PO Box 20027 70360 985-857-8808
Dr. Jules Boquet, dir. Fax 851-3116
St. Bernadette S 500/PK-7
309 Funderburk Ave 70364 985-872-3854
Angie Adams, prin. Fax 876-9654
St. Francis De Sales S 800/PK-7
PO Box 8034 70361 985-868-6646
Brenda Tanner, prin. Fax 851-5896
St. Gregory Barbarigo S 200/PK-7
441 6th St 70364 985-876-2038
Liz Scurto, prin. Fax 879-2789
St. Matthews Episcopal S 200/PK-7
266 Gabasse St 70360 985-872-5573
Cheryl Natherne, hdmstr. Fax 868-9850

Independence, Saint Helena, Pop. 1,718
Tangipahoa Parish SD
Supt. — See Amite
Independence ES 400/K-4
221 Tiger Ave 70443 985-878-4946
Cathy LeBlanc, prin. Fax 878-4827
Independence MS 300/5-8
300 W 2nd St 70443 985-878-4376
Malcolm Mizell, prin. Fax 878-4848

Mater Dolorosa S 200/PK-8
PO Box 380 70443 985-878-4295
Alfred Donaldson, prin. Fax 878-4888

Iota, Acadia, Pop. 1,399
Acadia Parish SD
Supt. — See Crowley
Iota ES 500/PK-5
470 W Kennedy Ave 70543 337-779-2581
Charles Barbier, prin. Fax 779-3489
Iota MS 200/6-8
426 S 5th St 70543 337-779-2536
Debra Seibert, prin. Fax 779-2594

St. Francis S 200/PK-8
490 Saint Joseph Ave 70543 337-779-2527
Louis Cramer, prin. Fax 779-2527

Iowa, Calcasieu, Pop. 2,591
Calcasieu Parish SD
Supt. — See Lake Charles
Watson S 900/PK-8
201 E First St 70647 337-582-3537
Pat Schooler, prin. Fax 582-7530

Jackson, East Feliciana, Pop. 3,774
East Feliciana Parish SD
Supt. — See Clinton
Jackson ES 400/PK-5
3505 Highway 10 70748 225-634-5933
Carolyn Davis, prin. Fax 634-2224
Jackson MS 200/6-8
3503 Highway 10 70748 225-634-5932
Allison El Koubi, prin. Fax 634-5955

Jeanerette, Iberia, Pop. 5,945
Iberia Parish SD
Supt. — See New Iberia
Jeanerette ES 300/K-6
600 Ira St 70544 337-276-6355
Athena Self, prin. Fax 276-7266
Jeanerette MS 200/7-8
609 Pellerin Rd 70544 337-276-4320
Cheryl Broussard, prin. Fax 276-7064
Saint Charles Street ES 300/PK-6
1921 Saint Charles St 70544 337-276-9712
J. M. Trotter, prin. Fax 276-9713

St. Joseph S 100/K-8
10917 Old Jeanerette Rd 70544 337-276-3615
Earl Price, prin. Fax 276-7659

Jefferson, Jefferson, Pop. 14,521
Jefferson Parish SD
Supt. — See Harvey
Jefferson ES 400/PK-5
4440 Jefferson Hwy 70121 504-733-9461
Carolyn Sanders-O'Hare, prin. Fax 733-8177
Riverdale MS 700/6-8
3900 Jefferson Hwy 70121 504-828-2706
Randy Bennett, prin. Fax 833-5125

St. Agnes S 200/PK-8
3410 Jefferson Hwy 70121 504-835-6486
Bridget Sinibaldi, prin. Fax 835-4295

Jena, LaSalle, Pop. 2,872
LaSalle Parish SD 2,700/PK-12
PO Box 90 71342 318-992-2161
Roy Breithaupt, supt. Fax 992-8457
www.lasallepsb.com
Good Pine MS 300/4-6
12642 Highway 84 W 71342 318-992-5665
Janet Tullos, prin. Fax 992-5508
Jena ES 500/PK-3
PO Box 880 71342 318-992-5175
Debra Mayo, prin. Fax 992-2397
Jena JHS 200/7-8
PO Box 920 71342 318-992-5815
June Fowler, prin. Fax 992-6392
Nebo S 200/PK-8
300 Highway 777 71342 318-992-4416
Deedra Zeagler, prin. Fax 992-8780
Other Schools – See Olla, Trout, Urania

Temple Christian Academy 100/PK-8
5933 Aimwell Rd 71342 318-992-2711
Dustin McAnn, prin. Fax 992-0145

Jennings, Jefferson Davis, Pop. 10,652
Jefferson Davis Parish SD 5,800/PK-12
PO Box 640 70546 337-824-1834
David Clayton, supt. Fax 824-9737
www.jeffersondavis.org
Hathaway S 500/PK-12
4040 Pine Island Hwy 70546 337-824-4452
Mona Miller, prin. Fax 824-2769
Jennings ES 600/3-6
620 Florence St 70546 337-824-4972
Dr. Kieran Coleman, prin. Fax 824-4989
Ward ES 500/PK-2
208 Shankland Ave 70546 337-824-1235
Suzanne Doucet, prin. Fax 824-3155
Other Schools – See Elton, Fenton, Lacassine, Lake Arthur, Roanoke, Welsh

Bethel Christian S 300/PK-12
15147 Highway 102 70546 337-824-0020
Sheila Reed, admin. Fax 824-0579
Our Lady Immaculate Catholic S 300/PK-8
600 Roberts Ave 70546 337-824-1743
Nicole Reeves, prin. Fax 824-1752

Jonesboro, Jackson, Pop. 3,743
Jackson Parish SD 2,100/PK-12
PO Box 705 71251 318-259-4456
Wayne Alford, supt. Fax 259-2527
www.jpsb.us/
Jonesboro-Hodge MS 300/3-6
440 Old Winnfield Rd 71251 318-259-6611
Sam Strozier, prin. Fax 259-9699
Southside ES 200/K-2
2105 S Polk Ave 71251 318-259-4489
Keith Henderson, prin. Fax 259-4489

Weston S 600/PK-12
213 Highway 505 71251 318-259-7313
Dr. Robin Potts, prin. Fax 259-1056
Other Schools – See Quitman

Jonesville, Catahoula, Pop. 2,316
Catahoula Parish SD
Supt. — See Harrisonburg
Central S 100/K-12
244 Larto Bayou Rd 71343 318-339-7574
Johnnie Adams, prin. Fax 339-7925
Jonesville ES 500/PK-4
1219 Cora Dr 71343 318-339-8588
Glenda Barker, prin. Fax 339-9260
Jonesville JHS 200/5-7
802 Johnson St 71343 318-339-9604
Janie Smith, prin. Fax 339-8289

Kaplan, Vermilion, Pop. 5,131
Vermilion Parish SD
Supt. — See Abbeville
Kaplan ES 600/PK-4
608 N Eleazar Ave 70548 337-643-7965
Karla Toups, prin. Fax 643-2821
Rost MS 400/5-8
112 W 6th St 70548 337-643-8545
David Dupuis, prin. Fax 643-7013

Maltrait Memorial S 100/K-8
1 Crusader Sq 70548 337-643-7765
Renee Meaux, prin. Fax 643-2516

Keithville, Caddo
Caddo Parish SD
Supt. — See Shreveport
Keithville S 1,100/PK-8
12201 Mansfield Rd 71047 318-925-1005
Mark Allen, prin. Fax 925-2691

Kelly, Caldwell
Caldwell Parish SD
Supt. — See Columbia
Kelly ES 100/K-6
PO Box 130 71441 318-649-7714
Kristy Dauzat, prin. Fax 649-0402

Kenner, Jefferson, Pop. 69,911
Jefferson Parish SD
Supt. — See Harvey
Alexander ES 600/PK-5
600 W Esplanade Ave 70065 504-469-7326
Mary Jenks, prin. Fax 464-1058
Audubon ES 400/PK-5
200 W Loyola Dr 70065 504-466-0525
Caroline Roques, prin. Fax 466-6314
Chateau Estates ES 500/PK-5
4121 Medoc Dr 70065 504-464-5662
Yvette Gauthreaux, prin. Fax 464-6819
Clancy School for the Arts 300/PK-5
2100 Maine Ave 70062 504-469-3664
Lisa Kendrick, prin. Fax 469-0216
Greenlawn Terrace ES 300/PK-5
1500 38th St 70065 504-468-1016
Katherine Croft, prin. Fax 468-5962
Roosevelt MS 500/6-8
3315 Maine Ave 70065 504-443-1361
Robert Simmons, prin. Fax 443-3425
Schneckenburger ES 400/PK-5
26 Earnest Ave 70065 504-443-1236
Diane Lonadier, prin. Fax 443-6321
Washington Montessori S 200/PK-5
606 Clay St 70062 504-464-9111
Mary Jean Gabler, prin. Fax 466-7420
Woods ES 200/PK-5
1037 31st St 70065 504-466-6252
Amelia Noel, prin. Fax 467-9441

Our Lady of Perpetual Help S 200/PK-8
531 Williams Blvd 70062 504-464-0531
Sr. Julie Glaeser, prin. Fax 464-0725
St. Elizabeth Ann Seton S 500/PK-8
4119 Saint Elizabeth Dr 70065 504-468-3524
Rev. David Defour, prin. Fax 469-6014

Kentwood, Tangipahoa, Pop. 2,171
Tangipahoa Parish SD
Supt. — See Amite
Chesbrough ES 400/PK-5
68495 Highway 1054 70444 985-229-6377
Andrew Edwards, prin. Fax 229-7234
Dillon ES 500/PK-6
1541 C B Temple Rd 70444 985-229-8225
Ashley Walker, prin. Fax 229-5699
Spring Creek ES 400/PK-6
72961 Highway 1061 70444 985-229-8363
Rod Lea, prin. Fax 229-3109

Kilbourne, West Carroll, Pop. 418
West Carroll Parish SD
Supt. — See Oak Grove
Kilbourne S 300/K-12
PO Box 339 71253 318-428-3721
Shelton Kavalir, prin. Fax 428-3860

Kinder, Allen, Pop. 2,104
Allen Parish SD
Supt. — See Oberlin
Kinder ES 500/PK-4
412 N 12th St 70648 337-738-2454
Lisa Boudreaux, prin. Fax 738-5526
Kinder MS 300/5-8
PO Box 610 70648 337-738-3223
Tracey Odom, prin. Fax 738-3425

New Hope Christian Academy 50/K-7
PO Box 1390 70648 337-738-5241
Kelley Langley, admin. Fax 738-3099

Krotz Springs, Saint Landry, Pop. 1,239
St. Landry Parish SD
Supt. — See Opelousas
Krotz Springs S 400/K-8
PO Box 456 70750 337-566-1524
Mary Miller, prin. Fax 566-3585

Labadieville, Assumption, Pop. 1,821
Assumption Parish SD
Supt. — See Napoleonville
Labadieville MS 400/5-8
PO Box 127 70372 985-526-4227
Susan Harrison, prin. Fax 526-4163
Labadieville PS 400/PK-4
3045 Highway 1 70372 985-526-8220
Rachel Dugas, prin. Fax 526-8558

Lacassine, Jefferson Davis
Jefferson Davis Parish SD
Supt. — See Jennings
Lacassine S 500/PK-12
PO Box 50 70650 337-588-4206
David Troutman, prin. Fax 588-4283

Lacombe, Saint Tammany, Pop. 6,523
St. Tammany Parish SD
Supt. — See Covington
Bayou Lacombe MS 200/4-6
PO Box 787 70445 985-882-5416
Patrick Woods, prin. Fax 882-0056
Chahta-Ima ES 300/K-3
PO Box 806 70445 985-882-7541
Deborah Rushing, prin. Fax 882-7567

Lafayette, Lafayette, Pop. 112,030
Lafayette Parish SD 29,900/PK-12
PO Box 2158 70502 337-521-7000
Burnell Lemoine, supt. Fax 233-0977
www.lpssonline.com
Acadian MS 600/5-8
4201 Moss St 70507 337-233-2496
Alvin Lasseigne, prin. Fax 235-6711
Alleman MS 900/5-8
600 Roselawn Blvd 70503 337-984-7210
Kathy Aloisio, prin. Fax 984-7212
Boucher ES 700/K-5
400 Patterson St 70501 337-234-8351
Sandra Billeaudeau, prin. Fax 233-8676
Breaux MS 700/6-8
1400 S Orange St 70501 337-234-2313
Loretta Caldwell, prin. Fax 234-1915
Broadmoor ES 700/K-4
609 Broadmoor Blvd 70503 337-984-3399
Cindy Duhon, prin. Fax 984-0194
Evangeline ES 700/PK-4
610 E Butcher Switch Rd 70507 337-237-3274
Madeleine Dowd McNulty, prin. Fax 232-0553
Faulk ES 500/PK-5
711 E Willow St 70501 337-233-5820
Carol Mays, prin. Fax 234-6856
Lafayette MS 400/6-8
1301 W University Ave 70506 337-234-4032
Monique Magee, prin. Fax 235-4971
Live Oak ES 700/K-5
3020 N University Ave 70507 337-896-9908
Christine Duay, prin. Fax 896-4092
Martin MS 800/5-8
401 Broadmoor Blvd 70503 337-984-9796
Bobby Badeaux, prin. Fax 984-9968
Montgomery ES 600/K-5
600 Foreman Dr 70506 337-981-2350
Nelda Broussard, prin. Fax 981-8632
Moss MS 500/6-8
805 Teurlings Dr 70501 337-289-1994
Ken Douet, prin. Fax 289-1997
Myrtle Place ES 200/K-5
1100 Myrtle Pl 70506 337-235-5224
Janice Moncrief, prin. Fax 232-9711
Ossun ES 800/K-5
400 Rue Scholastique 70507 337-896-3263
Kelli Clause, prin. Fax 896-8915
Plantation ES 600/K-5
1801 Kaliste Saloom Rd 70508 337-984-7462
Ann Hermann, prin. Fax 988-2802
Prairie ES 900/PK-5
2910 Ambassador Caffery Pkw 70506 337-984-3391
Gwen Lewis, prin. Fax 988-3609
Truman Montessori S 700/PK-PK
200 Clara St 70501 337-235-8096
Joan Daley, prin. Fax 237-6045
Woodvale ES 600/K-4
100 Leon Dr 70503 337-984-8011
Vera Shanklin, prin. Fax 988-3676
Other Schools – See Broussard, Carencro, Duson, Milton, Scott, Youngsville

---

Ascension Episcopal S 600/PK-12
1030 Johnston St 70501 337-233-9748
Patrick Dickens, hdmstr. Fax 269-9768
Cathedral Carmel S 800/PK-8
848 Saint John St 70501 337-235-5577
Kay Aillet, prin. Fax 261-9493
Family Life Christian Academy 100/PK-8
2223 Dulles Dr 70506 337-988-0032
Sara Aloisio, prin. Fax 988-1637
First Baptist Christian S 300/PK-8
201 W Convent St 70501 337-237-1546
Susan Emerson, prin. Fax 237-9970
Holy Family S 200/PK-6
200 Saint John St 70501 337-235-0267
Rogers Griffin, prin. Fax 235-0558
Immaculate Heart of Mary S 100/PK-8
800 12th St 70501 337-235-7843
Thomas Brown, prin. Fax 233-0070
Lafayette Christion Academy 600/PK-12
220 Portland Ave 70507 337-234-9860
Dan Savoie, prin. Fax 233-3555
Lafayette Lutheran S 100/PK-6
301 W Farrel Rd 70508 337-984-7860
Daniel Markel, hdmstr. Fax 984-5977
Our Lady of Fatima S 900/PK-8
2315 Johnston St 70503 337-235-2464
Herb Boasso, prin. Fax 235-1320
St. Genevieve ES 300/PK-5
201 Elizabeth Ave 70501 337-234-5257
Rebecca Trouille, prin. Fax 237-6065
St. Genevieve MS 200/6-8
1500 E Willow St 70501 337-266-5553
Julie Champagne, prin. Fax 266-5775
St. Mary Early Learning Center 200/PK-K
419 Doucet Rd 70503 337-984-3750
Amy Robideaux, prin. Fax 981-5445
St. Pius S 700/PK-8
205 E Bayou Pkwy 70508 337-237-3139
Donna Lemaire, prin. Fax 232-3455
SS. Leo & Seton S 500/PK-8
502 Saint Leo St 70501 337-234-5510
Ebrar Reaux, prin. Fax 234-3676
Westminster Christian Academy 400/PK-6
111 Goshen Ln 70508 337-988-6489
Merida Brooks, supt. Fax 988-6340

Lafitte, Jefferson, Pop. 1,507
Jefferson Parish SD
Supt. — See Harvey
Kerner ES 600/PK-6
4924 City Park Dr 70067 504-689-4136
Charliemae Bordelon, prin. Fax 689-7666

Lake Arthur, Jefferson Davis, Pop. 2,912
Jefferson Davis Parish SD
Supt. — See Jennings
Lake Arthur ES 600/PK-6
500 Mill Ave 70549 337-774-3323
Philip Byler, prin. Fax 774-3189

Lake Charles, Calcasieu, Pop. 70,555
Calcasieu Parish SD 31,400/PK-12
PO Box 800 70602 337-217-4000
Wayne Savoy, supt. Fax 217-4001
www.cpsb.org
Barbe ES 300/PK-5
400 Penn St 70601 337-433-4746
John Spikes, prin. Fax 439-9048
Brentwood ES 400/PK-5
3825 Brentwood St 70607 337-477-7081
Brent Washington, prin. Fax 474-4116
Clifton ES 300/PK-5
100 N Prater St 70601 337-433-5316
Henry Hicks, prin. Fax 436-3520
College Oaks ES 300/PK-5
3618 Ernest St 70605 337-477-4341
Diane Ethridge, prin. Fax 474-8669
Combre-Fondel ES 400/PK-5
2115 Fitzenrieter Rd 70601 337-433-7218
Harold Winey, prin. Fax 436-8371
Cooley Magnet ES 300/K-5
2711 Common St 70601 337-433-4506
Fritzi Fralick, prin. Fax 439-1446
Dolby ES 500/PK-5
817 Jefferson Dr 70605 337-477-4631
Pamela Quebodeaux, prin. Fax 477-4759
Fairview ES 500/PK-5
3955 Gerstner Memorial Blvd 70607 337-477-0615
Louana Brown, prin. Fax 477-1758
Gillis ES 800/PK-5
916 Topsy Rd 70611 337-855-2077
Stephanie Couste, prin. Fax 855-4692
Henry Heights ES 400/PK-5
3600 Louisiana Ave 70607 337-477-5020
Novella Miller, prin. Fax 477-7058
Johnson ES 400/PK-5
500 Malcolm St 70601 337-439-9985
Betty Sims, prin. Fax 439-6160
Kaufman ES 400/PK-5
301 Tekel Rd 70607 337-477-1577
Lawrence Primeaux, prin. Fax 474-6298
Kennedy ES 300/PK-5
2001 Russell St 70615 337-436-3591
Dinah Robinson, prin. Fax 433-0737
LeBleu Settlement ES 400/K-5
6509 Highway 3059 70615 337-582-7629
Jill Portie, prin. Fax 582-6789
Molo Magnet MS 400/6-8
2300 Medora St 70601 337-433-6785
James Wilson, prin. Fax 439-0787
Moss Bluff ES 900/PK-5
215 School St 70611 337-855-2103
Charles Caldarera, prin. Fax 855-3212
Moss Bluff MS 900/6-8
297 Park Rd 70611 337-217-3351
John Duhon, prin. Fax 217-8026
Nelson ES 600/K-5
1001 Country Club Rd 70605 337-477-1775
Jacqueline Smith, prin. Fax 474-6843
Oak Park ES 300/PK-5
2001 18th St 70601 337-478-2768
Melinda Hardy, prin. Fax 478-2774
Oak Park MS 600/6-8
2200 Oak Park Blvd 70601 337-478-3310
Martin Guillory, prin. Fax 474-0753
Prien Lake ES 600/K-5
3741 Nelson Rd 70605 337-477-5586
Irene Greathouse, prin. Fax 477-5580
Reynaud MS 300/6-8
745 S Shattuck St 70601 337-436-5729
Carolyn Thomas, prin. Fax 491-0963
St. John ES 700/K-5
5566 Elliott Rd 70605 337-479-1901
Sabrah Kingham, prin. Fax 479-1110
Watkins ES 300/PK-5
2501 7th Ave 70601 337-478-3929
Kay Victorian, prin. Fax 478-9496
Watson ES 400/PK-5
1300 5th St 70601 337-436-5029
Berna Dean Johnson, prin. Fax 436-6815

Welsh MS 1,300/6-8
1500 W Mcneese St 70605 337-477-6611
Marion Sarver, prin. Fax 474-0519
White MS 700/6-8
1000 E McNeese St 70607 337-477-1648
Christopher Fontenot, prin. Fax 478-7899
Wilson ES 200/PK-5
1400 Opelousas St 70601 337-436-7103
Kim Broussard, prin. Fax 436-7943
Other Schools – See Bell City, Dequincy, Iowa, Starks, Sulphur, Vinton, Westlake

Cameron Parish SD 1,200/PK-12
1027 Highway 384 70607 337-905-5784
Stephanie Rodrigue, supt. Fax 905-5097
www.camsch.org
Grand Lake S 600/PK-12
1039 Highway 384 70607 337-905-2231
David Duhon, prin. Fax 905-2961
Other Schools – See Cameron, Grand Chenier, Hackberry

Bishop Noland Episcopal Day S 400/PK-8
803 Division St 70601 337-433-5246
Frances Kay, admin. Fax 436-1248
Hamilton Christian Academy 400/PK-12
1415 8th St 70601 337-439-1178
Dr. Wayne McEntire, prin. Fax 494-1928
Immaculate Conception Cathedral S 400/PK-8
1536 Ryan St 70601 337-433-3497
Dinah Bradford, prin. Fax 433-5056
Lakewood Christian Academy 100/PK-12
2520 W Sale Rd 70605 337-477-0531
Ray Hoffpauir, prin. Fax 477-4675
Our Lady Queen of Heaven S 700/PK-8
3908 Creole St 70605 337-477-7349
JoAnn Wallwork, prin. Fax 477-7384
Sacred Heart S 100/PK-8
1100 Mill St 70601 337-436-3588
Dr. Kathleen Bellow, prin. Fax 433-1761
St. Margaret S 300/PK-8
2510 Enterprise Blvd 70601 337-436-7959
Brenda Dufrene, prin. Fax 436-9932
St. Theodore Holy Family Catholic S 100/PK-8
785 Sam Houston Jones Pkwy 70611 337-855-9465
Jennifer Bellon, prin. Fax 855-2809

Lake Providence, East Carroll, Pop. 4,584
East Carroll Parish SD 1,500/PK-12
PO Box 792 71254 318-559-2222
Dr. Voleria Millikin, supt. Fax 559-3864
www.e-carrollschools.org
Griffin Middle Academy 300/6-8
1205 Charles D Jones Blvd 71254 318-559-1395
Janice Harris, prin. Fax 559-0679
Monticello HS 300/K-12
1046 Highway 577 71254 318-552-6366
Flora Watson, prin. Fax 552-7658
Northside ES 300/PK-5
328 Regenold St 71254 318-559-2887
James Burrell, prin. Fax 559-3896
Southside ES 400/PK-5
PO Box 128 71254 318-559-0325
Theola Chatman, prin. Fax 559-5853

Briarfield Academy 200/PK-12
301 Riddle Ln 71254 318-559-2360
Berton Kelly, prin. Fax 559-2360

Laplace, Saint John the Baptist, Pop. 24,194
St. John The Baptist Parish SD
Supt. — See Reserve
East St. John S 800/PK-8
400 Ory Dr 70068 985-536-8450
Jerry Galloway, prin. Fax 536-2040
Lake Pontchartrain S 900/PK-8
3328 New Highway 51 70068 985-652-2003
Margaret Hastings, prin. Fax 652-2989
LaPlace S 1,000/K-8
393 Greenwood Dr 70068 985-652-5552
Alison Cupit, prin. Fax 652-3979
Ory Communication Arts Magnet S 500/K-8
182 W 5th St 70068 985-651-3700
Teri Noel, prin. Fax 651-3712
Watkins ES K-5
944 Highway 628 70068 985-652-1593
Antoinette Robinet, prin. Fax 652-1578

Ascension of Our Lord S 400/PK-8
1809 Greenwood Dr 70068 985-652-4532
Amy Dimaggio, prin. Fax 651-5151
St. Joan of Arc S 600/PK-8
412 Fir St 70068 985-652-6310
Larry Bourgeois, prin. Fax 652-6390

Larose, Lafourche, Pop. 5,772
Lafourche Parish SD
Supt. — See Thibodaux
Larose Lower ES 300/PK-2
175 Richardel Dr 70373 985-693-3445
Rachel Crosby, prin. Fax 693-3256
Larose Upper ES 300/3-5
PO Box 1370 70373 985-693-7597
Tammy Shaw, prin. Fax 693-8141

Holy Rosary S 300/PK-8
PO Box 40 70373 985-693-3342
Joan LeBouef, prin. Fax 693-3348

Lawtell, Saint Landry
St. Landry Parish SD
Supt. — See Opelousas
Lawtell S 600/K-8
PO Box 238 70550 337-543-2315
William Thibodeaux, prin. Fax 543-7901

Lecompte, Rapides, Pop. 1,338
Rapides Parish SD
Supt. — See Alexandria

Raymond ES 100/PK-6
PO Box 429 71346 318-776-5489
Kelli Welch, prin. Fax 776-9459

Leesville, Vernon, Pop. 6,160
Vernon Parish SD 9,600/PK-12
201 Belview Rd 71446 337-239-3401
Jackie Self, supt. Fax 238-5777
www.vpsb.k12.la.us
East Leesville ES 500/PK-1
203 Belview Rd 71446 337-239-4966
Ramona Bennett, prin. Fax 239-7082
Hicks S 300/PK-12
1296 Hicks School Rd 71446 337-239-9645
Randy Lansdale, prin. Fax 239-6149
Leesville JHS 600/7-8
480 Berry Ave 71446 337-239-3874
Barbara Stainback, prin. Fax 238-4113
Pickering ES 700/PK-6
116 Lebleu Rd 71446 337-537-3394
Dwain Ducote, prin. Fax 537-2293
South Polk ES 500/2-4
1665 Louisiana Ave 71459 337-537-8120
Charles Balthrop, prin. Fax 537-8211
Vernon MS 500/5-6
PO Box 46 71496 337-238-1505
Cassandra Wilson, prin. Fax 239-2291
West Leesville ES 500/2-4
1200 Abe Allen Memorial Dr 71446 337-239-2330
Joan Simmons, prin. Fax 239-0979
Other Schools – See Anacoco, Evans, Fort Polk, Hornbeck, Pitkin, Rosepine, Simpson

---

Faith Training Christian Academy 300/PK-12
603 E Mechanic St 71446 337-239-1055
Richard Reese, prin. Fax 239-1044

Lena, Rapides
Rapides Parish SD
Supt. — See Alexandria
Northwood S 700/PK-12
8830 Highway 1 N 71447 318-793-8021
Donald Welch, prin. Fax 793-8503

Leonville, Saint Landry, Pop. 1,014
St. Landry Parish SD
Supt. — See Opelousas
Leonville S 600/K-8
PO Box 30 70551 337-879-2385
Ronald Lalonde, prin. Fax 879-7914

Livingston, Livingston, Pop. 1,577
Livingston Parish SD 22,400/PK-12
PO Box 1130 70754 225-686-7044
Bill Spear, supt. Fax 686-3052
www.lpsb.org
Doyle ES 600/PK-6
PO Box 130 70754 225-686-2416
Diane Smith, prin. Fax 686-1500
Frost S 300/K-8
19672 LA Highway 42 70754 225-698-3780
Gene Hampton, prin. Fax 698-3126
Other Schools – See Albany, Denham Springs, French Settlement, Holden, Maurepas, Springfield, Walker, Watson

Lockport, Lafourche, Pop. 2,596
Lafourche Parish SD
Supt. — See Thibodaux
Lockport Lower ES 400/PK-2
1421 Crescent Ave 70374 985-532-2846
Myra Ougel, prin. Fax 532-2820
Lockport MS 400/6-8
720 Main St 70374 985-532-2597
Nancy Curole, prin. Fax 532-2833
Lockport Upper ES 300/3-5
201 School St 70374 985-532-3223
Ann Hodson-Foret, prin. Fax 532-6353

Holy Savior S 300/PK-8
201 Church St 70374 985-532-2536
Annette Parfait, prin. Fax 532-2269

Logansport, DeSoto, Pop. 1,681
DeSoto Parish SD
Supt. — See Mansfield
Logansport ES 400/PK-6
PO Box 489 71049 318-697-4873
Terri Foley, prin. Fax 697-6507
Stanley S 400/PK-12
14323 Highway 84 71049 318-697-2664
Carolyn Phillips, prin. Fax 697-5984

Longville, Beauregard
Beauregard Parish SD
Supt. — See Deridder
South Beauregard ES 700/K-5
12378 Highway 171 70652 337-725-6302
Debbie Habetz, prin. Fax 725-3837

Loranger, Tangipahoa
Tangipahoa Parish SD
Supt. — See Amite
Loranger ES 800/PK-4
PO Box 530 70446 985-878-4538
Deborah Browning, prin. Fax 878-4864
Loranger MS 600/5-8
PO Box 469 70446 985-878-9455
Andre Pellerin, prin. Fax 878-4907

Loreauville, Iberia, Pop. 950
Iberia Parish SD
Supt. — See New Iberia
Loreauville ES 600/PK-6
PO Box 425 70552 337-229-6363
Gannon Dooley, prin. Fax 229-6861

Luling, Saint Charles, Pop. 2,803
St. Charles Parish SD 9,400/PK-12
13855 River Rd 70070 985-785-6289
Dr. Rodney Lafon, supt. Fax 785-1025
www.stcharles.k12.la.us
Lakewood ES 600/4-6
501 E Heather Dr 70070 985-785-1161
Kevin Barney, prin. Fax 785-2426
Luling ES 700/PK-5
904 Sugarhouse Rd 70070 985-785-6086
Ajit Pethe, prin. Fax 785-9933
Mimosa Park ES 500/1-3
222 Birch St 70070 985-785-8266
Michele deBruler, prin. Fax 785-1299
Smith MS 300/6-8
281 Sugarland Pkwy 70070 985-331-1018
Nicole LeBeauf, prin. Fax 331-9385
Songy K 200/PK-K
523 E Heather Dr 70070 985-785-0299
Paula Walsh, prin. Fax 785-0529
Other Schools – See Des Allemands, Destrehan, Norco, Paradis, Saint Rose

Lutcher, Saint James, Pop. 3,598
St. James Parish SD 4,100/PK-12
PO Box 338 70071 225-258-4500
Alonzo Luce Ph.D., supt. Fax 869-8845
www.stjames.k12.la.us
Lutcher ES 200/PK-6
PO Box P 70071 225-869-3661
Mary Carpenter, prin. Fax 869-9404
Other Schools – See Convent, Gramercy, Paulina, Saint James, Vacherie

Madisonville, Saint Tammany, Pop. 744
St. Tammany Parish SD
Supt. — See Covington
Madisonville ES 600/K-3
317 Highway 1077 70447 985-845-3671
Lauren Spencer, prin. Fax 845-1393
Madisonville JHS 600/4-8
PO Box 850 70447 985-845-3355
Fran Shea, prin. Fax 845-9018

Mamou, Evangeline, Pop. 3,433
Evangeline Parish SD
Supt. — See Ville Platte
Mamou ES 600/PK-4
1205 4th St 70554 337-468-3123
Cynthia Ardoin, prin. Fax 468-2722

Mandeville, Saint Tammany, Pop. 11,632
St. Tammany Parish SD
Supt. — See Covington
Fontainebleau JHS 800/7-8
100 Hurricane Aly 70471 985-875-7501
Dr. Timothy Schneider, prin. Fax 875-7650
Lake Harbor MS 600/4-6
1700 Viola St 70448 985-674-4440
Susan Patin, prin. Fax 674-6762
Magnolia Trace ES 900/K-3
1405 Highway 1088 70448 985-626-8238
Melanie Edwards, prin. Fax 626-0209
Mandeville ES 500/K-3
519 Massena St 70448 985-626-3950
Elizabeth Laine, prin. Fax 674-0886
Mandeville JHS 600/7-8
639 Carondelet St 70448 985-626-4428
Mary Ann Cucchiara, prin. Fax 674-0401
Mandeville MS 700/4-6
2525 Soult St 70448 985-626-8778
Kim Wood, prin. Fax 626-1640
Monteleone JHS 400/7-8
63000 Blue Marlin Dr 70448 985-951-8088
Donna Addison, prin. Fax 951-8083
Pontchartrain ES 900/K-3
1500 W Causeway Approach 70471 985-626-3748
Dr. Kathleen Wiseman, prin. Fax 626-4231
Tchefuncte MS 800/4-6
1530 W Causeway Approach 70471 985-626-7118
Laura Norsworthy, prin. Fax 674-0773
Woodlake ES 700/K-3
1620 Livingston St 70448 985-626-8842
Dr. Jean Krieger, prin. Fax 624-9404

Cedarwood S 400/PK-7
607 Heavens Dr 70471 985-845-7111
Mindy Gibbons, prin. Fax 845-0669
Mary Queen of Peace Catholic S 400/PK-7
1515 W Causeway Approach 70471 985-674-2466
Dr. Jan Daniel Lancaster, prin. Fax 674-1441
Our Lady of the Lake S 800/PK-7
316 Lafitte St 70448 985-626-5678
Frank Smith, prin. Fax 626-4337

Mangham, Richland, Pop. 563
Richland Parish SD
Supt. — See Rayville
Mangham ES 400/PK-5
419 Hixson St 71259 318-248-2575
Sandi Jones, prin. Fax 248-2273
Mangham JHS 200/6-8
PO Box 428 71259 318-248-2729
Connie Williams, prin. Fax 248-2931

Mansfield, DeSoto, Pop. 5,504
DeSoto Parish SD 4,200/PK-12
201 Crosby St 71052 318-872-2836
Walter Lee, supt. Fax 872-1324
www.desotopsb.com
Mansfield ES 400/PK-5
1915 McArthur Dr 71052 318-872-1772
Joyce Spears, prin. Fax 871-0512
Mansfield MS 400/6-8
1915 McArthur Dr 71052 318-872-1309
Grayson Collins, prin. Fax 872-1319
Other Schools – See Logansport, Pelican, Stonewall

Many, Sabine, Pop. 2,809
Sabine Parish SD 3,800/PK-12
PO Box 1079 71449 318-256-9228
Dorman Jackson, supt. Fax 256-0105
www.sabine.k12.la.us
Many ES 400/PK-3
265 Middle Creek Rd 71449 318-256-3450
Connie Ammons, prin. Fax 256-0190
Many JHS 400/4-8
1801 Natchitoches Hwy 71449 318-256-3573
Madeline Owens, prin. Fax 256-9619
Other Schools – See Converse, Florien, Negreet, Noble, Pleasant Hill, Zwolle

Maringouin, Iberville, Pop. 1,210
Pointe Coupee Parish SD
Supt. — See New Roads
Valverda ES 600/PK-6
1653 Valverda Rd 70757 225-637-2695
Major Swindler, prin. Fax 637-2595

Marion, Union, Pop. 784
Union Parish SD
Supt. — See Farmerville
Marion S 400/PK-12
3062 Taylor St 71260 318-292-4410
Nikki Cranford, prin. Fax 292-4422

Marksville, Avoyelles, Pop. 5,707
Avoyelles Parish SD 5,100/PK-12
221 Tunica Dr W 71351 318-253-5982
Dwayne Lemoine, supt. Fax 253-5178
www.avoyellespsb.com
Marksville ES 800/PK-6
430 W Waddil St 71351 318-253-7464
Cathy Brouillette, prin. Fax 253-9818
Other Schools – See Bunkie, Cottonport, Effie, Plaucheville, Simmesport

Marrero, Jefferson, Pop. 36,100
Jefferson Parish SD
Supt. — See Harvey
Ames ES 300/PK-5
500 Pine St 70072 504-347-0254
Esther Robertson, prin. Fax 347-0597
Ellender MS 700/6-8
4501 E Ames Blvd 70072 504-341-9469
Frank Rawle, prin. Fax 348-0054
Estelle ES 1,000/PK-5
2800 Barataria Blvd 70072 504-347-3727
Jackie Daniilidis, prin. Fax 340-4014
Janet ES 600/PK-5
2500 Bent Tree Blvd 70072 504-340-0487
Karen Doyle, prin. Fax 341-0548
Lincoln ES 200/PK-5
1429 Ames Blvd 70072 504-340-8489
Yelitza Gray, prin. Fax 347-1506
Marrero MS 700/6-8
4100 7th St 70072 504-341-5842
Randi Hindman, prin. Fax 341-0004
Ruppel Academy for Advanced Studies 50/5-7
2820 Mount Kennedy Dr 70072 504-347-4739
Londa Foster, prin. Fax 348-3707
Truman MS 1,000/6-8
5417 Ehret Rd 70072 504-341-0961
Carl Nini, prin. Fax 347-4497
Wall ES 500/PK-5
2001 Bonnie Ann Dr 70072 504-340-4941
Cathy Pierce, prin. Fax 341-5094

Concordia Lutheran S 200/PK-8
6700 Westbank Expy 70072 504-347-4155
Debra Sweeden, admin. Fax 348-9345
Conquering Word Christian Academy 200/PK-12
812 Avenue F 70072 504-328-2273
Carolyn Treaudo Ph.D., prin. Fax 328-2204
Faith Academy 200/PK-8
6216 6th Ave 70072 504-340-2894
Beverly Thompson, prin. Fax 340-0920
Immaculate Conception S 800/PK-8
601 Avenue C 70072 504-347-4409
Sr. Lise Parent, prin. Fax 341-2766
Visitation of Our Lady S 700/PK-8
3520 Ames Blvd 70072 504-347-3377
Carolyn Levet, prin. Fax 341-5378

Marthaville, Natchitoches
Natchitoches Parish SD
Supt. — See Natchitoches
Marthaville S 300/PK-8
PO Box 148 71450 318-472-6141
Terry Williams, prin. Fax 472-6592

Maurepas, Livingston
Livingston Parish SD
Supt. — See Livingston
Maurepas S 400/K-12
PO Box 39 70449 225-695-6111
Steve Vampran, prin. Fax 695-3265

Maurice, Vermilion, Pop. 731
Vermilion Parish SD
Supt. — See Abbeville
Picard ES 500/PK-6
203 S Albert St 70555 337-893-3887
Wendy Stoute, prin. Fax 893-3850

Melville, Saint Landry, Pop. 1,365
St. Landry Parish SD
Supt. — See Opelousas
Melville S 200/PK-8
PO Box 485 71353 337-623-4688
Willie Haynes, prin. Fax 623-3467

Meraux, Saint Bernard, Pop. 8,849
St. Bernard Parish SD
Supt. — See Chalmette
Davies ES, 4101 Mistrot St 70075 900/PK-5
Donna Schultz, prin. 504-267-7890

Trist MS 6-8
1 Pirates Cv 70075 504-872-9402
Denise Pritchard, prin. Fax 872-9426

Mermentau, Acadia, Pop. 702
Acadia Parish SD
Supt. — See Crowley
Mermentau S 200/PK-7
PO Box 250 70556 337-824-1943
Melvyn Smith, prin. Fax 824-1958

Mer Rouge, Morehouse, Pop. 686
Morehouse Parish SD
Supt. — See Bastrop
Delta S 400/K-8
PO Box 162 71261 318-647-3443
Cynthia Clark, prin. Fax 647-5631

Merryville, Beauregard, Pop. 1,162
Beauregard Parish SD
Supt. — See Deridder
Merryville S 500/K-12
7061 Highway 110 W 70653 337-825-8046
Kimberly Joshlin, prin. Fax 825-6443

Metairie, Jefferson, Pop. 145,500
Jefferson Parish SD
Supt. — See Harvey
Adams MS 700/6-8
5525 Henican Pl 70003 504-887-5240
Cheryl Milam, prin. Fax 887-0173
Airline Park ES 400/PK-5
6201 Camphor St 70003 504-888-0969
Lynda McVille, prin. Fax 454-6281
Birney ES 400/PK-5
4829 Hastings St 70006 504-885-1054
Patricia Favaloro, prin. Fax 888-3314
Bissonet Plaza ES 500/PK-5
6818 Kawanee Ave 70003 504-887-0470
Brenda Breithaupt, prin. Fax 887-5693
Bridgedale ES 300/PK-5
808 Zinnia Ave 70001 504-888-6807
Stephanie Sara, prin. Fax 454-8788
Bunche Academy for HS Prep 200/6-8
8101 Simon St 70003 504-737-3132
Jan Somoza, prin. Fax 737-7606
Dolhonde ES 400/PK-5
219 Severn Ave 70001 504-837-5370
Mathilde Wimberly, prin. Fax 834-1256
Ellis ES 400/PK-5
801 Brockenbraugh Ct 70005 504-833-7254
Julie Berner, prin. Fax 833-7255
Green Park ES 400/PK-5
1409 N Upland Ave 70003 504-466-0205
Anna Bordlee, prin. Fax 469-3978
Harris MS 700/6-8
911 Elise Ave 70003 504-733-0867
Otis Guichet, prin. Fax 733-0953
Hearst ES 500/PK-5
5208 Wabash St 70001 504-887-8814
Keith Mayeaux, prin. Fax 885-9117
Keller ES 400/PK-5
5301 Irving St 70003 504-887-3836
Sandra Doland, prin. Fax 455-1866
Maggiore ES 400/PK-5
2504 Maine Ave 70003 504-467-5609
Gloria Willis, prin. Fax 467-3729
Matas ES 300/PK-5
1201 Elise Ave 70003 504-733-6200
Patricia Helmstetter, prin. Fax 734-8520
Meisler MS 900/6-8
3700 Cleary Ave 70002 504-888-5832
Glenn Fallon, prin. Fax 888-5855
Metairie Academy for Advanced Studies 400/PK-5
201 Metairie Rd 70005 504-833-5539
Helen Blanke, prin. Fax 838-6241
Riviere ES 200/PK-5
1564 Lake Ave 70005 504-835-8439
Marc Milano, prin. Fax 835-8943

Atonement Lutheran S 200/PK-8
6500 Riverside Dr 70003 504-887-0225
Douglas Molin, prin. Fax 887-0225
Crescent City Christian S 400/PK-12
4828 Utica St 70006 504-885-4700
Bill Rigsby, admin. Fax 885-4703
Ecole Classique S 400/PK-12
5236 Glendale St 70006 504-887-3507
Sal Frederico, hdmstr. Fax 887-8140
Kehoe-France Day S 700/PK-8
720 Elise Ave 70003 504-733-0472
Frank France, prin. Fax 733-0477
Memorial Baptist Christian S 200/1-8
5701 Veterans Memorial Blvd 70003 504-887-0533
Dr. Gerald Pember, prin. Fax 887-0610
Metairie Park Country Day S 600/PK-12
300 Park Rd 70005 504-837-5204
Carolyn Chandler, hdmstr. Fax 837-0015
Our Lady of Divine Providence S 400/PK-8
917 N Atlanta St 70003 504-466-0591
Elvina DiBartolo, prin. Fax 466-0671
Ridgewood Prepatatory S 300/PK-12
201 Pasadena Ave 70001 504-835-2545
M. J. Montgomery, hdmstr. Fax 837-1864
St. Angela Merici S 500/PK-8
835 Melody Dr 70002 504-835-8491
Colleen Remont, prin. Fax 835-4463
St. Ann S 800/PK-8
4921 Meadowdale St 70006 504-455-8383
Susan Kropog, prin. Fax 455-9572
St. Benilde S 300/PK-8
1801 Division St 70001 504-833-9894
Vickie Helmstetter, prin. Fax 834-4380
St. Catherine of Siena S 1,100/PK-7
400 Codifer Blvd 70005 504-831-1166
Frances Dee Tarantino, prin. Fax 833-8982
St. Christopher S 900/PK-8
3900 Derbigny St 70001 504-837-6871
Ruth Meche, prin. Fax 834-0522
St. Clement of Rome S 500/PK-8
3978 W Esplanade Ave S 70002 504-888-0386
Michael Genevay, prin. Fax 885-8273
St. Edward the Confessor S 600/PK-8
4901 W Metairie Ave 70001 504-888-6353
Sr. Mary Charbonnet, prin. Fax 456-0960
St. Francis Xavier S 400/PK-8
215 Betz Pl 70005 504-833-1471
Barbara Martin, prin. Fax 833-1498
St. Louis King of France S 300/PK-8
1600 Lake Ave 70005 504-833-8224
Pamela Schott, prin. Fax 838-9938
St. Martin's Episcopal S 600/PK-12
225 Green Acres Rd 70003 504-733-0353
Dr. Jeffrey Beedy, hdmstr. Fax 736-8800
St. Mary Magdalen S 500/PK-8
6421 W Metairie Ave 70003 504-733-1433
Bonnie Gaspard, prin. Fax 736-0727
St. Philip Neri S 700/PK-8
6600 Kawanee Ave 70003 504-887-5600
Dr. Carol Stack, prin. Fax 456-6857
Torah Academy 50/PK-8
4141 W Esplanade Ave N 70002 504-456-6429
Dr. David Kaufman, prin. Fax 888-7558
Victory Christian Academy 200/1-8
5708 Airline Dr 70003 504-733-5087
Michelle Nichols, prin. Fax 734-3381

Milton, Lafayette
Lafayette Parish SD
Supt. — See Lafayette
Milton S 700/K-8
PO Box 239 70558 337-856-5826
Suzanne Kebodeaux, prin. Fax 856-9941

Minden, Webster, Pop. 13,281
Webster Parish SD 7,000/PK-12
PO Box 520 71058 318-377-7052
Wayne Williams, supt. Fax 377-4114
www.websterpsb.org
Harper ES 400/PK-5
618 Germantown Rd 71055 318-377-7548
Jeri Melancon, prin. Fax 377-7552
Jones ES 400/PK-5
620 District Dr 71055 318-377-1815
Levester Mills, prin. Fax 377-5257
Phillips MS 200/6-6
811 Durwood Dr 71055 318-377-0315
Linda Hudson, prin. Fax 377-0049
Richardson ES 500/PK-5
515 W Todd St 71055 318-377-2213
Ronnie Rhymes, prin. Fax 377-2219
Stewart ES 300/PK-5
215 N Middle Landing Rd 71055 318-377-0830
Dusty Rowland, prin. Fax 377-0883
Webster JHS 400/7-8
700 E Union St 71055 318-377-3847
Elena Black, prin. Fax 377-1943
Other Schools – See Cotton Valley, Doyline, Dubberly, Sarepta, Shongaloo, Springhill

---

Glenbrook S 300/K-12
1674 Country Club Cir 71055 318-377-2135
Darden Gladney, admin. Fax 377-0578

Monroe, Ouachita, Pop. 51,914
Monroe City SD 8,800/PK-12
PO Box 4180 71211 318-325-0601
Dr. James Dupree, supt. Fax 323-2864
www.mcschools.net/
Berg Jones Lane ES 400/PK-5
3000 Burg Jones Ln 71202 318-325-8982
Lisa Wilmore, prin. Fax 325-2302
Carroll Magnet JHS 400/7-8
2913 Renwick St 71201 318-322-1683
Angela Manning Ph.D., prin. Fax 322-0833
Carver ES 400/PK-6
1700 Orange St 71202 318-322-4245
Valeria Benson, prin. Fax 323-4592
Clark Magnet ES 500/PK-6
1207 Washington St 71201 318-322-8976
Christie Taylor, prin. Fax 338-7983
Cypress Point University ES 500/PK-6
6701 Mosswood Dr 71203 318-345-5666
Ann Cook, prin. Fax 345-3224
Faulk ES 300/PK-6
2110 Jackson St 71202 318-322-1300
Robert Curtis Johnson, prin. Fax 387-7803
Foster ES 400/PK-6
1310 Richwood Road 1 71202 318-325-7979
Addie Morehouse, prin. Fax 329-9275
Hall ES 400/PK-2
1000 Plum St 71202 318-322-8501
Lametria Robinson, prin. Fax 361-0928
Humble ES 400/PK-6
3800 Westminister Ave 71201 318-325-7659
David Claxton, prin. Fax 361-9448
Jefferson Upper ES 200/3-5
1001 Pecan St 71202 318-410-1378
Jacqueline Anderson, prin. Fax 387-2863
King MS 700/6-8
3716 Nutland Rd 71202 318-387-1825
Debbie Blue, prin. Fax 325-4285
Lee JHS 500/7-8
1600 N 19th St 71201 318-323-1143
Whitney Martin, prin. Fax 325-5236
Lexington ES 500/PK-6
1900 Lexington Ave 71201 318-322-9753
Lynn Hodge, prin. Fax 361-5170
Lincoln ES 500/PK-6
4200 Elm St 71203 318-322-9533
Janet Davis, prin. Fax 323-2596
Ruffin ES 500/PK-5
1801 Parkview Dr 71202 318-322-3447
Sylvia Brass, prin. Fax 322-5951

Ouachita Parish SD 18,800/PK-12
PO Box 1642 71210 318-388-2711
Dr. Robert Webber, supt. Fax 338-2221
www.opsb.net
Hayes ES 600/PK-6
3631 Old Sterlington Rd 71203 318-343-4560
Pamela Smith, prin. Fax 343-4573
Lakeshore ES 600/PK-6
550 Balboa Dr 71203 318-343-1173
Scott Crain, prin. Fax 345-0870
Ouachita JHS 700/7-8
5500 Blanks St 71203 318-345-5100
Marsha Dell Baker, prin. Fax 345-3308
Richwood JHS 300/7-8
5901 Highway 165 Byp 71202 318-651-0200
Tereatha Chisley, prin. Fax 398-9825
Robinson ES 500/PK-6
5101 Reddix Ln 71202 318-322-1784
Felicia Conway-Sledge, prin. Fax 325-3639
Shady Grove ES 500/PK-6
2304 Ticheli Rd 71202 318-323-9941
Jerlyn Bobo, prin. Fax 388-4470
Swartz Lower ES 500/K-2
235 Swartz School Rd 71203 318-343-8883
Judith Manning, prin. Fax 343-2932
Swartz Upper ES 500/3-6
400 Lincoln Hill Dr 71203 318-343-1723
Mary Skelton, prin. Fax 343-5087
Swayze ES 400/PK-6
2400 Burg Jones Ln 71202 318-325-1357
Marquita Bowman, prin. Fax 387-9532
Other Schools – See Calhoun, Sterlington, West Monroe

Grace Episcopal S 300/PK-8
1400 N 4th St 71201 318-322-5837
Dave Rath Ph.D., hdmstr. Fax 322-6956
Jesus the Good Shepherd S 300/K-6
900 Good Shepherd Ln 71201 318-325-8569
Lisa Patrick, prin. Fax 325-9730
Ouachita Christian S 700/PK-12
7065 Highway 165 N 71203 318-325-6000
William Stokes, hdmstr. Fax 387-7000
Our Lady of Fatima S 200/PK-6
3202 Franklin St 71201 318-387-1851
Donna Eichhorn, prin. Fax 325-7595
River Oaks S 400/PK-12
600 Finks Hideaway Rd 71203 318-343-4185
Dr. William Middleton, prin. Fax 343-1107

Montegut, Terrebonne, Pop. 1,784
Terrebonne Parish SD
Supt. — See Houma
Montegut ES 200/PK-4
1137 Highway 55 70377 985-594-3657
Stacy Whitney, prin. Fax 594-5941
Montegut MS 500/5-8
138 Dolphin St 70377 985-594-5886
Kim Vauclin, prin. Fax 594-9666
Pointe-Aux-Chenes ES 200/PK-4
1236 Highway 665 70377 985-594-2131
Dawn Lafont, prin. Fax 594-6849

Monterey, Concordia
Concordia Parish SD
Supt. — See Vidalia
Monterey S 500/PK-12
PO Box 127 71354 318-386-2214
Neeva Sibley, prin. Fax 386-7356

Montgomery, Grant, Pop. 823
Grant Parish SD
Supt. — See Colfax
Verda ES 300/PK-6
2580 Highway 122 71454 318-646-3146
Paxton Teddlie, prin. Fax 646-3146

Mooringsport, Caddo, Pop. 811
Caddo Parish SD
Supt. — See Shreveport
Mooringsport ES 300/PK-5
PO Box 310 71060 318-222-5214
Debra Kurkiewicz, prin. Fax 996-7676

Moreauville, Avoyelles, Pop. 934

Sacred Heart S 300/PK-8
PO Box 179 71355 318-985-2772
Sr. Anthony Castellani, prin. Fax 985-2164

Morgan City, Saint Mary, Pop. 11,930
Assumption Parish SD
Supt. — See Napoleonville
Bayou L'Ourse PS 200/PK-4
216 Lark Dr 70380 985-631-9268
Darlene Prince, prin. Fax 631-2011

St. Martin Parish SD
Supt. — See Saint Martinville
Stephensville S 200/PK-8
3243 Highway 70 70380 985-385-1366
Mary Wyble, prin. Fax 385-1369

St. Mary Parish SD
Supt. — See Centerville
Bayou Vista ES 400/PK-5
1155 Delmar Rd 70380 985-395-3758
Clair Guarisco, prin. Fax 395-8862
Maitland ES 300/PK-5
1907 Federal Ave 70380 985-384-4986
Tonia Verrette, prin. Fax 384-4989
Morgan City JHS 600/6-8
911 Marguerite St 70380 985-384-5922
Kenneth Holmes, prin. Fax 385-4170
Norman ES 200/PK-5
900 Spruce St 70380 985-384-0877
Elaine Cureton, prin. Fax 385-0889
Shannon ES 200/K-5
409 Brashear Ave 70380 985-385-4970
Rebecca Harris, prin. Fax 385-4971

Wyandotte ES 300/PK-5
2 Glenwood St 70380 985-384-0724
Barbara Leleux, prin. Fax 384-1590

Holy Cross S 400/PK-6
2100 Cedar St 70380 985-384-1933
Mamie Bergeron, prin. Fax 384-3270
Immanuel Christian S 200/PK-8
901 Fig St 70380 985-385-2129
Gwen Ross, admin. Fax 385-3041

Morrow, Saint Landry
St. Landry Parish SD
Supt. — See Opelousas
Morrow S 100/K-8
PO Box 320 71356 318-346-7851
Sandra Gamache, prin. Fax 346-7811

Morse, Acadia, Pop. 749
Acadia Parish SD
Supt. — See Crowley
Morse S 200/PK-7
PO Box 247 70559 337-783-5391
Linda Wilkerson, prin. Fax 783-5391

Mount Airy, Saint John the Baptist
St. John The Baptist Parish SD
Supt. — See Reserve
Garyville/Mt. Airy Math/Science Magnet S 600/K-8
240 Highway 54 70076 985-535-5400
Kelli Joseph, prin. Fax 535-5017

Mount Hermon, Washington
Washington Parish SD
Supt. — See Franklinton
Mount Hermon S 500/PK-12
36119 Highway 38 70450 985-877-4642
Ruth Stoudenmier, prin. Fax 877-4710

Napoleonville, Assumption, Pop. 689
Assumption Parish SD 4,200/PK-12
4901 Highway 308 70390 985-369-7251
Earl Martinez, supt. Fax 369-2530
www.assumptionschools.com
Napoleonville MS 300/5-8
4847 Highway 1 70390 985-369-6587
Angela Gregoire, prin. Fax 369-6595
Napoleonville PS 400/PK-4
185 Highway 1008 70390 985-369-6396
Jessica Thibodeaux, prin. Fax 369-9926
Other Schools – See Belle Rose, Labadieville, Morgan City, Pierre Part

Natalbany, Tangipahoa, Pop. 1,289
Tangipahoa Parish SD
Supt. — See Amite
Midway ES 700/PK-2
PO Box 69 70451 985-345-2376
Roxanne Patti, prin. Fax 345-3107
Natalbany ES 500/3-5
PO Box 9 70451 985-345-0854
JoAnn Whitmer, prin. Fax 345-3246

Natchitoches, Natchitoches, Pop. 17,701
Natchitoches Parish SD 7,000/PK-12
PO Box 16 71458 318-352-2358
Dr. Elwanda Murphy, supt. Fax 352-8138
www.nat.k12.la.us/
East Natchitoches S 400/4-8
1001 E 5th St 71457 318-352-4516
Carolyn Benefield, prin. Fax 352-4515
Natchitoches Magnet S 100/1-8
3707 University Pkwy 71457 318-357-1252
Julee Wright, prin. Fax 354-1122
NSU Elementary Lab S 300/PK-5
NSU Campus Easton W 71497 318-357-6973
Melanie McCain, prin. Fax 357-6979
NSU Middle Lab S 200/6-8
Tec Pod Bldg NSU 71497 318-357-4509
Ben LaGrone, prin. Fax 357-4260
Parks S 600/PK-8
800 Koonce St 71457 318-352-2764
Alvin Brossette, prin. Fax 352-1948
Vaughn S 600/PK-8
1500 Gold St 71457 318-352-2369
Cynthia Cole, prin. Fax 352-0565
Weaver ES 600/PK-3
520 Saint Maurice Ln 71457 318-352-3623
Laura McClain, prin. Fax 352-7319
Other Schools – See Campti, Cloutierville, Goldonna, Marthaville, Provencal

St. Mary's S 400/PK-12
PO Box 2070 71457 318-352-8394
Alan Powers, prin. Fax 352-5798

Negreet, Sabine
Sabine Parish SD
Supt. — See Many
Negreet S 500/PK-12
PO Box 14 71460 318-256-2349
Dan Salter, prin. Fax 256-5868

Newellton, Tensas, Pop. 1,346
Tensas Parish SD
Supt. — See Saint Joseph
Newellton S 200/PK-8
400 Verona St 71357 318-467-5063
Mary Johnson, prin. Fax 467-5108

New Iberia, Iberia, Pop. 32,495
Iberia Parish SD 12,900/PK-12
PO Box 200 70562 337-365-2341
Dale Henderson, supt. Fax 365-6996
www.iberia.k12.la.us
Anderson Street MS 500/7-8
1059 Anderson St 70560 337-365-3932
James Russell, prin. Fax 367-8285
Belle Place MS 500/7-8
4110 Loreauville Rd 70563 337-364-2141
Curtis Coquat, prin. Fax 365-9463

Caneview ES PK-6
5301 Highway 90 E 70560 337-369-6517
Dorothy Small, prin.
Center Street ES 400/K-6
1520 Center St 70560 337-369-9059
Linda Foreman, prin. Fax 369-9719
Coteau ES 600/K-6
2414 Coteau Rd 70560 337-369-3653
Connie Roberson, prin. Fax 369-9571
Daspit Road ES 500/K-6
1103 Daspit Rd 70563 337-364-2371
Kenneth Brantley, prin. Fax 364-8313
Dodson Street ES 400/PK-6
420 Dodson St 70563 337-369-3738
Sidney Leger, prin. Fax 365-1663
Hopkins Street ES 300/K-6
1200 S Hopkins St 70560 337-369-9687
Pamela Richardson, prin. Fax 369-9872
Iberia MS 600/7-8
613 Weeks Island Rd 70560 337-364-3927
Michael Bonin, prin. Fax 365-9681
Jefferson Island Rd ES PK-6
6007 Jefferson Island Rd 70560 337-365-1120
Deborah Viator, prin.
Johnston Street ES 300/K-6
400 Johnston St 70560 337-369-3560
Pam Landry, prin. Fax 369-9301
Live Oak Preschool 100/PK-PK
809 W Main St 70560 337-365-5013
Patricia Douglass, prin. Fax 369-3395
Magnolia ES 300/PK-6
3116 E Admiral Doyle Dr 70560 337-369-6120
Janis Wilson, prin. Fax 369-7311
North Lewis Street ES 600/PK-6
604 N Lewis St 70563 337-369-6132
Patricia Breaux, prin. Fax 367-9327
North Street ES 400/PK-6
121 N North St 70560 337-369-6636
Terry Magar, prin. Fax 369-6394
Park ES 300/PK-6
201 Gilbert Dr 70560 337-369-6189
Evelyn Louis, prin. Fax 365-6738
Pesson Addition ES 500/PK-6
619 Broussard St 70560 337-369-9907
Willie Mae Jefferson, prin. Fax 369-9950
Sugarland ES 500/K-6
2403 Jefferson Island Rd 70560 337-365-9624
Virginia Lewis, prin. Fax 364-8074
Other Schools – See Delcambre, Jeanerette, Loreauville

Assembly Christian S 200/PK-12
4219 E Admiral Doyle Dr 70560 337-364-4340
Armand Prentiss, prin. Fax 364-8310
Epiphany S 200/PK-5
303 W Main St 70560 337-364-6841
Cheryl Boutte Ph.D., hdmstr. Fax 365-8209
Highland Baptist Christian S 400/PK-12
708 Angers St 70563 337-364-2273
Janie Lamothe, admin. Fax 369-6303
St. Edward S 400/PK-3
175 Porter St 70560 337-369-6764
Dave Cavalier, prin. Fax 369-9534

New Orleans, Orleans, Pop. 454,863
Orleans Parish SD 7,400/PK-12
3520 General Degaulle Dr 70114 504-304-5660
Darryl Kilbert, supt. Fax 309-2865
www.nops.k12.la.us
Bethune S 300/PK-6
4040 Eagle St 70118 504-896-4001
Mary Smith, prin. Fax 896-4003
Franklin Math-Science ES 500/PK-6
1116 Jefferson Ave 70115 504-304-3932
Charlotte Matthew, prin. Fax 304-6257

Recovery SD 22,100/PK-12
1641 Poland Ave 70117 504-373-6200
Paul Vallas, supt. Fax 309-3647
www.nolapublicschools.net/
Banneker S 400/PK-8
421 Burdette St 70118 504-373-6203
Cheryllyn Branche, prin. Fax 862-5194
Bauduit S 300/PK-8
3649 Laurel St 70115 504-373-6224
Williette Wallace, prin. Fax 896-4003
Carver S, 3019 Higgins Blvd 70126 300/PK-8
Sharon Warren, prin. 504-373-6225
Coghill S, 5500 Piety Dr 70126 500/PK-8
Aisha Jones, prin. 504-373-6237
Craig S 400/PK-8
5316 Michoud Blvd 70129 504-373-6298
Sean Goodwin, prin. Fax 662-0404
Dibert S 300/PK-8
4217 Orleans Ave 70119 504-373-6205
Keith Bartlett, prin. Fax 488-4091
Drew S 600/PK-8
3819 Saint Claude Ave 70117 504-373-6208
Marc Merriman, prin. Fax 941-5309
Gentilly Terrace S 300/PK-8
4720 Painters St 70122 504-373-6240
Charlotte Tillman, prin.
Gregory S 200/PK-8
1700 Pratt Dr 70122 504-373-6229
Troy Washington, prin. Fax 286-7698
Habans S 300/PK-8
3819 Herschel St 70114 504-373-4590
Olga Johnson-Walters, prin. Fax 366-3410
Harney S 400/PK-8
2503 Willow St 70113 504-373-6230
Eileen Williams, prin. Fax 891-6919
Henderson S 300/PK-8
1912 L B Landry Ave 70114 504-373-6210
Beverly Johnson-Jelks, prin. Fax 361-8273
Johnson S 300/PK-8
1800 Monroe St 70118 504-373-6212
Wanda Brooks, prin. Fax 861-5943
Julian Leadership Academy 200/PK-8
2701 Lawrence St 70114 504-361-4828
Annette Hagan, prin.

Laurel S, 820 Jackson Ave 70130 600/PK-8
Janet Johnson, prin. 504-373-6213
Live Oak S, 3128 Constance St 70115 400/PK-8
Pamela Randall, prin. 504-373-6214
Livingston ES, 7301 Dwyer Rd 70126 400/6-8
Katrinia Horton, prin. 504-373-6232
Marshall MS, 4621 Canal St 70119 100/7-8
Ronald Alyer, prin. 504-220-4619
Reed S, 5552 Read Blvd 70127 400/PK-8
Daphyne Burnett, prin. 504-373-6221
Schaumburg S, 9501 Grant St 70127 600/PK-8
Josette Ripoll, prin. 504-373-6234
Washington Transitional S 200/6-8
1201 S Roman St 70125 504-373-6200
Cory Thames, prin.
Williams ES, 11755 Dwyer Rd 70128 400/PK-8
Kelly Batiste, prin. 504-373-6221
Williams ES 200/PK-8
3127 Martin Luther King Jr 70125 504-373-6218
Karen Bryan, prin.

Academy of the Sacred Heart 200/5-8
4521 Saint Charles Ave 70115 504-891-1943
Kim Duckworth, prin. Fax 891-2755
Academy of the Sacred Heart Lower 300/PK-4
4521 Saint Charles Ave 70115 504-269-1230
Kay Higginbotham, prin. Fax 896-7899
Bishop McManus Academy 100/PK-12
8801 Chef Menteur Hwy 70127 504-246-5121
Owen McManus, hdmstr. Fax 246-5564
Calvary Baptist S 100/PK-8
2401 General Degaulle Dr 70114 504-367-6465
Bernice Davis, admin. Fax 367-6632
Cathedral Academy 200/PK-8
820 Dauphine St 70116 504-525-3860
Sr. Mary Hession, prin. Fax 525-3193
Christian Brothers S 300/5-7
8 Friederichs Ave 70124 504-486-6770
Joey Scaffidi, prin. Fax 486-1053
Ecole Bilingue de la Nouvelle S 200/PK-5
821 General Pershing St 70115 504-896-4500
Cissy Rowley, dir. Fax 896-9610
Good Shepherd Nativity Mission S 100/K-7
353 Baronne St 70112 504-598-9399
Karen Ranatza, prin. Fax 598-9346
Holy Ghost S 300/PK-8
2035 Toledano St 70115 504-899-6782
Sr. Angela Smith, prin. Fax 899-6782
Holy Name of Jesus S 500/PK-8
6325 Cromwell Pl 70118 504-861-1466
Courtney Wolbrette, prin. Fax 861-1480
Holy Name of Mary S 200/PK-8
502 Olivier St 70114 504-361-4004
Joseph Bach, prin. Fax 361-4044
Holy Rosary Academy 100/PK-6
3368 Esplanade Ave 70119 504-482-7173
Michael Binder, prin. Fax 482-7229
McGehee S 400/PK-12
2343 Prytania St 70130 504-561-1224
Eileen Powers, prin. Fax 525-7910
Newman S 900/PK-12
1903 Jefferson Ave 70115 504-899-5641
T.J. Locke, hdmstr. Fax 896-8597
New Orleans Adventist Academy 50/K-10
4500 Gawain Dr 70127 504-240-2227
Resurrection of Our Lord S 200/PK-8
4861 Rosalia Dr 70127 504-243-2257
Dr. Si Nguyen, prin. Fax 241-5532
St. Alphonsus S 100/PK-2
2001 Constance St 70130 504-523-6594
Sr. Monica Ellerbusch, prin. Fax 523-8769
St. Andrew's Episcopal S 100/PK-8
8012 Oak St 70118 504-861-3743
Merrill Hall, hdmstr. Fax 861-3973
St. Andrew the Apostle S 800/PK-8
3131 Eton St 70131 504-394-4171
Nancy Hernandez, prin. Fax 391-3627
St. Anthony of Padua S 300/PK-7
4601 Cleveland Ave 70119 504-488-4426
Sr. Ruth Angelette, prin. Fax 488-5373
St. Benedict the Moor S 100/PK-4
5010 Piety Dr 70126 504-288-2745
Drue Dumas, prin. Fax 282-9386
St. Dominic S 500/PK-8
6326 Memphis St 70124 504-482-4123
Adrianne LeBlanc, prin. Fax 486-3870
St. George's Episcopal S 300/PK-8
923 Napoleon Ave 70115 504-891-5509
Dr. Robert Eichberger, hdmstr. Fax 895-1225
St. Joan of Arc S 300/PK-8
919 Cambronne St 70118 504-861-2887
Dionne Frost, prin. Fax 866-9588
St. John Lutheran S 50/PK-3
3937 Canal St 70119 504-488-6641
Bethany Gonski, prin. Fax 482-2101
St. Leo the Great S 300/PK-6
1501 Abundance St 70119 504-943-1482
Carmel Mire, prin. Fax 944-5895
St. Marys Academy 600/K-12
6905 Chef Menteur Hwy 70126 504-245-0200
Sr. Jennie Jones, prin. Fax 245-0422
St. Paul Lutheran S 200/PK-8
2624 Burgundy St 70117 504-947-1773
Charles Schiller, prin. Fax 945-3743
St. Paul's Episcopal S 100/PK-8
6249 Canal Blvd 70124 504-488-1319
Merry Sorrells, hdmstr. Fax 304-8315
St. Peter Claver S 300/PK-8
1020 N Prieur St 70116 504-822-8191
Vanessa Chavis, prin. Fax 822-2692
St. Pius X S 300/PK-8
6600 Spanish Fort Blvd 70124 504-282-2811
Pamela Fulham, prin. Fax 282-3043
St. Rita S 300/PK-8
65 Fontainebleau Dr 70125 504-866-1777
Sr. Annette Baxley, prin. Fax 861-8512

St. Stephen S 300/PK-8
1027 Napoleon Ave 70115 504-891-1927
Peggy LeBlanc, prin. Fax 891-1928
Stuart Hall S for Boys 300/PK-7
2032 S Carrollton Ave 70118 504-861-1954
Dr. Elizabeth LaForge, prin. Fax 861-5389
Trinity Episcopal S 300/PK-8
1315 Jackson Ave 70130 504-525-8661
Rev. Michael Kuhn, hdmstr. Fax 523-4837
Ursuline Academy S 300/PK-7
2635 State St 70118 504-866-5260
Kimberly Shankle, prin. Fax 866-5293
Waldorf S of New Orleans 50/PK-8
517 Soraparu St Apt 101 70130 504-891-8686
Amber Rosean, admin. Fax 525-3223

New Roads, Pointe Coupee, Pop. 4,790
Pointe Coupee Parish SD 2,400/PK-12
PO Box 579 70760 225-638-8674
Dr. Daniel Rawls, supt. Fax 638-3904
Rosenwald ES 500/PK-5
1100 New Roads St 70760 225-638-6341
Karla Jack, prin. Fax 638-7148
Other Schools – See Batchelor, Maringouin, Rougon

Catholic ES of Pointe Coupee 400/PK-6
304 Napoleon St 70760 225-638-9313
Melissa Cline, prin. Fax 638-9953
False River Academy 700/PK-12
201 Major Pkwy 70760 225-638-3783
Kenneth LeBeau, prin. Fax 638-8555

Noble, Sabine, Pop. 266
Sabine Parish SD
Supt. — See Many
Ebarb S 400/PK-12
5340 Highway 482 71462 318-645-9402
Victor Sepulvado, prin. Fax 645-4689

Norco, Saint Charles, Pop. 3,385
St. Charles Parish SD
Supt. — See Luling
Norco ES 4-6 300/4-6
102 5th St 70079 985-764-7079
Kelli Oertling, prin. Fax 764-7962
Norco ES K-3 400/PK-3
102 5th St 70079 985-764-2787
Steven Guitterrez, prin. Fax 764-2875

Sacred Heart of Jesus S 200/PK-8
453 Spruce St 70079 985-764-9958
Cheryl Orillion, prin. Fax 764-0041

Oakdale, Allen, Pop. 7,981
Allen Parish SD
Supt. — See Oberlin
Oakdale ES 600/PK-4
1515 Highway 1153 71463 318-335-0690
Kay Randolph, prin. Fax 335-2823
Oakdale MS 400/5-8
124 S 13th St 71463 318-335-1558
Linda Thompson, prin. Fax 335-4690

Oak Grove, West Carroll, Pop. 2,044
West Carroll Parish SD 1,900/PK-12
314 E Main St 71263 318-428-2378
Kent Davis, supt. Fax 428-3775
www.wcpsb.com
Goodwill S 100/K-8
1638 Highway 2 71263 318-428-2972
Glen Kelly, prin. Fax 428-2919
Oak Grove ES 400/PK-6
206 Tiger Dr 71263 318-428-4810
Kenneth Herring, prin. Fax 428-4884
Other Schools – See Epps, Forest, Kilbourne

Oberlin, Allen, Pop. 1,869
Allen Parish SD 4,200/PK-12
PO Box C 70655 337-639-4311
Michael Doucet, supt. Fax 639-2346
www.allen.k12.la.us
Oberlin ES 400/PK-6
PO Box E 70655 337-639-2241
Ronald Meaux, prin. Fax 639-5561
Other Schools – See Elizabeth, Grant, Kinder, Oakdale, Reeves

Oil City, Caddo, Pop. 1,189
Caddo Parish SD
Supt. — See Shreveport
Oil City ES 400/PK-6
PO Box 488 71061 318-995-6654
Thomas M. Irvin, prin. Fax 995-5317

Olla, LaSalle, Pop. 1,359
LaSalle Parish SD
Supt. — See Jena
Olla-Standard ES 400/PK-5
PO Box 1188 71465 318-495-5163
Debbie Gauthier, prin. Fax 495-5272

Opelousas, Saint Landry, Pop. 22,897
St. Landry Parish SD 14,600/PK-12
PO Box 310 70571 337-948-3657
Michael Nassif, supt. Fax 942-0204
www.slp.k12.la.us
Creswell ES 300/PK-6
1218 Leo St 70570 337-942-4459
Francis Richard, prin. Fax 942-4892
Grolee ES 500/K-6
1540 W Grolee St 70570 337-942-3130
Glenn Doucet, prin. Fax 942-2332
Northeast ES 500/PK-6
1125 Mamie St 70570 337-942-5390
Leroy Miller, prin. Fax 942-5390
North ES 400/PK-6
308 W Martin Luther King Dr 70570 337-948-6284
Matthew Scruggins, prin. Fax 942-2629
Opelousas JHS 700/7-8
730 S Market St 70570 337-942-4957
Ryan Hooks, prin. Fax 942-2659

Park Vista ES 700/K-6
PO Box 2059 70571 337-942-7456
Ulysse Joubert, prin. Fax 948-7352
Plaisance S 400/PK-8
3264 Highway 167 70570 337-826-3335
Larry Watson, prin. Fax 826-7062
St. Landry Accelerated Transition S 50/7-8
152 Violet Dr 70570 337-948-4763
Karen Domengeaux, prin. Fax 948-9792
South Street ES 400/K-6
409 E South St 70570 337-942-8127
Mary Miller, prin. Fax 942-3386
Southwest ES 400/PK-6
1203 Burr St 70570 337-942-9892
Judy Frank, prin. Fax 942-1763
Other Schools – See Arnaudville, Eunice, Grand Coteau, Krotz Springs, Lawtell, Leonville, Melville, Morrow, Palmetto, Port Barre, Sunset, Washington

---

Acadiana Preparatory S 200/PK-12
1592 E Prudhomme St 70570 337-948-6551
David Barham, prin. Fax 948-1006
Opelousas Catholic S 700/K-12
428 E Prudhomme St 70570 337-942-5404
Perry Fontenot, prin. Fax 942-5922
Westminster Christian Academy 1,000/PK-12
186 Westminster Dr 70570 337-948-8607
Merida Brooks, supt. Fax 948-8983

Paincourtville, Assumption, Pop. 1,550

St. Elizabeth Interparochial S 300/PK-8
PO Box M 70391 985-369-7402
Paula Simoneaux, prin. Fax 369-1527

Palmetto, Saint Landry, Pop. 185
St. Landry Parish SD
Supt. — See Opelousas
Palmetto S 100/PK-8
PO Box 200 71358 337-623-4482
Pauline Vidrine, prin. Fax 623-3939

Paradis, Saint Charles
St. Charles Parish SD
Supt. — See Luling
Martin MS 600/7-8
434 South St 70080 985-758-7579
Erin Raiford, prin. Fax 758-7570
Vial ES 400/3-6
510 Louisiana St 70080 985-758-2771
Tamika Green, prin. Fax 758-2773

Parks, Saint Martin, Pop. 540
St. Martin Parish SD
Supt. — See Saint Martinville
Parks MS 400/5-8
1010A Saint Louis Dr 70582 337-845-4753
Henry Derouselle, prin. Fax 845-5532
Parks PS 500/PK-4
1034 Main St 70582 337-845-4663
Bonnie Thibodeaux, prin. Fax 845-4198

Patterson, Saint Mary, Pop. 5,152
St. Mary Parish SD
Supt. — See Centerville
Patterson JHS 600/4-8
1101 1st St 70392 985-395-6772
Molly Stadalis, prin. Fax 395-6773
Watts ES 500/PK-3
PO Box 639 70392 985-395-5976
Nikki Fryou, prin. Fax 395-2588

Paulina, Saint James
St. James Parish SD
Supt. — See Lutcher
Paulina ES 500/PK-6
PO Box 99 70763 225-869-3639
Hollie Folse, prin. Fax 869-5290

St. Peter Chanel Interparochial S 200/PK-8
2590 LA 44 70763 225-869-5778
Joanna Foltz, prin. Fax 869-8131

Pearl River, Saint Tammany, Pop. 2,044
St. Tammany Parish SD
Supt. — See Covington
Creekside JHS 600/6-8
65434 Highway 41 70452 985-863-5882
Lisa Virga, prin. Fax 863-7658
Little Pearl ES PK-K
63829 Highway 11 70452 985-892-2276
Dr. April Whitfield, prin.
Riverside ES 700/K-5
38480 Sullivan Dr 70452 985-863-3141
Mary Lou Jordan, prin. Fax 863-9811
Sixth Ward ES 300/K-5
72360 Highway 41 70452 985-863-7126
Dr. Mary Biernacki, prin. Fax 863-2074

Pelican, DeSoto
DeSoto Parish SD
Supt. — See Mansfield
Pelican All Saints S 200/PK-12
200 All Saints Rd 71063 318-755-2318
Tamekia Smith, prin. Fax 755-2066

Pierre Part, Assumption, Pop. 3,053
Assumption Parish SD
Supt. — See Napoleonville
Pierre Part S 800/PK-8
3321 Highway 70 S 70339 985-252-6359
Anna Mabile, prin. Fax 252-3918

Pine Prairie, Evangeline, Pop. 1,211
Evangeline Parish SD
Supt. — See Ville Platte
Pine Prairie S 800/PK-12
PO Box 200 70576 337-599-2300
Glenn Lafleur, prin. Fax 599-2003

Pineville, Rapides, Pop. 14,083
Rapides Parish SD
Supt. — See Alexandria
Barron ES 800/PK-6
3655 Holloway Rd 71360 318-445-6860
Karla Tollett, prin. Fax 445-6850
Goff ES 300/PK-6
6900 Shreveport Hwy 71360 318-640-3416
Shannon Dewitt, prin. Fax 640-3425
Moore ES 200/PK-K, 6-6
207 Griffith St 71360 318-445-7151
Alyson Johnson, prin. Fax 445-7156
Pineville ES 400/PK-6
835 Main St 71360 318-442-8154
Randal Nethery, prin. Fax 442-8172
Pineville JHS 600/7-8
501 Edgewood Dr 71360 318-640-0512
Columbus Goodman, prin. Fax 640-9692
Ruby-Wise ES 400/PK-6
5279 Old Marksville Hwy 71360 318-443-6089
Duane Urbina, prin. Fax 443-5709

Alpine Christian S 100/PK-7
7215 Shreveport Hwy 71360 318-640-3804
Cindy LaCaze, admin. Fax 640-4645
Cenla Christian Academy 400/K-12
2900 Donahue Ferry Rd 71360 318-640-4787
Clara McNeely, prin. Fax 640-0697

Pitkin, Vernon
Vernon Parish SD
Supt. — See Leesville
Pitkin S 600/PK-12
PO Box 307 70656 318-358-3121
Kevin Lambright, prin. Fax 358-3580

Plain Dealing, Bossier, Pop. 1,057
Bossier Parish SD
Supt. — See Benton
Martin ES 300/PK-5
600 S Perrin St 71064 318-326-7800
Alan Herring, prin. Fax 326-7804
Plain Dealing MS 100/6-8
300 E Vance St 71064 318-326-7780
Aubrey Sayes, prin. Fax 326-7788

Plain Dealing Christian Academy 100/PK-12
200 Garrett St 71064 318-326-5823
Betty Thurman, admin. Fax 326-5907

Plaquemine, Iberville, Pop. 6,717
Iberville Parish SD 3,400/PK-12
PO Box 151 70765 225-687-4341
Dr. P. Edward Cancienne, supt. Fax 687-5408
www.ipsb.net
Crescent S 700/K-8
62575 Bayou Rd 70764 225-659-2437
Kathleen Schmit, prin. Fax 659-2696
Iberville ES 400/2-6
58650 Iron Farm Rd 70764 225-687-2217
Mary Delores Thibodeaux, prin. Fax 687-2266
Other Schools – See Rosedale, Saint Gabriel, White Castle

St. John S 600/PK-8
58645 Saint Clement Ave 70764 225-687-6616
Bernardine Legendre, prin. Fax 687-6280

Plaucheville, Avoyelles, Pop. 278
Avoyelles Parish SD
Supt. — See Marksville
Plaucheville ES 600/PK-6
School Loop 50 71362 318-922-3311
Fax 922-3608

St. Joseph S 400/PK-12
PO Box 59 71362 318-922-3401
Br. Anthony Dugas, prin. Fax 922-3776

Pleasant Hill, Sabine, Pop. 719
Sabine Parish SD
Supt. — See Many
Pleasant Hill S 300/PK-12
PO Box 8 71065 318-796-3670
Dale Skinner, prin. Fax 796-2644

Pollock, Grant, Pop. 379
Grant Parish SD
Supt. — See Colfax
Pollock ES 600/PK-6
4001 Highway 8 71467 318-765-3511
Rebecca Durand, prin. Fax 765-3762

Ponchatoula, Tangipahoa, Pop. 5,784
Tangipahoa Parish SD
Supt. — See Amite
Cooper S 700/K-8
42350 Highway 445 70454 985-542-6182
Anthony Sciortino, prin. Fax 542-8096
Perrin Early Learning Center 300/PK-K
350 W Ash St 70454 985-386-9734
Patricia Foster, prin. Fax 386-3069
Ponchatoula JHS 700/7-8
315 E Oak St 70454 985-370-5322
Gwendolyn Barsley, prin. Fax 370-5327
Reeves ES 700/3-4
18026 Sisters Rd 70454 985-386-6433
Mae Stilley, prin. Fax 386-9620
Tucker Memorial ES 700/1-2
310 S 3rd St 70454 985-386-6449
Amber Gardner, prin. Fax 386-9663
Vinyard ES 700/5-6
40105 Dunson Rd 70454 985-386-6364
Theresa Hamilton, prin. Fax 386-2553

St. Joseph S 300/PK-8
175 N 8th St 70454 985-386-6421
Dr. Gerard Toups, prin. Fax 386-0560

Port Allen, West Baton Rouge, Pop. 5,062
West Baton Rouge Parish SD 3,500/PK-12
3761 Rosedale Rd 70767 225-343-8309
David Corona, supt. Fax 387-2101
www.wbrschools.net
Chamberlin ES 200/K-3
6024 Section Rd 70767 225-627-6691
Charlotte Blanchard, prin. Fax 627-9306
Cohn ES 300/2-4
805 N 14th St 70767 225-343-7164
Kaye French, prin. Fax 383-8587
Devall MS 300/4-8
11851 N River Rd 70767 225-627-4268
John Currier, prin. Fax 627-4278
Port Allen ES 200/PK-1
609 Rosedale Rd 70767 225-343-7586
Michelle Kauffman, prin. Fax 343-4607
Port Allen MS 300/5-8
610 Rosedale Rd 70767 225-383-5777
Christina Anderson, prin. Fax 346-5030
Other Schools – See Brusly

Holy Family S 400/K-8
335 N Jefferson Ave 70767 225-344-4100
Brenda Fremin, prin. Fax 344-1928
Sharon Baptist Academy 100/PK-8
9433 Section Rd 70767 225-627-4145
Shawn Ostoj, prin. Fax 627-6994

Port Barre, Saint Landry, Pop. 2,318
St. Landry Parish SD
Supt. — See Opelousas
Port Barre ES 500/K-4
PO Box 310 70577 337-585-6172
Mazie Taylor, prin. Fax 585-3646
Port Barre MS 400/5-8
PO Box 69 70577 337-585-7256
William Edgar Duplechain, prin. Fax 585-2290

Port Sulphur, Plaquemines, Pop. 3,523
Plaquemines Parish SD
Supt. — See Belle Chasse
South Plaquemines ES 300/PK-6
315 Civic Dr 70083 504-595-6415
Theresita Ancar, prin. Fax 564-1335

Prairieville, Ascension
Ascension Parish SD
Supt. — See Donaldsonville
Galvez MS 700/5-8
42018 Highway 933 70769 225-621-2424
Linda Embry, prin. Fax 621-2434
Galvez PS 800/PK-4
16093 Henderson Bayou Rd 70769 225-621-2444
Deborah Capello, prin. Fax 621-2447
Oak Grove PS 1,000/K-5
17550 Old Jefferson Hwy 70769 225-621-2360
Terri Tate, prin. Fax 621-2370
Prairieville ES K-5
40228 Parker Rd 70769 225-391-7400
Carol Smith, prin. Fax 391-7401
Prairieville MS 500/6-8
16200 Highway 930 70769 225-621-2340
Diane Gautreau, prin. Fax 673-4883

St. John PS 200/PK-1
37407 Duplessis Rd 70769 225-677-8238
Tina Schexnaydre, prin. Fax 647-7814

Pride, East Baton Rouge
East Baton Rouge Parish SD
Supt. — See Baton Rouge
Northeast ES 800/PK-6
16477 Pride Port Hudson Rd 70770 225-654-5113
Mary Dominique, prin. Fax 654-6538

Princeton, Bossier
Bossier Parish SD
Supt. — See Benton
Princeton ES 600/4-5
1895 Winfield Rd 71067 318-549-5750
Emma Jordan, prin. Fax 549-5763

Provencal, Natchitoches, Pop. 704
Natchitoches Parish SD
Supt. — See Natchitoches
Provencal S 500/PK-8
PO Box 429 71468 318-472-6174
Willa Freeman, prin. Fax 472-9642

Quitman, Jackson, Pop. 165
Jackson Parish SD
Supt. — See Jonesboro
Quitman S 500/PK-12
PO Box 38 71268 318-259-2698
Steve Shovan, prin. Fax 259-1139

Raceland, Lafourche, Pop. 5,564
Lafourche Parish SD
Supt. — See Thibodaux
Raceland Lower ES 400/PK-2
PO Box 529 70394 985-537-6837
Valerie Bourgeois, prin. Fax 537-4375
Raceland MS 700/6-8
PO Box C 70394 985-537-5140
Ann Danos, prin. Fax 537-5182
Raceland Upper ES 400/3-5
PO Box 370 70394 985-537-5142
Bernita DeVille, prin. Fax 537-5354

St. Marys Nativity S 300/PK-8
3492 Nies St 70394 985-537-7544
Marissa Bagala, prin. Fax 537-4020

Rayne, Acadia, Pop. 8,516
Acadia Parish SD
Supt. — See Crowley
Armstrong MS 400/6-8
700 Martin Luther King Blvd 70578 337-334-3377
Marshall Thibodeaux, prin. Fax 334-2681
Central Rayne K 200/PK-K
507 N Polk St 70578 337-334-3669
Patsy Cart, prin. Fax 334-8783
Mire S 500/PK-8
5484 Mire Hwy 70578 337-873-6602
Melanie Venable, prin. Fax 873-4620
Petitjean ES 500/1-3
4039 Crowley Rayne Hwy 70578 337-334-9501
Kimberly Cummins, prin. Fax 334-9517
South Rayne ES 200/4-5
101 E Branche St 70578 337-334-3610
Amy Whatley, prin. Fax 334-4993

Vermilion Parish SD
Supt. — See Abbeville
Indian Bayou S 200/PK-8
1603 LA Highway 700 70578 337-334-4070
Howard Guillory, prin. Fax 334-4237

Rayne Catholic S 400/PK-8
407 S Polk St 70578 337-334-5657
Fred Menard, prin. Fax 334-3301

Rayville, Richland, Pop. 4,014
Richland Parish SD 3,400/PK-12
PO Box 599 71269 318-728-5964
Dr. Cathy Stockton, supt. Fax 728-6366
www.richland.k12.la.us
Holly Ridge S 200/K-8
2306 Highway 183 71269 318-728-6495
Clovis Christman, prin. Fax 728-6465
Rayville ES 500/PK-5
124 Learning Pl 71269 318-728-2029
Gloria Gallman, prin. Fax 728-2099
Rayville JHS 200/6-8
225 Highway 3048 71269 318-728-3618
Tony Guirlando, prin. Fax 728-9374
Other Schools – See Delhi, Mangham, Start

Riverfield Academy 300/PK-12
115 Wood St 71269 318-728-3281
Marie Miller, prin. Fax 728-3285

Reeves, Allen, Pop. 210
Allen Parish SD
Supt. — See Oberlin
Reeves S 300/PK-12
13770 Highway 113 70658 337-666-2414
Cherie Nichols, prin. Fax 666-2812

Reserve, Saint John the Baptist, Pop. 8,847
St. John The Baptist Parish SD 6,600/PK-12
PO Box AL 70084 985-536-1106
Courtney Millet Ph.D., supt. Fax 536-1109
www.stjohn.k12.la.us
Fifth Ward S 500/K-8
158 Panther Dr 70084 985-536-4221
Kendria Spears, prin. Fax 536-1706
Other Schools – See Edgard, Garyville, Laplace, Mount Airy

Our Lady of Grace S 300/PK-8
780 Highway 44 70084 985-536-4291
Camille Treaudo, prin. Fax 536-4250
Reserve Christian S 300/PK-12
PO Box AA 70084 985-536-2418
Rod Aguillard, prin. Fax 479-3135
Riverside Academy 800/PK-12
332 Railroad Ave 70084 985-536-4246
Heidi Tomeny-Duhe, prin. Fax 536-2127
St. Peter S 200/PK-8
188 W 7th St 70084 985-536-4296
Terri Jacob, prin. Fax 536-4305

Ridgecrest, Concordia, Pop. 734
Concordia Parish SD
Supt. — See Vidalia
Ridgecrest S 200/1-8
200 Robert Webber Dr 71334 318-757-2135
Nancy Anders, prin. Fax 757-4651

Ringgold, Bienville, Pop. 1,567
Bienville Parish SD
Supt. — See Arcadia
Ringgold ES 300/PK-6
4044 Bienville Rd Ste A 71068 318-894-2911
Donald Calloway, prin. Fax 894-2912

River Ridge, Jefferson, Pop. 14,800
Jefferson Parish SD
Supt. — See Harvey
Hazel Park/Hilda Knoff ES 300/PK-5
8809 Jefferson Hwy 70123 504-737-6163
Karen Bucher, prin. Fax 738-9153

Curtis Christian S 800/K-12
10125 Jefferson Hwy 70123 504-737-4621
Larry Manguno, prin. Fax 737-7326
St. Matthew the Apostle S 600/PK-8
10021 Jefferson Hwy 70123 504-737-4604
Jill Grabert, prin. Fax 738-7985

Roanoke, Jefferson Davis
Jefferson Davis Parish SD
Supt. — See Jennings
Welsh-Roanoke JHS 200/6-8
PO Box 9 70581 337-753-2317
Kenneth Lasserre, prin. Fax 753-2245

Rosedale, Iberville, Pop. 727
Iberville Parish SD
Supt. — See Plaquemine
North Iberville S 400/PK-12
PO Box 200 70772 225-625-2522
Wyvetta Parker, prin. Fax 625-2559

Roseland, Tangipahoa, Pop. 1,227
Tangipahoa Parish SD
Supt. — See Amite

Roseland ES 300/PK-6
PO Box 860 70456 985-748-9307
Brenda Johnson, prin. Fax 748-9250

Rosepine, Vernon, Pop. 1,321
Vernon Parish SD
Supt. — See Leesville
Rosepine ES 700/PK-6
PO Box 578 70659 337-463-4203
Charles Lewis, prin. Fax 463-4246

Rougon, Pointe Coupee
Pointe Coupee Parish SD
Supt. — See New Roads
Rougon S 400/PK-8
PO Box 626 70773 225-627-4291
Ted David, prin. Fax 627-5111

Ruston, Lincoln, Pop. 20,667
Lincoln Parish SD 6,600/PK-12
410 S Farmerville St 71270 318-255-1430
Danny Bell, supt. Fax 255-3203
www.lincolnschools.org/
Cypress Springs ES 400/K-5
1040 Saratoga St 71270 318-255-0791
Doris Lewis, prin. Fax 255-0596
Glen View ES 600/K-5
1601 Bittersweet Ave 71270 318-255-5724
Lisa Mangum, prin. Fax 255-5744
Hillcrest ES 400/K-5
301 E Kentucky Ave 71270 318-255-0550
Patrice Hilton, prin. Fax 255-0578
Lewis ES 300/6-6
1000 Mitchell Ave 71270 318-255-5963
Sonja Walker, prin. Fax 251-1947
Phillips Lab S 300/K-8
PO Box 10168 71272 318-257-3469
Dr. Carynn Wiggins, prin. Fax 257-3676
Ruston ES 400/PK-5
200 N Bernard St 71270 318-255-4714
Pam Harris, prin. Fax 255-4728
Ruston JHS 600/7-8
481 Tarbutton Rd 71270 318-251-1601
Tim Nutt, prin. Fax 254-5235
Other Schools – See Choudrant, Dubach, Grambling, Simsboro

Bethel Christian S 100/PK-12
2901 Winona Dr 71270 318-255-1112
Sarah Ingram, admin. Fax 513-1113
Cedar Creek S 600/PK-12
2400 Cedar Creek Dr 71270 318-255-7707
Connie Bradford, prin. Fax 251-2846
Wildflower Montessori S 100/PK-8
700 Woodward Ave 71270 318-251-1590
Angie Borden, prin. Fax 251-1576

Saint Amant, Ascension
Ascension Parish SD
Supt. — See Donaldsonville
Lake S 1,000/K-8
14185 Highway 431 70774 225-621-2470
Jay Benoit, prin. Fax 621-2476
Saint Amant MS 600/5-8
44317 Highway 429 70774 225-621-2600
Christy Bourgeois, prin. Fax 621-2593
Saint Amant PS 800/PK-4
44365 Highway 429 70774 225-621-2626
Christie Crooks, prin. Fax 621-2613

Saint Bernard, Saint Bernard
St. Bernard Parish SD
Supt. — See Chalmette
Gauthier ES PK-5
2214 Bobolink Dr 70085 504-272-0700
Lisa Young, prin. Fax 272-0710
Saint Bernard MS 6-7
2601 Torres Dr 70085 504-301-2000
Susan Deffes, prin.

Saint Francisville, West Feliciana, Pop. 1,672
West Feliciana Parish SD 2,400/PK-12
PO Box 1910 70775 225-635-3891
Lloyd Lindsey, supt. Fax 635-0108
www.wfpsb.org
Bains ES 600/2-5
PO Box 1940 70775 225-635-3272
Dorothy Temple, prin. Fax 635-3303
Bains Lower ES 500/PK-1
PO Box 2130 70775 225-635-4696
Joyce Edwards, prin. Fax 635-5345
West Feliciana MS 600/6-8
PO Box 690 70775 225-635-3898
Darryl Powell, prin. Fax 635-6925
Other Schools – See Tunica

Saint Gabriel, Iberville, Pop. 5,527
Iberville Parish SD
Supt. — See Plaquemine
East Iberville S 500/PK-12
3285 Highway 75 70776 225-642-5410
Maria DeLouise, prin. Fax 642-9607

Saint James, Saint James
St. James Parish SD
Supt. — See Lutcher
Fifth Ward ES 200/PK-6
8184 Villavaso St 70086 225-473-9537
Clara Harris, prin. Fax 473-3799

Saint Joseph, Tensas, Pop. 1,222
Tensas Parish SD 800/PK-12
PO Box 318 71366 318-766-3269
Carol Johnson, supt. Fax 766-3634
www.tensas.k12.la.us/
Tensas ES 300/PK-6
892 Highway 8976 71366 318-766-3346
Demetria Dix, prin. Fax 766-3377
Other Schools – See Newellton

Tensas Academy 200/PK-12
PO Box 555 71366 318-766-4384
Bonnie Adcock, prin. Fax 766-3559

Saint Martinville, Saint Martin, Pop. 6,993
St. Martin Parish SD 8,200/PK-12
PO Box 859 70582 337-394-6261
Richard Lavergne, supt. Fax 394-6387
www.stmartin.k12.la.us
Catahoula S 300/PK-8
1016A Catahoula School Hwy 70582 337-394-3641
Annette Baudoin, prin. Fax 394-3632
Early Learning Center 300/PK-1
1004 S Martin Luther King 70582 337-394-4763
Jessica Landry, prin. Fax 394-6115
St. Martinville ES 500/2-5
716 N Main St 70582 337-394-6254
Charee Leblanc, prin. Fax 394-8018
St. Martinville JHS 400/6-8
7190 Main Hwy 70582 337-394-4764
Frederick Wiltz, prin. Fax 394-9619
Other Schools – See Breaux Bridge, Cecilia, Morgan City, Parks

---

Trinity Catholic S 400/PK-8
242 Gary St 70582 337-394-6693
Rosemary Pierre, prin. Fax 394-3394

Saint Rose, Saint Charles, Pop. 6,259
St. Charles Parish SD
Supt. — See Luling
Cammon MS 400/6-8
234 Pirate Dr 70087 504-467-4536
Sylvia Zeno, prin. Fax 468-3873
Saint Rose ES 600/PK-5
230 Pirate Dr 70087 504-464-9254
Merlyna Adams, prin. Fax 468-8064

Saline, Bienville, Pop. 287
Bienville Parish SD
Supt. — See Arcadia
Saline S 300/PK-12
PO Box 129 71070 318-576-3215
Kenneth Heron, prin. Fax 576-9068

Sarepta, Webster, Pop. 916
Webster Parish SD
Supt. — See Minden
Sarepta S 500/K-12
6041 Highway 2 71071 318-847-4301
William Franklin, prin. Fax 847-4891

Schriever, Terrebonne, Pop. 4,958
Terrebonne Parish SD
Supt. — See Houma
Caldwell MS 600/4-7
445 Highway 311 70395 985-868-2565
Karen Bourgeois, prin. Fax 448-3963
Schriever ES 600/PK-3
2052 W Main St 70395 985-868-1199
Peggy Marcel, prin. Fax 446-1323

Scott, Lafayette, Pop. 8,120
Lafayette Parish SD
Supt. — See Lafayette
James Arts & Tech ES 800/PK-5
1500 W Willow St 70583 337-234-0461
Dana Schmersahl, prin. Fax 264-1607
Judice ES 300/PK-1
PO Box 237 70583 337-235-2486
Rosemary Landry, prin. Fax 269-0133
Scott MS 900/5-8
116 Marie St 70583 337-235-9698
Dr. John Pate, prin. Fax 235-9805
Westside ES 400/2-4
912 Delhomme Ave 70583 337-232-6984
Lisa Thomas, prin. Fax 233-7438

SS. Peter & Paul S PK-3
1301 Old Spanish Trail 70583 337-504-3400
Patricia Sonnier, prin. Fax 233-4868

Shongaloo, Webster, Pop. 160
Webster Parish SD
Supt. — See Minden
Shongaloo S 300/K-12
229 Highway Alt 2 71072 318-846-2541
Cynthia Hair, prin. Fax 846-2891

Shreveport, Caddo, Pop. 198,874
Caddo Parish SD 42,800/PK-12
PO Box 32000 71130 318-603-6300
Gerald Dawkins Ph.D., supt. Fax 631-5241
www.caddo.k12.la.us/
Arthur Circle ES 500/PK-5
261 Arthur Ave 71105 318-861-3537
Walter Smithey, prin. Fax 869-3395
Atkins ES 500/PK-5
7611 Saint Vincent Ave 71106 318-868-2810
Al Graham, prin. Fax 861-7778
Barrett ES 300/PK-5
2600 Barret St 71104 318-425-5042
Dr. Joanne Hood, prin. Fax 424-1364
Bethune Middle Academy - Laurel St 6-6
1730 Laurel St 71103 318-226-4957
Betty Jordan, prin. Fax 226-0122
Bethune MS 400/7-8
4331 Henry St 71109 318-636-6336
Perry Daniel, prin. Fax 636-6812
Bickham MS 700/6-8
7240 Old Mooringsport Rd 71107 318-929-4106
Shannon Wall, prin. Fax 929-2416
Blanchard ES 400/PK-5
402 Birch St 71107 318-929-2691
Meredith Haynes, prin. Fax 929-1702
Broadmoor MS Laboratory 600/6-8
441 Atlantic Ave 71105 318-861-2403
Kimberly Brun, prin. Fax 865-4142
Caddo Heights ES 600/PK-5
1702 Corbitt St 71108 318-636-9610
Dr. Cherry Burton, prin. Fax 636-7537
Caddo Learning Center 100/4-8
2550 Thomas E Howard Dr 71107 318-425-3411
Kenneth Coutee, prin. Fax 425-3414
Caddo Parish Magnet MS 1,300/6-8
7635 Cornelious Ln 71106 318-868-6588
Louis Cook, prin. Fax 865-6125
Central ES 200/PK-5
1627 Weinstock St 71103 318-222-5550
Eric Hill, prin. Fax 221-4699
Cherokee Park ES 300/PK-5
2010 E Algonquin Trl 71107 318-221-6782
Tyrone Burton, prin. Fax 221-1748
Claiborne Fundamental ES 400/K-5
2345 Claiborne Ave 71103 318-222-2580
Marilyn Johnson, prin. Fax 221-1680
Clark MS 600/6-8
351 Hearne Ave 71103 318-425-8742
Lewis McCulloch, prin. Fax 425-1151
Creswell ES 400/PK-5
2901 Creswell Ave 71104 318-222-5935
Tracey Harris, prin. Fax 674-8134
Eden Gardens Fundamental ES 500/K-5
626 Eden Blvd 71106 318-861-7654
Janice Hughes, prin. Fax 868-7213
Eighty-First Street ECE Center 200/PK-K
8108 Fairfield Ave 71106 318-865-3596
Niccie Johnson, prin. Fax 865-7519
Fairfield Magnet ES 400/K-5
6215 Fairfield Ave 71106 318-868-9826
Kathleen Barberousse, prin. Fax 861-0662
Forest Hill ES 800/PK-5
2005 Francais Dr 71118 318-686-1783
Oscar Killian, prin. Fax 688-4212
Hillsdale ES 500/PK-5
3860 Hutchinson St 71109 318-636-3484
Charlotte Bailey, prin. Fax 635-3931
Ingersoll ES 200/PK-5
401 N Holzman St 71101 318-222-5606
Jerry Paige, prin. Fax 227-8097
Judson Fundamental ES 500/PK-5
3809 Judson St 71109 318-635-1132
Doris Robinson, prin. Fax 635-1240
Lakeshore ES 600/PK-5
1807 San Jacinto St 71109 318-635-1325
Travis Smith, prin. Fax 635-1961
Linear MS 400/6-8
1845 Linear St 71107 318-221-1589
Dennis Redden, prin. Fax 221-0130
Linwood MS 600/6-8
401 W 70th St 71106 318-861-2401
Monica Jenkins-Moore, prin. Fax 865-1036
Midway Professional Development Center 300/PK-5
3840 Greenwood Rd 71109 318-636-1861
Priscilla Pullen, prin. Fax 636-3427
Mooretown Professional Development Ctr 300/PK-5
3913 Powell St 71109 318-631-7297
Melvin Ashley, prin. Fax 631-0195
North Highlands ES 500/PK-5
885 Poleman Rd 71107 318-221-6346
Cynthia Williams, prin. Fax 227-1426
Northside ES 500/PK-5
1950 Northside Rd 71107 318-221-3896
Jesse Scott, prin. Fax 425-3485
Oak Park ES 300/PK-5
4941 McDaniel Dr 71109 318-635-2141
Sabrina Brown, prin. Fax 635-3055
Pine Grove ES 400/PK-5
1800 Caldwell St 71107 318-424-7191
Linda Henderson, prin. Fax 425-2539
Queensborough ES 300/PK-5
2701 Catherine St 71109 318-631-8784
Beverly Cole, prin. Fax 631-7357
Ridgewood MS 700/6-8
2001 Ridgewood Dr 71118 318-686-0383
Dr. Gerald Burrow, prin. Fax 686-0390
Riverside ES 500/PK-5
625 Dixie Garden Dr 71105 318-865-3576
Christy Terrill, prin. Fax 865-3721
Shreve Island ES 800/PK-5
836 Sewanee Pl 71105 318-869-2335
Charles Lowder, prin. Fax 861-2256
Smith ES 300/PK-5
3000 Dr Mrtn Luther King Dr 71107 318-424-3610
Cindy Frazier Ph.D., prin. Fax 424-5195
Southern Hills ES 700/PK-5
9075 Kingston Rd 71118 318-686-1974
Donna Leone, prin. Fax 688-4459
South Highlands Magnet ES 500/PK-5
831 Erie St 71106 318-865-5119
Keith Burton, prin. Fax 861-6264
Steere ES 400/PK-5
4009 Youree Dr 71105 318-865-5675
Kim Derrick, prin. Fax 861-7823
Summerfield ES 700/PK-5
3131 Ardis Taylor Dr 71118 318-686-1930
Lane Hunnicutt, prin. Fax 688-6960
Summer Grove ES 600/PK-5
2955 Bert Kouns Industrl Lp 71118 318-686-1754
Pamela Bloomer, prin. Fax 688-6971
Sunset Acres ES 500/PK-5
6514 W Canal Blvd 71108 318-631-7121
Stacey Jamison, prin. Fax 636-5185
Timmons ES 300/PK-5
1410 Greenwood Mrngsport Rd 71107 318-929-3950
Mary McWherter, prin. Fax 929-7178
Turner S 1,200/PK-8
5904 W 70th St 71129 318-688-4380
Charles Washington, prin. Fax 671-5230
University ES 900/PK-5
9900 Smitherman Dr 71115 318-797-2240
Paula Nelson, prin. Fax 797-0894
Walnut Hill S 1,500/PK-8
9360 Woolworth Rd 71129 318-687-6610
Albert Hardison, prin. Fax 688-6522

Werner Park ES 500/PK-5
2715 Corbitt St 71108 318-635-9633
Deborah Alexander, prin. Fax 621-9846
West Shreveport ES 400/PK-5
2226 Murphy St 71103 318-222-3397
Shirley Pierson, prin. Fax 227-8486
Westwood ES 500/PK-5
7325 Jewella Ave 71108 318-686-5489
Rudgerick Brown, prin. Fax 688-7802
Williams Stoner Hill ES 300/PK-5
2127 C E Galloway Blvd 71104 318-222-5317
Michelle Franklin, prin. Fax 222-8710
Youree Drive MS 1,000/6-8
6008 Youree Dr 71105 318-868-5324
Victor Mainiero, prin. Fax 861-5086
Other Schools – See Belcher, Keithville, Mooringsport, Oil City, Vivian

Calvary Baptist Academy 1,200/PK-12
9333 Linwood Ave 71106 318-687-4923
Rhonda Honea, prin. Fax 687-4925
Colquitt Christian Academy 50/K-8
3233 Colquitt Rd 71118 318-686-8913
Evangel Christian Academy 700/K-12
7425 Broadacres Rd 71129 318-688-7061
Albert Dean, prin. Fax 688-7322
First Baptist Church S 300/PK-8
533 Ockley Dr 71106 318-869-2361
Dr. James Gillespie, hdmstr. Fax 869-0125
Montessori S for Shreveport 200/PK-8
2605 C E Galloway Blvd 71104 318-861-6777
Angie Day, prin. Fax 865-5793
Our Lady Blessed Sacrament Academy 50/PK-K
2932 Murphy St 71103 318-222-5051
Sr. John Jackson, prin. Fax 222-5840
St. John Berchmans S 200/PK-8
947 Jordan St 71101 318-221-6005
Jo Cazes, prin. Fax 425-0648
St. Joseph S 400/PK-8
1210 Anniston Ave 71105 318-865-3585
Susan Belanger, prin. Fax 868-1859
St. Marks Cathedral S 300/PK-8
2785 Fairfield Ave 71104 318-221-7454
T. P. Aggarwal, admin. Fax 221-7060
Southfield S 400/PK-8
1100 Southfield Rd 71106 318-868-5375
Jeff Stokes, prin. Fax 869-0890
University Christian Preparatory S 100/PK-12
4800 Old Mooringsport Rd 71107 318-221-2697
John Lewis, prin. Fax 221-2790

Sicily Island, Catahoula, Pop. 446
Catahoula Parish SD
Supt. — See Harrisonburg
Martin JHS 100/PK-PK, 5-
PO Box 338 71368 318-389-5651
Phyllis Parker, prin. Fax 389-5651
Sicily Island ES 100/K-4
PO Box 207 71368 318-389-5560
Marguerita Krause, prin. Fax 389-5196

Simmesport, Avoyelles, Pop. 2,211
Avoyelles Parish SD
Supt. — See Marksville
Riverside ES 600/PK-6
549 Norwood St 71369 318-941-2699
Delores Rabalais, prin. Fax 941-2140

Simpson, Vernon, Pop. 522
Vernon Parish SD
Supt. — See Leesville
Simpson S 300/PK-12
PO Box 8 71474 337-383-7810
David Lewis, prin. Fax 383-7655

Simsboro, Lincoln, Pop. 664
Lincoln Parish SD
Supt. — See Ruston
Simsboro S 500/K-12
1 Tiger Dr 71275 318-247-6265
Earlene Jackson, prin. Fax 247-6276

Singer, Beauregard
Beauregard Parish SD
Supt. — See Deridder
Singer S 300/K-12
153 Highway 110 E 70660 337-463-5908
Dennis Burk, prin. Fax 463-0199

Slaughter, East Feliciana, Pop. 997
East Feliciana Parish SD
Supt. — See Clinton
Slaughter ES 300/PK-5
PO Box 60 70777 225-654-4527
Kimberly Glascock, prin. Fax 654-2838

Slidell, Saint Tammany, Pop. 26,840
St. Tammany Parish SD
Supt. — See Covington
Abney ES 700/K-5
825 Kostmayer Ave 70458 985-643-4044
Robert Alford, prin. Fax 847-9509
Alton ES 200/K-5
38276 N 5th Ave 70460 985-863-5353
Schanette Hebert, prin. Fax 863-5818
Bayou Woods ES 800/K-3
35614 Liberty Dr 70460 985-641-1901
Linda Bankston, prin. Fax 649-0923
Bonne Ecole ES 600/K-6
900 Rue Verand 70458 985-643-0674
April Owens Ph.D., prin. Fax 847-1299
Boyet JHS 700/7-8
59295 Rebel Dr 70461 985-643-3775
Mitchell Stubbs, prin. Fax 643-9470
Brock ES 200/K-5
259 Brakefield St 70458 985-643-5166
Rose Smith, prin. Fax 646-1798
Clearwood JHS 600/4-8
130 Clearwood Dr 70458 985-641-8200
Alan Bennett, prin. Fax 641-7122

Cypress Cove ES 700/K-1
540 S Military Rd 70461 985-641-3033
Lisa Dial, prin. Fax 641-8366
Florida Avenue ES 400/K-6
342 Florida Ave 70458 985-643-1605
Elaine Motte, prin. Fax 641-2917
Honey Island ES 600/2-3
500 S Military Rd 70461 985-641-3557
Mary Jane Smith, prin. Fax 649-0959
Little Oak MS 900/4-6
59241 Rebel Dr 70461 985-641-6510
Amy DiCarlo, prin. Fax 641-6511
Park MS 600/4-6
35708 Liberty Dr 70460 985-643-8593
Anthony Esposito, prin. Fax 649-3910
St. Tammany JHS 400/6-8
701 Cleveland Ave 70458 985-643-1592
Vincent DiCarlo, prin. Fax 643-5873
Slidell JHS 700/7-8
333 Pennsylvania Ave 70458 985-641-5914
Brennan McCurley, prin. Fax 641-6397
Whispering Forest ES 500/K-3
300 Spiehler Rd 70458 985-641-3400
Eric Sacks, prin. Fax 641-3424

Calvary Baptist S 400/PK-8
1615 Old Spanish Trl 70458 985-643-7224
Timothy Crabtree, admin. Fax 643-6196
First Baptist Christian S 300/1-12
4141 Pontchartrain Dr 70458 985-643-3725
Mona Nelson, admin. Fax 641-9205
Our Lady of Lourdes S 600/PK-8
345 Westchester Blvd 70458 985-643-3230
Robert Kiefer, prin. Fax 645-0648
St. Margaret Mary S 800/PK-8
1050 Robert Blvd 70458 985-643-4612
Robert Ohler, prin. Fax 643-4659
Slidell Christian Academy 50/PK-8
59344 N Pearl Dr 70461 985-641-3785
Robert Brown, prin. Fax 649-1960

Spearsville, Union, Pop. 149
Union Parish SD
Supt. — See Farmerville
Spearsville S 400/K-12
PO Box 18 71277 318-778-3752
David Gray, prin. Fax 778-3269

Springfield, Livingston, Pop. 406
Livingston Parish SD
Supt. — See Livingston
Springfield ES 500/PK-4
PO Box 9 70462 225-294-3398
Jeanie Windham, prin. Fax 294-6920
Springfield MS 400/4-8
PO Box 40 70462 225-294-3306
Linda Abels, prin. Fax 294-3307

Springhill, Webster, Pop. 5,237
Webster Parish SD
Supt. — See Minden
Browning ES 400/PK-2
505 Herrington Dr 71075 318-539-5663
Barbara Bridges, prin. Fax 539-9867
Brown Upper ES 100/3-5
804 4th St SW 71075 318-539-2818
Hugh Bradford, prin. Fax 539-5427

Starks, Calcasieu
Calcasieu Parish SD
Supt. — See Lake Charles
Starks S 400/PK-12
PO Box 69 70661 337-743-5341
Vickie Poole, prin. Fax 743-5458

Start, Richland
Richland Parish SD
Supt. — See Rayville
Start S 400/K-8
PO Box 146 71279 318-728-2074
Joyce Davis, prin. Fax 728-9291

Sterlington, Ouachita, Pop. 1,246
Ouachita Parish SD
Supt. — See Monroe
Smith ES 500/PK-6
206 High Ave 71280 318-665-2713
Dena Leggett, prin. Fax 665-2716

Stonewall, DeSoto, Pop. 1,888
DeSoto Parish SD
Supt. — See Mansfield
North DeSoto ES 300/3-5
PO Box 427 71078 318-925-1610
Bruce Burback, prin. Fax 925-2894
North DeSoto MS 400/6-8
PO Box 310 71078 318-925-4520
Keith Simmons, prin. Fax 925-4719
North DeSoto PS 500/PK-2
PO Box 410 71078 318-925-2383
Bruce Burback, prin. Fax 925-9373

Sulphur, Calcasieu, Pop. 19,608
Calcasieu Parish SD
Supt. — See Lake Charles
Frasch ES 500/K-5
540 S Huntington St 70663 337-527-6894
Tony McCardle, prin. Fax 528-3114
Henning ES 500/PK-5
774 Henning Dr 70663 337-528-2862
Greg Whiteard, prin. Fax 527-6915
Key ES 500/K-5
1201 E Burton St 70663 337-527-7566
Chuck Sullivan, prin. Fax 527-0679
LeBlanc MS 400/6-8
1100 N Crocker St 70663 337-527-5296
Thomas Finnie, prin. Fax 527-5297
Lewis MS 800/6-8
1752 Cypress St 70663 337-527-6178
Tony Dougherty, prin. Fax 528-3773

Maplewood S 1,000/PK-8
4401 Maplewood Dr 70663 337-625-5521
Margaret Goode, prin. Fax 625-8725
Perkins ES 300/PK-5
565 N Crocker St 70663 337-527-7401
Gloria Marcantel, prin. Fax 527-3937
Vincent ES 400/PK-5
1634 Beglis Pkwy 70663 337-625-3396
Paul Champagne, prin. Fax 625-3872
Vincent Settlement ES 600/PK-5
1072 Vincent Settlement Rd 70665 337-583-4148
Jean Hernandez, prin. Fax 583-7542

Our Lady's S 200/PK-8
1111 Cypress St 70663 337-527-7828
Lana Cooley, prin. Fax 528-3778
Parkview Baptist S 100/K-12
1623 Picard Rd 70663 337-527-7089

Summerfield, Claiborne
Claiborne Parish SD
Supt. — See Homer
Summerfield S 300/PK-12
PO Box 158 71079 318-927-3621
D'Arcy Stevens, prin. Fax 927-9160

Sunset, Saint Landry, Pop. 2,459
St. Landry Parish SD
Supt. — See Opelousas
Cankton S 300/K-8
602 Main St 70584 337-668-4465
Pam Helton, prin. Fax 668-4435
Sunset S 500/K-8
236 Church Hill St 70584 337-662-3194
Shirley James, prin. Fax 662-3478

Tallulah, Madison, Pop. 8,152
Madison Parish SD 2,200/PK-12
PO Box 1620 71284 318-574-3616
Samuel Dixon, supt. Fax 574-3667
www.madisonpsb.org/
Madison MS 500/6-8
900 W Askew St 71282 318-574-0933
Rosie Armstrong, prin. Fax 574-9919
Tallulah ES 500/PK-5
1100 Johnson St 71282 318-574-0732
Glenn Kline, prin. Fax 574-0489
Wright ES 700/PK-5
809 Wyche St 71282 318-574-4430
Gloria Watkins, prin. Fax 574-3029

Tallulah Academy-Delta Christian S 300/PK-12
700 Wood St 71282 318-574-2606
Donald Pennington, prin. Fax 574-3390

Terrytown, Jefferson, Pop. 23,787

Christ the King S 400/PK-8
2106 Deerfield Rd 70056 504-367-3601
Cindy Ruel, prin. Fax 367-3679

Theriot, Terrebonne
Terrebonne Parish SD
Supt. — See Houma
Dularge ES 200/PK-2
1327 Bayou Dularge Rd 70397 985-879-1629
Melynda Rodrigue, prin. Fax 879-4528

Thibodaux, Lafourche, Pop. 14,408
Lafourche Parish SD 14,600/PK-12
PO Box 879 70302 985-446-5631
Jo Ann Matthews, supt. Fax 446-0801
www.lafourche.k12.la.us
Bayou Boeuf ES 200/PK-5
4138 Highway 307 70301 985-633-2352
Kenn Robichaux, prin. Fax 633-2359
Chackbay ES 400/PK-5
101 School Ln 70301 985-633-2348
Robby Lee, prin. Fax 633-4710
East Thibodaux MS 400/6-8
802 E 7th St 70301 985-446-5616
Belinda Harry, prin. Fax 446-5610
Lafargue ES 600/PK-5
700 Plantation Rd 70301 985-447-9292
Arlene Adams, prin. Fax 447-4243
St. Charles ES 200/PK-5
1690 Highway 1 70301 985-446-6862
Barry Filce, prin. Fax 446-8591
Sixth Ward MS 300/6-8
PO Box 1236 70302 985-633-2449
Marla Tabor, prin. Fax 633-7373
South Thiboudaux ES 600/PK-5
200 Iris St 70301 985-446-8471
Diane Smith, prin. Fax 447-1792
Thibodaux ES 600/PK-5
700 E 7th St 70301 985-446-6116
Jimi Encalade, prin. Fax 447-8234
West Thiboudaux MS 500/6-8
1111 E 12th St 70301 985-446-6889
Edmond Adams, prin. Fax 447-1777
Other Schools – See Cut Off, Galliano, Golden Meadow, Houma, Larose, Lockport, Raceland

St. Genevieve S 500/K-7
807 Barbier Ave 70301 985-447-9291
Chris Knobloch, prin. Fax 447-9883
St. Joseph S 700/PK-7
501 Cardinal Dr 70301 985-446-1346
Gerard Rodrigue, prin. Fax 449-0760

Tickfaw, Tangipahoa, Pop. 642
Tangipahoa Parish SD
Supt. — See Amite
Nesom MS 400/6-8
PO Box 280 70466 985-345-2166
Maureen Terese, prin. Fax 345-3731

Trout, LaSalle
LaSalle Parish SD
Supt. — See Jena

Fellowship S 200/PK-8
1650 Highway 773 71371 318-992-5177
Gary Wilbanks, prin. Fax 992-0049

Tunica, West Feliciana
West Feliciana Parish SD
Supt. — See Saint Francisville
Tunica ES 100/PK-5
General Delivery 70782 225-655-4135
Shannon Hall, prin. Fax 655-4220

Urania, LaSalle, Pop. 685
LaSalle Parish SD
Supt. — See Jena
LaSalle JHS 200/6-8
PO Box 520 71480 318-495-3474
Steve Long, prin. Fax 495-3478

Vacherie, Saint James, Pop. 2,354
St. James Parish SD
Supt. — See Lutcher
Sixth Ward ES 400/PK-6
3245 Valcour Aime St 70090 225-265-3942
Judy Ezidore, prin. Fax 265-8609
Vacherie ES 300/2-6
13440 Highway 644 70090 225-265-3674
Julie Dauzat, prin. Fax 265-7263
Vacherie PS 200/PK-1
19177 Highway 643 70090 225-265-7747
Julie Dauzat, prin. Fax 265-1001

Vidalia, Concordia, Pop. 4,210
Concordia Parish SD 4,000/PK-12
PO Box 950 71373 318-336-4226
Loretta Blankenstein, supt. Fax 336-5875
www.cpsbla.us/
Vidalia JHS 400/6-8
210 Gillespie St 71373 318-336-6227
Whest Shirley, prin. Fax 336-6229
Vidalia Lower ES 500/PK-2
300 Stampley St 71373 318-336-6220
Doris Polk, prin. Fax 336-6214
Vidalia Upper ES 400/3-5
1 Concordia Ave 71373 318-336-6224
Darla Johnston, prin. Fax 336-8922
Other Schools – See Ferriday, Monterey, Ridgecrest

Ville Platte, Evangeline, Pop. 8,250
Evangeline Parish SD 6,100/PK-12
1123 Te Mamou Rd 70586 337-363-6651
Toni Hamlin, supt. Fax 363-8086
www.epsb.com
Bayou Chicot S 700/PK-8
4576 Highway 167 N 70586 337-461-2687
Delores Miller, prin. Fax 461-2601
Stephens Montessori S 100/PK-2
1500 Martin Luther King Dr 70586 337-363-4745
Janice Soileau, prin. Fax 363-6242
Vidrine S 400/PK-8
5094 Vidrine Rd 70586 337-363-4280
Sherral Tezeno, prin. Fax 363-6828
Ville Platte ES 700/PK-4
708 High School Dr 70586 337-363-3068
Sally Moreaux, prin. Fax 363-7317
Other Schools – See Basile, Chataignier, Mamou, Pine Prairie

Christian Heritage Academy 200/PK-12
607 Prosper St 70586 337-363-7690
Steven Sawtelle, admin. Fax 363-7699
Sacred Heart S 500/K-8
532 E Main St 70586 337-363-3322
Diane Fontenot, prin. Fax 363-3551

Vinton, Calcasieu, Pop. 3,173
Calcasieu Parish SD
Supt. — See Lake Charles
Vinton ES 500/PK-5
1610 Hampton St 70668 337-589-7365
Molly Beard, prin. Fax 589-6613
Vinton MS 200/6-8
900 Horridge St 70668 337-589-7567
Stephen Hardy, prin. Fax 589-7587

Emmanuel Christian Academy 50/PK-8
PO Box 906 70668 337-589-5354
W.J. Turpin, prin. Fax 589-1222

Violet, Saint Bernard, Pop. 8,574
St. Bernard Parish SD
Supt. — See Chalmette
Smith ES PK-5
6701 E Saint Bernard Hwy 70092 504-301-2000
Dedra Bailey, prin.

Vivian, Caddo, Pop. 3,866
Caddo Parish SD
Supt. — See Shreveport
Vivian S 700/PK-8
100 W Kentucky Ave 71082 318-375-3271
Jamie Tolbert, prin. Fax 375-2499

Waggaman, Jefferson, Pop. 9,405
Jefferson Parish SD
Supt. — See Harvey
Cherbonnier ES 400/PK-5
700 Dandelion Dr 70094 504-431-9740
Constance Grove, prin. Fax 431-1236
Rillieux ES 300/PK-5
7121 River Rd 70094 504-436-8336
Myrtle Weber, prin. Fax 436-1088

Walker, Livingston, Pop. 5,751
Livingston Parish SD
Supt. — See Livingston
Milton ES 500/K-5
PO Box 187 70785 225-664-9711
Arlene Wilson, prin. Fax 665-4415
North Corbin ES 500/K-5
PO Box 328 70785 225-686-9169
Glenda Newman, prin. Fax 686-9170
North Corbin JHS 6-8
32725 N Corbin Rd 70785 225-686-2038
Dennis DeLee, prin. Fax 686-2690
South Walker ES 600/K-5
13745 Milton Ln 70785 225-665-0446
Kenneth Fohne, prin. Fax 665-0816
Walker ES 500/PK-5
PO Box 188 70785 225-665-5534
Allison Raborn, prin. Fax 665-9951
Westside JHS 700/6-8
12615 Burgess Ave 70785 225-665-8259
Steve Link, prin. Fax 665-8283

Washington, Saint Landry, Pop. 1,057
St. Landry Parish SD
Supt. — See Opelousas
Grand Prairie S 300/PK-8
669 Highway 363 70589 337-826-3391
Charles Moore, prin. Fax 826-5674
Washington S 200/PK-7
1530 Highway 10 70589 337-826-3393
Mary Fontenot, prin. Fax 826-5276

Watson, Livingston
Livingston Parish SD
Supt. — See Livingston
Live Oak ES 700/PK-5
PO Box 620 70786 225-665-6702
Murrice Kevin Owen, prin. Fax 664-7910
Live Oak MS 1,000/6-8
PO Box 470 70786 225-664-3211
Fred London, prin. Fax 664-1551
South Live Oak Upper ES 200/3-5
PO Box 500 70786 225-667-9330
Patricia Davis, prin. Fax 667-2713

Welsh, Jefferson Davis, Pop. 3,310
Jefferson Davis Parish SD
Supt. — See Jennings
Welsh ES 600/PK-5
222 Bourgeois St 70591 337-734-2351
Arlene Heinen, prin. Fax 734-2704

Westlake, Calcasieu, Pop. 4,565
Calcasieu Parish SD
Supt. — See Lake Charles
Arnett MS 400/6-8
400 Sulphur Ave 70669 337-436-9657
Vance Richmond, prin. Fax 436-5745
Western Heights ES 300/PK-5
1100 Elizabeth St 70669 337-433-5779
Daniel Racca, prin. Fax 439-9298
Westwood ES 500/K-5
1900 Sampson St 70669 337-436-6882
Phyllis Hess, prin. Fax 436-6964

West Monroe, Ouachita, Pop. 13,038
Ouachita Parish SD
Supt. — See Monroe
Boley ES 200/PK-5
2213 Cypress St 71291 318-387-7378
Curtis Pate, prin. Fax 387-7465
Claiborne ES 700/PK-5
1011 Wallace Dean Rd 71291 318-396-8200
Kevin Welch, prin. Fax 396-8604
Crosley K 200/PK-K
700 Natchitoches St 71291 318-325-3634
Janice Comeaux, prin. Fax 322-7951
Drew ES 600/PK-5
1132 Ole Highway 15 71291 318-396-7186
Barbara Dykes, prin. Fax 397-1923
Good Hope MS 600/6-8
400 Good Hope Rd 71291 318-396-9693
Twainna Calhoun, prin. Fax 397-5110
Highland ES 200/PK-5
1501 Wellerman Rd 71291 318-396-1213
Tommy Comeaux, prin. Fax 397-1927
Kiroli ES 500/PK-5
700 Kiroli Rd 71291 318-396-1118
Carolyn Norris, prin. Fax 396-0804
Lenwil ES 400/PK-5
112 Arrant Rd 71292 318-323-3604
Edwin Davis, prin. Fax 323-7796
Pinecrest S 200/PK-8
3604 Highway 557 71292 318-325-4331
Mike Stone, prin. Fax 325-4459
Riser ES 400/PK-5
100 Price Dr 71292 318-387-0577
Nicole Zordan, prin. Fax 387-6801
Riser MS 500/6-8
100 Price Dr 71292 318-387-0567
Donnie Dampier, prin. Fax 387-9072
Riverbend ES 400/1-5
700 Austin Ave 71292 318-361-0155
Anthony Moore, prin. Fax 329-9614
Welch ES 500/PK-5
199 Caldwell Rd 71291 318-397-1100
Vance Smith, prin. Fax 397-1383
West Ridge MS 600/6-8
6977 Cypress St 71291 318-397-8444
James Aulds, prin. Fax 397-9376
Woodlawn ES 600/K-5
5946 Jonesboro Rd 71292 318-325-1578
Terry Hollingsworth, prin. Fax 325-1579
Woodlawn MS 300/6-8
175 Woodlawn School Rd 71292 318-325-1574
Charles Dykes, prin. Fax 325-9858

Claiborne Christian S 300/PK-12
334 Laird St 71291 318-396-7968
Amy Brooks, prin. Fax 397-0567
Northeast Baptist S 200/PK-12
5225 I 20 Service Rd 71292 318-325-2077
Anita Watson, prin. Fax 998-0193

Westwego, Jefferson, Pop. 10,489
Jefferson Parish SD
Supt. — See Harvey
Butler ES 500/PK-5
300 Fourth St 70094 504-341-1351
Denise Rehm, prin. Fax 347-2583
Live Oak Manor ES 300/PK-5
220 Acadia Dr 70094 504-431-7924
Dannie Becnel, prin. Fax 431-1116
Pitre ES 400/PK-5
1525 Spruce St 70094 504-341-6517
Julie Flattmann, prin. Fax 341-9527
Strehle ES 400/PK-5
178 Millie Dr 70094 504-436-1920
Patti Waddell, prin. Fax 436-9264
Westwego ES 300/PK-5
537 Avenue D 70094 504-341-1451
Dodie Plaisance, prin. Fax 341-4087
Worley MS 600/6-8
801 Spartan Ln 70094 504-348-4964
Hope Alello, prin. Fax 348-7057

Our Lady of Prompt Succor S 300/PK-8
531 Avenue A 70094 504-341-9505
Sr. Deborah Walker, prin. Fax 341-9508

White Castle, Iberville, Pop. 1,850
Iberville Parish SD
Supt. — See Plaquemine
Dorseyville ES 400/PK-6
PO Box 518 70788 225-545-3805
Jeanne Caballero, prin. Fax 545-2534

Winnfield, Winn, Pop. 5,307
Winn Parish SD 2,800/PK-12
PO Box 430 71483 318-628-6936
Steve Bartlett, supt. Fax 628-2582
www.winnpsb.org
Winnfield IS 300/4-5
400 S Saint John St 71483 318-628-3557
Steve Adams, prin. Fax 628-1247
Winnfield K 200/PK-K
1607 Maple St 71483 318-628-4134
Ethel Howell, prin. Fax 628-9841
Winnfield MS 400/6-8
685 Thomas Mill Rd 71483 318-628-2765
Kaye Kieffer, prin. Fax 628-1838
Winnfield PS 400/1-3
401 S Saint John St 71483 318-628-4105
Claudia Franks, prin. Fax 628-4108
Other Schools – See Atlanta, Calvin, Dodson

Winnsboro, Franklin, Pop. 4,991
Franklin Parish SD 3,300/PK-12
7293 Prairie Rd 71295 318-435-9046
Dr. Lanny Johnson, supt. Fax 435-3392
www.franklin.k12.la.us
Winnsboro ES 600/PK-5
1310 Warren St 71295 318-435-5066
Fay Phillips, prin. Fax 435-5063
Other Schools – See Baskin, Crowville, Fort Necessity, Gilbert

---

Franklin Academy 300/K-12
2110 Loop Rd 71295 318-435-9520
Phil Jackson, prin. Fax 435-9508

Youngsville, Lafayette, Pop. 5,289
Lafayette Parish SD
Supt. — See Lafayette
Gallet ES 900/K-5
2901 E Milton Ave 70592 337-856-1934
Virginia Bonvillian, prin. Fax 856-1918
Lindon ES 700/PK-4
603 Avenue B 70592 337-856-7261
Gina Cahee, prin. Fax 856-8957
Youngsville MS 700/5-8
PO Box 1049 70592 337-856-5961
Darrel Combs, prin. Fax 856-9945

Zachary, East Baton Rouge, Pop. 12,258
Zachary Community SD 3,800/PK-12
4656 Main St 70791 225-658-4969
H. Warren Drake, supt. Fax 658-4969
www.zacharyschools.org
Copper Mill ES 600/4-5
1300 Independence Blvd 70791 225-658-1288
Dewey Davis, prin. Fax 658-1298
Northwestern ES 700/PK-1
4200 Rollins Rd 70791 225-654-2786
Martha Davis, prin. Fax 654-6613
Northwestern MS 900/6-8
5200 E Central Ave 70791 225-654-9201
Debby Brian, prin. Fax 658-2025
Zachary ES 600/2-3
3775 Hemlock St 70791 225-654-4036
Patrick Jenkins, prin. Fax 654-8746

Zwolle, Sabine, Pop. 1,768
Sabine Parish SD
Supt. — See Many
Zwolle ES 500/PK-6
PO Box 548 71486 318-645-6294
Laura Ford, prin. Fax 645-4519

MAINE

MAINE DEPARTMENT OF EDUCATION
23 State House Station, Augusta 04333-0023
Telephone 207-624-6600
Fax 207-624-6700
Website http://www.maine.gov/education/index.shtml

Commissioner of Education Susan Gendron

MAINE BOARD OF EDUCATION
23 State House Station, Augusta 04333-0023

Chairperson Ann Weisleder

PUBLIC, PRIVATE AND CATHOLIC ELEMENTARY SCHOOLS

Acton, York
Acton SD 300/K-8
700 Milton Mills Rd 04001 207-636-2100
Brian Beeler, supt. Fax 636-4525
www.acton.k12.me.us/
Acton S 300/K-8
700 Milton Mills Rd 04001 207-636-2100
Sean Casey, prin. Fax 636-3045

Addison, Washington
MSAD 37
Supt. — See Harrington
Merritt S 100/K-8
518 Indian River Rd 04606 207-483-2229
Lorna Greene, prin. Fax 488-4572

Albion, Kennebec
MSAD 49
Supt. — See Fairfield
Albion ES 200/K-6
20 School St 04910 207-437-2616
Claudette Massey, prin. Fax 437-2001

Alexander, Washington
Union SD 106
Supt. — See Calais
Alexander S 100/K-8
1430 Airline Rd 04694 207-454-2623
Terry Charlton, prin. Fax 454-7760

Alfred, York
Regional School Unit 57
Supt. — See Waterboro
Alfred ES 200/K-5
PO Box 579 04002 207-324-3831
Virginia Drouin, prin. Fax 490-9732

Alton, Penobscot
Union SD 90
Supt. — See Milford
Alton ES 50/K-5
22 Argyle Rd 04468 207-394-2331
Nathan Dyer, prin. Fax 394-2331

Andover, Oxford
MSAD 44
Supt. — See Bethel
Andover ES 100/K-5
PO Box 70 04216 207-392-4381
Roger Sabin, prin. Fax 392-1500

Anson, Somerset
MSAD 74
Supt. — See North Anson
Schenck ES 100/PK-5
PO Box 317 04911 207-696-3100
Jean Butler, prin. Fax 696-3656

Arundel, York
Arundel SD 300/K-5
600 Limerick Rd 04046 207-282-5709
Alton Hadley, supt. Fax 283-2874
www.arundelschool.net
Day S 300/K-5
600 Limerick Rd 04046 207-284-4677
Thomas Parker, prin. Fax 284-5832

Ashland, Aroostook
MSAD 32 300/K-12
PO Box 289 04732 207-435-3661
Gehrig Johnson Ph.D., supt. Fax 435-8421
www.sad32.org/
Ashland Central ES 100/K-5
PO Box 449 04732 207-435-3511
Robert Hennessey, prin. Fax 435-8421

Athens, Somerset
MSAD 59
Supt. — See Madison
Athens S 200/PK-8
PO Box 167 04912 207-654-2561
Scott Mitchell, prin. Fax 654-2109

Auburn, Androscoggin, Pop. 23,602
Auburn SD 3,200/K-12
PO Box 800 04212 207-333-6600
Thomas Morrill, supt. Fax 333-6628
www.auburnschl.edu
Auburn MS 500/7-8
38 Falcon Dr 04210 207-333-6654
Kathleen Fuller-Cutler, prin. Fax 784-1359
East Auburn Community ES 100/K-6
15 Andrew Dr 04210 207-782-4142
Sue Dorris, prin. Fax 782-0173
Fairview ES 500/K-6
397 Minot Ave 04210 207-784-3559
Catherine Folan, prin. Fax 786-0787
Park Avenue ES K-6
161 Park Ave 04210 207-333-6657
Vickie Gaylord, prin. Fax 786-6782
Sherwood Heights ES 400/K-6
32 Sherwood Dr 04210 207-783-8526
Laura Shaw, prin. Fax 784-1574
Walton ES 200/K-6
92 Mary Carroll St 04210 207-784-1528
Michelle McClellan, prin. Fax 784-1520
Washburn ES 200/K-6
35 Lake Auburn Ave 04210 207-784-5467
Fax 784-5468

Augusta, Kennebec, Pop. 18,626
Augusta SD 2,600/PK-12
12 Gedney St 04330 207-626-2468
Cornelia Brown, supt. Fax 626-2444
www.augustaschools.org/
Farrington ES 400/K-6
249 Eastern Ave 04330 207-626-2480
Carolyn Neighoff, prin. Fax 626-2479
Gilbert ES, 1 Sunset Ave 04330 300/PK-6
Sue Dionne, prin. 207-626-2491
Hodgkins MS, 17 Malta St 04330 400/7-8
Kathryn Holliker, prin. 207-626-2490
Hussey ES 200/PK-6
12 Gedney St 04330 207-626-2461
Michelle Michaud, prin. Fax 626-2539
Lincoln ES 200/K-6
30 Lincoln St 04330 207-626-2483
Lori Bolster, prin. Fax 626-2535
Other Schools – See Georgetown

Unorganized Territories SD 200/PK-8
23 State House Sta 04333 207-624-6892
Shelley Lane, supt. Fax 624-6891
Other Schools – See Connor, Edmunds, Kingman, Sinclair

St. Michael S 400/PK-8
56 Sewall St 04330 207-623-3491
Jon Caron, prin. Fax 623-2971

Aurora, Hancock
Airline Community SD
Supt. — See Holden
Airline Community S 50/K-8
26 Great Pond Rd 04408 207-584-3012
Kathleen Salkaln, prin. Fax 584-5112

Baileyville, Washington
Union SD 107 600/PK-12
PO Box 580 04694 207-427-6913
Barry McLaughlin, supt. Fax 427-3166
Woodland ES 200/PK-6
23 Fourth Ave 04694 207-427-3882
Edna Smith, prin. Fax 427-3632
Other Schools – See Princeton

Bangor, Penobscot, Pop. 31,074
Bangor SD 3,900/K-12
73 Harlow St 04401 207-992-4150
Betsy Webb, supt. Fax 992-4163
www.bangorschools.net
Cohen MS 400/6-8
304 Garland St 04401 207-941-6230
Gary Gonyar, prin. Fax 941-6235
Doughty MS 400/6-8
143 5th St 04401 207-941-6220
Robert MacDonald, prin. Fax 947-7606
Downeast ES 300/K-3
100 Moosehead Blvd 04401 207-941-6240
Mary Williams, prin. Fax 941-6242
Fairmount ES 300/4-5
58 13th St 04401 207-941-6260
Ryan Enman, prin. Fax 941-6269
Fourteenth Street PS 100/K-3
224 14th St 04401 207-941-6350
Richard Fournier, prin. Fax 941-6289
Fruit Street PS 300/K-3
175 Fruit St 04401 207-941-6270
Timothy Babcock, prin. Fax 941-6270
Lincoln ES 200/K-3
45 Forest Ave 04401 207-941-6280
William Armstrong, prin. Fax 941-6282
Snow ES 300/4-5
435 Broadway 04401 207-941-6290
Stephen Bishop, prin. Fax 941-6299
Vine Street ES 200/K-3
66 Vine St 04401 207-941-6300
Timothy McCluskey, prin. Fax 992-2448

All Saints S - St. John Campus 100/4-8
PO Box 1749 04402 207-942-0955
Marcia Diamond, prin. Fax 942-2398
All Saints S - St. Mary Campus 200/PK-3
768 Ohio St 04401 207-947-7063
Marcia Diamond, prin. Fax 942-7356
Bangor Christian S 300/PK-12
1476 Broadway 04401 207-947-7356
Jim Frost, prin. Fax 262-9528
Penobscot Christian S 100/PK-8
1423 Ohio St 04401 207-947-2704
William MacDonald, hdmstr. Fax 942-7482

Bar Harbor, Hancock, Pop. 2,768
Union SD 98
Supt. — See Mount Desert
Conners/Emerson S 400/K-8
11 Eagle Lake Rd 04609 207-288-3631
Barbara Neilly, prin. Fax 288-3597

Bar Mills, York
MSAD 6 4,100/K-12
PO Box 38 04004 207-929-3831
Suzanne Lukas, supt. Fax 929-5955
www.sad6.k12.me.us
Other Schools – See Buxton, Hollis Center, Limington, Standish, Steep Falls

Bass Harbor, Hancock
Union SD 98
Supt. — See Mount Desert
Tremont S 100/K-8
119 Tremont Rd 04653 207-244-7777
Dianne Waters, prin. Fax 244-7023

Bath, Sagadahoc, Pop. 9,257
Regional School Unit 1 2,300/PK-12
39 Andrews Rd 04530 207-443-6601
William Shuttleworth, supt. Fax 443-8295
www.rsu1.org/
Bath MS 400/6-8
6 Old Brunswick Rd 04530 207-443-8270
Louis Solebello, prin. Fax 443-8273
Dike-Newell ES 300/K-2
3 Wright Dr 04530 207-443-8285
Sally Brown, prin. Fax 443-8288
Fisher-Mitchell ES 300/3-5
597 High St 04530 207-443-8265
Lawrence Dyer, prin. Fax 443-4167
Other Schools – See Phippsburg, West Bath, Woolwich

Beals, Washington
Union SD 103
Supt. — See Jonesport
Beals S 50/K-8
PO Box 220 04611 207-497-5449
Christopher Crowley, lead tchr. Fax 497-2334

Belfast, Waldo, Pop. 6,872
MSAD 34 1,800/K-12
PO Box 363 04915 207-338-1960
Bruce Mailloux, supt. Fax 338-4597
www.sad34.net
East Belfast ES 100/K-5
14 Swan Lake Ave 04915 207-338-4220
Jody Henderson, prin. Fax 338-5990
Howard MS 500/6-8
173 Lincolnville Ave 04915 207-338-3320
Kimberly Buckheit, prin. Fax 338-5588

Stevens ES 300/K-5
31 Elementary Ave 04915 207-338-3510
Susan Inman, prin. Fax 338-4091
Other Schools – See Morrill, Northport, Searsmont, Swanville

Belgrade, Kennebec
MSAD 47
Supt. — See Oakland
Belgrade Central ES 300/PK-5
158 Depot Rd 04917 207-495-2321
Catherine Gordon, prin. Fax 495-2723

Benton, Kennebec
MSAD 49
Supt. — See Fairfield
Benton ES 700/1-6
68 School Dr 04901 207-453-4240
Suanne Giorgetti, prin. Fax 453-4242

Berwick, York
MSAD 60
Supt. — See North Berwick
Hussey PS 400/K-4
PO Box 1156 03901 207-698-4465
Audra Beauvais, prin. Fax 698-5069
Knowlton S 400/5-6
8 Noble Ln 03901 207-698-1188
Ron Robert, prin. Fax 698-4401
Noble MS 500/7-8
46 Cranberry Meadow Rd 03901 207-698-1320
Daniel Baker, prin. Fax 698-4400

Bethel, Oxford
MSAD 44 1,000/K-12
21 Philbrook St 04217 207-824-2185
David Murphy Ed.D., supt. Fax 824-2725
www.sad44.org
Crescent Park ES 300/K-5
19 Crescent St 04217 207-824-2839
Levi Brown, prin. Fax 824-0265
Telstar MS 300/6-8
284 Walkers Mills Rd 04217 207-824-2136
Sandra Schroeder, prin. Fax 824-0496
Other Schools – See Andover, Bryant Pond

Biddeford, York, Pop. 22,072
Biddeford SD 2,400/K-12
PO Box 1865 04005 207-282-8280
Sarah-Jane Poli, supt. Fax 284-7956
www.biddschools.org
Biddeford IS 4-5
335 Hill St 04005 207-282-5957
Debra Kenney, prin. Fax 282-8289
Biddeford MS 700/6-8
25 Tiger Way 04005 207-282-6400
Charles Lomonte, prin. Fax 282-7983
Biddeford PS 600/1-3
320 Hill St 04005 207-282-8285
Joan Warren, prin. Fax 286-9225
Kennedy Memorial ES 200/K-K
64 West St 04005 207-282-4134
Paulette Bonneau, prin. Fax 284-7199

St. James S 400/PK-8
25 Graham St 04005 207-282-4084
Patricia Berthiaume, prin. Fax 286-3693

Bingham, Somerset, Pop. 1,071
MSAD 13 300/K-12
PO Box 649 04920 207-672-5502
N. Kenneth Smith, supt. Fax 672-5502
www.sad13.k12.me.us/
Quimby MS 100/5-8
PO Box 649 04920 207-672-5500
Linda MacKenzie, prin. Fax 672-5502
Other Schools – See Moscow

Blue Hill, Hancock
Union SD 93 400/PK-8
PO Box 630 04614 207-374-9927
Arthur Wittine, supt. Fax 374-2951
Blue Hill Consolidated S 200/K-8
60 High St 04614 207-374-2202
Freddie Cole, prin. Fax 374-2919
Other Schools – See Brooksville, Castine, Penobscot

Bay S 100/PK-8
PO Box 950 04614 207-374-2187
Fax 374-5717

Boothbay Harbor, Lincoln, Pop. 1,267
SU 49/Boothbay-Boothbay Harbor Cmmnty SD 900/K-12
51 Emery Ln 04538 207-633-2874
Eileen King, supt. Fax 633-5458
Boothbay Region S 400/K-8
238 Townsend Ave 04538 207-633-5097
Mark Tess, prin. Fax 633-7130
Other Schools – See Edgecomb, Southport

Bowdoin, Sagadahoc
MSAD 75
Supt. — See Topsham
Bowdoin Central ES 200/K-5
1460 Main St 04287 207-666-5779
George Jenkins, prin. Fax 666-3139

Bowdoinham, Sagadahoc
MSAD 75
Supt. — See Topsham
Bowdoinham Community ES 200/K-5
23 Cemetery Rd 04008 207-666-5546
Diane Stahl, prin. Fax 666-3160

Bradford, Penobscot
MSAD 64
Supt. — See Corinth
Bradford ES 100/K-2
641 Main Rd 04410 207-327-1112
Judith Marvin, prin. Fax 327-1112

Bradley, Penobscot
Union SD 90
Supt. — See Milford
Rand ES 100/K-5
55 Highland Ave 04411 207-827-2508
Cheryl Leonard, prin. Fax 827-2508

Brewer, Penobscot, Pop. 9,138
Brewer SD 1,700/PK-12
49 Capri St 04412 207-989-3160
Daniel Lee, supt. Fax 989-8622
www.breweredu.org/
Brewer MS 300/6-8
5 Somerset St 04412 207-989-8640
William Leithiser, prin. Fax 989-8635
Capri Street S 50/PK-K
49 Capri St 04412 207-989-8620
Janet McIntosh, prin. Fax 989-8622
State Street ES 200/4-5
131 State St 04412 207-989-3244
Bill Leithiser, prin. Fax 989-8632
Washington Street ES 300/1-3
100 Washington St 04412 207-989-8660
Janet McIntosh, prin. Fax 989-8662

Bridgton, Cumberland, Pop. 2,195
MSAD 61 1,800/K-12
900 Portland Rd 04009 207-647-3048
Patrick Phillips, supt. Fax 647-5682
www.sad61.k12.me.us/
Stevens Brook ES 300/K-5
14 Frances Bell Dr 04009 207-647-5675
Cheryl Turpin, prin. Fax 647-8172
Other Schools – See Naples, Sebago

Brooklin, Hancock
Union SD 76
Supt. — See Sargentville
Brooklin S 100/K-8
PO Box 120 04616 207-359-2133
Halina Nawrot, prin. Fax 359-2303

Brooks, Waldo
MSAD 3
Supt. — See Unity
Morse Memorial ES 100/K-5
PO Box 37 04921 207-722-3636
Matthew Houghton, prin. Fax 722-3052

Brooksville, Hancock
Union SD 93
Supt. — See Blue Hill
Brooksville S 100/PK-8
1527 Coastal Rd 04617 207-326-8500
Corinne Pert, prin. Fax 326-9195

Brownville, Piscataquis
MSAD 41
Supt. — See Milo
Brownville ES 100/K-6
774 Main Rd 04414 207-965-8184
Christine Beres, prin. Fax 965-8363

Brunswick, Cumberland, Pop. 14,683
Brunswick SD 3,300/K-12
35 Union St 04011 207-319-1900
Paul Perzanoski, supt. Fax 725-1700
www.brunswick.k12.me.us/
Brunswick JHS 700/6-8
65 Columbia Ave 04011 207-319-1930
John Paige, prin. Fax 721-0602
Coffin ES 500/K-5
20 Barrows St 04011 207-319-1950
Walter Wallace, prin. Fax 725-1704
Hawthorn ES 100/1-5
46 Federal St 04011 207-319-1960
Jean Skorapa, prin. Fax 725-1706
Jordan Acres ES 500/K-5
75 Jordan Ave 04011 207-319-1970
Scott Snedden, prin. Fax 725-1707
Longfellow ES 300/K-5
21 Longfellow Ave 04011 207-319-1980
Gregory Scott, prin. Fax 725-1701

St. Johns S 200/PK-8
39 Pleasant St 04011 207-725-5507
Andree Tostevin, prin. Fax 798-4792

Bryant Pond, Oxford
MSAD 44
Supt. — See Bethel
Woodstock ES 100/K-5
224 Rumford Ave 04219 207-665-2228
Jolene Littlehale, prin. Fax 665-2229

Forestdale SDA S 50/K-9
27 Perkins Valley Rd 04219 207-674-2934
Fax 674-2934

Bucksport, Hancock, Pop. 2,989
Regional School Unit 25 1,300/PK-12
62 Mechanic St 04416 207-469-7311
James Boothby, supt. Fax 469-6640
www.rsu25.org/
Bucksport MS 300/5-8
100 Miles Ln 04416 207-469-6647
Thomas Jandreau, prin. Fax 469-2068
Jewett S 100/K-K
66 Bridge St 04416 207-469-6644
Marcelle Marble, prin. Fax 469-6646
Miles Lane ES 200/1-4
52 Miles Ln 04416 207-469-6666
Marcelle Marble, prin. Fax 469-6659
Other Schools – See Orland

Burnham, Waldo
MSAD 53
Supt. — See Pittsfield
Burnham Village ES 100/K-K
61 Troy Rd 04922 207-487-5622
Faye Anderson, prin.

Buxton, York
MSAD 6
Supt. — See Bar Mills
Bonny Eagle MS 1,000/6-8
92 Sokokis Trl 04093 207-929-3833
Ansel Stevens, prin. Fax 929-9181
Hanson ES 100/4-5
932 Long Plains Rd 04093 207-929-3835
Donald Gnecco, prin. Fax 929-9152
Jack Memorial ES 200/K-2
290 Parker Farm Rd 04093 207-929-3830
Donald Gnecco, prin. Fax 929-9152
Jewett S 300/2-5
24 Groveville Rd 04093 207-929-3836
Donald Gnecco, prin. Fax 929-9152
Libby ES 100/K-1
94 Main St 04093 207-929-3837
Donald Gnecco, prin. Fax 929-9166

Living Waters Christian S 100/PK-12
197 Parker Farm Rd 04093 207-727-4499
Denise Wingfield, prin. Fax 727-4422

Calais, Washington, Pop. 3,308
Union SD 106 800/PK-12
32 Blue Devil Hl 04619 207-454-7561
James Underwood, supt. Fax 454-2516
Calais ES 300/PK-6
53 Garfield St 04619 207-454-2000
Peter Perkins, prin. Fax 454-2708
Other Schools – See Alexander, Robbinston

Camden, Knox, Pop. 4,022
MSAD 28 900/K-8
7 Lions Ln 04843 207-236-3358
Patricia Hopkins, supt. Fax 236-7810
www.fivetowns.net
Camden-Rockport MS 400/5-8
34 Knowlton St 04843 207-236-7805
Maria Libby, prin. Fax 236-7815
Other Schools – See Rockport

Canaan, Somerset
MSAD 54
Supt. — See Skowhegan
Canaan ES 200/PK-6
178 Main St 04924 207-474-3901
Steven Swindells, prin. Fax 474-6385

Cape Elizabeth, Cumberland, Pop. 8,854
Cape Elizabeth SD 1,700/K-12
PO Box 6267 04107 207-799-2217
Alan Hawkins, supt. Fax 799-2914
www.cape.k12.me.us
Cape Elizabeth MS 600/5-8
14 Scott Dyer Rd 04107 207-799-8176
Steven Connolly, prin. Fax 767-0832
Pond Cove ES 500/K-4
12 Scott Dyer Rd 04107 207-799-7339
Thomas Eismeier, prin. Fax 799-8171

Caribou, Aroostook, Pop. 8,308
Eastern Aroostook Regional Sch Unit 39 2,000/PK-12
628 Main St 04736 207-496-6311
Franklin McElwain, supt. Fax 498-3261
www.rsu39.org
Caribou MS 500/5-8
21 Glenn St 04736 207-493-4240
Susan White, prin. Fax 493-4243
Hilltop ES 300/K-2
19 Marshall Ave 04736 207-493-4250
Jane Kilcollins, prin. Fax 493-4247
Teague Park ES 300/PK-PK, 3-
59 Glenn St 04736 207-493-4248
Tanya Belanger, prin. Fax 493-4262
Other Schools – See Limestone

Carmel, Penobscot
MSAD 23 600/PK-8
44 Plymouth Rd 04419 207-848-5173
John Backus, supt. Fax 848-5196
www.sad23.k12.me.us
Caravel MS 200/6-8
520 Irish Rd 04419 207-848-3615
Rhonda Sperrey, prin. Fax 848-0884
Carmel ES 200/PK-5
50 Plymouth Rd 04419 207-848-3383
Candice Devlin, prin. Fax 848-3113
Other Schools – See Levant

Castine, Hancock
Union SD 93
Supt. — See Blue Hill
Adams S 100/K-8
PO Box 29 04421 207-326-8608
Todd Nelson, prin. Fax 326-0665

Chelsea, Kennebec
Sheepscot Valley Regional School Unit 12
Supt. — See Whitefield
Chelsea S 200/K-8
566 Togus Rd 04330 207-582-2214
Andrew Doiron, prin. Fax 588-2489

Cherryfield, Washington
MSAD 37
Supt. — See Harrington
Cherryfield S 100/K-8
85 School St 04622 207-546-7949
Michele Janes, prin. Fax 546-7949

Monhegan Plt SD, 2 Elm St 04622 50/K-8
Bruce Ives, supt. 207-546-7325
Other Schools – See Monhegan

Cliff Island, See Portland
Portland SD
Supt. — See Portland
Cliff Island ES 50/K-5
PO Box 7 04019 207-766-2885
Gwen Smith, prin. Fax 766-2134

Clinton, Kennebec, Pop. 1,485
MSAD 49
Supt. — See Fairfield
Clinton ES 300/K-6
75 Morrison Ave 04927 207-426-2181
Stephen Soule, prin. Fax 426-9166

Columbia Falls, Washington
MSAD 37
Supt. — See Harrington
Columbia Falls S 100/K-8
PO Box 130 04623 207-483-2920
Michele Janes, prin. Fax 483-2920

Connor, Aroostook
Unorganized Territories SD
Supt. — See Augusta
Connor Consolidated ES 50/PK-6
1581 Van Buren Rd, 207-496-4521
Barbara Dechaine, prin. Fax 496-0012

Corinna, Penobscot
Regional School Unit 19
Supt. — See Newport
Corinna ES 200/PK-4
PO Box 411 04928 207-278-4263
Richard Fernald, prin. Fax 278-4265

Corinth, Penobscot
MSAD 64 1,300/K-12
408 Main St 04427 207-285-3334
Daniel Higgins, supt. Fax 285-4343
msad64.dcix.net
Central MS 300/6-8
PO Box 19 04427 207-285-3177
Jonathan Perry, prin. Fax 285-4350
Morison Memorial S 200/3-5
386 Main St 04427 207-285-3301
Shirley Wright, prin. Fax 285-3021
Other Schools – See Bradford, Hudson, Kenduskeag, Stetson

Cornish, York
MSAD 55
Supt. — See Hiram
Cornish ES 100/K-4
17 School St 04020 207-625-4393
Rebecca Carpenter, prin. Fax 625-3220

Ossipee Valley Christian S 100/PK-12
1890 North Rd 04020 207-793-4005
Susan Smith, admin. Fax 793-2904

Cornville, Somerset
MSAD 54
Supt. — See Skowhegan
Cornville ES 100/K-6
1192 W Ridge Rd 04976 207-474-3944
Debra Primmerman, prin. Fax 474-0665

Cumberland Center, Cumberland, Pop. 1,890
MSAD 51 2,100/PK-12
PO Box 6A 04021 207-829-4800
Robert Hasson, supt. Fax 829-4802
www.msad51.org
Drowne Road IS 200/3-3
12 Drowne Rd 04021 207-829-2250
Karen Bubar, prin. Fax 829-2253
Greely MS 600/6-8
351 Tuttle Rd 04021 207-829-4815
Kim Brandt, prin. Fax 829-4819
Wilson ES 300/PK-2
353 Tuttle Rd 04021 207-829-4825
Susan Robbins, prin. Fax 829-2254
Other Schools – See North Yarmouth

Cushing, Knox
MSAD 50
Supt. — See Thomaston
Cushing Community ES 100/K-4
54 Cross Rd 04563 207-354-2312
Beth Chamberlin, prin. Fax 354-0014

Cutler, Washington
Union SD 134
Supt. — See Machias
Bay Ridge S 50/K-8
PO Box 240 04626 207-259-3347
Darlene Wheeler, prin. Fax 259-3812

Damariscotta, Lincoln, Pop. 1,567
Great Salt Bay Community SD 400/K-8
767 Main St Ste 1A 04543 207-563-3044
Robert Bouchard, supt. Fax 563-8276
Great Salt Bay Community S 400/K-8
559 Main St 04543 207-563-3091
Jeffrey Boston, prin. Fax 563-6974

Long Island SD 50/K-5
128 Pine Ridge Rd 04543 207-766-4414
David Gaul, supt. Fax 766-4414
Other Schools – See Long Island

Union SD 74 500/K-8
767 Main St 04543 207-563-3044
Robert Bouchard, supt. Fax 563-8276
www.schoolunion74.org/
Other Schools – See Nobleboro, Pemaquid, South Bristol

Danforth, Washington
East Range Community SD 50/K-8
31A Houlton Rd 04424 207-448-2882
Fax 448-7235
Other Schools – See Topsfield

MSAD 14 200/PK-12
31A Houlton Rd 04424 207-448-2882
William Dobbins, supt. Fax 448-7235
www.eastgrandschool.org
East Grand S 200/PK-12
31 Houlton Rd 04424 207-448-2260
David Apgar, prin. Fax 448-7880

Union SD 108 50/PK-8
31A Houlton Rd 04424 207-448-2882
William Dobbins, supt. Fax 448-7235
Other Schools – See Vanceboro

Dayton, York
Union SD 7
Supt. — See Saco
Dayton Consolidated ES 200/K-5
21 Clarks Mills Rd 04005 207-499-2283
Janice Toomey, prin. Fax 499-7356

Dedham, Hancock
Dedham SD 200/PK-8
2065 Main Rd, 207-843-4314
Daniel Lee Ed.D., supt. Fax 843-4315
www.dedhamschool.net
Dedham S 200/PK-8
2065 Main Rd, 207-843-6498
Katherine Lawson, prin. Fax 843-4330

Deer Isle, Hancock
Deer Isle - Stonington Community SD
Supt. — See Sargentville
Deer Isle - Stonington S 300/K-8
249 N Deer Isle Rd 04627 207-348-6301
Catherine Ring, prin. Fax 348-6304

Denmark, Oxford
MSAD 72
Supt. — See Fryeburg
Denmark ES 100/K-5
637 W Main St 04022 207-452-2360
Mark Schrader, prin. Fax 452-2372

Dexter, Penobscot, Pop. 2,650
MSAD 46 1,000/K-12
10 Spring St 04930 207-924-5262
Kevin Jordan, supt. Fax 924-7660
www.msad46.org
Dexter MS 200/5-8
62 Abbott Hill Rd 04930 207-924-5571
Juliana Richard, prin. Fax 924-7668
Dexter PS 300/K-4
60 Abbott Hill Rd 04930 207-924-7671
Terry Wood, prin. Fax 924-7683
Other Schools – See Exeter, Garland

Dixfield, Oxford, Pop. 1,300
Regional School Unit 10 2,900/PK-12
33 Nash St 04224 207-562-7254
Thomas Ward Ed.D., supt. Fax 562-7059
www.msad21.org
Dirigo MS 300/5-8
45 Middle School Dr 04224 207-562-7552
Celena Ranger, prin. Fax 562-8329
Other Schools – See Mexico, Peru, Rumford, Sumner

Dixfield SDA S K-8
PO Box 605 04224 207-562-8262

Dover Foxcroft, Piscataquis, Pop. 3,077
MSAD 68 700/K-8
63 Harrison Ave Ste C 04426 207-564-2421
Ann Bridge, supt. Fax 564-3487
www.sad68.com/
Se Do Mo Cha ES 300/K-4
63 Harrison Ave 04426 207-564-2521
Wilma Lombardi, prin. Fax 564-6529
Se Do Mo Cha MS 300/5-8
63 Harrison Ave 04426 207-564-8376
Jay Robinson, prin. Fax 564-6531
Other Schools – See Monson

Dresden, Lincoln
Regional School Unit 2
Supt. — See Hallowell
Dresden ES 100/K-5
86 Cedar Grove Rd 04342 207-737-2559
Martha Witham, prin. Fax 737-4392

Durham, Androscoggin
Union SD 30
Supt. — See Lisbon
Durham S 300/K-8
654 Hallowell Rd 04222 207-353-9333
William Pidden, prin. Fax 353-2731

Dyer Brook, Aroostook
Southern Aroostook Community SD 400/K-12
922 Dyer Brook Rd, 207-757-8223
Terry Comeau, supt. Fax 757-8257
www.sacs.csd109.k12.me.us/
Southern Aroostook Community S 400/K-12
922 Dyer Brook Rd, 207-757-8206
Jon Porter, prin. Fax 757-8257

Eagle Lake, Aroostook
MSAD 27
Supt. — See Fort Kent
Eagle Lake S 100/PK-8
PO Box 190 04739 207-444-5213
Larry Murphy, prin. Fax 444-5213

Eastbrook, Hancock
Regional School Unit 24
Supt. — See Ellsworth
Cave Hill S 100/K-8
1205 Eastbrook Rd 04634 207-565-3638
Jeffery Fish, prin. Fax 565-2370

East Machias, Washington
East Machias SD
Supt. — See Machias

Elm Street S 200/PK-8
PO Box 229 04630 207-255-8692
Tony Maker, prin. Fax 255-5800

East Millinocket, Penobscot, Pop. 2,075
Millinocket SD 700/K-12
45 North St Ste 2 04430 207-746-3500
Sara Alberts, supt. Fax 746-3516
Other Schools – See Millinocket

Union SD 113 500/K-12
45 North St Ste 2 04430 207-746-3500
Sara Alberts, supt. Fax 746-3516
Myrick ES 200/K-4
6 1/2 Beech St 04430 207-746-3520
Ronnee Johnston, prin. Fax 746-3518
Other Schools – See Medway

Easton, Aroostook
Easton SD 200/PK-12
PO Box 126 04740 207-488-7700
Franklin Keenan, supt. Fax 488-2840
Easton ES 100/PK-6
PO Box 126 04740 207-488-7701
Franklin Keenan, prin. Fax 488-2840

Eastport, Washington, Pop. 1,594
Union SD 104 500/PK-12
102 High St 04631 207-853-2567
Terry Lux, supt. Fax 853-6260
Eastport S 100/PK-8
100 High St 04631 207-853-6252
Lovina Wormell, prin. Fax 853-6264
Other Schools – See Pembroke, Perry

East Waterboro, York
Regional School Unit 57
Supt. — See Waterboro
Massabesic MS 600/6-8
134 Old Alfred Rd 04030 207-247-6121
Mark Fisher, prin. Fax 247-8621
Waterboro ES 600/K-5
PO Box 438 04030 207-247-6126
Mark Petersen, prin. Fax 247-6127

Eddington, Penobscot
MSAD 63
Supt. — See Holden
Eddington ES 200/K-4
440 Main Rd 04428 207-843-6010
Don Spencer, prin. Fax 843-4317

Edgecomb, Lincoln
SU 49/Boothbay-Boothbay Harbor Cmmnty SD
Supt. — See Boothbay Harbor
Edgecomb Eddy ES 100/K-6
157 Boothbay Rd 04556 207-882-5515
Lisa Clarke, dean Fax 882-5948

Edmunds, Washington
Unorganized Territories SD
Supt. — See Augusta
Edmunds Consolidated S 100/PK-8
21 Harrison Rd, 207-726-4478
Martha Livingstone, prin. Fax 726-0932

Eliot, York
MSAD 35 1,800/PK-12
180 Depot Rd 03903 207-439-2438
Jeffrey Bearden, supt. Fax 439-2531
www.msad35.net/
Eliot ES 200/PK-3
1298 State Rd 03903 207-439-9004
Maureen Goering, prin. Fax 439-5380
Other Schools – See South Berwick

Tidewater S 100/PK-8
PO Box 420 03903 207-439-7911
Martha Coombs, admin. Fax 439-9599

Ellsworth, Hancock, Pop. 7,021
Regional School Unit 24 2,600/K-12
248 State St Ste 11A 04605 207-667-8136
Katrina Kane, supt. Fax 667-6493
169.244.34.8/rsu24/
Beech Hill S 100/K-8
105 Otis Rd 04605 207-537-2203
Deborah Metzler, prin. Fax 537-3127
Knowlton ES 200/K-3
160 State St 04605 207-667-8074
Amy Peterson-Roper, prin. Fax 667-8045
Lamoine Consolidated S 100/K-8
53 Lamoine Beach Rd 04605 207-667-8578
Val Perkins, prin. Fax 667-3860
Moore ES 200/4-7
125 State St 04605 207-667-6261
Jim Newett, prin. Fax 667-6263
Other Schools – See Eastbrook, Hancock, Steuben, Sullivan, Surry, Trenton, Winter Harbor

---

Acadia Christian S 100/PK-12
171 Bar Harbor Rd 04605 207-664-0182
Renee Clark, prin. Fax 667-0197

Embden, Somerset
MSAD 74
Supt. — See North Anson
Embden ES 50/2-5
797 Embden Pond Rd 04958 207-566-7302
Jean Butler, prin. Fax 566-5903

Etna, Penobscot
Regional School Unit 19
Supt. — See Newport
Etna-Dixmont S 300/K-8
2100 Dixmont Rd 04434 207-234-2491
Cynthia Alexander, prin. Fax 234-4190

Exeter, Penobscot
MSAD 46
Supt. — See Dexter

Exeter Consolidated ES — 50/3-5
PO Box 30 04435 — 207-379-2291
Juliana Richard, prin. — Fax 379-2292

Fairfield, Kennebec, Pop. 2,794
MSAD 49 — 2,500/PK-12
8 School St 04937 — 207-453-4200
Dean Baker, supt. — Fax 453-4208
www.sad49.k12.me.us/
Fairfield K — 100/PK-K
63 High St 04937 — 207-453-4220
Claudette Massey, prin. — Fax 453-4218
Lawrence JHS — 400/7-8
7 School St 04937 — 207-453-4200
Roberta Hersom, prin. — Fax 453-4214
Other Schools – See Albion, Benton, Clinton

Kennebec Montessori S — 100/PK-3
38 Sheridan Rd 04937 — 207-453-6055
Rebecca Green, prin. — Fax 453-6055

Falmouth, Cumberland, Pop. 7,610
Falmouth SD — 2,000/K-12
51 Woodville Rd 04105 — 207-781-3200
George Entwistle, supt. — Fax 781-5711
www.falmouthschools.org
Falmouth MS — 700/5-8
52 Woodville Rd 04105 — 207-781-3740
Sue Palfrey, prin. — Fax 781-7423
Lunt ES — 300/K-2
74 Lunt Rd 04105 — 207-781-7424
John Flaherty, prin. — Fax 781-8066
Plummer-Motz ES — 300/3-4
192 Middle Rd 04105 — 207-781-3988
Karen Boffa, prin. — Fax 781-2077

Friends S of Portland — 100/PK-8
1 Mackworth Is 04105 — 207-781-6321
James Grumbach, hdmstr.

Farmingdale, Kennebec, Pop. 2,070
Regional School Unit 2
Supt. — See Hallowell
Hall-Dale MS — 200/6-8
111 Maple St 04344 — 207-622-4162
Steven Lavoie, prin. — Fax 622-7515

Farmington, Franklin, Pop. 4,197
Mt. Blue Regional SD — 2,500/K-12
115 Learning Ln 04938 — 207-778-6571
Michael Cormier, supt. — Fax 778-4160
www.mtbluersd.org/
Cascade Brook ES — 300/4-6
162 Learning Ln 04938 — 207-778-4821
Nicole Goodspeed, prin. — Fax 778-5809
Mallet ES — 400/K-3
113 Quebec St 04938 — 207-778-3529
Tracy Williams, prin. — Fax 778-5823
Mt. Blue MS — 400/7-8
269 Middle St 04938 — 207-778-3511
Gary Oswald, prin. — Fax 778-5810
Other Schools – See New Sharon, Wilton

Fayette, Kennebec
Fayette SD — 100/PK-5
2023 Main St, — 207-685-4770
Briane Coulthard, supt. — Fax 685-4756
fayette.maranacook.org
Fayette Central ES — 100/PK-5
2023 Main St, — 207-685-4770
Briane Coulthard, prin. — Fax 685-4756

Fort Fairfield, Aroostook, Pop. 1,729
MSAD 20 — 600/PK-12
28 High School Dr Ste B 04742 — 207-473-4455
Marc Gendron, supt. — Fax 473-4095
www.msad20.org/
Fort Fairfield ES — 300/PK-5
76 Brunswick Ave 04742 — 207-472-3290
Suzanne Parks, prin. — Fax 472-3282

Fort Kent, Aroostook, Pop. 2,123
MSAD 27 — 1,100/PK-12
23 W Main St Ste 101 04743 — 207-834-3189
Dr. Patrick O'Neill, supt. — Fax 834-3395
www.sad27.k12.me.us/
Fort Kent S — 500/PK-8
108 Pleasant St 04743 — 207-834-3456
Gary Stevens, prin. — Fax 834-5169
Other Schools – See Eagle Lake, Saint Francis, Wallagrass

Frankfort, Waldo
MSAD 56
Supt. — See Searsport
Frankfort ES — 100/K-5
112 N Searsport Rd 04438 — 207-223-5723
Devora Kamys, prin. — Fax 223-5715

Freeport, Cumberland, Pop. 1,829
Freeport SD — 1,200/PK-12
17 West St 04032 — 207-865-0928
Elaine Tomaszewski, supt. — Fax 865-2855
www.freeportschooldistrict.com/
Freeport MS — 300/6-8
19 Kendall Ln 04032 — 207-865-6051
Kathleen Marquis-Girard, prin. — Fax 865-2902
Mast Landing ES — 300/3-5
116 Bow St 04032 — 207-865-4561
Holly Couturier, prin. — Fax 865-2855
Morse Street ES — 200/PK-2
21 Morse St 04032 — 207-865-6361
Cheryl White, prin. — Fax 865-2903

Merriconeag Waldorf S — 200/K-12
57 Desert Rd 04032 — 207-865-3900
Fax 865-6822

Pine Tree Academy — 100/PK-12
67 Pownal Rd 04032 — 207-865-4747
Fax 865-1768

Frenchboro, Hancock
Union SD 98
Supt. — See Mount Desert
Frenchboro S — 50/K-8
PO Box 39 04635 — 207-334-2944
Fax 334-2944

Frenchville, Aroostook
MSAD 33 — 300/PK-12
PO Box 9 04745 — 207-543-7334
Fern Desjardins, supt. — Fax 543-6242
www.msad33.org
Levesque ES — 200/PK-6
PO Box 489 04745 — 207-543-7302
Lisa Bernier, prin. — Fax 543-6185

Friendship, Knox
MSAD 40
Supt. — See Union
Friendship Village ES — 100/K-6
PO Box 100 04547 — 207-832-5057
Richard Blackman, prin. — Fax 832-7389

Fryeburg, Oxford, Pop. 1,580
MSAD 72 — 900/K-8
124 Portland St 04037 — 207-935-2600
Gary MacDonald, supt. — Fax 935-3787
www.msad72.k12.me.us/
Ockett MS — 300/6-8
25 Molly Ockett Dr 04037 — 207-935-2401
Sharon Burnell, prin. — Fax 935-4470
Snow ES — 200/K-5
11 Pine St 04037 — 207-935-2536
Jeanette Almy, prin. — Fax 935-8025
Other Schools – See Denmark, Lovell

Gardiner, Kennebec, Pop. 6,237
MSAD 11 — 2,300/PK-12
150 Highland Ave 04345 — 207-582-5346
Dr. Paul Knowles, supt. — Fax 582-8305
www.msad11.org
Gardiner Regional MS — 500/6-8
161 Cobbossee Ave 04345 — 207-582-1326
Todd Sanders, prin. — Fax 582-6823
Richards ES — 300/PK-2
279 Brunswick Ave 04345 — 207-582-3612
Karen Moody, prin. — Fax 582-3175
Other Schools – See Pittston, Randolph, South Gardiner, West Gardiner

Garland, Penobscot
MSAD 46
Supt. — See Dexter
Garland ES — 100/K-2
PO Box 129 04939 — 207-924-6942
Terry Wood, prin. — Fax 924-8896

Georgetown, Sagadahoc
Augusta SD
Supt. — See Augusta
Georgetown Central S — 100/K-6
PO Box 469 04548 — 207-371-2160
Theresa Lash, prin. — Fax 371-2595

Glenburn, See Bangor
Glenburn SD — 400/K-8
983 Hudson Rd 04401 — 207-942-4405
Douglas Smith, supt. — Fax 942-4250
www.glenburn.k12.me.us/
Glenburn S — 400/K-8
991 Hudson Rd 04401 — 207-947-8769
Tom Sullivan, prin. — Fax 947-3867

Glen Cove, Knox, Pop. 300

Riley S — 100/PK-9
PO Box 300 04846 — 207-596-6405
Glenna Plaisted, dir. — Fax 596-7200

Gorham, Cumberland, Pop. 3,618
Gorham SD — 2,600/K-12
75 South St Ste 2 04038 — 207-222-1000
Theodore Sharpe, supt. — Fax 839-5003
www.gorhamschools.org/
Gorham MS — 700/6-8
106 Weeks Rd 04038 — 207-222-1220
Robert Riley, prin. — Fax 839-4092
Narragansett ES — 300/K-2
284 Main St 04038 — 207-222-1250
Bradley Smith, prin. — Fax 839-5021
Village ES — 600/3-5
12 Robie St 04038 — 207-222-1300
Brian Porter, prin. — Fax 839-5029
White Rock ES — 100/K-2
10 N Gorham Rd 04038 — 207-222-1050
Margaret Evans, prin. — Fax 892-9539

Gray, Cumberland
MSAD 15 — 2,000/K-12
14 Shaker Rd 04039 — 207-657-3335
Victoria Burns, supt. — Fax 657-2040
www.msad15.org/
Gray-New Gloucester MS — 500/6-8
31 Libby Hill Rd 04039 — 207-657-4994
Sherry Levesque, prin. — Fax 657-5219
Russell ES — 200/K-2
8 Gray Park 04039 — 207-657-4929
Daniel Joseph, prin. — Fax 657-2286
Other Schools – See New Gloucester

Greenbush, Penobscot
Union SD 90
Supt. — See Milford
Dunn S — 200/PK-8
129 Military Rd 04418 — 207-826-2000
Denise Hamlin, prin. — Fax 826-2001

Greene, Androscoggin
MSAD 52
Supt. — See Turner
Greene Central ES — 400/K-6
41 Main St 04236 — 207-946-5681
Thomas Martellone, prin. — Fax 946-3281

Greenville, Piscataquis, Pop. 1,601
Union SD 60 — 300/K-12
PO Box 100 04441 — 207-695-3708
Heather Perry, supt. — Fax 695-3709
www.ghslakers.org
Nickerson ES — 100/K-5
PO Box 100 04441 — 207-695-2745
Rebecca Brown, prin. — Fax 695-4614
Other Schools – See Shirley Mills

Guilford, Piscataquis, Pop. 1,082
MSAD 4 — 800/PK-12
25 Campus Dr 04443 — 207-876-3444
Paul Stearns, supt. — Fax 876-3446
www.sad4.com/
Guilford PS — 100/2-3
31 High St 04443 — 207-876-4590
Julie Orton, prin. — Fax 876-4627
Piscataquis Community MS — 300/4-8
25 Campus Dr 04443 — 207-876-4301
Virginia Rebar, prin. — Fax 876-4291
Other Schools – See Parkman

Hallowell, Kennebec, Pop. 2,535
Regional School Unit 2 — 2,300/PK-12
7 Reed St 04347 — 207-622-6351
Don Siviski, supt. — Fax 622-7866
www.halldale.org/
Hall-Dale ES — 300/K-5
26 Garden Ln 04347 — 207-623-8677
Thomas Leonard, prin. — Fax 623-6246
Other Schools – See Dresden, Farmingdale, Monmouth, Richmond

Hampden, Penobscot, Pop. 3,895
MSAD 22 — 2,200/PK-12
24 Main Rd N 04444 — 207-862-3255
Richard Lyons, supt. — Fax 862-2789
www.sad22.us/
McGraw ES — 200/PK-2
20 Main Rd N 04444 — 207-862-3830
Marianne Deraps, prin. — Fax 862-5649
Reeds Brook MS — 400/6-8
28A Main Rd S 04444 — 207-862-3540
Thomas Ingraham, prin. — Fax 862-3551
Weatherbee ES — 300/3-5
22 Main Rd N 04444 — 207-862-3254
Regan Nickels, prin. — Fax 862-3141
Other Schools – See Newburgh, Winterport

Hancock, Hancock
Regional School Unit 24
Supt. — See Ellsworth
Hancock S — 200/K-8
PO Box 37 04640 — 207-422-9024
Michael Hammer, prin. — Fax 422-6568

Harmony, Somerset
Harmony SD — 100/K-8
PO Box 100 04942 — 207-683-2211
Gilbert Reynolds, supt. — Fax 683-5241
Harmony S — 100/K-8
PO Box 100 04942 — 207-683-2211
Michael Tracy, prin. — Fax 683-5241

Harpswell, Cumberland
MSAD 75
Supt. — See Topsham
Harpswell Islands ES — 100/K-5
308 Harpswell Islands Rd 04079 — 207-729-5177
Michael Estes, prin. — Fax 725-7567
West Harpswell ES — 100/K-5
9 Ash Point Rd 04079 — 207-833-5961
Michael Estes, prin. — Fax 833-6483

Harrington, Washington
MSAD 37 — 800/K-12
PO Box 79 04643 — 207-483-2734
David Beal, supt. — Fax 483-6051
www.sad37.com
Harrington S — 100/K-8
1227 US Highway 1A 04643 — 207-483-6681
Ronald Ramsay, prin. — Fax 483-4589
Other Schools – See Addison, Cherryfield, Columbia Falls, Milbridge

Harrison, Cumberland
MSAD 17
Supt. — See Oxford
Harrison ES — 200/K-6
309 Naples Rd 04040 — 207-583-2357
Kim Ramharter, prin. — Fax 583-9149

Hartland, Somerset, Pop. 1,038
Regional School Unit 19
Supt. — See Newport
Hartland Consolidated ES — 200/PK-4
62 Elm St 04943 — 207-938-4456
Denise Kimball, prin. — Fax 938-5148
Somerset Valley MS — 200/5-8
45 Blake St 04943 — 207-938-4770
Don Roux, prin. — Fax 938-2114

Hebron, Oxford
MSAD 17
Supt. — See Oxford
Hebron Station S — 100/K-6
884 Station Rd 04238 — 207-966-3323
Tiffany Karnes, prin. — Fax 966-3142

Hermon, See Bangor
Hermon SD — 1,200/PK-12
31 Billings Rd 04401 — 207-848-4000
Patricia Duran, supt. — Fax 848-5226
www.hermon.net

Hermon ES 400/PK-4
235 Billings Rd 04401 207-848-4000
Barbara Libby, prin. Fax 848-2100
Hermon MS 300/5-8
29 Billings Rd 04401 207-848-4000
James Russell, prin. Fax 848-2163

Northstar Christian S 50/1-8
42 Orion Way 04401 207-848-2331
Susan Strickland, prin. Fax 848-7314

Hiram, Oxford
MSAD 55 800/K-12
137 S Hiram Rd 04041 207-625-2490
Sylvia Pease, supt. Fax 625-7065
www.sad55.org/
Sacopee Valley MS 5-8
137 S Hiram Rd 04041 207-625-2450
Bob Griffin, prin. Fax 625-2465
South Hiram ES 200/K-4
213 S Hiram Rd 04041 207-625-8116
Suzanne Day, prin. Fax 625-8399
Other Schools – See Cornish, Parsonsfield, West Baldwin

Holden, Penobscot
Airline Community SD 50/K-8
202 Kidder Hill Rd 04429 207-843-7851
David Anderson, supt. Fax 843-7295
Other Schools – See Aurora

MSAD 63 600/K-8
202 Kidder Hill Rd 04429 207-843-7851
David Anderson, supt. Fax 843-7295
www.sad63.net/
Holbrook MS 300/5-8
202 Kidder Hill Rd 04429 207-843-7769
Richard Modery, prin. Fax 843-4328
Holden ES 200/K-4
590 Main Rd 04429 207-843-7828
David Anderson, prin. Fax 843-4329
Other Schools – See Eddington

Hollis Center, York
MSAD 6
Supt. — See Bar Mills
Hollis S 300/K-5
554 River Rd 04042 207-929-3838
Diane Gagne, prin. Fax 929-9166

Hope, Knox
Union SD 69 500/K-8
PO Box 2007 04847 207-763-3818
Dr. Deborah Stewart, supt. Fax 763-4262
Hope S 100/K-8
34 Highfield Rd 04847 207-785-4081
Carol Hathorne, prin. Fax 785-2671
Other Schools – See Lincolnville, Union

Houlton, Aroostook, Pop. 5,627
MSAD 29 1,300/PK-12
PO Box 190 04730 207-532-6555
Stephen Fitzpatrick, supt. Fax 532-6481
www.sad29.k12.me.us/
Houlton ES 400/PK-3
60 South St 04730 207-532-2285
Candace Crane, prin. Fax 521-0360
Houlton JHS 200/7-8
7 Bird St 04730 207-532-6551
Martin Bouchard, prin. Fax 532-6282
Houlton Southside ES 300/4-6
65 South St 04730 207-532-6027
Jason Tarr, prin. Fax 521-0356
Other Schools – See Monticello

MSAD 70 600/PK-12
175 Hodgdon Mills Rd 04730 207-532-3015
Robert McDaniel, supt. Fax 532-2679
Mill Pond S 400/PK-8
175 Hodgdon Mills Rd 04730 207-532-9228
Loreen Wiley, prin. Fax 532-4090

Greater Houlton Christian Academy 200/PK-12
27 School St 04730 207-532-0736
Mark B. Jago, hdmstr. Fax 532-9553

Howland, Penobscot, Pop. 1,304
MSAD 31 700/K-12
23 Cross St 04448 207-732-3112
Jerry White, supt. Fax 732-3390
www.msad31.com/
Hichborn MS 100/6-8
23 Cross St 04448 207-732-3113
Carol Marcinkus, prin. Fax 732-4085
Other Schools – See West Enfield

Hudson, Penobscot
MSAD 64
Supt. — See Corinth
Hudson ES 100/3-4
2150 Hudson Rd 04449 207-327-1444
Amanda Green, prin. Fax 327-1444

Isle au Haut, Knox
Isle Au Haut SD
Supt. — See Sargentville
Isle Au Haut Rural S 50/K-8
PO Box 56B 04645 207-335-2521

Islesboro, Waldo
Islesboro SD 100/K-12
PO Box 118 04848 207-734-6723
Thomas Comiciotto, supt. Fax 734-8159
www.islesboro-central.islesboro.k12.me.us
Islesboro Central S 100/K-12
PO Box 118 04848 207-734-2251
Heather Knight, prin. Fax 734-8159

Islesford, Hancock
Union SD 98
Supt. — See Mount Desert
Islesford S, PO Box 8 04646 50/K-8
Carol MacRae, prin. 207-244-3961

Jackman, Somerset
MSAD 12 200/K-12
606 Main St 04945 207-668-7749
Heather Perry, supt. Fax 668-4482
www.sad12.com/
Forest Hills Consolidated S 200/K-12
PO Box 239 04945 207-668-5291
Denise Plante, prin. Fax 668-4482

Jay, Franklin
Jay SD 800/K-12
31 Community Dr 04239 207-897-3936
Robert Wall, supt. Fax 897-5431
www.jayschools.org/
Jay ES 300/K-4
12 Tiger Dr 04239 207-897-5719
Chris Hollingsworth, prin. Fax 897-6375
Jay MS 200/5-8
23 Community Dr 04239 207-897-4319
Scott Albert, prin. Fax 897-3513

Jefferson, Lincoln
Union SD 132
Supt. — See Windsor
Jefferson Village S 200/K-8
47 Washington Rd 04348 207-549-7491
Norman Nelson, prin. Fax 549-5011

Jonesboro, Washington
Union SD 102
Supt. — See Machias
Jonesboro S 100/K-8
56 School Rd 04648 207-434-2602
Gregory Marsh, prin. Fax 434-2600

Jonesport, Washington
Union SD 103 200/K-8
127 Snare Creek Ln 04649 207-497-2154
Colleen Haskell, supt. Fax 497-2703
www.union103.org/
Jonesport S 100/K-8
139 Snare Creek Ln 04649 207-497-2830
Robert Alley, lead tchr. Fax 497-5912
Other Schools – See Beals

Kenduskeag, Penobscot
MSAD 64
Supt. — See Corinth
Kenduskeag ES 200/K-2
4067 Broadway 04450 207-884-7979
Judith Marvin, prin. Fax 884-7979

Kennebunk, York, Pop. 4,206
Regional School Unit 21 2,300/PK-12
87 Fletcher St 04043 207-985-1100
Andrew Dolloff, supt. Fax 985-1104
www.rsu21.net/
Kennebunk ES 300/PK-3
177 Alewive Rd 04043 207-985-2791
Sara Zito, prin. Fax 985-6082
Kennebunk MS 600/6-8
60 Thompson Rd 04043 207-467-8004
Jeff Rodman, prin. Fax 467-9059
Sea Road ES 300/4-5
71 Sea Rd 04043 207-985-1105
Kevin Crowley, prin. Fax 985-4274
Other Schools – See Kennebunkport

Kennebunkport, York, Pop. 1,100
Regional School Unit 21
Supt. — See Kennebunk
Kennebunkport Consolidated ES 200/K-5
25 School St 04046 207-967-5998
Kathy Pence, prin. Fax 985-5179

Kingfield, Franklin
MSAD 58
Supt. — See Phillips
Kingfield S 200/K-8
102 Salem Rd 04947 207-265-4132
Marco Aliberti, prin. Fax 265-2010

Kingman, Penobscot
Unorganized Territories SD
Supt. — See Augusta
Kingman ES 50/PK-5
25 Park St 04451 207-765-2500
Deborah Wood, prin. Fax 765-2008

Kittery, York, Pop. 5,151
Kittery SD 1,100/K-12
200 Rogers Rd 03904 207-439-6819
Larry Littlefield, supt. Fax 439-5407
www.kitteryschools.org/
Frisbee ES 200/3-5
120 Rogers Rd 03904 207-439-1122
Pat Garnis, prin. Fax 439-5846
Shapleigh MS 200/6-8
43 Stevenson Rd 03904 207-439-2572
Fax 439-9958
Other Schools – See Kittery Point

Kittery Point, York, Pop. 1,093
Kittery SD
Supt. — See Kittery
Mitchell PS 200/K-2
7 Mitchell School Ln 03905 207-439-1707
David Foster, prin. Fax 439-9198

Lagrange, Penobscot
MSAD 41
Supt. — See Milo
Cook ES 50/K-5
22 Howland Rd 04453 207-943-2196
Lynn Weston, prin. Fax 943-2196

Lebanon, York
MSAD 60
Supt. — See North Berwick
Lebanon ES 500/K-5
53 Upper Guinea Rd 04027 207-457-1299
Thomas Ledue, prin. Fax 457-1829

Lee, Penobscot
MSAD 30 200/PK-8
31 Winn Rd 04455 207-738-2665
Michael Lambert, supt. Fax 738-2010
www.msad30.org/
Mt. Jefferson JHS 100/6-8
61 Winn Rd 04455 207-738-2866
Pamela Hamilton, prin. Fax 738-3817
Other Schools – See Winn

Leeds, Androscoggin
MSAD 52
Supt. — See Turner
Leeds Central ES 200/K-6
1185 Route 106 04263 207-524-5151
Pamela Doyen, prin. Fax 524-2184

Levant, Penobscot
MSAD 23
Supt. — See Carmel
Smith ES 200/K-5
169 S Levant Rd 04456 207-884-7444
Lorri Day, prin. Fax 884-6201

Lewiston, Androscoggin, Pop. 36,050
Lewiston SD 4,500/K-12
36 Oak St 04240 207-795-4100
Leon Levesque, supt. Fax 753-6413
www.lewistonpublicschools.org/
Farwell ES 300/K-6
110 Farwell St 04240 207-795-4110
Linda St. Andre, prin. Fax 753-6407
Lewiston MS 700/7-8
75 Central Ave 04240 207-795-4180
Maureen Lachapelle, prin. Fax 753-1789
Longley ES 300/K-6
145 Birch St 04240 207-795-4120
Thomas Hood, prin. Fax 795-4122
Martel ES 300/K-6
880 Lisbon St 04240 207-795-4130
Stephen Whitfield, prin. Fax 753-6408
McMahon ES 500/K-6
151 N Temple St 04240 207-795-4140
Althea Walker, prin. Fax 795-4146
Montello ES 700/K-6
407 East Ave 04240 207-795-4150
Deborah Goding, prin. Fax 795-4176
Pettingill ES 300/K-6
409 College St 04240 207-795-4160
David Bartlett, prin. Fax 753-6409

Central Maine Christian Academy 100/PK-12
390 Main St 04240 207-777-0007
Patricia St. Hilaire, admin. Fax 777-0007
Trinity S 400/PK-5
17 Baird Ave 04240 207-783-9323
Paul Yarnevich, prin. Fax 783-9491
Trinity S 100/6-8
393 Main St 04240 207-784-8811
Paul Yarnevich, prin. Fax 783-9522
Vineyard Christian S 100/PK-12
PO Box 1610 04241 207-784-9500
Fax 777-3076

Liberty, Waldo
MSAD 3
Supt. — See Unity
Walker Memorial ES 100/K-5
PO Box 117 04949 207-589-4208
Carol McGovern, prin. Fax 589-3421

Limestone, Aroostook, Pop. 1,245
Caswell SD 50/PK-8
1025 Van Buren Rd 04750 207-325-4611
William Dobbins, supt. Fax 325-3371
Barnes S 50/PK-8
1025 Van Buren Rd 04750 207-325-4611
Fax 325-3371

Eastern Aroostook Regional Sch Unit 39
Supt. — See Caribou
Limestone Community S 300/PK-12
93 High St 04750 207-325-4742
Leland Caron, prin. Fax 325-4969

Limington, York
MSAD 6
Supt. — See Bar Mills
Emery Jr Memorial S 200/K-5
908 Cape Rd 04049 207-637-2056
Stephen Winger, prin. Fax 637-3716

Lincoln, Penobscot, Pop. 3,399
MSAD 67 1,300/PK-12
PO Box 250 04457 207-794-6500
Michael Marcinkus, supt. Fax 794-2600
www.sad67.k12.me.us/
Burr ES 400/PK-4
23 Ella P Burr St 04457 207-794-3014
Michael Bisson, prin. Fax 794-2602
Mattanawcook JHS 400/5-8
41 School St 04457 207-794-8935
Larry Malone, prin. Fax 794-2601
Other Schools – See Mattawamkeag

Greater Lincoln Christian Academy 50/K-6
PO Box 597 04457 207-794-6867
Cindy Priest, admin.

Lincolnville, Waldo
Union SD 69
Supt. — See Hope
Lincolnville Central S 200/K-8
523 Hope Rd 04849 207-763-3366
Paul Russo, prin. Fax 763-3455

Lisbon, See Lisbon Falls
Union SD 30 1,700/K-12
19 Gartley St 04250 207-353-6711
Shannon Welsh Ed.D., supt. Fax 353-3032
www.union30.org/
Lisbon Community ES 600/K-5
33 Mill St 04250 207-353-4132
Carlene Iverson, prin. Fax 353-4815
Other Schools – See Durham, Lisbon Falls

Lisbon Falls, Androscoggin, Pop. 4,674
Union SD 30
Supt. — See Lisbon
Sugg MS 300/6-8
4 Sugg Dr 04252 207-353-3055
Richard Green, prin. Fax 353-3053

Litchfield, Kennebec, Pop. 275
Union SD 44
Supt. — See Wales
Libby-Tozier ES 100/K-3
466 Academy Rd 04350 207-268-4137
Christine Lajoie-Cameron, prin. Fax 268-2680
Ricker MS 200/4-8
573 Richmond Rd 04350 207-268-4136
Christine Lajoie-Cameron, prin. Fax 268-4318

Livermore, See Livermore Falls
MSAD 36
Supt. — See Livermore Falls
Livermore ES 400/K-5
107 Gibbs Mill Rd 04253 207-897-3355
Jeannine Backus, prin. Fax 897-3690

Livermore Falls, Androscoggin, Pop. 1,935
MSAD 36 1,000/K-12
9 Cedar St 04254 207-897-6722
Terry Despres, supt. Fax 897-2362
www.sad36.org/
Livermore Falls MS 300/6-8
1 Highland Ave 04254 207-897-2121
Ted Finn, prin. Fax 897-9377
Other Schools – See Livermore

Long Island, See Portland
Long Island SD
Supt. — See Damariscotta
Long Island ES 50/K-5
Fern Ave 04050 207-766-4414
David Gaul, lead tchr. Fax 766-4414

Lovell, Oxford
MSAD 72
Supt. — See Fryeburg
New Suncook ES 200/K-5
PO Box H 04051 207-925-6711
Rhonda Poliquin, prin. Fax 925-1168

Lubec, Washington
MSAD 19 200/K-12
44 South St 04652 207-733-5573
Michael Buckley, supt. Fax 733-2004
Lubec Consolidated S 200/K-12
44 South St 04652 207-733-5591
Peter Doak, prin. Fax 733-2004

Lyman, York
Regional School Unit 57
Supt. — See Waterboro
Lyman ES 300/K-5
39 Schoolhouse Rd 04002 207-499-7228
Kevin Perkins, prin. Fax 499-2981

Machias, Washington, Pop. 1,773
East Machias SD 200/PK-8
291 Court St 04654 207-255-6585
Scott Porter, supt. Fax 255-8054
Other Schools – See East Machias

Union SD 102 500/K-12
291 Court St 04654 207-255-6585
Scott Porter, supt. Fax 255-8054
Gaffney S 300/K-8
15 Rose Gaffney Rd 04654 207-255-3411
Mitchell Look, prin. Fax 255-0346
Other Schools – See Jonesboro, Wesley

Union SD 134 200/PK-8
291 Court St 04654 207-255-6585
Scott Porter, supt. Fax 255-8054
www.union134.org/
Other Schools – See Cutler, Machiasport, Whiting

Machiasport, Washington
Union SD 134
Supt. — See Machias
Ft. O'Brien S 100/PK-8
PO Box 37 04655 207-255-4575
Beverly Taylor, prin. Fax 255-3190

Madawaska, Aroostook, Pop. 3,653
Madawaska SD 700/PK-12
328 Saint Thomas St Ste 201 04756 207-728-3346
William Fowler, supt. Fax 728-7823
www.madawaskaschools.org/
Madawaska ES 300/PK-5
353 11th Ave 04756 207-728-3635
Ginette Albert, prin. Fax 728-3444

Madison, Somerset, Pop. 2,956
MSAD 59 1,000/PK-12
55 Weston Ave 04950 207-696-3323
Michael Gallagher, supt. Fax 696-5631
www.sad59.k12.me.us/
Madison ES 300/PK-4
43 Learners Ln 04950 207-696-3911
Alan Mikal, prin. Fax 696-5642
Madison JHS 300/5-8
205 Main St 04950 207-696-3381
Bonnie Levesque, prin. Fax 696-5640
Other Schools – See Athens, Starks

Manchester, Kennebec
Regional School Unit 38
Supt. — See Readfield
Manchester ES 200/K-5
PO Box 217 04351 207-622-2949
William Wilson, prin. Fax 622-0616

Mapleton, Aroostook
MSAD 1
Supt. — See Presque Isle
Mapleton ES 200/K-5
1642 Main St 04757 207-764-1589
Gail Gibson, prin. Fax 764-6429

Mars Hill, Aroostook, Pop. 1,717
MSAD 42 400/PK-12
PO Box 1006 04758 207-425-3771
Roger Shaw, supt. Fax 429-8461
www.cahs.sad42.k12.me.us/
Fort Street ES 200/PK-6
PO Box 509 04758 207-429-8514
Frederick Boyd, prin. Fax 429-8462

Matinicus, Knox, Pop. 117
MSAD 65
Supt. — See North Haven
Matinicus S 50/K-8
PO Box 194 04851 207-366-3526

Mattawamkeag, Penobscot
MSAD 67
Supt. — See Lincoln
Troutt ES 100/PK-4
PO Box 35 04459 207-736-2750
Michael Bisson, prin. Fax 736-2751

Mechanic Falls, Androscoggin, Pop. 2,388
Union SD 29
Supt. — See Poland
Elm Street S 300/K-8
129 Elm St 04256 207-345-3381
Mary Martin, prin. Fax 346-6224

Medway, Penobscot
Union SD 113
Supt. — See East Millinocket
Medway MS 200/5-8
25 Middle School Dr 04460 207-746-3470
Kevin Towle, prin. Fax 746-9435

Mexico, Oxford, Pop. 2,302
Regional School Unit 10
Supt. — See Dixfield
Meroby ES 300/K-5
21 Cross St 04257 207-364-3715
Scott Drown, prin. Fax 369-0146
Mountain Valley MS 300/6-8
58 Highland Ter 04257 207-364-7926
Ryan Casey, prin. Fax 364-5608

Milbridge, Washington
MSAD 37
Supt. — See Harrington
Milbridge S 100/K-8
39 Washington St 04658 207-546-2210
Ronald Ramsey, prin. Fax 546-7399

Milford, Penobscot, Pop. 2,228
Union SD 90 600/PK-8
78 Main Rd 04461 207-827-8061
Alan Smith, supt. Fax 827-1513
www.union90.org/
Libby S 300/K-8
13 School St 04461 207-827-2252
Lynn Silk, prin. Fax 827-5454
Other Schools – See Alton, Bradley, Greenbush

Millinocket, Penobscot, Pop. 6,922
Millinocket SD
Supt. — See East Millinocket
Granite Street ES 200/K-5
191 Granite St 04462 207-723-6425
Linda MacDonald, prin. Fax 723-6425
Millinocket MS 200/6-8
199 State St 04462 207-723-6415
Jed Petsinger, prin. Fax 723-6437

Milo, Piscataquis, Pop. 2,129
MSAD 41 800/K-12
37 W Main St 04463 207-943-7317
Shirley Wright, supt. Fax 943-5314
msad41.us/
Milo ES 300/K-6
18 Belmont St 04463 207-943-2122
Cathryn Knox, prin. Fax 943-5330
Other Schools – See Brownville, Lagrange

Minot, Androscoggin
Union SD 29
Supt. — See Poland
Minot Consolidated S 300/K-8
23 Shaw Hill Rd 04258 207-346-6471
Margaret Pitts, prin. Fax 345-9535

Monhegan, Lincoln
Monhegan Plt SD
Supt. — See Cherryfield
Monhegan Island S 50/K-8
PO Box 8 04852 207-594-5895

Monmouth, Kennebec
Regional School Unit 2
Supt. — See Hallowell
Cottrell ES 200/K-3
169 Academy Rd 04259 207-933-4426
Deborah Emery, prin. Fax 933-7279
Monmouth MS 300/4-8
PO Box 240 04259 207-933-9002
Stephen Philbrook, prin. Fax 933-7252

Monroe, Waldo
MSAD 3
Supt. — See Unity
Monroe ES 100/K-5
36 W Main St 04951 207-525-3504
Matthew Houghton, prin. Fax 525-8599

Monson, Piscataquis
MSAD 68
Supt. — See Dover Foxcroft
Monson ES 50/K-5
35 Greenville Rd 04464 207-997-3737
Wilma Lombardi, prin. Fax 997-2981

Monticello, Aroostook
MSAD 29
Supt. — See Houlton
Wellington ES 100/PK-3
36 School St 04760 207-538-9495
Nancy Wright, prin. Fax 538-9160

Morrill, Waldo, Pop. 644
MSAD 34
Supt. — See Belfast
Weymouth ES 100/K-2
2 S Main St 04952 207-342-5300
Laura Miller, prin. Fax 342-5301

Moscow, Somerset
MSAD 13
Supt. — See Bingham
Moscow ES 100/K-4
125 Canada Rd 04920 207-672-5572
Linda MacKenzie, prin. Fax 672-3003

Mount Desert, Hancock
Union SD 98 1,600/K-12
PO Box 60 04660 207-288-5049
Robert Liebow, supt. Fax 288-5071
www.u98.k12.me.us/
Other Schools – See Bar Harbor, Bass Harbor, Frenchboro, Islesford, Northeast Harbor, Southwest Harbor, Swans Island

Mount Vernon, Kennebec
Regional School Unit 38
Supt. — See Readfield
Mount Vernon ES 100/PK-5
1507 North Rd 04352 207-293-2261
William Wilson, prin. Fax 293-3205

Naples, Cumberland
MSAD 61
Supt. — See Bridgton
Lake Region MS 300/6-8
204 Kansas Rd 04055 207-647-8403
Peter Mortenson, prin. Fax 647-0991
Songo Locks ES 300/K-5
25 Songo School Rd 04055 207-693-6828
June Conley, prin. Fax 693-4000

Newburgh, Penobscot
MSAD 22
Supt. — See Hampden
Newburgh ES 100/K-3
2220 Western Ave 04444 207-234-2781
Mary Smith, prin. Fax 234-2786

New Gloucester, Cumberland
MSAD 15
Supt. — See Gray
Dunn ES 400/3-5
667 Morse Rd 04260 207-657-5050
Bruce Beasley, prin. Fax 688-3012
Memorial ES 200/K-2
86 Intervale Rd 04260 207-926-4322
Donna Beeley, prin. Fax 926-4324

Newport, Penobscot, Pop. 1,843
Regional School Unit 19 2,500/PK-12
PO Box 40 04953 207-368-5091
William Braun, supt. Fax 368-2192
www.rsu19.org/
Newport ES 300/PK-4
142 Elm St 04953 207-368-4470
Randy Gould, prin. Fax 368-3274
Sebasticook Valley MS 300/5-8
337 Williams Rd 04953 207-368-4592
Fredrick Johnston, prin. Fax 368-4598
Other Schools – See Corinna, Etna, Hartland, Palmyra, Saint Albans

New Sharon, Franklin
Mt. Blue Regional SD
Supt. — See Farmington
Cape Cod Hill ES 200/K-6
516 Cape Cod Hill Rd 04955 207-778-3031
Cheryl Pike, prin. Fax 778-6910

New Sweden, Aroostook
Union SD 122
Supt. — See Woodland
New Sweden S 100/PK-8
113 Westmanland Rd 04762 207-896-5541
Gail Maynard, prin. Fax 896-3023

New Vineyard, Franklin

New Life Christian S 50/K-12
PO Box 242 04956 207-778-9065
Herman Ellis, prin. Fax 778-9065

Nobleboro, Lincoln
Union SD 74
Supt. — See Damariscotta
Nobleboro Central S 200/K-8
194 Center St 04555 207-563-3437
Mark Deblois, prin. Fax 563-3437

Damariscotta Montessori S 100/PK-8
93 Center St 04555 207-563-2168
Arthur DeLorenzo, prin.

Norridgewock, Somerset, Pop. 1,496
MSAD 54
Supt. — See Skowhegan
Millstream ES 300/PK-6
PO Box 98 04957 207-634-3121
Cecile Tobey, prin. Fax 634-4294

Riverview Memorial S 50/K-10
201 Mercer Rd 04957 207-634-2641
Trevor Schlisner, prin. Fax 634-2641

North Anson, Somerset
MSAD 74 800/PK-12
56 N Main St 04958 207-635-2727
Kenneth Smith Ed.D., supt. Fax 635-3599
www.sad74.k12.me.us
Carrabec Community S 300/K-8
PO Box 187 04958 207-635-2209
Dr. Regina Campbell, prin. Fax 635-2048
Other Schools – See Anson, Embden, Solon

North Berwick, York, Pop. 1,568
MSAD 60 3,100/K-12
PO Box 819 03906 207-676-2234
Paul Andrade, supt. Fax 676-3229
www.sad60.k12.me.us
North Berwick ES 300/K-5
PO Box 609 03906 207-676-9811
Shelley MacDonnell, prin. Fax 676-3213
Other Schools – See Berwick, Lebanon

Northeast Harbor, Hancock
Union SD 98
Supt. — See Mount Desert
Mt. Desert S 200/K-8
PO Box 308 04662 207-276-3348
Scott McFarland, prin. Fax 276-5830

North Haven, Knox
MSAD 65, PO Box 449 04853 50/K-8
Jerry White, supt. 207-867-4450
Other Schools – See Matinicus

MSAD 7 100/PK-12
93 Pulpit Harbor Rd 04853 207-867-4707
Thomas Marx, supt. Fax 867-4438
nhcsxserve.sad7.k12.me.us/
North Haven Community S 100/PK-12
93 Pulpit Harbor Rd 04853 207-867-4707
A. Barney Hallowell, prin. Fax 867-4438

Northport, Waldo
MSAD 34
Supt. — See Belfast
Drinkwater ES 100/K-5
56 Bayside Rd 04849 207-338-3430
Joanne Henderson, prin. Fax 338-5985

North Yarmouth, Cumberland
MSAD 51
Supt. — See Cumberland Center
North Yarmouth Memorial ES 300/4-5
120 Memorial Hwy 04097 207-829-5555
Becky Foley, prin. Fax 829-2706

Norway, Oxford, Pop. 3,023
MSAD 17
Supt. — See Oxford
Rowe ES 400/K-6
219 Main St 04268 207-743-5183
George Sincerbeaux, prin. Fax 743-5324

Oakland, Kennebec, Pop. 3,510
MSAD 47 2,600/PK-12
41 Heath St 04963 207-465-7384
James Morse Ed.D., supt. Fax 465-9130
www.msad47.org/
Atwood PS 200/PK-2
19 Heath St 04963 207-465-3411
Jennifer Haney, prin. Fax 465-9133
Messalonskee MS 600/6-8
33 School Bus Dr 04963 207-465-2167
Mark Hatch, prin. Fax 465-9683
Williams ES 200/3-5
55 Pleasant St 04963 207-465-2965
Kathy Harris-Smedberg, prin. Fax 465-4985
Other Schools – See Belgrade, Sidney

Old Orchard Beach, York, Pop. 7,789
Old Orchard Beach SD 1,000/PK-12
28 Jameson Hill Rd 04064 207-934-5751
John Turcotte, supt. Fax 934-1917
www.oobschools.org
Jameson ES 300/PK-3
28 Jameson Hill Rd 04064 207-934-2891
Michael Pulsifer, prin. Fax 934-3710
Loranger MS 400/4-8
148 Saco Ave 04064 207-934-2361
Lloyd Crocker, prin. Fax 934-3712

Old Town, Penobscot, Pop. 7,792
Regional School Unit 34 1,400/K-12
156 Oak St Ste 2 04468 207-827-7171
David Walker, supt. Fax 827-3922
www.rsu34.org/
Leonard MS 300/6-8
156 Oak St 04468 207-827-3900
John Keane, prin. Fax 827-3922
Old Town ES 500/K-5
576 Stillwater Ave 04468 207-827-1544
Jeanna Tuell, prin. Fax 827-1549

Orland, Hancock
Regional School Unit 25
Supt. — See Bucksport
Orland Consolidated S 200/PK-8
PO Box 9 04472 207-469-2272
Ivan Braun, prin. Fax 469-7815

Orono, Penobscot, Pop. 9,789
Union SD 87 1,000/K-12
18 Goodridge Dr 04473 207-866-5521
Kelly Clenchy, supt. Fax 866-7111
www.orono.u87.k12.me.us/
Adams ES 300/K-5
10 Goodridge Dr 04473 207-866-2151
Paula McHugh, prin. Fax 866-3664
Orono MS 100/6-8
14 Goodridge Dr 04473 207-866-2350
Robert Lucy, prin. Fax 866-7111
Other Schools – See Veazie

Orrington, Penobscot
Orrington SD 91 400/K-8
19 School St 04474 207-825-3364
Allan Snell, supt. Fax 825-3393
Center Drive S 400/K-8
17 School St 04474 207-825-3310
Roy Allen, prin. Fax 825-4525

Calvary Chapel Christian S 100/PK-12
154 River Rd 04474 207-991-9684
Dennis Harvey, prin. Fax 989-0687

Otisfield, Oxford
MSAD 17
Supt. — See Oxford
Otisfield Community ES 100/K-6
416 Powhatan Rd 04270 207-627-4208
Linda Park, prin. Fax 627-4208

Owls Head, Knox
MSAD 5
Supt. — See Rockland
Owls Head Central ES 100/2-5
54 Ash Point Dr 04854 207-594-5650
Sally Carleton, prin. Fax 594-4105

Oxford, Oxford, Pop. 1,284
MSAD 17 3,300/K-12
1570 Main St Ste 11 04270 207-743-8972
Mark Eastman Ed.D., supt. Fax 743-2878
www.sad17.k12.me.us/
Oxford ES 400/K-6
PO Box 839 04270 207-539-4456
Alan Struck, prin. Fax 539-2922
Other Schools – See Harrison, Hebron, Norway, Otisfield, South Paris, Waterford, West Paris

Palermo, Waldo
Sheepscot Valley Regional School Unit 12
Supt. — See Whitefield
Palermo Consolidated S 100/K-8
501 Route 3 04354 207-993-2352
Gregory Potter, prin. Fax 993-2354

Palmyra, Somerset
Regional School Unit 19
Supt. — See Newport
Palmyra Consolidated ES 100/PK-4
4 Madawaska Rd 04965 207-938-4544
Amanda Hersey, prin. Fax 938-4546

Parkman, Piscataquis
MSAD 4
Supt. — See Guilford
McKusick ES 100/PK-1
619 State Hwy 150 04443 207-876-2656
Julie Orton, prin. Fax 876-4363

Parsonsfield, York
MSAD 55
Supt. — See Hiram
Morrill ES 50/K-4
634 North Rd 04047 207-625-4842
Clayton Neidlinger, prin. Fax 625-8852

Peaks Island, See Portland
Portland SD
Supt. — See Portland
Peaks Island ES 50/K-5
4 Church Ave 04108 207-766-2528
Gwen Smith, prin. Fax 766-5619

Pemaquid, Lincoln
Union SD 74
Supt. — See Damariscotta
Bristol Consolidated S 200/K-8
2153 Bristol Rd 04558 207-677-2678
Jennifer Ribeiro, prin. Fax 677-2678

Pembroke, Washington
Union SD 104
Supt. — See Eastport
Charlotte S 50/PK-8
1006 Ayers Jct Rd 04666 207-454-2668
Peggy Lingley, prin. Fax 454-7399
Pembroke S 100/PK-8
36 US Route 1 04666 207-726-5564
Deborah Jamieson, prin. Fax 726-5139

Penobscot, Hancock
Union SD 93
Supt. — See Blue Hill
Penobscot S 100/K-8
PO Box 60 04476 207-326-9421
G. Allen Cole, prin. Fax 326-9422

Perry, Washington
Union SD 104
Supt. — See Eastport
Perry S 100/PK-8
1587 US Route 1 04667 207-853-2522
Arlo Smith, prin. Fax 853-4539

Peru, Oxford, Pop. 1,541
Regional School Unit 10
Supt. — See Dixfield
Dirigo ES PK-5
117 Auburn Rd 04290 207-562-4207
Kathy Richard, prin. Fax 562-8775

Phillips, Franklin
MSAD 58 900/K-12
1401 Rangeley Rd 04966 207-639-2086
Quenten Clark, supt. Fax 639-5120
www.sad58.k12.me.us/
Phillips S 200/K-8
1401 Rangeley Rd 04966 207-639-2909
Quenten Clark, prin. Fax 639-4139
Other Schools – See Kingfield, Stratton, Strong

Phippsburg, Sagadahoc
Regional School Unit 1
Supt. — See Bath
Phippsburg ES 200/PK-6
1047 Main Rd 04562 207-389-1514
Kari Babcock, prin. Fax 389-1516

Pittsfield, Somerset, Pop. 3,222
MSAD 53 800/PK-8
293 Hartland Ave 04967 207-487-5107
Michael Gallagher, supt. Fax 487-6310
www.msad53.org/
Manson Park ES 100/PK-1
179 Lancey St 04967 207-487-2281
Faye Anderson, prin.
Vickery ES 200/2-4
170 School St 04967 207-487-5575
Faye Anderson, prin. Fax 487-6155
Warsaw MS 300/5-8
167 School St 04967 207-487-5145
George Nevens, prin. Fax 487-4511
Other Schools – See Burnham

Pittston, Kennebec
MSAD 11
Supt. — See Gardiner
Pittston Consolidated ES 200/K-5
1023 School St, 207-582-6268
Shelly Simpson, prin. Fax 582-6334

Poland, Androscoggin
Union SD 29 1,700/K-12
1146 Maine St 04274 207-998-2727
Dennis Duquette, supt. Fax 998-2753
www.poland-hs.u29.k12.me.us/union29/union29.html
Poland Community ES 400/K-6
1250 Maine St 04274 207-998-4915
Ayesha Farag-Davis, prin. Fax 998-4998
Whittier MS 100/7-8
1457 Maine St 04274 207-998-5400
Ayesha Farag-Davis, prin. Fax 998-5060
Other Schools – See Mechanic Falls, Minot

Portland, Cumberland, Pop. 63,889
Portland SD 6,500/K-12
196 Allen Ave 04103 207-874-8100
James Morse, supt. Fax 874-8199
www.portlandschools.org
Clifford ES 300/K-5
180 Falmouth St 04102 207-874-8180
Beverly Coursey, prin. Fax 756-8496
East End Community S K-5
195 North St 04101 207-874-8100
Carol Dayn, prin. Fax 874-8234
Hall ES 500/K-5
23 Orono Rd 04102 207-874-8205
Kelly Hasson, prin. Fax 874-8243
King MS 500/6-8
92 Deering Ave 04102 207-874-8140
Michael McCarthy, prin. Fax 874-8290
Lincoln MS 400/6-8
522 Stevens Ave 04103 207-874-8145
Steven Nolan, prin. Fax 874-8288
Longfellow ES 300/K-5
432 Stevens Ave 04103 207-874-8195
Dawn Carrigan, prin. Fax 874-8284
Lyseth ES 500/K-5
175 Auburn St 04103 207-874-8215
Lenore Williams, prin. Fax 874-8218
Moore MS 600/6-8
171 Auburn St 04103 207-874-8150
Lee Crocker, prin. Fax 874-8272
Presumpscot ES 200/K-5
69 Presumpscot St 04103 207-874-8220
Cynthia Loring, prin. Fax 874-8286
Reiche Community ES 300/K-5
166 Brackett St 04102 207-874-8175
Marcia Gendron, prin. Fax 874-8177
Riverton ES 400/K-5
1600 Forest Ave 04103 207-874-8210
Nancy Kopack, prin. Fax 874-8271
Other Schools – See Cliff Island, Peaks Island

Breakwater S 100/PK-8
856 Brighton Ave 04102 207-772-8689
David Sullivan, hdmstr. Fax 772-1327
Cathedral S 200/PK-8
14 Locust St 04101 207-775-1491
Sr. Theresa Rand, prin. Fax 828-3989
Levey Day S 50/PK-5
400 Deering Ave 04103 207-774-7676
Elinor Miller, hdmstr. Fax 699-2780
St. Brigid S 200/PK-8
695 Stevens Ave 04103 207-797-7073
Lori Ann Lee, prin. Fax 797-7078
Waynflete S 600/PK-12
360 Spring St 04102 207-774-5721
Mark Segar, prin. Fax 772-4782

Pownal, Cumberland
MSAD 62 200/PK-8
587 Elmwood Rd 04069 207-688-4832
Elaine Tomaszewski, supt. Fax 688-4872
www.pownalschool.org/
Pownal S 200/PK-8
587 Elmwood Rd 04069 207-688-4832
Peter Buckley, prin. Fax 688-4872

Presque Isle, Aroostook, Pop. 9,377
MSAD 1 1,900/PK-12
PO Box 1118 04769 207-764-4101
Gehrig Johnson, supt. Fax 764-4103
www.sad1.org/
Pine Street ES 200/PK-2
50 Pine St 04769 207-764-8104
Loretta Clark, prin. Fax 768-3446
Presque Isle MS 400/6-8
569 Skyway St 04769 207-764-4474
Anne Blanchard, prin. Fax 768-3447
Skyway Education Learning Center 100/PK-PK
1 Skyspot Ln 04769 207-764-1289
Zippel ES 300/K-5
42 Griffin St 04769 207-764-8106
Sharon Brown, prin. Fax 768-3089
Other Schools – See Mapleton

Cornerstone Christian Academy 50/PK-6
PO Box 743 04769 207-768-6222
Troy McCrum, prin. Fax 768-6224

Princeton, Washington
Union SD 107
Supt. — See Baileyville
Princeton S 100/PK-8
289 Main St 04668 207-796-2253
Sue LaPlant, prin. Fax 796-8014

Randolph, Kennebec, Pop. 1,949
MSAD 11
Supt. — See Gardiner
Hamlin ES 100/K-5
17 School St 04346 207-582-4252
Lynn Izzi, prin. Fax 582-1696

Rangeley, Franklin
Union SD 37 200/K-12
PO Box 97 04970 207-864-3313
Philip Richardson, supt. Fax 864-2451
Rangeley Lakes Regional S 200/K-12
PO Box 97 04970 207-864-3311
Sharon Connally, prin. Fax 864-2451

Raymond, Cumberland
Windham Raymond RSU 14
Supt. — See Windham
Jordan-Small MS 200/5-8
423 Webbs Mills Rd 04071 207-655-4743
Randolph Crockett, prin. Fax 655-6952
Raymond ES 300/K-4
434 Webbs Mills Rd 04071 207-655-8672
Norma Richard, prin. Fax 655-8664

Readfield, Kennebec
Regional School Unit 38 1,400/PK-12
45 Millard Harrison Dr 04355 207-685-3336
Richard Abramson, supt. Fax 685-4703
www.maranacook.org/
Maranacook Community MS 300/6-8
2100 Millard Harrison Dr 04355 207-685-3128
Mary Callan, prin. Fax 685-9876
Readfield ES 200/K-5
84 South Rd 04355 207-685-4406
Cheryl Hasenfus, prin. Fax 685-5521
Other Schools – See Manchester, Mount Vernon, Wayne

Richmond, Sagadahoc, Pop. 1,775
Regional School Unit 2
Supt. — See Hallowell
Buker ES 300/PK-5
28 High St 04357 207-737-4748
Deborah Soule, prin. Fax 737-2563

Robbinston, Washington
Union SD 106
Supt. — See Calais
Robbinston S 100/K-8
904 US Rte 1 04671 207-454-3694
John Owen, prin. Fax 454-2441

Rockland, Knox, Pop. 7,658
MSAD 5 1,400/K-12
28 Lincoln St 04841 207-596-6620
Judith Lucarelli Ed.D., supt. Fax 596-2004
www.msad5.org
MacDougal ES 100/K-1
338 Broadway 04841 207-596-2005
Todd Martin, prin. Fax 594-1210
Rockland District MS 300/6-8
30 Broadway 04841 207-596-2020
Deborah Folsom, prin. Fax 596-2026
South ES 300/2-5
100 Holmes St 04841 207-596-2008
Jane Moore, prin. Fax 546-2025
Other Schools – See Owls Head, South Thomaston

Pen Bay Christian S 100/PK-8
1 Waldo Ave 04841 207-596-6460
Linda Curtis-Brawn, admin. Fax 594-5093

Rockport, Knox
MSAD 28
Supt. — See Camden
Rockport ES 400/K-4
PO Box 9 04856 207-236-7807
Jan Staples, prin. Fax 230-1061

Ashwood Waldorf S 100/PK-8
180 Park St 04856 207-236-8021
Jody Spanglet, prin. Fax 230-2423

Rumford, Oxford, Pop. 5,419
Regional School Unit 10
Supt. — See Dixfield
Rumford ES 300/K-5
121 Lincoln Ave 04276 207-364-8155
Anne Chamberlin, prin. Fax 369-9446

SS. Athanasius & John S 100/PK-8
115 Maine Ave 04276 207-364-2528
Barbara Pelletier, prin. Fax 364-3713

Sabattus, Androscoggin
Union SD 44
Supt. — See Wales
Sabattus Central S 300/3-8
40 Ball Park Rd 04280 207-375-6961
Beverly Coursey, prin. Fax 375-8871
Sabattus PS 200/K-2
36 No Name Pond Rd 04280 207-375-4525
Beverly Coursey, prin. Fax 375-8154

Saco, York, Pop. 18,230
Union SD 7 2,100/K-8
90 Beach St 04072 207-284-4505
Michael LaFortune, supt. Fax 284-5951
www.saco.org
Burns ES 600/3-5
135 Middle Street Ext 04072 207-284-5081
Terry Young, prin. Fax 284-0282
Fairfield ES 300/K-2
75 Beach St 04072 207-282-1322
Maureen McMullin, prin. Fax 284-1751
Saco MS 700/6-8
40 Buxton Rd 04072 207-282-4181
Richard Talbot, prin. Fax 286-1807
Young ES 300/K-2
36 Tasker St 04072 207-284-7053
Peter Harrison, prin. Fax 282-1510
Other Schools – See Dayton

Notre Dame De Lourdes S 100/PK-8
50 Beach St 04072 207-283-3111
Barbara Ann Arnoldo Ed.D., prin. Fax 286-2750

Saint Albans, Somerset
Regional School Unit 19
Supt. — See Newport
St. Albans Consolidated ES 100/K-4
129 Hartland Rd 04971 207-938-4581
Amanda Hersey, prin. Fax 938-5530

Saint Francis, Aroostook
MSAD 27
Supt. — See Fort Kent
Saint Francis S 100/PK-8
PO Box 99 04774 207-398-3107
Wendy Perreault, prin. Fax 398-3101

Sanford, York, Pop. 10,296
Sanford SD 3,300/K-12
917 Main St Ste 200 04073 207-324-2810
Elizabeth St. Cyr, supt. Fax 324-5742
www.sanford.org
Emerson ES 100/1-3
975 Main St 04073 207-324-3322
John Leggett, prin. Fax 459-4900
Lafayette ES 100/1-3
69 Brook St 04073 207-324-4160
John Leggett, prin. Fax 490-0346
Sanford JHS 600/7-8
708 Main St 04073 207-324-3114
Becky Brink, prin. Fax 490-5139
Smith ES 200/K-3
248 Twombley Rd 04073 207-324-7586
Sharon Remick, prin. Fax 324-2646
Willard ES 500/4-6
668 Main St 04073 207-324-8454
Charles Potter, prin. Fax 490-5130
Other Schools – See Springvale

St. Thomas S 200/PK-6
69 North Ave 04073 207-324-5832
Norman Provost, prin. Fax 324-2549

Sargentville, Hancock
Deer Isle - Stonington Community SD 400/K-12
712 Reach Rd 04673 207-359-8400
Robert Webster, supt. Fax 359-8451
Other Schools – See Deer Isle

Isle Au Haut SD 50/K-8
712 Reach Rd 04673 207-359-8400
Robert Webster, supt. Fax 359-8451
Other Schools – See Isle au Haut

Union SD 76 200/K-8
712 Reach Rd 04673 207-359-8400
Robert Webster, supt. Fax 359-8451
Other Schools – See Brooklin, Sedgwick

Scarborough, Cumberland, Pop. 2,586
Scarborough SD 3,300/K-12
PO Box 370 04070 207-730-4100
David Doyle, supt. Fax 730-4104
www.scarborough.k12.me.us
Blue Point ES 300/K-2
174 Pine Point Rd 04074 207-730-5300
Susan Helms, prin. Fax 730-5331
Eight Corners ES 200/K-2
22 Mussey Rd 04074 207-730-5200
Anne Marley, prin. Fax 730-5229
Pleasant Hill ES 200/K-2
143 Highland Ave 04074 207-730-5250
Kelly Mullen-Martin, prin. Fax 730-5251
Scarborough MS 800/6-8
21 Quentin Dr 04074 207-730-4800
Jo Anne Sizemore, prin. Fax 730-4804
Wentworth IS 800/3-5
9 Wentworth Dr 04074 207-730-4600
Anne Dexter, prin. Fax 730-4607

Searsmont, Waldo
MSAD 34
Supt. — See Belfast
Ames ES 100/3-5
165 New England Rd 04973 207-342-5100
Laura Miller, prin. Fax 342-5061

Searsport, Waldo, Pop. 1,151
MSAD 56 800/K-12
6 Mortland Rd 04974 207-548-6643
Ray Freve, supt. Fax 548-2310
www.msad56.org/
Searsport District MS 200/6-8
26 Mortland Rd 04974 207-548-2311
Gregg Palmer, prin. Fax 548-2352
Searsport ES 200/K-5
30 Mortland Rd 04974 207-548-2317
Erin Woodsome, prin. Fax 548-2329
Other Schools – See Frankfort, Stockton Springs

Sebago, Cumberland
MSAD 61
Supt. — See Bridgton
Sebago ES 100/K-5
283 Sebago Rd 04029 207-787-3701
Fax 787-2472

Sedgwick, Hancock
Union SD 76
Supt. — See Sargentville
Sedgwick S 100/K-8
272 Snows Cove Rd 04676 207-359-5002
Donald Buckingham, prin. Fax 359-5071

Shapleigh, York, Pop. 1,911
Regional School Unit 57
Supt. — See Waterboro
Shapleigh Memorial ES 200/K-5
467 Shapleigh Corner Rd 04076 207-636-1751
Cynthia Kostis, prin. Fax 636-2980

Shirley Mills, Piscataquis
Union SD 60
Supt. — See Greenville
Shirley ES 50/K-5
PO Box 148 04485 207-695-2895
Joyce Lessard, lead tchr. Fax 695-2895

Sidney, Kennebec
MSAD 47
Supt. — See Oakland
Bean ES 300/PK-5
2896 Middle Rd 04330 207-547-3395
Nancy Reynolds, prin. Fax 547-4438

Sinclair, Aroostook
Unorganized Territories SD
Supt. — See Augusta
Therriault ES 50/PK-6
PO Box 62 04779 207-543-7553
Cathy Marshall, prin. Fax 543-7570

Skowhegan, Somerset, Pop. 6,990
MSAD 54 2,600/PK-12
196 W Front St 04976 207-474-9508
Brent Colbry, supt. Fax 474-7422
www.msad54.org/
Bloomfield ES 300/1-4
140 Academy Cir 04976 207-474-6221
Patricia Watts, prin. Fax 474-7427
North ES 100/PK-1
33 Jewett St 04976 207-474-2907
Jean Pillsbury, prin. Fax 474-8648
Skowhegan Area MS 400/7-8
155 Academy Cir 04976 207-474-3339
Bruce Mochamer, prin. Fax 474-9588
Smith ES 200/4-6
40 Heselton St 04976 207-474-9822
Kathleen Harvey, prin. Fax 474-3772
Other Schools – See Canaan, Cornville, Norridgewock

Solon, Somerset
MSAD 74
Supt. — See North Anson
Solon ES 100/K-5
PO Box 146 04979 207-643-2491
Jean Butler, prin. Fax 643-2718

Somerville, Lincoln
Sheepscot Valley Regional School Unit 12
Supt. — See Whitefield
Somerville S 50/K-8
665 Patricktown Rd Ste 2 04348 207-549-7181
Fred Small, prin. Fax 549-3273

South Berwick, York
MSAD 35
Supt. — See Eliot
Central ES 400/PK-3
197 Main St 03908 207-384-2333
Vicki Stewart, prin. Fax 384-2678
Marshwood Great Works S 400/4-5
49 Academy St 03908 207-384-4010
Gerald Burnell, prin. Fax 384-4035

Berwick Academy 600/K-12
31 Academy St 03908 207-384-2164
Gregory Schneider, hdmstr. Fax 384-3332
Seacoast Christian S 100/PK-12
PO Box 325 03908 207-384-5759
Roy Reynolds, admin. Fax 384-2303

South Bristol, Lincoln
Union SD 74
Supt. — See Damariscotta
South Bristol S 100/K-8
2024 State Route 129 04568 207-644-8177
Scott White, prin. Fax 644-8170

South China, Kennebec
Union SD 52
Supt. — See Winslow
China MS 300/5-8
773 Lakeview Dr 04358 207-445-1500
Carl Gartley, prin. Fax 445-3278

China PS 300/K-4
763 Lakeview Dr 04358 207-445-1550
Carl Gartley, prin. Fax 445-3541

South Gardiner, See Gardiner
MSAD 11
Supt. — See Gardiner
River View Community ES 200/3-5
PO Box 9 04359 207-582-3402
Al Ghoreyeb, prin. Fax 582-8674

South Paris, Oxford, Pop. 2,320
MSAD 17
Supt. — See Oxford
Oxford Hills MS 500/7-8
100 Pine St 04281 207-743-5946
Troy Eastman, prin. Fax 743-8048
Paris ES K-6
4 Hathaway Rd 04281 207-743-7802
Jane Fahey, prin. Fax 744-0318

Oxford Hills Christian Academy 50/K-12
10 E Main St 04281 207-743-5970
Nancy Hanson, admin. Fax 743-5577

Southport, Lincoln
SU 49/Boothbay-Boothbay Harbor Cmmnty SD
Supt. — See Boothbay Harbor
Southport Central ES 50/K-6
PO Box 279 04576 207-633-3132
Michael McGuire, prin. Fax 633-9850

South Portland, Cumberland, Pop. 23,742
South Portland SD 3,100/K-12
130 Wescott Rd 04106 207-871-0555
Suzanne Godin, supt. Fax 871-0559
www.spsd.org
Brown ES 300/K-5
37 Highland Ave 04106 207-799-5196
Margaret Hawkins, prin. Fax 767-7742
Dyer ES 200/K-5
52 Alfred St 04106 207-799-4845
Colleen Fleming-Osborne, prin. Fax 767-7716
Kaler ES 200/K-5
165 S Kelsey St 04106 207-799-3214
Diane Lang, prin. Fax 767-7728
Mahoney MS 300/6-8
240 Ocean St 04106 207-799-7386
Kathy Germani, prin. Fax 767-7731
Memorial MS 300/6-8
120 Wescott Rd 04106 207-773-5629
Megan Welter, prin. Fax 772-4597
Skillin ES 400/K-5
180 Wescott Rd 04106 207-773-7375
Lucretia Buckley, prin. Fax 775-2904
Small ES 300/K-5
87 Thompson St 04106 207-799-7676
Bonnie Hicks, prin. Fax 767-7738

Greater Portland Christian S 100/K-12
1338 Broadway 04106 207-767-5123
Mary Willink, prin. Fax 767-5124
Holy Cross S 200/PK-8
436 Broadway 04106 207-799-6661
Martha Corkey, prin. Fax 799-8345

South Thomaston, Knox
MSAD 5
Supt. — See Rockland
Butler ES 100/K-2
PO Box 146 04858 207-594-7666
Patricia Snow, prin. Fax 594-4036

Southwest Harbor, Hancock
Union SD 98
Supt. — See Mount Desert
Pemetic S 200/K-8
PO Box 255 04679 207-244-5502
Dianne Helprin, prin. Fax 244-0367

Springvale, York, Pop. 3,542
Sanford SD
Supt. — See Sanford
Lamb ES 400/K-6
233 Shaws Ridge Rd 04083 207-324-8481
Deborah Gaudreau, prin. Fax 490-5144

Stacyville, Penobscot
MSAD 25 400/K-12
PO Box 20, 207-365-4272
John Doe, supt. Fax 365-4334
www.khs.msad25.k12.me.us/
Katahdin ES 200/K-6
PO Box 10, 207-365-4285
Christine Cunningham, prin. Fax 365-7606

Standish, Cumberland
MSAD 6
Supt. — See Bar Mills
Jack ES 200/4-5
15 Northeast Rd 04084 207-642-4885
Virginia Day, prin. Fax 637-3716
Libby ES 300/K-4
45 Fort Hill Rd 04084 207-642-2500
Virginia Day, prin. Fax 642-7898

Starks, Somerset
MSAD 59
Supt. — See Madison
Starks ES 50/PK-1
57 Anson Rd 04911 207-696-5111
Malcolm Watts, prin. Fax 696-0885

Steep Falls, Cumberland
MSAD 6
Supt. — See Bar Mills
Steep Falls ES 100/K-3
781 Boundary Rd 04085 207-675-3321
Stephen Winger, prin. Fax 642-7898

Stetson, Penobscot
MSAD 64
Supt. — See Corinth
Stetson ES 100/K-4
394 Village Rd 04488 207-296-2571
Dawn Nickerson, prin. Fax 296-2571

Steuben, Washington
Regional School Unit 24
Supt. — See Ellsworth
Lewis S 100/K-8
15 Village Rd 04680 207-546-2430
Darlene Falabella, prin. Fax 546-2774

Stockton Springs, Waldo
MSAD 56
Supt. — See Searsport
Stockton Springs ES 100/K-5
113 Church St 04981 207-567-3264
Linda Bowe, prin. Fax 567-3641

Stratton, Franklin
MSAD 58
Supt. — See Phillips
Stratton S 100/K-8
PO Box 10 04982 207-246-2283
Lorrie Arruda, prin. Fax 246-6598

Strong, Franklin
MSAD 58
Supt. — See Phillips
Strong S 200/K-8
110 N Main St 04983 207-684-3521
Felecia Pease, prin. Fax 684-3340

Sullivan, Hancock
Regional School Unit 24
Supt. — See Ellsworth
Mountain View S 300/K-8
542 Bert Gray Rd 04664 207-422-3200
William Dove, prin. Fax 422-6881

Sumner, Oxford
Regional School Unit 10
Supt. — See Dixfield
Hartford-Sumner ES 300/PK-6
145 Main St 04292 207-388-2681
Ryan Wilkins, prin. Fax 388-2882

Surry, Hancock
Regional School Unit 24
Supt. — See Ellsworth
Surry S, 754 N Bend Rd 04684 100/K-8
Elizabeth Ehrlenbach, prin. 207-667-9358

Swans Island, Hancock
Union SD 98
Supt. — See Mount Desert
Swans Island S 50/K-8
PO Box 13 04685 207-526-4300
G. Keith, prin. Fax 526-4501

Swanville, Waldo
MSAD 34
Supt. — See Belfast
Nickerson ES 100/K-5
18 Town House Rd 04915 207-338-1858
Abigail Frost, prin. Fax 338-5302

Tenants Harbor, Knox
MSAD 50
Supt. — See Thomaston
St. George S 200/K-8
PO Box 153 04860 207-372-6312
Larry Schooley, prin. Fax 372-6900

Thomaston, Knox, Pop. 2,445
MSAD 50 1,000/K-12
12 Starr St 04861 207-354-2555
Judith Harvey, supt. Fax 354-2564
www.msad50.org/
Libby ES 200/K-4
13 Valley St 04861 207-354-6464
Beth Chamberlin, prin. Fax 354-2574
Thomaston MS 200/5-8
65 Watts Ln 04861 207-354-6353
Mary-Alice McLean, prin. Fax 354-6238
Other Schools – See Cushing, Tenants Harbor

Thorndike, Waldo
MSAD 3
Supt. — See Unity
Mt. View ES 200/K-5
573 Mount View Rd 04986 207-568-7541
Peter Weston, prin. Fax 568-3896
Mt. View JHS 200/6-8
575 Mount View Rd 04986 207-568-7561
Aaron McCullough, prin. Fax 568-7590

Topsfield, Washington
East Range Community SD
Supt. — See Danforth
East Range II S 50/K-8
187 School Rd 04490 207-796-2665
Fax 796-2421

Topsham, Sagadahoc, Pop. 6,147
MSAD 75 3,000/K-12
50 Republic Ave 04086 207-729-9961
J. Michael Wilhelm Ed.D., supt. Fax 725-9354
www.link75.org/
Mt. Ararat MS 700/6-8
66 Republic Ave 04086 207-729-2950
Brenda Brown, prin. Fax 729-2964
Williams-Cone ES 300/K-5
19 Perkins St 04086 207-725-4391
Steve Ciembroniewicz, prin. Fax 725-6408
Woodside ES 400/K-5
42 Barrows Dr 04086 207-725-1243
Rick Dedek, prin. Fax 721-9206
Other Schools – See Bowdoin, Bowdoinham, Harpswell

Trenton, Hancock
Regional School Unit 24
Supt. — See Ellsworth
Trenton S 100/K-8
51 School Rd 04605 207-667-8447
Gary Bosk, prin. Fax 667-0146

Troy, Waldo
MSAD 3
Supt. — See Unity
Troy Central ES 100/K-5
PO Box 30 04987 207-948-2280
Laura Gabriel, prin. Fax 948-5211

Turner, Androscoggin
MSAD 52 2,200/PK-12
486 Turner Ctr Rd 04282 207-225-3795
Darlene Burdin, supt. Fax 225-5608
www.msad52.org
Tripp MS 300/7-8
65 Matthews Way 04282 207-225-3261
Robert Kahler, prin. Fax 225-2102
Turner ES 300/4-6
91 Matthews Way 04282 207-225-3620
Karen Slusser, prin. Fax 225-4559
Turner PS 300/PK-3
59 Cobb Rd 04282 207-225-3655
Theresa Gillis, prin. Fax 225-3989
Other Schools – See Greene, Leeds

Union, Knox
MSAD 40 1,700/K-12
1070 Heald Hwy 04862 207-785-2277
Frank Boynton, supt. Fax 785-3119
shakespeare.mvhs.sad40.k12.me.us
Union ES 100/K-6
1070 Heald Hwy 04862 207-785-4330
Deborah Howard, prin. Fax 785-2277
Other Schools – See Friendship, Waldoboro, Warren, Washington

Union SD 69
Supt. — See Hope
Appleton Village S 100/K-8
737 Union Rd 04862 207-785-4504
Joy Baker, prin. Fax 785-3036

Unity, Waldo
MSAD 3 1,400/K-12
74 School St 04988 207-948-6136
Joseph Mattos, supt. Fax 948-2678
www.msad3.org
Unity ES 100/K-5
84 School St 04988 207-948-3881
Laura Gabriel, prin. Fax 948-2089
Other Schools – See Brooks, Liberty, Monroe, Thorndike, Troy

Van Buren, Aroostook, Pop. 2,759
MSAD 24 300/PK-12
169 Main St Ste 101 04785 207-868-2746
Clayton Belanger, supt. Fax 868-5420
Gateway S 200/PK-8
110 School Dr 04785 207-868-2733
Clayton Belanger, prin. Fax 868-2723

Vanceboro, Washington
Union SD 108
Supt. — See Danforth
Vanceboro S 50/PK-8
High St 04491 207-788-3835
Fax 788-3835

Vassalboro, Kennebec
Union SD 52
Supt. — See Winslow
Vassalboro Community S 500/K-8
1116 Webber Pond Rd 04989 207-923-3100
Kevin Michaud, prin. Fax 923-3104

Veazie, See Bangor
Union SD 87
Supt. — See Orono
Veazie Community S 200/K-8
1040 School St 04401 207-947-6573
Scott Nichols, prin. Fax 974-6570

Vinalhaven, Knox
MSAD 8 200/K-12
22 Arcola Ln 04863 207-863-4800
Mark Hurvitt, supt. Fax 863-4572
www.vinalhavenschool.org/
Vinalhaven S 200/K-12
22 Arcola Ln 04863 207-863-4800
Mike Felton, prin. Fax 863-4572

Waldoboro, Lincoln, Pop. 1,420
MSAD 40
Supt. — See Union
Medomak MS 7-8
318 Manktown Rd 04572 207-832-5028
Ben Vail, prin. Fax 832-5710
Miller ES 400/K-6
145 Kalers Corner St 04572 207-832-2103
Julia Levensaler, prin. Fax 832-2101

Wales, Androscoggin
Union SD 44 1,000/K-8
971 Gardiner Rd 04280 207-375-4273
Robert Connors, supt. Fax 375-2522
www.schoolunion44.org/
Wales Central S 200/K-8
175 Centre Rd 04280 207-375-6995
Brian Albert, prin. Fax 375-6087
Other Schools – See Litchfield, Sabattus

Wallagrass, Aroostook
MSAD 27
Supt. — See Fort Kent
Wallagrass ES 100/PK-6
PO Box 9 04781 207-834-5114
Julia Kelly, prin. Fax 834-6569

Warren, Knox
MSAD 40
Supt. — See Union
Warren Community ES 300/K-6
117 Eastern Rd 04864 207-273-2001
Ann Kirkpatrick, prin. Fax 273-3207

Washburn, Aroostook
MSAD 45 400/PK-12
33 School St 04786 207-455-8301
Ed Buckley, supt. Fax 455-8217
www.msad45.net/
Washburn District S 300/PK-8
33 School St 04786 207-455-4504
Ricky Bragg, prin. Fax 455-4506

Washington, Knox
MSAD 40
Supt. — See Union
Prescott Memorial ES 100/K-6
100 Waldoboro Rd 04574 207-845-2424
Richard Blackman, prin. Fax 845-2748

Waterboro, York
Regional School Unit 57 3,300/K-12
86 West Rd 04087 207-247-3221
Frank Sherburne, supt. Fax 247-3477
fc.sad57.k12.me.us/
Other Schools – See Alfred, East Waterboro, Lyman, Shapleigh, West Newfield

Waterford, Oxford
MSAD 17
Supt. — See Oxford
Waterford Memorial ES 100/K-6
148 Valley Rd 04088 207-583-4418
Margaret Emery, prin. Fax 674-3084

Waterville, Kennebec, Pop. 15,621
Waterville SD 1,800/K-12
25 Messalonskee Ave 04901 207-873-4281
Eric Haley, supt. Fax 872-5531
www.wtvl.k12.me.us
Hall ES 300/4-5
27 Pleasant St 04901 207-872-8071
Harriet Trafford, prin. Fax 872-6129
Mitchell ES 500/K-3
58 Drummond Ave 04901 207-873-0695
Allan Martin, prin. Fax 872-6172
Waterville JHS 400/6-8
100 W River Rd 04901 207-873-2144
Mick Roy, prin. Fax 873-5752

Mt. Merici S 200/PK-6
152 Western Ave 04901 207-873-3773
Susan Cote, prin. Fax 873-6377
Temple Academy 100/PK-12
60 W River Rd 04901 207-873-5325
James McSpadden, prin. Fax 692-2659

Wayne, Kennebec
Regional School Unit 38
Supt. — See Readfield
Wayne ES 100/K-5
48 Pond Rd 04284 207-685-3634
Cheryl Hasenfus, prin. Fax 685-9172

Wells, York
Wells-Ogunquit Community SD 1,400/K-12
PO Box 578 04090 207-646-8331
Edward McDonough, supt. Fax 646-0314
www.wocsd.org/
Wells ES 500/K-4
PO Box 429 04090 207-646-5953
Marianne Horne, prin. Fax 646-2592
Wells JHS 400/5-8
PO Box 310 04090 207-646-5142
Christopher Chessie, prin. Fax 646-2899

Wesley, Washington
Union SD 102
Supt. — See Machias
Wesley S 50/K-8
13 Whining Pines Dr 04686 207-255-3263
Kenneth Johnson, prin. Fax 255-0902

West Baldwin, Cumberland
MSAD 55
Supt. — See Hiram
Baldwin Consolidated ES 100/K-4
536 Pequawket Trl 04091 207-625-4076
Shelley Lemieux, prin. Fax 625-8094

West Bath, Sagadahoc
Regional School Unit 1
Supt. — See Bath
West Bath ES 100/K-6
126 New Meadows Rd 04530 207-443-9145
Emily Thompson, prin. Fax 443-6305

Westbrook, Cumberland, Pop. 16,108
Westbrook SD 2,400/K-12
117 Stroudwater St 04092 207-854-0800
Stan Sawyer, supt. Fax 854-0809
www.westbrookschools.org
Congin ES 300/3-5
410 Bridge St 04092 207-854-0844
Peter Lancia, prin. Fax 854-0846
Oxford-Cumberland Canal ES 200/3-5
102 Glenwood Ave 04092 207-854-0840
Jeremy Ray, prin. Fax 854-0855
Pride's Corner ES 200/K-2
375 Pride St 04092 207-797-5222
Janet Crawford, prin. Fax 878-5996
Saccarappa ES 200/K-2
110 Huntress Ave 04092 207-854-0847
Kathryn Hersom, prin. Fax 854-0849
Wescott JHS 600/6-8
426 Bridge St 04092 207-854-0830
Brian Mazjanis, prin. Fax 854-0858

West Enfield, Penobscot
MSAD 31
Supt. — See Howland
Enfield Station ES 300/K-5
561 Hammett Rd 04493 207-732-4141
Laura Cook, prin. Fax 732-5319

West Gardiner, Kennebec
MSAD 11
Supt. — See Gardiner
Thompson ES 200/PK-5
309 Spears Corner Rd 04345 207-724-3930
Donna McGibney, prin. Fax 724-3934

West Newfield, York
Regional School Unit 57
Supt. — See Waterboro
Line ES 300/K-5
818 Water St 04095 207-793-4100
Patricia Durgin, prin. Fax 793-2425

West Paris, Oxford
MSAD 17
Supt. — See Oxford
Gray ES 100/2-6
170 Main St 04289 207-674-2332
Melanie Ellsworth, prin. Fax 674-3084
Legion Memorial PS 50/K-1
20 Kingsbury St 04289 207-674-2671
Melanie Ellsworth, prin. Fax 674-3084

Whitefield, Lincoln
Sheepscot Valley Regional School Unit 12 1,700/K-12
69 Augusta Rd 04353 207-549-3261
Gregory Potter, supt. Fax 549-3082
www.svrsu.org/
Whitefield S 200/K-8
164 Grand Army Rd 04353 207-549-7691
Ronald Cote, prin. Fax 549-4566
Other Schools – See Chelsea, Palermo, Somerville, Windsor, Wiscasset

Whiting, Washington
Union SD 134
Supt. — See Machias
Whiting Village S 50/K-8
145 US Rte 1 04691 207-733-4617
Scott Johnson, prin. Fax 733-7582

Wilton, Franklin, Pop. 2,453
Mt. Blue Regional SD
Supt. — See Farmington
Academy Hill ES 200/3-6
585 Depot St 04294 207-645-4488
Darlene Paine, prin. Fax 645-3844
Cushing ES 100/K-2
585 Depot St 04294 207-645-2442
Darlene Paine, prin. Fax 645-5102

Windham, Cumberland, Pop. 13,020
Windham Raymond RSU 14 3,200/K-12
228 Windham Center Rd 04062 207-892-1800
Sanford Prince, supt. Fax 892-1805
www.windham.k12.me.us
Manchester ES 400/4-5
709 Roosevelt Trl 04062 207-892-1830
Cynthia Curtis, prin. Fax 892-1834
Windham MS 600/6-8
408 Gray Rd 04062 207-892-1820
Harold Shortsleeve, prin. Fax 892-1826
Windham PS 600/K-3
404 Gray Rd 04062 207-892-1840
Dr. Kyle Rhoads, prin. Fax 892-1838
Other Schools – See Raymond

Windham Christian Academy 100/PK-12
1051 Roosevelt Trl 04062 207-892-2244
Roy Mickelson, prin. Fax 893-1289

Windsor, Kennebec
Sheepscot Valley Regional School Unit 12
Supt. — See Whitefield
Windsor S 300/K-8
366 Ridge Rd 04363 207-445-2356
Robert Moody, prin. Fax 445-3494

Union SD 132 200/K-8
320 Griffin Rd 04363 207-549-1010
Francis Boynton, supt. Fax 549-1015
Other Schools – See Jefferson

Winn, Penobscot
MSAD 30
Supt. — See Lee
Lee/Winn ES 100/PK-5
1009 Route 168 04495 207-738-3060
Pamela Hamilton, prin. Fax 738-3070

Winslow, Kennebec, Pop. 5,436
Union SD 52 2,300/PK-12
20 Dean St 04901 207-872-1960
Hugh Riordan, supt. Fax 859-2405
www.su52.org/
Winslow ES 400/PK-5
285 Benton Ave 04901 207-872-1967
Steven Frank, prin. Fax 873-6522
Winslow JHS 300/6-8
6 Danielson St 04901 207-872-1973
Kevin Michaud, prin. Fax 872-1977
Other Schools – See South China, Vassalboro

St. John S 100/PK-5
15 S Garand St 04901 207-872-7115
Valerie Wheeler, prin. Fax 872-2500

Winter Harbor, Hancock
Regional School Unit 24
Supt. — See Ellsworth
Peninsula Community S 200/K-8
PO Box 99 04693 207-963-2292
Cathy Lewis, prin. Fax 963-5951

Winterport, Waldo, Pop. 1,274
MSAD 22
Supt. — See Hampden
Smith ES 300/K-5
319 S Main St 04496 207-223-4282
Carla Leathem, prin. Fax 223-2267
Wagner MS 200/6-8
54 Mountainview Dr 04496 207-223-4309
Dale Williams, prin. Fax 223-4325

Winthrop, Kennebec, Pop. 2,819
Winthrop SD 900/PK-12
17A Highland Ave 04364 207-377-2296
Stephen Cottrell, supt. Fax 377-2708
www.winthrop.k12.me.us
Winthrop ES 400/PK-5
23 Highland Ave 04364 207-377-2241
Jeffrey Ladd, prin. Fax 377-4671
Winthrop MS 200/6-8
400 Rambler Rd 04364 207-377-2249
Karen Criss, prin. Fax 377-3667

Wiscasset, Lincoln, Pop. 1,233
Sheepscot Valley Regional School Unit 12
Supt. — See Whitefield
Wiscasset ES 300/K-4
146 Gardiner Rd 04578 207-882-7585
Cheryl McKeagney, prin. Fax 882-5239
Wiscasset MS 200/5-8
83 Federal St 04578 207-882-7767
Linda Bleile, prin. Fax 882-8279

Woodland, Aroostook, Pop. 1,287
Union SD 122 200/PK-8
843 Woodland Center Rd 04736 207-498-8436
John Hedman, supt. Fax 498-6349
Woodland S 100/PK-8
844 Woodland Center Rd 04736 207-496-2981
Susan Schloeman, prin. Fax 496-6913
Other Schools – See New Sweden

Woolwich, Sagadahoc, Pop. 2,570
Regional School Unit 1
Supt. — See Bath
Woolwich Central S 300/K-8
137 Nequasset Rd 04579 207-443-9739
Thomas Soule, prin. Fax 443-9792

Yarmouth, Cumberland, Pop. 3,338
Yarmouth SD 1,400/K-12
101 McCartney St 04096 207-846-5586
Ken Murphy Ed.D., supt. Fax 846-2339
www.yarmouth.k12.me.us
Harrison MS 400/5-8
220 McCartney St 04096 207-846-2499
Bruce Brann, prin. Fax 846-2489
Rowe ES 200/K-1
52 School St 04096 207-846-3771
Catherine Glaude, prin. Fax 846-2325
Yarmouth ES 300/2-4
121 McCartney St 04096 207-846-3391
Elizabeth Lane, prin. Fax 846-2330

York, York, Pop. 9,818
York SD 1,800/K-12
469 US Route 1 03909 207-363-3403
Henry Scipione, supt. Fax 363-5602
www.yorkschools.org/
Coastal Ridge ES 300/2-4
1 Coastal Ridge Rd 03909 207-363-1800
Sean Murphy, prin. Fax 363-1816
Village ES 300/K-2
124 York St 03909 207-363-4870
Ruth Dealy, prin. Fax 363-1818
York MS 600/5-8
30 Organug Rd 03909 207-363-4214
Stephen Bishop, prin. Fax 363-1815

Brixham Montessori Friends S 100/PK-6
18 Brickyard Ct 03909 207-351-2700
Alica Johnson-Grafe, hdmstr.

MARYLAND

MARYLAND DEPARTMENT OF EDUCATION
200 W Baltimore St, Baltimore 21201-2595
Telephone 410-767-0600
Fax 410-333-6033
Website http://www.marylandpublicschools.org

Superintendent of Schools Nancy Grasmick

MARYLAND BOARD OF EDUCATION
200 W Baltimore St, Baltimore 21201-2595

President James DeGraffenreidt

PUBLIC, PRIVATE AND CATHOLIC ELEMENTARY SCHOOLS

Aberdeen, Harford, Pop. 14,305
Harford County SD
Supt. — See Bel Air
Aberdeen MS 1,200/6-8
111 Mount Royal Ave 21001 410-273-5510
Chandra Krantz, prin. Fax 273-5542
Bakerfield ES 400/PK-5
36 Baker St 21001 410-273-5518
Monique Phillip, prin. Fax 273-5547
Hall's Cross Roads ES 400/PK-5
203 E Bel Air Ave 21001 410-273-5524
Gwendolyn Benjamin-Jones, prin. Fax 273-5555
Lisby ES at Hillsdale 300/PK-5
810 Edmund St 21001 410-273-5530
Patricia Chenworth, prin. Fax 273-5561

St. Joan of Arc S 200/K-8
230 S Law St 21001 410-575-7319
Dr. Jane Towery, prin. Fax 272-1959

Abingdon, Harford
Harford County SD
Supt. — See Bel Air
Abingdon ES 600/PK-5
399 Singer Rd 21009 410-638-3910
Kathleen Burr, prin. Fax 638-3914
James ES 500/K-5
1 Laurentum Pkwy 21009 410-638-3900
Raymond Schmalzer, prin. Fax 638-3906
Paca/Old Post Road ES 900/PK-5
2706 Philadelphia Rd 21009 410-612-1566
Gail Dunlap, prin. Fax 612-1587

New Covenant Christian S 200/K-9
128 Saint Marys Church Rd 21009 443-512-0771
Jason Van Bemmel, hdmstr. Fax 569-3846

Accident, Garrett, Pop. 340
Garrett County SD
Supt. — See Oakland
Accident ES 200/PK-5
534 Accident Bittinger Rd 21520 301-746-8863
Karen DeVore, prin. Fax 746-8570
Northern MS 400/6-8
371 Pride Pkwy 21520 301-746-8165
William Carlson, prin. Fax 746-8865

Accokeek, Prince George's, Pop. 4,477
Prince George's County SD
Supt. — See Upper Marlboro
Burroughs MS 700/6-8
14400 Berry Rd 20607 301-203-3200
George Covington, prin. Fax 203-3207
Ferguson ES 500/K-5
14600 Berry Rd 20607 301-203-1140
Monique Davis, prin. Fax 203-1135

Adamstown, Frederick
Frederick County SD
Supt. — See Frederick
Carroll Manor ES 500/PK-5
5624 Adamstown Rd 21710 240-236-3800
Kevin Cuppett, prin. Fax 236-3801

Adelphi, Prince George's, Pop. 13,524
Prince George's County SD
Supt. — See Upper Marlboro
Adelphi ES 400/K-6
8820 Riggs Rd 20783 301-431-6250
Jane Ennis, prin. Fax 408-5524
Buck Lodge MS 700/7-8
2611 Buck Lodge Rd 20783 301-431-6290
Sandra Jimenez, prin. Fax 445-8404
Cherokee Lane ES 400/K-6
9000 25th Ave 20783 301-445-8415
Jack St. Clair, prin. Fax 445-8442
Cool Spring ES 300/K-6
8910 Riggs Rd 20783 301-431-6200
Fran Tolbert, prin. Fax 445-8467
Jones ES 600/K-6
2405 Tecumseh St 20783 301-408-7900
Elizabeth Harriday, prin. Fax 408-7904

Annapolis, Anne Arundel, Pop. 36,300
Anne Arundel County SD 73,400/PK-12
2644 Riva Rd 21401 410-222-5000
Kevin Maxwell Ph.D., supt. Fax 222-5602
www.aacps.org/
Annapolis ES 200/PK-5
180 Green St 21401 410-222-1600
Susan Myers, prin. Fax 222-1601
Annapolis MS 400/6-8
1399 Forest Dr 21403 410-267-8658
Carolyn Burton-Page, prin. Fax 267-8924
Bates MS 600/6-8
701 Chase St 21401 410-263-0270
Diane Bragdon, prin. Fax 263-0295
Cape St. Claire ES 700/K-5
931 Blue Ridge Dr, 410-222-1685
Donna Pergerson, prin. Fax 222-1672
Eastport ES 200/PK-5
420 Fifth St 21403 410-222-1605
Lynne Evans, prin. Fax 222-1609
Georgetown East ES 300/PK-5
111 Dogwood Rd 21403 410-222-1610
Michelle Batten, prin.
Germantown ES 400/PK-5
1411 Cedar Park Rd 21401 410-222-1615
Walter Reap, prin. Fax 222-1617
Hillsmere ES 400/K-5
3052 Arundel on the Bay Rd 21403 410-222-1622
Christopher Wooleyhand, prin. Fax 295-0479
Mills-Parole ES 400/K-5
103 Chinquapin Round Rd 21401 410-222-1626
Alfreda Adams, prin.
Rolling Knolls ES 400/PK-5
1985 Valley Rd 21401 410-222-5820
Jane Taylor, prin. Fax 222-5828
Tyler Heights ES 300/PK-5
200 Janwall St 21403 410-222-1630
Faye Daniel, prin. Fax 222-1683
West Annapolis ES 200/K-5
210 Annapolis St 21401 410-222-1635
Christine Stockett, prin. Fax 222-1654
Windsor Farm ES 500/K-5
591 Broadneck Rd, 410-222-1690
Randall Rice, prin. Fax 222-8681
Other Schools – See Arnold, Baltimore, Crofton, Crownsville, Davidsonville, Deale, Edgewater, Fort Meade, Gambrills, Glen Burnie, Hanover, Jessup, Laurel, Linthicum Heights, Lothian, Millersville, Odenton, Pasadena, Severn, Severna Park, Shady Side, Tracys Landing

---

Annapolis Area Christian S 1,000/PK-12
716 Bestgate Rd 21401 410-266-8251
David Castle, supt. Fax 573-6866
Chesapeake Montessori S 100/PK-5
30 Old Mill Bottom Rd N, 410-757-4740
Deborah Bricker, hdmstr. Fax 757-8770
Key S 700/PK-12
534 Hillsmere Dr 21403 410-263-9231
Marcella Yedid, hdmstr. Fax 280-5516
Montessori International Childrens House 100/PK-6
1641 N Winchester Rd, 410-757-7789
Jean Burgess, dir. Fax 974-4610
St. Anne's S of Annapolis 300/PK-8
3112 Arundel on the Bay Rd 21403 410-263-8650
Frances Lukens, prin. Fax 280-8720
St. Margaret's Day S 100/PK-K
1605 Pleasant Plains Rd, 410-757-2333
Tricia Hallberg, dir. Fax 757-5334
St. Martin's Lutheran S 200/PK-8
1120 Spa Rd 21403 410-269-1955
Jane Daugherty, prin. Fax 280-2024
St. Mary S 900/K-8
111 Duke of Gloucester St 21401 410-263-2869
Margaret Dammeyer, prin. Fax 269-6513

Arnold, Anne Arundel, Pop. 20,261
Anne Arundel County SD
Supt. — See Annapolis
Arnold ES 400/K-5
90 Church Rd 21012 410-222-1670
Rosemary Biggart, prin. Fax 222-1672
Belvedere ES 500/PK-5
360 Broadwater Rd 21012 410-975-9432
Susan Errichiello, prin. Fax 975-9830
Broadneck ES 600/K-5
470 Shore Acres Rd 21012 410-222-1680
Alison Lee, prin.
Magothy River MS 800/6-8
241 Peninsula Farm Rd Ste 1 21012 410-544-0926
Christopher Mirenzi, prin. Fax 544-1867
Severn River MS 800/6-8
241 Peninsula Farm Rd Ste 2 21012 410-544-0922
June Eyet, prin. Fax 315-8006

Arnold Christian Academy 100/K-8
365 Jones Station Rd 21012 410-544-1882
Sue Maksim, prin. Fax 544-5765
Chesapeake Academy 300/PK-5
1185 Baltimore Annapolis Bl 21012 410-647-9612
Jason Scheurle, hdmstr. Fax 647-6088

Ashton, Montgomery

Mater Amoris Montessori S 100/PK-6
PO Box 97 20861 301-774-7468
Charlotte Shea, admin. Fax 774-5232

Avenue, Saint Mary's

Holy Angels-Sacred Heart S 100/PK-8
21335 Colton Point Rd 20609 301-769-3389
Dr. Janice Walthour, prin. Fax 769-4948

Baldwin, Baltimore
Baltimore County SD
Supt. — See Towson
Carroll Manor ES 300/PK-5
4434 Carroll Manor Rd 21013 410-887-5947
John Kroh, prin. Fax 887-5948

Baltimore, Baltimore, Pop. 635,815
Anne Arundel County SD
Supt. — See Annapolis
Belle Grove ES 200/PK-5
4502 Belle Grove Rd 21225 410-222-6589
Adrienne Taylor, prin. Fax 222-6500
Brooklyn Park ES 300/PK-5
200 14th Ave 21225 410-222-6590
Donald Leuschner, prin. Fax 222-6581
Brooklyn Park MS 600/6-8
200 Hammonds Ln 21225 410-636-2967
Maisha Gillins, prin.
Park ES 400/PK-5
201 E 11th Ave 21225 410-222-6593
Walter Jackson, prin. Fax 222-6596

Baltimore CSD 70,600/PK-12
200 E North Ave 21202 410-396-8700
Dr. Andres Alonso, admin. Fax 396-8898
www.bcps.k12.md.us
Abbottston ES 300/PK-5
1300 Gorsuch Ave 21218 410-984-2685
Angela Faltz, prin.
Arlington S 500/PK-8
3705 W Rogers Ave 21215 410-396-0567
Terrelle Gray, prin. Fax 396-0072
Armistead Gardens S 400/PK-8
5001 E Eager St 21205 410-396-9090
Sofia Glasson, prin. Fax 488-6270
Arundel S 300/PK-8
2400 Round Rd 21225 410-396-1379
Matthew Carpenter, prin. Fax 396-1836
Barclay S 400/PK-8
2900 Barclay St 21218 410-396-6387
Jenny Heinbaugh, prin. Fax 396-6200
Barrister ES 300/PK-7
1327 Washington Blvd 21230 410-396-5973
Bridgett Dean, prin. Fax 545-3272
Bay-Brook S 400/PK-8
4301 10th St 21225 410-396-1357
Ann Custis, prin. Fax 396-8430
Beechfield S 700/PK-8
301 S Beechfield Ave 21229 410-396-0525
Rene Browning, prin. Fax 396-0426
Belmont ES 400/PK-5
1406 N Ellamont St 21216 410-396-0579
Mary LaMartina, prin. Fax 545-7841
Bentalou ES 200/PK-2
220 N Bentalou St 21223 410-396-1385
Mary Ann Winterling, prin. Fax 545-7878

Brehms Lane ES 600/PK-5
3536 Brehms Ln 21213 410-396-9150
Andre Spencer, prin. Fax 396-5999

Brent S 200/PK-8
100 E 26th St 21218 410-396-6509
Jacqueline Scofield, prin. Fax 396-6038

Callaway ES 300/K-5
3701 Fernhill Ave 21215 410-396-0604
Joyce Middleton, prin. Fax 545-7847

Calverton S 700/PK-8
1100 Whitmore Ave 21216 410-396-0581
Tanya Green, prin. Fax 545-7849

Carter S 300/PK-8
820 E 43rd St 21212 410-396-6271
Deborah Barton, prin. Fax 323-7624

Cecil ES 400/PK-5
2000 Cecil Ave 21218 410-396-6385
Roxanne Forr, prin. Fax 396-7193

Cherry Hill S 400/PK-8
801 Bridgeview Rd 21225 410-396-1392
Tifini Stewart, prin. Fax 396-7586

Chinquapin MS 800/6-8
900 Woodbourne Ave 21212 410-396-6424
Andre Parson, prin. Fax 396-0381

Coldstream Park S 400/PK-8
1400 Exeter Hall Ave 21218 410-396-6443
Edwin Saunders, prin. Fax 396-6206

Coleman ES 300/PK-5
2400 Windsor Ave 21216 410-396-0764
Brenda Allen, prin. Fax 225-3035

Coleridge-Taylor ES 300/PK-5
507 W Preston St 21201 410-396-0783
Sandra Graves, prin. Fax 396-0975

Cross Country S 500/PK-8
6100 Cross Country Blvd 21215 410-396-0602
Matthew Riley, prin. Fax 545-7850

Curtis Bay S 400/PK-8
4301 W Bay Ave 21225 410-396-1397
Barbara Pryor, prin. Fax 396-5263

Dickey Hill S 400/K-8
5025 Dickey Hill Rd 21207 410-396-0610
Joyce Hughes, prin. Fax 396-0017

Diggs-Johnson MS 500/6-8
1300 Herkimer St 21223 410-396-1572
Esther Wallace, prin. Fax 385-0340

Dunbar MS 600/6-8
500 N Caroline St 21205 410-396-9296
Mark Bongiovanni, prin. Fax 396-2954

Edgecombe Circle S 500/PK-8
2835 Virginia Ave 21215 410-396-0550
Herbert Miller, prin. Fax 545-7867

Edgewood ES 300/PK-5
1900 Edgewood St 21216 410-396-0532
Carol Green, prin. Fax 396-0681

Eutaw-Marshburn ES 400/PK-5
1624 Eutaw Pl 21217 410-396-0779
Marilyn Jackson, prin. Fax 396-0397

Fallstaff S 200/K-8
3801 Fallstaff Rd 21215 410-396-0682
Faith Hibbert, prin. Fax 545-1737

Farring S 400/PK-8
300 Pontiac Ave 21225 410-396-1404
Linda Brewster, prin. Fax 396-5218

Federal Hill ES 300/PK-5
1040 William St 21230 410-396-1207
Sharon Van Dyke, prin. Fax 396-3532

Fort Worthington ES 400/PK-5
2701 E Oliver St 21213 410-396-9161
Shaylin Todd, prin. Fax 396-6341

Franklin Square S 300/PK-8
1400 W Lexington St 21223 410-396-0795
Terry Patton, prin. Fax 396-0999

Frederick ES 300/PK-5
2501 Frederick Ave 21223 410-396-0830
Fax 396-8073

Furley ES 500/K-5
4633 Furley Ave 21206 410-396-9094
Barb Myers, prin. Fax 545-7844

Gardenville ES 300/K-5
5300 Belair Rd 21206 410-396-6382
Tammie McIntire-Miller, prin. Fax 396-8081

Garrett Heights S 400/PK-8
2800 Ailsa Ave 21214 410-396-6361
Yetty Goodlin, prin. Fax 396-0428

Garrison MS 600/6-8
3910 Barrington Rd 21207 410-396-0735
Isiah Hemphill, prin. Fax 545-7861

Gilmor ES 500/PK-6
1311 N Gilmor St 21217 410-462-2700
Ledonnis Hernandez, prin. Fax 462-6775

Glenmount S 700/K-8
6211 Walther Ave 21206 410-396-6366
Charlotte Williams, prin. Fax 396-6760

Govans ES 400/PK-5
5801 York Rd 21212 410-396-6396
Linda Taylor, prin. Fax 547-7840

Graceland Park-O'Donnell Heights S 200/K-8
6300 ODonnell St 21224 410-396-9083
Wayne Law, prin. Fax 396-9364

Grove Park S 300/PK-8
5545 Kennison Ave 21215 410-396-0822
Carla Jackson, prin. Fax 545-7845

Guilford S 300/K-8
4520 York Rd 21212 410-396-6358
Sheilah Myers, prin. Fax 396-6212

Gwynns Falls ES 500/PK-5
2700 Gwynns Falls Pkwy 21216 410-396-0638
Hartavia Johnson, prin. Fax 545-7853

Hamilton ES 300/PK-5
800 Poplar Grove St 21216 410-396-0520
Charlotte Jackson, prin. Fax 396-1803

Hamilton MS 800/6-8
5609 Sefton Ave 21214 410-396-6370
Michelle Ferris, prin. Fax 396-6561

Hamilton S 600/PK-8
6101 Old Harford Rd 21214 410-396-6375
William Murphy, prin. Fax 545-7870

Hampden S 300/PK-8
3608 Chestnut Ave 21211 410-396-6004
Margaret Shipley, prin. Fax 545-7774

Harford Heights ES 300/PK-5
1919 N Broadway 21213 410-396-9341
Nancy Faulkner, prin. Fax 396-9060

Harlem Park ES 300/PK-8
1401 W Lafayette Ave 21217 410-396-0633
Joyce Akintillo, prin. Fax 396-0619

Harris ES 400/PK-5
1400 N Caroline St 21213 410-396-1452
Loren McCaskill, prin. Fax 396-3019

Hazelwood S 600/K-8
4517 Hazelwood Ave 21206 410-396-9098
Sidney Twiggs, prin. Fax 545-7868

Henson ES 400/PK-5
1600 N Payson St 21217 410-396-0776
Carla Bragg, prin. Fax 396-7840

Highlandtown S PK-8
3223 E Pratt St 21224 410-396-9381
Nancy Fagan, prin. Fax 396-1178

Highlandtown S, 231 S Eaton St 21224 500/PK-8
Prentiss Moore, prin. 443-642-2792

Hilton ES 300/PK-5
3301 Carlisle Ave 21216 410-396-0634
Sonya Goodwyn, prin. Fax 396-0892

Holabird S 200/PK-8
1500 Imla St 21224 410-396-9086
Lindsay Krey, prin. Fax 396-7588

Howard ES 200/PK-5
2011 Linden Ave 21217 410-396-0837
Erma Jefferson, prin. Fax 396-0184

Hughes ES 200/PK-5
5011 Arbutus Ave 21215 410-396-7827
Gloria Pulley, prin. Fax 545-7864

Jefferson S 300/PK-8
605 Dryden Dr 21229 410-396-0534
Wendy Leisher, prin. Fax 545-7846

Johnson S 300/PK-8
100 E Heath St 21230 410-396-1575
James Dedinger, prin. Fax 545-7345

Johnston Square S 300/PK-8
1101 Valley St 21202 410-396-1477
Laura Lyde, prin. Fax 396-5251

Kelson S 400/PK-8
701 Gold St 21217 410-396-0800
Federico Adams, prin. Fax 396-0855

Key S 700/PK-8
1425 E Fort Ave 21230 410-396-1503
Mary Booker, prin. Fax 545-6720

King S 600/PK-8
3750 Greenspring Ave 21211 410-396-0756
Sharon Bullock, prin. Fax 396-0576

Lakeland S 600/PK-8
2921 Stranden Rd 21230 410-396-1406
Jacqueline Ferris, prin. Fax 396-0015

Lakewood ES 200/PK-2
2625 E Federal St 21213 410-396-9158
Iris Harris, prin. Fax 276-5083

Lemmel MS 800/6-8
2801 N Dukeland St 21216 410-396-0664
Quianna Cooke, prin. Fax 225-9457

Liberty ES 400/PK-5
3901 Maine Ave 21207 410-396-0571
Beverly Woolford, prin. Fax 396-0396

Lockerman-Bundy ES 200/PK-5
301 N Pulaski St 21223 410-396-1364
Cynthia Cunningham, prin. Fax 545-7877

Lyndhurst ES 300/PK-5
621 Wildwood Pkwy 21229 410-396-0503
Tanya Wilson, prin. Fax 396-0439

March MS, 2050 N Wolfe St 21213 6-8
Diane Brown, prin. 443-984-3699

McHenry ES 300/PK-5
31 S Schroeder St 21223 410-396-1621
Judith Dixon, prin. Fax 396-1668

Medfield Heights ES 300/PK-5
4300 Buchanan Ave 21211 410-396-6460
Ramon Japzon, prin. Fax 545-7873

Moravia Park S 800/PK-8
6201 Frankford Ave 21206 410-396-9096
Barbara Sawyer, prin. Fax 396-8075

Morrell Park S 300/K-8
2601 Tolley St 21230 410-396-3426
Sean Conley, prin. Fax 396-0016

Morse ES 400/PK-5
424 S Pulaski St 21223 410-396-1355
Michael Cheatham, prin. Fax 396-0466

Mosher ES 300/PK-5
2400 W Mosher St 21216 410-396-0506
Cascelia Spears, prin. Fax 396-7841

Mt. Royal S 800/PK-8
121 McMechen St 21217 410-396-0864
Carolyn Freeland, prin. Fax 396-0309

Mount Washington ES 300/PK-5
1801 Sulgrave Ave 21209 410-396-6354
Sue Torr, prin. Fax 396-0147

Nicholas ES 300/PK-5
201 E 21st St 21218 410-396-4525
Iris Murdock, prin. Fax 396-5975

North Bend S 400/PK-8
181 N Bend Rd 21229 410-396-0376
Patricia Burrell, prin. Fax 396-0380

Northeast MS 600/6-8
5001 Moravia Rd 21206 410-396-9220
Wanda Young, prin. Fax 396-1680

Northwood ES 600/K-5
5201 Loch Raven Blvd 21239 410-396-6377
Edward English, prin. Fax 545-7852

Paca ES 700/PK-5
200 N Lakewood Ave 21224 410-396-9148
Stacy Place, prin. Fax 545-7838

Patapsco S 400/PK-8
844 Roundview Rd 21225 410-396-1400
Marvin Darden, prin. Fax 396-8631

Pimlico S 600/PK-8
4849 Pimlico Rd 21215 410-396-0876
Orrester Shaw, prin. Fax 396-0925

Pinderhughes ES 200/PK-5
1200 N Fremont Ave 21217 410-396-0761
Brenda Hubbard, prin. Fax 396-0342

Pitts-Ashburton S 500/K-8
3935 Hilton Rd 21215 410-396-0636
Lucy Miller, prin. Fax 396-0206

Roach ES 300/PK-5
3434 Old Frederick Rd 21229 410-396-0511
Sheila Hale, prin. Fax 396-0740

Rodman ES 400/PK-5
3510 W Mulberry St 21229 410-396-0508
Jerome Butler, prin. Fax 396-0702

Rodwell ES 300/PK-5
3501 Hillsdale Rd 21207 410-396-0940
Saundra Adams, prin. Fax 396-0854

Rogers S 300/PK-8
100 N Chester St 21231 410-396-9300
Lily McElveen, prin. Fax 396-9164

Rognell Heights S 400/K-8
4300 Sidehill Rd 21229 410-396-0528
Ivy Hill, prin. Fax 396-8456

Roland Park S 1,200/K-8
5207 Roland Ave 21210 410-396-6420
Carolyn Cole, prin. Fax 396-7662

Ruhrah S 300/PK-8
701 Rappolla St 21224 410-396-9125
Mary Donnelly, prin. Fax 396-8105

Sinclair Lane ES 500/PK-5
3880 Sinclair Ln 21213 410-396-9117
Roxanne Thorn-Lumpkins, prin. Fax 545-7525

Southeast MS 300/6-8
6820 Fait Ave 21224 410-396-9291
Vickie Lawson, prin. Fax 284-4947

Stadium S, 1300 Gorsuch Ave 21218 200/4-8
Ronald Shelly, dir. 443-984-2682

Steuart Hill Academy 100/6-8
30 S Gilmor St 21223 410-396-1387
Marsha Powell, prin. Fax 396-6953

Templeton ES 600/PK-5
1200 Pennsylvania Ave 21217 410-462-9560
Ken Cherry, prin. Fax 462-3824

Tench Tilghman S 300/PK-8
600 N Patterson Park Ave 21205 410-396-9247
Charletta Generette, prin. Fax 396-9451

Tubman ES 200/PK-5
1807 Harlem Ave 21217 410-396-1362
Fax 396-0080

Violetville S 400/K-8
1207 Pine Heights Ave 21229 410-396-1416
Catherine Reinholdt, prin. Fax 396-0838

Walk ES 800/PK-5
1235 Sherwood Ave 21239 410-396-6380
Edna Greer, prin. Fax 396-6294

Washington ES, 800 Scott St 21230 200/PK-5
Susan Burgess, prin. 410-396-1445

Washington MS 600/6-8
1301 McCulloh St 21217 410-396-7734
William Bailey, prin. Fax 396-0552

Waverly S 700/PK-8
3400 Ellerslie Ave 21218 410-396-6394
Brenda Abrams, prin. Fax 396-6161

West Baltimore MS 900/6-8
201 N Bend Rd 21229 410-396-0700
Eugene Qui, prin. Fax 396-7700

Westport Academy 400/PK-8
2401 Nevada St 21230 410-396-3396
Felecia Irick, prin.

Westside ES 300/PK-5
2235 N Fulton Ave 21217 410-396-0628
Fax 545-7862

Windsor Hills S 200/PK-8
4001 Alto Rd 21216 410-396-0595
Carmen Holmes, prin. Fax 545-7843

Winston MS 500/6-8
1101 Winston Ave 21212 410-396-6356
Eldon Thomas, prin. Fax 532-6584

Woodhome S 500/K-8
7300 Moyer Ave 21234 410-396-6398
Christine Skowronski, prin. Fax 396-7792

Woodson S 400/PK-8
2501 Seabury Rd 21225 410-396-1366
Patrick Harris, prin. Fax 396-3062

Yorkwood ES 500/PK-5
5931 Yorkwood Rd 21239 410-396-6364
Deborah Sharpe, prin. Fax 396-6262

Baltimore County SD
Supt. — See Towson

Arbutus ES 300/PK-5
1300 Sulphur Spring Rd 21227 410-887-1400
Karen Benny, prin. Fax 887-1401

Arbutus MS 900/6-8
5525 Shelbourne Rd 21227 410-887-1402
Kendra Johnson, prin. Fax 536-1164

Baltimore Highlands ES 500/PK-5
4200 Annapolis Rd 21227 410-887-0919
Rosemarie Kincannon, prin. Fax 789-2502

Battle Grove ES 300/PK-5
7828 Saint Patricia Ln 21222 410-887-7500
Jennifer Severson, prin. Fax 887-7501

Bear Creek ES 500/PK-5
1601 Melbourne Rd 21222 410-887-7007
Cheryl Thim, prin. Fax 887-7111

Bedford ES 300/PK-5
7407 Dorman Dr 21208 410-887-1200
Laverne Goins, prin. Fax 887-1201

Berkshire ES 300/PK-5
7431 Poplar Ave 21224 410-887-7008
Vicky Ciulla, prin. Fax 284-5345

Campfield ECC 200/PK-PK
6834 Alter St 21207 410-887-1227
Nashae Bennett, prin. Fax 887-1230

Carney ES 500/PK-5
3131 E Joppa Rd 21234 410-887-5228
Eileen Roberta, prin. Fax 887-5229

Chadwick ES 400/PK-5
1918 Winder Rd 21244 410-887-1300
Bonnie Hess, prin. Fax 277-9837

Charlesmont ES 300/PK-5
7800 W Collingham Dr 21222 410-887-7004
Marsha Ayres, prin. Fax 887-7355

Chase ES 400/PK-5
11701 Eastern Ave 21220 410-887-5940
Sharon Whitlock, prin. Fax 887-5941

Chesapeake Terrace ES 200/PK-5
2112 Lodge Farm Rd 21219 410-887-7505
Renee Johnson, prin. Fax 887-7555

Colgate ES 300/PK-5
401 51st St 21224 410-887-7010
Kevin Connelly, prin. Fax 887-7012
Cromwell Valley Magnet ES 400/K-5
825 Providence Rd 21286 410-887-4888
Darlene Morrison, prin. Fax 887-4889
Deep Creek ES 500/PK-5
1101 E Homberg Ave 21221 410-887-0110
Darla Evans, prin. Fax 391-6547
Deep Creek MS 800/6-8
1000 S Marlyn Ave 21221 410-887-0112
Anissa Brown-Dennis, prin. Fax 391-6534
Dogwood ES 500/K-5
7215 Dogwood Rd 21244 410-887-6808
Betty Pettiford, prin. Fax 298-2720
Dumbarton MS 900/6-8
300 Dumbarton Rd Ste 1 21212 410-887-3176
Nancy Fink, prin. Fax 887-3176
Dundalk ES 500/PK-5
2717 Playfield St 21222 410-887-7013
Barbara McLennan, prin. Fax 284-2204
Dundalk MS 500/6-8
7400 Dunmanway 21222 410-887-7018
John Foley, prin. Fax 887-7284
Eastwood Center Magnet ES 100/K-5
428 Westham Way 21224 410-887-7034
Joan Brauner, prin. Fax 887-7035
Edgemere ES 500/PK-5
7201 N Point Rd 21219 410-887-7507
Robert Findley, prin. Fax 887-7508
Edmondson Heights ES 600/PK-5
1600 Langford Rd 21207 410-887-0818
David Parker, prin. Fax 869-0240
Elmwood ES 500/PK-5
531 Dale Ave 21206 410-887-5232
Sharon Ward, prin. Fax 887-5233
Featherbed Lane S 600/PK-8
6700 Richardson Rd 21207 410-887-1302
Tiffany Livingstone, prin. Fax 277-9879
Fort Garrison ES 400/K-5
3310 Woodvalley Dr 21208 410-887-1203
Susan Herschfeld, prin. Fax 887-1204
Fullerton ES 500/PK-5
4400 Fullerton Ave 21236 410-887-5234
Susan Biscoe, prin. Fax 887-5235
Glenmar ES 400/PK-5
9700 Community Rd 21220 410-887-0127
Susan Wilken, prin. Fax 391-6130
Golden Ring MS 800/6-8
6700 Kenwood Ave 21237 410-887-0130
Kevin Roberts, prin. Fax 682-6750
Grange ES 400/PK-5
2000 Church Rd 21222 410-887-7043
Rosalie Daddura, prin. Fax 288-0415
Gunpowder ES 500/PK-5
9540 Holiday Manor Rd 21236 410-887-5121
Christine Smith, prin. Fax 887-5122
Halstead Academy 500/PK-5
1111 Halstead Rd 21234 410-887-3210
Jill Carter, prin. Fax 887-3220
Harford Hills ES 400/PK-5
8902 Old Harford Rd 21234 410-887-5236
Carol Mohsberg, prin. Fax 887-5237
Hawthorne ES 400/PK-5
125 Kingston Rd 21220 410-887-0138
Gerry DePetris, prin. Fax 686-8368
Hebbville ES 500/PK-5
3335 Washington Ave 21244 410-887-0708
Annie Gordon, prin. Fax 887-0709
Hillcrest ES 600/PK-5
1500 Frederick Rd 21228 410-887-0820
Teresa McVey, prin. Fax 887-0821
Holabird MS 700/6-8
1701 Delvale Ave 21222 410-887-7049
Susan Melton, prin. Fax 887-7275
Johnnycake ES 600/PK-5
5910 Craigmont Rd 21228 410-887-0823
Mary Maddox, prin. Fax 887-1048
Lansdowne ES 400/PK-5
2301 Alma Rd 21227 410-887-1408
Jane Lichter, prin. Fax 887-1468
Lansdowne MS 700/6-8
2400 Lansdowne Rd 21227 410-887-1411
Nicole Norris, prin. Fax 887-1412
Loch Raven Technical Academy 700/6-8
8101 Lasalle Rd 21286 410-887-3518
Linda Wilson, prin. Fax 821-6398
Logan ES 500/PK-5
7601 Dunmanway 21222 410-887-7052
Tracy Robinson, prin. Fax 282-6357
Mars Estates ES 400/PK-5
1500 E Homberg Ave 21221 410-887-0154
Linda Chapin, prin. Fax 887-0156
Martin Boulevard ES 300/PK-5
210 Riverton Rd 21220 410-887-0158
Karen Donoho, prin. Fax 391-7266
McCormick ES 400/PK-5
5101 Hazelwood Ave 21206 410-887-0500
Kevin Lindsey, prin. Fax 887-0504
Middleborough ES 300/PK-5
313 West Rd 21221 410-887-0160
Laurie Kourtesis, prin. Fax 887-0161
Middle River MS 800/6-8
800 Middle River Rd 21220 410-887-0165
Walter Mills, prin. Fax 887-0167
Middlesex ES 500/PK-5
142 Bennett Rd 21221 410-887-0170
Dr. Susan Smith, prin. Fax 887-0469
Milbrook ES 300/PK-5
4300 Crest Heights Rd 21215 410-887-1225
Christina Byers, prin. Fax 887-6744
Norwood ES 600/PK-5
1700 Delvale Ave 21222 410-887-7055
Patrice Goldys, prin. Fax 887-7057
Oakleigh ES 500/PK-5
1900 White Oak Ave 21234 410-887-5238
Sylvia Lemons, prin. Fax 887-5239
Old Court MS 600/6-8
4627 Old Court Rd 21208 410-887-0742
I. Lynette Woodley, prin. Fax 887-0670

Oliver Beach ES 300/PK-5
12912 Cunninghill Cove Rd 21220 410-887-5943
Mary Ann Rigopoulos, prin. Fax 887-5944
Orems ES 300/PK-5
711 Highvilla Rd 21221 410-887-0172
Marcia Wolf, prin. Fax 887-0173
Parkville MS 1,100/6-8
8711 Avondale Rd 21234 410-887-5250
Murray Parker, prin. Fax 887-5315
Perry Hall ES 500/PK-5
9021 Belair Rd 21236 410-887-5105
Donna Bergin, prin. Fax 887-5106
Perry Hall MS 1,500/6-8
4300 Ebenezer Rd 21236 410-887-5100
Allen Zink, prin. Fax 887-5152
Pikesville MS 900/6-8
7701 7 Mile Ln 21208 410-887-1207
Maria Talarigo, prin. Fax 887-1259
Pine Grove ES 500/PK-5
2701 Summit Ave 21234 410-887-5267
Richard Weber, prin. Fax 887-5268
Pine Grove MS 1,100/6-8
9200 Old Harford Rd 21234 410-887-5270
Sandra Reid, prin. Fax 668-5237
Powhatan ES 300/PK-5
3300 Kelox Rd 21207 410-887-1330
Yasmin Stokes, prin. Fax 277-0402
Red House Run ES 500/PK-5
1717 Weyburn Rd 21237 410-887-0506
Drue Whitney, prin. Fax 887-0507
Relay ES 400/PK-5
5885 Selford Rd 21227 410-887-1426
Heidi Miller, prin. Fax 887-1434
Riverview ES 500/PK-5
3298 Kessler Rd 21227 410-887-1428
Cheryl Jones, prin. Fax 887-1465
Rodgers Forge ES 500/K-5
250 Dumbarton Rd 21212 410-887-3582
Susan Deise, prin. Fax 832-5431
Sandalwood ES 500/PK-5
900 S Marlyn Ave 21221 410-887-0174
Phillip Byers, prin. Fax 391-6349
Sandy Plains ES 500/PK-5
8330 Kavanagh Rd 21222 410-887-7070
Harry Walker, prin. Fax 887-7107
Scotts Branch ES 500/K-5
8220 Tawnmoore Rd 21244 410-887-0761
Joyce Schultz, prin. Fax 887-0675
Seneca ES 400/PK-5
545 Carrollwood Rd 21220 410-887-5945
Charlene Behnke, prin. Fax 887-5946
Seven Oaks ES 400/PK-5
9220 Seven Courts Dr 21236 410-887-6257
Carol Wingard, prin. Fax 256-0379
Shady Spring ES 600/PK-5
8868 Goldenwood Rd 21237 410-887-0509
Kenneth Dunaway, prin. Fax 886-7619
Southwest Academy 900/6-8
6200 Johnnycake Rd 21207 410-887-0825
Karen Barnes, prin. Fax 887-0829
Sparrows Point MS 500/6-8
7400 N Point Rd 21219 410-887-7524
E. Donald Weglein, prin. Fax 477-6953
Stemmers Run MS 800/6-8
201 Stemmers Run Rd 21221 410-887-0177
John Ward, prin. Fax 918-1787
Stoneleigh ES 500/PK-5
900 Pemberton Rd 21212 410-887-3600
Christine Warner, prin. Fax 887-3601
Stricker MS 800/6-8
7855 Trappe Rd 21222 410-887-7038
Deborah Klaus, prin. Fax 285-1864
Sudbrook Magnet MS 1,000/6-8
4300 Bedford Rd 21208 410-887-6720
Sharon Robbins, prin. Fax 887-6737
Summit Park ES 300/PK-5
6920 Diana Rd 21209 410-887-1210
Diane Richmond, prin. Fax 887-1256
Sussex ES 300/PK-5
515 S Woodward Dr 21221 410-887-0182
Thomas Bowser, prin. Fax 887-0183
Victory Villa ES 300/PK-5
500 Compass Rd E 21220 410-887-0184
Kathleen East, prin. Fax 391-8594
Villa Cresta ES 500/PK-5
2600 Rader Ave 21234 410-887-5275
Kathleen Bishop, prin. Fax 887-5277
Wellwood International S 500/K-5
2901 Smith Ave 21208 410-887-1212
William Burke, prin. Fax 887-1213
Westchester ES 500/K-5
2300 Old Frederick Rd 21228 410-887-1088
Marguerite DeCrispino, prin. Fax 887-1089
Westowne ES 500/PK-5
401 Harlem Ln 21228 410-887-0854
Patricia Vogel, prin. Fax 887-0856
Winand ES 500/PK-5
8301 Scotts Level Rd 21208 410-887-0763
Wanda Better-Davis, prin. Fax 887-0730
Windsor Mill MS 6-8
8300 Windsor Mill Rd 21244 410-887-0618
Deborah Phelps, prin. Fax 496-1308
Winfield ES 400/K-5
8300 Carlson Ln 21244 410-887-0766
Lisa Dingle, prin. Fax 496-3275
Woodbridge ES 400/PK-5
1410 Pleasant Valley Dr 21228 410-887-0857
Nellie Slater, prin. Fax 887-0912
Woodlawn MS 700/6-8
3033 Saint Lukes Ln 21207 410-887-1304
Damien Ingram, prin. Fax 298-4352
Woodmoor ES 600/PK-5
3200 Elba Dr 21207 410-887-1318
Edith Howard, prin. Fax 887-1320

Archbishop Borders S 200/PK-8
201 S Conkling St 21224 410-276-6534
Catherine Marshall, prin. Fax 276-6915
Arlington Baptist S 200/K-12
3030 N Rolling Rd 21244 410-655-9300
Dennis Layton, admin. Fax 496-3901

Baltimore Actors Theatre Conservatory 50/K-12
300 Dumbarton Rd Ste 2 21212 410-337-8519
Walter Anderson, hdmstr. Fax 337-8582
Baltimore Christian S 100/K-5
505 E 42nd St 21218 410-435-5072
Rachel Ballad Ph.D., prin. Fax 435-8656
Baltimore Junior Academy 100/PK-8
3006 W Cold Spring Ln 21215 410-542-6758
Dorine Robinson, prin. Fax 542-7412
Baltimore-White Marsh SDA S 50/K-8
7427 Rossville Blvd 21237 410-663-1819
Heather Hastick, prin. Fax 663-9009
Bethlehem Christian Day S 200/PK-8
4815 Hamilton Ave 21206 410-488-8963
Fax 488-2689
Beth Tfiloh Dahan Community S 900/PK-12
3300 Old Court Rd 21208 410-486-1905
Zipora Schorr, dir. Fax 415-6348
Bnos Yisroel S of Baltimore 300/PK-8
5713 Park Heights Ave 21215 443-524-3200
Boys Latin S of Maryland 700/K-12
822 W Lake Ave 21210 410-377-5192
Christopher Post, hdmstr. Fax 377-4312
Bryn Mawr S 900/PK-12
109 W Melrose Ave 21210 410-323-8800
Maureen Walsh, hdmstr. Fax 377-8963
Calvary Lutheran S 100/PK-5
2625 E Northern Pkwy 21214 410-426-4302
Linda Gast, prin. Fax 426-7590
Calvert S 500/PK-8
105 Tuscany Rd 21210 410-243-6054
Andrew Martire, hdmstr. Fax 243-0384
Cardinal Shehan S 400/PK-8
5407 Loch Raven Blvd 21239 410-433-2775
Paula Redman, prin. Fax 323-6131
Catholic Community S 200/PK-8
300 E Gittings St 21230 410-685-6155
Sr. Vicki Staub, prin. Fax 685-0692
Church of the Redeemer Parrish Day S 100/PK-K
5603 N Charles St 21210 410-435-9510
Fax 435-9195
Day S at Baltimore Hebrew 200/PK-8
7401 Park Heights Ave 21208 410-764-1867
Gerri Chizeck, hdmstr. Fax 764-8138
Emmanuel Lutheran S 100/K-8
929 Ingleside Ave 21228 410-744-0015
Delbert Riemer, prin. Fax 744-1199
Father Charles Hall MS - St. Edwards 100/6-8
2848 W Lafayette Ave 21216 410-566-1231
Kathleen Filippelli, prin. Fax 566-0097
Father Charles Hall S - St. Peter Claver 100/PK-5
1526 N Fremont Ave 21217 410-225-7555
Kathleen Filippelli, prin. Fax 225-7721
First English Lutheran Preschool & K 100/PK-K
3807 N Charles St 21218 410-235-5887
Forbush S 300/PK-12
PO Box 6815 21285 410-938-4400
James Truscello, dir. Fax 938-4421
Friends S of Baltimore 1,000/PK-12
5114 N Charles St 21210 410-649-3200
Matthew Micciche, hdmstr. Fax 649-3213
Gilman S 1,000/K-12
5407 Roland Ave 21210 410-323-3800
John Schmick, hdmstr. Fax 864-2812
Greater Youth Christian Academy 50/PK-7
200 N Bentalou St 21223 410-945-7300
Dr. Denise Folks, prin. Fax 945-3275
Heritage Montessori S 100/PK-6
9515 Belair Rd 21236 410-529-0374
Melodie Sachs, hdmstr. Fax 529-8534
John Paul Regional S 200/PK-8
6946 Dogwood Rd 21244 410-944-0367
Theresa Brooks, prin. Fax 265-5316
Krieger Schechter Day S 500/K-8
8100 Stevenson Rd 21208 410-486-8640
Dr. Paul Schneider, hdmstr. Fax 486-6106
Mayfield Christian Preschool PK-PK
3300 Norman Ave 21213 410-243-6254
Kevin Frye, prin. Fax 243-6222
Mother Mary Lange Catholic S 300/PK-8
4410 Frankford Ave 21206 410-488-4848
Sr. Rita Proctor, prin. Fax 325-4003
Mother Seton Academy 100/6-8
724 S Ann St 21231 410-563-2833
Sr. Eileen Clinton, prin. Fax 563-7353
Mt. Pleasant Christian S 100/PK-8
6000 Radecke Ave 21206 410-325-4827
Dr. Brenda Haynes, dir. Fax 325-2655
Mt. Zion Baptist Christian S 200/PK-12
2000 E Belvedere Ave 21239 410-426-2309
Our Lady of Fatima S 200/PK-8
6410 E Pratt St 21224 410-633-5268
Paul Llufrio, prin. Fax 633-5882
Our Lady of Hope / St. Luke S 300/PK-8
8003 N Boundary Rd 21222 410-288-2793
Sr. Irene Pryle, prin. Fax 288-2850
Our Lady of Mt. Carmel S 600/PK-8
1702 Old Eastern Ave 21221 410-686-0859
Lisa Shipley, prin. Fax 686-4916
Our Lady of Victory S 500/PK-8
4416 Wilkens Ave 21229 410-242-3688
Thomas Riddle, prin. Fax 242-8867
Park S 900/PK-12
2425 Old Court Rd 21208 410-339-7070
Daniel Paradis, hdmstr. Fax 339-4125
Pilgrim Lutheran S 50/PK-5
7200 Liberty Rd 21207 410-484-9240
Sadie Henriques, prin. Fax 484-6692
Purpose & Potential Christian Arts Acad 100/PK-12
5532 Harford Rd 21214 410-444-2899
Patricia Matthews, prin. Fax 444-1434
Queen of Peace/St. Katharine S 300/PK-8
1201 N Rose St 21213 410-327-4738
Angela Calamari, prin. Fax 327-1835
Rabbi Benjamin Steinberg MS 300/6-8
6300 Smith Ave 21209 443-548-7700
Rock City Church Academy 50/K-5
1607 Cromwell Bridge Rd 21234 410-882-2217
Rosemary Gruver, admin. Fax 882-7163

Roland Park Country S 700/K-12
5204 Roland Ave 21210 410-323-5500
Jean Waller-Brune, hdmstr. Fax 323-2164
Sacred Heart of Mary S 200/PK-8
6726 Youngstown Ave 21222 410-633-7040
Pamela Waters, prin. Fax 633-7644
St. Agnes S 400/PK-8
603 Saint Agnes Ln 21229 410-747-4070
Susan Banks, prin. Fax 747-0138
St. Ambrose S 200/K-8
4506 Park Heights Ave 21215 410-664-2373
Pamela Sanders, prin. Fax 664-0857
St. Bernardine S 200/K-8
3601 Old Frederick Rd 21229 410-624-5088
Dr. Antoinette Lyles, prin. Fax 947-5439
St. Casimir S 200/PK-8
1035 S Kenwood Ave 21224 410-342-2681
Melanie Conley, prin. Fax 342-5715
St. Clare S 300/PK-8
716 Myrth Ave 21221 410-687-7787
Dorothy Williams, prin. Fax 687-2715
St. Clement Mary Hofbauer S 300/PK-8
1216 Chesaco Ave 21237 410-686-3316
Gary Rand, prin. Fax 686-6198
St. Francis of Assisi S 300/PK-8
3617 Harford Rd 21218 410-467-1683
J. Kevin Frye, prin. Fax 467-9449
St. Ignatius Loyola Academy 100/6-8
740 N Calvert St 21202 410-539-8268
Jeffrey Sindler, prin. Fax 539-4821
St. Joseph S 500/PK-8
8416 Belair Rd 21236 410-256-8026
Phyllis Karko, prin. Fax 529-7234
St. Mary of the Assumption S 200/PK-8
5502 York Rd 21212 410-435-5850
Elizabeth Phelan, prin. Fax 435-1256
St. Michael the Archangel S 400/PK-8
10 Willow Ave 21206 410-668-8797
Patricia Kelly, prin. Fax 663-9277
St. Paul Lutheran S 100/PK-5
2001 Old Frederick Rd 21228 410-747-1924
Norman Giguere, prin. Fax 747-7248
St. Peter's Christian Day S 100/PK-5
7910 Belair Rd 21236 410-665-4521
Carole Hengen, prin. Fax 665-4521
St. Pius X S 400/PK-8
6432 York Rd 21212 410-427-7400
Geraldine Morrison, prin. Fax 372-0552
St. Rose of Lima S 200/PK-8
410 E Jeffrey St 21225 410-355-1050
Madeline Hobik, prin. Fax 355-2408
St. Thomas Aquinas S 200/PK-8
3710 Roland Ave 21211 410-889-4618
Sr. Marie Gustatus, prin. Fax 889-1956
St. Ursula S 700/K-8
8900 Harford Rd 21234 410-665-3533
Sr. Joan Kelly, prin. Fax 661-1620
St. William of York S 200/PK-8
600 Cooks Ln 21229 410-945-1442
Noreen Hefner, prin. Fax 945-4036
School of Cathedral of Mary our Queen 400/K-8
111 Amberly Way 21210 410-464-4100
Sr. Josephann Wagoner, prin. Fax 464-4137
Shrine of the Sacred Heart S 200/PK-8
5800 Smith Ave 21209 410-542-7406
Martha Pierorazio, prin. Fax 664-1463
Sisters Academy of Baltimore 50/5-7
139 1st Ave 21227 410-242-1212
Sr. Debra Liesen, prin. Fax 242-5104
SS. James & John / Queen of Peace S 300/PK-5
1012 Somerset St 21202 410-342-3222
LaUanah Cassell, prin. Fax 732-1323
Talmudical Academy 700/K-12
4445 Old Court Rd 21208 410-484-6600
Fax 484-5717
Unselds S 100/PK-8
250 S Hilton St 21229 410-947-1110
Waldorf S of Baltimore 200/PK-10
4801 Tamarind Rd 21209 410-367-6808
Pat Whitehead, admin. Fax 664-4221
Yeshivat Rambam/Maimonides Academy 400/PK-12
6300 Park Heights Ave 21215 410-358-6091
Dr. Rita Shloush, hdmstr. Fax 358-4229

Bel Air, Harford, Pop. 10,014
Harford County SD 38,300/PK-12
102 S Hickory Ave 21014 410-838-7300
Robert Tomback, supt. Fax 893-2478
www.hcps.org/
Bel Air ES 500/PK-5
30 E Lee St 21014 410-638-4160
Robin Payne, prin. Fax 638-4320
Bel Air MS 1,400/6-8
99 Idlewild St 21014 410-638-4140
Sean Abel, prin. Fax 638-4144
Emmorton ES 500/K-5
2502 S Tollgate Rd 21015 410-638-3920
Margaret Kirk, prin. Fax 638-3926
Fountain Green ES 600/K-5
517 S Fountain Green Rd 21015 410-638-4220
Stacey Gerringer, prin. Fax 638-4347
Hickory ES 700/K-5
2100 Conowingo Rd 21014 410-638-4170
Jeanette Jennings, prin. Fax 638-4172
Homestead/Wakefield ES 800/PK-5
900 S Main St Bldg B 21014 410-638-4175
Dale Hunsinger, prin. Fax 638-4319
Prospect Mill ES 800/K-5
101 Prospect Mill Rd 21015 410-638-3817
G.C. Beehler, prin. Fax 638-3816
Ring Factory ES 500/K-5
1400 Emmorton Rd 21014 410-638-4186
H. Earl Gaskins, prin. Fax 638-4318
Southampton MS 1,500/6-8
1200 Moores Mill Rd 21014 410-638-4150
Barb Canavan, prin. Fax 638-4305
Other Schools – See Aberdeen, Abingdon, Belcamp, Churchville, Darlington, Edgewood, Fallston, Forest Hill, Havre de Grace, Jarrettsville, Joppa, Pylesville, Street, White Hall

---

Awakening Child Montessori S 100/PK-1
604 Yarmouth Ln 21014 410-836-0833
Gaye Novak, prin.
Bel Forest Christian Academy 100/PK-8
603 Vale Rd 21014 410-838-6074
James Harned, admin. Fax 836-8694
Harford Day S 300/PK-8
715 Moores Mill Rd 21014 410-838-4848
Susan Harris, hdmstr. Fax 836-5918
St. Margaret MS 300/6-8
1716A E Churchville Rd 21015 410-877-9660
Jane Dean, prin. Fax 420-9322
St. Margaret S 600/PK-5
205 N Hickory Ave 21014 410-879-1113
Jane Dean, prin. Fax 838-5879

Belcamp, Harford, Pop. 900
Harford County SD
Supt. — See Bel Air
Church Creek ES 600/PK-5
4299 Church Creek Rd 21017 410-273-5550
Kim Spence, prin. Fax 273-5558

Beltsville, Prince George's, Pop. 14,476
Prince George's County SD
Supt. — See Upper Marlboro
Beltsville ES 600/K-6
4300 Wicomico Ave 20705 301-572-0630
Steve Beegle, prin. Fax 572-0671
Calverton ES 600/K-6
3400 Beltsville Rd 20705 301-572-0640
Mary Tschudy, prin. Fax 572-0673
Fuchs ECC 400/PK-PK
11011 Cherry Hill Rd 20705 301-572-0600
Diedra Tramel, prin. Fax 572-0602
King MS 700/7-8
4545 Ammendale Rd 20705 301-572-0650
Robin Wiltison, prin. Fax 572-0668
Vansville ES PK-6
6813 Ammendale Way 20705 301-931-2830
Tom Smith, prin. Fax 931-2840

Beltsville Adventist S 200/K-8
4230 Ammendale Rd 20705 301-937-2933
Wendy Pega, prin. Fax 595-2431
Hope Christian Academy 50/PK-4
11416 Cedar Ln 20705 301-595-4955
Robyn Watts, dir.
St. Joseph S 200/PK-8
11011 Montgomery Rd 20705 301-937-7154
Andrew Currier, prin. Fax 937-1467

Berlin, Worcester, Pop. 3,711
Worcester County SD
Supt. — See Newark
Berlin IS 700/4-6
309 Franklin Ave 21811 410-632-5320
John Gaddis, prin. Fax 632-5329
Buckingham ES 500/PK-4
100 Buckingham Rd 21811 410-632-5300
Roger Pacella, prin. Fax 632-5309
Decatur MS 600/7-8
9815 Seahawk Rd 21811 410-641-2846
Mel Ross, prin. Fax 641-3274
Showell ES 400/PK-3
11318 Showell School Rd 21811 410-632-5350
Paula Jones, prin. Fax 632-5359

Most Blessed Sacrament Catholic S 200/K-8
11242 Race Track Rd 21811 410-208-1600
Amelia Mike, prin. Fax 208-4957
Worcester Preparatory S 600/PK-12
508 S Main St 21811 410-641-3575
Dr. Barry Tull, hdmstr. Fax 641-3586

Berwyn Heights, Prince George's, Pop. 3,068
Prince George's County SD
Supt. — See Upper Marlboro
Berwyn Heights ES 400/K-6
6200 Pontiac St 20740 240-684-6210
Dr. Karen Singer, prin. Fax 684-6216

Bethesda, Montgomery, Pop. 55,277
Montgomery County SD
Supt. — See Rockville
Ashburton ES 600/PK-5
6314 Lone Oak Dr 20817 301-571-6959
Charlene Eroh, prin. Fax 897-2517
Bannockburn ES 400/K-5
6520 Dalroy Ln 20817 301-320-6555
Kim Bosnic, prin. Fax 320-6559
Bells Mill ES 500/PK-5
5701 Grosvenor Ln 20814 301-571-6920
Jerri Oglesby, prin. Fax 571-6924
Bethesda ES 400/K-5
7600 Arlington Rd 20814 301-657-4979
Lisa Seymour, prin. Fax 657-4973
Bradley Hills ES 400/K-5
8701 Hartsdale Ave 20817 301-571-6966
Sandra Reece, prin. Fax 571-6969
Burning Tree ES 500/K-5
7900 Beech Tree Rd 20817 301-320-6510
Nancy Erdrich, prin. Fax 320-6538
Carderock Springs ES 300/PK-5
7000 Radnor Rd 20817 301-469-1034
Susan Thompson, prin. Fax 469-1115
North Bethesda MS 700/6-8
8935 Bradmoor Dr 20817 301-571-3883
Alton Sumner, prin. Fax 571-3881
Pyle MS 1,300/6-8
6311 Wilson Ln 20817 301-320-6540
Michael Zarchin, prin. Fax 320-6647
Seven Locks ES 300/K-5
9500 Seven Locks Rd 20817 301-469-1038
Rebecca Gordon, prin. Fax 469-1041
Westbrook ES 300/K-5
5110 Allan Ter 20816 301-320-6506
John Ewald, prin. Fax 320-6615
Westland MS 1,000/6-8
5511 Massachusetts Ave 20816 301-320-6515
Daniel Vogelman, prin. Fax 320-7054
Wood Acres ES 600/K-5
5800 Cromwell Dr 20816 301-320-6502
Marita Sherburne, prin. Fax 320-6536
Wyngate ES 500/K-5
9300 Wadsworth Dr 20817 301-571-6979
Barbara Leister, prin. Fax 571-3870

Harbor S 100/PK-2
7701 Bradley Blvd 20817 301-365-1100
Valaida Wise, hdmstr. Fax 365-7491
Holton-Arms S 700/3-12
7303 River Rd 20817 301-365-5300
Susanna Jones, hdmstr. Fax 365-6085
Landon S 700/3-12
6101 Wilson Ln 20817 301-320-3200
David Armstrong, prin. Fax 320-2787
Little Flower S 300/PK-8
5601 Massachusetts Ave 20816 301-320-3273
Sr. Rosemaron Rynn, prin. Fax 320-2867
Lycee Rochambeau 1,100/PK-12
9600 Forest Rd 20814 301-530-8260
Gilles Jospeh, prin. Fax 564-5779
Mater Dei S 200/1-8
9600 Seven Locks Rd 20817 301-365-2700
Edward Williams, prin. Fax 365-2710
Norwood S 500/K-8
8821 River Rd 20817 301-365-2595
Richard Ewing, hdmstr. Fax 365-7644
Our Lady of Lourdes S 200/PK-8
7500 Pearl St 20814 301-654-5376
Patricia McGann, prin. Fax 654-2568
Primary Day S 100/PK-2
7300 River Rd 20817 301-365-4355
Louise Plumb, dir. Fax 469-8611
St. Bartholomew S 200/K-8
6900 River Rd 20817 301-229-5586
Kathleen Miller, prin. Fax 229-8654
St. Jane De Chantel S 500/K-8
9525 Old Georgetown Rd 20814 301-530-1221
Elizabeth Hamilton, prin. Fax 530-1688
Stone Ridge S of the Sacred Heart 700/PK-12
9101 Rockville Pike 20814 301-657-4322
Catherine Karrels, hdmstr. Fax 657-4393
Washington Episcopal S 300/PK-8
5600 Little Falls Pkwy 20816 301-652-7878
Stuart Work, hdmstr. Fax 652-7255
Washington Waldorf S 300/PK-12
4800 Sangamore Rd 20816 301-229-6107
Natalie Adams, hdmstr. Fax 229-9379
Woods Academy 300/PK-8
6801 Greentree Rd 20817 301-365-3080
Mary Worch, hdmstr. Fax 469-6439

Bladensburg, Prince George's, Pop. 7,918
Prince George's County SD
Supt. — See Upper Marlboro
Bladensburg ES 500/K-6
4915 Annapolis Rd 20710 301-985-1450
Rhonda Pitts, prin. Fax 985-1457
Port Towns ES 600/PK-6
4351 58th Ave 20710 301-985-1480
Lisa Farabaugh, prin. Fax 985-1470
Rogers Heights ES 600/K-6
4301 58th Ave 20710 301-985-1860
Barbara Bottoms, prin. Fax 985-1868

Bloomington, Garrett
Garrett County SD
Supt. — See Oakland
Bloomington S 100/K-8
PO Box 158 21523 301-359-0331
Connie Uphold, prin. Fax 359-0331

Boonsboro, Washington, Pop. 2,982
Washington County SD
Supt. — See Hagerstown
Boonsboro ES 600/K-5
5 Campus Ave 21713 301-766-8013
J. Scott Woods, prin. Fax 432-4359
Boonsboro MS 800/6-8
1 J H Wade Dr 21713 301-766-8038
Paul Engle, prin. Fax 432-2644
Greenbrier ES 300/K-5
21222 San Mar Rd 21713 301-766-8170
Elaine Semler, prin. Fax 745-3321

Bowie, Prince George's, Pop. 53,878
Prince George's County SD
Supt. — See Upper Marlboro
Chapel Forge ECC 400/PK-PK
12711 Milan Way 20715 301-805-2740
Elyse Hurley, prin. Fax 805-6672
Heather Hills ES 400/K-6
12605 Heming Ln 20716 301-805-2730
Patsy Hosch, prin. Fax 805-2733
High Bridge ES 300/K-6
7011 High Bridge Rd 20720 301-805-2690
Charles Eller, prin. Fax 805-2693
Kenilworth ES 500/K-6
12520 Kembridge Dr 20715 301-805-6600
Chris Mills, prin. Fax 805-6605
Northview ES K-6
3700 Northview Dr 20716 301-218-1520
Judith Bissett, prin. Fax 218-3071
Ogle MS 800/6-8
4111 Chelmont Ln 20715 301-805-2641
Kathleen Brady, prin. Fax 805-6674
Pointer Ridge ES 600/K-6
1110 Parkington Ln 20716 301-390-0220
Mary Stephenson, prin. Fax 390-0281
Rockledge ES 500/K-6
7701 Laurel Bowie Rd 20715 301-805-2720
Pamela Landry, prin. Fax 805-2718
Tasker MS 800/7-8
4901 Collington Rd 20715 301-805-2660
Karen Coley, prin. Fax 805-2663
Tulip Grove ES 400/K-6
2909 Trainor Ln 20715 301-805-2680
Brian Boudoin, prin. Fax 805-6689
Whitehall ES 400/PK-6
3901 Woodhaven Ln 20715 301-805-1000
Jerenze Campbell, prin. Fax 805-1006

Yorktown ES 500/K-6
7301 Race Track Rd 20715 301-805-6610
Cheryl Archer-Hughes, prin. Fax 805-6626

Belair Baptist Christian Academy 100/K-12
PO Box 796 20718 301-262-0578
Dr. Gary Kohl, admin. Fax 262-0578
Bowie Montessori Children's House 300/PK-8
5004 Randonstone Ln 20715 301-262-3566
Anne Riley, admin. Fax 262-3566
Cornerstone Christian Academy 300/PK-8
16010 Annapolis Rd 20715 301-262-7683
Stephen Rhoades, admin. Fax 262-5200
Grace Christian S 400/K-8
7210 Race Track Rd 20715 301-262-0158
Evelyn Nunes, dir. Fax 262-4156
Greater Mt. Nebo Christian Academy 50/PK-4
1001 Old Mitchellville Rd 20716 301-249-5142
Sonya Hamilton, prin. Fax 249-5143
Patuxent Montessori S 100/PK-6
14210 Old Stage Rd 20720 301-464-4506
Suzanne Damadio, admin. Fax 464-8792
St. Pius X K at Sacred Heart K-K
16501 Annapolis Rd 20715 301-262-0203
Jean Allman, dir.
St. Pius X Regional S 800/K-8
14710 Annapolis Rd 20715 301-262-0203
Robert Love, prin. Fax 805-8875
Victory Christian Academy 50/PK-3
13701 Annapolis Rd 20720 301-352-3407
Margaret Adeyokunnu, admin. Fax 352-7226

Bradshaw, Baltimore

St. Stephen S 300/PK-8
8028 Bradshaw Rd 21087 410-592-7617
Mary Patrick, prin. Fax 592-7330

Brandywine, Prince George's, Pop. 1,406
Prince George's County SD
Supt. — See Upper Marlboro
Baden ES 300/PK-6
13601 Baden Westwood Rd 20613 301-888-1188
Dr. Charlene Johnson, prin. Fax 888-2205
Brandywine ES 400/K-6
14101 Brandywine Rd 20613 301-372-0100
Thomas Couteau, prin. Fax 372-0729
Gwynn Park MS 600/7-8
8000 Dyson Rd 20613 301-372-0120
Frederick Rivers, prin. Fax 372-0119

Brookeville, Montgomery, Pop. 127
Montgomery County SD
Supt. — See Rockville
Greenwood ES 600/K-5
3336 Gold Mine Rd 20833 301-924-3145
Cheryl Bunyan, prin. Fax 924-3296

Brooklandville, Baltimore

St. Paul's S for Boys 900/PK-12
PO Box 8100 21022 410-825-4400
Thomas Reid, hdmstr. Fax 427-0390
St. Paul's S for Girls 500/K-12
PO Box 8100 21022 410-823-6323
Monica M. Gillespie Ph.D., hdmstr. Fax 828-7238

Brunswick, Frederick, Pop. 5,242
Frederick County SD
Supt. — See Frederick
Brunswick ES 500/PK-5
400 Central Ave 21716 240-236-2900
Drenna Reineck, prin. Fax 236-2901
Brunswick MS 600/6-8
301 Cummings Dr 21716 240-236-5400
Brian Vasquenza, prin. Fax 236-5401

Bryantown, Charles
Charles County SD
Supt. — See La Plata
Martin ES 600/PK-5
6315 Olivers Shop Rd 20617 301-274-3182
Sabrina Robinson-Taylor, prin. Fax 274-3765

St. Mary S 200/PK-8
13735 Notre Dame Pl 20617 301-932-6883
Sharon Caniglia, prin. Fax 274-0626

Burtonsville, Montgomery, Pop. 5,853
Montgomery County SD
Supt. — See Rockville
Banneker MS 800/6-8
14800 Perrywood Dr 20866 301-989-5747
Samuel A. Rivera, prin. Fax 879-1032
Burtonsville ES 600/K-5
15516 Old Columbia Pike 20866 301-989-5654
Melissa Smith, prin. Fax 989-5707

Resurrection Church Preschool 100/PK-PK
3315 Greencastle Rd 20866 301-236-9529
Patricia Sullivan, prin.

California, Saint Mary's, Pop. 7,626

Starmaker Learning Center 50/PK-3
23443 Cottonwood Pkwy 20619 301-863-7740
Lynn Ennis, admin. Fax 863-6659

Callaway, Saint Mary's

King's Christian Academy 300/K-12
20738 Point Lookout Rd 20620 301-994-3080
Sarah Patterson, admin. Fax 994-3087

Cambridge, Dorchester, Pop. 11,089
Dorchester County SD 4,700/PK-12
PO Box 619 21613 410-228-4747
Fred Hildenbrand, supt. Fax 228-1847
www.dcps.k12.md.us
Choptank ES 300/PK-5
1103 Maces Ln 21613 410-228-4950
Jennifer Ruark, prin. Fax 221-1497
Maces Lane MS 500/6-8
1101 Maces Ln 21613 410-228-2111
Tom Gebert, prin. Fax 221-5278
Maple ES 300/PK-5
5225 Egypt Rd 21613 410-228-8577
Susan Piavis, prin. Fax 221-6584
Sandy Hill ES 400/PK-5
1503 Glasgow St 21613 410-228-7979
Michelle Ruark, prin. Fax 228-8738
Other Schools – See Church Creek, Hurlock, Secretary, Vienna

Cambridge Christian Academy 50/K-8
612 Locust St 21613 410-228-1188
Patricia Larsen, prin. Fax 228-1183
Countryside Christian S 100/PK-12
5333 Austin Rd 21613 410-228-0574
Phillip Sutton, prin. Fax 221-8659

Camp Springs, Prince George's, Pop. 16,392

Progressive Christian Academy 300/PK-12
5408 Brinkley Rd 20748 301-449-3160
Rev. Don Massey, admin. Fax 449-0382
St. Philip the Apostle S 300/PK-8
5414 Henderson Way 20746 301-423-4740
Linda Cullinan, prin. Fax 423-4716

Capitol Heights, Prince George's, Pop. 4,313
Prince George's County SD
Supt. — See Upper Marlboro
Bayne ES 500/K-6
7010 Walker Mill Rd 20743 301-499-7020
Joyce Phillips, prin. Fax 808-4499
Bradbury Heights ES 400/PK-6
1401 Glacier Ave 20743 301-817-0570
Denise Lynch, prin. Fax 817-0577
Brooks ES 400/PK-6
1301 Brooke Rd 20743 301-817-0480
Anita Stoddard, prin. Fax 817-0954
Capitol Heights ES 200/K-6
601 Suffolk Ave 20743 301-817-0494
Brenda White, prin. Fax 817-0931
Carmody Hills ES 400/K-6
401 Jadeleaf Ave 20743 301-808-8180
Rolaetta Alford, prin. Fax 808-8188
Gray ES 500/K-6
4949 Addison Rd 20743 301-636-8400
Cheryl Franklin, prin. Fax 636-8409
Hall ES 700/PK-6
5200 Marlboro Pike 20743 301-817-2933
Glenda Washington, prin. Fax 817-2946
Howard ES 300/PK-6
4400 Shell St 20743 301-817-0460
Herman Whaley, prin. Fax 817-0935
Seat Pleasant ES 200/K-6
6411 G St 20743 301-925-2330
Kassandra Lassiter, prin. Fax 925-2337
Walker Mill MS 600/7-8
800 Karen Blvd 20743 301-808-4055
Gorman Brown, prin. Fax 808-4039

Free Gospel Christian Academy 50/K-8
4703 Marlboro Pike 20743 301-420-2461
Dr. Lorraine Driggers, admin. Fax 516-9717
SACRED Life Academy for Boys 50/K-8
7230 Central Ave 20743 301-350-7360
Vermelle Greene, prin. Fax 350-0632

Cascade, Washington
Washington County SD
Supt. — See Hagerstown
Cascade ES 200/PK-5
14519 Pennersville Rd 21719 301-766-8066
Rose Pellegrino, prin. Fax 241-4037

Catonsville, Baltimore, Pop. 39,820
Baltimore County SD
Supt. — See Towson
Catonsville ES 400/PK-5
615 Frederick Rd 21228 410-887-0800
Linda Miller, prin. Fax 887-1050
Catonsville MS 700/6-8
2301 Edmondson Ave 21228 410-887-0803
Michael Thorne, prin. Fax 887-1036

St. Mark S 600/PK-8
26 Melvin Ave 21228 410-744-6560
Mary Jo Warthen, prin. Fax 747-3188

Cecilton, Cecil, Pop. 485
Cecil County SD
Supt. — See Elkton
Cecilton ES 300/PK-5
251 W Main St 21913 410-275-1000
Gail Mink, prin. Fax 275-1271

Centreville, Queen Anne's, Pop. 2,660
Queen Anne's County SD 7,400/PK-12
202 Chesterfield Ave 21617 410-758-2403
Dr. Carol Williamson, supt. Fax 758-8207
www.qacps.k12.md.us
Centreville ES 400/PK-2
213 Homewood Ave 21617 410-758-1320
Jean Cupani, prin. Fax 758-4443
Centreville MS 600/6-8
231 Ruthsburg Rd 21617 410-758-0883
Bonnie Dixon, prin. Fax 758-4447
Kennard ES 400/3-5
420 Little Kidwell Ave 21617 410-758-1166
Michele Hampton, prin. Fax 758-3317
Other Schools – See Church Hill, Grasonville, Stevensville, Sudlersville

Chaptico, Saint Mary's
St. Mary's County SD
Supt. — See Leonardtown
Dynard ES 500/PK-5
23510 Bushwood Rd 20621 301-769-4804
Kim Summers, prin. Fax 769-4808

Charlestown, Cecil, Pop. 1,091
Cecil County SD
Supt. — See Elkton
Charlestown ES 200/PK-5
550 Baltimore St 21914 410-996-6240
Linda Haske, prin. Fax 996-6242

Chesapeake Beach, Calvert, Pop. 3,463
Calvert County SD
Supt. — See Prince Frederick
Beach ES 500/PK-5
7900 Old Bayside Rd 20732 410-257-1513
Michael Shisler, prin. Fax 257-0502

Chesapeake City, Cecil, Pop. 802
Cecil County SD
Supt. — See Elkton
Bohemia Manor MS 500/6-8
2757 Augustine Herman Hwy 21915 410-885-2095
Berkeley Orr, prin. Fax 885-2485
Chesapeake City ES 300/K-5
214 3rd St 21915 410-885-2085
Elsie Harrigan, prin. Fax 885-2644

Chester, Queen Anne's

Kent Island Christian S 50/K-7
PO Box 260 21619 410-643-9203
Bernadette Wright, prin. Fax 643-9208

Chestertown, Kent, Pop. 4,673
Kent County SD 2,400/PK-12
215 Washington Ave 21620 410-778-1595
A. Barbara Wheeler, supt. Fax 778-6193
www.kent.k12.md.us
Chestertown MS 300/5-8
402 E Campus Ave 21620 410-778-1771
Ed Silver, prin. Fax 778-6541
Garnett ES 200/PK-4
320 Calvert St 21620 410-778-6890
Cheryl Vauls, prin. Fax 778-5707
Other Schools – See Galena, Millington, Rock Hall, Worton

Kent S 200/PK-8
6788 Wilkins Ln 21620 410-778-4100
Michael Schuler, hdmstr. Fax 778-7357

Cheverly, Prince George's, Pop. 6,668
Prince George's County SD
Supt. — See Upper Marlboro
Hoyer Montessori S 100/PK-PK
2300 Belleview Ave 20785 301-925-1986
Dr. Lynnette Whitt, prin. Fax 925-1994
Spellman ES 400/K-6
3324 64th Ave 20785 301-925-1944
Susan Holiday, prin. Fax 925-1951

St. Ambrose S 300/PK-8
6310 Jason St 20785 301-773-0223
Dian Carter, prin. Fax 773-9647

Chevy Chase, Montgomery, Pop. 2,776
Montgomery County SD
Supt. — See Rockville
Chevy Chase ES 500/3-6
4015 Rosemary St 20815 301-657-4994
Jody Smith, prin. Fax 657-4980
North Chevy Chase ES 300/3-6
3700 Jones Bridge Rd 20815 301-657-4950
Gary Bartee, prin. Fax 951-6658
Rock Creek Forest ES 500/PK-5
8330 Grubb Rd 20815 301-650-6410
David Chia, prin. Fax 650-6477
Somerset ES 400/K-5
5811 Warwick Pl 20815 301-657-4985
Laurie Gross, prin. Fax 951-6656

Childs, Cecil

Mt. Aviat Academy 300/PK-8
399 Childs Rd 21916 410-398-2206
Sr. John Elizabeth Callaghan, prin. Fax 398-8063

Church Creek, Dorchester, Pop. 84
Dorchester County SD
Supt. — See Cambridge
South Dorchester S 200/PK-8
3485 Golden Hill Rd 21622 410-397-3434
Dwayne Abt, prin. Fax 397-3595

Church Hill, Queen Anne's, Pop. 542
Queen Anne's County SD
Supt. — See Centreville
Church Hill ES 300/PK-5
631 Main St 21623 410-556-6681
Janet Pauls, prin. Fax 556-6508

Churchville, Harford
Harford County SD
Supt. — See Bel Air
Churchville ES 400/K-5
2935 Level Rd 21028 410-638-3800
Thomas Smith, prin. Fax 638-3834

Clarksburg, Montgomery
Montgomery County SD
Supt. — See Rockville
Clarksburg ES 400/PK-5
13530 Redgrave Pl 20871 301-353-8060
Kwang-Ja Lee, prin. Fax 353-0878
Little Bennett ES PK-5
23930 Burdette Forest Rd 20871 301-540-5535
Shawn Miller, prin. Fax 540-5792
Rocky Hill MS 1,000/6-8
22401 Brick Haven Way 20871 301-353-8282
Steven Whiting, prin. Fax 601-3197

Clarksville, Howard
Howard County SD
Supt. — See Ellicott City
Clarksville ES 600/K-5
12041 Clarksville Pike 21029 410-313-7050
Brad Herling, prin. Fax 313-7054
Clarksville MS 700/6-8
6535 Trotter Rd 21029 410-313-7057
JoAnn Hutchens, prin. Fax 313-7061
Pointers Run ES 700/PK-5
6600 Trotter Rd 21029 410-313-7142
Darlene Fila, prin. Fax 313-7147

St. Louis S 500/K-8
12500 State Route 108 21029 410-531-6664
Theresa Weiss, prin. Fax 531-6690

Clear Spring, Washington, Pop. 467
Washington County SD
Supt. — See Hagerstown
Clear Spring ES 400/PK-5
12627 Broadfording Rd 21722 301-766-8074
Sharon Palm, prin. Fax 842-1390
Clear Spring MS 400/6-8
12628 Broadfording Rd 21722 301-766-8094
Deron Crawford, prin. Fax 842-3826

Clinton, Prince George's, Pop. 19,987
Prince George's County SD
Supt. — See Upper Marlboro
Clinton Grove ES 500/K-6
9420 Temple Hill Rd 20735 301-599-2414
Alisha Plater, prin. Fax 599-2412
Decatur MS 800/7-8
8200 Pinewood Dr 20735 301-449-4950
Barry Cyrus, prin. Fax 449-2105
Evans ES 500/K-6
6720 Old Alexandria Ferry 20735 301-599-2480
Dr. Debra Stone, prin. Fax 599-2561
Randall ES 700/PK-6
5410 Kirby Rd 20735 301-449-4980
Dr. Marilyn Goldsmith, prin. Fax 449-2124
Waldon Woods ES 600/K-6
10301 Thrift Rd 20735 301-599-2540
LaChon Winston, prin. Fax 599-2544

Grace Brethren Christian S 800/PK-12
6501 Surratts Rd 20735 301-868-1600
George Hornickel, dir. Fax 868-9475
St. John the Evangelist S 200/PK-8
8912 Old Branch Ave 20735 301-868-2010
Susan Scott, prin. Fax 856-8941
St. Mary S of Piscataway 200/K-8
13407 Piscataway Rd 20735 301-292-2522
Kathleen Pfaff, prin. Fax 292-2534

Cockeysville, Baltimore, Pop. 18,668
Baltimore County SD
Supt. — See Towson
Cockeysville MS 900/6-8
10401 Greenside Dr 21030 410-887-7626
Deborah Magness, prin. Fax 887-7628
Padonia International ES 300/PK-5
9834 Greenside Dr 21030 410-887-7646
Carolyn Wolf, prin. Fax 887-7647
Warren ES 300/K-5
900 Bosley Rd 21030 410-887-7665
Susan Eisenhart, prin. Fax 887-7666

St. Joseph S 500/K-8
105 Church Ln 21030 410-683-0600
Sr. Anne O'Donnell, prin. Fax 628-6814

College Park, Prince George's, Pop. 25,171
Prince George's County SD
Supt. — See Upper Marlboro
Hollywood ES 400/K-6
9811 49th Ave 20740 301-513-5900
Barbara Caskey, prin. Fax 513-5383
Paint Branch ES 300/PK-6
5101 Pierce Ave 20740 301-513-5300
Jay Teston, prin. Fax 513-5303

Berwyn Baptist S 200/PK-8
4720 Cherokee St 20740 301-474-1561
Friends Community S 200/K-8
5901 Westchester Park Dr 20740 301-441-2100
Larry Clements, hdmstr. Fax 441-2105
Holy Redeemer S 300/K-8
4902 Berwyn Rd 20740 301-474-3993
Maria Bovich, prin. Fax 441-8137

Columbia, Howard, Pop. 88,254
Howard County SD
Supt. — See Ellicott City
Atholton ES 400/K-5
6700 Seneca Dr 21046 410-313-6853
Heidi Balter, prin. Fax 313-7410
Bryant Woods ES 400/K-5
5450 Blue Heron Ln 21044 410-313-6859
Sean Martin, prin. Fax 313-6864
Clemens Crossing ES 500/K-5
10320 Quarterstaff Rd 21044 410-313-6866
David Larner, prin. Fax 313-6869
Cradlerock S 900/K-8
6700 Cradlerock Way 21045 410-313-7601
Jason McCoy, prin. Fax 313-7610
Guilford ES 500/K-5
7335 Oakland Mills Rd 21046 410-880-5930
Genee Varlack, prin. Fax 880-5935
Harper's Choice MS 600/6-8
5450 Beaverkill Rd 21044 410-313-6929
C. Stephen Wallis, prin. Fax 313-5612
Jeffers Hill ES 400/K-5
6000 Tamar Dr 21045 410-313-6872
Pamela Butler, prin. Fax 313-6875
Longfellow ES 400/K-5
5470 Hesperus Dr 21044 410-313-6879
Cathy Nowack, prin. Fax 313-7106
Oakland Mills MS 500/6-8
9540 Kilimanjaro Rd 21045 410-313-6937
Cynthia Dillon, prin. Fax 313-7447
Phelps Luck ES 600/K-5
5370 Old Stone Ct 21045 410-313-6886
Pam Akers, prin. Fax 313-6889
Running Brook ES 300/PK-5
5215 W Running Brook Rd 21044 410-313-6893
Troy Todd, prin. Fax 313-6898
Steven's Forest ES 300/K-5
6045 Stevens Forest Rd 21045 410-313-6900
Ron Morris, prin. Fax 313-6903
Swansfield ES 500/K-5
5610 Cedar Ln 21044 410-313-6907
Jonathan Davis, prin. Fax 313-6910
Talbott Springs ES 400/K-5
9550 Basket Ring Rd 21045 410-313-6915
Nancy Thompson, prin. Fax 313-6921
Thunder Hill ES 300/K-5
9357 Mellenbrook Rd 21045 410-313-6922
John Birus, prin. Fax 313-6926
Waterloo ES 600/PK-5
5940 Waterloo Rd 21045 410-313-5014
Sue Webster, prin. Fax 313-5017
Wilde Lake MS 500/6-8
10481 Cross Fox Ln 21044 410-313-6957
Scott Conroy, prin. Fax 313-6963

Atholton Adventist S 200/PK-10
6520 Martin Rd 21044 410-740-2425
Marilynn Peeke, prin. Fax 740-2545
Children's Manor Montessori S 100/PK-K
9008 Red Branch Rd 21045 410-730-3100
Dr. Pradip Ghosh, prin. Fax 461-6850
Columbia Academy 300/PK-8
10350 Old Columbia Rd 21046 410-312-7413
Colleen Bakhsh, dir. Fax 312-7416
Gan Israel S 50/PK-1
770 Howes Ln 21044 410-740-2424

Conowingo, Cecil
Cecil County SD
Supt. — See Elkton
Conowingo ES 600/PK-5
471 Rowlandsville Rd 21918 410-996-6040
Cindy Fitzpatrick, prin. Fax 996-6059

Cooksville, Howard

Woodmont Academy 300/PK-8
2000 Woodmont Ln 21723 443-574-8100
John Farrell, prin. Fax 465-9162

Cordova, Talbot
Talbot County SD
Supt. — See Easton
Chapel District ES 400/PK-5
11430 Cordova Rd 21625 410-822-2391
Elizabeth Cassidy, prin. Fax 822-2039

Cresaptown, Allegany, Pop. 4,586
Allegany County SD
Supt. — See Cumberland
Cresaptown ES 300/K-5
13202 6th Ave 21502 301-729-0212
Roxanne Reuse, prin. Fax 729-1264

Calvary Christian Academy 300/PK-12
PO Box 5154 21505 301-729-0791
Geoff Wheeler, prin. Fax 729-1648

Crisfield, Somerset, Pop. 2,808
Somerset County SD
Supt. — See Westover
Woodson ES PK-5
281A Woodson School Rd 21817 410-968-1295
Lilly Welch, prin. Fax 968-1420

Crofton, Anne Arundel, Pop. 12,781
Anne Arundel County SD
Supt. — See Annapolis
Crofton ES 700/K-5
1405 Duke of Kent Dr 21114 410-222-5800
Donna O'Shea, prin. Fax 222-5802
Crofton Meadows ES 400/K-5
2020 Tilghman Dr 21114 410-721-9453
Janine Robinson, prin. Fax 721-5821
Crofton MS 900/6-8
2301 Davidsonville Rd 21114 410-793-0280
Sharon Hansen, prin. Fax 793-0295
Crofton Woods ES 500/K-5
1750 Urby Dr 21114 410-222-5805
John Barzal, prin.
Nantucket ES 700/K-5
2350 Nantucket Dr 21114 410-451-6120
Diana Strohecker, prin.

Crownsville, Anne Arundel, Pop. 1,514
Anne Arundel County SD
Supt. — See Annapolis
South Shore ES 200/K-5
1376 Fairfield Loop Rd 21032 410-222-3865
Linda Ferrara, prin. Fax 923-6730

Indian Creek Lower/Middle S 500/PK-8
680 Evergreen Rd 21032 410-923-3660
Anne Chambers, hdmstr. Fax 923-3884

Cumberland, Allegany, Pop. 20,915
Allegany County SD 8,100/PK-12
PO Box 1724 21501 301-759-2000
Dr. William AuMiller, supt. Fax 759-2039
www.boe.allconet.org
Bel Air ES 200/PK-5
14401 Barton Blvd SW 21502 301-729-2992
Autumn Eirich, prin. Fax 729-5024
Braddock MS 600/6-8
909 Holland St 21502 301-777-7990
Danny Carter, prin. Fax 777-9741
Cash Valley ES 300/PK-5
10601 Cash Valley Rd NW 21502 301-724-6632
Jackie Enright, prin. Fax 724-5297
Humbird ES 300/PK-5
120 E Mary St 21502 301-724-8842
Frank Billard, prin. Fax 759-4506
Northeast ES 300/K-5
11001 Forest Ave NE 21502 301-724-3285
Kerry Kelly, prin. Fax 724-7308
South Penn ES 500/PK-5
500 E 2nd St 21502 301-777-1755
Stephen Wilson, prin. Fax 777-1334
Washington MS 700/6-8
200 N Massachusetts Ave 21502 301-777-5360
Harry Smith, prin. Fax 777-8452
West Side ES 300/PK-5
425 Paca St 21502 301-724-0340
John Logsdon, prin. Fax 724-1651
Other Schools – See Cresaptown, Flintstone, Frostburg, La Vale, Lonaconing, Mount Savage, Westernport

---

Bishop Walsh S 600/PK-12
700 Bishop Walsh Rd 21502 301-724-5360
Samuel Torres, prin. Fax 722-0555
Lighthouse Christian Academy 100/PK-10
2020 Bedford St 21502 301-777-7375
Sheri Aspito, admin. Fax 777-3497

Damascus, Montgomery, Pop. 9,817
Montgomery County SD
Supt. — See Rockville
Baker MS 500/7-8
25400 Oak Dr 20872 301-253-7010
Louise Worthington, prin. Fax 253-7020
Clearspring ES 600/PK-5
9930 Moyer Rd 20872 301-253-7004
B. Gayle Mollet, prin. Fax 972-9027
Damascus ES 300/K-5
10201 Bethesda Church Rd 20872 301-253-7080
Rebecca Jones, prin. Fax 253-8717
Rockwell ES 400/PK-5
24555 Cutsail Dr 20872 301-253-7088
Cheryl Ann Clark, prin. Fax 253-7084

Darlington, Harford
Harford County SD
Supt. — See Bel Air
Darlington ES 100/K-5
2119 Shuresville Rd 21034 410-638-3700
Brenda Taylor, prin. Fax 638-3701

Darnestown, Montgomery

Mary of Nazareth S 500/PK-8
14131 Seneca Rd 20874 301-869-0940
Michael Friel, prin. Fax 869-0942

Davidsonville, Anne Arundel
Anne Arundel County SD
Supt. — See Annapolis
Davidsonville ES 500/K-5
962 W Central Ave 21035 410-222-1655
Jean Marie Hofstetter, prin. Fax 222-1682

Dayton, Howard
Howard County SD
Supt. — See Ellicott City
Dayton Oaks ES PK-5
4691 Ten Oaks Rd 21036 410-313-1571
Kimberlyn Pratesi, prin. Fax 313-1572

Deale, Anne Arundel, Pop. 4,151
Anne Arundel County SD
Supt. — See Annapolis
Deale ES 300/K-5
759 Masons Beach Rd 20751 410-222-1695
Melissa Brown, prin. Fax 222-1696

Deal Island, Somerset
Somerset County SD
Supt. — See Westover
Deal Island ES 100/PK-5
23275 Lola Wheatley Rd 21821 410-784-2449
Karen Linamen, prin. Fax 784-2411

Delmar, Wicomico, Pop. 2,290
Wicomico County SD
Supt. — See Salisbury
Delmar ES 800/PK-5
811 S 2nd St 21875 410-677-5178
Christopher Nunzio, prin. Fax 677-5184

Denton, Caroline, Pop. 3,252
Caroline County SD 5,500/PK-12
204 Franklin St 21629 410-479-1460
Dr. Edward Shirley, supt. Fax 479-0108
cl.k12.md.us
Denton ES 600/PK-5
303 Sharp Rd 21629 410-479-1660
Robin Daubach, prin. Fax 479-4220
Lockerman MS 800/6-8
410 Lockerman St 21629 410-479-2760
Dale Brown, prin. Fax 479-3594
Other Schools – See Federalsburg, Greensboro, Preston, Ridgely

---

Wesleyan Christian S 200/PK-12
PO Box 118 21629 410-479-2292
Regina Cook, prin. Fax 479-3294

Derwood, Montgomery
Montgomery County SD
Supt. — See Rockville
Sequoyah ES 400/K-5
17301 Bowie Mill Rd 20855 301-840-5335
Dr. Barbara Jasper, prin. Fax 840-5356

Dickerson, Montgomery
Montgomery County SD
Supt. — See Rockville
Monocacy ES 200/K-5
18801 Barnesville Rd 20842 301-972-7990
Cynthia Duranko, prin. Fax 972-7995

Barnesville S 200/PK-8
21830 Peach Tree Rd 20842 301-972-0341
John Huber, hdmstr. Fax 972-4076

District Heights, Prince George's, Pop. 6,296
Prince George's County SD
Supt. — See Upper Marlboro
Berkshire ES 300/PK-6
6201 Surrey Square Ln 20747 301-817-0314
Pearl Harmon, prin. Fax 817-0936
Claggett ES 200/PK-6
2001 Addison Rd S 20747 301-499-7050
Chandra Brown, prin. Fax 499-7060
Concord ES 300/K-6
2004 Concord Ln 20747 301-817-0488
Dr. Maria Smith, prin. Fax 817-0922
District Heights ES 400/K-6
2200 County Rd 20747 301-817-0484
Angela Mason, prin. Fax 817-0561
Key ES 400/K-6
2301 Scott Key Dr 20747 301-817-7970
Yetta Gilchrist, prin. Fax 817-7979

Easton, Talbot, Pop. 13,447
Talbot County SD 4,000/PK-12
PO Box 1029 21601 410-822-0330
Dr. Karen Salmon, supt. Fax 820-4260
www.talbotschools.org/
Easton ES - Dobson PK-1
305 Glenwood Ave 21601 410-822-0550
David Stofa, prin. Fax 822-9508
Easton ES - Moton 600/2-5
307 Glenwood Ave 21601 410-822-0686
David Stofa, prin. Fax 822-1890
Easton MS 800/6-8
201 Peach Blossom Ln 21601 410-822-2910
Corey Devaric, prin. Fax 822-7210
Other Schools – See Cordova, Saint Michaels, Tilghman, Trappe

Chesapeake Christian S 200/PK-12
1009 N Washington St 21601 410-822-7600
Keith Maxwell, admin. Fax 819-6974
Country S 300/K-8
716 Goldsborough St 21601 410-822-1935
Neil Mufson, hdmstr. Fax 822-1971
SS. Peter & Paul S 500/PK-8
900 High St 21601 410-822-2251
Connie Webster, prin. Fax 820-0136

Edgewater, Anne Arundel
Anne Arundel County SD
Supt. — See Annapolis
Central ES 600/K-5
130 Stepney Ln 21037 410-222-1075
Janice Haberlein, prin. Fax 222-1078
Central MS 1,000/6-8
221 Central Ave E 21037 410-956-5800
Mildred Beall, prin. Fax 956-1266
Edgewater ES 400/K-5
121 Washington Rd 21037 410-222-1660
Barry Fader, prin. Fax 222-1663
Mayo ES 300/K-5
1260 Mayo Ridge Rd 21037 410-222-1666
Steve Baran, prin. Fax 956-0070

Edgewood, Harford, Pop. 23,903
Harford County SD
Supt. — See Bel Air
Deerfield ES 600/PK-5
2307 Willoughby Beach Rd 21040 410-612-1535
Celeste Klima, prin. Fax 612-1573
Edgewood ES 400/PK-5
2100 Cedar Dr 21040 410-612-1540
Lisa Sundquist, prin. Fax 612-2013
Edgewood MS 1,200/6-8
2311 Willoughby Beach Rd 21040 410-612-1518
Dr. Lawrence Rudolph, prin. Fax 612-1523

Eldersburg, Carroll, Pop. 9,720

St. Stephen's Classical Christian Acad 100/K-12
2275 Liberty Rd 21784 410-795-1249
John Dykes, hdmstr. Fax 795-8820

Elkridge, Howard, Pop. 12,953
Howard County SD
Supt. — See Ellicott City
Deep Run ES 600/PK-5
6925 Old Waterloo Rd 21075 410-313-5000
Cindy Hankin, prin. Fax 313-5005
Elkridge ES 500/K-5
7075 Montgomery Rd 21075 410-313-5006
Diane Mumford, prin. Fax 596-1574
Elkridge Landing MS 700/6-8
7085 Montgomery Rd 21075 410-313-5040
Thomas Saunders, prin. Fax 313-5045
Mayfield Woods MS 500/6-8
7950 Red Barn Way 21075 410-313-5022
Susan Griffith, prin. Fax 313-5029
Rockburn ES 600/PK-5
6145 Montgomery Rd 21075 410-313-5030
Lauren Bauer, prin. Fax 313-5036

St. Augustine S 300/PK-8
5990 Old Washington Rd 21075 410-796-3040
Patricia Schratz, prin. Fax 579-1165

Elkton, Cecil, Pop. 14,466
Cecil County SD 16,300/PK-12
201 Booth St 21921 410-996-5400
Henry Shaffer, supt. Fax 996-5454
www.ccps.org
Cecil Manor ES 500/PK-5
971 Elk Mills Rd 21921 410-996-5090
Denisa Sopa, prin. Fax 996-5647
Cherry Hill MS 500/6-8
2535 Singerly Rd 21921 410-996-5020
Justin Zimmerman, prin. Fax 996-5435
Elk Neck ES 400/K-5
41 Racine School Rd 21921 410-996-5030
John Turner, prin. Fax 996-5648
Elkton MS 700/6-8
615 North St 21921 410-996-5010
Elizabeth Cronin, prin. Fax 996-5639
Gilpin Manor ES 400/PK-5
203 Newark Ave 21921 410-996-5040
Jennifer Hammer, prin. Fax 996-5412
Holly Hall ES 500/PK-5
233 White Hall Rd 21921 410-996-5050
James Orr, prin. Fax 996-5408
Kenmore ES 300/K-5
2475 Singerly Rd 21921 410-996-5060
Rose Clark, prin. Fax 996-5467
Leeds ES 400/PK-5
615 Deaver Rd 21921 410-996-5070
Alan Loman, prin. Fax 996-5290
Thomson Estates ES 500/PK-5
203 E Thomson Dr 21921 410-996-5080
Thomas Marinelli, prin. Fax 996-5272
Other Schools – See Cecilton, Charlestown, Chesapeake City, Conowingo, North East, Perryville, Port Deposit, Rising Sun

Elkton Christian Academy 500/PK-12
144 Appleton Rd 21921 410-398-6444
Dr. Gary Frasier, admin. Fax 392-0397
Immaculate Conception S 300/K-8
452 Bow St 21921 410-398-2636
Mary Kirkwood, prin. Fax 398-1190

Ellicott City, Howard, Pop. 56,397
Howard County SD 47,500/PK-12
10910 State Route 108 21042 410-313-6600
Dr. Sydney Cousin, supt. Fax 313-6833
www.hcpss.org
Bellows Spring ES 600/K-5
8125 Old Stockbridge Dr 21043 410-313-5057
Jacqueline Klamerus, prin. Fax 313-5060
Bonnie Branch MS 700/6-8
4979 Ilchester Rd 21043 410-313-2580
Carolyn Jameson, prin. Fax 313-2586
Burleigh Manor MS 700/6-8
4200 Centennial Ln 21042 410-313-2507
Claire Hafets, prin. Fax 313-2513
Centennial Lane ES 600/K-5
3825 Centennial Ln 21042 410-313-2800
Florence Hu, prin. Fax 313-2804
Dunloggin MS 600/6-8
9129 Northfield Rd 21042 410-313-2831
Cher Jones, prin. Fax 313-2530
Ellicott Mills MS 700/6-8
4445 Montgomery Rd 21043 410-313-2839
Michael Goins, prin. Fax 313-2845
Folly Quarter MS 600/6-8
13500 Triadelphia Rd 21042 410-313-1506
Rick Wilson, prin. Fax 313-1509
Hollifield Station ES 800/PK-5
8701 Stonehouse Dr 21043 410-313-2550
Lisa Booth, prin. Fax 313-2557
Ilchester ES 600/PK-5
4981 Ilchester Rd 21043 410-313-2524
John Morningstar, prin. Fax 313-2527
Manor Woods ES 600/K-5
11575 Frederick Rd 21042 410-313-7165
James Weisner, prin. Fax 313-7170
Northfield ES 600/K-5
9125 Northfield Rd 21042 410-313-2806
Steve Meconi, prin. Fax 313-2810
Patapsco MS 700/6-8
8885 Old Frederick Rd 21043 410-313-2848
Jennifer Peduzzi, prin. Fax 313-2852
St. John's Lane ES 700/K-5
2960 Saint Johns Ln 21042 410-313-2813
Deborah Jagoda, prin. Fax 313-2817
Triadelphia Ridge ES 400/K-5
13400 Triadelphia Rd 21042 410-313-2560
Chanel Morris, prin. Fax 313-2566
Veterans ES K-5
4355 Montgomery Rd 21043 410-313-1700
Robert Bruce, prin.
Waverly ES 700/PK-5
10220 Wetherburn Rd 21042 410-313-2819
Kathy Jacobs, prin. Fax 313-2824
Worthington ES 600/K-5
4570 Round Hill Rd 21043 410-313-2825
Katherine Orlando, prin. Fax 313-2829
Other Schools – See Clarksville, Columbia, Dayton, Elkridge, Fulton, Glenwood, Jessup, Laurel, Marriottsville, West Friendship, Woodbine

Childrens Manor Montessori S 200/PK-5
4465 Montgomery Rd 21043 410-461-6070
Dr. Pradip Ghosh, prin. Fax 461-6850
Crossroads SDA S 50/K-8
PO Box 126 21041 866-715-7752
Karohn Young, prin. Fax 498-2933
Glenelg Country S 800/PK-12
12793 Folly Quarter Rd 21042 410-531-8600
Greg Ventre, hdmstr. Fax 531-1882
Our Lady of Perpetual Help S 200/K-8
4801 Ilchester Rd 21043 410-744-4251
Nancy Malloy, prin. Fax 788-5210
Resurrection / St. Paul S 500/K-8
3155 Paulskirk Dr 21042 410-461-9111
Karen Murphy, prin. Fax 461-8621
St. John's Parish Day S 400/PK-5
9130 Frederick Rd 21042 410-465-7644
Tiffany Rath, dir. Fax 465-7748
Trinity S 300/K-8
4985 Ilchester Rd 21043 410-744-1524
Sr. Catherine Phelps, prin. Fax 744-1225

Emmitsburg, Frederick, Pop. 2,369
Frederick County SD
Supt. — See Frederick
Emmitsburg ES 300/PK-5
300 S Seton Ave 21727 240-236-1750
Kathy Golightly, prin. Fax 236-1751

Mother Seton S 400/PK-8
100 Creamery Rd 21727 301-447-3161
Sr. Joanne Goecke, prin. Fax 447-3914

Essex, Baltimore, Pop. 39,078
Baltimore County SD
Supt. — See Towson
Essex ES 400/PK-5
100 Mace Ave 21221 410-887-0117
Amy Grabner, prin. Fax 887-0118

Ewell, Somerset
Somerset County SD
Supt. — See Westover
Ewell ES 50/PK-7
4005 Smith Island Rd 21824 410-968-0280
Janet Evans, prin. Fax 968-0280

Fallston, Harford, Pop. 5,730
Harford County SD
Supt. — See Bel Air
Fallston MS 1,200/6-8
2303 Carrs Mill Rd 21047 410-638-4129
Joseph Mascari, prin. Fax 638-4237
Youths Benefit ES 900/K-5
1901 Fallston Rd 21047 410-638-4190
Angela Morton, prin. Fax 638-4193

Federalsburg, Caroline, Pop. 2,637
Caroline County SD
Supt. — See Denton
Federalsburg ES 400/PK-5
302 S University Ave 21632 410-754-5344
Helen Schmidt, prin. Fax 754-5504
Richardson MS 400/6-8
25390 Richardson Rd 21632 410-754-5263
Susan McCandless, prin. Fax 754-5695

Finksburg, Carroll
Carroll County SD
Supt. — See Westminster
Sandymount ES 500/K-5
2222 Old Westminster Pike 21048 410-751-3215
Monica Smith, prin. Fax 751-3925

Flintstone, Allegany
Allegany County SD
Supt. — See Cumberland
Flintstone ES 200/K-5
22000 National Pike NE 21530 301-478-2434
Sharon Morgan, prin. Fax 777-0612

Forest Hill, Harford
Harford County SD
Supt. — See Bel Air
Forest Hill ES 600/PK-5
2407 Rocks Rd 21050 410-638-4166
Belinda Cole, prin. Fax 638-4234
Forest Lakes ES 600/K-5
100 Osborne Pkwy 21050 410-638-4262
Christine Langrehr, prin. Fax 638-4265

Advent Lutheran S 50/K-5
2230 Rock Spring Rd 21050 410-838-4892
Paul Bickel, prin. Fax 838-6087

Forestville, Prince George's, Pop. 16,731
Prince George's County SD
Supt. — See Upper Marlboro
Jackson MS 700/7-8
3500 Regency Pkwy 20747 301-817-0310
Nathaniel Laney, prin. Fax 817-0339
Longfields ES 400/K-6
3300 Newkirk Ave 20747 301-817-0455
Jeffrey Holmes, prin. Fax 817-0934
Massie ES 600/K-6
3301 Regency Pkwy 20747 301-669-1120
Michelle Lambert, prin. Fax 669-6536
North Forestville ES 300/PK-6
2311 Ritchie Rd 20747 301-499-7098
Melissa Ellis, prin. Fax 808-4488

Children of Promise Christian Academy 50/PK-7
7808 Marlboro Pike 20747 301-516-3800
Frank Brown, admin. Fax 516-4002
Mt. Calvary S 200/PK-8
6704 Marlboro Pike 20747 301-735-5262
Darcy Tomko, prin. Fax 736-5044
Our Savior's S 50/PK-6
3111 Forestville Rd 20747 301-420-5076
Elizabeth Cottrell, admin. Fax 420-4153

Fort Meade, Anne Arundel, Pop. 12,509
Anne Arundel County SD
Supt. — See Annapolis
MacArthur MS 1,100/6-8
3500 Rockenbach Rd 20755 410-674-0032
Reginald Farrare, prin. Fax 674-8021
Manor View ES 500/K-5
2900 MacArthur Rd 20755 410-222-6504
Anita Dempsey, prin. Fax 222-6513
Meade Heights ES 600/PK-5
1925 Reece Rd 20755 410-222-6509
Susan Gallagher, prin. Fax 519-1277
Meade MS 800/6-8
1103 26th St 20755 410-674-2355
Eddie Scott, prin. Fax 674-6590
Pershing Hill ES 200/K-5
7600 29th Division Rd 20755 410-222-6519
Tasheka Sellman, prin. Fax 222-6527
West Meade ES, 7722 Ray St 20755 300/PK-5
Carole Janesko, prin. 410-222-6545

Fort Washington, Prince George's, Pop. 24,032
Prince George's County SD
Supt. — See Upper Marlboro
Apple Grove ES 500/K-6
7400 Bellefield Ave 20744 301-449-4966
Beth Linn, prin. Fax 449-2106
Avalon ES 400/K-6
7302 Webster Ln 20744 301-449-4970
Dianne Bruce, prin. Fax 449-2114

Dent ES 300/K-6
2700 Corning Ave 20744 301-702-3850
Lu Shun Dewberry, prin. Fax 702-7574
Fort Foote ES 500/PK-6
8300 Oxon Hill Rd 20744 301-749-4230
Sonia Beckford, prin. Fax 749-4236
Ft. Washington Forest ES 200/K-6
1300 Fillmore Rd 20744 301-203-1123
Dr. Margaret Stroman, prin. Fax 203-1129
Gourdine MS 600/7-8
8700 Allentown Rd 20744 301-449-4940
Leatriz Covington, prin. Fax 449-4948
Indian Queen ES 400/K-6
9551 Fort Foote Rd 20744 301-749-4250
Diane Fingers, prin. Fax 749-4252
Oxon Hill MS 700/7-8
9570 Fort Foote Rd 20744 301-749-4270
Byron Williams, prin. Fax 749-4286
Potomac Landing ES 400/K-6
12500 Fort Washington Rd 20744 301-203-1114
Richard Mosby, prin. Fax 203-3226
Rose Valley ES 300/K-6
9800 Jacqueline Dr 20744 301-449-4990
Michelle Powell-Larkin, prin. Fax 449-4766
Tayac Academy 300/K-5
8600 Allentown Rd 20744 301-449-4840
Saundra Mayo-Carr, prin. Fax 449-4785

Beddow S 100/PK-6
8600 Loughran Rd 20744 301-567-0330
National Christian Academy 400/PK-12
6700 Bock Rd 20744 301-567-9507
Andrew Stewart, prin. Fax 567-7438

Frederick, Frederick, Pop. 57,907
Frederick County SD 37,700/PK-12
115 E Church St 21701 301-696-6910
Dr. Linda Burgee, supt. Fax 696-6848
www.fcps.org
Ballenger Creek ES 500/PK-5
5250 Kingsbrook Dr 21703 240-236-2500
Paul Smith, prin. Fax 236-2501
Ballenger Creek MS 800/6-8
5525 Ballenger Creek Pike 21703 240-236-5700
Mita Badshah, prin. Fax 236-5701
Centerville ES 700/K-5
3601 Carriage Hill Dr 21704 240-566-0100
Stephen Raff, prin. Fax 566-0101
Crestwood MS 500/6-8
7100 Foxcroft Dr 21703 240-566-9000
Kathleen Hartsock, prin. Fax 566-9001
Hillcrest ES 500/PK-5
1285 Hillcrest Dr 21703 240-236-3200
Grason Jackson, prin. Fax 236-3201
Johnson MS 600/6-8
1799 Schifferstadt Blvd 21701 240-236-4900
Michelle Concepcion, prin. Fax 236-4901
Lincoln ES 400/PK-5
250 Madison St 21701 240-236-2650
Ann Reever, prin. Fax 236-2651
Monocacy ES 500/PK-5
7421 Hayward Rd 21702 240-236-1400
Jason Anderson, prin. Fax 236-1401
Monocacy MS 700/6-8
8009 Opossumtown Pike 21702 240-236-4700
Everett Warren, prin. Fax 236-4701
North Frederick ES 600/PK-5
1001 Motter Ave 21701 240-236-2000
Kathy Prichard, prin. Fax 236-2001
Orchard Grove ES 500/PK-5
5898 Hannover Dr 21703 240-236-2400
Cheryl Crawford, prin. Fax 236-2401
Parkway ES 200/PK-5
300 Carroll Pkwy 21701 240-236-2600
Sunora Knill-Wilbar, prin. Fax 236-2601
Spring Ridge ES 600/PK-5
9051 Ridgefield Dr 21701 240-236-1600
Deborah Thackston, prin. Fax 236-1601
Tuscarora ES 600/K-5
6321 Lambert Ct 21703 240-566-0000
Tracy Hilliard, prin. Fax 566-0001
Urbana ES 600/PK-5
3554 Urbana Pike 21704 240-236-2200
Jan Hollenbeck, prin. Fax 236-2201
Waverley ES 500/PK-5
201 Waverley Dr 21702 240-236-3900
Barbara Nash, prin. Fax 236-3901
West Frederick MS 800/6-8
515 W Patrick St 21701 240-236-4000
Daniel Lippy, prin. Fax 236-4050
Whittier ES 600/K-5
2400 Whittier Dr 21702 240-236-3100
John Festerman, prin. Fax 236-3101
Yellow Springs ES 400/K-5
8717 Yellow Springs Rd 21702 240-236-1700
Donna Hauver, prin. Fax 236-1701
Other Schools – See Adamstown, Brunswick, Emmitsburg, Ijamsville, Jefferson, Keymar, Libertytown, Middletown, Monrovia, Mount Airy, Myersville, New Market, Sabillasville, Thurmont, Walkersville, Woodsboro

---

Banner S 200/PK-10
1730 N Market St 21701 301-695-9320
Les McLean Ed.D., hdmstr. Fax 695-9336
Frederick Adventist S 100/K-8
6437 Jefferson Pike 21703 301-663-0363
Robin Correia, prin. Fax 698-8226
Good Shepherd Lutheran K 100/PK-K
1415 W 7th St 21702 301-695-5855
New Life Christian S 200/K-12
5909 Jefferson Pike 21703 301-663-8418
Don Lewis, prin. Fax 698-1583
St. John Regional S 600/PK-8
8414 Opossumtown Pike 21702 301-662-6722
Karen Smith, prin. Fax 695-7024
Visitation Academy 100/PK-8
200 E 2nd St 21701 301-662-2814
Susan Chase, prin. Fax 695-8549

Wee Folk S, 35 E Church St 21701 100/PK-PK
JoAnne Pritchett, dir. 301-663-5117

Freeland, Baltimore
Baltimore County SD
Supt. — See Towson
Prettyboy ES 400/PK-5
19810 Middletown Rd 21053 410-887-1900
Stacey Durkovic, prin. Fax 887-1901

Friendsville, Garrett, Pop. 518
Garrett County SD
Supt. — See Oakland
Friendsville ES 100/PK-5
PO Box 59 21531 301-746-5100
Kent Huber, prin. Fax 746-5065

Frostburg, Allegany, Pop. 7,958
Allegany County SD
Supt. — See Cumberland
Beall ES 400/PK-5
3 E College Ave 21532 301-689-3636
Robert Stevenson, prin. Fax 689-8006
Frost ES 200/K-5
260 Shaw St 21532 301-689-5168
Kim Smith, prin. Fax 689-1735

Garrett County SD
Supt. — See Oakland
Route 40 ES 200/PK-5
17764 National Pike 21532 301-689-6132
Candy Dolan-Opel, prin. Fax 687-0261

St. Michael S 100/PK-5
56 E Main St 21532 301-689-2155
Kathryn Black, prin. Fax 687-0119

Fruitland, Wicomico, Pop. 3,953
Wicomico County SD
Supt. — See Salisbury
Fruitland IS 400/3-5
208 W Main St 21826 410-677-5805
Kristina Gosnell, prin. Fax 677-5890
Fruitland PS 300/PK-2
301 N Division St 21826 410-677-5171
Darrel Morris, prin. Fax 677-5176

Fulton, Howard
Howard County SD
Supt. — See Ellicott City
Fulton ES 700/PK-5
11600 Scaggsville Rd 20759 410-880-5957
Karen Roby, prin. Fax 880-5969
Lime Kiln MS 600/6-8
11650 Scaggsville Rd 20759 410-880-5988
Brenda Thomas, prin. Fax 880-5996

Gaithersburg, Montgomery, Pop. 57,698
Montgomery County SD
Supt. — See Rockville
Brown Station ES 400/PK-5
851 Quince Orchard Blvd 20878 301-840-7172
Jan Riley, prin. Fax 840-7175
Carson ES 600/PK-5
100 Tschiffely Square Rd 20878 301-840-5333
Lawrence D. Chep, prin. Fax 840-5366
Darnestown ES 400/PK-5
15030 Turkey Foot Rd 20878 301-840-7157
Laura Colgary, prin. Fax 548-7527
Diamond ES 400/K-5
4 Marquis Dr 20878 301-840-7177
Carol Lange, prin. Fax 840-4506
Dufief ES 400/PK-5
15001 Dufief Dr 20878 301-279-4980
Dorothy Reitz, prin. Fax 279-4983
Fields Road ES 500/PK-5
1 School Dr 20878 301-840-7131
Kathryn Rupp, prin. Fax 548-7523
Flower Hill ES 500/PK-5
18425 Flower Hill Way 20879 301-840-7161
Lamar Whitmore, prin. Fax 840-7165
Forest Oak MS 800/6-8
651 Saybrooke Oaks Blvd 20877 301-670-8242
John Burley, prin. Fax 840-5322
Gaithersburg ES 500/PK-5
35 N Summit Ave 20877 301-840-7136
Niki Hazel, prin. Fax 548-7524
Gaithersburg MS 500/7-8
2 Teachers Way 20877 301-840-4554
Carol Goddard, prin. Fax 840-4570
Goshen ES 600/K-5
8701 Warfield Rd 20882 301-840-8165
Linda King, prin. Fax 840-8167
Jones Lane ES 500/PK-5
15110 Jones Ln 20878 301-840-8160
Carole Sample, prin. Fax 840-8162
Lakelands Park MS 900/6-8
1200 Main St 20878 301-670-1400
Joseph Sacco, prin. Fax 670-1418
Laytonsville ES 500/K-5
21401 Laytonsville Rd 20882 301-840-7145
Hilarie Rooney, prin. Fax 840-7147
Marshall ES 500/PK-5
12260 McDonald Chapel Dr 20878 301-670-8282
Pamela Nazzaro, prin. Fax 670-8256
Montgomery Village MS 700/6-8
19300 Watkins Mill Rd 20886 301-840-4660
Dr. Edgar Malker, prin. Fax 840-6388
Resnik ES 600/PK-5
7301 Hadley Farms Dr 20879 301-670-8200
Dr. Roy Settles, prin. Fax 840-7135
Ridgeview MS 500/7-8
16600 Raven Rock Dr 20878 301-840-4770
Dr. Carol Levine, prin. Fax 840-4679
Rosemont ES 500/PK-5
16400 Alden Ave 20877 301-840-7123
James Sweeney, prin. Fax 548-7512
Shady Grove S 600/K-8
8100 Midcounty Hwy 20877 301-548-7540
Eileen Dempsey, prin. Fax 548-7535
South Lake ES 500/PK-5
18201 Contour Rd 20877 301-840-7141
Nicole Priestly, prin. Fax 840-4549

Stedwick ES 600/PK-5
10631 Stedwick Rd 20886 301-840-7187
Dr. Margaret Pastor, prin. Fax 548-7532
Strawberry Knoll ES 500/PK-5
18820 Strawberry Knoll Rd 20879 301-840-7112
E. Frank Kaplan, prin. Fax 840-7114
Summit Hall ES 500/PK-5
101 W Deer Park Rd 20877 301-840-7127
Keith Jones, prin. Fax 548-7543
Travilah ES 500/K-5
13801 Dufief Mill Rd 20878 301-840-7153
Susan Shenk, prin. Fax 670-8230
Washington Grove ES 400/PK-5
8712 Oakmont St 20877 301-840-7120
Susan Barranger, prin. Fax 840-4523
Watkins Mill ES 500/PK-5
19001 Watkins Mill Rd 20886 301-840-7181
Stephanie Spencer, prin. Fax 840-5319
Whetstone ES 600/PK-5
19201 Thomas Farm Rd 20886 301-840-7191
Vicky Casey, prin. Fax 840-7185
Woodfield ES 400/K-5
24200 Woodfield Rd 20882 301-253-7085
Gayle Starr, prin. Fax 972-2084

Church of the Redeemer Christian S 300/PK-8
19425 Woodfield Rd 20879 240-238-1500
Dr. Patrick Malone, dir. Fax 238-1489
Covenant Life S 300/K-12
7503 Muncaster Mill Rd 20877 301-869-4500
Jamie Leach, hdmstr. Fax 948-4920
Ets Chaiyim S 50/K-7
20101 Woodfield Rd 20882 301-216-9592
Yvonne Roush, prin. Fax 216-9594
Mother of God S 200/K-8
20501 Goshen Rd 20879 301-990-2088
Eileen Smith, prin. Fax 947-0574
St. Martin of Tours S 200/K-8
115 S Frederick Ave 20877 301-990-2441
Sr. Sharon Mihm, prin. Fax 990-2688

Galena, Kent, Pop. 473
Kent County SD
Supt. — See Chestertown
Galena MS 200/5-8
114 S Main St 21635 410-648-5132
John Voshell, prin. Fax 648-6881

Gambrills, Anne Arundel
Anne Arundel County SD
Supt. — See Annapolis
Four Seasons ES 700/PK-5
979 Waugh Chapel Rd 21054 410-222-6501
Sharon Ferralli, prin. Fax 222-6503

Barr SDA S 50/1-8
2365 Bell Branch Rd 21054 410-451-0078
Roger Stull, prin. Fax 721-4910
School of the Incarnation 700/K-8
2601 Symphony Ln 21054 410-519-2285
Dr. Barbara Edmonson, prin. Fax 519-2286

Garrett Park, Montgomery, Pop. 942

Holy Cross S 200/PK-8
PO Box 249 20896 301-949-0053
Elizabeth Turner, prin. Fax 949-5074

Germantown, Montgomery, Pop. 55,419
Montgomery County SD
Supt. — See Rockville
Cedar Grove ES 500/K-5
24001 Ridge Rd 20876 301-253-7000
Lee Derby, prin. Fax 540-5736
Clemente MS 1,100/6-8
18808 Waring Station Rd 20874 301-601-0344
Shawn Joseph, prin. Fax 601-0370
Clopper Mill ES 400/PK-5
18501 Cinnamon Dr 20874 301-353-8065
Stephanie Curry, prin. Fax 353-8068
Daly ES 500/PK-5
20301 Brandermill Dr 20876 301-353-0939
Nora Dietz, prin. Fax 353-0872
Fox Chapel ES 600/PK-5
19315 Archdale Rd 20876 301-353-8055
Diana Zabetakis, prin. Fax 353-0873
Germantown ES 300/K-5
19110 Liberty Mill Rd 20874 301-353-8050
Amy Bryant, prin. Fax 601-0393
Great Seneca Creek ES PK-5
13010 Dairymaid Dr 20874 301-353-8500
Gregory Edmundson, prin. Fax 515-3044
King MS 700/6-8
13737 Wisteria Dr 20874 301-353-8080
Marc Cohen, prin. Fax 601-0399
Kingsview MS 800/6-8
18909 Kingsview Rd 20874 301-601-4611
Elizabeth Thomas, prin. Fax 601-4610
Lake Seneca ES 300/PK-5
13600 Wanegarden Dr 20874 301-353-0929
Teri Johnson, prin. Fax 353-0932
Matsunaga ES 800/PK-5
13902 Bromfield Rd 20874 301-601-4350
Judy Brubaker, prin. Fax 601-4358
McAuliffe ES 600/PK-5
12500 Wisteria Dr 20874 301-353-0910
Loretta Favret, prin. Fax 353-0923
McNair ES 600/PK-5
13881 Hopkins Rd 20874 301-353-0854
Eileen Macfarlane, prin. Fax 353-0964
Neelsville MS 800/6-8
11700 Neelsville Church Rd 20876 301-353-8064
Dollye McClain, prin. Fax 353-8094
Ride ES 500/PK-5
21301 Seneca Crossing Dr 20876 301-353-0994
Christopher Wynne, prin. Fax 601-0349
Waters Landing ES 600/K-5
13100 Waters Landing Dr 20874 301-353-0915
William Poole, prin. Fax 601-0392

Butler S 200/PK-8
15951 Germantown Rd 20874 301-977-6600
Fax 977-2419

Covenant Christian S 100/PK-1
18901 Waring Station Rd 20874 301-444-0250
Dr. Hei-Jung Kim, prin. Fax 444-0251

Glenarden, Prince George's, Pop. 6,380
Prince George's County SD
Supt. — See Upper Marlboro
Glenarden Woods ES 500/K-6
7801 Glenarden Pkwy 20706 301-925-1300
Cecelia Jones-Bowlding, prin. Fax 925-1304
Woods ES 600/PK-6
3000 Church St 20706 301-925-2840
Michelle Williams, prin. Fax 925-2844

Glen Arm, Baltimore

Trinity Church Day S 100/PK-K
12400 Manor Rd 21057 410-592-7423
Lynn Abplanalp, dir. Fax 592-7938

Glen Burnie, Anne Arundel, Pop. 38,922
Anne Arundel County SD
Supt. — See Annapolis
Corkran MS 700/6-8
7600 Quarterfield Rd 21061 410-222-6493
Debbie Montgomery, prin. Fax 761-3853
Cromwell ES 300/1-5
525 Wellham Ave 21061 410-222-6920
Karen Markovic, prin. Fax 222-6923
Ferndale ECC 100/PK-K
105 Packard Ave 21061 410-222-6927
Lisa Rice, prin. Fax 222-6929
Freetown ES 400/PK-5
7904 Freetown Rd 21060 410-222-6900
Shirley Moaney, prin.
Glen Burnie Park ES 300/K-5
500 Marlboro Rd 21061 410-222-6400
Brenda Care, prin. Fax 222-6418
Glendale ES 500/PK-5
105 Carroll Rd 21060 410-222-6404
Richard Chilipko, prin. Fax 222-6471
Hilltop ES, 415 Melrose Ave 21061 500/PK-5
Louise DeJesu, prin. 410-222-6409
Lee ES 500/K-5
400 A St SW 21061 410-222-6435
Mary Wagner, prin. Fax 222-6437
Marley ES 500/PK-5
715 Cooper Rd 21060 410-222-6414
Donna Williman, prin. Fax 222-6413
Marley MS 800/6-8
10 Davis Ct 21060 410-761-0934
Kevin Buckley, prin. Fax 761-0736
North Glen ES 200/PK-5
615 W Furnace Branch Rd 21061 410-222-6416
Julie Little-McVearry, prin. Fax 222-6419
Oakwood ES 200/PK-5
330 Oak Manor Dr 21061 410-222-6420
Nancy Knouse, prin. Fax 222-6421
Point Pleasant ES 500/PK-5
1035 Dumbarton Rd 21060 410-222-6425
Lisa Koennel, prin. Fax 222-6459
Rippling Woods ES 600/PK-5
530 Nolfield Dr 21061 410-222-6440
Gwen Atkinson, prin. Fax 969-1240
Solley ES 600/PK-5
7608 Solley Rd 21060 410-222-6473
Robert Wagner, prin. Fax 222-6467
Southgate ES 500/K-5
290 Shetlands Ln 21061 410-222-6445
Jane George, prin.
Woodside ES 300/PK-5
160 Funke Rd 21061 410-222-6910
Anthony Alston, prin. Fax 222-6917

St. Paul's Lutheran S 400/PK-8
308 Oak Manor Dr 21061 410-766-5790
Fax 766-8758
Slade Edu-Care Center 900/PK-PK
124 Dorsey Rd 21061 410-766-2024
Deborah Gielner, dir. Fax 766-7399
Slade Regional Catholic S 900/K-8
120 Dorsey Rd 21061 410-766-7130
Gregory Jones, prin. Fax 787-0594

Glenn Dale, Prince George's, Pop. 9,689
Prince George's County SD
Supt. — See Upper Marlboro
Glenn Dale ES 600/K-6
6700 Glenn Dale Rd 20769 301-805-2750
Lia Thompson, prin. Fax 805-2753

Holy Trinity Episcopal Day S 600/PK-8
11902 Daisy Ln 20769 301-464-3215
Marcy Cathey, hdmstr. Fax 464-9725
Reid Temple Christian Academy 100/PK-5
11400 Glenn Dale Blvd 20769 301-860-6570
Dr. Donnette Dais, admin. Fax 860-6571

Glenwood, Howard
Howard County SD
Supt. — See Ellicott City
Bushy Park ES 700/PK-5
14601 Carrs Mill Rd 21738 410-313-5500
Rebecca Straw, prin. Fax 313-5505
Glenwood MS 700/6-8
2680 Route 97 21738 410-313-5520
Dave Brown, prin. Fax 313-5534

Glyndon, Baltimore

Sacred Heart S 800/PK-8
PO Box 3672 21071 410-833-0857
Sherri Wright, prin. Fax 833-0914

Grantsville, Garrett, Pop. 593
Garrett County SD
Supt. — See Oakland
Grantsville ES 200/K-5
PO Box 9 21536 301-746-8662
Matthew Eggleston, prin. Fax 746-8662

Grasonville, Queen Anne's, Pop. 2,439
Queen Anne's County SD
Supt. — See Centreville
Grasonville ES 400/PK-5
5435 Main St 21638 410-827-8070
Roberta Leaverton, prin. Fax 827-4695

Great Mills, Saint Mary's
St. Mary's County SD
Supt. — See Leonardtown
Greenview Knolls ES 500/PK-5
45711 Military Ln 20634 301-863-4095
Elizabeth Servello, prin. Fax 863-4099

Little Flower S 300/PK-8
20410 Point Lookout Rd 20634 301-994-0404
Marsha Stewart, prin. Fax 994-2055

Greenbelt, Prince George's, Pop. 22,242
Prince George's County SD
Supt. — See Upper Marlboro
Greenbelt ES 600/K-6
66 Ridge Rd 20770 301-513-5911
Kimberly Seidel, prin. Fax 513-5319
Greenbelt MS 700/7-8
8950 Edmonston Rd 20770 301-513-5040
Judy Austin, prin. Fax 513-5097
Springhill Lake ES 500/K-6
6060 Springhill Dr 20770 301-513-5996
Linda Sherwood, prin. Fax 513-5314

St. Hugh S 200/K-8
145 Crescent Rd 20770 301-474-4071
Tiffani James, prin. Fax 474-3950

Greensboro, Caroline, Pop. 1,944
Caroline County SD
Supt. — See Denton
Greensboro ES 600/PK-5
625 N Main St 21639 410-482-6251
Keri Hutchins, prin. Fax 482-8880

Hagerstown, Washington, Pop. 38,326
Washington County SD 21,100/PK-12
PO Box 730 21741 301-766-2800
Dr. Elizabeth Morgan, supt. Fax 766-2829
www.wcboe.k12.md.us
Bester ES 600/PK-5
30 Memorial Blvd E 21740 301-766-8001
Kristi Bachtell, prin. Fax 797-3464
Conococheague ES 300/K-5
12408 Learning Ln 21740 301-766-8102
Ryan Hench, prin. Fax 582-5721
Doub ES 300/PK-5
1221 S Potomac St 21740 301-766-8130
Betsy Donohoe, prin. Fax 791-4291
Eastern ES 600/K-5
1320 Yale Dr 21742 301-766-8122
Ellen Hayes, prin. Fax 739-5066
Fountaindale ES 300/PK-4
901 Northern Ave 21742 301-766-8156
Kerry Rowe, prin. Fax 745-3041
Fountain Rock ES 400/K-5
17145 Lappans Rd 21740 301-766-8146
Michael Telemeco, prin. Fax 223-5759
Funkstown S for Early Childhood Ed 300/PK-2
23 Funkstown Rd 21740 301-766-8162
Susan Burger, prin. Fax 791-4113
Hicks MS 700/6-8
1321 S Potomac St 21740 301-766-8110
Duane McNairn, prin. Fax 766-8116
Lincolnshire ES 500/PK-5
17545 Lincolnshire Rd 21740 301-766-8206
Cathy Scuffins, prin. Fax 582-0428
Northern MS 700/5-8
701 Northern Ave 21742 301-766-8258
Peggy Pugh, prin. Fax 797-5887
Old Forge ES 400/K-5
21615 Old Forge Rd 21742 301-766-8273
Dana Peake, prin. Fax 745-6130
Pangborn Boulevard ES 500/K-5
195 Pangborn Blvd 21740 301-766-8282
Richard Gehrman, prin. Fax 797-5905
Paramount ES 500/K-5
19410 Longmeadow Rd 21742 301-766-8289
Theresa Williamson, prin. Fax 791-4263
Potomac Heights ES 300/K-5
301 E Magnolia Ave 21742 301-766-8305
Kathy Kelsey, prin. Fax 739-9353
Robinwood ECC 100/PK-PK
11402 Robinwood Dr 21742 301-791-4332
Jessica Wilkenson, lead tchr. Fax 791-4395
Rockland Woods ES K-5
18201 Rockland Dr 21740 301-766-8485
Kathy Stiles, prin. Fax 766-8498
Salem Avenue ES 500/PK-4
1323 Salem Ave 21740 301-766-8313
Thomas Garner, prin. Fax 791-4382
Western Heights MS 600/5-8
1300 Marshall St 21740 301-766-8403
Dr. Stephen Tarason, prin. Fax 766-8540
Winter Street ES 300/PK-4
59 Winter St 21740 301-766-8439
Matthew Semler, prin. Fax 745-5449
Other Schools – See Boonsboro, Cascade, Clear Spring, Hancock, Knoxville, Maugansville, Sharpsburg, Smithsburg, Williamsport

Broadfording Christian Academy 400/PK-12
13535 Broadfording Church 21740 301-797-8886
William Wyand, supt. Fax 797-3155
Grace Academy 400/PK-12
13321 Cearfoss Pike 21740 301-733-2033
Jack Appleby, hdmstr. Fax 733-4706
Heritage Academy 200/PK-12
12215 Walnut Pt W 21740 301-582-2600
Carl Gibbs, prin. Fax 582-2603

Mt. Aetna SDA S 100/PK-8
10207 Crystal Falls Dr 21740 301-824-3875
Paradise Mennonite S 200/1-10
19308 Air View Rd 21742 301-733-1368
St. Mary S 300/K-8
218 W Washington St 21740 301-733-1184
Patricia McDermott, prin. Fax 745-4997

Halethorpe, Baltimore
Baltimore County SD
Supt. — See Towson
Halethorpe ES 400/PK-5
4300 Maple Ave 21227 410-887-1406
Jill Bordenick, prin. Fax 887-7407

Ascension S 200/PK-8
4601 Maple Ave 21227 410-242-2020
Virginia Bahr, prin. Fax 242-2384
Mt. Providence Child Development Ctr 50/PK-K
701 Gun Rd 21227 410-247-0449
Sr. M. Concetta Melton, dir.

Hampstead, Carroll, Pop. 5,451
Carroll County SD
Supt. — See Westminster
Hampstead ES 600/PK-5
3737 Shiloh Rd 21074 410-751-3420
Jacalyn Powell, prin. Fax 751-3438
North Carroll MS 700/6-8
2401 Hanover Pike 21074 410-751-3440
Carl Snook, prin. Fax 751-3464
Shiloh MS 800/6-8
3675 Willow St 21074 410-386-4570
James Carver, prin. Fax 386-4579
Spring Garden ES 600/K-5
700 Boxwood Dr 21074 410-751-3433
Kimberly Renfro, prin. Fax 751-3475

Hancock, Washington, Pop. 1,736
Washington County SD
Supt. — See Hagerstown
Hancock ES 200/PK-5
290 W Main St 21750 301-766-8178
Michelle Gest, prin. Fax 678-5698

Hanover, Anne Arundel
Anne Arundel County SD
Supt. — See Annapolis
Hebron-Harman ES 500/PK-5
7660 Ridge Chapel Rd 21076 410-222-6930
Susan Bachmann, prin. Fax 222-6932

Havre de Grace, Harford, Pop. 11,884
Harford County SD
Supt. — See Bel Air
Havre De Grace ES 400/PK-5
600 S Juniata St 21078 410-939-6616
Renee Villareal, prin. Fax 939-6632
Havre De Grace MS 600/6-8
401 Lewis Ln 21078 410-939-6608
Glenn Jensen, prin. Fax 939-6613
Meadowvale ES 600/PK-5
910 Graceview Dr 21078 410-939-6622
A. Blaine Hawley, prin. Fax 939-6635
Roye-Williams ES 500/PK-5
201 Oakington Rd 21078 410-273-5536
Susan Osborn, prin. Fax 273-5559

Hebron, Wicomico, Pop. 1,022
Wicomico County SD
Supt. — See Salisbury
Westside IS 400/2-5
8000 Quantico Rd 21830 410-677-5118
Pamela Mitchell, prin. Fax 677-5138

Helen, Saint Mary's
St. Mary's County SD
Supt. — See Leonardtown
Brent MS 900/6-8
29675 Point Lookout Rd 20635 301-884-4635
Mike Egan, prin. Fax 884-8937

Mother Catherine Spalding S 200/K-8
38833 Chaptico Rd 20635 301-884-3165
Susan Fatka, prin. Fax 472-4469

Hollywood, Saint Mary's
St. Mary's County SD
Supt. — See Leonardtown
Hollywood ES 600/PK-5
44345 Joy Chapel Rd 20636 301-373-4350
Jennifer Gilman, prin. Fax 373-4355

St. John S 200/K-8
PO Box 69 20636 301-373-2142
Patricia Suit, prin. Fax 373-4500

Huntingtown, Calvert
Calvert County SD
Supt. — See Prince Frederick
Huntingtown ES 600/PK-5
4345 Huntingtown Rd 20639 410-535-7212
Ramona Crowley, prin. Fax 535-7224
Plum Point ES 700/K-5
1245 Plum Point Rd 20639 410-535-7391
Joyce King, prin. Fax 535-7327
Plum Point MS 800/6-8
1475 Plum Point Rd 20639 410-535-7400
Zachary Seawell, prin. Fax 535-7413

Calverton S 400/PK-12
300 Calverton School Rd 20639 410-535-0216
Daniel Hildebrand, hdmstr. Fax 535-6934
Good News Preschool PK-PK
885 Cox Rd 20639 410-414-8304
Karen Burns, dir. Fax 535-9057

Hurlock, Dorchester, Pop. 2,003
Dorchester County SD
Supt. — See Cambridge

Hurlock ES 400/PK-5
301 Charles St 21643 410-943-3303
Regina Teat, prin. Fax 943-8917
North Dorchester MS 400/6-8
5745 Cloverdale Rd 21643 410-943-3322
Vaughn Evans, prin. Fax 943-3797

Hyattsville, Prince George's, Pop. 16,677
Prince George's County SD
Supt. — See Upper Marlboro
Chavez ES 200/K-6
6609 Riggs Rd 20782 301-853-5694
Jose Taboada, prin. Fax 853-5696
Chillum ES 200/K-6
1420 Chillum Rd 20782 301-853-0825
Sheila Jefferson, prin. Fax 853-0857
Hyattsville ES 400/K-6
5311 43rd Ave 20781 301-209-5800
Jeanne Washburn, prin. Fax 985-1499
Hyattsville MS 800/7-8
6001 42nd Ave 20781 301-209-5830
Gail Golden, prin. Fax 209-5849
Langley Park/McCormick ES 400/K-6
8201 15th Ave 20783 301-445-8423
Amy Stout, prin. Fax 445-8425
Lewisdale ES 500/K-6
2400 Banning Pl 20783 301-445-8433
Melissa Glee-Woodard, prin. Fax 431-5654
Orem MS 700/7-8
6100 Editors Park Dr 20782 301-853-0840
Richard Jackson, prin. Fax 853-0839
Parks ES K-6
6111 Ager Rd 20782 301-445-8090
Tracey Adesegun, prin. Fax 445-8099
Ridgecrest ES 600/K-6
6120 Riggs Rd 20783 301-853-0820
Daniel Heller, prin. Fax 853-0861
University Park ES 600/K-6
4315 Underwood St 20782 301-985-1898
Brenda Foxx, prin. Fax 927-1181
Woodridge ES 400/PK-6
5001 Flintridge Dr 20784 301-918-8585
Carol Dimmie, prin. Fax 918-4462

Concordia Lutheran S 200/PK-8
3799 E West Hwy 20782 301-927-0266
Dr. David Falkner, admin. Fax 699-0071
Paint Branch Montessori S 50/PK-6
3215 Powder Mill Rd 20783 301-937-2244
Fax 937-2266
Peters Adventist S 100/PK-8
6303 Riggs Rd 20783 301-559-6710
Fax 559-6444
St. Jerome S 400/PK-8
5207 42nd Pl 20781 301-277-4568
Joyce Volpini, prin. Fax 779-2428
St. Mark the Evangelist S 300/PK-8
7501 Adelphi Rd 20783 301-422-7440
Charles Russell, prin. Fax 422-7710

Hydes, Baltimore

St. John the Evangelist S 300/PK-8
13311 Long Green Pike 21082 410-592-9585
Genevieve Delcher, prin. Fax 817-4548

Ijamsville, Frederick, Pop. 350
Frederick County SD
Supt. — See Frederick
Oakdale ES 500/PK-5
9850 Old National Pike 21754 240-236-3300
Elizabeth Little, prin. Fax 236-3301
Oakdale MS 600/6-8
9840 Old National Pike 21754 240-236-5500
Neal Case, prin. Fax 236-5501
Urbana MS 6-8
3511 Pontius Ct 21754 240-566-9200
Frank Vetter, prin. Fax 566-9201
Windsor Knolls MS 600/6-8
11150 Windsor Rd 21754 240-236-5000
Nancy Doll, prin. Fax 236-5001

Friends Meeting S 100/PK-8
3232 Green Valley Rd 21754 301-798-0288
Annette Breiling, hdmstr. Fax 798-0299

Indian Head, Charles, Pop. 3,642
Charles County SD
Supt. — See La Plata
Henson MS 900/6-8
3535 Livingston Rd 20640 301-375-8550
Ronald Stup, prin. Fax 375-9216
Indian Head ES 400/PK-5
4200 Indian Head Hwy 20640 301-743-5454
Toni Melton-Trainor, prin. Fax 743-5080
Parks ES 600/PK-5
3505 Livingston Rd 20640 301-375-7444
Kristin Shields, prin. Fax 375-9106
Smallwood MS 600/6-8
4990 Indian Head Hwy 20640 301-743-5422
Cynthia Baker, prin. Fax 753-8421

Potomac Heights Christian Academy 100/PK-8
37 Glymont Rd Unit A 20640 301-753-9350
Garland Foreman, admin. Fax 743-5400
St. Mary Star of the Sea S 100/K-8
6485 Indian Head Hwy 20640 301-283-6151
Henry Wroblewski, prin. Fax 283-4368

Jarrettsville, Harford, Pop. 2,148
Harford County SD
Supt. — See Bel Air
Jarrettsville ES 400/K-5
3818 Norrisville Rd 21084 410-692-7800
Richard Russell, prin. Fax 692-7801
North Bend ES 400/PK-5
1445 N Bend Rd 21084 410-692-7815
Steven Hardy, prin. Fax 692-7826

Jefferson, Frederick
Frederick County SD
Supt. — See Frederick
Valley ES 500/PK-5
3519 Jefferson Pike 21755 240-236-3000
Tess Blumenthal, prin. Fax 236-3001

Jessup, Howard, Pop. 6,537
Anne Arundel County SD
Supt. — See Annapolis
Jessup ES 500/PK-5
2900 Elementary School Ln 20794 410-222-6490
Ava Tasker, prin. Fax 222-6492

Howard County SD
Supt. — See Ellicott City
Bollman Bridge ES 600/PK-5
8200 Savage Guilford Rd 20794 410-880-5920
Monterey Morrell, prin. Fax 880-5923
Patuxent Valley MS 700/6-8
9151 Vollmerhausen Rd 20794 410-880-5840
Robert Motley, prin. Fax 880-5846

Joppa, Harford, Pop. 11,084
Harford County SD
Supt. — See Bel Air
Joppatowne ES 500/PK-5
407 Trimble Rd 21085 410-612-1546
Christopher Cook, prin. Fax 612-1578
Magnolia ES 500/PK-5
901 Trimble Rd 21085 410-612-1553
Patricia Mason, prin. Fax 612-1576
Magnolia MS 900/6-8
299 Fort Hoyle Rd 21085 410-612-1525
Melissa Mickey, prin. Fax 612-1598
Riverside ES 600/PK-5
211 Stillmeadow Dr 21085 410-612-1560
Creighton Leizear, prin. Fax 612-1559

Chesapeake Christian S 100/K-12
900 Trimble Rd 21085 410-679-8815
Lisa Gordon, admin. Fax 679-8825
Mountain Christian S 300/K-8
1824 Mountain Rd 21085 410-877-7333
Nadine Wellington, dir. Fax 877-4151
Trinity Lutheran S 300/PK-8
1100 Philadelphia Rd 21085 410-679-4000
Rev. John Austin, hdmstr. Fax 679-3472

Kensington, Montgomery, Pop. 1,920
Montgomery County SD
Supt. — See Rockville
Garrett Park ES 400/K-5
4810 Oxford St 20895 301-929-2170
Elaine Baxter, prin. Fax 929-2008
Kensington-Parkwood ES 500/PK-5
4710 Saul Rd 20895 301-571-6949
Barbara Liess, prin. Fax 571-6953
Newport Mill MS 600/6-8
11311 Newport Mill Rd 20895 301-929-2244
Panagiota Tsonis, prin. Fax 929-2274
Rock View ES 500/PK-5
3901 Denfeld Ave 20895 301-929-2002
Kyle Heatwole, prin. Fax 929-5986

Grace Episcopal Day S 200/1-8
9411 Connecticut Ave 20895 301-949-5860
Carol Franek, hdmstr. Fax 949-8398
Holy Redeemer S 400/PK-8
9715 Summit Ave 20895 301-942-3701
Harrian Walker, prin. Fax 942-4981

Keymar, Frederick
Frederick County SD
Supt. — See Frederick
New Midway ES 3-5
12226 Woodsboro Pike 21757 240-236-1500
Cynthia Houston, prin. Fax 236-1501

Kingsville, Baltimore, Pop. 3,550
Baltimore County SD
Supt. — See Towson
Kingsville ES 300/PK-5
7300 Sunshine Ave 21087 410-887-5949
Susan Felts, prin. Fax 887-5950

Open Bible Christian Academy 200/PK-12
13 Open Bible Way 21087 410-593-9940
William Trautman, hdmstr. Fax 593-9942
St. Paul's Lutheran S 200/PK-8
12022 Jerusalem Rd 21087 410-592-8100
William Osbourn, prin. Fax 592-3282

Kitzmiller, Garrett, Pop. 288
Garrett County SD
Supt. — See Oakland
Kitzmiller ES 100/PK-5
288 W Main St 21538 301-453-3101
Richard Stevens, prin. Fax 453-3210

Knoxville, Washington
Washington County SD
Supt. — See Hagerstown
Pleasant Valley ES 200/K-5
1707 Rohrersville Rd 21758 301-766-8297
Cheryl Lannon, prin. Fax 432-8777

Landover, Prince George's, Pop. 5,052
Prince George's County SD
Supt. — See Upper Marlboro
Carroll ES 300/PK-6
1400 Nalley Ter 20785 301-925-1955
Peter Thompson, prin. Fax 925-1961
Columbia Park ES 300/K-6
1901 Kent Village Dr 20785 301-925-1322
Michelle Tyler-Skinner, prin. Fax 925-1327
Dodge Park ES 400/PK-6
3401 Hubbard Rd 20785 301-883-4220
Judith White, prin. Fax 883-4223
Gholson MS 900/7-8
900 Nalley Rd 20785 301-883-8390
Jeffrey Parker, prin. Fax 883-8394
Henson ES 200/K-6
7910 Scott Rd 20785 301-925-2320
Michelle Pegram, prin. Fax 925-2324
Highland Park ES 400/K-6
6501 Lowland Dr 20785 301-333-0980
Lori Ellis, prin. Fax 333-0992
Kenmoor ES 300/K-6
3211 82nd Ave 20785 301-925-1970
Rodney Henderson, prin. Fax 925-2364
Kenmoor MS 700/7-8
2500 Kenmoor Dr 20785 301-925-2300
Maha Fadli, prin. Fax 925-2317
Oakcrest ES 400/K-6
929 Hill Rd 20785 301-808-8870
Wanda Robinson, prin. Fax 808-8869
Paca ES 400/K-6
7801 Sheriff Rd 20785 301-925-1330
Dorothy Clowers, prin. Fax 925-1338
Pullen S 800/K-8
700 Brightseat Rd 20785 301-808-8160
Pamela Lucas, prin. Fax 808-8166
Rice ES 500/K-6
950 Nalley Rd 20785 301-636-6340
Mattie Turman, prin. Fax 636-6344

Highland Park Christian Academy 300/PK-6
6801 Sheriff Rd 20785 301-773-4079
Connie Cowley, dir. Fax 773-2626
Jericho Christian Academy 400/PK-12
8500 Jericho City Dr 20785 301-333-9400
Joel Peebles, hdmstr. Fax 333-0521
SHABACH Christian Academy 300/PK-9
3600 Brightseat Rd 20785 301-772-8590
Etrulia Lee, supt. Fax 773-6282

Landover Hills, Prince George's, Pop. 1,589
Prince George's County SD
Supt. — See Upper Marlboro
Cooper Lane ES 400/K-6
3817 Cooper Ln 20784 301-925-1350
Laverne Wilson, prin. Fax 925-2360
Glenridge ES 600/PK-6
7200 Gallatin St 20784 301-918-8740
Gloria McCoy, prin. Fax 918-8547

Ascension Lutheran S 200/K-8
7415 Buchanan St 20784 301-577-0500
Jack Bartels, prin. Fax 577-9558
St. Mary S 300/PK-8
7207 Annapolis Rd 20784 301-577-0031
Susan Varrone, prin. Fax 577-5485
Washington United Christian Academy 100/PK-12
4610 69th Ave 20784 301-807-9397
Abraham Moses, prin. Fax 772-3999

Lanham Seabrook, Prince George's, Pop. 16,792
Prince George's County SD
Supt. — See Upper Marlboro
Gaywood ES 500/K-6
6701 97th Ave 20706 301-918-8730
Sonya Harris, prin. Fax 918-8560
Goddard French Immersion S 500/K-8
9850 Good Luck Rd 20706 301-918-3515
Kona Facia-Nepay, prin. Fax 918-8670
Goddard Montessori S 500/PK-8
9850 Good Luck Rd 20706 301-918-3515
Suzanne Johnson, prin. Fax 918-8670
Johnson MS 1,000/7-8
5401 Barker Pl 20706 301-918-8680
Omar Gobourne, prin. Fax 918-8688
Magnolia ES 400/K-6
8400 Nightingale Dr 20706 301-918-8770
Phyllis Gillens, prin. Fax 918-8772
McHenry ES 600/K-6
8909 McHenry Ln 20706 301-918-8760
Jane Handlesman, prin. Fax 918-8638
Reed ES 400/K-6
9501 Greenbelt Rd 20706 301-918-8716
Gwendolyn Jefferson, prin. Fax 918-8559
Seabrook ES 400/PK-6
6001 Seabrook Rd 20706 301-918-8542
Clareta Spinks, prin. Fax 918-8543

Lanham Christian S 300/PK-12
8400 Good Luck Rd 20706 301-552-9102
Gene Pinkard, hdmstr. Fax 552-2021
Lighthouse Christian Academy 50/PK-8
6310 Cipriano Rd 20706 301-552-3179
Sherise Webb, admin. Fax 552-7199
St. Matthias Apostle S 200/PK-8
9473 Annapolis Rd 20706 301-577-9412
Patricia Wilson, prin. Fax 577-2060

La Plata, Charles, Pop. 8,442
Charles County SD 25,300/PK-12
PO Box 2770 20646 301-932-6610
James Richmond, supt. Fax 932-6651
www.ccboe.com
Matula ES 600/PK-5
6025 Radio Station Rd 20646 301-934-5412
Timothy Rosin, prin. Fax 934-5414
Mitchell ES 600/PK-5
400 Willow Ln 20646 301-934-4687
Linda Gill, prin. Fax 753-1649
Somers MS 1,200/6-8
300 Willow Ln 20646 301-934-4663
Stephanie Wesolowski, prin. Fax 934-2982
Other Schools – See Bryantown, Indian Head, Marbury, Nanjemoy, Newburg, Pomfret, Waldorf

---

Archbishop Neale S 500/PK-8
104 Port Tobacco Rd 20646 301-934-9595
Margaret Howard, prin. Fax 934-8610
Grace Lutheran S 200/PK-8
1200 Charles St 20646 301-932-0963
Ruth Blackwell, prin. Fax 934-1459

Largo, Prince George's, Pop. 9,475

Divine Peace Lutheran S 50/1-8
1500 Brown Station Rd 20774 301-350-4522
Joshua Roth, prin. Fax 350-2420

Laurel, Prince George's, Pop. 22,125
Anne Arundel County SD
Supt. — See Annapolis
Brock Bridge ES 500/K-5
405 Brock Bridge Rd 20724 301-498-6280
Joan Briscoe, prin. Fax 776-0128
Maryland City ES 300/PK-5
3359 Crumpton S 20724 301-725-4256
Karen Soneira, prin.

Howard County SD
Supt. — See Ellicott City
Forest Ridge ES 500/K-5
9550 Gorman Rd 20723 410-880-5950
Allan Olchowski, prin. Fax 880-5956
Gorman Crossing ES 500/K-5
9999 Winter Sun Rd 20723 410-880-5900
Cheryl Logan, prin. Fax 880-5902
Hammond ES 500/K-5
8110 Aladdin Dr 20723 410-880-5890
Judith Bland, prin. Fax 880-5895
Hammond MS 700/6-8
8110 Aladdin Dr 20723 410-880-5830
Kerry McGowan, prin. Fax 880-5837
Laurel Woods ES 500/K-5
9250 N Laurel Rd 20723 410-880-5960
Peggy Dumler, prin. Fax 880-5964
Murray Hill MS 700/6-8
9989 Winter Sun Rd 20723 410-880-5897
Donyall Dickey, prin. Fax 317-5048

Prince George's County SD
Supt. — See Upper Marlboro
Bond Mill ES 600/K-6
16001 Sherwood Ave 20707 301-497-3600
Justin Fitzgerald, prin. Fax 497-3606
Deerfield Run ES 500/K-6
13000 Laurel Bowie Rd 20708 301-497-3610
Thomas Tucker, prin. Fax 497-3615
Eisenhower MS 800/7-8
13725 Briarwood Dr 20708 301-497-3620
Charoscar Coleman, prin. Fax 497-3637
Harrison ES 400/K-6
13200 Larchdale Rd 20708 301-497-3650
Patricia Haith-Bellgrave, prin. Fax 497-7217
Laurel ES 400/K-5
516 Montgomery St 20707 301-497-3660
Melinda Lee, prin. Fax 497-3657
Montpelier ES 700/K-6
9200 Muirkirk Rd 20708 301-497-3670
Carla Furlow, prin. Fax 497-5431
Oaklands ES 500/K-6
13710 Laurel Bowie Rd 20708 301-497-3110
Audrey Briscoe, prin. Fax 497-3114
Scotchtown Hills ES 600/PK-6
15950 Dorset Rd 20707 301-497-3994
Tracie Prevost, prin. Fax 498-6421

Augsburg Academy 50/PK-8
13800 Old Gunpowder Rd 20707 240-786-0283
Rev. Arthur Hebbeler, hdmstr.
Brown Montessori S 100/PK-3
9450 Madison Ave 20723 301-498-0604
Ellen Komesarook, admin.
Faith Baptist Christian S 200/PK-8
12700 Claxton Dr 20708 301-497-4490
Esther Marsh, prin. Fax 776-3277
First Baptist S of Laurel 300/PK-8
15002 First Baptist Ln 20707 301-490-1076
Francie Wallace, admin. Fax 725-3414
Pallotti Early Learning Center 100/PK-K
113 Saint Marys Pl 20707 301-776-6471
Mia Laughlin, dir. Fax 776-2694
St. Mary of the Mills S 500/K-8
106 Saint Marys Pl 20707 301-498-1433
James Pavlacka, prin. Fax 498-1170

La Vale, Allegany, Pop. 4,694
Allegany County SD
Supt. — See Cumberland
Parkside ES 300/PK-5
50 Parkside Blvd, 301-729-0085
Patti Stevenson, prin. Fax 729-0176

Leonardtown, Saint Mary's, Pop. 2,075
St. Mary's County SD 16,400/PK-12
PO Box 641 20650 301-475-5511
Dr. Michael Martirano, supt. Fax 475-4262
www.smcps.org/
Leonardtown ES 500/PK-5
22885 Duke St 20650 301-475-0250
Denise Eichel, prin. Fax 475-0254
Leonardtown MS 1,100/6-8
24015 Point Lookout Rd 20650 301-475-0230
Lisa Bachner, prin. Fax 475-0237
Other Schools – See Chaptico, Great Mills, Helen, Hollywood, Lexington Park, Loveville, Mechanicsville, Park Hall, Ridge, Tall Timbers

Father Andrew White S 300/PK-8
PO Box 1756 20650 301-475-9795
Linda Maloney, prin. Fax 475-3537

Lexington Park, Saint Mary's, Pop. 9,943
St. Mary's County SD
Supt. — See Leonardtown
Carver ES 400/PK-5
46155 Carver School Blvd 20653 301-863-4076
Annette Wood, prin. Fax 862-1217
Esperanza MS 900/6-8
22790 Maple Rd 20653 301-863-4016
Jill Snyder-Mills, prin. Fax 863-4020
Green Holly ES 600/PK-5
46060 Millstone Landing Rd 20653 301-863-4064
Paul Fancella, prin. Fax 863-4072
Lexington Park ES 400/PK-5
46763 S Shangri La Dr 20653 301-863-4085
Susie Fowler, prin. Fax 863-4089
Spring Ridge MS 800/6-8
19856 Three Notch Rd 20653 301-863-4031
Maureen Montgomery, prin. Fax 863-4035
Town Creek ES 300/K-5
45805 Dent Dr 20653 301-863-4044
Kathryn Miluski, prin. Fax 863-4048

Libertytown, Frederick
Frederick County SD
Supt. — See Frederick
Liberty ES 400/PK-5
11820 Liberty Rd 21762 240-236-1800
Gerald DeGrange, prin. Fax 236-1801

Linthicum Heights, Anne Arundel, Pop. 2,980
Anne Arundel County SD
Supt. — See Annapolis
Lindale MS, 415 Andover Rd 21090 900/6-8
George Lindley, prin. 410-691-4344
Linthicum ES, 101 School Ln 21090 400/K-5
Frances Nussle, prin. 410-222-6935
Overlook ES 200/K-5
401 Hampton Rd 21090 410-222-6585
Kristie Battista, prin. Fax 636-0548

Friendship Adventist S 50/K-8
901 Andover Rd 21090 410-859-9909
Mary Brown, lead tchr. Fax 859-0866
St. Philip Neri S 400/K-8
6401 S Orchard Rd 21090 410-859-1212
Shirley Wise, prin. Fax 859-5480

Lonaconing, Allegany, Pop. 1,164
Allegany County SD
Supt. — See Cumberland
Georges Creek ES 400/PK-5
15600 Lwr Georges Crk Rd SW 21539 301-463-6202
Daniel Clark, prin. Fax 463-3124
Westmar MS 300/6-8
16915 Lower Georges Creek 21539 301-463-5751
Toby Eirich, prin. Fax 359-8049

Lothian, Anne Arundel
Anne Arundel County SD
Supt. — See Annapolis
Lothian ES 500/PK-5
5175 Solomons Island Rd 20711 410-222-1697
Melissa Brown, prin. Fax 222-1699
Southern MS 800/6-8
5235 Solomons Island Rd 20711 410-222-1659
Jason Dykstra, prin. Fax 867-0231

Arundel Bay Christian Academy 200/PK-8
968C Lower Pindell Rd 20711 301-952-0123
Terry Zink, admin. Fax 952-0073

Loveville, Saint Mary's
St. Mary's County SD
Supt. — See Leonardtown
Banneker ES 700/PK-5
27180 Point Lookout Rd 20656 301-475-0260
Debra Bowling, prin. Fax 475-0262

Lusby, Calvert
Calvert County SD
Supt. — See Prince Frederick
Appeal IS 400/3-5
11655 H G Trueman Rd 20657 410-535-7800
Bernadette Stephenson, prin. Fax 326-6996
Dowell ES 700/PK-5
12680 H G Trueman Rd 20657 410-535-7802
Jennifer Young, prin. Fax 535-7803
Mill Creek MS 600/6-8
12200 Margaret Taylor Rd 20657 410-535-7824
Darrel Prioleau, prin. Fax 257-7829
Patuxent ES 400/PK-2
35 Appeal Ln 20657 410-535-7830
Dennis Vogel, prin. Fax 326-0828
Southern MS 700/6-8
9615 H G Trueman Rd 20657 410-535-7877
Sylvia Lawson, prin. Fax 535-7879

Lutherville, Baltimore, Pop. 16,442
Baltimore County SD
Supt. — See Towson
Hampton ES 400/PK-5
1115 Charmuth Rd 21093 410-887-3205
Patricia Kaiser, prin. Fax 887-3209
Lutherville Laboratory ES 500/PK-5
1700 York Rd 21093 410-887-7800
Steve Buettner, prin. Fax 887-7804
Ridgely MS 1,100/6-8
121 E Ridgely Rd 21093 410-887-7650
Susan Evans, prin. Fax 887-7834

Dayspring Christian Academy 100/PK-8
2122 W Joppa Rd 21093 410-821-5876
Judith Hengst, admin. Fax 821-7656
Montessori S 300/PK-8
10807 Tony Dr 21093 410-321-8555
Albert Swartz, hdmstr. Fax 321-8566
St. Paul's Lutheran K 100/PK-K
1609 Kurtz Ave 21093 410-252-3867

Manchester, Carroll, Pop. 3,557
Carroll County SD
Supt. — See Westminster
Ebb Valley ES PK-5
3100 Swiper Dr 21102 410-386-1550
Robert Mitchell, prin. Fax 386-1555
Manchester ES 600/K-5
3224 York St 21102 410-751-3410
Martin Tierney, prin. Fax 751-3439

Marbury, Charles, Pop. 1,244
Charles County SD
Supt. — See La Plata
Gale-Bailey ES 500/PK-5
4740 Pisgah Marbury Rd 20658 301-743-5491
Carolyn Richardson, prin. Fax 743-2119

Mardela Springs, Wicomico, Pop. 360
Wicomico County SD
Supt. — See Salisbury
Northwestern ES 300/PK-5
9975 Sharptown Rd 21837 410-677-5808
Kirby Bryson, prin. Fax 677-5850

Barren Creek Christian Academy 50/K-12
25845 Ocean Gtwy 21837 410-341-0023
Edwin Cade, admin.

Marriottsville, Howard
Howard County SD
Supt. — See Ellicott City
Mount View MS 700/6-8
12101 Woodford Dr 21104 410-313-5545
Kathy McKinley, prin. Fax 313-5551

Maugansville, Washington
Washington County SD
Supt. — See Hagerstown
Maugansville ES 300/K-5
18023 Maugans Ave 21767 301-766-8230
Archie VanNorden, prin. Fax 665-1086

Mechanicsville, Saint Mary's
St. Mary's County SD
Supt. — See Leonardtown
Dent ES 500/K-5
37840 New Market Turner Rd 20659 301-472-4500
Barbara Eddy, prin. Fax 472-4503
Mechanicsville ES 300/PK-5
28585 Three Notch Rd 20659 301-472-4800
Barbara Abell, prin. Fax 472-4809
Oakville ES 400/PK-5
26410 Three Notch Rd 20659 301-373-4365
Tenina Reeves, prin. Fax 373-4369
White Marsh ES 300/K-5
29090 Thompson Corner Rd 20659 301-472-4600
Luchrisha Flowers, prin. Fax 472-4604

Middle River, Baltimore, Pop. 24,616

Our Lady Of Mt. Carmel Children's Center PK-PK
10001 Bird River Rd 21220 410-687-8513
Lisa Shipley, prin. Fax 687-7338

Middletown, Frederick, Pop. 2,860
Frederick County SD
Supt. — See Frederick
Middletown ES 400/3-5
201 E Green St 21769 240-236-1100
Suzanne O'Toole, prin. Fax 236-1150
Middletown MS 900/6-8
100 High St 21769 240-236-4200
Donna Faith, prin. Fax 236-4250
Middletown PS PK-2
403 Franklin St 21769 240-566-0200
Mark Pritts, prin. Fax 566-0201

Millersville, Anne Arundel
Anne Arundel County SD
Supt. — See Annapolis
Millersville ES 400/K-5
1601 Millersville Rd 21108 410-222-3800
Tammy Brendle, prin. Fax 222-3802
Old Mill MS North 900/6-8
610 Patriot Ln 21108 410-969-5950
Sean McElhaney, prin.
Old Mill MS South 800/6-8
620 Patriot Ln 21108 410-969-7000
William Goodman, prin. Fax 969-5157
Shipley's Choice ES 400/K-5
310 Governor Stone Pkwy 21108 410-222-3851
Rocco Ferretti, prin. Fax 222-3885

Millington, Kent, Pop. 371
Kent County SD
Supt. — See Chestertown
Millington ES 200/PK-4
172 Sassafras St 21651 410-928-3141
Tracey Rodney, prin. Fax 928-5235

Mitchellville, Prince George's, Pop. 12,593
Prince George's County SD
Supt. — See Upper Marlboro
Just MS 1,000/7-8
1300 Campus Way N 20721 301-808-4040
Carlton Carter, prin. Fax 808-4050
Kingsford ES 700/K-6
1401 Enterprise Rd 20721 301-390-0260
Paulette Watkins, prin. Fax 390-0274
Lake Arbor ES 800/K-6
10205 Lake Arbor Way 20721 301-808-5940
Stephen Greene, prin. Fax 808-5960
Woodmore ES 600/K-6
12500 Woodmore Rd 20721 301-390-0239
Jill Walker, prin. Fax 390-0277

Mitchellville Montessori S 100/PK-4
12112 Central Ave 20721 301-249-9187
Gloria Panton-Harvey, prin. Fax 249-9742
Woodstream Christian Academy 400/PK-12
9800 Lottsford Rd 20721 301-883-8160
Marlyn Hinkle, admin. Fax 883-8169

Monkton, Baltimore
Baltimore County SD
Supt. — See Towson
Hereford MS 1,000/6-8
712 Corbett Rd 21111 410-887-7902
Cathryn Walrod, prin. Fax 887-7904

St. James Academy 400/K-8
3100 Monkton Rd 21111 410-771-4816
Elizabeth Legenhausen Ed.D., prin. Fax 771-4842

Monrovia, Frederick
Frederick County SD
Supt. — See Frederick
Green Valley ES — 500/K-5
11501 Fingerboard Rd 21770 — 240-236-3400
Leigh Warren, prin. — Fax 236-3401
Kemptown ES — 600/PK-5
3456 Kemptown Church Rd 21770 — 240-236-3500
Steve Parsons, prin. — Fax 236-3501

Montgomery Village, Montgomery, Pop. 38,051

Living Grace Christian S — 50/K-6
20300 Pleasant Ridge Dr 20886 — 301-840-9830
Daniel Switzer, prin. — Fax 840-8005

Mount Airy, Carroll, Pop. 8,375
Carroll County SD
Supt. — See Westminster
Mount Airy ES — 500/3-5
405 N Main St 21771 — 301-751-3540
Deborah Bunker, prin. — Fax 751-3543
Mount Airy MS — 600/6-8
102 Watersville Rd 21771 — 301-751-3554
Virginia Savell, prin. — Fax 751-3556
Parr's Ridge ES — 300/PK-2
202 Watersville Rd 21771 — 410-751-3559
Ann Blonkowski, prin. — Fax 549-7221

Frederick County SD
Supt. — See Frederick
Twin Ridge ES — 600/PK-5
1106 Leafy Hollow Cir 21771 — 240-236-2300
DeVeda Coley, prin. — Fax 236-2301

Mount Airy Christian Academy — 300/K-12
16700 Old Frederick Rd 21771 — 410-489-4321
Vicky Webster, admin. — Fax 489-4492

Mount Rainier, Prince George's, Pop. 8,751
Prince George's County SD
Supt. — See Upper Marlboro
Mount Rainier ES — 300/K-6
4011 32nd St 20712 — 301-985-1810
Janet Reed, prin. — Fax 985-1814
Stone ES — 700/PK-6
4500 34th St 20712 — 301-985-1890
Helen Smith, prin. — Fax 927-1153

Mount Savage, Allegany
Allegany County SD
Supt. — See Cumberland
Mount Savage S — 400/PK-12
13201 New School Rd NW 21545 — 301-264-3220
Gary Llewellyn, prin. — Fax 264-4015

Myersville, Frederick, Pop. 1,509
Frederick County SD
Supt. — See Frederick
Myersville ES — 500/K-5
Lushbaugh Way 21773 — 240-236-1900
Susan Kreiger, prin. — Fax 236-1901
Wolfsville ES — 200/PK-5
12520 Wolfsville Rd 21773 — 240-236-2250
Lynnea Richards, prin. — Fax 236-2251

Nanjemoy, Charles
Charles County SD
Supt. — See La Plata
Mt. Hope/Nanjemoy ES — 300/PK-5
9275 Ironsides Rd 20662 — 301-246-4383
Annie Blount, prin. — Fax 246-9453

Newark, Worcester
Worcester County SD — 6,700/PK-12
6270 Worcester Hwy 21841 — 410-632-5000
Jon Andes, supt. — Fax 632-0364
www.worcesterk12.com/
Other Schools – See Berlin, Ocean City, Pocomoke City, Snow Hill

Newburg, Charles
Charles County SD
Supt. — See La Plata
Higdon ES — 500/PK-5
12872 Rock Point Rd 20664 — 301-934-4091
Peggy Mertes, prin. — Fax 934-1718
Piccowaxen MS — 500/6-8
12834 Rock Point Rd 20664 — 301-934-1977
Kenneth Schroeck, prin. — Fax 934-1628

New Carrollton, Prince George's, Pop. 12,818
Prince George's County SD
Supt. — See Upper Marlboro
Carroll MS — 1,000/7-8
6130 Lamont Dr 20784 — 301-918-8640
Eric Wood, prin. — Fax 918-8646
Carrollton ES — 600/K-6
8300 Quintana St 20784 — 301-918-8708
John Enkiri, prin. — Fax 918-8710
Frost ES — 300/PK-6
6419 85th Ave 20784 — 301-918-8792
Dr. Renita Alexander-Spriggs, prin. — Fax 918-8566
Lamont ES — 500/K-6
7101 Good Luck Rd 20784 — 301-513-5205
Sharon Porter, prin. — Fax 513-5271

New Market, Frederick, Pop. 463
Frederick County SD
Supt. — See Frederick
Deer Crossing ES — 600/PK-5
10601 Finn Dr 21774 — 240-236-5900
Karen Hopson, prin. — Fax 236-5901
New Market ES — 500/PK-5
93 W Main St 21774 — 240-236-1300
Cindy Alvarado, prin. — Fax 236-1301
New Market MS — 800/6-8
125 W Main St 21774 — 240-236-4600
Gwendolyn Dorsey, prin. — Fax 236-4650

New Windsor, Carroll, Pop. 1,359
Carroll County SD
Supt. — See Westminster
New Windsor MS — 400/6-8
1000 Green Valley Rd 21776 — 410-751-3355
Donald Bell, prin. — Fax 751-3358

North East, Cecil, Pop. 2,817
Cecil County SD
Supt. — See Elkton
Bay View ES — 600/PK-5
910 N East Rd 21901 — 410-996-6230
Richard Edwards, prin. — Fax 996-6233
North East ES — 500/PK-5
301 E Thomas Ave 21901 — 410-996-6220
Georgia Clark, prin. — Fax 996-6302
North East MS — 800/6-8
200 E Cecil Ave 21901 — 410-996-6210
Al Volpe, prin. — Fax 996-6236

Tome S — 500/K-12
581 S Maryland Ave 21901 — 410-287-2050
Dr. F. Darcy Williams, hdmstr. — Fax 287-8999

North Potomac, Montgomery, Pop. 18,456
Montgomery County SD
Supt. — See Rockville
Stone Mill ES — 600/PK-5
14323 Stonebridge View Dr 20878 — 301-279-4975
Kimberly Williams, prin. — Fax 279-4979

Nottingham, Baltimore

Tabernacle Christian S — 100/PK-8
8855 Belair Rd 21236 — 410-256-2225
Glenn Hyatt, admin. — Fax 256-8566

Oakland, Garrett, Pop. 1,896
Garrett County SD — 4,600/PK-12
40 S 2nd St 21550 — 301-334-8900
Wendell Teets, supt. — Fax 334-7621
www.ga.k12.md.us/
Broad Ford ES — 400/K-5
607 Harvey Winters Dr 21550 — 301-334-9445
Suzanne Sincell, prin. — Fax 334-5774
Crellin ES — 100/PK-5
115 Kendall Dr 21550 — 301-334-4704
Dana McCauley, prin. — Fax 334-4704
Dennett Road ES — 300/PK-5
770 Dennett Rd 21550 — 301-334-3452
Gary Galloway, prin. — Fax 334-4936
Southern MS — 700/6-8
605 Harvey Winters Dr 21550 — 301-334-8881
Jane Wildesen, prin. — Fax 334-2315
Swan Meadow S — 100/1-8
6709 Garrett Hwy 21550 — 301-334-2059
Virginia Craig, prin. — Fax 334-6335
Yough Glades ES — 300/PK-5
70 Wolf Acres Dr 21550 — 301-334-3334
Keith Harvey, prin. — Fax 334-6992
Other Schools – See Accident, Bloomington, Friendsville, Frostburg, Grantsville, Kitzmiller

Mountaintop SDA S — K-8
16335 Garrett Hwy 21550 — 301-387-9532

Ocean City, Worcester, Pop. 7,049
Worcester County SD
Supt. — See Newark
Ocean City ES — 500/PK-4
12828 Center Dr 21842 — 410-632-5370
Irene Kordick, prin. — Fax 632-5379

Odenton, Anne Arundel, Pop. 12,833
Anne Arundel County SD
Supt. — See Annapolis
Arundel MS — 1,000/6-8
1179 Hammond Ln 21113 — 410-674-6900
Shawn Ashworth, prin. — Fax 674-6593
Odenton ES — 400/K-5
1290 Odenton Rd 21113 — 410-222-6514
Maurine Larkin, prin. — Fax 222-6516
Piney Orchard ES — 700/K-5
2641 Strawberry Lake Way 21113 — 410-672-7591
Karen Bailey, prin. — Fax 672-7173
Seven Oaks ES — 600/PK-5
1905 Town Center Dr 21113 — 410-222-0937
Lisa Leitholf, prin.
Waugh Chapel ES — 400/K-5
840 Sunflower Dr 21113 — 410-222-6542
Joyce Sims, prin. — Fax 222-6963

Olney, Montgomery, Pop. 23,019
Montgomery County SD
Supt. — See Rockville
Belmont ES — 400/K-5
19528 Olney Mill Rd 20832 — 301-924-3140
Peter Bray, prin. — Fax 924-3233
Brooke Grove ES — 400/K-5
2700 Spartan Rd 20832 — 301-924-3154
Gail West, prin. — Fax 924-3161
Farquhar MS — 700/6-8
16915 Batchellors Forest Rd 20832 — 301-924-3100
Scott Murphy, prin. — Fax 924-3152
Olney ES — 600/PK-5
3401 Queen Mary Dr 20832 — 301-924-3126
Dr. Joan O'Brien, prin. — Fax 570-1094
Parks MS — 1,000/6-8
19200 Olney Mill Rd 20832 — 301-924-3180
Sarah Pinkney-Murkey, prin. — Fax 924-3288

Olney Adventist Preparatory S — 100/K-8
4100 Olney Laytonsville Rd 20832 — 301-570-2500
Kimberlie Hogan, prin. — Fax 570-0400
St. John's Episcopal S — 300/K-8
3427 Olney Laytonsville Rd 20832 — 301-774-6804
John Zurn, hdmstr. — Fax 774-2375
St. Peter S — 400/K-8
2900 Olney Sandy Spring Rd 20832 — 301-774-9112
Carol Mikoni, prin. — Fax 924-6698
Washington Christian Academy — 300/K-12
16227 Batchellors Forest Rd 20832 — 301-390-0429
Larry Danner, hdmstr. — Fax 559-0115

Owings, Calvert
Calvert County SD
Supt. — See Prince Frederick
Mt. Harmony ES — 600/K-5
900 W Mount Harmony Rd 20736 — 410-257-1611
Elizabeth Gebelein, prin. — Fax 257-1628
Northern MS — 800/6-8
2954 Chaneyville Rd 20736 — 410-257-1622
Karen Burnett, prin. — Fax 257-1623
Windy Hill ES — 700/PK-5
9550 Boyds Turn Rd 20736 — 410-257-1539
Kelley Adams, prin. — Fax 257-1541
Windy Hill MS — 800/6-8
9560 Boyds Turn Rd 20736 — 410-257-1560
Nancy Miller, prin. — Fax 257-1556

Cardinal Hickey Academy — 200/K-8
1601 W Mount Harmony Rd 20736 — 410-286-0404
Sr. Mary Cox, prin. — Fax 286-6334

Owings Mills, Baltimore, Pop. 9,474
Baltimore County SD
Supt. — See Towson
Deer Park ES — 500/PK-5
9809 Lyons Mill Rd 21117 — 410-887-0723
Iris Steele, prin. — Fax 887-0724
New Town ES — 500/PK-5
4924 New Town Blvd 21117 — 410-887-1541
Beth Strauss, prin. — Fax 887-1544
Owings Mills ES — 600/PK-5
10824 Reisterstown Rd 21117 — 410-887-1710
Chet Scott, prin. — Fax 887-1712
Timber Grove ES — 600/PK-5
701 Academy Ave 21117 — 410-887-1714
Leslie Dunn, prin. — Fax 887-1566

Bais Yaakov Girls S — 500/PK-5
11111 Park Heights Ave 21117 — 410-363-3300
Christ the King Academy — 50/K-5
515 Academy Ave 21117 — 410-356-3488
Betty Dorsey, prin. — Fax 356-3400
Garrison Forest S — 600/PK-12
300 Garrison Forest Rd 21117 — 410-363-1500
G. Peter O'Neill, hdmstr. — Fax 363-8441
Jemicy S — 1-7
11 Celadon Rd 21117 — 410-653-2700
Ben Shifrin, hdmstr. — Fax 653-1972
Liberty Christian S — 300/K-8
11303 Liberty Rd 21117 — 410-655-5527
Steven Kennedy, prin. — Fax 655-0209
McDonogh S — 1,300/K-12
PO Box 380 21117 — 410-363-0600
Charles Britton, hdmstr. — Fax 581-4777
Ruxton Country S — 200/K-8
11202 Garrison Forest Rd 21117 — 443-544-3000
Stephen Barker, hdmstr. — Fax 544-3010
Yeshivas Kochav Yitzchak — 500/K-8
35 Rosewood Ln 21117 — 410-654-3500

Oxon Hill, Prince George's, Pop. 35,355
Prince George's County SD
Supt. — See Upper Marlboro
Barnaby Manor ES — 500/PK-6
2411 Owens Rd 20745 — 301-702-7560
Rhonda Gladden, prin. — Fax 702-7529
Flintstone ES — 400/PK-6
800 Comanche Dr 20745 — 301-749-4210
Sana Sims, prin. — Fax 749-4215
Forest Heights ES — 200/K-6
200 Talbert Dr 20745 — 301-749-4220
Theresa Merrifield, prin. — Fax 749-4224
Glassmanor ES — 200/K-6
1011 Marcy Ave 20745 — 301-749-4240
Diane Jones, prin. — Fax 749-4242
Hanson French Immersion S — K-8
6360 Oxon Hill Rd 20745 — 301-749-4780
Dr. Lysianne Essama, prin. — Fax 749-4054
Hanson Montessori S — 500/PK-8
6360 Oxon Hill Rd 20745 — 301-749-4052
Sherra Chappelle, prin. — Fax 749-4054
Owens Road ES — 200/K-6
1616 Owens Rd 20745 — 301-702-3860
Dr. Patricia Payne, prin. — Fax 702-3863
Oxon Hill ES — 400/K-6
7701 Livingston Rd 20745 — 301-749-4290
Cynthia Best-Goring, prin. — Fax 749-4295
Valley View ES — 500/PK-6
5500 Danby Ave 20745 — 301-749-4350
JoAnn Spruell, prin. — Fax 749-4354

St. Columba S — 300/K-8
7800 Livingston Rd 20745 — 301-567-6212
Tina Magnaye, prin. — Fax 567-6907

Park Hall, Saint Mary's
St. Mary's County SD
Supt. — See Leonardtown
Park Hall ES — 500/PK-5
20343 Hermanville Rd 20667 — 301-863-4054
Katherine Norton, prin. — Fax 863-4050

Parkton, Baltimore
Baltimore County SD
Supt. — See Towson
Seventh District ES — 400/K-5
20300 York Rd 21120 — 410-887-1902
Leslie Brooks, prin. — Fax 887-1903

Our Lady of Grace S — 200/K-8
18310 Middletown Rd 21120 — 410-329-6956
Byrdie Ricketts, prin. — Fax 357-5793

Pasadena, Anne Arundel, Pop. 10,012
Anne Arundel County SD
Supt. — See Annapolis
Bodkin ES — 500/K-5
8320 Ventnor Rd 21122 — 410-437-0464
Charles Jansky, prin. — Fax 437-0845
Chesapeake Bay MS — 1,400/6-8
4804 Mountain Rd 21122 — 410-437-2400
M. Jacques Smith, prin. — Fax 437-9920

Fort Smallwood ES 400/PK-5
1720 Poplar Ridge Rd 21122 410-222-6450
Ed Johnson, prin. Fax 222-6452
Fox MS 800/6-8
7922 Outing Ave 21122 410-437-5512
Kevin Dennehy, prin. Fax 360-1511
High Point ES 600/K-5
924 Duvall Hwy 21122 410-222-6454
Timothy Merritt, prin. Fax 222-6456
Jacobsville ES 500/K-5
3801 Mountain Rd 21122 410-222-6460
Sharon Herring, prin. Fax 222-6498
Lake Shore ES 300/K-5
4804 Mountain Rd 21122 410-222-6465
Donna Spencer, prin. Fax 222-6468
Pasadena ES 300/K-5
401 E Pasadena Rd 21122 410-222-6573
Janis Horn, prin. Fax 222-6576
Riviera Beach ES 300/K-5
8515 Jenkins Rd 21122 410-222-6469
Kathleen Panagopulos, prin.
Sunset ES 500/PK-5
8572 Fort Smallwood Rd 21122 410-222-6478
Antoinette Carr, prin. Fax 222-6482

Gibson Island Country S 100/PK-5
5191 Mountain Rd 21122 410-255-5370
Laura Kang, prin. Fax 255-0416
St. Jane Frances S 600/PK-8
8513 Saint Jane Dr 21122 410-255-4750
Michelle Jones, prin. Fax 360-6720

Perry Hall, Baltimore, Pop. 22,723
Baltimore County SD
Supt. — See Towson
Chapel Hill ES 600/PK-5
5200 E Joppa Rd 21128 410-887-5119
Jonna Hundley, prin. Fax 887-5119
Joppa View ES 600/PK-5
8727 Honeygo Blvd 21128 410-887-5065
Victoria Layman, prin. Fax 887-5066

Perry Hall Christian S 300/PK-12
3919 Schroeder Ave 21128 410-256-4886
Gary Heinke, admin. Fax 256-5451

Perryville, Cecil, Pop. 3,770
Cecil County SD
Supt. — See Elkton
Perryville ES 400/PK-5
901 Maywood Ave 21903 410-996-6020
Hinda Smith, prin. Fax 996-6024
Perryville MS 700/6-8
850 Aiken Ave 21903 410-996-6010
R. Joseph Buckley, prin. Fax 996-6048

Good Shepherd S 200/K-8
800 Aiken Ave 21903 410-642-6265
Scott Nicodemus, prin. Fax 642-6522
Susquehanna SDA S 50/1-8
36 Blythedale Rd 21903 410-378-4343

Phoenix, Baltimore, Pop. 500
Baltimore County SD
Supt. — See Towson
Jacksonville ES 500/PK-5
3400 Hillendale Heights Rd 21131 410-887-7880
Deborah Glinowiecki, prin. Fax 683-8919

Pikesville, Baltimore, Pop. 24,815
Baltimore County SD
Supt. — See Towson
Woodholme ES 500/K-5
300 Mount Wilson Ln 21208 410-887-6700
Maralee Clark, prin. Fax 887-6762

Pittsville, Wicomico, Pop. 1,188
Wicomico County SD
Supt. — See Salisbury
Pittsville S 500/PK-8
34404 Old Ocean City Rd 21850 410-677-5811
Michael Cody, prin. Fax 677-5895

Pocomoke City, Worcester, Pop. 3,909
Worcester County SD
Supt. — See Newark
Pocomoke ES 400/PK-3
2119 Pocomoke Beltway 21851 410-632-5130
Todd Hall, prin. Fax 632-5139
Pocomoke MS 400/4-8
800 8th St 21851 410-632-5150
Caroline Bloxom, prin. Fax 632-5159

Pomfret, Charles
Charles County SD
Supt. — See La Plata
Craik ES 500/PK-5
7725 Marshall Corner Rd 20675 301-934-4270
Penny Berg-Nye, prin. Fax 934-8096

Poolesville, Montgomery, Pop. 5,498
Montgomery County SD
Supt. — See Rockville
Poole MS 400/6-8
17014 Tom Fox Ave 20837 301-972-7979
Richard Bishop, prin. Fax 972-7982
Poolesville ES 400/PK-5
19565 Fisher Ave 20837 301-972-7960
Darlyne McEleney, prin. Fax 972-7963

Port Deposit, Cecil, Pop. 693
Cecil County SD
Supt. — See Elkton
Bainbridge ES 200/PK-5
41 Preston Dr 21904 410-996-6030
Pamela Thomey, prin. Fax 996-6033

Lighthouse Christian Academy 200/PK-12
7 Pleasant View Church Rd 21904 410-378-3279
Fax 658-3004

Port Republic, Calvert
Calvert County SD
Supt. — See Prince Frederick
Mutual ES 600/PK-5
1455 Ball Rd 20676 410-535-7700
Lisa Wisniewski, prin. Fax 535-7701

Potomac, Montgomery, Pop. 44,822
Montgomery County SD
Supt. — See Rockville
Cabin John MS 1,000/6-8
10701 Gainsborough Rd 20854 301-469-1150
Dr. Paulette Smith, prin. Fax 469-1003
Wayside ES 500/K-5
10011 Glen Rd 20854 301-279-8484
Yong-Mi Kim, prin. Fax 279-8486

Bullis S 600/3-12
10601 Falls Rd 20854 301-299-8500
Thomas Farquhar, hdmstr. Fax 299-9050
Fourth Presbyterian S 100/PK-8
10701 S Glen Rd 20854 301-765-8133
John Murray, hdmstr. Fax 765-0821
German S Washington DC 600/PK-12
8617 Chateau Dr 20854 301-365-4400
Klaus-Dieter Bloch, hdmstr. Fax 365-3905
Heights S 400/3-12
10400 Seven Locks Rd 20854 301-365-4300
Alvaro de Vicente, hdmstr. Fax 365-4303
Lone Oak Montessori S 200/PK-6
10201 Democracy Blvd 20854 301-656-8608
Patricia Swann, dir. Fax 469-0036
Manor Montessori S 300/PK-4
PO Box 60691 20859 301-299-7400
Kathy Damico, dir. Fax 299-7908
McLean S of Maryland 500/K-12
8224 Lochinver Ln 20854 301-299-8277
Darlene Pierro, hdmstr. Fax 299-1639
Muslim Community S 200/PK-12
7917 Montrose Rd 20854 301-340-6713
Dr. Mohammad Paryavi, hdmstr. Fax 340-7339
Our Lady of Mercy S 300/K-8
9222 Kentsdale Dr 20854 301-365-4477
Joan Hosmer, prin. Fax 365-3423
St. Andrews Lower S - Potomac Village 100/PK-5
10033 River Rd 20854 301-365-2642
Patricia Talbert Smith, hdmstr. Fax 299-0412
St. James Children's S 100/PK-K
11815 Seven Locks Rd 20854 301-762-3246
Fax 762-4076

Preston, Caroline, Pop. 582
Caroline County SD
Supt. — See Denton
Preston ES 400/PK-5
255 Main St 21655 410-673-2552
John Lischner, prin. Fax 673-7301

Prince Frederick, Calvert, Pop. 1,885
Calvert County SD 17,100/PK-12
1305 Dares Beach Rd 20678 410-535-1700
Jack Smith, supt. Fax 535-7476
www.calvertnet.k12.md.us
Barstow ES PK-5
295 J W Williams Rd 20678 443-486-4770
Donna House, prin. Fax 535-4069
Calvert ES 600/PK-5
1450 Dares Beach Rd 20678 410-535-7311
Laurie Haynie, prin. Fax 535-7473
Calvert MS 500/6-8
435 Solomons Island Rd N 20678 410-535-7355
Bruce Hutchinson, prin. Fax 535-7356
Other Schools – See Chesapeake Beach, Huntingtown, Lusby, Owings, Port Republic, Saint Leonard, Sunderland

---

Christian Beginnings Preschool 50/PK-PK
105 Vianney Ln 20678 410-535-0223
Marie Chrzanowski, dir. Fax 535-4442

Princess Anne, Somerset, Pop. 2,800
Somerset County SD
Supt. — See Westover
Greenwood ES 300/K-5
11412 Dryden Rd 21853 410-651-0931
Cheryl O'Neal, prin. Fax 651-4091
Princess Anne ES 400/PK-5
11576 Lankford Ave 21853 410-651-0481
Lynette Johnson, prin. Fax 651-4286

Pylesville, Harford
Harford County SD
Supt. — See Bel Air
North Harford ES 500/PK-5
120 Pylesville Rd 21132 410-638-3670
Frances M. Haslup, prin. Fax 638-3675
North Harford MS 1,100/6-8
112 Pylesville Rd 21132 410-638-3658
Karl Wickman, prin. Fax 638-3669

Quantico, Wicomico
Wicomico County SD
Supt. — See Salisbury
Westside PS 200/PK-1
6046 Quantico Rd 21856 410-677-5117
Glendon Jones, prin. Fax 677-5860

Randallstown, Baltimore, Pop. 30,870
Baltimore County SD
Supt. — See Towson
Church Lane ES Technology 500/K-5
3820 Fernside Rd 21133 410-887-0717
Judith Devlin, prin. Fax 496-0473
Deer Park Magnet MS 1,200/6-8
9830 Winands Rd 21133 410-887-0726
Penelope Martin, prin. Fax 887-0704
Hernwood ES 500/PK-5
9919 Marriottsville Rd 21133 410-887-0732
Dr. Cathy Gantz, prin. Fax 521-7679
Randallstown ES 400/PK-5
9013 Liberty Rd 21133 410-887-0746
Lois Stokes, prin. Fax 887-0747

Colonial Christian Academy 100/PK-5
9411 Liberty Rd 21133 410-521-7191
Courtney Lewis, prin. Fax 521-7193
Holy Family S 200/K-8
9535 Liberty Rd 21133 410-922-3677
Angela Rebbert, prin. Fax 521-9764

Reisterstown, Baltimore, Pop. 19,314
Baltimore County SD
Supt. — See Towson
Cedarmere ES 500/PK-5
17 Nicodemus Rd 21136 410-887-1100
Stephen Coco, prin. Fax 887-6920
Chatsworth ES 400/PK-5
222 New Ave 21136 410-887-1103
Nancy Casalena, prin. Fax 887-1109
Franklin ES 500/PK-5
33 Cockeys Mill Rd 21136 410-887-1111
Joyce Albert, prin. Fax 887-6947
Franklin MS 1,400/6-8
10 Cockeys Mill Rd 21136 410-887-1114
Lynn Wolf, prin. Fax 517-2548
Glyndon ES 500/PK-5
445 Glyndon Dr 21136 410-887-1130
Janice Lane, prin. Fax 887-1131
Reisterstown ES 500/K-5
223 Walgrove Rd 21136 410-887-1133
Barbara Shields, prin. Fax 887-6925

Ridge, Saint Mary's
St. Mary's County SD
Supt. — See Leonardtown
Ridge ES 300/PK-5
49430 Airedele Rd 20680 301-872-0200
Sandra Kerner, prin. Fax 872-0205

St. Michael S 100/PK-8
PO Box 259 20680 301-872-5454
Lila Hofmeister, prin. Fax 872-4047

Ridgely, Caroline, Pop. 1,354
Caroline County SD
Supt. — See Denton
Ridgely ES 500/PK-5
118 N Central Ave 21660 410-634-2105
Andrea Berry-Opher, prin. Fax 634-1789

Rising Sun, Cecil, Pop. 1,785
Cecil County SD
Supt. — See Elkton
Calvert ES 300/K-5
79 Brick Meeting House Rd 21911 410-658-5335
Anthony Petinga, prin. Fax 658-9130
Rising Sun ES 700/PK-5
500 Hopewell Rd 21911 410-658-5925
Carol Roberts, prin. Fax 658-7999
Rising Sun MS 700/6-8
289 Pearl St 21911 410-658-5535
Diana Rudolph, prin. Fax 658-9173

Riverdale, Prince George's, Pop. 5,120
Prince George's County SD
Supt. — See Upper Marlboro
Beacon Heights ES 400/K-6
6929 Furman Pkwy 20737 301-918-8700
Lynne Stuewe, prin. Fax 918-8707
Riverdale ES 500/K-6
5006 Riverdale Rd 20737 301-985-1850
Carol Cantu, prin. Fax 927-1166
Templeton ES 500/K-6
6001 Carters Ln 20737 301-985-1880
Marlowe Blount-Rich, prin. Fax 985-1876
Wirt MS 700/7-8
62nd Pl and Tuckerman St 20737 301-985-1720
Prentice Christian, prin. Fax 985-1440

Rock Hall, Kent, Pop. 2,566
Kent County SD
Supt. — See Chestertown
Rock Hall ES 200/PK-4
5608 Boundary Ave 21661 410-639-2265
Brenda Rose, prin. Fax 639-2997
Rock Hall MS 100/5-8
21203 W Sharp St 21661 410-639-2279
Gary McCulloch, prin. Fax 639-2998

Rockville, Montgomery, Pop. 57,402
Montgomery County SD 131,800/PK-12
850 Hungerford Dr 20850 301-279-3381
Jerry Weast Ed.D., supt. Fax 279-3205
www.montgomeryschoolsmd.org
Barnsley ES 600/K-5
14516 Nadine Dr 20853 301-460-2121
Kristin Alban, prin. Fax 460-2172
Beall ES 600/PK-5
451 Beall Ave 20850 301-279-8460
Troy Boddy, prin. Fax 279-4999
Beverly Farms ES 600/K-5
8501 Post Oak Rd 20854 301-469-1050
Dr. Beth Brown, prin. Fax 469-1058
Brookhaven ES 400/PK-5
4610 Renn St 20853 301-460-2140
Robert Grundy, prin. Fax 460-2460
Candlewood ES 300/K-5
7210 Osprey Dr 20855 301-840-7167
Dr. Linda Sheppard, prin. Fax 840-7171
Cashell ES 300/K-5
17101 Cashell Rd 20853 301-924-3130
Maureen Stamoulis, prin. Fax 924-3132
Cold Spring ES 400/K-5
9201 Falls Chapel Way 20854 301-279-8480
Martin Barnett, prin. Fax 279-3226
College Gardens ES 500/K-5
1700 Yale Pl 20850 301-279-8470
Dr. Albert Dupont, prin. Fax 279-8473
Fallsmead ES 500/K-5
1800 Greenplace Ter 20850 301-279-4984
R. Kevin Payne, prin. Fax 279-3040
Farmland ES 600/PK-5
7000 Old Gate Rd 20852 301-230-5919
Katherine Smith, prin. Fax 230-5424

Flower Valley ES 500/PK-5
4615 Sunflower Dr 20853 301-924-3135
Wilma Holmes, prin. Fax 924-6789
Frost MS 1,100/6-8
9201 Scott Dr 20850 301-279-3949
Dr. Joey Jones, prin. Fax 279-3956
Hoover MS 1,000/6-8
8810 Postoak Rd 20854 301-469-1010
Billie Jean Bensen, prin. Fax 469-1013
Key MS 800/6-8
6300 Tilden Ln 20852 301-770-8015
Eric Minus, prin. Fax 230-5441
Lakewood ES 600/K-5
2534 Lindley Ter 20850 301-279-8465
Robin Malcotti, prin. Fax 460-2113
Luxmanor ES 300/K-5
6201 Tilden Ln 20852 301-230-5914
Ryan Forkert, prin. Fax 230-5917
Maryvale ES 600/PK-5
1000 1st St 20850 301-279-4990
Kimberly Kimber, prin. Fax 279-4993
Meadow Hall ES 300/PK-5
951 Twinbrook Pkwy 20851 301-279-4988
Cabell Lloyd, prin. Fax 517-5887
Mill Creek Towne ES 500/PK-5
17700 Park Mill Dr 20855 301-840-7149
Kenneth Marcus, prin. Fax 460-2113
Parkland MS 700/6-8
4610 W Frankfort Dr 20853 301-438-5700
Dr. Benjamin OuYang, prin. Fax 460-2699
Potomac ES 500/K-5
10311 River Rd 20854 301-469-1042
Linda Goldberg, prin. Fax 469-1025
Redland MS 700/6-8
6505 Muncaster Mill Rd 20855 301-840-4680
Robert Sinclair, prin. Fax 840-4688
Ritchie Park ES 400/K-5
1514 Dunster Rd 20854 301-279-8475
Bonnie Dougherty, prin. Fax 517-5047
Rock Creek Valley ES 400/PK-5
5121 Russett Rd 20853 301-460-2195
Catherine Jasperse, prin. Fax 460-2128
Tilden MS 600/7-8
11211 Old Georgetown Rd 20852 301-230-5930
Jennifer Baker, prin. Fax 230-5991
Twinbrook ES 500/PK-5
5911 Ridgway Ave 20851 301-230-5925
Karen Johnson, prin. Fax 230-5929
West MS 1,000/6-8
651 Great Falls Rd 20850 301-279-3979
Nanette Poirier, prin. Fax 517-8216
Wheaton Woods ES 500/PK-5
4510 Faroe Pl 20853 301-929-2018
Dr. Judith Lewis, prin. Fax 929-6974
Wood MS 800/6-8
14615 Bauer Dr 20853 301-460-2150
Eugenia Dawson, prin. Fax 460-2159
Other Schools – See Bethesda, Brookeville, Burtonsville, Chevy Chase, Clarksburg, Damascus, Derwood, Dickerson, Gaithersburg, Germantown, Kensington, North Potomac, Olney, Poolesville, Potomac, Sandy Spring, Silver Spring, Takoma Park

---

Berman Hebrew Academy 700/PK-12
13300 Arctic Ave 20853 301-962-9400
Dr. Joshua Levisohn, hdmstr. Fax 962-3991
Christ Episcopal S 200/PK-8
109 S Washington St 20850 301-424-6550
Carol Shabe, hdmstr. Fax 424-3516
Franklin S 300/PK-K
10500 Darnestown Rd 20850 301-279-2799
Pamela Trumble, prin. Fax 762-4544
Green Acres S 300/PK-8
11701 Danville Dr 20852 301-881-4100
Neal Brown Ed.D., hdmstr. Fax 881-3319
Montrose Christian S 400/PK-12
5100 Randolph Rd 20852 301-770-5335
Sheree Pilgrim, hdmstr. Fax 871-7345
St. Elizabeth S 500/K-8
917 Montrose Rd 20852 301-881-1824
Vincent Spadoni, prin. Fax 881-6035
St. Jude Catholic S 400/PK-8
4820 Walbridge St 20853 301-946-7888
Mary Ellen Jordan, prin. Fax 929-8927
St. Mary S 300/PK-8
600 Veirs Mill Rd 20852 301-762-4179
Sr. Carol Rigali, prin. Fax 762-9550
St. Patrick S 100/K-8
4101 Norbeck Rd 20853 301-929-9672
Susan Milloy-Splendido, prin. Fax 929-1474
St. Raphael's S PK-3
1513 Dunster Rd 20854 301-762-2143
Teri Dwyer, prin. Fax 762-4991
Smith Jewish Day S 800/K-6
1901 E Jefferson St 20852 301-881-1400
Jonathan Cannon, hdmstr. Fax 984-7834

Sabillasville, Frederick
Frederick County SD
Supt. — See Frederick
Sabillasville ES 100/K-5
16210 Sabillasville Rd # B 21780 240-236-6000
Karen Locke, prin. Fax 236-6001

Saint Leonard, Calvert
Calvert County SD
Supt. — See Prince Frederick
Saint Leonard ES 700/PK-5
5370 Saint Leonard Rd 20685 410-535-7714
Toni Chapman, prin. Fax 535-7726

Saint Michaels, Talbot, Pop. 1,139
Talbot County SD
Supt. — See Easton
St. Michaels ES 300/PK-6
100 Seymour Ave 21663 410-745-2882
James Redman, prin. Fax 745-2473

Salisbury, Wicomico, Pop. 26,295
Wicomico County SD 13,700/PK-12
PO Box 1538 21802 410-677-4400
Dr. John Fredericksen, supt. Fax 677-4444
www.wcboe.org
Beaver Run ES 400/PK-2
31481 Old Ocean City Rd 21804 410-677-5101
William Curtis, prin. Fax 677-3477
Bennett MS 900/6-8
200 E College Ave 21804 410-677-5140
C. Michael Johnson, prin. Fax 677-5133
Chipman ES 300/PK-2
711 Lake St 21801 410-677-5814
Deborah Emge, prin. Fax 677-5882
Early Learning Center PK-PK
1101 Robert St 21804 410-344-6051
Melissa Eiler, coord. Fax 334-6061
East Salisbury ES 400/3-5
1201 Old Ocean City Rd 21804 410-677-5803
Lillie Giddens, prin. Fax 677-5872
Glen Avenue ES 300/3-5
1615 Glen Avenue Ext 21804 410-677-5806
Michael Collins, prin. Fax 677-5840
North Salisbury ES 500/3-5
1213 Emerson Ave 21801 410-677-5807
Janet Veditz, prin. Fax 677-5835
Pemberton ES 600/PK-5
1300 Pemberton Dr 21801 410-677-5809
Scott Thorpe, prin. Fax 677-5848
Pinehurst ES 400/PK-5
520 S Pinehurst Ave 21801 410-677-5810
Curtis Twilley, prin. Fax 677-5858
Prince Street ES 400/PK-5
400 Prince St 21804 410-677-5813
Wauchilue Jackson-Snyder, prin. Fax 677-5865
Salisbury MS 900/6-8
607 Morris St 21801 410-677-5149
Amy Eskridge, prin. Fax 677-5122
West Salisbury ES 300/PK-2
1321 West Rd 21801 410-677-5816
Melva Wright, prin. Fax 677-5870
Wicomico MS 700/6-8
635 E Main St 21804 410-677-5145
Jon Shearer, prin. Fax 677-5197
Other Schools – See Delmar, Fruitland, Hebron, Mardela Springs, Pittsville, Quantico, Willards

---

St. Francis de Sales S 300/K-8
500 Camden Ave 21801 410-749-9907
Mark Record, prin. Fax 749-9507
Salisbury Christian S 600/PK-12
807 Parker Rd 21804 410-546-0661
Rev. James Fox, hdmstr. Fax 546-4674
Salisbury S 400/PK-12
6279 Hobbs Rd 21804 410-742-4464
Dr. Fred Neill, hdmstr. Fax 546-2310

Sandy Spring, Montgomery, Pop. 3,092
Montgomery County SD
Supt. — See Rockville
Sherwood ES 500/K-5
1401 Olney Sandy Spring Rd 20860 301-924-3195
Jerrold Perlot, prin. Fax 924-3294

Sandy Spring Friends S 600/PK-12
16923 Norwood Rd 20860 301-774-7455
Ken Smith, hdmstr. Fax 924-1115

Savage, Howard, Pop. 9,669

Bethel Christian Academy 300/PK-8
PO Box 406 20763 301-725-4673
Alice Green, prin. Fax 617-9277

Secretary, Dorchester, Pop. 501
Dorchester County SD
Supt. — See Cambridge
Warwick ES 300/PK-5
PO Box 549 21664 410-943-8151
Susan Price, prin. Fax 943-8152

Severn, Anne Arundel, Pop. 24,499
Anne Arundel County SD
Supt. — See Annapolis
Quarterfield ES 400/PK-5
7967 Quarterfield Rd 21144 410-222-6430
Jennifer Green, prin. Fax 222-6432
Ridgeway ES 600/K-5
1440 Evergreen Rd 21144 410-222-6524
Vickie Wardell, prin.
Severn ES 400/K-5
838 Reece Rd 21144 410-551-6220
Veronica Williams, prin. Fax 551-6223
Van Bokkelen ES 400/PK-5
1140 Reece Rd 21144 410-222-6535
Leonard Massie, prin.

Calvary Chapel Christian Academy 100/K-12
8064 New Cut Rd 21144 410-969-5101
Barbara Fridy, prin. Fax 969-7729

Severna Park, Anne Arundel, Pop. 28,507
Anne Arundel County SD
Supt. — See Annapolis
Benfield ES, 365 Lynwood Dr 21146 500/K-5
Teresa Sacchetti, prin. 410-222-6555
Jones ES, 122 Hoyle Ln 21146 300/K-5
Kathleen Fitzgerald, prin. 410-222-6565
McKinsey ES 600/K-5
175 Arundel Beach Rd 21146 410-222-6560
Donna Ruhsam, prin. Fax 544-3249
Oak Hill ES 400/PK-5
34 Truck House Rd 21146 410-222-6568
Deneen Houghton, prin. Fax 222-6570
Severna Park ES 300/K-5
6 Riggs Ave 21146 410-222-6577
Janice Tourre, prin. Fax 222-6522
Severna Park MS 1,400/6-8
450 Jumpers Hole Rd 21146 410-647-7900
Sharon Morell, prin. Fax 431-5376

St. John the Evangelist S 500/K-8
669 Ritchie Hwy 21146 410-647-2283
Sr. Linda Larsen, prin. Fax 431-5438
St. Martin's In The Field Day S 300/PK-8
375A Benfield Rd 21146 410-647-7055
Sharon Holsclaw, hdmstr. Fax 647-7411

Shady Side, Anne Arundel, Pop. 4,107
Anne Arundel County SD
Supt. — See Annapolis
Shady Side ES 400/K-5
4859 Atwell Rd 20764 410-222-1621
Deborah Short, prin. Fax 867-4941

Sharpsburg, Washington, Pop. 674
Washington County SD
Supt. — See Hagerstown
Sharpsburg ES 300/K-5
17525 Shepherdstown Pike 21782 301-766-8321
Carl Stark, prin. Fax 432-8974

Silver Spring, Montgomery, Pop. 76,540
Montgomery County SD
Supt. — See Rockville
Arcola ES K-5
1820 Franwall Ave 20902 301-649-8590
Eric Wilson, prin. Fax 649-8592
Argyle MS 700/6-8
2400 Bel Pre Rd 20906 301-460-2400
Dr. Debra Mugge, prin. Fax 460-2423
Bel Pre ES 300/PK-2
13801 Rippling Brook Dr 20906 301-460-2145
Carmen van Zutphen, prin. Fax 460-2148
Briggs-Chaney MS 900/6-8
1901 Rainbow Dr 20905 301-989-6000
Kimberly Johnson, prin. Fax 989-6020
Broad Acres ES 500/PK-5
710 Beacon Rd 20903 301-431-7616
Michael Bayewitz, prin. Fax 431-7691
Burnt Mills ES 300/PK-5
11211 Childs St 20901 301-649-8192
Lisa Thomas, prin. Fax 649-8097
Cannon Road ES 400/K-5
901 Cannon Rd 20904 301-989-5662
Dr. Judith Theiss, prin. Fax 989-5692
Cloverly ES 500/K-5
800 Briggs Chaney Rd 20905 301-989-5770
Melissa Brunson, prin. Fax 879-1035
Cresthaven ES 300/K-5
1234 Cresthaven Dr 20903 301-431-7622
Kafi Berry, prin. Fax 431-7651
Drew ES 500/PK-5
1200 Swingingdale Dr 20905 301-989-6030
Gail Scott-Parizer, prin. Fax 879-1033
Eastern MS 800/6-8
300 University Blvd E 20901 301-650-6650
Charlotte Boucher, prin. Fax 650-6657
East Silver Spring ES 200/PK-3
631 Silver Spring Ave 20910 301-650-6420
Adrienne Morrow, prin. Fax 650-6424
Fairland ES 500/K-5
14315 Fairdale Rd 20905 301-989-5658
Tillie Garfinkel, prin. Fax 989-5769
Forest Knolls ES 500/K-5
10830 Eastwood Ave 20901 301-649-8060
Donald Masline, prin. Fax 649-8196
Galway ES 700/PK-5
12612 Galway Dr 20904 301-595-2930
Shahid Muhammad, prin. Fax 902-1221
Georgian Forest ES 400/PK-5
3100 Regina Dr 20906 301-460-2170
Aara Davis, prin. Fax 460-2477
Glenallan ES 400/K-5
12520 Heurich Rd 20902 301-929-2014
Ronnie Fields, prin. Fax 929-2016
Glen Haven ES 600/PK-5
10900 Inwood Ave 20902 301-649-8051
Dr. Joanne Smith, prin. Fax 649-8540
Greencastle ES 600/PK-5
13611 Robey Rd 20904 301-595-2940
Andrew Winter, prin. Fax 902-1222
Harmony Hills ES 500/PK-5
13407 Lydia St 20906 301-929-2157
Robin Weaver, prin. Fax 962-5976
Highland ES 600/PK-5
3100 Medway St 20902 301-929-2040
Raymond Myrtle, prin. Fax 929-2042
Highland View ES 300/PK-5
9010 Providence Ave 20901 301-650-6426
Anne Dardarian, prin. Fax 650-6506
Jackson Road ES 500/PK-5
900 Jackson Rd 20904 301-989-5650
Sally Ann Macias, prin. Fax 879-1054
Kemp Mill ES 600/PK-5
411 Sisson St 20902 301-649-8046
Floyd Starnes, prin. Fax 649-8216
Lee MS 500/6-8
11800 Monticello Ave 20902 301-649-8100
Joseph Rubens, prin. Fax 649-8110
Loiederman MS 800/6-8
12701 Goodhill Rd 20906 301-929-2282
Alison Serino, prin. Fax 962-5993
Montgomery Knolls ES 400/PK-2
807 Daleview Dr 20901 301-431-7667
Deann Collins, prin. Fax 431-7669
New Hampshire Estates ES 400/PK-3
8720 Carroll Ave 20903 301-431-7607
Jane Litchko, prin. Fax 431-7644
Nix ES PK-5
1100 Corliss St 20903 301-422-5070
Annette Ffolkes, prin. Fax 422-5072
Oakland Terrace ES 600/K-5
2720 Plyers Mill Rd 20902 301-929-2161
Cheryl Pulliam, prin. Fax 929-6910
Oak View IS 200/4-6
400 E Wayne Ave 20901 301-650-6434
Peggy Salazar, prin. Fax 650-6527
Page ES 400/PK-5
13400 Tamarack Rd 20904 301-989-5672
Debra Berner, prin. Fax 879-1036

Pine Crest ES 300/PK-5
201 Woodmoor Dr 20901 301-649-8066
Meredith Casper, prin. Fax 649-8194
Rosemary Hills ES 400/PK-2
2111 Porter Rd 20910 301-650-6400
Ralph Viggiano, prin. Fax 650-6404
Shriver ES PK-5
12518 Greenly St 20906 301-929-4426
Janet Dunn, prin. Fax 929-4428
Silver Spring International MS 700/6-8
313 Wayne Ave 20910 301-650-6544
Victoria Parcan, prin. Fax 649-8005
Sligo Creek ES 600/K-5
500 Schuyler Rd 20910 301-562-2722
Diantha Swift, prin. Fax 562-2717
Sligo MS 600/6-8
1401 Dennis Ave 20902 301-649-8121
Richard Rhodes, prin. Fax 649-8145
Stonegate ES 400/PK-5
14811 Notley Rd 20905 301-989-5668
Audra Fladung, prin. Fax 989-5671
Strathmore ES 400/3-5
3200 Beaverwood Ln 20906 301-460-2135
Robert Dodd, prin. Fax 460-2137
Takoma Park MS 900/6-8
7611 Piney Branch Rd 20910 301-650-6444
Renay Johnson, prin. Fax 230-5924
Viers Mill ES 500/PK-5
11711 Joseph Mill Rd 20906 301-929-2165
Matthew Devan, prin. Fax 929-6977
Weller Road ES 500/PK-5
3301 Weller Rd 20906 301-929-2010
Michaele Manaigo, prin. Fax 929-2284
Westover ES 300/K-5
401 Hawkesbury Ln 20904 301-989-5676
Dr. Patricia Kelly, prin. Fax 989-5679
White Oak MS 800/6-8
12201 New Hampshire Ave 20904 301-989-5780
Virginia de los Santos, prin. Fax 989-5696
Woodlin ES 500/K-5
2101 Luzerne Ave 20910 301-650-6440
Sarah Sirgo, prin. Fax 650-6425

Barrie S 400/PK-12
13500 Layhill Rd 20906 301-576-2800
Tim Trautman, hdmstr. Fax 576-2803
Calvary Lutheran S 100/K-8
9545 Georgia Ave 20910 301-589-4001
Michael Gall, prin. Fax 589-4012
Faith Arts Academy 100/PK-6
13618 Layhill Rd 20906 301-438-2012
Dominique Harris, admin. Fax 977-2411
Forcey Christian S 400/PK-8
2130 E Randolph Rd 20904 301-622-2281
Zeke Wharton, admin. Fax 622-0204
Grace Episcopal Day S 100/PK-K
9115 Georgia Ave 20910 301-585-3513
Carol Franek, hdmstr. Fax 585-5240
Hebrew Day S 100/K-6
1840 University Blvd W 20902 301-649-5400
Rabbi David Serkin, prin. Fax 649-9599
St. Andrew Apostle S 400/PK-8
11602 Kemp Mill Rd 20902 301-649-3555
Kathleen Kilty, prin. Fax 649-2352
St. Bernadette S 500/K-8
80 University Blvd E 20901 301-593-5611
Cheryl Wood, prin. Fax 593-9042
St. Camillus S 300/PK-8
1500 Saint Camillus Dr 20903 301-434-2344
Tobias Harkleroad, prin. Fax 434-7726
St. John the Baptist S 300/K-8
12319 New Hampshire Ave 20904 301-622-3076
Marianne Moore, prin. Fax 622-2453
St. John the Evangelist S 200/PK-8
10201 Woodland Dr 20902 301-681-7656
Sr. Kathleen Lannak, prin. Fax 681-0745
St. Michael the Archangel S 200/K-8
824 Wayne Ave 20910 301-585-6873
Dawn Clemens, prin. Fax 587-1142
Spencerville Adventist Academy 300/K-12
15930 Good Hope Rd 20905 301-421-9101
Brian Kittleson, prin. Fax 421-0007
Thornton Friends S 50/6-8
10309 New Hampshire Ave 20903 301-622-9033
Norman Maynard, hdmstr. Fax 622-4786
Torah S of Greater Washington 200/K-6
2010 Linden Ln 20910 301-962-8003
Rabbi Yitzchak Charner, hdmstr. Fax 962-9755

Smithsburg, Washington, Pop. 2,859
Washington County SD
Supt. — See Hagerstown
Smithsburg ES 400/K-5
67 N Main St 21783 301-766-8329
Jessica Scarberry-Price, prin. Fax 824-4462
Smithsburg MS 700/6-8
68 N Main St 21783 301-766-8353
Michael Kuhaneck, prin. Fax 824-5147

Snow Hill, Worcester, Pop. 2,323
Worcester County SD
Supt. — See Newark
Snow Hill ES 400/PK-3
515 Coulbourne Ln 21863 410-632-5210
Denise Shorts, prin. Fax 632-5219
Snow Hill MS 400/4-8
522 Coulbourne Ln 21863 410-632-5240
Janet Simpson, prin. Fax 632-5249

Solomons, Calvert

Our Lady Star of the Sea S 200/K-8
PO Box 560 20688 410-326-3171
Sr. Rosella Summe, prin. Fax 326-9478

Sparks, Baltimore
Baltimore County SD
Supt. — See Towson
Sparks ES 500/K-5
601 Belfast Rd 21152 410-887-7900
Sharon Kearney, prin. Fax 472-3190

Springdale, Prince George's
Prince George's County SD
Supt. — See Upper Marlboro
Ardmore ES 500/K-6
9301 Ardwick Ardmore Rd 20774 301-925-1311
Georgette Gregory, prin. Fax 925-1318

Stevensville, Queen Anne's, Pop. 1,862
Queen Anne's County SD
Supt. — See Centreville
Bayside ES 400/2-5
301 Church St 21666 410-643-6181
Carol Kamp, prin. Fax 643-6685
Kent Island ES 200/PK-1
110 Elementary Way 21666 410-643-2392
David Dulac, prin. Fax 643-9354
Matapeake ES 500/PK-5
651 Romancoke Rd 21666 410-643-3105
Lawrence Dunn, prin. Fax 643-3711
Matapeake MS 6-8
671 Romancoke Rd 21666 410-643-7330
Leigh Veditz, prin. Fax 643-7445
Stevensville MS 800/6-8
610 Main St 21666 410-643-3194
Sean Kenna, prin. Fax 643-3046

Street, Harford
Harford County SD
Supt. — See Bel Air
Dublin ES 300/PK-5
1527 Whiteford Rd 21154 410-638-3703
Michael Steeg, prin. Fax 638-3707

Harford Friends S 50/1-8
PO Box 200 21154 410-452-5507
Jonathan Huxtable, prin. Fax 452-5537

Sudlersville, Queen Anne's, Pop. 394
Queen Anne's County SD
Supt. — See Centreville
Sudlersville ES 400/PK-5
300 S Church St 21668 410-438-3164
Dr. Lloyd Taylor, prin. Fax 438-3551
Sudlersville MS 300/6-8
201 N Church St 21668 410-438-3151
Kevin Kintop, prin. Fax 438-3489

Eastern Shore Junior Academy 50/PK-10
407 Dudley Corners Rd 21668 410-505-4074
Fax 438-3778

Suitland, Prince George's, Pop. 33,515
Prince George's County SD
Supt. — See Upper Marlboro
Beanes ES 500/PK-6
5108 Dianna Dr 20746 301-817-0533
Peter Miller, prin. Fax 817-0982
Drew-Freeman MS 900/7-8
2600 Brooks Dr 20746 301-817-0900
Charles Wilson, prin. Fax 817-0915
Foulois ES 300/K-6
4601 Beauford Rd 20746 301-817-0300
Dr. Veonca Richardson, prin. Fax 817-0941
Morningside ES 200/K-6
6900 Ames St 20746 301-817-0544
Ezekial Bloyce, prin. Fax 817-0956
Princeton ES 300/K-6
6101 Baxter Dr 20746 301-702-7650
Cynthia Rodgers, prin. Fax 702-7658
Skyline ES 200/K-6
6311 Randolph Rd 20746 301-817-0535
Mark Dennison, prin. Fax 817-0953
Suitland ES 600/PK-6
4650 Homer Ave 20746 301-817-3770
Andre Walker, prin. Fax 817-3791

Renaissance Christian Academy 200/PK-8
2101 Shadyside Ave 20746 301-568-8171
Dr. Karen Scott, prin. Fax 516-7742

Sunderland, Calvert
Calvert County SD
Supt. — See Prince Frederick
Sunderland ES 500/K-5
150 Clyde Jones Rd 20689 410-257-1501
Karen Vogel, prin. Fax 257-7569

Sykesville, Carroll, Pop. 4,440
Carroll County SD
Supt. — See Westminster
Carrolltowne ES 500/PK-5
6542 Ridge Rd 21784 410-751-3530
Theresa Ball, prin. Fax 751-3534
Eldersburg ES 500/K-5
1021 Johnsville Rd 21784 410-751-3520
Michael Eisenklam, prin. Fax 751-3553
Freedom District ES 600/K-5
5626 Sykesville Rd 21784 410-751-3525
Richard Huss, prin. Fax 751-3598
Linton Springs ES 500/PK-5
375 Ronsdale Rd 21784 410-751-3280
Vicki Winner, prin. Fax 751-3285
Mechanicsville ES 600/K-5
3838 Sykesville Rd 21784 410-751-3510
Nicholas Shockney, prin. Fax 751-3516
Oklahoma Road MS 900/6-8
6300 Oklahoma Rd 21784 410-751-3600
Catherine Hood, prin. Fax 751-3604
Piney Ridge ES 500/K-5
6315 Freedom Ave 21784 410-751-3535
Karen Covino, prin. Fax 751-3537
Sykesville MS 900/6-8
7301 Springfield Ave 21784 410-751-3545
Thomas Eckenrode, prin. Fax 751-3573

Takoma Park, Montgomery, Pop. 18,540
Montgomery County SD
Supt. — See Rockville
Piney Branch ES 300/4-6
7510 Maple Ave 20912 301-891-8000
Bertram Generlette, prin. Fax 891-8011

Rolling Terrace ES 600/PK-5
705 Bayfield St 20912 301-431-7600
Jennifer Connors, prin. Fax 431-7643
Takoma Park ES 300/PK-3
7511 Holly Ave 20912 301-650-6414
Zadia Gadsden, prin. Fax 650-6526

Prince George's County SD
Supt. — See Upper Marlboro
Carole Highlands ES 600/PK-6
1610 Hannon St 20912 301-431-5660
Lita Kelly, prin. Fax 431-5670

Andrews S 200/PK-8
117 Elm Ave 20912 301-270-1400
David Waller, prin. Fax 270-1403
Sligo Adventist S 200/PK-8
8300 Carroll Ave 20912 301-434-1417
Larry Rich, prin. Fax 434-4680

Tall Timbers, Saint Mary's
St. Mary's County SD
Supt. — See Leonardtown
Piney Point ES 600/PK-5
44550 Tall Timbers Rd 20690 301-994-2205
Kathy Woodford, prin. Fax 994-2207

Taneytown, Carroll, Pop. 5,453
Carroll County SD
Supt. — See Westminster
Northwest MS 600/6-8
99 Kings Dr 21787 410-751-3270
Amy Gromada, prin. Fax 751-3275
Taneytown ES 500/PK-5
100 Kings Dr 21787 410-751-3260
Rose Mattavi, prin. Fax 751-3532

Temple Hills, Prince George's, Pop. 6,865
Prince George's County SD
Supt. — See Upper Marlboro
Allenwood ES 500/K-6
6300 Harley Ln 20748 301-702-3930
Kaye Stumb, prin. Fax 702-7598
Chase ES 300/K-6
5700 Fisher Rd 20748 301-702-7660
Marie Jackson, prin. Fax 702-7631
Hillcrest Heights ES 400/K-6
4305 22nd Pl 20748 301-702-3800
Phyllis Hayes, prin. Fax 702-3807
Marshall MS 800/7-8
4909 Brinkley Rd 20748 301-702-7540
Kristil Fossett, prin. Fax 702-7555
Middleton Valley ES 300/K-6
4815 Dalton St 20748 301-702-3820
Lynne Todd, prin. Fax 702-7572
Overlook ES 300/PK-5
3298 Curtis Dr 20748 301-702-3831
Patricia Lowery, prin. Fax 702-3839
Panorama ES 500/K-5
2002 Callaway St 20748 301-702-3870
Patricia Roache, prin. Fax 702-7600
Shugart MS 600/6-8
2000 Callaway St 20748 301-702-3950
Michael Robinson, prin. Fax 702-3957
Stoddert MS 800/6-8
2501 Olson St 20748 301-702-7500
Mark Bickerstaff, prin. Fax 702-7515

Holy Family S 200/PK-8
2200 Callaway St 20748 301-894-2323
Mary Hawkins, prin. Fax 894-7100

Thurmont, Frederick, Pop. 6,036
Frederick County SD
Supt. — See Frederick
Lewistown ES 200/K-5
11119 Hessong Bridge Rd 21788 240-236-3750
Amy Schwiegerath, prin. Fax 236-3751
Thurmont ES 400/3-5
805 E Main St 21788 240-236-0900
Kate Krietz, prin. Fax 236-0901
Thurmont MS 700/6-8
408 E Main St 21788 240-236-5100
Barbara Keiling, prin. Fax 236-5101
Thurmont PS 300/PK-2
7989 Rocky Ridge Rd 21788 240-236-2800
Debra Myers, prin. Fax 236-2801

Tilghman, Talbot
Talbot County SD
Supt. — See Easton
Tilghman ES 100/K-5
21374 Foster Ave 21671 410-886-2391
Joyce Crow, prin. Fax 886-2149

Timonium, See Lutherville
Baltimore County SD
Supt. — See Towson
Pinewood ES 500/PK-5
200 Rickswood Rd 21093 410-887-7663
Kathryn Arnold, prin. Fax 252-1962
Pot Spring ES 500/K-5
2410 Spring Lake Dr 21093 410-887-7648
Jane Martin, prin. Fax 887-7649
Timonium ES 400/PK-5
2001 Eastridge Rd 21093 410-887-7661
Donna Scaccio, prin. Fax 887-7662

Towson, Baltimore, Pop. 51,793
Baltimore County SD 103,800/PK-12
6901 N Charles St 21204 410-887-4554
Dr. Joe Hairston, supt. Fax 887-4309
www.bcps.org
Pleasant Plains ES 500/PK-6
8300 Pleasant Plains Rd 21286 410-887-3549
Maureen Partilla, prin. Fax 887-8088
Riderwood ES 500/PK-5
1711 Landrake Rd 21204 410-887-3568
Kathy DeHart, prin. Fax 887-4667

Other Schools – See Baldwin, Baltimore, Catonsville, Cockeysville, Essex, Freeland, Halethorpe, Kingsville, Lutherville, Monkton, Owings Mills, Parkton, Perry Hall, Phoenix, Pikesville, Randallstown, Reisterstown, Sparks, Timonium, Upperco, White Marsh

---

Ascension Lutheran K 200/PK-K
7601 York Rd 21204 410-825-1725
Immaculate Conception S 500/PK-8
112 Ware Ave 21204 410-427-4801
Madeline Meaney, prin. Fax 427-4895
Immaculate Heart of Mary S 500/PK-8
8501 Loch Raven Blvd 21286 410-668-8466
Amy Belz, prin. Fax 668-6171

Tracys Landing, Anne Arundel
Anne Arundel County SD
Supt. — See Annapolis
Traceys ES 300/K-5
20 Deale Rd 20779 410-222-1633
Theresa Zablonski, prin. Fax 867-3709

Trappe, Talbot, Pop. 1,137
Talbot County SD
Supt. — See Easton
White Marsh ES 200/PK-5
4322 Lovers Ln 21673 410-476-3144
Marcia Sprankle, prin. Fax 476-5187

Union Bridge, Carroll, Pop. 1,085
Carroll County SD
Supt. — See Westminster
Wolfe ES 400/PK-5
119 N Main St 21791 410-751-3307
Robin Townsend, prin. Fax 751-3309

Upperco, Baltimore
Baltimore County SD
Supt. — See Towson
Fifth District ES 300/PK-5
3725 Mount Carmel Rd 21155 410-887-1726
Carole Quental, prin. Fax 374-5625

Upper Marlboro, Prince George's, Pop. 683
Prince George's County SD 122,800/PK-12
14201 School Ln 20772 301-952-6000
John Deasy Ph.D., supt. Fax 952-1383
www.pgcps.org
Arrowhead ES 400/K-6
2300 Sansbury Rd 20774 301-499-7071
Douglas Anthony, prin. Fax 499-7074
Kettering ES 400/PK-5
11000 Layton St 20774 301-808-5977
Janie Talbert, prin. Fax 808-5973
Kettering MS 700/7-8
65 Herrington Dr 20774 301-808-4060
Maurice Wright, prin. Fax 808-5920
Madison MS 1,000/7-8
7300 Woodyard Rd 20772 301-599-2422
Kyle Bacon, prin. Fax 599-2562
Marlton ES 500/K-6
8506 Old Colony Dr S 20772 301-952-7780
Carol Pica, prin. Fax 952-7718
Mattaponi ES 500/K-6
11701 Duley Station Rd 20772 301-599-2442
Dr. Janice Hay, prin. Fax 599-2449
Melwood ES 700/K-6
7100 Woodyard Rd 20772 301-599-2500
Carrington Smith, prin. Fax 599-2507
Patuxent ES 600/K-6
4410 Bishopmill Dr 20772 301-952-7700
Judy Dent, prin. Fax 952-7723
Perrywood ES 700/K-6
501 Watkins Park Dr 20774 301-218-3040
Carolyn Poole, prin. Fax 218-3050
Rosaryville ES 700/K-6
9925 Rosaryville Rd 20772 301-599-2490
Rhonda Green, prin. Fax 599-2494
Williams ES 500/K-6
9601 Prince Pl 20774 301-499-3373
Dr. Kenneth Newby, prin. Fax 808-4487
Other Schools – See Accokeek, Adelphi, Beltsville, Berwyn Heights, Bladensburg, Bowie, Brandywine, Capitol Heights, Cheverly, Clinton, College Park, District Heights, Forestville, Fort Washington, Glenarden, Glenn Dale, Greenbelt, Hyattsville, Landover, Landover Hills, Lanham Seabrook, Laurel, Mitchellville, Mount Rainier, New Carrollton, Oxon Hill, Riverdale, Springdale, Suitland, Takoma Park, Temple Hills

---

Capitol Christian Academy 200/PK-12
610 Largo Rd 20774 301-336-2200
Tom O'Connor, admin. Fax 336-6704
Clinton Christian S 600/PK-12
6707 Woodyard Rd 20772 301-599-9600
Travis Crutchfield, admin. Fax 599-9603
Concordia Lutheran S 100/PK-K
10201 Old Indian Head Rd 20772 301-372-6763
Beverly Wiggins, dir. Fax 372-1954
Excellence Christian S 200/PK-10
9010 Frank Tippett Rd 20772 301-868-1873
Joseph Crisp, prin. Fax 868-1877
Henson Valley Montessori S 300/PK-8
13400 Edgemeade Rd 20772 301-449-4442
Sherri Jones, hdmstr. Fax 449-6695
Kingdom Christian Academy 50/PK-8
529 Commerce Dr 20774 301-218-7656
Valerie Royster, prin. Fax 390-8410
Riverdale Baptist S 800/PK-12
1133 Largo Rd 20774 301-249-7000
Terry Zink, admin. Fax 249-3425
St. Mary of the Assumption S 300/K-8
4610 Largo Rd 20772 301-627-4170
Steven Showalter, prin. Fax 627-6383

Vienna, Dorchester, Pop. 301
Dorchester County SD
Supt. — See Cambridge
Vienna ES 200/PK-5
4905 Ocean Gateway Rt 731 21869 410-376-3151
Linda Wilson, prin. Fax 376-3623

Waldorf, Charles, Pop. 15,058
Charles County SD
Supt. — See La Plata
Barnhart ES 600/PK-5
4800 Lancaster Cir 20603 301-645-9053
Kimberly Hairston, prin. Fax 645-8970
Berry ES 700/PK-5
10155 Berry Rd 20603 301-638-2330
Darryll Evans, prin. Fax 638-3659
Brown ES 500/PK-5
421 University Dr 20602 301-645-1330
Marvin Jones, prin. Fax 374-9489
Daniel of St. Thomas Jenifer ES 600/PK-5
2820 Jenifer School Ln 20603 301-932-9603
Thadine Wright, prin. Fax 374-9496
David MS 6-8
2495 Davis Rd 20603 301-638-0858
Wendell Martin, prin. Fax 638-3562
Diggs ES PK-5
2615 Davis Rd 20603 301-638-7202
Sandra McDuffie, prin. Fax 638-7214
Hanson MS 900/6-8
12350 Vivian Adams Dr 20601 301-645-4520
Deborah Hile, prin. Fax 870-1182
Malcolm ES 600/PK-5
14760 Poplar Hill Rd 20601 301-645-2691
Wilhelmina Pugh, prin. Fax 638-0054
Mattawoman MS 900/6-8
10145 Berry Rd 20603 301-645-7708
William Wise Ed.D., prin. Fax 638-0043
Middleton ES 400/PK-5
1109 Copley Ave 20602 301-645-3338
Gregory Miller, prin. Fax 645-0931
Mudd ES 400/PK-5
820 Stone Ave 20602 301-645-3686
Robert Opiekun, prin. Fax 374-9581
Neal ES PK-5
12105 Saint Georges Dr 20602 301-638-2617
Carol Leveillee, prin. Fax 638-4054
Ryon ES 600/PK-5
12140 Vivian Adams Dr 20601 301-645-3090
Virginia McGraw, prin. Fax 374-9583
Stoddert MS 800/6-8
2040 Saint Thomas Dr 20602 301-645-1334
Sue DelaCruz, prin. Fax 870-1183
Turner ES 500/PK-5
1000 Bannister Cir 20602 301-645-4828
Kathleen Morgan, prin. Fax 374-9587
Wade ES 800/K-5
2300 Smallwood Dr W 20603 301-932-4304
Amy DiSabatino, prin. Fax 645-8793

Grace Brethren Christian S 500/PK-12
13000 Zekiah Dr 20601 301-645-0406
Lloyd Chadwick, dir. Fax 645-7463
Our Lady's Little Christians Preschool PK-PK
100 Village St 20602 301-645-7112
Neida Billard, dir. Fax 645-3635
St. Peters S 300/PK-8
3310 Saint Peters Dr 20601 301-843-1955
Judith DeLucco, prin. Fax 843-6371

Walkersville, Frederick, Pop. 5,593
Frederick County SD
Supt. — See Frederick
Glade ES 600/PK-5
9525 Glade Rd 21793 240-236-2100
Karen Miller, prin. Fax 236-2101
Walkersville ES 500/PK-5
83 W Frederick St 21793 240-236-1000
Stephanie Brown, prin. Fax 236-1050
Walkersville MS 900/6-8
55 W Frederick St 21793 240-236-4400
Valda Valbrun, prin. Fax 236-4401

Westernport, Allegany, Pop. 2,020
Allegany County SD
Supt. — See Cumberland
Westernport ES 300/PK-5
172 Church St 21562 301-359-0511
Gary Stein, prin. Fax 359-0411

West Friendship, Howard
Howard County SD
Supt. — See Ellicott City
West Friendship ES 300/K-5
12500 State Route 144 21794 410-313-5512
Corita Oduyoye, prin. Fax 313-5514

Westminster, Carroll, Pop. 17,761
Carroll County SD 27,800/PK-12
125 N Court St 21157 410-751-3000
Dr. Charles Ecker, supt. Fax 751-3031
www.carrollk12.org/
Carroll ES 300/K-5
3719 Littlestown Pike 21158 410-751-3211
Patricia Heacock, prin. Fax 751-3934
Cranberry Station ES 500/PK-5
505 N Center St 21157 410-386-4440
Judith Walker, prin. Fax 386-4444
Friendship Valley ES 400/K-5
1100 Gist Rd 21157 410-751-3650
Patricia Dorsey, prin. Fax 751-3655
Moton ES 500/PK-5
1413 Washington Rd 21157 410-751-3610
Pamela Meyers, prin. Fax 751-3927
Runnymede ES 500/PK-5
3000 Langdon Dr 21158 410-751-3203
Tammy Richards, prin. Fax 751-3930
Westminster East MS 700/6-8
121 Longwell Ave 21157 410-751-3656
Mary Swack, prin. Fax 751-3660
Westminster ES 600/K-5
811 Uniontown Rd 21158 410-751-3222
Tracy Belski, prin. Fax 751-3926
Westminster West MS 1,100/6-8
60 Monroe St 21157 410-751-3661
Thomas Hill, prin. Fax 751-3667
Winchester ES 500/PK-5
70 Monroe St 21157 410-751-3230
Joseph Dorsey, prin. Fax 751-3929
Winfield ES 700/PK-5
4401 Salem Bottom Rd 21157 410-751-3242
Cynthia Bell, prin. Fax 751-3243
Other Schools – See Finksburg, Hampstead, Manchester, Mount Airy, New Windsor, Sykesville, Taneytown, Union Bridge

---

Carroll Christian S 300/PK-12
550 Baltimore Blvd 21157 410-876-3838
Michael Cole, admin. Fax 876-7766
Carroll Lutheran S 100/K-8
1738 Old Taneytown Rd 21158 410-848-1050
Bronson Jones, prin. Fax 848-0614
Crest Lane SDA S 50/K-8
328 Crest Ln 21157 410-840-4240
Nancy Thomas, admin.
Faith Christian S 100/PK-12
30 N Cranberry Rd 21157 410-848-8875
Sandra Smith, prin. Fax 848-9051
Montessori S of Westminster 200/PK-9
1055 Montessori Dr 21158 410-848-6283
Nancy Title, dir. Fax 848-3217
St. John S 200/K-8
45 Monroe St 21157 410-876-7228
Patricia Brink, prin. Fax 848-2822

Westover, Somerset
Somerset County SD 2,600/PK-12
7982A Tawes Campus Dr 21871 410-651-1616
Dr. Karen-Lee Brofee, supt. Fax 651-2931
www.somerset.k12.md.us
Somerset 6-7 IS 400/6-7
7970 Tawes Campus Dr 21871 410-621-0160
Lisa Hopkins, prin. Fax 621-0166
Other Schools – See Crisfield, Deal Island, Ewell, Princess Anne

---

Holly Grove Christian S 500/PK-12
7317 Mennonite Church Rd 21871 410-957-0222
Michael Rohrer, prin. Fax 957-4250

Wheaton, Montgomery

Evergreen S 100/PK-6
10700 Georgia Ave 20902 301-942-5979
Marcia Jacques, prin. Fax 946-0311
St. Catherine LaBoure S 300/PK-8
11811 Claridge Rd 20902 301-946-1717
Beverly Consilvio, prin. Fax 946-9572

White Hall, Harford
Harford County SD
Supt. — See Bel Air
Norrisville ES 200/K-5
5302 Norrisville Rd 21161 410-692-7810
Duane Wallace, prin. Fax 692-7812

White Marsh, Baltimore, Pop. 8,183
Baltimore County SD
Supt. — See Towson
Vincent Farm ES K-5
6019 Ebenezer Rd 21162 410-887-2983
Anne Gold, prin. Fax 335-4054

White Plains, Charles, Pop. 3,560

Southern Maryland Christian Academy 300/PK-12
PO Box 1668 20695 301-870-2550
Colleen Gaines, prin. Fax 934-2855

Willards, Wicomico, Pop. 959
Wicomico County SD
Supt. — See Salisbury
Willards ES 300/PK-2
36161 Richland Rd 21874 410-677-5819
Regina Rando, prin. Fax 677-5830

Williamsport, Washington, Pop. 2,135
Washington County SD
Supt. — See Hagerstown
Hickory ES 300/PK-5
11101 Hickory School Rd 21795 301-766-8198
Amy Norris, prin. Fax 582-5799
Springfield MS 800/6-8
334 Sunset Ave 21795 301-766-8389
Jennifer Ruppenthal, prin. Fax 766-8401
Williamsport ES 500/K-5
1 S Clifton Dr 21795 301-766-8415
Jana Palmer, prin. Fax 223-4142

Gateway Christian Academy 100/PK-12
PO Box 590 21795 301-582-4595
Renee Wyand, prin. Fax 223-5972

Woodbine, Howard
Howard County SD
Supt. — See Ellicott City
Lisbon ES 500/K-5
15901 Frederick Rd 21797 410-313-5506
Jayne Diggs, prin. Fax 313-5508

Woodsboro, Frederick, Pop. 912
Frederick County SD
Supt. — See Frederick
Woodsboro ES 200/PK-2
101 Liberty Rd 21798 240-236-3700
Bonna Loverock, prin. Fax 236-3701

Worton, Kent
Kent County SD
Supt. — See Chestertown
Worton ES 200/PK-4
11085 Worton Rd 21678 410-778-2164
Ken Hudock, prin. Fax 778-3803

MASSACHUSETTS

MASSACHUSETTS DEPARTMENT OF EDUCATION

75 Pleasant St, Malden 02148-4906
Telephone 781-388-3000
Fax 781-388-3770
Website http://www.doe.mass.edu

Commissioner of Education Mitchell Chester

MASSACHUSETTS BOARD OF EDUCATION

75 Pleasant St, Malden 02148-4906

Chairperson Maura Banta

PUBLIC, PRIVATE AND CATHOLIC ELEMENTARY SCHOOLS

Abington, Plymouth, Pop. 13,817

Abington SD 2,200/PK-12
1 Ralph Hamlin Ln 02351 781-982-2150
Peter Schafer, supt. Fax 982-2157
www.abington.k12.ma.us

Abington ECC 400/PK-2
1 Ralph Hamlin Ln 02351 781-982-2185
Ann Harper, prin. Fax 982-2157

Center ES 200/3-6
65 Thaxter Ave 02351 781-982-2195
Marilyn Weber, prin. Fax 982-0053

Frolio JHS 400/7-8
1071 Washington St 02351 781-982-2170
Jeffrey Knight, prin. Fax 982-2173

North ES 200/3-6
171 Adams St 02351 781-982-2190
Matthew MacCurtain, prin. Fax 982-0054

Woodsdale ES 400/3-6
128 Chestnut St 02351 781-982-2180
Amy Scolaro, prin. Fax 982-2180

St. Bridget S 300/PK-8
455 Plymouth St 02351 781-878-8482
Joseph Cirigliano, prin. Fax 878-6566

Acton, Middlesex

Acton SD 2,500/K-6
16 Charter Rd 01720 978-264-4700
Stephen Mills, supt. Fax 264-3340
ab.mec.edu

Conant ES 500/K-6
80 Taylor Rd 01720 978-266-2550
Christine Price, prin. Fax 266-2509

Douglas ES 500/K-6
21 Elm St 01720 978-266-2560
Christopher Whitbeck, prin. Fax 266-2500

Gates ES 500/K-6
75 Spruce St 01720 978-266-2570
Lynne Newman, prin. Fax 263-2573

McCarthy-Towne ES 500/K-6
11 Charter Rd 01720 978-264-4700
David Krane, prin. Fax 264-4098

Merriam ES 600/K-6
11 Charter Rd 01720 978-264-4700
Ed Kaufman, prin. Fax 264-3356

Acton-Boxborough Regional SD 2,900/7-12
16 Charter Rd 01720 978-264-4700
William Ryan, supt. Fax 263-8409
ab.mec.edu

Grey JHS 1,000/7-8
16 Charter Rd 01720 978-264-4700
Craig Hardimon, prin. Fax 266-2535

Acushnet, Bristol, Pop. 3,170

Acushnet SD 1,000/PK-8
708 Middle Rd 02743 508-998-0260
Stephen Donovan, supt. Fax 998-0262
www.acushnetschools.us

Acushnet ES 500/PK-4
800 Middle Rd 02743 508-998-0255
Jennifer Cummings, prin. Fax 998-0259

Ford MS 500/5-8
708 Middle Rd 02743 508-998-0265
Timothy Plante, prin. Fax 998-7316

St. Francis Xavier S 200/PK-8
223 Main St 02743 508-995-4313
Donald Pelletier, prin. Fax 995-0456

Adams, Berkshire, Pop. 6,356

Adams-Cheshire Regional SD
Supt. — See Cheshire

Adams Memorial MS 300/6-8
30 Columbia St 01220 413-743-0554
Kimberly Roberts-Morandi, prin. Fax 743-8424

Plunkett ES 500/K-5
14 Commercial St 01220 413-743-0876
Kristen Gordon, prin. Fax 743-8406

St. Stanislaus Kostka S 100/PK-8
108 Summer St 01220 413-743-1091
Sr. Jaqueline Kazanowski, prin.

Agawam, Hampden, Pop. 28,599

Agawam SD
Supt. — See Feeding Hills

Agawam MS 700/5-6
68 Main St 01001 413-789-1400
Marc Costanzi, prin. Fax 789-7337

Clark ES 400/K-4
65 Oxford St 01001 413-821-0576
Sandra Howard, prin. Fax 821-0594

Phelps ES 400/K-4
689 Main St 01001 413-821-0587
Teresa Urbinati, prin. Fax 786-0497

Robinson Park ES 400/K-4
65 Begley St 01001 413-821-0584
Cynthia Palazzi, prin. Fax 786-9793

Allston, See Boston

Boston SD
Supt. — See Boston

Gardner Pilot Academy 300/PK-5
30 Athol St 02134 617-635-8365
Erica Herman, prin. Fax 635-7812

Jackson/Mann S 600/K-8
40 Armington St 02134 617-635-8532
Joanne Russell, prin. Fax 635-8543

Amesbury, Essex, Pop. 12,109

Amesbury SD 2,300/PK-12
10 Congress St 01913 978-388-0507
Charles Chaurette, supt. Fax 388-8315
www.ci.amesbury.ma.us

Amesbury ES 400/PK-4
20 S Hampton Rd 01913 978-388-3659
Walter Helliesen, prin. Fax 388-4961

Amesbury MS 800/5-8
220 Main St 01913 978-388-0515
Michael Curry, prin. Fax 388-1626

Cashman ES 400/PK-4
193 Lions Mouth Rd 01913 978-388-4407
Peter Hoyt, prin. Fax 388-4479

Amherst, Hampshire, Pop. 17,824

Amherst SD 1,400/K-6
170 Chestnut St 01002 413-362-1810
Helen Vivian, supt. Fax 549-9811
www.arps.org/

Crocker Farm ES 300/K-6
280 West St 01002 413-362-1600
Michael Morris, prin. Fax 256-0835

Fort River ES 500/K-6
70 S East St 01002 413-253-9731
Raymond Sharick, prin. Fax 256-5941

Marks Meadow Laboratory S 200/K-6
813 N Pleasant St 01002 413-362-1305
Nicholas Yaffe, prin. Fax 549-0473

Wildwood ES 400/K-6
71 Strong St 01002 413-549-6300
Matthew Behnke, prin. Fax 549-9519

Amherst-Pelham SD 1,900/7-12
170 Chestnut St 01002 413-362-1810
Helen Vivian, supt. Fax 549-9811
www.arps.org/

Amherst Regional MS 600/7-8
170 Chestnut St 01002 413-362-1850
Glenda Cresto, prin. Fax 549-9812

Pelham SD 100/K-6
170 Chestnut St 01002 413-362-1810
Helen Vivian, supt. Fax 549-9811
www.arps.org
Other Schools – See Pelham

Amherst Montessori S 100/PK-5
27 Pomeroy Ln 01002 413-253-3101
Tamara Balis, prin. Fax 253-1620

Common S 100/PK-6
PO Box 2248 01004 413-256-8989
Robert Lichtenstein, dir. Fax 253-1671

Andover, Essex, Pop. 8,242

Andover SD 6,000/PK-12
36 Bartlet St 01810 978-623-8501
Claudia Bach Ed.D., supt. Fax 623-8505
www.aps1.net

Andover West MS 500/6-8
98 Shawsheen Rd 01810 978-623-8700
Steve Murray, prin. Fax 623-8720

Bancroft ES 500/K-5
15 Bancroft Rd 01810 978-623-8880
Francine Goldstein, prin. Fax 623-8888

Doherty MS 600/6-8
50 Bartlet St 01810 978-623-8750
Theresa McGuinness, prin. Fax 623-8770

High Plain ES 500/K-5
333 High Plain Rd 01810 978-623-8900
Pamela Lathrop, prin. Fax 623-8904

Sanborn ES 400/K-5
90 Lovejoy Rd 01810 978-623-8860
Patricia Barrett, prin. Fax 623-8866

Shawsheen ES 200/PK-2
18 Magnolia Ave 01810 978-623-8850
Moira O'Brien, prin. Fax 623-8851

South ES 600/K-5
55 Woburn St 01810 978-623-8830
Colleen McBride, prin. Fax 623-8840

West ES 600/K-5
58 Beacon St 01810 978-623-8800
Liz Roos, prin. Fax 623-8802

Wood Hill MS 400/6-8
11 Cross St 01810 978-623-8925
Patrick Bucco, prin. Fax 623-8929

Andover S of Montessori 200/PK-8
400 S Main St 01810 978-475-2299
Peg Roberts, hdmstr. Fax 475-1290

Kadima Community Day S 50/PK-2
41 Central St 01810 978-475-5510
Michael Jacobson, prin. Fax 475-5077

Pike S 400/PK-9
34 Sunset Rock Rd 01810 978-475-1197
John Waters, hdmstr. Fax 475-3014

St. Augustine S 400/PK-8
26 Central St 01810 978-475-2414
Ann Kendall, prin. Fax 470-1327

Aquinnah, Dukes

Up-Island Regional SD
Supt. — See Vineyard Haven

Chilmark ES 100/PK-5
8 State Rd 02535 508-645-2562
Diane Gandy, prin. Fax 645-2460

Arlington, Middlesex, Pop. 42,000

Arlington SD 4,500/K-12
869 Massachusetts Ave 02476 781-316-3502
Kathleen Bodie, supt. Fax 316-3509
www.arlington.k12.ma.us

Bishop ES 400/K-5
25 Columbia Rd 02474 781-316-3792
Stephen Carme, prin. Fax 316-3747

Brackett ES 400/K-5
66 Eastern Ave 02476 781-316-3702
Stephanie Zerchykov, prin. Fax 316-3710

Dallin ES 300/K-5
185 Florence Ave 02476 781-316-3721
Wallis Raemer, prin. Fax 316-3727

Hardy ES 300/K-5
52 Lake St 02474 781-316-3781
Deborah D'Amico, prin. Fax 316-3717

Ottoson MS 1,000/6-8
63 Acton St 02476 781-316-3744
Timothy Ruggere, prin. Fax 641-5436

Peirce ES 200/K-5
85 Blossom St 02474 781-316-3736
Robert Penta, prin. Fax 316-3728

Stratton ES 300/K-5
180 Mountain Ave 02474 781-316-3754
Alan Brown, prin. Fax 641-5454

Thompson ES 300/K-5
60 N Union St 02474 781-316-3768
Sheryl Donovan, prin. Fax 641-6471

Covenant S 50/K-8
9 Westminster Ave 02474 781-643-5511
Brian Emmet, hdmstr. Fax 643-4588
Ellis S, 41 Foster St 02474 200/PK-5
Deanne Benson, hdmstr. 781-641-5987
St. Agnes S 400/PK-8
39 Medford St 02474 781-643-9031
Helen Blinstrub, prin. Fax 643-2834

Ashburnham, Worcester
Ashburnham-Westminster Regional SD 2,500/PK-12
11 Oakmont Dr 01430 978-827-1434
Mr. Michael Zapantis, supt. Fax 827-5969
www.awrsd.org
Briggs ES 500/PK-5
96 Williams Rd 01430 978-827-5750
Candace Wright, prin. Fax 827-1411
Overlook MS 600/6-8
10 Oakmont Dr 01430 978-827-1425
Philip Saisa, prin. Fax 827-1423
Other Schools – See Westminster

Ashby, Middlesex
North Middlesex SD
Supt. — See Townsend
Ashby ES 300/PK-5
911 Main St 01431 978-386-7266
Anne Cromwell-Gapp, prin. Fax 386-0973

Ashfield, Franklin
Mohawk Trail SD
Supt. — See Shelburne Falls
Sanderson Academy 100/K-6
808 Cape St 01330 413-628-4404
B. Litchfield, prin. Fax 628-4697

Ashland, Middlesex, Pop. 12,066
Ashland SD 2,700/PK-12
87 W Union St 01721 508-881-0150
Dr. Richard Hoffmann, supt. Fax 881-0161
www.ashland.k12.ma.us
Ashland MS 600/6-8
87 W Union St 01721 508-881-0167
Kevin Carney, prin. Fax 881-0169
Mindess S 600/3-5
90 Concord St 01721 508-881-0166
Arlene Argir, prin. Fax 881-0153
Pittaway S 300/K-K
75 Central St 01721 508-881-0199
Beverly Kirton, prin. Fax 881-0193
Warren ES 400/PK-PK, 1-
73 Fruit St 01721 508-881-0188
Jane Mason, prin. Fax 881-0191

MetroWest Christian Academy 100/PK-5
PO Box 229 01721 508-881-7404
Charlie Legassey, prin. Fax 881-3020

Athol, Worcester, Pop. 8,732
Athol-Royalston SD 1,800/PK-12
PO Box 968 01331 978-249-2400
Anthony Polito, supt. Fax 249-2402
www.athol-royalstonschools.org
Athol-Royalston MS 500/5-8
1062 Pleasant St 01331 978-249-2430
John Doty, prin. Fax 249-0055
Pleasant Street ES 300/PK-5
1060 Pleasant St 01331 978-249-2405
Erica Brouillet, prin. Fax 249-7212
Riverbend ES 200/K-5
174 Riverbend St 01331 978-249-2415
Bobbie French, prin. Fax 249-2428
Sanders Street ES 100/K-3
314 Sanders St 01331 978-249-2410
Elizabeth Ervin, prin. Fax 249-7213
Other Schools – See Royalston

Attleboro, Bristol, Pop. 43,382
Attleboro SD 5,900/PK-12
100 Rathbun Willard Dr 02703 508-222-0012
Pia Durkin Ph.D., supt. Fax 223-1577
www.attleboroschools.com
Brennan MS 600/5-8
320 Rathbun Willard Dr 02703 508-222-6260
Karen Saltzman, prin. Fax 223-1555
Coelho MS 600/5-8
99 Brown St 02703 508-761-7551
Reza Sarkarati, prin. Fax 399-6506
Early Learning Center 100/PK-K
7 James St 02703 508-223-1563
Joan Mullen, prin. Fax 223-1589
Fine ES 400/K-4
790 Oakhill Ave 02703 508-222-1419
Carrie Glenn, prin. Fax 226-0255
Studley ES 500/K-4
299 Rathbun Willard Dr 02703 508-222-2621
Jennella Porter, prin. Fax 226-0419
Thacher ES 300/K-4
7 James St 02703 508-226-4162
Elaine Sabra, prin. Fax 226-4165
Wamsutta MS 600/5-8
300 Locust St 02703 508-223-1540
Karol Coffin, prin. Fax 226-2087
Willett ES 400/K-4
32 Watson Ave 02703 508-222-0286
Catherine Zinni, prin. Fax 223-1536
Other Schools – See South Attleboro

St. John Evangelist S 300/K-8
13 Hodges St 02703 508-222-5062
Sr. Mary Jane Holden, prin. Fax 223-1737

Auburn, Worcester, Pop. 15,005
Auburn SD 2,300/K-12
5 West St 01501 508-832-7755
Maryellen Brunelle, supt. Fax 832-7757
www.auburn.k12.ma.us
Auburn MS 600/6-8
10 Swanson Rd 01501 508-832-7722
Joseph Gagnon, prin. Fax 832-8655
Bancroft ES 300/3-5
3 Vinal St 01501 508-832-7744
Kathy Goldstein, prin. Fax 832-7732
Bryn Mawr ES 200/K-2
35 Swanson Rd 01501 508-832-7733
Patricia Haggerty, prin. Fax 832-7734
Pakachoag S 300/3-5
110 Pakachoag St 01501 508-832-7788
Fax 832-7787
Stone ES 300/K-2
10 Church St 01501 508-832-7766
Elizabeth Chase, prin. Fax 832-7767

Auburndale, See Newton
Newton SD
Supt. — See Newtonville
Burr ES 300/K-5
171 Pine St 02466 617-559-9360
Cynthia Bencal, prin. Fax 552-5562
Williams ES 300/K-5
141 Grove St 02466 617-559-6480
Christine Moynihan, prin. Fax 559-2013

Avon, Norfolk, Pop. 4,558
Avon SD 800/PK-12
Patrick Clark Dr 02322 508-588-0230
Dr. Margaret Frieswyk, supt. Fax 559-1081
www.avon.k12.ma.us/
Butler ES 400/PK-6
1 Patrick Clark Dr 02322 508-587-7009
Debra Swain, prin. Fax 583-7193

Ayer, Middlesex, Pop. 2,889
Ayer SD 1,100/PK-12
141 Washington St 01432 978-772-8600
George Frost, supt. Fax 772-7444
www.ayer.k12.ma.us
Ayer MS 300/6-8
141 Washington St 01432 978-772-8600
Don Parker, prin. Fax 772-8643
Page Hilltop ES 400/PK-5
115 Washington St 01432 978-772-8600
Fred Deppe, prin. Fax 772-8631

Baldwinville, Worcester, Pop. 1,795
Narragansett Regional SD 1,700/PK-12
462 Baldwinville Rd 01436 978-939-5661
Roseli Weiss Ed.D., supt. Fax 939-5179
www.nrsd.org/
Baldwinville ES 200/K-4
16 School St 01436 978-939-5318
Joanna Cackett, prin. Fax 939-4438
Narragansett MS 600/5-8
460 Baldwinville Rd 01436 978-393-5928
Rob Rouleau, prin. Fax 939-8422
Other Schools – See East Templeton, Phillipston, Templeton

Barnstable, Barnstable, Pop. 48,854

Trinity Christian Academy 100/PK-12
979 Mary Dunn Rd 02630 508-790-0114
Merrilynn Grodecki, hdmstr. Fax 790-1293

Barre, Worcester, Pop. 1,094
Quabbin SD 3,200/PK-12
872 South St 01005 978-355-4668
Cheryl Duval, supt. Fax 355-6756
www.qrsd.org/
Quabbin Regional MS 600/7-8
800 South St 01005 978-355-5042
Susanne Musnicki, prin. Fax 355-6104
Ruggles Lane ES 500/K-6
105 Ruggles Ln 01005 978-355-2934
Fax 355-2870
Other Schools – See Gilbertville, Hubbardston, New Braintree, Oakham

Becket, Berkshire
Central Berkshire Regional SD
Supt. — See Dalton
Becket Washington ES 100/PK-5
12 Maple St 01223 413-623-8757
Deborah White, prin. Fax 684-6161

Bedford, Middlesex, Pop. 12,996
Bedford SD 2,100/K-12
97 McMahon Rd 01730 781-275-7588
Maureen Lacroix, supt. Fax 275-0885
www.bedford.k12.ma.us
Davis ES 300/K-2
414 Davis Rd 01730 781-275-6804
Jennifer Brown, prin. Fax 275-7639
Glenn MS 500/6-8
99 McMahon Rd 01730 781-275-3201
P. Jayne Vilandenis, prin. Fax 275-7632
Lane ES 500/3-5
66 Sweetwater Ave 01730 781-275-7606
Robert Ackerman, prin. Fax 275-4722

Belchertown, Hampshire, Pop. 2,339
Belchertown SD 2,500/PK-12
PO Box 841 01007 413-323-0456
Dr. Judy Houle, supt. Fax 323-0448
www.belchertownps.org
Chestnut Hill Community MS 600/4-6
59 State St 01007 413-323-0437
Brian Cameron, prin. Fax 323-0438
Cold Spring K 100/PK-K
57 S Main St 01007 413-323-0428
Robert Kuhn, prin. Fax 323-0493
Jabish MS 400/7-8
62 N Washington St 01007 413-323-0433
Thomas Ruscio, prin. Fax 323-0450
Swift River ES 600/1-3
57 State St 01007 413-323-0472
Robert Kuhn, prin. Fax 323-0492

Bellingham, Norfolk, Pop. 4,535
Bellingham SD 2,600/PK-12
60 Harpin St 02019 508-883-1706
David Fischer, supt. Fax 883-0180
www.bellingham.k12.ma.us
Bellingham ECC 50/PK-PK
338 Hartford Ave 02019 508-966-2512
Pamela Fuhrman, dir.
Macy ES 300/K-4
60 Monique Dr 02019 508-966-0244
Jaime Dorr, prin. Fax 966-3365
Memorial MS 800/5-8
130 Blackstone St 02019 508-883-2330
Elaine D'Alfonso, prin. Fax 883-2037
South District ES 400/K-4
70 Harpin St 02019 508-883-8001
Kathryn Wilson, prin. Fax 883-5081
Stallbrook ES 300/K-4
342 Hartford Ave 02019 508-966-0451
Helen Chamides, prin. Fax 966-4679

Belmont, Middlesex, Pop. 24,720
Belmont SD 3,700/K-12
644 Pleasant St 02478 617-993-5401
Dr. George Entwistle, supt. Fax 993-5409
www.belmont.k12.ma.us
Burbank ES 300/K-4
266 School St 02478 617-484-3411
Christine Francis, prin. Fax 484-2050
Butler ES 300/K-4
90 White St 02478 617-484-3519
Michael McAllister, prin. Fax 484-7921
Chenery MS 1,100/5-8
95 Washington St 02478 617-484-3900
Deborah Alexander, prin. Fax 484-3676
Wellington ES 400/K-4
121 Orchard St 02478 617-484-8668
Amy Wagner, prin. Fax 484-1790
Winn Brook ES 400/K-4
97 Waterhouse Rd 02478 617-484-0306
Janet Carey, prin. Fax 484-2657

Belmont Day S 300/PK-8
55 Day School Ln 02478 617-484-3078
Lenesa Leana, hdmstr. Fax 489-1942

Berkley, Bristol
Berkley SD 1,000/PK-8
21 N Main St 02779 508-822-5220
Thomas Lynch, supt. Fax 823-1772
Berkley Community ES 600/PK-4
59 S Main St 02779 508-822-9550
Jennifer Francisco, prin. Fax 822-3773
Berkley MS 400/5-8
21 N Main St 02779 508-884-9434
Kimberly Hebert, prin. Fax 823-1772

Berlin, Worcester
Berlin SD
Supt. — See Boylston
Berlin Memorial ES 200/K-6
34 South St 01503 978-838-2417
Carol Bradley, prin. Fax 838-2395

Bernardston, Franklin
Pioneer Valley SD
Supt. — See Northfield
Bernardston ES 200/PK-6
37 School Rd 01337 413-648-9356
R. Scott Lyman, prin. Fax 648-5404

Beverly, Essex, Pop. 39,876
Beverly SD 4,200/PK-12
502 Cabot St 01915 978-921-6100
James Hayes Ed.D., supt. Fax 922-6597
www.beverlyschools.org/index2.shtm
Ayers/Ryal Side ES 400/PK-5
40 Woodland Ave 01915 978-921-6116
Suzanne Charochak, prin. Fax 921-1995
Briscoe MS 900/6-8
7 Sohier Rd 01915 978-921-6103
Matthew Poska, prin. Fax 927-7781
Centerville ES 300/K-5
17 Hull St 01915 978-921-6120
Karla Pressman, prin. Fax 921-8571
Cove ES 500/PK-5
20 Eisenhower Ave 01915 978-921-6121
Stacy Bucyk, prin. Fax 921-8551
Hannah ES 300/K-5
41R Brimbal Ave 01915 978-921-6126
Susan Snyder, prin. Fax 921-6084
North Beverly ES 300/K-5
48 Putnam St 01915 978-921-6130
Jennifer Flewelling, prin. Fax 921-4007

Beacon Christian Academy 100/PK-8
35 Conant St 01915 978-921-2888
Kathy Ely, prin. Fax 921-5888
Cape Ann Waldorf S 200/PK-8
668 Hale St 01915 978-927-8811
Susan White, admin. Fax 927-5237
Harborlight Montessori S 300/PK-8
243 Essex St 01915 978-922-1008
Susan Egan, hdmstr. Fax 922-0594
St. John the Evangelist S 200/K-8
111 New Balch St 01915 978-922-0048
Karen McCarthy, prin. Fax 927-6694
St. Mary Star of the Sea S 200/PK-8
13 Chapman St 01915 978-927-3259
Kevin Cushman, prin. Fax 927-7170
Shore Country Day S 500/PK-9
545 Cabot St 01915 978-927-1700
Lawrence Griffin, prin. Fax 927-1822

Stoneridge Childrens Montessori S 200/PK-8
290 Hale St 01915 978-927-0700
Alan Feldman, prin. Fax 922-3088
Urquhart S 200/K-8
74 Hart St 01915 978-927-1064
Raymond Nance, hdmstr. Fax 921-0060

Billerica, Middlesex, Pop. 37,609
Billerica SD 6,100/K-12
365 Boston Rd 01821 978-436-9500
Anthony Serio, supt. Fax 436-9595
www.billerica.mec.edu
Ditson ES 600/K-5
39 Cook St 01821 978-436-9530
William Downing, prin. Fax 436-9537
Hajjar ES 600/K-5
59 Rogers St 01862 978-436-9550
Anthony Larosa, prin. Fax 436-9556
Kennedy ES 500/K-5
20 Kimbrough Rd 01821 978-436-9560
David Marble, prin. Fax 436-9567
Locke MS 700/6-8
110 Allen Rd 01821 978-436-9420
Tracy Sands, prin. Fax 436-9424
Marshall MS 900/6-8
15 Floyd St 01821 978-436-9440
Roland Boucher, prin. Fax 439-1242
Parker ES 400/K-5
52 River St 01821 978-436-9570
Mary Wittenhagen, prin. Fax 436-9573
Vining ES 300/K-5
121 Lexington Rd 01821 978-436-9580
Maureen O'Hara, prin. Fax 436-9587
Other Schools – See North Billerica

Blackstone, Worcester, Pop. 8,023
Blackstone-Millville Regional SD 2,000/PK-12
175 Lincoln St 01504 508-883-4400
Christine Tyrie, supt. Fax 883-9892
www.bmrsd.net
Hartnett MS 500/6-8
35 Federal St 01504 508-876-0190
Gabrielle Abrams, prin. Fax 876-0198
Kennedy ES 300/K-3
200 Lincoln St 01504 508-876-0118
Everett Campbell, prin. Fax 876-0140
Maloney ES 200/4-5
200 Lincoln St 01504 508-876-0119
Everett Campbell, prin. Fax 876-0158
Other Schools – See Millville

Blandford, Hampden
Gateway SD
Supt. — See Huntington
Blandford ES 100/K-4
1 Russell Stage Rd 01008 413-685-3150
Joanne Blocker, prin. Fax 848-0139

Bolton, Worcester
Nashoba Regional SD 3,300/PK-12
50 Mechanic St 01740 978-779-0539
Michael Wood Ed.D., supt. Fax 779-5537
www.nrsd.net
Sawyer S 800/PK-8
100 Mechanic St 01740 978-779-5155
Ken Tucker, prin. Fax 779-0121
Other Schools – See Lancaster, Stow

Boston, Suffolk, Pop. 559,034
Boston SD 54,800/PK-12
26 Court St 02108 617-635-9000
Dr. Carol Johnson, supt. Fax 635-9059
www.bostonpublicschools.org/
Blackstone ES 600/PK-5
380 Shawmut Ave 02118 617-635-8471
Mildred Ruiz-Allen, prin. Fax 635-7975
Eliot S 200/K-8
16 Charter St 02113 617-635-8545
Traci Griffith, prin. Fax 635-8550
Farragut ES 200/K-5
10 Fenwood Rd 02115 617-635-8450
Rosemary Harmon, prin. Fax 635-8452
Hurley ES 300/PK-5
70 Worcester St 02118 617-635-8489
Marjorie Soto, prin. Fax 635-6868
Quincy ES 700/PK-5
885 Washington St 02111 617-635-8497
Suzanne Lee, prin. Fax 635-7778
Other Schools – See Allston, Brighton, Charlestown, Dorchester, East Boston, Hyde Park, Jamaica Plain, Mattapan, Roslindale, Roxbury, South Boston, West Roxbury

---

Advent S 200/PK-6
15 Brimmer St 02108 617-742-0520
Nancy Frohlich, hdmstr. Fax 723-2207
Cathedral S 200/K-8
595 Harrison Ave 02118 617-422-0042
Sr. Dorothy Burns, prin. Fax 422-0119
Kingsley Montessori S 200/PK-6
26 Exeter St 02116 617-226-4900
Renee DuChainey-Farkes, prin. Fax 247-1417
Learning Project S 100/K-6
107 Marlborough St 02116 617-266-8427
Michael McCord, hdmstr. Fax 266-3543
Parkside Christian Academy 100/PK-8
215 Forest Hills St 02130 617-522-1841
Michael Dixon, hdmstr. Fax 524-9583
Park Street S 100/PK-6
67 Brimmer St 02108 617-523-7577
Tracy Bradley, hdmstr. Fax 523-7576
St. John S 200/PK-8
9 Moon St 02113 617-227-3143
Sr. Eileen Harvey, prin. Fax 227-2188

Bourne, Barnstable, Pop. 1,284
Bourne SD 2,000/PK-12
36 Sandwich Rd 02532 508-759-0660
Edmond LaFleur, supt. Fax 759-1107
www.bourne.k12.ma.us
Bournedale ES PK-4
41 Ernest Valeri Rd 02532 508-743-0434
Jeanne Holland, prin. Fax 743-3801
Bourne MS 800/5-8
77 Waterhouse Rd 02532 508-759-0690
Mary Childress, prin. Fax 759-0695
Peebles ES 500/1-4
70 Trowbridge Rd 02532 508-759-0680
Debra Howard, prin. Fax 759-0683

Boxborough, Middlesex, Pop. 3,343
Boxborough SD 500/PK-6
493 Massachusetts Ave 01719 978-263-4569
Dr. Curtis Bates, supt. Fax 263-0477
www.boxboroughschool.org
Blanchard Memorial ES 500/PK-6
493 Massachusetts Ave 01719 978-263-4569
Maryellen Driscoll, prin. Fax 263-0477

Boxford, Essex, Pop. 2,072
Boxford SD 900/PK-6
28 Middleton Rd 01921 978-887-0771
Bernard Creeden Ed.D., supt. Fax 887-8042
www.tritownschoolunion.com
Cole ES 300/PK-2
26 Middleton Rd 01921 978-887-2856
Kathryn Nikas, prin. Fax 887-0703
Spofford Pond ES 600/3-6
31 Spofford Rd 01921 978-352-8616
Lawrence Fliegelman, prin. Fax 352-7855

Middleton SD 800/PK-6
28 Middleton Rd 01921 978-887-0771
Bernard Creeden Ed.D., supt. Fax 887-8042
www.tritownschoolunion.com
Other Schools – See Middleton

Topsfield SD 700/PK-6
28 Middleton Rd 01921 978-887-0771
Bernard Creeden Ed.D., supt. Fax 887-8042
www.tritownschoolunion.com
Other Schools – See Topsfield

Boxford Academy 100/PK-5
PO Box 223 01921 978-887-8390
Martha Thompson, hdmstr. Fax 887-5180

Boylston, Worcester
Berlin SD 200/K-6
215 Main St 01505 508-869-2837
Brian McDermott Ph.D., supt. Fax 869-0023
www.bbrsd.org
Other Schools – See Berlin

Boylston SD 400/K-6
215 Main St 01505 508-869-2837
Brian McDermott, supt. Fax 869-0023
www.mec.edu/bbps
Boylston ES 400/K-6
200 Sewall St 01505 508-869-2200
Daniel Deneen, prin. Fax 869-6914

Bradford, See Haverhill
Haverhill SD
Supt. — See Haverhill
Bradford ES 600/K-5
118 Montvale St 01835 978-374-2443
Michael Rossi, prin. Fax 374-0529

Braintree, Norfolk, Pop. 33,800
Braintree SD 5,100/K-12
348 Pond St 02184 781-380-0130
Dr. Peter Kurzberg, supt. Fax 380-0146
www.braintreeschools.org/
East MS 700/6-8
305 River St 02184 781-380-0170
Kristen St. George, prin. Fax 848-4522
Flaherty ES 400/K-5
99 Lakeside Dr 02184 781-380-0180
Mary Struzziero, prin. Fax 380-0184
Highlands ES 400/K-5
144 Wildwood Ave 02184 781-380-0190
Nancy Pelletier, prin. Fax 380-0128
Hollis ES 500/K-5
482 Washington St 02184 781-380-0120
Timothy MacDonald, prin. Fax 380-0122
Liberty ES 400/K-5
49 Proctor Rd 02184 781-380-0210
Joyce Radiches, prin. Fax 380-0213
Morrison ES 400/K-5
260 Liberty St 02184 781-380-0230
John Riordan, prin. Fax 380-0233
Ross ES 300/K-5
20 Hayward St 02184 781-380-0240
Donna Bonarrigo, prin. Fax 380-0243
South MS 600/6-8
232 Peach St 02184 781-380-0160
Edward McDonough, prin. Fax 380-0164

Meeting House Montessori S 100/PK-5
25 Brow Ave 02184 781-356-7877
Caren Chevalier-Putnam, dir. Fax 356-6744
St. Francis of Assisi S 300/PK-8
850 Washington St 02184 781-848-0842
Vittoria DeBenedictis, prin. Fax 356-5309
South Shore SDA S 50/1-8
250 Washington St 02184 781-356-7794

Brewster, Barnstable, Pop. 1,818
Brewster SD
Supt. — See Orleans

Eddy ES 300/3-5
2298 Main St 02631 508-896-4531
Keith Gauley, prin. Fax 896-4529
Stony Brook ES 200/PK-2
384 Underpass Rd 02631 508-896-4545
Denise Fronius, prin. Fax 896-4081

Bridgewater, Plymouth, Pop. 7,242
Bridgewater-Raynham Regional SD 4,100/PK-12
166 Mount Prospect St 02324 508-279-2140
Dr. George Guasconi, supt.
www.bridge-rayn.org
Bridgewater MS 7-8
166 Mount Prospect St 02324 508-279-2100
Angela Watson, prin. Fax 279-2104
Mitchell ES 700/PK-3
500 South St 02324 508-279-2120
Brian Lynch, prin. Fax 279-2133
Williams IS 500/4-6
200 South St 02324 508-697-6968
Nancy Kirk, prin. Fax 697-6775
Other Schools – See Raynham

Brighton, See Boston
Boston SD
Supt. — See Boston
Baldwin Early Learning Center 200/PK-1
121 Corey Rd 02135 617-635-8409
Graciela Hopkins, prin. Fax 635-9544
Edison MS 500/6-8
60 Glenmont Rd 02135 617-635-8436
Mary Driscoll, prin. Fax 635-8446
Garfield ES 200/K-5
95 Beechcroft St 02135 617-635-8351
Louise Kuhlman, prin. Fax 635-8353
Hamilton ES 100/K-5
198 Strathmore Rd 02135 617-635-8388
Yolanda Burnett, prin. Fax 635-9557
Lyon S 100/K-8
50 Beechcroft St 02135 617-635-7945
Deborah Rooney, prin. Fax 635-7949
Winship ES 200/PK-5
54 Dighton St 02135 617-635-8399
Antonio Barbosa, prin. Fax 635-8403

St. Columbkille S 200/K-8
25 Arlington St 02135 617-254-3110
Dr. Michael McCarthy, hdmstr. Fax 254-3161
Shaloh House Jewish Day S 100/PK-8
29 Chestnut Hill Ave 02135 617-787-2200
Rabbi Dan Rodkin, dir. Fax 787-4693

Brimfield, Hampden
Brimfield SD
Supt. — See Fiskdale
Brimfield ES 400/PK-6
22 Wales Rd 01010 413-245-7337
Brian Ledbetter, prin. Fax 245-4110

Brockton, Plymouth, Pop. 94,632
Brockton SD 12,700/PK-12
43 Crescent St 02301 508-580-7511
Dr. Matthew Malone, supt. Fax 580-7513
www.bpsma.org/
Angelo ES 500/K-5
472 N Main St 02301 508-894-4501
Ryan Powers, prin. Fax 894-4500
Arnone Community ES 700/K-6
135 Belmont St 02301 508-894-4440
Colleen Proudler, prin. Fax 894-4464
Ashfield ES, 225 Coe Rd 02302 100/PK-PK, 6-
Barbara Lovell, prin. 508-580-7268
Baker ES K-5
45 Quincy St 02302 508-894-4427
Donna Haymes, prin. Fax 894-4472
Brookfield ES 500/K-5
135 Jon Dr 02302 508-580-7257
Kathleen Moran, prin. Fax 580-7073
Davis S 800/K-8
380 Plain St 02302 508-580-7360
Darlene Campbell, prin. Fax 580-7074
Downey ES 500/K-5
55 Electric Ave 02302 508-580-7221
Diane Gosselin, prin. Fax 580-7075
East JHS 600/6-8
464 Centre St 02302 508-580-7351
Violet LeMar, prin. Fax 580-7090
George ES K-5
180 Colonel Bell Dr 02301 508-580-7913
Vilma Gonzalez, prin. Fax 580-7917
Hancock ES 600/K-5
125 Pearl St 02301 508-580-7252
Marcia Andrade-Serpa, prin. Fax 580-7079
Huntington ES 400/K-5
1121 Warren Ave 02301 508-580-7235
June Saba, prin. Fax 580-7081
Kennedy ES 500/K-5
900 Ash St 02301 508-580-7278
Brian Rogan, prin. Fax 580-7082
North MS 500/6-8
108 Oak St 02301 508-580-7371
Sean Ahern, prin. Fax 580-7088
Plouffe MS 200/5-8
250 Crescent St 02302 508-894-4301
Michelle Nessralla, prin. Fax 894-4300
Raymond S 700/K-7
125 Oak St 02301 508-580-7364
Carol McGrath, prin. Fax 580-7085
South MS 600/6-8
105 Keith Avenue Ext 02301 508-580-7311
Kevin Karo, prin. Fax 580-7089
West MS 600/6-8
271 West St 02301 508-580-7381
Clifford Murray, prin. Fax 580-7307

Brockton Christian S 100/PK-8
1367 Main St 02301 508-588-4669
Karen Hodges, prin. Fax 588-4684
Brockton SDA S 50/K-8
PO Box 7544 02303 508-586-9955
Convelle Morton, prin. Fax 586-9956
Trinity Catholic Academy - Lower Campus 300/PK-3
631 N Main St 02301 508-583-6231
Pauline Labouliere, prin. Fax 583-6336
Trinity Catholic Academy - Upper Campus 200/4-8
37 Erie Ave 02302 508-583-6225
Patrick Hart, prin. Fax 583-6229

Brookfield, Worcester
Brookfield SD
Supt. — See Fiskdale
Brookfield ES 300/PK-6
37 Central St 01506 508-867-8774
Kathleen Hosterman, prin. Fax 867-0320

Brookline, Norfolk, Pop. 57,600
Brookline SD 6,100/PK-12
333 Washington St 02445 617-730-2403
Dr. William Lupini, supt. Fax 730-2108
www.brookline.k12.ma.us/
Devotion S 700/PK-8
345 Harvard St 02446 617-879-4400
Gerardo Martinez, prin. Fax 739-7501
Driscoll S 400/PK-8
64 Westbourne Ter 02446 617-879-4250
James Parziale, prin. Fax 739-7502
Lawrence S 500/PK-8
27 Francis St 02446 617-879-4300
Rick Rogers, prin. Fax 879-4390
Lincoln S 500/PK-8
19 Kennard Rd 02445 617-879-4600
Timothy McGillicuddy, prin. Fax 739-7505
Lynch Center 100/PK-PK
599 Brookline Ave 02445 617-739-7516
Patricia Vonnegut, prin. Fax 264-6429
Pierce S 600/K-8
50 School St 02446 617-730-2580
Pipier Smith-Mumford, prin. Fax 264-6468
Runkle S 500/PK-8
50 Druce St 02445 617-879-4650
Joseph Connolly, prin. Fax 739-7675
Other Schools – See Chestnut Hill

Dexter S 400/PK-12
20 Newton St 02445 617-522-5544
Fax 522-8166
Maimonides S 600/K-12
34 Philbrick Rd 02445 617-232-4452
Nathan Katz, dir. Fax 566-2061
New England Hebrew Academy 200/PK-12
9 Prescott St 02446 617-731-5330
Fax 277-0752
Park S 500/PK-9
171 Goddard Ave 02445 617-277-2456
Jerrold Katz, prin. Fax 232-1261
St. Mary of the Assumption S 200/PK-8
67 Harvard St 02445 617-566-7184
Maureen Jutras, prin. Fax 731-4078
Southfield S 400/PK-12
10 Newton St 02445 617-522-6980
William Phinney, hdmstr. Fax 522-8166
Torah Academy 200/K-8
11 Williston Rd 02445 617-731-3196
Rabbi Dovid Winkler, dir. Fax 731-1042

Burlington, Middlesex, Pop. 23,302
Burlington SD 3,500/K-12
123 Cambridge St 01803 781-270-1800
Dr. Eric Conti, supt. Fax 270-1773
www.burlington.mec.edu
Fox Hill ES 500/K-5
1 Fox Hill Rd 01803 781-270-1791
Ellen Johnson, prin. Fax 229-5909
Memorial ES 200/K-5
125 Winn St 01803 781-270-1721
Karen Rickershauser, prin. Fax 229-5751
Pine Glen ES 400/K-5
1 Pine Glen Way 01803 781-270-1712
Jane Dwyer, prin. Fax 229-5793
Simonds MS 800/6-8
114 Winn St 01803 781-270-1781
Richard Connors, prin. Fax 229-4980
Wyman ES 600/K-5
41 Terrace Hall Ave 01803 781-270-1701
Susan Astone, prin. Fax 229-5667

Mount Hope Christian S 300/PK-5
3 McGinnis Dr 01803 781-272-1014
Elaine Driscoll, prin. Fax 272-3830

Buzzards Bay, Barnstable, Pop. 3,250

St. Margaret Regional S 200/K-8
143 Main St 02532 508-759-2213
Paul Hudson, prin. Fax 759-8776
Waldorf S of Cape Cod 100/PK-8
85 Cotuit Rd 02532 508-759-7499
Gary Cannon, admin. Fax 759-7383

Byfield, Essex
Triton Regional SD 3,300/PK-12
112 Elm St 01922 978-465-2397
Sandra Halloran, supt. Fax 465-8599
www.trsd.net
Triton Regional MS 500/7-8
112 Elm St 01922 978-463-5845
Jared Fulgoni, prin. Fax 465-6868
Other Schools – See Newbury, Rowley, Salisbury

Cambridge, Middlesex, Pop. 100,135
Cambridge SD 5,600/PK-12
159 Thorndike St 02141 617-349-6494
Dr. Jeffrey Young, supt. Fax 349-6496
www.cpsd.us
Amigos S 300/K-8
100 Putnam Ave 02139 617-349-6567
Deborah Sercombe, prin. Fax 349-6833
Baldwin S 400/K-8
28 Sacramento St 02138 617-349-6525
Rebecca Vyduna, prin. Fax 349-4407
Cambridgeport S 300/K-8
89 Elm St 02139 617-349-6587
Jennifer Ford, prin. Fax 349-6511
Fletcher-Maynard Academy 200/PK-8
225 Windsor St 02139 617-349-6588
Robin Harris, prin. Fax 349-6595
Graham and Parks S 400/K-8
44 Linnaean St 02138 617-349-6577
Sarah Fiarman, prin. Fax 349-6590
Haggerty ES 300/K-6
110 Cushing St 02138 617-349-6555
Janelle Bradshaw, prin. Fax 349-6034
Kennedy-Longfellow S 400/K-8
158 Spring St 02141 617-349-6841
Kathleen Conway, prin. Fax 349-6852
King Open S 500/K-8
850 Cambridge St 02141 617-349-6540
Timothy Groves, prin. Fax 349-6548
King S 200/K-8
100 Putnam Ave 02139 617-349-6562
Gerald Yung, prin. Fax 349-6565
Morse S 300/PK-8
40 Granite St 02139 617-349-6575
Patricia Beggy, prin. Fax 349-6571
Peabody S 400/PK-8
70 Rindge Ave 02140 617-349-6530
Joellen Scannell, prin. Fax 349-6531
Tobin Montessori S 300/PK-8
197 Vassal Ln 02138 617-349-6600
Seth Lewis-Levin, prin. Fax 349-6890

Boston Archdiocesan Choir S 100/5-8
29 Mount Auburn St 02138 617-868-8658
Sherry Kenney, prin. Fax 354-7092
Buckingham Browne & Nichols MS 200/7-8
80 Gerrys Landing Rd 02138 617-800-2336
Rebecca Upham, hdmstr. Fax 491-5159
Buckingham Browne & Nichols S 300/PK-6
80 Gerrys Landing Rd 02138 617-800-2461
Rebecca Upham, hdmstr. Fax 497-8804
Cambridge Friends S 200/PK-8
5 Cadbury Rd 02140 617-354-3880
Peter Sommer, hdmstr. Fax 876-1815
Cambridge Montessori S 200/PK-8
161 Garden St 02138 617-492-3410
David B. Harris, hdmstr. Fax 576-5154
Fayerweather Street S 200/PK-8
765 Concord Ave 02138 617-876-4746
Edward Kuh, hdmstr. Fax 520-6700
International School of Boston 500/PK-12
45 Matignon Rd 02140 617-499-1451
John Larner, hdmstr. Fax 499-1454
St. Peter S 200/K-8
96 Concord Ave 02138 617-547-0101
Mary Jo Keaney, prin. Fax 441-8911
Shady Hill S 500/PK-8
178 Coolidge Hl 02138 617-520-5260
Bruce Shaw, dir. Fax 520-9387

Canton, Norfolk, Pop. 18,530
Canton SD 2,900/PK-12
960 Washington St 02021 781-821-5060
John D'Auria Ed.D., supt. Fax 575-6500
www.cantonma.org
Galvin MS 700/6-8
55 Pecunit St 02021 781-821-5070
Thomas LaLiberte, prin. Fax 575-6509
Hansen ES 400/1-5
25 Pecunit St 02021 781-821-5085
William Griffin, prin. Fax 821-4271
Kennedy ES 400/1-5
100 Dedham St 02021 781-821-5080
Jennifer Henderson, prin. Fax 575-6543
Luce ES 500/PK-5
45 Independence St 02021 781-821-5075
Robie Peter, prin. Fax 575-6528

St. John the Evangelist S 200/PK-8
696 Washington St 02021 781-828-2130
Charlotte Kelly, prin. Fax 828-7563

Carlisle, Middlesex
Carlisle SD 800/PK-8
83 School St 01741 978-369-6550
Marie Doyle, supt. Fax 371-2400
www.carlisle.mec.edu/
Carlisle S 800/PK-8
83 School St 01741 978-369-4102
Joyce Mehaffey, prin. Fax 371-2400

Carver, Plymouth
Carver SD 1,900/PK-12
3 Carver Square Blvd 02330 508-866-6160
Elizabeth Sorrell, supt. Fax 866-2920
www.carver.org
Carver ES 500/3-5
PO Box 327 02330 508-866-6220
Candace Weiler, prin. Fax 866-6887
Carver MS 500/6-8
60 S Meadow Rd 02330 508-866-6130
Scott Knief, prin. Fax 866-6880
Washburn PS 400/PK-2
PO Box 327 02330 508-866-6210
Candace Weiler, prin. Fax 866-6845

Centerville, Barnstable, Pop. 9,190
Barnstable SD
Supt. — See Hyannis
Centerville ES 300/PK-4
658 Bay Ln 02632 508-790-9890
Matthew Scheufele, prin. Fax 790-9895

Charlemont, Franklin
Hawlemont Regional SD
Supt. — See Shelburne Falls
Hawlemont Regional ES 100/K-6
10 School St 01339 413-339-8316
Joanne Giguere, prin. Fax 339-5760

Mohawk Trail SD
Supt. — See Shelburne Falls
Heath ES 100/PK-6
18 Jacobs Rd 01339 413-337-5307
Anne Mislak, prin. Fax 337-5507

Charlestown, See Boston
Boston SD
Supt. — See Boston
Edwards MS 400/6-8
28 Walker St 02129 617-635-8516
Jeffrey Riley, prin. Fax 635-8522
Harvard-Kent ES 400/PK-5
50 Bunker Hill St 02129 617-635-8358
Richard Martin, prin. Fax 635-8364
Warren-Prescott S 400/K-8
50 School St 02129 617-635-8346
Domenic Amara, prin. Fax 635-9454

Charlton, Worcester
Dudley-Charlton Regional SD
Supt. — See Dudley
Charlton ES 300/PK-1
9 Burlingame Rd 01507 508-248-7774
Lori Pacheco, prin. Fax 248-7003
Charlton MS 800/5-8
2 Oxford Rd 01507 508-248-1423
Dean Packard, prin. Fax 248-1418
Heritage ES 600/2-4
34 Oxford Rd 01507 508-248-4884
John Prouty, prin. Fax 248-1109

Chatham, Barnstable, Pop. 1,916
Chatham SD 700/PK-12
425 Crowell Rd 02633 508-945-5130
Mary Ann Lanzo, supt. Fax 945-5133
www.chatham.k12.ma.us
Chatham ES 300/PK-4
147 Depot Rd 02633 508-945-5135
Gaylene Heppe, prin. Fax 945-5138
Chatham MS 200/5-8
425 Crowell Rd 02633 508-945-5148
Lisa Sjostrom, prin. Fax 945-5143

Chelmsford, Middlesex, Pop. 33,858
Chelmsford SD 5,300/PK-12
230 North Rd 01824 978-251-5100
Donald Yeoman Ed.D., supt. Fax 251-5110
www.chelmsford.k12.ma.us/
Byam ES 500/K-4
25 Maple Rd 01824 978-251-5144
Jane Gilmore, prin. Fax 251-5150
Center ES 400/K-4
84 Billerica Rd 01824 978-251-5155
Christopher Raymond, prin. Fax 251-5160
McCarthy MS 900/5-8
250 North Rd 01824 978-251-5122
Frank Tiano, prin. Fax 251-5130
Parker MS 700/5-8
75 Graniteville Rd 01824 978-251-5133
Denise Rainis, prin. Fax 251-5140
South Row ES 400/K-4
250 Boston Rd 01824 978-251-5177
Irene Hannigan, prin. Fax 251-5180
Other Schools – See North Chelmsford

Chelsea, Suffolk, Pop. 32,518
Chelsea SD 5,100/PK-12
500 Broadway 02150 617-466-4477
Thomas Kingston, supt. Fax 889-8361
chelseaschools.com
Berkowitz ES 400/1-4
300 Crescent Ave 02150 617-889-8486
Sheila Harrison, prin. Fax 889-8646
Browne S 400/5-8
180 Walnut St 02150 617-889-8652
Debra McElroy, prin. Fax 889-8459
Clark Avenue S 600/5-8
8 Clark Ave 02150 617-466-5100
Linda Breau, prin. Fax 889-7539
Hooks ES 400/1-4
300 Crescent Ave 02150 617-889-8450
Adele Lubarsky, prin. Fax 889-8647
Kelly ES 400/1-4
300 Crescent Ave 02150 617-889-8483
Timothy Howard, prin. Fax 889-8644
Shurtleff ECC 400/PK-K
99 Hawthorne St 02150 617-466-5150
Jacqueline Bevere, prin. Fax 889-8425
Sokolowski ES 400/1-4
300 Crescent Ave 02150 617-889-8464
Jeffrey Bryson, prin. Fax 889-8470
Wright S 500/5-8
180 Walnut St 02150 617-466-5240
Donna Covino, prin. Fax 889-8463

St. Rose S 200/PK-8
580 Broadway 02150 617-884-2626
Mary Anne Babineau, prin. Fax 889-2354

Cheshire, Berkshire
Adams-Cheshire Regional SD 1,600/PK-12
125 Savoy Rd 01225 413-743-2939
Alfred Skrocki, supt. Fax 743-4135
www.acrsd.net
Cheshire ES 300/PK-6
191 Church St 01225 413-743-2298
Pamela St. John, prin. Fax 743-8423
Other Schools – See Adams

Chester, Hampden
Gateway SD
Supt. — See Huntington
Chester ES 100/PK-4
325 Middlefield Rd 01011 413-685-1360
Joanne Blocker, prin. Fax 354-9618

Chesterfield, Hampshire
Chesterfield-Goshen SD
Supt. — See Westhampton
New Hingham Regional ES 200/PK-6
30 Smith Rd 01012 413-296-0000
Michael Fredette, prin. Fax 296-0003

Chestnut Hill, See Newton
Brookline SD
Supt. — See Brookline
Baker S 700/PK-8
205 Beverly Rd 02467 617-879-4500
Mary Brown, prin. Fax 879-4505
Heath S 400/PK-8
100 Eliot St 02467 617-879-4570
Mildred Katz, prin. Fax 739-7570

Brimmer and May S 400/PK-12
69 Middlesex Rd 02467 617-566-7462
Anne Reenstierna, hdmstr. Fax 734-5147
Chestnut Hill S 300/PK-6
428 Hammond St 02467 617-566-4394
Dr. Steven Tobolsky, hdmstr. Fax 738-6602
Mt. Alvernia Academy 300/PK-6
20 Manet Rd 02467 617-527-7540
Joan Sullivan, prin. Fax 527-7995

Chicopee, Hampden, Pop. 54,680
Chicopee SD 7,700/PK-12
180 Broadway St 01020 413-594-3410
Richard Rege, supt. Fax 594-3552
www.chicopee.mec.edu/
Barry ES 400/K-5
44 Connell St 01020 413-594-3425
David Drugan, prin. Fax 594-3468
Belcher ES 200/K-2
10 Southwick St 01020 413-594-3526
Jon Ferris, prin. Fax 594-3469
Bellamy MS 1,000/6-8
314 Pendleton Ave 01020 413-594-3527
Matthew Francis, prin. Fax 594-1837
Bowe ES 400/PK-5
115 Hampden St 01013 413-594-3431
Samuel Karlin, prin. Fax 594-1848
Bowie ES 400/K-5
80 DARE Way 01022 413-594-3532
Norman Burgess, prin. Fax 594-3590
Fairview MS 800/6-8
26 Memorial Ave 01020 413-594-3501
Lynn Clark, prin. Fax 594-3509
Lambert-Lavoie ES 300/K-5
99 Kendall St 01020 413-594-3444
Ginger Coleman, prin. Fax 594-3513
Litwin ES 400/K-5
135 Litwin Ln 01020 413-594-3545
Jordana Harper-Ewert, prin. Fax 594-3547
Selser ES 400/K-5
12 DARE Way 01022 413-594-3449
Irene Lemieux, prin. Fax 594-1863
Stefanik ES 400/K-5
720 Meadow St 01013 413-594-3464
Jennifer Dold, prin. Fax 594-3462
Streiber Memorial ES 300/K-5
40 Streiber Dr 01020 413-594-3446
January Wilson, prin. Fax 594-3480
Szetela Early Childhood S 200/PK-PK
66 Macek Dr 01013 413-594-3597
Janet Reid, prin. Fax 594-3596

Holy Name S 200/PK-8
63 South St 01013 413-592-6857
Patricia Kern, prin. Fax 598-0150
St. Joan of Arc-St. George S 300/PK-8
587 Grattan St 01020 413-533-1475
Paula Jenkins, prin. Fax 533-1418
St. Stanislaus S 400/PK-8
534 Front St 01013 413-592-5135
Sr. Cecelia Haier, prin. Fax 598-0187

Clarksburg, Berkshire, Pop. 1,745
Clarksburg SD
Supt. — See North Adams
Clarksburg S 200/K-8
777 W Cross Rd 01247 413-663-8735
Karen Gallese, prin. Fax 663-8629

Clinton, Worcester, Pop. 7,943
Clinton SD 1,900/PK-12
150 School St 01510 978-365-4200
Gerald Gaw, supt. Fax 365-5037
clinton.k12.ma.us
Clinton ES 700/PK-4
100 Church St 01510 978-365-4230
Geraldine Sargent, prin. Fax 368-7209
Clinton MS 600/5-8
100 W Boylston St 01510 978-365-4220
Michael Vetros, prin. Fax 368-7256

Cohasset, Norfolk, Pop. 7,075
Cohasset SD 1,300/PK-12
143 Pond St 02025 781-383-6111
Denise Walsh Ed.D., supt. Fax 383-6507
www.cohassetk12.org
Deer Hill ES 300/3-5
208 Sohier St 02025 781-383-6115
Jennifer de Chiara Ph.D., prin. Fax 383-6791
Osgood ES 300/PK-2
210 Sohier St 02025 781-383-6117
Janet Sheehan, prin. Fax 383-0255

Colrain, Franklin
Mohawk Trail SD
Supt. — See Shelburne Falls
Colrain Central ES 100/PK-6
22 Jacksonville Rd 01340 413-624-3451
Anne Mislak, prin. Fax 624-3452

Concord, Middlesex, Pop. 4,700
Concord SD 1,800/K-8
120 Meriam Rd 01742 978-318-1500
Diana Rigby, supt. Fax 318-1537
www.concordpublicschools.net
Alcott ES 400/K-5
93 Laurel St 01742 978-318-9544
Sharon Young, prin. Fax 371-2000
Concord MS 600/6-8
835 Old Marlboro Rd 01742 978-318-1380
Arthur Unobskey, prin. Fax 318-1392
Thoreau ES 400/K-5
29 Prairie St 01742 978-318-1300
Robert Colantuono, prin. Fax 318-1308
Willard ES 400/K-5
185 Powder Mill Rd 01742 978-318-1340
Patricia Fernandes, prin. Fax 318-1348

Fenn S 300/4-9
516 Monument St 01742 978-369-5800
Gerard Ward, hdmstr. Fax 371-7520
Nashoba Brooks S 300/PK-8
200 Strawberry Hill Rd 01742 978-369-4591
Kay Cowan, hdmstr. Fax 371-2597

Conway, Franklin
Conway SD
Supt. — See South Deerfield
Conway ES 200/PK-6
24 Fournier Rd 01341 413-369-4239
Dr. Judy Siciliano, prin. Fax 369-4017

Cotuit, Barnstable, Pop. 2,364
Barnstable SD
Supt. — See Hyannis
Cotuit ES 100/3-4
140 Old Oyster Rd 02635 508-428-0268
Karen Stonely, prin. Fax 428-3679

Cummington, Hampshire
Central Berkshire Regional SD
Supt. — See Dalton
Berkshire Trail ES 100/PK-5
2 Main St 01026 413-634-5327
Laura Dumouchel, prin. Fax 634-0271

Cuttyhunk, Dukes
Gosnold SD
Supt. — See Rehoboth
Cuttyhunk S 50/PK-8
PO Box 164 02713 508-997-5408
Margaret Martin, prin. Fax 990-3318

Dalton, Berkshire, Pop. 7,155
Central Berkshire Regional SD 2,100/PK-12
PO Box 299 01227 413-684-0320
James Stankiewicz, supt. Fax 684-1520
www.cbrsd.org
Craneville ES 500/K-5
71 Park Ave 01226 413-684-0209
Kathy Buckley, prin. Fax 684-0584
Nessacus Regional MS 500/6-8
35 Fox Rd 01226 413-684-0780
Gerard Dery, prin. Fax 684-4214
Other Schools – See Becket, Cummington, Hinsdale

St. Agnes S 200/PK-8
30 Carson Ave 01226 413-684-3143
Theresa Dudziak, prin. Fax 684-3124

Danvers, Essex, Pop. 24,174
Danvers SD 3,600/PK-12
64 Cabot Rd 01923 978-777-4539
Lisa Dana, supt. Fax 777-8931
www.danvers.mec.edu
Great Oak ES 400/PK-5
76 Pickering St 01923 978-774-2533
Matthew Fusco, prin. Fax 777-1471
Highlands ES 300/K-5
190 Hobart St 01923 978-774-5011
Elizabeth Matthews, prin. Fax 777-5821
Holten-Richmond MS 900/6-8
57 Conant St 01923 978-774-8590
Michael Cali, prin. Fax 762-8686
Riverside ES 300/PK-5
95 Liberty St 01923 978-774-5010
Violetta Powers, prin. Fax 774-7850
Smith ES 300/K-5
15 Lobao Dr 01923 978-774-1350
Sharon Burrill, prin. Fax 774-1351
Thorpe ES 300/K-5
1 Avon Rd 01923 978-774-6946
Rita Ward, prin. Fax 739-4417

St. Mary of the Annunciation S 500/PK-8
14 Otis St 01923 978-774-0307
Molly Kelley, prin. Fax 750-4852

Dedham, Norfolk, Pop. 23,782
Dedham SD 2,700/PK-12
100 Whiting Ave 02026 781-326-5622
June Doe, supt. Fax 320-0193
www.dedham.k12.ma.us
Avery ES 200/1-5
123 High St 02026 781-326-5354
Clare Sullivan, prin. Fax 326-5899
Dedham MS 700/6-8
70 Whiting Ave 02026 781-326-6900
Debra Gately, prin. Fax 461-0354
Early Childhood Education Center 100/PK-K
322 Sprague St 02026 781-451-5978
Heidi Dineen, prin. Fax 326-6445
Greenlodge ES 300/1-5
191 Greenlodge St 02026 781-326-5622
Kathleen Kiewlicz, prin. Fax 461-0034
Oakdale ES 400/1-5
137 Cedar St 02026 781-326-5351
Holli Armstrong, prin. Fax 326-8945
Riverdale ES 200/1-5
143 Needham St 02026 781-326-5350
Doris Claypool, prin. Fax 461-0183

Dedham Country Day S 200/PK-8
90 Sandy Valley Rd 02026 781-329-0850
Nicholas Thacher, prin. Fax 329-0551

Deerfield, Franklin

Bement S 200/K-9
94 Old Main St 01342 413-774-7061
Shelley Jackson, hdmstr. Fax 774-7863

Dighton, Bristol
Dighton-Rehoboth Regional SD
Supt. — See North Dighton
Dighton ES 500/PK-4
1250 Somerset Ave 02715 508-669-4245
Sandra Cummings, prin. Fax 669-4248
Dighton MS 400/5-8
1250R Somerset Ave 02715 508-669-4200
Michael Cichon, prin. Fax 669-4210

Dorchester, See Boston
Boston SD
Supt. — See Boston
Clap ES 100/K-5
35 Harvest St 02125 617-635-8672
Mary Tormey-Hamilton, prin. Fax 635-6389
Dever ES 500/K-5
325 Mount Vernon St 02125 617-635-8694
Vivian Swoboda, prin. Fax 635-8097
Dickerman ES 200/K-5
206 Magnolia St 02121 617-635-8253
Jessica Bolt, prin. Fax 635-8255
East Zone-ELC 100/PK-1
370 Columbia Rd 02125 617-635-8604
Corrinna Horton, dir. Fax 635-8575
Everett ES 300/PK-5
71 Pleasant St 02125 617-635-8778
Nicole Mack, prin. Fax 635-8780
Fifield ES 300/K-5
25 Dunbar Ave 02124 617-635-8618
Craig Lankhorst, prin. Fax 635-8621
Frederick Pilot MS 600/6-8
270 Columbia Rd 02121 617-635-1650
Debra Socia, prin. Fax 635-1637
Greenwood S 400/PK-8
189 Glenway St 02121 617-635-8710
Isabel Mendez, prin. Fax 635-8713
Harbor S 300/6-8
11 Charles St 02122 617-635-6365
Amy Marx, prin. Fax 635-6367
Holland ES 700/K-5
85 Olney St 02121 617-635-8832
Michelle O'Connell, prin. Fax 635-8838
Holmes ES 200/PK-5
40 School St 02124 617-635-8681
Catherine Constant, prin. Fax 635-8685
Kenny ES 200/PK-5
19 Oakton Ave 02122 617-635-8789
Suzanne Federspiel, prin. Fax 635-8791
King MS 300/6-8
100 Maxwell St 02124 617-635-8212
Ruby Ababio-Fernandez, prin. Fax 635-9356
Lee Academy 100/PK-1
155 Talbot Ave 02124 617-635-6619
Genteen Jean-Michel, prin. Fax 635-6618
Lee ES 400/PK-5
155 Talbot Ave 02124 617-635-8687
Kimberly Curtis, prin. Fax 635-8692
Marshall ES 600/PK-5
35 Westville St 02124 617-635-8810
Teresa Harvey-Jackson, prin. Fax 635-8815
Mather ES 500/PK-5
1 Parish St 02122 617-635-8757
Emily Cox, prin. Fax 635-8762
McCormack MS 700/6-8
315 Mount Vernon St 02125 617-635-8657
DaQuall Graham, prin. Fax 635-9788
Murphy S 900/PK-8
1 Worrell St 02122 617-635-8781
Vera Johnson, prin. Fax 635-8787
O'Hearn ES 200/PK-5
1669 Dorchester Ave 02122 617-635-8725
William Henderson, prin. Fax 635-8728
Russell ES 300/K-5
750 Columbia Rd 02125 617-635-8803
Tamara Blake, prin. Fax 635-9768
Shaw ES 300/PK-5
429 Norfolk St 02124 617-635-8719
Maudlin Wright, prin. Fax 635-8721
Stone ES 100/PK-5
22 Regina Rd 02124 617-635-8773
Patricia Niles-Randolph, prin. Fax 635-8777

Trotter ES 500/PK-5
135 Humboldt Ave 02121 617-635-8225
Mairead Nolan, prin. Fax 635-7915
Wilson MS 400/6-8
18 Croftland Ave 02124 617-635-8827
Claudette Mulligan-Gates, prin. Fax 635-6414
Winthrop ES 300/PK-5
35 Brookford St 02125 617-635-8379
Emily Shamieh, prin. Fax 635-9396

Epiphany S 100/5-8
154 Centre St 02124 617-326-0425
Rev. John Finley, hdmstr. Fax 326-0424
Notre Dame Montessori S PK-K
265 Mount Vernon St 02125 617-282-0101
Sr. Elizabeth A. Calcagni, prin. Fax 436-7273
Pope John Paul II Academy 200/PK-8
239 Neponset Ave 02122 617-825-6262
Catherine Cameron, prin. Fax 288-3432
Pope John Paul II Academy 200/PK-8
197 Centre St 02124 617-282-2577
Thomas Vennochi, prin. Fax 282-2014
Pope John Paul II Academy 200/PK-8
2214 Dorchester Ave 02124 617-296-1210
Kim Mahoney, prin. Fax 296-0144
Pope John Paul II Academy 200/PK-8
100 Savin Hill Ave 02125 617-265-0019
Mary Russo, dir. Fax 298-2926
Pope John Paul II Academy PK-8
790 Columbia Rd 02125 617-265-7110
Claire Sheridan, prin. Fax 288-1372
St. Brendan S 200/PK-8
29 Rita Rd 02124 617-282-3388
Ellen Leary, prin. Fax 822-9152

Douglas, Worcester
Douglas SD 1,500/PK-12
21 Davis St 01516 508-476-7901
Nancy Lane, supt. Fax 476-3719
www.douglas.k12.ma.us/
Douglas ECC 200/PK-PK
PO Box 610 01516 508-476-4034
Denise O'Connell, prin. Fax 476-4032
Douglas ES 200/K-2
17 Gleason Ct 01516 508-476-2154
Kimberly Taylor, prin. Fax 476-4041
Douglas IS 500/3-7
21 Davis St 01516 508-476-3332
Damian Sugrue, dir. Fax 476-1604

Dover, Norfolk, Pop. 2,163
Dover SD 600/K-5
157 Farm St 02030 508-785-0036
Fax 785-2239
www.doversherborn.org
Chickering ES 600/K-5
28 Cross St 02030 508-785-0480
Kirk Downing, prin. Fax 785-9748

Dover-Sherborn SD 1,100/6-12
157 Farm St 02030 508-785-0036
Valerie Spriggs, supt. Fax 785-2239
www.doversherborn.org
Dover-Sherborn Regional MS 500/6-8
155 Farm St 02030 508-785-0635
Frederick Randall, prin. Fax 785-0796

Sherborn SD 500/PK-5
157 Farm St 02030 508-785-0036
Fax 785-2239
www.doversherborn.org
Other Schools – See Sherborn

Charles River S 200/PK-8
PO Box 339 02030 508-785-0068
Catherine Gately, prin. Fax 785-8290

Dracut, Middlesex, Pop. 25,594
Dracut SD 4,000/PK-12
2063 Lakeview Ave 01826 978-957-2660
W. Spencer Mullin, supt. Fax 957-2682
www.dracutpublicschools.net
Brookside ES 500/PK-4
1560 Lakeview Ave 01826 978-957-0716
Gian Criscitiello, prin. Fax 957-9726
Campbell ES 500/PK-4
1021 Methuen St 01826 978-459-6186
Deborah Koniowka, prin. Fax 459-9780
Englesby IS 700/5-6
1580 Lakeview Ave 01826 978-957-9745
Robert Young, prin. Fax 957-8449
Greenmont Avenue ES 300/K-4
37 Greenmont Ave 01826 978-453-1797
David Hill, prin. Fax 453-8739
Lakeview JHS 700/7-8
1570 Lakeview Ave 01826 978-957-3330
Theresa Rogers, prin. Fax 957-4075
Parker Avenue ES 200/K-4
77 Parker Ave 01826 978-957-3102
Spiros Sintros, prin. Fax 957-7684

Dudley, Worcester, Pop. 3,700
Dudley-Charlton Regional SD 4,000/PK-12
68 Dudley Oxford Rd 01571 508-943-6888
Sean Gilrein, supt. Fax 943-1077
www.dcrsd.org/
Dudley ES 400/2-4
16 School St 01571 508-943-3351
Terri Caffelle, prin. Fax 949-3305
Dudley MS 600/5-8
70 Dudley Oxford Rd 01571 508-943-2224
Gregg Desto, prin. Fax 949-0720
Mason Road ES 100/K-1
20 Mason Rd 01571 508-943-4312
Theodore Dono, prin. Fax 949-1005
Other Schools – See Charlton

Dunstable, Middlesex
Groton Dunstable Regional SD
Supt. — See Groton
Swallow / Union ES 300/K-4
522 Main St 01827 978-649-7281
Peter Myerson, prin. Fax 649-5078

Duxbury, Plymouth, Pop. 1,637
Duxbury SD 3,200/PK-12
130 Saint George St 02332 781-934-7600
Susan Skeiber, supt. Fax 934-7644
www.duxbury.k12.ma.us
Alden ES 800/3-5
130 Saint George St 02332 781-934-7630
Christopher Trombly, prin. Fax 934-7636
Chandler ES 600/PK-2
93 Chandler St 02332 781-934-7680
Deborah Zetterberg, prin. Fax 934-7675
Duxbury MS 800/6-8
130 Saint George St 02332 781-934-7640
Blake Dalton, prin. Fax 934-7608

Bay Farm Montessori Academy 200/PK-6
145 Loring St 02332 781-934-7101
Kevin Clark, dir. Fax 934-7102
Good Shepherd Christian Academy 100/PK-8
2 Tremont St 02332 781-934-6007
Jay Lowder, prin. Fax 934-7049

East Boston, See Boston
Boston SD
Supt. — See Boston
Adams ES 200/PK-5
165 Webster St 02128 617-635-8383
Margarita Ruiz, prin. Fax 635-7822
Alighieri ES 100/K-5
37 Gove St 02128 617-635-8529
Anthony Valdez, prin. Fax 635-7691
Bradley ES 200/PK-5
110 Beachview Rd 02128 617-635-8422
Anne Kelly, prin. Fax 635-6927
East Boston Early Education Center 200/PK-1
135 Gove St 02128 617-635-6456
Olga Frechon, prin. Fax 635-8864
Guild ES 300/PK-5
195 Leyden St 02128 617-635-8523
Simon Ho, prin. Fax 635-8526
Kennedy ES 200/PK-5
343 Saratoga St 02128 617-635-8466
Marice Diakite, prin. Fax 635-8469
McKay S 600/K-8
122 Cottage St 02128 617-635-8510
Marco Curnen, prin. Fax 635-8515
O'Donnell ES 200/K-5
33 Trenton St 02128 617-635-8454
Robert Martin, prin. Fax 635-8459
Otis ES 300/K-5
218 Marion St 02128 617-635-8372
Leo Flanagan, prin. Fax 635-8376
Umana MS Academy 600/6-8
312 Border St 02128 617-635-8481
Dr. Jose Salgado, prin. Fax 635-9595

East Boston Central Catholic S 200/K-8
69 London St 02128 617-567-7456
Maryann Manfredonia, prin. Fax 567-9559
St. Mary Star of the Sea S 100/K-8
58 Moore St 02128 617-567-6609
Joan Lawrence, prin. Fax 567-5757

East Bridgewater, Plymouth, Pop. 11,104
East Bridgewater SD 2,300/PK-12
11 Plymouth St 02333 508-378-8200
Margaret Strojny Ph.D., supt. Fax 378-8225
www.ebps.net
Central ES 700/PK-3
107 Central St 02333 508-378-8204
Gina Williams, prin. Fax 378-8229
Mitchell MS 1,000/4-8
435 Central St 02333 508-378-8209
Stanley Piltch, prin. Fax 378-8228

East Brookfield, Worcester, Pop. 1,396
Spencer-East Brookfield SD
Supt. — See Spencer
East Brookfield ES 200/PK-6
410 E Main St 01515 508-885-8536
Mark Andrews, prin. Fax 885-8571

East Falmouth, Barnstable, Pop. 5,577
Falmouth SD 3,900/PK-12
340 Teaticket Hwy 02536 508-548-0151
Marc Dupuis, supt. Fax 457-9032
www.falmouth.k12.ma.us
East Falmouth ES 300/PK-4
33 Davisville Rd 02536 508-548-1052
Samuel Slarskey, prin. Fax 548-0301
Other Schools – See Falmouth, North Falmouth, Teaticket

Heritage Christian Academy 50/PK-8
655 Boxberry Hill Rd 02536 508-564-6341
Joseph Giampietro, prin. Fax 564-6343

East Freetown, Bristol
Freetown SD
Supt. — See Lakeville
Freetown ES 500/PK-4
43 Bullock Rd 02717 508-763-5121
Robert Frizelle, prin. Fax 763-3986

Eastham, Barnstable
Eastham SD
Supt. — See Orleans
Eastham ES 200/K-5
200 School House Rd 02642 508-255-0808
Susan Glass Helman, prin. Fax 240-5403

Easthampton, Hampshire, Pop. 16,004
Easthampton SD 1,700/PK-12
50 Payson Ave Ste 200 01027 413-529-1500
Deborah Carter, supt. Fax 529-1567
www.easthampton.k12.ma.us
Center ES 200/K-4
9 School St 01027 413-529-1540
Robert Orlando, prin. Fax 529-1547
Maple ES 300/PK-4
7 Chapel St 01027 413-529-1550
Thomas Luce, prin. Fax 529-1599
Pepin ES 200/K-4
4 Park St 01027 413-529-1545
Robert Orlando, prin. Fax 529-1594
White Brook MS 500/5-8
200 Park St 01027 413-529-1530
Allison Rebello, prin. Fax 529-1534

East Longmeadow, Hampden, Pop. 13,367
East Longmeadow SD 2,600/K-12
180 Maple St 01028 413-525-5450
Dr. Edward Costa, supt. Fax 525-5456
www.eastlongmeadowma.gov/schools.htm
Birchland Park MS 700/6-8
50 Hanward Hl 01028 413-525-5480
Kathleen Hill, prin. Fax 525-5320
Mapleshade ES 300/3-5
175 Mapleshade Ave 01028 413-525-5485
Brenda Houle, prin. Fax 525-5321
Meadow Brook ES 400/K-2
607 Parker St 01028 413-525-5470
Judith Fletcher, prin. Fax 525-5405
Mountain View ES 300/3-5
77 Hampden Rd 01028 413-525-5490
Carolyn Wallace, prin. Fax 525-5405

East Sandwich, Barnstable, Pop. 3,171
Sandwich SD 3,800/PK-12
365 Quaker Meeting House Rd 02537 508-888-1054
Dr. Mary Johnson, supt. Fax 888-9505
www.sandwich.k12.ma.us
Oak Ridge S 1,000/K-8
260 Quaker Meeting House Rd 02537 508-833-0111
Thomas Daniels, prin. Fax 888-0911
Other Schools – See Forestdale, Sandwich

East Taunton, See Taunton
Taunton SD
Supt. — See Taunton
East Taunton ES 600/K-4
58R W Stevens St 02718 508-821-1330
Dr. Sheila Reardon, prin. Fax 821-1334
Martin MS 800/5-8
131 Caswell St 02718 508-821-1250
Michael Byron, prin. Fax 821-1273

East Templeton, Worcester
Narragansett Regional SD
Supt. — See Baldwinville
East Templeton ES 100/3-4
PO Box 299 01438 978-632-0557
Angelo Garofalo, prin. Fax 630-1863

East Walpole, Norfolk, Pop. 3,800
Walpole SD
Supt. — See Walpole
Bird MS 400/6-8
625 Washington St 02032 508-660-7226
Bridget Gough, prin. Fax 660-7229
Old Post Road ES 500/K-5
99 Old Post Rd 02032 508-660-7219
Stephen Fortin, prin. Fax 660-3114

East Weymouth, Norfolk
Weymouth SD
Supt. — See Weymouth
Adams MS 700/5-8
89 Middle St 02189 781-335-1100
Zeffro Gianetti, prin. Fax 340-2544
Chapman MS 1,300/5-8
1051 Commercial St 02189 781-337-4500
Sheila Fisher, prin. Fax 340-2594

Edgartown, Dukes
Edgartown SD
Supt. — See Vineyard Haven
Edgartown S 300/K-8
35 Robinson Rd 02539 508-627-3316
John Stevens, prin. Fax 627-7983

Erving, Franklin
Erving SD 200/PK-6
18 Pleasant St 01344 413-423-3337
Joan Wickman Ed.D., supt. Fax 423-3236
www.union28.org
Erving ES 200/PK-6
28 Northfield Rd 01344 413-423-3326
Charlene Galenski, prin. Fax 423-3648

Leverett SD 200/PK-6
18 Pleasant St 01344 413-423-3337
Joan Wickman, supt. Fax 423-3236
Other Schools – See Leverett

New Salem-Wendell SD 200/PK-6
18 Pleasant St 01344 413-423-3337
Joan Wickman, supt. Fax 423-3236
www.swiftriverschool.org/
Other Schools – See New Salem

Shutesbury SD 200/PK-6
18 Pleasant St 01344 413-423-3337
Joan Wickman, supt. Fax 423-3236
www.shutesburyschool.org
Other Schools – See Shutesbury

Essex, Essex, Pop. 1,507
Manchester Essex Regional SD
Supt. — See Manchester

Essex ES 300/K-6
12 Story St 01929 978-768-7324
Eric Gordon, prin. Fax 768-2502

Everett, Middlesex, Pop. 36,837
Everett SD 5,100/PK-12
121 Vine St 02149 617-389-7950
Frederick Foresteire, supt. Fax 394-2408
www.everett.k12.ma.us/
English S 600/PK-8
105 Woodville St 02149 617-394-5013
Laurence Arinello, prin. Fax 389-5116
Keverian S 700/K-8
20 Nichols St 02149 617-394-5020
John Obremski, prin. Fax 394-5028
Lafayette S 800/K-8
117 Edith St 02149 617-394-2450
Kevin Shaw, prin. Fax 387-5207
Parlin S 700/K-8
587 Broadway 02149 617-394-2480
Erick Naumann, prin. Fax 389-5827
Webster S PK-3
30 Dartmouth St 02149 617-394-5040
Joan Feudo, prin. Fax 394-5043
Whittier S 400/K-8
337 Broadway 02149 617-394-2410
Helen MacLaughlin, prin. Fax 389-5073

St. Anthony S 300/PK-8
54 Oakes St 02149 617-389-2448
Maria Giggie, prin. Fax 389-3769

Fairhaven, Bristol, Pop. 16,132
Fairhaven SD 1,900/PK-12
128 Washington St 02719 508-979-4000
Dr. Robert Baldwin, supt. Fax 979-4149
www.fairhavenps.org/
East Fairhaven ES 200/PK-5
2 New Boston Rd 02719 508-979-4058
Geraldine Lucas, prin. Fax 979-4143
Hastings MS 500/6-8
30 School St 02719 508-979-4063
Dr. Bonny Gifford, prin. Fax 979-4068
Rogers ES 200/PK-5
100 Pleasant St 02719 508-979-4075
Wendy Williams, prin. Fax 979-4142
Wood ES 300/K-5
60 Sconticut Neck Rd 02719 508-979-4073
Amy Hartley-Matteson, prin. Fax 979-4111

St. Joseph S 200/PK-8
100 Spring St 02719 508-996-1983
Julie Varieka, prin. Fax 996-1998

Fall River, Bristol, Pop. 91,802
Fall River SD 7,900/PK-12
417 Rock St 02720 508-675-8420
Dr. Nicholas Fischer, supt. Fax 675-8462
www.fallriverschools.org/
Borden ES 500/PK-5
1400 President Ave 02720 508-675-8202
Marie Woollam, prin. Fax 675-8259
Doran ES 400/K-5
101 Fountain St 02721 508-675-8225
Maria Pontes, prin. Fax 235-2608
Fonseca ES, 160 N Wall St 02723 K-5
Elaine Sabra, prin. 508-675-8177
Greene ES 600/PK-5
409 Cambridge St 02721 508-675-8325
Vivian Kuss, prin. Fax 675-8328
Kuss MS 500/6-8
290 Rock St 02720 508-675-8335
Nancy Mullen, prin. Fax 675-1984
LeTourneau ES 200/K-5
323 Anthony St 02721 508-675-8290
Barbara Allard, prin. Fax 235-2613
Lord MS 700/6-8
151 Amity St 02721 508-675-8208
Debra Decarlo, prin. Fax 675-8253
Morton MS 700/6-8
376 President Ave 02720 508-675-8340
Karlene Ross, prin. Fax 675-8414
Silvia ES 600/PK-5
1899 Meridian St 02720 508-675-9811
Denise Ward, prin. Fax 675-8314
Talbot MS 600/6-8
124 Melrose St 02723 508-675-8350
Elizabeth Coogan, prin. Fax 675-8356
Tansey ES 300/K-5
711 Ray St 02720 508-675-8206
Elizabeth Almeida, prin. Fax 675-4530
Watson ES 200/K-5
935 Eastern Ave 02723 508-675-8240
Nancy Martin-Bernier, prin. Fax 235-2674

East Gate Christian Academy 100/PK-12
397 Bay St 02724 508-730-1735
Dr. Ronald Bernier, hdmstr. Fax 674-6166
Espirito Santo S 300/PK-8
143 Everett St 02723 508-672-2229
Louise Kane, prin. Fax 672-7724
Holy Name S 200/PK-8
850 Pearce St 02720 508-674-9131
Dr. Patricia Wardell, prin. Fax 679-0571
Holy Trinity S 200/PK-8
64 Lamphor St 02721 508-673-6772
Brenda Gagnon, prin. Fax 730-1864
St. Michael S 200/K-8
209 Essex St 02720 508-678-0266
Sr. Marie Baldi, prin. Fax 324-4433
St. Stanislaus S 100/PK-8
PO Box 300 02724 508-674-6771
Jean Willis, prin. Fax 677-1622
SS. Peter & Paul S 200/PK-8
240 Dover St 02721 508-672-7258
Kathleen Burt, prin. Fax 674-6042

Falmouth, Barnstable, Pop. 4,047
Falmouth SD
Supt. — See East Falmouth
Lawrence MS 600/7-8
113 Lakeview Ave 02540 508-548-0606
Paul Fay, prin. Fax 457-9778
Morse Pond MS 600/5-6
323 Jones Rd 02540 508-548-7300
Jane Manzelli, prin. Fax 457-1810
Mullen-Hall ES 400/K-4
130 Katherine Lee Bates Rd 02540 508-548-0220
Donna Noonan, prin. Fax 457-5404

Feeding Hills, Hampden, Pop. 5,450
Agawam SD 4,300/K-12
1305 Springfield St Ste 1 01030 413-821-0548
Mary Czajkowski Ed.D., supt. Fax 789-1835
www.agawampublicschools.org
Agawam JHS 700/7-8
1305 Springfield St Ste 2 01030 413-821-0561
Norman Robbins, prin. Fax 786-4240
Granger ES 400/K-4
31 S Westfield St 01030 413-821-0581
Tari Thomas, prin. Fax 821-0595
Other Schools – See Agawam

Fiskdale, Worcester, Pop. 2,189
Brimfield SD 400/PK-6
320 Brookfield Rd 01518 508-347-3077
Daniel Durgin, supt. Fax 347-2697
www.tantasqua.org
Other Schools – See Brimfield

Brookfield SD 300/PK-6
320A Brookfield Rd 01518 508-347-3077
Daniel Durgin, supt. Fax 347-2697
www.tantasqua.org
Other Schools – See Brookfield

Holland SD 300/PK-6
320 Brookfield Rd 01518 508-347-3077
Daniel Durgin, supt. Fax 347-2697
www.tantasqua.org
Other Schools – See Holland

Sturbridge SD 900/PK-6
320 Brookfield Rd 01518 508-347-5977
Daniel Durgin, supt. Fax 347-2697
www.tantasqua.org
Other Schools – See Sturbridge

Tantasqua SD 1,900/7-12
320 Brookfield Rd 01518 508-347-3077
Daniel Durgin, supt. Fax 347-2697
www.tantasqua.org
Tantasqua Regional JHS 600/7-8
320 Brookfield Rd 01518 508-347-7381
Jennifer Lundwall, prin. Fax 347-3994

Wales SD 200/PK-6
320A Brookfield Rd 01518 508-347-3077
Daniel Durgin, supt. Fax 347-2697
www.tantasqua.org
Other Schools – See Wales

Fitchburg, Worcester, Pop. 40,045
Fitchburg SD 4,500/PK-12
376 South St 01420 978-345-3200
Andre Ravenelle, supt. Fax 348-2305
www.fitchburg.k12.ma.us
Crocker ES 500/K-4
200 Bigelow Rd 01420 978-345-3290
Terri Grattan, prin. Fax 345-3233
Longsjo MS 500/5-8
98 Academy St 01420 978-343-2146
Craig Chalifoux, prin. Fax 348-2323
McKay Campus ES 400/PK-4
67 Rindge Rd 01420 978-665-3187
Ruth Joseph, prin. Fax 665-3523
Memorial MS 700/5-8
615 Rollstone St 01420 978-345-3295
Francis Thomas, prin. Fax 343-2121
Reingold ES 500/K-4
70 Reingold Ave 01420 978-345-3287
Judy Roy, prin. Fax 343-2132
South Street ES 600/PK-4
376 South St 01420 978-348-2300
Lisa Bryant, prin. Fax 345-3292

Applewild S 300/K-9
120 Prospect St 01420 978-342-6053
Christopher Williamson, hdmstr. Fax 345-5059
Messiah Lutheran Preschool 50/PK-PK
750 Rindge Rd 01420 978-345-5954
Fax 345-5954

St. Anthony S 300/PK-8
123 Salem St 01420 978-345-7785
John Ginnity, prin. Fax 342-5110
St. Bernard S 200/PK-8
254 Summer St 01420 978-342-1948
David Farnsworth, prin. Fax 342-1153

Florence, See Northampton
Northampton SD
Supt. — See Northampton
Finn Ryan Road ES 300/K-5
498 Ryan Rd 01062 413-587-1550
Margaret Riddle, prin. Fax 587-1561
Kennedy MS 700/6-8
100 Bridge Rd 01062 413-587-1489
Lesley Wilson, prin. Fax 587-1495

Florida, Berkshire
Florida SD
Supt. — See North Adams
Abbott Memorial S 100/PK-8
56 N County Rd 01247 413-664-6023
Heidi Dugal, prin. Fax 663-3593

Forestdale, Barnstable, Pop. 2,833
Sandwich SD
Supt. — See East Sandwich
Forestdale S 900/K-8
151 Route 130 02644 508-477-6600
Douglas Jenkins, prin. Fax 477-7665

Foxboro, Norfolk, Pop. 5,706
Foxborough SD 2,900/PK-12
60 South St 02035 508-543-1660
Dr. Christopher Martes, supt. Fax 543-4793
www.foxborough.k12.ma.us
Ahern MS 900/5-8
111 Mechanic St 02035 508-543-1610
Susan Abrams, prin. Fax 543-1613
Burrell ES 300/PK-4
16 Morse St 02035 508-543-1605
Michele McCarthy, prin. Fax 698-2196
Igo ES 500/PK-4
70 Carpenter St 02035 508-543-1680
Ingrid Allardi, prin. Fax 543-1699
Taylor ES 300/K-4
196 South St 02035 508-543-1607
Peter Regan, prin. Fax 543-3261

Living Waters Christian Academy 100/PK-8
115 Mechanic St 02035 508-543-6500
Katrina Joseph, admin. Fax 543-5124
Sage S 200/PK-8
171 Mechanic St 02035 508-543-9619
Katherine Windsor, hdmstr. Fax 543-1152

Framingham, Middlesex, Pop. 67,300
Framingham SD 8,000/PK-12
14 Vernon St Ste 201 01701 508-626-9117
Dr. Eugene Thayer, supt. Fax 626-9119
www.framingham.k12.ma.us
Barbieri ES 500/K-5
100 Dudley Rd 01702 508-626-9187
Minerva Gonzalez, prin. Fax 626-9176
BLOCKS Preschool @ King 300/PK-PK
454 Water St 01701 508-877-9521
Rosario Alvarez-O'Neil, prin. Fax 788-1059
Brophy ES 400/K-5
575 Pleasant St 01701 508-626-9158
Margaret Doyle, prin. Fax 628-1305
Cameron MS 500/6-8
215 Elm St 01701 508-879-2290
Judith Kelly, prin. Fax 788-3560
Dunning ES 500/K-5
48 Frost St 01701 508-626-9155
Deborah Del Dotto, prin. Fax 628-1363
Fuller MS 600/6-8
31 Flagg Dr 01702 508-620-4956
Juan Rodriguez, prin. Fax 628-1308
Hemenway ES 600/K-5
729 Water St 01701 508-626-9149
Dr. Carolyn Burke, prin. Fax 877-2262
McCarthy ES 500/K-5
8 Flagg Dr 01702 508-626-9161
Joan Vodoklys, prin. Fax 626-9106
Potter Road ES 400/K-5
492 Potter Rd 01701 508-626-9110
Maria Iglesias, prin. Fax 877-1683
Stapleton ES 400/K-5
25 Elm St 01701 508-626-9143
William McDonald, prin. Fax 877-4908
Walsh MS 700/6-8
301 Brook St 01701 508-626-9180
Jay Cummings, prin. Fax 626-9167
Wilson ES 500/K-5
169 Leland St 01702 508-626-9164
Robin Welch, prin. Fax 620-2965

St. Bridget S 300/K-8
832 Worcester Rd 01702 508-875-0181
Roseanne Mungovan, prin. Fax 875-9552
St. Tarcisius S 200/PK-8
560 Waverly St 01702 508-872-8188
Mary Ellen Wyman, prin. Fax 872-2495
Summit Montessori S 100/PK-6
283 Pleasant St 01701 508-872-3630
Richard Eyster, hdmstr. Fax 872-3314

Franklin, Norfolk, Pop. 30,893
Franklin SD 6,200/PK-12
355 E Central St 02038 508-541-5243
Wayne Ogden, supt. Fax 533-0321
www.franklin.k12.ma.us
Franklin ECDC 200/PK-PK
224 Oak St 02038 508-541-8166
Karen Seyfried, prin. Fax 541-8254
Jefferson ES 500/K-5
628 Washington St 02038 508-541-2140
Jane Hyman, prin. Fax 541-2124
Keller ES 600/K-5
500 Lincoln St 02038 508-553-0322
Mary Jane Wiles, prin. Fax 541-2109
Kennedy Memorial ES 600/K-5
551 Pond St 02038 508-541-5260
Joan Toye, prin. Fax 541-5260
Mann MS 600/6-8
224 Oak St 02038 508-553-0322
Anne Bergen, prin. Fax 541-7071
Oak Street ES 500/K-5
224 Oak St 02038 508-541-7890
Corine Minkle, prin. Fax 541-8047
Parmenter ES 400/K-5
235 Wachusett St 02038 508-541-5281
Judith Bassignani, prin. Fax 553-0894
Remington MS 500/6-8
628 Washington St 02038 508-541-2130
Paul Peri, prin. Fax 541-2124
Sullivan MS 500/6-8
500 Lincoln St 02038 508-553-0322
Beth Wittcoff, prin. Fax 542-2109

Thayer ES 300/PK-5
137 W Central St 02038 508-541-5263
Shirley Babcock, prin. Fax 553-0891

Cornerstone Christian Academy 100/K-8
40 Kenwood Cir 02038 508-520-2272
Amanda Irwin, hdmstr. Fax 520-7537

Gardner, Worcester, Pop. 20,908
Gardner SD 2,800/PK-12
70 Waterford St 01440 978-632-1000
Carol Daring Ph.D., supt. Fax 632-1164
www.gardnerk12.org
Elm Street ES 500/3-5
160 Elm St 01440 978-632-1673
Joyce Swedberg, prin. Fax 632-4382
Gardner MS 700/6-8
297 Catherine St 01440 978-632-1603
Chris Casavant, prin. Fax 632-4234
Sauter ES 200/1-3
130 Elm St 01440 978-632-5480
Cherie McComb, prin. Fax 632-1164
Waterford Street ES 300/PK-2
62 Waterford St 01440 978-632-1605
Paul Guerin, prin. Fax 632-4037

Our Lady of the Rosary S 300/PK-8
99 Nichols St 01440 978-632-8656
Dr. Paul Damour, prin. Fax 630-1433
Sacred Heart S 200/PK-8
53 Lynde St 01440 978-632-0950
Maureen Lapan, prin. Fax 630-2448

Georgetown, Essex
Georgetown SD 1,600/PK-12
51 North St 01833 978-352-5777
Carol Jacobs, supt. Fax 352-5778
www.georgetown.k12.ma.us
Penn Brook ES 500/2-5
68 Elm St 01833 978-352-5785
Dr. Donna Tanner, prin. Fax 352-5787
Perley ES 300/PK-1
51 North St 01833 978-352-5780
Gail Korpusik, prin. Fax 352-5782

Gilbertville, Worcester
Quabbin SD
Supt. — See Barre
Hardwick ES 300/K-6
531 Lower Rd 01031 413-477-6351
Janeth Williams, prin. Fax 477-6409

Gill, Franklin, Pop. 1,583
Gill-Montague SD
Supt. — See Turners Falls
Gill ES 100/K-6
48 Boyle Rd, 413-863-3255
Rita Detweiler, prin. Fax 863-3268

Gloucester, Essex, Pop. 30,713
Gloucester SD 3,800/PK-12
6 School House Rd 01930 978-281-9800
Christopher Farmer, supt. Fax 281-9899
www.gloucesterschools.com
Beeman Memorial ES 200/K-5
138 Cherry St 01930 978-281-9825
Ellen Sibley, prin. Fax 282-3011
East Gloucester ES 200/K-5
8 Davis St 01930 978-281-9830
Gregg Bach, prin. Fax 281-9864
Fuller ES 600/PK-5
4 School House Rd 01930 978-281-9840
Sue Ellen Hogan, prin. Fax 281-9861
O'Maley MS 800/6-8
32 Cherry St 01930 978-281-9850
Michael Tracy, prin. Fax 281-9890
Plum Cove ES 100/K-4
15 Hickory St 01930 978-282-3030
Tammy Morgan, prin. Fax 282-3006
Veterans Memorial ES 200/K-5
11 Webster St 01930 978-281-9820
Cherylann Parker, prin. Fax 281-9717
West Parish ES 400/K-5
10 Concord St 01930 978-281-9835
James Gutstadt, prin. Fax 281-9886

Faith Christian S 50/PK-8
384 Washington St 01930 978-283-8856
Donald Lodge, prin. Fax 283-8856
St. Ann S 100/PK-8
60 Prospect St 01930 978-283-3455
Sr. Judy O'Brien, prin. Fax 282-1686

Grafton, Worcester
Grafton SD 2,500/PK-12
30 Providence Rd Ste 2 01519 508-839-5421
Joseph Connors Ph.D., supt. Fax 839-7618
www.grafton.k12.ma.us
Grafton ES 700/3-5
105 Millbury St 01519 508-839-0757
Brenda Plainte, prin. Fax 839-7458
Grafton MS 600/6-8
60 North St 01519 508-839-5420
Richard Lind, prin. Fax 839-8528
Other Schools – See North Grafton, South Grafton

Touchstone Community S 100/PK-8
54 Leland St 01519 508-839-0038
Donald Grace, hdmstr. Fax 839-7331

Granby, Hampshire, Pop. 1,327
Granby SD 1,100/PK-12
387 E State St 01033 413-467-7193
Patricia Stevens, supt. Fax 467-3909
www.granbyschoolsma.org/
East Meadow ES 300/4-6
393 E State St 01033 413-467-7199
James Pietras, prin. Fax 467-3909
West Street ES 300/PK-3
14 West St 01033 413-467-9235
Pamela McCauley, prin. Fax 467-7163

Granville, Hampden
Granville SD
Supt. — See Southwick
Granville Village S 200/PK-8
409 Main Rd 01034 413-357-6626
Anna Ohlson, prin. Fax 357-6009

Great Barrington, Berkshire, Pop. 2,810
Berkshire Hills SD
Supt. — See Stockbridge
Monument Valley Regional MS 400/5-8
313 Monument Valley Rd 01230 413-644-2300
Jane Furey, prin. Fax 644-2394
Muddy Brook Regional ES 400/PK-4
318 Monument Valley Rd 01230 413-644-2350
Denise Hardie, prin. Fax 644-2395

Great Barrington Rudolf Steiner S 200/PK-8
35 W Plain Rd 01230 413-528-4015
Marilyn Ruppart, admin. Fax 528-6410

Greenfield, Franklin, Pop. 14,016
Greenfield SD 1,200/PK-12
141 Davis St 01301 413-772-1311
Susan Hollins, supt. Fax 774-7940
www.gpsk12.org/
Academy for Learning at North Parish 50/PK-PK
15 Place Ter 01301 413-772-1390
Joan Schell, dir. Fax 772-1337
Federal ES 200/K-4
125 Federal St 01301 413-772-1380
Joan Schell, prin. Fax 772-1319
Greenfield MS 400/4-8
195 Federal St 01301 413-772-1360
Gary Tashjian, prin. Fax 772-1367
Newton ES 100/K-3
70 Shelburne Rd 01301 413-772-1370
Joan Schell, prin. Fax 772-1332

Cornerstone Christian S 100/PK-8
385 Chapman St 01301 413-772-1063
Sandra Peck, prin. Fax 772-5728
Greenfield Center S 100/K-8
71 Montague City Rd 01301 413-773-1700
Charlie Spencer, prin. Fax 774-1135
Holy Trinity S 100/PK-8
10 Beacon St 01301 413-773-3831
Arlene Ashby, prin. Fax 774-7794

Groton, Middlesex, Pop. 1,044
Groton Dunstable Regional SD 2,700/PK-12
PO Box 729 01450 978-448-5505
Alan Genovese, supt. Fax 448-9402
www.gdrsd.org
Boutwell S 100/PK-K
PO Box 730 01450 978-448-2297
Russell Hoyt, prin. Fax 448-8459
Groton Dunstable Regional MS 900/5-8
PO Box 727 01450 978-448-6155
Steven Silverman, prin. Fax 448-1201
Roche ES 600/K-4
PO Box 738 01450 978-448-6665
Ruthann Goguen, prin. Fax 448-3988
Other Schools – See Dunstable

Country Day S of the Holy Union 200/K-8
14 Main St 01450 978-448-5646
Sr. Yvette Ladurantaye, prin. Fax 448-2392

Groveland, Essex, Pop. 5,214
Pentucket SD
Supt. — See West Newbury
Bagnall ES 700/PK-6
253 School St 01834 978-372-8856
Elaine Champion, prin. Fax 521-8956

Hadley, Hampshire
Hadley SD 700/PK-12
125 Russell St 01035 413-586-0822
Dr. Nicholas Young, supt. Fax 582-6453
www.hadleyschools.org
Hadley ES 400/PK-6
21 River Dr 01035 413-584-5011
Phillip DiPietro, prin. Fax 582-6457

Hartsbrook S 300/PK-12
193 Bay Rd 01035 413-584-3198
Fax 586-9438

Halifax, Plymouth
Halifax SD
Supt. — See Kingston
Halifax ES 600/K-6
464 Plymouth St 02338 781-293-2581
Claudia Motta, prin. Fax 293-6589

Hampden, Hampden
Hampden-Wilbraham SD
Supt. — See Wilbraham
Burgess MS 300/5-8
85 Wilbraham Rd 01036 413-566-8950
Noel Pixley, prin. Fax 566-2163
Green Meadows ES 300/K-4
38 North Rd 01036 413-566-3263
Deborah Thompson, prin. Fax 566-2089

Hancock, Berkshire
Hancock SD
Supt. — See Richmond
Hancock ES 50/PK-6
3080 Hancock Rd 01237 413-738-5676
Sarah Madden, prin. Fax 738-5338

Hanover, Plymouth, Pop. 11,912
Hanover SD 2,700/PK-12
188 Broadway 02339 781-878-0786
Kristine Nash Ed.D., supt. Fax 871-3374
www.hanoverschools.org
Cedar ES 600/PK-4
265 Cedar St 02339 781-878-7228
Fred Morris, prin. Fax 878-1968
Center ES 300/PK-2
65 Silver St 02339 781-826-2631
Jane A. Degrenier, prin. Fax 826-0765
Hanover MS 900/5-8
45 Whiting St 02339 781-871-1122
Charles Egan, prin. Fax 871-8792
Sylvester ES 200/3-4
495 Hanover St 02339 781-826-3844
Jane A. Degrenier, prin. Fax 829-5098

Master's Academy 100/K-12
1075 Washington St 02339 781-826-2110
David McGee, prin. Fax 826-3110

Hanscom AFB, See Bedford
Lincoln SD
Supt. — See Lincoln
Hanscom MS 300/4-8
6 Ent Rd 01731 781-274-0050
Mark Kaufman, prin. Fax 274-7329
Hanscom PS 300/PK-3
6 Ent Rd 01731 781-274-7721
Randy Davis, prin. Fax 274-6414

Hanson, Plymouth, Pop. 2,188
Whitman-Hanson SD
Supt. — See Whitman
Hanson MS 500/6-8
111 Liberty St 02341 781-618-7575
Martin Geoghegan, prin. Fax 618-8815
Indian Head ES 500/3-5
720 Indian Head St 02341 781-618-7065
Elaine White, prin. Fax 618-7094
Maquan ES 400/PK-2
38 School St 02341 781-618-7060
Ellen Stockdale, prin. Fax 618-7097

Harvard, Worcester
Harvard SD 1,300/K-12
39 Mass Ave 01451 978-456-4140
Dr. Thomas Jefferson, supt. Fax 456-8592
www.psharvard.org
Harvard ES 500/K-5
27 Mass Ave 01451 978-456-4145
Mary Beth Banios, prin. Fax 456-4146

Harwich, Barnstable
Harwich SD 1,400/K-12
81 Oak St 02645 508-430-7200
Dr. Carolyn Cragin, supt. Fax 430-7205
www.harwich.edu
Harwich ES 600/K-5
263 South St 02645 508-430-7216
Samuel Hein, prin. Fax 430-7232
Harwich MS 300/6-8
204 Sisson Rd 02645 508-430-7212
John Riley, prin. Fax 430-7230

Hatfield, Hampshire, Pop. 1,234
Hatfield SD 400/PK-12
34 School St 01038 413-247-5641
Patrice Dardenne, supt. Fax 247-0201
www.hatfieldpublicschools.net/
Hatfield ES 200/PK-6
33 Main St 01038 413-247-5010
Jennifer Chapin, prin. Fax 247-0482

Haverhill, Essex, Pop. 60,242
Haverhill SD 6,800/PK-12
4 Summer St Ste 104 01830 978-374-3400
Raleigh Buchanan Ed.D., supt. Fax 373-1535
www.haverhill-ps.org/
Consentino MS 600/6-8
685 Washington St 01832 978-374-5775
Mary Malone, prin. Fax 374-3442
Crowell ES 100/K-2
26 Belmont Ave 01830 978-374-3473
Raleigh Buchanan, prin. Fax 374-3489
Golden Hill ES 500/K-5
140 Boardman St 01830 978-374-5794
Bonnie Antkowiak, prin. Fax 374-3454
Greenleaf ES 300/K-2
58 Chadwick St 01835 978-374-3487
Larry Marino, prin. Fax 374-3437
Hunking MS 400/6-8
98 Winchester St 01835 978-374-5787
Larry Marino, prin. Fax 372-5890
Moody S 200/PK-K
59 Margin St 01832 978-374-3459
Judith Zaino, dir. Fax 374-3496
Nettle MS 400/6-8
150 Boardman St 01830 978-374-5792
Gerald Kayo, prin. Fax 374-3441
Pentucket Lake ES 600/K-5
252 Concord St 01830 978-374-2421
Jennifer Roberts, prin. Fax 374-0392
Tilton ES 500/K-4
70 Grove St 01832 978-374-3475
Mary Maranto, prin. Fax 374-3440
Walnut Square ES 100/K-2
645 Main St 01830 978-374-3471
Larry Marino, prin. Fax 374-3486
Whittier MS 400/6-8
256 Concord St 01830 978-374-5782
Elizabeth Kitsos, prin. Fax 372-5999
Other Schools – See Bradford

Sacred Hearts S 300/K-8
31 S Chestnut St 01835 978-372-5451
Kathleen Blain, prin. Fax 372-1110
St. Joseph S 400/PK-8
56 Oak Ter 01832 978-521-4256
Carol Simone, prin. Fax 521-2613

Hingham, Plymouth, Pop. 5,454
Hingham SD 3,700/PK-12
220 Central St 02043 781-741-1500
Dorothy Galo, supt. Fax 749-7457
www.hinghamschools.com/
Foster ES 600/K-5
55 Downer Ave 02043 781-741-1520
Deborah Stellar, prin. Fax 741-1522
Hingham MS 900/6-8
1103 Main St 02043 781-741-1550
Roger Boddie, prin. Fax 749-6297
Plymouth River ES 600/K-5
200 High St 02043 781-741-1530
Charles Cormier, prin. Fax 741-1533
South ES 700/PK-5
831 Main St 02043 781-741-1540
Anthony Keady, prin. Fax 749-5673

Derby Academy 300/PK-8
56 Burditt Ave 02043 781-749-0746
Andrea Archer, hdmstr. Fax 740-2542
Old Colony Montessori S 100/PK-3
20 Derby St 02043 781-749-3698
Michael Walker, admin. Fax 741-8859
St. Paul S 300/PK-8
18 Fearing Rd 02043 781-749-2407
Cynthia Duggan, prin. Fax 749-8053

Hinsdale, Berkshire
Central Berkshire Regional SD
Supt. — See Dalton
Kittredge ES 200/PK-5
80 Maple St 01235 413-655-2525
Deborah White, prin. Fax 655-0184

Holbrook, Norfolk, Pop. 11,041
Holbrook SD 1,400/PK-12
227 Plymouth St 02343 781-767-1226
Susan Martin, supt. Fax 767-1312
www.holbrook.k12.ma.us/
Kennedy ES 500/PK-3
339 Plymouth St 02343 781-767-4600
Barbara McLaughlin, prin. Fax 767-7273
South ES 300/4-6
719 S Franklin St 02343 781-767-0211
Julie Hamilton, prin. Fax 767-4054

St. Joseph S 300/PK-8
143 S Franklin St 02343 781-767-1544
Anne Clough, prin. Fax 767-3975

Holden, Worcester, Pop. 14,628
Wachusett Regional SD
Supt. — See Jefferson
Davis Hill ES 500/K-5
80 Jamieson Rd 01520 508-829-1754
Mark Aucoin, prin. Fax 829-2057
Dawson ES 500/PK-5
155 Salisbury St 01520 508-829-6828
Patricia Scales, prin. Fax 829-6801
Mayo ES 500/K-5
351 Bullard St 01520 508-829-3203
Judith Evans, prin. Fax 829-5216
Mountview MS 700/6-8
270 Shrewsbury St 01520 508-829-5577
Preston Shaw, prin. Fax 829-3711

Holden Christian Academy 100/PK-8
279 Reservoir St 01520 508-829-4418
Susan Hayward, prin. Fax 829-4665

Holland, Hampden, Pop. 1,331
Holland SD
Supt. — See Fiskdale
Holland ES 300/PK-6
28 Sturbridge Rd 01521 413-245-9644
Andrew Samuelson, prin. Fax 245-4417

Holliston, Middlesex, Pop. 12,926
Holliston SD 2,700/PK-12
370 Hollis St 01746 508-429-0654
Bradford Jackson, supt. Fax 429-0653
www.holliston.k12.ma.us/
Adams MS 700/6-8
323 Woodland St 01746 508-429-0657
Peter Botelho, prin. Fax 429-0690
Miller ES 600/3-5
235 Woodland St 01746 508-429-0667
David Keim, prin. Fax 429-3684
Placentino ES 500/PK-3
235 Woodland St 01746 508-429-0647
Linda Weene, prin. Fax 429-0691

Holyoke, Hampden, Pop. 39,958
Holyoke SD 5,400/PK-12
57 Suffolk St Ste 101 01040 413-534-2005
Dr. Eduardo Carballo, supt. Fax 534-2297
www.hps.holyoke.ma.us
Donahue S 500/K-8
210 Whiting Farms Rd 01040 413-534-2069
Luz Perez, prin. Fax 534-2309
Kelly S 500/K-8
216 West St 01040 413-534-2078
Chad Mazza, prin. Fax 534-2303
McMahon S 300/K-8
75 Kane Rd 01040 413-534-2062
Hilary Russell, prin. Fax 534-2290
Metcalf Preschool 200/PK-PK
2019 Northampton St 01040 413-534-2104
Gina Roy, prin. Fax 534-2141
Morgan S 500/K-8
596 S Bridge St 01040 413-534-2083
Paula Fitzgerald, prin. Fax 534-2148
Peck S 200/K-8
1916 Northampton St 01040 413-534-2040
Paul Hyry, prin. Fax 532-8563
Sullivan S 600/K-8
400 Jarvis Ave 01040 413-534-2060
John Breish, prin. Fax 534-2304
White S 500/K-8
1 Jefferson St 01040 413-534-2058
Ellen Jackson, prin. Fax 534-2293

Blessed Sacrament S 300/PK-8
21 Westfield Rd 01040 413-536-2236
Anne Heston, prin. Fax 534-0795
First Lutheran S 100/PK-8
1810 Northampton St 01040 413-532-4272
Fax 534-4239
Mater Dolorosa S 300/PK-8
25 Maple St 01040 413-532-2831
Sr. Corinne Gurka, prin. Fax 532-8588

Hopedale, Worcester, Pop. 3,961
Hopedale SD 1,300/PK-12
25 Adin St 01747 508-634-2220
Dr. Patricia Ruane, supt. Fax 478-1471
www.hopedale.k12.ma.us
Bright Beginnings Center 100/PK-PK
6 Park St 01747 508-634-2213
Susan Mulready, dir. Fax 634-2232
Memorial ES 700/K-6
6 Prospect St 01747 508-634-2214
Joanne Finnegan, prin. Fax 634-0695

Hopkinton, Middlesex, Pop. 2,305
Hopkinton SD 3,100/PK-12
89 Hayden Rowe St 01748 508-417-9360
John Phelan Ed.D., supt. Fax 497-9833
www.hopkinton.k12.ma.us
Center ES 300/K-1
11 Ash St 01748 508-497-9875
Jen Parson, prin. Fax 497-9878
Elmwood ES 500/2-3
14 Elm St 01748 508-497-9860
Ilene Silver, prin. Fax 497-9862
Hopkins ES 600/4-5
104 Hayden Rowe St 01748 508-497-9824
Martha Starr, prin. Fax 435-0314
Hopkinton MS 800/6-8
88 Hayden Rowe St 01748 508-497-9830
William Lynch Ed.D., prin. Fax 497-9803
Hopkinton Preschool PK-PK
88 Hayden Rowe St Ste B 01748 508-497-9806
William Lynch, prin.

Hubbardston, Worcester
Quabbin SD
Supt. — See Barre
Hubbardston Center ES 500/K-6
8 Elm St 01452 978-928-4487
Maureen Donelan, prin. Fax 928-4487

Hudson, Middlesex, Pop. 14,267
Hudson SD 2,800/PK-12
155 Apsley St 01749 978-567-6100
Stephen Dlott, supt. Fax 567-6103
www.hudson.k12.ma.us
Farley ES 500/1-5
119 Cottage St 01749 978-567-6153
Sharon MacDonald, prin. Fax 567-6162
Forest Avenue ES 500/PK-5
138 Forest Ave 01749 978-567-6190
Jodi Fortuna, prin. Fax 567-6202
Hubert K 200/K-K
119 Broad St 01749 978-567-6130
Mary McCarthy, prin. Fax 567-6142
Kennedy MS 400/6-7
201 Manning St 01749 978-567-6210
George Calnan, prin. Fax 567-6232
Mulready ES 300/1-5
306 Cox St 01749 978-567-6170
Charlene Cook, prin. Fax 567-6182

St. Michael S 200/PK-8
18 High St 01749 978-562-2917
Patricia Delaney, prin. Fax 562-3293

Hull, Plymouth, Pop. 10,466
Hull SD 1,200/PK-12
180 Harborview Rd 02045 781-925-0771
Kathleen Tyrell, supt. Fax 925-0615
www.town.hull.ma.us
Jacobs ES 500/PK-5
180 Harborview Rd 02045 781-925-4400
Donna Tobin, prin. Fax 925-2938
Memorial MS 300/6-8
81 Central Ave 02045 781-925-2040
Lynda Feeney, prin. Fax 925-8002

Huntington, Hampshire
Gateway SD 1,100/PK-12
12 Littleville Rd 01050 413-685-1000
Dr. David Hopson, supt. Fax 667-8739
www.grsd.org
Gateway Regional MS 200/5-6
12 Littleville Rd 01050 413-685-1200
Todd Gazda, prin. Fax 667-5669
Littleville ES 200/PK-4
4 Littleville Rd 01050 413-685-1300
Joanne Blocker, prin. Fax 667-5734
Other Schools – See Blandford, Chester, Russell, Worthington

Hyannis, Barnstable, Pop. 14,120
Barnstable SD 4,400/PK-12
PO Box 955 02601 508-862-4953
Dr. Patricia Grenier, supt. Fax 790-6454
www.barnstable.k12.ma.us/
Barnstable Early Learning Center 100/PK-PK
744 W Main St 02601 508-775-2770
David Thomas, dir. Fax 775-2565
Barnstable MS 900/7-8
895 Falmouth Rd 02601 508-790-6460
Lisa Chen, prin. Fax 790-6435
Hyannis East ES 300/K-4
165 Bearses Way 02601 508-790-6485
Thomas Larrabee, prin. Fax 790-6432
Hyannis West ES 300/K-4
549 W Main St 02601 508-790-6480
Patricia Sullivan, prin. Fax 790-6433
Other Schools – See Centerville, Cotuit, Marstons Mills, Osterville, West Barnstable

---

St. Francis Xavier Prep S 300/5-8
33 Cross St 02601 508-771-7200
Robert Deburro, hdmstr. Fax 771-7233

Hyde Park, See Boston
Boston SD
Supt. — See Boston
Channing ES 300/PK-5
35 Sunnyside St 02136 617-635-8722
Deborah Dancy, prin. Fax 635-8564
Greenwood ES 400/K-5
612 Metropolitan Ave 02136 617-635-8665
Ida Weldon, prin. Fax 635-8671
Grew ES 200/K-5
40 Gordon Ave 02136 617-635-8715
Ronald Jackson, prin. Fax 635-8718
Rogers MS 500/6-8
15 Everett St 02136 617-635-8700
Andrew Bott, prin. Fax 635-8708
Roosevelt S 300/K-8
95 Needham Rd 02136 617-635-8676
Emily Glasgow, prin. Fax 635-8679

Indian Orchard, See Springfield
Springfield SD
Supt. — See Springfield
Indian Orchard ES 600/PK-5
95 Milton St 01151 413-787-7255
Deborah Beglane, prin. Fax 787-7283

Ipswich, Essex, Pop. 4,132
Ipswich SD 2,100/PK-12
1 Lord Sq 01938 978-356-2935
Richard Korb, supt. Fax 356-0445
www.ipswichschools.org
Doyon Memorial ES 500/PK-5
216 Linebrook Rd 01938 978-356-5506
Kenneth Cooper, prin. Fax 356-8574
Ipswich MS 500/6-8
130 High St 01938 978-356-3535
Cheryl Forster, prin. Fax 412-8169
Winthrop ES 500/PK-5
65 Central St 01938 978-356-2976
Sheila McAdams, prin. Fax 356-8739

Jamaica Plain, See Boston
Boston SD
Supt. — See Boston
Agassiz ES 600/PK-5
20 Child St 02130 617-635-8198
Maria Cordon, prin. Fax 635-7835
Curley S 600/K-8
493 Centre St 02130 617-635-8239
Jeffrey Slater, prin. Fax 635-8184
Hennigan ES 500/K-5
200 Heath St 02130 617-635-8264
Eleanor Perry, prin. Fax 635-8271
Kennedy ES 400/K-5
7 Bolster St 02130 617-635-8127
Eileen Morales, prin. Fax 635-8130
Manning ES 200/K-5
130 Louders Ln 02130 617-635-8102
Sarah Stone, prin. Fax 635-9348
West Zone-ELC 100/K-1
200 Heath St 02130 617-635-8275
Eunice DaSilva Fernandes, prin. Fax 635-9370
Young Achievers Science and Math S 300/K-8
25 Walk Hill St 02130 617-635-6804
Virginia Chalmers, prin. Fax 635-6811

Our Lady of Lourdes S 200/K-8
54 Brookside Ave 02130 617-524-6136
Janice Wilson, prin. Fax 522-2966

Jefferson, Worcester
Wachusett Regional SD 6,600/PK-12
1745 Main St 01522 508-829-1670
Thomas Pandiscio Ed.D., supt. Fax 829-1680
www.wrsd.net
Other Schools – See Holden, Paxton, Princeton, Rutland, Sterling

Kingston, Plymouth, Pop. 4,774
Halifax SD 600/K-6
250 Pembroke St 02364 781-585-4313
John Tuffy, supt. Fax 585-2994
www.silverlake.mec.edu
Other Schools – See Halifax

Kingston SD 1,000/K-6
250 Pembroke St 02364 781-585-4313
John Tuffy, supt. Fax 585-2994
www.silverlake.mec.edu
Kingston ES 300/K-2
150 Main St 02364 781-585-3821
Paula Bartosiak, prin. Fax 582-3858

Kingston IS 700/3-6
65 Second Brook St 02364 781-585-0472
Robert Hodge, prin. Fax 585-0053

Plympton SD 200/K-6
250 Pembroke St 02364 781-585-4313
John Tuffy, supt. Fax 585-2994
www.silverlake.mec.edu
Other Schools – See Plympton

Silver Lake Regional SD 1,700/7-12
250 Pembroke St 02364 781-585-4313
John Tuffy, supt. Fax 585-2994
www.silverlake.mec.edu
Silver Lake Regional MS 600/7-8
256 Pembroke St 02364 781-582-3555
Dennis Azevedo, prin. Fax 582-3599

Sacred Heart ES 500/PK-6
329 Bishops Hwy 02364 781-585-2114
Sr. Ann Connolly, prin. Fax 585-6993

Lakeville, Plymouth
Freetown SD 500/PK-4
98 Howland Rd 02347 508-923-2000
Dr. Stephen Furtado, supt. Fax 923-9960
Other Schools – See East Freetown

Freetown-Lakeville SD 1,900/4-12
98 Howland Rd 02347 508-923-2000
Dr. Stephen Furtado, supt. Fax 923-9960
www.freelake.org/
Freetown-Lakeville IS 300/4-5
112 Howland Rd 02347 508-923-3506
Megan Beaubien, prin. Fax 947-0266
Freetown-Lakeville MS 800/6-8
96 Howland Rd 02347 508-923-3518
David Patota, prin. Fax 946-2050

Lakeville SD 600/PK-4
98 Howland Rd 02347 508-923-2000
Dr. Stephen Furtado, supt. Fax 923-9960
www.freelake.org/
Assawompset ES 500/PK-3
232 Main St 02347 508-947-1403
Laurie Hunter, prin. Fax 947-7068
Austin IS 200/4-4
112 Howland Rd 02347 508-923-3506
Megan Beaubein, prin. Fax 947-0266

Mullein Hill Christian Academy 100/PK-8
111 Highland Rd 02347 508-946-4566
Barbara Priestly, prin. Fax 947-1637

Lancaster, Worcester
Nashoba Regional SD
Supt. — See Bolton
Burbank MS 200/6-8
1 Hollywood Dr 01523 978-365-4558
Patrick Perkins, prin. Fax 365-6882
Rowlandson ES 500/PK-5
103 Hollywood Dr 01523 978-368-8482
Sean O'Shea, prin. Fax 368-8730

Lanesboro, Berkshire
Richmond SD 200/PK-8
188 Summer St 01237 413-442-2229
William Ballen, supt. Fax 447-9958
Other Schools – See Richmond

Williamstown-Lanesboro SD 71
Supt. — See Williamstown
Lanesboro ES 300/PK-6
188 Summer St 01237 413-443-0027
Ellen Boshe, prin. Fax 447-9958

Berkshire Hills SDA S 50/1-8
900 Cheshire Rd 01237 413-443-7777
Fax 443-7777

Lawrence, Essex, Pop. 71,314
Lawrence SD 9,100/PK-12
255 Essex St 01840 978-975-5900
Dr. Wilfredo Laboy, supt. Fax 975-5904
www.lawrence.k12.ma.us
Arlington ES 500/K-4
150 Arlington St 01841 978-975-5926
Elizabeth Qualter, prin. Fax 975-4004
Arlington MS 5-8
150 Arlington St 01841 978-975-5930
Juan Rodriguez, prin. Fax 975-4004
Breen ECC 200/PK-K
114 Osgood St 01843 978-975-5932
Norma Micheroni, prin. Fax 687-6643
Bruce S 700/1-8
135 Butler St 01841 978-975-5935
Sharon Godbold, prin. Fax 685-8009
Frost ES K-4
33 Hamlet St 01843 978-975-5941
Patricia Weir, prin. Fax 685-3668
Frost MS 400/5-8
33 Hamlet St 01843 978-975-5941
Ellen Baranowski, prin. Fax 685-3668
Guilmette ES 1-4
80 Bodwell St 01841 978-686-8810
Lori Butterfield, prin. Fax 686-6740
Guilmette MS 500/5-8
80 Bodwell St 01841 978-722-8270
Ian Gosselin, prin. Fax 880-4317
Hennessey ES 200/PK-1
122 Hancock St 01841 978-975-5950
Judith Alaimo, prin. Fax 975-1899
Lawlor ECC 200/K-K
41 Lexington St 01841 978-975-5956
Ada Ramos, prin. Fax 681-0963
Leahy ES 500/K-5
100 Erving Ave 01841 978-975-5959
Patricia Mariano, prin. Fax 975-1835

Leonard MS 400/6-8
60 Allen St 01840 978-975-5962
Fax 975-7965
Oliver S 600/1-8
233 E Haverhill St 01841 978-975-5966
Donna Dooley, prin. Fax 975-7980
Parthum ES 600/K-4
255 E Haverhill St 01841 978-691-7200
Sharman Sullivan, prin. Fax 975-2196
Parthum MS 5-8
255 E Haverhill St 01841 978-691-7200
Peter Lefebre, prin. Fax 975-2196
Rollins ECC, 451 Howard St 01841 PK-K
James O'Keefe, prin. 978-722-8190
South Lawrence East ES 1-4
165 Crawford St 01843 978-975-5970
Mary Toomey, prin. Fax 975-2780
South Lawrence East MS 600/5-8
165 Crawford St 01843 978-975-5970
Fax 975-2780
Tarbox ES 300/K-5
59 Alder St 01841 978-975-5983
Martha Duffy, prin. Fax 725-6089
Wetherbee S 600/K-8
75 Newton St 01843 978-975-5986
Colleen Lennon, prin. Fax 975-4297

Blessed Stephen Bellesini Academy 100/5-8
94 Bradford St 01840 978-989-0004
Julie DeFillippo, dir. Fax 989-9404
Esperanza Academy S of Hope 5-8
198 Garden St 01840 978-686-4673
Laurie Bottiger, hdmstr. Fax 681-1591
Our Lady of Good Counsel S 200/K-8
526 Lowell St 01841 978-682-9761
Maureen Cocchiaro, prin. Fax 686-1988
St. Mary of the Assumption S 200/PK-8
301 Haverhill St 01840 978-685-2091
Vina Troianello, prin. Fax 688-7244
St. Patrick S 400/PK-8
101 Parker St 01843 978-683-5822
Sr. Lucy Veilleux, prin. Fax 683-1165

Lee, Berkshire, Pop. 2,020
Lee SD 900/PK-12
480 Pleasant St Ste 102 01238 413-243-0276
Jason McCandless, supt. Fax 243-4995
www.lee.k12.ma.us/
Lee ES 400/PK-6
310 Greylock St 01238 413-243-0336
Kimberly Lohse, prin. Fax 243-8216

St. Marys S 100/PK-8
115 Orchard St 01238 413-243-1079
Joan Davis, prin. Fax 243-1022

Leeds, See Northampton
Northampton SD
Supt. — See Northampton
Leeds ES 300/K-5
20 Florence St 01053 413-587-1531
Kathleen Malynoski, prin. Fax 587-1539

Leicester, Worcester, Pop. 10,191
Leicester SD 1,800/PK-12
1078 Main St 01524 508-892-7040
Paul Soojian, supt. Fax 892-7043
www.leicester.k12.ma.us/
Leicester Memorial ES 400/3-5
11 Memorial Dr 01524 508-892-7048
Greg Martineau, prin. Fax 892-7052
Leicester MS 500/6-8
70 Winslow Ave 01524 508-892-7055
Matthew Young, prin. Fax 892-7047
Leicester PS 400/PK-2
170 Paxton St 01524 508-892-7050
Doris Whitworth, prin. Fax 892-7053

Lenox, Berkshire, Pop. 1,687
Lenox SD 800/PK-12
6 Walker St Ste 3 01240 413-637-5550
Marianne Young, supt. Fax 637-5559
www.lenoxps.org
Morris ES 400/PK-5
129 West St 01240 413-637-5570
Timothy Lee, prin. Fax 637-5511

Berkshire County Christian S 100/PK-8
PO Box 1980 01240 413-637-2474
Christine Novak, prin. Fax 637-8336

Leominster, Worcester, Pop. 41,804
Leominster SD 5,400/PK-12
24 Church St 01453 978-534-7700
Dr. Nadine Binkley, supt. Fax 534-7775
www.leominster.mec.edu/
Appleseed ES 700/K-5
845 Main St 01453 978-534-7765
Margaret O'Hearn-Curran, prin. Fax 534-7776
Bennett K 200/PK-K
145 Pleasant St 01453 978-534-7704
James Reilly, prin. Fax 534-7769
Fall Brook ES 600/K-5
25 DeCicco Dr 01453 978-534-7745
John Mendes, prin. Fax 466-9825
Northwest ES 600/K-5
45 Stearns Ave 01453 978-534-7756
Steven Mammone, prin. Fax 534-7779
Priest Street K 300/K-K
115 Priest St 01453 978-534-7761
James Reilly, prin. Fax 534-7770
Samoset MS 500/6-8
100 DeCicco Dr 01453 978-534-7725
Donna Pierce, prin. Fax 466-7421

Samoset Preschool 50/PK-PK
100 DeCicco Dr 01453 978-537-3383
James Reilly, prin. Fax 537-4879
Sky View MS 500/6-8
500 Kennedy Way 01453 978-534-7780
Kathleen Ciccolini, prin. Fax 840-8600
Southeast ES 100/K-5
95 Viscoloid Ave 01453 978-534-7751
Elizabeth Pratt, prin. Fax 460-8603

St. Anna S 200/PK-8
213 Lancaster St 01453 978-534-4770
Danielle Colvert, prin. Fax 466-1167
St. Leo S 300/PK-8
120 Main St 01453 978-537-1007
Carolyn Polselli, prin. Fax 537-7420

Leverett, Franklin
Leverett SD
Supt. — See Erving
Leverett ES 200/PK-6
85 Montague Rd 01054 413-548-9144
Anne Ross, prin. Fax 548-8148

Lexington, Middlesex, Pop. 30,600
Lexington SD 6,200/PK-12
146 Maple St 02420 781-861-2550
Paul Ash Ph.D., supt. Fax 863-5829
lps.lexingtonma.org
Bowman ES 500/K-5
9 Philip Rd 02421 781-861-2500
Mary Anton-Oldenburg, prin. Fax 861-2315
Bridge ES 500/K-5
55 Middleby Rd 02421 781-861-2510
Jade Reitman, prin. Fax 861-9257
Clarke MS 700/6-8
17 Stedman Rd 02421 781-861-2450
Steven Flynn, prin. Fax 674-2043
Diamond MS 800/6-8
99 Hancock St 02420 781-861-2460
Joanne Hennessy, prin. Fax 274-0174
Estabrook ES 400/K-5
117 Grove St 02420 781-861-2520
Martha Batten, prin. Fax 862-5610
Fiske ES 300/K-5
55 Adams St 02420 781-541-5001
Nancy Peterson, prin. Fax 541-5008
Harrington ES 400/PK-5
328 Lowell St 02420 781-860-0012
Elaine Mead, prin. Fax 860-5818
Hastings ES 500/K-5
7 Crosby Rd 02421 781-860-5800
Louise Lipsitz, prin. Fax 860-5242

Armenian Sisters Academy 100/PK-8
20 Pelham Rd 02421 781-861-8303
Sr. Cecile Keghiayan, prin. Fax 862-8479
Lexington Montessori S 200/PK-8
130 Pleasant St 02421 781-862-8571
Aline Gery, hdmstr. Fax 674-0079
Waldorf S 300/PK-8
739 Massachusetts Ave 02420 781-863-1062
Fax 863-7221

Leyden, Franklin, Pop. 662
Pioneer Valley SD
Supt. — See Northfield
Rhodes ES 100/PK-6
7 Brattleboro Rd 01301 413-772-6245
Stacey Jenkins, prin. Fax 772-1030

Lincoln, Middlesex, Pop. 2,850
Lincoln SD 1,200/PK-8
Ballfield Rd 01773 781-259-9409
Michael Brandmeyer, supt. Fax 259-9246
www.lincnet.org/
Lincoln S 700/PK-8
6 Ballfield Rd 01773 781-259-9404
Sharon Hobbs, prin. Fax 259-2637
Other Schools – See Hanscom AFB

Littleton, Middlesex, Pop. 2,867
Littleton SD 1,400/PK-12
PO Box 1486 01460 978-486-8951
Diane Bemis, supt. Fax 486-9581
www.littletonps.org/
Littleton MS 300/6-8
55 Russell St 01460 978-486-8938
Kevin Moran, prin. Fax 952-4547
Russell Street ES 400/3-5
55 Russell St 01460 978-486-3134
Jane Hall, prin. Fax 952-4547
Shaker Lane ES 300/PK-2
35 Shaker Ln 01460 978-486-3959
Richard Faherty, prin. Fax 952-4550

Oak Meadow Montessori S 300/PK-8
2 Old Pickard Ln 01460 978-486-9874
David Stettler, hdmstr. Fax 486-3269

Longmeadow, Hampden, Pop. 15,467
Longmeadow SD 3,200/PK-12
127 Grassy Gutter Rd 01106 413-565-4200
E. Jahn Hart, supt. Fax 565-4215
www.longmeadow.k12.ma.us/
Blueberry Hill ES 600/PK-5
275 Blueberry Hill Rd 01106 413-565-4280
Marie Pratt, prin. Fax 565-4283
Center ES 400/K-5
837 Longmeadow St 01106 413-565-4290
Donna Hutton, prin. Fax 565-4292
Glenbrook MS 400/6-8
110 Cambridge Cir 01106 413-565-4250
Michael Sullivan, prin. Fax 565-4277
Williams MS 400/6-8
410 Williams St 01106 413-565-4260
Chris Collins, prin. Fax 565-4254

Wolf Swamp Road ES 400/K-5
62 Wolf Swamp Rd 01106 413-565-4270
Kimberly Stillwell, prin. Fax 565-4273

Heritage Academy 100/K-8
594 Converse St Ste A 01106 413-567-1517
Dr. Deborah Starr, dir. Fax 567-2167
Lubavitcher Yeshiva Academy 100/PK-8
1148 Converse St 01106 413-567-8665
Rabbi Noah Kosofsky, prin. Fax 567-2233
St. Mary's Academy 200/PK-8
56 Hopkins Pl 01106 413-567-0907
Joan MacDonald, prin. Fax 567-7695

Lowell, Middlesex, Pop. 103,111
Lowell SD 12,800/PK-12
43 Highland St 01852 978-937-7604
Chris Scott, supt. Fax 446-7436
www.lowell.k12.ma.us/
Bailey ES 500/PK-4
175 Campbell Dr 01851 978-937-7644
Rich Perry, prin. Fax 459-5314
Bartlett ES 200/PK-4
79 Wannalancit St 01854 978-937-8968
Grace Wai, prin. Fax 441-3745
Butler MS 500/5-8
1140 Gorham St 01852 978-937-8973
Eilish Connaughton, prin. Fax 937-2819
Daley MS 700/5-8
150 Fleming St 01851 978-937-8981
Liam Skinner, prin. Fax 937-7610
Greenhalge ES 400/PK-4
149 Ennell St 01850 978-937-7670
LeeAnn Conners, prin. Fax 441-3724
Lincoln ES 500/PK-4
300 Chelmsford St 01851 978-937-2846
Sandra Dunning, prin. Fax 937-2855
MacAuliffe ES 400/PK-4
570 Beacon St 01850 978-937-2838
Jason DiCarlo, prin. Fax 937-2845
McAvinnue ES 500/PK-4
131 Mammoth Rd 01854 978-937-2871
Kelly Clough, prin. Fax 937-2880
Moody ES 200/K-4
158 Rogers St 01852 978-937-7673
Cheryl Cunningham, prin. Fax 937-7606
Morey ES 400/PK-4
130 Pine St 01851 978-937-7662
Jason McCrevan, prin. Fax 937-7663
Murkland ES 500/PK-4
350 Adams St 01854 978-937-2826
Marianne Bond, prin. Fax 937-2835
Pawtucketville Memorial ES 500/PK-4
425 W Meadow Rd 01854 978-937-7667
Alison Corner, prin. Fax 441-3732
Pyne S of Arts 400/PK-8
145 Boylston St 01852 978-937-7639
William Manoloupolos, prin. Fax 446-0942
Reilly ES 400/K-4
115 Douglas Rd 01852 978-937-7652
Margaret Shepherd, prin. Fax 446-7432
Robinson MS 500/5-8
110 June St 01850 978-937-8974
Robert Murphy, prin. Fax 937-8988
Shaughnessy ES 400/PK-4
1158 Gorham St 01852 978-937-7657
Linda Lee, prin. Fax 446-7074
Stoklosa MS 600/5-8
560 Broadway St 01854 978-937-7604
Stephen Gross, prin. Fax 275-6343
Sullivan MS 600/5-8
150 Draper St 01852 978-937-8993
Edith LaBran, prin. Fax 937-3278
Wang MS 600/5-8
365 W Meadow Rd 01854 978-937-7683
Gayle Feeney, prin. Fax 937-7680
Washington ES 200/PK-4
795 Wilder St 01851 978-937-7635
Matthew Stahl, prin. Fax 937-7636

Community Christian Academy 200/PK-12
105R Princeton Blvd 01851 978-934-9414
Rev. Raffoul Najem, admin. Fax 453-1506
Franco American S 300/K-8
357 Pawtucket St 01854 978-458-0308
Sr. Lorraine Richard, prin. Fax 458-0308
Hellenic American Academy 100/PK-6
41 Broadway St 01854 978-453-5422
Douglas Anderson, prin. Fax 970-3554
Immaculate Conception S 200/PK-8
218 E Merrimack St 01852 978-454-5339
Jean Murphy, prin. Fax 454-6593
St. Jeanne d'Arc S 400/K-8
68 Dracut St 01854 978-453-4114
Sr. Prescille Malo, prin. Fax 454-8304
St. Louis S 400/K-8
77 Boisvert St 01850 978-458-7594
Kristyna Dumais, prin. Fax 454-9289
St. Margaret S 300/K-8
486 Stevens St 01851 978-453-8491
Sr. Loretta Fleming, prin. Fax 453-1358
St. Michael S 400/K-8
21 6th St 01850 978-453-9511
Mary Chisholm, prin. Fax 454-4104
St. Patrick S 200/K-8
311 Adams St 01854 978-458-4232
Sr. Joanne Sullivan, prin. Fax 458-4233

Ludlow, Hampden, Pop. 18,820
Ludlow SD 2,300/PK-12
63 Chestnut St 01056 413-583-8372
Theresa Kane Ed.D., supt. Fax 583-5666
www.ludlowps.org
Baird MS 700/6-8
1 Rooney Rd 01056 413-583-5685
Sheryl Stanton, prin. Fax 583-5636
Chapin Street Campus 100/2-3
766 Chapin St 01056 413-583-5031
Lisa Dakin, prin. Fax 583-5627
East Street Campus 100/PK-1
508 East St 01056 413-589-9121
Brett Bishop, prin. Fax 593-5629
Ludlow ECC 100/PK-PK
54 Winsor St 01056 413-583-4480
Irene Ryan, dir. Fax 583-3160
Veterans Park Campus 200/4-5
486 Chapin St 01056 413-583-5695
Susan Dukeshire, prin. Fax 583-5630

St. John the Baptist S 200/PK-8
217 Hubbard St 01056 413-583-8550
Shelly Rose, prin. Fax 589-0544

Lunenburg, Worcester, Pop. 1,694
Lunenburg SD 1,700/PK-12
1033 Massachusetts Ave 01462 978-582-4100
Loxi Jo Calmes, supt. Fax 582-4103
www.lunenburgonline.com/
Lunenburg PS 300/PK-2
1401 Massachusetts Ave 01462 978-582-4122
Cyndy Daukantas, prin. Fax 582-4173
Passios ES 400/3-5
1025 Massachusetts Ave 01462 978-582-4105
Christine Bonci, prin. Fax 582-4108
Turkey Hill MS 400/6-8
129 Northfield Rd 01462 978-582-4110
Sara Lane, prin. Fax 582-4109

Twin City Christian S 300/PK-12
194 Electric Ave 01462 978-582-4901
Carrol Conley, admin. Fax 582-4978

Lynn, Essex, Pop. 88,792
Lynn SD 13,700/PK-12
90 Commercial St 01905 781-593-1680
Catherine Latham, supt. Fax 477-7487
www.lynnschools.org/
Aborn ES 200/K-5
409 Eastern Ave 01902 781-477-7320
Anne Graul, prin. Fax 581-1058
Breed MS 1,100/6-8
90 OCallaghan Way 01905 781-477-7330
Frederick Dupuis, prin. Fax 581-6985
Brickett ES 300/K-5
123 Lewis St 01902 781-477-7333
Debra Ruggiero, prin. Fax 596-2665
Callahan ES 400/K-5
200 OCallaghan Way 01905 781-477-7340
Edward Turmenne, prin. Fax 581-9248
Cobbet ES 500/K-5
40 Franklin St 01902 781-477-7341
Brian Fay, prin. Fax 477-7341
Connery ES 500/PK-5
50 Elm St 01905 781-477-7344
Patricia Riley, prin. Fax 477-7451
Drewicz ES 400/PK-5
34 Hood St 01905 781-477-7350
Bernadette Stamm, prin. Fax 477-7353
Ford S 800/PK-8
49 Hollingsworth St 01902 781-477-7375
Claire Crane, prin. Fax 477-7378
Harrington ES 400/PK-5
21 Dexter St 01902 781-477-7380
Michael Molnar, prin. Fax 477-7383
Hood ES 400/K-5
24 Oakwood Ave 01902 781-477-7390
Joseph Cole, prin. Fax 593-9746
Ingalls ES 500/PK-8
1 Collins Street Ter 01902 781-477-7400
Kimberlee Powers, prin. Fax 477-7398
Lincoln-Thomson ES 200/K-5
115 Gardiner St 01905 781-477-7460
Helen Mihos, prin. Fax 477-7459
Lynn Woods ES 100/K-5
31 Trevett Ave 01904 781-477-7433
Ellen Fritz, prin. Fax 477-7435
Marshall MS 900/6-8
19 Porter St 01902 781-477-7360
Richard Cowdell, prin. Fax 477-7355
Pickering MS 600/6-8
70 Conomo Ave 01904 781-477-7440
Robert Murphy, prin. Fax 477-7202
Sewell-Anderson ES 200/K-5
25 Ontario St 01905 781-477-7444
Patricia Mallett, prin. Fax 477-7446
Shoemaker ES 400/PK-5
26 Regina Rd 01904 781-477-7450
Linda Mann, prin. Fax 477-7454
Sisson ES 400/K-5
58 Conomo Ave 01904 781-477-7455
Jane Franklin, prin. Fax 268-0550
Tracy ES 200/K-5
35 Walnut St 01905 781-477-7466
Mary Dill, prin. Fax 477-7465

North Shore Christian S 100/PK-8
26 Urban St 01904 781-599-2040
Martin Trice, hdmstr. Fax 595-7444
Sacred Heart S 200/K-8
581 Boston St 01905 781-592-7581
Joanne Eagan, prin. Fax 595-9948
St. Pius V S 400/K-8
28 Bowler St 01904 781-593-8292
Paul Maestranzi, prin. Fax 593-6973

Lynnfield, Essex, Pop. 11,274
Lynnfield SD 2,300/PK-12
55 Summer St 01940 781-334-5800
Robert Hassett, supt. Fax 334-5802
www.lynnfield.k12.ma.us/
Huckleberry Hill ES 400/K-4
5 Knoll Rd 01940 781-334-5835
Marybeth Shea, prin. Fax 334-7205
Lynnfield MS 700/5-8
505 Main St 01940 781-334-5810
Stephen Ralston, prin. Fax 334-7203
Lynnfield Preschool PK-K
525 Salem St 01940 781-581-5140
Janet Barry, prin. Fax 581-5231
Summer Street ES 500/PK-4
262 Summer St 01940 781-334-5830
Jane Tremblay, prin. Fax 334-5817

Messiah Lutheran S 100/PK-K
708 Lowell St 01940 781-334-6591
Joanne Penta, dir. Fax 334-6557
Our Lady of the Assumption S 500/PK-8
40 Grove St 01940 781-599-4422
Dr. Joan Shea-Desmond, prin. Fax 599-9280

Malden, Middlesex, Pop. 55,871
Malden SD 6,200/PK-12
200 Pleasant St 02148 781-397-7204
Sidney Smith, supt. Fax 397-7276
www.malden.mec.edu
Beebe S 900/K-8
401 Pleasant St 02148 781-388-0621
Susan Vatalaro, prin. Fax 388-0623
Ferryway S 900/K-8
150 Cross St 02148 781-388-0655
Thomas DeVito, prin. Fax 388-0657
Forestdale S 600/K-8
74 Sylvan St 02148 781-397-7326
Sally Orme, prin. Fax 397-1517
Linden S 800/K-8
29 Wescott St 02148 781-397-7218
Dael Angelico-Hart, prin. Fax 397-1512
Malden ECC 300/PK-K
257 Mountain Ave 02148 781-397-7025
Anne O'Connell-Hanifan, prin. Fax 321-3495
Salemwood S 1,000/K-8
529 Salem St 02148 781-388-0643
Jonathan Ponds, prin. Fax 388-0645

Cheverus Centennial S 400/PK-8
30 Irving St 02148 781-324-6584
Susan Degnan, prin. Fax 324-3322

Manchester, Essex, Pop. 5,286
Manchester Essex Regional SD 900/K-12
36 Lincoln St 01944 978-526-4919
Dr. Marcia O'Neil, supt. Fax 526-7585
www.mersd.org
Manchester Essex Regional MS 200/7-8
36 Lincoln St 01944 978-526-2022
Beth Raucci, prin.
Manchester Memorial ES 400/K-6
43 Lincoln St 01944 978-526-1908
Jack Mara, prin. Fax 526-2060
Other Schools – See Essex

Brookwood S 400/PK-8
1 Brookwood Rd 01944 978-526-4500
John Peterman, hdmstr. Fax 526-9303
Landmark S North Campus 100/2-8
PO Box 1489 01944 978-526-7531
Robert Kahn, dir. Fax 526-1482

Mansfield, Bristol, Pop. 7,170
Mansfield SD 4,600/K-12
2 Park Row 02048 508-261-7500
Brenda Hodges, supt. Fax 261-7509
www.mansfieldschools.com
Jordan/Jackson ES 1,200/3-5
255 East St 02048 508-261-7520
Kathleen Podesky, prin. Fax 261-7528
Qualters MS 1,200/6-8
240 East St 02048 508-261-7530
Mary Mega, prin. Fax 261-7535
Robinson ES 700/K-2
245 East St 02048 508-261-7510
Mary Gentili, prin. Fax 337-9340

Hands-On Montessori S 100/PK-4
12 Creeden St 02048 508-339-4667
Emily Miller, prin. Fax 339-4315
St. Mary's Catholic S 200/K-8
330 Pratt St 02048 508-339-4800
Joanne Riley, prin. Fax 337-2603

Marblehead, Essex, Pop. 19,971
Marblehead SD 3,000/PK-12
9 Widger Rd 01945 781-639-3141
Dr. Paul Dulac, supt. Fax 639-3149
www.marbleheadschools.org
Bell ES 400/PK-3
40 Baldwin Rd 01945 781-639-3170
Stephen Medeiros, prin. Fax 639-3173
Coffin ES 200/2-3
1 Turner Rd 01945 781-639-3180
Sean Satterfield, prin. Fax 639-3182
Eveleth S 50/K-K
3 Brook Rd 01945 781-639-3195
Mary Devlin, prin. Fax 639-3192
Gerry ES 200/K-1
50 Elm St 01945 781-639-3185
Sean Satterfield, prin. Fax 639-3182
Glover ES 200/1-3
9 Maple St 01945 781-639-3190
Mary Devlin, prin. Fax 639-3192
Marblehead Veterans MS 500/7-8
217 Pleasant St 01945 781-639-3120
Libby Moore, prin. Fax 639-3130
Village S 600/4-6
93 Village St 01945 781-639-3159
Michael Hanna, prin. Fax 639-9423

Cohen Hillel Academy 200/K-8
6 Community Rd 01945 781-639-2880
Ken Schulman, hdmstr. Fax 631-2832
Tower S 300/PK-8
75 W Shore Dr 01945 781-631-5800
Peter Philip, prin. Fax 631-2292

Marion, Plymouth, Pop. 1,426
Marion SD
Supt. — See Mattapoisett
Sippican ES 500/PK-6
16 Spring St 02738 508-748-0100
Edwin Fava, prin. Fax 748-1953

Marlboro, Middlesex

New Covenant Christian S 100/K-8
204 Main St 01752 508-485-6844
Judi Pinkerton, dir. Fax 485-6814

Marlborough, Middlesex, Pop. 37,444
Marlborough SD 3,500/PK-12
17 Washington St 01752 508-460-3509
Mary Carlson, supt. Fax 485-1142
www.mps-edu.org
ECC 100/PK-PK
17 Washington St 01752 508-460-3502
Tina Betley, prin. Fax 460-3547
Jaworek ES 400/K-3
444 Hosmer St 01752 508-460-3506
Mary Murphy, prin. Fax 460-3709
Kane ES 400/K-3
520 Farm Rd 01752 508-460-3507
John Collins, prin. Fax 460-3588
Marlborough MS 700/4-7
25 Union St 01752 508-460-3502
Daniel Hanneken, prin. Fax 460-3597
Richer ES 300/K-3
80 Foley Rd 01752 508-460-3504
Joanne Stocklin, prin. Fax 460-3586

Immaculate Conception S 200/PK-8
25 Washington Ct 01752 508-460-3401
Martha McCook, prin. Fax 460-6003
Our Lady Preschool Learning Ctr 100/PK-PK
197 Pleasant St 01752 508-481-0654
Sr. Jeanne Allard, prin. Fax 481-0663
St. Anne Montessori S 50/PK-PK
720 Boston Post Rd E 01752 508-597-7416
Kathleen Finn, prin. Fax 597-1403

Marshfield, Plymouth, Pop. 4,002
Marshfield SD 4,700/PK-12
76 S River St 02050 781-834-5000
Middleton McGoodwin Ed.D., supt. Fax 834-5070
www.mpsd.org/
Eames ES 400/K-5
165 Eames Way 02050 781-834-5090
William Campia, prin. Fax 834-5094
Furnace Brook MS 1,100/6-8
500 Furnace St 02050 781-834-5020
Alfred Makein, prin. Fax 834-5899
Martinson ES 500/PK-5
275 Forest St 02050 781-834-5025
Thomas Kilduff, prin. Fax 834-5003
South River ES 500/PK-5
59 Hatch St 02050 781-834-5030
Linda Loiselle, prin. Fax 834-5071
Webster ES 400/PK-5
1456 Ocean St 02050 781-834-5045
Edward Mitchell, prin. Fax 834-5072
Winslow ES 500/PK-5
60 Regis Rd 02050 781-834-5060
Dennis Oakman, prin. Fax 834-5075

Marstons Mills, Barnstable, Pop. 8,017
Barnstable SD
Supt. — See Hyannis
Marstons Mills ES 200/PK-2
2095 Main St 02648 508-428-2090
Karen Stonely, prin. Fax 428-2185

Mashpee, Barnstable
Mashpee SD 1,900/K-12
150A Old Barnstable Rd 02649 508-539-1500
Ann Bradshaw, supt. Fax 477-5805
www.mashpee.k12.ma.us
Coombs ES 300/K-2
152 Old Barnstable Rd 02649 508-539-1520
Donna Zaeske, prin. Fax 539-1530
Mashpee MS 300/7-8
500 Old Barnstable Rd 02649 508-539-3600
Steven Babbitt, prin.
Quashnet S 600/3-6
150 Old Barnstable Rd 02649 508-539-1550
Patricia DeBoer, prin. Fax 539-1556

Mattapan, See Boston
Boston SD
Supt. — See Boston
Chittick ES 300/K-5
154 Ruskindale Rd 02126 617-635-8652
Michelle Burnett-Herndon, prin. Fax 635-6925
Ellison-Parks Early Education S 200/PK-1
108 Babson St 02126 617-635-7680
Nora Toney, prin. Fax 635-6491
Lewenberg MS 400/6-8
20 Outlook Rd 02126 617-635-8623
Andy Tuite, prin. Fax 635-9947
Mattahunt ES 500/PK-5
100 Hebron St 02126 617-635-8792
Gloria J. Woods, prin. Fax 635-8799
Mildred Avenue MS 600/6-8
5 Mildred Ave 02126 617-635-1645
Kris Taylor, prin. Fax 635-1641
Taylor ES 500/PK-5
1060 Morton St 02126 617-635-8731
Elie Jean-Louis, prin. Fax 635-6877

Berea SDA Academy 100/K-8
800 Morton St 02126 617-436-8301
Grafton Jones, prin. Fax 436-8304
Pope John Paul II Academy 200/PK-8
120 Babson St 02126 617-296-1161
Maryanne Martinelli, prin. Fax 296-1659

Mattapoisett, Plymouth, Pop. 2,949
Marion SD 500/PK-6
135 Marion Rd 02739 508-758-2772
Dr. William Cooper, supt. Fax 758-2802
www.oldrochester.org
Other Schools – See Marion

Mattapoisett SD 500/PK-6
135 Marion Rd 02739 508-758-2772
Dr. William Cooper, supt. Fax 758-2802
www.oldrochester.org
Center ES 300/PK-3
17 Barstow St 02739 508-758-2521
Rosemary Bowen, prin. Fax 758-3153
Old Hammondtown ES 200/4-6
20 Shaw St 02739 508-758-6241
Matthew D'Andrea, prin. Fax 758-4667

Old Rochester Regional SD 1,200/7-12
135 Marion Rd 02739 508-758-2772
Dr. William Cooper, supt. Fax 758-2802
www.oldrochester.org
Old Rochester Regional JHS 500/7-8
133 Marion Rd 02739 508-758-4928
Kevin Brogioli, prin. Fax 758-6021

Rochester SD 600/PK-6
135 Marion Rd 02739 508-758-2772
Dr. William Cooper, supt. Fax 758-2802
www.oldrochester.org
Other Schools – See Rochester

Maynard, Middlesex, Pop. 10,325
Maynard SD 1,200/PK-12
12 Bancroft St 01754 978-897-2222
Dr. Mark Masterson, supt. Fax 897-4610
web.maynard.ma.us/schools/
Fowler MS 500/4-8
3 Tiger Dr 01754 978-897-6700
Robert Brooks, prin. Fax 897-5737
Green Meadow ES 400/PK-3
5 Tiger Dr 01754 978-897-8246
Bernadette McLaughlin, prin. Fax 897-8298

Medfield, Norfolk, Pop. 5,985
Medfield SD 2,900/PK-12
459 Main St Fl 3 02052 508-359-2302
Robert Maguire, supt. Fax 359-9829
www.medfield.net
Blake MS 700/6-8
24 Pound St 02052 508-359-2396
Robert Parga, prin. Fax 359-0134
Dale Street S 500/4-5
45 Adams St 02052 508-359-5538
Kim Cave, prin. Fax 359-1419
Memorial S 300/PK-1
59 Adams St 02052 508-359-5135
Andrea Trasher, prin. Fax 359-1419
Wheelock S 500/2-3
17 Elm St 02052 508-359-6055
Patricia Allen, prin. Fax 359-6174

Medford, Middlesex, Pop. 53,523
Medford SD 4,600/PK-12
489 Winthrop St 02155 781-393-2442
Roy Belson, supt. Fax 393-2322
www.medford.k12.ma.us
Andrews MS 500/6-8
3000 Mystic Valley Pkwy 02155 781-393-2228
Timothy Blake, prin. Fax 395-8128
Brooks ES 500/K-5
388 High St 02155 781-393-2166
Michael Simon, prin. Fax 393-2174
Columbus ES 400/K-5
37 Hicks Ave 02155 781-393-2177
Joan Yaeger, prin. Fax 393-2187
McGlynn ES 500/PK-5
3002 Mystic Valley Pkwy 02155 781-393-2333
Patricia Buker, prin. Fax 393-5462
McGlynn MS 500/6-8
3004 Mystic Valley Pkwy 02155 781-393-2333
Jacob Edwards, prin. Fax 393-5462
Roberts ES 500/PK-5
35 Court St 02155 781-393-2155
Kirk Johnson, prin. Fax 393-2158

St. Clement S 200/PK-12
579 Boston Ave 02155 617-393-5600
Robert Chevrier, prin. Fax 396-3230
St. Francis of Assisi S 200/PK-8
1 Saint Clare Rd 02155 781-395-9170
Michael McCabe, prin. Fax 306-0044
St. Joseph S 500/PK-8
132 High St 02155 781-396-3636
Sr. Maureen Hunt, prin. Fax 396-5478
St. Raphael S 400/PK-8
516 High St 02155 781-483-3373
Paul Madden, prin. Fax 483-3097

Medway, Norfolk, Pop. 9,931
Medway SD 2,700/PK-12
45 Holliston St 02053 508-533-3222
Dr. Judith Evans, supt. Fax 533-3226
www.medwayschools.org
Burke ES 100/PK-K
16 Cassidy Ln 02053 508-533-3242
Leigh Ann Becker, prin. Fax 533-3261
McGovern ES 400/1-2
9 Lovering St 02053 508-533-3243
Wendy Rocha, prin. Fax 533-3263
Medway MS 900/5-8
45 Holliston St 02053 508-533-3230
Joanne Senier-LaBarre, prin. Fax 533-3257
Memorial ES 400/3-4
16 Cassidy Ln 02053 508-533-3266
Leigh Ann Becker, prin. Fax 533-3261

Melrose, Middlesex, Pop. 26,365
Melrose SD 3,500/PK-12
360 Lynn Fells Pkwy 02176 781-662-2000
Joseph Casey, supt. Fax 979-2149
www.melroseschools.com
ECC 200/PK-K
16 Franklin St 02176 781-979-2260
Jennifer Corduck, dir. Fax 979-2261
Hoover ES 300/K-5
37 Glendower Rd 02176 781-979-2181
Dennet Sidell, prin. Fax 979-2183
Lincoln ES 400/K-5
80 W Wyoming Ave 02176 781-979-2250
Brent Conway, prin. Fax 979-2259
Mann ES 300/K-5
40 Damon Ave 02176 781-979-2191
Jeffrey Strasnick, prin. Fax 979-2194
Melrose MS 800/6-8
350 Lynn Fells Pkwy 02176 781-979-2102
Thomas Brow, prin. Fax 979-2104
Roosevelt ES 300/K-5
253 Vinton St 02176 781-979-2270
Kerry Clery, prin. Fax 979-2275
Winthrop ES 400/K-5
162 1st St 02176 781-979-2280
Bryna Lakin-Davis, prin. Fax 979-2281

St. Mary of the Annunciation S 400/PK-8
4 Myrtle St 02176 781-665-5037
Cindy Boyle, prin. Fax 665-7321

Mendon, Worcester
Mendon-Upton Regional SD 2,100/PK-12
PO Box 5 01756 508-634-1585
Antonio Fernandes, supt. Fax 634-1582
mu-regional.k12.ma.us
Clough ES 300/PK-4
10 North Ave 01756 508-634-1580
Vincent Rozen, prin. Fax 634-1576
Miscoe Hill S 700/5-8
148 North Ave 01756 508-634-1590
Roseanne Kurposka, prin. Fax 634-1576
Other Schools – See Upton

Bethany Christian Academy 100/PK-12
15 Cape Rd 01756 508-634-8171
Cheri McCutchen, admin. Fax 478-4706

Merrimac, Essex
Pentucket SD
Supt. — See West Newbury
Donaghue ES 400/3-6
24 Union Street Ext 01860 978-346-8921
Robert Harrison, prin. Fax 346-7839
Sweetsir ES 300/PK-2
104 Church St 01860 978-346-8319
Patricia Messina, prin. Fax 346-7844

Methuen, Essex, Pop. 44,609
Methuen SD 6,800/PK-12
10 Ditson Pl 01844 978-722-6000
Jeanne Whitten Ed.D., supt. Fax 722-6002
www.methuen.k12.ma.us
Comprehensive Grammar S 1,000/PK-8
100 Howe St 01844 978-722-9052
Brandi Kwong, prin. Fax 722-9053
Marsh Grammar S 1,200/PK-8
309 Pelham St 01844 978-722-9077
Timothy Lannan, prin. Fax 722-9078
Tenney Grammar S 1,300/PK-8
75 Pleasant St 01844 978-722-9027
James Giuca, prin. Fax 722-9028
Timony Grammar S 1,300/PK-8
45 Pleasant View St 01844 978-722-9002
Judith Scannell, prin. Fax 722-9003

Fellowship Christian Academy 100/PK-12
1 Fellowship Way 01844 978-686-9373
Presentation of Mary Montessori 100/PK-PK
209 Lawrence St 01844 978-686-4462
Sr. Jacqueline Lambert, prin. Fax 975-1998
St. Monica S 200/K-8
212 Lawrence St 01844 978-686-1801
Beth Ingenieri, prin. Fax 686-3582

Middleboro, Plymouth, Pop. 6,837
Middleborough SD 3,300/PK-12
30 Forest St 02346 508-946-2000
Robert Sullivan, supt. Fax 946-2004
www.middleboro.k12.ma.us
Burkland IS 900/3-5
41 Mayflower Ave 02346 508-946-2040
Louise Snyder, prin. Fax 946-2029
Goode ES 600/1-2
31 Mayflower Ave 02346 508-946-2045
Anita Rodriguez, prin. Fax 946-8851
Memorial ECC PK-K
219 N Main St 02346 508-946-2032
Virginia Levesque, prin. Fax 946-2030
Nichols MS 900/6-8
112 Tiger Dr 02346 508-946-2020
Scott Kellett, prin. Fax 946-2019

Fuller S, 6 Plympton St 02346 50/K-3
Margaret McKenna, hdmstr. 508-715-4256

Middleton, Essex, Pop. 4,921
Middleton SD
Supt. — See Boxford
Fuller Meadow ES 400/PK-3
143 S Main St 01949 978-750-4756
Malvena Baxter, prin. Fax 777-3352
Howe-Manning ES 300/4-6
26 Central St 01949 978-774-3519
Michelle Fitzpatrick, prin. Fax 774-4959

Milford, Worcester, Pop. 23,339
Milford SD 3,900/PK-12
31 W Fountain St 01757 508-478-1100
Robert Tremblay, supt. Fax 478-1459
www.milford.ma.us/schools.htm
Brookside ES 300/K-2
110 Congress St 01757 508-478-1177
Kathleen Kay, prin. Fax 634-2375
Memorial ES 300/K-2
12 Walnut St 01757 508-478-1689
Francis Anderson, prin. Fax 478-1696
Milford MS East 300/8-8
45 Main St 01757 508-478-1170
Craig Consigli, prin. Fax 634-2381
Shining Star ECC 100/PK-PK
31 W Fountain St 01757 508-478-1483
Lisa Burns, prin. Fax 478-1459
Stacy MS 1,000/5-7
66 School St 01757 508-478-1180
Nancy Angelini, prin. Fax 634-2370
Woodland ES 600/3-4
10 N Vine St 01757 508-478-1186
Linda Ashley, prin. Fax 473-4280

Milford Catholic S 200/PK-6
11 E Main St 01757 508-473-7303
Andrea Tavaskas, prin. Fax 478-4902

Millbury, Worcester, Pop. 12,228
Millbury SD 1,800/PK-12
12 Martin St 01527 508-865-9501
Susan Hitchcock, supt. Fax 865-0888
www.millbury.k12.ma.us
Elmwood Street ES 500/PK-3
40 Elmwood St 01527 508-865-5241
Susan Frederick, prin. Fax 865-0888
Shaw ES 400/4-6
58 Elmwood St 01527 508-865-3541
Riitta Bolton, prin. Fax 865-3430

Assumption S 200/PK-8
17 Grove St 01527 508-865-5404
Dr. Rita Bernard, prin. Fax 581-8974

Millis, Norfolk, Pop. 4,081
Millis SD 1,200/PK-12
245 Plain St 02054 508-376-7000
Nancy Gustafson, supt. Fax 376-7020
www.millis.k12.ma.us/
Brown ES 500/PK-4
5 Park Rd 02054 508-376-7003
Jeffrey Wolff, prin. Fax 376-7038
Millis MS 400/5-8
245 Plain St 02054 508-376-7014
Andrew Zitoli, prin. Fax 376-7020

Woodside Montessori Academy 100/PK-8
350 Village St 02054 508-376-5320
Kathleen Gasbarro, hdmstr. Fax 376-4200

Mill River, Berkshire
Southern Berkshire Regional SD
Supt. — See Sheffield
New Marlborough Central ES 100/PK-4
PO Box 280 01244 413-229-8754
Thomas McGuire, prin. Fax 229-7872

Millville, Worcester
Blackstone-Millville Regional SD
Supt. — See Blackstone
Millville ES 400/PK-5
122 Berthelette Way 01529 508-876-0177
Eileen Tetreault, prin. Fax 883-0339

Milton, Norfolk, Pop. 27,000
Milton SD 3,700/PK-12
25 Gile Rd 02186 617-696-4808
Mary Gormley, supt. Fax 696-5099
www.edline.net/pages/Milton_Public_Schools
Collicot ES 400/PK-5
80 Edge Hill Rd 02186 617-696-4282
Gerard Schultz, prin. Fax 698-3577
Cunningham ES 400/K-5
44 Edge Hill Rd 02186 617-696-4285
Christine Gerber, prin. Fax 698-3473
Glover ES 500/K-5
255 Canton Ave 02186 617-696-4288
Dore Korschun, prin. Fax 698-2346
Pierce MS 900/6-8
451 Central Ave 02186 617-696-4568
James Jette, prin. Fax 698-2238
Tucker ES 400/PK-5
187 Blue Hills Pkwy 02186 617-696-4291
Drew Echelson, prin. Fax 698-3374

Delphi Academy 100/PK-9
564 Blue Hill Ave 02186 617-333-9610
Corrine Perkins, prin. Fax 333-9613
Milton Academy 1,000/K-12
170 Centre St 02186 617-898-1798
Todd Bland, hdmstr. Fax 898-1700
St. Agatha S 400/K-8
440 Adams St 02186 617-696-3548
Maureen Simmons, prin. Fax 696-6288
St. Mary of the Hills S 400/K-8
250 Brook Rd 02186 617-698-2464
Pamela Vasta, prin. Fax 696-9346
Thacher Montessori S 200/PK-8
1425 Blue Hill Ave 02186 617-361-2522
Fred Catlin, hdmstr. Fax 364-0911

Monson, Hampden, Pop. 2,101
Monson SD 1,600/PK-12
PO Box 159 01057 413-267-4150
Linda Denault, supt. Fax 267-9168
www.monsonschools.com
Granite Valley MS 500/5-8
21 Thompson St 01057 413-267-4155
Cheryl Clarke, prin. Fax 267-4624
Quarry Hill Community S 600/PK-4
43 Margaret St 01057 413-267-4160
Neil Gile, prin. Fax 267-4154

Montague, Franklin
Gill-Montague SD
Supt. — See Turners Falls
Great Falls MS 200/6-8
224 Turnpike Rd 01351 413-863-7300
Donna Fitzpatrick, prin. Fax 863-7354

Monterey, Berkshire
Southern Berkshire Regional SD
Supt. — See Sheffield
Monterey K 50/K-K
Main St 01245 413-229-8754
Thomas McGuire, prin. Fax 229-3211

Nahant, Essex, Pop. 3,828
Nahant SD 200/PK-6
290 Castle Rd 01908 781-581-1600
Joseph Lisi, supt. Fax 581-0440
www.johnsonschool.org/
Johnson ES 200/PK-6
290 Castle Rd 01908 781-581-1600
Diane Mulcahy, prin. Fax 581-0440

Nantucket, Nantucket, Pop. 3,069
Nantucket SD 1,200/K-12
10 Surfside Rd 02554 508-228-7285
Robert Pellicone, supt. Fax 325-5318
www.npsk.org
Nantucket ES 500/K-5
30 Surfside Rd 02554 508-228-7290
John Miller, prin. Fax 325-5342
Peirce MS 300/6-8
10 Surfside Rd 02554 508-228-7283
Caryl Toole, prin. Fax 325-7597

Nantucket New S 100/PK-8
PO Box 2021 02584 508-228-8569
David Provost, hdmstr. Fax 825-9811

Natick, Middlesex, Pop. 30,700
Natick SD 4,500/PK-12
13 E Central St 01760 508-647-6500
Peter Sanchioni, supt. Fax 647-6506
www.natickps.org/
Bennett-Hemenway ES 500/PK-4
22 E Evergreen Rd 01760 508-647-6580
Ian Kelly, prin. Fax 652-9951
Brown ES 400/PK-4
1 Jean Burke Dr 01760 508-647-6660
Edward Quigley, prin. Fax 647-6668
Johnson ES 200/K-4
99 S Main St 01760 508-647-6680
Karen Ghilani, prin. Fax 647-6688
Kennedy MS 500/5-8
165 Mill St 01760 508-647-6650
Rosemary Vickery, prin. Fax 647-6658
Lilja ES 400/K-4
41 Bacon St 01760 508-647-6570
Barbara Brown, prin. Fax 647-6572
Memorial ES 400/K-4
107 Eliot St 01760 508-647-6590
Beverly McCloskey, prin. Fax 647-6598
Wilson MS 800/5-8
22 Rutledge Rd 01760 508-647-6670
Anna Nolin, prin. Fax 647-6678

Eliot Montessori S 100/K-8
6 Auburn St 01760 508-655-7333
Bill O'Hearn, prin. Fax 655-3867
Westgate Christian Academy 100/PK-8
90 Oak St 01760 508-315-3152
Rev. Larry Loring, hdmstr. Fax 315-3155

Needham, Norfolk, Pop. 29,200
Needham SD 4,800/PK-12
1330 Highland Ave 02492 781-455-0400
Daniel Gutekanst, supt. Fax 455-0417
www.needham.k12.ma.us/
Broadmeadow ES 500/K-5
120 Broad Meadow Rd 02492 781-455-0448
Emily Gaberman, prin. Fax 455-0851
High Rock S, 77 Ferndale Rd 02492 6-6
Jessica Downey, prin. 781-455-0455
Mitchell ES 400/K-5
187 Brookline St 02492 781-455-0466
Dr. Michael Schwinden, prin. Fax 455-0871
Newman ES 600/PK-5
1155 Central Ave 02492 781-455-0416
Rita Bissonnette-Clark, prin. Fax 453-2523
Pollard MS 1,100/6-8
200 Harris Ave 02492 781-455-0480
Glenn Brand, prin. Fax 455-0413
Other Schools – See Needham Heights

Haddad MS 200/6-8
110 May St 02492 781-449-0133
Jane Abel, prin. Fax 449-8096
St. Joseph S 400/K-5
90 Pickering St 02492 781-444-4459
Paul Kelly, prin. Fax 444-0822

Needham Heights, Norfolk
Needham SD
Supt. — See Needham
Eliot ES 400/K-5
135 Wellesley Ave 02494 781-455-0452
Suzanne Wilcox, prin. Fax 455-0852
Hillside ES 400/K-5
28 Glen Gary Rd 02494 781-455-0461
Michael Kascak, prin. Fax 455-0857

New Bedford, Bristol, Pop. 93,102
New Bedford SD 12,600/PK-12
455 County St 02740 508-997-4511
Dr. Portia Bonner, supt. Fax 997-0298
www.newbedfordschools.org
Ashley ES 300/K-5
122 Rochambeau St 02745 508-997-4511
Karen Meyer, prin. Fax 995-9707
Brooks ES 300/K-5
212 Nemasket St 02740 508-997-4511
Kevin Sullivan, prin. Fax 991-3659
Campbell ES 200/PK-5
145 Essex St 02745 508-997-4511
Lisa Andrade, prin. Fax 991-7483
Carney ES 500/PK-5
247 Elm St 02740 508-997-4511
Raymond Letendre, prin. Fax 990-2879
Congdon ES 300/K-5
50 Hemlock St 02740 508-997-4511
Steven Machado, prin. Fax 999-3959
DeValles ES 300/K-5
120 Katherine St 02744 508-997-4511
Cynthia Trinidad, prin. Fax 999-4034
Dunbar ES 100/K-5
338 Dartmouth St 02740 508-997-4511
Susan Campinha Beck, prin. Fax 984-1279
Gomes ES 700/PK-5
286 S 2nd St 02740 508-997-4511
Martha Kay, prin. Fax 990-1840
Hannigan ES 200/K-5
33 Emery St 02744 508-997-4511
Arthur Dutra, prin. Fax 984-5660
Hathaway ES, 256 Court St 02740 300/K-5
Bart Lush, prin. 508-997-4511
Hayden/McFadden ES 500/PK-5
361 Cedar Grove St 02746 508-997-4511
Suzanne Scallin, prin. Fax 979-4664
Keith MS 700/6-8
225 Hathaway Blvd 02740 508-997-4511
Deborah Cimo, prin. Fax 996-2040
Kempton ES 100/K-5
135 Shawmut Ave 02740 508-997-4511
Richard Desrosiers, prin. Fax 984-1451
Lincoln ES 200/K-5
445 Ashley Blvd 02745 508-997-4511
Jo Anne Hodgson, prin. Fax 995-7933
Normandin MS 1,200/6-8
81 Felton St 02745 508-997-4511
Jeanne Bonneau, prin. Fax 995-6975
Ottiwell ES, 26 Madeira Ave 02746 300/PK-5
Eugene Sladewski, prin. 508-997-4511
Pacheco ES 300/PK-5
251 Mount Pleasant St 02746 508-997-4511
Marcia Faucher, prin. Fax 994-7241
Parker ES 400/PK-5
705 County St 02740 508-997-4511
Sunita Mehrotra, prin. Fax 994-4063
Phillips Avenue ES 100/K-5
249 Phillips Ave 02746 508-997-4511
Timothy Rumberger, prin.
Pulaski ES, 1097 Braley Rd 02745 600/PK-5
Jamie Camacho, prin. 508-997-4511
Rodman ES 100/K-5
497 Mill St 02740 508-997-4511
Tammy Morgan, prin. Fax 997-1567
Roosevelt MS 800/6-8
119 Frederick St 02744 508-997-4511
Darcy Fernandes, prin. Fax 997-1198
Swift ES 200/K-5
2203 Acushnet Ave 02745 508-997-4511
Debra Letendre, prin. Fax 998-0887
Taylor ES 200/K-5
620 Brock Ave 02744 508-997-4511
Matthew Riley, prin. Fax 991-7483
Winslow ES 200/K-5
561 Allen St 02740 508-997-4511
Paula Bailey, prin. Fax 999-0489

Holy Family-Holy Name S 300/PK-8
91 Summer St 02740 508-993-3547
Cecilia Felix, prin. Fax 993-8277
Nazarene Christian Academy 200/PK-12
764 Hathaway Rd 02740 508-992-7944
Rev. Jon Helm, hdmstr. Fax 994-1457
St. Mary S 200/PK-8
115 Illinois St 02745 508-995-3696
Daphne Costa, prin. Fax 998-0840
SS. James & John S 300/PK-8
180 Orchard St 02740 508-996-0534
Cristina Raposo, prin. Fax 996-3087
SS. Joseph & Therese S 200/PK-8
35 Kearsarge St 02745 508-995-2264
Sherri Swainamer, prin. Fax 995-0038

New Braintree, Worcester
Quabbin SD
Supt. — See Barre
New Braintree Grade S 100/K-6
15 Memorial Dr 01531 508-867-2553
Patricia Worthington, prin. Fax 867-3331

Newbury, Essex
Triton Regional SD
Supt. — See Byfield
Newbury ES 600/PK-6
63 Hanover St 01951 978-465-5353
Sylvia Jordan, prin. Fax 463-3070

Newburyport, Essex, Pop. 17,414
Newburyport SD 1,800/PK-12
70 Low St 01950 978-465-4457
Deirdre Farrell, supt. Fax 462-3495
www.newburyport.k12.ma.us/
Bresnahan ES 300/1-3
333 High St 01950 978-465-4431
Kristina Davis, prin. Fax 465-0410
Brown S 100/PK-K
40 Milk St 01950 978-465-4435
Margo Perriello, prin. Fax 465-5776
Molin Upper ES 4-5
70 Low St 01950 978-465-4445
Lori Gallivan, prin. Fax 465-7699
Nock MS 500/6-8
70 Low St 01950 978-465-4447
Barry Hopping, prin. Fax 465-4074

Immaculate Conception S 300/PK-8
1 Washington St 01950 978-465-7780
Mary Reardon, prin. Fax 234-7331

New Salem, Franklin
New Salem-Wendell SD
Supt. — See Erving
Swift River ES 200/PK-6
201 Wendell Rd 01355 978-544-6926
Sheila Hunter, prin. Fax 544-2253

Newton, Middlesex, Pop. 83,158
Newton SD
Supt. — See Newtonville
Bigelow MS 500/6-8
42 Vernon St 02458 617-552-7800
Todd Harrison, prin. Fax 552-7752
Lincoln-Eliot ES 300/K-5
191 Pearl St 02458 617-559-9540
Catheryn Charner-Laird, prin. Fax 552-5558
Oak Hill MS 600/6-8
130 Wheeler Rd 02459 617-559-9200
Henry Van Putten, prin. Fax 552-5547
Underwood ES 300/K-5
101 Vernon St 02458 617-559-9660
Dr. David Castelline, prin. Fax 552-5552

Jackson S 300/K-6
200 Jackson Rd 02458 617-969-1537
Susan Niden, prin. Fax 244-8596
Rashi S 300/K-8
15 Walnut Park 02458 617-969-4444
Matthew King, prin. Fax 969-9949
Walnut Park Montessori S 100/PK-PK
47 Walnut Park 02458 617-969-9208
Mary Rockett, hdmstr. Fax 969-6408

Newton Center, See Newton
Newton SD
Supt. — See Newtonville
Bowen ES 400/K-5
280 Cypress St 02459 617-559-9330
Ruth Chapman, prin. Fax 552-7363
Brown MS 700/6-8
125 Meadowbrook Rd 02459 617-559-6900
John Jordan, prin. Fax 552-7729
Mason-Rice ES 400/K-5
149 Pleasant St 02459 617-559-9570
Mark Springer, prin. Fax 552-7315
Memorial-Spaulding ES 400/K-5
250 Brookline St 02459 617-559-9600
Donette Wilson-Wood, prin. Fax 552-7944
Ward ES 200/K-5
10 Dolphin Rd 02459 617-559-6450
Audrey Peller, prin. Fax 552-5563

Newton Montessori S 100/PK-8
80 Crescent Ave 02459 617-969-4488
Ellen Kelley, hdmstr. Fax 969-4430
Solomon Schechter Day S Greater Boston 200/K-3
60 Stein Cir 02459 617-964-7765
Arnold Zar-Kessler, hdmstr. Fax 964-8693
Solomon Schechter Day S Greater Boston 300/4-8
125 Wells Ave 02459 617-928-9100
Arnold Zar-Kessler, hdmstr. Fax 928-9108

Newton Highlands, See Newton
Newton SD
Supt. — See Newtonville
Countryside ES 400/K-5
191 Dedham St 02461 617-559-9450
Emily Ostrower, prin. Fax 552-5583

Newtonville, See Newton
Newton SD 11,600/PK-12
100 Walnut St 02460 617-559-6100
Dr. Jeffrey Young, supt. Fax 559-6101
www.newton.k12.ma.us/
Cabot ES 400/K-5
229 Cabot St 02460 617-559-9400
James Swaim, prin. Fax 552-5584
Day MS 700/6-8
21 Minot Pl 02460 617-559-9100
Gina Healy, prin. Fax 559-9103
Mann ES 400/K-5
687 Watertown St 02460 617-559-9510
Joseph Russo, prin. Fax 559-2004
Newton ECC 200/PK-PK
100 Walnut St 02460 617-559-6050
Lisa Robinson, dir. Fax 559-6026
Other Schools – See Auburndale, Newton, Newton Center, Newton Highlands, Waban, West Newton

Norfolk, Norfolk
King Philip SD 2,000/7-12
18 King St 02056 508-520-7991
Richard Robbat, supt. Fax 520-2044
www.kingphilip.org
King Philip Regional MS North 800/7-8
18 King St 02056 508-541-7324
Dr. Susan Gilson, prin. Fax 541-3467

Norfolk SD 900/PK-6
70 Boardman St 02056 508-528-1225
Don LeClerc, supt. Fax 528-3739
www.norfolk.k12.ma.us/
Day ES 300/PK-2
232 Main St 02056 508-541-5475
Linda Balfour, prin. Fax 541-5482
Freeman-Centennial IS 600/3-6
70 Boardman St 02056 508-528-1266
Lucia Godfrey, prin. Fax 541-5495

North Adams, Berkshire, Pop. 14,010
Clarksburg SD 200/K-8
98 Church St 01247 413-664-9292
Jon Lev, supt. Fax 664-9942
Other Schools – See Clarksburg

Florida SD 100/PK-8
98 Church St 01247 413-664-9292
Jon Lev, supt. Fax 664-9942
Other Schools – See Florida

North Adams SD 1,800/PK-12
191 E Main St Ste 1 01247 413-662-3225
James Montepare, supt. Fax 662-3212
www.napsk12.org/
Brayton ES 400/PK-5
20 Barbour St 01247 413-662-3260
Linda Reardon, prin. Fax 662-3293
Conte MS 400/6-8
24 N Church St 01247 413-662-3200
Diane Ryczek, prin. Fax 662-3212
Greylock ES 200/K-5
100 Phelps Ave 01247 413-662-3255
Sandra Cote, prin. Fax 662-3033
Sullivan ES 300/K-5
151 Kemp Ave 01247 413-662-3250
Shelley Fachini, prin. Fax 662-3032

Northampton, Hampshire, Pop. 28,715
Northampton SD 2,800/PK-12
212 Main St Rm 200 01060 413-587-1327
Isabelina Rodriguez, supt. Fax 587-1318
www.nps.northampton.ma.us
Bridge Street ES 300/K-5
2 Parsons St 01060 413-587-1460
Johanna McKenna, prin. Fax 587-1474
Jackson Street ES 400/PK-5
120 Jackson St 01060 413-587-1510
Gwen Agna, prin. Fax 587-1524
Other Schools – See Florence, Leeds

Lander-Grinspoon Academy 100/K-6
257 Prospect St 01060 413-584-6622
Suzanne Atkins, prin. Fax 586-7550
Montessori S of Northhampton 100/PK-6
51 Bates St 01060 413-586-4538
Susan Swift, hdmstr. Fax 586-7047
Smith College Campus S 300/K-6
33 Prospect St 01063 413-585-3270
Cathy Reid, prin. Fax 585-3285

North Andover, Essex, Pop. 22,792
North Andover SD 4,600/PK-12
43 High St 01845 978-794-1503
Dr. Vincent Marini, supt. Fax 794-0231
www.northandoverpublicschools.com/
Atkinson ES 300/K-5
111 Phillips Brooks Rd 01845 978-794-0124
Greg Landry, prin. Fax 794-2454
Franklin ES 500/PK-5
2 Cypress Ter 01845 978-794-1990
Pamela Lathrop, prin. Fax 682-0240
Kittredge ES 300/K-5
601 Main St 01845 978-794-1688
Richard Cushing, prin. Fax 794-2514
North Andover MS 1,100/6-8
495 Main St 01845 978-794-1870
Joan McQuade, prin. Fax 794-3619
Sargent ES 600/PK-5
300 Abbott St 01845 978-725-3673
Elizabeth Kline, prin. Fax 725-3678
Thomson ES 400/K-5
266 Waverley Rd 01845 978-794-1545
Gregg Gilligan, prin. Fax 794-2508

St. Michael S 500/PK-8
80 Maple Ave 01845 978-686-1862
Susan Reidy Gosselin, prin. Fax 688-5144

North Attleboro, Bristol, Pop. 16,178
North Attleborough SD 4,700/PK-12
6 Morse St 02760 508-643-2100
Richard Smith, supt. Fax 643-2110
www.naschools.net
Allen Avenue ES 200/K-4
290 Allen Ave 02760 508-643-2165
Gideon Gaudette, prin. Fax 643-2183
Amvet Boulevard ES 400/K-5
70 Amvet Blvd 02760 508-643-2155
Mary Alice Gruppi, prin. Fax 643-2184
Community S 400/K-5
45 S Washington St 02760 508-643-2148
Thomas Labonte, prin. Fax 643-2179
Early Learning Center 100/PK-PK
25 School St 02760 508-643-2145
Sheila Burgess, prin. Fax 643-2188
Falls ES 300/K-5
2 Jackson St 02763 508-643-2170
George Gagnon, prin. Fax 643-2185
Martin ES 600/K-5
37 Landry Ave 02760 508-643-2140
Michael Luce, prin. Fax 643-2186
North Attleboro MS 1,200/6-8
564 Landry Ave 02760 508-643-2130
Victoria Ekk, prin. Fax 643-2134
Roosevelt Avenue ES 200/K-5
108 Roosevelt Ave 02760 508-643-2151
John Quinn, prin. Fax 643-2187

St. Mary-Sacred Heart S 200/K-8
57 Richards Ave 02760 508-695-3072
Denise Peixoto, prin. Fax 695-9074

North Billerica, Middlesex, Pop. 5,400
Billerica SD
Supt. — See Billerica
Dutile ES 500/K-5
10 Biagiotti Way 01862 978-436-9540
Patricia Tobin, prin. Fax 436-9548

Northborough, Worcester, Pop. 5,761
Northborough-Southborough SD
Supt. — See Southborough
Lincoln Street ES 300/K-5
76 Lincoln St 01532 508-351-7030
Jean Fitzgerald, prin. Fax 351-7033
Melican MS 600/6-8
145 Lincoln St 01532 508-351-7020
Patricia Montimurro, prin. Fax 351-7006
Peaslee ES 300/K-5
31 Maple St 01532 508-351-7035
Scott Bazydlo, prin. Fax 351-7037
Proctor ES 300/K-5
26 Jefferson Rd 01532 508-351-7040
Margaret Donohoe, prin. Fax 351-7007
Zeh ES 400/PK-5
33 Howard St 01532 508-351-7048
Susan Whitten, prin. Fax 393-5125

St. Bernadette S 500/PK-8
266 Main St 01532 508-351-9905
Deborah O'Neil, prin. Fax 351-2941

North Brookfield, Worcester, Pop. 2,635
North Brookfield SD 700/K-12
10 New School Dr 01535 508-867-9821
Erin Nosek, supt. Fax 867-8148
www.nbschools.org/
North Brookfield ES 400/K-6
10 New School Dr 01535 508-867-8326
Deborah Peterson, prin. Fax 867-6255

North Chelmsford, Middlesex
Chelmsford SD
Supt. — See Chelmsford
Harrington ES 600/PK-4
120 Richardson Rd 01863 978-251-5166
Colleen Beaudoin, prin. Fax 251-5170

Keystone Montessori S 100/PK-4
73 Princeton St 01863 978-251-2929
Cary Williams, prin. Fax 251-0809

North Dartmouth, Bristol, Pop. 8,000
Dartmouth SD
Supt. — See South Dartmouth
Dartmouth MS 1,000/6-8
366 Slocum Rd 02747 508-997-9333
Darren Doane, prin. Fax 999-7720
Potter ES 500/K-5
185 Cross Rd 02747 508-996-8250
Heidi Brooks, prin. Fax 990-0250
Quinn ES 600/PK-5
529 Hawthorn St 02747 508-997-3178
Lorraine Granda, prin. Fax 997-6257

Friends Academy 200/PK-8
1088 Tucker Rd 02747 508-999-1356
Andrew Rodin, prin. Fax 997-0117

North Dighton, Bristol
Dighton-Rehoboth Regional SD 3,300/PK-12
2700 Regional Rd 02764 508-252-5000
Kathleen Montagano, supt. Fax 252-5024
www.drregional.org/
Other Schools – See Dighton, Rehoboth

North Easton, Bristol, Pop. 4,400
Easton SD 2,900/PK-12
PO Box 359 02356 508-230-3200
Dr. William Simmons, supt. Fax 238-3563
www.easton.k12.ma.us/
Easton MS 600/6-8
98 Columbus Ave 02356 508-230-3222
John Giuggio, prin. Fax 230-0198
Moreau Hall ES 200/K-2
360 Washington St 02356 508-230-3235
Robert Smith, prin. Fax 238-3237
Olmsted S 300/3-5
101 Lothrop St 02356 508-230-3205
Dr. Gary Mazzola, prin. Fax 238-3244
Parkview S 300/K-2
50 Spooner St 02356 508-230-3230
Vanessa Beauchaine, prin. Fax 230-3249
Richardson S 300/3-5
101 Lothrop St 02356 508-230-3227
Patrick Lucier, prin. Fax 238-3244
Other Schools – See South Easton

North Falmouth, Barnstable, Pop. 2,625
Falmouth SD
Supt. — See East Falmouth

North Falmouth ES 400/PK-4
62 Old Main Rd 02556 508-563-2334
Sue Driscoll, prin. Fax 564-7525

Northfield, Franklin, Pop. 1,322
Pioneer Valley SD 1,100/PK-12
97 F Sumner Turner Rd 01360 413-498-2911
Dayle Doiron, supt. Fax 498-0045
www.pioneervalley.k12.ma.us
Northfield ES 300/PK-6
104 Main St 01360 413-498-5842
Thomas King, prin. Fax 498-5459
Other Schools – See Bernardston, Leyden, Warwick

North Grafton, Worcester, Pop. 3,100
Grafton SD
Supt. — See Grafton
North Grafton ES 200/PK-2
46 Waterville St 01536 508-839-5483
Michelle Tynan, prin. Fax 839-1073

North Quincy, See Quincy
Quincy SD
Supt. — See Quincy
Atlantic MS 500/6-8
86 Hollis Ave 02171 617-984-8727
Maureen MacNeil, prin. Fax 984-8646
Montclair ES 300/K-5
8 Belmont St 02171 617-984-8708
Renee Lalumiere, prin. Fax 984-8719
Parker ES 300/K-5
148 Billings Rd 02171 617-984-8710
Maryann Palmer, prin. Fax 984-8624
Squantum ES 300/K-5
50 Huckins Ave 02171 617-984-8706
Stephen Sylvia, prin. Fax 984-8857

Sacred Heart S 300/PK-8
370 Hancock St 02171 617-328-3830
Katherine Hunter, prin. Fax 328-6438

North Reading, Middlesex, Pop. 12,002
North Reading SD 2,700/K-12
19 Sherman Rd 01864 978-664-7810
David Troughton, supt. Fax 664-0252
ps.north-reading.k12.ma.us/
Batchelder ES 500/K-5
175 Park St 01864 978-664-7814
Sean Killeen, prin. Fax 664-3178
Hood ES 500/K-5
298 Haverhill St 01864 978-664-7816
Glen McKay, prin. Fax 664-7805
Little ES 400/K-5
7 Barberry Rd 01864 978-664-7820
William Lecesse, prin. Fax 664-3081
North Reading MS 600/6-8
19 Sherman Rd 01864 978-664-7806
John Faucher, prin. Fax 276-0679

North Weymouth, Norfolk
Weymouth SD
Supt. — See Weymouth
Johnson ECC, 70 Pearl St 02191 PK-PK
Victoria Silberstein, prin. 781-335-0191
Wessagusset PS 400/K-4
75 Pilgrim Rd 02191 781-335-2210
Jean McLean, prin. Fax 335-4379

St. Jerome S 200/K-8
598 Bridge St 02191 781-335-1235
Sheila Kukstis, prin. Fax 340-0256

Norton, Bristol, Pop. 1,899
Norton SD 2,900/PK-12
64 W Main St 02766 508-285-0100
Patricia Ansay, supt. Fax 285-0199
www.edline.net/pages/Norton_Public_Schools
Norton MS 800/6-8
215 W Main St 02766 508-285-0140
Chris Baratta, prin. Fax 286-9457
Nourse ES 400/PK-3
38 Plain St 02766 508-285-0110
Danielle Klingaman, prin. Fax 285-0109
Solmonese ES 500/K-3
315 W Main St 02766 508-285-0120
Riitta Bolton, prin. Fax 285-0130
Yelle ES 500/4-5
64 W Main St 02766 508-285-0190
Lisa Farrell, prin. Fax 285-0187

New Testament Christian S 200/PK-12
1 New Taunton Ave 02766 508-285-9771
Lynne Brennan, prin. Fax 285-6775

Norwell, Plymouth
Norwell SD 2,300/PK-12
322 Main St 02061 781-659-8800
Donald Beaudette Ed.D., supt. Fax 659-8805
www.norwellschools.org
Cole ES 600/PK-5
81 High St 02061 781-659-8823
Garry Pelletier, prin. Fax 659-7089
Norwell MS 500/6-8
328 Main St 02061 781-659-8814
Derek Sulc, prin. Fax 659-8822
Vinal ES 600/PK-5
102 Old Oaken Bucket Rd 02061 781-659-8820
Annette Bailey, prin. Fax 659-8812

Norwood, Norfolk, Pop. 28,500
Norwood SD 3,200/PK-12
PO Box 67 02062 781-762-6804
John Moretti, supt. Fax 762-0229
www.norwood.k12.ma.us/
Balch ES 300/1-5
PO Box 67 02062 781-762-0694
John Condlin, prin. Fax 255-5610
Callahan ES 200/1-5
PO Box 67 02062 781-762-0693
Robert Griffin, prin. Fax 255-5611
Cleveland ES 300/1-5
PO Box 67 02062 781-762-6522
Scott Williams, prin. Fax 255-7317
Coakley MS 800/6-8
PO Box 67 02062 781-762-7880
Zeff Gianetti, prin. Fax 255-5630
Oldham ES 200/1-5
PO Box 67 02062 781-769-2417
Wesley Manaday, prin. Fax 255-7007
Prescott ES 200/1-5
PO Box 67 02062 781-762-6497
Brianne Killion, prin. Fax 255-7028
Willett ECC 100/PK-K
PO Box 67 02062 781-762-6805
Virginia Ceruti, prin. Fax 762-7245

St. Catherine of Siena S 500/K-8
249 Nahatan St 02062 781-769-5354
Gretchen Hawley, prin. Fax 769-7905
South Area Solomon Schechter Day S 200/K-8
1 Commerce Way 02062 781-769-7555
Jane Cohen, hdmstr. Fax 769-5553

Oak Bluffs, Dukes
Oak Bluffs SD
Supt. — See Vineyard Haven
Oak Bluffs S 400/K-8
PO Box 1325 02557 508-693-0951
Laury Binney, prin. Fax 693-5189

Oakham, Worcester
Quabbin SD
Supt. — See Barre
Oakham Center ES 300/PK-6
1 Deacon Allen Dr 01068 508-882-3392
Patricia Worthington, prin. Fax 882-0101

Onset, Plymouth, Pop. 1,461
Wareham SD
Supt. — See Wareham
Hammond ES 100/PK-K
PO Box 191 02558 508-291-3565
Joan Seamans, prin. Fax 291-3546

Orange, Franklin, Pop. 3,791
Orange SD 600/K-6
131 W Main St 01364 978-544-6763
Dr. Paul Burnim, supt. Fax 544-3450
www.orange-elem.org/
Butterfield S 200/5-6
94 S Main St 01364 978-544-6136
Robert Haigh, prin. Fax 544-1121
Dexter Park ES 200/3-4
1 Dexter St 01364 978-544-6080
Enver Softic, prin. Fax 544-1123
Fisher Hill ES 200/K-2
59 Dexter St 01364 978-544-0018
Jennifer Haggerty, prin. Fax 544-5703

Orleans, Barnstable, Pop. 1,699
Brewster SD 500/PK-5
78 Eldridge Park Way 02653 508-255-8800
Michael Gradone, supt. Fax 240-2351
www.nausetschools.org
Other Schools – See Brewster

Eastham SD 200/K-5
78 Eldridge Park Way 02653 508-255-8800
Michael Gradone, supt. Fax 240-2351
www.nausetschools.org
Other Schools – See Eastham

Nauset SD 1,600/6-12
78 Eldridge Park Way 02653 508-255-8800
Michael Gradone, supt. Fax 240-2351
www.nausetschools.org
Nauset Regional MS 500/6-8
70 S Orleans Rd 02653 508-255-0016
Greg Baecker, prin. Fax 240-1105

Orleans SD 200/K-5
78 Eldridge Park Way 02653 508-255-8800
Michael Gradone, supt. Fax 240-2351
www.nausetschools.org
Orleans ES 200/K-5
46 Eldridge Park Way 02653 508-255-0380
Diane Carreiro, prin. Fax 255-7943

Wellfleet SD 100/PK-5
78 Eldridge Park Way 02653 508-255-8800
Michael Gradone, supt. Fax 240-2351
www.nausetschools.org
Other Schools – See Wellfleet

Osterville, Barnstable, Pop. 2,911
Barnstable SD
Supt. — See Hyannis
Osterville ES 200/K-2
350 Bumps River Rd 02655 508-428-6638
Donna Forloney, prin. Fax 428-6174

Bayberry Christian S 50/1-8
2736 Falmouth Rd 02655 508-428-9178
Jennifer Case, prin. Fax 428-8921
Cape Cod Academy 400/K-12
PO Box 469 02655 508-428-5400
Clark Daggett, prin. Fax 428-0701

Otis, Berkshire
Farmington River Regional SD 100/PK-6
PO Box 679 01253 413-269-4466
Joanne Austin, supt. Fax 269-7659
www.farmingtonriverelementary.com
Farmington River ES 100/PK-6
PO Box 679 01253 413-269-4466
Jeffrey Hatch, prin. Fax 269-7659

Oxford, Worcester, Pop. 5,969
Oxford SD 2,200/PK-12
5 Sigourney St 01540 508-987-6050
Ernest Boss, supt. Fax 987-6054
www.oxps.org
Barton ES 400/K-4
25 Depot Rd 01540 508-987-6066
Norman Yvon, prin. Fax 987-2364
Chaffee ES 500/PK-4
9 Clover St 01540 508-987-6057
Nancy Fournier, prin. Fax 987-5828
Oxford MS 700/5-8
497 Main St 01540 508-987-6074
Katherine Hackett, prin. Fax 987-2588

Oak Hill Christian S 50/PK-8
PO Box 277 01540 508-987-0287
Casandra Bergeron, admin. Fax 987-6156

Palmer, Hampden, Pop. 4,069
Palmer SD 1,800/PK-12
24 Converse St Ste 1 01069 413-283-2650
Dr. Gerald Fournier, supt. Fax 283-2655
www.palmerschools.org
Converse MS 500/5-7
24 Converse St Ste 3 01069 413-283-8109
David Stetkiewicz, prin. Fax 283-2655
Old Mill Pond ES 600/PK-4
4107 Main St 01069 413-283-4300
Mary Lou Callahan, prin. Fax 283-2619

Paxton, Worcester
Wachusett Regional SD
Supt. — See Jefferson
Paxton Center S 500/K-8
19 West St 01612 508-798-8576
Bobbie French, prin. Fax 754-6569

Peabody, Essex, Pop. 51,239
Peabody SD 6,400/PK-12
21 Johnson St 01960 978-536-6500
C. Milton Burnett, supt. Fax 536-6504
www.peabody.k12.ma.us/
Brown ES 400/K-5
150 Lynn St 01960 978-536-4100
Elaine Metropolis, prin. Fax 536-4180
Burke ES 400/K-5
127 Birch St 01960 978-536-5400
Judith McNiff, prin. Fax 536-5410
Carroll ES 500/K-5
60 Northend St 01960 978-536-4200
Cara Murtagh, prin. Fax 536-4215
Center ES 400/K-5
18 Irving St 01960 978-536-5475
Madeline Roy, prin. Fax 536-5490
Higgins MS 1,500/6-8
1 King St 01960 978-536-4800
Todd Bucey, prin. Fax 536-4810
McCarthy S 300/PK-5
76 Lake St 01960 978-536-5625
Amy Sullivan, prin. Fax 536-6545
South Memorial ES 400/PK-5
16 Maple Street Ext 01960 978-536-5700
Maryellen McGrath, prin. Fax 536-5710
Welch ES 300/PK-5
50 Swampscott Ave 01960 978-536-5775
Monique Nappi, prin. Fax 536-5845
West Memorial ES 300/K-5
15 Bow St 01960 978-536-5850
Susan Cassidy, prin. Fax 536-5860

St. John the Baptist S 500/PK-8
19 Chestnut St 01960 978-531-0444
Maureen Kelleher, prin. Fax 531-3569

Pelham, Hampshire
Pelham SD
Supt. — See Amherst
Pelham ES 100/K-6
45 Amherst Rd 01002 413-253-3595
Rena Moore, prin. Fax 253-4108

Pembroke, Plymouth
Pembroke SD 3,400/PK-12
72 Pilgrim Rd 02359 781-829-1178
Frank Hackett, supt. Fax 826-1182
www.pembrokepublicschools.org/
Bryantville ES 600/K-6
29 Gurney Dr 02359 781-293-5411
Catherine Glaude, prin. Fax 294-4662
Hobomock ES 700/K-6
81 Learning Ln 02359 781-294-0911
Donna McGarrigle, prin. Fax 293-1281
North Pembroke ES 700/PK-6
72 Pilgrim Rd 02359 781-826-5115
Jean Selines, prin. Fax 826-4851
Pembroke Community MS 500/7-8
559 School St 02359 781-294-0911
Margaret Szostak, prin. Fax 294-0916

Pepperell, Middlesex, Pop. 2,350
North Middlesex SD
Supt. — See Townsend
Fitzpatrick ES 500/PK-2
45 Main St 01463 978-433-2787
Dr. Pauline Cormier, prin. Fax 433-8880
Nissitissit MS 500/6-8
33 Chase Ave 01463 978-433-0114
Michael Tikonoff, prin. Fax 433-0118
Varnum Brook ES 500/3-5
10 Hollis St 01463 978-433-6722
Ralph Slavik, prin. Fax 433-8140

Petersham, Worcester
Petersham SD 100/K-6
PO Box 148 01366 978-724-3363
Dr. Patricia Martin, supt. Fax 724-6687
www.petershamcenterschool.org/
Petersham Center ES 100/K-6
PO Box 148 01366 978-724-3363
Rebecca Phillips, prin. Fax 724-6687

Phillipston, Worcester, Pop. 1,485
Narragansett Regional SD
Supt. — See Baldwinville
Phillipston Memorial ES 200/PK-4
20 The Cmn 01331 978-249-4969
Joanna Cackett, prin. Fax 249-5526

Pittsfield, Berkshire, Pop. 43,860
Pittsfield SD 6,400/PK-12
269 1st St 01201 413-499-9512
Dr. Howard Eberwein, supt. Fax 448-2643
www.pittsfield.net/
Allendale ES 300/K-5
180 Connecticut Ave 01201 413-448-9650
Carl Ameen, prin. Fax 499-4766
Capeless ES 300/PK-5
86 Brooks Ave 01201 413-448-9665
Susan Burt, prin. Fax 496-9449
Conte Community ES 400/PK-5
200 W Union St 01201 413-448-9660
Donna Leep, prin. Fax 448-9692
Crosby ES 400/PK-5
517 West St 01201 413-448-9670
Lisa Buchinski, prin. Fax 443-9520
Egremont ES 500/K-5
84 Egremont Ave 01201 413-448-9655
Judith Rush, prin. Fax 442-0886
Herberg MS 800/6-8
501 Pomeroy Ave 01201 413-448-9640
Christopher Jacoby, prin. Fax 448-9644
Morningside Community ES 400/PK-5
100 Burbank St 01201 413-448-9690
Joseph Curtis, prin. Fax 443-8907
Reid MS 700/6-8
950 North St 01201 413-448-9620
Morgan Williams, prin. Fax 443-1587
Stearns ES 200/K-5
75 Lebanon Ave 01201 413-499-9554
Jean Bednarski, prin. Fax 499-9514
Williams ES 300/K-5
50 Bushey Rd 01201 413-448-9680
Fax 448-9831

St. Mark S 200/PK-7
400 Columbus Ave Ste 1 01201 413-442-6040
Margaret Skowron, prin. Fax 448-5645

Plainville, Norfolk, Pop. 6,871
Plainville SD 700/PK-6
68 Messenger St 02762 508-699-1300
David Raiche, supt. Fax 699-1302
www.plainville.k12.ma.us
Jackson ES 400/PK-3
68 Messenger St 02762 508-699-1304
Anne Houle, prin. Fax 696-1303
Wood ES 300/4-6
72 Messenger St 02762 508-699-1312
Margaret Myers, prin. Fax 699-1317

Plymouth, Plymouth, Pop. 7,258
Plymouth SD 7,300/PK-12
253 S Meadow Rd 02360 508-830-4300
Gary Maestas, supt. Fax 746-1873
www.plymouthschools.com
Cold Spring ES 200/K-5
25 Alden St 02360 508-830-4335
David Sinclair, prin. Fax 830-4328
Federal Furnace ES 500/PK-5
860 Federal Furnace Rd 02360 508-830-4360
Margaret McKay, prin. Fax 830-4362
Hedge ES 200/K-5
258 Standish Ave 02360 508-830-4340
Adam Blaisdell, prin. Fax 830-4341
Indian Brook ES 500/K-4
1181 State Rd 02360 508-830-4370
Daniel Harold, prin. Fax 830-4373
Manomet ES 300/K-5
70 Manomet Point Rd 02360 508-830-4380
Patrick Fraine, prin. Fax 830-4387
Morton ES 600/PK-5
6 Lincoln St 02360 508-830-4320
Dona Mahoney, prin. Fax 830-4324
Mt. Pleasant S 100/PK-PK
22A Whiting St 02360 508-830-4343
Mary Mello, dir. Fax 746-1779
Plymouth Community IS 1,300/5-8
117 Long Pond Rd 02360 508-830-4450
Brian Palladino, prin. Fax 830-4464
Plymouth South MS 800/5-8
488 Long Pond Rd 02360 508-224-2725
John Siever, prin. Fax 224-5660
South ES 500/K-4
178 Bourne Rd 02360 508-830-4390
Ellen Gunning, prin. Fax 830-4398
West ES 400/K-5
170 Plympton Rd 02360 508-830-4350
Cynthia Silva, prin. Fax 830-4442

New Testament Christian S 100/2-12
1120 Long Pond Rd 02360 508-888-1889
Dr. Paul Jehle, prin. Fax 833-0920

Plympton, Plymouth
Plympton SD
Supt. — See Kingston
Dennett ES 200/K-6
80 Crescent St 02367 781-585-3659
Philip Holt, prin. Fax 585-3872

Prides Crossing, See Beverly

Landmark S 400/2-12
PO Box 227 01965 978-236-3010
Robert Broudo, hdmstr. Fax 921-0361

Princeton, Worcester
Wachusett Regional SD
Supt. — See Jefferson
Prince S 400/K-8
170 Sterling Rd 01541 978-464-2110
Mary Cringan, prin. Fax 464-2112

Master's Christian Academy 100/PK-8
PO Box 1125 01541 978-464-0622
Chad Lorion, prin. Fax 464-5622

Provincetown, Barnstable, Pop. 3,374
Provincetown SD 200/PK-12
2 Mayflower Ln 02657 508-487-5000
Jessica Waugh, supt. Fax 487-5098
www.edline.net/pages/Provincetown_Public_Schools
Veterans Memorial ES 100/PK-6
2 Mayflower Ln 02657 508-487-5020
Floriano Pavao, prin. Fax 487-5090

Quincy, Norfolk, Pop. 90,250
Quincy SD 8,400/PK-12
70 Coddington St 02169 617-984-8700
Dr. Richard DeCristofaro, supt. Fax 984-8965
www.quincypublicschools.com
Atherton Hough ES 200/K-5
1084 Sea St 02169 617-984-8797
Dorothy Greene, prin. Fax 984-8653
Beechwood Knoll ES 300/K-5
225 Fenno St 02170 617-984-8781
Diane O'Keefe, prin. Fax 984-8636
Bernazzani ES 300/K-5
701 Furnace Brook Pkwy 02169 617-984-8713
Peter Dionne, prin. Fax 984-8657
Broad Meadows MS 300/6-8
50 Calvin Rd 02169 617-984-8723
Lawrence Taglieri, prin. Fax 984-8834
Central MS 600/6-8
1012 Hancock St 02169 617-984-8725
Jen Fay-Beers, prin. Fax 984-8661
Chiesa ECC PK-PK
100 Brooks Ave 02169 617-984-8777
Ruth Witmer, prin. Fax 984-8764
Lincoln-Hancock Community ES 300/K-4
300 Granite St 02169 617-984-8715
Ruth Witmer, prin. Fax 984-8808
Marshall ES 400/K-4
200 Moody St Ext 02169 617-984-8721
Philip Connolly, prin. Fax 984-8609
Merrymount ES 300/K-5
4 Agawam Rd 02169 617-984-8762
Ann Pegg, prin. Fax 984-8909
Point Webster MS 300/5-8
60 Lancaster St 02169 617-984-6600
James McGuire, prin. Fax 984-6609
Snug Harbor Community ES 400/PK-5
333 Palmer St 02169 617-984-8763
Daniel Gilbert, prin. Fax 984-8645
Sterling MS 300/5-8
444 Granite St 02169 617-984-8729
Christine Barrett, prin. Fax 984-8640
Wollaston ES 300/PK-5
205 Beale St 02170 617-984-8791
James Hennessy, prin. Fax 984-8629
Other Schools – See North Quincy

Djerf Christian Preschool & Kindergarten 100/PK-K
65 Roberts St 02169 617-472-2960
Montessori S of Quincy 100/PK-6
101 Adams St 02169 617-773-8200
Rosine Afshar, admin. Fax 773-2359
St. Ann S 400/PK-8
1 Saint Anns Rd 02170 617-471-9071
Sr. Catherine Lee, prin. Fax 328-3128
St. Mary S 100/K-8
121 Crescent St 02169 617-773-5237
Anne Dailey, prin. Fax 786-9199

Randolph, Norfolk, Pop. 31,200
Randolph SD 3,100/1-12
40 Highland Ave 02368 781-961-6205
Dr. Richard Silverman, supt. Fax 961-6295
Donovan ES 400/1-6
123 Reed St 02368 781-961-6248
Samuel Bertolino, prin. Fax 961-6266
Kennedy ES 500/1-6
20 Hurley Dr 02368 781-961-6211
Nancy Connelly, prin. Fax 961-6268
Lyons ES 300/1-6
60 Vesey Rd 02368 781-961-6252
Fax 961-6264
Randolph Community MS 600/7-8
225 High St 02368 781-961-6243
John Sheehan, prin. Fax 961-6286
Young ES 300/1-6
30 Lou Courtney Dr 02368 781-961-6256
Helen Deranian, prin. Fax 961-6292

Raynham, Bristol, Pop. 2,100
Bridgewater-Raynham Regional SD
Supt. — See Bridgewater
Laliberte ES 500/2-4
777 Pleasant St 02767 508-824-2731
Dennis Bray, prin. Fax 824-2746
Merrill ES 200/PK-1
687 Pleasant St 02767 508-824-2490
Kathryn Tripp, prin. Fax 880-6720
Raynham MS 700/5-8
420 Titicut Rd 02767 508-977-0504
David Thomson, prin. Fax 977-0659

Reading, Middlesex, Pop. 22,539
Reading SD 4,300/K-12
82 Oakland Rd 01867 781-944-5800
Patrick Schettini J.D., supt. Fax 942-9149
www.reading.k12.ma.us/
Barrows ES 400/K-5
16 Edgemont Ave 01867 781-942-9166
Karen Callan, prin. Fax 942-9119
Birch Meadow ES 400/K-5
27 Arthur B Lord Dr 01867 781-944-2335
Eric Sprung, prin. Fax 942-9164
Coolidge MS 400/6-8
89 Birch Meadow Dr 01867 781-942-9158
Craig Martin, prin. Fax 942-9118
Eaton ES 500/K-5
365 Summer Ave 01867 781-942-9161
Patricia de Garavilla, prin. Fax 942-9053
Killam ES 500/K-5
333 Charles St 01867 781-944-7831
Catherine Giles, prin. Fax 942-9186
Parker MS 600/6-8
45 Temple St 01867 781-944-1236
Douglas Lyons, prin. Fax 942-9008
Wood End ES 400/K-5
85 Sunset Rock Ln 01867 781-942-5420
Richard Davidson, prin. Fax 942-5428

Readville, Suffolk

St. Anne S 100/PK-8
20 Como Rd 02136 617-361-3563
Grace Alexander, prin. Fax 361-8280

Rehoboth, Bristol
Dighton-Rehoboth Regional SD
Supt. — See North Dighton
Beckwith MS 600/5-8
330R Winthrop St 02769 508-252-5080
Debra Pincince, prin. Fax 252-5082
Palmer River ES 600/PK-4
326 Winthrop St 02769 508-252-5100
Linda McSweeney, prin. Fax 252-5110

Gosnold SD 50/PK-8
16 Williams St 02769 508-252-4272
Russell Latham, supt. Fax 252-4272
Other Schools – See Cuttyhunk

Cedar Brook SDA S 50/PK-8
24 Ralsie Rd 02769 508-252-3930
Dausele Vieira, prin. Fax 252-4378

Revere, Suffolk, Pop. 45,807
Revere SD 4,200/PK-12
101 School St 02151 781-286-8226
Dr. Paul Dakin, supt. Fax 286-8221
www.revereps.mec.edu
Anthony MS 6-8
107 Newhall St 02151 781-388-7520
Christopher Malone, prin. Fax 388-7521
Beachmont S 300/K-5
15 Everard Ave 02151 781-286-8316
Rosemarie O'Connor, prin. Fax 286-8293
Garfield Magnet ES PK-5
176 Garfield Ave 02151 781-286-8296
Salvatore Cammarata, prin. Fax 286-8128
Garfield Magnet MS 500/6-8
176 Garfield Ave 02151 781-286-8298
Patricia Massa, prin. Fax 286-3557
Lincoln ES 400/K-5
68 Tuckerman St 02151 781-286-8270
Ramona Repucci, prin. Fax 286-8315
McKinley ES 400/K-5
65 Yeamans St 02151 781-286-8284
Elizabeth Anton, prin. Fax 286-8289
Revere ES 300/K-5
15 Everard Ave 02151 781-286-8278
Barbara Kelly, prin. Fax 485-2740
Rumney Marsh Academy 6-8
140 American Legion Hwy 02151 781-388-3500
Cindy Evans, prin. Fax 485-8443
Whelan Memorial ES 600/PK-5
107 Newhall St 02151 781-388-7510
John Macero, prin. Fax 388-7511

Immaculate Conception S 200/K-8
127 Winthrop Ave 02151 781-284-0519
Josephine Felice, prin. Fax 284-3805

Richmond, Berkshire
Hancock SD 50/PK-6
1831 State Rd 01254 413-698-4001
William Ballen, supt. Fax 698-4003
www.hancockschool.org/
Other Schools – See Hancock

Richmond SD
Supt. — See Lanesboro
Richmond Consolidated S 200/PK-8
1831 State Rd 01254 413-698-2207
Jenevra Strock, prin. Fax 698-3199

Rochester, Plymouth
Rochester SD
Supt. — See Mattapoisett
Rochester Memorial ES 600/PK-6
16 Pine St 02770 508-763-2049
Joseph Ryan, prin. Fax 763-2623

Rockland, Plymouth, Pop. 16,123
Rockland SD 2,300/K-12
34 MacKinlay Way 02370 781-878-3893
John Retchless, supt. Fax 982-1483
www.rockland.mec.edu/
Esten ES 400/1-5
733 Summer St 02370 781-878-8336
Carol McGrath, prin. Fax 871-8451

Jefferson ES 200/K-5
93 George St 02370 781-871-8400
Gerald Kohn, prin. Fax 871-8449
Memorial Park ES 400/1-5
1 Brian Duffy Way 02370 781-878-1367
Janice Sheehan, prin. Fax 871-8450
Rogers MS 600/6-8
100 Taunton Ave 02370 781-878-4341
Paul Stanish, prin. Fax 871-8448

Calvary Chapel Academy 100/PK-12
PO Box 409 02370 781-871-1043
Richard Colello, hdmstr. Fax 792-3902
Holy Family S 400/PK-8
6 Delprete Ave 02370 781-878-1154
Paul Swett, prin. Fax 982-2485

Rockport, Essex, Pop. 5,448
Rockport SD 1,000/PK-12
24 Jerdens Ln 01966 978-546-1200
Susan King Ph.D., supt. Fax 546-1205
rockport.k12.ma.us
Rockport ES 400/PK-5
34 Jerdens Ln 01966 978-546-1220
Shawn Maguire, prin. Fax 546-8140
Rockport MS 200/6-8
26 Jerdens Ln 01966 978-546-1250
Charles Symonds, prin. Fax 546-1205

Roslindale, See Boston
Boston SD
Supt. — See Boston
Bates ES 300/K-5
426 Beech St 02131 617-635-8064
Kelly Hung, prin. Fax 635-8068
Conley ES 200/PK-5
450 Poplar St 02131 617-635-8099
Kathleen Armstrong, prin. Fax 635-6417
Haley ES 300/K-5
570 American Legion Hwy 02131 617-635-8169
Ross Wilson, prin. Fax 635-8173
Irving MS 700/6-8
105 Cummins Hwy 02131 617-635-8072
James Watson, prin. Fax 635-9363
Mozart ES 100/PK-5
236 Beech St 02131 617-635-8082
James Brewer, prin. Fax 635-8087
Philbrick ES 100/PK-5
40 Philbrick St 02131 617-635-8069
Laurie Carr, prin. Fax 635-7927
Sumner ES 500/PK-5
15 Basile St 02131 617-635-8131
Lourdes Santiago, prin. Fax 635-8136

Sacred Heart S 400/PK-8
1035 Canterbury St 02131 617-323-2500
Monica Haldiman, prin. Fax 325-7151

Rowe, Franklin
Rowe SD
Supt. — See Shelburne Falls
Rowe ES 100/K-6
86 Pond Rd 01367 413-339-8381
Robert Clancy, prin. Fax 339-8621

Rowley, Essex, Pop. 1,144
Triton Regional SD
Supt. — See Byfield
Pine Grove ES 600/PK-6
191 Main St 01969 978-948-2520
Arthur Beane, prin. Fax 948-2980

Roxbury, See Boston
Boston SD
Supt. — See Boston
Dearborn MS 400/6-8
35 Greenville St 02119 617-635-8412
Carroll Blake, prin. Fax 635-8419
Ellis ES 300/K-5
302 Walnut Ave 02119 617-635-8257
Carlos Gibb, prin. Fax 635-8262
Emerson ES 200/K-5
6 Shirley St 02119 617-635-8507
C. Sura O'Mard-Gentle, prin. Fax 635-6320
Hale ES 200/K-5
51 Cedar St 02119 617-635-8205
Sandra Mitchell-Woods, prin. Fax 635-8558
Haynes Early Education Center 200/PK-1
263 Blue Hill Ave 02119 617-635-6446
Valerie Gumes, prin. Fax 635-9795
Hernandez S 400/PK-8
61 School St 02119 617-635-8187
Margarita Muniz, prin. Fax 635-8190
Higginson ES 200/PK-5
160 Harrishof St 02119 617-635-8247
Joy Oliver, prin. Fax 635-8252
Lewis MS 300/6-8
131 Walnut Ave 02119 617-635-8137
Ronald Spratling, prin. Fax 635-6341
Mason ES 200/PK-5
150 Norfolk Ave 02119 617-635-8405
Harolyn Bowden, prin. Fax 635-8406
Mendell ES 100/K-5
164 School St 02119 617-635-8234
Karen Cahill, prin. Fax 635-8238
Mission Hill S 200/K-8
67 Alleghany St 02120 617-635-6384
Ayla Gavins, prin. Fax 635-6419
Orchard Gardens S 600/K-8
906 Albany St 02119 617-635-1660
Norman Townsend, prin. Fax 635-1634
Timilty MS 600/6-8
205 Roxbury St 02119 617-635-8109
Valeria Lowe-Barehmi, prin. Fax 635-8115
Tobin S 400/K-8
40 Smith St 02120 617-635-8393
Cheryl Harris, prin. Fax 635-7900

Our Lady Perpetual Help S 200/PK-8
94 Saint Alphonsus St 02120 617-442-2660
Maura Bradley, prin. Fax 442-3775
St. Patrick S 200/PK-8
131 Mount Pleasant Ave 02119 617-427-3881
Mary Lanata, prin. Fax 427-4529

Royalston, Worcester
Athol-Royalston SD
Supt. — See Athol
Royalston Community ES 100/PK-6
96 Winchendon Rd 01368 978-249-2900
Elizabeth Ervin, prin. Fax 249-4110

Russell, Hampden
Gateway SD
Supt. — See Huntington
Russell ES 100/K-4
155 Highland Ave 01071 413-685-1380
Joanne Blocker, prin. Fax 862-3228

Rutland, Worcester, Pop. 2,145
Wachusett Regional SD
Supt. — See Jefferson
Central Tree MS 300/5-8
281 Main St 01543 508-886-0073
C. Erik Githmark, prin. Fax 886-0141
Glenwood ES K-4
65 Glenwood Rd 01543 508-886-0385
Anthony Gasbarro, prin. Fax 886-0892
Naquag ES 300/K-4
285 Main St 01543 508-886-2901
Dixie Herbst, prin. Fax 886-2803

Sagamore, Barnstable, Pop. 2,589

Bridgeview S 100/PK-6
PO Box 270 02561 508-888-3567
Sandra Nickerson, prin. Fax 888-4940

Salem, Essex, Pop. 41,756
Salem SD 4,400/PK-12
29 Highland Ave 01970 978-740-1212
Dr. William Cameron, supt. Fax 740-3083
www.salem.k12.ma.us/
Bates ES 300/K-5
53 Liberty Hill Ave 01970 978-740-1250
Thomas LaValley, prin. Fax 740-1255
Bentley ES 300/K-5
25 Memorial Dr 01970 978-740-1260
Nancy Pelletier, prin. Fax 740-1164
Bowditch S 500/K-8
79 Willson St 01970 978-740-1290
Ana Hanton, prin. Fax 740-1180
Carlton ES 100/K-5
10 Skerry St 01970 978-740-1280
Philip Burke, prin. Fax 740-1283
Collins MS 800/6-8
29 Highland Ave 01970 978-740-1191
Mary Manning, prin. Fax 740-1183
Mann Laboratory ES 200/K-5
33 Loring Ave 01970 978-542-6220
Diane O'Donnell, prin. Fax 542-8332
Salem ECC 100/PK-PK
25 Memorial Dr 01970 978-740-1260
Nancy Pelletier, prin. Fax 740-1164
Saltonstall ES 300/K-6
211 Lafayette St 01970 978-740-1297
Margaret Howard, prin. Fax 740-1288
Witchcraft Heights ES 400/K-5
1 Frederick St 01970 978-740-1271
Mark Higgins, prin. Fax 825-3451

Phoenix S, 89 Margin St 01970 50/K-8
Betsey Sargent, hdmstr. 978-741-0870
St. Joseph S 200/PK-8
160 Federal St 01970 978-744-4773
Lou Ann Melino, prin. Fax 744-7237

Salisbury, Essex, Pop. 3,729
Triton Regional SD
Supt. — See Byfield
Salisbury ES 600/PK-6
100 Lafayette Rd 01952 978-463-5852
James Montanari, prin. Fax 463-8149

Sandwich, Barnstable, Pop. 2,998
Sandwich SD
Supt. — See East Sandwich
Wing S 900/PK-8
33 Water St 02563 508-888-1343
Matthew Bridges, prin. Fax 888-1082

Sandwich Montessori S 50/PK-6
284 Cotuit Rd 02563 508-888-4222
Virginia Collier, prin. Fax 888-4222

Saugus, Essex, Pop. 26,200
Saugus SD 3,100/PK-12
23 Main St 01906 781-231-5000
Richard Langlois, supt. Fax 233-9424
www.saugus.k12.ma.us
Belmonte MS 800/6-8
25 Dow St 01906 781-231-5052
Geoff Bruno, prin. Fax 233-5665
Lynnhurst ES 300/K-5
443 Walnut St 01906 781-231-5079
Sue Carney, prin. Fax 233-9420
Oaklandvale ES 200/K-5
266 Main St 01906 781-231-5082
Kathleen Stanton, prin. Fax 231-5085
Veterans Memorial ES 600/PK-5
39 Hurd Ave 01906 781-231-8166
Uri Harel, prin. Fax 231-8502
Waybright ES 300/PK-5
25 Talbot St 01906 781-231-5087
Linda Arsenault, prin. Fax 231-5090

Savoy, Berkshire
Savoy SD 100/PK-5
26 Chapel Rd 01256 413-743-1992
Jon Lev, supt. Fax 743-1114
Savoy ES 100/PK-5
26 Chapel Rd 01256 413-743-1992
Marjorie Senecal, prin. Fax 743-1114

Scituate, Plymouth, Pop. 5,180
Scituate SD 3,100/K-12
606 Chief Justice Cushing 02066 781-545-8759
Susan Martin, supt. Fax 545-6291
www.scituate.k12.ma.us/
Cushing ES 400/K-6
1 Aberdeen Dr 02066 781-545-8770
Mary Ohrenberger, prin. Fax 545-8776
Gates IS 500/7-8
327 First Parish Rd 02066 781-545-8760
Richard Blake, prin. Fax 545-8767
Hatherly ES 400/K-6
72 Ann Vinal Rd 02066 781-545-8780
Mari-An Fitzmaurice, prin. Fax 545-8786
Jenkins ES 600/K-6
54 Vinal Ave 02066 781-545-4910
John Willis, prin. Fax 545-8509
Wampatuck ES 400/K-6
266 Tilden Rd 02066 781-545-8790
Linda Whitney, prin. Fax 545-8797

Inly S 300/PK-8
46 Watch Hill Dr 02066 781-545-5544
Donna Luther, hdmstr. Fax 545-6522

Seekonk, Bristol, Pop. 13,046
Seekonk SD 2,200/PK-12
25 Water Ln 02771 508-399-5106
Dr. Emile Chevrette, supt. Fax 399-5128
seekonk.sharpschool.com/
Aitken ES 500/PK-5
165 Newman Ave 02771 508-336-5230
Nancy Gagliardi, prin. Fax 336-0324
Hurley MS 600/6-8
650 Newman Ave 02771 508-761-7570
Joan Fargnoli, prin. Fax 336-9630
Martin ES 500/PK-5
445 Cole St 02771 508-336-7558
Kevin Madden, prin. Fax 336-0309

Seekonk Christian Academy 100/K-8
95 Sagamore Rd 02771 508-336-4110
Brent Gilliam, hdmstr. Fax 336-5789

Sharon, Norfolk, Pop. 5,893
Sharon SD 3,500/PK-12
1 School St 02067 781-784-1570
Barbara Dunham Ed.D., supt. Fax 784-1573
www.sharon.k12.ma.us
Cottage Street ES 500/K-5
30 Cottage St 02067 781-784-1580
John Marcus, prin. Fax 784-0374
East ES 500/PK-5
45 Wilshire Dr 02067 781-784-1551
Judith Freedberg Ed.D., prin. Fax 784-7403
Heights ES 600/K-5
454 S Main St 02067 781-784-1595
Lisa Lamore, prin. Fax 784-1599
Sharon MS 800/6-8
75 Mountain St 02067 781-784-1560
Kevin O'Rourke, prin. Fax 784-8432

Chabad Day S 100/PK-12
162 N Main St 02067 781-784-4269
Sara Wolosow, prin. Fax 634-0485
Striar Hebrew Academy 100/PK-6
100 Ames St 02067 781-784-8724
Rabbi M. Mendel Lewitin, hdmstr. Fax 793-0654

Sheffield, Berkshire
Southern Berkshire Regional SD 900/PK-12
PO Box 339 01257 413-229-8778
Michael Singleton Ed.D., supt. Fax 229-2913
sbrsd.org
Undermountain ES 400/PK-6
PO Box 326 01257 413-229-8754
Thomas McGuire, prin. Fax 228-3211
Other Schools – See Mill River, Monterey, South Egremont

Shelburne Falls, Franklin, Pop. 1,996
Hawlemont Regional SD 100/K-6
24 Ashfield Rd 01370 413-625-0192
Michael Buoniconti, supt. Fax 625-0196
www.hawlemont.mtrsd.k12.ma.us/site/
Other Schools – See Charlemont

Mohawk Trail SD 1,300/PK-12
24 Ashfield Rd 01370 413-625-0192
Michael Buoniconti, supt. Fax 625-0196
www.mohawkschools.org
Buckland-Shelburne ES 200/PK-6
75 Mechanic St 01370 413-625-2521
Clayton Connor, prin. Fax 625-2034
Other Schools – See Ashfield, Charlemont, Colrain

Rowe SD 100/K-6
24 Ashfield Rd 01370 413-625-0192
Michael Buoniconti, supt. Fax 625-0196
www.mohawkschools.org/
Other Schools – See Rowe

Sherborn, Middlesex
Sherborn SD
Supt. — See Dover
Pine Hill ES 500/PK-5
10 Pine Hill Ln 01770 508-655-0630
Veronica Kenney, prin. Fax 655-2763

Shirley, Middlesex, Pop. 1,559
Shirley SD 700/PK-8
34 Lancaster Rd 01464 978-425-2630
Malcolm Reid, supt. Fax 425-2639
www.shirley-ma.gov
Center Preschool 50/PK-PK
34 Lancaster Rd 01464 978-425-2630
Suzanne Mahoney, prin. Fax 425-2639
Shirley MS 300/5-8
1 Hospital Rd 01464 978-425-2630
Brian Haas, prin. Fax 425-0474
White ES 400/PK-4
34 Lancaster Rd 01464 978-425-2630
Suzanne Mahoney, prin. Fax 425-2638

Shrewsbury, Worcester, Pop. 25,900
Shrewsbury SD 5,400/PK-12
100 Maple Ave 01545 508-841-8400
Joseph Sawyer, supt. Fax 841-8490
schools.shrewsbury-ma.gov
Beal ECC 100/K-1
1 Maple Ave 01545 508-841-8860
Alice Brennan, prin. Fax 841-8862
Coolidge ES 300/K-4
1 Florence St 01545 508-841-8880
Amy Clouter, prin. Fax 841-8883
Floral Street ES 700/1-4
57 Floral St 01545 508-841-8720
Todd Curtis, prin. Fax 841-8721
Oak MS 1,000/7-8
45 Oak St 01545 508-841-1200
Christopher Starczewski, prin. Fax 841-1223
Parker Road Preschool PK-PK
15 Parker Rd 01545 508-841-8646
Mary Lammi, dir. Fax 841-8661
Paton ES 400/1-4
58 Grafton St 01545 508-841-8626
Jayne Wilkin, prin. Fax 841-8627
Sherwood MS 1,000/5-6
30 Sherwood Ave 01545 508-841-8670
Jane Lizotte, prin. Fax 841-8671
Spring Street ES 400/K-4
123 Spring St 01545 508-841-8700
Brian Mabie, prin. Fax 841-8701

Lilliput ECC 300/PK-2
18 Grafton St 01545 508-842-0430
Linda Sullivan, prin. Fax 842-1857
St. Mary S 300/PK-8
16 Summer St 01545 508-842-1601
Joan Barry, prin. Fax 845-1535
Shrewsbury Montessori S 200/PK-6
55 Oak St 01545 508-842-2116
Margaret Smetana, prin. Fax 845-2491

Shutesbury, Franklin
Shutesbury SD
Supt. — See Erving
Shutesbury ES 200/PK-6
23 W Pelham Rd 01072 413-259-1212
Robert Mahler, prin. Fax 259-1531

Somerset, Bristol, Pop. 17,655
Somerset SD 2,900/PK-12
580 Whetstone Hill Rd 02726 508-324-3100
Richard Medeiros, supt. Fax 324-3104
www.somerset.k12.ma.us/
Chace Street ES 300/PK-5
538 Chace St 02726 508-324-3160
Judy Richardson, prin. Fax 324-3163
North ES 500/K-5
580 Whetstone Hill Rd 02726 508-324-3170
Irene Fortin, prin. Fax 324-3174
Somerset MS 600/6-8
1141 Brayton Ave 02726 508-324-3140
Pauline Camara, prin. Fax 324-3145
South ES 200/K-5
700 Read St 02726 508-324-3180
Wendy Morin, prin. Fax 324-3182
Wilbur ES 200/K-5
816 Brayton Point Rd 02725 508-324-3190
Joan DeAngelis, prin. Fax 324-3192

Somerville, Middlesex, Pop. 74,963
Somerville SD 4,400/PK-12
181 Washington St 02143 617-625-6600
Anthony Pierantozzi, supt. Fax 625-4731
www.somerville.k12.ma.us
Argenziano S at Lincoln Park K-8
290 Washington St 02143 617-625-6600
Dorothy Rudolph, prin. Fax 629-5221
Brown ES 200/K-6
201 Willow Ave 02144 617-625-6600
Thelma Davis, prin. Fax 625-4258
Capuano ECC 200/PK-K
150 Glen St 02145 617-625-6600
Pamela Holmes, prin. Fax 628-6159
East Somerville Community S 600/K-8
8 Bonair St 02145 617-625-6600
Holly Hatch, prin. Fax 666-9587
Healey S 500/K-8
5 Meacham St 02145 617-625-6600
Michael Sabin, prin. Fax 776-5401
Kennedy S 500/K-8
5 Cherry St 02144 617-625-6600
Dr. Anne Foley, prin. Fax 776-8224
West Somerville Neighborhood S 300/K-8
177 Powder House Blvd 02144 617-625-6600
Pauline Lampropoulos, prin. Fax 666-7676
Winter Hill Community S 500/K-8
115 Sycamore St 02145 617-625-6600
Stephen Tuccelli, prin. Fax 623-8492

St. Catherine of Genoa S 200/PK-8
192 Summer St 02143 617-666-9116
Marian Burns, prin. Fax 623-9161

Southampton, Hampshire
Southampton SD
Supt. — See Westhampton
Norris ES 500/PK-6
34 Pomeroy Meadow Rd 01073 413-527-0811
William Collins, prin. Fax 527-4795

South Attleboro, See Attleboro
Attleboro SD
Supt. — See Attleboro
Hill-Roberts ES 500/K-4
80 Roy Ave 02703 508-399-7560
Matthew Joseph, prin. Fax 399-7284

Dayspring Christian Academy 400/PK-8
1052 Newport Ave 02703 508-761-5552
Frank Rydwansky, prin. Fax 761-3577

Southborough, Worcester
Northborough-Southborough SD 4,700/PK-12
53 Parkerville Rd 01772 508-486-5115
Dr. Charles Gobron, supt. Fax 486-5123
www.nsboro.k12.ma.us/
Finn ES 200/PK-1
60 Richards Rd 01772 508-485-3176
Mary Ryan, prin. Fax 229-4449
Neary ES 400/4-5
53 Parkerville Rd 01772 508-481-2300
Joanne Irish, prin. Fax 229-4460
Trottier MS 500/6-8
49 Parkerville Rd 01772 508-485-2400
Linda Murdock, prin. Fax 481-1506
Woodward Memorial S 300/2-3
28 Cordaville Rd 01772 508-229-1250
James Randell, prin. Fax 229-0623
Other Schools – See Northborough

Fay S 400/1-9
48 Main St 01772 508-485-0100
Robert Gustavson, hdmstr. Fax 485-5381

South Boston, See Boston
Boston SD
Supt. — See Boston
Condon ES 700/PK-5
200 D St 02127 617-635-8608
Ann Garofalo, prin. Fax 635-8611
Gavin MS 500/6-8
215 Dorchester St 02127 617-635-8817
Alexander Mathews, prin. Fax 635-8826
Perkins ES 200/K-5
50 Burke St 02127 617-635-8601
Barney Brawer, prin. Fax 635-9774
Perry ES 200/PK-5
745 E 7th St 02127 617-635-8840
Mary Dotson, prin. Fax 635-6387
Tynan ES 300/K-5
650 E 4th St 02127 617-635-8641
Carlene Shavis, prin. Fax 635-9758

Gate of Heaven S 200/PK-8
609 E 4th St 02127 617-268-8431
Sr. Patricia McCarthy, prin. Fax 268-5131
St. Brigid S 200/PK-5
866 E Broadway 02127 617-268-2326
Nancy Carr, prin. Fax 268-7269

Southbridge, Worcester, Pop. 13,631
Southbridge SD 1,900/K-12
41 Elm St Ste 11 01550 508-764-5414
Dale Hanley, supt. Fax 764-8325
www.southbridge.k12.ma.us/
Charlton Street ES 400/2-3
220 Charlton St 01550 508-764-5475
Bryant Montigny, prin. Fax 764-5491
Eastford Road ES 200/K-1
120 Eastford Rd 01550 508-764-5460
Betsy Cooper, prin. Fax 764-5495
Wells JHS 600/6-8
82 Marcy St 01550 508-764-5440
Jason DeFalco, prin. Fax 764-5496
West Street ES 400/4-5
156 West St 01550 508-764-5470
Joany Santa, prin. Fax 764-5493

Trinity Catholic Academy 200/PK-8
11 Pine St 01550 508-765-5991
Madeleine Brouillard, prin. Fax 765-0017

South Dartmouth, Bristol, Pop. 9,850
Dartmouth SD 3,800/PK-12
8 Bush St 02748 508-997-3391
Stephen Russell, supt. Fax 991-4184
www.dartmouth.k12.ma.us/
Demello ES 400/K-5
654 Dartmouth St 02748 508-996-6750
Cathy Maccini, prin. Fax 990-2519
Other Schools – See North Dartmouth

South Deerfield, Franklin, Pop. 1,906
Conway SD 200/PK-6
219 Christian Ln 01373 413-665-1155
Regina Nash Ed.D., supt. Fax 665-8506
www.cgs.conway.ma.us/
Other Schools – See Conway

Deerfield SD 500/PK-6
219 Christian Ln 01373 413-665-1155
Regina Nash Ed.D., supt. Fax 665-8506
www.des.deerfield.ma.us
Deerfield ES 500/PK-6
21 Pleasant St 01373 413-665-1131
Kevin Kelly, prin. Fax 665-2747

Sunderland SD 200/PK-6
219 Christian Ln 01373 413-665-1155
Regina Nash Ed.D., supt. Fax 665-8506
www.ses.sunderland.ma.us/
Other Schools – See Sunderland

Whately SD 100/PK-6
219 Christian Ln 01373 413-665-1155
Regina Nash Ed.D., supt. Fax 665-8506
www.wes.whately.ma.us
Other Schools – See Whately

South Dennis, Barnstable, Pop. 3,559
Dennis-Yarmouth SD
Supt. — See South Yarmouth
Wixon MS 500/4-8
901 Route 134 02660 508-398-7695
Carole Eichner, prin. Fax 398-7608

South Easton, Bristol
Easton SD
Supt. — See North Easton
Center S 300/PK-2
388 Depot St 02375 508-230-3233
Debra Dicenso, prin. Fax 230-3240

South Egremont, Berkshire
Southern Berkshire Regional SD
Supt. — See Sheffield
South Egremont ES 50/K-1
Main St 01258 413-229-8754
Thomas McGuire, prin. Fax 528-1430

South Grafton, Worcester, Pop. 2,700
Grafton SD
Supt. — See Grafton
South Grafton ES 300/K-2
90 Main St 01560 508-839-5484
Doreen Parker, prin. Fax 839-5432

South Hadley, Hampshire, Pop. 5,400
South Hadley SD 2,100/PK-12
116 Main St Ste 202 01075 413-538-5060
Gus Sayer, supt. Fax 532-6284
www.shschools.com
Mosier ES 500/2-4
101 Mosier St 01075 413-538-5077
Jill Pasquini-Torchia, prin. Fax 538-6922
Plains ES 200/PK-1
267 Granby Rd 01075 413-538-5068
Jillayne Flanders, prin. Fax 538-8712
Smith MS 700/5-8
100 Mosier St 01075 413-538-5074
Erica Faginski, prin. Fax 538-5003

South Hamilton, Essex, Pop. 2,750
Hamilton-Wenham SD
Supt. — See Wenham
Cutler ES 300/K-5
237 Asbury St 01982 978-468-5330
Jennifer Clifford, prin. Fax 468-5314
Miles River MS 500/6-8
787 Bay Rd 01982 978-468-0362
Matthew Fox, prin. Fax 468-8454
Winthrop ES 400/PK-5
325 Bay Rd 01982 978-468-5340
Carrie Vaich, prin. Fax 468-5315

South Lancaster, Worcester, Pop. 1,772

Browning S 200/PK-8
PO Box 1129 01561 978-368-8544
Ron Huff, prin. Fax 365-2244

South Walpole, Norfolk
Walpole SD
Supt. — See Walpole
Boyden ES 400/K-5
1852 Washington St 02071 508-660-7216
Michael Stanton, prin. Fax 660-7217

South Weymouth, Norfolk
Weymouth SD
Supt. — See Weymouth
Hamilton PS 400/K-4
400 Union St 02190 781-335-2122
Susan Kerrigan, prin. Fax 335-3552
Talbot PS 300/K-4
277 Ralph Talbot St 02190 781-335-7250
Garry Pelletier, prin. Fax 337-8228

St. Francis Xavier S 400/PK-8
234 Pleasant St 02190 781-335-6868
Sr. Teresa Vesey, prin. Fax 331-4192

Southwick, Hampden
Granville SD 200/PK-8
86 Powder Mill Rd 01077 413-569-5391
John Barry, supt. Fax 569-1711
Other Schools – See Granville

Southwick-Tolland SD 1,800/PK-12
86 Powder Mill Rd 01077 413-569-5391
John Barry, supt. Fax 569-1711
www.strsd.southwick.ma.us/
Powder Mill MS 600/5-8
94 Powder Mill Rd 01077 413-569-5951
Ronald Peloquin, prin. Fax 569-1710
Woodland ES 600/PK-4
80 Powder Mill Rd 01077 413-569-6598
Kimberly Saso, prin. Fax 569-1721

South Yarmouth, Barnstable, Pop. 10,358
Dennis-Yarmouth SD 3,700/PK-12
296 Station Ave 02664 508-398-7600
Carol Woodbury, supt. Fax 398-7622
www.dy-regional.k12.ma.us/
MacArthur ES 300/PK-3
1175 Route 28 02664 508-398-7685
Peter Crowell, prin. Fax 398-7603

Station Avenue ES 300/K-3
276 Station Ave 02664 508-760-5600
Lisa Whelan, prin. Fax 760-5601
Other Schools – See South Dennis, West Dennis, West Yarmouth

St. Pius X S 200/PK-8
321 Wood Rd 02664 508-398-6112
John Regan, prin. Fax 398-6113

Spencer, Worcester, Pop. 6,306
Spencer-East Brookfield SD 2,100/PK-12
306 Main St 01562 508-885-8500
Ralph Hicks Ed.D., supt. Fax 885-8504
www.ultranet.com/~seb
Knox Trail JHS 300/7-8
73 Ash St 01562 508-885-8550
Mark Wilson, prin. Fax 885-8557
Lake Street ES 400/1-3
17 Lake St 01562 508-885-8517
Debora Zablocki, prin. Fax 885-8519
Maple Street S 100/PK-K
68 Maple St 01562 508-885-8529
Cynthia Ahearn, prin. Fax 885-8547
Wire Village S 400/4-6
60 Paxton Rd 01562 508-885-8524
Linda Crewe, prin. Fax 885-8546
Other Schools – See East Brookfield

Springfield, Hampden, Pop. 151,732
Springfield SD 25,100/PK-12
195 State St 01103 413-787-7100
Dr. Alan Ingram, supt. Fax 787-7171
www.sps.springfield.ma.us
Balliet ES 300/K-5
111 Seymour Ave 01109 413-787-7446
Gwen Page, prin. Fax 787-7531
Beal ES 300/K-5
285 Tiffany St 01108 413-787-7544
Linda Fenlason, prin. Fax 787-7363
Boland ES 600/PK-5
426 Armory St 01104 413-750-2511
Thomas O'Brien, prin. Fax 750-2396
Bowles ES 300/K-5
24 Bowles Park 01104 413-787-7334
Luisa Rivera, prin. Fax 750-2885
Bradley ES 600/K-5
22 Mulberry St 01105 413-787-7475
Beverly Brown, prin. Fax 750-2214
Brightwood ES 400/K-5
471 Plainfield St 01107 413-787-7238
Fax 787-7477
Brookings S 500/K-8
367 Hancock St 01105 413-787-7200
Fax 787-7394
Brunton ES 500/PK-5
1801 Parker St 01128 413-787-7444
Fax 787-7205
Chestnut Accelerated MS 1,200/6-8
355 Plainfield St 01107 413-750-2333
Anthony Davila, prin. Fax 750-2351
DeBerry ES 300/K-5
670 Union St 01109 413-787-7582
Mary Worthy, prin. Fax 787-6824
Dorman ES 200/K-5
20 Lydia St 01109 413-787-7554
Shannon Collins, prin. Fax 787-7771
Dryden Memorial ES 300/PK-5
190 Surrey Rd 01118 413-787-7248
Ann Dryden, prin. Fax 750-2314
Duggan MS 800/6-8
1015 Wilbraham Rd 01109 413-787-7410
Jonathan Swan, prin. Fax 750-2209
Ells ES 200/PK-5
319 Cortland St 01109 413-787-7345
Jose Irizarry, prin. Fax 787-7344
Forest Park MS 1,000/6-8
46 Oakland St 01108 413-787-7420
Bonnie Osgood, prin. Fax 787-7419
Freedman ES 200/K-5
90 Cherokee Dr 01109 413-787-7443
Gloria Williams, prin. Fax 750-2367
Gerena ES 600/PK-5
200 Birnie Ave 01107 413-787-7320
Analida Munera, prin. Fax 750-2661
Glenwood ES 300/K-5
50 Morison Ter 01104 413-787-7527
Rhonda Stowell, prin. Fax 787-7468
Glickman ES 300/K-5
120 Ashland Ave 01119 413-750-2756
Martha Kelliher, prin. Fax 750-2765
Harris ES 500/PK-5
58 Hartford Ter 01118 413-787-7254
Deborah Lantaigne, prin. Fax 787-7333
Homer Street ES 300/K-5
43 Homer St 01109 413-787-7526
Linda Wilson, prin. Fax 750-2752
Johnson ES 700/PK-5
55 Catharine St 01109 413-787-6687
Francine Pina-Council, prin. Fax 787-6697
Kennedy MS 600/6-8
1385 Berkshire Ave 01151 413-787-7510
Bonnie Elliston, prin. Fax 787-7561
Kensington Avenue ES 300/K-5
31 Kensington Ave 01108 413-787-7522
Margaret Thompson, prin. Fax 787-7374
Kiley MS 900/6-8
180 Cooley St 01128 413-787-7240
Kenneth Luce, prin. Fax 787-7247
Liberty ES 300/K-5
962 Carew St 01104 413-787-7299
John Doty, prin. Fax 750-2331
Lincoln ES 400/K-5
732 Chestnut St 01107 413-787-7314
Diane Gagnon, prin. Fax 787-7364
Lynch ES 300/K-5
315 N Branch Pkwy 01119 413-787-7250
Tara Clark, prin. Fax 750-2165
Pottenger ES 400/K-5
1435 Carew St 01104 413-787-7266
Valerie Williams, prin. Fax 787-7006
Sumner Avenue ES 500/PK-5
45 Sumner Ave 01108 413-787-7430
Lisa Bakowski, prin. Fax 787-6229
Talmadge ES 300/K-5
1395 Allen St 01118 413-787-7249
Elizabeth Crowley, prin. Fax 750-2743
Van Sickle MS 1,100/6-8
1170 Carew St 01104 413-750-2887
Cheryl Despirt-Lambert, prin. Fax 750-2972
Walsh ES 400/K-5
50 Empress Ct 01129 413-787-7448
Mary Ellen Petruccelli, prin. Fax 750-2171
Warner ES 300/PK-5
493 Parker St 01129 413-787-7258
Dr. Ann Stennett, prin. Fax 750-2213
Washington ES 300/K-5
141 Washington St 01108 413-787-7551
Kathleen Sullivan, prin. Fax 787-7742
White Street ES 400/K-5
300 White St 01108 413-787-7543
Geraldine Barrett, prin. Fax 787-7349
Zanetti S 500/PK-8
59 Howard St 01105 413-787-7400
Sandra Wyner Andrew, prin. Fax 787-7701
Other Schools – See Indian Orchard

Academy Hill S 100/K-8
1190 Liberty St 01104 413-788-0300
Jake Giessman, hdmstr. Fax 781-4806
Pioneer Valley Christian S 300/PK-12
965 Plumtree Rd 01119 413-782-8031
Timothy Duff, hdmstr. Fax 782-8033
Pioneer Valley Montessori S 100/PK-6
1524 Parker St 01129 413-782-3108
Molly Reynolds, prin. Fax 782-3109
St. Michael's Academy 400/PK-8
99 Wendover Rd 01118 413-782-5246
Nelly deCarvalho, hdmstr. Fax 782-8137
Springfield SDA Jr Academy 50/K-8
797 State St 01109 413-731-2220
Danette Walcott, prin. Fax 731-2227

Sterling, Worcester
Wachusett Regional SD
Supt. — See Jefferson
Chocksett MS 400/5-8
40 Boutelle Rd 01564 978-422-6552
Margaret Morgan, prin. Fax 422-7720
Houghton ES 400/K-4
32 Boutelle Rd 01564 978-422-2333
Anthony Cipro, prin. Fax 422-2301

Stockbridge, Berkshire
Berkshire Hills SD 1,500/PK-12
PO Box 617 01262 413-298-4017
Donna Moyer, supt. Fax 298-4672
www.bhrsd.org
Other Schools – See Great Barrington

Berkshire Country Day S 200/PK-9
55 Interlaken Rd 01262 413-637-0755
Paul Lindenmaier, hdmstr. Fax 637-8927

Stoneham, Middlesex, Pop. 22,203
Stoneham SD 2,900/PK-12
149 Franklin St 02180 781-279-3800
Dr. Les Olson, supt. Fax 279-3818
www.stonehamschools.net/
Central ES 400/K-5
36 Pomeworth St 02180 781-279-3860
Lawrence MacElhiney, prin. Fax 279-3861
Colonial Park ES 300/PK-5
30 Avalon Rd 02180 781-279-3890
Margaret Burke, prin. Fax 279-3892
Hood ES 300/K-5
70 Oak St 02180 781-279-3870
Alice Reilly, prin. Fax 438-8697
South ES 400/PK-5
11 Summer St 02180 781-279-3880
Nick Leonardos, prin. Fax 279-2104
Stoneham MS 600/6-8
101 Central St 02180 781-279-3840
Christopher Banos, prin. Fax 279-3843

Edgewood/Greater Boston Academy 100/PK-12
108 Pond St 02180 781-438-4253
Rondi Aastrup, prin. Fax 438-6857
St. Patrick S 200/K-8
20 Pleasant St 02180 781-438-2593
Arthur Swanson, prin. Fax 438-2543

Stoughton, Norfolk, Pop. 27,500
Stoughton SD 4,000/PK-12
232 Pearl St 02072 781-344-4000
Anthony Sarno, supt. Fax 344-6417
www.stoughtonschools.org/
Dawe ES 400/K-5
131 Pine St 02072 781-344-7007
David Barner, prin. Fax 344-8271
Gibbons ES 400/K-5
235 Morton St 02072 781-344-7008
Lynne Jardin, prin. Fax 344-2653
Hansen ES 300/K-5
1800 Central St 02072 781-344-7006
Faye Polillio, prin. Fax 344-4927
Jones ECC 100/PK-PK
137 Walnut St 02072 781-344-1003
Mark Chitty, prin. Fax 344-2782
O'Donnell MS 900/6-8
211 Cushing St 02072 781-344-7002
Wayne Hester, prin. Fax 297-5263
South ES 300/K-5
171 Ash St 02072 781-344-7004
Mark Chitty, prin. Fax 344-2876
West ES 300/K-5
1322 Central St 02072 781-344-7006
Brendan Dearborn, prin. Fax 344-2973

Shaloh House Preschool 50/PK-K
50 Ethyl Way 02072 781-344-6334
Marilyn Rabinovitz, dir. Fax 344-8174

Stow, Middlesex
Nashoba Regional SD
Supt. — See Bolton
Center S 300/3-5
403 Great Rd 01775 978-897-0290
Gregory Irvine, prin. Fax 461-0525
Hale MS 300/6-8
55 Hartley Rd 01775 978-897-4788
Fax 897-3631
Pompositticut ES 300/K-2
511 Great Rd 01775 978-897-5774
Gregory Irvine, prin. Fax 461-0525

Sturbridge, Worcester, Pop. 2,093
Sturbridge SD
Supt. — See Fiskdale
Burgess ES 900/PK-6
45 Burgess School Rd 01566 508-347-7041
Daniel Carlson, prin. Fax 347-8237

Sudbury, Middlesex
Sudbury SD 3,100/K-8
40 Fairbank Rd Ste C 01776 978-443-1058
John Brackett, supt. Fax 443-9001
www.sudbury.k12.ma.us
Curtis MS 1,000/6-8
22 Pratts Mill Rd 01776 978-443-1071
Stephen Lambert, prin. Fax 443-1098
Haynes ES 400/K-5
169 Haynes Rd 01776 978-443-1093
Kim Swain, prin. Fax 443-7513
Loring ES 600/K-5
80 Woodside Rd 01776 978-579-0870
Jeffery Dees, prin. Fax 579-0890
Nixon ES 500/K-5
472 Concord Rd 01776 978-443-1080
Joni Jay, prin. Fax 443-0282
Noyes ES 500/K-5
280 Old Sudbury Rd 01776 978-443-1085
Annette Doyle, prin. Fax 443-6310

Apple Valley Montessori S 100/PK-6
142 North Rd 01776 978-287-4000
Audrey Newton, dir. Fax 371-8999

Sunderland, Franklin
Sunderland SD
Supt. — See South Deerfield
Sunderland ES 200/PK-6
Swampfield Dr 01375 413-665-1151
Penny Spearance, prin. Fax 665-4545

Sutton, Worcester
Sutton SD 1,500/PK-12
383 Boston Rd 01590 508-581-1600
Cecilia DiBella, supt. Fax 865-6463
www.suttonschools.net/
Sutton Early Learning 300/PK-2
409 Boston Rd 01590 508-581-1610
Lauren Dubeau, prin. Fax 865-3628
Sutton ES 400/3-5
383 Boston Rd 01590 508-581-1620
Michael Breault, prin. Fax 865-3628
Sutton MS 400/6-8
409 Boston Rd 01590 508-581-1630
Deborah Cimo, prin. Fax 865-6463

Swampscott, Essex, Pop. 13,650
Swampscott SD 2,100/K-12
207 Forest Ave 01907 781-596-8800
Matthew Malone Ed.D., supt. Fax 599-2502
www.swampscott.k12.ma.us/
Clarke ES 200/K-4
100 Middlesex Ave 01907 781-596-8812
Lois Longin, prin. Fax 581-5556
Hadley ES 200/K-4
24 Redington St 01907 781-596-8847
Sandra Rivers, prin. Fax 596-5298
Stanley ES 300/K-4
10 Whitman Rd 01907 781-596-8837
Pamela Angelakis, prin. Fax 592-9500
Swampscott MS 500/5-8
207 Forest Ave 01907 781-596-8820
Ralph Watson Ed.D., prin. Fax 593-2126

Swansea, Bristol
Swansea SD 2,100/PK-12
1 Gardners Neck Rd 02777 508-675-1195
Stephen Flanagan, supt. Fax 672-1040
www.swanseaschools.org
Brown ES 200/3-5
29 Gardners Neck Rd 02777 508-675-7892
Elizabeth White, prin. Fax 646-4411
Case JHS 600/6-8
195 Main St 02777 508-675-0116
Robert Monteiro, prin. Fax 646-4413
Gardner ES 300/K-2
10 Church St 02777 508-675-7899
Douglas Benoit, prin. Fax 646-4410
Hoyle ES 300/PK-2
70 Community Ln 02777 508-679-4049
William Courville, prin. Fax 646-4407

Luther ES 200/3-5
100 Pearse Rd 02777 508-675-7499
Christine Panarese, prin. Fax 646-4408

New England Christian Academy 200/PK-12
271 Sharps Lot Rd 02777 508-676-3011
Frederick Poulin, prin. Fax 646-0392

Taunton, Bristol, Pop. 56,251
Taunton SD 8,000/PK-12
110 County St 02780 508-821-1101
Dr. Julie Hackett, supt. Fax 821-1177
www.tauntonschools.org
Barnum K 200/PK-K
25 Barnum St 02780 508-821-1282
Mary Jane Webster, prin. Fax 821-1352
Bennett ES 400/K-4
41 N Walker St 02780 508-821-1245
Fax 821-1353
Chamberlain ES 400/K-4
480 Norton Ave 02780 508-821-3216
Paul Moccia, prin. Fax 821-3877
Friedman MS 900/5-8
500 Norton Ave 02780 508-821-1493
John Cabral, prin. Fax 821-3185
Galligan ES 300/K-4
15 Sheridan St 02780 508-821-1295
Mike Ferrari, prin. Fax 821-1355
Hopewell ES 300/K-4
16 Monroe St 02780 508-821-1240
Thomas Quigley, prin. Fax 821-1356
Leddy ES 200/K-4
36 2nd St 02780 508-821-1275
Fax 821-1366
Maxham ES 200/K-4
141 Oak St 02780 508-821-1265
Rebecca Couet, prin. Fax 821-1274
Mulcahey MS 500/5-8
28 Clifford St 02780 508-821-1255
Christel Torres, prin. Fax 821-1360
Parker MS 500/5-8
50 Williams St 02780 508-821-1111
Manuel Fernandez, prin. Fax 821-1361
Pole ES 400/1-4
215 Harris St 02780 508-821-1260
Barbara McGuire, prin. Fax 821-1363
Summer Street K 100/K-K
66 Summer St 02780 508-821-1301
Fax 821-1365
Walker ES 200/K-4
145 Berkley St 02780 508-821-1285
Michele Sharpe, prin. Fax 821-1364
Other Schools – See East Taunton

Our Lady of Lourdes S 100/K-5
52 1st St 02780 508-822-3746
Lincoln DeMoura, prin. Fax 822-1450
St. Mary S 400/PK-5
106 Washington St 02780 508-822-9480
Brian Cote, prin. Fax 822-7164
Taunton Catholic MS 200/5-8
61 Summer St 02780 508-822-0491
Margaret Menear, prin. Fax 824-0469
Villa Fatima Preschool 100/PK-PK
90 County St 02780 508-880-7447
Sr. Elizabeth Hayes, prin. Fax 823-0825

Teaticket, Barnstable, Pop. 1,856
Falmouth SD
Supt. — See East Falmouth
Teaticket ES 400/PK-4
45 Maravista Avenue Ext 02536 508-548-1550
Michael Arth, prin. Fax 540-4383

Templeton, Worcester
Narragansett Regional SD
Supt. — See Baldwinville
Templeton Center ES 200/K-2
PO Box 306 01468 978-939-8892
Angelo Garofalo, prin. Fax 939-1211

Tewksbury, Middlesex, Pop. 11,000
Tewksbury SD 4,700/PK-12
139 Pleasant St 01876 978-640-7800
Christine McGrath, supt. Fax 640-7804
www.tewksbury.k12.ma.us
Center S 100/PK-PK
139 Pleasant St 01876 978-640-7818
Jan Fuller, prin. Fax 640-7820
Dewing ES 500/K-4
1469 Andover St 01876 978-640-7858
Robert Laroche, prin. Fax 640-7862
Heath-Brook ES 500/K-4
165 Shawsheen St 01876 978-640-7865
Rosamond Dorrence, prin. Fax 640-7869
North Street ES 400/K-4
133 North St 01876 978-640-7875
Pauline King, prin. Fax 640-7879
Ryan ES 800/5-6
135 Pleasant St 01876 978-640-7880
Kevin McArdle, prin. Fax 640-7888
Trahan ES 400/PK-4
12 Salem Rd 01876 978-640-7870
Edward Foster, prin. Fax 640-7874
Wynn MS 800/7-8
1 Griffin Way 01876 978-640-7846
John Donoghue, prin. Fax 640-7850

Topsfield, Essex, Pop. 2,711
Masconomet SD 2,100/7-12
20 Endicott Rd 01983 978-887-2323
Claire Sheff Kohn, supt. Fax 887-3573
www.masconomet.org
Masconomet Regional MS 700/7-8
20 Endicott Rd 01983 978-887-2323
Catherine Cullinane, prin. Fax 887-1991

Topsfield SD
Supt. — See Boxford
Proctor ES 300/4-6
60 Main St 01983 978-887-1530
Kerry Kaplon, prin. Fax 887-1531
Steward ES 400/PK-3
261 Perkins Row 01983 978-887-1538
Trudy Dooner, prin. Fax 887-7462

Townsend, Middlesex, Pop. 1,164
North Middlesex SD 4,200/PK-12
23 Main St 01469 978-597-8713
Maureen Marshall, supt. Fax 597-6534
nmiddlesex.mec.edu
Hawthorne Brook MS 600/6-8
64 Brookline St 01469 978-597-6914
Pamela Miller, prin. Fax 597-0354
Spaulding Mem ES 300/PK-2
1 Whitcomb St 01469 978-597-0380
Becky Janda, prin. Fax 597-0386
Squannacook ES 400/3-5
66 Brookline St 01469 978-597-3085
Christine Morassi, prin. Fax 597-0285
Other Schools – See Ashby, Pepperell

Truro, Barnstable
Truro SD 100/PK-6
PO Box 2029 02666 508-487-1558
Brian Davis, supt. Fax 487-4289
www.truromass.org
Truro Central ES 100/PK-6
PO Box 2029 02666 508-487-1558
Brian Davis, prin. Fax 487-4289

Turners Falls, Franklin, Pop. 4,731
Gill-Montague SD 900/PK-12
35 Crocker Ave 01376 413-863-9324
Carl Ladd, supt. Fax 863-4560
www.gmrsd.org
Hillcrest ES 100/PK-K
30 Griswold St 01376 413-863-9526
Christine Jutres, prin. Fax 863-4560
Sheffield ES 200/1-5
43 Crocker Ave 01376 413-863-9326
Elizabeth Musgrave, prin. Fax 863-3259
Other Schools – See Gill, Montague

Tyngsboro, Middlesex
Tyngsborough SD 2,000/PK-12
50 Norris Rd 01879 978-649-7488
Dr. Darrell Lockwood, supt. Fax 649-7199
www.tyngsboroughps.org/
Tyngsboro ES 900/PK-5
205 Westford Rd 01879 978-649-1990
Elizabeth Devine, prin. Fax 649-2004
Tyngsboro MS 500/6-8
50 Norris Rd 01879 978-649-3115
Donald Ciampa, prin. Fax 649-8673

Academy of Notre Dame ES 500/PK-8
180 Middlesex Rd 01879 978-649-7611
Sr. Mary Duke, prin. Fax 649-2909

Upton, Worcester, Pop. 2,347
Mendon-Upton Regional SD
Supt. — See Mendon
Memorial ES 400/PK-4
69 Main St 01568 508-529-1082
Ruth Danforth, prin. Fax 634-1576

Uxbridge, Worcester, Pop. 3,400
Uxbridge SD 1,900/PK-12
21 S Main St 01569 508-278-8648
Daniel Stefanilo, supt. Fax 278-8612
uxbridgeschools.com
Taft ES 800/PK-4
16 Granite St 01569 508-278-8643
Paula Montesi, prin. Fax 278-8646
Whitin MS 600/5-8
120 Granite St 01569 508-278-8640
Ron Farrar, prin. Fax 278-8639

Our Lady of the Valley S 200/K-8
75 Mendon St 01569 508-278-5851
Marilyn Willand, prin. Fax 278-0391

Vineyard Haven, Dukes, Pop. 1,762
Edgartown SD 300/K-8
4 Pine St 02568 508-627-3316
James Weiss Ed.D., supt. Fax 627-7983
www.mvyps.org
Other Schools – See Edgartown

Oak Bluffs SD 400/K-8
4 Pine St 02568 508-693-2007
James Weiss Ed.D., supt. Fax 693-3190
www.mv.k12.ma.us/
Other Schools – See Oak Bluffs

Tisbury SD 300/PK-8
4 Pine St 02568 508-693-2007
James Weiss Ed.D., supt. Fax 693-3190
www.mv.k12.ma.us/
Tisbury S 300/PK-8
PO Box 878 02568 508-696-6500
Richard Smith, prin. Fax 696-7437

Up-Island Regional SD 300/PK-8
4 Pine St 02568 508-693-2007
James Weiss Ed.D., supt. Fax 693-3190
www.mvyps.org/
Other Schools – See Aquinnah, West Tisbury

Waban, See Newton
Newton SD
Supt. — See Newtonville
Angier ES 400/K-5
1697 Beacon St 02468 617-559-9300
Loreta Lamberti, prin. Fax 559-2014

Zervas ES 300/K-5
30 Beethoven Ave 02468 617-559-6750
Stephen Griffin, prin. Fax 552-5546

Wakefield, Middlesex, Pop. 24,825
Wakefield SD 3,400/K-12
60 Farm St 01880 781-246-6400
Joan Landers, supt. Fax 245-9164
www.wakefield.k12.ma.us/
Dolbeare ES 500/K-4
340 Lowell St 01880 781-246-6480
Phyllis Dubina, prin. Fax 246-6372
Galvin JHS 1,100/5-8
525 Main St 01880 781-246-6410
Paula Mullen, prin. Fax 224-5009
Greenwood ES 300/K-4
1030 Main St 01880 781-246-6460
Deborah Collura, prin. Fax 224-5082
Walton ES 200/K-4
40 Western Ave 01880 781-246-6494
Deborah Collura, prin. Fax 246-6429
Woodville ES 400/K-4
30 Farm St 01880 781-246-6469
Brian Middleton-Cox, prin. Fax 224-5006

Odyssey Day S, 11 Paul Ave 01880 100/PK-8
Lori Conway, hdmstr. 781-245-6050
St. Joseph S 200/K-8
15 Gould St 01880 781-245-2081
Joseph Sullivan, prin. Fax 245-0084

Wales, Hampden
Wales SD
Supt. — See Fiskdale
Wales ES 200/PK-6
PO Box 247 01081 413-245-7748
Richard Zinkus, prin. Fax 245-4422

Walpole, Norfolk, Pop. 5,495
Walpole SD 3,900/PK-12
135 School St 02081 508-660-7200
Lincoln Lynch, supt. Fax 668-1167
www.walpole.ma.us
Elm Street ES 500/PK-5
415 Elm St 02081 508-660-7374
Mary Grinavic, prin. Fax 660-7379
Feeney Preschool PK-PK
415 Elm St 02081 508-660-7374
Jennifer Bernard, prin. Fax 660-7379
Fisher ES 500/K-5
65 Gould St 02081 508-660-7234
Colleen Duggan, prin. Fax 660-7233
Johnson MS 500/6-8
111 Robbins Rd 02081 508-660-7242
Sandra Esmond, prin. Fax 660-7240
Other Schools – See East Walpole, South Walpole

Blessed Sacrament S 500/PK-8
808 East St 02081 508-668-2336
Russell Wilson, prin. Fax 668-7944

Waltham, Middlesex, Pop. 59,556
Waltham SD 4,700/PK-12
617 Lexington St 02452 781-314-5440
Dr. Peter Azar, supt. Fax 314-5411
www.city.waltham.ma.us/school/index.html
Fitzgerald ES 300/K-5
140 Beal Rd 02453 781-314-5680
Alice Shull, prin. Fax 314-5691
Kennedy MS 500/6-8
655 Lexington St 02452 781-314-5560
John Cawley, prin. Fax 314-5571
MacArthur ES 400/K-5
494 Lincoln St 02451 781-314-5720
Anthony Colannino, prin. Fax 314-5731
McDevitt MS 500/6-8
75 Church St 02452 781-314-5590
Brad Morgan, prin. Fax 314-5601
Northeast ES 400/PK-5
70 Putney Ln 02452 781-314-5740
Nadine Stein, prin. Fax 314-5751
Plympton ES 300/K-5
20 Farnsworth St 02451 781-314-5760
Peter Silverman, prin. Fax 314-5771
Stanley ES 500/PK-5
250 South St 02453 781-314-5620
Tom LeFort, prin. Fax 314-5631
Whittemore ES 200/K-5
30 Parmenter Rd 02453 781-314-5780
Deborah Butts, prin. Fax 314-5791

Bartlett S 100/PK-6
1841 Trapelo Rd 02451 781-890-1865
Grace Cavallo, hdmstr. Fax 890-5566
Our Lady Comforter Afflicted S 200/PK-8
920 Trapelo Rd 02452 781-899-0353
Chandra Minor, prin. Fax 891-8734
St. Jude S 200/K-8
175 Main St 02453 781-899-3644
Sr. Katherine Caughey, prin. Fax 899-3644

Ware, Hampshire, Pop. 6,533
Ware SD 1,000/PK-12
PO Box 240 01082 413-967-4271
Dr. Mary-Elizabeth Beach, supt. Fax 967-9580
www.warepublicschools.com
Koziol ES 400/PK-3
4 Gould Rd 01082 413-967-6236
Marlene DiLeo, prin. Fax 967-4203
Ware MS 200/4-6
239 West St 01082 413-967-6903
Robert Warren, prin. Fax 967-3182

St. Mary S 100/PK-8
60 South St 01082 413-967-9936
Paula Moran, prin. Fax 967-8217

Wareham, Plymouth, Pop. 19,232
Wareham SD 2,900/PK-12
54 Marion Rd Ste 1 02571 508-291-3500
Barry Rabinovitch, supt. Fax 291-3578
www.warehamps.org/district/index.htm
Decas ES 600/K-5
760 Main St 02571 508-291-3530
Andanilza Miranda, prin. Fax 291-3533
Minot Forest ES 500/1-5
63 Minot Ave 02571 508-291-3555
Joan Seamans, prin. Fax 291-3529
Wareham MS 800/6-8
4 Viking Dr 02571 508-291-3550
Howard Gilmore, prin. Fax 291-3580
Other Schools – See Onset

Warren, Worcester, Pop. 1,516
Quaboag Regional SD 1,500/PK-12
PO Box 1538 01083 413-436-9256
Edward Malvey, supt. Fax 436-9738
www.quaboag.org
Other Schools – See West Brookfield, West Warren

Warwick, Franklin, Pop. 200
Pioneer Valley SD
Supt. — See Northfield
Warwick Community ES 100/PK-6
41 Winchester Rd 01378 978-544-6310
Ellen Edson, prin. Fax 544-6356

Watertown, Middlesex, Pop. 32,303
Watertown SD 2,400/K-12
30 Common St 02472 617-926-7700
Dr. Ann Koufman-Frederick, supt. Fax 923-1234
www.watertown.k12.ma.us
Cunniff ES 300/K-5
246 Warren St 02472 617-926-7726
Stephen Billhardt, prin. Fax 924-0420
Hosmer ES 500/K-5
1 Concord Rd 02472 617-926-7740
William McCarthy, prin. Fax 926-3259
Lowell ES 400/K-5
175 Orchard St 02472 617-926-7770
Darilyn Donovan, prin. Fax 926-2676
Watertown MS 500/6-8
68 Waverley Ave 02472 617-926-7783
James Carter, prin. Fax 926-5407

Atrium S 100/K-6
69 Grove St 02472 617-923-4156
Stephen Middlebrook, dir. Fax 923-1061
JCDS Bostons Jewish Community Day S 200/K-8
57 Stanley Ave 02472 617-972-1733
Ruth Gass, hdmstr. Fax 972-1736
Perkins School for the Blind 200/PK-12
175 N Beacon St 02472 617-924-3434
Steven Rothstein, pres.
Rosary Academy Learning Center 100/PK-PK
2 Rosary Dr 02472 617-923-1935
Sr. Judith Ward, dir. Fax 923-2993
St. Stephens Armenian S 100/K-5
47 Nichols Ave 02472 617-926-6979
Houry Boyamian M.Ed., prin. Fax 923-8299

Wayland, Middlesex, Pop. 2,500
Wayland SD 2,400/K-12
PO Box 408 01778 508-358-3774
Gary Burton, supt. Fax 358-7708
www.wayland.k12.ma.us
Claypit Hill ES 400/1-5
Adams Ln 01778 508-358-7401
Debbie Bearse, prin. Fax 358-3793
Happy Hollow ES 300/1-5
63 Pequot Rd 01778 508-358-2120
James Lee, prin. Fax 358-3761
Loker ES 100/K-K
47 Loker St 01778 508-655-0331
James Lee, prin. Fax 650-4007
Wayland MS 700/6-8
201 Main St 01778 508-655-6670
John Kavaleski, prin. Fax 655-2548

Webster, Worcester, Pop. 11,849
Webster SD 1,700/K-12
PO Box 430 01570 508-943-0104
Gregory Ciardi Ph.D., supt. Fax 949-2364
www.webster-schools.org
Park Avenue ES 300/K-2
58 Park Ave 01570 508-943-4554
Philip Benincasa, prin. Fax 949-1668
Webster MS 600/3-6
75 Poland St 01570 508-943-1922
Jason Phelps, prin. Fax 949-2648

St. Anne S 200/PK-8
PO Box 818 01570 508-943-2735
Sr. Constance Bayeur, prin. Fax 943-6215
St. Joseph S 100/PK-8
47 Whitcomb St 01570 508-943-0378
Don Cushing, prin. Fax 949-0581
St. Louis S 200/K-8
48 Negus St 01570 508-943-0257
Katherine Kelly, prin. Fax 943-0257

Wellesley, Norfolk, Pop. 26,600
Wellesley SD 4,600/PK-12
40 Kingsbury St 02481 781-446-6210
Bella Wong, supt. Fax 446-6207
www.wellesley.mec.edu/
Bates ES 400/K-5
116 Elmwood Rd 02481 781-446-6260
Michael Spencer, prin. Fax 263-1520
Fiske ES 400/PK-5
45 Hastings St 02481 781-446-6265
Elaine Harold, prin. Fax 263-1519
Hardy ES 300/K-5
293 Weston Rd 02482 781-446-6270
MaryBeth Kinkead, prin. Fax 263-1523
Hunnewell ES 300/K-5
28 Cameron St 02482 781-446-6275
Sheryl Boris-Schacter, prin. Fax 263-1525
Schofield ES 400/K-5
27 Cedar St 02481 781-446-6280
David Wilkins, prin. Fax 263-1527
Sprague ES 400/K-5
401 School St 02482 781-263-1965
Donna Dankner, prin. Fax 263-1963
Upham ES 300/K-5
35 Wynnewood Rd 02481 781-446-6285
Tracey Mara, prin. Fax 263-1507
Wellesley MS 1,000/6-8
50 Kingsbury St 02481 781-446-6235
Joshua Frank, prin. Fax 446-6208

St. Paul S 200/K-8
10 Atwood St 02482 781-235-1510
Karen McLaughlin, prin. Fax 235-4620
Tenacre Country Day S 200/PK-6
78 Benvenue St 02482 781-235-2282
Christian Elliot, hdmstr. Fax 237-7057

Wellesley Hills, Norfolk

St. John the Evangelist S 200/PK-6
9 Ledyard St 02481 781-235-0300
Kathleen Aldridge, prin. Fax 207-5379

Wellfleet, Barnstable
Wellfleet SD
Supt. — See Orleans
Wellfleet ES 100/PK-5
100 Lawrence Rd 02667 508-349-3101
Patricia Kent, prin. Fax 349-1377

Wenham, Essex, Pop. 4,212
Hamilton-Wenham SD 2,200/PK-12
5 School St 01984 978-468-5310
Dr. Marinel McGrath, supt. Fax 468-7889
www.hw-regional.k12.ma.us
Buker ES 200/K-5
1 School St 01984 978-468-5324
Brian O'Donoghue, prin. Fax 468-5329
Other Schools – See South Hamilton

Notre Dame Children's Class S 100/PK-2
74 Grapevine Rd 01984 978-468-1340
Sr. Barbara Beauchamp, prin. Fax 468-0166

West Barnstable, Barnstable, Pop. 1,508
Barnstable SD
Supt. — See Hyannis
West Barnstable ES 200/K-4
2463 Main St 02668 508-362-4949
Frank Gigliotti, prin. Fax 362-1740

Westborough, Worcester, Pop. 3,917
Westborough SD 3,500/PK-12
PO Box 1152 01581 508-836-7700
Dr. Anne Towle, supt. Fax 836-7704
www.westborough.org
Armstrong ES 400/K-3
50 West St 01581 508-836-7760
John Mendes, prin. Fax 836-7723
Fales ES 300/K-3
50 Eli Whitney St 01581 508-836-7770
Maryann Stannart, prin. Fax 836-7773
Gibbons MS 500/7-8
20 Fisher St 01581 508-836-7740
Dr. David Fredette, prin. Fax 836-7744
Hastings ES 400/PK-3
111 E Main St 01581 508-836-7750
Pattie Berkey, prin. Fax 836-7755
Mill Pond IS 800/4-6
6 Olde Hickory Path 01581 508-836-7780
Irene Hatherley, prin. Fax 836-7788

West Boylston, Worcester, Pop. 6,611
West Boylston SD 1,100/PK-12
125 Crescent St 01583 508-835-2917
Thomas J. Kane, supt. Fax 835-8992
www.wbschools.com
Edwards ES 500/PK-5
70 Crescent St 01583 508-835-4461
Thomas Caruso, prin. Fax 835-4119

West Bridgewater, Plymouth
West Bridgewater SD 1,200/PK-12
2 Spring St 02379 508-894-1230
Dr. Patricia Oakley, supt. Fax 894-1232
wbridgewaterschools.com
Howard / Spring Street ES 300/4-6
70 Howard St 02379 508-894-1250
Mark Bodwell, prin. Fax 894-1253
MacDonald ES 300/1-3
164 N Elm St 02379 508-894-1240
Linda Dubin, prin. Fax 894-1242
Spring Street S 100/PK-K
2 Spring St Ste 1 02379 508-894-1236
Linda Dubin, prin. Fax 894-1232

New England Baptist Academy 100/PK-12
560 N Main St 02379 508-584-5188

West Brookfield, Worcester, Pop. 1,419
Quaboag Regional SD
Supt. — See Warren
West Brookfield ES 300/PK-6
PO Box 386 01585 508-867-4655
Jennifer Mandeville, prin. Fax 867-9208

Warren SDA S 50/K-8
1570 Southbridge Rd 01585 413-436-9245
Fax 436-9245

West Dennis, Barnstable, Pop. 2,307
Dennis-Yarmouth SD
Supt. — See South Yarmouth
Baker ES 400/PK-3
810 Main St 02670 508-398-7690
Kevin Depin, prin. Fax 398-7693

Westfield, Hampden, Pop. 40,525
Westfield SD 6,000/PK-12
22 Ashley St 01085 413-572-6403
Shirley Alvira, supt. Fax 572-6518
www.k12.westfield.ma.us/
Fort Meadow ECC 200/PK-PK
35 White St 01085 413-572-6422
James Kane, prin. Fax 572-6540
Franklin Avenue ES 200/K-5
22 Franklin Ave 01085 413-572-6424
Leslie Clark-Yvon, prin. Fax 572-6424
Gibbs ES 200/K-5
50 W Silver St 01085 413-572-6418
Maggie Adams, prin. Fax 572-6446
Highland ES 300/K-5
34 Western Ave 01085 413-572-6428
Linda Carrier, prin. Fax 572-6849
Juniper Park ES 300/K-3
715 Western Ave 01085 413-572-6505
James Kane, prin. Fax 572-1396
Munger Hill ES 400/K-5
33 Mallard Ln 01085 413-572-6520
Carla Lussier, prin. Fax 562-0875
North MS 800/6-8
350 Southampton Rd 01085 413-572-6441
Eileen Jachym, prin. Fax 572-1669
Paper Mill ES 400/K-5
148 Paper Mill Rd 01085 413-572-6519
Susan Dargie, prin. Fax 572-0687
Southampton Road ES 400/K-5
330 Southampton Rd 01085 413-572-6435
Kathleen MacLean, prin. Fax 572-6873
South MS 700/6-8
30 W Silver St 01085 413-568-1900
Ronald Rix, prin. Fax 572-4892

St. Mary S 200/PK-8
35 Bartlett St 01085 413-568-2388
Sr. Christine Lavoie, prin. Fax 568-7460
Westfield Christian Academy 100/K-8
866 North Rd 01085 413-572-2748
Benjamin Timakov, prin. Fax 572-0037

Westford, Middlesex
Westford SD 4,800/PK-12
23 Depot St 01886 978-692-5560
Everett Olsen, supt. Fax 392-4497
westfordk12.us/
Abbot S 400/3-5
25 Depot St 01886 978-692-5580
Rose Vetere, prin. Fax 692-9587
Blanchard MS 600/6-8
14 West St 01886 978-692-5582
Jessica Huizenga, prin. Fax 692-5598
Crisafulli ES 400/3-5
13 Robinson Rd 01886 978-392-4483
Julie Vincentsen, prin. Fax 392-8581
Day ES 400/3-5
75 E Prescott St 01886 978-692-5591
Kevin Regan, prin. Fax 692-8476
Millennium Preschool PK-PK
23 Depot St 01886 978-692-5565
Diane Pelletier, prin. Fax 392-4497
Miller ES 300/K-2
1 Mitchell Way 01886 978-392-4476
Sarah Mullavey, prin. Fax 692-5502
Nabnasset S 200/K-2
99 Plain Rd 01886 978-692-5583
Susan DuBois, prin. Fax 392-9618
Robinson S 300/K-2
60 Concord Rd 01886 978-692-5586
Denise Arvidson, prin. Fax 692-5133
Stony Brook MS 700/6-8
9 Farmers Way 01886 978-692-2708
Peter Cohen, prin. Fax 692-5391

Westhampton, Hampshire
Chesterfield-Goshen SD 200/PK-6
19 Stage Rd 01027 413-527-7200
Dr. Barbara Ripa, supt. Fax 529-9497
Other Schools – See Chesterfield

Southampton SD 500/PK-6
19 Stage Rd 01027 413-527-7200
Barbara Ripa, supt. Fax 529-9497
www.wmnorris.com/
Other Schools – See Southampton

Westhampton SD 100/PK-6
19 Stage Rd 01027 413-527-7200
Barbara Ripa, supt. Fax 529-9497
www.westhamptonelementaryschool.org/
Westhampton ES 100/PK-6
37 Kings Hwy 01027 413-527-0561
Deane Bates, prin. Fax 529-9753

Williamsburg SD 100/K-6
19 Stage Rd 01027 413-527-7200
Dr. Barbara Ripa, supt. Fax 529-9497
www.burgy.org/schools/
Other Schools – See Williamsburg

West Harwich, Barnstable, Pop. 1,200

Holy Trinity S 100/PK-5
245 Route 28 02671 508-432-8216
Linda Mattson, prin. Fax 432-9349

Westminster, Worcester
Ashburnham-Westminster Regional SD
Supt. — See Ashburnham
Meetinghouse ES 200/PK-1
8 South St 01473 978-874-0163
Patricia Marquis, prin. Fax 874-7305
Westminster ES 400/2-5
9 Academy Hill Rd 01473 978-874-2043
Patricia Marquis, prin. Fax 874-7308

Wachusett Hill Christian S 50/PK-8
100 Colony Rd 01473 978-874-6432
Edie Conrad, prin.

West Newbury, Essex
Pentucket SD 3,400/PK-12
22 Main St 01985 978-363-2280
Paul Livingston Ed.D., supt. Fax 363-1165
www.prsd.org
Page ES 500/PK-6
694 Main St Ste 7 01985 978-363-2672
Lizabeth Perry, prin. Fax 363-2234
Pentucket Regional MS 500/7-8
20 Main St 01985 978-363-2957
Robin Wilson, prin. Fax 363-2720
Other Schools – See Groveland, Merrimac

West Newton, See Newton
Newton SD
Supt. — See Newtonville
Franklin ES 400/K-5
125 Derby St 02465 617-559-9500
Amy Kelly, prin. Fax 552-5521
Peirce ES 300/K-5
170 Temple St 02465 617-559-9630
Eva Thompson, prin. Fax 552-7318

Fessenden S 500/K-9
250 Waltham St 02465 617-964-5350
Peter Drake, hdmstr. Fax 630-2303

Weston, Middlesex, Pop. 10,200
Weston SD 2,400/PK-12
89 Wellesley St 02493 781-529-8080
Cheryl Maloney, supt. Fax 529-8097
www.westonschools.org/
Country ES 400/PK-3
10 Alphabet Ln 02493 781-529-8020
Stephen Shaw, prin. Fax 529-8113
Field ES 400/4-5
99 School St 02493 781-529-8000
Matthew Lucey, prin. Fax 529-8012
Weston MS 500/6-8
456 Wellesley St 02493 781-529-8060
John Gibbons, prin. Fax 529-8072
Woodland ES 400/K-3
12 Alphabet Ln 02493 781-529-8100
Debra Dunn, prin. Fax 529-8111

Meadowbrook S of Weston 300/PK-8
10 Farm Rd 02493 781-894-1193
Stephen Hinds, hdmstr. Fax 894-0557

West Peabody, Essex

Covenant Christian Academy 200/PK-12
83 Pine St 01960 978-535-7100
Tom Stoner, hdmstr. Fax 535-7123

Westport, Bristol, Pop. 13,852
Westport Community SD 1,800/PK-12
17 Main Rd 02790 508-636-1137
Dr. Linda Galton, supt. Fax 636-1146
www.westportschools.org
Macomber K 100/PK-K
154 Gifford Rd 02790 508-678-8671
Susan Wilkinson, prin. Fax 673-4284
Westport ES 500/1-4
380 Old County Rd 02790 508-636-1075
Alec Ciminello, prin. Fax 636-1077
Westport MS 700/5-8
400 Old County Rd 02790 508-636-1090
James Gibney, prin. Fax 636-7413

Montessori S of the Angels 100/PK-8
PO Box 1570 02790 508-636-0200
Alice Levesque, prin. Fax 636-7200

West Roxbury, See Boston
Boston SD
Supt. — See Boston
Beethoven ES 300/K-5
5125 Washington St 02132 617-635-8149
Eileen Nash, prin. Fax 635-8155
Kilmer S 300/K-8
35 Baker St 02132 617-635-8060
Jerome Doherty, prin. Fax 635-8063
Lyndon S 500/K-8
20 Mount Vernon St 02132 617-635-6824
Kate Johnson, coord. Fax 635-6828
Ohrenberger ES 400/K-5
175 W Boundary Rd 02132 617-635-8157
Steven Zrike, prin. Fax 635-8163

Holy Name S 500/PK-6
535 W Roxbury Pkwy 02132 617-325-9338
Linda Workman, prin. Fax 325-7885
St. Theresa S 400/PK-8
40 Saint Theresa Ave 02132 617-323-1050
Jane Gibbons, prin. Fax 323-8118

West Springfield, Hampden, Pop. 27,989
West Springfield SD 3,700/PK-12
26 Central St Ste 33 01089 413-263-3290
Dr. Suzanne Marotta, supt. Fax 739-8748
www.wsps.org
Ashley K 50/PK-K
88 Massasoit Ave 01089 413-263-3323
Shelly St. George, prin. Fax 827-0404
Coburn ES 400/1-5
115 Southworth St 01089 413-263-3363
Colleen Marcus, prin. Fax 781-2604
Fausey ES 400/1-5
784 Amostown Rd 01089 413-263-3314
Martha Tighe, prin. Fax 781-6973
Memorial ES 200/1-5
201 Norman St 01089 413-263-3333
Jeffrey Udall, prin. Fax 747-5535
Mittineague ES 100/1-5
26 2nd St 01089 413-263-3327
Paul Heath, prin. Fax 739-1718
Tatham ES 200/1-5
61 Laurel Rd 01089 413-263-3330
Susan Mulvaney, prin. Fax 739-1587
West Springfield MS 900/6-8
31 Middle School Dr 01089 413-263-3406
Thomas McNulty, prin. Fax 781-0965

St. Thomas Apostle S 400/PK-8
75 Pine St 01089 413-739-4131
Sr. Lillian Reilly, prin. Fax 731-8768

West Tisbury, Dukes
Up-Island Regional SD
Supt. — See Vineyard Haven
West Tisbury S 300/PK-8
PO Box 250 02575 508-696-7738
Michael Halt, prin. Fax 696-7739

West Warren, Worcester
Quaboag Regional SD
Supt. — See Warren
Warren Community ES 500/PK-6
PO Box 446 01092 413-436-5983
Theodore Brown, prin. Fax 436-9743

Westwood, Norfolk, Pop. 12,557
Westwood SD 3,000/PK-12
220 Nahatan St 02090 781-326-7500
John Antonucci, supt. Fax 326-8154
www.westwood.k12.ma.us
Deerfield ES 200/K-5
72 Deerfield Ave 02090 781-326-7500
Allen Cameron, prin. Fax 320-0189
Downey ES 300/PK-5
250 Downey St 02090 781-326-7500
Debra Gallagher, prin. Fax 329-7642
Hanlon ES 200/K-5
790 Gay St 02090 781-326-7500
Elizabeth Herlihy, prin. Fax 326-2702
Jones ES 400/K-5
80 Martha Jones Rd 02090 781-326-7500
Peggy Scott, prin. Fax 255-9277
Sheehan ES 300/K-5
549 Pond St 02090 781-326-7500
Kristen Evans, prin. Fax 769-8046
Thurston MS 700/6-8
850 High St 02090 781-326-7500
Allison Borchers, prin. Fax 326-2709
Westwood Integrated Preschool PK-PK
200 Nahatan St 02090 781-326-7500
Nichole Rich, prin. Fax 461-9782

West Yarmouth, Barnstable, Pop. 5,409
Dennis-Yarmouth SD
Supt. — See South Yarmouth
Mattacheese MS 600/6-8
400 Higgins Crowell Rd 02673 508-778-7979
Mary Wollak, prin. Fax 778-7987
Small ES 400/4-5
440 Higgins Crowell Rd 02673 508-778-7975
Emily Mezzetti, prin. Fax 778-4456

Weymouth, Norfolk, Pop. 53,900
Weymouth SD 6,600/PK-12
111 Middle St 02189 781-335-1460
MaryJo Livingstone, supt. Fax 335-8777
www.weymouth.ma.us/schools/index.asp
Academy Avenue PS 300/K-4
94 Academy Ave 02189 781-335-4717
James Lucia, prin. Fax 340-2514
Murphy PS 300/K-4
417 Front St 02188 781-335-2000
Ann Barry, prin. Fax 340-2517
Nash PS 200/K-4
1003 Front St 02190 781-340-2506
Susan Nutting, prin. Fax 340-2534
Pingree PS 300/K-4
1250 Commercial St 02189 781-337-2974
Marianne Weiner, prin. Fax 340-2518
Seach PS 400/K-4
770 Middle St 02188 781-335-7589
Deborah St. Ives, prin. Fax 335-3098
Other Schools – See East Weymouth, North Weymouth, South Weymouth

First Baptist Christian S 100/PK-8
40 West St 02190 781-335-6232
Elaine Allshouse, admin. Fax 335-7901
Sacred Heart S 300/PK-8
75 Commercial St 02188 781-335-6010
Mary Ferrucci, prin. Fax 331-7936
South Shore Christian Academy 200/PK-12
45 Broad St 02188 781-331-4340
Theodore Chamberlain, hdmstr. Fax 331-9956

Whately, Franklin
Whately SD
Supt. — See South Deerfield
Whately ES 100/PK-6
PO Box 158 01093 413-665-7826
Dr. Sue Hogan, prin. Fax 665-0428

Whitinsville, Worcester, Pop. 5,639
Northbridge SD 2,400/PK-12
87 Linwood Ave 01588 508-234-8156
Henry O'Donnell, supt. Fax 234-8469
www.nps.org/
Balmer ES 500/PK-4
21 Crescent St 01588 508-234-8161
John Zywien, prin. Fax 234-0808
Northbridge ES 300/PK-4
30 Cross St 01588 508-234-6346
Maureen Rossetti, prin. Fax 234-8499
Northbridge MS 800/5-8
171 Linwood Ave 01588 508-234-8718
Michael Gauthier, prin. Fax 234-9718

Whitinsville Christian S 600/PK-12
279 Linwood Ave 01588 508-234-8211
Lance Engbers, hdmstr. Fax 234-0624

Whitman, Plymouth, Pop. 13,240
Whitman-Hanson SD 4,200/PK-12
610 Franklin St 02382 781-618-7000
Ruth Gilbert-Whitner Ed.D., supt. Fax 618-7099
www.whrsd.k12.ma.us
Conley ES 500/PK-5
100 Forest St 02382 781-618-7050
Karen Downey, prin. Fax 618-7092
Duval ES 600/K-5
60 Regal St 02382 781-618-7055
Julie Stimpson, prin. Fax 618-7096
Whitman MS 600/6-8
100 Corthell Ave 02382 781-618-7035
George Ferro, prin. Fax 618-7091
Other Schools – See Hanson

Wilbraham, Hampden, Pop. 3,352
Hampden-Wilbraham SD 3,600/PK-12
621 Main St 01095 413-596-3884
Martin O'Shae, supt. Fax 599-1328
www.hwrsd.org
Memorial ES 300/2-6
310 Main St 01095 413-596-6821
Marguerite Myers-Killeen, prin. Fax 596-6669
Mile Tree ES 200/PK-1
625 Main St 01095 413-596-6921
Rosemary Brosnan, prin. Fax 596-9319
Soule Road ES 300/2-6
300 Soule Rd 01095 413-596-9311
Mary Goodwin, prin. Fax 599-1742
Stony Hill ES 300/2-6
675 Stony Hill Rd 01095 413-599-1950
Sherrill Caruana, prin. Fax 596-4497
Wilbraham MS 400/7-8
466 Stony Hill Rd 01095 413-596-9061
Stephen Hale, prin. Fax 596-9382
Other Schools – See Hampden

Williamsburg, Hampshire
Williamsburg SD
Supt. — See Westhampton
Dunphy ES 100/4-6
1 Petticoat Hill Rd 01096 413-268-8421
Fred Venne, prin. Fax 268-8420
James ES 50/K-3
16 Main St 01096 413-268-8424
Fred Venne, prin. Fax 268-8420

Williamstown, Berkshire, Pop. 4,791
Williamstown-Lanesboro SD 71 800/PK-6
115 Church St 01267 413-458-5707
Rose Ellis, supt. Fax 458-3287
Williamstown ES 500/PK-6
115 Church St 01267 413-458-5707
Stephen Johnson, prin. Fax 458-3287
Other Schools – See Lanesboro

Pine Cobble S 200/PK-9
163 Gale Rd 01267 413-458-4680
Nicholas Edgerton, hdmstr. Fax 458-8174

Wilmington, Middlesex, Pop. 17,654
Wilmington SD 3,600/PK-12
161 Church St 01887 978-694-6000
Joanne Benton, supt. Fax 694-6005
www.wilmington.k12.ma.us
Boutwell Early Education Center 50/PK-K
17 Boutwell St 01887 978-694-6070
Robert Appolloni, prin. Fax 694-6009
North IS 300/4-5
320 Salem St 01887 978-694-6040
Frank Ferriero, prin. Fax 694-6043
Shawsheen ES 400/1-3
298 Shawsheen Ave 01887 978-694-6030
Robert Appolloni, prin. Fax 694-6036
West IS 300/4-5
22 Carter Ln 01887 978-694-6050
Dennis Shaw, prin. Fax 694-6052
Wildwood Early Education Center 50/PK-K
182 Wildwood St 01887 978-694-6010
Joel Sanderson, prin. Fax 694-6008
Wilmington MS 1,000/6-8
25 Carter Ln 01887 978-694-6080
Christine McMenimen, prin. Fax 694-6085
Woburn Street ES 500/1-3
227 Woburn St 01887 978-694-6020
Joel Sanderson, prin. Fax 694-6014

Abundant Life Christian S 200/PK-8
173 Church St 01887 978-657-8710
Patti Hobart, admin. Fax 658-2739

Winchendon, Worcester, Pop. 4,316
Winchendon SD 1,500/PK-12
175 Grove St 01475 978-297-0031
Brooke Clenchy Ed.D., supt. Fax 297-5250
www.winchendonk12.org
Marvin ECC PK-PK
89 Ash St 01475 978-297-3436
Suzanne Michel, coord. Fax 297-0631
Memorial S 400/K-3
32 Elmwood Rd 01475 978-297-1305
Christina Littlewood, prin. Fax 297-3944
Toy Town ES 400/4-6
175 Grove St 01475 978-297-2005
J. Leonard Mackey, prin. Fax 297-3011

Winchester, Middlesex, Pop. 20,267
Winchester SD 3,900/PK-12
154 Horn Pond Brook Rd 01890 781-721-7004
William McAlduff, supt. Fax 721-0016
www.winchester.k12.ma.us
Ambrose ES 400/K-5
27 High St 01890 781-721-7012
Lisa McManus, prin. Fax 721-5605
Lincoln ES 400/K-5
161 Mystic Valley Pkwy 01890 781-721-2296
Kate Scanlon, prin. Fax 721-7040
Lynch ES 400/PK-5
10 Brantwood Rd 01890 781-721-7013
Stephen Goodwin, prin. Fax 721-4480
McCall MS 900/6-8
458 Main St 01890 781-721-7026
Evander French, prin. Fax 721-0886
Muraco ES 400/K-5
33 Bates Rd 01890 781-721-7030
Laurie Kirby, prin. Fax 721-0244
Vinson-Owen ES 300/K-5
75 Johnson Rd 01890 781-721-7019
Guido Sabelli, prin. Fax 721-2681

St. Mary S 200/PK-5
162 Washington St 01890 781-729-5515
Elaine O'Reilly, prin. Fax 729-1352

Winthrop, Suffolk, Pop. 18,127
Winthrop SD 1,900/PK-12
45 Pauline St 02152 617-846-5500
Dr. Steven Jenkins, supt. Fax 539-0891
www.winthrop.k12.ma.us
Cummings ES 500/3-5
40 Hermon St 02152 617-846-5543
Brian Gill, prin. Fax 846-6559
Gorman-Ft. Banks ES 300/PK-2
101 Kennedy Rd 02152 617-846-5509
Ilene Pearson, prin. Fax 539-0271
Winthrop MS 500/6-8
151 Pauline St 02152 617-846-5507
Zoe Haskell, prin. Fax 539-1115

Woburn, Middlesex, Pop. 37,147
Woburn SD 4,400/K-12
55 Locust St 01801 781-937-8233
Mark Donovan Ed.D., supt. Fax 937-3805
woburnpublicschools.com/
Altavesta ES 200/K-5
990 Main St 01801 781-937-8235
Wendy Sprague, prin. Fax 937-8273
Clapp/Goodyear ES 200/K-5
40 Hudson St 01801 781-937-8236
Christine Kelley, prin. Fax 937-8272
Hurld ES 200/K-5
75 Bedford Rd 01801 781-937-8238
Eileen Mills, prin. Fax 937-8270
Joyce JHS 500/6-8
55 Locust St 01801 781-937-8233
Thomas Qualey Ph.D., prin. Fax 937-8279
Kennedy JHS 500/6-8
41 Middle St 01801 781-937-8230
Carl Nelson, prin. Fax 937-8223
Linscott-Rumford ES 300/K-5
86 Elm St 01801 781-937-8239
Ernie Wells, prin. Fax 937-8269
Reeves ES 400/K-5
240 Lexington St 01801 781-937-8240
James White, prin. Fax 937-8268
Shamrock ES 200/K-5
60 Green St 01801 781-937-8241
Wayne Clark, prin. Fax 937-8267
White ES 300/K-5
36 Bow St 01801 781-937-8242
Peter Roketenetz, prin. Fax 937-8266
Wyman ES 200/K-5
679 Main St 01801 781-937-8243
Paul McQuilkin, prin. Fax 937-8265

St. Charles S 400/PK-8
8 Myrtle St 01801 781-935-4635
Rita Masotta, prin. Fax 935-3121

Worcester, Worcester, Pop. 175,898
Worcester SD 23,500/PK-12
20 Irving St 01609 508-799-3116
Dr. Melinda Boone, supt. Fax 799-3119
www.wpsweb.com
Belmont Street Community ES 400/PK-6
170 Belmont St 01605 508-799-3588
Susan Proulx, prin. Fax 799-8204
Burncoat MS 600/7-8
135 Burncoat St 01606 508-799-3390
Lisa Houlihan, prin. Fax 799-8207
Burncoat Street Preparatory S 200/K-6
526 Burncoat St 01606 508-799-3537
Deborah Frank, prin. Fax 799-8205
Canterbury Street Magnet ES 400/PK-6
129 Canterbury St 01603 508-799-3484
Elizabeth Army, prin. Fax 799-8208
Chandler Community ES 300/PK-6
114 Chandler St 01609 508-799-3572
Mark Berthiaume, prin. Fax 799-8209
Chandler Magnet ES 300/PK-6
525 Chandler St 01602 508-799-3452
Ivone Perez, prin. Fax 799-8210
City View ES 500/PK-6
80 Prospect St 01605 508-799-3670
Albert Ganem, prin. Fax 799-3521
Claremont Academy 800/PK-12
15 Claremont St 01610 508-799-3077
Fax 799-8202
Clark Street Developmental Learning S 300/PK-6
280 Clark St 01606 508-799-3545
Marie Morse, prin. Fax 799-8212
Columbus Park Preparatory Academy 400/PK-6
75 Lovell St 01603 508-799-3490
Jessica Boss, prin. Fax 799-8213
Elm Park Community ES 400/PK-6
23 N Ashland St 01609 508-799-3568
Ruthann Melancon, prin. Fax 799-8216
Flagg Street ES 400/K-6
115 Flagg St 01602 508-799-3522
Dr. Sheila Graham, prin. Fax 799-8217
Forest Grove MS 900/7-8
495 Grove St 01605 508-799-3420
Mark Williams, prin. Fax 799-8218
Gates Lane S of International Studies 700/PK-6
1238 Main St 01603 508-799-3488
Ann Swenson, prin. Fax 799-8219
Goddard Science Technical ES 700/PK-6
14 Richards St 01603 508-799-3594
Marion Guerra, prin. Fax 799-8258
Grafton Street ES 400/PK-6
311 Grafton St 01604 508-799-3478
Mary McKiernan, prin. Fax 799-8222
Heard Street Discovery Academy 300/K-6
200 Heard St 01603 508-799-3525
Thomas Brindisi, prin. Fax 799-8226
Hiatt Magnet ES 500/PK-6
772 Main St 01610 508-799-3601
Patricia Gaudette, prin. Fax 799-8261
Lake View ES 300/K-6
133 Coburn Ave 01604 508-799-3536
Margaret Bondar, prin. Fax 799-8228
Lincoln Street ES 200/PK-6
549 Lincoln St 01605 508-799-3504
MaryBeth Pulsifer, prin. Fax 799-8229
May Street ES 300/K-6
265 May St 01602 508-799-3520
Luke Robert, prin. Fax 799-8230
McGrath ES 200/PK-6
493 Grove St 01605 508-799-3584
Nancy Dahlstrom, prin. Fax 799-8235
Midland Street ES 200/K-6
18 Midland St 01602 508-799-3548
Dr. Patricia McCullough, prin. Fax 799-8231
Nelson Place ES 400/K-6
35 Nelson Pl 01605 508-799-3506
Malachi Kelley, prin. Fax 799-8257
Norrback Avenue ES 500/PK-6
44 Malden St 01606 508-799-3500
Dr. Karrie Allen, prin. Fax 799-8234
Quinsigamond ES 600/PK-6
14 Blackstone River Rd 01607 508-799-3502
Debbie Mitchell, prin. Fax 799-3517
Rice Square ES 400/PK-6
76 Massasoit Rd 01604 508-799-3556
Kathleen Valeri, prin. Fax 799-8240
Roosevelt ES 600/PK-6
1006 Grafton St 01604 508-799-3482
Ellen Kelley, prin. Fax 799-8241
Sullivan MS 900/7-8
140 Apricot St 01603 508-799-3350
Robert Jennings, prin. Fax 799-8244
Tatnuck Magnet ES 500/K-6
1083 Pleasant St 01602 508-799-3554
Thomas Pappas, prin. Fax 799-8245
Thorndyke Road ES 400/PK-6
30 Thorndyke Rd 01606 508-799-3550
Margaret Doyle, prin. Fax 799-8246
Union Hill ES 300/K-6
1 Chapin St 01604 508-799-3600
Denise Bahosh, prin. Fax 799-8247
Vernon Hill ES 400/K-6
211 Providence St 01607 508-799-3630
Irene Logan, prin. Fax 799-8248
Wawecus Road ES 200/K-6
20 Wawecus Rd 01605 508-799-3527
Paula Proctor, prin. Fax 799-8249
West Tatnuck ES 300/PK-6
300 Mower St 01602 508-799-3596
Steven Soldi, prin. Fax 799-8250
Worcester Arts Magnet ES 300/PK-6
315 Saint Nicholas Ave 01606 508-799-3575
Susan O'Neil, prin. Fax 799-8243
Worcester East MS 700/7-8
420 Grafton St 01604 508-799-3430
Rose Dawkins, prin. Fax 799-8251

Bancroft S 600/K-12
110 Shore Dr 01605 508-853-2640
Scott Reisinger, hdmstr. Fax 853-7824
Our Lady Angels S 300/PK-8
1220 Main St 01603 508-752-5609
Doreen Albert, prin. Fax 798-9634
St. Marys S 100/K-6
50 Richland St 01610 508-753-0484
Corey Maloney, prin. Fax 767-1384
St. Peter Central S 400/PK-8
865 Main St 01610 508-791-6496
Meg Kursonis, prin. Fax 770-0818
St. Stephen S 200/PK-8
355 Grafton St 01604 508-755-3209
Elizabeth Drake, prin. Fax 770-1052
Venerini Academy 400/PK-8
23 Edward St 01605 508-753-3210
Sr. Sandra Napier, prin. Fax 754-6050
Worcester SDA S 50/1-8
2 Airport Dr 01602 508-753-4732
Yeshiva Academy of Worcester 100/PK-12
22 Newton Ave 01602 508-752-0904
Rabbi Hershel Fogelman, dean Fax 799-7413

Worthington, Hampshire
Gateway SD
Supt. — See Huntington
Conwell ES 100/PK-4
147 Huntington Rd 01098 413-685-1370
Joanne Blocker, prin. Fax 238-4247

Wrentham, Norfolk
Wrentham SD 1,100/PK-6
120 Taunton St 02093 508-384-5439
Jeffrey Marsden, supt. Fax 384-5444
www.wrentham.k12.ma.us
Delaney ES 600/PK-3
120 Taunton St 02093 508-384-5430
Melissa Peterson, prin. Fax 384-5444
Roderick ES 500/4-6
120 Taunton St 02093 508-384-5435
Stephen Grenham, prin. Fax 384-5444

MICHIGAN

MICHIGAN DEPARTMENT OF EDUCATION
608 W Allegan St, Lansing 48933-1524
Telephone 517-373-3324
Fax 517-335-4565
Website http://www.michigan.gov/mde

Superintendent of Public Instruction Michael Flanagan

MICHIGAN BOARD OF EDUCATION
608 W Allegan St, Lansing 48933-1524

President Kathleen Straus

INTERMEDIATE SCHOOL DISTRICTS (ISD)

Allegan Area ESA
Mark Dobias, supt. 269-673-2161
310 Thomas St, Allegan 49010 Fax 673-2361
www.alleganaesa.org/

Alpena-Montmorency-Alcona ESD
Brian Wilmot, supt. 989-354-3101
2118 US Highway 23 S Fax 356-3385
Alpena 49707
www.amaesd.k12.mi.us

Barry ISD
Jeff Jennette, supt. 269-945-9545
535 W Woodlawn Ave Fax 945-2575
Hastings 49058
www.barryisd.org

Bay-Arenac ISD
Michael R. Dewey, supt. 989-686-4410
4228 2 Mile Rd, Bay City 48706 Fax 667-3286
www.baisd.net

Berrien County ISD
Jeffrey Siegel, supt. 269-471-7725
711 Saint Joseph Ave Fax 471-2941
Berrien Springs 49103
www.berrienresa.org

Branch ISD
Michael Beckwith, supt. 517-279-5730
370 Morse St, Coldwater 49036 Fax 279-5766
www.branch-isd.org

Calhoun ISD
Terance Lunger, supt. 269-781-5141
17111 G Dr N, Marshall 49068 Fax 781-7071
www.calhounisd.org

Charlevoix-Emmet ISD
Mark Eckhardt, supt. 231-547-9947
8568 Mercer Rd, Charlevoix 49720 Fax 547-5621
www.charemisd.org

Cheboygan-Otsego-Presque Isle ISD
Mary Vratanina, supt. 231-238-9394
6065 Learning Ln Fax 238-8551
Indian River 49749
www.copesd.org/

Clare-Gladwin RESD
Sheryl Presler, supt. 989-386-3851
4041 E Mannsiding Rd Fax 386-3238
Clare 48617
www.cgresd.net/

Clinton County RESA
Lawrence Lloyd, supt. 989-224-6831
1013 S US Highway 27 Ste A Fax 224-9574
Saint Johns 48879
www.ccresa.org

C.O.O.R. ISD
Robert Jones, supt. 989-275-9555
PO Box 827, Roscommon 48653 Fax 275-5881
www.coorisd.k12.mi.us

Copper Country ISD
Dennis Harbour, supt. 906-482-4250
PO Box 270, Hancock 49930 Fax 482-1931
www.copperisd.org

Delta-Schoolcraft ISD
Michael Koster, supt. 906-786-9300
2525 3rd Ave S, Escanaba 49829 Fax 786-9318
www.dsisd.k12.mi.us

Dickinson-Iron ISD
Johanna Ostwald, supt. 906-779-2690
1074 Pyle Dr, Kingsford 49802 Fax 779-2669
www.diisd.org

Eastern Upper Peninsula ISD
Peter Everson, supt., PO Box 883 906-632-3373
Sault Sainte Marie 49783 Fax 632-1125
www.eupisd.com/

Eaton ISD
Albert Widner, supt. 517-543-5500
1790 Packard Hwy Fax 543-6633
Charlotte 48813
www.eaton.k12.mi.us/

Genesee ISD
Thomas Svitkovich Ed.D., supt. 810-591-4400
2413 W Maple Ave, Flint 48507 Fax 591-7570
www.geneseeisd.org

Gogebic-Ontonagon ISD
Bruce Mayle, supt. 906-575-3438
PO Box 218, Bergland 49910 Fax 575-3373
www.goisd.org/

Gratiot-Isabella RESD
Jan Amsterburg, supt. 989-875-5101
PO Box 310, Ithaca 48847 Fax 875-7531
www.giresd.net/

Hillsdale ISD
Robert W. Henthorne, supt. 517-437-0990
310 W Bacon St, Hillsdale 49242 Fax 439-4388
www.hillsdale-isd.org

Huron ISD
Robert Colby, supt. 989-269-6406
711 E Soper Rd, Bad Axe 48413 Fax 269-9218
www.hisd.k12.mi.us

Ingham ISD
Stanley Kogut, supt. 517-676-1051
2630 W Howell Rd, Mason 48854 Fax 676-1277
www.inghamisd.org

Ionia County ISD
Robert Kjolhede, supt. 616-527-4900
2191 Harwood Rd, Ionia 48846 Fax 527-4731
www.ioniaisd.org/

Iosco RESA
Thomas Caldwell, supt. 989-362-3006
27 N Rempert Rd Fax 362-9076
Tawas City 48763
www.ioscoresa.net/

Jackson County ISD
John Graves, supt. 517-768-5200
6700 Browns Lake Rd Fax 787-2026
Jackson 49201
www.jcisd.org

Kalamazoo RESA
Ronald Fuller, supt. 269-385-1500
1819 E Milham Ave Fax 381-9423
Kalamazoo 49002
www.kresa.org

Kent ISD
Kevin Konarska, supt. 616-364-1333
2930 Knapp St NE Fax 364-1488
Grand Rapids 49525
www.kentisd.org

Lapeer County ISD
Joseph Keena, supt. 810-664-5917
1996 W Oregon St, Lapeer 48446 Fax 664-1011
www.lcisd.k12.mi.us

Lenawee ISD
Stephen Krusich, supt. 517-265-2119
4107 N Adrian Hwy, Adrian 49221 Fax 265-7405
www.lisd.us/

Lewis Cass ISD
John Ostrowski, supt. 269-445-6204
61682 Dailey Rd, Cassopolis 49031 Fax 445-2981
www.lewiscassisd.org

Livingston ESA
Scott Menzel, supt. 517-546-5550
1425 W Grand River Ave Fax 546-7047
Howell 48843
www.livingstonesa.org

Macomb ISD
Michael DeVault, supt. 586-228-3300
44001 Garfield Rd Fax 286-1523
Clinton Township 48038
www.misd.net

Manistee ISD
Charlene Myers, supt. 231-723-4264
772 E Parkdale Ave Fax 398-3036
Manistee 49660
www.manistee.org

Marquette-Alger RESA
Steven Peffers, supt. 906-226-5100
321 E Ohio St, Marquette 49855 Fax 226-5134
www.maresa.org

Mason-Lake ISD
Jeanne Oakes, supt. 231-757-3716
2130 W US Highway 10 Fax 757-2406
Ludington 49431
www.mlisd.k12.mi.us

Mecosta-Osceola ISD
Curtis Finch, supt., 15760 190th Ave 231-796-3543
Big Rapids 49307 Fax 796-3300
www.moisd.org

Menominee ISD
Lawrence Godwin, supt. 906-863-5665
1201 41st Ave, Menominee 49858 Fax 863-7776
www.mc-isd.org

Midland County ESA
Clark Volz, supt. 989-631-5890
3917 Jefferson Ave, Midland 48640 Fax 631-4361
www.mcesa.k12.mi.us

Monroe County ISD
Donald Spencer, supt. 734-242-5799
1101 S Raisinville Rd Fax 242-0567
Monroe 48161
misd.k12.mi.us/

Montcalm Area ISD
Dr. Scott Koenigsknecht, supt. 989-831-5261
PO Box 367, Stanton 48888 Fax 831-8727
www.maisd.com

Muskegon Area ISD
Susan Meston, supt. 231-777-2637
630 Harvey St, Muskegon 49442 Fax 773-3498
www.muskegonisd.org

Newaygo County RESA
Lori Clark, supt. 231-924-0381
4747 W 48th St, Fremont 49412 Fax 924-8910
www.ncresa.org/

Oakland ISD
Vickie Markavitch, supt. 248-209-2000
2111 Pontiac Lake Rd Fax 209-2206
Waterford 48328
www.oakland.k12.mi.us

Oceana ISD
Jeanne Oakes, supt. 231-873-5651
844 S Griswold St, Hart 49420 Fax 873-5779
oceanaisd.com

Ottawa Area ISD
Karen McPhee, supt. 616-738-8940
13565 Port Sheldon St Fax 738-8946
Holland 49424
www.oaisd.org

Saginaw ISD
Richard Syrek, supt. 989-399-7473
6235 Gratiot Rd, Saginaw Fax 793-1571
www.sisd.cc/

St. Clair County RESA
Dan DeGrow, supt. 810-364-8990
PO Box 1500, Marysville 48040 Fax 364-7474
www.sccresa.org/

St. Joseph County ISD
Barbara Marshall, supt. 269-467-5400
62445 Shimmel Rd Fax 467-4309
Centreville 49032
www.sjcisd.org

Sanilac ISD
Timothy Edwards Ph.D., supt. 810-648-4700
175 E Aitken Rd, Peck 48466 Fax 648-5784
www.sanilac.k12.mi.us

Shiawassee RESD
John Hagel, supt. 989-743-3471
1025 N Shiawassee St Fax 743-6477
Corunna 48817
www.sresd.org/

Traverse Bay Area ISD
Michael Hill, supt. 231-922-6200
PO Box 6020, Traverse City 49696 Fax 922-6270
www.tbaisd.k12.mi.us

Tuscola ISD
Carol Socha, supt. 989-673-2144
1385 Cleaver Rd, Caro 48723 Fax 673-5366
www.tisd.k12.mi.us

Van Buren ISD
Jeffrey Mills, supt. 269-674-8091
490 S Paw Paw St Fax 674-8030
Lawrence 49064
www.vbisd.org/

Washtenaw ISD
William Miller, supt. 734-994-8100
PO Box 1406, Ann Arbor 48106 Fax 994-2203
www.wash.k12.mi.us/

Wayne RESA
Christopher Wigent, supt. 734-334-1300
PO Box 807, Wayne 48184 Fax 334-1760
www.resa.net

Wexford-Missaukee ISD
Scott Crosby, supt. 231-876-2260
9907 E 13th St, Cadillac 49601 Fax 876-2261
www.wmisd.org

PUBLIC, PRIVATE AND CATHOLIC ELEMENTARY SCHOOLS

Ada, Kent
Forest Hills SD
Supt. — See Grand Rapids
Ada ES 400/K-4
731 Ada Dr SE 49301 616-493-8940
Judi Scholten, prin. Fax 493-8947
Ada Vista ES 400/K-4
7192 Bradfield Ave SE 49301 616-493-8970
Jesus Santillan, prin. Fax 493-8979
Central MS 700/7-8
5810 Ada Dr SE 49301 616-493-8750
Nancy Flink, prin. Fax 493-8764
Central Woodlands 5/6 S 600/5-6
400 Alta Dale Ave SE 49301 616-493-8790
Robynn McKinney, prin. Fax 493-8795
Eastern MS 400/7-8
2200 Pettis Ave NE 49301 616-493-8850
David Washburn, prin. Fax 493-8839
Goodwillie Environmental S 100/5-6
8400 2 Mile Rd NE 49301 616-493-8633
David Ellis, prin. Fax 682-1428

Ada Christian S 700/PK-8
6206 Ada Dr SE 49301 616-676-1289
Judith DeJong, prin. Fax 676-9216
St. Patrick S 100/K-8
4333 Parnell Ave NE 49301 616-691-8833
Sean Donovan, prin. Fax 691-6309

Addison, Lenawee, Pop. 611
Addison Community SD 700/PK-12
219 N Comstock St 49220 517-547-6123
Eileen Grant-Ball, supt. Fax 547-3838
scnc.addison.k12.mi.us
Gray Early Learning Center 200/PK-2
219 N Comstock St 49220 517-547-6124
Judy Britsch, prin. Fax 547-3838
Panther ES 100/3-6
219 N Comstock St 49220 517-547-6125
Judith Britsch, prin. Fax 547-3838

Adrian, Lenawee, Pop. 21,784
Adrian SD 3,500/K-12
785 Riverside Ave Ste 1 49221 517-263-2115
Christopher Timmis, supt. Fax 265-5381
www.adrian.k12.mi.us
Adrian MS 5-6 500/5-6
340 E Church St 49221 517-265-8122
Matt Schwartz, prin. Fax 264-1365
Adrian MS 7-8 500/7-8
615 Springbrook Ave 49221 517-263-0543
Mike Perez, prin. Fax 265-5984
Alexander ES 400/K-4
520 Cherry St 49221 517-263-9533
Jeff Petterson, prin. Fax 265-3633
Lincoln ES 300/K-4
158 S Scott St 49221 517-265-8544
Marcie Brown, prin. Fax 265-8923
Michener ES 300/K-4
104 Dawes Ave 49221 517-263-9002
Deb Risner, prin. Fax 265-9296
Prairie ES 300/K-4
2568 Airport Rd 49221 517-265-5082
Deb Agnew, prin. Fax 265-8310

Madison SD 1,300/PK-12
3498 Treat Hwy 49221 517-265-1840
James Hartley, supt. Fax 265-5635
www.madison.k12.mi.us
Madison ES 600/PK-5
3498 Treat Hwy 49221 517-263-0744
Deborah Scharp, prin. Fax 265-1849
Madison MS 300/6-8
3498 Treat Hwy 49221 517-263-0743
Brad Anschuetz, prin. Fax 265-5635

Tecumseh SD
Supt. — See Tecumseh
Sutton ES 400/K-4
2780 Sutton Rd 49221 517-423-2367
Debra Langmeyer, prin. Fax 423-1302

Lenawee Christian S 500/PK-12
111 Wolf Creek Hwy 49221 517-265-7590
Ronald Evans, supt. Fax 265-6558
St. Joseph Academy 200/PK-8
1267 E Siena Heights Dr 49221 517-263-4898
Sr. Patricia Fischer, prin. Fax 265-6240
St. Stephen Lutheran S 100/K-8
632 S Madison St 49221 517-263-1775
Neil Neumann, prin. Fax 263-1775

Akron, Tuscola, Pop. 452
Akron-Fairgrove SD
Supt. — See Fairgrove
Akron-Fairgrove ES 200/K-6
PO Box 279 48701 989-691-5141
Rebecca Crosby, prin. Fax 691-1022

Alanson, Emmet, Pop. 811
Alanson SD 400/K-12
7400 North St 49706 231-548-2261
Jeffrey Liedel, supt. Fax 548-2132
www.alansonvikings.net/
Littlefield S 300/K-8
7400 North St 49706 231-548-2261
Joyce Green, prin. Fax 548-2165

Alba, Antrim
Alba SD 200/PK-12
PO Box 10 49611 231-584-2000
Derrel Kent, supt. Fax 584-2001
www.albaschool.org/
Alba S 200/PK-12
PO Box 10 49611 231-584-2000
Derrel Kent, prin. Fax 584-2001

Albion, Calhoun, Pop. 9,348
Albion SD 1,300/PK-12
1418 Cooper St 49224 517-629-9166
Frederick Clarke, supt. Fax 629-8209
www.albion.k12.mi.us
Caldwell ES 200/PK-K
1100 N Berrien St 49224 517-629-7474
Henderson Harris, prin. Fax 630-3300
Harrington ES 200/1-4
100 S Clark St 49224 517-629-2435
Craig Wilson, prin. Fax 630-3310
Washington Gardner MS 300/5-8
401 E Michigan Ave 49224 517-629-9448
Derrick Crum, prin. Fax 629-8257

Algonac, Saint Clair, Pop. 4,598
Algonac Community SD 2,100/K-12
1216 Saint Clair Blvd 48001 810-794-9364
Michael Sharrow, supt. Fax 794-0040
www.algonac.k12.mi.us
Algonac ES 200/K-5
1300 Saint Clair Blvd 48001 810-794-4991
Melissa Hanners, prin. Fax 794-8871
Algonquin MS 500/6-8
9185 Marsh Rd 48001 810-794-9317
Abe Leaver, prin. Fax 794-8872
Millside ES 300/K-5
1904 Mill St 48001 810-794-8880
Martha Szymanski, prin. Fax 794-8870
Other Schools – See Ira

Allegan, Allegan, Pop. 4,963
Allegan SD 2,900/PK-12
550 5th St 49010 269-673-5431
Kevin Harness, supt. Fax 673-5463
www.alleganps.org/
Dawson ES 300/PK-5
125 Elm St 49010 269-673-6925
Joe James, prin. Fax 686-8138
North Ward ES 300/K-5
440 River St 49010 269-673-6003
Ron Orr, prin. Fax 686-8093
Pine Trails ES 400/K-5
2950 Center St 49010 269-673-5379
Dave Kanine, prin. Fax 673-1989
West Ward ES 300/K-5
630 Vernon St 49010 269-673-7000
Harry Dalm, prin. Fax 673-1987
White MS 700/6-8
3300 115th Ave 49010 269-673-2241
George Mohr, prin. Fax 686-0309

Allendale, Ottawa, Pop. 6,950
Allendale SD 1,700/PK-12
10505 Learning Ln 49401 616-892-5570
Daniel Jonker, supt. Fax 895-6690
www.allendale.k12.mi.us
Allendale MS 400/6-8
7161 Pleasant View Ct 49401 616-892-5595
Rocky Thompson, prin. Fax 895-9111
Evergreen ES 200/PK-3
10690 Learning Ln 49401 616-892-3465
Steve VanderPloeg, prin. Fax 892-5798
Oakwood IS 4-5
10505 Learning Ln 49401 616-892-3475
Doug Bol, prin. Fax 892-5517
Springview ES 300/PK-3
10690 Learning Ln 49401 616-892-3470
Jill Wilson, prin. Fax 895-9191

Allendale Christian S 200/PK-8
11050 64th Ave 49401 616-895-5108
Alice Spaanstra, prin. Fax 895-5109

Allen Park, Wayne, Pop. 28,083
Allen Park SD 3,700/K-12
9601 Vine Ave 48101 313-827-2150
Dr. John Sturock, supt. Fax 827-2151
www.apps.k12.mi.us
Allen Park MS 900/6-8
8401 Vine Ave 48101 313-827-2200
Michael Dawson, prin. Fax 827-2251
Arno ES 500/K-5
7500 Fox Ave 48101 313-827-1050
Susan Vokal, prin. Fax 827-1085
Bennie ES 400/K-5
17401 Champaign Rd 48101 313-827-1300
Cathryne Goulet, prin. Fax 827-1342
Lindemann ES 500/K-5
9201 Carter Ave 48101 313-827-1150
Dr. Janine Hall, prin. Fax 827-1185

Melvindale-Northern Allen Park SD
Supt. — See Melvindale
Rogers ES 200/K-1
5000 Shenandoah Ave 48101 313-389-3345
Lisa Tafelski, prin. Fax 277-5405

Cabrini S 500/K-8
15300 Wick Rd 48101 313-928-6610
Patricia Pollick, prin. Fax 928-8502
Inter City Baptist S 300/K-12
4700 Allen Rd 48101 313-928-6900
James Hubbard, prin. Fax 928-7310
Montessori Children's Center 200/PK-6
4141 Laurence Ave 48101 313-382-2777
Jane Adams, prin. Fax 382-4838
Mt. Hope Lutheran S 50/PK-PK
5323 Southfield Rd 48101 313-565-9140
Jackie Fults, dir. Fax 565-2426

Alma, Gratiot, Pop. 9,260
Alma SD 2,200/PK-12
1500 Pine Ave 48801 989-463-3111
Don Pavlik, supt. Fax 466-2943
www.almaschools.net
Alma MS 500/6-8
1700 Pine Ave 48801 989-463-3111
Carolyn Studley, prin. Fax 466-7612
Hillcrest ES 300/2-3
515 E Elizabeth St 48801 989-463-3111
Tom Neuenfeldt, prin. Fax 466-2852
Luce Road ECC 200/PK-1
6265 N Luce Rd 48801 989-463-3111
Donalynn Ingersoll, prin. Fax 466-6087
Pine Avenue ES 300/4-5
1065 Pine Ave 48801 989-463-3111
Carrie Akin, prin. Fax 466-5038

Good Shephard ECC 50/PK-K
7400 N Begole Rd 48801 989-463-3056
Susan Eich, prin. Fax 463-8513
St. Mary S 100/PK-6
220 W Downie St 48801 989-463-4579
Lisa Seeley, prin. Fax 463-8297

Almont, Lapeer, Pop. 2,874
Almont Community SD 1,700/K-12
401 Church St 48003 810-798-8561
Steven Zott, supt. Fax 798-2367
www.almont.k12.mi.us
Almont ES 400/3-5
401 Church St 48003 810-798-8467
James Jenuwine, prin. Fax 798-8744
Almont MS 500/6-8
4624 Kidder Rd 48003 810-798-3578
Thomas English, prin. Fax 798-3549
Orchard PS 300/K-2
4664 Kidder Rd 48003 810-798-7019
James Jenuwine, prin. Fax 798-3530

Alpena, Alpena, Pop. 10,792
Alpena SD 4,700/K-12
2373 Gordon Rd 49707 989-358-5040
Brent Holcomb, supt. Fax 358-5041
www.alpenaschools.com
Besser ES 400/K-6
375 Wilson St 49707 989-358-5100
Pam Sornberger, prin. Fax 358-5105
Hinks ES 300/K-6
7667 US Highway 23 N 49707 989-358-5560
Tim Wedge, prin. Fax 358-5565
Lincoln ES 200/K-6
309 W Lake St 49707 989-358-5900
Pauline Burnham, prin. Fax 358-5905
Sunset ES 200/K-6
1421 Hobbs Dr 49707 989-358-5840
Tim Wedge, prin. Fax 358-5845
Thunder Bay JHS 800/7-8
3500 S 3rd Ave 49707 989-358-5400
Steve Genschaw, prin. Fax 358-5499
White ES 400/K-6
201 N Ripley Blvd 49707 989-358-5950
Melissa Schaedig, prin. Fax 358-5955
Other Schools – See Herron, Lachine, Ossineke

All Saints Catholic S 100/PK-6
500 N 2nd Ave 49707 989-354-4911
Mary Lightner, prin. Fax 354-3752
Alpena SDA S 50/K-8
4029 US Highway 23 S 49707 989-356-2932
Sarah Taylor, prin.
Immanuel Lutheran S 100/PK-8
355 Wilson St 49707 989-354-4805
Pamela White, prin. Fax 358-1102

Alto, Kent
Caledonia Community SD
Supt. — See Caledonia
Kettle Lake ES 400/K-5
8451 Garbow Dr SE 49302 616-868-6113
Chris Warren, prin. Fax 868-0021

Lowell Area SD
Supt. — See Lowell
Alto ES 400/K-5
6150 Bancroft Ave SE 49302 616-987-2600
Randy Fleenor, prin. Fax 987-2611

Ann Arbor, Washtenaw, Pop. 113,271
Ann Arbor SD 16,700/PK-12
PO Box 1188 48106 734-994-2200
Dr. Todd Roberts, supt. Fax 994-2414
www.aaps.k12.mi.us/
Abbot ES 300/K-5
2670 Sequoia Pkwy 48103 734-994-1901
Pati Barnes, prin. Fax 994-4717
Allen ES 400/K-5
2560 Towner Blvd 48104 734-997-1210
Joan Fitzgibbon, prin. Fax 997-1257
Angell ES 300/K-5
1608 S University Ave 48104 734-994-1907
Gary Court, prin. Fax 994-8938
Ann Arbor Preschool 200/PK-PK
2775 Boardwalk St 48104 734-994-2303
Connie Toigo, prin. Fax 994-2895
Bach ES 300/K-5
600 W Jefferson St 48103 734-994-1949
Shelley Bruder, prin. Fax 994-8239
Bryant ES 200/K-2
2150 Santa Rosa Dr 48108 734-997-1212
Dr. Luther Corbitt, prin. Fax 997-1231
Burns Park ES 400/K-5
1414 Wells St 48104 734-994-1919
Kathy Morhous, prin. Fax 994-1548
Carpenter ES 300/K-5
4250 Central Blvd 48108 734-997-1214
Ron Collins, prin. Fax 997-1226
Clague MS 700/6-8
2616 Nixon Rd 48105 734-994-1976
Cynthia Leaman, prin. Fax 994-1645

Dicken ES 400/K-5
2135 Runnymede Blvd 48103 734-994-1928
Michael Madison, prin. Fax 997-1884
Eberwhite ES 300/K-5
800 Soule Blvd 48103 734-994-1934
Debi Wagner, prin. Fax 996-3014
Forsythe MS 600/6-8
1655 Newport Rd 48103 734-994-1985
Janet Schwamb, prin. Fax 994-5749
Haisley ES 400/K-5
825 Duncan St 48103 734-994-1937
MaryAnne Jaeger, prin. Fax 994-1371
King ES 400/K-5
3800 Waldenwood Dr 48105 734-994-1940
Kevin Karr, prin. Fax 997-1258
Lakewood ES 300/K-5
344 Gralake Ave 48103 734-994-1953
Patrick O'Neill, prin. Fax 997-1952
Lawton ES 500/K-5
2250 S 7th St 48103 734-994-1946
Ruth Williams, prin. Fax 994-2597
Logan ES 400/K-5
2685 Traver Blvd 48105 734-994-1807
Terra Webster, prin. Fax 994-1473
Mitchell ES 300/K-5
3550 Pittsview Dr 48108 734-997-1216
Kathleen Scarnecchia, prin. Fax 997-1228
Northside ES 300/K-5
912 Barton Dr 48105 734-994-1958
Monica Harrold, prin. Fax 997-1232
Pattengill ES 300/3-5
2100 Crestland St 48104 734-994-1961
Che Carter, prin. Fax 994-1276
Pittsfield ES 300/K-5
2543 Pittsfield Blvd 48104 734-997-1218
Carol Shakarian, prin. Fax 997-1229
Scarlett MS 600/6-8
3300 Lorraine St 48108 734-997-1220
Benjamin Edmondson, prin. Fax 997-1885
Slauson MS 800/6-8
1019 W Washington St 48103 734-994-2004
Christopher Curtis, prin. Fax 994-1681
Tappan MS 800/6-8
2251 E Stadium Blvd 48104 734-994-2011
Jazz Parks, prin. Fax 997-1873
Thurston ES 400/K-5
2300 Prairie St 48105 734-994-1970
Patricia Manley, prin. Fax 994-1742
Wines ES 400/K-5
1701 Newport Rd 48103 734-994-1973
Janette Jackson, prin. Fax 996-3023

Ann Arbor Christian S 200/K-8
5500 Whitmore Lake Rd 48105 734-741-4948
Thom Ritzema, prin. Fax 929-6629
Ann Arbor Hills Child Development Center 100/PK-2
2775 Bedford Rd 48104 734-971-3080
Ramelle Alexander, prin.
Ann Arbor SDA S 50/1-8
2796 Packard St 48108 734-971-5570
Lloyd Smith, prin. Fax 929-0820
Christian Montessori S of Ann Arbor 100/PK-8
5225 Jackson Rd 48103 734-332-9600
Erin Milligan, prin. Fax 213-6207
Daycroft Montessori PS 100/PK-K
100 Oakbrook Dr 48104 734-930-0333
Michele Buchanan, prin. Fax 930-0312
Daycroft Montessori S 100/K-6
1095 N Zeeb Rd 48103 734-662-3335
Diane Mukkala, prin. Fax 662-3360
Doughty Montessori S 50/PK-K
416 S Ashley St 48103 734-663-8050
Sherry Doughty, prin. Fax 663-4813
Emerson S 400/K-8
5425 Scio Church Rd 48103 734-665-9005
Patricia Adams, prin. Fax 665-8126
Go Like the Wind S 300/PK-9
3540 Dixboro Ln 48105 734-747-7422
Doug Collier, admin. Fax 747-6560
Hebrew Day S 100/K-5
2937 Birch Hollow Dr 48108 734-971-4633
Dina Shtull-Leber, hdmstr. Fax 971-6204
Michigan Islamic Academy 200/PK-12
2301 Plymouth Rd 48105 734-665-8882
Nabila Gomaa, prin. Fax 665-9058
St. Francis of Assisi S 400/K-8
2270 E Stadium Blvd 48104 734-821-2200
Sara Collins, prin. Fax 821-2202
St. Paul Lutheran S 200/PK-8
495 Earhart Rd 48105 734-665-0604
Bradley Massey, prin. Fax 665-7809
St. Thomas the Apostle S 300/PK-8
540 Elizabeth St 48104 734-769-0911
Anthony Moskus, prin. Fax 769-9078
Spiritus Sanctus Academy 100/PK-8
4101 E Joy Rd 48105 734-996-3855
Sr. John Rasmussen, prin. Fax 996-4270
Steiner S of Ann Arbor 300/PK-8
2775 Newport Rd 48103 734-995-4141
Peggy Wilson, admin. Fax 995-4383
Summers-Knoll S 50/PK-8
2015 Manchester Rd 48104 734-971-7991
Joanna Hastings, prin. Fax 971-9663

Armada, Macomb, Pop. 1,650
Armada Area SD 1,900/PK-12
74500 Burk St 48005 586-784-2112
Arnold Kummerow, supt. Fax 784-4268
www.macomb.k12.mi.us/armada
Armada MS 500/6-8
23550 Armada Center Rd 48005 586-784-2500
William Zebelian, prin. Fax 784-8650
Krause Early ES 300/PK-2
23900 Armada Center Rd 48005 586-784-2600
Susan Curry, prin. Fax 784-9147
Krause Later ES 500/3-5
23900 Armada Center Rd 48005 586-784-2640
Kurt Sutton, prin. Fax 784-9147

Arnold, Marquette
Wells Township SD 50/K-8
PO Box 108 49819 906-238-4200
Jacqueline Cole, supt. Fax 238-4200
Wells Township S 50/K-8
PO Box 108 49819 906-238-4200
Jacqueline Cole, prin. Fax 238-4200

Ashley, Gratiot, Pop. 521
Ashley Community SD 300/K-12
PO Box 6 48806 989-847-4000
Tim Hughes, supt. Fax 847-3500
www.bearnet.net
Ashley ES 200/K-6
PO Box 6 48806 989-847-2102
Tom Saylor, prin. Fax 847-4204

Athens, Calhoun, Pop. 1,075
Athens Area SD 800/K-12
304 E South St 49011 269-729-5427
Dr. Randall Davis, supt. Fax 729-9610
www.athensk12.org
Athens MS 200/5-8
515 E Williams St 49011 269-729-5421
Richard Franklin, prin. Fax 729-9613
Other Schools – See East Leroy

Factoryville Christian S 50/PK-12
33650 Factoryville Rd 49011 269-729-4203
Fred Goebert, admin. Fax 729-4182

Atlanta, Montmorency
Atlanta Community SD 400/K-12
PO Box 619 49709 989-785-4877
Teresa Stauffer, supt. Fax 785-2611
www.atlanta.k12.mi.us
Atlanta Community S 400/K-12
PO Box 619 49709 989-785-4785
Teresa Staffer, prin. Fax 785-2588

Atlantic Mine, Houghton
Stanton Township SD 100/K-8
50870 Holman School Rd 49905 906-482-2797
Paul Saaranen, supt. Fax 487-5928
www.stanton.k12.mi.us
Holman S 100/K-8
50870 Holman School Rd 49905 906-482-2797
Paul Saaranen, prin. Fax 487-5928

Auburn, Bay, Pop. 2,057
Bay City SD
Supt. — See Bay City
Auburn ES 500/K-5
301 E Midland Rd 48611 989-662-4921
Mary Goedert, prin. Fax 662-2205
Forest ECC 50/K-K
2169 W Midland Rd 48611 989-496-3430
Sheri Zimmerman, prin. Fax 496-0221
Western MS 800/6-8
500 W Midland Rd 48611 989-662-4489
Dale Dunham, prin. Fax 662-0185

Auburn Area Catholic S 100/PK-5
114 W Midland Rd 48611 989-662-6431
Tia Hahn, prin. Fax 662-3391
Grace Lutheran S 50/K-8
303 Ruth St 48611 989-662-4791
Peter Fredrich, prin. Fax 662-0091
Zion Lutheran S 100/PK-8
1557 Seidlers Rd 48611 989-662-4264
Dennis Schmidt, prin. Fax 662-7052

Auburn Hills, Oakland, Pop. 21,011
Avondale SD 3,900/PK-12
2940 Waukegan St 48326 248-537-6000
Dr. George Heitsch, supt. Fax 537-6005
www.avondale.k12.mi.us
Auburn ES 400/PK-4
2900 Waukegan St 48326 248-537-6500
Marsha Wharton, prin. Fax 537-6505
Graham ES 300/K-4
2450 Old Salem Rd 48326 248-537-6800
David Pass, prin. Fax 537-6805
Other Schools – See Rochester Hills, Troy

Pontiac SD
Supt. — See Pontiac
Rogers ES 400/K-6
2600 Dexter Rd 48326 248-451-7850
Bettye Clark, prin. Fax 451-7862

Auburn Hills Christian S 300/PK-12
3655 N Squirrel Rd 48326 248-373-3399
Scott Wickson, prin. Fax 373-2001
Oakland Christian S 600/PK-12
3075 Shimmons Rd 48326 248-373-2700
Randall Speck, admin. Fax 373-9255

Au Gres, Arenac, Pop. 982
Au Gres-Sims SD 500/K-12
PO Box 648 48703 989-876-7150
Gary Marchel, supt. Fax 876-6752
www.ags-schools.org
Au Gres-Sims ES 200/K-5
PO Box 648 48703 989-876-7158
Fax 876-4684

Augusta, Kalamazoo, Pop. 852
Galesburg-Augusta Community SD
Supt. — See Galesburg
Galesburg-Augusta IS 200/4-5
600 W Michigan Ave 49012 269-484-2030
Martha Hymer, prin. Fax 731-2196
Galesburg-Augusta MS 300/6-8
750 W Van Buren St 49012 269-484-2020
Jeremy Mansfield, prin. Fax 731-4138

Avoca, Saint Clair
Yale SD
Supt. — See Yale
Avoca ES 300/K-5
PO Box 365 48006 810-324-2660
Nancy LePla, prin. Fax 324-2843

Bad Axe, Huron, Pop. 3,246
Bad Axe SD 1,300/K-12
760 S Van Dyke Rd 48413 989-269-9938
James Wencel, supt. Fax 269-2739
www.badaxeps.org/
Bad Axe IS 300/3-5
404 Hatchet Dr 48413 989-269-2736
Peter Batzer, prin. Fax 803-9097
Bad Axe JHS 300/6-8
750 S Van Dyke Rd 48413 989-269-2735
Gregory Newland, prin. Fax 269-9001
Greene PS 300/K-2
309 N Outer Dr 48413 989-269-2737
Peter Batzer, prin. Fax 803-9096

Bloomfield Township SD 7F 50/K-8
2072 N Verona Rd 48413 989-269-2110
Jennifer Eugster, supt. Fax 269-2110
www.huroncountyruralschools.com/
Rapson S 50/K-8
2072 N Verona Rd 48413 989-269-2110
Jennifer Eugster, prin. Fax 269-2110

Church SD 50/K-8
2927 Crockard Rd 48413 989-269-7772
Fax 269-3022
www.huroncountyruralschools.com/church/index.html
Church S 50/K-8
2927 Crockard Rd 48413 989-269-7772
David Phelps, prin. Fax 269-3022

Colfax Township SD 1F 50/K-8
1509 N Van Dyke Rd 48413 989-269-8853
Fax 269-7245
www.huroncountyruralschools.com/bigburning/index.html
Big Burning S 50/K-8
1509 N Van Dyke Rd 48413 989-269-8853
Michelle Daniels, lead tchr. Fax 269-7245

Sigel Township SD 3 50/K-8
4151 Section Line Rd 48413 989-269-8944
Fax 269-8937
www.huroncountyruralschools.com/adams/index.html
Adams S 50/K-8
4151 Section Line Rd 48413 989-269-8944
Jessica Tenbusch, prin. Fax 269-8937

Verona Mills SD 1F 50/K-8
3487 School St 48413 989-269-7054
Kathy Cregeur, lead tchr. Fax 269-9033
www.huroncountyruralschools.com/veronamills/index.htm
Verona Mills S 50/K-8
3487 School St 48413 989-269-7054
Kathy Cregeur, lead tchr. Fax 269-9033

Baldwin, Lake, Pop. 1,157
Baldwin Community SD 600/PK-12
525 4th St 49304 231-745-4791
Randall Howes, supt. Fax 745-3240
www.baldwin.k12.mi.us
Baldwin ES 300/PK-6
525 4th St 49304 231-745-3261
Stiles Simmons, prin. Fax 745-7481
Baldwin JHS 100/7-8
525 4th St 49304 231-745-4683
Jim Sibley, prin. Fax 745-2898

Bancroft, Shiawassee, Pop. 609
Durand Area SD
Supt. — See Durand
Bills ES 100/K-5
251 W Prior Rd 48414 989-634-5388
Christa Bowman, prin. Fax 634-5740

Bangor, Van Buren, Pop. 1,882
Bangor SD 1,300/K-12
801 W Arlington St 49013 269-427-6800
Ron Parker, supt. Fax 427-8274
www.bangorvikings.org
Bangor MS 300/6-8
803 W Arlington St 49013 269-427-6824
Jim Greydanus, prin. Fax 427-8274
Bangor PS 200/K-2
12 N Walnut St 49013 269-427-6848
Maurice Scott, prin. Fax 427-6174
South Walnut ES 300/3-5
309 S Walnut St 49013 269-427-6863
Jeremy Davison, prin. Fax 427-9377

Bangor Township SD 8 50/K-8
35594 66th St 49013 269-427-8562
Jeffrey Mills, supt.
www.vbisd.org
Wood S, 35594 66th St 49013 50/K-8
Connie Hollis, prin. 269-427-8562

Trinity Lutheran S 50/K-8
115 E Monroe St 49013 269-427-7102
Kevin Lemke, prin. Fax 427-1024

Baraga, Baraga, Pop. 1,252
Baraga Area SD 500/K-12
PO Box 428 49908 906-353-6664
Norman McKindles, supt. Fax 353-7454
www.baragaschools.org
La Tendresse ES 200/3-6
PO Box 428 49908 906-353-6664
Jennifer Lynn, prin. Fax 353-7454
Other Schools – See Pelkie

Barryton, Mecosta, Pop. 385
Chippewa Hills SD
Supt. — See Remus
Barryton ES 300/PK-5
19701 30th Ave 49305 989-382-5311
Lynell Inman-Crosby, prin. Fax 382-5387

Bath, Clinton
Bath Community SD 1,000/K-12
PO Box 310 48808 517-641-6721
Jake Huffman, supt. Fax 641-6958
www.bath.k12.mi.us
Bath ES 400/K-5
PO Box 310 48808 517-641-6771
Mary Larson, prin. Fax 641-7288
Bath MS 200/6-8
PO Box 310 48808 517-641-6781
Lorenda Jonas, prin. Fax 641-4996

Battle Creek, Calhoun, Pop. 53,202
Battle Creek SD 6,100/PK-12
3 Van Buren St W 49017 269-965-9500
Dr. Charles Coleman, supt. Fax 965-9474
www.battlecreekpublicschools.org
Coburn ES 200/K-5
39 Fairhome Ave 49015 269-965-9730
Kim Jankowski, prin. Fax 965-9732
Dudley ES 200/K-5
308 Roosevelt Ave W, 269-965-9720
Tamara Jamierson, prin. Fax 965-9724
Franklin ES 200/K-5
20 Newark Ave 49014 269-965-9693
Debra Norman, prin. Fax 965-9696
Fremont ES 300/K-5
115 Emmett St E 49017 269-965-9715
Debra Hulsey, prin. Fax 965-9715
Kellogg ES 400/PK-5
306 Champion St, 269-965-9773
Chandra Youngblood, prin. Fax 965-9780
Kellogg MS 600/6-8
60 Van Buren St W 49017 269-965-9655
Bobbi Morehead, prin. Fax 965-9789
LaMora Park ES 200/K-5
65 Woodlawn Ave N, 269-965-9725
Tim Allen, prin. Fax 965-7007
Northwestern MS 400/6-8
176 Limit St, 269-965-9607
Matt Montange, prin. Fax 965-9525
Urbandale ES 300/K-5
123 Bedford Rd N, 269-965-9735
Brendal Hatley, prin. Fax 964-7438
Valley View ES 300/PK-5
960 Avenue A, 269-965-9760
Deborah Bordner, prin. Fax 965-9764
Verona ES 300/K-5
825 Capital Ave NE 49017 269-965-9710
Garth Cooper, prin. Fax 965-9712
Other Schools – See Springfield

Harper Creek Community SD 2,600/K-12
7454 B Dr N 49014 269-441-6550
John Severson, supt. Fax 979-5310
www.harpercreek.net
Beadle Lake ES 300/K-4
8175 C Dr N 49014 269-964-3341
Ben Barkema, prin. Fax 962-4748
Harper Creek MS 800/5-8
7290 B Dr N 49014 269-441-4750
Cristine Eyre, prin. Fax 979-4613
Sonoma ES 300/K-4
4640 B Dr S 49015 269-979-1107
Cyndi Mead, prin. Fax 979-6246
Wattles Park ES 300/K-4
132 Wattles Rd S 49014 269-973-5551
Wendy VanGeison, prin. Fax 963-1174

Lakeview SD 3,600/K-12
15 Arbor St 49015 269-565-2400
Cindy Ruble, supt. Fax 565-2408
www.lakeviewspartans.org
Lakeview MS 1,200/5-8
300 28th St S 49015 269-565-3900
Nkenge Bergan, prin. Fax 565-3908
Minges Brook ES 400/K-4
435 Lincoln Hill Dr 49015 269-565-4500
Laura Williams, prin. Fax 565-4508
Prairieview ES 200/K-4
1675 Iroquois Ave 49015 269-565-4600
Carol Disler, prin. Fax 565-4608
Riverside ES 300/K-4
650 Riverside Dr 49015 269-565-4700
Denise Myers, prin. Fax 565-4708
Westlake ES 400/K-4
1184 24th St S 49015 269-565-4900
Jim Owen, prin. Fax 565-4908

Pennfield SD 1,900/K-12
8587 Pennfield Rd 49017 269-961-9781
Ben Laser, supt. Fax 961-9799
www.pennfield.net/
Pennfield Dunlap ES 300/3-5
8587 Pennfield Rd 49017 269-961-9789
Dirk VanDiver, prin. Fax 961-9756
Pennfield MS 500/6-8
8587 Pennfield Rd 49017 269-961-9784
Christina Feneley, prin. Fax 441-5535
Pennfield North ES 200/K-2
8587 Pennfield Rd 49017 269-961-9797
Mary Ann DeVries, prin. Fax 961-9765
Pennfield Purdy ES 200/K-2
8587 Pennfield Rd 49017 269-961-9795
Jane Haudek, prin. Fax 961-9764

Battle Creek Christian S 100/PK-8
1035 Wagner Dr 49017 269-963-0649
Barb Hesselink, admin. Fax 963-7936
Battle Creek SDA Academy 100/K-12
480 Parkway Dr, 269-965-1278
Eric Velez, prin. Fax 965-3250
Calhoun Christian S 100/PK-12
20 Woodrow Ave S 49015 269-965-5560
Tangi Olds, admin. Fax 965-8038
Cross Creek Christian S 100/K-4
114 Minges Rd E 49015 269-964-0401
Fax 966-1142
St. Joseph MS 100/6-8
44 25th St N 49015 269-963-4935
Marcy Arnson, prin. Fax 963-5590
St. Joseph S 400/PK-5
47 23rd St N 49015 269-965-7749
Patricia Riley, prin. Fax 965-0790

Bay City, Bay, Pop. 34,879
Bangor Township SD 2,600/PK-12
3359 E Midland Rd 48706 989-684-8121
Dr. Tina Kerr, supt. Fax 684-6000
www.bangorschools.org
Bangor Central S 400/K-5
208 State Park Dr 48706 989-684-8891
Margy Dewey, prin. Fax 686-8211
Bangor Lincoln S 300/K-5
2771 N Euclid Ave 48706 989-686-7639
Diane Hurley, prin. Fax 686-8213
Bangor North Preschool 100/PK-PK
504 Revilo Rd 48706 989-686-7649
Thomas Matuszewski, prin. Fax 686-8217
Bangor West Central S 300/K-5
3175 Wilder Rd 48706 989-684-3373
Thomas Matuszewski, prin. Fax 686-8214
McAuliffe MS 600/6-8
3281 Kiesel Rd 48706 989-686-7640
Diana Tuttle, prin. Fax 686-7633

Bay City SD 9,100/K-12
910 N Walnut St 48706 989-686-9700
Douglas Newcombe, supt. Fax 686-1047
www.bcschools.net
Hampton ES 500/K-5
1908 W Youngs Ditch Rd 48708 989-893-1100
Robert Jansen, prin. Fax 893-6347
Handy MS 1,200/6-8
601 Blend St 48706 989-684-1723
Matt Schmidt, prin. Fax 684-1960
Kolb ES 400/K-5
305 W Crump St 48706 989-893-9518
Brian DuFresne, prin. Fax 893-0462
Linsday ES 400/K-5
607 Lasalle St 48706 989-684-0692
Deborah VanSumeren, prin. Fax 684-8760
MacGregor ES 500/K-5
1012 Fremont St 48708 989-892-1558
Amy Luczak, prin. Fax 892-8651
Mackensen ES 300/K-5
5535 Dennis Dr 48706 989-684-4958
John Folsom, prin. Fax 684-8598
McAlear Sawden ES 600/K-5
2300 Midland Rd 48706 989-684-7702
Mike Connors, prin. Fax 684-6464
Washington ES 400/K-5
1821 McKinley St 48708 989-894-2744
Judy Cox, prin. Fax 894-5870
Other Schools – See Auburn

Bethel Lutheran S 100/PK-8
749 N Pine Rd 48708 989-892-4508
Douglas Dast, prin. Fax 892-5668
Faith Lutheran S 200/PK-8
3033 Wilder Rd 48706 989-684-3448
Daniel Stoelting, prin. Fax 684-3545
Holy Family MS 100/6-8
2307 S Monroe St Ste 200 48708 989-892-8332
John Hoving, prin. Fax 892-8727
Holy Trinity S 100/PK-5
1004 S Wenona St 48706 989-892-3018
Terrie DeWaele, prin. Fax 892-0793
Immanuel Lutheran S 200/PK-8
247 N Lincoln St 48708 989-893-8521
Patricia Hambaum, prin. Fax 893-4172
St. James S 100/PK-5
715 14th St 48708 989-892-4371
Sr. Julie Gatza, prin. Fax 892-7567
St. John Lutheran S 100/PK-8
210 S Alp St 48706 989-684-6442
Michael Falk, prin. Fax 684-6442
St. John Lutheran S 100/PK-8
1664 Amelith Rd 48706 989-686-0176
Jennifer Enge, prin. Fax 686-2169
St. Paul Lutheran S 100/PK-8
6094 Westside Saginaw Rd 48706 989-684-4450
Jerry Eisman, prin. Fax 684-0882
St. Stanilaus S 100/PK-5
900 S Grant St 48708 989-893-5085
Christine Szatkowski, prin. Fax 893-2352
Trinity Lutheran S 100/PK-8
20 E Salzburg Rd 48706 989-662-4891
Henry Pickelmann, prin. Fax 662-6173
Trinity Lutheran S 100/K-8
2515 Broadway St 48708 989-894-2092
Ryan Hill, prin. Fax 894-2870
Zion Lutheran S 100/PK-8
1707 S Kiesel St 48706 989-893-5793
Janet LaRocque, prin. Fax 893-4633

Bear Lake, Manistee, Pop. 331
Bear Lake SD 400/K-12
7748 Cody St 49614 231-864-3133
Michael Matesich, supt. Fax 864-3434
www.bearlake.k12.mi.us
Bear Lake ES 200/K-6
7748 Cody St 49614 231-864-3133
Marci Augenstein, prin. Fax 864-3434

Beaver Island, Charlevoix
Beaver Island Community SD 100/K-12
37895 Kings Hwy 49782 231-448-2744
Kathleen McNamara, supt. Fax 448-2919
www.beaverisland.k12.mi.us
Beaver Island Community S 100/K-12
37895 Kings Hwy 49782 231-448-2744
Kathleen McNamara, prin. Fax 448-2919

Beaverton, Gladwin, Pop. 1,118
Beaverton Rural SD 1,500/PK-12
PO Box 529 48612 989-246-3000
Joan Cashin, supt. Fax 435-7631
www.brs.cgresd.net
Beaverton MS 500/4-8
PO Box 529 48612 989-246-3020
Jeffrey Budge, prin. Fax 246-3420
Beaverton Preschool 50/PK-PK
PO Box 529 48612 989-246-3000
Joan Cashin, prin. Fax 435-7631
Beaverton PS 400/K-3
PO Box 529 48612 989-246-3040
Ron Morley, prin. Fax 246-3210

Belding, Ionia, Pop. 5,895
Belding Area SD 2,100/PK-12
1975 Orchard St 48809 616-794-4700
Charles Barker, supt. Fax 794-4730
www.bas-k12.org/
Belding MS 500/6-8
410 Ionia St 48809 616-794-4400
Fax 794-4420
ECC 50/PK-PK
1975 Orchard St 48809 616-794-4731
Leslie Mount, prin. Fax 794-4734
Ellis ES 300/K-2
100 W Ellis Ave 48809 616-794-4100
Andrew Feuerstein, prin. Fax 794-4142
Woodview ES 500/3-5
450 Orchard St 48809 616-794-4750
Mike Burde, prin. Fax 794-4790

Faith Community Christian S 50/K-6
9614 Fisk Rd 48809 616-794-3451
Tricia McGovern, prin. Fax 794-2469

Bellaire, Antrim, Pop. 1,146
Bellaire SD 400/K-12
204 W Forrest Home Ave 49615 231-533-8141
James Emery, supt. Fax 533-6797
www.bellairepublicschools.com/
Bellaire S 200/K-8
204 W Forrest Home Ave 49615 231-533-8916
Kristi Poel, prin. Fax 533-9214

Belleville, Wayne, Pop. 3,853
Lincoln Consolidated SD
Supt. — See Ypsilanti
Hoffman ES 300/K-5
50700 Willow Rd 48111 734-484-3150
Carol McCoy, prin. Fax 484-3155

Van Buren SD
Supt. — See Ypsilanti
Edgemont ES 500/K-5
125 S Edgemont St 48111 734-697-8002
Karen Mida, prin. Fax 697-6588
Elwell ES 300/K-5
17601 Elwell Rd 48111 734-697-8277
Sandra Peer, prin. Fax 697-6789
Haggerty ES 500/K-5
13770 Haggerty Rd 48111 734-697-8483
Michelle Briegel, prin. Fax 697-6399
North MS 800/6-8
47097 McBride Ave 48111 734-697-9171
Dianne Tilson, prin. Fax 697-6573
Savage ES 500/K-5
42975 Savage Rd 48111 734-699-5050
Aleisha Pitt, prin. Fax 697-6520
South MS 600/6-8
45201 Owen St 48111 734-697-8711
Michelle Herring, prin. Fax 697-6576
Tyler ES 500/K-5
42200 Tyler Rd 48111 734-699-5818
Barbara Santo, prin. Fax 697-6521

Bellevue, Eaton, Pop. 1,375
Bellevue Community SD 500/K-12
201 West St 49021 269-763-9432
Scott Belt, supt. Fax 763-3101
www.bellevue-schools.com/
Bellevue ES 200/K-6
201 West St 49021 269-763-9435
Karyn Hall, prin. Fax 763-3091

Belmont, Kent
Rockford SD
Supt. — See Rockford
Belmont ES 400/K-5
6097 Belmont Ave NE 49306 616-863-6362
William Armitage, prin. Fax 863-6356

Assumption BVM S 200/K-8
6393 Belmont Ave NE 49306 616-361-5483
Michael Miceli, prin. Fax 361-2553

Benton Harbor, Berrien, Pop. 10,749
Benton Harbor Area SD 3,400/PK-12
PO Box 1107 49023 269-605-1000
Carole Schmidt, supt. Fax 605-1010
www.bhas.org
Boynton Montessori Program 200/K-6
1700 E Britain Ave 49022 269-605-1800
Micole Dyson, prin. Fax 605-1803
Britain ES 300/PK-5
209 E Britain Ave 49022 269-605-2000
Larry Gavin, prin. Fax 605-2003
Creative Arts\Gifted & Talented Academy 200/K-5
1995 Union Ave 49022 269-605-1900
Lori Kuntz, prin. Fax 605-1903
Fair Plain Renaissance MS 400/6-8
120 E Napier Ave 49022 269-605-0658
Freddie McGee, prin. Fax 605-1403
Fair Plain West ES 300/K-5
1901 Fairplain Ave 49022 269-605-2200
George Jones, prin. Fax 605-2203
Hull MS 400/6-8
1716 Territorial Rd 49022 269-605-1500
Karen Mitchell, prin. Fax 605-1503

McCord ES 300/K-5
465 S Mccord St 49022 269-605-1600
Stephanie Rockette, prin. Fax 605-1603
Morton ES 300/K-5
267 N Hull Ave 49022 269-605-2500
Greg Mauchmar, prin. Fax 605-2503
Sorter ES 200/K-5
1421 Pipestone Rd 49022 269-605-2600
Andrew Stansberry, prin. Fax 605-2603
Stump ECC PK-PK
1651 Nickerson Ave 49022 269-605-2700
Patricia Robinson, prin. Fax 605-2703

Dowagiac UNSD
Supt. — See Dowagiac
Sister Lakes ES 300/K-5
68701 M 152 49022 269-424-3101
Matt Severin, prin. Fax 944-1811

Brookview S 200/PK-8
501 Zollar Dr 49022 269-925-3544
George Barfield, hdmstr. Fax 925-3525

Benzonia, Benzie, Pop. 476
Benzie County Central SD 2,000/K-12
9222 Homestead Rd 49616 231-882-9654
David Micinski, supt. Fax 882-9121
www.benzie.k12.mi.us
Benzie Central JHS 300/7-8
9300 Homestead Rd 49616 231-882-4498
David Clasen, prin. Fax 882-7627
Crystal Lake ES 200/K-5
7048 Severence St 49616 231-882-4641
Monica Deloney, prin. Fax 882-7829
Other Schools – See Honor, Interlochen, Thompsonville

Berkley, Oakland, Pop. 15,089
Berkley SD
Supt. — See Oak Park
Anderson MS 600/6-8
3205 Catalpa Dr 48072 248-837-8200
Vince Gigliotti, prin. Fax 546-0696
Angell ES 400/K-5
3849 Beverly Blvd 48072 248-837-8500
Chris Sandoval, prin. Fax 546-0848
Pattengill ES 400/K-5
3540 Morrison Ave 48072 248-837-8700
Daryl Robbins, prin. Fax 435-0184
Rogers ES 400/K-5
2265 Hamilton Ave 48072 248-837-8800
S. Lundquist-Schiller, prin. Fax 546-0634

Our Lady of La Salette S 200/PK-8
2219 Coolidge Hwy 48072 248-542-3757
Carol Smith, prin. Fax 582-9787

Berrien Springs, Berrien, Pop. 1,951
Berrien Springs SD 1,600/PK-12
1 Sylvester Ave 49103 269-471-2891
James Bermingham, supt. Fax 471-2590
www.homeoftheshamrocks.org
Berrien Springs MS 400/6-8
1 Sylvester Ave 49103 269-471-2796
Ryan Pesce, prin. Fax 471-2590
Mars ES 300/PK-2
1 Sylvester Ave 49103 269-471-1836
Michael Shembarger, prin. Fax 471-8855
Sylvester ES 300/3-5
1 Sylvester Ave 49103 269-471-7198
Mike Shembarger, prin. Fax 471-8856

Murdoch S 300/K-8
200 Garland Ave 49104 269-471-3225
Sunimal Kulasekere, prin. Fax 471-6115
Trinity Lutheran S 100/PK-8
9123 George Ave 49103 269-473-1811
Deborah Wedde, prin. Fax 473-2322
Village SDA S 200/K-8
409 W Mars St 49103 269-473-5121
John Chen, prin. Fax 473-2830

Bessemer, Gogebic, Pop. 1,957
Bessemer City SD 500/PK-12
301 E Sellar St 49911 906-667-0802
Mark Johnson, supt. Fax 667-0318
www.bessemer.k12.mi.us
Washington ES 200/PK-6
301 E Sellar St 49911 906-663-4515
Gene Goss, prin. Fax 667-0318

Bluff View Christian S 50/K-8
507 E Cinnebar St 49911 906-663-6959
Merrie Hellman, prin.

Beverly Hills, Oakland, Pop. 10,086
Birmingham SD
Supt. — See Birmingham
Berkshire MS 800/6-8
21707 W 14 Mile Rd 48025 248-203-4702
Jim Moll, prin. Fax 203-4802
Beverly ES 300/PK-5
18305 Beverly Rd 48025 248-203-3164
Jennifer Martella, prin. Fax 203-3165
Greenfield ES 300/K-5
31200 Fairfax Ave 48025 248-203-3217
Donald Tobe, prin. Fax 203-3218

Detroit Country Day MS Hillview Campus 400/6-8
22400 Hillview Ln 48025 248-646-7985
Glen Shilling, hdmstr. Fax 646-3459
Our Lady Queen of Martyrs S 300/PK-8
32460 Pierce St 48025 248-642-2616
Peter Ferguson, prin. Fax 642-2713

Big Bay, Marquette
Powell Township SD 50/PK-8
PO Box 160 49808 906-345-9355
Jill Bevins, supt. Fax 345-9936
www.powell.maresa.k12.mi.us
Powell Township S 50/PK-8
PO Box 160 49808 906-345-9355
Jill Bevins, prin. Fax 345-9936

Big Rapids, Mecosta, Pop. 10,704
Big Rapids SD 1,500/PK-12
21034 15 Mile Rd 49307 231-796-2627
Thomas Langdon, supt. Fax 592-0639
www.brps.k12.mi.us
Big Rapids MS 400/5-8
500 N Warren Ave 49307 231-796-9965
Russ Greenleaf, prin. Fax 592-3494
Brookside ES 200/2-4
210 Escott St 49307 231-796-8323
Tim Buckingham, prin. Fax 592-3496
Eastwood ECC 50/PK-1
410 N 3rd Ave 49307 231-796-5556
Marty Aldrich, coord. Fax 592-8502
Riverview ES 100/2-4
509 Willow Ave 49307 231-796-2550
Renee Kent, prin. Fax 592-8501

St. Mary S 100/PK-8
927 Marion Ave 49307 231-796-6731
Barbara Borth, prin. Fax 796-9293
St. Peter's Lutheran S 100/PK-8
408 W Bellevue St 49307 231-796-8782
David Truog, prin. Fax 796-1186

Bingham Farms, Oakland, Pop. 1,012
Birmingham SD
Supt. — See Birmingham
Bingham Farms ES 300/K-5
23400 W 13 Mile Rd 48025 248-203-3350
Russell Facione, prin. Fax 203-3394

Birch Run, Saginaw, Pop. 1,719
Birch Run Area SD 1,800/K-12
12400 Church St 48415 989-624-9307
Wayne Wright, supt. Fax 624-5081
www.birchrun.k12.mi.us
Greene MS 600/5-8
8225 Main St 48415 989-624-5821
Scott Preston, prin. Fax 624-8507
North ES 500/K-4
12440 Church St 48415 989-624-9011
Heidii Periard, prin. Fax 624-8504

Birmingham, Oakland, Pop. 19,081
Birmingham SD 8,000/PK-12
550 W Merrill St 48009 248-203-3000
David Larson, supt. Fax 203-3007
www.birmingham.k12.mi.us
Derby MS 800/6-8
1300 Derby Rd 48009 248-203-5000
Deborah Hubbell, prin. Fax 203-4948
Pierce ES 500/K-5
1829 Pierce St 48009 248-203-4337
James Lalik, prin. Fax 203-4393
Quarton ES 400/K-5
771 Chesterfield Ave 48009 248-203-3428
Jill Ghiardi-Coignet, prin. Fax 203-3425
Other Schools – See Beverly Hills, Bingham Farms, Bloomfield Hls, Troy

---

Eton Academy 200/K-12
1755 E Melton Rd 48009 248-642-1150
Peter Pullen, hdmstr. Fax 642-3670
Holy Name S 400/PK-8
680 Harmon St 48009 248-644-2722
Mary Grady, prin. Fax 644-1191
Our Shepherd Lutheran S 200/PK-8
1658 E Lincoln St 48009 248-645-0551
Janet McLoughlin, prin. Fax 645-2427
Roeper S 200/6-8
1051 Oakland Ave 48009 248-203-7300
Emery Pence, hdmstr. Fax 203-7350

Blanchard, Isabella
Montabella Community SD
Supt. — See Edmore
Montabella ES 300/PK-6
1456 N County Line Rd 49310 989-561-2345
Shelly Millis, prin. Fax 561-5377

Blissfield, Lenawee, Pop. 3,256
Blissfield Community SD 1,200/K-12
630 S Lane St 49228 517-486-2205
Scott Moellenberndt, supt. Fax 486-5701
www.blissfieldschools.us/
Blissfield MS 300/6-8
1305 Beamer Rd 49228 517-486-4420
Mark Willson, prin. Fax 486-4758
South ES 500/K-5
640 S Lane St 49228 517-486-2811
Delinda Crane, prin. Fax 486-3348

Bloomfield Hls, Oakland, Pop. 3,851
Birmingham SD
Supt. — See Birmingham
Birmingham Covington S 600/3-8
1525 Covington Rd, 248-203-4425
Adam Hartley, prin. Fax 203-4433
Harlan ES 300/K-5
3595 N Adams Rd, 248-203-3265
Embekka Thompson, prin. Fax 203-3269
West Maple ES 600/K-5
6275 Inkster Rd, 248-851-2667
Laura Mahler, prin. Fax 203-5109

Bloomfield Hills SD 4,900/PK-12
4175 Andover Rd, 248-341-5400
Steven Gaynor, supt. Fax 341-5449
www.bloomfield.org
Bloomfield Hills MS 500/5-8
4200 Quarton Rd, 248-341-6000
Kaarin Averill, prin. Fax 341-6099
Conant ES 300/PK-4
4100 Quarton Rd, 248-341-7000
Pam Balas, prin. Fax 341-7099
East Hills MS 500/5-8
2800 Kensington Rd, 248-341-6200
Chris Delgado, prin. Fax 341-6299
Eastover ES 300/K-4
1101 Westview Rd, 248-341-7100
Letitia Tappin, prin. Fax 341-7199
Way ES 300/K-4
765 W Long Lake Rd, 248-341-7800
Adam Scher, prin. Fax 341-7899
Other Schools – See Orchard Lake, West Bloomfield

Academy of the Sacred Heart 600/PK-12
1250 Kensington Rd, 248-646-8900
Sr. Bridget Bearss, prin. Fax 646-4143
Cranbrook S 1,600/PK-12
PO Box 801, 248-645-3602
Arlyce Seibert, dir. Fax 645-3524
Detroit Country Day S Maple Road Campus 300/PK-2
3003 W Maple Rd, 248-433-1050
Glen Shilling, hdmstr. Fax 433-3729
Detroit Country Day S Village Campus 200/3-5
3600 Bradway Blvd, 248-647-2522
Glen Shilling, hdmstr. Fax 647-8206
Roeper S 300/PK-5
PO Box 329, 248-203-7300
Randall Dunn, hdmstr. Fax 203-7350
St. Hugo of the Hills S 800/K-8
380 E Hickory Grove Rd, 248-642-6131
Sr. Margaret Van Velzen, prin. Fax 642-4457
St. Regis S 500/K-8
3691 Lincoln Rd, 248-646-2686
Christopher Ciagne, prin. Fax 644-0944

Bloomingdale, Van Buren, Pop. 511
Bloomingdale SD 1,400/K-12
PO Box 217 49026 269-521-3900
Brett Geier, supt. Fax 521-3907
www.bdalecards.org/
Bloomingdale ES 400/K-5
PO Box 217 49026 269-521-3935
Deborah Paquette, prin. Fax 521-3949
Bloomingdale MS 300/6-8
PO Box 217 49026 269-521-3950
Steven Sikkenga, prin. Fax 521-3958
Other Schools – See Pullman

Boon, Wexford
Cadillac Area SD
Supt. — See Cadillac
Forest View ES 300/K-5
7840 S 25 Rd 49618 231-876-5100
Bob Kellogg, prin. Fax 876-5121

Boyne City, Charlevoix, Pop. 3,292
Boyne City SD 1,200/K-12
321 S Park St Ste 1 49712 231-439-8190
Robert Alger, supt. Fax 439-8195
www.boyne.k12.mi.us
Boyne City ES 500/K-4
930 Brockway St 49712 231-439-8300
Fred Sitkins, prin. Fax 439-8251
Boyne City MS 300/5-8
1025 Boyne Ave 49712 231-439-8200
Karen Sherwood, prin. Fax 439-8233

Boyne Falls, Charlevoix, Pop. 347
Boyne Falls SD 300/K-12
PO Box 356 49713 231-549-2211
Gary Urman, supt. Fax 549-2922
www.boynefalls.org
Boyne Falls S 300/K-12
PO Box 356 49713 231-549-2212
Paul Zagata, prin. Fax 549-2922

Breckenridge, Gratiot, Pop. 1,318
Breckenridge Community SD 1,000/K-12
PO Box 217 48615 989-842-3182
Sean McNatt, supt. Fax 842-3625
breck.edzone.net/
Breckenridge ES 400/K-5
PO Box 217 48615 989-842-3182
Kimberly Thompson, prin. Fax 842-5655
Breckenridge MS 200/6-8
PO Box 217 48615 989-842-3182
Sheila Pilmore, prin. Fax 842-3186

Brethren, Manistee
Kaleva Norman Dickson SD 900/K-12
4400 Highbridge Rd 49619 231-477-5353
Michael Matesich, supt. Fax 477-5240
www.knd.k12.mi.us
Brethren MS 100/7-8
4400 Highbridge Rd 49619 231-477-5354
Marlen Cordes, prin. Fax 477-5351
Other Schools – See Kaleva, Wellston

Bridgeport, Saginaw, Pop. 8,569
Bridgeport-Spaulding Community SD 1,900/PK-12
PO Box 657 48722 989-777-1770
Desmon Daniel, supt. Fax 777-4720
www.bscs.k12.mi.us
Bridgeport-Spaulding MS 300/7-8
4221 Bearcat Blvd 48722 989-777-0440
David Hurst, prin. Fax 777-2284
Other Schools – See Saginaw

Bridgeport Baptist Academy 100/K-12
PO Box 249 48722 989-777-6811
John Howell, prin. Fax 777-7376

Bridgman, Berrien, Pop. 2,449
Bridgman SD 1,000/K-12
9964 Gast Rd 49106 269-466-0271
Kevin Ivers, supt. Fax 466-0221
www.bridgmanschools.com
Bridgman ES 300/K-4
3891 Lake St 49106 269-466-0241
John Wittmuss, prin. Fax 466-0248

Reed MS | 300/5-8
10254 California 49106 | 269-465-5410
Lori Graves, prin. | Fax 466-0393

Immanuel Lutheran S | 100/PK-5
PO Box 26 49106 | 269-465-3351
Marie Watson, prin. | Fax 465-6409

Brighton, Livingston, Pop. 7,139
Brighton Area SD | 7,000/K-12
125 S Church St 48116 | 810-299-4000
James Craig, supt. | Fax 299-4092
bas.k12.mi.us/
Hawkins ES | 600/1-5
8900 Lee Rd 48116 | 810-299-3900
Jack Yates, prin. | Fax 299-3910
Hilton ES | 500/1-5
9600 Hilton Rd 48114 | 810-299-3950
Angela Geise, prin. | Fax 299-3960
Hornung ES | 600/1-5
4680 Bauer Rd 48116 | 810-299-4450
Susan Johnson, prin. | Fax 299-4460
Lindbom ES | 500/1-5
1010 State St 48116 | 810-299-4400
Kay Short, prin. | Fax 299-4410
Maltby MS | 800/6-8
4740 Bauer Rd 48116 | 810-299-3600
Scott Brenner, prin. | Fax 299-3610
Miller ECC | 600/K-K
850 Spencer Rd 48116 | 810-299-3800
Kay Nicholas, prin. | Fax 299-3810
Scranton MS | 800/6-8
8415 Maltby Rd 48116 | 810-299-3700
Henry Vecchioni, prin. | Fax 299-3710
Spencer Road ES | 400/K-5
10639 Spencer Rd 48114 | 810-299-4350
Mary Williams, prin. | Fax 299-4360

Hartland Consolidated SD
Supt. — See Howell
Hartland Farms IS | 800/5-6
581 Taylor Rd 48114 | 810-626-2500
Keenan Simpson, prin. | Fax 626-2501
Lakes ES | 400/K-4
687 Taylor Rd 48114 | 810-626-2700
Lindsay Smither, prin. | Fax 626-2701

Cornerstone Christian S | 100/K-8
9455 Hilton Rd 48114 | 810-494-4040
Nancy Brownsey, prin. | Fax 494-4041
Holy Spirit Catholic S | 50/PK-8
9565 Musch Rd 48116 | 810-231-9199
Anna Piccirillo Loewe, prin. | Fax 231-6129
Mapletree Montessori Academy | 100/PK-4
2944 S Old US Highway 23 48114 | 810-225-8321
Patricia Cherry, prin. | Fax 632-3061
St. Patrick S | 400/K-8
1001 Orndorf Dr 48116 | 810-229-7946
Jeanine Kenny, prin. | Fax 229-6206
Shepherd of the Lakes S | 200/PK-5
2101 S Hacker Rd 48114 | 810-227-6473
Ronald Beardsley, prin. | Fax 227-3566

Brimley, Chippewa
Brimley Area SD | 500/K-12
7134 S M 221 49715 | 906-248-3219
Alan Kantola, supt. | Fax 248-3220
www.eup.k12.mi.us/brimley/
Brimley ES | 300/K-6
7134 S M 221 49715 | 906-248-3217
Peter Routhier, prin. | Fax 248-5594

Britton, Lenawee, Pop. 678
Britton-Macon Area SD | 500/K-12
201 College Ave 49229 | 517-451-4581
Charles Pelham, supt. | Fax 451-8595
www.britton-macon.us/
Britton-Macon S | 500/K-12
201 College Ave 49229 | 517-451-4581
John Eisley, prin. | Fax 451-8595

Bronson, Branch, Pop. 2,346
Bronson Community SD | 1,200/K-12
215 W Chicago St 49028 | 517-369-3257
Bob Walter, supt. | Fax 369-2802
www.bronson.k12.mi.us
Anderson ES | 200/K-2
335 E Corey St 49028 | 517-369-3234
Dixie Koenemann, prin. | Fax 369-2190
Chicago Street ES | 200/5-6
501 E Chicago St 49028 | 517-369-3250
Mark Heifner, prin. | Fax 369-2280
Ryan ES | 200/3-4
461 Rudd St 49028 | 517-369-3254
Mark Heifner, prin. | Fax 369-2260

St. Marys Assumption S | 100/PK-8
204 Albers Rd 49028 | 517-369-4625
Sharon Alexander, prin. | Fax 369-1652

Brooklyn, Jackson, Pop. 1,363
Columbia SD | 1,800/K-12
11775 Hewitt Rd 49230 | 517-592-6641
Brent Beamish, supt. | Fax 592-8090
www.columbiaschooldistrict.org
Brooklyn ES | 400/K-5
320 School St 49230 | 517-592-6632
Debra Powell, prin. | Fax 592-3337
Columbia MS | 400/6-8
321 School St 49230 | 517-592-2181
Greg Meschke, prin. | Fax 592-3447
Other Schools – See Cement City

Brown City, Sanilac, Pop. 1,310
Brown City Community SD | 1,100/K-12
PO Box 160 48416 | 810-346-2781
Jerry Steigerwald, supt. | Fax 346-3762
www.bc.k12.mi.us

Brown City ES | 500/K-6
PO Box 160 48416 | 810-346-2781
Douglas Muxlow, prin. | Fax 346-2601

Brownstown, See Flat Rock
Woodhaven-Brownstown SD | 5,200/K-12
24975 Van Horn Rd 48134 | 734-783-3300
Barbara Lott, supt. | Fax 783-3316
www.woodhaven.k12.mi.us
Brownstown MS | 800/6-7
20135 Inkster Rd 48174 | 734-783-3400
Michael Prescott, prin. | Fax 783-3407
Gudith ES | 400/K-5
22700 Sibley Rd, | 734-783-5386
Jackie Pfalzer, prin. | Fax 783-5389
Wegienka ES | 400/K-5
23925 Arsenal Rd 48134 | 734-783-3367
Ann LaPointe, prin. | Fax 783-3372
Other Schools – See Woodhaven

Brownstown Twp, Wayne
Gibraltar SD
Supt. — See Woodhaven
Hunter ES | 400/PK-5
21320 Roche Rd 48183 | 734-379-6390
Els Ferguson, prin. | Fax 379-6391

Buchanan, Berrien, Pop. 4,531
Buchanan Community SD | 1,800/PK-12
401 W Chicago St 49107 | 269-695-8401
Diana Davis, supt. | Fax 695-8450
www.buchananschools.com
Buchanan MS | 400/6-8
610 W 4th St 49107 | 269-695-8406
Mark Kurland, prin. | Fax 695-8459
Moccasin ES | 400/PK-5
410 Moccasin St 49107 | 269-695-8408
Mark Nixon, prin. | Fax 695-8427
Ottawa ES | 300/K-5
109 Ottawa St 49107 | 269-695-8409
Karin Falkenstein, prin. | Fax 695-8426
Stark ES | 200/K-5
502 Claremont St 49107 | 269-695-8407
Karla Hurlbutt, prin. | Fax 695-8436

Buckley, Wexford, Pop. 565
Buckley Community SD | 400/K-12
PO Box 38 49620 | 231-269-3325
Steve Prissel, supt. | Fax 269-3833
www.buckleyschools.com
Buckley Community S | 400/K-12
PO Box 38 49620 | 231-269-3325
Todd Kulawiak, prin. | Fax 269-3833

Burr Oak, Saint Joseph, Pop. 771
Burr Oak Community SD | 300/K-12
PO Box 337 49030 | 269-489-2213
Terry Conklin, supt. | Fax 489-5198
www.remc12.k12.mi.us/burr-oak/
Burr Oak ES | 100/K-6
PO Box 337 49030 | 269-489-5181
Raymond Bohm, prin. | Fax 489-5198

Burt, Saginaw, Pop. 1,169
Chesaning UNSD
Supt. — See Chesaning
Albee ES | 200/K-4
11540 Bueche Rd 48417 | 989-770-4600
Colleen Nixon, prin. | Fax 770-4641

Burton, Genesee, Pop. 30,916
Atherton Community SD | 1,000/K-12
3354 S Genesee Rd 48519 | 810-591-9182
Mark Madden, supt. | Fax 591-1926
www.athertonschools.org
Atherton MS | 300/4-8
3444 S Genesee Rd 48519 | 810-591-0604
Jamie Johnston, prin. | Fax 591-9456
Van Y ES | 300/K-3
2400 Clarice Ave 48519 | 810-591-0850
Robert Steinhaus, prin. | Fax 591-9191

Bendle SD | 1,100/PK-12
3420 Columbine Ave 48529 | 810-591-2501
John Angle, supt. | Fax 591-2210
www.bendleschools.org
Bendle MS | 300/6-8
2294 E Bristol Rd 48529 | 810-591-3385
Scott Williams, prin. | Fax 591-2540
South Bendle ES | 200/PK-2
4341 Larkin Dr 48529 | 810-591-0620
John Krolewski, prin. | Fax 591-2520
West Bendle ES | 300/3-5
4020 Cerdan Dr 48529 | 810-591-0880
Tom Meszaros, prin. | Fax 591-9011

Bentley Community SD | 700/K-12
1170 N Belsay Rd 48509 | 810-591-9100
John Schantz, supt. | Fax 591-9102
www.bentleyschools.org/bentleycs/site/default.asp
Barhitte ES | 300/K-6
6080 Roberta St 48509 | 810-591-9661
Debra McCollum, prin. | Fax 591-9198

Carman-Ainsworth Community SD
Supt. — See Flint
Dillon ES | 300/K-3
1197 E Schumacher St 48529 | 810-591-3590
Gina Ryan, prin. | Fax 591-3835

Kearsley Community SD
Supt. — See Flint
Weston ES | 200/K-1
2499 Cashin St 48509 | 810-591-8483
Doris Goetz, prin. | Fax 591-8485

Faithway Christian S | 200/PK-12
1225 S Center Rd 48509 | 810-743-0055
Gail Scott, admin. | Fax 743-0033
Genesee Christian S | 400/PK-12
1223 S Belsay Rd 48509 | 810-743-3108
Robert Buchalski, prin. | Fax 743-3230

Good Shepherd Lutheran S | 50/K-8
5496 Lippincott Blvd 48519 | 810-742-1131
David Backus, prin. | Fax 742-9907
St. Thomas More Academy | 100/K-12
6456 E Bristol Rd 48519 | 810-742-2411
Dan Le Blanc, prin. | Fax 742-4803
Valley Christian Academy | 200/PK-12
3266 S Genesee Rd 48519 | 810-742-4500
Sam Pace, admin. | Fax 742-4537

Byron, Shiawassee, Pop. 582
Byron Area SD | 1,300/K-12
312 W Maple St 48418 | 810-266-4881
Daniel Scow, supt. | Fax 266-5723
www.byron.k12.mi.us
Byron ES | 600/K-5
401 E Maple St 48418 | 810-266-4671
Penny Kentish-McWilliams, prin. | Fax 266-5011
Byron MS | 300/6-8
312 W Maple St 48418 | 810-266-4422
Steve Vowles, prin. | Fax 266-4151

Byron Center, Kent
Byron Center SD | 2,900/K-12
8542 Byron Center Ave SW 49315 | 616-878-6100
Daniel Takens, supt. | Fax 878-6120
www.bcpsk12.net
Brown ES | 300/K-4
8064 Byron Center Ave SW 49315 | 616-878-6200
Barb Johnson, prin. | Fax 878-6220
Byron Center West MS | 500/7-8
8654 Homerich Ave SW 49315 | 616-878-6500
Mike Spahr, prin. | Fax 878-6520
Countryside ES | 300/K-4
8200 Eastern Ave SE 49315 | 616-878-6900
Carla Kauffman, prin. | Fax 878-6920
Marshall ES | 400/K-4
1756 64th St SW 49315 | 616-531-6300
Kevin Macina, prin. | Fax 878-6320
Nickels IS | 500/5-6
8638 Byron Center Ave SW 49315 | 616-878-6400
Thomas Trout, prin. | Fax 878-6420

Wayland UNSD | 2,800/K-12
500 100th St SW 49315 | 269-792-2181
Eivor Swan, supt. | Fax 877-0520
web.wayland.k12.mi.us/wus
Other Schools – See Dorr, Wayland

Byron Center Christian S | 400/PK-8
8840 Byron Center Ave SW 49315 | 616-878-3347
Glen Hendricks, prin. | Fax 878-0019
St. Mary's Visitation S | 100/PK-6
2455 146th Ave SW 49315 | 616-681-9607
Gail Lewis, prin. | Fax 681-9919
Zion Christian S | 200/PK-12
7555 Byron Center Ave SW 49315 | 616-878-9472
Tom Kwekel, prin. | Fax 878-9473

Cadillac, Wexford, Pop. 10,167
Cadillac Area SD | 3,300/K-12
421 S Mitchell St 49601 | 231-876-5000
Paul Liabenow, supt. | Fax 876-5021
www.vikingnet.org
Franklin ES | 300/K-5
505 Lester St 49601 | 231-876-5200
Joy Beth Hicks, prin. | Fax 876-5221
Kenwood ES | 300/K-5
1700 Chestnut St 49601 | 231-876-5300
James Hunt, prin. | Fax 876-5321
Lincoln ES | 200/K-5
125 Ayer St 49601 | 231-876-5400
Scott Hanson, prin. | Fax 876-5421
Mackinaw Trail MS | 500/6-7
8401 Mackinaw Trl 49601 | 231-876-5600
Andy Brown, prin. | Fax 876-5621
McKinley ES | 200/K-5
601 E North St 49601 | 231-876-5500
Jennifer Wilhelm, prin. | Fax 876-5521
Other Schools – See Boon

Cadillac Heritage Christian S | 100/PK-12
1706 Wright St 49601 | 231-775-4272
William Goodwill, admin. | Fax 775-2999
Northview SDA S | 50/1-8
202 N Carmel St 49601 | 231-775-3622
Lanette Brandow, prin. | Fax 775-6233
St. Ann S | 200/PK-7
800 W 13th St 49601 | 231-775-1301
R. Craig King, prin. | Fax 775-0161

Caledonia, Kent, Pop. 1,278
Caledonia Community SD | 3,700/PK-12
9753 Duncan Lake Ave SE 49316 | 616-891-8185
Jerry Phillips, supt. | Fax 891-9253
www.caledonia.k12.mi.us
Caledonia ES | 400/PK-5
9770 Duncan Lake Ave SE 49316 | 616-891-8181
Randy Rodriguez, prin. | Fax 891-7019
Duncan Lake ECC | 50/PK-PK
9751 Duncan Lake Ave SE 49316 | 616-891-6220
Janel Switzer, prin. | Fax 891-6229
Duncan Lake MS | 400/6-8
9757 Duncan Lake Ave SE 49316 | 616-891-1380
Cheryl Davis, prin. | Fax 891-0833
Dutton ES | 400/PK-5
3820 68th St SE 49316 | 616-698-8982
Darrell Kingsbury, prin. | Fax 698-2117
Emmons Lake ES | 400/K-5
8950 Kraft Ave SE 49316 | 616-528-8100
Tony Silveri, prin. | Fax 528-8104
Kraft Meadows MS | 400/6-8
9230 Kraft Ave SE 49316 | 616-891-8649
Brian Leatherman, prin. | Fax 891-7013
Other Schools – See Alto

Kentwood SD
Supt. — See Kentwood
Explorer ES 500/K-5
2307 68th St SE 49316 616-554-0302
Donald Dahlquist, prin. Fax 554-0970

Dutton Christian S 500/PK-8
6729 Hanna Lake Ave SE 49316 616-698-8660
Daniel Netz, admin. Fax 698-2281

Calumet, Houghton, Pop. 812
Calumet-Laurium-Keweenaw SD 1,500/K-12
57070 Mine St 49913 906-337-0311
Darryl Pierce, supt. Fax 337-1406
clkschools.org
CLK ES 600/K-5
57070 Mine St 49913 906-337-0311
Karyn King, prin. Fax 337-5408
Washington MS 300/6-8
57070 Mine St 49913 906-337-0311
Michael Steber, prin. Fax 337-5406

Camden, Hillsdale, Pop. 542
Camden-Frontier SD 600/K-12
4971 W Montgomery Rd 49232 517-368-5991
Wendy Moore, supt. Fax 368-5959
www.cfss.org/
Camden Frontier ES 300/K-5
4971 W Montgomery Rd 49232 517-368-5258
Wendy Moore, prin. Fax 368-5950
Camden Frontier MS 100/6-8
4971 W Montgomery Rd 49232 517-368-5255
Mark Hubbard, prin. Fax 368-5950

Canton, Wayne, Pop. 81,500
Plymouth-Canton Community SD
Supt. — See Plymouth
Bentley ES 500/K-5
1100 S Sheldon Rd 48188 734-397-6360
Jerold Meier, prin. Fax 397-6347
Discovery MS 1,000/6-8
45083 Hanford Rd 48187 734-416-2880
Roche LaVictor, prin. Fax 416-2895
Dodson ES 600/K-5
205 N Beck Rd 48187 734-981-8003
Dan Carr, prin. Fax 981-9202
Eriksson ES 500/K-5
1275 N Haggerty Rd 48187 734-981-5560
Kevin Learned, prin. Fax 981-2740
Field ES 600/K-5
1000 S Haggerty Rd 48188 734-397-6330
Peter Kudlak, prin. Fax 397-6334
Gallimore ES 500/K-5
8375 N Sheldon Rd 48187 734-416-3150
Kimberly May, prin. Fax 416-7670
Hoben ES 500/K-5
44680 Saltz Rd 48187 734-981-8670
Dr. E. Vartanian-Gibbs, prin. Fax 981-7405
Hulsing ES 400/K-5
8055 Fleet St 48187 734-416-6150
Carolyn Washington, prin. Fax 455-9530
Miller ES 300/K-5
43721 Hanford Rd 48187 734-416-4800
Lynn Haire, prin. Fax 416-4801
Tonda ES 600/K-5
46501 Warren Rd 48187 734-416-6100
Kurt Tyszkiewicz, prin. Fax 416-2018
Workman ES 700/K-5
250 N Denton Rd 48187 734-582-6705
Dr. James Burt, prin. Fax 844-6526

Wayne-Westland Community SD
Supt. — See Westland
Walker-Winter ES 400/K-5
39932 Michigan Ave 48188 734-419-2780
Pauline Koulouberis, prin. Fax 595-2578

Agape Christian Academy 200/PK-12
PO Box 87770 48187 734-394-0357
Mark Moore, prin. Fax 394-0206
All Saints S 600/PK-8
48735 Warren Rd 48187 734-459-2490
Debrah Davidson, prin. Fax 459-0981
Crescent Academy International 400/PK-8
40440 Palmer Rd 48188 734-729-1000
Sommieh Uddin, prin. Fax 729-1004
Plymouth Christian Academy 600/PK-12
43065 Joy Rd 48187 734-459-3505
Dr. David Butler, hdmstr. Fax 459-9997
St. Michael Christian S 50/PK-3
7000 N Sheldon Rd 48187 734-459-9720
Karolynn O'Neill, prin. Fax 459-2311
Schoolhouse Montessori - Canton 100/PK-3
6215 N Canton Center Rd 48187 734-416-1849
Lisa Ahwal, prin.

Capac, Saint Clair, Pop. 2,233
Capac Community SD 1,600/PK-12
403 N Glassford St 48014 810-395-4321
Jerry Jennex, supt. Fax 395-4858
www.capac.k12.mi.us
Capac ES 500/PK-4
351 W Kempf Ct 48014 810-395-3636
Kathy Kish, prin. Fax 395-8086
Capac MS 400/5-7
201 N Neeper St 48014 810-395-3750
Matthew Drake, prin. Fax 395-4098

Carleton, Monroe, Pop. 2,874
Airport Community SD 3,200/PK-12
11270 Grafton Rd 48117 734-654-2414
Henry Schafer, supt. Fax 654-3424
www.acspublic.com/
Eyler ES 300/PK-5
1335 Carleton Rockwood Rd 48117 734-654-2121
Douglas Monthei, prin. Fax 654-9535
Sterling ES 300/K-5
160 Fessner Rd 48117 734-654-6846
Leslie Varsogea, prin. Fax 654-9480

Wagar MS 800/6-8
11200 Grafton Rd 48117 734-654-6205
Josephine Brish, prin. Fax 654-0057
Other Schools – See Newport, South Rockwood

St. Patrick S 100/K-8
2970 W Labo Rd 48117 734-654-2522
Ruth Meiring, prin. Fax 654-8532

Carney, Menominee, Pop. 220
Carney-Nadeau SD 300/K-12
PO Box 68 49812 906-639-2000
Steven Martin, supt. Fax 639-2176
www.cnps.us
Carney-Nadeau S 300/K-12
PO Box 68 49812 906-639-2171
Steven Martin, prin. Fax 639-2176

Caro, Tuscola, Pop. 4,193
Caro Community SD 1,900/K-12
301 N Hooper St 48723 989-673-3160
Neil Beckwith, supt. Fax 673-6248
www.caro.k12.mi.us
Caro MS 500/6-8
299 N Hooper St 48723 989-673-3167
JoAnn Nordstrom, prin. Fax 673-1225
McComb ES 300/K-2
303 N Hooper St 48723 989-673-3169
David Wheeler, prin. Fax 673-3883
Schall ES 500/3-5
325 E Frank St 48723 989-673-3168
Susan Chambers, prin. Fax 672-4684

Carson City, Montcalm, Pop. 1,197
Carson City-Crystal Area SD 1,100/K-12
PO Box 780 48811 989-584-3138
Robert Swanson, supt. Fax 584-3539
www.carsoncity.k12.mi.us
Carson City ES 300/K-5
PO Box 780 48811 989-584-3130
Jan Ellis, prin. Fax 584-6612
Carson City MS 300/6-8
PO Box 780 48811 989-584-3903
Charles Larkins, prin. Fax 584-3259
Other Schools – See Crystal

Carsonville, Sanilac, Pop. 493
Carsonville-Port Sanilac SD 600/K-12
100 N Goetze Rd 48419 810-657-9393
Harold Titus, supt. Fax 657-9060
www.carsport.k12.mi.us
Carsonville-Port Sanilac ES 300/K-6
4115 E Chandler St 48419 810-657-9318
Brenda Cutler, prin. Fax 657-8966

Casco, Saint Clair
Anchor Bay SD 6,400/K-12
5201 County Line Rd Ste 100 48064 586-725-2861
Leonard Woodside, supt. Fax 725-0290
www.anchorbay.misd.net
MacDonald ES 200/K-5
5201 County Line Rd 48064 586-648-2522
Sherri Milton-Hoffman, prin. Fax 727-0967
Other Schools – See Chesterfield, Ira, New Baltimore

Caseville, Huron, Pop. 887
Caseville SD 100/K-12
PO Box 1068 48725 989-856-2940
Dr. Dan Tighe, supt. Fax 856-3095
www.caseville.k12.mi.us
Caseville S 100/K-12
PO Box 1068 48725 989-856-7192
Ken Ewald, prin. Fax 856-8641

Cass City, Tuscola, Pop. 2,606
Cass City SD 1,300/PK-12
4868 Seeger St 48726 989-872-2200
Ronald Wilson, supt. Fax 872-5015
www.casscity.k12.mi.us
Campbell ES 400/PK-4
6627 Rose St 48726 989-872-2158
Aaron Fernald, prin. Fax 872-3910
Cass City MS 500/5-8
4805 Ale St 48726 989-872-4397
Jeff Hartel, prin. Fax 872-2990

Cassopolis, Cass, Pop. 1,840
Cassopolis SD 1,000/K-12
63700 Brick Church Rd 49031 269-445-0500
Gregory Weatherspoon, supt. Fax 445-0505
www.cassopolis.k12.mi.us
Adams ES 400/3-6
101 S East St 49031 269-445-0530
Dee Melville-Voss, prin. Fax 445-0521
Squires Early ES 200/K-2
725 Center St 49031 269-445-0516
Tracy Hertsel, prin. Fax 445-8857

Calvin Center SDA S 50/1-8
19084 Brownsville Rd 49031 269-476-2218
Norman Usher, prin. Fax 476-2614

Cedar Lake, Montcalm

Cedar Lake SDA S 100/K-8
PO Box 218 48812 989-427-5614
Karen Gotshall, prin. Fax 427-0012

Cedar Springs, Kent, Pop. 3,234
Cedar Springs SD 3,600/PK-12
204 E Muskegon St 49319 616-696-1204
Fax 696-3755
www.csredhawks.org
Cedar Springs ES Beach Campus 400/2-4
204 E Muskegon St 49319 616-696-0350
Jane Hendrickson, prin. Fax 696-3182
Cedar Springs ES Cedar View Campus 700/2-4
204 E Muskegon St 49319 616-696-9102
Anne Kostus, prin. Fax 696-3177

Cedar Springs MS 500/7-8
204 E Muskegon St 49319 616-696-9100
Ken See, prin. Fax 696-3109
Cedar Trails ES 300/PK-1
204 E Muskegon St 49319 616-696-9884
Jennifer Harper, prin. Fax 696-3104
Red Hawk ES 500/5-6
204 E Muskegon St 49319 616-696-7330
Mike Duffy, prin. Fax 696-3123

Cedarville, Mackinac
Les Cheneaux Community SD 300/K-12
PO Box 366 49719 906-484-2256
Rod Goehmann, supt. Fax 484-2072
eup.k12.mi.us/les_cheneaux
Cedarville ES 100/K-5
PO Box 366 49719 906-484-2256
Amy Scott, prin. Fax 484-7811

Cement City, Jackson, Pop. 440
Columbia SD
Supt. — See Brooklyn
Miller ES 400/K-5
130 Jackson St 49233 517-592-2157
Geoffrey Bontrager, prin. Fax 592-3432

Center Line, Macomb, Pop. 8,308
Center Line SD 2,600/PK-12
26400 Arsenal 48015 586-510-2000
Terry Follbaum, supt. Fax 510-2019
www.clps.org
Miller ES 300/K-5
23855 Lawrence 48015 586-510-2500
Barbara Klimek, prin. Fax 510-2509
Wolfe MS 700/6-8
8640 McKinley 48015 586-510-2300
Amy Maruca, prin. Fax 510-2319
Other Schools – See Warren

St. Clement S 200/PK-8
8155 Ritter 48015 586-757-7500
Michelle Shepard, prin. Fax 757-4724

Central Lake, Antrim, Pop. 988
Central Lake SD 400/K-12
PO Box 128 49622 231-544-3141
Steve Paliewicz, supt. Fax 544-2903
clps.k12.mi.us
Central Lake ES 200/K-5
PO Box 128 49622 231-544-5221
Todd Derenzy, prin. Fax 544-6061

Centreville, Saint Joseph, Pop. 1,555
Centreville SD 1,000/K-12
PO Box 158 49032 269-467-5220
William Miller, supt. Fax 467-5226
cpschools.org
Centreville ES 500/K-6
PO Box 158 49032 269-467-5200
Becky Stauffer, prin. Fax 467-5209
Centreville MS 200/7-8
PO Box 158 49032 269-467-5205
Barbara Lester, prin. Fax 467-4864

Charlevoix, Charlevoix, Pop. 2,776
Charlevoix SD 1,100/K-12
104 E Saint Marys Dr 49720 231-547-3200
Chet Janik, supt. Fax 547-0556
www.rayder.net
Charlevoix ES 300/K-4
13513 Division Ave 49720 231-547-3215
Richard Swenor, prin. Fax 547-3150
Charlevoix MS 400/5-8
108 E Garfield Ave 49720 231-547-3206
Keith Haske, prin. Fax 547-3244

St. Mary S 100/PK-6
1005 Bridge St 49720 231-547-9441
Keisha Veryser, prin. Fax 547-6658

Charlotte, Eaton, Pop. 9,069
Charlotte SD 2,900/K-12
378 State St 48813 517-541-5100
Nancy Hipskind, supt. Fax 541-5105
www.charlottenet.org
Charlotte MS 1,000/5-8
1068 Carlisle Hwy 48813 517-541-5700
Wayne Brown, prin. Fax 541-5705
Galewood ES 200/K-4
512 E Lovett St 48813 517-541-5770
Fax 541-5775
Parkview ES 300/K-4
301 E Kalamo Hwy 48813 517-543-5780
Kim Caudell, prin. Fax 541-5785
Washington ES 300/K-4
525 High St 48813 517-541-5170
Therese Edwards, prin. Fax 541-5175

Charlotte SDA S 50/1-8
1510 S Cochran Rd 48813 517-543-9491
Ben Zork, prin.
St. Mary S 100/K-5
905 Saint Marys Blvd 48813 517-543-3460
Mary Beecy, prin. Fax 543-9798

Chassell, Houghton
Chassell Township SD 300/K-12
PO Box 140 49916 906-523-4691
Michael Gaunt, supt. Fax 523-4969
www.cts.k12.mi.us/
Chassell Township S 300/K-12
PO Box 140 49916 906-523-4491
George Stockero, prin. Fax 523-4969

Cheboygan, Cheboygan, Pop. 5,191
Cheboygan Area SD 1,700/K-12
504 Division St 49721 231-627-4436
Dan Bauer, supt. Fax 627-9105
www.cheboygan.k12.mi.us/

Cheboygan MS 500/5-8
905 W Lincoln Ave 49721 231-627-7103
Mark Dombroski, prin. Fax 627-4151
East ES 300/2-4
440 Garfield Ave 49721 231-627-5211
Sandra Jeannotte, prin. Fax 627-5211
West ES 100/K-1
512 Pine St 49721 231-627-2362
Cathleen Stone, prin. Fax 627-2362

Bishop Baraga S 200/PK-8
623 W Lincoln Ave 49721 231-627-5608
Kitty LeBlance, prin. Fax 627-6048
Cornerstone Christian S 50/PK-8
900 S Western Ave 49721 231-627-2160
Sally Agee, admin. Fax 627-2360

Chelsea, Washtenaw, Pop. 4,801
Chelsea SD 2,600/K-12
500 Washington St 48118 734-433-2200
David Killips, supt. Fax 433-2218
www.chelsea.k12.mi.us
Beach MS 400/7-8
445 Mayer Dr 48118 734-433-2202
Patrick Little, prin. Fax 433-2212
North Creek ES 400/K-2
699 McKinley St 48118 734-433-2203
Marcus Kaemming, prin. Fax 433-2213
Pierce Lake ES 400/3-4
275 N Freer Rd 48118 734-433-2204
Lucille Stieber, prin. Fax 433-2214
South Meadows ES 400/5-6
335 Pierce St 48118 734-433-2205
Lisa Nickel, prin. Fax 433-2215

Chesaning, Saginaw, Pop. 2,463
Chesaning UNSD 1,900/K-12
PO Box 95 48616 989-845-7020
Donald Barnes, supt. Fax 845-3722
www.chesaningschools.net
Big Rock ES 400/K-4
920 E Broad St 48616 989-845-2430
Jan Krause, prin. Fax 845-5872
Chesaning MS 600/5-8
431 N 4th St 48616 989-845-7040
Michael McGough, prin. Fax 845-5335
Other Schools – See Burt, Oakley

Our Lady of Perpetual Help S 100/PK-8
802 Lockwood St 48616 989-845-6338
Keith Valentine, prin. Fax 845-6338
Zion Evangelical Lutheran S 50/PK-8
796 Hampton St 48616 989-845-2377
Paul Jacobs, prin. Fax 845-5699

Chesterfield, Macomb
Anchor Bay SD
Supt. — See Casco
Great Oaks ES 500/K-5
32900 24 Mile Rd 48047 586-725-2038
Kathy Elias, prin. Fax 725-4014

L'Anse Creuse SD
Supt. — See Harrison Township
Carkenord ES 500/K-5
27100 24 Mile Rd 48051 586-493-5230
Sara O'Hara, prin. Fax 493-5235
Chesterfield ES 400/K-5
25925 23 Mile Rd 48051 586-493-5240
Susan Strickler, prin. Fax 493-5245
Green ES 500/K-5
47260 Sugarbush Rd 48047 586-493-5280
Eileen Hielscher, prin. Fax 493-5285
Higgins ES 500/PK-5
29901 24 Mile Rd 48051 586-493-5210
Wayne Wrona, prin. Fax 493-5215
L'Anse Creuse MS East 800/6-8
30300 Hickey Rd 48051 586-493-5200
Mike VanCamp, prin. Fax 493-5205

Clare, Clare, Pop. 3,233
Clare SD 1,400/PK-12
201 E State St 48617 989-386-9945
Greg McMillan, supt. Fax 386-6055
www.clare.k12.mi.us/
Clare ES 400/PK-4
201 E State St 48617 989-386-3438
Jeanie Mishler, prin. Fax 386-1215
Clare MS 500/5-8
201 E State St 48617 989-386-9979
Steve Newkirk, prin. Fax 386-4008

St. Cecilia S 100/PK-6
106 E Wheaton Ave 48617 989-386-9862
Kyle Welter, prin. Fax 386-3550

Clarkston, Oakland, Pop. 980
Clarkston Community SD 7,900/PK-12
6389 Clarkston Rd 48346 248-623-5400
Albert Roberts, supt. Fax 623-5450
ww2.clarkston.k12.mi.us/
Bailey Lake ES 500/K-5
8051 Pine Knob Rd 48348 248-623-5300
Glenn Gualtieri, prin. Fax 623-5305
Clarkston ES 400/K-5
6589 Waldon Rd 48346 248-623-5100
Dana Pennanen, prin. Fax 623-5144
Independence ES 600/K-5
6850 Hubbard Rd 48348 248-623-5500
Chris Turner, prin. Fax 623-5554
North Sashabaw ES 400/K-5
5290 Maybee Rd 48346 248-623-4100
Debra Latozas, prin. Fax 623-4105
Pine Knob ES 500/K-5
6020 Sashabaw Rd 48346 248-623-3900
Valerie Grimes, prin. Fax 623-3905
Sashabaw MS 1,200/6-7
5565 Pine Knob Rd 48346 248-623-4200
Linda Foran, prin. Fax 623-4205

Springfield Plains ES 600/PK-5
8650 Holcomb Rd 48348 248-623-3800
K.C. Leh, prin. Fax 623-3805
Other Schools – See Davisburg

Cedarcrest Academy 200/PK-8
8970 Dixie Hwy 48348 248-625-7270
Bette Moen, dir. Fax 625-7212
Everest Academy 400/PK-8
5935 Clarkston Rd 48348 248-620-3390
Richard Copland, prin. Fax 620-3942
Oakland Christian S 100/PK-3
6300 Clarkston Rd 48346 248-625-1324
Erin Akers, prin. Fax 625-7406
Springfield Christian Academy 100/K-12
8585 Dixie Hwy 48348 248-625-9760
Patrick Wagner, dir. Fax 625-9640

Clarksville, Ionia, Pop. 318
Lakewood SD
Supt. — See Lake Odessa
Clarksville ES 100/K-5
PO Box 110 48815 616-693-2175
Cindy Trebian, prin. Fax 693-3302

Clawson, Oakland, Pop. 12,337
Clawson SD 1,500/K-12
626 Phillips Ave 48017 248-655-4400
Cheryl Rogers, supt. Fax 655-4422
www.clawson.k12.mi.us
Clawson MS 300/6-8
150 John M Ave 48017 248-655-4250
John Dickinson, prin. Fax 655-4251
Kenwood ES 200/K-5
240 Nahma Ave 48017 248-655-3838
Virginia Mantela, prin. Fax 655-3802
Schalm ES 500/K-5
940 N Selfridge Blvd 48017 248-655-4949
Patricia Pell, prin. Fax 655-4947

Guardian Angels S 300/K-8
521 E 14 Mile Rd 48017 248-588-5545
Sharon Hammerschmidt, prin. Fax 589-7356

Climax, Kalamazoo, Pop. 748
Climax-Scotts Community SD 600/K-12
372 S Main St 49034 269-746-2400
Douglas Newington, supt. Fax 746-4374
www.csschools.net
Other Schools – See Scotts

Clinton, Lenawee, Pop. 2,354
Clinton Community SD 1,000/K-12
341 E Michigan Ave 49236 517-456-6501
David Pray, supt. Fax 456-4324
www.clinton.k12.mi.us/
Clinton ES 500/K-5
200 E Franklin St 49236 517-456-6504
Marcia Wright, prin. Fax 456-8201
Clinton MS 200/6-8
100 E Franklin St 49236 517-456-6507
Donald Dunham, prin. Fax 456-4997

Clinton Township, Macomb, Pop. 95,648
Chippewa Valley SD 13,000/K-12
19120 Cass Ave 48038 586-723-2000
Mark Deldin, supt. Fax 723-2001
www.chippewavalleyschools.org
Algonquin MS 600/6-8
19150 Briarwood Ln 48036 586-723-3500
Walter Kozlowski, prin. Fax 723-3501
Cherokee ES 600/K-5
42900 Rivergate Dr 48038 586-723-4800
Pamela Jones, prin. Fax 723-4801
Erie ES 500/K-5
42276 Romeo Plank Rd 48038 586-723-5400
Dr. Gerard Evanski, prin. Fax 723-5401
Huron ES 400/K-5
15800 Terra Bella St 48038 586-723-5800
J. Scott Burns, prin. Fax 723-5801
Miami ES 400/K-5
41290 Kentvale Dr 48038 586-723-6000
Craig Bulgrin, prin. Fax 723-6001
Ottawa ES 400/K-5
18601 Millar Rd 48036 586-723-6600
Duane Lockhart, prin. Fax 723-6601
Wyandot MS 600/6-8
39490 Garfield Rd 48038 586-723-4200
Darleen Sims, prin. Fax 723-4201
Other Schools – See Macomb, Mount Clemens

Clintondale Community SD 3,500/PK-12
35100 Little Mack Ave 48035 586-791-6300
George Sassin, supt. Fax 790-7643
www.clintondale.k12.mi.us
Clintondale MS 600/6-8
35300 Little Mack Ave 48035 586-791-6300
Don Sikora, prin. Fax 790-7642
McGlinnen ES 400/K-5
21415 Sunnyview St 48035 586-791-3400
Cathy LaMont, prin. Fax 790-7639
Parker ES 400/PK-5
22055 Quinn Rd 48035 586-791-6900
Karen Hessler, prin. Fax 790-7641
Rainbow ES 200/K-5
33749 Wurfel St 48035 586-791-3500
Simonne Silage, prin. Fax 790-7640

Fraser SD
Supt. — See Fraser
Disney ES 300/K-6
36155 Kelly Rd 48035 586-439-6400
Jennifer McGuire, prin. Fax 439-6401
Salk ES 500/K-6
17601 15 Mile Rd 48035 586-439-6800
Denis Metty, prin. Fax 439-6801

L'Anse Creuse SD
Supt. — See Harrison Township
Tenniswood ES 400/K-5
23450 Glenwood St 48035 586-493-5640
Karen Nelson, prin. Fax 493-5645

Faith Christian S 200/PK-12
23130 Remick Dr 48036 586-783-9630
Matt Fenton, prin. Fax 783-9628
St. Luke Lutheran S 200/PK-8
21400 S Nunneley Rd 48035 586-791-1151
David Kleimola, prin. Fax 791-1591
St. Thecla S 400/K-8
20762 S Nunneley Rd 48035 586-791-2170
Sr. M. Kathleen White, prin. Fax 791-2356
Trinity Lutheran S 200/PK-8
38900 Harper Ave 48036 586-468-8511
Gordon Kennedy, prin. Fax 468-1226

Clio, Genesee, Pop. 2,619
Clio Area SD 3,500/PK-12
430 N Mill St 48420 810-591-0500
Fay Latture, supt. Fax 591-0140
www.clioschools.org
Carter MS 1,100/5-8
300 Upland Dr 48420 810-591-0503
Neil Bedell, prin. Fax 591-8148
Edgerton ES 400/K-4
11218 N Linden Rd 48420 810-591-7650
Eileen Kerr, prin. Fax 591-8162
Garner ES 400/K-4
10271 N Clio Rd 48420 810-591-1871
Michael Lytle, prin. Fax 591-8163
Lacure ES 500/PK-4
12167 N Lewis Rd 48420 810-591-1950
John Lanyi, prin. Fax 591-8168

Coldwater, Branch, Pop. 10,783
Coldwater Community SD 3,200/PK-12
401 Sauk River Dr 49036 517-279-5910
Dr. Dale Martin, supt. Fax 279-7651
www.coldwaterschools.org/
Jefferson ES 400/K-5
255 N Clay St 49036 517-279-5970
Douglas Bower, prin. Fax 279-2332
Lakeland ES 300/PK-5
519 Otis Rd 49036 517-238-2105
Seth Parker, prin. Fax 238-4022
Larsen ES 400/PK-5
25 Parkhurst Ave 49036 517-279-5960
Audrey Burgher, prin. Fax 279-2516
Legg MS 800/6-8
175 Green St 49036 517-279-5940
Terry Emery, prin. Fax 279-5945
Lincoln ES 300/PK-5
70 Tibbits St 49036 517-279-5975
James Garnett, prin. Fax 279-5977

St. Charles S 100/PK-5
79 Harrison St 49036 517-279-0404
Carlene Sosinski, prin. Fax 278-0505
St. Paul Lutheran S 50/PK-5
95 W State St 49036 517-278-8061
Karen Quade, prin. Fax 279-6232
Woodland SDA S 50/1-9
128 E Barnhart Rd 49036 517-278-4650
Catherine Buell, prin. Fax 639-3995

Coleman, Midland, Pop. 1,266
Coleman Community SD 700/K-12
PO Box 522 48618 989-465-6060
Keely Mounger, supt. Fax 465-9853
www.colemanschools.net
Coleman ES 400/K-6
PO Box 522 48618 989-465-6179
Mary Jo Fachting, prin. Fax 465-9852

Coloma, Berrien, Pop. 1,524
Coloma Community SD 1,800/PK-12
PO Box 550 49038 269-468-2424
Terry Ann Boguth, supt. Fax 468-2440
www.ccs.coloma.org
Coloma ES 200/2-4
PO Box 550 49038 269-468-2420
Daryl Ost, prin. Fax 468-2434
Coloma MS 500/5-7
PO Box 550 49038 269-468-2415
Scott Pauley, prin. Fax 468-2445
Little Learners Preschool 50/PK-PK
PO Box 550 49038 269-468-2430
Victoria Born, dir. Fax 468-2436
Washington ES 100/PK-1
PO Box 550 49038 269-468-2430
William Dygert, prin. Fax 468-2436

Colon, Saint Joseph, Pop. 1,189
Colon Community SD 800/K-12
400 Dallas St 49040 269-432-3442
Lloyd Kirby, supt. Fax 432-2577
www.colonschools.org
Colon ES 400/K-6
328 E State St 49040 269-432-2121
Jason Messenger, prin. Fax 432-9341
Other Schools – See Leonidas

Columbiaville, Lapeer, Pop. 817
LakeVille Community SD
Supt. — See Otisville
Columbiaville ES 400/3-5
4775 Pine St 48421 810-538-3420
Margaret Allen-Quaderer, prin. Fax 793-6516

Commerce Township, Oakland, Pop. 26,955
Huron Valley SD
Supt. — See Highland
Country Oaks ES 600/K-5
5070 S Duck Lake Rd 48382 248-684-8075
Debbie Devers, prin. Fax 684-8275

Oak Valley MS 700/6-8
4200 White Oak Trl 48382 248-684-8101
Scott Lindberg, prin. Fax 684-8105

Walled Lake Consolidated SD
Supt. — See Walled Lake
Commerce ES 600/K-5
520 Farr St 48382 248-956-3900
Dennis Graham, prin. Fax 956-3905
Smart MS 1,000/6-8
8500 Commerce Rd 48382 248-956-3500
Mindy MoeKouris, prin. Fax 956-3505

Comstock Park, Kent, Pop. 6,530
Comstock Park SD 2,500/PK-12
PO Box 800 49321 616-254-5001
Ethan Ebenstein, supt. Fax 784-5404
www.cppschools.com
Greenridge ES 300/PK-K
PO Box 825 49321 616-254-5700
Stacy Reehl, prin. Fax 785-9829
Mill Creek MS 500/6-8
PO Box 850 49321 616-254-5100
August Harju, prin. Fax 785-2464
Pine Island ES 500/3-5
PO Box 902 49321 616-254-5500
Troy Reehl, prin. Fax 785-4176
Stoney Creek ES 400/1-2
PO Box 901 49321 616-254-5600
Robert Fidler, prin. Fax 785-9853

Kenowa Hills SD
Supt. — See Grand Rapids
Alpine ES 400/K-4
4730 Baumhoff Ave NW 49321 616-784-0884
Jason Snyder, prin. Fax 784-1228

Holy Trinity S 200/PK-8
1304 Alpine Church Rd NW 49321 616-784-0696
Kathy Rand, prin. Fax 988-9415

Concord, Jackson, Pop. 1,112
Concord Community SD 1,000/K-12
PO Box 338 49237 517-524-8850
Robert Bada, supt. Fax 524-8613
www.ccs.k12.mi.us
Concord ES 400/K-5
PO Box 338 49237 517-524-6650
Tony Hutchins, prin. Fax 524-7680
Concord MS 200/6-8
PO Box 338 49237 517-524-8854
Michael Corey, prin. Fax 524-7324

Conklin, Ottawa

St. Joseph S 100/PK-8
18768 8th Ave 49403 616-899-5300
Shannon Saxton-Murphy, prin. Fax 899-5491
Trinity Lutheran S 100/PK-5
1401 Harding St 49403 616-899-2152
Gordon Kennedy, prin. Fax 899-2930

Constantine, Saint Joseph, Pop. 2,161
Constantine SD 1,400/K-12
1 Falcon Dr 49042 269-435-8900
Charles Frisbie, supt. Fax 435-8980
www.constps.org
Constantine MS 400/6-8
260 W 6th St 49042 269-435-8940
Jean Logan, prin. Fax 435-8982
Eastside ES 200/K-2
935 White Pigeon Rd 49042 269-435-8960
Kristin Flynn, prin. Fax 435-8984
Riverside ES 300/3-5
600 W 6th St 49042 269-435-8950
Craig Badman, prin. Fax 435-8983

Cooks, Delta
Big Bay de Noc SD 300/K-12
8928 00.25 Rd 49817 906-644-2773
John Peterson, supt. Fax 644-2615
www.bigbayschool.com
Big Bay de Noc S 300/K-12
8928 00.25 Rd 49817 906-644-2773
Julie Peterson, prin. Fax 644-2615

Coopersville, Ottawa, Pop. 4,222
Coopersville Area SD 2,300/K-12
198 East St 49404 616-997-3200
Kevin O'Neill, supt. Fax 997-3214
www.coopersvillebroncos.org/
Coopersville East ES 500/3-5
198 East St 49404 616-997-3100
Martin Alexander, prin. Fax 997-3114
Coopersville JHS 600/6-8
198 East St 49404 616-997-3400
Ryan Pfahler, prin. Fax 997-3414
Coopersville West ES 400/K-2
198 East St 49404 616-997-3300
Rich Salo, prin. Fax 997-3314

Lamont Christian S 100/PK-8
5260 Leonard St 49404 616-677-1757
Tom Mulder, prin. Fax 677-2935
St. Michael S 100/PK-6
17150 88th Ave 49404 616-837-6346
Pete Emmerson, prin. Fax 837-7893

Copper Harbor, Keweenaw
Grant Township SD 2 50/K-8
PO Box 74 49918 906-289-4447
Diane Trudgeon, supt. Fax 289-4447
www.copperharborschool.org/
Grant Township S 50/K-8
PO Box 74 49918 906-289-4447
Diane Trudgeon, prin. Fax 289-4447

Corunna, Shiawassee, Pop. 3,377
Corunna SD 2,400/PK-12
124 N Shiawassee St 48817 989-743-6338
Dr. Mark Miller, supt. Fax 743-4474
www.corunna.k12.mi.us
Corunna MS 600/6-8
400 N Comstock St 48817 989-743-5641
John Fattal, prin. Fax 743-8761
Meyer ES 400/K-5
100 Hastings St 48817 989-743-4404
Kathy Hurley, prin. Fax 743-8854
Peacock ES 300/K-5
505 E McArthur St 48817 989-743-4464
Sean McLaughlin, prin. Fax 743-4924
Other Schools – See Vernon

Covert, Van Buren
Covert SD 700/PK-12
35323 M 140 Hwy 49043 269-764-3701
Dr. Stephanie Burrage, supt. Fax 764-8598
www.covertps.org
Covert ES 300/PK-5
35323 M 140 Hwy 49043 269-764-3721
Leadriane Roby, prin. Fax 764-8598
Covert MS 200/6-8
35323 M 140 Hwy 49043 269-764-3741
Craig LeSuer, prin. Fax 764-8598

Croswell, Sanilac, Pop. 2,548
Croswell-Lexington SD 2,300/PK-12
5407 Peck Rd 48422 810-679-1000
Kevin Miller, supt. Fax 679-1005
www.croslex.org
Croswell-Lexington MS 500/5-8
5485 Peck Rd 48422 810-679-1400
Dale Ann Ogden, prin. Fax 679-1405
Frostick ES 300/PK-4
57 S Howard Ave 48422 810-679-1100
Julie Western, prin. Fax 679-1105
Geiger S 400/PK-K
57 S Howard Ave 48422 810-679-1100
Julie Western, prin. Fax 679-1105
Other Schools – See Lexington

Crystal, Montcalm
Carson City-Crystal Area SD
Supt. — See Carson City
Crystal ES 200/K-5
PO Box 86 48818 989-584-6927
Bob Naumann, prin. Fax 584-6917

Crystal Falls, Iron, Pop. 1,649
Forest Park SD 600/K-12
801 Forest Pkwy 49920 906-875-6761
Tom Jayne, supt. Fax 875-4660
Forest Park ES 200/K-5
801 Forest Pkwy 49920 906-875-3131
Becky Taylor, prin. Fax 875-4660

Custer, Mason, Pop. 322
Mason County Eastern SD 500/K-12
18 S Main St 49405 231-757-3733
Ellen Bonter, supt. Fax 757-9671
mceschools.com
Mason County Eastern ES 200/K-5
18 S Main St 49405 231-757-3733
Connie Robinson, prin. Fax 757-9671

Dansville, Ingham, Pop. 437
Dansville SD 900/K-12
PO Box 187 48819 517-623-6120
Ronald Stoneman, supt. Fax 623-6719
www.dansville.org
Dansville ES 400/K-5
PO Box 187 48819 517-623-6120
Faith Norman, prin. Fax 623-6665
Dansville MS 200/6-8
PO Box 187 48819 517-623-6120
Terry Jones, prin. Fax 623-6719

Davisburg, Oakland
Clarkston Community SD
Supt. — See Clarkston
Andersonville ES 500/K-5
10350 Andersonville Rd 48350 248-623-5200
D. Bruce Martin, prin. Fax 623-5205

Holly Area SD
Supt. — See Holly
Davisburg ES 400/K-5
12003 Davisburg Rd 48350 248-328-3500
Barbara Bloom, prin. Fax 328-3504

Davison, Genesee, Pop. 5,372
Davison Community SD 5,500/K-12
PO Box 319 48423 810-591-0801
R. Clay Perkins, supt. Fax 591-7813
www.davisonschools.org/
Central ES 600/1-4
600 S State Rd 48423 810-591-0818
Shelly Fenner-Krasny, prin. Fax 591-0830
Davison MS 800/7-8
600 S Dayton St 48423 810-591-0848
Ken Nuss, prin. Fax 591-2754
Gates ES 500/1-4
2359 S Irish Rd 48423 810-591-5001
Theresa Wendt, prin. Fax 591-5016
Hahn IS 800/5-6
500 S Dayton St 48423 810-591-0530
Holly Halabicky, prin. Fax 591-1120
Hill ES 300/K-4
404 Aloha St 48423 810-591-0839
Lance Harper, prin. Fax 591-9490
Siple ES 400/K-4
9286 E Coldwater Rd 48423 810-591-5104
Martha Morris, prin. Fax 591-5102
Thomson ES 400/K-1
617 E Clark St 48423 810-591-0911
Sandra Hynes, prin. Fax 591-0905

Faith Baptist S 300/PK-12
7306 E Atherton Rd 48423 810-653-9661
Larry Nagengast, prin. Fax 658-0087

Dearborn, Wayne, Pop. 94,090
Dearborn SD 16,800/PK-12
18700 Audette St 48124 313-827-3020
Brian Whiston, supt. Fax 827-3137
www.dearbornschools.org
Becker ES 300/PK-5
10821 Henson St 48126 313-827-6950
Nada Fouani, prin. Fax 827-6955
Bryant MS 700/6-8
460 N Vernon St 48128 313-827-2900
Shannon Peterson, prin. Fax 827-2905
Cotter ECC 300/PK-PK
13020 Osborne St 48126 313-827-6150
Intissar Naraji, coord. Fax 827-6155
DuVall ES 200/K-5
22561 Beech St 48124 313-827-2750
Glenn Maleyko, prin. Fax 827-2755
Ford ES 600/K-5
16140 Driscoll St 48126 313-827-4700
Kathleen Kocher, prin. Fax 827-4705
Ford ES 600/K-5
14749 Alber St 48126 313-827-6400
Mohmoud Abu-Rus, prin. Fax 827-6405
Geer Park ES 300/K-5
14767 Prospect St 48126 313-827-2300
Andrea Awada, prin. Fax 827-2305
Haigh ES 400/K-5
601 N Silvery Ln 48128 313-827-6200
Patricia Buoy, prin. Fax 827-6205
Howard ES 300/K-5
1611 N York St 48128 313-827-6350
Andrew Denison, prin. Fax 827-6355
Lindbergh ES 300/K-5
500 N Waverly St 48128 313-827-6300
Pamela DeNeen, prin. Fax 827-6305
Long ES 200/K-5
3100 Westwood St 48124 313-827-6100
Veronica Jakubus, prin. Fax 827-6105
Lowrey S 700/K-8
6601 Jonathon St 48126 313-827-1800
Samir Makki, prin. Fax 827-1805
Maples ES 500/K-5
6801 Mead St 48126 313-827-6450
Lisa Napolitan, prin. Fax 827-6455
McCollough / Unis S 700/K-8
7801 Maple St 48126 313-827-1700
Rita Rauch, prin. Fax 827-1705
McDonald ES 400/K-5
10151 Diversey St 48126 313-827-6700
Megdieh Jawad, prin. Fax 827-6705
Miller ES 500/PK-5
4824 Lois St 48126 313-827-6850
Rose Aldubaily, prin. Fax 827-6855
Nowlin ES 200/PK-5
23600 Penn St 48124 313-827-6900
Larry Simon, prin. Fax 827-6905
Oakman ES 300/K-5
7545 Chase Rd 48126 313-827-6500
Radewin Awada, prin. Fax 827-6505
Salina ES 300/PK-3
2700 Ferney St 48120 313-827-6550
Nadia Youmans, prin. Fax 827-6555
Salina IS 500/4-8
2623 Salina St 48120 313-827-6600
Majed Fadlallan, prin. Fax 827-6605
Smith MS 600/6-8
23851 Yale St 48124 313-827-2800
Scott Casebolt, prin. Fax 827-2805
Snow ES 300/K-5
2000 Culver Ave 48124 313-827-6250
Kathleen Klee, prin. Fax 827-6255
Stout MS 700/6-8
18500 Oakwood Blvd 48124 313-827-4600
Julia Maconochie, prin. Fax 827-4605
Whitmore-Bolles ES 300/PK-5
21501 Whitmore St 48124 313-827-6800
Jill Chochol, prin. Fax 827-6805
Woodworth MS 700/6-8
4951 Ternes St 48126 313-827-7100
Troy Patterson, prin. Fax 827-7105
Other Schools – See Dearborn Heights

Dearborn Christian S 100/PK-8
21360 Donaldson St 48124 313-563-1240
Robert DeRoo, prin. Fax 563-4348
Divine Child S 700/1-8
25001 Herbert Weier Dr 48128 313-562-1090
Sr. Cecilia Bondy, prin. Fax 562-9306
Emmanuel Lutheran S 100/PK-8
22425 Morley Ave 48124 313-561-6265
Paul Baerwolf, prin. Fax 565-4330
Guardian Lutheran S 200/PK-8
24544 Cherry Hill St 48124 313-274-3665
Walter Krone, prin. Fax 274-2076
Muslim American Youth Academy 400/PK-8
19500 Ford Rd 48128 313-436-3300
Albert Harp, prin. Fax 436-7909
Sacred Heart S 300/K-8
22513 Garrison St 48124 313-561-9192
Lisa Powaser, prin. Fax 561-1598

Dearborn Heights, Wayne, Pop. 56,176
Crestwood SD 3,500/PK-12
1501 N Beech Daly Rd 48127 313-278-0903
Dr. Laurine VanValkenburg, supt. Fax 278-4774
www.csdm.k12.mi.us/
Highview ES 300/PK-4
25225 Richardson St 48127 313-278-8390
Dee Levine, prin. Fax 792-0204
Hillcrest ES 400/K-4
7500 N Vernon St 48127 313-278-0425
Marilee Camerer, prin. Fax 792-0202

Kinloch ES 500/K-4
1505 Kinloch St 48127 313-278-4482
Dianne Laura, prin. Fax 792-0203
Riverside MS 1,100/5-8
25900 W Warren St 48127 313-792-0201
Mary Kerwin, prin. Fax 792-0201

Dearborn Heights SD 7 2,900/K-12
20629 Annapolis St 48125 313-278-1900
Jeffrey Bartold, supt. Fax 278-1413
www.resa.net/district7
Bedford ES 300/K-5
4650 Croissant St 48125 313-278-3544
Catherine Williams, prin. Fax 278-1980
Best JHS 700/6-8
22201 Powers Ave 48125 313-278-6200
Jon Znamierowski, prin. Fax 278-2470
Madison ES 300/K-5
4950 Madison St 48125 313-292-2883
Linda Zibbell, prin. Fax 292-3608
Pardee ES 300/K-5
4650 Pardee Ave 48125 313-292-7300
William Murphy, prin. Fax 292-3606
Polk ES 400/K-5
4651 Polk St 48125 313-278-4455
Mark Brenton, prin. Fax 563-7189

Dearborn SD
Supt. — See Dearborn
River Oaks ES 300/K-5
20755 Ann Arbor Trl 48127 313-827-6750
Youssef Mosallam, prin. Fax 827-6755

Westwood Community SD 1,600/K-12
3335 S Beech Daly St 48125 313-565-1900
Dr. Ernando Minghine, supt. Fax 565-3162
www.westwood.k12.mi.us
Thorne IS 300/3-5
25251 Annapolis St 48125 313-292-1600
Jean Schoenberger, prin. Fax 292-4282
Thorne PS 300/K-2
25251 Annapolis St 48125 313-292-2440
Maureen Molloy, prin. Fax 292-4273
Other Schools – See Inkster

Christus Victor Learning Center 50/PK-PK
25535 Ford Rd 48127 313-278-8879
Debbie Haelterman, dir. Fax 278-8112
Dearborn Heights Montessori Center 200/PK-8
466 N John Daly Rd 48127 313-359-3000
Kay Neff, prin. Fax 359-3003
St. Anselm S 200/PK-8
17700 W Outer Dr 48127 313-563-3430
Stephanie Tozer, prin. Fax 563-2435
St. Linus S 200/PK-8
6466 N Evangeline St 48127 313-274-5320
Dena Jayson, prin. Fax 562-2821
St. Sabina S 200/K-8
8147 Arnold St 48127 313-274-5628
Sr. Juanita Szymanski, prin. Fax 274-5618
St. Sebastian S 200/PK-8
20700 Colgate St 48125 313-563-6640
Sr. Geraldine Kaczynski, prin. Fax 563-6641

Decatur, Van Buren, Pop. 1,890
Decatur SD 1,000/PK-12
110 Cedar St 49045 269-423-6800
Dr. Elizabeth Godwin, supt. Fax 423-6849
www.raiderpride.org/
Davis ES 400/PK-4
409 N Phelps St 49045 269-423-6950
Anne Olsen, prin. Fax 423-6999
Decatur MS 400/5-8
405 N Phelps St 49045 269-423-6900
Larry Smith, prin. Fax 423-6949

Deckerville, Sanilac, Pop. 928
Deckerville Community SD 700/K-12
2633 Black River St 48427 810-376-3615
Donald Schelke, supt. Fax 376-3115
www.deckerville.k12.mi.us
Deckerville ES 400/K-6
2633 Black River St 48427 810-376-9785
Allen Hosler, prin. Fax 376-3115

Deerfield, Lenawee, Pop. 968
Deerfield SD 400/K-12
PO Box 217 49238 517-447-3215
Larry Shilling, supt. Fax 447-3282
www.deerfieldpublicschools.org/
Deerfield S 400/K-12
PO Box 217 49238 517-447-3015
Michael Bowman, prin. Fax 447-3282

Deerton, Alger
Autrain-Onota SD 50/PK-6
PO Box 105 49822 906-343-6632
Mary Alice Boone, supt. Fax 343-6633
www.autrainonota.maresa.k12.mi.us/
Autrain-Onota ES 50/PK-6
PO Box 105 49822 906-343-6632
Mary Alice Boone, prin. Fax 343-6633

Delton, Barry
Delton Kellogg SD 1,600/K-12
327 N Grove St 49046 269-623-9200
Cynthia Vujea, supt. Fax 623-9225
www.dkschools.org/
Delton Kellogg ES 500/K-4
327 N Grove St 49046 269-623-9275
Steve Scoville, prin. Fax 623-9291
Delton Kellogg MS 500/5-8
6325 Delton Rd 49046 269-623-9229
Diane Talo, prin. Fax 623-9259

De Tour Village, Chippewa, Pop. 416
De Tour Area SD 200/K-12
PO Box 429 49725 906-297-2421
Rod Goehmann, supt. Fax 297-3403
eup.k12.mi.us/detour/index.html
De Tour ES 100/K-5
PO Box 429 49725 906-297-2011
Angela Reed, prin. Fax 297-3403
Other Schools – See Drummond Island

Detroit, Wayne, Pop. 886,671
Detroit SD 98,100/PK-12
3011 W Grand Blvd 48202 313-873-7450
Connie Calloway Ph.D., supt. Fax 873-7433
www.detroitk12.org
Academy of the Americas 700/PK-8
5680 Konkel St 48210 313-596-7640
Naomi Khalil, prin. Fax 596-7652
Bagley ES 400/PK-6
8100 Curtis St 48221 313-494-7175
Peggy Williams, prin. Fax 494-7173
Barbour Magnet MS 500/6-8
4209 Seneca St 48214 313-866-2300
Deborah Manciel, prin. Fax 866-2262
Barton ES 400/PK-5
8530 Joy Rd 48204 313-873-0655
Freddie Neal, prin. Fax 873-0755
Beard ECC 100/PK-K
840 Waterman St 48209 313-849-3183
Brenda Phillips, prin. Fax 849-5010
Beckham Academy 600/PK-5
9860 Park Dr 48213 313-852-8500
Sandra Morgan, prin. Fax 852-8511
Bennett ES 500/PK-5
2111 Mullane St 48209 313-849-3585
Antonia Gonzales, prin. Fax 849-1169
Bethune Academy 700/PK-8
10825 Fenkell St 48238 313-873-9460
Pamela Askew, prin. Fax 873-9459
Birney ES 300/K-6
4055 Richton St 48204 313-873-7240
Sandra Rall, prin. Fax 873-9909
Blackwell Institute 600/PK-8
9330 Shoemaker St 48213 313-866-4391
Patricia Hines, prin. Fax 866-4386
Bow ES 500/PK-5
19801 Prevost St 48235 313-852-0500
Ernestine Woodward, prin. Fax 852-0508
Boynton S 400/PK-8
12800 Visger St 48217 313-386-5530
Deborah Hurst, prin. Fax 386-1276
Brewer ES 500/PK-5
12450 Hayes St 48205 313-866-0404
Brenda Carethers, prin. Fax 866-2017
Brown Academy 800/PK-6
11530 E Outer Dr 48224 313-886-2611
Nancy Ross, prin. Fax 886-2860
Bunche ES 200/PK-5
2601 Ellery St 48207 313-866-7926
Marvin Franklin, prin. Fax 866-7943
Burns ES 400/PK-5
14350 Terry St 48227 313-852-0534
Charlene Harper, prin. Fax 852-0539
Burt ES 300/PK-6
20710 Pilgrim St 48223 313-494-7487
Carol Garland, prin. Fax 494-7718
Burton International S 600/PK-8
1333 Pine St 48201 313-596-3800
John T. Wilson, prin. Fax 596-3807
Butzel S 400/PK-8
2301 Van Dyke St 48214 313-866-7400
Margaret Wilson, prin. Fax 866-7382
Campbell ES 300/PK-5
2301 E Alexandrine St 48207 313-494-2052
Charlene White-Bryant, prin. Fax 494-7878
Carleton ES 500/K-5
11724 Casino St 48224 313-866-8322
Rachel Anderson, prin. Fax 866-8333
Carstens ES 300/K-5
2592 Coplin St 48215 313-852-8070
Dr. Theresa Mattison, prin. Fax 852-8075
Carver S 600/PK-8
18701 Paul St 48228 313-240-6622
Ronald Peart, prin. Fax 240-8741
Cerveny MS 300/6-8
15850 Strathmoor St 48227 313-866-9600
Gladys Stoner, prin. Fax 866-9626
Chrysler ES 200/K-5
1445 E Lafayette St 48207 313-494-8440
Linda Whitaker, prin. Fax 494-8367
Clark ES 300/PK-5
15755 Bremen St 48224 313-417-9340
Cindy Lang, prin. Fax 417-9345
Clemente ES 700/PK-5
1551 Beard St 48209 313-849-3489
Helena Lazo, prin. Fax 849-6304
Clinton ES 300/PK-5
8145 Chalfonte St 48238 313-873-5705
Janet Glenn, prin. Fax 873-9613
Clippert Academy 400/5-8
1981 McKinstry St 48209 313-849-5009
Kim Gonzalez, prin. Fax 849-5740
Coffey S 500/K-8
17210 Cambridge Ave 48235 313-852-0582
Omega Mostyn, prin. Fax 852-0589
Columbus MS 500/6-8
18025 Brock St 48205 313-866-2070
Alvin Wood, prin. Fax 866-2098
Cooke ES 300/PK-6
18800 Puritan St 48223 313-494-7458
Arthur Flowers, prin. Fax 494-7759
Coolidge ES 400/PK-5
16501 Elmira St 48227 313-852-1000
Yvette Pinchem-Stewart, prin. Fax 852-1010
Courtis S 400/K-8
8100 W Davison 48238 313-873-0250
Walter Stokely, prin. Fax 873-0249
Crary ES 400/PK-5
16164 Asbury Park 48235 313-852-0612
Dannis White, prin. Fax 852-0617
Davison ES 600/PK-6
2800 E Davison St 48212 313-252-3118
Diane Holland, prin. Fax 866-0919

Detroit Open S 300/PK-8
24601 Frisbee St 48219 313-494-7601
Gretchen Pitts-Sykes, prin. Fax 494-7605
Dixon S 600/K-8
19500 Tireman St 48228 313-582-1330
Ora Beard, prin. Fax 582-3953
Dossin ES 300/PK-6
16650 Glendale St 48227 313-866-9390
Linda Porter-King, prin. Fax 866-9386
Drew Academy 500/K-8
9600 Wyoming St 48204 313-873-6880
Gerlma Johnson, prin. Fax 873-0114
Duffield S 400/PK-8
2715 Macomb St 48207 313-494-8350
Kenneth Jenkins, prin. Fax 494-8354
Durfee S 500/PK-8
2470 Collingwood St 48206 313-252-3070
Jacquline Ensley, prin. Fax 866-0914
Earhart MS 600/6-8
1000 Scotten St 48209 313-849-3945
Geraldo Vasquez, prin. Fax 849-4746
Edison ES 300/PK-5
17045 Grand River Ave 48227 313-852-1066
Beverly Green, prin. Fax 852-1060
Edmonson ES 300/PK-5
1300 W Canfield St 48201 313-494-2242
Clarence Hayes, prin. Fax 494-1113
Ellington Conservatory of Music/Art 600/K-8
8030 E Outer Dr 48213 313-866-2860
Yolanda Herbert, prin. Fax 866-2866
Elmdale ES 200/K-5
12844 Elmdale St 48213 313-852-8533
Jacqueline McNeal, prin. Fax 852-8532
Emerson ES 300/PK-5
18240 Huntington Rd 48219 313-831-9689
Julienne Akins, prin. Fax 831-9699
Farwell MS 600/5-8
19955 Fenelon St 48234 313-866-3700
Laverne Jordan, prin. Fax 866-3632
Fisher Magnet S 500/PK-8
15600 E State Fair St 48205 313-866-2670
Linda McIntosh, prin. Fax 866-2667
Fitzgerald S 700/PK-8
8145 Puritan St 48238 313-494-3830
Lachelle Williams, prin. Fax 494-3829
Fleming ES 400/PK-5
18501 Waltham St 48205 313-852-8557
Ronnie Sims, prin. Fax 852-8559
Foreign Language Immersion S 600/K-8
6501 W Outer Dr 48235 313-651-2400
Ineala Chambers, prin. Fax 651-2401
Gardner ES 300/PK-5
6528 Mansfield St 48228 313-581-4615
Karen Doneghy, prin. Fax 581-4582
Garvey Academy 300/K-8
7701 Sylvester St 48214 313-866-5770
James Hearn, prin. Fax 866-8384
Glazer ES 300/PK-5
2001 La Belle St 48238 313-852-1500
Bennie Glenn, prin. Fax 852-1499
Gompers ES 300/PK-5
20601 W Davison St 48223 313-494-7495
Bobbie Milner, prin. Fax 494-7636
Greenfield Union S 500/PK-8
420 W 7 Mile Rd 48203 313-866-2999
Beverly Campbell, prin. Fax 866-2362
Guyton ES 300/PK-6
355 Philip St 48215 313-866-3063
Debra Kelly-McGill, prin. Fax 866-3066
Hally Magnet MS 600/6-8
2585 Grove St 48221 313-494-3939
Rita Davis, prin. Fax 494-7089
Hamilton ES 300/K-5
14223 Southampton St 48213 313-866-4505
Tracy Johnson, prin. Fax 866-4493
Hanstein ES 300/PK-5
4290 Marseilles St 48224 313-417-9370
Bernadine Carroll, prin. Fax 417-9296
Harding ES 300/PK-5
14450 Burt Rd 48223 313-494-7606
Sharon Harvell, prin. Fax 494-7610
Harms ES 400/PK-5
2400 Central St 48209 313-849-3492
Karen White, prin. Fax 849-4690
Heilmann Park ES 500/PK-5
15510 E State Fair St 48205 313-642-4854
Yvette Little, prin. Fax 642-4855
Heilmann Park MS 700/6-8
19035 Crusade St 48205 313-866-7233
Cheryl Harshaw, prin. Fax 866-7329
Henderson Lower ES 300/K-4
9600 Mettetal St 48227 313-866-9363
Marian Jennings-Jones, prin. Fax 866-9333
Henderson Upper S 600/5-8
16101 W Chicago St 48228 313-852-0512
Karyne Johnson, prin. Fax 852-0523
Holcomb ES 300/PK-5
18100 Bentler St 48219 313-494-7498
Kimberly Davis, prin. Fax 494-7499
Holmes S 400/K-8
8950 Crane St 48213 313-866-5644
Dr. Delores Harris, prin. Fax 866-2299
Holmes S 400/PK-8
4833 Ogden St 48210 313-582-4300
Stephen Black, prin. Fax 582-7861
Houghton ES 300/PK-5
16745 Lamphere St 48219 313-494-7615
Cecelia Muhammad, prin. Fax 537-6659
Howe ES 500/PK-5
2600 Garland St 48214 313-642-4801
Russell Covington, prin. Fax 642-4802
Hughes Academy 300/K-8
19900 McIntyre St 48219 313-831-9182
Angela Broaden, prin. Fax 831-9195
Hutchinson ES 400/PK-6
5221 Montclair St 48213 313-852-9900
Stanley Johnson, prin. Fax 852-9911

Hutchins S 300/K-8
6050 Linwood St 48208 313-596-3502
Dr. Virginia Clay, prin. Fax 596-3500
Jamieson ES 400/PK-6
2900 W Philadelphia St 48206 313-596-0910
David Harris, prin. Fax 596-0794
Jemison School of Choice 600/PK-8
16400 Tireman St 48228 313-584-5525
Sheila Jenkins, prin. Fax 584-4807
Jordan S 600/PK-8
3901 Margareta St 48221 313-494-7300
Marcia Morrow, prin. Fax 494-7304
Joyce ES 400/PK-5
8411 Sylvester St 48214 313-866-7545
Diane Goins, prin. Fax 866-8068
King Academic and Performing Arts Acad 500/PK-6
16800 Cheyenne St 48235 313-494-7347
Vivian Hughes-Norde, prin. Fax 494-3962
Law S 600/PK-8
19411 Cliff St 48234 313-866-3400
Frano Ivezaj, prin. Fax 866-6200
Lessenger S 400/K-8
8401 Trinity St 48228 313-945-1330
Bettie Reid, prin. Fax 945-1557
Lodge ES 200/PK-5
24325 Bennett St 48219 313-494-7591
Nazarene Banks, prin. Fax 494-7655
Logan ES 600/K-5
3811 Cicotte St 48210 313-596-0100
Mauro Cruz, prin. Fax 596-0077
Loving ES 200/PK-5
1000 Lynn St 48211 313-252-3028
Eddie Huwitte, prin. Fax 866-0989
Ludington Magnet MS 600/5-8
19355 Edinborough Rd 48219 313-494-7549
Alora Comer-Maxwell, prin. Fax 494-7707
MacDowell ES 400/PK-6
4201 W Outer Dr 48221 313-494-7310
Mildred Davis, prin. Fax 494-7349
Macomb ES 300/PK-5
12021 Evanston St 48213 313-866-8282
Willie Trotter, prin. Fax 866-8288
Malcom X Academy 500/PK-8
3550 John C Lodge Fwy 48201 313-494-2219
Freda Dawson, prin. Fax 494-2302
Mann ES 400/PK-5
19625 Elmira St 48228 313-866-9580
Gwendolyn Frencher, prin. Fax 866-9587
Marquette S 700/PK-8
6145 Canyon St 48236 313-417-9360
Dwana Brown, prin. Fax 881-3398
Marshall ES 500/PK-5
1255 E State Fair 48203 313-866-7711
Cleo Moody, prin. Fax 866-7722
Marshall ES 400/PK-6
15531 Linwood St 48238 313-494-8820
Willye Jean Pearsall, prin. Fax 494-7294
Mason ES 400/K-5
19635 Mitchell St 48234 313-866-3600
E. Wilson, prin. Fax 866-3609
Maybury ES 500/PK-5
4410 Porter St 48209 313-849-2014
Ellen Snedeker, prin. Fax 849-2016
McColl ES 300/PK-5
20550 Cathedral St 48228 313-852-0708
Ruby Windhom, prin. Fax 852-0676
McFarlane ES 400/PK-5
8900 Cheyenne St 48228 313-873-5700
Carolyn Freeman, prin. Fax 873-1355
McKenny ES 400/PK-6
20833 Pembroke Ave 48219 313-494-7594
Patricia Smith, prin. Fax 494-7720
McNair MS 400/6-8
4180 Marlborough St 48215 313-417-8898
John White, prin. Fax 417-8796
Munger S 200/K-6
5525 Martin St 48210 313-596-3565
Wendy Shirley, prin. Fax 596-3561
Murphy S 500/K-8
23901 Fenkell St 48223 313-494-7585
Corey Pitts, prin. Fax 494-7550
Neinas ES 500/K-5
6021 Mcmillan St 48209 313-849-3701
Alberta Lyons, prin. Fax 849-4733
Nichols S 300/K-8
3000 Burns St 48214 313-852-0800
Dr. Granada Peterson, prin. Fax 852-0811
Noble S 500/PK-8
8646 Fullerton St 48238 313-873-0377
James Ellison, prin. Fax 873-0398
Nolan MS 500/6-8
1150 E Lantz St 48203 313-866-7730
Daryl McDuffie, prin. Fax 866-7725
Northwest ECC 50/PK-K
13735 W 7 Mile Rd 48235 313-494-7344
Ingrid Haywood, prin. Fax 494-7345
Owen Academy 500/K-8
2001 Martin Luther King Jr 48208 313-596-3780
Calvin Patillo, prin. Fax 596-3783
Parker S 400/PK-8
12744 Elmira St 48227 313-873-0260
Ledora Scott, prin. Fax 873-7983
Pasteur ES 300/PK-6
19811 Stoepel St 48221 313-494-7314
Sharon Lawson, prin. Fax 494-7313
Phoenix Multicultural Academy 400/PK-8
7735 Lane St 48209 313-849-2419
Norma Hernandez, prin. Fax 849-1170
Priest ES 700/PK-5
7840 Wagner St 48210 313-849-3705
Beverly Tolliver, prin. Fax 849-4824
Pulaski S 500/K-8
19725 Strasburg St 48205 313-866-7022
Dr. Ethel Jones, prin. Fax 866-7011
Richard S 500/K-8
13840 Lappin St 48205 313-245-3581
Karen Dudley, prin. Fax 245-3155

Robeson Academy 700/PK-8
2701 Fenkell St 48238 313-494-8100
Dr. Jeanette Collins, prin. Fax 494-7287
Robinson MS 400/6-8
13000 Essex Ave 48215 313-866-5500
Sharon Lee, prin. Fax 866-5580
Rutherford ES 300/K-5
16411 Curtis St 48235 313-852-0709
Miriam Adams, prin. Fax 852-0702
Sampson Academy 300/PK-8
4700 Tireman St 48204 313-596-4750
Dr. Sabrina Smith-Campbell, prin. Fax 596-4748
Schulze ES 600/PK-6
10700 Santa Maria St 48221 313-340-4400
Brenda Lyons, prin. Fax 340-4401
Scott MS 900/6-8
18400 Hoover St 48205 313-866-6700
Beverly Butler, prin. Fax 866-2693
Sherrill S 500/PK-8
7300 Garden St 48204 313-873-6723
Maxine Hankins-Cain, prin. Fax 873-6411
Spain S 800/PK-8
3700 Beaubien St 48201 313-494-2081
Ronald Alexander, prin. Fax 494-1508
Stark ES of Technology 200/K-5
12611 Avondale St 48215 313-866-5940
Cynthia Watt, prin. Fax 866-5947
Stephens ES 400/PK-6
6006 Seneca St 48213 313-852-0826
Deborah Sinclair, prin. Fax 852-0828
Stewart S 300/PK-8
13120 Wildemere St 48238 313-252-3050
Mary Wright, prin. Fax 866-0912
Taft MS 500/6-8
19501 Berg Rd 48219 313-494-7577
Naomi Lewis, prin. Fax 494-7538
Thirkell ES 400/PK-5
7724 14th St 48206 313-596-0990
Clara Smith, prin. Fax 596-0982
Trix S 500/K-8
13700 Bringard Dr 48205 313-852-8644
Wesley Ganson, prin. Fax 866-8655
Turning Point Academy 300/K-12
12300 Linnhurst St 48205 313-866-2200
Janet Brooks, prin. Fax 866-2082
Twain S 200/PK-8
12001 Gleason St 48217 313-388-0401
Margaret Scales, prin. Fax 388-0008
Van Zile ES 500/PK-5
2915 E Outer Dr 48234 313-368-8444
Marva Johnson, prin. Fax 368-1507
Vernor ES 400/K-6
13726 Pembroke Ave 48235 313-494-7342
Elizabeth Nevels, prin. Fax 494-7341
Vetal S 500/PK-8
14200 Westwood St 48223 313-852-0710
Eric George, prin. Fax 852-0771
Wayne ES 400/PK-5
10633 Courville St 48224 313-866-0400
Theresa Matthews, prin. Fax 866-2022
Webster ES 300/PK-5
1450 25th St 48216 313-849-3709
Salma Abou-Elkhair, prin. Fax 849-4684
Westside Multicultural Academy 400/PK-8
4700 Vinewood St 48208 313-596-4939
Regina Randall, prin. Fax 456-8001
White ES 600/PK-6
5161 Charles St 48212 313-866-3595
Vernice Gains, prin. Fax 866-3476
Wilkins ES 600/K-6
12400 Nashville St 48205 313-852-8600
Milton Andrews, prin. Fax 245-3567
Winterhalter S 700/K-8
12121 Broadstreet Ave 48204 313-873-8440
Randolph Gear, prin. Fax 873-8366
Wright ES 600/PK-5
19299 Berg Rd 48219 313-538-3024
Silvia Green, prin. Fax 538-3049
Young ES 600/PK-5
15771 Hubbell St 48227 313-852-0725
Sharon Mills-Sanford, prin. Fax 852-0732
Other Schools – See Redford

Bethany Lutheran S 100/PK-8
11475 E Outer Dr 48224 313-885-0180
Gerald Heuer, prin. Fax 885-1680
Christ the King S 200/PK-8
16800 Trinity St 48219 313-532-1213
Roseanne Jodway, prin. Fax 532-1050
Cornerstone S - Grove Campus 400/PK-7
13436 Grove St 48235 313-862-2352
Joyce Stephens, prin. Fax 862-2462
Cornerstone S - Nevada MS 200/6-8
6861 E Nevada St 48234 313-892-1860
Dennis Wrosch, prin. Fax 892-1861
Cornerstone S - Nevada PS 400/PK-5
6861 E Nevada St 48234 313-892-1860
Monica Thompson, prin. Fax 892-1091
Detroit Urban Lutheran S 300/K-12
8181 Greenfield Rd 48228 313-582-9900
R. David Siefker, prin. Fax 582-0817
Detroit Waldorf S 100/PK-8
2555 Burns St 48214 313-822-0300
Linda Brooks, prin. Fax 822-4030
Friends S in Detroit 100/PK-8
1100 Saint Aubin St 48207 313-259-6722
Dwight Wilson, hdmstr. Fax 259-8066
Gesu S 200/PK-8
17139 Oak Dr 48221 313-863-4677
John Champion, prin. Fax 862-4395
Giving Tree Montessori S 100/PK-3
4351 Marseilles St 48224 313-881-2255
Bonnie Surrell, admin. Fax 881-2316
Holy Redeemer S 200/K-8
1711 Junction St 48209 313-841-5230
Sr. E. Fleckenstein, prin. Fax 841-3640

Most Holy Trinity S 100/PK-6
1229 Labrosse St 48226 313-961-8855
Kathleen McBride, prin. Fax 961-5797
Our Lady of Guadalupe MS 50/5-8
4100 Martin St 48210 313-894-2228
Lisa Pacholski, prin. Fax 894-2271
St. Bartholomew S 100/K-8
20001 Wexford St 48234 313-366-3640
Sharon Perko, prin. Fax 366-0257
St. Cecilia S 100/PK-8
6327 Burlingame St 48204 313-933-2400
Darlisa Rickman, prin. Fax 933-9332
St. John Lutheran S 50/PK-8
4950 Oakman Blvd 48204 313-933-8928
Paul Schmidt, prin. Fax 933-5842
St. Scholastica S 100/K-8
17351 Southfield Fwy 48235 313-532-1916
Faye Vaughn, prin. Fax 532-0140
St. Timothy Lutheran S 50/PK-2
19400 Evergreen Rd 48219 313-535-1971
Sammie Tolbert, prin. Fax 535-9732
Temple of Faith Baptist S 50/K-6
9351 Forrer St 48228 313-835-8889
Gloria Newton, admin. Fax 836-0458
Westside Christian Academy 100/PK-12
9540 Bramell 48239 313-255-5760
Darryl Ounanian, prin. Fax 255-0809

De Witt, Clinton, Pop. 4,499
De Witt SD 3,000/K-12
PO Box 800, 517-668-3000
Tina Templin, supt. Fax 668-3018
www.dewitt.edzone.net
De Witt JHS 500/7-8
PO Box 800, 517-668-3200
Lori Webb, prin. Fax 668-3255
Fuerstenau ECC 200/K-K
PO Box 800, 517-668-3460
Keith Cravotta, prin. Fax 668-3484
Herbison Woods ES 500/5-6
PO Box 800, 517-668-3300
Mark Bensinger, prin. Fax 668-3355
Schavey Road ES 500/1-2
PO Box 800, 517-668-3500
David Potter, prin. Fax 668-3555
Scott ES 400/3-4
PO Box 800, 517-668-3400
Ruth Foster, prin. Fax 668-3455

Dexter, Washtenaw, Pop. 3,198
Dexter Community SD 3,400/K-12
7714 Ann Arbor St 48130 734-424-4100
Rob Glass, supt. Fax 424-4112
www.dexterschools.org/
Bates ES 300/K-2
2704 Baker Rd 48130 734-424-4130
Roger Moore, prin. Fax 424-4139
Cornerstone ES 300/K-2
7480 Dan Hoey Rd 48130 734-424-4120
Craig McCalla, prin. Fax 424-4129
Creekside IS 600/5-6
2615 Baker Rd 48130 734-424-4160
Mollie Sharrar, prin. Fax 424-4169
Mill Creek MS 600/7-8
7305 Dexter Ann Arbor Rd 48130 734-424-4150
Jami Bronson, prin. Fax 424-4159
Wylie ES 600/3-4
3060 Kensington St 48130 734-424-4140
Paula Thomas, prin. Fax 424-4149

Dimondale, Eaton, Pop. 1,346
Holt SD
Supt. — See Holt
Dimondale ES 300/K-4
PO Box 159 48821 517-694-6411
James Cooper, prin. Fax 694-6472

Dollar Bay, Houghton
Dollar Bay-Tamarack City SD 300/K-12
PO Box 371 49922 906-482-5800
Jan Quarless, supt. Fax 487-5931
www.dollarbay.k12.mi.us
Davis ES 200/K-6
PO Box 371 49922 906-482-5849
William Rivest, prin. Fax 487-5931

Dorr, Allegan
Hopkins SD
Supt. — See Hopkins
Sycamore ES 400/K-5
2163 142nd Ave 49323 616-681-9189
Amy Mielke, prin. Fax 681-0154

Wayland UNSD
Supt. — See Byron Center
Dorr ES 300/K-4
4159 18th St 49323 616-681-9637
Gregory Rutten, prin. Fax 681-0765

St. Stanislaus S 100/PK-8
1861 136th Ave 49323 269-793-7204
Ann Miller, prin. Fax 793-3264

Douglas, Allegan, Pop. 1,196
Saugatuck SD 600/PK-12
PO Box 818 49406 269-857-1444
Rolfe Timmerman Ph.D., supt. Fax 857-1448
www.saugatuck.k12.mi.us
Douglas ES 300/PK-5
PO Box 818 49406 269-857-2139
Teya Lober, prin. Fax 857-4487

Dowagiac, Cass, Pop. 5,955
Dowagiac UNSD 2,100/PK-12
206 Main St 49047 269-782-4400
Peg Stowers, supt. Fax 782-3152
www.dowagiacschools.org
Dowagiac MS 400/6-8
57072 Riverside Dr 49047 269-782-4440
Michael Frazier, prin. Fax 782-4449

Gage ES 300/K-5
301 Oak St 49047 269-782-4460
Marcy Hendress, prin. Fax 782-2382
Hamilton ES 200/K-5
614 Spruce St 49047 269-782-4450
Heather Nash, prin. Fax 782-9205
Inside Track Preschool PK-PK
301 Oak St 49047 269-782-4484
Marcy Hendress, prin. Fax 782-2382
Kincheloe ES 200/K-5
25121 Gage St 49047 269-782-4464
Dawn Conner, prin. Fax 782-8985
Other Schools – See Benton Harbor

St. John Lutheran S 50/PK-8
603 McCleary St 49047 269-782-3771
Nathan Buch, prin. Fax 782-0403

Drummond Island, Chippewa, Pop. 500
De Tour Area SD
Supt. — See De Tour Village
Drummond Island ES 50/K-6
PO Box 39 49726 906-493-5225
Angela Reed, prin. Fax 493-6030

Dryden, Lapeer, Pop. 813
Dryden Community SD 800/K-12
3866 Rochester Rd 48428 810-796-9534
Thomas Goulette, supt. Fax 796-3698
www.dryden.k12.mi.us
Dryden ES 400/K-6
3835 N Mill Rd 48428 810-796-2201
Todd Bidlack, prin. Fax 796-9621

Dundee, Monroe, Pop. 3,892
Dundee Community SD 1,600/PK-12
420 Ypsilanti St 48131 734-529-2350
Ronald Tarrant, supt. Fax 529-5606
www.dundeecommunityschools.org
Dundee ES 500/PK-4
420 Ypsilanti St 48131 734-529-2350
Maury Geiger, prin. Fax 529-5606
Dundee MS 500/5-8
420 Ypsilanti St 48131 734-529-2350
Jeff LaRoux, prin. Fax 529-5606

Durand, Shiawassee, Pop. 3,868
Durand Area SD 1,900/PK-12
310 N Saginaw St 48429 989-288-2681
Cindy Weber, supt. Fax 288-3553
durand.k12.mi.us/
Durand MS 400/6-8
9550 E Lansing Rd 48429 989-288-3435
Barb Birchmeier, prin. Fax 288-5563
Kerr ES 200/3-5
9591 E Monroe Rd 48429 989-288-2805
James Dell, prin. Fax 288-3461
Neal ES 200/PK-2
930 W Main St 48429 989-288-2016
Michael Cooney, prin. Fax 288-3603
Other Schools – See Bancroft, Lennon

Eagle, Clinton, Pop. 123
Grand Ledge SD
Supt. — See Grand Ledge
Wacousta ES 400/K-5
9135 W Herbison Rd 48822 517-925-5940
Scott Eckhart, prin. Fax 925-5970

East China, Saint Clair, Pop. 3,216
East China SD 5,100/K-12
1585 Meisner Rd 48054 810-676-1018
Rodney Green, supt. Fax 676-1037
www.ecsd.us
Pine River ES 400/K-5
3575 King Rd 48054 810-676-1050
Joyce Lemmer, prin. Fax 676-1060
Other Schools – See Fair Haven, Marine City, Saint Clair

East Jordan, Charlevoix, Pop. 2,338
East Jordan SD 1,200/K-12
PO Box 399 49727 231-536-3131
Robert Hansen, supt. Fax 536-3310
www.ejps.org/
East Jordan ES 500/K-5
PO Box 399 49727 231-536-7564
Cal Prins, prin. Fax 536-3379
East Jordan MS 300/6-8
PO Box 399 49727 231-536-2823
Matthew Stevenson, prin. Fax 536-0051

East Lansing, Ingham, Pop. 46,419
East Lansing SD 3,400/K-12
841 Timberlane St Ste A 48823 517-333-7420
David Chapin, supt. Fax 333-7470
www.elps.k12.mi.us
Donley ES 300/K-4
2961 E Lake Lansing Rd 48823 517-333-7370
Mercy Kinzer, prin. Fax 333-5090
Glencairn ES 200/5-6
939 N Harrison Rd 48823 517-333-7930
Jo Preston, prin. Fax 333-5091
MacDonald MS 500/7-8
1601 Burcham Dr 48823 517-333-7600
Cliff Seybert, prin. Fax 333-5098
Marble ES 300/K-4
729 N Hagadorn Rd 48823 517-333-7860
Ruth Riddle, prin. Fax 333-5092
Pinecrest ES 300/K-4
1811 Pinecrest Dr 48823 517-333-7870
Cynthia Blakeslee, prin. Fax 333-5093
Red Cedar ES 200/K-4
1110 Narcissus Dr 48823 517-333-5060
Mindy Emerson, prin. Fax 333-5094
Whitehills ES 300/5-6
621 Pebblebrook Ln 48823 517-333-7900
Andrew Wells, prin. Fax 333-5096

Okemos SD
Supt. — See Okemos
Wardcliff ES 300/K-5
5150 Wardcliff Dr 48823 517-337-1346
Noelle Palasty, prin. Fax 337-0170

St. Thomas Aquinas S 400/K-8
915 Alton Rd 48823 517-332-0813
Rod Murphy, prin. Fax 332-9490
Stepping Stones Montessori S 100/PK-6
1370 Beech St 48823 517-336-0422
Meg Thomas, prin. Fax 336-0423

East Leroy, Calhoun
Athens Area SD
Supt. — See Athens
East Leroy ES 300/K-4
4320 K Dr S 49051 269-729-5419
Walter Dubbeld, prin. Fax 729-9648

Eastpointe, Macomb, Pop. 33,180
East Detroit SD 4,700/PK-12
15115 Deerfield Ave 48021 586-445-4400
Bruce Kefgen, supt. Fax 445-4427
www.eastdetroit.org
Bellview ES 300/K-5
15800 Bell Ave 48021 586-445-4630
Rosemary Monsour, prin. Fax 445-4629
Crescentwood ES 200/K-5
14500 Crescentwood Ave 48021 586-445-4635
Fran Hobbs, prin. Fax 445-4638
Forest Park ES 300/K-5
18361 Forest Ave 48021 586-445-4640
Susan Lenz, prin. Fax 445-4673
Kantner Preschool PK-PK
17363 Toepfer Dr 48021 586-445-4453
Kelly Garrison, dir. Fax 445-4649
Kelly MS 600/6-8
24701 Kelly Rd 48021 586-445-4570
Ira Hamden, prin. Fax 445-4582
Oakwood MS 600/6-8
14825 Nehls Ave 48021 586-445-4600
Gerald St. Onge, prin. Fax 445-4612
Pleasantview ES 300/K-5
16501 Toepfer Dr 48021 586-445-4650
Jerry Tait, prin. Fax 445-4653
Woodland ES 300/K-5
23750 David Ave 48021 586-445-4665
Susan Miller, prin. Fax 445-4669
Other Schools – See Warren

South Lake SD
Supt. — See Saint Clair Shores
Koepsell Education Center 300/K-6
21760 Raven Ave 48021 586-435-1500
Diane Boehm, prin. Fax 445-4322

St. Peter Lutheran S 200/PK-8
23000 Gratiot Ave 48021 586-771-2809
John Kutz, prin. Fax 777-0347
St. Thomas Lutheran S 200/PK-8
23801 Kelly Rd 48021 586-772-3372
Roy Leidich, prin. Fax 772-6265

East Tawas, Iosco, Pop. 2,852

Holy Family S 100/K-6
411 Wilkinson St 48730 989-362-5651
Linda Howe, prin. Fax 362-9077

Eaton Rapids, Eaton, Pop. 5,266
Eaton Rapids SD 2,200/PK-12
912 Greyhound Dr 48827 517-663-8155
Dr. William DeFrance, supt. Fax 663-2236
www.erpsk12.org/
Eaton Rapids MS 500/7-8
815 Greyhound Dr 48827 517-663-8151
Stephen Dembowski, prin. Fax 663-0625
Greyhound IS 500/4-6
805 Greyhound Dr 48827 517-663-9192
Russ Olejownik, prin. Fax 663-9181
Lockwood ES 100/PK-1
810 Greyhound Dr 48827 517-663-8194
Julie Powers, prin. Fax 663-6836
Northwestern ES 100/2-3
400 Dexter Rd 48827 517-663-2571
Shawn Towsley, prin. Fax 663-2229

St. Peter S 100/K-8
515 E Knight St 48827 517-663-1799
Kathleen Christesen, prin. Fax 663-3799

Eau Claire, Berrien, Pop. 643
Eau Claire SD 800/K-12
PO Box 398 49111 269-461-6947
D. Stefan Jaggi, supt. Fax 461-0089
www.eauclairepublicschools.com/
Eau Claire MS 200/6-8
7450 Hochberger Rd 49111 269-461-0083
Chris Porter, prin. Fax 461-0065
Lybrook ES 400/K-5
6238 W Main St 49111 269-461-6191
Dao Noi Down, prin. Fax 461-6662

Eau Claire SDA S 50/1-8
6562 Naomi Rd 49111 269-944-4132
James Gray, prin. Fax 944-4132

Eben Junction, Alger
Superior Central SD 400/K-12
PO Box 148 49825 906-439-5531
Pamela Morris, supt. Fax 439-5734
superiorcentralschools.org/
Superior Central S 400/K-12
PO Box 148 49825 906-439-5532
Pamela Morris, prin. Fax 439-5243

Ecorse, Wayne, Pop. 10,757
Ecorse SD 1,200/PK-12
4024 W Jefferson Ave 48229 313-294-4750
Emma Epps, supt. Fax 294-4769
204.39.0.221/
Bunche ES 300/PK-3
503 Hyacinthe St 48229 313-294-4710
Leslie Coleman, prin. Fax 294-4719
Grandport MS 300/4-7
4536 6th St 48229 313-294-4720
Nancy DeLeon, prin. Fax 383-3125

Edenville, Midland

Edenville SDA S, PO Box 189 48620 50/1-8
Jerry Murray, prin. 989-689-3505

Edmore, Montcalm, Pop. 1,258
Montabella Community SD 600/PK-12
PO Box 349 48829 989-427-5148
Ronald Farrell, supt. Fax 427-3828
www.montabella.com
Other Schools – See Blanchard

Edwardsburg, Cass, Pop. 1,114
Edwardsburg SD 2,400/K-12
69410 Section St 49112 269-663-3055
Sherman Ostrander, supt. Fax 663-6485
www.edwardsburgpublicschools.org/
Eagle Lake ES 400/2-3
69410 Section St 49112 269-663-1040
James Hendress, prin. Fax 663-7653
Edwardsburg IS 400/4-5
69410 Section St 49112 269-663-1063
Daniel Nommay, prin. Fax 663-2156
Edwardsburg MS 600/6-8
69410 Section St 49112 269-663-1031
Anthony Koontz, prin. Fax 663-8638
Edwardsburg PS 200/K-1
69410 Section St 49112 269-663-1037
Debora Crouch, prin. Fax 663-8361

Elk Rapids, Antrim, Pop. 1,710
Elk Rapids SD 1,600/K-12
707 E 3rd St 49629 231-264-8692
Jon Hoover, supt. Fax 264-6538
www.erschools.com
Cherryland MS 400/6-8
707 E 3rd St 49629 231-264-8991
Jon Hoover, prin. Fax 264-9370
Lakeland ES 400/K-5
616 Buckley St 49629 231-264-8289
Terry Starr, prin. Fax 264-6132
Other Schools – See Williamsburg

Ellsworth, Antrim, Pop. 466
Ellsworth Community SD 300/K-12
9467 Park St 49729 231-588-2544
Lynn Spearing, supt. Fax 588-6183
www.ellsworth.k12.mi.us/
Ellsworth Community S 300/K-12
9467 Park St 49729 231-588-2544
Lynn Spearing, prin. Fax 588-6183

Ebenezer Christian S 50/PK-8
PO Box 158 49729 231-588-2111
Jennifer Finnigan, dir. Fax 588-2111

Elsie, Clinton, Pop. 1,005
Ovid-Elsie Area SD 1,800/K-12
8989 E Colony Rd 48831 989-834-2271
Wayne Petroelje, supt. Fax 862-5887
www.oe.k12.mi.us/
Knight ES 400/K-6
215 N Tyler Dr 48831 989-862-5170
Matt Airgood, prin. Fax 862-5995
Ovid-Elsie MS 300/7-8
8989 E Colony Rd 48831 989-834-2271
Jerry Goosen, prin. Fax 862-4463
Other Schools – See Ovid

Emmett, Saint Clair, Pop. 246
Yale SD
Supt. — See Yale
Farrell-Emmett ES 300/K-5
3300 Kinney Rd 48022 810-384-1300
Robert Watson, prin. Fax 384-8010

Engadine, Mackinac
Engadine Consolidated SD 300/K-12
W13920 Melville St 49827 906-477-6313
Stu Hobbs, supt. Fax 477-6643
www.eup.k12.mi.us/engadine
Engadine ES 100/K-6
W13920 Melville St 49827 906-477-6351
Angie McArthur, coord. Fax 477-6643

Erie, Monroe
Mason Consolidated SD 1,400/PK-12
2400 Mason Eagle Dr 48133 734-848-9304
David Drewyor, supt. Fax 848-3975
www.eriemason.k12.mi.us
Central ES 500/PK-5
2400 Mason Eagle Dr 48133 734-848-5595
Debra McCain, prin. Fax 848-2933
Mason MS 300/6-8
2400 Mason Eagle Dr 48133 734-848-4944
Tom McGarry, prin. Fax 848-0035

St. Joseph S 100/PK-8
2238 Manhattan St 48133 734-848-6985
Sr. Jean Walczak, prin. Fax 848-8215

Escanaba, Delta, Pop. 12,679
Escanaba Area SD 2,700/K-12
1500 Ludington St 49829 906-786-5411
Michele Burley, supt. Fax 786-0106
www.escanabaschool.com
Escanaba MS 400/7-8
1500 Ludington St 49829 906-786-7462
Catherine Johnson, prin. Fax 786-5958

Franklin ES 200/K-6
612 2nd Ave S 49829 906-786-9203
Linda Pearl, prin. Fax 789-8167
Lemmer ES 300/K-6
700 S 20th St 49829 906-786-5333
Matthew Johnson-Reeves, prin. Fax 789-8169
Soo Hill ES 300/K-6
5219 18th Rd 49829 906-786-7035
Paulette Wickham, prin. Fax 789-8163
Webster ES 300/K-6
1209 N 19th St 49829 906-786-6118
Linda Pearl, prin. Fax 789-8165

Escanaba SDA S 50/K-8
210 S Lincoln Rd 49829 906-786-3039
Janice Tirzmalis, prin.
Holy Name Central S 300/PK-8
409 S 22nd St 49829 906-786-7550
Joe Carlson, prin. Fax 786-7582

Essexville, Bay, Pop. 3,590
Essexville-Hampton SD 1,800/K-12
303 Pine St 48732 989-894-9700
John Mertz, supt. Fax 894-9705
www.e-hps.net
Bush ES 100/K-1
800 Nebobish St 48732 989-894-9760
Joan Douglas, prin. Fax 894-9739
Cramer JHS 500/6-8
313 Pine St 48732 989-894-9740
James Glasgow, prin. Fax 894-9720
Hughes ES 300/4-5
805 Langstaff St 48732 989-894-9750
Steve Estes, prin. Fax 894-9774
Verellen ES 300/2-3
612 W Borton Rd 48732 989-894-9770
Barry Kenniston, prin. Fax 894-9759

St. John the Evangelist S 100/PK-5
619 Main St 48732 989-892-0363
Sue Grzegorczyk, prin. Fax 892-0350

Evart, Osceola, Pop. 1,734
Evart SD 1,200/K-12
PO Box 917 49631 231-734-5594
Howard Hyde, supt. Fax 734-2931
www.evart.k12.mi.us/
Evart ES 400/K-4
515 N Cedar St 49631 231-734-5595
Carol Phelps, prin. Fax 734-3218
Evart MS 300/5-8
321 N Hemlock St 49631 231-734-4222
Sue Lenahan, prin. Fax 734-2931

Ewen, Ontonagon
Ewen-Trout Creek SD 300/K-12
14312 Airport Rd 49925 906-988-2350
Lee Lindberg, supt. Fax 988-2549
www.etc.k12.mi.us/
Ewen-Trout Creek ES 100/K-6
14312 Airport Rd 49925 906-988-2365
Lee Lindberg, prin. Fax 988-2549

Fairgrove, Tuscola, Pop. 619
Akron-Fairgrove SD 400/K-12
PO Box 217 48733 989-693-6163
Joseph Candela, supt. Fax 693-6560
www.a-f.k12.mi.us
Other Schools – See Akron

Fair Haven, Saint Clair, Pop. 1,505
East China SD
Supt. — See East China
Palms ES 200/K-5
6101 Palms Rd 48023 810-676-1350
Robbie Kafcas, prin. Fax 676-1360

Immaculate Conception S 200/PK-8
7043 Church Rd 48023 586-725-0078
Kathleen Steele, prin. Fax 725-8240

Fairview, Oscoda
Fairview Area SD 300/K-12
1879 E Miller Rd 48621 989-848-7000
James Wilcoxen, supt. Fax 848-7070
www.fairview.k12.mi.us
Fairview S 200/K-8
1879 E Miller Rd 48621 989-848-7009
Raymond Poellet, prin. Fax 848-7073

Farmington, Oakland, Pop. 10,035
Farmington SD 11,800/PK-12
32500 Shiawassee Rd 48336 248-489-3349
Susan Zurvalec, supt. Fax 489-3348
www.farmington.k12.mi.us
Farmington ECC PK-PK
30415 Shiawassee Rd 48336 248-489-3373
Kirsten Jules, coord. Fax 489-3378
Flanders ES 300/K-5
32600 Flanders St 48336 248-489-3673
Rosemarie Simon, prin. Fax 489-3681
Gill ES 500/K-5
21195 Gill Rd 48335 248-489-3690
Mark Morawski, prin. Fax 489-3480
Longacre ES 400/K-5
34850 Arundel Dr 48335 248-489-3733
Barbara Lafer, prin. Fax 489-3730
Other Schools – See Farmington Hills, West Bloomfield

Our Lady of Sorrows S 700/PK-8
24040 Raphael Rd 48336 248-476-0977
Mariann Lupinacci, prin. Fax 615-5567
St. Fabian S 400/K-6
32200 W 12 Mile Rd 48334 248-553-2750
Keiren Stoller, prin. Fax 848-3035
St. Paul Lutheran S 200/PK-8
20815 Middlebelt Rd 48336 248-474-2488
David Kusch, prin. Fax 474-1945

Farmington Hills, Oakland, Pop. 80,223
Farmington SD
Supt. — See Farmington
Alameda ECC 100/PK-PK
32400 Alameda St 48336 248-489-3808
Nancy Ely, prin. Fax 489-3810
Beechview ES 400/K-5
26850 Westmeath Ct 48334 248-489-3655
Sharon Cooper, prin. Fax 489-3659
Dunckel MS 700/6-8
32800 W 12 Mile Rd 48334 248-489-3577
Allen Archer, prin. Fax 489-3590
East MS 800/6-8
25000 Middlebelt Rd 48336 248-489-3601
Ken Sanders, prin. Fax 489-3606
Forest ES 400/K-5
34545 Old Timber Rd 48331 248-785-2068
Jon Manier, prin. Fax 788-2002
Grace ES 300/K-5
29040 Shiawassee Rd 48336 248-489-3747
Pam Green, prin. Fax 489-3752
Highmeadow Common Campus ES 300/1-5
30175 Highmeadow Rd 48334 248-785-2070
Dyanne Sanders, prin. Fax 737-9135
Hillside ES 600/K-5
36801 W 11 Mile Rd 48335 248-489-3773
Kathy Smith, prin. Fax 489-3781
Lanigan ES 500/K-5
23800 Tuck Rd 48336 248-489-3722
Robert Kauffman, prin. Fax 489-3742
Power MS 700/6-8
34740 Rhonswood St 48335 248-489-3622
Robert Kovar, prin. Fax 489-3628
Warner MS 600/6-8
30303 W 14 Mile Rd 48334 248-785-2030
Mark Watson, prin. Fax 855-2831
Wood Creek ES 300/K-5
28400 Harwich Dr 48334 248-785-2077
Fax 851-1526
Wooddale ES 300/K-5
34275 Oak Forest Dr 48331 248-489-3766
Fax 489-3555

Art Start Montessori Academy 100/PK-4
31195 W 13 Mile Rd 48334 248-626-2850
Suman Kapila, dir. Fax 626-0952
Hillel Day S 600/K-8
32200 Middlebelt Rd 48334 248-851-3220
Steve Freedman, hdmstr. Fax 851-5095
Maria Montessori Center 100/PK-8
32450 W 13 Mile Rd 48334 248-851-9695
Thomas Kerbawy, prin.
Red Hill Montessori S 100/PK-4
29001 W 13 Mile Rd 48334 248-851-4166
Leila Charlesworth, prin. Fax 851-4237

Farwell, Clare, Pop. 850
Farwell Area SD 1,400/K-12
371 E Main St 48622 989-588-9917
David Peterson, supt. Fax 588-6440
www.farwellschools.net/
Farwell ES 400/K-4
268 E Ohio St 48622 989-588-9916
Diane Wilberding, prin. Fax 588-0158
Farwell MS 500/5-8
500 E Ohio St 48622 989-588-9915
Catheryn Gross, prin. Fax 588-3337

Felch, Dickinson
North Dickinson County SD 400/K-12
W6588 State Highway M69 49831 906-542-9281
Claude Siders, supt. Fax 542-6950
www.go-nordics.com
North Dickinson S 400/K-12
W6588 State Highway M69 49831 906-542-9281
Dan Nurmi, prin. Fax 542-6950

Fennville, Allegan, Pop. 1,446
Fennville SD 1,500/K-12
5 Memorial Dr 49408 269-561-7331
Dirk Weeldreyer, supt. Fax 561-5792
www.fennvilleschools.org/
Fennville Lower ES 300/K-2
8 North St 49408 269-561-7231
Kathy Kirby, prin. Fax 561-2356
Fennville MS 300/6-8
1 Memorial Dr 49408 269-561-7341
Jody Martin, prin. Fax 561-2143
Fennville Upper ES 300/3-5
8 North St 49408 269-561-7236
Wendy Dubuisson, prin. Fax 561-7271

Fenton, Genesee, Pop. 11,946
Fenton Area SD 3,400/K-12
3100 Owen Rd 48430 810-591-4701
Peggy Yates, supt. Fax 591-4705
www.fenton.k12.mi.us
Fenton IS 500/5-6
404 W Ellen St 48430 810-591-8300
Trevor Alward, prin. Fax 591-8305
North Road ES 400/K-4
525 North Rd 48430 810-591-1500
Melody Strang, prin. Fax 591-1505
Schmidt MS 600/7-8
3255 Donaldson Dr 48430 810-591-7700
Pete Vance, prin. Fax 591-7705
State Road ES 300/K-4
1161 State Rd 48430 810-591-2400
Barry Tiemann, prin. Fax 591-2405
Tomek-Eastern ES 400/K-4
600 4th St 48430 810-591-6800
Patricia Baldwin, prin. Fax 591-6805

Lake Fenton Community SD 1,600/K-12
11425 Torrey Rd 48430 810-591-4141
Ralph Coaster, supt. Fax 591-9866
lake-fenton.k12.mi.us
Lake Fenton MS 400/6-8
11425 Torrey Rd 48430 810-591-2209
Dan Ferguson, prin. Fax 591-8475
Torrey Hills IS 400/3-5
12410 Torrey Rd 48430 810-591-3617
Kathleen Conover, prin. Fax 591-3550
West Shore ES 300/K-2
3076 Lahring Rd 48430 810-591-6542
Denise Rodgers, prin. Fax 591-5399

St. John the Evangelist S 500/K-8
514 Lincoln St 48430 810-629-6551
Ted Havens, prin. Fax 629-2213

Ferndale, Oakland, Pop. 21,460
Ferndale SD 4,200/PK-12
2920 Burdette St 48220 248-586-8652
Gary Meier, supt. Fax 586-8655
www.ferndaleschools.org
Coolidge IS 300/4-6
2521 Bermuda St 48220 248-586-8758
Gail Snoddy, prin. Fax 586-8754
Ferndale MS 500/7-8
725 Pinecrest Dr 48220 248-586-8830
Dawn Warren, prin. Fax 586-8834
Grant ECC 50/PK-PK
21131 Garden Ln 48220 248-586-8820
Denise Stevens, dir. Fax 586-8819
Roosevelt PS 400/K-3
2610 Pinecrest Dr 48220 248-586-8803
Dina Krause, prin. Fax 586-8804
Other Schools – See Oak Park

Hazel Park SD
Supt. — See Hazel Park
Webb ES 300/K-5
2100 Woodward Hts 48220 248-658-5900
James Knapp, prin. Fax 544-5316

Fife Lake, Grand Traverse, Pop. 466
Forest Area Community SD 900/PK-12
7741 Shippy Rd SW 49633 231-369-4191
John Smith, supt. Fax 369-4153
www.forestarea.k12.mi.us
Fife Lake ES 200/3-5
7741 Shippy Rd SW 49633 231-879-3362
M. R. Gillooly, prin. Fax 879-4825
Forest Area MS 200/6-8
7741 Shippy Rd SW 49633 231-369-2867
M.J. Grajewski, prin. Fax 369-3618
Other Schools – See South Boardman

Flat Rock, Wayne, Pop. 9,560
Flat Rock Community SD 1,800/K-12
28639 Division St 48134 734-535-6500
Russell Pickell, supt. Fax 535-6501
www.flatrockschools.org
Barnes ES 400/3-5
24925 Meadows Ave 48134 734-535-6800
Ronald Smith, prin. Fax 535-6801
Bobcean ES 300/K-2
28300 Evergreen St 48134 734-535-6900
Joan Donaldson, prin. Fax 535-6901
Simpson MS 500/6-8
24900 Meadows Ave 48134 734-535-6700
Blaine Armstrong, prin. Fax 535-6701

Flint, Genesee, Pop. 118,551
Beecher Community SD 1,700/PK-12
1020 W Coldwater Rd 48505 810-591-9200
Jerri Lynn Williams, supt. Fax 591-5755
www.beecherschools.org/
Tucker ES 400/K-6
G5159 Summit St 48505 810-591-9361
Diana Castle, coord. Fax 591-6190
Other Schools – See Mount Morris

Carman-Ainsworth Community SD 4,900/K-12
G3475 W Court St 48532 810-591-3700
William Haley, supt. Fax 591-3323
www.carman.k12.mi.us
Carman-Ainsworth MS 1,300/6-8
1409 W Maple Ave 48507 810-591-3500
Kevin Summey, prin. Fax 591-3594
Dye ES 400/K-5
1174 S Graham Rd 48532 810-591-3229
Detra Fields, prin. Fax 591-3310
Randels ES 600/K-5
6022 Brobeck St 48532 810-591-3250
Bonnie Haffajee, prin. Fax 591-3225
Woodland ES 300/K-5
G-3493 Beveridge Rd 48532 810-591-3270
Maria Cox, prin. Fax 591-3265
Other Schools – See Burton, Swartz Creek

Flint Community SD 13,500/PK-12
923 E Kearsley St 48503 810-760-1000
Linda Thompson, supt. Fax 760-6790
www.flintschools.org
Anderson ES 300/PK-6
G3248 Mackin Rd 48504 810-760-1614
Napoleon Demps, prin. Fax 760-5191
Brownell ES 300/PK-6
6302 Oxley Dr 48504 810-760-1643
Valeria Shepard, prin. Fax 760-1538
Bryant ES 500/PK-6
201 E Pierson Rd 48505 810-760-7254
Grant Whitehead, prin. Fax 760-1522
Bunche ES 300/PK-6
4121 M L King Ave 48505 810-760-1700
Ed Walthers, prin. Fax 760-5101
Carpenter Road ES 300/PK-6
6901 N Webster Rd 48505 810-760-1709
Kimberly Cross, prin. Fax 760-5099
Civic Park ES 400/PK-6
1402 W Dayton St 48504 810-760-1441
Brenda Greer, prin. Fax 760-5395
Coolidge ES 400/PK-6
3615 Van Buren Ave 48503 810-760-1422
James Bracy, prin. Fax 760-7035
Dort ES 300/PK-6
601 E Witherbee St 48505 810-760-1450
Curtis Speights, prin. Fax 760-5499

Doyle-Ryder ES 500/PK-6
1040 N Saginaw St 48503 810-760-5266
Shirley Henderson, prin. Fax 760-5118
Durant-Tuuri-Mott ES 500/PK-6
1518 W 3rd Ave 48504 810-760-1594
Daniel Berezny, prin. Fax 760-7729
Eisenhower ES 300/PK-6
1235 Pershing St 48503 810-760-1607
Patti Davis, prin. Fax 760-7457
Freeman ES 400/PK-6
4001 Ogema Ave 48507 810-760-1797
June Alexander, prin. Fax 760-6882
Garfield ES 300/PK-6
301 E McClellan St 48505 810-760-1677
Mary Madden, prin. Fax 760-7013
Holmes MS 100/7-8
6602 Oxley Dr 48504 810-760-1620
Cheryl Adkins, prin. Fax 760-5346
King ECC 200/PK-K
520 W Rankin St 48505 810-760-1344
Lauren Chom, prin. Fax 760-7006
Manley K 400/PK-K
3002 Farley St 48507 810-760-1841
Linda Burroughs, prin. Fax 760-7299
McKinley MS 800/7-8
4501 Camden Ave 48507 810-760-1356
Lavern Bond, prin. Fax 760-5104
Merrill ES 200/PK-6
1501 W Moore St 48504 810-760-1633
Carl Evans, prin. Fax 760-5131
Neithercut ES 500/PK-6
2010 Crestbrook Ln 48507 810-760-1359
Marcia James, prin. Fax 760-5133
Pierce ES 600/PK-6
1101 W Vernon Dr 48503 810-760-1386
Kathlene Chapman, prin. Fax 760-7147
Potter ES 500/PK-6
2500 N Averill Ave 48506 810-760-1813
Tony Sitko, prin. Fax 760-5156
Scott ES 400/PK-6
1602 S Averill Ave 48503 810-760-1805
Sherry Baker, prin. Fax 760-1808
Stewart ES 200/PK-6
1950 Burr Blvd 48503 810-760-1573
Sherry Anderson, prin. Fax 760-5153
Summerfield ES 400/PK-6
1360 Milbourne Ave 48504 810-760-1550
Phyllis McCree, prin. Fax 760-4061
Washington ES 500/PK-6
1400 N Vernon Ave 48506 810-760-1381
Maria Hope, prin. Fax 760-4065
Wilkins ES 200/PK-6
121 E York Ave 48505 810-760-1693
Diana Wright, prin. Fax 760-5158
Williams ES 300/PK-6
3501 Minnesota Ave 48506 810-760-1658
Karen Krohn, prin. Fax 760-7019

Kearsley Community SD 3,300/PK-12
4396 Underhill Dr 48506 810-591-8000
Jeffry Morgan, supt. Fax 591-8421
www.kearsley.k12.mi.us
Armstrong MS 900/6-8
6161 Hopkins Rd 48506 810-591-9929
Patti Yorks, prin. Fax 591-9944
Buffey ES 300/2-5
4235 Crosby Rd 48506 810-591-9922
Casey Killingbeck, prin. Fax 591-9924
Burgtorf ECC PK-PK
4160 Underhill Dr 48506 810-591-3585
Julie Dinnan, dir. Fax 591-3595
Dowdall ES 400/2-5
3333 Shillelagh Dr 48506 810-591-2274
Annette Miller, prin. Fax 591-2276
Fiedler ES 300/2-5
6317 Nightingale Dr 48506 810-591-9925
Kelly Fisher, prin. Fax 591-9927
Other Schools – See Burton

Westwood Heights SD 900/PK-12
3400 N Jennings Rd 48504 810-591-0870
Dr. Deborah Hunter-Harvill, supt. Fax 591-0898
www.hamadyhawks.net
Hamady MS 300/6-8
3223 W Carpenter Rd 48504 810-591-0895
Cresynthia Devereaux, prin. Fax 591-5140
McMonagle ES 200/PK-5
3484 N Jennings Rd 48504 810-591-5145
Salli Stevens, prin. Fax 591-5149

Fairhaven SDA S 50/1-8
1379 Louis Ave 48505 810-785-4024
John Adeogun, prin. Fax 785-6207
First Flint SDA S 50/1-8
G4285 Beecher Rd 48532 810-732-0230
Gayle Stevens, prin. Fax 732-0065
Holy Rosary S 100/K-8
5191 Richfield Rd 48506 810-736-4220
Fax 736-1064
St. John Vianney S 300/PK-8
2319 Bagley St 48504 810-235-5687
Kathleen Slattery, prin. Fax 235-2811
St. Mark Lutheran S 100/PK-8
5073 Daly Blvd 48506 810-736-6910
Mark Schallhorn, prin. Fax 736-6096
St. Paul Lutheran S 200/PK-8
402 S Ballenger Hwy 48532 810-239-6733
Mary Buck, prin. Fax 239-5466
St. Pius X S 200/PK-8
G3139 Hogarth Ave 48532 810-235-8572
R.J. Kaplan, prin. Fax 235-2675

Flushing, Genesee, Pop. 8,110
Flushing Community SD 4,200/PK-12
522 N McKinley Rd 48433 810-591-1180
Barbara Goebel, supt. Fax 591-0656
www.flushing.k12.mi.us
Central ES 500/1-6
525 Coutant St 48433 810-591-1901
Bob Chase, prin. Fax 591-0669
Elms ES 500/1-6
6125 N Elms Rd 48433 810-591-7350
John Hagens, prin. Fax 591-0690
Flushing ECC 50/PK-K
409 Chamberlain St 48433 810-591-2326
Kaye Brisson, prin. Fax 591-0699
Flushing MS 800/7-8
8100 Carpenter Rd 48433 810-591-2800
Andrew Schmidt, prin. Fax 591-0148
Seymour ES 500/1-6
3088 N Seymour Rd 48433 810-591-5150
Joseph Reinfelder, prin. Fax 591-0595
Springview ES 400/1-6
1233 Springview Dr 48433 810-591-8550
Kasey Cronin, prin. Fax 591-8555

St. Robert Bellarmine S 300/PK-8
214 E Henry St 48433 810-659-2503
Susan Sharp, prin. Fax 659-4002

Fort Gratiot, Saint Clair, Pop. 8,968
Port Huron Area SD
Supt. — See Port Huron
Edison ES 400/PK-5
3559 Pollina Ave 48059 810-984-6507
Mary Ann Wiegand, prin. Fax 989-2740
Fort Gratiot MS 700/6-8
3985 Keewahdin Rd 48059 810-984-6544
Debra Ladensack, prin. Fax 385-1624
Keewahdin ES 400/K-5
4801 Lakeshore Rd 48059 810-984-6517
Gerald Weaver, prin. Fax 385-2916

Fowler, Clinton, Pop. 1,081
Fowler SD 500/PK-12
PO Box 408 48835 989-593-2296
Neil Hufnagel, supt. Fax 593-2125
www.fps.k12.mi.us
Waldron S 400/PK-8
PO Box 408 48835 989-593-2160
Kristine Naumann, prin. Fax 593-2125

Most Holy Trinity MS 100/4-8
11144 W Kent St 48835 989-593-2616
Anne Hufnagel, prin. Fax 593-2801

Fowlerville, Livingston, Pop. 3,132
Fowlerville Community SD 2,300/K-12
PO Box 769 48836 517-223-6000
Ed Alverson, supt. Fax 223-6022
www.fvl.k12.mi.us
Fowlerville JHS 500/6-8
PO Box 769 48836 517-223-6003
Tom Tannar, prin. Fax 223-6199
Kreeger ES 400/3-5
PO Box 769 48836 517-223-6006
Jan Fleck, prin. Fax 223-6388
Smith ES 400/K-2
PO Box 769 48836 517-223-6005
Jim Kitchen, prin. Fax 223-6444

Frankenmuth, Saginaw, Pop. 4,803
Frankenmuth SD 1,200/K-12
941 E Genesee St 48734 989-652-9958
Mary Anne Ackerman, supt. Fax 652-9780
www.frankenmuth.k12.mi.us/
List ES 400/K-4
805 E Genesee St 48734 989-652-6187
Adele Martin, prin. Fax 652-7255
Rittmueller MS 300/5-8
965 E Genesee St 48734 989-652-6119
Martin Mattlin, prin. Fax 652-2921

St. Lorenz Lutheran S 500/PK-8
140 Churchgrove Rd 48734 989-652-6141
Michael Bender, prin. Fax 652-9071

Frankfort, Benzie, Pop. 1,493
Frankfort-Elberta Area SD 600/K-12
534 11th St 49635 231-352-4641
Thomas Stobie, supt. Fax 352-5066
www.frankfort.k12.mi.us
Frankfort ES 300/K-6
613 Leelanau Ave 49635 231-352-7601
Jeffrey Tousley, prin. Fax 352-5066

Franklin, Oakland, Pop. 2,958

Huda S 300/PK-8
32220 Franklin Rd 48025 248-626-0900
Azra Ali, prin. Fax 626-7146

Fraser, Macomb, Pop. 15,095
Fraser SD 5,100/PK-12
33466 Garfield Rd 48026 586-439-7000
Richard Repicky, supt. Fax 439-7001
www.fraser.k12.mi.us/
Edison ES 500/K-6
17470 Sewel 48026 586-439-6500
Dr. Kristi Weiss, prin. Fax 439-6501
Eisenhower ES 500/K-6
31275 Eveningside 48026 586-439-6600
Stephen Zielinski, prin. Fax 439-6601
Emerson ES 400/K-6
32151 Danna 48026 586-439-6700
K. Madeleine, prin. Fax 439-6701
Richards MS 800/7-8
33500 Garfield Rd 48026 586-439-7400
Jeffrey Wood, prin. Fax 439-7401
Other Schools – See Clinton Township, Roseville

St. John Lutheran S 200/PK-8
16339 E 14 Mile Rd 48026 586-294-8740
David Waltz, prin. Fax 294-9565

Freeland, Saginaw, Pop. 1,421
Freeland Community SD 1,600/K-12
710 Powley Dr 48623 989-695-5527
Matthew Cairy, supt. Fax 695-5789
www.freeland.k12.mi.us
Freeland ES 500/3-6
710 Powley Dr 48623 989-695-5371
Tim Parson, prin. Fax 695-5789
Freeland Learning Center 200/K-2
307 S 3rd St 48623 989-695-5721
Beverly Beyer, prin. Fax 695-2508
Freeland MS 300/7-8
8250 Webster Rd 48623 989-692-4032
Christopher Arrington, prin. Fax 692-4034

Free Soil, Mason, Pop. 180
Free Soil Community SD 50/K-8
8480 N Democrat St 49411 231-464-5651
Ronald Nurnberger, supt. Fax 464-5337
www.freesoil.net
Free Soil Community S 50/K-8
8480 N Democrat St 49411 231-464-5651
Sharon Spencer, prin. Fax 464-5337

Fremont, Newaygo, Pop. 4,256
Fremont SD 2,500/K-12
220 W Pine St 49412 231-924-2350
John Kingsnorth Ph.D., supt. Fax 924-5264
www.fremont.net
Daisy Brook ES 400/4-5
502 N Division Ave 49412 231-924-4380
Nancy Sparks, prin. Fax 924-9117
Fremont MS 600/6-8
500 Woodrow St 49412 231-924-0230
Carolyn Hummel, prin. Fax 924-9149
Pathfinder ES 500/1-3
109 W 44th St 49412 231-924-7230
Bob Cassiday, prin. Fax 924-7231
Pine Street Primary Center 200/K-K
450 E Pine St 49412 231-924-3530
Nancy Sparks, prin. Fax 924-9284

Newaygo County RESA 200/
4747 W 48th St 49412 231-924-0381
Lori Clark, supt. Fax 924-8910
www.ncresa.org/
Fremont Center PK-PK
4575 W 48th St 49412 231-924-5820
Eva Houseman, dir.
Other Schools – See Newaygo

Fremont Christian S 200/PK-8
208 Hillcrest Ave 49412 231-924-2740
Joseph Fox, prin. Fax 924-1240

Fruitport, Muskegon, Pop. 1,087
Fruitport Community SD 3,100/PK-12
3255 Pontaluna Rd 49415 231-865-4100
Fax 865-3393
www.fruitportschools.net
Edgewood ES 500/PK-5
3255 Pontaluna Rd 49415 231-865-3171
Amy Upham, prin. Fax 865-4085
Fruitport MS 700/6-8
3113 Pontaluna Rd 49415 231-865-3128
Ellen Beal, prin. Fax 865-4086
Other Schools – See Muskegon

Calvary Christian S 200/PK-12
5873 Kendra Rd 49415 231-865-2141
Tom Kapanka, admin. Fax 865-8730

Gaines, Genesee, Pop. 363
Swartz Creek Community SD
Supt. — See Swartz Creek
Gaines ES 300/K-5
300 Lansing St 48436 810-591-1076
Michael Gibbons, prin. Fax 591-1099

Galesburg, Kalamazoo, Pop. 1,926
Galesburg-Augusta Community SD 1,100/PK-12
1076 N 37th St 49053 269-484-2000
Doug Newington, supt. Fax 484-2001
www.gacsnet.org
Galesburg-Augusta PS 300/PK-3
315 W Battle Creek St 49053 269-484-2040
Christopher Hurley, prin. Fax 484-2041
Other Schools – See Augusta

Galien, Berrien, Pop. 578
Galien Township SD 200/PK-8
PO Box 248 49113 269-545-3364
Jon Garcia, supt. Fax 545-2483
www.remc11.k12.mi.us./galien
Galien MS 50/6-8
PO Box 248 49113 269-545-3365
Jonathan Garcia, prin. Fax 545-2483
Wolford ES 100/PK-5
PO Box 248 49113 269-545-3365
Jonathan Garcia, prin. Fax 545-2483

Garden City, Wayne, Pop. 28,960
Garden City SD 5,300/K-12
1333 Radcliff St 48135 734-762-6311
Michelle Cline, supt. Fax 762-6310
www.gardencityschools.com
Douglas ES 500/K-6
6400 Hartel St 48135 734-762-8450
Alexander McNeece, prin. Fax 762-8535
Farmington ES 400/K-6
33411 Marquette St 48135 734-762-8460
Kristopher O'Leary, prin. Fax 762-8536
Garden City MS 800/7-8
1851 Radcliff St 48135 734-762-8400
Brian Sumner, prin. Fax 762-8532
Lathers ES 500/K-6
28351 Marquette St 48135 734-762-8490
Susan Ford, prin. Fax 762-8539

Memorial ES 500/K-6
30001 Marquette St 48135 734-762-8480
Mary Pantier, prin. Fax 762-8538
Ruff ES 500/K-6
30300 Maplewood St 48135 734-762-8470
Jan Blumberg, prin. Fax 762-8537

St. Dunstan S 100/K-8
1615 Belton St 48135 734-425-4380
Don Lipinski, prin. Fax 425-8411
St. Raphael S 300/K-8
31500 Beechwood St 48135 734-425-9771
Jeanine Kenny, prin. Fax 427-8895

Gaylord, Otsego, Pop. 3,730
Gaylord Community SD 3,100/K-12
615 S Elm Ave 49735 989-705-3080
Cheryl Wojtas, supt. Fax 732-6029
www.gaylordschools.com
Gaylord IS 700/4-6
240 E 4th St 49735 989-731-0856
Rich Marshall, prin. Fax 732-6475
Gaylord MS 500/7-8
600 E 5th St 49735 989-731-0848
Gerald Belanger, prin. Fax 732-2632
North Ohio ES 300/K-3
912 N Ohio Ave 49735 989-731-2648
Dan Vaara, prin. Fax 731-3387
South Maple ES 400/K-3
650 E 5th St 49735 989-731-0648
Therese Hansen, prin. Fax 731-0095

Grace Baptist Christian S 100/PK-12
PO Box 177 49734 989-732-5676
Chad Vest, prin. Fax 731-1122
Otsego Christian S 100/PK-7
PO Box 1365 49734 989-732-8333
Karla Hawkins, admin. Fax 705-7713
St. Mary Cathedral S 300/PK-12
321 N Otsego Ave 49735 989-732-5801
Cynthia Pineda, prin. Fax 732-2085

Genesee, Genesee
Genesee SD 900/PK-12
PO Box 220 48437 810-591-1650
Jeff Rohrer, supt. Fax 591-1646
www.geneseeschools.org
Haas ES 500/PK-6
7347 N Genesee Rd 48437 810-591-2101
Joseph Perrera, prin. Fax 591-1656

Gibraltar, Wayne, Pop. 5,191
Gibraltar SD
Supt. — See Woodhaven
Parsons ES 500/PK-5
14473 Middle Gibraltar Rd 48173 734-379-7050
Belinda Livingston, prin. Fax 379-7051
Shumate MS 900/6-8
30448 W Jefferson Ave 48173 734-379-7600
Brad Coon, prin. Fax 379-2370

Gladstone, Delta, Pop. 5,255
Gladstone Area SD 1,500/K-12
400 S 10th St 49837 906-428-2417
Dr. Jay Kulbertis, supt. Fax 789-8457
www.gladstoneschools.com
Cameron ES 200/K-2
803 29th St 49837 906-428-2314
Karl Dollhopf, prin. Fax 789-8502
Gladstone MS 400/6-8
300 S 10th St 49837 906-428-2295
Dave Ballard, prin. Fax 789-8404
Jones ES 300/3-5
400 S 10th St 49837 906-428-3660
Karl Dollhopf, prin. Fax 789-8464

Gladwin, Gladwin, Pop. 3,018
Gladwin Community SD 1,800/K-12
401 N Bowery Ave 48624 989-426-9255
Rick Seebeck, supt. Fax 426-5981
www.gcsnet.org
Gladwin ES 300/K-2
600 W 1st St 48624 989-426-7771
Marcene Damitz, prin. Fax 426-6036
Gladwin IS 400/3-5
780 W 1st St 48624 989-426-4531
Joe Cote, prin. Fax 426-6037
Gladwin JHS 500/6-8
401 N Bowery Ave 48624 989-426-3808
Clair Wetmore, prin. Fax 426-6038

Sacred Heart S 100/PK-8
330 N Silverleaf St 48624 989-426-8574
Lorraine Dunn, prin. Fax 426-5770
Skeels Christian S 100/PK-12
3956 N M 18 48624 989-426-2054
Mary Owens, admin. Fax 426-4527

Glenn, Allegan
Glenn SD 50/K-6
PO Box 68 49416 269-673-2161
Michael O'Connor, supt. Fax 673-2361
www.glennpublicschool.org
Glenn ES 50/K-6
PO Box 68 49416 269-227-3411
Michael O'Connor, prin. Fax 673-2361

Glennie, Alcona
Oscoda Area SD
Supt. — See Oscoda
Glennie ES 50/PK-5
4932 Bamfield Rd 48737 989-735-2261
Jane Negro, prin. Fax 735-2410

Gobles, Van Buren, Pop. 807
Gobles SD 1,100/K-12
PO Box 412 49055 269-628-5618
Brenda Wilson, supt. Fax 628-5306
www.gobles.org/
Gobles ES 500/K-6
PO Box 412 49055 269-628-2131
Terry Breen, prin. Fax 628-2824
Gobles MS 100/7-8
PO Box 412 49055 269-628-5680
Chris Miller, prin. Fax 628-5768

Gobles Jr. Academy 50/1-10
32110 6th Ave 49055 269-628-2704
Thomas Coffee, prin. Fax 628-7314

Goodrich, Genesee, Pop. 1,567
Goodrich Area SD 2,100/K-12
8029 Gale Rd 48438 810-591-2250
Larry Allen, supt. Fax 591-2550
www.goodrich.k12.mi.us/
Goodrich MS 500/6-8
7480 Gale Rd 48438 810-591-4210
Jerry Lawrason Ph.D., prin. Fax 636-7879
Oaktree ES 500/3-5
7500 Gale Rd 48438 810-591-5200
Elizabeth Wallberg, prin. Fax 591-5210
Reid ES 300/K-2
7501 Seneca St 48438 810-591-3455
Paul Minns, prin. Fax 636-2622

Grand Blanc, Genesee, Pop. 7,898
Grand Blanc Community SD 7,300/PK-12
11920 S Saginaw St 48439 810-591-6000
Dr. Michael Newton, supt. Fax 591-6018
www.grandblancschools.org
Anderson ES 300/K-2
5290 Leroy St 48439 810-591-5829
Barbara Watkins, prin. Fax 591-5833
Brendel ES 400/K-5
223 Bush St 48439 810-591-6137
Rachel Turner, prin. Fax 591-6149
City S 100/K-8
11920 S Saginaw St 48439 810-591-6078
Tia Dale, prin. Fax 591-6095
Cook ES 300/K-5
4434 E Cook Rd 48439 810-591-7910
Judy Webber, prin. Fax 591-7916
Grand Blanc MS East 900/6-8
6100 Perry Rd 48439 810-591-4696
Jodi Kruse, prin. Fax 591-0242
Grand Blanc MS West 900/6-8
1515 E Reid Rd 48439 810-591-7309
Jeff Neall, prin. Fax 591-0182
Indian Hill ES 400/K-5
11240 Woodbridge Dr 48439 810-591-4100
Sarah Stone, prin. Fax 591-4101
Mason ES 400/3-5
4455 E Cook Rd 48439 810-591-7840
Sonya James, prin. Fax 591-7811
McGrath ES 400/3-5
5288 Todd St 48439 810-591-5827
Cheryl Hemond, prin. Fax 591-5824
Myers ES 600/K-5
6085 Sun Valley Dr 48439 810-591-3000
Lonnie Vallie, prin. Fax 591-3002
Perry Learning Center 200/PK-K
11920 S Saginaw St 48439 810-591-6078
Tia Dale, dir. Fax 591-6095
Reid ES 500/K-5
2103 E Reid Rd 48439 810-591-7121
Brian Scieszka, prin. Fax 591-7179

Holy Family S 500/PK-8
215 Orchard St 48439 810-694-9072
Michele Jahn, prin. Fax 694-9405

Grand Haven, Ottawa, Pop. 10,586
Grand Haven Area SD 5,900/PK-12
1415 S Beechtree St 49417 616-850-5015
Keith Konarska, supt. Fax 850-5010
www.ghaps.org
Ferry ES 400/PK-5
1050 Pennoyer Ave 49417 616-850-5300
Harry Weller, prin. Fax 850-5310
Griffin ES 400/K-5
1700 S Griffin St 49417 616-850-5500
Debra Mann, prin. Fax 850-5510
Lakeshore MS 500/6-8
900 Cutler St 49417 616-850-6500
Julia Houle, prin. Fax 850-6510
Peach Plains ES 400/PK-5
15849 Comstock St 49417 616-850-5800
Kate Drake, prin. Fax 850-5810
Robinson ES 400/K-5
11801 120th Ave 49417 616-850-5900
Jeff Marcus, prin. Fax 850-5910
Rosy Mound ES 400/K-5
14016 Lakeshore Dr 49417 616-850-6700
Kevin Blanding, prin. Fax 850-6710
White ES 400/K-5
1400 Wisconsin Ave 49417 616-850-5700
Valerie Livingston, prin. Fax 850-5710
White Pines MS 700/6-8
1400 S Griffin St 49417 616-850-6300
Mike Shelton, prin. Fax 850-6310
Other Schools – See Spring Lake

Grand Haven Christian S 300/PK-8
1102 Grant Ave 49417 616-842-5420
Richard Geertsma, prin. Fax 842-6850
St. John Lutheran S 100/PK-8
525 Taylor Ave 49417 616-842-0260
Laura Harvey, admin. Fax 842-0934
St. Patrick Preschool PK-PK
901 Columbus Ave 49417 616-842-8230
Wendy DeWent, dir. Fax 842-1174

Grand Ledge, Eaton, Pop. 7,768
Grand Ledge SD 5,300/K-12
220 Lamson St 48837 517-925-5400
Steve Matthews Ed.D., supt. Fax 925-5409
www.glps.k12.mi.us/
Beagle MS 500/6-8
600 W South St 48837 517-925-5480
Charles Phillips, prin. Fax 925-5523
Greenwood ES 300/K-5
310 Greenwood St 48837 517-925-5600
Susan Friend, prin. Fax 925-5633
Hayes MS 700/6-8
12620 Nixon Rd 48837 517-925-5680
Chris Groves, prin. Fax 925-5730
Holbrook ES 300/K-5
615 Jones St 48837 517-925-5640
Mark Christman, prin. Fax 925-5667
Neff ES 400/K-5
950 Jenne St 48837 517-925-5740
Edward Armstrong, prin. Fax 925-5772
Willow Ridge ES 500/K-5
12840 Nixon Rd 48837 517-925-5775
Michael Johnson, prin. Fax 925-5811
Other Schools – See Eagle, Lansing

Oneida Township SD 3 50/K-5
8981 Oneida Rd 48837 517-627-7005
Fax 627-5569

Strange ES 50/K-5
8981 Oneida Rd 48837 517-627-7005
Nancy Ewing, prin. Fax 627-5569

St. Michael S 100/PK-8
325 Edwards St 48837 517-627-2167
Mitzi Luttrull, prin. Fax 627-1289

Grand Marais, Alger
Burt Township SD 100/K-12
PO Box 338 49839 906-494-2543
Penny Barney, supt. Fax 494-2522
Burt Township S 100/K-12
PO Box 338 49839 906-494-2521
Seth Hoopingarner, prin. Fax 494-2522

Grand Rapids, Kent, Pop. 193,780
East Grand Rapids SD 3,000/K-12
2915 Hall St SE 49506 616-235-3535
Dr. Sara Shubel, supt. Fax 235-6730
www.egrps.org/
Breton Downs ES 400/K-5
2500 Boston St SE 49506 616-235-7552
Wendy Van Zegeren, prin. Fax 235-6733
East Grand Rapids MS 600/6-8
2425 Lake Dr SE 49506 616-235-7551
J. Peter Stuursma, prin. Fax 235-7587
Lakeside ES 500/K-5
2325 Hall St SE 49506 616-235-7553
Linda Kehm, prin. Fax 235-3915
Wealthy ES 500/K-5
1961 Lake Dr SE 49506 616-235-7550
Heidi Christiansen, prin. Fax 235-3918

Forest Hills SD 9,400/K-12
6590 Cascade Rd SE 49546 616-493-8800
Daniel Behm, supt. Fax 493-8560
www.fhps.us
Collins ES 400/K-4
4368 Heather Ln SE 49546 616-493-8900
Karen Johnson, prin. Fax 493-8909
Knapp Forest ES 700/K-6
4243 Knapp Valley Dr NE 49525 616-493-8980
Margaret Fellinger, prin. Fax 493-8989
Meadow Brook ES 400/K-4
1450 Forest Hill Ave SE 49546 616-493-8740
Larry Mathews, prin. Fax 493-8749
Northern Hills MS 500/7-8
3775 Leonard St NE 49525 616-493-8650
Nancy Susterka, prin. Fax 493-8686
Northern Trails 5/6 S 400/5-6
3777 Leonard St NE 49525 616-493-8990
Craig Mears, prin. Fax 493-8995
Orchard View ES 500/K-6
2770 Leffingwell Ave NE 49525 616-493-8930
Matt Hanichen, prin. Fax 493-8939
Pine Ridge ES 400/K-4
3250 Redford Dr SE 49546 616-493-8910
David Ellis, prin. Fax 493-8919
Thornapple ES 400/K-4
6932 Bridgewater Dr SE 49546 616-493-8920
Greg Shubel, prin. Fax 493-8929
Other Schools – See Ada

Grand Rapids SD 19,600/PK-12
PO Box 117 49501 616-819-2000
Bernard Taylor Ed.D., supt. Fax 819-2104
www.grpublicschools.org/
Aberdeen ES 200/K-5
928 Aberdeen St NE 49505 616-819-2868
Lynda Walker, prin. Fax 819-1111
Alexander ES 200/K-5
1010 Alexander St SE 49507 616-819-2213
Stephanie Davis, prin. Fax 819-2220
Alger MS 600/6-8
921 Alger St SE 49507 616-819-6200
Michael Ghareeb, prin. Fax 819-6201
Brookside ES 400/K-5
2505 Madison Ave SE 49507 616-819-2242
Ann Lasotta, prin. Fax 819-6059
Buchanan ES 400/PK-5
1775 Buchanan Ave SW 49507 616-819-2252
Yolanda Valenzuela, prin. Fax 819-2249
Burton ES 400/K-5
2133 Buchanan Ave SW 49507 616-819-2262
Margarita Hernandez, prin. Fax 819-2284
Burton MS 400/6-8
2133 Buchanan Ave SW 49507 616-819-2269
Robert Evans, prin. Fax 819-2282
Campau Park ES 200/K-5
50 Antoine St SW 49507 616-819-2290
Cynthia Jones, prin. Fax 819-2291
Campus ES 300/K-5
710 Benjamin Ave SE 49506 616-819-3525
Fax 819-3526

Center of Economicology 6-8
2420 Coit Ave NE 49505 616-819-2955
Dale Hovenkamp, prin. Fax 819-3672
Chavez ES 400/K-5
1205 Grandville Ave SW 49503 616-819-2560
Ana Aleman-Putnam, prin. Fax 819-2556
Coit Creative Arts Academy 200/K-5
617 Coit Ave NE 49503 616-819-2390
Jerry McComb, prin. Fax 819-4209
Congress ES 200/PK-5
940 Baldwin St SE 49506 616-819-2201
JoAnn Riemersma, prin. Fax 819-2203
Covell ES 300/K-5
1417 Covell Ave NW 49504 616-819-2411
Tricia Shenefield, prin. Fax 819-2414
Dickinson ES 200/K-5
448 Dickinson St SE 49507 616-819-2505
Dorothy Johnson, prin. Fax 819-2502
East Leonard ES 200/K-5
410 Barnett St NE 49503 616-819-2525
Mike Meyer, prin. Fax 819-2528
Ford MS 400/6-8
851 Madison Ave SE 49507 616-819-2640
Emmanuel Armstrong, prin. Fax 819-2660
Frost Environmental Science Academy 500/K-8
1460 Laughlin Dr NW 49504 616-819-2550
Pam Wells, prin. Fax 819-2184
Grand Rapids Montessori S 400/PK-8
111 College Ave NE 49503 616-819-2405
Jerry Bentley, prin. Fax 819-2406
Harrison Park ES 500/PK-5
1440 Davis Ave NW 49504 616-819-2565
Mike Nassar, prin. Fax 819-2567
Harrison Park MS 300/6-8
1440 Davis Ave NW 49504 616-819-2570
Jackie Bell, prin. Fax 819-2571
Ken-O-Sha Park ES 200/K-5
1353 Van Auken St SE 49508 616-819-2696
Gary Harmon, prin. Fax 819-3461
Kent Hills ES 200/PK-5
1445 Emerald Ave NE 49505 616-819-2727
Dr. Michele Coyne, prin. Fax 819-2726
King Leadership Academy 500/PK-8
645 Logan St SE 49503 616-819-2600
Carrie Tellerico, prin. Fax 819-2596
Mulick Park ES 300/K-5
1761 Rosewood Ave SE 49506 616-819-2810
Jamie McCabe, prin. Fax 819-2817
North Park ES 100/K-5
3375 Cheney Ave NE 49525 616-819-2848
Fax 819-2849
North Park Montessori Academy 100/PK-6
3375 Cheney Ave NE 49525 616-819-2848
Fax 819-2849
Palmer ES 300/PK-5
309 Palmer St NE 49505 616-819-2929
Rich Miller, prin. Fax 819-2928
Ridgemoor ECC 200/PK-PK
2555 Inverness Rd SE 49546 616-819-2950
Ann Zoellner, admin. Fax 819-2952
Riverside 6th Grade Academy 300/6-6
2420 Coit Ave NE 49505 616-819-2955
Mitchell Balingit, prin. Fax 819-3672
Riverside MS 500/7-8
265 Eleanor St NE 49505 616-819-2969
Mitchell Balingit, prin. Fax 819-2981
Shawmut Hills ES 200/K-5
2550 Burritt St NW 49504 616-819-3055
Steve VanHammen, prin. Fax 819-3056
Shawnee Tech/Math/Science Academy 300/PK-5
2036 Chesaning Dr SE 49506 616-819-3062
Barbara Todd, prin. Fax 819-3065
Sherwood Park Global Studies S 500/K-8
3859 Chamberlain Ave SE 49508 616-819-3095
Michelle Ghareeb, prin. Fax 819-3099
Sibley ES 500/PK-5
947 Sibley St NW 49504 616-819-3100
Mary Ann Prisichenko, prin. Fax 819-3108
Southeast Academic Center 300/K-8
1250 Sigsbee St SE 49506 616-819-3077
Fax 819-3080
Southwest Community Campus 700/PK-8
801 Oakland Ave SW 49503 616-819-2947
Carmen Fernandez, prin. Fax 819-3630
Stocking ES 400/PK-5
863 7th St NW 49504 616-819-3130
Kathy Sainz, prin. Fax 819-3134
University Preparatory Academy 6-8
409 Lafayette Ave SE 49503 616-819-1010
Michael Ghareeb, prin. Fax 819-1011
Westwood MS 500/6-8
1524 Mount Mercy Dr NW 49504 616-819-3322
Pam Orgeck, prin. Fax 819-3301
Zoo ES 100/6-6
1300 Fulton St W 49504 616-819-3344
Pam Wells, prin. Fax 819-3345

Grandville SD
Supt. — See Grandville
Cummings ES 400/K-6
4261 Schoolcraft St SW, 616-254-6040
Scott Merkel, prin. Fax 254-6043

Kelloggsville SD 2,300/PK-12
242 52nd St SE 49548 616-538-7460
Samuel Wright, supt. Fax 530-8194
www.kvilleps.org
East Kelloggsville S 400/K-5
4656 Jefferson Ave SE 49548 616-532-1580
Eric Schilthuis, prin. Fax 532-7487
Kelloggsville ECC 100/PK-PK
977 44th St SW 49509 616-532-1585
Kathleen Stuby, prin. Fax 532-7437
Kelloggsville MS 500/6-8
4650 Division Ave S 49548 616-532-1575
Timothy Reeves, prin. Fax 532-1579
Southeast Kelloggsville S 300/K-5
240 52nd St SE 49548 616-532-1590
Paula Dykstra, prin. Fax 532-7750
West Kelloggsville S 300/K-5
4555 Magnolia Ave SW 49548 616-532-1595
Jeffrey Owen, prin. Fax 532-7475

Kenowa Hills SD 3,400/K-12
2325 4 Mile Rd NW 49544 616-784-2511
Tom Martin, supt. Fax 784-8323
khps.org
Fairview ES 200/K-4
2396 Hillside Dr NW 49544 616-363-3879
Tim Carlson, prin. Fax 363-9099
Kenowa Hills IS 500/5-6
4252 3 Mile Rd NW, 616-453-6351
Erich Harmsen, prin. Fax 453-9686
Kenowa Hills MS 600/7-8
3950 Hendershot Ave NW 49544 616-785-3225
Ruth Posthumus, prin. Fax 784-2404
Walker Station ES 200/K-4
3971 Richmond Ct NW, 616-791-9757
Judy Burtch, prin. Fax 791-1431
Zinser ES 200/K-4
1234 Kinney Ave NW, 616-453-2461
Eric Vermeulen, prin. Fax 453-4828
Other Schools – See Comstock Park, Marne

Kentwood SD
Supt. — See Kentwood
Hamilton ES 300/K-5
3303 Breton Rd SE 49512 616-245-2203
Cindy Charles, prin. Fax 245-3577

Northview SD 3,300/PK-12
4365 Hunsberger Ave NE 49525 616-363-6861
Norman Taylor, supt. Fax 363-9609
www.nvps.net
Crossroads MS 500/7-8
4400 Ambrose Ave NE 49525 616-361-3430
F. Andrew Scogg, prin. Fax 363-7868
East Oakview ES 500/K-4
3940 Suburban Shores Dr NE 49525 616-361-3460
Jerry Klekotka, prin. Fax 361-3458
Highlands MS 400/5-6
4645 Chandy Dr NE 49525 616-361-3440
Dan Duba, prin. Fax 365-6171
North Oakview ES 400/PK-4
4300 Costa Ave NE 49525 616-361-3450
Cindi O'Connor, prin. Fax 365-6161
West Oakview ES 200/K-4
3880 Stuyvesant Ave NE 49525 616-361-3470
Tricia Hampel, prin. Fax 361-3492

All Saints Academy - ES Campus 100/PK-4
2233 Diamond Ave NE 49505 616-364-9453
Christine Burns, prin. Fax 361-6991
All Saints Academy - MS Campus 100/5-8
1110 4 Mile Rd NE 49525 616-363-7725
Christine Burns, prin. Fax 363-3086
Creston Christian S 200/PK-5
1031 Page St NE 49505 616-574-6500
Chip Jenkins, prin. Fax 451-9252
Evergreen Christian S 100/PK-5
1031 Page St NE 49505 616-574-6500
Chip Jenkins, prin. Fax 451-9252
Grand Rapids Christian MS 400/6-8
1875 Rosewood Ave SE 49506 616-574-6350
Mary Broene, prin. Fax 574-6316
Grand Rapids Hebrew Academy 50/PK-7
2615 Michigan St NE 49506 616-957-0770
Grand Rapids SDA Academy 200/K-12
1151 Oakleigh Rd NW 49504 616-791-9797
Debra Barr, prin. Fax 791-7242
Holy Name of Jesus S 100/K-8
1650 Godfrey Ave SW 49509 616-243-1126
Rosa Fraga, prin. Fax 243-0862
Holy Spirit S 400/PK-8
2222 Lake Michigan Dr NW 49504 616-453-2772
Sharon Grant, prin. Fax 453-0018
Hope Protestant Reformed Christian S 300/K-9
1545 Wilson Ave SW, 616-453-9717
Ron Koole, prin. Fax 453-9907
Immaculate Heart of Mary S 400/PK-8
1951 Plymouth Ave SE 49506 616-241-4633
Kathleen Vafadari, prin. Fax 241-4418
Immanuel-St. James Lutheran S 200/PK-8
2066 Oakwood Ave NE 49505 616-454-2216
Karen McCarty, prin. Fax 454-4227
Legacy Christian ES 300/PK-5
520 68th St SE 49548 616-455-0310
Jill Ellens, prin. Fax 455-6162
Legacy Christian MS 200/6-8
67 68th St SW 49548 616-455-3860
Vince Bonnema, prin. Fax 455-1960
Millbrook Christian S 300/PK-5
3662 Poinsettia Ave SE 49508 616-574-6000
Mark Krommendyk, prin. Fax 452-9107
North Hills Classical Academy 100/K-12
2777 Knapp St NE 49525 616-365-0525
Peter VandeBrake, hdmstr. Fax 365-3683
NorthPointe Christian ES 200/PK-6
540 Russwood St NE 49505 616-363-4869
Gordon Nickel, prin. Fax 363-5977
Oakdale Christian S 300/PK-5
1050 Fisk St SE 49507 616-574-5700
Eric Burgess, prin. Fax 245-6661
Our Savior Lutheran S 100/PK-8
1916 Ridgewood Ave SE 49506 616-949-0710
Barry Blomquist, prin. Fax 975-7840
Plymouth Christian S 200/PK-6
1000 Ball Ave NE 49505 616-458-4367
David Engelsma, prin. Fax 458-8532
Potter's House S 300/PK-8
810 Van Raalte Dr SW 49509 616-241-5202
Deb Hoeft, admin. Fax 241-9331
Sacred Heart of Jesus S 100/PK-8
1200 Dayton St SW 49504 616-459-0948
Christine Peplinski, prin. Fax 459-0899
St. Andrew S 100/PK-8
302 Sheldon Blvd SE 49503 616-451-8463
Fax 451-2354
St. Anthony of Padua S 400/PK-8
2510 Richmond St NW 49504 616-453-8229
Julie Whelan, prin. Fax 453-8053
St. Paul the Apostle S 200/PK-8
2750 Burton St SE 49546 616-949-1690
Lori Salva, prin. Fax 949-0836
St. Stephen S 300/PK-8
740 Gladstone Dr SE 49506 616-243-8998
Cindy Thomas, prin. Fax 243-0451
St. Thomas the Apostle S 300/PK-8
1429 Wilcox Park Dr SE 49506 616-458-4228
David Faber, prin. Fax 458-4583
Stepping Stones Montessori S 100/PK-6
1110 College Ave NE 49503 616-451-8627
Libby Kreiner, hdmstr. Fax 451-0145
West Side Christian S 400/PK-8
955 Westend Ave NW 49504 616-453-3925
Vernon Groenendyk, prin. Fax 453-4150

Grandville, Kent, Pop. 16,711
Grandville SD 5,700/K-12
3839 Prairie St SW 49418 616-254-6550
Ronald Caniff, supt. Fax 254-6559
www.grandville.k12.mi.us
Central ES 200/K-6
4052 Prairie St SW 49418 616-254-6010
Michelle Carter, prin. Fax 254-6013
Century Park Learning Center 400/K-6
5710 Kenowa Ave SW 49418 616-254-6820
Tonia Shoup, prin. Fax 254-6823
East ES 300/K-6
3413 30th St SW 49418 616-254-6080
William Cheevers, prin. Fax 254-6083
Grand View ES 600/K-6
3701 52nd St SW 49418 616-254-6120
Jean Carroll-Hamilton, prin. Fax 254-6123
Grandville MS 900/7-8
3535 Wilson Ave SW 49418 616-254-6610
Theresa Waterbury, prin. Fax 254-6613
South ES 400/K-6
3650 Navaho St SW 49418 616-254-6210
Chuck Schultz, prin. Fax 254-6213
West ES 300/K-6
3777 Aaron Ave SW 49418 616-254-6250
David Martini, prin. Fax 254-6253
Other Schools – See Grand Rapids

Calvin Christian MS 200/7-8
3740 Ivanrest Ave SW 49418 616-531-7400
John Kramer, prin. Fax 531-7402
Grandville Christian S 300/PK-6
3934 Wilson Ave SW 49418 616-538-9710
Timothy Steenstra, prin. Fax 538-3553
Pride & Joy Preschool PK-PK
4109 40th St SW 49418 616-538-2600
Amy Dukesherer, dir. Fax 538-6340

Grant, Newaygo, Pop. 885
Grant SD 2,200/PK-12
148 Elder St 49327 231-834-5621
Scott Bogner, supt. Fax 834-7146
www.grantps.net
Grant ES 400/2-4
160 E State Rd 49327 231-834-5678
Joel Schuitema, prin. Fax 834-9002
Grant MS 700/5-8
96 E 120th St 49327 231-834-5910
Lance Jones, prin. Fax 834-9029
Grant PS 200/PK-2
103 Elder St 49327 231-834-7382
Renae Galsterer, prin. Fax 834-5707

Grant Christian S 100/PK-8
12931 Poplar Ave 49327 231-834-8445
Melissa Sutter, prin. Fax 834-8445

Grass Lake, Jackson, Pop. 1,171
Grass Lake Community SD 1,100/K-12
899 S Union St 49240 517-522-5540
Brad Hamilton, supt. Fax 522-8195
www.grasslakeschools.com
Grass Lake MS 300/6-8
1000 Grass Lake Rd 49240 517-522-5550
Jeanene Satterthwaite, prin. Fax 522-4775
Long ES 400/K-5
829 S Union St 49240 517-522-5590
Michelle Clark, prin. Fax 522-8789

Grayling, Crawford, Pop. 1,943
Crawford AuSable SD 1,800/PK-12
1135 N Old 27 49738 989-344-3500
Joseph Powers, supt. Fax 348-6822
www.casdk12.net/
AuSable PS 300/PK-2
306 Plum St 49738 989-344-3650
Barbara Mick, prin. Fax 348-3544
Grayling ES 400/3-5
1000 E Michigan Ave 49738 989-344-3600
Melissa Stone, prin. Fax 348-4782
Grayling MS 400/6-8
500 Spruce St 49738 989-344-3550
Jeffrey Branch, prin. Fax 348-7045

Grayling SDA S 50/K-8
2468 Camp AuSable Rd 49738 989-348-2501
Russell Hayner, prin.

Greenville, Montcalm, Pop. 8,306
Greenville SD 3,900/K-12
1414 Chase St 48838 616-754-3686
Peter Haines, supt. Fax 754-5374
www.greenville.k12.mi.us
Baldwin Heights ES 600/K-5
821 W Oak St 48838 616-754-3643
Jeff Wright, prin. Fax 754-0272
Cedar Crest ES 400/K-5
622 S Cedar St 48838 616-754-3641
Gretchen Baarman, prin. Fax 754-0338

Greenville MS 900/6-8
1321 Chase St 48838 616-754-9361
Leigh Acker, prin. Fax 754-2901
Lincoln Heights ES 500/K-5
12420 Lincoln Lake Rd NE 48838 616-754-9167
Michelle Blaszczynski, prin. Fax 754-0469
Walnut Hills ES 300/K-5
712 N Walnut St 48838 616-754-3688
Susan Ayres, prin. Fax 754-0484

St. Charles S 100/K-8
502 S Franklin St 48838 616-754-3416
Margaret Karpus, prin. Fax 754-9262

Grosse Ile, Wayne, Pop. 9,781
Grosse Ile Township SD 2,000/K-12
23276 E River Rd 48138 734-362-2555
Dena Dardzinski, supt. Fax 362-2594
www.gischools.org/
Grosse Ile MS 500/6-8
23270 E River Rd 48138 734-362-2500
David Tucker, prin. Fax 362-2596
Meridian ES 400/K-5
26700 Meridian Rd 48138 734-362-2700
Diane Sanford, prin. Fax 362-2796
Parke Lane ES 500/K-5
21610 Parke Ln 48138 734-362-2600
Pat Nordstrom, prin. Fax 362-2696

Grosse Pointe, Wayne, Pop. 5,426
Grosse Pointe SD 8,800/K-12
389 Saint Clair St 48230 313-432-3000
Dr. C. Suzanne Klein, supt. Fax 432-3002
www.gpschools.org
Barnes ECC 50/K-K
20090 Morningside Dr 48236 313-432-3800
Susan Banner, prin. Fax 432-3802
Brownell MS 700/6-8
260 Chalfonte Ave 48236 313-432-3900
Dr. Michael Dib, prin. Fax 432-3902
Defer ES 500/K-5
15425 Kercheval Ave 48230 313-432-4000
Ronald Wardie, prin. Fax 432-4002
Ferry ES 500/K-5
748 Roslyn Rd 48236 313-432-4100
Gloria Hinz, prin. Fax 432-4102
Kerby ES 400/K-5
285 Kerby Rd 48236 313-432-4200
Maureen Bur, prin. Fax 432-4202
Maire ES 400/K-5
740 Cadieux Rd 48230 313-432-4300
Kathleen Satut, prin. Fax 432-4302
Mason ES 300/K-5
1640 Vernier Rd 48236 313-432-4400
Elaine Middlekauf, prin. Fax 432-4402
Monteith ES 600/K-5
1275 Cook Rd 48236 313-432-4500
Keith Howell, prin. Fax 432-4502
Parcells MS 800/6-8
20600 Mack Ave 48236 313-432-4600
Mark Mulholland, prin. Fax 432-4602
Pierce MS 600/6-8
15430 Kercheval Ave 48230 313-432-4700
Gary Buslepp, prin. Fax 432-4702
Richard ES 400/K-5
176 McKinley Ave 48236 313-432-4900
M. MacDonald-Barrett, prin. Fax 432-4902
Trombly ES 300/K-5
820 Beaconsfield Ave 48230 313-432-5000
Walter Fitzpatrick, prin. Fax 432-5002
Other Schools – See Harper Woods

Grosse Pointe Academy 400/PK-8
171 Lake Shore Rd 48236 313-886-1221
Phil Demartini, hdmstr. Fax 886-1418
Our Lady Star of the Sea S 500/PK-8
467 Fairford Rd 48236 313-884-1070
Michael Reece, prin. Fax 884-0406
St. Clare of Montefalco S 300/PK-8
16231 Charlevoix St 48230 313-647-5100
Sr. Kathy Avery, prin. Fax 647-5105
St. Paul on the Lake S 500/PK-8
170 Grosse Pointe Blvd 48236 313-885-3430
Mary Miller, prin. Fax 885-9357
University Liggett S 500/PK-12
1045 Cook Rd 48236 313-884-4444
Joseph Healy, prin. Fax 884-1775
University Liggett S 100/6-8
850 Briar Cliff Dr 48236 313-886-4220
Motoko Maegawa, prin. Fax 417-8002

Gwinn, Marquette, Pop. 2,370
Gwinn Area Community SD 1,400/K-12
50 W State Highway M35 49841 906-346-9283
Michael Maino, supt. Fax 346-3616
www.gwinn.k12.mi.us
Gilbert ES 300/K-6
250 W Iron St 49841 906-346-5726
Sandra Petrovich, prin. Fax 346-6744
Gwinn MS 200/7-8
135 W Granite St 49841 906-346-5914
Kimberly Van Drese, prin. Fax 346-6213
Sawyer ES 400/K-6
411 Scorpion Rd 49841 906-346-5567
Kristen Peterson, prin. Fax 346-7126

Hale, Iosco
Hale Area SD 700/K-12
200 W Main St 48739 989-728-7661
Rhonda Provoast, supt. Fax 728-2406
www.halemichigan.net/school.html
Hale Area MS 200/5-8
311 N Washington St 48739 989-728-3551
Vince LaCavera, prin. Fax 728-9551
Hale ES 200/K-4
311 N Washington St 48739 989-728-3551
Vince LaCavera, prin. Fax 728-9551

Hamilton, Allegan
Hamilton Community SD 2,600/K-12
4815 136th Ave 49419 269-751-5148
Scott Karpak, supt. Fax 751-7116
www.hamiltonschools.us
Bentheim ES 300/K-5
4057 38th St 49419 269-751-5335
Dan Scoville, prin. Fax 751-7537
Hamilton ES 500/K-5
3472 Lincoln Rd 49419 269-751-5413
Fax 751-7554
Hamilton MS 600/6-8
4845 136th Ave 49419 269-751-4436
Scott Smith, prin. Fax 751-8560
Other Schools – See Holland

Hamtramck, Wayne, Pop. 21,994
Hamtramck SD 2,700/PK-12
PO Box 12012 48212 313-872-9270
Thomas Niczay, supt. Fax 872-8679
www.hamtramck.k12.mi.us
Dickinson East ES 600/1-6
3385 Norwalk St 48212 313-873-9437
Nayal Maktari, prin. Fax 871-0511
Dickinson West ES 400/1-6
2650 Caniff St 48212 313-873-0177
Mohammad Hussein, prin. Fax 871-2360
Hamtramck ECC 100/PK-K
11680 McDougall St 48212 313-891-3200
Christine Salata, prin. Fax 366-0786
Holbrook ES 200/1-6
2361 Alice St 48212 313-872-3203
Michael Zygmontowicz, prin. Fax 871-2366
Kosciuszko MS 400/7-8
2333 Burger St 48212 313-365-4625
Nuo Ivezaj, prin. Fax 365-4760

Al-Ikhlas Training Academy 200/K-12
12555 McDougall St 48212 313-369-0880
Jaha Rashid, prin. Fax 369-0881

Hancock, Houghton, Pop. 4,223
Hancock SD 900/K-12
417 Quincy St 49930 906-487-5925
Monica Healy, supt. Fax 487-5216
www.hancock.k12.mi.us
Barkell ES 400/K-5
1201 N Elevation St 49930 906-487-9030
Bruce Matson, prin. Fax 487-9041
Hancock MS 200/6-8
417 Quincy St 49930 906-487-5923
Monica Healy, prin. Fax 487-5924

Hanover, Jackson, Pop. 432
Hanover-Horton SD
Supt. — See Horton
Hanover-Horton ES 500/K-5
131 Fairview St 49241 517-563-0103
Cindy Casad, prin. Fax 563-0160

Harbor Beach, Huron, Pop. 1,719
Harbor Beach Community SD 700/K-12
402 S 5th St 48441 989-479-3261
Ron Kraft, supt. Fax 479-9881
www.harborbeach.k12.mi.us/
Harbor Beach ES 200/K-4
402 S 5th St 48441 989-479-3261
Denise Kish, prin. Fax 479-9881
Harbor Beach MS 200/5-8
402 S 5th St 48441 989-479-3261
Denise Kish, prin. Fax 479-9881

Sigel Township SD 4 50/K-8
5754 Section Line Rd 48441 989-479-9266
Robert Colby, supt.
www.huroncountyruralschools.com/
Eccles S, 5754 Section Line Rd 48441 50/K-8
Robert Colby, prin. 989-479-9266

Sigel Township SD 6 50/K-8
4499 Kipper Rd 48441 989-269-7863
Robert Colby, supt. Fax 269-7863
www.huroncountyruralschools.com/kipper/index.html
Kipper S 50/K-8
4499 Kipper Rd 48441 989-269-7863
Robert Colby, prin. Fax 269-7863

Our Lady of Lake Huron S 100/PK-8
222 Court St 48441 989-479-3427
David Mausolf, prin. Fax 479-3335
Zion Lutheran S 100/PK-8
299 Garden St 48441 989-479-3615
Cynthia Brown, prin. Fax 479-6551

Harbor Springs, Emmet, Pop. 1,594
Harbor Springs SD 1,100/PK-12
800 S State Rd 49740 231-526-4545
Mark Tompkins, supt. Fax 526-4544
www.harborps.org
Blackbird ES 200/PK-2
421 E Lake St 49740 231-526-4600
Karey Scholten, prin. Fax 526-4630
Harbor Springs MS 300/6-8
800 S State Rd 49740 231-526-4700
Wil Cwikiel, prin. Fax 526-4760
Shay ES 200/3-5
175 E Lake St 49740 231-526-4500
Karey Scholten, prin. Fax 526-4534

Harbor Light Christian S 100/PK-12
8333 Clayton Rd 49740 231-347-7859
Loren Vannest, admin. Fax 347-7703

Harper Woods, Wayne, Pop. 13,621
Grosse Pointe SD
Supt. — See Grosse Pointe
Poupard ES 400/K-5
20655 Lennon St 48225 313-432-4800
Penny Stocks, prin. Fax 432-4802

Harper Woods SD 1,200/K-12
20225 Beaconsfield St 48225 313-245-3000
Fax 839-1249
www.hwschools.org
Beacon ES 400/K-3
19475 Beaconsfield St 48225 313-245-3000
Janet Gottsleben, prin. Fax 371-4170
Harper Woods MS 200/7-8
20225 Beaconsfield St 48225 313-245-3000
Heather Blum, prin. Fax 839-4360
Tyrone ES 300/4-6
19525 Tyrone St 48225 313-245-3000
Cheryl VanDerlinden, prin. Fax 884-1057

Harris, Menominee
Bark River-Harris SD 700/K-12
PO Box 350 49845 906-466-9981
Russell Pirlot, supt. Fax 466-2925
www.dsisd.k12.mi.us/barkriver
Bark River-Harris ES 400/K-6
PO Box 350 49845 906-466-5334
Scott Brant, prin. Fax 466-2925

Harrison, Clare, Pop. 2,083
Harrison Community SD 1,500/K-12
PO Box 529 48625 989-539-7871
Thomas House, supt. Fax 539-7491
www.cgresd.net/hcs
Harrison MS 300/7-8
PO Box 529 48625 989-539-7194
Richard Foote, prin. Fax 539-0460
Hillside ES 400/3-6
PO Box 529 48625 989-539-6902
Barbara Elliott, prin. Fax 539-4322
Larson ES 100/K-2
PO Box 529 48625 989-539-3259
Julie Rosekrans, prin. Fax 539-4316

Harrison Township, Macomb, Pop. 24,685
L'Anse Creuse SD 11,200/PK-12
36727 Jefferson Ave 48045 586-783-6300
Dr. DiAnne Pellerin, supt. Fax 783-6310
www.lc-ps.org
Graham ES 400/PK-5
25555 Crocker Blvd 48045 586-783-6460
Sally Bergmann, prin. Fax 783-6466
L'Anse Creuse MS Central 600/6-8
38000 Reimold St 48045 586-783-6430
Patricia Rabenburg, prin. Fax 783-6437
L'Anse Creuse MS South 600/6-8
34641 Jefferson Ave 48045 586-493-5620
Greg Dixon, prin. Fax 493-5625
Lobbestael ES 400/K-5
38495 Prentiss St 48045 586-783-6450
Pamela Leidlein, prin. Fax 783-6456
South River ES 500/K-5
27733 S River Rd 48045 586-783-6480
Laura Holbert, prin. Fax 783-6486
Yacks ES 500/K-5
34700 Union Lake Rd 48045 586-493-5630
Betty Kozma, prin. Fax 493-5635
Other Schools – See Chesterfield, Clinton Township, Macomb

Hart, Oceana, Pop. 1,996
Hart SD 1,100/PK-12
301 Johnson St W 49420 231-873-6214
Peter Moss, supt. Fax 873-6244
www.hart.k12.mi.us
Hart MS 300/6-8
308 Johnson St W 49420 231-873-6320
Steven Sanocki, prin. Fax 873-0245
Hart Upper ES 300/2-5
306 Johnson St W 49420 231-873-6330
Mari Fox, prin. Fax 873-5162
Spitler ES 100/PK-1
302 Johnson St W 49420 231-873-6340
Dyanne Mullen, prin. Fax 873-7042

Oceana Christian S 100/PK-8
3258 N 72nd Ave 49420 231-873-2514
Jean Riley, admin. Fax 873-5096

Hartford, Van Buren, Pop. 2,433
Hartford SD 1,400/K-12
115 School St 49057 269-621-7000
David Levstek, supt. Fax 621-3887
www.hartford-schools.org
Hartford MS 300/6-8
141 School St 49057 269-621-7200
John Visser, prin. Fax 621-7260
Red Arrow ES 300/K-5
15 S East St 49057 269-621-7400
John Busch, prin. Fax 621-7460
Woodside ES 300/K-5
395 Woodside Dr 49057 269-621-7300
Donna Johnson, prin. Fax 621-7360

Hartland, Livingston
Hartland Consolidated SD
Supt. — See Howell
Creekside ES 400/K-4
PO Box 408 48353 810-626-2600
Tracey Sahouri, prin. Fax 626-2601
Hartland MS 900/7-8
3250 Hartland Rd 48353 810-626-2400
Steve Livingway, prin. Fax 626-2401
Round ES 400/K-4
11550 Hibner Rd 48353 810-626-2800
David Minsker, prin. Fax 626-2801
Village ES 500/K-4
10632 Hibner Rd 48353 810-626-2850
William Cain, prin. Fax 626-2851

Child of Christ Lutheran S 100/PK-8
3375 Fenton Rd 48353 248-887-3836
Steve Burger, prin. Fax 889-8279

Haslett, Ingham, Pop. 10,230
Haslett SD 2,700/K-12
5593 Franklin St 48840 517-339-8242
Michael Duda, supt. Fax 339-1360
www.haslett.k12.mi.us/
Haslett MS 600/6-8
1535 Franklin St 48840 517-339-8233
Andy Pridgeon, prin. Fax 339-4837
Murphy ES 400/2-5
1875 Lake Lansing Rd 48840 517-339-8253
Diane Lindbert, prin. Fax 339-4830
Ralya ES 400/2-5
5645 School St 48840 517-339-8202
Judy Tegreeny, prin. Fax 339-7359
Wilkshire ECC 200/K-1
5750 Academic Way 48840 517-339-8208
Gail Hicks, prin. Fax 339-4832

Hastings, Barry, Pop. 7,166
Hastings Area SD 3,000/PK-12
232 W Grand St 49058 269-948-4400
Richard Satterlee, supt. Fax 948-4425
www.hassk12.org
Central ES 400/PK-5
509 S Broadway St 49058 269-948-4423
Christopher Cooley, prin. Fax 948-4449
Hastings MS 800/6-8
232 W Grand St 49058 269-948-4404
Michael Karasinski, prin. Fax 945-6101
Northeastern ES 300/K-5
519 E Grant St 49058 269-948-4421
Terry Sedlar, prin. Fax 948-4502
Southeastern ES 200/K-5
1300 S East St 49058 269-948-4419
Judy Johnson, prin. Fax 948-4504
Star ES 300/K-5
1900 Star School Rd 49058 269-948-4442
Amy Tebo, prin. Fax 948-4448

Barry County Christian S 100/PK-12
2999 McKeown Rd 49058 269-948-2151
Ken Oosterhouse, admin. Fax 948-2795
Hastings SDA S, 888 Terry Ln 49058 50/1-8
Ann Barrett, prin. 269-945-3896
St. Rose of Lima S 100/PK-6
707 S Jefferson St 49058 269-945-3164
Bernadette Norris, prin. Fax 945-0005

Hazel Park, Oakland, Pop. 18,391
Hazel Park SD 3,600/PK-12
1620 E Elza Ave 48030 248-658-5200
Victor Mayo Ed.D., supt. Fax 544-5443
www.hazelpark.k12.mi.us/
Hazel Park JHS 600/6-8
22770 Highland Ave 48030 248-658-2300
Douglas Esler, prin. Fax 658-2305
Hoover ES 200/PK-5
23720 Hoover Ave 48030 248-658-5300
Leslie Baker, prin. Fax 586-5831
United Oaks ES 300/PK-5
1015 E Harry Ave 48030 248-658-2400
Mark Brown, prin. Fax 542-3530
Webster ES 200/PK-5
431 W Jarvis Ave 48030 248-658-5550
Kathleen Borowicz, prin. Fax 544-5421
Other Schools – See Ferndale

Hemlock, Saginaw, Pop. 1,601
Hemlock SD 1,300/K-12
PO Box 260 48626 989-642-5282
Rudy Godefroidt, supt. Fax 642-2773
www.hemlock.k12.mi.us
Hemlock ES 200/K-2
PO Box 260 48626 989-642-5221
G. Madaleno, prin. Fax 642-4146
Hemlock MS 300/6-8
PO Box 260 48626 989-642-5253
Terry Keyser, prin. Fax 642-8239
Ling ES 300/3-5
PO Box 260 48626 989-642-5235
G. Madaleno, prin. Fax 642-8008

St. John Lutheran S 50/K-8
2290 Pretzer Rd 48626 989-642-5178
Aaron Hartwig, prin.
St. Peter Lutheran S 200/PK-8
2440 N Raucholz Rd 48626 989-642-5659
Lester Altevogt, prin. Fax 642-9053

Hermansville, Menominee
North Central Area SD 400/PK-12
PO Box 159 49847 906-498-7737
Andrew Hongisto, supt. Fax 498-2235
www.ncajets.org
North Central ES 200/PK-6
PO Box 159 49847 906-498-7737
Andrew Hongisto, prin. Fax 498-2235

Herron, Alpena
Alpena SD
Supt. — See Alpena
Wilson ES 200/K-6
4999 Herron Rd 49744 989-358-5700
Jean Kowalski, prin. Fax 358-5705

Hesperia, Oceana, Pop. 987
Hesperia Community SD 1,100/K-12
PO Box 338 49421 231-854-6185
Dean Havelka, supt. Fax 854-1586
www.hesp.net
Hesperia MS 300/5-8
PO Box 338 49421 231-854-6475
Nancy Cairnduff, prin. Fax 854-6096
St. Clair ES 400/K-4
PO Box 338 49421 231-854-6615
Jennifer Roth, prin. Fax 854-6075

Hickory Corners, Kalamazoo
Gull Lake Community SD
Supt. — See Richland
Kellogg ES 300/K-3
9594 N 40th St 49060 269-488-5070
Amie McCaw, prin. Fax 488-5071

Highland, Oakland
Huron Valley SD 10,200/PK-12
2390 S Milford Rd 48357 248-684-8000
Jacquelyn Johnston, supt. Fax 684-8235
www.huronvalley.k12.mi.us
Apollo Center 50/PK-PK
2029 N Milford Rd 48357 248-684-8040
Julie Conn, admin. Fax 684-8286
Heritage ES 600/K-5
219 Watkins Blvd 48357 248-684-8190
Frank Bateman, prin. Fax 684-8193
Highland ES 300/K-5
300 W Livingston Rd 48357 248-684-8070
Bruce Bendure, prin. Fax 684-8269
Highland MS 600/6-8
305 N John St 48357 248-684-8080
Martin Lindberg, prin. Fax 684-8186
Spring Mills ES 500/K-5
3150 Harvey Lake Rd 48356 248-684-8130
Randy Muffley, prin. Fax 684-8189
Other Schools – See Commerce Township, Milford, White Lake

Highland Park, Wayne, Pop. 15,430
Highland Park SD 3,400/PK-12
20 Bartlett St 48203 313-957-3000
Arthur Carter Ed.D., supt. Fax 868-4950
www.hipark.k12.mi.us/
Barber Focus S 500/K-8
45 E Buena Vista St 48203 313-957-3005
Sontoya LaShore, prin. Fax 868-0485
Cortland Academy 300/PK-5
138 Cortland St 48203 313-957-3003
Gayna Evans, prin. Fax 868-0487
Ford Academy 700/PK-8
131 Pilgrim St 48203 313-957-3004
Patricia Dicks-Arnell, prin. Fax 868-0481

Hillman, Montmorency, Pop. 679
Hillman Community SD 600/K-12
26042 M 32 S 49746 989-742-2908
Jack Richards, supt. Fax 742-3376
hillman.amaesd.k12.mi.us
Hillman ES 300/K-6
26042 M 32 S 49746 989-742-4537
Shawn Olson, prin. Fax 742-4509

Hillsdale, Hillsdale, Pop. 7,904
Hillsdale Community SD 1,700/PK-12
30 S Norwood Ave 49242 517-437-4401
Richard Ames, supt. Fax 439-4194
www.hillsdaleschools.org
Bailey ES 300/1-2
59 S Manning St 49242 517-437-7369
Shawn Vondra, prin. Fax 437-4319
Davis MS 400/6-8
30 N West St 49242 517-439-4326
Jackie Wickham, prin. Fax 437-1195
Gier ES 400/3-5
175 Spring St 49242 517-437-7347
Scott Siakel, prin. Fax 437-5641
Mauck ES 50/PK-K
113 E Fayette St 49242 517-437-2717
Lois Foster, prin. Fax 437-5644

Hillsdale Academy 200/K-12
1 Academy Ln 49242 517-439-8644
Kenneth Calvert, prin. Fax 607-2794

Holland, Ottawa, Pop. 34,429
Hamilton Community SD
Supt. — See Hamilton
Blue Star ES 300/K-5
3846 58th St 49423 269-751-5630
Tim Lyman, prin. Fax 751-2901
Sandyview ES 100/K-5
4317 46th St 49423 269-751-5372
Barbara Ferguson, prin. Fax 751-5089

Holland SD 3,900/PK-12
156 W 11th St 49423 616-494-2000
Brian Davis, supt. Fax 392-8225
www.hollandpublicschools.org/
East S 600/K-7
373 E 24th St 49423 616-494-2425
Nery Garcia, prin. Fax 355-0674
Holland ECC 200/PK-PK
925 Central Ave 49423 616-494-2650
Ellen Westveer, prin. Fax 393-7653
Holland Heights ES 300/K-7
856 E 12th St 49423 616-494-2750
Kevin Derr, prin. Fax 393-7566
Jefferson ES 500/K-7
282 W 30th St 49423 616-494-2500
Rick Muniz, prin. Fax 393-7569
West ES 500/K-7
500 W 24th St 49423 616-494-2350
Dana Loveland, prin. Fax 393-7544

West Ottawa SD 7,900/K-12
1138 136th Ave 49424 616-738-5700
Dr. Patricia Koeze, supt. Fax 738-5792
www.westottawa.net
Glerum ES 300/K-5
342 W Lakewood Blvd 49424 616-395-2200
Michelle Williams, prin. Fax 395-2291
Great Lakes ES 600/K-5
3200 152nd Ave 49424 616-738-6300
Gerald McDowell, prin. Fax 738-6391
Harbor Lights MS 1,000/6-8
1024 136th Ave 49424 616-738-6700
Jeri Start, prin. Fax 738-6791
Lakeshore ES 400/K-5
3765 N 168th Ave 49424 616-786-1400
Dr. Randall Busscher, prin. Fax 786-1491
Lakewood ES 400/K-5
2134 W Lakewood Blvd 49424 616-786-1300
Jacquelyn DelRaso, prin. Fax 786-1391
Macatawa Bay MS 700/6-8
3700 140th Ave 49424 616-786-2000
Michael Fine, prin. Fax 786-2091
North Holland ES 300/K-5
11946 New Holland St 49424 616-786-1500
Karen Abraham, prin. Fax 786-1591
Pine Creek ES 400/K-5
1184 136th Ave 49424 616-786-1600
Rita Nowling, prin. Fax 786-1691
Waukazoo ES 600/K-5
1294 W Lakewood Blvd 49424 616-786-1800
Jennifer Cook, prin. Fax 786-1891
Woodside ES 600/K-5
2591 N Division Ave 49424 616-786-1900
Lisa Neumann, prin. Fax 786-1991
Other Schools – See West Olive

Calvary S of Holland 300/PK-12
518 Plasman Ave 49423 616-396-4494
Paul Davis, admin. Fax 396-0326
Corpus Christi S 200/PK-8
12100 Quincy St 49424 616-994-9864
Joanne Jones, prin. Fax 994-9870
Holland SDA S 50/K-8
11385 Ottogan St 49423 616-396-5941
Frances Robinson, prin. Fax 396-5941
North Shore Christian MS 200/6-8
556 Butternut Dr 49424 616-820-4055
Gary Dewey, lead tchr. Fax 820-4060
Pine Ridge Christian S 200/3-5
623 W 40th St 49423 616-820-3505
Timothy Howell, prin. Fax 820-3510
Rose Park Christian S 400/PK-5
556 Butternut Dr 49424 616-820-4055
Sally Van Hemert, prin. Fax 820-4060
South Olive Christian S 50/PK-8
6230 120th Ave 49424 616-875-8224
Carla Zastrow, prin. Fax 875-2287
South Shore Christian MS 200/6-8
850 Ottawa Ave 49423 616-820-3205
Mark Van Dyke, prin. Fax 820-3210
South Side Christian S 300/PK-2
913 Pine Ave 49423 616-820-3535
Laura Kos, prin. Fax 820-3540

Holly, Oakland, Pop. 6,375
Holly Area SD 4,200/K-12
920 Baird St 48442 248-328-3140
R. Kent Barnes, supt. Fax 328-3145
www.has-k12.org/
Holly ES 400/K-5
801 E Maple St 48442 248-328-3600
Beth Hunter, prin. Fax 328-3604
Patterson ES 500/K-5
3231 Grange Hall Rd 48442 248-328-3700
Dennis Inhulsen, prin. Fax 328-3704
Pioneer ES 400/K-5
7110 Milford Rd 48442 248-328-3800
Michael Beattie, prin. Fax 328-3804
Richter IS 300/6-6
920 Baird St 48442 248-328-3030
Matthew Olson, prin. Fax 328-3034
Sherman MS 600/7-8
14470 N Holly Rd 48442 248-328-3400
Matthew Olson, prin. Fax 328-3404
Other Schools – See Davisburg

Adelphian Jr. Academy 50/K-10
PO Box 208 48442 248-634-9481
Diane Barlow, prin. Fax 634-9222

Holt, Ingham, Pop. 11,744
Holt SD 6,000/K-12
5780 Holt Rd 48842 517-694-0401
Dr. Johnny Scott, supt. Fax 694-1335
www.hpsk12.net/
Elliott ES 400/K-4
4200 Bond Ave 48842 517-699-2106
Francine Minnick, prin. Fax 699-3409
Holt JHS 1,000/7-8
1784 Aurelius Rd 48842 517-694-7117
Marshall Perkins, prin. Fax 694-3535
Hope MS 400/5-6
2020 Park Ln 48842 517-699-2194
Dean Manikas, prin. Fax 699-3442
Horizon ES 400/K-4
5776 Holt Rd 48842 517-694-4224
David Hornak, prin. Fax 699-3427
Midway ES 400/K-4
4552 Spahr St 48842 517-694-0444
Pam Crookedacre, prin. Fax 699-3417
Sycamore ES 400/K-4
4429 Sycamore St 48842 517-699-2185
Melissa Usiak, prin. Fax 699-3449
Washington Woods MS 400/5-6
2055 S Washington Rd 48842 517-699-0250
Scott Martin, prin. Fax 699-3438
Wilcox ES 300/K-4
1650 Laurelwood Dr 48842 517-699-0249
Traci Heuhs, prin. Fax 699-3422
Other Schools – See Dimondale

Capitol City Baptist S 100/PK-12
5100 Willoughby Rd 48842 517-694-6122
Brian Ogle, prin. Fax 694-3344
Holt Lutheran S 100/PK-12
2418 Aurelius Rd 48842 517-694-3182
Janice Poellet, prin. Fax 694-6371

Holton, Muskegon
Holton SD 1,100/K-12
PO Box 159 49425 231-821-1700
John Fazer, supt. Fax 821-1724
www.holton.k12.mi.us/

Holton ES 400/K-4
PO Box 159 49425 231-821-1825
Carol Dawson, prin. Fax 821-1849
Holton MS 300/5-8
PO Box 159 49425 231-821-1775
Kelli-Ann Rich, prin. Fax 821-1824

Homer, Calhoun, Pop. 1,819
Homer Community SD 900/K-12
403 S Hillsdale St 49245 517-568-4461
Robert Ridgeway, supt. Fax 568-4468
www.homer.k12.mi.us/
Fletcher ES 300/K-4
403 S Hillsdale St 49245 517-568-4452
Rick Cooley, prin. Fax 568-5651
Homer MS 300/5-8
403 S Hillsdale St 49245 517-568-4456
Scott Salow, prin. Fax 568-4831

Honor, Benzie, Pop. 297
Benzie County Central SD
Supt. — See Benzonia
Platte River ES 300/K-6
11434 Main St 49640 231-325-3063
Phil Cook, prin. Fax 325-2905

Hopkins, Allegan, Pop. 572
Hopkins SD 1,700/K-12
PO Box 278 49328 269-793-7261
Chris Stephens, supt. Fax 793-3154
www.hpsvikings.org
Hopkins ES 400/K-5
400 S Clark St 49328 269-793-7286
Mary Howard, prin. Fax 793-3154
Hopkins MS 400/6-8
215 S Clark St 49328 269-793-7407
Ken Szczepanski, prin. Fax 793-4086
Other Schools – See Dorr

St. Paul's Lutheran S 50/K-8
2912 24th St 49328 269-793-7481
Michael Smith, prin. Fax 793-7648

Horton, Jackson
Hanover-Horton SD 1,300/K-12
237 Farview St 49246 517-563-0100
Linda Brian, supt. Fax 563-0150
www.hhsd.k12.mi.us
Hanover-Horton MS 300/6-8
10000 Moscow Rd 49246 517-563-0102
Denise Dennison, prin. Fax 563-9140
Other Schools – See Hanover

Houghton, Houghton, Pop. 7,076
Houghton-Portage Township SD 1,300/K-12
1603 Gundlach Rd 49931 906-482-0451
William Polkinghorne, supt. Fax 487-9764
www.houghton.k12.mi.us/
Houghton ES 500/K-5
203 W Jacker Ave 49931 906-482-0456
Doreen Klingbeil, prin. Fax 487-5941
Houghton MS 300/6-8
1603 Gundlach Rd 49931 906-482-4871
James Luoma, prin. Fax 483-2566

Houghton Lake, Roscommon, Pop. 3,353
Houghton Lake Community SD 1,600/K-12
6001 W Houghton Lake Dr 48629 989-366-2000
Peter Injasoulian, supt. Fax 366-2070
www.hlcs.k12.mi.us/index.shtml
Collins ES 400/K-3
4451 W Houghton Lake Dr 48629 989-366-2024
Pam Akin, prin. Fax 366-2077
Houghton Lake MS 500/4-7
4441 W Houghton Lake Dr 48629 989-366-2018
Susan Tyer, prin. Fax 366-2078

Howard City, Montcalm, Pop. 1,617
Tri County Area SD
Supt. — See Sand Lake
Edgerton Upper ES 200/4-5
412 Edgerton St 49329 231-937-4391
Susan Wanner, prin. Fax 937-7077
MacNaughton ES 400/K-3
415 Cedar 49329 231-937-4380
Allen Cumings, prin. Fax 937-4442
Tri County MS 500/6-8
21350 Kendaville Rd 49329 231-937-4318
Kurt Mabie, prin. Fax 937-6319

Howell, Livingston, Pop. 9,757
Hartland Consolidated SD 5,300/K-12
9525 E Highland Rd 48843 810-626-2100
Janet Sifferman, supt. Fax 626-2101
www.hartlandschools.us/
Other Schools – See Brighton, Hartland

Howell SD 8,400/K-12
411 N Highlander Way 48843 517-548-6234
Theodore Gardella, supt. Fax 548-6229
www.howellschools.com
Challenger ES 500/K-5
1066 W Grand River Ave 48843 517-548-6375
Deborah Madeja, prin. Fax 545-1436
Highlander Way MS 1,100/6-8
511 N Highlander Way 48843 517-548-6252
Sandra Moore, prin. Fax 545-1455
Hutchings ES 500/K-5
3503 Bigelow Rd, 517-548-1127
John Clay, prin. Fax 548-2155
Latson ES 500/K-5
1201 S Latson Rd 48843 517-548-6319
Kari Naghtin, prin. Fax 545-1426
Northwest ES 500/K-5
1233 Bower St 48843 517-548-6297
Kara Cotton, prin. Fax 545-1433
Southeast ES 500/K-5
861 E Sibley St 48843 517-548-6283
Melanie Post, prin. Fax 545-1431
Southwest ES 600/K-5
915 Gay St 48843 517-548-6288
Jill Hilla, prin. Fax 545-1432
Three Fires MS 900/6-8
4125 Crooked Lake Rd 48843 517-548-6387
Sue Muntz, prin. Fax 548-7524
Voyager ES 600/K-5
1450 Byron Rd 48843 517-552-7500
Jason Feig, prin. Fax 552-7519

Hidden Springs Christian S 100/K-8
5860 N Latson Rd, 517-546-2417
Mary Scott, prin. Fax 546-9951
St. Joseph S 400/PK-8
425 E Washington St 48843 517-546-0090
Kathleen Freeman, prin. Fax 546-8939

Hudson, Lenawee, Pop. 2,415
Hudson Area SD 1,100/K-12
781 N Maple Grove Ave 49247 517-448-8912
Kathryn Malnar Ed.D., supt. Fax 448-8570
www.hudson.k12.mi.us
Hudson MS 200/6-8
771 N Maple Grove Ave 49247 517-445-8912
Mike Osborne, prin. Fax 448-5702
Lincoln ES 500/K-5
746 N Maple Grove Ave 49247 517-448-8912
Cindy Godfrey, prin. Fax 448-5801

Sacred Heart S 100/PK-7
208 S Market St 49247 517-448-6405
April McCaskey, prin. Fax 448-2401

Hudsonville, Ottawa, Pop. 7,052
Hudsonville SD 5,100/PK-12
3886 Van Buren St 49426 616-669-1740
Nicholas Ceglarek, supt. Fax 669-4878
www.hudsonville.k12.mi.us
Alward ES 400/PK-5
3811 Port Sheldon St 49426 616-669-6700
Jay Dekker, prin. Fax 662-1470
Baldwin Street MS 700/6-8
3835 Baldwin St 49426 616-669-7750
David Powers, prin. Fax 669-7755
Bauer ES 400/PK-5
8136 48th Ave 49426 616-669-6824
Dorothy VanderJagt, prin. Fax 669-4897
Forest Grove ES 200/PK-5
1645 32nd Ave 49426 616-896-9429
John Gillette, prin. Fax 896-1370
Georgetown ES 400/PK-5
3909 Baldwin St 49426 616-797-9797
Theresa Reagan, prin. Fax 797-9929
Jamestown ES 400/PK-5
3291 Lincoln St 49426 616-896-9375
Jack DeLeeuw, prin. Fax 896-1375
Park ES 400/PK-5
5525 Park Ave 49426 616-669-1970
Brian Field, prin. Fax 669-4899
Riley Street MS 400/6-8
2745 Riley St 49426 616-896-1920
Bill Ross, prin. Fax 896-1925
South ES 300/PK-5
3400 Allen St 49426 616-669-9362
Mark Heagle, prin. Fax 662-1471

Beaverdam Christian S 100/PK-8
5181 64th Ave 49426 616-875-8340
Stephanie Miedema, prin. Fax 875-3777
Freedom Baptist S 400/PK-12
6340 Autumn Dr 49426 616-669-2270
Tony Clymer, supt. Fax 669-2410
Heritage Christian S 500/K-9
4900 40th Ave 49426 616-669-1773
Brian Kuiper, prin. Fax 669-4257
Hudsonville Christian MS 300/6-8
3925 Van Buren St 49426 616-669-7487
Dan Pott, prin. Fax 669-2031
Hudsonville Christian S 700/PK-5
3435 Oak St 49426 616-669-6689
Karen Ophoff, prin. Fax 669-7491

Huntington Woods, Oakland, Pop. 5,928
Berkley SD
Supt. — See Oak Park
Burton ES 400/K-5
26315 Scotia Rd 48070 248-837-8600
Beth Krehbiel, prin. Fax 546-0279

Ida, Monroe
Ida SD 1,600/K-12
3145 Prairie St 48140 734-269-3110
Marv Dick, supt. Fax 269-2294
www.idaschools.org
Ida ES 500/K-4
7900 Ida St 48140 734-269-3805
Tamie Rawlings, prin. Fax 269-1334
Ida MS 600/5-8
3145 Prairie St 48140 734-269-2220
Sheldon Wiens, prin. Fax 269-2576

Imlay City, Lapeer, Pop. 3,850
Imlay City Community SD 2,300/PK-12
634 W Borland Rd 48444 810-724-2765
Dr. Gary Richards, supt. Fax 724-4307
www.imlay.k12.mi.us/
Borland ES 500/3-5
500 W Borland Rd 48444 810-724-9813
Bill Kalmar, prin. Fax 724-9894
Imlay City MS 600/6-8
495 W 1st St 48444 810-724-9811
Erik Mason, prin. Fax 724-9896
Weston ES 400/PK-2
275 Weston St 48444 810-724-9812
Eric Whitney, prin. Fax 724-9895

Imlay City Christian S 100/PK-8
7197 E Imlay City Rd 48444 810-724-5695
Robert Reitsma, prin. Fax 724-5355

Indian River, Cheboygan
Inland Lakes SD 1,100/K-12
4363 S Straits Hwy 49749 231-238-6868
Mary Jo Dismang, supt. Fax 238-4181
www.inlandlakes.org
Inland Lakes ES 400/K-4
4363 S Straits Hwy 49749 231-238-6868
Carolyn Sackett, prin. Fax 238-4981
Inland Lakes MS 300/5-8
4363 S Straits Hwy 49749 231-238-6868
Mike VanVuren, prin. Fax 238-4872

Inkster, Wayne, Pop. 28,870
Inkster SD 1,700/PK-12
29115 Carlysle St 48141 734-722-5310
Thomas Maridada, supt. Fax 722-2150
www.inksterschools.org/
Baylor-Woodson ES 300/3-5
28865 Carlysle St 48141 734-467-5697
Beverly Gerhard, prin. Fax 722-8675
Blanchette MS 400/6-8
1771 Henry Ruff Rd 48141 734-326-7041
Mischa Bashir, prin. Fax 722-5402
Meek-Milton ES 300/PK-2
28865 Carlysle St 48141 734-326-6940
Darryl Love, prin. Fax 728-1528

Wayne-Westland Community SD
Supt. — See Westland
Hicks ES 300/K-5
100 Helen St 48141 734-419-2660
Akeya Murphy, prin. Fax 563-8450

Westwood Community SD
Supt. — See Dearborn Heights
Daly ES 200/K-5
25824 Michigan Ave 48141 313-565-0016
Glen Taylor, prin. Fax 565-2359
Tomlinson MS 50/6-8
25912 Annapolis St 48141 313-565-1900
Robert Brooks, prin. Fax 565-0920

Peterson-Warren Academy 100/K-12
PO Box 888 48141 313-565-5808
Juanita Martin, prin. Fax 565-7784

Interlochen, Grand Traverse
Benzie County Central SD
Supt. — See Benzonia
Lake Ann ES 300/K-5
19375 Bronson Lake Rd 49643 231-275-7730
Gail Wheeler, prin. Fax 275-7735

Traverse City Area SD
Supt. — See Traverse City
Interlochen Community ES 300/PK-5
3113 M 137 49643 231-933-5920
Paul Bauer, prin. Fax 933-5941

Ionia, Ionia, Pop. 12,336
Berlin Township SD 3 50/K-8
6679 S State Rd 48846 616-527-2569
Robert Kjolhede, supt. Fax 527-8460
Coon S 50/K-8
6679 S State Rd 48846 616-527-2569
David Schwartz, prin. Fax 527-8460

Easton Twp SD 6 50/K-5
1779 Haynor Rd 48846 616-527-0089
Kris Deatsman, supt. Fax 527-4494
Haynor ES 50/K-5
1779 Haynor Rd 48846 616-527-0089
Kris Deatsman, prin. Fax 527-4494

Ionia SD 3,100/K-12
250 E Tuttle Rd 48846 616-527-9280
Patricia Batista, supt. Fax 527-8846
www.ioniaschools.org
Boyce ES 300/K-5
3550 N State Rd 48846 616-527-0571
Stacey Bovee, prin. Fax 527-8003
Emerson ES 200/K-5
645 Hackett St 48846 616-527-8018
Mitch Mercer, prin. Fax 527-1741
Ionia MS 700/6-8
438 Union St 48846 616-527-0040
Cheri Meier, prin. Fax 527-3380
Jefferson ES 300/K-5
420 N Jefferson St 48846 616-527-2740
Matt Vogel, prin. Fax 527-8002
Rather ES 300/K-5
380 E Tuttle Rd 48846 616-527-1720
Darin Magley, prin. Fax 527-8004
Other Schools – See Muir

Ionia Township SD 2 50/K-5
2120 N State Rd 48846 616-527-0787
Fax 527-4731
North LeValley ES 50/K-5
2120 N State Rd 48846 616-527-0787
Linda Emelander, lead tchr. Fax 527-4731

Ionia SDA S, 721 Elmwood Dr 48846 50/K-8
Jeff Thompson, prin. 616-527-1971
SS. Peter & Paul S 100/PK-8
317 Baldie St 48846 616-527-3561
Julie Palmer, prin. Fax 527-3562

Ira, Saint Clair
Algonac Community SD
Supt. — See Algonac
Fair Haven ES 200/K-5
8361 Broadbridge Rd 48023 586-725-7911
Jennifer Weaver, prin. Fax 725-0971

Anchor Bay SD
Supt. — See Casco
Maconce ES 200/K-5
6300 Church Rd 48023 586-725-0284
Carol Selby, prin. Fax 725-2037

Iron Mountain, Dickinson, Pop. 8,173
Iron Mountain SD 1,300/PK-12
217 Izzo Marriucci Way 49801 906-779-2600
Dennis Chartier, supt. Fax 779-2676
www.imschools.org
Central ES 200/K-5
301 W Hughitt St 49801 906-779-2620
Robert Strang, prin. Fax 779-2634
Central MS 300/6-8
301 E Hughitt St 49801 906-779-2620
Robert Strang, prin. Fax 779-2634
East ES 100/K-5
800 E E St 49801 906-779-2624
Scott McClure, prin. Fax 779-2637
North ES 200/PK-5
900 5th St 49801 906-779-2626
Scott McClure, prin. Fax 779-2636

Dickinson Area S 200/PK-8
406 W B St 49801 906-774-2277
Patricia Covitz, prin. Fax 774-8704
Pine Mountain Christian SDA S 50/K-8
N3770 Pine Mountain Rd 49801 906-779-7640
Jay Hellman, prin.

Iron River, Iron, Pop. 3,112
West Iron County SD 1,000/PK-12
601 Garfield Ave 49935 906-265-9218
Christopher Thomson, supt. Fax 265-9736
www.westiron.org
Stambaugh ES 300/PK-4
700 Washington Ave 49935 906-265-6141
Carol Brunswick, prin. Fax 265-9810
West Iron County Upper ES 5-6
3257 US Highway 2 49935 906-265-5188
Carol Brunswick, dir. Fax 265-0026

Ironwood, Gogebic, Pop. 5,728
Ironwood Area SD 1,100/PK-12
650 E Ayer St 49938 906-932-0200
James Rayner, supt. Fax 932-9915
www.ironwood.k12.mi.us/
Norrie ES 200/3-5
401 Alfred Wright Blvd 49938 906-932-3110
Bruce KerKove, prin. Fax 932-1889
Sleight ES 200/PK-2
108 E Arch St 49938 906-932-1531
Bruce KerKove, prin. Fax 932-0973

All Saints Catholic Academy 100/PK-6
106 S Marquette St 49938 906-932-3200
Roberta Fabbri, prin. Fax 932-1019

Ishpeming, Marquette, Pop. 6,507
Ishpeming SD 1 900/PK-12
319 E Division St 49849 906-485-5501
Stephen Piereson, supt. Fax 485-1422
www.ishpemingschools.com
Birchview ES 200/K-4
663 Poplar St 49849 906-485-6341
Brian Veale, prin. Fax 485-5925
Central ES 100/PK-PK
324 E Pearl St 49849 906-486-9521
Brian Veale, prin. Fax 485-6077
Phelps IS 300/5-8
700 E North St 49849 906-486-4438
Charleen Willey, prin. Fax 486-6549

NICE Community SD 1,100/K-12
300 S Westwood Dr 49849 906-485-1021
Michael Haynes, supt. Fax 485-4095
www.nice.k12.mi.us/
Aspen Ridge ES 400/K-5
350 Aspen Ridge School Rd 49849 906-485-3175
Scott Hall, prin. Fax 485-3182
Aspen Ridge MS 300/6-8
350 Aspen Ridge School Rd 49849 906-485-3176
Dennis Tasson, prin. Fax 485-3182

Ithaca, Gratiot, Pop. 3,101
Ithaca SD 1,400/K-12
710 N Union St 48847 989-875-3700
Charles Schnetzler, supt. Fax 875-4538
www.ithacaschools.net
Ithaca MS 300/7-8
710 N Union St 48847 989-875-3373
Steven Netzley, prin. Fax 875-2500
North ES 400/3-6
201 E Arcada St 48847 989-875-3047
Kathleen Paul, prin. Fax 875-4701
South ES 200/K-2
400 Webster St 48847 989-875-4741
Terri Brown, prin. Fax 875-8701

Ithaca SDA S 50/K-8
937 N Pine River St 48847 989-875-4961
Deborah Curran, prin.

Jackson, Jackson, Pop. 34,879
East Jackson Community SD 1,500/K-12
1404 N Sutton Rd 49202 517-764-2090
Bruce Van Eyck, supt. Fax 764-6033
ejs.k12.mi.us/
East Jackson Memorial ES 300/K-5
345 N Dettman Rd 49202 517-784-7131
Beth Murphy, prin. Fax 784-6160
East Jackson MS 300/6-8
4340 Walz Rd 49201 517-764-6010
Heather Jacobs, prin. Fax 764-6081
Robinson ES 300/K-5
5400 Seymour Rd 49201 517-764-1810
Jackie Murray, prin. Fax 764-6085

Jackson SD 6,400/PK-12
522 Wildwood Ave 49201 517-841-2200
Daniel Evans, supt. Fax 789-8056
www.jpsk12.org/
Bennett ES 400/K-6
820 Bennett St 49202 517-841-2730
Scott Hutchins, prin. Fax 768-5901
Cascades ES 200/K-2
1200 S Wisner St 49203 517-841-3900
Ed Peterson, prin. Fax 768-5902
Dibble ES 300/K-6
3450 Kibby Rd 49203 517-841-3970
Pamela Perlos, prin. Fax 768-5903
Frost ES 800/K-6
1226 S Wisner St 49203 517-841-2600
Jennifer Oswalt, prin. Fax 768-6045
Hunt ES 600/PK-6
1143 N Brown St 49202 517-841-2610
M. Raczkowski-Shannon, prin. Fax 768-5900
MS at Parkside 900/7-8
2400 4th St 49203 517-841-2300
William Patterson, prin. Fax 768-5968
McCulloch ES 100/PK-5
216 E Biddle St 49203 517-841-3940
Frances Reeves, prin. Fax 768-5906
Northeast ES 600/PK-6
1024 Fleming Ave 49202 517-841-2500
Derry Sims, prin. Fax 768-5911
Sharp Park S 200/PK-4
766 Park Rd 49203 517-841-2860
Ellen Seguin, prin. Fax 784-1325

Northwest Community SD 3,200/PK-12
4000 Van Horn Rd 49201 517-569-2247
Emily Kress, supt. Fax 569-2395
www.nsd.k12.mi.us
Flora List ES 300/PK-1
6900 Rives Junction Rd 49201 517-569-2247
Lorri McAlpine, prin. Fax 569-3908
Kidder MS 800/6-8
6700 Rives Junction Rd 49201 517-569-2247
Dan Brooks, prin. Fax 569-2931
Northwest ES 500/4-5
3757 Lansing Ave 49202 517-789-6159
Kip O'Leary, prin. Fax 789-8467
Parnall ES 500/2-3
3737 Lansing Ave 49202 517-768-4500
Valerie Shelters, prin. Fax 768-4505

Vandercook Lake SD 1,200/K-12
1000 E Golf Ave 49203 517-782-9044
Anthony Hollow, supt. Fax 788-3690
www.vandyschools.org
Townsend ES 500/K-5
1005 Floyd Ave 49203 517-784-6133
Paul Chilcote, prin. Fax 788-3695

Jackson Catholic MS 300/7-8
915 Cooper St 49202 517-784-3385
Anthony Shaughnessy, prin. Fax 782-7883
Jackson Christian ES 200/PK-5
801 Halstead Blvd 49203 517-784-6161
Aaron Metzcar, prin. Fax 784-6322
Jackson Christian MS 100/6-8
4200 Lowe Rd 49203 517-783-2658
Todd Barney, prin. Fax 783-4235
Jackson SDA S 50/1-8
3600 County Farm Rd 49201 517-787-1280
Ashley Johnson, prin. Fax 787-1280
Queen of Miraculous Medals S 300/K-6
811 S Wisner St 49203 517-782-2664
Ruth Benner, prin. Fax 782-3570
St. John the Evangelist S 200/K-6
405 E North St 49202 517-784-1714
Kathy Tarnacki, prin. Fax 788-5382
St. Mary Star of the Sea S 200/PK-6
116 E Wesley St 49201 517-784-8811
Julia Hurlburt, prin. Fax 788-3425
Trinity Lutheran S 100/PK-8
4900 McCain Rd 49201 517-750-2105
Lee Erfourth, prin. Fax 750-9945

Jenison, Ottawa, Pop. 17,882
Jenison SD 4,600/PK-12
8375 20th Ave 49428 616-457-8890
Thomas TenBrink, supt. Fax 457-8898
www.jpsonline.org/
Bauerwood ES 500/K-6
1443 Bauer Rd 49428 616-457-1408
Crystal Morse, prin. Fax 457-8491
Bursley ES 400/K-6
1195 Port Sheldon St 49428 616-457-2200
Rane Garcia, prin. Fax 457-8489
ECC 50/PK-PK
800 Connie St 49428 616-457-1406
Lee Westervelt, prin. Fax 457-8492
Jenison JHS 700/7-8
8295 20th Ave 49428 616-457-1402
Brandon Graham, prin. Fax 457-8090
Pinewood ES 400/K-6
2405 Chippewa St 49428 616-457-1407
Cynthia Sinclair, prin. Fax 457-8490
Rosewood ES 500/K-6
2370 Tyler St 49428 616-669-0011
Lloyd Gingerich, prin. Fax 669-5980
Sandy Hill ES 400/K-6
1990 Baldwin St 49428 616-457-1404
Kathy Keehn, prin. Fax 457-8493

Jenison Christian S 400/PK-8
7726 Graceland Dr 49428 616-457-3301
Charles Pasma, prin. Fax 457-1430

Johannesburg, Otsego
Johannesburg-Lewiston Area SD 900/K-12
10854 M 32 E 49751 989-732-1773
James Hilgendorf, supt. Fax 732-6556
www.jlas.org
Johannesburg S 300/K-8
10854 M 32 E 49751 989-731-2040
Thomas Hausbeck, prin. Fax 732-6556
Other Schools – See Lewiston

Jonesville, Hillsdale, Pop. 2,293
Jonesville Community SD 1,200/PK-12
202 Wright St 49250 517-849-9075
Michael Potts, supt. Fax 849-2434
www.jonesvilleschools.org
Jonesville MS 300/6-8
401 E Chicago St 49250 517-849-3210
Penny Snyder, prin. Fax 849-3213
Williams ES 500/PK-5
440 Adrian Rd 49250 517-849-9175
Johanna Curson, prin. Fax 849-7306

Kalamazoo, Kalamazoo, Pop. 72,700
Comstock SD 2,200/PK-12
3010 Gull Rd 49048 269-388-9461
Dr. Sandy Standish, supt. Fax 388-9481
www.comstockps.org
Comstock Northeast MS 600/6-8
1423 N 28th St 49048 269-388-9433
Kelley Howard, prin. Fax 388-9664
East ES 100/4-5
175 Hunt St 49048 269-388-9449
Wesley Seeley, prin. Fax 388-9661
Green Meadow ES 200/K-3
6171 E MN Ave 49048 269-388-9440
Michael Campbell, prin. Fax 388-9663
North ES 300/PK-3
3100 N 26th St 49048 269-388-9455
Heather Yankovich, prin. Fax 388-9660

Kalamazoo SD 10,500/K-12
1220 Howard St 49008 269-337-0100
Michael Rice, supt. Fax 337-0149
www.kalamazoopublicschools.com
Arcadia ES 300/K-6
932 Boswell Ln 49006 269-337-0530
Sandy VanErkel, prin. Fax 372-9871
Edison Environmental Science Academy 300/K-5
924 Russell St 49001 269-337-0550
Chuck Tansey, prin. Fax 337-1621
Greenwood ES 100/K-3
3501 Moreland St 49001 269-337-0560
Sara Glendenning, prin. Fax 337-1622
Hillside MS 500/7-8
1941 Alamo Ave 49006 269-337-0570
Gloria Foster-Wimbley, prin. Fax 337-1618
Indian Prairie ES 200/K-3
3546 Grand Prairie Rd 49006 269-337-0590
Gwenn Mathews, prin. Fax 337-1623
King-Westwood ES 500/K-6
1100 Nichols Rd 49006 269-337-0610
Judy D'Arcangelis, prin. Fax 337-1624
Lincoln International Studies ES 600/K-6
912 N Burdick St 49007 269-337-0640
Kimberly Parker-Devauld, prin. Fax 337-1626
Maple Magnet MS 600/7-8
922 W Maple St 49008 269-337-0730
Kevin Doerfler, prin. Fax 337-1633
Milwood ES 500/K-5
3400 Lovers Ln 49001 269-337-0660
Chuck Pearson, prin. Fax 337-1627
Milwood Magnet MS 600/6-8
2916 Konkle St 49001 269-337-0670
Kevin Campbell, prin. Fax 337-1628
Northeastern ES 400/K-6
2433 Gertrude St 49048 269-337-0690
Sue Chartier, prin. Fax 337-1629
Northglade Montessori Magnet ES 300/K-6
1914 Cobb Ave 49007 269-337-0700
Dr. Terina Harvey, prin. Fax 337-1630
Parkwood-Upjohn ES 400/K-6
2321 S Park St 49001 269-337-0720
Carol Steiner, prin. Fax 337-1632
Prairie Ridge ES K-6
2294 S 9th St 49009 269-337-0540
Jillian George, prin. Fax 372-9839
Spring Valley ES 400/K-6
3530 Mount Olivet Rd 49004 269-337-0750
Susan Wager-Dameron, prin. Fax 337-1634
Washington Writers' Academy 300/K-5
1919 Portage St 49001 269-337-0770
John Klein, prin. Fax 337-1635
Winchell ES 500/K-6
2316 Winchell Ave 49008 269-337-0780
Michael Hughes, prin. Fax 337-1636
Woods Lake Magnet ES 500/K-5
3215 Oakland Dr 49008 269-337-0790
William Hawkins, prin. Fax 337-1637
Woodward ES for Technology & Research 400/K-6
606 Stuart Ave 49007 269-337-0810
Mary Beth Yankee, prin. Fax 337-1638

Otsego SD
Supt. — See Otsego
Alamo ES 300/K-5
8184 N 6th St 49009 269-692-6150
Melissa Koenig, prin. Fax 692-6144

Parchment SD
Supt. — See Parchment
North ES 300/K-5
5535 Keyes Dr 49004 269-488-1400
Marcy Patterson, prin. Fax 488-1410
Northwood ES 200/K-5
600 Edison St 49004 269-488-1300
Sarah Johnson, prin. Fax 488-1310

Plainwell Community SD
Supt. — See Plainwell
Cooper ES 300/K-5
7559 N 14th St 49009 269-349-2674
Bradley Wyant, prin. Fax 345-5111

Gagie S 300/K-8
615 Fairview Ave 49008 269-342-8008
Sandra Gagie, prin. Fax 342-1064
Heritage Christian Academy 300/K-12
6312 Quail Run Dr 49009 269-372-1400
James Wessing, admin. Fax 372-6018

Kalamazoo Christian East ES 100/PK-5
5196 Comstock Ave 49048 269-343-0202
Richard Van Donselaar, prin. Fax 343-0327
Kalamazoo Christian MS 200/6-8
3333 S Westnedge Ave 49008 269-343-3645
Jeff Blamer, prin. Fax 343-4649
Kalamazoo Christian West ES 300/PK-5
3800 S 12th St 49009 269-544-2332
Marc Verkaik, prin. Fax 544-2391
Kalamazoo Country Day S 200/PK-8
4221 E Milham Ave 49002 269-329-0116
Sheilla Bridenstine, prin. Fax 329-1850
Kalamazoo Jr. Academy 50/K-8
1601 Nichols Rd 49006 269-342-8943
William Crawford, prin. Fax 492-1459
Montessori S 100/PK-5
750 Howard St 49008 269-349-3248
Pamela Boudreau, prin. Fax 349-1480
Providence Christian S 100/K-9
100 Pratt Rd 49001 269-385-4889
Jacqueline Markus, admin. Fax 385-4889
St. Augustine S 300/K-8
600 W Michigan Ave 49007 269-349-1945
Andra Zommers, prin. Fax 349-1085
St. Monica S 400/PK-8
530 W Kilgore Rd 49008 269-345-2444
Rebecca Reits, prin. Fax 345-8534

Kaleva, Manistee, Pop. 502
Kaleva Norman Dickson SD
Supt. — See Brethren
Kaleva ES 200/K-6
9208 Kauko 49645 231-362-3591
Keith Shearer, prin. Fax 362-2360

Kalkaska, Kalkaska, Pop. 2,205
Excelsior Township SD 1 100/K-8
5521 M 72 NE 49646 231-258-2934
Fax 258-4103
www.crawfordschool.com
Crawford S 100/K-8
5521 M 72 NE 49646 231-258-2934
Karen Hart, lead tchr. Fax 258-4103

Kalkaska SD 1,600/PK-12
PO Box 580 49646 231-258-9109
Lee Sandy, supt. Fax 258-4474
www.kpschools.com/
Birch Street ES 400/PK-3
PO Box 580 49646 231-258-8629
Jessica Ziecina, prin. Fax 258-3579
Cherry Street IS 200/4-5
PO Box 580 49646 231-258-9146
John Gross, prin. Fax 258-5149
Kalkaska MS 400/6-8
PO Box 580 49646 231-258-4040
Diane Swoverland, prin. Fax 258-3576
Other Schools – See Rapid City

Kawkawlin, Bay

St. Bartholomew Lutheran S 100/K-8
1033 E Beaver Rd 48631 989-684-6751
Mark Boileau, prin. Fax 684-0071
St. Valentine S 50/K-6
1010 9 Mile Rd 48631 989-662-6966
Robin Honard, prin. Fax 662-6964

Keego Harbor, Oakland, Pop. 2,791
West Bloomfield SD
Supt. — See West Bloomfield
Roosevelt ES 400/K-5
2065 Cass Lake Rd 48320 248-865-6620
Thomas Shelton, prin. Fax 865-6621

Kent City, Kent, Pop. 1,074
Kent City Community SD 1,100/PK-12
200 N Clover St 49330 616-678-7714
William Smith, supt. Fax 678-4320
www.kentcityschools.org
Kent City ES 300/PK-5
29 College St 49330 616-678-4181
Doug Greer, prin. Fax 678-7785
Kent City MS 300/6-8
285 N Main St 49330 616-678-4214
Greg Apkarian, prin. Fax 678-5099

Algoma Christian S 200/PK-12
PO Box 220 49330 616-678-7480
Daniel Beach, admin. Fax 678-7484

Kentwood, Kent, Pop. 46,491
Kentwood SD 9,000/PK-12
5820 Eastern Ave SE 49508 616-455-4400
Scott Palczewski, supt. Fax 455-4476
www.kentwoodps.org
Bowen ES 300/K-5
4483 Kalamazoo Ave SE 49508 616-455-5220
Sullie Wright, prin. Fax 455-6991
Brookwood ES 400/K-5
5465 Kalamazoo Ave SE 49508 616-455-0030
Sandy Lauritzen, prin. Fax 455-5778
Challenger ES 300/K-5
2475 52nd St SE 49508 616-698-2524
Mark Bea, prin. Fax 698-9089
Crestwood MS 600/6-8
2674 44th St SE 49512 616-455-1200
John Keenoy, prin. Fax 455-2338
Discovery ES 400/K-5
2461 60th St SE 49508 616-871-1080
Deb McNally, prin. Fax 871-1081
Endeavor ES 400/PK-5
5757 E Paris Ave SE 49512 616-554-5241
Valerie Pearce, prin. Fax 554-5244
Glenwood ES 300/K-5
912 Silverleaf St SE 49508 616-455-2510
Kari Anama, prin. Fax 455-0320
Meadowlawn ES 300/PK-5
4939 Burgis Ave SE 49508 616-534-4608
Mike Pickard, prin. Fax 534-2512

Pinewood MS 900/6-8
2100 60th St SE 49508 616-455-1224
Dave Chesney, prin. Fax 455-2054
Southwood ES 400/K-5
630 66th St SE 49548 616-455-7230
Jeff Overkleeft, prin. Fax 455-7220
Townline ES 200/K-5
100 60th St SE 49548 616-538-4120
Karen Friberg, prin. Fax 538-8770
Valleywood MS 600/6-8
1110 50th St SE 49508 616-538-7670
Mindy Westra, prin. Fax 538-9301
Other Schools – See Caledonia, Grand Rapids

St. Mark Lutheran S 200/PK-8
1934 52nd St SE 49508 616-281-7892
Joel Bahr, prin. Fax 281-1543

Kimball, Saint Clair, Pop. 7,247
Port Huron Area SD
Supt. — See Port Huron
Indian Woods ES 400/PK-5
4975 W Water St 48074 810-984-6515
Cheryl Rogers, prin. Fax 989-2790
Kimball ES 200/PK-5
5801 Griswold Rd 48074 810-984-6519
Shelley Harding, prin. Fax 989-2768

New Life Christian Academy 200/PK-12
5517 Griswold Rd 48074 810-367-3770
Lee Ann Shimmel, admin. Fax 367-2249

Kinde, Huron, Pop. 503
North Huron SD 500/K-12
21 Main St 48445 989-874-4100
Martin Prout, supt. Fax 874-4109
www.nhuron.org
North Huron ES 200/K-6
69 Michigan St 48445 989-874-4103
Jacquie Johnson, prin. Fax 874-4128

Kingsford, Dickinson, Pop. 5,565
Breitung Township SD 1,700/K-12
2000 W Pyle Dr 49802 906-779-2650
Craig Allen, supt. Fax 779-9017
www.kingsford.org
Kingsford MS 400/6-8
445 Hamilton Ave 49802 906-779-2680
David Holmes, prin. Fax 774-1354
Woodland ES 600/K-5
2000 W Pyle Dr 49802 906-779-2685
Darren Petschar, prin. Fax 779-7701

Dickinson-Iron ISD 100/
1074 Pyle Dr 49802 906-779-2690
Johanna Ostwald, supt. Fax 779-2669
www.diisd.org
Willis ECC, 245 Balsam St 49802 100/PK-PK
Casey McCormick, dir. 906-779-2695

Kingsley, Grand Traverse, Pop. 1,524
Kingsley Area SD 1,400/K-12
402 Fenton St 49649 231-263-5262
Lynn Gullekson, supt. Fax 263-5282
www.kingsley.k12.mi.us/
Kingsley Area ES 400/K-4
402 Fenton St 49649 231-263-5262
Karl Hartman, prin. Fax 263-3813
Kingsley Area MS 500/5-8
402 Fenton St 49649 231-263-5262
Ken Knudsen, prin. Fax 263-4623

St. Mary of Hannah S 100/PK-6
2912 W M 113 49649 231-263-5288
Lisa Swartz-Medina, prin. Fax 263-5288

Kingston, Tuscola, Pop. 442
Kingston Community SD 700/PK-12
5790 State St 48741 989-683-2294
Joseph Murphy, supt. Fax 683-2644
www.kingston.k12.mi.us
Kingston ES 400/PK-6
3644 Ross St 48741 989-683-2284
Mike Rea, prin. Fax 683-3318

Lachine, Alpena
Alpena SD
Supt. — See Alpena
Long Rapids ES 200/K-6
12595 Long Rapids Rd 49753 989-358-5730
Jean Kowalski, prin. Fax 358-5735

Laingsburg, Shiawassee, Pop. 1,270
Laingsburg Community SD 1,300/PK-12
205 S Woodhull Rd 48848 517-651-2705
Richard Dunham, supt. Fax 651-9075
www.laingsburg.k12.mi.us/
Early Childhood Ed Center 100/PK-PK
320 E Grand River Rd 48848 517-651-3100
Gregory Kingdon, prin. Fax 651-3101
Laingsburg ES 500/K-5
117 Prospect St 48848 517-651-5067
Connie Schindewolf, prin. Fax 651-2615
Laingsburg MS 300/6-8
112 High St 48848 517-651-5034
Gregory Kingdon, prin. Fax 651-6213

Lake City, Missaukee, Pop. 940
Lake City Area SD 1,200/K-12
PO Box 900 49651 231-839-4333
Harry Ashton, supt. Fax 839-5219
www.lakecityschools.net
Lake City Lower ES 300/K-2
PO Box 900 49651 231-839-7162
Carol Thula, prin. Fax 839-6680
Lake City MS 300/6-8
PO Box 900 49651 231-839-7163
Dave Swanson, prin. Fax 839-6042

Lake City Upper ES 200/3-5
PO Box 900 49651 231-839-2665
Kay Gill, prin. Fax 839-6029

Lakeland, Livingston
Pinckney Community SD
Supt. — See Pinckney
Lakeland ES 400/K-4
PO Box 770 48143 810-225-6700
Sean LaRosa, prin. Fax 225-6705

Lake Leelanau, Leelanau

St. Mary S 200/PK-12
PO Box 340 49653 231-256-9636
Mark Gaubatz, prin. Fax 256-7239

Lake Linden, Houghton, Pop. 1,044
Lake Linden-Hubbell SD 500/K-12
601 Calumet St 49945 906-296-6211
Randall Roberts, supt. Fax 296-0943
www.lakelinden.k12.mi.us
Lake Linden Hubbell ES 300/K-6
601 Calumet St 49945 906-296-6221
Craig Sundblad, prin. Fax 296-0305

Lake Odessa, Ionia, Pop. 2,288
Lakewood SD 2,200/K-12
639 Jordan Lake St 48849 616-374-8043
Michael O'Mara, supt. Fax 374-8858
www.lakewoodps.org
West ES 400/K-5
812 Washington Blvd 48849 616-374-8842
Tim McMillen, prin. Fax 374-1499
Other Schools – See Clarksville, Sunfield, Woodland

Lakewood Christian S 50/PK-8
7766 N Velte Rd 48849 616-374-7944
Fax 374-7947
St. Edward Preschool PK-PK
531 Jordan Lake St 48849 616-374-8809
Fredia Prysock, coord. Fax 374-1559

Lake Orion, Oakland, Pop. 2,756
Lake Orion Community SD 7,800/PK-12
315 N Lapeer St 48362 248-693-5400
Kenneth Gutman, supt. Fax 693-5466
www.lakeorion.k12.mi.us/
Orion Oaks ES 600/PK-5
1255 Joslyn Rd 48360 248-393-0010
Brian Kaplan, prin. Fax 393-0018
Paint Creek ES 600/K-5
2800 Indianwood Rd 48362 248-814-1724
Lauren Sanborn, prin. Fax 814-0209
Pine Tree ES 500/K-5
590 Pine Tree Rd 48362 248-693-5470
Diane Dunaskiss, prin. Fax 693-5319
Scripps MS 600/6-8
385 E Scripps Rd 48360 248-693-5440
Dan Haas, prin. Fax 693-5301
Sims ES 400/K-5
465 E Jackson St 48362 248-693-5460
Jennifer Goethals, prin. Fax 693-5322
Stadium Drive ES 500/K-5
244 Stadium Dr 48360 248-693-5475
Dr. Jesse Baker, prin. Fax 693-5318
Waldon MS 600/6-8
2509 Waldon Rd 48360 248-391-1100
Randy Groya, prin. Fax 391-5452
Webber ES 500/K-5
3191 W Clarkston Rd 48362 248-391-0400
Sarah Manzo, prin. Fax 391-5460
Other Schools – See Oakland, Orion

Divine Grace Lutheran S 100/PK-8
3000 S Lapeer Rd 48359 248-391-2811
Paul Hoffman, prin. Fax 391-7649
Good Shepherd Lutheran S 100/PK-7
1950 S Baldwin Rd 48360 248-391-7244
Marilyn Campbell, prin. Fax 391-0558
Lake Orion Baptist S 100/K-12
255 E Scripps Rd 48360 248-693-6203
Tony Bryson, prin. Fax 693-6177
Oak Hollow Christian SDA S 50/K-8
120 Manitou Ln 48362 248-693-1224
Tamie Hasty, prin.
St. Joseph S 400/K-8
703 N Lapeer Rd 48362 248-693-6215
Sr. Theresa Darga, prin. Fax 693-0958

Lakeport, Saint Clair
Port Huron Area SD
Supt. — See Port Huron
Lakeport ES 300/K-5
3835 Franklin St 48059 810-984-6521
Lea Gourlay, prin. Fax 385-2918

St. Edward on the Lake S 100/PK-5
6995 Lakeshore Rd 48059 810-385-4461
Helen Casper, prin. Fax 385-6070

Lakeview, Montcalm, Pop. 1,122
Lakeview Community SD 1,600/PK-12
123 5th St 48850 989-352-6226
Dr. Dixie Pope, supt. Fax 352-8245
www.lakeviewschools.net
Bright Start ES 300/PK-2
9497 Paden Rd 48850 989-352-8404
Gary Jensen, prin. Fax 352-7021
Lakeview ES 400/3-5
125 5th St 48850 989-352-8016
Timothy Erspamer, prin. Fax 352-8245
Lakeview MS 400/6-8
516 Washington St 48850 989-352-8016
Kyle Hamlin, prin. Fax 352-6710

Lambertville, Monroe, Pop. 7,860
Bedford SD
Supt. — See Temperance

Douglas Road ES 400/K-6
6875 Douglas Rd 48144 734-850-6700
Rose Nearpass, prin. Fax 850-6799
Monroe Road ES 700/K-6
7979 Monroe Rd 48144 734-850-6800
Thea Kirkwood, prin. Fax 850-6899

L Anse, Baraga, Pop. 2,147
L'Anse Area SD 800/K-12
201 N 4th St 49946 906-524-6121
Ray Pasquali, supt. Fax 524-6001
www.laschools.k12.mi.us
L'Anse MS 200/6-8
201 N 4th St 49946 906-524-5390
Robert Willman, prin. Fax 524-0345
Sullivan ES 300/K-5
201 N 4th St 49946 906-524-7365
Tom Sprague, prin. Fax 524-0277

Sacred Heart S 100/PK-6
433 Baraga Ave 49946 906-524-5157
Anne Schumer, prin. Fax 524-5154

Lansing, Ingham, Pop. 115,518
Grand Ledge SD
Supt. — See Grand Ledge
Delta Center ES 400/K-5
305 S Canal Rd 48917 517-925-5540
David Averill, prin. Fax 925-5579

Lansing SD 14,100/PK-12
519 W Kalamazoo St 48933 517-755-1000
Dr. T.C. Wallace, supt. Fax 755-1019
www.lansingschools.net/
Attwood ES 300/K-5
915 Attwood Dr 48911 517-755-1210
Patricia Fitzpatrick, prin. Fax 755-1219
Averill ES 300/K-5
3201 Averill Dr 48911 517-755-1220
Rosa Thill, prin. Fax 755-1229
Bingham ES 200/K-5
121 S Bingham St 48912 517-755-1240
Dr. Freya Rivers, prin. Fax 755-1249
Cavanaugh ES 300/K-5
300 W Cavanaugh Rd 48910 517-755-1250
Mary Henry, prin. Fax 755-1259
Cumberland ES 300/PK-5
2801 Cumberland Rd 48906 517-755-1280
Nanette Kuhlmann, prin. Fax 755-1289
Elmhurst ES 200/PK-5
2400 Pattengill Ave 48910 517-755-1290
Sue Sulzman, prin. Fax 755-1299
Fairview ES 200/K-5
815 N Fairview Ave 48912 517-755-1310
Terry Baker, prin. Fax 755-1319
Forest View ES 300/PK-5
3119 Stoneleigh Dr 48910 517-755-1330
Layla Ahmad, prin. Fax 755-1339
Gardner MS 900/6-8
333 Dahlia Dr 48911 517-755-1120
Norm Gear, prin. Fax 755-1129
Gier Park ES 300/K-5
401 E Gier St 48906 517-755-1360
Mara Lud, prin. Fax 755-1369
Kendon ES 300/K-5
827 Kendon Dr 48910 517-755-1450
Martha Rusesky, prin. Fax 755-1459
Lewton ES 300/K-5
2000 Lewton Pl 48911 517-755-1460
Teri Bernero, prin. Fax 755-1469
Lyons ES 300/K-5
2901 Lyons Ave 48910 517-755-1480
Tony Forsthoefel, prin. Fax 755-1489
Mt. Hope ES 400/K-5
1215 E Mount Hope Ave 48910 517-755-1550
Donna Old, prin. Fax 755-1559
North ES 400/K-5
333 E Miller Rd 48911 517-755-1710
Shelley Barlow, prin. Fax 755-1719
Otto MS 800/6-8
500 E Thomas St 48906 517-755-1150
Sandra Noecker, prin. Fax 755-1159
Pattengill MS 600/6-8
626 Marshall St 48912 517-755-1130
Kirk Sulzman, prin. Fax 755-1139
Pleasant View Magnet S 500/K-8
4501 Pleasant Grove Rd 48910 517-755-1600
Madeline Shanahan, prin. Fax 755-1609
Post Oak ES 300/K-5
2320 Post Oak Ln 48912 517-755-1610
Camela Diaz, prin. Fax 755-1619
Reo ES 300/K-5
1221 Reo Rd 48910 517-755-1620
Kim Johnson-Ray, prin. Fax 755-1629
Rich MS 700/6-8
2600 Hampden Dr 48911 517-755-1160
Linda Angel-Weinberg, prin. Fax 755-1169
Riddle ES 300/K-5
221 Huron St 48915 517-755-1720
Betty Javoroski, prin. Fax 755-1729
Sheridan Road ES 300/K-5
16900 Cedar St 48906 517-755-1630
Ginny Acheson, prin. Fax 755-1639
Wainwright Leadership Magnet ES 200/K-6
4200 Wainwright Ave 48911 517-755-1660
LaDonna Mask, prin. Fax 755-1669
Wexford Montessori Magnet ES 300/PK-6
5217 Wexford Rd 48911 517-755-1740
Nabila Boctor, prin. Fax 755-1749
Willow ES 300/K-5
1012 W Willow St 48915 517-755-1680
Connie Nickson, prin. Fax 755-1689
Woodcreek ES 300/K-5
4000 Woodcreek Ln 48911 517-755-1700
Delsa Chapman, prin. Fax 755-1709

Waverly Community SD 3,100/PK-12
515 Snow Rd 48917 517-321-7265
Thomas Pillar, supt. Fax 321-8577
web.waverly.k12.mi.us/index.cfm
Colt ES 300/PK-4
4344 W Michigan Ave 48917 517-323-3777
Dr. Margaret Baldwin, prin. Fax 323-9813
Elmwood ES 200/K-4
1533 Elmwood Rd 48917 517-321-3383
Valerie Hendrickson-Carr, prin. Fax 321-9318
Waverly East IS 500/5-6
3131 W Michigan Ave 48917 517-484-8830
Michael Moreno, prin. Fax 485-4008
Waverly MS 500/7-8
620 Snow Rd 48917 517-321-7240
Vincent Perkins, prin. Fax 321-5789
Winans ES 300/K-4
5601 W Michigan Ave 48917 517-321-2371
Shawn Talifarro, prin. Fax 323-1840
Windemere View ES 200/K-4
1500 Boynton Dr 48917 517-321-3543
Vickie Tisdale, prin. Fax 321-9592

Emanuel First Lutheran S 100/K-8
1001 N Capitol Ave 48906 517-485-4547
Daniel Hosbach, prin. Fax 484-7484
Greater Lansing Adventist S 100/K-10
5330 W St Joe Hwy 48917 517-321-5565
Chad Bernard, prin. Fax 321-5580
Immaculate Heart/St. Casimir S 200/PK-8
3830 Rosemont St 48910 517-882-6631
Angela Johnston, prin. Fax 882-5536
Lansing Christian S 700/PK-12
3405 Belle Chase Way 48911 517-882-5779
Pam Campbell, supt. Fax 882-5849
Montessori Childrens House 200/PK-6
2100 W Saint Joseph St 48915 517-482-9191
Maureen Newton, prin. Fax 482-0011
New Covenant Christian S 100/PK-12
PO Box 80737 48908 517-323-8903
Jim Ryckman, prin. Fax 323-0421
Our Saviour Lutheran S 100/PK-8
7910 E St Joe Hwy 48917 517-882-3550
Jim Landskroener, prin. Fax 882-3477
Resurrection S 200/PK-8
1527 E Michigan Ave 48912 517-487-0439
Jon VonAchen, prin. Fax 487-3198
St. Gerard S 600/PK-8
4433 W Willow Hwy 48917 517-321-6126
Michelle Piecuch, prin. Fax 323-8046
St. Therese S 100/K-8
2620 Turner St 48906 517-482-1634
Christopher Smith, prin. Fax 482-1635

Lapeer, Lapeer, Pop. 9,370
Lapeer Community SD 6,900/PK-12
250 2nd St 48446 810-667-2401
Debbie Thompson, supt. Fax 667-2411
www.lapeerschools.org
Cramton Kids & Company 50/PK-PK
333 Denville Blvd 48446 810-667-2454
Ann Robb, coord. Fax 245-1090
Elba/Seaton ES - Elba Campus 300/PK-3
300 N Elba Rd 48446 810-667-2436
Cynthia Niblack, prin. Fax 667-2463
Elba/Seaton ES - Seaton Campus 200/4-6
5065 Coldwater Rd 48446 810-793-6264
Cynthia Niblack, prin. Fax 793-6477
Lynch ES 400/PK-6
2035 Roods Lake Rd 48446 810-667-2448
William Slater, prin. Fax 667-2473
Maple Grove ES 400/PK-6
2020 Imlay City Rd 48446 810-667-2444
Paul Dombrowski, prin. Fax 667-2467
Mayfield ES 500/PK-6
302 Plum Creek Rd 48446 810-667-2442
Heather Vance, prin. Fax 667-2468
Schickler ES 500/PK-6
2020 W Oregon St 48446 810-667-2440
Michelle Bradford, prin. Fax 667-2469
Turrill ES 400/PK-6
785 S Elm St 48446 810-667-2438
Jenny Torok, prin. Fax 667-2470
Zemmer JHS 600/7-7
1920 W Oregon St 48446 810-667-2413
John Dunlop, prin. Fax 667-2483
Other Schools – See Metamora

Bishop Kelley Memorial S 200/PK-8
926 W Nepessing St 48446 810-664-5011
Anne Estelle, prin. Fax 664-5606
St. Paul Lutheran S 200/PK-8
90 Millville Rd 48446 810-664-0046
Raymond Sturm, prin. Fax 245-4082

Lawrence, Van Buren, Pop. 1,030
Lawrence SD 800/PK-12
650 W Saint Joseph St 49064 269-674-8233
John Overley, supt. Fax 674-8206
www.lawrenceschools.cc
Lawrence ES 400/PK-6
648 W Saint Joseph St 49064 269-674-8231
Susan McQueen, prin. Fax 674-3545

Lawton, Van Buren, Pop. 1,852
Lawton Community SD 1,100/PK-12
101 Primary Way 49065 269-624-7900
Joseph Trimboli, supt. Fax 624-6489
www.lawtoncs.org
Lawton ES 500/PK-5
101 Primary Way 49065 269-624-4241
Chris Rice, prin. Fax 624-5604
Lawton MS 300/6-8
101 Primary Way 49065 269-624-4581
Tim Cerven, prin. Fax 624-5206

Leland, Leelanau
Leland SD 500/K-12
PO Box 498 49654 231-256-9857
Michael Hartigan, supt. Fax 256-9844
mail.leland.k12.mi.us
Leland S 500/K-12
PO Box 498 49654 231-256-9857
Jason Stowe, prin. Fax 256-9844

Lennon, Shiawassee, Pop. 505
Durand Area SD
Supt. — See Durand
Knight ES 200/K-5
900 Oak St 48449 810-621-3252
Lorraine Thayer, prin. Fax 621-3119

Leonard, Oakland, Pop. 332
Oxford Community SD
Supt. — See Oxford
Leonard ES 300/K-5
335 E Elmwood 48367 248-969-5300
Dianna Zink, prin. Fax 969-5310

Romeo Community SD
Supt. — See Romeo
Hamilton-Parsons ES 300/K-5
69875 Dequindre Rd 48367 586-752-0280
Robert Maedel, prin. Fax 752-0421

Leonidas, Saint Joseph
Colon Community SD
Supt. — See Colon
Leonidas S 50/K-8
30945 Church St 49066 269-496-7385
Jason Messenger, prin. Fax 432-9341

Le Roy, Osceola, Pop. 266
Pine River Area SD 1,300/K-12
17445 Pine River Rd 49655 231-829-3141
Jim Ganger, supt. Fax 829-4410
www.pineriver.org/
Le Roy ES 200/K-2
408 W Gilbert St 49655 231-768-4481
Barb Parmenter, prin. Fax 768-4048
Pine River MS 300/6-8
17445 Pine River Rd 49655 231-829-4064
Darrell Holmes, prin. Fax 829-3041
Other Schools – See Luther, Tustin

Leslie, Ingham, Pop. 2,268
Leslie SD 1,300/K-12
432 N Main St 49251 517-589-8200
Corey Netzley, supt. Fax 589-5340
www.lesliek12.net/
Leslie MS 400/5-8
400 Kimball St 49251 517-589-8218
John Denney, prin. Fax 589-5714
Woodworth ES 400/K-4
212 Pennsylvania St 49251 517-589-5151
Maureen Packer, prin. Fax 589-5548

Lewiston, Montmorency
Johannesburg-Lewiston Area SD
Supt. — See Johannesburg
Lewiston S 300/K-8
PO Box 417 49756 989-786-2253
Rick Holt, prin. Fax 786-5315

Lexington, Sanilac, Pop. 1,096
Croswell-Lexington SD
Supt. — See Croswell
Meyer ES 300/PK-4
7201 Lake St 48450 810-679-1200
Donna Barrier, prin. Fax 679-1205

Lincoln, Alcona, Pop. 352
Alcona Community SD 1,000/K-12
PO Box 249 48742 989-736-6212
Shawn Thornton, supt. Fax 736-6261
www.edline.net/pages/Alcona_CS
Alcona ES 400/K-5
PO Box 249 48742 989-736-8146
Sharon Fairchild, prin. Fax 736-7031
Alcona MS 300/6-8
PO Box 249 48742 989-736-8534
Terrence Allison, prin. Fax 736-3184

Lincoln Park, Wayne, Pop. 38,237
Lincoln Park SD 5,200/PK-12
1650 Champaign Rd 48146 313-389-0200
Randall Kite, supt. Fax 389-1322
www.resa.net/lincolnpark
Carr ES 300/K-6
3901 Ferris Ave 48146 313-389-0230
Steve Massengill, prin. Fax 388-9869
Crowley Center 200/PK-PK
2000 Pagel Ave 48146 313-389-0259
Debbie Kitson, prin. Fax 928-8212
Foote ES 300/K-6
3250 Abbott Ave 48146 313-389-0216
Cheryl Irving, prin. Fax 389-0997
Hoover ES 300/K-6
3750 Howard St 48146 313-389-0207
Daphne Springer, prin. Fax 388-0278
Keppen ES 300/K-6
661 Mill St 48146 313-389-0232
Terry Dangerfield, prin. Fax 389-3522
LaFayette ES 500/K-6
1360 Lafayette Blvd 48146 313-389-0224
Craig Stanczyk, prin. Fax 389-0749
Lincoln Park MS 800/7-8
2800 Lafayette Blvd 48146 313-389-0757
Tara Randall, prin. Fax 389-0761
Mixter ES 200/K-6
3301 Electric Ave 48146 313-389-0228
Stefanie Hayes, prin. Fax 388-6611
Paun ES 300/K-6
2821 Bailey Ave 48146 313-389-0218
Walter Gates, prin. Fax 388-2955
Raupp ES 300/K-6
1351 Ethel Ave 48146 313-389-0226
Bernard Falahee, prin. Fax 388-6429

Christ the Good Shepherd S 200/PK-8
1590 Riverbank St 48146 313-386-0633
Tom Caruso, prin. Fax 928-1326

Linden, Genesee, Pop. 3,452
Linden Community SD 2,800/K-12
7205 Silver Lake Rd 48451 810-591-0980
Edward Koledo, supt. Fax 591-5587
www.lindenschools.org
Central ES 400/K-5
7199 Silver Lake Rd 48451 810-591-8410
Linda Tottingham, prin. Fax 591-7316
Hyatt ES 500/K-5
325 Stan Eaton Dr 48451 810-591-8180
Brian Boudreau, prin. Fax 591-4377
Linden ES 300/K-5
400 S Bridge St 48451 810-591-9130
Linda Blakey, prin. Fax 591-9143
Linden MS 700/6-8
15425 Lobdell Rd 48451 810-591-0712
Julie Brown, prin. Fax 591-0155

Linwood, Bay
Pinconning Area SD
Supt. — See Pinconning
Linwood ES 200/K-6
517 W Center St 48634 989-697-5711
Mark Abenth, prin. Fax 697-5707

St. Anne S 100/PK-6
317 W Center St 48634 989-697-3100
Robin Honard, prin. Fax 697-5901

Litchfield, Hillsdale, Pop. 1,429
Litchfield Community SD 500/K-12
210 Williams St 49252 517-542-2388
Tom Bartol, supt. Fax 542-2580
www.litchfieldschools.com/
Litchfield ES 200/K-5
210 Williams St 49252 517-542-2356
Monte Bishop, prin. Fax 542-2650

Livonia, Wayne, Pop. 97,977
Clarenceville SD 1,900/PK-12
20210 Middlebelt Rd 48152 248-919-0400
Pamela Swert, supt. Fax 919-0430
www.clarenceville.k12.mi.us
Botsford ES 400/PK-5
19515 Lathers St 48152 248-919-0402
Joe Schiffman, prin. Fax 919-0442
Clarenceville MS 400/6-8
20210 Middlebelt Rd 48152 248-919-0406
Kathleen Guntzviller, prin. Fax 919-0436
Grandview ES 400/K-5
19814 Louise St 48152 248-919-0404
Ellen Demray, prin. Fax 919-0434

Livonia SD 16,900/PK-12
15125 Farmington Rd 48154 734-744-2500
Dr. Randy Liepa, supt. Fax 744-2571
www.livoniapublicschools.org/
Buchanan ES 400/K-4
16400 Hubbard St 48154 734-744-2690
Marjorie Moore, prin. Fax 744-2692
Cass ES 300/K-4
34633 Munger St 48154 734-744-2695
Marcia Kreger, prin. Fax 744-2697
Cleveland ES 500/K-4
28030 Cathedral St 48150 734-744-2700
Michael Daraskavich, prin. Fax 744-2702
Coolidge ES 500/K-4
30500 Curtis Rd 48152 248-744-2705
Ann Kalec, prin. Fax 744-2707
Emerson MS 900/7-8
29100 W Chicago St 48150 734-744-2665
Ann Owen, prin. Fax 744-2667
Frost MS 900/7-8
14041 Stark Rd 48154 734-744-2670
Christina Berry, prin. Fax 744-2672
Garfield ES 300/K-4
10218 Arthur St 48150 734-744-2715
William Green, prin. Fax 744-2717
Grant ES 600/K-4
9300 Hubbard St 48150 734-744-2720
Marla Feldman, prin. Fax 744-2722
Holmes MS 900/7-8
16200 Newburgh Rd 48154 734-744-2675
Eric Stromberg, prin. Fax 744-2677
Hoover ES 500/K-4
15900 Levan Rd 48154 734-744-2730
Andrea Oquist, prin. Fax 744-2732
Jackson ECC 100/PK-PK
32025 Lyndon St 48154 734-744-2813
Gayle Fedoronko, prin. Fax 744-2814
Kennedy ES 400/K-4
14201 Hubbard St 48154 734-744-2745
DeAnn Urso, prin. Fax 744-2747
Randolph ES 400/K-4
14470 Norman St 48154 734-744-2770
Danielle Daniels, prin. Fax 744-2772
Riley ES 900/5-6
15555 Henry Ruff St 48154 734-744-2680
Cynthia Scott, prin. Fax 744-2682
Roosevelt ES 400/K-4
30200 Lyndon St 48154 734-744-2775
Kay DePerro, prin. Fax 744-2777
Rosedale ES 300/K-4
36651 Ann Arbor Trl 48150 734-744-2800
Tammy Spangler-Timm, prin. Fax 744-2802
Webster ES 100/K-4
32401 Pembroke St 48152 734-744-2795
Shellie Moore, prin. Fax 744-2797
Other Schools – See Westland

Peace Lutheran S 100/PK-8
9415 Merriman Rd 48150 734-422-6930
David Wilson, prin. Fax 422-0790

St. Edith S 300/K-8
15089 Newburgh Rd Ste 1 48154 734-464-1250
Sr. Mary Margaret Kijek, prin. Fax 464-6765
St. Genevieve S 300/PK-8
28933 Jamison St 48154 734-425-4420
Betty Flack, prin. Fax 458-3915
St. Michael S 800/K-8
11300 Fairfield St 48150 734-421-7360
Sr. Mary Carolyn Ratkowski, prin. Fax 466-9713
St. Paul Lutheran S 200/PK-8
17810 Farmington Rd 48152 734-421-9022
Charles Buege, prin. Fax 261-2760

Lowell, Kent, Pop. 4,140
Lowell Area SD 3,700/K-12
300 High St 49331 616-987-2500
Gregory Pratt, supt. Fax 987-2511
www.lowellschools.com/
Bushnell ES 100/K-1
700 Elizabeth St 49331 616-987-2650
Karen Burd, prin. Fax 987-2661
Cherry Creek ES 500/2-5
12675 Foreman St 49331 616-987-2700
Shelli Otten, prin. Fax 987-2711
Lowell MS 900/6-8
750 Foreman St 49331 616-987-2800
Linda Warren, prin. Fax 987-2811
Murray Lake ES 400/K-5
3275 Alden Nash Ave NE 49331 616-987-2750
Brent Noskey, prin. Fax 987-2761
Other Schools – See Alto

Ludington, Mason, Pop. 8,292
Ludington Area SD 1,900/PK-12
809 E Tinkham Ave 49431 231-845-7303
Cal DeKuiper, supt. Fax 843-4930
www.lasd.net
DeJonge MS 400/6-8
706 E Tinkham Ave 49431 231-845-3810
Melissa Bansch, prin. Fax 845-3814
Foster ES 100/3-5
505 E Foster St 49431 231-845-3820
Michael Ritter, prin. Fax 845-0146
Franklin ES 200/K-2
721 Anderson St 49431 231-845-3830
Andrea Large, prin. Fax 843-8567
Lakeview ES 200/K-2
502 W Haight St 49431 231-845-3840
Carol Nelson, prin. Fax 845-0788
Pere Marquette ECC 50/PK-PK
1115 S Madison St 49431 231-845-3850
Carol Nelson, prin. Fax 843-9680

Covenant Christian S 100/PK-8
243 N Stiles Rd 49431 231-845-9183
Richard Ambrose, prin. Fax 845-9058
Ludington Area Catholic S 200/PK-6
700 E Bryant Rd 49431 231-843-3188
Collin Thompson, prin. Fax 843-2052

Luther, Lake, Pop. 343
Pine River Area SD
Supt. — See Le Roy
Luther ES 100/K-5
900 N State St 49656 231-797-5201
Jim Ganger, prin. Fax 797-5663

Mc Bain, Missaukee, Pop. 747
McBain Rural Agricultural SD 1,100/PK-12
107 E Maple St 49657 231-825-2165
Michael Harris, supt. Fax 825-2119
www.mcbain.org/
Mc Bain ES 500/PK-5
107 E Maple St 49657 231-825-2021
Pat Smith, prin. Fax 825-2119
Mc Bain MS 300/6-8
107 E Maple St 49657 231-825-8041
Gail Loeks, prin. Fax 825-2119

Northern Michigan Christian S 300/PK-12
128 S Martin St 49657 231-825-2492
Rick Klooster, supt. Fax 825-2371

Mackinac Island, Mackinac, Pop. 491
Mackinac Island SD 100/K-12
PO Box 340 49757 906-847-3377
Dr. Roger Schrock, supt. Fax 847-3773
mackinac.eup.k12.mi.us
Mackinac Island S 100/K-12
PO Box 340 49757 906-847-3377
Dr. Roger Schrock, prin. Fax 847-3773

Mackinaw City, Emmet, Pop. 862
Mackinaw City SD 200/K-12
609 W Central Ave 49701 231-436-8211
Jeffrey Curth, supt. Fax 436-5434
www.mackcity.k12.mi.us
Mackinaw City S 200/K-12
609 W Central Ave 49701 231-436-8211
William Alexander, prin. Fax 436-5434

Macomb, Macomb, Pop. 22,714
Chippewa Valley SD
Supt. — See Clinton Township
Cheyenne ES 700/K-5
47600 Heydenreich Rd 48044 586-723-5000
Don Brosky, prin. Fax 723-5001
Fox ES 600/K-5
17500 Millstone Dr 48044 586-723-5600
Darlene Wade, prin. Fax 723-5601
Iroquois MS 1,000/6-8
48301 Romeo Plank Rd 48044 586-723-3700
James Capoferi, prin. Fax 723-3701
Mohawk ES 600/K-5
48101 Romeo Plank Rd 48044 586-723-6200
Geraldine Marturano, prin. Fax 723-6201
Ojibwa ES 600/K-5
46950 Heydenreich Rd 48044 586-723-6400
John Rose, prin. Fax 723-6401

Seneca MS 1,300/6-8
47200 Heydenreich Rd 48044 586-723-3900
Todd Distelrath, prin. Fax 723-3901
Sequoyah ES 600/K-5
18500 24 Mile Rd 48042 586-723-7000
Ted Zotos, prin. Fax 723-2001
Shawnee ES 500/K-5
21555 Vesper Dr 48044 586-723-6800
Christine Robershaw, prin. Fax 723-6801

L'Anse Creuse SD
Supt. — See Harrison Township
Atwood ES 600/K-5
45690 North Ave 48042 586-493-5250
Lou Ann Fanning, prin. Fax 493-5255
L'Anse Creuse MS North 700/6-8
46201 Fairchild Rd 48042 586-493-5260
John Da Via, prin. Fax 493-5265

Utica Community SD
Supt. — See Sterling Heights
Beck Centennial ES 700/K-6
54600 Hayes Rd 48042 586-797-3900
Sally Klatt, prin. Fax 797-3901
Ebeling ES 700/PK-6
15970 Haverhill Dr 48044 586-797-4700
Denise Bailey, prin. Fax 797-4701

Immanuel Lutheran S 600/PK-8
47120 Romeo Plank Rd 48044 586-286-7076
Robert Christian, prin. Fax 286-4243
St. Peter Lutheran S 600/PK-8
17051 24 Mile Rd 48042 586-781-9296
Terry Davis, prin. Fax 781-9726

Madison Heights, Oakland, Pop. 30,251
Lamphere SD 2,500/K-12
31201 Dorchester Ave 48071 248-589-1990
Marsha Pando, supt. Fax 589-2618
www.lamphere.k12.mi.us
Edmonson ES 300/K-5
621 E Katherine Ave 48071 248-547-5342
Sharon Stephens, prin. Fax 547-6444
Hiller ES 300/K-5
400 E La Salle Ave 48071 248-589-0406
Curtis Benham, prin. Fax 589-2055
Lessenger ES 200/K-5
30150 Campbell Rd 48071 248-589-0556
Jane Jurvis, prin. Fax 589-8853
Page MS 600/6-8
29615 Tawas St 48071 248-589-3428
Douglas Kelley, prin. Fax 545-1870
Simonds ES 300/K-5
30000 Rose St 48071 248-547-5292
Rhonda Mienko, prin. Fax 547-8635

Madison SD 1,500/K-12
26524 John R Rd 48071 248-399-7800
Gary Vettori, supt. Fax 399-2229
www.madisonschools.k12.mi.us/
Edison ES 200/K-5
27321 Hampden St 48071 248-542-3414
David Hurnevich, prin. Fax 542-1756
Halfman ES 300/K-5
25601 Couzens Ave 48071 248-543-4433
Joanne Vader, prin. Fax 543-9323
Wilkinson MS 300/6-8
26524 John R Rd 48071 248-399-0455
Tony Morse, prin. Fax 399-1965

Mancelona, Antrim, Pop. 1,386
Mancelona SD 1,000/K-12
PO Box 739 49659 231-587-9764
Jeffery DiRosa, supt. Fax 587-9500
www.mancelonaschools.org/
Mancelona ES 400/K-4
PO Box 739 49659 231-587-8661
Trent Naumcheff, prin. Fax 587-8699
Mancelona MS 300/5-8
PO Box 739 49659 231-587-9869
Chad Culver, prin. Fax 587-0615

Manchester, Washtenaw, Pop. 2,240
Manchester Community SD 1,200/K-12
410 City Rd 48158 734-428-9711
Shawn Lewis-Lakin Ph.D., supt. Fax 428-9188
www.mcs.k12.mi.us
Klager ES 400/K-4
405 Ann Arbor St 48158 734-428-8321
Jennifer Mayes, prin. Fax 428-7962
Manchester MS 400/5-8
710 City Rd 48158 734-428-7442
Shanna Spickard, prin. Fax 428-9264

Manistee, Manistee, Pop. 6,656
Manistee Area SD 1,700/K-12
550 Maple St Ste 2 49660 231-723-3521
Robert Olsen, supt. Fax 723-1507
www.honoredstudents.org
Jefferson ES 300/K-3
515 Bryant Ave 49660 231-723-9285
Kevin Schmutzler, prin. Fax 723-2021
Kennedy ES 200/4-5
610 E Parkdale Ave 49660 231-723-9242
Kenn Kott, prin. Fax 398-2011
Madison ES 200/K-3
1309 Madison Rd 49660 231-723-5212
Cheryl Matson, prin. Fax 723-1607
Manistee MS 400/6-8
550 Maple St 49660 231-723-3271
Matt Kieffer, prin. Fax 723-5879

Manistee Catholic Central S 300/PK-12
1200 US Highway 31 S 49660 231-723-2529
Edward Kolanowski, prin. Fax 723-0669
Trinity Lutheran S 100/PK-8
420 Oak St 49660 231-723-8700
David Moehring, prin. Fax 723-9755

Manistique, Schoolcraft, Pop. 3,460
Manistique Area SD 800/K-12
100 N Cedar St 49854 906-341-4300
John Chandler, supt. Fax 341-2374
www.manistique.k12.mi.us
Emerald ES 100/K-5
100 N Cedar St 49854 906-341-4313
Jason Lockwood, prin. Fax 341-4323
Manistique MS 300/6-8
100 N Cedar St 49854 906-341-4300
Butch Yurk, prin. Fax 341-8473

St. Francis de Sales S 100/PK-6
210 Lake St 49854 906-341-5512
Kitty Lovell, prin. Fax 341-5512

Manton, Wexford, Pop. 1,219
Manton Consolidated SD 1,100/K-12
105 5th St 49663 231-824-6411
J. Mark Parsons, supt. Fax 824-4101
www.mantonschools.org/schools
Manton ES 400/K-4
105 5th St 49663 231-824-6413
Catherine Smart, prin. Fax 824-6804
Manton MS 400/5-8
105 5th St 49663 231-824-6401
Susan Ingram, prin. Fax 824-4121

Maple City, Leelanau
Glen Lake Community SD 800/K-12
3375 W Burdickville Rd 49664 231-334-3061
Joan Groening, supt. Fax 334-6255
www.glenlake.k12.mi.us
Glen Lake ES 400/K-6
3375 W Burdickville Rd 49664 231-334-3061
Kim Wright, prin. Fax 334-6255

Marcellus, Cass, Pop. 1,111
Marcellus Community SD 1,000/K-12
PO Box 48 49067 269-646-7655
Ronald Herron, supt. Fax 646-2700
www.marcelluscs.org/
Marcellus ES 300/K-4
PO Box 48 49067 269-646-9209
Melinda Bohan, prin. Fax 646-5014
Marcellus MS 300/5-8
PO Box 48 49067 269-646-3158
Phillip McAndrew, prin. Fax 646-2438

Howardsville Christian S 200/K-12
53441 Bent Rd 49067 269-646-9367
Ric Gilson, admin. Fax 646-7006

Marine City, Saint Clair, Pop. 4,475
East China SD
Supt. — See East China
Belle River ES 300/K-5
1601 Chartier Rd 48039 810-676-1150
Patti Andrea, prin. Fax 676-1160
Marine City MS 600/6-8
6373 King Rd 48039 810-676-1201
Kevin Rhein, prin. Fax 676-1225

Holy Cross S 100/K-8
618 S Water St 48039 810-765-3591
Amanda Lund, prin. Fax 765-9074

Marion, Osceola, Pop. 837
Marion SD 700/K-12
PO Box O 49665 231-743-2486
Charles Chase, supt. Fax 743-2890
marion.k12.mi.us
Marion ES 300/K-6
PO Box O 49665 231-743-6251
Greg Mikulich, prin. Fax 743-2955

Marlette, Sanilac, Pop. 2,070
Marlette Community SD 700/K-12
3197 Sterling St 48453 989-635-7425
Duane Lange, supt. Fax 635-7103
Marlette ES 300/K-6
6230 Euclid St 48453 989-635-7427
Michael Distelrath, prin. Fax 635-7103

Our Savior Lutheran S 100/PK-5
6770 Marlette St 48453 989-635-7994
Eric Kilmer, prin. Fax 635-8306

Marne, Ottawa
Kenowa Hills SD
Supt. — See Grand Rapids
Marne ES 100/K-4
14141 State St 49435 616-677-1222
Cindy Ruscett, coord. Fax 677-1611

Marquette, Marquette, Pop. 20,581
Marquette Area SD 2,900/K-12
1201 W Fair Ave 49855 906-225-4200
Jon Hartwig, supt. Fax 225-5340
www.mapsnet.org
Bothwell MS 700/6-8
1200 Tierney St 49855 906-225-4262
William Saunders, prin. Fax 225-4229
Cherry Creek ES 200/K-4
1111 Ortman Rd 49855 906-225-4399
Donna Koskiniemi, prin. Fax 225-4326
Graveraet IS 200/5-5
611 N Front St 49855 906-225-4302
Tamra Bott, prin. Fax 225-4312
Sandy Knoll ES 300/K-4
401 N 6th St 49855 906-225-4281
Kevin Hooper, prin. Fax 225-4335
Superior Hills ES 200/K-4
1201 S McClellan Ave 49855 906-225-4295
Michael Woodard, prin. Fax 225-4339
Vandenboom Child Development Center 50/K-K
1175 Erie Ave 49855 906-225-4320
Fax 225-4319

Crossroads Christian Academy 50/K-5
219 Silver Creek Rd 49855 906-249-2030
Willa Vallin, prin. Fax 249-5562
Father Marquette MS 100/5-8
414 W College Ave 49855 906-226-7912
Karen Ogles, prin. Fax 225-9962
Father Marquette S 200/PK-4
500 S 4th St 49855 906-225-1129
Jacalyn Wright, prin. Fax 225-1987

Marshall, Calhoun, Pop. 7,363
Mar Lee SD 300/K-8
21236 H Dr N 49068 269-781-5412
William Le Tarte, supt. Fax 781-9471
www.remc12.k12.mi.us/marlee
Mar Lee S 300/K-8
21236 H Dr N 49068 269-781-5412
Fax 781-9471

Marshall SD 2,500/K-12
100 E Green St 49068 269-781-1257
Dr. Randall Davis, supt. Fax 789-1813
www.marshall.k12.mi.us/
Gordon ES 300/K-4
400 N Gordon St 49068 269-781-1270
Linda Bennink, prin. Fax 789-3700
Hughes ES 300/K-4
103 W Hughes St 49068 269-781-1275
Thomas Hanson, prin. Fax 789-3704
Marshall MS 700/5-8
100 E Green St 49068 269-781-1251
David Turner, prin. Fax 781-6621
Walters ES 400/K-4
705 N Marshall Ave 49068 269-781-1280
Susan Townsend, prin. Fax 789-3703

Martin, Allegan, Pop. 421
Martin SD 600/K-12
PO Box 241 49070 269-672-7194
D.G. Alexander, supt. Fax 672-7116
www.martinpublicschools.org/
Brandon ES 300/K-5
PO Box 241 49070 269-672-7253
Julie Boyle, prin. Fax 672-5138

East Martin Christian S 100/K-8
516 118th Ave 49070 269-672-5722
Keith Fennema, prin. Fax 672-5736

Marysville, Saint Clair, Pop. 10,042
Marysville SD 2,700/K-12
1111 Delaware Ave 48040 810-364-7731
John Silveri, supt. Fax 364-3150
www.marysville.k12.mi.us/
Gardens ES 500/K-5
1076 6th St 48040 810-364-7141
Karen Curley, prin. Fax 364-2987
Marysville IS 600/6-8
400 Collard Dr 48040 810-364-6336
John Sazehn, prin. Fax 364-4456
Morton ES 300/K-5
920 Lynwood St 48040 810-364-2990
Kathleen Schmitt, prin. Fax 364-5983
Washington ES 500/K-5
905 16th St 48040 810-364-7101
Tracie Eschenburg, prin. Fax 364-2986

Mason, Ingham, Pop. 7,985
Mason SD 2,800/K-12
118 W Oak St 48854 517-676-2484
James Harvey, supt. Fax 676-6058
www.mason.k12.mi.us/
Alaiedon ES 300/K-5
1723 Okemos Rd 48854 517-676-6499
Lisa Francisco, prin. Fax 676-0283
Mason MS 700/6-8
235 Temple St 48854 517-676-6514
Daniel McConeghy, prin. Fax 676-0287
North Aurelius ES 300/K-5
115 N Aurelius Rd 48854 517-676-6506
Gina Stanley, prin. Fax 676-0293
Steele ES 300/K-5
531 Steele St 48854 517-676-6510
Kathleen Dean, prin. Fax 676-0295

Mattawan, Van Buren, Pop. 2,838
Mattawan Consolidated SD 3,400/K-12
56720 Murray St 49071 269-668-3361
James Weeldreyer, supt. Fax 668-2372
www.mattawanschools.org/
Mattawan Early ES 600/K-2
56720 Murray St 49071 269-668-3361
Derek Wheaton, prin. Fax 668-3364
Mattawan Later ES 800/3-5
56720 Murray St 49071 269-668-3361
Christie Enstrom-West, prin. Fax 668-3363
Mattawan MS 900/6-8
56720 Murray St 49071 269-668-3361
Chip Schuman, prin. Fax 668-3188

Mayville, Tuscola, Pop. 1,034
Mayville Community SD 1,100/PK-12
6250 Fulton St 48744 989-843-6115
William Hartzell, supt. Fax 843-6988
www.mayville.k12.mi.us
Mayville ES 500/PK-5
106 Orchard St 48744 989-843-6115
Martin Blackmer, prin. Fax 843-7218
Mayville MS 200/6-8
6210 Fulton St 48744 989-843-6115
Rhonda Blackburn, prin. Fax 843-7209

Mecosta, Mecosta, Pop. 453
Chippewa Hills SD
Supt. — See Remus
Mecosta ES 300/PK-5
555 W Main St 49332 231-972-7477
Chi Ethridge, prin. Fax 972-4005

Melvindale, Wayne, Pop. 10,612
Melvindale-Northern Allen Park SD 2,600/K-12
18530 Prospect St 48122 313-389-3300
Cora Kelly, supt. Fax 389-3312
www.melnap.k12.mi.us
Allendale ES 800/2-5
3201 Oakwood Blvd 48122 313-389-4664
Robert Bateman, prin. Fax 389-8713
Strong MS 700/6-8
3303 Oakwood Blvd 48122 313-389-3330
Dr. Kim Soranno-Bond, prin. Fax 389-2077
Other Schools – See Allen Park

Memphis, Saint Clair, Pop. 1,123
Memphis Community SD
Supt. — See Riley
Memphis ES 400/K-5
PO Box 201 48041 810-392-2125
Nancy Thomson, prin. Fax 392-2324

Mendon, Saint Joseph, Pop. 933
Mendon Community SD 700/K-12
148 Kirby Rd 49072 269-496-9940
Sue Bombrys, supt. Fax 496-8234
www.mendonschools.org
Mendon ES 300/K-5
306 Lane St 49072 269-496-2175
Kristi O'Brian, prin. Fax 496-7021
Mendon MS 200/6-8
148 Kirby Rd 49072 269-496-8491
Jay Peterson, prin. Fax 496-8234

Menominee, Menominee, Pop. 8,753
Menominee Area SD 1,700/PK-12
1230 13th St 49858 906-863-9951
Erik Bergh, supt. Fax 863-1171
www.menominee.k12.mi.us/
Blesch IS 400/4-6
1200 11th Ave 49858 906-863-4466
Peggy Tafelski, prin. Fax 863-1171
Central ES 100/PK-1
2101 18th Ave 49858 906-863-3605
Anders Hill, prin. Fax 863-3554
Lincoln ES 300/2-3
2701 17th St 49858 906-863-6617
Deborah Kroll, prin. Fax 863-8858
Menominee JHS 300/7-8
2101 18th St 49858 906-863-9929
Mike Cattani, prin. Fax 863-8883

Menominee Catholic Central S 200/PK-8
1406 10th Ave 49858 906-863-3190
Beth Horn, prin. Fax 863-3990

Merrill, Saginaw, Pop. 758
Merrill Community SD 800/PK-12
555 W Alice St 48637 989-643-7261
John Searles, supt. Fax 643-5570
saginawmerrill.mi.schoolwebpages.com
Merrill ES 400/PK-5
555 W Alice St 48637 989-643-7283
Pam Schomaker, prin. Fax 643-5249
Merrill MS 200/6-8
555 W Alice St 48637 989-643-7247
Christine Garno, prin. Fax 643-5971

Mesick, Wexford, Pop. 463
Mesick Consolidated SD 800/K-12
PO Box 275 49668 231-885-1200
Dennis Stratton, supt. Fax 885-1234
www.mesick.org
Jewett ES 300/K-4
PO Box 275 49668 231-885-1211
Linda Salling, prin. Fax 885-2475
Mesick MS 300/5-8
PO Box 275 49668 231-885-1207
Deann Jenkins, prin. Fax 885-2544

Metamora, Lapeer, Pop. 502
Lapeer Community SD
Supt. — See Lapeer
Murphy ES 400/PK-6
1100 Pratt Rd 48455 810-678-2201
Scott Warren, prin. Fax 678-3393

Michigan Center, Jackson, Pop. 4,863
Michigan Center SD 1,300/PK-12
400 S State St 49254 517-764-5778
David Tebo, supt. Fax 764-5790
www.mcps.k12.mi.us
Arnold ES 200/K-2
400 S State St 49254 517-764-5700
Kelly McCloughan, prin. Fax 764-6623
Keicher ES 400/3-6
400 S State St 49254 517-764-5200
Johanna Pscodna, prin. Fax 764-6624
Preschool/Child Care PK-PK
400 S State St 49254 517-764-3380
Kim Trudell, prin. Fax 764-6620

Our Lady of Fatima S 100/PK-6
911 Napoleon Rd 49254 517-764-2563
Colleen McNeal, prin. Fax 990-6780

Middleton, Gratiot
Fulton SD 800/PK-12
8060 Ely Hwy 48856 989-236-7300
Raymond Mungall, supt. Fax 236-7660
www.fulton.edzone.net
Fulton ES 400/PK-6
8060 Ely Hwy 48856 989-236-7234
Paul Avery, prin. Fax 236-5607
Fulton MS 100/7-8
8060 Ely Hwy 48856 989-236-7232
Daymond Grifka, prin. Fax 236-7628

Middleville, Barry, Pop. 2,790
Thornapple-Kellogg SD 2,700/PK-12
10051 Green Lake Rd 49333 269-795-3313
Gary Rider, supt. Fax 795-5401
www.tkschools.org/

Lee ES 400/2-3
840 W Main St 49333 269-795-9747
Tim Shaw, prin. Fax 795-5587

McFall ES 200/PK-1
509 W Main St 49333 269-795-3637
Jon Washburn, prin. Fax 795-5554

Page ES 400/4-5
3675 Bender Rd 49333 269-795-7944
Dona Raymer, prin. Fax 795-5501

Thornapple-Kellogg MS 700/6-8
10375 Green Lake Rd 49333 269-795-3349
Mike Birely, prin. Fax 795-5455

Midland, Midland, Pop. 41,760

Bullock Creek SD 1,800/K-12
1420 S Badour Rd 48640 989-631-9022
John Hill, supt. Fax 631-2882
www.bcreek.k12.mi.us

Bullock Creek ES 200/K-2
1037 S Poseyville Rd 48640 989-832-8691
Todd Gorsuch, prin. Fax 832-4014

Bullock Creek MS 400/6-8
644 S Badour Rd 48640 989-631-9260
Craig Carmoney, prin. Fax 832-4018

Floyd ES 400/K-5
725 S 8 Mile Rd 48640 989-832-2081
Rod Dishaw, prin. Fax 832-4029

Pine River ES 200/3-5
1894 E Pine River Rd 48640 989-631-5121
Debbie Bradford, prin. Fax 832-4017

Midland SD 9,300/K-12
600 E Carpenter St 48640 989-923-5001
Carl Ellinger, supt. Fax 923-5003
www.mps.k12.mi.us

Adams ES 500/K-5
1005 Adams Dr 48642 989-923-6037
Dan Macek, prin. Fax 923-6035

Carpenter ES 200/K-5
1407 W Carpenter St 48640 989-923-6411
Linda Lipsitt, prin. Fax 923-6410

Central MS 600/6-8
305 E Reardon St 48640 989-923-5571
Jeffrey Hall, prin. Fax 923-5518

Chestnut Hill ES 400/K-5
3900 Chestnut Hill Dr 48642 989-923-6634
Tracy Renfro, prin. Fax 923-6630

Chippewassee ES 200/K-5
919 Smith Rd 48640 989-923-6836
Linda Lipsitt, prin. Fax 923-6876

Cook ES 300/K-5
5500 Perrine Rd 48640 989-923-7013
Jim Huber, prin. Fax 923-7041

Eastlawn ES 200/K-5
115 Eastlawn Dr 48640 989-923-7112
Greg Matheson, prin. Fax 923-7110

Jefferson MS 800/6-8
800 W Chapel Ln 48640 989-923-5873
Michael Decker, prin. Fax 923-5800

Longview ES 200/K-5
337 Lemke St 48642 989-923-7214
Greg Matheson, prin. Fax 923-7210

Mills ES 100/K-5
3329 E Baker Rd 48642 989-923-7339
Susan Johnson, prin. Fax 923-7300

Northeast MS 900/6-8
1305 E Sugnet Rd 48642 989-923-5772
Janet Greif, prin. Fax 923-5780

Parkdale ES 300/K-5
1609 Eastlawn Dr 48642 989-923-7515
Bonnie Westervelt, prin. Fax 923-7500

Plymouth ES 400/K-5
1105 E Sugnet Rd 48642 989-923-7616
Bridget Hockemeyer, prin. Fax 923-7665

Siebert ES 500/K-5
5700 Siebert St 48640 989-923-7835
Brad Vander Vliet, prin. Fax 923-7875

Woodcrest ES 400/K-5
5500 Drake St 48640 989-923-7940
Jeff Pennex, prin. Fax 923-7919

Blessed Sacrament S 200/PK-5
3109 Swede Ave 48642 989-835-6777
LeeAnn Berg, prin. Fax 835-2451

Calvary Baptist Academy 400/PK-12
6100 Perrine Rd 48640 989-832-3341
David Warren, admin. Fax 832-7443

Good Shepherd Lutheran S 50/K-8
907 Mattes Dr 48642 989-835-4181
Timothy Thies, prin. Fax 835-4181

Midland Christian S 100/PK-12
4417 W Wackerly St 48640 989-835-9881
Eric Vanderhoof, prin. Fax 835-5201

St. Brigid S 100/K-8
130 W Larkin St 48640 989-835-9481
Maureen Becker, prin. Fax 835-9141

St. John Lutheran S 100/PK-8
505 E Carpenter St 48640 989-835-7041
Jonathan Pickelmann, prin. Fax 835-2443

Milan, Monroe, Pop. 5,376

Milan Area SD 2,200/K-12
100 Big Red Dr 48160 734-439-5050
Bryan Girbach, supt. Fax 439-5083
www.milanareaschools.org/

Milan MS 600/6-8
920 North St 48160 734-439-5200
William Brown, prin. Fax 439-5288

Paddock ES 300/K-2
707 Marvin St 48160 734-439-5100
Tonya Saragoza, prin. Fax 439-5160

Symons ES 500/3-5
432 S Platt Rd 48160 734-439-5300
Nancy Tetens, prin. Fax 439-5303

Milford, Oakland, Pop. 6,587

Huron Valley SD
Supt. — See Highland

Baker ES 200/K-5
716 Union St 48381 248-684-8010
Teri Thompson, prin. Fax 684-8011

Johnson ES 400/K-5
515 General Motors Rd 48381 248-684-8020
Larry Johnson, prin. Fax 684-8023

Kurtz ES 400/K-5
1350 Kurtz Dr 48381 248-684-8025
Dale Phillips, prin. Fax 684-8024

Muir MS 600/6-8
425 George St 48381 248-684-8060
Gayle Lizzet, prin. Fax 684-8068

Christ Lutheran Preschool & K 100/PK-K
620 General Motors Rd 48381 248-684-6773
Jacqueline Read, prin. Fax 684-0895

West Highland Christian Academy 50/K-12
1116 S Hickory Ridge Rd 48380 248-887-6698
Jan Grimm, prin. Fax 887-4645

Millersburg, Presque Isle, Pop. 257

Onaway Area SD
Supt. — See Onaway

Millersburg ES 100/K-4
Main St 49759 989-733-4083
Nancy Miiller, prin. Fax 733-4354

Millington, Tuscola, Pop. 1,115

Millington Community SD 1,400/K-12
8780 Dean Dr 48746 989-871-5227
Lawrence Kroswek, supt. Fax 871-5260
www.mcsdistrict.com

Kirk ES 400/K-4
8664 Dean Dr 48746 989-871-5270
Gloria Rubis, prin. Fax 871-5217

Meachum JHS 500/5-8
8537 Gleason St 48746 989-871-5269
Gary Iwinski, prin. Fax 871-5249

St. Paul Lutheran S 300/PK-8
4941 Center St 48746 989-871-4581
Elaine Bickel, prin. Fax 871-5573

Mio, Oscoda, Pop. 1,886

Mio-AuSable SD 700/K-12
1110 W 8th St 48647 989-826-2400
Christina Siwik, supt. Fax 826-2415
www.mio.k12.mi.us

Mio-Ausable ES 400/K-6
1110 W 8th St 48647 989-826-2430
Teresa Cole, prin. Fax 826-2415

Mio-AuSable MS 100/7-8
1110 W 8th St 48647 989-826-2481
James Gendernalik, prin. Fax 826-2416

Moline, Allegan

Moline Christian S 300/PK-8
PO Box 130 49335 616-877-4688
Kevin Sall, prin. Fax 877-4689

Monroe, Monroe, Pop. 21,791

Jefferson SD 2,300/PK-12
2400 N Dixie Hwy 48162 734-289-5550
Craig Haugen, supt. Fax 289-5574
www.jefferson.k12.mi.us/

Hurd Road ECC 400/PK-PK
1960 E Hurd Rd 48162 734-289-5580
Betsy Bender, dir. Fax 289-5581

Jefferson 5/6 ES 5-6
5102 N Stoney Creek Rd 48162 734-289-5578
Michael Petty, prin. Fax 289-5560

Jefferson MS 400/7-8
5102 N Stoney Creek Rd 48162 734-289-5565
Stephen Kinsland, prin. Fax 289-5596

Sodt ES 300/K-4
2888 Nadeau Rd 48162 734-289-5575
Sharon Brighton, prin. Fax 289-5600
Other Schools – See Newport

Monroe SD 6,000/PK-12
PO Box 733 48161 734-265-3000
David Taylor, supt. Fax 265-3001
www.monroe.k12.mi.us

Christiancy ES 300/PK-6
306 Lincoln Ave 48162 734-265-4200
Mary Ann Cyr, prin. Fax 265-4201

Custer ES 800/PK-6
5003 W Albain Rd 48161 734-265-4300
JoAnn Weeks, prin. Fax 265-4301

Hollywood ES 200/PK-6
1135 Riverview Ave 48162 734-265-4500
Ryan Starr, prin. Fax 265-4501

Lincoln ES 300/PK-6
908 E 2nd St 48161 734-265-4600
Pamela Sica, prin. Fax 265-4601

Manor ES 400/PK-6
1731 W Lorain St 48162 734-265-4700
Kelly McMahon, prin. Fax 265-4701

Monroe MS 700/7-8
503 Washington St 48161 734-265-4000
Ryan McLeod, prin. Fax 265-4001

Raisinville ES 400/PK-6
2300 N Raisinville Rd 48162 734-265-4800
Julie Everly, prin. Fax 265-4801

Riverside ES 200/PK-6
77 N Roessler St 48162 734-265-4900
Mari Treece, prin. Fax 265-4901

South Monroe ES 200/PK-6
15488 Eastwood St 48161 734-265-5000
Mari Treece, prin. Fax 265-5001

Waterloo ES 300/PK-6
1933 S Custer Rd 48161 734-265-5100
Lisa McLaughlin, prin. Fax 265-5101

Holy Ghost Lutheran S 100/PK-8
3563 Heiss Rd 48162 734-242-0509
Eric Heins, prin. Fax 242-2701

Meadow Montessori S 200/PK-12
1670 S Raisinville Rd 48161 734-241-9496
Catharine Calder, hdmstr. Fax 241-0829

St. John the Baptist S 200/K-8
521 S Monroe St 48161 734-241-1670
Cheryl Tibai, prin. Fax 241-8782

St. Mary S 200/K-8
151 N Monroe St 48162 734-241-3377
Mary Ann Lapinski, prin. Fax 241-0497

St. Michael the Archangel S 200/K-8
510 W Front St 48161 734-241-3923
Karen Pilon, prin. Fax 241-7314

Trinity Lutheran S 200/PK-8
315 Scott St 48161 734-241-1160
John Hilken, prin. Fax 241-6293

Zion Lutheran S 100/PK-8
186 Cole Rd 48162 734-242-1378
Kyle Gut, prin. Fax 242-7049

Montague, Muskegon, Pop. 2,339

Montague Area SD 1,400/PK-12
4882 Stanton Blvd 49437 231-893-1515
David Sipka, supt. Fax 894-6586
www.montague.k12.mi.us

Chisholm MS 400/6-8
4700 Stanton Blvd 49437 231-894-5617
Gary Beaudoin, prin. Fax 894-5728

Oehrli ES 500/PK-5
4859 Knudsen St 49437 231-894-9018
Jeff Henderson, prin. Fax 894-8177

Montrose, Genesee, Pop. 1,552

Montrose Community SD 1,600/PK-12
PO Box 3129 48457 810-591-7267
Mark Kleinhans, supt. Fax 591-7268
www.montrose.k12.mi.us

Carter ES 500/PK-4
PO Box 3129 48457 810-591-8842
Pete Carey, prin. Fax 591-7283

Kuehn-Haven MS 500/5-8
PO Box 3129 48457 810-591-8832
Edward Graham, prin. Fax 591-7282

Morenci, Lenawee, Pop. 2,352

Morenci Area SD 900/PK-12
500 Page St 49256 517-458-7501
Kyle Griffith, supt. Fax 458-7821
www.morenci.k12.mi.us

Morenci ES 300/PK-4
517 E Locust St 49256 517-458-7504
Mary Fisher, dean Fax 458-6364

Morenci MS 200/5-8
304 Page St 49256 517-458-7506
Kay Johnson, prin. Fax 458-3379

Morley, Mecosta, Pop. 501

Morley Stanwood Community SD 1,600/K-12
4700 Northland Dr 49336 231-856-4392
Linda Myers, supt. Fax 856-4180
morleystanwood.org

Morley ES 300/K-4
151 7th St 49336 231-856-7684
Clark Huntey, prin. Fax 856-0139

Morley-Stanwood MS 500/5-8
4808 Northland Dr 49336 231-856-4550
Kim Colby, prin. Fax 856-0136
Other Schools – See Stanwood

Morrice, Shiawassee, Pop. 888

Morrice Area SD 600/K-12
691 Purdy Ln 48857 517-625-3142
Bruce Burger, supt. Fax 625-3866
www.morrice.k12.mi.us

Morrice ES 300/K-6
111 E Mason 48857 517-625-3141
Brian Eddy, prin. Fax 625-3866

Mount Clemens, Macomb, Pop. 17,053

Chippewa Valley SD
Supt. — See Clinton Township

Clinton Valley ES 400/K-5
1260 Mulberry St 48043 586-723-5200
Greg Finlayson, prin. Fax 723-5201

Mount Clemens Community SD 2,100/PK-12
167 Cass Ave 48043 586-469-6100
Dr. Charles Muncatchy, supt. Fax 469-5569
www.mtcps.org

King Jr Academy 200/K-6
400 Clinton River Dr 48043 586-469-3100
Sharon Gryzenia, prin. Fax 469-7006

Macomb Early Learning Center 100/PK-PK
11 Grand Ave 48043 586-461-3700
Yvonne McQueen, prin. Fax 469-7096

Mount Clemens JHS 300/7-8
161 Cass Ave 48043 586-461-3300
Mike Bruce, prin. Fax 469-7066

Seminole Academy 500/K-6
1500 Mulberry St 48043 586-461-3900
Janice Hooks, prin. Fax 469-7027

Washington Academy 400/K-6
196 N Rose St 48043 586-461-3800
George Loder, prin. Fax 469-7027

Montessori Stepping Stones 100/PK-6
174 Cass Ave 48043 586-465-4260
Diane Aitken, prin. Fax 783-9412

St. Mary S 600/PK-8
105 Market St 48043 586-468-4570
Tina Forsythe, prin. Fax 468-6454

Mount Morris, Genesee, Pop. 3,321

Beecher Community SD
Supt. — See Flint

Beecher MS 300/7-8
6255 Neff Rd 48458 810-591-9281
Darrell Ross, prin. Fax 591-6911

Dailey ES 500/PK-6
6236 Neff Rd 48458 810-591-9300
Rodney Prewitt, prin. Fax 591-5632

Mount Morris Consolidated SD 2,900/K-12
12356 Walter St 48458 810-591-8760
Lisa Hagel, supt. Fax 591-7469
www.mtmorrisschools.org
Montague ES 300/K-5
344 W Mount Morris St 48458 810-591-3750
Rebekah Dupuis, prin. Fax 591-8079
Moore ES 300/K-5
1201 Wisner St 48458 810-591-6090
John Strickert, prin. Fax 591-8077
Mount Morris JHS 400/6-8
12356 Walter St 48458 810-591-7100
Susan Carlson, prin. Fax 591-7105
Pinehurst ES 300/K-5
1013 Pinehurst Blvd 48458 810-591-2760
Scott Holman, prin. Fax 591-8070

St. Mary S 100/PK-8
11208 N Saginaw St 48458 810-686-4790
Dennis Winchester, prin. Fax 686-4749

Mount Pleasant, Isabella, Pop. 26,253
Beal City SD 700/PK-12
3117 Elias Rd 48858 989-644-3901
William Chilman, supt. Fax 644-5847
www.edzone.net/bealcity/
Mayes ES 400/PK-6
3117 Elias Rd 48858 989-644-2740
Diane Saltarelli, prin. Fax 644-5847

Mount Pleasant SD 3,800/K-12
720 N Kinney Ave 48858 989-775-2300
Joseph Pius, supt. Fax 775-2309
www.mtpleasant.edzone.net
Fancher ES 300/5-6
801 S Kinney Ave 48858 989-775-2230
Linda Boyd, prin. Fax 775-2234
Ganiard ES 400/K-4
101 S Adams St 48858 989-775-2240
Marcy Stout, prin. Fax 775-2244
McGuire ES 200/5-6
4883 E Crosslanes St 48858 989-775-2260
Lisa Bergman, prin. Fax 775-2264
Pullen ES 400/K-4
251 S Brown St 48858 989-775-2270
Diane Falsetta, prin. Fax 775-2274
Vowles ES 300/K-4
1560 Watson Rd 48858 989-775-2280
Terry Hutchins, prin. Fax 775-2284
West IS 500/7-8
440 S Bradley St 48858 989-775-2220
Luke Stefanovsky, prin. Fax 775-2229
Other Schools – See Rosebush

Mount Pleasant SDA S 50/1-8
1730 E Pickard Rd 48858 989-773-3231
Tamara Draves, prin.
Sacred Heart Academy 300/PK-6
200 S Franklin St 48858 989-773-9530
Denny Starnes, prin. Fax 772-9056
Saginaw Chippewa Academy 200/PK-8
7498 E Broadway Rd 48858 989-775-4453
Leanne Barton, prin. Fax 775-4450
St. Joseph the Worker S 100/1-6
2091 N Winn Rd 48858 989-644-3970
Mary Hauck, prin. Fax 644-6968

Muir, Ionia, Pop. 644
Ionia SD
Supt. — See Ionia
Twin Rivers ES 200/K-5
435 Lou Lemke Ln 48860 989-855-3333
Dayna Ellis, prin. Fax 855-2074

Munising, Alger, Pop. 2,386
Munising SD 800/K-12
411 Elm Ave 49862 906-387-2251
Barbara Hase, supt. Fax 387-5416
www.mps-up.com
Central ES 400/K-6
124 E Chocolay St 49862 906-387-2102
Dee Jay Paquette, prin. Fax 387-4774

Munising SDA S, PO Box 68 49862 50/1-8
Daisy Nieman, prin. 906-387-2942

Muskegon, Muskegon, Pop. 39,919
Fruitport Community SD
Supt. — See Fruitport
Beach ES 400/PK-5
2741 Heights Ravenna Rd 49444 231-773-8996
Julie VanBergen, prin. Fax 777-3455
Shettler ES 500/PK-5
2187 Shettler Rd 49444 231-737-7595
Norman Heerema, prin. Fax 733-1328

Mona Shores SD
Supt. — See Norton Shores
Campbell ES 400/PK-5
1355 Greenwich Rd 49441 231-755-2550
Nathan Smith, prin. Fax 759-1260

Muskegon SD 5,500/PK-12
349 W Webster Ave 49440 231-720-2000
Colin Armstrong, supt. Fax 720-2050
www.muskegon.k12.mi.us/
Bluffton ES 200/K-5
1875 Waterworks Rd 49441 231-720-2170
Jerry Johnson, prin. Fax 720-2179
Bunker JHS 600/6-8
2312 Denmark St 49441 231-720-2300
Paul Kurdziel, prin. Fax 720-2325
Marquette ES 400/PK-5
480 Bennett St 49442 231-720-2600
Gay Monroe, prin. Fax 720-2658
McLaughlin ES 300/PK-5
125 Catherine Ave 49442 231-720-2750
Alina Fortenberry, prin. Fax 720-2791
Moon ES 400/PK-5
1826 Hoyt St 49442 231-720-2700
Kristina Precious, prin. Fax 720-2735
Nelson ES 300/PK-5
550 W Grand Ave 49441 231-720-2200
Anne Norwood, prin. Fax 720-2215
Nims ES 400/K-5
1161 W Southern Ave 49441 231-720-2660
LaKisha Williams, prin. Fax 720-2695
Oakview ES 400/PK-5
1420 Madison St 49442 231-720-2450
Pam Johnson, prin. Fax 720-2490
Steele JHS 500/6-8
1150 Amity Ave 49442 231-720-3000
Duane Cook, prin. Fax 720-3025

Oakridge SD 1,800/PK-12
275 S Wolf Lake Rd 49442 231-788-7100
Tom Livezey, supt. Fax 788-7114
www.oakridgeschools.org
Oakridge ECC 50/PK-K
1050 Carr Rd 49442 231-788-7150
Shelley Peets, dir. Fax 788-7154
Oakridge Lower ES 400/1-3
5290 Bryn Mawr Pl 49442 231-788-7600
Shelley Peets, prin. Fax 788-7614
Oakridge MS 300/7-8
251 S Wolf Lake Rd 49442 231-788-7400
Jonathan Fitzpatrick, prin. Fax 788-7414
Oakridge Upper ES 400/4-6
481 S Wolf Lake Rd 49442 231-788-7500
Mary Galsterer, prin. Fax 788-7514

Orchard View SD 2,800/PK-12
35 S Sheridan Dr 49442 231-760-1300
Patricia Walstra, supt. Fax 760-1323
www.orchardview.org
Cardinal ES 800/2-5
2310 Marquette Ave 49442 231-760-1700
Pam Snow, prin. Fax 760-1655
Orchard View Early ES 400/PK-1
2820 MacArthur Rd 49442 231-760-1850
Susan Fuller, prin. Fax 760-1673
Orchard View MS 600/6-8
35 S Sheridan Dr 49442 231-760-1500
Jim Nielsen, prin. Fax 760-1506

Reeths-Puffer SD 3,900/PK-12
991 W Giles Rd 49445 231-744-4736
Stephen Cousins, supt. Fax 744-9497
www.reeths-puffer.org/
Central ES 400/K-4
1807 W Giles Rd 49445 231-744-1693
Mike Lyons, prin. Fax 744-0507
McMillan ES 300/K-4
2885 Hyde Park Rd 49445 231-766-3443
Ann White, prin. Fax 744-2906
Reeths-Puffer ES 400/PK-4
1404 N Getty St 49445 231-744-4777
Greg Helmer, prin. Fax 744-2815
Reeths-Puffer IS 600/5-6
1500 N Getty St 49445 231-744-9280
Lee Andrews, prin. Fax 744-7922
Other Schools – See North Muskegon, Twin Lake

Michigan Dunes Montessori S 100/PK-1
5248 Henry St 49441 231-798-7293
Claire Chiasson, prin. Fax 798-4586
Muskegon Catholic Central S 200/PK-8
1145 W Laketon Ave 49441 231-755-2201
Penny Johnson, prin. Fax 755-2744
Muskegon Christian S 200/PK-8
1220 Eastgate St 49442 231-773-3221
Dan DeKam, prin. Fax 773-1647
Muskegon SDA S 50/K-8
3050 Evanston Ave 49442 231-773-8866
Cleo Benedict, prin.
West Shore Lutheran S 100/PK-8
3225 Roosevelt Rd 49441 231-755-1048
William Hutton, prin. Fax 755-6942

Muskegon Heights, Muskegon, Pop. 11,821
Muskegon Heights SD 2,100/PK-12
2603 Leahy St 49444 231-830-3200
Dana Bryant, supt. Fax 830-3560
www.mhpsnet.org
Edgewood ES 400/K-6
3028 Howden St 49444 231-830-3250
Edward Causey, prin. Fax 830-3576
Glendale ECC 200/PK-K
3001 Jefferson St 49444 231-830-3300
Celestine Parker, prin. Fax 830-3573
King ES 300/K-6
160 E Barney Ave 49444 231-830-3450
Marvin Nash, prin. Fax 830-3578
Loftis ES 200/K-6
2301 6th St 49444 231-830-3400
Rosie Holmes, prin. Fax 830-3575
Muskegon Heights MS 300/7-8
55 E Sherman Blvd 49444 231-830-3600
Bernard Colton, prin. Fax 830-3572
Roosevelt ES 200/K-6
525 W Summit Ave 49444 231-830-3500
Jaronique Benjamin, prin. Fax 830-3574

Napoleon, Jackson, Pop. 1,332
Napoleon Community SD 1,500/K-12
PO Box 308 49261 517-536-8667
James Graham, supt. Fax 536-8006
www.napoleonschools.org
Eby ES 600/K-5
PO Box 308 49261 517-536-8667
Pam Barnes, prin. Fax 536-8029
Napoleon MS 400/6-8
PO Box 308 49261 517-536-8667
Shelley Jusick, prin. Fax 536-8005

Nashville, Barry, Pop. 1,705
Maple Valley SD
Supt. — See Vermontville
Fuller Street ES 300/PK-3
251 Fuller St 49073 517-852-9468
Jason Miller, prin. Fax 852-1640

Negaunee, Marquette, Pop. 4,471
Negaunee SD 1,300/K-12
101 S Pioneer Ave 49866 906-475-4157
Jim Derocher, supt. Fax 475-5107
www.negaunee.k12.mi.us/
Lakeview ES 500/K-5
200 Croix St 49866 906-475-7803
Joe Meyskens, prin. Fax 475-5764
Negaunee MS 300/6-8
102 W Case St 49866 906-475-7866
Dan Skewis, prin. Fax 475-6408

Newaygo, Newaygo, Pop. 1,685
Newaygo County RESA
Supt. — See Fremont
Neway Center, 585 Fremont St 49337 100/PK-PK
Eva Houseman, dir. 231-652-1638

Newaygo SD 1,700/K-12
PO Box 820 49337 231-652-6984
Larry Lethorn, supt. Fax 652-6505
www.newaygo.net
Matson Upper ES 400/3-5
PO Box 820 49337 231-652-2100
Steve Bush, prin. Fax 652-9705
Newaygo MS 400/6-8
PO Box 820 49337 231-652-1285
Troy Lindley, prin. Fax 652-9704
Wilsie ES 300/K-2
PO Box 820 49337 231-652-6371
Mary Kay Yonker, prin. Fax 652-9706

New Baltimore, Macomb, Pop. 11,165
Anchor Bay SD
Supt. — See Casco
Anchor Bay MS North 800/6-8
52805 Ashley Dr 48047 586-725-7373
Tim Brisbois, prin. Fax 725-6760
Anchor Bay MS South 700/6-8
48650 Sugarbush Rd 48047 586-949-4510
Douglas Glassford, prin. Fax 949-4739
Ashley ES 500/K-5
52347 Ashley St 48047 586-725-2801
Cathy Pennington, prin. Fax 725-4426
Lighthouse ES 600/K-5
51880 Washington St 48047 586-725-6404
Tom Huber, prin. Fax 725-4016
Naldrett ES 200/K-5
47800 Sugarbush Rd 48047 586-949-1212
Kathlynn Markel, prin. Fax 598-7666
Schmidt ES 300/K-5
33700 Hooker Rd 48047 586-725-7541
Anne Berglund, prin. Fax 725-7590
Sugarbush ES 300/K-5
48400 Sugarbush Rd 48047 586-598-7660
Marie DeWitte, prin. Fax 598-7671

Newberry, Luce, Pop. 1,598
Tahquamenon Area SD 700/PK-12
700 Newberry Ave 49868 906-293-3226
Alice Walker, supt. Fax 293-3709
eup.k12.mi.us/tahquamenon
Newberry ES 300/PK-6
700 Newberry Ave 49868 906-293-5153
Meg Hobbs, prin. Fax 293-3709

New Boston, Wayne
Huron SD 2,500/K-12
32044 Huron River Dr 48164 734-782-2441
Richard Naughton, supt. Fax 783-0338
www.huronschools.org
Brown ES 400/1-5
25485 Middlebelt Rd 48164 734-782-2716
Patrick Bevier, prin. Fax 783-0326
Miller ES 400/1-5
18955 Hannan Rd 48164 734-753-4421
Lynn James, prin. Fax 753-4270
Renton JHS 600/6-8
31578 Huron River Dr 48164 734-782-2483
Kurt Mrocko, prin. Fax 783-0327
Sunnyside K Center 200/K-K
24820 Merriman Rd 48164 734-782-1162
Lou Ann Matsos, lead tchr. Fax 782-7216

St. John Lutheran S 100/PK-8
28320 Waltz Rd 48164 734-654-6366
John Hinck, prin. Fax 654-3675
St. Stephen S 200/K-8
18800 Huron River Dr 48164 734-753-4175
Sr. M. Thaddea Meyers, prin. Fax 753-4579

New Buffalo, Berrien, Pop. 2,274
New Buffalo Area SD 700/K-12
1112 E Clay St 49117 269-469-6010
Michael Lindley, supt. Fax 469-3315
www.nbas.org/
New Buffalo ES 200/K-5
12291 Lubke Rd 49117 269-469-6060
Joshua Traughber, prin. Fax 469-6065
New Buffalo MS 100/6-8
1112 E Clay St 49117 269-469-6003
William Welling, prin. Fax 469-6017

St. Mary of the Lake S 200/PK-8
704 W Merchant St 49117 269-469-1515
Kathleen Kelly, prin. Fax 469-3772

New Era, Oceana, Pop. 475
Shelby SD
Supt. — See Shelby
New Era ES 100/1-5
2752 Hillcrest Dr 49446 231-861-2662
Todd Kraai, prin. Fax 861-6203

New Era Christian S — 100/PK-8
1901 Oak Ave 49446 — 231-861-5450
David Wagner, prin. — Fax 861-5450

New Haven, Macomb, Pop. 4,708
New Haven Community SD — 1,100/PK-12
PO Box 482000 48048 — 586-749-5123
Dr. James Avery, supt. — Fax 749-6307
newhaven.misd.net/
New Haven ES — 500/PK-4
PO Box 482000 48048 — 586-749-8360
Aaron Sutherland, prin. — Fax 749-8365
Other Schools – See Ray

New Hudson, Oakland
South Lyon Community SD
Supt. — See South Lyon
Dolsen ES — 400/K-5
56775 Rice St 48165 — 248-573-8400
James Soubly, prin. — Fax 573-8371

New Lothrop, Shiawassee, Pop. 598
New Lothrop Area SD — 800/PK-12
PO Box 339 48460 — 810-638-5091
John Strycker, supt. — Fax 638-7277
www.newlothrop.k12.mi.us
New Lothrop ES — 500/PK-6
PO Box 279 48460 — 810-638-5026
David Harnish, prin. — Fax 638-7289

Newport, Monroe
Airport Community SD
Supt. — See Carleton
Niedermeier ES — 300/K-5
8400 Newport South Rd 48166 — 734-586-2676
Angela Schaal, prin. — Fax 586-3342

Jefferson SD
Supt. — See Monroe
North ES — 400/K-4
8281 N Dixie Hwy 48166 — 734-586-6784
Millie Grow, prin. — Fax 586-8854

St. Charles S — 200/PK-8
8125 Swan Creek Rd 48166 — 734-586-2531
Karen Johnson, prin. — Fax 586-3900

Niles, Berrien, Pop. 11,738
Brandywine Community SD — 1,100/K-12
1830 S 3rd St 49120 — 269-684-7150
John Jarpe, supt. — Fax 684-8998
brandywine.schoolfusion.us/
Brandywine ES — 400/3-6
2428 S 13th St 49120 — 269-684-8574
Tim Bagby, prin. — Fax 684-8924
Merritt ES — 200/K-2
1620 Lasalle Ave 49120 — 269-684-6511
Karen Weimer, prin. — Fax 684-8940

Niles Community SD — 4,200/PK-12
111 Spruce St 49120 — 269-683-0732
Douglas Law, supt. — Fax 684-6337
www.nilesschools.org
Ballard ES — 700/K-5
1601 W Chicago Rd 49120 — 269-683-5900
Amy DeVos, prin. — Fax 684-9527
Eastside ES — 400/K-5
315 N 14th St 49120 — 269-683-2585
David Eichenberg, prin. — Fax 684-9529
Ellis ES — 200/K-1
2740 Mannix St 49120 — 269-683-4635
Barbara Garrard, prin. — Fax 684-9539
Howard ES — 400/2-5
2788 Mannix St 49120 — 269-683-4633
Barbara Garrard, prin. — Fax 684-9534
Northside Child Development Center — 300/PK-K
2020 N 5th St 49120 — 269-683-1982
Cindy Wickham, prin. — Fax 684-9542
Oak Manor ES — 300/6-6
1 Tyler St 49120 — 269-683-7484
Robin Hadrick, prin. — Fax 684-9532
Ring Lardner MS — 600/7-8
801 N 17th St 49120 — 269-683-6610
Douglas Langmeyer, prin. — Fax 684-9524

Niles Adventist S — 50/PK-8
110 N Fairview Ave 49120 — 269-683-5444
Denise Kidder, prin. — Fax 683-9885
St. Mary S — 100/PK-6
217 S Lincoln Ave 49120 — 269-683-9191
Marie Doyle, prin. — Fax 683-6612

North Adams, Hillsdale, Pop. 500
North Adams-Jerome SD — 500/K-12
4555 Knowles Rd 49262 — 517-287-4214
Christopher Voisin, supt. — Fax 287-4722
www.najps.org
North Adams-Jerome ES — 300/K-6
4555 1/2 Knowles Rd 49262 — 517-287-4278
Joni Leininger, prin. — Fax 287-4275

North Branch, Lapeer, Pop. 1,008
North Branch Area SD — 2,200/K-12
PO Box 3620 48461 — 810-688-3570
Alan Piwinski, supt. — Fax 688-4344
nbbroncos.net
Fox ES — 400/5-6
PO Box 3620 48461 — 810-688-3284
Ann Wood, prin. — Fax 688-7051
North Branch ES — 500/K-4
PO Box 3620 48461 — 810-688-3041
Wendy Spivy, prin. — Fax 688-7010
North Branch MS — 500/7-8
PO Box 3620 48461 — 810-688-4431
John Sherman, prin. — Fax 688-4344

North Muskegon, Muskegon, Pop. 4,012
North Muskegon SD — 900/K-12
1600 Mills Ave 49445 — 231-719-4100
Mr. John Weaver, supt. — Fax 744-0739
www.nmps.k12.mi.us
North Muskegon ES — 400/K-5
1600 Mills Ave 49445 — 231-719-4200
Mitri Zainea, prin. — Fax 744-0739
North Muskegon MS — 200/6-8
1507 Mills Ave 49445 — 231-719-4110
James VanBergen, prin. — Fax 744-0739

Reeths-Puffer SD
Supt. — See Muskegon
Reeths-Puffer MS — 700/7-8
1911 W Giles Rd 49445 — 231-744-4721
Rob Renes, prin. — Fax 744-6049

Northport, Leelanau, Pop. 651
Northport SD — 200/K-12
PO Box 188 49670 — 231-386-5153
John Hoeffler, supt. — Fax 386-9838
Northport S — 200/K-12
PO Box 188 49670 — 231-386-5153
John Hoeffler, prin. — Fax 386-9838

Northville, Oakland, Pop. 6,311
Northville SD — 7,000/K-12
501 W Main St 48167 — 248-349-3400
Leonard Rezmierski, supt. — Fax 347-6928
www.northville.k12.mi.us/
Amerman ES — 600/K-5
847 N Center St 48167 — 248-344-8405
Stephen Anderson, prin. — Fax 380-4019
Hillside MS — 800/6-8
775 N Center St 48167 — 248-344-8493
James Cracraft, prin. — Fax 334-8480
Meads Mill MS — 900/6-8
16700 Franklin Rd, — 248-344-8435
Sue Meyer, prin. — Fax 334-1830
Moraine ES — 500/K-5
46811 8 Mile Rd 48167 — 248-344-8473
Denise Bryan, prin. — Fax 344-8408
Ridge Wood ES — 600/K-5
49775 6 Mile Rd, — 248-349-7602
Alicia Parsons, prin. — Fax 349-4147
Silver Springs ES — 400/K-5
19801 Silver Spring Dr 48167 — 248-344-8410
Scott Snyder, prin. — Fax 344-8404
Winchester ES — 500/K-5
16141 Winchester Dr, — 248-344-8415
Pat Messing, prin. — Fax 344-8402
Other Schools – See Novi

Northville Christian S — 400/PK-8
41355 6 Mile Rd, — 248-348-9031
Ken Storey, prin. — Fax 348-5423
Our Lady of Victory S — 400/K-8
132 Orchard Dr 48167 — 248-349-3610
Paula Nemeth, prin. — Fax 380-7247
St. Paul's Lutheran S — 100/PK-8
201 Elm St 48167 — 248-349-3146
Carl Hall, prin. — Fax 349-7493

Norton Shores, Muskegon, Pop. 23,479
Mona Shores SD — 4,000/PK-12
3374 McCracken St 49441 — 231-780-4751
Terry Babbitt, supt. — Fax 780-2099
www.monashores.net
Churchill ES — 400/PK-5
961 Porter Rd 49441 — 231-798-1276
Mark Platt, prin. — Fax 798-2012
Lincoln Park ES — 400/PK-5
2951 Leon St 49441 — 231-755-1257
Ray McLeod, prin. — Fax 759-2427
Mona Shores MS — 1,000/6-8
1700 Woodside Rd 49441 — 231-759-8506
Fax 755-0514
Ross Park ES — 400/PK-5
121 Randall Rd 49441 — 231-798-1773
Dan Cwayna, prin. — Fax 798-8741
Other Schools – See Muskegon

Norway, Dickinson, Pop. 2,973
Norway-Vulcan Area SD — 900/PK-12
300 Section St 49870 — 906-563-9552
Randall Van Gasse, supt. — Fax 563-5169
www.norway.k12.mi.us
Norway ES, 300 Section St 49870 — 300/PK-4
Brad Grayvold, prin. — 906-563-9543
Vulcan MS, 300 Section St 49870 — 300/5-8
Donald Byczek, prin. — 906-563-9563

Holy Spirit Central S — 50/PK-8
PO Box 187 49870 — 906-563-8817
Elizabeth Stack, prin. — Fax 563-8854

Novi, Oakland, Pop. 53,115
Northville SD
Supt. — See Northville
Thornton Creek ES — 400/K-5
46180 W 9 Mile Rd 48374 — 248-344-8475
Sharon Irvine, prin. — Fax 344-8423

Novi Community SD — 6,300/K-12
25345 Taft Rd 48374 — 248-449-1200
Peter Dion, supt. — Fax 449-1219
www.novi.k12.mi.us
Deerfield ES — 500/K-4
26500 Wixom Rd 48374 — 248-449-1700
Richard Njus, prin. — Fax 449-1709
Novi Meadows ES — 500/5-6
25549 Taft Rd 48374 — 248-449-1250
Lisa Fenchol, prin. — Fax 449-1259
Novi Meadows ES — 500/6-6
25299 Taft Rd 48374 — 248-449-1270
David Ascher, prin. — Fax 449-1279
Novi MS — 1,000/7-8
49000 W 11 Mile Rd 48374 — 248-449-1600
Milan Obrenovich, prin. — Fax 449-1619

Novi Woods ES — 400/K-4
25195 Taft Rd 48374 — 248-449-1230
Pam Quitiquit, prin. — Fax 449-1239
Orchard Hills ES — 500/K-4
41900 Quince Dr 48375 — 248-449-1400
Paul LePlae, prin. — Fax 449-1419
Parkview ES — 500/K-4
45825 W 11 Mile Rd 48374 — 248-449-1220
Jenifer Michos, prin. — Fax 449-1229
Village Oaks ES — 400/K-4
23333 Willowbrook 48375 — 248-449-1300
Susan Burnham, prin. — Fax 449-1319

Walled Lake Consolidated SD
Supt. — See Walled Lake
Hickory Woods ES — 500/PK-5
30655 Novi Rd 48377 — 248-956-2600
Patricia Werner, prin. — Fax 956-2605
Meadowbrook ES — 500/K-5
29200 Meadowbrook Rd 48377 — 248-956-2700
Dr. Christopher Peal, prin. — Fax 956-2705

Franklin Road Christian S — 300/K-12
40800 W 13 Mile Rd 48377 — 248-668-7100
Rev. Timothy Gambino, supt. — Fax 668-7101

Oakland, Oakland
Lake Orion Community SD
Supt. — See Lake Orion
Oakview MS — 600/6-8
917 Lake George Rd 48363 — 248-693-0321
Alice Seppanen, prin. — Fax 693-5419

Rochester Community SD
Supt. — See Rochester
Delta Kelly ES — 500/K-5
3880 Adams Rd 48363 — 248-726-3500
Marsha Andres, prin. — Fax 726-3505

Eagle Creek Academy — 100/PK-8
3739 Kern Rd 48363 — 248-475-9999
Catherine Rondeau, prin. — Fax 475-1616

Oakley, Saginaw, Pop. 336
Chesaning UNSD
Supt. — See Chesaning
Brady ES — 200/K-4
17295 S Hemlock Rd 48649 — 989-845-7060
Colleen Nixon, prin. — Fax 845-5858

Christ Lutheran S — 50/K-8
16070 W Brady Rd 48649 — 989-845-2611
Alan Schaffer, prin.

Oak Park, Oakland, Pop. 31,194
Berkley SD — 4,200/PK-12
14700 Lincoln St 48237 — 248-837-8000
Michael Simeck, supt. — Fax 544-5835
www.berkley.k12.mi.us
Norup International S — 600/K-8
14450 Manhattan St 48237 — 248-837-8300
Jamii Hitchcock, prin. — Fax 547-5558
Other Schools – See Berkley, Huntington Woods

Ferndale SD
Supt. — See Ferndale
Kennedy ES — 400/K-6
24220 Rosewood St 48237 — 248-586-8777
Nancy DeRousha, prin. — Fax 586-8780

Oak Park SD — 4,400/PK-12
13900 Granzon St 48237 — 248-336-7700
Dr. Sandra Harris, supt. — Fax 336-7738
www.oakparkschools.org
Einstein ES — 600/K-5
14001 Northend Ave 48237 — 248-336-7640
Gregory Church, prin. — Fax 336-7648
Key ES — 500/K-5
23400 Jerome St 48237 — 248-336-7610
Dr. JoAnn Wright, prin. — Fax 336-7618
Lessenger ECC — 100/PK-2
12901 Albany St 48237 — 248-336-7650
Brenda Snow, prin. — Fax 336-7658
Pepper ES — 400/K-5
24301 Church St 48237 — 248-336-7680
Dr. Carol Johnson, prin. — Fax 336-7688
Roosevelt MS — 600/6-7
23261 Scotia Rd 48237 — 248-336-7620
William Washington, prin. — Fax 336-7638

Beth Jacob School for Girls — 300/K-12
14390 W 10 Mile Rd 48237 — 248-544-9070
Shulamis Rubinfeld, prin. — Fax 544-4662

Okemos, Ingham, Pop. 20,216
Okemos SD — 4,200/K-12
4406 Okemos Rd 48864 — 517-349-1418
Cheryl Kreger Ed.D., supt. — Fax 349-6235
www.okemosschools.net/
Bennett Woods ES — 400/K-5
2650 Bennett Rd 48864 — 517-351-0115
Jeri Mifflin, prin. — Fax 351-1912
Central ES — 200/K-5
4406 Okemos Rd 48864 — 517-349-4440
Robert Greenhoe, prin. — Fax 349-9833
Chippewa MS — 500/6-8
4000 Okemos Rd 48864 — 517-349-4460
John Hood, prin. — Fax 347-9824
Cornell ES — 400/K-5
4371 Cornell Rd 48864 — 517-349-0100
Tara Fry, prin. — Fax 349-2080
Edgewood Montessori S — 200/K-5
1826 Osage Dr 48864 — 517-349-1070
Sue Hallman, prin. — Fax 349-0099
Hiawatha ES — 400/K-5
1900 Jolly Rd 48864 — 517-347-6766
Gary Kinzer, prin. — Fax 347-6770
Kinawa MS — 500/6-8
1900 Kinawa Dr 48864 — 517-349-9220
Barbara Hoevel, prin. — Fax 347-4189

Other Schools – See East Lansing

Montessori Radmoor S 200/PK-6
2745 Mount Hope Rd 48864 517-351-3655
Susan Hyatt, admin. Fax 351-3957
St. Martha S 200/PK-8
1100 W Grand River Ave 48864 517-349-3322
Francie Herring, prin. Fax 349-3322

Olivet, Eaton, Pop. 1,789
Olivet Community SD 1,300/K-12
255 1st St 49076 269-749-9129
David Campbell, supt. Fax 749-9701
www.olivetschools.org
Olivet MS 500/4-8
255 1st St 49076 269-749-9953
Mary Barkley, prin. Fax 749-9701
Persons ES 300/K-3
4425 W Butterfield Hwy 49076 269-749-4611
Sarah Scott, prin. Fax 749-4621

Onaway, Presque Isle, Pop. 961
Onaway Area SD 800/K-12
4549 M 33 49765 989-733-4970
Bob Szymoniak, supt. Fax 733-4889
www.onawayschools.com/
Onaway ES 300/K-5
4549 M 33 49765 989-733-4900
Nancy Miller, prin. Fax 733-4949
Onaway MS 200/6-8
4549 M 33 49765 989-733-4850
Bob Szymoniak, prin. Fax 733-4899
Other Schools – See Millersburg

Onaway SDA S 50/K-8
PO Box 156 49765 989-733-8600
Grace Ivey, prin. Fax 733-9916

Onekama, Manistee, Pop. 634
Onekama Consolidated SD 400/K-12
5016 Main St 49675 231-889-4251
Kevin Hughes, supt. Fax 889-3720
www.onekama.k12.mi.us
Onekama ES 200/K-5
5016 Main St 49675 231-889-5521
Gina Hagen, prin. Fax 889-9567

Onsted, Lenawee, Pop. 1,021
Onsted Community SD 1,700/K-12
PO Box 220 49265 517-467-2174
Mark Haag, supt. Fax 467-2026
www.onsted.k12.mi.us
Onsted ES 700/K-5
PO Box 220 49265 517-467-2166
Marsha Davis, prin. Fax 467-6293
Onsted MS 400/6-8
PO Box 220 49265 517-467-2168
Thomas Durbin, prin. Fax 467-6907

Ontonagon, Ontonagon, Pop. 1,637
Ontonagon Area SD 500/K-12
301 Greenland Rd 49953 906-884-4963
Gray Webber, supt. Fax 884-2057
www.oasd.k12.mi.us
Ontonagon Area ES 200/K-5
301 Greenland Rd 49953 906-884-4422
Jim Bobula, lead tchr. Fax 884-2942

Orchard Lake, Oakland
Bloomfield Hills SD
Supt. — See Bloomfield Hls
Lone Pine ES 200/PK-3
3100 Lone Pine Rd 48323 248-341-7300
Mary Hillberry, prin. Fax 341-7399

Our Lady of Refuge S 300/K-8
3750 Commerce Rd 48324 248-682-3422
Sally Chaney, prin. Fax 683-2265

Orion, Oakland, Pop. 24,076
Lake Orion Community SD
Supt. — See Lake Orion
Carpenter ES 500/K-5
2290 Flintridge St 48359 248-391-3500
Kerri Anderson, prin. Fax 391-5461

Ortonville, Oakland, Pop. 1,509
Brandon SD 3,600/K-12
1025 S Ortonville Rd 48462 248-627-1800
Lorrie McMahon, supt. Fax 627-4533
www.brandon.k12.mi.us
Belle Ann ES 300/K-4
155 E Glass Rd 48462 248-627-1860
Mark Rodak, prin. Fax 627-5715
Brandon Fletcher IS 500/5-6
300 South St 48462 248-627-1840
Jeffrey Beane, prin. Fax 627-7028
Brandon MS 600/7-8
609 S Ortonville Rd 48462 248-627-1830
Dr. William Snyder, prin. Fax 627-7201
Harvey-Swanson ES 500/K-4
209 Varsity Dr 48462 248-627-1850
Dr. Helen Clemetsen, prin. Fax 627-1858
Oakwood ES 300/K-4
2839 Oakwood Rd 48462 248-627-1880
Kristy Spann, prin. Fax 627-1888

Oscoda, Iosco, Pop. 1,061
Oscoda Area SD 1,300/PK-12
3550 E River Rd 48750 989-739-2033
Christine Beardsley, supt. Fax 739-2325
www.oscodaschools.org
Cedar Lake ES 300/PK-2
4950 Cedar Lake Rd 48750 989-739-5491
Jane Negro, prin. Fax 739-0670
Richardson S 300/3-8
3630 E River Rd 48750 989-739-9173
Charles Negro, prin. Fax 739-2510
Other Schools – See Glennie

Ossineke, Alpena, Pop. 1,091
Alpena SD
Supt. — See Alpena
Sanborn ES 300/K-6
12170 US Highway 23 S 49766 989-358-5800
Eric Cardwell, prin. Fax 358-5805

Otisville, Genesee, Pop. 845
LakeVille Community SD 1,800/PK-12
11107 Washburn Rd 48463 810-591-6525
Vickie Luoma, supt. Fax 591-6538
www.lakevilleschools.org/
Lakeville MS 500/6-8
11107 Washburn Rd 48463 810-591-3945
Kathy Schlaud, prin. Fax 591-6632
Otisville ES 100/PK-K
11107 Washburn Rd 48463 810-591-3132
Stephanie Stiles, prin. Fax 631-6050
Other Schools – See Columbiaville, Otter Lake

Otsego, Allegan, Pop. 3,941
Otsego SD 2,200/PK-12
400 Sherwood St 49078 269-692-6066
Dennis Patzer, supt. Fax 692-6074
www.otsegops.org/
Dix Street ES 300/PK-5
503 Dix St 49078 269-692-6099
Timothy Allard, prin. Fax 692-6130
Otsego MS 600/6-8
540 Washington St 49078 269-692-6199
Bill Houseman, prin. Fax 692-6203
Washington Street ES 300/PK-5
538 Washington St 49078 269-692-6069
Heather Badders, prin. Fax 692-6123
Other Schools – See Kalamazoo

Ostego Baptist Academy 50/PK-8
247 E Allegan St 49078 269-694-6738
Joseph Delinski, admin.
Peace Evangelical Lutheran S 50/K-4
805 S Wilmott St 49078 269-694-6104
Jason Thiel, prin.
St. Margaret S 100/K-8
736 S Farmer St 49078 269-694-2951
Charles Heidelberg, prin. Fax 694-4520

Ottawa Lake, Monroe
Whiteford Agricultural SD 800/K-12
6655 Consear Rd 49267 734-856-1443
Larry Shilling, supt. Fax 854-6463
www.whiteford.k12.mi.us
Whiteford ES 300/K-5
6655 Consear Rd 49267 734-856-1443
Kimberly Wegener, prin. Fax 856-4724
Whiteford MS 200/6-8
6655 Consear Rd 49267 734-856-1443
Kelli Tuller, prin. Fax 856-2564

Otter Lake, Lapeer, Pop. 428
LakeVille Community SD
Supt. — See Otisville
Otter Lake ES 200/1-2
6313 Hart Lake Rd 48464 810-538-3640
Stephanie Stiles, prin. Fax 793-1854

Ovid, Clinton, Pop. 1,439
Ovid-Elsie Area SD
Supt. — See Elsie
Leonard ES 400/K-6
732 Mabbit Rd 48866 989-834-5029
Ryan Cunningham, prin. Fax 834-5242

Owendale, Huron, Pop. 279
Owendale-Gagetown Area SD 200/K-12
7166 E Main St 48754 989-678-4261
Dana Compton, supt. Fax 678-4284
www.owengage.org/
Owendale-Gagetown ES 100/K-5
7166 E Main St 48754 989-678-4141
Dana Compton, prin. Fax 678-0920

Owosso, Shiawassee, Pop. 15,422
Owosso SD 3,700/PK-12
PO Box 340 48867 989-723-8131
Fax 723-7777
www.owosso.k12.mi.us
Bentley Bright Beginnings ECC 200/PK-PK
1375 W North St 48867 989-725-5770
Hattie Hanycz, dir. Fax 729-5694
Bryant ES 400/K-6
925 Hampton St 48867 989-723-4355
Stephen Brooks, prin. Fax 729-5666
Central ES 300/K-6
600 W Oliver St 48867 989-723-2790
Dr. Andrea Tuttle, prin. Fax 723-3046
Emerson ES 600/K-6
515 E Oliver St 48867 989-725-7361
Mark Erickson, prin. Fax 729-5451
Owosso MS 600/7-8
219 N Water St 48867 989-723-3460
Rich Collins, prin. Fax 729-5760
Roosevelt ECC 100/PK-PK
201 N Brooks St 48867 989-723-3918
Becky Wilkinson, dir. Fax 723-7663
Washington ES 400/K-6
645 Alger Ave 48867 989-725-5821
Chris Perry, prin. Fax 729-5440

Owosso SDA S 50/K-8
1215 Summit St 48867 989-723-6562
Darlene Huckabay, prin. Fax 725-1054
St. Paul S 200/K-8
718 W Main St 48867 989-725-7766
Merry Jane Robertson, prin. Fax 725-9824
Salem Lutheran S 100/PK-8
520 W Stewart St 48867 989-725-2234
Anthony Perry, prin. Fax 725-2429

Oxford, Oakland, Pop. 3,564
Oxford Community SD 4,100/K-12
105 Pontiac St 48371 248-969-5000
William Skilling, supt. Fax 969-5016
www.oxford.k12.mi.us
Axford ES 200/K-2
74 Mechanic St 48371 248-969-5050
Joyce Brasington, prin. Fax 969-5099
Clear Lake ES 500/K-5
2085 W Drahner Rd 48371 248-969-5200
Sue Hannant, prin. Fax 969-5216
Lakeville ES 400/K-5
1400 E Lakeville Rd 48371 248-969-1850
Kristy Gibson-Marshall, prin. Fax 969-1855
Oxford ES 400/3-5
109 Pontiac St 48371 248-969-5075
Jeff Brown, prin. Fax 969-5085
Oxford MS 1,000/6-8
1420 E Lakeville Rd 48371 248-969-1800
Kenneth Weaver, prin. Fax 969-1840
Other Schools – See Leonard

Kingsbury Country Day S 100/PK-8
5000 Hosner Rd 48370 248-628-2571
Tom Mecsey, prin. Fax 628-3612

Painesdale, Houghton
Adams Township SD 400/K-12
PO Box 37 49955 906-482-0599
Patrick Rozich, supt. Fax 487-5999
www.adams.k12.mi.us
Other Schools – See South Range

Palo, Ionia
Palo Community SD 100/PK-6
PO Box 338 48870 989-637-4359
Robert Kjohede, supt. Fax 637-4727
palocommunityschools.schools.officelive.com/
Palo Community S 100/PK-6
PO Box 338 48870 989-637-4359
Denise Weber-Herrmann, lead tchr. Fax 637-4727

Paradise, Chippewa
Whitefish Township Community SD 100/K-12
PO Box 58 49768 906-492-3353
Patrick Rowley, supt. Fax 492-3254
whitefish.eup.k12.mi.us/
Whitefish Township S 100/K-12
PO Box 58 49768 906-492-3353
Patrick Rowley, prin. Fax 492-3254

Parchment, Kalamazoo, Pop. 1,813
Parchment SD 1,900/K-12
520 N Orient St 49004 269-488-1050
Matthew Miller, supt. Fax 488-1060
www.parchmentschools.org
Parchment Central ES 300/K-5
516 N Orient St 49004 269-488-1000
Julia Kaemming, prin. Fax 488-1010
Parchment MS 400/6-8
307 N Riverview Dr 49004 269-488-1200
George Stamas, prin. Fax 488-1210
Other Schools – See Kalamazoo

Paris, Newaygo
Big Jackson SD 50/K-6
4020 13 Mile Rd 49338 231-796-8947
James Jacobson, supt. Fax 796-2921
bigjackson.ncats.net/
Big Jackson ES 50/K-6
4020 13 Mile Rd 49338 231-796-8947
James Jacobson, prin. Fax 796-2921

Parma, Jackson, Pop. 879
Western SD 3,000/K-12
1400 S Dearing Rd 49269 517-841-8100
William Coale Ph.D., supt. Fax 841-8801
www.westernschools.org/
Parma ES 400/K-5
385 Elizabeth St 49269 517-841-8600
Susan Haney, prin. Fax 841-8806
Western MS 700/6-8
1400 S Dearing Rd 49269 517-841-8300
Christopher Rugh, prin. Fax 841-8803
Other Schools – See Spring Arbor

Paw Paw, Van Buren, Pop. 3,328
Paw Paw SD 2,300/K-12
119 Johnson Rd 49079 269-657-8800
Mark Bielang, supt. Fax 657-7292
www.ppps.org
Paw Paw Early ES 300/K-2
512 W North St 49079 269-657-8810
Dawn Thompson, prin. Fax 657-7418
Paw Paw Later ES 500/3-5
612 W North St 49079 269-657-8820
Mary Puckett, prin. Fax 657-7399
Paw Paw MS 600/6-8
313 W Michigan Ave 49079 269-657-8870
Donald Barnhouse, prin. Fax 657-5011

St. Mary S 100/PK-5
508 E Paw Paw St 49079 269-657-3750
Connie Cooley, prin. Fax 657-4260
Trinity Lutheran S 100/PK-8
725 Pine St 49079 269-657-5921
Deanna Hindenach, prin. Fax 657-3359

Peck, Sanilac, Pop. 587
Peck Community SD 600/K-12
222 E Lapeer St 48466 810-378-5171
David Bush, supt. Fax 378-5116
www.peck.k12.mi.us
Peck ES 300/K-6
222 E Lapeer St 48466 810-378-5200
Michelle Warren, prin. Fax 378-5116

Pelkie, Baraga
Baraga Area SD
Supt. — See Baraga

Pelkie ES 100/K-2
Pelkie Rd 49958 906-353-6664
Jennifer Lynn, prin. Fax 353-7508

Pellston, Emmet, Pop. 798
Pellston SD 500/K-12
172 Park St 49769 231-539-8682
William Tebbe, supt. Fax 539-8838
www.pellstonschools.org/
Pellston ES 300/K-5
172 Park St 49769 231-539-8421
Frank Schneider, prin. Fax 539-8118

Pentwater, Oceana, Pop. 984
Pentwater SD 200/K-12
600 Park St 49449 231-869-4100
Jake Huffman, supt. Fax 869-4535
www.pentwater.k12.mi.us
Pentwater S 200/K-12
600 Park St 49449 231-869-4100
Jake Huffman, prin. Fax 869-4535

Perry, Shiawassee, Pop. 2,052
Perry SD 1,900/PK-12
PO Box 900 48872 517-625-3108
Jacklyn Hurd, supt. Fax 625-6256
www.perry.k12.mi.us
Perry ES 500/PK-5
PO Box 900 48872 517-625-3101
Mike Judd, prin. Fax 625-5003
Perry MS 500/6-8
PO Box 900 48872 517-625-6196
Dan Hare, prin. Fax 625-0120
Other Schools – See Shaftsburg

Petersburg, Monroe, Pop. 1,138
Summerfield SD 900/K-12
17555 Ida West Rd 49270 734-279-1035
John Hewitt, supt. Fax 279-1448
www.summerfield.k12.mi.us
Summerfield ES 400/K-6
232 E Elm St 49270 734-279-1013
Jodi Bucher, prin. Fax 279-1017
Summerfield MS 100/7-8
232 E Elm St 49270 734-279-1013
Jodi Bucher, prin. Fax 279-1017

Petoskey, Emmet, Pop. 6,198
Petoskey SD 3,000/K-12
1130 Howard St 49770 231-348-2100
John Scholten, supt. Fax 348-2342
www.petoskeyschools.org
Central ES 300/K-5
410 State St 49770 231-348-2110
Dale Lewis, prin. Fax 348-2402
Lincoln ES 300/K-5
616 Connable Ave 49770 231-348-2120
Thomas VanDeventer, prin. Fax 348-2471
Montessori ES 50/1-5
1560 E Mitchell Rd 49770 231-347-5331
Kim Maves, admin. Fax 347-4304
Ottawa ES 400/K-5
871 Kalamazoo Ave 49770 231-348-2130
Ruth Goldsmith, prin. Fax 348-2302
Petoskey MS 700/6-8
801 Northmen Dr 49770 231-348-2150
David Gracy, prin. Fax 348-2234
Sheridan ES 300/K-5
1415 Howard St 49770 231-348-2140
Joel Donaldson, prin. Fax 348-2444

Petoskey Montessori S 100/PK-6
1560 E Mitchell Rd 49770 231-347-5331
Fax 347-4304
Petoskey SDA S 50/K-8
1404 Howard St 49770 231-347-2560
Lorene Yount, prin.
St. Francis Xavier S 200/K-8
414 Michigan St 49770 231-347-3651
Phyllis Daily, prin. Fax 347-3610

Pewamo, Ionia, Pop. 564
Pewamo-Westphalia SD
Supt. — See Westphalia
Pewamo ES 100/K-6
430 W Jefferson St 48873 989-593-3488
George Heckman, prin. Fax 593-4118

St. Joseph S 100/2-8
PO Box 38 48873 989-593-3400
Pat O'Mara, prin. Fax 593-3400

Pickford, Chippewa
Pickford SD 400/K-12
PO Box 278 49774 906-647-6285
Keith Krahnke, supt. Fax 647-3706
pickford.eup.k12.mi.us/
Pickford ES 200/K-6
PO Box 278 49774 906-647-6245
Jan Rairigh, prin. Fax 647-7720

Pigeon, Huron, Pop. 1,130
Elkton-Pigeon-Bay Port Laker SD 1,000/K-12
6136 Pigeon Rd 48755 989-453-4600
Robert Smith, supt. Fax 453-4609
www.lakerschools.org/
Laker ES 400/K-5
6436 Pigeon Rd 48755 989-453-4600
Kevin Green, prin. Fax 453-4629
Laker MS 200/6-8
6136 Pigeon Rd 48755 989-453-4600
Brian Keim, prin. Fax 453-4609

Cross Lutheran S 100/PK-8
200 Ruppert St 48755 989-453-3330
Craig Lehrke, prin. Fax 453-3331
St. John Lutheran S 50/K-8
7379 Berne Rd 48755 989-453-2861
Alan Selbig, prin. Fax 453-2884

Pinckney, Livingston, Pop. 2,435
Pinckney Community SD 4,600/K-12
2130 E MI 36 48169 810-225-3900
Daniel Danosky, supt. Fax 225-3905
www.pcs.k12.mi.us
Country ES 400/K-4
2939 E MI 36 48169 810-225-6600
Carrie Fosselman, prin. Fax 225-6605
Farley Hill ES 500/K-4
8110 Farley Rd 48169 810-225-6400
Lynda Henderson, prin. Fax 225-6405
Navigator S 700/5-6
2150 E MI 36 48169 810-225-5300
Stacey Urbin, prin. Fax 225-5305
Pathfinder S 800/7-8
2100 E MI 36 48169 810-225-5200
Richard Todd, prin. Fax 225-5205
Pinckney ES 300/K-4
935 W MI 36 48169 810-225-5800
Yvonne Taylor, prin. Fax 225-5805
Other Schools – See Lakeland

Light of the World Academy 100/PK-4
1740 E MI 36 48169 734-878-3301
Fax 878-6026
Livingston Christian S 200/PK-12
550 E Hamburg St 48169 734-878-9818
Theodore Nast, admin. Fax 878-9830
St. Mary S 200/PK-8
10601 Dexter Pinckney Rd 48169 734-878-5616
Veronica Kinsey, prin. Fax 878-2383

Pinconning, Bay, Pop. 1,349
Pinconning Area SD 1,800/K-12
605 W 5th St 48650 989-879-4556
Darren Kroczaleski, supt. Fax 879-4705
www.pasd.org/
Central ES 400/K-6
605 W 5th St 48650 989-879-2301
John Sanford, prin. Fax 879-2740
Mt. Forest ES 200/K-6
4197 N 11 Mile Rd 48650 989-879-2798
Keith Wetters, prin. Fax 879-7237
Pinconning Area MS 300/7-8
605 W 5th St 48650 989-879-2311
Mark Fuhrmanm, prin. Fax 879-7258
Other Schools – See Linwood

St. Michael S 100/PK-8
310 E 2nd St 48650 989-879-3063
Robin Honard, prin. Fax 879-3626

Pittsford, Hillsdale
Pittsford Area SD 700/K-12
9304 Hamilton Rd 49271 517-523-3481
Andrew Shaw, supt. Fax 523-3467
www.pas.k12.mi.us/
Pittsford ES 400/K-6
9304 Hamilton Rd 49271 517-523-3481
Andrew Shaw, prin. Fax 523-3467

Prattville SDA S 50/1-8
5085 S Waldron Rd 49271 517-523-4143
Barbara Hinkley, prin.

Plainwell, Allegan, Pop. 3,996
Plainwell Community SD 2,900/PK-12
600 School Dr 49080 269-685-5823
Susan Wakefield, supt. Fax 685-1108
www.plainwellschools.org
Gilkey ES 400/PK-5
707 S Woodhams St 49080 269-685-2424
Beth Green, prin. Fax 685-9742
Plainwell MS 700/6-8
720 Brigham St 49080 269-685-5813
Tammi Lawrence, prin. Fax 685-2099
Starr ES 600/K-5
601 School Dr 49080 269-685-5835
Laurie Lanphear, prin. Fax 685-2027
Other Schools – See Kalamazoo

Plymouth, Wayne, Pop. 9,100
Plymouth-Canton Community SD 18,500/K-12
454 S Harvey St 48170 734-416-2700
Dr. Craig Fiegel, supt. Fax 416-4932
www.pccs.k12.mi.us
Allen ES 500/K-5
11100 N Haggerty Rd 48170 734-416-3050
Marcia Moore, prin. Fax 416-4816
Bird ES 500/K-5
220 S Sheldon Rd 48170 734-416-3100
Susan Kelty, prin. Fax 455-9521
Central MS 900/6-8
650 Church St 48170 734-416-2990
Anthony Ruela, prin. Fax 416-7699
East MS 800/6-8
1042 S Mill St 48170 734-416-4950
Amy Potts, prin. Fax 416-4949
Farrand ES 400/K-5
41400 Greenbriar Ln 48170 734-582-6900
Dana Jones, prin. Fax 420-7022
Fiegel ES 400/K-5
39750 Joy Rd 48170 734-416-6030
James Johnson, prin. Fax 416-6031
Isbister ES 600/K-5
9300 N Canton Center Rd 48170 734-416-6050
Lee Harrison, prin. Fax 416-7681
Pioneer MS 800/6-8
46081 Ann Arbor Rd W 48170 734-416-2770
Philip Freeman, prin. Fax 416-7569
Smith ES 500/K-5
1298 McKinley St 48170 734-416-4850
Jill Cantin, prin. Fax 455-9522
West MS 800/6-8
44401 W Ann Arbor Trl 48170 734-416-7550
Clint Smiley, prin. Fax 416-7648
Other Schools – See Canton

Metropolitan SDA Jr Academy 50/K-10
15585 N Haggerty Rd 48170 734-420-4044
David Tripp, prin. Fax 420-3710
Our Lady of Good Counsel S 600/K-8
1151 William St 48170 734-453-3053
Kathleen Reilly, prin. Fax 357-5331
St. Peter Lutheran S 100/PK-8
1309 Penniman Ave 48170 734-453-0460
Ryan Roth, prin. Fax 453-3598
Spiritus Sanctus Academy 200/K-8
10450 Joy Rd 48170 734-414-8430
Sr. Mary Handwerker, prin. Fax 414-8495

Pointe Aux Pins, Mackinac
Bois Blanc Pines SD 50/K-8
PO Box 876 49775 231-634-7225
Fax 634-7225
Pines S 50/K-8
PO Box 876 49775 231-634-7225
Wendy Spray, lead tchr. Fax 634-7225

Pontiac, Oakland, Pop. 67,331
Pontiac SD 8,300/PK-12
47200 Woodward Ave 48342 248-451-6800
Linda Paramore, supt. Fax 451-6890
www.pontiac.k12.mi.us
Alcott ES 400/K-6
460 W Kennett Rd 48340 248-451-7910
Shana Burnett, prin. Fax 451-7924
Crofoot ES 400/K-6
250 W Pike St 48341 248-451-7930
Fax 451-7949
Emerson ES 400/K-6
859 Emerson Ave 48340 248-451-7700
Roselyn Northcross, prin. Fax 451-7715
Franklin ES 200/K-6
661 Franklin Rd 48341 248-451-7720
Elberta Stephens, prin. Fax 451-7738
Frost Preschool PK-PK
723 Cottage St 48342 248-451-7770
Fax 451-7776
Herrington ES 400/K-6
541 Bay St 48342 248-451-7790
Pamela Farris, prin. Fax 451-7805
Jefferson MS 500/7-8
600 Motor St 48341 248-451-7620
Wendy Fitzpatrick, prin. Fax 451-7631
LeBaron ES 300/K-6
1033 Barkell St 48340 248-451-7810
Donna Dulaney, prin. Fax 451-7823
Lincoln MS 400/7-8
131 Hillside Dr 48342 248-451-7650
Gloria Hill, prin. Fax 451-7670
Longfellow ES 300/K-6
31 N Astor St 48342 248-451-7830
Kelley Williams, prin. Fax 451-7841
Madison MS 500/7-8
1275 N Perry St 48340 248-451-8010
Arlee Ewing, prin. Fax 451-8034
Owen-Kennedy ES 400/K-6
1700 Baldwin Ave 48340 248-451-7870
Fax 451-7885
Whitman ES 300/K-6
125 E Montcalm St 48342 248-451-7950
Iraida Garcia, prin. Fax 451-7963
Other Schools – See Auburn Hills

Marist Academy 300/6-8
1300 Giddings Rd 48340 248-373-5371
Sandra Favrow, prin. Fax 373-4707

Portage, Kalamazoo, Pop. 45,277
Portage SD 8,300/K-12
8111 S Westnedge Ave 49002 269-323-5000
Marsha Wells, supt. Fax 323-5001
www.portageps.org
Amberly ES 500/K-5
6637 Amberly St 49024 269-323-5900
Mary Daoust, prin. Fax 323-5990
Angling Road ES 400/K-5
5340 Angling Rd 49024 269-323-6000
Karen Witvoet, prin. Fax 323-6090
Central ES 400/K-5
8422 S Westnedge Ave 49002 269-323-6100
Susan Roberts, prin. Fax 323-6190
Haverhill ES 400/K-5
6633 Haverhill Ave 49024 269-323-6200
David Nicolette, prin. Fax 323-6290
Lake Center ES 500/K-5
10011 Portage Rd 49002 269-323-6300
Mark Root, prin. Fax 323-6390
Moorsbridge ES 600/K-5
7361 Moorsbridge Rd 49024 269-323-6400
Nancy Haas, prin. Fax 323-6490
North MS 600/6-8
5808 Oregon Ave 49024 269-323-5700
Celeste Shelton-Harris, prin. Fax 323-5790
Portage Central MS 700/6-8
8305 S Westnedge Ave 49002 269-323-5600
David Babcock, prin. Fax 323-5690
12th Street ES 400/K-5
6501 S 12th St 49024 269-323-6500
Ron Jones, prin. Fax 323-6590
West MS 700/6-8
7145 Moorsbridge Rd 49024 269-323-5800
Larry Killips, prin. Fax 323-5890
Woodland ES 500/K-5
1401 Woodland Dr 49024 269-323-6600
Susan O'Donnell, prin. Fax 323-6690

St. Michael Lutheran S 200/PK-8
7211 Oakland Dr 49024 269-327-0512
Greg Johnson, prin. Fax 327-3148

Port Hope, Huron, Pop. 288
Port Hope Community SD 100/K-12
7840 Portland Rd 48468 989-428-4151
Larry Johnson, supt. Fax 428-4153
www.porthope.k12.mi.us
Port Hope S 100/K-12
7840 Portland Rd 48468 989-428-4151
Donn Pitts, prin. Fax 428-4153

St. John Lutheran S 50/PK-8
PO Box 206 48468 989-428-4811
Paula Ceplecha, prin. Fax 428-4811

Port Huron, Saint Clair, Pop. 31,501
Port Huron Area SD 10,200/PK-12
PO Box 5013 48061 810-984-3101
Thomas Shorkey, supt. Fax 984-6606
www.phasd.us/
Central MS 700/6-8
200 32nd St 48060 810-984-6533
Eddie Kindle, prin. Fax 989-2709
Chippewa MS 600/6-8
2800 Chippewa Trl 48060 810-984-6539
Terry Stoneburner, prin. Fax 989-2712
Cleveland ES 200/K-5
2801 Vanness St 48060 810-984-6500
Mary Jo Smith, prin. Fax 989-2736
Crull ES 500/PK-5
2615 Hancock St 48060 810-984-6504
Debra Barr, prin. Fax 989-2733
Garfield ES 400/K-5
1221 Garfield St 48060 810-984-6509
Gary Bates, prin. Fax 989-2743
Holland Woods MS 500/6-8
1617 Holland Ave 48060 810-984-6548
Ethan Barden, prin. Fax 989-2713
Michigamme ES 500/K-5
2855 Michigan Rd 48060 810-984-6523
Thomas Navarro, prin. Fax 989-2789
Roosevelt ES 400/K-5
1112 20th St 48060 810-984-6525
Ruth Barnes, prin. Fax 989-2762
Wilson ES 400/K-5
834 Chestnut St 48060 810-984-6530
Donnilee Hernandez, prin. Fax 989-2771
Other Schools – See Fort Gratiot, Kimball, Lakeport

St. Mary/McCormick Academy 200/PK-8
1429 Ballentine St 48060 810-982-7906
Deborah Krueger, prin. Fax 987-8255
Trinity Lutheran S 100/PK-8
1517 10th St 48060 810-984-2501
Kenneth Hass, prin. Fax 982-3906

Portland, Ionia, Pop. 3,822
Portland SD 1,900/K-12
1100 Ionia Rd 48875 517-647-4161
Charles Dumas, supt. Fax 647-2975
www.portlandk12.org
Oakwood ES 300/K-2
500 Oak St 48875 517-647-2991
Lisa Riffle, prin. Fax 647-4479
Portland MS 500/6-8
745 Storz St 48875 517-647-2985
Bill Carlton, prin. Fax 647-2820
Westwood ES 500/3-5
883 Cross St 48875 517-647-2989
James Walter, prin. Fax 647-1790

St. Patrick S 300/PK-12
122 N West St 48875 517-647-7551
Randy Hodge, prin. Fax 647-4545

Posen, Presque Isle, Pop. 282
Posen Consolidated SD 9 300/K-12
PO Box 187 49776 989-766-2573
Dru Milliron, supt. Fax 766-2519
www.posen.k12.mi.us
Posen Consolidated ES 200/K-6
PO Box 187 49776 989-766-2573
Dru Milliron, prin. Fax 766-2519

Potterville, Eaton, Pop. 2,205
Potterville SD 900/K-12
420 N High St 48876 517-645-2662
William Eis, supt. Fax 645-0092
www.pps.k12.mi.us/
Potterville ES 300/K-4
426 N High St 48876 517-645-2525
Gerard Schneider, prin. Fax 645-0256
Potterville MS 300/5-8
424 N High St 48876 517-645-4777
Michael Hugan, prin. Fax 645-0091

Prudenville, Roscommon, Pop. 1,513

Our Lady of the Lake S 100/PK-8
PO Box 800 48651 989-366-5592
Brenda Doral, prin. Fax 366-1348

Pullman, Allegan
Bloomingdale SD
Supt. — See Bloomingdale
Pullman ES 300/K-5
5582 South Ave 49450 269-236-5235
Patrick Creagan, prin. Fax 236-5307

Quincy, Branch, Pop. 1,657
Quincy Community SD 1,300/PK-12
1 Educational Pkwy 49082 517-639-7141
Joseph Lopez, supt. Fax 639-4273
www.quincyschools.org
Jennings ES 300/3-5
44 E Liberty St 49082 517-639-4719
Penny Brockway, prin. Fax 639-3205
Jennings PS 200/PK-2
44 E Liberty St 49082 517-639-9885
Ron Olmsted, prin. Fax 639-3461

Quincy MS 300/6-8
32 Fulton St 49082 517-639-4201
David Spalding, prin. Fax 639-3701

Rapid City, Kalkaska
Kalkaska SD
Supt. — See Kalkaska
Rapid City ES 100/K-5
5258 River St NW 49676 231-331-6121
Melissa Heller, prin. Fax 331-4910

Rapid River, Delta
Rapid River SD 500/K-12
PO Box 68 49878 906-474-6411
Terri Mileski, supt. Fax 474-9903
www.rapidriver.k12.mi.us
Rapid River ES 200/K-5
PO Box 68 49878 906-474-6411
William Warning, prin. Fax 474-9903

Ravenna, Muskegon, Pop. 1,238
Ravenna SD 1,100/K-12
12322 Stafford St 49451 231-853-2231
John Van Loon, supt. Fax 853-2193
www.ravennaschools.org
Beechnau ES 500/K-5
12322 Stafford St 49451 231-853-2258
Susan Sharp, prin. Fax 853-6889
Ravenna MS 200/6-8
2700 S Ravenna Rd 49451 231-853-2268
Jason Mellema, prin. Fax 853-2629

St. Catherine S 100/K-6
PO Box 216 49451 231-853-6743
Sr. Peter Mary Korson, prin. Fax 853-8673

Ray, Macomb
New Haven Community SD
Supt. — See New Haven
New Haven MS 300/5-8
24125 26 Mile Rd 48096 586-749-3401
David Rayes, prin. Fax 749-8338

Reading, Hillsdale, Pop. 1,104
Reading Community SD 900/K-12
223 Strong St 49274 517-283-2166
Mike Potts, supt. Fax 283-3519
www.rcsk12.org
Reynolds ES 500/K-6
221 Strong St 49274 517-283-2188
Tim Davis, prin. Fax 283-3973

Redford, Wayne, Pop. 51,100
Detroit SD
Supt. — See Detroit
Ann Arbor Trail S 500/PK-8
7635 Chatham 48239 313-274-8560
Deborah Ferguson, prin. Fax 274-8074

Redford Union SD 3,800/PK-12
18499 Beech Daly Rd 48240 313-242-6000
Donna Rhodes, supt. Fax 242-6025
www.redfordu.k12.mi.us
Beck Education Center 100/PK-PK
27100 Bennett 48240 313-242-3500
Neil Thomas, dir. Fax 242-3505
Bulman ES 500/2-5
15995 Delaware Ave 48239 313-242-3600
Susan Stanley, prin. Fax 242-3605
Hilbert MS 800/6-8
26440 Puritan 48239 313-242-4000
Susan Shelton, prin. Fax 242-4005
MacGowan ES 200/K-1
18255 Kinloch 48240 313-242-3800
Kathy Robbins, prin. Fax 242-3805
Stuckey ES 500/2-5
26000 Fargo 48240 313-242-3900
Robert Hanley, prin. Fax 242-3905

South Redford SD 3,400/K-12
26141 Schoolcraft 48239 313-535-4000
Linda Hicks Ed.D., supt. Fax 535-1059
southredford.net
Addams ES 300/K-5
14025 Berwyn 48239 313-532-8064
Carol Lindman, prin. Fax 532-2585
Fisher ES 400/K-5
10000 Crosley 48239 313-532-2455
Brian Galdes, prin. Fax 532-5602
Jefferson ES 300/K-5
26555 Westfield 48239 313-937-2330
Deborah Greenwood, prin. Fax 937-0654
Pierce MS 800/6-8
25605 Orangelawn 48239 313-937-8880
Jason Riggs, prin. Fax 937-9486
Vandenberg ES 400/K-5
24901 Cathedral 48239 313-532-0300
Syndee Malek, prin. Fax 532-0327

Cornerstone S - Redford Campus 300/PK-8
11685 Appleton 48239 313-592-6061
Scott Cairo, prin. Fax 242-5156
Hosanna-Tabor Lutheran S 100/PK-8
9600 Leverne 48239 313-937-2233
David Kusch, prin. Fax 937-2173
St. Robert Bellarmine S 200/K-8
27201 W Chicago 48239 313-937-1655
Nancy Kuszczak, prin. Fax 937-9795
St. Valentine S 200/PK-8
25875 Hope 48239 313-533-7149
Rachel Damuth, prin. Fax 533-3060

Reed City, Osceola, Pop. 2,418
Reed City Area SD 1,600/K-12
829 S Chestnut St Ste A 49677 231-832-2201
Steven Westhoff, supt. Fax 832-2202
www.reedcity.k12.mi.us
Norman ES 600/K-5
338 W Lincoln Ave 49677 231-832-5548
David Vander Goot, prin. Fax 832-6194

Reed City MS 400/6-8
233 W Church Ave 49677 231-832-6174
Tim Webster, prin. Fax 832-6180

Trinity Lutheran S 100/PK-8
139 W Church Ave 49677 231-832-5186
James Smith, prin. Fax 832-0107

Reese, Tuscola, Pop. 1,365
Reese SD 1,000/PK-12
PO Box 389 48757 989-868-9864
Storm Lairson, supt. Fax 868-9570
www.reese.k12.mi.us/
Reese ES 300/PK-4
PO Box 389 48757 989-868-4561
Gary Grysko, prin. Fax 868-4446
Reese MS 300/5-8
PO Box 389 48757 989-868-4157
Gary Grysko, prin. Fax 868-1609

St. Elizabeth S 100/PK-8
PO Box 392 48757 989-868-4108
M. Gabriela Costoya, prin. Fax 868-0060
Trinity Lutheran S 100/PK-8
9858 North St 48757 989-868-4501
Jane Dohrmann, prin. Fax 868-4769

Remus, Mecosta
Chippewa Hills SD 2,600/PK-12
3226 Arthur Rd 49340 989-967-2000
Shirley Howard, supt. Fax 967-2009
www.chsd.us
Chippewa Hills IS 500/6-8
3102 Arthur Rd 49340 989-967-2200
Bob Grover, prin. Fax 967-2209
Chippewa Hills Remus ES 200/PK-5
350 E Wheatland Ave 49340 989-967-8230
John Zolynsky, prin. Fax 967-8534
Other Schools – See Barryton, Mecosta, Weidman

St. Michael S 100/PK-6
8944 50th Ave 49340 989-967-3681
Mary Schoner, prin. Fax 967-3061

Republic, Marquette
Republic-Michigamme SD 200/K-12
227 Maple St 49879 906-376-2277
Vicki Lempinen, supt. Fax 376-8299
www.republicmichigamme.maisd.k12.mi.us
Republic-Michigamme S 200/K-12
227 Maple St 49879 906-376-2277
Vicki Lempinen, prin. Fax 376-8299

Richland, Kalamazoo, Pop. 707
Gull Lake Community SD 2,600/K-12
11775 E D Ave 49083 269-488-5000
Christopher Rundle, supt. Fax 488-5000
www.gulllakecs.org
Gull Lake MS 500/6-8
9550 M 89 49083 269-488-5040
David Alban, prin. Fax 488-5051
Richland ES 400/K-3
9476 M 89 49083 269-488-5080
Deb Linden, prin. Fax 488-5081
Ryan IS 400/4-5
9562 M 89 49083 269-488-5060
Dee Stamats, prin. Fax 488-5061
Other Schools – See Hickory Corners

Richmond, Macomb, Pop. 5,607
Richmond Community SD 1,900/PK-12
68931 S Main St 48062 586-727-3565
Patrick Bird, supt. Fax 727-2098
www.richmond.misd.net/
Lee ES 500/PK-4
68399 S Forest Ave 48062 586-727-2509
Jim Benoit, prin. Fax 727-9223
Richmond MS 600/5-8
35250 Division Rd 48062 586-727-7552
Keith Bartels, prin. Fax 727-2545

St. Augustine S 200/PK-8
67901 Howard St 48062 586-727-9365
Gerald Bagierek, prin. Fax 727-3760
St. Peter Lutheran S 200/PK-8
37601 31 Mile Rd 48062 586-727-9080
George Kovtun, prin. Fax 727-3370

Richville, Tuscola

St. Michael Lutheran S 200/PK-8
PO Box 185 48758 989-868-4809
Kevin Hendrikson, prin. Fax 868-4288

Riley, Saint Clair
Memphis Community SD 1,100/K-12
34110 Bordman Rd 48041 810-392-2151
Dr. David Symington, supt. Fax 392-3614
www.memphisk12.org/
Memphis JHS 200/6-8
34130 Bordman Rd 48041 810-392-2131
Kenneth Reygaert, prin. Fax 392-2513
Other Schools – See Memphis

River Rouge, Wayne, Pop. 9,202
River Rouge SD 1,300/PK-12
1460 Coolidge Hwy 48218 313-297-9600
Carlos Lopez Ed.D., supt. Fax 297-6525
www.rrouge.k12.mi.us/
Sabbath Preparatory Academy 300/K-8
340 Frazier St 48218 313-297-9654
Brandon Cox, prin. Fax 297-5695
Visger Preparatory Academy 300/PK-5
11121 W Jefferson Ave 48218 313-297-9648
Tammy Hubbard, prin. Fax 297-5694
White K Preparatory Academy 100/PK-K
550 Eaton St 48218 313-297-9600
Carlos Lopez Ed.D., prin. Fax 297-6525

Riverside, Berrien

Hagar Township SD 6 100/K-8
PO Box 133 49084 269-849-1343
Sally Woods, supt. Fax 849-3512
www.remc11.k12.mi.us/~rside
Riverside S 100/K-8
PO Box 133 49084 269-849-1343
Sally Woods, prin. Fax 849-3512

Riverview, Wayne, Pop. 12,744

Riverview Community SD 2,600/K-12
13425 Colvin St Ste 1, 734-285-9660
Dennis Desmarais, supt. Fax 285-9822
www.riverviewschools.com
Forest ES 400/K-5
19400 Hampton St, 734-479-2550
Allen Gaggini, prin. Fax 479-2912
Huntington ES 300/K-5
17752 Kennebec St, 734-283-4820
Susan King, prin. Fax 285-6650
Memorial ES 400/K-5
13425 Colvin St Ste 2, 734-285-4080
Nancy Holloway, prin. Fax 285-6664
Seitz MS 600/6-8
17800 Kennebec St, 734-285-2043
Fred Keier, prin. Fax 285-6649

Rochester, Oakland, Pop. 11,209

Rochester Community SD 14,400/K-12
501 W University Dr 48307 248-726-3000
Dave Pruneau, supt. Fax 726-3105
www.rochester.k12.mi.us/
Baldwin ES 500/K-5
4325 Bannister Rd 48306 248-726-3200
Denise Bereznoff, prin. Fax 726-3205
Brewster ES 300/K-5
1535 Brewster Rd 48306 248-726-3300
Teresa DiMaria, prin. Fax 726-3305
Hamlin ES 500/K-5
270 W Hamlin Rd 48307 248-726-3600
Gary Cornish, prin. Fax 726-3605
Hampton ES 500/K-5
530 Hampton Cir 48307 248-726-3700
Charles Rowland, prin. Fax 726-3705
Hart MS 1,100/6-8
6500 Sheldon Rd 48306 248-726-4500
David Hurst, prin. Fax 726-4505
Hugger ES 500/K-5
5050 Sheldon Rd 48306 248-726-3800
Debi Fragomeni, prin. Fax 726-3805
McGregor ES 400/K-5
1101 1st St 48307 248-726-4000
Sharen Howard, prin. Fax 726-4005
Meadow Brook ES 400/K-5
2350 Munster Rd 48309 248-726-4100
Maria Etienne, prin. Fax 726-4105
Musson ES 400/K-5
3500 Dutton Rd 48306 248-726-4200
Victoria Righter, prin. Fax 726-4205
North Hill ES 500/K-5
1385 Mahaffy Ave 48307 248-726-4300
Michael Behrmann, prin. Fax 726-4305
Reuther JHS 700/6-8
1430 E Auburn Rd 48307 248-726-4700
Cheryl Gambaro, prin. Fax 726-4705
Van Hoosen JHS 800/6-8
1339 N Adams Rd 48306 248-726-4900
Stephen Cook, prin. Fax 726-4905
Other Schools – See Oakland, Rochester Hills

Holy Family Regional S - North Campus 500/K-3
1240 Inglewood Ave 48307 248-656-1234
Sr. Karen Hawver, prin. Fax 656-3494
Living Word Lutheran S 200/PK-8
3838 N Rochester Rd 48306 248-651-9474
Stacy Hoeft, prin. Fax 651-8349
St. John Lutheran S 300/PK-8
1011 W University Dr 48307 248-402-8050
Mychal Thom, prin. Fax 402-8001

Rochester Hills, Oakland, Pop. 69,995

Avondale SD
Supt. — See Auburn Hills
Avondale Meadows Upper ES 600/5-6
1435 W Auburn Rd 48309 248-537-6400
Dianne Shepich, prin. Fax 537-6405
Avondale MS 600/7-8
1445 W Auburn Rd 48309 248-537-6300
Todd Robinson, prin. Fax 537-6305
Deerfield ES 300/K-4
3600 Crooks Rd 48309 248-537-6700
John Pagel, prin. Fax 537-6705

Rochester Community SD
Supt. — See Rochester
Brooklands ES 500/K-5
480 E Auburn Rd 48307 248-726-3400
Denise Holub, prin. Fax 726-3405
Long Meadow ES 500/K-5
450 Allston Dr 48309 248-726-3900
April Wuest, prin. Fax 726-3905
University Hills ES 400/K-5
600 Croydon Rd 48309 248-726-4400
Amy Grande, prin. Fax 726-4405
West JHS 900/6-8
500 Old Perch Rd 48309 248-726-5000
Mike Dillon, prin. Fax 726-5005

Brookfield Academy 300/PK-8
1263 S Adams Rd 48309 248-375-1700
Dawn McComb, prin. Fax 375-1020
Holy Family Regional S - South Campus 600/4-8
2633 John R Rd 48307 248-299-3798
Sr. Karen Hawver, prin. Fax 299-3843
Oakland Steiner S 100/PK-8
3976 S Livernois Rd 48307 248-299-8755
Katherine Thivierge, prin. Fax 299-3614
Rochester Hills Christian S 300/PK-12
3300 S Livernois Rd 48307 248-852-0585
Karen Patton, prin. Fax 852-4757

Rock, Delta

Mid Peninsula SD 300/K-12
5055 Saint Nicholas 31st Rd 49880 906-359-4387
Mike Loy, supt. Fax 359-4167
midpen.dsisd.net/
Mid Peninsula S 300/K-12
5055 Saint Nicholas 31st Rd 49880 906-359-4390
Bethney Bergh, prin. Fax 359-4167

Rockford, Kent, Pop. 5,062

Rockford SD 7,500/PK-12
350 N Main St 49341 616-863-6320
Michael Shibler Ph.D., supt. Fax 866-1911
www.rockfordschools.org
Cannonsburg ES 200/K-5
4894 Sturgis Ave NE 49341 616-863-6344
Maggie Thelen, prin. Fax 863-6357
Crestwood ES 500/K-5
6350 Courtland Dr NE 49341 616-863-6346
Doug Hoogerland, prin. Fax 863-6359
East Rockford MS 900/6-8
8615 9 Mile Rd NE 49341 616-863-6140
Dan Warren, prin. Fax 863-6565
Lakes ES 500/K-5
6849 Young Ave NE 49341 616-863-6340
Blake Bowman, prin. Fax 863-6358
Meadow Ridge ES 400/PK-5
8100 Courtland Dr NE 49341 616-863-6342
Julie Devereaux, prin. Fax 866-7593
North Rockford MS 900/6-8
397 E Division St 49341 616-863-6300
Lissa Weidenfeller, prin. Fax 866-5998
Parkside ES 300/K-5
156 Lewis St 49341 616-863-6360
Sharon Wells, prin. Fax 866-2327
Roguewood ES 400/K-5
3900 Kroes St NE 49341 616-863-6374
Michael Hibbeln, prin. Fax 866-7132
Valley View ES 400/K-5
405 Summit Ave NE 49341 616-863-6366
Robert Siegel, prin. Fax 866-5995
Other Schools – See Belmont

Our Lady of Consolation S 200/PK-8
4865 11 Mile Rd NE 49341 616-866-2427
Kevin Varner, prin. Fax 866-5475
Rockford Christian S 200/PK-8
6060 Belding Rd NE 49341 616-574-6400
Jan VanderWerp, prin. Fax 874-9932

Rockwood, Wayne, Pop. 3,411

Gibraltar SD
Supt. — See Woodhaven
Chapman ES 500/PK-5
31500 Olmstead Rd 48173 734-379-6380
Susan Andrade, prin. Fax 379-6381

St. Mary S 200/K-8
32447 Church St 48173 734-379-9285
Kevin Dufresne, prin. Fax 379-9088

Rogers City, Presque Isle, Pop. 3,201

Rogers City Area SD 600/K-12
251 W Huron Ave 49779 989-734-9100
Daniel Byrne, supt. Fax 734-7428
www.rcas.k12.mi.us
Rogers City ES 200/K-5
532 W Erie St 49779 989-734-9150
Daniel Byrne, prin. Fax 734-9165

St. Ignatius S 100/1-8
545 S Third St 49779 989-734-3443
Amy Rabeau, prin. Fax 734-7671
St. John Lutheran S 100/K-8
145 N Fifth St 49779 989-734-3580
Kenneth Schroeder, prin. Fax 734-2120

Romeo, Macomb, Pop. 3,815

Romeo Community SD 5,300/K-12
316 N Main St 48065 586-752-0200
Joseph Beck, supt. Fax 752-0228
www.romeo.k12.mi.us
Moore ES 400/K-5
209 Dickenson St 48065 586-752-0260
Fax 752-0468
Romeo MS 700/6-8
297 Prospect St 48065 586-752-0240
Sam Argiri, prin. Fax 752-0256
Other Schools – See Leonard, Washington

Romulus, Wayne, Pop. 23,853

Romulus Community SD 4,000/PK-12
36540 Grant St 48174 734-532-1600
Carl Weiss, supt. Fax 532-1611
www.romulus.net/
Barth ES 500/PK-6
38207 Barth St 48174 734-532-1250
Diane Golka, prin. Fax 532-1251
Cory ES 300/K-6
35200 Smith Rd 48174 734-532-1300
Dorothy West, prin. Fax 532-1301
Halecreek ES 400/K-6
16200 Harrison 48174 734-532-1350
Jason Salhaney, prin. Fax 532-1351
Merriman ES 300/K-6
15303 Merriman Rd 48174 734-532-1400
Kay Williams, prin. Fax 532-1401
Romulus ES 400/K-6
32200 Beverly Rd 48174 734-532-1450
Marjie McAnally, prin. Fax 532-1451
Romulus MS 700/7-8
37300 Wick Rd 48174 734-532-1700
Phyllis Adkins, prin. Fax 532-1701
Wick ES 300/K-6
36900 Wick Rd 48174 734-532-1500
Shavonna Johnson, prin. Fax 532-1501

Roscommon, Roscommon, Pop. 1,105

Gerrish-Higgins SD 1,800/K-12
PO Box 825 48653 989-275-6600
Dr. Millie Mellgren, supt. Fax 275-8227
www.ghsd.net/
Roscommon ES 400/K-4
PO Box 825 48653 989-275-6610
JoEllen McNitt, prin. Fax 275-4745
Roscommon MS 600/5-8
PO Box 825 48653 989-275-6640
Ron Alden, prin. Fax 275-6053
Other Schools – See Saint Helen

Rosebush, Isabella, Pop. 341

Mount Pleasant SD
Supt. — See Mount Pleasant
Rosebush ES 200/K-4
3771 N Mission Rd 48878 989-433-2962
Mike Ross, prin. Fax 433-5801

Rose City, Ogemaw, Pop. 715

West Branch-Rose City Area SD 2,400/K-12
515 Harrington St 48654 989-343-2000
David Marston, supt. Fax 343-2006
www.wbrc.k12.mi.us/
Rose City ES 200/K-4
PO Box 407 48654 989-343-2280
Jill Retherford, prin. Fax 343-2299
Rose City MS 200/5-8
PO Box 407 48654 989-343-2250
Jill Retherford, prin. Fax 343-2299
Other Schools – See West Branch

Roseville, Macomb, Pop. 47,708

Fraser SD
Supt. — See Fraser
Dooley ECC 50/PK-PK
16170 Canberra St 48066 586-439-7600
Jean DeBruyn, prin. Fax 439-7601
Twain ES 400/K-6
30601 Calahan Rd 48066 586-439-6900
Ed Skowneski, prin. Fax 439-6901

Roseville Community SD 6,100/K-12
18975 Church St 48066 586-445-5505
John Kment, supt. Fax 771-1772
www.rcs.misd.net
Alumni Memorial ES 300/K-6
29725 John J St 48066 586-445-5740
Andrea Glynn, prin. Fax 445-5723
Arbor ES 200/K-6
19140 Meier St 48066 586-445-5745
David Van Houten, prin. Fax 445-5809
Dort ES 400/K-6
16225 Dort St 48066 586-445-5750
Charles Felker, prin. Fax 445-5753
Eastland ES 200/K-6
16221 Frazho Rd 48066 586-445-5755
Shawn Wightman, prin. Fax 445-5764
Fountain ES 400/K-6
16850 Wellington Ave 48066 586-445-5765
Judy Claseman, prin. Fax 445-5769
Huron Park ES 600/K-6
18530 Marquette St 48066 586-445-5780
Daniel Schultz, prin. Fax 445-5784
Kaiser ES 400/K-6
16700 Wildwood St 48066 586-445-5785
Wayne Johnson, prin. Fax 445-5789
Lincoln ES 300/K-6
16435 Chestnut St 48066 586-445-5790
Cathy McPherson, prin. Fax 445-5843
Patton ES 200/K-6
18851 Mckinnon St 48066 586-445-5795
Faye Bucci, prin. Fax 293-2881

Bethlehem Lutheran S 50/PK-PK
29675 Gratiot Ave 48066 586-777-9130
Kristyn Letwin, dir. Fax 777-1788

Royal Oak, Oakland, Pop. 58,299

Royal Oak SD 5,500/PK-12
1123 Lexington Blvd 48073 248-435-8400
Thomas Moline, supt. Fax 435-6170
www.royaloakschools.com
Addams ES 600/PK-5
2222 W Webster Rd 48073 248-288-3100
Judith Juneau, prin. Fax 288-3144
Keller ES 400/K-5
1505 N Campbell Rd 48067 248-542-6500
John Houghton, prin. Fax 541-1260
Northwood ES 300/K-5
926 W 12 Mile Rd 48073 248-541-0229
Carole Benedict, prin. Fax 541-4709
Oakland ES 300/K-5
2415 Brockton Ave 48067 248-542-4406
Dave Pontzious, prin. Fax 542-9289
Oak Ridge ES 400/K-5
506 E 13 Mile Rd 48073 248-588-8353
Zoe Marcus, prin. Fax 588-0750
Royal Oak MS 1,300/6-8
709 N Washington Ave 48067 248-541-7100
Cecilia Boyer, prin. Fax 541-0408
Upton ES 300/K-5
4400 Mandalay Ave 48073 248-549-4968
Sharon Ivascu, prin. Fax 549-0013

St. Dennis S 200/PK-8
1415 N Stephenson Hwy 48067 248-398-6555
Ed McCulloch, prin. Fax 398-2878
St. Mary S 200/PK-8
628 S Lafayette Ave 48067 248-545-2140
Gregory Carnacchi, prin. Fax 545-2303
St. Paul Lutheran S 100/PK-8
508 S Williams St 48067 248-546-6555
Eric Pittman, prin. Fax 546-8096

Shrine Academy — 100/7-8
3500 W 13 Mile Rd 48073 — 248-549-2925
Gabrielle Erken, prin. — Fax 549-2953
Shrine Catholic ES — 600/PK-6
1621 Linwood Ave 48067 — 248-541-4622
Sharon Dixon, prin. — Fax 541-6969

Rudyard, Chippewa
Rudyard Area SD — 700/K-12
PO Box 246 49780 — 906-478-3771
Nathan Bootz, supt. — Fax 478-3912
rudyard.eup.k12.mi.us/
Rudyard MS, PO Box 246 49780 — 200/4-8
Richard Smith, prin. — 906-478-3710
Turner-Howson ES — 200/K-3
PO Box 246 49780 — 906-478-4551
Bill Goetz, prin. — Fax 478-4600

Rudyard Christian S — 50/1-5
10702 W 17 Mile Rd 49780 — 906-478-3910
Joanna Spotts, lead tchr.

Saginaw, Saginaw, Pop. 58,361
Bridgeport-Spaulding Community SD
Supt. — See Bridgeport
Atkins ES — 900/1-6
3675 Southfield Dr 48601 — 989-777-1600
Charles Lesser, prin. — Fax 777-4652
White K — 100/PK-K
3650 Southfield Dr 48601 — 989-777-2811
Jennifer McDonald, prin. — Fax 746-0318

Buena Vista SD — 1,000/PK-12
705 N Towerline Rd 48601 — 989-755-2184
Dr. Sharron Norman, supt. — Fax 755-0286
www.bvsd.us
Brunkow ES — 200/2-5
3000 S 24th St 48601 — 989-777-5830
Betty Chaney, prin. — Fax 777-7164
Doerr Child Development Center — 200/PK-1
3200 Perkins St 48601 — 989-755-5421
Theresa Doyle, admin. — Fax 755-5145
Ricker MS — 300/6-8
1925 S Outer Dr 48601 — 989-753-6438
Helen Jiles, prin. — Fax 753-4953

Carrollton SD — 1,500/K-12
3211 Carla Dr 48604 — 989-754-1475
Craig Douglas, supt. — Fax 754-1470
www2.carrollton.k12.mi.us/
Carrollton ES — 400/2-5
3211 Carla Dr 48604 — 989-754-2425
Marc Jaremba, prin. — Fax 754-2427
Carrollton MS — 400/6-8
3211 Carla Dr 48604 — 989-753-9704
Tiffany Peterson, prin. — Fax 754-1470
Griffith ES — 200/K-1
3211 Carla Dr 48604 — 989-754-2425
Marc Jaremba, prin. — Fax 754-2427

Saginaw SD — 9,500/PK-12
550 Millard St 48607 — 989-399-6500
Thomas Barris, supt. — Fax 399-6635
www.spsd.net
Central MS — 500/6-8
1010 Hoyt Ave 48607 — 989-399-5300
Ramont Roberts, prin. — Fax 399-5315
Coulter ES — 100/PK-5
1450 Bridgeton Rd 48601 — 989-399-4050
Lynne George, prin. — Fax 399-4055
Eddy S — 500/K-8
1000 Cathay St 48601 — 989-399-5250
Trent Mosley, prin. — Fax 399-5255
Handley S - P.C.A.T. — 400/PK-5
224 N Elm St 48602 — 989-399-4250
Beverly Bowman, prin. — Fax 399-4255
Heavenrich ES — 400/PK-5
2435 Perkins St 48601 — 989-399-4300
Carol Selby, prin. — Fax 399-4305
Herig ES — 300/PK-5
1905 Houghton Ave 48602 — 989-399-4350
Susan Duran, prin. — Fax 399-4355
Houghton ES — 300/PK-5
1604 Johnson St Ste 1 48601 — 989-399-4450
Peggie Hall, prin. — Fax 399-4455
Jerome ES — 300/PK-5
1515 Sweet St 48602 — 989-399-4500
Lisa Tran, prin. — Fax 399-4505
Kempton ES — 400/K-5
3040 Davenport Ave 48602 — 989-399-4600
Dianne Willer-Dalton, prin. — Fax 399-4605
Longfellow ES — 200/PK-5
1314 Brown St 48601 — 989-399-4650
Janice Anderson, prin. — Fax 399-4655
Loomis ES — 400/PK-5
2001 Limerick St 48601 — 989-399-4750
Wilson Smith, prin. — Fax 399-4755
Merrill Park ES — 300/PK-5
1800 Grout St 48602 — 989-399-4800
Sandra Buckley, prin. — Fax 399-4805
Miller ES — 300/PK-5
2020 Brockway St 48602 — 989-399-4850
Donna Block, prin. — Fax 399-4855
Rouse ES — 200/PK-5
435 Randolph St 48601 — 989-399-5000
Ericka Taylor, prin. — Fax 399-5005
Stone ES — 300/PK-5
1006 State St 48602 — 989-399-5100
Sylvia Trevino, prin. — Fax 399-5105
Thompson MS — 800/6-8
3021 Court St 48602 — 989-399-5600
Mit Foley, prin. — Fax 399-5615
Webber S — 400/K-8
2600 Prescott Ave 48601 — 989-399-5700
Lillian Jones-Thomas, prin. — Fax 399-5715
Zilwaukee S — 400/PK-8
500 W Johnson St 48604 — 989-399-5200
Sheri Bledsoe, prin. — Fax 399-5205

Saginaw Township Community SD — 5,300/PK-12
PO Box 6278 48608 — 989-797-1800
Jerry Seese Ed.D., supt. — Fax 797-1801
stcs.org
Arrowwood ES — 500/PK-5
5410 Seidel Rd, — 989-797-1835
Sandra Braun, prin. — Fax 799-5140
Hemmeter ES — 300/K-5
1890 Hemmeter Rd, — 989-797-1832
Ron Helmer, prin. — Fax 797-1854
Plainfield ES — 300/K-5
2775 Shattuck Rd 48603 — 989-799-7630
Sandra Galko, prin. — Fax 797-1855
Sherwood ES — 500/K-5
3870 Shattuck Rd 48603 — 989-799-2382
Janet Kennelly, prin. — Fax 797-1856
Weiss ES — 300/K-5
4645 Weiss St 48603 — 989-793-5226
Mina Burns, prin. — Fax 797-1857
Westdale ES — 200/K-5
705 S Center Rd, — 989-797-1827
Karen Volk, prin. — Fax 797-1858
White Pine MS — 1,200/6-8
505 N Center Rd, — 989-797-1814
Bonnie Eaves, prin. — Fax 797-1859

Swan Valley SD — 1,800/PK-12
8380 OHern Rd 48609 — 989-921-3701
David Moore, supt. — Fax 921-3705
www.swanvalley.k12.mi.us
Havens ES — 300/PK-5
457 Van Wormer Rd 48609 — 989-921-4201
David Essmann, prin. — Fax 921-4205
Shields ES — 400/K-5
6900 Stroebel Rd 48609 — 989-921-4701
Dennis Miner, prin. — Fax 921-4705
Swan Valley MS — 400/6-8
453 Van Wormer Rd 48609 — 989-921-2601
Karsten Schlenter, prin. — Fax 921-2605

Bethlehem Lutheran S — 200/PK-8
2777 Hermansau Rd 48604 — 989-755-1146
Ronald Dressler, prin. — Fax 755-3969
Community Baptist Christian S — 100/PK-12
8331 Gratiot Rd 48609 — 989-781-2340
Vicki Torrey, prin. — Fax 781-1344
Good Shepherd ECC — 100/PK-K
5335 Brockway Rd, — 989-793-8252
Wendy Butler, prin. — Fax 793-9525
Grace Christian S — 100/PK-12
4619 Mackinaw Rd 48603 — 989-793-2129
Sharon Gamber, prin. — Fax 793-2125
Holy Cross Lutheran S — 200/PK-8
610 Court St 48602 — 989-793-9795
Roger Wolter, prin. — Fax 793-7441
Immanuel Lutheran S — 100/PK-8
8220 E Holland Rd 48601 — 989-754-4285
Dennis Neumeyer, prin. — Fax 754-0454
Peace Lutheran S — 300/PK-8
3161 Lawndale Rd 48603 — 989-792-2581
Gary Campbell, prin. — Fax 792-8266
St. Helen S — 200/PK-8
2415 N Charles St 48602 — 989-792-7781
Virginia Guevara Beer, prin. — Fax 792-1612
St. Paul Lutheran S — 100/PK-8
2745 W Genesee Ave 48602 — 989-799-3271
Michael Hein, prin. — Fax 799-1713
St. Stephen S — 300/PK-8
1300 Malzahn St 48602 — 989-793-2811
David Szymanowski, prin. — Fax 793-8463
St. Thomas Aquinas S — 400/PK-8
2136 Berberovich Dr 48603 — 989-792-2361
Sr. Ann de Guise, prin. — Fax 792-0411
SS. Peter & Paul S — 100/PK-8
4735 W Michigan Ave, — 989-799-9006
Sr. Kathleen Stafford, prin. — Fax 799-2341
Tri-City SDA S — 50/1-8
3955 Kochville Rd 48604 — 989-790-2508
Laura Muir, prin. — Fax 790-3721

Saint Charles, Saginaw, Pop. 2,169
Saint Charles Community SD — 1,200/K-12
891 W Walnut St 48655 — 989-865-9961
Michael Wallace, supt. — Fax 865-6185
www.stccs.org
Saint Charles ES — 500/K-5
801 W Walnut St 48655 — 989-865-9210
Jim Rundborg, prin. — Fax 865-2449
Thurston MS — 300/6-8
893 W Walnut St 48655 — 989-865-9927
Patricia Sowle, prin. — Fax 865-2429

Saint Clair, Saint Clair, Pop. 5,881
East China SD
Supt. — See East China
Eddy ES — 400/K-5
301 N 9th St 48079 — 810-676-1550
John Fitzmaurice, prin. — Fax 676-1560
Gearing ES — 400/K-5
200 N Carney Dr 48079 — 810-676-1650
Lynda Crandall, prin. — Fax 676-1660
Saint Clair MS — 700/6-8
4335 Yankee Rd 48079 — 810-676-1800
Michael Alley, prin. — Fax 676-1825

St. Mary S — 200/PK-8
800 Orchard St 48079 — 810-329-4150
Marilynn Pavlov, prin. — Fax 329-5705

Saint Clair Shores, Macomb, Pop. 61,896
Lake Shore SD — 3,300/K-12
28850 Harper Ave 48081 — 586-285-8480
Christopher Loria, supt. — Fax 285-8463
www.lakeshoreschools.org
Kennedy MS — 800/6-8
23101 Masonic Blvd 48082 — 586-285-8800
Pam Vermiglio, prin. — Fax 285-8804
Masonic Heights ES — 400/K-5
22100 Masonic Blvd 48082 — 586-285-8500
George Lewis, prin. — Fax 285-8504
Rodgers ES — 500/K-5
21601 Lanse St 48081 — 586-285-8600
Martha Kliebert, prin. — Fax 285-8604
Violet ES — 400/K-5
22020 Violet St 48082 — 586-285-8700
Elizabeth Netschke, prin. — Fax 285-8704

Lakeview SD — 3,000/K-12
20300 Statler St 48081 — 586-445-4000
Karl Paulson, supt. — Fax 445-4029
www.lakeview.misd.net
Ardmore ES — 300/K-5
27001 Greater Mack Ave 48081 — 586-445-4160
Kathy Simonelli, prin. — Fax 445-4524
Greenwood ES — 300/K-5
27900 Joan St 48081 — 586-445-4178
Diane Hickens, prin. — Fax 445-4181
Harmon ES — 300/K-5
24800 Harmon St 48080 — 586-445-4184
Amy Gaglio, prin. — Fax 445-4526
Jefferson MS — 700/6-8
27900 Rockwood St 48081 — 586-445-4130
David Lavender, prin. — Fax 445-4041
Princeton ES — 300/K-5
20300 Statler St 48081 — 586-445-4190
M. Nowakowski, prin. — Fax 445-4399

South Lake SD — 2,200/K-12
23101 Stadium Dr 48080 — 586-435-1600
Deborah Thompson, supt. — Fax 445-4202
www.solake.org
Avalon ES — 300/K-6
20000 Avalon St 48080 — 586-435-1000
Jeanne Poleski, prin. — Fax 445-4358
Elmwood ES — 400/K-6
22700 California St 48080 — 586-435-1100
Timothy Jalkanen, prin. — Fax 445-4338
South Lake MS — 400/7-8
21621 California St 48080 — 586-435-1300
Richard Norsigian, prin. — Fax 778-3151
Other Schools – See Eastpointe

St. Germaine S — 300/PK-8
28250 Rockwood St 48081 — 586-771-0890
Julie DeGrez, prin. — Fax 779-3667
St. Isaac Jogues S — 400/PK-8
21100 Madison St 48081 — 586-771-3525
Patricia Domagala, prin. — Fax 778-8183
St. Joan of Arc S — 500/PK-8
22415 Overlake St 48080 — 586-775-8370
Donald Ancypa, prin. — Fax 447-3574

Saint Helen, Roscommon, Pop. 2,390
Gerrish-Higgins SD
Supt. — See Roscommon
Saint Helen ES — 200/K-4
1350 N Saint Helen Rd 48656 — 989-275-6690
Kathy Rees, prin. — Fax 389-4850

Saint Ignace, Mackinac, Pop. 2,535
Moran Township SD — 100/K-8
W1828 Gros Cap Rd 49781 — 906-643-7970
William Peltier, supt. — Fax 643-7240
morantwp.eup.k12.mi.us
Gros Cap S — 100/K-8
W1828 Gros Cap Rd 49781 — 906-643-7970
Monica Silet, prin. — Fax 643-7240

Saint Ignace Area SD — 700/K-12
W429 Portage St 49781 — 906-643-8145
Mike Springsteen, supt. — Fax 643-0247
stignace.eup.k12.mi.us/
Saint Ignace ES — 200/K-4
W429 Portage St 49781 — 906-643-8500
Kari Visnaw, prin. — Fax 643-0247
Saint Ignace MS — 200/5-8
W429 Portage St 49781 — 906-643-7822
Gregg Fettig, prin. — Fax 643-7873

Saint Johns, Clinton, Pop. 7,513
Saint Johns SD — 3,300/K-12
PO Box 230 48879 — 989-227-4050
Robert Kudwa, supt. — Fax 227-4099
www.stjohns.edzone.net
East Essex ES — 100/K-2
5531 W Lowe Rd 48879 — 989-227-4100
Dr. Roberta Glaser, prin. — Fax 227-4799
East Olive ES — 200/K-5
2583 Green Rd 48879 — 989-227-4800
Pat Steinhoff-Lokey, prin. — Fax 227-4899
Eureka ES — 100/3-5
7550 N Welling Rd 48879 — 989-227-4900
Dr. Roberta Glaser, prin. — Fax 227-4999
Gateway North ES — 300/K-5
915 N Lansing St 48879 — 989-227-4600
Gretchen Baarman, prin. — Fax 227-4699
Oakview South ES — 400/K-5
1400 S Clinton Ave 48879 — 989-227-4500
Sharon Chalker, prin. — Fax 227-4599
Riley ES — 300/K-5
5935 W Pratt Rd 48879 — 989-227-5100
Melissa Dawes, prin. — Fax 227-5199
Saint Johns MS — 800/6-8
900 W Townsend Rd 48879 — 989-227-4300
Dennis Toth, prin. — Fax 227-4399

St. Joseph S — 300/K-6
201 E Cass St 48879 — 989-224-2421
Tomi Ann Schultheiss, prin. — Fax 224-1900
St. Peter Lutheran S — 100/PK-8
8982 Church Rd 48879 — 989-224-3113
David Bremer, prin. — Fax 224-8962

Saint Joseph, Berrien, Pop. 8,656
Saint Joseph SD 2,800/K-12
3275 Lincoln Ave 49085 269-926-3100
Allen Skibbe, supt. Fax 926-3103
sjschools.org/
Brown ES 300/K-5
2831 Garden Ln W 49085 269-926-3500
Craig Hubble, prin. Fax 926-3503
Clark ES 500/K-5
515 E Glenlord Rd 49085 269-926-3600
Michelle Allen, prin. Fax 926-3603
Lincoln ES 400/K-5
1102 Orchard Ave 49085 269-926-3700
Michael Wagner, prin. Fax 926-3703
Upton MS 600/6-8
800 Maiden Ln 49085 269-926-3400
Chad Mandarino, prin. Fax 926-3403

Grace Lutheran S 100/PK-8
404 E Glenlord Rd 49085 269-429-4951
David Snyder, prin. Fax 429-4797
Lake Michigan Catholic MS 100/6-8
915 Pleasant St 49085 269-983-2511
John Berlin, prin. Fax 983-0883
Lake Michigan Catholic S 300/PK-5
3165 Washington Ave 49085 269-429-0227
Jody Maher, prin. Fax 429-1461
Trinity Lutheran S 300/PK-8
613 Court St 49085 269-983-3056
Julian Petzold, prin. Fax 983-0037

Saint Louis, Gratiot, Pop. 5,445
Saint Louis SD 1,100/PK-12
113 E Saginaw St 48880 989-681-2545
Joann Spry, supt. Fax 681-5894
www.stlouisschools.net
Knause ECC 200/PK-2
121 I and K St 48880 989-681-3535
Sandy Russell, prin. Fax 681-3387
Nikkari ES 300/3-5
301 W State St 48880 989-681-5131
Carl Sztuczko, prin. Fax 681-4228
Nurnberger MS 300/6-8
312 Union St 48880 989-681-5155
Kristi Teall, prin. Fax 681-4658

Salem, Washtenaw
South Lyon Community SD
Supt. — See South Lyon
Salem ES 400/K-5
7806 Salem Rd 48175 248-573-8450
John Brickey, prin. Fax 573-8440

Saline, Washtenaw, Pop. 8,826
Saline Area SD 5,100/PK-12
200 N Ann Arbor St 48176 734-429-8000
Scot Graden, supt. Fax 429-8028
www.salineschools.com
Harvest ES 500/1-4
1155 Campus Pkwy 48176 734-944-8901
Les Sharon, prin. Fax 944-8902
Heritage S 900/5-6
290 Woodland Dr 48176 734-944-8970
Betty Rosen-Leacher, prin. Fax 944-8983
Houghton ES 100/PK-1
555 Mills Rd 48176 734-944-8960
Jesse Stevenson, prin. Fax 944-8965
Pleasant Ridge ES 500/1-4
229 Pleasant Ridge Dr 48176 734-944-8940
Sheila Light, prin. Fax 944-8945
Saline MS 900/7-8
7190 N Maple Rd 48176 734-429-8070
David Raft, prin. Fax 429-8076
Woodland Meadows ES 400/1-4
350 Woodland Dr 48176 734-944-8985
Wanda Killips, prin. Fax 944-8999

Washtenaw Christian Academy 300/PK-12
7200 Moon Rd 48176 734-429-7733
Amy Houpt, prin. Fax 944-8343

Sand Creek, Lenawee
Sand Creek Community SD 900/K-12
6518 Sand Creek Hwy 49279 517-436-3108
Steven Laundra, supt. Fax 436-3143
www.sc-aggies.us
McGregor ES 500/K-6
6850 Sand Creek Hwy 49279 517-436-3121
Micki Berg, prin. Fax 436-3143

Sand Lake, Montcalm, Pop. 512
Tri County Area SD 2,300/K-12
PO Box 79 49343 616-636-5454
James Scholten M.A., supt. Fax 636-5677
www.tricountyschools.com
Sand Lake ES 400/K-5
15 7th St 49343 616-636-5669
Krystyna Sweeney, prin. Fax 636-4894
Other Schools – See Howard City

Sandusky, Sanilac, Pop. 2,694
Sandusky Community SD 1,100/K-12
191 E Pinetree Ln 48471 810-648-3400
Martha Essenmacher, supt. Fax 648-5113
www.sandusky.k12.mi.us
Maple Valley ES 400/K-5
138 Maple Valley St 48471 810-648-2488
Adam Lulis, prin. Fax 648-5211
Sandusky MS 300/6-8
395 S Sandusky Rd 48471 810-648-3300
Fred Hicks, prin. Fax 648-5221

Sanford, Midland, Pop. 930
Meridian SD 1,300/PK-12
3361 N Meridian Rd 48657 989-687-3200
Douglas Fillmore, supt. Fax 687-3222
www.merps.k12.mi.us
Meridian ES 400/K-4
3353 N Meridian Rd 48657 989-687-3500
Sarah Barratt, prin. Fax 687-3490
Meridian JHS 500/5-8
3475 N Meridian Rd 48657 989-687-3360
Kent Boxey, prin. Fax 687-3364
Sanford ECC PK-PK
2534 N West River Rd 48657 989-687-3455
Julie Sheets, dir. Fax 687-3458

Saranac, Ionia, Pop. 1,332
Saranac Community SD 1,100/K-12
88 Pleasant St 48881 616-642-1400
Jeanette Adams, supt. Fax 642-1405
www.saranac.k12.mi.us
Harker MS 300/6-8
234 Vosper St 48881 616-642-1300
Josh Leader, prin. Fax 642-1305
Saranac ES 400/K-5
250 Pleasant St 48881 616-642-1200
Connie Hamilton, prin. Fax 642-1205

Sault Sainte Marie, Chippewa, Pop. 15,300
Sault Sainte Marie Area SD 2,700/PK-12
876 Marquette Ave 49783 906-635-6609
Daniel Reattoir Ed.D., supt. Fax 635-6642
sault.eup.k12.mi.us
Lincoln ES 400/PK-5
810 E 5th Ave 49783 906-635-6626
Dan Barry, prin. Fax 635-6666
Sault Sainte Marie MS 600/6-8
684 Marquette Ave 49783 906-635-6604
Timothy Hall, prin. Fax 635-3841
Soo Township ES 300/PK-5
5788 S M 129 49783 906-635-6630
Diane Chevillot, prin. Fax 635-6668
Washington ES 300/K-5
1200 Ryan Ave 49783 906-635-6629
Edward Chevillot, prin. Fax 635-6669

Immanuel Lutheran S 50/K-8
615 Washington Way 49783 906-632-2640
Josiah Stoering, prin. Fax 632-2640
St. Mary S 100/K-8
360 Maple St 49783 906-635-6141
Maria Farney, prin. Fax 635-6934

Sawyer, Berrien
River Valley SD
Supt. — See Three Oaks
Chikaming ES 100/K-5
13742 Three Oaks Rd 49125 269-426-4204
Garry Lange, prin. Fax 426-8491

Trinity Lutheran S 100/PK-8
PO Box 247 49125 269-426-3151
Shirley Brazinsky, prin. Fax 426-3151

Schoolcraft, Kalamazoo, Pop. 1,504
Schoolcraft Community SD 1,100/K-12
629 E Clay St 49087 269-488-7390
Douglas Knobloch, supt. Fax 488-7391
www.schoolcraftschools.org
Schoolcraft Early ES 200/K-2
629 E Clay St 49087 269-488-7200
Cynthia Stull, prin. Fax 488-7211
Schoolcraft MS 200/7-8
629 E Clay St 49087 269-488-7300
Douglas Maltby, prin. Fax 488-7303
Schoolcraft Upper ES 300/3-6
629 E Clay St 49087 269-488-7250
Douglas Ryskamp, prin. Fax 488-7269

Scotts, Kalamazoo
Climax-Scotts Community SD
Supt. — See Climax
Climax-Scotts ES 200/PK-5
11250 QR Ave E 49088 269-497-2100
Jan Lee, prin. Fax 497-2127

Vicksburg Community SD
Supt. — See Vicksburg
Tobey ES 400/PK-5
8551 Long Lake Dr E 49088 269-321-1600
Mike Barwegen, prin. Fax 321-1655

Scottville, Mason, Pop. 1,273
Mason County Central SD 1,600/PK-12
300 W Broadway Ave 49454 231-757-3713
Jeff Mount, supt. Fax 757-5716
www.mccschools.com
Mason County Central MS 500/5-8
310 W Beryl St 49454 231-757-3724
Kevin Kimes, prin. Fax 757-4820
Mason County Central Upper ES 400/3-5
505 W Maple Ave 49454 231-757-5720
Chris Etchison, prin. Fax 757-1059
Scottville ES 200/K-2
201 W Maple Ave 49454 231-757-4701
Randy Fountain, prin. Fax 757-4810
Victory ECC 50/PK-PK
4171 N Stiles Rd 49454 231-843-2410
Angie Hood, prin. Fax 845-1717

Sebewaing, Huron, Pop. 1,861
Unionville-Sebewaing SD 1,000/K-12
2203 Wildner Rd 48759 989-883-2360
John Walker, supt. Fax 883-9021
main.think-usa.org/
Unionville-Sebewaing MS 200/5-8
2203 Wildner Rd 48759 989-883-3140
Mark Gainforth, prin. Fax 883-9469
Other Schools – See Unionville

Christ the King Lutheran S 200/PK-8
612 E Bay St 48759 989-883-3730
David Kumm, prin. Fax 883-3556
New Salem Lutheran S 50/1-8
214 E Grove St 48759 989-883-3880
Paul Pappenfuss, prin. Fax 883-3880

Shaftsburg, Shiawassee
Perry SD
Supt. — See Perry
Shaftsburg ES 400/PK-5
7320 Beard Rd 48882 517-675-5115
Laura Zdybel, prin. Fax 675-5024

Shelby, Oceana, Pop. 1,971
Shelby SD 1,500/PK-12
525 N State St 49455 231-861-5211
Dana McGrew, supt. Fax 861-5416
hs.shelby.k12.mi.us/
Benona ES 100/1-5
2692 S 40th Ave 49455 231-861-4089
Donna Hieftje, prin. Fax 861-4490
ECC PK-K
155 E 6th St 49455 231-861-6629
Valerie Church-McHugh, prin. Fax 861-6764
Read ES 300/1-5
155 E 6th St 49455 231-861-5541
Fred Osborn, prin. Fax 861-6764
Shelby MS 400/6-8
525 N State St 49455 231-861-4521
Vaughn White, prin. Fax 861-0415
Other Schools – See New Era

Shelby Township, Macomb, Pop. 69,500
Utica Community SD
Supt. — See Sterling Heights
Beacon Tree ES 600/K-6
55885 Schoenherr Rd 48315 586-797-7300
Gail Clor, prin. Fax 797-7301
Crissman ES 600/K-6
53550 Wolf Dr 48316 586-797-4300
LouAnne Pisha, prin. Fax 797-4301
Duncan ES 700/K-6
14500 26 Mile Rd 48315 586-797-4600
Sharon Coil, prin. Fax 797-4601
Ewell ES 600/PK-6
51041 Shelby Rd 48316 586-797-4800
Vivian Constand, prin. Fax 797-4801
Monfort ES 600/K-6
6700 Montgomery Dr 48316 586-797-5700
Greg Seader, prin. Fax 797-5701
Morgan ES 400/K-6
53800 Mound Rd 48316 586-797-5800
Patrick Zott, prin. Fax 797-5801
Roberts ES 600/K-6
2400 Belle View Dr 48316 586-797-6100
Christine Ferber, prin. Fax 797-6101
Switzer ES 600/K-6
53200 Shelby Rd 48316 586-797-6400
Carol Pollack, prin. Fax 797-6401
West Utica ES 500/K-6
5415 W Utica Rd 48317 586-797-6600
Karen Zimmerman, prin. Fax 797-6601

Peace Lutheran S 200/PK-8
6580 24 Mile Rd 48316 586-739-2431
Jared Weiss, prin. Fax 731-8935

Shepherd, Isabella, Pop. 1,379
Shepherd SD 1,600/K-12
PO Box 219 48883 989-828-5520
Terrance Baker, supt. Fax 828-5679
www.edzone.net/~shepherd
Shepherd ES 500/K-5
168 E Maple St 48883 989-828-5998
Tom Ryan, prin. Fax 828-6947
Shepherd MS 400/6-8
150 E Hall St 48883 989-828-6605
Phyllis Hall, prin. Fax 828-6578
Other Schools – See Winn

Sheridan, Montcalm, Pop. 713
Central Montcalm SD
Supt. — See Stanton
Sheridan ES 300/PK-3
289 Saint Clair St 48884 989-831-2500
Rick Heitmeyer, prin. Fax 831-2510

Beth Haven Baptist Academy 100/K-12
1158 W Carson City Rd 48884 989-291-0555
Kevin Crowell, prin. Fax 248-3110

Skanee, Baraga
Arvon Township SD 50/K-6
21798 Skanee Rd 49962 906-524-7336
Fax 524-7394
www.arvontownshipschool.org
Skanee ES 50/K-6
21798 Skanee Rd 49962 906-524-7336
Mary Henry, prin. Fax 524-7394

Sodus, Berrien
Sodus Township SD 5 100/K-8
4439 River Rd 49126 269-925-6757
Fax 925-3144
www.remc11.k12.mi.us/river/
River S 100/K-8
4439 River Rd 49126 269-925-6757
Andres Velez, prin. Fax 925-3144

South Boardman, Kalkaska
Forest Area Community SD
Supt. — See Fife Lake
South Boardman ES 200/PK-2
5210 Boardman Rd SW 49680 231-369-2841
M.R. Gillooly, prin. Fax 369-4301

Southfield, Oakland, Pop. 76,818
Southfield SD 9,100/PK-12
24661 Lahser Rd, 248-746-8500
Wanda Cook-Robinson Ph.D., supt. Fax 746-8540
www.southfield.k12.mi.us
Adler ES 400/K-5
19100 Filmore St 48075 248-746-8870
Janet Jones, prin. Fax 746-8946

Birney MS — 800/6-8
27225 Evergreen Rd 48076 — 248-746-8800
Shawn Shackelford, prin. — Fax 352-0709
Brace-Lederle S — 800/K-8
18575 W 9 Mile Rd 48075 — 248-746-8730
Vicki Bayne-Perry, prin. — Fax 746-8854
Bussey Preschool — 50/PK-PK
19080 W 12 Mile Rd 48076 — 248-746-7350
Dr. Bailie Rosenthal, prin. — Fax 746-7354
Eisenhower ES — 400/K-5
24500 Larkins St, — 248-746-8780
Gretchen Sykes-Pitts, prin. — Fax 746-8822
Leonhard ES — 400/K-5
20900 Independence Dr 48076 — 248-746-8855
Sharon Lewis, prin. — Fax 746-8942
Levey MS — 600/6-8
25300 W 9 Mile Rd, — 248-746-8740
Rita Teague, prin. — Fax 746-8718
MacArthur K-8 University Academy — 100/K-8
24501 Fredrick St, — 248-746-8590
Bobbie Hentrel, prin. — Fax 746-8944
McIntyre ES — 400/K-5
19600 Saratoga Blvd 48076 — 248-746-7365
Kimberly Beckwith, prin. — Fax 746-7663
Schoenhals ES — 300/K-5
16500 Lincoln Dr 48076 — 248-746-7440
Paula Whitted-Lightsey, prin. — Fax 372-2543
Stevenson ES — 500/K-5
27777 Lahser Rd 48034 — 248-746-8840
Dianna Kirkland, prin. — Fax 746-8945
Thompson MS — 600/6-8
16300 Lincoln Dr 48076 — 248-746-7400
Josha Talison, prin. — Fax 746-7493
Vandenberg ES — 400/K-5
16100 Edwards Ave 48076 — 248-746-7375
Teri John, prin. — Fax 746-7617

Akiva Hebrew Day S — 300/PK-12
21100 W 12 Mile Rd 48076 — 248-386-1625
Teri Giannetti, prin. — Fax 386-1632
Early Impressions S — 100/PK-1
25000 W 10 Mile Rd, — 248-357-1740
Nancy Sallen, prin. — Fax 357-6361
Southfield Christian S — 600/K-12
28650 Lahser Rd 48034 — 248-357-3660
Margie Baldwin, prin. — Fax 357-5271
Yeshiva Beth Yehuda — 200/PK-8
15751 Lincoln Dr 48076 — 248-557-9380
Susan Colbert, dean — Fax 557-6838
Yeshivas Darchei Torah S — 300/K-12
21550 W 12 Mile Rd 48076 — 248-948-1080
Sara Kahn, prin. — Fax 948-1825

Southgate, Wayne, Pop. 29,572
Southgate Community SD — 5,800/K-12
13305 Reeck Rd Ste 100 48195 — 734-246-4600
David Peden, supt. — Fax 283-6791
www.southgateschools.com
Allen ES — 300/K-5
16500 McCann St 48195 — 734-246-4644
Timothy Flint, prin. — Fax 246-7277
Chormann ES — 300/K-5
15500 Howard St 48195 — 734-246-4650
Jill Pastor, prin. — Fax 246-7850
Fordline ES — 300/K-5
14775 Fordline St 48195 — 734-246-4640
Renne Chilson, prin. — Fax 246-7259
Gerisch MS — 800/6-7
12601 Mccann St 48195 — 734-246-4623
Eric Carlson, prin. — Fax 246-7299
Grogan ES — 400/K-5
13300 Burns St 48195 — 734-246-4642
Timothy Barlage, prin. — Fax 246-7269
North Pointe ES — 400/K-5
18635 Bowie St 48195 — 734-246-4638
Robert Wolsek, prin. — Fax 287-9467
Shelters ES — 400/K-5
12600 Fordline St 48195 — 734-246-4631
Glenn Perry, prin. — Fax 246-4653

Christ the King Lutheran S — 200/PK-8
15600 Trenton Rd 48195 — 734-285-9697
Michael Rosin, prin. — Fax 285-5275
St. Pius X S — 300/PK-8
14141 Pearl St 48195 — 734-284-6500
Michelle Seward, prin. — Fax 285-6525

South Haven, Van Buren, Pop. 5,157
South Haven SD — 2,100/PK-12
600 Elkenburg St 49090 — 269-637-0520
Robert Black, supt. — Fax 637-3025
www.shps.org
Baseline MS — 500/6-8
7357 Baseline Rd 49090 — 269-637-0530
John Weiss, prin. — Fax 639-9689
Lincoln ES — 300/PK-3
500 Elkenburg St 49090 — 269-637-0540
Carey Frost, prin. — Fax 639-8267
Maple Grove ES — 300/K-3
72399 12th Ave 49090 — 269-637-0549
Chip Jenkins, prin. — Fax 637-0550
North Shore ES — 300/4-5
7320 N Shore Dr 49090 — 269-637-0560
LaTonya Gill, prin. — Fax 639-9689

St. Basil S — 100/K-8
94 Superior St 49090 — 269-637-3529
Patricia Slasinski, prin. — Fax 639-1242
St. Paul Lutheran S — 50/K-8
718 Arbor Ct 49090 — 269-637-4459
Joseph Greefkes, prin. — Fax 639-7109

South Lyon, Oakland, Pop. 11,040
South Lyon Community SD — 7,300/K-12
345 S Warren St 48178 — 248-573-8127
William Pearson, supt. — Fax 437-8686
www.slcs.us
Bartlett ES — 400/K-5
350 School St 48178 — 248-573-8300
Stacy Cooper, prin. — Fax 573-8320
Brummer ES — 500/K-5
9919 N Rushton Rd 48178 — 248-573-8520
Dr. Mary Brun, prin. — Fax 573-8521
Centennial MS — 700/6-8
62500 9 Mile Rd 48178 — 248-573-8600
David Phillips, prin. — Fax 573-8611
Hardy ES — 500/K-5
24650 Collingwood Dr 48178 — 248-573-8650
Kim Raginia, prin. — Fax 573-8660
Kent Lake ES — 500/K-5
30181 Kent Lake Rd 48178 — 248-573-8350
Kim Dancer, prin. — Fax 486-0412
Millennium MS — 900/6-8
61526 9 Mile Rd 48178 — 248-573-8200
Maureen Altermatt, prin. — Fax 573-8231
Sayre ES — 500/K-5
23000 Valerie St 48178 — 248-573-8500
Jennifer Murphy, prin. — Fax 437-3826
Other Schools – See New Hudson, Salem

South Range, Houghton, Pop. 701
Adams Township SD
Supt. — See Painesdale
South Range ES — 200/K-6
PO Box 69 49963 — 906-482-4430
Kim Harris, prin. — Fax 487-5948

South Rockwood, Monroe, Pop. 1,590
Airport Community SD
Supt. — See Carleton
Ritter ES — 300/K-5
5650 Carleton Rockwood Rd 48179 — 734-379-5335
Robert Culter, prin. — Fax 379-0701

Sparta, Kent, Pop. 4,046
Sparta Area SD — 1,800/PK-12
465 S Union St 49345 — 616-887-8253
Kent Swinson, supt. — Fax 887-9958
www.spartaschools.org
Appleview ES — 3-5
240 E Spartan Dr 49345 — 616-887-1743
Kris Vydareny, prin. — Fax 887-7509
Ridgeview ES — 200/K-2
560 W Spartan Dr 49345 — 616-887-8218
Deb Dufour, prin. — Fax 887-1928
Sparta MS — 700/6-8
480 S State St 49345 — 616-887-8211
Joel Stoner, prin. — Fax 887-1080
White ECC — 50/PK-PK
1655 12 Mile Rd NW 49345 — 616-887-0068
Fax 887-7503

Spring Arbor, Jackson, Pop. 2,010
Western SD
Supt. — See Parma
Bean ES — 400/K-5
3201 Noble Rd 49283 — 517-841-8400
Michael Ykimoff, prin. — Fax 841-8804
Warner ES — 400/K-5
118 Star Rd 49283 — 517-841-8500
Joshua Cooper, prin. — Fax 841-8805

Springfield, Calhoun, Pop. 5,203
Battle Creek SD
Supt. — See Battle Creek
Springfield MS — 400/5-8
1023 Avenue A, — 269-965-9640
Jane Berger, prin. — Fax 962-2486

Spring Lake, Ottawa, Pop. 2,383
Grand Haven Area SD
Supt. — See Grand Haven
Lake Hills ES — 300/K-5
18181 Dogwood Dr 49456 — 616-850-5600
Susan Mueller, prin. — Fax 850-5610

Spring Lake SD — 2,100/PK-12
345 Hammond St 49456 — 616-846-5500
Dennis Furton, supt. — Fax 846-9830
www.spring-lake.k12.mi.us
Holmes ES — 300/PK-4
426 River St 49456 — 616-846-5504
Mary Keeton, prin. — Fax 847-7934
Jeffers ES — 300/PK-4
14429 Leonard Rd 49456 — 616-846-5503
Tom Koops, prin. — Fax 847-7928
Spring Lake IS — 300/5-6
345 Hammond St 49456 — 616-846-6845
Ben Lewakowski, prin. — Fax 847-7580
Spring Lake MS — 400/7-8
345 Hammond St 49456 — 616-846-5502
Scott Ely, prin. — Fax 847-7913

St. Mary S — 200/K-8
421 E Exchange St 49456 — 616-842-1282
Michael Devitt, prin. — Fax 842-8048

Springport, Jackson, Pop. 682
Springport SD — 1,100/K-12
PO Box 100 49284 — 517-857-3495
Randall Cook, supt. — Fax 857-4179
www.springportschools.net
Springport ES — 500/K-5
PO Box 100 49284 — 517-857-3465
Janis Sanford, prin. — Fax 857-3499
Springport MS — 200/6-8
PO Box 100 49284 — 517-857-3445
Tanya Overweg, prin. — Fax 857-3453

Standish, Arenac, Pop. 2,036
Standish-Sterling Community SD — 1,800/PK-12
3789 Wyatt Rd 48658 — 989-846-3670
Michael Dodge, supt. — Fax 846-7890
www.standish-sterling.org
Standish ES — 400/K-4
583 E Cedar St 48658 — 989-846-4103
Roger Fritz, prin. — Fax 846-3383
Standish-Sterling MS — 600/5-8
3789 Wyatt Rd 48658 — 989-846-4526
Beverly Skinner, prin. — Fax 846-4529
Other Schools – See Sterling

Stanton, Montcalm, Pop. 1,527
Central Montcalm SD — 1,900/PK-12
PO Box 9 48888 — 989-831-5243
Jacob Helms, supt. — Fax 831-5580
www.qualityschool.org
Central Montcalm MS — 300/7-8
1480 S Sheridan Rd 48888 — 989-831-2200
Fax 831-2210
Central Montcalm Upper ES — 400/4-6
PO Box 9 48888 — 989-831-2300
Susan Koster, prin. — Fax 831-2310
Stanton ES — 300/PK-3
710 N State St 48888 — 989-831-2400
Martin Combs, prin. — Fax 831-2410
Other Schools – See Sheridan

Stanwood, Mecosta, Pop. 206
Morley Stanwood Community SD
Supt. — See Morley
Stanwood ES — 300/K-4
156 N Front St 49346 — 231-823-2211
Douglas Beemer, prin. — Fax 823-3027

Stephenson, Menominee, Pop. 835
Stephenson Area SD — 700/K-12
PO Box 509 49887 — 906-753-2221
Roger Cole, supt. — Fax 753-4676
www.stephenson.k12.mi.us
Stephenson ES — 200/2-5
PO Box 307 49887 — 906-753-2223
Julee Nordin, prin. — Fax 753-2864
Other Schools – See Wallace

Sterling, Arenac, Pop. 511
Standish-Sterling Community SD
Supt. — See Standish
Sterling ES — 300/PK-4
PO Box 560 48659 — 989-654-2367
Clinton Potts, prin. — Fax 654-2138

Sterling Heights, Macomb, Pop. 128,034
Utica Community SD — 29,500/PK-12
11303 Greendale Dr 48312 — 586-797-1000
Christine Johns Ed.D., supt. — Fax 797-1001
www.uticak12.org/
Bemis JHS — 1,000/7-8
12500 19 Mile Rd 48313 — 586-797-2500
Joyce Spade, prin. — Fax 797-2501
Browning ES — 500/K-6
12500 19 Mile Rd 48313 — 586-797-4000
Tricia Hassell, prin. — Fax 797-4001
Burr ES — 400/K-6
41460 Ryan Rd 48314 — 586-797-4100
Suzanne Palte, prin. — Fax 797-4101
Collins ES — 400/K-6
12900 Grand Haven Dr 48312 — 586-797-4200
Brad Suggs, prin. — Fax 797-4201
DeKeyser ES — 400/K-6
39600 Atkinson Dr 48313 — 586-797-4400
Don Santilli, prin. — Fax 797-4401
Dresden ES — 500/PK-6
11400 Delvin Dr 48314 — 586-797-4500
Michelle VanDeKerkhove, prin. — Fax 797-4501
Graebner ES — 600/PK-6
41875 Saal Rd 48313 — 586-797-5000
Linda Schneider-Rediske Ed.D., prin. — Fax 797-5001
Harvey ES — 400/K-6
41700 Montroy Dr 48313 — 586-797-5100
Lisa Fontaine, prin. — Fax 797-5101
Havel ES — 500/K-6
41855 Schoenherr Rd 48313 — 586-797-5200
Kathleen Chimunatto, prin. — Fax 797-5201
Kidd ES — 500/K-6
38397 Gladstone Dr 48312 — 586-797-5300
Jason Ellis, prin. — Fax 797-5301
Magahay ES — 400/K-6
44700 Oleander Dr 48313 — 586-797-5400
Stephen Slancik, prin. — Fax 797-5401
Messmore ES — 300/K-6
8742 Dill Dr 48312 — 586-797-5600
Robert Wilcox, prin. — Fax 797-5601
Oakbrook ES — 500/PK-6
12060 Greenway Dr 48312 — 586-797-5900
Brian Shepard, prin. — Fax 797-5901
Plumbrook ES — 400/K-6
39660 Spalding Dr 48313 — 586-797-6000
Sue Balcueva, prin. — Fax 797-6001
Schuchard ES — 600/K-6
2900 Holly Dr 48310 — 586-797-6200
Karen Monahan, prin. — Fax 797-6201
Schwarzkoff ES — 700/K-6
8401 Constitution Blvd 48313 — 586-797-6300
Michael Hardy, prin. — Fax 797-6301
Walsh ES — 500/PK-6
38901 Dodge Park Rd 48312 — 586-797-6500
Lou Misovski, prin. — Fax 797-6501
Other Schools – See Macomb, Shelby Township, Utica

Warren Consolidated SD
Supt. — See Warren
Angus ES — 400/K-5
3180 Hein Dr 48310 — 586-825-2780
Lisa Fisk, prin. — Fax 698-4321
Black ES — 400/K-5
14100 Heritage Rd 48312 — 586-825-2840
Mary Caruso, prin. — Fax 698-4326
Carleton JHS — 600/6-8
8900 15 Mile Rd 48312 — 586-825-2590
Stephen Bigelow, prin. — Fax 698-4286
Fillmore ES — 400/K-5
8655 Irving Rd 48312 — 586-825-2860
Heather Shabnell, prin. — Fax 698-4336
Flynn JHS — 700/6-8
2899 Fox Hill Dr 48310 — 586-825-2900
Douglas Babcock, prin. — Fax 698-4304

Grissom JHS 700/6-8
35701 Ryan Rd 48310 586-825-2560
Shaun Greene-Beebe, prin. Fax 698-4313
Harwood ES 400/K-5
4900 Southlawn Dr 48310 586-825-2650
Kerry Keener, prin. Fax 698-4346
Hatherly ES 400/K-5
35201 Davison St 48310 586-825-2880
Joseph Konal, prin. Fax 698-4351
Holden ES 400/K-5
37565 Calka Dr 48310 586-825-2670
Cheryl Priemer, prin. Fax 698-4356
Jefferson ES 400/K-5
37555 Carol Dr 48310 586-825-2680
Jennifer Davis, prin. Fax 698-4361
Willow Woods ES 300/K-5
11001 Daniel Dr 48312 586-825-2850
Melissa Hardy, prin. Fax 698-4390

Parkway Christian S 500/PK-12
14500 Metropolitan Pkwy 48312 586-446-9900
Richard Mallino, admin. Fax 446-9904
St. Paul Lutheran S 100/PK-8
42681 Hayes Rd 48313 586-247-4645
Luther Kell, prin. Fax 247-4427
Sterling Christian S 100/PK-12
33380 Ryan Rd 48310 586-268-5420
Dwight Schultz, prin. Fax 795-0929

Stevensville, Berrien, Pop. 1,164
Lakeshore SD 2,900/PK-12
5771 Cleveland Ave 49127 269-428-1400
Donald Frank, supt. Fax 428-1574
www.lakeshoreschools.k12.mi.us
Hollywood ES 400/PK-5
143 E John Beers Rd 49127 269-428-1414
Marcy White, prin. Fax 428-1578
Lakeshore MS 700/6-8
1459 W John Beers Rd 49127 269-428-1408
William Shepard, prin. Fax 428-1571
Roosevelt ES 400/K-5
2000 El Dorado Dr 49127 269-428-1416
Marcia Bowman, prin. Fax 428-1576
Stewart ES 400/K-5
2750 Orchard Ln 49127 269-428-1418
Kathleen Boyle, prin. Fax 428-1580

Christ Lutheran S 200/PK-8
4333 Cleveland Ave 49127 269-429-7111
Charles Strohacker, prin. Fax 429-3788
St. Paul Lutheran S 100/K-8
2673 W John Beers Rd 49127 269-429-1546
Ronald Schleef, prin. Fax 429-0172

Stockbridge, Ingham, Pop. 1,279
Stockbridge Community SD 1,600/K-12
305 W Elizabeth St 49285 517-851-7188
Bruce Brown, supt. Fax 851-8334
panthernet.net
Heritage ES 400/3-5
222 Western St 49285 517-851-8600
James Kelly, prin. Fax 851-4676
Smith ES 300/K-2
100 Price Ave 49285 517-851-7735
Michelle Ruh, prin. Fax 851-4721
Stockbridge MS 400/6-8
305 W Elizabeth St 49285 517-851-8149
Sean Williams, prin. Fax 851-8334

Sturgis, Saint Joseph, Pop. 11,134
Nottawa Community SD 100/K-8
26438 M 86 49091 269-467-7153
Marcia Griffin, supt. Fax 467-6069
Nottawa S 100/K-8
26438 M 86 49091 269-467-7153
Marcia Griffin, prin. Fax 467-6069

Sturgis SD 3,100/K-12
107 W West St 49091 269-659-1500
Robert Olsen, supt. Fax 659-1584
www.sturgisps.org/
Congress ES 300/K-2
421 E Congress St 49091 269-659-1565
Teresa Belote, prin. Fax 659-1567
Eastwood ES 700/3-5
909 S Franks Ave 49091 269-659-1560
Robert Matkin, prin. Fax 659-1555
Sturgis MS 700/6-8
1400 E Lafayette St 49091 269-659-1550
Eric Anderson, prin. Fax 659-1553
Wall ES 300/K-2
702 E Lafayette St 49091 269-659-1570
Nicole Airgood, prin. Fax 659-1589
Wenzel ES 200/K-2
403 S Park St 49091 269-659-1575
Teresa Belote, prin. Fax 659-8161

Lake Area Christian S 50/PK-12
63590 Borgert Rd 49091 269-651-5135
Dean Miller, admin. Fax 651-8648
St. John Lutheran S 50/K-8
1108 E Lafayette St 49091 269-651-3240
Jerome Wolff, prin.
Trinity Lutheran S 200/PK-8
406 S Lakeview Ave 49091 269-651-4245
Paul Kosman, prin. Fax 651-2909

Sunfield, Eaton, Pop. 595
Lakewood SD
Supt. — See Lake Odessa
Sunfield ES 200/K-5
PO Box 249 48890 517-566-8110
Ann Haglund, prin. Fax 566-8770

Suttons Bay, Leelanau, Pop. 590
Suttons Bay SD 800/PK-12
PO Box 367 49682 231-271-8604
Michael Murray, supt. Fax 271-8691
www.suttonsbay.k12.mi.us
Suttons Bay ES 300/PK-4
PO Box 367 49682 231-271-8601
Roger Arvo, prin. Fax 271-8691
Suttons Bay MS 100/5-8
PO Box 367 49682 231-271-8602
Benjamin Lantz, prin. Fax 271-8691
Suttons Bay Montessori ES 50/PK-6
PO Box 367 49682 231-271-8609
Lyn Bahle, dir. Fax 271-8691

Swartz Creek, Genesee, Pop. 5,341
Carman-Ainsworth Community SD
Supt. — See Flint
Rankin ES 300/K-5
G-3459 Mundy Ave 48473 810-591-4605
Barton Zachrich, prin. Fax 591-8440

Swartz Creek Community SD 4,300/PK-12
8354 Cappy Ln 48473 810-591-2381
Dr. Jeff Pratt, supt. Fax 591-2784
www.swartzcreek.org
Crapo Child Development Center PK-PK
8197 Miller Rd 48473 810-591-4373
Lynn Cavett, dir. Fax 591-4343
Dieck ES 400/K-5
2239 Van Vleet Rd 48473 810-591-5271
Bruce Fuller, prin. Fax 591-5273
Elms Road ES 500/K-5
3259 Elms Rd 48473 810-591-1250
Mary Deschaine, prin. Fax 591-1274
Morrish ES 500/K-5
5055 Maple Ave 48473 810-591-3702
Rod Hetherton, prin. Fax 591-0580
Swartz Creek MS 1,000/6-8
8230 Crapo St 48473 810-591-1705
Kevin Klaeren, prin. Fax 591-1712
Syring ES 300/K-5
5300 Oakview Dr 48473 810-591-1301
Jane Flarity-Gram, prin. Fax 591-1303
Other Schools – See Gaines

Genesee Academy 200/PK-9
9447 Corunna Rd 48473 810-635-3890
Erum Mohiuddin, prin. Fax 635-3687

Tawas City, Iosco, Pop. 1,952
Tawas Area SD 1,500/K-12
245 W M 55 48763 989-984-2250
Donald Vernon, supt. Fax 984-2253
www.tawas.net
Bolen ES 400/K-3
211 S Plank Rd 48763 989-984-2200
Eugene Kauffman, prin. Fax 984-2203
Tawas Area MS 300/7-8
255 W M 55 48763 989-984-2150
William Grusecki, prin. Fax 984-2165
Tawas City ES 300/4-6
825 2nd St 48763 989-984-2300
Jeffrey Hutchison, prin. Fax 984-2303

Emanuel Lutheran S 100/1-8
216 North St W 48763 989-362-3622
Dennis Friske, prin. Fax 362-3622

Taylor, Wayne, Pop. 64,962
Taylor SD 9,300/PK-12
23033 Northline Rd 48180 734-374-1200
Bethany Iverson, supt. Fax 287-6083
www.taylorschools.net/
Eureka Heights ES 500/K-6
25125 Eureka Rd 48180 734-946-6597
Kristine Kunzi, prin. Fax 946-6591
Fischer ES 300/K-6
8882 Beech Daly Rd 48180 313-295-5793
Dennis Joyce, prin. Fax 295-8374
Holland ES 400/K-6
10201 Holland Rd 48180 313-295-5795
Sue Massucci, prin. Fax 295-8375
Hoover MS 500/7-8
27101 Beverly Rd 48180 313-295-5775
Teresa Winnie, prin. Fax 295-8354
Johnson Preschool Center 300/PK-PK
20701 Wohlfeil St 48180 313-295-5798
Dannielle McGuire, prin. Fax 295-8376
Kinyon ES 400/K-6
10455 Monroe Blvd 48180 313-295-5802
Brian Theil, prin. Fax 295-8377
McDowell ES 400/K-6
22929 Brest 48180 734-374-1240
Richard Kunzi, prin. Fax 374-1290
Moody ES 500/K-6
8280 Hipp St 48180 313-295-5807
Michelle Tocco, prin. Fax 295-8358
Myers ES 500/K-6
16201 Lauren St 48180 734-946-6602
Diedre Zockheem, prin. Fax 955-6847
Randall ES 500/K-6
8699 Robert St 48180 313-295-5809
Diane Allen, prin. Fax 295-8336
Sixth Grade Academy 400/6-6
13500 Pine St 48180 734-374-1227
Michelle Hernandez, prin. Fax 374-1577
Taylor Parks ES 400/K-6
20614 Pinecrest St 48180 734-374-1246
Diane Downie, prin. Fax 388-0655
West MS 700/7-8
10575 William St 48180 313-295-5783
Michael Wiltse, prin. Fax 291-2203

Baptist Park S 200/PK-12
12501 Telegraph Rd 48180 734-287-2720
Roger Cook, admin. Fax 287-2184
Oakwood Jr. Academy 50/K-8
26300 Goddard Rd 48180 313-291-6790
Miriam Troup, prin. Fax 291-5483
St. Alfred S 200/K-8
9540 Telegraph Rd 48180 313-291-0247
Ann Tonissen, prin. Fax 291-2162
St. John Lutheran S 50/PK-8
13115 Telegraph Rd 48180 734-287-3866
Rev. Richard Zeile, prin. Fax 287-0532

Tecumseh, Lenawee, Pop. 8,863
Tecumseh SD 3,400/K-12
212 N Ottawa St 49286 517-424-7318
Michael McAran, supt. Fax 423-3847
tps.k12.mi.us
Herrick Park ES 200/K-4
600 Herrick Park Dr 49286 517-423-2324
Robyn Francis, prin. Fax 423-1401
Patterson ES 300/K-4
401 N Van Buren St 49286 517-423-3331
Edward Manuszek, prin. Fax 423-1301
Tecumseh Acres ES 300/K-4
500 S Adrian St 49286 517-423-9744
Carl Lewandowski, prin. Fax 423-1400
Tecumseh MS 1,000/5-8
307 N Maumee St 49286 517-423-1105
Rick Hilderley, prin. Fax 423-1300
Other Schools – See Adrian

Lenawee SDA S 50/1-8
6801 S Occidental Rd 49286 517-423-5885
Fred Goliath, prin.

Tekonsha, Calhoun, Pop. 706
Tekonsha Community SD 300/K-12
245 S Elm St 49092 517-767-4121
Thomas Cameron, supt. Fax 767-3465
www.tekonsha.k12.mi.us
Perrine ES 100/K-4
327 Catherine St 49092 517-767-4123
Joe Huepenbecker, prin. Fax 767-3465

Temperance, Monroe, Pop. 6,542
Bedford SD 5,300/K-12
1623 W Sterns Rd 48182 734-850-6000
Ted Magrum, supt. Fax 850-6099
www.bedford.k12.mi.us
Bedford JHS 900/7-8
8405 Jackman Rd 48182 734-850-6200
Mary Zaums, prin. Fax 850-6299
Jackman Road ES 500/K-6
8008 Jackman Rd 48182 734-850-6600
Sherry Farnan, prin. Fax 850-6699
Smith Road ES 400/K-6
1135 Smith Rd 48182 734-850-6400
Carol Perz, prin. Fax 850-6499
Temperance Road ES 600/K-6
1575 W Temperance Rd 48182 734-850-6500
Bob Harris, prin. Fax 850-6599
Other Schools – See Lambertville

St. Anthony S 100/PK-8
4609 Saint Anthony Rd 48182 734-854-1160
Frances Sweet, prin. Fax 854-4622
State Line Christian S 300/K-12
6320 Lewis Ave 48182 734-847-6774
Josh Newbold, prin. Fax 847-4968

Thompsonville, Manistee, Pop. 456
Benzie County Central SD
Supt. — See Benzonia
Betsie Valley ES 200/K-5
17936 Cadillac Hwy 49683 231-378-4164
Patti Yauck, prin. Fax 378-2538

Three Oaks, Berrien, Pop. 1,768
River Valley SD 700/PK-12
15480 Three Oaks Rd 49128 269-756-9541
Robert Schroeder, supt. Fax 756-6631
www.rivervalleyschools.org/
Three Oaks ES 200/PK-5
100 Oak St 49128 269-756-9050
Garry Lange, prin. Fax 756-1420
Other Schools – See Sawyer

Three Rivers, Saint Joseph, Pop. 7,342
Three Rivers Community SD 2,800/K-12
851 6th Avenue Rd 49093 269-279-1100
Roger Rathburn, supt. Fax 279-5584
www.trschools.org
Andrews ES 200/K-5
200 S Douglas Ave 49093 269-279-1140
Cheryl Riley, prin. Fax 278-8106
Hoppin ES 300/K-5
415 N Main St 49093 269-279-1142
Sue Potts, prin. Fax 278-6096
Norton ES 300/K-5
59692 Arthur L Jones Rd 49093 269-244-1144
Lois Millet, prin. Fax 244-0500
Park ES 400/K-5
53806 Wilbur Rd 49093 269-279-1143
Fred Matusik, prin. Fax 278-7122
Three Rivers MS 700/6-8
1101 Jefferson St 49093 269-279-1130
Chad Cottingham, prin. Fax 279-1139

Immaculate Conception S 100/PK-5
601 S Douglas Ave 49093 269-273-2085
Jean Crillo, prin. Fax 273-1925

Toivola, Houghton
Elm River Township SD 50/K-6
3999 Winona Rd 49965 906-288-3751
Dennis Harbour, supt. Fax 288-3074
www.elmriver.k12.mi.us/
Elm River ES 50/K-6
3999 Winona Rd 49965 906-288-3751
Mike Aubin, lead tchr. Fax 288-3074

Traverse City, Grand Traverse, Pop. 14,513
Traverse City Area SD 8,300/PK-12
412 Webster St 49686 231-933-1725
Jim Feil, supt. Fax 933-1726
www.tcaps.net

Blair ES 300/PK-5
1625 Sawyer Rd 49684 231-933-5700
Sharon Dionne, prin. Fax 933-5703
Central ES 400/PK-5
301 W 7th St 49684 231-933-5600
Robert Peters, prin. Fax 933-5617
Cherry Knoll ES 300/PK-5
1800 3 Mile Rd N 49686 231-933-8940
Chris Parker, prin. Fax 933-8943
Courtade ES 200/PK-5
1111 Rasho Rd 49686 231-933-5800
Caroline Wacker, prin. Fax 933-5803
Eastern ES 300/K-5
1600 Eastern Ave 49686 231-933-1660
Susan Zell, prin. Fax 933-1682
Long Lake ES 200/PK-5
7738 N Long Lake Rd 49684 231-933-7800
Terri Sheldon, prin. Fax 933-7822
Montessori S at Glenn Loomis 300/PK-6
1009 S Oak St 49684 231-933-5608
Angela Camp, dir. Fax 933-3655
Old Mission Peninsula ES 200/PK-5
2735 Island View Rd 49686 231-933-7420
Patty Olson, prin. Fax 933-7442
Silver Lake ES 300/PK-5
5858 Culver Rd 49684 231-933-5760
Terry Smith, prin. Fax 933-5789
Traverse City East MS 800/6-8
1776 3 Mile Rd N 49686 231-933-7300
Glenn Solowiej, prin. Fax 933-6998
Traverse City West MS 900/6-8
3950 Silver Lake Rd 49684 231-933-8200
Pam Alfieri, prin. Fax 933-8205
Traverse Heights ES 200/PK-5
933 Rose St 49686 231-933-6500
Jessica Ziecina, prin. Fax 933-6503
Westwoods ES 300/PK-5
1500 Fisher Rd 49684 231-933-7970
Sander Scott, prin. Fax 933-8520
Willow Hill ES 300/PK-5
1250 Hill St 49684 231-933-8540
Colleen Smith, prin. Fax 933-8572
Other Schools – See Interlochen

Children's House 200/PK-6
5363 N Long Lake Rd 49684 231-929-9325
M. Shane, prin. Fax 929-9384
Holy Angels S 300/PK-2
130 E 10th St 49684 231-946-5961
Lori Phillips, prin. Fax 946-1878
Immaculate Conception S 200/3-5
218 Vine St 49684 231-947-1252
Matthew Bauman, prin. Fax 947-2508
St. Elizabeth Ann Seton MS 200/6-8
1601 3 Mile Rd N 49686 231-932-4810
Janet Troppman, prin. Fax 932-4814
Traverse Bay Christian S 100/PK-6
1895 Keystone Rd N 49686 231-929-9504
Jason Harding, admin. Fax 929-4237
Traverse City Christian ES PK-5
1514 Birmley Rd 49686 231-946-5276
Steve Stargardt, prin. Fax 946-3244
Traverse City SDA S 50/K-8
2055B 4 Mile Rd N 49686 231-947-4640
Steven Champion, prin.
Trinity Lutheran S 100/PK-8
1003 S Maple St 49684 231-946-2721
Dr. Daniel Dockery, prin. Fax 946-4796

Trenton, Wayne, Pop. 19,311
Trenton SD 3,000/K-12
2603 Charlton Rd 48183 734-676-8600
Dr. John Savel, supt. Fax 676-4851
www.trenton.k12.mi.us
Anderson ES 600/K-5
2600 Harrison Ave 48183 734-676-2177
Kathleen Gibson, prin. Fax 692-6354
Arthurs MS 700/6-8
4000 Marian Dr 48183 734-676-8700
Stephanie O'Connor, prin. Fax 676-7364
Hedke ES 400/K-5
3201 Marian Dr 48183 734-692-4563
Vince Porreca, prin. Fax 692-6355
Taylor ES 300/K-5
3700 Benson St 48183 734-676-6711
Janice Misko, prin. Fax 692-6356

St. Joseph S 200/K-8
2675 3rd St 48183 734-676-2565
Wanda Rovenskie, prin. Fax 676-9744

Troy, Oakland, Pop. 81,168
Avondale SD
Supt. — See Auburn Hills
Woodland ES 400/PK-4
6465 Livernois Rd 48098 248-537-6900
Amy Price, prin. Fax 537-6905

Birmingham SD
Supt. — See Birmingham
Pembroke ES 300/K-5
955 Eton Dr 48084 248-203-3888
Colette Ivey, prin. Fax 203-3920

Troy SD 11,900/PK-12
4400 Livernois Rd 48098 248-823-4000
Dr. Barbara Fowler, supt. Fax 823-4013
www.troy.k12.mi.us
Baker MS 600/6-8
1291 Torpey Dr 48083 248-823-4600
Larry Hahn, prin. Fax 823-4613
Barnard ES 500/K-5
3601 Forge Dr 48083 248-823-4300
Mary Haezebrouck, prin. Fax 823-4313
Bemis ES 500/K-5
3571 Northfield Pkwy 48084 248-823-4100
Janet Keeling, prin. Fax 823-4113
Boulan Park MS 700/6-8
3570 Northfield Pkwy 48084 248-823-4900
Jo Kwasny, prin. Fax 823-4913
Costello ES 400/K-5
1333 Hamman Dr 48085 248-823-3700
Gary Wood, prin. Fax 823-3713
Hamilton ES 400/K-5
5625 Northfield Pkwy 48098 248-823-4400
Dr. Pamela Mathers, prin. Fax 823-4413
Hill ES 400/K-5
4600 Forsyth Dr 48085 248-823-3500
Janice Brzezinski, prin. Fax 823-3513
Larson MS 700/6-8
2222 E Long Lake Rd 48085 248-823-4800
Dennis Seppanen, prin. Fax 823-4813
Leonard ES 500/PK-5
4401 Tallman Dr 48085 248-823-3300
Jerry Cottone, prin. Fax 823-3313
Martell ES 400/K-5
5666 Livernois Rd 48098 248-823-3800
Lois Byrne, prin. Fax 823-3813
Morse ES 400/K-5
475 Cherry Dr 48083 248-823-3200
Judith Hunsberger, prin. Fax 823-3213
Schroeder ES 400/K-5
3541 Jack Dr 48084 248-823-3600
Brian Canfield, prin. Fax 823-3613
Smith MS 700/6-8
5835 Donaldson Dr 48085 248-823-4700
Joseph Hosang, prin. Fax 823-4713
Troy Union ES 500/K-5
1340 E Square Lake Rd 48085 248-823-3100
Dr. Ronald O'Hara, prin. Fax 823-3113
Wass ES 400/K-5
2340 Willard Dr 48085 248-823-3900
Dr. Don VanDenBerghe, prin. Fax 823-3913
Wattles ES 400/K-5
3555 Ellenboro Dr 48083 248-823-3400
Dr. Judith Garrett, prin. Fax 823-3413

Warren Consolidated SD
Supt. — See Warren
Susick ES 400/K-5
2200 Castleton Dr 48083 586-825-2665
Ellen Kozich, prin. Fax 698-4376

Bethany Christian S 200/K-12
2601 John R Rd 48083 248-689-4821
Philip Fitzgerald, prin. Fax 689-3441
Brookfield Academy 300/PK-5
3950 Livernois Rd 48083 248-689-9565
Lisa Luther, prin. Fax 689-3335
Christian Leadership Academy 100/K-12
3668B Livernois Rd 48083 248-457-1510
Robin Schmidt, hdmstr. Fax 457-1520
Schoolhouse Montessori Academy 100/K-4
3305 Crooks Rd 48084 248-649-6149
Sherri Roberts, prin. Fax 649-6130
Troy Adventist Academy 50/K-8
2777 Crooks Rd 48084 248-649-3122
Rosemary Avila, prin. Fax 643-0805

Tustin, Osceola, Pop. 235
Pine River Area SD
Supt. — See Le Roy
Tustin ES 200/3-5
107 Bremer St 49688 231-829-3251
Kelly Buckmaster, prin. Fax 829-3300

Twining, Arenac, Pop. 183
Arenac Eastern SD 200/PK-12
PO Box 98 48766 989-867-4234
Rocky Aldrich, supt. Fax 867-4241
www.arenaceastern.org
Arenac Eastern S 200/PK-12
PO Box 98 48766 989-867-4234
Rocky Aldrich, prin. Fax 867-4241

Twin Lake, Muskegon, Pop. 1,328
Reeths-Puffer SD
Supt. — See Muskegon
Twin Lake ES 300/PK-4
3175 5th St 49457 231-828-6891
Wanda Groeneveld, prin. Fax 828-5028

Ubly, Sanilac, Pop. 819
Ubly Community SD 800/K-12
2020 Union St 48475 989-658-8202
Kenneth Sweeney, supt. Fax 658-2361
bearcat.ubly.k12.mi.us/
Ubly S 500/K-6
2020 Union St 48475 989-658-8261
Joel Brandel, prin. Fax 658-8564

Union City, Branch, Pop. 1,776
Union City Community SD 1,100/PK-12
430 Saint Joseph St 49094 517-741-8091
Patrick Kreger, supt. Fax 741-5205
www.unioncityschools.org/
Union City ES 300/PK-4
430 Saint Joseph St 49094 517-741-8191
Lori Vaccaro, prin. Fax 741-8415
Union City MS 400/5-8
430 Saint Joseph St 49094 517-741-5381
Brandon Bruce, prin. Fax 741-8513

Unionville, Tuscola, Pop. 594
Unionville-Sebewaing SD
Supt. — See Sebewaing
Unionville-Sebewaing ES 400/K-4
7835 N Unionville Rd 48767 989-883-9147
Elizabeth Treiber, prin. Fax 883-9193

Utica, Macomb, Pop. 4,913
Utica Community SD
Supt. — See Sterling Heights
Flickinger ES 400/K-6
45400 Vanker Ave 48317 586-797-4900
James Steere, prin. Fax 797-4901
Wiley ES 600/PK-6
47240 Shelby Rd 48317 586-797-6700
Chris Cassin, prin. Fax 797-6701

St. Lawrence S 800/K-8
44429 Utica Rd 48317 586-731-0135
Christine Lee, prin. Fax 731-5393
Trinity Lutheran S 500/PK-8
45160 Van Dyke Ave 48317 586-731-4490
Thomas Wrege, prin. Fax 731-1071

Vanderbilt, Otsego, Pop. 597
Vanderbilt Area SD 200/K-12
947 Donovan St 49795 989-983-2561
John Palmer, supt. Fax 983-3051
www.vanderbilt.k12.mi.us
Vanderbilt Area S 200/K-12
947 Donovan St 49795 989-983-2561
John Palmer, prin. Fax 983-3051

Vassar, Tuscola, Pop. 2,776
Vassar SD 1,700/PK-12
220 Athletic St 48768 989-823-8535
T. Palmer, supt. Fax 823-7823
www.vassar.k12.mi.us
Central ES 400/3-6
220 Athletic St 48768 989-823-8566
Phil Marcy, prin. Fax 823-7516
Townsend North ES 200/PK-2
220 Athletic St 48768 989-823-7722
Cheryl Weirauch, prin. Fax 823-7513
Vassar JHS 200/7-8
220 Athletic St 48768 989-823-8533
Paul Wojno, prin. Fax 823-7823

Juniata Christian S 100/K-12
5656 Washburn Rd 48768 989-843-5326
Lyle Ohman, prin.
St. Luke's Lutheran S 50/K-8
1056 Wels Ln 48768 989-823-8400
John Lange, prin. Fax 823-8400

Vermontville, Eaton, Pop. 797
Maple Valley SD 1,600/PK-12
11090 Nashville Hwy 49096 517-852-9699
Kim Kramer, supt. Fax 852-5076
mvs.k12.mi.us
Maplewood ES 300/4-6
170 Seminary St 49096 517-726-0600
Fred Davenport, prin. Fax 726-0070
Other Schools – See Nashville

Vernon, Shiawassee, Pop. 823
Corunna SD
Supt. — See Corunna
Reed ES 300/PK-5
201 E Washington Ave 48476 989-288-4094
Margy Dewey, prin. Fax 288-0945

Vestaburg, Montcalm
Vestaburg Community SD 800/K-12
7188 Avenue B 48891 989-268-5353
Donald Myers, supt. Fax 268-5852
www.vcs-k12.net
Vestaburg ES 300/K-5
7188 Avenue B 48891 989-268-5284
Kerry Kelly, prin. Fax 268-5898
Vestaburg MS 200/6-8
7188 Avenue B 48891 989-268-5883
Jeff Beal, prin. Fax 268-5898

Vicksburg, Kalamazoo, Pop. 2,189
Vicksburg Community SD 2,700/PK-12
PO Box 158 49097 269-321-1000
Charles Glaes, supt. Fax 321-1055
www.vicksburgcommunityschools.org/
Indian Lake ES 300/PK-5
11901 S 30th St 49097 269-321-1400
Rick Szabla, prin. Fax 321-1455
Sunset Lake ES 500/PK-5
201 N Boulevard St 49097 269-321-1500
Patricia Moreno, prin. Fax 321-1555
Vicksburg MS 600/6-8
348 E Prairie St 49097 269-321-1300
Greg Tibbetts, prin. Fax 321-1355
Other Schools – See Scotts

Wakefield, Gogebic, Pop. 1,956
Wakefield-Marenisco SD 300/K-12
715 Putnam St 49968 906-224-9421
Lawrence Kapugia, supt. Fax 224-1771
www.wmschools.org
Wakefield-Marenisco S 300/K-12
715 Putnam St 49968 906-224-7211
Carrie Nyman, prin. Fax 224-1771

Waldron, Hillsdale, Pop. 577
Waldron Area SD 100/K-12
13380 Waldron Rd 49288 517-286-6251
William Stitt, supt. Fax 286-6254
www.waldron.k12.mi.us/
Waldron S 100/K-12
13380 Waldron Rd 49288 517-286-6251
William Stitt, prin. Fax 286-6254

Walkerville, Oceana, Pop. 265
Walkerville SD 400/PK-12
PO Box 68 49459 231-873-4850
Philip Espinoza, supt. Fax 873-5615
www.walkerville.k12.mi.us
Walkerville ES 200/PK-5
PO Box 68 49459 231-873-5727
Philip Espinoza, prin. Fax 873-5642

Wallace, Menominee
Stephenson Area SD
Supt. — See Stephenson
Mellen ES 100/K-1
PO Box 37 49893 906-788-4218
Julee Nordin, prin. Fax 788-4301

Walled Lake, Oakland, Pop. 6,919
Walled Lake Consolidated SD 15,500/PK-12
850 Ladd Rd Bldg D 48390 248-956-2000
William Hamilton Ed.D., supt. Fax 956-2123
www.walledlake.k12.mi.us
Geisler MS 900/6-8
46720 W Pontiac Trl 48390 248-956-2900
Colleen Sturgill, prin. Fax 956-2905
Glengary ES 500/K-5
3070 Woodbury St 48390 248-956-3100
Beth Timlin, prin. Fax 956-3105
Guest ES 400/K-5
1655 Decker Rd 48390 248-956-3300
Dr. George Culbert, prin. Fax 956-3305
Oakley Park ES 400/K-5
2015 E Oakley Park Rd 48390 248-956-4100
Susan Matz, prin. Fax 956-4105
Walled Lake ES 500/K-5
1055 W West Maple Rd 48390 248-956-4300
Linda Day, prin. Fax 956-4305
Other Schools – See Commerce Township, Novi, West Bloomfield, White Lake, Wixom

---

Lakes Area Montessori S 100/PK-5
8605 Richardson Rd 48390 248-360-0500
Usha Mangrulkar, prin. Fax 737-9517
St. Matthew Lutheran S 300/PK-8
2040 S Commerce Rd 48390 248-624-7677
Susan Palka, prin. Fax 624-0685
St. William S 200/K-8
135 Oflaherty St 48390 248-669-4440
Linda Jackson, prin. Fax 669-2245

Warren, Macomb, Pop. 135,311
Center Line SD
Supt. — See Center Line
Crothers ES 200/K-5
27401 Campbell Rd 48093 586-510-2400
Eve Kaltz, prin. Fax 510-2409
Peck ES 300/K-5
11300 Engleman Rd 48089 586-510-2600
JoAnne Elkin, prin. Fax 510-2609
Roose ES 200/K-5
25310 Masch Ave 48091 586-510-2700
Greg Oke, prin. Fax 510-2709
Warren ECC 50/PK-PK
24580 Cunningham Ave 48091 586-510-2800
Tammy Schwinke, coord. Fax 510-2809

East Detroit SD
Supt. — See Eastpointe
Roosevelt ES 200/K-5
14200 Stephens Rd 48089 586-445-4655
Judy Helms, prin. Fax 445-4659

Fitzgerald SD 2,800/PK-12
23200 Ryan Rd 48091 586-757-1750
Barbara VanSweden, supt. Fax 758-0991
www.fitz.k12.mi.us
Chatterton MS 600/6-8
24333 Ryan Rd 48091 586-757-6650
Marcia Keast, prin. Fax 758-0928
Fitzgerald ECC PK-PK
24077 Warner Ave 48091 586-757-3343
Theresa Swalec, admin. Fax 759-1160
Mound Park ES 400/K-5
5356 Toepfer Rd 48091 586-757-7590
Sean DeSarbo, prin. Fax 758-0935
Schofield ES 400/K-5
21555 Warner Ave 48091 586-757-5150
Donna Anderson, prin. Fax 758-0941
Westview ES 400/K-5
24077 Warner Ave 48091 586-757-5520
Denise Kluck, prin. Fax 758-0946

Van Dyke SD 3,000/K-12
23500 Mac Arthur Blvd 48089 586-758-8333
Kathleen Spaulding, supt. Fax 759-9408
www.macomb.k12.mi.us/vandyke
Carlson ES 300/K-6
12355 Mruk Ave 48089 586-758-8345
Sharon Bienkowski, prin. Fax 758-7397
Kennedy ES 300/K-6
11333 Kaltz Ave 48089 586-758-8349
Angela Wright, prin. Fax 758-7394
Lincoln MS 600/7-8
22500 Federal Ave 48089 586-758-8320
Alena Zachery, prin. Fax 758-8322
McKinley ES 300/K-6
13173 Toepfer Rd 48089 586-758-8366
Marcia Powell, prin. Fax 778-7240
Washington ES 400/K-6
11400 Continental Ave 48089 586-758-8369
Darleen Loef, prin. Fax 758-7382

Warren Consolidated SD 15,200/K-12
31300 Anita Dr 48093 586-825-2400
Dr. Robert Livernois, supt. Fax 698-4095
www.wcskids.net
Beer MS 700/6-8
3200 Martin Rd 48092 586-574-3175
Annette Lauria, prin. Fax 698-4277
Carter MS 900/6-8
12000 Masonic Blvd 48093 586-825-2620
Dr. Kathleen Szuminski, prin. Fax 698-4295
Cromie ES 600/K-5
29797 Gilbert Dr 48093 586-574-3160
Shirley Matuszewski, prin. Fax 698-4331
Green Acres ES 500/K-5
4655 Holmes Dr 48092 586-825-2890
Marianne Ochalek, prin. Fax 698-4341
Lean ES 400/K-5
2825 Girard Dr 48092 586-574-3230
Mark Corless, prin. Fax 698-4366
Siersma ES 500/K-5
3100 Donna Ave 48091 586-574-3174
Vera Ivezaj, prin. Fax 698-4371
Wilde ES 300/K-5
32343 Bunert Rd 48088 586-294-8490
Matt Guinn, prin. Fax 698-4380
Wilkerson ES 500/K-5
12100 Masonic Blvd 48093 586-825-2550
Keith Karpinski, prin. Fax 698-4385
Other Schools – See Sterling Heights, Troy

Warren Woods SD 3,200/K-12
12900 Frazho Rd 48089 586-439-4400
Stacey Denewith-Fici, supt. Fax 353-0545
warrenwoods.misd.net
Briarwood ES 400/K-5
14100 Leisure Dr 48088 586-439-4404
Mary Tewksbury, prin. Fax 445-6335
Pinewood ES 400/K-5
14411 Bade Dr 48088 586-439-4405
Jonathon Wennstrom, prin. Fax 778-3520
Warren Woods MS 700/6-8
13400 E 12 Mile Rd 48088 586-439-4403
Jennifer McFarlane, prin. Fax 574-9830
Westwood ES 500/K-5
11999 Martin Rd 48093 586-439-4406
Cynthia Duby, prin. Fax 573-4813

Crown of Life Lutheran S 50/PK-8
25065 Eureka Dr 48091 586-427-6579
Daniel Nolte, prin. Fax 427-6579
Immaculate Conception Ukranian S 200/K-12
29500 Westbrook Ave 48092 586-574-2480
Alexandra Lawrin, prin. Fax 574-3497
Macomb Christian S 300/PK-12
28501 Lorraine Ave 48093 586-751-8980
Beverly Edwards, prin. Fax 751-7946
Peace Lutheran S 100/PK-8
11701 E 12 Mile Rd 48093 586-751-8011
Kregg Fritsch, prin. Fax 751-8558
St. Anne S 600/K-8
5920 Arden Ave 48092 586-264-2911
Anthony Sahadi, prin. Fax 264-4533
Warren Jr. Academy 50/1-8
12100 E 13 Mile Rd 48093 586-573-4740
Delores Qualls, prin. Fax 573-3788
Warren Woods Christian S 200/PK-8
14000 E 13 Mile Rd 48088 586-772-8787
Beth Denhart, admin. Fax 772-9078

Washington, Macomb
Romeo Community SD
Supt. — See Romeo
Hevel ES 400/K-5
12700 29 Mile Rd 48094 586-752-5951
Mike Phillips, prin. Fax 752-6008
Indian Hills ES 400/K-5
8401 29 Mile Rd 48095 586-752-0290
Bob Smith, prin. Fax 752-0467
Powell MS 700/6-8
62100 Jewell Rd 48094 586-752-0270
Jeffrey LaPerriere, prin. Fax 752-0276
Washington ES 500/K-5
58230 Van Dyke Rd 48094 586-781-5563
Fax 752-0470

Cross of Glory Lutheran S 100/PK-8
61095 Campground Rd 48094 586-781-9870
Douglas Fillner, prin. Fax 781-9870
Krambrooke-Griffin Academy 100/PK-8
59025 Van Dyke Rd 48094 586-992-0410
Kathy Kram, dir. Fax 992-0420

Waterford, Oakland, Pop. 74,500
Waterford SD 11,600/PK-12
1150 Scott Lake Rd 48328 248-682-7800
Robert Neu, supt. Fax 706-4862
www.waterford.k12.mi.us
Adams ES 400/K-5
3810 Clintonville Rd 48329 248-673-8900
Lynn Bigelman, prin. Fax 674-6319
Beaumont ES 400/K-5
6532 Elizabeth Lake Rd 48327 248-682-6822
Jan McCartan, prin. Fax 738-4723
Burt ES 400/K-5
581 S Winding Dr 48328 248-682-5110
Mary Barghahn, prin. Fax 738-4726
Cooley ES 400/K-5
2000 Highfield Rd 48329 248-673-0300
Sue Walton, prin. Fax 674-6322
Crary MS 800/6-8
501 N Cass Lake Rd 48328 248-682-9300
Craig Blomquist, prin. Fax 682-0220
Donelson Hills ES 400/K-5
2690 Wewoka Rd 48328 248-682-9530
Karen Gomez, prin. Fax 738-4703
Grayson ES 400/K-5
3800 W Walton Blvd 48329 248-674-0200
Laura Smith, prin. Fax 674-6383
Haviland ES 300/K-5
5305 Cass Elizabeth Rd 48327 248-682-2620
Angela Novotny, prin. Fax 738-4798
Knudsen ES 400/PK-5
5449 Crescent Rd 48327 248-682-7300
Catherine Force, prin. Fax 738-4711
Mason MS 900/6-8
3835 W Walton Blvd 48329 248-674-2281
Cheryl Ellsworth, prin. Fax 673-3718
Pierce MS 900/6-8
5145 Hatchery Rd 48329 248-674-0331
Yvonne Dixon, prin. Fax 674-4222
Riverside ES 400/K-5
5280 Farm Rd 48327 248-674-0805
Bill Gesaman, prin. Fax 674-7686
Sandburg ES 300/K-5
1355 Merry Rd 48328 248-674-0221
Jan Tirrell, prin. Fax 674-1658
Schoolcraft ES 400/K-5
6400 Maceday Dr 48329 248-623-6211
Cheryl Pocius, prin. Fax 623-2635
Stepanski ECC 400/K-K
6010 Hatchery Rd 48329 248-666-9593
Joan Mulcahy, prin. Fax 666-8669
Waterford Village ES 300/K-5
4241 Steffin Rd 48329 248-623-1091
Steve Garrison, prin. Fax 623-1186
Other Schools – See White Lake

Brookfield Academy 100/PK-5
2490 Airport Rd 48327 248-673-0008
Lisa Winkel, prin. Fax 673-8163
Marist Academy - St. Benedict Campus 200/PK-5
60 S Lynn Ave 48328 248-682-5580
Diana Atkins, prin. Fax 681-3635
Our Lady of the Lakes S 400/PK-8
5501 Dixie Hwy 48329 248-623-0340
Julie Sartori, prin. Fax 623-2274
St. Stephen Lutheran S 100/PK-8
4860 Midland Ave 48329 248-673-5906
Kristen Nelson-McKenzie, prin. Fax 673-4826
Waterford SDA S 50/K-8
5725 Pontiac Lake Rd 48327 248-682-6262
Susan Meseraull, prin. Fax 682-7164

Watersmeet, Gogebic
Watersmeet Township SD 200/K-12
PO Box 217 49969 906-358-4504
George Peterson, supt. Fax 358-4713
www.watersmeet.k12.mi.us/
Watersmeet Township S 200/K-12
PO Box 217 49969 906-358-4555
George Peterson, prin. Fax 358-3036

Watervliet, Berrien, Pop. 1,801
Watervliet SD 1,200/K-12
450 E Red Arrow Hwy 49098 269-463-5566
Robert Gabel, supt. Fax 463-6809
www.watervliet.k12.mi.us/
North ES 300/3-5
287 W Baldwin Ave 49098 269-463-6755
Kevin Schooley, prin. Fax 463-7616
South ES 200/K-2
433 Lucinda Ln 49098 269-463-6749
Darla Campbell, prin. Fax 463-7614
Watervliet MS 300/6-8
450 E Red Arrow Hwy 49098 269-463-0342
Dave Armstrong, prin. Fax 463-0325

Grace Christian S 200/PK-12
325 N M 140 49098 269-463-5545
Jonathan Kohns Ed.D., admin. Fax 463-5739
St. Joseph S 100/PK-6
188 Lucinda Ln 49098 269-463-3941
David Loebach, prin. Fax 463-4525

Wayland, Allegan, Pop. 3,948
Wayland UNSD
Supt. — See Byron Center
Baker ES 300/K-2
507 W Sycamore St 49348 269-792-9208
Celeste Diehm, prin. Fax 792-1104
Pine Street ES 400/5-6
201 Pine St 49348 269-792-1127
Jennifer Moushegian, prin. Fax 792-1103
Steeby ES 200/3-4
435 E Superior St 49348 269-792-2281
Patrick Coughlin, prin. Fax 792-1100
Wayland Union MS 500/7-8
701 Wildcat Dr 49348 269-792-2306
Carolyn Whyte, prin. Fax 792-1102

St. Therese S 100/PK-6
430 S Main St 49348 269-792-2016
Jane Gee, prin. Fax 792-6778

Wayne, Wayne, Pop. 18,589
Wayne-Westland Community SD
Supt. — See Westland
Franklin MS 700/6-8
33555 Annapolis St 48184 734-419-2400
Darlene Scott, prin. Fax 595-2401
Hoover ES 300/K-5
5400 4th St 48184 734-419-2670
Jennifer Curry, prin. Fax 595-2498
Roosevelt/McGrath ES 400/K-5
36075 Currier St 48184 734-419-2720
Linda Hammond, prin. Fax 595-2126
Taft-Galloway ES 400/K-5
4035 Gloria St 48184 734-419-2760
Stephanie Ormsby, prin. Fax 595-2574
Vandenberg ES 200/K-5
32101 Stellwagen St 48184 734-419-2770
Kim Murphy, prin. Fax 595-2584

St. Mary S 300/K-8
34516 W Michigan Ave 48184 734-721-1240
Jaylee Lynch, prin. Fax 467-7381
St. Michael Lutheran S 200/PK-8
3003 Hannan Rd 48184 734-728-3315
Harvey Schmit, prin. Fax 728-9569

Webberville, Ingham, Pop. 1,497
Webberville Community SD 700/K-12
309 E Grand River Rd 48892 517-521-3422
Brian Friddle, supt. Fax 521-4139
www.webbervilleschools.org
Webberville ES 300/K-6
202 N Main St 48892 517-521-3071
Suzi Slater, prin. Fax 521-1028

Weidman, Isabella, Pop. 696
Chippewa Hills SD
Supt. — See Remus
Weidman ES 300/PK-5
3311 N School Rd 48893 989-644-3430
Shirley Howard, prin. Fax 644-5113

Wellston, Manistee
Kaleva Norman Dickson SD
Supt. — See Brethren

Wellston ES 300/K-6
17345 6th St 49689 231-848-4244
Keith Shearer, prin. Fax 848-4297

West Bloomfield, Oakland, Pop. 67,200
Bloomfield Hills SD
Supt. — See Bloomfield Hls
West Hills MS 400/4-8
2601 Lone Pine Rd 48323 248-341-6100
Heidi Kattula, prin. Fax 341-6199

Farmington SD
Supt. — See Farmington
Eagle ES 400/K-5
29410 W 14 Mile Rd 48322 248-785-2045
Arnie Rubin, prin. Fax 626-5118

Walled Lake Consolidated SD
Supt. — See Walled Lake
Keith ES 600/K-5
2800 Keith Rd 48324 248-956-3700
Suzanne Cowles, prin. Fax 956-3705
Maple ES 500/K-5
7389 W Maple Rd 48322 248-956-3200
Susan Schreiber, prin. Fax 956-3205
Pleasant Lake ES 500/K-5
4900 Halsted Rd 48323 248-956-2800
Andrew Dale, prin. Fax 681-9950
Twin Beach ES 300/PK-5
7149 Oakley Park 48323 248-956-4200
Jeff Drewno, prin. Fax 956-4205
Walnut Creek MS 900/6-8
7601 Walnut Lake Rd 48323 248-956-2400
Joan Heinz, prin. Fax 956-2405

West Bloomfield SD 6,600/K-12
5810 Commerce Rd 48324 248-865-6420
Dr. JoAnn Andrees, supt. Fax 865-6481
www.westbloomfield.k12.mi.us/
Abbott MS 800/6-8
3380 Orchard Lake Rd 48324 248-865-3670
Amy Hughes, prin. Fax 865-3671
Doherty ES 500/K-5
3575 Walnut Lake Rd 48323 248-865-6020
Susan Crocker, prin. Fax 865-6021
Ealy ES 500/K-5
5475 W Maple Rd 48322 248-865-6210
Dr. David DeYoung, prin. Fax 865-6211
Green ES 500/K-5
4500 Walnut Lake Rd 48323 248-865-6370
Katherine Sheiko, prin. Fax 865-6371
Gretchko ES 200/K-1
5300 Greer Rd 48324 248-865-6570
Sally Drummond, prin. Fax 865-6571
Orchard Lake MS 800/6-8
6000 Orchard Lake Rd 48322 248-865-4480
Sonja James, prin. Fax 865-4481
Scotch ES 700/2-5
5959 Commerce Rd 48324 248-865-3280
Jeremey Whan, prin. Fax 865-3281
Other Schools – See Keego Harbor

Bloomfield Maples Montessori S 100/PK-3
6201 W Maple Rd 48322 248-737-9516
Usha Mangrulkar, prin. Fax 737-9517
Brookfield Academy 100/PK-5
2965 Walnut Lake Rd 48323 248-626-6665
Kelly Randazzo, prin. Fax 626-3690

West Branch, Ogemaw, Pop. 1,905
West Branch-Rose City Area SD
Supt. — See Rose City
Surline ES 500/K-4
PO Box 308 48661 989-343-2190
Gail Hughey, prin. Fax 343-2200
Surline MS 600/5-8
PO Box 308 48661 989-343-2140
Patsy Marchel, prin. Fax 343-2239

Ogemaw Hills Christian S 100/PK-6
2106 S Gray Rd 48661 989-345-2084
Carol Powell, admin. Fax 345-2094
St. Joseph S 100/K-8
935 W Houghton Ave 48661 989-345-0220
Lorrene Spaulding, prin. Fax 345-3030

Westland, Wayne, Pop. 85,623
Livonia SD
Supt. — See Livonia
Cooper ES 800/5-6
28550 Ann Arbor Trl 48185 734-744-2710
Heidi Frazer-Cherry, prin. Fax 744-2712
Hayes ES 400/K-4
30600 Louise St 48185 734-744-2725
Dr. Ernest Terry, prin. Fax 744-2727
Johnson ES 700/5-6
8400 N Hix Rd 48185 734-744-2740
Richard Steele, prin. Fax 744-2742

Wayne-Westland Community SD 13,700/PK-12
36745 Marquette St 48185 734-419-2000
Dr. Gregory Baracy, supt. Fax 595-2123
www.wwcsd.net/
Adams MS 700/6-8
33475 Palmer Rd 48186 734-419-2380
John Besek, prin. Fax 595-2374
Edison ES 400/K-5
34505 Hunter Ave 48185 734-419-2600
Barbara Hastings, prin. Fax 595-2368
Elliott ES 300/K-5
30800 Bennington St 48186 734-419-2610
Johnnye Summerville Ed.D., prin. Fax 595-2430
Graham ES 400/K-5
1255 S John Hix St 48186 734-419-2620
Dan Briody, prin. Fax 595-2483
Hamilton ES 300/K-5
1031 S Schuman St 48186 734-419-2650
April Quasarano, prin. Fax 595-2488
Jefferson-Barns ES 200/K-5
32150 Dorsey St 48186 734-419-2680
Laura Beckman, prin. Fax 595-2553
Kettering ES 400/K-5
1200 S Hubbard St 48186 734-419-2690
Paula Hotaling Ph.D., prin. Fax 595-2554
Lincoln ES 300/K-5
33800 Grand Traverse St 48186 734-419-2700
Jennifer Munson, prin. Fax 595-2558
Madison ES 400/K-5
1075 S Carlson St 48186 734-419-2710
Sandy Kingston, prin. Fax 595-2559
Marshall MS 900/6-8
35100 Bay View St 48186 734-419-2277
Paul Salah Ph.D., prin. Fax 595-2588
Patchin ES 400/K-5
6420 N Newburgh Rd 48185 734-419-2740
Molly Funk, prin. Fax 595-2569
Schweitzer ES 400/K-5
2601 Treadwell St 48186 734-419-2750
Mary Anne Garzon, prin. Fax 595-2564
Stevenson MS 800/6-8
38501 Palmer Rd 48186 734-419-2350
Ginny O'Brien, prin. Fax 595-2692
Stottlemyer ECC 500/PK-PK
34801 Marquette St 48185 734-419-2645
Ron Barratt, prin. Fax 595-2573
Wildwood ES 300/K-5
500 N Wildwood St 48185 734-419-2790
Amy McCusker, prin. Fax 595-2579
Other Schools – See Canton, Inkster, Wayne

St. Damian S 200/PK-8
29891 Joy Rd 48185 734-427-1680
Mary Stempin, prin. Fax 427-1272
St. John Lutheran S 100/PK-8
2602 S Wayne Rd 48186 734-721-4650
Lori Bartholomew, prin. Fax 721-4650
St. Matthew Lutheran S 200/PK-8
5885 N Venoy Rd 48185 734-425-0261
Judy Schwaegerle, prin. Fax 425-7932

West Olive, Ottawa
West Ottawa SD
Supt. — See Holland
Sheldon Woods ES 200/K-5
15050 Blair St 49460 616-786-1700
Karen Abraham, prin. Fax 786-1791

Westphalia, Clinton, Pop. 835
Pewamo-Westphalia SD 300/K-12
5101 S Clintonia Rd 48894 989-587-5100
Ronald Simon, supt. Fax 587-5120
www.pw.k12.mi.us
Other Schools – See Pewamo

St. Mary S 300/1-6
209 N Westphalia St 48894 989-587-3702
Raymond Rzepecki, prin. Fax 587-3706

White Cloud, Newaygo, Pop. 1,432
White Cloud SD 1,100/PK-12
PO Box 1003 49349 231-689-6820
Tim Rossler, supt. Fax 689-3210
www.whitecloud.net
Jones ES 100/PK-1
PO Box 1002 49349 231-689-1295
Lorie Watson, prin. Fax 689-3208
White Cloud MS 300/6-8
PO Box 1001 49349 231-689-2181
Tom Cameron, prin. Fax 689-3339
White Cloud Upper ES 400/2-5
PO Box 1007 49349 231-689-2300
Lorie Watson, prin. Fax 689-2323

Whitehall, Muskegon, Pop. 2,839
Whitehall SD 2,000/PK-12
541 E Slocum St 49461 231-893-1005
Darlene Dongvillo, supt. Fax 894-6450
www.whitehall.k12.mi.us
Ealy ES 500/3-5
425 E Sophia St 49461 231-893-1040
David Rodgers, prin. Fax 894-9060
Shoreline ES 300/PK-2
205 E Market St 49461 231-893-1050
David Hundt, prin. Fax 893-4705
Whitehall MS 500/6-8
401 S Elizabeth St 49461 231-893-1030
Dale McKenzie, prin. Fax 894-6844

White Lake, Oakland, Pop. 22,608
Huron Valley SD
Supt. — See Highland
Brooks ES 300/K-5
1000 Hill Rd 48383 248-684-8050
Steven Chisik, prin. Fax 676-8460
Lakewood ES 400/K-5
1500 Bogie Lake Rd 48383 248-684-8030
Julie Bedford, prin. Fax 684-8069
Oxbow ES 400/K-5
100 Oxbow Lake Rd 48386 248-684-8085
Peg Berry, prin. Fax 676-8436
White Lake MS 600/6-8
1450 Bogie Lake Rd 48383 248-684-8004
Paul Gmelin, prin. Fax 676-8437

Walled Lake Consolidated SD
Supt. — See Walled Lake
Dublin ES 500/K-5
425 Farnsworth St 48386 248-956-3800
Dr. Ronald Thorin, prin. Fax 956-3805

Waterford SD
Supt. — See Waterford
Houghton ES 400/K-5
8080 Elizabeth Lake Rd 48386 248-698-9230
Ray Nester, prin. Fax 698-9146

St. Patrick S 500/K-8
9040 Hutchins St 48386 248-698-3240
Carol Budchuck, prin. Fax 698-4339

White Pigeon, Saint Joseph, Pop. 1,599
White Pigeon Community SD 800/K-12
410 Prairie Ave 49099 269-483-7676
Ronald Drzewicki, supt. Fax 483-2256
www.wpcschools.org
Central ES 400/K-6
305 E Hotchin Ave 49099 269-483-7107
Nicole Airgood, prin. Fax 483-8742
White Pigeon MS 100/7-8
410 Prairie Ave 49099 269-483-7679
Patrick West, prin. Fax 483-2256

Whitmore Lake, Washtenaw, Pop. 3,251
Whitmore Lake SD 1,200/K-12
8845 Main St 48189 734-449-4464
Kimberley Hart, supt. Fax 449-5336
www.wlps.net/
Whitmore Lake ES 400/K-4
1077 Barker Rd 48189 734-449-2051
Mary Anne Waters, prin. Fax 449-9376
Whitmore Lake MS 400/5-8
8877 Main St 48189 734-449-4715
Michael Benczarski, prin. Fax 449-1042

Whittemore, Iosco, Pop. 462
Whittemore-Prescott Area SD 1,000/PK-12
PO Box 250 48770 989-756-2500
Ted Matuszak, supt. Fax 756-2278
www.wpas.net/
Whittemore-Prescott ECC 100/PK-K
PO Box 250 48770 989-756-4120
Marilyn Herriman, prin. Fax 756-4407
Whittemore-Prescott ES 400/1-4
8878 Prescott Rd 48770 989-756-2881
Marilyn Herriman, prin. Fax 756-3097
Whittemore-Prescott JHS 200/5-8
8878 Prescott Rd 48770 989-873-4986
Dorothy Miller, prin. Fax 873-6096

Williamsburg, Grand Traverse
Elk Rapids SD
Supt. — See Elk Rapids
Mill Creek ES 300/K-5
9039 Old M 72 49690 231-267-9955
Margaret Antcliff, prin. Fax 267-5215

Williamston, Ingham, Pop. 3,790
Williamston Community SD 1,800/PK-12
418 Highland St 48895 517-655-4361
Joel Raddatz, supt. Fax 655-7500
www.gowcs.net/
Discovery ES 200/PK-2
350 Highland St 48895 517-655-2855
Bronwyn Cobb, prin. Fax 655-7504
Explorer ES 400/3-5
416 Highland St 48895 517-655-2174
Brian DeRath, prin. Fax 655-7503
Williamston MS 500/6-8
3845 Vanneter Rd 48895 517-655-4668
Christine Sermak, prin. Fax 655-7502

Memorial Lutheran S 100/K-8
2070 E Sherwood Rd 48895 517-655-1402
Joshua Pederson, prin. Fax 655-1402
St. Mary S 100/PK-5
220 N Cedar St 48895 517-655-4038
Katherine White, prin. Fax 655-3855

Wilson, Menominee, Pop. 1,391

Wilson Jr. Academy 50/1-10
N13925 County Road 551 49896 906-639-2566
Scott Johnson, prin. Fax 639-2566

Winn, Isabella
Shepherd SD
Supt. — See Shepherd
Winn ES 200/K-5
PO Box 338 48896 989-866-2250
Kim Stegman, prin. Fax 866-2740

Wixom, Oakland, Pop. 13,384
Walled Lake Consolidated SD
Supt. — See Walled Lake
Banks MS 900/6-8
1760 Charms Rd 48393 248-956-2200
Mark Hess, prin. Fax 956-2205
Loon Lake ES 500/K-5
2151 Loon Lake Rd 48393 248-956-4000
Robert Furca, prin. Fax 956-4005
Wixom ES 600/K-5
301 N Wixom Rd 48393 248-956-3400
Alec Bender, prin. Fax 956-3405

Wixom Christian S 100/PK-12
620 N Wixom Rd 48393 248-624-4362
Brad Stille, admin. Fax 624-1068

Wolverine, Cheboygan, Pop. 352
Wolverine Community SD 400/K-12
PO Box 219 49799 231-525-8201
Susan Denise, supt. Fax 525-8591
www.wolverine.k12.mi.us
Wolverine Community ES 200/K-6
PO Box 219 49799 231-525-8252
Susan Denise, prin. Fax 525-8591

Woodhaven, Wayne, Pop. 13,354
Gibraltar SD 3,700/PK-12
19370 Vreeland Rd 48183 734-379-6350
Fax 379-6353
www.gibdist.net
Weiss ES 300/PK-5
26631 Reaume St 48183 734-379-7060
Cindy Hoffman, prin. Fax 379-7061

Other Schools – See Brownstown Twp, Gibraltar, Rockwood

Woodhaven-Brownstown SD
Supt. — See Brownstown
Bates ES 500/K-5
22811 Gudith Rd 48183 734-692-2217
Paul Elsey, prin. Fax 692-2235
Erving ES 500/K-5
24175 Hall Rd 48183 734-692-2212
Matthew Czajkowski, prin. Fax 692-2211
Yake ES 500/K-5
16400 Carter Rd 48183 734-692-2230
Andrea Stevenson, prin. Fax 692-2234

Woodland, Barry, Pop. 501
Lakewood SD
Supt. — See Lake Odessa
Lakewood MS 500/6-8
8699 Brown Rd 48897 616-374-2400
David Nisbet, prin. Fax 374-2424
Woodland ES 200/K-5
223 W Broadway St 48897 269-367-4935
Michelle Sharp, prin. Fax 367-4771

Wyandotte, Wayne, Pop. 26,940
Wyandotte SD 4,300/PK-12
PO Box 130 48192 734-759-5000
Dr. Patricia Cole, supt. Fax 759-6009
www.wyandotte.org
Garfield ES 300/PK-5
340 Superior Blvd 48192 734-759-5500
Cindy Wright, prin. Fax 759-5509
Jefferson ES 300/PK-5
1515 15th St 48192 734-759-5600
Carol Makuch, prin. Fax 759-5609
Monroe ES 300/K-5
1501 Grove St 48192 734-759-5800
Vicki Wilson, prin. Fax 759-5809
Taft ES 300/PK-5
891 Goddard St 48192 734-759-5900
Kelly Kazmierski, prin. Fax 759-5909
Washington ES 300/PK-5
1440 Superior Blvd 48192 734-759-6100
Kristin McMaster, prin. Fax 759-6109
Wilson MS 600/6-8
1275 15th St 48192 734-759-5300
Thomas Kell, prin. Fax 759-5309

Our Lady of Mt. Carmel S 200/PK-8
2609 10th St 48192 734-285-5520
Timothy Scanlon, prin. Fax 285-9245
Wyandotte Consolidated S 100/K-8
3051 4th St 48192 734-285-2030
David McCarney, prin. Fax 285-0327

Wyoming, Kent, Pop. 70,122
Godfrey-Lee SD 1,500/PK-12
1324 Burton St SW 49509 616-241-4722
Jack Wallington, supt. Fax 241-4707
www.godfrey-lee.k12.mi.us
Godfrey ES 300/3-5
1920 Godfrey Ave SW 49509 616-243-0533
Jane Dykhouse, prin. Fax 475-6618
Lee ECC 400/PK-2
961 Joosten St SW 49509 616-452-8703
Bruce Clapp, prin. Fax 475-6628
Lee MS 300/6-8
1335 Lee St SW 49509 616-452-3297
David Britten, prin. Fax 475-6619

Godwin Heights SD 2,000/PK-12
15 36th St SW 49548 616-252-2090
Valdis Gailitis, supt. Fax 252-2232
www.godwinschools.org
Godwin Heights MS 300/7-8
111 36th St SE 49548 616-252-2070
Dan Vandermeulen, prin. Fax 252-2075
North Godwin ES 300/K-6
161 34th St SW 49548 616-252-2010
William Fetterhoff, prin. Fax 252-2011
South Godwin ES 300/K-6
28 Bellevue St SE 49548 616-252-2020
Mary Lang, prin. Fax 252-2021
West Godwin ES 400/PK-6
3546 Clyde Park Ave SW 49509 616-252-2030
Chad Tolson, prin. Fax 252-2031

Wyoming SD 4,500/PK-12
3575 Gladiola Ave SW, 616-530-7550
Jon Felske, supt. Fax 530-7557
www.wyoming.k12.mi.us
Gladiola ES 400/K-5
3500 Gladiola Ave SW, 616-530-7596
Bruce Cook, prin. Fax 249-7623
Huntington Woods ECC 400/PK-PK
4334 Byron Center Ave SW, 616-530-7561
Harry Knol, dir. Fax 249-7656
Jackson Park IS 200/5-6
1331 33rd St SW 49509 616-530-7540
Kirk Bloomquist, prin. Fax 249-7659
Newhall MS 500/7-8
1840 38th St SW, 616-530-7590
Adrian Lamar, prin. Fax 249-7673
Oriole Park ES 400/K-6
1420 40th St SW 49509 616-530-7558
Craig Hoekstra, prin. Fax 249-7624
Parkview ES 400/K-5
2075 Lee St SW, 616-530-7572
Andrea van der Laan, prin. Fax 249-7625
Taft ES 300/K-5
2700 Taft Ave SW, 616-530-7548
John Blackburn, prin. Fax 249-7699
West ES 300/K-5
3600 Byron Center Ave SW, 616-530-7533
Michael Sturm, prin. Fax 249-7606

Adams Protestant Reformed Christian S 200/K-9
5539 Byron Center Ave SW, 616-531-0748
David Harbach, prin. Fax 531-5172
Calvin Christian S 200/PK-6
601 36th St SW 49509 616-531-2700
Bob Van Wieren, prin. Fax 531-9340
Holy Trinity Evangelical Lutheran S 100/PK-8
4201 Burlingame Ave SW 49509 616-538-1122
Larry Sellnow, prin. Fax 538-1122
St. John Vianney Preschool PK-PK
900 Floyd St SW 49509 616-534-5392
Kelly Robertston, prin. Fax 532-8224
St. John Vianney S 300/K-8
4101 Clyde Park Ave SW 49509 616-532-7001
Tom Priest, prin. Fax 532-1884
Tri-Unity Christian ES 200/PK-6
2222 44th St SW, 616-530-6096
Debra Blanker, admin. Fax 530-6384

Yale, Saint Clair, Pop. 1,993
Yale SD 2,300/K-12
198 School Dr 48097 810-387-4274
Frank Johnson, supt. Fax 387-4418
www.yale.k12.mi.us
Yale ES 400/K-5
200 School Dr 48097 810-387-3231
Suzanne Guttowsky, prin. Fax 387-9413
Yale JHS 600/6-8
198 School Dr 48097 810-387-3231
Joseph Haynes, prin. Fax 387-9207
Other Schools – See Avoca, Emmett

Emanuel-Redeemer Lutheran S 50/K-9
11089 Yale Rd 48097 810-387-2906
Joel Neumann, prin. Fax 387-2906

Ypsilanti, Washtenaw, Pop. 21,832
Lincoln Consolidated SD 5,200/PK-12
8970 Whittaker Rd 48197 734-484-7000
Lynn Cleary, supt. Fax 484-1212
lincoln.k12.mi.us
Brick ES 700/1-5
8970 Whittaker Rd 48197 734-484-7031
Donald Goven, prin. Fax 484-7049
Childs ES 500/K-5
7300 Bemis Rd 48197 734-484-7035
Jeffery Petzak, prin. Fax 484-7048
Lincoln ECC 50/PK-PK
8850 Whittaker Rd 48197 734-484-7070
Mary Aldridge, dir. Fax 484-7047
Lincoln MS 1,200/6-8
8744 Whittaker Rd 48197 734-484-7033
Michael Furnas, prin. Fax 484-7088
Model K 400/K-K
8850 Whittaker Rd 48197 734-484-7045
Mary Aldrich, prin. Fax 484-7047
Redner ES 500/1-5
8888 Whittaker Rd 48197 734-484-7061
David Northrop, prin. Fax 484-7064
Other Schools – See Belleville

Van Buren SD 6,400/K-12
3110 S Grove St 48198 734-697-9123
Pete Lazaroff, supt. Fax 482-3306
www.vanburenschools.net
Rawsonville ES 400/K-5
3110 S Grove St 48198 734-482-9845
Susan Farber, prin. Fax 482-3306
Other Schools – See Belleville

Willow Run Community SD 2,400/K-12
235 Spencer Ln 48198 734-481-8200
Dr. Doris Hope-Jackson, supt. Fax 481-8151
www.wrcs.k12.mi.us/
Cheney Academy of Math & Science 200/K-8
1500 Stamford Rd 48198 734-481-8270
Kelly Webb, prin. Fax 481-8174
Ford ES 200/1-5
2440 E Clark Rd 48198 734-481-8275
Joe Ann Allen, prin. Fax 481-8186
Holmes ES 400/K-5
1255 Holmes Rd 48198 734-481-8280
Rosalind Coffey, prin. Fax 481-8175
Kaiser ES 200/K-5
670 Onandago St 48198 734-481-8284
Laura Lisiscki, prin. Fax 481-8172
Kettering ES 200/K-5
1633 Knowles St 48198 734-481-8288
Delores Jenkins, prin. Fax 481-8179
Willow Run MS 600/6-8
235 Spencer Ln 48198 734-481-8125
Larry Gray, prin. Fax 481-8170

Ypsilanti SD 4,100/PK-12
1885 Packard Rd 48197 734-714-1218
Dr. James Hawkins, supt. Fax 714-1220
www.ypsd.org
Adams ES 300/1-5
503 Oak St 48198 734-714-1650
Connie Thompson, prin. Fax 714-1653
Chapelle ES 300/1-5
111 S Wallace Blvd 48197 734-714-1700
Joe Guillen, prin. Fax 714-1717
East MS 400/6-8
510 Emerick St 48198 734-714-1400
Candice Churchwell, prin. Fax 714-1423
Erickson ES 400/1-5
1427 Levona St 48198 734-714-1600
Kevin Carney, prin. Fax 714-1603
Estabrook ES 400/1-5
1555 W Cross St 48197 734-714-1900
Pat DeRossett, prin. Fax 714-1903
Perry Child Development Center 400/PK-K
550 Perry St 48197 734-714-1750
C. Sharine Buddin, prin. Fax 714-1754
West MS 500/6-8
105 N Mansfield St 48197 734-714-1300
Monica Merritt, prin. Fax 714-1303

Calvary Christian Academy 200/K-12
1007 Ecorse Rd 48198 734-482-1990
Cathy White, prin. Fax 484-5118
Huron Valley Catholic S 200/PK-8
1300 N Prospect Rd 48198 734-483-0366
Timothy Kotyuk, prin. Fax 483-0372

Zeeland, Ottawa, Pop. 5,532
Zeeland SD 4,800/PK-12
PO Box 110 49464 616-748-3000
Gary Feenstra, supt. Fax 748-3035
www.zps.org/
Cityside MS 700/6-8
320 E Main Ave 49464 616-748-3200
Jon Voss, prin. Fax 748-3210
Creekside MS 400/6-8
179 W Roosevelt Ave 49464 616-748-3300
Greg Eding, prin. Fax 748-3325
Lincoln ES 400/1-5
60 E Lincoln Ave 49464 616-748-3350
Tom DeGraaf, prin. Fax 772-7374
New Groningen ES 400/1-5
10542 Chicago Dr 49464 616-748-3375
James Schoettle, prin. Fax 772-7389
Quincy ES 300/K-5
10155 Quincy St 49464 616-748-4700
Ellen Kontowicz, prin. Fax 748-4705
Roosevelt ES 400/1-5
175 W Roosevelt Ave 49464 616-748-3050
Judy Bierlein, prin. Fax 748-3016
Woodbridge ES 400/1-5
9110 Woodbridge St 49464 616-748-3400
Mike Dalman, prin. Fax 748-1436
Zeeland ECC 50/PK-K
140 W McKinley Ave 49464 616-748-3275
Mary Colton, prin. Fax 748-1428

Borculo Christian S 100/PK-8
6830 96th Ave 49464 616-875-8152
Randy Hazenberg, prin. Fax 875-2236
Zeeland Christian S 600/PK-8
334 W Central Ave 49464 616-772-2609
William Van Dyk, prin. Fax 772-2706

MINNESOTA

MN DEPARTMENT OF EDUCATION
1500 Highway 36 W, Roseville 55113-4035
Telephone 651-582-8200
Website cfl.state.mn.us

Commissioner of Education   Alice Seagren

PUBLIC, PRIVATE AND CATHOLIC ELEMENTARY SCHOOLS

Ada, Norman, Pop. 1,555
Ada-Borup SD 2854   500/PK-12
604 W Thorpe Ave 56510   218-784-5300
Gerald Hansen, supt.   Fax 784-3475
www.ada.k12.mn.us
Ada ES   200/PK-4
209 6th St W 56510   218-784-5303
Ollen Church, prin.   Fax 784-2039
Other Schools – See Borup

Adams, Mower, Pop. 782
Southland SD 500   700/K-12
PO Box 351 55909   507-582-3283
Steve Sallee, supt.   Fax 582-7813
www.isd500.k12.mn.us
Southland MS   200/6-8
PO Box 351 55909   507-582-3568
Ryan Luft, prin.   Fax 582-7813
Other Schools – See Rose Creek

Sacred Heart S   100/1-8
PO Box 249 55909   507-582-3120
Shawn Kennedy, prin.   Fax 582-1033

Adrian, Nobles, Pop. 1,231
Adrian SD 511   700/PK-12
PO Box 40 56110   507-483-2266
Roger Graff, supt.   Fax 483-2342
www.adrianschool.net
Adrian ES   300/PK-5
PO Box 40 56110   507-483-2225
Russell Lofthus, prin.   Fax 483-2461
Adrian MS   200/6-8
PO Box 40 56110   507-483-2232
Tim Christensen, prin.   Fax 483-2375

Aitkin, Aitkin, Pop. 1,997
Aitkin SD 1   1,300/PK-12
306 2nd St NW 56431   218-927-2115
Bernie Novak, supt.   Fax 927-4234
www.aitkin.k12.mn.us
Rippleside ES   700/PK-6
225 2nd Ave SW 56431   218-927-4838
Allan Albertson, prin.   Fax 927-4234
Other Schools – See Palisade

Albany, Stearns, Pop. 2,007
Albany SD 745   1,700/PK-12
PO Box 330 56307   320-845-2171
Dr. Scott Thielman, supt.   Fax 845-4017
www.albany.k12.mn.us
Albany ES   600/PK-6
PO Box 330 56307   320-845-2161
Ann Schultz, prin.   Fax 845-2165
Albany JHS   200/7-8
PO Box 330 56307   320-845-2171
Charles Griffith, prin.   Fax 845-4017
Avon ES   400/PK-6
PO Box 330 56307   320-356-7346
Jean Weis-Clough, prin.   Fax 356-2241

Holy Family S   100/K-6
PO Box 675 56307   320-845-2011
Bonnie Massmann, prin.   Fax 845-7380

Albert Lea, Freeborn, Pop. 17,915
Albert Lea SD 241   3,500/K-12
211 W Richway Dr 56007   507-379-4800
Mike Funk, supt.   Fax 379-4898
albertlea.k12.mn.us
Halverson ES   400/K-6
707 E 10th St 56007   507-379-4900
Delano Stein, prin.   Fax 379-4958
Hawthorne ES   400/K-6
1000 E Hawthorne St 56007   507-379-4960
Corrine Tims, prin.   Fax 379-5018
Lakeview ES   500/K-6
902 Abbott St 56007   507-379-5020
Jean Jordan, prin.   Fax 379-5078
Sibley ES   400/K-6
1501 W Front St 56007   507-379-5080
Ross Williams, prin.   Fax 379-5138
Southwest MS   500/7-8
1601 W Front St 56007   507-379-5240
Marsha Langseth, prin.   Fax 379-5338

St. Theodore S   100/K-6
323 E Clark St 56007   507-373-9657
Fax 373-9657

Albertville, Wright, Pop. 5,733
Saint Michael-Albertville SD 885   3,800/PK-12
11343 50th St NE 55301   763-497-3180
Dr. Marcia Ziegler, supt.   Fax 497-6588
www.stma.k12.mn.us
Albertville PS   100/PK-K
5386 Main Ave NE 55301   763-497-2688
Ann Foucault, prin.   Fax 497-6593
Other Schools – See Saint Michael

Alden, Freeborn, Pop. 634
Alden-Conger ISD 242   400/K-12
PO Box 99 56009   507-874-3240
Joe Guanella, supt.   Fax 874-2747
www.alden-conger.org
Alden-Conger ES   200/K-5
PO Box 99 56009   507-874-3240
Joe Guanella, dean   Fax 874-2747

Alexandria, Douglas, Pop. 10,603
Alexandria SD 206   3,900/K-12
PO Box 308 56308   320-762-2141
Dr. Terry Quist, supt.   Fax 762-2765
www.alexandria.k12.mn.us
Lincoln ES   600/K-6
1120 Lark St 56308   320-762-2146
Brendan Bogart, prin.   Fax 762-7777
Voyager ES   600/K-6
PO Box 339 56308   320-762-5437
Dana Christenson, prin.   Fax 762-7979
Woodland ES   400/K-6
1410 McKay Ave S Ste 101 56308   320-762-3300
Scott Heckert, prin.   Fax 762-3301
Other Schools – See Carlos, Garfield, Miltona

St. Marys S   200/K-6
421 Hawthorne St 56308   320-763-5861
Troy Sladek, prin.   Fax 763-7992
Zion Lutheran S   200/PK-8
300 Lake St 56308   320-763-4842
Lynn Peffer, prin.   Fax 763-3676

Andover, Anoka, Pop. 29,745
Anoka-Hennepin SD 11
Supt. — See Coon Rapids
Andover ES   1,100/K-5
14950 Hanson Blvd NW 55304   763-506-1700
Dorothy Olsen, prin.   Fax 506-1703
Crooked Lake ES   500/K-5
2939 Bunker Lake Blvd NW 55304   763-506-2100
Cheryl Kortuem, prin.   Fax 506-2103
Oak View MS   1,300/6-8
15400 Hanson Blvd NW 55304   763-506-5600
Jinger Gustafson, prin.   Fax 506-5603
Rum River ES   800/K-5
16950 Verdin St NW 55304   763-506-8200
Deb Shepard, prin.   Fax 506-8203

Bunker Hills Academy   100/K-12
3210 Bunker Lake Blvd NW 55304   763-421-3530
Gary Peterson, supt.   Fax 421-3151
Meadow Creek Christian S   700/PK-12
3037 Bunker Lake Blvd NW 55304   763-427-4595
Scott Thune, supt.   Fax 427-3398

Angle Inlet, Lake of the Woods
Warroad SD 690
Supt. — See Warroad
Angle Inlet ES   50/K-6
17606 Inlet Rd NW 56711   218-223-4161
Nick Smieja, prin.

Annandale, Wright, Pop. 2,996
Annandale SD 876   1,700/K-12
PO Box 190 55302   320-274-5602
Steve Niklaus, supt.   Fax 274-5978
www.annandale.k12.mn.us
Annandale MS   600/5-8
PO Box 190 55302   320-274-8226
Tim Prom, prin.   Fax 274-5978
Bendix ES   500/K-4
PO Box 190 55302   320-274-8218
Tracy Reimer, prin.   Fax 274-8470

Anoka, Anoka, Pop. 17,608
Anoka-Hennepin SD 11
Supt. — See Coon Rapids
Enich K   200/K-K
2740 Wingfield Ave 55303   763-506-2400
Marilyn McKeehen, prin.   Fax 506-2403
Franklin ES   400/K-5
215 W Main St 55303   763-506-2600
Vicki Spindler, prin.   Fax 506-2603
Lincoln ES   300/K-5
540 South St 55303   763-506-3100
Sheryl Ray, prin.   Fax 506-3103
Moore MS   1,100/6-8
1523 5th Ave 55303   763-506-5000
Kathy Baufield, prin.   Fax 506-5003
Sandburg MS   900/6-8
1902 2nd Ave 55303   763-506-6000
Tom Hagerty, prin.   Fax 506-6003
Washington ES   400/1-5
2171 6th Ave 55303   763-506-4600
Janel Wahlin, prin.   Fax 506-4603
Wilson ES   500/K-5
1025 Sunny Ln 55303   763-506-4700
Diane Henning, prin.   Fax 506-4703

Anoka Adventist Christian S   50/K-8
1035 Lincoln St 55303   763-421-6710
Minnesota Renaissance S   100/PK-8
1333 5th Ave 55303   763-323-0741
Daniel Van Bogart, prin.   Fax 427-3976
Mt. Olive Christian Preschl & Kindrgrten   200/PK-K
700 Western St 55303   763-421-9048
Linda Stroming, dir.   Fax 576-9626
St. Stephen S   400/K-8
506 Jackson St 55303   763-421-3236
Rebecca Gustafson, prin.   Fax 712-7433

Appleton, Swift, Pop. 2,870
Lac Qui Parle Valley SD 2853
Supt. — See Madison
Appleton/Milan ES   100/PK-4
349 S Edquist St 56208   320-289-1114
Renae Tostenson, prin.   Fax 289-1334

Apple Valley, Dakota, Pop. 49,856
Rosemount-Apple Valley-Eagan ISD 196
Supt. — See Rosemount
Cedar Park ES   500/K-5
7500 Whitney Dr 55124   952-431-8360
John Garcia, prin.   Fax 431-8365
Diamond Path ES   500/K-5
14455 Diamond Path 55124   952-423-7695
Lynn Hernandez, prin.   Fax 423-7694
Falcon Ridge MS   1,200/6-8
12900 Johnny Cake Ridge Rd 55124   952-431-8760
Noel Mehus, prin.   Fax 431-8770
Greenleaf ES   700/K-5
13333 Galaxie Ave 55124   952-431-8270
Michelle deKam Palmieri, prin.   Fax 431-8274
Highland ES   500/K-5
14001 Pilot Knob Rd 55124   952-423-7595
Chad Ryburn, prin.   Fax 423-7665
Scott Highlands MS   800/6-8
14011 Pilot Knob Rd 55124   952-423-7581
Daniel Wilharber, prin.   Fax 423-7601
Southview ES   700/K-5
1025 Whitney Dr 55124   952-431-8370
Rhonda Smith, prin.   Fax 431-8377
Valley MS   1,000/6-8
900 Garden View Dr 55124   952-431-8300
Dave McKeag, prin.   Fax 431-8313
Westview ES   500/K-5
225 Garden View Dr 55124   952-431-8380
Karen Toomey, prin.   Fax 431-8338

Arden Hills, Ramsey, Pop. 9,780
Mounds View SD 621
Supt. — See Shoreview
Valentine Hills ES   500/K-5
1770 County Road E2 W 55112   651-621-7800
Nathan Flansburg, prin.   Fax 621-7805

Argyle, Marshall, Pop. 630
Stephen-Argyle Central SD 2856
Supt. — See Stephen
Stephen-Argyle ES   200/PK-6
PO Box 279 56713   218-437-6616
Chris Mills, prin.   Fax 437-6617

Arlington, Sibley, Pop. 2,063
Sibley East SD 2310   1,200/PK-12
PO Box 1000 55307   507-964-2292
Stephen Jones, supt.   Fax 964-8224
www.sibleyeast.org/
Sibley East ES Arlington Campus   300/K-6
PO Box 1000 55307   507-964-8225
Mari Lu Martens, prin.   Fax 964-8245
Other Schools – See Gaylord

St. Paul S   100/K-8
510 W Adams St 55307   507-964-2397
Eric Kaesermann, prin.   Fax 964-2397

Ashby, Grant, Pop. 449
Ashby SD 261   300/K-12
PO Box 30 56309   218-747-2257
Allan Jensen, supt.   Fax 747-2289
www.ashby.k12.mn.us

Ashby ES 100/K-6
PO Box 30 56309 218-747-2257
Tom Otte, prin. Fax 747-2289

Atwater, Kandiyohi, Pop. 1,047
ACGC SD 2396
Supt. — See Grove City
ACGC North ES 200/K-4
302 2nd St S 56209 320-974-8841
Dave Oehrlein, prin. Fax 974-8410

St. John Lutheran S 50/K-6
19911 56th Ave NE 56209 320-974-8982
Marlena Ressie, prin. Fax 974-8983

Audubon, Becker, Pop. 458
Lake Park Audubon ISD 2889
Supt. — See Lake Park
Lake Park Audubon ES 400/K-6
PO Box 338 56511 218-439-3301
Sam Skaaland, prin. Fax 439-3318

Aurora, Saint Louis, Pop. 1,751
Mesabi East SD 2711 900/PK-12
601 N 1st St W 55705 218-229-3321
Shawn Northey, supt. Fax 229-3736
www.mesabieast.k12.mn.us/
Mesabi East ES 500/PK-6
601 N 1st St W 55705 218-229-3321
Sam Wilkes, prin. Fax 229-3736

Austin, Mower, Pop. 23,469
Austin SD 492 4,200/K-12
401 3rd Ave NW 55912 507-433-0966
Dr. Bruce Anderson, supt. Fax 433-0950
www.austin.k12.mn.us
Banfield ES 400/1-5
301 17th St SW 55912 507-437-6623
Deb Meyer, prin. Fax 437-1599
Ellis MS 900/6-8
1700 4th Ave SE 55912 507-433-8800
Katie Berglund, prin. Fax 433-7330
Neveln ES 400/1-5
1918 E Oakland Ave 55912 507-437-6669
Jean McDermott, prin. Fax 437-1307
Southgate ES 400/1-5
1601 19th Ave SW 55912 507-433-4624
Mark Randall, prin. Fax 437-9542
Sumner ES 300/1-5
805 8th Ave NW 55912 507-433-3425
Edwina Harder, prin. Fax 433-2618
Woodson Kindergarten Center 400/K-K
1601 4th St SE 55912 507-433-4422
Jayne Gibson, prin.

Austin S 200/PK-6
511 4th Ave NW 55912 507-433-8859
Mary Holtorf, dir. Fax 433-6630
Holy Cross Lutheran S 50/PK-PK
300 16th St NE 55912 507-433-7844
Fax 437-2107

Babbitt, Saint Louis, Pop. 1,616
Saint Louis County SD 2142
Supt. — See Virginia
Babbitt S 200/PK-12
30 South Dr 55706 218-827-3101
Gary Friedlieb, prin. Fax 827-3103

Badger, Roseau, Pop. 476
Badger SD 676 200/PK-12
PO Box 68 56714 218-528-3201
Gwen Borgen, supt. Fax 528-3366
www.badger.k12.mn.us
Badger ES 100/PK-6
PO Box 68 56714 218-528-3201
Gwen Borgen, prin. Fax 528-3366

Bagley, Clearwater, Pop. 1,205
Bagley SD 162 1,100/PK-12
202 Bagley Ave NW 56621 218-694-6184
Laine Larson, supt. Fax 694-3221
www.bagley.k12.mn.us/
Bagley ES 600/PK-6
202 Bagley Ave NW 56621 218-694-6528
Don Nordlund, prin. Fax 694-3450

Barnesville, Clay, Pop. 2,295
Barnesville SD 146 800/K-12
PO Box 189 56514 218-354-2217
Scott Loeslie, supt. Fax 354-7260
www.barnesville.k12.mn.us/
Barnesville ES 400/K-6
PO Box 189 56514 218-354-2300
Todd Henrickson, prin. Fax 354-7797

Barnum, Carlton, Pop. 614
Barnum SD 91 700/PK-12
3675 County Road 140 55707 218-389-6978
David Bottem, supt. Fax 389-3259
www.barnum.k12.mn.us
Barnum ES 400/PK-6
3813 E North St 55707 218-389-6976
Tom Cawcutt, prin. Fax 389-3259

Barrett, Grant, Pop. 346
West Central Area SD 2342 800/PK-12
301 County Road 2 56311 320-528-2650
Patrick Westby, supt. Fax 528-2279
www.westcentralareaschools.net
Other Schools – See Elbow Lake, Kensington

Battle Lake, Otter Tail, Pop. 778
Battle Lake SD 542 500/K-12
402 W Summit St 56515 218-864-5215
Rick Bleichner, supt. Fax 864-8651
www.battlelake.k12.mn.us/
Battle Lake ES 300/K-6
402 W Summit St 56515 218-864-5217
Rick Bleichner, prin. Fax 864-0919

Baudette, Lake of the Woods, Pop. 1,029
Lake of the Woods SD 390 600/PK-12
PO Box 310 56623 218-634-2735
Steve Wymore, supt. Fax 634-2467
www.blw.k12.mn.us/
Lake of the Woods ES 300/PK-6
PO Box 310 56623 218-634-2056
Jeff Nelson, prin. Fax 634-2467

Baxter, Crow Wing, Pop. 7,400
Brainerd SD 181
Supt. — See Brainerd
Baxter ES 400/K-4
5546 Fairview Rd 56425 218-454-6400
Steve Lundberg, prin. Fax 454-9317
Forestview MS 2,100/5-8
12149 Knollwood Dr 56425 218-454-6000
Donna Whalen, prin. Fax 454-6687

Family of Christ Lutheran S 100/PK-7
6785 Woida Rd 56425 218-829-9020
Paul Koehler, prin. Fax 829-9020
Lake Region Christian S 200/PK-12
7398 Fairview Rd 56425 218-828-1226
Steve Ogren, prin. Fax 828-1643

Bayport, Washington, Pop. 3,249
Stillwater Area SD 834
Supt. — See Stillwater
Andersen ES 400/K-6
309 4th St N 55003 651-351-6600
Mark Drommerhausen, prin. Fax 351-6695

Beaver Creek, Rock, Pop. 260
Hills-Beaver Creek SD 671
Supt. — See Hills
Hills-Beaver Creek ES 200/PK-6
PO Box 49 56116 507-673-2541
Todd Holthaus, prin. Fax 673-2550

Becker, Sherburne, Pop. 3,868
Becker SD 726 2,500/PK-12
12000 Hancock St SE 55308 763-261-4502
Steven Dooley, supt. Fax 261-4559
www.becker.k12.mn.us
Becker IS 700/3-5
12000 Hancock St SE 55308 763-261-4504
E. Bid Heidorf, prin. Fax 261-5799
Becker MS 600/6-8
12000 Hancock St SE 55308 763-261-6300
Nancy Helmer, prin. Fax 261-6306
Becker PS 500/PK-2
12000 Hancock St SE 55308 763-261-6330
Dale Christensen, prin. Fax 261-6340

Belle Plaine, Scott, Pop. 4,546
Belle Plaine SD 716 1,400/PK-12
130 S Willow St 56011 952-873-2400
Kelly Smith, supt. Fax 873-6909
www.belleplaine.k12.mn.us/
Belle Plaine Chatfield ES 300/PK-2
330 S Market St 56011 952-873-2401
Matt Hillmann, prin. Fax 873-2598
Belle Plaine JHS 200/7-8
220 S Market St 56011 952-873-2403
Lowell Hoffman, prin. Fax 378-2420
Belle Plaine Oak Crest ES 500/3-6
1101 W Commerce Dr 56011 952-873-2402
JoAnne Tierney, prin. Fax 378-2430

Our Lady of the Prairie S 100/PK-6
215 N Chestnut St 56011 952-873-6564
Dawn Kincs, prin. Fax 873-6717
Trinity Lutheran S 100/PK-8
500 W Church St 56011 952-873-6320
Daniel Whitney, prin. Fax 873-6545

Bellingham, Lac qui Parle, Pop. 190
Bellingham SD 371 100/K-12
522 1st St 56212 320-568-2118
Ray Seiler, supt. Fax 568-2230
Bellingham ES 100/K-6
522 1st St 56212 320-568-2118
Gloria Letrud, prin. Fax 568-2230

Bemidji, Beltrami, Pop. 13,296
Bemidji SD 31 4,500/K-12
3300 Gillett Dr NW 56601 218-333-3100
Dr. James Hess, supt. Fax 333-3129
www.bemidji.k12.mn.us
Bemidji MS 1,000/6-8
3300 Gillett Dr NW 56601 218-333-3215
Drew Hildenbrand, prin. Fax 333-3333
Central ES 200/K-5
3300 Gillett Dr NW 56601 218-333-3220
Patricia Welte, prin. Fax 333-3205
Lincoln ES 500/K-5
3300 Gillett Dr NW 56601 218-333-3250
Thomas Kusler, prin. Fax 333-3480
May ES 400/K-5
3300 Gillett Dr NW 56601 218-333-3240
William Burwell, prin. Fax 333-3244
Northern ES 500/K-5
3300 Gillett Dr NW 56601 218-333-3260
Bruce Anderson, prin. Fax 333-3263
Smith ES 300/K-5
3300 Gillett Dr NW 56601 218-333-3290
Patricia Welte, prin. Fax 333-3296
Solway ES 200/K-5
3300 Gillett Dr NW 56601 218-467-3232
Tami Wesely, prin. Fax 467-3490

Heartland Christian Academy 100/PK-8
9914 Heartland Cir NW 56601 218-751-1751
Dr. Robert Roach, prin. Fax 333-0260
St. Mark Lutheran S 50/1-7
2220 Anne St NW 56601 218-444-9635
Nathan Bitter, prin. Fax 444-3939

St. Philips S 300/PK-8
620 Beltrami Ave NW 56601 218-444-4938
Carol Rettinger, prin. Fax 444-1379

Benson, Swift, Pop. 3,189
Benson SD 777 700/PK-12
1400 Montana Ave 56215 320-843-2710
Lee Westrum, supt. Fax 843-2262
www.benson.k12.mn.us
Benson IS 5-8
1400 Montana Ave 56215 320-843-2710
Brad Johnson, prin. Fax 843-2262
Northside ES 300/PK-4
1800 Nevada Ave 56215 320-842-2717
Dennis Laumeyer, prin. Fax 843-5300

Bertha, Todd, Pop. 448
Bertha-Hewitt SD 786 500/K-12
PO Box 8 56437 218-924-2500
Robert Sieling, supt. Fax 924-3252
www.bertha-hewitt.k12.mn.us/
Bertha ES 200/K-6
PO Box 8 56437 218-924-3213
Diane Teigland, prin. Fax 924-3252

Bigfork, Itasca, Pop. 455
Grand Rapids SD 318
Supt. — See Grand Rapids
Bigfork ES 100/K-6
PO Box 228 56628 218-743-3444
Scott Patrow, prin. Fax 743-3443

Big Lake, Sherburne, Pop. 8,804
Big Lake SD 727 3,300/PK-12
501 Minnesota Ave 55309 763-262-2536
Jonathan Miller, supt. Fax 262-2539
www.biglake.k12.mn.us
Big Lake MS 800/6-8
601 Minnesota Ave 55309 763-262-2567
Glenn Evans, prin. Fax 262-2563
Independence ES 800/K-5
701 Minnesota Ave 55309 763-262-2537
Kay Miles, prin. Fax 262-2533
Liberty ES 700/PK-5
17901 205th Ave NW 55309 763-262-8100
Julie LeCaptain, prin. Fax 262-8185

Birchdale, Koochiching
South Koochiching-Rainy River ISD 363
Supt. — See Northome
Indus ES 100/K-6
8560 Highway 11 56629 218-634-2425
Lynn Jennissen, prin. Fax 634-1334

Bird Island, Renville, Pop. 1,176
BOLD SD 2534
Supt. — See Olivia
BOLD-Bird Island ES 400/K-6
110 S 9th St 55310 320-365-3551
Kip Lynk, prin. Fax 365-3515

St. Mary S 100/K-8
PO Box 500 55310 320-365-3693
Tracy Bertrand, prin. Fax 365-3142

Blackduck, Beltrami, Pop. 755
Blackduck SD 32 700/PK-12
PO Box 550 56630 218-835-5200
Robert Doetsch, supt. Fax 835-4491
www.blackduck.k12.mn.us/
Blackduck ES 400/PK-6
PO Box 550 56630 218-835-5300
Robert Doetsch, prin. Fax 835-5351

Blaine, Anoka, Pop. 54,084
Anoka-Hennepin SD 11
Supt. — See Coon Rapids
Jefferson ES 600/K-5
11331 Jefferson St NE 55434 763-506-2900
Kimberly Pavlovich, prin. Fax 506-2903
Johnsville ES 600/K-5
991 125th Ave NE 55434 763-506-3000
Neil Klund-Schubert, prin. Fax 506-3003
Madison ES 500/K-5
650 Territorial Rd NE 55434 763-506-3300
Susan Donovan, prin. Fax 506-3303
Roosevelt MS 1,200/6-8
650 125th Ave NE 55434 763-506-5800
Greg Blodgett, prin. Fax 506-5803
University Avenue ES 500/K-5
9901 University Ave NE 55434 763-506-4500
Tami Van Overbeke, prin. Fax 506-4503

Spring Lake Park SD 16
Supt. — See Minneapolis
Westwood IS 600/4-5
701 91st Ave NE 55434 763-784-8551
Tom Larson, prin. Fax 783-5395
Westwood MS 1,000/6-8
711 91st Ave NE 55434 763-784-8625
Paula Hoff, prin. Fax 786-7815

Calvin Christian S 200/K-8
8966 Pierce St NE 55434 763-785-0135
Jack Shields, prin. Fax 795-9148
Northside Christian S 100/PK-8
804 131st Ave NE 55434 763-755-3993
David Reid, admin. Fax 755-4405
Way of the Shepherd Montessori S 100/PK-6
13200 Central Ave NE 55434 763-862-9110
Jean Bemis, admin. Fax 276-0146

Blooming Prairie, Steele, Pop. 1,962
Blooming Prairie SD 756 800/PK-12
202 4th Ave NW 55917 507-583-4426
Barry Olson, supt. Fax 583-7952
www.blossoms.k12.mn.us
Blooming Prairie ES 400/PK-6
123 2nd St NW 55917 507-583-6615
Sandra Grenell, prin. Fax 583-4415

Bloomington, Hennepin, Pop. 81,164
Bloomington SD 271 — 10,300/K-12
1350 W 106th St 55431 — 952-681-6400
Les Fujitake, supt. — Fax 681-6401
www.bloomingtonschools.info/
Hillcrest Community ES — 400/K-5
9301 Thomas Rd S 55431 — 952-681-5300
Paul Schullo, prin. — Fax 681-5301
Indian Mounds ES — 400/K-5
9801 11th Ave S 55420 — 952-681-6000
Joan Maland, prin. — Fax 681-6001
Normandale Hills ES — 500/K-5
9501 Toledo Ave S 55437 — 952-806-7000
Andrew Vollmuth, prin. — Fax 806-7001
Oak Grove ES — 400/K-5
1301 W 104th St 55431 — 952-681-6800
Raymond Yu, prin. — Fax 681-6801
Oak Grove MS — 900/6-8
1300 W 106th St 55431 — 952-681-6600
Brian Ingemann, prin. — Fax 681-6601
Olson ES — 500/K-5
4501 W 102nd St 55437 — 952-806-8800
Paul Meyer, prin. — Fax 806-8801
Olson MS — 800/6-8
4551 W 102nd St 55437 — 952-806-8600
Thomas Lee, prin. — Fax 806-8601
Poplar Bridge ES — 500/K-5
8401 Palmer Ave S 55437 — 952-681-5400
Dr. Gail Swor, prin. — Fax 681-5401
Ridgeview ES — 300/K-5
9400 Nesbitt Ave S 55437 — 952-806-7100
Steve Abrahamson, prin. — Fax 806-7101
Valley View ES — 500/K-5
351 E 88th St 55420 — 952-681-5700
Paul Helberg, prin. — Fax 681-5701
Valley View MS — 700/6-8
8900 Portland Ave S 55420 — 952-681-5800
Andrew Kubas, prin. — Fax 681-5801
Washburn ES — 500/K-5
8401 Xerxes Ave S 55431 — 952-681-5500
Jon Millerhagen, prin. — Fax 681-5501
Westwood ES — 400/K-5
3701 W 108th St 55431 — 952-806-7200
Carolyn Hartwigsen, prin. — Fax 806-7201

Bethany Academy — 300/K-12
4300 W 98th St 55437 — 952-831-8686
Robin Sovine, supt. — Fax 831-9568
Bloomington Lutheran S — 200/PK-8
10600 Bloomington Ferry Rd 55438 — 952-941-9047
Kurt Schmidt, prin. — Fax 941-1242
Living Hope Lutheran S — 100/PK-8
10600 Bloomington Ferry Rd 55438 — 952-445-1785
Kurt Schmidt, prin. — Fax 445-1822
Mt. Hope-Redemption Lutheran S — 100/PK-8
927 E Old Shakopee Rd 55420 — 952-881-0036
David Polzin, prin. — Fax 881-0036
Nativity of the BVM S — 400/K-8
9901 E Bloomington Fwy 55420 — 952-881-8160
Barb Castagna, prin. — Fax 881-3032
TLC Early Learning Center — 100/PK-K
11000 France Ave S 55431 — 952-884-7955

Blue Earth, Faribault, Pop. 3,452
Blue Earth Area ISD 2860 — 1,200/K-12
315 E 6th St 56013 — 507-526-3188
Dale Brandsoy, supt. — Fax 526-2432
www.blueearth.k12.mn.us
Blue Earth Area MS — 300/6-8
315 E 6th St 56013 — 507-526-3115
Melissa McGuire, prin. — Fax 526-2432
Blue Earth ES — 400/K-5
315 E 6th St 56013 — 507-526-3090
Kevin Grant, prin. — Fax 526-2432
Other Schools – See Winnebago

Granada - Huntley - East Chain SD 2536
Supt. — See Granada
Granada - Huntley - East Chain ES — 100/PK-6
395 280th Ave 56013 — 507-773-4203
Robert Grant, prin. — Fax 773-4215

Bluffton, Otter Tail, Pop. 208

SonRise Christian S, PO Box 65 56518 — 50/PK-9
Rev. Todd Orr, admin. — 218-385-3774

Borup, Norman, Pop. 89
Ada-Borup SD 2854
Supt. — See Ada
Borup IS — 100/5-6
PO Box 8 56519 — 218-582-3333
Ollen Church, prin. — Fax 861-6515

Bovey, Itasca, Pop. 661
Greenway SD 316
Supt. — See Coleraine
Connor-Jasper MS — 500/4-8
PO Box 40 55709 — 218-245-2661
Dennis Perreault, prin. — Fax 245-3483

Braham, Isanti, Pop. 1,574
Braham SD 314 — 900/K-12
531 Elmhurst Ave S 55006 — 320-396-3313
Craig Schultz, supt. — Fax 396-3068
Braham Area ES — 500/K-6
528 8th St SW 55006 — 320-396-3316
Randy Pauly, prin. — Fax 396-3317

Brainerd, Crow Wing, Pop. 13,684
Brainerd SD 181 — 6,400/PK-12
804 Oak St 56401 — 218-454-6900
Steve Razidlo, supt. — Fax 454-6901
www.isd181.org/
Garfield ES — 400/PK-4
1120 10th Ave NE 56401 — 218-454-6450
Jane Fritscher, prin. — Fax 454-6421
Harrison ES — 200/K-4
1515 Oak St 56401 — 218-454-6500
Jeff Devaney, prin. — Fax 454-6501
Lowell ES — 300/K-4
704 3rd Ave NE 56401 — 218-454-6550
Todd Sauer, prin. — Fax 454-6551
Riverside ES — 400/K-4
220 NW 3rd St 56401 — 218-454-6800
Cathy Engler, prin. — Fax 454-6801
Other Schools – See Baxter, Nisswa

Oak Street Christian S — 50/1-8
2822 Oak St 56401 — 218-828-9660
St. Francis of the Lakes S — 200/PK-8
817 Juniper St 56401 — 218-829-2344
Deborah Euteneuer, prin. — Fax 829-4157

Brandon, Douglas, Pop. 419
Brandon SD 207 — 300/PK-12
PO Box 185 56315 — 320-524-2263
Mark Westby, supt. — Fax 524-2228
www.brandon.k12.mn.us
Brandon ES — 200/PK-6
PO Box 185 56315 — 320-524-2263
Mark Westby, prin. — Fax 524-2228

Breckenridge, Wilkin, Pop. 3,373
Breckenridge SD 846 — 900/PK-12
810 Beede Ave 56520 — 218-643-6822
Warren Schmidt, supt. — Fax 641-4035
www.breckenridge.k12.mn.us
Breckenridge ES — 400/PK-5
810 Beede Ave 56520 — 218-643-6681
Donald Schill, prin. — Fax 643-5021
Breckenridge MS — 200/6-8
810 Beede Ave 56520 — 218-643-6681
Donald Schill, prin. — Fax 643-5021

St. Marys S — 100/PK-8
210 4th St N 56520 — 218-643-5443
Linda Johnson, prin. — Fax 643-5443

Brewster, Nobles, Pop. 492
Brewster SD 513 — 100/PK-6
PO Box 309 56119 — 507-842-5951
John Cselovszki, supt. — Fax 842-5365
Brewster ES — 100/PK-6
PO Box 309 56119 — 507-842-5951
John Cselovszki, prin. — Fax 842-5365

Brooklyn Center, Hennepin, Pop. 27,551
Anoka-Hennepin SD 11
Supt. — See Coon Rapids
Evergreen Park ES — 500/K-5
7020 Dupont Ave N 55430 — 763-506-2500
Gwen Dillenburg, prin. — Fax 506-2503

Brooklyn Center SD 286 — 1,500/PK-12
6500 Humboldt Ave N 55430 — 763-561-2120
Fax 560-2647
www.brookcntr.k12.mn.us/
Brown ES — 800/PK-6
1500 59th Ave N 55430 — 763-561-4480
Randal Koch, prin. — Fax 560-1674

Osseo SD 279
Supt. — See Maple Grove
Garden City ES — 400/K-6
3501 65th Ave N 55429 — 763-561-9768
Todd Tischer, prin. — Fax 549-2360
Willow Lane ECC — 300/PK-PK
7020 Perry Ave N 55429 — 763-585-7300
John Norlander, coord. — Fax 585-7303

Robbinsdale SD 281
Supt. — See New Hope
Northport ES — 400/K-5
5421 Brooklyn Blvd 55429 — 763-504-7800
Patrick Smith, prin. — Fax 504-7809

St. Alphonsus S — 200/K-8
7031 Halifax Ave N 55429 — 763-561-5101
Robert Terry, prin. — Fax 561-0336

Brooklyn Park, Hennepin, Pop. 68,550
Anoka-Hennepin SD 11
Supt. — See Coon Rapids
Monroe ES — 500/K-5
901 Brookdale Dr 55444 — 763-506-3600
Rose Wippler, prin. — Fax 506-3603
Riverview ES — 400/K-5
1400 93rd Ave N 55444 — 763-506-4200
Kari Rock, prin. — Fax 506-4203

Osseo SD 279
Supt. — See Maple Grove
Birch Grove S for the Arts — 600/K-6
4690 Brookdale Dr N 55443 — 763-561-1374
Jeff Zastrow, prin. — Fax 549-2300
Crest View ES — 400/K-6
8200 Zane Ave N 55443 — 763-561-5165
Suzette Erickson, prin. — Fax 549-2323
Edinbrook ES — 800/K-6
8925 Zane Ave N 55443 — 763-493-4737
John Groenke, prin. — Fax 391-8400
Fair Oaks ES — 300/K-3
5600 65th Ave N 55429 — 763-533-2246
Phil Sadler, prin. — Fax 549-2350
Palmer Lake ES — 700/K-6
7300 W Palmer Lake Dr 55429 — 763-561-1930
Tommy Watson, prin. — Fax 549-2400
Park Brook ES — 300/K-6
7400 Hampshire Ave N 55428 — 763-561-6870
Scott Taylor, prin. — Fax 549-2410
Woodland ES — 800/K-6
4501 Oak Grove Pkwy N 55443 — 763-315-6400
Linda Perdaems, prin. — Fax 315-6401
Zanewood Community S — 500/K-6
7000 Zane Ave N 55429 — 763-561-9077
Carol Rowan, prin. — Fax 549-2440

St. Vincent De Paul S — 400/K-8
9050 93rd Ave N 55445 — 763-425-3970
Kathleen O'Hara, prin. — Fax 425-2674

Brooten, Stearns, Pop. 623
Belgrade-Brooten-Elrosa SD 2364 — 700/PK-12
PO Box 39 56316 — 320-346-2278
Matt Bullard, supt. — Fax 346-2589
bbe.k12.mn.us
Belgrade-Brooten-Elrosa ES — 400/PK-6
PO Box 39 56316 — 320-346-2278
Rick Gossen, prin. — Fax 346-2589

Browerville, Todd, Pop. 721
Browerville SD 787 — 500/PK-12
PO Box 185 56438 — 320-594-2272
Robert Schaefer, supt. — Fax 594-8105
www.browerville.k12.mn.us/
Browerville ES — 200/PK-6
PO Box 185 56438 — 320-594-2272
Tom Oven, prin. — Fax 594-8105

Christ the King S — 100/PK-6
PO Box 186 56438 — 320-594-6114
Paula Becker, prin. — Fax 594-6114

Brownsdale, Mower, Pop. 713
Hayfield SD 203
Supt. — See Hayfield
Brownsdale ES — 100/PK-3
PO Box 160 55918 — 507-567-2244
Diana Orr, prin. — Fax 567-2432

Browns Valley, Traverse, Pop. 631
Browns Valley SD 801 — 100/PK-8
PO Box N 56219 — 320-695-2103
Brenda Reed, supt. — Fax 695-2868
www.brownsvalley.k12.mn.us/
Browns Valley ES — 100/PK-4
PO Box N 56219 — 320-695-2103
Brenda Reed, prin. — Fax 695-2868
Browns Valley MS — 100/5-8
PO Box N 56219 — 320-695-2103
Brenda Reed, prin. — Fax 695-2868

Buffalo, Wright, Pop. 13,290
Buffalo SD 877 — 4,900/K-12
214 1st Ave NE 55313 — 763-682-5200
Jim Bauck, supt. — Fax 682-8785
www.buffalo.k12.mn.us
Buffalo Community MS — 1,300/6-8
1300 Highway 25 N 55313 — 763-682-8200
Julie Swaggert, prin. — Fax 682-8209
Discovery ES — 200/K-5
301 2nd Ave NE 55313 — 763-682-8400
Michelle Robinson, prin. — Fax 682-8444
Northwinds ES — K-5
1111 7th Ave NW 55313 — 763-682-8800
Gail Feneis, prin. — Fax 682-8805
Parkside ES — 400/K-5
207 3rd St NE 55313 — 763-682-8500
Michelle Robinson, prin. — Fax 682-8577
Tatanka ES — 400/K-5
703 8th St NE 55313 — 763-682-8600
Don Metzler, prin. — Fax 682-8671
Other Schools – See Hanover, Montrose

St. Francis Xavier S — 200/PK-6
219 19th St NW 55313 — 763-684-0075
Kim Zumbusch, prin. — Fax 684-5377

Buffalo Lake, Renville, Pop. 762
Buffalo Lake-Hector SD 2159
Supt. — See Hector
Buffalo Lake-Hector ES — 200/PK-5
PO Box 278 55314 — 320-833-5311
Dr. Rick Clark, prin. — Fax 833-5312

Burnsville, Dakota, Pop. 59,159
Burnsville-Eagan-Savage ISD 191 — 10,100/K-12
100 River Ridge Ct 55337 — 952-707-2000
Randall Clegg, supt. — Fax 707-2002
www.isd191.org
Byrne ES — 500/K-6
11608 River Hills Dr 55337 — 952-707-3500
Paul McDowall, prin. — Fax 707-3502
Gideon Pond ES — 400/K-6
613 E 130th St 55337 — 952-707-3000
Laura Pierce, prin. — Fax 707-3002
Neill ES — 500/K-6
13409 Upton Ave S 55337 — 952-707-3100
Pat Flynn, prin. — Fax 707-3102
Sioux Trail ES — 500/K-6
2801 River Hills Dr 55337 — 952-707-3300
Taber Akin, prin. — Fax 707-3302
Sky Oaks ES — 600/K-6
100 E 134th St 55337 — 952-707-3700
Kaye Fecke, prin. — Fax 707-3702
Vista View ES — 600/K-6
13109 County Road 5 55337 — 952-707-3400
Susan Risius, prin. — Fax 707-3402
Other Schools – See Eagan, Savage

Rosemount-Apple Valley-Eagan ISD 196
Supt. — See Rosemount
Echo Park ES — 600/K-5
14100 County Road 11 55337 — 952-431-8390
Sally Soliday, prin. — Fax 431-8333

Good Shepherd Lutheran S — 100/PK-8
151 County Road 42 E 55306 — 952-953-0690
George Traucht, prin. — Fax 891-3469
Southview Christian S — 50/K-9
15304 County Road 5 55306 — 952-898-2727
Rayleen Hansen, prin. — Fax 898-0457

Butterfield, Watonwan, Pop. 526
Butterfield SD 836 200/K-12
PO Box 189 56120 507-956-2771
Lisa Shellum, supt. Fax 956-3431
butterfield.k12.mn.us/
Butterfield ES 100/K-6
PO Box 189 56120 507-956-2771
Lisa Shellum, prin. Fax 956-3431

Byron, Olmsted, Pop. 4,509
Byron SD 531 1,500/PK-12
1887 2nd Ave NW 55920 507-775-2383
Wendy Shannon Ph.D., supt. Fax 775-2385
bears.byron.k12.mn.us
Byron ES 500/PK-4
501 10th Ave NE 55920 507-775-6620
Abe Rodemeyer, prin. Fax 775-7225
Byron MS 500/5-8
601 4th St NW 55920 507-775-2189
Shelley Balkan, prin. Fax 775-2825

Caledonia, Houston, Pop. 2,939
Caledonia SD 299 800/PK-12
511 W Main St 55921 507-725-3053
Bruce Thomas, supt. Fax 725-3558
www.cps.k12.mn.us/
Caledonia Area MS 200/6-8
825 N Warrior Ave 55921 507-725-3316
Paul DeMorett, prin. Fax 725-3319
Caledonia ES 300/PK-5
511 W Main St 55921 507-725-5205
Connie Hesse, prin. Fax 725-3558

St. John's Lutheran S 100/PK-8
720 N Marshall St 55921 507-725-3412
Jonathan Hahm, prin. Fax 725-3049
St. Mary S 200/PK-8
308 E South St 55921 507-725-3355
Gail Trocinski, prin. Fax 725-8355

Cambridge, Isanti, Pop. 7,198
Cambridge-Isanti SD 911 4,000/PK-12
625A Main St N 55008 763-689-6188
Bruce Novak, supt. Fax 689-6200
www.cambridge.k12.mn.us
Cambridge IS 3-5
428 2nd Ave NW 55008 763-691-6600
Scott Peterson, prin. Fax 691-6699
Cambridge MS 600/6-8
31374 Xylite St NE 55008 763-552-6300
Charlie Burroughs, prin. Fax 552-6399
Cambridge PS 600/PK-2
310 Elm St N 55008 763-691-6500
Chris Grote, prin. Fax 691-6599
Other Schools – See Isanti

Cambridge Christian S 200/PK-12
2211 Main St S 55008 763-689-3806
Mark DeJong, supt. Fax 689-3807

Campbell, Wilkin, Pop. 232
Campbell-Tintah SD 852 100/PK-12
PO Box 8 56522 218-630-5311
Wayne Olson, supt. Fax 630-5881
www.campbell.k12.mn.us
Campbell-Tintah S 100/PK-12
PO Box 8 56522 218-630-5311
Wayne Olson, prin. Fax 630-5881

Canby, Yellow Medicine, Pop. 1,784
Canby SD 891 600/PK-12
307 1st St W 56220 507-223-2001
Loren Hacker, supt. Fax 223-2011
www.canbymn.org/
Canby ES 300/PK-6
307 1st St W 56220 507-223-2003
Sandi Arndt, prin. Fax 223-2013

St. Peter S 100/K-6
410 Ring Ave N 56220 507-223-7729
Sandra Kollar, prin. Fax 223-7178

Cannon Falls, Goodhue, Pop. 3,914
Cannon Falls SD 252 1,200/PK-12
820 Minnesota St E 55009 507-263-6800
Todd Sesker, supt. Fax 263-2555
www.cannonfallsschools.com
Cannon Falls ES 600/PK-6
1020 Minnesota St E 55009 507-263-4226
Neil Koven, prin. Fax 263-4888

St. Paul S 50/K-8
30289 59th Avenue Way 55009 507-263-4589
Nathaniel Kallies, prin. Fax 263-4589

Carlos, Douglas, Pop. 415
Alexandria SD 206
Supt. — See Alexandria
Carlos ES 100/K-6
PO Box 128 56319 320-852-7181
Lisa Pikop, prin. Fax 852-7538

Carlton, Carlton, Pop. 795
Carlton SD 93 600/PK-12
PO Box 310 55718 218-384-4225
Scott Hoch, supt. Fax 384-3543
www.carlton.k12.mn.us
South Terrace ES 200/PK-5
PO Box 620 55718 218-384-4728
B. J. Berg, prin. Fax 384-4039

Carver, Carver, Pop. 2,268
Eastern Carver County SD 112
Supt. — See Chaska
East Union ES 200/1-5
15655 County Road 43 55315 952-556-6800
Greg Lange, prin. Fax 556-6809

Cass Lake, Cass, Pop. 867
Cass Lake-Bena SD 115 1,100/PK-12
208 Central Ave NW 56633 218-335-2204
Carl Remmers, supt. Fax 335-2614
www.clbs.k12.mn.us
Cass Lake-Bena ES 400/PK-4
15 4th St NW 56633 218-335-2201
Patti Haasch, prin. Fax 335-8538
Cass Lake-Bena MS 300/5-8
15314 State Highway 371 NW 56633 218-335-7851
Clyde Hadrava, prin. Fax 335-1194

Cedar, Anoka
Saint Francis SD 15
Supt. — See Saint Francis
Cedar Creek Community ES 1,000/K-5
21108 Polk St NE 55011 763-213-8780
Darin Hahn, prin. Fax 434-7679
East Bethel Community ES 500/K-5
21210 Polk St NE 55011 763-213-8900
Angie Scardigli, prin. Fax 434-7627

Centerville, Anoka, Pop. 3,765
Centennial SD 12
Supt. — See Circle Pines
Centerville ES 600/K-5
1721 Westview Ave 55038 763-792-5800
Robert Stevens, prin. Fax 792-5850

Champlin, Hennepin, Pop. 23,302
Anoka-Hennepin SD 11
Supt. — See Coon Rapids
Champlin ES 400/1-5
111 Dean Ave W 55316 763-506-2000
Todd Protivinsky, prin. Fax 506-2003
Jackson MS 2,300/6-8
6000 109th Ave N 55316 763-506-5200
Tom Sullivan, prin. Fax 506-5203
Oxbow Creek ES 1,000/1-5
6505 109th Ave N 55316 763-506-3800
Rolf Carlsen, prin. Fax 506-3803
Park View ECC 400/K-K
6100 109th Ave N 55316 763-506-3900
Marilyn McKeehen, prin. Fax 506-3903

Chandler, Murray, Pop. 256

Chandler Christian S 50/K-8
410 5th St 56122 507-677-2358
Calvin Hoekstra, prin. Fax 677-2358

Chanhassen, Carver, Pop. 23,229
Eastern Carver County SD 112
Supt. — See Chaska
Bluff Creek ES 500/K-5
2300 Coulter Blvd 55317 952-556-6600
Joan MacDonald, prin. Fax 556-6609
Chanhassen ES 600/K-5
7600 Laredo Dr 55317 952-556-6700
Matt Dorschner, prin. Fax 556-6709

Chapel Hill Academy 400/K-8
306 W 78th St 55317 952-949-9014
Kathy Tweeten, admin. Fax 949-3871
St. Hubert S 700/K-8
8201 Main St 55317 952-934-6003
Martha Laurent, prin. Fax 906-1229

Chaska, Carver, Pop. 22,820
Eastern Carver County SD 112 8,600/K-12
11 Peavey Rd 55318 952-556-6100
David Jennings, supt. Fax 556-6109
www.district112.org
Chaska ES 600/K-5
1800 N Chestnut St 55318 952-556-6300
Roger Hunt, prin. Fax 556-6309
K Center 600/K-K
110600 Village Rd 55318 952-556-6400
Greg Lange, prin. Fax 556-6409
Chaska MS East 1,000/6-8
1600 Park Ridge Dr 55318 952-556-7600
James Bach, prin. Fax 556-7609
Chaska MS West 900/6-8
140 Engler Blvd 55318 952-556-7400
Sheryl Hough, prin. Fax 556-7409
Clover Ridge ES 600/1-5
114000 Hundertmark Rd 55318 952-556-6900
June Johnson, prin. Fax 556-6909
Jonathan ES 600/K-5
110300 Pioneer Trl W 55318 952-556-6500
Nancy Wittman-Beltz, prin. Fax 556-6509
Pioneer Ridge MS 700/6-8
1085 Pioneer Trl 55318 952-556-7800
Dana Miller, prin. Fax 556-7809
Other Schools – See Carver, Chanhassen, Victoria

Guardian Angels S 300/PK-8
217 W 2nd St 55318 952-227-4010
Nancy Ronhovde, prin. Fax 227-4050
St. John's Lutheran S 300/PK-8
300 E 4th St 55318 952-448-2526
Jack Pallas, prin. Fax 448-9500

Chatfield, Fillmore, Pop. 2,462
Chatfield SD 227 900/PK-12
205 Union St NE 55923 507-867-4210
Don Hainlen, supt. Fax 867-3147
www.chatfield.k12.mn.us/
Chatfield ES 500/PK-6
405 Main St S 55923 507-867-4521
James Borgschatz, prin. Fax 867-4525

St. Paul Lutheran S 50/PK-8
128 Fillmore St SE 55923 507-867-4604
Rhonda Dedor, prin.

Chisago City, Chisago, Pop. 3,071
Chisago Lakes SD 2144
Supt. — See Lindstrom
Chisago Lakes PS 500/PK-3
11009 284th St 55013 651-213-2200
Brenda Schell, prin. Fax 213-2250
Lakeside ES 500/3-5
10345 Wyoming Ave 55013 651-213-2300
Warren Retzlaff, prin. Fax 213-2350

Chisago Lakes Baptist S 100/K-12
9387 Wyoming Trl 55013 651-257-4587
Alan Hodak, prin. Fax 257-3888

Chisholm, Saint Louis, Pop. 4,701
Chisholm SD 695 700/PK-12
300 3rd Ave SW 55719 218-254-5726
James Varichak, supt. Fax 254-3741
www.chisholm.k12.mn.us
Chisholm ES 200/4-6
300 3rd Ave SW 55719 218-254-5726
Richard Aldrich, prin. Fax 254-3741
Vaughan ES 200/PK-3
1000 1st Ave NE 55719 218-254-5726
James Varichak, prin. Fax 254-3741

Chokio, Stevens, Pop. 441
Chokio-Alberta SD 771 100/K-12
PO Box 68 56221 320-324-7131
Ray Farwell, supt. Fax 324-2731
Chokio-Alberta S 100/K-12
PO Box 68 56221 320-324-7131
Ray Farwell, prin. Fax 324-2731

Circle Pines, Anoka, Pop. 5,356
Centennial SD 12 6,800/K-12
4707 North Rd 55014 763-792-6000
Dr. Paul Stremick, supt. Fax 792-6050
www.isd12.org
Centennial ES 500/K-5
4657 North Rd 55014 763-792-5300
Kathleen Kaiser, prin. Fax 792-5350
Golden Lake ES 400/K-5
1 School Rd 55014 763-792-5900
Fax 792-5950
Other Schools – See Centerville, Lino Lakes

Clara City, Chippewa, Pop. 1,353
MACCRAY SD 2180 600/K-12
PO Box 690 56222 320-847-2154
Greg Schmidt, supt. Fax 847-3239
www.maccray.k12.mn.us/
Other Schools – See Maynard, Raymond

Clarissa, Todd, Pop. 602
Eagle Valley SD 2759
Supt. — See Eagle Bend
Eagle Valley ES 200/PK-6
PO Box 468 56440 218-756-3631
Mark Lundin, prin. Fax 756-2560

Clarkfield, Yellow Medicine, Pop. 879
Yellow Medicine East SD 2190
Supt. — See Granite Falls
Hagg ES 100/K-6
PO Box 338 56223 320-669-4424
Stacy Hinz, prin. Fax 669-4828

Clearbrook, Clearwater, Pop. 536
Clearbrook-Gonvick SD 2311 500/K-12
16770 Clearwater Lake Rd 56634 218-776-3112
Allen Ralston, supt. Fax 776-3117
www.cgbearzone.com
Clearbrook-Gonvick ES 300/K-6
16770 Clearwater Lake Rd 56634 218-776-3112
Allen Ralston, prin. Fax 776-3117

Clear Lake, Sherburne, Pop. 441
Saint Cloud Area SD 742
Supt. — See Saint Cloud
Clearview ES 400/K-6
7310 State Highway 24 55319 320-743-2241
Paula Foley, prin. Fax 743-4407

Cleveland, LeSueur, Pop. 707
Cleveland SD 391 400/PK-12
PO Box 310 56017 507-931-5953
Brian Phillips, supt. Fax 931-9088
cleveland.k12.mn.us/
Cleveland ES 200/PK-6
PO Box 310 56017 507-931-5953
Dawn Brown, prin. Fax 931-9088

Climax, Polk, Pop. 243
Climax-Shelly SD 592 100/PK-12
PO Box 67 56523 218-857-2385
Norman Baumgarn, supt. Fax 857-3544
www.climax.k12.mn.us
Climax-Shelly S 100/PK-12
PO Box 67 56523 218-857-2385
Nancy Newcomb, prin. Fax 857-3544

Clinton, Big Stone, Pop. 415
Clinton-Graceville-Beardsley SD 2888 400/K-12
PO Box 361 56225 320-325-5282
Mary Smidt, supt. Fax 325-5509
www.graceville.k12.mn.us
Clinton-Graceville-Beardsley ES 200/K-6
PO Box 361 56225 320-325-5224
Mary Smidt, prin. Fax 325-5509
Lismore Colony S, PO Box 361 56225 50/K-8
Mary Smidt, prin. 320-325-5583
Other Schools – See Graceville

Cloquet, Carlton, Pop. 11,476
Cloquet SD 94 2,100/PK-12
302 14th St 55720 218-879-6721
Kenneth Scarbrough, supt. Fax 879-6724
www.cloquet.k12.mn.us
Churchill ES 500/PK-5
515 Granite St 55720 218-879-3308
David Wangen, prin. Fax 879-1514

Cloquet MS 500/6-8
509 Carlton Ave 55720 218-879-3328
Tom Brenner, prin. Fax 879-4175
Washington ES 400/K-5
801 12th St 55720 218-879-3369
Randy Thudin, prin. Fax 879-3360

Cloquet Christian Academy 100/PK-12
1705 Wilson Ave 55720 218-879-2536
Jason Peterson, admin. Fax 879-3334
Queen of Peace S 100/PK-5
102 4th St 55720 218-879-8516
Sr. Therese Gutting, prin. Fax 879-8930

Cohasset, Itasca, Pop. 2,508
Grand Rapids SD 318
Supt. — See Grand Rapids
Cohasset ES 300/K-4
450 Columbus Ave 55721 218-327-5860
Sean Martinson, prin. Fax 327-5861

Cokato, Wright, Pop. 2,700
Dassel-Cokato SD 466 2,300/PK-12
PO Box 1700 55321 320-286-4100
Jeff Powers, supt. Fax 286-4101
www.dc.k12.mn.us
Cokato ES 500/PK-4
PO Box 1300 55321 320-286-4100
Lorene Force, prin. Fax 286-4131
Dassel-Cokato MS 700/5-8
PO Box 1500 55321 320-286-4100
Gary Johnson, prin. Fax 286-4176
Other Schools – See Dassel

Cold Spring, Stearns, Pop. 3,646
Rocori SD 750 2,300/PK-12
534 5th Ave N 56320 320-685-4901
Scott Staska, supt. Fax 685-4906
www.rocori.k12.mn.us/
Cold Spring ES 600/PK-6
601 Red River Ave N 56320 320-685-7534
Eric Skanson, prin. Fax 685-4962
Rocori MS 400/7-8
533 Main St 56320 320-685-3296
Cheryl Schmidt, prin. Fax 685-3448
Other Schools – See Richmond, Rockville

St. Boniface S 300/PK-6
501 Main St 56320 320-685-3541
Sr. Sharon Waldoch, prin. Fax 685-8194

Coleraine, Itasca, Pop. 1,041
Greenway SD 316 1,100/PK-12
PO Box 195 55722 218-245-6500
Rochelle Van Den Heuvel, supt. Fax 245-6507
www.greenway.k12.mn.us/
Vandyke ES 300/PK-3
PO Box 570 55722 218-245-2510
Jolene Landwer, prin. Fax 245-6602
Other Schools – See Bovey, Marble

Cologne, Carver, Pop. 1,197

St. Bernard S 100/PK-6
300 Church St E 55322 952-466-5917
Sr. Jancy Nedumkallel, prin. Fax 466-5917
Zion Lutheran S 100/PK-8
14735 County Road 153 55322 952-466-3379
Fax 466-2703

Columbia Heights, Anoka, Pop. 18,110
Columbia Heights SD 13 2,900/K-12
1440 49th Ave NE 55421 763-528-4500
Kathy Kelly, supt. Fax 571-9203
www.colheights.k12.mn.us
Central MS 600/6-8
900 49th Ave NE 55421 763-586-4701
Mary Bussman, prin. Fax 528-4707
Highland ES 500/K-5
1500 49th Ave NE 55421 763-528-4400
Michele DeWitt, prin. Fax 528-4407
Valley View ES 400/K-5
800 49th Ave NE 55421 763-528-4200
Scott Tryggeseth, prin. Fax 528-4207
Other Schools – See Fridley

Immaculate Conception S 200/PK-8
4030 Jackson St NE 55421 763-788-9065
Richard Krainz, prin. Fax 788-9066

Comfrey, Brown, Pop. 354
Comfrey SD 81 200/K-12
305 Ochre St W 56019 507-877-3491
Wayne Olson, supt. Fax 877-3492
comfreyed.org
Comfrey ES 100/K-6
305 Ochre St W 56019 507-877-3491
Wayne Olson, prin. Fax 877-3492

Cook, Saint Louis, Pop. 622
Saint Louis County SD 2142
Supt. — See Virginia
Cook S 200/PK-12
306 E Vermilion Blvd 55723 218-666-5221
Kevin Abrahamson, prin. Fax 666-5223

Coon Rapids, Anoka, Pop. 62,417
Anoka-Hennepin SD 11 39,200/K-12
11299 Hanson Blvd NW 55433 763-506-1000
Dennis Carlson, supt. Fax 506-1003
www.anoka.k12.mn.us
Adams ES 500/K-5
8989 Sycamore St NW 55433 763-506-1600
Jeremy Tammi, prin. Fax 506-1603
Bye ES 500/K-5
11931 Crooked Lake Blvd NW 55433 763-506-3700
Alice Shea, prin. Fax 506-3703
Coon Rapids MS 1,500/6-8
11600 Raven St NW 55433 763-506-4800
Annette Ziegler, prin. Fax 506-4803
Eisenhower ES 400/K-5
151 Northdale Blvd NW 55448 763-506-2300
Ranae Case-Evenson, prin. Fax 506-2303
Hamilton ES 400/K-5
1374 111th Ave NW 55433 763-506-2700
Diane Merritt, prin. Fax 506-2703
Hoover ES 500/K-5
2369 109th Ave NW 55433 763-506-2800
David Ollanketo, prin. Fax 506-2803
Jacob ES 400/K-5
1700 Coon Rapids Blvd NW 55433 763-506-3200
Anissa Cravens, prin. Fax 506-3203
Mississippi ES 500/K-5
10620 Direct River Dr NW 55433 763-506-3500
Mark Hansen, prin. Fax 506-3503
Northdale MS 1,300/6-8
11301 Dogwood St NW 55448 763-506-5400
Laurie Jacklitch, prin. Fax 506-5403
Sand Creek ES 600/K-5
12156 Olive St NW 55448 763-506-4300
Paul Anderson, prin. Fax 506-4303
Sorteberg ES 400/K-5
11400 Magnolia St NW 55448 763-506-4400
Marcia Beyer, prin. Fax 506-4403
Other Schools – See Andover, Anoka, Blaine, Brooklyn Center, Brooklyn Park, Champlin, Dayton, Ham Lake, Ramsey

---

Cross of Christ Lutheran S 100/K-8
9931 Foley Blvd NW 55433 763-786-0641
Jason Hahn, prin. Fax 792-0484
Epiphany S 600/K-8
11001 Hanson Blvd NW 55433 763-754-1750
Jane Carroll, prin. Fax 862-4350

Corcoran, Hennepin, Pop. 5,683

St. John Lutheran S 200/PK-8
9141 County Road 101 55340 763-420-2426
Gary Volberding, prin. Fax 420-7198

Cosmos, Meeker, Pop. 574
ACGC SD 2396
Supt. — See Grove City
ACGC South ES 100/PK-4
320 Saturn St N 56228 320-877-7231
Sherri Broderius, prin. Fax 877-7441

Cottage Grove, Washington, Pop. 32,553
South Washington County SD 833 13,500/K-12
7362 E Point Douglas Rd S 55016 651-458-6300
Mark Porter, supt. Fax 458-6318
www.sowashco.k12.mn.us
Armstrong ES 400/K-5
8855 Inwood Ave S 55016 651-768-4100
Tom Berg, prin. Fax 768-4111
Cottage Grove ES 600/K-5
7447 65th St S 55016 651-768-5800
Carl Aegler, prin. Fax 768-5899
Cottage Grove MS 700/6-8
9775 Indian Blvd S 55016 651-768-6800
Elise Block, prin. Fax 768-6828
Crestview/Nuevas Fronteras ES 400/K-5
7830 80th St S 55016 651-768-3800
Rich Romano, prin. Fax 768-3888
Grey Cloud ES 500/K-5
9525 Indian Blvd S 55016 651-768-4200
Laura Loshek, prin. Fax 768-4242
Hillside ES 500/K-5
8177 Hillside Trl S 55016 651-768-4000
Erin Shadick, prin. Fax 768-4004
Pine Hill ES 400/K-5
9015 Hadley Ave S 55016 651-768-3900
Terry Lizakowski, prin. Fax 768-3940
Other Schools – See Newport, Saint Paul Park, Woodbury

Cotton, Saint Louis
Saint Louis County SD 2142
Supt. — See Virginia
Cotton S 100/PK-12
PO Box 187 55724 218-482-3232
Jeffrey Carey, prin. Fax 482-3233

Cottonwood, Lyon, Pop. 1,123
Lakeview SD 2167 600/PK-12
PO Box 107 56229 507-423-5164
Chris Fenske, supt. Fax 423-5568
www.lakeview2167.com
Lakeview ES 300/PK-6
PO Box 107 56229 507-423-5164
Philip Lienemann, prin. Fax 423-5568

Courtland, Nicollet, Pop. 575

Immanuel Lutheran S 100/PK-8
50605 478th St 56021 507-359-2534
Dan Erdman, prin. Fax 359-3288

Cromwell, Carlton, Pop. 201
Cromwell-Wright SD 95 300/PK-12
PO Box 7 55726 218-644-3737
Herbert Hilinski, supt. Fax 644-3992
www.cromwellwright.k12.mn.us
Cromwell-Wright ES 200/PK-6
PO Box 7 55726 218-644-3716
Nathan Libbon, prin. Fax 644-3992

Crookston, Polk, Pop. 7,929
Crookston SD 593 1,400/K-12
402 Fisher Ave Ste 593 56716 218-281-5313
Wayne Gilman, supt. Fax 281-3505
www.crookston.k12.mn.us
Highland S 500/3-7
801 Central Ave N 56716 218-281-5600
Travis Thorvilson, prin. Fax 281-6166
Washington ES 300/K-2
724 University Ave 56716 218-281-2762
Denice Oliver, prin. Fax 281-2784

Cathedral S 100/K-6
702 Summit Ave 56716 218-281-1735
Adam Hollingsworth, prin. Fax 281-1747
Our Savior Lutheran S 100/PK-7
217 S Broadway 56716 218-281-5191
Sandra Trittin, prin.

Crosby, Crow Wing, Pop. 2,222
Crosby-Ironton SD 182 1,200/PK-12
711 Poplar St 56441 218-545-8801
Jamie Skjeveland, supt. Fax 545-8836
www.ci.k12.mn.us
Cuyuna Range ES 600/PK-6
711 Poplar St 56441 218-545-8803
Mindy Jezierski, prin. Fax 545-8858

Crystal, Hennepin, Pop. 21,645
Robbinsdale SD 281
Supt. — See New Hope
Forest ES 500/K-5
6800 47th Ave N 55428 763-504-7900
Connie Grumdahl, prin. Fax 504-7909
Neill ES 400/K-5
6600 Medicine Lake Rd 55427 763-504-7400
Heather Hanson, prin. Fax 504-7409

St. Raphael S 200/PK-8
7301 Bass Lake Rd 55428 763-504-9450
Dorothy Bialke, prin. Fax 504-9460

Cyrus, Pope, Pop. 282
Cyrus SD 611 100/K-6
PO Box 38 56323 320-795-2216
Tom Knoll, supt. Fax 795-2426
www.cyrus.k12.mn.us
Cyrus Math Science & Technology ES 100/K-6
PO Box 38 56323 320-795-2217
Dorothy Jenum, prin. Fax 795-2426

Dakota, Winona, Pop. 322

St. John's Lutheran S 100/PK-8
42685 County Road 12 55925 507-643-6440
Mark Kutz, prin. Fax 643-6007

Dassel, Meeker, Pop. 1,268
Dassel-Cokato SD 466
Supt. — See Cokato
Dassel ES 400/PK-4
PO Box 368 55325 320-286-4100
Rob Nudell, prin. Fax 286-4151

Dawson, Lac qui Parle, Pop. 1,448
Dawson-Boyd SD 378 500/PK-12
848 Chestnut St 56232 320-769-2955
Brad Madsen, supt. Fax 769-4502
dawsonboydschools.org/
Stevens ES 200/PK-6
848 Chestnut St 56232 320-769-4590
Valorie Tuff, prin. Fax 769-2001

Dayton, Hennepin, Pop. 4,622
Anoka-Hennepin SD 11
Supt. — See Coon Rapids
Dayton ES 600/1-5
12000 S Diamond Lake Rd 55327 763-506-2200
Joan Iserman, prin. Fax 506-2203

Deer River, Itasca, Pop. 924
Deer River SD 317 900/PK-12
PO Box 307 56636 218-246-2420
Matt Grose, supt. Fax 246-8948
www.isd317.org
King ES 400/PK-6
PO Box 307 56636 218-246-8860
Amy Galatz, prin. Fax 246-8897

Delano, Wright, Pop. 4,551
Delano SD 879 2,000/PK-12
700 Elm Ave E Ste 2 55328 763-972-3365
John Sweet, supt. Fax 972-6706
www.delano.k12.mn.us
Delano ES 600/PK-4
678 Tiger Dr 55328 763-972-3365
Darren Schuler, prin. Fax 972-6199
Delano MS 700/5-8
700 Elm Ave E Ste 2 55328 763-972-3365
Renee Klinkner, prin. Fax 972-6706

Mount Olive Lutheran S 100/PK-8
435 Bridge Ave E 55328 763-972-2442
Scott Loberger, prin. Fax 972-8139
St. Peter S 100/PK-6
PO Box 470 55328 763-972-2528
Nicole Belpedio, prin. Fax 972-6177

Dent, Otter Tail, Pop. 188
Perham-Dent SD 549
Supt. — See Perham
Dent ES 100/K-4
PO Box 157 56528 218-346-5437
Kari Yates, prin. Fax 758-2010

Detroit Lakes, Becker, Pop. 7,914
Detroit Lakes SD 22 2,600/PK-12
PO Box 766 56502 218-847-9271
Doug Froke, supt. Fax 847-9273
www.dlschools.net/www/index.php
Detroit Lakes MS 600/6-8
510 11th Ave 56501 218-847-9228
Michael Suckert, prin. Fax 847-0057
Roosevelt ES 600/PK-5
510 11th Ave 56501 218-847-1106
Jerry Hanson, prin. Fax 847-1305

Rossman ES 500/PK-5
1221 Rossman Ave 56501 218-847-9268
Sanford Nelson, prin. Fax 847-1481

Adventist Christian S 50/1-8
404 Richwood Rd 56501 218-846-9764
Faith Christian S 50/K-3
24688 County Highway 6 56501 218-847-7375
Gina Kinney, admin. Fax 844-6054
Holy Rosary S 200/PK-8
1043 Lake Ave 56501 218-847-5306
Kathleen Klindt, prin. Fax 847-6367

Dilworth, Clay, Pop. 3,452
Dilworth-Glyndon-Felton SD 2164 1,300/PK-12
PO Box 188 56529 218-287-2371
Randy Bruer, supt. Fax 287-2709
www.dgf.k12.mn.us
Dilworth ES 400/PK-6
PO Box 188 56529 218-287-2100
Peggy Hanson, prin. Fax 287-2709
Dilworth-Glyndon-Felton JHS 200/7-8
PO Box 188 56529 218-287-2148
Colleen Houglum, prin. Fax 287-2709
Other Schools – See Glyndon

Dodge Center, Dodge, Pop. 2,524
Triton SD 2125 1,100/PK-12
813 W Highway St 55927 507-374-2192
Robert Kelly, supt. Fax 374-6524
www.triton.k12.mn.us/
Triton ES 500/PK-5
813 W Highway St 55927 507-374-2258
Nancy Stuckey, prin. Fax 374-2208
Triton MS, 813 W Highway St 55927 300/6-8
Craig Schlichting, prin. 507-374-2192

Grace Lutheran S 50/PK-4
404 Central Ave N 55927 507-633-2253
Patricia Marquardt, dir. Fax 633-2783
Maranatha Adventist S 50/1-8
700 10th Ave NW 55927 507-374-6353

Duluth, Saint Louis, Pop. 84,896
Duluth SD 709 8,800/PK-12
215 N 1st Ave E 55802 218-336-8752
Keith Dixon, supt. Fax 336-8773
www.duluth.k12.mn.us
Congdon Park ES 500/K-5
3116 E Superior St 55812 218-336-8825
Deb Rickard, prin. Fax 336-8829
Early Childhood Family Education 200/PK-PK
215 N 1st Ave E 55802 218-336-8744
Marci Hoff, dir. Fax 733-2091
Grant Magnet ES 200/K-5
1027 N 8th Ave E 55805 218-733-2156
Stephanie Heilig, prin. Fax 733-2159
Homecroft ES 300/K-5
4784 Howard Gnesen Rd 55803 218-728-7446
William Gronseth, prin. Fax 728-7490
Lakewood ES 300/K-5
5207 N Tischer Rd 55804 218-336-8870
Kristin Teberg, prin. Fax 336-8874
Lester Park ES 300/2-5
315 N 54th Ave E 55804 218-525-0804
Bonnie Wolden, prin. Fax 525-0806
Lincoln Park S 400/K-8
2424 W 5th St 55806 218-733-2046
Cher Obst, prin. Fax 733-2056
Lowell Music Magnet ES 500/K-5
2000 Rice Lake Rd 55811 218-733-2164
Jerry Maki, prin. Fax 733-2167
MacArthur ES 500/K-5
727 N Central Ave 55807 218-628-4881
Deb Sauter, prin. Fax 628-4885
Morgan Park MS 500/6-8
1243 88th Ave W 55808 218-626-4512
Denise Clairmont, prin. Fax 626-4520
Nettleton Magnet ES 400/K-5
108 E 6th St 55805 218-733-2172
Stephanie Heilig, prin. Fax 733-2175
Rockridge ES 200/K-1
4849 Ivanhoe St 55804 218-525-0821
Bonnie Wolden, prin. Fax 525-0826
Stowe ES 400/K-5
715 101st Ave W 55808 218-336-8965
Terry Cottingham, prin. Fax 336-8969
Woodland MS 700/6-8
201 Clover St 55812 218-728-7456
Gina Kleive, prin. Fax 728-7460

Proctor SD 704
Supt. — See Proctor
Bay View ES 400/PK-5
8708 Vinland St 55810 218-628-4949
Jon Larson, prin. Fax 628-4951
Pike Lake ES 100/3-5
5682 Martin Rd 55811 218-729-8214
William Gritzmacher, prin. Fax 729-8215

Holy Rosary S 300/K-8
2802 E 4th St 55812 218-724-8565
Jesse Murray, prin. Fax 724-6201
Lakeview Christian Academy 200/PK-12
155 W Central Entrance 55811 218-723-8844
Diane Goldberg, admin. Fax 722-7850
St. James S 200/PK-8
715 N 57th Ave W 55807 218-624-1511
Bill VanLoh, prin. Fax 624-3435
St. John's S 100/PK-6
1 W Chisholm St 55803 218-724-9392
Peggy Frederickson, prin. Fax 724-9368
St. Michael's Lakeside S 100/PK-6
4628 Pitt St 55804 218-525-1931
Amy Flaig, prin. Fax 525-0296
Stone Ridge Christian S 50/1-8
115 E Orange St 55811 218-722-7535

Eagan, Dakota, Pop. 63,665
Burnsville-Eagan-Savage ISD 191
Supt. — See Burnsville
Rahn ES 400/K-6
4424 Sandstone Dr 55122 952-707-3600
Doug Steele, prin. Fax 707-3602

Rosemount-Apple Valley-Eagan ISD 196
Supt. — See Rosemount
Black Hawk MS 1,000/6-8
1540 Deerwood Dr 55122 651-683-8521
Richard Wendorff, prin. Fax 683-8527
Dakota Hills MS 1,300/6-8
4183 Braddock Trl Ste 1 55123 651-683-6800
Trevor Johnson, prin. Fax 683-6858
Deerwood ES 500/K-5
1480 Deerwood Dr 55122 651-683-6801
Miles Haugen, prin. Fax 683-6808
Glacier Hills ES 400/K-5
3825 Glacier Hls 55123 651-683-8570
Jeff Holten, prin. Fax 683-8577
Northview ES 600/K-5
965 Diffley Rd 55123 651-683-6820
Kathy Carl, prin. Fax 683-6819
Oak Ridge ES 600/K-5
4350 Johnny Cake Ridge Rd 55122 651-683-6970
Lisa Hannon, prin. Fax 683-6873
Pinewood ES 600/K-5
4300 Dodd Rd 55123 651-683-6980
Cris Town, prin. Fax 683-6870
Red Pine ES 800/K-5
530 Red Pine Ln 55123 651-423-7870
Gary Anger, prin. Fax 423-7875
Thomas Lake ES 500/K-5
4350 Thomas Lake Rd 55122 651-683-6890
Mary Jelenik, prin. Fax 683-6884
Woodland ES 500/K-5
945 Wescott Rd 55123 651-683-6990
Lisa Carlson, prin. Fax 683-6883

West St. Paul-Mendota Hts-Eagan SD 197
Supt. — See Mendota Heights
Pilot Knob ES 300/PK-4
1436 Lone Oak Rd 55121 651-405-2788
Tom Benson, prin. Fax 454-1569

Faithful Shepherd S 600/K-8
3355 Columbia Dr 55121 651-406-4747
John Boone, prin. Fax 406-4743
Living Word Academy 50/1-6
4300 Nicols Rd 55122 651-456-0001
Dr. Kathy Gjesfeld, prin. Fax 994-6901
Tesseract S 200/PK-6
3800 Tesseract Pl 55122 651-454-0604
Charles McGill, prin. Fax 454-6627
Trinity Lone Oak Lutheran S 200/PK-8
2950 Highway 55 55121 651-454-1139
Sean Martens, prin. Fax 454-0109

Eagle Bend, Todd, Pop. 590
Eagle Valley SD 2759 300/PK-12
PO Box 299 56446 218-738-6442
Jim Madsen, supt. Fax 738-6493
www.evps.k12.mn.us
Other Schools – See Clarissa

Eagle Lake, Blue Earth, Pop. 2,028
Mankato SD 77
Supt. — See Mankato
Eagle Lake ES 300/K-5
PO Box 129 56024 507-257-3530
Ginnette Kearney, prin. Fax 257-3867

East Grand Forks, Polk, Pop. 7,734
East Grand Forks SD 595 1,600/PK-12
PO Box 151 56721 218-773-3494
David Pace, supt. Fax 773-7408
www.egf.k12.mn.us/
Central MS 400/6-8
PO Box 151 56721 218-773-1141
Lon Ellingson, prin. Fax 773-9112
New Heights ES 300/PK-2
PO Box 151 56721 218-773-0908
Luther Meyer, prin. Fax 773-3150
South Point ES 400/3-5
PO Box 151 56721 218-773-1149
Suraya Driscoll, prin. Fax 773-4392

Riverside Christian S 100/PK-8
610 2nd Ave NE 56721 218-773-1770
Jane Hellekson, admin. Fax 773-4322
Sacred Heart S 200/PK-6
117 4th St NW 56721 218-773-1579
David Andrys, prin. Fax 773-0318

Eden Prairie, Hennepin, Pop. 60,649
Eden Prairie SD 272 8,900/PK-12
8100 School Rd 55344 952-975-7000
Melissa Krull Ph.D., supt. Fax 975-7012
www.edenpr.org
Cedar Ridge ES 800/K-4
8905 Braxton Dr 55347 952-975-7800
Marilee Hoch, prin. Fax 975-7820
Central Kindergarten 50/K-K
8100 School Rd 55344 952-975-7200
Carol Meyer, prin. Fax 975-7220
Central MS 1,600/7-8
8025 School Rd 55344 952-975-7300
Joe Epping, prin. Fax 975-7320
Eagle Heights Spanish Immersion S PK-3
8104 School Rd 55344 952-975-7200
Larry Leebens, prin.
Eden Lake ES 800/K-4
12000 Anderson Lakes Pkwy 55344 952-975-8400
Charles Richter, prin. Fax 975-8420
Forest Hills ES 500/K-4
13708 Holly Rd 55346 952-975-8600
Connie Hytjan, prin. Fax 975-8620
Oak Point IS 1,500/5-6
13400 Staring Lake Pkwy 55347 952-975-7600
Arnette Bell, prin. Fax 975-7620
Prairie View ES 600/K-4
17255 Peterborg Rd 55346 952-975-8800
Carol Meyer, prin. Fax 975-8820

International School of Minnesota 500/PK-12
6385 Beach Rd 55344 952-918-1800
Susan Berg, dir. Fax 918-1801

Eden Valley, Meeker, Pop. 925
Eden Valley-Watkins SD 463 900/PK-12
298 Brooks St N 55329 320-453-2900
Larry Peterson, supt. Fax 453-5600
www.evw.k12.mn.us
Eden Valley ES 400/K-6
901 Stearns Ave E 55329 320-453-2900
Robert Pederson, prin. Fax 453-6457
Watkins K 100/PK-K
901 Stearns Ave E 55329 320-453-2900
Robert Pederson, prin. Fax 453-6457

Edgerton, Pipestone, Pop. 976
Edgerton SD 581 300/PK-12
PO Box 28 56128 507-442-7881
Leroy Domagala, supt. Fax 442-8541
edgertonpublic.com
Edgerton ES 100/PK-6
PO Box 28 56128 507-442-7881
Brian Gilbertson, prin. Fax 442-8541

Edgerton Christian S 200/K-8
PO Box 210 56128 507-442-6181
Randy Pfeifle, prin. Fax 442-3019

Edina, Hennepin, Pop. 45,567
Edina SD 273 7,300/K-12
5701 Normandale Rd Ste 1 55424 952-848-3900
Ric Dressen, supt. Fax 848-3901
www.edina.k12.mn.us
Concord ES 600/K-5
5900 Concord Ave 55424 952-848-4300
Rick Sansted, prin. Fax 848-4301
Cornelia ES 500/K-5
7000 Cornelia Dr 55435 952-848-4600
Chris Holden, prin. Fax 848-4601
Countryside ES 600/K-5
5701 Benton Ave 55436 952-848-4700
Julie Hatzung, prin. Fax 848-4701
Creek Valley ES 500/K-5
6401 Gleason Rd 55439 952-848-3200
Kari Dahlquist, prin. Fax 848-3201
Highlands ES 500/K-5
5505 Doncaster Way 55436 952-848-4500
Peter Hodne, prin. Fax 848-4501
Normandale ES 500/K-5
5701 Normandale Rd 55424 952-848-4100
John Devine, prin. Fax 848-4101

Calvin Christian S 300/K-8
4015 Inglewood Ave S 55416 952-927-5304
Steven Groen, prin. Fax 927-4628
Our Lady of Grace S 600/K-8
5051 Eden Ave 55436 952-929-5463
Maureen Trenary, prin. Fax 929-8170
St. Peter Lutheran S 100/PK-6
5421 France Ave S 55410 952-927-8400
Fax 926-6545

Elbow Lake, Grant, Pop. 1,225
West Central Area SD 2342
Supt. — See Barrett
West Central Area North ES 200/PK-6
411 1st St SE 56531 218-685-4477
Jim Houseman, prin. Fax 685-4149

Elgin, Wabasha, Pop. 938
Plainview-Elgin-Millville ISD 2899
Supt. — See Plainview
Plainview-Elgin-Millville IS 100/4-6
210 2nd St SW 55932 507-876-2213
Clark Olstad, prin. Fax 876-2296
Plainview-Elgin-Millville JHS 100/7-8
70 1st St SE 55932 507-876-2521
Clark Olstad, prin. Fax 876-2110

Elko, Scott, Pop. 533
New Prague Area SD 721
Supt. — See New Prague
Eagle View ES K-5
25600 Nevada Ave 55020 952-758-6000
Mark Randall, prin. Fax 758-6099

Elk River, Sherburne, Pop. 21,329
Elk River Area SD 728 10,000/K-12
815 Highway 10 55330 763-241-3400
Mark Bezek, supt. Fax 241-3407
www.elkriver.k12.mn.us
Lincoln ES 600/K-5
600 School St NW 55330 763-241-3480
Donna Williams, prin. Fax 241-3481
Meadowvale ES 700/K-5
12701 Elk Lake Rd NW 55330 763-241-3470
David Hauer, prin. Fax 241-3471
Otsego ES 700/K-5
8125 NE River Rd 55330 763-241-3494
Erin Talley, prin. Fax 241-3496
Parker ES 600/K-5
500 School St NW 55330 763-241-3500
Mike Malmberg, prin. Fax 241-3501
Salk MS 600/6-8
11970 Highland Rd NW 55330 763-241-3455
Julie Athman, prin. Fax 241-3456
Twin Lakes ES K-5
10051 191st Ave NW 55330 763-274-7242
Dan Collins, prin. Fax 274-7243

VandenBerge MS 600/6-8
948 Proctor Ave NW 55330 763-241-3450
Clair Olson, prin. Fax 241-3451
Other Schools – See Rogers, Zimmerman

Rivers Christian Academy 100/K-12
829 School St NW 55330 763-441-6594
St. Andrew S 300/K-6
428 Irving Ave NW 55330 763-441-2216
Kari Staples, prin. Fax 441-1146
St. John Lutheran S 200/PK-8
9231 Viking Blvd NW 55330 763-441-6616
Fax 441-9858

Ellendale, Steele, Pop. 649
NRHEG SD 2168
Supt. — See New Richland
NRHEG S 400/PK-8
600 School St S 56026 507-684-3183
Paul Cyr, prin. Fax 684-2108

Ellsworth, Nobles, Pop. 521
Ellsworth SD 514 100/PK-12
PO Box 8 56129 507-967-2242
George Berndt, supt. Fax 967-2588
www.ellsworth.mntm.org
Ellsworth S 100/PK-12
PO Box 8 56129 507-967-2151
George Berndt, prin. Fax 967-2588

Ely, Saint Louis, Pop. 3,633
Ely SD 696 300/PK-12
600 E Harvey St 55731 218-365-6166
Dr. Donald Langan, supt. Fax 365-6138
www.ely.k12.mn.us
Ely Public S 300/PK-12
600 E Harvey St 55731 218-365-6166
Joselyn Murphy, prin. Fax 365-6138

Erskine, Polk, Pop. 416
Win-E-Mac SD 2609 500/K-12
23130 345th St SE 56535 218-687-2236
Dan Parent, supt. Fax 563-2902
www.win-e-mac.k12.mn.us
Win-E-Mac ES 200/K-6
23130 345th St SE 56535 218-687-2236
Kevin McKeever, prin. Fax 563-2902

Esko, Carlton
Esko SD 99 1,100/PK-12
PO Box 10 55733 218-879-2969
Aaron Fischer, supt. Fax 879-7490
www.esko.k12.mn.us/
Winterquist ES 600/PK-6
PO Box 10 55733 218-879-3361
Brian Harker, prin. Fax 879-7490

Evansville, Douglas, Pop. 554
Evansville SD 208 200/PK-12
PO Box 40 56326 218-948-2241
John Kraker, supt. Fax 948-2441
www.evansville.k12.mn.us/
Evansville ES 100/PK-6
PO Box 40 56326 218-948-2241
John Kraker, prin. Fax 948-2441

Eveleth, Saint Louis, Pop. 3,661
Eveleth-Gilbert SD 2154 1,200/PK-12
801 Jones St 55734 218-744-7701
Deborah Hilde, supt. Fax 744-4381
isd2154.k12.mn.us
Franklin ES 500/PK-6
801 Jones St 55734 218-744-7710
Lynn Bol, prin. Fax 744-4381
Other Schools – See Gilbert

Excelsior, Hennepin, Pop. 2,294
Minnetonka SD 276
Supt. — See Minnetonka
Excelsior ES 500/K-5
441 Oak St 55331 952-401-5650
Lee Drolet, prin. Fax 401-5657
Minnetonka West MS 900/6-8
6421 Hazeltine Blvd 55331 952-401-5300
Bill Jacobson, prin. Fax 401-5350
Minnewashta ES 500/K-5
26350 Smithtown Rd 55331 952-401-5500
Cindy Andress, prin. Fax 401-5506

Our Savior Lutheran S 100/PK-8
23290 Highway 7 55331 952-474-5181
Mickey Bloom, prin. Fax 470-1985
St. John the Baptist S 200/PK-8
638 Mill St 55331 952-474-5812
Mike Moch, prin. Fax 401-8778
Spring Hill S 100/PK-8
471 3rd St 55331 952-449-0040
Fax 380-3546

Eyota, Olmsted, Pop. 1,708
Dover-Eyota SD 533 1,100/PK-12
615 South Ave SE 55934 507-545-2125
Bruce Klaehn, supt. Fax 545-2349
www.desch.org
Dover-Eyota ES 600/PK-6
27 Knowledge Rd SE 55934 507-545-2632
Jeanne Svobodny, prin. Fax 545-2841

Fairfax, Renville, Pop. 1,279
GFW SD 2365
Supt. — See Gibbon
GFW MS 200/5-8
PO Box 489 55332 507-426-7251
Ralph Fairchild, prin. Fax 426-7425

Prairie Lutheran MS 50/5-8
PO Box 130 55332 507-426-7755
Macord Johnson, prin. Fax 426-8372

Fairmont, Martin, Pop. 10,505
Fairmont Area SD 2752 1,600/K-12
115 S Park St 56031 507-238-4234
Harlow Hanson, supt. Fax 235-4050
fairmont.k12.mn.us
Budd ES 300/K-2
1001 Albion Ave 56031 507-235-9874
Richard Truman, prin. Fax 235-4521
Five Lakes ES 500/3-6
714 Victoria St 56031 507-238-4487
Jim Davison, prin. Fax 235-4652

St. James Lutheran S 100/PK-8
108 S James St 56031 507-436-5289
Charles Lieder, prin. Fax 436-5547
St. John Vianney S 100/PK-6
911 S Prairie Ave 56031 507-235-5304
Joan Schaffer, prin. Fax 235-9099
St. Paul Lutheran S 200/PK-8
201 Oxford St 56031 507-238-9492
Gerald Bergt, prin. Fax 238-9492

Falcon Heights, Ramsey, Pop. 5,469
Roseville Area SD 623
Supt. — See Roseville
Falcon Heights ES 400/K-6
1393 Garden Ave 55113 651-646-0021
Paul Charest, prin. Fax 646-7183

Faribault, Rice, Pop. 22,047
Faribault SD 656 3,900/PK-12
PO Box 618 55021 507-333-6016
Robert Stepaniak, supt. Fax 333-6077
www.faribault.k12.mn.us/
Faribault MS 900/6-8
704 17th St SW 55021 507-333-6300
Jennifer Backer, prin. Fax 333-6400
Jefferson ES 600/K-5
922 Home Pl 55021 507-333-6500
Brad Palmer, prin. Fax 333-6544
Lincoln ES 500/PK-5
510 Lincoln Ave NW 55021 507-333-6600
Mark Wergeland, prin. Fax 333-6642
McKinley ECC PK-K
PO Box 618 55021 507-333-6800
Judy Covert, prin. Fax 333-6802
Roosevelt ES 600/K-5
925 Parshall St 55021 507-333-6700
Terry Ronayne, prin. Fax 333-6734

Divine Mercy Catholic S 300/PK-6
15 3rd Ave SW 55021 507-334-7706
Robert Seidel, prin. Fax 332-2669
Faribault Lutheran S - Peace Campus 100/K-2
213 6th Ave SW 55021 507-334-9270
Karen Fuchs, prin. Fax 334-1726
Faribault Lutheran S - Trinity Campus 100/3-8
526 4th St NW 55021 507-334-7982
Karen Fuchs, prin. Fax 334-4208
Parkside SDA S 50/1-8
1390 Albers Path 55021 507-334-6588

Farmington, Dakota, Pop. 17,740
Farmington SD 192 4,100/K-12
421 Walnut St 55024 651-463-5000
Dr. Bradley Meeks, supt. Fax 463-5010
www.farmington.k12.mn.us
Akin Road ES 600/K-5
5231 195th St W 55024 651-460-1700
Karen Bergman, prin. Fax 460-1710
Boeckman MS 6-8
800 Denmark Ave 55024 651-460-1400
Barb Duffrin, prin. Fax 460-1410
Dodge MS 400/6-8
4200 208th St W 55024 651-460-1500
Chris Bussmann, prin. Fax 460-1510
Farmington ES 700/K-5
500 Maple St 55024 651-463-9000
Ben Januschka, prin. Fax 463-9010
Meadowview ES 600/K-5
6100 195th St W 55024 651-460-3100
Jon Reid, prin. Fax 460-3110
North Trail ES 700/K-5
5580 170th St W 55024 651-460-1800
Steven Geis, prin. Fax 460-1810
Riverview ES K-5
4100 208th St W 55024 651-460-1600
Kim Grengs, prin. Fax 460-1610

Christian Life S 200/PK-12
6300 212th St W 55024 651-463-4545
Pastor Darin Kindle, admin. Fax 463-8353

Fergus Falls, Otter Tail, Pop. 13,722
Fergus Falls SD 544 1,900/PK-12
1519 Pebble Lake Rd 56537 218-998-0544
Gerald Ness, supt. Fax 998-3952
www.fergusfalls.k12.mn.us
Adams ES 100/1-2
301 W Bancroft Ave 56537 218-998-0544
Scott Colbeck, prin. Fax 998-3961
Cleveland ES 100/3-5
919 Northern Ave 56537 218-998-0544
Scott Colbeck, prin. Fax 998-3945
Early Childhood Family Education PK-K
724 W Laurel Ave 56537 218-998-0935
Stacy McAllister, dir. Fax 998-3952
Fergus Falls MS 700/6-8
601 Randolph Ave 56537 218-998-0544
Dean Monke, prin. Fax 998-3943
McKinley ES 100/K-K, 4-4
724 W Laurel Ave 56537 218-998-0544
Scott Colbeck, prin. Fax 998-0547

Morning Son Christian S 200/PK-6
1319 N Cleveland Ave 56537 218-736-2477
Kathy Austvold, prin. Fax 739-9374

Our Lady of Victory S 200/PK-6
426 W Cavour Ave 56537 218-736-6661
Sandy Carpenter, prin. Fax 736-4407
Trinity Lutheran S 50/PK-6
1150 W Cavour Ave 56537 218-736-5847
Fax 739-3667

Fertile, Polk, Pop. 866
Fertile-Beltrami SD 599 500/PK-12
PO Box 648 56540 218-945-6933
Brian Clarke, supt. Fax 945-6934
fertilebeltrami.k12.mn.us/FBSchool/Home/home.htm
Fertile-Beltrami ES 200/PK-6
PO Box 648 56540 218-945-6983
Brian Clarke, prin. Fax 945-6934

Finlayson, Pine, Pop. 323
East Central SD 2580 700/PK-12
61085 State Highway 23 55735 320-245-2289
Jeffrey Peura, supt. Fax 245-5453
www.eastcentral.k12.mn.us
East Central ES 400/PK-5
61085 State Highway 23 55735 320-245-2931
Jeffrey Peura, prin. Fax 245-2448

Hinckley-Finlayson SD 2165
Supt. — See Hinckley
Finlayson ES 100/PK-6
PO Box 180 55735 320-233-7611
Larry Edgerton, prin. Fax 233-6148

Fisher, Polk, Pop. 417
Fisher SD 600 300/K-12
313 Park Ave 56723 218-891-4105
David Vik, supt. Fax 891-4251
www.fisher.k12.mn.us
Fisher ES 100/K-6
313 Park Ave 56723 218-891-4105
Tami Newhouse, coord. Fax 891-4251

Floodwood, Saint Louis, Pop. 503
Floodwood SD 698 400/PK-12
PO Box 287 55736 218-476-2285
Palmer Anderson, supt. Fax 476-2813
www.floodwood.k12.mn.us/
Floodwood ES 200/PK-6
PO Box 287 55736 218-476-2285
Robert Bestul, prin. Fax 476-2813

Foley, Benton, Pop. 2,373
Foley SD 51 1,600/PK-12
PO Box 297 56329 320-968-7175
Dr. Fred Nolan, supt. Fax 968-8608
foley.k12.mn.us
Foley ES 400/PK-3
PO Box 197 56329 320-968-7286
Maria Erlandson, prin. Fax 968-8467
Foley MS 700/4-8
PO Box 297 56329 320-968-6251
Brad Kelvington, prin. Fax 968-8608

St. John S 100/PK-6
PO Box 368 56329 320-968-7972
Mary Sabin, prin. Fax 968-9956

Forest Lake, Washington, Pop. 17,353
Forest Lake SD 831 7,300/K-12
6100 210th St N 55025 651-982-8100
Linda Madsen, supt. Fax 982-8114
www.forestlake.k12.mn.us
Central Montessori ES 200/K-6
200 4th St SW 55025 651-982-8270
Gayle McGrane, prin. Fax 982-3172
Columbus ES 400/K-6
17345 Notre Dame St NE 55025 651-982-8900
Neal Fox, prin. Fax 982-8957
Forest Lake ES 300/K-6
408 4th St SW 55025 651-982-3200
Jeffrey Ion, prin. Fax 982-3299
Forest View ES 600/K-6
620 4th St SW 55025 651-982-8200
Dr. Janet Palmer, prin. Fax 982-8260
Other Schools – See Lino Lakes, Scandia, Wyoming

St. Peter S 300/PK-6
1250 S Shore Dr 55025 651-982-2215
Ann Laird, prin. Fax 982-2230

Foreston, Mille Lacs, Pop. 507

Faith Christian S 100/PK-12
11818 160th Ave 56330 320-294-5501
Marilyn Miller, admin. Fax 294-5197

Fosston, Polk, Pop. 1,515
Fosston SD 601 700/PK-12
301 1st St E 56542 218-435-6335
Gene Paulson, supt. Fax 435-1663
www.fosston.k12.mn.us
Magelssen ES 400/PK-6
700 1st St E 56542 218-435-6036
Gregory Bruce, prin. Fax 435-6414

Franklin, Renville, Pop. 493
Cedar Mountain SD 2754
Supt. — See Morgan
Cedar Mountain ES 200/K-6
PO Box 38 55333 507-557-2251
Patti Machart, prin. Fax 557-2116

Frazee, Becker, Pop. 1,396
Frazee-Vergas SD 23 1,000/PK-12
305 N Lake St 56544 218-334-3181
Deron Stender, supt. Fax 334-3182
www.frazee.k12.mn.us/
Frazee ES 500/PK-6
305 N Lake St 56544 218-334-3181
Brian Koslofsky, prin. Fax 334-2115

Freeport, Stearns, Pop. 469

Sacred Heart S 100/PK-6
PO Box 38 56331 320-836-2591
Fax 836-2142

Fridley, Anoka, Pop. 26,515
Columbia Heights SD 13
Supt. — See Columbia Heights
North Park ES 500/K-5
5575 Fillmore St NE 55432 763-528-4300
Jeff Cacek, prin. Fax 528-4307

Fridley SD 14 2,400/K-12
6000 Moore Lake Dr W 55432 763-502-5000
Mark Robertson, supt. Fax 502-5040
www.fridley.k12.mn.us
Fridley MS 800/5-8
6100 Moore Lake Dr W 55432 763-502-5400
Margaret Leibfried, prin. Fax 502-5440
Hayes ES 300/K-4
615 Mississippi St NE 55432 763-502-5200
John Piotraschke, prin. Fax 502-5240
Stevenson ES 400/K-4
6080 E River Rd 55432 763-502-5300
Daryl Vossler, prin. Fax 502-5340

Spring Lake Park SD 16
Supt. — See Minneapolis
Woodcrest ES 300/K-3
880 Osborne Rd NE 55432 763-784-9293
Judi Kahoun, prin. Fax 783-5217

Fulda, Murray, Pop. 1,272
Fulda SD 505 400/PK-12
410 N College Ave 56131 507-425-2514
Luther Onken, supt. Fax 425-2001
www.fps.mntm.org
Fulda ES 200/PK-6
303 N Lafayette Ave 56131 507-425-2581
Gregg Slaathaug, dean Fax 425-2001

St. Paul Lutheran S 100/PK-8
208 3rd St NE 56131 507-425-2169
Leah Olson, prin.

Garfield, Douglas, Pop. 297
Alexandria SD 206
Supt. — See Alexandria
Garfield ES 200/K-6
PO Box 158 56332 320-834-2261
Lisa Pikop, prin. Fax 834-2260

Gary, Norman, Pop. 207
Norman County East SD 2215
Supt. — See Twin Valley
Norman County East ES 200/PK-6
301 2nd Ave E 56545 218-356-8222
Dean Krogstad, admin. Fax 356-8794

Gaylord, Sibley, Pop. 2,194
Sibley East SD 2310
Supt. — See Arlington
Sibley East ES Gaylord Campus 300/PK-6
PO Box 356 55334 507-237-3318
Mari Lu Martens, prin. Fax 237-3300

Immanuel Lutheran S 50/K-8
PO Box 448 55334 507-237-2804
Fax 237-2804

Gibbon, Sibley, Pop. 764
GFW SD 2365 800/PK-12
323 E 11th St 55335 507-834-9813
Stephen Malone, supt. Fax 834-6264
www.gfw.k12.mn.us
GFW ES 300/PK-4
323 E 11th St 55335 507-834-6501
Ralph Fairchild, prin. Fax 834-6503
Other Schools – See Fairfax

Prairie Lutheran ES 100/PK-4
1322 1st Ave 55335 507-834-6136
Macord Johnson, prin. Fax 426-8372
St. Peter Lutheran S 50/K-8
63872 240th St 55335 507-834-6676
Fax 834-6676

Gilbert, Saint Louis, Pop. 1,772
Eveleth-Gilbert SD 2154
Supt. — See Eveleth
Eveleth-Gilbert JHS 200/7-8
Summit St 55741 218-741-7773
Nate Hanson, prin. Fax 741-7504
Shean ES 200/K-6
Summit St 55741 218-744-7773
Nate Hanson, prin. Fax 741-7504

Glencoe, McLeod, Pop. 5,553
Glencoe-Silver Lake SD 2859 1,500/PK-12
1621 16th St E 55336 320-864-2498
Chris Sonju, supt. Fax 864-6320
www.gsl.k12.mn.us
Baker ES 200/PK-2
1621 16th St E 55336 320-864-2501
Debbie Morris, prin. Fax 864-2682
Lincoln JHS 300/7-8
1621 16th St E 55336 320-864-2401
Lon Jorgensen, prin. Fax 864-2475
Other Schools – See Silver Lake

First Evangelical Lutheran S 100/PK-8
1015 14th St E 55336 320-864-3317
Craig Kohls, prin. Fax 864-3317
St. Pius X S 100/PK-6
1103 10th St E 55336 320-864-3214
Kathryn Morgan, prin. Fax 864-5163

Glenville, Freeborn, Pop. 701
Glenville-Emmons SD 2886 400/K-12
PO Box 38 56036 507-448-2889
Mark Roubinek, supt. Fax 448-2836
www.geschools.com
Glenville-Emmons ES 200/K-6
240 2nd Ave SW 56036 507-448-3334
Sue Gillard, prin. Fax 448-2045

Glenwood, Pope, Pop. 2,564
Minnewaska SD 2149 1,000/PK-12
25122 State Highway 28 56334 320-239-4800
Gregory Ohl, supt. Fax 239-1360
www.minnewaska.k12.mn.us
Minnewaska Area ES 400/PK-4
409 4th St SE 56334 320-634-4567
Patrick Falk, prin. Fax 239-1380

Glyndon, Clay, Pop. 1,168
Dilworth-Glyndon-Felton SD 2164
Supt. — See Dilworth
Glyndon-Felton ES 300/PK-6
513 Parke Ave S 56547 218-498-2265
Shannon Dahlberg, prin. Fax 498-2488

Golden Valley, Hennepin, Pop. 20,003
Hopkins SD 270
Supt. — See Hopkins
Meadowbrook ES 600/K-6
5430 Glenwood Ave 55422 952-988-5100
Greta Evans-Becker, prin. Fax 988-5115

Robbinsdale SD 281
Supt. — See New Hope
Noble ES 400/K-5
2601 Noble Ave N 55422 763-504-4000
Lori Sundberg, prin. Fax 504-4009

Good Shepherd S 300/K-6
145 Jersey Ave S 55426 763-545-4285
Thomas Zellmer, prin. Fax 545-1896
King of Grace Lutheran S 200/PK-8
6000 Duluth St 55422 763-546-3131
Allen Labitsky, prin. Fax 540-0028

Goodhue, Goodhue, Pop. 929
Goodhue SD 253 600/PK-12
510 3rd Ave 55027 651-923-4447
Robert Bangston, supt. Fax 923-4083
www.goodhue.k12.mn.us
Goodhue ES 300/PK-6
510 3rd Ave 55027 651-923-4447
Mark Opsahl, prin. Fax 923-4083

St. John Lutheran S 50/K-8
36639 County 4 Blvd 55027 651-923-4773
Emily Babinec, prin. Fax 923-5015

Goodridge, Pennington, Pop. 107
Goodridge SD 561 200/K-12
PO Box 195 56725 218-378-4133
Galen Clow, supt. Fax 378-4142
www.goodridge.k12.mn.us/
Goodridge ES 100/K-6
PO Box 195 56725 218-378-4134
Andrew Almos, prin. Fax 378-4142

Good Thunder, Blue Earth, Pop. 570
Maple River SD 2135
Supt. — See Mapleton
Maple River West ES 200/PK-5
PO Box 306 56037 507-278-3039
Deanne Rengstorf, prin. Fax 278-4266

Graceville, Big Stone, Pop. 574
Clinton-Graceville-Beardsley SD 2888
Supt. — See Clinton
Big Stone Colony S 50/K-8
26051 Big Stone Colony Rd 56240 320-748-7117
Mary Smidt, prin.

Granada, Martin, Pop. 305
Granada - Huntley - East Chain SD 2536 300/PK-12
PO Box 17 56039 507-447-2211
Randy Grupe, supt. Fax 447-2214
www.ghec.k12.mn.us
Other Schools – See Blue Earth

Grand Marais, Cook, Pop. 1,426
Cook County SD 166 400/K-12
101 W 5th St 55604 218-387-2271
Beth Schwarz, supt. Fax 387-1093
www.cookcountyschools.org/
Sawtooth Mountain ES 200/K-5
101 W 5th St 55604 218-387-1273
Gwen Carman, prin. Fax 387-9667

Grand Meadow, Mower, Pop. 946
Grand Meadow SD 495 300/K-12
PO Box 68 55936 507-754-5318
Joseph Brown, supt. Fax 754-5608
www.gm.k12.mn.us/
Grand Meadow ES 100/K-5
PO Box 68 55936 507-754-5310
David Stadum, prin. Fax 754-5608
Grand Meadow MS 100/6-8
PO Box 68 55936 507-754-5318
Joseph Brown, prin. Fax 754-5608

Grand Rapids, Itasca, Pop. 8,277
Grand Rapids SD 318 3,500/PK-12
820 NW 1st Ave 55744 218-327-5700
Joe Silko, supt. Fax 327-5702
www.isd318.org
Early Childhood Family Education PK-PK
820 NW 1st Ave 55744 218-327-5850
Sue Hoeft, dir. Fax 327-5851
Elkington MS 700/5-8
1000 NE 8th Ave 55744 218-327-5800
Brent Brunetta, prin. Fax 327-5801
Forest Lake ES 300/K-4
715 NW 7th Ave 55744 218-327-5870
Ranae Seykora, prin. Fax 327-5871
Murphy ES 300/K-4
822 NE 5th Ave 55744 218-327-5880
Patricia Anderson, prin. Fax 327-5881
Southwest ES 300/K-4
601 SW 7th St 55744 218-327-5890
Ken Decoster, prin. Fax 327-5891
Other Schools – See Bigfork, Cohasset

St. Joseph's S 200/PK-6
614 NW 2nd Ave 55744 218-326-6232
Teresa Matetich, prin. Fax 326-6034

Granite Falls, Yellow Medicine, Pop. 2,988
Yellow Medicine East SD 2190 1,000/K-12
450 9th Ave 56241 320-564-4081
Allen Stoeckman, supt. Fax 564-4781
isd2190.org/
Raney ES 400/K-6
555 7th St 56241 320-564-4427
Stacy Hinz, prin. Fax 564-4082
Other Schools – See Clarkfield

Greenbush, Roseau, Pop. 770
Greenbush-Middle River SD 2683 500/PK-12
PO Box 70 56726 218-782-2231
Ron Ruud, supt. Fax 782-3141
www.middleriver.k12.mn.us/
Greenbush ES 100/PK-5
PO Box 70 56726 218-782-2232
Eldon Sparby, prin. Fax 782-2165
Other Schools – See Middle River

Grey Eagle, Todd, Pop. 337
Long Prairie-Grey Eagle SD 2753
Supt. — See Long Prairie
Grey Eagle ES 100/PK-6
304 State St E 56336 320-285-5300
Paul Weinzierl, prin. Fax 285-5301

Grove City, Meeker, Pop. 600
ACGC SD 2396 700/PK-12
27250 Minnesota Highway 4 56243 320-857-2271
Sherri Broderius, supt. Fax 857-2989
www.acgc.k12.mn.us
Other Schools – See Atwater, Cosmos

Grygla, Marshall, Pop. 233
Grygla SD 447 200/PK-12
PO Box 18 56727 218-294-6155
Galen Clow, supt. Fax 294-6766
www.grygla.k12.mn.us/
Grygla ES 100/PK-6
PO Box 18 56727 218-294-6155
Patti Johnson, prin. Fax 294-6766

Hallock, Kittson, Pop. 1,087
Kittson Central SD 2171 300/PK-12
PO Box 670 56728 218-843-3682
Bruce Jensen, supt. Fax 843-2856
kittson.k12.mn.us
Other Schools – See Kennedy, Saint Vincent

Hamburg, Carver, Pop. 543

Emanuel Lutheran S 100/PK-8
18155 County Road 50 55339 952-467-2780
Dean Scheele, prin. Fax 467-2907

Ham Lake, Anoka, Pop. 14,774
Anoka-Hennepin SD 11
Supt. — See Coon Rapids
McKinley ES 700/K-5
1740 Constance Blvd NE 55304 763-506-3400
Mark VanVoorhis, prin. Fax 506-3403

Hampton, Dakota, Pop. 613

St. Mary S - New Trier S 50/PK-5
8433 239th St E 55031 651-437-5546
Patricia Ziegenbein, prin. Fax 437-3764
St. Mathias S 50/PK-5
23335 Northfield Blvd 55031 651-437-5282
Dawn Conway, prin. Fax 437-3427

Hancock, Stevens, Pop. 694
Hancock SD 768 300/K-12
PO Box 367 56244 320-392-5622
Jerry Martinson, supt. Fax 392-5156
Hancock ES 100/K-6
PO Box 367 56244 320-392-5622
Jerry Martinson, prin. Fax 392-5156

Hanover, Wright, Pop. 2,264
Buffalo SD 877
Supt. — See Buffalo
Hanover ES 500/K-5
274 Labeaux Ave 55341 763-682-0823
Jeff Olson, prin. Fax 682-0868

Hastings, Dakota, Pop. 20,910
Hastings SD 200 5,000/K-12
1000 11th St W 55033 651-437-6111
Tim Collins, supt. Fax 437-1928
www.hastings.k12.mn.us
Hastings MS 1,200/6-8
1000 11th St W 55033 651-438-0705
Mark Zuzek, prin. Fax 438-0707
Kennedy ES 600/1-5
1175 Tyler St 55033 651-438-0811
Nancy Techam, prin. Fax 438-0613
McAuliffe ES 500/1-5
1601 12th St W 55033 651-438-0862
Elaine Bell, prin. Fax 437-0617
Pinecrest ES 600/1-5
975 12th St W 55033 651-438-0832
Roger Esser, prin. Fax 438-0614

Tilden K 300/K-K
855 3rd St W 55033 651-438-0850
Diane Smith, prin. Fax 438-0615

Pine Harbor Christian Academy 100/PK-8
11125 West Point Douglas Rd 55033 651-438-2259
Karla Schommer, admin. Fax 437-9039
St. Elizabeth Ann Seton S 400/PK-8
600 Tyler St 55033 651-437-3098
Rita Humbert, prin. Fax 438-3377

Hawley, Clay, Pop. 1,892
Hawley SD 150 900/K-12
PO Box 608 56549 218-483-4647
Phil Jensen, supt. Fax 483-3510
www.hawley.k12.mn.us/
Hawley ES 400/K-6
PO Box 608 56549 218-483-3316
Wayne LePard, prin. Fax 483-4638
Spring Prairie S 50/K-12
PO Box 608 56549 218-483-3316
Wayne LePard, prin. Fax 483-4638

Hayfield, Dodge, Pop. 1,370
Hayfield SD 203 900/PK-12
9 6th Ave SE 55940 507-477-3235
Ron Evjen, supt. Fax 477-3230
www.hayfield.k12.mn.us/
Hayfield ES 300/K-6
9 6th Ave SE 55940 507-477-3236
Annette Freiheit, prin. Fax 477-3204
Other Schools – See Brownsdale

Hector, Renville, Pop. 1,140
Buffalo Lake-Hector SD 2159 600/PK-12
PO Box 307 55342 320-848-2233
Dr. Rick Clark, supt. Fax 848-2401
blh.k12.mn.us
Other Schools – See Buffalo Lake

Henderson, Sibley, Pop. 936
Le Sueur-Henderson SD 2397
Supt. — See Le Sueur
Hilltop ES 100/K-5
PO Box 457 56044 507-665-5900
William Bjorndahl, prin. Fax 248-3838

Hendricks, Lincoln, Pop. 677
Hendricks SD 402 200/PK-6
PO Box 137 56136 507-275-3116
Bruce Houck, supt. Fax 275-3150
www.lincolnhi.org
Lincoln HI ES 200/PK-6
PO Box 137 56136 507-275-3115
Judy Pearson, prin. Fax 275-3150

Hendrum, Norman, Pop. 304
Norman County West SD 2527 300/PK-12
PO Box 39 56550 218-861-5800
Ollen Church, supt. Fax 861-6223
www.ncw.k12.mn.us
Norman County West ES 200/PK-6
PO Box 39 56550 218-861-5800
Ollen Church, prin. Fax 861-6223

Henning, Otter Tail, Pop. 812
Henning SD 545 400/PK-12
500 School Ave 56551 218-583-2927
Dean Souter, supt. Fax 583-2312
www.henning.k12.mn.us
Henning ES 200/PK-6
500 School Ave 56551 218-583-2927
Thomas Williams, prin. Fax 583-2312

Herman, Grant, Pop. 425
Herman-Norcross SD 264 100/K-12
PO Box 288 56248 320-677-2291
Tom Knoll, supt. Fax 677-2412
herman.mn.schoolwebpages.com
Herman ES 100/K-6
PO Box 288 56248 320-677-2291
Steve Wymore, prin. Fax 677-2412

Hermantown, Saint Louis, Pop. 8,861
Hermantown SD 700 1,900/K-12
4307 Ugstad Rd 55811 218-729-9313
Brad Johnson, supt. Fax 729-9315
www.hermantown.k12.mn.us
Hermantown ES 400/K-3
5365 W Arrowhead Rd 55811 218-729-6891
Debra Tabor, prin. Fax 729-9870
Hermantown MS 800/4-8
4289 Ugstad Rd 55811 218-729-6690
David Radovich, prin. Fax 729-9890

Heron Lake, Jackson, Pop. 766
Heron Lake-Okabena SD 330
Supt. — See Okabena
Southwest Star Concept ES 100/PK-6
PO Box 378 56137 507-793-2307
Fax 793-2557

Hibbing, Saint Louis, Pop. 16,509
Hibbing SD 701 2,400/K-12
800 E 21st St 55746 218-263-4850
Robert Belluzzo, supt. Fax 262-0494
www.hibbing.k12.mn.us
Greenhaven ES 200/K-2
323 E 37th St 55746 218-263-8322
Kathleen Antilla, prin. Fax 263-7855
Lincoln ES 700/3-6
1114 E 23rd St 55746 218-262-1089
Morley Reimer, prin. Fax 262-4810
Washington ES 300/K-2
2100 12th Ave E 55746 218-263-8393
Kathleen Antilla, prin. Fax 263-8113

Assumption S 200/PK-6
2310 7th Ave E 55746 218-263-3054
Susan Scipioni, prin. Fax 263-5058

Victory Christian Academy 100/PK-6
4220 3rd Ave W 55746 218-262-6550
Darcie Norton, admin. Fax 262-0695

Hill City, Aitkin, Pop. 462
Hill City SD 2 300/PK-12
500 Ione Ave 55748 218-697-2394
Scott Vedbraaten, supt. Fax 697-2594
www.hillcity.k12.mn.us/
Hill City ES 200/PK-6
500 Ione Ave 55748 218-697-2394
Dean Yocum, prin. Fax 697-2594

Hills, Rock, Pop. 595
Hills-Beaver Creek SD 671 300/PK-12
PO Box 547 56138 507-962-3240
David Deragisch, supt. Fax 962-3238
www.hbcpatriots.com
Other Schools – See Beaver Creek

Hills Christian S 50/K-8
PO Box 27 56138 507-962-3297
Myrna Haak, prin. Fax 962-3297

Hinckley, Pine, Pop. 1,440
Hinckley-Finlayson SD 2165 1,100/PK-12
PO Box 308 55037 320-384-6277
Jack Almos, supt. Fax 384-6135
www.hf.k12.mn.us/
Hinckley ES 500/PK-6
PO Box 308 55037 320-384-6443
Larry Edgerton, prin. Fax 384-6425
Other Schools – See Finlayson

Hokah, Houston, Pop. 595

St. Peter S 100/PK-8
PO Box 357 55941 507-894-4375
Rachel Fishel, prin. Fax 894-4375

Holdingford, Stearns, Pop. 710
Holdingford SD 738 1,000/PK-12
PO Box 250 56340 320-746-2196
John Haas, supt. Fax 746-2274
www.edline.net/pages/Holdingford_Public_Schools
Holdingford ES 500/PK-6
PO Box 250 56340 320-746-2221
Mark Messman, prin. Fax 746-8174

Hollandale, Freeborn, Pop. 284

Hollandale Christian S 100/K-8
203 Central Ave S 56045 507-889-3321
Lisa Vos, prin. Fax 889-3321

Hopkins, Hennepin, Pop. 16,825
Hopkins SD 270 7,400/K-12
1001 Highway 7 55305 952-988-4000
John Schultz, supt. Fax 988-4020
www.hopkins.k12.mn.us
Eisenhower ES 600/K-6
1001 Highway 7 55305 952-988-4300
Terri Siquenza, prin. Fax 988-4314
Smith ES 500/K-6
801 Minnetonka Mills Rd 55343 952-988-4200
Jody De St. Hubert, prin. Fax 988-4195
Other Schools – See Golden Valley, Minnetonka

Blake S 600/PK-12
110 Blake Rd S 55343 952-988-3400
John Gulla, hdmstr. Fax 988-3455
St. John the Evangelist S 100/PK-6
1503 Boyce St 55343 952-935-7787
Sr. Patricia Beckman, prin. Fax 938-2724

Houston, Winona, Pop. 1,001
Houston SD 294 1,200/PK-12
306 W Elm St 55943 507-896-5323
Kim Ross, supt. Fax 896-3452
www.houston.k12.mn.us
Houston ES 200/PK-6
310 S Sherman St 55943 507-896-5323
Richard Bartz, prin. Fax 896-3222

Howard Lake, Wright, Pop. 1,957
Howard Lake-Waverly-Winsted SD 2687 900/PK-12
PO Box 708 55349 320-543-3521
Brad Sellner, supt. Fax 543-3590
www.hlww.k12.mn.us
Howard Lake MS 300/5-8
PO Box 708 55349 320-543-3501
Jim Schimelpfenig, prin. Fax 543-3590
Other Schools – See Waverly, Winsted

St. James Lutheran S 200/PK-8
1000 6th St 55349 320-543-2630
Gregory Bauman, prin. Fax 543-3063

Hugo, Washington, Pop. 9,683
Stillwater Area SD 834
Supt. — See Stillwater
Withrow ES 200/K-6
10158 122nd St N 55038 651-351-8800
Lynn Bormann, prin. Fax 351-8804

White Bear Lake Area SD 624
Supt. — See White Bear Lake
Oneka ES 500/K-5
4888 Heritage Pkwy 55038 651-288-1800
Teresa Dahlem, prin. Fax 288-1899

Hutchinson, McLeod, Pop. 13,722
Hutchinson SD 423 2,800/PK-12
30 Glen St NW 55350 320-587-2860
Daron VanderHeiden, supt. Fax 587-4590
www.hutch.k12.mn.us
Hutchinson MS 600/6-8
1365 S Grade Rd SW 55350 320-587-2854
Todd Grina, prin. Fax 587-2857

Hutchinson Park ES 900/2-5
100 Glen St SW 55350 320-587-2837
Dan Olberg, prin. Fax 587-4821
Hutchinson West PS 300/PK-1
875 School Rd SW 55350 320-587-4470
Anne Broderius, prin. Fax 587-0735

Immanuel S 50/K-8
20917 Walden Ave 55350 320-587-4858
Justin Groth, prin. Fax 587-4858
Northwoods S 50/K-8
95 Academy Ln NW 55350 320-234-5994
Carlene Lang, prin.
Our Savior's Lutheran S 100/PK-8
800 Bluff St NE 55350 320-587-3319
Leland Huebner, prin. Fax 234-7861
St. Anastasia S 200/PK-6
400 Lake St SW 55350 320-587-2490
Jody Stoffels, prin. Fax 234-6756
St. John Lutheran S 50/K-6
60929 110th St 55350 320-587-4851
Robin Kruse, prin. Fax 587-4851

International Falls, Koochiching, Pop. 6,332
International Falls SD 361 1,100/K-12
1515 11th St 56649 218-283-8468
Don Langan, supt. Fax 283-8104
www.isd361.k12.mn.us
Falls ES 500/K-K, 3-6
1414 15th St 56649 218-283-3487
Gerry Hilfer, prin. Fax 283-3133
West End ES, 1515 11th St 56649 1-2
Gerry Hilfer, prin. 218-283-2219

St. Thomas Aquinas S 100/PK-8
810 5th St 56649 218-283-3430
Michael Gerard, prin. Fax 283-3553

Inver Grove Heights, Dakota, Pop. 33,182
Inver Grove Heights Community ISD 199 3,300/PK-12
2990 80th St E 55076 651-306-7800
Dr. Deirdre Wells, supt. Fax 306-7295
www.invergrove.k12.mn.us
Hilltop ES 400/PK-5
3201 68th St E 55076 651-306-7400
Thomas Barker, prin. Fax 306-7444
Inver Grove Heights MS 800/6-8
8167 Cahill Ave 55076 651-306-7200
Jane Stevenson, prin. Fax 306-7152
Pine Bend ES 500/K-5
9875 Inver Grove Trl 55076 651-306-7701
Ruth Ann Moore, prin. Fax 306-7739
Salem Hills ES 300/PK-5
5899 Babcock Trl 55077 651-306-7300
Jean Vogel, prin. Fax 306-7321

Iron, Saint Louis, Pop. 135
Saint Louis County SD 2142
Supt. — See Virginia
Cherry S 200/PK-12
3943 Tamminen Rd 55751 218-258-8991
John Metsa, prin. Fax 258-8993

Isanti, Isanti, Pop. 5,167
Cambridge-Isanti SD 911
Supt. — See Cambridge
Isanti IS 3-5
101 9th Ave NE 55040 763-552-8800
Mark Ziebarth, prin. Fax 552-8899
Isanti MS 500/6-8
201 Centennial Dr 55040 763-691-8661
Timothy Truebenbach, prin. Fax 691-8662
Isanti PS 400/PK-2
301 County Road 5 W 55040 763-691-8778
Kristine Stueve, prin. Fax 691-8700
Minnesota Center S 100/6-8
201 Centennial Dr 55040 763-691-8661
Timothy Truebenbach, prin. Fax 691-8677
School for all Seasons 200/K-5
101 9th Ave NE 55040 763-552-8800
Mark Ziebarth, prin. Fax 552-8899

Isle, Mille Lacs, Pop. 873
Isle SD 473 600/K-12
PO Box 25 56342 320-676-3146
Michael Conner, supt. Fax 676-3966
www.isle.k12.mn.us
Nyquist ES 300/K-6
PO Box 54 56342 320-676-3494
Dean Kapsner, dean Fax 676-3966

Jackson, Jackson, Pop. 3,454
Jackson County Central SD 2895 1,200/PK-12
PO Box 119 56143 507-847-3608
Todd Meyer, supt. Fax 847-3078
www.jccschools.com/
Riverside ES 400/PK-5
820 Park St 56143 507-847-5963
Dan Beert, prin. Fax 846-4398
Other Schools – See Lakefield

Janesville, Waseca, Pop. 2,148
Janesville-Waldorf-Pemberton SD 2835 500/PK-12
PO Box 389 56048 507-234-5478
Richard Orcutt, supt. Fax 234-5796
www.jwp.k12.mn.us
Janesville-Waldorf-Pemberton ES 200/PK-3
PO Box L 56048 507-234-6360
Sherry Trahms, prin. Fax 234-5330
Other Schools – See Waldorf

Trinity Lutheran S 200/PK-8
501 N Main St 56048 507-231-6646
Wade Stockman, prin. Fax 234-6751

Jeffers, Cottonwood, Pop. 383
Red Rock Central SD 2884
Supt. — See Lamberton

Red Rock Central ES 200/PK-5
PO Box 68 56145 507-628-5521
Dr. John Brennan, lead tchr. Fax 628-5546

Jordan, Scott, Pop. 5,120
Jordan SD 717 1,400/PK-12
500 Sunset Dr 55352 952-492-6200
Kirk Nelson, supt. Fax 492-4445
www.jordan.k12.mn.us
Jordan ES 500/PK-4
815 Sunset Dr 55352 952-492-2336
Stacy DeCorsey, prin. Fax 492-4446
Jordan MS 500/5-8
500 Sunset Dr 55352 952-492-2332
Lance Chambers, prin. Fax 492-4450

St. John the Baptist S 200/PK-6
215 Broadway St N 55352 952-492-2030
Bonita Jungels, prin. Fax 492-3211

Karlstad, Kittson, Pop. 722
Tri-County SD 2358 200/PK-12
PO Box 178 56732 218-436-2261
Ron Ruud, supt. Fax 436-2263
www.tricounty.k12.mn.us
Karlstad ES 100/PK-6
PO Box 178 56732 218-436-2374
Dave Sorgaard, prin. Fax 436-3422

Kasson, Dodge, Pop. 5,333
Kasson-Mantorville SD 204 1,900/PK-12
101 16th St NE 55944 507-634-1100
Peter Grant, supt. Fax 634-6661
www.komets.k12.mn.us
Kasson-Mantorville ES 700/PK-4
604 16th St NE 55944 507-634-1234
Marsha Groth, prin. Fax 634-1240
Kasson-Mantorville MS 300/7-8
105 16th St NE 55944 507-634-4030
Alan Hodge, prin. Fax 634-6485
Other Schools – See Mantorville

Keewatin, Itasca, Pop. 1,105
Nashwauk-Keewatin SD 319
Supt. — See Nashwauk
Keewatin ES 300/PK-6
300 W 3rd Ave 55753 218-778-6511
John Klarich, prin. Fax 885-2909

Kelliher, Beltrami, Pop. 302
Kelliher SD 36 300/PK-12
PO Box 259 56650 218-647-8286
Tim Lutz, supt. Fax 647-8660
www.kelliher.k12.mn.us
Kelliher ES 100/PK-5
PO Box 259 56650 218-647-8286
Shelly DeJean, prin. Fax 647-8660

Kennedy, Kittson, Pop. 228
Kittson Central SD 2171
Supt. — See Hallock
Kittson Central ES 200/PK-6
306 3rd St W 56733 218-674-4136
Bruce Jensen, prin. Fax 674-4154

Kensington, Douglas, Pop. 272
West Central Area SD 2342
Supt. — See Barrett
West Central Area South ES 200/PK-6
31 Central Ave N 56343 320-965-2724
Jim Houseman, prin. Fax 965-2264

Kenyon, Goodhue, Pop. 1,665
Kenyon-Wanamingo SD 2172
Supt. — See Wanamingo
Kenyon-Wanamingo MS 300/5-8
400 6th St 55946 507-789-6186
Matt Ryan, dean Fax 789-6188

Kerkhoven, Swift, Pop. 711
Kerkhoven-Murdock-Sunburg SD 775 600/PK-12
PO Box 168 56252 320-264-1411
Martin Heidelberger, supt. Fax 264-1410
www.kms.k12.mn.us
Other Schools – See Murdock

Kimball, Stearns, Pop. 687
Kimball SD 739 800/PK-12
PO Box 368 55353 320-398-5585
John Tritabaugh, supt. Fax 398-5595
www.kimball.k12.mn.us/
Kimball ES 400/PK-6
PO Box 368 55353 320-398-5425
Jon Clark, prin. Fax 398-5433

Holy Cross of Pearl Lake S 100/PK-6
10672 County Road 8 55353 320-398-7885
Ann Moran, prin. Fax 398-7873

La Crescent, Houston, Pop. 5,095
La Crescent-Hokah SD 300 900/PK-12
703 S 11th St 55947 507-895-4484
David Krenz, supt. Fax 895-8560
www.isd300.k12.mn.us
La Crescent-Hokah ES 500/PK-5
504 S Oak St 55947 507-895-4428
Ron Wilke, prin. Fax 895-4470
La Crescent MS 400/6-8
1301 Lancer Dr 55947 507-895-4474
Ben Barton, prin. Fax 895-8597

Crucifixion S 100/K-6
420 S 2nd St 55947 507-895-4402
Robert Formanek, prin. Fax 895-4403

Lake Benton, Lincoln, Pop. 667
Lake Benton SD 404 100/K-6
PO Box 158 56149 507-368-4241
Loy Woelber, supt. Fax 368-4477
www.lakebentonschool.org/
Lake Benton ES 100/K-6
PO Box 158 56149 507-368-4241
Ryan Nielson, prin. Fax 368-4477

Pipestone Area SD 2689
Supt. — See Pipestone
Heartland S 50/K-8
2171 100th Ave 56149 507-368-9585
Don Plahn, prin. Fax 368-9518

Lake City, Wabasha, Pop. 5,282
Lake City SD 813 1,400/PK-12
PO Box 454 55041 651-345-2198
Clayton Hovda, supt. Fax 345-3709
www.lake-city.k12.mn.us
Bluff View ES 700/PK-6
PO Box 454 55041 651-345-4551
James Borgschatz, prin. Fax 345-2781

St. John Lutheran S 100/K-8
516 W Chestnut St 55041 651-345-4092
Kurt Maciejczak, prin. Fax 345-4002

Lake Crystal, Blue Earth, Pop. 2,516
Lake Crystal Wellcome Memorial SD 2071 800/PK-12
PO Box 160 56055 507-726-2323
Les Norman, supt. Fax 726-2334
www.isd2071.k12.mn.us
Lake Crystal Wellcome Memorial ES 400/PK-6
PO Box 810 56055 507-726-2320
Sharon Schindle, prin. Fax 726-2003

Lake Elmo, Washington, Pop. 7,615
Stillwater Area SD 834
Supt. — See Stillwater
Lake Elmo ES 700/K-6
11030 Stillwater Blvd N 55042 651-351-6700
Andrew Fields, prin. Fax 351-6797

Lakefield, Jackson, Pop. 1,698
Jackson County Central SD 2895
Supt. — See Jackson
Jackson County Central MS 300/6-8
PO Box 338 56150 507-662-6625
Kari Wilkinson, prin. Fax 662-5083
Pleasantview ES 100/PK-5
PO Box 754 56150 507-662-6218
Larry Tractow, prin. Fax 662-6690

Immanuel Lutheran S 100/K-8
PO Box 750 56150 507-662-5860
Jonathan Leonard, prin. Fax 662-5820

Lakeland, Washington, Pop. 1,865
Stillwater Area SD 834
Supt. — See Stillwater
Afton-Lakeland ES 500/K-6
475 Saint Croix Trl S 55043 651-351-6500
Tom Hobert, prin. Fax 351-6595

Lake Park, Becker, Pop. 830
Lake Park Audubon ISD 2889 600/K-12
PO Box 479 56554 218-238-5914
Dale Hogie, supt. Fax 238-5643
www.lakeparkaudubon.com
Other Schools – See Audubon

Lakeville, Dakota, Pop. 51,484
Lakeville Area SD 194 10,900/K-12
8670 210th St W 55044 952-232-2000
Gary Amoroso, supt. Fax 469-6054
www.isd194.k12.mn.us
Century MS 800/6-8
18610 Ipava Ave 55044 952-232-2300
Catherine Gillach, prin. Fax 469-6103
Cherry View ES 600/K-5
8600 175th St W 55044 952-232-3200
John Beal, prin. Fax 469-7245
Crystal Lake ES 500/K-5
16250 Ipava Ave 55044 952-232-3000
Bill Mack, prin. Fax 469-7314
Eastview ES 700/K-5
18060 Ipava Ave 55044 952-232-2900
Richard Oscarson, prin. Fax 469-7644
Huddleston ES 400/K-5
9569 175th St W 55044 952-232-3100
Amy Schmidt, prin. Fax 469-7280
Kennedy ES 500/K-5
21240 Holyoke Ave 55044 952-232-2800
Mary Jo Hanson, prin. Fax 469-7248
Kenwood Trail JHS 800/6-8
19455 Kenwood Trl 55044 952-232-3800
Kate Eisenthal, prin. Fax 469-3508
Lake Marion ES 600/K-5
19875 Dodd Blvd 55044 952-232-2700
John Braun, prin. Fax 469-7180
Lakeview ES 600/K-5
20500 Jacquard Ave 55044 952-232-2600
Terry Lind, prin. Fax 469-7270
McGuire MS 1,000/6-8
21220 Holyoke Ave 55044 952-232-2200
Joshua Alexander, prin. Fax 469-7224
Oak Hills ES 500/K-5
8640 165th St W 55044 952-232-2500
Wade Labatte, prin. Fax 469-6304
Orchard Lake ES 300/K-5
16531 Klamath Trl 55044 952-232-2100
Karen Roos, prin. Fax 469-7331

All Saints S 300/K-8
19795 Holyoke Ave 55044 952-469-3332
Jan Heuman, prin. Fax 469-4484
Glory Academy 50/K-10
9995 170th St W 55044 952-898-3079
Dean Engelman, prin.

Lamberton, Redwood, Pop. 805
Red Rock Central SD 2884 500/PK-12
PO Box 278 56152 507-752-7361
Dr. John Brennan, supt. Fax 752-6133
www.rrcnet.org
Other Schools – See Jeffers

Lancaster, Kittson, Pop. 328
Lancaster SD 356 200/PK-12
PO Box 217 56735 218-762-5400
Bradley Homstad, supt. Fax 762-5512
www.lancaster.k12.mn.us/
Lancaster ES 100/PK-6
PO Box 217 56735 218-762-5400
Bradley Homstad, prin. Fax 762-5512

Lanesboro, Fillmore, Pop. 767
Lanesboro SD 229 400/PK-12
100 Kirkwood St E 55949 507-467-2229
Jeff Boggs, supt. Fax 467-3026
www.lanesboro.k12.mn.us
Lanesboro ES 200/PK-6
100 Kirkwood St E 55949 507-467-2229
James Semmen, prin. Fax 467-3026

Laporte, Hubbard, Pop. 150
Laporte SD 306 300/PK-12
315 Main St W 56461 218-224-2288
Harvey Johnson, supt. Fax 224-2905
www.laporte.k12.mn.us
Laporte ES 100/PK-6
315 Main St W 56461 218-224-2288
Gregg Parks, prin. Fax 224-2905

Le Center, LeSueur, Pop. 2,308
Le Center SD 392 500/PK-12
150 W Tyrone St 56057 507-357-6802
Tony Boyer, supt. Fax 357-4825
lc.k12.mn.us
Le Center ES 200/PK-3
160 Mill Ave 56057 507-357-6807
Deb Dwyer, prin. Fax 357-4155

Leota, Nobles, Pop. 300

Leota Christian S, PO Box 278 56153 50/K-8
Brian Tschettier, admin. 507-443-5501

Le Roy, Mower, Pop. 917
Le Roy SD 499 300/PK-12
PO Box 1000 55951 507-324-5743
Larry Tompkins, supt. Fax 324-5149
www.leroy.k12.mn.us
Le Roy-Ostrander ES 200/PK-6
PO Box 1000 55951 507-324-5786
Aaron Hungerholt, prin. Fax 324-5004

Lester Prairie, McLeod, Pop. 1,601
Lester Prairie SD 424 500/PK-12
131 Hickory St N 55354 320-395-2521
Greg East, supt. Fax 395-4204
www.lp.k12.mn.us
Lester Prairie ES 200/PK-6
131 Hickory St N 55354 320-395-2909
Pamela Lukens, prin. Fax 395-4204

Le Sueur, LeSueur, Pop. 4,257
Le Sueur-Henderson SD 2397 1,100/PK-12
115 1/2 N 5th St Ste 200 56058 507-665-4600
David Johnson, supt. Fax 665-6858
www.isd2397.k12.mn.us
Park ES 400/PK-5
115 N 5th St 56058 507-665-4700
William Bjorndahl, prin. Fax 665-8819
Other Schools – See Henderson

St. Anne S 100/K-6
511 N 4th St 56058 507-665-2489
Kathy Segna, prin. Fax 665-3811

Lewiston, Winona, Pop. 1,485
Lewiston-Altura SD 857 800/PK-12
100 County Road 25 55952 507-523-2191
Bruce Montplaisir, supt. Fax 523-3460
www.lewalt.k12.mn.us
Lewiston-Altura ES 300/PK-4
105 S Fremont St 55952 507-523-2194
David Riebel, prin. Fax 523-2609
Lewiston-Altura IS 100/5-6
325 1st Ave N 55952 507-796-6851
David Riebel, prin. Fax 796-5127

Immanuel Lutheran S 100/PK-8
22591 County Road 25 55952 507-523-3143
Kevin Meyer, prin. Fax 523-1049
St. John Lutheran S 100/K-8
PO Box 9 55952 507-523-2508
David Menges, prin. Fax 523-3472

Lindstrom, Chisago, Pop. 3,934
Chisago Lakes SD 2144 3,400/PK-12
13750 Lake Blvd 55045 651-213-2000
Michael McLoughlin, supt. Fax 213-2050
www.chisagolakes.k12.mn.us
Chisago Lakes MS 900/6-8
13750 Lake Blvd 55045 651-213-2400
John Menard, prin. Fax 213-2051
Other Schools – See Chisago City, Taylors Falls

Lino Lakes, Anoka, Pop. 19,424
Centennial SD 12
Supt. — See Circle Pines
Blue Heron ES 600/K-5
405 Elm St 55014 763-792-6200
Dan Melde, prin. Fax 792-6250
Centennial MS 1,700/6-8
399 Elm St 55014 763-792-5400
Jerry Meschke, prin. Fax 792-5450

Rice Lake ES 700/K-5
575 Birch St 55014 763-792-5700
Warren Buerkley, prin. Fax 792-5750

Forest Lake SD 831
Supt. — See Forest Lake
Lino Lakes ES 400/K-6
725 Main St 55014 651-982-8850
Jan Masterson, prin. Fax 982-8891

Litchfield, Meeker, Pop. 6,658
Litchfield SD 465 1,700/PK-12
114 N Holcombe Ave Ste 100 55355 320-693-2444
William Wold, supt. Fax 593-6528
www.litchfield.k12.mn.us
Lake Ripley ES 400/PK-3
100 W Pleasure Dr 55355 320-693-2436
Gregg Zender, prin. Fax 593-0227
Litchfield MS 400/6-8
340 E 10th St 55355 320-693-2441
Patrick Devine, prin. Fax 593-3485
Wagner ES 300/4-5
307 E 6th St 55355 320-693-2824
Gregg Zender, prin. Fax 593-0280

St. Philip S 100/K-5
225 E 3rd St 55355 320-693-6283
Diana McCarney, prin. Fax 593-4783

Little Canada, Ramsey, Pop. 9,543
Roseville Area SD 623
Supt. — See Roseville
Roseville Area MS 800/7-8
15 County Road B2 E 55117 651-482-5280
Juanita Hoskins, prin. Fax 482-5299

St. John the Evangelist S 300/PK-8
2621 McMenemy St 55117 651-484-3038
Mary Kay Rowan, prin. Fax 481-1355

Little Falls, Morrison, Pop. 8,139
Little Falls SD 482 2,500/K-12
1001 5th Ave SE 56345 320-632-2002
Curt Tryggestad, supt. Fax 632-2012
www.lfalls.k12.mn.us
Lincoln ES 300/K-5
300 6th St SW 56345 320-616-6200
Rande Smith, prin. Fax 616-2144
Lindbergh ES 600/K-5
101 9th St SE 56345 320-616-3200
Jill Griffith-McRaith, prin. Fax 616-3210
Little Falls Community MS 500/6-8
1000 1st Ave NE 56345 320-616-4200
Nathan Swenson, prin. Fax 616-4210
Other Schools – See Randall

Mary of Lourdes MS 200/5-8
205 3rd St NW 56345 320-632-6742
Paul Scheiffert, prin. Fax 632-3556
Mary of Lourdes S 200/PK-4
307 4th St SE 56345 320-632-5408
Maria Heymans-Becker, prin. Fax 632-3556

Littlefork, Koochiching, Pop. 714
Littlefork-Big Falls SD 362 200/PK-12
700 Main St 56653 218-278-6614
Fred Seybert, supt. Fax 278-6615
www.isd362.k12.mn.us
Littlefork-Big Falls S 200/PK-12
700 Main St 56653 218-278-6614
Fred Seybert, prin. Fax 278-6615

Long Lake, Hennepin, Pop. 1,827
Orono SD 278 2,400/K-12
PO Box 46 55356 952-449-8300
Dr. Karen Orcutt, supt. Fax 449-8399
www.orono.k12.mn.us
Orono IS 600/3-5
PO Box 136 55356 952-449-8470
Paula Martin, prin. Fax 449-8479
Orono MS 600/6-8
PO Box 16 55356 952-449-8450
Dr. Patricia Wroten, prin. Fax 449-8453
Orono Schumann ES 400/K-2
PO Box 6 55356 952-449-8480
Connie Fladeland, prin. Fax 449-8499

Long Prairie, Todd, Pop. 2,944
Long Prairie-Grey Eagle SD 2753 1,200/PK-12
205 2nd St S 56347 320-732-2194
Jon Kringen, supt. Fax 732-3791
www.lpge.k12.mn.us/
Long Prairie ES 400/PK-5
205 2nd St S 56347 320-732-2194
Paul Weinzierl, prin. Fax 732-0961
Long Prairie MS 300/6-8
205 2nd St S 56347 320-732-2194
Paul Weinzierl, prin. Fax 732-2844
Other Schools – See Grey Eagle

St. Mary of Mount Carmel S 100/PK-6
425 Central Ave 56347 320-732-3478
Brenda Gugglberger, prin. Fax 732-8023

Longville, Cass, Pop. 191
Northland Community SD 118
Supt. — See Remer
Longville ES 100/K-6
PO Box 117 56655 218-363-2020
Mary Wilke, prin. Fax 363-9000

Lonsdale, Rice, Pop. 2,409
Montgomery-Lonsdale SD 394
Supt. — See Montgomery
Montgomery-Lonsdale ES East PK-4
1000 Idaho St SW 55046 507-744-3900
Dave Dooley, prin. Fax 744-3902

Loretto, Hennepin, Pop. 608

Academy of SS. Peter & Paul 100/PK-8
150 Railway St E 55357 763-479-0540
Sarah Windlow, prin. Fax 479-4046
Salem Lutheran S 100/PK-8
9615 Pioneer Trl 55357 763-498-7283
Matthew Meitner, prin. Fax 498-7835

Luverne, Rock, Pop. 4,466
Luverne SD 2184 1,200/PK-12
709 N Kniss Ave 56156 507-283-8088
Gary Fisher, supt. Fax 283-9681
www.isd2184.net/
Luverne ES 600/PK-5
709 N Kniss Ave 56156 507-283-4497
Stacy Gillette, prin. Fax 283-9681
Luverne MS 300/6-8
709 N Kniss Ave 56156 507-283-4491
Donna Judson, prin. Fax 283-9681

Lyle, Mower, Pop. 576
Lyle SD 497 200/PK-12
700 E 2nd St 55953 507-325-4146
Jerry Reshetar, supt. Fax 325-4611
www.lyle.k12.mn.us
Lyle ES 100/PK-5
700 E 2nd St 55953 507-325-2201
Royce Helmbrecht, prin. Fax 325-4611

Lynd, Lyon, Pop. 384
Lynd SD 415 100/PK-8
PO Box 68 56157 507-865-4404
Bruce Houck, supt. Fax 865-4621
Lynd S 100/PK-8
PO Box 68 56157 507-865-4404
Bruce Houck, prin. Fax 865-4621

Mabel, Fillmore, Pop. 743
Mabel-Canton SD 238 300/PK-12
PO Box 337 55954 507-493-5423
Marcia Love, supt. Fax 493-5425
www.mabelcanton.k12.mn.us/
Mabel-Canton ES 100/PK-6
PO Box 337 55954 507-493-5422
Jeffrey Nolte, prin. Fax 493-5425

Mc Gregor, Aitkin, Pop. 405
Mc Gregor ISD 4 400/PK-12
PO Box 160, 218-768-2111
Paul Grams, supt. Fax 768-3901
www.mcgregor.k12.mn.us
Mc Gregor ES 200/PK-6
PO Box 160, 218-768-2111
Paul Grams, prin. Fax 768-3901

Madelia, Watonwan, Pop. 2,218
Madelia SD 837 600/PK-12
320 Buck Ave SE 56062 507-642-3232
Brian Grenell, supt. Fax 642-3622
www.madelia.k12.mn.us
Madelia ES 300/PK-6
121 E Main St 56062 507-642-3234
Mary Hanson, prin. Fax 642-8893

St. Marys S 50/PK-6
223 1st St NE 56062 507-642-3324
John DeZeeuw, prin. Fax 642-3899

Madison, Lac qui Parle, Pop. 1,654
Lac Qui Parle Valley SD 2853 900/PK-12
2860 291st Ave 56256 320-752-4200
Brad Madsen, supt. Fax 752-4401
www.lqpv.org/
Lac Qui Parle Valley MS 100/5-6
2860 291st Ave 56256 320-752-4200
Scott Sawatzky, prin. Fax 752-4409
Madison-Marietta-Nassau ES 100/PK-4
316 W 4th St 56256 320-598-7528
Kipp Stender, prin. Fax 598-3001
Other Schools – See Appleton

Madison Lake, Blue Earth, Pop. 906

All Saints S 50/PK-4
PO Box 158 56063 507-243-3819
Shelley Shultz, prin. Fax 243-4485

Mahnomen, Mahnomen, Pop. 1,176
Mahnomen SD 432 600/PK-12
PO Box 319 56557 218-935-2211
Walter Aanenson, supt. Fax 935-5921
www.mahnomen.k12.mn.us/
Mahnomen ES 300/PK-6
PO Box 319 56557 218-935-2581
Ramona Miller, prin. Fax 935-5951

St. Michaels S 100/PK-6
501 1st St SW 56557 218-935-5222
Kathy Klindt, prin. Fax 935-5222

Mahtomedi, Washington, Pop. 8,017
Mahtomedi SD 832 2,900/K-12
1520 Mahtomedi Ave 55115 651-407-2000
Dr. Mark Wolak, supt. Fax 407-2025
www.mahtomedi.k12.mn.us
Anderson ES 600/3-5
666 Warner Ave S 55115 651-407-2300
Kirsten Bouwens, prin. Fax 407-2325
Mahtomedi MS 800/6-8
8100 75th St N 55115 651-407-2200
Dr. Sharon Zweber, prin. Fax 407-2225
Wildwood ES 400/K-2
535 Warner Ave N 55115 651-407-2400
Mark Hamre, prin. Fax 407-2425

St. Andrew's Academy 100/K-6
900 Stillwater Rd 55115 651-379-5299
Ed Cavin, hdmstr. Fax 426-1716

St. Jude of the Lake S 300/PK-8
600 Mahtomedi Ave 55115 651-426-2562
Sally Hermes, prin. Fax 653-3662

Mankato, Blue Earth, Pop. 34,976
Mankato SD 77 6,900/K-12
PO Box 8741 56002 507-387-1868
Sheri Allen, supt. Fax 387-4257
www.isd77.k12.mn.us
Bridges Community ES 100/K-6
820 Hubbell Ave 56001 507-387-2800
Robin Courrier, prin. Fax 387-3143
Franklin ES 600/K-6
1000 N Broad St 56001 507-345-4287
Leslie Koppendrayer, prin. Fax 345-4801
Jefferson ES 200/K-5
100 James Ave 56001 507-388-5480
Linda Kilander, prin. Fax 388-8440
Kennedy ES 500/K-5
2600 E Main St 56001 507-387-2122
Travis Olson, prin. Fax 387-1665
Mankato East JHS 500/7-8
2600 Hoffman Rd 56001 507-345-6625
Rich Dahman, prin. Fax 387-2890
Roosevelt ES 300/K-5
600 Owatonna St 56001 507-345-4285
Richard Lund, prin. Fax 345-1374
Washington ES 400/K-5
1100 Anderson Dr 56001 507-345-3059
Will Remmert, prin. Fax 345-7198
Other Schools – See Eagle Lake, North Mankato

Fitzgerald MS 200/4-8
110 N 5th St 56001 507-388-9344
William Schumacher, prin. Fax 388-2750
Immanuel Lutheran S 100/K-12
421 N 2nd St 56001 507-345-3027
Karl Olmanson, prin. Fax 345-1562
Loyola MS, 110 N 5th St 56001 4-8
William Schumacher, prin. 507-388-9344
Loyola S 700/PK-12
145 Good Counsel Dr 56001 507-388-2997
Bette Blaisdell, prin. Fax 388-3081
Mt. Olive Lutheran S 100/K-8
1123 Marsh St 56001 507-345-7927
Larry Rude, prin. Fax 345-7463
Risen Savior Lutheran S 50/K-8
502 W 7th St 56001 507-388-6624
Ryan Jaeger, prin. Fax 388-2831

Mantorville, Dodge, Pop. 1,180
Kasson-Mantorville SD 204
Supt. — See Kasson
Kasson-Mantorville IS 300/5-6
PO Box 97 55955 507-635-2631
Alan Hodge, prin. Fax 635-5720

Maple Grove, Hennepin, Pop. 59,756
Osseo SD 279 19,700/PK-12
11200 93rd Ave N 55369 763-391-7000
Susan Hintz, supt. Fax 391-7070
www.district279.org
Arbor View ECC 100/PK-PK
9401 Fernbrook Ln N 55369 763-585-7330
Gayle Southwell, coord. Fax 391-8762
Basswood ES 800/K-6
15425 Bass Lake Rd 55311 763-494-3858
Dennis Palm, prin. Fax 315-7660
Cedar Island ES 300/K-3
6777 Hemlock Ln N 55369 763-425-5855
Dan Wald, prin. Fax 315-7680
Elm Creek ES 500/K-6
9830 Revere Ln N 55369 763-425-0577
Jim Meyer, prin. Fax 315-7690
Fernbrook ES 700/K-6
9661 Fernbrook Ln N 55369 763-420-8888
Wendy Biallas, prin. Fax 391-8420
Oak View ES 300/4-6
6710 E Fish Lake Rd 55369 763-425-1881
Ann Mock, prin. Fax 391-8686
Rice Lake ES 400/K-6
13755 89th Ave N 55369 763-420-4220
Mark French, prin. Fax 315-7370
Rush Creek ES 700/K-6
8801 County Road 101 N 55311 763-494-4549
Don Johnson, prin. Fax 315-7360
Weaver Lake Science Math & Technology S 600/K-6
15900 Weaver Lake Rd 55311 763-420-3337
Gretchen Peel, prin. Fax 391-8880
Other Schools – See Brooklyn Center, Brooklyn Park

Heritage Christian Academy 600/PK-12
15655 Bass Lake Rd 55311 763-463-2200
Dave Pauli, admin. Fax 463-2299
Shepherd Care Lutheran S 50/PK-PK
11875 W Eagle Lake Dr 55369 763-493-3623
Susanne Herrlin, prin. Fax 425-0622

Maple Lake, Wright, Pop. 1,878
Maple Lake SD 881 1,000/PK-12
PO Box 760 55358 320-963-3171
Mark Redemske, supt. Fax 963-3170
www.maplelake.k12.mn.us
Maple Lake ES 500/PK-6
PO Box 788 55358 320-963-3024
Kris Harlan, prin. Fax 963-6584

St. Timothy S 100/K-6
241 Star St E 55358 320-963-3417
Fax 963-8804

Mapleton, Blue Earth, Pop. 1,653
Maple River SD 2135 900/PK-12
PO Box 515 56065 507-524-3918
Willis Schoeb, supt. Fax 524-4882
www.isd2135.k12.mn.us/

Maple River MS 100/6-8
PO Box 515 56065 507-524-3918
Dan Anderson, prin. Fax 524-3638
Other Schools – See Good Thunder, Minnesota Lake

Maplewood, Ramsey, Pop. 35,085
North St. Paul-Maplewood-Oakdale SD 622
Supt. — See North Saint Paul
Carver ES 600/K-5
2680 Upper Afton Rd E 55119 651-702-8200
Peter Olson-Skog, prin. Fax 702-8291
Glenn MS 800/6-8
1560 County Road B E 55109 651-748-6300
Mike Redmond, prin. Fax 748-6391
Maplewood MS 800/6-8
2410 Holloway Ave E 55109 651-748-6500
Ruthanne Strohn, prin. Fax 748-6591
Weaver ES 500/K-5
2135 Birmingham St 55109 651-748-7000
Judy Jemtrud, prin. Fax 748-7091

Roseville Area SD 623
Supt. — See Roseville
Edgerton ES 400/K-6
1929 Edgerton St 55117 651-772-2565
Becky Berkas, prin. Fax 772-1510

Saint Paul SD 625
Supt. — See Saint Paul
Harambee Magnet S 400/K-5
30 County Road B E 55117 651-379-2500
Kristine Black, prin. Fax 379-2590

Gethsemane Lutheran S 100/K-8
2410 Stillwater Rd E 55119 651-739-7540
Judy Hinck, prin. Fax 578-0610
Presentation of Mary S 200/PK-8
1695 Kennard St 55109 651-777-5877
Brian Ragatz, prin. Fax 777-8283
St. Jerome S 200/PK-8
384 Roselawn Ave E 55117 651-771-8494
Laureen Sherman, prin. Fax 771-3466

Marble, Itasca, Pop. 678
Greenway SD 316
Supt. — See Coleraine
Marble ECC 50/PK-PK
PO Box 10 55764 218-247-7306
Jolene Landwer, dir. Fax 245-6612

Marine on Saint Croix, Washington, Pop. 579
Stillwater Area SD 834
Supt. — See Stillwater
Marine ES 100/K-6
550 Pine St 55047 651-351-8870
Lynn Bormann, prin. Fax 351-8877

Marshall, Lyon, Pop. 12,291
Marshall SD 413 1,700/K-12
401 S Saratoga St 56258 507-537-6924
Klint Willert, supt. Fax 537-6931
www.swmn.org
Marshall MS 200/5-8
401 S Saratoga St 56258 507-537-6938
Mary Kay Thomas, prin. Fax 537-6942
Park Side ES 300/K-2
1300 E Lyon St 56258 507-537-6948
Heidi Critchley, prin. Fax 537-6953
West Side ES 300/3-4
500 S 4th St 56258 507-537-6962
Heidi Critchley, prin. Fax 537-6966

Holy Redeemer S 300/K-8
501 S Whitney St 56258 507-532-6642
Carol DeSmet, prin. Fax 532-2636
Marshall Area Christian S 100/K-8
PO Box 751 56258 507-532-2762
Russell Oglesby, prin. Fax 337-0019
Samuel Lutheran S 50/K-8
500 Village Dr 56258 507-532-2162
John Festerling, prin. Fax 532-2162

Mayer, Carver, Pop. 1,139

Zion Lutheran S 100/PK-8
209 Bluejay Ave 55360 952-657-2339
Fax 657-2337

Maynard, Chippewa, Pop. 370
MACCRAY SD 2180
Supt. — See Clara City
MACCRAY West ES 100/K-6
PO Box 276 56260 320-367-2396
Doug Runia, prin. Fax 367-2399

Mazeppa, Wabasha, Pop. 784
Zumbrota-Mazeppa SD 2805 1,100/PK-12
PO Box 222 55956 507-843-4080
Richard Meyerhofer, supt. Fax 843-4086
www.zmschools.us/
Zumbrota-Mazeppa MS 400/5-8
343 3rd Ave NE 55956 507-843-2165
David Fleming, prin. Fax 843-5853
Other Schools – See Zumbrota

Medford, Steele, Pop. 1,164
Medford ISD 763 800/PK-12
750 2nd Ave SE 55049 507-451-5250
Gary Hanson, supt. Fax 451-6474
www.medford.k12.mn.us/
Medford ES 400/PK-6
750 2nd Ave SE 55049 507-451-5250
Mark Ristau, prin. Fax 451-6474

Melrose, Stearns, Pop. 3,145
Melrose SD 740 1,400/PK-12
546 N 5th Ave E 56352 320-256-4224
Tom Rich, supt. Fax 256-4311
www.melrose.k12.mn.us
Melrose ES 500/PK-5
566 N 5th Ave E 56352 320-256-3617
Gregory Seawell, prin. Fax 256-4311
Melrose MS 300/6-8
546 N 5th Ave E 56352 320-256-4224
Randy Bergquist, prin. Fax 256-4311

St. John-St. Andrew S 100/K-6
115 E County Road 13 56352 320-987-3133
Jeri Bachel, prin. Fax 987-3306
St. Marys S 200/PK-6
320 S 5th Ave E 56352 320-256-4257
Robert Doyle, prin. Fax 256-4208

Menahga, Wadena, Pop. 1,197
Menahga SD 821 700/PK-12
PO Box 160 56464 218-564-4141
Jerry Nesland, supt. Fax 564-5401
www.menahga.k12.mn.us
Menahga ES 400/PK-6
PO Box 160 56464 218-564-4141
Joleen DeLaHunt, prin. Fax 564-4502

Mendota Heights, Dakota, Pop. 11,338
West St. Paul-Mendota Hts-Eagan SD 197 4,500/PK-12
1897 Delaware Ave 55118 651-681-2300
Jay Haugen, supt. Fax 681-9102
isd197.org
Friendly Hills MS 600/5-8
701 Mendota Heights Rd 55120 651-905-4100
Joni Hagebock, prin. Fax 905-4101
Mendota ES 300/PK-4
1979 Summit Ln 55118 651-405-2451
Steve Goldade, prin. Fax 405-2891
Somerset ES 300/PK-4
1355 Dodd Rd 55118 651-405-2631
Mary Bowman, prin. Fax 405-2632
Other Schools – See Eagan, West Saint Paul

Convent of the Visitation S 600/PK-12
2455 Visitation Dr 55120 651-683-1700
Dawn Nichols, hdmstr. Fax 454-7144

Middle River, Marshall, Pop. 314
Greenbush-Middle River SD 2683
Supt. — See Greenbush
Greenbush-Middle River JHS 100/6-8
PO Box 130 56737 218-222-3310
Sharon Schultz, prin. Fax 222-3314
Middle River ES 100/PK-5
PO Box 130 56737 218-222-3310
Sharon Schultz, prin. Fax 222-3314

Milaca, Mille Lacs, Pop. 2,954
Milaca SD 912 1,800/PK-12
500 Highway 23 W 56353 320-982-7210
Jerry Hansen, supt. Fax 982-7179
www.milaca.k12.mn.us/
Milaca ES 800/PK-6
500 Highway 23 W 56353 320-982-7301
Steve Voshell, prin. Fax 982-7178

Community Christian S 100/PK-8
208 E Main St 56353 320-369-4239
Fax 369-4346

Milroy, Redwood, Pop. 256
Milroy SD 635 50/K-8
PO Box 10 56263 507-336-2563
William Delaney, supt. Fax 336-2568
www.milroy.k12.mn.us/
Milroy S 50/K-8
PO Box 10 56263 507-336-2563
William Delaney, prin. Fax 336-2568

Miltona, Douglas, Pop. 308
Alexandria SD 206
Supt. — See Alexandria
Miltona ES 100/K-6
PO Box 113 56354 218-943-2371
Lisa Pikop, prin. Fax 943-5140

Minneapolis, Hennepin, Pop. 372,811
Minneapolis SD 1 31,700/PK-12
807 Broadway St NE 55413 612-668-0000
William Green Ph.D., supt. Fax 668-0195
www.mpls.k12.mn.us
Afrocentric Academy 400/6-8
1500 James Ave N 55411 612-668-1798
Ellen Stewart, prin. Fax 668-1770
Andersen ES 400/K-5
2727 10th Ave S 55407 612-668-4200
Denise Wells, prin. Fax 668-4210
Andersen Open S 700/PK-8
1098 Andersen Ln 55407 612-668-4250
Denise Wells, prin. Fax 668-4260
Anishinabe Academy 300/PK-8
2225 E Lake St 55407 612-668-0880
Steve Couture, prin. Fax 668-0890
Anthony MS 500/6-8
5757 Irving Ave S 55419 612-668-3240
Jackie Hanson, prin. Fax 668-3250
Anwatin MS 500/6-8
256 Upton Ave S 55405 612-668-2450
Cecelia Saddler, prin. Fax 668-2460
Armatage ES 400/PK-5
2501 W 56th St 55410 612-668-3180
Joan Franks, prin. Fax 668-3190
Bancroft ES 400/K-5
1315 E 38th St 55407 612-668-3550
Judi Golden, prin. Fax 668-3560
Barton Open S 800/K-8
4237 Colfax Ave S 55409 612-668-3580
Steve DeLapp, prin. Fax 668-3590
Bethune Community ES 200/PK-5
919 Emerson Ave N 55411 612-668-2550
Renee James, prin. Fax 668-2560
Bryn Mawr Community ES 200/PK-5
252 Upton Ave S 55405 612-668-2500
Renee Montague, prin. Fax 668-2510
Burroughs Community ES 500/K-5
1601 W 50th St 55419 612-668-3280
Tim Cadotte, prin. Fax 668-3290
Cityview Performing Arts Magnet S 500/K-8
3350 N 4th St 55412 612-668-2270
Laura Cavender, prin. Fax 668-2280
Dowling Urban Environmental ES 500/K-5
3900 W River Pkwy 55406 612-668-4410
Joe Rossow, prin. Fax 668-4420
Emerson Spanish Immersion S 600/K-8
1421 Spruce Pl 55403 612-668-3610
Mark Quinn, prin. Fax 668-3620
Field Community MS 500/5-8
4645 4th Ave S 55419 612-668-3640
Steve Norlin-Weaver, prin. Fax 668-3661
Folwell MS 300/6-8
3611 20th Ave S 55407 612-668-4550
Luis Ortega, prin. Fax 668-4560
Green Central Park S 600/K-8
3416 4th Ave S 55408 612-668-3730
Jan Parrish, prin. Fax 668-3740
Hale Community ES 500/K-4
1220 E 54th St 55417 612-668-3760
Bob Brancale, prin. Fax 668-3770
Hall International ES 200/PK-5
1601 Aldrich Ave N 55411 612-668-2650
Bennice Young, prin. Fax 668-2660
Hiawatha Community ES 300/K-5
4201 42nd Ave S 55406 612-668-4610
Rosalind Robbins, prin. Fax 668-4620
Hmong International Academy K-8
2410 Girard Ave N 55411 612-668-2110
Chai Lee, prin. Fax 668-2115
Jefferson Community S 600/PK-8
1200 W 26th St 55405 612-668-2720
Ray Aponte, prin. Fax 668-2730
Johnson Community S 500/PK-8
807 27th Ave N 55411 612-668-2930
Mark Bonine, prin. Fax 668-2940
Kenny Community ES 300/PK-5
5720 Emerson Ave S 55419 612-668-3340
Bill Gibbs, admin. Fax 668-3350
Kenwood Community Performing Arts ES 300/K-5
2013 Penn Ave S 55405 612-668-2760
Susan Craig, prin. Fax 668-2770
Lake Harriet Community Lower ES 200/PK-2
4030 Chowen Ave S 55410 612-668-3210
Mary Rynchek, prin. Fax 668-3220
Lake Harriet Community Upper ES 600/3-8
4912 Vincent Ave S 55410 612-668-3310
Mary Rynchek, prin. Fax 668-3320
Lake Nokomis S - Keewaydin Campus 200/4-8
5209 30th Ave S 55417 612-668-4670
Jane Ellis, prin. Fax 668-4680
Lake Nokomis S - Wenonah Campus 300/K-3
5625 23rd Ave S 55417 612-668-5040
Joan Hultman, prin. Fax 668-5050
Laney Community S 400/K-8
3333 Penn Ave N 55412 612-668-2200
David Branch, prin. Fax 668-2210
Lind ES 300/K-4
5025 Bryant Ave N 55430 612-668-2020
Aura Wharton-Beck, prin. Fax 668-2030
Longfellow Community ES 300/PK-5
3017 E 31st St 55406 612-668-4700
Lillie Pang, prin. Fax 668-4710
Loring Community ES 300/K-5
2600 44th Ave N 55412 612-668-2060
Jane Thompson, prin. Fax 668-2070
Lyndale ES 300/PK-5
312 W 34th St 55408 612-668-4000
Ossie Brooks James, prin. Fax 668-4010
Marcy Open S 600/K-8
415 4th Ave SE 55414 612-668-1020
Donna Andrews, prin. Fax 668-1030
Northeast MS 500/6-8
2955 Hayes St NE 55418 612-668-1500
Padmini Udupa, prin. Fax 668-1510
Northrop Urban Environmental ES 400/K-5
4315 31st Ave S 55406 612-668-4520
Kathy Alvig, prin. Fax 668-4530
Olson Upper Academy 400/5-8
1607 51st Ave N 55430 612-668-1640
Karon Cunningham, prin. Fax 668-1650
Park View Montessori ES 300/K-6
252 Upton Ave S 55405 612-668-2540
Dorothy Washington, prin. Fax 668-2535
Pillsbury Math/Science/Technology ES 500/PK-5
2250 Garfield St NE 55418 612-668-1530
Pao Vue, prin. Fax 668-1540
Pratt Community ES 100/K-5
66 Malcolm Ave SE 55414 612-668-1122
Annie Wade, admin. Fax 668-1110
Ramsey International Fine Arts S 1,000/K-8
1 W 49th St 55419 612-668-4040
Karen Hart, prin. Fax 668-4050
Sanford MS 400/6-8
3524 42nd Ave S 55406 612-668-4900
Meredith Davis, prin. Fax 668-4910
Seward Montessori S 800/PK-8
2309 28th Ave S 55406 612-668-4950
Marilyn Levine, prin. Fax 668-4960
Sheridan International Fine Arts S 700/K-8
1201 University Ave NE 55413 612-668-1130
Jean Neuman, prin. Fax 668-1140
Sullivan Community Center 700/PK-8
3100 E 28th St 55406 612-668-5000
Greg Beyer, prin. Fax 668-5010
Waite Park Community ES 400/K-5
1800 34th Ave NE 55418 612-668-1600
Lois Shapiro, prin. Fax 668-1610
Whittier International ES 300/PK-5
315 W 26th St 55404 612-668-4170
Shawn Harris-Berry, prin. Fax 668-4180

Windom Open S 300/K-8
5821 Wentworth Ave 55419 612-668-3370
Tami VanOverbeke, prin. Fax 668-3380

Spring Lake Park SD 16 3,600/K-12
1415 81st Ave NE 55432 763-786-5570
Don Helmstetter, supt. Fax 784-7838
www.springlakeparkschools.org
Northpoint ES K-3
2350 124th Ct NE 55449 763-754-9700
Mike Callahan, prin. Fax 754-9701
Other Schools – See Blaine, Fridley, Spring Lake Park

Wayzata SD 284 9,700/PK-12
210 County Road 101 N 55447 952-745-5000
Dr. Chace Anderson, supt. Fax 745-5091
www.wayzata.k12.mn.us
Other Schools – See Plymouth, Wayzata

Annunciation S 400/K-8
525 W 54th St 55419 612-823-4394
Sandy Nesvig, prin. Fax 824-0998
Ascension S 200/K-8
1726 Dupont Ave N 55411 612-521-3609
Dorwatha Woods, prin. Fax 522-3862
Breck S 1,200/PK-12
123 Ottawa Ave N 55422 763-381-8100
Edward Kim, hdmstr. Fax 381-8288
Carondelet Catholic S 300/K-8
3210 W 51st St 55410 612-927-8673
Becky Farber, prin. Fax 927-7426
City of Lakes Waldorf S 200/PK-8
2344 Nicollet Ave 55404 612-767-1550
Fax 767-1551
Hope Academy 200/K-8
2300 Chicago Ave 55404 612-721-6294
Russ Gregg, prin. Fax 722-9048
Lake Country S 200/PK-9
3755 Pleasant Ave 55409 612-827-3707
Paulette Zoe, prin. Fax 827-1332
Maranatha Christian Academy 700/PK-12
4021 Thomas Ave N 55412 612-588-2850
Brian Sullivan, admin. Fax 588-7854
Minnehaha Academy 600/PK-8
4200 W River Pkwy 55406 612-721-3359
Dean Erickson, prin. Fax 728-7777
Our Lady of Peace S 200/K-8
5435 11th Ave S 55417 612-823-8253
Dr. Lori Glynn, prin. Fax 824-7328
Pilgrim Lutheran S 100/PK-8
3901 1st Ave S 55409 612-825-5375
Michelle Cambrice, dean Fax 822-3239
Pope John Paul II Catholic S 100/K-8
1630 4th St NE 55413 612-789-8851
Deb King, prin. Fax 789-8773
Risen Christ S 300/K-8
1120 E 37th St 55407 612-822-5329
Liz Ramsey, prin. Fax 729-2336
St. Charles Borromeo S 300/K-8
2727 Stinson Blvd 55418 612-781-2643
John Hartnett, prin. Fax 787-1110
St. Elizabeth Seton S 100/K-8
5140 Fremont Ave N 55430 612-529-7781
Karen Meskill, prin. Fax 529-3343
St. Helena S 200/K-8
3200 E 44th St 55406 612-729-9301
Jane Hileman, prin. Fax 729-6016
San Miguel MS 50/6-8
3800 Pleasant Ave 55409 612-870-1109
Sr. Mary Willette, prin. Fax 870-1224
Trinity Lutheran S 100/PK-8
1115 E 19th St 55404 612-871-2353
Sarah Wippich, prin. Fax 871-6550
Woodcrest Baptist Academy 200/K-12
6875 University Ave NE 55432 763-571-6410
Fax 571-3978

Minneota, Lyon, Pop. 1,377
Minneota SD 414 500/K-12
PO Box 98 56264 507-872-6532
Dan Deitte, supt. Fax 872-5172
www.minneotaschools.org/
Minneota ES 200/K-6
PO Box 98 56264 507-872-6122
Harlen Ulrich, prin. Fax 872-5172

St. Edward S 100/1-8
210 W 4th St 56264 507-872-6391
Lori Rangaard, prin. Fax 872-5263

Minnesota Lake, Faribault, Pop. 659
Maple River SD 2135
Supt. — See Mapleton
Maple River East ES 100/K-5
PO Box 218 56068 507-462-3348
James Bisel, prin. Fax 462-3219

Minnetonka, Hennepin, Pop. 50,045
Hopkins SD 270
Supt. — See Hopkins
Gatewood ES 600/K-6
14900 Gatewood Dr 55345 952-988-5250
Donna Montgomery, prin. Fax 988-5276
Glen Lake ES 500/K-6
4801 Woodridge Rd 55345 952-988-5200
Beth Potter, prin. Fax 988-5199
Tanglen ES 600/K-6
10901 Hillside Ln W 55305 952-988-4900
Gail Lewis-Miller, prin. Fax 988-4871

Minnetonka SD 276 7,500/K-12
5621 County Rd 101 55345 952-401-5000
Dennis Peterson, supt. Fax 401-5083
www.minnetonka.k12.mn.us
Clear Springs ES 500/K-5
5701 County Rd 101 55345 952-401-6950
Curt Carpenter, prin. Fax 401-6955
Groveland ES 400/K-5
17310 Minnetonka Blvd 55345 952-401-5600
David Parker, prin. Fax 401-5606
Minnetonka East MS 900/6-8
17000 Lake Street Ext 55345 952-401-5200
Pete Dymit, prin. Fax 401-5268
Scenic Heights ES 500/K-5
5650 Scenic Heights Dr 55345 952-401-5400
Joe Wacker, prin. Fax 401-5412
Other Schools – See Excelsior, Wayzata

Immaculate Heart of Mary S 300/PK-8
13505 Excelsior Blvd 55345 952-935-0004
Cheri Gardner, prin. Fax 935-2031
Minnetonka Christian Academy 100/K-12
3500 Williston Rd 55345 952-935-4497
Ken Rannow, prin. Fax 935-4498

Minnetrista, Hennepin, Pop. 5,501
Westonka SD 277 2,200/PK-12
5901 Sunnyfield Rd E 55364 952-491-8000
Kevin Borg, supt. Fax 491-8012
www.westonka.k12.mn.us
Other Schools – See Mound

Montevideo, Chippewa, Pop. 5,365
Montevideo SD 129 1,200/PK-12
2001 William Ave 56265 320-269-8833
Dr. Luther Heller, supt. Fax 269-8834
www.montevideoschools.com
Montevideo MS 400/5-8
2001 William Ave 56265 320-269-6431
Brenda Vatthauer, prin. Fax 269-8834
Ramsey ES 200/K-2
501 Hamilton Ave 56265 320-269-6584
Sarah Lieber, dean Fax 269-6585
Sanford ES 100/PK-PK, 3-
412 S 13th St 56265 320-269-6538
Sarah Lieber, dean Fax 269-6539

Montgomery, LeSueur, Pop. 3,076
Montgomery-Lonsdale SD 394 900/PK-12
101 2nd St NE 56069 507-364-8100
Corey Lunn, supt. Fax 364-8103
www.montlonsdale.k12.mn.us
Montgomery-Lonsdale ES West 300/PK-4
700 4th St NW 56069 507-364-8119
Dave Dooley, prin. Fax 364-8411
Montgomery-Lonsdale IS 200/5-6
101 2nd St NE 56069 507-364-8118
Alan Fitterer, prin. Fax 364-8103
Other Schools – See Lonsdale

Most Holy Redeemer S 100/PK-8
205 Vine Ave W 56069 507-364-7383
Sr. Mary Margaret Murphy, prin. Fax 364-5964

Monticello, Wright, Pop. 10,882
Monticello SD 882 3,600/PK-12
302 Washington St 55362 763-272-2000
James Johnson, supt. Fax 272-2009
www.monticello.k12.mn.us
Little Mountain ES 700/PK-5
9350 Fallon Ave NE 55362 763-272-2600
Joe Dockendorf, prin. Fax 272-2609
Monticello MS 900/6-8
800 E Broadway St 55362 763-272-2100
Jeff Scherber, prin. Fax 272-2109
Pinewood ES 800/PK-5
1010 W Broadway St 55362 763-272-2400
Brad Sanderson, prin. Fax 272-2409

Montrose, Wright, Pop. 2,246
Buffalo SD 877
Supt. — See Buffalo
Montrose ES 400/K-5
100 2nd St S 55363 763-682-8350
Gary Theis, prin. Fax 682-8350

Moorhead, Clay, Pop. 34,081
Moorhead SD 152 4,900/K-12
2410 14th St S 56560 218-284-3330
Lynne Kovash, supt. Fax 284-3332
www.moorhead.k12.mn.us
Asp ES 600/K-5
910 11th St N 56560 218-284-6300
Kevin Kopperud, prin. Fax 284-6333
Hopkins ES 600/K-5
2020 11th St S 56560 218-284-4300
Dr. Mary Jo Schmid, prin. Fax 284-4333
Horizon MS 1,200/6-8
3601 12th Ave S 56560 218-284-7300
Lori Lockhart, prin. Fax 284-7333
Reinertsen ES 700/K-5
1201 40th Ave S 56560 218-284-5300
Anne Moyano, prin. Fax 284-5333

Park Christian S 400/PK-12
300 17th St N 56560 218-236-0500
John Bole, supt. Fax 236-7301
Red River Valley Academy 50/PK-6
1015 30th Ave S 56560 218-287-0415
Dr. Terrijann Dahlberg, prin. Fax 287-0416
St. Joseph S 200/PK-7
202 10th St S 56560 218-233-0553
Leslie Honebrink, prin. Fax 291-9479

Moose Lake, Carlton, Pop. 2,551
Moose Lake SD 97 800/PK-12
PO Box 489 55767 218-485-4435
Timothy Caroline, supt. Fax 485-8110
www.mooselake.k12.mn.us
Moose Lake ES 400/PK-6
PO Box 489 55767 218-485-4834
Kraig Konietzko, prin. Fax 485-4351

Mora, Kanabec, Pop. 3,449
Mora SD 332 1,600/PK-12
400 Maple Ave E 55051 320-679-6200
Douglas Conboy, supt. Fax 679-6209
www.mora.k12.mn.us
Fairview ES 300/PK-2
707 McLean St 55051 320-679-6260
Cheryl Bjerk, prin. Fax 679-6259
Trailview S 400/3-6
200 E 9th St 55051 320-679-6240
Mark Antonson, prin. Fax 679-6258

Morgan, Redwood, Pop. 846
Cedar Mountain SD 2754 400/K-12
PO Box 188 56266 507-249-5990
Robert Tews, supt. Fax 249-3149
www.cms.mntm.org/
Other Schools – See Franklin

St. Michael S 50/PK-6
PO Box 459 56266 507-249-3192
Patty McCauley, prin. Fax 249-2557

Morris, Stevens, Pop. 5,091
Morris SD 769 900/PK-12
201 S Columbia Ave 56267 320-589-4840
Scott Monson, supt. Fax 589-3203
www.morris.k12.mn.us
Morris ES 500/PK-6
151 S Columbia Ave 56267 320-589-1250
Brad Korn, prin. Fax 589-3920

St. Marys S 100/K-6
411 Colorado Ave 56267 320-589-1704
Jennifer Grammond, prin. Fax 589-1703

Morristown, Rice, Pop. 1,021
Waterville-Elysian-Morristown SD 2143
Supt. — See Waterville
Morristown ES 100/5-6
PO Box 278 55052 507-685-4222
Bernardine Sauter, prin. Fax 685-2420
Waterville-Elysian-Morristown JHS 200/7-8
PO Box 278 55052 507-685-4222
Bernardine Sauter, prin. Fax 685-2420

Trinity Lutheran S 50/K-8
10500 215th St W 55052 507-685-2200
Warren Schmidt, prin.

Motley, Morrison, Pop. 667
Staples-Motley ISD 2170
Supt. — See Staples
Motley ES 100/PK-5
PO Box 68 56466 218-352-6170
Gwynne Gildow, prin. Fax 352-6508
Motley-Staples MS 300/6-8
PO Box 68 56466 218-352-6170
Mark Schmitz, prin. Fax 352-6508

Mound, Hennepin, Pop. 9,416
Westonka SD 277
Supt. — See Minnetrista
Grandview MS 500/5-7
1881 Commerce Blvd 55364 952-491-8300
Christy Zachow, prin. Fax 491-8303
Hilltop PS 400/PK-4
5700 Game Farm Rd E 55364 952-491-8500
Nancy Benz, prin. Fax 491-8503
Shirley Hills PS 400/PK-4
2450 Wilshire Blvd 55364 952-491-8400
Ann Swanson, prin. Fax 491-8403

Our Lady of the Lake S 200/PK-8
2411 Commerce Blvd 55364 952-472-1284
Ellen Feuling, prin. Fax 472-9152

Mounds View, Ramsey, Pop. 12,106
Mounds View SD 621
Supt. — See Shoreview
Edgewood MS 600/6-8
5100 Edgewood Dr 55112 651-621-6600
Penny Howard, prin. Fax 621-6605
Pinewood ES 500/K-5
5500 Quincy St 55112 763-621-7500
William Book, prin. Fax 621-7505

Mountain Iron, Saint Louis, Pop. 2,945
Mountain Iron-Buhl SD 712 600/PK-12
5720 Marble Ave 55768 218-735-8271
John Klarich, supt. Fax 735-8244
www.mib.k12.mn.us
Merritt ES 300/PK-6
5529 Emerald Ave 55768 218-741-4809
John Klarich, prin. Fax 741-1930

Mountain Lake, Cottonwood, Pop. 2,008
Mountain Lake SD 173 500/PK-12
PO Box 400 56159 507-427-2325
William Strom, supt. Fax 427-3047
www.mountainlake.k12.mn.us
Mountain Lake ES 300/PK-6
PO Box 400 56159 507-427-2325
Karl Wassman, prin. Fax 427-3047

Mountain Lake Christian S 100/PK-12
PO Box 478 56159 507-427-2010
John Newton, admin. Fax 427-3123

Murdock, Swift, Pop. 291
Kerkhoven-Murdock-Sunburg SD 775
Supt. — See Kerkhoven
Murdock ES 300/PK-6
PO Box 46 56271 320-875-2441
Jeff Keil, prin. Fax 875-2226

Nashwauk, Itasca, Pop. 897
Nashwauk-Keewatin SD 319 600/PK-12
400 2nd St 55769 218-885-2705
Mark Adams, supt. Fax 885-2905
Other Schools – See Keewatin

Nett Lake, Saint Louis
Nett Lake SD 707 100/K-6
13090 Westley Rd 55772 218-757-3102
Teresa Strong, supt. Fax 757-3330
www.nettlake.k12.mn.us/
Nett Lake ES 100/K-6
13090 Westley Rd 55772 218-757-3102
Teresa Strong, prin. Fax 757-3330

Nevis, Hubbard, Pop. 376
Nevis SD 308 500/PK-12
PO Box 138 56467 218-652-3500
Steven Rassier, supt. Fax 652-3505
www.nevis.k12.mn.us
Nevis ES 300/PK-6
PO Box 138 56467 218-652-3500
Sharon Hadrava, prin. Fax 652-3505

New Brighton, Ramsey, Pop. 20,738
Mounds View SD 621
Supt. — See Shoreview
Bel Air ES 700/K-5
1800 5th St NW 55112 651-621-6300
Richard Skinner, prin. Fax 621-6305
Highview MS 800/6-8
2300 7th St NW 55112 651-621-6700
Mona Fadness, prin. Fax 621-6705
Sunnyside ES 500/K-5
2070 County Road H 55112 651-621-7600
Paul Good, prin. Fax 621-7605

St. John the Baptist S 400/K-8
845 2nd Ave NW 55112 651-633-1522
Sue Clausen, prin. Fax 633-7404

Newfolden, Marshall, Pop. 344
Marshall County Central SD 441 400/K-12
PO Box 189 56738 218-874-8530
Ronald Paggen, supt. Fax 874-8581
www.newfolden.k12.mn.us/
Newfolden ES 100/4-6
PO Box 189 56738 218-874-8805
James Hodny, prin. Fax 874-8581
Other Schools – See Viking

New Germany, Carver, Pop. 326

St. Mark Lutheran S 50/PK-8
211 Adams Ave S 55367 952-353-2464
Dan Wacker, prin. Fax 353-2464

New Hope, Hennepin, Pop. 20,296
Robbinsdale SD 281 10,500/K-12
4148 Winnetka Ave N 55427 763-504-8000
Aldo Sicoli, supt. Fax 504-8979
www.rdale.org
Meadow Lake ES 500/K-5
8525 62nd Ave N 55428 763-504-7700
Kim Hiel, prin. Fax 504-7709
Robbinsdale Spanish Immersion ES 500/K-5
8808 Medicine Lake Rd 55427 763-504-4400
Jane Byrne, prin. Fax 504-4409
Sonnesyn ES 600/K-5
3421 Boone Ave N 55427 763-504-7600
James Calhoun, prin. Fax 504-7609
Other Schools – See Brooklyn Center, Crystal, Golden Valley, Plymouth, Robbinsdale

Holy Trinity Lutheran S K-8
4240 Gettysburg Ave N 55428 763-533-0600
Dennis Klatt, admin.

New London, Kandiyohi, Pop. 1,196
New London-Spicer SD 345 1,400/K-12
PO Box 430 56273 320-354-2252
Paul Carlson, supt. Fax 354-9001
nls.k12.mn.us
New London-Spicer MS 500/5-8
PO Box 430 56273 320-354-2252
Trish Perry, prin. Fax 354-4244
Prairie Woods ES 400/K-4
PO Box 430 56273 320-354-2252
Sonya Peterson, prin. Fax 354-2093

Newport, Washington, Pop. 3,654
South Washington County SD 833
Supt. — See Cottage Grove
Newport ES 300/K-5
851 6th Ave 55055 651-768-4300
Aaron Krueger, prin. Fax 768-4333

New Prague, Scott, Pop. 6,439
New Prague Area SD 721 2,400/K-12
410 Central Ave N 56071 952-758-1700
Craig Menozzi, supt. Fax 758-1799
www.np.k12.mn.us
Falcon Ridge ES 500/K-5
1200 Columbus Ave N 56071 952-758-1600
Barbara Wilson, prin. Fax 758-1699
New Prague MS 800/6-8
721 Central Ave N 56071 952-758-1400
Tim Dittberner, prin. Fax 758-1499
Raven Stream ES K-5
300 11th Ave NW 56071 952-758-1500
Pat Pribyl, prin. Fax 758-1599
Other Schools – See Elko

St. Wenceslaus S 300/K-8
227 Main St E 56071 952-758-3133
Kim Doyle, prin. Fax 758-2958

New Richland, Waseca, Pop. 1,159
NRHEG SD 2168 1,000/PK-12
PO Box 427 56072 507-465-3205
Kevin Wellen, supt. Fax 465-8633
www.nrheg.k12.mn.us
NRHEG ES 200/PK-5
PO Box 427 56072 507-465-3205
Paul Sparby, prin. Fax 465-8633
Other Schools – See Ellendale

New Ulm, Brown, Pop. 13,619
New Ulm SD 88 1,700/PK-12
15 N State St 56073 507-359-8401
Harold Remme, supt. Fax 359-8406
www.newulm.k12.mn.us/
Jefferson ES 500/PK-3
318 S Payne St 56073 507-359-8460
Pamela Kirsch, prin. Fax 359-3728
Washington ES 400/4-6
910 14th St N 56073 507-359-8490
Bill Sprung, prin. Fax 359-1329

Holy Trinity MS 200/5-8
515 N State St 56073 507-354-4311
Shelly Bauer, prin. Fax 354-7071
St. Anthony S 200/PK-4
514 N Washington St 56073 507-354-2928
Shelly Bauer, prin. Fax 354-7029
St. Paul's Lutheran S 300/PK-8
126 S Payne St 56073 507-354-2329
Dale Markgraf, prin. Fax 354-6893

New York Mills, Otter Tail, Pop. 1,186
New York Mills SD 553 700/PK-12
PO Box 218 56567 218-385-4201
Todd Cameron, supt. Fax 385-2551
www.nymills.k12.mn.us
New York Mills ES 400/PK-6
PO Box 218 56567 218-385-2553
Greg Esala, prin. Fax 385-2551

Nicollet, Nicollet, Pop. 991
Nicollet SD 507 200/K-12
PO Box 108 56074 507-232-3411
Tony Boyer, supt. Fax 232-3536
isd507.k12.mn.us
Nicollet S 200/K-12
PO Box 108 56074 507-232-3448
Theresa Sorenson, prin. Fax 232-3536

Trinity Lutheran S 50/K-8
PO Box 137 56074 507-232-3888
David Duncan, prin. Fax 232-9878

Nisswa, Crow Wing, Pop. 2,068
Brainerd SD 181
Supt. — See Brainerd
Nisswa ES 200/PK-4
5533 County Road 18 56468 218-961-6860
Erin Herman, prin. Fax 961-6861

North Branch, Chisago, Pop. 10,234
North Branch ISD 138 3,500/PK-12
PO Box 370 55056 651-674-1000
Dr. Deb Henton, supt. Fax 674-1010
www.northbranch.k12.mn.us
Early Childhood Center 100/PK-PK
PO Box 370 55056 651-674-1220
Kerry Moberg, dir. Fax 674-1210
North Branch MS 900/6-8
PO Box 370 55056 651-674-1300
Todd Tetzlaff, prin. Fax 674-1310
North Branch PS 300/K-1
PO Box 370 55056 651-674-1200
Jan Ashlin, prin. Fax 674-1210
Sunrise River ES 1,000/2-5
PO Box 370 55056 651-674-1100
Jason Hartmann, prin. Fax 674-1110

Trinity Christian S 300/PK-5
38460 Lincoln Trl 55056 651-674-7042
Nichole Laven, prin. Fax 674-7048

Northfield, Rice, Pop. 18,671
Northfield SD 659 3,800/PK-12
1400 Division St S 55057 507-663-0629
L. Chris Richardson Ph.D., supt. Fax 663-0611
www.nfld.k12.mn.us
Bridgewater ES 500/K-5
401 Jefferson Pkwy 55057 507-664-3300
Nancy Antoine, prin. Fax 664-3308
Greenvale Park ES 500/K-5
700 Lincoln Pkwy 55057 507-645-3500
David Craft, prin. Fax 645-3505
Longfellow S 50/PK-PK
201 Orchard St S 55057 507-645-1200
Gary Lewis, prin. Fax 645-1250
Northfield MS 900/6-8
2200 Division St S 55057 507-663-0650
Jeff Pesta, prin. Fax 663-0660
Sibley ES 500/K-5
1400 Maple St 55057 507-645-3470
Scott Sannes, prin. Fax 645-3469

St. Dominic S 200/K-8
216 Spring St N 55057 507-645-8136
Vicki Marvin, prin. Fax 645-8818

North Mankato, Nicollet, Pop. 12,078
Mankato SD 77
Supt. — See Mankato
Dakota Meadows JHS 500/7-8
1900 Howard Dr W 56003 507-387-5077
Carmen Strahan, prin. Fax 387-1119
Garfield ES 300/6-6
320 Garfield Ave 56003 507-387-4400
Tom Schueneman, prin. Fax 387-3960

Hoover ES 500/K-5
1524 Hoover Dr 56003 507-388-5202
Dan Kamphoff, prin. Fax 388-8432
Monroe ES 500/K-5
441 Monroe Ave 56003 507-387-7889
Al Lawrence, prin. Fax 387-4027

North Oaks, Ramsey, Pop. 4,141
Mounds View SD 621
Supt. — See Shoreview
Chippewa MS 1,000/6-8
5000 Hodgson Rd, 651-621-6400
Sheila Eller, prin. Fax 621-6405

Northome, Koochiching, Pop. 220
South Koochiching-Rainy River ISD 363 400/K-12
PO Box 465 56661 218-897-5275
Bob Jaszczak, supt. Fax 897-5280
www.northome.k12.mn.us
Northome ES 100/K-6
PO Box 465 56661 218-897-5275
Shannon Avenson, prin. Fax 897-5280
Other Schools – See Birchdale

North Saint Paul, Ramsey, Pop. 12,568
North St. Paul-Maplewood-Oakdale SD 622 10,900/K-12
2520 12th Ave E 55109 651-748-7410
Patricia Phillips, supt. Fax 748-7413
www.isd622.org/
Cowern ES 400/K-5
2131 Margaret St N 55109 651-748-6800
Sonya Czerepak, prin. Fax 748-6891
Richardson ES 400/K-5
2615 1st St N 55109 651-748-6900
Pat Steingruebl, prin. Fax 748-6991
Webster ES 300/K-5
2170 7th Ave E 55109 651-748-7100
Sara Palodichuk, prin. Fax 748-7191
Other Schools – See Maplewood, Oakdale

Christ Lutheran S 200/K-8
2475 17th Ave E 55109 651-777-1450
Mark Dobberstein, prin. Fax 748-0723
St. Peter S 400/PK-8
2620 Margaret St N 55109 651-777-3091
Cecilia Crowley, prin. Fax 777-7750

Norwood Young America, Carver, Pop. 3,317
Central ISD 108 1,100/PK-12
PO Box 247 55368 952-467-7000
Brian Corlett, supt. Fax 467-7003
www.central.k12.mn.us
Central ES 500/PK-5
PO Box 367 55368 952-467-7300
Andrew Wilkins, prin. Fax 467-7303
Central MS 200/6-8
PO Box 247 55368 952-467-7200
Ron Erpenbach, prin. Fax 467-7203

Oakdale, Washington, Pop. 27,389
North St. Paul-Maplewood-Oakdale SD 622
Supt. — See North Saint Paul
Castle ES 500/K-5
6675 50th St N 55128 651-748-6700
Kerri Town, prin. Fax 748-6791
Eagle Point ES 400/K-5
7850 15th St N 55128 651-702-8300
Kathy Nadeau, prin. Fax 702-8391
Oakdale ES 500/K-5
821 Glenbrook Ave N 55128 651-702-8500
Peter Mau, prin. Fax 702-8591
Skyview Community ES 600/K-5
1100 Heron Ave N 55128 651-702-8100
Carol Erickson, prin. Fax 702-8191
Skyview Community MS 900/6-8
1100 Heron Ave N 55128 651-702-8000
Thomas Harrold, prin. Fax 702-8091

Transfiguration S 400/K-8
6135 15th St N 55128 651-501-2220
Ted Zarembski, prin. Fax 739-1550

Ogema, Becker, Pop. 147
Waubun SD 435
Supt. — See Waubun
Ogema ES 300/PK-4
PO Box 68 56569 218-473-6174
Mitch Anderson, prin. Fax 983-4200

Ogilvie, Kanabec, Pop. 477
Ogilvie SD 333 600/K-12
333 School Dr 56358 320-272-5000
Ed Harris, supt. Fax 272-5072
www.ogilvie.k12.mn.us
Ogilvie ES 300/K-6
333 School Dr 56358 320-272-5050
DuWayne Hass, prin. Fax 272-5072

Okabena, Jackson, Pop. 179
Heron Lake-Okabena SD 330 300/PK-12
PO Box 97 56161 507-853-4507
Becky Cselovszki, supt. Fax 853-4642
www.ssc.mntm.org
Other Schools – See Heron Lake

Olivia, Renville, Pop. 2,504
BOLD SD 2534 900/K-12
701 9th St S 56277 320-523-1031
Tom Farrell, supt. Fax 523-2399
www.bold.k12.mn.us
Other Schools – See Bird Island

Onamia, Mille Lacs, Pop. 916
Onamia SD 480 700/K-12
35465 125th Ave 56359 320-532-4174
John Varner, supt. Fax 532-4658
www.onamia.k12.mn.us
Onamia ES 300/K-6
35465 125th Ave Ste 2 56359 320-532-4174
Larry Jallen, prin. Fax 532-4359

Orr, Saint Louis, Pop. 247
Saint Louis County SD 2142
Supt. — See Virginia
Orr S 100/PK-12
PO Box 307 55771 218-757-3225
John Jirik, dean Fax 757-3666

Ortonville, Big Stone, Pop. 2,011
Ortonville SD 2903 300/PK-12
200 Trojan Dr 56278 320-839-6181
Jeffrey Taylor, supt. Fax 839-3708
www.ortonville.k12.mn.us
Ortonville S 300/PK-12
200 Trojan Dr 56278 320-839-6183
Joel Stattelman, prin. Fax 839-2499

Osakis, Douglas, Pop. 1,568
Osakis SD 213 700/PK-12
PO Box X 56360 320-859-2191
Gregg Allen, supt. Fax 859-2835
www.osakispublicschools.org/
Osakis ES 400/PK-6
PO Box X 56360 320-859-2193
Pat Ryan, prin. Fax 859-2835

St. Agnes S 100/PK-6
PO Box O 56360 320-859-2130
Tammy Boushek, prin. Fax 859-5850

Owatonna, Steele, Pop. 24,133
Owatonna SD 761 5,000/K-12
515 W Bridge St 55060 507-444-8600
Tom Tapper, supt. Fax 444-8688
www.owatonna.k12.mn.us/
Lincoln ES 600/K-5
747 Havana Rd 55060 507-444-8110
Teri Preisler, prin. Fax 444-8199
McKinley ES 500/K-5
423 14th St NE 55060 507-444-8210
Bob Olson, prin. Fax 444-8299
Owatonna JHS 700/7-8
500 15th St NE 55060 507-444-8710
Kyle DeKam, prin. Fax 444-8799
Washington ES 500/K-5
338 E Main St 55060 507-444-8310
Mary Baier, prin. Fax 444-8399
Willow Creek IS 400/6-6
1050 22nd St NE 55060 507-444-8510
Mary Trapp, prin. Fax 444-8599
Wilson ES 500/K-5
325 Meadow Ln 55060 507-444-8410
Amy LaDue, prin. Fax 444-8499

Owatonna Christian S 100/PK-12
265 26th St NE 55060 507-451-3495
Shawn Smith, prin. Fax 451-3762
St. Isidore S 50/PK-5
9970 SE 24th Ave 55060 507-451-5876
Jenny Deml, lead tchr. Fax 451-5159
St. Marys S 400/PK-8
730 S Cedar Ave 55060 507-446-2300
Gerald Kent, prin. Fax 446-2304

Palisade, Aitkin, Pop. 119
Aitkin SD 1
Supt. — See Aitkin
Palisade ES 50/K-4
PO Box 45 56469 218-845-2406
Allan Albertson, prin. Fax 845-2208

Parkers Prairie, Otter Tail, Pop. 998
Parkers Prairie ISD 547 600/PK-12
PO Box 46 56361 218-338-6011
Kent Baldry, supt. Fax 338-4077
www.isd547.com
Parkers Prairie ES 300/PK-6
PO Box 46 56361 218-338-4079
Caryl Gordy, prin. Fax 338-4078

Park Rapids, Hubbard, Pop. 3,445
Park Rapids SD 309 1,500/PK-12
301 Huntsinger Ave 56470 218-237-6500
Glenn Chiodo, supt. Fax 237-6519
www.parkrapids.k12.mn.us
Century ES 500/PK-4
501 Helten Ave 56470 218-237-6200
Mitchell Peterson, prin. Fax 237-6248
Century MS 500/5-8
501 Helten Ave 56470 218-237-6300
Bruce Gravalin, prin. Fax 237-6349

Paynesville, Stearns, Pop. 2,243
Paynesville SD 741 900/PK-12
217 W Mill St 56362 320-243-3410
Todd Burlingame, supt. Fax 243-7525
www.paynesvilleschools.com/
Paynesville ES 500/PK-5
205 W Mill St 56362 320-243-3725
Debra Gillman, prin. Fax 243-7525

Pelican Rapids, Otter Tail, Pop. 2,357
Pelican Rapids SD 548 1,100/PK-12
PO Box 642 56572 218-863-5910
Deborah Wanek, supt. Fax 863-5915
www.pelicanrapids.k12.mn.us
Viking ES 500/PK-6
PO Box 642 56572 218-863-2911
Crystal Thorson, prin. Fax 863-5358

Pequot Lakes, Crow Wing, Pop. 1,874
Pequot Lakes SD 186 1,500/PK-12
30805 Olson St 56472 218-568-4996
Rick Linnell, supt. Fax 568-5259
pequotlakes.k12.mn.us/
Eagle View ES 500/PK-5
30805 Olson St 56472 218-562-6100
Donald Lenzen, prin. Fax 562-6106
Pequot Lakes MS 400/6-8
30805 Olson St 56472 218-568-9357
Randy Hansen, prin. Fax 568-9202

Perham, Otter Tail, Pop. 2,711
Perham-Dent SD 549 1,500/PK-12
200 5th St SE 56573 218-346-4501
Tamara Uselman, supt. Fax 346-4506
www.perham.k12.mn.us
Heart of Lake ES 400/PK-4
810 2nd Ave SW 56573 218-346-5437
Kari Yates, prin. Fax 346-4634
Prairie Wind MS 500/5-8
480 Coney St W 56573 218-346-1700
Scott Bjerke, prin. Fax 346-1704
Other Schools – See Dent

St. Henry S 100/K-6
253 2nd St SW 56573 218-346-6190
Jason Smith, prin. Fax 346-6190
St. Paul Lutheran S 100/PK-6
500 6th Ave SW 56573 218-346-2300
Bonnie Stohs, prin. Fax 346-2306

Peterson, Fillmore, Pop. 220
Rushford-Peterson SD 239
Supt. — See Rushford
Rushford-Peterson MS 100/6-8
PO Box 8 55962 507-875-2238
Brad Johnson, prin. Fax 875-2316

Pierz, Morrison, Pop. 1,316
Pierz SD 484 1,000/PK-12
112 Kamnic St 56364 320-468-6458
George Weber, supt. Fax 468-6408
www.pierz.k12.mn.us
Pioneer ES 500/PK-6
66 Kamnic St 56364 320-468-6458
Galen Swoboda, prin. Fax 468-2841

Holy Trinity S 200/PK-6
PO Box 427 56364 320-468-6446
Debra Meyer-Myrum, prin. Fax 468-6446

Pillager, Cass, Pop. 480
Pillager SD 116 800/PK-12
323 E 2nd St 56473 218-746-3772
Chuck Arns, supt. Fax 746-4236
www.pillager.k12.mn.us/
Pillager ECC PK-PK
323 E 2nd St 56473 218-746-3075
Betty Doss, dir. Fax 746-2188
Pillager ES 400/PK-6
323 E 2nd St 56473 218-746-3557
Wanda Bell, prin. Fax 746-3406

Pine City, Pine, Pop. 3,323
Pine City SD 578 1,500/K-12
1400 Main St S 55063 320-629-4000
Darwin Bostic, supt. Fax 629-4070
www.pinecity.k12.mn.us
Pine City ES 700/K-6
700 6th Ave SW 55063 320-629-4200
David Arola, prin. Fax 629-4205

St. Mary's S 100/PK-6
815 6th Ave SW 55063 320-629-3953
Rev. David Forsman, prin. Fax 629-1438

Pine Island, Goodhue, Pop. 3,170
Pine Island SD 255 800/K-12
PO Box 398 55963 507-356-8326
Chris Bates, supt. Fax 356-8827
www.pineisland.k12.mn.us
Pine Island S 400/K-8
PO Box 398 55963 507-356-2488
Darren Overton, prin. Fax 356-8827

Pine River, Cass, Pop. 958
Pine River-Backus SD 2174 1,000/PK-12
PO Box 610 56474 218-587-4720
Catherine Bettino, supt. Fax 587-4120
www.prbackus.k12.mn.us
Pine River-Backus ES 500/PK-6
PO Box 610 56474 218-587-4447
Jackie Bruns, prin. Fax 587-8390

Pipestone, Pipestone, Pop. 4,161
Pipestone Area SD 2689 1,200/PK-12
1401 7th St SW 56164 507-825-5861
Jim Lentz, supt. Fax 825-6718
pas.k12.mn.us
Brown ES 200/PK-1
701 7th St SE 56164 507-825-6756
Don Plahn, prin. Fax 825-6749
Hill ES 200/2-4
900 6th Ave SW 56164 507-825-6763
Don Plahn, prin. Fax 825-6757
Pipestone MS 400/5-8
1401 7th St SW 56164 507-825-5861
Ray Staatz, prin. Fax 825-6729
Other Schools – See Lake Benton

Plainview, Wabasha, Pop. 3,296
Plainview-Elgin-Millville ISD 2899 900/PK-12
500 W Broadway 55964 507-534-3651
Gary Kuphal, supt. Fax 534-3907
www.pem.k12.mn.us/
Plainview-Elgin-Millville ES 300/PK-3
500 W Broadway 55964 507-534-4232
W. Lynn Bastian, prin. Fax 534-3907
Other Schools – See Elgin

Immanuel Lutheran S 100/PK-8
45 W Broadway 55964 507-534-2108
Alvin Lutringer, prin.

Plummer, Red Lake, Pop. 271
Plummer SD 628 200/K-6
PO Box 7 56748 218-465-4222
James Guetter, supt. Fax 465-4225
www.rlccelementary.org/
Red Lake County Central ES 200/K-6
PO Box 7 56748 218-465-4222
Randy Pederson, prin. Fax 465-4225

Plymouth, Hennepin, Pop. 69,701
Robbinsdale SD 281
Supt. — See New Hope
Plymouth MS 1,100/6-8
10011 36th Ave N 55441 763-504-7100
Bruce Beidelman, prin. Fax 504-7131
Zachary Lane ES 500/K-5
4350 Zachary Ln N 55442 763-504-7300
Randy Moberg, prin. Fax 504-7309

Wayzata SD 284
Supt. — See Minneapolis
Birchview ES 600/K-5
425 Ranchview Ln N 55447 763-745-5300
Tom Koch, prin. Fax 745-5391
Gleason Lake ES 700/PK-5
310 County Rd 101 N 55447 763-745-5400
Mary McKasy, prin. Fax 745-5491
Greenwood ES 600/K-5
18005 Medina Rd, 763-745-5500
Ginny Clark, prin. Fax 745-5591
Kimberly Lane ES 600/K-5
17405 Old Rockford Rd, 763-745-5600
Gary Kipling, prin. Fax 745-5691
Oakwood ES 500/K-5
17340 County Road 6 55447 763-745-5700
Dennis Grasmick, prin. Fax 745-5791
Plymouth Creek ES 600/K-5
16005 41st Ave N, 763-745-5800
Karla Thompson, prin. Fax 745-5891
Sunset Hill ES 600/K-5
13005 Sunset Trl 55441 763-745-5900
Karen Keffeler, prin. Fax 745-5991
Wayzata Central MS 900/6-8
305 Vicksburg Ln N 55447 763-745-6000
Steven Root, prin. Fax 745-6091
Wayzata East MS 700/6-8
12000 Ridgemount Ave W 55441 763-745-6200
Paul Paetzel, prin. Fax 745-6291

Providence Academy 800/PK-12
15100 Schmidt Lake Rd, 763-258-2500
Dr. Todd Flanders, hdmstr. Fax 258-2501

Ponemah, Beltrami, Pop. 704
Red Lake SD 38
Supt. — See Redlake
Ponemah S 200/PK-8
PO Box 39 56666 218-554-7337
John Klinke, prin. Fax 554-7442

Ponsford, Becker
Pine Point SD 25 100/K-8
PO Box 8 56575 218-573-4100
Bonita Gurno, supt. Fax 573-4128
www.pinepoint.k12.mn.us
Pine Point S 100/K-8
PO Box 8 56575 218-573-4100
Jason Luksik, prin. Fax 573-4128

Preston, Fillmore, Pop. 1,377
Fillmore Central SD 2198 600/PK-12
PO Box 50 55965 507-765-3845
Myrna Luehmann, supt. Fax 765-3636
www.fillmorecentral.k12.mn.us/
Fillmore Central ES 200/PK-4
PO Box 50 55965 507-765-3809
Myrna Luehmann, prin. Fax 765-2367
Fillmore Central MS 200/5-8
PO Box 50 55965 507-765-3843
Myrna Luehmann, prin. Fax 765-2367

Princeton, Mille Lacs, Pop. 4,694
Princeton SD 477 3,300/PK-12
706 1st St 55371 763-389-2422
Mark Sleeper, supt. Fax 389-9142
www.princeton.k12.mn.us
North ES 800/3-5
1202 7th Ave N 55371 763-389-6802
John Beach, prin. Fax 389-6850
Princeton MS 800/6-8
1100 4th Ave N 55371 763-389-6705
Richard Lahn, prin. Fax 389-6737
South ES 600/PK-2
805 8th Ave S 55371 763-389-6901
Gregory Finck, prin. Fax 389-6920

Prinsburg, Kandiyohi, Pop. 446

Central Minnesota Christian S 300/PK-12
PO Box 98 56281 320-978-8700
Peter Van Der Puy, supt. Fax 978-6797

Prior Lake, Scott, Pop. 22,168
Prior Lake - Savage Area SD 719 5,500/K-12
PO Box 539 55372 952-226-0000
Dr. Sue Gruver, supt. Fax 226-0059
www.priorlake-savage.k12.mn.us
Edgewood S 300/K-K
PO Box 539 55372 952-226-0900
Deb Williams, prin. Fax 226-0949
Five Hawks ES 600/K-5
PO Box 539 55372 952-226-0100
Tim Bell, prin. Fax 226-0149
Grainwood ES 400/K-5
PO Box 539 55372 952-226-0300
Patrick Glynn, prin. Fax 226-0349
Hidden Oaks MS 900/6-8
PO Box 539 55372 952-226-0700
Sasha Kuznetsov, prin. Fax 226-0749
Jeffers Pond ES K-5
PO Box 539 55372 952-226-0600
Cindy Solberg, prin. Fax 226-0649

Twin Oaks MS 6-8
PO Box 539 55372 952-226-0500
Dan Edwards, prin. Fax 226-0549
Westwood ES 600/K-5
PO Box 539 55372 952-226-0400
Pam Winfield, prin. Fax 226-0449
Other Schools – See Savage

St. Michael S 600/PK-8
16280 Duluth Ave SE 55372 952-447-2124
Patrick Fox, prin. Fax 447-2132
St. Paul's Lutheran S 100/PK-6
5634 Luther Rd SE 55372 952-447-2117
Belinda Granlund, prin. Fax 447-2119

Proctor, Saint Louis, Pop. 2,779
Proctor SD 704 1,700/PK-12
131 9th Ave 55810 218-628-4934
John Engelking, supt. Fax 628-4937
www.proctor.k12.mn.us
Jedlicka MS 400/6-8
131 9th Ave 55810 218-628-4926
Kim Belcastro, prin. Fax 628-4932
Other Schools – See Duluth, Saginaw

St. Rose S 100/PK-6
2 6th Ave 55810 218-624-0818
Nicole Pearson, prin. Fax 624-0984

Ramsey, Anoka, Pop. 22,074
Anoka-Hennepin SD 11
Supt. — See Coon Rapids
Ramsey ES 1,100/1-5
15000 Nowthen Blvd NW 55303 763-506-4000
Jeffrey Clusiau, prin. Fax 506-4003

Randall, Morrison, Pop. 627
Little Falls SD 482
Supt. — See Little Falls
Knight ES 100/K-5
PO Box 185 56475 320-616-5200
Maxine Strege, prin. Fax 749-2147

Randolph, Dakota, Pop. 341
Randolph SD 195 500/PK-12
PO Box 38 55065 507-263-2151
Michael Kelley, supt. Fax 645-5950
www.randolph.k12.mn.us
Randolph ES 300/PK-6
PO Box 38 55065 507-263-2151
Matt Rutledge, prin. Fax 645-5950

Raymond, Kandiyohi, Pop. 766
MACCRAY SD 2180
Supt. — See Clara City
MACCRAY East ES 200/K-6
PO Box 215 56282 320-967-4281
Doug Runia, prin. Fax 967-4283

Redlake, Beltrami, Pop. 1,068
Red Lake SD 38 1,200/PK-12
PO Box 499 56671 218-679-3353
Brent Gish, supt. Fax 679-2321
www.redlake.k12.mn.us
Red Lake ES 400/K-5
PO Box 499 56671 218-679-3329
Jean Whitefeather, prin. Fax 679-3644
Red Lake MS 200/6-8
PO Box 499 56671 218-679-2700
Gregory Ferrin, prin. Fax 679-2733
Other Schools – See Ponemah

St. Marys Mission S 100/1-6
PO Box 189 56671 218-679-3388
Al Yarnott, prin. Fax 679-2231

Red Lake Falls, Red Lake, Pop. 1,590
Red Lake Falls SD 630 400/PK-12
PO Box 399 56750 218-253-2139
Joel Young, supt. Fax 253-2135
www.redlakefalls.k12.mn.us
Hughes ES 200/PK-6
PO Box 399 56750 218-253-2161
Jan Anderson, prin. Fax 253-4479

St. Joseph S 50/PK-6
PO Box 400 56750 218-253-2188
Geraldine Cyr, prin. Fax 253-2195

Red Wing, Goodhue, Pop. 15,799
Red Wing SD 256 2,600/K-12
2451 Eagle Ridge Dr 55066 651-385-4500
Stan Slessor, supt. Fax 385-4510
www.redwing.k12.mn.us
Burnside ES 600/3-5
5001 Learning Ln 55066 651-385-4700
Sheila Beckner, prin. Fax 385-4710
Sunnyside ES 400/K-2
1669 Southwood Ave 55066 651-385-4570
Patti Roberts, prin. Fax 385-4576
Twin Bluff MS 700/6-8
2120 Twin Bluff Rd 55066 651-385-4530
Nancy Glasenapp, prin. Fax 385-4540

Concordia-Immanuel Lutheran S 50/K-5
1805 Bush St 55066 651-388-3839
Fax 388-3891
River Bluff Christian S 50/1-8
4652 Highway 61 N 55066 651-388-9175
St. John Lutheran S 50/K-8
421 East Ave 55066 651-388-2611
Benjamin Bain, prin. Fax 388-8325
St. Joseph S 100/PK-5
469 12th St 55066 651-388-9493
Brenda Balzer, prin. Fax 385-0769

Redwood Falls, Redwood, Pop. 5,272
Redwood Area SD 2897 1,200/PK-12
100 George Ramseth Dr 56283 507-644-3531
Rick Ellingworth, supt. Fax 644-3057
redwood.mntm.org
Gray ES 400/PK-4
201 McPhail Dr 56283 507-644-2627
Stephanie Perry, prin. Fax 644-8138
Redwood Valley MS 400/5-8
100 George Ramseth Dr 56283 507-644-3521
Wade Mathers, prin. Fax 644-3057

St. John Lutheran S 100/PK-8
119 W Broadway St 56283 507-637-3502
David Gartner, prin. Fax 637-3502

Remer, Cass, Pop. 385
Northland Community SD 118 500/PK-12
316 Main St E Rm 200 56672 218-566-2351
Mike Doro, supt. Fax 566-3199
www.isd118.k12.mn.us
Remer ES 200/PK-6
316 Main St E Rm 500 56672 218-566-2353
Mary Wilke, prin. Fax 566-3199
Other Schools – See Longville

Renville, Renville, Pop. 1,282
Renville County West SD 2890 600/K-12
PO Box 338 56284 320-329-8362
Lance Bagstad, supt. Fax 329-3271
www.rcw.k12.mn.us
Other Schools – See Sacred Heart

Rice, Benton, Pop. 1,038
Sauk Rapids-Rice SD 47
Supt. — See Sauk Rapids
Rice ES 400/PK-5
PO Box 25 56367 320-393-2177
Nate Swenson, prin. Fax 393-2140

Richfield, Hennepin, Pop. 33,497
Richfield SD 280 3,700/K-12
7001 Harriet Ave 55423 612-798-6000
Robert Slotterback, supt. Fax 798-6057
www.richfield.k12.mn.us
Centennial ES 300/K-2
7315 Bloomington Ave 55423 612-798-6800
LeeAnn Wise, prin. Fax 798-6827
Richfield IS 800/3-5
7020 12th Ave S 55423 612-798-6600
Eric Paulson, prin. Fax 798-6664
Richfield MS 900/6-8
7461 Oliver Ave S 55423 612-798-6400
Stephen West, prin. Fax 798-6427
Sheridan Hills ES 300/K-2
6400 Sheridan Ave S 55423 612-798-6900
Joey Page, prin. Fax 798-6927

Blessed Trinity S - Nicollet Campus 200/4-8
6720 Nicollet Ave 55423 612-869-5200
Sue Kerr, prin. Fax 767-2191
Blessed Trinity S - Penn Campus 200/PK-3
7540 Penn Ave S 55423 612-866-6906
Kim Doyle, prin. Fax 869-0277
Mt. Calvary Lutheran S 100/PK-8
6541 16th Ave S 55423 612-869-9441
Stephen Schrader, prin. Fax 866-6005

Richmond, Stearns, Pop. 1,255
Rocori SD 750
Supt. — See Cold Spring
Richmond ES 200/K-6
34 2nd St NE 56368 320-597-2016
Rochelle Wagner, prin. Fax 597-2955

SS. Peter & Paul S 100/K-6
PO Box 189 56368 320-597-2565
Jacqueline Walz, prin. Fax 597-4385

Robbinsdale, Hennepin, Pop. 13,331
Robbinsdale SD 281
Supt. — See New Hope
Lakeview ES 400/K-5
4110 Lake Drive Ave N 55422 763-504-4100
Nichole Rens, prin. Fax 504-4109
Robbinsdale MS 800/6-8
3730 Toledo Ave N 55422 763-504-4800
Tom Henderlite, prin. Fax 504-4831

Sacred Heart S 200/PK-8
4050 Hubbard Ave N 55422 763-537-1329
Karen Bursey, prin. Fax 537-1486

Rochester, Olmsted, Pop. 94,950
Rochester ISD 535 14,100/PK-12
615 7th St SW 55902 507-328-3000
Romain Dallemand, supt. Fax 328-4212
www.rochester.k12.mn.us
Adams MS, 1525 31st St NW 55901 1,100/6-8
Richard Jones, prin. 507-328-5700
Bamber Valley ES 800/PK-5
2001 Bamber Valley Rd SW 55902 507-328-3030
Becky Gerdes, prin.
Bishop ES, 406 36th Ave NW 55901 500/K-5
Jacque Peterson, prin. 507-328-3100
Churchill ES, 2240 7th Ave NE 55906 200/K-2
Joyce Dammer, prin. 507-328-3150
Elton Hills ES 400/K-5
1421 Elton Hills Dr NW 55901 507-328-3200
Paul Ehling, prin.
Folwell ES, 603 15th Ave SW 55902 300/K-5
Todd Kieffer, prin. 507-328-3220
Franklin Montessori ES 200/K-5
1801 9th Ave SE 55904 507-328-3300
Jean Murphy, prin.
Friedell MS, 1200 S Broadway 55904 300/6-8
Monica Bowler, prin. 507-328-5650
Gage East K, 930 40th St NW 55901 50/PK-K
Kim McDonald, prin. 507-328-3430
Gage ES, 1300 40th St NW 55901 1-5
Kim McDonald, prin. 507-328-3400
Hoover ES 200/3-5
369 Elton Hills Dr NW 55901 507-328-3450
Joyce Dammer, prin.
Jefferson ES 500/K-5
1201 10th Ave NE 55906 507-328-3500
Brenda Wichmann, prin.
Kellogg MS, 503 17th St NE 55906 1,000/6-8
Dwight Jennings, prin. 507-328-5800
Lincoln S, 1122 8th Ave SE 55904 400/K-8
James Sonju, prin. 507-328-3550
Longfellow ES 300/K-5
1615 Marion Rd SE 55904 507-328-3600
Les Ernster, prin.
Pinewood ES 300/K-5
1900 Pinewood Rd SE 55904 507-328-3630
Roxanne Nauman, prin.
Riverside Central ES 500/K-5
506 5th Ave SE 55904 507-328-3700
Christine Smith, prin.
Sunset Terrace ES 600/PK-5
1707 19th Ave NW 55901 507-328-3770
Judy Goldstein, prin.
Washington ES 400/K-5
1200 11th Ave NW 55901 507-328-3800
Linda Stockwell, prin.
Willow Creek MS 1,000/6-8
2425 11th Ave SE 55904 507-328-5900
Jeffrey Elstad, prin.

Greene Valley SDA S 50/1-8
7240 Dresser Dr NE 55906 507-282-7981
Holy Spirit S 300/K-8
5455 50th Ave NW 55901 507-288-8818
Matthew Klebe, prin. Fax 288-5155
Resurrection Lutheran S 100/K-8
4520 19th Ave NW 55901 507-285-9735
Philip Zahn, prin. Fax 285-9724
Rochester Central Lutheran S 300/PK-8
2619 9th Ave NW 55901 507-289-3267
Henry Pahlkotter, prin. Fax 287-6588
Rochester Montessori S 100/K-6
5099 7th St NW 55901 507-288-8725
Patrick Sheedy, dir. Fax 288-4186
St. Francis of Assisi S 500/PK-8
318 11th Ave SE 55904 507-288-4816
Barb Plenge, prin. Fax 288-4815
St. John S 300/K-8
424 W Center St 55902 507-282-5248
Suzanne Lagerwaard, prin. Fax 282-1343
St. Pius X S 200/PK-4
1205 12th Ave NW 55901 507-282-5161
Don Valentine, prin. Fax 282-5107
Schaeffer Academy 400/K-12
2700 Schaeffer Ln NE 55906 507-286-1050
Keith Phillips, hdmstr. Fax 282-3823

Rockford, Wright, Pop. 3,808
Rockford SD 883 1,500/PK-12
6051 Ash St 55373 763-477-9165
Michael Smith, supt. Fax 477-5833
www.rockford.k12.mn.us
Rockford ES 600/PK-5
PO Box 69 55373 763-477-5837
Brenda Petersmeyer, prin. Fax 477-5025
Rockford MS 400/6-8
PO Box 189 55373 763-477-5831
Marie Flanary, prin. Fax 477-5832

Rockville, Stearns, Pop. 2,488
Rocori SD 750
Supt. — See Cold Spring
Clark ES 200/K-6
PO Box 37 56369 320-251-8651
Rochelle Wagner, prin. Fax 251-8430

Rogers, Hennepin, Pop. 6,042
Elk River Area SD 728
Supt. — See Elk River
Hassan ES 600/K-5
14055 Orchid Ave 55374 763-274-7230
Heidi Adamson, prin. Fax 274-7231
Rogers ES 500/K-5
12521 Main St 55374 763-241-3462
Phil Schreifels, prin. Fax 428-8475
Rogers MS 900/6-8
20855 141st Ave N 55374 763-241-3550
Nancy Elsmore, prin. Fax 241-3518

Mary Queen of Peace S 200/PK-6
21201 Church Ave 55374 763-428-2355
Patrick Gallivan, prin. Fax 428-2062

Rollingstone, Winona, Pop. 644
Winona Area SD 861
Supt. — See Winona
Rollingstone Community ES 100/PK-4
61 Main St 55969 507-689-2171
Sonia Hanson, prin. Fax 689-2934

Roseau, Roseau, Pop. 2,814
Roseau SD 682 1,300/PK-12
509 3rd St NE 56751 218-463-1471
Larry Guggisberg, supt. Fax 463-3243
www.roseau.k12.mn.us/
Roseau ES 600/PK-6
509 3rd St NE 56751 218-463-2746
Gary Olson, prin. Fax 463-1016

Rose Creek, Mower, Pop. 352
Southland SD 500
Supt. — See Adams
Southland ES 200/K-5
PO Box 157 55970 507-437-3214
Randy Juhl, prin. Fax 433-2368

Rosemount, Dakota, Pop. 19,311
Rosemount-Apple Valley-Eagan ISD 196 26,200/K-12
3455 153rd St W 55068 651-423-7700
Jane Berenz, supt. Fax 423-7633
www.district196.org
Parkview ES 500/K-5
6795 Gerdine Path W 55068 952-431-8350
Pam Haldeman, prin. Fax 431-8346
Rosemount ES 600/K-5
3155 143rd St W 55068 651-423-7690
Tom Idstrom, prin. Fax 423-7668
Rosemount MS 1,100/6-8
3135 143rd St W 55068 651-423-7570
Mary Thompson, prin. Fax 423-7664
Shannon Park ES 700/K-5
13501 Shannon Pkwy 55068 651-423-7670
Michael Guthrie, prin. Fax 423-7667
Other Schools – See Apple Valley, Burnsville, Eagan

Christian Heritage Academy 100/PK-8
17297 Glacier Way 55068 952-953-4155
Gail Wolfe, prin. Fax 997-1543
First Baptist Schools 100/K-12
14400 Diamond Path W 55068 651-423-2271
Dr. David Clear, hdmstr. Fax 423-4471
St. Joseph S 200/K-8
14355 S Robert Trl 55068 651-423-1658
Thomas Joseph, prin. Fax 423-6616

Roseville, Ramsey, Pop. 32,079
Roseville Area SD 623 6,300/K-12
1251 County Road B2 W 55113 651-635-1600
Dr. John Thein, supt. Fax 635-1659
www.isd623.org
Brimhall ES 600/K-6
1744 County Road B W 55113 651-638-1958
Penny Bidne, prin. Fax 638-9007
Central Park ES 400/K-6
535 County Road B2 W 55113 651-481-9951
Florence Odegard, prin. Fax 481-7128
Parkview Center S 700/K-8
701 County Road B W 55113 651-487-4360
Kristen Olson, prin. Fax 487-4379
Other Schools – See Falcon Heights, Little Canada, Maplewood, Saint Paul, Shoreview

King of Kings Lutheran S 100/K-8
2330 Dale St N 55113 651-484-9206
Daniel Kuball, prin. Fax 484-4346
North Heights Christian Academy 200/K-12
2701 Rice St 55113 651-797-7900
Jeffrey Taylor, prin. Fax 484-8636
St. Rose of Lima S 300/PK-8
2072 Hamline Ave N 55113 651-646-3832
Greg Pizzolato, prin. Fax 647-6437

Rothsay, Wilkin, Pop. 508
Rothsay SD 850 100/K-12
123 2nd St NW 56579 218-867-2117
Mary Donohue Stetz, supt. Fax 867-2376
www.rothsay.k12.mn.us
Rothsay S 100/K-12
123 2nd St NW 56579 218-867-2116
Mary Donohue Stetz, prin. Fax 867-2376

Royalton, Morrison, Pop. 919
Royalton SD 485 700/PK-12
PO Box 5 56373 320-584-5531
Dr. John Franzoia, supt. Fax 584-5218
www.royalton.k12.mn.us
Royalton ES 400/PK-6
PO Box 138 56373 320-584-5551
Philipp Gurbada, prin. Fax 584-5552

Rush City, Chisago, Pop. 2,986
Rush City SD 139 1,000/K-12
PO Box 566 55069 320-358-4855
Vern Koepp, supt. Fax 358-1351
www.rushcity.k12.mn.us
Jacobson ES 500/K-6
PO Box 566 55069 320-358-4724
Melody Tenhoff, prin. Fax 358-1361

Rushford, Fillmore, Pop. 1,786
Rushford-Peterson SD 239 600/PK-12
PO Box 627 55971 507-864-7785
Charles Ehler, supt. Fax 864-2085
www.r-pschools.com
Rushford-Peterson ES 200/PK-3
PO Box 627 55971 507-864-7787
Charles Ehler, prin. Fax 864-2085
Other Schools – See Peterson

Russell, Lyon, Pop. 342
R T R ISD 2902
Supt. — See Tyler
R T R MS 100/6-8
PO Box 310 56169 507-823-4371
James Burns, prin. Fax 823-4657

Ruthton, Pipestone, Pop. 263
R T R ISD 2902
Supt. — See Tyler
R T R ES 200/PK-5
PO Box B 56170 507-658-3301
Amy Christensen, prin. Fax 658-3589

Sacred Heart, Renville, Pop. 526
Renville County West SD 2890
Supt. — See Renville
Renville County West ES 300/K-6
PO Box 10 56285 320-765-2241
Bill Adams, prin. Fax 765-2252

Saginaw, Saint Louis
Proctor SD 704
Supt. — See Proctor
Caribou Lake ES 100/K-2
6279 Industrial Rd 55779 218-729-8802
Jon Larson, prin. Fax 729-6771

Saint Louis County SD 2142
Supt. — See Virginia
Albrook S 200/PK-12
7427 Seville Rd 55779 218-729-8322
Kristy Berlin, prin. Fax 729-8808

Saint Anthony, Hennepin, Pop. 7,915
Saint Anthony-New Brighton SD 282 1,600/PK-12
3303 33rd Ave NE 55418 612-706-1000
Rod Thompson, supt. Fax 706-1020
www.stanthony.k12.mn.us
Saint Anthony MS 400/6-8
3303 33rd Ave NE 55418 612-706-1030
Shirley Gregoire, prin. Fax 706-1040
Wilshire Park ES 600/PK-5
3600 Highcrest Rd NE 55418 612-706-1200
Kari Page, prin. Fax 706-1240

Saint Augusta, Stearns

St. Mary Help of Christians S 100/K-6
24560 County Road 7, 320-251-3937
Bonnie VanHeel, prin.
St. Wendelin S 100/PK-6
22776 State Highway 15, 320-251-9175
Lynn Rasmussen, prin. Fax 654-9030

Saint Charles, Winona, Pop. 3,393
Saint Charles SD 858 1,000/PK-12
600 E 6th St 55972 507-932-4423
Thomas Ames, supt. Fax 932-4700
www.scschools.net
Saint Charles ES 500/PK-6
925 Church Ave 55972 507-932-4910
Allen Rasmussen, prin. Fax 932-4912

Saint Clair, Blue Earth, Pop. 813
Saint Clair SD 75 600/PK-12
PO Box 99 56080 507-245-3501
Tom Bruels, supt. Fax 245-3517
www.isd75.k12.mn.us/
Saint Clair ES 400/PK-6
PO Box 99 56080 507-245-3533
Susan Owens, dean Fax 245-3378

Saint Cloud, Stearns, Pop. 59,458
Saint Cloud Area SD 742 9,000/PK-12
1000 44th Ave N 56303 320-253-9333
Steven Jordahl, supt. Fax 529-4343
www.isd742.org
Lincoln ES 300/K-6
336 5th Ave SE 56304 320-251-6343
Hugh Skaja, prin. Fax 251-9488
Madison ES 500/K-5
2805 9th St N 56303 320-252-4665
Daniel Anderson, prin. Fax 252-6971
North JHS 600/6-8
1212 29th Ave N 56303 320-251-2159
Robert Huot, prin. Fax 251-7350
Oak Hill Community ES 800/K-6
2600 County Road 136 56301 320-251-7936
Tina Lahr, prin. Fax 251-5233
Roosevelt ECC 200/PK-PK
3015 3rd St N 56303 320-253-5828
Marj Hawkins, dir. Fax 253-5828
South JHS 800/7-8
1120 15th Ave S 56301 320-251-1322
Eric Williams, prin. Fax 251-2911
Talahi Community ES 600/K-6
1321 University Dr SE 56304 320-251-7551
Jason Scherber, prin. Fax 251-5042
Westwood ES 500/K-6
5800 Ridgewood Rd 56303 320-253-1350
Janet Knoll, prin. Fax 253-7794
Other Schools – See Clear Lake, Saint Joseph, Waite Park

Prince of Peace Lutheran S 200/PK-8
4770 County Road 120 56303 320-251-1477
Bob Wolter, prin. Fax 251-8996
St. Augustine & St. Marys Cathedral S 200/PK-6
428 2nd St SE 56304 320-251-2376
Pat Lindeman, prin. Fax 529-3222
Saint Cloud Christian S 300/K-12
430 3rd Ave NE 56304 320-252-8182
MaryJo Froemming, admin. Fax 656-9678
St. Elizabeth Ann Seton IS 100/4-6
2410 1st St N 56303 320-251-6231
Tom Troness, prin. Fax 251-0664
St. Elizabeth Ann Seton PS 100/K-3
1615 11th Ave S 56301 320-251-1988
Tom Troness, prin. Fax 229-2149
SS. Peter Paul & Michael MS 200/5-8
1215 11th Ave N 56303 320-251-5295
Sharon Bichler, prin. Fax 251-5295
SS. Peter Paul & Michael S 300/PK-4
925 30th Ave N 56303 320-251-4737
Sharon Bichler, prin. Fax 253-7110

Saint Francis, Anoka, Pop. 6,449
Saint Francis SD 15 5,400/K-12
4115 Ambassador Blvd NW 55070 763-753-7040
Edward Saxton, supt. Fax 753-4693
www.stfrancis.k12.mn.us
Saint Francis ES 700/K-5
22919 Saint Francis Blvd NW 55070 763-213-8670
Kathy Kohnen, prin. Fax 753-5180
Saint Francis MS 1,300/6-8
23026 Ambassador Blvd NW 55070 763-213-8500
Dale Johnson, prin. Fax 753-3821
Other Schools – See Cedar

Trinity Lutheran S 100/K-12
3812 229th Ave NW 55070 763-753-1234
Ken Koch, prin. Fax 753-1774
Zion Lutheran S 100/PK-6
7515 269th Ave NW 55070 763-856-2099
Gary Carlson, prin.

Saint James, Watonwan, Pop. 4,592
Saint James SD 840 1,100/PK-12
500 8th Ave S 56081 507-375-5974
Nordy Nelson, supt. Fax 375-7143
www.stjames.k12.mn.us
Saint James Armstrong IS 300/4-6
500 8th Ave S 56081 507-375-3321
Tony Faith, prin. Fax 375-3323
Saint James Northside ES 400/PK-3
500 8th Ave S 56081 507-375-3325
Connie Finnern, prin. Fax 375-3327

St. Paul's Lutheran S 50/K-8
315 9th St S 56081 507-375-3809
Philip Haefner, prin. Fax 375-3809

Saint Joseph, Stearns, Pop. 5,089
Saint Cloud Area SD 742
Supt. — See Saint Cloud
Kennedy S 400/K-8
1300 Jade Rd 56374 320-363-7791
Diane Moeller, prin. Fax 529-4336

St. Joseph Lab S 200/PK-6
32 W Minnesota St 56374 320-363-7769
Karl Terhaar, prin. Fax 363-7760

Saint Louis Park, Hennepin, Pop. 44,114
Saint Louis Park SD 283 3,900/K-12
6425 W 33rd St 55426 952-928-6000
Debra Bowers, supt. Fax 928-6020
www.slpschools.org
Aquila ES 300/K-3
8500 W 31st St 55426 952-928-6500
Shelley Nielsen, prin. Fax 928-6466
Cedar Manor IS 400/4-6
9400 Cedar Lake Rd S 55426 952-928-6555
Freida Bailey, prin. Fax 928-6565
Hobart ES 300/K-3
6500 W 26th St 55426 952-928-6600
Frank Johnson, prin. Fax 928-6643
Lindgren IS 300/4-6
4801 W 41st St 55416 952-928-6700
Ann Sullivan, prin. Fax 928-6716
Park Spanish Immersion ES 600/K-6
6300 Walker St 55416 952-928-6759
Gerry Lukaska, prin. Fax 928-6753
Saint Louis Park JHS 600/7-8
2025 Texas Ave S 55426 952-928-6300
Les Bork, prin. Fax 928-6383

Groves Academy 200/1-12
3200 Highway 100 S 55416 952-920-6377
John Alexander, hdmstr. Fax 920-2068
Holy Family Academy 200/PK-8
5925 W Lake St 55416 952-925-9193
Ann Coone, prin. Fax 925-5298
Minneapolis Jewish Day S 400/K-8
4330 Cedar Lake Rd S 55416 952-381-3500
Dr. Ray Levi, hdmstr. Fax 381-3501
Torah Academy 300/PK-8
2800 Joppa Ave S 55416 952-920-6630
Fax 922-7844
Westwood ECC 100/PK-K
9001 Cedar Lake Rd S 55426 952-545-5624
Marilyn Stalheim, dir. Fax 545-0251

Saint Michael, Wright, Pop. 12,850
Saint Michael-Albertville SD 885
Supt. — See Albertville
Big Woods ES 800/1-5
13470 Frankfort Pkwy NE 55376 763-497-8025
Lee Brown, prin. Fax 497-6563
Fieldstone ES 1-5
5255 Jansen Ave NE 55376 763-497-0904
Jeanette Aanerud, prin.
Saint Michael-Albertville MS 1,000/6-8
4862 Naber Ave NE 55376 763-497-2655
Jennifer Kelly, prin. Fax 497-6591
Saint Michael ES 700/1-5
101 Central Ave W 55376 763-497-4882
Sheila Bichler, prin. Fax 497-6592

St. Michael S 300/K-6
14 Main St N 55376 763-497-3887
Jennifer Haller, prin. Fax 497-9159

Saint Paul, Ramsey, Pop. 280,404
Roseville Area SD 623
Supt. — See Roseville
Little Canada ES 400/K-6
400 Eli Rd 55117 651-490-1353
Garin Bogenholm, prin. Fax 490-1436

Saint Paul SD 625 38,100/PK-12
360 Colborne St 55102 651-767-8100
Dr. Meria Carstarphen, supt. Fax 293-8586
www.spps.org
Adams Spanish Immersion Magnet ES 600/K-6
615 Chatsworth St S 55102 651-298-1595
Judy Kaufmann, prin. Fax 298-1598
Aerospace at Cleveland S 400/7-8
1000 Walsh St 55106 651-293-8880
Troy Vincent, prin. Fax 293-8888
Aerospace at Farnsworth ES 400/PK-4
1290 Arcade St 55106 651-293-8675
Troy Vincent, prin. Fax 293-8679
American Indian Magnet S 300/PK-6
1075 3rd St E 55106 651-778-3100
Brenda Peltier, prin. Fax 778-3101
Ames ES 300/PK-6
1760 Ames Pl 55106 651-293-8970
Delores Henderson, prin. Fax 293-8976
Battle Creek Environmental Magnet S 600/K-6
60 Ruth St S 55119 651-293-8850
Eleanor Clemmons, prin. Fax 293-5396

Battle Creek MS 700/7-8
2121 N Park Dr 55119 651-293-8960
Jocelyn Sims, prin. Fax 293-8866
Capitol Hill Magnet S 1,000/1-8
560 Concordia Ave 55103 651-325-2500
Louis Mariucci, prin. Fax 325-2501
Chelsea Heights ES 400/K-6
1557 Huron St 55108 651-293-8790
Jill Gebeke, prin. Fax 293-8793
Cherokee Heights West Side S 500/PK-6
694 Charlton St 55107 651-293-8610
Sharon Hendrix, prin. Fax 293-8617
Como Park ES 500/PK-6
780 Wheelock Pkwy W 55117 651-293-8820
Christine Vang, prin. Fax 293-8828
Crossroads ES 300/K-6
543 Front Ave 55117 651-767-8540
Celeste Carty, prin. Fax 312-9003
Daytons Bluff ES 300/PK-6
262 Bates Ave 55106 651-293-8915
Andrew Collins, prin. Fax 771-3428
Eastern Heights ES 300/PK-6
2001 Margaret St 55119 651-293-8870
Jayne Ropella, prin. Fax 293-8982
Expo for Excellence Magnet S 500/PK-6
540 Warwick St 55116 651-290-8384
Darren Yerama, prin. Fax 293-8639
Four Seasons A+ ES 300/K-6
340 Colborne St 55102 651-290-7595
Howard Wilson, prin. Fax 293-6575
Franklin Music Magnet ES 400/K-6
690 Jackson St, 651-293-8620
Katherine Burks, prin. Fax 293-8968
Frost Lake Magnet ES 500/K-6
1505 Hoyt Ave E 55106 651-293-8930
Annamarie Erbes, prin. Fax 293-8932
Galtier Magnet ES 300/K-6
1317 Charles Ave 55104 651-293-8710
Adrian Pendelton, prin. Fax 293-8973
Groveland Park ES 400/K-6
2045 Saint Clair Ave 55105 651-293-8760
Rebecca Pederson, prin. Fax 293-8653
Hancock/Hamline Magnet ES 600/K-6
1599 Englewood Ave 55104 651-293-8715
Marjorie Abrams, prin. Fax 293-8718
Hayden Heights ES 400/PK-6
1863 Clear Ave 55119 651-293-8815
Kristine Peterson, prin. Fax 293-8977
Hazel Park MS 600/7-8
1140 White Bear Ave N 55106 651-293-8920
Coleman McDonough, prin. Fax 228-3609
Highland Park ES 400/K-6
1700 Saunders Ave 55116 651-293-8770
Teresa Ciccarelli, prin. Fax 293-8983
Highland Park JHS 800/7-8
975 Snelling Ave S 55116 651-293-8950
Charlene Hoff, prin. Fax 293-8953
Highwood Hills ES 300/PK-6
2188 Londin Ln E 55119 651-293-8875
Patricia Rosenbaum, prin. Fax 293-5296
Hill Montessori Magnet S 400/PK-6
998 Selby Ave 55104 651-293-8720
Yeu Vang, prin. Fax 298-1586
Humboldt JHS 400/7-8
640 Humboldt Ave 55107 651-293-8630
Tim Williams, prin. Fax 293-6660
Jackson Preparatory Magnet ES 500/PK-6
437 Edmund Ave 55103 651-293-8650
Patrick Bryan, prin. Fax 228-7742
Johnson Achievement ES 300/PK-6
740 York Ave 55106 651-793-7300
Frank Feinberg, prin. Fax 793-7310
L'Etoile Dunord French Immersion ES 400/K-6
1363 Bush Ave 55106 651-221-1480
Fatima Lawson, prin. Fax 221-1487
Linwood A+ ES 400/K-6
1023 Osceola Ave 55105 651-293-6606
Steve Unowsky, prin. Fax 293-6605
Longfellow Magnet ES 300/PK-6
318 Moore St 55104 651-293-8725
Mark Vandersteen, prin. Fax 293-5286
Mann ES 300/K-6
2001 Eleanor Ave 55116 651-293-8965
Jim Litwin, prin. Fax 293-8985
Maxfield Magnet ES 400/K-6
380 Victoria St N 55104 651-293-8680
Belinda Green, prin. Fax 293-5306
Mays International Magnet S 300/K-6
560 Concordia Ave 55103 651-325-2400
Kate Flynn, prin. Fax 325-2401
Mississippi Magnet ES 500/K-6
1575 L Orient St 55117 651-293-8840
Andy Xiong, prin. Fax 293-8843
Monroe Achievement + Community S 400/K-8
810 Palace Ave 55102 651-293-8690
Steve Unowsky, prin. Fax 293-8699
Murray JHS 800/7-8
2200 Buford Ave 55108 651-293-8740
Winston Tucker, prin. Fax 293-8742
Museum Magnet S 300/K-6
560 Concordia Ave 55103 651-325-2600
Tyrone Brookins, prin. Fax 325-2601
Nokomis Montessori Magnet S 400/PK-6
985 Ruth St N 55119 651-293-8857
Melissa McCollor, prin. Fax 293-5464
North End ES 400/K-6
27 Geranium Ave E 55117 651-293-8795
Hamilton Bell, prin. Fax 293-8798
Phalen Lake ES 600/K-6
1089 Cypress St 55106 651-293-8935
Catherine Rich, prin. Fax 293-8978
Prosperity Heights ES 300/K-6
1305 Prosperity Ave 55106 651-293-8695
Aly Xiong, prin. Fax 293-8799
Ramsey JHS 700/7-8
1700 Summit Ave 55105 651-293-8860
Bruce Maeda, prin. Fax 298-1587

Randolph Heights ES 400/K-6
348 Hamline Ave S 55105 651-293-8780
Nancy Flynn, prin. Fax 293-8986
Riverview West Side S of Excellence 200/K-6
271 Belvidere St E 55107 651-293-8665
Elizabeth Heffernan, prin. Fax 293-5303
Roosevelt West Side S of Excellence 500/K-6
160 Isabel St E 55107 651-293-8655
Scott Tryggeseth, prin. Fax 293-5304
Saint Anthony Park ES 400/K-6
2180 Knapp St 55108 651-293-8735
Ann Johnson, prin. Fax 293-8737
Saint Paul Open S 400/K-12
90 Western Ave S 55102 651-293-8670
Todd Bartholomy, prin. Fax 293-5308
Sheridan ES 300/K-6
525 White Bear Ave N 55106 651-293-8745
Shoua Moua, prin. Fax 290-8391
Vento ES 400/K-6
409 Case Ave, 651-293-8685
Darrell Rivard, prin. Fax 293-8688
Washington Technology Magnet MS 600/7-8
1041 Marion St 55117 651-293-8830
Mike McCollor, prin. Fax 228-4331
Webster Magnet ES 700/K-6
707 Holly Ave 55104 651-293-8625
Lori Simon, prin. Fax 293-8669
Wellstone S 400/PK-6
65 Kellogg Blvd E 55101 651-290-8354
Christine Osorio, prin. Fax 290-8357
World Culture & Languages Magnet S 300/K-6
1075 3rd St E 55106 651-778-3200
Mary Weyandt, prin. Fax 778-3101
Other Schools – See Maplewood

Capital City Adventist Christian S 50/PK-8
1220 McKnight Rd S 55119 651-739-7484
Fax 739-6383
Central Lutheran S 200/PK-8
775 Lexington Pkwy N 55104 651-645-8649
Jacqueline Illian, dir. Fax 645-8640
Christ's Household of Faith S 100/K-12
355 Marshall Ave 55102 651-265-3400
Friends S of Minnesota 200/K-8
1365 Englewood Ave 55104 651-917-0636
Lili Herbert, hdmstr. Fax 917-0708
Highland Catholic S 400/K-8
2017 Bohland Ave 55116 651-690-2477
Jane Schmidt, prin. Fax 699-1869
Holy Childhood S 100/K-8
1435 Midway Pkwy 55108 651-644-2791
Chuck Wollmering, prin. Fax 917-8797
Holy Spirit S 300/K-8
515 Albert St S 55116 651-698-3353
Dr. Mary Adrian, prin. Fax 698-1605
Lubavitcher Cheder S 100/PK-8
1758 Ford Pkwy 55116 651-698-0556
Maternity of Mary-St. Andrew S 200/PK-8
592 Arlington Ave W 55117 651-489-1459
Melissa Dan, prin. Fax 489-3560
Minnesota Waldorf S 200/PK-8
70 County Road B E 55117 651-487-6700
Fax 487-6800
Mounds Park Academy 700/PK-12
2051 Larpenteur Ave E 55109 651-777-2555
Michael Downs, hdmstr. Fax 777-8633
Nativity of Our Lord S 800/PK-8
1900 Stanford Ave 55105 651-699-1311
Margo Weiberg, prin. Fax 696-5420
St. Agnes S 400/K-12
530 Lafond Ave 55103 651-228-1161
James Morehead, prin. Fax 228-1158
St. Bernard S 400/PK-12
170 Rose Ave W 55117 651-489-1338
Jennifer Cassidy, prin. Fax 488-9466
St. Francis & St. James United S 100/K-8
486 View St 55102 651-228-1167
Gail Rappe, prin. Fax 228-0169
St. John Lutheran S 50/PK-8
771 Margaret St 55106 651-776-8861
Tony Drkula, prin. Fax 774-0803
St. Mark S 300/PK-8
1983 Dayton Ave 55104 651-644-3380
Molly Whinnery, prin. Fax 644-1923
St. Matthew S 100/K-8
497 Humboldt Ave 55107 651-224-6912
Doug Lieser, dir. Fax 602-0489
St. Pascal Baylon S 200/K-8
1757 Conway St 55106 651-776-0092
Marty Weisbeck, prin. Fax 774-9152
St. Paul Academy & Summit S 300/K-5
1150 Goodrich Ave 55105 651-698-2451
Bryn Roberts, hdmstr. Fax 296-9470
St. Peter Claver S 100/K-8
1060 Central Ave W 55104 651-646-1797
Teresa Mardenborough, prin. Fax 647-5394
St. Thomas More S 300/K-8
1065 Summit Ave 55105 651-224-4836
Patrick Lofton, prin. Fax 224-0097
Talmud Torah of St. Paul 100/K-8
768 Hamline Ave S 55116 651-698-8807
Sara Lynn Newberger, prin. Fax 698-8912
Trinity Catholic S 100/PK-8
835 5th St E 55106 651-776-2763
Sandy Krekeler, prin. Fax 772-4847

Saint Paul Park, Washington, Pop. 5,028
South Washington County SD 833
Supt. — See Cottage Grove
Oltman MS 400/6-8
1020 3rd St 55071 651-768-3500
Becky Schroeder, prin. Fax 768-3555
Pullman ES 400/K-5
1260 Selby Ave 55071 651-768-3600
Ed Ross, prin. Fax 768-3666

Hope Christian Academy 100/K-12
920 Holley Ave Ste 2 55071 651-459-6438
Randy Krussow, prin. Fax 769-2108
St. Andrew Lutheran S 100/PK-8
1001 Holley Ave 55071 651-459-3021
Eric Oakland, prin. Fax 459-3021

Saint Peter, Nicollet, Pop. 10,162
Saint Peter SD 508 1,300/K-12
100 Lincoln Dr 56082 507-934-5703
Jeffrey Olson, supt. Fax 934-2805
www.stpeterschools.org
North IS 400/3-6
815 N 9th St 56082 507-934-3260
Karen Coblentz, prin. Fax 934-1865
South ES 200/K-2
1405 S 7th St 56082 507-934-2754
Nancy Kluck, prin. Fax 934-4830

Ireland S 100/K-6
PO Box 522 56082 507-931-2810
Sr. Therese Collison, prin. Fax 931-9179
St. Peter S 100/PK-8
427 W Mulberry St 56082 507-931-1866
James Bakken, prin. Fax 934-8013

Saint Vincent, Kittson, Pop. 110
Kittson Central SD 2171
Supt. — See Hallock
Kittson Central St. Vincent S 50/K-8
911 Pacific Ave 56755 218-823-6215
Bruce Jensen, prin. Fax 843-2856

Sandstone, Pine, Pop. 2,519

Harvest Christian S 50/PK-9
PO Box 646 55072 320-245-5330
John Schutt, admin. Fax 245-5330

Sartell, Stearns, Pop. 12,668
Sartell-St Stephen SD 748 2,900/PK-12
212 3rd Ave N 56377 320-656-3715
Dr. Dale Gasser, supt. Fax 656-3765
www.sartell.k12.mn.us
Oak Ridge ES 500/PK-4
1111 27th St N 56377 320-258-3693
Randy Husmann, prin. Fax 258-3694
Pine Meadow ES 500/K-4
1029 5th St N 56377 320-253-8303
Greg Johnson, prin. Fax 656-3766
Sartell MS 1,000/5-8
627 3rd Ave N 56377 320-253-2200
Michael Spanier, prin. Fax 253-1403

St. Francis Xavier S 200/PK-6
PO Box 150 56377 320-252-9940
Linda Wilfahrt, prin. Fax 259-7090

Sauk Centre, Stearns, Pop. 3,915
Sauk Centre SD 743 1,100/PK-12
903 State Rd 56378 320-352-2284
Dan Brooks, supt. Fax 352-3404
Sauk Centre ES 400/PK-6
890 State Rd 56378 320-352-6521
Karen Maschler, prin. Fax 352-3404

Holy Family S 200/K-6
231 Sinclair Lewis Ave 56378 320-352-6535
Lynn Peterson, prin. Fax 352-6537

Sauk Rapids, Benton, Pop. 11,523
Sauk Rapids-Rice SD 47 3,600/PK-12
1833 Osauka Rd 56379 320-253-4703
Greg Vandal, supt. Fax 255-1914
www.isd47.org
Mississippi Heights ES 600/PK-5
1003 4th St S 56379 320-252-0122
Jean Clark, prin. Fax 252-0656
Pleasant View ES 500/PK-5
1009 6th Ave N 56379 320-253-0506
Sue Paasch, prin. Fax 253-1444
Sauk Rapids-Rice MS 900/6-8
901 1st St S 56379 320-654-9073
Larry Stracke, prin. Fax 259-8909
Other Schools – See Rice

Petra Lutheran S 50/PK-8
1049 1st Ave N 56379 320-251-0158
Lydia Eberhardt, prin.
Sacred Heart S 200/K-6
PO Box 127 56379 320-251-2854
Erin Hatlestad, prin. Fax 251-0705

Savage, Scott, Pop. 26,581
Burnsville-Eagan-Savage ISD 191
Supt. — See Burnsville
Bishop ES 600/K-6
14400 OConnell Rd 55378 952-707-3900
Rob Nelson, prin. Fax 707-3902
Hidden Valley ES 700/K-6
13875 Glendale Rd 55378 952-707-3800
Jon Bonneville, prin. Fax 707-3802
Savage ES 600/K-6
4819 W 126th St 55378 952-707-3200
Jeremy Willey, prin. Fax 707-3202

Prior Lake - Savage Area SD 719
Supt. — See Prior Lake
Glendale ES 600/K-5
6601 Connelly Pkwy 55378 952-226-0200
Sam Richardson, prin. Fax 226-0249
Redtail Ridge ES 100/K-5
15200 Hampshire Ave 55378 952-226-8003
Barb Yetzer, prin. Fax 226-8049

St. John the Baptist S 800/PK-8
12508 Lynn Ave 55378 952-890-6604
Beth Behnke, prin. Fax 890-9481

Scandia, Washington
Forest Lake SD 831
Supt. — See Forest Lake
Scandia ES 500/K-6
14351 Scandia Trl N 55073 651-982-3300
Julianne Greiman, prin. Fax 982-3349

Sebeka, Wadena, Pop. 680
Sebeka SD 820 500/PK-12
PO Box 249 56477 218-837-5101
Dave Fjeldheim, supt. Fax 837-5967
www.sebeka.com
Sebeka ES 300/PK-6
PO Box 249 56477 218-837-5101
Dave Fjeldheim, prin. Fax 837-5967

Shakopee, Scott, Pop. 31,233
Shakopee SD 720 4,400/K-12
505 Holmes St S 55379 952-496-5000
Jon McBroom, supt. Fax 445-8446
www.shakopee.k12.mn.us
Eagle Creek ES K-5
6855 Woodward Ave 55379 952-496-5922
Elizabeth Bergen, prin. Fax 496-5935
Pearson ES 600/K-5
917 Dakota St S 55379 952-496-5862
Doug Schleif, prin. Fax 496-5862
Red Oak ES 800/K-5
7700 Old Carriage Ct 55379 952-496-5952
Mitch Perrine, prin. Fax 496-5952
Shakopee MS 6-7
1137 Marschall Rd 55379 952-496-5702
Michael Neubeck, prin.
Sun Path ES 400/K-5
2250 17th Ave E 55379 952-496-5892
Patrick Leonard, prin. Fax 496-5852
Sweeney ES 500/K-5
1001 Adams St S 55379 952-496-5952
Dave Orlowsky, prin. Fax 496-5832

Shakopee Area Catholic S 800/PK-8
2700 17th Ave E 55379 952-445-3387
Dr. Scott Breimhorst, prin. Fax 445-7256

Sherburn, Martin, Pop. 1,060
Martin County West SD 2448
Supt. — See Welcome
Sherburn ES 300/K-4
PO Box 100 56171 507-764-4461
Dale Harbitz, prin. Fax 764-3651

Shoreview, Ramsey, Pop. 26,855
Mounds View SD 621 9,700/K-12
350 Highway 96 W 55126 651-621-6000
Dan Hoverman, supt. Fax 621-6046
www.moundsviewschools.org
Island Lake ES 600/K-5
3555 Victoria St N 55126 651-621-7000
Todd Durand, prin. Fax 621-7005
Turtle Lake ES 800/K-5
1141 Lepak Ct 55126 651-621-7700
Craig Sundberg, prin. Fax 621-7705
Other Schools – See Arden Hills, Mounds View, New Brighton, North Oaks

Roseville Area SD 623
Supt. — See Roseville
Williams ES 400/K-6
955 County Road D W 55126 651-482-8624
Stacie Stanley, prin. Fax 482-0801

Oak Hill Montessori S 200/PK-8
4665 Hodgson Rd 55126 651-484-8242
Kathryn Anderson, hdmstr. Fax 484-4130
St. Odilia S 600/K-8
3495 Victoria St N 55126 651-484-3364
Robert Grose, prin. Fax 415-3395

Silver Bay, Lake, Pop. 1,982
Lake Superior SD 381
Supt. — See Two Harbors
Kelley ES 200/PK-6
137 Banks Blvd 55614 218-226-4437
George Starkovich, prin. Fax 226-4860

Silver Lake, McLeod, Pop. 784
Glencoe-Silver Lake SD 2859
Supt. — See Glencoe
Lakeside ES 500/3-6
229 Lake Ave 55381 320-864-2501
Debbie Morris, prin. Fax 327-3122

Holy Family S 100/K-6
PO Box 346 55381 320-327-2356
Cathy Millerbernd, prin. Fax 327-6355

Slayton, Murray, Pop. 1,953
Murray County Central SD 2169 700/PK-12
2420 28th St 56172 507-836-6183
Steve Jones, supt. Fax 836-6375
www.mcc.mntm.org
Murray County Central ES 400/PK-6
2640 Forest Ave 56172 507-836-6450
Sally Berg, prin. Fax 836-6610

Sleepy Eye, Brown, Pop. 3,478
Sleepy Eye SD 84 700/PK-12
400 4th Ave SW 56085 507-794-7903
Arla Dockter, supt. Fax 794-5404
www.sleepyeyeschools.com
Sleepy Eye ES 300/PK-6
400 4th Ave SW 56085 507-794-7905
Adam Kluver, prin. Fax 794-5457

St. John's Lutheran S 100/PK-8
216 3rd Ave SE 56085 507-794-6200
Kurk Kramer, prin. Fax 794-6202
St. Mary S 200/PK-6
104 Saint Marys St NW 56085 507-794-6141
Mary Gangelhoff, prin. Fax 794-4841

South Saint Paul, Dakota, Pop. 19,787
South St. Paul SD 6 3,000/PK-12
104 5th Ave S 55075 651-457-9400
Patty Heminover, supt. Fax 457-9485
www.sspps.org
Kaposia Education Center ES 600/PK-6
1225 1st Ave S 55075 651-451-9260
John Laliberte, prin. Fax 457-9453
Lincoln Center ES 800/PK-6
357 9th Ave N 55075 651-457-9426
Connie Garling, prin. Fax 457-9423

Holy Trinity S 200/PK-8
745 6th Ave S 55075 651-455-8557
Daniel Gleason, prin. Fax 455-7600
St. John Vianney S 100/PK-6
1815 Bromley Ave 55075 651-451-8395
Patrick Gannon, prin. Fax 451-1864

Springfield, Brown, Pop. 2,135
Springfield SD 85 600/PK-12
12 Burns Ave 56087 507-723-4283
Keith Kottke, supt. Fax 723-6407
www.springfield.mntm.org/
Springfield ES 300/PK-6
12 Burns Ave 56087 507-723-4286
Jeff Kuehn, prin. Fax 723-4289

St. Raphael S 100/K-6
20 W Van Dusen St 56087 507-723-4135
John Dezeeuw, prin. Fax 723-5409

Spring Grove, Houston, Pop. 1,281
Spring Grove SD 297 300/K-12
PO Box 626 55974 507-498-3221
James Busta, supt. Fax 498-3470
Spring Grove ES 200/K-6
PO Box 626 55974 507-498-3223
Nancy Gulbranson, prin. Fax 498-3470

Spring Lake Park, Anoka, Pop. 6,699
Spring Lake Park SD 16
Supt. — See Minneapolis
Park Terrace ES 400/K-3
8301 Terrace Rd NE 55432 763-784-8983
Claudia Hagberg, prin. Fax 783-5820

Prince of Peace Lutheran S 100/PK-8
7700 Monroe St NE 55432 763-786-1755
Gail Petroff, prin. Fax 786-2473

Spring Valley, Fillmore, Pop. 2,480
Kingsland SD 2137 700/PK-12
705 N Section Ave 55975 507-346-7276
Darrin Strosahl, supt. Fax 346-7278
www.kingsland.k12.mn.us
Kingsland ES 200/PK-4
705 N Section Ave 55975 507-346-7276
Jim Hecimovich, prin. Fax 346-7278
Other Schools – See Wykoff

Staples, Todd, Pop. 3,121
Staples-Motley ISD 2170 1,400/PK-12
202 Pleasant Ave NE 56479 218-894-2430
Mark Schmitz, supt. Fax 894-1828
www.isd2170.k12.mn.us/
Staples ES 400/PK-5
1025 4th St NE 56479 218-894-2433
Gwynne Gildow, prin. Fax 894-1545
Other Schools – See Motley

Sacred Heart S 100/PK-6
324 4th St NE 56479 218-894-2077
Jim Opelia, prin. Fax 894-2994

Stephen, Marshall, Pop. 672
Stephen-Argyle Central SD 2856 400/PK-12
PO Box 68 56757 218-478-3315
Chris Mills, supt. Fax 478-3537
www.sac.k12.mn.us/
Other Schools – See Argyle

Stewartville, Olmsted, Pop. 5,494
Stewartville SD 534 1,700/PK-12
500 4th St SW 55976 507-533-1438
Dr. David Thompson, supt. Fax 533-4012
ssd.k12.mn.us
Bonner ES 400/K-3
526 5th Ave SE 55976 507-533-1500
David Nystuen, prin. Fax 533-4836
Central IS 300/4-5
301 2nd St SW 55976 507-533-1400
Eldon Anderson, prin. Fax 533-6114
Early Childhood Learning Center PK-PK
101 5th St NE 55976 507-533-1424
Stewartville MS 400/6-8
500 4th St SW 55976 507-533-1666
Joe Jezierski, prin. Fax 533-1021

Stillwater, Washington, Pop. 17,378
Stillwater Area SD 834 8,500/K-12
1875 Greeley St S 55082 651-351-8301
Keith Ryskoski, supt. Fax 351-8380
www.stillwater.k12.mn.us
Lily Lake ES 600/K-6
2003 Willard St W 55082 651-351-6800
Malinda Lansfeldt, prin. Fax 351-6895
Oak Park ES 400/K-6
6355 Osman Ave N 55082 651-351-8600
Dawn Wiegand, prin. Fax 351-8635
Rutherford ES 600/K-6
115 Rutherford Rd 55082 651-351-6400
Stephen Gorde, prin. Fax 351-6495
Stonebridge ES 500/K-6
900 Owens St N 55082 651-351-8700
Heather Nelson, prin. Fax 351-8790
Other Schools – See Bayport, Hugo, Lake Elmo, Lakeland, Marine on Saint Croix

---

St. Croix Catholic S 500/PK-8
621 3rd St S 55082 651-439-5581
Cressy Epperly, prin. Fax 439-8360
St. Croix Montessori 100/PK-6
177 Neal Ave N 55082 651-436-2603
Sheri Rylicki, hdmstr. Fax 436-1170
Salem Lutheran S 200/PK-8
14940 62nd St N 55082 651-439-7831
David Noack, prin. Fax 439-0035

Swanville, Morrison, Pop. 344
Swanville SD 486 400/PK-12
PO Box 98 56382 320-547-2431
Gene Harthan, supt. Fax 547-2576
Swanville ES 200/PK-6
PO Box 98 56382 320-547-2431
Dennis Saurer, prin. Fax 547-2576

Taylors Falls, Chisago, Pop. 1,011
Chisago Lakes SD 2144
Supt. — See Lindstrom
Taylors Falls ES 400/K-5
648 West St 55084 651-213-2100
Joe Thimm, prin. Fax 213-2150

Thief River Falls, Pennington, Pop. 8,377
Thief River Falls SD 564 1,900/PK-12
230 Labree Ave S 56701 218-681-8711
Laine Larson, supt. Fax 681-3252
Challenger ES 800/PK-5
601 County Road 61 56701 218-681-2345
Patrick Marolt, prin. Fax 681-3252
Franklin MS 500/6-8
300 Spruce Ave S 56701 218-681-8813
Bob Wayne, prin. Fax 681-4771

St. Bernards S 100/PK-5
117 Knight Ave N 56701 218-681-1539
Sr. Kathy Kuchar, prin. Fax 681-2261
St. John Lutheran S 50/PK-6
15671 158th St NE 56701 218-681-7753
Ila Anderson, prin. Fax 681-7753

Tower, Saint Louis, Pop. 469
Saint Louis County SD 2142
Supt. — See Virginia
Tower-Soudan S 100/PK-12
PO Box 469 55790 218-753-4040
Fax 753-6461

Tracy, Lyon, Pop. 2,089
Tracy SD 2904 700/PK-12
934 Pine St 56175 507-629-5500
David Marlette, supt. Fax 629-5507
tracy.k12.mn.us
Tracy ES 300/PK-6
700 S 4th St 56175 507-629-5518
Brad Gustafson, prin. Fax 629-5525

St. Mary S 50/K-6
225 6th St 56175 507-629-3270
Juliana Neuman, prin. Fax 629-3518

Trimont, Martin, Pop. 712
Martin County West SD 2448
Supt. — See Welcome
Martin County West JHS 100/7-8
PO Box 408 56176 507-639-2081
Allison Schmidt, prin. Fax 639-2091
Trimont ES 100/K-K, 5-6
PO Box 408 56176 507-639-2071
Allison Schmidt, prin. Fax 639-2091

Truman, Martin, Pop. 1,201
Truman SD 458 400/K-12
PO Box 276 56088 507-776-2111
John Larson, supt. Fax 776-3379
www.truman.k12.mn.us
Truman ES 200/K-6
PO Box 276 56088 507-776-2775
Brian Shanks, prin. Fax 776-3379

St. Paul Lutheran S 100/PK-8
114 E 4th St N 56088 507-776-6541
William Wachholz, prin. Fax 776-3060

Twin Valley, Norman, Pop. 822
Norman County East SD 2215 400/PK-12
PO Box 420 56584 218-584-5151
Dean Krogstad, supt. Fax 584-5170
nce.k12.mn.us/
Other Schools – See Gary

Two Harbors, Lake, Pop. 3,533
Lake Superior SD 381 1,500/PK-12
1640 Highway 2 55616 218-834-8201
Phil Minkkinen, supt. Fax 834-8239
www.isd381.k12.mn.us/
Minnehaha ES 400/PK-5
421 7th St 55616 218-834-8221
Pat Driscoll, prin. Fax 834-8247
Other Schools – See Silver Bay

Tyler, Lincoln, Pop. 1,118
R T R ISD 2902 600/PK-12
PO Box 659 56178 507-247-5913
Bruce Houck, supt. Fax 247-3876
www.rtrschools.org
Other Schools – See Russell, Ruthton

Ulen, Clay, Pop. 561
Ulen-Hitterdal SD 914 300/K-12
PO Box 389 56585 218-596-8853
Allen Zenor, supt. Fax 596-8610
www.ulenhitterdal.k12.mn.us
Ulen-Hitterdal ES 200/K-6
PO Box 389 56585 218-596-8853
Kent Henrickson, prin. Fax 596-8610

Underwood, Otter Tail, Pop. 325
Underwood SD 550 500/PK-12
100 Southern Ave E 56586 218-826-6101
Gary Sletten, supt. Fax 826-6310
www.underwood.k12.mn.us
Underwood ES 300/PK-6
100 Southern Ave E 56586 218-826-6101
John Hamann, prin. Fax 826-6310

Upsala, Morrison, Pop. 413
Upsala SD 487 400/PK-12
PO Box 190 56384 320-573-2174
Earl Mathison, supt. Fax 573-2173
www.upsala.k12.mn.us
Upsala ES 200/PK-6
PO Box 190 56384 320-573-2175
Tim Pahl, prin. Fax 573-2173

Vadnais Heights, Ramsey, Pop. 12,586
White Bear Lake Area SD 624
Supt. — See White Bear Lake
Vadnais Heights ES 500/K-5
3645 Centerville Rd 55127 651-653-2858
Sara Svir, prin. Fax 653-2860

Vermillion, Dakota, Pop. 421

St. John the Baptist S 100/PK-5
111 Main St W 55085 651-437-2644
Sr. Tresa Margret, prin. Fax 437-9006

Verndale, Wadena, Pop. 554
Verndale SD 818 400/PK-12
411 SW Brown St 56481 218-445-5184
James Madsen, supt. Fax 445-5185
www.verndale.k12.mn.us
Verndale ES 200/PK-6
411 SW Brown St 56481 218-445-5184
Paul Brownlow, prin. Fax 445-5185

Victoria, Carver, Pop. 5,702
Eastern Carver County SD 112
Supt. — See Chaska
Victoria ES 500/K-5
9300 Red Fox Dr 55386 952-556-3000
Nancy Wittman, prin. Fax 556-3009

Viking, Marshall, Pop. 92
Marshall County Central SD 441
Supt. — See Newfolden
Viking ES 100/K-3
PO Box 10 56760 218-523-4425
James Hodny, prin. Fax 523-4428

Virginia, Saint Louis, Pop. 8,666
Saint Louis County SD 2142 1,100/PK-12
1701 N 9th Ave 55792 218-749-8130
Charles Rick, supt. Fax 749-8133
www.isd2142.k12.mn.us/
Other Schools – See Babbitt, Cook, Cotton, Iron, Orr, Saginaw, Tower

Virginia SD 706 1,500/PK-12
411 S 5th Ave 55792 218-742-3901
Phillip Johnson, supt. Fax 742-3960
www.virginia.k12.mn.us/
Parkview Learning Center 300/PK-3
411 S 5th Ave 55792 218-742-3802
Michael Krebsbach, prin. Fax 741-8522
Roosevelt ES 300/4-6
411 S 5th Ave 55792 218-742-3943
William Spelts, prin. Fax 741-8522

Marquette S 100/PK-6
311 3rd St S 55792 218-741-6811
Georgia Brown Epp, prin. Fax 741-2158

Wabasha, Wabasha, Pop. 2,553
Wabasha-Kellogg SD 811 600/PK-12
2113 Hiawatha Dr E 55981 651-565-3559
Jim Freihammer, supt. Fax 565-2769
www.wabasha-kellogg.k12.mn.us/
Wabasha-Kellogg ES 300/PK-6
2113 Hiawatha Dr E 55981 651-565-3559
Jon Stern, prin. Fax 565-2769

St. Felix S 100/PK-6
130 3rd St E 55981 651-565-4446
Marsha Stenzel, prin. Fax 565-0244

Wabasso, Redwood, Pop. 656
Wabasso SD 640 400/PK-12
PO Box 69 56293 507-342-5114
Ted Suss, supt. Fax 342-5203
www.wabassoschool.com
Wabasso ES 200/PK-6
PO Box 69 56293 507-342-5114
Ted Suss, prin. Fax 342-5203

St. Anne S 100/K-6
PO Box 239 56293 507-342-5389
Mary Franta, prin. Fax 342-5156

Waconia, Carver, Pop. 8,692
Waconia SD 110 2,700/PK-12
512 Industrial Blvd 55387 952-442-0600
Nancy Rajanen, supt. Fax 442-0609
www.waconia.k12.mn.us
Bayview ES 500/K-4
24 S Walnut St 55387 952-442-0630
Chuck Anderson, prin. Fax 442-0609
Clearwater MS 900/5-8
1650 Community Dr 55387 952-442-0650
Peter Gustafson, prin. Fax 442-0659
Southview ES 500/PK-4
225 W 4th St 55387 952-442-0620
Khuzana DeVaan, prin. Fax 442-0629

St. Joseph S 400/PK-8
41 E 1st St 55387 952-442-4500
Maggie Smith, prin. Fax 442-3719
Trinity Lutheran S 400/PK-8
601 E 2nd St 55387 952-442-4165
Randy Ash, prin. Fax 442-4644

Wadena, Wadena, Pop. 4,107
Wadena-Deer Creek SD 2155 1,100/PK-12
600 Colfax Ave SW 56482 218-632-2155
Virginia Dahlstrom, supt. Fax 632-2199
www.wdc2155.k12.mn.us
Wadena-Deer Creek ES 500/PK-6
600 Colfax Ave SW 56482 218-632-2400
Louis Rutten, prin. Fax 632-2499

St. Ann S 50/PK-6
519 2nd St SE 56482 218-631-2631
Eileen Weber, prin. Fax 632-5612

Waite Park, Stearns, Pop. 6,832
Saint Cloud Area SD 742
Supt. — See Saint Cloud
Discovery ES 600/K-6
700 7th St S 56387 320-251-7770
Joni Olson, prin. Fax 251-1827

St. Joseph S 100/PK-6
108 6th Ave N 56387 320-251-4741
Kathleen Peters Cziok, prin. Fax 230-2161

Waldorf, Waseca, Pop. 238
Janesville-Waldorf-Pemberton SD 2835
Supt. — See Janesville
Janesville-Waldorf-Pemberton IS 100/4-6
PO Box 218 56091 507-239-2176
Mike Francis, prin. Fax 239-2195

Walker, Cass, Pop. 1,170
Walker-Hackensack-Akeley SD 113 700/PK-12
PO Box 4000 56484 218-547-1311
Wallace Schoeb, supt. Fax 547-4298
www.wha.k12.mn.us
Walker-Hackensack-Akeley ES 400/PK-6
PO Box 4000 56484 218-547-4261
Lee Furuseth, prin. Fax 547-4367

Immanuel Lutheran S 50/PK-8
PO Box 307 56484 218-547-4139
Janna Kietzman, prin. Fax 547-4139

Walnut Grove, Redwood, Pop. 561
Westbrook-Walnut Grove SD 2898
Supt. — See Westbrook
Walnut Grove ES 100/PK-4
PO Box 278 56180 507-859-2141
Paul Olson, prin. Fax 859-2329
Westbrook-Walnut Grove MS 200/5-8
PO Box 278 56180 507-859-2141
Paul Olson, prin. Fax 859-2329

Wanamingo, Goodhue, Pop. 1,043
Kenyon-Wanamingo SD 2172 900/PK-12
225 3rd Ave 55983 507-824-2211
Jeff Evert, supt. Fax 824-2212
www.kw.k12.mn.us/
Kenyon-Wanamingo ES 300/PK-4
225 3rd Ave 55983 507-824-2211
Jeff Evert, prin. Fax 824-2212
Other Schools – See Kenyon

Warren, Marshall, Pop. 1,630
Warren-Alvarado-Oslo SD 2176 500/PK-12
224 E Bridge Ave 56762 218-745-5393
Bryan Thygeson, supt. Fax 745-5886
www.wao.k12.mn.us
Warren ES 200/PK-6
224 E Bridge Ave 56762 218-745-4441
Kirk Thorstenson, prin. Fax 745-7659

Warroad, Roseau, Pop. 1,699
Warroad SD 690 1,200/PK-12
510 Cedar Ave NW 56763 218-386-1472
Craig Oftedahl, supt. Fax 386-1909
www.warroad.k12.mn.us
Warroad ES 200/PK-3
510 Cedar Ave NW 56763 218-386-1776
Nick Smieja, prin. Fax 386-1785
Warroad MS 400/4-8
510 Cedar Ave NW 56763 218-386-1877
Brad Nash, prin. Fax 386-2179
Other Schools – See Angle Inlet

Waseca, Waseca, Pop. 9,445
Waseca SD 829 1,800/PK-12
501 Elm Ave E 56093 507-835-2500
John Rokke, supt. Fax 835-1161
www.waseca.k12.mn.us
Hartley ES 300/PK-3
605 7th St NE 56093 507-835-2248
Michelle Krell, prin. Fax 835-3187
Waseca IS 400/4-6
501 Elm Ave E 56093 507-835-3000
Patrick Glynn, prin. Fax 835-1161
Waseca JHS 300/7-8
400 19th Ave NW 56093 507-835-1048
Bill Bunkers, prin. Fax 835-1063

Sacred Heart Childrens House 100/PK-PK
400 2nd Ave NW 56093 507-835-1044
Pauline Holeman, dir. Fax 835-4149
Sacred Heart S 200/K-4
308 Elm Ave W 56093 507-835-2780
LeAnn Dahle, prin. Fax 833-1498

Watertown, Carver, Pop. 3,932
Watertown-Mayer SD 111 1,300/PK-12
1001 Highway 25 Shls NW 55388 952-955-0480
Karsten Anderson, supt. Fax 955-0481
www.wm.k12.mn.us/
Watertown-Mayer ES 400/1-5
500 Paul Ave 55388 952-955-0300
Pat Hittle, dean Fax 955-0301
Watertown-Mayer MS 400/6-8
1001 Highway 25 Shls NW 55388 952-955-0400
Jonathon Anderson, dean Fax 955-0481
Watertown-Mayer PS PK-K
313 Angel Ave NW 55388 952-955-0200
Suzanne Busacker, prin. Fax 955-0201

Christ Community Lutheran S 100/PK-8
512 County Road 10 NW 55388 952-955-1419
Jeff Bohelke, prin. Fax 955-1424

Waterville, LeSueur, Pop. 1,881
Waterville-Elysian-Morristown SD 2143 700/PK-12
500 Paquin St E 56096 507-362-4432
Joel Whitehurst, supt. Fax 362-4561
www.wem.k12.mn.us/
Waterville-Elysian ES 200/PK-4
500 Paquin St E 56096 507-362-4439
Randy Mediger, prin. Fax 362-4762
Other Schools – See Morristown

Waubun, Mahnomen, Pop. 392
Waubun SD 435 600/PK-12
PO Box 98 56589 218-473-6171
Mitch Anderson, supt. Fax 473-6191
www.waubun.k12.mn.us
Waubun ES 100/5-6
PO Box 98 56589 218-473-6174
Helen Kennedy, prin. Fax 983-4200
Other Schools – See Ogema

Waverly, Wright, Pop. 952
Howard Lake-Waverly-Winsted SD 2687
Supt. — See Howard Lake
Humphrey ES 200/PK-4
PO Box 248 55390 763-658-4424
Jennifer Olson, prin. Fax 658-4497

Wayzata, Hennepin, Pop. 3,941
Minnetonka SD 276
Supt. — See Minnetonka
Deephaven ES 500/K-5
4452 Vinehill Rd 55391 952-401-6900
Bryan McGinley, prin. Fax 401-6906

Wayzata SD 284
Supt. — See Minneapolis
Wayzata West MS 700/6-8
149 Barry Ave N 55391 952-745-6400
Susan Sommerfeld, prin. Fax 745-6491

Blake S - Highcroft Campus 300/PK-5
301 Peavey Ln 55391 952-988-3550
Julie Vang, prin. Fax 988-3555
Calvary Memorial Christian S 100/PK-8
2420 Dunwoody Ave 55391 952-471-0023
Glenn Heinsch, prin. Fax 471-8512
Holy Name of Jesus S 300/K-6
155 County Road 24 55391 952-473-3675
Randall Vetsch, prin. Fax 745-3499
Redeemer Lutheran S 200/PK-8
115 Wayzata Blvd W 55391 952-473-5356
William Souza, prin. Fax 473-3295
St. Bartholomew S 200/PK-6
630 Wayzata Blvd E 55391 952-473-6189
Sr. Carol Bongaarts, prin. Fax 473-0980
St. Therese S 300/K-8
18323 Minnetonka Blvd 55391 952-473-4355
Laura Porter-Jones, prin. Fax 261-0630

Webster, Rice

Holy Cross S 200/PK-8
6100 37th St W 55088 952-652-6100
Lisa Reichelt, prin. Fax 652-6102

Welcome, Martin, Pop. 681
Martin County West SD 2448 800/K-12
PO Box 268 56181 507-728-8276
Randy Grupe, supt. Fax 728-8278
www.martin.k12.mn.us
Welcome ES 50/K-K
PO Box 268 56181 507-728-8609
Dale Harbitz, prin. Fax 728-8921
Other Schools – See Sherburn, Trimont

Wells, Faribault, Pop. 2,485
United South Central SD 2134 600/PK-12
250 2nd Ave SW 56097 507-553-3134
Jerry Jensen, supt. Fax 553-5929
www.usc.k12.mn.us
United South Central ES 300/PK-6
250 2nd Ave SW 56097 507-553-5810
Tracy Frank, prin. Fax 553-5929

St. Casimir S 100/K-8
330 2nd Ave SW 56097 507-553-5822
Joanne Tibodeau, prin. Fax 553-5391

Westbrook, Cottonwood, Pop. 762
Westbrook-Walnut Grove SD 2898 600/PK-12
PO Box 129 56183 507-274-5450
Loy Woelber, supt. Fax 274-6113
Westbrook ES 100/PK-4
344 8th St 56183 507-274-5500
William Richards, prin. Fax 274-6113
Other Schools – See Walnut Grove

West Saint Paul, Dakota, Pop. 19,070
West St. Paul-Mendota Hts-Eagan SD 197
Supt. — See Mendota Heights
Garlough ES 300/PK-4
1740 Charlton St 55118 651-403-8100
Susan Powell, prin. Fax 405-2989
Heritage MS 700/5-8
121 Butler Ave W 55118 651-905-4000
Chris Hiti, prin. Fax 905-4001
Moreland ES 400/PK-4
217 Moreland Ave W 55118 651-405-2531
Peter Otterson, prin. Fax 405-2508

Crown of Life Lutheran S 100/K-8
115 Crusader Ave W 55118 651-451-3832
Daniel Plath, prin. Fax 451-7579
St. Joseph S 700/K-8
1138 Seminole Ave 55118 651-457-8550
Jane Nordin, prin. Fax 457-0780
St. Michael S 100/K-8
335 Hurley Ave E 55118 651-457-2510
Maryanna Charley, prin. Fax 457-5049

Wheaton, Traverse, Pop. 1,488
Wheaton Area SD 803 400/PK-12
1700 3rd Ave S 56296 320-563-8283
Daniel Posthumus, supt. Fax 563-4218
www.wheaton.k12.mn.us
Pearson ES 200/PK-5
710 4th Ave N 56296 320-563-8191
Daniel Posthumus, prin. Fax 563-4636

White Bear Township, See White Bear Lake
White Bear Lake Area SD 624
Supt. — See White Bear Lake
Otter Lake ES 600/K-5
1401 County Road H2, White Bear Lake MN 55110
651-653-2831
Max DeRaad, prin. Fax 653-2833

White Bear Lake, Ramsey, Pop. 23,733
White Bear Lake Area SD 624 7,500/PK-12
4855 Bloom Ave 55110 651-407-7500
Dr. Michael Lovett, supt. Fax 407-7566
www.whitebear.k12.mn.us
Birch Lake ES 300/K-5
1616 Birch Lake Ave 55110 651-653-2776
Dan Schmidt, prin. Fax 653-2778
Central MS 1,100/6-8
4857 Bloom Ave 55110 651-653-2888
Noel Schmidt, prin. Fax 653-2885
Lakeaires ES 400/K-5
3963 Van Dyke St 55110 651-653-2809
Cary Krusemark, prin. Fax 653-2811
Lincoln ES 400/K-5
1961 6th St 55110 651-653-2820
Dan Schmidt, prin. Fax 653-2822
Normandy Park Education Center 100/PK-PK
2482 County Road F E 55110 651-653-3100
Margie McMahon, admin. Fax 653-3155
Parkview ES 500/K-5
2530 Spruce Pl 55110 651-653-2847
Barbara Kearn, prin. Fax 653-2849
Sunrise Park MS 50/6-8
2399 Cedar Ave 55110 651-653-2700
David Law, prin. Fax 653-2716
Willow Lane ES 400/K-5
3375 Willow Ave 55110 651-773-6170
Barbara Kearn, prin. Fax 773-6176
Other Schools – See Hugo, Vadnais Heights, White Bear Township

---

Magnuson Christian S 100/K-4
4000 Linden St 55110 651-429-5349
Louann Lindbeck, dir. Fax 429-3942
St. Mary of the Lake S 400/PK-8
4690 Bald Eagle Ave 55110 651-429-7771
Mary Fritz, prin. Fax 429-9539
St. Pius X-Holy Family S 300/PK-8
3878 Highland Ave 55110 651-429-5338
Kathleen Groettum, prin. Fax 429-9359
White Bear Montessori S 100/PK-6
1201 County Road E E 55110 651-429-3710
Heather Petersen, hdmstr. Fax 429-2927

Willmar, Kandiyohi, Pop. 18,183
Willmar SD 347 3,000/K-12
611 5th St SW 56201 320-231-8500
Jerry Kjergaard, supt. Fax 231-1061
www.willmar.k12.mn.us
Kennedy ES 600/K-5
824 7th St NW 56201 320-214-6688
Scott Hisken, prin. Fax 235-9536
Roosevelt ES 400/K-5
1800 19th Ave SW 56201 320-231-8470
Patricia Dols, prin. Fax 231-1170
Willmar MS 600/6-8
201 Willmar Ave SE 56201 320-214-6000
Mark Miley, prin. Fax 235-1254

Community Christian S 300/PK-10
1300 19th Ave SW 56201 320-235-0592
Del Brouwer, admin. Fax 235-0620

Willow River, Pine, Pop. 379
Willow River SD 577 400/PK-12
PO Box 66 55795 218-372-3131
Lynette Maas, supt. Fax 372-3132
www.willowriver.k12.mn.us
Willow River ES 200/PK-6
PO Box 66 55795 218-372-3131
Scott Anderson, prin. Fax 372-3132

Windom, Cottonwood, Pop. 4,416
Windom SD 177 1,000/K-12
PO Box C177 56101 507-831-6901
Wayne Wormstadd, supt. Fax 831-6919
www.windom.k12.mn.us
Windom MS 300/5-8
PO Box C177 56101 507-831-6910
Tom Farrell, prin. Fax 831-6909
Winfair ES 300/K-4
PO Box C177 56101 507-831-6925
Tom Farrell, prin. Fax 831-6932

Winnebago, Faribault, Pop. 1,419
Blue Earth Area ISD 2860
Supt. — See Blue Earth
Winnebago ES 100/K-5
132 1st Ave SE 56098 507-893-3176
Kevin Grant, prin. Fax 893-4592

Winona, Winona, Pop. 26,587
Winona Area SD 861 3,700/PK-12
903 Gilmore Ave 55987 507-494-0861
Paul Durand, supt. Fax 494-0863
www.winona.k12.mn.us
Central ES 100/K-4
317 Market St 55987 507-494-2251
Jack Kaehler, prin. Fax 494-2250
Goodview ES 200/PK-4
5100 W 9th St 55987 507-494-2400
Marianne Texley, prin. Fax 494-2401
Jefferson ES 300/K-4
1268 W 5th St 55987 507-494-2000
Sonia Hanson, prin. Fax 494-2010
Madison ES 200/K-4
515 W Wabasha St 55987 507-494-2200
Judy Davis, prin. Fax 494-2201
Washington-Kosciusko ES 300/K-4
365 Mankato Ave 55987 507-494-2100
Jack Kaehler, prin. Fax 494-2101
Winona MS 1,100/5-8
1570 Homer Rd 55987 507-494-1000
Sharon Suchla, prin. Fax 494-1002
Other Schools – See Rollingstone

Cathedral S 100/1-3
352 Center St 55987 507-452-4936
Scott Walker, prin. Fax 454-1473
Cotter JHS 100/7-8
1115 W Broadway St 55987 507-453-5366
Dave Forney, prin. Fax 453-5806
St. Martins Lutheran S 100/PK-8
253 Liberty St 55987 507-452-6928
Fax 452-8992
St. Marys S 100/PK-K
1315 W Broadway St 55987 507-452-2890
Scott Walker, prin. Fax 452-2898
St. Matthew Lutheran S 100/PK-8
756 W Wabasha St 55987 507-454-3083
Philip Moll, prin. Fax 452-1676
St. Stanislaus MS 200/4-6
602 E 5th St 55987 507-452-3766
Scott Walker, prin. Fax 452-5497

Winsted, McLeod, Pop. 2,367
Howard Lake-Waverly-Winsted SD 2687
Supt. — See Howard Lake
Winsted ES 200/PK-4
PO Box 160 55395 320-485-2190
Jennifer Olson, prin. Fax 485-4183

Holy Trinity S 300/PK-12
PO Box 38 55395 320-485-2182
Bill Tschida, prin. Fax 485-4283

Woodbury, Washington, Pop. 52,479
South Washington County SD 833
Supt. — See Cottage Grove
Bailey ES 600/K-5
4125 Woodlane Dr 55129 651-768-4800
Molly Roeske, prin. Fax 768-4849
Lake MS 800/6-8
3133 Pioneer Dr 55125 651-768-6400
Todd Hochman, prin. Fax 768-6428
Liberty Ridge ES 700/K-5
11395 Eagle View Blvd 55129 651-768-5900
Mike Moore, prin. Fax 768-5905
Middleton ES 600/K-5
9105 Lake Rd 55125 651-768-4900
Julie Nielsen, prin. Fax 768-4950
Red Rock ES 700/K-5
3311 Commonwealth Ave 55125 651-768-5600
Andy Caflisch, prin. Fax 768-5672
Royal Oaks ES 500/K-5
7335 Steepleview Rd 55125 651-768-4700
Theresa Blume, prin. Fax 768-4777
Valley Crossing Community S K-6
9900 Park Xing 55125 651-702-5700
Mary Anderson, prin. Fax 702-5770
Woodbury ES 500/K-5
1251 School Dr 55125 651-768-4600
Kristine Schaefer, prin. Fax 768-4646
Woodbury MS 600/6-8
1425 School Dr 55125 651-768-4500
Kari Lopez, prin. Fax 768-4567

New Life Academy 700/PK-12
6758 Bailey Rd 55129 651-459-4121
Terry Campbell, admin. Fax 459-6194
St. Ambrose S 600/K-8
4125 Woodbury Dr 55129 651-768-3000
Matt Metz, prin. Fax 768-3080
Woodbury K 200/PK-K
7380 Afton Rd 55125 651-739-5146
Dorothy Blaisdell, prin. Fax 739-3536

Worthington, Nobles, Pop. 11,092
Worthington SD 518 1,900/PK-12
1117 Marine Ave 56187 507-372-2172
John Landgaard, supt. Fax 372-2174
www.isd518.net
Prairie ES 800/PK-5
1700 1st Ave SW 56187 507-727-1250
Paul Besel, prin. Fax 727-1255
Worthington MS 500/6-8
1401 Crailsheim Dr 56187 507-376-4174
Dr. Clete Lipetzky, prin. Fax 372-1424

St. Marys S 100/K-6
1206 8th Ave 56187 507-376-5236
Barbara Daly, prin. Fax 376-6159
Worthington Christian S 100/PK-8
1770 Eleanor St 56187 507-376-4861
Cindy Vogel, prin. Fax 376-4185

Wrenshall, Carlton, Pop. 349
Wrenshall SD 100 400/PK-12
PO Box 68 55797 218-384-4274
Rick Herman, supt. Fax 384-4293
www.wrenshall.k12.mn.us/
Wrenshall ES 200/PK-6
PO Box 68 55797 218-384-4274
Sue Frank, prin. Fax 384-4293

Wykoff, Fillmore, Pop. 448
Kingsland SD 2137
Supt. — See Spring Valley
Kingsland MS 200/5-8
PO Box 96 55990 507-352-2731
Jim Hecimovich, prin. Fax 352-6071

St. John Lutheran S 50/PK-8
PO Box 189 55990 507-352-4671
Karl Peterman, prin. Fax 352-7671

Wyoming, Chisago, Pop. 3,820
Forest Lake SD 831
Supt. — See Forest Lake
Linwood ES 500/K-6
21900 Typo Creek Dr NE 55092 651-982-1900
Roche Martin, prin. Fax 982-1955
Wyoming ES 600/K-6
25701 Forest Blvd Ste N 55092 651-982-8000
Michael Conway, prin. Fax 982-8067

Young America, Carver, Pop. 1,659

St. John Lutheran S 200/PK-8
27 1st St NW 55397 952-467-3461
Erlen Schroeder, prin. Fax 467-2937

Zimmerman, Sherburne, Pop. 4,724
Elk River Area SD 728
Supt. — See Elk River
Westwood ES 600/3-5
13651 4th Ave S 55398 763-274-3180
Gary Bachmann, prin. Fax 274-3181
Zimmerman ES 400/K-6
25959 4th St W 55398 763-241-3475
Susan Johnston, prin. Fax 241-3476

Zumbrota, Goodhue, Pop. 2,966
Zumbrota-Mazeppa SD 2805
Supt. — See Mazeppa
Zumbrota-Mazeppa ES 400/PK-4
799 Mill St 55992 507-732-7848
Erick Enger, prin. Fax 732-4522

Christ Lutheran S 50/K-8
223 E 5th St 55992 507-732-5367
Karl Mantzke, prin. Fax 732-7641

MISSISSIPPI

MISSISSIPPI DEPARTMENT OF EDUCATION
PO Box 771, Jackson 39205-0771
Telephone 601-359-3513
Fax 601-359-3242
Website http://www.mde.k12.ms.us

Superintendent of Education John Jordan

MISSISSIPPI BOARD OF EDUCATION
PO Box 771, Jackson 39205-0771

Chairperson William Jones

PUBLIC, PRIVATE AND CATHOLIC ELEMENTARY SCHOOLS

Aberdeen, Monroe, Pop. 6,227
Aberdeen SD 1,500/PK-12
PO Box 607 39730 662-369-4682
Chester Leigh, supt. Fax 369-0987
www.aberdeen.k12.ms.us
Aberdeen ES 200/PK-1
PO Box 607 39730 662-369-4782
Angelia Bluitt, prin. Fax 369-0980
Aberdeen MS 200/4-5
PO Box 607 39730 662-369-4715
Bobby Eiland, prin. Fax 369-3201
Belle ES 200/2-3
PO Box 607 39730 662-369-2649
Terry Cox, prin. Fax 369-4986
Shivers JHS 300/7-8
PO Box 607 39730 662-369-6241
Teresa Price, prin. Fax 369-3207
Other Schools – See Prairie

Ackerman, Choctaw, Pop. 1,631
Choctaw County SD 1,700/PK-12
PO Box 398 39735 662-285-4022
Donna Shea, supt. Fax 285-4049
www.choctaw.k12.ms.us/
Ackerman ES 600/PK-6
8475 MS Highway 15 39735 662-285-4052
Glen Blaine, prin. Fax 285-4099
Other Schools – See French Camp, Weir

Amory, Monroe, Pop. 7,415
Amory SD 1,700/K-12
PO Box 330 38821 662-256-5991
Dr. Gearl Loden, supt. Fax 256-6302
www.amoryschools.com/
Amory MS 500/6-8
700 2nd Ave N 38821 662-256-5658
Cheryl Moore, prin. Fax 256-6304
East Amory ES 400/3-5
1530 Concord Ave 38821 662-256-7191
Brian Jones, prin. Fax 256-1647
West Amory ES 300/K-2
704 111th St 38821 662-256-2601
Leigh Todd, prin. Fax 256-1643

Monroe County SD 2,400/K-12
PO Box 209 38821 662-257-2176
Scott Cantrell, supt. Fax 257-2181
www.mcsd.us/
Hatley S 1,000/K-12
60286 Hatley Rd 38821 662-256-4563
Van Pearson, prin. Fax 256-5626
Other Schools – See Hamilton, Smithville

Anguilla, Sharkey, Pop. 813
South Delta SD
Supt. — See Rolling Fork
South Delta MS 300/6-8
PO Box 487 38721 662-873-6535
James Tankson, prin. Fax 873-6073

Arcola, Washington, Pop. 525
Hollandale SD
Supt. — See Hollandale
Chambers MS 100/7-8
PO Box 396 38722 662-827-2438
Fax 827-7168

Deer Creek S 200/K-12
PO Box 376 38722 662-827-5165
F. E. Allegrezza, admin. Fax 827-5128

Ashland, Benton, Pop. 564
Benton County SD 1,200/K-12
PO Box 247 38603 662-224-6252
Patrick Washington, supt. Fax 224-3607
www.benton.k12.ms.us
Ashland ES 300/K-5
768 Lamar Rd 38603 662-224-6622
Margie Childers, prin. Fax 224-3613
Ashland JHS 6-8
PO Box 368 38603 662-224-6485
John Bostick, prin. Fax 224-3609
Other Schools – See Hickory Flat

Avon, Washington
Western Line SD 1,800/K-12
PO Box 50 38723 662-335-7186
Larry Green, supt. Fax 378-2285
www.westernline.org
Riverside ES 500/K-6
PO Box 130 38723 662-335-4528
Becky Avis, prin. Fax 332-5921
Riverside K K-K
PO Box 50 38723 662-332-7675
Cathy Magee, prin. Fax 332-7694
Other Schools – See Greenville

Baldwyn, Lee, Pop. 3,352
Baldwyn SD 900/K-12
107 W Main St 38824 662-365-1000
Harvey Brooks, supt. Fax 365-1003
baldwyn.ms.schoolwebpages.com/
Baldwyn ES 400/K-4
515 Bender Cir 38824 662-365-1010
Joe Blassingame, prin. Fax 365-1034
Baldwyn MS 300/5-8
452 N Fourth St 38824 662-365-1015
Ronnie Hill, prin. Fax 365-1029

Bassfield, Jefferson Davis, Pop. 287
Jefferson Davis County SD
Supt. — See Prentiss
Carver ES 500/K-6
PO Box 460 39421 601-943-5251
Cathy Anderson, prin. Fax 943-5151

Batesville, Panola, Pop. 7,708
South Panola SD 4,200/PK-12
209 Boothe St 38606 662-563-9361
Dr. Keith Shaffer, supt. Fax 563-6077
www.southpanola.k12.ms.us
Batesville ES 300/PK-1
110 College St 38606 662-563-4596
LaSherry Irby, prin. Fax 563-0028
Batesville IS 600/2-3
200 College St 38606 662-563-7834
Elizabeth Ferguson, prin. Fax 563-3462
Batesville JHS 900/6-8
507 Tiger Dr 38606 662-563-4503
Leslie Busby, prin. Fax 563-6038
Batesville MS 600/4-5
509 Tiger Dr 38606 662-563-1924
Willie Chapman, prin. Fax 563-3808
Other Schools – See Pope

North Delta S 400/PK-12
330 Green Wave Ln 38606 662-563-4536
John Howell, hdmstr. Fax 563-5690

Bay Saint Louis, Hancock, Pop. 9,433
Bay St. Louis-Waveland SD 1,400/K-12
201 Carroll Ave 39520 228-467-6621
Kim Stasny, supt. Fax 466-4895
www.bwsd.org/
Bay-Waveland MS 400/5-8
600 Pine St 39520 228-463-0315
Cherie Labat, prin. Fax 467-5872
North Bay ES 200/K-2
740 Dunbar Ave 39520 228-467-4757
Frances Weiler, prin. Fax 466-0286
Second Street ES 100/3-4
400 N 2nd St 39520 228-467-4052
Myron Labat, prin. Fax 467-5872
Other Schools – See Waveland

Hancock County SD
Supt. — See Kiln
South Hancock ES 500/K-5
6590 Lakeshore Rd 39520 228-467-4655
Jan White, prin. Fax 467-0618

Holy Trinity S 400/PK-6
301 S Second St 39520 228-467-5158
Janet Buras, prin. Fax 467-9742

Bay Springs, Jasper, Pop. 2,194
West Jasper Consolidated SD 1,700/K-12
PO Box 610 39422 601-764-2280
Kaye Patrick, supt. Fax 764-4490
www.westjasper.k12.ms.us/
Bay Springs ES 400/K-4
PO Box 927 39422 601-764-2016
Ola Jones, prin. Fax 764-6757
Bay Springs MS 300/5-8
PO Box 587 39422 601-764-3378
George Duke, prin. Fax 764-2329
Other Schools – See Stringer

Sylva-Bay Academy 300/K-12
PO Box J 39422 601-764-2157
Dr. Lavahn Moss, hdmstr. Fax 764-6755

Beaumont, Perry, Pop. 976
Perry County SD
Supt. — See New Augusta
Beaumont S 300/K-8
1300 Beaumont Brooklyn Rd 39423 601-784-3393
Rebecca Bull, prin. Fax 784-9374

Belden, Lee

Tupelo Christian Preparatory S 500/PK-12
5440 Endville Rd 38826 662-844-8604
David Culpepper, hdmstr. Fax 844-8620

Belmont, Tishomingo, Pop. 1,965
Tishomingo County Special Municipal SD
Supt. — See Iuka
Belmont S 1,000/K-12
PO Box 250 38827 662-454-7924
Mark Hood, prin. Fax 454-7611

Belzoni, Humphreys, Pop. 2,541
Humphreys County SD 1,600/K-12
PO Box 678 39038 662-247-6000
Bonnie Horton, supt. Fax 247-6004
Greene ES 400/K-3
401 Fourth St 39038 662-247-6080
Mary Ann Washington, prin. Fax 247-6084
Humphreys JHS 300/7-8
700 Cohn St 39038 662-247-6050
Elliot Wheeler, prin. Fax 247-6054
McNair Upper ES 400/4-6
910 Church St 39038 662-247-6060
Ora Smith, prin. Fax 247-6064

Humphreys Academy 200/K-12
PO Box 179 39038 662-247-1572
Hal Bridges, admin. Fax 247-2776

Benoit, Bolivar, Pop. 584
Benoit SD 300/PK-12
PO Box 189 38725 662-742-3287
Dr. Beverly Culley, supt. Fax 742-3149
Brooks S 300/PK-12
PO Box 8 38725 662-742-3257
Brenda Hopson, prin. Fax 742-3498

Benton, Yazoo

Benton Academy 200/K-12
PO Box 308 39039 662-673-9722
Cindy Shipp, prin. Fax 673-9090

Bentonia, Yazoo, Pop. 501
Yazoo County SD
Supt. — See Yazoo City
Bentonia/Gibbs ES 600/K-6
PO Box 247 39040 662-755-2270
Dana Guthrie, prin. Fax 755-9966

Biloxi, Harrison, Pop. 50,209
Biloxi Public SD 3,700/K-12
PO Box 168 39533 228-374-1810
Paul Tisdale, supt. Fax 436-5171
www.biloxischools.net
Beauvoir ES 300/K-5
2003 Lawrence St 39531 228-436-5131
Melanie Nelson, prin. Fax 388-4350

Biloxi JHS 400/7-8
1424 Father Ryan Ave 39530 228-435-1421
Carl Fantroy, prin. Fax 435-1426
Davis ES 300/K-5
340 Saint Mary Blvd 39531 228-436-5110
Aline Balius, prin. Fax 374-6837
Gorenflo ES 100/K-5
771 Elder St 39530 228-436-5145
Tina Thompson, prin. Fax 374-6224
Michel 6th Grade S 400/6-6
1440 Father Ryan Ave 39530 228-435-4540
Vera Robertson, prin. Fax 374-5119
Nichols ES 100/K-5
590 Division St 39530 228-436-4648
Melissa Nance, prin. Fax 374-5819
North Bay ES 700/K-5
1825 Popps Ferry Rd 39532 228-435-6166
Laurie Pitre, prin. Fax 436-5185
Popps Ferry ES 500/K-5
364 Nelson Rd 39531 228-436-5135
Patti Hughes, prin. Fax 388-2313

Harrison County SD
Supt. — See Gulfport
North Woolmarket S 800/K-8
16237 Old Woolmarket Rd 39532 228-396-3674
Christy Buchanan, prin. Fax 396-3444
Woolmarket ES 400/K-6
12513 John Lee Rd 39532 228-392-5640
Vicki Williams, prin. Fax 392-9868

Jackson County SD
Supt. — See Vancleave
St. Martin ES North 300/K-3
16308 Lemoyne Blvd 39532 228-392-1387
Christopher Williams, prin. Fax 392-6805

Cedar Lake Christian Academy 300/PK-8
11555 Cedar Lake Rd 39532 228-392-9389
Billy Wise, prin. Fax 396-2006
Gulf Coast SDA S 50/K-8
13301 Highway 67 39532 228-392-5727
Nativity BVM S 200/PK-6
1046 Beach Blvd 39530 228-432-2269
Sr. Mary Jo Mike, prin. Fax 432-9421
Our Lady of Fatima S 300/PK-6
320 Jim Money Rd 39531 228-388-3602
Susan Bass, prin. Fax 385-1140

Blue Mountain, Tippah, Pop. 713
South Tippah SD
Supt. — See Ripley
Blue Mountain S 300/K-12
408 W Mill St 38610 662-685-4706
Eddie Conner, prin. Fax 685-4706

Blue Springs, Union, Pop. 153
Union County SD
Supt. — See New Albany
East Union S 800/K-12
1548 Highway 9 S 38828 662-534-6920
Tim Carter, prin. Fax 534-6542

Bogue Chitto, Lincoln, Pop. 689
Lincoln County SD
Supt. — See Brookhaven
Bogue Chitto S 600/K-12
385 Monticello St 39629 601-734-2723
Bill McGehee, prin. Fax 734-6020

Bolton, Hinds, Pop. 611
Hinds County SD
Supt. — See Raymond
Bolton/Edwards S 600/K-8
9700 I 20 39041 601-866-2522
Marnetta McIntyre, prin. Fax 866-2524

Booneville, Prentiss, Pop. 8,585
Booneville SD 1,300/K-12
PO Box 358 38829 662-728-2171
Rickey Neaves, supt. Fax 728-4940
www.booneville.k12.ms.us
Anderson ES 400/K-4
111 Anderson St 38829 662-728-5465
Beverly Hill, prin. Fax 728-2959
Booneville MS 400/5-8
300A W George E Allen Dr 38829 662-728-5843
Terry King, prin. Fax 728-2427

Prentiss County SD 2,200/K-12
PO Box 179 38829 662-728-4911
Matt Smith, supt. Fax 728-2000
www2.mde.k12.ms.us/5900/
Hills Chapel S 500/K-8
8 County Road 2371 38829 662-728-5181
Annette Bishop, prin. Fax 728-1773
Jumpertown S 300/K-12
717 Highway 4 W 38829 662-728-6378
Anthony Michael, prin. Fax 728-9420
Thrasher S 400/K-12
167 County Road 1040 38829 662-728-5233
Rivers Stroup, prin. Fax 728-8107
Other Schools – See Marietta, Wheeler

Boyle, Bolivar, Pop. 677
Cleveland SD
Supt. — See Cleveland
Bell ES 300/PK-6
PO Box 368 38730 662-843-4572
Jessica Tyson, prin. Fax 843-1719

Brandon, Rankin, Pop. 19,390
Rankin County SD 15,700/K-12
PO Box 1359 39043 601-825-5590
Dr. Lynn Weathersby, supt. Fax 825-2618
www.rcsd.ms
Brandon ES 1,100/3-5
125 Overby St 39042 601-825-4706
Sue Townsend, prin. Fax 824-9574

Brandon MS 1,100/6-8
408 S College St 39042 601-825-5998
Charles Frazier, prin. Fax 825-8402
Highland Bluff ES K-5
5970 Highway 25 39047 601-825-5590
Dr. Barbara McCool, prin.
Northshore ES 600/K-5
110 N Shore Pkwy 39047 601-992-5279
Rita Arender, prin. Fax 992-5359
Oakdale ES 600/K-5
171 Oakdale Rd 39047 601-992-5442
Janet Smith, prin. Fax 992-5429
Pisgah ES 500/K-6
125 Pisgah High Rd 39047 601-829-2937
Bobby Taylor, prin. Fax 829-1099
Rouse ES 800/K-2
151 Boyce Thompson Dr 39042 601-825-5437
Kelli Adcock, prin. Fax 824-1081
Other Schools – See Florence, Flowood, Pelahatchie, Puckett, Richland

---

Good Shepherd Lutheran S 50/PK-4
PO Box 5013 39047 601-992-4752
Carolyn Sawyer, dir.
Pinelake Christian S 300/K-6
6073 Highway 25 39047 601-829-4599
Terry Thompson, dir. Fax 829-3136

Brookhaven, Lincoln, Pop. 9,907
Brookhaven SD 2,700/PK-12
PO Box 540 39602 601-833-6661
Lea Barrett Ed.D., supt. Fax 833-4154
www.brookhaven.k12.ms.us
Alexander JHS 500/7-8
713 Beauregard St 39601 601-833-7549
Rod Henderson, prin. Fax 835-5467
Brookhaven ES 400/3-4
300 S Church St 39601 601-833-3139
Delores Gearing, prin. Fax 833-8170
Lipsey MS 400/5-6
412 Drury Ln 39601 601-833-6148
Rob McCreary, prin. Fax 835-3968
Martin ES 500/PK-2
420 Vivian Merritt St 39601 601-833-7359
Danita Hobbs, prin. Fax 835-3964

Lincoln County SD 3,000/K-12
PO Box 826 39602 601-835-0011
Terry Brister, supt. Fax 833-3030
lcsd.k12.ms.us/
Enterprise S 800/K-12
1601 Highway 583 SE 39601 601-833-7284
Shannon Eubanks, prin. Fax 835-1261
Star S 900/K-12
1880 Highway 550 NW 39601 601-833-3473
Robin Case, prin. Fax 833-1254
West Lincoln S 700/K-12
948 Jackson Liberty Dr SW 39601 601-833-4600
Jason Case, prin. Fax 833-9909
Other Schools – See Bogue Chitto

Brookhaven Academy 400/K-12
PO Box 3339 39603 601-833-4041
Dr. Miller Hammill, hdmstr. Fax 833-1846

Brooklyn, Forrest
Forrest County SD
Supt. — See Hattiesburg
South Forrest S 700/K-8
8 Burborne St 39425 601-545-7714
Charles Lewis, prin. Fax 544-3002

Brooksville, Noxubee, Pop. 1,151
Noxubee County SD
Supt. — See Macon
Wilson ES 300/K-6
PO Box E 39739 662-738-5557
DJ Ward, prin. Fax 738-5286

Bruce, Calhoun, Pop. 2,032
Calhoun County SD
Supt. — See Pittsboro
Bruce Lower ES 400/PK-3
PO Box 579 38915 662-983-3373
Angie Weldon, prin. Fax 983-3375
Bruce Upper ES 200/4-6
PO Box 1159 38915 662-983-3366
Linda White, prin. Fax 983-3376

Buckatunna, Wayne
Wayne County SD
Supt. — See Waynesboro
Buckatunna S 500/K-8
PO Box 60 39322 601-648-2501
Ronnie Crane, prin. Fax 648-2519

Burnsville, Tishomingo, Pop. 1,040
Tishomingo County Special Municipal SD
Supt. — See Iuka
Burnsville S 500/K-8
23 Washington St 38833 662-427-9226
Roger Moore, prin. Fax 427-9521

Byhalia, Marshall, Pop. 716
Marshall County SD
Supt. — See Holly Springs
Byhalia ES 500/K-5
172 Highway 309 N 38611 662-838-6980
Sonya Cross, prin. Fax 838-3941
Byhalia MS 400/6-8
172 Highway 309 N 38611 662-838-2591
Kerry Reid, prin. Fax 838-5141

Caledonia, Lowndes, Pop. 974
Lowndes County SD
Supt. — See Columbus
Caledonia ES 700/K-5
99 Confederate Dr 39740 662-356-2050
Roger Hill, prin. Fax 356-2065

Caledonia MS 500/6-8
105 Confederate Dr 39740 662-356-2042
Karen Pittman, prin. Fax 356-2045

Calhoun City, Calhoun, Pop. 1,815
Calhoun County SD
Supt. — See Pittsboro
Calhoun City ES 500/PK-5
PO Box H 38916 662-628-5111
Lisa Langford, prin. Fax 628-6270

Calhoun Academy 200/PK-12
PO Box C 38916 662-412-2087
Cameron Wright, hdmstr. Fax 412-2081

Camden, Madison
Madison County SD
Supt. — See Flora
Camden ES 200/K-5
PO Box 130 39045 662-468-2833
Susan Adam, prin. Fax 468-3695

Canton, Madison, Pop. 12,507
Canton SD 3,000/K-12
403 Lincoln St 39046 601-859-4110
Dwight Luckett, supt. Fax 859-4023
www.cantonschools.net/
Canton ES 500/3-5
740 E Academy St 39046 601-859-2400
Dorothy Smith, prin. Fax 859-6955
Canton S of Arts & Sciences 500/K-5
357 Old Yazoo City Rd 39046 601-855-7819
LaShunda Catchings, prin. Fax 855-7823
McNeal ES 400/K-2
364 Martin Luther King Dr 39046 601-859-3654
Michael Ellis, prin. Fax 859-6956
Nichols MS 800/6-8
529 Mace St 39046 601-859-3741
Henry Dorsey, prin. Fax 859-6561

Madison County SD
Supt. — See Flora
Branson ES 300/K-5
3903 Highway 16 E 39046 601-859-2743
Marilyn Naron, prin. Fax 859-0173
Madison Crossing ES 500/K-5
300 Yandell Rd 39046 601-898-7710
Dr. Martha D'Amico, prin. Fax 898-7709
Madison Crossing MS 200/6-8
300 Yandell Rd 39046 601-898-7702
Brad Peets, prin. Fax 898-7709
Northeast Madison MS 300/6-8
820 Sulphur Springs Rd 39046 601-855-2406
Dr. Earnest Ward, prin. Fax 859-7615

Canton Academy 300/K-12
PO Box 116 39046 601-859-5231
Curt McCain, prin. Fax 859-5232
Holy Child Jesus S 100/PK-6
315 Garrett St 39046 601-859-4168
Felicia Jackson-Stewart, prin. Fax 859-4140

Carriere, Pearl River
Pearl River County SD 2,900/K-12
7441 Highway 11 39426 601-798-7744
Dennis Penton, supt. Fax 798-3527
www.prc.k12.ms.us/
Pearl River Central Lower ES 500/K-2
116 Alphabet Ave 39426 601-799-4519
Dr. Sharon Guepet, prin. Fax 799-0356
Pearl River Central MS 800/6-8
7391 Highway 11 39426 601-798-5654
Nileve Quave, prin. Fax 798-2822
Pearl River Central Upper ES 700/3-5
1592 Henleyfield McNeill Rd 39426 601-798-2864
Missy Holston, prin. Fax 799-0356

Carrollton, Carroll, Pop. 397
Carroll County SD 1,000/K-12
PO Box 256 38917 662-237-9276
Billy Joe Ferguson, supt. Fax 237-9703
www.ccs-ms.org/
Other Schools – See North Carrollton, Vaiden

Carroll Academy 400/K-12
PO Box 226 38917 662-237-6858
Carl Blaylock, hdmstr. Fax 237-9231

Carthage, Leake, Pop. 4,771
Leake County SD 3,100/K-12
PO Box 478 39051 601-267-4579
Monte Ladner, supt. Fax 267-5283
www.leakesd.k12.ms.us
Carthage ES 700/K-5
603 Highway 16 W 39051 601-267-9148
Elizabeth Jenkins, prin. Fax 267-5904
Carthage JHS 400/6-8
801 Martin Luther King Dr 39051 601-267-8909
Haywood Hannah, prin. Fax 267-5902
Edinburg S 500/K-12
673 Mars Hill Rd 39051 601-267-7137
Billy Wilbanks, prin. Fax 267-3007
Thomastown S 400/K-12
7100 Highway 429 39051 601-267-7896
Calvin Melton, prin. Fax 298-1295
Other Schools – See Walnut Grove

St. Ann Learning Center PK-PK
207 Red Dog Rd 39051 601-267-7191
Fax 267-8972

Cedarbluff, Clay
Clay County SD
Supt. — See West Point
West Clay County ES 200/K-6
9414 Joe Stevens Rd 39741 662-494-2350
Sandra Murray, prin. Fax 494-4824

Centreville, Wilkinson, Pop. 1,591
Wilkinson County SD
Supt. — See Woodville
Finch ES 300/PK-5
PO Box 130 39631 601-645-5081
Willie McCray, prin. Fax 645-6358
Winans MS 400/6-8
PO Box 610 39631 601-645-0008
Fax 645-0170

Centreville Academy 300/K-12
PO Box 70 39631 601-645-5912
Lea Hurst, prin. Fax 645-5940

Charleston, Tallahatchie, Pop. 2,054
East Tallahatchie Consolidated SD 1,400/K-12
411 E Chestnut St 38921 662-647-5524
William Tribble, supt. Fax 647-3720
www.etsd.k12.ms.us
Charleston ES 300/K-3
412 E Chestnut St 38921 662-647-2679
Fax 647-2381
Charleston MS 600/4-8
411 E Chestnut St 38921 662-647-5486
Fax 647-2396

Strider Academy 200/K-12
3698 MS Highway 32 Central 38921 662-647-5833
Joe Bradshaw, hdmstr. Fax 647-5702

Clara, Wayne
Wayne County SD
Supt. — See Waynesboro
Clara S 500/K-8
PO Box 90 39324 601-735-2065
Donna Hopkins, prin. Fax 735-3633

Clarksdale, Coahoma, Pop. 19,297
Clarksdale Municipal SD 3,500/K-12
PO Box 1088 38614 662-627-8500
Dennis Dupree, supt. Fax 627-8542
www.cmsd.k12.ms.us/
Hall IV ES 300/K-5
PO Box 1088 38614 662-627-8590
Toya Harrell-Matthews, prin. Fax 627-8542
Heidelberg ES 300/K-5
PO Box 1088 38614 662-627-8577
Suzanne Ryals, prin. Fax 627-8548
Higgins MS 500/6-8
PO Box 1088 38614 662-627-8550
Reginald Griffin, prin. Fax 627-8543
Kirkpatrick ES 300/K-5
PO Box 1088 38614 662-627-8588
SuzAnne Walton, prin. Fax 627-8526
Oakhurst MS 400/6-8
PO Box 1088 38614 662-627-8560
Linda Downing, prin. Fax 627-8512
Oliver ES 400/K-5
PO Box 1088 38614 662-627-8605
Sharon Montgomery, prin. Fax 627-8547
Stampley ES 300/K-5
PO Box 1088 38614 662-627-8570
Barbara Akon, prin. Fax 627-8569
Washington ES 300/K-5
PO Box 1088 38614 662-627-8567
Dorothy Johnson, prin. Fax 627-7355

Coahoma County SD 1,700/K-12
PO Box 820 38614 662-624-5448
Pauline Rhoads, supt. Fax 624-5512
www.coahoma.k12.ms.us
Sherard ES 200/K-6
3105 Bobo Sherard Rd 38614 662-624-4629
Florence Crocroft, prin. Fax 624-4629
Other Schools – See Friars Point, Jonestown, Lyon

Lee Academy 500/PK-12
415 Lee Dr 38614 662-627-7891
Ricky Weiss, prin. Fax 627-7896
Presbyterian Day S 100/PK-6
944 Catalpa St 38614 662-627-7761
Patsy Lawrence, admin. Fax 627-1943
St. Elizabeth S 100/PK-6
150 Florence Ave 38614 662-624-4239
Elizabeth Scarbrough, prin. Fax 624-2072
St. Georges Episcopal S 100/K-6
1040 W 2nd St 38614 662-624-4376
Bernie Winkel, admin. Fax 624-4314

Cleveland, Bolivar, Pop. 12,818
Cleveland SD 3,100/PK-12
305 Merritt Dr 38732 662-843-3529
Jacquelyn Thigpen Ed.D., supt. Fax 843-9731
www.cleveland.k12.ms.us/
Cypress Park ES 300/K-6
725 S Martin Luther King Dr 38732 662-846-6152
Angela Silas Towers, prin. Fax 846-7820
Green JHS 300/7-8
205 N Bolivar Ave 38732 662-843-2456
Robert Montesi, prin. Fax 843-6820
Nailor ES 200/PK-6
600 Cross St 38732 662-843-4528
Lester Fisher, prin. Fax 843-2293
Parks ES 400/PK-6
1301 Terrace Rd 38732 662-843-3166
Lisa Bramuchi, prin. Fax 843-3155
Pearman ES 300/K-6
420 Robinson Dr 38732 662-843-4484
Johnnie Shumpert, prin. Fax 843-4484
Smith MS 200/7-8
715 S Martin Luther King Dr 38732 662-843-4355
Jim Washington, prin. Fax 843-7334
Other Schools – See Boyle

Bayou Academy 200/PK-12
PO Box 417 38732 662-843-3708
Robert Foust, admin. Fax 843-9618

Presbyterian Day S 200/PK-6
1100 W Highway 8 38732 662-843-8698
Diane Burd, hdmstr. Fax 843-8686

Clinton, Hinds, Pop. 26,017
Clinton SD 4,500/K-12
PO Box 300 39060 601-924-7533
Phillip Burchfield, supt. Fax 924-6345
www.clintonpublicschools.com
Clinton JHS 800/7-8
711 Lakeview Dr 39056 601-924-0619
Anthony Goins, prin. Fax 924-7703
Clinton Park ES 400/K-1
501 Arrow Dr 39056 601-924-5205
Suzanne Hollingshead, prin. Fax 925-6237
Eastside ES 800/4-5
201 Easthaven Dr 39056 601-924-7261
Cindy Hamil, prin. Fax 925-9005
Lovett MS 400/6-6
2002 W Northside Dr 39056 601-924-5664
Richard Burge, prin. Fax 924-3778
Northside ES 700/2-3
1111 Old Vicksburg Rd 39056 601-924-7531
Joy Tyner, prin. Fax 925-4028

Mount Salus Christian S 400/K-12
PO Box 240 39060 601-924-6652
Morris Richards, admin. Fax 924-6661

Coffeeville, Yalobusha, Pop. 947
Coffeeville SD 600/K-12
16849 Okahoma St 38922 662-675-8941
Eddie Anderson, supt. Fax 675-5004
www.coffeevilleschools.org/
Coffeeville ES 400/K-7
16849 Okahoma St 38922 662-675-2721
William Austin, prin. Fax 675-5007

Coldwater, Tate, Pop. 1,649
Tate County SD
Supt. — See Senatobia
Coldwater S 400/K-8
340 Peyton Rd Ste C 38618 662-622-5561
Kelvin Knox, prin. Fax 622-7253
East Tate ES 500/K-4
6832 E Tate Rd 38618 662-562-4688
Kaye Adams, prin. Fax 560-0881

Collins, Covington, Pop. 2,761
Covington County SD 3,100/K-12
PO Box 1269 39428 601-765-8247
Isaac Sanford, supt. Fax 765-4102
www.cov.k12.ms.us/
Carver MS 400/5-8
PO Box 757 39428 601-765-4908
Pauline Fairley, prin. Fax 765-4100
Collins ES 400/K-4
PO Box 160 39428 601-765-4383
Jamie Rogers, prin. Fax 765-4105
Hopewell ES 300/K-6
824 Hopewell Rd 39428 601-765-8568
Angela Palmer, prin. Fax 765-9486
Other Schools – See Mount Olive, Seminary

Columbia, Marion, Pop. 6,408
Columbia SD 1,700/K-12
613 Bryan Ave 39429 601-736-2366
Dr. Marietta James, supt. Fax 736-2653
www.columbiaschools.org
Columbia ES 300/4-5
401 Mary St 39429 601-736-2362
Wendy Bracey, prin. Fax 736-5891
Columbia PS 500/K-3
501 Dale St 39429 601-736-2216
Loren Monk, prin. Fax 731-3764
Jefferson MS 400/6-8
611 Owens St 39429 601-736-2786
Raymond Powell, prin. Fax 731-3762

Marion County SD 2,400/PK-12
1010 Highway 13 N Ste 2 39429 601-736-7193
Fax 736-6274
www.marionk12.org
East Marion ES 200/4-6
527 E Marion School Rd 39429 601-731-1498
Dr. Portia Hull, prin. Fax 731-2037
East Marion PS 300/PK-3
527 E Marion School Rd 39429 601-736-7290
Angie Pradat, prin. Fax 736-7157
Other Schools – See Foxworth

Columbia Academy 500/K-12
1548 Highway 98 E 39429 601-736-6418
H. Tom Porter, hdmstr. Fax 736-0098

Columbus, Lowndes, Pop. 24,425
Columbus Municipal SD 4,300/PK-12
PO Box 1308 39703 662-241-7400
Dr. Del Phillips, supt. Fax 241-7453
www.columbuscityschools.org/
Cook ES 400/K-4
2217 7th Ave N 39701 662-241-7180
Lois Kappler, prin. Fax 241-7182
Fairview ES 200/K-4
225 Airline Rd 39702 662-241-7140
Billie Smith, prin. Fax 241-7141
Franklin Academy ES 400/K-4
501 3rd Ave N 39701 662-241-7150
Patricia Overstreet, prin. Fax 241-7152
Hunt IS 700/5-6
924 20th St N 39701 662-241-7160
Tamela Barr, prin. Fax 241-7164
Lee MS 700/7-8
1815 Military Rd 39701 662-241-7300
Cindy Wamble, prin. Fax 241-7305
Sale ES 200/K-4
520 Warpath Rd 39702 662-241-7260
Nancy Bragg, prin. Fax 241-7262

Stokes-Beard ES 300/PK-4
311 Martin Luther King Dr 39701 662-241-7270
Pamela Lenoir, prin. Fax 241-7272

Lowndes County SD 5,100/K-12
1053 Highway 45 S 39701 662-244-5000
Michael Halford, supt. Fax 244-5043
www.lowndes.k12.ms.us/
New Hope ES 1,100/K-5
199 Enlow Dr 39702 662-244-4760
Joe York, prin. Fax 244-4775
New Hope MS 700/6-8
462 Center Rd 39702 662-244-4740
Sam Allison, prin. Fax 244-4758
West Lowndes ES 200/K-5
1000 Gilmer Wilburn Rd 39701 662-244-5050
Robert Sanders, prin. Fax 328-2912
West Lowndes MS 200/6-8
1380 Motley Rd 39701 662-244-5060
Cynthia McMath, prin. Fax 327-4857
Other Schools – See Caledonia

Annunciation Catholic S 100/PK-6
223 N Browder St 39702 662-328-4479
Barbara Calland, prin. Fax 328-0430
Emmaus S 50/1-8
1030 Bennett Ave 39702 662-241-7264
Heritage Academy 700/K-12
625 Magnolia Ln 39705 662-327-5272
Tommy Gunn, admin. Fax 327-2226

Como, Panola, Pop. 1,321
North Panola SD
Supt. — See Sardis
Como ES 300/K-5
200 Lewers St 38619 662-526-0396
Ben Lundy, prin. Fax 526-5259
North Panola JHS 300/6-8
526 Lewers St 38619 662-526-5938
Demond Radcliff, prin. Fax 526-5990

Corinth, Alcorn, Pop. 14,256
Alcorn SD 3,500/K-12
PO Box 1420 38835 662-286-5591
Stacy Suggs, supt. Fax 286-7713
www.alcorn.k12.ms.us
Biggersville ES 200/K-6
571A Highway 45 38834 662-286-6593
Gina Smith, prin. Fax 286-5735
Kossuth ES 500/K-4
14 County Road 604 38834 662-286-2761
Van Carpenter, prin. Fax 286-6875
Kossuth MS 500/5-8
17 County Road 604 38834 662-286-7093
Fred Jackson, prin. Fax 286-6837
Other Schools – See Glen, Rienzi

Corinth SD 1,700/K-12
1204 N Harper Rd 38834 662-287-2425
Edward Lee Childress, supt. Fax 286-1885
www.corinth.k12.ms.us
Corinth JHS 300/7-8
1000 E 5th St 38834 662-286-1261
Brian Knippers, prin. Fax 287-0296
East Corinth ES 500/2-4
1200 Meeks St 38834 662-286-5245
Denise Webb, prin. Fax 287-0298
South Corinth IS 300/5-6
700 Crater St 38834 662-287-2285
Dave Jennings, prin. Fax 286-2276
West Corinth ES 200/K-1
200 Wenasoga Rd 38834 662-286-2348
Denise Webb, prin. Fax 287-0374

Corinth SDA S, 42 CR 278 38834 50/1-8
George Reed, lead tchr. 662-286-3600

Crenshaw, Panola, Pop. 924
North Panola SD
Supt. — See Sardis
Crenshaw ES 200/K-5
PO Box 250 38621 662-382-5803
Michael Britt, prin. Fax 382-7122

Crystal Springs, Copiah, Pop. 5,913
Copiah County SD
Supt. — See Hazlehurst
Crystal Springs ES 400/PK-3
213 Newton St 39059 601-892-4795
Cheryl Haynes, prin. Fax 892-4789
Crystal Springs MS 800/4-8
2092 S Pat Harrison Dr 39059 601-892-2722
Adren McCoy, prin. Fax 892-9949

Decatur, Newton, Pop. 1,426
Newton County SD 1,700/K-12
PO Box 97 39327 601-635-2317
Pat Ross, supt. Fax 635-4025
www.newton.k12.ms.us
Newton County ES 800/K-5
PO Box 249 39327 601-635-2956
Danny Lindsley, prin. Fax 635-4074

Newton County Academy 200/PK-12
PO Box 25 39327 601-635-2756
Mike Tucker, admin. Fax 635-3525

De Kalb, Kemper, Pop. 923
Kemper County SD 1,300/PK-12
PO Box 219 39328 601-743-2657
Jackie Pollock, supt. Fax 743-9297
kemper.k12.ms.us/
West Kemper ES 500/PK-6
PO Box 250 39328 601-743-2432
Wendy Wade, prin. Fax 743-4232
Other Schools – See Scooba

Kemper Academy 200/K-12
149 Walnut Ave 39328 601-743-2232
Jerry Jones, admin. Fax 743-9627

D Iberville, Harrison, Pop. 7,868
Harrison County SD
Supt. — See Gulfport
D'Iberville ES 500/K-4
4540 Brodie Rd, 228-392-2803
Dana Trochessett, prin. Fax 392-0557
D'Iberville MS 500/5-8
3320 Warrior Dr, 228-392-1746
Dean Scarbrough, prin. Fax 392-9948

Sacred Heart S 100/PK-6
10482 Lemoyne Blvd, 228-392-4180
Jane Sema, prin. Fax 392-4859

Drew, Sunflower, Pop. 2,215
Drew SD 600/K-12
286 W Park Ave 38737 662-745-6657
Dr. Earlcine Carter, supt. Fax 745-6630
www.drew.k12.ms.us/
Hunter MS 200/5-8
10 Swoope Rd 38737 662-745-8940
Sam Evans, prin. Fax 745-6630
James ES 300/K-4
400 South Blvd 38737 662-745-8892
Devoice Morris, prin. Fax 745-6630

North Sunflower Academy 200/K-12
148 Academy Rd 38737 662-756-2547
Herman Coats, admin. Fax 756-2580

Duncan, Bolivar, Pop. 558
North Bolivar SD
Supt. — See Shelby
Brooks ES 200/K-3
PO Box 168 38740 662-398-4060
Fredrick Ford, prin. Fax 395-2247

Dundee, Tunica
Tunica County SD
Supt. — See Tunica
Dundee ES 200/PK-5
12910 Old Highway 61 S 38626 662-363-1810
Dexter Green, prin. Fax 363-1695

Durant, Holmes, Pop. 2,845
Durant SD 500/K-12
5 W Madison St 39063 662-653-3175
Glennie Carlisle, supt. Fax 653-6151
www.durant.k12.ms.us/
Durant ES 300/K-6
PO Box 669 39063 662-653-3176
Willie Dale, prin. Fax 653-6342

Holmes County SD
Supt. — See Lexington
Williams-Sullivan ES 100/K-5
14494 Highway 51 39063 662-653-6218
Charles Lacy, prin. Fax 653-6519

Ecru, Pontotoc, Pop. 1,015
Pontotoc County SD
Supt. — See Pontotoc
North Pontotoc ES 700/K-5
8324 Highway 15 N 38841 662-489-5613
Lisa Lucius, prin. Fax 489-9162
North Pontotoc MS 400/6-8
8324 Highway 15 N 38841 662-489-2479
Libby Young, prin. Fax 489-2985

Ellisville, Jones, Pop. 3,735
Jones County SD 6,200/K-12
5204 Highway 11 N 39437 601-649-5201
Steve Thrasher, supt. Fax 649-1613
www.jones.k12.ms.us/
South Jones ES 400/4-6
27 Warrior Rd 39437 601-477-3577
Charles King, prin. Fax 477-2700
Other Schools – See Laurel, Moselle

Enterprise, Clarke, Pop. 454
Enterprise SD 900/K-12
503 S River Rd 39330 601-659-7965
Arthur McMillan, supt. Fax 659-3254
www.esd.k12.ms.us/
Enterprise ES 300/K-4
103 Short St 39330 601-659-7613
Patsy Smith, prin. Fax 659-7371
Enterprise MS 300/5-8
105 Short St 39330 601-659-7722
Steven Gunn, prin. Fax 659-7722

Escatawpa, Jackson, Pop. 3,902
Moss Point SD
Supt. — See Moss Point
Escatawpa ES 500/K-6
4208 Jamestown Rd 39552 228-474-3300
Joan Pettaway, prin. Fax 474-3396

Eupora, Webster, Pop. 2,265
Webster County SD 1,800/PK-12
95 Clark Ave 39744 662-258-5921
Jimmy Pittman, supt. Fax 258-3134
www.webster.k12.ms.us/
Eupora ES 500/PK-6
1 Naron Ave 39744 662-258-6735
Michael Adkins, prin. Fax 258-3129
Other Schools – See Mathiston

Falkner, Tippah, Pop. 208
North Tippah SD
Supt. — See Tiplersville
Falkner ES 300/K-6
PO Box 146 38629 662-837-3947
Fax 837-0082

Fayette, Jefferson, Pop. 2,133
Jefferson County SD 1,600/K-12
PO Box 157 39069 601-786-3721
John Dickey, supt. Fax 786-8441
www.jcpsd.net
Jefferson County ES 400/K-4
430 Highway 33 39069 601-786-6003
Rosetta Hammett, prin. Fax 786-2274
Jefferson County JHS 200/7-8
468 Highway 33 39069 601-786-3900
Michael Brown, prin. Fax 786-2273
Jefferson County Upper ES 200/5-6
442 Highway 33 39069 601-786-3658
Claudine Middleton, prin. Fax 786-3527

Flora, Madison, Pop. 1,478
Madison County SD 10,000/K-12
PO Box 159 39071 601-879-3000
Michael Kent, supt. Fax 879-3039
www.madison-schools.com/
East Flora ES 400/K-5
PO Box J 39071 601-879-8724
Christi Hollingshead, prin. Fax 879-3158
East Flora MS 100/6-8
PO Box J 39071 601-879-3809
William White, prin. Fax 879-3158
Other Schools – See Camden, Canton, Madison, Ridgeland

Tri-County Academy 300/K-12
PO Box K 39071 601-879-8517
Mark Johnson, hdmstr. Fax 879-3373

Florence, Rankin, Pop. 3,063
Rankin County SD
Supt. — See Brandon
Florence ES 500/3-5
285 Highway 469 N 39073 601-845-8164
Michelle Nowlin, prin. Fax 845-1582
Florence MS 500/6-8
123 Beverly Dr 39073 601-845-2862
Beverly Weathersby, prin. Fax 845-2114
McLaurin ES 700/K-6
2693 Star Rd 39073 601-845-2127
Amanda Stocks, prin. Fax 845-3251
Steen's Creek ES 400/K-2
300 Highway 469 N 39073 601-845-5724
Cindy Ponder, prin. Fax 845-3549

Flowood, Rankin, Pop. 6,762
Rankin County SD
Supt. — See Brandon
Flowood ES 500/K-5
102 Winners Cir 39232 601-992-6277
Dr. Kathy Martin, prin. Fax 992-2468
Northwest ES 500/K-5
500 Vine Dr 39232 601-992-0924
Dr. Charlotte Young, prin. Fax 992-7112
Northwest MS 1,100/6-8
1 Paw Print Pl 39232 601-992-1329
Jacob McEwen, prin. Fax 992-1347

St. Paul Learning Center PK-PK
5969 Highway 25 39232 601-992-2876
Ellen Treadaway, dir. Fax 992-8741
University Christian S 300/K-12
1240 Luckney Rd 39232 601-992-5333
Pam Ulrich, hdmstr. Fax 992-5320

Forest, Scott, Pop. 6,029
Forest Municipal SD 1,400/K-12
325 Cleveland St 39074 601-469-3250
Raymond Clark, supt. Fax 469-3101
www.forest.k12.ms.us/
Forest ES 500/K-4
513 Cleveland St 39074 601-469-3073
Pam Jones, prin. Fax 469-8252
Hawkins MS 500/5-8
803 E Oak St 39074 601-469-1474
Fletcher Harges, prin. Fax 469-8251

Scott County SD 3,600/K-12
100 E First St 39074 601-469-3861
Frank McCurdy, supt. Fax 469-3874
www.scott.k12.ms.us
Scott Central S 900/K-12
2415 Old Jackson Rd 39074 601-469-4883
Dr. Janet McLin, prin. Fax 469-3746
Other Schools – See Lake, Morton, Sebastopol

Foxworth, Marion
Marion County SD
Supt. — See Columbia
West Marion ES 400/4-6
2 W Marion St 39483 601-731-2076
Libby Aaron, prin. Fax 731-7938
West Marion PS 400/K-3
PO Box 6 39483 601-736-3713
Tammy Fairburn, prin. Fax 731-2091

French Camp, Choctaw, Pop. 389
Choctaw County SD
Supt. — See Ackerman
French Camp S 200/PK-8
300 Church St 39745 662-547-5329
Johnnie Henderson, prin. Fax 547-7119

Friars Point, Coahoma, Pop. 1,405
Coahoma County SD
Supt. — See Clarksdale
Friars Point ES 300/K-6
PO Box 600 38631 662-383-2477
Sherry Coleman, prin. Fax 383-2477

Fulton, Itawamba, Pop. 4,102
Itawamba County SD 3,100/PK-12
605 S Cummings St 38843 662-862-2159
Teresa McNeese, supt. Fax 862-4713
www.itawamba.k12.ms.us/

Dorsey Attendance Center 400/PK-8
1 Dorsey School Rd 38843 662-862-3663
Mark Hitt, prin. Fax 862-7210
Itawamba Attendance Center 900/PK-8
488 Little Indian Rd 38843 662-862-4641
Kenny Goralczyk, prin. Fax 862-4396
Other Schools – See Golden, Mantachie, Tremont

Gallman, Copiah

Copiah Academy 600/K-12
PO Box 125 39077 601-892-3770
Carol Rigby, hdmstr. Fax 892-6222

Gautier, Jackson, Pop. 16,846
Pascagoula SD
Supt. — See Pascagoula
College Park ES 400/K-5
2617 Ladnier Rd 39553 228-522-8829
Suzanne Ros, prin. Fax 522-8830
Gautier ES 200/K-5
505 Magnolia Tree Dr 39553 228-522-8824
Michelle Richmond, prin. Fax 522-8825
Gautier MS 800/6-8
1920 Graveline Rd 39553 228-522-8806
Christy Reimsnyder, prin. Fax 522-8813
Martin Bluff ES 400/K-5
1306 Roys Rd 39553 228-522-8850
Dr. Vickie Tiblier, prin. Fax 522-8852
Singing River ES 500/K-5
4601 Gautier Vancleave Rd 39553 228-522-8835
Dr. Frank Catchings, prin. Fax 522-8839

Glen, Alcorn, Pop. 294
Alcorn SD
Supt. — See Corinth
Alcorn Central ES 400/K-4
20 County Road 254 38846 662-286-6899
Joe Horton, prin. Fax 287-6487
Alcorn Central MS 500/5-8
8A County Road 254 38846 662-286-3674
Dan Burcham, prin. Fax 286-6712
Glendale ES 200/K-6
PO Box 69 38846 662-286-2734
Robert Strickland, prin. Fax 287-7702

Gloster, Amite, Pop. 1,060
Amite County SD
Supt. — See Liberty
Gloster S 400/K-8
PO Box 220 39638 601-225-9913
Melessa Walker, prin. Fax 225-7939

Golden, Itawamba, Pop. 202
Itawamba County SD
Supt. — See Fulton
Fairview Attendance Center 200/K-8
66 Fairview School Rd 38847 662-585-3127
Derek Shumpert, prin. Fax 585-3139

Goodman, Holmes, Pop. 1,220
Holmes County SD
Supt. — See Lexington
Goodman-Pickens ES 300/K-5
3877 Highway 51 39079 662-468-2116
Lillian Mitchell, prin. Fax 468-2786

Greenville, Washington, Pop. 38,724
Greenville SD 6,900/PK-12
PO Box 1619 38702 662-334-7000
Joyce McNair, supt. Fax 334-7021
gvillepublicschools.org/
Akin ES 500/PK-6
361 Bowman Blvd 38701 662-334-7161
Mary Stone, prin. Fax 334-2847
Armstrong ES 300/PK-6
528 Redbud St 38701 662-334-7121
Norma McDavid, prin. Fax 334-7120
Boyd ES 600/PK-6
1021 S Colorado St 38703 662-334-7166
Reva Pree, prin. Fax 334-2872
Coleman MS 600/7-8
400 Highway 1 N 38701 662-334-7036
Dianne Zanders, prin. Fax 334-7040
Darling ES 200/PK-6
242 S Broadway St 38701 662-334-7141
Arthur Johnson, prin. Fax 334-7023
Fulwiler ES 300/PK-6
699 Dublin St 38703 662-334-7111
Betty Johnson, prin. Fax 334-2846
Manning ES 400/PK-6
430 Highway 1 N 38701 662-334-7116
David Wolfe, prin. Fax 334-2877
McBride ES 200/PK-6
438 N Poplar St 38701 662-334-7136
Myrna Harris, prin. Fax 334-2874
Solomon MS 500/7-8
556 Bowman Blvd 38701 662-334-7050
Bynarozelle Mitchell, prin. Fax 334-7053
Stern Enhancement S 400/K-6
522 McAllister St 38701 662-334-7131
Michael McNeece, prin. Fax 378-1821
Trigg ES 400/PK-6
3004 Lincoln Dr 38703 662-334-7177
Tamalyn Williams, prin. Fax 334-7176
Webb ES 300/PK-6
600 S Harvey St 38701 662-334-7146
Dorothy Chatman, prin. Fax 334-2879
Weddington ES 500/PK-6
668 Sampson Rd 38701 662-334-7101
Debra Reeves, prin. Fax 334-2863

Western Line SD
Supt. — See Avon
O'Bannon ES 400/K-6
PO Box 5816 38704 662-332-4830
Kathryn Livingston, prin. Fax 334-1956

Greenville Christian S 200/K-12
PO Box 4398 38704 662-332-0946
Keith Aycock, hdmstr. Fax 332-0948
Our Lady of Lourdes S 200/PK-6
1600 E Reed Rd 38703 662-334-3287
Michelle Gardiner, prin. Fax 332-9877
Washington S 800/PK-12
1605 E Reed Rd 38703 662-334-4096
Rodney Brown, hdmstr. Fax 332-0434

Greenwood, LeFlore, Pop. 17,344
Greenwood SD 3,100/PK-12
401 Howard St 38930 662-453-4231
Dr. Margie Pulley, supt. Fax 455-7409
www.greenwood.k12.ms.us/
Bankston ES 300/K-6
1312 Grand Blvd 38930 662-455-7421
Kirby Love, prin. Fax 455-7473
Davis ES 600/K-6
400 Cotton St 38930 662-455-7430
Deborah Cole, prin. Fax 455-7497
Greenwood MS 500/7-8
1200 Garrard Ave 38930 662-455-3661
Lorita Harris, prin. Fax 455-5559
Threadgill ES 600/PK-6
1001 Broad St 38930 662-455-7440
Cassandra Hart, prin. Fax 455-7413
Williams ES 300/K-6
1300 Carrollton Ave 38930 662-455-7445
Brenda Brown, prin. Fax 455-7448

Leflore County SD 2,800/K-12
1901 Highway 82 W 38930 662-453-8566
Ms. Willie Jean Hall, supt. Fax 459-7265
www.leflorecountyschools.org
Brown ES 300/K-3
3827 County Road 363 38930 662-453-8622
Ezzard Beane, prin. Fax 453-8623
East MS 400/4-8
208 Meadowbrook Rd 38930 662-453-9182
Valerie Reed, prin. Fax 451-7734
Elzy ES 400/K-6
604 Elzy Ave 38930 662-453-9677
Jackie Lewis, prin. Fax 455-0139
Other Schools – See Itta Bena

Pillow Academy 800/PK-12
69601 Highway 82 W 38930 662-453-1266
Termie Land, hdmstr. Fax 455-6484
St. Francis of Assisi S 100/PK-6
2607 Highway 82 E 38930 662-453-9511
Sr. Carol Seidl, prin. Fax 453-9060

Grenada, Grenada, Pop. 14,569
Grenada SD 4,100/K-12
PO Box 1940 38902 662-226-1606
Dr. David Daigneault, supt. Fax 226-7994
www.gsd.k12.ms.us/
Grenada ES 1,000/K-3
250 Pender Dr 38901 662-226-2584
Paul Portera, prin. Fax 227-4497
Grenada MS 1,100/6-8
28 Jones Rd 38901 662-226-5135
Tim Wilder, prin. Fax 227-6106
Grenada Upper ES 700/4-5
500 Pender Dr 38901 662-226-2818
Teresa Jackson, prin. Fax 227-6107

Kirk Academy 400/PK-12
PO Box 1008 38902 662-226-2791
Embree Bolton, hdmstr. Fax 226-9066

Gulfport, Harrison, Pop. 72,464
Gulfport SD 5,300/K-12
2001 Pass Rd 39501 228-865-4600
Glen East, supt. Fax 865-1918
www.gulfportschools.org/
Anniston Avenue ES 500/K-5
2314 Jones St 39507 228-896-6309
Carol Payne, prin. Fax 896-3124
Bayou View ES 500/K-5
4898 Washington Ave 39507 228-865-4625
Sandra Wilks, prin. Fax 865-1928
Bayou View MS 700/6-8
212 43rd St 39507 228-865-4633
Bryan Caldwell, prin. Fax 867-1967
Central ES 500/K-5
1043 Pass Rd 39501 228-865-4642
Cindy DeFrances, prin. Fax 865-0281
Gaston Point ES 500/K-5
1526 Mills Ave 39501 228-865-4656
Dr. Wanda Bradley, prin. Fax 865-4701
Gulfport Central MS 600/6-8
1310 42nd Ave 39501 228-870-1035
Mike Battle, prin. Fax 870-1041
Pass Road ES 300/K-5
37 Pass Rd 39507 228-865-4659
Kenny Hudson, prin. Fax 863-1549
West ES 400/K-5
4051 15th St 39501 228-870-1025
Scott Powell, prin. Fax 870-1032

Harrison County SD 11,100/K-12
11072 Highway 49 39503 228-539-6500
Henry Arledge, supt. Fax 539-6507
www.harrison.k12.ms.us/
Bel Aire ES 600/K-6
10531 Klein Rd 39503 228-832-7436
Sherry Washburn, prin. Fax 832-5388
Crossroads ES, 10453 Klein Rd 39503 K-6
Wanda Morra, prin. 228-832-6711
Harrison Central ES 600/K-3
15451 Dedeaux Rd 39503 228-832-2701
Pam McInnis, prin. Fax 831-5357
Lizana ES 600/K-6
15341 Lizana School Rd 39503 228-832-1592
Debra Spiers, prin. Fax 831-5354

Lyman ES 500/K-6
14222 Old Highway 49 39503 228-832-2257
George Black, prin. Fax 831-5345
North Gulfport 7th & 8th Grade S 900/7-8
4715 Illinois Ave 39501 228-864-8944
Patsy Brewer, prin. Fax 863-7326
Orange Grove IS 500/4-6
11391 Old Highway 49 39503 228-832-2322
Shelly Holmes, prin. Fax 831-5347
Three Rivers ES 700/K-6
13500 Three Rivers Rd 39503 228-831-5359
Tracy Sellers, prin. Fax 831-5361
Other Schools – See Biloxi, D Iberville, Pass Christian, Saucier

Christian Collegiate Academy 300/PK-12
12200 Dedeaux Rd 39503 228-832-4585
John Hartsell, prin. Fax 832-3290
St. James S 400/PK-6
603 West Ave 39507 228-896-6631
Jennifer Broadus, prin. Fax 896-6638
St. John S 200/PK-6
2415 17th St 39501 228-863-1606
Cindy Hahn, prin. Fax 863-9677
Westminster Academy 200/PK-7
5003 Lawson Ave 39507 228-868-1312
Dr. Brenda Stiles, prin. Fax 868-1320

Guntown, Lee, Pop. 1,311
Lee County SD
Supt. — See Tupelo
Guntown MS 700/6-8
PO Box 8 38849 662-348-8800
Steven Havens, prin. Fax 348-8810

Hamilton, Monroe
Monroe County SD
Supt. — See Amory
Hamilton S 700/K-12
40201 Hamilton Rd 39746 662-343-8307
Mark Howell, prin. Fax 343-5813

Hattiesburg, Forrest, Pop. 47,176
Forrest County SD 2,500/K-12
PO Box 1977 39403 601-545-6055
Debbie Burt, supt. Fax 545-6054
www.forrest.k12.ms.us/
Dixie S 700/K-8
790 Elks Lake Rd 39401 601-582-4890
Dale Coleman, prin. Fax 582-5277
North Forrest ES 300/K-6
702 Eatonville Rd 39401 601-584-6466
Jon Greer, prin. Fax 544-1779
Rawls Springs ES 200/K-6
10 Archie Smith Rd 39402 601-268-2217
Kelly Lambert, prin. Fax 264-7256
Travillion S 200/K-6
316 Travillion Rd 39401 601-584-9303
Christopher Furdge, prin. Fax 582-5785
Other Schools – See Brooklyn

Hattiesburg SD 4,300/K-12
PO Box 1569 39403 601-582-5078
Annie Wimbish Ed.D., supt. Fax 582-6666
www.hpsd.k12.ms.us/
Burger MS 700/7-8
174 WSF Tatum Dr Ext 39401 601-582-0536
Robert Williams, prin. Fax 582-0572
Burney ES 400/K-6
901 Ida Ave 39401 601-582-5291
Deborah Smith, prin. Fax 583-7325
Christian ES 400/K-6
2207 W 7th St 39401 601-583-0662
Debra Large, prin. Fax 582-6083
Hawkins ES 300/K-6
526 Forrest St 39401 601-583-4311
Malcolm Cobb, prin. Fax 583-8840
Rowan ES 400/K-6
500 Martin Luther King Ave 39401 601-583-0960
Michelle Johnson, prin. Fax 582-0227
Thames ES 500/K-6
2900 Jamestown Rd 39402 601-582-6655
Carrie Hornsby, prin. Fax 582-6084
Woodley ES 400/K-6
2006 Oferral St 39401 601-583-8112
Felicia Morris, prin. Fax 582-6081

Lamar County SD
Supt. — See Purvis
Oak Grove Lower ES 800/2-3
1762 Old Highway 24 39402 601-268-3862
Teresa Jenny, prin. Fax 268-8852
Oak Grove MS 1,000/6-8
2543 Old Highway 24 39402 601-264-4634
Terry Ingram, prin. Fax 264-0160
Oak Grove Primary ES K-1
70 Leaf Ln 39402 601-261-3380
Dahlia Landers, prin. Fax 261-3393
Oak Grove Upper ES 700/4-5
1760 Old Highway 24 39402 601-264-6724
Debbie Dabbs, prin. Fax 264-6771

Alpha Christian S 200/K-12
PO Box 1361 39403 601-583-3144
Fax 544-4090
Presbyterian Christian ES 500/K-6
3901 Lincoln Rd 39402 601-268-3867
Scott Griffith, prin. Fax 268-9868
Sacred Heart S 500/PK-12
608 Southern Ave 39401 601-583-8683
Brian McCrory, prin. Fax 583-8684

Hazlehurst, Copiah, Pop. 4,372
Copiah County SD 2,700/PK-12
254 W Gallatin St 39083 601-894-1341
Rickey Clopton, supt. Fax 894-2634
www.copiahcounty.org/School%20District.htm
Other Schools – See Crystal Springs, Wesson

Hazlehurst CSD 1,600/PK-12
119 Robert McDaniel Dr 39083 601-894-1152
Jay Norals, supt. Fax 894-3170
www.hazlehurst.k12.ms.us
Hazlehurst ES 600/PK-4
136 School Dr 39083 601-894-3742
Dr. Billy Brown, prin. Fax 894-3960
Hazlehurst MS 500/5-8
112 School Dr 39083 601-894-3463
Marvin Davis, prin. Fax 894-2629

Heidelberg, Jasper, Pop. 810
East Jasper Consolidated SD 1,200/K-12
PO Box E 39439 601-787-3281
Dr. Gwendolyn Page, supt. Fax 787-3410
www.eastjasper.k12.ms.us
Berry ES 700/K-6
PO Box O 39439 601-787-2607
Diane Hales, prin. Fax 787-2662

Heidelberg Academy 200/K-12
PO Box Q 39439 601-787-4589
Patricia Green, hdmstr. Fax 787-3371

Hernando, DeSoto, Pop. 9,890
DeSoto County SD 25,600/K-12
5 E South St 38632 662-429-5271
Milton Kuykendall, supt. Fax 429-4198
www.desotocountyschools.org/
Hernando ES 300/K-1
455 Riley St 38632 662-429-4160
Barbara Jepsen, prin. Fax 429-4114
Hernando Hills ES 600/2-3
570 McIngvale Rd 38632 662-429-9117
Stephanie Gilder, prin. Fax 429-3607
Hernando MS 700/6-8
700 Dilworth Ln 38632 662-429-4154
Jerry Darnell, prin. Fax 429-4189
Oak Grove Central ES 500/4-5
893 W Oak Grove Rd 38632 662-429-4180
Dr. Janice Barton, prin. Fax 429-1423
Other Schools – See Horn Lake, Lake Cormorant, Olive Branch, Southaven, Walls

Hickory Flat, Benton, Pop. 542
Benton County SD
Supt. — See Ashland
Hickory Flat S 600/K-12
1005 Spruce St 38633 662-333-7731
Robert Keenum, prin. Fax 333-4127

Hollandale, Washington, Pop. 3,189
Hollandale SD 800/K-12
PO Box 128 38748 662-827-2276
Willie Amos, supt. Fax 827-5261
www.hollandale.k12.ms.us
Sanders ES 500/K-6
PO Box 366 38748 662-827-2024
Fax 827-2056
Other Schools – See Arcola

Holly Springs, Marshall, Pop. 8,014
Holly Springs SD 1,600/K-12
840 Highway 178 E 38635 662-252-2183
Irene Walton, supt. Fax 252-7718
www.hssd.k12.ms.us
Holly Springs IS 500/3-6
210 W Valley Ave 38635 662-252-2329
Debbie Jeffries, prin. Fax 252-7740
Holly Springs JHS 300/7-8
325 E Falconer Ave 38635 662-252-7737
Louise Sanders-Tate, prin. Fax 252-7751
Holly Springs PS 300/K-2
405 S Maury St 38635 662-252-1768
Joseph Stone, prin. Fax 252-7732

Marshall County SD 2,700/K-12
158 E College Ave 38635 662-252-4271
Dan Ranolph, supt. Fax 252-5129
www.mcs.k12.ms.us/
Byers S 300/K-12
4178 Highway 72 38635 662-851-7826
Dixie Pye, prin. Fax 851-4027
Galena S 200/K-8
4202 Highway 4 W 38635 662-564-2229
Charlie Hall, prin. Fax 564-2231
Other Schools – See Byhalia, Potts Camp

Holy Family S 200/PK-8
395 West St 38635 662-252-1612
Mille Smith, prin. Fax 252-3694
Marshall Academy 400/PK-12
100 Academy Dr 38635 662-252-3449
Jane Hubbard, admin. Fax 252-4510

Horn Lake, DeSoto, Pop. 22,151
DeSoto County SD
Supt. — See Hernando
Horn Lake ES 400/K-2
6341 Ridgewood Rd 38637 662-393-4608
Cindy Dunning, prin. Fax 393-0216
Horn Lake IS 1,100/3-5
6585 Horn Lake Rd 38637 662-280-7075
Vickie Bullock, prin. Fax 280-7067
Horn Lake MS 1,000/6-8
6125 Hurt Rd 38637 662-393-7443
Van Alexander, prin. Fax 342-5039
Shadow Oaks ES 400/K-2
3780 Shadow Oaks Pkwy 38637 662-393-4585
Traci Suiter, prin. Fax 342-1035

Houlka, Chickasaw, Pop. 553
Chickasaw County SD 500/PK-12
PO Box 480 38850 662-568-3333
Kathy Davis, supt. Fax 568-2993
chickasaw.k12.ms.us/
Houlka S 500/PK-12
510 Griffin Ave 38850 662-568-2772
William Cotton, prin. Fax 568-7931

Houston, Chickasaw, Pop. 3,980
Houston SD 1,700/K-12
PO Box 351 38851 662-456-3332
Dr. Steve Coker, supt. Fax 456-5259
www.houston.k12.ms.us
Houston Lower ES 300/K-2
123 S Starkville Rd 38851 662-456-3323
Emily Speck, prin. Fax 456-5876
Houston MS 500/6-8
PO Box 192 38851 662-456-5174
Tony Horton, prin. Fax 456-2254
Houston Upper ES 500/3-5
452 Pittsboro St 38851 662-456-2797
Shannon Eaton, prin. Fax 456-5840

Hurley, Jackson
Jackson County SD
Supt. — See Vancleave
East Central Lower ES 400/K-2
PO Box 13 39555 228-588-7060
Mary Tanner, prin. Fax 588-7071
East Central Upper ES 600/3-5
PO Box 13 39555 228-588-7019
Lynn Brewer, prin. Fax 588-7046

Independence, Tate
Tate County SD
Supt. — See Senatobia
Independence MS 500/5-8
505 Sycamore Rd, 662-233-0250
Malinda White, prin. Fax 233-0253

Indianola, Sunflower, Pop. 11,321
Indianola SD 1,700/K-12
702 Highway 82 E 38751 662-887-5654
Dr. King Rush, supt. Fax 887-4850
www.indianolaschools.org/
Carver Upper ES 300/3-5
404 Jefferson St 38751 662-887-2353
Karen Blumenberg, prin. Fax 887-7086
Lockard ES 200/K-2
302 College Ave 38751 662-887-2554
Stanley Lott, prin. Fax 887-7710
Merritt MS 400/6-8
705 Kinlock Rd 38751 662-887-1449
Glenda Shedd, prin. Fax 887-5247

Sunflower County SD 1,800/K-12
PO Box 70 38751 662-887-4919
Peirce McIntosh, supt. Fax 887-7051
www.sunflower.k12.ms.us/
Other Schools – See Inverness, Moorhead, Ruleville, Sunflower

---

Indianola Academy 500/PK-12
PO Box 967 38751 662-887-2025
Sammy Henderson, hdmstr. Fax 887-3117
Restoration Ministries Christian Academy 100/K-12
PO Box 1001 38751 662-887-2040
Richard Jenkins, admin. Fax 887-2040

Inverness, Sunflower, Pop. 1,061
Sunflower County SD
Supt. — See Indianola
Inverness S 200/K-8
1101 Oak St 38753 662-265-5752
Patricia Boyd, prin. Fax 265-0027

Itta Bena, LeFlore, Pop. 2,019
Leflore County SD
Supt. — See Greenwood
LeFlore County ES 600/K-6
PO Box 564 38941 662-254-6225
Carl Palmer, prin. Fax 254-7942

Iuka, Tishomingo, Pop. 2,987
Tishomingo County Special Municipal SD 3,300/K-12
1620 Paul Edmondson Dr 38852 662-423-3206
Malcolm Kuykendall, supt. Fax 424-9820
www.tishomingo.k12.ms.us
Iuka ES 400/K-4
1500 Whitehouse Rd 38852 662-423-9290
Dr. Tina Joslin, prin. Fax 423-7315
Iuka MS 400/5-8
507 W Quitman St 38852 662-423-3316
Jimmy Smith, prin. Fax 423-2426
Other Schools – See Belmont, Burnsville, Tishomingo

Jackson, Hinds, Pop. 177,977
Hinds County SD
Supt. — See Raymond
Gary Road ES 600/K-2
7241 Gary Rd 39272 601-373-1319
Martha Stringer, prin. Fax 346-4165
Gary Road IS 1,000/3-5
7255 Gary Rd 39272 601-372-8150
Kim Davenport, prin. Fax 372-5028

Jackson SD 30,100/PK-12
PO Box 2338 39225 601-960-8700
Lonnie Edwards Ph.D., supt. Fax 960-8713
www.jackson.k12.ms.us
Baker Magnet ES 300/K-5
300 E Santa Clair St 39212 601-371-4327
Dr. Shauna Nicholson-Johnson, prin. Fax 371-4371
Barr ES 200/PK-5
1593 W Capitol St 39203 601-960-5336
Dr. Limmie Flowers, prin. Fax 960-5428
Blackburn MS 500/6-8
1311 W Pearl St 39203 601-960-5329
Bobby Brown, prin. Fax 360-2601
Boyd Magnet ES 400/K-5
4531 Broadmeadow Dr 39206 601-987-3504
Julia Harris Brown, prin. Fax 987-3682
Bradley ES 200/K-5
2601 Ivanhoe Ave 39213 601-987-3507
Dionne Woody, prin. Fax 987-4979
Brinkley MS 500/6-8
3535 Albermarle Rd 39213 601-987-3573
Dr. Leroy Pope, prin. Fax 987-3746
Brown ES 300/PK-5
146 E Ash St 39202 601-960-5326
Jason Sargent, prin. Fax 960-4043
Casey ES 300/K-5
2101 Lake Cir 39211 601-987-3510
Leslie Coleman, prin. Fax 987-4944
Chastain MS 1,200/6-8
4650 Manhattan Rd 39206 601-987-3550
Victor Ellis, prin. Fax 987-4930
Clausell ES 500/K-5
3330 Harley St 39209 601-960-5319
Mitchell Shears, prin. Fax 360-2693
Davis Magnet ES 300/K-5
750 N Congress St 39202 601-960-5333
Dr. Jane Everly, prin. Fax 592-2494
Dawson ES 200/K-5
4215 Sunset Dr 39213 601-987-3513
Yavonka McGee, prin. Fax 987-3683
French ES 300/K-5
311 Joel Ave 39209 601-960-5316
Sebrena Brown, prin. Fax 592-2495
Galloway ES 400/PK-5
186 Idlewild St 39203 601-960-5313
Erica Bradley, prin. Fax 360-2657
George ES 200/K-5
1020 Hunter St 39204 601-960-5339
Mary Ann Bailey, prin. Fax 360-2694
Green ES 400/K-5
610 Forest Ave 39206 601-987-3519
Marilyn Clark, prin. Fax 987-4938
Hardy MS 600/6-8
545 Ellis Ave 39209 601-960-5362
Dr. Nehru Brown, prin. Fax 360-2686
Hopkins ES 600/K-5
170 John Hopkins Rd 39209 601-923-2540
Vicki Conley, prin. Fax 923-0556
Isable ES 400/PK-5
1716 Isable St 39204 601-960-5310
Theresa Green, prin. Fax 360-2695
Johnson ES 400/PK-5
1339 Oak Park Dr 39213 601-987-3501
Faith Strong, prin. Fax 987-4971
Key ES 400/K-5
699 W Mcdowell Rd 39204 601-371-4333
Elaine Woods, prin. Fax 371-4374
Lake ES 500/PK-5
472 Mount Vernon Ave 39209 601-960-5308
Althea Johnson, prin. Fax 960-5449
Lee ES 400/K-5
330 Judy St 39212 601-371-4336
Dr. Eric Cook, prin. Fax 371-1102
Lester ES 300/K-5
2350 Oakhurst Dr 39204 601-371-4339
Dr. Douglas Scott, prin. Fax 371-4737
Marshall ES 400/K-5
2909 Oak Forest Dr 39212 601-371-4342
Tony Yarber, prin. Fax 371-4729
McLeod ES 400/K-5
1616 Sandlewood Pl 39211 601-987-3597
Courtney Sheriff, prin. Fax 956-3948
McWillie S 400/K-9
4851 McWillie Cir 39206 601-987-3709
Dr. Margrit Wallace, prin. Fax 987-4960
North Jackson ES 500/K-5
650 James M Davis Dr 39206 601-987-3528
Pamela Franklin, prin. Fax 987-4976
Northwest Jackson MS 700/6-8
7020 Highway 49 N 39213 601-987-3609
Dr. Edward Buck, prin. Fax 987-4975
Oak Forest ES 500/K-5
1831 Smallwood St 39212 601-371-4330
Michael Coco, prin. Fax 371-4702
Pecan Park ES 500/K-5
415 Claiborne Ave 39209 601-960-5444
Wanda Quon, prin. Fax 592-2490
Peeples MS 1,000/6-8
290 Treehaven Dr 39212 601-371-4345
Isaac Norwood, prin. Fax 371-4722
Poindexter ES 200/PK-5
1017 Robinson St 39203 601-960-5304
Yolanda Lloyd, prin. Fax 592-2493
Powell MS 900/6-8
3655 Livingston Rd 39213 601-987-3580
Dr. Valerie Bradley, prin. Fax 987-3583
Raines ES 300/K-5
156 N Flag Chapel Rd 39209 601-923-2544
Melissa McCray, prin. Fax 923-0555
Rowan MS 300/6-8
136 W Ash St 39202 601-960-5349
Tony Winters, prin. Fax 960-4046
Siwell Road MS 900/6-8
1983 N Siwell Rd 39209 601-923-2550
Dr. Josephine Kelly, prin. Fax 923-2570
Smith ES 400/K-5
3900 Parkway Ave 39213 601-987-3525
Mathis Sheriff, prin. Fax 987-3546
Spann ES 400/K-5
1615 Brecon Dr 39211 601-987-3532
Nicole Menotti, prin. Fax 987-3719
Sykes ES 400/K-5
3555 Simpson St 39212 601-371-4303
Eloise Jones, prin. Fax 371-4701
Timberlawn ES 500/K-5
1980 N Siwell Rd 39209 601-923-2556
Dr. Carrie Pillers, prin. Fax 923-0553
Van Winkle ES 500/K-5
1655 Whiting Rd 39209 601-923-2547
Wanda Bowen, prin. Fax 923-2566
Walton ES 600/PK-5
3200 Bailey Ave 39213 601-987-3591
Gwen Gardner, prin. Fax 987-4943
Watkins ES 400/K-5
3915 Watkins Dr 39206 601-987-3594
Dr. Michelle King, prin. Fax 987-3690
Whitten MS 800/6-8
210 Daniel Lake Blvd 39212 601-371-4309
Marvin Grayer, prin. Fax 371-4728
Wilkins ES 500/K-5
1970 Castle Hill Dr 39204 601-371-4306
Dr. Rachel Ellis, prin. Fax 371-4730
Woodville Heights ES 600/K-5
2930 Mcdowell Rd Ext 39204 601-371-4300
Amanda Thomas, prin. Fax 371-4372

Bowman S 100/PK-5
1217 Hattiesburg St 39209 601-352-5441
Ann Hardy, prin. Fax 352-5136
Christ Missionary & Industrial S 200/PK-12
PO Box 11159 39283 601-366-6413
Dr. Mary Seay, hdmstr. Fax 362-7864
Education Center S 200/1-12
4080 Old Canton Rd 39216 601-982-2812
Lynn Macon, prin. Fax 982-2827
Emmanuel Christian S 200/PK-6
1109 Cooper Rd 39212 601-371-2728
Rev. Jesse Horton, hdmstr. Fax 372-0560
First Presbyterian Church Day S 700/K-6
1390 N State St Ste A 39202 601-355-1731
Gary Herring, hdmstr. Fax 355-1739
Hillcrest Christian S 500/K-12
4060 S Siwell Rd 39212 601-372-0149
Dr. Tom Prather, hdmstr. Fax 371-8061
Jackson Academy 1,400/PK-12
PO Box 14978 39236 601-362-9676
Dr. Pat Taylor, hdmstr. Fax 364-5722
Mother Goose Christian Academy 300/PK-4
6543 Watkins Dr 39213 601-981-4678
Malcolm Cobb, hdmstr. Fax 981-4688
New Hope Christian S 300/PK-6
5202 Watkins Dr 39206 601-362-4776
Gerilynn Thomas, prin. Fax 362-0938
Rogers SDA S 50/K-8
1284 Forest Ave 39206 601-981-2648
St. Andrew's Episcopal S 500/PK-4
4120 Old Canton Rd 39216 601-987-9300
Dr. George Penick, hdmstr. Fax 987-9324
St. Richard S 500/PK-6
100 Holly Dr 39206 601-366-1157
Jules Michel, prin. Fax 366-4344
St. Therese S 100/PK-6
309 W McDowell Rd 39204 601-372-3323
Sr. Brenda Monahan, prin. Fax 372-3365
Word of Faith Academy 100/PK-7
4890 Clinton Blvd 39209 601-922-7217
Jocelyn Ford, admin. Fax 922-9337

Jonestown, Coahoma, Pop. 1,643
Coahoma County SD
Supt. — See Clarksdale
Jonestown ES 400/K-6
PO Box 26 38639 662-358-4496
Jennifer Pitts, prin. Fax 358-4491

Kilmichael, Montgomery, Pop. 735
Montgomery County SD
Supt. — See Winona
Montgomery County ES 200/K-6
PO Box 248 39747 662-262-4912
Patricia Cox, prin. Fax 262-4912

Kiln, Hancock, Pop. 1,262
Hancock County SD 4,400/K-12
17304 Highway 603 39556 228-255-0376
Alan Dedeaux, supt. Fax 255-0378
www.hancock.k12.ms.us
East Hancock ES 600/K-5
4221 Kiln Delisle Rd 39556 228-255-6637
Charles Rolison, prin. Fax 255-8372
Hancock MS 1,000/6-8
7070 Stennis Airport Rd 39556 228-467-1889
Dane Aube, prin. Fax 467-2812
Hancock North Central ES 700/K-5
6122 Cuevas Town Rd 39556 228-255-7641
Haleigh Cuevas, prin. Fax 255-1580
Other Schools – See Bay Saint Louis, Picayune

Kosciusko, Attala, Pop. 7,334
Attala County SD 1,300/PK-12
100 Courthouse Ste 3 39090 662-289-2801
Larry Stevens, supt. Fax 289-2804
www.attala.k12.ms.us/
Other Schools – See Mc Cool, Sallis

Kosciusko SSD 1,900/K-12
229 W Washington St 39090 662-289-4771
Dr. David Sistrunk, supt. Fax 289-1177
Kosciusko JHS 500/6-8
229 W Washington St 39090 662-289-3737
Patrick Henderson, prin. Fax 289-1177
Kosciusko Lower ES 200/K-1
229 W Washington St 39090 662-289-3364
Michelle Brown, prin. Fax 289-3364
Kosciusko Middle ES 300/2-3
229 W Washington St 39090 662-289-4653
Robert Simpson, prin. Fax 289-4653
Kosciusko Upper ES 300/4-5
229 W Washington St 39090 662-289-2264
Presley Tate, prin. Fax 289-2264

Presbyterian Day S 100/PK-8
603 Smythe St 39090 662-289-3322
Samuel LeVert, admin. Fax 289-3009

Lake, Newton, Pop. 404
Scott County SD
Supt. — See Forest
Lake Attendance Center 500/K-12
24442 Highway 80 39092 601-775-3248
Randy Martin, prin. Fax 775-3861
Lake MS 200/5-8
1770 E Scott Rd 39092 601-775-3614
Kathy Myers, prin. Fax 775-8830

Lake Cormorant, DeSoto
DeSoto County SD
Supt. — See Hernando

Lake Cormorant ES K-6
3285 Wilson Mill Rd 38641 662-781-1135
Thomas Spencer, prin.

Lambert, Quitman, Pop. 1,818
Quitman County SD
Supt. — See Marks
Quitman County ES 400/K-4
PO Box 175 38643 662-326-7186
Lela Westbrooks, prin. Fax 326-2494

Laurel, Jones, Pop. 18,298
Jones County SD
Supt. — See Ellisville
East Jones ES 700/K-6
108 Northeast Dr 39443 601-425-9799
Becky Stewart, prin. Fax 425-9118
Glade ES 400/K-6
990 Highway 15 S 39443 601-428-4265
Steve Musgrove, prin. Fax 425-5690
North Jones ES, 650 Trace Rd 39443 K-6
Robert Hill, prin. 601-426-6632
West Jones ES 800/K-6
5652 Highway 84 W 39443 601-763-4850
Mark Reddoch, prin. Fax 763-4853

Laurel SD 2,900/PK-12
PO Box 288 39441 601-649-6391
Dr. Glenn McGee, supt. Fax 649-6398
www.laurelschools.org
Davis Magnet ES 400/PK-6
1305 Martin Luther King Dr 39440 601-428-7782
Elaine Read, prin. Fax 425-3692
Jones MS 500/7-8
1125 N 5th Ave 39440 601-428-5312
Carl Michael Day, prin. Fax 426-6775
Mason ES 500/K-6
2726 Old Bay Springs Rd 39440 601-428-0393
David Jones, prin. Fax 649-2751
Oak Park Magnet S 600/PK-6
1205 Queensburg Ave 39440 601-428-5046
Jaymar Jackson, prin. Fax 649-6342
Stainton ES 400/K-6
795 S 19th Ave 39440 601-426-6437
Ruby Lovett, prin. Fax 649-2954

Laurel Christian S 400/PK-12
PO Box 8425 39441 601-649-3999
Rick Bartley, hdmstr. Fax 649-1027
St. Johns S 200/PK-6
520 N 5th Ave 39440 601-428-4350
Ronnie Jones, prin. Fax 428-0419

Leakesville, Greene, Pop. 1,007
Greene County SD 1,900/K-12
PO Box 1329 39451 601-394-2364
Richard Fleming, supt. Fax 394-5542
www.greene.k12.ms.us/
Leakesville ES 400/K-4
175 Annex Rd 39451 601-394-2493
Debbie McLeod, prin. Fax 394-5548
Leakesville JHS 300/5-8
PO Box 1479 39451 601-394-2495
Chris West, prin. Fax 394-5690
Other Schools – See Mc Lain, Richton

Learned, Hinds, Pop. 47

Rebul Academy 100/PK-12
5257 Learned Rd 39154 601-885-6802
Jack Rice, hdmstr. Fax 885-9550

Leland, Washington, Pop. 5,157
Leland SD 1,100/K-12
408 4th St 38756 662-686-5000
Ilean Richards, supt. Fax 686-5029
www2.mde.k12.ms.us/7612/
Leland ES 300/K-5
406 E 3rd St 38756 662-686-5013
Veronica Parish, prin. Fax 686-5043
Leland School Park S 500/1-8
200 Milam St 38756 662-686-5017
Gloria McCray, prin. Fax 686-5042

Lexington, Holmes, Pop. 1,941
Holmes County SD 2,700/K-12
PO Box 630 39095 662-834-2175
Powell Rucker, supt. Fax 834-9060
holmes.k12.ms.us/
Lexington ES 600/K-5
PO Box 309 39095 662-834-1333
Pearl Mabry, prin. Fax 834-4581
Marshall ES 400/K-5
12572 Highway 51 39095 662-235-5226
Bernell Saffold, prin. Fax 235-4895
McClain MS 400/6-8
PO Box 270 39095 662-834-0875
Shawn Terrell, prin. Fax 834-0617
Other Schools – See Durant, Goodman, Tchula

Central Holmes Christian S 200/PK-12
130 Robert E Lee Dr 39095 662-834-3011
Terry Cox, hdmstr. Fax 834-1011

Liberty, Amite, Pop. 686
Amite County SD 1,300/K-12
PO Box 378 39645 601-657-4361
Deborah Hopf, supt. Fax 657-4291
www.amite.k12.ms.us/
Liberty S 500/K-8
PO Box 308 39645 601-657-8311
William Brabham, prin. Fax 657-4365
Other Schools – See Gloster

Amite School Center 300/K-12
PO Box 354 39645 601-657-8896
Dan Brewer, hdmstr. Fax 657-4642

Long Beach, Harrison, Pop. 17,283
Long Beach SD 2,800/K-12
19148 Commission Rd 39560 228-864-1146
Carrolyn Hamilton, supt. Fax 863-3196
www.lbsdk12.com
Harper McCaughan ES 400/K-5
113 Quarles St 39560 228-863-0478
Eddie Holmes, prin. Fax 867-1786
Long Beach MS 700/6-8
204 N Cleveland Ave 39560 228-864-3370
Mary Jean Harvey, prin. Fax 867-1789
Quarles ES 400/K-5
111 Quarles St 39560 228-864-3946
Ken Sims, prin. Fax 868-6448
Reeves ES 400/K-5
214 St Augustine Dr 39560 228-864-9764
Lori Price, prin. Fax 867-1787

Coast Episcopal S 200/PK-6
5065 Espy Ave 39560 228-452-9442
Jim Seidule, hdmstr. Fax 452-9446
St. Vincent DePaul S 300/PK-6
4321 Espy Ave 39560 228-863-6876
Elizabeth Fortenberry, prin. Fax 863-9537

Louisville, Winston, Pop. 6,797
Louisville Municipal SD 2,700/K-12
PO Box 909 39339 662-773-3411
Harry Kemp, supt. Fax 773-4013
louisville.k12.ms.us/
Eiland MS 300/7-8
508 Camille Ave 39339 662-773-9001
James Brooks, prin. Fax 773-4016
Fair ES 400/K-3
310 N Columbus Ave 39339 662-773-5946
Penny Hill, prin. Fax 773-4012
Louisville ES 400/4-6
300 N Columbus Ave 39339 662-773-3258
Ella Smith, prin. Fax 773-4015
Waiya S 500/K-12
13937 Highway 397 39339 662-773-6770
Fax 773-6764
Other Schools – See Noxapater

Grace Christian S 100/PK-12
173 McLeod Rd 39339 662-773-8524
James Gregory, hdmstr. Fax 773-4308
Winston Academy 400/PK-12
PO Box 545 39339 662-773-3569
Farrell Rigby, prin. Fax 773-8373

Lucedale, George, Pop. 2,890
George County SD 4,100/K-12
5152 Main St 39452 601-947-6993
Dr. Barbara Massey, supt. Fax 947-8805
www.gcsd.us
Agricola ES 400/K-5
6165 Highway 613 39452 601-947-8447
Teresa Lawrence, prin. Fax 947-8218
Benndale ES 200/K-5
5204 Highway 26 W 39452 601-766-6341
Sheila Bexley, prin. Fax 945-2938
Central ES 500/K-5
14159 Highway 26 W 39452 601-947-2429
Kathy Sellers, prin. Fax 947-1421
George County MS 1,000/6-8
330 Church St 39452 601-947-3106
Patsy Horn, prin. Fax 947-6004
Lucedale ES 300/K-3
689 Church St 39452 601-947-3110
Tanya Beech, prin. Fax 947-9548
Lucedale IS 200/4-5
159 Mable St 39452 601-947-6065
Tony Williams, prin. Fax 947-6127
Rocky Creek ES 400/K-5
2183 Rocky Creek Rd 39452 601-947-3886
Roger McLeod, prin. Fax 766-9662

Lumberton, Lamar, Pop. 2,476
Lamar County SD
Supt. — See Purvis
Baxterville S 200/K-8
5531 Highway 13 39455 601-796-4483
Martha Smith, prin. Fax 796-5933

Lumberton SD 800/K-12
PO Box 551 39455 601-796-2441
Dr. Robert Walker, supt. Fax 796-2051
www.lumberton.k12.ms.us/
Lumberton S 600/K-8
PO Box 551 39455 601-796-3721
Dr. Linda Smith, prin. Fax 796-7903

Bass Christian S 50/1-8
74 Maranatha Cir 39455 601-794-8867

Lyon, Coahoma, Pop. 391
Coahoma County SD
Supt. — See Clarksdale
Lyon ES 300/K-6
2020 Roberson Rd 38645 662-624-8544
Sherley Fields, prin. Fax 624-8544

Mc Comb, Pike, Pop. 11,957
McComb SD 2,700/K-12
PO Box 868, 601-684-4661
Therese Palmertree, supt. Fax 249-4732
www.mccomb.k12.ms.us
Denman JHS 500/7-8
1211 Louisiana Ave, 601-684-2387
Larry Holmes, prin. Fax 249-3564
Higgins MS 500/5-6
1000 Elmwood St, 601-684-2038
Kelli Little, prin. Fax 249-4734
Kennedy ES 400/3-4
207 S Myrtle St, 601-684-2889
Katrina Hines, prin. Fax 249-4739

Otken ES 500/K-2
401 Montana Ave, 601-684-3749
Camita Nobles, prin. Fax 684-8304

Parklane Academy 900/K-12
1115 Parklane Dr, 601-684-7841
Fax 684-4166
St. Alphonsus S 200/PK-7
104 S 5th St, 601-684-1843
Tammy Mabile, prin. Fax 684-1831

Mc Cool, Attala, Pop. 167
Attala County SD
Supt. — See Kosciusko
Greenlee ES 400/PK-6
26050 Highway 12 39108 662-674-5263
Bryan Weaver, prin. Fax 674-5936

Mc Lain, Greene, Pop. 603
Greene County SD
Supt. — See Leakesville
Mc Lain S 200/K-8
PO Box 39 39456 601-753-2257
Charles Breland, prin. Fax 753-2237

Macon, Noxubee, Pop. 2,353
Noxubee County SD 2,100/PK-12
PO Box 540 39341 662-726-4527
Kevin Jones Ed.D., supt. Fax 726-2809
www.noxcnty.k12.ms.us
Liddell MS 500/5-8
PO Box 229 39341 662-726-4880
Dr. Pat Johnson-Scott, prin. Fax 726-5044
Nash ES 500/PK-4
PO Box 391 39341 662-726-5203
Lorene Cannon, prin. Fax 726-3431
Other Schools – See Brooksville, Shuqualak

Central Academy 200/PK-12
PO Box 231 39341 662-726-4817
Scott Wasdin, hdmstr. Fax 726-9711

Madden, Leake

Leake Academy 600/PK-12
PO Box 128 39109 601-267-4461
Jerry Crowe, hdmstr. Fax 267-6933

Madison, Madison, Pop. 16,737
Madison County SD
Supt. — See Flora
Madison Avenue Lower ES 400/K-2
1199 Madison Ave 39110 601-856-2951
Brenda Jones, prin. Fax 853-2726
Madison Avenue Upper ES 600/3-5
1209 Madison Ave 39110 601-856-6609
Rick Ross, prin. Fax 856-7679
Madison MS 1,300/6-8
1365 Mannsdale Rd 39110 601-605-4171
Ron Morrison, prin. Fax 853-2254
Madison Station ES 1,100/K-5
459 Reunion Pkwy 39110 601-856-6246
Beverly Johnston, prin. Fax 856-5321

Assisi Early Learning Center 200/PK-PK
4000 W Tidewater Ln 39110 601-856-9494
Sr. Paula Blouin, dir. Fax 856-2849
Madison Ridgeland Academy 800/K-12
7601 Old Canton Rd 39110 601-856-4455
Tommy Thompson, hdmstr. Fax 853-3835

Magee, Simpson, Pop. 4,294
Simpson County SD
Supt. — See Mendenhall
Magee ES 600/K-4
410 8th St NE 39111 601-849-3601
Ken Barron, prin. Fax 849-6207
Magee MS 500/5-8
300 1st St NE 39111 601-849-3334
Terrell Luckey, prin. Fax 849-6130

Magnolia, Pike, Pop. 2,079
South Pike SD 1,900/K-12
250 W Bay St 39652 601-783-0430
Dr. Bill Gunnell, supt. Fax 783-6733
www.southpike.org
Gordon ES 400/K-3
1175 N Clark Ave 39652 601-783-0434
Connie McNabb, prin. Fax 783-2055
Magnolia ES 300/4-6
1147 N Clark Ave 39652 601-783-0432
Blake Brewer, prin. Fax 783-2231
South Pike JHS 300/7-8
275 W Myrtle St 39652 601-783-0425
Joe Leavy, prin. Fax 783-2272
Other Schools – See Osyka

Mantachie, Itawamba, Pop. 1,134
Itawamba County SD
Supt. — See Fulton
Mantachie ES 600/PK-6
PO Box 38 38855 662-282-7536
Jamie Dill, prin. Fax 282-7167

Marietta, Prentiss, Pop. 248
Prentiss County SD
Supt. — See Booneville
Marietta S 300/K-8
42 County Road 4070 38856 662-728-4770
Sonya Thompson, prin. Fax 728-0965

Marks, Quitman, Pop. 1,893
Quitman County SD 1,100/K-12
PO Box E 38646 662-326-5451
Valmadge Towner, supt. Fax 326-3694
www.qcschools.org
Quitman County MS 300/5-8
PO Box 290 38646 662-326-6871
Roosevelt Ramsey, prin. Fax 326-6300

Other Schools – See Lambert

Delta Academy 200/PK-12
PO Box 70 38646 662-326-8164
Shirley Morris, admin. Fax 326-3201

Mathiston, Webster, Pop. 716
Webster County SD
Supt. — See Eupora
East Webster ES 500/K-6
230 South St 39752 662-263-8373
Jim Ray, prin. Fax 263-8386

Meadville, Franklin, Pop. 508
Franklin County SD 1,300/PK-12
PO Box 605 39653 601-384-2340
Grady Fleming Ph.D., supt. Fax 384-2393
www2.mde.k12.ms.us/1900/index.htm
Franklin Lower ES 300/PK-2
481 Highway 98 E 39653 601-384-5605
Marsha Webb, prin. Fax 384-3078
Franklin MS 300/6-8
236 Edison St S 39653 601-384-2441
Karen Tutor, prin. Fax 384-2085
Franklin Upper ES 300/3-5
409 Highway 98 E 39653 601-384-2940
Janet Carlock, prin. Fax 384-5885

Mendenhall, Simpson, Pop. 2,544
Simpson County SD 3,900/K-12
111 Education Ln 39114 601-847-8000
Joe Welch, supt. Fax 847-8001
www.simpson.k12.ms.us
Mendenhall ES 500/K-4
101 Circle Dr 39114 601-847-2621
Kathy Swalm, prin. Fax 847-7192
Mendenhall JHS 500/5-8
733 Dixie Ave 39114 601-847-2296
Janice Skiffer, prin. Fax 847-7175
Other Schools – See Magee, Pinola

Simpson County Academy 500/K-12
124 Academy Cir 39114 601-847-1395
Jack Henderson, prin. Fax 847-1338

Meridian, Lauderdale, Pop. 38,605
Lauderdale County SD 6,000/PK-12
PO Box 5498 39302 601-693-1683
Randy Hodges, supt. Fax 485-1748
www.lauderdale.k12.ms.us
Clarkdale S 900/K-12
7000 Highway 145 39301 601-693-4463
Cheryl Thomas, prin. Fax 483-6329
Northeast Lauderdale ES 700/PK-4
6750 Newell Rd 39305 601-485-4882
Teri Edwards, prin. Fax 482-5198
Northeast MS 700/5-8
7763 Highway 39 39305 601-483-3532
Billy Burnham, prin. Fax 485-0846
Southeast ES 500/K-4
2362 Long Creek Rd 39301 601-486-2500
Ryan Powell, prin. Fax 486-2515
Southeast MS 400/5-8
2535 Old Highway 19 SE 39301 601-485-5751
Kenny Neal, prin. Fax 485-2302
West Lauderdale ES 600/K-4
10350 Highway 495 39305 601-737-2279
Larry Vick, prin. Fax 737-8962

Meridian SD 5,000/K-12
PO Box 31 39302 601-483-6271
Charlie Kent, supt. Fax 484-4917
www.mpsd.k12.ms.us
Carver MS 400/6-7
900 44th Ave 39307 601-484-4487
Martha Walker, prin. Fax 484-3011
Crestwood ES 400/K-5
730 Crestwood Dr 39301 601-484-4971
Rhonda Holloman, prin. Fax 484-5194
Harris ES 400/K-5
3951 12th St 39307 601-484-4464
Wanda Kendrick, prin. Fax 484-4994
Magnolia MS 600/6-8
1350 24th St 39301 601-484-4060
Jonas Crenshaw, prin. Fax 484-5179
Northwest JHS 300/6-8
4400 32nd St 39307 601-484-4094
Kimberly Kendrick, prin. Fax 484-5180
Oakland Heights ES 600/K-5
601 59th Ave 39307 601-484-4983
Rosalind Operton, prin. Fax 484-4986
Parkview ES 400/K-5
1225 26th St 39305 601-484-4990
Lisa Barfield, prin. Fax 484-5192
Poplar Springs ES 400/K-5
4101 27th Ave 39305 601-484-4450
LaVonda Germany, prin. Fax 484-5189
West Hills ES 500/K-5
4100 32nd St 39307 601-484-4472
Owida Stuart, prin. Fax 484-5188

Calvary Christian S 200/PK-12
3917 7th St 39307 601-483-2305
Keith May, hdmstr. Fax 482-5376
Community Christian S 50/K-8
6256 Highway 39 N 39305 601-485-4515
Marie Knowles, prin. Fax 485-0715
Lamar S 500/PK-12
544 Lindley Rd 39305 601-482-1345
John Stephens, admin. Fax 482-7202
Russell Christian Academy PK-12
1844D Highway 11 And 80 39301 601-484-5888
Joey Knight, hdmstr. Fax 492-4054
St. Patrick S 100/PK-6
2700 Davis St 39301 601-482-6044
Julie Bordelon, prin. Fax 485-2762

Mize, Smith, Pop. 283
Smith County SD
Supt. — See Raleigh
Mize S 800/K-12
PO Box 187 39116 601-733-2242
David Burris, prin. Fax 733-2243

Monticello, Lawrence, Pop. 1,724
Lawrence County SD 2,200/K-12
346 Thomas E Jolly Dr W 39654 601-587-2506
Tony Davis, supt. Fax 587-2221
www.lawrence.k12.ms.us
Monticello ES 400/K-4
PO Box 339 39654 601-587-7609
Cindy Carr, prin. Fax 587-4167
Paige MS 400/5-8
1570 W Broad St 39654 601-587-2128
Dr. Lenard King, prin. Fax 587-7178
Topeka-Tilton S 300/K-8
853 Highway 27 39654 601-587-4895
John Bull, prin. Fax 587-2367
Other Schools – See Newhebron

Mooreville, Lee
Lee County SD
Supt. — See Tupelo
Mooreville ES 600/K-5
PO Box 60 38857 662-844-7105
Jimmy Weeks, prin. Fax 844-0777
Mooreville MS 400/6-8
PO Box 60 38857 662-680-4894
Craig Cherry, prin. Fax 680-4896

Moorhead, Sunflower, Pop. 2,472
Sunflower County SD
Supt. — See Indianola
Moorhead MS 100/6-8
PO Box 749 38761 662-246-5680
Miskia Davis, prin. Fax 246-5080
Rosser ES 300/K-5
PO Box 628 38761 662-246-5395
Angela Winters, prin. Fax 246-8018

Morton, Scott, Pop. 3,441
Scott County SD
Supt. — See Forest
Jack Upper MS 500/5-8
PO Box 500 39117 601-732-6977
Tanya Walker, prin. Fax 732-2242
Morton ES 500/K-4
265 E Second Ave 39117 601-732-8529
John Johnson, prin. Fax 732-1781

Moselle, Jones
Jones County SD
Supt. — See Ellisville
Moselle ES 500/K-6
PO Box 249 39459 601-582-7586
Edward Crosby, prin. Fax 582-7587

Moss Point, Jackson, Pop. 15,125
Jackson County SD
Supt. — See Vancleave
East Central MS 700/6-8
5404 Hurley Wade Rd 39562 228-588-7009
R. L. Watson, prin. Fax 588-7043

Moss Point SD 3,200/PK-12
4924 Church St 39563 228-475-0691
Lt. Col. Kim Staley, supt. Fax 474-3302
www.mosspointschools.org/
East Park ES 300/PK-6
4924 Church St 39563 228-475-9866
Evelyn Murphy, prin. Fax 474-7245
Hyatt ES 200/K-6
4924 Church St 39563 228-475-2171
Tommy Molden, prin. Fax 474-3395
Kreole ES 400/PK-6
4924 Church St 39563 228-475-3719
Tonya Hall, prin. Fax 474-3312
Magnolia JHS 500/7-8
4924 Church St 39563 228-475-1429
Robert Likely, prin. Fax 474-3397
Orange Lake ES 100/K-6
4924 Church St 39563 228-474-7377
Icyo Tolbert, prin. Fax 474-3308
West ES 200/PK-6
4924 Church St 39563 228-475-5656
Searcy Kay, prin. Fax 474-3307
Other Schools – See Escatawpa

Mound Bayou, Bolivar, Pop. 2,018
Mound Bayou SD 700/K-12
301 E Martin Luther King St 38762 662-741-2555
William Crockett, supt. Fax 741-2726
mbpsd.com/
Montgomery ES 300/K-6
PO Box 901 38762 662-741-2433
Willie Norwood, prin. Fax 741-2578

Mount Olive, Covington, Pop. 900
Covington County SD
Supt. — See Collins
Mt. Olive S 500/K-12
PO Box 309 39119 601-797-3939
Clay Anglin, prin. Fax 797-3980

Myrtle, Union, Pop. 558
Union County SD
Supt. — See New Albany
Myrtle S 600/K-12
1008 Hawk Ave 38650 662-988-2416
Vince Jordan, prin. Fax 988-2001
West Union S 600/K-12
1610 State Road 30 W 38650 662-534-4982
Paul Correro, prin. Fax 534-6716

Natchez, Adams, Pop. 16,966
Natchez-Adams SD 3,800/PK-12
10 Homochitto St 39120 601-445-2800
Dr. Anthony Morris, supt. Fax 445-2818
www.natchez.k12.ms.us/
Frazier PS 700/1-2
1445 George F West Sr Blvd 39120 601-445-2885
Vera Dunmore, prin. Fax 445-2497
Lewis MS 700/7-8
1221 N Dr ML King Jr St 39120 601-445-2927
Sekufele Lewanika, prin. Fax 445-2966
McLaurin ES 600/3-4
170 Sgt Prentiss Dr 39120 601-445-2953
Alice Morrison, prin. Fax 445-3003
Morgantown ES 600/5-6
101 Cottage Home Dr 39120 601-445-2917
Fred Marsalis, prin. Fax 445-2912
West PS 100/PK-K
161 Lewis Dr 39120 601-445-2891
Cynthia Idom, prin. Fax 445-3010

Adams County Christian S 400/PK-12
300 Chinquapin Ln 39120 601-442-1422
William Wade, admin. Fax 442-1477
Cathedral Unit S 600/PK-12
701 N Dr ML King Jr St 39120 601-442-2531
Patrick Sanguinetti, prin. Fax 442-0960
Holy Family ECC 100/PK-PK
8 Orange Ave 39120 601-442-3947
Ira Young, dir. Fax 442-3973
Trinity Episcopal Day S 400/PK-12
1 Mallan G Morgan Dr 39120 601-442-5424
Dr. Delecia Carey, hdmstr. Fax 442-3216

Nettleton, Itawamba, Pop. 2,019
Nettleton SD 1,200/K-12
PO Box 409 38858 662-963-2151
James Malone, supt. Fax 963-7407
www.nettletonschools.com/
Nettleton MS 500/4-8
PO Box 409 38858 662-963-7406
Van Ross, prin. Fax 963-7407
Nettleton PS 300/K-3
PO Box 409 38858 662-963-2360
Jennifer King, prin. Fax 963-7413

New Albany, Union, Pop. 8,009
New Albany SD 1,900/K-12
301 State Highway 15 N 38652 662-534-1800
Charles Garrett Ed.D., supt. Fax 534-3608
www.newalbany.k12.ms.us
New Albany ES 900/K-5
874 Sam T Barkley Dr 38652 662-534-1840
Lance Evans, prin. Fax 534-1843
New Albany MS 500/6-8
400 Apple St 38652 662-534-1820
Lecia Stubblefield, prin. Fax 534-1819

Union County SD 2,600/K-12
PO Box 939 38652 662-534-1960
Ken Basil, supt. Fax 534-1961
www.union.k12.ms.us
Ingomar S 600/K-12
1384 County Road 101 38652 662-534-2680
Kenny Roberts, prin. Fax 534-3624
Other Schools – See Blue Springs, Myrtle

New Augusta, Perry, Pop. 696
Perry County SD 1,400/K-12
PO Box 137 39462 601-964-3211
Gregory Dearman, supt. Fax 964-8204
www.perry.k12.ms.us/
New Augusta S 300/K-8
PO Box 197 39462 601-964-3226
Kevin Britt, prin. Fax 964-3229
Other Schools – See Beaumont, Petal

Newhebron, Lawrence, Pop. 381
Lawrence County SD
Supt. — See Monticello
New Hebron S 400/K-8
120 Main Avenue Ext 39140 601-694-2151
Ronnie Morgan, prin. Fax 587-2799

Newton, Newton, Pop. 3,700
Newton Municipal SD 1,000/K-12
205 School St 39345 601-683-2451
May Garvin, supt. Fax 683-7131
www.nmsd.k12.ms.us
Newton ES 400/K-4
301 W Tatum St 39345 601-683-3979
Barbara Ware, prin. Fax 683-7138
Pilate MS 300/5-8
531 E Church St 39345 601-683-3926
Shannon Ruffin, prin. Fax 683-7139

Nicholson, Pearl River
Picayune SD
Supt. — See Picayune
Nicholson ES 500/K-6
PO Box 919 39463 601-798-6309
Patrick Rutherford, prin. Fax 798-1558

North Carrollton, Carroll, Pop. 475
Carroll County SD
Supt. — See Carrollton
Marshall ES 400/K-6
PO Box 130 38947 662-237-6840
Laura Curry, prin. Fax 237-0080

Noxapater, Winston, Pop. 415
Louisville Municipal SD
Supt. — See Louisville
Noxapater S 400/K-12
220 W Alice St 39346 662-724-4241
Susan Stone, prin. Fax 724-4240

Ocean Springs, Jackson, Pop. 17,783
Jackson County SD
Supt. — See Vancleave

St. Martin ES East 500/K-3
7508 Rose Farm Rd 39564 228-875-3204
Judith Moore, prin. Fax 875-3155
St. Martin MS 500/6-8
10900 Yellow Jacket Rd 39564 228-818-4833
Stephanie Gruich, prin. Fax 818-0198
St. Martin Upper ES 500/4-5
10910 Yellow Jacket Rd 39564 228-818-2849
Valerie Martino, prin. Fax 818-0425

Ocean Springs SD 4,900/K-12
PO Box 7002 39566 228-875-7706
Robert Hirsch, supt. Fax 875-7708
www.ossdms.org/
Magnolia Park ES 600/K-4
PO Box 7002 39566 228-875-4263
Jeanne Lewis, prin. Fax 872-0017
Oak Park ES 500/K-4
PO Box 7002 39566 228-875-5847
Julia Platt, prin. Fax 875-3496
Ocean Springs MS 1,200/6-8
PO Box 7002 39566 228-872-6210
Jerry Twiggs, prin. Fax 872-9850
Pecan Park ES 500/K-4
PO Box 7002 39566 228-875-2851
Judy Illich, prin. Fax 875-0547
Taconi ES 400/5-5
PO Box 7002 39566 228-875-4367
Susan Dollar, prin. Fax 872-5048

St. Alphonsus S 300/PK-6
504 Jackson Ave 39564 228-875-5329
Dr. Pamala Rogers, prin. Fax 875-3584
St. John's Episcopal Preschool 100/PK-K
611 Rayburn Ave 39564 228-872-3343
Fax 875-4485

Okolona, Chickasaw, Pop. 2,955
Okolona SSD 800/K-12
105 N Church St 38860 662-447-2353
Paul Dobbs, supt. Fax 447-9955
okolona.k12.ms.us/
Okolona ES 400/K-6
411 W Main St 38860 662-447-5406
Ellis Orange, prin. Fax 447-2700

Olive Branch, DeSoto, Pop. 27,964
DeSoto County SD
Supt. — See Hernando
Center Hill ES 500/K-5
13662 Center Hill Rd 38654 662-890-7705
Rebecca Dearden, prin. Fax 890-7679
Chickasaw ES 600/2-3
6391 Chickasaw Dr 38654 662-895-6664
Selina Baker, prin. Fax 893-3434
Lewisburg ES 800/K-5
1717 Craft Rd 38654 662-895-8750
Gloria Hopkins, prin. Fax 895-8754
Olive Branch ES 200/K-1
9549 Pigeon Roost Rd 38654 662-895-2256
Sunnie Barkley, prin. Fax 893-3299
Olive Branch IS 500/4-5
8631 Pigeon Roost Rd 38654 662-893-1221
Claudette Smith, prin. Fax 893-1225
Olive Branch MS 900/6-8
6530 Blocker St 38654 662-895-4610
Mike McCoy, prin. Fax 895-7358
Overpark ES 600/K-5
8530 Forest Hill Irene Ln 38654 662-890-8745
Lisa Love, prin. Fax 890-3839
Pleasant Hill ES 700/K-5
7686 Pleasant Hill Rd 38654 662-890-9654
Jamie Loper, prin. Fax 890-9659

Osyka, Pike, Pop. 496
South Pike SD
Supt. — See Magnolia
Osyka ES 300/K-6
444 Amite St 39657 601-783-0427
Dalton Williams, prin. Fax 542-5350

Oxford, Lafayette, Pop. 13,618
Lafayette County SD 2,100/PK-12
100 Commodore Dr 38655 662-234-3271
W. Michael Foster, supt. Fax 236-3019
www.gocommodores.org
Lafayette ES 400/PK-2
150 Commodore Dr 38655 662-234-5627
Margaret Boyd, prin. Fax 238-7991
Lafayette MS 600/6-8
102 Commodore Dr 38655 662-234-1664
Rodney Flowers, prin. Fax 232-8736
Lafayette Upper ES 600/3-5
120 Commodore Dr 38655 662-236-3761
Thomas Tillman, prin. Fax 234-0291

Oxford SD 2,500/PK-12
224 Bramlett Blvd 38655 662-234-3541
Kim Stasny, supt. Fax 232-2862
www.oxford.k12.ms.us
Bramlett ES 400/PK-1
225 Bramlett Blvd 38655 662-234-2685
SuzAnne Liddell, prin. Fax 236-2775
Davidson ES 200/4-5
209 Common Wealth Blvd 38655 662-236-4870
Dr. Martha McLarty, prin. Fax 236-4874
Oxford ES 500/2-3
1637 Highway 30 E 38655 662-234-3497
Evelyn Smith, prin. Fax 236-7942
Oxford MS 500/6-8
501 Mrtin Luther King Jr Dr 38655 662-234-2288
Patrick Robinson, prin. Fax 234-0235

Oxford University S 100/PK-8
2402 S Lamar Blvd 38655 662-234-2200
Tis Dean, hdmstr. Fax 234-3505
Regents S of Oxford 100/PK-10
14 County Road 130 38655 662-232-1945
Robbie Hinton, hdmstr. Fax 232-8818

Pascagoula, Jackson, Pop. 25,173
Pascagoula SD 6,400/K-12
PO Box 250 39568 228-938-6491
Wayne Rodolfich, supt. Fax 938-6528
www.psd.ms
Arlington Heights ES 300/K-5
3511 Arlington St 39581 228-938-6552
Alison Block, prin. Fax 938-6551
Beach ES 100/K-5
633 Market St 39567 228-938-6428
Shirley Hunter, prin. Fax 696-6619
Central ES 200/K-5
1100 Dupont Ave 39567 228-938-6559
Catterria Payton, prin. Fax 696-6614
Cherokee ES 300/K-5
4102 Scovel Ave 39581 228-938-6547
Tina Bankston, prin. Fax 938-6201
Colmer MS 300/7-8
3112 Eden St 39581 228-938-6473
Wanda Fishburn, prin. Fax 938-6593
Eastlawn ES 400/K-5
2611 Ingalls Ave 39567 228-938-6431
Peggy Feinberg, prin. Fax 938-6433
Jackson ES 200/K-5
3203 Lanier Ave 39581 228-938-6554
Pam Rone, prin. Fax 938-6218
Lake ES 100/K-5
4504 Willow St 39567 228-938-6422
Greta Adams, prin. Fax 696-6618
Lott Sixth Grade Academy 100/6-6
2234 Pascagoula St 39567 228-938-6465
Dr. Shannon Vincent, prin. Fax 938-6463
Other Schools – See Gautier

Gateway Christian Academy K-8
1704 Belair St 39567 228-762-4144
Danny James, admin. Fax 762-4199
Resurrection S 300/PK-6
3704 Quinn Dr 39581 228-762-7207
Elizabeth Benefield, prin. Fax 762-0611

Pass Christian, Harrison, Pop. 6,851
Harrison County SD
Supt. — See Gulfport
Pineville ES 200/K-6
5192 Menge Ave 39571 228-452-4364
Jackie Graves, prin. Fax 452-4605

Pass Christian SD 1,400/K-12
6457 Kiln Delisle Rd 39571 228-255-6200
Sue Matheson Ed.D., supt. Fax 255-6204
www.pc.k12.ms.us/
DeLisle ES 300/3-5
6303 W Wittman Rd 39571 228-255-9681
Ramona Berry, prin. Fax 255-0607
Pass Christian ES 200/K-2
6303 W Wittman Rd 39571 228-255-9681
Meredith Bang, prin. Fax 452-1122
Pass Christian MS 400/6-8
6303 W Wittman Rd 39571 228-255-6219
Joe Nelson, prin.

Pearl, Rankin, Pop. 23,111
Pearl SD 3,500/K-12
PO Box 5750 39288 601-932-7921
Dr. John Ladner, supt. Fax 932-7929
www.pearl.k12.ms.us/
Northside ES 600/2-3
3600 Harle St 39208 601-932-7971
Nikki Smith, prin. Fax 932-7984
Pearl JHS 900/6-8
200 Mary Ann Dr 39208 601-932-7952
Karen Wilson, prin. Fax 932-7998
Pearl Lower ES 300/K-1
160 Mary Ann Dr 39208 601-932-7976
Canda Jackson, prin. Fax 932-7978
Pearl Upper ES 600/4-5
180 Mary Ann Dr 39208 601-932-7981
Joan Ishee, prin. Fax 932-7983

College Drive SDA S K-8
PO Box 5476 39288 601-933-0990
Park Place Christian Academy 300/PK-12
5701 Highway 80 E 39208 601-939-6229
Preston Gordon, admin. Fax 939-3276

Pelahatchie, Rankin, Pop. 1,490
Rankin County SD
Supt. — See Brandon
Pelahatchie ES 400/K-6
PO Box 599 39145 601-854-8060
Laura Brown, prin. Fax 854-8762

East Rankin Academy 800/PK-12
PO Box 509 39145 601-854-5691
Robert Gates, hdmstr. Fax 854-5893

Perkinston, Stone
Stone County SD
Supt. — See Wiggins
Perkinston ES 400/K-5
40 2nd St 39573 601-928-3380
Gwen Miller, prin. Fax 528-6008

Petal, Forrest, Pop. 10,088
Perry County SD
Supt. — See New Augusta
Runnelstown S 400/K-8
9214 Highway 42 39465 601-544-2811
Dale Goodin, prin. Fax 584-6565

Petal SD 3,600/K-12
PO Box 523 39465 601-545-3002
Dr. John Buchanan, supt. Fax 584-4700
www.petalschools.com
Petal ES 700/K-2
1179 Highway 42 39465 601-582-7454
Sue Turner, prin. Fax 584-9400

Petal MS 900/6-8
203 Highway 42 39465 601-584-6301
Michael Hogan, prin. Fax 584-4716
Petal Upper ES 800/3-5
400 Hillcrest Loop 39465 601-584-7660
Renee Evans, prin. Fax 545-1720

Pheba, Clay

Hebron Christian S 200/K-12
6230 Henryville Rd 39755 662-494-7513
Sam Pearson, prin. Fax 494-1002

Philadelphia, Neshoba, Pop. 7,618
Neshoba County SD 2,700/K-12
PO Box 338 39350 601-656-3752
George Shaw, supt. Fax 656-3789
www.neshoba.k12.ms.us/
Neshoba Central ES 1,200/K-5
1002 Saint Francis Dr 39350 601-656-2182
Lundy Brantley, prin. Fax 656-9922
Neshoba Central MS 700/6-8
1000 Saint Francis Dr 39350 601-656-4636
Jimmy Buchanan, prin. Fax 389-2989

Philadelphia SD 1,000/K-12
248 Byrd Ave N 39350 601-656-2955
Dr. Joseph White, supt. Fax 656-3141
www.philadelphia.k12.ms.us/
Philadelphia ES 600/K-6
406 Stribling St 39350 601-656-1623
LeeAnn Fulton, prin. Fax 656-1302
Philadelphia MS 200/7-8
248 Byrd Ave N 39350 601-656-6439
Steve Eiland, prin. Fax 656-5328

Picayune, Pearl River, Pop. 10,830
Hancock County SD
Supt. — See Kiln
West Hancock ES 500/K-5
23350 Highway 43 39466 228-586-6054
Katie Warren, prin. Fax 586-6055

Picayune SD 3,600/K-12
706 Goodyear Blvd 39466 601-798-3230
Dean Shaw, supt. Fax 798-1742
www.pcu.k12.ms.us/
Picayune JHS 600/7-8
702 Goodyear Blvd 39466 601-798-5449
James Williams, prin. Fax 799-4715
Roseland Park ES 500/K-6
1610 Gilcrease Ave 39466 601-798-6824
Vicki Vaughn, prin. Fax 798-1894
South Side ES 300/3-6
1500 Rosa St 39466 601-798-1105
Debra Smith, prin. Fax 798-6032
South Side Lower ES 200/K-2
400 S Beech St 39466 601-799-0683
Joaun Lee, prin. Fax 798-6371
West Side ES 500/K-6
111 Kirkwood St 39466 601-798-3625
Pamela Pigott, prin. Fax 798-1879
Other Schools – See Nicholson

Roseland Park Baptist Church Academy 200/PK-8
2132 Highway 11 N 39466 601-798-3918
Julia Fortenberry, dir. Fax 798-3889
St. Charles Borromeo S PK-4
1020 Fifth Aye 39466 601-799-0860
Ellen Loper, prin. Fax 798-4749
Union Baptist K 100/PK-K
1628 W Union Rd 39466 601-798-6470

Pinola, Simpson
Simpson County SD
Supt. — See Mendenhall
Simpson Central S 600/K-8
755 Simpson Highway 28 W 39149 601-847-2630
Glenn Harris, prin. Fax 847-0954

Pittsboro, Calhoun, Pop. 207
Calhoun County SD 2,600/PK-12
119 W Main St 38951 662-412-3152
Mike Moore, supt. Fax 412-3157
www.calhoun.k12.ms.us/
Other Schools – See Bruce, Calhoun City, Vardaman

Plantersville, Lee, Pop. 1,318
Lee County SD
Supt. — See Tupelo
Plantersville MS 300/5-8
PO Box 129 38862 662-842-4690
Bill Horton, prin. Fax 791-0491

Pontotoc, Pontotoc, Pop. 5,784
Pontotoc CSD 2,100/K-12
140 Education Dr 38863 662-489-3336
Conwell Duke, supt. Fax 489-7932
www.pontotoc.k12.ms.us
Cox ES 400/3-4
304 Clark St 38863 662-489-2454
Chad Spence, prin. Fax 489-6239
Pontotoc ES 400/K-2
145 Fred Dowdy Ave 38863 662-489-4973
Chad Chism, prin. Fax 489-8916
Pontotoc JHS 800/5-8
132 N Main St 38863 662-489-8360
Tony Cook, prin. Fax 489-8947

Pontotoc County SD 2,900/K-12
285 Highway 15 S 38863 662-489-3932
Kenneth Roye, supt. Fax 489-3922
www.pcsd.k12.ms.us/
South Pontotoc ES 600/K-5
1523 S Pontotoc Rd 38863 662-489-5941
Anna Guntharp, prin. Fax 489-1757
South Pontotoc MS 400/6-8
1523 S Pontotoc Rd 38863 662-489-3476
Scotty Collins, prin. Fax 489-6252
Other Schools – See Ecru

Pope, Panola, Pop. 245
South Panola SD
Supt. — See Batesville
Pope S 500/K-8
PO Box 59 38658 662-563-3732
Susan Vance, prin. Fax 563-0895

Poplarville, Pearl River, Pop. 2,663
Poplarville SSD 2,000/PK-12
302 S Julia St 39470 601-795-8477
Carl Merritt, supt. Fax 795-0712
poplarvilleschools.org/
Poplarville Lower ES 400/PK-2
804 S Julia St Ste A 39470 601-795-4736
Diane Herndon, prin. Fax 795-6568
Poplarville MS 500/6-8
6 Spirit Dr 39470 601-795-1350
Leah Stevens, prin. Fax 795-1351
Poplarville Upper ES 500/3-5
1 Todd Cir 39470 601-795-8303
Lynn Payne, prin. Fax 795-3104

Port Gibson, Claiborne, Pop. 1,765
Claiborne County SD 1,700/K-12
404 Market St 39150 601-437-4232
Annie Kilcrease Ph.D., supt. Fax 437-4409
www.claiborne.k12.ms.us/
Port Gibson MS 400/6-8
PO Box 567 39150 601-437-4251
Earl Taylor, prin. Fax 437-3099
Watson ES 700/K-5
880 Anthony St 39150 601-437-5070
Curtis Ross, prin. Fax 437-3044

Potts Camp, Marshall, Pop. 509
Marshall County SD
Supt. — See Holly Springs
Reid PS 200/K-3
160 W Pontotoc Ave 38659 662-333-7774
Leigh Anne Sanderson, prin. Fax 333-7775

Prairie, Monroe
Aberdeen SD
Supt. — See Aberdeen
Prairie ES 100/6-6
10200 Highway 382 39756 662-369-6372
Angela Irvin, prin. Fax 369-0205

Prentiss, Jefferson Davis, Pop. 1,061
Jefferson Davis County SD 2,000/K-12
PO Box 1197 39474 601-792-4267
Ike Haynes, supt. Fax 792-2251
www.jeffersondavis.k12.ms.us
Johnson ES 500/K-5
PO Box 1408 39474 601-792-8338
Mary West, prin. Fax 792-2656
Other Schools – See Bassfield

Prentiss Christian S 300/K-12
PO Box 1287 39474 601-792-8549
Danny Quick, prin. Fax 792-2560

Puckett, Rankin, Pop. 354
Rankin County SD
Supt. — See Brandon
Puckett ES K-6
PO Box 40 39151 601-825-6140
Donna Bishop, prin. Fax 825-0015

Purvis, Lamar, Pop. 2,445
Lamar County SD 6,300/K-12
PO Box 609 39475 601-794-1030
Ben Burnett, supt. Fax 794-1012
www.lamar.k12.ms.us
Purvis Lower ES K-2
5976 US Highway 11 39475 601-794-3302
Rita Downs, prin. Fax 794-3317
Purvis MS 300/6-8
PO Box 549 39475 601-794-1068
Linda Greer, prin. Fax 794-1069
Purvis Upper ES 200/3-5
PO Box 1150 39475 601-794-2959
Jennifer Moore, prin. Fax 794-1036
Other Schools – See Hattiesburg, Lumberton, Sumrall

Lamar Christian S 400/PK-12
PO Box 880 39475 601-794-0016
Louis Nicolosi, admin. Fax 794-3726

Quitman, Clarke, Pop. 2,388
Quitman SD 2,000/K-12
104 E Franklin St 39355 601-776-2186
Suzanne Hawley, supt. Fax 776-1051
www.qsd.k12.ms.us/
Quitman JHS 500/6-8
501 W Lynda St 39355 601-776-6243
Minnie Dace, prin. Fax 776-1288
Quitman Lower ES 400/K-2
101 E McArthur St 39355 601-776-6156
James Bounds, prin. Fax 776-1035
Quitman Upper ES 500/3-5
300 E Franklin St 39355 601-776-6123
Vince McLemore, prin. Fax 776-1043

Raleigh, Smith, Pop. 1,257
Smith County SD 3,100/K-12
PO Box 308 39153 601-782-4296
Jimmy Hancock, supt. Fax 782-9895
www.smith.k12.ms.us/
Raleigh ES 700/K-6
201 Whiteoak Ave 39153 601-782-9507
Kelly Chandler, prin. Fax 782-9366
Other Schools – See Mize, Taylorsville

Raymond, Hinds, Pop. 1,681
Hinds County SD 6,100/K-12
13192 Highway 18 39154 601-857-5222
Dr. Stephen Handley, supt. Fax 857-8548
www.hinds.k12.ms.us/
Carver MS 200/6-8
417 Palestine St 39154 601-857-5006
Lana Clark, prin. Fax 857-4935
Raymond ES 400/K-5
417 Palestine St 39154 601-857-0213
Amanda Cook, prin. Fax 857-4156
Other Schools – See Bolton, Jackson, Terry, Utica

Central Hinds Academy 300/K-12
2894 Raymond Bolton Rd 39154 601-857-5568
Steven Harrell, hdmstr. Fax 857-5082

Redwood, Warren
Vicksburg Warren SD
Supt. — See Vicksburg
Redwood ES 400/K-6
100 Redwood Rd 39156 601-636-4885
Charles Hanks, prin. Fax 636-7815

Richland, Rankin, Pop. 7,051
Rankin County SD
Supt. — See Brandon
Richland ES 300/K-2
200 Spell Dr 39218 601-939-4375
Tanya Crain, prin. Fax 939-1991
Richland Upper ES 600/3-6
175 Wilson Dr 39218 601-939-2288
Christopher Bates, prin. Fax 939-1946

Richton, Perry, Pop. 1,008
Greene County SD
Supt. — See Leakesville
Sand Hill S 400/K-8
39455 Highway 63 N 39476 601-989-2022
John Turner, prin. Fax 394-2021

Richton SD 800/K-12
PO Box 568 39476 601-788-6581
Kyle Nobles, supt. Fax 788-9391
Richton ES 400/K-6
PO Box 568 39476 601-788-6975
Vicki Olier, prin. Fax 788-6802

Ridgeland, Madison, Pop. 21,236
Madison County SD
Supt. — See Flora
Highland ES 500/3-5
330 Brame Rd 39157 601-853-8103
Dr. Cheryl Stone, prin. Fax 853-8109
Olde Towne MS 600/6-8
210 Sunnybrook Rd 39157 601-898-8730
Allen Lawrence, prin. Fax 853-8108
Smith ES 400/K-2
306 S Pear Orchard Rd 39157 601-856-6621
Kathy Rigsby, prin. Fax 853-2043

Christ Covenant S 200/K-6
752 S Pear Orchard Rd 39157 601-978-2272
Cathy Haynie, hdmstr. Fax 957-2766

Rienzi, Alcorn, Pop. 326
Alcorn SD
Supt. — See Corinth
Rienzi ES 200/K-6
21 School St 38865 662-462-5214
Stan Platt, prin. Fax 462-5004

Ripley, Tippah, Pop. 5,633
South Tippah SD 2,500/K-12
402 Greenlee Dr 38663 662-837-7156
Frank Campbell, supt. Fax 837-1362
www.stippah.k12.ms.us/
Pine Grove S 600/K-12
3510A County Road 600 38663 662-837-7789
Tony Elliott, prin. Fax 837-8179
Ripley ES 600/K-4
702 Terry St 38663 662-837-7203
Nedra Nabors, prin. Fax 837-1480
Ripley MS 500/5-8
718 S Clayton St 38663 662-837-7959
James Storey, prin. Fax 837-0251
Other Schools – See Blue Mountain

Robinsonville, Tunica
Tunica County SD
Supt. — See Tunica
Robinsonville ES 500/PK-5
7743 Old Highway 61 N 38664 662-357-1077
Wilner Bolden, prin. Fax 357-1087

Rolling Fork, Sharkey, Pop. 2,237
South Delta SD 1,200/PK-12
PO Box 219 39159 662-873-4302
Katherine Tankson, supt. Fax 873-4198
www.sdelta.org
South Delta ES 600/PK-5
138 Weathers Ave 39159 662-873-4849
Lucille Lovette, prin. Fax 873-6104
Other Schools – See Anguilla

Sharkey Issaquena Academy 300/K-12
272 Academy Dr 39159 662-873-4241
Fax 873-4637

Rosedale, Bolivar, Pop. 2,421
West Bolivar SD 1,000/K-12
PO Box 189 38769 662-759-3525
Henry Phillips, supt. Fax 759-6795
www.wbsd.k12.ms.us/
West Bolivar ES 300/K-4
PO Box 429 38769 662-759-3823
Latanya Calhoun, prin. Fax 759-6795
West Bolivar MS 300/5-8
PO Box 159 38769 662-759-3743
Larry Johnson, prin. Fax 759-6795

Ruleville, Sunflower, Pop. 2,935
Sunflower County SD
Supt. — See Indianola
Ruleville Central ES 400/K-5
410 L F Packer Dr 38771 662-756-2548
Kathern Barber, prin. Fax 756-2622
Ruleville MS 300/6-8
PO Box 129 38771 662-756-4698
Darron Edwards, prin. Fax 756-4902

Sallis, Attala, Pop. 108
Attala County SD
Supt. — See Kosciusko
Long Creek ES 300/PK-6
9534 Highway 429 39160 662-289-1630
Dietrick Harmon, prin. Fax 289-4020

Saltillo, Lee, Pop. 3,789
Lee County SD
Supt. — See Tupelo
Saltillo ES 700/3-5
PO Box 520 38866 662-869-2211
Coke Magee, prin. Fax 869-1620
Saltillo PS 500/K-2
PO Box 1525 38866 662-869-3724
Ken Smith, prin. Fax 869-3726

Sarah, Tate
Tate County SD
Supt. — See Senatobia
Strayhorn ES 500/K-6
3402 Highway 4 W 38665 662-562-8637
MeLynda Crockett, prin. Fax 562-8631

Sardis, Panola, Pop. 2,033
North Panola SD 1,600/K-12
PO Box 334 38666 662-487-2305
Fax 487-2050
www.northpanolaschools.org
Green Hill S 400/K-5
599 W Pearl 38666 662-487-1074
Lakeldra Pride, prin. Fax 487-2057
Other Schools – See Como, Crenshaw

Saucier, Harrison
Harrison County SD
Supt. — See Gulfport
Saucier ES 500/K-6
PO Box 460 39574 228-832-2440
Cynthia Grimes, prin. Fax 831-5343
West Wortham S 1,200/K-8
20199 W Wortham Rd 39574 228-831-1276
Heather Blenden, prin. Fax 539-5962

Scooba, Kemper, Pop. 597
Kemper County SD
Supt. — See De Kalb
East Kemper ES 300/PK-6
PO Box 97 39358 662-476-8423
Carol Newton, prin. Fax 476-8001

Sebastopol, Scott, Pop. 232
Scott County SD
Supt. — See Forest
Sebastopol Attendance Center 600/K-12
PO Box 86 39359 601-625-8654
Charles Brown, prin. Fax 625-9426

Seminary, Covington, Pop. 349
Covington County SD
Supt. — See Collins
Seminary S 1,100/K-12
PO Box 34 39479 601-722-3220
Ricky Shoemake, prin. Fax 722-9543

Senatobia, Tate, Pop. 6,869
Senatobia Municipal SD 1,500/K-12
104 McKie St 38668 662-562-4897
Michael Hood, supt. Fax 562-4996
www.senatobia.k12.ms.us/
Senatobia ES 300/K-2
403 W Gilmore St 38668 662-562-9613
Cedrick Jackson, prin. Fax 562-0372
Senatobia MS 400/3-6
301 Marvin St 38668 662-562-4420
Dr. Angie Brock, prin. Fax 562-7735

Tate County SD 2,800/K-12
107 Court St 38668 662-562-5861
Gary Walker, supt. Fax 562-8516
www.tcsd.k12.ms.us/
Other Schools – See Coldwater, Independence, Sarah

Magnolia Heights S 700/K-12
1 Chiefs Dr 38668 662-562-4491
Dr. Marvin Lishman, admin. Fax 562-0386

Shannon, Lee, Pop. 1,704
Lee County SD
Supt. — See Tupelo
Shannon ES 400/3-6
PO Box 7 38868 662-767-9514
Ida Brand, prin. Fax 767-8687
Shannon MS 7-8
PO Box 8 38868 662-767-3986
Ralph Green, prin. Fax 767-9981
Shannon PS 200/K-2
PO Box 469 38868 662-767-0135
Candace Moore, prin. Fax 767-0137

Shaw, Bolivar, Pop. 2,236
Shaw SD 600/K-12
PO Box 510 38773 662-754-2611
Dr. Cederick Ellis, supt. Fax 754-2612
www2.mde.k12.ms.us/0615/shdhot.htm
McEvans S 400/K-8
PO Box 560 38773 662-754-2611
Sharita Giles, prin. Fax 754-6630

Shelby, Bolivar, Pop. 2,701
North Bolivar SD 800/K-12
PO Box 28 38774 662-398-4000
Ronzy Humphrey, supt. Fax 398-7884
www.nbsd.k12.ms.us/

Shelby MS 300/4-7
PO Box 28 38774 662-398-4020
Joe Lordi, prin. Fax 398-4039
Other Schools – See Duncan

Shuqualak, Noxubee, Pop. 547
Noxubee County SD
Supt. — See Macon
Reed ES 100/K-6
PO Box 29 39361 662-793-4544
Dr. Susie Ussery, prin. Fax 793-4793

Smithville, Monroe, Pop. 879
Monroe County SD
Supt. — See Amory
Smithville S 600/K-12
PO Box 149 38870 662-651-4276
Chad O'Brian, prin. Fax 651-4163

Southaven, DeSoto, Pop. 38,840
DeSoto County SD
Supt. — See Hernando
DeSoto Central ES 1,000/K-5
2411 Central Pkwy 38672 662-349-6234
Brenda Wilkinson, prin. Fax 349-9387
Desoto Central MS 1,000/6-8
2611 Central Pkwy 38672 662-349-6660
Chad White, prin. Fax 349-1045
Greenbrook ES 1,000/K-5
730 Rasco Rd E 38671 662-342-2330
Patricia Moore, prin. Fax 342-9227
Southaven ES 500/K-5
8274 Claiborne Dr 38671 662-342-2289
Lenore Turner, prin. Fax 280-9873
Southaven IS 3-5
175 Rasco Rd E 38671 662-253-0123
Susan Williams, prin. Fax 253-0128
Southaven MS 1,300/6-8
899 Rasco Rd W 38671 662-280-0422
Levi Williams, prin. Fax 280-3613
Sullivan ES 1,000/K-5
7985 Southaven Cir W 38671 662-393-2919
Emily Ballard, prin. Fax 393-2920

Sacred Heart S 300/PK-8
5150 Tchulahoma Rd 38671 662-349-0900
Catherine Warwick, prin. Fax 349-0690
Southern Baptist Educational Center 1,200/PK-12
7400 Getwell Rd 38672 662-349-3096
David Manley, pres. Fax 349-4962

Starkville, Oktibbeha, Pop. 22,131
Oktibbeha County SD 900/K-12
105 Dr Douglas L Conner Dr 39759 662-323-1472
James Covington, supt. Fax 323-9614
www.oktibbeha.k12.ms.us
East Oktibbeha County ES 300/K-6
1884 16th Section Rd 39759 662-323-1462
Broderick Cochran, prin. Fax 324-8463
Other Schools – See Sturgis

Starkville SD 3,600/PK-12
401 Greensboro St 39759 662-324-4050
Judy Couey, supt. Fax 324-4068
www.starkville.k12.ms.us
Armstrong MS 600/7-8
303 McKee St 39759 662-324-4070
Bob Fuller, prin. Fax 324-4075
Emerson Family S PK-PK
1504 Louisville St 39759 662-324-4155
Joan Butler, prin. Fax 324-5011
Henderson IS 300/6-6
200 Highway 82 W 39759 662-324-4100
Timothy Bourne, prin. Fax 324-6958
Overstreet ES 400/3-3
307 S Jackson St 39759 662-324-4090
Lynn Shea, prin. Fax 324-4162
Sudduth ES 700/K-2
101 Greenfield St 39759 662-324-4150
Libby Mosley, prin. Fax 324-6137
Ward-Stewart ES 600/4-5
200 Highway 82 W 39759 662-324-4160
Diane Baker, prin. Fax 324-6957

Starkville Academy 1,000/PK-12
505 Academy Rd 39759 662-323-7814
Bobby Eiland, hdmstr. Fax 323-5480
Starkville Christian S 200/PK-12
303 Lynn Ln 39759 662-323-7453
Rev. Randall Witbeck, prin. Fax 323-7571

Steens, Lowndes

Immanuel Center for Christian Education 300/PK-12
6405 Military Rd 39766 662-328-7888
Bob Williford, admin. Fax 328-7750

Stringer, Jasper
West Jasper Consolidated SD
Supt. — See Bay Springs
Stringer S 700/K-12
PO Box 68 39481 601-428-5508
Margaret Pollard, prin. Fax 426-6760

Sturgis, Oktibbeha, Pop. 188
Oktibbeha County SD
Supt. — See Starkville
West Oktibbeha ES 200/K-6
2747 Sturgis Maben Rd 39769 662-465-7956
Dr. Gale Cook, prin. Fax 465-6470

Summit, Pike, Pop. 1,603
North Pike SD 1,900/K-12
1036 Jaguar Trl 39666 601-276-2216
Dr. Ben Cox, supt. Fax 276-3666
npsd.k12.ms.us/
North Pike ES 700/K-4
1052 Jaguar Trl 39666 601-276-2646
Bobbi Dunn, prin. Fax 276-2688
North Pike MS 700/5-8
2034 Highway 44 NE 39666 601-684-3283
Danny Rushing, prin. Fax 684-3269

Sumner, Tallahatchie, Pop. 384
West Tallahatchie SD
Supt. — See Webb
Bearden ES 500/K-6
PO Box 189 38957 662-375-8304
Sherry Ellington, prin. Fax 375-7234

Sumrall, Lamar, Pop. 1,163
Lamar County SD
Supt. — See Purvis
Sumrall ES 500/K-5
198 Todd Rd 39482 601-758-4289
Danny Sumrall, prin. Fax 758-4203
Sumrall MS 300/6-8
Highway 42 39482 601-758-4416
Julie Jones, prin. Fax 758-4148

Sunflower, Sunflower, Pop. 642
Sunflower County SD
Supt. — See Indianola
East Sunflower ES 200/K-6
212 E Claiborne St 38778 662-569-3137
Minola Fields, prin. Fax 569-3309

Taylorsville, Smith, Pop. 1,297
Smith County SD
Supt. — See Raleigh
Taylorsville S 900/K-12
PO Box 8 39168 601-785-2283
Yvonne Dees, prin. Fax 785-2282

Tchula, Holmes, Pop. 2,254
Holmes County SD
Supt. — See Lexington
Mileston MS 50/6-8
147 Head Start Rd 39169 662-235-5026
Jacqueline Saffold, prin. Fax 235-5136

Terry, Hinds, Pop. 701
Hinds County SD
Supt. — See Raymond
Byram MS 1,100/6-8
2009 Byram Bulldog Blvd 39170 601-372-4597
David Campbell, prin. Fax 346-2383

Tiplersville, Tippah
North Tippah SD 1,400/K-12
PO Box 65 38674 662-223-4384
Fax 223-5379
Other Schools – See Falkner, Walnut

Tishomingo, Tishomingo, Pop. 317
Tishomingo County Special Municipal SD
Supt. — See Iuka
Tishomingo S 400/K-8
PO Box 90 38873 662-438-6800
Van Roberts, prin. Fax 438-6321

Tremont, Itawamba, Pop. 396
Itawamba County SD
Supt. — See Fulton
Tremont Attendance Center 300/K-12
PO Box 9 38876 662-652-3391
Eddie Moore, prin. Fax 652-3994

Tunica, Tunica, Pop. 1,089
Tunica County SD 2,200/PK-12
PO Box 758 38676 662-363-2811
Jerry Gentry, supt. Fax 363-3061
www.tunica.k12.ms.us/
Tunica ES 500/PK-5
PO Box 1289 38676 662-363-1442
Jeffery Blackmon, prin. Fax 363-4221
Tunica MS 500/6-8
PO Box 967 38676 662-363-4224
Glenn Rogers, prin. Fax 357-1058
Other Schools – See Dundee, Robinsonville

Tunica Institute of Learning S 100/K-12
PO Box 966 38676 662-363-1051
Don Coker, hdmstr. Fax 363-2037

Tupelo, Lee, Pop. 35,673
Lee County SD 6,100/K-12
1280 College View St 38804 662-841-9144
Mike Scott, supt. Fax 680-6012
www.leecountyschools.us/
Other Schools – See Guntown, Mooreville, Plantersville, Saltillo, Shannon, Verona

Tupelo SD 7,000/PK-12
PO Box 557 38802 662-841-8850
Dr. Randy McCoy, supt. Fax 841-8887
www.tupeloschools.com/
Carver ES 300/4-6
910 N Green St 38804 662-841-8870
Kimberly Britton, prin. Fax 841-8877
Church Street ES 300/K-3
445 N Church St 38804 662-841-8880
Kay Collins, prin. Fax 841-8861
Joyner ES 300/K-3
1201 Joyner Ave 38804 662-841-8900
Brenda Johnson, prin. Fax 841-8903
King ECC 100/PK-PK
1402 N Green St 38804 662-840-5237
Anita Buchanan, prin. Fax 842-2609
Lawhon ES 400/K-3
140 Lake St 38804 662-841-8910
Carroll Christy, prin. Fax 840-1856
Lawndale ES 600/4-6
1563 Mitchell Rd 38801 662-841-8890
Terry Harbin, prin. Fax 840-1837
Milam ES 700/4-6
720 W Jefferson St 38804 662-841-8920
Travis Beard, prin. Fax 841-8929
Parkway ES 400/K-3
628 Rutherford Rd 38801 662-844-6303
Joan Dozier, prin. Fax 841-2957
Pierce Street ES 300/K-3
1008 Pierce St 38801 662-841-8940
Dr. Debbie Davis, prin. Fax 841-8959
Rankin ES 300/K-3
1908 Forrest St 38801 662-841-8950
Glenda Scott, prin. Fax 840-1826
Thomas Street ES 300/K-3
520 S Thomas St 38801 662-841-8960
Brenda Robinson, prin. Fax 841-8965
Tupelo MS 1,100/7-8
1009 Varsity Dr 38801 662-840-8780
Linda Clifton, prin. Fax 840-1831

Tylertown, Walthall, Pop. 1,898
Walthall County SD 2,400/K-12
814A Morse Ave 39667 601-876-3401
Danny McCallum, supt. Fax 876-6982
www.wcsd.k12.ms.us/
Dexter S 300/K-12
927 Highway 48 E 39667 601-876-3985
John Stephens, prin. Fax 876-5410
Salem S 600/K-12
881 Highway 27 N 39667 601-876-2580
Charles Boyd, prin. Fax 876-4155
Tylertown Lower ES 200/3-4
705 Broad St 39667 601-876-3350
Helen Magee, prin. Fax 876-3146
Tylertown PS 300/K-2
813 Ball Ave 39667 601-876-2149
Norman Hammon, prin. Fax 876-0066
Tylertown Upper ES 300/5-6
613 Broad St 39667 601-876-3561
Christian Graves, prin. Fax 222-1508

Union, Newton, Pop. 2,102
Union SD 300/K-12
PO Box 445 39365 601-774-9579
Michael McInnis, supt. Fax 774-0600
www.unioncity.k12.ms.us/
Union ES K-4
101 Forest St 39365 601-774-8250
Gene Cliburn, prin. Fax 774-8187
Union MS 5-8
115 James St 39365 601-774-5303
Brett Rigby, prin. Fax 774-9607

Utica, Hinds, Pop. 922
Hinds County SD
Supt. — See Raymond
Utica S 500/K-8
PO Box 329 39175 601-885-8765
David Adams, prin. Fax 885-2083

Vaiden, Carroll, Pop. 856
Carroll County SD
Supt. — See Carrollton
Hathorn ES 100/K-6
PO Box 658 39176 662-464-5411
Coretta Green, prin. Fax 464-8827

Vancleave, Jackson, Pop. 3,214
Jackson County SD 7,600/K-12
PO Box 5069 39565 228-826-1757
Dr. Barry Amacker, supt. Fax 826-3393
www.jcsd.k12.ms.us/
Vancleave ES 400/K-2
12602 Highway 57 39565 228-826-5982
Amy Peterson, prin. Fax 826-2689
Vancleave MS 600/6-8
4725 Bull Dog Ln 39565 228-826-5902
Jill Davis, prin. Fax 826-1421
Vancleave Upper ES 600/3-5
13901 Highway 57 39565 228-826-4581
Penny Westfaul, prin. Fax 826-2015
Other Schools – See Biloxi, Hurley, Moss Point, Ocean Springs

Vardaman, Calhoun, Pop. 1,019
Calhoun County SD
Supt. — See Pittsboro
Vardaman ES 400/PK-6
PO Box 267 38878 662-682-7799
Deedee Lee, prin. Fax 682-7734

Vaughan, Yazoo
Yazoo County SD
Supt. — See Yazoo City
Linwood ES 300/K-6
3439 Vaughan Rd 39179 662-673-9191
Shundria Shaffer, prin. Fax 673-9163

Verona, Lee, Pop. 3,379
Lee County SD
Supt. — See Tupelo
Verona S 400/K-4
PO Box 579 38879 662-566-7266
Temeka Shannon, prin. Fax 566-4247

Vicksburg, Warren, Pop. 25,752
Vicksburg Warren SD 8,500/K-12
1500 Mission 66 39180 601-638-5122
Dr. James Price, supt. Fax 631-2819
www.vwsd.k12.ms.us
Beechwood ES 600/K-6
999 Highway 27 39180 601-638-3875
Jack Grogan, prin. Fax 631-2869
Bovina ES K-6
5 Willow Creek Dr 39183 601-619-4453
Miki Ginn, prin. Fax 619-4455
Bowmar Avenue ES 500/K-6
912 Bowmar Ave 39180 601-636-2486
Tammy Burris, prin. Fax 631-2853
Dana Road ES 500/K-3
1247 Dana Rd 39180 601-619-2340
Dr. Ethel Lassiter, prin. Fax 619-2343
Sherman Avenue ES 500/K-3
2145 Sherman Ave 39183 601-638-2409
Ray Hume, prin. Fax 638-5169

South Park ES 500/K-6
6530 Nailor Rd 39180 601-636-0176
Dr. Wanda Fears, prin. Fax 636-2501
Vicksburg IS 600/3-6
1245 Dana Rd 39180 601-638-4199
Sharon Williams, prin. Fax 638-4416
Vicksburg JHS 800/7-8
1533 Baldwin Ferry Rd 39180 601-636-1966
Michael Winters, prin. Fax 631-2830
Warren Central IS 600/3-6
2147 Sherman Ave 39183 601-638-5656
Dr. Edward Wiggins, prin. Fax 638-6358
Warren Central JHS 800/7-8
1630 Baldwin Ferry Rd 39180 601-638-3981
Cedric Magee, prin. Fax 631-2839
Warrenton ES 500/K-6
809 Belva Dr 39180 601-636-7549
Dr. Janice Hatcher, prin. Fax 638-6191
Other Schools – See Redwood

Campus Preparatory Christian S 100/K-12
400 Evans St 39180 601-631-0014
Porters Chapel Academy 200/K-12
3460 Porters Chapel Rd 39180 601-638-3733
Lynn Baker M.Ed., hdmstr. Fax 638-6311
St. Francis Xavier S 400/PK-6
1200 Hayes St 39183 601-636-4824
Jennifer Henry, prin. Fax 631-0430

Walls, DeSoto, Pop. 452
DeSoto County SD
Supt. — See Hernando
Walls ES 700/K-5
6131 Delta View Rd 38680 662-781-1280
Rebecca Kelley, prin. Fax 781-3918

Walnut, Tippah, Pop. 759
North Tippah SD
Supt. — See Tiplersville
Chalybeate S 300/K-8
PO Box 401 38683 662-223-4311
Fax 223-5362
Walnut S 500/K-12
280 Commerce Ave 38683 662-223-6471
Fax 223-5275

Walnut Grove, Leake, Pop. 1,260
Leake County SD
Supt. — See Carthage
South Leake ES 400/K-6
1280 School St 39189 601-253-2324
Jimmy Henderson, prin. Fax 253-2325

Water Valley, Yalobusha, Pop. 3,822
Water Valley SD 1,200/K-12
PO Box 788 38965 662-473-1203
Sammy Higdon, supt. Fax 473-1225
www.wvsd.k12.ms.us
Davidson ES 600/K-6
PO Box 808 38965 662-473-1110
Chester Drewrey, prin. Fax 473-2277

Waveland, Hancock, Pop. 7,227
Bay St. Louis-Waveland SD
Supt. — See Bay Saint Louis
Waveland ES 200/K-3
1101 Saint Joseph St 39576 228-467-6630
Donna Torres, prin. Fax 466-0489

Waynesboro, Wayne, Pop. 5,719
Wayne County SD 3,700/K-12
810 Chickasawhay St 39367 601-735-4871
Robert Dean, supt. Fax 735-4872
www.wayne.k12.ms.us
Beat Four S 400/K-8
5090 Highway 84 39367 601-735-2124
Belinda Singleton, prin. Fax 735-6311
Waynesboro ES 600/K-4
1022 Azalea Dr 39367 601-735-2205
Mary Jo Britton, prin. Fax 735-6314
Waynesboro MS 600/5-8
155 Wayne St 39367 601-735-3159
DeJuan Walley, prin. Fax 735-6316
Other Schools – See Buckatunna, Clara

Wayne Academy 200/K-12
PO Box 308 39367 601-735-2921
Wendell Barr, admin. Fax 735-2117

Webb, Tallahatchie, Pop. 540
West Tallahatchie SD 1,000/K-12
PO Box 129 38966 662-375-9291
Howard Hollins, supt. Fax 375-9294
www2.mde.k12.ms.us/6812/index.htm
Other Schools – See Sumner

Weir, Choctaw, Pop. 530
Choctaw County SD
Supt. — See Ackerman
Weir S 500/PK-12
351 Marion Kelley Dr 39772 662-547-7062
Glen Beard, prin. Fax 547-7074

Wesson, Copiah, Pop. 1,692
Copiah County SD
Supt. — See Hazlehurst
Wesson S 1,000/K-12
1048 Grove St 39191 601-643-2221
Ronald Greer, prin. Fax 643-2458

West Point, Clay, Pop. 11,582
Clay County SD 200/K-6
PO Box 759 39773 662-494-2915
Mae Brewer, supt. Fax 495-2050
www.clay.k12.ms.us/
Other Schools – See Cedarbluff

West Point SD 3,600/PK-12
PO Box 656 39773 662-494-4242
Steve Montgomery, supt. Fax 494-8605
www.westpoint.k12.ms.us/
Bryan Preschool 100/PK-PK
510 Calhoun St 39773 662-494-6051
Susan Watts, prin. Fax 495-6207
Central S 500/5-6
634 E Westbrook St 39773 662-495-2418
Reita Humphries, prin. Fax 494-0060
Church Hill ES 500/1-2
400 W Church Hill Rd 39773 662-494-5900
Jane Tackett, prin. Fax 495-2434
East Side K 400/K-K
813 E Broad St 39773 662-494-4691
Susan Watts, prin. Fax 495-6203
Fifth Street JHS 600/7-8
PO Box 776 39773 662-494-2191
Alvin Taylor, prin. Fax 494-2432
South Side ES 500/3-4
400 Union Dr 39773 662-495-6216
Burnell McDonald, prin. Fax 494-2434

Oak Hill Academy 500/PK-12
800 N Eshman Ave 39773 662-494-5043
Bill Miley, hdmstr. Fax 494-0487

Wheeler, Prentiss
Prentiss County SD
Supt. — See Booneville
Wheeler S 500/K-12
PO Box 98 38880 662-365-2629
Todd Swinney, prin. Fax 365-2535

Wiggins, Stone, Pop. 4,463
Stone County SD 2,400/K-12
214 Critz St N 39577 601-928-7247
James Morrison, supt. Fax 928-5122
stoneweb.stone.k12.ms.us
Stone ES 700/K-5
1652 Central Ave E 39577 601-928-5473
Jackie Spruill, prin. Fax 928-5122
Stone MS 700/6-8
532 Central Ave E 39577 601-928-4876
Mike Gavin, prin. Fax 928-6440
Other Schools – See Perkinston

Winona, Montgomery, Pop. 4,934
Montgomery County SD 400/K-12
PO Box 687 38967 662-283-4533
Sammie McCaskill, supt. Fax 283-4584
www.mcsd.ms/
Other Schools – See Kilmichael

Winona SD 1,200/K-12
218 Fairground St 38967 662-283-3731
John Buchanan Ph.D., supt. Fax 283-1003
www.winonaschools.net/
Winona ES 600/K-6
513 S Applegate St 38967 662-283-4129
Paul Lawrence, prin. Fax 283-1066

Winona Christian S 300/PK-12
1014 S Applegate St 38967 662-283-1169
James Hodges, admin. Fax 283-3333

Woodville, Wilkinson, Pop. 1,162
Wilkinson County SD 1,400/PK-12
PO Box 785 39669 601-888-3582
Timothy Scott, supt. Fax 888-3133
www2.mde.k12.ms.us/7900
Wilkinson County ES 400/PK-5
PO Box 1197 39669 601-888-4331
Frances Alexander, prin. Fax 888-6335
Other Schools – See Centreville

Wilkinson County Christian Academy 300/K-12
PO Box 977 39669 601-888-4313
Fax 888-3588

Yazoo City, Yazoo, Pop. 11,879
Yazoo City Municipal SD 2,600/PK-12
1133 Calhoun Ave 39194 662-746-2125
Rebecca Turner-Berry, supt. Fax 746-9210
www.yazoocity.k12.ms.us/
McCoy ES 700/2-4
1835 School Dr 39194 662-746-5800
Mary Golliday, prin. Fax 746-8608
Webster Street ES 300/PK-1
622 E Fourth St 39194 662-746-4093
David Starling, prin. Fax 716-0258
Woolfolk MS 900/5-8
209 E Fifth St 39194 662-746-2904
Elease Lee, prin. Fax 746-8609

Yazoo County SD 1,700/K-12
PO Box 1088 39194 662-746-4672
Dr. Jack Nicholson, supt. Fax 746-9270
www.yazoo.k12.ms.us
Yazoo County JHS 300/7-8
6781 Highway 49 Frontage Rd 39194 662-746-1596
Gloria Washington, prin. Fax 746-1616
Other Schools – See Bentonia, Vaughan

Covenant Christian S 100/K-6
PO Box 1108 39194 662-746-8855
Vicki Foster, admin. Fax 746-8887
Manchester Academy 400/PK-12
2132 Gordon Ave 39194 662-746-5913
Bryan Dendy, hdmstr. Fax 746-5108

MISSOURI

MISSOURI DEPARTMENT OF EDUCATION
PO Box 480, Jefferson City 65102-0480
Telephone 573-751-4212
Fax 573-751-1179
Website http://www.dese.mo.gov

Commissioner of Education Chris Nicastro

MISSOURI BOARD OF EDUCATION
PO Box 480, Jefferson City 65102-0480

President David Liechti

PUBLIC, PRIVATE AND CATHOLIC ELEMENTARY SCHOOLS

Adrian, Bates, Pop. 1,839
Adrian R-III SD 700/K-12
PO Box 98 64720 816-297-2710
Dr. Kirk Eidson, supt. Fax 297-2980
www.adrian.k12.mo.us/
Adrian ES 400/K-6
PO Box 98 64720 816-297-2158
Brian Borgmeyer, prin. Fax 297-2980

Advance, Stoddard, Pop. 1,216
Advance R-IV SD 400/K-12
PO Box 370 63730 573-722-3581
Michael Redman, supt. Fax 722-9886
www.advance.k12.mo.us/default.asp
Advance ES 200/K-6
PO Box 370 63730 573-722-3564
Shannon Garner, prin. Fax 722-5366

Affton, Saint Louis, Pop. 21,106

Christ Memorial Lutheran S 100/PK-PK
9712 Tesson Ferry Rd 63123 314-631-0992
Wilma Griffith, prin. Fax 631-8583

Albany, Gentry, Pop. 1,832
Albany R-III SD 500/PK-12
101 W Jefferson St 64402 660-726-3911
Bryan Prewitt, supt. Fax 726-5841
www.albany.k12.mo.us
Albany MS 100/6-8
101 W Jefferson St 64402 660-726-3912
James Boothe, prin. Fax 726-5841
George ES 200/PK-5
202 S East St 64402 660-726-5621
Sandra Seipel, prin. Fax 726-4107

Alexandria, Clark, Pop. 169
Clark County R-I SD
Supt. — See Kahoka
Running Fox ES 200/PK-5
RR 1 Box 170 63430 660-754-6766
Ryan Bergeson, prin. Fax 754-6725

Alma, Lafayette, Pop. 378
Santa Fe R-X SD 400/K-12
PO Box 197 64001 660-674-2238
Dr. Douglas Wright, supt. Fax 674-2239
schoolweb.missouri.edu/santafe.k12.mo.us/
Other Schools – See Waverly

Trinity Lutheran S 100/PK-8
PO Box 257 64001 660-674-2444
Rob Tebbenkamp, prin. Fax 674-2747

Altenburg, Perry, Pop. 315
Altenburg SD 48 100/K-8
PO Box 127 63732 573-824-5857
Bleau Deckerd, supt. Fax 824-5122
Altenburg S 100/K-8
PO Box 127 63732 573-824-5857
Bleau Deckerd, prin. Fax 824-5122

Alton, Oregon, Pop. 648
Alton R-IV SD 800/K-12
RR 2 Box 2180 65606 417-778-7216
Sheila Wheeler, supt. Fax 778-6394
www.alton.k12.mo.us/
Alton ES 400/K-6
RR 2 Box 2181 65606 417-778-7217
Shane Benson, prin. Fax 778-7865

Amazonia, Andrew, Pop. 287
Savannah R-III SD
Supt. — See Savannah
Amazonia ES 100/K-6
845 6th St 64421 816-475-2161
Aimee Addington, prin. Fax 475-2504

Amoret, Bates, Pop. 217
Miami R-I SD 200/K-12
RR 1 Box 418 64722 660-267-3480
Leonard Tourtillott, supt. Fax 267-3630
www.miami-eagles.k12.mo.us/
Miami ES 100/K-6
RR 1 Box 418 64722 660-267-3495
Mike Dorband, prin. Fax 267-3630

Anderson, McDonald, Pop. 1,902
McDonald County R-I SD 3,900/PK-12
100 Mustang Dr 64831 417-845-3321
Randall Smith, supt. Fax 845-6972
www.mcdonaldco.k12.mo.us/
Anderson ES 800/PK-6
512 Chapman St 64831 417-845-3488
Judith Harper, prin. Fax 845-7042
Anderson MS 200/7-8
100 Red Bird Ln 64831 417-845-3488
Ken Anders, prin. Fax 845-7406
Other Schools – See Noel, Pineville, Rocky Comfort, South West City

Annapolis, Iron, Pop. 298
South Iron R-I SD 400/PK-12
210 School St 63620 573-598-4241
Donald Wakefield, supt. Fax 598-4210
www.schoolweb.missouri.edu/southiron.k12.mo.us/
South Iron ES 200/PK-6
210 School St 63620 573-598-4240
Cristie Ayers, prin. Fax 598-1163

Appleton City, Saint Clair, Pop. 1,318
Appleton City R-II SD 400/K-12
408 W 4th St 64724 660-476-2161
Dr. Steve Beckett, supt. Fax 476-5564
appletoncity.k12.mo.us/
Appleton City ES 200/K-5
408 W 4th St 64724 660-476-2024
Jane Delaney, prin. Fax 476-5564

Hudson R-IX SD 100/K-8
RR 3 Box 32-1 64724 660-476-5467
Karen Warmbrodt, supt. Fax 476-5527
Hudson S 100/K-8
RR 3 Box 32-1 64724 660-476-5467
Karen Warmbrodt, prin. Fax 476-5527

Archie, Cass, Pop. 958
Archie R-V SD 600/PK-12
PO Box 106 64725 816-293-5312
Sean Smith, supt. Fax 293-5712
Cass County ES 300/PK-6
PO Box 106 64725 816-293-5312
Pam Caskey, prin. Fax 293-5712

Arnold, Jefferson, Pop. 20,413
Fox C-6 SD 11,600/PK-12
745 Jeffco Blvd 63010 636-296-8000
Dr. Dianne Brown, supt. Fax 282-5170
www.fox.k12.mo.us
Earl ECC 200/PK-PK
849 Jeffco Blvd 63010 636-282-5184
Carla Duffey, prin. Fax 282-6982
Fox ES 600/K-6
739 Jeffco Blvd 63010 636-296-3396
Lisa Sell, prin. Fax 282-1468
Fox MS 500/7-8
743 Jeffco Blvd 63010 636-296-5077
Greg Ervin, prin. Fax 282-5171
Lone Dell ES 500/PK-6
2500 Tomahawk Dr 63010 636-282-1470
Luann Domek, prin. Fax 282-1474
Meremec Heights ES 600/PK-6
1340 W Outer 21 Rd 63010 636-296-4385
Randy Gilman, prin. Fax 282-1472
Ridgewood MS 500/7-8
1401 Ridgewood School Rd 63010 636-282-1459
Kristen Pelster, prin. Fax 282-5193
Rockport Heights ES 600/K-6
3871 Jeffco Blvd 63010 636-464-2010
Janine Hueter, prin. Fax 464-0390
Sherwood ES 500/PK-6
1769 Missouri State Rd 63010 636-296-1413
Colleen Cole, prin. Fax 282-1475
Simpson ES 600/K-6
3585 Vogel Rd 63010 636-282-1480
Bryan Clark, prin. Fax 282-5174
Other Schools – See Fenton, Imperial

Holy Child S 300/PK-8
2316 Church Rd 63010 636-296-0055
Joann Coyle, prin. Fax 296-5639

St. John's Lutheran S 200/PK-8
3511 Jeffco Blvd 63010 636-464-7303
Scott Osbourn, prin. Fax 464-8424

Ash Grove, Greene, Pop. 1,491
Ash Grove R-IV SD 900/K-12
100 N Maple Ln 65604 417-751-2534
Don Christensen, supt. Fax 751-2283
www.ashgrove.k12.mo.us/
Ash Grove ES 300/K-6
100 N Maple Ln 65604 417-751-2533
Sheila Cox-Hines, prin. Fax 751-2283
Other Schools – See Bois D Arc

Ashland, Boone, Pop. 2,175
Southern Boone County R-I SD 1,400/K-12
PO Box 168 65010 573-657-2147
Charlotte Miller, supt. Fax 657-5513
schoolweb.missouri.edu/ashland.k12.mo.us/
Southern Boone County ES 300/3-5
PO Box 168 65010 573-657-2145
Brandi Fatherley, prin. Fax 657-5510
Southern Boone County MS 300/6-8
PO Box 168 65010 573-657-2146
Robert Simpson, prin. Fax 657-5519
Southern Boone County PS 300/K-2
PO Box 168 65010 573-657-2148
Scott Salmons, prin. Fax 657-4236

Atlanta, Macon, Pop. 453
Atlanta C-3 SD 200/K-12
PO Box 367 63530 660-239-4212
William Perkins, supt. Fax 239-4205
www.atlanta.k12.mo.us/
Atlanta ES 100/K-6
PO Box 367 63530 660-239-4211
Brent Doolin, prin. Fax 239-4205

Augusta, Saint Charles, Pop. 221
Washington SD
Supt. — See Washington
Augusta ES 200/PK-6
5541 Locust St 63332 636-231-2400
Stan Ponder, prin. Fax 231-2405

Aurora, Lawrence, Pop. 7,307
Aurora R-VIII SD 1,400/PK-12
409 W Locust St 65605 417-678-3373
Dan Decker, supt. Fax 678-4043
www.hdnet.k12.mo.us
Aurora JHS 300/7-8
500 W Olive St 65605 417-678-3630
Bill Kirby, prin. Fax 678-2487
Pate ECC 300/PK-2
400 Terrace Dr 65605 417-678-1552
Sandra Thrasher, prin. Fax 678-3491
Robinson ES 200/3-4
1034 S Lincoln Ave 65605 417-678-7436
Paula Seal, prin. Fax 678-6554
Robinson IS 5-6
1044 S Lincoln Ave 65605 417-678-5651
Shawn Page, prin. Fax 678-8900

Auxvasse, Callaway, Pop. 996
North Callaway County R-I SD
Supt. — See Kingdom City
Auxvasse S 400/K-8
PO Box 8 65231 573-386-2217
Amy James, prin. Fax 386-2039

Ava, Douglas, Pop. 3,078
Ava R-I SD 1,500/PK-12
PO Box 338 65608 417-683-4717
Dr. Andrew Underwood, supt. Fax 683-6329
www.avaschools.k12.mo.us/
Ava ES 500/PK-4
PO Box 338 65608 417-683-5450
Diana Premer, prin. Fax 683-9010
Ava MS 400/5-8
PO Box 338 65608 417-683-3835
Brad Plackemeier, prin. Fax 683-9101

Plainview R-VIII SD 100/K-8
RR 3 Box 145 65608 417-683-2046
Brenda Jenkins, supt. Fax 683-3222
Plainview S 100/K-8
RR 3 Box 145 65608 417-683-2046
Brenda Jenkins, prin. Fax 683-3222

Ava Victory Academy 100/PK-12
PO Box 608 65608 417-683-6630
Daniel Letzinger, admin. Fax 683-1402

Avilla, Jasper, Pop. 142
Avilla R-XIII SD 200/K-8
PO Box 7 64833 417-246-5330
Scott Blake, supt. Fax 246-5432
www.avillapanthers.org
Avilla S 200/K-8
PO Box 7 64833 417-246-5330
Scott Blake, prin. Fax 246-5432

Bakersfield, Ozark, Pop. 286
Bakersfield R-IV SD 400/PK-12
PO Box 38 65609 417-284-7333
Jackie Estes, supt. Fax 284-7335
www.bakersfield.k12.mo.us
Bakersfield ES 200/PK-5
PO Box 38 65609 417-284-7593
Sandra Barnes, prin. Fax 284-7335

Ballwin, Saint Louis, Pop. 30,481
Parkway C-2 SD
Supt. — See Chesterfield
Claymont ES 400/K-5
405 Country Club Dr 63011 314-415-6150
Aaron Wills, prin. Fax 415-6162
ECC PK-PK
14605 Clayton Rd 63011 314-415-6950
Pat Teich, dir. Fax 415-6956
Hanna Woods ES 400/K-5
720 Hanna Rd 63021 314-415-6300
Dr. Jackie Frisbee, prin. Fax 415-6312
Oak Brook ES 500/K-5
510 Big Bend Rd 63021 314-415-6550
Chris Shirley, prin. Fax 415-6562
Parkway Southwest MS 800/6-8
701 Wren Ave 63021 314-415-7300
Chelsea Watson, prin. Fax 415-7334
Sorrento Springs ES 400/K-5
390 Tumulty Dr 63021 314-415-6800
Rhonda Saitta, prin. Fax 415-6812
Wren Hollow ES 400/K-5
655 Wren Ave 63021 314-415-6850
Mary Johnston, prin. Fax 415-6862

Rockwood R-VI SD
Supt. — See Eureka
Ballwin ES 500/K-5
400 Jefferson Ave 63021 636-207-2533
Julie Gay, prin. Fax 207-2536
Crestview MS 1,200/6-8
16025 Clayton Rd 63011 636-207-2520
Dr. Jill Scheulen, prin. Fax 207-2529
Ridge Meadows ES 600/K-5
777 Ridge Rd 63021 636-207-2661
Amy Digman, prin. Fax 207-2666
Selvidge MS 700/6-8
235 New Ballwin Rd 63021 636-207-2622
Sean Stryhal, prin. Fax 207-2632
Westridge ES 400/K-5
908 Crestland Dr 63011 636-207-2572
Dr. Meg Brooks, prin. Fax 207-2577
Woerther ES 500/K-5
314 New Ballwin Rd 63021 636-207-2674
Jane Levy, prin. Fax 207-2681

Holy Infant S 900/K-8
248 New Ballwin Rd 63021 636-227-0802
Sr. Rosario Delaney, prin. Fax 227-9184
Hope Montessori Academy - Ballwin 200/PK-4
2809 Barrett Station Rd 63021 314-984-8111
Stacie Walck, prin. Fax 984-8838
Linda Vista S 100/PK-8
930 Kehrs Mill Rd 63011 636-532-3315
Maureen Wuestling, prin. Fax 532-2578
Twin Oaks Christian S 300/PK-8
1230 Big Bend Rd 63021 636-861-1901
Jean Zoet, hdmstr. Fax 861-2084

Barnard, Nodaway, Pop. 250
South Nodaway County R-IV SD 200/PK-12
209 Morehouse St 64423 660-652-3221
Terry Hutchings, supt. Fax 652-3413
missouri.ihigh.com/southnodaway
Other Schools – See Guilford

Barnhart, Jefferson, Pop. 4,911
Windsor C-1 SD
Supt. — See Imperial
Freer ES 400/K-3
1800 Hanover Ln 63012 636-464-2951
Charles Bouzek, prin. Fax 464-4471

Battlefield, Greene, Pop. 3,612
Springfield R-XII SD
Supt. — See Springfield
Wilson's Creek IS 500/5-6
4035 W Weaver Rd 65619 417-523-7800
Karyn Christy, prin. Fax 523-7995

Beaufort, Franklin
Union R-XI SD
Supt. — See Union
Beaufort ES 400/K-6
3200 Highway 50 63013 573-484-3221
Meg Vogel, prin. Fax 484-4145

Belgrade, Washington
Valley R-VI SD
Supt. — See Caledonia
Belgrade ES 100/K-2
18437 Delbridge Rd 63622 573-766-5689
Rebecca Jenkins, prin. Fax 766-5229

Bell City, Stoddard, Pop. 453
Bell City R-II SD 300/K-12
25254 Walnut St 63735 573-733-4444
Rhonda Niemczyk, supt. Fax 733-4114
www.bellcity.k12.mo.us/
Bell City ES 100/K-6
25254 Walnut St 63735 573-733-4444
Patresa Eakin, prin. Fax 733-4114

Belle, Maries, Pop. 1,348
Maries County R-II SD 800/PK-12
PO Box 819 65013 573-859-3800
Dr. Ted Spessard, supt. Fax 859-3883
www.mariesr2.org/
Belle ES 400/PK-5
PO Box 819 65013 573-859-3326
Magdalyn Ames, prin. Fax 859-3883
Other Schools – See Bland

Belleview, Iron
Belleview R-III SD 100/K-8
27431 Highway 32 63623 573-697-5702
Lawrence Naeger, supt. Fax 697-5701
Belleview S 100/K-8
27431 Highway 32 63623 573-697-5702
Lawrence Naeger, prin. Fax 697-5701

Bellflower, Montgomery, Pop. 414
Montgomery County R-II SD
Supt. — See Montgomery City
Bellflower ES 100/PK-5
406 S Walnut St 63333 573-929-3211
Debby Guile, prin. Fax 929-3444

Bel Nor, Saint Louis, Pop. 1,704
Normandy SD
Supt. — See Saint Louis
Bel-Nor ES 200/K-3
3101 Nordic Dr 63121 314-493-0140
Netra Taylor, prin. Fax 493-0150

Bel Ridge, Saint Louis, Pop. 3,232
Normandy SD
Supt. — See Saint Louis
Bel Ridge ES 200/4-6
8930 Boston Ave 63121 314-493-0850
Sonya Murray, prin. Fax 493-0870

Belton, Cass, Pop. 24,140
Belton SD 124 4,800/PK-12
110 W Walnut St 64012 816-348-1000
Dr. Kenneth Southwick, supt. Fax 348-1068
www.beltonschools.org
Cambridge ES 500/K-4
109 W Cambridge Rd 64012 816-348-1008
Michelle Biondo, prin. Fax 348-1093
Gladden ES 400/K-4
405 Westover Rd 64012 816-348-1015
Ken McCrary, prin. Fax 348-1530
Grace ECC 300/PK-PK
614 Mill St 64012 816-348-1514
Rhonda Hardee, prin. Fax 348-1565
Hillcrest ES 400/K-4
106 S Hillcrest Rd 64012 816-348-1023
Bryce Johnson, prin. Fax 348-1505
Kentucky Trail ES K-4
8301 E 163rd St 64012 816-348-1100
Carrie Bachmeier, prin. Fax 348-1105
Mill Creek Upper ES 700/5-6
308 S Cleveland Ave 64012 816-348-1576
Kimberly Mauck, prin. Fax 348-1595
Scott ES 400/K-4
310 S Scott Ave 64012 816-348-1005
Starr Rich, prin. Fax 348-1545
Yeokum MS 700/7-8
613 Mill St 64012 816-348-1042
Michele Norman, prin. Fax 348-1534

Heartland Family S 200/PK-12
810 S Cedar St 64012 816-331-1000
Dr. Trey Dimsdale, supt. Fax 322-2782

Benton, Scott, Pop. 729
Kelso C-7 SD 100/PK-8
1016 State Highway A 63736 573-545-3357
William Rogers, supt. Fax 545-4356
kelsoc-7.k12.mo.us/
Kelso S 100/PK-8
1016 State Highway A 63736 573-545-3357
William Rogers, prin. Fax 545-4356

Scott County R-IV SD 1,000/K-12
4035 State Highway 77 63736 573-545-3887
Don Moore, supt. Fax 545-3929
kelly.k12.mo.us/
Scott County ES 400/K-5
4035 State Highway 77 63736 573-545-3541
Fara Jones, prin. Fax 545-3452
Scott County MS 200/6-8
4035 State Highway 77 63736 573-545-3541
Jeremy Siebert, prin. Fax 545-4386

St. Denis S 100/1-8
PO Box 189 63736 573-545-3017
Karen Powers, prin. Fax 545-9185

Berkeley, Saint Louis, Pop. 9,631
Ferguson-Florissant R-II SD
Supt. — See Florissant
Airport ES 300/K-6
8249 Airport Rd 63134 314-524-3872
Rosetta Patton, prin. Fax 524-3879
Berkeley MS 400/7-8
8300 Frost Ave 63134 314-524-3883
Winston Rogers, prin. Fax 524-3885

Holman ES 200/K-6
8811 Harold Dr 63134 314-428-9695
Dr. Donna Thurman, prin. Fax 428-9792

Bernie, Stoddard, Pop. 1,801
Bernie R-XIII SD 600/PK-12
516 W Main Ave 63822 573-293-5333
Robin Ritchie, supt. Fax 293-5731
www.bernie.k12.mo.us
Bernie ES 400/PK-6
121 S Spiker St 63822 573-293-5335
Tommie Ellenburg, prin. Fax 293-6124

Bethany, Harrison, Pop. 3,060
South Harrison County R-II SD 900/PK-12
PO Box 445 64424 660-425-8044
Larry Linthacum, supt. Fax 425-7050
www.shr2.k12.mo.us
South Harrison County ECC 100/PK-PK
PO Box 445 64424 660-425-7539
Rhonda Price, prin. Fax 425-4478
South Harrison County R-II ES 400/K-6
PO Box 445 64424 660-425-8061
Dana Seymour, prin. Fax 425-2130

Bevier, Macon, Pop. 729
Bevier C-4 SD 200/K-12
400 Bloomington St 63532 660-773-6611
Joan Patrick, supt. Fax 773-6955
Bevier S 200/K-8
400 Bloomington St 63532 660-773-6611
Lisa Keen, prin. Fax 773-5565

Billings, Christian, Pop. 1,142
Billings R-IV SD 500/K-12
118 W Mount Vernon Rd 65610 417-744-2623
Cynthia Brandt, supt. Fax 744-4545
www.billings.k12.mo.us
Billings ES 200/K-6
118 W Mount Vernon Rd 65610 417-744-2552
Allan Brown, prin. Fax 744-4357

Birch Tree, Shannon, Pop. 619
Mountain View-Birch Tree R-III SD
Supt. — See Mountain View
Birch Tree ES 200/PK-6
PO Box 300 65438 573-292-3106
Robert Bennett, prin. Fax 292-4421

Bismarck, Saint Francois, Pop. 1,558
Bismarck R-V SD 600/PK-12
PO Box 257 63624 573-734-6111
Dr. Damon Gamble, supt. Fax 734-2957
schoolweb.missouri.edu/bismarck.k12.mo.us
Bismarck ES 400/PK-6
PO Box 257 63624 573-734-6111
Karen Hodges, prin. Fax 734-2957

Blackwater, Cooper, Pop. 197
Blackwater R-II SD 100/PK-8
PO Box 117 65322 660-846-2461
Gary Dunn, supt. Fax 846-2431
Blackwater S 100/PK-8
PO Box 117 65322 660-846-2461
Gary Dunn, prin. Fax 846-2431

Bland, Gasconade, Pop. 571
Maries County R-II SD
Supt. — See Belle
Maries County MS 200/6-8
PO Box 10 65014 573-646-3912
Bobbie Jo Lewis, prin. Fax 646-3148

Bloomfield, Stoddard, Pop. 1,888
Bloomfield R-XIV SD 800/PK-12
PO Box 650 63825 573-568-4564
Dr. Nicholas Thiele, supt. Fax 568-4565
www.bloomfieldschooldistrict.blogspot.com/
Bloomfield S 500/PK-8
PO Box 650 63825 573-568-4562
Kelly Renfroe, prin. Fax 568-4563

Bloomsdale, Sainte Genevieve, Pop. 434
St. Genevieve County R-II SD
Supt. — See Sainte Genevieve
Bloomsdale ES 300/K-5
6279 Highway 61 63627 573-883-4500
Lorie Zuspann, prin. Fax 483-3535

St. Agnes S 200/PK-8
PO Box 154 63627 573-483-2506
Pat Kirk, prin. Fax 483-9303

Blue Eye, Stone, Pop. 97
Blue Eye R-V SD 700/PK-12
PO Box 105 65611 417-779-5332
Dan Ray, supt. Fax 779-2151
www.blueeye.k12.mo.us
Blue Eye ES 300/PK-4
PO Box 105 65611 417-779-4318
Michael Fransen, prin. Fax 779-3268
Blue Eye MS 200/5-8
PO Box 105 65611 417-779-4299
Craig Linson, prin. Fax 779-4526

Morningside S 50/1-12
180 Grace Chapel Rd 65611 417-779-9000
Randy Brown, supt.

Blue Springs, Jackson, Pop. 53,099
Blue Springs R-IV SD 13,500/K-12
1801 NW Vesper St 64015 816-224-1300
Dr. Paul Kinder, supt. Fax 224-1310
www.bluesprings-schools.net
Brittany Hill MS 800/6-8
2701 NW 1st St 64014 816-224-1700
Dallas Truex, prin. Fax 224-1704
Bryant ES 500/K-5
1101 SE Sunnyside School Rd 64014 816-224-1340
Dr. Cathy Paul, prin. Fax 224-1343

Cordill-Mason ES 500/K-5
4001 SW Christiansen Dr 64014 816-224-1370
Alan Michelson, prin. Fax 224-1372
Franklin ES 500/K-5
111 NE Roanoke Dr 64014 816-224-1390
Jill Johnston, prin. Fax 224-1396
Lewis ES 500/K-5
717 NW Park Rd 64015 816-224-1345
Kelly Flax, prin. Fax 224-1347
Moreland Ridge MS 900/6-8
900 SW Bishop Dr 64015 816-224-1800
Kevin Grover, prin. Fax 224-1805
Nowlin ES 400/K-5
5020 NW Valley View Rd 64015 816-224-1355
Deborah Curtis, prin. Fax 224-1359
Smith ES 400/K-5
1609 SW Clark Rd 64015 816-224-1375
Jan Castle, prin. Fax 224-1378
Sunny Pointe ES 500/K-5
3920 S R D Mize Rd 64015 816-224-7800
Steve Goddard, prin. Fax 224-7804
Sunny Vale MS 700/6-8
3930 S R D Mize Rd 64015 816-224-1330
Beverly Leonard, prin. Fax 224-1309
Ultican ES 400/K-5
1813 W Main St 64015 816-224-1365
Jill Sherman, prin. Fax 224-1490
Walker ES 400/K-5
201 SE Sunnyside School Rd 64014 816-224-1380
Greg Johnson, prin. Fax 224-1461
Young ES 400/K-5
505 SE Shamrock Ln 64014 816-224-1335
Douglas Nielsen, prin. Fax 224-1492
Other Schools – See Independence, Lees Summit

Plaza Heights Christian Academy 200/PK-12
1500 SW Clark Rd 64015 816-228-0670
Michael Hart, admin. Fax 229-4092
St. John LaLande ECC 50/PK-PK
700 NW Range St 64015 816-229-8343
Molly McAnerney, prin. Fax 229-8343
St. John LaLande S 400/PK-8
801 NW R D Mize Rd 64015 816-228-5895
Natalie Helm, prin. Fax 228-8979
Timothy ECC 100/PK-PK
425 NW R D Mize Rd 64014 816-228-5300
Patty Koogler, dir. Fax 228-5323
Timothy Lutheran S 100/K-7
205 NW 16th St 64015 816-228-5300
Ed Kuerschner, prin. Fax 874-4025

Bois D Arc, Greene
Ash Grove R-IV SD
Supt. — See Ash Grove
Bois D'Arc ES 200/K-6
10315 W State Highway T 65612 417-742-2203
Mary Mays, prin. Fax 742-4460

Bolivar, Polk, Pop. 10,179
Bolivar R-I SD 2,400/PK-12
524 W Madison St 65613 417-326-5291
Dr. Steve Morgan, supt. Fax 326-3562
www.bolivar.k12.mo.us/
Bolivar IS 500/3-5
1300 N Hartford Ave 65613 417-777-5160
Laura Boyd, prin. Fax 777-5434
Bolivar MS 600/6-8
604 W Jackson St 65613 417-326-3811
Shane Dublin, prin. Fax 326-8277
Bolivar PS 500/PK-2
706 N Leonard Pl 65613 417-326-5247
Mary Gregory, prin. Fax 326-2394

Polk County Christian S 100/PK-10
PO Box 303 65613 417-777-2330
Paula Bogart, admin. Fax 777-5723

Bonne Terre, Saint Francois, Pop. 6,520
North St. Francois County R-I SD 2,500/PK-12
300 Berry Rd 63628 573-358-2247
Yancy Poorman, supt. Fax 358-2377
www.ncsd.k12.mo.us/
North County PS 300/K-2
405 Hillcrest St 63628 573-358-3600
Kathryn Bockman, prin. Fax 358-7475
Preschool Center 100/PK-PK
405 Hillcrest St 63628 573-358-3600
Kathryn Bockman, prin. Fax 358-7475
Other Schools – See Desloge

St. Joseph S 50/PK-6
20 Saint Joseph St 63628 573-358-5947
Karen Basden, prin. Fax 358-5947

Bonnots Mill, Osage

St. Mary S 50/1-8
1641 Highway C 65016 573-897-2567
Sr. Celly Amparano, prin. Fax 897-4143

Boonville, Cooper, Pop. 8,669
Boonville R-I SD 1,500/PK-12
736 Main St 65233 660-882-7474
Mark Ficken, supt. Fax 882-5721
www.boonville.k12.mo.us/
Barton ES 400/3-5
814 Locust St 65233 660-882-6527
Susan Williams, prin. Fax 882-2473
Cole PS 100/K-2
1700 W Ashley Rd 65233 660-882-2744
Leslie Reardon, prin. Fax 882-2898
Elliott MS 300/6-8
700 Main St 65233 660-882-6649
Neal Randol, prin. Fax 882-8646

SS. Peter & Paul S 200/PK-8
502 7th St 65233 660-882-2589
Alan Lammers, prin. Fax 882-2476

Bosworth, Carroll, Pop. 388
Bosworth R-V SD 100/PK-12
102 E Eldridge St 64623 660-534-7311
Lachrissa Smith, supt. Fax 534-7409
www.bosworthr-v.k12.mo.us/
Bosworth ES 100/PK-6
102 E Eldridge St 64623 660-534-7311
Cindy Beltz, prin. Fax 534-7409

Bourbon, Crawford, Pop. 1,408
Crawford County R-I SD 1,100/PK-12
1444 S Old Highway 66 65441 573-732-4426
Dr. Thomas Sharp, supt. Fax 732-4545
www.warhawks.k12.mo.us/
Bourbon ES 500/PK-4
357 Jost St 65441 573-732-5365
Patricia Thompson, prin. Fax 732-3196
Bourbon MS 300/5-8
363 Jost St 65441 573-732-4424
Dena Smith, prin. Fax 732-4425

Bourbon SDA S 50/K-8
750 Old Highway 66 65441 573-732-5531
J. L. Meek, prin. Fax 732-5531

Bowling Green, Pike, Pop. 5,185
Bowling Green R-I SD 1,400/K-12
700 W Adams St 63334 573-324-5441
Michael Gray, supt. Fax 324-2439
www.bgschools.k12.mo.us
Bowling Green ES 400/K-5
700 W Adams St 63334 573-324-2331
David Wehde, prin. Fax 324-2439
Bowling Green MS 300/6-8
700 W Adams St 63334 573-324-2181
Kimberlee Pafford, prin. Fax 324-2181
Other Schools – See Frankford

Pike County Christian S 50/K-9
12682 Highway U 63334 573-324-5769
Frank Welch, admin. Fax 324-5769
St. Clement S 100/K-8
21493 Highway 161 63334 573-324-2166
Dr. Larry Twellman, prin. Fax 324-6159

Bradleyville, Taney, Pop. 84
Bradleyville R-I SD 200/K-12
PO Box 20 65614 417-796-2288
Joe Combs, supt. Fax 796-2289
Bradleyville ES 100/K-6
PO Box 20 65614 417-796-2288
Nona Norwine, prin. Fax 796-2289

Branson, Taney, Pop. 7,010
Branson R-IV SD 3,300/PK-12
400 Cedar Ridge Dr 65616 417-334-6541
Dr. Doug Hayter, supt. Fax 334-6619
www.branson.k12.mo.us
Branson ES East 300/2-4
308 Cedar Ridge Dr 65616 417-334-5137
Diana Cutbirth, prin. Fax 336-3652
Branson ES West 600/2-4
396 Cedar Ridge Dr 65616 417-334-5135
Mike Dawson, prin. Fax 336-6079
Branson IS 600/5-6
766 Buchanan Rd 65616 417-332-3201
Susan Bell, prin. Fax 332-3224
Branson JHS 600/7-8
263 Buccaneer Dr 65616 417-334-3087
Brad Swofford, prin. Fax 336-3913
Branson PS 50/PK-1
402 Cedar Ridge Dr 65616 417-336-1887
Michelle Collins, prin. Fax 336-1889

Brashear, Adair, Pop. 272
Adair County R-II SD 200/K-12
205 W Dewey St 63533 660-323-5272
Don Wilburn, supt. Fax 323-5250
brashear.k12.mo.us
Adair County R-II ES 100/K-6
205 W Dewey St 63533 660-323-5272
Shelly Shipman, prin. Fax 323-5250

Braymer, Caldwell, Pop. 962
Braymer C-4 SD 400/PK-12
400 Bobcat Ave 64624 660-645-2284
Thomas Anderson, supt. Fax 645-2780
www.brayc4.k12.mo.us/
Braymer ES 200/PK-6
400 Bobcat Ave 64624 660-645-2284
Lyndsey Hall, prin. Fax 645-2780

Breckenridge, Caldwell, Pop. 462
Breckenridge R-I SD 100/K-12
400 W Colfax St 64625 660-644-5715
John Dunham, supt. Fax 644-5710
Breckenridge ES 100/K-6
400 W Colfax St 64625 660-644-5715
Brent Skinner, prin. Fax 644-5710

Brentwood, Saint Louis, Pop. 7,365
Brentwood SD 800/K-12
90 Yorkshire Lane Ct 63144 314-962-4507
Charles Penberthy, supt. Fax 962-7302
www.brentwood.k12.mo.us
Brentwood MS 200/6-8
9127 White Ave 63144 314-962-8238
Julie Sperry, prin. Fax 968-8724
McGrath ES 200/K-5
2350 Saint Clair Ave 63144 314-962-6824
Kathleen Behrmann, prin. Fax 962-6541
Twain ES 100/K-5
8636 Litzsinger Rd 63144 314-962-0613
Karen Smith, prin. Fax 963-7724

St. Mary Magdelen S 200/K-8
8750 Magdalen Ave 63144 314-961-0149
Marlise Albert, prin. Fax 961-7208

Bridgeton, Saint Louis, Pop. 15,259
Pattonville R-III SD
Supt. — See Saint Ann
Bridgeway ES 300/K-5
11635 Oakbury Ct 63044 314-213-8012
Victoria Nienhuis, prin. Fax 213-8612

Bronaugh, Vernon, Pop. 248
Bronaugh R-VII SD 200/PK-12
527 E 6th St 64728 417-922-3211
Patricia Phillips, supt. Fax 922-3308
www.bronaugh.k12.mo.us/
Bronaugh ES 100/PK-6
527 E 6th St 64728 417-922-3211
Jacob Sherwood, prin. Fax 922-3308

Brookfield, Linn, Pop. 4,506
Brookfield R-III SD 1,100/PK-12
124A N Pershing Dr 64628 660-258-7443
Dr. Paul Barger, supt. Fax 258-4711
www.brookfield.k12.mo.us
Brookfield ES 500/PK-4
128 N Pershing Dr 64628 660-258-2241
Dr. Ernest Raney, prin. Fax 258-2243
Brookfield MS 200/5-8
126 N Pershing Dr 64628 660-258-7335
Melinda Wilbeck, prin. Fax 258-2190

Broseley, Butler
Twin Rivers R-X SD 1,000/K-12
PO Box 146 63932 573-328-4321
Mike Stevenson, supt. Fax 328-1070
www.tr10.us/
Other Schools – See Fisk, Qulin

Brunswick, Chariton, Pop. 895
Brunswick R-II SD 300/PK-12
1008 County Rd 65236 660-548-3550
David Figg, supt. Fax 548-3029
schoolweb.missouri.edu/brunswick.k12.mo.us/
Brunswick ES 200/PK-6
1008 County Rd 65236 660-548-3777
Susan Duncan, prin. Fax 548-3029

Bucklin, Linn, Pop. 496
Bucklin R-II SD 100/K-12
26832 Highway 129 64631 660-695-3555
Steve Coulson, supt. Fax 695-3345
www.bucklin.k12.mo.us/
Bucklin R-II S 100/K-12
26832 Highway 129 64631 660-695-3225
Steve Coulson, prin. Fax 695-3345

Buckner, Jackson, Pop. 2,724
Fort Osage R-I SD
Supt. — See Independence
Buckner ES 400/K-4
013 S Sibley St 64016 816-650-7300
Patrick Farnan, prin. Fax 650-7305

Buffalo, Dallas, Pop. 3,006
Dallas County R-I SD 1,700/PK-12
309 W Commercial St 65622 417-345-2222
Gary Arthaud, supt. Fax 345-8446
www.dallasr1.k12.mo.us/
Buffalo MS 600/5-8
926 Truman 65622 417-345-2335
Matt Nimmo, prin. Fax 345-5968
Mallory ES 400/K-4
315 S Hickory St 65622 417-345-2350
Wendy Moeller, prin. Fax 345-5080
Other Schools – See Long Lane

Bunceton, Cooper, Pop. 357
Cooper County R-IV SD 200/K-12
PO Box 110 65237 660-427-5347
Mary Battles, supt. Fax 427-5348
bunceton.k12.mo.us
Bunceton ES 100/K-6
PO Box 110 65237 660-427-5415
Connie Kunze, prin. Fax 427-5348

Zion Lutheran S 50/1-8
17321 Lone Elm Rd 65237 660-838-6307
Marsha Toellner, prin.

Bunker, Reynolds, Pop. 437
Bunker R-III SD 200/K-12
PO Box 365 63629 573-689-2507
Jane Reeves, supt. Fax 689-2011
Bunker ES 100/K-6
PO Box 365 63629 573-689-2211
Deena Swyers, prin. Fax 689-2011

Burlington Junction, Nodaway, Pop. 613
West Nodaway R-I SD 300/PK-12
PO Box 260 64428 660-725-4613
Gary Battles, supt. Fax 725-4300
www.wnrockets.com/
West Nodaway R-1 ES 100/PK-6
PO Box 260 64428 660-725-4126
Nancy Greeley, prin. Fax 725-4300

Butler, Bates, Pop. 4,249
Ballard R-II SD 100/K-12
RR 1 Box 497 64730 816-297-2656
Rick Stark, supt. Fax 297-4002
Ballard ES 100/K-6
RR 1 Box 497 64730 816-297-2656
John Siebeneck, prin. Fax 297-4002

Butler R-V SD 1,100/PK-12
420 S Fulton St 64730 660-679-0653
Alan Stauffacher, supt. Fax 679-6626
butler.k12.mo.us
Butler ES 600/PK-6
4 N High St 64730 660-679-6591
Dennis Page, prin. Fax 679-6626

Cabool, Texas, Pop. 2,140
Cabool R-IV SD 800/PK-12
PO Box 613 65689 417-962-3153
Wesley Davis, supt. Fax 962-5043
www.cabool.k12.mo.us/index.html
Cabool ES 300/PK-4
PO Box 613 65689 417-962-3153
Paul Landman, prin. Fax 962-5293
Cabool MS 200/5-8
PO Box 613 65689 417-962-3153
Gary Flippin, prin. Fax 962-0078

Cadet, Washington
Kingston SD K-14 800/K-12
10047 Diamond Rd 63630 573-438-4982
Gary Milner, supt. Fax 438-8813
www.kingston.k12.mo.us/
Kingston ES 300/K-5
10047 Diamond Rd 63630 573-438-4982
Maria Boyer, prin. Fax 438-8814
Kingston MS 200/6-8
10047 Diamond Rd 63630 573-438-4982
Thomas Gotsch, prin. Fax 438-1212

Cainsville, Harrison, Pop. 373
Cainsville R-I SD 100/PK-12
PO Box 108 64632 660-893-5213
Richard Smith, supt. Fax 893-5713
Cainsville ES 100/PK-6
PO Box 108 64632 660-893-5214
Mike Booth, prin. Fax 893-5713

Cairo, Randolph, Pop. 304
Northeast Randolph County R-IV SD 400/K-12
301 W Martin St 65239 660-263-2788
Richard Morelock, supt. Fax 263-5735
Northeast ES 200/K-5
301 W Martin St 65239 660-263-2828
Melva Gipson, prin. Fax 263-5735

Caledonia, Washington, Pop. 163
Valley R-VI SD 500/K-12
1 Viking Dr 63631 573-779-3446
Steve Yount, supt. Fax 779-3505
www.valley.k12.mo.us/
Caledonia ES 100/3-6
1 Viking Dr 63631 573-779-3332
Rebecca Jenkins, prin. Fax 779-3562
Other Schools – See Belgrade

Calhoun, Henry, Pop. 508
Calhoun R-VIII SD 200/PK-12
409 S College St 65323 660-694-3422
Kyle Powell, supt. Fax 694-3501
Calhoun ES 100/PK-6
409 S College St 65323 660-694-3422
Janette Lawson, prin. Fax 694-3501

California, Moniteau, Pop. 4,137
Moniteau County R-I SD 1,200/K-12
211 S Owen St Ste B 65018 573-796-2145
Marty Albertson, supt. Fax 796-6123
www.californiak12.org/
California ES 500/K-5
101 S Owen St 65018 573-796-2161
Terri Steffes, prin. Fax 796-8650
California MS 300/6-8
211 S Owen St 65018 573-796-2146
Matt Abernathy, prin. Fax 796-8257

Callao, Macon, Pop. 279
Callao C-8 SD 50/K-8
PO Box A 63534 660-768-5541
Debra Lawrence, supt. Fax 768-5699
Callao S 50/K-8
PO Box A 63534 660-768-5541
Debra Lawrence, prin. Fax 768-5699

Camden Point, Platte, Pop. 547
North Platte County R-I SD
Supt. — See Dearborn
North Platte ES 200/PK-3
300 Scout St 64018 816-280-3422
Cathy Hubble, prin. Fax 445-3764

Camdenton, Camden, Pop. 3,061
Camdenton R-III SD 3,500/PK-12
PO Box 1409 65020 573-346-9213
Dr. Maurice Overlander, supt. Fax 346-9211
camdenton.k12.mo.us/
Camdenton MS 700/7-8
PO Box 1409 65020 573-346-9257
Sean Kirksey, prin. Fax 346-9288
Dogwood ES 500/PK-2
PO Box 1409 65020 573-346-9239
Melissa Salsman, prin. Fax 346-9291
Hawthorn ES 3-4
PO Box 1409 65020 573-317-3450
Todd Shockley, prin. Fax 317-3452
Oak Ridge IS 600/5-6
PO Box 1409 65020 573-346-9280
Terry Jacob, prin. Fax 346-9286
Other Schools – See Osage Beach, Sunrise Beach

Cameron, Clinton, Pop. 9,141
Cameron R-I SD 1,600/PK-12
423 N Chestnut St 64429 816-632-2170
Dr. Ronald White, supt. Fax 632-2612
www.cameron.k12.mo.us/
Cameron MS 500/5-8
915 Park Ave 64429 816-632-2185
Dwight Sanders, prin. Fax 632-3752
Parkview ES 600/PK-4
602 S Harris St 64429 816-632-7212
Clark Dauner, prin. Fax 632-7973

Campbell, Dunklin, Pop. 1,872
Campbell R-II SD 700/PK-12
801 S State Highway 53 63933 573-246-2133
Darrell Wilburn, supt. Fax 246-3212
www.campbell.k12.mo.us
Campbell ES 400/PK-6
801 S State Highway 53 63933 573-246-3109
Linda Barkley, prin. Fax 246-2245

St. Teresa S 100/PK-8
40648 State Highway JJ 63933 573-328-4197
Janet Kuper, prin. Fax 328-4197

Canton, Lewis, Pop. 2,502
Canton R-V SD 500/PK-12
200 S 4th St 63435 573-288-5216
David Tramel, supt. Fax 288-5442
canton.k12.mo.us/
Canton ES 300/PK-6
200 S 4th St 63435 573-288-5216
Darla Gaus, prin. Fax 288-5442

Cape Girardeau, Cape Girardeau, Pop. 36,204
Cape Girardeau SD 63 4,000/PK-12
301 N Clark St 63701 573-335-1867
Dr. James Welker, supt. Fax 334-2817
cape.k12.mo.us
Blanchard ES 300/K-4
1829 N Sprigg St 63701 573-335-3030
Dr. Barbara Kohlfeld, prin. Fax 334-1319
Central JHS 600/7-8
205 Caruthers St 63701 573-334-2923
Roy Merideth, prin. Fax 335-7173
Central MS 600/5-6
1900 Thilenius St 63701 573-334-6281
Mark Kiehne, prin. Fax 334-1557
Clippard ES 300/K-4
2860 Hopper Rd 63701 573-334-5720
Sydney Herbst, prin. Fax 334-1067
Franklin ES 200/K-4
215 N Louisiana St 63701 573-335-5456
Rhonda Dunham, prin. Fax 334-1140
Jefferson ES 300/PK-4
520 S Minnesota St 63703 573-334-2030
Mark Cook, prin. Fax 334-1159
Schrader ES 300/K-4
1360 Randol Ave 63701 573-335-5310
Ruthann Orr, prin. Fax 334-3871

Jackson R-II SD
Supt. — See Jackson
Gordonville ES 50/K-3
653 State Highway Z 63701 573-243-9580
Shauna Criddle, prin. Fax 243-9580

Nell Holcomb R-IV SD 300/K-8
6547 State Highway 177 63701 573-334-3644
Darryl Pannier, supt. Fax 334-9552
www.nellholcomb.k12.mo.us/
Holcomb S 300/K-8
6547 State Highway 177 63701 573-334-3644
Mary Boeller, prin. Fax 334-9552

Cape Christian S 100/PK-8
1855 Perryville Rd 63701 573-335-8333
Beverly Smart, prin. Fax 335-7157
Eagle Ridge Christian S 100/PK-12
4210 State Highway K 63701 573-339-1335
Janice Margrabe, admin. Fax 339-1390
St. Marys Cathedral S 300/K-8
210 S Sprigg St 63703 573-335-3840
Carol Strattman, prin. Fax 335-4142
St. Vincent De Paul S 400/K-8
1919 Ritter Dr 63701 573-334-9594
Kay Glastetter, prin. Fax 334-0425
Trinity Lutheran S 200/PK-8
55 N Pacific St 63701 573-334-1068
Diane Maurer, prin. Fax 334-5081

Cardwell, Dunklin, Pop. 751
Southland C-9 SD 400/PK-12
500 S Main St 63829 573-654-3574
Raymond Lasley, supt. Fax 654-3575
Southland ES 200/PK-6
500 S Main St 63829 573-654-3564
Alicia Shaw, prin. Fax 654-3565

Carl Junction, Jasper, Pop. 6,483
Carl Junction R-I SD 2,900/K-12
206 S Roney St 64834 417-649-7026
Phillip Cook, supt. Fax 649-6594
www.cj.k12.mo.us
Carl Junction IS 800/4-6
206 S Roney St 64834 417-649-7011
Connie Godwin, prin. Fax 649-7248
Carl Junction JHS 500/7-8
206 S Roney St 64834 417-649-7246
Debra Elbrader, prin. Fax 649-0022
Carl Junction PS 2-3 500/2-3
206 S Roney St 64834 417-649-7034
Carolyn Porter, prin. Fax 649-6566
Carl Junction PS K-1 300/K-1
206 S Roney St 64834 417-649-7045
Kari Arehart, prin. Fax 649-7981

Carrollton, Carroll, Pop. 4,012
Carrollton R-VII SD 900/PK-12
103 E 9th St 64633 660-542-2769
Dr. Judith DeLany, supt. Fax 542-3416
www.trojans.k12.mo.us/
Adams ES 400/PK-6
207 E 9th St 64633 660-542-2535
Nancy Schmidt, prin. Fax 542-3692
Carrollton JHS 200/7-8
300 E 9th St 64633 660-542-3472
Brent Dobbins, prin. Fax 542-3169

Carterville, Jasper, Pop. 1,916
Webb City R-VII SD
Supt. — See Webb City
Carterville ES 100/K-4
210 E Hall St 64835 417-673-6080
Kristine McCulley, prin. Fax 673-6081

Carthage, Jasper, Pop. 13,096
Carthage R-IX SD 3,000/PK-12
710 Lyon St 64836 417-359-7000
Blaine Henningsen, supt. Fax 359-7004
www.carthage.k12.mo.us
Carthage JHS 600/7-8
714 S Main St 64836 417-359-7050
Ron Wallace, prin. Fax 359-7057
Carthage MS 5-6
827 E Centennial Ave 64836 417-359-7246
Robin Jones, prin. Fax 359-7408
Columbian ES 400/PK-4
1015 W Macon St 64836 417-359-7060
Sonia Resa, prin. Fax 359-8979
Fairview ES 400/PK-4
1201 E Fairview Ave 64836 417-359-7070
Ronna Patterson, prin. Fax 359-7074
Pleasant Valley ES 100/K-4
652 County Road 180 64836 417-359-7085
Brenten Byrd, prin. Fax 359-7084
Steadley ES 400/K-4
1814 W Fir Rd 64836 417-359-7065
Bob Goltra, prin. Fax 359-7069
Twain ES 200/K-4
1435 S Main St 64836 417-359-7080
Laurel Rosenthal, prin. Fax 359-7079

St. Ann Catholic S 100/PK-6
1156 Grand Ave 64836 417-358-2674
Bonnie Schaeffer, prin. Fax 358-8976

Caruthersville, Pemiscot, Pop. 6,450
Caruthersville SD 18 1,400/PK-12
1711 Ward Ave 63830 573-333-6100
J.J. Bullington, supt. Fax 333-6108
www.cps18.org
Caruthersville ES 600/PK-5
900 Washington Ave 63830 573-333-6133
Claire Wallace, prin. Fax 333-6137
Caruthersville MS 300/6-8
1705 Ward Ave 63830 573-333-6120
Matt Hodges, prin. Fax 333-1835

Pemiscot County R-III SD 100/K-8
1727 County Highway 536 63830 573-333-1856
Anthony Hartsfield, supt. Fax 333-1857
r3.k12.mo.us
Hamlett S 100/K-8
1727 County Highway 536 63830 573-333-1856
Anthony Hartsfield, prin. Fax 333-1857

Cassville, Barry, Pop. 3,095
Cassville R-IV SD 2,000/PK-12
1501 Main St 65625 417-847-2221
Jim Orrell, supt. Fax 847-4009
wildcats.cassville.k12.mo.us/
Cassville IS 400/3-5
1501 Main St 65625 417-847-4010
Jill Lecompte, prin. Fax 847-4008
Cassville MS 500/6-8
1501 Main St 65625 417-847-3136
Eric White, prin. Fax 847-3156
Thomas ES 400/PK-2
1501 Main St 65625 417-847-2445
Catherine Weaver, prin. Fax 847-2462

Catawissa, Franklin
Meramec Valley R-III SD
Supt. — See Pacific
Nike ES 100/K-5
2264 Highway AP 63015 636-271-1444
Ketina Armstrong, prin. Fax 271-1447

Cedar Hill, Jefferson, Pop. 1,966
Northwest R-I SD
Supt. — See High Ridge
Cedar Hill IS 200/5-6
6471 Cedar Hill Rd 63016 636-274-3415
Aaron Kohler, prin. Fax 274-5729

Center, Ralls, Pop. 637
Ralls County R-II SD 800/PK-12
21622 Highway 19 63436 573-267-3397
Deanette Jarman, supt. Fax 267-3538
rallsr2.k12.mo.us/
Center ES 100/PK-5
601 E Hawkins St 63436 573-267-3341
Delores Woodhurst, prin. Fax 267-3567
Twain JHS 200/6-8
21622 Highway 19 63436 573-267-3397
Cherrie Allen, prin. Fax 267-3538
Other Schools – See New London

Centerview, Johnson, Pop. 258
Johnson County R-VII SD 600/PK-12
92 NW State Route 58 64019 660-656-3316
Dr. Phil Wright, supt. Fax 656-3633
crs.k12.mo.us
Crest Ridge ES 300/PK-5
94 NW State Route 58 64019 660-656-3315
Edith Jones, prin. Fax 656-3411
Crest Ridge MS 200/6-8
92 NW State Route 58 64019 660-656-3843
Gary Manning, prin. Fax 656-3633

Johnson County Christian Academy 100/PK-8
401 S Walnut St 64019 660-656-3307
Liz Deno, admin. Fax 656-3320

Centerville, Reynolds, Pop. 174
Centerville R-I SD 100/K-8
PO Box 99 63633 573-648-2285
Bobbie Meinershagen, supt. Fax 648-2282
Centerville S 100/K-8
PO Box 99 63633 573-648-2285
Bobbie Meinershagen, prin. Fax 648-2282

Centralia, Boone, Pop. 3,657
Centralia R-VI SD 1,200/PK-12
635 S Jefferson St 65240 573-682-3561
Darin Ford, supt. Fax 682-2181
www.centralia.k12.mo.us
Boren MS 400/5-8
110 N Jefferson St 65240 573-682-2617
Vincent Matlick, prin. Fax 682-1500
Chance ES 400/PK-4
510 S Rollins St 65240 573-682-2014
Sandra Dorr, prin. Fax 682-1369

Sunnydale Adventist S 50/K-8
6979 Audrain Road 9139 65240 573-682-2811

Chadwick, Christian
Chadwick R-I SD 200/K-12
7090 State Highway 125 S 65629 417-634-3588
Dr. William Wheeler, supt. Fax 634-2668
www.chadwick.k12.mo.us/
Chadwick ES 100/K-6
7090 State Highway 125 S 65629 417-634-3588
Dana Comstock, prin. Fax 634-2668

Chaffee, Scott, Pop. 3,006
Chaffee R-II SD 600/PK-12
517 W Yoakum Ave 63740 573-887-3532
Ken Latham, supt. Fax 887-3926
Chaffee ES 300/PK-6
408 Elliott Ave 63740 573-887-3244
Michele Williams, prin. Fax 887-6493

St. Ambrose S 100/K-8
419 S 3rd St 63740 573-887-6711
Susan Long, prin. Fax 887-6711

Chamois, Osage, Pop. 473
Osage County R-I SD 200/K-12
614 S Poplar St 65024 573-763-5666
Ryan Nowlin, supt. Fax 763-5686
www.chamois.k12.mo.us
Osage County ES 100/K-6
614 S Poplar St 65024 573-763-5446
Dee Luker, prin. Fax 763-5686

Charleston, Mississippi, Pop. 5,129
Charleston R-I SD 1,000/K-12
PO Box 39 63834 573-683-3776
Kevin Miller, supt. Fax 683-2909
charleston.k12.mo.us/
Charleston MS 300/6-8
PO Box 39 63834 573-683-3346
Jason Roberts, prin. Fax 683-2909
Hearnes ES 400/K-5
PO Box 39 63834 573-683-3728
Fax 683-2909

St. Henry S 100/K-8
306 Court St 63834 573-683-6218
Alice Harvell, prin. Fax 683-4124

Chesterfield, Saint Louis, Pop. 47,020
Parkway C-2 SD 18,400/PK-12
455 N Woods Mill Rd 63017 314-415-8100
Robert Malito Ph.D., supt. Fax 415-8009
www.pkwy.k12.mo.us/
Green Trails ES 500/K-5
170 Portico Dr 63017 314-415-6250
Sean Doherty, prin. Fax 415-6262
Highcroft Ridge ES 400/K-5
15380 Highcroft Dr 63017 314-415-6400
Simone Wilson, prin. Fax 415-6419
Parkway Central MS 900/6-8
471 N Woods Mill Rd 63017 314-415-7800
Michael Baugus, prin. Fax 415-7834
Parkway West MS 900/6-8
2312 Baxter Rd 63017 314-415-7400
Linda Lelonek, prin. Fax 415-7409
River Bend ES 300/K-5
224 River Valley Dr 63017 314-415-6650
Bonnie McCracken, prin. Fax 415-6669
Shenandoah Valley ES 400/K-5
15399 Appalachian Trl 63017 314-415-6750
Bruce Hunter, prin. Fax 415-6762
Other Schools – See Ballwin, Creve Coeur, Manchester, Maryland Heights

Rockwood R-VI SD
Supt. — See Eureka
Chesterfield ES 500/K-5
17700 Wild Horse Creek Rd 63005 636-537-4342
Jodi Davidson, prin. Fax 537-4347
Kehrs Mill ES 600/K-5
2650 Kehrs Mill Rd 63017 636-537-4359
Margaret Lucero, prin. Fax 537-4363
Rockwood Center ECC 300/PK-PK
2730 Valley Rd 63005 636-207-2600
Marie Wohlert, dir. Fax 207-2607
Wild Horse ES 500/K-5
16695 Wild Horse Creek Rd 63005 636-537-4398
Karen Kieffer, prin. Fax 537-4388

Ascension S 500/K-8
238 Santa Maria Dr 63005 636-532-1151
Cathie Wayland, prin. Fax 532-6502
Chesterfield Day S 400/PK-6
1100 White Rd 63017 314-469-6622
Dennis Guilliams, hdmstr. Fax 469-7889
Chesterfield Montessori S 200/PK-6
14000 Ladue Rd 63017 314-469-7150
Anita Chastain, admin. Fax 469-7851
Gateway Academy 400/PK-12
17815 Wild Horse Creek Rd 63005 636-519-9099
Denise Cress, dir. Fax 519-1621
Incarnate Word S 400/K-8
13416 Olive Blvd 63017 314-576-5366
Michael Welling, prin. Fax 576-2046
West County Christian S 100/K-8
13431 N Outer 40 Rd 63017 314-579-9610
Janet Gregory, prin. Fax 579-0500
Westwood Jr. Academy 50/PK-10
16601 Wild Horse Creek Rd 63005 636-519-8222

Chilhowee, Johnson, Pop. 340
Chilhowee R-IV SD 200/K-12
101 Highway 2 64733 660-678-2511
Stephen Pope, supt. Fax 678-5711
www.chilhowee.k12.mo.us
Chilhowee ES 100/K-6
101 Highway 2 64733 660-678-4511
Renae Gregory, prin. Fax 678-5711

Shawnee R-III SD 100/K-8
1193 N Highway 13 64733 660-885-3620
Nancy Akert, supt. Fax 885-3620
Shawnee S 100/K-8
1193 N Highway 13 64733 660-885-3620
Nancy Akert, prin. Fax 885-3620

Chillicothe, Livingston, Pop. 8,686
Chillicothe R-II SD 1,800/K-12
PO Box 530 64601 660-646-4566
Dr. Linda Gray Smith, supt. Fax 646-6508
www.chillicotheschools.org/
Central ES 300/4-5
321 Elm St 64601 660-646-2359
Philip Pohren, prin. Fax 646-3832
Chillicothe MS 400/6-8
1529 Calhoun St 64601 660-646-1916
Bryan Copple, prin. Fax 646-5065
Dewey ES 100/K-1
905 Dickinson St 64601 660-646-4255
Pam Brobst, prin. Fax 646-0801
Field ES 300/2-3
1100 Oak St 64601 660-646-2909
Paula Grozinger, prin. Fax 646-6286

Bishop Hogan Memorial S 100/PK-8
1114 Trenton St 64601 660-646-0705
Fr. Tom Hermes, prin. Fax 646-0705

Chula, Livingston, Pop. 201
Livingston County R-III SD 100/PK-8
PO Box 40 64635 660-639-3135
Sara Littrell, supt. Fax 639-2171
Livingston County S 100/PK-8
PO Box 40 64635 660-639-3135
Sara Littrell, prin. Fax 639-2171

Clarence, Shelby, Pop. 906
Shelby County R-IV SD
Supt. — See Shelbina
Clarence ES 100/PK-5
206 N Shelby St 63437 660-699-3302
Karla Matlock, prin. Fax 699-2168

Clarksburg, Moniteau, Pop. 390
Clarksburg C-2 SD 100/K-8
401 S Highway H 65025 573-787-3511
Bonnie Aaron, supt. Fax 787-3667
schoolweb.missouri.edu/clarksburg.k12.mo.us/
Clarksburg S 100/K-8
401 S Highway H 65025 573-787-3511
Bonnie Aaron, prin. Fax 787-3667

Clarksville, Pike, Pop. 512
Pike County R-III SD 600/PK-12
28176 Highway WW 63336 573-242-3546
Terry Robertson, supt. Fax 485-2393
www.clopton.k12.mo.us
Clopton ES 300/PK-6
28176 Highway WW 63336 573-485-2488
Mark Harvey, prin. Fax 485-2393

Clarkton, Dunklin, Pop. 1,280
Clarkton C-4 SD 400/PK-12
PO Box 637 63837 573-448-3712
Philip Harrison, supt. Fax 448-5182
www.clarktonschools.org/
Clarkton ES 200/PK-6
PO Box 637 63837 573-448-3712
William Thornton, prin. Fax 448-5182

Clayton, Saint Louis, Pop. 16,061
Clayton SD 2,700/PK-12
2 Mark Twain Cir 63105 314-854-6000
Dr. Don Senti, supt. Fax 854-6094
www.clayton.k12.mo.us
Captain ES 300/K-5
6345 Northwood Ave 63105 314-854-6100
Sandra Rosell, prin. Fax 854-6190
Family Center 100/PK-PK
301 Gay Ave 63105 314-854-6900
Debbie Reilly, dir. Fax 854-6940
Glenridge ES 400/K-5
7447 Wellington Way 63105 314-854-6200
Beth Scott, prin. Fax 854-6290
Meramec ES 400/K-5
400 S Meramec Ave 63105 314-854-6300
Annette Isselhard, prin. Fax 854-6390
Wydown MS 600/6-8
6500 Wydown Blvd 63105 314-854-6400
Mary Ann Goldberg, prin. Fax 854-6491

Cleveland, Cass, Pop. 674
Midway R-I SD 600/K-12
5801 State Route 2 64734 816-250-2994
David Copeland, supt. Fax 899-2823
www.midway.k12.mo.us
Midway ES 300/K-6
5801 State Route 2 64734 816-250-2994
Susan Tinich, prin. Fax 899-2823

Clever, Christian, Pop. 1,242
Clever R-V SD 800/PK-12
103 S Public Ave 65631 417-743-4800
Richard Henson, supt. Fax 743-4802
www.clever.k12.mo.us
Clever ES 300/PK-3
400 W Brown St 65631 417-743-4810
Rebecca Bernard, prin. Fax 743-4812
Clever MS 200/6-8
401 W Inman Rd 65631 417-743-4820
Benjy Fenske, prin. Fax 743-4802
Clever Upper ES 100/4-5
103 S Public Ave 65631 417-743-4815
Jeremy Thompson, prin. Fax 743-4802

Clifton Hill, Randolph, Pop. 129
Westran R-I SD
Supt. — See Huntsville
Westran MS 100/6-8
622 Harlan St 65244 660-261-4511
Mike Aulbur, prin. Fax 261-4292

Climax Springs, Camden, Pop. 85
Climax Springs R-IV SD 200/PK-12
119 Nort Dr 65324 573-347-3905
Michael Diekmann, supt. Fax 347-9931
csprings.k12.mo.us/
Climax Springs ES 100/PK-6
119 Nort Dr 65324 573-347-3005
Mary Gerriets, prin. Fax 347-9933

Clinton, Henry, Pop. 9,414
Clinton SD 124 1,700/PK-12
701 S 8th St 64735 660-885-2237
William Biggerstaff, supt. Fax 885-7033
clinton.k12.mo.us
Clinton ECC PK-PK
701 S 8th St 64735 660-885-5845
Wendy Faulconer, coord. Fax 885-7033
Clinton MS 400/6-8
701 S 8th St 64735 660-885-3353
Andy Ford, prin. Fax 885-4826
Henry ES 600/K-5
701 S 8th St 64735 660-885-5585
Mary Young, prin. Fax 885-2784

Davis R-XII SD 50/PK-8
227 SW Highway T 64735 660-885-2629
Deborah Day, supt. Fax 885-2648
Davis S 50/PK-8
227 SW Highway T 64735 660-885-2629
Deborah Day, prin. Fax 885-2648

Leesville R-IX SD 100/K-8
823 SE Highway 7 64735 660-477-3406
Lori Rowe, supt. Fax 477-9362
Leesville S 100/K-8
823 SE Highway 7 64735 660-477-3406
Lori Rowe, prin. Fax 477-9362

Clinton Christian Academy 100/PK-8
271 W Division Rd 64735 660-890-2111
Timothy Slagle, admin. Fax 885-2191
Holy Rosary S 100/PK-8
400 E Wilson St 64735 660-885-4412
Doug McMillan, prin. Fax 885-5791

Coffey, Daviess, Pop. 144
North Daviess R-III SD
Supt. — See Jameson
North Daviess ES 100/PK-6
PO Box 139 64636 660-533-2515
Becky Morris, prin. Fax 533-4515

Cole Camp, Benton, Pop. 1,160
Cole Camp R-I SD 800/K-12
500 S Keeney St 65325 660-668-4427
Dr. Jerry Cochran, supt. Fax 668-4703
Cole Camp ES 300/K-5
500 S Keeney St 65325 660-668-3011
Cheryl Petersen, prin. Fax 668-4703
Cole Camp MS 200/6-8
500 S Keeney St 65325 660-668-3502
Tyler Clark, prin. Fax 668-4703

Lutheran School Association 100/K-8
204 E Butterfield Trl 65325 660-668-4614
Larry Andersen, prin. Fax 668-2456

Columbia, Boone, Pop. 91,814
Columbia SD 93 16,600/PK-12
1818 W Worley St 65203 573-214-3400
Dr. Phyllis Chase, supt. Fax 214-3401
www.columbia.k12.mo.us/
Benton ES 300/PK-5
1410 Hinkson Ave 65201 573-214-3610
Troy Hogg, prin. Fax 214-3611
Blue Ridge ES 500/PK-5
3700 Woodland Dr 65202 573-214-3580
Timothy Majerus, prin. Fax 214-3581
Cedar Ridge ES 200/K-5
1100 S Roseta Ave 65201 573-214-3510
Diana Demoss, prin. Fax 214-3511
Derby Ridge ES 600/PK-5
4000 Derby Ridge Dr 65202 573-214-3270
Tina Windett, prin. Fax 214-3271
Fairview ES 500/K-5
909 S Fairview Rd 65203 573-214-3590
Fax 214-3591

Field ES 300/PK-5
1010 Rangeline St 65201 573-214-3620
Dr. Carol Garman, prin. Fax 214-3621
Gentry MS 700/6-7
4200 Bethel St 65203 573-214-3240
Janice Morris, prin. Fax 214-3241
Grant ES 300/K-5
10 E Broadway 65203 573-214-3520
Beverly Borduin, prin. Fax 214-3521
Keeley ES 600/K-5
201 Park De Ville Dr 65203 573-214-3570
Elaine Hassemer, prin. Fax 214-3571
Lange MS 800/6-7
2201 Smiley Ln 65202 573-214-3250
Shelly Adams, prin. Fax 214-3251
Lee ES 300/K-5
1208 Locust St 65201 573-214-3530
Dr. Teresa Van Dover, prin. Fax 214-3531
Midway Heights ES 300/K-5
8130 Highway 40 W 65202 573-214-3540
Anne Billington, prin. Fax 214-3541
Mill Creek ES 600/K-5
2200 W Nifong Blvd 65203 573-214-3280
Mary Sue Gibson, prin. Fax 214-3281
New Haven ES 300/K-5
3301 New Haven Ave 65201 573-214-3640
Cynthia Giovanini, prin. Fax 214-3641
Parkade ES 500/PK-5
111 Parkade Blvd 65202 573-214-3630
Amy Watkins, prin. Fax 214-3631
Ridgeway ES 200/K-5
107 E Sexton Rd 65203 573-214-3550
Marsha Baclesse, prin. Fax 214-3551
Rock Bridge ES 400/PK-5
5151 S Highway 163 65203 573-214-3290
Mary Korth-Lloyd, prin. Fax 214-3291
Russell Boulevard ES 600/PK-5
1800 W Rollins Rd 65203 573-214-3650
Dr. Edward Schumacher, prin. Fax 214-3651
Shepard Boulevard ES 500/K-5
2616 Shepard Blvd 65201 573-214-3660
Jonetta Weaver, prin. Fax 214-3661
Smithton MS 900/6-7
3600 W Worley St 65203 573-214-3260
Dr. Craig Martin, prin. Fax 214-3261
Two Mile Prairie ES 300/K-5
5450 N Route Z 65202 573-214-3560
Larry Jones, prin. Fax 214-3561
West Boulevard ES 300/PK-5
319 West Blvd N 65203 573-214-3670
Peter Stieplemann, prin. Fax 214-3671

Childrens House of Columbia 100/PK-3
915 Maryland Ave 65201 573-443-2825
Mary Windmiller, prin. Fax 874-4056
Christian Fellowship S 300/PK-12
4600 Christian Fellowshp Rd 65203 573-445-8565
Dr. Rick Mueller, admin. Fax 445-8564
College Park Christian Academy 50/PK-9
1114 College Park Dr 65203 573-445-6315
Sandra Blackburn, prin. Fax 445-6113
Columbia Catholic S 600/K-8
817 Bernadette Dr 65203 573-445-6516
Linda Garner, prin. Fax 445-9887
Columbia Independent S 200/K-12
1200 E Broadway 65215 573-815-5960
Scott Gibson, hdmstr.
Good Shepherd Lutheran S 100/K-7
2201 W Rollins Rd 65203 573-445-5878
Fax 445-4078
Trinity Lutheran Child Learning Center 50/PK-K
2201 W Rollins Rd 65203 573-445-1014
Fax 445-4078

Conception Junction, Nodaway, Pop. 197
Jefferson C-123 SD 200/PK-12
37614 US Highway 136 64434 660-944-2316
Rob Dowis, supt. Fax 944-2315
www.jc123.k12.mo.us/
Jefferson ES 100/PK-6
37614 US Highway 136 64434 660-944-2417
Jane Walter, prin. Fax 944-2315

Concordia, Lafayette, Pop. 2,413
Concordia R-II SD 500/PK-12
PO Box 879 64020 660-463-7235
Mary Beth Scherer, supt. Fax 463-1326
www.concordia.k12.mo.us
Concordia ES 300/PK-6
PO Box 879 64020 660-463-2261
Joe Beydler, prin. Fax 463-2413

St. Paul Lutheran S 200/PK-8
407 S Main St 64020 660-463-7654
Lori Flenner, prin. Fax 463-7173

Conway, Laclede, Pop. 774
Laclede County R-I SD 900/K-12
726 W Jefferson Ave 65632 417-589-2951
Dr. Chris Berger, supt. Fax 589-3202
www.conwayschooldistrict.com
Conway JHS 100/7-8
726 W Jefferson Ave 65632 417-589-8147
Ricky Lowrance, prin. Fax 589-2500
Ezard ES 500/K-6
209 S Shiloh Ave 65632 417-589-2171
Cindy Hawkins, prin. Fax 589-8251

Cooter, Pemiscot, Pop. 437
Cooter R-IV SD 300/K-12
PO Box 218 63839 573-695-3312
William Crowder, supt. Fax 695-3073
Cooter ES 100/K-6
PO Box 218 63839 573-695-4584
Jerry Hatley, prin. Fax 695-2542

Cosby, Andrew, Pop. 146
Avenue City R-IX SD 100/K-8
18069 Highway 169 64436 816-662-2305
Jerry Archer, supt. Fax 662-3201
schoolweb.missouri.edu/avenuecity.k12.mo.us/
Avenue City S 100/K-8
18069 Highway 169 64436 816-662-2305
Becky Grimes, prin. Fax 662-3201

Country Club, Andrew, Pop. 1,897
Savannah R-III SD
Supt. — See Savannah
Glenn ES 300/K-6
12401 County Road 438, 816-279-4533
Vance Vanderwerken, prin. Fax 279-0540

Cowgill, Caldwell, Pop. 257
Cowgill R-VI SD 50/K-6
PO Box 49 64637 660-255-4415
John Ross, supt. Fax 255-4224
Cowgill S 50/K-6
PO Box 49 64637 660-255-4415
John Ross, prin. Fax 255-4224

Craig, Holt, Pop. 297
Craig R-III SD 100/K-12
402 N Ward St 64437 660-683-5351
Michael Leach, supt. Fax 683-5431
www.schoolweb.missouri.edu/craigr3.k12.mo.us
Craig ES 50/K-6
402 N Ward St 64437 660-683-5431
Terry Petersen, prin. Fax 683-5769

Crane, Stone, Pop. 1,442
Crane R-III SD 700/K-12
PO Box 405 65633 417-723-5300
Tyler Laney, supt. Fax 723-5551
www.crane.k12.mo.us
Crane ES 300/K-4
PO Box 405 65633 417-723-5780
Patricia Pearson, prin. Fax 723-5551
Crane MS 200/5-8
PO Box 405 65633 417-723-8177
Karla Snook, prin. Fax 723-5551

Creighton, Cass, Pop. 350
Sherwood Cass R-VIII SD 900/PK-12
PO Box 98 64739 660-499-2834
Freddie Doherty, supt. Fax 499-2624
sherwood.k12.mo.us
Sherwood ES 400/PK-5
PO Box 98 64739 660-499-2202
Lori Hernandez, prin. Fax 499-2865
Sherwood MS 200/6-8
PO Box 98 64739 660-499-2239
Brenda Koch, prin. Fax 499-2585

Creve Coeur, Saint Louis, Pop. 16,975
Ladue SD
Supt. — See Saint Louis
Spoede ES 500/K-5
425 N Spoede Rd 63141 314-432-4438
Connie Brawley, prin. Fax 432-6098

Parkway C-2 SD
Supt. — See Chesterfield
Bellerive ES 400/K-5
666 Rue De Fleur Dr 63141 314-415-6050
Deborah McMillan, prin. Fax 415-6062
Craig ES 500/K-5
1492 Craig Rd, Saint Louis MO 63146 314-415-6200
Nicole Evans, prin. Fax 415-6212
Mason Ridge ES 400/K-5
715 S Mason Rd 63141 314-415-6450
Michael Schmerold, prin. Fax 415-6462
Parkway Northeast MS 1,000/6-8
181 Coeur De Ville Dr 63141 314-415-7100
Kim Brandon, prin. Fax 415-7113
Ross ES 500/K-5
1150 Ross Ave, Saint Louis MO 63146
314-415-6700
Lisa Greenstein, prin. Fax 415-6712

Pattonville R-III SD
Supt. — See Saint Ann
Willow Brook ES 300/K-5
11022 Schuetz Rd, Saint Louis MO 63146
314-213-8018
Montize Aaron, prin. Fax 213-8618

St. Monica S 300/K-8
12132 Olive Blvd 63141 314-434-2173
Kathy Hunt, prin. Fax 434-7689
St. Richard S 100/K-8
11211 Schuetz Rd, Saint Louis MO 63146
314-872-3152
Julie Smith, prin. Fax 872-0931

Crocker, Pulaski, Pop. 1,010
Crocker R-II SD 600/PK-12
PO Box 488 65452 573-736-5000
Dr. Jim Bogle, supt. Fax 736-5924
www.crocker.k12.mo.us/
Crocker ES 300/PK-6
PO Box 488 65452 573-736-5000
Doug Jacobson, prin. Fax 736-2688

Crystal City, Jefferson, Pop. 4,508
Crystal City SD 47 700/K-12
1100 Mississippi Ave 63019 636-937-4411
Ronald Swafford, supt. Fax 937-2512
www.crystal.k12.mo.us/
Crystal City S 400/K-8
600 Mississippi Ave 63019 636-937-4017
Nicholle Ruess, prin. Fax 937-2229

Cuba, Crawford, Pop. 3,447
Crawford County R-II SD 1,300/K-12
1 Wildcat Pride Dr 65453 573-885-2534
Waymon Boast, supt. Fax 885-3900
www.cuba.k12.mo.us/
Cuba ES 500/K-4
1 Wildcat Pride Dr 65453 573-885-2534
Diane Haggard, prin. Fax 885-3123
Cuba MS 400/5-8
1 Wildcat Pride Dr 65453 573-885-2534
Patricia Tavenner, prin. Fax 885-6278

Holy Cross S 100/PK-8
407 School Ave 65453 573-885-4727
Cate Sanazaro, prin. Fax 885-3501

Dadeville, Dade, Pop. 224
Dadeville R-II SD 200/K-12
PO Box 188 65635 417-995-2201
Matt Bushey, supt. Fax 995-2110
Dadeville ES 100/K-6
PO Box 188 65635 417-995-2201
Mike Linehan, prin. Fax 995-2110

Dardenne Pr, Saint Charles, Pop. 967

Immaculate Conception S - Dardenne 700/K-8
2089 Hanley Rd, 636-561-4450
Janet Eaton, prin. Fax 625-9020

Dearborn, Platte, Pop. 531
North Platte County R-I SD 700/PK-12
212 W 6th St 64439 816-450-3511
Dr. Jeffrey Sumy, supt. Fax 992-8727
www.nplatte.k12.mo.us/
North Platte JHS 100/7-8
212 W 6th St 64439 816-450-3350
Karl Matt, prin. Fax 992-3665
Other Schools – See Camden Point, Edgerton

Deepwater, Henry, Pop. 505
Lakeland R-III SD 500/PK-12
12530 Lakeland School Dr 64740 417-644-2223
Ryan Huff, supt. Fax 644-2316
www.lakelandschools.com/index.html
Lakeland ES 300/PK-6
12530 Lakeland School Dr 64740 417-644-2281
Patricia Munsterman, prin. Fax 644-2316

Deering, Pemiscot, Pop. 130
Delta C-7 SD 200/K-12
PO Box 297 63840 573-757-6648
James Williams, supt. Fax 757-9691
www.schoolweb.missouri.edu/deltac7.k12.mo.us/
Delta C-7 ES 100/K-6
PO Box 297 63840 573-757-6615
Kenny Copley, prin. Fax 757-6201

De Kalb, Buchanan, Pop. 258
Buchanan County R-IV SD 400/PK-12
702 Main St 64440 816-685-3160
Lane Novinger, supt. Fax 685-3203
www.bcr4.k12.mo.us/
Other Schools – See Rushville

Delta, Cape Girardeau, Pop. 536
Delta R-V SD 300/PK-12
PO Box 787 63744 573-794-2500
Nate Crowden, supt. Fax 794-2504
deltarv.k12.mo.us
Delta ES 200/PK-6
PO Box 219 63744 573-794-2440
Mary Livingston, prin. Fax 794-2504

Desloge, Saint Francois, Pop. 5,143
North St. Francois County R-I SD
Supt. — See Bonne Terre
North County IS 500/5-6
801 E Elm St 63601 573-431-1358
Jason Samples, prin. Fax 518-0569
North County MS 500/7-8
406 E Chestnut St 63601 573-431-6700
Brenda Medley, prin. Fax 431-5203
Parkside ES 200/3-4
100 N Parkside St 63601 573-431-3300
Janet Moak, prin. Fax 431-0250

De Soto, Jefferson, Pop. 6,552
Desoto SD 73 2,700/PK-12
610 Vineland School Rd 63020 636-586-1000
Andrew Arbeitman, supt. Fax 586-1009
www.desoto.k12.mo.us
Athena ES 600/K-6
3775 Athena School Rd 63020 636-586-1020
Alex Mahn, prin. Fax 586-1029
De Soto JHS 400/7-8
731 Amvets Dr 63020 636-586-1030
Dan Hoehn, prin. Fax 586-1039
Little Dragons Preschool PK-PK
1812 Rock Rd 63020 636-337-8847
Trish Burkeen, dir. Fax 586-1009
Vineland ES 700/K-6
650 Vineland School Rd 63020 636-586-1010
Adam A. Grindstaff, prin. Fax 586-1019

Sunrise R-IX SD 400/K-8
4485 Sunrise School Rd 63020 636-586-6660
Clay Whitener, supt. Fax 586-3192
www.sunrise-r9.com/
Sunrise S 400/K-8
4485 Sunrise School Rd 63020 636-586-6660
Lori England, prin. Fax 586-3192

St. Rose of Lima S 100/PK-8
523 S 4th St 63020 636-337-7855
Imogene Renick, prin. Fax 337-2394

Dexter, Stoddard, Pop. 7,596
Dexter R-XI SD 1,900/PK-12
1031 Brown Pilot Ln 63841 573-614-1000
Dr. Kenneth Jackson, supt. Fax 614-1002
dexter.k12.mo.us/
Central ES 500/3-5
1213 Central Dr 63841 573-614-1020
Cynthia E. Bowman, prin. Fax 614-1021

Hill MS 400/6-8
1107 Brown Pilot Ln 63841 573-614-1010
Dr. Roger Alsup, prin. Fax 614-1012
Southwest ES 400/PK-2
915 W Grant St 63841 573-614-1015
Sherry Mathews, prin. Fax 614-1017

Diamond, Newton, Pop. 846
Diamond R-IV SD 1,000/K-12
PO Box 68 64840 417-325-5186
Patricia Wilson, supt. Fax 325-5338
www.diamondwildcats.org/
Diamond ES 400/K-4
PO Box 68 64840 417-325-5189
Melissa Massey, prin. Fax 325-5187
Diamond MS 300/5-8
PO Box 68 64840 417-325-5336
Danny DeWitt, prin. Fax 325-5333

Dittmer, Jefferson
Northwest R-I SD
Supt. — See High Ridge
Maple Grove ES 400/K-4
7887 Dittmer Ridge Rd 63023 636-274-5327
Melissa Daniel, prin. Fax 274-0413

Dixon, Pulaski, Pop. 1,548
Dixon R-I SD 1,100/PK-12
PO Box A 65459 573-759-7163
Dawna Burrow, supt. Fax 759-2506
www.dixonr1.yhti.net/
Dixon ES 500/PK-5
PO Box A 65459 573-759-7163
Joyce Shepherd, prin. Fax 759-2952
Dixon MS 300/6-8
PO Box A 65459 573-759-7163
Jim Brown, prin. Fax 759-6627

Doniphan, Ripley, Pop. 1,924
Doniphan R-I SD 1,500/PK-12
309 Pine St 63935 573-996-3819
Kevin Sandlin, supt. Fax 996-5865
www.doniphanr1.k12.mo.us
Doniphan ES 600/PK-5
603 E Summit St 63935 573-996-3523
Mark Thompson, prin. Fax 996-5675
Doniphan MS 400/6-8
651 E Summit St 63935 573-996-3614
Dr. Tim Hager, prin. Fax 996-4525

Ripley County R-IV SD 200/K-8
HC 7 Box 51 63935 573-996-7118
Ligie Waddell, supt. Fax 996-7484
lonestar.k12.mo.us
Ripley County S 200/K-8
HC 7 Box 51 63935 573-996-7118
Ligie Waddell, prin. Fax 996-7484

Dora, Ozark
Dora R-III SD 300/PK-12
PO Box 14 65637 417-261-2346
Jeffrey Chappell, supt. Fax 261-2673
www.dora.org
Dora ES 100/PK-6
PO Box 14 65637 417-261-2337
Sherry Anstine, prin. Fax 261-2673

Drexel, Bates, Pop. 1,115
Drexel R-IV SD 300/K-12
PO Box 860 64742 816-657-4715
Dr. Judy Stivers, supt. Fax 657-4798
www.drexel.k12.mo.us/
Drexel ES 200/K-6
PO Box 860 64742 816-619-2468
Jeff Levy, prin. Fax 657-4798

Duenweg, Jasper, Pop. 1,068
Joplin R-VIII SD
Supt. — See Joplin
Duenweg ES 100/K-5
202 Malloy Cir 64841 417-625-5330
Teresa Adams, prin. Fax 625-5334

Eagleville, Harrison, Pop. 326
North Harrison R-III SD 200/PK-12
12023 Fir St 64442 660-867-5222
Nancy Parman, supt. Fax 867-5263
www.nhr3.net
North Harrison ES 100/PK-5
12023 Fir St 64442 660-867-5214
Sherry Henson, prin. Fax 867-3397

East Lynne, Cass, Pop. 312
East Lynne SD 40 200/PK-8
PO Box 108 64743 816-626-3511
Bill Redinger, supt. Fax 869-3505
East Lynne S 200/PK-8
PO Box 108 64743 816-626-3511
Bill Redinger, prin. Fax 869-3505

Easton, Buchanan, Pop. 253
East Buchanan County C-1 SD
Supt. — See Gower
East Buchanan MS 200/6-8
301 N County Park Rd 64443 816-473-2451
Douglas Miller, prin. Fax 473-2604

East Prairie, Mississippi, Pop. 3,117
East Prairie R-II SD 1,100/PK-12
304 E Walnut St 63845 573-649-3562
Scott Downing, supt. Fax 649-5455
www.eprairie.k12.mo.us
Doyle ES 300/PK-2
402 N Washington St 63845 573-649-2272
Mellisa Heath, prin. Fax 649-5671
East Prairie JHS 200/7-8
210 E Washington St 63845 573-649-9368
Eva Hinshaw, prin. Fax 649-9370
Martin ES 300/3-6
510 Wilkinson St 63845 573-649-3521
Donna Smith, prin. Fax 649-9260

Edgar Springs, Phelps, Pop. 188
Phelps County R-III SD 200/K-8
17790 State Route M 65462 573-435-6293
Kay McMurtrey, supt. Fax 435-9489
Phelps County S 200/K-8
17790 State Route M 65462 573-435-6293
Kay McMurtrey, prin. Fax 435-9489

Edgerton, Platte, Pop. 546
North Platte County R-I SD
Supt. — See Dearborn
North Platte IS 100/4-6
900 Lewis St 64444 816-790-3622
Cathy Boyd, prin. Fax 227-3719

Edina, Knox, Pop. 1,162
Knox County R-I SD 600/PK-12
RR 3 Box 59 63537 660-397-2228
D.J. Leverton, supt. Fax 397-3998
www.knox.k12.mo.us/
Knox County ES 300/PK-6
RR 3 Box 59 63537 660-397-2285
Marty Strange, prin. Fax 397-3316

Edwards, Benton
Warsaw R-IX SD
Supt. — See Warsaw
South ES 200/PK-5
23395 Highway 7 65326 660-438-5976
Amie Breshears, prin. Fax 438-5976

Eldon, Miller, Pop. 4,934
Eldon R-I SD 1,900/PK-12
112 S Pine St 65026 573-392-8000
Matt Davis, supt. Fax 392-8080
www.eldon.k12.mo.us/
Eldon MS 300/7-8
1400 N Grand Ave 65026 573-392-8020
Shaun Fischer, prin. Fax 392-9151
Eldon Upper ES 400/4-6
409 E 15th St 65026 573-392-6364
Denise Harwood, prin. Fax 392-9152
South ES 500/PK-3
1210 S Maple St 65026 573-392-8030
Steve Rhine, prin. Fax 392-9152

El Dorado Springs, Cedar, Pop. 3,849
El Dorado Springs R-II SD 1,300/PK-12
901 S Grand Ave 64744 417-876-3112
Roger Barnes, supt. Fax 876-2128
www.eldo.k12.mo.us/
El Dorado Springs ES 600/PK-5
901 S Grand Ave 64744 417-876-3112
Tracy Lanser, prin. Fax 876-0613
El Dorado Springs MS 300/6-8
901 S Grand Ave 64744 417-876-3112
Brad Stewart, prin. Fax 876-2128

El Dorado Christian S 200/PK-12
1600 S Ohio St 64744 417-876-2201
Amy Castor, prin. Fax 876-4913

Ellington, Reynolds, Pop. 1,013
Southern Reynolds County R-II SD 600/PK-12
1 School St 63638 573-663-3591
Dr. Mike Redlich, supt. Fax 663-2412
www.ellington.k12.mo.us/
Southern Reynolds County ES 300/PK-6
1 School St 63638 573-663-2293
Caroline Bouma, prin. Fax 663-2144

Ellisville, Saint Louis, Pop. 9,353
Rockwood R-VI SD
Supt. — See Eureka
Ellisville ES 600/K-5
1425 Froesel Dr 63011 636-207-2548
Dr. Allison Loy, prin. Fax 207-2553
Green Pines ES 500/K-5
16543 Green Pines Dr 63011 636-458-7255
Jane Brown, prin. Fax 458-7262

St. Clare of Assisi S 500/K-8
15668 Clayton Rd 63011 636-227-8654
Marie Sinnett, prin. Fax 394-0359
St. John Lutheran S 300/PK-8
15800 Manchester Rd 63011 636-779-2325
Spencer Peregoy, prin. Fax 394-6274

Ellsinore, Carter, Pop. 363
East Carter County R-II SD 900/PK-12
24 S Herren Ave 63937 573-322-5625
Dr. Daniel Slack, supt. Fax 322-8586
www.ecarter.k12.mo.us
East Carter County R-II ES 400/PK-5
24 S Herren Ave 63937 573-322-5325
Carol Metz, prin. Fax 322-5325
East Carter County R-II MS 300/6-8
24 S Herren Ave 63937 573-322-5420
Richard Sullivan, prin. Fax 322-5420

Elsberry, Lincoln, Pop. 2,417
Elsberry R-II SD 800/K-12
PO Box 106 63343 573-898-5554
Larry Flanagan, supt. Fax 898-3140
schoolweb.missouri.edu/elsberry.k12.mo.us/
Cannon ES 300/K-4
PO Box 106 63343 573-898-5554
Cyril Heintzelman, prin. Fax 898-2977
Cannon MS 300/5-8
PO Box 106 63343 573-898-5554
Kenny Youmans, prin. Fax 898-5825

Eminence, Shannon, Pop. 550
Eminence R-I SD 300/PK-12
PO Box 730 65466 573-226-3251
Kevin Goddard, supt. Fax 226-3250
eminence.echalk.com/
Eminence ES 200/PK-6
PO Box 730 65466 573-226-3281
Dyle Stephens, prin. Fax 226-3802

Essex, Stoddard, Pop. 530
Richland R-I SD 300/K-12
24456 State Highway 114 63846 573-283-5332
Michael Kiehne, supt. Fax 283-5798
www.richland.k12.mo.us/
Richland ES 100/K-6
24456 State Highway 114 63846 573-283-5310
Lori Scheeter, prin. Fax 283-5108

Eugene, Cole, Pop. 159
Cole County R-V SD 700/K-12
14803 Highway 17 65032 573-498-4000
Mark Blythe, supt. Fax 498-4090
www.coler-v.k12.mo.us/
Eugene ES 300/K-6
14803 Highway 17 65032 573-498-4002
Dan Smith, prin. Fax 498-4090

Our Lady of Snows S 100/PK-8
276 Highway H 65032 573-498-3574
Gayle Trachsel, prin. Fax 498-3776

Eureka, Saint Louis, Pop. 8,957
Rockwood R-VI SD 22,400/PK-12
111 E North St 63025 636-938-2200
Dr. Craig Larson, supt. Fax 938-2251
www.rockwood.k12.mo.us
Blevins ES 500/K-5
25 E North St 63025 636-938-2150
Sharon Jackson, prin. Fax 938-2170
Eureka ES 300/K-5
442 W 4th St 63025 636-938-2452
Brian Gentz, prin. Fax 938-2457
Geggie ES 500/K-5
430 Bald Hill Rd 63025 636-938-2458
Dr. Mary Kleekamp, prin. Fax 938-2460
Other Schools – See Ballwin, Chesterfield, Ellisville, Fenton, Glencoe, Grover

---

Sacred Heart S 200/PK-8
350 E 4th St 63025 636-938-4602
Monica Wilson, prin. Fax 938-5802
St. Mark's Lutheran S 200/PK-8
500 Meramec Blvd 63025 636-938-4432
Sue Templeton, prin. Fax 938-6464

Everton, Dade, Pop. 322
Everton R-III SD 200/K-12
211 E School St 65646 417-535-2221
Chuck Adams, supt. Fax 535-4105
www.evertontigers.org
Everton ES 100/K-6
211 E School St 65646 417-535-2221
Dana Dreier, prin. Fax 535-4105

Ewing, Lewis, Pop. 453
Lewis County C-1 SD 1,000/PK-12
PO Box 366 63440 573-209-3217
Jacqueline Ebeling, supt. Fax 209-3318
www.lewis.k12.mo.us
Other Schools – See Lewistown

Excelsior Springs, Clay, Pop. 11,472
Excelsior Springs SD 40 3,000/PK-12
PO Box 248 64024 816-630-9200
James Horton, supt. Fax 630-9203
tigernet.estigers.k12.mo.us/
Elkhorn ES 300/K-5
PO Box 248 64024 816-630-9270
Brian Herndon, prin. Fax 630-9274
Excelsior Springs MS 700/6-8
PO Box 248 64024 816-630-9230
William Bielefeld, prin. Fax 630-9236
Lewis ES 400/PK-5
PO Box 248 64024 816-630-9290
Christina Compton, prin. Fax 630-9295
Westview ES 500/K-5
PO Box 248 64024 816-630-9260
Rita Linhart, prin. Fax 630-9265

Exeter, Barry, Pop. 737
Exeter R-VI SD 300/K-12
101 Locust St 65647 417-835-2922
Tina Nolan, supt. Fax 835-3201
www.exeter.k12.mo.us/
Exeter S 200/K-8
101 Locust St 65647 417-835-8001
Tamra Kester, prin. Fax 835-3201

Fairfax, Atchison, Pop. 622
Fairfax R-III SD 200/PK-12
500 E Main St 64446 660-686-2421
Ed Defenbaugh, supt. Fax 686-2848
www.fairfaxk12mo.us/
Fairfax ES 100/PK-6
500 E Main St 64446 660-686-2851
Dustin Barnes, prin. Fax 686-2848

Fair Grove, Greene, Pop. 1,283
Fair Grove R-X SD 1,200/K-12
PO Box 367 65648 417-759-2233
John Link, supt. Fax 759-7150
www.fairgrove.k12.mo.us
Fair Grove ES 400/K-4
PO Box 367 65648 417-759-2555
Kelly Sutherland, prin. Fax 759-7634
Fair Grove MS 400/5-8
PO Box 367 65648 417-759-2556
Charity Rael, prin. Fax 759-9053

Fair Play, Polk, Pop. 439
Fair Play R-II SD 400/K-12
301 N Walnut St 65649 417-654-2231
Renee Sagaser, supt. Fax 654-5028
www.fairplay.k12.mo.us/
Fair Play ES 200/K-6
301 N Walnut St 65649 417-654-2233
Betty Spitler, prin. Fax 654-2233

Falcon, Laclede
Gasconade C-4 SD 100/K-8
32959 Highway 32 65470 417-532-4821
Mickey Bowers, supt. Fax 532-0615
www.gasconadec4.k12.mo.us
Gasconade S 100/K-8
32959 Highway 32 65470 417-532-4821
Mickey Bowers, prin. Fax 532-0615

Farmington, Saint Francois, Pop. 15,176
Farmington R-VII SD 3,800/PK-12
PO Box 570 63640 573-701-1300
Dr. W. L. Sanders, supt. Fax 701-1309
www.farmington.k12.mo.us
Farmington MS 600/7-8
506 S Fleming St 63640 573-701-1330
Dorothy Winslow, prin. Fax 701-1339
Jefferson ES 300/1-4
9 Summit Dr 63640 573-701-1360
Sheryl Robinson, prin. Fax 701-1369
Johns ECC 100/PK-PK
510 S Franklin St 63640 573-701-1390
Barbara Guiley, dir. Fax 701-1399
Lincoln IS 500/5-6
708 S Fleming St 63640 573-701-1340
Shirley Bieser, prin. Fax 701-1349
Roosevelt ES 400/1-4
1040 Forster St 63640 573-701-1345
Janice Rohrer, prin. Fax 701-1348
Truman K 200/K-K
209 W College St 63640 573-701-1370
Barbara Guiley, prin. Fax 701-1379
Washington-Franklin ES 400/1-4
409 N Washington St 63640 573-701-1350
Angie Winch, prin. Fax 701-1359

St. Joseph S 100/K-8
501 Sainte Genevieve Ave 63640 573-756-6312
Jacqueline Whitworth, prin. Fax 756-0738
St. Paul Lutheran S 200/PK-8
608 E Columbia St 63640 573-756-5147
Duane Giesselmann, prin. Fax 756-8669

Faucett, Buchanan
Mid-Buchanan County R-V SD 700/K-12
3221 State Route H SE 64448 816-238-1646
John James, supt. Fax 238-4150
www.midbuchanan.k12.mo.us
Mid-Buchanan ES 300/K-6
3221 State Route H SE 64448 816-238-1646
Reesa Smiddy, prin. Fax 238-2029

Fayette, Howard, Pop. 2,701
Fayette R-III SD 700/PK-12
705 Lucky St 65248 660-248-2153
Russ Brock, supt. Fax 248-3702
www.fayette.k12.mo.us/
Clark MS 100/6-8
704 Lucky St 65248 660-248-3800
Kevin Beeler, prin. Fax 248-2610
Daly ES 300/PK-5
702 Lucky St 65248 660-248-3200
Brett Frerking, prin. Fax 248-3702

Fenton, Saint Louis, Pop. 4,376
Fox C-6 SD
Supt. — See Arnold
Guffey ES 500/K-6
400 13th St 63026 636-343-7662
Jackie Waller, prin. Fax 343-7664

Rockwood R-VI SD
Supt. — See Eureka
Bowles ES 300/K-5
501 Bowles Ave 63026 636-305-2736
David Cobb, prin. Fax 305-2740
Kellison ES 500/K-5
1626 Hawkins Rd 63026 636-861-7760
Dr. Tracy Edwards, prin. Fax 861-7761
Rockwood South MS 1,000/6-8
1628 Hawkins Rd 63026 636-861-7723
Dr. Linda Miller, prin. Fax 861-7730
Stanton ES 400/K-5
1430 Flora Del Dr 63026 636-861-7766
Matt Miller, prin. Fax 861-7767
Uthoff Valley ES 500/K-5
1600 Uthoff Dr 63026 636-305-2717
Connie Browning, prin. Fax 305-2721

Our Savior Lutheran S 200/PK-8
1500 San Simeon Way 63026 636-343-7511
Jim House, prin. Fax 343-4921
St. Paul S 400/K-8
465 New Smizer Mill Rd 63026 636-343-4333
Pam Brown, prin. Fax 343-1769

Ferguson, Saint Louis, Pop. 21,458
Ferguson-Florissant R-II SD
Supt. — See Florissant
Central ES 300/K-6
201 Wesley Ave 63135 314-521-4981
Ronald Stedman, prin. Fax 521-4983
Griffith ES 300/K-6
200 Day Dr 63135 314-521-5971
Robin Witherspoon, prin. Fax 521-2820
Hamilton ES 300/K-6
401 Powell Ave 63135 314-521-6755
Kathy Steinmann, prin. Fax 521-6757
Johnson-Wabash ES 500/K-6
685 January Ave 63135 314-524-0280
Suzette Simms, prin. Fax 524-1149
Walnut Grove ES 500/K-6
1248 N Florissant Rd 63135 314-524-8922
Aline Phillips, prin. Fax 524-3052

Blessed Teresa of Calcutta S 200/PK-8
150 N Elizabeth Ave 63135 314-522-3888
Jennifer Stutsman, prin. Fax 521-3173

Festus, Jefferson, Pop. 10,905
Festus R-VI SD 2,900/K-12
1515 Midmeadow Ln 63028 636-937-4920
Dr. Randy Sheriff, supt. Fax 937-8525
www2.csd.org/festus/
Festus ES 700/K-3
1500 Midmeadow Ln 63028 636-937-4063
Darin Siefert, prin. Fax 937-7870
Festus IS 700/4-6
1501 Midmeadow Ln 63028 636-937-4750
Laura Borman, prin. Fax 937-6106
Festus MS 500/7-8
1717 W Main St 63028 636-937-5417
Stacie Stryhal, prin. Fax 937-4171

Jefferson County R-VII SD 800/PK-12
1250 Dooling Hollow Rd 63028 636-937-9188
Dr. J. Thomas Guenzler, supt. Fax 937-9189
www.jr7.k12.mo.us/
Danby-Rush Tower MS 200/6-8
1250 Dooling Hollow Rd 63028 636-937-9188
Kim Weik, prin. Fax 937-9189
Plattin PS 300/PK-2
2400 R-7 School Rd 63028 636-937-7170
Tina Basler, prin. Fax 937-7985
Telegraph IS 200/3-5
1265 Dooling Hollow Rd 63028 636-937-6530
Cynthia Holdinghausen, prin. Fax 937-6835

Our Lady S 200/PK-8
1599 Saint Marys Ln 63028 636-931-2963
Cathy Whitlock, prin. Fax 933-2230

Fisk, Butler, Pop. 369
Twin Rivers R-X SD
Supt. — See Broseley
Fisk S 400/K-8
PO Box 547 63940 573-967-3607
Clinton Salyer, prin. Fax 967-3679

Florissant, Saint Louis, Pop. 51,812
Ferguson-Florissant R-II SD 12,800/PK-12
1005 Waterford Dr 63033 314-506-9000
Jeffrey Spiegel, supt. Fax 506-9010
www.fergflor.org/
Combs ES 300/K-6
300 Saint Jean St 63031 314-831-0411
Adrienne Bland, prin. Fax 831-0414
Commons Lane ES 400/K-6
2700 Derhake Rd 63033 314-831-0440
Dr. Barbara Wright, prin. Fax 831-0474
Cross Keys MS 1,000/7-8
14205 Cougar Dr 63033 314-506-9700
David Watkins, prin. Fax 506-9701
Duchesne ES 400/K-6
100 S New Florissant Rd 63031 314-831-1911
Katie Sanders, prin. Fax 831-1914
Early Education Center 600/PK-PK
1005 Waterford Dr 63033 314-506-9066
Joy Rouse, dir. Fax 506-9080
Halls Ferry ES 400/K-6
13585 New Halls Ferry Rd 63033 314-831-1022
Lisa Troesser-Hazel, prin. Fax 831-1024
Parker Road ES 400/K-6
2800 Parker Rd 63033 314-831-2644
Jo Ann Clay, prin. Fax 831-2648
Robinwood ES 300/K-6
955 Derhake Rd 63033 314-831-4633
Kerry McDaniel, prin. Fax 831-4656
Wedgwood ES 600/K-6
14275 New Halls Ferry Rd 63033 314-831-4551
Alexandra Gwydir, prin. Fax 831-4607
Other Schools – See Berkeley, Ferguson, Saint Louis

Hazelwood SD 18,000/PK-12
15955 New Halls Ferry Rd 63031 314-953-5000
Dr. Mary Piper, supt. Fax 953-5085
www.hazelwoodschools.org/
Barrington ES 400/K-5
15600 Old Halls Ferry Rd 63034 314-953-4050
Dr. Beverly Boyd, prin. Fax 953-4063
Brown ES 400/K-5
3325 Chicory Creek Ln 63031 314-953-4100
William Heckel, prin. Fax 953-4113
Cold Water ES 400/K-5
1105 Wiethaupt Rd 63031 314-953-4150
Dr. Crista Warner, prin. Fax 953-4163
Hazelwood Central MS 6-8
13450 Old Jamestown Rd 63033 314-953-7400
Robert Lawrence, prin. Fax 953-7413
Hazelwood East ECC PK-PK
12555 Partridge Run Dr 63033 314-953-7600
Dr. Cornetta Mendoza, coord. Fax 741-4450
Hazelwood North MS 6-8
4420 Vaile Ave 63034 314-953-7500
Dr. Laurie Birkenmeier, prin. Fax 953-7513
Hazelwood Northwest MS 1,200/6-8
1605 Shackelford Rd 63031 314-953-5500
Willicia Hobbs, prin. Fax 953-5513
Hazelwood Central ECC PK-PK
15955 New Halls Ferry Rd 63031 314-953-4950
Debbie Dill, prin. Fax 953-4963
Jamestown ES 300/K-5
13750 Old Jamestown Rd 63033 314-953-4300
Dr. Lisa Strauther, prin. Fax 953-4313
Jana ES 500/K-5
405 Jana Dr 63031 314-953-4350
Sheilah Fitzgerald, prin. Fax 953-4363
Jury ES 300/K-5
11950 Old Halls Ferry Rd 63033 314-953-4400
Mary Shaw, prin. Fax 953-4463
Lawson ES 300/K-5
1830 Charbonier Rd 63031 314-953-4550
Dr. Betty Scheller, prin. Fax 953-4563
Lusher ES 400/K-5
2015 Mullanphy Ln 63031 314-953-4600
Dr. Julie Melton, prin. Fax 953-4613

McCurdy ES 400/K-5
975 Lindsay Ln 63031 314-953-4650
Dr. Jane McKinney, prin. Fax 953-4663
Townsend ES 300/K-5
6645 Parker Rd 63033 314-953-4800
Lois Taylor, prin. Fax 953-4813
Walker ES 300/K-5
1250 Humes Ln 63031 314-953-4900
Dr. Eric Arbetter, prin. Fax 953-4913
Other Schools – See Hazelwood, Saint Louis

Atonement Lutheran S 300/PK-8
1285 N New Florissant Rd 63031 314-837-1252
Mark Briggs, prin. Fax 837-6754
North County Christian S 500/PK-12
845 Dunn Rd 63031 314-972-6227
Ken Rankin, admin. Fax 972-6220
Sacred Heart K 100/PK-K
751 N Jefferson St 63031 314-837-6939
Mary Kay Gladbach, prin. Fax 837-6954
Sacred Heart S 300/1-8
501 Saint Louis St 63031 314-831-3372
Lois Vollmer, prin. Fax 831-2844
St. Angela Merici S 300/PK-8
3860 N US Highway 67 63034 314-831-8012
Mary Ann Kauffman, prin. Fax 839-5308
St. Ferdinand S 300/K-8
1735 Charbonier Rd 63031 314-921-2201
Jeanne Gearon, prin. Fax 921-2253
St. Norbert S 400/PK-8
16475 New Halls Ferry Rd 63031 314-839-0948
Pam Gilbert, prin. Fax 839-0948
St. Rose Philippine Duchesne S 300/PK-8
3500 Saint Catherine St 63033 314-921-3023
Ken Morr, prin. Fax 921-6724
St. Sabina S 200/PK-8
1625 Swallow Ln 63031 314-837-6524
Sr. Joan Galli, prin. Fax 837-3162
Salem Lutheran S 200/PK-8
5190 Parker Rd 63033 314-741-8220
Daniel Schwerin, prin. Fax 741-7242

Fordland, Webster, Pop. 746
Fordland R-III SD 600/PK-12
1230 School St 65652 417-738-2296
Brian Wilson, supt. Fax 767-4483
www.fordland.k12.mo.us
Fordland ES 300/K-5
252 North St 65652 417-738-2223
Marcia Chadwell, prin. Fax 767-4267
Fordland MS 100/6-8
1230 School St 65652 417-738-2119
Judy Kindall, prin. Fax 767-4483
Fordland Preschool PK-PK
241 Hill St 65652 417-767-2223
Marcia Chadwell, prin. Fax 767-4267

Forsyth, Taney, Pop. 1,706
Forsyth R-III SD 1,200/PK-12
PO Box 187 65653 417-546-6384
Dr. Brent Blevins, supt. Fax 546-2204
www.forsythr3.k12.mo.us/
Forsyth ES 500/PK-4
PO Box 187 65653 417-546-6381
Carol Hawkins, prin. Fax 546-2696
Forsyth MS 400/5-8
PO Box 187 65653 417-546-6382
Sandra Goss, prin. Fax 546-6943

Fort Leonard Wood, Pulaski, Pop. 15,863
Waynesville R-VI SD
Supt. — See Waynesville
Partridge ES 300/K-5
7078 Young St 65473 573-329-5888
George Lauritson, prin. Fax 329-6298
Pick ES 300/K-5
8478 Buckeye Ave 65473 573-329-6262
Hilary Bales, prin. Fax 329-6294
Thayer ES 200/K-5
4273 Thayer St 65473 573-329-6222
Mark Parker, prin. Fax 329-3252
Wood ES 200/K-6
7076 Pulaski Ave 65473 573-329-2311
Sonya Campbell, prin. Fax 329-2827

Frankford, Pike, Pop. 365
Bowling Green R-I SD
Supt. — See Bowling Green
Frankford ES 100/K-5
500 School St 63441 573-784-2550
Stephanie Bailey, prin. Fax 324-2550

Fredericktown, Madison, Pop. 4,035
Fredericktown R-I SD 1,800/PK-12
704 E Highway 72 63645 573-783-2570
Dr. Kelly Burlison, supt. Fax 783-7045
fredericktown.k12.mo.us/
Fredericktown ES 300/PK-2
419 Newberry St 63645 573-783-3477
Tenna Groom, prin. Fax 783-8038
Fredericktown IS 400/3-5
905 E Highway 72 63645 573-783-6455
Mary Moyers, prin. Fax 783-8033
Fredericktown MS 400/6-8
501 Park Dr 63645 573-783-6555
Scott Sikes, prin. Fax 783-8079

Freeburg, Osage, Pop. 439

Holy Family S 100/K-8
PO Box 156 65035 573-744-5200
Debbie Reinkemeyer, prin. Fax 744-5254
Sacred Heart S 100/1-8
4309 Highway U 65035 573-744-5898
Linda Neuner, prin. Fax 744-5761

Freistatt, Lawrence, Pop. 193

Trinity Lutheran S 100/PK-8
218 N Main St 65654 417-235-5931
Carol Kleibocker, prin. Fax 235-5931

Frohna, Perry, Pop. 201

Concordia Trinity Lutheran S 100/PK-8
10158 Highway C 63748 573-824-5218
Linda Dressler, prin. Fax 824-5250

Fulton, Callaway, Pop. 12,101
Fulton SD 58 2,200/PK-12
2 Hornet Dr 65251 573-642-2206
Dr. Jacque Cowherd, supt. Fax 642-1444
www.fulton.k12.mo.us/
Bartley ES 200/K-5
603 S Business 54 65251 573-642-5365
Connie Epperson, prin. Fax 592-0306
Bush ES 300/K-5
908 Wood St 65251 573-642-2877
Alexandria Engle, prin. Fax 642-5986
Fulton MS 500/6-8
403 E 10th St 65251 573-642-7221
Jeffrey Wright, prin. Fax 642-6282
McIntire ES 400/PK-5
706 Hickman Ave 65251 573-642-6472
Jennifer Houf, prin. Fax 592-0585

Kingdom Christian Academy 100/K-8
PO Box 695 65251 573-642-2117
Ann Taylor, admin. Fax 642-2022
St. Peter S 100/PK-8
700 State Road Z 65251 573-642-2839
Cynthia Loftus, prin. Fax 642-2839

Gainesville, Ozark, Pop. 607
Gainesville R-V SD 600/PK-12
HC 3 Box 170 65655 417-679-4260
Bill Looney, supt. Fax 679-4270
gainesville.mo.schoolwebpages.com
Gainesville ES 300/PK-6
PO Box 236 65655 417-679-4416
Mike Henry, prin. Fax 679-2077

Galena, Stone, Pop. 528
Galena R-II SD 600/PK-12
PO Box 286 65656 417-357-6027
Cynthia Allen, supt. Fax 357-0058
www.galena.k12.mo.us/
Galena-Abesville ES 300/PK-6
PO Box 286 65656 417-357-6378
Daniel Humble, prin. Fax 357-8807

Gallatin, Daviess, Pop. 1,776
Gallatin R-V SD 600/PK-12
602 S Olive St 64640 660-663-2171
James Ruse, supt. Fax 663-2559
gallatin.k12.mo.us
Searcy ES 300/PK-6
502 S Olive St 64640 660-663-2173
Toni Cox, prin. Fax 663-2559

Galt, Grundy, Pop. 275
Grundy County R-V SD 200/K-12
PO Box 6 64641 660-673-6511
Robert Deaver, supt. Fax 673-6523
Other Schools – See Humphreys

Garden City, Cass, Pop. 1,667

Training Center Christian S 100/PK-12
PO Box 200 64747 816-773-8367
Judy Williams, admin. Fax 862-6052

Gatewood, Ripley
Ripley County R-III SD 100/K-8
HC 6 Box 200 63942 573-255-3213
Kenneth Hunt, supt. Fax 255-3648
schoolweb.missouri.edu/ripleyr3.k12.mo.us/
Ripley County S 100/K-8
HC 6 Box 200 63942 573-255-3213
Kenneth Hunt, prin. Fax 255-3648

Gerald, Franklin, Pop. 1,238
Gasconade County R-II SD
Supt. — See Owensville
Gerald ES 300/K-5
PO Box 25 63037 573-764-3321
Dot Colter, prin. Fax 764-2183

Gideon, New Madrid, Pop. 1,019
Gideon SD 37 400/K-12
PO Box 227 63848 573-448-3911
Dr. David Hollingshead, supt. Fax 448-5197
gideon.k12.mo.us/
Gideon ES 200/K-6
PO Box 227 63848 573-448-3447
William Hoffman, prin. Fax 448-5153

Gilliam, Saline, Pop. 224
Gilliam C-4 SD 50/K-8
PO Box 8 65330 660-784-2225
Darrel Lee, supt. Fax 784-2238
Gilliam S 50/K-8
PO Box 8 65330 660-784-2225
Darrel Lee, prin. Fax 784-2238

Gilman City, Daviess, Pop. 383
Gilman City R-IV SD 200/PK-12
PO Box 45 64642 660-876-5221
David Cross, supt. Fax 876-5553
Gilman City ES 100/PK-6
PO Box 45 64642 660-876-5221
Connie Ward, prin. Fax 876-5553

Gladstone, Clay, Pop. 27,306
North Kansas City SD 74
Supt. — See Kansas City
Antioch MS 800/6-8
2100 NE 65th St 64118 816-413-6200
Robert Russell, prin. Fax 413-6205
Chapel Hill ES 500/K-5
3220 NE 67th Ter 64119 816-413-6600
Raylene Walsh, prin. Fax 413-6605
Linden West ES 500/K-5
7333 N Wyandotte St 64118 816-413-4750
Carla Forbes, prin. Fax 413-4755
Meadowbrook ES 500/K-5
6301 N Michigan Ave 64118 816-413-6700
Judy Wartick, prin. Fax 413-6705
Oakwood Manor ES 300/K-5
5900 N Flora Ave 64118 816-413-5250
Amy Casey, prin. Fax 413-5255

Glasgow, Howard, Pop. 1,205
Glasgow SD 300/PK-12
860 Randolph St 65254 660-338-2012
Michael Reynolds, supt. Fax 338-2610
www.glasgow.k12.mo.us/
Glasgow ES 100/PK-6
860 Randolph St 65254 660-338-2012
Sonya Fuemmeler, prin. Fax 338-2610

St. Marys S 100/K-8
501 3rd St 65254 660-338-2258
Kent Monnig, prin. Fax 338-9930

Glencoe, Saint Louis
Rockwood R-VI SD
Supt. — See Eureka
Babler ES 600/K-5
1955 Shepard Rd 63038 636-733-1175
Dr. Diane Metz, prin. Fax 458-7347
LaSalle Springs MS 900/6-8
3300 Highway 109 63038 636-938-2425
Deborah Brandt, prin. Fax 938-2434
Rockwood Valley MS 800/6-8
1220 Babler Park Dr 63038 636-458-7324
Andrew Loiterstein, prin. Fax 458-7325
Wildwood MS 800/6-8
17401 Manchester Rd 63038 636-458-7360
Dr. Gregory Batenhorst, prin. Fax 458-7372

St. Alban Roe S 500/PK-8
2005 Shepard Rd 63038 636-458-6084
Mary Chrapek, prin. Fax 405-3026

Glendale, Saint Louis, Pop. 5,595
Kirkwood R-VII SD
Supt. — See Kirkwood
North Glendale ES 400/1-5
765 N Sappington Rd 63122 314-213-6130
Todd Benben, prin. Fax 213-6173

Golden City, Barton, Pop. 918
Golden City R-III SD 300/PK-12
1208 Walnut St 64748 417-537-4900
Susan Whittle, supt. Fax 537-8717
Golden City ES 100/PK-6
1208 Walnut St 64748 417-537-4272
Paula Brous, prin. Fax 537-8717

Goodman, McDonald, Pop. 1,233
Neosho R-V SD
Supt. — See Neosho
Goodman ES 300/K-4
117 N School St 64843 417-364-7216
Dottie Smith, prin. Fax 451-8685

Gorin, Scotland, Pop. 131
Gorin R-III SD 50/PK-8
PO Box 98 63543 660-282-3282
Tina Townsend, supt. Fax 282-3219
Gorin S 50/PK-8
PO Box 98 63543 660-282-3282
Tina Townsend, prin. Fax 282-3219

Gower, Buchanan, Pop. 1,433
East Buchanan County C-1 SD 700/K-12
100 Smith St 64454 816-424-6466
Paul Mensching, supt. Fax 424-3511
www.ebs.k12.mo.us/
East Buchanan ES 300/K-5
100 Smith St 64454 816-424-3111
Terry Poindexter, prin. Fax 424-3511
Other Schools – See Easton

Graham, Nodaway, Pop. 186
Nodaway-Holt R-VII SD 300/PK-12
318 S Taylor St 64455 660-939-2137
Karma Coleman, supt. Fax 939-2200
www.asde.com/~nodholt/
Other Schools – See Maitland

Grain Valley, Jackson, Pop. 8,644
Grain Valley R-V SD 2,800/K-12
PO Box 304 64029 816-847-5006
Dr. Chris Small, supt. Fax 229-4831
www.grainvalley.k12.mo.us
Grain Valley MS 600/6-8
PO Box 304 64029 816-229-3499
Theresa Nelson, prin. Fax 847-5017
Matthews ES 500/K-5
PO Box 304 64029 816-229-4870
Kathy Ambrose, prin. Fax 847-5003
Prairie Branch ES 500/K-5
PO Box 304 64029 816-847-5070
Marc Snow, prin. Fax 847-5071
Sni-A-Bar ES 500/K-5
PO Box 304 64029 816-847-5020
Brad Welle, prin. Fax 847-5023
Stony Point ES K-5
PO Box 304 64029 816-847-7800
Scott Schmidt, prin. Fax 847-7802

Granby, Newton, Pop. 2,230
East Newton County R-VI SD 1,700/K-12
22808 E Highway 86 64844 417-472-6231
Tanya Vest, supt. Fax 472-3500
www.enr6.k12.mo.us
Granby S 700/K-8
PO Box 440 64844 417-472-6279
Mark Drake, prin. Fax 472-7115
Other Schools – See Stella

Grandview, Jackson, Pop. 24,549
Grandview C-4 SD 4,100/PK-12
13015 10th St 64030 816-316-5000
Dr. Ralph Teran, supt. Fax 316-5050
www.csd4.k12.mo.us
Belvidere ES 300/K-5
15200 White Ave 64030 816-316-5300
Liz Means, prin. Fax 316-5305
Butcher-Greene ES 200/K-5
5302 E 140th St 64030 816-316-5400
Cindy Langensand, prin. Fax 316-5445
Conn-West ES 300/PK-5
1100 High Grove Rd 64030 816-316-5225
Mary Moore, prin. Fax 316-5230
Grandview MS 700/6-8
12650 Manchester Ave 64030 816-316-5600
Cynthia Johnson, prin. Fax 316-5699
High Grove ES 300/K-5
2500 High Grove Rd 64030 816-316-5500
Rosey Brown, prin. Fax 316-5505
Meadowmere ES 400/K-5
7010 E 136th St 64030 816-316-5525
Lisa G. Walker, prin. Fax 316-5599
Other Schools – See Kansas City

Coronation Little Lambs ECC 50/PK-PK
13000 Bennington Ave 64030 816-761-8811
Jennifer Coots, dir. Fax 761-8812
Grandview Christian S 100/K-12
12340 Grandview Rd 64030 816-767-8630
Dean Barrett, admin. Fax 763-5029
Life-A-New Preparatory Academy 50/PK-5
12401 Byars Rd 64030 816-966-8989
Rachel Starks, prin. Fax 966-9533

Grant City, Worth, Pop. 826
Worth County R-III SD 400/K-12
510 East Ave 64456 660-564-3389
Matt Robinson, supt. Fax 564-2193
wc.k12.mo.us/index.html
Worth County ES 200/K-6
510 East Ave 64456 660-564-3320
Nancy Lewis, prin. Fax 564-2193

Gravois Mills, Morgan, Pop. 225
Morgan County R-II SD
Supt. — See Versailles
Morgan County South ES 65084 100/PK-3
Steve Rhine, prin. 573-372-6261
Fax 372-6261

Green City, Sullivan, Pop. 650
Green City R-I SD 300/PK-12
301 Northeast St 63545 660-874-4128
Donnie Campbell, supt. Fax 874-4515
www.greencity.k12.mo.us/
Green City ES 200/PK-6
301 Northeast St 63545 660-874-4126
Ann Gray, prin. Fax 874-5950

Greenfield, Dade, Pop. 1,299
Greenfield R-IV SD 500/K-12
410 College St 65661 417-637-5321
Cheryl Mack, supt. Fax 637-5805
greenfield.k12.mo.us/
Greenfield ES 300/K-6
409 N Montgomery St 65661 417-637-5921
Cheri Walters, prin. Fax 637-2844

Green Ridge, Pettis, Pop. 455
Green Ridge R-VIII SD 400/K-12
PO Box 70 65332 660-527-3315
Tim Lenz, supt. Fax 527-3299
greenridge.k12.mo.us
Green Ridge ES 200/K-6
PO Box 70 65332 660-527-3315
Wendy Brock, prin. Fax 527-3299

Greenville, Wayne, Pop. 446
Greenville R-II SD 800/PK-12
PO Box 320 63944 573-224-3844
Jim Morrison, supt. Fax 224-3412
www.bears.k12.mo.us
Greenville ES 300/PK-6
PO Box 320 63944 573-224-3617
Dolores Murray, prin. Fax 224-3819
Greenville JHS 100/7-8
PO Box 320 63944 573-224-3833
Rick Rainwater, prin. Fax 224-3580
Other Schools – See Williamsville

Greenwood, Jackson, Pop. 4,512
Lee's Summit R-VII SD
Supt. — See Lees Summit
Greenwood ES 400/K-6
805 W Main St 64034 816-986-1320
Teera Rogers, prin. Fax 986-1335

Grover, Saint Louis
Rockwood R-VI SD
Supt. — See Eureka
Fairway ES 600/K-5
480 Old Fairway Dr 63040 636-458-7300
Dr. Karen Hargadine, prin. Fax 458-7350
Pond ES 500/K-5
17200 Manchester Rd 63040 636-458-7264
Carlos Diaz-Granados, prin. Fax 458-7271

Grovespring, Wright
Hartville R-II SD
Supt. — See Hartville

Grovespring ES 100/K-6
PO Box 100 65662 417-462-3288
Kathy Claxton, prin. Fax 462-3144

Guilford, Nodaway, Pop. 84
South Nodaway County R-IV SD
Supt. — See Barnard
South Nodaway ES 100/PK-6
PO Box 75 64457 660-652-3718
Darbi Bauman, prin. Fax 652-3711

Hale, Carroll, Pop. 478
Hale R-I SD 200/PK-12
PO Box 248 64643 660-565-2417
Clinton Heussner, supt. Fax 565-2418
Hale ES 100/PK-6
PO Box 248 64643 660-565-2417
Kim Rodriguez, prin. Fax 565-2418

Half Way, Polk, Pop. 188
Halfway R-III SD 300/K-12
2150 Highway 32 65663 417-445-2351
Tim Boatwright, supt. Fax 445-2026
www.halfwayschools.org
Halfway ES 200/K-6
2150 Highway 32 65663 417-445-2215
Karla Spear, prin. Fax 445-6714

Hallsville, Boone, Pop. 955
Hallsville R-IV SD 900/PK-12
421 Hwy 124 E 65255 573-696-5512
John Robertson, supt. Fax 696-3606
www.hallsville.org/
Hallsville IS 300/2-5
411 Hwy 124 E 65255 573-696-5512
Daniel Lane, prin. Fax 696-8990
Hallsville MS 300/6-8
421 Hwy 124 E 65255 573-696-5512
Christopher Crane, prin. Fax 696-7238
Hallsville PS PK-1
6401 E Highway 124 65255 573-636-5512
Amber Hicks, prin. Fax 696-0729

Hamilton, Caldwell, Pop. 1,811
Hamilton R-II SD 700/PK-12
PO Box 128 64644 816-583-2134
Stephen Yost, supt. Fax 583-2139
www.hamilton.k12.mo.us/
Hamilton ES 300/PK-4
PO Box 128 64644 816-583-4811
Lana Crawford, prin. Fax 583-7919
Hamilton MS 200/5-8
PO Box 128 64644 816-583-2173
Troy Ford, prin. Fax 583-2686

New York R-IV SD 50/K-8
6061 NE State Route U 64644 816-583-2563
Debra Ellis, supt. Fax 583-4065
www.geocities.com/newyorkschool
New York S 50/K-8
6061 NE State Route U 64644 816-583-2563
Debra Ellis, prin. Fax 583-4065

Hannibal, Marion, Pop. 17,649
Hannibal SD 60 3,800/PK-12
4650 McMasters Ave 63401 573-221-1258
Dr. Jill Janes, supt. Fax 221-2994
www.hannibal.k12.mo.us
Field ES 300/PK-5
1405 Pearl St 63401 573-221-1050
Vicki Dudding, prin. Fax 221-0545
Hannibal MS 800/6-8
4700 Mcmasters Ave 63401 573-221-5840
Kenneth Treaster, prin. Fax 221-7779
Oakwood ES 300/PK-5
3716 Market St 63401 573-221-2747
Penny Strube, prin. Fax 221-3753
Stowell ES 300/PK-5
700 Fulton Ave 63401 573-221-0980
Brenda Zessin, prin. Fax 221-2994
Twain ES 300/PK-5
2714 Bird St 63401 573-221-0768
Karen S. Wheelan, prin. Fax 221-3726
Veterans ES 600/PK-5
790 N Veterans Rd 63401 573-221-0649
Beverly Walker, prin. Fax 221-1349

Holy Family Catholic S 200/PK-8
1113 Broadway 63401 573-221-0456
Melissa Millan, prin. Fax 221-6357
St. John's Lutheran S 100/PK-5
1317 Lyon St 63401 573-221-0215
Irene Brown, prin. Fax 221-8384

Hardin, Ray, Pop. 590
Hardin-Central C-2 SD 200/K-12
PO Box 548 64035 660-398-4394
Steven Andes, supt. Fax 398-4396
www.hardincentral.k12.mo.us/phpnuke/
Hardin-Central ES 100/K-6
PO Box 548 64035 660-398-4394
Julia Griggs, prin. Fax 398-4396

Harrisburg, Boone, Pop. 182
Harrisburg R-VIII SD 500/K-12
1000 S Harris St 65256 573-875-5604
Lynn Proctor, supt. Fax 875-8877
www.harrisburg.k12.mo.us
Harrisburg ES 300/K-6
221 S Harris St 65256 573-875-0290
Susan Twenter, prin. Fax 875-8572
Harrisburg MS 100/7-8
233 S Harris St 65256 573-817-5857
Steve Combs, prin. Fax 875-8936

Harrisonville, Cass, Pop. 9,790
Harrisonville R-IX SD 2,400/PK-12
503 S Lexington St 64701 816-380-2727
Douglas Van Zyl, supt. Fax 380-3134
www.harrisonvilleschools.org/
Harrisonville ECC 100/PK-K
500 Polar Ln 64701 816-380-4421
Rebecca Campbell, prin. Fax 884-2148
Harrisonville ES 500/1-3
101 Meghan Dr 64701 816-380-4131
Juana Weber, prin. Fax 884-2938
Harrisonville MS 600/6-8
601 S Highland Dr 64701 816-380-7654
Chris Grantham, prin. Fax 884-5733
McEowen ES 400/4-5
1901 S Halsey Ave 64701 816-380-4545
Dan Erholtz, prin. Fax 884-3046

Harrisonville Christian S East Campus 200/PK-4
1606 Chapel Dr 64701 816-380-3318
Al Sancken, admin. Fax 380-3040
Harrisonville Christian S West Campus 100/5-8
1202 S Commercial St 64701 816-884-6499
Al Sancken, admin. Fax 884-6479

Hartville, Wright, Pop. 603
Hartville R-II SD 800/PK-12
PO Box 460 65667 417-741-7676
Dr. Sharon Hayden, supt. Fax 741-7746
schoolweb.missouri.edu/hartville.k12.mo.us/
Hartville ES 300/PK-6
PO Box 460 65667 417-741-7141
Mark Piper, prin. Fax 741-7746
Other Schools – See Grovespring

Harviell, Butler
Neelyville R-IV SD
Supt. — See Neelyville
Hillview ES 200/K-6
11001 Highway 160 63945 573-989-3370
Sherri Ponder, prin. Fax 989-3975

Hawk Point, Lincoln, Pop. 524
Troy R-III SD
Supt. — See Troy
Hawk Point ES 100/K-5
PO Box 207 63349 636-338-4366
Matt Busekrus, prin. Fax 338-4566

Hayti, Pemiscot, Pop. 3,066
Hayti R-II SD 900/PK-12
PO Box 469 63851 573-359-6500
Thomas Tucker, supt. Fax 359-6502
www.edline.net/pages/hhs
Mathis ES 300/PK-3
PO Box 469 63851 573-359-6500
Lee Ann Wallace, prin. Fax 359-6509
Wallace ES 200/4-6
PO Box 469 63851 573-359-6500
Jeri Claire Crowder, prin. Fax 359-6511

Hazelwood, Saint Louis, Pop. 25,535
Hazelwood SD
Supt. — See Florissant
Armstrong ES 400/K-5
6255 Howdershell Rd 63042 314-953-4000
Dr. Amy Dittmar, prin. Fax 953-4013
Garrett ES 300/K-5
1400 Ville Rosa Ln 63042 314-953-4200
Dr. Crystal Reiter, prin. Fax 953-4213
Hazelwood West ECC PK-PK
5323 Ville Maria Ln 63042 314-953-7650
Patricia Adkins, prin. Fax 209-0348
Hazelwood West MS 900/6-8
12834 Missouri Bottom Rd 63042 314-953-5800
Dr. Allison Klouse, prin. Fax 953-5813
McNair ES 400/K-5
585 Coachway Ln 63042 314-953-4700
Dr. Brenda Rone, prin. Fax 953-4713
Russell ES 400/K-5
7350 Howdershell Rd 63042 314-953-4750
Patrick Lane, prin. Fax 953-4763

Alphabet Soup Academy 100/PK-8
8390 Latty Ave 63042 314-524-4272
Janet Strickland, prin. Fax 524-4271

Helena, Andrew
Savannah R-III SD
Supt. — See Savannah
Helena ES 100/K-6
21080 Osage St 64459 816-369-2865
Troy Dunn, prin. Fax 369-2404

Herculaneum, Jefferson, Pop. 3,172
Dunklin R-V SD 1,300/PK-12
PO Box 306 63048 636-479-5200
Stan Stratton, supt. Fax 479-6208
www.dunklin.k12.mo.us/
Senn-Thomas MS 400/5-8
200 Senn Tomas Dr 63048 636-479-5200
Tom Okruch, prin. Fax 479-7219
Other Schools – See Pevely

Christ the Vine S 50/PK-K
1615 Vine School Rd 63048 636-931-9900
Stephanie Miller, prin. Fax 931-9901

Hermann, Gasconade, Pop. 2,735
Gasconade County R-I SD 1,100/K-12
164 Blue Pride Dr 65041 573-486-2116
Chris Neale, supt. Fax 486-3032
www.hermann.k12.mo.us
Hermann ES 300/K-3
328 W 7th St 65041 573-486-3197
Steve Heidger, prin. Fax 486-3244
Hermann MS 400/4-8
164 Blue Pride Dr 65041 573-486-3121
Bonnie Hollaway, prin. Fax 486-5106

St. George S 200/PK-8
133 W 4th St 65041 573-486-5914
Julie Clingman, prin. Fax 486-1914

Hermitage, Hickory, Pop. 509
Hermitage R-IV SD 300/PK-12
PO Box 327 65668 417-745-6418
Shelly Aubuchon, supt. Fax 745-6475
www.hermitage.k12.mo.us/
Hermitage ES 200/PK-5
PO Box 327 65668 417-745-6277
Sharon Johnson, prin. Fax 745-6475
Hermitage MS 100/6-8
PO Box 327 65668 417-745-6417
Ed Vest, prin. Fax 745-6475

Higbee, Randolph, Pop. 652
Higbee R-VIII SD 200/K-12
PO Box 128 65257 660-456-7277
Ted Rathburn, supt. Fax 456-7278
Higbee ES 100/K-6
PO Box 128 65257 660-456-7206
Karl Janson, prin. Fax 456-7207

Higginsville, Lafayette, Pop. 4,660
Lafayette County C-1 SD 1,100/PK-12
805 W 31st St 64037 660-584-3631
Dr. David Lawrence, supt. Fax 584-2622
huskers.k12.mo.us
Grandview ES 500/PK-5
705 W 31st St 64037 660-584-7127
Ginger Cochran, prin. Fax 584-6094
Lafayette County MS 200/6-8
807b W 31st St 64037 660-584-7161
Gary Wheeler, prin. Fax 584-8666

Immanuel Lutheran S 100/PK-8
1500 Lipper Ave 64037 660-584-2854
Fax 584-5914

Highlandville, Christian, Pop. 921
Spokane R-VII SD 700/PK-12
167 Kentling Ave 65669 417-443-2200
Brent Depee, supt. Fax 443-2205
www.spokane.k12.mo.us
Highlandville ES 400/PK-5
PO Box 69 65669 417-443-3361
Jennifer Wheeler, prin. Fax 443-2013
Other Schools – See Spokane

High Point, Moniteau
High Point R-III SD 100/K-8
60909 Highway C 65042 660-489-2213
Tondelayo Westbrooks, admin. Fax 489-2412
High Point S 100/K-8
60909 Highway C 65042 660-489-2213
Tondelayo Westbrooks, prin. Fax 489-2412

High Ridge, Jefferson, Pop. 4,423
Northwest R-I SD 7,000/K-12
2843 Community Ln 63049 636-677-3473
Dr. Paul Ziegler, supt. Fax 677-5480
www.nwr1.k12.mo.us/
Brennan Woods ES 400/K-4
4630 Brennan Rd 63049 636-677-3400
Kim Quentin, prin. Fax 677-5440
High Ridge ES 400/K-4
2901 High Ridge Blvd 63049 636-677-3996
Susan Wingenbach, prin. Fax 376-4576
Murphy ES 400/K-4
2102 Valley Dr 63049 636-326-0577
Cynthia Spurgeon, prin. Fax 343-5786
North Jefferson IS 500/5-6
2109 Gravois Rd 63049 636-677-3577
Jeff Boyer, prin. Fax 677-5581
Other Schools – See Cedar Hill, Dittmer, House Springs

Hillsboro, Jefferson, Pop. 1,784
Grandview R-II SD 800/K-12
11470 Highway C 63050 636-944-3941
Dr. Michael Brown, supt. Fax 944-5239
www.grandviewr2.com
Grandview ES 300/K-5
11470 Highway C 63050 636-944-3291
Kimberly Bequette, prin. Fax 944-3870
Grandview MS 200/6-8
11470 Highway C 63050 636-944-3931
James Keeling, prin. Fax 944-5239

Hillsboro R-III SD 3,400/K-12
20 Hawk Dr 63050 636-789-0060
Beverly Schonhoff Ph.D., supt. Fax 789-3216
www.hillsboro.k12.mo.us/
Hillsboro ES 500/3-4
13 Hawk Dr 63050 636-789-0020
Jacqueline Kocurek, prin. Fax 789-3214
Hillsboro IS 600/5-6
10478 Business 21 63050 636-789-0030
Scott Readnour, prin. Fax 789-3213
Hillsboro JHS 600/7-8
12 Hawk Dr 63050 636-789-0020
Heath Allison, prin. Fax 789-3212
Hillsboro PS 500/K-2
101 Leon Hall Pkwy 63050 636-789-0050
Paul Suchland, prin. Fax 789-3215

Christian Outreach S 100/PK-12
4450 Outreach Dr 63050 636-797-3466
John Speropoulos, prin. Fax 789-2585
Good Shepherd S 100/PK-8
701 3rd St 63050 636-797-2300
Julie Connors, prin. Fax 797-2300

Holcomb, Dunklin, Pop. 697
Holcomb R-III SD 600/PK-12
PO Box 190 63852 573-792-3113
Jeff Bullock, supt. Fax 792-3118
holcomb.k12.mo.us/
Holcomb ES 400/PK-6
PO Box 190 63852 573-792-3550
Jason Skelton, prin. Fax 792-3490

Holden, Johnson, Pop. 2,543
Holden R-III SD 1,200/PK-12
1612 S Main St 64040 816-732-5568
Mike Ringen, supt. Fax 732-4336
schoolweb.missouri.edu/holden.k12.mo.us/
Holden MS 400/6-8
301 Eagle Dr 64040 816-732-4125
Mike Hough, prin. Fax 732-2009
South ES 400/PK-5
1903 S Market St 64040 816-732-6071
Robyn Sisk, prin. Fax 732-2008

Holliday, Monroe, Pop. 129
Holliday C-2 SD 100/K-8
PO Box 7038 65258 660-266-3412
Carol Hall, supt. Fax 266-3029
www.mcmsys.com/~holliday
Holliday S 100/K-8
PO Box 7038 65258 660-266-3412
Carol Hall, prin. Fax 266-3029

Hollister, Taney, Pop. 3,835
Hollister R-V SD 1,200/PK-12
1798 State Highway BB 65672 417-243-4005
Dr. Timothy Taylor, supt. Fax 334-2663
www.hollister.k12.mo.us/
Hollister ES 500/PK-4
1794 State Highway BB 65672 417-243-4025
Pamela Davis, prin. Fax 334-5152
Hollister JHS 200/7-8
1798 State Highway BB 65672 417-243-4055
Travis Shaw, prin. Fax 334-2663
Hollister MS 200/5-6
1798 State Highway BB 65672 417-243-4035
Mary Lou Combs, prin. Fax 336-5263

Trinity Christian Academy 100/PK-12
119 Myrtle Ave 65672 417-334-7084
Holly Gregory, prin. Fax 334-1794

Holt, Clay, Pop. 436

Northern Hills Christian Academy 100/K-8
17211 NE 180th St 64048 816-320-3204
Rick Collier, admin. Fax 320-3226

Holts Summit, Callaway, Pop. 3,384
Jefferson City SD
Supt. — See Jefferson City
Callaway Hills ES 300/K-5
2715 State Road AA 65043 573-896-5051
Ramona Dobson, prin. Fax 896-4054
North ES 400/K-5
285 S Summit Dr 65043 573-896-8304
Barb Martin, prin. Fax 896-4018

Hopkins, Nodaway, Pop. 561
North Nodaway County R-VI SD 300/PK-12
PO Box 260 64461 660-778-3411
Joan Bolon, supt. Fax 778-3210
www.nnr6.k12.mo.us/
Other Schools – See Pickering

Hornersville, Dunklin, Pop. 681
Senath-Hornersville C-8 SD
Supt. — See Senath
Senath-Hornersville MS 200/5-8
601 School St 63855 573-737-2455
Chad Morgan, prin. Fax 737-2456

House Springs, Jefferson
Northwest R-I SD
Supt. — See High Ridge
Cedar Springs ES 400/K-4
6922 Rivermont Trl 63051 636-671-3330
Kimm O'Connor, prin. Fax 671-7244
House Springs ES 500/K-4
4380 Gravois Rd 63051 636-671-3360
Gay Moore, prin. Fax 671-7269
House Springs IS 300/5-6
6180 Highway MM 63051 636-671-3382
Jenny Baugh, prin. Fax 671-1625
Northwest Valley MS 1,100/7-8
4300 Gravois Rd 63051 636-671-3470
Clint Freeman, prin. Fax 671-1535

Our Lady Queen of Peace S 300/K-8
4675 Notre Dame Dr 63051 636-671-0247
Debbie Clark, prin. Fax 671-0418

Houston, Texas, Pop. 2,005
Houston R-I SD 1,100/PK-12
423 W Pine St 65483 417-967-3024
Dan Vandiver, supt. Fax 967-4887
www.houston.k12.mo.us
Houston ES 500/PK-5
423 W Pine St 65483 417-967-3024
Leann Edington, prin. Fax 967-4885
Houston MS 200/6-8
423 W Pine St 65483 417-967-3024
Scott Dill, prin. Fax 967-5481

Wellspring Christian S 50/K-12
PO Box 248 65483 417-967-4735
Wilda Pingel, prin. Fax 967-4735

Houstonia, Pettis, Pop. 287
Pettis County R-V SD
Supt. — See Hughesville
Northwest ES 200/K-6
407 W Tuck St 65333 660-568-3315
Sharee Norfleet, prin. Fax 568-3394

Hughesville, Pettis, Pop. 181
Pettis County R-V SD 400/K-12
16215 Highway H 65334 660-827-0772
Charles Price, supt. Fax 827-7162
www.northwest.k12.mo.us
Other Schools – See Houstonia

Humansville, Polk, Pop. 986
Humansville R-IV SD 400/K-12
300 N Oak St 65674 417-754-2535
Mark Koca, supt. Fax 754-8565
www.humansville.k12.mo.us/
Humansville ES 200/K-6
300 N Oak St 65674 417-754-2221
Linda Meador, prin. Fax 754-8565

Hume, Bates, Pop. 346
Hume R-VIII SD 200/PK-12
PO Box 402 64752 660-643-7411
David Quick, supt. Fax 643-7506
Hume ES 100/PK-5
PO Box 402 64752 660-643-7411
Kenny Otto, prin. Fax 643-7506

Humphreys, Sullivan, Pop. 158
Grundy County R-V SD
Supt. — See Galt
Grundy County ES 100/K-6
PO Box 88 64646 660-673-6314
Lisa Fairley, prin. Fax 673-6346

Huntsville, Randolph, Pop. 1,625
Westran R-I SD 700/PK-12
210 W Depot St 65259 660-277-4429
Kelly Shelby, supt. Fax 277-4420
westran.k12.mo.us/
Westran ES 300/PK-5
210 W Depot St 65259 660-277-3666
Carl Brown, prin. Fax 277-4420
Other Schools – See Clifton Hill

Hurley, Stone, Pop. 160
Hurley R-I SD 300/K-12
PO Box 248 65675 417-369-3271
Doug Arnold, supt. Fax 369-2212
www.hurley.k12.mo.us/
Hurley ES 100/K-5
PO Box 248 65675 417-369-3271
Joshua Phillips, prin. Fax 369-2212

Iberia, Miller, Pop. 673
Iberia R-V SD 800/PK-12
PO Box 156 65486 573-793-6818
Deon Duncan, supt. Fax 793-6821
www.iberia.k12.mo.us/
Iberia ES 400/PK-6
PO Box 156 65486 573-793-6267
George Bunger, prin. Fax 793-6304

Imperial, Jefferson, Pop. 4,156
Fox C-6 SD
Supt. — See Arnold
Antonia ES 500/K-6
3901 Highway M 63052 636-942-2181
Mark Rudanovich, prin. Fax 942-3042
Hamrick ES 400/K-6
4525 E 4 Ridge Rd 63052 636-282-6930
Elizabeth Anderson, prin. Fax 282-6934
Hodge ES 400/K-6
2499 Prairie Hollow Rd 63052 636-282-6920
Theresa Jansen, prin. Fax 282-6984
Seckman ES 700/PK-6
2824 Seckman Rd 63052 636-296-2030
Christine Simokaitis, prin. Fax 282-5176
Seckman MS 800/7-8
2840 Seckman Rd 63052 636-296-5707
David Black, prin. Fax 296-5707

Windsor C-1 SD 2,800/K-12
6208 US Highway 61/67 63052 636-464-4400
Dr. Rudy Duran, supt. Fax 464-4454
windsorc1sd.schoolwires.com/
Windsor ES 300/K-2
6208 US Highway 61/67 63052 636-464-4408
Marsha Harris, prin. Fax 464-4470
Windsor IS 500/3-5
6208 US Highway 61/67 63052 636-464-4408
Sherri Strauser, prin. Fax 464-4470
Windsor MS 700/6-8
6208 US Highway 61/67 63052 636-464-4417
Mike Rickermann, prin. Fax 464-4473
Other Schools – See Barnhart

St. Joseph S 400/K-8
6024 Old Antonia Rd 63052 636-464-9027
Mary Smith, prin. Fax 464-8792

Independence, Jackson, Pop. 110,208
Blue Springs R-IV SD
Supt. — See Blue Springs
Yates ES 400/K-5
3600 S Davidson Ave 64055 816-224-1350
Rhonda Jacoby, prin. Fax 478-6137

Fort Osage R-I SD 4,700/K-12
2101 N Twyman Rd 64058 816-650-7000
Mark Enderle, supt. Fax 650-3888
www.fortosage.net
Blue Hills ES 400/K-4
2101 N Twyman Rd 64058 816-650-7440
Monica Shane, prin. Fax 650-7445
Cler-Mont ES 400/K-4
2101 N Twyman Rd 64058 816-650-7350
Julie Stout, prin. Fax 650-7355
Elm Grove ES 500/K-4
2101 N Twyman Rd 64058 816-650-7400
Pam Fore, prin. Fax 650-7405
Fire Prairie MS 700/5-6
2101 N Twyman Rd 64058 816-650-7158
Tim Gallagher, prin. Fax 650-7166
Indian Trails ES K-4
2101 N Twyman Rd 64058 816-650-7645
Emily Cross, prin. Fax 650-7694
Osage Trail MS 700/7-8
2101 N Twyman Rd 64058 816-650-7151
Nita McLean, prin. Fax 650-7152
Other Schools – See Buckner

Independence SD 30 14,300/PK-12
3225 S Noland Rd 64055 816-521-5300
Dr. Jim Hinson, supt. Fax 521-2999
www.indep.k12.mo.us
Benton ES 400/PK-5
429 S Leslie St 64050 816-521-2850
Leslie Hochspring, prin. Fax 521-2855
Bingham MS 700/6-8
1716 S Speck Rd 64057 816-521-5490
Charles Garner, prin. Fax 796-4880
Blackburn ES 600/PK-5
17302 E R D Mize Rd 64057 816-521-5395
Dr. David Hunt, prin. Fax 478-2508
Bridger MS 900/6-8
18200 E State Route 78 64057 816-521-5375
Belinda Woodson, prin. Fax 796-4812
Bryant ES 200/PK-5
827 W College St 64050 816-521-5400
Dr. Jon Pye, prin. Fax 521-2874
Fairmount ES 300/PK-5
120 N Cedar Ave 64053 816-521-5405
Jeff Anger, prin. Fax 254-7738
Glendale ES 500/PK-5
2611 S Lees Summit Rd 64055 816-521-5510
Todd Siebert, prin. Fax 521-2839
Hanthorn S 300/PK-PK
1511 S Kings Hwy 64055 816-521-5485
Sarah Monfore, prin. Fax 521-2765
Korte ES 500/PK-5
2437 S Hardy Ave 64052 816-521-5430
Dr. R.D. Mallams, prin. Fax 254-7416
Luff ES 300/PK-5
3700 S Delaware Ave 64055 816-521-5415
Toni Kilgore, prin. Fax 521-2842
Mill Creek ES 300/PK-5
2601 N Liberty St 64050 816-521-5420
Laura LaCroix, prin. Fax 521-2822
Nowlin MS 600/6-8
2800 S Hardy Ave 64052 816-521-5380
Jean Carton, prin. Fax 254-7975
Ott ES 400/PK-5
1525 N Noland Rd 64050 816-521-5435
Dr. Ronnee Laughlin, prin. Fax 521-2782
Pioneer Ridge MS 800/6-8
1656 S Speck Rd 64057 816-521-5385
Dr. Michael Weishaar, prin. Fax 796-4899
Procter ES 300/PK-5
1403 W Linden Ave 64052 816-521-5440
Deborah Marlowe, prin. Fax 521-2749
Randall ES 300/PK-5
509 N Jennings Rd 64056 816-521-5445
Cynthia Grant, prin. Fax 257-4102
Santa Fe Trail ES 300/PK-5
1301 Windsor St 64055 816-521-5450
Janet Gibbs, prin. Fax 521-2732
Southern ES 500/PK-5
4300 S Phelps Rd 64055 816-521-5475
Barb Allinder, prin. Fax 478-2533
Spring Branch ES 300/PK-5
20404 E Truman Rd 64056 816-521-5455
Janet Richards, prin. Fax 796-4823
Sycamore Hills ES 500/PK-5
15208 E 39th St S 64055 816-521-5465
Ann Laudwig, prin. Fax 478-2522
Three Trails ES 300/PK-5
11801 E 32nd St S 64052 816-521-5470
Dr. Susan Hendricks, prin. Fax 254-7169
Other Schools – See Sugar Creek

Englewood Christian Academy 300/PK-12
10628 E Winner Rd 64052 816-254-8313
Messiah Lutheran S 100/PK-8
613 S Main St 64050 816-254-9409
Ann Arndt, prin. Fax 254-9407
Nativity of Mary S 300/PK-8
10021 E 36th Ter S 64052 816-353-0284
Elizabeth Baker, prin. Fax 356-0286
St. Ann S 100/PK-8
10113 E Lexington Ave 64053 816-252-1024
Janet Spallo, prin. Fax 504-6234
St. Mark Preschool 50/PK-PK
3736 S Lees Summit Rd 64055 816-373-2600
Charlotte Davis, dir. Fax 373-3816

Ironton, Iron, Pop. 1,362
Arcadia Valley R-II SD 1,200/PK-12
750 Park Dr 63650 573-546-9700
Jim Carver, supt. Fax 546-7314
www.av.k12.mo.us
Arcadia Valley ES 400/PK-4
700 Park Dr 63650 573-546-9700
Laura Williams, prin. Fax 546-7388
Arcadia Valley MS 300/5-8
550 Park Dr 63650 573-546-9700
Kent Huddleston, prin. Fax 546-7304

Jackson, Cape Girardeau, Pop. 12,982
Jackson R-II SD 4,500/K-12
614 E Adams St 63755 573-243-9501
Ron Anderson, supt. Fax 243-9503
www.jacksonr2schools.com
Jackson MS 800/6-7
1651 W Independence St 63755 573-243-9543
Rodney Pensel, prin. Fax 243-9545
North ES 300/K-5
10730 State Hwy W 63755 573-243-9590
Shauna Criddle, prin. Fax 243-9591
Orchard Drive ES 400/K-3
1402 Orchard Dr 63755 573-243-9555
Clay Vangilder, prin. Fax 243-9559
South ES 500/K-5
1701 S Hope St 63755 573-243-9575
Bonnie Knowlan, prin. Fax 243-9574
West Lane ES 500/3-5
338 N West Ln 63755 573-243-9565
Cynthia Matthew, prin. Fax 243-9572
Other Schools – See Cape Girardeau, Millersville

Immaculate Conception S 300/K-8
300 S Hope St 63755 573-243-5013
Tamara Nenninger, prin. Fax 243-7216
St. Paul Lutheran S 400/PK-8
216 S Russell St 63755 573-243-5360
David Johnson, prin. Fax 243-4527

Jameson, Daviess, Pop. 123
North Daviess R-III SD 100/PK-12
413 E 2nd St 64647 660-828-4123
Becky Morris, supt. Fax 828-4122
www.ndaviess.k12.mo.us
Other Schools – See Coffey

Jamesport, Daviess, Pop. 516
Tri-County R-VII SD 200/K-12
904 W Auberry Grv 64648 660-684-6118
Dennis Croy, supt. Fax 684-6218
Tri-County ES 100/K-6
904 W Auberry Grv 64648 660-684-6117
Darla Chapman, prin. Fax 684-6218

Jamestown, Moniteau, Pop. 397
Jamestown C-1 SD 200/K-12
222 School St 65046 660-849-2141
James Deeken, supt. Fax 849-2600
Jamestown C-I ES 100/K-6
222 School St 65046 660-849-2141
Kevin Kohler, prin. Fax 849-2600

Jasper, Jasper, Pop. 1,037
Jasper County R-V SD 500/K-12
201 W Mercer St 64755 417-394-2416
Kathy Fall, supt. Fax 394-2394
www.jasper.k12.mo.us/
Jasper County ES 300/K-6
201 W Mercer St 64755 417-394-2301
Dave Davis, prin. Fax 394-2001

Jefferson City, Cole, Pop. 39,062
Blair Oaks R-II SD 900/K-12
6124 Falcon Ln 65101 573-636-2020
Dr. James Jones, supt. Fax 636-2202
www.blairoaks.k12.mo.us
Blair Oaks ES 400/K-6
6124 Falcon Ln 65101 573-634-2808
Lorie Winslow, prin. Fax 634-3240

Jefferson City SD 7,900/PK-12
315 E Dunklin St 65101 573-659-3000
Brian Mitchell, supt. Fax 659-3044
www.jcps.k12.mo.us
Belair ES 500/K-5
701 Belair Dr 65109 573-659-3155
Scott Salmons, prin. Fax 632-3492
Cedar Hill ES 400/K-5
1510 Vieth Dr 65109 573-659-3160
Lori Rost, prin. Fax 632-3493
East ES 300/K-5
1229 E McCarty St 65101 573-659-3165
Julia Martin, prin. Fax 632-3489
Gordon ES 300/K-5
1101 Jackson St 65101 573-659-3170
Suzanne Wilson, prin. Fax 659-3514
Jefferson MS 900/6-8
1201 Fairgrounds Rd 65109 573-659-3250
Roberta Hubbs, prin. Fax 659-3259
Lawson ES 400/PK-5
1105 Fairgrounds Rd 65109 573-659-3175
Stephen Saak, prin. Fax 632-3487
Lewis and Clark MS 900/6-8
325 Lewis and Clark Dr 65101 573-659-3200
Robert Steffes, prin. Fax 659-3209
Moreau Heights ES 400/K-5
1410 Hough Park St 65101 573-659-3180
Sheila Logan, prin. Fax 632-3495
Pioneer ES K-5
301 Pioneer Trail Dr 65109 573-632-3400
Estella Murphy, prin. Fax 632-3420
South ES 200/K-5
707 Linden Dr 65109 573-659-3185
Belinda Couty, prin. Fax 632-3497
West ES 400/K-5
100 Dix Rd 65109 573-659-3195
Marcia Heberle, prin. Fax 632-3496
Other Schools – See Holts Summit

Concord Christian S 50/PK-4
3212 Emerald Ln Ste 100 65109 573-634-3983
Paul Young, admin. Fax 634-7095
Immaculate Conception S 500/PK-8
1208 E McCarty St 65101 573-636-7680
Jill Struemph, prin. Fax 635-1833
Immanuel-Honey Creek Lutheran S 100/PK-8
8231 Tanner Bridge Rd 65101 573-496-3766
William Leech, prin. Fax 496-3766
St. Francis Xavier S 200/K-8
7307 Route M 65101 573-395-4612
Donna Frazier, prin. Fax 395-4302
St. Joseph Cathedral S 500/PK-8
2303 W Main St 65109 573-635-5024
Spencer Allen, prin. Fax 635-5238
St. Martin S 200/K-8
7206 Saint Martins Blvd 65109 573-893-3519
Cathy Wolters, prin. Fax 893-7404
St. Peter S 100/K-8
314 W High St 65101 573-636-8922
Dr. Joseph Gulino, prin. Fax 636-8410
St. Stanislaus S 200/PK-8
6410 Route W 65101 573-636-7802
Nancy Heberlie, prin. Fax 635-4782
Trinity Lutheran S 300/K-8
812 Stadium Blvd 65109 573-636-7807
Ken Hartman, prin. Fax 636-7348

Jennings, Saint Louis, Pop. 14,926
Jennings SD 3,100/PK-12
2559 Dorwood Dr 63136 314-653-8000
Clarence Holman, supt. Fax 653-8030
www.jenningsk12.net/index.html
Fairview IS 4-6
7051 Emma Ave 63136 314-653-8070
Penny Parker, prin. Fax 653-8075
Fairview PS 400/PK-3
7047 Emma Ave 63136 314-653-8070
Lavon Hardy, prin. Fax 653-8075
Gore ES 200/5-6
2545 Dorwood Dr 63136 314-653-8040
Delcina Bland, prin. Fax 653-8045
Hanrahan ES 200/4-6
8430 Lucas and Hunt Rd 63136 314-653-8190
Curt Wrisberg, prin. Fax 653-8197
Jennings JHS 600/7-8
8831 Cozens Ave 63136 314-653-8150
Dr. Richard Bass, prin. Fax 653-8168
Northview ES 400/K-4
8920 Cozens Ave 63136 314-653-8050
Chanua Ross, prin. Fax 653-8055
Woodland ES 300/K-3
8420 Sunbury Ave 63136 314-653-8170
Dr. Kathleen Kurz, prin. Fax 653-8173

Jonesburg, Montgomery, Pop. 707
Montgomery County R-II SD
Supt. — See Montgomery City
Jonesburg ES 100/PK-5
106 Smith Rd 63351 636-488-5923
Larry Geib, prin. Fax 488-3387

Joplin, Jasper, Pop. 47,183
Joplin R-VIII SD 7,500/PK-12
PO Box 128 64802 417-625-5200
Dr. C.J. Huff, supt. Fax 625-5210
www.joplin.k12.mo.us
Columbia ES 300/K-5
PO Box 128 64802 417-625-5325
Lori Musser, prin. Fax 625-5329
Duquesne ES 100/K-5
PO Box 128 64802 417-625-5335
Teresa Adams, prin. Fax 625-5339
Eastmorland ES 300/K-5
PO Box 128 64802 417-625-5340
Lisa Webb, prin. Fax 625-5344
Emerson ES 200/K-5
PO Box 128 64802 417-625-5345
Nila Vance, prin. Fax 625-5349
Floyd ES 500/K-5
PO Box 128 64802 417-625-5320
Douglas Adams, prin. Fax 625-5324
Irving ES 300/K-5
PO Box 128 64802 417-625-5350
Debra Fort, prin. Fax 625-5354
Jefferson ES 300/K-5
PO Box 128 64802 417-625-5355
Randy Randolph, prin. Fax 625-5216
McKinley ES 300/K-5
PO Box 128 64802 417-625-5365
Jennifer Doshier, prin. Fax 625-5369
Memorial MS 700/6-8
PO Box 128 64802 417-625-5250
Stephen Gilbreth, prin. Fax 625-5256
Norman ES 300/K-5
PO Box 128 64802 417-625-5360
Julie Munn, prin. Fax 625-5364
North MS 400/6-8
PO Box 128 64802 417-625-5270
Barbara D. Cox, prin. Fax 625-5273
Royal Heights ES 300/K-5
PO Box 128 64802 417-625-5370
Larry Masters, prin. Fax 625-5374
South MS 600/6-8
PO Box 128 64802 417-625-5280
Ron Mitchell, prin. Fax 625-5284
Stapleton ES 400/K-5
PO Box 128 64802 417-625-5375
Marilyn Alley, prin. Fax 625-5379
Washington Education Center 100/PK-PK
PO Box 128 64802 417-625-5290
Janet Earl, dir. Fax 625-5297
West Central ES 200/PK-5
PO Box 128 64802 417-625-5380
Denise Legore, prin. Fax 625-5384
Other Schools – See Duenweg

College Heights Christian S 600/PK-12
4311 Newman Rd 64801 417-782-4114
Daniel Lewis, prin. Fax 659-9092
Jefferson Independent Day S 200/PK-12
3401 Newman Rd 64801 417-781-5124
Bill Carter, hdmstr. Fax 781-1949
Martin Luther S 100/PK-8
2616 Connecticut Ave 64804 417-624-1403
Jeremy Schamber, prin. Fax 624-2774
St. Mary S 200/PK-5
505 W 25th St 64804 417-623-1465
Stephen Jones, prin. Fax 623-4749
St. Peter MS 100/6-8
802 Byers Ave 64801 417-624-5605
Greg Emory, prin. Fax 624-6254

Kahoka, Clark, Pop. 2,193
Clark County R-I SD 1,000/PK-12
427 W Chestnut St 63445 660-727-2377
Ritchie Kracht, supt. Fax 727-2035
www.clarkcounty.k12.mo.us/
Black Hawk ES 300/K-5
751 W Chestnut St 63445 660-727-3318
Julie Brotherton, prin. Fax 727-8017
Clark County MS 200/6-8
384 N Jefferson St 63445 660-727-3319
Jason Church, prin. Fax 727-3363
Other Schools – See Alexandria

Shiloh Christian S 50/K-12
RR 1 Box 68A 63445 573-853-4337
Ken Penfield, admin. Fax 853-4505

Kansas City, Jackson, Pop. 444,965
Center SD 58 2,500/PK-12
8701 Holmes Rd 64131 816-349-3300
Dr. Robert Bartman, supt. Fax 349-3431
www.center.k12.mo.us
Boone ES 300/K-5
8817 Wornall Rd 64114 816-349-3613
Dr. Sheryl Cochran, prin. Fax 349-3637
Center ECC 100/PK-PK
8817 Wornall Rd 64114 816-349-3700
Tamara Sandage, prin. Fax 349-3733
Center ES 200/K-5
8401 Euclid Ave 64132 816-349-3444
Dr. Zora Durham, prin. Fax 349-3441
Center MS 500/6-8
326 E 103rd St 64114 816-612-4000
Linda Williams, prin. Fax 612-4053
Indian Creek ES 300/K-5
9801 Grand Ave 64114 816-612-4250
Angela Price, prin. Fax 612-4287
Red Bridge ES 200/K-5
10781 Oak St 64114 816-612-4200
Danelle Marsden, prin. Fax 612-4205

Grandview C-4 SD
Supt. — See Grandview
Martin City S 600/K-8
201 E 133rd St 64145 816-316-5700
Dr. Barbara Schell, prin. Fax 316-5751

Hickman Mills C-I SD 6,900/K-12
9000 Old Santa Fe Rd 64138 816-316-7000
Dr. Marge Williams, supt. Fax 316-7020
www.hickmanmills.org
Burke ES 500/K-5
11115 Bennington Ave 64134 816-316-7750
Casey Klapmeyer, prin. Fax 316-7745
Dobbs ES 400/K-5
9400 Eastern Ave 64138 816-316-7800
Rodney Watson, prin. Fax 316-7805
Ervin JHS 800/6-8
10530 Greenwood Rd 64134 816-316-7600
Angie McConico, prin. Fax 316-7601
Ingels ES 400/K-5
11600 Food Ln 64134 816-316-7850
Lisa Smith, prin. Fax 316-7887
Johnson ES 300/K-5
10900 Marsh Ave 64134 816-316-7900
Roger Williams, prin. Fax 316-7928
Santa Fe ES 400/K-5
8908 Old Santa Fe Rd 64138 816-316-7950
Dr. Diana Swezy, prin. Fax 316-7988
Smith-Hale JHS 800/6-8
8925 Longview Rd 64134 816-316-7700
Jan Davis, prin. Fax 316-7704
Symington ES 300/K-5
8650 Ruskin Way 64134 816-316-8050
Gail White, prin. Fax 316-8051
Truman ES 400/K-5
9601 James A Reed Rd 64134 816-316-8100
Shaunda Fowler, prin. Fax 316-8111
Warford ES 300/K-5
11400 Cleveland Ave 64137 816-316-8150
Everlyn Williams, prin. Fax 316-8170

Kansas City SD 33 21,900/PK-12
1211 McGee St 64106 816-418-7000
Dr. Clive Coleman, supt. Fax 418-7631
www.kcmsd.net
ACE Collegium MS 6-8
3500 E Meyer Blvd 64132 816-418-1078
Marshall Peeples, prin. Fax 418-1080
Askew ES 200/PK-7
2630 Topping Ave 64129 816-418-2750
Dorothy Washington, prin. Fax 418-2760
Attucks ES 300/PK-7
2400 Prospect Ave 64127 816-418-3900
Sheila Danner, prin. Fax 418-3904
Banneker ES 300/PK-7
7050 Askew Ave 64132 816-418-1850
Deborah Johnson, prin. Fax 418-1860
Blenheim ES 200/PK-7
2411 E 70th Ter 64132 816-418-1550
Rebecca McKeel, prin. Fax 418-1560
Border Star Montessori ES 300/PK-6
6321 Wornall Rd 64113 816-418-5150
Tina Langston, prin. Fax 418-5165
Bryant ES 200/K-7
319 Westover Rd 64113 816-418-1500
Roxanne Pearce, prin. Fax 418-1510
Carver ES 200/K-7
4600 Elmwood Ave 64130 816-418-4925
Gustava Cooper-Baker, prin. Fax 418-4930
Central Magnet MS 200/8-8
3611 E Linwood Blvd 64128 816-418-2100
Joyce Jennings, prin. Fax 418-2115
Cook Montessori S 200/PK-PK
7302 Pennsylvania Ave 64114 816-418-1650
Donna Brown, prin. Fax 418-1662
Douglas ECC 500/PK-PK
2640 Belleview Ave 64108 816-418-6475
Catherine Renner, prin. Fax 418-6480
East S 600/PK-8
6400 E 23rd St 64129 816-418-3770
Dr. Wendy McNitt, prin. Fax 418-4803
Faxon Montessori ES 200/PK-6
1320 E 32nd Ter 64109 816-418-6525
Jeanne Mason, prin. Fax 418-6530
Foreign Language Academy 700/PK-8
3450 Warwick Blvd 64111 816-418-6000
Dr. Carol Allman, prin. Fax 418-6010
Franklin ES 300/PK-7
3400 Highland Ave 64109 816-418-6775
Mamie Keith, prin. Fax 418-6795

Garcia ES 500/K-7
1000 W 17th St 64108 816-418-8725
Bob Wilcox, prin. Fax 418-8730
Garfield ES 300/K-7
436 Prospect Ave 64124 816-418-3600
Dr. Gwendolyn Squires, prin. Fax 418-3610
Gladstone ES 600/K-7
335 N Elmwood Ave 64123 816-418-3950
Dr. Anne David, prin. Fax 418-3960
Graceland ES 200/PK-7
4101 E 53rd St 64130 816-418-2800
Dr. Patricia Nard, prin. Fax 418-2810
Hartman ES 200/PK-7
8111 Oak St 64114 816-418-1750
Dr. Jessie Kirksey, prin. Fax 418-1760
Holliday Montessori ES 400/PK-6
7227 Jackson Ave 64132 816-418-1950
Karen May, prin. Fax 418-1960
James ES 300/K-7
5810 Scarritt Ave 64123 816-418-3700
Renee Sweeden, prin. Fax 418-3710
Kansas City MS of the Arts 500/6-8
4848 Woodland Ave 64110 816-418-2400
Dr. Arlene Penner, prin. Fax 418-2415
King S 300/K-7
4201 Indiana Ave 64130 816-418-2475
Yvette Hayes, prin. Fax 418-2480
Knotts ES Magnet 300/K-7
5915 Park Ave 64130 816-418-1900
Dr. Gayle Hurst, prin. Fax 418-1910
Ladd ES 200/K-5
3640 Benton Blvd 64128 816-418-2850
Amelia Ragan, prin. Fax 418-2860
Lincoln College Prep MS 400/6-8
2012 E 23rd St 64127 816-418-3525
Kenneth Holstine, prin. Fax 418-3530
Longan ES 300/PK-7
3421 Cherry St 64109 816-418-6425
Martin Ngom, prin. Fax 418-6430
Longfellow ES Magnet 300/PK-7
2830 Holmes St 64109 816-418-5325
Douglas White, prin. Fax 418-5330
McCoy ES 300/PK-7
1524 White Ave 64126 816-418-3650
Dr. Jo Lynn Nemeth, prin. Fax 418-3665
Melcher ES 200/K-7
3958 Chelsea Ave 64130 816-418-6725
Shana Strawn, prin. Fax 418-6730
Moore ES 200/K-7
4510 E Linwood Blvd 64128 816-418-6825
Jo Greene, prin. Fax 418-6830
Northeast ES 400/K-7
4904 Independence Ave 64124 816-418-3400
Belinda Goolsby, prin. Fax 418-3447
Northeast MS 8-8
5008 Independence Ave 64124 816-418-3503
Tracy McClain, prin. Fax 418-3513
Paige S 500/PK-8
3301 E 75th St 64132 816-418-5050
James Jenkins, prin. Fax 418-5060
Phillips S 200/K-8
1619 E 24th Ter 64108 816-418-3750
Deloris Brown, prin. Fax 418-3760
Pinkerton ES 200/K-7
6409 Agnes Ave 64132 816-418-1600
Joyce White, prin. Fax 418-1610
Pitcher ES 300/PK-7
9915 E 38th Ter 64133 816-418-4550
Kim Johnson, prin. Fax 418-4560
Richardson ES 200/PK-7
3515 Park Ave 64109 816-418-2650
Lonnie Anthony, prin. Fax 418-2670
Scarritt ECC 400/PK-PK
3509 Anderson Ave 64123 816-418-3800
Stephanie Trugly, prin. Fax 418-3810
Swinney ES 400/K-7
1106 W 47th St 64112 816-418-6275
Cornelia Clark, prin. Fax 418-6280
Trailwoods S 400/PK-8
6201 E 17th St 64126 816-418-3250
Craig Waters, prin. Fax 418-3275
Troost ES 300/PK-7
1215 E 59th St 64110 816-418-1700
Judith Jordan, prin. Fax 418-1715
Weeks S 200/PK-PK
4201 Indiana Ave 64130 816-418-2550
Regina Hamilton, prin. Fax 418-2560
Westport MS 100/8-8
300 E 39th St 64111 816-418-2108
Sharon Fisher, prin. Fax 418-2115
West Rock Creek ES 300/K-7
8820 E 27th St 64129 816-418-4400
Jo Brandsgaard, prin. Fax 418-4404
Wheatley ES 200/PK-7
2415 Agnes Ave 64127 816-418-4825
Teresa May, prin. Fax 418-4830
Whittier ES 300/K-7
1012 Bales Ave 64127 816-418-3850
Alice Osborne, prin. Fax 418-3860
Woodland ES 300/K-7
711 Woodland Ave 64106 816-842-3775
Craig Rupert, prin. Fax 421-6528

Lee's Summit R-VII SD
Supt. — See Lees Summit
Summit Pointe ES K-6
13100 E 147th St 64149 816-986-2410
Dr. Heather Kenney, prin. Fax 986-4235

Liberty SD 53
Supt. — See Liberty
Early Childhood Education Center 200/PK-PK
9600 NE 79th St 64158 816-736-5324
Becky Gossett, prin. Fax 736-6781
Liberty Oaks ES 500/K-5
8150 N Farley Ave 64158 816-736-5600
Kaysie Wahlert, prin. Fax 736-5605

Shoal Creek ES 500/K-5
9000 NE Flintlock Rd 64157 816-736-7150
Michelle Schmitz, prin. Fax 736-7155

North Kansas City SD 74 17,400/PK-12
2000 NE 46th St 64116 816-413-5000
Dr. Thomas Cummings, supt. Fax 413-5005
www.nkcsd.k12.mo.us
Briarcliff ES 300/K-5
4100 N Briarcliff Rd 64116 816-413-4950
Chad Sutton, prin. Fax 413-4955
Chouteau ES 300/PK-5
3701 N Jackson Ave 64117 816-413-6760
Chris Daniels, prin. Fax 413-6765
Clardy ES 500/2-5
8100 N Troost Ave 64118 816-413-6800
Dr. David Cox, prin. Fax 413-6805
Davidson ES 300/K-5
5100 N Highland Ave 64118 816-413-4850
Leah Martisko, prin. Fax 413-4855
Eastgate MS 700/6-8
4700 NE Parvin Rd 64117 816-413-5800
Dr. Daniel Clemens, prin. Fax 413-5805
Fox Hill ES 600/K-5
545 NE 106th St 64155 816-413-6500
Gretchen Anderson, prin. Fax 413-6505
Gashland ES 100/K-1
500 NE 83rd St 64118 816-413-6870
Linda Greason, prin. Fax 413-6875
Gracemor ES 500/PK-5
5125 N Sycamore Ave 64119 816-413-6420
Cynthia Kupka, prin. Fax 413-6425
Lakewood ES 200/K-5
4624 N Norton Ave 64117 816-413-6570
Dr. Suzanne Boyer-Baker, prin. Fax 413-6575
Maple Park MS 800/6-8
5300 N Bennington Ave 64119 816-413-5700
Charlotte Sands, prin. Fax 413-5705
Maplewood ES 300/PK-5
6400 NE 52nd St 64119 816-413-4800
Robert Geist, prin. Fax 413-4805
Nashua ES 300/K-5
221 NE 114th St 64155 816-413-6960
Kathy D'Anza, prin. Fax 413-6965
New Mark MS 1,000/6-8
515 NE 106th St 64155 816-413-6300
Terri Stirlen, prin. Fax 413-6305
Northgate MS 700/6-8
2117 NE 48th St 64118 816-413-6100
Steve St. Louis, prin. Fax 413-6105
Northview ES 600/K-5
9201 N Indiana Ave 64156 816-413-6900
Mark Lewis, prin. Fax 413-6905
Ravenwood ES 300/K-5
5020 NE 58th St 64119 816-413-4600
Amanda Riedl, prin. Fax 413-4605
Topping ES 300/K-5
4433 N Topping Ave 64117 816-413-6660
Dana Miller, prin. Fax 413-6665
West Englewood ES 400/PK-5
1506 NW Englewood Rd 64118 816-413-4900
Lynda Casey, prin. Fax 413-4905
Winnwood ES 300/PK-5
4531 NE 44th Ter 64117 816-413-4650
Dr. Sara Cocolis, prin. Fax 413-4655
Other Schools – See Gladstone, North Kansas City, Pleasant Valley

Park Hill SD 9,600/K-12
7703 NW Barry Rd 64153 816-359-4000
Dr. Dennis Fisher, supt. Fax 359-4049
www.parkhill.k12.mo.us
Chinn ES 400/K-5
7100 N Chatham Ave 64151 816-359-4330
Shawn Fitzmorris, prin. Fax 359-4339
Congress MS 800/7-8
8150 N Congress Ave 64152 816-359-4230
Dr. Timothy Todd, prin. Fax 359-4219
English Landing ES 500/K-5
6500 NW Klamm Dr 64151 816-359-4370
Dr. Kerry Roe, prin. Fax 359-4379
Hawthorn ES 400/K-5
8200 N Chariton Ave 64152 816-359-4390
Sandy Hemaya, prin. Fax 359-4399
Lakeview MS 800/7-8
6720 NW 64th St 64151 816-359-4220
Becky Kiefer, prin. Fax 359-4229
Line Creek ES 500/K-5
5801 NW Waukomis Dr 64151 816-359-4320
Betsy Greim, prin. Fax 359-4329
Plaza MS 700/6-6
6501 NW 72nd St 64151 816-359-4210
Mike Brown, prin. Fax 359-4219
Prairie Point ES 500/K-5
8101 NW Belvidere Pkwy 64152 816-359-4380
Dr. Jennifer Corum, prin. Fax 359-4389
Renner ES 500/K-5
7401 NW Barry Rd 64153 816-359-4350
Teresa Tulipana, prin. Fax 359-4359
Southeast ES 500/K-5
5704 N Northwood Rd 64151 816-359-4360
Diane Simpson, prin. Fax 359-4369
Union Chapel ES 500/K-5
7100 NW Hampton Rd 64152 816-359-4310
Dr. Steven Archer, prin. Fax 359-4319
Other Schools – See Parkville

Platte County R-III SD
Supt. — See Platte City
Barry S 300/3-8
2001 NW 87th Ter 64154 816-436-9623
Rebecca Henshaw, prin. Fax 468-6046
Pathfinder ES K-2
1951 NW 87th Ter 64154 816-436-6670
Dr. Devin Doll, prin. Fax 436-2130

Raytown C-2 SD
Supt. — See Raytown
Eastwood Hills ES 300/K-5
5290 Sycamore Ave 64129 816-268-7210
Julie Whyte, prin. Fax 268-7215
Fleetridge ES 500/K-5
13001 E 55th St 64133 816-268-7220
Debbie Kingrey, prin. Fax 268-7225
Little Blue ES K-5
13900 E 61st St 64133 816-268-7740
Dr. Keith Gurley, prin. Fax 268-7745
Norfleet ES 500/K-5
6140 Norfleet Rd 64133 816-268-7240
Lori Kang, prin. Fax 268-7245
Raytown MS 1,100/6-8
4900 Pittman Rd 64133 816-268-7360
Dr. Georgetta May, prin. Fax 268-7365
Robinson ES 400/K-5
6707 Woodson Rd 64133 816-268-7260
Dr. Sandra Dickerson, prin. Fax 268-7265
Westridge ES 400/K-5
8500 E 77th St 64138 816-268-7290
Dea Bermudez, prin. Fax 268-7295

Barstow S 700/PK-12
11511 State Line Rd 64114 816-942-3255
Shane Foster, hdmstr. Fax 942-3227
Blue Ridge Christian S 300/PK-12
8524 Blue Ridge Blvd 64138 816-358-0950
Tony Ryff, supt. Fax 358-1138
Calvary Lutheran S 300/PK-8
8030 Ward Parkway Plz 64114 816-361-1200
Fax 361-5979
Christ the King Preschool 50/PK-PK
8510 Wornall Rd 64114 816-363-4888
Theresa Harris, dir. Fax 363-2889
Christ the King S 200/K-8
425 W 85th St 64114 816-363-1113
Jennifer Scanlon-Smith, prin. Fax 363-2889
Covenant Memorial Baptist Day S 50/PK-6
1115 Emanuel Cleaver II Blv 64110 816-756-3464
Faith Academy 100/PK-12
4300 N Corrington Ave 64117 816-455-2847
Donna Houpe, admin. Fax 455-8041
Glad Tidings Christian Academy 50/PK-K
PO Box 300932 64130 816-333-1054
Errolyn Fraser, admin. Fax 333-0396
Holy Cross Lutheran S 50/PK-PK
2003 NE Englewood Rd 64118 816-453-7211
Fax 452-8263
Holy Cross S 200/PK-8
121 N Quincy Ave 64123 816-231-8874
Jean Ferrara, prin. Fax 231-7258
Northland Christian ES 200/PK-6
4214 NW Cookingham Rd 64164 816-464-0555
Danny McCubbin, admin. Fax 464-0578
Notre Dame de Sion S of Kansas City 300/PK-8
3823 Locust St 64109 816-753-3810
Catherine Butel, prin. Fax 753-0806
Oakhill Day S 300/PK-8
7019 N Cherry St 64118 816-436-6228
Suzanne McCanles, hdmstr. Fax 436-0184
Our Lady of Guadalupe S 100/K-5
2310 Madison Ave 64108 816-221-2539
Connie Bowman, prin. Fax 283-3315
Our Lady of Peace S 200/PK-8
10526 Grandview Rd 64137 816-761-5605
Barbara McCormick, prin. Fax 761-2797
Our Lady of the Angels S 200/PK-8
4232 Mercier St 64111 816-931-1693
Mary Delac, prin. Fax 931-6713
Outreach Christian Education 100/PK-12
2900 NE Cates St 64117 816-455-5575
Kathy Taylor, prin. Fax 455-5168
Pembroke Hill S 500/PK-5
400 W 51st St 64112 816-936-1200
Steve Bellis, hdmstr. Fax 936-1208
St. Andrew the Apostle S 200/PK-8
6415 NE Antioch Rd 64119 816-454-7377
Sr. Leona Bax, prin. Fax 453-6393
St. Elizabeth S 500/PK-8
14 W 75th St 64114 816-523-7100
Sandra Kopp-Nickel, prin. Fax 523-2566
St. Gabriel ELC 100/PK-PK
4737 N Cleveland Ave 64117 816-453-4555
Lilly Winkeljohn, dir. Fax 453-6254
St. Gabriel S 200/K-8
4737 N Cleveland Ave 64117 816-453-4443
Judy Marsh, prin. Fax 453-6254
St. John Francis Regis ECC 50/PK-PK
8945 James A Reed Rd 64138 816-763-6566
Saundra Lanning, prin. Fax 761-2537
St. John Francis Regis S 300/K-8
8941 James A Reed Rd 64138 816-763-5837
Mary Bachkora, prin. Fax 966-1350
St. Patrick S 200/PK-8
1401 NE 42nd Ter 64116 816-453-0971
Julie Hess, prin. Fax 453-5451
St. Pauls Episcopal Day S 500/PK-8
4041 Main St 64111 816-931-8614
Elizabeth Barnes, hdmstr. Fax 931-6860
St. Peter S 600/PK-8
6400 Charlotte St 64131 816-523-4899
Janet Spallo, prin. Fax 523-1248
St. Stephen S 100/K-8
1001 Bennington Ave 64126 816-231-5227
Richard Soetaert, prin. Fax 231-2824
St. Therese ECC 200/PK-PK
7207 N State Route 9 64152 816-746-1500
Melissa Smitson, dir. Fax 741-0533
St. Therese S 600/K-8
7277 N State Route 9 64152 816-741-5400
Carol Hussin, prin. Fax 741-0533
St. Thomas More S 600/PK-8
11800 Holmes Rd 64131 816-942-5581
John O'Connor, prin. Fax 941-2450

Visitation S — 500/K-8
5134 Baltimore Ave 64112 — 816-531-6200
Vincent Cascone, prin. — Fax 531-8045

Kearney, Clay, Pop. 7,399
Kearney R-I SD — 2,800/K-12
1002 S Jefferson St 64060 — 816-628-4116
Dr. Chris Belcher, supt. — Fax 628-4074
www.kearney.k12.mo.us
Dogwood ES — 500/K-5
1400 Cedar Wood Pkwy 64060 — 816-903-1400
Janelle Norton, prin. — Fax 628-0016
Hawthorne ES — 200/K-5
1815 S Jefferson St 64060 — 816-628-4114
Sandra Peitzman, prin. — Fax 628-6476
Kearney ES — 300/K-5
902 S Jefferson St 64060 — 816-628-4113
Jeff Morrison, prin. — Fax 628-4132
Kearney MS — 300/6-7
200 E 5th St 64060 — 816-628-4115
Bart Woods, prin. — Fax 628-4424
Southview ES — 400/K-5
7 S Campus St 64060 — 816-628-4652
Melanie Brock, prin. — Fax 628-6173

Kelso, Scott, Pop. 523

St. Augustine S — 100/1-8
PO Box 97 63758 — 573-264-4644
Tracy Dumey, prin. — Fax 264-1475

Kennett, Dunklin, Pop. 11,028
Kennett SD 39 — 1,900/PK-12
510 College Ave 63857 — 573-717-1100
Jerry Noble, supt. — Fax 717-1016
www.kennett.k12.mo.us
ECC — 100/PK-PK
205 Wiggs St 63857 — 573-717-1145
Melissa Turner, prin. — Fax 717-1102
Kennett MS — 400/6-8
510 College Ave 63857 — 573-717-1105
Ward Billings, prin. — Fax 717-1106
Masterson ES — 300/K-2
1600 Ely St 63857 — 573-717-1115
Laurie L. McAtee, prin. — Fax 717-1115
South ES — 500/3-5
920 Kennett St 63857 — 573-717-1130
Kimberly Lowry, prin. — Fax 717-1130

Keytesville, Chariton, Pop. 516
Keytesville R-III SD — 200/PK-12
27247 Highway 5 65261 — 660-288-3767
Paul Vossler, supt. — Fax 288-3110
schoolweb.missouri.edu/keytesville.k12.mo.us/
Keytesville ES — 100/PK-6
27247 Highway 5 65261 — 660-288-3767
Rena Roth, prin. — Fax 288-3110

King City, Gentry, Pop. 944
King City R-I SD — 400/PK-12
PO Box 189 64463 — 660-535-4319
Bruce Skogland, supt. — Fax 535-4765
www.kingcity.k12.mo.us
King City ES — 200/PK-6
PO Box 189 64463 — 660-535-4712
Adrianne Workman, prin. — Fax 535-4965

Kingdom City, Callaway, Pop. 137
North Callaway County R-I SD — 1,300/K-12
2690 US Highway 54 65262 — 573-386-2214
Dr. Roy Moss, supt. — Fax 386-2169
nc.k12.mo.us
Hatton-McCredie S — 300/K-8
4171 County Road 240 65262 — 573-642-4333
Jenny Bilbro, prin. — Fax 642-5624
Other Schools – See Auxvasse, Williamsburg

Kingston, Caldwell, Pop. 300
Kingston SD 42 — 100/PK-8
139 E Lincoln St 64650 — 816-586-3111
Cinthia Barnes, supt. — Fax 586-3903
kingston42.k12.mo.us/
Kingston S — 100/PK-8
139 E Lincoln St 64650 — 816-586-3111
Cinthia Barnes, prin. — Fax 586-3903

Kingsville, Johnson, Pop. 260
Kingsville R-I SD — 300/K-12
PO Box 7 64061 — 816-597-3422
Kevin Coleman, supt. — Fax 597-3702
www.kingsville.k12.mo.us/
Kingsville ES — 100/K-6
PO Box 7 64061 — 816-597-3422
Angela Helms, prin. — Fax 597-3702

Kirbyville, Taney, Pop. 143
Kirbyville R-VI SD — 300/K-8
6225 E State Highway 76 65679 — 417-337-8913
Jerry Parrett, supt. — Fax 348-0794
www.kirbyville.k12.mo.us/
Kirbyville ES — 200/K-3
4278 E State Highway 76 65679 — 417-334-2757
Addie Gaines, prin. — Fax 336-2084
Kirbyville MS — 200/4-8
6225 E State Highway 76 65679 — 417-348-0444
J. Carless Osbourn, prin. — Fax 348-0525

Kirksville, Adair, Pop. 16,986
Kirksville R-III SD — 2,400/PK-12
1901 E Hamilton St 63501 — 660-665-7774
Patrick Williams, supt. — Fax 665-3281
www.kirksville.k12.mo.us
Kirksville MS — 600/6-8
1515 Cottage Grove Ave 63501 — 660-665-3793
Dr. Michael Mitchell, prin. — Fax 626-1418
Kirksville PS — 500/PK-2
1815 E Hamilton St 63501 — 660-665-5691
Tricia Reger, prin. — Fax 626-1421
Miller ES — 500/3-5
2010 E Normal Ave 63501 — 660-665-2834
Marianne Farr, prin. — Fax 626-1464

Faith Lutheran S — 100/PK-2
1820 S Baltimore St 63501 — 660-665-8166
Fax 627-0101
Mary Immaculate S — 100/K-8
712 E Washington St 63501 — 660-665-1006
Sr. Ruth Klauser, prin. — Fax 665-1006

Kirkwood, Saint Louis, Pop. 27,038
Kirkwood R-VII SD — 4,800/K-12
11289 Manchester Rd 63122 — 314-213-6101
Dr. Tom Williams, supt. — Fax 984-0002
www.kirkwoodschools.org
Keysor ES — 400/K-5
725 N Geyer Rd 63122 — 314-213-6120
Dr. Bryan Painter, prin. — Fax 213-6172
Nipher MS — 600/6-8
700 S Kirkwood Rd 63122 — 314-213-6180
Dr. Michele Condon, prin. — Fax 213-6178
North Kirkwood MS — 600/6-8
11287 Manchester Rd 63122 — 314-213-6170
Tim Cochran, prin. — Fax 213-6177
Robinson ES — 400/K-5
803 Couch Ave 63122 — 314-213-6140
Dr. Jacalyn Wheelehan, prin. — Fax 213-6174
Tillman ES — 400/K-5
230 Quan Ave 63122 — 314-213-6150
B.R. Rhoads, prin. — Fax 213-6175
Westchester ES — 400/K-5
1416 Woodgate Dr 63122 — 314-213-6160
Dr. Chris Clay, prin. — Fax 213-6176
Other Schools – See Glendale

Christ Community Lutheran S — 500/PK-8
110 W Woodbine Ave 63122 — 314-822-7774
Robert Cooksey, dir. — Fax 822-5472
St. Gerard Majella S — 400/K-8
2005 Dougherty Ferry Rd 63122 — 314-822-8844
Dr. Jane Koberlein, prin. — Fax 822-8588
St. Peter S — 500/PK-8
215 N Clay Ave 63122 — 314-821-0460
Dan Bauer, prin. — Fax 821-0833
Villa Di Maria Montessori S — 100/PK-6
1280 Simmons Ave 63122 — 314-822-2601
Nicole Cook, admin. — Fax 822-5711

Knob Noster, Johnson, Pop. 2,734
Knob Noster R-VIII SD — 1,600/PK-12
401 E Wimer St 65336 — 660-563-3186
Dr. Margret Anderson, supt. — Fax 563-3026
knobnoster.k12.mo.us/
Knob Noster ES — 400/PK-5
405 E Wimer St 65336 — 660-563-3019
Tracy Kunzinski, prin. — Fax 563-3781
Knob Noster MS — 400/6-8
211 E Wimer St 65336 — 660-563-2260
Dr. Jamie Burkhart, prin. — Fax 563-3274
Other Schools – See Whiteman AFB

Koshkonong, Oregon, Pop. 208
Oregon-Howell R-III SD — 300/K-12
PO Box 398 65692 — 417-867-5601
Luke Boyer, supt. — Fax 867-3757
koshkonong.k12.mo.us/
Koshkonong ES — 100/K-6
PO Box 398 65692 — 417-867-5601
David Kirk, prin. — Fax 867-3757

Labadie, Franklin
Washington SD
Supt. — See Washington
Labadie ES — 200/K-6
2749 Highway T 63055 — 636-231-2600
Glenda Leslie, prin. — Fax 231-2605

Laddonia, Audrain, Pop. 600
Community R-VI SD — 300/PK-12
35063 Highway BB 63352 — 573-492-6223
Arlen Provancha, supt. — Fax 492-6268
www.cr6.net/
Community ES — 100/PK-5
35063 Highway BB 63352 — 573-492-6223
Natalie Gibson, prin. — Fax 492-6268

Lake Ozark, Camden, Pop. 1,915
School of the Osage R-II SD — 1,600/PK-12
PO Box 1960 65049 — 573-365-4091
Dr. Mary Ann Johnson, supt. — Fax 365-5748
www.osage.k12.mo.us
Mills ES — 300/PK-2
PO Box 1960 65049 — 573-365-5341
Veronica Smith, prin. — Fax 365-5394
Other Schools – See Osage Beach

Lake Saint Louis, Saint Charles, Pop. 8,833
Wentzville R-IV SD
Supt. — See Wentzville
Duello ES — 500/K-5
1814 Duello Rd 63367 — 636-327-6050
Kathy Fisher, prin. — Fax 327-4211
Green Tree ES — 600/K-5
1000 Ronald Reagan Dr 63367 — 636-625-5600
Angela Politte, prin. — Fax 625-5610

Hope Montessori Academy — 100/PK-K
1799 Lake Saint Louis Blvd 63367 — 636-561-2811
Pamela Kenney, prin. — Fax 561-2895

Lamar, Barton, Pop. 4,602
Lamar R-I SD — 1,300/PK-12
202 W 7th St 64759 — 417-682-3527
Dr. Dennis Wilson, supt. — Fax 682-6013
www.lamar.k12.mo.us
East PS — 300/PK-2
202 W 7th St 64759 — 417-681-0613
Zach Harris, prin. — Fax 681-0652
Lamar MS — 300/6-8
202 W 7th St 64759 — 417-682-3548
Alan Ray, prin. — Fax 682-3420
West ES — 300/3-5
202 W 7th St 64759 — 417-682-3567
Sharon Brannon, prin. — Fax 682-9675

La Monte, Pettis, Pop. 1,062
La Monte R-IV SD — 400/PK-12
301 S Washington St 65337 — 660-347-5439
Joan Twidwell, supt. — Fax 347-5467
lamonte.k12.mo.us/
La Monte ES — 200/PK-6
201 S Washington St 65337 — 660-347-5621
Elizabeth Wilkerson, prin. — Fax 347-5467

La Plata, Macon, Pop. 1,442
La Plata R-II SD — 300/K-12
201 W Moore St 63549 — 660-332-7001
Steve Carvajal, supt. — Fax 332-7929
laplata.k12.mo.us
La Plata ES — 200/K-6
201 W Moore St 63549 — 660-332-7003
Lisa Coy, prin. — Fax 332-4881

Laquey, Pulaski
Laquey R-V SD — 700/PK-12
PO Box 130 65534 — 573-765-3716
Bob Boulware, supt. — Fax 765-4052
www.laquey.k12.mo.us/
Laquey R-V ES — 300/PK-5
PO Box 130 65534 — 573-765-3245
Linda Storie, prin. — Fax 765-5604
Laquey R-V MS — 200/6-8
PO Box 130 65534 — 573-765-3129
Jerry Stenson, prin. — Fax 765-4086

Laredo, Grundy, Pop. 249
Laredo R-VII SD — 50/K-8
PO Box C 64652 — 660-286-2225
Jean Dustman, supt. — Fax 286-2226
Laredo S — 50/K-8
PO Box C 64652 — 660-286-2225
Jean Dustman, prin. — Fax 286-2226

Latham, Moniteau
Moniteau County R-V SD — 100/K-8
PO Box 367 65050 — 660-458-6271
Tanya Brown, supt. — Fax 458-6604
Latham S — 100/K-8
PO Box 367 65050 — 660-458-6271
Tanya Brown, prin. — Fax 458-6604

Lathrop, Clinton, Pop. 2,328
Lathrop R-II SD — 900/K-12
700 East St 64465 — 816-528-7500
Dr. Chris Blackburn, supt. — Fax 528-7514
schoolweb.missouri.edu/lathrop.k12.mo.us
Lathrop ES — 400/K-5
700 Center St 64465 — 816-528-7700
Chauncey Rardon, prin. — Fax 528-7759
Lathrop MS — 200/6-8
612 Center St 64465 — 816-528-7600
Chris Fine, prin. — Fax 528-7637

Lawson, Ray, Pop. 2,406
Lawson R-XIV SD — 1,200/PK-12
PO Box 157 64062 — 816-580-7277
S. Craig Barker, supt. — Fax 296-7723
schoolweb.missouri.edu/lawson.k12.mo.us/
Lawson MS — 400/5-8
PO Box 157 64062 — 816-580-7279
Tammy Dunn, prin. — Fax 296-3164
Southwest ES — 400/PK-4
PO Box 157 64062 — 816-580-7272
Holly Simmons, prin. — Fax 296-3202

Leadwood, Saint Francois, Pop. 1,173
West St. Francois County R-IV SD — 1,000/PK-12
1124 Main St 63653 — 573-562-7535
Stacy Stevens, supt. — Fax 562-7510
westco.k12.mo.us/
West County MS — 200/6-8
1124 Main St 63653 — 573-562-7544
Kevin Coffman, prin. — Fax 562-7510
Other Schools – See Park Hills

Lebanon, Laclede, Pop. 13,336
Laclede County C-5 SD — 500/PK-8
16050 Highway KK 65536 — 417-532-4837
Jeff Plake, supt. — Fax 588-2100
www.jebc5.k12.mo.us/
Barber S — 500/PK-8
16050 Highway KK 65536 — 417-532-4837
Roger Moore, prin. — Fax 588-2100

Lebanon R-III SD — 4,400/PK-12
1310 E Route 66 65536 — 417-532-9141
Dr. Duane Widhalm, supt. — Fax 532-9492
www.lebanon.k12.mo.us
Boswell ES — 600/4-5
695 Millcreek Rd 65536 — 417-532-3091
Lael Hyde, prin. — Fax 532-4359
Esther ES — 500/PK-1
1200 Clark Ave 65536 — 417-532-3961
Sheila Moore, prin. — Fax 532-8063
Hillcrest Accelerated S — 300/6-6
301 Hoover St 65536 — 417-532-4681
Ed Elsea, prin. — Fax 533-3801
Lebanon JHS — 700/7-8
500 N Adams Ave 65536 — 417-532-9121
Craig Reeves, prin. — Fax 533-3805
Maplecrest ES — 700/2-3
901 Maple Ln 65536 — 417-532-2641
Tracy Klein, prin. — Fax 533-3802

Lees Summit, Jackson, Pop. 74,948
Blue Springs R-IV SD
Supt. — See Blue Springs

Chapel Lakes ES 400/K-5
3701 NE Independence Ave 64064 816-525-9100
Jason Woolf, prin. Fax 525-9502
Delta Woods MS 600/6-8
4401 NE Lakewood Way 64064 816-795-5830
Steve Cook, prin. Fax 795-5839
Spears ES 600/K-5
201 NE Anderson Dr 64064 816-478-9899
Renee Spaulding, prin. Fax 478-9799

Lee's Summit R-VII SD 16,600/PK-12
301 NE Tudor Rd 64086 816-986-1000
Dr. David McGehee, supt. Fax 986-1170
www.leesummit.k12.mo.us
Campbell MS 900/7-8
1201 NE Colbern Rd 64086 816-986-3175
Dr. Vicki Porter, prin. Fax 986-3245
Cedar Creek ES 500/K-6
2600 SW 3rd St 64081 816-986-1260
Lynn Lang, prin. Fax 986-1285
Great Beginnings Early Education Center 200/PK-PK
905 NE Bluestem Dr 64086 816-986-2460
Kerry Boehm, prin. Fax 986-2475
Hawthorn Hill ES 600/K-6
2801 SW Pryor Rd 64082 816-986-3380
Carol Germano, prin. Fax 986-3405
Hazel Grove ES 500/K-6
2001 NW Blue Pkwy 64064 816-986-3310
Dr. Chris Troester, prin. Fax 986-3335
Highland Park ES 500/K-6
400 SE Millstone Ave 64063 816-986-2250
Jodi Mallette, prin. Fax 986-2275
Lee's Summit ES 200/K-6
110 SE Green St 64063 816-986-3340
Katie Collier, prin. Fax 986-3355
Longview Farms ES 600/K-6
1001 SW Longview Park Dr 64081 816-986-4180
Dr. Ryan Rostine, prin. Fax 986-4205
Mason ES 300/K-6
27600 E Colbern Rd 64086 816-986-2330
Beth Ratty, prin. Fax 986-2355
Meadow Lane ES 600/K-6
1421 NE Independence Ave 64086 816-986-3250
Joy Brigman, prin. Fax 986-3275
Pleasant Lea ES 500/K-6
700 SW Persels Rd 64081 816-986-1230
Patricia Alexander, prin. Fax 986-1255
Pleasant Lea MS 900/7-8
630 SW Persels Rd 64081 816-986-1175
Janette Cooley, prin. Fax 986-1225
Prairie View ES 800/K-6
501 SE Todd George Pkwy 64063 816-986-2280
Tamara Asplund, prin. Fax 986-2325
Richardson ES 600/K-6
800 NE Blackwell Rd 64086 816-986-2220
Mary Naudet, prin. Fax 986-2245
Summit Lakes MS 800/7-8
3500 SW Windemere Dr 64082 816-986-1375
Lisa Jacques, prin. Fax 986-1435
Sunset Valley ES K-6
1850 SE Ranson Rd 64082 816-986-4240
Susan Romeo, prin.
Trailridge ES 600/K-6
3651 SW Windemere Dr 64082 816-986-1290
Pam Carpenter, prin. Fax 986-1305
Underwood ES 600/K-6
1125 NE Colbern Rd 64086 816-986-3280
Brian Sloan, prin. Fax 986-3295
Westview ES 400/K-6
200 NW Ward Rd 64063 816-986-1350
David Boulden, prin. Fax 986-1365
Woodland ES 600/K-6
12709 Smart Rd 64086 816-986-2360
Dr. Michael Pragman, prin. Fax 986-2385
Other Schools – See Greenwood, Kansas City

Lee's Summit Community Christian S 700/PK-12
1500 SW Jefferson St 64081 816-525-1480
Linda Harrelson, admin. Fax 525-5402
Our Lady of the Presentation ECC 200/PK-PK
100 NW Murray Rd 64081 816-251-1140
Cathy Koob, dir. Fax 251-1132
Our Lady of the Presentation S 400/K-8
150 NW Murray Rd 64081 816-251-1150
Jodi Briggs, prin. Fax 251-1155
Summit View Adventist S 1-8
12503 State Route 7 64086 816-697-3443

Leeton, Johnson, Pop. 626
Leeton R-X SD 400/PK-12
500 N Main St 64761 660-653-2301
Dr. William Nicely, supt. Fax 653-4315
www.leeton.k12.mo.us/
Leeton ES 200/PK-5
500 N Main St 64761 660-653-4731
Susan Crooks, prin. Fax 653-4315
Leeton MS 100/6-8
500 N Main St 64761 660-653-4314
Jeff Curley, prin. Fax 653-4315

Leopold, Bollinger
Leopold R-III SD 200/K-12
PO Box 39 63760 573-238-2211
Derek Urhahn, supt. Fax 238-9868
schoolweb.missouri.edu/leopold.k12.mo.us/
Leopold ES 100/K-6
PO Box 39 63760 573-238-2211
Keenan Kinder, prin. Fax 238-9868

Lesterville, Reynolds
Lesterville R-IV SD 300/PK-12
PO Box 120 63654 573-637-2201
Earlene Fox, supt. Fax 637-2279
www.lesterville.k12.mo.us/
Lesterville ES 100/PK-6
PO Box 120 63654 573-637-2201
Susan Myers, prin. Fax 637-2279

Lewistown, Lewis, Pop. 580
Lewis County C-1 SD
Supt. — See Ewing
Highland ES 600/PK-6
25189 Heritage Ave 63452 573-209-3586
Kirt Malone, prin. Fax 209-3370

Lexington, Lafayette, Pop. 4,632
Lexington R-V SD 1,000/PK-12
100 S Highway 13 64067 660-259-4369
Brad MacLaughlin, supt. Fax 259-4992
www.lexington.k12.mo.us
Bell ES 400/K-4
400 S 20th St 64067 660-259-4341
Linda Florence, prin. Fax 259-2040
ECC PK-PK
811 S Highway 13 Ste B 64067 660-259-4369
Michelle Roush, admin. Fax 259-4992
Lexington MS 300/5-8
1111 S 24th St 64067 660-259-4611
Joy Grimes, prin. Fax 259-2538

Liberal, Barton, Pop. 811
Liberal R-II SD 600/PK-12
PO Box 38 64762 417-843-5115
William Harvey, supt. Fax 843-6698
www.liberal.k12.mo.us/
Liberal ES 300/PK-5
PO Box 38 64762 417-843-5865
Leticia Fry, prin. Fax 843-5231
Liberal MS 100/6-8
PO Box 38 64762 417-843-6033
Margaret Gillard, prin. Fax 843-2403

Liberty, Clay, Pop. 29,042
Liberty SD 53 8,800/PK-12
650 Conistor Ln 64068 816-736-5300
Mike Brewer, supt. Fax 736-5306
www.liberty.k12.mo.us
Doniphan ES 400/K-5
1900 Clay Dr 64068 816-736-5400
Jay Niceswanger, prin. Fax 736-5403
Franklin ES 300/K-5
201 W Mill St 64068 816-736-5440
Andy Wright, prin. Fax 736-5443
Lewis & Clark ES 500/K-5
1407 Nashua Rd 64068 816-736-5430
Kyle Palmer, prin. Fax 736-5433
Liberty MS 800/6-7
1500 S Withers Rd 64068 816-736-5410
Dr. Mike Kimbrel, prin. Fax 736-5415
Manor Hill ES 400/K-5
1400 S Skyline Dr 64068 816-736-5460
Jeff Williams, prin. Fax 736-5464
Ridgeview ES 300/K-5
701 Thornton St 64068 816-736-5450
Vicki Ogden, prin. Fax 736-5454
Schumacher ES 500/K-5
425 Claywoods Pkwy 64068 816-736-5490
Mike Dye, prin. Fax 736-5494
South Valley MS 600/6-7
1000 Midjay Dr 64068 816-736-7180
Jill Mullen, prin. Fax 736-7185
Warren Hills ES 500/K-5
1251 Camille St 64068 816-736-5630
Steven Lumetta, prin. Fax 736-5635
Other Schools – See Kansas City

St. James S 400/PK-8
309 S Stewart Rd 64068 816-781-4428
Molly Doherty, prin. Fax 781-0747

Licking, Texas, Pop. 1,500
Licking R-VIII SD 900/PK-12
PO Box 179 65542 573-674-2911
Dr. John Hood, supt. Fax 674-4064
www.licking.k12.mo.us/
Licking ES 400/PK-6
PO Box 179 65542 573-674-3211
Sandra Aiken, prin. Fax 674-4064
Licking JHS 100/7-8
PO Box 149 65542 573-674-4891
Grant Crow, prin. Fax 674-4421

Lilbourn, New Madrid, Pop. 1,237
New Madrid County R-I SD
Supt. — See New Madrid
Lilbourn ES 300/PK-5
PO Box 605 63862 573-688-2593
Laurie Brittain, prin. Fax 688-2595

Lincoln, Benton, Pop. 1,103
Lincoln R-II SD 600/K-12
PO Box 39 65338 660-547-3514
Kevin Smith, supt. Fax 547-3729
www.lincoln.k12.mo.us/
Lincoln ES 300/K-6
PO Box 39 65338 660-547-2222
Rebecca Eifert, prin. Fax 547-3729

Linn, Osage, Pop. 1,424
Osage County R-II SD 700/PK-12
1212 E Main St 65051 573-897-4200
Mary Elsensohn, supt. Fax 897-3768
www.linn.k12.mo.us
Osage County ES 300/PK-6
1212 E Main St 65051 573-897-4226
Amy Cox, prin. Fax 897-3768

St. George S 200/K-8
PO Box 19 65051 573-897-3645
Sr. Celly Amparano, prin. Fax 897-2148

Lockwood, Dade, Pop. 962
Lockwood R-I SD 400/K-12
400 W 4th St 65682 417-232-4513
Bill Rogers, supt. Fax 232-4187
www.lockwoodschools.org/
Lockwood S 200/K-8
408 Locust St 65682 417-232-4528
Kenneth Hackney, prin. Fax 232-4875

Immanuel Lutheran S 100/PK-8
PO Box H 65682 417-232-4530
Judy MacLean, prin. Fax 232-4476

Lonedell, Franklin
Lonedell R-XIV SD 400/K-8
7466 Highway FF 63060 636-629-0401
Rolla Fraley, supt. Fax 629-5561
www.lonedell-bobcats.org/
Lonedell S 400/K-8
7466 Highway FF 63060 636-629-0401
Stephen Wunderlich, prin. Fax 629-5561

Lone Jack, Jackson, Pop. 697
Lone Jack C-6 SD 600/PK-12
201 W Lne Jack Lees Smmt Rd 64070 816-697-3539
Ronald Davies, supt. Fax 697-8869
www.lonejackc6.net
Lone Jack ES 200/PK-PK, 2-
600 N Bynum Rd 64070 816-697-2811
Jacqueline Duvall, prin. Fax 566-2473
Lone Jack PS 100/K-1
201 W Lne Jack Lees Smmt Rd 64070 816-697-3539
Jacqueline Duvall, prin. Fax 697-8869

Long Lane, Dallas
Dallas County R-I SD
Supt. — See Buffalo
Long Lane ES 100/PK-4
25 State Road P 65590 417-345-7749
Gina Hohensee, prin. Fax 345-6897

Loose Creek, Osage

Immaculate Conception S 100/K-8
PO Box 68 65054 573-897-3516
Rita Stiefermann, prin. Fax 897-4271

Louisiana, Pike, Pop. 3,881
Boncl R-X SD 50/K-8
23526 Pike 9247 63353 573-754-5412
Natalie Lilley, supt. Fax 754-7981
Boncl S 50/K-8
23526 Pike 9247 63353 573-754-5412
Natalie Lilley, prin. Fax 754-7981

Louisiana R-II SD 800/PK-12
3321 Georgia St 63353 573-754-4261
Dan Jones, supt. Fax 754-4319
www.schoolweb.missouri.edu/louisiana.k12.mo.us
Louisiana ES 300/PK-5
500 Haley Ave 63353 573-754-6904
Erik Melton, prin. Fax 754-3122
Louisiana MS 200/6-8
3321 Georgia St 63353 573-754-5340
Chuck Tophinke, prin. Fax 754-5377

Ludlow, Livingston, Pop. 198
Southwest Livingston County R-I SD 200/K-12
4944 Highway DD 64656 660-738-4433
John Locker, supt. Fax 738-4441
www.southwestr1.org/
Southwest Livingston County ES 100/K-6
4944 Highway DD 64656 660-738-4433
Barbara Kugler, prin. Fax 738-4441

Luray, Clark, Pop. 102
Luray SD 33 100/K-8
PO Box 248 63453 660-866-2222
Kim Clark, supt. Fax 866-2233
Luray S 100/K-8
PO Box 248 63453 660-866-2222
Kim Clark, prin. Fax 866-2233

Macks Creek, Camden, Pop. 284
Macks Creek R-V SD 300/PK-12
245 State Rd N 65786 573-363-5909
Donna Moffatt, supt. Fax 363-0127
mcreek.k12.mo.us/
Macks Creek ES 200/PK-6
245 State Rd N 65786 573-363-5977
Bonnie Gould, prin. Fax 363-0127

Macon, Macon, Pop. 5,428
Macon County R-I SD 1,200/PK-12
702 N Missouri St 63552 660-385-5719
Debbie Livingston, supt. Fax 385-7179
www.macon.k12.mo.us/
Macon County ES 500/PK-5
702 N Missouri St 63552 660-385-2118
Ernest Motley, prin. Fax 385-7689
Macon County MS 300/6-8
702 N Missouri St 63552 660-385-2189
Dustin Fanning, prin. Fax 385-7230

Immaculate Conception S 100/K-8
401 N Rubey St 63552 660-385-2711
Sr. Barbara Koch, prin. Fax 385-2839

Madison, Monroe, Pop. 562
Madison C-3 SD 300/PK-12
309 S Thomas St 65263 660-291-5115
Fred Weibling, supt. Fax 291-5006
www.schoolweb.missouri.edu/madisonc3.k12.mo.us/
Madison ES 200/PK-6
309 S Thomas St 65263 660-291-4515
Scott Salmons, prin. Fax 291-5006

Middle Grove C-1 SD 50/K-8
11476 Route M 65263 660-291-8583
Sharon Woods, supt. Fax 291-8584
Middle Grove S 50/K-8
11476 Route M 65263 660-291-8583
Sharon Woods, prin. Fax 291-8584

Maitland, Holt, Pop. 315
Nodaway-Holt R-VII SD
Supt. — See Graham
Nodaway-Holt ES 100/PK-6
409 Hickory St 64466 660-935-2514
Ethan Sickels, prin. Fax 935-2242

Malden, Dunklin, Pop. 4,635
Malden R-I SD 1,100/K-12
505 Burkhart St 63863 573-276-5794
Kenneth Cook, supt. Fax 276-5796
www.malden.k12.mo.us/
Malden ES 600/K-6
505 Burkhart St 63863 573-276-5791
Kent Luke, prin. Fax 276-5792

Malta Bend, Saline, Pop. 243
Malta Bend R-V SD 100/K-12
PO Box 10 65339 660-595-2371
Melissa Vesser, supt. Fax 595-2430
Malta Bend ES 100/K-5
PO Box 10 65339 660-595-2371
Roger Feagan, prin. Fax 595-2430

Manchester, Saint Louis, Pop. 18,970
Parkway C-2 SD
Supt. — See Chesterfield
Barretts ES 500/K-5
1780 Carman Rd 63021 314-415-6000
Tim Dutton, prin. Fax 415-6012
Carman Trails ES 400/K-5
555 S Weidman Rd 63021 314-415-6100
Chris Raeker, prin. Fax 415-6119
Henry ES 400/K-5
700 Henry Ave 63011 314-415-6350
Dr. Lynn Pott, prin. Fax 415-6362
Parkway South MS 700/6-8
760 Woods Mill Rd 63011 314-415-7200
Craig Fenner, prin. Fax 415-7213
Pierremont ES 400/K-5
1215 Dauphine Ln 63011 314-415-6600
Kathy Cain, prin. Fax 415-6612

Christ Prince of Peace S 400/K-8
417 Weidman Rd 63011 636-394-6840
Chris Einig, prin. Fax 594-0082
St. Joseph S 500/PK-8
555 Saint Joseph Ln 63021 636-391-1253
Jeanette Dandino, prin. Fax 391-1462

Mansfield, Wright, Pop. 1,352
Mansfield R-IV SD 700/PK-12
316 W Ohio St 65704 417-924-8458
Randy Short, supt. Fax 924-3427
www.mansfieldschool.net/
Mansfield JHS 200/6-8
316 W Ohio St 65704 417-924-8625
Gary Greene, prin. Fax 924-8789
Wilder ES 400/PK-5
414 W Ohio St 65704 417-924-3289
Nate Moore, prin. Fax 924-3280

Maplewood, Saint Louis, Pop. 8,808
Maplewood-Richmond Heights SD 1,000/PK-12
7539 Manchester Rd 63143 314-644-4400
Dr. Linda Henke, supt. Fax 781-3160
www.mrhsd.org/
Maplewood Richmond Heights ECC 100/PK-1
2801 Oakland Ave 63143 314-644-4405
Cyndi Hebenstreit, prin. Fax 781-1896
Other Schools – See Richmond Heights, Saint Louis

Marble Hill, Bollinger, Pop. 1,512
Woodland R-IV SD 800/K-12
RR 5 Box 3210 63764 573-238-3343
Dennis Parham, supt. Fax 238-2153
www.woodland.k12.mo.us/
Woodland ES 300/K-4
RR 5 Box 3210 63764 573-238-2822
Stan Seiler, prin. Fax 238-3319
Woodland MS 100/5-8
RR 5 Box 3210 63764 573-238-2663
Dan Schlief, prin. Fax 238-0186

New Salem Baptist Academy 100/PK-12
HC 64 Box 4220 63764 573-238-2643

Marceline, Linn, Pop. 2,405
Marceline R-V SD 700/K-12
400 E Santa Fe Ave 64658 660-376-3371
Gabe Edgar, supt. Fax 376-6001
www.marceline.k12.mo.us
Disney ES 300/K-5
420 E California Ave 64658 660-376-2166
Sarah Dunham, prin. Fax 376-6026
Marceline MS 200/6-8
314 E Santa Fe Ave 64658 660-376-2411
Brian Sherrow, prin. Fax 376-6016

Father McCartan Memorial S 100/K-8
327 S Kansas Ave 64658 660-376-3580
Kelly Ott, prin. Fax 376-2836

Marionville, Lawrence, Pop. 2,161
Marionville R-IX SD 800/K-12
PO Box 409 65705 417-258-7755
Larry Brown, supt. Fax 258-2564
www.marionville.us/
Marionville ES 400/K-6
PO Box 409 65705 417-258-2550
Christy Short, prin. Fax 258-2564

Marquand, Madison, Pop. 266
Marquand-Zion R-VI SD 200/K-12
PO Box A 63655 573-783-3388
Duane Schindler, supt. Fax 783-3067
Marquand ES 100/K-6
PO Box A 63655 573-783-3388
Pamela Moyers, prin. Fax 783-3067

Marshall, Saline, Pop. 12,403
Hardeman R-X SD 100/K-8
21051 Highway D 65340 660-837-3400
Kristy Forrester, admin. Fax 837-3411
Hardeman S 100/K-8
21051 Highway D 65340 660-837-3400
Paul Vaillancourt, admin. Fax 837-3411

Marshall SD 2,500/K-12
860 W Vest St 65340 660-886-7414
Dr. Craig Noah, supt. Fax 886-5641
www.marshallschools.com/
Benton ES 200/K-1
467 S Ellsworth Ave 65340 660-886-3993
Paige Clouse, prin. Fax 886-7188
Bueker MS 700/5-8
565 S Odell Ave 65340 660-886-6833
Lance Tobin, prin. Fax 886-7529
Eastwood ES 200/K-K, 3-3
313 E Eastwood St 65340 660-886-7100
John Angelhow, prin. Fax 886-3812
Northwest ES 200/K-K, 4-4
411 N Benton Ave 65340 660-886-2993
Janine Machholz, prin. Fax 886-3875
Southeast ES 200/K-K, 2-2
215 E Mitchell St 65340 660-886-2655
Randy Maupin, prin. Fax 886-6824

St. Peter S 200/PK-8
368 S Ellsworth Ave 65340 660-886-6390
Gary Littrell, prin. Fax 886-6606

Marshfield, Webster, Pop. 6,763
Marshfield R-I SD 2,800/PK-12
170 State Highway DD 65706 417-859-2120
Dr. Mark Mayo, supt. Fax 859-2193
www.mr1.k12.mo.us/
Hubble PS 200/PK-1
600 N Locust St 65706 417-859-2120
Leasha DeCamp, prin. Fax 859-7332
Marshfield JHS 700/6-8
660 N Locust St 65706 417-859-2120
Alan Thomas, prin. Fax 859-4970
Shook ES 500/4-5
180 State Highway DD 65706 417-859-2120
Robert Currier, prin. Fax 859-5186
Webster ES 500/2-3
650 N Locust St 65706 417-859-2120
Valerie Willis, prin. Fax 859-7333

Marthasville, Warren, Pop. 864
Washington SD
Supt. — See Washington
Marthasville ES 200/K-6
800 E Main St 63357 636-231-2650
Laura Bruckerhoff, prin. Fax 231-2605

St. Ignatius Loyola S 100/PK-8
19129 Mill Rd 63357 636-932-4444
Lori Koenig, prin. Fax 932-4479
St. Vincent S 100/K-8
13495 S State Highway 94 63357 636-433-2466
Marietta Stieber, prin. Fax 433-2924

Martinsburg, Audrain, Pop. 328

St. Joseph S 100/K-8
401 E Kellett St 65264 573-492-6283
Kay Robnett, prin. Fax 492-6346

Maryland Heights, Saint Louis, Pop. 26,544
Parkway C-2 SD
Supt. — See Chesterfield
McKelvey ES 600/K-5
1751 McKelvey Rd 63043 314-415-6500
Alli Rudich, prin. Fax 415-6512

Pattonville R-III SD
Supt. — See Saint Ann
Parkwood ES 400/K-5
3199 Parkwood Ln 63043 314-213-8015
Virginia Folk, prin. Fax 213-8615
Pattonville Heights MS 600/6-8
195 Fee Fee Rd 63043 314-213-8033
Scot Mosher, prin. Fax 213-8633
Remington Traditional S 400/K-8
102 Fee Fee Rd 63043 314-213-8016
Lisa Luna-Schwarz, prin. Fax 213-8616
Rose Acres ES 400/K-5
2905 Rose Acres Ln 63043 314-213-8017
Steve Vargo, prin. Fax 213-8617

Grace Christian Academy 200/PK-8
12463 Grace Church Rd 63043 314-291-6933
Larry Ketcham, prin. Fax 291-9854
Holy Spirit S 200/PK-8
3120 Parkwood Ln 63043 314-739-1934
Marybeth Chik, prin. Fax 739-7703

Maryville, Nodaway, Pop. 10,567
Maryville R-II SD 1,200/PK-12
1429 S Munn Ave 64468 660-562-3255
Vickie Miller, supt. Fax 562-4113
www.maryville.k12.mo.us/
Field ES 400/PK-4
418 E 2nd St 64468 660-562-3233
Steve Klotz, prin. Fax 562-2735
Maryville MS 400/5-8
525 W South Hills Dr 64468 660-562-3244
Kevin Pitts, prin. Fax 562-4130

St. Gregory Barbarigo S 200/PK-8
315 S Davis St 64468 660-582-2462
Susan Martin, prin. Fax 582-2496

Matthews, New Madrid, Pop. 552
New Madrid County R-I SD
Supt. — See New Madrid
Matthews ES 200/PK-5
PO Box 118 63867 573-471-0077
Don Phillips, prin. Fax 471-3410

Maysville, DeKalb, Pop. 1,165
Maysville R-I SD 600/K-12
PO Box 68 64469 816-449-2308
Robert Smith, supt. Fax 449-5678
maysville.k12.mo.us/
Maysville ES 300/K-6
PO Box 68 64469 816-449-2308
Stacy Blythe, prin. Fax 449-5678

Meadville, Linn, Pop. 443
Meadville R-IV SD 200/PK-12
PO Box 217 64659 660-938-4111
Kenneth Dudley, supt. Fax 938-4100
Meadville ES 100/PK-6
PO Box 217 64659 660-938-4112
Velma Trentham, prin. Fax 938-4100

Memphis, Scotland, Pop. 2,003
Scotland County R-I SD 600/PK-12
RR 3 Box 19A 63555 660-465-8531
David Shalley, supt. Fax 465-8636
scotland.k12.mo.us/
Scotland County ES 300/PK-6
RR 3 Box 19A 63555 660-465-8532
Rhonda McBee, prin. Fax 465-8636

Mendon, Chariton, Pop. 201
Northwestern R-I SD 200/PK-12
PO Box 43 64660 660-272-3201
William Jones, supt. Fax 272-3419
Northwestern ES 100/PK-4
PO Box 43 64660 660-272-3201
Ron Garber, prin. Fax 272-3419
Northwestern MS 100/5-8
PO Box 43 64660 660-272-3201
Ron Garber, prin. Fax 272-3738

Mercer, Mercer, Pop. 330
North Mercer County R-III SD 200/PK-12
PO Box 648 64661 660-382-4214
Dan Owens, supt. Fax 382-4236
www.northmercer.k12.mo.us
North Mercer ES 100/PK-6
PO Box 648 64661 660-382-4214
Kim Palmer, prin. Fax 382-4239

Mexico, Audrain, Pop. 11,018
Mexico SD 59 2,400/K-12
920 S Jefferson St 65265 573-581-3773
Tina Woolsey, supt. Fax 581-4410
www.mexicoschools.net/
Field ES 400/K-5
704 W Boulevard St 65265 573-581-5268
Christine Harper, prin. Fax 581-0690
Hawthorne ES 400/K-5
1250 W Curtis St 65265 573-581-3064
Lynn Becker, prin. Fax 581-3065
McMillan ES 200/K-5
1101 E Anderson St 65265 573-581-5029
Sharon Palmer, prin. Fax 581-3175
Mexico MS 600/6-8
1200 W Boulevard St 65265 573-581-4664
Linda Hensley, prin. Fax 581-8440

St. Brendan S 200/PK-8
620 S Clark St 65265 573-581-2443
Bill Gleeson, prin. Fax 581-2571

Miami, Saline, Pop. 157
Miami R-I SD 100/K-8
34520 N Highway 41 65344 660-852-3269
Lyle Best, supt. Fax 852-3259
Miami S 100/K-8
34520 N Highway 41 65344 660-852-3269
Lyle Best, prin. Fax 852-3259

Milan, Sullivan, Pop. 1,849
Milan C-2 SD 700/PK-12
373 S Market St 63556 660-265-4414
Bill Lewis, supt. Fax 265-4315
www.milan.k12.mo.us/
Milan ES 300/PK-4
373 S Market St 63556 660-265-4416
Jason Smith, prin. Fax 265-4315
Milan MS 200/5-8
373 S Market St 63556 660-265-4421
Tennille Banner, prin. Fax 265-4315

Miller, Lawrence, Pop. 792
Miller R-II SD 500/K-12
110 W 6th St 65707 417-452-3515
Dr. Anthony Rossetti, supt. Fax 452-2709
Central ES 200/K-6
303 W 2nd St 65707 417-452-3512
Peggy Jones, prin. Fax 452-3264

Round Grove Christian Academy 100/PK-8
877 N Highway U 65707 417-452-3670
Lori Bowles, lead tchr. Fax 452-2573

Millersville, Cape Girardeau
Jackson R-II SD
Supt. — See Jackson
Millersville ES 100/K-3
377 State Highway B 63766 573-243-9585
Rob French, prin. Fax 243-9585

Missouri City, Clay, Pop. 323
Missouri City SD 56 50/K-8
PO Box 259 64072 816-750-4391
Jay Jackson, supt. Fax 750-4394
www.mocity.k12.mo.us/
Missouri City S 50/K-8
PO Box 259 64072 816-750-4391
Jay Jackson, prin. Fax 750-4394

Moberly, Randolph, Pop. 13,921
Moberly SD 2,300/K-12
926 Kwix Rd 65270 660-269-2600
Mark Penny, supt. Fax 269-2611
moberly.k12.mo.us/
Gratz Brown ES 500/3-5
1320 Gratz Brown St 65270 660-269-2694
Della Bell, prin. Fax 269-8093
Moberly MS 500/6-8
920 Kwix Rd 65270 660-269-2680
Kelly Briscoe, prin. Fax 269-8519
North Park ES 200/K-2
909 Porter St 65270 660-269-2630
Parisa Stoddard, prin. Fax 269-8094
South Park ES 300/K-2
701 S 4th St 65270 660-269-2640
Tim Roth, prin. Fax 269-2695

Maranatha SDA S 50/5-8
1400 E McKinsey St 65270 660-263-8600
St. Pius X S 200/PK-8
210 S Williams St 65270 660-263-5500
William Hagedorn, prin. Fax 263-5744

Mokane, Callaway, Pop. 196
South Callaway County R-II SD 1,000/PK-12
10135 State Road C 65059 573-676-5225
Dr. Dustin Storm, supt. Fax 676-5134
www.sc.k12.mo.us/
South Callaway ES 400/PK-4
10135 State Road C 65059 573-676-5218
John Elliston, prin. Fax 676-5063
South Callaway MS 300/5-8
10135 State Road C 65059 573-676-5216
Michael Auer, prin. Fax 676-5347

Monett, Barry, Pop. 8,349
Monett R-I SD 1,600/PK-12
900 E Scott St 65708 417-235-7422
Dr. John Jungmann, supt. Fax 235-1415
hs1.monett.k12.mo.us/
Monett Central Park ES 3-4
1010 7th St 65708 417-354-2168
Annette Cozort, prin. Fax 354-2198
Monett ES 400/PK-2
400 Linden Ave 65708 417-235-3411
Susie Gasser, prin. Fax 235-3086
Monett IS 300/5-6
711 9th St 65708 417-235-6151
Peggy Bryan, prin. Fax 236-0248
Monett MS 300/7-8
710 9th St 65708 417-235-6228
Dr. Jonathan Apostol, prin. Fax 235-3278

St. Lawrence S 100/1-6
407 7th St 65708 417-235-3721
Rita Donica, prin. Fax 235-3721

Monroe City, Monroe, Pop. 2,556
Monroe City R-I SD 700/PK-12
401 US Highway 24/36 E 63456 573-735-4631
James Masters, supt. Fax 735-2413
www.monroe.k12.mo.us/
Monroe City ES 300/PK-5
420 N Washington St 63456 573-735-4632
Kim Shinn, prin. Fax 735-2413
Monroe City MS 200/6-8
430 N Washington St 63456 573-735-4742
Ty Crain, prin. Fax 735-2413

Holy Rosary S 200/K-8
620 S Main St 63456 573-735-2422
Sr. Suzanne Walker, prin. Fax 735-3091

Montgomery City, Montgomery, Pop. 2,513
Montgomery County R-II SD 1,400/PK-12
418 N Highway 19 63361 573-564-2278
Dr. Thomas Ward, supt. Fax 564-6182
www.mc-wildcats.org/
Montgomery City ES 400/PK-5
817 N Harper St 63361 573-564-3711
Kindra Weaver, prin. Fax 564-2136
Montgomery County MS 300/6-8
418 N Highway 19 63361 573-564-2253
Madonna Pund, prin. Fax 564-6182
Other Schools – See Bellflower, Jonesburg

Immaculate Conception S 50/PK-8
407 W 3rd St 63361 573-564-2679
Lisa Gruenfeld, prin. Fax 564-2305

Montrose, Henry, Pop. 431
Montrose R-XIV SD 100/K-12
307 E 2nd St 64770 660-693-4812
Scott Ireland, supt. Fax 693-4594
Montrose S 100/K-8
307 E 2nd St 64770 660-693-4812
Scott Ireland, prin. Fax 693-4594

St. Mary S 50/1-8
608 Kansas Ave 64770 660-693-4502
Sue Koehler, prin. Fax 693-4713

Morehouse, New Madrid, Pop. 960
Sikeston R-6 SD
Supt. — See Sikeston
Morehouse ES 200/K-4
420 S Carroll 63868 573-472-8885
Jeff Williams, prin. Fax 472-8885

Morrisville, Polk, Pop. 362
Marion C. Early R-V SD 800/K-12
5309 S Main Ave 65710 417-376-2255
Eric Kusse, supt. Fax 376-3243
mcearly.k12.mo.us
Early ES 300/K-5
5309 S Main Ave 65710 417-376-2215
Dr. Tammy Condren, prin. Fax 376-3243

Moscow Mills, Lincoln, Pop. 2,232
Troy R-III SD
Supt. — See Troy
Cappel ES 500/K-5
121 Hampel Rd 63362 636-356-4246
Rebecca Parks, prin. Fax 335-0016

Mound City, Holt, Pop. 1,110
Mound City R-II SD 300/PK-12
PO Box 247 64470 660-442-3737
Ken Eaton, supt. Fax 442-5941
Mound City ES 100/PK-6
PO Box 247 64470 660-442-5420
Jan Seitz, prin. Fax 442-5282

Mountain Grove, Wright, Pop. 4,594
Manes R-V SD 100/K-8
8939 Highway 95 65711 417-668-5313
Randy Adams, supt. Fax 668-5537
www.schoolweb.missouri.edu/manes.k12.mo.us/
Manes S 100/K-8
8939 Highway 95 65711 417-668-5313
Randy Adams, prin. Fax 668-5537

Mountain Grove R-III SD 1,400/K-12
PO Box 806 65711 417-926-3177
Bridget Williams, supt. Fax 926-3177
www.mgr3.k12.mo.us
Mountain Grove ES 500/K-4
PO Box 806 65711 417-926-3177
Missy Glenn, prin. Fax 926-7474
Mountain Grove MS 400/5-8
PO Box 806 65711 417-926-3177
J.T. Hale, prin. Fax 926-1673

Mountain View, Howell, Pop. 2,546
Mountain View-Birch Tree R-III SD 1,400/PK-12
PO Box 464 65548 417-934-2020
Jerry Nicholson, supt. Fax 934-5404
mvbt.k12.mo.us/
Liberty MS 200/7-8
PO Box 464 65548 417-934-2020
Walt Belcher, prin. Fax 934-1329
Mountain View ES 600/PK-6
PO Box 464 65548 417-934-2550
Loren Smith, prin. Fax 934-5417
Other Schools – See Birch Tree

Mount Vernon, Lawrence, Pop. 4,402
Mt. Vernon R-V SD 1,300/K-12
731 S Landrum St 65712 417-466-7573
Russ Cruzan, supt. Fax 466-7058
Mount Vernon ES 200/K-2
301 E Blaze Rd 65712 417-466-7512
Joana King, prin. Fax 466-7058
Mount Vernon IS 200/3-5
260 W Highway 174 65712 417-466-2312
Dulcie Price, prin.
Mount Vernon MS 400/6-8
731 S Landrum St 65712 417-466-3137
Robert Senninger, prin. Fax 466-7058

Myrtle, Oregon
Couch R-I SD 300/PK-12
RR 1 Box 1187 65778 417-938-4211
Tom Bull, supt. Fax 938-4267
www.couch.k12.mo.us/
Couch ES 100/PK-6
RR 1 Box 1187 65778 417-938-4215
Russell Deckard, prin. Fax 938-4267

Naylor, Ripley, Pop. 614
Naylor R-II SD 400/K-12
RR 2 Box 512 63953 573-399-2505
Stephen Cookson, supt. Fax 399-2874
schoolweb.missouri.edu/naylor.k12.mo.us/
Naylor ES 200/K-6
RR 2 Box 512 63953 573-399-2507
Sherry Burns, prin. Fax 399-2307

Neelyville, Butler, Pop. 503
Neelyville R-IV SD 700/PK-12
PO Box 8 63954 573-989-3813
Brad Hagood, supt. Fax 989-3434
neelyville.k12.mo.us/
Neelyville ES 200/PK-6
PO Box 8 63954 573-989-3814
Sherri Ponder, prin. Fax 989-3336
Other Schools – See Harviell

Neosho, Newton, Pop. 11,130
Neosho R-V SD 4,600/PK-12
511 S Neosho Blvd 64850 417-451-8600
Dr. Richard Page, supt. Fax 451-8604
www.neosho.k12.mo.us
Benton ES 600/K-4
1120 Carl Sweeney Rd 64850 417-451-8610
Glenda Condict, prin. Fax 451-8607
Carver ES 100/K-4
12350 Norway Rd 64850 417-451-8690
Satotha Burr, prin. Fax 451-8696
Central ES 300/K-4
301 Big Spring Dr 64850 417-451-8620
Jeff Freeland, prin. Fax 451-8624
Field K 200/PK-K
302 Smith Ave 64850 417-451-8630
Connie Bryant, prin. Fax 451-8633
Neosho JHS 300/8-8
511 S Neosho Blvd 64850 417-451-8660
Jenifer Cryer, prin. Fax 451-8687
Neosho MS 1,000/5-7
1420 Hale McGinty Dr 64850 417-451-8650
Doretta Fox, prin. Fax 451-8649
South ES 500/K-4
1111 Wornall St 64850 417-451-8640
Sandy Davidson, prin. Fax 451-8644
Other Schools – See Goodman

Westview C-6 SD 200/K-8
7441 Westview Rd 64850 417-776-2425
Jan Cox, supt. Fax 776-1994
Westview S 200/K-8
7441 Westview Rd 64850 417-776-2425
Jan Cox, prin. Fax 776-1994

Ozark Christian Academy 50/K-12
PO Box 786 64850 417-451-1100
Joyce Prihoda, prin. Fax 451-9902

Nevada, Vernon, Pop. 8,457
Nevada R-V SD 2,500/PK-12
800 W Hickory St 64772 417-448-2000
David Stephens, supt. Fax 448-2006
www.nevada.k12.mo.us
Benton ES 200/2-2
500 E Vernon St 64772 417-448-2070
Misti Raney, prin. Fax 448-2071
Bryan ES 300/PK-1
400 W Lee St 64772 417-448-2060
Deborah Spaur, prin. Fax 448-2067
Nevada MS 600/6-8
900 N Olive St 64772 417-448-2040
Tyson Beshore, prin. Fax 448-2048
Truman ES 600/3-5
901 W Ashland St 64772 417-448-2080
Diann Marti, prin. Fax 448-2085

Calvary Christian S 50/K-12
113 W Arch St 64772 417-667-4200
St. Mary S 50/PK-3
330 N Main St 64772 417-667-7517
Nancy Coffer, prin. Fax 667-7517

New Bloomfield, Callaway, Pop. 688
New Bloomfield R-III SD 800/PK-12
307 Redwood Dr 65063 573-491-3700
Michael Parnell, supt. Fax 491-3772
www.callaway.k12.mo.us
New Bloomfield ES 400/PK-6
307 Redwood Dr 65063 573-491-3700
Stacy Fick, prin. Fax 491-3439

Newburg, Phelps, Pop. 479
Newburg R-II SD 500/PK-12
PO Box C 65550 573-762-2211
Mike Bumgarner, supt. Fax 762-2512
www.newburg.k12.mo.us
Newburg ES 200/PK-6
PO Box C 65550 573-762-2721
Ronald Reagan, prin. Fax 762-2512

New Cambria, Macon, Pop. 223
Macon County R-IV SD 100/K-12
PO Box 70 63558 660-226-5615
Ron Garber, supt. Fax 226-5618
www.mcr4.k12.mo.us/
Macon County ES 100/K-6
PO Box 70 63558 660-226-5615
Carol Burstert, prin. Fax 226-5618

New Franklin, Howard, Pop. 1,113
New Franklin R-I SD 400/PK-12
412 W Broadway 65274 660-848-2141
Dr. Jeanie Gordon, supt. Fax 848-2226
www.nfranklin.k12.mo.us/
New Franklin ES 200/PK-5
412 W Broadway 65274 660-848-2112
Pam Chitwood, prin. Fax 848-3061

New Haven, Franklin, Pop. 1,950
Franklin County R-II SD 200/K-8
3128 Highway Y 63068 573-237-2414
Carol Laboube, supt. Fax 237-4838
www.franklincountyr2.k12.mo.us/
Franklin County S 200/K-8
3128 Highway Y 63068 573-237-2414
Carol Laboube, prin. Fax 237-4838

New Haven SD 500/K-12
100 Park Dr 63068 573-237-3231
Kyle Kruse, supt. Fax 237-5959
www.shamrocks.k12.mo.us/
New Haven ES 200/K-6
100 Park Dr 63068 573-237-2141
Kasi Meyer, prin. Fax 237-5959
New Haven MS 100/7-8
100 Park Dr 63068 573-237-2900
Dennis Carey, prin. Fax 237-5959

Washington SD
Supt. — See Washington
Campbellton ES 200/K-6
3693 Highway 185 63068 636-231-2450
Dr. Teri Alsadi, prin. Fax 231-2455

New London, Ralls, Pop. 992
Ralls County R-II SD
Supt. — See Center
New London ES 200/PK-5
1101 S Main St 63459 573-985-5371
Mike Griewing, prin. Fax 985-3936

New Madrid, New Madrid, Pop. 3,131
New Madrid County R-I SD 1,700/PK-12
310 US Highway 61 63869 573-688-2161
Bill Nance, supt. Fax 688-2169
www.newmadridco.k12.mo.us/
Central MS 400/6-8
308 US Highway 61 63869 573-688-2176
Thomas Drummond, prin. Fax 688-2245
New Madrid ES 400/PK-5
PO Box 130 63869 573-748-5568
Rand Amick, prin. Fax 748-5572
Other Schools – See Lilbourn, Matthews

Immaculate Conception S 50/PK-8
560 Powell Ave 63869 573-748-5123
Mary Shy, prin. Fax 748-5150

Newtown, Sullivan, Pop. 197
Newtown-Harris R-III SD 100/K-12
PO Box 128 64667 660-794-2245
W. Anderson, supt. Fax 794-2730
www.nhtigers.k12.mo.us/
Newtown-Harris ES 50/K-6
PO Box 128 64667 660-794-2245
Misty Foster, prin. Fax 794-2730

Niangua, Webster, Pop. 484
Niangua R-V SD 200/PK-12
301 Rumsey St 65713 417-473-6101
Andy Adams, supt. Fax 473-6124
Niangua ES 100/PK-6
301 Rumsey St 65713 417-473-6101
Lori Allen, prin. Fax 473-6124

Nixa, Christian, Pop. 15,925
Nixa R-II SD 4,800/PK-12
205 North St 65714 417-875-5400
Dr. Stephen Kleinsmith, supt. Fax 875-5428
www.nixa.k12.mo.us
Century ES 500/K-4
732 E North St 65714 417-724-3800
Jennifer Chastain, prin. Fax 725-7475
Espy ES 400/K-4
220 S Gregg Rd 65714 417-875-5650
Michelle Wilkerson, prin. Fax 725-7448
High Pointe ES K-4
900 Cheyenne Rd 65714 417-225-1600
Kevin Kopp, prin. Fax 225-1608
Inman ES 500/5-6
1300 N Nicholas Rd 65714 417-725-7460
April Hawkins, prin. Fax 725-7468
Main Street ES 400/PK-PK, 5-
301 S Main St 65714 417-724-4000
Josh Chastain, prin. Fax 724-4008
Mathews ES 500/K-4
605 S Gregg Rd 65714 417-725-7470
Patricia Sutherland, prin. Fax 725-7474
Nixa JHS 800/7-8
205 North St 65714 417-875-5430
Mark McGehee, prin. Fax 875-5426
Thomas ES 400/K-4
312 N Market St 65714 417-875-5600
Marilyn Hanna, prin. Fax 725-7424

Noel, McDonald, Pop. 1,515
McDonald County R-I SD
Supt. — See Anderson
Noel PS 200/PK-2
14762 W State Highway 90 64854 417-475-3900
Deborah Pearson, prin. Fax 475-3950
Noel S 400/3-8
318 Sulphur St 64854 417-451-7675
Carl Nichols, prin. Fax 475-6516

Norborne, Carroll, Pop. 792
Norborne R-VIII SD 200/K-12
PO Box 192 64668 660-593-3319
Douglas Carpenter, supt. Fax 593-3657
www.schoolweb.missouri.edu/norborne.k12.mo.us/
Norborne ES 100/K-5
PO Box 192 64668 660-593-3616
Verna Monk, prin. Fax 593-3657

Normandy, Saint Louis, Pop. 5,032
Normandy SD
Supt. — See Saint Louis
Garfield ES 300/K-6
6506 Wright Way 63121 314-493-0740
Carl Hudson, prin. Fax 493-0770
Lucas Crossing Elementary Complex 900/K-6
7837 Natural Bridge Rd 63121 314-493-0200
Kimberly Austin, prin. Fax 493-0270
Normandy MS 1,000/7-8
7855 Natural Bridge Rd 63121 314-493-0500
Bryan Cannon, prin. Fax 493-0560

St. Ann S 200/K-8
7532 Natural Bridge Rd 63121 314-381-0113
Mary Jo Reichenbach, prin. Fax 381-1367

North Kansas City, Clay, Pop. 5,388
North Kansas City SD 74
Supt. — See Kansas City
Crestview ES 500/PK-5
4327 N Holmes St 64116 816-413-4700
Kevin Kooi, prin. Fax 413-4705

Norwood, Wright, Pop. 576
Norwood R-I SD 400/K-12
675 N Hawk St 65717 417-746-4101
Don Forrest, supt. Fax 746-9950
www.norwood.k12.mo.us/
Norwood ES 200/K-4
675 N Hawk St 65717 417-746-4101
Dana Webb, prin. Fax 746-4804
Norwood MS 100/5-8
675 N Hawk St 65717 417-746-4101
Fred Vanbibber, prin. Fax 746-4804

Skyline R-II SD 100/PK-8
RR 2 Box 486 65717 417-683-4874
Jeanne Curtis, supt. Fax 683-5865
schoolweb.missouri.edu/skyline.k12.mo.us
Skyline S 100/PK-8
RR 2 Box 486 65717 417-683-4874
Jeanne Curtis, prin. Fax 683-5865

Novinger, Adair, Pop. 524
Adair County R-I SD 300/PK-12
600 Rombauer Ave 63559 660-488-6411
William Lake, supt. Fax 488-5400
www.novinger.k12.mo.us
Adair County ES 200/PK-6
600 Rombauer Ave 63559 660-488-6412
Connie Charles, prin. Fax 488-5400

Oak Grove, Jackson, Pop. 6,763
Oak Grove R-VI SD 2,000/PK-12
1305 SE Salem St 64075 816-690-4156
Dr. James Haley, supt. Fax 690-3031
www.oakgrove.k12.mo.us
Oak Grove ES 500/3-5
501 SE 12th St 64075 816-690-4153
Peggy West, prin. Fax 690-8561
Oak Grove MS 500/6-8
401 SE 12th St 64075 816-690-4154
Keith Roskens, prin. Fax 690-3976
Oak Grove PS 300/PK-2
500 SE 17th 64075 816-690-8770
Laura Oyler, prin. Fax 690-6984

Oak Ridge, Cape Girardeau, Pop. 208
Oak Ridge R-VI SD 400/K-12
PO Box 10 63769 573-266-3218
Dr. Gerald Landewee, supt. Fax 266-0133
Oak Ridge ES 200/K-6
PO Box 10 63769 573-266-3232
Adrian Eftink, prin. Fax 266-0133

Oakview, Clay, Pop. 386

St. Charles Borromeo S 500/PK-8
804 NE Shady Lane Dr 64118 816-436-1009
Mary Omecene, prin. Fax 436-6293

Odessa, Lafayette, Pop. 4,841
Odessa R-VII SD 2,100/K-12
701 S 3rd St 64076 816-633-5316
Dr. Forrest Bollow, supt. Fax 633-8582
www.odessa.k12.mo.us/
McQuerry ES 300/K-2
607 S 3rd St 64076 816-633-5334
Larry Hol, prin. Fax 633-5327
Odessa MS 700/5-8
607 S 5th St 64076 816-633-1500
Sherry Billings, prin. Fax 633-7101
Odessa Upper ES 300/3-4
310 S 1st St 64076 816-633-5396
Debora Schweikert, prin. Fax 633-4299

O Fallon, Saint Charles, Pop. 59,678
Francis Howell R-III SD
Supt. — See Saint Charles
Weldon ES 600/K-5
7370 Weldon Spring Rd, 636-851-5500
Cindi Crigler, prin. Fax 851-4136

Ft. Zumwalt R-II SD 18,200/K-12
110 Virgil St 63366 636-272-6620
Dr. Bernard DuBray, supt. Fax 980-1946
www.fz.k12.mo.us
Dardenne ES 500/K-5
2621 Highway K, 636-978-4001
Jill Hutcheson, prin. Fax 978-4012
Emge ES 400/K-5
250 Fallon Pkwy, 636-281-0261
Alex Tripamer, prin. Fax 281-0331
Forest Park ES 500/3-5
501 Sunflower Ln 63366 636-272-2704
Randall Gettman, prin. Fax 281-0007
Ft. Zumwalt North MS 1,100/6-8
210 Virgil St 63366 636-281-2356
Tim Jamieson, prin. Fax 281-0005
Ft. Zumwalt West MS 1,300/6-8
150 Waterford Crossing Dr, 636-272-6690
Jennifer Waters, prin. Fax 272-6361
Mount Hope ES 500/K-5
1099 Mount Hope Ln 63366 636-272-2717
Dr. Sandy Baner, prin. Fax 281-0003
Mudd ES 300/K-2
610 Prince Ruppert Dr 63366 636-272-2709
Sharon Ellerbrook, prin. Fax 281-0008
Ostmann ES 600/K-5
200 Meriwether Lewis Dr, 636-281-3382
Dr. Gregg Sartorius, prin. Fax 281-3372
Pheasant Point ES 600/K-5
3450 Pheasant Meadow Dr, 636-379-0173
Greg Cicotte, prin. Fax 980-3650
Rock Creek ES 700/K-5
8970 Mexico Rd 63366 636-980-1800
Deanne McCullough, prin. Fax 980-1653
Twin Chimneys ES 500/K-5
7396 Twin Chimneys Blvd, 636-240-0093
Denise Risner, prin. Fax 240-0095
Westhoff ES 600/K-5
900 Homefield Blvd 63366 636-272-6710
Jason Sefrit, prin. Fax 272-6351
Other Schools – See Saint Peters

Wentzville R-IV SD
Supt. — See Wentzville
Crossroads ES 700/K-5
7500 Highway N, 636-625-4537
Richard Beauchamp, prin. Fax 625-4447
Frontier MS 600/6-8
9233 Highway DD, 636-625-1026
Phil Ragusky, prin. Fax 625-1094
Prairie View ES 400/K-5
1550 Feise Rd, 636-625-2494
Matt Schulte, prin. Fax 625-2491

Assumption S - O'Fallon 500/K-8
203 W 3rd St 63366 636-240-4474
Genevieve Callier, prin. Fax 240-5795
First Baptist Christian Academy 400/PK-6
8750 Veterans Memorial Pkwy 63366 636-272-3220
Dr. Ray Patterson, prin. Fax 240-3067

Old Mines, Washington

St. Joachim S 100/PK-8
10121 Crest Rd 63630 573-438-3973
Joyce Politte, prin. Fax 438-3161

Old Monroe, Lincoln, Pop. 283

Immaculate Conception S 200/K-8
120 Maryknoll Rd 63369 636-661-5156
Susan Schutz, prin. Fax 661-5002

Olivette, Saint Louis, Pop. 7,455

Immanuel Lutheran S 200/PK-8
9733 Olive Blvd 63132 314-993-2394
Christine Dehnke, prin. Fax 993-0311

Oran, Scott, Pop. 1,259
Oran R-III SD 400/K-12
PO Box 250 63771 573-262-2330
Mitchell Wood, supt. Fax 262-2330
www.oran.k12.mo.us
Oran ES 200/K-6
PO Box 250 63771 573-262-3435
Travis Spane, prin. Fax 262-3874

Guardian Angel S 100/1-8
514 Church St 63771 573-262-3583
Michele Huffman, prin. Fax 262-3583

Oregon, Holt, Pop. 901
South Holt County R-I SD 300/K-12
201 S Barbour St 64473 660-446-2282
Bob Ottman, supt. Fax 446-2312
www.southholtr1.com
South Holt County ES 100/K-6
201 S Barbour St 64473 660-446-2356
Ted Quinlin, prin. Fax 446-2312

Orrick, Ray, Pop. 867
Orrick R-XI SD 400/PK-12
100 Kirkham St 64077 816-770-0094
Marcus Stucker, supt. Fax 496-2306
www.orrick.k12.mo.us
Orrick ES 200/PK-6
100 Kirkham St 64077 816-770-3922
Keri Cavanah, prin. Fax 496-3253

Osage Beach, Miller, Pop. 4,259
Camdenton R-III SD
Supt. — See Camdenton
Osage Beach ES 200/PK-4
4427 Highway 54 65065 573-348-2461
Renee Slack, prin. Fax 348-2820

School of the Osage R-II SD
Supt. — See Lake Ozark
Osage MS 300/6-8
635 Highway 42 65065 573-552-8326
Tony Slack, prin. Fax 552-8322
Osage Upper ES 400/3-5
626 Highway 42 65065 573-348-0004
Chris Wolf, prin. Fax 348-3058

Osborn, DeKalb, Pop. 448
Osborn R-0 SD 100/K-12
275 Clinton Ave 64474 816-675-2217
Laurie Mefford, supt. Fax 675-2222
schoolweb.missouri.edu/osborn.k12.mo.us/
Osborn ES 100/K-6
275 Clinton Ave 64474 816-675-2217
Laurie Mefford, prin. Fax 675-2222

Osceola, Saint Clair, Pop. 818
Osceola SD 600/PK-12
76 SE Highway WW 64776 417-646-8143
Aron Bennett, supt. Fax 646-8075
www.osceola.k12.mo.us
Osceola ES 300/PK-6
76 SE Highway WW 64776 417-646-8333
Chris McClimans, prin. Fax 646-8075

Otterville, Cooper, Pop. 486
Otterville R-VI SD 300/K-12
PO Box 177 65348 660-366-4391
Michael Scott, supt. Fax 366-4293
Otterville ES 100/K-6
PO Box 177 65348 660-366-4621
Raymond Kahrs, prin. Fax 366-4293

Overland, Saint Louis, Pop. 16,082
Normandy SD
Supt. — See Saint Louis
Washington ES 300/K-6
1730 N Hanley Rd 63114 314-493-0810
Elaine Woodson, prin. Fax 493-0820

Ritenour SD
Supt. — See Saint Louis
Iveland ES 500/K-5
1836 Dyer Ave 63114 314-493-6330
Sandy Wiley, prin. Fax 429-6721
Ritenour MS 700/6-8
2500 Marshall Ave 63114 314-493-6250
Ken Roumpos, prin. Fax 429-6726

Owensville, Gasconade, Pop. 2,544
Gasconade County R-II SD 1,700/K-12
PO Box 536 65066 573-437-2177
Fax 437-5808
owensville.k12.mo.us
Owensville ES 300/K-5
PO Box 536 65066 573-437-2171
Jennifer Hall, prin. Fax 437-5405
Owensville MS 400/6-8
PO Box 536 65066 573-437-2172
Teresa Ragan, prin. Fax 437-6704
Other Schools – See Gerald

Ozark, Christian, Pop. 15,265
Ozark R-VI SD 4,100/K-12
PO Box 166 65721 417-582-5900
Dr. Gordon Pace, supt. Fax 582-5960
www.ozark.k12.mo.us

East ES 400/K-4
PO Box 166 65721 417-582-5906
Kent Sappington, prin. Fax 582-5785
North ES 500/K-4
PO Box 166 65721 417-582-5904
Donna Ham, prin. Fax 582-4786
Ozark JHS 700/7-8
PO Box 166 65721 417-582-4701
Jeff Simpson, prin. Fax 582-4714
South ES 300/K-4
PO Box 166 65721 417-582-5905
Ryan Knight, prin. Fax 582-4886
Upper ES 800/5-6
PO Box 166 65721 417-582-5903
Chris Bauman, prin. Fax 582-4802
West ES K-4
PO Box 166 65721 417-582-5907
Mark Hedger, prin. Fax 582-5761

Pacific, Franklin, Pop. 7,098
Meramec Valley R-III SD 3,700/PK-12
126 N Payne St 63069 636-271-1400
Randy George, supt. Fax 271-1406
www.mvr3.k12.mo.us/
Meramec Valley ECC 100/PK-PK
2001 W Osage St 63069 636-271-1464
Lisa Weirich, prin. Fax 271-7829
Meramec Valley MS 600/6-7
195 N Indian Pride Dr 63069 636-271-1425
Russell Rowbottom, prin. Fax 271-1465
Riverbend MS 300/8-8
2085 Highway N 63069 636-271-1481
Gary Peck, prin. Fax 271-8080
Truman ES 300/K-5
101 Indian Warpath Dr 63069 636-271-1434
Marian Meinhardt, prin. Fax 271-1490
Zitzman ES 500/K-5
255 S Indian Pride Dr 63069 636-271-1440
Linda Pahl, prin. Fax 271-1443
Other Schools – See Catawissa, Robertsville, Villa Ridge

St. Bridget of Kildare S 100/PK-8
223 W Union St 63069 636-271-4533
Pat Herbst, prin. Fax 257-2504

Palmyra, Marion, Pop. 3,443
Palmyra R-I SD 1,100/K-12
PO Box 151 63461 573-769-2066
Eric Churchwell, supt. Fax 769-4218
schoolweb.missouri.edu/palmyra.k12.mo.us
Palmyra ES 400/K-4
PO Box 151 63461 573-769-3736
Connie Browning, prin. Fax 769-4113
Palmyra MS 400/5-8
PO Box 151 63461 573-769-2174
Lora Hillman, prin. Fax 769-4227

Paris, Monroe, Pop. 1,468
Paris R-II SD 600/PK-12
740 Cleveland St 65275 660-327-4112
Nancy Henke, supt. Fax 327-4290
paris.k12.mo.us/site/
Paris ES 300/PK-6
725 Cleveland St 65275 660-327-5116
Terri Udelhoven, prin. Fax 327-5074
Paris JHS 100/7-8
25678 Business Highway 24 65275 660-327-4563
Sally Eales, prin. Fax 327-4782

Park Hills, Saint Francois, Pop. 8,525
Central R-III SD 1,800/PK-12
200 High St 63601 573-431-2616
Dr. David Stevens, supt. Fax 431-2107
www.centralr3.org
Central ES 300/PK-2
900 Saint Francois Ave 63601 573-431-1300
Timothy McCoy, prin. Fax 431-8965
Central MS 500/6-8
801 Columbia St 63601 573-431-1322
Mike Harlow, prin. Fax 431-5393
West ES 400/3-5
403 W Fite St 63601 573-431-1302
Keith Groom, prin. Fax 431-2562

West St. Francois County R-IV SD
Supt. — See Leadwood
West County ES 500/PK-5
625 Chariton Ave 63601 573-562-7558
Todd Watson, prin. Fax 562-7510

Parkville, Platte, Pop. 5,116
Park Hill SD
Supt. — See Kansas City
Graden ES 500/K-5
8804 NW Highway 45 64152 816-359-4340
Dr. LuAnn Halverstadt, prin. Fax 359-4349

Parnell, Nodaway, Pop. 191
Northeast Nodaway County R-V SD
Supt. — See Ravenwood
Parnell ES 100/PK-6
PO Box 107 64475 660-986-2125
Linda Mattson, prin. Fax 986-2130

Pasadena Hills, Saint Louis, Pop. 1,122
Normandy SD
Supt. — See Saint Louis
Jefferson ES 300/K-6
4315 Cardwell Dr 63121 314-493-0100
Robin Vaulx-Williams, prin. Fax 493-0110

Patton, Bollinger
Meadow Heights R-II SD 600/K-12
RR 1 Box 2365 63662 573-866-0060
Rob Huff, supt. Fax 866-3240
www.meadowheights.k12.mo.us/
Meadow Heights ES 300/K-6
RR 1 Box 2365 63662 573-866-2611
Donna Bristow, prin. Fax 866-3719

Pattonsburg, Daviess, Pop. 243
Pattonsburg R-II SD 200/PK-12
PO Box 200 64670 660-367-2111
Cheryl Cornett, supt. Fax 367-4205
Pattonsburg ES 100/PK-6
PO Box 200 64670 660-367-4416
Holly Brady, prin. Fax 367-4205

Peculiar, Cass, Pop. 3,832
Raymore-Peculiar R-II SD 5,600/PK-12
PO Box 366 64078 816-892-1300
Jeff Kyle, supt. Fax 892-1380
www.raypec.k12.mo.us
Peculiar ES 400/K-4
PO Box 366 64078 816-892-1650
Rob Weida, prin. Fax 892-1655
Raymore-Peculiar MS 800/7-8
PO Box 366 64078 816-892-1550
David Mitchell, prin. Fax 892-1551
Shull ES 300/K-4
PO Box 366 64078 816-892-1600
Jerrod Fellhauer, prin. Fax 892-1601
Other Schools – See Raymore

Perryville, Perry, Pop. 7,935
Perry County SD 32 2,100/K-12
326 College St 63775 573-547-7500
Kevin Dunn, supt. Fax 547-8572
www.perryville.k12.mo.us
Perry County MS 700/5-8
326 College St 63775 573-547-7500
Velda Haertling, prin. Fax 547-1962
Perryville ES 700/K-4
326 College St 63775 573-547-7500
Jennifer Streiler, prin. Fax 547-6445

Immanuel Lutheran S 200/PK-8
225 W South St 63775 573-547-6161
William Unzicker, prin. Fax 547-8205
St. Vincent S 400/PK-6
1007 W Saint Joseph St 63775 573-547-6503
Elaine Blair, prin. Fax 547-4145

Pevely, Jefferson, Pop. 4,208
Dunklin R-V SD
Supt. — See Herculaneum
Pevely ES 500/PK-4
PO Box 327 63070 636-479-5200
Sherri Lindquist, prin. Fax 479-7804

Philadelphia, Marion
Marion County R-II SD 200/PK-12
PO Box 100 63463 573-439-5913
Dianna Hoenes, supt. Fax 439-5914
www.marion.k12.mo.us/
Marion County ES 100/PK-6
PO Box 100 63463 573-439-5913
Eric Spratt, prin. Fax 439-5914

Pickering, Nodaway, Pop. 149
North Nodaway County R-VI SD
Supt. — See Hopkins
North Nodaway ES 100/PK-5
PO Box 35 64476 660-927-3322
Brenda Dougan, prin. Fax 927-3482

Piedmont, Wayne, Pop. 1,975
Clearwater R-I SD 1,100/PK-12
RR 4 Box 1004 63957 573-223-7426
Blane Keel, supt. Fax 223-2932
Clearwater ES 400/PK-4
RR 4 Box 1004 63957 573-223-4812
Charles Brown, prin. Fax 223-7820
Clearwater MS 400/5-8
RR 4 Box 1004 63957 573-223-7724
Samuel Holmes, prin. Fax 223-3117

Pierce City, Lawrence, Pop. 1,442
Pierce City R-VI SD 800/PK-12
300 N Myrtle St 65723 417-476-2555
Russell Moreland, supt. Fax 476-5213
schoolweb.missouri.edu/piercecity.k12.mo.us/
Central ES 300/PK-5
PO Box E 65723 417-476-2255
Teresa Abramovitz, prin. Fax 476-5446
Pierce City MS 200/6-8
300 N Myrtle St 65723 417-476-2842
Gayla DeGraffenreid, prin. Fax 476-5405

St. Mary S 100/K-8
202 Front St 65723 417-476-2824
Sally Heidlage, prin. Fax 476-5103

Pilot Grove, Cooper, Pop. 739
Pilot Grove C-4 SD 300/PK-12
107 School St 65276 660-834-6915
Mark Pottorff, supt. Fax 834-6925
www.schoolweb.missouri.edu/pilotgrovec4.k12.mo.us/
Pilot Grove ES 100/PK-5
107 School St 65276 660-834-4115
Nicole Gizzie, prin. Fax 834-4401
Pilot Grove MS 100/6-8
107 School St 65276 660-834-4415
Randall Glenn, prin. Fax 834-4401

St. Joseph S 50/1-8
405 Harris St 65276 660-834-5600
Kent Monnig, prin. Fax 834-5601

Pine Lawn, Saint Louis, Pop. 4,092
Normandy SD
Supt. — See Saint Louis
Pine Lawn ES 300/K-6
2505 Kienlen Ave 63120 314-493-0700
Paula Sams, prin. Fax 493-0730

Pineville, McDonald, Pop. 868
McDonald County R-I SD
Supt. — See Anderson
Pineville PS 100/PK-2
340 Pleasant Ridge Rd 64856 417-223-3303
Donna Waters, prin. Fax 223-3305
Pineville S 200/3-8
202 E 8th St 64856 417-223-4346
Donna Waters, prin. Fax 223-4195
White Rock S 400/PK-8
119 White Rock Rd 64856 417-226-4446
Adam Lett, prin. Fax 226-4447

Plato, Texas, Pop. 65
Plato R-V SD 700/PK-12
PO Box A 65552 417-458-3333
V. Leon Slape, supt. Fax 458-4706
www.plato.k12.mo.us/
Plato ES 300/PK-5
PO Box A 65552 417-458-4700
Donnie Miller, prin. Fax 458-4706
Plato MS 100/6-8
PO Box A 65552 417-458-4980
Karissa McNiel, prin. Fax 458-4706

Platte City, Platte, Pop. 4,907
Platte County R-III SD 2,600/K-12
998 Platte Falls Rd 64079 816-858-5420
Dr. Mike Reik, supt. Fax 858-5593
www.plattecountyschooldistrict.com/index.htm
Paxton S 300/4-5
1601 Branch St 64079 816-858-5808
Chad Searcey, prin. Fax 858-5280
Platte City MS 500/6-8
900 Pirate Dr 64079 816-858-2036
Chris Miller, prin. Fax 858-3748
Rising Star K 200/K-K
1009 2nd St 64079 816-858-2167
Dr. Donna Hughes, prin. Fax 858-4361
Siegrist ES 500/1-3
1701 Branch St 64079 816-858-5977
Tolan Singer, prin. Fax 858-3942
Other Schools – See Kansas City

Platte Woods, Platte, Pop. 462

Luther Academy 100/K-9
6700 NW 72nd St 64151 816-734-1060
Kyle Karsten, prin. Fax 734-0485

Plattsburg, Clinton, Pop. 2,442
Clinton County R-III SD 900/PK-12
PO Box 287 64477 816-539-2183
Lacee Sell, supt. Fax 539-2412
ccr3.k12.mo.us
Clinton County R-III MS 300/5-8
PO Box 287 64477 816-539-3920
Debi Stewart, prin. Fax 539-2412
Ellis ES 300/PK-4
PO Box 287 64477 816-539-2187
Julie Ausmus, prin. Fax 539-3305

Pleasant Hill, Cass, Pop. 6,747
Pleasant Hill R-III SD 2,100/PK-12
318 Cedar St 64080 816-540-3161
Dr. Wesley Townsend, supt. Fax 540-5135
www.pleasanthillschools.com
Pleasant Hill ES 300/3-4
327 N Mckissock St 64080 816-540-2220
John Stahl, prin. Fax 987-2040
Pleasant Hill IS 300/5-6
1204 E 163rd St 64080 816-540-3156
Chandra Arbuckle, prin. Fax 987-6316
Pleasant Hill MS 300/7-8
1301 E Myrtle St 64080 816-540-2149
Jenny Bell, prin. Fax 987-2017
Pleasant Hill PS 400/PK-2
304 Eklund St 64080 816-540-2119
Sandra Haight, prin. Fax 987-2752

Pleasant Hope, Polk, Pop. 575
Pleasant Hope R-VI SD 900/K-12
PO Box 387 65725 417-267-2850
Tom Allen, supt. Fax 267-4373
www.phr6.com
Pleasant Hope ES 300/K-4
PO Box 387 65725 417-267-2277
Jessica Robertson, prin. Fax 267-4304
Pleasant Hope MS 300/5-8
PO Box 387 65725 417-267-7701
Jessica McIntyre, prin. Fax 267-9221

Pleasant Valley, Clay, Pop. 3,445
North Kansas City SD 74
Supt. — See Kansas City
Pleasant Valley ECC 200/PK-PK
6800 Sobbie Rd 64068 816-413-5650
Jennifer Beutel, dir. Fax 413-5655

Polo, Caldwell, Pop. 602
Mirabile C-1 SD 100/PK-8
2954 SW State Route D 64671 816-586-4129
Sheri Steinman, supt. Fax 586-2029
Mirabile S 100/PK-8
2954 SW State Route D 64671 816-586-4129
Sheri Steinman, prin. Fax 586-2029

Polo R-VII SD 400/K-12
300 W School St 64671 660-354-2326
Robert Newhart, supt. Fax 354-2910
polo.k12.mo.us/
Polo ES 100/K-4
300 W School St 64671 660-354-2200
Beverly Deis, prin. Fax 354-3162
Polo MS 100/5-8
300 W School St 64671 660-354-2200
Beverly Deis, prin. Fax 354-3162

Poplar Bluff, Butler, Pop. 16,912
Poplar Bluff R-I SD 4,800/PK-12
1110 N Westwood Blvd 63901 573-785-7751
Ernie Lawson, supt. Fax 785-0336
www.r1schools.org

Field ES 400/1-4
711 Nickey St 63901 573-785-4047
Jennifer Taylor, prin. Fax 785-4047

Kinyon ECC 200/PK-PK
910 Vine St 63901 573-785-6803
Jo Anne Westbrook, prin. Fax 785-2827

Lake Road ES 200/1-4
986 Highway AA 63901 573-785-4392
Brenda Allen, prin. Fax 778-0303

Oak Grove ES 400/1-4
3297 Oak Grove Rd 63901 573-785-6589
Mike Owen, prin. Fax 785-6589

O'Neal ES 500/1-4
2300 Baugh Ln 63901 573-785-3037
Lorenzo Sandlin, prin. Fax 785-3037

Poplar Bluff 5th & 6th Center 700/5-6
3209 Oak Grove Rd 63901 573-785-5566
Patty Robertson, prin. Fax 785-6748

Poplar Bluff JHS 700/7-8
550 N Westwood Blvd 63901 573-785-5602
Carla Henderson, prin. Fax 785-5602

Twain K 400/K-K
1235 N Main St 63901 573-785-4905
Carl Rosenquist, prin. Fax 785-4423

Sacred Heart S 300/PK-8
111 N 8th St 63901 573-785-5836
Gloria Wilson, prin. Fax 785-3908

Portageville, New Madrid, Pop. 3,071

North Pemiscot County R-I SD
Supt. — See Wardell

Ross ES 100/K-5
128 State Highway A 63873 573-359-0543
Tina Boatwright, prin. Fax 359-0930

Portageville SD 800/PK-12
904 King Ave 63873 573-379-3855
Toni Hall, supt. Fax 379-5817
portageville.k12.mo.us

Portageville ES 300/PK-4
904 King Ave 63873 573-379-5706
Sandra Mudd, prin. Fax 379-5873

Portageville MS 200/5-8
902 King Ave 63873 573-379-3853
Michael Eftink, prin. Fax 379-3159

St. Eustachius S 100/PK-8
214 W 4th St 63873 573-379-3525
Patricia Rone, prin. Fax 379-3525

Potosi, Washington, Pop. 2,709

Potosi R-III SD 2,200/PK-12
400 N Mine St 63664 573-438-5485
Randy Davis, supt. Fax 438-5487
www.potosir3.org/

Evans MS 400/7-8
303 S Lead St 63664 573-438-2101
Don Young, prin. Fax 438-4635

Potosi ES 600/PK-3
205 State Highway P 63664 573-438-2223
Carmen Litton, prin. Fax 438-4370

Trojan IS 500/4-6
367 Intermediate Dr 63664 573-436-8108
Kristy Hale, prin. Fax 436-8608

Prairie Home, Cooper, Pop. 225

Prairie Home R-V SD 200/K-12
301 Highway 87 65068 660-841-5296
Barbara Bancroft, supt. Fax 841-5513
www.prairiehome.k12.mo.us/

Prairie Home ES 100/K-6
301 Highway 87 65068 660-841-5296
Darin Nichols, prin. Fax 841-5513

Princeton, Mercer, Pop. 969

Princeton R-V SD 400/K-12
1008 E Coleman St 64673 660-748-3211
Alan Hamilton, supt. Fax 748-3212
www.tigertown.k12.mo.us/

Princeton ES 200/K-6
408 Ballew St 64673 660-748-3335
Dan Johnson, prin. Fax 748-3334

Purdin, Linn, Pop. 215

Linn County R-I SD 300/PK-12
PO Box 130 64674 660-244-5035
John Brinkley, supt. Fax 244-5025
www.linnr1.k12.mo.us

Linn County ES 100/PK-5
PO Box 130 64674 660-244-5035
Candi Ward, prin. Fax 244-5025

Purdy, Barry, Pop. 1,146

Purdy R-II SD 700/K-12
PO Box 248 65734 417-442-3216
Jerry Lingo, supt. Fax 442-3963
purdy.k12.mo.us/

Purdy ES 300/K-5
PO Box 248 65734 417-442-3217
Jeff Swadley, prin. Fax 442-7988

Purdy MS 200/6-8
PO Box 248 65734 417-442-7066
Janet Boys, prin. Fax 442-3963

Puxico, Stoddard, Pop. 1,150

Puxico R-VIII SD 900/PK-12
481 N Bedford St 63960 573-222-3762
Kyle Dare, supt. Fax 222-3137
www.puxico.k12.mo.us

Puxico ES 400/PK-5
481 N Bedford St 63960 573-222-3542
Jim Davis, prin. Fax 222-2441

Puxico JHS 200/6-8
481 N Bedford St 63960 573-222-3058
Stanley Crisel, prin. Fax 222-6373

Queen City, Schuyler, Pop. 646

Schuyler County R-I SD 700/K-12
PO Box 339 63561 660-766-2204
Robert Amen, supt. Fax 766-2400
www.schuyler.k12.mo.us

Schuyler County R-I ES 300/K-5
PO Box 248 63561 660-766-2296
Kirk Cohagan, prin. Fax 766-2400

Schuyler County R-I MS 100/6-8
PO Box 248 63561 660-766-2296
Kirk Cohagan, prin. Fax 766-2400

Qulin, Butler, Pop. 482

Twin Rivers R-X SD
Supt. — See Broseley

Qulin S 300/K-8
406 Connecticut St 63961 573-328-4444
Danny Rowland, prin. Fax 328-4246

Ravenwood, Nodaway, Pop. 439

Northeast Nodaway County R-V SD 200/PK-12
PO Box 206 64479 660-937-3112
Jeff Mehlenbacher, supt. Fax 937-3110
www.nen.k12.mo.us
Other Schools – See Parnell

Raymondville, Texas, Pop. 439

Raymondville R-VII SD 100/PK-8
PO Box 10 65555 417-457-6237
Nathan Holder, supt. Fax 457-6318
rville.k12.mo.us/

Raymondville S 100/PK-8
PO Box 10 65555 417-457-6237
Nathan Holder, prin. Fax 457-6318

Raymore, Cass, Pop. 15,530

Raymore-Peculiar R-II SD
Supt. — See Peculiar

Bridle Ridge IS 500/5-6
900 E 195th St 64083 816-892-1700
Jamie Mackender, prin. Fax 892-1701

Creekmoor ES 300/K-4
1501 Creekmoor Dr 64083 816-892-1875
Kelly Vines, prin. Fax 892-1876

Eagle Glen IS 400/5-6
100 S Fox Ridge Dr 64083 816-892-1750
Lisa Hatfield, prin. Fax 892-1751

Raymore ES 400/PK-4
500 S Madison St 64083 816-892-1925
Michelle Hofmann, prin. Fax 892-1926

Stonegate ES 400/K-4
900 S Fox Ridge Dr 64083 816-892-1900
Doug Becker, prin. Fax 892-1901

Timber Creek ES 400/K-4
310 E Calico Dr 64083 816-892-1950
Lovie Driskill, prin. Fax 892-1951

Bethlehem Lutheran S 50/PK-8
310 Johnston Pkwy 64083 816-322-3606
Terry Bird, prin. Fax 322-9673

Raytown, Jackson, Pop. 28,923

Raytown C-2 SD 8,900/PK-12
6608 Raytown Rd 64133 816-268-7000
Dr. Allan Markley, supt. Fax 268-7019
www.raytownschools.org/

Blue Ridge ES 400/PK-5
6410 Blue Ridge Blvd 64133 816-268-7200
David Trewhitt, prin. Fax 268-7205

Laurel Hills ES 400/K-5
5401 Lane Ave 64133 816-268-7230
Matt Miller, prin. Fax 268-7235

New Trails Early Learning Center 100/PK-PK
6325 Hunter St 64133 816-268-7430
Donna Denney, prin. Fax 268-7435

Raytown Central MS 6-8
10601 E 59th St 64133 816-268-7050
Andrea Mixon, prin. Fax 268-7055

Raytown South MS 1,000/6-8
8401 E 83rd St 64138 816-268-7380
Randy Thomas, prin. Fax 268-7385

Southwood ES 500/K-5
8015 Raytown Rd 64138 816-268-7280
Susan Emory, prin. Fax 268-7285

Spring Valley ES 500/K-5
8838 E 83rd St 64138 816-268-7270
Greg Owen, prin. Fax 268-7275
Other Schools – See Kansas City

Our Lady of Lourdes S 100/PK-8
8812 E Gregory Blvd 64133 816-353-7062
Steve Messerschmidt, prin. Fax 353-7650

Reeds Spring, Stone, Pop. 672

Reeds Spring R-IV SD 2,000/PK-12
22595 Main St 65737 417-272-8173
Michael Mason, supt. Fax 272-8656
www.wolves.k12.mo.us

DBS Preschool PK-PK
22595 Main St 65737 417-272-6015
Karen Kelly, prin. Fax 272-8656

Reeds Spring ES 500/2-4
300 Wolves Ln 65737 417-272-1735
Tonya Pettypiece, prin. Fax 272-1754

Reeds Spring MS 300/7-8
21016 Main St 65737 417-272-8245
Jason Webb, prin. Fax 272-8490

Reeds Spring PS 200/K-1
257 Elementary Rd 65737 417-272-3241
Karen Kelly, prin. Fax 272-3239

Reeds Springs IS 300/5-6
175 Elementary Rd 65737 417-272-8250
Jodi Gronvold, prin. Fax 272-1743

Renick, Randolph, Pop. 235

Renick R-V SD 200/PK-8
PO Box 37 65278 660-263-4886
Tara Lewis, supt. Fax 263-4249
www.renick.k12.mo.us/

Renick S 200/PK-8
PO Box 37 65278 660-263-4886
Tara Lewis, prin. Fax 263-4249

Republic, Greene, Pop. 10,637

Republic R-III SD 3,500/PK-12
518 N Hampton Ave 65738 417-732-3605
Dr. Vern Minor, supt. Fax 732-3609
www.republicschools.org/

ECC 200/PK-K
720 N Main Ave 65738 417-732-3670
Carol Lohkamp, prin. Fax 732-3679

Republic ES I 600/1-2
235 E Anderson St 65738 417-732-3610
Allan Brown, prin. Fax 732-3619

Republic ES II 600/3-4
234 E Anderson St 65738 417-732-3620
Tracey Hankins, prin. Fax 732-3629

Republic ES III 600/5-6
201 E State Highway 174 65738 417-732-3630
Darin Carter, prin. Fax 732-3639

Republic MS 600/7-8
518 N Hampton Ave 65738 417-732-3640
Pat Mithelavage, prin. Fax 732-3649

Revere, Clark, Pop. 116

Revere C-3 SD 100/PK-8
PO Box 300 63465 660-948-2621
Ryan Horner, supt. Fax 948-2623

Revere S 100/PK-8
PO Box 300 63465 660-948-2621
Ryan Horner, prin. Fax 948-2623

Rich Hill, Bates, Pop. 1,500

Rich Hill R-IV SD 400/K-12
703 N 3rd St 64779 417-395-2418
Terry Mayfield, supt. Fax 395-2407
www.richhill.k12.mo.us/

Rich Hill ES 200/K-6
320 E Poplar St 64779 417-395-2227
Garalene Pyatt, prin. Fax 395-2963

Richland, Pulaski, Pop. 1,776

Richland R-IV SD 700/PK-12
714 E Jefferson Ave 65556 573-765-3241
Joe Ridgeway, supt. Fax 765-5552
schoolweb.missouri.edu/richlandr4.k12.mo.us/

Richland ES 300/PK-6
714 E Jefferson Ave 65556 573-765-3812
Staci Brown, prin. Fax 765-5783

Richland JHS 100/7-8
714 E Jefferson Ave 65556 573-765-3711
Michele Hedges, prin. Fax 765-5552

Swedeborg R-III SD 50/K-8
17507 Highway T 65556 573-736-2735
Ryan Warnol, supt. Fax 736-5926
www.swedeborg.k12.mo.us

Swedeborg S 50/K-8
17507 Highway T 65556 573-736-2735
Ryan Warnol, prin. Fax 736-5926

Richmond, Ray, Pop. 6,075

Richmond R-XVI SD 1,600/PK-12
1017 E Main St 64085 816-776-6912
Jim Robins, supt. Fax 776-5554
richmond.k12.mo.us

Dear ES 100/PK-1
701 E Main St 64085 816-776-5401
Carole Garth, prin. Fax 776-2110

Richmond MS 400/6-8
715 S Wellington St 64085 816-776-5841
Damon Kizzire, prin. Fax 776-2788

Sunrise ES 500/2-5
401 Matt Waller Dr 64085 816-776-3059
Megan Owens, prin. Fax 776-2608

Richmond Heights, Saint Louis, Pop. 9,309

Maplewood-Richmond Heights SD
Supt. — See Maplewood

Maplewood Richmond Heights ES 400/2-6
1800 Princeton Pl 63117 314-644-4403
Kathy Stroud, prin. Fax 644-0315

Immacolata S 300/K-8
8910 Clayton Rd 63117 314-991-5700
Sam Latragna, prin. Fax 991-9354

Richwoods, Washington

Richwoods R-VII SD 200/PK-8
10788 State Highway A 63071 573-678-2257
John Westerman, supt. Fax 678-5207
www.schoolweb.missouri.edu/richwoods.k12.mo.us/

Richwoods S 200/PK-8
10788 State Highway A 63071 573-678-2257
John Westerman, prin. Fax 678-5207

Ridgeway, Harrison, Pop. 536

Ridgeway R-V SD 100/PK-12
305 Main St 64481 660-872-6813
Dr. Regina Knott, supt. Fax 872-6230

Ridgeway ES 100/PK-6
305 Main St 64481 660-872-6813
Dr. Regina Knott, prin. Fax 872-6230

Risco, New Madrid, Pop. 364

Risco R-II SD 200/K-12
PO Box 17 63874 573-396-5568
Dr. Stan Templeton, supt. Fax 396-5503
www.risco.k12.mo.us/

Risco ES 100/K-6
PO Box 17 63874 573-396-5501
Ron Cross, prin. Fax 396-5503

Robertsville, Franklin

Meramec Valley R-III SD
Supt. — See Pacific

Robertsville ES 200/K-5
4000 Highway N 63072 636-271-1448
Greta Franklin, prin. Fax 271-1450

Rock Port, Atchison, Pop. 1,343
Rock Port R-II SD 400/K-12
600 S Nebraska St 64482 660-744-6298
Alan Kerr, supt. Fax 744-5539
Rock Port ES 200/K-6
600 S Nebraska St 64482 660-744-6294
Jamie Evans, prin. Fax 744-5539

Rockville, Bates, Pop. 168

Zion Lutheran S, RR 1 Box 31 64780 50/1-8
JoAnne Walling, prin. 660-598-6213

Rocky Comfort, McDonald
McDonald County R-I SD
Supt. — See Anderson
Rocky Comfort S 200/K-8
14814 E State Highway 76 64861 417-223-4857
Cyndee Undernehr, prin. Fax 652-7366

Rogersville, Greene, Pop. 2,239
Logan-Rogersville R-VIII SD 1,900/PK-12
100 E Front St 65742 417-753-2891
Michael Tucker, supt. Fax 753-3063
logrog.net/
Logan-Rogersville MS 500/6-8
8225 E Farm Road 174 65742 417-753-2896
Richard McPheeters, prin. Fax 753-3182
Logan-Rogersville PS 200/PK-1
512 Sentry Dr 65742 417-881-2947
Toni Bass, prin. Fax 753-5027
Logan-Rogersville Upper ES 600/2-5
306 S Mill St 65742 417-753-2996
Teri Jernigan, prin. Fax 753-7033

Rolla, Phelps, Pop. 17,717
Rolla SD 31 3,800/PK-12
500A Forum Dr 65401 573-458-0100
Jerry Giger, supt. Fax 458-0105
rolla.k12.mo.us
Rolla MS 900/5-7
1111 Soest Rd 65401 573-458-0120
Monica Davis, prin. Fax 458-0124
Truman ES 400/K-4
1001 E 18th St 65401 573-458-0180
Darlene Bramel, prin. Fax 458-0185
Twain ES 300/K-4
1100 Mark Twain Dr 65401 573-458-0170
Jim Pritchett, prin. Fax 458-0175
Wyman ES 500/PK-4
402 Lanning Ln 65401 573-458-0190
Susan Bowles, prin. Fax 458-0195

Rolla Adventist S 50/K-8
810 Highway O 65401 573-364-2041
Betty Hay, prin.
Rolla-Immanuel Lutheran S 100/PK-7
807 W 11th St 65401 573-364-3915
Rick Krumland, prin. Fax 364-3945
St. Patrick S 200/PK-8
19 Saint Patrick Ln 65401 573-364-1162
Michael Brooks, prin. Fax 364-0679

Roscoe, Saint Clair, Pop. 112
Roscoe C-1 SD 100/K-8
PO Box 128 64781 417-646-2376
Jim Rhea, supt. Fax 646-2856
Roscoe S 100/K-8
PO Box 128 64781 417-646-2376
Jim Rhea, prin. Fax 646-2856

Rosebud, Gasconade, Pop. 373

Immanuel Lutheran S 50/PK-8
300 1st St N 63091 573-764-3495
Jim Johnston, prin.

Rosendale, Andrew, Pop. 184
North Andrew County R-VI SD 400/K-12
9120 Highway 48 64483 816-567-2965
Jim Shultz, supt. Fax 567-2096
schoolweb.missouri.edu/nandrew.k12.mo.us/
North Andrew ES 200/K-5
9120 Highway 48 64483 816-567-2527
Mark McDaniel, prin. Fax 567-2096
North Andrew MS 100/6-8
9120 Highway 48 64483 816-567-2525
Shannon Nolte, prin. Fax 567-2096

Rueter, Taney
Mark Twain R-VIII SD 100/K-8
37707 US Highway 160 65744 417-785-4323
Deborah Marsh, supt. Fax 785-9810
www.marktwain.k12.mo.us
Twain S 100/K-8
37707 US Highway 160 65744 417-785-4323
Deborah Marsh, prin. Fax 785-9810

Rushville, Buchanan, Pop. 268
Buchanan County R-IV SD
Supt. — See De Kalb
Rushville ES 200/PK-6
8681 SW State Route 116 64484 816-688-7777
Jennifer Dittemore, prin. Fax 688-7775

Russellville, Cole, Pop. 735
Cole County R-I SD 600/PK-12
13600 Route C 65074 573-782-3534
Jerry Hobbs, supt. Fax 782-3545
www.cole.k12.mo.us
Cole County R-I S 300/PK-8
13111 Park St 65074 573-782-4814
Steve Helton, prin. Fax 782-3435

Saint Albans, Franklin

Fulton School at St. Albans 200/PK-12
PO Box 78 63073 636-458-6688
Kara Douglass, hdmstr. Fax 458-6660

Saint Ann, Saint Louis, Pop. 13,408
Pattonville R-III SD 5,500/PK-12
11097 Saint Charles Rock Rd 63074 314-213-8500
Dr. Michael Fulton, supt. Fax 213-8601
www.psdr3.org
Briar Crest ES 200/K-5
2900 Adie Rd 63074 314-213-8011
Jerona Washington, prin. Fax 213-8611
Drummond ES 500/K-5
3721 Saint Bridget Ln 63074 314-213-8419
Jason Van Beers, prin. Fax 213-8619
Holman MS 600/6-8
11055 Saint Charles Rock Rd 63074 314-213-8032
Teisha Ashford, prin. Fax 213-8632
Pattonville Preschool PK-PK
11097 Saint Charles Rock Rd 63074 314-213-8100
Laurie Wenzel, admin. Fax 213-8630
Other Schools – See Bridgeton, Creve Coeur, Maryland Heights

Ritenour SD
Supt. — See Saint Louis
Buder ES 500/K-5
10350 Baltimore Ave 63074 314-493-6300
Chris Kilbride, prin. Fax 429-6734
Hoech MS 800/6-8
3312 Ashby Rd 63074 314-493-6200
Tim Streicher, prin. Fax 426-3837

Holy Trinity Catholic S 200/K-8
10901 Saint Henry Ln 63074 314-426-8966
Margaret Ahle, prin. Fax 428-7084
Hope Lutheran S 100/PK-8
10701 Saint Cosmas Ln 63074 314-429-0988
Nina Lavigne, prin. Fax 429-3809

Saint Charles, Saint Charles, Pop. 61,253
Francis Howell R-III SD 21,400/PK-12
4545 Central School Rd 63304 636-851-4000
Dr. Renee Schuster, supt. Fax 851-4093
www.fhsdschools.org
Barnwell MS 900/6-8
1035 Jungs Station Rd 63303 636-851-4100
David Eckhoff, prin. Fax 851-4095
Becky-David ES 800/K-5
1155 Jungs Station Rd 63303 636-851-4200
Sherri Brown, prin. Fax 851-4097
Castlio ES 800/K-5
1020 Dingledine Rd 63304 636-851-4300
Bridgett Niedringhaus, prin. Fax 851-4099
Central ES 700/K-5
4525 Central School Rd 63304 636-851-5700
Stacey King, prin. Fax 851-4104
Early Childhood Family Education Center 1,200/PK-PK
2555 Hackmann Rd 63303 636-851-6200
Susan Lane, prin. Fax 851-6202
Early Childhood Family Education Center 1,500/PK-PK
4535 Central School Rd 63304 636-851-6400
Marcia Birk, prin. Fax 851-4106
Harvest Ridge ES 600/K-5
1220 Harvest Ridge Dr 63303 636-851-5100
Brien McCarthy, prin. Fax 851-4128
Henderson ES 500/K-5
2501 Hackmann Rd 63303 636-851-5200
Jennette Barker, prin. Fax 851-4131
Hollenbeck MS 800/6-8
4555 Central School Rd 63304 636-851-5400
Woody Borgschulte, prin. Fax 851-4132
Saeger MS 800/6-8
5201 Highway N 63304 636-851-5600
Brian Schick, prin. Fax 851-4138
Other Schools – See O Fallon, Saint Peters, Weldon Spring, Wentzville

Orchard Farm R-V SD 1,200/K-12
2165 Highway V 63301 636-250-5000
Dr. Daniel Dozier, supt. Fax 250-5444
www.ofsd.k12.mo.us
Orchard Farm ES 500/K-5
2165 Highway V 63301 636-250-5200
Jerry Oetting, prin. Fax 250-5204
Orchard Farm MS 300/6-8
2165 Highway V 63301 636-250-5300
Marcia Cummins, prin. Fax 250-5306

St. Charles R-VI SD 4,100/K-12
400 N 6th St 63301 636-443-4000
Randal Charles, supt. Fax 443-4001
www.stcharles.k12.mo.us
Coverdell ES 300/K-4
2475 W Randolph St 63301 636-443-4600
Annette Hill, prin. Fax 443-4601
Hardin MS 400/7-8
1950 Elm St 63301 636-443-4300
Ed Gettemeier, prin. Fax 443-4301
Harris ES 500/K-4
2800 Old Muegge Rd 63303 636-443-4700
Melvin Bishop, prin. Fax 443-4701
Jefferson MS 200/5-6
2660 Zumbehl Rd 63301 636-443-4400
Kim Harris, prin. Fax 443-4401
Lincoln ES 200/K-4
625 S 6th St 63301 636-443-4650
Julie Williams, prin. Fax 443-4651
Monroe ES 400/K-4
2670 Zumbehl Rd 63301 636-443-4800
Susan Rhoads, prin. Fax 443-4801
Null ES 200/K-4
435 Yale Blvd 63301 636-443-4900
Gina Piccinni, prin. Fax 443-4901

Academy of the Sacred Heart 700/PK-8
619 N 2nd St 63301 636-946-6127
Kathleen Hopper, prin. Fax 949-6659
Campbell Montessori S 100/PK-6
3880 Shady Springs Ln 63301 636-477-8200
Miriam Gutting, dir. Fax 477-6075
Immanuel Lutheran S 500/PK-8
115 S 6th St 63301 636-946-0051
Rebecca Schmidt Ed.D., prin. Fax 946-0166
Living Word Christian S - Harvester ES 100/PK-6
4075 S Old Highway 94 63304 636-926-0042
James Drury, prin. Fax 926-0073
Messiah Lutheran S 300/PK-8
5911 S Highway 94 63304 636-329-1096
Mike Font, prin. Fax 329-1098
St. Charles Borromeo S 400/K-8
431 Decatur St 63301 636-946-2713
Ann Hoffman, prin. Fax 946-3096
St. Cletus S 300/K-8
2721 Zumbehl Rd 63301 636-946-7756
Rosann Doherty, prin. Fax 946-6526
St. Joseph S - Cottleville 900/K-8
1351 Motherhead Rd 63304 636-441-0055
Sr. Maria Christi, prin. Fax 441-9932
St. Peter S 200/K-8
201 1st Capitol Dr 63301 636-947-9669
Tammi Rohman, prin. Fax 946-3580
SS. Elizabeth & Robert S 400/K-8
1 Seton Ct 63303 636-946-6716
Bill Braun, prin. Fax 946-2670
SS. Joachim & Ann S 400/K-8
4110 McClay Rd 63304 636-441-4835
Deborah Pecher, prin. Fax 441-9534
Trinity Lutheran S 50/1-8
4689 N Highway 94 63301 636-250-3654
Esther Loeffler, prin. Fax 250-3354
Zion Lutheran S 300/PK-8
3866 Harvester Rd 63304 636-441-7424
Marc Debrick, prin. Fax 441-7424

Saint Clair, Franklin, Pop. 4,420
St. Clair R-XIII SD 2,300/K-12
905 Bardot St 63077 636-629-3500
Michael Murphy, supt. Fax 629-4466
stclair.fesdev.org
Murray ES 500/3-5
1044 School Dr 63077 636-629-3500
Debra Rufkahr, prin. Fax 629-8413
Saint Clair ES 400/K-2
895 Bardot St 63077 636-629-3500
Nadine Myers, prin. Fax 629-8413
Saint Clair JHS, 925 School Dr 63077 500/6-8
Steven Weinhold, prin. 636-629-3500

St. Clare S 100/PK-8
125 E Springfield Rd 63077 636-629-0413
Mary Hoffman, prin. Fax 629-1440

Sainte Genevieve, Sainte Genevieve, Pop. 4,666
St. Genevieve County R-II SD 2,000/K-12
375 N 5th St 63670 573-883-4500
Mikel Stewart, supt. Fax 883-5957
www.stegen.k12.mo.us
Sainte Genevieve ES 500/K-5
725 Washington St 63670 573-883-4500
Cheryl Bauman, prin. Fax 883-5957
Sainte Genevieve MS 500/6-8
211 N 5th St 63670 573-883-4500
John Boyd, prin. Fax 883-5957
Other Schools – See Bloomsdale

St. Joseph S 100/PK-5
11822 Zell Rd 63670 573-883-5097
Sr. Rita Ann Frey, prin. Fax 883-5097
Valle Catholic S 300/K-8
40A N 4th St 63670 573-883-2403
Sara Menard, prin. Fax 883-7413

Saint Elizabeth, Miller, Pop. 300
St. Elizabeth R-IV SD 200/PK-12
PO Box 68 65075 573-493-2246
Sid Doerhoff, supt. Fax 493-2380
www.ste.k12.mo.us/
Saint Elizabeth ES 100/PK-6
PO Box 68 65075 573-493-2246
Leroy Heckemeyer, prin. Fax 493-2380

Saint James, Phelps, Pop. 3,941
St. James R-I SD 1,700/PK-12
122 E Scioto St 65559 573-265-2300
Joy Tucker, supt. Fax 265-6126
www.stjschools.org/
James ES 600/PK-5
314 S Jefferson St 65559 573-265-2300
Kim Shockley, prin. Fax 265-1504
St. James MS 400/6-8
1 Tiger Dr 65559 573-265-2300
Kaaren Lepper, prin. Fax 265-6302

Saint Joseph, Buchanan, Pop. 72,663
St. Joseph SD 11,700/PK-12
925 Felix St 64501 816-671-4000
Melody Smith, supt. Fax 671-4470
www.sjsd.k12.mo.us
Bode MS 500/7-8
720 N Noyes Blvd 64506 816-671-4050
Roberta Dias, prin. Fax 671-4473
Coleman ES 500/K-6
3312 Beck Rd 64506 816-671-4100
Molly Pierce, prin. Fax 671-4101
Edison ES 300/PK-6
515 N 22nd St 64501 816-671-4110
Jennifer Patterson, prin. Fax 671-4477
Ellison ES 300/K-6
45 SE 85th Rd 64507 816-667-5316
Kim Siela, prin. Fax 667-5530
Field ES 300/K-6
2602 Gene Field Rd 64506 816-671-4130
Jo DeShon, prin. Fax 671-4478
Hall ES 300/K-6
2509 Duncan St 64507 816-671-4160
Heather Gladhart, prin. Fax 671-4162

Hosea ES 400/K-6
6401 Gordon Ave 64504 816-671-4180
Lindsey Minson, prin. Fax 671-4182
Humboldt ES 300/PK-6
1520 N 2nd St 64505 816-671-4190
Jeremy Burright, prin. Fax 671-4191
Hyde ES 400/K-6
509 Thompson Ave 64504 816-671-4210
Jeaneen Boyer, prin. Fax 671-4211
Lake Contrary ES 300/PK-6
1800 Alabama St 64504 816-671-4240
Jennee Barnes, prin. Fax 671-4481
Lindbergh ES 500/PK-6
2812 Saint Joseph Ave 64505 816-671-4250
Julie Gaddie, prin. Fax 671-4251
Neely ES 300/PK-6
1909 S 12th St 64503 816-671-4280
K. Jennifer Gaddie, prin. Fax 671-4484
Noyes ES 300/K-6
1415 N 26th St 64506 816-671-4290
Judith Long, prin. Fax 671-4291
Parkway ES 300/K-6
2900 Duncan St 64507 816-671-4310
Joni Owens, prin. Fax 671-4311
Pershing ES 300/K-6
2610 Blackwell Rd 64505 816-671-4320
Tara Wells, prin. Fax 671-4485
Pickett ES 300/PK-6
3923 Pickett Rd 64503 816-671-4330
Kevin Tedlock, prin. Fax 671-4486
Robidoux MS 400/7-8
4212 Saint Joseph Ave 64505 816-671-4350
Krista Sly, prin. Fax 671-4487
Skaith ES 400/K-6
4701 Schoolside Ln 64503 816-671-4370
Matthew Martz, prin. Fax 671-4488
Spring Garden MS 400/7-8
5802 S 22nd St 64503 816-671-4380
Lara Gilpin, prin. Fax 671-4489
Truman MS 400/7-8
3227 Olive St Ste 45 64507 816-671-4400
Beery Johnson, prin. Fax 671-4491
Twain ES 300/PK-6
705 S 31st St 64507 816-671-4270
Pam Kent, prin. Fax 671-4483
Webster ES 300/PK-6
1211 N 18th St 64501 816-671-4410
Lacey Adams, prin. Fax 671-4492

Co-Cathedral S 200/PK-8
518 N 11th St 64501 816-232-8486
Mary Burgess, prin. Fax 232-8793
Prescott SDA S 50/K-8
1405 Weisenborn Rd 64507 816-279-8591
St. Francis Xavier S 400/PK-8
2614 Seneca St 64507 816-232-4911
Denise Campbell, prin. Fax 364-0263
St. James S 200/PK-8
120 Michigan Ave 64504 816-238-0281
Sue Scalard, prin. Fax 238-1758
St. Joseph Christian S 400/PK-12
5401B Gene Field Rd 64506 816-279-3760
Lydia Zuidema, supt. Fax 279-3836
St. Paul Lutheran S 300/PK-8
4715 Frederick Ave 64506 816-279-1118
Ronnie Pister, prin. Fax 279-1114

Saint Louis, Saint Louis, Pop. 332,223
Affton SD 101 2,300/K-12
8701 MacKenzie Rd 63123 314-638-8770
Dr. Don Francis, supt. Fax 631-2548
www.affton.k12.mo.us
Gotsch IS 500/3-5
8348 S Laclede Station Rd 63123 314-842-1238
Brian Smith, prin. Fax 633-5991
Mesnier PS 400/K-2
6930 Weber Rd 63123 314-849-5566
Diane Renda, prin. Fax 633-5992
Rogers MS 600/6-8
7550 MacKenzie Rd 63123 314-351-9679
Jeff Remelius, prin. Fax 351-6381

Bayless SD 1,500/PK-12
4530 Weber Rd 63123 314-631-2244
Maureen Clancy-May, supt. Fax 544-6315
csd.org/schools/bayless/baylesshome.html#bsd
Bayless ES 300/PK-2
4530 Weber Rd 63123 314-256-8620
Gina Siebe, prin. Fax 544-6315
Bayless IS 500/3-6
4530 Weber Rd 63123 314-256-8640
Kim Stallons, prin. Fax 544-6315
Bayless JHS 200/7-8
4530 Weber Rd 63123 314-256-8690
Ron Tucker, prin. Fax 544-6315

Ferguson-Florissant R-II SD
Supt. — See Florissant
Bermuda ES 300/K-6
5835 Bermuda Dr 63121 314-524-4821
Alice Aldridge, prin. Fax 524-4827
Cool Valley ES 300/K-6
1351 S Florissant Rd 63121 314-521-5622
Ralph Moore, prin. Fax 521-5624
Ferguson MS 700/7-8
701 January Ave 63135 314-506-9600
Susan Kelly, prin. Fax 506-9601
Vogt ES 200/K-6
200 Church St 63135 314-521-6347
Karen van der Graaf, prin. Fax 521-5938

Hancock Place SD 1,700/PK-12
9101 S Broadway 63125 314-544-1300
Dr. Greg Clark, supt. Fax 631-3752
hancock.k12.mo.us
Hancock Place ES 800/PK-5
9101 S Broadway 63125 314-544-1300
Debbie Kyle, prin. Fax 544-4931
Hancock Place MS 400/6-8
243 W Ripa Ave 63125 314-544-6423
Scott Wilkerson, prin. Fax 544-6470

Hazelwood SD
Supt. — See Florissant
Arrowpoint ES 600/K-5
2017 Arrowpoint Dr 63138 314-953-5300
Lynette Jackson, prin. Fax 953-5313
Grannemann ES 400/K-5
2324 Redman Rd 63136 314-953-4250
Kamina Hunter, prin. Fax 953-4263
Hazelwood East MS 1,200/6-8
1865 Dunn Rd 63138 314-953-5700
Dr. Sonya Ptah, prin. Fax 953-5713
Hazelwood Southeast MS 6-8
918 Prigge Rd 63138 314-953-7700
Dr. Carol Fouse, prin. Fax 953-7713
Keeven ES 400/K-5
11230 Old Halls Ferry Rd 63136 314-953-4450
Sue Fields, prin. Fax 953-4463
Larimore ES 500/K-5
1025 Trampe Ave 63138 314-953-4500
Dr. Jean McClendon, prin. Fax 953-4513
Twillman ES 400/K-5
11831 Bellefontaine Rd 63138 314-953-4850
Dr. Brenda Harris, prin. Fax 953-4863

Ladue SD 3,500/PK-12
9703 Conway Rd 63124 314-994-7080
Marsha Chappelow, supt. Fax 994-0441
www.ladue.k12.mo.us
Conway ES 400/K-5
9900 Conway Rd 63124 314-993-2878
M. Lane Narvaez, prin. Fax 994-3988
Ladue ECC PK-PK
10601 Clayton Rd 63131 314-993-5724
Dawn Hogan-Lopez, dir. Fax 432-0980
Ladue MS 800/6-8
9701 Conway Rd 63124 314-993-3900
Cathy Richter, prin. Fax 997-8736
Old Bonhomme ES 400/K-5
9661 Old Bonhomme Rd 63132 314-993-0656
Cheryl Kirchgessner, prin. Fax 994-3987
Reed ES 400/K-5
9060 Ladue Rd 63124 314-991-1456
Chris Schreiner, prin. Fax 994-3981
Other Schools – See Creve Coeur

Lindbergh R-VIII SD 5,500/K-12
4900 S Lindbergh Blvd 63126 314-729-2480
Dr. Jim Simpson, supt. Fax 729-2482
www.lindbergh.k12.mo.us
Crestwood ES 300/K-5
1020 S Sappington Rd 63126 314-729-2430
Scott Taylor, prin. Fax 729-2432
Kennerly ES 400/K-5
10025 Kennerly Rd 63128 314-729-2440
Suzanne Christopher, prin. Fax 729-2442
Long ES 300/K-5
9021 Sappington Rd 63126 314-729-2450
Brian McKenney, prin. Fax 729-2452
Sappington ES 400/K-5
11011 Gravois Rd 63126 314-729-2460
Mary Hogan, prin. Fax 729-2462
Sperreng MS 1,300/6-8
12111 Tesson Ferry Rd 63128 314-729-2420
Dr. Jennifer Tiller, prin. Fax 729-2422
Truman ES 700/K-5
12225 Eddie and Park Rd 63127 314-729-2470
Megan Stryjewski, prin. Fax 729-2472

Maplewood-Richmond Heights SD
Supt. — See Maplewood
Maplewood Richmond Heights MS 200/7-8
7539 Manchester Rd 63143 314-644-4406
Steven Lawler, prin. Fax 781-4629

Mehlville R-IX SD 11,100/K-12
3120 Lemay Ferry Rd 63125 314-467-5000
Terry Noble, supt. Fax 467-5099
www.mehlvilleschooldistrict.com/
Beasley ES 300/K-5
3131 Koch Rd 63125 314-467-5400
Melody Gunn, prin. Fax 467-5499
Bernard MS 700/6-8
1054 Forder Rd 63129 314-467-6600
Phil Milligan, prin. Fax 467-6699
Bierbaum ES 600/K-5
2050 Union Rd 63125 314-467-5500
Kristy Roberts, prin. Fax 467-5599
Blades ES 500/K-5
5140 Patterson Rd 63129 314-467-7300
Tina Plummer, prin. Fax 467-7399
Buerkle MS 600/6-8
623 Buckley Rd 63125 314-467-6800
John Weber, prin. Fax 467-6899
Forder ES 400/K-5
623 W Ripa Ave 63125 314-467-5600
Scott Clark, prin. Fax 467-5699
Hagemann ES 400/K-5
6401 Hagemann Rd 63128 314-467-5700
Scott Andrews, prin. Fax 467-5799
Oakville ES 400/K-5
2911 Yaeger Rd 63129 314-467-5800
Chad Dickemper, prin. Fax 467-5899
Oakville MS 700/6-8
5950 Telegraph Rd 63129 314-467-7400
Mike Salsman, prin. Fax 467-7499
Point ES 500/K-5
6790 Telegraph Rd 63129 314-467-5900
Jim Walters, prin. Fax 467-5999
Rogers ES 400/K-5
7700 Fine Rd 63129 314-467-6300
Jeff Bresler, prin. Fax 467-6399
Trautwein ES 500/K-5
5011 Ambs Rd 63128 314-467-6400
Donna Wagener, prin. Fax 467-6499
Washington MS 500/6-8
5165 Ambs Rd 63128 314-467-7600
Adam Smith, prin. Fax 467-7699
Wohlwend ES 500/K-5
5966 Telegraph Rd 63129 314-467-6500
Dave Meschke, prin. Fax 467-6599

Normandy SD 4,900/PK-12
3855 Lucas and Hunt Rd 63121 314-493-0400
Dr. Stanton Lawrence, supt. Fax 493-0475
www.normandy.k12.mo.us
Normandy ECC / K Complex 100/PK-K
3417 Saint Thomas More Pl 63121 314-493-0880
Joyce Buck, prin. Fax 493-0890
Other Schools – See Bel Nor, Bel Ridge, Normandy, Overland, Pasadena Hills, Pine Lawn

Ritenour SD 6,200/PK-12
2420 Woodson Rd 63114 314-493-6010
Cheryl Compton, supt. Fax 426-7144
www.ritenour.k12.mo.us
ECC PK-PK
9330 Stansberry Ave 63134 314-493-6240
Karen Flavin, prin. Fax 429-3688
Kratz ES 500/K-5
4301 Edmundson Rd 63134 314-493-6360
Dorlita Adams, prin. Fax 429-6735
Marion ES 400/K-5
2634 Sims Ave 63114 314-493-6400
Janet Lesage, prin. Fax 429-6720
Marvin ES 500/K-5
3510 Woodson Rd 63114 314-493-6430
Mary Beth Fortney, prin. Fax 429-6737
Wyland ES 500/K-5
2200 Brown Rd 63114 314-493-6460
Kathy Pfeifer, prin. Fax 429-6728
Other Schools – See Overland, Saint Ann

Riverview Gardens SD 7,100/K-12
1370 Northumberland Dr 63137 314-869-2505
Dr. Rhonda Key, supt. Fax 869-6354
www.rgsd.org
Central MS 700/6-8
9800 Patricia Barkalow Dr 63137 314-869-2505
Cheketa Riddle, prin. Fax 388-6028
Danforth ES 400/K-5
1111 Saint Cyr Rd 63137 314-868-9524
Dr. Stacy Nichols, prin. Fax 388-6030
Gibson ES 400/K-5
9926 Fonda Dr 63137 314-869-8556
Cheri Gaston, prin. Fax 388-6032
Glasgow ES 400/K-5
10560 Renfrew Dr 63137 314-868-4680
Stacie Price, prin. Fax 388-6034
Highland ES 400/K-5
174 Shepley Dr 63137 314-868-4561
Dr. Nona Greenlee, prin. Fax 388-6036
Koch ES 400/K-5
1910 Exuma Dr 63136 314-868-3029
Jeff Cook, prin. Fax 388-6038
Lemasters ES 400/K-5
1825 Crown Point Dr 63136 314-868-8192
Janice Turnage, prin. Fax 388-6040
Lewis & Clark ES 300/K-5
10242 Prince Dr 63136 314-868-5205
Jason Brown, prin. Fax 388-6042
Meadows ES 400/K-5
9801 Edgefield Dr 63136 314-868-2454
Linda Show, prin. Fax 388-6044
Moline ES 500/K-5
9865 Winkler Dr 63136 314-868-9829
Michael Wallace, prin. Fax 388-6048
Westview MS 700/6-8
1950 Nemnich Rd 63136 314-867-0410
Dr. Valerie Robinson, prin. Fax 388-6055

St. Louis City SD 29,600/PK-12
801 N 11th St 63101 314-231-3720
Dr. Kelvin Adams, supt. Fax 345-2661
www.slps.org/
Adams ES 300/PK-6
1311 Tower Grove Ave 63110 314-535-3910
Jeanetta Stegall, prin. Fax 535-3949
Ames Visual/Perf Arts ES 300/PK-5
2900 Hadley St 63107 314-241-7165
Javeeta Parks, prin. Fax 231-1607
Ashland ES 500/PK-6
3921 N Newstead Ave 63115 314-385-4767
Cynthia Warren, prin. Fax 385-6129
Baden ES 300/PK-6
5814 Thekla Ave 63120 314-388-2477
Alila Barr, prin. Fax 388-9931
Blewett MS 200/6-8
1927 Cass Ave 63106 314-231-7738
Hollie Russell, prin. Fax 231-0073
Bryan Hill ES 200/PK-5
2128 E Gano Ave 63107 314-534-0370
Carole Johnson, prin. Fax 535-7864
Buder ES 400/PK-5
5319 Lansdowne Ave 63109 314-352-4343
Dr. Sally Bloom, prin. Fax 352-3150
Bunche International Studies MS 300/6-8
1118 S 7th St 63104 314-588-8750
Michelle McDaniel-Headd, prin. Fax 588-1510
Busch/Academic-Athletic Academy 300/6-8
5910 Clifton Ave 63109 314-352-1043
Robert Lescher, prin. Fax 352-3685
Carr Lane Visual & Performing Art MS 500/6-8
1004 N Jefferson Ave 63106 314-231-0413
Melba Davis, prin. Fax 241-1213
Clark ES 300/PK-6
1020 Union Blvd 63113 314-367-1505
Vickie Rogers, prin. Fax 367-3624
Clay ES 300/PK-5
3820 N 14th St 63107 314-231-9608
Donna Owens, prin. Fax 231-1660
Cole ES 300/PK-7
3935 Enright Ave 63108 314-533-0894
Stella Erondu, prin. Fax 533-4509

Columbia ES 300/PK-6
3120 Saint Louis Ave 63106 314-533-2750
Vrhonnee Brown, prin. Fax 534-4062
Compton-Drew ILC MS 500/6-8
5130 Oakland Ave 63110 314-652-9282
Susan Reid, prin. Fax 652-9371
Cote Brilliante ES 300/K-6
4908 Cote Brilliante Ave 63113 314-531-8680
Karen Jones, prin. Fax 531-7910
Dewey S International Studies 500/PK-5
6746 Clayton Ave 63139 314-645-4845
Dr. Ann Russek, prin. Fax 645-5926
Dunbar ES 300/PK-6
1415 N Garrison Ave 63106 314-533-2526
Carla Cunigan, prin. Fax 533-0269
Fanning MS Community Education Center 300/6-8
3417 Grace Ave 63116 314-772-1038
Verona Bowers, prin. Fax 772-0437
Farragut ES 300/PK-6
4025 Sullivan Ave 63107 314-531-1198
Joyce Wilks-Love, prin. Fax 531-5356
Ford ES 300/PK-6
1383 Clara Ave 63112 314-383-0836
Denise Segers, prin. Fax 383-0887
Froebel ES 400/PK-5
3709 Nebraska Ave 63118 314-771-3533
Mamie Womack, prin. Fax 771-3590
Gateway ES 500/PK-5
4 Gateway Dr 63106 314-241-8255
Dr. Rose Howard, prin. Fax 241-3159
Gateway MS 500/6-8
1200 N Jefferson Ave 63106 314-241-2295
Bruce Green, prin. Fax 241-7698
Hamilton ES 200/PK-5
5819 Westminster Pl 63112 314-367-0552
Todd Williams, prin. Fax 367-2392
Henry ES 200/PK-6
1220 N 10th St 63106 314-231-7284
Esperansa Veal, prin. Fax 231-0232
Herzog ES 300/K-7
5831 Pamplin Ave 63147 314-385-2212
Deirdre Jackson, prin. Fax 385-1925
Hickey ES 300/PK-5
3111 Cora Ave 63115 314-383-2550
Peggy Starks, prin. Fax 383-5164
Hodgen ES 200/PK-6
1616 California Ave 63104 314-771-2539
Vasilika Tsichlis, prin. Fax 771-2418
Jefferson ES 400/PK-6
1301 Hogan St 63106 314-231-2459
Roger Brock, prin. Fax 231-2905
Kennard Classical Jr Academy 300/PK-5
5031 Potomac St 63139 314-353-8875
Merry Denny, prin. Fax 351-0441
Laclede ES 300/PK-5
5821 Kennerly Ave 63112 314-385-0546
Sandy Wiley, prin. Fax 385-7294
Langston MS 300/6-8
5511 Wabada Ave 63112 314-383-2908
Rose Johnson, prin. Fax 385-4632
Lexington ES 300/PK-5
5030 Lexington Ave 63115 314-385-2522
Barbara Anderson, prin. Fax 385-4158
Long MS Community Education Center 400/6-8
5028 Morganford Rd 63116 314-481-3440
Alva Blue, prin. Fax 481-7329
L'Ouverture MS 200/6-8
3021 Hickory St 63104 314-664-3579
Juanita Jones, prin. Fax 664-7955
Lyon Academy 200/K-8
516 Loughborough Ave 63111 314-353-1353
Ingrid Iskali, prin. Fax 481-8625
Mallinckrodt ES 300/PK-5
6020 Pernod Ave 63139 314-352-9212
Betty Blanchard, prin. Fax 352-3142
Mann ES 300/PK-6
4047 Juniata St 63116 314-772-4545
Brian Zimmerman, prin. Fax 772-6348
Mason ES 300/PK-6
6031 Southwest Ave 63139 314-645-1201
Deborah Leto, prin. Fax 645-0884
Meramec ES 300/PK-5
2745 Meramec St 63118 314-353-7145
Jerome Woodson, prin. Fax 353-6783
Monroe ES 400/PK-6
3641 Missouri Ave 63118 314-776-7315
Gerald Arbini, prin. Fax 776-7339
Mullanphy Botanical Gardens ES 500/PK-6
4221 Shaw Blvd 63110 314-772-0994
Kenneth Blanton, prin. Fax 865-3759
Nance ES 300/PK-6
8959 Riverview Blvd 63147 314-867-0634
Monica Miller, prin. Fax 867-1006
Northwest MS 200/8-8
5140 Riverview Blvd 63120 314-385-4774
Valerie Carter, prin. Fax 385-3651
Oak Hill ES 400/PK-5
4300 Morganford Rd 63116 314-481-0420
Wanda Leflore, prin. Fax 481-2371
Peabody S 400/PK-8
1224 S 14th St 63104 314-241-1533
Chereyl Spann, prin. Fax 241-2805
Scruggs ES 400/PK-5
4611 S Grand Blvd 63111 314-752-0604
DeAndria Wallace, prin. Fax 752-3887
Shaw Visual/Performing Arts ES 300/K-5
5329 Columbia Ave 63139 314-776-5091
Marilyn Burress, prin. Fax 776-5124
Shenandoah ES 200/PK-5
3412 Shenandoah Ave 63104 314-772-7544
Sonya Wayne, prin. Fax 772-8581
Shepard ES 200/PK-6
3450 Wisconsin Ave 63118 314-776-3664
Carol Hall-Whittier, prin. Fax 664-3708
Sherman ES 200/PK-6
3942 Flad Ave 63110 314-776-2626
Shonta Smith, prin. Fax 776-3978

Sigel ES 200/PK-6
2050 Allen Ave 63104 314-771-0010
Christine McCoy, prin. Fax 771-4527
Simmons ES 300/PK-5
4318 Saint Louis Ave 63115 314-535-5844
Carey Cunningham, prin. Fax 535-0827
Stevens MS Community Education Center 300/6-8
1033 Whittier St 63113 314-533-8550
Larry Schleicher, prin. Fax 533-0306
Stix ECC 300/PK-2
647 Tower Grove Ave 63110 314-533-0874
Diane Dymond, prin. Fax 533-8262
Twain ES 300/PK-6
5316 Ruskin Ave 63115 314-381-1616
Dr. Bobbie Gines, prin. Fax 381-6926
Walbridge ES 400/PK-7
5000 Davison Ave 63120 314-383-1829
Ruth Banks, prin. Fax 383-2292
Washington ECC 50/PK-PK
2030 S Vandeventer Ave 63110 314-771-4041
Nahid Hashemi, prin. Fax 345-2482
Washington/Euclid Montessori ES 300/PK-5
1130 N Euclid Ave 63113 314-361-0432
Deadrienne Torrey, prin. Fax 361-2760
Wilkinson ECC 200/PK-2
1921 Prather Ave 63139 314-645-1202
Dr. Rosalyn Mason, prin. Fax 645-2618
Woerner ES 400/K-5
6131 Leona St 63116 314-481-8585
George Taubenheim, prin. Fax 351-2272
Woodward ES 300/PK-5
725 Bellerive Blvd 63111 314-353-1346
Candice Carter-Oliver, prin. Fax 353-5768

University City SD 3,600/PK-12
8136 Groby Rd 63130 314-290-4000
Joylynn Wilson, supt. Fax 725-7692
www.ucityschools.org
Jordan ES 300/K-6
8136 Groby Rd 63130 314-290-4360
Bonita Jamison, prin. Fax 993-6413
Other Schools – See University City

Webster Groves SD
Supt. — See Webster Groves
Bristol ES 300/K-5
20 Gray Ave 63119 314-963-6433
Nancy Zitzmann, prin. Fax 963-6438
Computer ES 100/K-5
701 N Rock Hill Rd 63119 314-963-6460
Kristin Denbow, prin. Fax 963-6471
Hixson MS 600/7-8
630 S Elm Ave 63119 314-963-6450
Jason Heisserer, prin. Fax 918-4624
Steger 6th Grade Center 300/6-6
701 N Rock Hill Rd 63119 314-963-6460
Kristin Denbow, prin. Fax 963-6471

Wellston SD 600/PK-12
6574 Saint Louis Ave 63121 314-290-7900
Dr. Charles Brown, supt. Fax 290-7905
www.wellston.k12.mo.us
Bishop MS 100/6-7
6310 Wellsmar Ave 63133 314-290-7600
Adrienne Reed, prin. Fax 290-7605
Central ES 200/1-5
6238 Ella Ave 63133 314-290-7200
Mary Hairston, prin. Fax 290-7205
Wellston ECC 100/PK-K
1635 Kienlen Ave 63133 314-290-7100
Crissie Kirkendall, dir. Fax 290-7105

Abiding Saviour Lutheran S 200/PK-8
4353 Butler Hill Rd 63128 314-892-4408
Laura Montgomery, prin. Fax 892-4469
Agape Academy 300/PK-8
7400 Olive Blvd 63130 314-725-5262
Donna Griffin, dir. Fax 725-0902
Andrews Academy 200/PK-6
888 N Mason Rd 63141 314-878-1883
Joe Patterson, hdmstr. Fax 878-0759
Assumption S - Mattese 400/K-8
4709 Mattis Rd 63128 314-487-6520
Cynthia Hasten, prin. Fax 487-3598
Bethel Lutheran S 50/PK-8
7001 Forsyth Blvd 63105 314-863-3111
Sandy Kalin, prin. Fax 863-3393
Cathedral Basilica S of St. Louis 100/PK-8
4430 Maryland Ave 63108 314-373-8250
Michel Wendell, prin. Fax 373-8289
Central Catholic / St. Nicholas S 300/PK-PK
1805 Lucas Ave 63103 314-421-1822
Sr. Gail Trippett, prin. Fax 231-0254
Central Catholic / St. Nicholas S 300/K-8
1106 N Jefferson Ave 63106 314-231-6254
Sr. Gail Trippett, prin. Fax 621-2666
Central Christian S 200/PK-6
700 S Hanley Rd 63105 314-727-4535
Joshua Crane, hdmstr. Fax 727-8006
Christ Light of the Nations S 300/PK-8
1650 Redman Rd 63138 314-741-0400
Sr. Mary Lawrence, prin. Fax 653-2531
City Acadmey 200/PK-6
4175 N Kingshighway Blvd 63115 314-382-0085
Don Danforth, pres. Fax 382-0228
Clayton Child Ctr/Clayton Academy 100/PK-8
1414 Bellevue Ave 63117 314-727-2643
Barbara Geno Ed.D., dir.
Community S 300/PK-6
900 Lay Rd 63124 314-991-0005
Matthew Gould Ph.D., hdmstr. Fax 991-1512
Covenant Christian S 100/PK-4
2145 N Ballas Rd 63131 314-787-1036
Rev. John Roberts, prin. Fax 432-3989
De LaSalle MS 50/6-8
4145 Kennerly Ave 63113 314-531-9820
Phil Pusateri, prin. Fax 531-4820

Epiphany of Our Lord S 200/PK-8
6576 Smiley Ave 63139 314-781-5626
Sharon Morgenthaler, prin. Fax 645-7166
Forsyth S 400/PK-6
6235 Wydown Blvd 63105 314-726-4542
Mike Vachow, hdmstr. Fax 726-0112
Freedom S 100/PK-4
1483 82nd Blvd 63132 314-432-7396
Odetta Fields, prin. Fax 432-6766
Grace Chapel Lutheran S 200/PK-8
10015 Lance Dr 63137 314-867-6564
Fax 868-2485
GreenPark Christian Academy 100/K-12
3635 Union Rd 63125 314-416-7000
Art Morgan, admin. Fax 416-1114
Green Park Lutheran S 300/K-8
4248 Green Park Rd 63125 314-544-4248
Dan Dueck, prin. Fax 544-0237
Hope Lutheran S 100/PK-8
5320 Brannon Ave 63109 314-832-1850
Deborah Dikeman, prin. Fax 832-0184
Immaculate Heart of Mary S 200/PK-8
4070 Blow St 63116 314-832-1678
Richard Danzeisen, prin. Fax 832-1627
King of Glory Lutheran S 100/PK-8
4293 Chippewa St 63116 314-865-1144
Fax 772-4210
Kirk of the Hills Christian Day S 400/PK-6
12928 Ladue Rd 63141 314-434-4349
Sue Pitzer, prin. Fax 434-0047
Life Christian S 50/PK-8
13001 Gravois Rd 63127 314-842-1781
Aleta Stuart, lead tchr. Fax 843-2731
Little Flower S 200/PK-8
1275 Boland Pl 63117 314-781-4995
Dr. Sharon Baumgartner, prin. Fax 781-9177
Loyola Academy 100/6-8
3851 Washington Blvd 63108 314-531-9091
Eric Clark, prin. Fax 531-3603
Marian MS 100/6-8
4130 Wyoming St 63116 314-771-7674
Christy Leming, prin. Fax 771-7679
Mary Institute/St. Louis Country Day S 1,200/PK-12
101 N Warson Rd 63124 314-993-5100
Lisa Lyle, hdmstr. Fax 995-7470
Miriam S 100/PK-8
501 Bacon Ave 63119 314-968-5225
John Holland M.Ed., dir. Fax 968-7338
Most Holy Trinity S 100/PK-8
1435 Mallinckrodt St 63107 314-231-9014
Dr. John Kosash, prin. Fax 436-9291
New City S 400/PK-6
5209 Waterman Blvd 63108 314-361-6411
Dr. Tom Hoerr, hdmstr. Fax 361-1499
Our Lady of Guadalupe S 200/PK-8
1115 S Florissant Rd 63121 314-524-1948
Margaret O'Brien, prin. Fax 522-8461
Our Lady of Providence S 200/K-8
8874 Pardee Rd 63123 314-842-2073
Clare Ortmeier, prin. Fax 843-8033
Our Lady of the Pillar S 200/K-8
403 S Lindbergh Blvd 63131 314-993-3353
Judith Talleur, prin. Fax 993-2172
Our Lady of the Presentation S 100/PK-8
8840 Tudor Ave 63114 314-428-8191
Kathryn Gilmartin, prin. Fax 423-1213
Our Redeemer Lutheran S 200/PK-8
9135 Shelley Ave 63114 314-427-3462
Fax 429-7081
Principia S 600/PK-12
13201 Clayton Rd 63131 314-434-2100
Marilyn Wallace, hdmstr. Fax 275-3583
Queen of all Saints S 500/K-8
6611 Christopher Dr 63129 314-846-0506
Cathy Johns, prin. Fax 846-4939
Rabbi Epstein Hebrew Academy 200/PK-8
1138 N Warson Rd 63132 314-994-7856
Rabbi Shmuel Kay, hdmstr. Fax 994-9437
River Roads Lutheran S 100/PK-8
8623 Church Rd 63147 314-388-0300
Yvonne Boyd, prin. Fax 388-3253
Rohan Woods S 100/PK-6
1515 Bennett Ave 63122 314-821-6270
Kelly Horn, hdmstr. Fax 821-6878
Rossman S 200/PK-6
12660 Conway Rd 63141 314-434-5877
Patricia Shipley, hdmstr. Fax 434-1668
Sacred Heart Villa PK-K
2108 Macklind Ave 63110 314-771-2224
Sr. Catherine Coleman, prin. Fax 771-1261
St. Ambrose S 300/K-8
5110 Wilson Ave 63110 314-772-1437
Sr. Carol Sansone, prin. Fax 771-4560
St. Catherine Laboure S 500/K-8
9750 Sappington Rd 63128 314-843-2819
Margaret Visconti, prin. Fax 843-7687
St. Cecilia S & Academy 100/PK-8
906 Eichelberger St 63111 314-353-2455
Jim Ford, prin. Fax 353-2114
St. Clement S 400/K-8
1508 Bopp Rd 63131 314-822-1903
Jean Grana, prin. Fax 822-8371
St. Dominic Savio S 200/PK-8
7748 MacKenzie Rd 63123 314-832-4161
Kathleen Wiseman, prin. Fax 352-6331
St. Francis Cabrini Academy 200/K-8
3022 Oregon Ave 63118 314-776-0883
Maureen DePriest, prin. Fax 776-4912
St. Francis of Assisi S 500/PK-8
4550 Telegraph Rd 63129 314-487-5736
Darrel Sturgill, prin. Fax 416-7118
St. Gabriel the Archangel S 500/K-8
4711 Tamm Ave 63109 314-353-1229
Dr. Ann Davis, prin. Fax 353-6737
St. Genevieve Du Bois S 200/K-8
1575 N Woodlawn Ave 63122 314-821-4245
Claudia Dougherty, prin. Fax 822-4881

St. James the Greater S 100/K-8
1360 Tamm Ave 63139 314-647-5244
Karen Battaglia, prin. Fax 647-8237
St. Joan of Arc S 200/K-8
5821 Pernod Ave 63139 314-752-4171
Deborah Dalay, prin. Fax 351-8562
St. John the Baptist S 400/PK-8
4170 Delor St 63116 314-481-6654
Kathleen Anger, prin. Fax 481-3179
St. Justin the Martyr S 200/K-8
11914 Eddie and Park Rd 63126 314-843-6447
Elizabeth Bartolotta, prin. Fax 843-9257
St. Katharine Drexel S 400/K-8
5831 S Kingshighway Blvd 63109 314-353-1451
Rebecca Finnegan, prin. Fax 351-8464
St. Louis Catholic Academy 200/PK-8
4720 Carter Ave 63115 314-389-0401
Sybil Selfe, prin. Fax 389-7042
St. Louis Unified S 50/PK-8
PO Box 3969 63136 314-869-7800
Fax 869-7801
St. Lucas Lutheran S 50/PK-K
7100 Morganford Rd 63116 314-351-7298
St. Luke's Lutheran S 100/PK-8
3415 Taft Ave 63111 314-832-0118
Fax 832-7074
St. Margaret Mary Alacoque S 600/K-8
4900 Ringer Rd 63129 314-487-1666
Marianne Freiling, prin. Fax 487-4475
St. Margaret of Scotland S 300/PK-8
3964 Castleman Ave 63110 314-776-7837
Julie Hesed, prin. Fax 776-7955
St. Mark S 300/K-8
4220 Ripa Ave 63125 314-743-8640
Jill Burkett, prin. Fax 743-8690
St. Martin of Tours S 200/K-8
618 W Ripa Ave 63125 314-544-5793
Aleta Marshall, prin. Fax 544-1892
St. Matthew Lutheran S 100/PK-8
5403 Wren Ave 63120 314-261-7708
Jonathon Lewis, prin. Fax 261-7707
St. Michael S 100/PK-6
6345 Wydown Blvd 63105 314-721-4422
Beth Mosher, hdmstr. Fax 721-4448
St. Paul Lutheran S 300/K-8
1300 N Ballas Rd 63131 314-822-2771
Janet Profilet, prin. Fax 822-6574
St. Raphael the Archangel S 200/K-8
6000 Jamieson Ave 63109 314-352-9474
Margaret Kenny, prin. Fax 351-7477
St. Roch S 200/PK-8
6040 Waterman Blvd 63112 314-721-2595
Gloria Openlander, prin. Fax 721-1656
St. Simon S 400/K-8
11019 Mueller Rd 63123 314-842-0181
Michael Talleur, prin. Fax 849-6355
St. Stephen Protomartyr S 200/K-8
3929 Wilmington Ave 63116 314-752-4700
Meghan Bohac, prin. Fax 752-5165
Salem Lutheran S 200/PK-8
5025 Lakewood Ave 63123 314-353-9242
Scott Akerson, prin. Fax 353-9328
Seven Holy Founders S 500/PK-8
6737 S Rock Hill Rd 63123 314-631-8149
Joel Lechner, prin. Fax 633-0129
Shining Rivers S 50/PK-8
915 N Elm Ave 63119 314-962-2129
Solomon Schechter Day S 200/K-8
348 S Mason Rd 63141 314-576-6177
Rabbi Allen Selis, hdmstr. Fax 576-3624
South City Community S 50/PK-1
620 N Grand Blvd 63103 314-374-0082
Rebekah Brown, hdmstr.
Torah Prep Boys S 100/2-8
609 N And South Rd 63130 314-727-3335
Torah Prep Girls S 100/PK-8
8659 Olive Blvd 63132 314-569-2929
Tower Grove Christian S 300/PK-12
4257 Magnolia Ave 63110 314-776-6473
Michael Gregory, admin. Fax 776-4867
Victory Christian S 100/K-8
10255 Musick Rd 63123 314-849-3425
David Talley, prin. Fax 849-5224
Villa Duchesne/Oak Hill S 400/PK-6
801 S Spoede Rd 63131 314-810-3552
Margaret Karl, prin. Fax 810-3594
Visitation Academy 200/PK-6
3020 N Ballas Rd 63131 314-625-9117
Mimi Francisco, prin. Fax 991-7747
Visitation Academy 100/7-8
3020 N Ballas Rd 63131 314-625-9100
Mary Ellen Schraeder, prin. Fax 432-7210
Wilson S 200/PK-6
400 De Mun Ave 63105 314-725-4999
Thad Falkner, hdmstr. Fax 725-5242
Word of Life Lutheran S 200/PK-8
6535 Eichelberger St 63109 314-832-1244
David Robinson, prin. Fax 832-0195

Saint Marys, Sainte Genevieve, Pop. 517

Sacred Heart S - Ozora 50/K-5
17740 State Rte N 63673 573-543-2997
Sr. Agnes Keena, prin. Fax 543-2209

Saint Paul, Saint Charles, Pop. 1,655

St. Paul S 200/PK-8
1235 Church Rd 63366 636-978-1900
Sharon Woelbling, prin. Fax 272-4966

Saint Peters, Saint Charles, Pop. 53,397
Francis Howell R-III SD
Supt. — See Saint Charles
Fairmount ES 800/K-5
1725 Thoele Rd 63376 636-851-4500
Casey Godfrey, prin. Fax 851-4107

Warren ES 600/K-5
141 Weiss Rd 63376 636-851-6100
Michele Hercules, prin. Fax 851-6209

Ft. Zumwalt R-II SD
Supt. — See O Fallon
DuBray MS 900/6-8
100 DuBray Dr 63376 636-279-7979
Mike Anderson, prin. Fax 278-4749
Ft. Zumwalt South MS 1,200/6-8
300 Knaust Rd 63376 636-281-0776
Dr. Monte Massey, prin. Fax 281-0006
Hawthorn ES 500/K-5
166 Boone Hills Dr 63376 636-928-5205
Kim Mckinley, prin. Fax 447-9216
Lewis & Clark ES 400/3-5
460 Mcmenamy Rd 63376 636-397-3111
Nelda Wetzel, prin. Fax 397-1454
Mid Rivers ES 500/K-5
7479 Mexico Rd 63376 636-278-2168
Carol Ransom, prin. Fax 278-2451
Progress South ES 800/K-5
201 Knaust Rd 63376 636-272-2721
Deb Yerkes, prin. Fax 281-0002
Saint Peters ES 300/K-2
400 Mcmenamy Rd 63376 636-397-3211
Debbie Mueller, prin. Fax 279-3416

All Saints S 400/K-8
5 Mcmenamy Rd 63376 636-397-1477
Rae Ann Keilty, prin. Fax 397-1477
Child of God Lutheran S 200/PK-6
650 Salt Lick Rd 63376 636-970-7080
Fax 970-7083
Living Word Christian S - Mid Rivers ES 200/PK-6
310 Cardinal Pl 63376 636-970-2398
James Drury, prin. Fax 278-9516
Willott Road Christian Academy 300/K-8
1610 Willott Rd 63376 636-926-3595
Steven Sparks, admin. Fax 447-8577

Saint Robert, Pulaski, Pop. 3,037
Waynesville R-VI SD
Supt. — See Waynesville
Freedom ES 1,100/3-6
286 Eastlawn Ave 65584 573-451-2100
Mike Morriss, prin. Fax 451-2101

Saint Thomas, Cole, Pop. 280

St. Thomas the Apostle S 100/PK-8
PO Box 211 65076 573-477-3322
Lora Boessen, prin. Fax 477-3700

Salem, Dent, Pop. 4,789
Dent-Phelps R-III SD 300/PK-8
27870 Highway C 65560 573-729-4680
Johnnie Brown, admin. Fax 729-8644
www.dentphelps.k12.mo.us/
Dent-Phelps S 300/PK-8
27870 Highway C 65560 573-729-4680
Victoria Brooker, prin. Fax 729-8644

Green Forest R-II SD 200/K-8
6111 Highway F 65560 573-729-3902
Kevin Prugh, supt. Fax 729-4842
Green Forest S 200/K-8
6111 Highway F 65560 573-729-3902
Kevin Prugh, prin. Fax 729-4842

North Wood R-IV SD 200/PK-8
3734 N Highway 19 65560 573-729-4607
Chris Welch, supt. Fax 729-8714
www.northwood.k12.mo.us
North Wood S 200/PK-8
3734 N Highway 19 65560 573-729-4607
Richard Hockersmith, prin. Fax 729-8714

Oak Hill R-I SD 100/PK-8
6200 S Highway 19 65560 573-729-5618
Rexanna Shackelford, supt. Fax 729-6982
Oak Hill S 100/PK-8
6200 S Highway 19 65560 573-729-5618
Rexanna Shackelford, prin. Fax 729-6982

Salem R-80 SD 1,400/K-12
1409 W Rolla Rd 65560 573-729-6642
Steve Bryant, supt. Fax 729-8493
www.salem.k12.mo.us/
Lynch ES 300/K-2
101 N Main St 65560 573-729-6611
Kriste Crocker, prin. Fax 729-2433
Salem Upper ES 300/3-6
1601 Doss Rd 65560 573-729-4812
Melanie Wisdom, prin. Fax 729-0284

New Harmony Christian Academy 100/PK-6
PO Box 724 65560 573-729-5991
Julie McNeal, admin. Fax 729-5661

Salisbury, Chariton, Pop. 1,635
Salisbury R-IV SD 500/K-12
PO Box 314 65281 660-388-6699
Todd Willhite, supt. Fax 388-6753
www.salisbury.k12.mo.us/
Salisbury ES 200/K-6
PO Box 314 65281 660-388-6611
Renee Henke, prin. Fax 388-6752

St. Joseph S 100/K-8
105 N Willie Ave 65281 660-388-5518
Janice Dubbert, prin. Fax 388-5518

Sarcoxie, Jasper, Pop. 1,340
Sarcoxie R-II SD 800/K-12
101 S 17th St 64862 417-548-3134
Mike Resa, supt. Fax 548-6165
www.sarcoxie.k12.mo.us/

Wildwood ES 400/K-5
214 S 11th St 64862 417-548-3421
Sharon Wooten, prin. Fax 548-6445

Savannah, Andrew, Pop. 4,925
Savannah R-III SD 2,400/K-12
PO Box 151 64485 816-324-3144
Donald Lawrence, supt. Fax 324-5594
www.savannah.k12.mo.us
Cline ES 600/K-5
808 W Price Ave 64485 816-324-3915
Kelly Warren, prin. Fax 324-6767
Savannah MS 500/6-8
701 W Chestnut St 64485 816-324-3126
Leisa Blair, prin. Fax 324-6397
Other Schools – See Amazonia, Country Club, Helena

Schell City, Vernon, Pop. 290
Northeast Vernon County R-I SD
Supt. — See Walker
Northeast Vernon County R-I ES 100/PK-6
PO Box 68 64783 417-432-3196
Kendall Ogburn, prin. Fax 432-3197

Scott City, Scott, Pop. 4,584
Scott City R-I SD 900/K-12
3000 Main St 63780 573-264-2381
Diann Bradshaw-Ulmer, supt. Fax 264-2206
scschools.k12.mo.us/
Scott City ES 300/K-4
3000 Main St 63780 573-264-2131
Courtney Kern, prin. Fax 264-4058
Scott City MS 200/5-8
3000 Main St 63780 573-264-2139
Michael Umfleet, prin. Fax 264-2599

St. Joseph Catholic S 50/PK-8
606 Sycamore St 63780 573-264-2600
Clifford Lankheit, prin. Fax 264-1325

Sedalia, Pettis, Pop. 20,430
Pettis County R-XII SD 200/PK-8
22675 Depot Rd 65301 660-826-5385
Verlin Tyler, supt. Fax 826-5452
www.pettisr12.k12.mo.us
Pettis County R-XII S 200/PK-8
22675 Depot Rd 65301 660-826-5385
Verlin Tyler, prin. Fax 826-5452

Sedalia SD 200 2,600/PK-12
2806 Matthew Dr 65301 660-829-6450
Dr. Harriet Wolfe, supt. Fax 827-8938
www.sedalia200.com
Hunt ES 400/K-4
600 S Warren Ave 65301 660-826-1058
Wade Norton, prin. Fax 829-0698
Mann ES 300/K-4
1100 W 16th St 65301 660-826-6441
William Betteridge, prin. Fax 829-0767
Parkview ES 400/K-4
1901 S New York Ave 65301 660-826-4947
Kelly Sobaski, prin. Fax 829-0873
Pettis County ECC 100/PK-PK
600 E 14th St 65301 660-827-8955
Grace Kendrick, prin. Fax 827-8957
Sedalia MS 300/5-6
2205 S Ingram Ave 65301 660-829-6500
Sara Pannier, prin. Fax 827-6112
Skyline ES 400/K-4
2505 W 32nd St 65301 660-826-8087
Kelly McFatrich, prin. Fax 829-0916
Washington ES 300/K-4
610 S Engineer Ave 65301 660-826-2216
Lisa Volk, prin. Fax 829-0982

Sacred Heart S 300/K-8
416 W 3rd St 65301 660-827-3800
Dr. Mark Register, prin. Fax 827-3806
St. Paul Lutheran S 100/PK-8
701 S Massachusetts Ave 65301 660-826-1925
John Nail, prin. Fax 826-1925
Sedalia Adventist Academy 50/K-8
29531 Highway 50 65301 660-827-4045

Senath, Dunklin, Pop. 1,641
Senath-Hornersville C-8 SD 800/PK-12
PO Box 370 63876 573-738-2669
Larry Wood, supt. Fax 738-9845
www.shs.k12.mo.us/
Senath-Hornersville ES 300/PK-4
PO Box 370 63876 573-738-2515
Cynthia Keating, prin. Fax 738-9845
Other Schools – See Hornersville

Seneca, Newton, Pop. 2,237
Seneca R-VII SD 1,600/K-12
914 Frisco St 64865 417-776-3426
Rick Cook, supt. Fax 776-2177
schoolweb.missouri.edu/seneca.k12.mo.us/
Seneca ES 600/K-5
1815 Saint Eugene St 64865 417-776-2785
Susan Barnes, prin. Fax 776-1508
Wells MS 400/6-8
925 Oneida St 64865 417-776-3911
Tony Simmons, prin. Fax 776-2673

Seymour, Webster, Pop. 1,960
Seymour R-II SD 900/PK-12
416 E Clinton Ave 65746 417-935-2287
Frank Rowles, supt. Fax 935-4060
schoolweb.missouri.edu/seymour.k12.mo.us/
Seymour ES 400/PK-5
425 E Center Ave 65746 417-935-2234
Kelly Lowe, prin. Fax 935-2083
Seymour MS 200/6-8
501 E Clinton Ave 65746 417-935-4626
Brian Bell, prin. Fax 935-2848

Shelbina, Shelby, Pop. 1,886
Shelby County R-IV SD 800/PK-12
4154 Highway 36 63468 573-588-4961
Rick Roberts, supt. Fax 588-2490
www.cardinals.k12.mo.us
Shelbina ES 200/PK-5
111 W College Ave 63468 573-588-2181
Susan See, prin. Fax 588-4982
Other Schools – See Clarence

Shelbyville, Shelby, Pop. 686
North Shelby SD 300/PK-12
3071 Highway 15 63469 573-633-2410
Larry Smoot, supt. Fax 633-2138
www.nshelby.k12.mo.us
North Shelby ES 200/PK-6
3071 Highway 15 63469 573-633-2401
Sharri Kemp, prin. Fax 633-2138

Sheldon, Vernon, Pop. 534
Sheldon R-VIII SD 200/PK-12
100 E Gene Lathrop Dr 64784 417-884-5113
Stephen Fox, supt. Fax 884-5331
www.sheldon.k12.mo.us
Sheldon ES 100/PK-6
100 E Gene Lathrop Dr 64784 417-884-5113
Tim Judd, prin. Fax 884-5331

Shell Knob, Barry
Shell Knob ESD 78 200/K-8
24400 State Highway 39 65747 417-858-6743
Shelly Fransen, supt. Fax 858-2202
www.sks.k12.mo.us/
Shell Knob S 200/K-8
24400 State Highway 39 65747 417-858-6743
Shelly Fransen, prin. Fax 858-2202

Shrewsbury, Saint Louis, Pop. 6,393

St. Michael the Archangel S 200/K-8
7630 Sutherland Ave 63119 314-647-7159
Nancy Haselhorst, prin. Fax 644-1433

Sikeston, Scott, Pop. 17,180
Scott County Central SD 400/PK-12
20794 US Highway 61 63801 573-471-2686
Dr. Joel Holland, supt. Fax 471-2029
scottcentral.k12.mo.us
Scott County Central ES 200/PK-6
20794 US Highway 61 63801 573-471-3511
Tim Thompson, prin. Fax 471-3515

Sikeston R-6 SD 3,100/K-12
1002 Virginia St 63801 573-472-2581
Stephen Borgsmiller, supt. Fax 472-2584
www.sikeston.k12.mo.us
Hunter ES 400/1-4
1002 Virginia St 63801 573-472-2200
Monica Ward, prin. Fax 472-3847
Matthews ES 300/1-4
1002 Virginia St 63801 573-471-0614
Angela Zorbas, prin. Fax 471-0614
Sikeston 5th and 6th Grade Center 600/5-6
1002 Virginia St 63801 573-471-0792
Chuck Mayes, prin. Fax 471-0793
Sikeston 7th and 8th Grade Center 300/7-8
1002 Virginia St 63801 573-471-1720
Cheryl Macke, prin. Fax 472-8884
Sikeston K 300/K-K
1002 Virginia St 63801 573-471-0653
Jennifer Hobeck, prin. Fax 471-0654
Southeast ES 300/1-4
1002 Virginia St 63801 573-472-0707
Kathy Sturgess, prin. Fax 471-1714
Other Schools – See Morehouse

Christian Academy 100/PK-6
210 S Kingshighway St 63801 573-481-0216
Jeannette Smith, admin. Fax 481-9485
St. Francis Xavier S 200/PK-8
106 N Stoddard St 63801 573-471-0841
Pierre Antoine, prin. Fax 471-9820

Silex, Lincoln, Pop. 232
Silex R-I SD 400/K-12
PO Box 46 63377 573-384-5227
Elaine Henderson, supt. Fax 384-5996
schoolweb.missouri.edu/silex.k12.mo.us/
Silex ES 200/K-6
PO Box 46 63377 573-384-5044
Melissa Orf, prin. Fax 384-5996

St. Alphonsus S - Milwood 100/K-8
25 Saint Alphonsus Rd 63377 573-384-5305
Ruby Karolczak, prin. Fax 384-6190

Slater, Saline, Pop. 1,954
Orearville R-IV SD 50/PK-8
32524 E Highway P 65349 660-529-2481
Dr. Marilyn Ehlert, supt. Fax 529-2454
Orearville S 50/PK-8
32524 E Highway P 65349 660-529-2481
Dr. Marilyn Ehlert, prin. Fax 529-2454

Slater SD 400/PK-12
515 Elm St 65349 660-529-2278
John McEachern, supt. Fax 529-2279
www.slaterpublicschools.net
Alexander S 300/PK-8
515 Elm St 65349 660-529-3132
Jean Dowell, prin. Fax 529-2279

Smithton, Pettis, Pop. 502
Smithton R-VI SD 600/K-12
505 S Myrtle Ave 65350 660-343-5316
Andy Henley, supt. Fax 343-5389
smithton.k12.mo.us
Smithton ES 300/K-6
505 S Myrtle Ave 65350 660-343-5317
Cindy Jorgenson, prin. Fax 343-5389

Smithville, Clay, Pop. 7,118
Smithville R-II SD 2,000/PK-12
655 S Commercial Ave 64089 816-532-0406
Dr. Robert Leachman, supt. Fax 532-4192
www.smithville.k12.mo.us/
Smithville MS 500/6-8
675 S Commercial Ave 64089 816-532-1122
Susan Hurst, prin. Fax 532-3210
Smithville PS 300/PK-2
600 Maple Ave 64089 816-532-0589
Bethany Case, prin. Fax 532-3158
Smithville Upper ES 500/3-5
695 S Commercial Ave 64089 816-532-4566
Terrill Kelly, prin. Fax 532-4409

South West City, McDonald, Pop. 868
McDonald County R-I SD
Supt. — See Anderson
Southwest City S 300/PK-8
PO Box 189 64863 417-762-3251
Deborah Wolin, prin. Fax 762-3165

Sparta, Christian, Pop. 1,226
Sparta R-III SD 800/PK-12
PO Box 160 65753 417-634-4284
Jeff Hyatt, supt. Fax 634-3156
www.sparta.k12.mo.us/
Sparta ES 400/PK-5
PO Box 160 65753 417-634-3223
Joy Finney, prin. Fax 634-5256
Sparta MS 200/6-8
PO Box 160 65753 417-634-5518
Shawn Poyser, prin. Fax 634-0091

Spickard, Grundy, Pop. 314
Spickard R-II SD 100/PK-8
105 N 4th St 64679 660-485-6121
Amy May, supt. Fax 485-6179
Spickard S 100/PK-8
105 N 4th St 64679 660-485-6121
Amy May, prin. Fax 485-6179

Spokane, Christian
Spokane R-VII SD
Supt. — See Highlandville
Spokane MS 200/6-8
PO Box 220 65754 417-443-3506
Pamila Rowe, prin. Fax 443-2069

Springfield, Greene, Pop. 150,298
Springfield R-XII SD 24,400/PK-12
940 N Jefferson Ave 65802 417-523-0000
Dr. Norman Ridder, supt. Fax 523-0196
www.springfieldpublicschoolsmo.org/
Bingham ES 400/K-5
2126 E Cherry St 65802 417-523-3400
Adam Meador, prin. Fax 523-3495
Bissett ES 300/K-5
3014 W Calhoun St 65802 417-523-2800
Marcie Stallcup, prin. Fax 523-2895
Bowerman ES 200/K-5
2148 N Douglas Ave 65803 417-523-1400
Jason Steingraber, prin. Fax 523-1495
Boyd ES 200/K-5
1409 N Washington Ave 65802 417-523-1500
James Grandon, prin. Fax 523-1595
Campbell ES 200/K-5
506 S Grant Ave 65806 417-523-3200
Jason Anderson, prin. Fax 523-3295
Carver MS 700/6-8
3325 W Battlefield St 65807 417-523-6800
Dr. Dan O'Reilly, prin. Fax 523-6895
Cherokee MS 700/6-8
420 E Farm Road 182 65810 417-523-7200
Bill Powers, prin. Fax 523-7295
Cowden ES 300/PK-5
2927 S Kimbrough Ave 65807 417-523-3500
Cherie Norman, prin. Fax 523-3595
Delaware ES 200/K-5
1505 S Delaware Ave 65804 417-523-3700
Beth Engelhart, prin. Fax 523-3795
Disney ES 600/K-5
4100 S Fremont Ave 65804 417-523-3600
Dr. Lynne Miller, prin. Fax 523-3695
Field ES 300/K-5
2120 E Barataria St 65804 417-523-4800
Nancy Colbaugh, prin. Fax 523-4895
Fremont ES 200/K-5
2814 N Fremont Ave 65803 417-523-1700
Susan McCollegan, prin. Fax 523-1795
Gray ES 600/K-4
2101 W Farm Road 182 65810 417-523-4000
Angela Carder, prin. Fax 888-2694
Harrison ES, 3055 W Kildee Ln 65810 100/K-5
Christine Mendel, prin. 417-523-5800
Hickory Hills ES 300/K-5
3429 E Trafficway St 65802 417-523-7100
Kelly Allison, prin. Fax 523-7195
Hickory Hills MS 500/6-8
3429 E Trafficway St 65802 417-523-7100
Kelly Allison, prin. Fax 523-7195
Holland ES 200/K-5
2403 S Holland Ave 65807 417-523-4100
Nicole Kimbrough, prin. Fax 523-4195
Jarrett MS 600/6-8
840 S Jefferson Ave 65806 417-523-6600
Marty Marsh, prin. Fax 523-6695
Jeffries ES 500/K-5
4051 S Scenic Ave 65807 417-523-3900
Liz Cooper, prin. Fax 523-3995
Mann ES 400/K-5
3745 S Broadway Ave 65807 417-523-4400
Teri Peterson, prin. Fax 523-4495
McBride ES 500/K-4
5005 S Farm Road 135 65810 417-523-4500
Bret Range, prin. Fax 523-4595
McGregor ES 300/K-5
1221 W Madison St 65806 417-523-5700
Jeff Thornsberry, prin. Fax 523-5795
Pershing ES 200/K-5
2120 S Ventura Ave 65804 417-523-2400
Natalie Cauldwell, prin. Fax 523-2495
Pershing MS 800/6-8
2120 S Ventura Ave 65804 417-523-2400
Dr. Kim Finch, prin. Fax 523-2495
Pipkin MS 500/6-8
1215 N Boonville Ave 65802 417-523-6000
Dr. Tim Zeigler, prin. Fax 523-6195
Pittman ES 300/K-5
2934 E Bennett St 65804 417-523-4700
Gary Tew, prin. Fax 523-4795
Pleasant View ES 200/K-5
2210 E State Highway AA 65803 417-523-2100
Julie Steiger, prin. Fax 523-2395
Pleasant View MS 400/6-8
2210 E State Highway AA 65803 417-523-2100
Julie Steiger, prin. Fax 523-2395
Portland ES 200/K-5
906 W Portland St 65807 417-523-4600
Lora Hopper, prin. Fax 523-4695
Reed MS 500/6-8
2000 N Lyon Ave 65803 417-523-6300
Dr. Debbie Grega, prin. Fax 523-6395
Robberson ES 300/PK-5
1100 E Kearney St 65803 417-523-1800
Kevin Huffman, prin. Fax 523-1895
Rountree ES 300/K-5
1333 E Grand St 65804 417-523-4900
David Martin, prin. Fax 523-4995
Sequiota ES 400/K-5
3414 S Mentor Ave 65804 417-523-5400
Kristi Johnson, prin. Fax 523-5495
Shady Dell ECC 50/PK-K
2757 E Division St 65803 417-523-1300
Melissa Riley, prin. Fax 523-1395
Sherwood ES 300/K-5
1813 S Scenic Ave 65807 417-523-3800
Lesa Haase, prin. Fax 523-3895
Study MS 400/6-8
2343 W Olive St 65802 417-523-6400
Jim Harvey, prin. Fax 523-6495
Sunshine ES 200/K-5
421 E Sunshine St 65807 417-523-5200
Rene Saner, prin. Fax 523-5295
Truman ES 300/PK-5
3850 N Farm Rd 159 65803 417-523-5100
Stephanie Young, prin. Fax 523-5195
Twain ES 500/K-5
2352 S Weaver Ave 65807 417-523-4300
Janell Bagwell, prin. Fax 523-4395
Watkins ES 300/PK-5
732 W Talmage St 65803 417-523-5000
Robert Reed, prin. Fax 523-5095
Weaver ES 300/K-5
1461 N Douglas Ave 65802 417-523-1200
Janelle Andrus, prin. Fax 523-1295
Weller ES 300/K-5
1630 N Weller Ave 65803 417-523-1900
Marilyn Monroe, prin. Fax 523-1995
Westport ES 500/PK-5
415 S Golden Ave 65802 417-523-3100
Dr. Nancy Brake, prin. Fax 523-3195
Wilder ES 400/K-5
2526 S Hillsboro Ave 65804 417-523-5300
Joe Callaway, prin. Fax 523-5395
Williams ES 300/PK-5
2205 W Kearney St 65803 417-523-2000
Jennifer Webb, prin. Fax 523-2095
York ES 200/K-5
2100 W Nichols St 65802 417-523-3000
Gary Danielson, prin. Fax 895-2149
Other Schools – See Battlefield

Willard R-II SD
Supt. — See Willard
Willard Central ES 400/K-4
2625 N Farm Rd 101 65802 417-831-4440
Shane Medlin, prin. Fax 831-2486
Willard South ES 300/K-4
4151 W Division St 65802 417-862-6308
Kara Crighton-Smith, prin. Fax 862-4266

Greenwood Laboratory S 300/K-12
901 S National Ave, 417-836-5124
Dr. Janice Duncan, dir. Fax 836-8449
Immaculate Conception S 500/PK-8
3555 S Fremont Ave 65804 417-881-7000
Paula Baird, prin. Fax 881-7087
New Covenant Academy 400/PK-12
3304 S Cox Ave 65807 417-887-9848
Cynthia Evans, supt. Fax 887-2419
St. Agnes S 300/PK-8
531 S Jefferson Ave 65806 417-866-5038
Jeanne Skahan, prin. Fax 866-2906
St. Elizabeth Ann Seton S 100/K-2
2200 W Republic Rd 65807 417-887-6056
Cheryl Hall, prin. Fax 866-2189
St. Joseph S 100/PK-8
515 W Scott St 65802 417-866-0667
Marilyn Batson, prin. Fax 866-2862
Springfield Lutheran S 300/PK-8
2852 S Dayton Ave 65807 417-883-5717
Paul Baker, prin. Fax 889-6218
Springfield SDA S 50/K-10
704 S Belview Ave 65802 417-862-0833

Stanberry, Gentry, Pop. 1,192
Stanberry R-II SD 400/PK-12
610 N Park St 64489 660-783-2136
Dr. Bruce Johnson, supt. Fax 783-2177
www.sr2.k12.mo.us/
Stanberry R-II ES 200/PK-6
610 N Park St 64489 660-783-2141
Bob Heddinger, prin. Fax 783-2177

Steele, Pemiscot, Pop. 2,169
South Pemiscot County R-V SD 800/K-12
611 Beasley Rd 63877 573-695-4426
Johnny Thompson, supt. Fax 695-4427
www.southpemiscot.com/
South Pemiscot ES 500/K-6
611 Beasley Rd 63877 573-695-3141
Patricia Farley, prin. Fax 695-7464

Steelville, Crawford, Pop. 1,454
Steelville R-III SD 1,000/PK-12
PO Box 339 65565 573-775-2175
Harvey Richards, supt. Fax 775-2179
steelville.k12.mo.us
Steelville ES 400/PK-4
PO Box 339 65565 573-775-2099
Suzanne Alexander, prin. Fax 775-4940
Steelville MS 300/5-8
PO Box 339 65565 573-775-2176
Matt Fridley, prin. Fax 775-2591

Stella, Newton, Pop. 187
East Newton County R-VI SD
Supt. — See Granby
Triway S 500/K-8
PO Box 208 64867 417-628-3227
Kern Sorrell, prin. Fax 628-3226

Stet, Carroll
Stet R-XV SD 100/K-12
18760 Cardinal Rd 64680 660-484-3122
Thomas Challender, supt. Fax 484-3124
Stet ES 100/K-6
18760 Cardinal Rd 64680 660-484-3122
Thomas Challender, prin. Fax 484-3124

Stewartsville, DeKalb, Pop. 746
Stewartsville C-2 SD 300/K-12
902 Buchanan St 64490 816-669-3792
Ono Monachino, supt. Fax 669-8125
www.geocities.com/stewartsvillec2/index.html
Stewartsville ES 100/K-6
902 Buchanan St 64490 816-669-3258
Monica Landess, prin. Fax 669-8125

Stockton, Cedar, Pop. 2,004
Stockton R-I SD 1,100/K-12
PO Box 190 65785 417-276-5143
Dr. Vicki Sandberg, supt. Fax 276-3765
www.stockton.k12.mo.us/
Stockton ES 400/K-4
PO Box 190 65785 417-276-3315
Patricia Steinmuller, prin. Fax 276-5946
Stockton MS 300/5-8
PO Box 190 65785 417-276-6161
Bill Crabtree, prin. Fax 276-4909

Stoutland, Laclede, Pop. 186
Stoutland R-II SD 500/PK-12
7584 State Road T 65567 417-286-3711
Eric Cooley, supt. Fax 286-3153
www.schoolweb.missouri.edu/stoutland/
Stoutland ES 300/PK-6
7584 State Road T 65567 417-286-3711
James Roberts, prin. Fax 286-4341

Stover, Morgan, Pop. 1,022
Morgan County R-I SD 700/PK-12
701 N Oak St 65078 573-377-2218
Tom Wales, supt. Fax 377-2952
mcr1.stovermo.com/
Morgan County R-I ES 200/PK-4
701 N Oak St 65078 573-377-2219
Shari Schulz, prin. Fax 377-2211
Morgan County R-I MS 200/5-8
701 N Oak St 65078 573-377-4284
Timothy Beydler, prin. Fax 377-4441

St. Paul Lutheran S 100/PK-8
PO Box 9 65078 573-377-2690
Debra Eckhoff, prin. Fax 377-2185

Strafford, Greene, Pop. 1,909
Strafford R-VI SD 1,100/K-12
201 W McCabe St 65757 417-736-7000
John Collins, supt. Fax 736-7016
straffordschools.net
Strafford ES 400/K-4
213 W McCabe St 65757 417-736-7000
Pam Holmes, prin. Fax 736-7018
Strafford MS 400/5-8
211 W McCabe St 65757 417-736-7000
Shane Pierce, prin. Fax 736-7019

Strasburg, Cass, Pop. 140
Strasburg C-3 SD 100/K-8
PO Box 244 64090 816-680-3333
Marvin Misemer, supt. Fax 865-3349
Strasburg S 100/K-8
PO Box 244 64090 816-680-3333
Marvin Misemer, prin. Fax 865-3349

Sturgeon, Boone, Pop. 913
Sturgeon R-V SD 400/K-12
210 W Patton St 65284 573-687-3515
Stan Ingraham, supt. Fax 687-2116
www.sturgeon.k12.mo.us/
Sturgeon ES 200/K-4
210 W Patton St 65284 573-687-3519
Shawn Schultz, prin. Fax 687-1226
Sturgeon MS 100/5-8
210 W Patton St 65284 573-687-2155
Jeff Carr, prin. Fax 687-1226

Success, Texas
Success R-VI SD 100/PK-8
10341 Highway 17 65570 417-967-2597
Randy Eagleman, supt. Fax 967-5774
Success S 100/PK-8
10341 Highway 17 65570 417-967-2597
Randy Eagleman, prin. Fax 967-5774

Sugar Creek, Jackson, Pop. 3,598
Independence SD 30
Supt. — See Independence
Sugar Creek ES 200/PK-5
11424 Gill St 64054 816-521-5460
Dr. Sharon Byrd, prin. Fax 254-3935

Sullivan, Franklin, Pop. 6,613
Spring Bluff R-XV SD 200/K-8
9374 Highway 185 63080 573-457-8302
Kay Bylo, supt. Fax 457-2070
Spring Bluff S 200/K-8
9374 Highway 185 63080 573-457-8302
Kay Bylo, prin. Fax 457-2070

Strain-Japan R-XVI SD 100/K-8
4640 Highway H 63080 573-627-3243
Dr. Marilyn Boeh, supt. Fax 627-3243
Strain-Japan S 100/K-8
4640 Highway H 63080 573-627-3243
Dr. Marilyn Boeh, prin. Fax 627-3243

Sullivan SD 2,100/PK-12
138 Taylor St 63080 573-468-5171
Dr. Mickie Shank, supt. Fax 468-7720
www.eagles.k12.mo.us
Sullivan ES 600/2-5
104 W Washington St 63080 573-468-5196
Gary Edler, prin. Fax 860-2436
Sullivan MS 400/6-8
1156 Elmont Rd 63080 573-468-5191
Jana Thornsberry, prin. Fax 860-2326
Sullivan PS 200/PK-1
1132 Elmont Rd 63080 573-468-5446
Cindy Carey, prin. Fax 468-6387

St. Anthony S 100/PK-8
119 W Springfield Rd 63080 573-468-4423
Sr. Joann Kuchler, prin. Fax 468-3428

Summersville, Texas, Pop. 555
Summersville R-II SD 400/K-12
PO Box 198 65571 417-932-4045
Mark Hampton, supt. Fax 932-5360
www.summersville.k12.mo.us/
Summersville ES 200/K-6
PO Box 198 65571 417-932-4613
Mary Holder, prin. Fax 932-5360

Sunrise Beach, Morgan, Pop. 389
Camdenton R-III SD
Supt. — See Camdenton
Hurricane Deck ES 100/PK-4
16594 N State Highway 5 65079 573-374-5369
Shawn Dandoy, prin. Fax 374-4416

Sweet Springs, Saline, Pop. 1,551
Sweet Springs R-VII SD 400/K-12
105 Main St 65351 660-335-4860
Boyd Jones, supt. Fax 335-4378
sweetsprings.k12.mo.us/
Sweet Springs ES 200/K-6
105 Main St 65351 660-335-6348
Donna Wright, prin. Fax 335-4378

Taneyville, Taney, Pop. 384
Taneyville R-II SD 200/K-8
302 Myrtle St 65759 417-546-5803
Tim Crawley, supt. Fax 546-6401
Taneyville S 200/K-8
302 Myrtle St 65759 417-546-5803
Scott Ewing, prin. Fax 546-6401

Tarkio, Atchison, Pop. 1,866
Tarkio R-I SD 400/K-12
312 S 11th St 64491 660-736-4161
Linda Blum, supt. Fax 736-4546
www.tarkio.k12.mo.us
Tarkio ES 200/K-6
1201 Pine St 64491 660-736-4177
Melanie Rucker, prin. Fax 736-9952

Thayer, Oregon, Pop. 2,171
Thayer R-II SD 700/PK-12
401 E Walnut St 65791 417-264-7261
Rod Priest, supt. Fax 264-4608
thayer.k12.mo.us/
Thayer ES 300/PK-6
365 E Walnut St 65791 417-264-3911
Gaylon Justus, prin. Fax 264-3956

Theodosia, Ozark, Pop. 253
Lutie R-VI SD 200/K-12
HC 4 Box 4775 65761 417-273-4274
Marty Witt, supt. Fax 273-4171
www.schoolweb.missouri.edu/lutie.k12.mo.us
Lutie ES 100/K-6
HC 4 Box 4775 65761 417-273-4274
Nancy Wray, prin. Fax 273-4171

Thornfield, Ozark
Thornfield R-I SD 100/K-8
HC 71 Box 102 65762 417-265-3212
Michael Wallace, supt. Fax 265-3729
Thornfield S 100/K-8
HC 71 Box 102 65762 417-265-3212
Michael Wallace, prin. Fax 265-3729

Tina, Carroll, Pop. 196
Tina-Avalon R-II SD 200/PK-12
11896 Highway 65 64682 660-622-4211
David Garber, supt. Fax 622-4210
tinaavalon.k12.mo.us/
Tina-Avalon ES 100/PK-6
11896 Highway 65 64682 660-622-4212
David Garber, prin. Fax 622-4210

Tipton, Moniteau, Pop. 3,142
Tipton R-VI SD 600/K-12
305 US Highway 50 E 65081 660-433-5520
Robert Brinkley, supt. Fax 433-5241
tipton.k12.mo.us/
Tipton ES 300/K-6
305 US Highway 50 E 65081 660-433-2213
Kelley Kohler, prin. Fax 433-2899

St. Andrew S 100/K-8
118 E Cooper St 65081 660-433-2232
Helen Franken, prin. Fax 433-5432

Town and Country, Saint Louis, Pop. 10,807

Churchill S 100/2-10
1021 Municipal Center Dr, 314-997-4343
Sandra Gilligan, dir. Fax 997-2760

Trenton, Grundy, Pop. 6,121
Pleasant View R-VI SD 100/PK-8
128 SE 20th St 64683 660-359-3438
Brian Robinson, supt. Fax 359-6925
Pleasant View S 100/PK-8
128 SE 20th St 64683 660-359-3438
Brian Robinson, prin. Fax 359-6925

Trenton R-IX SD 1,200/K-12
1607 Normal St 64683 660-359-3994
Becky Albrecht, supt. Fax 359-3995
www.trentonr9.k12.mo.us/
Rissler ES 400/K-4
804 W 4th Ter 64683 660-359-2228
Jennie Boon, prin. Fax 359-3778
Trenton MS 400/5-8
1417 Oklahoma Ave 64683 660-359-4328
Jamie Oram, prin. Fax 359-6554

Troy, Lincoln, Pop. 9,862
Troy R-III SD 4,200/PK-12
951 W College St 63379 636-462-6098
Terry Morrow, supt. Fax 528-2411
www.troy.k12.mo.us
Boone ES 500/K-5
1464 Boone St 63379 636-528-1560
Teri Stolle, prin. Fax 528-1563
Cuive Park ES K-5
100 Wieman Ln 63379 636-462-5218
Danielle Vogelsang, prin. Fax 462-5219
Early Childhood Education Center PK-PK
711 W College St 63379 636-528-3020
Kristin Clemons, prin. Fax 528-3021
Lincoln ES 400/K-5
1484 Boone St 63379 636-528-1990
Christina Garland, prin. Fax 528-1993
Main Street ES 500/K-5
51 Main St 63379 636-528-4809
Kristi Shinn, prin. Fax 528-2649
Troy MS 900/6-8
713 W College St 63379 636-528-7057
Jeff Swartz, prin. Fax 528-2199
Other Schools – See Hawk Point, Moscow Mills

First Baptist Christian Academy 100/K-7
1000 Elm Tree Rd 63379 636-528-5967
Karen Ryan, prin. Fax 528-8766
Sacred Heart S 300/K-8
110 Thompson Dr 63379 636-528-6684
Sr. Jeannette Fennewald, prin. Fax 528-3923

Tuscumbia, Miller, Pop. 223
Miller County R-III SD 200/K-12
PO Box 1 65082 573-369-2375
Dr. Jeff Koonce, supt. Fax 369-2833
www.tuscumbialions.com/
Miller County S 200/K-12
PO Box 1 65082 573-369-2375
Doug Kempker, prin. Fax 369-2833

Union, Franklin, Pop. 8,897
Union R-XI SD 2,700/K-12
PO Box 440 63084 636-583-8626
Dr. VeAnn Tilson, supt. Fax 583-2403
union.k12.mo.us
Central ES 500/K-3
PO Box 440 63084 636-583-3152
Deborah Stephens, prin. Fax 583-8173
Clark-Vitt ES 500/4-6
PO Box 440 63084 636-583-6997
Aaron Jones, prin. Fax 583-8517
Union MS 500/7-8
PO Box 440 63084 636-583-5855
Gary Menke, prin. Fax 583-6156
Other Schools – See Beaufort

Washington SD
Supt. — See Washington
Clearview ES 300/PK-6
1581 Clearview Rd 63084 636-231-2500
Dawn Hellebusch, prin. Fax 231-2505

Immaculate Conception S 300/PK-8
6 W State St 63084 636-583-2641
Thomas Stahlman, prin. Fax 583-3073

Union Star, DeKalb, Pop. 412
Union Star R-II SD 100/K-12
6132 NW State Route Z 64494 816-593-2294
Steve Thompson, supt. Fax 593-4427
star.k12.mo.us
Union Star ES 100/K-6
6132 NW State Route Z 64494 816-593-2294
Kim Hart, prin. Fax 593-4427

Unionville, Putnam, Pop. 1,981
Putnam County R-I SD 800/PK-12
803 S 20th St 63565 660-947-3361
Heath Halley, supt. Fax 947-2912
www.putnamcountyr1.net
Putnam County ES 400/PK-5
801 S 20th St 63565 660-947-2494
Marion Spase, prin. Fax 947-2912

Putnam County MS 200/6-8
802 S 18th St 63565 660-947-3237
Barbara Hodges, prin. Fax 947-2912

University City, Saint Louis, Pop. 37,170
University City SD
Supt. — See Saint Louis
Brittany Woods MS 600/7-8
8125 Groby Rd 63130 314-290-4280
Jamie Jordan, prin. Fax 997-1786
Delmar-Harvard ES 200/K-6
711 Kingsland Ave 63130 314-290-4390
Phyllis Fredericksen, prin. Fax 721-3206
Flynn Park ES 400/K-6
7220 Waterman Ave 63130 314-290-4420
DeAnn Blumberg, prin. Fax 727-8244
Goldstein Early Education Center 100/PK-PK
737 Kingsland Ave 63130 314-721-2965
Lucille Sibert, prin. Fax 721-2045
Hawthorne ES 300/K-6
1351 N Hanley Rd 63130 314-290-4200
Elliott Shostak, prin. Fax 862-5065
Jackson Park ES 300/K-6
7400 Balson Ave 63130 314-290-4450
Monica Hudson, prin. Fax 727-4478
Pershing ES 400/K-6
6761 Bartmer Ave 63130 314-290-4150
Herbert Buie, prin. Fax 725-3562

Christ the King S 200/PK-8
7324 Balson Ave 63130 314-725-5855
Susan Hooker, prin. Fax 725-5981
Our Lady of Lourdes S 300/K-8
7157 Northmoor Dr, 314-726-3352
Theresa Watson, prin. Fax 727-0503

Urbana, Hickory, Pop. 426
Hickory County R-I SD 800/K-12
RR 1 Box 838 65767 417-993-4241
Mark Beem, supt. Fax 993-4269
hickorycountyschools.net/
Skyline ES 300/K-4
RR 1 Box 838 65767 417-993-4225
Jason Pursley, prin. Fax 993-0216
Skyline MS 300/5-8
RR 1 Box 838 65767 417-993-4254
Daniel Roberts, prin. Fax 993-5948

Valley Park, Saint Louis, Pop. 6,405
Valley Park SD 1,000/PK-12
1 Main St 63088 636-923-3500
Dave Knes, supt. Fax 861-1002
www.vp.k12.mo.us
Valley Park ES 500/PK-5
1 Main St 63088 636-923-3500
Jan Humphrey, prin. Fax 225-4518
Valley Park MS 200/6-8
1 Main St 63088 636-923-3624
Dr. Tad Savage, prin. Fax 225-1529

Sacred Heart S 400/PK-8
12 Ann Ave 63088 636-225-3824
Joan Wojciechowski, prin. Fax 225-8941

Van Buren, Carter, Pop. 817
Van Buren R-I SD 500/PK-12
PO Box 550 63965 573-323-4281
Dr. Jeffrey Lindsey, supt. Fax 323-4297
schoolweb.missouri.edu/vanburen.k12.mo.us
Van Buren ES 200/PK-3
PO Box 550 63965 573-323-4266
Beverly Reed, prin. Fax 323-4537
Van Buren MS, PO Box 550 63965 100/4-8
Rick Johnson, prin. 573-333-4406

Vandalia, Audrain, Pop. 4,067
Van-Far R-I SD 600/K-12
2200 W US Highway 54 63382 573-594-6111
Chris Felmlee, supt. Fax 594-2878
www.vf.k12.mo.us
Van-Far ES 300/K-6
2122 Audrain Rd 557 63382 573-594-2731
Brian Meny, prin. Fax 594-2133

Verona, Lawrence, Pop. 720
Verona R-VII SD 400/K-12
PO Box 7 65769 417-498-2274
William Sweet, supt. Fax 498-6590
schoolweb.missouri.edu/verona.k12.mo.us/
Verona ES 200/K-6
PO Box 7 65769 417-498-6418
Jeannie Abeln, prin. Fax 498-6046

Versailles, Morgan, Pop. 2,662
Morgan County R-II SD 1,500/PK-12
913 W Newton St 65084 573-378-4231
Jeffery Carter, supt. Fax 378-5714
www.mcr2.k12.mo.us/
Morgan County ES 600/PK-5
913 W Newton St 65084 573-378-4272
Steve Rhine, prin. Fax 378-5164
Morgan County MS 400/6-8
913 W Newton St 65084 573-378-5432
Matt Unger, prin. Fax 378-6610
Other Schools – See Gravois Mills

Viburnum, Iron, Pop. 811
Iron County C-4 SD 500/K-12
PO Box 368 65566 573-244-5422
Doug Ruck, supt. Fax 244-3410
www.ironc4.k12.mo.us
Viburnum ES 300/K-6
PO Box 368 65566 573-244-5670
Deron Gibbs, prin. Fax 244-5767

Vienna, Maries, Pop. 635
Maries County R-I SD 600/PK-12
PO Box 218 65582 573-422-3304
Richard Spacek, supt. Fax 422-3185
www.mariesr1.k12.mo.us/
Vienna ES 300/PK-6
PO Box 218 65582 573-422-3365
Sherree Burkholder, prin. Fax 422-3185

Visitation S 100/K-8
PO Box 269 65582 573-422-3375
Linda Stuckenschneider, prin. Fax 422-3537

Villa Ridge, Franklin, Pop. 1,865
Meramec Valley R-III SD
Supt. — See Pacific
Coleman ES 500/K-5
4536 Coleman Rd 63089 636-742-2133
Cheryl Jackson, prin. Fax 742-2281

Crosspoint Christian S 100/PK-12
PO Box 100 63089 636-742-5380
Brian Brasher, admin. Fax 742-5917
St. John the Baptist S 200/PK-8
5579 Gildehaus Rd 63089 636-583-2392
Barbara Danner, prin. Fax 583-9341

Walker, Vernon, Pop. 279
Northeast Vernon County R-I SD 200/PK-12
216 E Leslie Ave 64790 417-465-2221
Charles Naas, supt. Fax 465-2388
www.nevcknights.org
Other Schools – See Schell City

Walnut Grove, Greene, Pop. 626
Walnut Grove R-V SD 300/K-12
PO Box 187 65770 417-788-2543
Dr. Aaron Cornman, supt. Fax 788-1254
www.wg.k12.mo.us/
Walnut Grove ES 100/K-6
PO Box 187 65770 417-788-2544
Christine Bowers, prin. Fax 788-1254

Wardell, Pemiscot, Pop. 262
North Pemiscot County R-I SD 300/K-12
PO Box 38 63879 573-628-3471
Terry Hamilton, supt. Fax 628-3472
Other Schools – See Portageville

Warrensburg, Johnson, Pop. 17,769
Warrensburg R-VI SD 3,300/PK-12
PO Box 638 64093 660-747-7823
Deborah Orr, supt. Fax 747-9615
warrensburg.k12.mo.us/r6/co.html
Reese S 50/PK-PK
301 W Market St 64093 660-747-2496
Chalice Jeffries, prin. Fax 747-2579
Ridge View ES 400/K-3
215 S Ridgeview Dr 64093 660-747-6013
Lorna Stanton, prin. Fax 747-3697
South East S 300/K-K
415 E Clark St 64093 660-747-9163
Nancy Rogers, prin. Fax 747-0250
Sterling ES 500/4-5
522 E Gay St 64093 660-747-7478
Monda Reynolds, prin. Fax 747-9400
Warren ES 400/1-3
105 S Maguire St 64093 660-747-7160
James Helmig, prin. Fax 747-8062
Warrensburg MS 700/6-8
640 E Gay St 64093 660-747-5612
Jim Elliott, prin. Fax 747-8779

Sacred Heart Preschool PK-PK
300 S Ridgeview Dr 64093 660-747-6154
Lesa Carroll, prin. Fax 747-7623

Warrenton, Warren, Pop. 6,612
Warren County R-III SD 2,300/K-12
302 Kuhl Ave 63383 636-456-6901
Dr. John Long, supt. Fax 456-7687
www.warrencor3.org
Black Hawk MS 700/6-8
300 Kuhl Ave 63383 636-456-6903
Stacy Ray, prin. Fax 456-1445
Boone ES 200/K-1
302 Kuhl Ave 63383 636-456-6905
Albert Slusser, prin. Fax 456-6900
Boone ES 500/4-5
836 South St 63383 636-456-6904
Rebecca Parks, prin. Fax 456-0481
Warrior Ridge ES 2-3
800 Warrior Ave 63383 636-456-6906
Bobbie Russell, prin. Fax 456-6996

Holy Rosary S 100/K-8
716 E Booneslick Rd 63383 636-456-3698
Michael Etter, prin. Fax 456-6181

Warsaw, Benton, Pop. 2,268
Warsaw R-IX SD 1,400/PK-12
PO Box 248 65355 660-438-7120
Brett Reese, supt. Fax 438-3749
www.warsaw.k12.mo.us/
Boise MS 300/6-8
PO Box 1750 65355 660-438-9079
Tim Thomas, prin. Fax 438-3749
Mercer K 100/K-K
PO Box 307 65355 660-438-7222
John Carleton, prin. Fax 438-5976
North ES 400/PK-PK, 1-
PO Box 307 65355 660-438-6260
John Carleton, prin. Fax 438-3817
Other Schools – See Edwards

Washburn, Barry, Pop. 468
Southwest R-V SD 900/PK-12
529 E Pineville Rd 65772 417-826-5410
Doug Lawyer, supt. Fax 826-5603
www.swr5.k12.mo.us
Southwest ES 300/PK-4
529 E Pineville Rd 65772 417-826-5411
Judy Randall, prin. Fax 826-5603
Southwest MS 300/5-8
529 E Pineville Rd 65772 417-826-5050
Beverly Bonner, prin. Fax 826-5603

Washington, Franklin, Pop. 14,136
Washington SD 4,200/PK-12
220 Locust St 63090 636-231-2000
Dr. Lori VanLeer, supt. Fax 239-3315
www.washington.k12.mo.us
Fifth Street ES 200/PK-6
100 W 5th St 63090 636-231-2550
Dr. Deborah Miles, prin. Fax 231-2555
South Point ES 500/PK-6
2300 Southbend Dr 63090 636-231-2700
Eric Lause, prin. Fax 231-2750
Washington MS 500/7-8
401 E 14th St 63090 636-231-2300
Ron Millheiser, prin. Fax 231-2305
Washington West ES 500/PK-6
1570 W 5th St 63090 636-390-9150
Kim Hunt, prin. Fax 390-9152
Other Schools – See Augusta, Labadie, Marthasville, New Haven, Union

---

Immanuel Lutheran S 300/PK-8
214 W 5th St 63090 636-239-1636
Alan Wunderlich, hdmstr. Fax 239-0589
Our Lady of Lourdes S 200/PK-8
950 Madison Ave 63090 636-239-5292
Margaret Burrus, prin. Fax 239-7682
St. Francis Borgia S 400/PK-8
225 Cedar St 63090 636-239-2590
Keith Branson, prin. Fax 239-3501
St. Gertrude S 400/PK-8
6520 Highway YY 63090 636-239-2347
Michael Newbanks, prin. Fax 239-3550

Waverly, Lafayette, Pop. 807
Santa Fe R-X SD
Supt. — See Alma
Santa Fe ES 200/K-6
703 W Walnut St 64096 660-493-2811
Amy Tieman, prin. Fax 493-2421

Waynesville, Pulaski, Pop. 3,511
Waynesville R-VI SD 5,000/PK-12
200 Fleetwood Dr 65583 573-774-6497
Dr. Judene Blackburn, supt. Fax 774-6491
waynesville.k12.mo.us
Waynesville East ES 600/PK-2
1501 State Route F 65583 573-774-6179
Debora Houchens, prin. Fax 774-2563
Waynesville MS 800/7-8
1001 Historic 66 W 65583 573-774-6198
Jess Grizzell, prin. Fax 774-6089
Other Schools – See Fort Leonard Wood, Saint Robert

Weaubleau, Hickory, Pop. 536
Weaubleau R-III SD 400/PK-12
509 N Center St 65774 417-428-3317
Jason Buckner, supt. Fax 428-3521
www.weaubleau.k12.mo.us/
Weaubleau ES 200/PK-6
509 N Center St 65774 417-428-3668
Eric Wilken, prin. Fax 428-3360

Webb City, Jasper, Pop. 10,764
Webb City R-VII SD 3,700/PK-12
411 N Madison St 64870 417-673-6000
Ronald Lankford, supt. Fax 673-6007
www.wccards.k12.mo.us/
Field ES 200/3-4
510 S Oronogo St 64870 417-673-6040
Tammy Thomas, prin. Fax 673-6041
Franklin ECC 100/PK-PK
404 Tracy St 64870 417-673-6070
Renee Goostree, prin. Fax 673-6007
James K 200/K-K
211 W Aylor St 64870 417-673-6075
Amanda Green, prin. Fax 673-6077
Truman ES 300/2-4
810 N Highway D 64870 417-673-6085
Kevin Cooper, prin. Fax 673-6087
Truman Primary Center K-1
800 N Highway D 64870 417-673-6055
Gail Sweet, prin.
Twain ES 200/3-4
1427 W Aylor St 64870 417-673-6050
Jan Shelley, prin. Fax 673-6051
Webb City JHS 600/7-8
807 W 1st St 64870 417-673-6030
Trey Moeller, prin. Fax 673-6037
Webb City MS 600/5-6
603 W Aylor St 64870 417-673-6045
Larry Shelley, prin. Fax 673-6048
Webster ES 400/1-2
700 N Main St 64870 417-673-6060
Bobbie Dykens, prin. Fax 673-6061
Other Schools – See Carterville

Webster Groves, Saint Louis, Pop. 22,896
Webster Groves SD 4,100/PK-12
400 E Lockwood Ave 63119 314-961-1233
Sarah Riss, supt. Fax 918-4023
www.webster.k12.mo.us
Avery ES 400/K-5
909 N Bompart Ave 63119 314-963-6425
Dr. Donald Furjes, prin. Fax 963-6490
Clark ES 300/K-5
9130 Big Bend Blvd 63119 314-963-6444
Bill Schiller, prin. Fax 963-6446
Early Childhood Education Center 100/PK-PK
222 W Cedar Ave 63119 314-968-5354
Marty Baker, dir. Fax 968-9259
Edgar Road ES 300/K-5
1131 Edgar Rd 63119 314-963-6472
Dr. Pam Retzlaff, prin. Fax 963-6477

Hudson ES 200/K-5
9825 Hudson Ave 63119 314-963-6466
Lisa Hilpert, prin. Fax 963-6478
Other Schools – See Saint Louis

Annunciation S 200/PK-8
16 W Glendale Rd 63119 314-961-7712
Cathy Davis, prin. Fax 961-2157
College S 300/PK-8
1 Newport Pl 63119 314-962-9355
Sheila Gurley, hdmstr. Fax 962-5078
Holy Redeemer S 200/PK-8
341 E Lockwood Ave 63119 314-962-8989
Wayne Schiefelbein, prin. Fax 962-3560
Mary Queen of Peace S 600/K-8
680 W Lockwood Ave 63119 314-961-2891
Michael Biggs, prin. Fax 961-7469

Weldon Spring, Saint Charles, Pop. 5,361
Francis Howell R-III SD
Supt. — See Saint Charles
Bryan MS 900/6-8
605 Independence Rd 63304 636-851-5800
Sue Hartman, prin. Fax 851-6208
Early Childhood Family Education Center 1,600/PK-PK
4810 Meadows Pkwy 63304 636-851-6000
Ellen Waterman, prin. Fax 851-6198
Howell MS 800/6-8
825 OFallon Rd 63304 636-851-4800
Amy Johnston, prin. Fax 851-4121
Independence ES 700/K-5
4800 Meadows Pkwy 63304 636-851-5900
Emily Allen, prin. Fax 851-6149

Wellington, Lafayette, Pop. 783
Wellington-Napoleon R-IX SD 500/K-12
PO Box 280 64097 816-934-2531
Jeff Ruskey, supt. Fax 934-8649
www.well-nap.k12.mo.us/
Wellington-Napoleon ES 200/K-6
PO Box 280 64097 816-240-2631
Melissa Register, prin. Fax 934-8649

Wellsville, Montgomery, Pop. 1,398
Wellsville Middletown R-I SD 500/PK-12
900 Burlington St 63384 573-684-2428
Duane Bennett, supt. Fax 684-2018
wmr1.k12.mo.us/
Wellsville ES 200/PK-6
900 Burlington St 63384 573-684-2047
Peter Nasir, prin. Fax 684-2018

Wentzville, Saint Charles, Pop. 17,988
Francis Howell R-III SD
Supt. — See Saint Charles
Boone ES 400/K-5
201 W Highway D 63385 636-851-4400
Kevin Armour, prin. Fax 851-4105

Wentzville R-IV SD 10,200/K-12
1 Campus Dr 63385 636-327-3800
Dr. Terry Adams, supt. Fax 327-8611
www.wentzville.k12.mo.us
Boone Trail ES 900/K-5
555 E Highway N 63385 636-327-3830
John Schulte, prin. Fax 327-3956
Heritage IS 800/3-5
601 Carr St 63385 636-327-3839
Laura Smith, prin. Fax 327-3957
Heritage PS 600/K-2
612 Blumhoff Ave 63385 636-327-3846
Geri Buss, prin. Fax 327-3958
Peine Ridge ES 400/K-5
1107 Peine Rd 63385 636-327-5110
Deanna Kitson, prin. Fax 327-5121
Wentzville MS 900/6-8
405 Campus Dr 63385 636-327-3815
Stacy Ray, prin. Fax 327-3954
Wentzville South MS 700/6-8
561 E Highway N 63385 636-327-3928
Scott Swift, prin. Fax 327-3955
Other Schools – See Lake Saint Louis, O Fallon

Immanuel Lutheran S 300/PK-8
317 W Pearce Blvd 63385 636-639-9887
Allison Dolak, prin. Fax 327-5054
St. Joseph S 100/PK-8
1410 Josephville Rd 63385 636-332-5672
Dwight Elmore, prin. Fax 332-8648
St. Patrick S 500/K-8
701 S Church St 63385 636-332-9913
Dianne Kelly, prin. Fax 332-4877
St. Theodore S 200/K-8
5059 Highway P 63385 636-639-1385
Joy Long, prin. Fax 639-1385

Weston, Platte, Pop. 1,644
West Platte County R-II SD 700/K-12
1103 Washington St 64098 816-640-2236
Kyle Stephenson, supt. Fax 386-2104
schoolweb.missouri.edu/wprii.k12.mo.us/index.htm
Central ES 300/K-6
1103 Washington St 64098 816-640-2811
Cecil Waddell, prin. Fax 386-5888

Westphalia, Osage, Pop. 331
Osage County R-III SD 800/PK-12
PO Box 37 65085 573-455-2375
Joe Scott, supt. Fax 455-9884
www.fatima.k12.mo.us/
Fatima ES 300/PK-6
PO Box 37 65085 573-455-2395
Sherry Bingaman, prin. Fax 455-9884

St. Joseph S 200/K-8
PO Box 205 65085 573-455-2339
James Skahan, prin. Fax 455-2287

West Plains, Howell, Pop. 11,348
Fairview R-XI SD 600/PK-8
4036 State Route K 65775 417-256-1063
Victor Williams, supt. Fax 256-8831
Fairview S 600/PK-8
4036 State Route K 65775 417-256-3868
Terrie Honeycutt, prin. Fax 256-0770

Glenwood R-VIII SD 300/PK-8
10286 State Route 17 65775 417-256-4849
Dr. R. A. Pendergrass, supt. Fax 257-2567
www.glenwood.k12.mo.us
Glenwood S 300/PK-8
10286 State Route 17 65775 417-256-4849
Karen Moffis, prin. Fax 257-2567

Howell Valley R-I SD 200/K-8
6461 State Route ZZ 65775 417-256-2268
Casus Baird, supt. Fax 257-2953
Howell Valley S 200/K-8
6461 State Route ZZ 65775 417-256-2268
Matthew Douglas, prin. Fax 256-5570

Junction Hill C-12 SD 200/K-8
8004 County Rd 3010 65775 417-256-4265
Heather Sexton, supt. Fax 256-3588
www.junctionhill.k12.mo.us
Junction Hill S 200/K-8
8004 County Rd 3010 65775 417-256-4265
Heather Sexton, prin. Fax 256-3588

Richards R-V SD 400/K-8
3461 County Road 1710 65775 417-256-5239
Jerry Premer, supt. Fax 256-3314
Richards ES 300/K-5
3461 County Road 1710 65775 417-256-5239
Melonie Bunn, prin. Fax 256-3314
Richards MS 100/6-8
3461 County Road 1710 65775 417-256-5239
Melonie Bunn, prin. Fax 256-3314

West Plains R-VII SD 2,400/K-12
613 W 1st St 65775 417-256-6150
Dr. Fred Czerwonka, supt. Fax 256-8616
wphs.k12.mo.us/
South Fork ES 100/K-6
3209 US Highway 160 65775 417-256-2836
Seth Huddleston, prin. Fax 255-1432
West Plains ES 500/K-4
1136 Allen St 65775 417-256-6150
Brad Owings, prin. Fax 256-2358
West Plains MS 500/5-8
730 E Olden St 65775 417-256-6150
Scott Smith, prin. Fax 256-8907

Faith Assembly Christian S 100/PK-12
PO Box 748 65775 417-256-1817
Roberta Jacobs, admin. Fax 257-2838

Wheatland, Hickory, Pop. 402
Wheatland R-II SD 300/K-12
PO Box 68 65779 417-282-6433
Robert McQuerter, supt. Fax 282-5733
www.wheatlandschool.com/
Wheatland R-II ES 100/K-6
PO Box 68 65779 417-282-5833
Artie Pearson, prin. Fax 282-5733

Wheaton, Barry, Pop. 732
Wheaton R-III SD 400/K-12
PO Box 249 64874 417-652-3914
Joe Layton, supt. Fax 652-7355
www.wheatonbulldogs.org/
Wheaton ES 200/K-6
PO Box 249 64874 417-652-7240
Eileen Ford, prin. Fax 652-7355

Whiteman AFB, Johnson, Pop. 4,174
Knob Noster R-VIII SD
Supt. — See Knob Noster
Whiteman AFB ES 400/PK-5
120 Houx Dr 65305 660-563-3028
Heidi Mackey, prin. Fax 563-3443

Wildwood, Saint Louis, Pop. 34,831

Hope Montessori Academy 200/PK-K
16554 Clayton Rd 63011 636-458-4540
Mary O'Boyle, prin. Fax 458-4541
Living Water Academy 100/PK-7
17770 Mueller Rd 63038 636-821-2308
Joe Brooks, admin. Fax 779-0011

Willard, Greene, Pop. 3,330
Willard R-II SD 4,000/K-12
460 Kime St 65781 417-742-2584
Dr. Kent Medlin, supt. Fax 742-2586
www.willard.k12.mo.us/
Willard East ES 400/K-4
518 Kime St 65781 417-742-4639
Melinda Miller, prin. Fax 685-0005
Willard IS 700/5-6
407 Farmer Rd 65781 417-742-4242
Tom Davis, prin. Fax 742-0139
Willard MS 700/7-8
205 S Miller Rd 65781 417-742-2588
Amy Sims, prin. Fax 742-3505
Willard North ES 400/K-4
409 Farmer Rd 65781 417-742-2597
Rhonda Bishop, prin. Fax 742-0139
Other Schools – See Springfield

Williamsburg, Callaway
North Callaway County R-I SD
Supt. — See Kingdom City
Williamsburg S 200/K-8
10500 Old US Highway 40 63388 573-254-3415
Nicole Kemp, prin. Fax 254-3859

Williamsville, Wayne, Pop. 373
Greenville R-II SD
Supt. — See Greenville
Williamsville ES 100/K-6
HC 1 Box 6M 63967 573-998-2313
Dolores Murray, prin. Fax 998-2339

Willow Springs, Howell, Pop. 2,116
Willow Springs R-IV SD 1,200/PK-12
215 W 4th St 65793 417-469-3260
Derrick Hutsell, supt. Fax 469-5127
www.willowspringsschool.com/
Willow Springs ES 500/PK-4
215 W 4th St 65793 417-469-2474
Donna Gossard, prin. Fax 469-4320
Willow Springs MS 400/5-8
215 W 4th St 65793 417-469-3211
Charlie Malam, prin. Fax 469-1229

Windsor, Henry, Pop. 3,265
Henry County R-I SD 700/PK-12
210 North St 65360 660-647-3533
Gordon Myers, supt. Fax 647-2711
henrycountyr1.k12.mo.us
Windsor ES 400/PK-6
501 S Main St 65360 660-647-5621
Brian Wishard, prin. Fax 647-5344

Winfield, Lincoln, Pop. 850
Winfield R-IV SD 1,500/K-12
701 W Elm St 63389 636-668-8188
Dr. Arnold Bell, supt. Fax 668-8641
www.winfield.k12.mo.us/
Winfield IS 400/3-5
701 W Elm St 63389 636-668-8300
Shanna Weber, prin. Fax 668-6056
Winfield MS 400/6-8
701 W Elm St 63389 636-668-8001
Jeff Haug, prin. Fax 668-6044
Winfield PS 200/K-2
701 W Elm St 63389 636-668-8195
Nancy Baker, prin. Fax 668-6259

Winona, Shannon, Pop. 1,317
Winona R-III SD 500/PK-12
PO Box 248 65588 573-325-8101
Scott Lindsey, supt. Fax 325-8447
www.winona.k12.mo.us
Winona S 400/PK-8
PO Box 248 65588 573-325-8101
Suzanne Bockman, prin. Fax 325-4345

Winston, Daviess, Pop. 253
Winston R-VI SD 200/PK-12
PO Box 38 64689 660-749-5456
Lisa Yost, supt. Fax 749-5432
Winston ES 100/PK-6
PO Box 38 64689 660-749-5459
Abby Smith, prin. Fax 749-5432

Wright City, Warren, Pop. 2,440
Wright City R-II SD 1,400/PK-12
90 Bell Rd 63390 636-745-7200
Chris Gaines, supt. Fax 745-3613
www.wrightcity.k12.mo.us/
Wright City ES 400/PK-4
100 Wildcat Dr 63390 636-745-7400
Juanita Deeker, prin. Fax 745-7411
Wright City MS 500/5-8
100 Bell Rd 63390 636-745-7300
Holly Redman, prin. Fax 745-7304

Liberty Christian Academy 100/K-12
PO Box 514 63390 636-745-0388
Dr. Rita Wildhaber, prin. Fax 745-0390

Zalma, Bollinger, Pop. 97
Zalma R-V SD 200/K-12
HC 2 Box 184 63787 573-722-5504
Darryl Sauer, supt. Fax 722-9870
Zalma ES 100/K-6
HC 2 Box 184 63787 573-722-3136
Linda Lemons, prin. Fax 722-9870

MONTANA

MONTANA OFFICE OF PUBLIC INSTRUCTION
PO Box 202501, Helena 59620-2501
Telephone 406-444-3095
Fax 406-444-2893
Website http://www.opi.state.mt.us

State Superintendent of Public Instruction Denise Juneau

MONTANA BOARD OF EDUCATION
PO Box 200601, Helena 59620-0601

Chairperson Patty Myers

COUNTY SUPERINTENDENTS OF SCHOOLS

Beaverhead County Office of Education
Emily Rebish, supt. 406-683-3737
2 S Pacific St, Dillon 59725 Fax 683-3769
Big Horn County Office of Education
Sandy Watts, supt. 406-665-9820
PO Box 908, Hardin 59034 Fax 665-9738
Blaine County Office of Education
Carol Elliot, supt. 406-357-3270
PO Box 819, Chinook 59523 Fax 357-2199
Broadwater County Office of Education
Rhonda Nelson, supt. 406-266-9215
515 Broadway St, Townsend 59644 Fax 266-3674
Carbon County Office of Education
Jerry Scott, supt. 406-446-1301
PO Box 116, Red Lodge 59068 Fax 446-9155
Carter County Office of Education
Marilyn Hutchinson, supt. 406-775-8721
PO Box 352, Ekalaka 59324 Fax 775-8703
Cascade County Office of Education
Jess Anderson, supt. 406-454-6776
121 4th St N Ste 1A Fax 454-6778
Great Falls 59401
Chouteau County Office of Education
Larry Stollfuss, supt. 406-622-3242
PO Box 459, Fort Benton 59442 Fax 622-3028
Custer County Office of Education
Doug Ellingson, supt. 406-874-3421
1010 Main St, Miles City 59301 Fax 874-3452
Daniels County Office of Education
Patricia McDonnell, supt. 406-487-2651
PO Box 67, Scobey 59263 Fax 487-5432
Dawson County Office of Education
Steve Engebretson, supt. 406-377-3963
207 W Bell St, Glendive 59330 Fax 377-2022
Deer Lodge County Office of Education
Michael O'Rourke, supt. 406-563-9178
800 Main St, Anaconda 59711 Fax 563-5476
Fallon County Office of Education
Brenda Wood, supt. 406-778-8182
PO Box 846, Baker 59313 Fax 778-2048
Fergus County Office of Education
Rhonda Long, supt. 406-535-3136
712 W Main St, Lewistown 59457 Fax 535-2819
Flathead County Office of Education
Marcia Sheffels, supt. 406-758-5720
800 S Main St, Kalispell 59901 Fax 758-5850
Gallatin County Office of Education
Mary Ellen Fitzgerald, supt. 406-582-3090
311 W Main St Rm 107 Fax 582-3093
Bozeman 59715
Garfield County Office of Education
Jessica McWilliams, supt. 406-557-6115
PO Box 28, Jordan 59337 Fax 557-6115
Glacier County Office of Education
Darryl Omsberg, supt. 406-873-2295
1210 E Main St, Cut Bank 59427 Fax 873-9103
Golden Valley County Office of Education
Jennae Mitchell, supt. 406-568-2342
107 Kemp St, Ryegate 59074 Fax 568-2428
Granite County Office of Education
Jo Ann Husbyn, supt. 406-859-7024
PO Box 520, Philipsburg 59858 Fax 859-3817
Hill County Office of Education
Shirley Isbell, supt. 406-265-5481
315 4th St, Havre 59501 Fax 265-5487
Jefferson County Office of Education
Garry Pace, supt. 406-225-4114
PO Box H, Boulder 59632 Fax 225-4149
Judith Basin County Office of Education
Julie Peevey, supt. 406-566-2277
PO Box 307, Stanford 59479 Fax 566-2211
Lake County Office of Education
Gale Decker, supt. 406-883-7262
106 4th Ave E, Polson 59860 Fax 883-7283
www.lakecounty-mt.org/schools
Lewis & Clark County Office of Education
Marsha Davis, supt. 406-447-8344
316 N Park Ave Ste 301 Fax 447-8370
Helena 59623
Liberty County Office of Education
Rachel Ghekiere, supt. 406-759-5216
PO Box 684, Chester 59522 Fax 759-5996
Lincoln County Office of Education
Ron Higgins, supt. 406-293-7781
418 Mineral Ave, Libby 59923 Fax 293-9794
Madison County Office of Education
Judi Osborn, supt. 406-843-4217
PO Box 247, Virginia City 59755 Fax 843-5261
McCone County Office of Education
Jackie Becker, supt. 406-485-3590
PO Box 180, Circle 59215 Fax 485-2689
Meagher County Office of Education
Helen Hanson, supt., PO Box 354 406-547-3612
White Sulphur Springs 59645 Fax 547-3388
Mineral County Office of Education
AnnaBelle Getz, supt. 406-822-3529
PO Box 100, Superior 59872 Fax 822-3579
Missoula County Office of Education
Rachel Vielleux, supt. 406-258-4860
438 W Spruce St, Missoula 59802 Fax 258-3973
Musselshell County Office of Education
Kathryn Pfister, supt. 406-323-1470
506 Main St, Roundup 59072 Fax 323-3303
Park County Office of Education
Ed Barich, supt., 414 E Callender St 406-222-4148
Livingston 59047 Fax 222-4199
Petroleum County Office of Education
Lisa Solf, supt. 406-429-5551
PO Box 226, Winnett 59087 Fax 429-6328
Phillips County Office of Education
Vivian Taylor, supt. 406-654-2010
PO Box 138, Malta 59538 Fax 654-1213
Pondera County Office of Education
Jo Stone, supt. 406-271-4055
20 4th Ave SW Ste 307 Fax 271-4070
Conrad 59425
Powder River County Office of Education
Charlotte Miller, supt. 406-436-2488
PO Box 718, Broadus 59317 Fax 436-2151
Powell County Office of Education
Jules Waber, supt. 406-846-3680
409 Missouri Ave Fax 846-2784
Deer Lodge 59722
Prairie County Office of Education
Jamie Smith, supt. 406-635-5577
PO Box 566, Terry 59349 Fax 635-5576
Ravalli County Office of Education
Ernie Jean, supt. 406-375-6522
215 S 4th St Ste B, Hamilton 59840 Fax 375-6523
Richland County Office of Education
Gail Anne Staffanson, supt. 406-433-1608
201 W Main St, Sidney 59270 Fax 433-3731
Roosevelt County Office of Education
Pat Stennes, supt. 406-653-6266
400 2nd Ave S, Wolf Point 59201 Fax 653-6203
Rosebud County Office of Education
Joby Parker, supt. 406-346-2537
PO Box 407, Forsyth 59327 Fax 346-7319
Sanders County Office of Education
Kathy McEldery, supt. 406-826-4288
PO Box 519, Plains 59859 Fax 826-4288
Sheridan County Office of Education
June Johnson, supt. 406-765-3403
100 W Laurel Ave Fax 765-2609
Plentywood 59254
Silver Bow County Office of Education
Edward Heard, supt. 406-497-6215
155 W Granite St, Butte 59701 Fax 497-6328
Stillwater County Office of Education
Judy Martin, supt. 406-322-8057
PO Box 1139, Columbus 59019 Fax 322-1118
Sweet Grass County Office of Education
Susan Metcalf, supt. 406-932-5147
PO Box 1310, Big Timber 59011 Fax 932-5112
Teton County Office of Education
Diane Inbody, supt. 406-466-2907
PO Box 610, Choteau 59422 Fax 466-2138
Toole County Office of Education
Boyd Jackson, supt. 406-424-8329
226 1st St S, Shelby 59474 Fax 424-8321
Treasure County Office of Education
Kathleen Thomas, supt. 406-342-5545
PO Box 429, Hysham 59038 Fax 342-5445
Valley County Office of Education
Lynne Nyquist, supt. 406-228-6226
501 Court Sq Ste 2 Fax 228-9027
Glasgow 59230
Wheatland County Office of Education
Susan Beley, supt. 406-632-4816
PO Box 637, Harlowton 59036 Fax 632-4880
Wibaux County Office of Education
Patricia Zinda, supt. 406-796-2481
PO Box 199, Wibaux 59353 Fax 796-2625
Yellowstone County Office of Education
A.J. Micheletti, supt. 406-256-6933
PO Box 35022, Billings 59107 Fax 256-6930
www.co.yellowstone.mt.us

PUBLIC, PRIVATE AND CATHOLIC ELEMENTARY SCHOOLS

Absarokee, Stillwater, Pop. 1,067
Absarokee SD 300/K-12
327 S Woodard Ave 59001 406-328-4583
Mike Reynolds, supt. Fax 328-4077
www.absarokee.k12.mt.us/
Absarokee ES 100/K-6
327 S Woodard Ave 59001 406-328-4581
Mike Reynolds, prin. Fax 328-4575
Absarokee MS 100/7-8
327 S Woodard Ave 59001 406-328-4583
Kevin Smith, prin. Fax 328-4077

Nye ESD 50/PK-6
PO Box 699 59001 406-328-6138
Nye ES, PO Box 699 59001 50/PK-6
Kathy Currie, lead tchr. 406-328-6138

Alberton, Mineral, Pop. 422
Alberton SD 200/K-12
PO Box 330 59820 406-722-4413
James Baldwin, supt. Fax 722-3040
Alberton ES 100/K-6
PO Box 330 59820 406-722-4413
Terry Falcon, prin. Fax 722-3040
Alberton MS 50/7-8
PO Box 330 59820 406-722-4413
Terry Falcon, prin. Fax 722-3040

Alder, Madison
Alder-Upper Ruby ESD 50/PK-8
PO Box 110 59710 406-842-5285
Fax 842-7149
Alder S 50/PK-8
PO Box 110 59710 406-842-5285
Lanaie Morgan, prin. Fax 842-7149

Anaconda, Deer Lodge, Pop. 10,093
Anaconda SD 1,000/PK-12
400 Main St 59711 406-563-6361
Dr. Tom Darnell, supt. Fax 563-6333
www.sd10.org
Dwyer ES 100/PK-2
1601 Tammany St 59711 406-563-7365
Stan Blaz, prin. Fax 563-5729
Lincoln ES 100/3-5
506 Chestnut St 59711 406-563-6141
Anthony Laughlin, prin. Fax 563-5639
Moodry JHS 300/6-8
3rd and Cherry 59711 406-563-6242
Sue Meredith, prin. Fax 563-5093

Arlee, Lake, Pop. 489
Arlee SD JT & 8 400/PK-12
PO Box 37 59821 406-726-3216
John Miller, supt. Fax 726-3940
www.arlee.k12.mt.us/
Arlee ES 200/PK-6
PO Box 37 59821 406-726-3216
Lisa Miller, prin. Fax 726-3940
Arlee JHS 100/7-8
PO Box 37 59821 406-726-3216
James Taylor, prin. Fax 726-3940

Ashland, Rosebud, Pop. 484
Ashland ESD 100/PK-8
PO Box 17 59003 406-784-2568
Matthew Kleinsasser, supt. Fax 784-6138

Ashland ES 50/PK-6
PO Box 17 59003 406-784-2568
Matthew Kleinsasser, prin. Fax 784-6138
Ashland MS 50/7-8
PO Box 17 59003 406-784-2568
Matthew Kleinsasser, prin. Fax 784-6138

St. Labre Catholic Academy 100/5-8
PO Box 216 59003 406-784-4500
Scott Gion, prin. Fax 784-4565
St. Labre Catholic ES 200/K-4
PO Box 216 59003 406-784-4500
Toni Wendt, prin. Fax 784-4565

Augusta, Lewis and Clark
Augusta SD 100/PK-12
PO Box 307 59410 406-562-3384
Pennie Hufford, supt. Fax 562-3898
Augusta ES 50/PK-6
PO Box 307 59410 406-562-3384
Pennie Hufford, prin. Fax 562-3898
Augusta MS 50/7-8
PO Box 307 59410 406-562-3384
Pennie Hufford, prin. Fax 562-3898

Avon, Powell
Avon ESD 50/K-8
PO Box 246 59713 406-492-6191
Fax 492-6191
Avon S 50/K-8
PO Box 246 59713 406-492-6191
Julie Shubin, lead tchr. Fax 492-6191

Babb, Glacier
Browning SD
Supt. — See Browning
Babb ES 59417 50/K-6
Laura Gervais, prin. 406-732-5539
Fax 732-9255

Bainville, Roosevelt, Pop. 151
Bainville SD 100/PK-12
PO Box 177 59212 406-769-2321
Brandy Hansen, supt. Fax 769-3291
www.bainvilleschool.k12.mt.us
Bainville ES 50/PK-6
PO Box 177 59212 406-769-2321
Rhiannon Beery, prin. Fax 769-3291
Bainville MS 50/7-8
PO Box 177 59212 406-769-2321
Rhiannon Beery, prin. Fax 769-3291

Baker, Fallon, Pop. 1,628
Baker SD 400/PK-12
PO Box 659 59313 406-778-3574
Donald Schillinger, supt. Fax 778-2785
www.baker.k12.mt.us/
Baker JHS 100/7-8
PO Box 659 59313 406-778-3329
David Breitbach, prin. Fax 778-2785
Lincoln ES 100/PK-3
PO Box 659 59313 406-778-2022
David Blake, prin. Fax 778-2445
Longfellow MS 50/4-6
PO Box 659 59313 406-778-2426
David Blake, prin. Fax 778-2445

Basin, Jefferson
Basin ESD 50/PK-6
PO Box 128 59631 406-225-3211
Basin ES, PO Box 128 59631 50/PK-6
Tammy Urich, lead tchr. 406-225-3211

Belfry, Carbon
Belfry SD 100/PK-12
PO Box 210 59008 406-664-3319
Les McCormick, supt. Fax 664-3274
Belfry ES 50/PK-6
PO Box 210 59008 406-664-3319
Les McCormick, prin. Fax 664-3274
Belfry MS 50/7-8
PO Box 210 59008 406-664-3319
Les McCormick, prin. Fax 664-3274

Belgrade, Gallatin, Pop. 7,033
Belgrade SD 2,900/PK-12
PO Box 166 59714 406-388-6951
Herbert Benz, supt. Fax 388-0122
www.belgrade.k12.mt.us
Belgrade IS 700/4-6
421 Spooner Rd 59714 406-388-3311
Janice Riebhoff, prin. Fax 388-1055
Belgrade MS 400/7-8
410 Triple Crown St 59714 406-388-1309
Julie Mickolio, prin. Fax 388-8894
Heck/Quaw ES 500/PK-3
308 N Broadway 59714 406-388-4104
Craig Cummings, prin. Fax 388-4577
Ridge View ES 400/K-3
117 Green Belt Dr 59714 406-388-4534
Mark Halgren, prin. Fax 388-4569

Pass Creek ESD 50/PK-8
3747 Pass Creek Rd 59714 406-388-6353
Fax 388-7978
Pass Creek S 50/PK-8
3747 Pass Creek Rd 59714 406-388-6353
Sid Rider, lead tchr.

Springhill ESD 50/PK-8
6020 Springhill Rd 59714 406-586-6485
Fax 586-6485
Springhill S 50/PK-8
6020 Springhill Rd 59714 406-586-6485
Linda Rice, lead tchr. Fax 586-6485

Belt, Cascade, Pop. 610
Belt SD 300/PK-12
PO Box 197 59412 406-277-3351
Calvin Johnson, supt. Fax 277-4466
www.beltschool.com
Belt ES 200/PK-6
PO Box 197 59412 406-277-3351
Kathleen Prody, prin. Fax 277-4466
Belt MS 100/7-8
PO Box 197 59412 406-277-3351
Kathleen Prody, prin. Fax 277-4466
Pleasant Valley S 50/K-8
PO Box 197 59412 406-277-3351
Kathleen Prody, prin. Fax 277-4466

Biddle, Powder River
Biddle ESD 50/PK-8
PO Box 397 59314 406-427-5290
Biddle S, PO Box 397 59314 50/PK-8
Tedi Jo Williams, lead tchr. 406-427-5290

Bigfork, Flathead
Bigfork SD 900/PK-12
PO Box 188 59911 406-837-7400
Russell Kinzer, supt. Fax 837-7407
bigfork.k12.mt.us/
Bigfork ES 400/PK-6
PO Box 188 59911 406-837-7412
Jackie Boshka, prin. Fax 837-7438
Bigfork MS 100/7-8
PO Box 188 59911 406-837-7412
Jackie Boshka, prin. Fax 837-7438

Swan Lake-Salmon Prairie ESD 50/PK-8
40224 Salmon Prairie Rd 59911 406-883-7262
Gale Decker, supt. Fax 883-7262
Salmon Prairie S 50/PK-8
744 Salmon Prairie Rd 59911 406-754-2245
Thomas Hubbard, lead tchr. Fax 754-2245

Swan River ESD 200/PK-8
1205 Swan Hwy 59911 406-837-4528
Fax 837-4055
swanriverschool.com
Swan River ES 100/PK-6
1205 Swan Hwy 59911 406-837-4528
Peter Loyda, prin. Fax 837-4055
Swan River MS 50/7-8
1205 Swan Hwy 59911 406-837-4528
Peter Loyda, prin. Fax 837-4055

Big Sandy, Chouteau, Pop. 643
Big Sandy SD 200/PK-12
PO Box 570 59520 406-378-2501
Sonny Broesder, supt. Fax 378-2275
Big Sandy JHS 50/7-8
PO Box 570 59520 406-378-2502
Sonny Broesder, prin. Fax 378-2275
Miley ES 100/PK-6
PO Box 570 59520 406-378-2406
Sonny Broesder, prin. Fax 378-2255

Warrick ESD, 29200 Warrick Rd 59520 50/PK-8
Larry Stollfuss, supt. 406-622-3242
Warrick S, 29200 Warrick Rd 59520 50/PK-8
Samaria Kirby, lead tchr. 406-386-2285

Big Timber, Sweet Grass, Pop. 1,725
Big Timber ESD 400/PK-8
PO Box 887 59011 406-932-5939
Gary Harkness, supt. Fax 932-4069
www.bigtimber-gs.k12.mt.us
Big Timber ES 300/PK-6
PO Box 887 59011 406-932-5939
Mark Ketcham, prin. Fax 932-4069
Big Timber MS 100/7-8
PO Box 887 59011 406-932-5939
Mark Ketcham, prin. Fax 932-4069

Mc Leod ESD 50/PK-8
346 Otter Creek Rd 59011 406-932-6164
Fax 932-6164

Other Schools – See Mc Leod

Billings, Yellowstone, Pop. 98,721
Billings SD 15,500/PK-12
415 N 30th St 59101 406-281-5065
Jack Copps, supt. Fax 281-6179
www.billingsschools.org/
Alkali Creek ES 400/PK-6
681 Alkali Creek Rd 59105 406-281-6200
Julia Mattson, prin. Fax 254-0162
Arrowhead ES 400/PK-6
2510 38th St W 59102 406-281-6201
Robin Bedford, prin. Fax 656-0169
Beartooth ES PK-6
1345 Elaine St 59105 406-281-6202
Cheryl Malia-McCall, prin. Fax 254-1123
Bench ES 400/PK-6
505 Milton Rd 59105 406-281-6203
John English, prin. Fax 254-1130
Big Sky ES 400/PK-6
3231 Granger Ave E 59102 406-281-6204
Sandie Mammenga, prin. Fax 656-0247
Bitterroot ES 400/PK-6
1801 Bench Blvd 59105 406-281-6205
Greg Senitte, prin. Fax 254-1155
Boulder ES 400/PK-6
2202 32nd St W 59102 406-281-6206
Jay Lemelin, prin. Fax 656-0287
Broadwater ES 300/PK-6
415 Broadwater Ave 59101 406-281-6207
Lee Kvilhaug, prin. Fax 254-0057
Burlington ES 300/PK-6
2135 Lewis Ave 59102 406-281-6208
Kyra Gaskill, prin. Fax 656-0357
Castle Rock MS 700/7-8
1441 Governors Blvd 59105 406-281-5800
Shaun Harrington, prin. Fax 254-1116
Central Heights ES 300/PK-6
120 Lexington Dr 59102 406-281-6209
Bob Barone, prin. Fax 656-0878
Eagle Cliffs ES 500/PK-6
1201 Kootenai Ave 59105 406-281-6210
Lorrie Wolverton, prin. Fax 254-1312
Highland ES 300/PK-6
729 Parkhill Dr 59102 406-281-6211
Carol Forney, prin. Fax 254-1412
James MS 500/7-8
1200 30th St W 59102 406-281-6100
Lance Orner, prin. Fax 281-6178
Lewis & Clark MS 600/7-8
1315 Lewis Ave 59102 406-281-5900
Steve Pomroy, prin. Fax 281-6177
McKinley ES 300/PK-6
820 N 31st St 59101 406-281-6212
Bert Reyes, prin. Fax 254-1225
Meadowlark ES 500/PK-6
221 29th St W 59102 406-281-6213
Kevin Croff, prin. Fax 656-0359
Miles Avenue ES 300/PK-6
1601 Miles Ave 59102 406-281-6214
Dr. Shanna Henry, prin. Fax 656-0625
Newman ES 300/PK-6
605 S Billings Blvd 59101 406-281-6215
Kim Anthony, prin. Fax 254-1675
Orchard ES 300/PK-6
120 Jackson St 59101 406-281-6216
Mark Venner, prin. Fax 254-1723
Poly Drive ES 300/PK-6
2410 Poly Dr 59102 406-281-6217
Pam Meier, prin. Fax 656-0649
Ponderosa ES 400/PK-6
4188 King Ave E 59101 406-281-6218
Lori Booke, prin. Fax 254-1825
Riverside MS 500/7-8
3700 Madison Ave 59101 406-281-6000
Rusty Martin, prin. Fax 255-3534
Rose Park ES 300/PK-6
1812 19th St W 59102 406-281-6219
Linda Bakken, prin. Fax 254-1404
Sandstone ES 400/PK-6
1440 Nutter Blvd 59105 406-281-6220
Stacy Lemelin, prin. Fax 254-1965
Washington ES 200/PK-6
1044 Cook Ave 59102 406-281-6221
Karen Ziegler, prin. Fax 254-1287

Blue Creek ESD 200/PK-6
3652 Blue Creek Rd 59101 406-259-0653
Dan Nelsen, supt. Fax 259-9378
www.bluecreek.k12.mt.us
Blue Creek ES 200/PK-6
3652 Blue Creek Rd 59101 406-259-0653
Cathi Rude, prin. Fax 259-9378

Canyon Creek ESD 200/PK-8
3139 Duck Creek Rd 59101 406-656-4471
Stephanie Long, supt. Fax 655-1031
www.canyoncreek.k12.mt.us/
Canyon Creek ES 100/PK-6
3139 Duck Creek Rd 59101 406-656-4471
Stephanie Long, prin. Fax 655-1031
Canyon Creek MS 50/7-8
3139 Duck Creek Rd 59101 406-656-4471
Stephanie Long, prin. Fax 655-1031

Elder Grove ESD 300/K-8
1532 S 64th St W 59106 406-656-2893
Tobin Novasio, supt. Fax 651-4346
Elder Grove ES 300/K-6
1532 S 64th St W 59106 406-656-2893
Monica Pugh, prin. Fax 651-4346
Elder Grove MS 100/7-8
1532 S 64th St W 59106 406-656-2893
Monica Pugh, prin. Fax 651-1987

Elysian ESD 100/PK-8
6416 Elysian Rd 59101 406-656-4101
Brenda Koch, supt. Fax 656-9941
Elysian ES 100/PK-6
6416 Elysian Rd 59101 406-656-4101
Brenda Koch, prin. Fax 656-9941
Elysian MS 50/7-8
6416 Elysian Rd 59101 406-656-4101
Brenda Koch, prin. Fax 656-9941

Independent ESD 300/PK-6
2907 Roundup Rd 59105 406-259-8109
Bill Laurent, supt. Fax 259-8541
Independent ES 300/PK-6
2907 Roundup Rd 59105 406-259-8109
Bill Laurent, prin. Fax 259-8541

Lockwood ESD 1,200/PK-8
1932 US Highway 87 E 59101 406-252-6022
Eileen Johnson, supt. Fax 259-2502
www.lockwood.k12.mt.us/
Lockwood IS 400/3-5
1932 US Highway 87 E 59101 406-248-3239
Dave Deboer, prin. Fax 245-8300
Lockwood MS 400/6-8
1932 US Highway 87 E 59101 406-259-0154
Mike Sullivan, prin. Fax 259-3832
Lockwood PS 400/PK-2
1932 US Highway 87 E 59101 406-252-2776
Michael Bowman, prin. Fax 256-0373

Morin ESD 50/PK-6
8824 Pryor Rd 59101 406-259-6093
Fax 259-6093
Morin ES 50/PK-6
8824 Pryor Rd 59101 406-259-6093
Tia Schacht, lead tchr. Fax 259-6093

Pioneer ESD 100/PK-6
1937 Dover Rd 59105 406-373-5357
Fax 373-5357
Pioneer ES 100/PK-6
1937 Dover Rd 59105 406-373-5357
Allison Nys, lead tchr. Fax 373-5357

Yellowstone Academy ESD 100/PK-8
1750 Ray of Hope Ln 59106 406-656-2198
Ed Zabrocki, supt. Fax 656-2328
Yellowstone Academy S 100/PK-8
1750 Ray of Hope Ln 59106 406-656-2198
Jim Snyder, prin. Fax 656-2328

Adelphi Christian Academy 100/PK-12
3212 1st Ave S 59101 406-294-9144
Patrick Deveney, hdmstr. Fax 294-9145
Billings Christian S 100/K-12
4519 Grand Ave 59106 406-656-9484
Paul Waggoner, prin. Fax 655-4880
Central Acres SDA S 50/1-8
3204 Broadwater Ave 59102 406-652-1799

St. Francis IS 200/3-5
1734 Yellowstone Ave 59102 406-656-2300
Chris Read, prin. Fax 656-2301
St. Francis PS 200/PK-2
511 Custer Ave 59101 406-259-6421
Karen Petermann, prin. Fax 245-0176
St. Francis Upper S 200/6-8
205 N 32nd St 59101 406-259-5037
Jim Stanton, prin. Fax 259-7981
Shiloh Christian Academy 50/PK-K
328 S Shiloh Rd 59106 406-652-3161
Trinity Lutheran S 200/K-8
2802 Belvedere Dr 59102 406-656-1021
Richard Thomas, prin. Fax 656-1936

Birney, Rosebud
Birney ESD 50/PK-8
PO Box 521 59012 406-984-6247
Fax 984-6247
Birney S 50/PK-8
PO Box 521 59012 406-984-6247
Fax 984-6247

Bloomfield, Dawson
Bloomfield ESD 50/PK-8
2285 Fas 470 59315 406-583-7575
Bloomfield S 50/PK-8
2285 Fas 470 59315 406-583-7575

Bonner, Missoula, Pop. 1,669
Bonner ESD 400/PK-8
PO Box 1004 59823 406-258-6151
Doug Ardiana, supt. Fax 258-6153
www.bonner.k12.mt.us
Bonner ES 300/PK-6
PO Box 1004 59823 406-258-6151
Brian Bessett, prin. Fax 258-6153
Bonner MS 100/7-8
PO Box 1004 59823 406-258-6151
Doug Ardiana, prin. Fax 258-6153

Potomac ESD 100/PK-8
29750 Potomac Rd 59823 406-244-5581
Fax 244-5840
www.blackfoot.net/~potomacschool
Potomac ES 100/PK-6
29750 Potomac Rd 59823 406-244-5581
Kim Kingston, lead tchr. Fax 251-7243
Potomac MS 50/7-8
29750 Potomac Rd 59823 406-244-5581
Kim Kingston, lead tchr. Fax 251-7243

Boulder, Jefferson, Pop. 1,436
Boulder ESD 200/PK-8
PO Box 838 59632 406-225-3740
Robert Klein, supt. Fax 225-3289
www.bgs.k12.mt.us/
Boulder ES 100/PK-6
PO Box 838 59632 406-225-3316
Dustin Shipman, prin. Fax 655-3140
Boulder MS 100/7-8
PO Box 838 59632 406-225-3316
Dustin Shipman, prin. Fax 225-9218

Box Elder, Hill
Box Elder SD 400/PK-12
PO Box 205 59521 406-352-4195
Robert Heppner, supt. Fax 352-3830
Box Elder ES 200/PK-6
PO Box 205 59521 406-352-3330
Dave Nelson, prin. Fax 352-3225
Box Elder MS 100/7-8
PO Box 205 59521 406-352-4195
Darrin Hannum, prin. Fax 352-3830

Rocky Boy SD 500/PK-12
235 Black Prarie St 59521 406-395-4291
Voyd St. Pierre, supt. Fax 395-4829
www.rockyboy.k12.mt.us
Rocky Boy ES 300/PK-6
235 Black Prarie St 59521 406-395-4474
Josephine Corcoran, prin. Fax 395-4829
Rocky Boy MS 100/7-8
235 Black Prarie St 59521 406-395-4270
James Capps, prin. Fax 395-4829

Bozeman, Gallatin, Pop. 33,535
Anderson ESD 200/PK-8
10040 Cottonwood Rd 59718 406-587-1305
Terry Vanderpan, supt. Fax 587-2501
www.andersonmt.org/
Anderson ES 200/PK-6
10040 Cottonwood Rd 59718 406-587-1305
Terry Vanderpan, prin. Fax 587-2501
Anderson MS 50/7-8
10040 Cottonwood Rd 59718 406-587-1305
Terry Vanderpan, prin. Fax 587-2501

Bozeman SD 5,400/PK-12
PO Box 520 59771 406-522-6001
Kirk Miller Ed.D., supt. Fax 522-6065
www.bozeman.k12.mt.us/
Chief Joseph MS 500/6-8
4255 Kimberwicke St 59718 406-522-6300
Diane Cashell, prin. Fax 522-6306
Dickinson ES 500/K-5
2435 Annie St 59718 406-522-6650
Sharon Navas, prin. Fax 522-6640
Hawthorne ES 300/K-5
114 N Rouse Ave 59715 406-522-6700
Robin Miller, prin. Fax 522-6730
Irving ES 300/K-5
611 S 8th Ave 59715 406-522-6600
James Bruggeman, prin. Fax 522-6690
Longfellow ES 300/K-5
516 S Tracy Ave 59715 406-522-6150
Randy Walthall, prin. Fax 522-6180
Morning Star ES 600/PK-5
830 W Arnold St 59715 406-522-6500
Nonnie Hughes, prin. Fax 522-6550
Sacajawea MS 700/6-8
3525 S 3rd Rd 59715 406-522-6470
Gordon Grissom, prin. Fax 522-6474
Whittier ES 300/PK-5
511 N 5th Ave 59715 406-522-6750
Jerry Bauer, prin. Fax 522-6780

Cottonwood ESD 50/K-8
13233 Cottonwood Rd 59718 406-763-4903
Cottonwood S 50/K-8
13233 Cottonwood Rd 59718 406-763-4903

LaMotte ESD 100/PK-8
841 Bear Canyon Rd 59715 406-586-2838
Fax 586-8626
LaMotte ES 100/PK-6
841 Bear Canyon Rd 59715 406-586-2838
LeeAnn Burke, prin. Fax 586-8626
LaMotte MS 50/7-8
841 Bear Canyon Rd 59715 406-586-2838
LeeAnn Burke, prin. Fax 585-8626

Malmborg ESD 50/PK-8
375 Jackson Creek Rd 59715 406-586-2759
Fax 586-5735
Malmborg S 50/PK-8
375 Jackson Creek Rd 59715 406-586-2759
Linda Trousil, lead tchr. Fax 586-5735

Monforton ESD 200/PK-8
6001 Monforton School Rd 59718 406-586-1557
Lynne Scalia, supt. Fax 587-5049
Monforton IS 100/3-6
6001 Monforton School Rd 59718 406-586-1557
Lynne Scalia, prin. Fax 587-5049
Monforton MS 50/7-8
6001 Monforton School Rd 59718 406-586-1557
Lynne Scalia, prin. Fax 587-5049
Monforton PS 50/PK-2
6001 Monforton School Rd 59718 406-586-1557
Lynne Scalia, prin. Fax 587-5049

Headwaters Academy 50/6-8
418 W Garfield St 59715 406-585-9997
Tim McWilliams, hdmstr. Fax 585-9992
Heritage Christian S 200/PK-12
4310 Durston Rd 59718 406-587-9311
Mathew Henry, admin. Fax 587-1838
Learning Circle Montessori S 100/K-6
3001 W Villard St 59718 406-585-3778
Danielle Stern, prin. Fax 522-9477
Middle Creek Montessori S 50/K-6
1572 Cobb Hill Rd 59718 406-587-3817
Nancy McNabb, prin. Fax 587-9698
Mount Ellis SDA S 50/K-8
3835 Bozeman Trail Rd 59715 406-587-5430
Petra Academy 100/K-12
100 Discovery Dr 59718 406-582-8165
Todd Hicks, hdmstr. Fax 556-8777

Brady, Pondera
Knees ESD 50/PK-8
21377 Brady Rd E 59416 406-627-2304
Knees S, 23831 Brady Rd E 59416 50/PK-8
Leah Conyers, lead tchr. 406-627-2304

Bridger, Carbon, Pop. 752
Bridger SD 200/PK-12
PO Box 467 59014 406-662-3533
John Ballard, supt. Fax 662-3076
www.bridger.k12.mt.us
Bridger ES 100/PK-6
PO Box 467 59014 406-662-3588
John Ballard, prin. Fax 662-3520
Bridger MS 50/7-8
PO Box 467 59014 406-662-3588
John Ballard, prin. Fax 662-3520

Broadus, Powder River, Pop. 445
Broadus SD 300/PK-12
PO Box 500 59317 406-436-2658
Richard Cameron, supt. Fax 436-2660
www.broadus.net/
Broadus ES 200/PK-6
PO Box 500 59317 406-436-2637
Rosalie Lundby, prin. Fax 436-2660
Broadus MS 100/7-8
PO Box 500 59317 406-436-2658
Jim Hansen, prin. Fax 436-2660

Broadview, Yellowstone, Pop. 150
Broadview SD 200/PK-12
PO Box 147 59015 406-667-2337
Rob Osborne, supt. Fax 667-2195
www.broadview.k12.mt.us/
Broadview ES 100/PK-6
PO Box 147 59015 406-667-2337
Rob Osborne, prin. Fax 667-2195
Broadview MS 50/7-8
PO Box 147 59015 406-667-2337
Rob Osborne, prin. Fax 667-2195

Brockton, Roosevelt, Pop. 243
Brockton SD 200/PK-12
PO Box 198 59213 406-786-3195
Richard Whitesell, supt. Fax 786-3121
www.brockton.k12.mt.us/
Gilligan ES 100/PK-6
PO Box 198 59213 406-786-3318
Fax 786-3400
Gilligan MS 50/7-8
PO Box 198 59213 406-786-3311
Fax 786-3377

Browning, Glacier, Pop. 1,078
Browning SD 1,900/PK-12
PO Box 610 59417 406-338-2715
Mary Johnson, supt. Fax 338-3200
www.bps.k12.mt.us/
Bergan ES 300/PK-1
PO Box 629 59417 406-338-2715
Chuck Pilling, prin. Fax 338-5607
Browning MS 200/7-8
PO Box 610 59417 406-338-2725
Julie Hayes, prin. Fax 338-5320
Chattin ES 300/2-3
PO Box 689 59417 406-338-2758
Wilma Mad Plume, prin. Fax 338-5625
Napi ES 400/4-6
PO Box 649 59417 406-338-2735
Dianne Magee, prin. Fax 338-3350
Other Schools – See Babb, Cut Bank

De LaSalle Blackfeet S 100/5-8
PO Box 1489 59417 406-338-5290
Br. Paul Ackerman, contact Fax 338-7900

Brusett, Garfield
Pine Grove ESD 50/PK-8
3646 Brusett Rd 59318 406-557-6115
Jessica McWilliams, supt.
Pine Grove S 50/PK-8
9 Seven Blackfoot Rd 59318 406-557-2782
Cindy Murphy, prin.

Butte, Silver Bow, Pop. 32,716
Butte SD 4,500/PK-12
111 N Montana St 59701 406-533-2500
Dr. Linda Reksten, supt. Fax 533-2525
www.butte.k12.mt.us
East MS 700/7-8
2600 Grand Ave 59701 406-533-2600
Larry Driscoll, prin. Fax 496-2670
Emerson ES 400/PK-6
1924 Phillips Ave 59701 406-533-2800
Evonne Holman, prin. Fax 533-2818
Hillcrest ES 400/K-6
3000 Continental Dr 59701 406-533-2850
Susan Johnson, prin. Fax 533-2858
Kennedy ES 300/K-6
1101 N Emmett Ave 59701 406-533-2450
Jennifer Luoma, prin. Fax 533-2457
Leary ES 300/K-6
1301 Four Mile View Rd 59701 406-533-2550
Jim O'Neill, prin. Fax 494-1216
West ES 400/K-6
1000 Steele St 59701 406-533-2700
Pat Kissell, prin. Fax 533-2717
Whittier ES 400/K-6
3000 Sherman Ave 59701 406-533-2890
Christy Johnson, prin. Fax 533-2929

Butte Central Catholic S 400/PK-8
100 Delaware Ave 59701 406-782-4500
Carolyn Trudnowski, prin. Fax 723-4845
Capstone Christian Academy 50/PK-12
PO Box 3074 59702 406-782-7777
Healey Apted, prin. Fax 782-7777
Silver Bow Montessori S 50/K-6
1800 Sunset Rd 59701 406-494-1033
Don Kronenberger, prin.

Bynum, Teton
Bynum ESD 50/K-8
PO Box 766 59419 406-469-2373
Fax 469-2253
Bynum S 50/K-8
PO Box 766 59419 406-469-2373
Susan Luinstra, lead tchr. Fax 469-2253

Canyon Creek, Lewis and Clark
Trinity ESD 50/PK-6
PO Box 523 59633 406-368-2230
Fax 368-2250
Trinity ES 50/PK-6
PO Box 523 59633 406-368-2230
Katrina Chaney, lead tchr. Fax 368-2250

Cardwell, Jefferson
Cardwell ESD 50/PK-8
80 MT Highway 359 59721 406-287-3321
Fax 287-3321
Cardwell S 50/PK-8
80 MT Highway 359 59721 406-287-3321
Nancy Veca, lead tchr. Fax 287-3321

Carter, Chouteau
Carter ESD 50/PK-8
PO Box 159 59420 406-734-5387
Carter S, PO Box 159 59420 50/PK-8
Marjorie Scott, lead tchr. 406-734-5387

Cascade, Cascade, Pop. 798
Cascade SD 400/PK-12
PO Box 529 59421 406-468-9383
June Sprout, supt. Fax 468-2212
www.cascade.k12.mt.us
Cascade ES 200/PK-6
PO Box 529 59421 406-468-2671
LouAnn Gay, prin. Fax 468-2212
Cascade JHS 100/7-8
PO Box 529 59421 406-468-2267
Dave Malloy, prin. Fax 468-2212

Charlo, Lake, Pop. 358
Charlo SD 300/PK-12
PO Box 10 59824 406-644-2207
Bill Colter, supt. Fax 644-2400
www.charlo.k12.mt.us/
Charlo ES 200/PK-6
PO Box 10 59824 406-644-2207
Clair Rasmussen, prin. Fax 644-2400
Charlo MS 100/7-8
PO Box 10 59824 406-644-2206
Clair Rasmussen, prin. Fax 644-2401

Chester, Liberty, Pop. 811
Chester-Joplin-Inverness SD 300/PK-12
PO Box 550 59522 406-759-5108
Calvin Moore, supt. Fax 759-7867
Chester-Joplin-Inverness ES 100/PK-6
PO Box 550 59522 406-759-5477
Pam Graff, prin. Fax 759-5867
Chester-Joplin-Inverness MS 50/7-8
PO Box 550 59522 406-759-5108
Pam Graff, prin. Fax 759-5867
Riverview S 50/K-8
PO Box 550 59522 406-759-5477
Pam Graff, prin. Fax 759-5867
Sage Creek S 50/K-8
PO Box 550 59522 406-759-5477
Pam Graff, prin. Fax 759-5867

Chinook, Blaine, Pop. 1,299
Bear Paw ESD 50/PK-8
29815 Clear Creek Rd 59523 406-395-4436

Bear Paw S 50/PK-8
29815 Clear Creek Rd 59523 406-395-4436
Haven Linder, lead tchr.

Chinook SD 400/PK-12
PO Box 1059 59523 406-357-2628
Jay Eslick, supt. Fax 357-2238
www.chinookschools.org
Chinook MS 100/7-8
PO Box 1059 59523 406-357-2237
Matt Molyneaux, prin. Fax 357-2238
Meadowlark ES 200/PK-6
PO Box 1059 59523 406-357-2033
Rita Surber, prin. Fax 357-3146
Other Schools – See Havre

Cleveland ESD 50/K-8
22820 Cleveland Rd 59523 406-357-3689
Cleveland S 50/K-8
9785 Peoples Creek Rd 59523 406-357-2018
Emily Evans, lead tchr.

Zurich ESD 50/PK-8
7405 Paradise Valley Rd 59523 406-357-4164
Fax 357-4299
Other Schools – See Zurich

Choteau, Teton, Pop. 1,738
Choteau SD 400/PK-12
204 7th Ave NW 59422 406-466-5303
Kevin St. John, supt. Fax 466-5305
Choteau ES 200/PK-6
102 7th Ave NW 59422 406-466-5364
Chuck Gameon, prin. Fax 466-5365
Choteau MS 100/7-8
204 7th Ave NW 59422 406-466-5303
Nate Achenbach, prin. Fax 466-5305

Circle, McCone, Pop. 584
Circle SD 200/K-12
PO Box 99 59215 406-485-2545
Mike Radakovich, supt. Fax 485-2332
Bo Peep PS 100/K-3
PO Box 99 59215 406-485-2140
Mike Radakovich, prin. Fax 485-2332
Redwater IS 100/4-6
PO Box 99 59215 406-485-2140
Mike Radakovich, prin. Fax 485-2332
Redwater MS 100/7-8
PO Box 99 59215 406-485-2140
Helen Murphy, prin. Fax 485-2332

Clancy, Jefferson
Clancy ESD 300/PK-8
PO Box 209 59634 406-933-5575
Robert Klein, supt. Fax 933-5715
www.clancy.k12.mt.us/
Clancy ES 200/PK-6
PO Box 209 59634 406-933-5575
Bruce Dunkle, prin. Fax 933-5715
Clancy MS 100/7-8
PO Box 209 59634 406-933-5575
Bruce Dunkle, prin. Fax 933-5715

Montana City ESD 400/PK-8
11 McClellan Creek Rd 59634 406-442-6779
Tony Kloker, supt. Fax 443-8875
Montana City ES 300/PK-5
11 McClellan Creek Rd 59634 406-442-6779
Tony Kloker, prin. Fax 443-8875
Montana City MS 100/6-8
11 McClellan Creek Rd 59634 406-442-6779
Kathy Kidder, prin. Fax 443-8875

Clinton, Missoula
Clinton ESD 200/K-8
PO Box 250 59825 406-825-3113
Mark Latrielle, supt. Fax 825-3114
Clinton ES 200/K-6
PO Box 250 59825 406-825-3113
Eric McBride, prin. Fax 825-3114
Clinton MS 50/7-8
PO Box 250 59825 406-825-3113
Eric McBride, prin. Fax 825-3114

Cohagen, Garfield
Cohagen ESD 50/PK-8
PO Box 113 59322 406-557-2771
Cohagen S, PO Box 113 59322 50/PK-8
Jessica McWilliams, prin. 406-557-2771

Colstrip, Rosebud, Pop. 2,331
Colstrip SD 700/PK-12
PO Box 159 59323 406-748-4699
Harry Cheff, supt. Fax 748-2268
www.colstrip.k12.mt.us/
Brattin MS 200/6-8
PO Box 159 59323 406-748-4699
Dinny Bennett, prin. Fax 748-3143
Pine Butte ES 300/PK-5
PO Box 159 59323 406-748-4699
Holly Bailey, prin. Fax 748-2551

Columbia Falls, Flathead, Pop. 4,440
Columbia Falls SD 2,500/PK-12
PO Box 1259 59912 406-892-6550
Michael Nicosia, supt. Fax 892-6552
www.sd6.k12.mt.us
Columbia Falls Grade 6 S 200/6-6
PO Box 1259 59912 406-892-6530
Dave Wick, prin. Fax 892-6528
Columbia Falls JHS 400/7-8
PO Box 1259 59912 406-892-6530
Dave Wick, prin. Fax 892-6528
Glacier Gateway ES 400/PK-5
PO Box 1259 59912 406-892-6540
Dorothea Wood, prin. Fax 892-6544
Ruder ES 500/K-5
PO Box 1259 59912 406-892-6570
Brenda Hoerner, prin. Fax 892-6563
Other Schools – See Hungry Horse

Deer Park ESD 100/PK-8
2105 Middle Rd 59912 406-892-5388
Fax 892-3504
Deer Park ES 100/PK-6
2105 Middle Rd 59912 406-892-5388
Dennis Haverlandt, prin. Fax 892-3504
Deer Park MS 50/7-8
2105 Middle Rd 59912 406-892-5388
Dennis Haverlandt, prin. Fax 892-3504

Columbus, Stillwater, Pop. 1,897
Columbus SD 700/PK-12
433 N 3rd St 59019 406-322-5373
Allan Sipes, supt. Fax 322-5028
www.columbus.k12.mt.us/
Columbus ES 300/PK-5
218 E 1st Ave N 59019 406-322-5372
Marlene Deis, prin. Fax 322-5371
Columbus MS 200/6-8
415 N 3rd St 59019 406-322-5375
Ron Osborne, prin. Fax 322-5376

Condon, Missoula
Swan Valley ESD 50/K-8
6423 MT Highway 83 59826 406-754-2320
Fax 754-2627
Swan Valley S 50/K-8
6423 MT Highway 83 59826 406-754-2320
Sue Patrick, lead tchr. Fax 754-2627

Conrad, Pondera, Pop. 2,600
Conrad SD 500/PK-12
215 S Maryland St 59425 406-278-5521
Lynn Utterback, supt. Fax 278-3630
www.edline.net/pages/Conrad_Public_Schools/
Meadowlark ES 200/PK-3
17 3rd Ave SW 59425 406-278-5620
Craig Barringer, prin. Fax 278-5621
Prairie View ES 4-5
220 N Wisconsin St 59425 406-278-5251
Greg Jensen, prin.
Utterback IS 50/6-6
24 2nd Ave SW 59425 406-278-3227
Craig Barringer, prin. Fax 271-2680
Utterback MS 100/7-8
24 2nd Ave SW 59425 406-278-3227
Craig Barringer, prin. Fax 271-2680

Miami ESD 50/PK-8
413 2nd Ave SW 59425 406-271-4055
Jo Stone, supt. Fax 271-4070
Miami S 50/PK-8
400 New Miami Colony Rd 59425 406-472-3325
Janice Hayworth, lead tchr.

Cooke City, Park
Cooke City ESD 50/K-8
PO Box 1070 59020 406-838-2285
Fax 838-2285
Cooke City S 50/K-8
PO Box 1070 59020 406-838-2285
Barbara Dempsey, lead tchr. Fax 838-2285

Corvallis, Ravalli
Corvallis SD 1,400/PK-12
PO Box 700 59828 406-961-4211
Daniel Sybrant, supt. Fax 961-5144
www.corvallis.k12.mt.us
Brown PS 500/PK-4
PO Box 700 59828 406-961-3261
Janice Stranahan, prin. Fax 961-5147
Corvallis JHS 200/7-8
PO Box 700 59828 406-961-3007
Rich Durgin, prin. Fax 961-5144
Thomas MS 200/5-6
PO Box 700 59828 406-961-3007
Rich Durgin, prin. Fax 961-8876

Crow Agency, Big Horn, Pop. 1,446
Hardin SD
Supt. — See Hardin
Crow Agency ES 200/K-5
Ammaachimuua St 59022 406-638-2252
Gene Grose, prin. Fax 638-3602

Culbertson, Roosevelt, Pop. 714
Culbertson SD 300/PK-12
PO Box 459 59218 406-787-6246
Larry Crowder, supt. Fax 787-6244
culbertsonschool.k12.mt.us
Culbertson ES 100/PK-6
PO Box 459 59218 406-787-6241
Jerry Waagen, prin. Fax 787-6244
Culbertson MS 50/7-8
PO Box 459 59218 406-787-6241
Jerry Waagen, prin. Fax 787-6244

Custer, Yellowstone
Custer SD 100/K-12
PO Box 69 59024 406-856-4117
Tim Dolphay, supt. Fax 856-4206
Custer ES 50/K-6
PO Box 69 59024 406-856-4117
Tim Dolphay, prin. Fax 856-4206
Custer MS 50/7-8
PO Box 69 59024 406-856-4117
Tim Dolphay, prin. Fax 856-4206

Cut Bank, Glacier, Pop. 3,167
Browning SD
Supt. — See Browning
Big Sky S 50/1-8
PO Box 147 59427 406-336-3790
Laura Gervais, prin. Fax 336-4690
Glendale S 50/1-8
PO Box 850 59427 406-336-2635
Laura Gervais, prin. Fax 336-2635

Cut Bank SD 800/PK-12
101 3rd Ave SE 59427 406-873-2229
Wade Johnson, supt. Fax 873-4691
www.cutbankschools.net
Cut Bank ES 400/PK-6
101 3rd Ave SE 59427 406-873-5513
Venus Dodson, prin. Fax 873-4691
Cut Bank JHS 100/7-8
101 3rd Ave SE 59427 406-873-4421
Don Paulson, prin. Fax 873-4691
Glacier S 50/1-8
101 3rd Ave SE 59427 406-336-2623
Don Paulson, prin. Fax 873-4691
Hidden Lake S 50/K-8
101 3rd Ave SE 59427 406-336-3695
Don Paulson, prin. Fax 873-4691

Mountain View ESD 50/PK-8
PO Box 1169 59427 406-336-2433
Fax 336-2434
Mountain View S 50/PK-8
PO Box 1169 59427 406-336-2433
Fax 336-2434

Darby, Ravalli, Pop. 835
Darby SD 400/PK-12
209 School Dr 59829 406-421-1305
Tim Bronk, supt. Fax 821-4977
www.darby.k12.mt.us/
Darby ES 200/PK-6
209 School Dr 59829 406-821-3643
Loyd Rennaker, prin. Fax 821-4977
Darby MS 100/7-8
209 School Dr 59829 406-821-3252
Dan Peters, prin. Fax 821-4977

Dayton, Lake
Upper West Shore ESD 50/PK-6
PO Box 195 59914 406-849-5484
Fax 849-5485
Dayton ES 50/PK-6
PO Box 195 59914 406-849-5484
Nichole Fant, lead tchr. Fax 849-5485

Decker, Big Horn
Spring Creek ESD 50/PK-8
PO Box 118 59025 406-757-2515
Fax 757-2247
Spring Creek S 50/PK-8
PO Box 118 59025 406-757-2515
Kari French, lead tchr. Fax 757-2247

Deer Lodge, Powell, Pop. 3,313
Deer Lodge ESD 500/PK-8
444 Montana Ave 59722 406-846-1553
Tom Cotton, supt. Fax 846-1599
Duvall MS 100/7-8
444 Montana Ave 59722 406-846-1684
Rick Chrisman, prin. Fax 846-1599
Speer ES 300/PK-6
444 Montana Ave 59722 406-846-2268
Rick Ashworth, prin. Fax 846-1599

Denton, Fergus, Pop. 288
Denton SD 100/PK-12
PO Box 1048 59430 406-567-2270
Bill Phillips, supt. Fax 567-2559
Denton ES 100/PK-6
PO Box 1048 59430 406-567-2370
Bill Phillips, prin. Fax 567-2559
Denton JHS 50/7-8
PO Box 1048 59430 406-567-2370
Bill Phillips, prin. Fax 567-2559

Dillon, Beaverhead, Pop. 3,988
Dillon ESD 700/PK-8
225 E Reeder St 59725 406-683-4311
Glen Johnson, supt. Fax 683-4312
www.dillonelem.k12.mt.us/
Dillon MS 200/6-8
14 Cottom Dr 59725 406-683-2368
Randy Shipman, prin. Fax 683-2369
Innes ES 100/PK-K
225 E Reeder St 59725 406-683-4311
Glen Johnson, prin. Fax 683-4312
Parkview ES 400/1-5
32 Cottom Dr 59725 406-683-2373
Greg Fitzgerald, prin. Fax 683-2374

Grant ESD 50/PK-8
811 E Orr St 59725 406-681-3143
Grant S, 811 E Orr St 59725 50/PK-8
Penny Huxtable, lead tchr. 406-681-3143

Jackson ESD 50/PK-8
19200 MT Highway 278 59725 406-834-3138
Fax 834-3204
Other Schools – See Jackson

Wisdom ESD 50/PK-8
19200 MT Highway 278 59725 406-689-3227
Fax 689-3217
Other Schools – See Wisdom

Divide, Silver Bow
Divide ESD 50/PK-8
PO Box 9 59727 406-267-3347
Divide S, PO Box 9 59727 50/PK-8
Judith Boyle, lead tchr. 406-267-3347

Dixon, Sanders
Dixon ESD 100/PK-8
PO Box 10 59831 406-246-3566
Fax 246-3379
Dixon ES 100/PK-6
PO Box 10 59831 406-246-3566
Mark Faroni, prin. Fax 246-3379
Dixon MS 50/7-8
PO Box 10 59831 406-246-3566
Mark Faroni, prin. Fax 246-3379

Dodson, Phillips, Pop. 110
Dodson SD 100/PK-12
PO Box 278 59524 406-383-4362
Frank Frickanisee, supt. Fax 383-4489
Dodson ES 50/PK-6
PO Box 278 59524 406-383-4362
Frank Frickanisee, prin. Fax 383-4489
Dodson MS 50/7-8
PO Box 278 59524 406-383-4362
Frank Frickanisee, prin. Fax 383-4489

Drummond, Granite, Pop. 332
Drummond SD 200/K-12
PO Box 349 59832 406-288-3281
Kitty Logan, supt. Fax 288-3299
Drummond ES 100/K-6
PO Box 349 59832 406-288-3283
Kitty Logan, prin. Fax 288-3299
Drummond MS 50/7-8
PO Box 349 59832 406-288-3283
Donn Livoni, prin. Fax 288-3299

Dupuyer, Pondera
Dupuyer ESD 50/PK-8
PO Box 149 59432 406-472-3297
Fax 472-3256
Dupuyer S 50/PK-8
PO Box 149 59432 406-472-3297
Lydia Mild, lead tchr. Fax 472-3256

Dutton, Teton, Pop. 372
Dutton/Brady SD 100/PK-12
101 2nd St NE 59433 406-476-3424
Tim Tharp, supt. Fax 476-3342
www.duttonbrady.com/
Dutton/Brady ES 100/PK-6
101 2nd St NE 59433 406-476-3201
Norma Clements, prin. Fax 476-3342
Dutton/Brady MS 50/7-8
101 2nd St NE 59433 406-476-3201
Norma Clements, prin. Fax 476-3342

East Glacier Park, Glacier
East Glacier Park SD 50/PK-8
PO Box 150 59434 406-226-5543
Fax 226-4269
East Glacier Park S 50/PK-8
PO Box 150 59434 406-226-5543
Karlona Sheppard, lead tchr. Fax 226-4269

East Helena, Lewis and Clark, Pop. 1,848
East Helena ESD 1,000/PK-8
PO Box 1280 59635 406-227-7700
Ron Whitmoyer, supt. Fax 227-5534
www.ehps.k12.mt.us
Eastgate ES 200/PK-1
PO Box 1280 59635 406-227-7770
Keith Obert, prin. Fax 227-8479
East Valley MS 400/6-8
PO Box 1280 59635 406-227-7740
Dan Rispens, prin. Fax 227-9730
Radley ES 400/2-5
PO Box 1280 59635 406-227-7710
Joseph McMahon, prin. Fax 227-7713

Ekalaka, Carter, Pop. 395
Carter County SD 100/PK-12
PO Box 458 59324 406-775-8767
Christina Schmid, supt. Fax 775-8766
Ekalaka ES 100/PK-6
PO Box 458 59324 406-775-8765
Christina Schmid, prin. Fax 775-8766
Ekalaka MS 50/7-8
PO Box 458 59324 406-775-8767
Christina Schmid, prin. Fax 775-8766

Elliston, Powell
Elliston ESD 27 50/PK-8
PO Box 160 59728 406-492-7676
Elliston S, PO Box 160 59728 50/PK-8
Brooks Phillips, lead tchr. 406-492-7676

Ennis, Madison, Pop. 973
Ennis SD 400/PK-12
PO Box 517 59729 406-682-4258
Douglas Walsh, supt. Fax 682-7751
www.ennisschools.org
Ennis ES 200/PK-6
PO Box 517 59729 406-682-4237
Brian Hilton, prin. Fax 682-7752
Ennis MS 100/7-8
PO Box 517 59729 406-682-4237
Brian Hilton, prin. Fax 682-7752

Eureka, Lincoln, Pop. 1,028
Eureka SD 700/PK-12
PO Box 2000 59917 406-297-5637
Jim Mepham, supt. Fax 297-2644
eureka.k12.mt.us
Eureka ES 300/PK-4
PO Box 2000 59917 406-297-5500
Cari Lucey, prin. Fax 297-2400
Eureka MS 100/5-8
PO Box 2000 59917 406-297-5600
Trevor Utter, prin. Fax 297-5653

Fairfield, Teton, Pop. 635
Fairfield SD 300/PK-12
PO Box 399 59436 406-467-2103
Dennis Davis, supt. Fax 467-2554
www.fairfield.k12.mt.us/
Fairfield ES 100/PK-6
PO Box 399 59436 406-467-2425
Courtney Bake, prin. Fax 467-2554
Fairfield MS 100/7-8
PO Box 399 59436 406-467-2425
Les Meyer, prin. Fax 467-2554

Golden Ridge ESD 50/PK-8
1374 US Highway 408 59436 406-467-2010
Fax 467-2190
Golden Ridge S 50/PK-8
1374 US Highway 408 59436 406-467-2010
Callie Kolste, lead tchr. Fax 467-2190

Greenfield ESD 100/PK-8
590 Mt Highway 431 59436 406-467-2433
Fax 467-3138
Greenfield ES 50/PK-6
590 Mt Highway 431 59436 406-467-2433
Paul Wilson, prin. Fax 467-3138
Greenfield MS 50/7-8
590 Mt Highway 431 59436 406-467-2433
Paul Wilson, prin. Fax 467-3138

Fairview, Richland, Pop. 666
Fairview SD 300/PK-12
PO Box 467 59221 406-742-5265
Matt Schriver, supt. Fax 742-3336
www.fairview.k12.mt.us/
Fairview ES 100/PK-6
PO Box 467 59221 406-742-5265
Luke Kloker, prin. Fax 742-8265
Fairview MS 50/7-8
PO Box 467 59221 406-742-5265
Luke Kloker, prin. Fax 742-8265

Fishtail, Stillwater
Fishtail ESD 50/PK-8
PO Box 75 59028 406-328-4277
Fax 328-4277
Fishtail S 50/PK-8
PO Box 75 59028 406-328-4277
Fax 328-4277

Florence, Ravalli
Florence-Carlton SD 800/PK-12
5602 Old US Highway 93 59833 406-273-6751
John McGee, supt. Fax 273-2802
www.florence.k12.mt.us
Florence-Carlton ES 400/PK-5
5602 Old US Highway 93 59833 406-273-6741
Christine Hulla, prin. Fax 273-2802
Florence-Carlton MS 100/6-8
5602 Old US Highway 93 59833 406-273-0587
Audrey Backus, prin. Fax 273-0545

Floweree, Chouteau
Benton Lake ESD 50/PK-8
17557 Bootlegger Trl 59440 406-452-9023
Benton Lake S 50/PK-8
17557 Bootlegger Trl 59440 406-452-9023
Dawn Dawson, lead tchr.

Forsyth, Rosebud, Pop. 1,888
Forsyth SD 400/PK-12
PO Box 319 59327 406-346-2796
David Shreeve, supt. Fax 346-7455
Forsyth ES 200/PK-6
PO Box 319 59327 406-346-2796
Kelly Anderson, prin. Fax 346-7797
Forsyth MS 100/7-8
PO Box 319 59327 406-346-2796
Doug Roberts, prin. Fax 346-9219

Fort Benton, Chouteau, Pop. 1,475
Ft. Benton SD 300/PK-12
PO Box 399 59442 406-622-5691
Scott Chauvet, supt. Fax 622-5691
www.fortbenton.k12.mt.us/
Fort Benton ES 100/PK-6
PO Box 399 59442 406-622-3761
Scott Chauvet, prin. Fax 622-5408
Fort Benton JHS 100/7-8
PO Box 399 59442 406-622-3213
Jim Howard, prin. Fax 622-5691

Fortine, Lincoln
Fortine ESD 100/PK-8
PO Box 96 59918 406-882-4531
Fax 882-4057
Fortine S 100/PK-8
PO Box 96 59918 406-882-4531
Dan Smith, prin. Fax 882-4057

Fort Shaw, Cascade
Sun River Valley SD
Supt. — See Simms
Cascade Colony S 50/K-8
Birdtail Creek Rd 59443 406-264-5104
Rick Danelson, prin. Fax 264-5265
Fort Shaw ES 100/PK-5
School Loop 59443 406-264-5651
Rick Danelson, prin. Fax 264-5146

Fort Smith, Big Horn, Pop. 270
Hardin SD
Supt. — See Hardin
Fort Smith ES 50/K-5
502 Avenue C 59035 406-666-2350
Fax 666-2305

Frazer, Valley, Pop. 403
Frazer SD 100/K-12
PO Box 488 59225 406-695-2241
Donald Johnson, supt. Fax 695-2243
Frazer ES 50/K-6
PO Box 488 59225 406-695-2241
Donald Johnson, prin. Fax 695-2243
Frazer MS 50/7-8
PO Box 488 59225 406-695-2241
Donald Johnson, prin. Fax 695-2243

Lustre ESD 50/PK-8
282 Lustre Rd 59225 406-392-5725
Fax 392-5780
Lustre S 50/PK-8
282 Lustre Rd 59225 406-392-5725
Vernelle Unrau, lead tchr. Fax 392-5780

Frenchtown, Missoula
Frenchtown SD 1,200/PK-12
PO Box 117 59834 406-626-2600
Randy Cline, supt. Fax 626-2605
www.frenchtown.k12.mt.us
Frenchtown ES 600/PK-6
PO Box 117 59834 406-626-2620
Cynthia Worrall, prin. Fax 626-2625
Frenchtown MS 200/7-8
PO Box 117 59834 406-626-2650
Jon Fimmel, prin. Fax 626-2605

Froid, Roosevelt, Pop. 191
Froid SD 100/K-12
PO Box 218 59226 406-766-2343
Roger Britton, supt. Fax 766-2206
Froid ES 50/K-6
PO Box 218 59226 406-766-2342
Roger Britton, prin. Fax 766-2206
Froid MS 50/7-8
PO Box 218 59226 406-766-2342
Roger Britton, prin. Fax 766-2206

Fromberg, Carbon, Pop. 492
Fromberg SD 200/PK-12
PO Box 189 59029 406-668-7611
Eldon Johnson, supt. Fax 668-7669
www.fromberg.k12.mt.us/
Fromberg ES 100/PK-6
PO Box 189 59029 406-668-7755
Eldon Johnson, prin. Fax 668-7602
Fromberg MS 50/7-8
PO Box 189 59029 406-668-7315
Eldon Johnson, prin. Fax 668-7669

Galata, Toole
Galata ESD 50/PK-7
PO Box 76 59444 406-432-2123
Fax 432-2155
Galata S 50/PK-7
PO Box 76 59444 406-432-2123
Fax 432-2155

Liberty ESD 50/PK-8
PO Box 78 59444 406-432-5265
Fax 432-2582
Liberty S 50/PK-8
PO Box 78 59444 406-432-5265
Fax 432-2582

Gallatin Gateway, Gallatin
Gallatin Gateway ESD 200/PK-8
PO Box 265 59730 406-763-4415
Kim DeBruycker, supt. Fax 763-4886
Gallatin Gateway ES 100/PK-6
PO Box 265 59730 406-763-4415
Kim DeBruycker, prin. Fax 763-4886
Gallatin Gateway MS 50/7-8
PO Box 265 59730 406-763-4415
Kim DeBruycker, prin. Fax 763-4886

Ophir ESD 100/PK-8
45465 Gallatin Rd 59730 406-995-4281
AnneMarie Mistretta, supt. Fax 995-2161
Ophir ES 100/PK-5
45465 Gallatin Rd 59730 406-995-4281
Andrea Johnson, prin. Fax 995-2161
Ophir MS 50/6-8
45465 Gallatin Rd 59730 406-995-4281
AnneMarie Mistretta, prin. Fax 995-2161

Gardiner, Park
Gardiner SD 200/PK-12
510 Stone St 59030 406-848-7261
Leland Stocker, supt. Fax 848-9489
www.gardiner.org/
Gardiner ES 100/PK-6
510 Stone St 59030 406-848-7563
Ken Ballagh, prin. Fax 848-9489
Gardiner MS 50/7-8
510 Stone St 59030 406-848-7563
Ken Ballagh, prin. Fax 848-9489

Garrison, Powell
Garrison ESD 50/K-6
33 School House Rd 59731 406-846-1043
Fax 846-2154
Garrison ES 50/K-6
33 School House Rd 59731 406-846-1043
Shirley Peters, lead tchr. Fax 846-2154

Geraldine, Chouteau, Pop. 258
Geraldine SD 100/PK-12
PO Box 347 59446 406-737-4311
Rodney Simpson, supt. Fax 737-4478
www.geraldine.k12.mt.us/
Geraldine ES 50/PK-6
PO Box 347 59446 406-737-4371
Rodney Simpson, prin. Fax 737-4478
Geraldine MS 50/7-8
PO Box 347 59446 406-737-4371
Rodney Simpson, prin. Fax 737-4478

Geyser, Judith Basin
Geyser SD 100/PK-12
PO Box 70 59447 406-735-4368
Dale Bernard, supt. Fax 735-4452
geyser.k12.mt.us
Geyser ES 50/PK-6
PO Box 70 59447 406-735-4358
Dale Bernard, prin. Fax 735-4452
Geyser MS 50/7-8
PO Box 70 59447 406-735-4368
Dale Bernard, prin. Fax 735-4452
Surprise Creek S 50/K-8
PO Box 70 59447 406-566-2269
Dale Bernard, prin. Fax 735-4452

Gildford, Hill
Gildford Colony ESD 50/PK-8
HC 74 Box 6 59525 406-376-3249
Gildford Colony S 50/PK-8
21719 Road 160 N 59525 406-376-3249
Ranae Mellgren, lead tchr.

North Star SD
Supt. — See Rudyard
North Star ES 100/PK-6
205 3rd St E 59525 406-355-4481
Ken Halverson, prin. Fax 355-4532

Glasgow, Valley, Pop. 3,018
Glasgow SD 800/PK-12
PO Box 28 59230 406-228-2406
Glenn Hageman, supt. Fax 228-2407
www.glasgow.k12.mt.us/
Glasgow IS 200/4-6
PO Box 28 59230 406-228-8268
Clint Croy, prin. Fax 228-8163
Glasgow MS 100/7-8
PO Box 28 59230 406-228-2485
Margaret Markle, prin. Fax 228-4061
Irle ES 200/PK-3
PO Box 28 59230 406-228-2419
Rachel Erickson, prin. Fax 228-8762

Glen, Beaverhead
Reichle ESD 50/PK-8
PO Box 320097 59732 406-835-2281
Fax 683-2691
Reichle S 50/PK-8
PO Box 320097 59732 406-835-2281
Sue Webster, lead tchr. Fax 683-2691

Glendive, Dawson, Pop. 4,670
Deer Creek ESD 50/PK-8
12 Rd 564 59330 406-687-3724
Deer Creek S, 12 Rd 564 59330 50/PK-8
Etta Herring, lead tchr. 406-687-3724

Glendive SD 1,200/PK-12
PO Box 701 59330 406-377-5293
Jim Germann, supt. Fax 377-6212
www.glendiveschools.com
Jefferson ES 200/K-4
PO Box 701 59330 406-377-4155
Don Idso, prin. Fax 377-8944
Lincoln ES 200/PK-4
PO Box 701 59330 406-377-2308
Steve Lynn, prin. Fax 377-2309
Washington MS 400/5-8
PO Box 701 59330 406-377-2356
Ross Farber, prin. Fax 377-2357

Valley View Christian S 50/1-8
264 Highway 200 S 59330 406-687-3472

Gold Creek, Powell
Gold Creek ESD 50/PK-8
PO Box 330011 59733 406-288-3560
Gold Creek S, PO Box 330011 59733 50/PK-8
Mary Fox, lead tchr. 406-288-3560

Grass Range, Fergus, Pop. 145
Ayers ESD 50/PK-8
PO Box 100 59032 406-428-2368
Fax 428-2368
Ayers S 50/PK-8
PO Box 100 59032 406-428-2368
Susan Seastrand, lead tchr. Fax 428-2368

Grass Range SD 100/PK-12
PO Box 58 59032 406-428-2122
Russell McKenna, supt. Fax 428-2235
Grass Range ES 50/PK-6
PO Box 58 59032 406-428-2341
Russell McKenna, prin. Fax 428-2235
Grass Range MS 50/7-8
PO Box 58 59032 406-428-2122
Russell McKenna, prin. Fax 428-2235

Great Falls, Cascade, Pop. 56,338
Deep Creek ESD 50/PK-6
1508 Millegan Rd 59405 406-866-3381
Deep Creek ES 50/PK-6
1508 Millegan Rd 59405 406-866-3381
Terry Clark, lead tchr.

Great Falls SD 10,600/PK-12
PO Box 2429 59403 406-268-6001
Cheryl Crawley, supt. Fax 268-6002
www.gfps.k12.mt.us
Chief Joseph ES 300/K-6
5305 3rd Ave S 59405 406-268-6675
Michelle Meredith, prin. Fax 268-6955
East MS 800/7-8
4040 Central Ave 59405 406-268-6500
Shelly Fagenstrom, prin. Fax 268-6524
Lewis & Clark ES 300/K-6
3800 1st Ave S 59405 406-268-6705
Vickie Donisthorpe, prin. Fax 268-7003
Lincoln ES 400/K-6
624 27th St S 59405 406-268-6800
Kathy Johnson, prin. Fax 268-6819
Longfellow ES 300/PK-6
1100 6th Ave S 59405 406-268-6845
Cal Gilbert, prin. Fax 268-7450
Loy ES 300/PK-6
501 57th St N 59405 406-268-6885
Ryan Hart, prin. Fax 268-6887
Meadowlark ES 500/K-6
2204 Fox Farm Rd 59404 406-268-7300
Kelly Maki, prin. Fax 268-7304
Morningside ES 300/K-6
4119 7th Ave N 59405 406-268-6960
Bill Salonen, prin. Fax 268-7480
Mountain View ES 400/PK-6
3420 15th Ave S 59405 406-268-7305
Carole McKittrick, prin. Fax 268-7336
North MS 800/7-8
2601 8th St NE 59404 406-268-6525
Jane Gregiore, prin. Fax 268-6575
Riverview ES 400/PK-6
100 Smelter Ave NW 59404 406-268-7015
Howard Corey, prin. Fax 268-7007
Roosevelt ES 300/K-6
2501 2nd Ave N 59401 406-268-7045
Rhonda Zobrak, prin. Fax 268-7077
Sacajawea ES 400/K-6
630 Sacajawea Dr 59404 406-268-7080
Rae Smith, prin. Fax 268-7114
Sunnyside ES 400/K-6
1800 19th St S 59405 406-268-7115
Kathryn McLean, prin. Fax 268-7421
Valley View ES 300/K-6
900 Avenue A NW 59404 406-268-7145
Rhonda McCarty, prin. Fax 268-7148
West ES 500/K-6
1205 1st Ave NW 59404 406-268-7180
Bobby Ingalls, prin. Fax 268-7227
Whittier ES 200/PK-6
305 8th St N 59401 406-268-7230
Mende Kloppel, prin. Fax 268-7423

Five Falls Christian S 50/K-8
3102 Flood Rd 59404 406-452-6883
Foothills Community Christian S 200/PK-12
2210 5th Ave N 59401 406-452-5276
John Peterson, admin. Fax 452-8606

Holy Spirit Catholic S 300/PK-8
2820 Central Ave 59401 406-761-5775
Roger Robbins, prin. Fax 761-5887
Our Lady of Lourdes S 300/PK-8
1305 5th Ave S 59405 406-452-0551
Sherri Schmitz, prin. Fax 761-7180

Greenough, Missoula
Sunset ESD 50/PK-8
5024 Sunset Hill Rd 59823 406-244-5542
Sunset S 50/PK-8
5024 Sunset Hill Rd 59823 406-244-5542

Greycliff, Sweet Grass
Greycliff ESD 50/PK-8
PO Box 65 59033 406-932-6641
Greycliff S, PO Box 65 59033 50/PK-8
Robin Thomas, lead tchr. 406-932-6641

Hall, Granite
Hall ESD 50/PK-8
PO Box 22 59837 406-859-3831
JoAnn Husbyn, supt. Fax 859-3817
Hall S, PO Box 22 59837 50/PK-8
Teresa Kielley, lead tchr. 406-288-3440

Hamilton, Ravalli, Pop. 4,443
Hamilton SD 1,600/PK-12
217 Daly Ave 59840 406-363-2280
Duby Santee, supt. Fax 363-1843
www.hsd3.org
Daly ES 400/2-5
208 Daly Ave 59840 406-363-2122
Eric Larson, prin. Fax 363-6494
Grantsdale ES 100/2-5
778 Grantsdale Rd 59840 406-363-1889
Kathleen Dent, prin. Fax 363-6231
Hamilton MS 400/6-8
209 S 5th St 59840 406-363-2121
Dan Kimzey, prin. Fax 363-7032
Washington ES 200/PK-1
225 N 5th St 59840 406-363-2144
Bradley Henson, prin. Fax 363-7420

Blodgett View Adventist S 50/PK-8
119 Westbridge Rd 59840 406-375-0733
Hamilton Christian Academy 100/PK-8
601 W Main St 59840 406-363-4534
Stephanie Beck, admin. Fax 375-0960

Hammond, Carter
Hawks Home ESD 50/K-8
20 Talcott Ln 59332 406-427-5438
Hammond S 50/K-8
10851 Highway 212 59332 406-427-5438
Barb Lapke, lead tchr.

Hardin, Big Horn, Pop. 3,510
Hardin SD 1,600/PK-12
585 W John Deere Rd 59034 406-665-1304
Albert Peterson, supt. Fax 665-2784
www.hardin.k12.mt.us
Hardin IS 300/3-5
631 5th St W 59034 406-665-6390
Larry Johnson, prin. Fax 665-1713
Hardin MS 300/6-8
611 5th St W 59034 406-665-6350
Scott Brokaw, prin. Fax 665-1409
Hardin PS 300/PK-2
314 3rd St W 59034 406-665-2505
Rocky Eggart, prin. Fax 665-2505
Other Schools – See Crow Agency, Fort Smith

Harlem, Blaine, Pop. 806
Harlem SD 600/PK-12
PO Box 339 59526 406-353-2289
Nancy Coleman, supt. Fax 353-2674
www.harlem-hs.k12.mt.us
Harlem ES 300/PK-6
PO Box 309 59526 406-353-2258
Joe Davis, prin. Fax 353-2892
Harlem MS 100/7-8
PO Box 339 59526 406-353-2287
Sally O'Leary, prin. Fax 353-2339

North Harlem Colony ESD 50/K-8
668 Hillcrest Rd 59526 406-353-2800
Fax 353-4746
North Harlem S 50/K-8
668 Hillcrest Rd 59526 406-353-2800
Robin Rhodes, lead tchr. Fax 353-4746

Fort Belknap Adventist S 50/1-8
17 Rodeo Dr 59526 406-353-4858

Harlowton, Wheatland, Pop. 941
Harlowton SD 300/PK-12
PO Box 288 59036 406-632-4822
Andrew Begger, supt. Fax 632-4416
www.harlowton.k12.mt.us/
Hillcrest ES 200/PK-6
PO Box 288 59036 406-632-4361
Aubrey Miller, prin. Fax 632-4744
Hillcrest MS 50/7-8
PO Box 288 59036 406-632-4361
Gregg Wasson, prin. Fax 632-4416

Harrison, Madison
Harrison SD 100/PK-12
PO Box 7 59735 406-685-3471
Darren Strauch, supt. Fax 685-3430
www.hhswildcats.com
Harrison ES 50/PK-6
PO Box 7 59735 406-685-3471
Darren Strauch, prin. Fax 685-3430
Harrison MS 50/7-8
PO Box 7 59735 406-685-3471
Darren Strauch, prin. Fax 685-3430

Havre, Hill, Pop. 9,390
Chinook SD
Supt. — See Chinook
Hartland S 50/K-8
2105 Woodpile Rd 59501 406-357-2033
Rita Surber, prin. Fax 357-3146

Cottonwood ESD 50/PK-8
24570 Road 415 N 59501 406-265-5481
Shirley Isbell, supt. Fax 394-2273
Cottonwood North S PK-8
24570 Road 415 N 59501 406-394-2313
Diane McLean, lead tchr.
Cottonwood West S 50/PK-8
24570 Road 415 N 59501 406-394-2273
Monica Groth, lead tchr. Fax 394-2273

Davey ESD 50/PK-8
PO Box 1829 59501 406-265-4506
Davey S, PO Box 1829 59501 50/PK-8
Denellda Barnekoff, lead tchr. 406-395-4461

Havre SD 2,000/K-12
PO Box 7791 59501 406-265-4356
Dennis Parman, supt. Fax 265-8460
www.havre.k12.mt.us/
Havre MS 400/6-8
1441 11th St W 59501 406-265-9613
Dustin Kraske, prin. Fax 265-4414
Highland Park ES North K-1
500 1st Ave 59501 406-265-2378
Denise Wheeler, prin. Fax 265-8460
Highland Park ES South 300/K-1
1207 Washington Ave 59501 406-265-5554
Denise Wheeler, prin. Fax 265-8460
Lincoln-McKinley ES 300/2-3
801 4th Ave 59501 406-265-9619
Karla Geda, prin. Fax 265-8460
Sunnyside ES 300/4-5
601 14th St 59501 406-265-9671
Jeff Blessum, prin. Fax 265-8460

Havre SDA S 50/1-8
4115 9th St W 59501 406-265-8312
St. Jude Thaddeus S 200/PK-8
430 7th Ave 59501 406-265-4613
Carol Ortman, prin. Fax 265-1315

Hays, Blaine, Pop. 333
Hays-Lodge Pole SD 200/PK-12
PO Box 110 59527 406-673-3120
Robert McLean, supt. Fax 673-3294
Hays-Lodge Pole MS 100/7-8
PO Box 110 59527 406-673-3120
Amy Snow, prin. Fax 673-3274
Lodge Pole ES 100/PK-6
PO Box 110 59527 406-673-3220
Amy Snow, prin. Fax 673-3274

St. Paul's Mission S, PO Box 40 59527 100/K-6
Sr. Helen Durso, prin. 406-673-3123

Heart Butte, Pondera, Pop. 499
Heart Butte SD 200/PK-12
PO Box 259 59448 406-338-3344
Lori Falcon, supt. Fax 338-2088
Heart Butte ES 100/PK-6
PO Box 259 59448 406-338-2200
Lori Falcon, prin. Fax 338-5832
Heart Butte MS 50/7-8
PO Box 259 59448 406-338-2200
Robin Kratz, prin. Fax 338-5832

Helena, Lewis and Clark, Pop. 27,383
Helena SD 8,000/K-12
55 S Rodney St 59601 406-324-2001
Dr. Bruce Messinger, supt. Fax 324-2035
www.helena.k12.mt.us/
Anderson MS 1,000/6-8
1200 Knight St 59601 406-324-2800
Bruce Campbell, prin. Fax 324-2801
Broadwater ES 300/K-5
900 Hollins Ave 59601 406-324-1130
Sue Johnson, prin. Fax 324-1131
Bryant ES 200/K-5
1529 Boulder Ave 59601 406-324-1200
Russell VanHook, prin. Fax 324-1201
Central ES 300/K-5
402 N Warren St 59601 406-324-1230
Merry Fahrman, prin. Fax 324-1231
Darcy ES 300/K-5
990 Lincoln Rd W 59602 406-324-1410
Brian Cummings, prin. Fax 324-1411
Four Georgians ES 500/K-5
555 W Custer Ave 59602 406-324-1300
Melinda Thompson, prin. Fax 324-1301
Hawthorne ES 200/K-5
430 Madison Ave 59601 406-324-1370
Dr. Deborah Jacobsen, prin. Fax 324-1371
Helena MS 700/6-8
1025 N Rodney St 59601 406-324-1000
Josh McKay, prin. Fax 324-1001
Jefferson ES 200/K-5
1023 E Broadway St 59601 406-324-2060
Lona Carter-Scanlon, prin. Fax 324-2061
Kessler ES 200/K-5
2420 Choteau St 59601 406-324-1700
Karen Stout-Suenram, prin. Fax 324-1701
Rossiter ES 500/K-5
1497 Sierra Rd E 59602 406-324-1500
Kareen Bangert, prin. Fax 324-1501
Smith ES 300/K-5
2320 5th Ave 59601 406-324-1530
Pam Wright, prin. Fax 324-1531
Warren ES 300/K-5
2690 York Rd 59602 406-324-1600
Tim McMahon, prin. Fax 324-1601

First Lutheran S 50/PK-2
2231 E Broadway St 59601 406-442-5367
Erin Lavender, prin. Fax 442-5285
Helena Christian S 100/K-12
1421 N Roberts St 59601 406-442-3821
Ray Fuller, supt. Fax 442-3821

Helmville, Powell
Helmville ESD 50/PK-8
PO Box 91 59843 406-793-5656
Helmville S, PO Box 91 59843 50/PK-8
Susan Graveley, lead tchr. 406-793-5656

Highwood, Chouteau
Highwood SD 100/PK-12
160 West St S 59450 406-733-2081
Becky Aaring, supt. Fax 733-2671
www.highwood.k12.mt.us
Highwood ES 50/PK-5
160 West St S 59450 406-733-2081
Becky Aaring, prin. Fax 733-2671
Highwood MS 50/6-8
160 West St S 59450 406-733-2081
Becky Aaring, prin. Fax 733-2671

Hinsdale, Valley
Hinsdale SD 100/K-12
PO Box 398 59241 406-364-2314
Julie Gaffney, supt. Fax 364-2205
Hinsdale ES 50/K-6
PO Box 398 59241 406-364-2314
Julie Gaffney, prin. Fax 364-2205
Hinsdale MS 50/7-8
PO Box 398 59241 406-364-2314
Julie Gaffney, prin. Fax 364-2205

Hobson, Judith Basin, Pop. 231
Hobson SD 100/PK-12
PO Box 410 59452 406-423-5483
Wesley Coy, supt. Fax 423-5260
www.hobson.k12.mt.us/
Hobson ES 100/PK-6
PO Box 410 59452 406-423-5483
Wesley Coy, prin. Fax 423-5260
Hobson MS 50/7-8
PO Box 410 59452 406-423-5483
Wesley Coy, prin. Fax 423-5260

Hot Springs, Sanders, Pop. 565
Hot Springs SD 200/PK-12
PO Box 1005 59845 406-741-3285
Larry Markuson, supt. Fax 741-3287
Hot Springs ES 100/PK-6
PO Box 1005 59845 406-741-2014
Sean Estill, prin. Fax 741-3287
Hot Springs MS 50/7-8
PO Box 1005 59845 406-741-2962
Larry Markuson, prin. Fax 741-3287

Hungry Horse, Flathead
Columbia Falls SD
Supt. — See Columbia Falls
Canyon ES 100/K-5
200 North St 59919 406-387-5323
Matt Fawcett, prin. Fax 387-5342

Hysham, Treasure, Pop. 262
Hysham SD 100/PK-12
PO Box 272 59038 406-342-5237
Larry Fink, supt. Fax 342-5257
Hysham ES 100/PK-6
PO Box 272 59038 406-342-5237
Larry Fink, prin. Fax 342-5257
Hysham MS 50/7-8
PO Box 272 59038 406-342-5237
Larry Fink, prin. Fax 342-5257

Ismay, Custer, Pop. 25
Cottonwood ESD 50/PK-8
876 Road 431 59336 406-772-5888
Fax 772-5671
Knowlton S 50/PK-8
876 Road 431 59336 406-772-5888
Lenora Phillips, lead tchr. Fax 772-5671

Jackson, Beaverhead
Jackson ESD
Supt. — See Dillon
Jackson S 50/PK-8
Main St 59736 406-834-3138
Teresa Murdoch, lead tchr. Fax 834-3204

Joliet, Carbon, Pop. 601
Joliet SD 400/PK-12
PO Box 590 59041 406-962-2200
Les Cabot, supt. Fax 962-3958
Joliet ES 200/PK-6
PO Box 590 59041 406-962-3541
Les Cabot, prin. Fax 962-3958
Joliet MS 100/7-8
PO Box 590 59041 406-962-3541
Marilyn Vukonich, prin. Fax 962-3958

Jordan, Garfield, Pop. 339
Big Dry Creek ESD 50/PK-8
489 S Sand Creek Rd 59337 406-557-6216
Big Dry S 50/PK-8
489 S Sand Creek Rd 59337 406-557-6216
Marisa O'Connor, lead tchr.

Jordan SD 100/PK-12
PO Box 409 59337 406-557-2259
Jennifer O'Connor, supt. Fax 557-2778
Jordan ES 100/PK-6
PO Box 409 59337 406-557-2259
Jennifer O'Connor, prin. Fax 557-2778
Jordan MS 50/7-8
PO Box 409 59337 406-557-2259
Jennifer O'Connor, prin. Fax 557-2778

Kester ESD 50/PK-8
2031 Haxby Rd 59337 406-557-6274
Fax 557-2890
Kester S 50/PK-8
2031 Haxby Rd 59337 406-557-6274
Fax 557-2890

Judith Gap, Wheatland, Pop. 145
Judith Gap SD 100/PK-12
PO Box 67 59453 406-473-2211
Frances Swensgard, supt. Fax 473-2250
www.judithgap.k12.mt.us/
Judith Gap ES 50/PK-6
PO Box 67 59453 406-473-2211
Frances Swensgard, prin. Fax 473-2250
Judith Gap MS 50/7-8
PO Box 67 59453 406-473-2211
Frances Swensgard, prin. Fax 473-2250

Kalispell, Flathead, Pop. 18,480
Cayuse Prairie ESD 200/K-8
897 Lake Blaine Rd 59901 406-756-4560
Rick Nadeau, supt. Fax 756-4570
Cayuse Prairie ES 100/K-6
897 Lake Blaine Rd 59901 406-756-4560
Rick Nadeau, prin. Fax 756-4570
Cayuse Prairie MS 50/7-8
897 Lake Blaine Rd 59901 406-756-4560
Rick Nadeau, prin. Fax 756-4570

Creston ESD 100/PK-6
4495 Montana 35 59901 406-755-2859
Fax 752-2859
Creston ES 100/PK-6
4495 Montana 35 59901 406-755-2859
Judith Hewitt, prin. Fax 752-2859

Evergreen ESD 800/PK-8
18 W Evergreen Dr 59901 406-751-1111
Joel Voytoski, supt. Fax 752-2307
East Evergreen ES 400/PK-4
18 W Evergreen Dr 59901 406-751-1121
Linda DeVoe, prin. Fax 751-1120
Evergreen JHS 200/7-8
18 W Evergreen Dr 59901 406-751-1131
Kim Anderson, prin. Fax 751-1134
Evergreen MS 200/5-6
18 W Evergreen Dr 59901 406-751-1131
Kim Anderson, prin. Fax 751-1134

Fair-Mont-Egan ESD 100/PK-8
797 Fairmont Rd 59901 406-755-7072
Christine Anthony, admin. Fax 755-7077
fair.mt.schoolwebpages.com
Fair-Mont-Egan ES 100/PK-6
797 Fairmont Rd 59901 406-755-7072
Christine Anthony, prin. Fax 755-7077
Fair-Mont-Egan MS 50/7-8
797 Fairmont Rd 59901 406-755-7072
Christine Anthony, prin. Fax 755-7077

Helena Flats ESD 200/K-8
1000 Helena Flats Rd 59901 406-257-2301
Paul Jenkins, supt. Fax 257-2304
Helena Flats ES 200/K-6
1000 Helena Flats Rd 59901 406-257-2301
Paul Jenkins, prin. Fax 257-2304
Helena Flats MS 100/7-8
1000 Helena Flats Rd 59901 406-257-2301
Paul Jenkins, prin. Fax 257-2304

Kalispell SD 3,800/PK-12
233 1st Ave E 59901 406-751-3434
Dr. Darlene Schottle, supt. Fax 751-3416
www.sd5.k12.mt.us
Edgerton ES 500/PK-5
1400 Whitefish Stage 59901 406-751-4040
Darren Schlepp, prin. Fax 751-4045
Elrod ES 300/K-5
412 3rd Ave W 59901 406-751-3700
Jeff Hornby, prin. Fax 751-3705
Hedges ES 300/K-5
827 4th Ave E 59901 406-751-4090
Casey Bertram, prin. Fax 751-4095
Kalispell MS 300/6-8
205 Northwest Ln 59901 406-751-3800
Barry Grace, prin. Fax 751-3805
Peterson ES 300/K-5
1119 2nd St W 59901 406-751-3737
Rick Anfenson, prin. Fax 751-3740
Russell ES 300/PK-5
227 W Nevada St 59901 406-751-3900
Bill Sullivan, prin. Fax 751-3905

Smith Valley ESD 200/PK-8
2901 US Highway 2 W 59901 406-756-4535
Fax 756-4534
Smith Valley ES 200/PK-6
2901 US Highway 2 W 59901 406-756-4535
Harold Welling, prin. Fax 756-4534
Smith Valley MS 50/7-8
2901 US Highway 2 W 59901 406-756-4535
Harold Welling, prin. Fax 756-4534

West Valley ESD 400/PK-8
2290 Farm To Market Rd 59901 406-755-7239
Todd Fiske, supt. Fax 755-7300
www.westvalleyschool.com
West Valley ES 200/PK-5
2290 Farm To Market Rd 59901 406-755-7239
Todd Fiske, prin. Fax 755-7300
West Valley MS 100/6-8
2290 Farm to Market Rd 59901 406-755-7239
Todd Fiske, prin. Fax 755-7300

Glacier Waldorf S 50/PK-2
PO Box 626 59903 406-755-2343
St. Matthews S 300/PK-8
602 S Main St 59901 406-752-6303
Gene Boyle, prin. Fax 756-8248
Stillwater Christian S 300/K-12
255 FFA Dr 59901 406-752-4400
Daniel Makowski, supt. Fax 755-4061
Trinity Lutheran S 200/PK-8
495 5th Avenue West N 59901 406-257-6716
David Hobus, prin. Fax 257-6717
Valley Adventist Christian S 50/K-8
1275 Helena Flats Rd 59901 406-752-0830
Clark McCrain, lead tchr. Fax 752-0850

Kila, Flathead
Kila ESD 100/K-8
PO Box 40 59920 406-257-2428
Fax 755-6663
www.kilaschool.com/
Kila ES 100/K-6
PO Box 40 59920 406-257-2428
Renee Boisseau, prin. Fax 755-6663
Kila MS 50/7-8
PO Box 40 59920 406-257-2428
Renee Boisseau, prin. Fax 755-6663

Kinsey, Custer
Kinsey ESD 100/PK-8
HC 46 Box 386 59338 406-232-2440
Fax 232-2440
Kinsey S 100/PK-8
HC 46 Box 396 59338 406-232-2440
Jackie Walby, lead tchr. Fax 232-2440

Lambert, Richland
Lambert SD 100/PK-12
PO Box 260 59243 406-774-3333
Steven Schwartz, supt. Fax 774-3335
Lambert ES 50/PK-6
PO Box 260 59243 406-774-3333
Steven Schwartz, prin. Fax 774-3335
Lambert MS 50/7-8
PO Box 260 59243 406-774-3333
Steven Schwartz, prin. Fax 774-3335

Lame Deer, Rosebud, Pop. 1,918
Lame Deer SD 600/PK-12
PO Box 96 59043 406-477-6305
Daniel Lantis, supt. Fax 477-6535
www.lamedeer.k12.mt.us/
Lame Deer ES 300/PK-6
PO Box 96 59043 406-477-6305
Jill Henzie, prin. Fax 477-8234
Lame Deer MS 100/7-8
PO Box 96 59043 406-477-8900
Veronica Small-Eastman, prin. Fax 477-8906

Laurel, Yellowstone, Pop. 6,342
Laurel SD 1,200/PK-12
410 Colorado Ave 59044 406-628-8623
Josh Middleton, supt. Fax 628-8625
www.laurel.k12.mt.us
Graff ES 100/3-4
417 E 6th St 59044 406-628-6916
Troy Zickefoose, prin. Fax 628-3497
Laurel MS 400/5-8
725 Washington Ave 59044 406-628-6919
Linda Filpula, prin. Fax 628-3350
West ES 100/PK-2
502 8th Ave 59044 406-628-6914
Dale Ahrens, prin. Fax 628-3447

Lavina, Golden Valley, Pop. 236
Lavina SD 100/PK-12
PO Box 290 59046 406-636-2761
Mark Allen, supt. Fax 636-4911
www.edline.net/pages/lavina_k-12_schools
Lavina ES 50/PK-6
PO Box 290 59046 406-636-2761
Mark Allen, prin. Fax 636-4911
Lavina MS 50/7-8
PO Box 290 59046 406-636-2761
Mark Allen, prin. Fax 636-4911

Lewistown, Fergus, Pop. 6,099
Deerfield ESD 50/PK-8
360 Deerfield Rd 59457 406-538-3852
Deerfield S, 360 Deerfield Rd 59457 50/PK-8
Traci Manseau, lead tchr. 406-538-3852

King Colony ESD 50/PK-8
2370 King Colony Rd 59457 406-538-9702
King Colony S 50/PK-8
2370 King Colony Rd 59457 406-538-9702
Kathleen Irwin, lead tchr.

Lewistown SD 1,400/PK-12
215 7th Ave S 59457 406-535-8777
Jason Butcher, supt. Fax 535-7292
www.lewistown.k12.mt.us
Garfield ES 200/3-4
215 7th Ave S 59457 406-535-2366
John Moffatt, prin. Fax 535-2367
Highland Park ES 300/PK-2
215 7th Ave S 59457 406-535-2555
Sharon Redfern, prin. Fax 535-2556
Lewis & Clark ES 200/5-6
215 7th Ave S 59457 406-535-2811
Matt Lewis, prin. Fax 535-2812
Lewistown JHS 200/7-8
215 7th Ave S 59457 406-535-5419
Jerry Feller, prin. Fax 535-2300

Spring Creek Colony ESD 50/PK-8
PO Box 1185 59457 406-538-8022
Fax 538-2819
Spring Creek Colony S 50/PK-8
PO Box 1185 59457 406-538-8022
Amie Talkington, lead tchr. Fax 538-2819

Libby, Lincoln, Pop. 2,648
Libby SD 1,400/PK-12
724 Louisiana Ave 59923 406-293-8811
K. Maki, supt. Fax 293-8812
libby.k12.mt.us/
Libby ES 300/PK-3
700 Idaho Ave 59923 406-293-8881
Marjorie O'Brien-Johnson, prin. Fax 293-8882
Libby MS 500/4-8
101 Ski Rd 59923 406-293-2763
Ron Goodman, prin. Fax 293-2862

Kootenai Valley Christian S 100/PK-8
1024 Montana Ave 59923 406-293-2303
Myresa Boulware, admin. Fax 293-2303
Libby Adventist Christian S 50/1-8
88 Airfield Rd 59923 406-293-8613
Nick Ratcliff, prin.

Lima, Beaverhead, Pop. 227
Lima SD 100/PK-12
PO Box 186 59739 406-276-3571
Stephen Henderson, supt. Fax 276-3571
Lima MS 50/7-8
PO Box 186 59739 406-276-3571
Stephen Henderson, prin. Fax 276-3571
Lima S 50/PK-6
PO Box 186 59739 406-276-3571
Stephen Henderson, prin. Fax 276-3571

Lincoln, Lewis and Clark
Lincoln SD — 200/PK-12
PO Box 39 59639 — 406-362-4201
Kathy Heisler, supt. — Fax 362-4030
www.lincolnlynx.com
Lincoln ES — 100/PK-6
PO Box 39 59639 — 406-362-4201
Laurie Maughan, prin. — Fax 362-4030
Lincoln MS — 50/7-8
PO Box 39 59639 — 406-362-4201
Laurie Maughan, prin. — Fax 362-4030

Lindsay, Dawson
Lindsay ESD — 50/PK-8
PO Box B 59339 — 406-584-7486
Lindsay S — 50/PK-8
PO Box B 59339 — 406-584-7486

Livingston, Park, Pop. 7,146
Arrowhead ESD — 100/PK-8
1489 E River Rd 59047 — 406-333-4359
Adam Galvin, supt. — Fax 333-4975
www.arrowheadschool.net
Arrowhead ES — 100/PK-6
1489 E River Rd 59047 — 406-333-4359
Adam Galvin, prin. — Fax 333-4975
Arrowhead MS — 50/7-8
1489 E River Rd 59047 — 406-333-4359
Adam Galvin, prin. — Fax 333-4975

Livingston SD — 1,500/PK-12
132 S B St 59047 — 406-222-0861
Andrew Anderson, supt. — Fax 222-7323
East Side ES — 300/K-5
401 View Vista Dr 59047 — 406-222-1773
Sandy Tangan, prin. — Fax 222-5243
Sleeping Giant MS — 300/6-8
301 View Vista Dr 59047 — 406-222-3292
Tena Versland, prin. — Fax 222-3512
Winans ES — 300/PK-5
1015 W Clark St 59047 — 406-222-0192
Jim Huntzicker, prin. — Fax 222-7239

Pine Creek ESD — 50/K-8
2575 E River Rd 59047 — 406-222-0059
Fax 222-0059
Pine Creek ES — 50/K-6
2575 E River Rd 59047 — 406-222-0059
Leah Shannon-Beye, lead tchr. — Fax 222-0059
Pine Creek MS — 50/7-8
2575 E River Rd 59047 — 406-222-0059
Leah Shannon-Beye, lead tchr. — Fax 222-0059

St. Marys Catholic S — 100/PK-8
511 S F St 59047 — 406-222-3303
Judy Jagodzinski, prin. — Fax 222-4662

Lodge Grass, Big Horn, Pop. 522
Lodge Grass SD — 400/PK-12
PO Box 810 59050 — 406-639-2304
Wallace Leider, supt. — Fax 639-2388
Lodge Grass ES — 200/PK-6
PO Box 810 59050 — 406-639-2333
Kenneth Deputee, prin. — Fax 639-2375
Lodge Grass MS — 100/7-8
PO Box 810 59050 — 406-639-2333
John Small, prin. — Fax 639-2388

Lolo, Missoula, Pop. 2,746
Lolo ESD — 600/PK-8
11395 US Highway 93 S 59847 — 406-273-0451
Michael Magone, supt. — Fax 273-2628
www.lolo.k12.mt.us/
Lolo ES — 400/PK-5
11395 US Highway 93 S 59847 — 406-273-6686
Alice Kupilik, prin. — Fax 273-2628
Lolo MS — 200/6-8
11395 US Highway 93 S 59847 — 406-273-6141
Dave Hansen, prin. — Fax 273-2628

Woodman ESD — 50/K-8
18470 Lolo Creek Rd 59847 — 406-273-6770
Fax 273-6659
Woodman ES — 50/K-6
18470 Lolo Creek Rd 59847 — 406-273-6770
Michelle Morgan, lead tchr. — Fax 273-6659
Woodman MS — 50/7-8
18470 Lolo Creek Rd 59847 — 406-273-6770
Louise Rhode, prin. — Fax 273-6659

Loring, Phillips
Malta SD
Supt. — See Malta
Loring Colony S — 50/K-8
Highway 191 59537 — 406-674-5525
Jeanne Engebretson, lead tchr. — Fax 654-2326

Luther, Carbon
Luther ESD
Supt. — See Red Lodge
Luther S — 50/PK-8
4 Luther Roscoe Rd 59068 — 406-446-2480
Janice Eckert, lead tchr. — Fax 446-2480

Mc Leod, Sweet Grass
Mc Leod ESD
Supt. — See Big Timber
Mc Leod S — 50/PK-8
1 Main St 59052 — 406-932-6164
Diana Baker, prin. — Fax 932-6164

Malta, Phillips, Pop. 1,922
Malta SD — 600/PK-12
PO Box 670 59538 — 406-654-1871
Kris Kuehn, supt. — Fax 654-2205
www.malta.k12.mt.us/
Malta ES — 200/PK-6
706 S 3rd Ave E 59538 — 406-654-2320
Theodore Schye, prin. — Fax 654-2326
Malta JHS — 100/7-8
S 9th St W 59538 — 406-654-2225
John Roberts, prin. — Fax 654-2226
Tallow Creek S — 50/K-8
28605 Content Rd 59538 — 406-658-2643
Jenny Crowder, prin. — Fax 654-2326
Other Schools – See Loring

Manhattan, Gallatin, Pop. 1,465
Amsterdam ESD — 100/K-6
6360 Camp Creek Rd 59741 — 406-282-7216
Fax 282-7724
Amsterdam ES — 100/K-6
6360 Camp Creek Rd 59741 — 406-282-7216
Jamie Wubben, lead tchr. — Fax 282-7724

Manhattan SD — 600/PK-12
PO Box 425 59741 — 406-284-6460
Jerry Pease, supt. — Fax 284-6853
Manhattan ES — 300/PK-6
PO Box 425 59741 — 406-284-3250
Scott Schumacher, prin. — Fax 284-4122
Manhattan MS — 100/7-8
PO Box 425 59741 — 406-284-3250
Scott Schumacher, prin. — Fax 284-4122

Manhattan Christian S — 300/PK-12
8000 Churchill Rd 59741 — 406-282-7261
Thomas Kamp, admin. — Fax 282-7701

Marion, Flathead
Marion ESD — 100/PK-8
205 Gopher Ln 59925 — 406-854-2333
Fax 854-2690
Marion ES — 100/PK-6
205 Gopher Ln 59925 — 406-854-2333
Mark Tollefson, prin. — Fax 854-2690
Marion MS — 50/7-8
205 Gopher Ln 59925 — 406-854-2333
Mark Tollefson, prin. — Fax 854-2690

Pleasant Valley ESD — 50/PK-8
7975 Pleasant Valley Rd 59925 — 406-758-5750
Marcia Scheffels, supt. — Fax 858-2250
Pleasant Valley S — 50/PK-8
7975 Pleasant Valley Rd 59925 — 406-858-2343
Teri Holmquist, prin. — Fax 858-2250

Martinsdale, Meagher
Lennep ESD — 50/PK-8
25 Lennep Rd 59053 — 406-572-3381
Fax 572-3381
Lennep S — 50/PK-8
25 Lennep Rd 59053 — 406-572-3381
Leah Tucker, lead tchr. — Fax 572-3381

Medicine Lake, Sheridan, Pop. 228
Medicine Lake SD — 100/PK-12
PO Box 265 59247 — 406-789-2211
David Kloker, supt. — Fax 789-2213
Medicine Lake ES — 100/PK-6
PO Box 265 59247 — 406-789-2211
Kathleen Waller, prin. — Fax 789-2213
Medicine Lake MS — 50/7-8
PO Box 265 59247 — 406-789-2211
Kathleen Waller, prin. — Fax 789-2213

Melrose, Silver Bow
Melrose ESD — 50/PK-8
PO Box 128 59743 — 406-835-2811
Melrose S, PO Box 128 59743 — 50/PK-8
Mary Smith, lead tchr. — 406-835-2811

Melstone, Musselshell, Pop. 137
Melstone SD — 100/PK-12
PO Box 97 59054 — 406-358-2352
Kelly Haaland, supt. — Fax 358-2346
Melstone ES — 50/PK-6
PO Box 97 59054 — 406-358-2352
Kelly Haaland, prin. — Fax 358-2346
Melstone MS — 50/7-8
PO Box 97 59054 — 406-358-2352
Kelly Haaland, prin. — Fax 358-2346

Melville, Sweet Grass
Melville ESD — 50/PK-8
PO Box 275 59055 — 406-537-4457
Melville S, PO Box 275 59055 — 50/PK-8
Patty Bell, lead tchr. — 406-537-4457

Miles City, Custer, Pop. 8,162
Kircher ESD — 50/PK-6
331 Kircher Creek Rd 59301 — 406-234-2761
Kircher ES — 50/PK-6
331 Kircher Creek Rd 59301 — 406-234-2761

Miles City SD — 1,600/PK-12
1604 Main St 59301 — 406-234-3840
Jack Regan, supt. — Fax 234-3147
garfieldweb.com/milescity/
Garfield ES — 300/PK-6
1015 Milwaukee St 59301 — 406-234-4310
Laurie Huffman, prin. — Fax 234-4311
Highland Park ES — 100/PK-3
716 Cale Ave 59301 — 406-234-3890
Larry Wilkerson, prin. — Fax 234-3892
Jefferson ES — 100/PK-3
106 N Strevell Ave 59301 — 406-234-2888
Larry Wilkerson, prin. — Fax 234-2889
Lincoln ES — 200/4-6
210 S Lake Ave 59301 — 406-234-1697
John Gorton, prin. — Fax 234-2081
Washington MS — 300/7-8
210 N 9th St 59301 — 406-234-2084
Jon Plowman, prin. — Fax 234-7403

SH ESD — 50/PK-8
HC 32 59301 — 406-421-5560
SH S, HC 32 59301 — 50/PK-8
David Fry, lead tchr. — 406-421-5560

Spring Creek ESD — 50/PK-8
HC 30 59301 — 406-554-3512
Other Schools – See Powderville

Trail Creek ESD — 50/PK-8
HC 40 Box 6591 59301 — 406-421-5503
Riverview S, HC 40 Box 6591 59301 — 50/PK-8
Tabitha Perry, lead tchr. — 406-421-5503

Sacred Heart S — 100/PK-8
519 N Center Ave 59301 — 406-234-3850
Bart Freese, prin. — Fax 234-5687

Missoula, Missoula, Pop. 62,923
DeSmet ESD — 100/PK-8
6355 Padre Ln 59808 — 406-549-4994
Fax 549-4994
DeSmet ES — 100/PK-6
6355 Padre Ln 59808 — 406-549-4994
Rose Woodford, prin. — Fax 549-4994
DeSmet MS — 50/7-8
6355 Padre Ln 59808 — 406-549-4994
Rose Woodford, prin. — Fax 549-4994

Hellgate ESD — 1,200/PK-8
2385 Flynn Ln 59808 — 406-728-5626
Dr. Doug Reisig, supt. — Fax 728-5636
www.hellgate.k12.mt.us
Hellgate ES — 800/PK-5
2385 Flynn Ln 59808 — 406-721-2160
Dr. Bruce Whitehead, prin. — Fax 728-5636
Hellgate MS — 400/6-8
2385 Flynn Ln 59808 — 406-721-2452
Nancy Singleton, prin. — Fax 728-0967

Missoula SD — 8,800/PK-12
215 S 6th St W 59801 — 406-728-2400
Alex Apostle, supt. — Fax 542-4009
www.mcps.k12.mt.us
Chief Charlo ES — 400/K-5
5600 Longview Dr 59803 — 406-542-4005
David Rott, prin. — Fax 721-2977
Cold Springs ES — 500/K-5
2625 Briggs St 59803 — 406-542-4010
Webb Harrington, prin. — Fax 542-4012
Franklin ES — 300/PK-5
1901 S 10th St W 59801 — 406-542-4020
Mike Williams, prin. — Fax 728-7373
Hawthorne ES — 400/K-5
2835 S 3rd St W 59804 — 406-542-4025
Steve McHugh, prin. — Fax 542-4027
Lewis & Clark ES — 500/K-5
2901 Park St 59801 — 406-542-4035
Jack Sturgis, prin. — Fax 542-4037
Lowell ES — 200/K-5
1200 Sherwood St 59802 — 406-542-4040
Cindy Christensen, prin. — Fax 542-4042
Meadow Hill MS — 500/6-8
4210 S Reserve St 59803 — 406-542-4045
Nick Carter, prin. — Fax 721-4418
Paxson ES — 400/K-5
101 Evans Ave 59801 — 406-542-4055
Roberta Stengel, prin. — Fax 542-4058
Porter MS — 500/6-8
2510 W Central Ave 59804 — 406-542-4060
Gail Chandler, prin. — Fax 542-4098
Rattlesnake ES — 400/PK-5
1220 Pineview Dr 59802 — 406-542-4050
Jerry Seidensticker, prin. — Fax 542-4059
Russell ES — 300/K-5
3216 S Russell St 59801 — 406-542-4080
Fax 721-7063
Washington MS — 600/6-8
645 W Central Ave 59801 — 406-542-4085
Robert Gearheart, prin. — Fax 721-7346

Target Range ESD — 400/PK-8
4095 South Ave W 59804 — 406-549-9239
George Linthicum, supt. — Fax 728-8841
www.target.k12.mt.us
Target Range ES — 300/PK-6
4095 South Ave W 59804 — 406-549-9239
Luke Laslovich, prin. — Fax 728-8841
Target Range MS — 100/7-8
4095 South Ave W 59804 — 406-549-9239
Ann Minckler, prin. — Fax 728-8841

Mountain View SDA S — 50/K-8
1010 Clements Rd 59804 — 406-543-6223
St. Joseph S — 300/K-8
503 Edith St 59801 — 406-549-1290
Rick Hyland, prin. — Fax 543-4034
Valley Christian S — 300/PK-12
2526 Sunset Ln 59804 — 406-549-0482
Chris Martineau, prin. — Fax 549-5047

Molt, Stillwater
Molt ESD — 50/K-8
PO Box 70 59057 — 406-669-3224
Fax 669-3224
Molt S — 50/K-8
PO Box 70 59057 — 406-669-3224
Debra Flynn, lead tchr. — Fax 669-3224

Moore, Fergus, Pop. 188
Moore SD — 100/PK-12
509 Highland Ave 59464 — 406-374-2231
Yvette Majerus, supt. — Fax 374-2490
www.moore.k12.mt.us
Moore ES — 50/PK-6
509 Highland Ave 59464 — 406-374-2231
Yvette Majerus, prin. — Fax 374-2490
Moore MS — 50/7-8
509 Highland Ave 59464 — 406-374-2231
Yvette Majerus, prin. — Fax 374-2490

Mosby, Garfield
Ross ESD, 1491 Old Stage Rd 59058 — 50/PK-8
Jessica McWilliams, supt. — 406-557-6115
Ross S, 1491 Old Stage Rd 59058 — 50/PK-8
Carol Smith, lead tchr. — 406-429-6501

Nashua, Valley, Pop. 303
Nashua SD — 100/PK-12
PO Box 170 59248 — 406-746-3411
Gary Fisher, supt. — Fax 746-3458
Nashua ES — 100/PK-6
PO Box 170 59248 — 406-746-3411
Gary Fisher, prin. — Fax 746-3458
Nashua MS — 50/7-8
PO Box 170 59248 — 406-746-3411
Gary Fisher, prin. — Fax 746-3458

Noxon, Sanders
Noxon SD — 200/K-12
300 Noxon Ave 59853 — 406-847-2442
Jackie Branum, supt. — Fax 847-2232

Noxon ES 100/K-6
300 Noxon Ave 59853 406-847-2442
Jackie Branum, prin. Fax 847-2232
Noxon MS 50/7-8
300 Noxon Ave 59853 406-847-2442
Kelly Moore, prin. Fax 847-2232

Opheim, Valley, Pop. 103
Opheim SD 100/PK-12
PO Box 108 59250 406-762-3214
Leroy Nelson, supt. Fax 762-3348
Opheim ES 50/PK-6
PO Box 108 59250 406-762-3214
Leroy Nelson, prin. Fax 762-3348
Opheim MS 50/7-8
PO Box 108 59250 406-762-3214
Leroy Nelson, prin. Fax 762-3348

Ovando, Powell
Ovando ESD 50/K-8
PO Box 176 59854 406-793-5722
Fax 793-5525
Ovando S 50/K-8
PO Box 176 59854 406-793-5722
Stacey Mannix, lead tchr. Fax 793-5525

Pablo, Lake, Pop. 1,298
Ronan SD
Supt. — See Ronan
Pablo ES 200/K-4
608 4th Ave E 59855 406-676-3390
Frank Ciez, prin. Fax 675-2833

Paradise, Sanders
Paradise ESD 50/PK-8
PO Box 126 59856 406-826-3344
Fax 826-5299
Paradise S 50/PK-8
PO Box 126 59856 406-826-3344
James LeClair, prin. Fax 826-5299

Park City, Stillwater
Park City SD 300/PK-12
PO Box 278 59063 406-633-2406
Dick Webb, supt. Fax 633-2913
Park City ES 200/PK-6
PO Box 278 59063 406-633-2350
Janet Southworth, prin. Fax 633-2913
Park City MS 100/7-8
PO Box 278 59063 406-633-2350
Thomas Gauthier, prin. Fax 633-2913

Pendroy, Teton
Pendroy ESD 50/PK-8
PO Box 65 59467 406-469-2387
Fax 469-2386
Pendroy S 50/PK-8
PO Box 65 59467 406-469-2387
Fax 469-2386

Philipsburg, Granite, Pop. 959
Philipsburg SD 200/PK-12
PO Box 400 59858 406-859-3232
Mike Cutler, supt. Fax 859-3674
pburg.k12.mt.us
Philipsburg ES 100/PK-6
PO Box 400 59858 406-859-3233
Dan Farnam, prin. Fax 859-3673
Philipsburg MS 50/7-8
PO Box 400 59858 406-859-3232
Dan Farnam, prin. Fax 859-3674

Plains, Sanders, Pop. 1,247
Plains SD 500/PK-12
PO Box 549 59859 406-826-3666
Richard Magera, supt. Fax 826-4439
www.plainsschools.net/
Plains ES 200/PK-6
PO Box 549 59859 406-826-3642
Jim Holland, prin. Fax 826-4439
Plains MS 100/7-8
PO Box 549 59859 406-826-3666
Larry McDonald, prin. Fax 826-4439

Plentywood, Sheridan, Pop. 1,774
Plentywood SD 400/PK-12
100 E Laurel Ave 59254 406-765-1803
Joe Bennett, supt. Fax 765-1195
www.plentywood.k12.mt.us/
Plentywood ES 200/PK-6
100 E Laurel Ave 59254 406-765-1803
Rob Pedersen, prin. Fax 765-1195
Plentywood MS 100/7-8
100 E Laurel Ave 59254 406-765-1803
Rob Pedersen, prin. Fax 765-1195

Plevna, Fallon, Pop. 131
Plevna SD 100/PK-12
PO Box 158 59344 406-772-5666
Jule Walker, supt. Fax 772-5548
www.plevna.k12.mt.us/
Plevna ES 50/PK-6
PO Box 158 59344 406-772-5666
Jule Walker, prin. Fax 772-5548
Plevna MS 50/7-8
PO Box 158 59344 406-772-5666
Jule Walker, prin. Fax 772-5548

Polson, Lake, Pop. 4,828
Polson SD 1,400/K-12
111 4th Ave E 59860 406-883-6355
David Whitesell, supt. Fax 883-6345
www.polson.k12.mt.us
Cherry Valley ES 100/K-1
111 4th Ave E 59860 406-883-6333
Elaine Meeks, prin. Fax 883-6332
Linderman ES 200/2-4
111 4th Ave E 59860 406-883-6229
Steve York, prin. Fax 883-6365
Polson MS 300/5-6
111 4th Ave E 59860 406-883-6335
Tom Digiallonardo, prin. Fax 883-6334
Polson MS 300/7-8
111 4th Ave E 59860 406-883-6335
Brian Adams, prin. Fax 883-6334

Valley View ESD 50/PK-6
42448 Valley View Rd 59860 406-883-7262
Gale Decker, supt. Fax 883-7262
Valley View ES 50/PK-6
42448 Valley View Rd 59860 406-883-2208
Susie Kayser, prin. Fax 883-2996

Poplar, Roosevelt, Pop. 904
Poplar SD 800/PK-12
PO Box 458 59255 406-768-3409
Charles Cook, supt. Fax 768-5510
www.poplar.k12.mt.us/
Poplar ES 300/PK-4
PO Box 458 59255 406-768-5601
Tom Granbois, prin. Fax 768-5616
Poplar IS 100/5-6
PO Box 458 59255 406-768-5602
Keith Erickson, prin. Fax 768-5604
Poplar JHS 200/7-8
PO Box 458 59255 406-768-5602
Keith Erickson, prin. Fax 768-5604

Powderville, Powder River
Spring Creek ESD
Supt. — See Miles City
Spring Creek S 50/PK-8
552 County Road 59345 406-554-3512
Lydianne Jurica, lead tchr.

Power, Teton
Power SD 100/PK-12
PO Box 155 59468 406-463-2251
Ken Kelly, supt. Fax 463-2360
www.power.k12.mt.us/
Power ES 100/PK-6
PO Box 155 59468 406-463-2251
Kelly Glass, prin. Fax 463-2360
Power MS 50/7-8
PO Box 155 59468 406-463-2251
Kelly Glass, prin. Fax 463-2360

Pryor, Big Horn, Pop. 654
Pryor SD 100/K-12
PO Box 229 59066 406-259-7329
Luke Enemy Hunter, supt. Fax 245-8938
Pryor ES 50/K-6
PO Box 229 59066 406-259-8011
Fax 252-9197
Pryor MS 50/7-8
PO Box 229 59066 406-259-7329
Dell Fritzler, prin. Fax 245-8938

St. Charles Mission S 100/PK-8
PO Box 29 59066 406-259-9976
Dell Fritzler, prin. Fax 259-7092

Ramsay, Silver Bow
Ramsay ESD 100/K-8
PO Box 105 59748 406-782-5470
Fax 723-8905
Ramsay ES 100/K-6
PO Box 105 59748 406-782-5470
Rosemary Garvey, prin. Fax 723-8905
Ramsay MS 50/7-8
PO Box 105 59748 406-782-5470
Rosemary Garvey, prin. Fax 723-8905

Rapelje, Stillwater
Rapelje SD 100/K-12
PO Box 89 59067 406-663-2215
Jerry Thompson, supt. Fax 663-2299
www.rapelje.k12.mt.us/
Rapelje ES 50/K-6
PO Box 89 59067 406-663-2215
Jerry Thompson, prin. Fax 663-2299
Rapelje MS 50/7-8
PO Box 89 59067 406-663-2215
Jerry Thompson, prin. Fax 663-2299

Red Lodge, Carbon, Pop. 2,401
Luther ESD 50/PK-8
1401 Red Lodge Creek Rd 59068 406-446-2480
Fax 446-2480
Other Schools – See Luther

Red Lodge SD 500/PK-12
PO Box 1090 59068 406-446-1804
Mark Brajcich, supt. Fax 446-2037
redlodge.schoolwires.com/redlodge/site/default.asp
Mountain View PS 100/PK-3
PO Box 1090 59068 406-446-1804
Doug Mann, prin. Fax 446-2037
Red Lodge MS 100/7-8
PO Box 1090 59068 406-446-2110
John Fitzgerald, prin. Fax 446-3975
Roosevelt IS 100/4-6
PO Box 1090 59068 406-446-2110
John Fitzgerald, prin. Fax 446-3975

Reedpoint, Stillwater
Reed Point SD 100/PK-12
PO Box 338 59069 406-326-2245
Dwain Haggard, supt. Fax 326-2339
www.reedpoint.k12.mt.us/
Reed Point ES 50/PK-6
PO Box 338 59069 406-326-2228
Dwain Haggard, prin. Fax 326-2339
Reed Point MS 50/7-8
PO Box 338 59069 406-326-2225
Dwain Haggard, prin. Fax 326-2339

Richey, Dawson, Pop. 179
Richey SD 100/K-12
PO Box 60 59259 406-773-5680
Brad Moore, supt. Fax 773-5554
www.richey.k12.mt.us/
Richey ES 50/K-6
PO Box 60 59259 406-773-5523
Brad Moore, prin. Fax 773-5554
Richey MS 50/7-8
PO Box 60 59259 406-773-5680
Brad Moore, prin. Fax 773-5554

Roberts, Carbon
Roberts SD 100/K-12
PO Box 78 59070 406-445-2421
Jeff Bermes, supt. Fax 445-2506
robertsschool.net
Roberts ES 100/K-6
PO Box 78 59070 406-445-2421
Jeff Bermes, prin. Fax 445-2506
Roberts MS 50/7-8
PO Box 78 59070 406-445-2421
Jeff Bermes, prin. Fax 445-2506

Ronan, Lake, Pop. 1,968
Ronan SD 1,300/PK-12
421 Andrew St NW 59864 406-676-3390
Andrew Holmlund, supt. Fax 676-3392
www.ronank12.edu/
Harvey ES 400/PK-5
421 Andrew St NW 59864 406-676-3390
Dave Marzolf, prin. Fax 676-3319
Ronan MS 300/6-8
421 Andrew St NW 59864 406-676-3390
Jim Gillhouse, prin. Fax 676-2852
Other Schools – See Pablo

Glacier View Christian S 50/1-8
36332 Mud Creek Ln 59864 406-676-5142

Rosebud, Rosebud
Rosebud SD 100/PK-12
PO Box 38 59347 406-347-5353
Ellis Parry, supt. Fax 347-5544
www.rosebudschooldist.com/
Rosebud ES 50/PK-6
PO Box 38 59347 406-347-5353
Ellis Parry, prin. Fax 347-5544
Rosebud MS 50/7-8
PO Box 38 59347 406-347-5353
Ellis Parry, prin. Fax 347-5544

Roundup, Musselshell, Pop. 1,916
Roundup SD 600/K-12
700 3rd St W 59072 406-323-1507
Chad Sealey, supt. Fax 323-1927
www.roundup.k12.mt.us
Central ES 300/K-6
600 1st St W 59072 406-323-1512
Vicki Begin, prin. Fax 323-1759
Roundup MS 100/7-8
525 6th Ave W 59072 406-323-2402
Jim Schladweiler, prin. Fax 323-1583

Roy, Fergus
Roy SD 100/K-12
PO Box 9 59471 406-464-2511
Dustin Sturm, supt. Fax 464-2561
Roy ES 50/K-6
PO Box 9 59471 406-464-2511
Dustin Sturm, prin. Fax 464-2561
Roy MS 50/7-8
PO Box 9 59471 406-464-2511
Dustin Sturm, prin. Fax 464-2561

Rudyard, Hill
North Star SD 200/PK-12
PO Box 129 59540 406-355-4481
Ken Halverson, supt. Fax 355-4532
www.northstar.k12.mt.us
North Star MS 50/7-8
PO Box 129 59540 406-355-4481
Ken Halverson, prin. Fax 355-4532
Other Schools – See Gildford

Ryegate, Golden Valley, Pop. 304
Ryegate SD 100/K-12
PO Box 129 59074 406-568-2211
Mike Lee, supt. Fax 568-2528
Ryegate ES 50/K-6
PO Box 129 59074 406-568-2211
Mike Lee, prin. Fax 568-2528
Ryegate MS 50/7-8
PO Box 129 59074 406-568-2211
Mike Lee, prin. Fax 568-2528

Saco, Phillips, Pop. 203
Saco SD 100/PK-12
PO Box 298 59261 406-527-3531
Gordon Hahn, supt. Fax 527-3479
www.sacoschools.k12.mt.us
Saco ES 50/PK-6
PO Box 298 59261 406-527-3531
Gordon Hahn, prin. Fax 527-3479
Saco MS 50/7-8
PO Box 298 59261 406-527-3531
Gordon Hahn, prin. Fax 527-3479

Saint Ignatius, Lake, Pop. 796
St. Ignatius SD 500/PK-12
PO Box 1540 59865 406-745-3811
Gerry Nolan, supt. Fax 745-4421
St. Ignatius ES 200/PK-5
PO Box 1540 59865 406-745-3811
Tammy Demien, prin. Fax 745-4070
St. Ignatius MS 100/6-8
PO Box 1540 59865 406-745-3811
Jason Sargent, prin. Fax 745-4060

Saint Regis, Mineral
Saint Regis SD 200/PK-12
PO Box K 59866 406-649-2427
Patty Kero, supt. Fax 649-2788
Saint Regis ES 100/PK-6
PO Box K 59866 406-649-2311
Don Almquist, prin. Fax 649-2788
Saint Regis MS 50/7-8
PO Box K 59866 406-649-2311
Don Almquist, prin. Fax 649-2788

Saint Xavier, Big Horn, Pop. 100

Pretty Eagle Catholic S 100/K-8
PO Box 257 59075 406-666-2215
Garla Williamson, prin. Fax 666-2245

Sand Coulee, Cascade
Centerville SD 200/PK-12
PO Box 100 59472 406-736-5167
Dennis Gerke, supt. Fax 736-5210
www.centerville.k12.mt.us/
Big Stone S 50/K-8
PO Box 100 59472 406-736-5167
Dennis Gerke, prin. Fax 736-5210
Centerville ES 100/PK-6
PO Box 100 59472 406-736-5167
Dennis Gerke, prin. Fax 736-5210
Centerville MS 50/7-8
PO Box 100 59472 406-736-5167
Matthew McCale, prin. Fax 736-5210

Sand Springs, Garfield
Sand Springs ESD 50/K-8
1706 S Fork Rd 59077 406-557-2774
Sand Springs S, PO Box 25 59077 50/K-8
Verna Jessen, lead tchr. 406-557-2774

Savage, Richland
Savage SD 100/PK-12
PO Box 110 59262 406-776-2317
Loren Dunk, supt. Fax 776-2260
Savage ES 50/PK-6
PO Box 110 59262 406-776-2317
John McNeil, prin. Fax 776-2260
Savage MS 50/7-8
PO Box 110 59262 406-776-2317
Loren Dunk, prin. Fax 776-2260

Scobey, Daniels, Pop. 991
Scobey SD 200/PK-12
PO Box 10 59263 406-487-2202
Dave Selvig, supt. Fax 487-2204
Scobey ES 100/PK-6
PO Box 10 59263 406-487-2202
Dave Selvig, prin. Fax 487-2204
Scobey MS 50/7-8
PO Box 10 59263 406-487-2202
George Rider, prin. Fax 487-2204

Seeley Lake, Missoula
Seeley Lake ESD 200/PK-8
PO Box 840 59868 406-677-2265
Suzanne Dobb, supt. Fax 677-2264
Seeley Lake ES 100/PK-6
PO Box 840 59868 406-677-2265
Suzanne Dobb, prin. Fax 677-2264
Seeley MS 100/7-8
PO Box 840 59868 406-677-2265
Suzanne Dobb, prin. Fax 677-2264

Shawmut, Wheatland
Shawmut ESD 50/PK-6
PO Box 65 59078 406-632-4430
Fax 632-4770
Shawmut ES 50/PK-6
PO Box 65 59078 406-632-4430
Atha Stagner, prin. Fax 632-4770

Shelby, Toole, Pop. 3,304
Shelby SD 300/PK-12
1010 Oilfield Ave 59474 406-434-2622
Matt Genger, supt. Fax 434-2959
www.shelby.k12.mt.us/
Rose S 50/PK-8
253 Union School Rd 59474 406-424-8910
Joe Rapkoch, prin. Fax 424-8933
Shelby ES PK-6
901 Valley St 59474 406-424-8910
Joe Rapkoch, prin. Fax 424-8933
Shelby MS 100/7-8
1001 Valley St 59474 406-424-8910
Shawn Clark, prin. Fax 434-7273

Shepherd, Yellowstone
Shepherd SD 900/PK-12
PO Box 8 59079 406-373-5461
Dan Jamieson, supt. Fax 373-5284
www.shepherd.k12.mt.us/
Shepherd ES 400/PK-6
PO Box 8 59079 406-373-5516
Brent Bassett, prin. Fax 373-5076
Shepherd MS 200/7-8
PO Box 8 59079 406-373-5873
Kenneth Poepping, prin. Fax 373-5648

Sheridan, Madison, Pop. 689
Sheridan SD 200/PK-12
PO Box 586 59749 406-842-5302
Kim Harding, supt. Fax 842-5391
www.sheridan.k12.mt.us/
Sheridan ES 100/PK-6
PO Box 586 59749 406-842-5302
Kim Harding, prin. Fax 842-5391
Sheridan MS 50/7-8
PO Box 586 59749 406-842-5302
Kim Harding, prin. Fax 842-5391

Sidney, Richland, Pop. 4,470
Brorson ESD 50/K-6
PO Box 145 59270 406-798-3361
Fax 798-3414
Brorson ES 50/K-6
PO Box 145 59270 406-798-3361
A. Thingstad, lead tchr. Fax 798-3414

Rau ESD 100/PK-6
12138 County Road 350 59270 406-482-1088
Fax 482-1016
Rau ES 100/PK-6
12138 County Road 350 59270 406-482-1088
Carolyn Koch, lead tchr. Fax 482-1016

Sidney SD 1,100/K-12
200 3rd Ave SE 59270 406-433-4080
Doug Sullivan, supt. Fax 433-4358
www.sidneyps.com
Sidney ES 500/K-5
200 3rd Ave SE 59270 406-433-5501
William Nankivel, prin. Fax 433-9186
Sidney MS 300/6-8
200 3rd Ave SE 59270 406-433-4050
Kelly Johnson, prin. Fax 433-4052

Simms, Cascade
Sun River Valley SD 300/PK-12
PO Box 380 59477 406-264-5111
Elaine Forrest, supt. Fax 264-5188
www.srvs.k12.mt.us
Other Schools – See Fort Shaw, Sun River

Somers, Flathead
Somers ESD 600/PK-8
PO Box 159 59932 406-857-3661
Teri Wing, supt. Fax 857-3144
www.somersdist29.org
Lakeside ES 400/PK-5
PO Box 159 59932 406-844-2208
John Thies, prin. Fax 844-4609
Somers MS 200/6-8
PO Box 159 59932 406-857-3661
Lori Schieffer, prin. Fax 857-3144

Springdale, Park
Springdale ESD 50/PK-8
PO Box 102 59082 406-932-6756
Fax 932-6704
Springdale S 50/PK-8
PO Box 102 59082 406-932-6756
Amy Jones, lead tchr. Fax 932-6704

Stanford, Judith Basin, Pop. 428
Stanford SD 100/PK-12
PO Box 506 59479 406-566-2265
Eric Gustafson, supt. Fax 566-2772
www.stanford.k12.mt.us/
Stanford ES 100/PK-6
PO Box 506 59479 406-566-2265
Eric Gustafson, prin. Fax 566-2772
Stanford MS 50/7-8
PO Box 506 59479 406-566-2265
Eric Gustafson, prin. Fax 566-2772

Stevensville, Ravalli, Pop. 1,855
Lone Rock ESD 300/PK-8
1112 Three Mile Creek Rd 59870 406-777-3314
Mark Anderson, supt. Fax 777-2770
www.lonerockschool.org/
Lone Rock ES 200/PK-6
1112 Three Mile Creek Rd 59870 406-777-3314
Dave Cluff, prin. Fax 777-2770
Lone Rock MS 100/7-8
1112 Three Mile Creek Rd 59870 406-777-3314
Dave Cluff, prin. Fax 777-2770

Stevensville SD 1,000/PK-12
300 Park St 59870 406-777-5481
Kent Kultgen, supt. Fax 777-1381
www.stevensville.k12.mt.us/
Stevensville ES 400/PK-6
300 Park St 59870 406-777-5613
Jaclyn Mavencamp, prin. Fax 777-5291
Stevensville JHS 100/7-8
300 Park St 59870 406-777-5533
Bob Connors, prin. Fax 777-5291

Sunburst, Toole, Pop. 346
Sunburst SD 200/K-12
PO Box 710 59482 406-937-2811
John Hvidsten, supt. Fax 937-2828
www.sunburstschools.net/
Hillside Colony S 50/K-8
PO Box 710 59482 406-937-2816
Dan Nau, prin. Fax 937-4444
Rimrock Colony S 50/K-8
PO Box 710 59482 406-937-2816
Dan Nau, prin. Fax 937-4444
Sunburst ES 100/K-6
PO Box 710 59482 406-937-2816
Dan Nau, prin. Fax 937-4444
Sunburst MS 50/7-8
PO Box 710 59482 406-937-2816
Dan Nau, prin. Fax 937-4444

Sun River, Cascade
Sun River Valley SD
Supt. — See Simms
Sun River MS 100/6-8
301 Largent St 59483 406-264-5330
Rick Danelson, prin. Fax 264-5333

Superior, Mineral, Pop. 910
Superior SD 400/K-12
PO Box 400 59872 406-822-3600
Wayne Stanley, supt. Fax 822-3601
www.sd3.k12.mt.us/
Superior ES 200/K-6
PO Box 400 59872 406-822-3600
Scott Kinney, prin. Fax 822-3601
Superior MS 100/7-8
PO Box 400 59872 406-822-4851
Allan Labbe, prin. Fax 822-4396

Terry, Prairie, Pop. 563
Terry SD 100/PK-12
PO Box 187 59349 406-635-5533
Charles Deisher, supt. Fax 635-5705
www.terry.k12.mt.us/
Terry ES 100/PK-6
PO Box 187 59349 406-635-5533
Charles Deisher, prin. Fax 635-5705
Terry MS 50/7-8
PO Box 187 59349 406-635-5595
Charles Deisher, prin. Fax 635-5705

Thompson Falls, Sanders, Pop. 1,392
Thompson Falls SD 600/K-12
PO Box 129 59873 406-827-3323
Jerry Pauli, supt. Fax 827-3020
Thompson Falls ES 200/K-6
PO Box 129 59873 406-827-3592
Jennifer Guthals, prin. Fax 827-0192
Thompson Falls MS 100/7-8
PO Box 129 59873 406-827-3593
Tom Holleran, prin. Fax 827-0306

Three Forks, Gallatin, Pop. 1,845
Three Forks SD 600/PK-12
212 E Neal St 59752 406-285-3216
John Overstreet, supt. Fax 285-3216
Three Forks ES 300/PK-6
212 E Neal St 59752 406-285-6830
Jerry Breen, prin. Fax 285-3216
Three Forks MS 100/7-8
210 E Neal St 59752 406-285-3503
Tom Blakely, prin. Fax 285-3503

Townsend, Broadwater, Pop. 1,950
Townsend SD 700/PK-12
201 N Spruce St 59644 406-266-5512
Brian Patrick, supt. Fax 266-4957
townsendps.schoolwires.com/townsendps/site/default.asp
Hazelton ES 400/PK-6
201 N Spruce St 59644 406-266-3942
Charles Smith, prin. Fax 266-4975
Townsend MS 100/7-8
201 N Spruce St 59644 406-266-4983
Brad Racht, prin. Fax 266-4966

Trego, Lincoln
Trego ESD 100/K-8
PO Box 10 59934 406-882-4713
Fax 882-4365
Trego S 100/K-8
PO Box 10 59934 406-882-4713
Dawn Black, lead tchr. Fax 882-4365

Trout Creek, Sanders
Trout Creek ESD 100/PK-8
4 School Ln 59874 406-827-3629
Daisy Carlsmith, admin. Fax 827-4185
www.troutcreekeagles.org/
Trout Creek ES 50/PK-6
4 School Ln 59874 406-827-3629
Daisy Carlsmith, lead tchr. Fax 827-4185
Trout MS 50/7-8
4 School Ln 59874 406-827-3629
Daisy Carlsmith, lead tchr. Fax 827-4185

Troy, Lincoln, Pop. 982
McCormick ESD 50/PK-8
1564 Old US Highway 2 N 59935 406-295-4982
Fax 295-6035
McCormick S 50/PK-8
1564 Old US Highway 2 N 59935 406-295-4982
Jennie Folkerts, lead tchr. Fax 295-6035

Troy SD 400/PK-12
PO Box 867 59935 406-295-4606
Brady Selle, supt. Fax 295-4802
Morrison ES 200/PK-6
PO Box 867 59935 406-295-4321
Lance Pearson, prin. Fax 295-8672
Troy MS 100/7-8
PO Box 867 59935 406-295-4520
Jeff Ralston, prin. Fax 295-5371

Yaak ESD 50/K-8
30117 Yaak River Rd 59935 406-295-4805
Fax 295-8805
Yaak S 50/K-8
30117 Yaak River Rd 59935 406-295-4805
Jennifer Smith, lead tchr. Fax 295-8805

Turner, Blaine
Turner SD 100/PK-12
PO Box 40 59542 406-379-2315
Terry Grant, supt. Fax 379-2398
www.turner.k12.mt.us
Turner ES 50/PK-6
PO Box 40 59542 406-379-2219
Terry Grant, prin. Fax 379-2398
Turner MS 50/7-8
PO Box 40 59542 406-379-2219
Terry Grant, prin. Fax 379-2398

Twin Bridges, Madison, Pop. 418
Twin Bridges SD 300/PK-12
PO Box 419 59754 406-684-5657
David Whitesell, supt. Fax 684-5458
www.twinbridges.k12.mt.us
Twin Bridges ES 100/PK-6
PO Box 419 59754 406-684-5613
Aaron Griffin, prin. Fax 684-5458
Twin Bridges MS 50/7-8
PO Box 419 59754 406-684-5613
Aaron Griffin, prin. Fax 684-5458

Ulm, Cascade
Ulm ESD 100/PK-8
PO Box 189 59485 406-866-3313
Fax 866-3209
Fair Haven Colony S 50/K-8
PO Box 189 59485 406-866-3313
Lauri Ingebrigtson, prin. Fax 866-3209
Ulm ES 50/PK-6
PO Box 189 59485 406-866-3313
Lauri Ingebritson, prin. Fax 866-3209
Ulm MS 50/7-8
PO Box 189 59485 406-866-3313
Lauri Ingebritson, prin. Fax 866-3209

Valier, Pondera, Pop. 472
Valier SD 200/PK-12
PO Box 528 59486 406-279-3613
John Dallum, supt. Fax 279-3764
Kingsbury Colony S 50/K-8
PO Box 528 59486 406-279-3613
John Dallum, prin. Fax 279-3764
Valier ES 100/PK-6
PO Box 528 59486 406-279-3314
John Dallum, prin. Fax 279-3510
Valier MS 50/7-8
PO Box 528 59486 406-279-3314
John Dallum, prin. Fax 279-3510

Vaughn, Cascade
Vaughn ESD 100/PK-8
PO Box 279 59487 406-965-2231
Dean Jardee, admin. Fax 965-3703
www.vaughnschool.com/
Vaughn ES 100/PK-6
PO Box 279 59487 406-965-2231
Dean Jardee, prin. Fax 965-3703

Vaughn MS 50/7-8
PO Box 279 59487 406-965-2231
Dean Jardee, prin. Fax 965-3703

Victor, Ravalli
Victor SD 300/PK-12
425 4th Ave 59875 406-642-3221
Orville Getz, supt. Fax 642-3446
www.victor.k12.mt.us/
Victor ES 100/PK-5
425 4th Ave 59875 406-642-3551
Orville Getz, prin. Fax 642-3446
Victor MS 100/6-8
425 4th Ave 59875 406-642-3221
Danny Johnston, prin. Fax 642-3446

Vida, McCone
Vida ESD 50/PK-8
200 Shell St 59274 406-525-3374
Jackie Becker, supt. Fax 525-3234
Prairie Elk Colony S PK-8
1436 Highway 528 59274 406-525-3438
Jackie Becker, prin. Fax 525-3030
Vida S 50/PK-8
200 Shell St 59274 406-525-3374
Jackie Becker, lead tchr. Fax 525-3234

Volborg, Custer
South Stacey ESD 50/PK-8
179 E Fork Otter Stacey Rd 59351 406-784-2256
Fax 784-2850
South Stacey S 50/PK-8
179 E Fork Otter Stacey Rd 59351 406-784-2256
Rebecca Wilson, lead tchr. Fax 784-2850

Westby, Sheridan, Pop. 148
Westby SD 100/PK-12
PO Box 109 59275 406-385-2258
Wayne Koterba, supt. Fax 385-2430
www.westbyschool.k12.mt.us/
Westby ES 50/PK-6
PO Box 109 59275 406-385-2225
Wayne Koterba, prin. Fax 385-2430
Westby MS 50/7-8
PO Box 109 59275 406-385-2225
Wayne Koterba, prin. Fax 385-2430

West Glacier, Flathead
West Glacier ESD 50/PK-6
PO Box 309 59936 406-888-5312
Fax 888-5141
West Glacier ES 50/PK-6
PO Box 309 59936 406-888-5312
Cortni King, prin. Fax 888-5141

West Yellowstone, Gallatin, Pop. 1,223
West Yellowstone SD 200/PK-12
PO Box 460 59758 406-646-7617
Brian Bagley, supt. Fax 646-7232
www.westyellowstone.k12.mt.us
West Yellowstone ES 100/PK-6
PO Box 460 59758 406-646-7617
Lael Calton, prin. Fax 646-7232
West Yellowstone MS 50/7-8
PO Box 460 59758 406-646-7617
Brian Bagley, prin. Fax 646-7232

Whitefish, Flathead, Pop. 7,067
Olney-Bissell ESD 100/PK-8
5955 Farm To Market Rd 59937 406-862-2828
Fax 862-2838
Bissell ES 100/PK-6
5955 Farm To Market Rd 59937 406-862-2828
Lona Everett, prin. Fax 862-2838
Bissell MS 50/7-8
5955 Farm to Market Rd 59937 406-862-2828
Lona Everett, prin. Fax 862-2838

Whitefish SD 1,600/PK-12
600 2nd St E 59937 406-862-8640
Jerry House, supt. Fax 862-1507
www.wfps.k12.mt.us
Muldown ES 600/PK-4
600 2nd St E 59937 406-862-8620
Jill Rocksund, prin. Fax 862-8630
Whitefish Central MS 300/5-8
600 2nd St E 59937 406-862-8650
Kerry Drown, prin. Fax 862-8664

Whitefish Christian Academy 100/PK-8
820 Ashar Ave 59937 406-862-5875
Kris Queen, admin. Fax 862-3515

Whitehall, Jefferson, Pop. 1,156
Whitehall SD 500/PK-12
PO Box 1109 59759 406-287-3455
Paula Johnston, supt. Fax 287-3843
Whitehall ES 200/PK-6
PO Box 1109 59759 406-287-3882
Luann Carroll, prin. Fax 287-5508
Whitehall JHS 100/7-8
PO Box 1109 59759 406-287-3882
Luann Carroll, prin. Fax 287-5508

White Sulphur Springs, Meagher, Pop. 1,017
White Sulphur Springs SD 100/PK-12
PO Box C 59645 406-547-3751
Andrew Lind, supt. Fax 547-3922
www.whitesulphur.k12.mt.us/
White Sulphur Springs ES PK-6
PO Box C 59645 406-547-3751
Andrew Lind, prin. Fax 547-3922
White Sulphur Springs MS 50/7-8
PO Box C 59645 406-547-3351
Paul Bartas, prin. Fax 547-2407

Whitewater, Phillips
Whitewater SD 100/PK-12
PO Box 46 59544 406-674-5418
Darin Cummings, supt. Fax 674-5460
www.whitewater.k12.mt.us
Whitewater ES 50/PK-6
PO Box 46 59544 406-674-5417
Darin Cummings, prin. Fax 674-5460
Whitewater MS 50/7-8
PO Box 46 59544 406-674-5417
Darin Cummings, prin. Fax 674-5460

Whitlash, Liberty
Whitlash ESD 50/PK-8
PO Box 91 59545 406-432-5153
Fax 432-5151
Whitlash S 50/PK-8
PO Box 91 59545 406-432-5153
Fax 432-5151

Wibaux, Wibaux, Pop. 505
Wibaux SD 200/PK-12
121 F St N 59353 406-796-2474
Renee Rasmussen, supt. Fax 796-2259
wchs.k12.mt.us/
Wibaux ES 100/PK-6
121 F St N 59353 406-796-2518
Janet Huisman, prin. Fax 796-2635
Wibaux JHS 50/7-8
121 F St N 59353 406-796-2474
Janet Huisman, prin. Fax 796-2259

Willow Creek, Gallatin
Willow Creek SD 100/PK-12
PO Box 189 59760 406-285-6991
D.K. Brooks, supt. Fax 285-6923
www.willowcreek.k12.mt.us/
Willow Creek ES 50/PK-6
PO Box 189 59760 406-285-6991
D.K. Brooks, prin. Fax 285-6923
Willow Creek MS 50/7-8
PO Box 189 59760 406-285-6991
D.K. Brooks, prin. Fax 285-6923

Wilsall, Park
Shields Valley SD 300/PK-12
PO Box 131 59086 406-578-2535
Erik Wilkerson, supt. Fax 578-2176
www.shieldsvalleyschools.org/
Shields Valley ES 100/PK-6
PO Box 131 59086 406-578-2535
Alan Peterson, prin. Fax 578-2176
Shields Valley MS 50/7-8
PO Box 131 59086 406-686-4621
Daniel Beck, prin. Fax 686-4937

Winifred, Fergus, Pop. 151
Winifred SD 100/PK-12
PO Box 109 59489 406-462-5349
Dustin Sturm, supt. Fax 462-5477
Winifred ES 50/PK-6
PO Box 109 59489 406-462-5349
Dustin Sturm, prin. Fax 462-5477
Winifred MS 50/7-8
PO Box 109 59489 406-462-5349
Dustin Sturm, prin. Fax 462-5477

Winnett, Petroleum, Pop. 176
Winnett SD 100/PK-12
PO Box 167 59087 406-429-2251
Dr. Clay Dunlap, supt. Fax 429-7631
Winnett ES 50/PK-6
PO Box 167 59087 406-429-2251
Dr. Clay Dunlap, prin. Fax 429-7631
Winnett MS 50/7-8
PO Box 167 59087 406-429-2251
Dr. Clay Dunlap, prin. Fax 429-7631

Wisdom, Beaverhead
Wisdom ESD
Supt. — See Dillon
Wisdom S 50/PK-8
43 Country Rd 59761 406-689-3227
Michele Conners, lead tchr. Fax 689-3217

Wise River, Beaverhead
Wise River ESD 50/PK-8
School House Rd 59762 406-832-3279
Fax 832-3180
Wise River S 50/PK-8
School House Rd 59762 406-832-3279
Barbara Gneiting, lead tchr. Fax 832-3214

Wolf Creek, Lewis and Clark
Auchard Creek ESD 50/PK-8
9605 US Highway 287 59648 406-562-3528
Fax 562-3722
Auchard Creek S 50/PK-8
9605 US Highway 287 59648 406-562-3528
Fax 562-3722

Wolf Creek ESD 50/PK-6
PO Box 200 59648 406-235-4241
Fax 235-4241
Wolf Creek ES 50/PK-6
PO Box 200 59648 406-235-4241
Nellene Hickel, lead tchr. Fax 235-4241

Wolf Point, Roosevelt, Pop. 2,623
Frontier ESD 100/PK-8
6996 Roy St 59201 406-653-2501
Christine Eggor, supt. Fax 653-2508
Frontier ES 100/PK-6
6996 Roy St 59201 406-653-2501
Wes Young, prin. Fax 653-2508
Frontier MS 50/7-8
6996 Roy St 59201 406-653-2501
Wes Young, prin. Fax 653-2508

Wolf Point SD 900/PK-12
220 4th Ave S 59201 406-653-2361
Timothy Cody, supt. Fax 653-1881
wolfpoint.k12.mt.us/
Northside IS 200/4-6
710 4th Ave N 59201 406-653-1653
Ann Beste-Guldborg, prin. Fax 653-2368
Southside ES 300/PK-3
415 4th Ave S 59201 406-653-1480
Eileen Karge, prin. Fax 653-1483
Wolf Point JHS 100/7-8
213 6th Ave S 59201 406-653-1200
Tony Holecek, prin. Fax 653-3104

Worden, Yellowstone
Huntley Project SD 700/PK-12
1477 Ash St 59088 406-967-2540
David Mahon, supt. Fax 967-3059
www.huntley.k12.mt.us/
Huntley Project ES 400/PK-6
1477 Ash St 59088 406-967-2540
Brent Lipp, prin. Fax 967-2547
Huntley Project MS 100/7-8
1477 Ash St 59088 406-967-2540
Frank Hollowell, prin. Fax 967-3054

Wyola, Big Horn
Wyola ESD 100/PK-8
PO Box 66 59089 406-343-2722
Dr. Linda Brown, supt. Fax 343-5901
www.wyola.k12.mt.us
Wyola ES 100/PK-6
PO Box 66 59089 406-343-2722
Jason Cummins, prin. Fax 343-5901
Wyola MS 50/7-8
PO Box 66 59089 406-343-2722
Jason Cummins, prin. Fax 343-5901

Zurich, Blaine
Zurich ESD
Supt. — See Chinook
Zurich S 50/PK-8
265 Park Rd 59547 406-357-4164
Colleen Overcast, lead tchr. Fax 357-4299

NEBRASKA

NEBRASKA DEPARTMENT OF EDUCATION
PO Box 94987, Lincoln 68509-4987
Telephone 402-471-2295
Fax 402-471-0117
Website http://www.nde.state.ne.us

Commissioner of Education Roger Breed

NEBRASKA BOARD OF EDUCATION
PO Box 94987, Lincoln 68509-4987

President Kandy Imes

EDUCATIONAL SERVICE UNITS (ESU)

ESU 1
Robert H. Uhing, admin. 402-287-2061
211 10th St, Wakefield 68784 Fax 287-2065
www.esu1.org/
ESU 2
Michael Ough, admin. 402-721-7710
PO Box 649, Fremont 68026 Fax 721-7712
www.esu2.org/
ESU 3
Douglas Kettelhut, admin. 402-597-4800
6949 S 110th St, La Vista 68128 Fax 597-4808
www2.esu3.org/esu3/
ESU 4
Jon Fisher, admin. 402-274-4354
PO Box 310, Auburn 68305 Fax 274-4356
www.esu4.org/
ESU 5
Al Schneider, admin. 402-223-5277
900 W Court St, Beatrice 68310 Fax 223-5279
www.esu5.org/
ESU 6
Dr. Dan Shoemake, admin. 402-761-3341
PO Box 748, Milford 68405 Fax 761-3279
www.esu6.org/
ESU 7
Dr. Norman Ronell, admin. 402-564-5753
2657 44th Ave, Columbus 68601 Fax 563-1121
www.esu7.org
ESU 8
Randall Peck, admin. 402-887-5041
PO Box 89, Neligh 68756 Fax 887-4604
www.esu8.org/
ESU 9
Calvin Loughran, admin. 402-463-5611
PO Box 2047, Hastings 68902 Fax 463-9555
www.esu9.org/
ESU 10
Wayne Bell, admin. 308-237-5927
PO Box 850, Kearney 68848 Fax 237-5920
www.esu10.org/
ESU 11
Ron Karr, admin. 308-995-6585
PO Box 858, Holdrege 68949 Fax 995-6587
www.esu11.org/
ESU 13
Jeff West, admin. 308-635-3696
4215 Avenue I, Scottsbluff 69361 Fax 635-0680
www.esu13.org/
ESU 15
Brent McMurtrey, admin. 308-334-5160
PO Box 398, Trenton 69044 Fax 334-5581
www.esu15.org
ESU 16
Margene Beatty, admin. 308-284-8481
PO Box 915, Ogallala 69153 Fax 284-8483
www.esu16.org/
ESU 17
Dennis Radford, admin. 402-387-1420
207 N Main St, Ainsworth 69210 Fax 387-1028
www.esu17.org/
ESU 18
David Myers, admin. 402-436-1610
PO Box 82889, Lincoln 68501 Fax 436-1620
www.lps.org/
ESU 19 402-557-2002
, 3215 Cuming St, Omaha 68131 Fax 557-2019
www.ops.org/

PUBLIC, PRIVATE AND CATHOLIC ELEMENTARY SCHOOLS

Adams, Gage, Pop. 486
Freeman SD 300/K-12
PO Box 259 68301 402-988-2525
Gary Hammack, supt. Fax 988-3475
www.freemanpublicschools.org/
Freeman ES 200/K-6
PO Box 259 68301 402-988-2525
Gary Hammack, prin. Fax 988-3475

Ainsworth, Brown, Pop. 1,717
Ainsworth SD 500/K-12
PO Box 65 69210 402-387-2333
Darrell Peterson, supt. Fax 387-0525
www.ainsworthschools.org/
Ainsworth ES 200/K-4
PO Box 65 69210 402-387-2083
Sarah Williams, prin. Fax 387-0525
Ainsworth MS 200/5-8
PO Box 65 69210 402-387-2082
Harvey Wewel, prin. Fax 387-0525

Albion, Boone, Pop. 1,672
Boone Central SD 600/K-12
PO Box 391 68620 402-395-2134
Larry Lambert, supt. Fax 395-2137
www.boonecentral.esu7.org/
Boone Central ES - Albion 200/K-5
PO Box 391 68620 402-395-2134
Timothy Hamilton, prin. Fax 395-2137
Other Schools – See Petersburg

St. Michael's S 100/PK-8
520 W Church St 68620 402-395-2926
Lisa Schumacher, prin. Fax 395-2926

Alda, Hall, Pop. 651
Wood River Rural SD
Supt. — See Wood River
Alda ES 50/K-5
PO Box 146 68810 308-382-4052
Laurel Roth, prin. Fax 382-4052

Allen, Dixon, Pop. 400
Allen Consolidated SD 200/K-12
PO Box 190 68710 402-635-2484
Dr. Katherine Meink, supt. Fax 635-2331
allenweb.esu1.org/
Allen ES 100/K-6
PO Box 190 68710 402-635-2484
Randy Kort, prin. Fax 635-2331

Alliance, Box Butte, Pop. 8,331
Alliance SD 1,600/K-12
1604 Sweetwater Ave 69301 308-762-5475
John McLane, supt. Fax 762-8249
www.allianceps.org/
Alliance MS 500/5-8
1100 Laramie Ave 69301 308-762-3079
Katie White, prin. Fax 762-7302
Emerson ES 300/K-2
700 Black Hills Ave 69301 308-762-4093
Susan Cummings, prin. Fax 762-8249
Grandview ES 200/2-4
615 Grand Ave 69301 308-762-4519
Steve Folchert, prin. Fax 762-8249

St. Agnes Academy 200/PK-8
1104 Cheyenne Ave 69301 308-762-2315
Stacey Romick-Imig, prin. Fax 762-7474

Alma, Harlan, Pop. 1,110
Alma SD 300/K-12
PO Box 170 68920 308-928-2131
Jon Davis, supt. Fax 928-2763
alma.k12.ne.us
Alma ES 200/K-6
PO Box 170 68920 308-928-2131
Jon Davis, prin. Fax 928-2763

Amherst, Buffalo, Pop. 269
Amherst SD 300/K-12
PO Box 8 68812 308-826-3131
Tom Moore, supt. Fax 826-4865
sites.amherst.k12.ne.us/
Amherst ES 100/K-6
PO Box 8 68812 308-826-3131
Tom Moore, prin. Fax 826-4865

Ansley, Custer, Pop. 493
Ansley SD 200/K-12
PO Box 370 68814 308-935-1121
Michael McCabe, supt. Fax 935-9103
Ansley ES 100/K-6
PO Box 370 68814 308-935-1121
Michael McCabe, prin. Fax 935-9103

Arapahoe, Furnas, Pop. 954
Arapahoe SD 300/K-12
PO Box 360 68922 308-962-5458
Damon McDonald, supt. Fax 962-7481
www.esu11.org/arapahoe/fp.html
Arapahoe ES 200/K-6
PO Box 360 68922 308-962-5459
Bob Braithwait, prin. Fax 962-7481

Arcadia, Valley, Pop. 337
Arcadia SD 100/K-12
PO Box 248 68815 308-789-6522
Michael McCabe, supt. Fax 789-6214
sites.arcadia.k12.ne.us/arcadia/
Arcadia ES 100/K-6
PO Box 248 68815 308-789-6522
Michael McCabe, prin. Fax 789-6214

Arlington, Washington, Pop. 1,192
Arlington SD 600/K-12
PO Box 580 68002 402-478-4173
Nathan Stineman, supt. Fax 478-4176
www.apseagles.org/
Arlington ES 300/K-6
PO Box 580 68002 402-478-4121
Chad Radke, prin. Fax 478-4176

St. Paul Lutheran S 100/K-8
8951 County Road 9 68002 402-478-4278
Barb Cook, prin. Fax 478-5378

Arnold, Custer, Pop. 618
Arnold SD 200/K-12
PO Box 399 69120 308-848-2226
Robert Brown, supt. Fax 848-2201
sites.arnold.k12.ne.us/arnoldhome/
Arnold ES 100/K-6
PO Box 399 69120 308-848-2226
Robert Brown, prin. Fax 848-2201

Arthur, Arthur, Pop. 123
Arthur County SD 100/K-12
PO Box 145 69121 308-764-2253
John Frates, supt. Fax 764-2206
Arthur Lower ES 50/K-4
PO Box 145 69121 308-764-2233
John Frates, prin. Fax 764-2206
Arthur Upper ES 50/5-6
PO Box 145 69121 308-764-2231
John Frates, prin. Fax 764-2206

Ashland, Saunders, Pop. 2,493
Ashland-Greenwood SD 900/PK-12
1225 Clay St 68003 402-944-2128
Craig Pease, supt. Fax 944-3310
www.agps.org/
Ashland-Greenwood ES 500/PK-6
1200 Boyd St 68003 402-944-7083
Teresa Bray, prin. Fax 944-3515
Ashland-Greenwood MS 100/7-8
1842 Furnas St 68003 402-944-2114
Ray Bentzen, prin. Fax 944-2116

Atkinson, Holt, Pop. 1,151
West Holt SD — 400/K-12
PO Box 457 68713 — 402-925-2890
William McAllister, supt. — Fax 925-2177
westholt.esu8.org
Atkinson S — 200/K-8
PO Box 457 68713 — 402-925-2848
Jenny Stracke, prin. — Fax 925-2177
Clover Cove S — 50/K-8
86604 468th Ave 68713 — 402-925-2421
Fax 925-2177
Ridgeway S — 50/K-8
47596 880th Rd 68713 — 402-925-2336
Fax 925-2177
Union S — 50/K-8
47572 887th Rd 68713 — 402-925-2435
Fax 925-2177

St. Joseph S — 50/K-8
PO Box 69 68713 — 402-925-2104
Rhonda Ketteler, prin. — Fax 925-2104

Auburn, Nemaha, Pop. 3,076
Auburn SD — 900/K-12
820 Central Ave Ste 1 68305 — 402-274-4830
Steve Schneider, supt. — Fax 274-5227
www.auburnpublicschools.org/
Auburn MS — 200/4-6
1713 J St 68305 — 402-274-4027
Sharon Pollard, prin. — Fax 274-4147
Calvert ES — 200/K-3
2103 O St 68305 — 402-274-4129
Sharon Pollard, prin. — Fax 274-4121

Aurora, Hamilton, Pop. 4,282
Aurora SD — 1,000/K-12
300 L St 68818 — 402-694-6923
Larry Ramaekers, supt. — Fax 694-5097
www.aurora.k12.ne.us/
Aurora ES — 500/K-5
300 L St 68818 — 402-694-3167
Mark Standage, prin. — Fax 694-5348
Aurora MS — 200/6-8
300 L St 68818 — 402-694-6915
Kenneth Thiele, prin. — Fax 694-3815

Axtell, Kearney, Pop. 708
Axtell Community SD — 300/K-12
PO Box 97 68924 — 308-743-2414
Thomas Sandberg, supt. — Fax 743-2417
Axtell ES — 100/K-6
PO Box 97 68924 — 308-743-2415
Thomas Sandberg, prin. — Fax 743-2417

Ayr, Adams, Pop. 103
Adams Central SD
Supt. — See Hastings
Ayr ES — 50/K-6
PO Box 91 68925 — 402-463-8844
Joe Cook, prin. — Fax 463-6344

Bancroft, Cuming, Pop. 490
Bancroft-Rosalie SD — 300/K-12
PO Box 129 68004 — 402-648-3337
Jon Cerny, supt. — Fax 648-3338
www.bancroft-rosalie.org/
Bancroft ES — 100/K-6
PO Box 129 68004 — 402-648-3336
Jon Cerny, prin. — Fax 648-3338
Bancroft JHS — 100/7-8
PO Box 129 68004 — 402-648-3336
Mike Sjuts, prin. — Fax 648-3338

Zion Lutheran S — 50/K-8
1710 20th Rd 68004 — 402-648-7534
Fax 648-7534

Bartlett, Wheeler, Pop. 115
Wheeler Central SD — 100/K-12
PO Box 68 68622 — 308-654-3273
Alan Ehlers, supt. — Fax 654-3237
teachers.esu8.org/WheelerCentral/
Wheeler Central ES #45 — 100/K-6
PO Box 68 68622 — 308-654-3273
Alan Ehlers, prin. — Fax 654-3237

Bartley, Red Willow, Pop. 348
Southwest SD 179 — 400/PK-12
PO Box 187 69020 — 308-692-3223
David Hendricks, supt. — Fax 692-3221
Southwest MS — 100/6-8
PO Box 187 69020 — 308-692-3223
Matt Springer, prin. — Fax 692-3351
Other Schools – See Indianola

Bassett, Rock, Pop. 660
Rock County SD — 200/K-12
PO Box 448 68714 — 402-684-3411
David Zumbahlen, supt. — Fax 684-3671
Bassett ES — 100/K-6
PO Box 407 68714 — 402-684-3855
Steve Camp, prin. — Fax 684-3808
Pony Lake S — 50/K-8
45597 866th Rd 68714 — 402-244-5450
Steve Camp, prin. — Fax 244-5201
Rose Community S — 50/K-8
85256 US Highway 183 68714 — 402-684-3469
Steve Camp, prin. — Fax 684-3469
Other Schools – See Newport

Battle Creek, Madison, Pop. 1,178
Battle Creek SD — 400/K-12
PO Box 100 68715 — 402-675-6905
Jay Bellar, supt. — Fax 675-1038
bcps.esu8.org/
Battle Creek ES — 200/K-6
PO Box 100 68715 — 402-675-8085
Kyle Finke, prin. — Fax 675-1038

St. John Lutheran S — 100/PK-8
PO Box 67 68715 — 402-675-3605
Valerie Snow, prin. — Fax 675-4445

Bayard, Morrill, Pop. 1,155
Bayard SD — 400/K-12
PO Box 607 69334 — 308-586-1325
Allen Gross, supt. — Fax 586-1638
Bayard ES — 200/K-6
PO Box 607 69334 — 308-586-1211
Dennis Dubry, prin. — Fax 586-1638

Beatrice, Gage, Pop. 12,890
Beatrice SD — 2,200/PK-12
320 N 5th St 68310 — 402-223-1500
Dale Kruse, supt. — Fax 223-1509
www.beatricepublicschools.org/
Beatrice MS — 500/6-8
215 N 5th St 68310 — 402-223-1545
Randy Schlueter, prin. — Fax 223-1547
Cedar ES — 200/K-5
201 Cedar St 68310 — 402-223-1585
Theresa Smith, prin. — Fax 223-1586
Lincoln ES — 200/K-5
500 N 19th St 68310 — 402-223-1575
Theresa Smith, prin. — Fax 223-1576
Paddock Lane ES — 300/PK-5
1300 N 14th St 68310 — 402-223-1566
Elizabeth Replogle, prin. — Fax 223-1595
Stoddard ES — 200/K-5
400 S 7th St 68310 — 402-223-1580
Elizabeth Replogle, prin. — Fax 223-1597

St. Joseph S — 100/K-6
420 N 6th St 68310 — 402-223-5033
Vickie Gilbert, lead tchr. — Fax 228-0100
St. Paul Lutheran S — 100/PK-5
930 Prairie Ln 68310 — 402-223-3414
Lonnie Duensing, prin. — Fax 223-3418

Beemer, Cuming, Pop. 717
West Point SD
Supt. — See West Point
Beemer ES — 50/K-6
815 3rd St 68716 — 402-528-3232
Dawn De Turk, prin. — Fax 528-7203

Bellevue, Sarpy, Pop. 47,334
Bellevue SD — 9,100/PK-12
1600 Highway 370 68005 — 402-293-4000
Dr. John Deegan, supt. — Fax 293-5002
www.bellevuepublicschools.org
Avery ES — 300/K-6
2107 Avery Rd E 68005 — 402-293-4460
Roberta Mitchell, prin. — Fax 293-5700
Barber ES — 200/PK-6
1402 Main St 68005 — 402-293-4560
Susan Fjelstad, prin. — Fax 293-5704
Belleaire ES — 300/K-6
1200 W Mission Ave 68005 — 402-293-4510
Jeanna Pestel, prin. — Fax 293-5706
Betz ES — 300/PK-6
605 W 27th Ave 68005 — 402-293-4585
Matthew Fenster, prin. — Fax 293-5702
Birchcrest ES — 400/K-6
1212 Fairfax Rd 68005 — 402-293-4635
Jason Farwell, prin. — Fax 293-5708
Central ES — 200/K-6
510 W 22nd Ave 68005 — 402-293-4685
Dr. Lori Thomas, prin. — Fax 293-5710
Fairview ES — 400/K-6
14110 Tregaron Dr 68123 — 402-827-5950
Robert Ingram, prin. — Fax 827-5948
Fontenelle MS — 700/7-8
701 Kayleen Dr 68005 — 402-293-4360
Doug Schaefer, prin. — Fax 293-4450
Ft. Crook ES — 300/K-6
12501 S 25th St 68123 — 402-293-4710
Laura Jackson, prin. — Fax 293-5712
Lawrence ES — 500/K-6
13204 S 29th St 68123 — 402-293-4880
Chrystal Frey, prin. — Fax 293-5716
LeMay ES — 300/K-6
2726 Kennedy Blvd 68123 — 402-293-4760
Dwayne Chism, prin. — Fax 293-5714
Lewis & Clark MS — 7-8
13502 S 38th St 68123 — 402-898-8760
Dr. Mike Smith, prin. — Fax 898-9018
Mission MS — 700/7-8
2202 Washington St 68005 — 402-293-4260
Laurie Hanna, prin. — Fax 293-4350
Sarpy ES — 300/PK-6
2908 Vandenberg Ave 68123 — 402-293-4795
Larry Wade, prin. — Fax 293-5719
Twin Ridge ES — 300/K-6
1400 Sunbury Dr 68005 — 402-293-4845
Talma Whitney, prin. — Fax 293-5721
Two Springs ES — 600/PK-6
3001 Spring Blvd 68123 — 402-293-5070
Paige Roberts, prin. — Fax 293-5723
Wake Robin ES — 400/K-6
700 Lincoln Rd 68005 — 402-293-4955
Chad Zavala, prin. — Fax 293-5725

Papillion-La Vista SD
Supt. — See Papillion
Anderson Grove ES — 200/PK-6
11820 S 37th St 68123 — 402-898-0479
Anne Harley, prin. — Fax 898-0481
Golden Hills ES — 300/PK-6
2912 Coffey Ave 68123 — 402-898-0459
Heidi Henningsen, prin. — Fax 898-0461

Bellevue Christian Academy — 100/K-8
1400 Harvell Dr 68005 — 402-898-4222
Teresa Winchell, prin. — Fax 291-5904

Cornerstone Christian S — 100/PK-8
3704 370 Plz 68123 — 402-292-1030
Teri Schrag, admin. — Fax 292-1030
Pilgrim Lutheran K — 50/K-K
2311 Fairview Rd 68123 — 402-293-2813
Julie Kyriss, dir. — Fax 292-7836
St. Mary S — 200/PK-8
903 W Mission Ave 68005 — 402-291-1694
William Huben, prin. — Fax 291-9667
St. Matthew the Evangelist S — 100/PK-8
12210 S 36th St 68123 — 402-291-2030
Janet Wilson, prin. — Fax 291-2047

Bellwood, Butler, Pop. 437
David City SD
Supt. — See David City
Bellwood ES — 100/PK-6
PO Box 100 68624 — 402-538-4805
Tom Jahde, prin. — Fax 538-2041

Benkelman, Dundy, Pop. 914
Dundy County-Straton SD — 400/PK-12
PO Box 586 69021 — 308-423-2738
Dr. Dallas Watkins, supt. — Fax 423-2711
204.234.184.9/
Benkelman S — 200/PK-8
PO Box 586 69021 — 308-423-2216
Michael Rotherham, prin. — Fax 423-2320
Other Schools – See Haigler, Stratton

Bennet, Lancaster, Pop. 681
Palmyra OR 1 SD
Supt. — See Palmyra
Bennet ES — 200/K-6
50 Dogwood St 68317 — 402-782-3535
Steven Robb, prin. — Fax 782-3545

Bennington, Douglas, Pop. 913
Bennington SD — 800/K-12
11620 N 156th St 68007 — 402-238-3044
Terry Haack, supt. — Fax 238-2185
www.benningtonschools.org/
Bennington ES — 400/K-6
11620 N 156th St 68007 — 402-238-2690
Shannon Thoendel, prin. — Fax 238-2185

Bertrand, Phelps, Pop. 791
Bertrand SD — 200/K-12
PO Box 278 68927 — 308-472-3427
Dr. Dennis Shipp, supt. — Fax 472-3429
www.esu11.org/bertrand/home.html
Bertrand ES — 100/K-6
PO Box 278 68927 — 308-472-3427
Michael Williams, prin. — Fax 472-3429

Big Springs, Deuel, Pop. 399
South Platte SD — 100/K-12
PO Box 457 69122 — 308-889-3622
David Spencer, supt. — Fax 889-3523
southplatte.ne.schoolwebpages.com/
South Platte ES — 100/K-6
PO Box 457 69122 — 308-889-3674
David Spencer, prin. — Fax 889-3674

Bladen, Webster, Pop. 275
Silver Lake SD
Supt. — See Roseland
Silver Lake ES Bladen — 100/K-6
PO Box 127 68928 — 402-756-1311
Daune Arntt, prin. — Fax 756-1313

Blair, Washington, Pop. 7,765
Blair Community SD — 2,100/PK-12
PO Box 288 68008 — 402-426-2610
Dr. Jane Stavem, supt. — Fax 426-3110
www.blairschools.org/
Blair Arbor Park ES — 300/4-5
PO Box 288 68008 — 402-426-2735
Mike Janssen, prin. — Fax 533-8110
Blair Deerfield ES, PO Box 288 68008 — PK-3
Beth Welke, prin. — 402-426-5123
Blair North ES — 200/K-3
PO Box 288 68008 — 402-426-3835
Amy Rogers, prin. — Fax 533-8355
Blair South ES — 200/K-3
PO Box 288 68008 — 402-426-2229
Amy Rogers, prin. — Fax 533-8355
Blair West ES — 200/K-3
PO Box 288 68008 — 402-426-3135
Beth Welke, prin. — Fax 533-8355
Otte Blair MS — 500/6-8
PO Box 288 68008 — 402-426-3678
James Sides, prin. — Fax 426-1788

Bloomfield, Knox, Pop. 1,049
Bloomfield SD — 200/PK-12
PO Box 308 68718 — 402-373-4800
Robert Marks, supt. — Fax 373-2712
bloomfield.esu1.org/
Bloomfield ES — 100/PK-6
PO Box 308 68718 — 402-373-4985
Kimberly Lingenfelter, prin. — Fax 373-2562

Blue Hill, Webster, Pop. 798
Blue Hill SD — 400/K-12
PO Box 217 68930 — 402-756-2085
Glen Larsen, supt. — Fax 756-2086
www.bluehillschools.org/
Blue Hill ES — 200/K-6
PO Box 217 68930 — 402-756-2085
Glen Larsen, prin. — Fax 756-2086

Blue Springs, Gage, Pop. 376
Southern SD 1
Supt. — See Wymore
Southern ES — 300/K-6
PO Box 158 68318 — 402-645-3359
Jerry Rempe, prin. — Fax 645-3740

Brady, Lincoln, Pop. 379
Brady SD 200/K-12
PO Box 68 69123 308-584-3317
Joyce Huffman, supt. Fax 584-3725
athena.esu16.org/~brady/
Brady ES 100/K-6
PO Box 68 69123 308-584-3317
Gerald Wallace, prin. Fax 584-3725

Brainard, Butler, Pop. 346
East Butler SD 300/K-12
PO Box 36 68626 402-545-2081
James Koontz, supt. Fax 545-2023
www.ebutler.esu7.org/eastbutler.html
Brainard ES 100/K-6
PO Box 36 68626 402-545-2081
James Koontz, prin. Fax 545-2023
Other Schools – See Dwight

Bridgeport, Morrill, Pop. 1,493
Bridgeport SD 63 600/K-12
PO Box 430 69336 308-262-1470
Kirk Nielsen, supt. Fax 262-1470
www.bridgeportschools.org/
Bridgeport ES 300/K-6
PO Box 430 69336 308-262-1574
Kevin Myers, prin. Fax 262-1414

Broken Bow, Custer, Pop. 3,311
Broken Bow SD 800/PK-12
323 N 7th Ave 68822 308-872-6821
Timothy Shafer, supt. Fax 872-2751
www.bbps.org/
Broken Bow MS 200/6-8
322 N 9th Ave 68822 308-872-6441
Ken Kujath, prin. Fax 872-2528
Broken Bow S - Round Hill 50/1-8
323 N 7th Ave 68822 308-872-6821
Kim Jonas, prin. Fax 872-2751
Custer ES 200/3-5
727 S 6th Ave 68822 308-872-2503
Kim Jonas, prin. Fax 872-6262
North Park ES 200/K-2
1135 N H St 68822 308-872-2982
Kim Jonas, prin. Fax 872-6349
SESC Preschool Tappan Valley PK-PK
44003 Road 801 68822 308-872-6542
Kim Jonas, prin.

Brownlee, Cherry
Thedford SD
Supt. — See Thedford
Brownlee ES, HC 58 Box 51 69166 50/K-6
Henry Eggert, prin. 308-748-2258

Bruning, Thayer, Pop. 262
Bruning-Davenport USD
Supt. — See Davenport
Bruning-Davenport ES 50/PK-1
PO Box 70 68322 402-353-4445
Michael Brown, prin. Fax 353-4445

Burwell, Garfield, Pop. 1,063
Burwell SD 300/PK-12
PO Box 670 68823 308-346-4150
Daniel Bird, supt. Fax 346-5430
sites.burwell.k12.ne.us/burwellelem/
Burwell ES 100/PK-6
PO Box 790 68823 308-346-4431
Jason Alexander, prin. Fax 346-5324
District 70 S 50/K-8
47017 Cedar River Rd 68823 308-348-2271
Jason Alexander, prin. Fax 346-4651
Richland S 50/K-8
PO Box 277 68823 308-346-4642
Jason Alexander, prin. Fax 346-4651

Butte, Boyd, Pop. 344
West Boyd SD
Supt. — See Spencer
West Boyd S - Butte Attendence Center 100/K-4
PO Box 139 68722 402-775-2201
Duane Lechtenberg, prin. Fax 775-2204

Cairo, Hall, Pop. 787
Centura SD 500/PK-12
PO Box 430 68824 308-485-4258
Kenneth Heinz, supt. Fax 485-4780
www.centura.k12.ne.us/
Centura ES 300/PK-6
PO Box 430 68824 308-485-4258
Cory Bohling, prin. Fax 485-4780

Callaway, Custer, Pop. 625
Callaway SD 200/K-12
101 N Needham St 68825 308-836-2272
Patrick Osmond, supt. Fax 836-2771
sites.callaway.k12.ne.us/
Callaway ES 100/K-6
101 N Needham St 68825 308-836-2272
Patrick Osmond, prin. Fax 836-2771
Other Schools – See Oconto

Cambridge, Furnas, Pop. 971
Cambridge SD 300/K-12
PO Box 100 69022 308-697-3322
Ronald Streit, supt. Fax 697-4880
www.esu11.org/cambridge/
Cambridge ES 200/K-6
PO Box 100 69022 308-697-3322
Donald Sackett, prin. Fax 697-4880

Cedar Bluffs, Saunders, Pop. 617
Cedar Bluffs SD 300/PK-12
PO Box 66 68015 402-628-2060
Joel Bohlken, supt. Fax 628-2005
www.cedarbluffsschools.org/
Cedar Bluffs ES 100/PK-6
PO Box 66 68015 402-628-2060
Joel Bohlken, prin. Fax 628-2005

Cedar Rapids, Boone, Pop. 371
Cedar Rapids SD 200/K-12
408 W Dayton St 68627 308-358-0640
Amy Malander, supt. Fax 358-0211
www.cedar.esu7.org/
Cedar Rapids ES 100/K-6
408 W Dayton St 68627 308-358-0640
Matthew Asche, prin. Fax 358-0211

Central City, Merrick, Pop. 2,891
Central City SD 800/PK-12
PO Box 57 68826 308-946-3055
Candace Conradt, supt. Fax 946-3149
home.centralcityps.org/
Central City ES 300/PK-4
PO Box 57 68826 308-946-3057
Darlene Darbro, prin. Fax 946-3149
Central City MS 200/5-8
PO Box 57 68826 308-946-3056
Richard Moore, prin. Fax 946-2124

Nebraska Christian S 200/PK-12
1847 Inskip Ave 68826 308-946-3836
Daniel Woods, admin. Fax 946-3837

Ceresco, Saunders, Pop. 899
Raymond Central SD
Supt. — See Raymond
Ceresco ES 100/K-5
PO Box 10 68017 402-665-3651
Dan Ingwersen, prin. Fax 665-2307

Chadron, Dawes, Pop. 5,320
Chadron SD 900/K-12
602 E 10th St 69337 308-432-0700
Sherlock Hirning, supt. Fax 432-0702
www.chadronschools.org/
Alpha S 50/K-8
60 Alpha Rd 69337 308-432-3824
Tom Detwiler, prin. Fax 432-0108
Chadron East Ward ES 200/K-4
732 Ann St 69337 308-432-0710
William Cogdill, prin. Fax 432-6985
Chadron MS 200/5-8
551 E 6th St 69337 308-432-0708
Lorrie Miller, prin. Fax 432-0720
Kenwood ES 100/K-4
450 Norfolk Ave 69337 308-432-0717
Lou Alcorn, prin. Fax 432-0715
Prairie Home S 50/K-8
91 Prairie Home Rd 69337 308-432-5243
Tom Detwiler, prin. Fax 432-0108
Trunk Butte S 50/K-8
5240 Highway 20 69337 308-432-3717
Tom Detwiler, prin. Fax 432-0108
Other Schools – See Whitney

Prairie View SDA S 50/K-8
602 Bordeaux St 69337 308-432-4228
Allen Muhlenbeck, admin. Fax 432-6517

Chambers, Holt, Pop. 312
Chambers SD 200/K-12
PO Box 218 68725 402-482-5233
Robert Hanger, supt. Fax 482-5234
chambers.esu8.org/
Chambers ES 100/K-6
PO Box 218 68725 402-482-5233
Robert Hanger, prin. Fax 482-5234

Chapman, Merrick, Pop. 331
Northwest SD
Supt. — See Grand Island
Chapman S 100/K-8
PO Box 206 68827 308-986-2215
Rahn Vander Hamm, prin. Fax 986-2726

Chappell, Deuel, Pop. 935
Creek Valley SD 300/K-12
PO Box 608 69129 308-874-2911
Ted Classen, supt. Fax 874-2602
creekvalleystorm.com/
Creek Valley ES 100/K-4
PO Box 608 69129 308-874-2911
Brent Christensen, prin. Fax 874-2602
Other Schools – See Lodgepole

Clarks, Merrick, Pop. 341
High Plains Community SD
Supt. — See Polk
High Plains ES at Clarks 100/K-3
PO Box 205 68628 308-548-2216
Karyee LeSuer, prin. Fax 548-2120
High Plains MS 100/6-8
PO Box 205 68628 308-548-2216
Karyee LeSuer, prin. Fax 548-2120

Clarkson, Colfax, Pop. 680
Clarkson SD 200/K-12
PO Box 140 68629 402-892-3454
Daniel Polk, supt. Fax 892-3455
teachers.esu7.org/clarkson/
Clarkson S 200/K-12
PO Box 140 68629 402-892-3454
Rich Lemburg, prin. Fax 892-3455

St. John Neumann S 50/1-6
PO Box 457 68629 402-892-3474
Ann Prokopec, lead tchr. Fax 892-3474

Clay Center, Clay, Pop. 813
Clay Center SD 200/PK-12
PO Box 125 68933 402-762-3561
Lee Sayer, supt. Fax 762-3200
www.claycenter.k12.ne.us/
Clay Center ES 100/PK-6
PO Box 125 68933 402-762-3561
Jim Bovee, prin. Fax 762-3200

Clearwater, Antelope, Pop. 357
Nebraska USD 1
Supt. — See Royal
Clearwater ES 100/K-6
PO Box 38 68726 402-485-2505
Mike Sanne, prin. Fax 485-2634

Cody, Cherry, Pop. 148
Cody-Kilgore SD 100/K-12
PO Box 216 69211 402-823-4190
Terry Hazard, supt. Fax 823-4275
Other Schools – See Kilgore

Valentine SD
Supt. — See Valentine
Cutcomb Lake S 50/K-8
HC 74 Box 6 69211 402-823-4208
Eva Westover, prin. Fax 376-8096

Coleridge, Cedar, Pop. 501
Coleridge Community SD 100/K-12
PO Box 37 68727 402-283-4844
Dr. Daniel Hoesing, supt. Fax 283-4230
coleridge.esu1.org/
Coleridge ES 50/K-6
PO Box 37 68727 402-283-4844
Stephanie Petersen, prin. Fax 283-4230

Columbus, Platte, Pop. 20,909
Columbus SD 3,400/K-12
PO Box 947 68602 402-563-7000
Dr. Paul Hillyer, supt. Fax 563-7005
www.columbuspublicschools.org
Centennial ES 400/K-5
500 Centennial St 68601 402-563-8180
Jackie Herink, prin. Fax 563-8185
Columbus MS 800/6-8
2410 16th St 68601 402-563-7060
Douglas Kluth, prin. Fax 563-7068
Emerson ES 300/K-5
2410 20th St 68601 402-563-7030
Sara Colford, prin. Fax 563-7035
Lost Creek ES 300/K-5
3772 33rd Ave 68601 402-563-7045
Jeff Bartels, prin. Fax 563-7047
North Park ES 300/K-5
2200 31st St 68601 402-563-7070
Robert Hausmann, prin. Fax 563-7072
West Park ES 300/K-5
4100 Adamy St 68601 402-563-7075
Paula Lawrence, prin. Fax 563-7077

Lakeview Community SD 800/K-12
3744 83rd St 68601 402-563-2345
Paul Calvert, supt. Fax 564-5209
www.lakeview.esu7.org/
Shell Creek S 200/K-8
16786 280th St 68601 402-564-8008
Patricia Meyer, prin. Fax 563-4552
Sunrise S 100/K-8
860 E 29th Ave 68601 402-564-4540
John Mlinar, prin. Fax 562-7530
Other Schools – See Platte Center

Christ Lutheran S 50/K-8
32312 122nd Ave 68601 402-564-3531
Dean Plummer, prin. Fax 564-5680
Columbus Christian S 100/PK-8
PO Box 924 68602 402-562-6470
Kathryn Wolfe, admin.
Columbus SDA Christian S K-8
4807 29th St 68601 402-563-2620
Shirley Smith, lead tchr.
Immanuel Lutheran S 200/PK-8
2865 26th Ave 68601 402-564-8423
Jody Timm, prin. Fax 564-1162
St. Anthony S 100/PK-6
1719 6th St 68601 402-564-4767
Norma Cremers, prin. Fax 564-5530
St. Bonaventure S 300/PK-6
1604 15th St 68601 402-564-7153
Cheryl Zoucha, prin. Fax 564-2587
St. Isidore S 200/PK-6
3821 20th St 68601 402-564-2604
Kevin Ingemansen, prin. Fax 564-8955
St. John Lutheran S 50/PK-8
39346 205th Ave 68601 402-285-0335
Fax 285-0335

Cook, Johnson, Pop. 309
Johnson County Central SD
Supt. — See Tecumseh
Johnson County Central ES - Cook 100/K-5
PO Box 255 68329 402-864-4181
Ron Skwarek, prin. Fax 864-2074
Johnson County Central MS 50/6-7
PO Box 255 68329 402-864-4181
Rich Bacon, prin. Fax 864-2074

Cozad, Dawson, Pop. 4,222
Cozad CSD 900/K-12
PO Box 15 69130 308-784-2745
John Grinde, supt. Fax 784-2728
cozadschools.cozad.k12.ne.us/
Cozad Early Education Center 100/K-K
420 W 14th St 69130 308-784-3381
Dale Henderson, prin.
Cozad ES 300/1-5
420 E 14th St 69130 308-784-3462
Dale Henderson, prin. Fax 784-2724
Cozad MS 200/6-8
1810 Meridian Ave 69130 308-784-2746
Todd Hilyard, prin. Fax 784-2606

Crawford, Dawes, Pop. 1,035
Crawford SD 300/PK-12
908 5th St 69339 308-665-1537
Dick Lesher, supt. Fax 665-1483
www.cpsrams.org/

Crawford ES 100/PK-6
908 5th St 69339 308-665-1928
Kathy Griesse, prin. Fax 665-1909

Creighton, Knox, Pop. 1,187
Creighton SD 400/K-12
PO Box 10 68729 402-358-3663
Fred Boelter, supt. Fax 358-3804
creighton.esu1.org/
Creighton ES 200/K-6
PO Box 10 68729 402-358-3348
Beata Rudloff, prin. Fax 358-3804

St. Ludger S 50/PK-6
410 Bryant Ave 68729 402-358-3501
Joyce Tunink, lead tchr. Fax 358-3559

Crete, Saline, Pop. 6,308
Crete SD 1,600/PK-12
920 Linden Ave 68333 402-826-5855
Kyle McGowan, supt. Fax 826-5120
www.creteschools.com
Crete ES 700/PK-5
920 Linden Ave 68333 402-826-5822
Bret Schroder, prin. Fax 826-2135
Crete MS 300/6-8
1700 Glenwood Ave 68333 402-826-5844
Kim Jacobson, prin. Fax 826-7789

St. James S 100/K-6
525 E 14th St 68333 402-826-2318
Sr. Mary Wesely, lead tchr. Fax 826-2318

Crofton, Knox, Pop. 710
Crofton Community SD 400/K-12
PO Box 429 68730 402-388-2440
Randall Anderson, supt. Fax 388-4265
www.croftonschools.com/
Crofton ES 200/K-6
PO Box 429 68730 402-388-4357
Susan Benak, prin. Fax 388-2457

St. Rose of Lima S 100/PK-8
1302 W 5th St 68730 402-388-4393
Scott Becker, lead tchr. Fax 388-4393

Crookston, Cherry, Pop. 94
Todd County SD 66-1
Supt. — See Mission, SD
Lakeview S 50/K-8
HC 78 Box 15 69212 605-429-3339
Bobbie Cox, lead tchr. Fax 429-3309

Valentine SD
Supt. — See Valentine
German Settlement S 50/K-8
PO Box 9 69212 402-425-3270
Eva Westover, prin. Fax 376-8096

Culbertson, Hitchcock, Pop. 559
Hitchcock County USD
Supt. — See Trenton
Culbertson ES 100/K-6
PO Box 128 69024 308-278-2131
John Kershaw, prin. Fax 278-3173

Curtis, Frontier, Pop. 736
Medicine Valley SD 200/K-12
PO Box 9 69025 308-367-4106
Alan Garey, supt. Fax 367-4108
www.mvraiders.org/
Medicine Valley ES 100/K-6
PO Box 65 69025 308-367-4210
Steven Gleisberg, prin. Fax 367-4108

Dakota City, Dakota, Pop. 1,880
South Sioux City SD
Supt. — See South Sioux City
Dakota City ES 200/K-5
1801 Locust St 68731 402-987-3363
Jo Ellen Nugent, prin. Fax 987-0629
Sioux Land Family Center 100/PK-PK
1401 Pine St 68731 402-494-1727
Katie Terry, dir. Fax 494-8754

Dalton, Cheyenne, Pop. 322
Leyton SD 300/K-12
PO Box 297 69131 308-377-2303
William Hakonson, supt. Fax 377-2304
Other Schools – See Gurley

Davenport, Thayer, Pop. 296
Bruning-Davenport USD 100/PK-12
PO Box 190 68335 402-364-2225
Trudy Clark, supt. Fax 364-2477
www.bruning.esu6.org/Homepage.htm
Bruning-Davenport ES 50/2-4
PO Box 190 68335 402-364-2225
Trudy Clark, prin. Fax 364-2477
Bruning-Davenport MS 50/5-8
PO Box 190 68335 402-364-2225
Trudy Clark, prin. Fax 364-2477
Other Schools – See Bruning

St. Peters Lutheran S 50/PK-8
PO Box 207 68335 402-364-2139
Sherry Burger, lead tchr.

David City, Butler, Pop. 2,558
David City SD 700/PK-12
750 D St 68632 402-367-4590
Jerry Phillips, supt. Fax 367-3479
www.davidcitypublicschools.org/
David City ES 300/PK-6
826 E St 68632 402-367-3779
Jim Bathen, prin. Fax 367-3783
Other Schools – See Bellwood

St. Marys S 200/PK-5
1026 N 5th St 68632 402-367-3669
Carm Fiala, prin. Fax 367-3703

Daykin, Jefferson, Pop. 167
Meridian SD 200/K-12
PO Box 190 68338 402-446-7265
Thomas Rother, supt. Fax 446-7246
www.meridian.esu6.k12.ne.us/
Meridian ES 100/K-6
PO Box 190 68338 402-446-7265
Thomas Rother, prin. Fax 446-7246

Deshler, Thayer, Pop. 790
Deshler SD 300/K-12
PO Box 547 68340 402-365-7272
Al Meier, supt. Fax 365-7560
www.deshler.esu6.k12.ne.us/
Deshler ES 100/K-6
PO Box 547 68340 402-365-7272
Al Meier, prin. Fax 365-7560

Deshler Lutheran S 100/K-8
PO Box 340 68340 402-365-7858
David Beikmann, prin. Fax 365-7858

De Witt, Saline, Pop. 577
Tri County SD 400/K-12
72520 Highway 103 68341 402-683-2015
Russell Finken, supt. Fax 683-2116
www.tricountyschools.org/
Tri County ES 200/K-6
72520 Highway 103 68341 402-683-4035
Scot Davis, prin. Fax 683-2116

Diller, Jefferson, Pop. 279
Diller-Odell SD
Supt. — See Odell
Diller-Odell ES 100/K-6
PO Box 8 68342 402-793-5170
Fax 793-5173

Dix, Kimball, Pop. 247
Potter-Dix SD
Supt. — See Potter
Potter-Dix ES 100/K-6
PO Box 149 69133 308-682-5226
Kevin Thomas, prin. Fax 682-5227

Dodge, Dodge, Pop. 683
Dodge SD 100/K-12
209 N Ash St 68633 402-693-2207
Randall Marymee, supt. Fax 693-2209
www.dodgepublicschools.org/
Dodge ES 100/K-6
209 N Ash St 68633 402-693-2207
Patty Novicki, prin. Fax 693-2209

St. Wenceslaus S 100/1-8
212 N Linden St 68633 402-693-2819
Stacy Uttecht, lead tchr. Fax 693-2819

Doniphan, Hall, Pop. 762
Doniphan-Trumbull SD 500/K-12
PO Box 300 68832 402-845-2282
Kirk Russell, supt. Fax 845-6688
www.dtcardinals.org
Doniphan-Trumbull ES 300/K-6
PO Box 300 68832 402-845-2730
Mary Yilk, prin. Fax 845-6688

Dorchester, Saline, Pop. 630
Dorchester SD 200/K-12
PO Box 7 68343 402-946-2781
Brian Redinger, supt. Fax 946-6271
www.dorchester.esu6.k12.ne.us/
Dorchester ES 100/K-6
PO Box 7 68343 402-946-2781
Mitch Kubicek, prin. Fax 946-6271

Dunning, Blaine, Pop. 90
Sandhills SD 100/K-12
PO Box 29 68833 308-538-2224
Charles Hafer, supt. Fax 538-2228
sites.sandhills.k12.ne.us/sandhillspanthers/
Other Schools – See Halsey

Dwight, Butler, Pop. 255
East Butler SD
Supt. — See Brainard
Dwight ES 100/K-6
PO Box 160 68635 402-566-2445
James Koontz, prin. Fax 545-2023

Eagle, Cass, Pop. 1,155
Waverly SD 145
Supt. — See Waverly
Eagle ES 200/K-5
600 S 1st St 68347 402-781-2210
Dottie Heusman, prin. Fax 781-2068

Elba, Howard, Pop. 239
Elba SD 100/K-12
PO Box 100 68835 308-863-2228
Gary Klahn, supt. Fax 863-2329
www.elba.k12.ne.us/
Elba ES 100/K-6
PO Box 100 68835 308-863-2228
John Hanson, prin. Fax 863-2329

Elgin, Antelope, Pop. 681
Elgin SD 200/K-12
PO Box 399 68636 402-843-2455
Gayla Fredrickson, supt. Fax 843-2475
elgineagles.org/
Elgin S 100/K-8
PO Box 399 68636 402-843-2455
Gayla Fredrickson, prin. Fax 843-2475

St. Boniface S 100/PK-6
PO Box B 68636 402-843-5460
Betty Getzfred, prin. Fax 843-5842

Elkhorn, Douglas, Pop. 8,192
Elkhorn SD 3,900/PK-12
20650 Glenn St 68022 402-289-2579
Steve Baker, supt. Fax 289-2585
www.elkhornweb.org/
Elkhorn Eary Education Center PK-PK
20650 Glenn St 68022 402-289-3790
Michele Stoecklin, dir. Fax 289-2585
Elkhorn MS 400/6-8
3200 N 207th Plz 68022 402-289-2428
Michael Tomjack, prin. Fax 289-1639
Fire Ridge ES 400/K-5
19660 Farnam St 68022 402-289-0735
Anne Doerr, prin. Fax 289-0741
Hillrise ES 300/K-5
20110 Hopper St 68022 402-289-2602
Ryan Lindquist, prin. Fax 289-1610
Skyline ES 300/K-5
400 S 210th St 68022 402-289-3433
Jan Peterson, prin. Fax 289-1652
Westridge ES 300/PK-5
3100 N 206th St 68022 402-289-2559
Troy Sidders, prin. Fax 289-5725
Other Schools – See Omaha

St. Patrick S 600/PK-8
PO Box 10 68022 402-289-5407
Don Ridder, prin. Fax 763-9530

Ellsworth, Sheridan
Gordon-Rushville SD
Supt. — See Gordon
Golden Spade S 50/1-8
1669 330th Trl 69340 308-282-1071
Jean Hensley, prin. Fax 282-1071

Elm Creek, Buffalo, Pop. 867
Elm Creek SD 300/K-12
PO Box 490 68836 308-856-4300
Larry Babcock, supt. Fax 856-4907
www.elmcreek.k12.ne.us/
Elm Creek ES 200/K-6
PO Box 490 68836 308-856-4300
Larry Babcock, prin. Fax 856-4907

Elmwood, Cass, Pop. 715
Elmwood-Murdock SD
Supt. — See Murdock
Elmwood-Murdock ES 200/K-6
400 W F St 68349 402-994-2125
Bruce Friedrich, prin. Fax 994-2078

Elwood, Gosper, Pop. 712
Elwood SD 300/K-12
PO Box 107 68937 308-785-2491
Richard Einspahr, supt. Fax 785-2322
www.esu11.org/elwood/elwhome.html
Elwood ES 100/K-6
PO Box 107 68937 308-785-2491
Richard Einspahr, prin. Fax 785-2322

Elyria, Valley, Pop. 50
Ord SD
Supt. — See Ord
Elyria S, 201 Benton St 68837 50/K-8
Jason Alexander, prin. 308-728-3390

Emerson, Dakota, Pop. 816
Emerson-Hubbard SD 400/K-12
PO Box 9 68733 402-695-2621
Thomas Becker, supt. Fax 695-2622
emersonhubbardschools.org/
Emerson-Hubbard ES 200/K-6
PO Box 9 68733 402-695-2654
Thomas Becker, prin. Fax 695-2622

Emmet, Holt, Pop. 72
O'Neill SD
Supt. — See O Neill
Emmet S 50/K-8
PO Box 68 68734 402-336-1428
Jennifer Hagen, prin. Fax 336-2198

Eustis, Frontier, Pop. 410
Eustis-Farnham SD 200/K-12
PO Box 9 69028 308-486-3991
Steve Sampy, supt. Fax 486-5350
Eustis ES 100/K-6
PO Box 9 69028 308-486-3991
Kyle Hemmerling, prin. Fax 486-5350

Ewing, Holt, Pop. 414
Ewing SD 100/K-12
PO Box 98 68735 402-626-7235
Dr. Katherine Meink, supt. Fax 626-7236
ewing.ne.schoolwebpages.com
Ewing ES 100/K-6
PO Box 98 68735 402-626-7235
Greg Appleby, prin. Fax 626-7236

Exeter, Fillmore, Pop. 679
Exeter-Milligan SD 300/PK-12
PO Box 139 68351 402-266-5911
Paul Sheffield, supt. Fax 266-4811
Exeter-Milligan ES 100/PK-6
PO Box 139 68351 402-266-5911
Mari Lyn Poppert, prin. Fax 266-4811
Other Schools – See Milligan

Fairbury, Jefferson, Pop. 4,020
Fairbury SD 900/PK-12
703 K St 68352 402-729-6104
Frederick J. Helmink, supt. Fax 729-6392
www.fairburyjeffs.org/
Central ES 200/PK-3
808 F St 68352 402-729-2418
Jeremy Christiansen, prin. Fax 729-2467

Jefferson IS 200/3-6
924 K St 68352 402-729-5041
Annette Weise, prin. Fax 729-5446

Fairfield, Clay, Pop. 441
South Central Nebraska Unified SD 600/PK-12
30671 Highway 14 68938 402-726-2151
Kent Miller, supt. Fax 726-2208
162.127.9.3:8080/scnud5/
Sandy Creek ES 200/PK-6
30671 Highway 14 68938 402-726-2412
Glen Moorhead, prin. Fax 726-2208
Other Schools – See Lawrence

Fairmont, Fillmore, Pop. 659
Fillmore Central SD
Supt. — See Geneva
Fillmore Central MS 200/5-8
PO Box 157 68354 402-268-3411
Jeremy Klein, prin. Fax 268-3491

Falls City, Richardson, Pop. 4,218
Falls City SD 900/PK-12
PO Box 129 68355 402-245-2825
Dr. Jon Habben, supt. Fax 245-2022
www.fctigers.org/
Falls City MS 200/6-8
PO Box 129 68355 402-245-3455
Rick Johnson, prin. Fax 245-2022
Falls City North ES 200/PK-2
2500 Chase St 68355 402-245-2712
Tim Heckenlively, prin. Fax 245-4005
Falls City South ES 200/3-5
1000 Fulton St 68355 402-245-4067
Rita Johansen, prin. Fax 245-3476
Maple Grove S 50/K-5
PO Box 129 68355 402-245-4889
Rita Johansen, prin. Fax 245-3476

Sacred Heart S 200/K-12
1820 Fulton St 68355 402-245-4151
Doug Goltz, prin. Fax 245-5217

Firth, Lancaster, Pop. 687
Norris SD 160 1,900/PK-12
25211 S 68th St 68358 402-791-0000
Roy Baker, supt. Fax 791-0025
www.norris160.org
Norris ES 700/PK-4
25211 S 68th St 68358 402-791-0030
Robert Brandt, prin. Fax 791-0025
Norris MS 600/5-8
25211 S 68th St 68358 402-791-0020
MaryJo Rupert, prin. Fax 791-0025

Fordyce, Cedar, Pop. 173

West Catholic S 50/1-6
PO Box 167 68736 402-357-3507
Monique Stubbs, lead tchr. Fax 357-3551

Fort Calhoun, Washington, Pop. 917
Fort Calhoun SD 600/K-12
PO Box 430 68023 402-468-5592
Gerald Beach, supt. Fax 468-5593
www.fortcalhounschools.org/
Fort Calhoun ES 300/K-6
PO Box 430 68023 402-468-5714
John McClarnen, prin. Fax 468-5593

Franklin, Franklin, Pop. 980
Franklin SD 300/K-12
1001 M St 68939 308-425-6283
Mike Lucas, supt. Fax 425-6553
www.esu11.org/franklin/franklin.home.html
Franklin ES 200/K-6
1001 M St 68939 308-425-6283
Shelley Kahrs, prin. Fax 425-6553

Fremont, Dodge, Pop. 25,314
Fremont SD 4,600/PK-12
130 E 9th St 68025 402-727-3000
Dr. Stephen Sexton, supt. Fax 727-3002
www.fpsweb.org
Bell Field ES 400/K-5
1240 E 11th St 68025 402-727-3178
Diane Bradford, prin. Fax 727-3040
Clarmar ES 200/K-5
1865 E 19th St 68025 402-727-3175
Byron McCune, prin. Fax 727-3041
Davenport ECC 100/PK-PK
940 Michael St 68025 402-727-3173
Theresa Muhle, admin. Fax 727-3042
Fremont MS 1,000/6-8
540 Johnson Rd 68025 402-727-3100
Gale Hamilton, prin. Fax 727-3963
Grant ES 200/K-5
226 N Grant St 68025 402-727-3171
Greg Borland, prin. Fax 727-3043
Howard ES 300/K-5
240 N Howard St 68025 402-727-3169
Kate Heineman, prin. Fax 727-3044
Linden ES 400/K-5
1250 N L St 68025 402-727-3150
Bob Robinson, prin. Fax 727-3046
Milliken Park ES 300/K-5
2950 Dale St 68025 402-727-3160
Susan Farkas, prin. Fax 727-3047
Platteville ES 100/K-5
1102 County Rd W 68025 402-721-1143
Jason Chicoine, prin. Fax 721-2438
Washington ES 300/K-5
515 S Broad St 68025 402-727-3164
Michael Aerni, prin. Fax 727-3049

Archbishop Bergan Catholic ES PK-3
441 N Union St 68025 402-721-9766
Katherine Griffen, prin. Fax 721-5366

Trinity Lutheran S 200/K-8
1546 N Luther Rd 68025 402-721-5959
James Knoepfel, prin. Fax 721-5537

Friend, Saline, Pop. 1,204
Friend SD 300/K-12
PO Box 67 68359 402-947-2781
Beth Johnsen, supt. Fax 947-2026
www.friend.esu6.org/
Friend ES 200/K-6
PO Box 67 68359 402-947-2781
Beth Johnsen, prin. Fax 947-2026

Fullerton, Nance, Pop. 1,259
Fullerton SD 300/K-12
PO Box 520 68638 308-536-2431
Jeffrey Anderson, supt. Fax 536-2432
teachers.esu7.org/fps/
Fullerton S 200/K-8
PO Box 520 68638 308-536-2431
Jeffrey Anderson, prin. Fax 536-2432

Geneva, Fillmore, Pop. 2,149
Fillmore Central SD 600/K-12
1410 L St 68361 402-759-4955
Mark Norvell, supt. Fax 759-4038
www.fcps.esu6.org/
Fillmore Central ES 200/K-4
225 N 17th St 68361 402-759-3184
Mark Wragge, prin. Fax 759-3110
Other Schools – See Fairmont

Grace Lutheran S 50/K-8
434 N 16th St 68361 402-759-4517
Rev. Matthew Zimpelmann, prin.

Genoa, Nance, Pop. 883
Twin River SD 500/K-12
PO Box 640 68640 402-993-2274
Donald Graff, supt. Fax 993-7718
www.esu7.org/~trweb/
Twin River ES at Genoa 200/K-6
PO Box 640 68640 402-993-2274
Tod Heier, prin. Fax 993-7718
Other Schools – See Silver Creek

Gering, Scotts Bluff, Pop. 7,767
Gering SD 1,900/PK-12
1800 8th St 69341 308-436-3125
Don Hague, supt. Fax 436-4301
www.geringschools.net
Cedar Canyon ES 100/K-6
190234 Carter Canyon Rd 69341 308-436-2004
Betty Smith, prin. Fax 436-7167
Geil ES 300/K-6
1600 D St 69341 308-436-2545
Mary Kay Haun, prin. Fax 436-4398
Gering JHS 400/7-8
800 Q St 69341 308-436-3123
Maurie Deines, prin. Fax 436-6010
Gering Preschool/Early Child Development 100/PK-PK
116 Terry Blvd 69341 308-632-8670
Becky Sorensen, prin.
Lincoln ES 300/K-6
1725 13th St 69341 308-436-2350
George Schlothauer, prin. Fax 436-3383
Northfield ES 300/PK-6
1900 Flaten Ave 69341 308-436-5555
Pam Barker, prin. Fax 436-4352

Gibbon, Buffalo, Pop. 1,753
Gibbon SD 600/K-12
PO Box 790 68840 308-468-6555
Larry Witt, supt. Fax 468-5164
Gibbon ES 300/K-6
PO Box 790 68840 308-468-6546
Debra Turner, prin. Fax 468-5164

Giltner, Hamilton, Pop. 400
Giltner SD 200/K-12
PO Box 160 68841 402-849-2238
John Poppert, supt. Fax 849-2440
www.giltner.k12.ne.us/
Giltner ES 100/K-6
PO Box 160 68841 402-849-2238
John Poppert, prin. Fax 849-2440

Gordon, Sheridan, Pop. 1,589
Gordon-Rushville SD 700/K-12
PO Box 530 69343 308-282-1322
Merrell Nelsen, supt. Fax 282-2207
www.grmustangs.org
Gordon ES 200/K-6
PO Box 530 69343 308-282-0216
Jean Hensley, prin. Fax 282-1512
Other Schools – See Ellsworth, Lakeside, Merriman, Rushville

Valentine SD
Supt. — See Valentine
Hart Lake S 50/K-8
HC 84 Box 94 69343 308-282-0793
Eva Westover, prin. Fax 376-8096
Willow Valley South S 50/K-8
HC 84 Box 67 69343 308-282-1561
Eva Westover, prin. Fax 376-8096

Gothenburg, Dawson, Pop. 3,692
Gothenburg SD 900/K-12
1322 Avenue I 69138 308-537-3651
Michael Teahon, supt. Fax 537-3965
gothenburg.k12.ne.us
Gothenburg ES 400/K-6
1311 Avenue G 69138 308-537-3651
James Widdifield, prin. Fax 537-3965

Grand Island, Hall, Pop. 44,546
Grand Island SD 8,200/PK-12
PO Box 4904 68802 308-385-5900
Dr. Stephen Joel, supt. Fax 385-5949
www.gips.org/

Barr MS 700/6-8
602 W Stolley Park Rd 68801 308-385-5875
Jeff Gilbertson, prin. Fax 385-5880
Dodge ES 500/K-5
641 S Oak St 68801 308-385-5889
Stephanie Schulte, prin. Fax 385-5141
Early Learning Center PK-PK
4360 W Capital Ave 68803 308-385-5655
Pam Dobrovolny, admin.
Engleman ES 300/K-5
1812 Mansfield Rd 68803 308-385-5902
Maureen Oman, prin. Fax 385-5726
Gates ES 400/PK-5
2700 W Louise St 68803 308-385-5892
Julie Martin, prin. Fax 385-5729
Howard ES 400/PK-5
502 W 9th St 68801 308-385-5916
Julie Schnitzler, prin. Fax 385-5959
Jefferson ES 300/PK-5
1314 W 7th St 68801 308-385-5922
Jeanna Fiala, prin. Fax 385-5711
Knickrehm ES 200/K-5
2013 N Oak St 68801 308-385-5927
Andrew Rinaldi, prin. Fax 385-5984
Lincoln ES 300/K-5
805 Beal St 68801 308-385-5924
Brad Wentzlaff, prin. Fax 385-5710
Newell ES 400/PK-5
2700 W 13th St 68803 308-385-5905
Bradley Wolfe, prin. Fax 385-5907
Seedling Mile ES 100/K-5
3208 E Seedling Mile Rd 68801 308-385-5910
Lee Wolfe, prin. Fax 385-5803
Shoemaker ES 200/K-5
4160 W Old Potash Hwy 68803 308-385-5936
Toni Palmer, prin. Fax 385-5986
Starr ES 200/K-5
315 Wyandotte St 68801 308-385-5882
John Hauser, prin. Fax 385-5954
Stolley Park ES 200/K-5
1700 W Stolley Park Rd 68801 308-385-5913
Carrie Kolar, prin. Fax 385-5722
Walnut MS 800/6-8
1600 N Custer Ave 68803 308-385-5990
Rod Foley, prin. Fax 385-5992
Wasmer ES 400/K-5
318 S Clark St 68801 308-385-5920
Betty Desaire, prin. Fax 385-5749
West Lawn ES 300/K-5
3022 College St 68803 308-385-5930
Jane Gloor, prin. Fax 385-5603
Westridge MS 300/6-8
4111 W 13th St 68803 308-385-5886
Dr. Dan Brosz, prin. Fax 385-5003

Northwest SD 1,400/K-12
2710 N North Rd 68803 308-385-6398
Bill Mowinkel, supt. Fax 385-6393
www.ginorthwest.org/
Cedar Hollow S 300/K-8
4900 S Engleman Rd 68803 308-385-6306
Stephen Morris, prin. Fax 385-6308
1 R S 200/K-8
3301 W One-R Rd 68803 308-385-6352
Scott Mazour, prin. Fax 385-6358
Other Schools – See Chapman, Saint Libory

Christ Lutheran S 50/K-8
1316 N Grand Island Ave 68803 308-381-2837
David Wietzke, admin. Fax 381-2837
Grand Island Christian S 50/PK-5
1804 State St 68803 308-384-2755
Tim Salcedo, prin. Fax 389-3286
Trinity Lutheran S 200/PK-8
208 W 13th St 68801 308-382-5274
Sandra Armstrong, prin. Fax 389-2418

Grant, Perkins, Pop. 1,145
Perkins County SD 400/K-12
PO Box 829 69140 308-352-4735
Tobin Buchanan, supt. Fax 352-4769
www.pcs.k12.ne.us/
Perkins County ES 200/K-5
PO Box 809 69140 308-352-4313
Terry Prante, prin. Fax 352-4955
Other Schools – See Madrid

Perkins County Christian S 50/K-10
PO Box 322 69140 308-352-4256
Jarret Malmkar, pres. Fax 326-4390

Greeley, Greeley, Pop. 511
Greeley-Wolbach SD 200/PK-12
PO Box 160 68842 308-428-3145
Lee Sayer, supt. Fax 428-5395
sites.greeley-wolbach.k12.ne.us/
Greeley-Wolbach ES 100/PK-6
PO Box 160 68842 308-428-3145
Todd Beck, prin. Fax 428-5395
Other Schools – See Wolbach

Gretna, Sarpy, Pop. 4,860
Gretna SD 2,300/K-12
11717 S 216th St 68028 402-332-3265
Kevin Riley, supt. Fax 332-5833
gretna.esu3.org/
Gretna ES 600/K-5
11717 S 216th St 68028 402-332-3341
Travis Lightle, prin. Fax 332-4601
Gretna MS 500/6-8
11717 S 216th St 68028 402-332-3048
Harvey Birky, prin. Fax 332-2931
Thomas ES 600/K-5
11717 S 216th St 68028 402-332-5578
Patricia Brownlee, prin. Fax 332-2959
Other Schools – See Omaha

Millard SD
Supt. — See Omaha
Reeder ES 700/K-5
19202 Chandler St 68028 402-715-6420
Suzanne Hinman, prin. Fax 715-6440

Gurley, Cheyenne, Pop. 230
Leyton SD
Supt. — See Dalton
Leyton S 100/K-8
PO Box 178 69141 308-884-2248
Gregory Brenner, prin. Fax 884-2300

Hadar, Pierce, Pop. 325

Immanuel Lutheran S 50/K-8
PO Box 190 68738 402-371-0685
Justin Ohm, prin.

Haigler, Dundy, Pop. 199
Dundy County-Straton SD
Supt. — See Benkelman
Haigler ES 50/K-6
PO Box 127 69030 308-297-3275
Michael Rotherham, prin. Fax 297-3375

Halsey, Thomas, Pop. 51
Sandhills SD
Supt. — See Dunning
Halsey ES 100/K-6
PO Box 98 69142 308-533-2204
Dale Hafer, prin. Fax 533-2204

Hampton, Hamilton, Pop. 439
Hampton SD 100/K-12
458 5th St 68843 402-725-3117
Holly Herzberg, supt. Fax 725-3334
www.hampton.k12.ne.us/
Hampton ES 100/K-6
458 5th St 68843 402-725-3233
Holly Herzberg, prin. Fax 725-3334

Hampton Lutheran S 100/PK-6
732 N 3rd St 68843 402-725-3347
Kathy Gloystein, prin. Fax 725-3341

Harrisburg, Banner
Banner County SD 200/K-12
PO Box 5 69345 308-436-5263
Lana Sides, supt. Fax 436-5252
schools.esu13.org/bannercounty/
Banner County ES 100/K-6
PO Box 5 69345 308-436-5263
Travis Miller, prin. Fax 436-5252

Harrison, Sioux, Pop. 277
Sioux County SD 100/K-12
PO Box 38 69346 308-668-2415
Brett Gies, supt. Fax 668-2260
schs.panesu.org/
Bodarc S 50/K-8
PO Box 38 69346 308-668-2249
Deb Brownfield, prin. Fax 635-2931
Harrison S 50/K-8
PO Box 38 69346 308-668-2336
Deb Brownfield, prin. Fax 668-2335
Panhandle S 50/K-8
PO Box 38 69346 308-668-2391
Deb Brownfield, prin. Fax 635-2931
Other Schools – See Marsland, Morrill

Hartington, Cedar, Pop. 1,587
Hartington SD 300/K-12
PO Box 75 68739 402-254-3947
Scott Swisher, supt. Fax 254-3945
hartington.esu1.org/
Hartington ES 100/K-6
PO Box 75 68739 402-254-3947
Lori Peitz, prin. Fax 254-3945

East Catholic S 100/PK-6
108 W 889 Rd 68739 402-357-2146
Monique Stubbs, lead tchr. Fax 357-3758
Holy Trinity S 200/K-6
PO Box 278 68739 402-254-6496
Terry Kathol, prin. Fax 254-3976

Harvard, Clay, Pop. 943
Harvard SD 200/K-12
PO Box 100 68944 402-772-2171
Larry Turnquist, supt. Fax 772-2204
Harvard ES 100/K-6
PO Box 100 68944 402-772-2171
Larry Turnquist, prin. Fax 772-2204

Hastings, Adams, Pop. 25,437
Adams Central SD 800/K-12
PO Box 1088 68902 402-463-3285
Shawn Scott, supt. Fax 463-6344
sites.esu9.org/adamscentral/
Adams County ES 15 100/K-6
1970 E 12th St 68901 402-463-6107
Joe Cook, prin. Fax 463-6107
Tri-View ES 50/K-6
1300 E Lochland Rd 68901 402-463-8326
Joseph Cook, prin. Fax 463-8467
Wallace ES 100/K-6
2975 S Baltimore Ave 68901 402-463-5090
Allyson Bohlen, prin. Fax 463-6006
Other Schools – See Ayr, Juniata

Hastings SD 2,900/PK-12
1924 W A St 68901 402-461-7500
Craig Kautz, supt. Fax 461-7509
www1.hastings.esu9.k12.ne.us/
Alcott ES 300/K-5
313 N Cedar Ave 68901 402-461-7580
Donald Gronemeyer, prin. Fax 461-7639
Hastings MS 400/6-8
201 N Marian Rd 68901 402-461-7520
Jeffrey Schneider, prin. Fax 461-7650
Hawthorne ES 300/PK-5
2200 W 9th St 68901 402-461-7540
Ann Auten, prin. Fax 461-7546
Lincoln ES 200/PK-5
720 S Franklin Ave 68901 402-461-7589
Andrew Heady, prin. Fax 461-7592
Longfellow ES 300/K-5
828 N Hastings Ave 68901 402-461-7584
Cathleen Cafferty, prin. Fax 461-7585
Morton ES 200/K-5
731 N Baltimore Ave 68901 402-461-7545
John Nelson, prin. Fax 461-7616
Watson ES 100/PK-5
1720 Crane Ave 68901 402-461-7593
Deborah Lee, prin. Fax 461-7636

St. Michael S 200/K-6
721 Creighton Ave 68901 402-462-6310
Sr. Bernard Simmons, prin. Fax 462-6035
Zion Lutheran S 100/PK-8
465 S Marian Rd 68901 402-462-5012
Fax 462-5375

Hayes Center, Hayes, Pop. 226
Hayes Center SD 200/K-12
PO Box 8 69032 308-286-5600
Kate Repass, supt. Fax 286-5629
www.hccardinals.org
Hayes Center ES 100/K-6
PO Box 8 69032 308-286-5601
Kristine Walker, prin. Fax 286-5630

Hay Springs, Sheridan, Pop. 585
Hay Springs SD 200/PK-12
PO Box 280 69347 308-638-4434
Ernest Griffiths, supt. Fax 638-7500
www.hshawks.com/
Hay Springs Early Childhood Development PK-PK
122 Main St 69347 308-638-7691
Kim Marx, admin.
Hay Springs ES 100/K-5
PO Box 280 69347 308-638-4434
Mikal Shalikow, prin. Fax 638-7500
Hay Springs MS 50/6-8
PO Box 280 69347 308-638-4434
Mikal Shalikow, prin. Fax 638-7500
Mirage Flats S 50/K-8
4346 440th Rd 69347 308-232-4517
Mikal Shalikow, prin. Fax 232-4647

Hebron, Thayer, Pop. 1,410
Thayer Central Community SD 400/K-12
PO Box 9 68370 402-768-6117
Drew Harris, supt. Fax 768-6110
www.thayercentral.org/
Thayer Central IS 100/3-6
PO Box 9 68370 402-768-7287
Kurk Wiedel, prin. Fax 768-2572
Thayer Central PS 100/K-2
PO Box 9 68370 402-768-6038
Kurk Wiedel, prin. Fax 768-2572

Hemingford, Box Butte, Pop. 916
Hemingford SD 300/PK-12
PO Box 217 69348 308-487-3328
Casper Ningen, supt. Fax 487-5215
www.hemingfordschools.org/
Hemingford ES 200/PK-6
PO Box 217 69348 308-487-3330
Ronald Foster, prin. Fax 487-5215

Henderson, York, Pop. 999
Heartland Community SD 300/K-12
1501 Front St 68371 402-723-4434
Norman Yoder, supt. Fax 723-4431
www.heartlandschools.org/
Heartland Community ES 100/K-6
1501 Front St 68371 402-723-4434
Cindy Huebert, prin. Fax 723-4431

Herman, Washington, Pop. 301
Tekamah-Herman SD
Supt. — See Tekamah
Herman ES 100/PK-6
PO Box 240 68029 402-456-7404
Chris Fleischman, prin. Fax 374-2155

Hershey, Lincoln, Pop. 568
Hershey SD 500/K-12
PO Box 369 69143 308-368-5574
Dr. Michael Cunning, supt. Fax 368-5570
webquests.esu16.org:8080/hershey/
Hershey ES 200/K-6
PO Box 369 69143 308-368-5572
Thomas Hain, prin. Fax 368-5570

Hildreth, Franklin, Pop. 352
Wilcox-Hildreth SD
Supt. — See Wilcox
Wilcox-Hildreth MS 100/6-8
PO Box 157 68947 308-938-3825
Roger Boyer, prin. Fax 938-5335

Holdrege, Phelps, Pop. 5,349
Holdrege SD 1,000/K-12
PO Box 2002 68949 308-995-8663
Cynthia Wendell, supt. Fax 995-6956
www.thedusters.org/
Franklin ES 200/K-4
PO Box 2002 68949 308-995-4269
LeRoy Walker, prin. Fax 995-5241
Holdrege ES R7 100/K-4
PO Bos 2002 68949 308-995-6179
LeRoy Walker, prin. Fax 995-6170
Holdrege MS 300/5-8
PO Box 2002 68949 308-995-5421
Russell Baker, prin. Fax 995-4970
Washington ES 200/K-4
PO Box 2002 68949 308-995-4339
Amber Porter, prin. Fax 995-4558

All Saints S 50/K-4
1206 Logan St 68949 308-995-4590
Fr. Thomas Lux, prin. Fax 995-2217

Homer, Dakota, Pop. 603
Homer Community SD 400/PK-12
PO Box 340 68030 402-698-2377
Russ Gade, supt. Fax 698-2379
homerweb.esu1.org/
Homer ES 200/PK-6
PO Box 340 68030 402-698-2377
Russ Gade, prin. Fax 698-2379

Hooper, Dodge, Pop. 798
Logan View SD 500/K-12
2163 County Road G 68031 402-654-3317
Steve Wilson, supt. Fax 654-3699
www.loganview.org/
Logan View ES 100/K-4
PO Box 446 68031 402-654-3315
William Kraus, prin. Fax 654-3515
Logan View IS 100/5-6
2187 County Road G 68031 402-654-3317
William Kraus, prin. Fax 654-2164

Immanuel Lutheran S 50/K-8
27053 County Road 12 68031 402-654-3663
Connie Eckert, prin. Fax 654-2814

Hoskins, Wayne, Pop. 263

Trinity Lutheran S 50/K-8
PO Box 100 68740 402-565-4517
Timothy Hemling, prin. Fax 565-4517

Howells, Colfax, Pop. 635
Howells SD 200/K-12
PO Box 159 68641 402-986-1621
Thomas McMahon, supt. Fax 986-1261
howellspublicschools.org/
Howells ES 50/K-6
PO Box 159 68641 402-986-1621
Dan Martin, prin. Fax 986-1261

Howells Community Catholic S 100/1-6
114 N 6th St 68641 402-986-1689
Mary Goodart, prin. Fax 986-1653

Humboldt, Richardson, Pop. 852
Humboldt Table Rock Steinauer SD 70 400/PK-12
810 Central Ave 68376 402-862-2235
Clinton Kimbrough, supt. Fax 862-3135
www.humboldt.esu6.org
Humboldt Table Rock Steinauer ES 100/PK-3
810 Central Ave 68376 402-862-2235
Laurie Kimbrough, prin. Fax 862-3135
Other Schools – See Table Rock

Humphrey, Platte, Pop. 768
Humphrey SD 200/PK-12
PO Box 278 68642 402-923-1230
Greg Sjuts, supt. Fax 923-1235
www.humphrey.esu7.org/
Humphrey ES 100/PK-6
PO Box 278 68642 402-923-1230
Marty Moser, prin. Fax 923-1235
Other Schools – See Lindsay

St. Francis S 200/K-12
300 S 7th St 68642 402-923-0818
Darron Arlt, prin. Fax 923-1590

Hyannis, Grant, Pop. 257
Hyannis Area Schools 100/K-12
PO Box 286 69350 308-458-2202
Raymond Davis, supt. Fax 458-2227
Hyannis ES 50/K-6
PO Box 109 69350 308-458-2297
Howard Gaffney, prin. Fax 458-2321

Imperial, Chase, Pop. 1,876
Chase County SD 500/K-12
PO Box 577 69033 308-882-4304
Matthew Fisher, supt. Fax 882-5629
Chase County S 300/K-8
PO Box 577 69033 308-882-4228
Nathan Vitosh, prin. Fax 882-5629

Indianola, Red Willow, Pop. 611
Southwest SD 179
Supt. — See Bartley
Southwest ES 100/PK-5
39145 Road 718 69034 308-364-2613
Carrie Rasmussen, prin. Fax 364-2508

Inman, Holt, Pop. 132
O'Neill SD
Supt. — See O Neill
Inman S 50/K-8
PO Box 48 68742 402-394-5454
Jennifer Hagen, prin. Fax 394-5455

Jackson, Dakota, Pop. 207
Ponca SD
Supt. — See Ponca
Jackson ES 100/K-6
PO Box 67 68743 402-632-4276
Bob Hayes, prin. Fax 632-5014

Johnson, Nemaha, Pop. 253
Johnson-Brock SD 200/K-12
PO Box 186 68378 402-868-5235
Arlan Andreesen, supt. Fax 868-4785
manila.esu4.org/JohnsonBrock/

Johnson ES 100/K-6
PO Box 186 68378 402-868-5235
Jacquelyn Kelsay, prin. Fax 868-4785

Juniata, Adams, Pop. 729
Adams Central SD
Supt. — See Hastings
Juniata ES 100/K-6
PO Box 157 68955 402-751-2245
Lonnie Abbott, prin. Fax 751-2711

Christ Lutheran S 100/K-8
13175 W 70th St 68955 402-744-4991
Dennis Rosenthal, prin. Fax 744-4971

Kearney, Buffalo, Pop. 28,958
Kearney SD 4,900/PK-12
310 W 24th St 68845 308-698-8000
Dr. Brian Maher, supt. Fax 698-8001
www.kearneypublicschools.org/
Bright Futures Preschool 100/PK-PK
910 E 34th St 68847 308-698-8233
Judy Witte, prin. Fax 698-8235
Bryant ES 200/K-5
1611 Avenue C 68847 308-698-8190
Mark Johnson, prin. Fax 698-8192
Central ES 200/K-5
300 W 24th St 68845 308-698-8040
Teresa Schnoor, prin. Fax 698-8053
Emerson ES 200/K-5
2705 Avenue E 68847 308-698-8270
David Townsend Ph.D., prin. Fax 698-8273
Glenwood ES 100/K-5
8105 9th Ave 68845 308-698-8240
Harold Jochum, prin. Fax 698-8244
Horizon MS 500/6-8
915 W 35th St 68845 308-698-8120
Kipp Petersen, prin. Fax 698-8143
Kenwood ES 200/K-5
1511 5th Ave 68845 308-698-8200
Jill Clevenger, prin. Fax 698-8202
Meadowlark ES 300/K-5
1010 E 53rd St 68847 308-698-8210
Mark Stute, prin. Fax 698-8215
Northeast ES 400/K-5
910 E 34th St 68847 308-698-8230
Joe Horky, prin. Fax 698-8235
Park ES 300/K-5
3000 7th Ave 68845 308-698-8280
Kathleen Mathews, prin. Fax 698-8283
Stone ES 50/K-5
2430 Cherry Ave 68847 308-234-9486
Harold Jochum, prin. Fax 237-6545
Sunrise MS 500/6-8
4611 Avenue N 68847 308-698-8150
Lance Fuller, prin. Fax 698-8152
Windy Hills ES 300/K-5
4211 20th Ave 68845 308-698-8220
Jerry Gloystein, prin. Fax 698-8224
Other Schools – See Riverdale

Faith Christian S of Kearney 50/K-8
4010 7th Ave 68845 308-236-8744
Andrew Falk, prin. Fax 237-4312
Zion Lutheran S 100/PK-8
PO Box 778 68848 308-234-3410
Anthony Splittgerber, lead tchr. Fax 236-8100

Kenesaw, Adams, Pop. 913
Kenesaw SD 300/K-12
PO Box 129 68956 402-752-3215
William Troshynski, supt. Fax 752-3579
www.kenesawschools.org/
Kenesaw ES 100/K-6
PO Box 129 68956 402-752-3215
William Troshynki, prin. Fax 752-3579

Kilgore, Cherry, Pop. 99
Cody-Kilgore SD
Supt. — See Cody
Cody-Kilgore ES 100/K-6
PO Box 58 69216 402-966-2291
Fax 966-2167

Kimball, Kimball, Pop. 2,341
Kimball SD 500/K-12
901 S Nadine St 69145 308-235-2188
Troy Unzicker, supt. Fax 235-3269
kimball.k12.ne.us/
Lynch ES 200/3-6
1000 E 6th St 69145 308-235-4696
Robert Alderson, prin. Fax 235-2227
West ES 100/K-2
301 S Howard St 69145 308-235-3671
Robert Alderson, prin. Fax 235-8371

Lakeside, Sheridan
Gordon-Rushville SD
Supt. — See Gordon
Lakeside S 50/1-8
3144 Charlton St 69351 308-762-3723
Lori Lissett, prin. Fax 762-9128

Laurel, Cedar, Pop. 924
Laurel-Concord SD 400/K-12
PO Box 8 68745 402-256-3133
Daniel Hoesing, supt. Fax 256-9465
www.laurel.esu1.org
Laurel-Concord ES 200/K-6
PO Box 8 68745 402-256-3730
Stephanie Petersen, prin. Fax 256-9465

La Vista, Sarpy, Pop. 15,692
Papillion-La Vista SD
Supt. — See Papillion
Hall ES 400/PK-6
7600 S 72nd St 68128 402-898-0455
Laurinda Petersen, prin. Fax 898-0457
La Vista JHS 700/7-8
7900 Edgewood Blvd 68128 402-898-0436
Thomas Furby, prin. Fax 898-0442
La Vista West ES 300/PK-6
7821 Terry Dr 68128 402-898-0463
Lisa Wood, prin. Fax 898-0465
Parkview Heights ES 300/K-6
7609 S 89th St 68128 402-898-0433
Pam Lowndes, prin. Fax 898-0435
Portal ES 300/K-6
9920 Brentwood Dr 68128 402-898-0425
Paul Bohn, prin. Fax 898-0426

Lawrence, Nuckolls, Pop. 297
South Central Nebraska Unified SD
Supt. — See Fairfield
Lawrence/Nelson ES 100/K-6
411 E 2nd St 68957 402-756-7013
Clayton Waddle, prin. Fax 756-7120

Sacred Heart S 50/K-8
PO Box 25 68957 402-756-7043
Rev. Loras Grell, prin. Fax 756-7409

Leigh, Colfax, Pop. 432
Leigh Community SD 200/K-12
PO Box 98 68643 402-487-2228
Grant Norgaard, supt. Fax 487-2607
www.esu7.org/~leiweb/leigh.html
Leigh ES 100/K-6
PO Box 98 68643 402-487-3301
Grant Norgaard, prin. Fax 487-2607

Lewellen, Garden, Pop. 244
Garden County SD
Supt. — See Oshkosh
Garden County JHS 100/5-8
PO Box 268 69147 308-778-5561
Jason Spady, prin. Fax 778-5568

Lewiston, Pawnee, Pop. 81
Lewiston SD 200/K-12
306 Tiger Ave 68380 402-865-4675
William McCoy, supt. Fax 865-4875
www.lewistonschool.org/
Lewiston ES 100/K-6
306 Tiger Ave 68380 402-865-4675
Fax 865-4875

Lexington, Dawson, Pop. 10,085
Lexington SD 2,800/PK-12
PO Box 890 68850 308-324-4681
Clarence Chessmore Ed.D., supt. Fax 324-2528
www.lex.esu10.org/
Bryan ES 200/K-5
1003 N Harrison St 68850 308-324-3762
Drew Welch, prin. Fax 324-7471
Early Learning Academy 200/PK-PK
1500 Plum Creek Pkwy 68850 308-324-8171
Robert Ripp, prin. Fax 324-2528
Lexington MS 600/6-8
1100 N Washington St 68850 308-324-2349
Dean Tickle, prin. Fax 324-6612
Morton ES 400/K-5
PO Box 820 68850 308-324-3764
Barry McFarland, prin. Fax 324-2138
Pershing ES 300/K-5
PO Box 840 68850 308-324-3765
Jerry Bergstrom, prin. Fax 324-2665
Sandoz ES 300/K-5
1711 N Erie St 68850 308-324-5540
Fred Evans, prin. Fax 324-2350

Lincoln, Lancaster, Pop. 239,213
Lincoln SD 31,700/PK-12
PO Box 82889 68501 402-436-1000
E. Susan Gourley Ph.D., supt. Fax 436-1084
www.lps.org/
Adams ES PK-5
7401 Jacobs Creek Dr 68512 402-436-1121
Cindy Schwaninger, prin.
Arnold ES 600/PK-5
5000 Mike Scholl St 68524 402-436-1120
Kathy Honeycutt, prin. Fax 458-3220
Beattie ES 400/PK-5
1901 Calvert St 68502 402-436-1123
Suzanne Reimers, prin. Fax 458-3223
Belmont ES 700/PK-5
3425 N 14th St 68521 402-436-1124
Mona Manley, prin. Fax 458-3224
Brownell ES 300/PK-5
6000 Aylesworth Ave 68505 402-436-1127
Chris Schefdore, prin. Fax 436-1117
Calvert ES 400/PK-5
3709 S 46th St 68506 402-436-1130
Michelle Suarez, prin. Fax 458-3230
Campbell ES 600/PK-5
2200 Dodge St 68521 402-436-1129
Rosemary Molvar, prin. Fax 458-3229
Cavett ES 600/PK-5
7701 S 36th St 68516 402-436-1131
Kathy Evasco, prin. Fax 458-3231
Clinton ES 500/PK-5
1520 N 29th St 68503 402-436-1132
Jo Theis, prin. Fax 458-3232
Culler MS 500/6-8
5201 Vine St 68504 402-436-1210
Dan Larson, prin. Fax 458-3210
Eastridge ES 200/K-5
6245 L St 68510 402-436-1135
Deborah Dabbert, prin. Fax 458-3235
Elliott ES 400/K-5
225 S 25th St 68510 402-436-1136
Dr. Deann Currin, prin. Fax 458-3236
Everett ES 500/PK-5
1123 C St 68502 402-436-1159
Jadi Miller, prin. Fax 436-1468
Fredstrom ES 500/K-5
5700 NW 10th St 68521 402-436-1140
Vicki Schulenberg, prin. Fax 436-1404
Goodrich MS 700/6-8
5130 Colfax Ave 68504 402-436-1213
Michael Henninger, prin. Fax 458-3213
Hartley ES 300/K-5
730 N 33rd St 68503 402-436-1139
Jeff Vercellino, prin. Fax 436-1191
Hill ES 600/K-5
5230 Tipperary Trl 68512 402-436-1142
Michelle Phillips, prin. Fax 458-3242
Holmes ES 500/PK-5
5230 Sumner St 68506 402-436-1143
Katherine Richter, prin. Fax 458-3243
Humann ES 700/PK-5
6720 Rockwood Ln 68516 402-436-1145
Randy Oltman, prin. Fax 436-1426
Huntington ES 500/PK-5
4601 Adams St 68504 402-436-1144
Rik Devney, prin. Fax 458-3244
Irving MS 800/6-8
2745 S 22nd St 68502 402-436-1214
Hugh McDermott, prin. Fax 458-3214
Kahoa ES 400/K-5
7700 Leighton Ave 68507 402-436-1147
Russell Reckewey, prin. Fax 458-3247
Kooser ES PK-5
7301 N 13th St 68521 402-436-1146
Ann Jablonski, prin. Fax 458-3246
Lakeview ES 200/K-5
300 Capitol Beach Blvd 68528 402-436-1149
Sudie Bock, prin. Fax 436-1438
Lefler MS 600/6-8
1100 S 48th St 68510 402-436-1215
Kelly Schrad, prin. Fax 458-3215
Lux MS 900/6-8
7800 High St 68506 402-436-1220
William Bucher, prin. Fax 458-3292
Maxey ES 700/PK-5
5200 S 75th St 68516 402-436-1153
Patrick Decker, prin. Fax 458-3253
McPhee ES 200/PK-5
820 Goodhue Blvd 68508 402-436-1150
Scott Nelson, prin. Fax 436-1442
Meadow Lane ES 500/PK-5
7200 Vine St 68505 402-436-1151
Tim Muggy, prin. Fax 458-3251
Mickle MS 700/6-8
2500 N 67th St 68507 402-436-1216
Gene Thompson, prin. Fax 458-3216
Morley ES 400/K-5
6800 Monterey Dr 68506 402-436-1154
Coni Schwartz, prin. Fax 436-1457
Norwood Park ES 200/K-5
4710 N 72nd St 68507 402-436-1155
Dr. Bill G. Thurmond, prin. Fax 458-3255
Park MS 800/6-8
855 S 8th St 68508 402-436-1212
Ryan Zabawa, prin. Fax 458-3212
Pershing ES 400/PK-5
6402 Judson St 68507 402-436-1160
Paula Baker, prin. Fax 436-1471
Pound MS 700/6-8
4740 S 45th St 68516 402-436-1217
Dr. Christopher Deibler, prin. Fax 458-3217
Prescott ES 300/PK-5
1930 S 20th St 68502 402-436-1161
Ruth Wylie, prin. Fax 458-3261
Pyrtle ES 400/K-5
721 Cottonwood Dr 68510 402-436-1162
Sandra Robertson, prin. Fax 458-3262
Randolph ES 400/K-5
1024 S 37th St 68510 402-436-1163
Dr. Wendy Bonaiuto, prin. Fax 458-3263
Riley ES 300/PK-5
5021 Orchard St 68504 402-436-1164
Molly Bates, prin. Fax 458-3264
Roper ES 700/PK-5
2323 S Coddington Ave 68522 402-436-1170
Daniel Navratil, prin. Fax 458-3270
Rousseau ES 500/K-5
3701 S 33rd St 68506 402-436-1165
Susan Braun, prin. Fax 458-3265
Saratoga ES 200/PK-5
2215 S 13th St 68502 402-436-1166
Kathy Fleming, prin. Fax 436-1506
Schoo MS 6-8
700 Penrose Dr 68521 402-436-1222
Dr. Linda Hix, prin. Fax 458-3222
Scott MS 900/6-8
2200 Pine Lake Rd 68512 402-436-1218
Dave Knudsen, prin. Fax 458-3218
Sheridan ES 400/K-5
3100 Plymouth Ave 68502 402-436-1167
Mary Kanter, prin. Fax 458-3267
West Lincoln ES 400/PK-5
630 W Dawes Ave 68521 402-436-1168
Scott Schwartz, prin. Fax 458-3268
Zeman ES 400/K-5
4900 S 52nd St 68516 402-436-1169
Donna Williams, prin. Fax 458-3108

Blessed Sacrament S 200/K-8
2500 S 17th St 68502 402-476-6202
Holly Kruger, prin. Fax 476-0232
Cathedral of Risen Christ S 400/K-8
3245 S 37th St 68506 402-489-9621
Tony Primavera, prin. Fax 488-9622
Christ S 100/PK-5
4325 Sumner St 68506 402-483-7774
Linda Becken, prin. Fax 483-7776
College View Academy 100/K-12
5240 Calvert St 68506 402-483-1181
David Branum, prin. Fax 483-5574

Faith Lutheran S 300/PK-6
8701 Adams St 68507 402-466-7402
Stuart Tietz, prin. Fax 466-3857
Good Shepherd Lutheran S 100/PK-8
3825 Wildbriar Ln 68516 402-423-7677
Rev. Thomas Obersat, admin. Fax 423-0984
Hyatt S 200/K-8
5140 Calvert St 68506 402-483-1181
Fax 483-5574
Lincoln Christian S 600/PK-12
5801 S 84th St 68516 402-488-8888
Mark Wilson, supt. Fax 486-4527
Messiah Lutheran S 300/PK-5
1800 S 84th St 68506 402-489-3024
Matthew Stueber, prin. Fax 489-3093
North American Martyrs S 500/K-8
1101 Isaac Dr 68521 402-476-7373
Sr. Patricia Heirigs, prin.
Parkview Christian S 300/PK-12
4400 N 1st St 68521 402-474-5820
Larry Frost, supt. Fax 474-5830
Sacred Heart S 200/K-8
530 N 31st St 68503 402-476-1783
Sr. Bernadette Radek, prin. Fax 476-3040
St. John the Apostle S 300/K-8
7601 Vine St 68505 402-486-1860
Dennis Martin, prin. Fax 486-4732
St. Joseph's S 600/K-8
1940 S 77th St 68506 402-489-0341
Sr. Mary Joseph Silbernick, prin. Fax 489-3260
St. Mark Lutheran S 50/K-8
3930 S 19th St 68502 402-423-1497
Matthew Kanzenbach, prin. Fax 423-1497
St. Mary S 100/K-8
1434 K St 68508 402-476-3987
Dr. Nina Beck, prin. Fax 476-0838
St. Patrick S 100/K-8
4142 N 61st St 68507 402-466-3710
Sr. Carol Kelly, prin. Fax 466-3572
St. Peter S 500/K-8
4500 Duxhall Dr 68516 402-421-6299
Sr. Mary Alma Linscott, prin. Fax 421-6507
St. Teresa S 300/K-8
616 S 36th St 68510 402-477-3358
Sr. Mary Cecilia Mills, prin. Fax 477-3361
Stone SDA S 50/1-8
3800 S 48th St 68506 402-486-2896
Joseph Allison, prin. Fax 486-2574
Trinity Lutheran S 200/PK-5
1200 N 56th St 68504 402-466-1800
Mervin Dehning, prin. Fax 466-1820

Lindsay, Platte, Pop. 270
Humphrey SD
Supt. — See Humphrey
Lindsay K 50/K-K
PO Box 62 68644 402-428-2409
Marty Moser, prin. Fax 923-1235

Holy Family S 100/1-12
PO Box 158 68644 402-428-3455
David Schindler, prin. Fax 428-3231

Litchfield, Sherman, Pop. 260
Litchfield SD 100/K-12
PO Box 167 68852 308-446-2244
Michael Gillming, supt. Fax 446-2244
sites.litchfield.k12.ne.us/
Litchfield ES 100/K-6
PO Box 167 68852 308-446-2244
Brad Stithem, prin. Fax 446-2244

Lodgepole, Cheyenne, Pop. 359
Creek Valley SD
Supt. — See Chappell
Creek Valley MS 100/5-8
PO Box 158 69149 308-483-5252
Katherine Urbanek, prin. Fax 483-5251

Loomis, Phelps, Pop. 375
Loomis SD 200/K-12
PO Box 250 68958 308-876-2111
Keith Fagot, supt. Fax 876-2372
Loomis ES 100/K-6
PO Box 250 68958 308-876-2111
Keith Fagot, prin. Fax 876-2372

Louisville, Cass, Pop. 1,073
Louisville SD 500/K-12
PO Box 489 68037 402-234-3585
Edward Kasl, supt. Fax 234-2141
www.louisvillepublicschools.org/
Louisville ES 200/K-5
PO Box 489 68037 402-234-4215
Cory Holl, prin. Fax 234-2141
Louisville MS 100/6-8
PO Box 489 68037 402-234-3585
Cindy Osterloh, prin. Fax 234-2141

Loup City, Sherman, Pop. 924
Loup City SD 300/K-12
PO Box 628 68853 308-745-0120
Caroline Winchester, supt. Fax 745-0130
www.loupcity.k12.ne.us/
Loup City S 200/K-6
PO Box 628 68853 308-745-1814
Caroline B. Winchester, prin. Fax 745-0130

Lynch, Boyd, Pop. 239
Lynch SD 100/K-12
PO Box 98 68746 402-569-2081
Ted Hillman, supt. Fax 569-2091
lynch.esu8.org/
Lynch ES 50/K-6
PO Box 98 68746 402-569-2081
Ted Hillman, prin. Fax 569-2091

Lyons, Burt, Pop. 912
Lyons-Decatur Northeast SD 300/PK-12
PO Box 526 68038 402-687-2363
Fred Hansen, supt. Fax 687-2472
www.lyonsdecaturschools.org/
Northeast ES 100/PK-6
PO Box 526 68038 402-687-2349
Fred Hansen, prin. Fax 687-2472

Mc Cook, Red Willow, Pop. 7,926
Mc Cook SD 1,500/K-12
700 W 7th St 69001 308-345-2510
Grant Norgaard, supt. Fax 345-2511
www.mccookbison.org/
Central ES 200/4-5
604 W 1st St 69001 308-345-3976
Dennis Berry, prin. Fax 345-3262
Mc Cook ES 400/K-3
1500 W 3rd St 69001 308-345-5681
Lynda Baumbach, prin. Fax 345-4948
Mc Cook JHS 300/6-8
800 W 7th St 69001 308-345-6940
Dennis Berry, prin. Fax 345-6941

St. Patrick S 100/K-8
PO Box 1040 69001 308-345-4546
Ellen Griffin, prin. Fax 345-4546

Mc Cool Junction, York, Pop. 388
Mc Cool Junction SD 200/K-12
PO Box 278 68401 402-724-2231
Curtis Cogswell, supt. Fax 724-2232
www.mccool.esu6.org/
Mc Cool Junction ES 100/K-6
PO Box 278 68401 402-724-2231
Curtis Cogswell, prin. Fax 724-2232

Macy, Thurston, Pop. 836
UMO N HO N Nation SD 400/PK-12
PO Box 280 68039 402-837-5622
Morris Bates, supt. Fax 837-5245
macyweb.esu1.org/
UMO N HO N Nation ES 200/PK-5
PO Box 280 68039 402-837-5622
Brenda Totten, prin. Fax 837-4194
UMO N HO N Nation MS 100/6-8
PO Box 280 68039 402-837-5622
Broderick Steed, prin. Fax 837-5245

Madison, Madison, Pop. 2,309
Madison SD 500/K-12
PO Box 450 68748 402-454-3336
David Melick, supt. Fax 454-2238
madison.esu8.org/
Madison ES 200/K-5
PO Box 450 68748 402-454-2656
Andrew Luebbe, prin. Fax 454-3978
Madison MS 100/6-8
PO Box 450 68748 402-454-3336
Harold Scott, prin. Fax 454-2238

St. Leonard S 100/PK-6
PO Box 368 68748 402-454-3525
Scott Olson, lead tchr. Fax 454-6533
Trinity Lutheran S 100/PK-8
PO Box 969 68748 402-454-2651
Annie Rumsey, prin. Fax 454-3476

Madrid, Perkins, Pop. 256
Perkins County SD
Supt. — See Grant
Perkins County MS 100/6-8
501 S Ford Ave 69150 308-326-4201
Terry Prante, prin. Fax 326-4231

Malcolm, Lancaster, Pop. 441
Malcolm SD 400/K-12
10004 NW 112th St 68402 402-796-2151
Gene Neddenriep, supt. Fax 796-2178
www.malcolmschools.esu6.org/
Westfall ES 200/K-6
10000 NW 112th St 68402 402-796-2151
Ryan Terwilliger, prin. Fax 796-2186

Marsland, Dawes, Pop. 10
Sioux County SD
Supt. — See Harrison
Pink S 50/K-8
1022 River Rd 69354 308-665-1964
Deb Brownfield, prin. Fax 665-1964

Maxwell, Lincoln, Pop. 323
Maxwell SD 300/PK-12
PO Box 188 69151 308-582-4585
Charles Hervert, supt. Fax 582-4584
Maxwell ES 100/PK-6
PO Box 188 69151 308-582-4585
Charles Hervert, prin. Fax 582-4584

Maywood, Frontier, Pop. 294
Maywood SD 200/K-12
PO Box 46 69038 308-362-4223
Jeffrey Koehler, supt. Fax 362-4454
webquests.esu16.org:8080/Maywood/
Maywood ES 100/K-6
PO Box 46 69038 308-362-4223
Jeffrey Koehler, prin. Fax 362-4454

Mead, Saunders, Pop. 623
Mead SD 200/K-12
PO Box 158 68041 402-624-2745
George Robertson, supt. Fax 624-2001
www.meadpublicschools.org/
Mead ES 100/K-6
PO Box 158 68041 402-624-6465
P.J. Quinn, prin. Fax 624-2001

Merna, Custer, Pop. 384
Anselmo-Merna SD 100/K-12
PO Box 68 68856 308-643-2224
Susan McNeil, supt. Fax 643-2243
sites.esu10.org/anselmomerna/
Anselmo-Merna S 100/K-12
PO Box 68 68856 308-643-2224
Darrin Max, prin. Fax 643-2243

Merriman, Cherry, Pop. 117
Gordon-Rushville SD
Supt. — See Gordon
Merriman S 50/K-8
PO Box 7 69218 308-684-3372
Merrill Nelson, prin. Fax 376-8096
Pioneer S 50/1-8
HC 75 Box 30A 69218 308-282-0419
Merrill Nelson, prin. Fax 376-8096

Milford, Seward, Pop. 2,053
Milford SD 700/PK-12
PO Box C 68405 402-761-3321
Kevin Wingard, supt. Fax 761-3322
www.milfordpublicschools.org/
Milford ES 300/PK-6
PO Box C 68405 402-761-2408
Penny Jans, prin. Fax 761-3322
Other Schools – See Pleasant Dale

Milligan, Fillmore, Pop. 299
Exeter-Milligan SD
Supt. — See Exeter
Exeter-Milligan ES 100/K-6
PO Box 40 68406 402-629-4265
Mari Lyn Poppert, prin. Fax 629-4293

Minatare, Scotts Bluff, Pop. 784
Minatare SD 200/K-12
PO Box 425 69356 308-783-1232
Charles Bunner, supt. Fax 783-2982
www.minatareschools.com/
Minatare ES 100/K-6
PO Box 425 69356 308-783-1255
Charles J. Bunner, prin. Fax 783-2982

Scottsbluff SD
Supt. — See Scottsbluff
Lake Minatare ES 100/K-5
280548 County Road K 69356 308-783-1134
Karen Johnson, prin. Fax 783-1574

Minden, Kearney, Pop. 2,913
Minden SD 800/PK-12
PO Box 301 68959 308-832-2440
Melissa Wheelock, supt. Fax 832-2567
www.mpschools.org/
Jones MS 300/4-8
PO Box 301 68959 308-832-2338
John Osgood, prin. Fax 832-3236
Minden East ES 200/K-3
PO Box 301 68959 308-832-2460
Mary Lieske, prin. Fax 832-2567
Minden Preschool 50/PK-PK
PO Box 301 68959 308-832-1666

Mitchell, Scotts Bluff, Pop. 1,796
Mitchell SD 600/K-12
1819 19th Ave 69357 308-623-1707
Kent Halley, supt. Fax 623-1330
www.mpstigers.com
Mitchell ES 300/K-6
1439 13th Ave 69357 308-623-2828
Kirk Kuxhausen, prin. Fax 623-1690

Morrill, Scotts Bluff, Pop. 941
Morrill SD 500/PK-12
PO Box 486 69358 308-247-3414
Stephen Osborn, supt. Fax 247-2196
schools.esu13.org/morrill/
Morrill ES 200/K-6
PO Box 486 69358 308-247-2176
Brian Hartwig, prin. Fax 247-2196
Tri Community Preschool PK-PK
PO Box 486 69358 308-247-2176
Dawn Terrell, dir. Fax 247-2491

Sioux County SD
Supt. — See Harrison
Chalk Butte S 50/K-8
321 S I Rd 69358 308-247-2811
Deb Brownfield, prin. Fax 635-2931

Mullen, Hooker, Pop. 497
Mullen SD 200/K-12
PO Box 127 69152 308-546-2223
Jeffery Hoesing, supt. Fax 546-2209
Mullen ES 100/K-6
PO Box 89 69152 308-546-2292
Jeffery Hoesing, prin. Fax 546-2423

Murdock, Cass, Pop. 273
Elmwood-Murdock SD 400/K-12
PO Box 407 68407 402-867-2341
Daniel Novak, supt. Fax 867-2009
www.elm.esu3.org/index.htm
Other Schools – See Elmwood

Murray, Cass, Pop. 494
Conestoga SD 600/PK-12
PO Box 184 68409 402-235-2992
Mark Sievering, supt. Fax 227-2992
www.conestogacougars.org/
Conestoga ES - Murray 300/PK-6
PO Box 68 68409 402-235-2341
Eric Dennis, prin. Fax 235-2345

Nebraska City, Otoe, Pop. 7,035
Nebraska City SD 1,400/PK-12
215 N 12th St 68410 402-873-6033
Dr. Jeffrey Edwards, supt. Fax 873-6030
www.nebcity.esu6.org

Hayward ES 300/3-5
306 S 14th St 68410 402-873-6641
Jason McNeely, prin. Fax 873-6674
Nebraska City MS 300/6-8
909 1st Corso 68410 402-873-5591
Jenny Powell, prin. Fax 873-5641
Northside ES 300/PK-2
1212 12th Ave 68410 402-873-5561
Haeven Pederson, prin. Fax 873-5562

Lourdes S 100/K-5
412 2nd Ave 68410 402-873-6154
Valerie Jo Able, prin. Fax 873-3154

Neligh, Antelope, Pop. 1,542
Neligh-Oakdale SD 400/K-12
PO Box 149 68756 402-887-4166
Ron Brandl, supt. Fax 887-5322
teachers.esu8.org/nohs/
Neligh-Oakdale ES 200/K-6
PO Box 149 68756 402-887-4166
Ronald Brandl, prin. Fax 887-5322

Nenzel, Cherry, Pop. 13
Valentine SD
Supt. — See Valentine
Taylor Lake S 50/K-8
HC 74 Box 26 69219 402-823-4386
Eva Westover, prin. Fax 376-8096

Newcastle, Dixon, Pop. 285
Newcastle SD 200/K-12
PO Box 187 68757 402-355-2231
Dan Hoesing, supt. Fax 355-2635
newcastle.esu1.org/
Newcastle ES 100/K-6
PO Box 187 68757 402-355-2231
Joseph Lefdal, prin. Fax 355-2635

Newman Grove, Madison, Pop. 774
Newman Grove SD 300/K-12
PO Box 370 68758 402-447-2721
Loren Pokorny, supt. Fax 447-2445
newman.esu8.org/
Newman Grove ES 100/K-6
PO Box 370 68758 402-447-6051
Loren Pokorny, prin. Fax 447-2445

Newport, Keya Paha, Pop. 89
Rock County SD
Supt. — See Bassett
Newport S 50/K-8
PO Box 276 68759 402-244-5225
Steve Camp, prin. Fax 244-5317

Niobrara, Knox, Pop. 358
Niobrara SD 100/K-12
247 N Highway 12 68760 402-857-3323
Margaret Sandoz, supt. Fax 857-3877
niobrara.esu1.org/uptodate.html
Niobrara ES 100/K-4
247 N Highway 12 68760 402-857-3323
Margaret Sandoz, prin. Fax 857-3877

Santee SD 100/K-12
206 Frazier Ave E 68760 402-857-2741
Bruce Blanchard, supt. Fax 857-2743
santeeweb.esu1.org/
Santee S 100/K-8
206 Frazier Ave E 68760 402-857-2741
France Blanchard, prin. Fax 857-2743

Norfolk, Madison, Pop. 23,946
Norfolk SD 3,900/PK-12
PO Box 139 68702 402-644-2500
Marlene Uhing Ed.D., supt. Fax 644-2506
www.norfolkpublicschools.org/
Bel Air ES 300/K-5
PO Box 139 68702 402-644-2539
Tim Kwapnioski, prin. Fax 644-2542
ECC 100/PK-PK
PO Box 139 68702 402-644-2583
Fax 644-2516
Grant ES 100/K-5
PO Box 139 68702 402-644-2543
Chad Boyer, prin. Fax 644-2545
Jefferson ES 200/K-5
PO Box 139 68702 402-644-2546
Trudie DePasquale, prin. Fax 644-2548
Lincoln ES 100/K-5
PO Box 139 68702 402-644-2550
Jo Roberts, prin. Fax 644-2552
Norfolk MS 500/6-7
PO Box 139 68702 402-644-2569
Michael Hart, prin. Fax 644-2576
Norfolk Montessori ES 100/PK-3
PO Box 139 68702 402-644-2556
Cory Worrell, prin. Fax 644-8768
Northern Hills ES 100/K-5
PO Box 139 68702 402-644-2553
Julie Curry, prin. Fax 644-2555
Sunny Meadow ES 100/K-6
PO Box 139 68702 402-371-9075
Chad Boyer, prin. Fax 379-1034
Washington ES 200/K-5
PO Box 139 68702 402-644-2557
Cory Worrell, prin. Fax 644-2560
Westside ES 200/K-5
PO Box 139 68702 402-644-2561
Jennifer Drahota, prin. Fax 644-2562
Woodland Park ES 200/K-5
PO Box 139 68702 402-644-2565
Scott Dodson, prin. Fax 644-2568

Christ Lutheran S 300/PK-8
511 S 5th St 68701 402-371-5536
Steven Stortz, prin. Fax 371-1288
Keystone Christian Academy 100/PK-9
715 W Madison Ave 68701 402-371-3531
Sharon Lotz, admin. Fax 371-4824
Sacred Heart S 400/PK-6
2301 W Madison Ave 68701 402-371-4584
Troy Berryman, prin. Fax 379-8129
St. Paul Lutheran S 100/PK-8
1010 Georgia Ave 68701 402-371-1233
Seth Fitzsimmons, prin. Fax 379-3646

North Bend, Dodge, Pop. 1,211
North Bend Central SD 500/K-12
PO Box 160 68649 402-652-3268
James Havelka, supt. Fax 652-8348
www.nbtigers.org/
North Bend ES 200/K-6
PO Box 220 68649 402-652-8122
Caryn Ziettlow, prin. Fax 652-3474

North Loup, Valley, Pop. 316
North Loup Scotia SD
Supt. — See Scotia
North Loup ES 100/K-6
PO Box 257 68859 308-496-3331
Deborah Kluthe, prin. Fax 245-9133

North Platte, Lincoln, Pop. 24,324
North Platte SD 4,100/K-12
PO Box 1557 69103 308-535-7100
Dr. David Engle, supt. Fax 535-5300
www.nppsd.org
Adams MS 600/6-8
1200 Mcdonald Rd 69101 308-535-7112
Todd Rhodes, prin. Fax 535-5309
Buffalo ES 200/K-5
1600 N Buffalo Bill Ave 69101 308-535-7130
Michael McPherron, prin. Fax 535-5363
Cody ES 300/K-5
2000 W 2nd St 69101 308-535-7132
Tom Coviello, prin. Fax 535-5364
Eisenhower ES 200/K-5
3900 W A St 69101 308-535-7134
Shane Alexander, prin. Fax 535-5365
Hall S 100/K-8
3199 N Studley Rd 69101 308-532-2470
Chris Vieyra, prin. Fax 534-5646
Jefferson ES 400/K-5
700 E 3rd St 69101 308-535-7136
Dr. Midge Mougey, prin. Fax 535-5366
Lake Maloney S 100/K-8
848 E Correction Line Rd 69101 308-532-9392
Ronald Parks, prin. Fax 534-4371
Lincoln ES 200/K-5
200 W 9th St 69101 308-535-7138
George Schere, prin. Fax 535-5367
Madison MS 200/6-8
1400 N Madison Ave 69101 308-535-7126
Tim Vanderheiden, prin. Fax 535-5303
McDonald ES 200/K-5
601 Mcdonald Rd 69101 308-535-7140
Mary Derby, prin. Fax 535-5368
Osgood ES 100/K-5
495 W State Farm Rd 69101 308-535-7144
Ron Parks, prin. Fax 535-5369
Washington ES 200/K-5
600 W 3rd St 69101 308-535-7142
Matt Irish, prin. Fax 535-5370

Mc Daid S 200/K-6
PO Box 970 69103 308-532-1874
Rick Carpenter, prin. Fax 532-8015
Our Redeemer Lutheran S 100/K-8
1400 E E St 69101 308-532-6421
Janet Livingston, prin. Fax 532-0295
Platte Valley Christian Academy 100/PK-8
1521 Rodeo Rd 69101 308-534-8883
Ben Miller, pres.

Oakland, Burt, Pop. 1,298
Oakland Craig SD 400/K-12
309 N Davis Ave 68045 402-685-5661
Joe Peitzmeier, supt. Fax 685-5697
ocknights.esu2.org/
Oakland Craig ES 200/K-6
400 N Brewster Ave 68045 402-685-5631
John Holys, prin. Fax 685-6734
Oakland Craig JHS 100/7-8
309 N Davis Ave 68045 402-685-5661
Rusty Droescher, prin. Fax 685-5697

Oconto, Custer, Pop. 138
Callaway SD
Supt. — See Callaway
Oconto ES 50/K-5
202 S Washington 68860 308-858-4491
Patrick Osmond, prin. Fax 858-4491

Odell, Gage, Pop. 336
Diller-Odell SD 300/K-12
PO Box 188 68415 402-766-4171
Darrell Vitosh, supt. Fax 766-4211
www.dillerodell.org/
Other Schools – See Diller

Ogallala, Keith, Pop. 4,696
Ogallala SD 1,000/K-12
205 E 6th St 69153 308-284-4060
Carl Dietz, supt. Fax 284-3981
www.opsd.org/
Ogallala MS 300/6-8
205 E 6th St 69153 308-284-4478
Greg Pavlik, prin. Fax 284-8129
Prairie View ES 200/3-5
801 E O St 69153 308-284-6087
Jim Jeffres, prin. Fax 284-3839
Progress ES 100/1-2
601 W B St 69153 308-284-3921
Jim Jeffres, prin. Fax 284-2937
West 5th K 100/K-K
500 W H St 69153 308-284-3866
Jim Jeffres, prin. Fax 284-2910

St. Luke S, 406 E 3rd St 69153 50/K-5
Sr. Loretta Krajewski, prin. 308-284-4841
St. Pauls Lutheran S 50/K-5
312 W 3rd St 69153 308-284-2944

Omaha, Douglas, Pop. 414,521
Elkhorn SD
Supt. — See Elkhorn
Elkhorn Ridge MS 500/6-8
17880 Marcy St 68118 402-334-9302
Kevin Riggert, prin. Fax 334-9378
Manchester ES K-5
2750 HWS Cleveland Blvd 68116 402-289-2590
Amy Christ, prin. Fax 289-2585
Spring Ridge ES 500/K-5
17830 Shadow Ridge Dr 68130 402-637-0204
Don Pechous, prin. Fax 637-0207

Gretna SD
Supt. — See Gretna
Palisades ES K-5
11717 S 216th St 68136 402-895-2194
Sallisue Hajek, prin. Fax 332-5833

Millard SD 21,100/PK-12
5606 S 147th St 68137 402-715-8200
Dr. Keith Lutz, supt. Fax 715-8409
www.mpsomaha.org
Abbott ES 400/PK-5
1313 N 156th Ave 68118 402-715-2900
Erik Chaussee, prin. Fax 715-2911
Ackerman ES 600/K-5
5110 S 156th St 68135 402-715-8420
Melissa Gilbert, prin. Fax 715-6193
Aldrich ES 400/K-5
506 N 162nd Ave 68118 402-715-2020
Susie Melliger, prin. Fax 715-2035
Andersen MS 800/6-8
15404 Adams St 68137 402-715-8440
Jeff Alfrey, prin. Fax 715-8410
Beadle MS 700/6-8
18201 Jefferson St 68135 402-715-6100
John Southworth, prin. Fax 715-6140
Black Elk ES 600/K-5
6708 S 161st Ave 68135 402-715-6200
Josh Fields, prin. Fax 715-6220
Bryan ES 400/K-5
5010 S 144th St 68137 402-715-8325
Brad Sullivan, prin. Fax 715-6194
Cather ES 400/K-5
3030 S 139th St 68144 402-715-1315
Paula Peal, prin. Fax 715-1432
Cody ES 300/PK-5
3320 S 127th St 68144 402-715-1320
Matthew Dominy, prin. Fax 715-1250
Cottonwood ES 300/K-5
615 Piedmont Dr 68154 402-715-1390
Nancy Nelson, prin. Fax 715-1428
Disney ES 300/K-5
5717 S 112th St 68137 402-715-2350
Bethany Case, prin. Fax 715-2358
Hitchcock ES 200/K-5
5809 S 104th St 68127 402-715-2255
Amanda Johnson, prin. Fax 715-1901
Holling Heights ES 400/K-5
6565 S 136th St 68137 402-715-8330
Terry Houlton, prin. Fax 715-6195
Kiewit MS 900/6-8
15650 Howard St 68118 402-715-1470
Lori Jasa, prin. Fax 715-1490
Millard Central MS 800/6-8
12801 L St 68137 402-715-8225
Beth Fink, prin. Fax 715-8574
Millard ES 400/K-5
14111 Blondo St 68164 402-715-2955
Carrie Novotny-Buss, prin. Fax 715-2970
Millard North MS 600/6-8
2828 S 139th St 68144 402-715-1280
Joan Wilson, prin. Fax 715-1275
Montclair ES 500/K-5
2405 S 138th St 68144 402-715-1295
Matt Rega, prin. Fax 715-1446
Morton ES 400/K-5
1805 S 160th St 68130 402-715-1290
Julie Bergstrom, prin. Fax 715-1311
Neihardt ES 600/PK-5
15130 Drexel St 68137 402-715-8360
Colleen Beckwith, prin. Fax 715-6191
Norris ES 300/K-5
12424 Weir St 68137 402-715-8340
Joyce Rozelle, prin. Fax 715-6119
Oaks ES 300/K-5
15228 Shirley St 68144 402-715-1386
Roberta Deremer, prin. Fax 715-1624
Reagan ES K-5
4440 S 198th Ave 68135 402-715-7100
Dr. Nila Nielsen, prin. Fax 715-7120
Rockwell ES 400/K-5
6370 S 140th Ave 68137 402-715-8246
Jerri Wesley, prin. Fax 715-6197
Rowher ES 500/K-5
17701 F St 68135 402-715-6225
Nancy Brosamle, prin. Fax 715-6240
Russell MS 800/6-8
5304 S 172nd St 68135 402-715-8500
Mitch Mollring, prin. Fax 715-8368
Sandoz ES 300/K-5
5959 Oak Hills Dr 68137 402-715-8345
Heidi Penke, prin. Fax 715-8367
Wheeler ES 600/K-5
6707 S 178th St 68135 402-715-6250
Andy DeFreece, prin. Fax 715-6270

Willowdale ES 400/K-5
16901 P St 68135 402-715-8280
Susan Kelley, prin. Fax 715-8580
Other Schools – See Gretna

Omaha SD 45,300/PK-12
3215 Cuming St 68131 402-557-2222
John Mackiel, supt. Fax 557-2019
www.ops.org
Adams ES 300/K-6
3420 N 78th St 68134 402-572-9072
Pamela Lang, prin. Fax 572-9075
Ashland Park-Robbins ES 1,100/PK-6
5050 S 51st St 68117 402-734-6001
Raymond Perrigo, prin. Fax 734-6210
Bancroft ES 700/PK-6
2724 Riverview Blvd 68108 402-344-7505
Andrea Eisner, prin. Fax 344-7695
Beals ES 400/PK-6
1720 S 48th St 68106 402-554-8570
Dr. LeDonna York, prin. Fax 554-8546
Belvedere Academy 500/PK-6
3775 Curtis Ave 68111 402-457-6630
Melissa Comine, prin. Fax 457-6609
Benson West ES 600/K-6
6652 Maple St 68104 402-554-8633
Terry Burton, prin. Fax 554-8616
Beveridge Magnet MS 700/7-8
1616 S 120th St 68144 402-557-4000
David Lavender, prin. Fax 557-4009
Boyd ES 400/PK-6
8314 Boyd St 68134 402-572-8928
Elaine Adams, prin. Fax 572-9001
Bryan MS 800/7-8
8210 S 42nd St 68147 402-557-4100
Robert Aranda, prin. Fax 557-4129
Buffet Magnet MS 600/5-8
14101 Larimore Ave 68164 402-561-6160
Dr. ReNae Kehrberg, prin. Fax 561-6170
Castelar ES 500/PK-6
2316 S 18th St 68108 402-344-7794
Nicole Goodman, prin. Fax 344-7884
Catlin Magnet ES 300/K-6
12736 Marinda St 68144 402-697-0414
Sharon Royers, prin. Fax 697-0016
Central Park ES 400/PK-6
4904 N 42nd St 68111 402-457-5277
Mary Austin, prin. Fax 457-5122
Chandler View ES 600/K-6
7800 S 25th St 68147 402-734-5705
Gregory Eversoll, prin. Fax 734-5609
Columbian ES 300/K-6
330 S 127th St 68154 402-697-1433
Kathy Nelson, prin. Fax 697-1273
Conestoga Magnet ES 300/K-6
2115 Burdette St 68110 402-344-7147
David Milan, prin. Fax 344-7195
Crestridge Magnet ES 400/K-6
818 Crestridge Rd 68154 402-697-1185
Patricia Schweer, prin. Fax 697-0969
Dodge ES 400/PK-6
3520 Maplewood Blvd 68134 402-572-9005
Emily Miller, prin. Fax 572-9049
Druid Hill ES 400/PK-6
4020 N 30th St 68111 402-451-8225
Cherice Williams, prin. Fax 457-6448
Dundee ES 500/K-6
310 N 51st St 68132 402-554-8424
Kaye Goetzinger, prin. Fax 554-0303
Edison ES 300/PK-6
2303 N 97th St 68134 402-392-7310
Alberta Nelson, prin. Fax 392-7357
Field Club ES 700/PK-6
3512 Walnut St 68105 402-344-7226
Jerome Meyer, prin. Fax 344-7395
Florence ES 300/K-6
7902 N 36th St 68112 402-457-5818
Craig McGee, prin. Fax 457-4722
Fontenelle ES 600/PK-6
3905 N 52nd St 68104 402-457-5905
Dr. Kathleen Peterson, prin. Fax 457-6525
Franklin ES 200/K-6
3506 Franklin St 68111 402-554-8508
Decua Jean-Baptiste, prin. Fax 554-8479
Fullerton Magnet ES 800/K-4
4711 N 138th St 68164 402-498-2787
Mark Suing, prin. Fax 498-0967
Gilder ES 400/K-6
3705 Chandler Rd W 68147 402-734-7334
Cassandra Boyd, prin. Fax 734-9973
Gomez Heritage ES 600/PK-4
5101 S 17th St 68107 402-557-4400
John Campin, prin. Fax 557-4429
Hale MS 400/7-8
6143 Whitmore St 68152 402-557-4200
Susan Colvin, prin. Fax 557-4229
Harrison ES 300/K-6
5304 Hamilton St 68132 402-554-8535
Shawn Hall, prin. Fax 553-2940
Hartman ES 400/PK-6
5530 N 66th St 68104 402-572-1966
Shelly Burghardt, prin. Fax 572-1653
Highland ES 500/PK-6
2625 Jefferson St 68107 402-734-5711
Gwen Foxall, prin. Fax 734-5821
Indian Hill ES 500/PK-6
3121 U St 68107 402-734-7574
Karma Cunningham, prin. Fax 734-1502
Jackson ES 200/PK-6
620 S 31st St 68105 402-344-7484
Donna Dobson, prin. Fax 344-7414
Jefferson ES 300/K-6
4065 Vinton St 68105 402-554-6590
Kimberly Lidgett, prin. Fax 553-2956
Joslyn ES 400/PK-6
11220 Blondo St 68164 402-496-5322
Elizabeth Kosch, prin. Fax 496-6293

Kellom ES 400/PK-6
1311 N 24th St 68102 402-344-0441
Eric Nelson, prin. Fax 344-0213
Kennedy ES 200/K-6
2906 N 30th St 68111 402-457-5520
Phyllis Brooks, prin. Fax 457-5031
King ES 300/PK-6
3706 Maple St 68111 402-457-5723
Sandra McGee, prin. Fax 457-4932
King Science Magnet MS 400/5-8
3720 Florence Blvd 68110 402-557-3720
Susan Christopherson, prin. Fax 557-4459
Lewis & Clark MS 600/7-8
6901 Burt St 68132 402-557-4300
Dr. Lisa Sterba, prin. Fax 557-4309
Liberty ES 600/PK-6
2021 Saint Marys Ave 68102 402-898-1697
Carri Hutcherson, prin. Fax 898-1698
Lothrop Magnet ES 300/PK-4
3300 N 22nd St 68110 402-457-5704
Rebecca Nichol, prin. Fax 457-7963
Marrs Magnet MS 400/5-8
5619 S 19th St 68107 402-557-4400
Pamela Cohn, prin. Fax 557-4429
Masters ES 300/K-6
5505 N 99th St 68134 402-572-1027
Jacqueline Weir, prin. Fax 572-0952
McMillan Magnet MS 700/7-8
3802 Redick Ave 68112 402-557-4500
Dr. Keith Bigsby, prin. Fax 557-4509
Miller Park ES 300/PK-6
5625 N 28th Ave 68111 402-457-5620
Vanessa Marisett, prin. Fax 457-5702
Minne Lusa ES 500/PK-6
2728 Ida St 68112 402-457-5611
Matt Piechota, prin. Fax 451-4971
Monroe MS 700/7-8
5105 Bedford Ave 68104 402-557-4600
Herman Colvin, prin. Fax 557-4609
Morton Magnet MS 500/5-8
4606 Terrace Dr 68134 402-557-4700
Matt Brandl, prin. Fax 557-4709
Mt. View ES 200/PK-6
5322 N 52nd St 68104 402-457-5117
Christy Payne, prin. Fax 457-5109
Norris MS 700/7-8
2235 S 46th St 68106 402-557-4800
Anita Harkins, prin. Fax 557-4809
Oak Valley ES 200/PK-6
3109 Pedersen Dr 68144 402-697-0690
Laura MacHolmes, prin. Fax 697-0769
Pawnee ES 600/K-6
7310 S 48th St 68157 402-734-5011
Sandra Bredfeldt, prin. Fax 734-1365
Picotte ES 600/K-6
14506 Ohio St 68116 402-496-8401
Denise McCown, prin. Fax 496-2108
Pinewood ES 300/PK-6
6717 N 63rd St 68152 402-561-6000
Pamela Johnson, prin. Fax 561-6009
Ponca ES 100/K-6
11300 N Post Rd 68112 402-457-6415
Barbara Wild, prin. Fax 457-6347
Prairie Wind ES 700/K-6
10908 Ellison Ave 68164 402-491-0859
Paula Knutzen-Peatrow, prin. Fax 491-0273
Rose Hill ES 300/K-6
5605 Corby St 68104 402-554-6797
Heather Harbison, prin. Fax 554-8406
Ryan ES 300/PK-6
1807 S 60th St 68106 402-554-8582
Janet Martin, prin. Fax 554-8576
Saratoga ES 200/PK-6
2504 Meredith Ave 68111 402-457-6427
Alina Bass Harvey, prin. Fax 457-6438
Sherman ES 300/PK-6
5618 N 14th Ave 68110 402-457-6711
Jodie Lenser, prin. Fax 457-7965
Skinner Magnet ES 600/K-6
4304 N 33rd St 68111 402-453-6857
Rios Gunter, prin. Fax 453-4864
Spring Lake Magnet Center 600/PK-4
4215 S 20th St 68107 402-734-1833
Susan Aguilera-Robles, prin. Fax 734-1715
Springville ES 200/K-6
7400 N 60th St 68152 402-572-0130
Norma Deeb, prin. Fax 572-9106
Standing Bear ES 300/K-6
15860 Taylor St 68116 402-827-4362
Lynnette Keyes, prin. Fax 827-4363
Sunny Slope ES 500/PK-6
10828 Old Maple Rd 68164 402-496-1810
Kim Whitehouse, prin. Fax 496-0840
Wakonda ES 300/PK-6
4845 Curtis Ave 68104 402-457-6737
Aaron Dailey, prin. Fax 457-6730
Walnut Hill ES 300/PK-6
4370 Hamilton St 68131 402-554-8644
Loraine Amill, prin. Fax 554-8638
Washington ES 200/K-6
5519 Mayberry St 68106 402-554-8690
Jean Gilreath, prin. Fax 554-1407
Western Hills Magnet ES 400/K-6
6523 Western Ave 68132 402-554-1510
Marjorie Reed-Schmid, prin. Fax 554-1409

Ralston SD
Supt. — See Ralston
Blumfield ES 300/K-6
10310 Mockingbird Dr 68127 402-331-0891
Dennis Moore, prin. Fax 331-1191
Meadows ES 300/K-6
9225 Berry St 68127 402-339-6655
Don Hooper, prin. Fax 331-1044
Mockingbird ES 300/PK-6
5100 S 93rd St 68127 402-331-6954
Katherine Boeve, prin. Fax 331-6403

Western ES 200/PK-6
6224 H St 68117 402-731-7477
Sheri Sessions, prin. Fax 731-0952

South Sarpy SD 46
Supt. — See Springfield
Westmont ES 300/K-6
13210 Glenn St 68138 402-895-9602
Brian Ferguson, prin. Fax 894-4876

Westside Community SD 5,700/PK-12
909 S 76th St 68114 402-390-2100
Jacquie Estee, supt. Fax 390-2136
www.westside66.org/
Hillside ES 400/PK-6
7500 Western Ave 68114 402-390-6450
Ruby Larson, prin. Fax 390-2165
Loveland ES 300/K-6
8201 Pacific St 68114 402-390-6455
Sondra Irish, prin. Fax 390-2162
Oakdale ES 300/PK-6
9801 W Center Rd 68124 402-390-6460
Marla Fries, prin. Fax 390-2164
Paddock Road ES 300/PK-6
3535 Paddock Rd 68124 402-390-6465
James Otto, prin. Fax 390-2161
Prairie Lane ES 300/PK-6
11444 Hascall St 68144 402-390-6470
Jennifer Harr, prin. Fax 390-6469
Rockbrook ES 300/PK-6
2514 S 108th St 68144 402-390-6475
Douglas Wragge, prin. Fax 390-2157
Sunset Hills ES 100/PK-6
9503 Walnut St 68124 402-390-6480
Andy Rikli Ed.D., prin. Fax 390-2160
Swanson ES 300/PK-6
8601 Harney St 68114 402-390-6485
Laura Croom, prin. Fax 390-2159
Westbrook ES K-6
1312 Robertson Dr 68114 402-390-6490
Cindy Vann, prin. Fax 390-2163
Westgate ES 300/PK-6
7802 Hascall St 68124 402-390-6495
Gary Ohm, prin. Fax 390-2156
Westside MS 900/7-8
8601 Arbor St 68124 402-390-6464
Steve Schrad, prin. Fax 390-6454

All Saints S 200/PK-8
1335 S 10th St 68108 402-346-5757
Marlan Burki, prin. Fax 346-8794
Assumption/Guadalupe S 50/PK-2
5221 S 23rd St 68107 402-731-1601
Cheryl Castle, prin. Fax 731-0519
Assumption/Guadalupe S 100/3-8
5602 S 22nd St 68107 402-734-4504
Cheryl Castle, prin. Fax 734-4505
Blessed Sacrament S 100/K-8
6316 N 30th St 68111 402-455-4030
Robert Laird, prin. Fax 455-6699
Brownell-Talbot S 500/PK-12
400 N Happy Hollow Blvd 68132 402-556-3772
Diane Desler, hdmstr. Fax 553-2994
Christ the King S 300/PK-8
831 S 88th St 68114 402-391-0977
Christopher Segrell, prin. Fax 391-2418
Concordia Academy 200/K-6
3504 S 108th St 68144 402-592-8005
Dean Raabe, prin. Fax 393-2487
Friedel Jewish Academy 50/K-6
335 S 132nd St 68154 402-334-0517
Ron Giller, prin. Fax 334-6455
Gethsemane Lutheran S 50/K-8
4040 N 108th St 68164 402-493-2550
Corey Pederson, prin. Fax 493-5427
Good Shepherd Lutheran S 100/PK-8
5071 Center St 68106 402-553-6760
Jeffrey Loberger, prin.
Holy Cross S 400/PK-8
1502 S 48th St 68106 402-551-3773
Terri Anderson, prin. Fax 556-1896
Holy Ghost S 200/PK-8
5302 S 52nd St 68117 402-731-5161
Dana Martin, prin. Fax 731-5174
Holy Name S 200/PK-8
2901 Fontenelle Blvd 68104 402-451-5403
Sofia Kock, prin. Fax 453-7950
Jesuit MS 100/4-8
2311 N 22nd St 68110 402-346-4464
Anthony Connelly, prin. Fax 341-1817
Kopecky Montessori S 300/PK-6
913 Leawood Dr 68154 402-393-1311
Dr. LaVonne Plambeck, dir. Fax 397-4958
Mary Our Queen S 500/K-8
3405 S 119th St 68144 402-333-8663
Kayleen Wallace, prin. Fax 334-3948
Montessori Children's Room 100/PK-5
7302 Burt St 68114 402-551-1440
Mary Anderson, prin. Fax 397-5417
Mt. Calvary Lutheran S 100/K-8
5529 Leavenworth St 68106 402-551-7020
Terri Kohtz, prin. Fax 551-7020
Omaha Christian Academy 300/PK-12
5612 L St 68117 402-399-9565
Gene Bentley, supt. Fax 399-0248
Omaha Memorial Adventist S 50/K-8
840 N 72nd St 68114 402-397-4642
Jerry Groeneweg, lead tchr. Fax 393-0125
Our Lady of Lourdes S 300/PK-8
2124 S 32nd Ave 68105 402-341-5604
William Kelly, prin. Fax 341-9957
Sacred Heart S 100/K-8
2205 Binney St 68110 402-455-5858
Matthew Ossenfort, prin. Fax 451-7480
St. Bernadette S 300/PK-8
7600 S 42nd St 68147 402-731-3033
Therese Nelson, prin. Fax 731-8735

St. Bernard S — 200/PK-8
3604 N 65th St 68104 — 402-553-4993
Ellie Seward, prin. — Fax 551-4939
St. Cecilia S — 300/PK-8
3869 Webster St 68131 — 402-556-6655
Paulette Rourke, prin. — Fax 556-9233
St. James-Seton S — 800/K-8
4720 N 90th St 68134 — 402-572-0339
Terry Crum, prin. — Fax 572-0347
St. Joan of Arc S — 100/PK-8
7430 Hascall St 68124 — 402-393-2314
Chris Vos, prin. — Fax 393-4405
St. Margaret Mary S — 600/K-8
123 N 61st St 68132 — 402-551-6663
Peggy Grennan, prin. — Fax 551-5631
St. Paul Lutheran S — 100/K-8
5020 Grand Ave 68104 — 402-451-2865
Linda Tripp, prin. — Fax 451-6816
St. Philip Neri S — 200/PK-8
8202 N 31st St 68112 — 402-455-8666
Richard Cuva, prin. — Fax 453-3620
St. Pius X-St. Leo S — 800/PK-8
6905 Blondo St 68104 — 402-551-6667
Joyce Gubbels, prin. — Fax 551-8123
St. Richard S — 100/PK-8
4318 Fort St 68111 — 402-451-0692
Catherine Barmettler, prin. — Fax 451-1489
St. Robert Bellarmine S — 600/PK-8
11900 Pacific St 68154 — 402-334-1929
Sandra Suiter, prin. — Fax 333-7188
St. Stanislaus S — 100/PK-8
4501 S 41st St 68107 — 402-731-0484
Gary Davis, prin. — Fax 733-4898
St. Stephen the Martyr S — 900/PK-8
16701 S St 68135 — 402-896-0754
Dr. David Peters, prin. — Fax 861-4640
St. Thomas More S — 300/PK-8
3515 S 48th Ave 68106 — 402-551-9504
Dr. Roseanne Williby, prin. — Fax 551-9507
St. Vincent de Paul S — 800/K-8
14330 Eagle Run Dr 68164 — 402-492-2111
Dr. Barbara Marchese, prin. — Fax 496-9933
St. Wenceslaus S — 800/K-8
15353 Pacific St 68154 — 402-330-4356
Mary McGuire, prin. — Fax 330-1476
SS. Peter & Paul S — 200/PK-8
3619 X St 68107 — 402-731-4713
Richard Leimbach, prin. — Fax 731-2633
Trinity Christian S — 500/K-8
15555 W Dodge Rd 68154 — 402-330-5724
Steve York, admin. — Fax 758-6980

O Neill, Holt, Pop. 3,721
O'Neill SD — 800/K-12
PO Box 230 68763 — 402-336-3775
Amy Shane, supt. — Fax 336-4890
oneill.esu8.org/
O'Neill ES — 400/K-6
PO Box 230, — 402-336-1400
Jennifer Widner, prin. — Fax 336-2651
Other Schools – See Emmet, Inman

St. Mary S — 300/PK-12
326 E Benton St, — 402-336-4455
Norman Hale, prin. — Fax 336-1281

Orchard, Antelope, Pop. 359
Nebraska USD 1
Supt. — See Royal
Orchard ES — 100/K-6
PO Box 269 68764 — 402-893-3215
Dale Martin, prin. — Fax 893-2065

Ord, Valley, Pop. 2,129
Ord SD — 500/K-12
320 N 19th St 68862 — 308-728-5013
Max Kroger, supt. — Fax 728-5108
www.ordps.org/
Ord ES — 200/K-6
820 S 16th St 68862 — 308-728-3331
Jason Alexander, prin. — Fax 728-3749
Vinton S, 47407 808th Rd 68862 — 50/K-8
Jason Alexander, prin. — 308-728-5667
Other Schools – See Elyria

St. Marys S, 527 N 20th St 68862 — 100/K-8
Cheryl Rongish, lead tchr. — 308-728-5389

Osceola, Polk, Pop. 902
Osceola SD — 300/K-12
PO Box 198 68651 — 402-747-3121
Ken Schroeder, supt. — Fax 747-3041
www.esu7.org/~oweb/osceola.html
Osceola ES — 100/K-6
PO Box 198 68651 — 402-747-2091
Jane Howerter, prin. — Fax 747-3041
Osceola MS — 100/7-8
PO Box 198 68651 — 402-747-3121
Clete Arasmith, prin. — Fax 747-3041

Polk County Christian S — 50/K-7
PO Box 177 68651 — 402-747-6561
Samuel Bell, supt. — Fax 747-6561

Oshkosh, Garden, Pop. 766
Garden County SD — 300/K-12
PO Box 230 69154 — 308-772-3242
Paula Sissel, supt. — Fax 772-3039
www.gardencountyschools.org/
Garden County ES — 100/K-4
PO Box 200 69154 — 308-772-3336
Paula Sissel, prin. — Fax 772-4059
Other Schools – See Lewellen

Osmond, Pierce, Pop. 746
Osmond SD — 300/K-12
PO Box 458 68765 — 402-748-3777
Steven Rinehart, supt. — Fax 748-3210
osmond.esu8.org/
Osmond ES — 100/K-6
PO Box 458 68765 — 402-748-3777
Jane Brummels, prin. — Fax 748-3210

St. Marys S — 50/1-8
PO Box 427 68765 — 402-748-3433
Joyce Tunink, prin. — Fax 748-3433

Overton, Dawson, Pop. 655
Overton SD — 300/PK-12
PO Box 310 68863 — 308-987-2424
Mark Aten, supt. — Fax 987-2349
www.ovr.esu10.k12.ne.us/
Overton ES — 200/PK-6
PO Box 310 68863 — 308-987-2424
Brian Fleischman, prin. — Fax 987-2349

Oxford, Furnas, Pop. 806
Southern Valley SD — 400/K-12
43739 Highway 89 68967 — 308-868-2222
Chuck Lambert, supt. — Fax 868-2223
southernvalley.esu11.org/sovalley/
Southern Valley ES — 100/K-6
43737 Highway 89 68967 — 308-868-2222
Stephen Billeter, prin. — Fax 868-2223

Palisade, Hitchcock, Pop. 377
Wauneta-Palisade SD
Supt. — See Wauneta
Palisade ES — 100/K-6
PO Box 329 69040 — 308-285-3232
Fax 285-3219

Palmer, Merrick, Pop. 458
Palmer SD — 200/K-12
PO Box 248 68864 — 308-894-3065
Gary Monter, supt. — Fax 894-8245
www.palmer.esu7.org/school/school.html
Palmer ES — 100/K-6
PO Box 248 68864 — 308-894-3065
Gary Monter, prin. — Fax 894-8245

Palmyra, Otoe, Pop. 543
Palmyra OR 1 SD — 500/K-12
PO Box 130 68418 — 402-780-5327
Clyde Childers, supt. — Fax 780-5328
www.districtor1.org/
Other Schools – See Bennet

Papillion, Sarpy, Pop. 20,431
Papillion-La Vista SD — 8,800/PK-12
420 S Washington St 68046 — 402-537-9998
Rick Black, supt. — Fax 537-6216
www.paplv.esu3.org
Bell ES, 7909 Reed St 68046 — K-6
Kathy Szczepaniak, prin. — 402-898-0408
Carriage Hill ES — 400/PK-6
400 Cedardale Rd 68046 — 402-898-0449
Dr. Debra Rodenburg, prin. — Fax 898-0453
Hickory Hill ES — 400/PK-6
1307 Rogers Dr 68046 — 402-898-0469
Troy Juracek, prin. — Fax 898-0472
Papillion JHS — 700/7-8
423 S Washington St 68046 — 402-898-0424
John McGill, prin. — Fax 898-0430
Patriot ES — PK-6
1701 Hardwood Dr 68046 — 402-898-0405
Mary Scarborough, prin. — Fax 898-0406
Rumsey Station ES — 600/K-6
110 Eagle Ridge Dr 68133 — 402-898-0475
Allison Kelberla, prin. — Fax 898-0418
Tara Heights ES — 400/PK-6
700 Tara Rd 68046 — 402-898-0445
Patricia Zeimet, prin. — Fax 898-0447
Trumble Park ES — 400/PK-6
500 Valley Rd 68046 — 402-898-0466
Kellen Czaplewski, prin. — Fax 898-0474
Walnut Creek ES — 600/PK-6
720 Fenwick St 68046 — 402-898-9630
Amy Wemhoff, prin. — Fax 898-9634
Other Schools – See Bellevue, La Vista

St. Columbkille S — 500/PK-8
224 E 5th St 68046 — 402-339-8706
Christine Overkamp, prin. — Fax 592-4147

Pawnee City, Pawnee, Pop. 946
Pawnee City SD — 300/K-12
PO Box 393 68420 — 402-852-2988
Wayne Koehler, supt. — Fax 852-2993
www.pawnee.esu6.org/
Pawnee City ES — 100/K-6
PO Box 393 68420 — 402-852-2988
Wayne Koehler, prin. — Fax 852-2993

Paxton, Keith, Pop. 548
Paxton Consolidated SD — 200/K-12
PO Box 368 69155 — 308-239-4283
Delbert Dack, supt. — Fax 239-4359
www.paxton.k12.ne.us/
Paxton ES — 100/K-6
PO Box 368 69155 — 308-239-4283
Delbert Dack, prin. — Fax 239-4359

Pender, Thurston, Pop. 1,165
Pender SD — 300/PK-12
PO Box 629 68047 — 402-385-3244
Joe Reinert, supt. — Fax 385-3342
www.penderschools.org/
Pender ES at Thurston — 200/PK-6
PO Box 629 68047 — 402-385-3244
Tim Olin, prin. — Fax 385-3342

Petersburg, Boone, Pop. 340
Boone Central SD
Supt. — See Albion
Boone Central MS — 100/6-8
PO Box 240 68652 — 402-386-5302
Mary Thieman, prin. — Fax 386-5464

St. John the Baptist S — 50/K-6
PO Box 208 68652 — 402-386-5472
Melinda Arkfeld, lead tchr.

Pierce, Pierce, Pop. 1,730
Pierce SD — 700/K-12
201 N Sunset St 68767 — 402-329-4677
Daniel Navrkal, supt. — Fax 329-4678
www.piercepublic.org/
Pierce ES — 300/K-6
211 N 7th St 68767 — 402-329-4302
Sharen Luhr, prin. — Fax 329-4186

Zion Lutheran S — 100/PK-8
520 E Main St 68767 — 402-329-4658
David Bliss, prin. — Fax 329-6406

Pilger, Stanton, Pop. 372
Wisner-Pilger SD
Supt. — See Wisner
Wisner-Pilger MS — 100/7-8
PO Box 325 68768 — 402-396-3566
David Ludwig, prin. — Fax 529-3477

Plainview, Pierce, Pop. 1,279
Plainview SD — 400/K-12
PO Box 638 68769 — 402-582-4993
David Hamm, supt. — Fax 582-4665
www.plainviewschools.org/
Plainview ES — 200/K-6
PO Box 638 68769 — 402-582-3808
David Hamm, prin. — Fax 582-4665

Zion Lutheran S — 50/PK-8
PO Box 159 68769 — 402-582-3312
Clee Wolske, lead tchr. — Fax 582-3912

Platte Center, Platte, Pop. 350
Lakeview Community SD
Supt. — See Columbus
Platte Center S — 100/K-8
PO Box 109 68653 — 402-246-3465
Patricia Meyer, prin. — Fax 246-3044

Plattsmouth, Cass, Pop. 7,023
Plattsmouth SD — 1,700/PK-12
1912 E Highway 34 68048 — 402-296-3361
Richard Hasty, supt. — Fax 296-2667
www.plattsmouthschools.org/
Plattsmouth ECC — 100/PK-PK
902 Main St 68048 — 402-296-5250
Jane Happe, dir. — Fax 296-5202
Plattsmouth ES — 600/K-4
1724 8th Ave 68048 — 402-296-4173
Claude Michel, prin. — Fax 296-2462
Plattsmouth MS — 500/5-8
1724 8th Ave 68048 — 402-296-3174
Mark Smith, prin. — Fax 296-2910

St. John the Baptist S — 200/K-8
500 S 18th St 68048 — 402-296-6230
Linda Isaacson, prin. — Fax 296-6961

Pleasant Dale, Seward, Pop. 243
Milford SD
Supt. — See Milford
Pleasant Dale ES — 50/K-6
418 Pine St 68423 — 402-795-3780
Penny Jans, prin. — Fax 761-3322

Pleasanton, Buffalo, Pop. 344
Pleasanton SD — 200/K-12
PO Box 190 68866 — 308-388-2041
Ronald Wymore, supt. — Fax 388-5502
www.pleasanton.k12.ne.us/
Pleasanton ES — 100/K-6
PO Box 190 68866 — 308-388-2041
Ronald Wymore, prin. — Fax 388-5502

Plymouth, Jefferson, Pop. 443

St. Paul Lutheran S — 50/K-8
PO Box 247 68424 — 402-656-4465
Thomas Plitzuweit, prin.

Polk, Polk, Pop. 301
High Plains Community SD — 300/K-12
PO Box 29 68654 — 402-765-2271
Stan Hendricks, supt. — Fax 765-3332
www.hpc.esu7.org/
High Plains ES at Polk — 50/4-5
PO Box 29 68654 — 402-765-2271
Cameron Hudson, prin. — Fax 765-3332
Other Schools – See Clarks

Immanuel Lutheran S — 50/K-8
2406 E 26th Rd 68654 — 402-765-7253
Lisa Lenz, lead tchr. — Fax 765-7253

Ponca, Dixon, Pop. 1,042
Ponca SD — 400/K-12
PO Box 568 68770 — 402-755-5700
William Thompson, supt. — Fax 755-5773
www.poncaschool.org/
Ponca ES — 200/K-6
PO Box 568 68770 — 402-755-5700
William Thompson, prin. — Fax 755-5773
Other Schools – See Jackson

Potter, Cheyenne, Pop. 411
Potter-Dix SD 200/K-12
PO Box 189 69156 308-879-4434
Kevin Thomas, supt. Fax 879-4566
www.pdcoyotes.com
Other Schools – See Dix

Prague, Saunders, Pop. 331
Prague SD 100/K-12
PO Box 98 68050 402-663-4388
Raymond Collins, supt. Fax 663-4312
www.praguepublicschools.org/
Prague ES 100/K-6
PO Box 98 68050 402-663-4388
Raymond Collins, prin. Fax 663-4312

Ralston, Douglas, Pop. 6,193
Ralston SD 3,200/PK-12
8545 Park Dr 68127 402-331-4700
Dr. Jerald Riibe, supt. Fax 331-4843
www.ralstonschools.org/
Ralston MS 500/7-8
8202 Lakeview St 68127 402-331-4701
Jason Buckingham, prin. Fax 331-5376
Seymour ES 200/K-6
4900 S 79th St 68127 402-331-0540
Shawna Mayer, prin. Fax 331-1099
Wildewood ES 200/K-6
8071 Ralston Ave 68127 402-331-6475
Janell Shain, prin. Fax 331-9099
Other Schools – See Omaha

St. Gerald S 400/K-8
7857 Lakeview St 68127 402-331-4223
Dave Garland, prin. Fax 331-4523

Randolph, Cedar, Pop. 888
Randolph SD 45 300/K-12
PO Box 755 68771 402-337-0252
Steven Rinehart, supt. Fax 337-0235
www.randolphpublic.org/
Randolph ES 100/K-6
PO Box 755 68771 402-337-0385
Pat Sweeney, prin. Fax 337-0410

Ravenna, Buffalo, Pop. 1,281
Ravenna SD 500/K-12
PO Box 8400 68869 308-452-3249
Dwaine Uttecht, supt. Fax 452-3172
ravenna.k12.ne.us/
Ravenna ES 200/K-6
PO Box 8400 68869 308-452-3202
Paul Anderson, prin. Fax 452-3172

Raymond, Lancaster, Pop. 195
Raymond Central SD 700/K-12
1800 W Agnew Rd 68428 402-785-2615
Paul Hull, supt. Fax 785-2097
www.rcentral.org
Other Schools – See Ceresco, Valparaiso

Red Cloud, Webster, Pop. 1,029
Red Cloud Community SD 300/K-12
334 N Cherry St 68970 402-746-3413
Joan Reznicek, supt. Fax 746-3690
www.redcloud.k12.ne.us/
Lincoln ES 100/K-6
334 N Cherry St 68970 402-746-3413
Joan Reznicek, prin. Fax 746-3690

Richland, Colfax, Pop. 89
Schuyler SD
Supt. — See Schuyler
Richland S 100/PK-8
595 Road 3 68601 402-564-6900
Dave Gibbons, prin. Fax 564-6900

Rising City, Butler, Pop. 381
Rising City SD 200/PK-12
PO Box 160 68658 402-542-2216
Daniel Alberts, supt. Fax 542-2265
www.risingcityschools.org/
Rising City ES 100/PK-6
PO Box 160 68658 402-542-2216
Michael Derr, prin. Fax 542-2265

Riverdale, Buffalo, Pop. 206
Kearney SD
Supt. — See Kearney
Riverdale ES 50/K-5
PO Box 9 68870 308-893-2481
Jim Grove, prin. Fax 893-2012

Roseland, Adams, Pop. 254
Silver Lake SD 200/K-12
PO Box 8 68973 402-756-6611
Jeffrey Walburn, supt. Fax 756-6613
www.silverlake.k12.ne.us
Other Schools – See Bladen

Royal, Antelope, Pop. 70
Nebraska USD 1 500/K-12
PO Box 98 68773 402-893-2068
William Kuester, supt. Fax 893-9949
neunified1.esu8.org/
Other Schools – See Clearwater, Orchard, Verdigre

Rushville, Sheridan, Pop. 902
Gordon-Rushville SD
Supt. — See Gordon
Extension S 50/K-8
7773 370th Trl 69360 308-862-4246
Lori Lissett, prin. Fax 282-2207
Gordon-Rushville MS 200/6-8
PO Box 590 69360 308-327-2491
Casey Slama, prin. Fax 327-2504
Rushville ES 100/K-5
PO Box 590 69360 308-327-2491
Casey Slama, prin. Fax 327-2504

Saint Edward, Boone, Pop. 757
Saint Edward SD 200/K-12
PO Box C 68660 402-678-2282
Kevin Lyons, supt. Fax 678-2284
teachers.esu7.org/stedweb/
Saint Edward ES 100/K-6
PO Box C 68660 402-678-2282
Kevin Lyons, prin. Fax 678-2284

Saint Libory, Howard
Northwest SD
Supt. — See Grand Island
Saint Libory S 100/K-8
435 Saint Paul Rd 68872 308-687-6475
Jeff Ellsworth, prin. Fax 687-6358

Zion Lutheran S 50/K-8
1655 Worms Rd 68872 308-687-6486
Charles Zehendner, admin. Fax 687-6486

Saint Paul, Howard, Pop. 2,257
Saint Paul SD 600/K-12
PO Box 325 68873 308-754-4433
Douglas Ackles, supt. Fax 754-5374
www.stpaul.k12.ne.us/
Saint Paul ES 300/K-6
PO Box 325 68873 308-754-4433
Kristen Uhrmacher, prin. Fax 754-5374

Sargent, Custer, Pop. 612
Sargent SD 200/K-12
PO Box 366 68874 308-527-4119
Robert Brown, supt. Fax 527-3332
sites.sargent.k12.ne.us/sargent/
Sargent ES 100/K-6
PO Box 366 68874 308-527-4119
Cory Grint, prin. Fax 527-3332

Schuyler, Colfax, Pop. 5,327
Schuyler SD 1,500/PK-12
401 Adam St 68661 402-352-3527
Robin Stevens, supt. Fax 352-5552
www.schuylercommunityschools.org/
Fisher's S 50/K-8
1098 Road J 68661 402-352-3700
Dave Gibbons, prin. Fax 352-3414
Schuyler North Ward ES 200/K-1
100 E 15th St 68661 402-352-2628
Darli Jo Vrba, prin. Fax 352-5976
Schuyler S 4R 50/K-8
697 Road 16 68661 402-352-2755
Dave Gibbons, prin. Fax 352-2755
Schuyler West Ward S 600/2-8
200 W 10th St 68661 402-352-5514
Stephan Grammer, prin. Fax 352-2644
Other Schools – See Richland

Scotia, Greeley, Pop. 287
North Loup Scotia SD 200/K-12
PO Box 307 68875 308-245-3201
Gene Haddix, supt. Fax 245-9133
Other Schools – See North Loup

Scottsbluff, Scotts Bluff, Pop. 14,814
Scottsbluff SD 2,700/PK-12
2601 Broadway 69361 308-635-6200
Dr. Gary Reynolds, supt. Fax 635-6217
www.sbps.net/
Bluffs MS 600/6-8
23rd and Broadway 69361 308-635-6270
Mike Mason, prin. Fax 635-6271
Lincoln Heights ES 200/PK-5
2214 Avenue C 69361 308-635-6252
Jodi Benson, prin. Fax 635-6251
Longfellow ES 300/PK-5
2003 5th Ave 69361 308-635-6262
Barbara Edwards, prin. Fax 635-6237
Roosevelt ES 300/K-5
1306 9th Ave 69361 308-635-6259
Nora Porupsky, prin. Fax 635-6258
Westmoor ES 300/K-5
1722 Avenue K 69361 308-635-6255
Charlotte Browning, prin. Fax 635-6233
Other Schools – See Minatare

Community Christian S 200/PK-8
511 W 14th St 69361 308-632-2230
Christopher Geary, prin. Fax 632-2230
St. Agnes S, 205 E 23rd St 69361 100/K-5
Sue Gerdan, prin. 308-632-6918
Valley View Christian S 50/K-8
415 W 31st St 69361 308-632-8804
Helen Rodrigue, lead tchr. Fax 632-8804

Scribner, Dodge, Pop. 968
Scribner-Snyder SD 200/K-12
PO Box L 68057 402-664-2567
Rick Kentfield, supt. Fax 664-2708
www.sstrojans.esu2.org/
Scribner ES 100/K-6
PO Box L 68057 402-664-2567
Rick Kentfield, prin. Fax 664-2708

Seward, Seward, Pop. 6,776
Seward SD 1,400/PK-12
410 South St 68434 402-643-2941
Greg Barnes, supt. Fax 643-4986
www.sewardpublicschools.org
Seward ES 500/PK-4
200 E Pinewood Ave 68434 402-643-2968
Lana Daws, prin. Fax 643-2969
Seward MS 400/5-8
237 S 3rd St 68434 402-643-2986
Kirk Gottschalk, prin. Fax 643-6686

St. John Lutheran S 100/K-8
877 N Columbia Ave 68434 402-643-4535
David Koopman, prin. Fax 643-4536

St. Vincent Depaul S 100/K-4
152 Pinewood Ave 68434 402-643-9525
Sr. Mary Bernadette Lenz, prin. Fax 643-2594

Shelby, Polk, Pop. 648
Shelby SD 300/K-12
PO Box 218 68662 402-527-5946
Larry Stick, supt. Fax 527-5133
www.shelby.esu7.org
Shelby ES 200/K-6
PO Box 218 68662 402-527-5946
Larry Stick, prin. Fax 527-5133

Shelton, Buffalo, Pop. 1,125
Shelton SD 300/K-12
PO Box 610 68876 308-647-6742
Kendall Steffensen, supt. Fax 647-5233
sites.shelton.k12.ne.us/sheltonpublic/
Shelton ES 200/K-6
PO Box 610 68876 308-647-6558
Tony Little, prin. Fax 647-5233

Shickley, Fillmore, Pop. 358
Shickley SD 100/K-12
PO Box 407 68436 402-627-3375
Evan Wieseman, supt. Fax 627-2003
www.shickleypublicschool.org/
Shickley ES 100/K-6
PO Box 407 68436 402-627-3085
Matt Koehler, prin. Fax 627-2003

Sidney, Cheyenne, Pop. 6,442
Sidney SD 1,200/K-12
2103 King St 69162 308-254-5855
John Hakonson, supt. Fax 254-5756
www.sidneyraiders.com/
Central ES 100/4-4
1110 16th Ave 69162 308-254-3642
Sheri Ehler, prin. Fax 254-5856
North Ward ES 200/2-3
434 16th Ave 69162 308-254-2114
Brent Jeffers, prin. Fax 254-5756
Sidney MS 200/7-8
1122 19th Ave 69162 308-254-5853
Brandon Ross, prin. Fax 254-5854
South Ward ES 200/K-1
2000 12th Ave 69162 308-254-3589
Brent Jeffers, prin. Fax 254-5756
West ES 200/5-6
2350 Osage St 69162 308-254-0960
Sheri Ehler, prin. Fax 254-5756

Silver Creek, Merrick, Pop. 428
Twin River SD
Supt. — See Genoa
Twin River ES at Silver Creek 100/K-6
PO Box 247 68663 308-773-2233
Tod Heier, prin. Fax 773-2234

South Sioux City, Dakota, Pop. 11,979
South Sioux City SD 3,600/PK-12
PO Box 158 68776 402-494-2425
Steve Rector, supt. Fax 494-3916
www.ssccardinals.org/
Cardinal ES 400/K-5
820 E 29th St 68776 402-494-1662
Al Agrimson, prin. Fax 494-1968
Covington ES 400/K-5
2116 A St 68776 402-494-4238
Susan Galvin, prin. Fax 494-6300
Harney ES 400/K-5
1001 Arbor Dr 68776 402-494-1446
Rebecca Eckhardt, prin. Fax 494-6303
Lewis & Clark ES 200/K-5
801 2nd Ave 68776 402-494-1917
Sheri Fillipi, prin. Fax 494-6301
South Sioux City MS 800/6-8
3625 G St 68776 402-494-3061
Tom McGuire, prin. Fax 494-8427
Swett ES 100/K-5
2300 C St 68776 402-494-3501
Laura Dandurand, prin. Fax 494-6302
Other Schools – See Dakota City

St. Michael S 100/K-8
1315 1st Ave 68776 402-494-1526
Julie Prusa, prin. Fax 494-4283

Spalding, Greeley, Pop. 502
Spalding SD 100/K-12
PO Box 220 68665 308-497-2431
Fax 497-2141
sites.spalding.k12.ne.us/
Spalding ES 100/K-6
PO Box 220 68665 308-497-2431
Stephanie Wlaschin, prin. Fax 497-2141

Spalding Academy 100/K-12
PO Box 310 68665 308-497-2103
Kevin Kirwan, prin. Fax 497-2105

Spencer, Boyd, Pop. 504
West Boyd SD 200/K-12
PO Box 109 68777 402-589-2040
Duane Lechtenberg, supt. Fax 589-2041
Other Schools – See Butte

Springfield, Sarpy, Pop. 1,497
South Sarpy SD 46 1,100/K-12
14801 S 108th St 68059 402-592-1300
Charles Chevalier, supt. Fax 597-8551
www.sarpy46.org/
Platteview Central JHS 200/7-8
14801 S 108th St 68059 402-339-5052
Ralph Glock, prin. Fax 339-3166
Springfield ES 300/K-6
765 Main St 68059 402-253-2245
Wesley Reed, prin. Fax 253-2003
Other Schools – See Omaha

Springview, Keya Paha, Pop. 217
Keya Paha County SD 100/K-12
PO Box 219 68778 402-497-3501
Rodger Lenhard, supt. Fax 497-4321
www.esu17.org/%7Ekphshome/index.html
Pleasant View S, PO Box 219 68778 50/K-8
Rodger Lenhard, prin. 402-497-3501
Spring View S, PO Box 219 68778 100/K-8
Rodger Lenhard, prin. 402-497-2621

Stanton, Stanton, Pop. 1,629
Stanton Community SD 400/K-12
PO Box 749 68779 402-439-2233
Michael Sieh, supt. Fax 439-2270
www.scs-ne.org/
Stanton ES 200/K-6
PO Box 749 68779 402-439-2639
Mary McKeon, prin. Fax 439-2270

St. John Lutheran S 50/K-8
PO Box 286 68779 402-439-2188
Nancy Aaberg, prin.

Staplehurst, Seward, Pop. 257

Our Redeemer Lutheran S 50/K-8
425 South St 68439 402-535-2251
John Garske, prin. Fax 535-2421

Stapleton, Logan, Pop. 288
Stapleton SD 200/PK-12
PO Box 128 69163 308-636-2252
Daniel Hutchison, supt. Fax 636-2618
Stapleton ES 100/PK-6
PO Box 128 69163 308-636-2252
Daniel Hutchison, prin. Fax 636-2618

Thedford SD
Supt. — See Thedford
Peaceful Plains Attendance Center 50/K-6
38250 Peaceful Plains Rd 69163 308-587-2395
Henry Eggert, prin. Fax 645-2618

Stella, Richardson, Pop. 207
SE Nebraska Consolidated SD 100/K-12
71829 642 Blvd 68442 402-883-2600
Michael Montgomery, supt. Fax 883-2020
www.southeast.esu6.org/
SE Nebraska Cons ES 50/K-6
71829 642 Blvd 68442 402-883-2600
Michael Montgomery, prin. Fax 883-2020

Sterling, Johnson, Pop. 495
Sterling SD 200/K-12
PO Box 39 68443 402-866-4761
Larry Harnisch, supt. Fax 866-4771
www.sterlingjets.org/
Sterling ES 100/K-6
PO Box 39 68443 402-866-4761
Fax 866-4771

Stratton, Hitchcock, Pop. 373
Dundy County-Straton SD
Supt. — See Benkelman
Stratton S 100/K-8
PO Box 324 69043 308-276-2281
Michael Rotherham, prin. Fax 276-2129

Stromsburg, Polk, Pop. 1,165
Cross County Community SD 300/K-12
PO Box 525 68666 402-764-2156
Rady Page, supt. Fax 764-2156
www.esu7.org/~stroweb/
Cross County ES - Stromsburg 100/K-5
PO Box 525 68666 402-764-3591
Trudy Samek, prin. Fax 764-2156

Stuart, Holt, Pop. 577
Stuart SD 200/K-12
PO Box 99 68780 402-924-3302
Robert Hanzlik, supt. Fax 924-3676
stuart.esu8.org/
Stuart ES 100/K-6
PO Box 99 68780 402-924-3302
Robert Hanzlik, prin. Fax 924-3676

Sumner, Dawson, Pop. 241
Sumner-Eddyville-Miller SD 200/K-12
PO Box 126 68878 308-752-2925
Mike Gillming, supt. Fax 752-2600
sites.sem.k12.ne.us/
SEM ES 100/K-6
PO Box 126 68878 308-752-2925
James Langin, prin. Fax 752-2600

Superior, Nuckolls, Pop. 1,903
Superior SD 400/K-12
PO Box 288 68978 402-879-3258
Charles Isom, supt. Fax 879-3022
North Ward ES 100/3-6
PO Box 288 68978 402-879-3025
Douglas Hoins, prin. Fax 879-4054
South Ward ES 100/K-2
PO Box 288 68978 402-879-4531
Douglas Hoins, prin. Fax 879-4054

Sutherland, Lincoln, Pop. 1,223
Sutherland SD 400/PK-12
PO Box 217 69165 308-386-4656
Brian Maschmann, supt. Fax 386-2426
Sutherland ES 200/PK-6
PO Box 217 69165 308-386-4656
Josie Floyd, prin. Fax 386-2426

Sutton, Clay, Pop. 1,394
Sutton SD 400/PK-12
PO Box 590 68979 402-773-5569
Dana Wiseman, supt. Fax 773-5578
sites.esu9.org/sutton/
Sutton ES 200/PK-6
PO Box 590 68979 402-773-4423
Elizabeth Ericson, prin. Fax 773-5578

Sutton Christian S, PO Box 321 68979 50/K-8
David Kauk, admin. 402-773-4845

Syracuse, Otoe, Pop. 1,835
Syracuse-Dunbar-Avoca SD 800/PK-12
PO Box P 68446 402-269-2383
Bradley Buller, supt. Fax 269-2224
www.sdarockets.org/
Syracuse ES 300/K-6
PO Box P 68446 402-269-2382
Roxanne Voorhees, prin. Fax 269-2224
Other Schools – See Unadilla

Table Rock, Pawnee, Pop. 249
Humboldt Table Rock Steinauer SD 70
Supt. — See Humboldt
Humboldt Table Rock Steinauer MS 100/4-8
PO Box F 68447 402-839-2085
Kari Cover, prin. Fax 839-2088

Taylor, Loup, Pop. 195
Loup County SD 100/K-12
PO Box 170 68879 308-942-6115
Wayne Ruppert, supt. Fax 942-6248
www.loupcounty.k12.ne.us/
Loup County ES 50/K-6
PO Box 170 68879 308-942-6115
Wayne Ruppert, prin. Fax 942-6248

Tecumseh, Johnson, Pop. 1,951
Johnson County Central SD 400/K-12
PO Box 338 68450 402-335-3320
Jack Moles, supt. Fax 335-3346
jccentral.org/
Johnson County Central ES - Tecumseh 200/K-5
PO Box 338 68450 402-335-3320
Ron Skwarek, prin. Fax 335-3346
Other Schools – See Cook

St. Andrew S 50/K-6
PO Box 386 68450 402-335-2234
Sr. Mary Ellen Auffert, prin. Fax 335-2246

Tekamah, Burt, Pop. 1,814
Tekamah-Herman SD 600/PK-12
112 N 13th St 68061 402-374-2157
Kevin Nolan, supt. Fax 374-2155
www.tekamah.esu2.org/
Tekamah ES 200/K-6
112 N 13th St 68061 402-374-2154
Chris Fleischman, prin. Fax 374-2155
Other Schools – See Herman

Thedford, Thomas, Pop. 180
Thedford SD 100/PK-12
PO Box 248 69166 308-645-2230
Henry Eggert, supt. Fax 645-2618
Thedford ES 50/PK-6
PO Box 248 69166 308-645-2214
Henry Eggert, prin. Fax 645-2618
Other Schools – See Brownlee, Stapleton

Tilden, Madison, Pop. 1,053
Elkhorn Valley SD 300/K-12
PO Box 430 68781 402-368-5301
Ken Navratil, supt. Fax 368-5338
falcon.esu8.org/
Elkhorn Valley ES 100/K-6
PO Box 430 68781 402-368-5301
Keith Leckron, prin. Fax 368-5338

Tobias, Saline, Pop. 158

Zion Lutheran S 50/PK-8
2245 County Road 400 68453 402-243-2354
Judy Bartels, prin. Fax 243-2354

Trenton, Hitchcock, Pop. 477
Hitchcock County USD 200/K-12
PO Box 368 69044 308-334-5575
Mike Apple, supt. Fax 334-5381
www.hcfalcons.org/
Other Schools – See Culbertson

Tryon, McPherson
McPherson County SD 100/K-12
PO Box 38 69167 308-587-2262
Joseph Sherwood, supt. Fax 587-2571
athena.esu16.org/~mchs/
Daly S 50/K-8
PO Box 38 69167 308-587-2479
Tryon S 50/K-8
PO Box 68 69167 308-587-2320
Fax 587-2320

Unadilla, Otoe, Pop. 340
Syracuse-Dunbar-Avoca SD
Supt. — See Syracuse
Unadilla S 100/PK-8
PO Box 98 68454 402-828-4655
Fax 828-2005

Utica, Seward, Pop. 825
Centennial SD 500/PK-12
PO Box 187 68456 402-534-2291
Tim DeWaard, supt. Fax 534-2291
www.centennialpublic.org/
Centennial ES 200/PK-6
PO Box 187 68456 402-534-2321
Mark Murphy, prin. Fax 534-2291

St. Paul Lutheran S 100/PK-8
1100 D St 68456 402-534-2121
Robert Brauer, prin. Fax 534-2100

Valentine, Cherry, Pop. 2,786
Todd County SD 66-1
Supt. — See Mission, SD
Klein S 50/K-8
803 N Moon St 69201 605-378-3854
Janen Epke, lead tchr. Fax 378-1111
Littleburg S 50/K-8
28406 301st St 69201 605-378-3881
Cindy Bachelor, lead tchr. Fax 378-1109

Valentine SD 800/K-12
431 N Green St 69201 402-376-2730
Jamie Isom, supt. Fax 376-2736
www.valentinecommunityschools.org/
Boardman Creek S 50/1-8
HC 32 Box 29 69201 402-376-3499
Eva Westover, prin. Fax 376-2623
Goose Creek S 50/1-8
HC 37 Box 59 69201 308-748-2294
Eva Westover, prin. Fax 376-8096
Kewanee S 50/1-8
PO Box 223 69201 402-376-1458
Eva Westover, prin. Fax 376-8096
Simeon S - East 50/K-8
HC 37 Box 22A 69201 402-376-2606
Eva Westover, prin. Fax 376-8096
Simeon S - West K-8
HC 32 Box 39 69201 402-376-1666
Eva Westover, prin. Fax 376-8096
Valentine ES 300/K-5
615 E 5th St 69201 402-376-3237
Cynthia Wobig, prin. Fax 376-1032
Valentine MS 200/6-8
239 N Wood St 69201 402-376-3367
Jeff Sayer, prin. Fax 376-3386
Other Schools – See Cody, Crookston, Gordon, Nenzel, Wood Lake

Zion Lutheran S 50/K-8
224 N Government St 69201 402-376-2745
Matthew Krenke, prin. Fax 376-1643

Valley, Douglas, Pop. 1,829
Douglas County West Community SD 600/K-12
PO Box 378 68064 402-359-2583
George Conrad, supt. Fax 359-4371
www.dcwest.org/
Douglas County West ES 200/K-4
PO Box 378 68064 402-359-2151
Duane Krusemark, prin. Fax 359-5421
Other Schools – See Waterloo

Valparaiso, Saunders, Pop. 598
Raymond Central SD
Supt. — See Raymond
Valparaiso ES 200/K-6
PO Box 68 68065 402-784-3301
Shelly Dostal, prin. Fax 784-3304

Verdigre, Knox, Pop. 486
Nebraska USD 1
Supt. — See Royal
Verdigre ES 100/K-6
204 2nd St 68783 402-668-2275
Chuck Kucera, prin. Fax 668-2276

Waco, York, Pop. 261

Trinity Lutheran S 50/K-8
401 Norval St 68460 402-728-5364
Philip Stern, prin. Fax 728-5433

Wahoo, Saunders, Pop. 4,063
Wahoo SD 900/PK-12
2201 N Locust St 68066 402-443-3051
Edward Rastovski, supt. Fax 443-4731
www.wahooschools.org/
Wahoo ES 400/K-5
2056 N Hackberry St 68066 402-443-4250
Jane Wiebold, prin. Fax 443-4731
Wahoo MS 200/6-8
2201 N Locust St 68066 402-443-3101
Jason Libal, prin. Fax 443-4731
Wahoo Preschool 50/PK-PK
2056 N Hackberry St 68066 402-443-4250
Jane Wiebold, prin. Fax 443-4731

St. Wenceslaus S 300/K-6
108 N Linden St 68066 402-443-3336
Mike Weiss, prin. Fax 443-5551

Wakefield, Dixon, Pop. 1,340
Wakefield SD 400/K-12
PO Box 330 68784 402-287-2012
Bill Heimann, supt. Fax 287-2014
www.wakefieldschools.org/
Wakefield ES 200/K-6
PO Box 330 68784 402-287-9892
Craig Patzel, prin. Fax 287-2014

Wallace, Lincoln, Pop. 321
Wallace SD 65 R 200/K-12
PO Box 127 69169 308-387-4323
Robert Porter, supt. Fax 387-4322
Wallace ES 100/K-6
PO Box 127 69169 308-387-4323
Robert Porter, prin. Fax 387-4322

Walthill, Thurston, Pop. 917
Walthill SD 300/K-12
PO Box 3C 68067 402-846-5432
Ed Stansberry, supt. Fax 846-5029
walthweb.esu1.org/
Walthill ES 200/K-6
PO Box 3C 68067 402-846-5432
Sandra Ostrand, prin. Fax 846-5029

Waterloo, Douglas, Pop. 506
Douglas County West Community SD
Supt. — See Valley

Douglas County West MS 200/5-8
800 N Front St 68069 402-779-2646
Tom Wicks, prin. Fax 779-2893

Wauneta, Chase, Pop. 577
Wauneta-Palisade SD 200/K-12
PO Box 368 69045 308-394-5700
Nelson Dahl, supt. Fax 394-5427
www.geocities.com/wauneta.geo
Wauneta ES 50/K-4
PO Box 368 69045 308-394-5700
Nelson Dahl, prin. Fax 394-5427
Wauneta Palisade JHS 50/7-8
PO Box 368 69045 308-394-5650
Randy Geier, prin. Fax 394-5427
Other Schools – See Palisade

Wausa, Knox, Pop. 587
Wausa SD 200/K-12
PO Box 159 68786 402-586-2255
Robert Marks Ed.D., supt. Fax 586-2406
wausaweb.esu1.org/
Wausa ES 100/K-6
PO Box 159 68786 402-586-2255
Bradley Hoesing, prin. Fax 586-2406

Waverly, Lancaster, Pop. 2,693
Waverly SD 145 1,500/K-12
PO Box 426 68462 402-786-2321
Robert Ziegler, supt. Fax 786-2799
www.dist145.esu6.org/
Hamlow ES 300/K-2
PO Box 426 68462 402-786-2341
Rodney Engel, prin. Fax 786-2396
Waverly IS 100/3-5
PO Box 426 68462 402-786-5340
Rodney Engel, prin. Fax 786-3385
Waverly MS 400/6-8
PO Box 426 68462 402-786-2348
Phillip Picquet, prin. Fax 786-2782
Other Schools – See Eagle

Villa Marie S 50/K-8
7205 N 112th St 68462 402-786-3625
Sr. Peggy Kucera, prin. Fax 488-6525

Wayne, Wayne, Pop. 5,163
Wayne SD 800/K-12
611 W 7th St 68787 402-375-3150
Fax 375-5251
schools.waynene.org/
Wayne MS 300/5-8
611 W 7th St 68787 402-375-2230
Timothy Krupicka, prin. Fax 375-2342
Wayne West ES 300/K-4
612 School View Dr 68787 402-375-3854
Daryl Schrunk, prin. Fax 375-1702

St. Mary S 50/PK-4
420 E 7th St 68787 402-375-2337
Robin Gamble, lead tchr. Fax 375-5782

Weeping Water, Cass, Pop. 1,118
Weeping Water SD 400/K-12
PO Box 206 68463 402-267-2445
Brian Gegg, supt. Fax 267-5217
www.weepingwaterps.org/
Weeping Water ES 200/K-6
PO Box 206 68463 402-267-2435
Gary Wockenfuss, prin. Fax 267-5217

Weston, Saunders, Pop. 307

St. John Nepomucene S 100/K-6
PO Box 10 68070 402-642-5234
Fran Vanak, lead tchr. Fax 642-5590

West Point, Cuming, Pop. 3,476
West Point SD 700/PK-12
1200 E Washington St 68788 402-372-5860
Theodore De Turk, supt. Fax 372-5458
www.wpcadets.org/
West Point ES 300/PK-6
1200 E Washington St 68788 402-372-5507
Lynn Pierce, prin. Fax 372-5318
Other Schools – See Beemer

Guardian Angels S 300/PK-8
408 E Walnut St 68788 402-372-5328
Sr. Mary Ann Tupy, prin. Fax 372-3563
St. Paul Lutheran S 100/PK-8
325 N Colfax St 68788 402-372-2355
Nancy Reppert, lead tchr. Fax 372-2742

Whitney, Dawes, Pop. 88
Chadron SD
Supt. — See Chadron
Whitney S 50/1-8
310 Elkhorn St 69367 308-667-1734
Tom Detwiler, prin. Fax 432-0108

Wilber, Saline, Pop. 1,799
Wilber-Clatonia SD 500/K-12
PO Box 487 68465 402-821-2266
David Rokusek, supt. Fax 821-3013
www.wilber-clatonia.org/
Wilber ES 300/K-6
PO Box 487 68465 402-821-2141
Allen Brozovsky, prin. Fax 821-3013

Wilcox, Kearney, Pop. 351
Wilcox-Hildreth SD 200/K-12
PO Box 190 68982 308-478-5265
Roger Boyer, supt. Fax 478-5260
Wilcox-Hildreth ES 100/K-5
PO Box 190 68982 308-478-5265
Victor Young, prin. Fax 478-5260
Other Schools – See Hildreth

Winnebago, Thurston, Pop. 798
Winnebago SD 400/K-12
PO Box KK 68071 402-878-2224
Dan Fehringer, supt. Fax 878-2472
winnebago.esu1.org/
Winnebago ES 300/K-6
PO Box KK 68071 402-878-2224
Tiffany Heese, prin. Fax 878-2472

St. Augustine Mission S 100/K-8
PO Box GG 68071 402-878-2291
David Korth, dir. Fax 878-2760

Winside, Wayne, Pop. 433
Winside SD 300/K-12
PO Box 158 68790 402-286-4466
Donavon Leighton, supt. Fax 286-4466
winside.esu1.org/
Winside ES 100/K-6
PO Box 158 68790 402-286-4466
Jeffrey Messersmith, prin. Fax 286-4466

Wisner, Cuming, Pop. 1,200
Wisner-Pilger SD 400/K-12
PO Box 580 68791 402-529-3249
Alan Harms, supt. Fax 529-3477
www.wisnerpilger.org/
Wisner-Pilger ES 200/K-6
PO Box 580 68791 402-529-6465
David Ludwig, prin. Fax 529-3477
Other Schools – See Pilger

Zion St. John Lutheran S 50/PK-8
998 6th Rd 68791 402-529-3348
Wende Carson, admin. Fax 529-3348

Wolbach, Greeley, Pop. 267
Greeley-Wolbach SD
Supt. — See Greeley
Greeley-Wolbach ES 100/PK-6
PO Box 67 68882 308-246-5231
Todd Beck, prin. Fax 246-5234
Greeley-Wolbach JHS 50/7-8
PO Box 67 68882 308-246-5232
Todd Beck, prin. Fax 246-5234

Wood Lake, Cherry, Pop. 72
Valentine SD
Supt. — See Valentine
Wood Lake S 50/K-8
PO Box 697 69221 402-967-3395
Eva Westover, prin. Fax 376-8096

Wood River, Hall, Pop. 1,200
Wood River Rural SD 600/K-12
PO Box 518 68883 308-583-2249
Cynthia Huff, supt. Fax 583-2395
www.woodriver.k12.ne.us/
Wood River ES 200/K-5
PO Box 488 68883 308-583-2525
Laurel Roth, prin. Fax 583-2668
Wood River MS 100/6-8
PO Box 518 68883 308-583-2249
Terry Zessin, prin. Fax 583-2395
Other Schools – See Alda

Wymore, Gage, Pop. 1,615
Southern SD 1 500/K-12
PO Box 237 68466 402-645-3326
William Shimeall, supt. Fax 645-8049
www.southernschools.org/
Other Schools – See Blue Springs

Wynot, Cedar, Pop. 175
Wynot SD 100/K-12
PO Box 157 68792 402-357-2121
Dan Hoesing, supt. Fax 357-2524
Wynot ES 50/K-4
PO Box 157 68792 402-357-2121
Richard Higgins, prin. Fax 357-2524
Wynot MS 50/5-8
PO Box 157 68792 402-357-2121
Richard Higgins, prin. Fax 357-2524

York, York, Pop. 7,888
York SD 1,200/K-12
2918 N Delaware Ave 68467 402-362-6655
Terrence Kenealy, supt. Fax 362-6943
york.ne.schoolwebpages.com
York ES 500/K-5
1501 Washington Ave 68467 402-362-1414
Kris Friesen, prin. Fax 362-5488
York MS 300/6-8
1730 N Delaware Ave 68467 402-362-6655
Brian Tonniges, prin. Fax 362-6831

Emmanuel-Faith Lutheran S 100/K-8
806 N Beaver Ave 68467 402-362-6575
John Seim, prin. Fax 362-5485
St. Joseph's S 100/K-8
428 N East Ave 68467 402-362-3021
Dawn Lewis, lead tchr. Fax 362-4067

Yutan, Saunders, Pop. 1,217
Yutan SD 500/K-12
1200 2nd St 68073 402-625-2243
Kevin Johnson, supt. Fax 625-2812
www.yutan.esu2.org/
Yutan ES 200/K-6
902 2nd St 68073 402-625-2141
Ryan Knippelmeyer, prin. Fax 625-2462

NEVADA

NEVADA DEPARTMENT OF EDUCATION
700 E Fifth St, Carson City 89701-5096
Telephone 775-687-9200
Fax 775-687-9101
Website http://www.doe.nv.gov/

Superintendent of Instruction Keith Rheault

NEVADA BOARD OF EDUCATION
700 E Fifth St, Carson City 89701-5096

President Anthony Ruggiero

PUBLIC, PRIVATE AND CATHOLIC ELEMENTARY SCHOOLS

Alamo, Lincoln
Lincoln County SD
Supt. — See Panaca
Pahranagat Valley ES 100/K-5
PO Box 170 89001 775-725-3351
Ken Higbee, prin. Fax 725-3355
Pahranagat Valley MS 100/6-8
PO Box 539 89001 775-725-3601
Ken Higbee, prin. Fax 725-3358

Amargosa Valley, Nye, Pop. 350
Nye County SD
Supt. — See Tonopah
Amargosa Valley S 200/K-8
777 E Amargosa Farm Rd 89020 775-372-5324
Karen Liberty, prin. Fax 372-5314

Austin, Lander
Lander County SD
Supt. — See Battle Mountain
Austin S 50/K-12
PO Box 160 89310 775-964-2467
Jim Rickley, prin. Fax 964-1206

Baker, White Pine
White Pine County SD
Supt. — See Ely
Baker ES 50/3-6
PO Box 120 89311 775-234-7333
Alan Hedges, prin. Fax 234-7157

Battle Mountain, Lander, Pop. 3,542
Lander County SD 1,000/K-12
PO Box 1300 89820 775-635-2886
Curtis Jordan, supt. Fax 635-5347
www.lander.k12.nv.us
Battle Mountain ES 100/K-3
PO Box 1390 89820 775-635-2889
Lorraine Sparks, prin. Fax 635-2889
Battle Mountain JHS 200/7-8
PO Box 1360 89820 775-635-2415
Fax 635-6118
Lemaire ES 300/4-6
PO Box 1420 89820 775-635-8114
Amy Nelson, prin. Fax 635-8803
Other Schools – See Austin

Beatty, Nye, Pop. 1,623
Nye County SD
Supt. — See Tonopah
Beatty S 100/K-8
PO Box 369 89003 775-553-2902
Nancy Hein, prin. Fax 553-2646

Blue Diamond, Clark
Clark County SD
Supt. — See Las Vegas
Blue Diamond ES 50/K-6
912 Village Ln 89004 702-875-4226
Shawn Paquette, prin. Fax 875-4053

Boulder City, Clark, Pop. 15,177
Clark County SD
Supt. — See Las Vegas
Garrett MS 600/6-8
1200 Avenue G 89005 702-799-8290
Jamey Hood, prin. Fax 799-8252
King ES 500/3-5
888 Adams Blvd 89005 702-799-8260
Anthony Gelsone, prin. Fax 799-8269
Mitchell ES 400/K-2
900 Avenue B 89005 702-799-8280
Louise Varvar, prin. Fax 799-8272

Grace Christian Academy 50/K-6
1150 Wyoming St 89005 702-293-3536
Marcia Harhay, admin. Fax 294-8050

Bunkerville, Clark
Clark County SD
Supt. — See Las Vegas
Bowler ES 500/K-5
451 Vincen Leavitt Ave 89007 702-346-1900
Michael Wilson, prin. Fax 346-1914

Caliente, Lincoln, Pop. 1,148
Lincoln County SD
Supt. — See Panaca
Caliente ES 200/K-6
PO Box 767 89008 775-726-3772
Pam Teel, prin. Fax 726-3880

Carlin, Elko, Pop. 2,083
Elko County SD
Supt. — See Elko
Carlin S 200/K-12
PO Box 730 89822 775-754-6317
Norm Mahlberg, prin. Fax 754-2175

Carson City, Carson City, Pop. 54,311
Carson City SD 8,300/K-12
PO Box 603 89702 775-283-2000
Richard Stokes, supt. Fax 283-2090
www.carsoncityschools.com
Bordewich/Bray ES 600/K-5
110 Thompson St 89703 775-283-2400
Valerie Dockery, prin. Fax 283-2490
Carson MS 1,100/6-8
1140 W King St 89703 775-283-2800
Sam Santillo, prin. Fax 283-2890
Eagle Valley MS 900/6-8
4151 E Fifth St 89701 775-283-2600
Christine Butson, prin. Fax 283-2690
Empire ES 600/K-5
1260 Monte Rosa Dr 89701 775-283-1100
Evelyn Allred, prin. Fax 283-1190
Fremont ES 600/K-5
1511 Firebox Rd 89701 775-283-1200
Mark VanVoorst, prin. Fax 283-1290
Fritsch ES 600/K-5
504 Bath St 89703 775-283-1400
Mary Garey, prin. Fax 283-1490
Seeliger ES 700/K-5
2800 S Saliman Rd 89701 775-283-2200
Lee Conley, prin. Fax 283-2290
Twain ES 700/K-5
2111 Carriage Crest Dr 89706 775-283-1000
Laura Austin, prin. Fax 283-1090

Douglas County SD
Supt. — See Minden
Jacks Valley ES 500/K-6
701 Jacks Valley Rd 89705 775-267-3267
Pam Gilmartin, prin. Fax 267-3211

Bethlehem Lutheran S 200/PK-8
1837 Mountain St 89703 775-882-5252
Lonnie Karges, prin. Fax 882-9278
Capital Christian S 300/PK-8
1600 Snyder Ave 89701 775-883-3009
Keith Squires, prin. Fax 883-3012
St. Teresa S 200/K-8
567 S Richmond Ave 89703 775-882-2079
Christine Perdomo, prin. Fax 882-6135

Crescent Valley, See Beowawe
Eureka County SD
Supt. — See Eureka
Crescent Valley ES 50/K-6
PO Box 211187 89821 775-468-0213
Ben Zunino, prin. Fax 468-2005

Dayton, Lyon, Pop. 2,217
Lyon County SD
Supt. — See Yerington
Dayton ES 600/K-5
285 Dayton Valley Rd 89403 775-246-6262
Cory Sandberg, prin. Fax 246-6264
Dayton IS 700/6-8
315 Dayton Valley Rd 89403 775-246-6250
Neal Freitas, prin. Fax 246-6253
Riverview ES K-5
1200 Ferretto Pkwy 89403 775-246-6170
Nolan Greenburg, prin. Fax 246-6299
Sutro ES 600/K-5
190 Dayton Village Pkwy 89403 775-246-6270
Cheryl Sample, prin. Fax 246-6276

Denio, Humboldt
Humboldt County SD
Supt. — See Winnemucca
Denio S 50/K-8
PO Box 76 89404 775-941-0376
Ray Parks, prin. Fax 941-0376

Duckwater, White Pine
Nye County SD
Supt. — See Tonopah
Duckwater S 50/K-8
2 Duckwater Rd 89314 775-863-0277
Lynette Huston, lead tchr. Fax 863-0149

Dyer, Esmeralda
Esmeralda County SD
Supt. — See Goldfield
Dyer S 50/K-8
PO Box 129 89010 775-572-3250
Fax 572-3310

Elko, Elko, Pop. 16,685
Elko County SD 8,700/K-12
PO Box 1012 89803 775-738-5196
Antoinette Cavanaugh, supt. Fax 738-5857
www.elko.k12.nv.us
Adobe MS 7-8
3375 Jennings Way 89801 775-738-3375
Mollie Keller, prin. Fax 738-3860
Elko Grammer S 2 500/K-6
1055 7th St 89801 775-738-7161
James Unger, prin. Fax 778-9144
Flag View IS 600/5-6
777 Country Club Dr 89801 775-738-7236
Todd Pehrson, prin. Fax 753-3876
Mountain View ES 800/K-6
3300 Argent Ave 89801 775-738-1844
Wendy Fluckey, prin. Fax 738-2561
Northside ES 600/K-6
1645 Sewell Dr 89801 775-738-7255
Toby Melver, prin. Fax 738-7251
Southside ES 600/K-6
501 S 9th St 89801 775-738-3731
Steven Cook, prin. Fax 738-9507
Other Schools – See Carlin, Jackpot, Montello, Owyhee, Ruby Valley, Spring Creek, Tuscarora, Wells, West Wendover

Ely, White Pine, Pop. 3,918
White Pine County SD 1,400/K-12
1135 Avenue C 89301 775-289-4851
Bob Dolezal, supt. Fax 289-3999
www.whitepine.k12.nv.us
Norman ES 400/K-5
1001 11th St E 89301 775-289-4847
Joseph Collins, prin. Fax 289-4850
White Pine County MS 300/6-8
844 Aultman St 89301 775-289-4841
Aaron Hansen, prin. Fax 289-1565
Other Schools – See Baker, Lund, Mc Gill

Eureka, Eureka
Eureka County SD 200/K-12
PO Box 249 89316 775-237-5373
Ben Zunino, supt. Fax 237-5014
www.eureka.k12.nv.us
Eureka ES 100/K-6
PO Box 249 89316 775-237-5700
Ben Zunino, prin. Fax 237-7026
Other Schools – See Crescent Valley

Fallon, Churchill, Pop. 8,103
Churchill County SD 3,900/PK-12
545 E Richards St 89406 775-423-5184
Dr. Carolyn Ross, supt. Fax 423-2959
www.churchill.k12.nv.us
Best ES 500/K-6
750 E Williams Ave 89406 775-423-3159
Keith Boone, prin. Fax 423-0407
Churchill County JHS 700/7-8
650 S Maine St 89406 775-423-7701
Jane Anderson, prin. Fax 423-8010
Lahontan ES 500/K-6
1099 Merton Dr 89406 775-423-1999
Mike Hogan, prin. Fax 423-8774

Northside Early Learning Center 50/PK-K
340 Venturacci Ln 89406 775-423-3463
Gregg Malkovich, prin. Fax 423-1240
Numa ES 500/K-6
601 Discovery Dr 89406 775-428-1996
Robert Freeman, prin. Fax 428-1699
West End ES 500/K-6
280 S Russell St 89406 775-423-2187
Kimi Melendy, prin. Fax 423-9581

Fallon SDA Church S 50/K-8
380 E Front St 89406 775-423-4185
Logos Christian Academy 100/K-12
665 Sheckler Rd 89406 775-428-1825
Tim Tucker, dir. Fax 428-6490

Fernley, Lyon, Pop. 11,342
Lyon County SD
Supt. — See Yerington
Cottonwood ES 700/K-5
925 Farm District Rd 89408 775-575-3414
Jake Chapin, prin. Fax 575-3417
East Valley ES K-5
4180 Farm District Rd 89408 775-575-3332
Claudia Fadness, prin. Fax 575-3342
Fernley ES 600/K-5
450 Hardie Ln 89408 775-575-3420
Billie Jo Hogan, prin. Fax 575-3428
Fernley IS 900/5-8
320 US Highway 95A S 89408 775-575-3390
Ryan Cross, prin. Fax 575-3394

Gabbs, Nye, Pop. 947
Nye County SD
Supt. — See Tonopah
Gabbs S 50/K-12
PO Box 147 89409 775-285-2692
Selway Mulkey, prin. Fax 285-2381

Gardnerville, Douglas, Pop. 2,177
Douglas County SD
Supt. — See Minden
Gardnerville ES 500/K-6
1290 Toler Ave 89410 775-782-5117
Shannon Brown, prin. Fax 782-2115
Meneley ES 600/K-6
1446 Muir Dr, 775-265-3154
Paula Zona, prin. Fax 265-7193
Scarselli ES 600/K-6
699 Long Valley Rd, 775-265-2222
Brandon Swain, prin. Fax 265-1218

Faith Christian Academy 100/K-8
1004 Dresslerville Rd, 775-265-0688
Jill Crandall, admin. Fax 265-0688
Pinenut S / Mt. Sierra Christian HS 100/PK-12
1788 Pinenut Rd 89410 775-782-6794
Kathryn Winebarger, admin. Fax 782-0187

Gerlach, Washoe
Washoe County SD
Supt. — See Reno
Johnson ES 50/K-5
555 E Sunset Blvd 89412 775-557-2326
Edna LaMarca, prin. Fax 557-2587

Goldfield, Esmeralda
Esmeralda County SD 100/K-8
PO Box 560 89013 775-485-6382
Robert Aumaugher, supt. Fax 485-3511
www.esmeralda.k12.nv.us/
Goldfield S 50/K-8
PO Box 560 89013 775-485-3215
Fax 485-3511
Other Schools – See Dyer, Silverpeak

Goodsprings, Clark
Clark County SD
Supt. — See Las Vegas
Goodsprings ES 50/K-6
385 San Pedro St 89019 702-874-1378
Mark Jones, prin. Fax 874-1404

Hawthorne, Mineral, Pop. 4,162
Mineral County SD 600/K-12
PO Box 1540 89415 775-945-2403
Dr. Paul Kirk, supt. Fax 945-3709
www.gohawthorne.com
Hawthorne S 400/K-8
PO Box 1060 89415 775-945-1000
Walt Hackford, prin. Fax 945-1009
Other Schools – See Schurz

Henderson, Clark, Pop. 232,146
Clark County SD
Supt. — See Las Vegas
Bartlett ES 700/K-5
1961 Wigwam Pkwy 89074 702-799-5750
Fax 799-5739
Brown JHS 1,100/6-8
307 Cannes St 89015 702-799-8900
Fax 799-3511
Burkholder MS 6-8
355 W Van Wagenen St 89015 702-799-8080
Jessie Phee, prin. Fax 799-8088
Cox ES 800/K-5
280 Clark Dr 89074 702-799-5730
David Westendorf, prin. Fax 799-5759
Dooley ES 500/K-5
1940 Chickasaw Dr, 702-799-8060
Nicole Lehman-Donadio, prin. Fax 799-8076
Galloway ES 800/K-5
701 Skyline Rd, 702-799-8920
Sharon Sneed, prin. Fax 799-8927
Gibson ES 700/K-5
271 Leisure Cir 89074 702-799-8730
Lisa Medina, prin. Fax 799-0791
Greenspun JHS 1,500/6-8
140 N Valle Verde Dr 89074 702-799-0920
Warren McKay, prin. Fax 799-0925
Hinman ES 500/K-5
450 E Merlayne Dr 89011 702-799-8990
Ann Heywood Angulo, prin. Fax 799-0599
Kesterson ES 700/K-5
231 Bailey Island Dr 89074 702-799-6300
Michele Wooldridge, prin. Fax 799-6306
Lamping ES 1,100/K-5
2551 Summit Grove Dr 89052 702-799-1330
Michael O'Dowd, prin. Fax 799-1347
Mack ES 600/K-5
3170 Laurel Ave 89014 702-799-7760
Nancy Heavey, prin. Fax 799-8795
Mannion MS 2,100/6-8
155 E Paradise Hills Dr, 702-799-3020
David Erbach, prin. Fax 799-3501
McCaw ES 700/K-5
330 Tin St 89015 702-799-8930
Jacqueline Walker, prin. Fax 799-8910
McDoniel ES 600/K-5
1831 Fox Ridge Dr 89014 702-799-7788
Holly Johnson-Troncoso, prin. Fax 799-0948
Miller MS 1,600/6-8
2400 Cozy Hill Cir 89052 702-799-2260
Tamathy Larnerd, prin. Fax 799-1309
Morrow ES 800/K-5
1070 Featherwood Ave 89015 702-799-3550
Miguel Rodrigues, prin. Fax 799-3556
Newton ES 700/K-5
571 Greenway Rd 89015 702-799-0500
Gwen Gibson, prin. Fax 799-0511
Roberts ES 900/K-5
227 Charter Oak St 89074 702-799-1320
Susan Karout, prin. Fax 799-1326
Sewell ES 600/K-5
700 E Lake Mead Pkwy 89015 702-799-8940
Carrie Larson, prin. Fax 799-8965
Smalley ES 800/K-5
304 E Paradise Hills Dr, 702-799-8090
Pamela Simone, prin. Fax 799-8094
Taylor ES 800/K-5
2655 Siena Heights Dr 89052 702-799-6892
Nicole Coloma, prin. Fax 799-2276
Taylor ES 500/K-5
144 Westminster Way 89015 702-799-8950
Janet Dobry, prin. Fax 799-8984
Thorpe ES 700/K-2
1650 Patrick Ln 89014 702-799-0740
Mark Dominguez, prin. Fax 799-0775
Treem ES 700/3-5
1698 Patrick Ln 89014 702-799-8760
Lee Esplin, prin. Fax 799-0916
Twitchell ES 800/K-5
2060 Desert Shadow Trl 89012 702-799-6860
Susan Smith, prin. Fax 799-6864
Vanderburg ES 800/K-5
2040 Desert Shadow Trl 89012 702-799-0540
Catherine Maggiore, prin. Fax 799-0546
Walker International ES 1,400/K-5
850 Scholar St, 702-799-0570
Celeste Oakes, prin. Fax 799-0537
Webb MS 500/6-8
2200 Reunion Ave 89052 702-799-1305
Paula Naegle, prin. Fax 799-1310
White MS 1,500/6-8
1661 Galleria Dr 89014 702-799-0777
Danielle Miller, prin. Fax 799-7690
Wolff ES 800/PK-5
1001 Seven Hills Dr 89052 702-799-2230
Deborah Harbin, prin. Fax 799-2257

Calvary Chapel Green Vlly Christian Acad 100/K-12
2615 W Horizon Ridge Pkwy 89052 702-456-2422
Williams Adams, dir. Fax 456-2515
Christ the Servant Lutheran K 100/PK-K
2 S Pecos Rd 89074 702-914-8782
Karen Forsythe, coord.
Foothills Montessori S 300/PK-8
1401 Amador Ln 89012 702-407-0790
Leanne Jorgensen, prin. Fax 407-0775
Green Valley Christian S 700/PK-12
711 N Valle Verde Dr 89014 702-454-4056
Deborah Ingalls, prin. Fax 454-6275
Henderson International S 1,000/PK-4
1051 Sandy Ridge Ave 89052 702-818-2100
Jolene Pruyt, admin. Fax 914-3555
Henderson International S 300/K-4
2150 Windmill Pkwy 89074 702-818-2100
Ron Bennett, hdmstr. Fax 897-7236
Lake Mead Christian Academy 700/PK-12
540 E Lake Mead Pkwy 89015 702-565-5831
Gayle Sue Blakeley, admin. Fax 566-6206

Imlay, Pershing
Pershing County SD
Supt. — See Lovelock
Imlay ES 50/K-6
PO Box 86 89418 775-538-7360
Shea Murphy, prin. Fax 538-7360

Incline Village, Washoe, Pop. 7,119
Washoe County SD
Supt. — See Reno
Incline ES 200/K-2
771 Southwood Blvd 89451 775-832-4240
Kathleen Watty, prin. Fax 832-4212
Incline ES 3-5
915 Northwood Blvd 89451 775-832-4250
Kathleen Watty, prin. Fax 832-4255
Incline MS 200/6-8
931 Southwood Blvd 89451 775-832-4220
Nichole Truax, prin. Fax 832-4210

Lake Tahoe S 100/K-9
995 Tahoe Blvd 89451 775-831-5828
Steven McKibben, hdmstr. Fax 831-5825

Indian Springs, Clark, Pop. 1,164
Clark County SD
Supt. — See Las Vegas
Indian Springs ES 100/K-5
PO Box 1088 89018 702-799-0932
Katherine Christensen, prin. Fax 879-3142
Indian Springs MS 100/6-8
400 Sky Rd 89018 702-799-0932
Katherine Christensen, prin. Fax 879-3142

Jackpot, Elko
Elko County SD
Supt. — See Elko
Jackpot S 100/K-12
PO Box 463 89825 775-755-2374
Brian Messmer, prin. Fax 755-2291

Las Vegas, Clark, Pop. 545,147
Clark County SD 307,200/PK-12
5100 W Sahara Ave 89146 702-799-5000
Walt Rulffes, supt. Fax 799-5125
www.ccsd.net/
Adams ES 500/K-5
580 Fogg St 89110 702-799-8800
Rebecca Johnson, prin. Fax 799-2115
Adcock ES 600/K-5
6350 Hyde Ave 89107 702-799-4185
Helen Carlson, prin. Fax 799-4172
Alamo ES 1,000/K-5
7455 El Camino Rd 89139 702-799-2590
Rodney Kissinger, prin. Fax 799-2622
Allen ES 700/K-5
8680 W Hammer Ln 89149 702-799-4580
Gary Prince, prin. Fax 799-4586
Bailey ES 800/K-5
4525 Jimmy Durante Blvd 89122 702-799-7510
Corean Mayorga, prin. Fax 799-7515
Bailey MS 1,600/6-8
2500 N Hollywood Blvd 89156 702-799-4811
Lisa Primas, prin. Fax 799-4807
Bass ES 900/PK-5
10377 Rancho Destino Rd, 702-799-2220
Sheila Jones-Mosley, prin. Fax 799-1372
Batterman ES 1,000/K-5
10135 W Quail Ave 89148 702-799-1920
Sandra Abston, prin. Fax 799-1912
Beatty ES 800/K-5
8685 Hidden Palms Pkwy 89123 702-799-5700
Craig VanTine, prin. Fax 799-5711
Becker MS 1,400/6-8
9151 Pinewood Hills Dr 89134 702-799-4460
Amy Smith, prin. Fax 799-4470
Beckley ES 900/K-5
3223 Glenhurst Dr 89121 702-799-7700
Jeanne Slama, prin. Fax 799-0792
Bell ES 1,000/K-5
2900 Wilmington Way 89102 702-799-5910
Timothy Adams, prin. Fax 799-5916
Bendorf ES 800/K-5
3550 Kevin St 89147 702-799-4440
Jerre Moore, prin. Fax 799-4319
Bilbray ES 900/K-5
9370 Brent Ln 89143 702-799-4646
Aalya Page, prin. Fax 799-4538
Bonner ES 700/K-5
765 Crestdale Ln 89144 702-799-6050
Deborah Franklin, prin. Fax 799-6056
Booker ES 300/K-5
2277 N Martin L King Blvd 89106 702-799-4720
Beverly Mathis, prin. Fax 799-4727
Bozarth ES K-5
7431 Egan Crest Dr 89149 702-799-6608
Rodney Saunders, prin. Fax 799-6618
Bracken ES 500/K-5
1200 N 27th St 89101 702-799-7095
Kathleen Decker, prin. Fax 799-7102
Brinley MS 1,200/6-8
2480 Maverick St 89108 702-799-4550
Sharon Beatty, prin. Fax 799-4549
Brookman ES 900/K-5
6225 E Washington Ave 89110 702-799-7250
Mary Dunlevy, prin. Fax 799-7241
Bryan ES 600/K-5
8050 Cielo Vista Ave 89128 702-799-1460
Stephen Piccininni, prin. Fax 799-1469
Bryan ES 800/K-5
8255 W Katie Ave 89147 702-799-1270
Cynthia Alamshaw, prin. Fax 799-1276
Bunker ES 600/K-5
6350 Peak Dr 89108 702-799-3420
Pauline Mills, prin. Fax 799-3476
Cadwallader MS 1,900/6-8
7775 Elkhorn Rd 89131 702-799-6692
Kathryn Singer, prin. Fax 799-4536
Cambeiro ES 600/K-5
2851 Harris Ave 89101 702-799-1700
Patricia Rosales, prin. Fax 799-1706
Canarelli MS 1,800/6-8
7808 S Torrey Pines Dr 89139 702-799-1340
Kristy Keller, prin. Fax 799-5715
Cannon JHS 1,000/6-8
5850 Euclid St 89120 702-799-5600
Elmer Manzanares, prin. Fax 799-5644
Carl ES 800/K-5
5625 Corbett St 89130 702-799-6650
Robert Bennett, prin. Fax 799-6659
Carson ES 300/K-5
1735 D St 89106 702-799-7113
Carolyn King, prin. Fax 799-0401
Cartwright ES 800/K-5
1050 E Gary Ave 89123 702-799-1350
Amy Siembida, prin. Fax 799-1356

Cashman MS 1,100/6-8
4622 W Desert Inn Rd 89102 702-799-5880
Misti Taton, prin. Fax 799-5947
Christensen ES 700/K-5
9001 Mariner Cove Dr 89117 702-799-4390
David Spitler, prin. Fax 799-1413
Conners ES 800/K-5
3810 Shadow Peak St 89129 702-799-1402
Patricia Blomstrom, prin. Fax 799-1414
Cortez ES 900/K-5
4245 E Tonopah Ave 89115 702-799-2180
Ariel Villalobos, prin. Fax 799-3219
Cortney JHS 1,500/6-8
5301 E Hacienda Ave 89122 702-799-2400
Teresa Holden, prin. Fax 799-2407
Cox ES 900/K-2
3855 Timberlake Dr 89115 702-799-4990
Cheryl Adler-Davis, prin. Fax 799-4997
Crestwood ES 700/K-5
1300 Pauline Way 89104 702-799-7890
Kalandra Sheppard, prin. Fax 799-7884
Culley ES 900/K-5
1200 N Mallard St 89108 702-799-4800
Ellen Stayman, prin. Fax 799-0611
Cunningham ES 1,000/K-5
4145 Jimmy Durante Blvd 89122 702-799-8780
Stacey Scott-Cherry, prin. Fax 799-0881
Dailey ES 700/K-5
2001 E Reno Ave 89119 702-799-5690
Jackie Lyons, prin. Fax 799-5698
Darnell ES 700/K-5
9480 W Tropical Pkwy 89149 702-799-6630
Patricia Cobb, prin. Fax 799-6651
Dearing ES 800/K-5
3046 Ferndale St 89121 702-799-7710
Wanda McCullough, prin. Fax 799-8798
Decker ES 900/K-5
3850 Redwood St 89103 702-799-5920
Mario Quinonez, prin. Fax 799-5924
Derfelt ES 500/K-5
1900 S Lisa Ln 89117 702-799-4370
Gregory Mingo, prin. Fax 799-4341
Deskin ES 800/K-5
4550 N Pioneer Way 89129 702-799-4600
Amy Yacobovsky, prin. Fax 799-4609
Detwiler ES 1,000/K-5
1960 Ferrell St 89106 702-799-1830
Teri Timpson, prin. Fax 799-3106
Diaz ES K-5
4450 E Owens Ave 89110 702-799-2120
Maribel McAdory, prin. Fax 799-2143
Diskin ES 900/K-5
4220 Ravenwood Dr 89147 702-799-5930
Elizabeth Smith, prin. Fax 799-5925
Dondero ES 700/K-5
4450 Ridgeville St 89103 702-799-5940
LeRoy Espinosa, prin. Fax 799-1210
Earl ES 900/K-5
1463 Marion Dr 89110 702-799-7310
Bonnie Townsend, prin. Fax 799-8817
Earl ES 700/K-5
6650 W Reno Ave 89118 702-799-8181
Sharlette Redick, prin. Fax 799-8188
Edwards ES 800/K-5
4551 Diamond Head Dr 89110 702-799-7320
Kristie Cole, prin. Fax 799-8890
Eisenberg ES 700/K-5
7770 W Delhi Ave 89129 702-799-4680
Ken Ligon, prin. Fax 799-4677
Escobedo MS 800/6-8
9501 Echelon Point Dr 89149 702-799-4560
Stefanie Machin, prin. Fax 799-4568
Faiss MS 1,000/6-8
9525 W Maule Ave 89148 702-799-6850
Joy Lea, prin. Fax 799-6852
Ferron ES 700/K-5
4200 Mountain Vista St 89121 702-799-7720
Christine Beaird, prin. Fax 799-0798
Fertitta MS 1,800/6-8
9905 W Mesa Vista Ave 89148 702-799-1900
Lisa Campbell, prin. Fax 799-5688
Fine ES K-5
6635 W Cougar Ave 89139 702-799-6882
Stephanie Taylor, prin. Fax 799-6889
Fong ES 700/K-5
2200 James Bilbray Dr 89108 702-799-4890
Jamie Agresti, prin. Fax 799-0694
Forbuss ES 900/K-5
8601 S Grand Canyon Dr, 702-799-6840
Shawn Paquette, prin. Fax 799-6844
Fremont MS 1,100/6-8
1100 E Saint Louis Ave 89104 702-799-5558
Antonio Rael, prin. Fax 799-5566
French ES 600/K-5
3235 E Hacienda Ave 89120 702-799-7730
Amy Graham, prin. Fax 799-0757
Frias ES 900/K-5
5800 Broken Top Ave 89141 702-799-2298
Valerie Rice, prin. Fax 799-6859
Fyfe ES 600/K-5
4101 W Bonanza Rd 89107 702-799-4191
Rick Winget, prin. Fax 799-0379
Garehime ES 700/K-5
3850 N Campbell Rd 89129 702-799-6000
Shelley Kresyman, prin. Fax 799-6012
Garside JHS 1,400/6-8
300 S Torrey Pines Dr 89107 702-799-4245
Stephanie Wong, prin. Fax 799-4296
Gehring ES 800/K-5
1155 E Richmar Ave 89123 702-799-6899
Sandra Brody, prin. Fax 799-6891
Gibson MS 1,200/6-8
3900 W Washington Ave 89107 702-799-4700
Linda Archambault, prin. Fax 799-4705
Givens ES 800/K-5
655 Park Vista Dr 89138 702-799-1430
Dale Slater, prin. Fax 799-1485

Goldfarb ES 800/K-5
1651 Orchard Valley Dr 89142 702-799-1550
Jacqueline Conarton, prin. Fax 799-1556
Goolsby ES 600/K-5
11175 W Desert Inn Rd 89135 702-799-2520
Lorraine Blume, prin. Fax 799-1233
Gragson ES 1,000/K-5
555 N Honolulu St 89110 702-799-7330
Annette Smith, prin. Fax 799-7339
Gray ES 500/K-5
2825 S Torrey Pines Dr 89146 702-799-5950
Carl Johnson, prin. Fax 799-5978
Griffith ES 500/K-5
324 Essex East Dr 89107 702-799-4200
George Anas, prin. Fax 799-0319
Guinn MS 1,000/6-8
4150 S Torrey Pines Dr 89103 702-799-5900
Georgia Taton, prin. Fax 799-5905
Hancock ES 500/K-5
1661 Lindell Rd 89146 702-799-4205
Susan Waters, prin. Fax 799-4183
Harmon ES 900/K-5
5351 Hillsboro Ln 89120 702-799-7740
Robert Solomon, prin. Fax 799-7748
Harney MS 1,700/6-8
1580 S Hollywood Blvd 89142 702-799-3240
Susan Echols, prin. Fax 799-3286
Harris ES 700/K-5
3620 S Sandhill Rd 89121 702-799-7750
Henry Rodda, prin. Fax 799-0785
Hayes ES 700/K-5
9620 W Twain Ave 89147 702-799-6030
Scott Bailey, prin. Fax 799-4466
Heard ES 700/K-5
42 Baer Dr 89115 702-799-4920
Traci Dyer, prin. Fax 799-4926
Heckethorn ES 600/K-5
5150 Whispering Sands Dr 89131 702-799-6690
Kari Scarlett, prin. Fax 799-6674
Herr ES 700/K-5
6475 Eagle Creek Ln 89156 702-799-8860
Howard Garrard, prin. Fax 799-8884
Hewetson ES 900/K-5
701 N 20th St 89101 702-799-7896
Lucille Keaton, prin. Fax 799-8526
Hickey ES 900/K-5
2450 N Hollywood Blvd 89156 702-799-1899
David Harcourt, prin. Fax 799-1612
Hill ES 700/3-5
560 E Eldorado Ln 89123 702-799-5720
Jacqueline Brown, prin. Fax 799-5719
Hoggard ES 400/K-5
950 N Tonopah Dr 89106 702-799-4740
Celese Rayford, prin. Fax 799-4884
Hollingsworth ES 900/K-5
1776 E Ogden Ave 89101 702-799-1660
Diana Cockrell, prin. Fax 799-1666
Hummel ES 800/K-5
9800 Placid St, 702-799-6810
Rick Darrington, prin. Fax 799-6803
Hyde Park MS 1,700/6-8
900 Hinson St 89107 702-799-4260
Kimberly Bauman, prin. Fax 799-0348
Iverson ES 1,100/K-5
1575 S Hollywood Blvd 89142 702-799-7260
Byron Green, prin. Fax 799-7329
Jacobson ES 600/K-5
8400 Boseck Dr 89145 702-799-4320
Deborah Palermo, prin. Fax 799-4359
Jeffers ES 800/K-5
2320 Clifford St 89115 702-799-2100
Wendy Roselinsky, prin. Fax 799-2110
Johnson JHS 1,300/6-8
7701 Ducharme Ave 89145 702-799-4480
Terry Ann Sobrero, prin. Fax 799-4497
Jydstrup ES 700/K-5
5150 Duneville St 89118 702-799-8140
Martha Slack, prin. Fax 799-8198
Kahre ES 600/K-5
7887 W Gowan Rd 89129 702-799-4660
Glenda Plaster, prin. Fax 799-4666
Katz ES 700/K-5
1800 Rock Springs Dr 89128 702-799-4330
Joan Lombard, prin. Fax 799-4306
Keller ES K-5
5445 Cedar Ave 89110 702-799-2140
Kerry Preston, prin. Fax 799-2145
Keller MS 1,500/6-8
301 Fogg St 89110 702-799-3220
April Key, prin. Fax 799-3226
Kelly ES 300/K-5
1900 J St 89106 702-799-4750
Patricia Harris, prin. Fax 799-0699
Kim ES 700/K-5
7600 Peace Way 89147 702-799-5990
Salwa Zaki, prin. Fax 799-5979
King ES 500/K-5
2260 Betty Ln 89156 702-799-7390
Judy Jordahl, prin. Fax 799-7299
Knudson MS 1,300/6-8
2400 Atlantic St 89104 702-799-7470
Northey Henderson, prin. Fax 799-0157
Lake ES 1,000/K-5
2904 Meteoro St, 702-799-5530
Larry McHargue, prin. Fax 799-0270
Lawrence JHS 1,400/6-8
4410 S Juliano Rd 89147 702-799-2540
Kathryn Mead, prin. Fax 799-2563
Leavitt MS 1,800/6-8
4701 Quadrel St 89129 702-799-4699
Keith Wipperman, prin. Fax 799-4528
Lied MS 1,500/6-8
5350 W Tropical Pkwy 89130 702-799-4620
Kimberly Bass-Davis, prin. Fax 799-4626
Long ES 800/K-5
2000 S Walnut Rd 89104 702-799-7456
Joyce Brooks, prin. Fax 799-7460

Lowman ES 800/K-2
4225 N Lamont St 89115 702-799-4930
Kathy Konowalow, prin. Fax 799-4927
Lummis ES 600/K-5
9000 Hillpointe Rd 89134 702-799-4380
Lisa McKenrick-Hanna, prin. Fax 799-4310
Lunt ES 600/K-5
2701 Harris Ave 89101 702-799-8360
Thelma Davis, prin. Fax 799-8372
Lynch ES 900/K-5
4850 Kell Ln 89115 702-799-8820
Deborah A. Slauzis, prin. Fax 799-8895
Mack MS 1,400/6-8
4250 Karen Ave 89121 702-799-2005
Joseph Murphy, prin. Fax 799-2412
Manch ES 700/3-5
4351 N Lamont St 89115 702-799-4900
Patricia Garcia, prin. Fax 799-4904
Martin MS 1,300/6-8
200 N 28th St 89101 702-799-7922
Mary Hafner, prin. Fax 799-7959
May ES 700/K-5
6350 W Washburn Rd 89130 702-799-4690
Mindi Martinez, prin. Fax 799-4544
McMillan ES 700/K-5
7000 Walt Lott Dr 89128 702-799-4350
Jerri Mausbach, prin. Fax 799-4307
McWilliams ES 800/K-5
1315 Hiawatha Rd 89108 702-799-4770
Randy Cheung, prin. Fax 799-3170
Mendoza ES 800/K-5
2000 S Sloan Ln 89142 702-799-8680
Brenton Lago, prin. Fax 799-7464
Miller ES 100/1-5
4851 E Lake Mead Blvd 89115 702-799-8830
Barbara Misday, prin. Fax 799-3259
Molasky JHS 1,500/6-8
7801 W Gilmore Ave 89129 702-799-3400
Daron Heilman, prin. Fax 799-3407
Monaco MS 1,400/6-8
1870 N Lamont St 89115 702-799-3670
Lawrence Russell, prin. Fax 799-3202
Moore ES 900/PK-5
491 N Lamb Blvd 89110 702-799-3270
Cheryl Butera, prin. Fax 799-3269
Mountain View ES 600/K-5
5436 Kell Ln 89156 702-799-7350
Alasha Woods, prin. Fax 799-7398
Neal ES 700/K-5
6651 W Azure Dr 89130 702-799-2200
Denise Murray, prin. Fax 799-4576
Ober ES 700/PK-5
3035 Desert Marigold Ln 89135 702-799-6077
Joanna Gerali, prin. Fax 799-6704
O'Callaghan MS 1,500/6-8
1450 Radwick Dr 89110 702-799-7340
Merry Sillitoe, prin. Fax 799-8870
O'Roarke ES K-5
8455 OHare Rd 89143 702-799-6600
Fredris Breen, prin. Fax 799-6612
Orr MS 1,000/6-8
1562 E Katie Ave 89119 702-799-5573
George Leavens, prin. Fax 799-0297
Paradise ES 600/K-5
900 Cottage Grove Ave 89119 702-799-5660
Maureen Stout, prin. Fax 895-2038
Park ES 800/K-5
931 Franklin Ave 89104 702-799-7904
Lorna Cervantes, prin. Fax 799-7949
Parson ES 600/K-5
4100 Thom Blvd 89130 702-799-4530
Toni Kuiper, prin. Fax 799-4540
Petersen ES 900/K-5
3650 Cambridge St, 702-799-1120
Susan Steaffens, prin. Fax 799-3397
Piggott ES 600/K-5
9601 Red Hills Rd 89117 702-799-4450
David Hudzick, prin. Fax 799-1410
Pittman ES 700/K-5
6333 Fargo Ave 89107 702-799-4213
David Frydman, prin. Fax 799-0315
Red Rock ES 600/K-5
408 Upland Blvd 89107 702-799-4223
Nadeen Archer, prin. Fax 799-4164
Reed ES 800/K-5
2501 Winwood St 89108 702-799-4777
Karen Bennett, prin. Fax 799-0680
Reedom ES K-5
10025 Rumrill St, 702-799-5702
Douglas Wilson, prin. Fax 799-5722
Rhodes ES 800/K-5
7350 Tealwood St 89131 702-799-3450
Darryl Wyatt, prin. Fax 799-3456
Ries ES 900/K-5
9805 Lindell Rd 89141 702-799-1240
Joseph Rekrut, prin. Fax 799-1275
Robison MS 1,200/6-8
825 Marion Dr 89110 702-799-7300
Elena Baker, prin. Fax 799-7302
Rogers ES 700/K-5
5535 S Riley St 89148 702-799-6870
Kip Krzmarzick, prin. Fax 799-2222
Rogich MS 1,600/6-8
235 N Pavilion Center Dr 89144 702-799-6040
Susan Harrison, prin. Fax 799-6094
Ronnow ES 1,000/K-5
1100 Lena St 89101 702-799-7159
Jonathan Herring, prin. Fax 799-7164
Ronzone ES 800/K-5
5701 Stacey Ave 89108 702-799-4780
Brett Booth, prin. Fax 799-4788
Roundy ES 700/K-5
2755 Mohawk St 89146 702-799-5890
George Knowles, prin. Fax 799-5899
Rowe ES 600/K-5
4338 S Bruce St 89119 702-799-5540
Beverly Hudson, prin. Fax 799-0299

Rundle ES 1,000/K-5
425 N Christy Ln 89110 702-799-7380
Laura Dickensheets, prin. Fax 799-7327
Saville MS 1,700/6-8
8101 N Torrey Pines Dr 89131 702-799-3460
Kathy Kulas, prin. Fax 799-4511
Sawyer MS 1,500/6-8
5450 Redwood St 89118 702-799-5980
Kim Friel, prin. Fax 799-5969
Scherkenbach ES 900/K-5
9371 Iron Mountain Rd 89143 702-799-3401
Karen Smallwood, prin. Fax 799-3433
Schofield MS 1,500/6-8
8625 Spencer St 89123 702-799-2290
Arthur Adams, prin. Fax 799-5717
Schorr ES 800/K-5
11420 Placid St, 702-799-1380
Kenneth Wronski, prin. Fax 799-1377
Silvestri JHS 1,500/6-8
1055 E Silverado Ranch Blvd, 702-799-2240
Robert Mars, prin. Fax 799-2247
Smith ES 800/PK-5
5150 E Desert Inn Rd 89122 702-799-3700
Clarence Ehler, prin. Fax 799-3711
Smith ES 500/K-5
7101 Pinedale Ave 89145 702-799-4300
John Haynal, prin. Fax 799-4436
Snyder ES 900/K-5
4317 E Colorado Ave 89104 702-799-3750
Traci Davis, prin. Fax 799-3723
Stanford ES 700/K-5
5350 Harris Ave 89110 702-799-7272
Debra Jones, prin. Fax 799-7303
Staton ES 800/PK-5
1700 Sageberry Dr 89144 702-799-6720
Martha Gardner, prin. Fax 799-6070
Steele ES 1,000/K-5
6995 W Eldorado Ln 89113 702-799-2201
Beverly Ashford, prin. Fax 799-2204
Sunrise Acres ES 800/K-5
211 N 28th St 89101 702-799-7912
Joanie Monroy, prin. Fax 799-8556
Tanaka ES 900/K-5
9135 W Maule Ave 89148 702-799-2504
Lea Chua, prin. Fax 799-1289
Tarkanian MS 1,100/6-8
5800 W Pyle Ave 89141 702-799-6801
Darren Sweikert, prin. Fax 799-6805
Tarr ES 600/K-5
9400 W Gilmore Ave 89129 702-799-6710
Michael Bishop, prin. Fax 799-4317
Tate ES 800/K-5
2450 Lincoln Rd 89115 702-799-7360
Mary Bowling, prin. Fax 799-7287
Thiriot ES 600/K-5
5700 W Harmon Ave 89103 702-799-2550
Patricia Schmidt, prin. Fax 799-2545
Thomas ES 700/K-5
1560 Cherokee Ln, 702-799-5550
Dennis Kubala, prin. Fax 799-1160
Thompson ES 1,000/K-5
7351 N Campbell Rd 89149 702-799-3430
Shawn Halland, prin. Fax 799-3432
Tobler ES 600/K-5
6510 Buckskin Ave 89108 702-799-4500
Scarlett Perryman, prin. Fax 799-4520
Tomiyasu ES 700/K-5
5445 Annie Oakley Dr 89120 702-799-7770
Renee Muraco, prin. Fax 799-0726
Twin Lakes ES 500/K-5
3300 Riverside Dr 89108 702-799-4790
Leary Adams, prin. Fax 799-4899
Ullom ES 700/K-5
4869 Sun Valley Dr 89121 702-799-7780
Belinda Jones, prin. Fax 799-0719
Vegas Verdes ES 800/K-5
4000 El Parque Ave 89102 702-799-5960
Margarita Garcia, prin. Fax 799-5975
Von Tobel MS 1,400/6-8
2436 N Pecos Rd 89115 702-799-7280
Rogelio Gonzalez, prin. Fax 799-7286
Ward ES 700/K-5
1555 E Hacienda Ave 89119 702-799-5650
Maria Chavez, prin. Fax 799-5658
Ward ES 1,000/K-5
5555 Horse Dr 89131 702-799-4501
Theresa Douglas, prin. Fax 799-4503
Warren ES 700/K-5
6451 Brandywine Way 89107 702-799-4233
Rosanna Gallagher, prin. Fax 799-0317
Wasden ES 600/K-5
2831 Palomino Ln 89107 702-799-4239
Scott DuChateau, prin. Fax 799-4252
Wengert ES 800/K-5
2001 Winterwood Blvd 89142 702-799-8600
Suhaila Mustafa, prin. Fax 799-0116
West Prep S 1,000/K-10
2050 Saphire Stone Ave 89106 702-799-3120
Mike Barton, prin. Fax 799-3126
Whitney ES 700/K-5
5005 Keenan Ave 89122 702-799-7790
Sherrie Gahn, prin. Fax 799-0933
Wiener ES 700/K-2
450 E Eldorado Ln 89123 702-799-5760
Krista Yarberry, prin. Fax 799-5770
Williams ES 300/K-5
1030 J St 89106 702-799-4760
Brenda McKinney, prin. Fax 799-4765
Woodbury MS 1,000/6-8
3875 E Harmon Ave 89121 702-799-7660
Greg Snelling, prin. Fax 799-0805
Woolley ES 800/3-5
3955 Timberlake Dr 89115 702-799-4970
Rick Ditondo, prin. Fax 799-4978
Wright ES 1,300/K-5
8425 Bob Fisk Ave, 702-799-5701
Betty Roqueni, prin. Fax 799-5708
Wynn ES 900/K-5
5655 Edna Ave 89146 702-799-8160
Ellen Bordinhao, prin. Fax 799-8146
Other Schools – See Blue Diamond, Boulder City, Bunkerville, Goodsprings, Henderson, Indian Springs, Laughlin, Logandale, Mesquite, Moapa, Mt Charleston, North Las Vegas, Overton, Sandy Valley, Searchlight

---

Adelson Educational Complex 200/PK-12
9700 Hillpointe Rd 89134 702-255-4500
Paul Schiffmann, admin. Fax 255-7232
All Saints Episcopal Day S PK-K
4201 W Washington Ave 89107 702-878-1205
Fax 878-1829
American Heritage Academy 100/K-8
6126 S Sandhill Rd Ste C 89120 702-949-5614
Eric Anderson, prin. Fax 949-0273
Calvary Chapel Christian S 600/K-12
7175 W Oquendo Rd 89113 702-248-8879
James Davis, supt. Fax 220-8694
Calvary Christian Learning Academy 100/K-5
2900 N Torrey Pines Dr 89108 702-655-1385
Kimberly Wright, admin. Fax 655-2932
Challenger S 500/PK-8
1725 E Serene Ave 89123 702-990-7300
Benjamin Celver, dir. Fax 492-0063
Challenger S 600/PK-8
9900 Isaac Newton Ln 89129 702-878-6418
Ashley Peace, prin. Fax 944-1709
Cornerstone Christian Academy 400/K-8
5825 Eldora Ave 89146 702-939-5050
James Whiddon, prin. Fax 507-0699
Cumorah Academy of Las Vegas 100/K-12
6000 W Oakey Blvd 89146 702-636-5577
April Taggart, prin. Fax 636-5570
Dawson S 700/PK-8
10845 W Desert Inn Rd 89135 702-949-3600
Michael Imperi, prin. Fax 838-1818
Desert Torah Academy 200/PK-8
1261 Arville St 89102 702-259-0777
Rabbi Moishe Rodman, prin. Fax 877-4700
Faith Community Lutheran Academy 300/K-5
2700 S Town Center Dr 89135 702-921-2777
Jerry Reinertson, prin. Fax 921-2730
First Good Shepard Lutheran S 200/K-6
301 S Maryland Pkwy 89101 702-382-8610
James Krafft, prin. Fax 384-2080
International Christian Academy 400/PK-8
8100 Westcliff Dr 89145 702-869-1109
Bob Mekus, prin. Fax 242-3206
Lamb of God Lutheran S 300/PK-5
6232 N Jones Blvd 89130 702-645-1626
Wayne Schmidt, prin. Fax 645-6031
Las Vegas Day S 600/PK-8
3275 Red Rock St 89146 702-362-1180
Neil Daseler, dir. Fax 362-0620
Las Vegas Junior Academy 100/K-10
6059 W Oakey Blvd 89146 702-871-7208
Arlyn Sundsted, prin. Fax 364-5456
Liberty Baptist Academy 200/K-12
6501 W Lake Mead Blvd 89108 702-647-4522
John Shorer, admin. Fax 647-8083
Meadows S 900/PK-12
8601 Scholar Ln 89128 702-254-1610
Carolyn Goodman, hdmstr. Fax 254-2452
Merryhill S at Spanish Trail 200/K-8
5055 S Durango Dr 89113 702-889-2803
Nicolette Utsinger, prin. Fax 889-2810
Merryhill S at Summerlin 200/K-7
2160 Snow Trl 89134 702-242-8838
Kimberly Roden, prin. Fax 242-8830
Montessori Visions Academy 100/PK-8
3551 E Sunset Rd 89120 702-451-9801
Lori Bossy, prin. Fax 451-0049
Mountain View Christian S 700/PK-12
3900 E Bonanza Rd 89110 702-452-1300
Crystal McClanahan, supt. Fax 452-0499
Mountain View Lutheran S 300/PK-6
9550 W Cheyenne Ave 89129 702-804-5291
Ross Chiles, prin. Fax 804-5293
Mt. Olive Lutheran S 100/K-8
3975 S Sandhill Rd 89121 702-451-1050
Frank Van Brocklin, prin. Fax 451-1050
Oasis Christian Academy 100/K-12
4824 E Desert Inn Rd 89121 702-777-0800
Darin Mauzy, admin. Fax 451-7074
Omar Haikal Islamic Academy 100/K-8
485 E Eldorado Ln 89123 702-614-9002
Doug Carden, prin. Fax 614-8002
Our Lady of Las Vegas S 700/PK-8
3046 Alta Dr 89107 702-878-6841
Phyllis Joyce, prin. Fax 880-5759
Redeemer Lutheran S 50/K-1
1730 N Pecos Rd 89115 702-642-5176
Patricia Davis, prin. Fax 642-3548
St. Anne S 300/PK-8
1813 S Maryland Pkwy 89104 702-735-2586
Dr. James Machinski, prin. Fax 735-8357
St. Elizabeth Ann Seton S 500/K-8
1807 Pueblo Vista Dr 89128 702-804-8328
Dr. Carey Roybal-Benson, prin. Fax 228-8906
St. Francis de Sales S 300/K-8
1111 N Michael Way 89108 702-647-2828
Catherine Thompson, prin. Fax 647-0284
St. Joseph's S 200/K-8
1300 E Bridger Ave 89101 702-384-6909
Lynda Ballard, prin. Fax 386-0249
St. Viator S 700/PK-8
4246 S Eastern Ave 89119 702-732-4477
Kathleen Daulton, prin. Fax 732-4418
Solomon Schecter Day S of Las Vegas 100/K-5
10700 Havenwood Ln 89135 702-804-1333
Jon Mitzmacher, hdmstr. Fax 804-1370
Southern Highlands Preparatory S 200/K-8
11500 Southern Highlands Pk 89141 702-617-6030
Tina Barone, admin. Fax 617-6031
Spring Valley Montessori S 100/PK-6
6940 Edna Ave 89117 702-362-9739
Susan Alcantara, prin. Fax 388-0900
Tree of Life Christian S 100/PK-6
6210 W Cheyenne Ave 89108 702-645-2415
Heather Raymondo, prin. Fax 658-1219
Trinity Christian S 200/PK-6
950 E Saint Louis Ave 89104 702-734-0562
Ronald Lee, prin. Fax 732-3469
Trinity International S 100/K-12
2525 Emerson Ave 89121 702-732-3957
Thurban Warrick, admin. Fax 784-0192
Word of Life Christian Academy 200/PK-12
3520 N Buffalo Dr 89129 702-645-1180
Kelly Marchello, prin. Fax 396-0293

Laughlin, Clark, Pop. 4,791
Clark County SD
Supt. — See Las Vegas
Bennett ES 400/K-5
2750 Needles Hwy 89029 702-298-3378
Lynne Ruegamer, prin. Fax 299-0405

Logandale, Clark
Clark County SD
Supt. — See Las Vegas
Bowler ES 700/K-5
1425 W Whipple Rd 89021 702-398-3233
Shawna Jessen, prin. Fax 398-3278

Lovelock, Pershing, Pop. 1,878
Pershing County SD 800/K-12
PO Box 389 89419 775-273-7819
Daniel Fox, supt. Fax 273-2668
www.pershing.k12.nv.us
Lovelock ES 300/K-5
PO Box 621 89419 775-273-2176
Shea Murphy, prin. Fax 273-1250
Pershing County MS 200/6-8
PO Box 1020 89419 775-273-1200
Richard Tree, prin. Fax 273-3191
Other Schools – See Imlay

Lund, White Pine
White Pine County SD
Supt. — See Ely
Lund ES 100/K-6
PO Box 129 89317 775-238-5200
Chris Cobb, prin. Fax 238-0208

Mc Dermitt, Humboldt, Pop. 373
Humboldt County SD
Supt. — See Winnemucca
Mc Dermitt ES 100/K-6
PO Box 98 89421 775-532-8761
Don Almquist, prin. Fax 532-8017

Mc Gill, White Pine, Pop. 1,258
White Pine County SD
Supt. — See Ely
Mc Gill ES 100/K-5
PO Box 1296 89318 775-235-7722
Alan Hedges, prin. Fax 235-7036

Mesquite, Clark, Pop. 13,523
Clark County SD
Supt. — See Las Vegas
Hughes MS 600/6-8
550 Hafen Ln 89027 702-346-3250
Clifford Hughes, prin. Fax 346-3095
Virgin Valley ES 700/K-5
200 Woodbury Ln 89027 702-346-5761
Cathy Davis, prin. Fax 346-5049

Minden, Douglas, Pop. 1,441
Douglas County SD 6,600/K-12
1638 Mono Ave 89423 775-782-5134
Carol Lark, supt. Fax 782-3162
www.dcsd.k12.nv.us
Minden ES 500/K-6
1170 Baler St 89423 775-782-5510
Ken Stoll, prin. Fax 782-5551
Pinon Hills ES 500/K-6
1638 Mono Ave 89423 775-267-3622
Romelle Cronin, prin. Fax 267-3846
Other Schools – See Carson City, Gardnerville, Zephyr Cove

Grace Christian Academy 100/K-8
2320 Heybourne Rd 89423 775-782-7811
Julie Henry, hdmstr. Fax 782-7768

Moapa, Clark
Clark County SD
Supt. — See Las Vegas
Perkins ES 200/K-5
PO Box 189 89025 702-864-2444
Kenneth Paul, prin. Fax 864-2566

Montello, Elko
Elko County SD
Supt. — See Elko
Montello S 50/1-8
PO Box 148 89830 775-776-2456
Dawn Hagness, prin. Fax 776-2456

Mt Charleston, Clark
Clark County SD
Supt. — See Las Vegas
Lundy ES 50/K-6
HC 38 Box 275, 702-872-5438
Katy Christensen, prin. Fax 872-0510

North Las Vegas, Clark, Pop. 176,635
Clark County SD
Supt. — See Las Vegas
Antonello ES 800/K-5
1101 W Tropical Pkwy 89031 702-799-8380
Kody Barto, prin. Fax 799-8355

Bridger MS 1,400/6-8
2505 N Bruce St 89030 702-799-7185
Deanna Kowal, prin. Fax 799-7074
Bruner ES 800/K-5
4289 Allen Ln 89032 702-799-0620
Catherine Conger, prin. Fax 799-0610
Cahlan ES 900/K-5
2801 Fort Sumter Dr 89030 702-799-7103
Wanda Renfrow, prin. Fax 799-0406
Cozine ES 900/K-5
5335 Coleman St 89031 702-799-0690
Samuel Rado, prin. Fax 799-0665
Craig ES 900/K-5
2637 E Gowan Rd 89030 702-799-4910
James Sesto, prin. Fax 799-4942
Cram MS 1,500/6-8
1900 W Deer Springs Way 89084 702-799-7020
Lori Sarabyn, prin. Fax 799-8346
Dickens ES 700/K-5
5550 Milan Peak St, 702-799-3878
Barbara Reininger, prin. Fax 799-3871
Elizondo ES 900/K-5
4865 Goldfield St 89031 702-799-1730
Alyson Jones, prin. Fax 799-1722
Findlay MS 1,400/6-8
333 W Tropical Pkwy 89031 702-799-3160
Ken Sobaszek, prin. Fax 799-3169
Fitzgerald ES 500/K-5
2651 Revere St 89030 702-799-0600
Laure Forsberg, prin. Fax 799-7045
Gilbert ES 400/K-5
2101 W Cartier Ave 89032 702-799-4730
Sharon Brewer, prin. Fax 799-4728
Goynes ES 1,100/K-5
3409 W Deer Springs Way 89084 702-799-1770
Jefferey Hybarger, prin. Fax 799-1721
Guy ES 800/K-5
4028 W La Madre Way 89031 702-799-3150
Diane Lewis, prin. Fax 799-3156
Hayden ES 1,000/K-5
150 W Rome Blvd 89084 702-799-3870
Ivy Burns, prin. Fax 799-3877
Herron ES 900/K-5
2421 Kenneth Rd 89030 702-799-7123
Kelly Sturdy, prin. Fax 799-8337
Johnston MS 1,400/6-8
5855 Lawrence St, 702-799-7001
Lisa Rustand, prin. Fax 799-7010
Lincoln ES 800/K-5
3010 Berg St 89030 702-799-7133
Keith France, prin. Fax 799-1724
Mackey ES 500/K-5
2726 Englestad St 89030 702-799-7139
Kemala Conley-Washington, prin. Fax 799-7132
Martinez ES 700/PK-5
350 Judson Ave 89030 702-799-3800
Felicia Kadlub, prin. Fax 799-3804
McCall ES 500/K-5
800 E Carey Ave 89030 702-799-7149
Maria Chairez, prin. Fax 799-7043
Perkins ES 600/K-5
3700 Shadow Tree St 89032 702-799-1805
Holly Jaacks, prin. Fax 799-1814
Priest ES 900/K-5
4150 Fuselier Dr 89032 702-799-6200
Linda Griffith, prin. Fax 799-4787
Scott ES K-5
5700 N Bruce St, 702-799-1766
Sharon Popolo, prin. Fax 799-1769
Sedway MS 1,500/6-8
3465 Engelstad St 89032 702-799-3880
Stanley Allen, prin. Fax 799-1785
Simmons ES 1,000/K-5
2328 Silver Clouds Dr 89031 702-799-1891
Christine Prosen, prin. Fax 799-1812
Smith MS 1,100/6-8
1301 E Tonopah Ave 89030 702-799-7080
Christine Ahrens, prin. Fax 799-7195
Squires ES 800/K-5
1312 E Tonopah Ave 89030 702-799-7169
Marcie McDonald, prin. Fax 799-7109
Swainston MS 1,500/6-8
3500 W Gilmore Ave 89032 702-799-4860
Lori Desiderato, prin. Fax 799-4806
Tartan ES 1,500/K-5
3030 E Tropical Pkwy, 702-799-4701
Katharine Braegger, prin. Fax 799-4707
Watson ES 800/K-5
5845 N Commerce St 89031 702-799-7040
Jennifer Newton, prin. Fax 799-7028
Wilhelm ES 1,100/K-5
609 W Alexander Rd 89032 702-799-1750
Chelsea Gibson, prin. Fax 799-1756
Williams ES 900/K-5
3000 E Tonopah Ave 89030 702-799-7179
Kristiena Rodeles, prin. Fax 799-8341
Wolfe ES 700/K-5
4027 W Washburn Rd 89031 702-799-1860
Sylvia Glass, prin. Fax 799-1869

St. Christopher S 200/K-8
1840 N Bruce St 89030 702-657-8008
Paul Mertzman, prin. Fax 642-2461
University Baptist Academy 100/K-12
3770 W Washburn Rd 89031 702-732-3385
Jorge Sanchez, contact Fax 734-0747

Orovada, Humboldt
Humboldt County SD
Supt. — See Winnemucca
Kings River S 50/K-8
134 Kings River Rd 89425 775-859-0352
Fax 859-0352
Orovada S 50/K-8
PO Box 85 89425 775-272-3333

Overton, Clark
Clark County SD
Supt. — See Las Vegas
Lyon MS 400/6-8
179 S Anderson St 89040 702-397-8610
Roderick Adams, prin. Fax 397-2754

Owyhee, Elko, Pop. 908
Elko County SD
Supt. — See Elko
Owyhee S 100/K-12
PO Box 100 89832 775-757-3400
Teola Blossom, prin. Fax 757-3663

Pahrump, Nye, Pop. 7,424
Nye County SD
Supt. — See Tonopah
Clarke MS 1,200/6-8
4201 N Blagg Rd 89060 775-727-5546
Jeff Skelton, prin. Fax 727-7104
Floyd ES PK-5
6181 Jane Ave 89061 775-751-4889
Holly Lepisto, prin. Fax 751-5094
Hafen ES 600/PK-5
7120 Hafen Ranch Rd 89061 775-751-4688
Terry Owens, prin. Fax 751-4686
Johnson ES 600/PK-5
900 Jack Rabbit St 89048 775-727-6619
DonaLee Descamps, prin. Fax 727-7885
Manse ES 500/PK-5
1020 E Wilson Rd 89048 775-727-5252
Evangeline Visser, prin. Fax 727-1526
Mt. Charleston ES 600/PK-5
1521 Idaho St 89048 775-727-7892
Timothy Wombaker, prin. Fax 727-7894

Community Christian Academy 100/K-8
PO Box 280 89041 775-751-9777
Renee Bell, admin. Fax 727-7548
New Hope Christian Academy 100/PK-12
781 West St 89048 775-751-1867
Julie Schmidt, admin. Fax 751-3387

Panaca, Lincoln
Lincoln County SD 1,100/K-12
PO Box 118 89042 775-728-4471
Clark Hardy, supt. Fax 728-4435
www.lincoln.k12.nv.us
Meadow Valley MS 100/7-8
PO Box 567 89042 775-728-4655
Marty Soderborg, prin. Fax 728-4302
Panaca ES 100/K-6
PO Box 307 89042 775-728-4446
Pete Peterson, prin. Fax 728-4470
Other Schools – See Alamo, Caliente, Pioche

Paradise Valley, See Paradise
Humboldt County SD
Supt. — See Winnemucca
Paradise Valley S 50/K-8
PO Box 33 89426 775-578-3382
Fax 578-3385

Pioche, Lincoln
Lincoln County SD
Supt. — See Panaca
Pioche ES 100/K-6
PO Box 30 89043 775-962-5832
Pete Peterson, prin. Fax 962-5257

Reno, Washoe, Pop. 203,550
Washoe County SD 59,700/K-12
PO Box 30425 89520 775-348-0200
Paul Dugan, supt. Fax 348-0304
www.washoe.k12.nv.us
Anderson ES 500/K-6
1055 Berrum Ln 89509 775-689-2500
Tom Wortman, prin. Fax 689-2502
Beck ES 500/K-6
1900 Sharon Way 89509 775-689-2520
Kristen Brown, prin. Fax 689-2598
Billinghurst MS 700/7-8
6685 Chesterfield Ln 89523 775-746-5870
Ken Cervantes, prin. Fax 746-5875
Booth ES 500/K-6
1450 Stewart St 89502 775-333-5140
Stacey Ting-Senini, prin. Fax 333-6053
Brown ES 800/K-6
13815 Spelling Ct, 775-851-5600
MaryEllen Arrascada, prin. Fax 851-5605
Cannan ES 600/K-6
2450 Cannan St 89512 775-353-5750
KayAnn Pilling, prin. Fax 353-5752
Caughlin Ranch ES 500/K-6
4885 Village Green Pkwy, 775-689-2600
Kelly Keane, prin. Fax 689-2535
Clayton MS 700/7-8
1295 Wyoming Ave 89503 775-746-5860
Carol Voss, prin. Fax 746-5864
Cold Springs MS 6-8
18235 Cody Ct, 775-677-5433
Roberta Duval, prin. Fax 677-5439
Corbett ES 400/K-6
1901 Villanova Dr 89502 775-333-5180
Fax 333-5184
Desert Heights ES 500/K-6
13948 Mount Bismark St 89506 775-677-5444
Dr. Mavis Leathley, prin. Fax 677-5449
Dodson ES 500/K-6
4355 Houston Dr 89502 775-689-2530
Don McHenry, prin. Fax 689-2531
Donner Springs ES 700/K-6
5125 Escuela Way 89502 775-689-2626
June Gronert, prin. Fax 689-2628
Double Diamond ES 800/K-6
1200 S Meadows Pkwy, 775-850-6212
Kristell Moller, prin. Fax 850-6215
Duncan ES 500/K-6
1200 Montello St 89512 775-333-5190
Mike Paul, prin. Fax 333-5193
Elmcrest ES 400/K-6
855 McDonald Dr 89503 775-746-5850
John Sutherland, prin. Fax 746-5852
Gomes ES 600/K-6
3870 Limkin St, 775-677-5440
Lisa Hansen, prin. Fax 677-5435
Gomm ES 500/K-6
4000 Mayberry Dr, 775-333-5000
Dave Christiansen, prin. Fax 333-5002
Hidden Valley ES 500/K-6
2115 Alphabet Dr 89502 775-857-3150
Bob LeVitt, prin. Fax 857-3153
Huffaker ES 600/K-6
980 Wheatland Rd 89511 775-689-2510
Ruth Williams, prin. Fax 689-2623
Hunsburger ES 700/K-6
2505 Crossbow Ct 89511 775-851-7095
Sally Scott, prin. Fax 850-6204
Hunter Lake ES 400/K-6
909 Hunter Lake Dr 89509 775-333-5040
Neil Schott, prin. Fax 333-5098
Lemmon Valley ES 700/K-6
255 W Patrician Dr 89506 775-677-5460
Kara Nelson, prin. Fax 677-5462
Lenz ES 500/K-6
2500 Homeland Dr 89511 775-851-5620
Teri Vaughan, prin. Fax 851-7080
Loder ES 600/K-6
600 Apple St 89502 775-689-2540
Debra Duty-Deery, prin. Fax 689-2594
Mathews ES 800/K-6
2750 Elementary Dr 89512 775-353-5950
Bob Deery, prin. Fax 353-5954
Melton ES 600/K-6
6575 Archimedes Ln 89523 775-746-7440
Mary Slagle, prin. Fax 746-7443
Mount Rose ES 300/K-6
915 Lander St 89509 775-333-5030
Karen Wallis, prin. Fax 333-5032
O'Brien MS 800/7-8
10500 Stead Blvd 89506 775-677-5420
Scott Grange, prin. Fax 677-5423
Peavine ES 400/K-6
1601 Grandview Ave 89503 775-746-5840
Doug Whitener, prin. Fax 746-5841
Pine MS 900/7-8
4800 Neil Rd 89502 775-689-2550
Brad Boudreau, prin. Fax 689-2539
Pleasant Valley ES 400/K-6
405 Surrey Dr, 775-849-0255
Carole Worthen, prin. Fax 849-2761
Sierra Vista ES 400/K-6
2001 Soaring Eagle Dr 89512 775-333-5080
Jonna AuCoin, prin. Fax 333-5008
Silver Lake ES 600/K-6
8719 Red Baron Blvd 89506 775-677-5400
Loretta Thomas, prin. Fax 677-5406
Smith ES 700/K-6
1070 Beckwourth Dr 89506 775-677-5410
Sanda Aird, prin. Fax 677-5413
Smithridge ES 600/K-6
4801 Neil Rd 89502 775-689-2560
Sheila Meibergen, prin. Fax 689-2507
Stead ES 800/K-6
10580 Stead Blvd 89506 775-677-5480
Don Angotti, prin. Fax 677-5483
Swope MS 800/7-8
901 Keele Dr 89509 775-333-5330
George Brown, prin. Fax 333-5083
Towles ES 400/K-6
2800 Kings Row 89503 775-746-5820
Edwin Heywood, prin. Fax 746-5822
Traner MS 500/7-8
1700 Carville Dr 89512 775-333-5130
Lauren Ford, prin. Fax 333-5135
Vaughn MS 700/7-8
1200 Bresson Ave 89502 775-333-5160
Dr. Ginny Knowles, prin. Fax 333-5118
Veterans Memorial ES 500/K-6
1200 Locust St 89502 775-333-5090
Gloria Geil, prin. Fax 333-5092
Warner ES 500/K-6
3075 Heights Dr 89503 775-746-5830
Larry Kuper, prin. Fax 746-5832
Westergard ES 600/K-6
1785 Ambassador Dr 89523 775-746-5800
William Chronister, prin. Fax 746-5803
Winnemucca ES 500/K-6
1349 Backer Way 89523 775-746-5810
Dr. Susan Frank, prin. Fax 746-5813
Other Schools – See Gerlach, Incline Village, Sparks, Sun Valley, Verdi, Wadsworth

---

Brookfield S 200/PK-8
6800 S McCarran Blvd 89509 775-825-0257
Katie Osgood, admin. Fax 825-3463
Church Academy 50/K-12
1205 N McCarran Blvd 89512 775-329-5848
Ron Poe, prin. Fax 329-3360
Little Flower S 300/K-8
1300 Casazza Dr 89502 775-323-2931
Karen Barreras, prin. Fax 323-2997
Mountain View Montessori S 200/PK-9
565 Zolezzi Ln 89511 775-852-6162
Mary Levy, dir. Fax 852-6553
Our Lady of the Snows S 300/K-8
1125 Lander St 89509 775-322-2773
Tim Fuetsch, prin. Fax 322-0827
Reno Christian Academy 100/K-9
PO Box 70723 89570 775-331-0909
Kim Troop, admin. Fax 331-5358
St. Albert the Great S 300/K-8
1255 Saint Alberts Dr 89503 775-747-3392
Patrick Perry, prin. Fax 747-6296

Silver State Adventist S 50/K-10
PO Box 11950 89510 775-322-0714

Round Mountain, Nye
Nye County SD
Supt. — See Tonopah
Round Mountain ES 200/K-5
PO Box 1429 89045 775-377-2236
Selway Mulkey, prin. Fax 377-2354

Ruby Valley, Elko, Pop. 37
Elko County SD
Supt. — See Elko
Ruby Valley S 50/1-8
HC 60 Box 620 89833 775-779-2289
Leslie Lotspeich, prin. Fax 779-2289

Sandy Valley, Clark
Clark County SD
Supt. — See Las Vegas
Sandy Valley ES 100/K-5
HC 31 Box 111 89019 702-723-5344
Mark Jones, prin. Fax 723-5251
Sandy Valley MS 100/6-8
HC 31 Box 111 89019 702-723-1800
Mark Jones, prin. Fax 723-1802

Schurz, Mineral, Pop. 617
Mineral County SD
Supt. — See Hawthorne
Schurz S 100/K-8
PO Box 70 89427 775-773-2323
Dr. Vivian Powell, prin. Fax 773-2275

Searchlight, Clark
Clark County SD
Supt. — See Las Vegas
Reid ES 50/K-5
300 Michael Wendell Way 89046 702-297-1224
Louise Varvar, prin. Fax 297-1767

Silverpeak, Esmeralda
Esmeralda County SD
Supt. — See Goldfield
Silverpeak S 50/K-8
PO Box 218 89047 775-937-2261
Fax 937-2308

Silver Springs, Lyon, Pop. 2,253
Lyon County SD
Supt. — See Yerington
Silver Springs ES 400/K-4
3900 W Spruce Ave 89429 775-577-5060
Pete Chapin, prin. Fax 577-5064
Silver Stage MS 400/5-8
3800 W Spruce Ave 89429 775-577-5050
Rob Jacobson, prin. Fax 577-5053

Smith, Lyon, Pop. 1,033
Lyon County SD
Supt. — See Yerington
Smith Valley ES 100/K-6
20 Day Ln 89430 775-465-2332
Keri Pommerening, prin. Fax 465-2681

Sparks, Washoe, Pop. 82,051
Storey County SD
Supt. — See Virginia City
Hillside ES 100/K-6
1250 Peri Ranch Rd 89434 775-342-0400
Marta Spandau, prin. Fax 342-0785

Washoe County SD
Supt. — See Reno
Beasley ES 700/K-6
2100 Canyon Pkwy 89436 775-626-5250
Bryan Myers, prin. Fax 626-5254
Diedrichsen ES 400/K-6
1735 Del Rosa Way 89434 775-353-5730
Dina Ciaramella, prin. Fax 353-5719
Dilworth MS 600/7-8
255 Prater Way 89431 775-353-5740
Bruce Meissner, prin. Fax 353-5584
Drake ES 400/K-6
2755 4th St 89431 775-353-5510
Jason Childs, prin. Fax 353-5512
Dunn ES 600/K-6
1135 O Callaghan Dr 89434 775-353-5520
Marla Mentaberry, prin. Fax 353-5522
Greenbrae ES 400/K-6
1840 4th St 89431 775-353-5530
Dr. Rose Kane, prin. Fax 353-5596
Hall ES K-6
185 Shelby Dr 89436 775-425-7755
Jeanne Ohl, prin. Fax 425-7756
Juniper ES 500/K-6
225 Queen Way 89431 775-353-5540
Bill Burt, prin. Fax 353-5759
Lincoln Park ES 500/K-6
201 Lincoln Way 89431 775-353-5570
Rosemary Pressler, prin. Fax 353-5797
Maxwell ES 400/K-6
2300 Rock Blvd 89431 775-353-5580
Denise Dufrene, prin. Fax 353-5763
Mendive MS 1,000/7-8
1900 Whitewood Dr 89434 775-353-5990
Mary Green, prin. Fax 353-5994
Mitchell ES 400/K-6
1216 Prater Way 89431 775-353-5590
Eileen Rountree, prin. Fax 353-5739
Moss ES 600/K-6
2200 Primio Way 89434 775-353-5507
Kristen McNeill, prin. Fax 353-5905
Risley ES 600/K-6
1900 Sullivan Ln 89431 775-353-5760
Muriel Dickey, prin. Fax 353-5762
Sepulveda ES K-6
5075 Ion Dr 89436 775-626-5257
Kathleen Diesner, prin. Fax 626-5258
Shaw MS 1,000/7-8
600 Eagle Canyon Dr, 775-425-7777
Dave Fullenwider, prin. Fax 425-7779
Smith ES 400/K-6
1925 F St 89431 775-353-5720
Richard Swanberg, prin. Fax 353-5927
Spanish Springs ES 600/K-6
100 Marilyn Mae Dr, 775-425-7710
Debbie O'Gorman, prin. Fax 425-7707
Sparks MS 700/7-8
2275 18th St 89431 775-353-5770
Andrew Yoxsimer, prin. Fax 353-5585
Sun Valley ES 600/K-6
5490 Leon Dr 89433 775-674-4420
Alyson Kendrick, prin. Fax 674-4423
Taylor ES 700/K-6
252 Egyptian Dr, 775-425-7700
Alan Reeder, prin. Fax 425-7704
Van Gorder ES 800/K-6
7650 Campello Dr 89436 775-425-7722
Troy Parks, prin. Fax 425-7725
Whitehead ES 400/K-6
3570 Waterfall Dr 89434 775-626-5200
Nancy Maldonado, prin. Fax 626-5202

Excel Christian S 100/K-12
2285 Oddie Blvd 89431 775-356-9995
Bonnie Krupa, admin. Fax 356-9527
Lamplight Christian S 100/K-8
780 E Lincoln Way 89434 775-329-7775
Paul Jachimiak, admin. Fax 530-9645
Legacy Christian ES 200/K-5
6255 Pyramid Way 89436 775-424-1777
Robert Morgan, prin. Fax 424-6670
Legacy Christian MS 100/6-8
1100 12th St 89431 775-358-1112
Robert Morgan, admin. Fax 358-5030

Spring Creek, Elko, Pop. 5,866
Elko County SD
Supt. — See Elko
Mound Valley S 50/1-8
HC 30 Box 348 89815 775-744-4382
Steven Cook, prin.
Sage ES 500/K-5
208 Boyd Kennedy Rd 89815 775-738-4711
Karen Agee, prin. Fax 753-4154
Spring Creek ES 600/K-5
7 Licht Pkwy 89815 775-753-6881
George Ozuna, prin. Fax 753-1074
Spring Creek MS 700/6-8
14650 Lamoille Hwy 89815 775-777-1688
Karen Branzell, prin. Fax 777-1738

Spring Creek Christian Academy 50/K-12
475 Diamondback Dr 89815 775-753-6700
Patrick Herman, prin. Fax 753-6898

Sun Valley, Washoe, Pop. 11,391
Washoe County SD
Supt. — See Reno
Allen ES 600/K-6
5155 McGuffey Rd 89433 775-674-4430
Laura Petersen, prin. Fax 677-4433
Bennett ES 500/K-6
5900 Sidehill Dr 89433 775-674-4444
Michael Henry, prin. Fax 674-4451
Palmer ES 600/K-6
5890 Klondike Dr 89433 775-674-4400
Dorothy Parks, prin. Fax 674-4417

Tonopah, Nye, Pop. 3,616
Nye County SD 6,200/PK-12
PO Box 113 89049 775-482-6258
Dr. William Roberts, supt. Fax 482-8573
www.nye.k12.nv.us
Silver Rim ES 100/K-2
PO Box 591 89049 775-482-9713
Gary Flood, prin. Fax 482-3375
Tonopah S 100/3-8
PO Box 1749 89049 775-482-6644
Gary Flood, prin. Fax 482-5717
Other Schools – See Amargosa Valley, Beatty, Duckwater, Gabbs, Pahrump, Round Mountain

Tuscarora, Elko
Elko County SD
Supt. — See Elko
Independence Valley S 50/1-8
HC 32 Box 110 89834 775-756-6508
Wendy Fluckey, prin. Fax 756-5598
Petan Ranch S 50/1-8
HC32 Box 450 89834 775-756-5562
Teola Blossom, prin. Fax 756-5589

Verdi, Washoe
Washoe County SD
Supt. — See Reno
Verdi ES 200/K-6
PO Box 309 89439 775-345-8100
Trish Gerbo, prin. Fax 345-7277

Virginia City, Storey
Storey County SD 500/K-12
PO Box C 89440 775-847-0983
Dr. Robert Slaby, supt. Fax 847-0989
www.storey.k12.nv.us
Gallagher ES 100/K-5
PO Box C 89440 775-847-0977
Michele Van Voorst, prin. Fax 847-0938
Virginia City MS 100/6-8
PO Box C 89440 775-847-0980
Todd Hess, prin. Fax 847-0913
Other Schools – See Sparks

Wadsworth, Washoe, Pop. 640
Washoe County SD
Supt. — See Reno
Natchez ES 100/K-6
PO Box 130 89442 775-351-1902
Rick Taylor, prin. Fax 575-1888

Wells, Elko, Pop. 1,295
Elko County SD
Supt. — See Elko
Wells S 100/K-12
PO Box 338 89835 775-752-3837
Leslie Lotspeich, prin. Fax 752-2470

West Wendover, Elko, Pop. 4,966
Elko County SD
Supt. — See Elko
West Wendover ES 700/K-6
PO Box 2400 89883 775-664-3100
Dawn Hagness, prin. Fax 664-2343

Winnemucca, Humboldt, Pop. 7,726
Humboldt County SD 3,300/K-12
310 E 4th St 89445 775-623-8100
Mike Bumgartner, supt. Fax 623-8102
www.humboldt.k12.nv.us
French Ford MS 500/5-6
5495 Palisade Dr 89445 775-623-8200
Robert Lindsay, prin. Fax 623-8210
Grass Valley ES 400/K-4
6465 Grass Valley Rd 89445 775-623-8150
Tim Conners, prin. Fax 623-8152
Sonoma Heights ES 500/K-4
1500 Melarkey St 89445 775-623-8165
Noel Morton, prin. Fax 623-8194
Winnemucca ES 300/K-4
522 Lay St 89445 775-623-8160
Dorene Kitras, prin. Fax 623-8176
Winnemucca JHS 500/7-8
451 Reinhart St 89445 775-623-8120
Ray Garrison, prin. Fax 623-8208
Other Schools – See Denio, Mc Dermitt, Orovada, Paradise Valley

Yerington, Lyon, Pop. 3,486
Lyon County SD 8,500/K-12
25 E Goldfield Ave 89447 775-463-6800
Caroline McIntosh, supt. Fax 463-6808
lyon.k12.nv.us
Yerington ES 500/K-4
112 N California St 89447 775-463-6844
Allan Ross, prin. Fax 463-6850
Yerington IS 500/5-8
215 Pearl St 89447 775-463-6833
Sean Moyle, prin. Fax 463-6840
Other Schools – See Dayton, Fernley, Silver Springs, Smith

Zephyr Cove, Douglas, Pop. 1,434
Douglas County SD
Supt. — See Minden
Zephyr Cove ES 200/K-6
PO Box 7 89448 775-588-4574
Nancy Cauley, prin. Fax 588-4572

NEW HAMPSHIRE

NEW HAMPSHIRE DEPT. OF EDUCATION
101 Pleasant St, Concord 03301-3852
Telephone 603-271-3494
Fax 603-271-1953
Website http://www.ed.state.nh.us

Commissioner of Education Virginia Barry

NEW HAMPSHIRE BOARD OF EDUCATION
101 Pleasant St, Concord 03301-3852

Chairperson John Lyons

SCHOOL ADMINISTRATIVE UNITS (SAU)

SAU 1
Dr. Richard Bergeron, supt. 603-924-3336
106 Hancock Rd Fax 924-6707
Peterborough 03458
www.conval.edu/

SAU 2
Dr. Phillip McCormack, supt. 603-279-7947
103 Main St Ste 2, Meredith 03253 Fax 279-3044
www.sau2.k12.nh.us/

SAU 3
John Moulis, supt. 603-752-6500
183 Hillside Ave, Berlin 03570 Fax 752-2528
www.sau3.org/

SAU 4
Marie Ross, supt. 603-744-5555
20 N Main St, Bristol 03222 Fax 744-6659
www.newfound.k12.nh.us

SAU 5
Howard Colter, supt. 603-868-5100
36 Coe Dr, Durham 03824 Fax 868-6668
www.orcsd.org

SAU 6
Jacqueline Guillette, supt. 603-543-4200
165 Broad St, Claremont 03743 Fax 543-4244
www.sau6.k12.nh.us/

SAU 7
Robert Mills, supt. 603-237-5571
21 Academy St, Colebrook 03576 Fax 237-5126

SAU 8
Dr. Christine Rath, supt. 603-225-0811
16 Rumford St, Concord 03301 Fax 226-2187
www.concord.k12.nh.us

SAU 9
Dr. Carl Nelson, supt. 603-447-8368
176A Main St, Conway 03818 Fax 447-8497

SAU 10
Mary Ellen Hannon, supt. 603-432-1210
18 S Main St, Derry 03038 Fax 432-1264
www.derry.k12.nh.us

SAU 11
Dr. John O'Connor, supt. 603-516-6800
61 Locust St Ste 409, Dover 03820 Fax 516-6809
www.dover.k12.nh.us/

SAU 12
Dr. Nathan Greenberg, supt. 603-432-6920
268 Mammoth Rd Fax 425-1049
Londonderry 03053

SAU 13
Dr. Gwen Poirer, supt. 603-539-2610
626 Plains Rd, Silver Lake 03875 Fax 539-9064

SAU 14
Barbara Munsey, supt. 603-679-5402
213 Main St, Epping 03042 Fax 679-1237

SAU 15
Dr. Charles Littlefield, supt. 603-622-3731
90 Farmer Rd, Hooksett 03106 Fax 669-4352

SAU 16
Michael Morgan, supt. 603-775-8653
30 Linden St, Exeter 03833 Fax 775-8673
www.sau16.org/

SAU 17
Dr. Keith Pfeifer, supt. 603-642-3688
178 Main St, Kingston 03848 Fax 642-7885

SAU 18
Jo Ellen Divoll, supt. 603-934-3108
119 Central St, Franklin 03235 Fax 934-3462

SAU 19
Stacy Buckley, supt. 603-497-4818
11 School St, Goffstown 03045 Fax 497-8425
www.goffstown.k12.nh.us

SAU 20
Paul Bousquet, supt. 603-466-3632
123 Main St, Gorham 03581 Fax 466-3870
www.sau20.org/

SAU 21
James Gaylord, supt. 603-926-8992
2 Alumni Dr, Hampton 03842 Fax 926-5157
www.sau21.k12.nh.us

SAU 23
Bruce Labs, supt. 603-787-2113
2975 Dartmouth College Hwy Fax 787-2118
North Haverhill 03774
www.sau23.k12.nh.us

SAU 24
Douglas White, supt. 603-428-3269
41 Liberty Hill Rd Bldg 5 Fax 428-3850
Henniker 03242

SAU 25
Timothy Mayes, supt. 603-472-3755
103 County Rd, Bedford 03110 Fax 472-2567
www.sau25.net/

SAU 26
Marjorie Chiafery, supt. 603-424-6200
36 McElwain St, Merrimack 03054 Fax 424-6229
www.merrimack.k12.nh.us

SAU 27
Dr. Elaine Cutler, supt. 603-578-3570
1 Highlander Ct, Litchfield 03052 Fax 578-1267

SAU 28
Dr. Frank Bass, supt. 603-425-1976
PO Box 510, Windham 03087 Fax 425-1719

SAU 29
Wayne Woolridge, supt. 603-357-9002
34 West St, Keene 03431 Fax 357-9012
www.sau29.k12.nh.us/

SAU 30
Robert Champlin, supt. 603-524-5710
PO Box 309, Laconia 03247 Fax 528-8442

SAU 31
Mark LaRoach, supt. 603-659-5020
186A Main St, Newmarket 03857 Fax 659-5022

SAU 32
Noelle Vitt, supt. 603-469-3442
92 Bonner Rd, Meriden 03770 Fax 469-3985

SAU 33
Dr. Jean Richards, supt. 603-895-4299
43 Harriman Hill Rd Fax 895-0147
Raymond 03077
www.raymond.k12.nh.us

SAU 34
Dr. Barbara Baker, supt. 603-464-4466
PO Box 2190, Deering 03244 Fax 464-4053
www.hdsd.org

SAU 35
Dr. Robert Patterson, supt. 603-444-3925
262 Cottage St Ste 230 Fax 444-6299
Littleton 03561
www.sau35.k12.nh.us

SAU 36
Dr. Louis Lafasciano, supt. 603-837-9363
14 King Sq, Whitefield 03598 Fax 837-2326
www.sau36.org

SAU 37
Dr. Thomas Brennan, supt. 603-624-6300
286 Commercial St Fax 624-6337
Manchester 03101
www.mansd.org

SAU 38
Dr. Kenneth Dassau, supt. 603-352-6955
600 Old Homestead Hwy Fax 358-6708
East Swanzey 03446
www.mrsd.org/

SAU 39
Dr. Mary Jennings, supt. 603-673-2690
PO Box 849, Amherst 03031 Fax 672-1786
www.sprise.com/

SAU 40
Robert Suprenant, supt. 603-673-2202
100 West St, Milford 03055 Fax 673-2237

SAU 41
Susan Hodgdon, supt. 603-465-7118
PO Box 1588, Hollis 03049 Fax 465-3933
www.sau41.k12.nh.us

SAU 42
Dr. Christopher Hottel, supt. 603-594-4300
PO Box 687, Nashua 03061 Fax 594-4350
www.nashua.edu

SAU 43
Dr. Marilyn Brannigan, supt. 603-863-3540
9 Depot St Ste 2, Newport 03773 Fax 863-5368

SAU 44
Dr. Michael Ludwell, supt. 603-942-1290
23 Mountain Ave Unit A Fax 942-1295
Northwood 03261

SAU 45
Michael Lancor, supt., PO Box 419 603-476-5247
Moultonborough 03254 Fax 476-8009
www.moultonborough.k12.nh.us

SAU 46
Dr. Michael Martin, supt. 603-753-6561
105 Community Dr Fax 753-6023
Penacook 03303

SAU 47
James O'Neill, supt. 603-532-8100
81 Fitzgerald Dr Unit 2 Fax 532-8165
Jaffrey 03452
www.sau47.k12.nh.us

SAU 48
Mark Halloran, supt. 603-536-1254
47 Old Ward Bridge Rd Fax 536-3545
Plymouth 03264
www.sau48.k12.nh.us/

SAU 49
John Robertson, supt. 603-569-1658
PO Box 190, Wolfeboro Falls 03896 Fax 569-6983
www.govwentworth.k12.nh.us

SAU 50
Dr. George Cushing, supt. 603-422-9572
48 Post Rd, Greenland 03840 Fax 422-9575
www.sau50.org

SAU 51
Dr. John Freeman, supt. 603-435-5526
175 Barnstead Rd Unit 3 Fax 435-5331
Pittsfield 03263
www.barnstead.k12.nh.us

SAU 52
Dr. Robert Lister, supt. 603-431-5080
50 Clough Dr, Portsmouth 03801 Fax 431-6753
www.cityofportsmouth.com/school/

SAU 53
Peter Warburton, supt. 603-485-5188
267 Pembroke St, Pembroke 03275 Fax 485-9529
www.sau53.org

SAU 54
Michael Hopkins, supt. 603-332-3678
150 Wakefield St Ste 8 Fax 335-7367
Rochester 03867
www.rochesterschools.com

SAU 55
Richard LaSalle, supt. 603-382-6119
30 Greenough Rd, Plaistow 03865 Fax 382-3334

SAU 56
Karen Soule, supt. 603-692-4450
51 W High St, Somersworth 03878 Fax 692-9100

SAU 57
Michael Dalahanty, supt. 603-893-7040
38 Geremonty Dr, Salem 03079 Fax 893-7080

SAU 58
Carl Ladd, supt. 603-636-1437
15 Preble St, Groveton 03582 Fax 636-6102
sau58.k12.nh.us

SAU 59
Dr. Tammy Davis, supt. 603-286-4116
433 W Main St, Northfield 03276 Fax 286-7402
www.winnisquam.k12.nh.us/Sau/index.htm

SAU 60
Dr. Debra Livingston, supt. 603-826-7756
PO Box 600, Charlestown 03603 Fax 826-4430

SAU 61
Michelle Langa, supt. 603-755-2627
356 Main St, Farmington 03835 Fax 755-2060

SAU 62
Barbara Tremblay, supt. 603-632-5563
PO Box 789, Enfield 03748 Fax 632-4181
mascoma.k12.nh.us

SAU 63
Dr. Leo Corriveau, supt. 603-878-8100
PO Box 1149, Wilton 03086 Fax 654-6691

SAU 64
William Lander, supt. 603-473-2326
39 Main St, Union 03887 Fax 473-2218
www.sau64.k12.nh.us

SAU 65
Jerome Frew, supt. 603-526-2051
169 Main St, New London 03257 Fax 526-2145

SAU 66
Dr. Brian Blake, supt. 603-746-5186
204 Maple St, Contoocook 03229 Fax 746-5714

SAU 67
Dr. Dean Cascadden, supt. 603-224-4728
32 White Rock Hill Rd, Bow 03304 Fax 224-4111

SAU 68
Michael Cosgriff, supt. 603-745-2051
PO Box 846, Lincoln 03251 Fax 745-2351
www.lin-wood.k12.nh.us

SAU 70
Wayne Gersen, supt. 603-643-6050
41 Lebanon St Ste 2 Fax 643-3073
Hanover 03755
www.sau70.org/

SAU 71
Dr. John Handfield, supt. 603-863-2420
29 School Rd, Lempster 03605 Fax 863-2451
SAU 72
Kathleen Holt, supt. 603-875-7890
252 Suncook Valley Rd Fax 875-0391
Alton 03809
www.alton.k12.nh.us
SAU 73
Dr. Paul DeMinico, supt. 603-527-9215
47 Cherry Valley Rd, Gilford 03249 Fax 527-9216
SAU 74
Dr. Henry Aliberti, supt. 603-664-2715
41 Province Ln, Barrington 03825 Fax 664-2609
www.barrington.k12.nh.us
SAU 75
Margaret Sullivan, supt. 603-863-9689
PO Box 287, Grantham 03753 Fax 863-9684
SAU 76
Dr. Gordon Schnare, supt. 603-795-4431
PO Box 117, Lyme 03768 Fax 795-9407
SAU 77
Karen Stewart, admin. 603-638-2800
PO Box 130, Monroe 03771 Fax 638-2031
SAU 78
Gail Keiling, supt. 603-353-2170
PO Box 153, Orford 03777 Fax 353-2189

SAU 79
John Fauci, supt. 603-267-9097
PO Box 309, Gilmanton 03237 Fax 267-9498
SAU 80
W. Michael Cozort, supt. 603-267-9223
58 School St, Belmont 03220 Fax 267-9225
www.shaker.k12.nh.us
SAU 81
Philip Bell, supt. 603-886-1235
20 Library St, Hudson 03051 Fax 886-1236
SAU 82
Dr. Victor Petzy, supt. 603-887-3621
22 Murphy Dr, Chester 03036 Fax 887-4961
www.chesteracademy.org/
SAU 83
Normand Tanguay, supt. 603-895-6903
5 Hall Rd Unit 1, Fremont 03044 Fax 895-6905
SAU 84
Dorothy Danforth, supt. 603-444-5215
102 School St, Littleton 03561 Fax 444-3015
www.littletonschools.org/
SAU 85
Brendan Minnihan, supt. 603-763-4627
68 Main St, Sunapee 03782 Fax 763-4718
www.sunapee.k12.nh.us/

SAU 86
Dr. William Compton, supt. 603-435-1510
PO Box 250 Fax 435-1511
Center Barnstead 03225
SAU 88
Dr. Michael Harris, supt. 603-448-1634
84 Hanover St, Lebanon 03766 Fax 448-0602
www.lebanon.k12.nh.us
SAU 97
Amy Morin, supt. 603-356-5535
91 Samuel Hale Dr Fax 356-5535
Hales Location 03860
SAU 98
, Commisioners Office 603-246-3321
West Stewartstown 03597
SAU 201
David Smith, hdmstr. 603-942-5531
907 1st NH Tpke Fax 942-7537
Northwood 03261
www.coebrownacademy.com
SAU 202
Mary Anderson, hdmstr. 603-437-5200
5 Pinkerton St, Derry 03038 Fax 432-5328
www.pinkertonacademy.net
SAU 301
Paul Bartolomucci, supt. 603-875-3800
242 Suncook Valley Rd Fax 875-8200
Alton 03809
www.pmhschool.com

PUBLIC, PRIVATE AND CATHOLIC ELEMENTARY SCHOOLS

Acworth, Sullivan
Fall Mountain Regional SD
Supt. — See Charlestown
Acworth ES 50/1-4
PO Box 69 03601 603-835-2270
Gail Rowe, prin. Fax 835-6218

Allenstown, Merrimack
Allenstown SD
Supt. — See Pembroke
Allenstown ES 200/K-5
30 Main St 03275 603-485-9574
Theresa Kenney, prin. Fax 485-1805
Dupont MS 200/6-8
10 1/2 School St 03275 603-485-4474
Fax 485-1806

Alstead, Cheshire
Fall Mountain Regional SD
Supt. — See Charlestown
Alstead S 100/K-4
PO Box 670 03602 603-835-2482
Gail Rowe, prin. Fax 835-9096
Vilas MS 100/5-8
PO Box 670 03602 603-835-6351
Gail Rowe, prin. Fax 835-2052

Alton, Belknap
Alton SD 600/PK-8
252 Suncook Valley Rd 03809 603-875-7890
Kathleen Holt, supt. Fax 875-0391
www.alton.k12.nh.us
Alton Central S 600/PK-8
PO Box 910 03809 603-875-7500
Jean Kuras, prin. Fax 875-0380

Amherst, Hillsborough
Amherst SD 1,600/K-8
PO Box 849 03031 603-673-2690
Dr. Mary Jennings, supt. Fax 672-1786
www.sprise.com
Amherst MS 800/5-8
PO Box 966 03031 603-673-8944
Porter Dodge, prin. Fax 673-6774
Clark ES 300/K-1
PO Box 420 03031 603-673-2343
Gerry St. Amand, prin. Fax 673-5114
Wilkins ES 600/1-4
PO Box 420 03031 603-673-4411
Gerry St. Amand, prin. Fax 672-0968

Mont Vernon SD 200/K-6
PO Box 849 03031 603-673-2690
Dr. Mary Jennings, supt. Fax 672-1786
Other Schools – See Mont Vernon

Country Village Montessori S 50/PK-4
2 Overlook Dr 03031 603-672-3882
Claire Doody, dir.

Andover, Merrimack
Andover SD
Supt. — See Penacook
Andover S 300/K-8
PO Box 87 03216 603-735-5494
Jane Slayton, prin. Fax 735-6108

Antrim, Hillsborough, Pop. 1,325
Contoocook Valley SD
Supt. — See Peterborough
Antrim ES 200/PK-4
10 School St 03440 603-588-6371
Gib West, prin. Fax 588-6972
Great Brook MS 400/5-8
16 School St 03440 603-588-6630
G. Bruce West, prin. Fax 588-3207

Ashland, Grafton
Ashland SD
Supt. — See Meredith
Ashland S 200/K-8
16 Education Dr 03217 603-968-7622
William Tirone, prin. Fax 968-3167

Atkinson, Rockingham
Timberlane Regional SD
Supt. — See Plaistow
Atkinson Academy 500/PK-5
17 Academy Ave 03811 603-362-5521
Kathie Dayotis, prin. Fax 362-5842

Auburn, Rockingham
Auburn SD
Supt. — See Hooksett
Auburn Village S 600/1-8
11 Eaton Hill Rd 03032 603-483-2769
Anita Johnson, prin. Fax 483-5144

Barrington, Strafford
Barrington SD 1,000/PK-8
41 Province Ln 03825 603-664-2715
Dr. Henry Aliberti, supt. Fax 664-2609
www.barrington.k12.nh.us
Barrington ES 500/PK-4
347 Route 125 03825 603-664-2641
Mary Maxfield, prin. Fax 664-5271
Barrington MS 400/5-8
20 Haley Dr 03825 603-664-2127
Michael Tursi, prin. Fax 664-5739

Good Shepherd S 100/PK-12
37 Province Ln 03825 603-664-2742
Emily Meehan, hdmstr. Fax 664-7196

Bartlett, Carroll
Bartlett SD
Supt. — See Conway
Bartlett S 300/K-8
PO Box 396 03812 603-374-2331
Joseph Voci, prin. Fax 374-1941

Bath, Grafton
Bath SD
Supt. — See North Haverhill
Bath Village ES 100/K-6
PO Box 141 03740 603-747-2004
Michael Amsden, prin. Fax 747-3260

Bedford, Hillsborough
Bedford SD 2,000/PK-12
103 County Rd 03110 603-472-3755
Timothy Mayes, supt. Fax 472-2567
www.sau25.net/
Lurgio MS 7-8
47 Nashua Rd Unit A 03110 603-310-9100
Edward Joyce, prin. Fax 472-5090
McKelvie IS 300/5-6
108 Liberty Hill Rd 03110 603-472-3951
Michael Fournier, prin. Fax 472-4503
Memorial ES 500/PK-4
55 Old Bedford Rd 03110 603-627-1776
Pamela Ilg, prin. Fax 644-5122
Riddle Brook ES 600/K-4
230 New Boston Rd 03110 603-471-1082
Molly McCarthy, prin. Fax 472-7879
Woodbury ES 600/K-4
180 County Rd 03110 603-622-0431
Kenneth Williams, prin. Fax 644-5128

Belmont, Belknap
Shaker Regional SD 1,500/PK-12
58 School St 03220 603-267-9223
W. Michael Cozort, supt. Fax 267-9225
www.shaker.k12.nh.us
Belmont ES 400/PK-4
26 Best St 03220 603-267-6568
Emily Spear, prin. Fax 267-6136
Belmont MS 400/5-8
38 School St 03220 603-267-9220
Aaron Pope, prin. Fax 267-9221
Other Schools – See Canterbury

Berlin, Coos, Pop. 10,097
Berlin SD 1,300/K-12
183 Hillside Ave 03570 603-752-6500
Corinne Cascadden, supt. Fax 752-2528
www.sau3.org/
Berlin JHS 300/7-8
200 State St 03570 603-752-5311
Beverly Dupont, prin. Fax 752-8580
Brown ES 100/K-2
190 Norway St 03570 603-752-1471
Amy Huter, prin. Fax 752-8581
Hillside ES 300/3-6
183 Hillside Ave 03570 603-752-5328
Beverly Dupont, prin. Fax 752-2528

Bethlehem, Grafton
Bethlehem SD
Supt. — See Littleton
Bethlehem ES 200/K-6
2297 Main St 03574 603-869-5842
Susan Herzog, prin. Fax 869-2482

Profile SD
Supt. — See Littleton
Profile JHS 100/7-8
691 Profile Rd 03574 603-823-7411
Michael Kelley, prin. Fax 823-7490

Boscawen, Merrimack
Merrimack Valley SD
Supt. — See Concord
Boscawen ES 300/PK-5
1 Best Ave 03303 603-753-6512
Tracy Murch, prin. Fax 753-8140

Bow, Merrimack
Bow SD 1,800/PK-12
32 White Rock Hill Rd 03304 603-224-4728
Dr. Dean Cascadden, supt. Fax 224-4111
www.bownet.org
Bow ES 500/PK-4
22 Bow Center Rd 03304 603-225-3049
Deborah Gibbens, prin. Fax 228-2205
Bow Memorial MS 600/5-8
20 Bow Center Rd 03304 603-225-3212
Kirk Spofford, prin. Fax 228-2228

Bradford, Merrimack
Kearsarge Regional SD
Supt. — See New London
Kearsarge Regional ES - Bradford 200/K-5
PO Box 435 03221 603-938-5959
James Spadaro, prin. Fax 938-5096
Sutton Central ES 100/K-5
28 Newbury Rd 03221 603-927-4215
Steven Potoczak, prin. Fax 927-4055

Brentwood, Rockingham
Brentwood SD
Supt. — See Exeter
Swasey ES 400/PK-5
355 Middle Rd 03833 603-642-3487
Joan Ostrowski, prin. Fax 642-6825

Bristol, Grafton, Pop. 1,483
Newfound Area SD 1,500/PK-12
20 N Main St 03222 603-744-5555
Marie Ross, supt. Fax 744-6659
www.newfound.k12.nh.us
Bridgewater-Hebron Village ES 200/PK-5
25 School House Ln 03222 603-744-6969
Mary Moriarty, prin. Fax 744-9747
Bristol ES 200/K-5
55 School St 03222 603-744-2761
Fax 744-2520
Newfound Memorial MS 400/6-8
155 N Main St 03222 603-744-8162
Eric Chase, prin. Fax 744-8037
Other Schools – See Danbury, New Hampton

Brookline, Hillsborough
Brookline SD
Supt. — See Hollis
Douglass Academy 300/4-6
PO Box 480 03033 603-673-0122
Lorraine Wenger, prin. Fax 673-7384
Maghakian Memorial S 300/K-3
PO Box 68 03033 603-673-4640
Lidia Desrochers, prin. Fax 673-4785

Campton, Grafton
Campton SD
Supt. — See Plymouth
Campton S 300/PK-8
1110 NH Route 175 03223 603-726-3931
James George, prin. Fax 726-8081

Canaan, Grafton
Mascoma Valley Regional SD
Supt. — See Enfield
Canaan ES 300/PK-4
PO Box 18 03741 603-523-4312
Sharyn Orvis, prin. Fax 523-8872
Indian River MS 500/5-8
45 Royal Rd 03741 603-632-4357
Rebecca Cummins, prin. Fax 632-4262

Candia, Rockingham
Candia SD
Supt. — See Hooksett

Moore S 500/K-8
12 Deerfield Rd 03034 603-483-2251
Robert St. Cyr, prin. Fax 483-2536

Canterbury, Merrimack
Shaker Regional SD
Supt. — See Belmont
Canterbury ES 100/K-5
15 Baptist Hill Rd 03224 603-783-9944
Mary Morrison, prin. Fax 783-4981

Center Barnstead, Belknap
Barnstead SD 600/PK-8
PO Box 250 03225 603-435-5526
Dr. William Compton, supt. Fax 435-5331
www.barnstead.k12.nh.us
Barnstead S 600/PK-8
PO Box 289 03225 603-269-5161
Timothy Rice, prin. Fax 269-2632

Center Conway, Carroll
Conway SD
Supt. — See Conway
Pine Tree ES 200/K-6
183 Mill St 03813 603-447-2882
Laura Jawitz, prin. Fax 447-6838

Center Ossipee, Carroll
Governor Wentworth Regional SD
Supt. — See Wolfeboro
Ossipee Central ES 300/PK-6
PO Box 68 03814 603-539-4589
Elizabeth Hertzfeld, prin. Fax 539-4390

Center Sandwich, Carroll
Inter-Lakes Cooperative SD
Supt. — See Meredith
Sandwich Central ES 100/K-6
28 Squam Lake Rd 03227 603-284-7712
John Hansen, prin. Fax 284-6104

Center Tuftonboro, Carroll
Governor Wentworth Regional SD
Supt. — See Wolfeboro
Tuftonboro Central ES 200/K-6
PO Box 118 03816 603-569-2050
Cathy Koukal, prin. Fax 569-8276

Charlestown, Sullivan, Pop. 1,173
Fall Mountain Regional SD 1,800/PK-12
PO Box 600 03603 603-826-7756
Dr. Debra Livingston, supt. Fax 826-4430
www.fall-mountain.k12.nh.us
Charlestown ES 300/K-5
PO Box 325 03603 603-826-3694
Paula Stevens, prin. Fax 826-3905
Charlestown MS 200/6-8
PO Box 325 03603 603-826-7711
Paula Stevens, prin. Fax 826-3102
North Charlestown Community ES 100/1-5
509 River Rd 03603 603-826-3986
Paula Stevens, prin. Fax 826-3186
Other Schools – See Acworth, Alstead, Langdon, North Walpole, Walpole

Chester, Rockingham
Chester SD 700/PK-8
22 Murphy Dr 03036 603-887-3621
Dr. Victor Petzy, supt. Fax 887-7586
www.chesteracademy.org/
Chester Academy 700/PK-8
22 Murphy Dr 03036 603-887-3621
Leslie Leahy, prin. Fax 887-4961

Chesterfield, Cheshire
Chesterfield SD
Supt. — See Keene
Chesterfield Central S 400/K-8
PO Box 205 03443 603-363-8301
Sharyn D'Eon, prin. Fax 363-8406

Chichester, Merrimack
Chichester SD
Supt. — See Pembroke
Chichester Central S 300/K-8
219 Main St 03258 603-798-5651
Pamela Stiles, prin. Fax 798-3230

Claremont, Sullivan, Pop. 13,388
Claremont SD 2,000/PK-12
165 Broad St 03743 603-543-4200
Jacqueline Guillette, supt. Fax 543-4244
www.sau6.k12.nh.us
Bluff ES 200/PK-5
1 Summit Rd 03743 603-543-4273
Linda Brenneman, prin. Fax 542-3703
Claremont MS 400/6-8
107 South St 03743 603-543-4250
Robert Edson, prin. Fax 543-4289
Disnard ES 300/K-5
160 Hanover St 03743 603-543-4260
Joanne Petelle, prin. Fax 543-4262
Maple Avenue ES 400/PK-5
210 Maple Ave 03743 603-543-4270
Catherine Davignon, prin.

Cornish SD 100/K-8
165 Broad St 03743 603-543-4200
Jacqueline Guillette, supt. Fax 543-4244
www.sau6.k12.nh.us/
Other Schools – See Cornish

Unity SD 100/K-8
165 Broad St 03743 603-543-4200
Jacqueline Guillette, supt. Fax 543-4244
Other Schools – See Newport

Claremont Christian Academy 50/K-12
97 Maple Ave 03743 603-542-8759
Marc Proch, dir. Fax 542-8759

Colebrook, Coos
Colebrook SD 500/K-12
21 Academy St 03576 603-237-5571
Robert Mills, supt. Fax 237-5126
www.colebrook.k12.nh.us/
Colebrook S 300/K-8
27 Dumont St 03576 603-237-4801
Mary Jolles, prin. Fax 237-5246

Pittsburg SD 200/K-12
21 Academy St 03576 603-237-5571
Robert Mills, supt. Fax 237-5126
Other Schools – See Pittsburg

Stewartstown SD 100/K-8
21 Academy St 03576 603-237-5571
Robert Mills, supt. Fax 237-5126
Other Schools – See West Stewartstown

Concord, Merrimack, Pop. 42,336
Concord SD 5,300/PK-12
16 Rumford St 03301 603-225-0811
Dr. Christine Rath, supt. Fax 226-2187
www.concord.k12.nh.us
Beaver Meadow ES 400/K-5
40 Sewalls Falls Rd 03301 603-225-0853
Roger Brooks, prin. Fax 225-0857
Broken Ground ES 400/3-5
123 Portsmouth St 03301 603-225-0855
Susan Lauze, prin. Fax 225-0869
Conant ES 400/PK-5
152 South St 03301 603-225-0827
Deborah McNeish, prin. Fax 225-0829
Dame ES 300/K-2
14 Canterbury Rd 03301 603-225-0830
Edward Barnwell, prin. Fax 225-0851
Eastman ES 100/PK-2
15 Shawmut St 03301 603-225-0858
Fax 225-0861
Kimball ES 300/K-5
17 N Spring St 03301 603-225-0840
Susan Noyes, prin. Fax 225-0839
Rumford ES 200/PK-5
40 Thorndike St 03301 603-225-0836
Fax 225-0838
Rundlett MS 1,100/6-8
144 South St 03301 603-225-0862
George Rogers, prin. Fax 226-3288
Walker ES 200/PK-5
4 Church St 03301 603-225-0844
Fax 226-1473

Merrimack Valley SD 2,800/PK-12
105 Community Dr 03303 603-753-6561
Dr. Michael Martin, supt. Fax 753-6023
fc.mvsd.k12.nh.us/
Loudon ES 400/K-5
7039 School St, Loudon NH 03307 603-783-4400
Thomas Laliberte, prin. Fax 783-4222
Other Schools – See Boscawen, Penacook, Salisbury, Webster

Capital Christian S K-8
PO Box 4087 03302 603-224-3641
Cliff Gleason, hdmstr.
Concord Christian Academy 200/PK-12
PO Box 3664 03302 603-228-8888
Thomas Englund, hdmstr. Fax 228-9988
St. John Regional S 200/K-8
61 S State St 03301 603-225-3222
Michele McKenna, prin. Fax 225-0195
Shaker Road S 200/K-9
131 Shaker Rd 03301 603-224-0161
Fax 226-0257
Trinity Christian S 200/K-12
80 Clinton St 03301 603-225-5410
Peter Flint, prin. Fax 225-3235

Contoocook, Merrimack, Pop. 1,334
Hopkinton SD 1,100/PK-12
204 Maple St 03229 603-746-5186
Dr. Brian Blake, supt. Fax 746-5714
www.hopkintonschools.org/
Hopkinton MS 200/7-8
297 Park Ave 03229 603-746-4167
Steven Chamberlin, prin. Fax 746-5109
Maple Street ES 200/4-6
194 Maple St 03229 603-746-4195
Michael Bessette, prin. Fax 746-6863
Other Schools – See Hopkinton

Hopkinton Independent S 100/PK-8
20 Beech Hill Rd 03229 603-226-4662
Heather Harwood, prin. Fax 228-5734

Conway, Carroll, Pop. 1,604
Bartlett SD 300/K-8
176A Main St 03818 603-447-8368
Dr. Carl Nelson, supt. Fax 447-8497
www.kennett.k12.nh.us/
Other Schools – See Bartlett

Conway SD 2,000/K-12
176A Main St 03818 603-447-8368
Dr. Carl Nelson, supt. Fax 447-8497
www.kennett.k12.nh.us
Conway ES 300/K-6
160 Main St 03818 603-447-3369
Brian Hastings, prin. Fax 447-6981
Kennett MS 300/7-8
176 Main St 03818 603-447-6364
Kevin Richard, prin. Fax 447-6842
Other Schools – See Center Conway, North Conway

Jackson SD 100/K-6
176A Main St 03818 603-447-8368
Dr. Carl Nelson, supt. Fax 447-8497
Other Schools – See Jackson

Cady Memorial S 50/K-8
1257 E Main St 03818 603-447-6298
Fax 447-6298
White Mountain Waldorf S 100/K-8
PO Box 1069 03818 603-447-3168
Fax 447-4433

Cornish, Sullivan
Cornish SD
Supt. — See Claremont
Cornish S 100/K-8
274 Town House Rd 03745 603-675-5891
Mary Bronga, prin. Fax 675-6279

Croydon, Sullivan
Croydon SD
Supt. — See Newport
Croydon Village ES 50/K-3
889 NH Route 10 03773 603-863-2080
Kim Doty, prin. Fax 863-7178

Danbury, Merrimack
Newfound Area SD
Supt. — See Bristol
Danbury ES 100/K-5
20 Daffodil Ln 03230 603-768-3434
Ann Holloran, prin. Fax 768-9802

Danville, Rockingham
Timberlane Regional SD
Supt. — See Plaistow
Danville ES 400/PK-5
23 School St 03819 603-382-5554
Nancy Hart, prin. Fax 382-1680

Deerfield, Rockingham
Deerfield SD
Supt. — See Pembroke
Deerfield Community S 500/PK-8
66 North Rd 03037 603-463-7422
Paul Yergeau, prin. Fax 463-2839

Deering, Hillsborough
Hillsboro-Deering Cooperative SD 1,400/PK-12
2300 2nd NH Tpke 03244 603-464-4466
Dr. Barbara Baker, supt. Fax 464-4053
www.hdsd.org
Other Schools – See Hillsborough

Washington SD 100/K-5
PO Box 2190 03244 603-464-4466
Dr. Barbara Baker, supt. Fax 464-4053
www.hdsd.org
Other Schools – See Washington

Derry, Rockingham, Pop. 20,446
Derry Cooperative SD 3,900/PK-PK, 1-
18 S Main St 03038 603-432-1210
Mary Ellen Hannon, supt. Fax 432-1264
www.derry.k12.nh.us
Barka ES 600/1-5
21 Eastgate Rd 03038 603-434-2430
Daniel LaFleur, prin. Fax 432-2305
Derry Early Education Program 100/PK-PK
5 Hood Rd 03038 603-437-5942
Jayne Boyle, dir. Fax 432-1227
Derry Village S 400/1-5
28 S Main St 03038 603-432-1233
Stephen Miller, prin. Fax 432-1235
East Derry Memorial ES 500/1-5
18 Dubeau Dr 03038 603-432-1260
Thomas Poliseno, prin. Fax 437-3575
Grinnell ES 400/1-5
6 Grinnell Rd 03038 603-432-1238
Mary Hill, prin. Fax 432-8717
Hood Memorial MS 900/6-8
5 Hood Rd 03038 603-432-1224
Austin Garofalo, prin. Fax 432-1227
South Range ES 300/1-5
1 Drury Ln 03038 603-432-1219
Matthew Olsen, prin. Fax 432-1221
West Running Brook MS 700/6-8
1 W Running Brook Ln 03038 603-432-1250
Leslie Saucier, prin. Fax 432-1243

Calvary Christian S 200/PK-12
145 Hampstead Rd 03038 603-434-1501
Frank Garland, admin. Fax 437-8096
Derry Montessori S 50/PK-6
65 E Broadway 03038 603-432-8345
Donna Compagna, dir. Fax 432-7978
St. Thomas Aquinas S 200/PK-8
PO Box 387 03038 603-432-2712
Paul Rakiey, prin. Fax 432-2179

Dover, Strafford, Pop. 28,486
Dover SD 4,100/PK-12
61 Locust St Ste 409 03820 603-516-6800
Dr. John O'Connor, supt. Fax 516-6809
www.dover.k12.nh.us
Dover MS 1,100/5-8
16 Daley Dr 03820 603-516-7200
Lawrence DeYoung, prin. Fax 516-5747
Garrison ES 400/K-4
50 Garrison Rd 03820 603-516-6752
Dustin Gray, prin. Fax 516-6742
Horne Street ES 500/K-4
78 Horne St 03820 603-516-6756
Malcolm Forsman, prin. Fax 516-6766
Woodman Park ES 500/PK-4
11 Towle Ave 03820 603-516-6700
Patrick Boodey, prin. Fax 516-6703

Portsmouth Christian Academy 700/PK-12
20 Seaborne Dr 03820 603-742-3617
Brian Bell, hdmstr. Fax 750-0490
St. Mary Academy 400/PK-8
222 Central Ave 03820 603-742-3299
Cynthia Kuder, prin. Fax 743-3483

Dublin, Cheshire
Contoocook Valley SD
Supt. — See Peterborough
Dublin Consolidated ES 100/K-5
1177 Main St 03444 603-563-8332
Mary Clark, prin. Fax 563-3465

Dublin Christian Academy 100/K-12
PO Box 521 03444 603-563-8505
Kevin Moody, prin. Fax 563-8008

Dunbarton, Merrimack, Pop. 1,759
Dunbarton SD
Supt. — See Goffstown

Dunbarton ES 200/K-6
20 Robert Rogers Rd 03046 603-774-3181
Carol Thibaudeau, prin. Fax 774-3186

Durham, Strafford, Pop. 9,236
Oyster River Cooperative SD 2,100/K-12
36 Coe Dr 03824 603-868-5100
Howard Colter, supt. Fax 868-6668
www.orcsd.org
Oyster River MS 700/5-8
1 Coe Dr 03824 603-868-2155
Jay Richard, prin. Fax 868-3469
Other Schools – See Lee, Madbury

East Kingston, Rockingham
East Kingston SD
Supt. — See Exeter
East Kingston ES 200/K-5
5 Andrews Ln 03827 603-642-3511
James Eaves, prin. Fax 642-6338

East Lempster, Sullivan
Goshen-Lempster Cooperative SD
Supt. — See Lempster
Goshen-Lempster Coop S 200/K-8
29 School Rd 03605 603-863-1080
Thomas Fitzgerald, prin. Fax 863-2451

East Rochester, See Rochester
Rochester SD
Supt. — See Rochester
East Rochester ES 300/PK-5
773 Portland St 03868 603-332-2146
Teresa Bailey, prin. Fax 335-7368

East Swanzey, Cheshire
Hinsdale SD 700/PK-12
600 Old Homestead Hwy 03446 603-352-6955
Dr. Kenneth Dassau, supt. Fax 358-6708
www.mrsd.org
Other Schools – See Hinsdale

Monadnock Regional SD 2,300/PK-12
600 Old Homestead Hwy 03446 603-352-6955
Dr. Kenneth Dassau, supt. Fax 358-6708
www.mrsd.org
Cutler ES 300/4-6
31 S Winchester St 03446 603-352-3383
Joseph Smith, prin. Fax 352-0815
Monadnock Regional MS 300/7-8
580 Old Homestead Hwy 03446 603-352-6575
Linda Sutton, prin. Fax 357-6520
Mt. Caesar ES 400/PK-3
585 Old Homestead Hwy 03446 603-352-4797
Elizabeth Tatro, prin. Fax 352-1713
Other Schools – See Fitzwilliam, Gilsum, Sullivan, Troy

Winchester SD 300/PK-8
600 Old Homestead Hwy 03446 603-352-6955
Dr. Kenneth Dassau, supt. Fax 358-6708
www.mrsd.org
Other Schools – See Winchester

Effingham, Carroll
Governor Wentworth Regional SD
Supt. — See Wolfeboro
Effingham ES 100/K-6
6 Partridge Cove Rd 03882 603-539-6032
Lisa Clegg, prin. Fax 539-4511

Enfield, Grafton, Pop. 1,560
Mascoma Valley Regional SD 1,500/PK-12
PO Box 789 03748 603-632-5563
Barbara Tremblay, supt. Fax 632-4181
www.mascoma.k12.nh.us/
Enfield ES 200/PK-4
PO Box 329 03748 603-632-4231
Justin Benna, prin. Fax 632-5482
Other Schools – See Canaan

Epping, Rockingham, Pop. 1,384
Epping SD 1,100/PK-12
213 Main St 03042 603-679-5402
Barbara Munsey, supt. Fax 679-1237
www.sau14.org
Epping ES 500/PK-5
17 Prospect St 03042 603-679-8018
Mark Vallone, prin. Fax 679-9822
Epping MS 200/6-8
33 Prescott Rd 03042 603-679-2544
Lyn Healy, prin. Fax 679-5514

Epsom, Merrimack
Epsom SD
Supt. — See Pembroke
Epsom Central S 500/K-8
282 Black Hall Rd 03234 603-736-9331
Patrick Connors, prin. Fax 736-8703

Pathfinder Academy 100/PK-8
59 Sawyer Ave 03234 603-736-8555
Wayne Anderson, prin. Fax 736-5888

Errol, Coos
Errol SD
Supt. — See Gorham
Errol Consolidated S 50/K-8
PO Box 129 03579 603-482-3341
Kathleen Urso, prin. Fax 482-3722

Exeter, Rockingham, Pop. 9,556
Brentwood SD 400/PK-5
30 Linden St 03833 603-775-8653
Michael Morgan, supt. Fax 775-8673
www.sau16.org/
Other Schools – See Brentwood

East Kingston SD 200/K-5
30 Linden St 03833 603-775-8653
Michael Morgan, supt. Fax 775-8673
www.sau16.org/
Other Schools – See East Kingston

Exeter Region Cooperative SD 3,000/6-12
30 Linden St 03833 603-775-8653
Michael Morgan, supt. Fax 775-8673
www.sau16.org/
Other Schools – See Stratham

Exeter SD 1,000/PK-5
30 Linden St 03833 603-775-8653
Michael Morgan, supt. Fax 775-8673
www.sau16.org/
Lincoln Street ES 500/3-5
25 Lincoln St 03833 603-775-8860
Richard Keays, prin. Fax 775-8968
Main Street ES 500/PK-2
40 Main St 03833 603-775-8946
Steven Adler, prin. Fax 775-8964

Kensington SD 200/K-5
30 Linden St 03833 603-775-8653
Michael Morgan, supt. Fax 775-8673
www.sau16.org
Kensington ES 200/K-5
122 Amesbury Rd 03833 603-772-5705
Barbara Switzer, prin. Fax 775-0502

Newfields SD 200/K-5
30 Linden St 03833 603-775-8653
Michael Morgan, supt. Fax 775-8673
www.sau16.org/
Other Schools – See Newfields

Stratham SD 600/PK-5
30 Linden St 03833 603-775-8653
Michael Morgan, supt. Fax 775-8673
www.sau16.org/
Other Schools – See Stratham

Farmington, Strafford, Pop. 3,567
Farmington SD 1,400/PK-12
356 Main St 03835 603-755-2627
Michelle Langa, supt. Fax 755-2060
www.sau61.com/
Valley View ES 400/PK-3
79 Thayer Dr 03835 603-755-4757
Cynthia Sparks, prin. Fax 755-4738
Wilson Memorial MS 500/4-8
51 School St 03835 603-755-2181
Clayton Lewis, prin. Fax 755-9473

Fitzwilliam, Cheshire
Monadnock Regional SD
Supt. — See East Swanzey
Emerson ES 200/PK-6
27 Rhododendron Rd 03447 603-585-6611
Karen Craig, prin. Fax 585-9287

Francestown, Hillsborough
Contoocook Valley SD
Supt. — See Peterborough
Francestown ES 100/K-4
PO Box 179 03043 603-547-2976
Mary Ellen Stanley, prin. Fax 547-2636

Franconia, Grafton
Lafayette Regional SD
Supt. — See Littleton
Lafayette Regional ES 100/K-6
149 Main St 03580 603-823-7741
Gordon Johnk, prin. Fax 823-5452

Franklin, Merrimack, Pop. 8,763
Franklin SD 1,400/PK-12
119 Central St 03235 603-934-3108
Jo Ellen Divoll, supt. Fax 934-3462
www.franklin.k12.nh.us/
Franklin MS 400/5-8
200 Sanborn St 03235 603-934-5828
James Friel, prin. Fax 934-2432
Franklin Preschool 50/PK-PK
115 Central St 03235 603-934-5441
Deborah Dalton, lead tchr. Fax 934-3462
Rowell ES 200/3-4
12 Rowell Dr 03235 603-934-5116
Kevin Barbour, prin. Fax 934-7452
Other Schools – See West Franklin

Hill SD 100/K-6
119 Central St 03235 603-934-3108
Jo Ellen Divoll, supt. Fax 934-3462
www.franklin.k12.nh.us
Other Schools – See Hill

Freedom, Carroll
Freedom SD
Supt. — See Silver Lake
Freedom ES 100/PK-6
40 Loon Lake Rd 03836 603-539-2077
Corinne Rocco, prin. Fax 539-5782

Fremont, Rockingham
Fremont SD 500/PK-8
5 Hall Rd Unit 1 03044 603-895-6903
Normand Tanguay, supt. Fax 895-6905
Ellis S 500/PK-8
432 Main St 03044 603-895-2511
William Marston, prin. Fax 895-1106

Gilford, Belknap
Gilford SD 1,400/K-12
47 Cherry Valley Rd 03249 603-527-9215
Dr. Paul DeMinico, supt. Fax 527-9216
www.sau.gilford.k12.nh.us
Gilford ES 400/K-4
76 Belknap Mountain Rd 03249 603-524-1661
Sandra McGonagle, prin. Fax 528-0041
Gilford MS 400/5-8
72 Alvah Wilson Rd 03249 603-527-2460
James Kemmerer, prin. Fax 527-2461

Gilmanton, Belknap
Gilmanton SD 400/K-8
PO Box 309, 603-267-9097
John Fauci, supt. Fax 267-9498
www.gilmanton.k12.nh.us/

Gilmanton S 400/K-8
1386 NH Route 140, 603-364-5681
Carol Locke, prin. Fax 364-7311

Gilsum, Cheshire
Monadnock Regional SD
Supt. — See East Swanzey
Gilsum ES 50/4-6
PO Box 38 03448 603-352-2226
David Mousette, prin. Fax 352-2901
Gilsum K K-K
PO Box 38 03448 603-352-2226
David Mousette, prin. Fax 352-2901

Goffstown, Hillsborough, Pop. 14,621
Dunbarton SD 200/K-6
11 School St 03045 603-497-4818
Stacy Buckley, supt. Fax 497-8425
www.goffstown.k12.nh.us
Other Schools – See Dunbarton

Goffstown SD 3,000/PK-12
11 School St 03045 603-497-4818
Stacy Buckley, supt. Fax 497-8425
www.goffstown.k12.nh.us
Glen Lake S PK-K
251 Elm St 03045 603-497-3550
Leslie Doster, prin. Fax 497-3660
Maple Avenue ES 500/1-4
16 Maple Ave 03045 603-497-3330
Marc Boyd, prin. Fax 497-5624
Mountain View MS 1,000/5-8
41 Lauren Ln 03045 603-497-8288
James Hunt, prin. Fax 497-4987
Other Schools – See Manchester

New Boston SD 500/PK-6
11 School St 03045 603-497-4818
Stacy Buckley, supt. Fax 497-8425
www.goffstown.k12.nh.us
Other Schools – See New Boston

Villa Augustina S 300/PK-8
208 S Mast St 03045 603-497-2361
Charles Lawrence, prin. Fax 497-5981

Gonic, Strafford
Rochester SD
Supt. — See Rochester
Gonic ES 200/K-5
10 Railroad Ave 03839 603-332-6487
Gwen Rhodes, prin. Fax 332-2004

St. Leo K, 59 Main St 03839 50/PK-K
Linda Carr, prin. 603-332-9840

Gorham, Coos, Pop. 1,910
Errol SD 50/K-8
123 Main St 03581 603-466-3632
Paul Bousquet, supt. Fax 466-3870
www.sau20.org/
Other Schools – See Errol

Gorham Randolph Shelburne Cooperative SD 600/K-12
123 Main St 03581 603-466-3632
Paul Bousquet, supt. Fax 466-3870
www.sau20.org/
Fenn ES 200/K-5
169 Main St 03581 603-466-3334
Karen Cloutier, prin. Fax 466-3109
Gorham MS 100/6-8
120 Main St 03581 603-466-2776
Keith Parent, prin. Fax 466-3111

Milan SD 100/PK-6
123 Main St 03581 603-466-3632
Paul Bousquet, supt. Fax 466-3870
www.sau20.org/
Other Schools – See Milan

Grantham, Sullivan
Grantham SD 200/K-6
PO Box 287 03753 603-863-9689
Keith Pfeifer, supt. Fax 863-9684
www.grantham.k12.nh.us/
Grantham Village ES 200/K-6
75 Learning Dr 03753 603-863-1681
Kurt Gergler, prin. Fax 863-8377

Greenfield, Hillsborough
Contoocook Valley SD
Supt. — See Peterborough
Greenfield ES 100/PK-4
860 Forest Rd 03047 603-547-3334
Timothy Iwanowicz, prin. Fax 547-2647
Pierce ES 100/K-4
PO Box 149 03047 603-588-2131
Pamela Campbell, prin. Fax 588-3802

Greenland, Rockingham
Greenland SD 400/K-8
48 Post Rd 03840 603-422-9572
Dr. George Cushing, supt. Fax 422-9575
www.sau50.org/gcs_district_profile.html
Greenland Central S 400/K-8
70 Post Rd 03840 603-431-6723
Peter Smith, prin. Fax 430-7683

New Castle SD 100/K-6
48 Post Rd 03840 603-422-9572
Dr. George Cushing, supt. Fax 422-9575
www.sau50.org
Other Schools – See New Castle

Newington SD 50/K-6
48 Post Rd 03840 603-422-9572
Dr. George Cushing, supt. Fax 422-9575
www.sau50.org
Other Schools – See Newington

Rye SD 500/PK-8
48 Post Rd 03840 603-422-9572
Dr. George Cushing, supt. Fax 422-9575
www.sau50.org
Other Schools – See Rye

Greenville, Hillsborough, Pop. 1,135
Mascenic Regional SD
Supt. — See New Ipswich
Greenville ES 100/1-4
16 Adams St 03048 603-878-1411
Marion Saari, prin. Fax 878-1411

Groveton, Coos, Pop. 1,255
Northumberland SD 400/K-12
15 Preble St 03582 603-636-1437
Carl Ladd, supt. Fax 636-6102
www.sau58.org
Groveton ES 200/K-6
36 Church St 03582 603-636-1806
Rosanna Moran, prin. Fax 636-6253

Stark SD 50/K-6
15 Preble St 03582 603-636-1437
Carl Ladd, supt. Fax 636-6102
sau58.k12.nh.us
Other Schools – See Stark

Stratford SD 100/K-12
15 Preble St 03582 603-636-1437
Carl Ladd, supt. Fax 636-6102
sau58.k12.nh.us
Other Schools – See North Stratford

Hampstead, Rockingham
Hampstead SD
Supt. — See Plaistow
Hampstead Central ES 500/PK-4
21 Emerson Ave 03841 603-329-6326
Dillard Collins, prin. Fax 329-4323
Hampstead MS 500/5-8
28 School St 03841 603-329-6743
Patricia Grassbaugh, prin. Fax 329-4120

Hampstead Academy 300/PK-8
320 East Rd 03841 603-329-4406
Keith Wheeler, hdmstr. Fax 329-7124

Hampton, Rockingham, Pop. 7,989
Hampton Falls SD 300/K-8
2 Alumni Dr 03842 603-926-8992
James Gaylord, supt. Fax 926-5157
www.sau21.k12.nh.us
Other Schools – See Hampton Falls

Hampton SD 1,300/PK-8
2 Alumni Dr 03842 603-926-8992
James Gaylord, supt. Fax 926-5157
www.sau21.org/
Hampton Academy 500/6-8
29 Academy Ave 03842 603-926-2000
Chris Sousa, prin. Fax 926-1855
Hampton Centre ES 400/PK-2
53 Winnacunnet Rd 03842 603-926-8706
Nancy Andrews, prin. Fax 926-1177
Marston IS 400/3-5
4 Marston Way 03842 603-926-8708
David O'Connor, prin. Fax 926-7896

North Hampton SD 500/PK-8
2 Alumni Dr 03842 603-926-8992
James Gaylord, supt. Fax 926-5157
Other Schools – See North Hampton

Seabrook SD 900/PK-8
2 Alumni Dr 03842 603-926-8992
James Gaylord, supt. Fax 926-5157
www.sau21.org/
Other Schools – See Seabrook

South Hampton SD 100/K-8
2 Alumni Dr 03842 603-926-8992
James Gaylord, supt. Fax 926-5157
www.sau21.k12.nh.us
Other Schools – See South Hampton

Sacred Heart S 300/PK-8
289 Lafayette Rd 03842 603-926-3254
Catherine Smith, prin. Fax 929-1109

Hampton Falls, Rockingham
Hampton Falls SD
Supt. — See Hampton
Akerman S 300/K-8
8 Exeter Rd 03844 603-926-2539
Judith Deshaies, prin. Fax 929-3708

Seacoast Academy 6-8
356 Exeter Rd 03844 603-339-0556
Scott Votey, hdmstr. Fax 225-7884

Hancock, Hillsborough
Contoocook Valley SD
Supt. — See Peterborough
Hancock ES 100/K-4
10 Elementary Ln 03449 603-525-3303
Jeanie West, prin. Fax 525-3864

Hanover, Grafton, Pop. 6,538
Dresden SD 1,200/6-12
41 Lebanon St Ste 2 03755 603-643-6050
Wayne Gersen, supt. Fax 643-3073
www.sau70.org/
Richmond MS 400/6-8
63 Lyme Rd 03755 603-643-6040
James Nourse, prin. Fax 643-0662

Hanover SD 500/K-6
41 Lebanon St Ste 2 03755 603-643-6050
Wayne Gersen, supt. Fax 643-3073
www.sau70.org/
Ray ES 500/K-5
26 Reservoir Rd 03755 603-643-6655
A. Bruce Williams, prin. Fax 643-0658

Harrisville, Cheshire, Pop. 981
Harrisville SD
Supt. — See Keene
Wells Memorial ES 100/K-6
235 Chesham Rd 03450 603-827-3272
Emily Hartshorne, prin. Fax 827-3073

Henniker, Merrimack, Pop. 1,693
Henniker SD 500/PK-8
41 Liberty Hill Rd Bldg 5 03242 603-428-3269
Douglas White, supt. Fax 428-3850
henniker.k12.nh.us
Henniker Community S 500/PK-8
51 Western Ave 03242 603-428-3476
Ralph Peterson, prin. Fax 428-8271

Stoddard SD 50/K-5
41 Liberty Hill Rd Bldg 5 03242 603-428-3269
Douglas White, supt. Fax 428-3850
Other Schools – See Stoddard

Weare SD 1,200/PK-8
41 Liberty Hill Rd Bldg 5 03242 603-428-3269
Douglas White, supt. Fax 428-3850
sau24.k12.nh.us
Other Schools – See Weare

Hill, Merrimack
Hill SD
Supt. — See Franklin
Blake ES 100/K-6
32 Crescent St 03243 603-934-2245
Wayne VanGorden, prin. Fax 934-5582

Hillsborough, Hillsborough, Pop. 1,826
Hillsboro-Deering Cooperative SD
Supt. — See Deering
Hillsboro-Deering ES 600/PK-5
4 Hillcat Dr 03244 603-464-1110
Ellen Klein, prin. Fax 464-4385
Hillsboro-Deering MS 400/6-8
6 Hillcat Dr 03244 603-464-1120
Richard Nannicelli, prin. Fax 464-5759

Hinsdale, Cheshire, Pop. 1,718
Hinsdale SD
Supt. — See East Swanzey
Hinsdale ES 400/PK-6
12 School St 03451 603-336-5332
Jurg Jenzer, prin. Fax 336-7522
Hinsdale JHS 100/7-8
49 School St 03451 603-336-5984
John Sullivan, prin. Fax 336-7497

Holderness, Grafton
Holderness SD
Supt. — See Plymouth
Holderness Central S 200/K-8
3 School Rd 03245 603-536-2538
William Van Bennekum, prin. Fax 536-1772

Hollis, Hillsborough
Brookline SD 600/K-6
PO Box 1588 03049 603-465-7118
Susan Hodgdon, supt. Fax 465-3933
www.sau41.k12.nh.us
Other Schools – See Brookline

Hollis SD 800/PK-6
PO Box 1588 03049 603-465-7118
Susan Hodgdon, supt. Fax 465-3933
www.hollis.k12.nh.us
Hollis PS 400/PK-3
36 Silver Lake Rd 03049 603-465-2260
Elizabeth Allen, prin. Fax 465-3243
Hollis Upper ES 400/4-6
12 Drury Ln 03049 603-465-9182
Candice Fowler, prin. Fax 465-9068

Hollis/Brookline Cooperative SD 1,400/7-12
PO Box 1588 03049 603-465-7118
Susan Hodgdon, supt. Fax 465-3933
www.sau41.k12.nh.us
Hollis/Brookline MS 500/7-8
25 Main St 03049 603-465-2223
Patricia Goyette, prin. Fax 465-7523

Hooksett, Merrimack, Pop. 2,573
Auburn SD 600/1-8
90 Farmer Rd 03106 603-622-3731
Dr. Charles Littlefield, supt. Fax 669-4352
Other Schools – See Auburn

Candia SD 500/K-8
90 Farmer Rd 03106 603-622-3731
Dr. Charles Littlefield, supt. Fax 669-4352
Other Schools – See Candia

Hooksett SD 1,500/PK-8
90 Farmer Rd 03106 603-622-3731
Dr. Charles Littlefield, supt. Fax 669-4352
www.hooksett.k12.nh.us/
Cawley MS 500/6-8
89 Whitehall Rd 03106 603-485-9959
Ronald Pedro, prin. Fax 485-5291
Hooksett Memorial S 500/3-5
5 Memorial Dr 03106 603-485-9890
Carol Soucy, prin. Fax 485-8574
Underhill ES 500/PK-2
2 Sherwood Dr 03106 603-623-7233
William Estey, prin. Fax 623-5896

Hopkinton, Merrimack
Hopkinton SD
Supt. — See Contoocook
Martin ES 300/PK-3
271 Main St 03229 603-746-3473
William Carozza, prin. Fax 746-6803

Hudson, Hillsborough, Pop. 7,626
Hudson SD 4,200/PK-12
20 Library St 03051 603-886-1235
Philip Bell, supt. Fax 886-1236
www.sau81.org/
Hills Garrison ES 500/1-5
190 Derry Rd 03051 603-881-3930
Marilyn Martellini, prin. Fax 881-3933
Hudson Memorial MS 1,000/6-8
1 Memorial Dr 03051 603-886-1240
Susan Nadeau, prin. Fax 883-1252
Library Street ES 200/1-5
22 Library St 03051 603-886-1255
Scott Baker, prin. Fax 595-1514

Nottingham West ES 700/PK-5
10 Pelham Rd 03051 603-595-1570
Peter Durso, prin. Fax 595-1515
Smith ES 200/1-5
33 School St 03051 603-886-1248
Scott Baker, prin. Fax 886-1239

Presentation of Mary Academy 400/K-8
182 Lowell Rd 03051 603-889-6054
Sr. Maria Rosa, prin. Fax 595-8504

Jackson, Carroll
Jackson SD
Supt. — See Conway
Jackson ES 100/K-6
PO Box J 03846 603-383-6861
Gayle Dembowski, prin. Fax 383-0827

Jaffrey, Cheshire, Pop. 2,558
Jaffrey-Rindge Cooperative SD 1,700/PK-12
81 Fitzgerald Dr Unit 2 03452 603-532-8100
James O'Neill, supt. Fax 532-8165
www.sau47.k12.nh.us
Jaffrey ES 400/PK-5
18 School St 03452 603-532-8355
Susan Shaw-Sarles, prin. Fax 532-4091
Jaffrey-Rindge MS 400/6-8
1 Conant Way 03452 603-532-8122
Richard Haywood, prin. Fax 532-8124
Other Schools – See Rindge

St. Patrick S 100/K-8
70 Main St 03452 603-532-7676
Sr. Cecile Provost, prin. Fax 532-7476

Jefferson, Coos
White Mountains Regional SD
Supt. — See Whitefield
Jefferson ES 100/PK-5
PO Box 100 03583 603-586-4363
Sherri Gregory, prin. Fax 586-4540

Keene, Cheshire, Pop. 22,778
Chesterfield SD 400/K-8
34 West St 03431 603-357-9002
Wayne Woolridge, supt. Fax 357-9012
www.sau29.k12.nh.us/
Other Schools – See Chesterfield

Harrisville SD 100/K-6
34 West St 03431 603-357-9002
Wayne Woolridge, supt. Fax 357-9012
www.sau29.k12.nh.us/
Other Schools – See Harrisville

Keene SD 3,700/PK-12
34 West St 03431 603-357-9002
Wayne Woolridge, supt. Fax 357-9012
www.sau29.k12.nh.us/
Daniels ES 200/K-5
179 Maple Ave 03431 603-352-8012
Patricia Yoerger, prin. Fax 357-3329
Franklin ES 200/PK-5
217 Washington St 03431 603-352-1712
William Harris, prin. Fax 357-9015
Fuller ES 300/K-5
422 Elm St 03431 603-352-1245
Loren Wilder, prin. Fax 357-9031
Keene MS 700/6-8
17 Washington St 03431 603-357-9023
Dorothy Frazier, prin. Fax 357-9045
Symonds ES 300/K-5
79 Park Ave 03431 603-352-3405
Richard Cate, prin. Fax 357-9018
Wheelock ES 200/PK-5
24 Adams St 03431 603-352-2244
Gwen Mitchell, prin. Fax 357-9028

Marlborough SD 200/K-8
34 West St 03431 603-357-9002
Wayne Woolridge, supt. Fax 357-9012
www.sau29.k12.nh.us/
Other Schools – See Marlborough

Marlow SD 50/K-6
34 West St 03431 603-357-9002
Wayne Woolridge, supt. Fax 357-9012
www.sau29.k12.nh.us/
Other Schools – See Marlow

Nelson SD 100/K-6
34 West St 03431 603-357-9002
Wayne Woolridge, supt. Fax 357-9012
www.sau29.k12.nh.us/
Other Schools – See Nelson

Westmoreland SD 200/K-8
34 West St 03431 603-357-9002
Wayne Woolridge, supt. Fax 357-9012
www.sau29.k12.nh.us/
Other Schools – See Westmoreland

Monadnock Waldorf S 200/PK-8
98 S Lincoln St 03431 603-357-4442
Fax 357-2955
St. Joseph S 100/PK-8
92 Wilson St 03431 603-355-2720
Sr. Laura Della Santa, prin. Fax 358-5465
Trinity Christian S 100/PK-8
100 Maple Ave 03431 603-352-9403
Gary Dresser, admin. Fax 358-3405

Kingston, Rockingham
Sanborn Regional SD 1,900/PK-12
178 Main St 03848 603-642-3688
Dr. Brian Blake, supt. Fax 642-7885
sanborn.k12.nh.us
Bakie ES 500/PK-5
179 Main St 03848 603-642-5272
Debora Bamforth, prin. Fax 642-8906
Other Schools – See Newton

Laconia, Belknap, Pop. 17,060
Laconia SD 2,300/PK-12
PO Box 309 03247 603-524-5710
Robert Champlin, supt. Fax 528-8442
www.laconia.k12.nh.us
Elm Street ES 300/PK-5
478 Elm St 03246 603-524-4113
Eric Johnson, prin. Fax 528-1249
Memorial MS 500/6-8
150 McGrath St 03246 603-524-4632
James McCollum, prin. Fax 528-8675
Pleasant Street ES 300/K-5
350 Pleasant St 03246 603-524-2168
Charles Dodson, prin. Fax 528-8452
Woodland Heights ES 400/PK-5
225 Winter St 03246 603-524-8733
Lisa Green-Barber, prin. Fax 528-8688

Holy Trinity S 100/K-8
50 Church St 03246 603-524-3156
John Fortier, prin. Fax 524-4454
Laconia Christian S 100/PK-12
1386 Meredith Center Rd 03246 603-524-3250
Rick Duba, prin. Fax 524-3285

Lancaster, Coos, Pop. 1,859
White Mountains Regional SD
Supt. — See Whitefield
Lancaster S 500/PK-8
51 Bridge St 03584 603-788-4924
Patricia McLean, prin. Fax 788-2216

Landaff, Grafton
Landaff SD
Supt. — See Littleton
Landaff Blue ES 50/K-3
813 Mill Brook Rd 03585 603-838-6416
Claire Cochrane, lead tchr.

Langdon, Sullivan
Fall Mountain Regional SD
Supt. — See Charlestown
Fall Mountain Preschool 50/PK-PK
144 Fmrhs Rd 03602 603-835-6314
Tammy Vittum, dir. Fax 835-6314
Porter ES 50/1-4
111 Village Rd 03602 603-835-2260
Gail Rowe, prin. Fax 835-9097

Lebanon, Grafton, Pop. 12,606
Lebanon SD 1,500/PK-12
84 Hanover St 03766 603-448-1634
Dr. Michael Harris, supt. Fax 448-0602
www.lebanon.k12.nh.us
Hanover Street ES 100/K-4
193 Hanover St 03766 603-448-2945
Scott Bouranis, prin. Fax 448-0615
Lebanon JHS 300/7-8
75 Bank St 03766 603-448-3056
Andrew Mellow, prin. Fax 448-0616
Other Schools – See West Lebanon

Lee, Strafford
Oyster River Cooperative SD
Supt. — See Durham
Mast Way ES 400/K-4
23 Mast Rd, 603-659-3001
Kristen Gallo, prin. Fax 659-8612

Lempster, Sullivan
Goshen-Lempster Cooperative SD 200/K-8
29 School Rd 03605 603-863-2420
Dr. John Handfield, supt. Fax 863-2451
Other Schools – See East Lempster

Lincoln, Grafton
Lincoln-Woodstock Cooperative SD 200/K-12
PO Box 846 03251 603-745-2051
Michael Cosgriff, supt. Fax 745-2351
www.lin-wood.k12.nh.us
Lin-Wood S 200/K-12
PO Box 97 03251 603-745-2214
Robert Nelson, prin. Fax 745-6797

Lisbon, Grafton, Pop. 1,246
Lisbon Regional SD
Supt. — See Littleton
Lisbon Regional S 200/K-12
24 Highland Ave 03585 603-838-5506
Stephen Sexton, prin. Fax 838-5012

Litchfield, Hillsborough
Litchfield SD 1,700/PK-12
1 Highlander Ct 03052 603-578-3570
Dr. Elaine Cutler, supt. Fax 578-1267
Griffin Memorial ES 500/PK-4
229 Charles Bancroft Hwy 03052 603-424-0078
Martin Schlichter, prin. Fax 424-2677
Litchfield MS 600/5-8
19 McElwain Dr 03052 603-424-0566
Thomas Lecklider, prin. Fax 424-1296

St. Francis of Assisi S 100/K-6
9 Saint Francis Way 03052 603-424-3312
Shannon Dannible, prin. Fax 424-9128
Tabernacle Christian S 100/K-12
242 Derry Rd 03052 603-883-6310

Littleton, Grafton, Pop. 4,633
Bethlehem SD 200/K-6
262 Cottage St Ste 230 03561 603-444-3925
Dr. Robert Patterson, supt. Fax 444-6299
www.bethlehem.k12.nh.us/
Other Schools – See Bethlehem

Lafayette Regional SD 100/K-6
262 Cottage St Ste 230 03561 603-444-3925
Dr. Robert Patterson, supt. Fax 444-6299
www.lafayetteregional.org/
Other Schools – See Franconia

Landaff SD 50/K-3
262 Cottage St Ste 230 03561 603-444-3925
Dr. Robert Patterson, supt. Fax 444-6299
www.sau35.org/blueschool.htm
Other Schools – See Landaff

Lisbon Regional SD 200/K-12
262 Cottage St Ste 230 03561 603-444-3925
Dr. Robert Patterson, supt. Fax 444-6299
www.lisbon.k12.nh.us/
Other Schools – See Lisbon

Littleton SD 900/K-12
102 School St 03561 603-444-5215
Dorothy Danforth, supt. Fax 444-3015
www.littletonschools.org/
Bronson JHS 100/7-8
96 School St 03561 603-444-3361
Judy Boulet, prin. Fax 444-3009
Lakeway ES 500/K-6
325 Union St 03561 603-444-2831
Richard Bidgood, prin. Fax 444-3009

Profile SD 300/7-12
262 Cottage St Ste 230 03561 603-444-3925
Dr. Robert Patterson, supt. Fax 444-6299
www.profile.k12.nh.us/
Other Schools – See Bethlehem

Londonderry, Rockingham, Pop. 10,114
Londonderry SD 5,400/PK-12
268C Mammoth Rd 03053 603-432-6920
Nathan Greenberg, supt. Fax 425-1049
www.londonderry.org
Londonderry MS 1,300/6-8
313 Mammoth Rd 03053 603-432-6925
Andrew Corey, prin. Fax 432-0714
Moose Hill S 400/PK-K
150 Pillsbury Rd 03053 603-437-5855
Richard Zacchilli, prin. Fax 437-3709
North Londonderry ES 600/1-5
19 Sanborn Rd 03053 603-432-6933
Richard Zacchilli, prin. Fax 425-1006
South Londonderry ES 600/1-5
88 South Rd 03053 603-432-6956
Linda Boyd, prin. Fax 425-1004
Thornton ES 700/1-5
275 Mammoth Rd 03053 603-432-6937
Carol Mack, prin. Fax 425-1005

St. Marks K, 1 South Rd 03053 50/PK-K
Jackie LeCompte, dir. 603-432-1506

Lyme, Grafton
Lyme SD 200/K-8
PO Box 117 03768 603-795-4431
Dr. Gordon Schnare, supt. Fax 795-9407
www.lymeschool.org/
Lyme S 200/K-8
PO Box 60 03768 603-795-2125
Jeffrey Valence, prin. Fax 795-4719

Crossroads Academy 100/K-8
95 Dartmouth College Hwy 03768 603-795-3111
Jean Behnke, prin. Fax 795-4329

Lyndeborough, Hillsborough
Lyndeborough SD
Supt. — See Wilton
Lyndeborough Central ES 100/1-6
192 Forest Rd 03082 603-654-9381
Susan Tussing, prin. Fax 654-6884

Madbury, Strafford
Oyster River Cooperative SD
Supt. — See Durham
Moharimet ES 400/K-4
11 Lee Rd, 603-742-2900
Dennis Harrington, prin. Fax 742-7569

Madison, Carroll
Madison SD
Supt. — See Silver Lake
Madison ES 200/K-6
2069 Village Rd 03849 603-367-4642
Cynthia Hyatt, prin. Fax 367-8784

Manchester, Hillsborough, Pop. 109,691
Goffstown SD
Supt. — See Goffstown
Bartlett ES 200/1-4
689 Mast Rd 03102 603-623-8088
David Bousquet, prin. Fax 644-8488

Manchester SD 17,200/PK-12
286 Commercial St 03101 603-624-6300
Thomas Brennan Ph.D., supt. Fax 624-6337
www.mansd.org
Bakersville ES 300/K-5
20 Elm St 03101 603-624-6312
Judith Adams, prin. Fax 624-6431
Beech Street ES 600/K-5
333 Beech St 03103 603-624-6314
Elinor Murphy, prin. Fax 628-6139
Deitch Early Learning Program 200/PK-PK
555 Auburn St 03103 603-624-6325
Pat Storm, prin. Fax 624-6425
Gossler Park ES 400/K-5
99 Sullivan St 03102 603-624-6327
James Adams, prin. Fax 624-6392
Green Acres ES 600/PK-5
100 Aurore Ave 03109 603-624-6330
Richard Norton, prin. Fax 624-6284
Hallsville ES 300/K-5
275 Jewett St 03103 603-624-6332
James Davenport, prin. Fax 624-6432
Highland/Goffes Falls ES 500/K-5
2021 Goffs Falls Rd 03103 603-624-6334
James Paul, prin. Fax 624-6345
Hillside MS 900/6-8
112 Reservoir Ave 03104 603-624-6352
Steven Donohue, prin. Fax 628-6049
Jewett ES 400/PK-5
130 S Jewett St 03103 603-624-6336
Christina Battistelli, prin. Fax 624-6434
McDonough ES 600/K-5
550 Lowell St 03104 603-624-6373
Kenneth DiBenedetto, prin. Fax 665-6692
McLaughlin MS 900/6-8
290 S Mammoth Rd 03109 603-628-6247
Barry Albert, prin. Fax 628-6274
Northwest ES 700/K-5
300 Youville St 03102 603-624-6321
Shelly Larochelle, prin. Fax 624-6319
Parker-Varney ES 500/K-5
223 James A Pollock Dr 03102 603-624-6338
Phil Callanan, prin. Fax 624-6399
Parkside MS 800/6-8
75 Parkside Ave 03102 603-624-6356
Dawn Pirog, prin. Fax 624-6355
Smyth Road ES 400/PK-5
245 Bruce Rd 03104 603-624-6340
Jennifer Briggs, prin. Fax 624-6433
Southside MS 900/6-8
140 S Jewett St 03103 603-624-6359
Larry George, prin. Fax 624-6361
Webster ES 500/K-5
2519 Elm St 03104 603-624-6344
Helene Stanley, prin. Fax 628-6059
Weston ES 600/K-5
1066 Hanover St 03104 603-624-6347
Lizabeth MacDonald, prin. Fax 624-6375
Wilson ES 500/K-5
401 Wilson St 03103 603-624-6350
Linda Durand, prin. Fax 624-6395

Mt. St. Mary Academy 200/PK-6
2291 Elm St 03104 603-623-3155
Patricia Baldissard, prin. Fax 621-9254
Mount Zion Christian S 200/PK-12
132 Titus Ave 03103 603-606-7930
Robert Carter, hdmstr. Fax 606-7935
St. Anthony of Padua S 200/PK-6
148 Belmont St 03103 603-622-0414
Gerard Bergeron, prin. Fax 669-5212
St. Augustine Preschool 50/PK-K
383 Beech St 03103 603-623-8800
Crystal Elie, dir. Fax 626-1517
St. Benedict Academy 100/K-6
85 3rd St 03102 603-669-3932
Sr. Elizabeth Roy, prin. Fax 669-3932
St. Casimir S 200/K-8
456 Union St 03103 603-623-6411
Sr. Frances Bonczar, prin. Fax 623-3236
St. Catherine S 300/PK-6
206 North St 03104 603-622-1711
Sr. Janet Belcourt, prin. Fax 624-4935
St. Joseph Regional JHS 200/7-8
460 Pine St 03104 603-624-4811
Pauline Martineau, prin. Fax 624-6670
St. Marie Child Care Center 100/PK-K
133 Wayne St 03102 603-668-2356
Terry Cody, prin. Fax 666-4732

Marlborough, Cheshire, Pop. 1,211
Marlborough SD
Supt. — See Keene
Marlborough S 200/K-8
23 School St 03455 603-876-4465
Karen Parsells, prin. Fax 876-4302

Marlow, Cheshire
Marlow SD
Supt. — See Keene
Perkins ES 50/K-6
919 NH Route 10 03456 603-446-3307
Phyllis Peterson, prin. Fax 446-7323

Meredith, Belknap, Pop. 1,654
Ashland SD 200/K-8
103 Main St Ste 2 03253 603-279-7947
Dr. Phillip McCormack, supt. Fax 279-3044
www.ashland.k12.nh.us/
Other Schools – See Ashland

Inter-Lakes Cooperative SD 1,200/PK-12
103 Main St Ste 2 03253 603-279-7947
Dr. Phillip McCormack, supt. Fax 279-3044
www.interlakes.org/
Inter-Lakes ES 400/PK-4
21 Laker Ln 03253 603-279-7968
Steven Kelley, prin. Fax 279-6344
Inter-Lakes MS 400/5-8
1 Laker Ln 03253 603-279-5312
Everett Bennett, prin. Fax 279-5310
Other Schools – See Center Sandwich

Meriden, Sullivan
Plainfield SD 300/K-8
92 Bonner Rd 03770 603-469-3442
Noelle Vitt, supt. Fax 469-3985
Plainfield S 300/K-8
92 Bonner Rd 03770 603-469-3250
Ellen Langsner, prin. Fax 469-3985

Merrimack, Hillsborough, Pop. 22,156
Merrimack SD 4,700/PK-12
36 McElwain St 03054 603-424-6200
Marjorie Chiafery, supt. Fax 424-6229
www.merrimack.k12.nh.us
Mastricola ES 400/K-4
7 School St 03054 603-424-6218
John Fabrizio, prin. Fax 424-6239
Mastricola Upper ES 700/5-6
26 Baboosic Lake Rd 03054 603-424-6221
Marsha McGill, prin. Fax 424-6323
Merrimack MS 800/7-8
31 Madeline Bennett Ln 03054 603-424-6289
Deborah Woolflein, prin. Fax 423-1109
Reeds Ferry ES 600/PK-4
15 Lyons Rd 03054 603-424-6215
Kimberly Yarlott, prin. Fax 424-6238
Thorntons Ferry ES 600/K-4
134 Camp Sargent Rd 03054 603-889-1577
Bridey Bellemare, prin. Fax 598-9821

Grace Christian S 50/K-6
PO Box 11 03054 603-424-2552
Nancy Busch, prin. Fax 429-1424

South Merrimack Christian Academy — 200/K-12
517 Boston Post Rd 03054 — 603-595-0955
Brian Burbach, prin. — Fax 598-7085

Milan, Coos
Milan SD
Supt. — See Gorham
Milan Village ES — 100/PK-6
11 Bridge St 03588 — 603-449-3306
David Backler, prin. — Fax 449-2509

Milford, Hillsborough, Pop. 8,015
Milford SD — 2,600/PK-12
100 West St 03055 — 603-673-2202
Robert Suprenant, supt. — Fax 673-2237
Heron Pond ES — 800/2-5
80 Heron Pond Rd 03055 — 603-673-1811
Peter Bonaccorsi, prin. — Fax 459-0814
Jacques Memorial ES — 300/PK-1
9 Elm St 03055 — 603-673-4434
John Foss, prin. — Fax 459-0814
Milford MS — 600/6-8
33 Osgood Rd 03055 — 603-673-5221
Anthony DeMarco, prin. — Fax 673-5221

Milford Christian Academy — 100/1-12
273 Elm St 03055 — 603-673-9324
Paul Sontag, prin. — Fax 672-4539

Milton, Strafford
Milton SD
Supt. — See Union
Milton ES — 300/K-5
8 School St 03851 — 603-652-4539
Stephanie Hillis, prin. — Fax 652-9431
Nute JHS — 200/6-8
22 Elm St 03851 — 603-652-4591
Robert Bickford, prin. — Fax 652-9926

Monroe, Grafton
Monroe SD — 100/PK-8
PO Box 130 03771 — 603-638-2800
Karen Stewart, supt. — Fax 638-2031
Monroe Consolidated S — 100/PK-8
PO Box 130 03771 — 603-638-2800
Karen Stewart, prin. — Fax 638-2031

Mont Vernon, Hillsborough
Mont Vernon SD
Supt. — See Amherst
Mont Vernon ES — 200/K-6
PO Box 98 03057 — 603-673-5141
Gail Westergren, prin. — Fax 672-1924

Moultonborough, Carroll
Moultonborough SD — 700/PK-12
PO Box 419 03254 — 603-476-5247
Michael Lancor, supt. — Fax 476-8009
www.moultonborough.k12.nh.us
Moultonborough Academy — 100/7-8
PO Box 228 03254 — 603-476-5517
Andrew Coppinger, prin. — Fax 476-5153
Moultonborough Central ES — 300/PK-6
PO Box 149 03254 — 603-476-5535
Scott Laliberte, prin. — Fax 476-2409

Nashua, Hillsborough, Pop. 87,321
Nashua SD — 12,700/PK-12
PO Box 687 03061 — 603-594-4300
Dr. Christopher Hottel, supt. — Fax 594-4350
www.nashua.edu
Amherst Street ES — 300/K-5
71 Amherst St 03064 — 603-594-4385
Pat Snow, prin. — Fax 594-4470
Bicentennial ES — 600/PK-5
296 E Dunstable Rd 03062 — 603-594-4382
Kyle Langille, prin. — Fax 594-4389
Birch Hill ES — 500/K-5
17 Birch Hill Dr 03063 — 603-594-4340
Mark Lucas, prin. — Fax 594-4342
Broad Street ES — 300/PK-5
390 Broad St 03063 — 603-594-4404
Christine Breen, prin. — Fax 882-2332
Charlotte Avenue ES — 500/K-5
48 Charlotte Ave 03064 — 603-594-4334
Thaiadora Dorow, prin. — Fax 594-4336
Crisp ES — 400/PK-5
50 Arlington St 03060 — 603-594-4390
Jane Quigley, prin. — Fax 594-4395
Elm Street MS — 1,300/6-8
117 Elm St 03060 — 603-594-4322
Colette Valade, prin. — Fax 594-4370
Fairgrounds ES — 600/K-5
37 Blanchard St 03060 — 603-594-4318
Chuck Healey, prin. — Fax 594-4348
Fairgrounds MS — 900/6-8
27 Cleveland St 03060 — 603-594-4393
John Nelson, prin. — Fax 594-4355
Ledge Street ES — 500/K-5
139 Ledge St 03060 — 603-594-4337
Janet Valeri, prin. — Fax 594-4344
Main Dunstable ES — 600/K-5
20 Whitford Rd 03062 — 603-594-4400
Christopher M. Gosselin, prin. — Fax 594-4369
Mt. Pleasant ES — 300/K-5
10 Manchester St 03064 — 603-594-4331
Mary Tintle, prin. — Fax 594-4417
New Searles ES — 400/PK-5
39 Shady Ln 03062 — 603-594-4409
Jay Harding, prin. — Fax 891-5504
Pennichuck MS — 800/6-8
207 Manchester St 03064 — 603-594-4308
Paul F. Asbell, prin. — Fax 594-4413
Purple Panthers Preschool — PK-PK
36 Riverside Dr 03062 — 603-589-4311
Jean Godlewski, prin. — Fax 589-8722
Sunset Heights ES — 400/K-5
15 Osgood Rd 03060 — 603-594-4387
Philip Schappler, prin. — Fax 594-4349

Infant Jesus S — 200/K-6
3 Crown St 03060 — 603-889-2649
Estelle LaFleur, prin. — Fax 594-9117

Nashua Catholic Regional JHS — 300/7-8
6 Bartlett Ave 03064 — 603-883-6707
Thomas Kelleher, prin. — Fax 594-8955
Nashua Christian Academy — 200/K-12
8 Franklin St 03064 — 603-889-8892
Christine Urban, prin. — Fax 821-7451
St. Christopher S — 300/PK-6
20 Cushing Ave 03064 — 603-882-7442
Jack Daniels, prin. — Fax 594-9253
World Schools — 300/PK-6
138 Spit Brook Rd 03062 — 603-888-1982
Kathy Nelson, dir. — Fax 888-5880

Nelson, Cheshire
Nelson SD
Supt. — See Keene
Nelson ES — 100/K-6
441 Granite Lake Rd 03457 — 603-847-3408
Sheila Vara, prin. — Fax 847-9612

New Boston, Hillsborough
New Boston SD
Supt. — See Goffstown
New Boston Central ES — 500/PK-6
15 Central School Rd 03070 — 603-487-2211
Richard Matthews, prin. — Fax 487-2215

New Castle, Rockingham
New Castle SD
Supt. — See Greenland
Trefethen ES — 100/K-6
PO Box 228 03854 — 603-436-5416
Lynn Zacharias, prin. — Fax 427-1918

New Durham, Strafford
Governor Wentworth Regional SD
Supt. — See Wolfeboro
New Durham ES — 200/K-6
PO Box 212 03855 — 603-859-2061
Barbara Reed, prin. — Fax 859-5308

Newfields, Rockingham
Newfields SD
Supt. — See Exeter
Newfields ES — 200/K-5
9 Piscassic Rd 03856 — 603-772-5555
Dennis W. Dobe, prin. — Fax 658-0401

New Hampton, Belknap
Newfound Area SD
Supt. — See Bristol
New Hampton Community ES — 100/K-5
191 Main St 03256 — 603-744-3221
Ann Holloran, prin. — Fax 744-3450

Newington, Rockingham, Pop. 990
Newington SD
Supt. — See Greenland
Newington ES — 50/K-6
133 Nimble Hill Rd 03801 — 603-436-1482
Helen Rist, prin. — Fax 427-0692

New Ipswich, Hillsborough
Mascenic Regional SD — 1,200/1-12
30 Tricnit Rd Unit 5 03071 — 603-731-0160
Dr. Leo Corriveau, supt. — Fax 654-6691
www.mascenic.org
Appleton ES — 100/3-4
72 Academy Rd 03071 — 603-878-2814
Marion Saari, prin. — Fax 878-2814
Boynton MS — 500/5-8
500 Turnpike Rd 03071 — 603-878-4800
Thomas Starratt, prin. — Fax 878-0525
New Ipswich Central ES — 100/1-2
571 Turnpike Rd 03071 — 603-878-2108
Marion Saari, prin. — Fax 878-2108
Other Schools – See Greenville

Our Redeemer Lutheran S — 50/K-K
PO Box 387 03071 — 603-878-1837
Fax 878-0891

New London, Merrimack
Kearsarge Regional SD — 2,100/K-12
169 Main St 03257 — 603-526-2051
Jerome Frew, supt. — Fax 526-2145
www.kearsarge.org
Kearsarge Regional ES - New London — 400/K-5
64 Cougar Ct 03257 — 603-526-4737
Kevin Johnson, prin. — Fax 526-8675
Other Schools – See Bradford, North Sutton, Warner

Newmarket, Rockingham, Pop. 4,917
Newmarket SD — 900/PK-12
186 Main St 03857 — 603-659-5020
Mark LaRoach, supt. — Fax 659-5022
Newmarket ES — 500/PK-5
243 S Main St 03857 — 603-659-2276
Scott Thompson, prin. — Fax 659-4716

Newport, Sullivan, Pop. 3,772
Croydon SD — 50/K-3
9 Depot St Ste 2 03773 — 603-863-3540
Dr. Marilyn Brannigan, supt. — Fax 863-5368
Other Schools – See Croydon

Newport SD — 1,200/K-12
9 Depot St Ste 2 03773 — 603-863-3540
Dr. Marilyn Brannigan, supt. — Fax 863-5368
newport.k12.nh.us/
Newport MS — 300/6-8
245 N Main St 03773 — 603-863-2414
Barry Connell, prin. — Fax 863-0887
Richards ES — 300/K-3
21 School St 03773 — 603-863-3710
Patricia Warren, prin. — Fax 863-3895
Towle IS — 200/4-5
86 N Main St 03773 — 603-863-2050
Kathryn Niboli, prin. — Fax 863-3390

Unity SD
Supt. — See Claremont
Unity S — 100/K-8
864 2nd NH Tpke 03773 — 603-542-5888
Maynard Baldwin, prin. — Fax 543-4211

Newton, Rockingham
Sanborn Regional SD
Supt. — See Kingston
Sanborn Regional Memorial ES — 300/K-5
31 W Main St 03858 — 603-382-5251
Jonathan VanderEls, prin. — Fax 382-1466
Sanborn Regional MS — 400/6-8
31 W Main St Ste A 03858 — 603-382-6226
Alexander Rutherford, prin. — Fax 382-9771

North Conway, Carroll, Pop. 2,032
Conway SD
Supt. — See Conway
Fuller ES — 300/K-6
51 Pine St 03860 — 603-356-5381
Mark Zangari, prin. — Fax 356-9382

Northfield, Merrimack
Winnisquam Regional SD
Supt. — See Tilton
Southwick IS — 300/3-5
50 Zion Hill Rd 03276 — 603-286-3611
Richard Hines, prin. — Fax 286-3526
Union Sanborn ES — 300/PK-2
5 Elm St 03276 — 603-286-4332
Timothy Neville, prin. — Fax 286-2153

North Hampton, Rockingham
North Hampton SD
Supt. — See Hampton
North Hampton S — 500/PK-8
201 Atlantic Ave 03862 — 603-964-5501
Peter Sweet, prin. — Fax 964-9018

North Haverhill, Grafton
Bath SD — 100/K-6
2975 Dartmouth College Hwy 03774 — 603-787-2113
Bruce Labs, supt. — Fax 787-2118
www.sau23.k12.nh.us
Other Schools – See Bath

Haverhill Cooperative SD — 800/PK-12
2975 Dartmouth College Hwy 03774 — 603-787-2113
Bruce Labs, supt. — Fax 787-2118
www.sau23.k12.nh.us
Haverhill Cooperative MS — 300/4-8
175 Morrill Dr 03774 — 603-787-2100
Brent Walker, prin. — Fax 787-6117
Other Schools – See Woodsville

Piermont SD — 100/K-8
2975 Dartmouth College Hwy 03774 — 603-787-2113
Bruce Labs, supt. — Fax 787-2118
www.sau23.k12.nh.us/PVS/home.htm
Other Schools – See Piermont

Warren SD — 100/K-6
2975 Dartmouth College Hwy 03774 — 603-787-2113
Bruce Labs, supt. — Fax 787-2118
www.sau23.k12.nh.us
Other Schools – See Warren

North Stratford, Coos
Stratford SD
Supt. — See Groveton
Stratford S — 100/K-12
19 School St 03590 — 603-922-3387
James Shallow, prin. — Fax 922-3303

North Sutton, Merrimack
Kearsarge Regional SD
Supt. — See New London
Kearsarge Regional MS — 500/6-8
PO Box 269 03260 — 603-927-2100
Donald West, prin. — Fax 927-4731

North Walpole, Cheshire
Fall Mountain Regional SD
Supt. — See Charlestown
North Walpole ES — 100/2-4
17 Cray Rd 03609 — 603-445-5450
Samuel Jacobs, prin. — Fax 445-1955

Northwood, Rockingham
Northwood SD — 500/K-8
23 Mountain Ave Unit A 03261 — 603-942-1290
Michael Ludwell Ph.D., supt. — Fax 942-1295
www.northwood.k12.nh.us/
Northwood S — 500/K-8
511 1st NH Tpke 03261 — 603-942-5488
Esther Asbell, prin. — Fax 942-5746

Nottingham SD — 500/K-8
569 1st NH Tpke 03261 — 603-942-1290
Judy McGann, supt. — Fax 942-1295
www.nottingham.k12.nh.us
Other Schools – See Nottingham

Strafford SD — 500/K-8
23 Mountain Ave Unit A 03261 — 603-942-1290
Dr. Michael Ludwell, supt. — Fax 942-1295
Other Schools – See Strafford

Nottingham, Rockingham
Nottingham SD
Supt. — See Northwood
Nottingham S — 500/K-8
245 Stage Rd 03290 — 603-679-5632
Michelle Carvalho, prin. — Fax 679-1617

Ossipee, Carroll

Cornerstone Christian Academy — 100/PK-8
129 Route 28 03864 — 603-539-8636
Greg Swenson, hdmstr. — Fax 539-8637

Pelham, Hillsborough
Pelham SD
Supt. — See Windham
Pelham ES — 900/1-5
61 Marsh Rd 03076 — 603-635-8875
Alicia LaFrance, prin. — Fax 635-8922
Pelham Memorial MS — 500/6-8
59 Marsh Rd 03076 — 603-635-2321
Catherine Pinsonneault, prin. — Fax 635-2369

St. Patrick S 200/K-8
16 Main St 03076 603-635-2941
Roger Dumont, prin. Fax 635-9800

Pembroke, Merrimack, Pop. 6,561
Allenstown SD 400/K-8
267 Pembroke St 03275 603-485-5188
Peter Warburton, supt. Fax 485-9529
www.sau53.org
Other Schools – See Allenstown

Chichester SD 300/K-8
267 Pembroke St 03275 603-485-5188
Peter Warburton, supt. Fax 485-9529
www.sau53.org
Other Schools – See Chichester

Deerfield SD 500/PK-8
267 Pembroke St 03275 603-485-5188
Peter Warburton, supt. Fax 485-9529
www.sau53.org
Other Schools – See Deerfield

Epsom SD 500/K-8
267 Pembroke St 03275 603-485-5188
Peter Warburton, supt. Fax 485-9529
www.sau53.org
Other Schools – See Epsom

Pembroke SD 1,900/K-12
267 Pembroke St 03275 603-485-5188
Peter Warburton, supt. Fax 485-9529
www.sau53.org
Pembroke Hill ES 300/2-4
300 Belanger Dr 03275 603-485-9000
Ryan Quinn, prin. Fax 485-8872
Pembroke Village ES 200/K-1
30 High St 03275 603-485-1807
Ryan Quinn, prin. Fax 485-1811
Three Rivers MS 400/5-8
243 Academy Rd 03275 603-485-9539
Deborah Bulkley, prin. Fax 485-1829

Penacook, See Concord
Andover SD 300/K-8
105 Community Dr 03303 603-753-6561
Dr. Michael Martin, supt. Fax 753-6023
www.andover.k12.nh.us/aemshome.htm
Other Schools – See Andover

Merrimack Valley SD
Supt. — See Concord
Merrimack Valley MS 600/6-8
14 Allen St 03303 603-753-6336
Mary Estee, prin. Fax 753-8107
Penacook ES 400/PK-5
60 Village St 03303 603-753-4891
G. Linda McAllister, prin. Fax 753-6419

Peterborough, Hillsborough, Pop. 2,685
Contoocook Valley SD 3,100/PK-12
106 Hancock Rd 03458 603-924-3336
Dr. Richard Bergeron, supt. Fax 924-6707
www.conval.edu
Peterborough ES 400/K-4
17 High St 03458 603-924-3828
Susan Copley, prin. Fax 924-4193
South Meadow MS 500/5-8
108 Hancock Rd 03458 603-924-7105
Richard Dunning, prin. Fax 924-2064
Other Schools – See Antrim, Dublin, Francestown, Greenfield, Hancock, Temple

Piermont, Grafton
Piermont SD
Supt. — See North Haverhill
Piermont Village S 100/K-8
PO Box 98 03779 603-272-5881
Jonann Torsey, prin. Fax 272-9203

Pittsburg, Coos
Pittsburg SD
Supt. — See Colebrook
Pittsburg S 100/K-8
12 School St 03592 603-538-6536
Kirsten Windsinger, prin. Fax 538-6996

Pittsfield, Merrimack, Pop. 1,717
Pittsfield SD 700/PK-12
175 Barnstead Rd Unit 3 03263 603-435-5526
Dr. John Freeman, supt. Fax 435-5331
Pittsfield ES 400/PK-6
34 Bow St 03263 603-435-8432
Doug Kilmister, prin. Fax 435-7358
Pittsfield MS 100/7-8
23 Oneida St 03263 603-435-6701
Rick Gremlitz, prin. Fax 435-7087

Plaistow, Rockingham
Hampstead SD 1,100/PK-8
30 Greenough Rd 03865 603-382-6119
Richard LaSalle, supt. Fax 382-3334
www.hampstead.k12.nh.us
Other Schools – See Hampstead

Timberlane Regional SD 4,500/PK-12
30 Greenough Rd 03865 603-382-6119
Richard LaSalle, supt. Fax 382-3334
www.timberlane.net/
Pollard ES 600/PK-5
120 Main St 03865 603-382-7146
Michelle Auger, prin. Fax 382-2782
Timberlane Regional MS 1,100/6-8
44 Greenough Rd 03865 603-382-7131
Michael Hogan, prin. Fax 382-2781
Other Schools – See Atkinson, Danville, Sandown

St. Luke the Evangelist Preschool 100/PK-K
8 Atkinson Depot Rd 03865 603-382-9783
Jean Lanctot, prin. Fax 382-1113

Plymouth, Grafton, Pop. 3,967
Campton SD 300/PK-8
47 Old Ward Bridge Rd 03264 603-536-1254
Mark Halloran, supt. Fax 536-3545
Other Schools – See Campton

Holderness SD 200/K-8
47 Old Ward Bridge Rd 03264 603-536-1254
Mark Halloran, supt. Fax 536-3545
www.sau48.org/schoolih/holderness.html
Other Schools – See Holderness

Plymouth SD 400/PK-8
47 Old Ward Bridge Rd 03264 603-536-1254
Mark Halloran, supt. Fax 536-3545
Plymouth S 400/PK-8
43 Old Ward Bridge Rd 03264 603-536-1152
Julie Flynn, prin. Fax 536-9085

Rumney SD 200/K-8
47 Old Ward Bridge Rd 03264 603-536-1254
Mark Halloran, supt. Fax 536-3545
www.russell.sau48.k12.nh.us/
Other Schools – See Rumney

Thornton SD 200/K-8
47 Old Ward Bridge Rd 03264 603-536-1254
Mark Halloran, supt. Fax 536-3545
www.thornton.sau48.k12.nh.us/
Other Schools – See Thornton

Waterville Valley SD 50/K-8
47 Old Ward Bridge Rd 03264 603-536-1254
Mark Halloran, supt. Fax 536-3545
www.wves.sau48.org/
Other Schools – See Waterville Valley

Wentworth SD 100/K-8
47 Old Ward Bridge Rd 03264 603-536-1254
Mark Halloran, supt. Fax 536-3545
Other Schools – See Wentworth

Portsmouth, Rockingham, Pop. 20,674
Portsmouth SD 2,600/PK-12
50 Clough Dr 03801 603-431-5080
Dr. Robert Lister, supt. Fax 431-6753
www.portsmouth.k12.nh.us
Dondero ES 300/K-5
32 Van Buren Ave 03801 603-436-2231
Jill LeMay, prin. Fax 427-2329
Little Harbour ES 400/K-5
50 Clough Dr 03801 603-436-1708
Robin Burdick, prin. Fax 427-2306
New Franklin ES 300/K-5
1 Franklin Dr 03801 603-436-0910
George Shea, prin. Fax 427-2335
Portsmouth Early Education Program 50/PK-PK
100 Campus Dr Ste 21 03801 603-422-8228
Beth Setear, dir. Fax 422-8230
Portsmouth MS 500/6-8
155 Parrott Ave 03801 603-436-5781
John Stokel, prin. Fax 427-2326

St. Patrick S 100/PK-8
125 Austin St 03801 603-436-0739
Sr. Mary Joan Walsh, prin. Fax 436-1569

Raymond, Rockingham, Pop. 2,516
Raymond SD 1,600/PK-12
43 Harriman Hill Rd 03077 603-895-4299
Dr. Jean Richards, supt. Fax 895-0147
www.raymond.k12.nh.us
Gove MS 400/5-8
1 Stephen K Batchelder Pkwy 03077 603-895-3394
Ellen Small, prin. Fax 895-9856
Lamprey River ES 600/PK-4
33 Old Manchester Rd 03077 603-895-3117
Daniel LeGallo, prin. Fax 895-9627

Rindge, Cheshire
Jaffrey-Rindge Cooperative SD
Supt. — See Jaffrey
Rindge Memorial ES 400/PK-5
58 School St 03461 603-899-3363
John Stone, prin. Fax 899-9816

Hampshire Country S 50/3-12
28 Patey Cir 03461 603-899-3325
William Dickerman, hdmstr. Fax 899-6521

Rochester, Strafford, Pop. 30,004
Rochester SD 4,800/PK-12
150 Wakefield St Ste 8 03867 603-332-3678
Michael Hopkins, supt. Fax 335-7367
www.rochesterschools.com
Allen ES 400/K-5
23 Granite St 03867 603-332-2280
Robert Hanson, prin. Fax 335-7381
Chamberlain Street ES 400/K-5
65 Chamberlain St 03867 603-332-5258
Stephen LeClair, prin. Fax 335-3098
Loud ES, 5 Cocheco Ave 03868 100/K-3
Maureen Oakman, prin. 603-332-6486
Maple Street ES, 27 Maple St 03867 100/K-4
Barbara McDowell, prin. 603-332-6481
McClelland ES 400/K-5
59 Brock St 03867 603-332-2180
Arlene Walker, prin. Fax 335-7369
Rochester MS 1,100/6-8
47 Brock St 03867 603-332-4090
Valerie McKenney, prin. Fax 332-9384
School Street ES, 13 School St 03867 100/K-4
Nancy Booth, prin. 603-332-6483
Other Schools – See East Rochester, Gonic

St. Elizabeth Seton S 200/K-8
16 Bridge St 03867 603-332-4803
Suzanne Boutin, prin. Fax 332-2915

Rollinsford, Strafford
Rollinsford SD
Supt. — See Somersworth
Rollinsford ES 200/K-6
487 Locust St 03869 603-742-2351
William Furbush, prin. Fax 749-5629

Rumney, Grafton
Rumney SD
Supt. — See Plymouth
Russell S 200/K-8
195 School St 03266 603-786-9591
Peter Helgerson, prin. Fax 786-9626

Rye, Rockingham
Rye SD
Supt. — See Greenland
Rye ES 300/PK-5
461 Sagamore Rd 03870 603-436-4731
Patricia Richardson, prin. Fax 431-6702
Rye JHS 200/6-8
501 Washington Rd 03870 603-964-5591
Christopher Pollet, prin. Fax 964-3881

Salem, Rockingham, Pop. 27,400
Salem SD 5,300/PK-12
38 Geremonty Dr 03079 603-893-7040
Michael Delahanty, supt. Fax 893-7052
www.salemschooldistrictnh.com
Barron ES 400/1-5
55 Butler St 03079 603-893-7067
Anthony Dinardo, prin. Fax 893-7068
Fisk ES 400/PK-5
14 Main St 03079 603-893-7051
Susan Rhodes, prin. Fax 893-7052
Haigh ES 200/1-5
24 School St 03079 603-893-7064
Christine Honey-Nadeau, prin. Fax 893-7065
Lancaster ES 300/1-5
54 Millville St 03079 603-893-7059
Adam Pagliarulo, prin. Fax 893-7059
North Salem ES 400/1-5
140 Zion Hill Rd 03079 603-893-7062
Janice Wilkins, prin.
Soule ES 200/1-5
173 S Policy St 03079 603-893-7053
Anna Parrill, prin. Fax 898-0218
Woodbury MS 1,200/6-8
206 Main St 03079 603-893-7055
Maura Palmer, prin. Fax 898-0634

St. Joseph Preschool 50/PK-PK
40 Main St 03079 603-893-5232
Catherine McDonough, dir. Fax 893-9236
St. Joseph Regional S 300/K-8
40 Main St 03079 603-893-6811
Ruth Hassett, prin. Fax 893-6811
Salem Christian S 100/PK-8
101 School St 03079 603-893-4289
Eldon Long, prin. Fax 893-9534

Salisbury, Merrimack
Merrimack Valley SD
Supt. — See Concord
Salisbury ES 100/K-5
6 Whittemore Rd 03268 603-648-2206
Sandra Davis, prin. Fax 648-2529

Sanbornton, Belknap
Winnisquam Regional SD
Supt. — See Tilton
Sanbornton Central ES 200/K-5
PO Box 109 03269 603-286-8223
Sandra Sterling, prin. Fax 286-2151

Sant Bani S 200/K-12
19 Ashram Rd 03269 603-934-4240
Kent Bicknell Ed.D., prin. Fax 934-2970

Sanbornville, Carroll
Wakefield SD
Supt. — See Union
Paul S 500/1-8
60 Taylor Way 03872 603-522-8891
Patrick Troy, prin. Fax 522-6143
Union ES, 60 Taylor Way 03872 50/K-K
Patrick Troy, prin. 603-473-2716

Sandown, Rockingham
Timberlane Regional SD
Supt. — See Plaistow
Sandown Central ES 200/4-5
295 Main St 03873 603-887-3648
Douglas Rolph, prin. Fax 887-3635
Sandown North ES 200/K-3
23 Stagecoach Rd 03873 603-887-8505
Jo Ann Georgian, prin. Fax 887-8509

Seabrook, Rockingham
Seabrook SD
Supt. — See Hampton
Seabrook ES 500/PK-4
256 Walton Rd 03874 603-474-2252
Jeni Mosca, prin. Fax 474-3504
Seabrook MS 400/5-8
256 Walton Rd 03874 603-474-9221
Jeni Mosca, prin. Fax 474-8020

Silver Lake, Carroll
Freedom SD 100/PK-6
626 Plains Rd 03875 603-539-2610
Dr. Gwen Poirier, supt. Fax 539-9064
Other Schools – See Freedom

Madison SD 200/K-6
626 Plains Rd 03875 603-539-2610
Dr. Gwen Poirier, supt. Fax 539-9064
Other Schools – See Madison

Tamworth SD 200/K-8
626 Plains Rd 03875 603-539-2610
Dr. Gwen Poirier, supt. Fax 539-9064
Other Schools – See Tamworth

Somersworth, Strafford, Pop. 11,720
Rollinsford SD 200/K-6
51 W High St 03878 603-692-4450
Karen Soule, supt. Fax 692-9100
Other Schools – See Rollinsford

Somersworth SD 1,800/PK-12
51 W High St 03878 603-692-4450
Karen Soule, supt. Fax 692-9100
www.sau56.org/
Hilltop ES 200/1-4
17 Grand St 03878 603-692-2435
Jerry Gregoire, prin. Fax 692-9115
Maple Wood ES 500/PK-4
184 Maple Street Ext 03878 603-692-3331
Caroline Butler, prin. Fax 692-4600
Somersworth MS 500/5-8
7 Memorial Dr 03878 603-692-2126
Paul Maskwa, prin. Fax 692-9101

Tri-City Christian Academy 300/PK-12
150 W High St 03878 603-692-2093
Paul Edgar, admin. Fax 692-6305

South Hampton, Rockingham, Pop. 740
South Hampton SD
Supt. — See Hampton
South Hampton Barnard S 100/K-8
219 Main Ave 03827 603-394-7744
Barbara Knapp, prin. Fax 394-0267

Amesbury SDA S 50/1-8
285 Main Ave 03827 603-394-9970

Stark, Coos
Stark SD
Supt. — See Groveton
Stark Village S 50/K-6
1192 Stark Hwy 03582 603-636-1092
Shelli Roberts, prin. Fax 636-1081

Stoddard, Cheshire
Stoddard SD
Supt. — See Henniker
Faulkner ES 50/K-5
PO Box 365 03464 603-446-3348
Mark Taft, prin. Fax 446-3638

Strafford, Strafford
Strafford SD
Supt. — See Northwood
Strafford S 500/K-8
22 Roller Coaster Rd Unit 1 03884 603-664-2842
Richard Jenisch, prin. Fax 664-5269

Stratham, Rockingham
Exeter Region Cooperative SD
Supt. — See Exeter
Cooperative MS 1,300/6-8
100 Academic Way 03885 603-775-8700
Thomas O'Malley, prin. Fax 775-0151

Stratham SD
Supt. — See Exeter
Stratham Memorial ES 600/PK-5
39 Gifford Farm Rd 03885 603-772-5413
Thomas Fosher, prin. Fax 772-0021

Cornerstone S 100/PK-8
146 High St 03885 603-772-4349
Lee Ann Robertson, hdmstr. Fax 772-4349

Sullivan, Cheshire, Pop. 706
Monadnock Regional SD
Supt. — See East Swanzey
Sullivan Central ES 50/1-3
PO Box 188 03445 603-847-3441
David Mousette, prin. Fax 847-3441

Sunapee, Sullivan
Sunapee SD 500/K-12
68 Main St 03782 603-763-4627
Brendan Minnihan, supt. Fax 763-4718
www.sunapee.k12.nh.us/
Sunapee Central ES 200/K-5
22 School St 03782 603-763-5675
Alan Pullman, prin. Fax 763-9627
Sunapee MS 100/6-8
10 North Rd 03782 603-763-5615
Sean Moynihan, prin. Fax 763-3055

Mount Royal Academy 100/K-12
26 Seven Hearths Ln 03782 603-763-9010
David Thibault, hdmstr. Fax 763-5390

Tamworth, Carroll
Tamworth SD
Supt. — See Silver Lake
Brett S 200/K-8
881 Tamworth Rd 03886 603-323-7271
Noel DeSousa, prin. Fax 323-7454

Temple, Hillsborough
Contoocook Valley SD
Supt. — See Peterborough
Temple ES 100/K-4
830 NH Route 45 03084 603-878-1955
Niki McGettigan, prin. Fax 878-2506

Thornton, Grafton
Thornton SD
Supt. — See Plymouth
Thornton Central S 200/K-8
1886 NH Route 175, 603-726-8904
Jonathan Bownes, prin. Fax 726-3801

Tilton, Belknap, Pop. 3,081
Winnisquam Regional SD 1,700/PK-12
433 W Main St 03276 603-286-4116
Dr. Tammy Davis, supt. Fax 286-7402
www.winnisquam.k12.nh.us
Winnisquam Regional MS 400/6-8
76 Winter St 03276 603-286-7143
Pamela Miller, prin. Fax 286-7410
Other Schools – See Northfield, Sanbornton

Troy, Cheshire
Monadnock Regional SD
Supt. — See East Swanzey
Troy ES 200/K-6
44 School St 03465 603-242-7741
David Dahl, prin. Fax 242-9710

Union, Carroll
Milton SD 700/K-12
39 Main St 03887 603-473-2326
William Lander, supt. Fax 473-2218
Other Schools – See Milton

Wakefield SD 500/K-8
39 Main St 03887 603-473-2326
William Lander, supt. Fax 473-2218
Other Schools – See Sanbornville

Walpole, Cheshire, Pop. 3,304
Fall Mountain Regional SD
Supt. — See Charlestown
Walpole MS 200/5-8
PO Box 549 03608 603-756-4728
Samuel Jacobs, prin. Fax 756-3343
Walpole PS 100/K-1
PO Box 549 03608 603-756-4241
Samuel Jacobs, prin. Fax 756-4131

Warner, Merrimack
Kearsarge Regional SD
Supt. — See New London
Simonds ES 200/K-5
PO Box 250 03278 603-456-2241
Judith Pellettieri, prin. Fax 456-3084

Warren, Grafton
Warren SD
Supt. — See North Haverhill
Warren Village ES 100/K-6
11 School St 03279 603-764-5538
Rose Darrow, prin. Fax 764-9382

Washington, Sullivan
Washington SD
Supt. — See Deering
Washington ES 100/K-5
337 Millen Pond Rd 03280 603-495-3463
Suzanne A. Lull, lead tchr. Fax 495-0140

Waterville Valley, Grafton
Waterville Valley SD
Supt. — See Plymouth
Waterville Valley S 50/K-8
PO Box 275 03215 603-236-4700
M. Gail Hannigan, prin. Fax 236-2018

Weare, Hillsborough
Weare SD
Supt. — See Henniker
Center Woods ES 600/PK-4
14 Center Rd 03281 603-529-4500
Jude Chauvette, prin. Fax 529-0446
Weare MS 600/5-8
16 East Rd 03281 603-529-7555
Mark Willis, prin. Fax 529-0464

Webster, Merrimack
Merrimack Valley SD
Supt. — See Concord
Webster ES 100/K-5
936 Battle St 03303 603-648-2467
Sandra Davis, prin. Fax 648-2439

Wentworth, Grafton
Wentworth SD
Supt. — See Plymouth
Wentworth S 100/K-8
PO Box 139 03282 603-764-5811
Keith Charpentier, prin. Fax 764-9973

West Franklin, Merrimack
Franklin SD
Supt. — See Franklin
Smith ES 300/K-2
41 Daniel Webster Dr 03235 603-934-4144
R. Michael Hoyt, prin. Fax 934-7449

West Lebanon, See Lebanon
Lebanon SD
Supt. — See Lebanon
Mt. Lebanon ES 200/PK-4
5 White Ave 03784 603-298-8202
Michael Foxall, prin. Fax 298-6433
Seminary Hill ES 100/5-6
20 Seminary Hl 03784 603-298-8500
Martha Langill, prin. Fax 298-6430

Estabrook S 50/1-8
101 Maple St 03784 603-298-8475
Fax 298-8475

Westmoreland, Cheshire
Westmoreland SD
Supt. — See Keene
Westmoreland S 200/K-8
40 Glebe Rd 03467 603-399-4421
Meredith Cargill, prin. Fax 399-7107

Pioneer Junior Academy 50/1-12
13 Mount Gilboa Rd 03467 603-399-4803

West Stewartstown, Coos
Stewartstown SD
Supt. — See Colebrook
Stewartstown Community S 100/K-8
PO Box 120 03597 603-246-7082
Melissa Loper, prin. Fax 246-3311

Whitefield, Coos, Pop. 1,041
White Mountains Regional SD 1,400/PK-12
14 King Sq 03598 603-837-9363
Dr. Louis Lafasciano, supt. Fax 837-2326
www.sau36.org
Whitefield S 300/K-8
PO Box 128 03598 603-837-3088
Ellen Turcotte, prin. Fax 837-9161
Other Schools – See Jefferson, Lancaster

Wilton, Hillsborough, Pop. 1,165
Lyndeborough SD 100/1-6
PO Box 1149 03086 603-878-8100
Dr. Leo Corriveau, supt. Fax 654-6691
Other Schools – See Lyndeborough

Wilton SD 300/K-6
PO Box 1149 03086 603-878-8100
Leo Corriveau, supt. Fax 654-6691
www.florencerideout.net/
Rideout ES 300/K-6
PO Box 430 03086 603-654-6714
Kenneth Griffin, prin. Fax 654-2018

Wilton-Lyndeborough SD 400/7-12
PO Box 1149 03086 603-878-8100
Leo Corriveau, supt. Fax 654-6691
www.wlcwarriors.net/
Wilton-Lyndeborough MS 100/7-8
PO Box 255 03086 603-654-6123
Jon Ingram, prin. Fax 654-2104

Pine Hill Waldorf S 200/PK-8
77 Pine Hill Dr 03086 603-654-6003
Suzan Moffett, admin. Fax 654-5012

Winchester, Cheshire, Pop. 1,735
Winchester SD
Supt. — See East Swanzey
Winchester S 300/PK-8
85 Parker St 03470 603-239-4721
David Funkhouser, prin. Fax 239-4968

Windham, Rockingham
Pelham SD 2,200/1-12
PO Box 510 03087 603-425-1976
Dr. Frank Bass, supt. Fax 425-1719
www.pelhamsd.org
Other Schools – See Pelham

Windham SD 1,600/PK-PK, 1-
PO Box 510 03087 603-425-1976
Dr. Frank Bass, supt. Fax 425-1719
www.windhamsd.org
Golden Brook S 400/1-2
112 Lowell Rd Ste B 03087 603-898-9586
Deb Armfield, prin. Fax 870-9030
Windham Center ES 600/3-5
2 Lowell Rd 03087 603-432-7312
Andrew Derosiers, prin. Fax 432-1189
Windham MS 600/6-8
112 Lowell Rd Ste A 03087 603-893-2636
Kori Becht, prin. Fax 870-9007
Windham-Pelham Preschool 50/PK-PK
21 Haverhill Rd 03087 603-425-1976
Tina McCoy, prin. Fax 425-1719

Wolfeboro, Carroll, Pop. 2,783
Governor Wentworth Regional SD 2,700/PK-12
140 Pine Hill Rd 03894 603-569-1658
John Robertson, supt. Fax 569-6983
www.govwentworth.k12.nh.us
Carpenter ES 300/K-3
PO Box 659 03894 603-569-3457
Janice Brooks, prin. Fax 569-8111
Crescent Lake S 200/4-6
75 McManus Rd 03894 603-569-0223
Jackleen Roberts, prin. Fax 569-4839
Kingswood Regional MS 500/7-8
404 S Main St 03894 603-569-3689
Kirkland Ross, prin. Fax 569-8113
Other Schools – See Center Ossipee, Center Tuftonboro, Effingham, New Durham

Woodsville, Grafton, Pop. 1,122
Haverhill Cooperative SD
Supt. — See North Haverhill
Woodsville ES 200/PK-3
206 Central St 03785 603-747-3363
Kathleen Clark, prin. Fax 747-3247

NEW JERSEY

NEW JERSEY DEPARTMENT OF EDUCATION
PO Box 500, Trenton 08625-0500
Telephone 609-292-4469
Fax 609-777-4099
Website http://www.state.nj.us/education

Commissioner of Education Lucille Davy

NEW JERSEY BOARD OF EDUCATION
100 River View Plz #CN500, Trenton 08611

President Josephine Hernandez

COUNTY SUPERINTENDENTS OF SCHOOLS

Atlantic County Office of Education
Mr. Thomas Dowd, supt. 609-625-0004
6260 Old Harding Hwy Ste 1 Fax 625-6539
Mays Landing 08330
www.aclink.org/education/homepage.asp

Bergen County Office of Education
Dr. Aaron Graham, supt. 201-336-6875
1 Bergen County Plz Ste 350 Fax 336-6880
Hackensack 07601

Burlington County Office of Education
Dr. Lester Richens, supt. 609-265-5060
2 Academy Dr, Westampton 08060 Fax 265-5922

Camden County Office of Education
Peggy Nicolosi, supt. 856-401-2400
PO Box 200, Blackwood 08012 Fax 401-2410

Cape May County Office of Education
Terrence Crowley, supt., 4 Moore Rd 609-465-1283
Cape May Court House Fax 465-2094

Cumberland County Office of Education
Michael Elwell, supt. 856-451-0211
19 Landis Ave, Bridgeton 08302 Fax 455-9523

Essex County Office of Education
Dr. Lawrence Feinsod, supt. 973-395-4677
7 Glenwood Ave Ste 404 Fax 395-4696
East Orange 07017

Gloucester County Office of Education
Dr. H. Mark Stanwood, supt. 856-468-6500
1492 Tanyard Rd, Sewell 08080 Fax 468-9115
www.co.gloucester.nj.us

Hudson County Office of Education
Dr. Timothy Brennan, supt. 201-319-3850
595 Newark Ave, Jersey City 07306 Fax 319-3650

Hunterdon County Office of Education
Christine Harttraft, supt. 908-788-1414
PO Box 2900, Flemington 08822 Fax 788-1457
www.co.hunterdon.nj.us/schools.htm

Mercer County Office of Education
Dr. Samuel Stewart, supt. 609-588-5884
1075 Old Trenton Rd Fax 588-5878
Trenton 08690

Middlesex County Office of Education
Dr. Patrick Piegari, supt. 732-249-2900
1460 Livingston Ave Fax 296-0683
North Brunswick 08902

Monmouth County Office of Education
Carole Morris, supt. 732-431-7816
60 Neptune Blvd Fl 2 Fax 776-7237
Neptune 07753

Morris County Office of Education
Dr. Kathleen Serafino, supt. 973-285-8332
PO Box 900, Morristown 07963 Fax 285-8341

Ocean County Office of Education
Dr. Bruce Greenfield, supt. 732-929-2078
212 Washington St Fax 506-5336
Toms River 08753

Passaic County Office of Education
Dr. Robert Gilmartin, supt. 973-569-2110
501 River St, Paterson 07524 Fax 754-0241

Salem County Office of Education
Robert Bumpus, supt. 856-339-8611
164 Route 45, Salem 08079 Fax 935-6290

Somerset County Office of Education
David Livingston, supt. 908-541-5700
PO Box 3000, Somerville 08876 Fax 722-6902

Sussex County Office of Education
Frank Dragotta, supt. 973-579-6996
262 White Lake Rd, Sparta 07871 Fax 579-6476
www.sussex.nj.us/

Union County Office of Education
Dr. Carmen Centuolo, supt. 908-654-9860
300 North Ave E, Westfield 07090 Fax 654-9869

Warren County Office of Education
Dr. Kevin Brennan, supt. 908-475-0464
1500A State Route 57 W Fax 475-1457
Washington 07882
www.warrennet.org/wcdoe/

PUBLIC, PRIVATE AND CATHOLIC ELEMENTARY SCHOOLS

Aberdeen, Monmouth, Pop. 17,038
Matawan-Aberdeen Regional SD 3,700/PK-12
1 Crest Way 07747 732-705-4003
Dr. Richard O'Malley, supt. Fax 290-0751
www.marsd.org/
Cambridge Park S PK-PK
1 Crest Way 07747 732-705-4000
Wayne Spells, prin.
Lloyd Road ES 600/4-5
401 Lloyd Rd 07747 732-705-5700
Patricia O'Keefe, prin. Fax 566-2975
Strathmore ES 500/K-3
282 Church St 07747 732-705-5900
Kenneth Smith, prin. Fax 290-8463
Other Schools – See Cliffwood, Matawan

Absecon, Atlantic, Pop. 7,989
Absecon CSD 800/K-8
800 Irelan Ave 08201 609-641-5375
James Giaquinto, supt. Fax 641-8692
www.abseconschools.org
Attales MS 400/5-8
800 Irelan Ave 08201 609-641-5375
Lynne Gale, prin. Fax 641-8692
Marsh ES 400/K-4
800 Irelan Ave 08201 609-641-5375
Joseph Giardina, prin. Fax 641-8692

Allamuchy, Warren, Pop. 2,764
Allamuchy Township SD 400/K-8
20 Johnsonburg Rd 07820 908-852-1894
Dr. Timothy Frederiks, supt. Fax 852-9816
www.aes.k12.nj.us
Allamuchy S 400/K-8
20 Johnsonburg Rd 07820 908-852-1894
Seth Cohen, prin. Fax 852-9816

Allendale, Bergen, Pop. 6,754
Allendale SD 1,000/K-8
100 Brookside Ave 07401 201-327-2020
Jerilyn Caprio Ed.D., supt. Fax 785-9735
www.allendaleschoolsnj.com
Brookside MS 600/4-8
100 Brookside Ave 07401 201-327-2021
Bruce Winkelstein, prin. Fax 825-6553
Hillside ES 400/K-3
89 Hillside Ave 07401 201-825-6565
Anastasia Maroulis, prin. Fax 236-8481

Allentown, Monmouth, Pop. 1,858
Upper Freehold Regional SD 2,300/PK-12
27 High St 08501 609-259-7292
Dr. Richard Fitzpatrick, supt. Fax 259-0881
www.ufrsd.net
Upper Freehold Regional ES 700/PK-4
27 High St 08501 609-259-7369
Kelly Huggins, prin. Fax 208-1411
Upper Freehold Regional MS 500/5-8
27 High St 08501 609-259-7369
Mark Guterl, prin. Fax 208-1411

Allenwood, Monmouth, Pop. 1,400
Wall Township SD
Supt. — See Wall
Allenwood ES 500/K-5
3301 Allenwood Lakewood Rd 08720 732-556-2150
William Carson, prin. Fax 223-6259

Shore Christian Academy 100/PK-8
PO Box 515 08720 732-938-3565
Fax 938-4729

Alloway, Salem, Pop. 1,371
Alloway Township SD 500/PK-8
PO Box 327 08001 856-935-1622
Robert Bazzel, supt. Fax 935-3017
www.alloway.k12.nj.us
Alloway Township S 500/PK-8
PO Box 327 08001 856-935-1622
Janis Gansert, prin. Fax 935-3017

Alpha, Warren, Pop. 2,455
Alpha SD 300/K-8
817 North Blvd 08865 908-454-5000
Donna Medea, admin. Fax 454-4347
alphapublicschool.com
Alpha S 300/K-8
817 North Blvd 08865 908-454-5000
Donna Medea, admin. Fax 454-4347

Alpine, Bergen, Pop. 2,368
Alpine SD 100/K-8
500 Hillside Ave 07620 201-768-8255
Dr. Kathleen Semergieff, supt. Fax 768-7855
www.alpineschool.org
Alpine S 100/K-8
500 Hillside Ave 07620 201-768-8255
Dr. Kathleen Semergieff, prin. Fax 768-7855

Andover, Sussex, Pop. 661

Tranquility Adventist S 50/PK-8
3 Academy Ln 07821 908-852-1391
Fax 852-4710

Annandale, Hunterdon, Pop. 1,074

Immaculate Conception S 500/PK-8
314 Old Allerton Rd 08801 908-735-6334
Annamarie Reilly, prin. Fax 238-0724

Asbury, Hunterdon
Bethlehem Township SD 600/K-8
940 Iron Bridge Rd 08802 908-537-4044
Dr. Carol Conger, supt. Fax 537-4309
www.btschools.org
Conley ES 300/K-4
940 Iron Bridge Rd 08802 908-537-4044
Dr. Nancy Lubarsky, prin. Fax 537-7224
Hoppock MS 300/5-8
280 Asbury West Portal Rd 08802 908-479-6336
Edward Keegan, prin. Fax 479-1021

Asbury Park, Monmouth, Pop. 16,624
Asbury Park SD 2,200/PK-12
603 Mattison Ave Ste 3 07712 732-776-2606
Denise Love, supt. Fax 774-8067
www.asburypark.k12.nj.us/
Asbury Park MS 500/6-8
1200 Bangs Ave 07712 732-776-2559
Howard Mednick, prin. Fax 776-7503
Bangs Avenue ES 400/K-5
1300 Bangs Ave 07712 732-776-2545
Kathy Baumgardner, prin. Fax 775-1428
Bradley ES 300/PK-5
1100 3rd Ave 07712 732-776-3100
Dr. Leslie Brian, prin. Fax 776-2284
Marshall ES 500/K-5
600 Monroe Ave 07712 732-776-2660
Roberta Beauford, prin. Fax 775-5067

Our Lady of Mt. Carmel S 200/K-8
1212 1st Ave 07712 732-775-8989
Sr. Jude Boyce, prin. Fax 775-0108

Atco, Camden
Waterford Township SD
Supt. — See Waterford Works
Atco ES 200/K-1
2162 Cooper Rd 08004 856-767-4200
Jennifer Boulden, prin. Fax 768-5497
Richards ES 300/2-3
934 Lincoln Ave 08004 856-767-2421
Dr. Will Maddox, prin. Fax 753-1032

Winslow Township SD 6,000/PK-12
30 Cooper Folly Rd 08004 856-767-2850
Dr. Daniel Swirsky, supt. Fax 767-4782
www.winslow-schools.com
Winslow Township MS 1,300/6-8
30 Cooper Folly Rd 08004 856-767-7222
Kurt Marella, prin. Fax 767-5411
Other Schools – See Berlin, Blue Anchor, Sicklerville

Assumption S 200/1-8
2122 Cooper Rd 08004 856-767-0569
Paul Ricci, prin. Fax 768-8910

Atlantic City, Atlantic, Pop. 40,368
Atlantic City SD 6,100/PK-12
1300 Atlantic Ave 08401 609-343-7200
Fredrick Nickles, supt. Fax 345-3268
www.acboe.org/
Chelsea Heights ES 300/K-7
4101 Filbert Ave 08401 609-343-7272
Kenneth Flood, prin. Fax 344-7668
King S 600/PK-8
1700 Marmora Ave 08401 609-343-7380
Debra Brown, prin. Fax 343-1647
New Jersey Avenue ES 300/PK-6
35 N New Jersey Ave 08401 609-343-7290
Sylvia Stewart, prin. Fax 343-6573
New York Ave S 600/PK-8
411 N New York Ave 08401 609-343-7280
James Knox, prin. Fax 345-2603
Richmond Ave S 100/K-6
30 N Brighton Ave 08401 609-343-7200
Gabrielle Caldwell, prin. Fax 344-0974
Sovereign Avenue S 600/K-6
111 N Sovereign Ave 08401 609-343-7260
Medina Peyton, prin. Fax 343-1583
Texas Avenue S 400/K-8
2523 Arctic Ave 08401 609-343-7350
Rosetta Johnson, prin. Fax 343-0016
Uptown S Complex 700/K-8
323 Madison Ave 08401 609-344-8809
LaKecia Hyman, prin. Fax 449-0346
Venice Park ES 50/PK-PK
1601 Penrose Ave 08401 609-343-7270
Debra Brown, prin. Fax 347-9598

New Hope Christian Academy 100/PK-3
715 Baltic Ave 08401 609-344-2737
Rev. John Howard, supt. Fax 344-2771
Our Lady Star of the Sea S 300/PK-8
15 N California Ave 08401 609-345-0648
Sr. Mary Shamus Zehrer, prin. Fax 344-0248

Atlantic Highlands, Monmouth, Pop. 4,625
Atlantic Highlands SD 300/K-6
140 1st Ave 07716 732-291-2020
Christopher Rooney, supt. Fax 872-9117
www.ahes.k12.nj.us
Atlantic Highlands ES 300/K-6
140 1st Ave 07716 732-291-2020
Christopher Rooney, prin. Fax 872-9117

Middletown Township SD
Supt. — See Middletown
Navesink ES 200/K-5
151 Monmouth Ave 07716 732-291-0289
Charlene O'Hagan, prin.

Mother Teresa Regional S 200/PK-8
55 South Ave 07716 732-291-1050
Melissa Molloy, prin. Fax 872-2293

Audubon, Camden, Pop. 9,047
Audubon SD 1,200/PK-12
350 Edgewood Ave 08106 856-547-1325
Donald Borden, supt. Fax 546-8550
www.audubon.k12.nj.us/
Haviland Avenue ES 100/PK-2
240 S Haviland Ave 08106 856-546-4922
Dr. Carleene Slowik, prin. Fax 547-1248
Mansion Avenue ES 200/3-6
300 Mansion Ave 08106 856-546-4926
Theodore Clarke, prin. Fax 547-1483

Avalon, Cape May, Pop. 2,133
Avalon SD 100/1-8
235 32nd St 08202 609-967-7544
David Rauenzahn, supt. Fax 967-3109
web.mac.com/avalonelementaschool/avalonweb07-08/Welcome.html
Avalon S 100/1-8
235 32nd St 08202 609-967-7544
Stacey LaRocca-Tracy, admin. Fax 967-3109

Avenel, Middlesex, Pop. 15,504
Woodbridge Township SD
Supt. — See Woodbridge
Avenel MS 700/6-8
85 Woodbine Ave 07001 732-396-7020
Gary Kuzniak, prin. Fax 574-0573
Avenel Street ES 400/K-5
230 Avenel St 07001 732-602-8504
Dara Kurlander, prin. Fax 855-9586
Woodbine Avenue ES 300/K-5
89 Woodbine Ave 07001 732-602-8523
Mary Jane Small, prin. Fax 855-0650

Avon by the Sea, Monmouth, Pop. 2,189
Avon Borough SD 100/K-8
505 Lincoln Ave 07717 732-775-4328
Helen Payne, supt. Fax 775-0761
www.avonschool.com/
Avon S 100/K-8
505 Lincoln Ave 07717 732-775-4328
Helen Payne, prin. Fax 775-0761

Barnegat, Ocean, Pop. 1,160
Barnegat Township SD 2,900/K-12
550 Barnegat Blvd N 08005 609-698-5800
Robert Mahon, supt. Fax 698-6638
www.bts.k12.nj.us
Brackman MS 800/6-8
600 Barnegat Blvd N 08005 609-698-5880
Stephen Nichol, prin. Fax 698-7965
Collins ES 600/K-5
570 Barnegat Blvd N 08005 609-698-5832
George Delaporte, prin. Fax 698-5843
Donahue ES, 200 Bengal Blvd 08005 K-5
George Chidiac, prin. 609-698-9634
Dunfee ES 300/K-5
128 Barnegat Blvd S 08005 609-698-5826
Katherine Makela, prin. Fax 698-2083
Horbelt ES 400/K-5
104 Burr St 08005 609-660-7500
Scott Kiewe, prin. Fax 660-7501

Barrington, Camden, Pop. 7,050
Barrington Borough SD 600/K-8
311 Reading Ave 08007 856-547-8467
Dr. Loyola Garcia, supt. Fax 547-5533
www.barringtonschools.net/
Woodland MS 200/6-8
1 School Ln 08007 856-547-8402
Patricia Moore, prin. Fax 522-1248
Other Schools – See Haddonfield

Castle Academy 200/PK-8
60 E Gloucester Pike 08007 856-546-5901

Basking Ridge, Somerset, Pop. 4,000
Bernards Township SD 5,200/K-12
101 Peachtree Rd 07920 908-204-2600
Dr. Valerie Goger, supt. Fax 766-7641
www.bernardsboe.com/
Annin MS 1,200/6-8
70 Quincy Rd 07920 908-204-2610
Karen Hudock, prin. Fax 204-0244
Cedar Hill ES 500/K-5
100 Peachtree Rd 07920 908-204-2633
Joseph Mollica, prin. Fax 204-1956
Mount Prospect ES 700/K-5
111 Hansom Rd 07920 908-470-1600
Judith Slutzky, prin. Fax 470-1610
Oak Street ES 600/K-5
70 W Oak St 07920 908-204-2565
Dr. Jane Costa, prin. Fax 204-9289
Other Schools – See Liberty Corner

Albrook S 200/PK-6
361 Somerville Rd 07920 908-580-0661
Anita Albers, dir. Fax 580-0785
Mendham Country Day S 200/PK-6
PO Box 167 07920 908-766-3323
Barbara Rogers, prin. Fax 766-1484
St. James S 400/PK-8
PO Box 310 07920 908-766-4774
Jeremiah Kenny, prin. Fax 766-4432

Bay Head, Ocean, Pop. 1,259
Bay Head SD 100/K-8
145 Grove St 08742 732-892-0668
Dr. John Ravally, supt. Fax 892-6427
www.bayheadschool.org
Bay Head S 100/K-8
145 Grove St 08742 732-892-0668
Walter Therien, prin. Fax 892-6427

Bayonne, Hudson, Pop. 59,987
Bayonne SD 8,200/PK-12
669 Avenue A 07002 201-858-5800
Dr. Patricia McGeehan, supt. Fax 858-6289
www.bhs.bboed.org/
Bailey S 600/PK-8
75 W 10th St 07002 201-858-5824
James McCabe, prin. Fax 858-6246
Donohoe S 400/PK-8
25 E 5th St 07002 201-858-5969
Nancy Ruane, prin. Fax 858-3720
Harris S 600/PK-8
135 Avenue C 07002 201-858-5945
Tom Fogu, prin. Fax 436-5169
Lincoln S 400/PK-8
208 Prospect Ave 07002 201-858-5973
Dennis Degnan Ed.D., prin. Fax 858-6246
Mann S 500/PK-8
25 W 38th St 07002 201-858-5979
Charles Costello, prin. Fax 243-4283
Midtown Community S 1,000/PK-8
550 Avenue A 07002 201-858-5984
Christina Mercun, prin. Fax 858-4584
Public S 14 200/4-8
33 E 24th St 07002 201-858-6281
Janice Lo Re, prin. Fax 436-5079
Robinson S 600/PK-8
95 W 31st St 07002 201-858-5964
Kevin Moran, prin. Fax 858-5845
Vroom S 400/PK-8
18 W 26th St 07002 201-858-5956
Maryann Connelly, prin. Fax 858-5562
Washington S 500/PK-8
191 Avenue B 07002 201-858-5990
Peter Anastas, prin. Fax 436-0256
Wilson S 600/PK-8
101 W 56th St 07002 201-858-5996
Dr. Catherine Quinn, prin. Fax 339-8513

All Saints Academy 200/PK-8
19 W 13th St 07002 201-437-2888
Sr. Eileen Wust, prin. Fax 437-3088
Beacon Christian Academy 100/K-8
100 E 22nd St 07002 201-437-5056
Fax 437-5059

Bayville, Ocean
Berkeley Township SD 1,700/K-6
53 Central Pkwy 08721 732-269-2909
Joseph Vicari Ed.D., supt. Fax 269-4487
www.berkeleytwpschools.com
Bayville ES 400/K-4
356 Atlantic City Blvd 08721 732-269-1300
Arleen Lippincott, prin. Fax 237-2142
Berkeley Township ES 500/5-6
10 Emory Ave 08721 732-269-2909
James Roselli, prin.
Potter ES 400/K-4
60 Veeder Ln 08721 732-269-5700
Jeffery Zito, prin. Fax 269-3044
Worth ES 400/K-4
57 Central Pkwy 08721 732-269-1700
Daniel Prima, prin. Fax 237-2159

Central Regional SD 2,100/7-12
509 Forest Hills Pkwy 08721 732-269-1100
T. Parlapanides, supt. Fax 237-8872
www.centralreg.k12.nj.us
Central Regional MS 700/7-8
509 Forest Hills Pkwy 08721 732-269-1100
Joseph Firetto, prin. Fax 269-7723

Beach Haven, Ocean, Pop. 1,352
Beach Haven Borough SD 100/PK-6
700 N Beach Ave 08008 609-492-7411
Dr. Patricia Daggy, supt. Fax 492-5657
Beach Haven ES 100/PK-6
700 N Beach Ave 08008 609-492-7411
Dr. Patricia Daggy, prin. Fax 492-5657

Beachwood, Ocean, Pop. 10,738
Toms River Regional SD
Supt. — See Toms River
Beachwood ES 600/K-5
901 Berkeley Ave 08722 732-505-5820
James Ricotta, prin. Fax 341-1659
Toms River IS South 1,100/6-8
1675 Pinewald Rd 08722 732-818-8570
Paul Gluck, prin. Fax 818-7512

Bedminster, Somerset
Bedminster Township SD 600/K-8
234 Somerville Rd 07921 908-234-0768
Dr. Andrew Rinko, supt. Fax 234-2318
www.bedminsterschool.org
Bedminster Township S 600/K-8
234 Somerville Rd 07921 908-234-0768
Christine McCann, prin. Fax 234-2318

Belford, Monmouth, Pop. 6,000
Middletown Township SD
Supt. — See Middletown
Bayview ES 400/K-5
300 Leonardville Rd 07718 732-787-3590
John Andl, prin.

Belleville, Essex, Pop. 36,300
Belleville SD 4,300/K-12
102 Passaic Ave 07109 973-450-3500
Melindo Persi, supt. Fax 450-3504
www.belleville.k12.nj.us/
Belleville ES 3 300/K-6
230 Joralemon St 07109 973-450-3530
Lucyn Demikoff, prin. Fax 450-3084
Belleville ES 4 300/K-6
30 Magnolia St 07109 973-450-3540
Paula Cummis, prin. Fax 450-5463
Belleville ES 5 300/K-6
149 Adelaide St 07109 973-450-3450
Dennis Villano, prin. Fax 844-1424
Belleville ES 7 400/K-6
20 Passaic Ave 07109 973-450-3470
Marilyn Hawthorne, prin. Fax 844-1421
Belleville ES 8 500/K-6
183 Union Ave 07109 973-450-3480
Joseph Petrillo, prin. Fax 844-1428
Belleville ES 9 100/K-6
301 Ralph St 07109 973-450-3490
Nanette Rotonda, prin. Fax 450-3488
Belleville ES 10 100/K-6
527 Belleville Ave 07109 973-450-3510
Dr. Marilyn McGrath, prin. Fax 844-1433
Belleville MS 700/7-8
279 Washington Ave 07109 973-450-3532
Carmine Guinta, prin. Fax 450-5001

Newark SD
Supt. — See Newark
Elliott Street S @ St. Anthony 3-4
25 N 7th St 07109 – Eva Ortiz, prin. 973-450-9333

St. Peter S 300/PK-8
152 William St 07109 973-759-3143
Marilyn Castellano, prin. Fax 759-4160

Bellmawr, Camden, Pop. 11,159
Bellmawr Borough SD 1,000/K-8
256 Anderson Ave 08031 856-931-3620
Annette Castiglione, supt. Fax 931-9326
bellmawrschools.org
Bellmawr Park ES 300/K-4
29 Peach Rd 08031 856-931-6272
Elizabeth Calabria, prin. Fax 931-1322
Bell Oaks MS 400/5-8
256 Anderson Ave 08031 856-931-6273
Anthony Farinelli, prin. Fax 931-9326
Burke ES 200/K-4
112 S Black Horse Pike 08031 856-931-6362
Frank Jankowski, prin. Fax 931-1417

Belmar, Monmouth, Pop. 5,962
Belmar SD 500/PK-8
1101 Main St 07719 732-681-2388
Paul Shappirio, supt. Fax 681-8709
www.belmar.k12.nj.us/

Belmar S 500/PK-8
1101 Main St 07719 732-681-2388
Paul Shappirio, prin. Fax 681-5334

Chrismont Montessori Academy 50/PK-6
503 7th Ave 07719 732-681-5641
Dr. Collyn Swanson, prin. Fax 280-3637
St. Rose S 400/K-8
605 6th Ave 07719 732-681-5555
Bill Roberts, prin. Fax 681-5890

Belvidere, Warren, Pop. 2,732
Belvidere SD 900/K-12
809 Oxford St 07823 908-475-6600
Dirk Swaneveld, supt. Fax 475-6619
www.belvideresd.org
Oxford Street MS 200/4-8
807 Oxford St 07823 908-475-4001
Karl Rice, prin. Fax 475-6619
Third Street ES 100/K-3
300 3rd St 07823 908-475-0104
Sandra Szabocsik, prin. Fax 475-3521

White Township SD 400/K-8
565 County Road 519 07823 908-475-4773
Linda Heilman, admin. Fax 475-3627
www.warrennet.org/whiteschool/
White Township S 400/K-8
565 County Road 519 07823 908-475-4773
Linda Heilman, admin. Fax 475-3627

Bergenfield, Bergen, Pop. 26,056
Bergenfield SD 3,500/K-12
100 S Prospect Ave 07621 201-385-8202
Dr. Michael Kuchar, supt. Fax 384-2914
www.bergenfield.org/
Brown MS 900/6-8
130 S Washington Ave 07621 201-385-8847
Seamus Regan, prin. Fax 385-0219
Franklin ES 400/K-5
2 N Franklin Ave 07621 201-385-8581
Rosemary LaGamma, prin. Fax 385-9708
Hoover ES 200/K-5
293 Murray Hill Ter 07621 201-385-8582
Peter Monchino, prin. Fax 385-0946
Jefferson ES 200/K-5
200 Hickory Ave 07621 201-385-8804
Hugh Beattie, prin. Fax 385-9389
Lincoln ES 300/K-5
115 Highview Ave 07621 201-385-8759
Steven Kaminsky, prin. Fax 385-9838
Washington ES 300/K-5
49 S Summit St 07621 201-385-8771
Dr. Ronald Kopec, prin. Fax 385-3703

Transfiguration Academy - Lower 100/PK-4
10 Bradley Ave 07621 201-384-3627
Sr. Madeline Hanson, prin. Fax 384-0293
Yeshivat Noam 200/PK-K
139 S Washington Ave 07621 201-439-1919
Rabbi Chaim Hagler, prin. Fax 439-1688

Berkeley Heights, Union, Pop. 11,980
Berkeley Heights SD 2,800/PK-12
345 Plainfield Ave 07922 908-464-1718
Judith Rattner, supt. Fax 464-1728
www.bhpsnj.org/
Columbia MS 600/6-8
345 Plainfield Ave 07922 908-464-1600
Frank Geiger, prin. Fax 464-0017
Hughes ES 300/2-5
446 Snyder Ave 07922 908-464-1717
Fax 464-1783
McMillin ECC 400/PK-1
651 Mountain Ave 07922 908-464-5583
Anne Corley-Hand, prin. Fax 464-5398
Mountain Park ES 300/2-5
55 Fairfax Dr 07922 908-464-1713
Jonathan Morisseau, prin. Fax 665-0969
Woodruff ES 200/2-5
55 Briarwood Dr W 07922 908-464-1723
Patricia Gasparini, prin. Fax 464-3369

Berlin, Camden, Pop. 7,844
Berlin Borough SD 800/PK-8
215 S Franklin Ave 08009 856-767-6785
Dr. James Lavender, supt. Fax 767-2465
www.bcsberlin.k12.nj.us
Berlin Community S 800/PK-8
215 S Franklin Ave 08009 856-767-0129
Kathleen Conaway, prin. Fax 767-2465

Winslow Township SD
Supt. — See Atco
Winslow Township Upper ES 5 600/3-5
130 Oak Leaf Rd 08009 856-728-9445
Cynthia Reid, prin. Fax 875-5402

Our Lady of Mt. Carmel Regional S 300/K-8
1 N Cedar Ave 08009 856-767-1751
Sr. Mary Ellen Tucker, prin. Fax 767-1293

Bernardsville, Somerset, Pop. 7,612
Somerset Hills SD 2,000/K-12
25 Olcott Ave 07924 908-630-3011
Peter Miller, supt. Fax 953-0567
www.shsd.org/
Bedwell ES 700/K-4
141 Seney Dr 07924 908-204-1920
Amy Phelan, prin. Fax 204-0481
Bernardsville MS 600/5-8
141 Seney Dr 07924 908-204-1916
Dr. Lynn Kratz, prin. Fax 953-2184

St. Elizabeth S 200/PK-8
30 Seney Dr 07924 908-766-0244
William Venezia, prin. Fax 766-5273

Beverly, Burlington, Pop. 2,670
Beverly CSD 200/PK-8
601 Bentley Ave 08010 609-387-2200
Dr. Brian Gross, supt. Fax 387-4447
Beverly S 200/PK-8
601 Bentley Ave 08010 609-387-2200
Dr. Brian Gross, prin. Fax 387-4447

Blackwood, Camden, Pop. 5,120
Gloucester Township SD 7,500/K-8
17 Erial Rd 08012 856-227-1400
Thomas Seddon, supt. Fax 228-1422
www.gloucestertownshipschools.org/
Blackwood ES 600/K-5
260 Erial Rd 08012 856-227-9510
Kim Capone, prin. Fax 228-2005
Chews ES 800/K-5
600 Somerdale Rd 08012 856-783-6607
Tracy Elwell, prin. Fax 783-8696
Glen Landing MS 900/6-8
85 Little Gloucester Rd 08012 856-227-3534
Suzanne Schultes, prin. Fax 228-5260
Gloucester Township ES 300/K-5
270 S Black Horse Pike 08012 856-227-8845
Joseph Gentile, prin. Fax 228-4366
Lewis MS 700/6-8
875 Erial Rd 08012 856-227-8400
Alan Gansert, prin. Fax 228-5130
Loring-Flemming ES 700/K-5
135 Little Gloucester Rd 08012 856-227-4045
Patricia Ferrier, prin. Fax 228-4666
Other Schools – See Erial, Glendora, Sicklerville

Our Lady of Hope Regional S 400/K-8
420 S Black Horse Pike 08012 856-227-4442
Sr. Paula Randow, prin. Fax 401-1622

Blairstown, Warren
Blairstown Township SD 700/K-6
PO Box E 07825 908-362-6111
Mark Saalfield, supt. Fax 362-9638
www.blairstownelem.net
Blairstown ES 700/K-6
PO Box E 07825 908-362-6111
Rosemary Goodman, prin. Fax 362-9638

Bloomfield, Essex, Pop. 48,200
Bloomfield Township SD 5,300/PK-12
155 Broad St 07003 973-680-8555
Frank Digesere, supt. Fax 680-0263
www.bloomfield.k12.nj.us
Berkeley ES 400/PK-6
351 Bloomfield Ave 07003 973-680-8540
Pat Pelikan, prin. Fax 743-0307
Bloomfield MS 800/7-8
60 Huck Rd 07003 973-680-8620
Salvatore Goncalves, prin. Fax 338-6523
Brookdale ES 300/K-6
1230 Broad St 07003 973-680-8520
Ruthann Cherence, prin. Fax 338-0704
Carteret ES 400/K-6
158 Grove St 07003 973-680-8580
Gina Rosamilia, prin. Fax 743-5310
Demarest ES 400/K-6
465 Broughton Ave 07003 973-680-8510
Mary Todaro, prin. Fax 893-9547
Fairview ES 500/K-6
376 Berkeley Ave 07003 973-680-8550
Salvatore DeSimone, prin. Fax 743-9782
Franklin ES 300/K-6
85 Curtis St 07003 973-680-8560
Marianne Abbasso, prin. Fax 743-0249
Oak View ES 300/PK-6
150 Garrabrant Ave 07003 973-680-8590
Julia Andriolo, prin. Fax 893-0534
Watsessing ES 300/K-6
71 Prospect St 07003 973-680-8570
Louis Clerico, prin. Fax 566-9135

St. Thomas the Apostle S 400/PK-8
50 Byrd Ave 07003 973-338-8505
Joan Ferraer, prin. Fax 338-9565

Bloomingdale, Passaic, Pop. 7,654
Bloomingdale SD 600/PK-8
31 Captolene Ave 07403 973-838-3282
Fredda Rosenberg Ed.D., supt. Fax 838-6397
www.bloomingdaleschools.org
Bergen MS 300/5-8
225 Glenwild Ave 07403 973-838-4835
Dr. Fredda Rosenberg, prin. Fax 283-1893
Day ES 100/PK-1
225 Rafkind Rd 07403 973-838-1311
Cheryl Mallen, prin. Fax 283-1476
Donald ES 200/2-4
29 Captolene Ave 07403 973-838-5353
Sharon Biggs, prin. Fax 838-3195

Bloomsbury, Hunterdon, Pop. 886
Bloomsbury SD 100/K-8
20 Main St 08804 908-479-4414
Michael Slattery, admin. Fax 479-1631
www.bburyes.com
Bloomsbury S 100/K-8
20 Main St 08804 908-479-4414
Michael Slattery, prin. Fax 479-1631

Blue Anchor, Atlantic
Winslow Township SD
Supt. — See Atco
Winslow Township ES 1 400/PK-2
413 Inskip Rd 08037 609-561-8300
Dr. Marianne Gaffney, prin. Fax 704-1032

Bogota, Bergen, Pop. 8,150
Bogota SD 1,200/K-12
1 Henry C Luthin Pl 07603 201-441-4800
John Hynes, supt. Fax 489-5759
bogotaboe.com
Bixby ES 300/K-6
25 Fischer Ave 07603 201-441-4834
Linda Gattuso, prin. Fax 525-1313
Steen ES 300/K-6
152 W Main St 07603 201-342-6446
Robert Watts, prin. Fax 342-6446

St. Joseph S 200/K-8
131 E Fort Lee Rd 07603 201-487-8641
James Newman, prin. Fax 487-7405
Trinity Lutheran S 100/PK-1
167 Palisade Ave 07603 201-487-3580
Cynthia Keohane, prin. Fax 487-1748

Boonton, Morris, Pop. 8,555
Boonton SD 1,200/K-12
434 Lathrop Ave 07005 973-335-3994
Christine Johnson, supt. Fax 335-8281
www.boontonschools.org
Boonton MS 100/7-8
306 Lathrop Ave 07005 973-335-9700
Augustus Modla, prin. Fax 402-5135
Hill ES 200/4-6
435 Lathrop Ave 07005 973-316-9235
Jennifer Aquino, prin. Fax 402-9375
School Street ES 300/K-3
724 Birch St 07005 973-316-9225
Robert Sutter, prin. Fax 402-9283

Boonton Township SD 500/K-8
11 Valley Rd 07005 973-334-4162
Dr. Roseann Humphrey, supt. Fax 334-0035
www.rvsnj.org
Rockaway Valley S 500/K-8
11 Valley Rd 07005 973-334-4162
Roseann Humphrey, prin. Fax 334-0035

Parsippany-Troy Hills Township SD
Supt. — See Parsippany
Intervale ES 300/K-5
60 Pitt Rd 07005 973-263-7075
Christopher Waack, prin. Fax 331-7150

Our Lady of Mt. Carmel S 200/PK-7
205 Oak St 07005 973-334-2777
Gladys Driscoll, prin. Fax 334-0975

Bordentown, Burlington, Pop. 3,989
Bordentown Regional SD 2,200/K-12
318 Ward Ave 08505 609-298-0025
Dr. Constance Bauer, supt. Fax 298-2515
www.bordentown.k12.nj.us
Barton ES 200/K-3
100 Crosswicks St 08505 609-298-0676
Daniel Riether, prin. Fax 324-2898
Bordentown Regional MS 500/6-8
50 Dunns Mill Rd 08505 609-298-0674
Robert Walder, prin. Fax 291-1929
McFarland IS 400/4-5
87 Crosswicks St 08505 609-291-7192
Dr. Norine Gerepka, prin. Fax 291-7199
Muschal ES 500/K-3
323 Ward Ave 08505 609-298-2600
Edward Chmiel, prin. Fax 324-1788

Holy Cross Lutheran S 100/PK-PK
280 Crosswicks Rd 08505 609-298-2880
Kathy Schroeder, dir. Fax 298-1411
St. Mary S 200/PK-8
30 Elizabeth St 08505 609-298-1448
Michael Rosenberg, prin. Fax 298-3803

Bound Brook, Somerset, Pop. 10,168
Bound Brook Borough SD 1,400/PK-12
337 W 2nd St 08805 732-652-7920
Dr. Edward Hoffman, supt. Fax 271-9097
www.bbrook.k12.nj.us
Lafayette ES 300/3-5
50 W High St 08805 732-652-7930
Janet Kellman, prin. Fax 271-5783
LaMonte ES 200/PK-2
337 W 2nd St 08805 732-652-7932
Janet Kellman, prin. Fax 748-8524
LaMonte ES Annex 200/PK-2
330 W 2nd St 08805 732-652-7934
Janet Kellman, prin.
Smalley MS 300/6-8
163 Cherry Ave 08805 732-652-7940
Edward Gordon, prin. Fax 271-4879

Holy Family Academy 200/PK-8
120 E 2nd St 08805 732-356-1151
Judith Clayton, prin. Fax 356-6844

Bradley Beach, Monmouth, Pop. 4,782
Bradley Beach SD 200/PK-8
515 Brinley Ave 07720 732-775-4413
Dr. Wayne Turner, supt. Fax 775-2463
www.bbes.org/
Bradley Beach S 200/PK-8
515 Brinley Ave 07720 732-775-4413
Dr. Wayne Turner, prin. Fax 775-2463

Branchburg, Somerset
Branchburg Township SD 1,900/K-8
240 Baird Rd 08876 908-722-3265
Kenneth Knops, supt. Fax 526-6144
www.branchburg.k12.nj.us
Branchburg Central MS 700/6-8
220 Baird Rd 08876 908-526-1415
William Feldman, prin. Fax 526-7486
Old York ES 300/3-5
580 Old York Rd 08876 908-725-2828
Matthew Barbosa, prin. Fax 725-2434
Stony Brook ES 300/3-5
136 Cedar Grove Rd 08876 908-722-2400
Frank Altmire, prin. Fax 722-4201
Other Schools – See Neshanic Station

Branchville, Sussex, Pop. 844
Frankford Township SD 700/PK-8
4 Pines Rd 07826 973-948-3727
Braden Hirsch, supt. Fax 948-2907
www.frankfordschool.org
Frankford Township S 700/PK-8
2 Pines Rd 07826 973-948-3727
Braden Hirsch, prin. Fax 948-6593

Brick, Ocean, Pop. 78,300
Brick Township SD 10,200/PK-12
101 Hendrickson Ave 08724 732-785-3000
Mary Ann Ceres, supt. Fax 840-9089
www.brickschools.org/
Brick Primary Learning Center 700/PK-K
224 Chambersbridge Rd 08723 732-262-2590
Rochelle Sheiman, prin. Fax 920-3417
Drum Point Road ES 500/1-5
41 Drum Point Rd 08723 732-262-2570
Susan Genco, prin. Fax 262-2795
Herbertsville ES 300/1-5
2282 Lanes Mill Rd 08724 732-785-3080
Patricia LoRusso, prin. Fax 458-5252
Lake Riviera MS 1,100/6-8
171 Beaverson Blvd 08723 732-262-2600
Susan McNamara, prin. Fax 477-0392
Lanes Mill Road ES 500/1-5
1891 Lanes Mill Rd 08724 732-785-3060
Jeffrey Luckenbach, prin. Fax 458-3830
Midstreams ES 500/1-5
500 Midstreams Rd 08724 732-785-3070
Gertrude Davis-Rebelo, prin. Fax 899-9528
Osbornville ES 300/1-5
218 Drum Point Rd 08723 732-262-2560
Maureen Higgins, prin. Fax 262-3813
Veteran's Memorial ES 600/1-5
103 Hendrickson Ave 08724 732-785-3052
Dr. Alyce Anderson, prin. Fax 785-5654
Veteran's Memorial MS 1,400/6-8
105 Hendrickson Ave 08724 732-785-3030
John VanDerslice, prin. Fax 458-9777
Young ES 800/1-5
43 Drum Point Rd 08723 732-262-2580
Susan Novelli, prin. Fax 477-0390

St. Dominic S 600/PK-8
250 Old Squan Rd 08724 732-840-1412
Carol Bathmann, prin. Fax 840-6457

Bridgeton, Cumberland, Pop. 23,959
Bridgeton SD 4,300/PK-12
PO Box 657 08302 856-455-8030
Dr. H. Victor Gilson, supt. Fax 451-0815
www.bridgeton.k12.nj.us/
Broad Street S 800/K-8
251 W Broad St 08302 856-455-8030
Steven Morris, prin. Fax 453-7684
Buckshutem Road S 300/K-8
550 Buckshutem Rd 08302 856-455-8030
Dr. Celeste Merriweather, prin. Fax 453-8225
Cherry Street S 400/K-8
20 Cherry St 08302 856-455-8030
Sam Hull, prin. Fax 453-2851
ExCEL S 6-8
7 Washington St 08302 856-455-8030
Roy Dawson Ed.D., prin. Fax 459-0280
Foster ECC 400/PK-PK
550 Buckshutem Rd 08302 856-455-8030
Darlene Grusemeyer, prin. Fax 453-8776
Indian Avenue S 600/K-8
399 Indian Ave 08302 856-455-8030
Rebecca Guess, prin. Fax 455-7706
Quarter Mile Lane S 400/K-8
300 Quarter Mile Ln 08302 856-455-8030
Susan Little, prin. Fax 453-8225
West Avenue S 500/K-8
51 N West Ave 08302 856-455-8030
Roy Dawson Ed.D., prin. Fax 451-4935

Fairfield Township SD 300/PK-8
375 Gouldtown Woodruff Rd 08302 856-453-1882
John Klug, supt. Fax 153-7148
www.fairfield.k12.nj.us
Fairfield Township S 300/PK-8
375 Gouldtown Woodruff Rd 08302 856-453-1882
Tanya Clark, prin. Fax 453-7148

Hopewell Township SD 500/K-8
122 Sewall Rd 08302 856-451-9203
Dr. Terry Van Zoeren, supt. Fax 451-9420
www.hopewellcrest.org
Hopewell Crest S 500/K-8
122 Sewall Rd 08302 856-451-9203
Dr. Terry Van Zoeren, prin. Fax 451-9420

Stow Creek Township SD 100/K-8
11 Gum Tree Corner Rd 08302 856-455-1717
Donna Levick, supt. Fax 455-0833
Stow Creek Township S 100/K-8
11 Gum Tree Corner Rd 08302 856-455-1717
Donna Levick, prin. Fax 455-0833

Bridgeton Christian S 100/PK-8
27 Central Ave 08302 856-455-1733
Glen Clement, admin. Fax 453-7729
Cohansey SDA S 50/K-8
256 Pecks Corner Cohansey 08302 856-451-3437
Woodland Country Day S 200/PK-8
1216 Roadstown Rd 08302 856-453-8499
Cosmo Terrigno, hdmstr. Fax 453-1648

Bridgewater, Somerset, Pop. 36,400
Bridgewater-Raritan Regional SD 9,000/PK-12
PO Box 6030 08807 908-685-2777
J. Michael Schilder Ed.D., supt. Fax 231-8496
www.brrsd.k12.nj.us
Adamsville ES 500/PK-4
400 Union Ave 08807 908-526-6440
Mitzi Morillo, prin. Fax 725-0610
Bradley Gardens ES 400/K-4
148 Pine St 08807 908-725-8444
Barbara Sutterlin, prin. Fax 725-0614
Bridgewater-Raritan MS 1,500/7-8
PO Box 6933 08807 908-231-8661
Nancy Mahoney, prin. Fax 575-0847
Crim ES 500/K-4
1300 Crim Rd 08807 908-231-1022
Margaret Kerr, prin. Fax 725-0640
Eisenhower IS 800/5-6
791 Eisenhower Ave 08807 908-231-0230
Joseph Diskin, prin. Fax 231-1079
Hamilton ES 500/K-4
PO Box 6030 08807 908-575-0050
Dr. Lorraine Lotowycz, prin. Fax 658-3481
Hillside IS 700/5-6
844 Brown Rd 08807 908-231-1905
Teresa Pennington, prin. Fax 231-1083
Milltown ES 600/K-4
611 Milltown Rd 08807 908-927-9510
Matthew Lembo, prin. Fax 927-9524
Van Holten ES 500/K-4
360 Van Holten Rd 08807 908-231-1220
George Rauh, prin. Fax 231-1065
Other Schools – See Raritan

Raritan Valley Montessori S 100/PK-6
120 Finderne Ave 08807 908-595-2900
Leslie Meldrum, hdmstr. Fax 595-2925
St. Bernard Preschool and K 100/PK-K
500 US Highway 22 08807 908-725-0552
Barbara Turse, prin. Fax 725-4524

Brielle, Monmouth, Pop. 4,878
Brielle Borough SD 700/K-8
605 Union Ln 08730 732-528-6400
Christine Carlson, supt. Fax 528-0810
www.brielle.k12.nj.us
Brielle S 700/K-8
605 Union Ln 08730 732-528-6400
Joseph Torrone, prin. Fax 528-0810

Brigantine, Atlantic, Pop. 12,861
Brigantine CSD 800/K-8
PO Box 947 08203 609-266-7671
Dr. Robert Previti, supt. Fax 266-4748
www.brigantine.atlnet.org
Brigantine ES 400/K-4
PO Box 947 08203 609-264-9501
Donald Marrandino, prin. Fax 264-0767
Brigantine North MS 400/5-8
PO Box 947 08203 609-266-3603
William Gussie, prin. Fax 266-7062

Brooklawn, Camden, Pop. 2,315
Brooklawn SD 300/K-8
301 Haakon Rd 08030 856-456-4039
Dr. John Kellmayer, supt. Fax 456-7980
www.alicecostello.com/
Costello S 300/K-8
301 Haakon Rd 08030 856-456-4039
Dr. John Kellmayer, prin. Fax 456-7980

Brookside, Morris
Mendham Township SD 900/K-8
18 W Main St 07926 973-543-7107
Kristopher Harrison, supt. Fax 543-5537
www.mendhamtwp.org
Mendham Township ES 500/K-4
18 W Main St 07926 973-543-7107
Michael Craver, prin. Fax 543-4631
Mendham Township MS 400/5-8
16 Washington Valley Rd 07926 973-543-2505
Dr. Patrick Ciccone, prin. Fax 543-0701

Browns Mills, Burlington, Pop. 11,429
Pemberton Township SD
Supt. — See Pemberton
Crichton ES 600/PK-5
2 Learning Way 08015 609-893-8141
Norman Adams, prin. Fax 893-0517
Denbo ES 300/K-5
1 Learning Way 08015 609-893-8141
Delores Sanchez, prin. Fax 893-8256
Haines ES 100/6-6
125 Trenton Rd Bldg B 08015 609-893-8141
John Schmidt, prin. Fax 893-0676
Harker-Wylie ES 300/PK-3
125 Trenton Rd Bldg C 08015 609-893-8141
Pam Kelly, prin. Fax 735-0118
Stackhouse ES 200/PK-3
125 Trenton Rd Bldg A 08015 609-893-8141
Margaret Duncan, prin. Fax 735-0083

Budd Lake, Morris, Pop. 7,272
Mt. Olive Township SD 4,800/K-12
89 US Highway 46 07828 973-691-4008
Larrie Reynolds Ph.D., supt. Fax 691-4022
www.mtoliveboe.org
Mt. Olive MS 1,200/6-8
160 Wolfe Rd 07828 973-691-4006
Dr. Tracey Severns, prin. Fax 691-4029
Sandshore Road ES 500/K-5
498 Sand Shore Rd 07828 973-691-4003
Robert Allen, prin. Fax 691-4027
Stephens ES 600/K-5
99 Sunset Dr 07828 973-691-4002
Gayle Dierks, prin. Fax 691-4030
Other Schools – See Flanders

Buena, Atlantic, Pop. 3,848
Buena Regional SD 2,400/K-12
PO Box 309 08310 856-697-0800
Walter Whitaker, supt. Fax 697-4963
www.buena.k12.nj.us/
Milanesi ES 300/K-5
880 Harding Hwy 08310 856-697-0605
Anna Bettini, prin. Fax 697-3412
Other Schools – See Landisville, Minotola, Newfield, Williamstown

Burlington, Burlington, Pop. 9,791
Burlington CSD 1,700/PK-12
518 Locust Ave 08016 609-387-5874
Patricia Doloughty, supt. Fax 386-6971
www.burlington-nj.net
Boudinot ES 100/K-2
213 Ellis St 08016 609-387-5867
Sherry Knight, prin. Fax 387-3162
Lawrence ES 200/PK-2
315 Barclay St 08016 609-387-5859
Deborah Banecker, prin. Fax 387-3096
Smith ES 300/PK-2
250 Farner Ave 08016 609-387-5854
Jean Stewart, prin. Fax 747-0758
Watts IS 300/3-6
550 High St 08016 609-387-5834
Robert Williams, prin. Fax 387-8509

Burlington Township SD 3,300/PK-12
PO Box 428 08016 609-387-3955
Dr. Christopher Manno, supt. Fax 239-2192
www.burltwpsch.org/
BTMS @ Springside 7-8
1600 Burlington Byp 08016 609-699-4021
Lawrence Penny, prin. Fax 699-4022
Fountain Woods ES 1,200/3-6
601 Fountain Ave 08016 609-387-1799
John Johnson, prin. Fax 387-1735
Young ES 1,000/PK-2
1203 Neck Rd 08016 609-386-3520
Denise King, prin. Fax 239-3532

Doane Academy 200/PK-12
350 Riverbank 08016 609-386-3500
John McGee, hdmstr. Fax 386-5878
Life Center Academy 300/PK-12
2045 Columbus Rd 08016 609-499-2100
Robert Newman, dean Fax 499-4905
St. Paul S 500/K-8
250 James St 08016 609-386-1645
Sr. Peter Damian, prin. Fax 386-1345

Butler, Morris, Pop. 8,091
Butler SD 1,100/K-12
38 Bartholdi Ave 07405 973-492-2000
Mario Cardinale, supt. Fax 492-1016
www.butlerboe.org
Butler MS 300/5-8
30 Pearl Pl 07405 973-492-2079
Andrea Vladichak, prin. Fax 492-9774
Decker ES 300/K-4
98 Decker Rd 07405 973-492-2037
Virginia Scala, prin. Fax 492-8679

St. Anthony of Padua S 200/PK-8
57 Bartholdi Ave 07405 973-838-0854
Felicia Goodness, prin. Fax 838-1460

Caldwell, Essex, Pop. 7,489
Caldwell-West Caldwell SD
Supt. — See West Caldwell
Cleveland MS, 36 Academy Rd 07006 600/6-8
Casey Shorter, prin. 973-228-9115
Jefferson ES, 85 Prospect St 07006 300/K-5
Timothy Ayers, prin. 973-228-5994
Lincoln ES, 18 Crane St 07006 200/K-5
C.R. Williams, prin. 973-228-3987

North Caldwell SD
Supt. — See North Caldwell
Grandview ES 400/K-3
35 Hamilton Dr E 07006 973-228-0510
Michael Stefanelli, prin. Fax 228-0913

Trinity Academy 600/PK-8
235 Bloomfield Ave 07006 973-226-3386
Joseph San Giancomo, prin. Fax 226-6548

Califon, Hunterdon, Pop. 1,055
Califon SD 100/K-8
6 School St 07830 908-832-2828
Kathleen Prystash Ed.D., supt. Fax 832-6719
www.califonschool.org
Califon S 100/K-8
6 School St 07830 908-832-2828
Kathleen Prystash, prin. Fax 832-6719

Lebanon Township SD 800/K-8
70 Bunnvale Rd 07830 908-638-4521
Judith Burd, supt. Fax 638-5511
www.lebtwpk8.org
Valley View ES 400/K-4
400 County Road 513 07830 908-832-2175
Michael Gorombey, prin. Fax 832-6280
Woodglen MS 400/5-8
70 Bunnvale Rd 07830 908-638-4111
Michael Rubright, prin. Fax 638-8418

Tewksbury Township SD 800/PK-8
173 County Road 517 07830 908-439-2010
William Petrick, supt. Fax 439-2655
www.tewksburyschools.org
Old Turnpike MS 300/PK-PK, 5-
171 County Road 517 07830 908-439-2010
William Petrick, prin. Fax 439-3160
Tewksbury ES 500/K-4
109 Fairmount Rd E 07830 908-832-2594
James Miller, prin. Fax 832-6296

Camden, Camden, Pop. 80,010
Camden CSD 12,600/PK-12
201 N Front St 08102 856-966-2000
Dr. B. LeFra Young, supt. Fax 966-2138
www.camden.k12.nj.us
Bonsall S 600/PK-8
1575 Mount Ephraim Ave 08104 856-966-5088
Deborah Olusa, prin. Fax 756-0294

Catto ES 100/1-5
3100 Westfield Ave 08105 856-966-4097
Robin Wyche, prin. Fax 756-0273
Coopers Poynt S 500/PK-8
201 State St 08102 856-966-5370
Sandra Sims-Foster, prin. Fax 756-0334
Cramer ES 700/PK-4
2800 Mickle St 08105 856-966-8910
Andrea Surratt, prin. Fax 756-0328
Cream S 600/K-8
1875 Mulford St 08104 856-966-4760
Joyous Carey, prin. Fax 963-8274
Davis ES 800/PK-6
3425 Cramer St 08105 856-966-8920
Sharon Woodridge, prin. Fax 963-8379
Early Childhood Developement Center 100/PK-PK
1602 Pine St 08103 856-966-8901
Thomas Rowan, prin. Fax 963-8267
East Camden MS 400/5-8
3064 Stevens St 08105 856-966-5111
Merry Ellerbee, prin. Fax 964-9791
Forest Hill ES 200/1-6
1625 Wildwood Ave 08103 856-966-8930
Brian Medley, prin. Fax 963-8609
Hatch MS 300/6-8
1875 Park Blvd 08103 856-966-5122
Dr. Faith Hartee, prin. Fax 964-0778
Lanning Square S @ Broadway 300/PK-2
501 S Broadway 08103 856-966-5365
Katrina McCombs, prin. Fax 756-0285
Lanning Square S @ Fetters 100/3-6
1020 S 3rd St 08103 856-966-5511
Katrina McCombs, prin. Fax 963-0017
McGraw ES 300/PK-5
3051 Fremont Ave 08105 856-966-8960
V. Pearson-Hunter, prin. Fax 963-8065
Molina ES 600/PK-6
601 Vine St 08102 856-966-8970
John Donohue, prin. Fax 342-6930
Morgan Village MS 400/5-8
1000 Morgan Blvd 08104 856-966-5330
Louis Mason, prin. Fax 964-8443
Parkside ES 200/K-5
1227 Kenwood Ave 08103 856-966-8977
Claudia Cream, prin. Fax 342-8204
Powell ES 200/PK-3
1000 Linden St 08102 856-966-8982
Janice Taylor, prin. Fax 342-7940
Pyne Poynt MS 300/4-8
800 Erie St 08102 856-966-5360
El Rikr Valentino, prin. Fax 964-8462
Sharp ES 400/PK-5
928 N 32nd St 08105 856-966-8988
Evelyn Ruiz, prin. Fax 342-8103
Sumner ES 400/PK-4
1600 S 8th St 08104 856-966-8908
Janis Kauffman, prin. Fax 342-6855
Veterans Memorial MS 400/5-8
800 N 26th St 08105 856-966-5090
Ellen Anderson, prin. Fax 541-5141
Washington ES 300/PK-5
1033 Cambridge Ave 08105 856-966-5278
Malcolm Adler, prin. Fax 964-9764
Whittier ES 200/K-5
740 Chestnut St 08103 856-966-8999
Marilyn Allen, prin. Fax 966-9771
Wiggins ES 500/PK-6
400 Mount Vernon St 08103 856-966-5120
Danette Sapowsky, prin. Fax 964-9782
Wilson ES 300/K-4
855 Woodland Ave 08104 856-966-8940
Kathleen Avant, prin. Fax 964-9560
Yorkship S 600/PK-8
1200 Collings Rd 08104 856-966-5110
Carolyn Morgan, prin. Fax 964-9650

Holy Name S 100/PK-8
700 N 5th St 08102 856-365-7930
Patricia Quinter, prin. Fax 365-8041
Sacred Heart S 200/K-8
404 Jasper St 08104 856-963-1341
Janet Williams, prin. Fax 963-3551
St. Anthony of Padua S 200/K-8
2824 River Rd 08105 856-966-6791
Anna Mae Muryasz, prin. Fax 966-1616
St. Joseph Pro Cathedral S 300/K-8
2907 Federal St 08105 856-964-4336
Frances Montgomery, prin. Fax 964-1080
San Miguel S 50/6-8
836 S 4th St 08103 856-342-6707
James Hoban, prin. Fax 342-6708

Cape May, Cape May, Pop. 3,760
Cape May CSD 100/K-6
921 Lafayette St 08204 609-884-8485
Victoria Zelenak, supt. Fax 884-7037
www.capemaycityschool.org
Cape May City ES 100/K-6
921 Lafayette St 08204 609-884-8485
Fax 884-7037

Lower Cap May Regional SD 1,700/7-12
687 Route 9 08204 609-884-3475
Jack Pfizenmayer, supt. Fax 884-7067
lcmrschool.org/lcmr/index.htm
Teitelman MS 600/7-8
687 Route 9 08204 609-884-3475
Eugene Sole, prin. Fax 884-4311

Lower Township ESD 1,900/PK-6
834 Seashore Rd 08204 609-884-9400
Joseph Cirrinicione, supt. Fax 884-9418
www.lowertwpschools.com
Abrams ES 500/3-4
714 Town Bank Rd 08204 609-884-9420
Barbara Dalrymple, prin. Fax 884-9421

Mitnick PS 500/1-2
905 Seashore Rd 08204 609-884-9470
Sherry Bosch, prin. Fax 898-9481
Sandman Consolidated ES 500/5-6
838 Seashore Rd 08204 609-884-9410
Denise LaBov, prin. Fax 884-9412
Other Schools – See Villas

Our Lady Star of the Sea S 200/K-8
520 Lafayette St 08204 609-884-4437
Donna DiPasquale, prin. Fax 898-4253

Cape May Court House, Cape May, Pop. 4,426
Dennis Township SD 700/K-8
601 Hagen Rd, 609-861-0549
George Papp, supt. Fax 861-1833
dennistwpschools.org
Dennis Township PS 200/K-2
601 Hagen Rd, 609-861-2821
Dr. Joseph LaRosa, prin. Fax 861-1567
Other Schools – See Dennisville

Middle Township SD 2,800/PK-12
216 S Main St, 609-465-1800
Michael Kopakowski, supt. Fax 465-7058
www.middletwp.k12.nj.us/
Middle Township ES 1 700/PK-2
215 Eldredge Rd, 609-463-1900
Catherine Kelly, prin. Fax 463-1901
Middle Township ES 2 500/3-5
101 W Pacific Ave, 609-465-1828
Doug Penkethman, prin. Fax 463-1909
Middle Township MS 4 600/6-8
300 E Pacific Ave, 609-465-1834
Amos Kraybill, prin. Fax 465-5524

Bishop McHugh Regional S 300/K-8
2221 N Route 9, 609-624-1900
Barbara Byrne, prin. Fax 624-9696
Cape Christian Academy 100/PK-12
10 Oyster Rd, 609-465-4132
James Patterson, admin. Fax 465-0170

Carlstadt, Bergen, Pop. 6,018
Carlstadt SD 300/PK-8
550 Washington St 07072 201-672-3000
Stephen Kollinok, supt. Fax 672-9845
www.carlstadt.org
Carlstadt S 300/PK-8
550 Washington St 07072 201-672-3000
Pat Civitello, prin. Fax 672-9845

Carneys Point, Salem, Pop. 7,686
Penns Grove-Carneys Point Regional SD
Supt. — See Penns Grove
Field Street ES 600/1-3
144 Field St 08069 856-299-0170
Roy Webb, prin. Fax 299-1833
Lafayette-Pershing ES 300/PK-K
237 Shell Rd 08069 856-299-3230
Mary Carter, prin. Fax 299-2180

Bishop Guilfoyle Regional S 200/PK-8
350 Georgetown Rd 08069 856-299-0400
Kathryn Chesnut, prin. Fax 299-6556

Carteret, Middlesex, Pop. 21,460
Carteret Borough SD 3,800/PK-12
599 Roosevelt Ave 07008 732-541-8960
Kevin Ahearn, supt. Fax 541-0433
www.carteretschools.org
Carteret MS 800/6-8
300 Carteret Ave 07008 732-541-8960
Mary Spiga, prin. Fax 541-0483
Columbus ES 600/PK-5
1 Carteret Ave 07008 732-541-8960
Christian Zimmer, prin. Fax 541-4245
Hale ES 600/PK-5
678 Roosevelt Ave 07008 732-541-8960
Rose Diaz, prin. Fax 969-8694
Minue ES 700/PK-5
83 Post Blvd 07008 732-541-8960
Cheryl Bolinger, prin. Fax 969-3902

St. Joseph S 200/PK-8
865 Roosevelt Ave 07008 732-541-7111
Roseann Johnson, prin. Fax 541-0676

Cedar Grove, Essex, Pop. 12,053
Cedar Grove Township SD 1,600/K-12
520 Pompton Ave 07009 973-239-1550
Dr. Gene Polles, supt. Fax 239-2994
www.cedargrove.k12.nj.us
Cedar Grove Memorial MS 500/5-8
500 Ridge Rd 07009 973-239-2646
Lawrence Neugebauer, prin. Fax 857-2003
North End ES 300/K-4
122 Stevens Ave 07009 973-256-1454
John Murray, prin. Fax 256-8224
South End ES 300/K-4
16 Harper Ter 07009 973-239-2116
Richard Norman, prin. Fax 239-5419

St. Catherine of Siena S 300/PK-8
39 E Bradford Ave 07009 973-239-6968
Celine Kerwin, prin. Fax 239-1008

Cedarville, Cumberland
Lawrence Township SD 500/PK-8
225 Main St 08311 856-447-4237
Ralph Scazafabo, supt. Fax 447-3446
www.lawrence.k12.nj.us
Powell S 500/PK-8
225 Main St 08311 856-447-4237
Ralph Scazafabo, prin. Fax 447-3446

Chatham, Morris, Pop. 8,439
School District of the Chathams 3,400/K-12
58 Meyersville Rd 07928 973-635-5656
James O'Neill, supt. Fax 701-0146
www.chatham-nj.org/coin
Chatham MS 800/6-8
480 Main St 07928 973-635-7200
Robert Accardi, prin. Fax 635-7190
Lafayette ES 600/4-5
221 Lafayette Ave 07928 973-635-8694
Cheryl Caggiano, prin. Fax 701-9153
Milton Avenue ES 300/K-3
16 Milton Ave 07928 973-635-0851
Marion McCarthy, prin. Fax 635-2116
Southern Boulevard ES 500/K-3
192 Southern Blvd 07928 973-635-5450
Ralph Pesapane, prin. Fax 635-4022
Washington Avenue ES 300/K-3
102 Washington Ave 07928 973-635-8962
Mary Quigley, prin. Fax 635-9062

Chatham Day S 200/PK-8
700 Shunpike Rd 07928 973-410-0400
Dr. Pamela Fiander, hdmstr. Fax 410-0401
Montessori Children's Academy of Chatham 100/PK-5
286 Main St 07928 973-665-0071
Harriet McCarter, dir. Fax 665-0081
St. Patrick S 400/PK-8
45 Chatham St 07928 973-635-4623
Marian Hobbie, prin. Fax 635-2311

Chatsworth, Burlington
Woodland Township SD 200/PK-8
PO Box 477 08019 609-726-1230
William Randazzo, supt. Fax 726-9037
Chatsworth S 200/PK-8
PO Box 477 08019 609-726-1230
William Randazzo, prin. Fax 726-9037

Cherry Hill, Camden, Pop. 70,100
Cherry Hill Township SD 11,300/K-12
PO Box 5015 08034 856-429-5600
Dr. David Campbell, supt. Fax 354-1864
www.cherryhill.k12.nj.us/
Barton ES 500/K-5
315 Rhode Island Ave 08002 856-667-3303
Farrah Koonce, prin. Fax 667-7968
Beck MS 900/6-8
936 Cropwell Rd 08003 856-424-4505
Dr. Dennis Perry, prin. Fax 424-8602
Carusi MS 900/6-8
315 Roosevelt Dr 08002 856-667-1220
Kirk Rickansrud, prin. Fax 779-0613
Cooper ES 300/K-5
1960 Greentree Rd 08003 856-424-4554
Mary Kline, prin. Fax 751-0974
Harte ES 300/K-5
1909 Queen Ann Rd 08003 856-795-0515
John Cafagna, prin. Fax 795-7090
Johnson ES 400/K-5
500 Kresson Rd 08034 856-428-8848
Karen Rockhill, prin. Fax 795-7132
Kilmer ES 400/K-5
2900 Chapel Ave W 08002 856-667-3903
Kwame Morton, prin. Fax 667-8516
Kingston ES 400/K-5
320 Kingston Rd 08034 856-667-0986
Stanley Scheckman, prin. Fax 667-0343
Knight ES 400/K-5
140 Old Carriage Rd 08034 856-428-0830
George Guy, prin. Fax 428-0972
Mann ES 300/K-5
150 Walt Whitman Blvd 08003 856-428-1144
Robert Sweeney, prin. Fax 428-7168
Paine ES 300/K-5
4001 Church Rd 08034 856-667-1350
Susan Weinman, prin. Fax 755-1491
Rosa International MS 800/6-8
485 Browning Ln 08003 856-616-8787
Ed Canzanese, prin. Fax 616-0904
Sharp ES 300/K-5
300 Old Orchard Rd 08003 856-424-1550
Robert Homer, prin. Fax 424-6577
Stockton ES 400/K-5
200 Wexford Dr 08003 856-424-1505
Eloisa DeJesus-Woodruff, prin. Fax 761-0367
Woodcrest ES 500/K-5
400 Cranford Rd 08003 856-429-2058
Beth Kob, prin. Fax 216-9073

Baptist Regional S 100/K-6
1721 Springdale Rd 08003 856-424-1209
Lynn Conahan, admin. Fax 424-6172
Kings Christian S 400/PK-12
5 Carnegie Plz 08003 856-489-6720
Dr. Rebecca Stiegel, hdmstr. Fax 489-6727
Living Faith Christian Academy 100/K-12
202 Park Blvd 08002 856-665-5507
Gail Lewis, prin. Fax 665-5601
Politz Day S 200/PK-8
720 Cooper Landing Rd 08002 856-667-1013
Rabbi Avraham Glustein, hdmstr. Fax 667-2010
Resurrection Regional Catholic S 300/PK-8
402 Kings Hwy N Ste A 08034 856-667-3034
Camille Forrest, prin. Fax 667-9160

Chesilhurst, Camden, Pop. 1,865
Chesilhurst Borough SD 100/PK-6
511 Edwards Ave 08089 856-767-5451
Abdi Gass, supt. Fax 767-1431
Foster ES, 511 Edwards Ave 08089 100/PK-6
Abdi Gass, prin. 856-767-5451

Chester, Morris, Pop. 1,653
Chester Township SD 1,400/K-8
415 State Route 24 Ste 11 07930 908-879-7373
Dr. Christina VanWoert, supt. Fax 879-5887
www.chester-nj.org

Black River MS 500/6-8
North Rd 07930 908-879-6363
Robert Mullen, prin. Fax 879-9085
Bragg ES 500/3-5
250 State Route 24 07930 908-879-5324
Daniel Johnson, prin. Fax 879-5438
Dickerson PS 400/K-2
250 State Route 24 07930 908-879-5313
Melissa Fair, prin. Fax 879-9018

Chesterfield, Burlington
Chesterfield Township SD 300/K-6
295 Bordentown Chstrfeld Rd, 609-298-6900
Walter Keiss, supt. Fax 298-7884
www.chesterfieldschool.com
Chesterfield ES 300/K-6
295 Bordentown Chstrfeld Rd, 609-298-6900
Walter Keiss, prin. Fax 298-7884

Meadow View Junior Academy 100/K-10
241 Bordentown Chstrfeld Rd, 609-298-1122
Sadrail Saint-Ulysse, prin. Fax 298-7550

Cinnaminson, Burlington, Pop. 14,583
Cinnaminson Township SD 2,500/K-12
PO Box 224 08077 856-829-7600
Salvatore Illuzzi, supt. Fax 786-9618
www.cinnaminson.com
Cinnaminson MS 500/6-8
312 N Fork Landing Rd 08077 856-786-8012
Gay Moceri, prin. Fax 786-1860
New Albany ES 500/K-2
2701 New Albany Rd 08077 856-786-2284
Robert Maher, prin. Fax 786-3763
Rush IS 500/3-5
1200 Wynwood Dr 08077 856-829-7778
Eugene Porco, prin. Fax 303-0218

St. Charles Borromeo S 300/K-8
2500 Branch Pike 08077 856-829-2778
Diane Kinnevy, prin. Fax 829-2159
Westfield Friends S 200/PK-8
2201 Riverton Rd 08077 856-829-0895
William Probsting, hdmstr. Fax 829-9320

Clark, Union, Pop. 14,629
Clark Township SD 2,300/K-12
365 Westfield Ave 07066 732-574-9600
Renae LaPrete, supt. Fax 574-1456
www.clarkschools.org
Hehnly ES 500/K-5
590 Raritan Rd 07066 732-381-8100
Shirley Bergin, prin. Fax 381-9359
Kumpf MS 500/6-8
59 Mildred Ter 07066 732-381-0400
Jennifer Feeley, prin. Fax 381-0262
Valley Road ES 400/K-5
150 Valley Rd 07066 732-388-7900
Joseph Beltramba, prin. Fax 388-6209

Featherbed Lane S of Clark 200/PK-5
801 Featherbed Ln 07066 732-388-7063
Barbara Faria, dir. Fax 388-7063
St. Agnes S 200/PK-8
342 Madison Hill Rd 07066 732-381-0850
Sr. Claire Ouimet, prin. Fax 381-1745
St. John the Apostle S 400/PK-8
Valley Rd 07066 732-388-1360
Sr. Donna O'Brien, prin. Fax 388-0775

Clarksburg, Monmouth
Millstone Township SD
Supt. — See Millstone
Millstone Township PS PK-2
18 Schoolhouse Rd 08510 732-786-0950
Gina Villana, prin.

Clayton, Gloucester, Pop. 7,447
Clayton SD 1,300/PK-12
300 W Chestnut St 08312 856-881-8700
Cleve Bryan, supt. Fax 863-8196
www.clayton.k12.nj.us
Clayton MS 200/7-8
350 E Clinton St 08312 856-881-8702
Nikolaos Koutsogianni, prin. Fax 863-0808
Simmons ES 700/PK-6
300 W Chestnut St 08312 856-881-8704
Patrice Taylor, prin. Fax 307-0924

St. Michael the Archangel Regional S 200/K-8
51 W North St 08312 856-881-0067
Janice Bruni, prin. Fax 881-4064

Clementon, Camden, Pop. 4,944
Clementon Borough SD 500/PK-8
4 Audubon Ave 08021 856-783-2300
Michael Adams, supt. Fax 783-8929
www.clementonschool.org
Clementon S 500/PK-8
4 Audubon Ave 08021 856-783-2300
Lynn Marcus, prin. Fax 783-8929

Children of Promise Christian S 100/PK-7
165 White Horse Pike 08021 856-309-9600
Aughtney Khan, prin. Fax 309-8991

Cliffside Park, Bergen, Pop. 23,035
Cliffside Park SD 2,200/PK-12
525 Palisade Ave 07010 201-313-2310
Michael Romagnino, supt. Fax 943-7050
www.cliffsidepark.edu
Cliffside Park ES 3 200/K-6
397 Palisade Ave 07010 201-313-2330
John Brunelli, prin. Fax 313-9488
Cliffside Park ES 4 300/K-6
27 Columbia Ave 07010 201-313-2340
Christine Giancola, prin. Fax 313-0397
Cliffside Park ES 5 100/K-6
214 Day Ave 07010 201-313-2350
Michael Bucco, prin. Fax 313-5642
Cliffside Park S 6 600/K-8
440 Oakdene Ave 07010 201-313-2360
Lorraine Morrow, prin. Fax 313-5814
Early Learning Center PK-K
263 Lafayette Ave 07010 201-313-8940
Janet Merrill, prin. Fax 313-4617

Cliffwood, Monmouth, Pop. 1,500
Matawan-Aberdeen Regional SD
Supt. — See Aberdeen
Cliffwood ES 300/K-3
422 Cliffwood Ave 07721 732-705-5600
Kelly Bera, prin. Fax 566-2837
Matawan Aberdeen MS 900/6-8
469 Matawan Ave 07721 732-705-5400
Kathleen Olsen, prin. Fax 765-0894

Cliffwood Beach, Middlesex, Pop. 3,543
Old Bridge Township SD
Supt. — See Matawan
Cooper ES 200/K-5
160 Birchwood Dr 07735 732-290-3881
Dr. Susanne Miskiewicz, prin. Fax 583-7109

Clifton, Passaic, Pop. 79,922
Clifton SD, PO Box 2209 07015 9,800/K-12
Richard Tardalo, supt. 973-470-2260
www.clifton.k12.nj.us
Columbus MS 1,200/6-8
350 Piaget Ave 07011 973-470-2360
Mark Tietjen, prin. Fax 470-2365
Public S 1 300/K-5
158 Park Slope 07011 973-470-2370
Luca Puzzo, prin. Fax 253-3237
Public S 2 300/K-5
1270 Van Houten Ave 07013 973-470-2380
Linette Shyers, prin. Fax 458-8325
Public S 3 300/K-5
365 Washington Ave 07011 973-470-2390
Nancy Latzoni, prin. Fax 478-2576
Public S 4 200/K-5
194 W 2nd St 07011 973-470-2382
David Montroni, prin. Fax 253-3286
Public S 5 300/K-5
136 Valley Rd 07013 973-470-2386
Shelia Gershenoff Ed.D., prin. Fax 357-2184
Public S 8 200/K-5
41 Oak St 07014 973-470-2393
Steven Cruz, prin. Fax 458-9249
Public S 9 200/K-5
25 Brighton Rd 07012 973-470-2396
Michele Cecere, prin. Fax 458-8416
Public S 11 400/K-5
147 Merselis Ave 07011 973-470-2401
Greg Dickey, prin. Fax 340-7205
Public S 12, 165 Clifton Ave 07011 600/K-5
Maria Parham-Talley, prin. 973-470-2404
Public S 13 400/K-5
782 Van Houten Ave 07013 973-470-2410
Marilyn Torley, prin. Fax 458-9253
Public S 14 200/K-5
99 Saint Andrews Blvd 07012 973-470-2411
Evelyn Sherman, prin. Fax 458-9216
Public S 15 300/K-5
700 Gregory Ave 07011 973-470-2418
Jennifer Montesano, prin. Fax 458-9238
Public S 16 200/K-5
755 Grove St 07013 973-470-2420
Michelle Christadore, prin. Fax 773-7834
Public S 17, 361 Lexington Ave 07011 500/K-5
Anthony Orlando, prin. 973-458-6017
Wilson MS 1,100/6-8
1400 Van Houten Ave 07013 973-470-2350
William Hahn, prin. Fax 470-2607

Sacred Heart S 200/PK-8
43 Clifton Ave 07011 973-546-4695
Sr. Maryann Kasica, prin. Fax 546-8774
St. Andrew the Apostle S 200/PK-8
418 Mount Prospect Ave 07012 973-473-3711
Sr. Margaret Murphy, prin. Fax 473-6611
St. Brendan S 400/PK-8
154 E 1st St 07011 973-772-1149
Monica Ramos, prin. Fax 772-5547
St. Clare S 200/PK-8
39 Allwood Rd 07014 973-777-7582
Sr. Joseph Nelida, prin. Fax 473-0127
St. Philip the Apostle S 400/PK-8
797 Valley Rd 07013 973-779-4700
Barbara Zito, prin. Fax 779-2959

Clinton, Hunterdon, Pop. 2,621
Clinton Town SD 500/K-8
10 School St 08809 908-735-8512
John Alfieri, supt. Fax 735-5895
www.cpsnj.org
Clinton Public S 500/K-8
10 School St 08809 908-735-8512
Richard Katz, prin. Fax 735-5895

Clinton Township SD
Supt. — See Lebanon
Clinton Township MS 400/7-8
34 Grayrock Rd 08809 908-238-9141
Gerard Dalton, prin. Fax 238-9376
Spruce Run ES 300/PK-1
27 Belvidere Ave 08809 908-735-7916
Ken Wark, prin. Fax 735-2213

Crossroads Christian Academy 200/PK-8
9 Pittstown Rd 08809 908-735-5501
Gayle Picinich, prin. Fax 735-7517

Closter, Bergen, Pop. 8,669
Closter SD 1,200/K-8
340 Homans Ave 07624 201-768-3001
Joanne Newberry, supt. Fax 768-1903
www.nvnet.org/k8/closter
Hillside ES 600/K-4
340 Homans Ave 07624 201-768-3860
Sylvan Hershey, prin. Fax 768-6770
Tenakill MS 600/5-8
275 High St 07624 201-768-1332
Alfred Baffa, prin. Fax 784-0726

Collingswood, Camden, Pop. 14,083
Collingswood Borough SD 1,800/K-12
200 Lees Ave 08108 856-962-5732
Scott Oswald, supt. Fax 962-5723
collingswood.k12.nj.us
Collingswood MS 300/7-8
414 W Collings Ave 08108 856-962-5702
John McMullin, prin. Fax 962-5751
Garfield ES 100/K-6
480 Haddon Ave 08108 856-962-5705
Thomas Santo, prin. Fax 962-5705
Newbie ES 200/K-6
2 E Browning Rd 08108 856-962-5706
Mary Bezanis, prin. Fax 962-5718
Tatem ES 200/K-6
265 Lincoln Ave 08108 856-962-5704
Joseph Gurcsik, prin. Fax 962-5574
Zane North ES 200/K-6
801 Stokes Ave 08108 856-962-5703
Thomas Santo, prin. Fax 962-5712
Other Schools – See West Collingswood

Good Shepherd Regional S 100/PK-8
100 Lees Ave 08108 856-858-1562
Donald Garecht, prin. Fax 854-2943

Colonia, Middlesex, Pop. 18,238
Woodbridge Township SD
Supt. — See Woodbridge
Claremont Avenue ES 400/K-5
90 Claremont Ave 07067 732-499-6547
Joanne Springer, prin. Fax 574-1634
Colonia MS 600/6-8
100 Delaware Ave 07067 732-396-7000
Gregg Miller, prin. Fax 574-0772
Lynn Crest ES 400/K-5
98 Ira Ave 07067 732-499-6558
Scott Osborne, prin. Fax 396-1874
Oak Ridge Heights ES 300/K-5
720 Inman Ave 07067 732-499-6553
Joseph D'Orsi, prin. Fax 574-1746
Pennsylvania Avenue ES 300/K-5
80 N Pennsylvania Ave 07067 732-499-6566
Denise O'Donaghue-Smith, prin. Fax 574-1841

St. John Vianney S 600/PK-8
420 Inman Ave 07067 732-388-1662
Carol Woodburn, prin. Fax 388-1003

Colts Neck, Monmouth
Colts Neck Township SD 1,500/K-8
70 Conover Rd 07722 732-946-0055
Ross Kasun, supt. Fax 946-4792
www.coltsneckschools.org
Cedar Drive MS 600/6-8
73 Cedar Dr 07722 732-946-0055
Collin Rigby, prin. Fax 462-4108
Conover PS 400/K-2
56 Conover Rd 07722 732-946-0055
Tricia Barr, prin. Fax 332-9501
Conover Road ES 500/3-5
80 Conover Rd 07722 732-946-0055
Jeffrey Huguenin, prin. Fax 332-0146

Columbus, Burlington
Mansfield Township SD 700/K-6
200 Mansfield Rd E 08022 609-298-2037
Diane Bacher, supt. Fax 298-5365
www.mansfieldschool.com
Hydock ES 300/K-2
19 Locust Ave 08022 609-298-0308
Jennifer Ferro, prin. Fax 298-1341
Mansfield Township ES 400/3-6
200 Mansfield Rd E 08022 609-298-2037
Joseph Langowski, prin.

Northern Burlington County Regional SD 1,700/7-12
160 Mansfield Rd E 08022 609-298-3900
Dr. James Sarruda, supt. Fax 298-3154
www.nburlington.com
Northern Burlington County Regional JHS 600/7-8
180 Mansfield Rd E 08022 609-298-3900
Eric Barnett, prin. Fax 291-1563

Cranbury, Middlesex
Cranbury Township SD 600/K-8
23 N Main St 08512 609-395-1700
John Haney, supt. Fax 860-9655
www.cranburyschool.org
Cranbury S 600/K-8
23 N Main St 08512 609-395-1700
John Haney, prin. Fax 860-9655

Cranford, Union, Pop. 22,624
Cranford Township SD 3,500/K-12
132 Thomas St 07016 908-709-6202
Dr. Gayle Carrick, supt. Fax 272-7735
www.cranfordschools.org
Bloomingdale Avenue ES 200/K-2
200 Bloomingdale Ave 07016 908-709-6969
Regina Gavin, prin. Fax 709-9138
Brookside Place ES 400/K-5
700 Brookside Pl 07016 908-709-6244
Michael Klimko, prin. Fax 709-6724
Hillside Avenue S 600/K-8
125 Hillside Ave 07016 908-709-6229
Curt Fogas Ed.D., prin. Fax 709-6752

Livingston Avenue ES 200/3-5
75 Livingston Ave 07016 908-709-6248
Dineen Seeley, prin. Fax 709-6748
Orange Avenue S 700/3-8
901 Orange Ave 07016 908-709-6257
Michelle Vella, prin. Fax 272-3025
Walnut Avenue ES 200/K-2
370 Walnut Ave 07016 908-709-6253
Angelo Paternoster, prin. Fax 709-6754

Calvary Nursery S 100/PK-PK
108 Eastman St 07016 908-272-3962
Stacy Nick-Casey, dir. Fax 276-2419
St. Michael S 400/PK-8
100 Alden St 07016 908-276-9425
Sandy Miragliotta, prin. Fax 276-4371

Cresskill, Bergen, Pop. 8,449
Cresskill SD 1,700/K-12
1 Lincoln Dr 07626 201-567-5919
Dr. Loretta Bellina, supt. Fax 567-7976
Bryan ES 600/K-6
51 Brookside Ave 07626 201-569-1191
Phyllis Weinberger, prin. Fax 569-3367
Merritt Memorial ES 400/K-6
91 Dogwood Ln 07626 201-569-8381
Joseph Donnelly, prin. Fax 569-3862

St. Therese of Lisieux S 200/PK-8
220 Jefferson Ave 07626 201-568-4296
Sr. Helene Byrne, prin. Fax 568-3179

Dayton, Middlesex, Pop. 4,321
South Brunswick Township SD
Supt. — See North Brunswick
Indian Fields ES 700/K-5
359 Ridge Rd 08810 732-329-1043
Mark Daniels, prin. Fax 274-1234
Indian Fields ES at Dayton K-2
310 Georges Rd 08810 732-329-6812
Mark Daniels, prin. Fax 329-1891

Deal, Monmouth, Pop. 1,043
Deal Borough SD 100/K-8
201 Roseld Ave 07723 732-531-0480
Dr. Anthony Moro, supt. Fax 531-1908
www.dealschool.org
Deal S 100/K-8
201 Roseld Ave 07723 732-531-0480
Dr. Anthony Moro, prin. Fax 531-1908

Delair, Camden
Pennsauken Township SD
Supt. — See Pennsauken
Delair ES 300/K-4
850 Derousse Ave 08110 856-662-6164
Martin Slater, prin. Fax 317-0362

Delanco, Burlington, Pop. 3,316
Delanco Township SD 400/K-8
1301 Burlington Ave 08075 856-461-1905
Walter Bowyer, supt. Fax 461-1627
www.delanco.com
Pearson ES 200/K-5
1301 Burlington Ave 08075 856-461-1976
Barbara Behnke, prin. Fax 461-4419
Walnut Street MS 100/6-8
411 Walnut St 08075 856-461-0874
John Cogan, prin. Fax 461-6903

Delaware, Warren
Knowlton Township SD 300/K-6
PO Box 227 07833 908-475-5118
Sharon Mooney, supt. Fax 475-1141
www.knowltonschool.com
Knowlton Township ES 300/K-6
PO Box 227 07833 908-475-5118
Sharon Mooney, prin. Fax 475-1141

Delran, Burlington, Pop. 13,178
Delran Township SD 2,700/K-12
52 Hartford Rd 08075 856-461-6800
Dr. George Sharp, supt. Fax 461-6125
www.delranschools.org/
Delran IS 600/3-5
20 Creek Rd 08075 856-764-5100
Jennifer Lowe, prin. Fax 764-5315
Delran MS 600/6-8
905 S Chester Ave 08075 856-461-8822
Melanie Goodwin, prin. Fax 461-0311
Millbridge ES 600/K-2
282 Conrow Rd 08075 856-461-2900
Judith Thourot, prin. Fax 461-0866

Montessori Academy of NJ 100/PK-8
28 Conrow Rd 08075 856-461-2121
Ellen Fox, admin. Fax 461-6835

Demarest, Bergen, Pop. 5,005
Demarest SD 700/K-8
568 Piermont Rd 07627 201-768-6060
Gregg Hauser, supt. Fax 767-9122
www.nvnet.org/k8/demarest/index.html
County Road ES 100/K-1
130 County Rd 07627 201-768-6256
Gladys Grossman, prin. Fax 768-1285
Demarest MS 300/5-8
568 Piermont Rd 07627 201-768-6061
Michael Fox, prin. Fax 768-9122
Emerson ES 200/2-4
15 Columbus Rd 07627 201-784-2084
Gladys Grossman, prin. Fax 784-6093

Dennisville, Cape May
Dennis Township SD
Supt. — See Cape May Court House
Dennis Township ES 200/3-5
165 Academy Rd 08214 609-861-2821
Dr. Joseph LaRosa, prin. Fax 861-1567
Dennis Township MS 300/6-8
165 Academy Rd 08214 609-861-2821
James DiCarlo, prin. Fax 861-5229

Denville, Morris, Pop. 13,812
Denville Township SD 1,900/K-8
501 Openaki Rd 07834 973-983-6530
Dr. Drucilla Clark, supt. Fax 366-2481
www.denville.org
Lakeview ES 700/K-5
44 Cooper Rd 07834 973-983-6540
Beth Baisley, prin. Fax 366-4345
Riverview ES 500/K-5
33 Saint Marys Pl 07834 973-983-6545
Diane Burton, prin. Fax 627-3681
Valleyview MS 600/6-8
320 Diamond Spring Rd 07834 973-983-6535
Joseph Novak, prin. Fax 627-0632

St. Marys S 100/PK-8
100 Route 46 07834 973-627-2606
Sr. M. Aurelia Cerny, prin. Fax 627-9316

Deptford, Gloucester
Deptford Township SD 4,100/PK-12
2022 Good Intent Rd 08096 856-232-2700
Dr. Joseph Canataro, supt. Fax 227-7473
www.deptford.k12.nj.us/
Central ECC 500/PK-1
1447 Delsea Dr 08096 856-384-8750
Maria Gioffre, prin. Fax 686-9829
Good Intent ES 400/2-6
1555 Good Intent Rd 08096 856-232-2737
Kim Matthews, prin. Fax 227-8014
Lake Tract ES 400/2-6
690 Iszard Rd 08096 856-686-2240
Kathleen Klausner, prin. Fax 845-3057
Other Schools – See Sewell, Wenonah, Westville

Delaware Valley Junior Academy 50/K-8
240 Sickle Ln 08096 856-227-0513

Dorothy, Atlantic
Weymouth Township SD 200/K-8
PO Box 231 08317 609-476-2412
Dr. Donna Van Horn, supt. Fax 476-3966
Weymouth Township S 200/K-8
PO Box 231 08317 609-476-2412
Dr. Donna Van Horn, prin. Fax 476-3966

Dover, Morris, Pop. 18,441
Dover Town SD 2,800/PK-12
100 Grace St 07801 973-989-2000
Robert Becker, supt. Fax 989-1662
www.dover-nj.org
Academy Street ES 500/K-6
14 Academy St 07801 973-989-2030
Deborah D'Urso, prin. Fax 989-6270
East Dover ES 500/K-6
302 E McFarlan St 07801 973-989-2055
Robert Franks, prin. Fax 361-2117
East Dover MS 400/7-8
302 E McFarlan St 07801 973-989-2040
Robert Franks, prin. Fax 361-2117
North Dover ES 500/PK-6
51 Highland Ave 07801 973-989-2020
Kathryn Rutan, prin. Fax 361-1841

Rockaway Township SD
Supt. — See Hibernia
Birchwood ES 300/K-5
1 Art St 07801 973-361-7080
Sylvia Ziegler, prin. Fax 361-8739
O'Brien ES 300/K-5
418 Mineral Springs Rd 07801 973-361-7330
Craig Wilson, prin. Fax 361-8537

Dumont, Bergen, Pop. 17,474
Dumont SD 2,600/K-12
25 Depew St 07628 201-387-3082
Emanuele Triggiano, supt. Fax 387-0259
www.dumontnj.org
Grant ES 400/K-5
100 Grant Ave 07628 201-387-3050
Dr. Kevin Donohue, prin. Fax 384-7148
Honiss S 700/K-8
31 Depew St 07628 201-387-3020
Karen Bennett, prin. Fax 387-8109
Lincoln ES 200/K-5
80 Prospect Ave 07628 201-387-3040
Emanuele Triggiano, prin. Fax 384-0422
Selzer S 500/K-8
435 Prospect Ave 07628 201-387-3030
Dr. James Kennedy, prin. Fax 384-1005

Dunellen, Middlesex, Pop. 6,994
Dunellen SD 1,100/K-12
High & Lehigh Sts 08812 732-968-3226
Pio Pennisi, supt. Fax 968-3513
www.dunellenschools.org/
Faber ES 500/K-5
400 High St 08812 732-968-5311
Robert Altmire, prin. Fax 968-4243
Lincoln MS 300/6-8
411 First St 08812 732-968-0885
Joseph Moran, prin. Fax 968-3138

Eastampton, Burlington
Eastampton Township SD 400/K-8
1 Student Dr 08060 609-267-9172
Robert Krastek, supt. Fax 267-7895
www.eastampton.k12.nj.us
Eastampton Township S 400/K-8
1 Student Dr 08060 609-267-9172
Robert Krastek, prin. Fax 261-3338

Timothy Christian Academy 200/PK-8
1341 Woodlane Rd 08060 609-261-9578
Paul Gardiner, dir. Fax 261-7122

East Brunswick, Middlesex, Pop. 47,400
East Brunswick Township SD 8,800/PK-12
760 State Route 18 08816 732-613-6705
Dr. Jo Ann Magistro, supt. Fax 698-9871
www.ebnet.org
Bowne-Munro ES 300/K-5
120 Main St 08816 732-613-6810
Joyce Boley, prin. Fax 257-0029
Brook ES 400/K-5
48 Sullivan Way 08816 732-613-6870
Christine Raymond, prin. Fax 249-5913
Central ES 400/PK-5
371 Cranbury Rd 08816 732-613-6820
Nicole Tibbetts, prin. Fax 254-2624
Chittick ES 600/K-5
5 Flagler St 08816 732-613-6830
Stephen Decker, prin. Fax 390-0172
Frost ES 500/K-5
65 Frost Ave 08816 732-613-6850
Beth Warren, prin. Fax 257-2034
Hammarskjold MS 1,400/6-7
200 Rues Ln 08816 732-613-6892
Michael Gaskell, prin. Fax 651-7135
Irwin ES 500/K-5
71 Race Track Rd 08816 732-613-6840
Ronald Lieberman, prin. Fax 257-7021
Memorial ES 400/K-5
14 Innes Rd 08816 732-613-6860
Pam Mayo, prin. Fax 613-1985
Warnsdorfer ES 500/PK-5
9 Hardenburg Ln 08816 732-613-6880
Maurie Grafas, prin. Fax 613-1548

Cornerstone Christian S 200/PK-8
100 Hardenburg Ln 08816 732-422-7066
Susan Howarth, prin. Fax 422-0398
St. Bartholomew S 400/PK-8
470 Ryders Ln 08816 732-254-7105
Ruth Mazzarella, prin. Fax 254-6352
Solomon Schechter Day S 200/K-8
511 Ryders Ln 08816 732-238-7971
Dr. Howard Rosenblatt, hdmstr. Fax 238-7531

East Hanover, Morris, Pop. 9,926
East Hanover Township SD 1,100/K-8
20 School Ave 07936 973-887-2112
Larry Santos, supt. Fax 887-2773
www.easthanoverschools.org/
Central ES 400/3-5
400 Ridgedale Ave 07936 973-887-0358
Douglas Dresher, prin. Fax 887-6565
East Hanover MS 400/6-8
477 Ridgedale Ave 07936 973-887-8810
Joseph Ricca, prin. Fax 887-5079
Smith ES 400/K-2
27 Green Dr 07936 973-887-5650
Melissa Falcone, prin. Fax 887-6407

St. Rose of Lima Academy 300/PK-8
316 Ridgedale Ave 07936 973-887-6990
Sheila Tomlinson, prin. Fax 887-8655

East Newark, Hudson, Pop. 2,262
East Newark SD 200/PK-8
501 N 3rd St 07029 973-481-6800
Salvatore Montagna, supt. Fax 485-1344
eastnewarkschool.org/
East Newark S 200/PK-8
501 N 3rd St 07029 973-481-6800
Richard Corbett, prin. Fax 485-1344

East Orange, Essex, Pop. 68,190
East Orange SD 8,800/PK-12
715 Park Ave 07017 973-266-5760
Dr. Clarence Hoover, supt. Fax 678-4865
www.eastorange.k12.nj.us
Barry-Garvin MicroSociety S 200/1-5
1 Grove Pl 07017 973-266-5890
Dr. Howard Walker, prin. Fax 672-2403
Bowser S of Excellence 800/PK-5
180 Lincoln St 07017 973-414-4170
Brian Heaphy, prin. Fax 414-4182
Carver Institute 500/PK-5
135 Glenwood Ave 07017 973-266-5860
Loretta Onyeani, prin. Fax 266-2495
Cochran Academy 300/K-5
190 Midland Ave 07017 973-395-5975
Deborah Harvest, prin. Fax 395-5980
Costley MS 500/6-8
116 Hamilton St 07017 973-266-5660
Amaila Trono, prin. Fax 266-2956
Fourth Avenue ES 300/K-5
199 4th Ave 07017 973-266-2957
Sharon Vincent, prin. Fax 673-1374
Gibson ECC 200/PK-K
490 William St 07017 973-266-7017
R. Carolyn Cahoon, prin. Fax 395-5990
Glenwood Campus MS 6-8
135 Glenwood Ave 07017 973-674-4200
Dr. Stephen Cowan, prin. Fax 674-4626
Healy MS 400/6-8
116 Hamilton St 07017 973-266-5670
Dr. Robert Morgan, prin. Fax 675-5094
Houston Academy 500/K-8
215 Dodd St 07017 973-266-5880
Henry Hamilton, prin. Fax 673-1466
Hughes ES 500/PK-5
160 Rhode Island Ave 07018 973-266-5870
Annie Jackson, prin. Fax 414-4196
Jackson Academy 300/K-5
106 Prospect St 07017 973-266-5895
Gladys Calhoun, prin. Fax 266-5569
L'Ouverture ES 300/PK-5
330 Central Ave 07018 973-266-5940
David Johnson, prin. Fax 677-2470
Parks Academy 300/K-6
98 Greenwood Ave 07017 973-266-5950
Norman Stanley, prin. Fax 414-4197

Truth MS 500/6-8
116 Hamilton St 07017 973-266-5665
Vincent Stallings, prin. Fax 395-3586
Tyson Community S of Fine & Perfrmg Arts K-8
45 N Arlington Ave 07017 973-414-9222
Passion Moss-Hasan, prin.
Wahlstrom ECC 200/PK-K
340 Prospect St 07017 973-395-1210
Fidelia Sturdivant, prin. Fax 395-1215
Warwick Institute 500/PK-5
120 Central Ave 07018 973-266-5930
Gloria Watson, prin. Fax 266-5935

Ahlus Sunnah S 200/PK-12
215 N Oraton Pkwy 07017 973-672-4124
Fax 672-3919
Holy Trinity S 50/PK-K
153 Glenwood Ave 07017 973-677-3131
Jamas Children's University 100/PK-12
86 Washington St 07017 973-678-7033
Joan Williams, prin. Fax 678-1894
Our Lady Help of Christian S 300/PK-8
23 N Clinton St 07017 973-677-1546
Sr. Patricia Hogan, prin. Fax 677-3939
St. Joseph S 400/K-8
115 Telford St 07018 973-674-2326
Marion Alexander, prin. Fax 674-7718

East Rutherford, Bergen, Pop. 8,960
East Rutherford SD 700/PK-8
Grove St and Uhland St 07073 201-804-3100
Fax 804-3131
www.erboe.net/
Faust MS 300/5-8
Grove St and Uhland St 07073 201-804-3110
Henry Srednicki Ph.D., prin. Fax 804-3131
McKenzie ES 400/PK-4
135 Carlton Ave 07073 201-531-1235
Susan Loeb, prin. Fax 531-1491

St. Joseph S 200/PK-8
20 Hackensack St 07073 201-939-3193
Frances Alberta, prin. Fax 939-1913

East Windsor, Mercer, Pop. 22,353
East Windsor Regional SD
Supt. — See Hightstown
Drew ES 600/K-5
70 Twin Rivers Dr N 08520 609-443-7820
Darlene Nemeth, prin. Fax 443-7891
Kreps MS 1,100/6-8
5 Kent Ln 08520 609-443-7767
Avis Leverett, prin. Fax 443-8972
McKnight ES 700/K-5
58 Twin Rivers Dr 08520 609-443-7800
Gayle Parker, prin. Fax 443-7852

Namias Shalom Torah Academy 100/PK-8
639 Abbington Dr 08520 609-443-4877

Eatontown, Monmouth, Pop. 14,088
Eatontown SD 1,100/K-8
5 Grant Ave 07724 732-542-1310
Barbara Struble, supt. Fax 578-0017
www.eatontown.org
Meadowbrook ES 300/K-6
65 Wyckoff Rd 07724 732-542-2777
Valerie Cioffi, prin. Fax 935-0813
Memorial MS 200/7-8
7 Grant Ave 07724 732-542-5013
Ron Danielson, prin. Fax 389-1364
Vetter ES 300/K-6
3 Grant Ave 07724 732-542-4644
Scott McCue, prin. Fax 389-2205
Woodmere ES 300/K-6
65 Raleigh Ct 07724 732-542-3388
Joe Polinski, prin. Fax 544-1560

Torah Academy of Monmouth County 200/PK-8
1 Meridian Rd 07724 732-460-1700

Edgewater, Bergen, Pop. 9,646
Edgewater SD 400/PK-6
251 Undercliff Ave 07020 201-945-4106
Dr. Ted Blumstein, supt. Fax 945-4104
www.evgschool.org
Van Gelder ES 400/PK-6
251 Undercliff Ave 07020 201-945-4106
Dr. Ted Blumstein, prin. Fax 945-4104

Edgewater Park, Burlington, Pop. 8,388
Edgewater Park Township SD 800/K-8
25 Washington Ave 08010 609-877-2124
Scott Streckbein, supt. Fax 877-3941
www.edgewaterpark.k12.nj.us
Magowan ES 400/K-4
405 Cherrix Ave 08010 609-877-1430
Betsy Miles, prin. Fax 877-8956
Ridgeway MS 300/5-8
300 Delanco Rd 08010 609-871-3434
Joseph Corn, prin. Fax 871-2434

Edison, Middlesex, Pop. 99,500
Edison Township SD 13,600/K-12
312 Pierson Ave 08837 732-452-4900
John DiMuzio, supt. Fax 452-4993
edisonpublicschools.org/
Adams MS 800/6-8
1081 New Dover Rd 08820 732-452-2920
Dr. MaryAnn Banks, prin. Fax 452-2922
Franklin ES 600/K-5
2485 Woodbridge Ave 08817 732-650-5300
Steven Preville, prin. Fax 650-5302
Hoover MS 800/6-8
174 Jackson Ave 08837 732-452-2940
Lou Figueroa, prin. Fax 452-2949
Jefferson MS 800/6-8
450 Division St 08817 732-650-5290
Antoinette Emden, prin. Fax 652-5295
King ES 600/K-5
285 Tingley Ln 08820 732-452-2980
Diane Wilton, prin. Fax 452-2982
Lincoln ES 700/K-5
53 Brookville Rd 08817 732-650-5270
Fax 650-5275
Lindeneau ES 600/K-5
50 Blossom St 08817 732-650-5320
Rosemary Shutz, prin. Fax 650-5322
Madison IS 500/3-5
838 New Dover Rd 08820 732-452-2960
Michael Duggan, prin. Fax 452-2964
Madison PS 500/K-2
840 New Dover Rd 08820 732-452-2990
Regina Foxx, prin. Fax 452-2994
Marshall ES 500/K-5
15 Cornell St 08817 732-650-5370
Gerald Young, prin. Fax 650-5376
Menlo Park ES 800/K-5
155 Monroe Ave 08820 732-452-2910
Patricia Cotoia, prin. Fax 452-2911
Monroe ES 400/K-5
7 Sharp Rd 08837 732-452-2970
Lynda Zapoticzny, prin. Fax 452-2975
Washington ES 500/K-5
153 Winthrop Rd 08817 732-650-5280
Anne-Marie Griffin-Ussak, prin. Fax 650-5283
Wilson MS 800/6-8
50 Woodrow Wilson Dr 08820 732-452-2870
Daniel Donnelly, prin. Fax 452-2876
Woodbrook ES 800/K-5
15 Robin Rd 08820 732-452-2901
Nicole Cirillo, prin. Fax 452-2904

Rabbi Pesach Raymon Yeshiva 400/K-8
2 Harrison St 08817 732-572-5052
St. Helena S 300/PK-8
930 Grove Ave 08820 732-549-6234
Sr. Mary Charles Wienckoski, prin. Fax 549-6205
St. Matthew S 200/PK-8
100 Seymour Ave 08817 732-985-6633
Eileen Sullivan, prin. Fax 985-7748
Wardlaw-Hartridge S 400/PK-12
1295 Inman Ave 08820 908-754-1882
Andrew Webster, hdmstr. Fax 754-9678
Yeshivat Netivot Montessori 100/PK-4
91 Jefferson Blvd 08817 732-985-4626
Rivky Ross, prin.

Egg Harbor City, Atlantic, Pop. 4,497
Egg Harbor City SD 500/PK-8
527 Philadelphia Ave 08215 609-965-1034
John Gilly, supt. Fax 965-6719
www.ehcs.k12.nj.us
Rittenberg MS 200/5-8
528 Philadelphia Ave 08215 609-965-1034
Jack Griffith, prin. Fax 965-4742
Spragg ES 300/PK-4
601 Buffalo Ave 08215 609-965-1034
Adrienne Shulby, prin. Fax 965-3651

Galloway Township SD
Supt. — See Galloway
Pomona K Learning Center 200/K-K
400 S Genoa Ave 08215 609-748-1250
Sharon Kurtz, prin. Fax 965-4267

Washington Township SD 100/K-8
2436 Route 563 08215 609-965-3520
Richard Goldberg, supt. Fax 965-6330
Green Bank S 100/K-8
2436 Route 563 08215 609-965-3520
Fax 965-6330

Pilgrim Academy 400/K-12
301 W Moss Mill Rd 08215 609-965-2866
Christopher Storr, hdmstr. Fax 965-3379

Egg Harbor Township, Atlantic
Egg Harbor Township SD 6,100/PK-12
13 Swift Ave 08234 609-646-7911
Dr. Scott McCartney, supt. Fax 383-8749
www.eht.k12.nj.us
Alder Avenue MS 600/6-8
25 Alder Ave 08234 609-383-3366
Margaret Quinn Peretti, prin. Fax 383-1492
Davenport ES 600/PK-3
2501 Spruce Ave 08234 609-645-3550
Louis DellaBarca, prin. Fax 645-1116
Fernwood Avenue MS 1,300/6-8
4034 Fernwood Ave 08234 609-383-3355
James Battersby, prin. Fax 383-0628
Miller ES 600/4-5
2 Alder Ave 08234 609-407-2500
Marjorie Fopeano, prin. Fax 383-3297
Slaybaugh ES 500/PK-3
11 Swift Ave 08234 609-927-8222
Dennis Burd, prin. Fax 927-0038
Swift ES 400/PK-3
5 Swift Ave 08234 609-927-4141
Pedro Bretones, prin. Fax 927-9099

Atlantic Christian S 400/PK-12
391 Zion Rd 08234 609-653-1199
Ron Mansdorfer, admin. Fax 653-1435
Trocki Hebrew Academy 50/PK-12
6814 Black Horse Pike 08234 609-383-8484

Elizabeth, Union, Pop. 125,809
Elizabeth SD 18,900/PK-12
500 N Broad St 07208 908-436-5000
Pablo Munoz, supt. Fax 436-6133
www.elizabeth.k12.nj.us
Antao S 200/PK-8
1014 S Elmora Ave 07202 908-436-4860
Michael Webb, prin. Fax 436-4880
Battin S 400/PK-8
300 S Broad St 07202 908-436-6300
Ben Candelino, prin. Fax 436-6293
Butler S 800/PK-8
501 Union Ave 07208 908-436-5900
Francisco Cuesta, prin. Fax 436-5886
Columbus S 500/PK-8
511 3rd Ave 07202 908-436-5730
AnnaMarie Gil, prin. Fax 436-5718
de Lafayette S 900/PK-8
1071 Julia St 07201 908-436-5600
Deborah Brady, prin. Fax 436-5595
Duarte - Marti S, 25 1st St 07206 PK-8
Gladys Castellanos, prin. 908-436-3950
Edreira Academy 500/PK-8
631 Westminster Ave 07208 908-436-5970
Joseph Engesser, prin. Fax 436-5954
Einstein Academy 800/PK-8
919 N Broad St 07208 908-436-6900
Linda Seniszyn, prin. Fax 436-6920
Elmora S 500/PK-8
638 Magie Ave 07208 908-436-5650
Caroline Cespedes, prin. Fax 436-5645
Franklin S 400/PK-8
248 Ripley Pl 07206 908-436-5700
Arlene Paige, prin. Fax 436-5678
Hamilton MS 700/6-8
310 Cherry St 07208 908-436-6100
Francisco Cuesta, prin. Fax 436-6082
Holmes S 400/PK-8
436 1st Ave 07206 908-436-6070
Manuel Gonzalez, prin. Fax 436-6052
Hudson S 500/PK-8
525 1st Ave 07206 908-436-5930
Dora Kuznitz, prin. Fax 436-5921
King ECC 300/PK-PK
130 Trumbull St 07206 908-436-6450
Liteove Tighe, prin. Fax 436-6449
LaCorte-Peterstown S 600/PK-8
700 2nd Ave 07202 908-436-6230
Jacqueline Jennings, prin. Fax 436-6220
Lincoln S 900/PK-8
50 Grove St 07202 908-436-5828
Philip Gomez, prin. Fax 436-5810
Madison-Monroe S 500/PK-8
1091 North Ave 07201 908-436-5770
Aaron Goldblatt, prin. Fax 436-5756
Marshall S 200/PK-8
521 Magnolia Ave 07206 908-436-5800
Dr. Thelma Hurd, prin. Fax 436-5781
Morris S 400/PK-8
860 Cross Ave 07208 908-436-6000
Lyle Moseley, prin. Fax 436-5987
Pantoja S, 505 Morris Ave 07208 PK-8
Carlos Lucio, prin. 908-436-3900
Reagan Leadership Academy 700/PK-8
730 Pennsylvania Ave 07201 908-436-6950
Arlene Campbell, prin. Fax 436-6959
Reilly S, 436 1st Ave 07206 200/2-8
Jennifer Cedeno, prin. 908-436-4860
Roosevelt S 900/PK-8
650 Bayway Ave 07202 908-436-6270
Ann Remus, prin. Fax 436-6253
Scott S 500/PK-8
125 Madison Ave 07201 908-436-6150
Hollis Mendes, prin. Fax 436-6141
Smith ECC 300/PK-PK
1000 S Elmora Ave 07202 908-436-6380
Kathy DiProfio, prin. Fax 436-6364
Stewart ECC 300/PK-PK
544 Pennsylvania Ave 07201 908-436-6410
Rafael Cortes, prin. Fax 436-6442
Washington S 1,000/PK-8
250 Broadway 07206 908-436-5555
Belinda Abruzzese, prin. Fax 436-5538
Wilson S 700/PK-8
529 Edgar Rd 07202 908-436-6200
Daniel Manies, prin. Fax 436-6191

Blessed Sacrament S 200/PK-8
1086 North Ave 07201 908-352-8629
Sr. Ursula Butler, prin. Fax 352-7934
Evangel Day S 100/PK-K
656 N Broad St 07208 908-353-2422
Akosua Asare, dir. Fax 353-4033
Jewish Educational Center 500/PK-12
330 Elmora Ave 07208 908-355-4850
Rabbi Elazar Teitz, dean Fax 289-5245
St. Anthony S 200/PK-8
227 Center St 07202 908-352-7419
Sr. Charitina Frabizio, prin. Fax 352-7062
St. Genevieve S 300/PK-8
209 Princeton Rd 07208 908-355-3355
Catherine Coyle, prin. Fax 355-1460
St. Mary of the Assumption S 200/K-8
237 S Broad St 07202 908-355-0717
Mary Mancini, prin. Fax 355-3136
Trinity Christian Academy 100/PK-12
417 Pennington St 07202 908-352-9725
Averil Bernard, prin. Fax 352-3970

Elmer, Salem, Pop. 1,379
Elmer Borough SD 100/PK-4
PO Box 596 08318 856-358-6761
Dr. Stephen Berkowitz, supt. Fax 358-7550
www.elmerschool.com
Elmer ES 100/PK-4
PO Box 596 08318 856-358-6761
Dr. Stephen Berkowitz, prin. Fax 358-7550

Elmwood Park, Bergen, Pop. 18,905
Elmwood Park SD 2,100/K-12
60 E 53rd St 07407 201-796-8700
Joseph Casapulla, supt. Fax 703-9337
www.epps.org/

Gantner Avenue ES 300/K-5
99 Roosevelt Ave 07407 201-794-2984
Stephen Bender, prin. Fax 703-4292
Gilbert Avenue ES 300/K-5
151 Gilbert Ave 07407 201-794-2988
Thomas Fedor, prin. Fax 475-0074
Memorial MS 500/6-8
375 River Dr 07407 201-794-2823
Richard Tomko, prin. Fax 791-3438
Sixteenth Avenue ES 300/K-5
85 16th Ave 07407 201-794-2992
Dominick Silla, prin. Fax 791-2616

St. Leo S 300/PK-8
300 Market St 07407 201-796-5156
Elizabeth Pinto, prin. Fax 796-2092

Elwood, Atlantic, Pop. 1,487
Mullica Township SD 700/K-8
PO Box 318 08217 609-561-3868
Richard Goldberg, supt. Fax 561-7133
www.mullica.k12.nj.us
Mullica Township ES 300/K-4
PO Box 318 08217 609-561-3868
Kevin Dugan, prin. Fax 561-7133
Mullica Township MS 300/5-8
PO Box 318 08217 609-561-3868
Brenda Harring-Marro, prin. Fax 561-7133

Emerson, Bergen, Pop. 7,334
Emerson SD 1,100/PK-12
131 Main St 07630 201-599-4178
Dr. Vincent Taffaro, supt. Fax 599-4160
www.emerson.k12.nj.us
Emerson Memorial ES 300/PK-2
1 Haines Ave 07630 201-599-7580
Jessica Espinoza, prin. Fax 262-1400
Villano ES 300/3-6
175 Linwood Ave 07630 201-262-4049
Barnet Ostrowsky, prin. Fax 599-7579

Assumption Academy 200/PK-8
35 Jefferson Ave 07630 201-262-0300
Heather Muller, prin. Fax 262-5910

Englewood, Bergen, Pop. 26,207
Englewood CSD 2,300/PK-12
12 Tenafly Rd 07631 201-862-6000
Dr. Richard Segall, supt. Fax 569-6099
www.epsd.org
Bergen Family Center 100/PK-K
44 Armory St 07631 201-568-0817
Barbara Berger, dir. Fax 568-0913
Cleveland ES 300/1-5
325 Tenafly Rd 07631 201-862-6155
Michael Brown, prin. Fax 816-0593
Dismus MS 400/6-8
325 Tryon Ave 07631 201-862-6025
Peter Elbert, prin. Fax 833-9103
Lincoln ES 300/2-5
51 W Englewood Ave 07631 201-862-6167
Marsha Howard, prin. Fax 871-9278
Quarles K 200/PK-K
155 Davison Pl 07631 201-862-6113
Arnold White, prin. Fax 871-4751

Dwight-Englewood S 900/PK-12
315 E Palisade Ave 07631 201-569-9500
Dr. Rodney DeJarnett, hdmstr. Fax 569-1676
Moriah S of Englewood 900/PK-8
53 S Woodland St 07631 201-567-0208
Dr. Elliot Prager, prin. Fax 567-7402
Morrow S 500/PK-8
435 Lydecker St 07631 201-568-5566
David Lowry, hdmstr. Fax 568-1209
St. Cecilia Interparochial S 200/PK-8
85 W Demarest Ave 07631 201-568-2615
Ann Walsh, prin. Fax 568-7071

Englewood Cliffs, Bergen, Pop. 5,738
Englewood Cliffs SD 400/K-8
143 Charlotte Pl 07632 201-567-7292
Dominic Mucci, supt. Fax 567-2738
www.englewoodcliffs.org
North Cliff ES 100/K-2
642 Floyd St 07632 201-568-4770
Joseph Spano, prin. Fax 568-9874
Upper S 300/3-8
143 Charlotte Pl 07632 201-567-6151
Joseph Spano, prin. Fax 541-8672

Japanese Children's Society 100/K-6
8 W Bayview Ave 07632 201-945-5151

Englishtown, Monmouth, Pop. 1,790
Manalapan-Englishtown Regional SD 4,800/PK-8
54 Main St 07726 732-786-2500
John Marciante Ph.D., supt. Fax 786-2542
www.mers.k12.nj.us
Other Schools – See Manalapan

Erial, Camden, Pop. 2,500
Gloucester Township SD
Supt. — See Blackwood
Lilley ES 700/K-5
1275 Williamstown Erial Rd 08081 856-875-4045
Angela Rose-Bounds, prin. Fax 728-3028
Union Valley ES 700/K-5
1300 Jarvis Rd 08081 856-309-5031
Michael Bohonko, prin. Fax 309-5193

Erial Christian S 200/PK-8
1725 New Brooklyn Rd 08081 856-346-0105
Sandy Gainsford, prin. Fax 346-8100

Essex Fells, Essex, Pop. 2,103
Essex Fells SD 300/PK-6
102 Hawthorne Rd 07021 973-226-0505
Raymond Hyman, supt. Fax 226-0451
www.efsk-6.org
Essex Fells ES 300/PK-6
102 Hawthorne Rd 07021 973-226-0505
Raymond Hyman, prin. Fax 226-0451

Estell Manor, Atlantic, Pop. 1,723
Estell Manor CSD 200/K-8
128 Cape May Ave 08319 609-476-2267
John Cressey, supt. Fax 476-4205
www.estellmanorschool.com
Estell Manor S 200/K-8
128 Cape May Ave 08319 609-476-2267
John Cressey, prin. Fax 476-4205

Ewing, Mercer, Pop. 36,000
Ewing Township SD 3,600/K-12
1331 Lower Ferry Rd 08618 609-538-9800
Michael Nitti, supt. Fax 538-0041
www.ewing.k12.nj.us
Antheil ES 600/K-5
339 Ewingville Rd 08638 609-538-9800
Joan Zuckerman, prin. Fax 883-4604
Fisher MS 900/6-8
1325 Lower Ferry Rd 08618 609-538-9800
Barbara Brower, prin. Fax 637-9753
Lore ES 500/K-5
13 Westwood Dr 08628 609-538-9800
Patricia Womelsdorf, prin. Fax 883-1027
Parkway ES 400/K-5
446 Parkway Ave 08618 609-538-9800
Nicole Harris, prin. Fax 637-9721

Villa Victoria Academy - Lower 100/PK-6
376 W Upper Ferry Rd 08628 609-883-5760
Sr. Alice Ivanyo, prin. Fax 882-8421

Fairfield, Essex, Pop. 7,615
Fairfield Township SD 700/PK-6
15 Knoll Rd 07004 973-227-5586
Dr. Mary Kildow, supt. Fax 227-2964
Churchill ES 300/4-6
233 Fairfield Rd 07004 973-227-2638
Mary Kildrow, prin. Fax 227-8994
Stevenson ES 400/PK-3
15 Knoll Rd 07004 973-227-2120
John Smalta, prin. Fax 227-3676

Fair Haven, Monmouth, Pop. 5,899
Fair Haven Borough SD 1,000/PK-8
224 Hance Rd 07704 732-747-2294
Kathleen Cronin, supt. Fax 747-7441
www.fairhaven.edu
Knollwood MS 500/4-8
224 Hance Rd 07704 732-747-0320
Thomas Famulary, prin. Fax 747-7441
Sickles ES 400/PK-3
25 Willow St 07704 732-741-6151
Marion Carolan, prin. Fax 741-1397

Fair Lawn, Bergen, Pop. 31,408
Fair Lawn SD 4,500/K-12
37-01 Fair Lawn Ave 07410 201-794-5500
Bruce Watson, supt. Fax 797-9296
www.fairlawnschools.org/
Forrest ES 300/K-5
10-00 Hopper Ave 07410 201-794-5565
Dr. Howard Schechter, prin. Fax 791-4427
Jefferson MS 700/6-8
35-01 Morlot Ave 07410 201-703-2240
Dr. John Dunay, prin. Fax 475-9185
Lyncrest ES 200/K-5
9-04 Morlot Ave 07410 201-794-5555
Maria Corso, prin. Fax 796-0536
Memorial MS 400/6-8
12-00 1st St 07410 201-794-5470
John Immerman, prin. Fax 703-2237
Milnes ES 400/K-5
8-01 Philip St 07410 201-794-5550
Dr. Wallace Dimson, prin. Fax 791-4608
Radburn ES 400/K-5
18-00 Radburn Rd 07410 201-794-5480
Natalie Lacatena, prin. Fax 797-7398
Warren Point ES 400/K-5
30-07 Broadway 07410 201-794-5570
Peter McGinness, prin. Fax 475-0614
Westmoreland ES 200/K-5
16-50 Parmelee Ave 07410 201-794-5490
Linda Cobb, prin. Fax 794-8621

St. Anne S 300/K-8
1-30 Summit Ave 07410 201-796-3353
Loretta Stachiotti, prin. Fax 796-9058

Fairview, Bergen, Pop. 13,565
Fairview SD 900/PK-8
130 Hamilton Ave 07022 201-943-1699
Louis DeLisio, supt. Fax 941-1195
Annex S, 130 Hamilton Ave 07022 100/K-8
Angela Penna, prin. 201-943-0564
Fairview ES 3, 403 Cliff St 07022 300/1-5
Lea Turro, prin. 201-943-0563
Lincoln S 500/PK-8
Anderson and Day Ave 07022 201-943-0561
Angela Penna, prin.

Our Lady of Grace S 300/PK-8
400 Kamena St 07022 201-945-8300
Sr. Alice D'Onofrio, prin. Fax 945-4580

Far Hills, Somerset, Pop. 919

Far Hills Country Day S 400/PK-8
PO Box 8 07931 908-766-0622
Jayne Geiger, hdmstr. Fax 766-6705

School of the Hills 50/PK-9
3545 US Highway 206 07931 908-781-5535
Patricia Mercer, prin. Fax 781-6773

Farmingdale, Monmouth, Pop. 1,572
Farmingdale Borough SD 200/PK-8
PO Box 706 07727 732-938-9611
Cheri Ellen Crowl, supt. Fax 938-2317
www.farmingdaleschool.com
Farmingdale S 200/PK-8
PO Box 706 07727 732-938-9611
Cheri Ellen Crowl, prin. Fax 938-2317

Howell Township SD 6,500/K-8
200 Squankum Yellowbrook Rd 07727 732-751-2480
Dr. Enid Golden, supt. Fax 919-1060
www.howell.k12.nj.us
Ardena ES 300/K-5
355 Adelphia Rd 07727 732-751-2485
Dr. Deborah Pennell, prin. Fax 938-5947
Griebling ES 500/K-5
130 Havens Bridge Rd 07727 732-751-2487
Nancy Rupp, prin. Fax 462-2985
Howell Township MS North 900/6-8
501 Squankum Yellowbrook Rd 07727 732-919-0095
Joe Isola, prin. Fax 919-1008
Other Schools – See Freehold, Howell

Flagtown, Somerset

Cherry Blossom Montessori S 100/PK-5
20 Equator Ave 08821 908-369-4436
Leslie Meldrum, prin. Fax 369-0891

Flanders, Morris, Pop. 1,200
Mt. Olive Township SD
Supt. — See Budd Lake
Mountain View ES 600/K-5
118 Clover Hill Dr 07836 973-927-2201
Ronald Marina, prin. Fax 927-2202
Tinc Road ES 600/K-5
24 Tinc Rd 07836 973-927-2203
Dr. Richard Fair, prin. Fax 927-2200

Flemington, Hunterdon, Pop. 4,171
Flemington-Raritan Regional SD 3,500/K-8
50 Court St 08822 908-284-7561
Gregory Nolan, supt. Fax 284-7514
www.frsd.k12.nj.us/
Barley Sheaf ES 500/K-4
80 Barley Sheaf Rd 08822 908-284-7584
Karen Gabruk, prin. Fax 284-7587
Case MS 800/7-8
301 Case Blvd 08822 908-284-5100
Robert Castellano, prin. Fax 284-5144
Desmares ES 400/K-4
16 Old Clinton Rd 08822 908-284-7540
Carol Howell, prin. Fax 284-7548
Hunter ES 500/K-4
8 Dayton Rd 08822 908-284-7620
Dr. Rebecca Hutto, prin. Fax 284-7630
Reading-Fleming IS 700/5-6
50 Court St 08822 908-284-7504
Kathleen Suchorsky, prin. Fax 284-7518
Other Schools – See Ringoes

St. Paul Christian S 100/PK-2
201 State Route 31 08822 908-782-3979
Pam Meyer, dir. Fax 782-1633

Florence, Burlington, Pop. 8,564
Florence Township SD 1,300/K-12
201 Cedar St 08518 609-499-4600
Dr. Louis Talarico, supt. Fax 499-9679
www.florence.k12.nj.us
Riverfront S 400/4-8
500 E Front St 08518 609-499-4647
Theresa Elias, prin. Fax 499-8356
Other Schools – See Roebling

Florham Park, Morris, Pop. 12,626
Florham Park SD 900/K-8
PO Box 39 07932 973-822-3880
Dr. William Ronzitti, supt. Fax 822-0716
www.fpks.org
Briarwood ES 300/K-2
151A Briarwood Rd 07932 973-822-3884
Dr. Sharon Maricle, prin. Fax 822-0289
Brooklake ES 400/3-5
235 Brooklake Rd 07932 973-822-3888
Susan Tietjen, prin. Fax 822-1577
Ridgedale MS 300/6-8
71 Ridgedale Ave 07932 973-822-3855
Mark Majeski, prin. Fax 822-7963

Holy Family S 200/PK-8
17 Lloyd Ave 07932 973-377-4181
James Singagliese, prin. Fax 377-0273

Folsom, Atlantic, Pop. 1,972
Folsom SD 400/PK-8
1357 Mays Landing Rd 08037 609-561-8666
Jean Rishel, supt. Fax 567-8751
www.folsomschool.org
Folsom S 400/PK-8
1357 Mays Landing Rd 08037 609-561-8666
Jean Rishel, prin. Fax 567-3021

Fords, Middlesex, Pop. 14,392
Woodbridge Township SD
Supt. — See Woodbridge
Ford Avenue ES 300/K-5
186 Ford Ave 08863 732-417-5414
Cathie Bedosky, prin. Fax 417-2156
Fords MS 600/6-8
100 Fanning St 08863 732-417-5400
Cynthia Lagunovich, prin. Fax 417-2159

Lafayette Estates ES 300/K-5
500 Ford Ave 08863 732-417-5425
Dr. Robert Zega, prin. Fax 346-0708

Our Lady of Peace S 300/PK-8
PO Box 69 08863 732-738-7464
John Donza, prin. Fax 738-0026
Our Redeemer Lutheran S 100/PK-8
28 S 4th St 08863 732-738-7470
Carol Johnson, prin. Fax 738-6547

Forked River, Ocean, Pop. 4,243
Lacey Township SD
Supt. — See Lanoka Harbor
Forked River ES 500/K-5
110 Lacey Rd 08731 609-971-2080
Eric Fiedler, prin. Fax 242-1081
Lacey Township MS 800/6-8
660 Denton Ave 08731 609-242-2100
James Handschuch, prin. Fax 242-2114

Fort Dix, Burlington, Pop. 10,205
Pemberton Township SD
Supt. — See Pemberton
Fort Dix ES 100/K-4
1199 Juliustown Rd 08640 609-893-8141
Tamara Garbutt, prin. Fax 723-5213

Fort Lee, Bergen, Pop. 37,175
Fort Lee SD 3,400/K-12
255 Whiteman St 07024 201-585-4610
Raymond Bandlow, supt. Fax 585-0691
www.fortlee-boe.net
Cole MS 500/7-8
467 Stillwell Ave 07024 201-585-4660
Rosemarie Giacomelli, prin. Fax 585-1688
Fort Lee ES 1 500/K-6
250 Hoym St 07024 201-585-4620
Joan Costantino, prin. Fax 585-8082
Fort Lee ES 2 400/K-6
2047 Jones Rd 07024 201-585-4630
Priscilla Church, prin. Fax 585-8972
Fort Lee ES 3 500/K-6
2405 2nd St 07024 201-585-4640
Robert Kravitz, prin. Fax 585-1488
Fort Lee ES 4 500/K-6
1193 Anderson Ave 07024 201-585-4650
Peter Emr, prin. Fax 585-1546

Christ the Teacher S 300/PK-8
359 Whiteman St 07024 201-944-0421
Sr. Rosemarie Bartnicki, prin. Fax 944-6293

Franklin, Sussex, Pop. 5,233
Franklin Borough SD 500/K-8
50 Washington Ave 07416 973-827-9775
Dr. Thomas Turner, supt. Fax 827-6522
www.fboe.org/
Franklin S 500/K-8
50 Washington Ave 07416 973-827-9775
Patricia Pfeil, prin. Fax 827-6522

Hardyston Township SD
Supt. — See Hamburg
Hardyston ES 500/K-5
50 State Rt 23 07416 973-823-7000
John Brennan, prin. Fax 827-6845

Immaculate Conception S 200/PK-8
65 Church St 07416 973-827-3777
David Carr, prin. Fax 827-8728

Franklin Lakes, Bergen, Pop. 11,302
Franklin Lakes SD 1,400/K-8
490 Pulis Ave 07417 201-891-1856
Roger Bayersdorfer, supt. Fax 891-9333
www.franklinlakes.k12.nj.us/
Colonial Road ES 300/K-5
749 Colonial Rd 07417 201-337-0336
Patricia Pollack, prin. Fax 337-1512
Franklin Avenue MS 500/6-8
755 Franklin Ave 07417 201-891-0202
Marco Cera, prin. Fax 848-5190
High Mountain Road ES 300/K-5
765 High Mountain Rd 07417 201-891-4433
Helen Attenello, prin. Fax 891-1689
Woodside Avenue ES 300/K-5
305 Woodside Ave 07417 201-891-5600
Dominick Rotante, prin. Fax 891-1483

Academy of the Most Blessed Sacrament 300/PK-8
785 Franklin Lakes Rd 07417 201-891-4250
JoAnn Mathews, prin. Fax 847-9227

Franklin Park, Somerset
Franklin Township SD
Supt. — See Somerset
Franklin Park ES 1,000/PK-4
30 Eden St 08823 732-297-5666
Eileen Brett, prin. Fax 297-5834

Franklinville, Gloucester
Delsea Regional SD 1,700/7-12
PO Box 405 08322 856-694-0100
Frank Borelli, supt. Fax 694-4417
www.delsearegional.us/
Delsea Regional MS 600/7-8
PO Box 405 08322 856-694-0100
Piera Gravenor, prin. Fax 694-4417

Franklin Township SD 1,400/K-6
3228 Coles Mill Rd 08322 856-629-9500
Michael Kozak, supt. Fax 629-1486
www.franklintwpschools.org
Janvier ES 600/K-2
1532 Pennsylvania Ave 08322 856-629-0431
Anthony Ettore, prin. Fax 629-1486

Reutter ES 400/3-6
2150 Delsea Dr 08322 856-694-0223
Robert Weigelt, prin. Fax 629-1486
Other Schools – See Newfield

Freehold, Monmouth, Pop. 11,439
Freehold Borough SD 1,300/PK-8
280 Park Ave 07728 732-761-2100
Elizabeth O'Connell, supt. Fax 462-8954
www.freeholdboro.k12.nj.us
Freehold IS 400/6-8
280 Park Ave 07728 732-761-2156
Nelson Ribon, prin. Fax 761-2181
Freehold Learning Center 500/PK-5
30 Dutch Lane Rd 07728 732-761-2239
Donna Johnson, prin. Fax 577-7029
Park Avenue ES 400/K-5
280 Park Ave 07728 732-761-2124
Joe Jerabek, prin. Fax 761-2161

Freehold Township SD 4,500/PK-8
384 W Main St 07728 732-866-8400
William Setaro Ed.D., supt. Fax 761-1809
www.freeholdtwp.k12.nj.us/
Applegate ES 500/K-5
47 Jean Brennan Dr 07728 732-431-5460
Rebecca Montgomery, prin. Fax 294-4853
Barkalow MS 800/6-8
498 Stillwells Corner Rd 07728 732-431-4403
John Soviero, prin. Fax 294-5560
Catena ES 600/K-5
275 Burlington Rd 07728 732-431-4430
Cathleen Areman, prin. Fax 294-5684
Donovan ES 500/K-5
237 Stonehurst Blvd 07728 732-431-3321
Jennifer Benbrook, prin. Fax 308-9238
Early Childhood Learning Center 50/PK-K
510 Stillwells Corner Rd 07728 732-866-6858
Penny Goldstein, prin. Fax 308-9204
Eisenhower MS 800/6-8
279 Burlington Rd 07728 732-431-3910
Dianne Brethauer, prin. Fax 294-7180
Errickson ES 600/K-5
271 Elton Adelphia Rd 07728 732-431-8022
James McCartney, prin. Fax 308-4541
West Freehold ES 600/K-5
100 Castranova Way 07728 732-431-5101
Edward Aldarelli, prin. Fax 308-9627

Howell Township SD
Supt. — See Farmingdale
Adelphia ES 500/K-5
495 Adelphia Rd 07728 732-919-1553
Alysson Keelen, prin. Fax 780-7714
Memorial MS 600/6-8
458 Adelphia Rd 07728 732-919-1085
Chuck Welsh, prin. Fax 751-0325

Providence Christian Academy 50/PK-6
61 Georgia Rd 07728 732-462-2347
Nadean Sheppard, admin. Fax 462-3085
St. Rose of Lima S 500/PK-8
51 Lincoln Pl 07728 732-462-2646
Sr. Patricia Doyle, prin. Fax 462-0331

Frenchtown, Hunterdon, Pop. 1,503
Frenchtown Borough SD 100/K-8
902 Harrison St 08825 908-996-2751
Rick Falkenstein, supt. Fax 996-3599
www.frenchtownschool.org/
Frenchtown S 100/K-8
902 Harrison St 08825 908-996-2751
Rick Falkenstein, prin. Fax 996-3599

Kingwood Township SD 500/PK-8
880 County Road 519 08825 908-996-2941
Laura Hartner, supt. Fax 996-7268
www.kingwoodschool.org
Kingwood Township S 500/PK-8
880 County Road 519 08825 908-996-2941
Kenneth Foy, prin. Fax 996-7268

Galloway, Atlantic
Galloway Township SD 3,600/K-8
101 S Reeds Rd 08205 609-748-1250
Douglas Groff, supt. Fax 748-1796
www.gtps.k12.nj.us
Galloway Township MS 900/7-8
100 S Reeds Rd 08205 609-748-1250
Dr. Donald Gross, prin.
Oceanville K Learning Center 100/K-K
259 S New York Rd 08205 609-748-1250
Sharon Kurtz, prin.
Rann ES 600/1-6
515 S 8th Ave 08205 609-748-1250
John Gibson, prin. Fax 652-1740
Reeds Road ES 600/1-6
103 S Reeds Rd 08205 609-748-1250
Dr. William Zipparo, prin. Fax 748-6564
Rogers ES 500/1-6
105 S Reeds Rd 08205 609-748-1250
Robin Moore, prin. Fax 748-6563
Smithville ES 600/1-6
37 Old Port Republic Rd 08205 609-748-1250
Dr. Kathie Hathaway, prin. Fax 748-6566
Other Schools – See Egg Harbor City

Assumption Regional S 300/K-8
146 S Pitney Rd 08205 609-652-7134
Mary Schurtz, prin. Fax 652-2544

Garfield, Bergen, Pop. 29,772
Garfield SD 4,100/PK-12
125 Outwater Ln 07026 973-340-5000
Nicholas Perrapato, supt. Fax 340-4620
www.garfield.k12.nj.us/
Columbus ES 400/K-6
147 Cedar St 07026 973-340-5038
Peter DeFranco, prin. Fax 340-6851

Garfield ECC 400/PK-PK
241 Ray St 07026 973-253-6600
Frank D'Amico, prin. Fax 478-0976
Garfield MS 600/6-8
175 Lanza Ave 07026 973-272-7020
Marilyn Martorano, prin. Fax 340-1767
Irving ES 300/K-6
12 Madonna Pl 07026 973-340-5034
Diane Freed, prin. Fax 340-4028
Lincoln ES 300/K-6
111 Palisade Ave 07026 973-340-5036
Frank Passucci, prin. Fax 365-1194
Madison ES 200/K-6
62 Alpine St 07026 973-340-5039
Dora D'Amico, prin. Fax 340-1963
Roosevelt ES 400/K-6
225 Lincoln Pl 07026 973-340-5037
Margarita Pennisi, prin. Fax 340-1037
Wilson ES 400/K-6
205 Outwater Ln 07026 973-340-5035
Doreen Velardi, prin. Fax 340-2463

Garwood, Union, Pop. 4,145
Garwood SD 400/PK-8
500 East St 07027 908-789-0165
T. Quigley, supt. Fax 789-0779
www.garwoodschools.org
Lincoln S 300/1-8
400 2nd Ave 07027 908-789-0331
Mary Emmons, prin. Fax 789-2970
Washington S 100/PK-K
500 East St 07027 908-789-0165
T. Quigley, prin. Fax 789-0779

Gibbsboro, Camden, Pop. 2,468
Gibbsboro SD 300/PK-8
37 Kirkwood Rd 08026 856-783-1140
Dr. James Lavender, supt. Fax 783-9155
www.gibbsboroschool.org
Gibbsboro S 300/PK-8
37 Kirkwood Rd 08026 856-783-1140
Dr. James Lavender, prin. Fax 783-9155

Gibbstown, Gloucester, Pop. 3,902
Greenwich Township SD 500/PK-8
415 Swedesboro Rd 08027 856-224-4920
Francine Marteski Ed.D., supt. Fax 224-5761
www.greenwich.k12.nj.us
Greenwich Township ES 300/PK-4
255 W Broad St 08027 856-224-4900
Susan McAlary, prin. Fax 423-7945
Nehaunsey MS 200/5-8
415 Swedesboro Rd 08027 856-224-4920
Alisa Whitcraft, prin. Fax 224-5765

Gaurdian Angels Regional S 200/K-8
150 S School St 08027 856-423-9440
Sr. Jerilyn Einstein, prin. Fax 423-9445

Gillette, Morris
Long Hill Township SD 1,100/K-8
759 Valley Rd 07933 908-647-1200
Rene Rovtar, supt. Fax 647-1200
www.longhill.org
Gillette ES 200/K-1
759 Valley Rd 07933 908-647-2313
Karen Wetherell Ed.D., prin. Fax 647-4969
Other Schools – See Millington, Stirling

Gladstone, Somerset, Pop. 2,086

Gill St. Bernard's S 700/PK-12
PO Box 604 07934 908-234-1611
Sidney Rowell, hdmstr. Fax 234-1715

Glassboro, Gloucester, Pop. 19,290
Elk Township SD 300/K-6
100 Unionville Rd 08028 856-881-4551
Frank Borelli, supt. Fax 881-3278
www.elk.k12.nj.us/
Aura ES 300/K-6
100 Unionville Rd 08028 856-881-4551
Ronnie Ginsberg, prin. Fax 881-3278

Glassboro SD 2,300/PK-12
560 Bowe Blvd 08028 856-652-2700
Dr. Mark Silverstein, supt. Fax 881-0884
www.glassboroschools.us
Bowe ES 500/4-6
7 Ruth H Mancuso Ln 08028 856-652-2700
Kriston Matthews, prin. Fax 589-0869
Bullock ES 500/1-3
370 New St E 08028 856-652-2700
Joseph DePalma, prin. Fax 881-7587
Glassboro IS 300/7-8
202 Delsea Dr N 08028 856-652-2700
Marianne Carver, prin. Fax 881-3751
Rodgers ECC 300/PK-K
301 Georgetown Rd 08028 856-652-2700
Barbara Raines, prin. Fax 881-1670

Ambassador Christian Academy 100/PK-8
535 Mullica Hill Rd 08028 856-881-3669
Wellington Watts, prin. Fax 881-3827

Glendora, Camden, Pop. 5,201
Gloucester Township SD
Supt. — See Blackwood
Glendora ES 300/K-5
201 Station Ave 08029 856-939-4704
David Hinlicky, prin. Fax 939-6552

Glen Ridge, Essex, Pop. 7,020
Glen Ridge SD 1,800/PK-12
12 High St 07028 973-429-8302
Kenneth Rota, supt. Fax 429-5750
www.glenridge.org

Forest Avenue S — 200/PK-2
287 Forest Ave 07028 — 973-429-8308
Deborah Fitzpatrick, prin. — Fax 429-2908
Linden Avenue S — 300/PK-2
205 Linden Ave 07028 — 973-429-8301
Joseph Caravela, prin. — Fax 429-3243
Ridgewood Avenue S — 600/3-6
235 Ridgewood Ave 07028 — 973-429-8306
Dirk Phillips, prin. — Fax 743-7181

Glen Rock, Bergen, Pop. 11,457
Glen Rock SD — 2,400/K-12
620 Harristown Rd 07452 — 201-445-7700
David Verducci, supt. — Fax 389-5019
www.glenrocknj.org/
Byrd ES — 200/K-5
640 Doremus Ave 07452 — 201-445-7700
Linda Weber, prin. — Fax 389-5025
Central ES — 300/K-5
600 S Maple Ave 07452 — 201-445-7700
Vito D'Alconzo, prin. — Fax 389-5030
Coleman ES — 300/K-5
100 Pinelynn Rd 07452 — 201-445-7700
Dawn Cappadona, prin. — Fax 389-5039
Glen Rock MS — 600/6-8
400 Hamilton Ave 07452 — 201-445-7700
Edward Thompson, prin. — Fax 389-5042
Hamilton ES — 300/K-5
380 Harristown Rd 07452 — 201-445-7700
Irene Pierides, prin. — Fax 670-6529

Academy of Our Lady S — 500/PK-8
180 Rodney St 07452 — 201-445-0622
Patricia Keenaghan, prin. — Fax 445-8345

Gloucester City, Camden, Pop. 11,582
Gloucester City SD — 2,000/PK-12
520 Cumberland St 08030 — 856-456-7000
Paul Spaventa, supt. — Fax 742-8815
www.gcsd.k12.nj.us
Cold Springs ES — 800/PK-3
1194 Market St 08030 — 856-456-7000
Martin O'Connor, prin. — Fax 456-2160
Costello ES — 300/4-6
520 Cumberland St 08030 — 856-456-7000
Kenneth Wagstaff, prin. — Fax 456-1254

St. Mary S — 300/PK-8
340 Cumberland St 08030 — 856-456-0913
Gail Corey, prin. — Fax 456-7382

Great Meadows, Warren, Pop. 1,108
Great Meadows Regional SD — 1,000/K-8
PO Box 74 07838 — 908-637-6576
Jason Bing, supt. — Fax 637-6356
www.gmrsd.com
Great Meadows Regional MS — 400/6-8
273 US Highway 46 07838 — 908-637-4584
Bud Beavers, prin. — Fax 637-4492
Independence Central ES — 400/K-5
281 US Highway 46 07838 — 908-637-4351
Danielle Hamblin, prin. — Fax 637-8935
Liberty Township ES — 300/K-5
334 Mountain Lake Rd 07838 — 908-637-4115
Ernest Batha, prin. — Fax 637-6008

Green Brook, Somerset
Green Brook Township SD — 1,000/K-8
132 Jefferson Ave 08812 — 732-968-1171
Stephanie Bilenker, supt. — Fax 968-1869
www.gbtps.org
Feldkirchner ES — 400/K-3
105 Andrew St 08812 — 732-968-1052
Armand Lamberti, prin. — Fax 968-0791
Green Brook MS — 500/4-8
132 Jefferson Ave 08812 — 732-968-1051
Linda Pollard, prin. — Fax 752-1086

Greendell, Sussex
Green Township SD — 500/PK-8
PO Box 14 07839 — 973-300-3800
Barry Worman, supt. — Fax 383-5705
www.greenhills.org
Green Hills S — 500/PK-8
PO Box 14 07839 — 973-300-3800
Bryan Hensz, prin. — Fax 383-5705

Greenwich, Cumberland
Greenwich Township SD — 100/K-8
839 Ye Greate St 08323 — 856-451-5513
Nancy Nosta, supt. — Fax 451-4476
www.greenwichnj.org
Goodwin S — 100/K-8
839 Ye Greate St 08323 — 856-451-5513
Nancy Nosta, prin. — Fax 451-4476

Guttenberg, Hudson, Pop. 10,885
Guttenberg SD — 900/PK-8
301 69th St 07093 — 201-861-3100
Dr. Joseph Ramos, supt. — Fax 861-1348
www.guttenberg.k12.nj.us
Klein S — 900/PK-8
301 69th St 07093 — 201-861-3100
Pedro Garrido, prin. — Fax 861-1348

Hackensack, Bergen, Pop. 43,735
Hackensack SD — 4,900/PK-12
355 State St 07601 — 201-646-7830
Dr. Edward Kliszus, supt. — Fax 646-7827
www.hackensackschools.org
Fairmount ES — 500/PK-4
105 Grand Ave 07601 — 201-646-7890
Joseph Cicchelli, prin. — Fax 342-7249
5ive 6ix S — 600/5-6
321 State St 07601 — 201-646-8170
Joy Dorsey-Whiting, prin. — Fax 646-1529
Hackensack MS — 700/7-8
360 Union St 07601 — 201-646-7842
Andrea Parchment, prin. — Fax 646-7840
Hillers ES — 400/PK-4
56 Longview Ave 07601 — 201-646-7870
Dr. Kathryn Podovano, prin. — Fax 646-0114
Jackson Avenue ES — 400/PK-4
405 Jackson Ave 07601 — 201-646-7991
Robert Corrado, prin. — Fax 931-0135
Parker ES — 400/PK-4
261 Maple Hill Dr 07601 — 201-646-8020
Lillian Whitaker, prin. — Fax 457-9573

Holy Trinity S — 300/PK-8
43 Maple Ave 07601 — 201-489-6870
Sr. Janet Roddy, prin. — Fax 489-2981
St. Francis of Assisi S — 200/PK-8
100 S Main St 07601 — 201-488-8862
Patricia Vrindten, prin. — Fax 525-0498

Hackettstown, Warren, Pop. 9,375
Hackettstown SD — 1,900/PK-12
PO Box 465 07840 — 908-850-6500
Robert Gratz, supt. — Fax 850-4985
www.hackettstown.org
Hackettstown MS — 400/5-8
500 Washington St 07840 — 908-852-8554
Marie Griffin, prin. — Fax 850-6544
Hatchery Hill ES — 300/PK-4
398 5th Ave 07840 — 908-852-8550
Sandra Machacek, prin. — Fax 850-1286
Willow Grove ES — 200/K-4
601 Willow Grove St 07840 — 908-852-2805
John Sarcone, prin. — Fax 852-7431

St. Mary S — 200/PK-8
159 Liberty St 07840 — 908-852-4791
Marilyn Walsh, prin. — Fax 852-4180

Haddonfield, Camden, Pop. 11,591
Barrington Borough SD
Supt. — See Barrington
Avon ES — 400/K-5
862 Mercer Dr 08033 — 856-547-6632
Anthony Arcodia, prin. — Fax 522-1125

Haddon Township SD
Supt. — See Westmont
Stoy ES — 200/PK-5
206 Briarwood Ave 08033 — 856-869-7725
Charles Warfield, prin. — Fax 869-7728
Van Sciver ES — 200/PK-5
625 Rhoads Ave 08033 — 856-869-7730
Don Pullano, prin.

Haddonfield Borough SD — 2,300/K-12
1 Lincoln Ave 08033 — 856-429-4130
Alan Fegley, supt. — Fax 354-2179
www.haddonfield.k12.nj.us
Central ES — 300/K-5
3 Lincoln Ave 08033 — 856-429-5851
Roger Bowley, prin. — Fax 429-2006
Haddon ES — 400/K-5
501 W Redman Ave 08033 — 856-429-0811
Craig Ogelby, prin. — Fax 429-8906
Haddonfield MS — 600/6-8
5 Lincoln Ave 08033 — 856-429-5851
Noah Tennant, prin. — Fax 429-2006
Tatem ES — 300/K-5
1 Glover Ave 08033 — 856-429-0902
Gino Priolo, prin. — Fax 427-2844

Christ the King Regional S — 300/PK-8
164 Hopkins Ave 08033 — 856-429-2084
Fax 429-4959
Haddonfield Friends S — 200/PK-8
47 N Haddon Ave 08033 — 856-429-6786
Sharon Dreese, hdmstr. — Fax 429-6376

Haddon Heights, Camden, Pop. 7,427
Haddon Heights SD — 1,200/K-12
316A 7th Ave 08035 — 856-547-1412
Dr. Nancy Hacker, supt. — Fax 547-3868
hhsd.k12.nj.us
Atlantic Avenue ES — 100/K-6
21 E Atlantic Ave 08035 — 856-547-0630
Jane McGovern, prin. — Fax 546-4657
Glenview Avenue ES — 200/K-6
1700 Sycamore St 08035 — 856-547-7647
Samuel Sassano, prin. — Fax 546-9566
Seventh Avenue ES — 100/K-6
316 7th Ave 08035 — 856-547-0610
Jane McGovern, prin. — Fax 546-2891

St. Rose of Lima S — 400/K-8
300 Kings Hwy 08035 — 856-546-6166
Steven Hogan, prin. — Fax 546-6601

Hainesport, Burlington
Hainesport Township SD — 600/K-8
PO Box 538 08036 — 609-265-8050
Dr. Mark Silverstein, supt. — Fax 265-8051
www.hainesport.k12.nj.us
Hainesport Township S — 600/K-8
PO Box 538 08036 — 609-267-1316
James Morrow, prin. — Fax 702-0142

Haledon, Passaic, Pop. 8,398
Haledon SD — 1,000/PK-8
70 Church St 07508 — 973-389-2841
Dr. Ray Kwak, supt. — Fax 790-3506
www.haledon.org
Haledon S — 1,000/PK-8
91 Henry St 07508 — 973-790-9000
Paul Iantosca, prin. — Fax 790-3506

Hamburg, Sussex, Pop. 3,567
Hamburg Borough SD — 300/K-8
30 Linwood Ave 07419 — 973-827-7570
Steven Engravalle, supt. — Fax 827-3624
www.hamburgschool.com/
Hamburg S — 300/K-8
30 Linwood Ave 07419 — 973-827-7570
Steven Engravalle, admin. — Fax 827-3624

Hardyston Township SD — 700/K-8
183 Wheatsworth Rd 07419 — 973-823-7000
Anthony Norod, supt. — Fax 823-7011
www.htps.org
Hardyston MS — 300/6-8
183 Wheatsworth Rd 07419 — 973-823-7000
Anthony Norod, prin. — Fax 823-7011
Other Schools – See Franklin

Prince of Peace Early Learning Center — 100/PK-K
PO Box 5 07419 — 973-827-5080
Christie Smith, prin. — Fax 827-5163

Hamilton, Mercer
Hamilton Township SD — 12,500/K-12
90 Park Ave 08690 — 609-631-4100
Neil Bencivengo, supt. — Fax 631-4103
www.hamilton.k12.nj.us
Crockett MS — 800/6-8
2631 Kuser Rd 08691 — 609-631-4149
Barbara Panfili, prin. — Fax 631-4116
Greenwood ES — 200/K-5
2069 Greenwood Ave 08609 — 609-631-4151
Lorraine Persiani, prin. — Fax 631-4118
Grice MS — 900/6-8
901 Whitehorse Hamilton Sq 08610 — 609-631-4152
David Innocenzi, prin. — Fax 631-4119
Kisthardt ES — 300/K-5
215 Harcourt Dr 08610 — 609-631-4153
Charlene Williams-Folsom, prin. — Fax 631-4120
Klockner ES — 200/K-5
830 Klockner Rd 08619 — 609-631-4154
Sharon Young, prin. — Fax 631-4121
Kuser ES — 300/K-5
70 Newkirk Ave 08629 — 609-631-4155
Roberto Kesting, prin. — Fax 631-4123
Lalor ES — 200/K-5
25 Barnt Deklyn Rd 08610 — 609-631-4156
Jay Morris, prin. — Fax 631-4124
Langtree ES — 300/K-5
2080 Whatley Rd 08690 — 609-631-4157
Peggy Gens, prin. — Fax 631-4125
McGalliard ES — 300/K-5
1600 Arena Dr 08610 — 609-631-4158
Cynthia Dacey, prin. — Fax 631-4126
Morgan ES — 400/K-5
37 Stamford Rd 08619 — 609-631-4160
Regina McIntyre, prin. — Fax 631-4128
Reynolds MS — 1,100/6-8
2145 Yrdvll Hamilton Squ Rd 08690 — 609-631-4162
Joseph Slavin, prin. — Fax 631-4130
Robinson ES — 400/K-5
495 Gropp Ave 08610 — 609-631-4163
Gary Mattia, prin. — Fax 631-4131
Sayen ES — 300/K-5
3333 Nottingham Way 08690 — 609-631-4164
Nancy Whalen, prin. — Fax 631-4132
Sunnybrae ES — 300/K-5
166 Elton Ave 08620 — 609-631-4166
Dr. William Fizzano, prin. — Fax 631-4135
University Heights/Morrison ES — 400/K-5
645 Paxson Ave 08619 — 609-631-4167
Donald Constantino, prin. — Fax 631-4136
Wilson ES — 400/K-5
600 E Park Ave 08610 — 609-631-4169
Joan Gray, prin. — Fax 631-4139
Yardville ES — 300/K-5
450 Yardville Allentown Rd 08620 — 609-631-4170
Karen Folis, prin. — Fax 631-4140
Other Schools – See Hamilton Square, Mercerville, Yardville

St. Gregory the Great S — 500/K-8
4680 Nottingham Way 08690 — 609-587-1131
Joan Pramberger, prin. — Fax 587-0322
Trenton Catholic Academy — 300/K-8
177 Leonard Ave 08610 — 609-586-5888
Anne Reap, prin. — Fax 631-9295

Hamilton Square, Mercer, Pop. 26,873
Hamilton Township SD
Supt. — See Hamilton
Alexander ES — 400/K-5
20 Robert Frost Dr 08690 — 609-631-4148
Suzanne Stevenson, prin. — Fax 631-4112

Faith Christian S — 200/PK-8
2111 Kuser Rd 08690 — 609-585-3353
Theodore Martens, admin. — Fax 581-2038

Hammonton, Atlantic, Pop. 13,585
Hammonton SD — 3,200/PK-12
PO Box 631 08037 — 609-567-7000
Mary Lou DeFrancisco, supt. — Fax 561-3567
www.hammontonps.org/
Hammonton ECC — 500/PK-1
601 N 4th St 08037 — 609-567-6693
Marlou Welsh, prin. — Fax 567-6399
Hammonton MS — 600/7-8
75 N Liberty St 08037 — 609-567-7007
Gene Miller, prin. — Fax 561-3974
Sooy ES — 800/2-6
601 N 4th St 08037 — 609-567-7070
Kristina Erman, prin. — Fax 704-1201

St. Joseph Regional S — 400/K-8
133 N 3rd St 08037 — 609-704-2400
Sr. Helen Sanchez, prin. — Fax 561-4940

Hampton, Hunterdon, Pop. 1,608
Hampton Borough SD — 200/K-8
32-41 South St 08827 — 908-537-4101
Joanna Hughes, supt. — Fax 537-6871
www.hamptonelementary.com/

Hampton S 200/K-8
32-41 South St 08827 908-537-4101
Joanna Hughes, prin. Fax 537-6871

Union Township SD 600/PK-8
165 Perryville Rd 08827 908-735-5511
Jeffrey Bender, supt. Fax 735-6657
www.uniontwpschool.org
Union Township ES 300/PK-4
149 Perryville Rd 08827 908-735-5511
Jeffrey Bender, prin. Fax 730-7591
Union Township MS 300/5-8
165 Perryville Rd 08827 908-735-5511
Frances Suchovic, prin. Fax 735-6657

Harrington Park, Bergen, Pop. 4,906
Harrington Park SD 700/K-8
191 Harriot Ave 07640 201-768-5700
Adam Fried Ed.D., supt. Fax 768-1487
www.hpsd.org
Harrington Park S 700/K-8
191 Harriot Ave 07640 201-768-5700
Brian Gatens, prin. Fax 768-1487

Harrison, Hudson, Pop. 14,060
Harrison SD, 430 William St 07029 1,800/K-12
Anthony Comprelli, supt. 973-483-4627
www.harrison.k12.nj.us
Lincoln ES, 221 Cross St 07029 800/K-5
Jo Ann Botch, prin. 973-483-6400
Washington MS, 1 N 5th St 07029 400/6-8
Alan Doffont, prin. 973-483-2285

Holy Cross S 200/PK-8
15 Frank E Rodgers Blvd S 07029 973-481-0340
Maria Barreiros, prin. Fax 481-0488

Harrisonville, Gloucester
South Harrison Township SD 300/K-6
PO Box 112 08039 856-769-0855
David Datz, supt. Fax 769-5426
www.southharrison.k12.nj.us
South Harrison ES 300/K-6
PO Box 112 08039 856-769-0855
David Datz, prin. Fax 769-5426

Hasbrouck Heights, Bergen, Pop. 11,643
Hasbrouck Heights SD 1,500/K-12
379 Boulevard 07604 201-288-6150
Joseph Luongo, supt. Fax 288-0289
www.hhschools.org
Euclid ES 300/K-5
1 Burton Ave 07604 201-288-2138
Linda Simmons, prin. Fax 727-1409
Hasbrouck Heights MS 300/6-8
365 Boulevard 07604 201-393-8190
Edward Bolcar, prin. Fax 288-2083
Lincoln ES 400/K-5
302 Burton Ave 07604 201-288-2365
Steven Forte, prin. Fax 393-8183

Corpus Christi S 400/PK-8
215 Kipp Ave 07604 201-288-0614
Michelle Murillo, prin. Fax 288-8332

Haskell, See Wanaque
Wanaque SD 1,000/K-8
973A Ringwood Ave 07420 973-835-8200
Dr. Richard Weisenfeld, supt. Fax 835-1316
www.wanaque.k12.nj.us
Haskell S 400/K-8
973 Ringwood Ave 07420 973-835-8200
Lynda D'Angiolillo, prin. Fax 835-3690
Other Schools – See Wanaque

St. Francis of Assisi S 200/PK-8
1 Father Hayes Dr 07420 973-835-3268
Laurie LaGuardia, prin. Fax 616-7644

Haworth, Bergen, Pop. 3,414
Haworth SD 500/K-8
205 Valley Rd 07641 201-384-5526
Raymond Albano, supt. Fax 384-8619
www.haworth.org
Haworth S 500/K-8
205 Valley Rd 07641 201-384-5526
Bert Diaz, prin. Fax 384-8619

Hawthorne, Passaic, Pop. 18,268
Hawthorne SD 2,300/PK-12
PO Box 2 07507 973-427-1300
Dr. Richard Spirito, supt. Fax 427-1757
www.hawthorne.k12.nj.us
Jefferson ES 200/PK-5
233 Goffle Hill Rd 07506 973-423-6480
Rosanne Zagatta, prin. Fax 423-6429
Lincoln MS 500/6-8
230 Hawthorne Ave 07506 973-423-6460
Douglas Alexander, prin. Fax 427-5393
Roosevelt ES 600/K-5
50 Roosevelt Ave 07506 973-423-6485
Joseph Brislin, prin. Fax 427-9335
Washington ES 200/K-5
176 Mohawk Ave 07506 973-423-6495
Michelle Gadaleta, prin. Fax 636-2094

Hawthorne Christian Academy 500/K-12
2000 State Rt 208 07506 973-423-3331
Donald J.Klingen, hdmstr. Fax 238-1718
St. Anthony S 200/PK-8
270 Diamond Bridge Ave 07506 973-423-1818
Sr. Marisa DeRose, prin. Fax 423-6065

Hazlet, Monmouth, Pop. 21,976
Hazlet Township SD 2,200/PK-12
421 Middle Rd 07730 732-264-8402
Dr. William George, supt. Fax 264-1599
www.hazlet.org

Beers Street ES 100/5-6
610 Beers St 07730 732-264-1107
Marc Natanagara, prin. Fax 264-1081
Cove Road ES 100/5-6
8 Cove Rd 07730 732-264-5050
Nicholas Sardone, prin. Fax 264-5826
Hazlet MS 500/7-8
1639 Union Ave 07730 732-264-0940
Colleen Rafter, prin. Fax 264-0571
Lillian Drive ES 100/1-4
28 Lillian Dr 07730 732-787-2332
Sarah O'Neill, prin. Fax 495-9332
Middle Road ES 200/1-4
305 Middle Rd 07730 732-264-9012
Loretta Zimmer, prin. Fax 203-2146
Raritan Valley ES 200/1-4
37 Cresci Blvd 07730 732-264-1333
Errol Bottani, prin. Fax 264-6600
Sycamore Drive Early Childhood Lrng Ctr 50/PK-K
37 Sycamore Dr 07730 732-264-2180
Elaine Hayden, prin. Fax 264-0182

Hewitt, Passaic
West Milford Township SD
Supt. — See West Milford
Upper Greenwood Lake ES 400/K-6
41 Henry Rd 07421 973-853-4466
Daniel Novak, prin. Fax 853-1233

Our Lady Queen of Peace S 100/K-8
1905 Union Valley Rd 07421 973-728-9339
Eugene Hewitt, prin. Fax 728-6850

Hibernia, Morris, Pop. 200
Rockaway Township SD 2,700/K-8
PO Box 500 07842 973-627-8200
Dr. Gary Vitta, supt. Fax 627-7968
www.morris.k12.nj.us/rocktwp
Other Schools – See Dover, Rockaway, Wharton

High Bridge, Hunterdon, Pop. 3,770
High Bridge SD 400/K-8
50 Thomas St 08829 908-638-4103
Dr. William Caldwell, supt. Fax 638-4211
www.hbschools.org
High Bridge ES 300/K-5
40 Fairview Ave 08829 908-638-4105
Paul Nigro, prin. Fax 638-5260
High Bridge MS 100/6-8
50 Thomas St 08829 908-638-4101
Dr. William Caldwell, prin. Fax 638-4211

Highland Park, Middlesex, Pop. 14,268
Highland Park SD 1,300/PK-12
435 Mansfield St 08904 732-572-6990
Frances Wood, supt. Fax 393-1174
www.highlandpark.k12.nj.us
Bartle ES 300/2-5
435 Mansfield St 08904 732-572-4100
Lauren Fraser, prin. Fax 572-6446
Highland Park MS 200/6-8
102 N 5th Ave 08904 732-572-2400
Richard Horowitz, prin. Fax 819-7041
Irving PS 300/PK-1
121 S 11th Ave 08904 732-572-1205
Nancy Romano, prin. Fax 572-3709

Highlands, Monmouth, Pop. 4,998
Highlands Borough SD 200/PK-6
360 State Route 36 07732 732-872-1476
Maryann Galassetti, supt. Fax 872-0973
www.highlandselementary.org/
Highlands ES 200/PK-6
360 State Route 36 07732 732-872-1476
Maryann Galassetti, prin. Fax 872-0973

Hightstown, Mercer, Pop. 5,293
East Windsor Regional SD 4,800/PK-12
25A Leshin Ln 08520 609-443-7717
Ronald Bolandi, supt. Fax 443-7704
www.eastwindsorregionalschools.com/
Black ES 500/K-5
371 Stockton St 08520 609-443-7816
Heidi Franzo, prin. Fax 443-7809
Rogers ES 500/PK-5
380 Stockton St 08520 609-443-7833
Robert Dias, prin. Fax 443-7835
Other Schools – See East Windsor

Hillsborough, Somerset
Hillsborough Township SD 7,300/PK-12
379 S Branch Rd 08844 908-369-0030
Edward Forsthoffer Ed.D., supt. Fax 369-8286
www.hillsborough.k12.nj.us
Amsterdam ES 500/K-4
301 Amsterdam Dr 08844 908-874-3700
Mary Ann Mullady, prin. Fax 874-6101
Auten Road IS 1,200/5-6
281 Auten Rd 08844 908-371-1690
Matthew Hoffman, prin. Fax 371-1614
Hillsborough ES 500/K-4
435 US Highway 206 08844 908-874-4777
Michael Volpe, prin. Fax 874-3693
Hillsborough MS 1,200/7-8
260 Triangle Rd 08844 908-874-3420
Joseph Trybulski, prin. Fax 874-3492
Sunnymead ES 400/K-4
55 Sunnymeade Rd 08844 908-722-4747
Tammy Jenkins, prin. Fax 575-1459
Triangle ES 400/K-4
156 S Triangle Rd 08844 908-874-3470
Lisa Heisel, prin. Fax 874-8563
Woodfern ES 500/K-4
425 Woodfern Rd 08844 908-369-4554
Anthony Caparoso, prin. Fax 369-0781
Woods Road ES 400/PK-4
401 S Woods Rd 08844 908-874-3460
Jodi Howe, prin. Fax 874-0496

Hillsdale, Bergen, Pop. 10,089
Hillsdale SD 1,400/PK-8
32 Ruckman Rd 07642 201-664-0282
Anthony DeNorchia, supt. Fax 664-9049
www.hillsdaleschools.com
Meadowbrook ES 400/PK-4
50 Piermont Ave 07642 201-664-8088
Rick Spirito, prin. Fax 664-6132
Smith ES 400/K-4
1000 Hillsdale Ave 07642 201-664-1188
Angela Iskenderian, prin. Fax 664-6354
White MS 700/5-8
120 Magnolia Ave 07642 201-664-0286
Noreen Hajinlian, prin. Fax 664-2715

St. John Academy 500/PK-8
460 Hillsdale Ave 07642 201-664-6364
Elizabeth Viola, prin. Fax 664-8096

Hillside, Union, Pop. 21,044
Hillside Township SD 2,900/K-12
195 Virginia St 07205 908-352-7664
Michael Roth, supt. Fax 282-5831
www.hillsidek12.org
Coolidge ES 200/3-6
614 Tillman St 07205 908-352-7664
Sharon Festante, prin. Fax 282-5835
Hurden-Looker ES 400/3-6
1261 Liberty Ave 07205 908-352-7664
Alphonsus Platt, prin. Fax 282-5845
Krumbiegel MS 400/7-8
145 Hillside Ave 07205 908-352-7664
Martin Dickerson Ed.D., prin. Fax 282-5840
Morris ECC 700/K-2
143 Coe Ave 07205 908-352-7664
Tracey Wolff, prin. Fax 282-5850
Washington ES 200/3-6
1530 Leslie St 07205 908-352-7664
Christine Sidwa, prin. Fax 282-5855

Hillside Catholic Academy 200/PK-8
397 Columbia Ave 07205 908-686-6740
Michael Butchko, prin. Fax 686-3819
Trinity Temple Academy 100/PK-8
1500 Maple Ave 07205 973-923-7568
Fax 923-2976

Hoboken, Hudson, Pop. 39,900
Hoboken SD, 1115 Clinton St 07030 1,700/PK-12
John Raslowsky, supt. 201-356-3600
www.hoboken.k12.nj.us
Brandt MS 200/7-8
215 9th St 07030 201-356-3690
Edith Vega, prin. Fax 356-3697
Calabro ES, 524 Park Ave 07030 100/K-5
Linda Palumbo, prin. 201-356-3670
Connors ES 300/K-6
201 Monroe St 07030 201-356-3680
Linda Erbe, prin. Fax 356-3686
Wallace ES 400/PK-5
1100 Willow Ave 07030 201-356-3650
Charles Tortorella, prin. Fax 356-3655

All Saints Episcopal Day S 100/PK-5
707 Washington St 07030 201-792-0736
Jill Singleton, hdmstr. Fax 792-1595
Hoboken Catholic Academy 300/PK-8
555 7th St 07030 201-963-9535
Rose Perry, prin. Fax 963-1256
Mustard Seed S 200/K-8
422 Willow Ave 07030 201-653-5548
Christine Metzger, hdmstr. Fax 653-4751
Stevens Cooperative S 200/PK-8
301 Garden St Ste 4 07030 201-792-3688
Zoe Hauser, hdmstr. Fax 792-0826

Ho Ho Kus, Bergen, Pop. 3,995
Ho-Ho-Kus SD 700/PK-8
70 Lloyd Rd 07423 201-652-4555
Deborah Ferrara, supt. Fax 652-2824
www.hohokus.org
Ho Ho Kus S 700/PK-8
70 Lloyd Rd 07423 201-652-4555
Alexis Eckert, prin. Fax 652-2824

Holmdel, Monmouth
Holmdel Township SD 3,400/K-12
PO Box 407 07733 732-946-1800
Barbara Duncan, supt. Fax 946-1875
www.holmdelschools.org
Indian Hill ES 800/4-6
735 Holmdel Rd 07733 732-946-1045
Brian Schillaci, prin. Fax 946-7610
Satz MS 600/7-8
24 Crawfords Corner Rd 07733 732-946-1808
Arthur Howard, prin. Fax 834-0089
Village ES 900/K-3
67 McCampbell Rd 07733 732-946-1820
Elizabeth Giacobbe, prin. Fax 946-1831

Little Lambs of the Good Shepherd 50/PK-K
PO Box 658 07733 732-842-1911
St. Benedict S 500/K-8
165 Bethany Rd 07733 732-264-5578
Mary Ellen Lilly, prin. Fax 264-8679

Hopatcong, Sussex, Pop. 16,001
Hopatcong Borough SD 2,300/K-12
PO Box 1029 07843 973-398-8801
Dr. Charles Maranzano, supt. Fax 398-1961
www.hopatcongschools.org/
Durban Avenue ES 400/4-5
PO Box 1029 07843 973-398-8805
Brian Byrne, prin. Fax 398-0971
Hopatcong MS 600/6-8
PO Box 1029 07843 973-398-8804
Jeffrey Hallenbeck, prin. Fax 398-4184

Maxim ES | 300/K-1
PO Box 1029 07843 | 973-398-8807
Tracey Hensz, prin. | Fax 398-7408
Tulsa Trail ES | 300/2-3
PO Box 1029 07843 | 973-398-8806
Jeffrey Nesnay, prin. | Fax 398-0970

Hope, Warren
Hope Township SD | 200/K-8
PO Box 293 07844 | 908-459-4242
Al Annunziata, admin. | Fax 459-5553
www.hope-elem.org
Hope Township S | 200/K-8
PO Box 293 07844 | 908-459-4242
Al Annunziata, prin. | Fax 459-5553

Hopewell, Mercer, Pop. 2,036
Hopewell Valley Regional SD
Supt. — See Pennington
Hopewell ES | 500/K-5
35 Princeton Ave 08525 | 609-737-4000
Christine Laquidara, prin. | Fax 466-8095

Howell, Monmouth
Howell Township SD
Supt. — See Farmingdale
Aldrich ES | 400/K-5
615 Aldrich Rd 07731 | 732-751-2483
Drew Smith, prin. | Fax 363-9164
Greenville ES | 500/K-5
210 Ramtown Greenville Rd 07731 | 732-202-1745
Wilma Cubero, prin. | Fax 458-5456
Howell Township MS South | 1,000/6-8
1 Kuzminski Way 07731 | 732-836-1327
Thomas Feaster, prin. | Fax 836-0698
Land O Pines ES | 500/K-5
1 Thompson Way 07731 | 732-751-2489
Sandra DeYonker, prin. | Fax 905-8505
Newbury ES | 400/K-5
179 Newbury Rd 07731 | 732-751-2491
James Quinn, prin. | Fax 364-0866
Ramtown ES | 500/K-5
216 Ramtown Greenville Rd 07731 | 732-751-2493
Dr. Laurie Bandlow, prin. | Fax 458-6773
Taunton ES | 400/K-5
41 Taunton Dr 07731 | 732-751-2497
Diana Rochon, prin. | Fax 364-4678

Monmouth Academy | 100/K-12
152 Lanes Mill Rd 07731 | 732-364-2812
Barbara Anastos, dir. | Fax 364-4004
St. Veronica S | 400/K-8
4219 US Highway 9 07731 | 732-364-4130
Sr. Cheree Power, prin. | Fax 363-4932
Solomon Schecter Academy | 100/PK-8
395 Kent Rd 07731 | 732-370-1767
Ricki Budelman, prin. | Fax 370-2122

Irvington, Essex, Pop. 60,600
Irvington Township SD | 7,200/PK-12
1 University Pl 07111 | 973-399-6800
Ethel Davion, supt. | Fax 372-3724
www.irvington.k12.nj.us
Augusta Preschool Academy | 300/PK-PK
96 Augusta St 07111 | 973-399-0524
Dr. Wilma Crespo, prin. | Fax 399-0527
Chancellor Avenue ES | 700/K-5
844 Chancellor Ave 07111 | 973-399-6858
Sandra Boon-Gibbs, prin. | Fax 375-2488
Chancellor South ES | 200/K-5
36 Mount Vernon Ave 07111 | 973-399-6875
Stacy Love, prin. | Fax 371-6875
Florence Avenue ES | 700/K-5
1324 Springfield Ave 07111 | 973-399-6862
James Washington, prin. | Fax 399-6965
Grove Street ES | 400/K-5
602 Grove St 07111 | 973-399-6867
Eugene Harris, prin. | Fax 399-2442
Irvington Preschool Academy | 100/PK-PK
1064 Clinton Ave 07111 | 973-399-6888
Rose Gordon, prin. | Fax 399-8193
Madison Avenue ES | 500/K-5
163 Madison Ave 07111 | 973-399-6870
Julie Slattery, prin. | Fax 399-7768
Marshall ES | 300/K-5
141 Montgomery Ave 07111 | 973-416-3821
Richard Graves, prin. | Fax 416-3807
Mt. Vernon Avenue ES | 400/K-5
54 Mount Vernon Ave 07111 | 973-399-6875
Burnett Davis, prin. | Fax 371-6875
Union Avenue MS | 700/6-8
427 Union Ave 07111 | 973-399-6885
Ronald Bligh, prin. | Fax 373-0734
University ES | 400/K-5
1 University Pl 07111 | 973-399-6826
Henry Sosnowski, prin. | Fax 373-0734
University MS | 600/6-8
255 Myrtle Ave 07111 | 973-399-6879
Shakuur Sabuur, prin. | Fax 351-1025

Good Shepherd Academy | 200/PK-8
285 Nesbit Ter 07111 | 973-375-0659
Thomas Scalea, prin. | Fax 373-4882
St. Leo/Sacred Heart S | 200/PK-8
123 Myrtle Ave 07111 | 973-372-7555
Sr. Carina Okeke, prin. | Fax 416-8819

Iselin, Middlesex, Pop. 16,141
Woodbridge Township SD
Supt. — See Woodbridge
Indiana Avenue ES | 400/K-5
256 Indiana Ave 08830 | 732-602-8518
Dr. Samuel Fancera, prin. | Fax 283-2637
Iselin MS | 700/6-8
900 Woodruff St 08830 | 732-602-8450
Jared Rumage, prin. | Fax 750-4861
Kennedy Park ES | 300/K-5
150 Goodrich St 08830 | 732-602-8424
Jill Osborne, prin. | Fax 283-2864
Mascenik ES | 300/K-5
300 Benjamin Ave 08830 | 732-602-8526
Beatrice Moskowitz, prin. | Fax 283-2665

St. Cecelia S | 200/PK-8
45 Wilus Way 08830 | 732-283-2824
Sr. Margaret Mary Hanlon, prin. | Fax 283-5023

Island Heights, Ocean, Pop. 1,861
Island Heights SD | 100/K-6
PO Box 329 08732 | 732-929-1222
John Lichtenberg, supt. | Fax 929-9563
www.islandheights.k12.nj.us
Island Heights ES | 100/K-6
PO Box 329 08732 | 732-929-1222
John Lichtenberg, prin. | Fax 929-9563

Jackson, Ocean, Pop. 800
Jackson Township SD | 9,700/K-12
151 Don Connor Blvd 08527 | 732-833-4600
Thomas Gialanella, supt. | Fax 833-4609
www.jacksonsd.org
Crawford-Rodriguez ES | 700/K-5
1025 Larsen Rd 08527 | 732-833-4690
Robert Rotante, prin. | Fax 833-4759
Elms ES | 800/K-5
780 Patterson Rd 08527 | 732-833-4680
Daniel Baginski, prin. | Fax 833-4739
Goetz MS | 1,300/6-8
835 Patterson Rd 08527 | 732-833-4610
Faith Lessig, prin. | Fax 833-4749
Holman ES | 700/K-5
125 Manhattan St 08527 | 732-833-4620
Theresa Licitra, prin. | Fax 833-4789
Johnson ES | 600/K-5
1021 Larsen Rd 08527 | 732-833-4640
Al Giambrone, prin. | Fax 833-4769
McAuliffe MS | 1,000/6-8
35 S Hope Chapel Rd 08527 | 732-833-4701
Kevin Dieugenio, prin. | Fax 833-4729
Rosenauer ES | 400/K-5
60 Citadel Dr 08527 | 732-833-4630
Michael Raymond, prin. | Fax 833-4779
Switlik ES | 1,000/K-5
75 W Veterans Hwy 08527 | 732-833-4650
Terrence Kenney, prin. | Fax 928-3714

Jesus Harvest Time Academy | 50/PK-6
404 Freehold Rd 08527 | 732-928-9540
Toniann Pena, prin. | Fax 928-9540
St. Aloysius S | 400/PK-8
935 Bennetts Mills Rd 08527 | 732-370-1515
Elizabeth O'Connor, prin. | Fax 370-3555

Jamesburg, Middlesex, Pop. 6,521
Jamesburg SD | 600/PK-8
13 Augusta St 08831 | 732-521-0303
Dr. Gail Verona, supt. | Fax 521-1267
www.jamesburg.org
Breckwedel MS | 200/6-8
13 Augusta St 08831 | 732-521-0640
Dr. Gail Verona, prin. | Fax 521-1267
Kennedy ES | 500/PK-5
28 Front St 08831 | 732-521-0400
Albert Perno, prin. | Fax 605-0571

Jersey City, Hudson, Pop. 239,614
Jersey City SD | 26,100/PK-12
346 Claremont Ave 07305 | 201-915-6202
Dr. Charles Epps, supt. | Fax 915-6084
www.jcboe.org/
Barnes S | 500/PK-8
91 Astor Pl 07304 | 201-915-6420
Annie Graham, prin. | Fax 333-7316
Bradford S | 400/PK-8
96 Sussex St 07302 | 201-915-6450
Terry Watkins-Williams, prin. | Fax 434-5158
Brensinger S | 1,200/PK-8
600 Bergen Ave 07304 | 201-915-6120
Magda Savino, prin. | Fax 434-2824
Conti S | 700/PK-8
182 Merseles St 07302 | 201-714-4300
Myrna Weglarz, prin. | Fax 659-5717
Conwell ES | 500/PK-5
111 Bright St 07302 | 201-915-6100
Ruth Hernandez-Vega, prin. | Fax 413-5118
Conwell MS | 700/6-8
107 Bright St 07302 | 201-946-5740
Wallace DeFelippo, prin. | Fax 209-1293
Copernicus ES | 600/PK-5
3385 John F Kennedy Blvd 07307 | 201-714-4340
Anne Butler, prin. | Fax 222-0949
Cordero S | 700/PK-8
158 Erie St 07302 | 201-714-4390
Marvin Strynar, prin. | Fax 222-9055
Culbreth S | 500/PK-6
153 Union St 07304 | 201-915-6430
Sharon Abbruscato, prin. | Fax 333-7255
DeFuccio S | 400/PK-8
214 Plainfield Ave 07306 | 201-915-6560
Esther Lawz, prin. | Fax 915-6563
Gandhi S | 1,400/PK-8
143 Romaine Ave 07306 | 201-915-6490
Jeanette Ayala, prin. | Fax 435-8514
Jersey City ES 20 | 600/PK-5
160 Danforth Ave 07305 | 201-915-6470
Jorge Fernandez, prin. | Fax 333-1464
Jersey City ES 33 | 400/PK-4
362 Union St 07304 | 201-915-6540
Frank Piccillo, prin. | Fax 433-4232
Jersey City S 8 | 700/PK-5
96 Franklin St 07307 | 201-714-4320
Marissa Migliozzi, prin. | Fax 659-7274
Jersey City S 34 | 700/PK-8
1830 John F Kennedy Blvd 07305 | 201-915-6550
Christine Myrlak, prin. | Fax 915-6553
Kennedy ES | 300/PK-5
222 Mercer St 07302 | 201-915-6410
Wendy Perez, prin. | Fax 433-7721
King S | 800/PK-8
886 Bergen Ave 07306 | 201-915-6521
Chester Kaminski, prin. | Fax 418-8582
Martin S | 300/7-8
59 Wilkinson Ave 07305 | 201-915-6590
Donald Howard, prin. | Fax 915-6596
McAuliffe S | 800/K-8
167 Hancock Ave 07307 | 201-714-4360
Norma Fernandez, prin. | Fax 656-0225
Murray S | 1,000/PK-8
339 Stegman Pkwy 07305 | 201-915-6620
Sandra Jones, prin. | Fax 333-6044
Nolan MS | 600/6-8
88 Gates Ave 07305 | 201-915-6570
Anna Ortiz-Rivas, prin. | Fax 369-3749
Nunnery S | 500/PK-5
123 Claremont Ave 07305 | 201-915-6520
Susan Harbace, prin. | Fax 433-2920
Sullivan ES | 800/PK-5
171 Seaview Ave 07305 | 201-915-6530
Gary Murphy, prin. | Fax 332-7147
Wakeman S | 700/PK-5
100 Saint Pauls Ave 07306 | 201-714-4310
Nicholas Capodice, prin. | Fax 659-5992
Watters S | 1,000/PK-8
220 Virginia Ave 07304 | 201-915-6510
Edwin Rivera, prin. | Fax 433-3150
Webb S | 500/PK-5
264 Van Horne St 07304 | 201-915-6481
Ismael Aponte, prin. | Fax 521-0909
Williams MS | 6-8
222 Laidlaw Ave 07306 | 201-714-8342
Susan Decker, prin. | Fax 659-6457
Young S | 700/PK-6
135 Stegman St 07305 | 201-369-3724
Joanna Veloz, prin. | Fax 433-6939
Zampella S | 1,000/K-8
201 North St 07307 | 201-714-4350
Sandra Frierson, prin. | Fax 420-9082

Al-Ghazaly S | 200/PK-6
17 Park St 07304 | 201-433-5002
| Fax 332-5207
First Christian Pentecostal Academy | 100/PK-8
PO Box 314 07303 | 201-413-1136
Olga Rosario, admin. | Fax 432-6214
Full Will of God Christian Academy | 50/1-12
84 Martin Luther King Jr Dr 07305 | 201-433-6278
Rev. Harold Daniels, supt. | Fax 938-1481
Genesis Academy | 100/PK-8
PO Box 367 07303 | 201-798-0642
Donna Kelly, prin. | Fax 798-1408
Montessori School of Jersey City | 50/PK-4
17 Erie St 07302 | 201-432-6300
Edith Jarquin, prin.
Our Lady of Czestochowa S | 300/PK-8
248 Marin Blvd 07302 | 201-434-2405
Mary Baier, prin. | Fax 434-6068
Our Lady of Mercy S | 300/PK-8
254 Bartholdi Ave 07305 | 201-434-4091
Victoria Hayes, prin. | Fax 434-8405
Our Lady of Victories S | 200/PK-8
240 Ege Ave 07304 | 201-434-4040
Patricia Byrnes, prin. | Fax 434-5356
Resurrection S | 200/PK-8
189 Brunswick St 07302 | 201-653-1699
Sr. Eleanor Uhl, prin. | Fax 418-9019
Sacred Heart S | 200/K-8
183 Bayview Ave 07305 | 201-332-7111
Sr. Frances Salemi, prin. | Fax 332-7160
St. Aloysius S | 300/PK-8
721 W Side Ave 07306 | 201-433-4270
Helen O'Connell, prin. | Fax 433-6916
St. Anne S | 200/PK-8
255 Congress St 07307 | 201-659-0450
Gina Iacona, prin. | Fax 659-1836
St. Joseph S | 200/PK-8
509 Pavonia Ave 07306 | 201-653-0128
John Richards, prin. | Fax 222-5324
St. Nicholas S | 300/PK-8
118 Ferry St 07307 | 201-659-5948
Sr. Ellen Fischer, prin. | Fax 798-6868
St. Patrick S/Assumption/All Saints S | 400/PK-8
509 Bramhall Ave 07304 | 201-433-4664
| Fax 433-0935
Waterfront Montessori | 100/PK-5
150 Warren St Ste 108 07302 | 201-333-5600
Karen Westman, dir. | Fax 333-5009

Jobstown, Burlington
Springfield Township SD | 300/K-6
2146 Jacksonville Jobstown 08041 | 609-723-2479
Dr. Beth Godett, supt. | Fax 723-6112
www.springfieldschool.org/
Springfield Township ES | 300/K-6
2146 Jacksonville Jobstown 08041 | 609-723-2479
Dr. Beth Godett, prin. | Fax 723-6112

Johnsonburg, Warren
Frelinghuysen Township SD | 200/K-6
PO Box 421 07846 | 908-362-6319
Dr. Dwight Klett, admin. | Fax 362-5730
www.fts.k12.nj.us
Frelinghuysen Township ES | 200/K-6
PO Box 421 07846 | 908-362-6319
Dr. Dwight Klett, prin. | Fax 362-5730

Keansburg, Monmouth, Pop. 10,619
Keansburg Borough SD | 1,900/PK-12
100 Palmer Pl 07734 | 732-787-2007
Nicholas Eremita, supt. | Fax 495-6714
www.keansburg.k12.nj.us

Bolger MS — 500/5-8
100 Palmer Pl 07734 — 732-787-2007
Craig Palmer, prin. — Fax 495-7906
Caruso ES — 200/3-4
81 Francis Pl 07734 — 732-787-2007
Elaine Feyereisen, prin. — Fax 787-5791
Port Monmouth Road ES — 700/PK-2
142 Port Monmouth Rd 07734 — 732-787-2007
Donna Glomb, prin. — Fax 787-7536

Kearny, Hudson, Pop. 38,771
Kearny SD — 5,300/PK-12
100 Davis Ave 07032 — 201-955-5021
Robert Mooney, supt. — Fax 955-0544
www.kearnyschools.com/
Franklin S — 900/PK-8
100 Davis Ave 07032 — 201-955-5020
Robert Sprague, prin. — Fax 955-0139
Garfield ES — 500/PK-6
360 Belgrove Dr 07032 — 201-955-5090
Nicholas Testa, prin. — Fax 246-1340
Lincoln S — 700/PK-8
121 Beech St 07032 — 201-955-5095
Paul Reitemeyer, prin. — Fax 997-2590
Roosevelt ES — 400/PK-6
733 Kearny Ave 07032 — 201-955-5100
James DiGuglielmo, prin. — Fax 991-7523
Schuyler S — 400/PK-8
644 Forest St 07032 — 201-955-5105
Kathleen Tutak, prin. — Fax 997-4875
Washington S — 600/PK-8
80 Belgrove Dr 07032 — 201-955-5110
Mary Costello, prin. — Fax 246-1129

Kearny Christian Academy — 100/PK-12
22 Wilson Ave 07032 — 201-998-0788
Jane Botelho, admin. — Fax 998-1102
St. Stephen S — 300/PK-8
131 Midland Ave 07032 — 201-991-3271
Madeline O'Sullivan, prin. — Fax 991-7829

Kendall Park, Middlesex, Pop. 7,127
South Brunswick Township SD
Supt. — See North Brunswick
Brunswick Acres ES — 500/K-5
41 Kory Dr 08824 — 732-297-6621
Joseph Anzek, prin. — Fax 940-2014
Cambridge ES — 500/K-5
35 Cambridge Rd 08824 — 732-297-2941
Glenn Famous, prin. — Fax 940-2030
Constable ES — 500/K-5
29 Constable Rd 08824 — 732-297-2488
Richard Chromey, prin. — Fax 297-7807
Greenbrook ES — 400/K-5
23 Roberts St 08824 — 732-297-2480
Patricia Holliday, prin. — Fax 940-2028

St. Augustine of Canterbury S — 500/PK-8
45 Henderson Rd 08824 — 732-297-6042
Sr. Mary Louise Shulas, prin. — Fax 297-7062

Kenilworth, Union, Pop. 7,743
Kenilworth SD — 1,300/PK-12
426 Boulevard 07033 — 908-276-1644
Dr. Lloyd Leschuk, supt. — Fax 276-7598
www.kenilworthschools.com
Harding ES — 600/PK-6
426 Boulevard 07033 — 908-276-5936
Kathleen Murphy, prin. — Fax 276-1993

St. Theresa S — 400/PK-8
540 Washington Ave 07033 — 908-276-7220
Sr. Theresa Samson, prin. — Fax 709-1103

Keyport, Monmouth, Pop. 7,505
Keyport SD — 1,100/PK-12
335 Broad St 07735 — 732-264-2840
Dr. C. Dan Blachford, supt. — Fax 888-3343
www.keyportschools.org/
Central ES — 600/PK-7
335 Broad St 07735 — 732-264-0561
Anthony Rapolla, prin. — Fax 264-0561

Kinnelon, Morris, Pop. 9,631
Kinnelon Borough SD — 2,200/K-12
109 Kiel Ave 07405 — 973-838-1418
James Opiekun, supt. — Fax 838-5527
www.kinnelonpublicschools.org/
Kiel ES — 400/K-2
115 Kiel Ave 07405 — 973-838-0611
Patricia Hart, prin. — Fax 838-6338
Miller MS — 500/6-8
117 Kiel Ave 07405 — 973-838-5250
Nancy Elmezzi, prin. — Fax 838-3998
Stonybrook ES — 500/3-5
118 Boonton Ave 07405 — 973-838-1881
Jodi Mulholland, prin. — Fax 838-7575

Our Lady of the Magnificat S — 200/PK-8
2 Miller Rd 07405 — 973-838-6222
Phyllis Sisco, prin. — Fax 838-0409

Lafayette, Sussex
Lafayette Township SD — 300/K-8
178 Beaver Run Rd 07848 — 973-875-3344
Keith Neuhs, supt. — Fax 875-3066
www.ltes.org
Lafayette Township S — 300/K-8
178 Beaver Run Rd 07848 — 973-875-3344
David Astor, prin. — Fax 875-3066

Lake Hiawatha, Morris
Parsippany-Troy Hills Township SD
Supt. — See Parsippany
Knollwood ES — 300/K-5
445 Knoll Rd 07034 — 973-263-7060
Susan Raymond, prin. — Fax 331-7153
Lake Hiawatha ES — 300/PK-5
1 Lincoln Ave 07034 — 973-263-4344
Tom Nolan, prin. — Fax 263-4346

Lake Hopatcong, Morris, Pop. 3,000
Jefferson Township SD — 3,500/K-12
28 Bowling Green Pkwy 07849 — 973-663-5780
Kathaleen Fuchs Ph.D., supt. — Fax 663-2790
www.jefftwp.org/
Briggs ES — 300/1-2
1 Jefferson Dr 07849 — 973-663-0900
Randi DeBrito, prin. — Fax 663-7853
Drummond K — 100/K-K
31 State Route 181 07849 — 973-663-0760
Randi DeBrito, prin. — Fax 663-7855
Other Schools – See Oak Ridge, Wharton

Lakehurst, Ocean, Pop. 2,683
Lakehurst SD, 301 Union Ave 08733 — 400/K-8
Kevin Carroll, supt. — 732-657-5741
www.lakehurstschool.org/
Lakehurst S, 301 Union Ave 08733 — 400/K-8
Scott McCue, prin. — 732-657-5741

Lakewood, Ocean, Pop. 38,800
Lakewood Township SD — 5,000/PK-12
1771 Madison Ave 08701 — 732-905-3633
Eugenia Lawson, supt. — Fax 905-3687
www.lakewood.k12.nj.us/
Clarke ES — 900/PK-6
455 Manetta Ave 08701 — 732-905-3620
Yvonne Marti de Daniels, prin. — Fax 905-3623
Clifton Avenue ES — 700/PK-6
625 Clifton Ave 08701 — 732-905-3650
Anne Luick, prin. — Fax 905-3653
Lakewood MS — 700/7-8
755 Somerset Ave 08701 — 732-905-3600
Annette Maldonado, prin. — Fax 905-3695
Oak Street ES — 900/K-6
75 Oak St 08701 — 732-905-3670
Dr. Sheldon Boxer, prin. — Fax 901-2703
Spruce Street ES — 600/PK-6
90 Spruce St 08701 — 732-905-3660
Gail Schwartz, prin. — Fax 905-3663

Bais Faiga S Gratter Building — 700/PK-2
100 Park Ave S 08701 — 732-367-6708
Bais Reuven Kamenitz — 200/PK-8
41 Henry St 08701 — 732-363-0579
Bais Rivka Rochel — 900/PK-8
285 River Ave 08701 — 732-367-4855
Bais Rochel — 400/K-8
115 Carey St 08701 — 732-905-1251
Bais Tova — 500/PK-6
555 Oak St 08701 — 732-901-3913
Bais Yaakov S — 100/K-8
419 5th St 08701 — 732-534-5160
Bnos Bina — 200/K-8
1 E 13th St 08701 — 732-730-1259
Bnos Bracha — 100/K-3
763 River Ave 08701 — 732-905-3030
Bnos Melech of Lakewood — 100/PK-3
685 River Ave 08701 — 732-364-5911
Bnos Rivka — 200/PK-6
1690 Oak St 08701 — 732-370-0100
Gittel Bresler, prin. — Fax 370-0121
Bnos Yaakov S — 500/PK-8
2 Kent Rd 08701 — 732-363-1400
Calvary Academy — 300/PK-12
1133 E County Line Rd 08701 — 732-363-3633
Melissa Payne, prin. — Fax 363-7337
Chinuch L'Banos S — 100/K-2
212 Main St 08701 — 732-367-9255
Holy Family S — 400/PK-8
1141 E County Line Rd 08701 — 732-363-4771
Dr. Robert Andrews, prin. — Fax 363-3146
Lakewood Cheder S — 3,400/K-8
PO Box 838 08701 — 732-364-1552
Lakewood Cheder S — 7-8
520 James St 08701 — 732-370-6460
Lakewood Cheder S Bais Faga — 1,200/3-8
350 Courtney Rd 08701 — 732-363-5070
Talmud Torah Beis Avrohon — 400/K-8
915 New Hampshire Ave 08701 — 732-363-0040
Talmud Torah Ohr Elchonon — 100/PK-6
805 Cross St 08701 — 732-730-2820
Rabbi Menachem Spiegel, dean — Fax 730-2830
Tashbar S of Lakewood — 200/PK-8
655 Princeton Ave 08701 — 732-905-1111
Tiferes Bais Yaakov S — 500/PK-8
170 Oberlin Ave N 08701 — 732-364-0466
United Talmudical Academy/Satmar Chedar — 200/K-9
800 Princeton Ave 08701 — 732-370-8757
Yeshiva Bais Hatorah — 300/PK-8
1815 Swarthmore Ave 08701 — 732-370-7580
Yeshiva Ketanah of Lakewood — 600/K-8
120 2nd St 08701 — 732-363-0303
Yeshiva Keter Torah — 200/K-10
209 2nd St 08701 — 732-961-9731
Yeshiva Masoras Avos — 200/K-8
23 Congress St S 08701 — 732-942-7522
Yeshiva Nesivos Ohr — 200/K-6
525 Oberlin Ave S 08701 — 732-961-1000
Yeshiva Orchos Chaim — 400/PK-8
PO Box 963 08701 — 732-370-0799
Yeshiva Tiferes Torah — 400/PK-8
PO Box 420 08701 — 732-370-9889

Lambertville, Hunterdon, Pop. 3,840
Lambertville SD — 200/PK-6
200 N Main St 08530 — 609-397-0183
Dr. Todd Fay, supt. — Fax 397-4607
www.lpschool.org
Lambertville ES — 200/PK-6
200 N Main St 08530 — 609-397-0183
Gail Tress, prin. — Fax 397-4607
West Amwell Township SD — 300/K-6
1417 Route 179 08530 — 609-397-0819
Dr. Todd Fay, supt. — Fax 397-4350
www.westamwellschool.org/
West Amwell Township ES — 300/K-6
1417 Route 179 08530 — 609-397-0819
Lynne Meara, prin. — Fax 397-4350

Hunterdon Christian Academy — 100/PK-12
638 Brunswick Pike 08530 — 609-397-9553
Shannon Nusser, prin. — Fax 397-4119
Jesus S — 100/PK-K
44 Bridge St 08530 — 609-397-0593
Sr. Marie Conaughton, prin. — Fax 397-8713

Landing, Morris, Pop. 3,000
Roxbury Township SD
Supt. — See Succasunna
Nixon ES — 300/K-4
275 Mount Arlington Blvd 07850 — 973-398-2564
Elizabeth Azar, prin. — Fax 398-3341

Landisville, See Buena
Buena Regional SD
Supt. — See Buena
Donini ES — 200/K-3
210 N Franklin St 08326 — 856-697-0085
Matthew Mazzoni, prin. — Fax 697-2392

Notre Dame Regional S - Landisville — 200/K-8
601 S Central Ave 08326 — 856-697-3456
Dr. Mary Alimenti, prin. — Fax 697-5114

Lanoka Harbor, Ocean
Lacey Township SD — 4,400/K-12
PO Box 216 08734 — 609-971-2000
Richard Starodub, supt. — Fax 242-9406
www.laceyschools.org/home.aspx
Cedar Creek ES — 600/K-5
PO Box 313 08734 — 609-971-5850
Jacqueline Ranuska, prin. — Fax 971-2846
Lanoka Harbor ES — 600/K-5
PO Box 186 08734 — 609-971-2090
Rosemarie Bond, prin. — Fax 971-0968
Mill Pond ES — 400/K-5
PO Box 197 08734 — 609-971-2070
Susan Gallagher, prin. — Fax 971-2057
Other Schools – See Forked River

Laurel Springs, Camden, Pop. 1,939
Laurel Springs SD — 200/K-6
623 Grand Ave 08021 — 856-783-1086
Dr. Albert Brown, supt. — Fax 784-0474
www.laurelspringschool.org
Laurel Springs ES — 200/K-6
623 Grand Ave 08021 — 856-783-1086
Kathleen Westerby, prin.

Laurence Harbor, Middlesex, Pop. 6,361
Old Bridge Township SD
Supt. — See Matawan
Memorial ES — 400/K-5
11 Ely Ave 08879 — 732-290-3876
Martha Simon, prin. — Fax 583-9431

Lavallette, Ocean, Pop. 2,747
Lavallette Borough SD — 100/K-8
105 Brooklyn Ave 08735 — 732-793-7722
Dr. Peter Morris, supt. — Fax 830-1604
www.lavallettek12.org/lavallette
Lavallette S — 100/K-8
105 Brooklyn Ave 08735 — 732-793-7722
Dr. Peter Morris, prin. — Fax 830-1604

Lawnside, Camden, Pop. 2,778
Lawnside Borough SD — 300/K-8
426 E Charleston Ave 08045 — 856-546-4850
Patricia Montgomery Ed.D., supt. — Fax 310-0901
www.lawnside.k12.nj.us
Lawnside S — 300/K-8
426 E Charleston Ave 08045 — 856-546-4850
Patricia Montgomery Ed.D., prin. — Fax 310-0901

Lawrenceville, Mercer, Pop. 6,446
Lawrence Township SD — 3,800/PK-12
2565 Princeton Pike 08648 — 609-671-5500
Philip Meara, supt. — Fax 883-4225
www.ltps.org
Eldridge Park ES — 200/PK-3
55 Lawn Park Ave 08648 — 609-671-5560
Kathy Robbins, prin. — Fax 637-0782
Franklin ES — 400/PK-3
2939 Princeton Pike 08648 — 609-671-5540
William Buss, prin. — Fax 530-1659
Lawrence IS — 800/4-6
66 Eggerts Crossing Rd 08648 — 609-671-5530
Jonathan Dauber, prin. — Fax 637-0783
Lawrence MS — 600/7-8
2455 Princeton Pike 08648 — 609-671-5520
Andrew Zuckerman, prin. — Fax 637-0768
Lawrenceville ES — 300/PK-3
40 Craven Ln 08648 — 609-671-5570
Judith McLaughlin, prin. — Fax 637-0769
Slackwood ES — 300/PK-3
2060 Princeton Pike 08648 — 609-671-5580
Patricia Wendell Ph.D., prin. — Fax 392-6175

Princeton Junior S — 100/PK-5
90 Fackler Rd 08648 — 609-924-8126
Peter Rapelye, hdmstr. — Fax 924-7456
St. Ann S — 300/PK-8
34 Rossa Ave 08648 — 609-882-8077
John McKenna, prin. — Fax 882-0327

Layton, Sussex
Sandyston-Walpack Township SD — 200/K-6
PO Box 128 07851 — 973-948-4450
Martin Sumpman, supt. — Fax 948-4492
www.sandystonwalpack.org

Sandyston-Walpack Consolidated ES 200/K-6
PO Box 128 07851 973-948-4450
Martin Sumpman, prin. Fax 948-4492

Lebanon, Hunterdon, Pop. 1,749
Clinton Township SD 1,200/PK-8
PO Box 362 08833 908-236-7235
Dennis Fyffe, supt. Fax 236-6358
www.ctsd.k12.nj.us
McGaheran ES 200/2-3
63 Allerton Rd 08833 908-735-5151
Mary Postma, prin. Fax 730-7744
Round Valley S 200/4-6
128 Cokesbury Rd 08833 908-236-6341
Judith Hammond, prin. Fax 236-2847
Other Schools – See Clinton

Lebanon Borough SD 100/K-6
6 Maple St 08833 908-236-7235
Dominic Costanzo, supt. Fax 236-7645
lbsd.schoolwires.com
Lebanon Borough ES 100/K-6
6 Maple St 08833 908-236-2448
Dominic Costanzo, prin. Fax 236-7670

Acorn Montessori S 200/PK-6
1222 State Route 31 08833 908-730-8986
Bobbi Cecio, prin. Fax 730-6797

Leonardo, Monmouth, Pop. 3,788
Middletown Township SD
Supt. — See Middletown
Bayshore MS 700/6-8
834 Leonardville Rd 07737 732-291-1380
Carol Force, prin.
Leonardo ES, 14 Hosford Ave 07737 300/K-5
Katherine Sidoti, prin. 732-291-1330

Leonia, Bergen, Pop. 8,853
Leonia SD 1,600/K-12
570 Grand Ave 07605 201-947-5200
Dr. Bernard Josefsberg, supt. Fax 947-4782
www.leoniaschools.org
Leonia MS 400/6-8
500 Broad Ave 07605 201-461-9100
Mark Toback, prin. Fax 461-1510
Scott ES 600/K-5
100 Highland St 07605 201-592-6023
Andrea Freeman, prin. Fax 592-6915

St. John the Evangelist S 200/PK-8
260 Harrison St 07605 201-944-4361
Sr. Mary Kelly, prin. Fax 944-2195

Liberty Corner, Somerset
Bernards Township SD
Supt. — See Basking Ridge
Liberty Corner ES 500/K-5
61 Church St 07938 908-204-2550
Dr. Kathleen Pecoraro, prin. Fax 647-2425

Lincoln Park, Morris, Pop. 10,899
Lincoln Park Borough SD 900/K-8
92 Ryerson Rd 07035 973-696-5500
James Grube, supt. Fax 696-9273
www.lincolnparkboe.org
Lincoln Park ES 500/K-4
274 Pine Brook Rd 07035 973-696-5530
Susan Grillo, prin. Fax 696-5321
Lincoln Park MS 400/5-8
90 Ryerson Rd 07035 973-696-5520
Michael Meyer, prin. Fax 872-8930

Lincroft, Monmouth, Pop. 6,193
Middletown Township SD
Supt. — See Middletown
Lincroft ES 500/K-5
729 Newman Springs Rd 07738 732-741-5838
Luigi Laugelli, prin. Fax 741-3382

Oak Hill Academy 400/PK-8
347 Middletown Lincroft Rd 07738 732-530-1343
Joseph Pacelli, prin. Fax 530-0045
St. Leo the Great S 500/K-8
550 Newman Springs Rd 07738 732-741-3133
Joanne Kowit, prin. Fax 741-2241

Linden, Union, Pop. 40,014
Linden SD 5,900/PK-12
2 E Gibbons St 07036 908-486-2800
Rocco Tomazic Ed.D., supt. Fax 486-6331
www.linden.k12.nj.us
McManus MS 700/6-8
300 Edgewood Rd 07036 908-486-7751
John Kolibas, prin. Fax 587-0607
Public S 1 400/3-5
728 N Wood Ave 07036 908-486-2668
Dona Preston, prin. Fax 925-7287
Public S 2 300/PK-5
1700 S Wood Ave 07036 908-862-3287
Kcyronne Zahir, prin. Fax 862-3856
Public S 4 500/PK-4
1602 Dill Ave 07036 908-486-3286
Anthony Cataline, prin. Fax 925-7284
Public S 5 300/PK-2
1014 Bower St 07036 908-486-2666
Jacqueline White-Bryant, prin. Fax 925-7335
Public S 6 300/PK-5
19 E Morris Ave 07036 908-862-3003
Danny Robertozzi, prin. Fax 862-3862
Public S 8 300/PK-5
500 W Blancke St 07036 908-862-4397
Christine Lospinoso, prin. Fax 862-3868
Public S 9 300/PK-5
1401 Deerfield Ter 07036 908-486-5164
James Iozzi, prin. Fax 925-7281
Public S 10 300/PK-5
2801 Highland Ave 07036 908-486-2043
Joseph Picaro, prin. Fax 925-7369

Soehl MS 600/6-8
300 E Henry St 07036 908-486-0550
Diana Braisted, prin. Fax 486-3478

SS. Elizabeth & Mary Academy 200/PK-8
170 Hussa St 07036 908-486-2507
Eileen Sullivan, prin. Fax 486-1757

Lindenwold, Camden, Pop. 17,265
Lindenwold SD 2,800/PK-12
801 Egg Harbor Rd 08021 856-783-0276
Geraldine Carroll, supt. Fax 435-5887
www.lindenwold.k12.nj.us/
Lindenwold ES 4 700/PK-4
900 E Gibbsboro Rd 08021 856-783-0405
Dana Lawrence, prin. Fax 782-2299
Lindenwold ES 5 800/PK-4
550 Chews Landing Rd 08021 856-784-4063
Richard Taibi, prin. Fax 782-2293
Lindenwold MS 700/5-8
40 White Horse Ave 08021 856-346-3330
J. Scott Strong, prin. Fax 346-0554

Linwood, Atlantic, Pop. 7,398
Linwood CSD 1,000/PK-8
51 Belhaven Ave 08221 609-926-6703
Thomas Baruffi Ed.D., supt. Fax 926-6705
www.linwoodschools.org/
Belhaven MS 500/5-8
51 Belhaven Ave 08221 609-926-6700
Frank Rudnesky Ed.D., prin. Fax 926-6705
Seaview ES 500/PK-4
2015 Wabash Ave 08221 609-926-6726
Susan Speirs, prin. Fax 926-6729

Little Egg Harbor Township, Ocean, Pop. 13,333
Little Egg Harbor Township SD 1,500/K-6
307 Frog Pond Rd 08087 609-296-1719
Dr. Frank Kasyan, supt. Fax 296-3225
Little Egg Harbor IS 800/3-6
305 Frog Pond Rd 08087 609-296-1719
Fax 296-4156
Mitchell ES 600/K-2
950 N Green St 08087 609-296-7131
Constance Fugere, prin. Fax 296-0849

Little Falls, Passaic, Pop. 11,294
Little Falls Township SD 800/K-8
560 Main St 07424 973-256-1034
Bruce deLyon, supt. Fax 256-6542
www.lfnjschools.org/
Little Falls ES 2 300/K-2
78 Long Hill Rd 07424 973-256-1386
Michael Ryan, prin. Fax 256-1610
Little Falls ES 3 200/3-4
560 Main St 07424 973-812-9512
Dr. Bruce deLyon, prin. Fax 256-6542
Little Falls MS 1 400/5-8
36 Stevens Ave 07424 973-256-1033
Gary Borges, prin. Fax 785-4857

Little Ferry, Bergen, Pop. 10,775
Little Ferry SD 900/PK-8
130 Liberty St 07643 201-641-6192
Frank Scarafile, supt. Fax 641-6604
www.littleferry.k12.nj.us
Memorial S 700/2-8
130 Liberty St 07643 201-641-6186
Miriam Bair, prin. Fax 641-3245
Washington PS 200/PK-1
123 Liberty St 07643 201-641-6760
Carmen Holster, prin. Fax 641-4072

Little Silver, Monmouth, Pop. 6,137
Little Silver Borough SD 800/K-8
124 Willow Dr 07739 732-741-2188
Dr. Carolyn Kossack, supt. Fax 741-3644
www.littlesilverschools.org/lss
Markham Place MS 400/5-8
95 Markham Pl 07739 732-741-7112
Dennis Morolda, prin. Fax 741-3562
Point Road ES 400/K-4
357 Little Silver Point Rd 07739 732-741-4022
Pamela Albert, prin. Fax 741-2384

Mastro Montessori Academy 100/PK-6
36 Birch Ave 07739 732-842-5816
Elizabeth Bradbury, dir.

Livingston, Essex, Pop. 27,500
Livingston Township SD 5,400/K-12
11 Foxcroft Dr 07039 973-535-8000
Brad Draeger, supt. Fax 535-1254
www.livingston.org
Burnet Hill ES 400/K-5
25 Byron Pl 07039 973-535-8000
Deborah Cook, prin. Fax 535-9529
Collins ES 400/K-5
67 Martin Rd 07039 973-535-8000
Jeffrey Truppo, prin. Fax 535-9586
Harrison ES 500/K-5
148 N Livingston Ave 07039 973-535-8000
Cynthia Healy, prin. Fax 716-9138
Heritage MS 800/7-8
20 Foxcroft Dr 07039 973-535-8000
Pat Boland, prin. Fax 597-9492
Hillside ES 400/K-5
98 Belmont Dr 07039 973-535-8000
Bernadette Pilchman, prin. Fax 535-8747
Mt. Pleasant ES 400/K-5
11 Broadlawn Dr 07039 973-535-8000
John Hopton, prin. Fax 535-8791
Mt. Pleasant MS 400/6-6
11 Broadlawn Dr 07039 973-535-8000
Louis Melchor, prin. Fax 535-8742
Riker Hill ES 500/K-5
31 Blackstone Dr 07039 973-535-8000
Jo E. Tandler, prin. Fax 740-1356

Aquinas Academy 300/PK-8
388 S Livingston Ave 07039 973-992-1587
Sr. Lena Picillo, prin. Fax 992-1742
Kushner Hebrew Academy 500/PK-8
110 S Orange Ave 07039 973-597-1115
Susan Dworken, hdmstr. Fax 597-3363

Lodi, Bergen, Pop. 24,310
Lodi SD 3,100/PK-12
8 Hunter St 07644 973-778-4620
Frank Quatrone, supt. Fax 778-6393
www.lodi.k12.nj.us
Columbus ES 300/K-5
370 Westervelt Pl 07644 973-478-0514
Vincent Di Chiara, prin. Fax 478-7753
Hilltop ES 400/PK-5
200 Woodside Ave 07644 973-778-1213
Glenn Focarino, prin. Fax 471-5729
Jefferson MS 700/6-8
75 1st St 07644 973-478-8662
Robert Sciolaro, prin. Fax 478-0358
Roosevelt ES 100/PK-5
435 Passaic Ave 07644 973-777-8511
Joseph Dispoto, prin. Fax 249-0840
Washington ES 400/PK-5
310 Main St 07644 973-777-8513
Emil Carafa, prin. Fax 777-2075
Wilson ES 300/PK-5
80 Union St 07644 973-473-8189
Linda Masullo, prin. Fax 471-7345

Logan, Gloucester
Logan Township SD 900/PK-8
110 School Ln 08085 856-467-5133
John Herbst, supt. Fax 467-9012
www.logan.k12.nj.us
Center Square S 200/PK-1
100 Peachwood Dr 08085 856-294-0145
Robert Fisicaro, prin. Fax 294-0151
Logan S 700/2-8
110 School Ln 08085 856-467-5133
Robert Fisicaro, prin. Fax 467-9012

Long Branch, Monmouth, Pop. 32,091
Long Branch SD 2,700/PK-12
540 Broadway 07740 732-571-2868
Joseph Ferraina, supt. Fax 229-0797
www.longbranch.k12.nj.us
Anastasia ES 600/PK-5
92 7th Ave 07740 732-571-3396
Loretta Johnson, prin. Fax 222-8469
Clark ES 300/3-5
192 Garfield Ave 07740 732-571-4677
Lea Trester, prin. Fax 571-1693
Conrow Preschool 300/PK-PK
335 Long Branch Ave 07740 732-222-4539
Cecilia Sweeting-Level, prin. Fax 222-2001
Ferraina ECC 400/PK-PK
80 Avenel Blvd 07740 732-571-4150
Margaret Matthews, prin. Fax 483-0239
Gregory ES 300/PK-5
201 Monmouth Ave 07740 732-222-7048
John Peri, prin. Fax 222-2807
Leadership Academy 6-8
350 Indiana Ave 07740 732-229-5533
Laurie Cancalosi, prin. Fax 229-4898
Morris Ave S 400/K-2
318 Morris Ave 07740 732-571-3139
Bonita Potter-Brown, prin. Fax 870-1911
Science and Computer Technology Academy 6-8
364 Indiana Ave 07740 732-229-5533
Francisco Rodriguez, prin. Fax 229-4898
West End ES 300/PK-5
132 W End Ave 07740 732-222-3215
Janet Lynn Dudick, prin. Fax 222-6953

Children of the King Academy 100/PK-3
167 Cedar Ave 07740 732-571-2223
Patricia Leone, dir. Fax 571-2223
Power of Christ Gospel Academy 50/K-6
PO Box 565 07740 732-870-3324
Gloria James, dir. Fax 870-8961
Seashore S 200/PK-8
345 2nd Ave 07740 732-222-6464
Charlotte Schatzow, prin. Fax 222-7101

Long Valley, Morris, Pop. 1,744
Washington Township SD 3,100/PK-8
53 W Mill Rd 07853 908-876-4172
John Sakala Ed.D., supt. Fax 876-9392
www.wtschools.org
Cucinella ES 700/PK-5
470 Naughright Rd 07853 908-850-3161
Richard Papera, prin. Fax 684-4874
Flocktown Road ES 300/3-5
90 Flocktown Rd 07853 908-852-1376
Dr. Nancy Canning, prin. Fax 850-0853
Kossmann ES 600/K-2
90 Flocktown Rd 07853 908-850-1010
Dr. Nancy Canning, prin. Fax 850-0401
Long Valley MS 1,000/6-8
51 W Mill Rd 07853 908-876-3434
Mark Ippolito, prin. Fax 876-3436
Old Farmers Road ES 400/K-5
51 Old Farmers Rd 07853 908-876-3865
Dr. Marie Roberts, prin. Fax 876-9506

Lumberton, Burlington
Lumberton Township SD 1,700/K-8
33 Municipal Dr 08048 609-267-1406
Frank Logandro, supt. Fax 267-0002
www.lumberton.k12.nj.us/
Ashbrook ES 400/2-3
33 Municipal Dr 08048 609-518-0030
Scott Dailey, prin. Fax 784-5101
Bobby's Run ES 400/4-5
32 Dimsdale Dr 08048 609-702-5555
Scott Heino, prin. Fax 702-1463

Lumberton MS 600/6-8
30 Dimsdale Dr 08048 609-265-0123
Patricia Hutchinson, prin. Fax 265-0476
Walther ES 300/K-1
56 Chestnut St 08048 609-267-1404
Janet Horan, prin. Fax 267-6038

Lyndhurst, Bergen, Pop. 18,262
Lyndhurst Township SD 2,200/PK-12
420 Fern Ave 07071 201-438-5683
Joseph Abate, supt. Fax 896-2118
www.lyndhurstschools.net
Columbus ES 100/K-5
640 Lake Ave 07071 201-896-2074
Joseph Vastola, prin. Fax 933-3078
Franklin S 200/K-8
360 Stuyvesant Ave 07071 201-896-2077
Kathy Stopherd, prin. Fax 933-3106
Jefferson S 200/K-8
336 Lake Ave 07071 201-896-2065
Peggy Romano, prin. Fax 933-3112
Lincoln S 200/K-8
281 Ridge Rd 07071 201-438-5683
Joseph Vastola, prin. Fax 438-5786
Roosevelt S 400/K-8
530 Stuyvesant Ave 07071 201-896-2068
Peter Strumolo, prin. Fax 933-3143
Washington S 300/PK-8
709 Ridge Rd 07071 201-896-2072
Nicholas Coffaro, prin. Fax 933-3173

Sacred Heart S 300/PK-8
620 Valley Brook Ave 07071 201-939-4277
Margaret Smiriga, prin. Fax 939-0534

Mc Guire AFB, Burlington, Pop. 7,580
North Hanover Township SD
Supt. — See Wrightstown
Atlantis ES 200/1-2
3 School Rd 08641 609-723-5550
Julie Fluet, prin. Fax 723-5586
Columbia ES 200/3-4
1 School Rd 08641 609-723-5900
Robert Scranton, prin. Fax 723-6810
Discovery K 300/PK-K
2 School Rd 08641 609-723-5700
Charles Bednarik, prin. Fax 723-2196

Madison, Morris, Pop. 15,918
Madison SD 2,100/PK-12
359 Woodland Rd 07940 973-593-3100
Richard Noonan, supt. Fax 301-2170
www.madisonpublicschools.org
Central Avenue ES 400/K-5
51 Central Ave 07940 973-593-3173
Philip Kennedy, prin. Fax 514-2070
Kings Road ES 200/K-5
215 Kings Rd 07940 973-593-3178
Kathleen Koop, prin. Fax 966-1927
Madison JHS 400/6-8
285 Main St 07940 973-593-3149
Glen Lampa, prin. Fax 966-1908
Sabatini ES 300/PK-5
359 Woodland Rd 07940 973-593-3182
Michael Post, prin. Fax 966-1925

St. Vincent the Martyr S 400/PK-6
26 Green Village Rd 07940 973-377-1104
Virginia Feury-Gagnon, prin. Fax 377-2632

Magnolia, Camden, Pop. 4,389
Magnolia Borough SD 400/PK-8
420 N Warwick Rd 08049 856-783-6343
Dr. Warren Pross, supt. Fax 783-4651
www.magnoliaschools.org/
Magnolia S 400/PK-8
420 N Warwick Rd 08049 856-783-2996
Ralph Johnson, prin. Fax 566-9736

Mahwah, Bergen, Pop. 17,905
Mahwah Township SD 3,300/PK-12
60 Ridge Rd 07430 201-762-2400
Charles Montesano, supt. Fax 529-1287
www.mahwah.k12.nj.us
Kilmer ES 600/4-5
80 Ridge Rd 07430 201-762-2270
Ruth Gillman, prin. Fax 529-4754
Lenape Meadows ES 400/PK-3
160 Ridge Rd 07430 201-762-2260
Christine Zimmermann, prin. Fax 529-6821
Ramapo Ridge MS 800/6-8
150 Ridge Rd 07430 201-762-2380
Brian Miller, prin. Fax 529-6790
Ross ES 300/K-3
20 Malcolm Rd 07430 201-762-2250
Catherine Bennett, prin. Fax 529-4150
Washington ES 300/K-3
39 Fardale Ave 07430 201-762-2240
Patricia Hanratty, prin. Fax 529-2759

Young World Day S 200/PK-5
585 Wyckoff Ave 07430 201-327-3888
Kimberly Watkins, prin. Fax 327-2416

Manahawkin, Ocean, Pop. 1,594
Southern Regional SD 4,000/7-12
105 Cedar Bridge Rd 08050 609-597-9481
Craig Henry, supt. Fax 978-0298
www.srsd.net
Southern Regional MS 900/7-8
75 Cedar Bridge Rd 08050 609-597-9481
Lorraine Airey, prin. Fax 978-8209

Stafford Township SD 2,200/PK-6
775 E Bay Ave 08050 609-978-5700
Ronald Meinders, supt. Fax 978-0807
www.staffordschools.org
McKinley Avenue ES 600/3-4
1000 McKinley Ave 08050 609-978-5700
Margaret Hoffman, prin. Fax 978-5737
Meinders Primary Learning Ctr 300/PK-K
1000 McKinley Ave 08050 609-978-5700
Susan D'Alessandro, prin. Fax 978-8393
Ocean Acres ES 400/1-2
489 Nautilus Dr 08050 609-978-5700
Deborah Addesso, prin. Fax 607-1983
Oxycocus ES 200/1-2
250 N Main St 08050 609-978-5700
Carl Krushinski, prin. Fax 978-5739
Stafford IS 600/5-6
1000 Mckinley Ave 08050 609-978-5700
William Wilkinson, prin. Fax 978-5738

All Saints Regional S 400/PK-8
400 Doc Cramer Blvd 08050 609-597-3800
Sr. Jeannette Daily, prin. Fax 597-2223
Lighthouse Christian Academy 100/PK-6
400 Beach Ave Ste B 08050 609-597-3915
Alice Hazeltine, prin. Fax 597-9659

Manalapan, Monmouth
Manalapan-Englishtown Regional SD
Supt. — See Englishtown
Clark Mills ES 600/1-5
34 Gordons Corner Rd 07726 732-786-2720
Stephanie Kraft, prin. Fax 786-2730
Dawes Early Learning Center 500/PK-K
38 Gordons Corner Rd 07726 732-786-2830
Melissa Foy, prin. Fax 786-2840
Lafayette Mills ES 300/1-5
66 Maxwell Ln 07726 732-786-2700
Gregory Duffy, prin. Fax 786-2710
Manalapan-Englishtown MS 1,400/7-8
155 Millhurst Rd 07726 732-786-2650
Robert Williams, prin. Fax 786-2660
Milford Brook ES 600/1-5
20 Glo Bar Ter 07726 732-786-2780
Kimberly Pickus, prin. Fax 786-2790
Pine Brook ES 300/6-6
155 Pease Rd 07726 732-786-2800
Michael D'Anna, prin. Fax 786-2810
Taylor Mills ES 500/1-5
77 Gordons Corner Rd 07726 732-786-2760
Kerry Marsala, prin. Fax 786-2770
Wemrock Brook ES 600/1-5
118 Millhurst Rd 07726 732-786-2600
Jacqueline Martin, prin. Fax 786-2610

Manasquan, Monmouth, Pop. 6,201
Manasquan SD 1,700/K-12
169 Broad St 08736 732-528-8800
Geraldine Margin, supt. Fax 223-6286
www.manasquanboe.org/
Manasquan S 700/K-8
168 Broad St 08736 732-528-8810
Colleen Graziano, prin. Fax 223-9736

Atlantis Preparatory S 300/PK-1
1904 Atlantic Ave 08736 732-528-5437
Donna Fortney, dir. Fax 223-1507
St. Denis S 200/PK-8
119 Virginia Ave 08736 732-223-4928
Trudy Bonavita, prin. Fax 223-1807

Manchester, Ocean
Manchester Township SD
Supt. — See Whiting
Manchester Township ES 500/K-5
101 N Colonial Dr 08759 732-323-9600
Dr. Frances Scudese, prin. Fax 323-9820
Manchester Township MS 700/6-8
2759 Ridgeway Rd 08759 732-657-1717
Thomas Baxter, prin. Fax 657-0326
Ridgeway ES 500/K-5
2861 Ridgeway Rd 08759 732-323-0800
Diane Pedroza, prin. Fax 323-9812

Mantua, Gloucester
Mantua Township SD
Supt. — See Sewell
Centre City ES 500/K-4
301 Columbus Dr 08051 856-468-2100
Joy Oliva, prin. Fax 468-7530
Tomlin ES 600/K-6
393 Main St 08051 856-468-0818
Robert Preziosi, prin. Fax 468-7174

Manville, Somerset, Pop. 10,404
Manville Borough SD 1,300/PK-12
410 Brooks Blvd 08835 908-231-8500
Dr. Donald Burkhardt, supt. Fax 707-3963
www.manvilleschools.org
Batcho IS, 100 N 13th Ave 08835 300/6-8
Dr. James Brunn, prin. 908-231-8521
Roosevelt ES, 410 Brooks Blvd 08835 200/4-5
Michael Magliacano, prin. 908-231-6809
Weston ES, 600 Newark Ave 08835 400/PK-3
Donald Frank, prin. 908-231-8548

Christ the King S 100/PK-8
99 N 13th Ave 08835 908-526-1339
Christine Benson, prin. Fax 526-3541

Maple Shade, Burlington, Pop. 19,211
Maple Shade Township SD 2,000/K-12
170 Frederick Ave 08052 856-779-1750
Michael Livengood, supt. Fax 779-1054
www.mapleshade.org/
Steinhauer ES 300/5-6
25 N Fellowship Rd 08052 856-779-7323
Cathy McElroy, prin. Fax 779-2921

Wilkins ES 300/3-4
34 W Mill Rd 08052 856-779-1129
Beth Norcia, prin. Fax 321-9217
Yocum ES 500/K-2
748 N Forklanding Rd 08052 856-779-7423
Daniel Gaffney, prin. Fax 779-7598

Our Lady of Perpetual Help S 300/PK-8
236 E Main St 08052 856-779-7526
Donna Satkowski, prin. Fax 667-3083

Maplewood, Essex, Pop. 21,756
South Orange-Maplewood SD 6,000/K-12
525 Academy St 07040 973-762-5600
Brian Osborne, supt. Fax 378-9464
www.somsd.k12.nj.us
Boyden ES 400/K-5
274 Boyden Ave 07040 973-378-5209
Mark Quiles, prin. Fax 378-5244
Clinton ES 500/K-5
27 Berkshire Rd 07040 973-378-7686
Patricia O'Neil, prin. Fax 378-5241
Jefferson ES 400/3-5
518 Ridgewood Rd 07040 973-378-7696
Maryrose Caulfield-Sloan, prin. Fax 378-7692
Maplewood MS 700/6-8
7 Burnett St 07040 973-378-7660
Kristopher Harrison, prin. Fax 378-5247
Tuscan ES 500/K-5
25 Harvard Ave 07040 973-378-5221
Malikah Majeed, prin. Fax 378-7626
Other Schools – See South Orange

St. Joseph S 300/PK-8
240 Franklin Ave 07040 973-761-4033
Susan Jurevich, prin. Fax 761-6705

Margate City, Atlantic, Pop. 8,666
Margate City SD 600/PK-8
8103 Winchester Ave 08402 609-822-1686
Theresa DeFranco, supt. Fax 822-3399
www.margateschools.org
Ross IS 200/3-5
101 N Haverford Ave 08402 609-822-2080
Michelle Carney-Ray, prin. Fax 822-3489
Tighe MS 200/6-8
7804 Amherst Ave 08402 609-822-2353
Kerri McGinley Ed.D., prin. Fax 822-8456
Union Avenue ES 200/PK-2
9001 Winchester Ave 08402 609-822-2391
John DiNicola, prin. Fax 822-1986

Marlboro, Monmouth
Marlboro Township SD 5,900/PK-8
1980 Township Dr 07746 732-972-2000
Dr. David Abbott, supt. Fax 972-2003
www.marlboro.k12.nj.us
Defino Central ES 800/1-5
175 State Route 79 N 07746 732-972-2099
Dr. Sandra Morris, prin. Fax 332-0521
Dugan ES 700/1-5
48 Topanemus Rd 07746 732-972-2110
Yolande Allen, prin. Fax 617-9736
Marlboro ES 700/1-5
100 School Rd W 07746 732-972-2095
Dr. Jonathan Shutman, prin. Fax 972-3429
Marlboro MS 1,200/6-8
355 County Road 520 07746 732-972-2100
Patricia Nieliwocki, prin. Fax 972-6765
Other Schools – See Morganville

Solomon Schecter Day S 200/PK-8
PO Box 203 07746 732-431-5525
Cory Chargo, dir. Fax 431-2562

Marlton, Burlington, Pop. 10,228
Evesham Township SD 4,800/K-8
25 S Maple Ave 08053 856-983-1800
Patricia Lucas, supt. Fax 983-2939
www.evesham.k12.nj.us
Beeler ES 400/K-5
60 Caldwell Ave 08053 856-988-0619
Tami Aronow, prin. Fax 988-0495
DeMasi ES 300/K-5
199 Evesboro Medford Rd 08053 856-988-0777
Virginia Grossman, prin. Fax 988-1691
DeMasi MS 700/6-8
199 Evesboro Medford Rd 08053 856-988-0777
Virginia Grossman, prin. Fax 596-1571
Evans ES 500/K-5
400 Route 73 S 08053 856-988-0675
Lou Casanova, prin. Fax 988-7755
Jaggard ES 400/K-5
2 Wescott Rd 08053 856-988-0679
Susan Screnci, prin. Fax 988-7788
Marlton ES 500/K-5
190 Tomlinson Mill Rd 08053 856-988-9811
Julio Feldman, prin. Fax 988-9812
Marlton MS 1,100/6-8
150 Tomlinson Mill Rd 08053 856-988-0684
Gary Hoffman, prin. Fax 988-9327
Rice ES 400/K-5
50 Crown Royale Pkwy 08053 856-988-0685
Geralyn Kennedy, prin. Fax 988-7799
Van Zant ES 500/K-5
270 Conestoga Dr 08053 856-988-0687
Rosemary McMullen, prin. Fax 988-8989

Joyful Noise Christian S 100/PK-K
55 E Main St 08053 856-983-1630
Laura Dolan, dir. Fax 983-1814
Marlton Christian Academy 100/K-6
625 E Main St 08053 856-988-8503
Gregory Phelps, prin. Fax 988-1523
St. Joan of Arc S 400/K-8
101 Evans Rd 08053 856-983-0774
Sr. Patricia Pycik, prin. Fax 983-3278

Marmora, Cape May
Upper Township SD
Supt. — See Petersburg
Upper Township ES 400/4-5
50 N Old Tuckahoe Rd 08223 609-390-1242
Dr. James Burke, prin. Fax 390-3003
Upper Township PS 500/K-3
130 N Old Tuckahoe Rd 08223 609-390-2242
Carla Bittner, prin. Fax 390-2390

Martinsville, Somerset

Pingry S 1,100/K-12
PO Box 366 08836 908-647-5555
Nathaniel Conard, hdmstr. Fax 647-5035

Matawan, Monmouth, Pop. 8,819
Matawan-Aberdeen Regional SD
Supt. — See Aberdeen
Ravine Drive ES 400/K-3
170 Ravine Dr 07747 732-705-5800
Patricia Janover, prin. Fax 566-6423

Old Bridge Township SD 9,600/K-12
4207 Highway 516 07747 732-290-3976
Dr. Simon Bosco, supt. Fax 441-3816
www.oldbridgeadmin.org
Cheesequake ES 300/K-5
111 State Route 34 07747 732-360-4552
Dr. Joanne Feldman, prin. Fax 316-9353
Other Schools – See Cliffwood Beach, Laurence Harbor, Old Bridge, Parlin

Mays Landing, Atlantic, Pop. 2,090
Hamilton Township SD 3,100/PK-8
1876 Dr Dennis Foreman Dr 08330 609-476-6300
Michelle Cappelluti, supt. Fax 625-4847
www.hamiltonschools.org
Davies MS 1,000/6-8
1876 Dr Dennis Foreman Dr 08330 609-625-6600
Michael Muldoon, prin. Fax 625-2267
Hess S 1,400/PK-PK, 2-
700 Babcock Rd 08330 609-625-6600
Jennifer Baldwin, prin. Fax 625-8346
Shaner Memorial ES 600/K-1
5801 3rd St 08330 609-625-6600
Russell Clark, prin. Fax 625-8346

St. Vincent DePaul S 200/K-8
5809 Main St 08330 609-625-1565
Linda Pirolli, prin. Fax 625-4703

Maywood, Bergen, Pop. 9,442
Maywood SD 800/PK-8
452 Maywood Ave 07607 201-845-9110
Dr. Robert Otinsky, supt. Fax 845-7146
www.maywoodschools.org
Maywood Avenue MS 500/4-8
452 Maywood Ave 07607 201-845-9110
Michael Jordan, prin. Fax 291-1917
Memorial ES 300/PK-3
764 Grant Ave 07607 201-845-9113
Raymond Bauer, prin. Fax 845-0657

Medford, Burlington
Medford Township SD 3,000/K-8
128 Route 70 Ste 1 08055 609-654-6416
Joseph Del Rossi Ed.D., supt. Fax 654-7436
www.medford.k12.nj.us/
Allen ES, 24 Allen Ave 08055 400/K-5
Jane Hower, prin. 609-654-4203
Chairville ES, 36 Chairville Rd 08055 400/K-5
Richard Lacovara, prin. 609-654-9610
Cranberry Pines ES 500/K-5
400 Fairview Rd 08055 856-983-2861
Lucas Coesfeld, prin.
Haines S 300/6-6
162 Stokes Rd 08055 609-654-4056
Brooke Farrow, prin. Fax 654-4717
Kirby's Mill ES, 151 Hartford Rd 08055 400/K-5
Mark Damon, prin. 609-953-7014
Medford Township Memorial MS 700/7-8
55 Mill St 08055 609-654-7707
Phillip Petru, prin. Fax 654-7297
Taunton Forge ES 400/K-5
32 Evergreen Trl 08055 609-654-6723
Sherry Weinberg, prin.

St. Mary of the Lakes S 500/PK-8
196 Route 70 08055 609-654-2546
Nina Hoover, prin. Fax 654-8125

Medford Lakes, Burlington, Pop. 4,185
Medford Lakes Borough SD 500/PK-8
135 Mudjekeewis Trl 08055 609-654-0991
Dr. James Lynch, supt. Fax 654-7629
www.medford-lakes.k12.nj.us
Neeta S 300/3-8
44 Neeta Trl 08055 609-654-5155
Carole Ramage, prin. Fax 953-8258
Nokomis S 200/PK-2
135 Mudjekeewis Trl 08055 609-654-0991
Carole Ramage, prin. Fax 654-7629

Mendham, Morris, Pop. 5,172
Mendham Borough SD 700/PK-8
12 Hilltop Rd 07945 973-543-2295
Dr. Janie Edmonds, supt. Fax 543-2805
www.mendhamboro.org
Hilltop ES 400/PK-4
12 Hilltop Rd 07945 973-543-4251
Robert Marold, prin. Fax 543-2805
Mountain View MS 300/5-8
100 Dean Rd 07945 973-543-7075
Patricia Lambert, prin. Fax 543-7993

St. Joseph S 300/K-8
8 W Main St 07945 973-543-7474
Helen Kelly, prin. Fax 543-7817

Mercerville, Mercer
Hamilton Township SD
Supt. — See Hamilton
Mercerville ES 400/K-5
60 Regina Ave 08619 609-631-4159
Joyce Palumbo, prin. Fax 631-4127

Our Lady of Sorrows S 300/PK-8
3800 E State Street Ext 08619 609-587-4140
Teresa Carrick, prin. Fax 584-8853

Merchantville, Camden, Pop. 3,820
Merchantville SD 300/PK-8
130 S Centre St 08109 856-663-1091
Christian Swanson, supt. Fax 486-9755
www.merchantville.k12.nj.us
Merchantville S 300/PK-8
130 S Centre St 08109 856-663-1091
Christian Swanson, prin. Fax 486-9755

St. Peter S 300/K-8
51 W Maple Ave 08109 856-665-5879
Maureen Lesniak, prin. Fax 665-4943

Metuchen, Middlesex, Pop. 13,383
Metuchen SD 2,000/PK-12
16 Simpson Pl 08840 732-321-8700
T. Pollifrone-Sinatra, supt. Fax 321-6567
www.metuchenschools.org/metuchen
Campbell S 600/1-4
24 Durham Ave 08840 732-321-8777
Robert Gugliara, prin. Fax 767-9324
Edgar MS 600/5-8
49 Brunswick Ave 08840 732-321-8770
Katherine Glutz, prin. Fax 452-0571
Moss S 100/PK-K
16 Simpson Pl 08840 732-321-8700
Paul Pineiro, prin. Fax 321-1285

Woodbridge Township SD
Supt. — See Woodbridge
Menlo Park Terrace ES 400/K-5
19 Maryknoll Rd 08840 732-417-5419
Sharon McGreevey, prin. Fax 549-8329

Metuchen Christian Academy 200/K-8
130 Whitman Ave 08840 732-549-7854
Fax 549-6686
St. Francis Cathedral S 500/PK-8
528 Main St 08840 732-548-3107
Barbara Stevens, prin. Fax 548-5760

Mickleton, Gloucester
East Greenwich Township SD 700/K-6
559 Kings Hwy 08056 856-423-0412
Joseph Conroy, supt. Fax 224-9337
www.eastgreenwich.k12.nj.us
Clark ES 300/K-2
7 Quaker Rd 08056 856-423-0613
Joshua Meyer, prin. Fax 423-9186
Mickle ES 400/3-6
559 Kings Hwy 08056 856-423-0412
Loretta Savidge, prin. Fax 423-9337

Middlesex, Middlesex, Pop. 13,938
Middlesex Borough SD 2,000/K-12
300 John F Kennedy Dr 08846 732-317-6000
Dr. James Baker, supt. Fax 317-6006
www.middlesex.k12.nj.us
Hazelwood ES 100/K-3
800 Hazelwood Ave 08846 732-317-6000
Shirley Ekberg, prin. Fax 317-6003
Mauger MS 800/4-8
Fisher Ave 08846 732-317-6000
Robert Heidt, prin. Fax 317-6002
Parker ES 200/K-3
150 S Lincoln Ave 08846 732-317-6000
Maureen Hughes, prin. Fax 317-6001
Watchung ES 200/K-3
1 Fisher Ave 08846 732-317-6000
Kathryn Diskin, prin. Fax 317-6004

Our Lady of Mt. Virgin S 300/PK-8
450 Drake Ave 08846 732-356-6560
Ann Major, prin. Fax 356-7860

Middletown, Monmouth, Pop. 24,000
Middletown Township SD 9,800/K-12
59 Tindall Rd 07748 732-671-3850
Karen Bilbao, supt. Fax 615-9351
www.middletownk12.org/
Middletown Village ES 400/K-5
145 Kings Hwy 07748 732-671-0267
Karen Zupancic, prin.
New Monmouth ES 400/K-5
121 New Monmouth Rd 07748 732-671-5317
Linda Chadwick, prin.
Nut Swamp ES 600/K-5
925 Nutswamp Rd 07748 732-671-5795
Anne Facendo, prin. Fax 671-3529
Ocean Avenue ES 300/K-5
235 Ocean Ave 07748 732-787-0092
Diane Cantillo, prin.
Thompson MS 1,000/6-8
1001 Middletown Lincroft Rd 07748 732-671-2212
Patrick Houston, prin.
Other Schools – See Atlantic Highlands, Belford, Leonardo, Lincroft, New Monmouth, Port Monmouth, Red Bank

---

King of Kings S 200/PK-K
250 Harmony Rd 07748 732-615-0220
Barbara Hines, dir. Fax 615-0220

Midland Park, Bergen, Pop. 6,952
Midland Park Borough SD 900/K-12
31 Highland Ave 07432 201-444-1400
William Heebink Ph.D., supt. Fax 444-3051
www.midlandparkschools.k12.nj.us
Godwin ES K-2
41 E Center St 07432 201-445-5350
Fax 652-5709
Highland Avenue ES 400/3-6
31 Highland Ave 07432 201-445-3880
Joseph Desiderio, prin. Fax 444-3051

Eastern Christian S 300/PK-4
25 Baldin Dr 07432 201-445-6150
Sandra Bottge, prin. Fax 445-0488

Milford, Hunterdon, Pop. 1,215
Holland Township SD 600/K-8
710 Milford Warren Glen Rd 08848 908-995-2401
Dr. George Petty, supt. Fax 995-2011
hts.k12.nj.us
Holland Township ES 300/K-4
710 Milford Warren Glen Rd 08848 908-995-2401
Nancy Yard, prin. Fax 995-2011
Holland Township MS 300/5-8
710 Milford Warren Glen Rd 08848 908-995-2401
Nancy Yard, prin. Fax 995-2011

Milford Borough SD 100/K-8
7 Hillside Ave 08848 908-995-4349
Edward Stoloski, supt. Fax 995-2813
www.milfordpublicschool.com
Milford S 100/K-8
7 Hillside Ave 08848 908-995-4349
Maggie Culley, prin. Fax 995-2813

Millburn, Essex, Pop. 18,630
Millburn Township SD 4,500/K-12
434 Millburn Ave 07041 973-376-3600
Dr. Richard Brodow, supt. Fax 912-9396
www.millburn.org
Millburn MS 1,000/6-8
25 Old Short Hills Rd 07041 973-379-2600
Michael Cahill, prin. Fax 912-0939
South Mountain ES 300/K-5
2 Southern Slope Dr 07041 973-921-1394
Anna Stefanelli, prin. Fax 921-1365
Wyoming ES 300/K-5
55 Myrtle Ave 07041 973-761-1619
George Dixon, prin. Fax 763-4128
Other Schools – See Short Hills

Millington, Morris
Long Hill Township SD
Supt. — See Gillette
Millington S 500/2-5
91 Northfield Rd 07946 908-647-2312
Jennifer Dawson, prin. Fax 647-4917

Millstone, Monmouth
Millstone Township SD 1,000/PK-8
5 Dawson Ct 08535 732-786-0950
Dr. Mary Anne Donahue, supt. Fax 792-0951
www.millstone.k12.nj.us/
Millstone Township ES 400/3-5
308 Millstone Rd, 732-786-0950
Brandy Worth, prin. Fax 446-5342
Millstone Township MS 600/6-8
5 Dawson Ct, 732-786-0950
Michelle Vella, prin.
Other Schools – See Clarksburg

Milltown, Middlesex, Pop. 7,130
Milltown SD 700/K-8
80 Violet Ter 08850 732-214-2360
Dr. Linda Madison, supt. Fax 214-2376
www.milltownps.org
Kilmer S 400/4-8
21 W Church St 08850 732-214-2370
Janet Ferlazzo, prin. Fax 214-2378
Parkview ES 300/K-3
80 Violet Ter 08850 732-214-2360
Dr. Linda Madison, prin. Fax 214-2376

Our Lady of Lourdes S 200/PK-8
44 Cleveland Ave 08850 732-828-1951
Sr. Maria Gruszka, prin. Fax 828-7871

Millville, Cumberland, Pop. 27,886
Millville SD 6,200/PK-12
PO Box 5010 08332 856-327-7575
Dr. Shelly Schneider, supt. Fax 825-1545
www.millvillenj.gov/schools/home/
Bacon ES 300/K-5
501 S 3rd St 08332 856-327-6101
Harry Tillotson, prin. Fax 327-7964
Child Family Center 600/PK-PK
1100 Coombs Rd 08332 856-293-2170
JoAnn Burns, prin. Fax 293-2174
Holly Heights ES 500/K-5
2509 E Main St 08332 856-293-2200
Gregg Merritt, prin. Fax 327-8738
Lakeside MS 1,100/6-8
2 N Sharp St 08332 856-293-2420
Thomas Denning, prin. Fax 825-7588
Mt. Pleasant ES 200/K-5
100 Carmel Rd 08332 856-327-6131
Arlene Jenkins, prin. Fax 327-3913
Rieck Avenue ES 500/K-5
339 Rieck Ave 08332 856-327-6093
Dr. Brian Robinson, prin. Fax 327-6088
Silver Run ES 500/K-5
301 Silver Run Rd 08332 856-327-6121
Dr. Pamela Moore, prin. Fax 327-3598
Wood ES 300/K-5
700 Archer St 08332 856-293-2245
William Sheridan, prin. Fax 825-8592

St. Mary Magdalen S 200/PK-8
7 W Powell St 08332 856-825-3600
Sr. Rosa Ojeda, prin. Fax 825-9119

Mine Hill, Morris, Pop. 3,333
Mine Hill Township SD 400/K-6
42 Canfield Ave 07803 973-366-0590
Richard Bitondo, supt. Fax 366-3881
www.minehillsch.org
Canfield Avenue ES 400/K-6
42 Canfield Ave 07803 973-366-0590
Gregory Hobaugh, prin. Fax 366-3881

Minotola, See Buena
Buena Regional SD
Supt. — See Buena
Cleary MS 500/6-8
1501 Central Ave 08341 856-697-0100
Kenneth Nelson, prin. Fax 697-9580

Monmouth Beach, Monmouth, Pop. 3,593
Monmouth Beach Borough SD 300/K-8
7 Hastings Pl 07750 732-222-6139
Neil Frankenfield, supt. Fax 222-2395
Monmouth Beach S 300/K-8
7 Hastings Pl 07750 732-222-6139
Fax 222-2395

Monmouth Junction, Middlesex, Pop. 1,570
South Brunswick Township SD
Supt. — See North Brunswick
Brooks Crossing ES 800/K-5
50 Deans Rhode Hall Rd 08852 732-821-7478
Gary Abbamont, prin. Fax 821-7429
Brooks Crossing ES at Deans K-1
848 Georges Rd 08852 732-297-3581
Gary Abbamont, prin. Fax 348-4465
Crossroads North MS 900/6-8
635 Georges Rd 08852 732-329-4191
Judith Black, prin. Fax 329-1907
Crossroads South MS 1,200/6-8
195 Major Rd 08852 732-329-4633
Raymond Tucholski, prin. Fax 329-1906
Monmouth Junction ES 400/K-5
630 Ridge Rd 08852 732-329-6981
Maribeth Edmunds, prin. Fax 329-1892

Noor Ul-Iman S 500/PK-12
PO Box 271 08852 732-329-1306
Janet Nazif, prin. Fax 329-8703

Monroe Township, Middlesex
Monroe Township SD 4,800/K-12
423 Buckelew Ave 08831 732-521-2111
Joseph King, supt. Fax 521-2719
monroe.k12.nj.us
Applegarth MS 700/7-8
227 Applegarth Rd 08831 609-655-0604
Jeff Gorman, prin. Fax 655-4314
Barclay Brook ES 700/K-2
358 Buckelew Ave 08831 732-521-1000
Carol Schwalje, prin. Fax 656-9082
Brookside ES 900/3-6
370 Buckelew Ave 08831 732-521-1101
Dori Alvich, prin. Fax 521-6022
Mill Lake ES 600/K-3
115 Monmouth Rd 08831 732-251-5336
Lynn Barberi, prin. Fax 251-8525
Oak Tree ES K-6
226 Applegarth Rd 08831 609-655-7642
Dennis Ventrello, prin.
Woodland ES 500/4-6
42 Harrison Ave 08831 732-251-1177
Victor Soriano, prin. Fax 251-1563

Monroeville, Salem
Upper Pittsgrove Township SD 400/K-8
235 Pine Tavern Rd 08343 856-358-8163
Robert Bazzel, supt. Fax 358-0319
www.ups.k12.nj.us
Upper Pittsgrove S 400/K-8
235 Pine Tavern Rd 08343 856-358-8163
Robert Bazzel, prin. Fax 358-1024

Montague, Sussex
Montague SD 300/K-6
475 US Highway 206 07827 973-293-7131
Janice Hodge, supt. Fax 293-3391
montagueschool.org/
Montague ES 300/K-6
475 US Highway 206 07827 973-293-7131
Janice Hodge, prin. Fax 293-3391

Montclair, Essex, Pop. 39,200
Montclair SD 6,400/K-12
22 Valley Rd 07042 973-509-4000
Dr. Frank Alvarez, supt. Fax 509-0586
www.montclair.k12.nj.us/
Bradford ES 400/K-5
87 Mount Hebron Rd 07043 973-509-4155
Catherine Vitone, prin. Fax 509-9523
Edgemont ES 300/K-5
20 Edgemont Rd 07042 973-509-4162
Adunni Anderson, prin. Fax 655-0489
Glenfield MS 600/6-8
25 Maple Ave 07042 973-509-4171
Alex Anemone, prin. Fax 509-4179
Hillside ES 600/3-5
54 Orange Rd 07042 973-509-4200
Michael Chiles, prin. Fax 509-1448
Mt. Hebron MS 600/6-8
173 Bellevue Ave 07043 973-509-4220
Dr. Mark Jennings, prin. Fax 509-4218
Nishuane ES 500/K-2
32 Cedar Ave 07042 973-509-4222
Felice Harrison, prin. Fax 746-8865
Northeast ES 400/K-5
603 Grove St 07043 973-509-4242
Katherine Lindsay, prin. Fax 509-1386
Rand S 400/K-5
176 N Fullerton Ave 07042 973-509-4255
Dr. Barbara Elder Weller, prin. Fax 746-4162
Renaissance MS 200/6-8
17 Munn St 07042 973-509-5741
Charles Cobb, prin. Fax 509-5752
Watchung ES 400/K-5
14 Garden St 07042 973-509-4259
Gail Clarke, prin. Fax 509-1344

Lacordaire Academy 100/PK-8
153 Lorraine Ave 07043 973-746-2660
Lauren Mazzari, admin. Fax 783-6804
Montclair Cooperative S 200/PK-8
65 Chestnut St 07042 973-783-4955
Bruce Kanze, hdmstr. Fax 783-1316
Montclair Kimberley Academy 200/PK-3
224 Orange Rd 07042 973-746-9800
Thomas Nammack, hdmstr. Fax 509-9670
Montclair Kimberley Academy 400/4-8
201 Valley Rd 07042 973-746-9800
Thomas Nammack, hdmstr. Fax 509-7950
St. Cassian S 200/PK-8
190 Lorraine Ave 07043 973-746-1636
Mary Cassels, prin. Fax 746-3271

Montvale, Bergen, Pop. 7,306
Montvale SD 1,000/PK-8
47 Spring Valley Rd 07645 201-391-1662
Lawrence Hughes, supt. Fax 391-8935
www.montvale.k12.nj.us
Fieldstone MS 500/5-8
47 Spring Valley Rd 07645 201-391-9000
Dr. Paul Semendinger, prin. Fax 391-8935
Memorial ES 500/PK-4
53 W Grand Ave 07645 201-391-2900
Dr. Nancy Drabik, prin. Fax 391-1330

Montville, Morris, Pop. 15,600
Montville Township SD
Supt. — See Pine Brook
Lazar MS 1,000/6-8
123 Changebridge Rd 07045 973-331-7140
John Gallucci, prin. Fax 331-9279
Mason ES 400/K-5
5 Shawnee Trl 07045 973-331-7135
Dr. Stephanie Adams, prin. Fax 331-9425
Valley View ES 400/K-5
30 Montgomery Ave 07045 973-331-7125
Dr. Patricia Kennedy, prin. Fax 331-9427

St. Pius X S 300/PK-8
24 Changebridge Rd 07045 973-335-1253
Sr. June Morrissey, prin. Fax 335-2392
Trinity Christian S 200/PK-12
160 Changebridge Rd 07045 973-334-1785
Douglas Prol, prin. Fax 334-9282

Moonachie, Bergen, Pop. 2,812
Moonachie SD 200/PK-8
20 W Park St 07074 201-641-5833
Mark Solimo, supt. Fax 641-3723
www.rlcraig.org
Craig S 200/PK-8
20 W Park St 07074 201-641-5833
Mark Solimo, prin. Fax 641-3723

Moorestown, Burlington, Pop. 13,242
Moorestown Township SD 4,300/K-12
803 N Stanwick Rd 08057 856-778-6600
John Bach, supt. Fax 235-0961
www.mtps.com
Allen III MS 700/7-8
801 N Stanwick Rd 08057 856-778-6620
Carole Butler, prin. Fax 727-9309
Baker ES 400/K-3
139 W Maple Ave 08057 856-778-6630
David Tate, prin. Fax 778-4412
Moorestown Upper ES 1,000/4-6
325 Bortons Landing Rd 08057 856-793-0333
Kim Jackson, prin. Fax 793-0363
Roberts ES 300/K-3
290 Crescent Ave 08057 856-778-6635
Dr. Fred Johnson, prin. Fax 778-4426
South Valley ES 500/K-3
210 S Stanwick Rd 08057 856-778-6640
Dr. Leisa Karanjia, prin. Fax 727-4357

Moorestown Friends S 700/PK-12
110 E Main St 08057 856-235-2900
Laurence Van Meter, hdmstr. Fax 235-6684
Our Lady of Good Counsel S 500/PK-8
23 W Prospect Ave 08057 856-235-7885
Jerome McGowan, prin. Fax 235-2570

Morganville, Monmouth
Marlboro Township SD
Supt. — See Marlboro
Holmes ES 600/1-5
48 Menzel Ln 07751 732-972-2080
Michael Ettore, prin. Fax 617-1361
Marlboro Early Learning Center 400/PK-K
171 Tennent Rd 07751 732-972-7100
Kathryn Arabia, prin. Fax 972-2493
Marlboro Memorial MS 900/6-8
71 Nolan Rd 07751 732-972-7115
Dr. Joanmarie Penney, prin. Fax 972-7118
Robertsville ES 700/1-5
36 Menzel Ln 07751 732-972-2044
Stephen Shifrinson, prin. Fax 617-0275

Shalom Torah Academy 200/PK-8
70 Amboy Rd 07751 732-536-0911

Morris Plains, Morris, Pop. 5,629
Hanover Township SD
Supt. — See Whippany
Mountview Road ES 300/K-5
30 Mountview Rd 07950 973-515-2424
Theodora Spina, prin. Fax 539-0628
Morris Plains SD 600/PK-8
500 Speedwell Ave 07950 973-538-1650
Vicki Pede, supt. Fax 540-1983
www.morris.k12.nj.us/mps/MPS%20Website/indexeve.html
Borough MS 400/3-8
500 Speedwell Ave 07950 973-538-1650
Rosalie Haller, prin. Fax 538-8367
Mountain Way ES 200/PK-2
205 Mountain Way 07950 973-538-0339
Lindsay Nahm, prin. Fax 538-0405

Morris SD
Supt. — See Morristown
Vail ES, 125 Speedwell Ave 07950 300/K-2
Anita Barber, prin. 973-292-2080

Parsippany-Troy Hills Township SD
Supt. — See Parsippany
Littleton ES 500/K-5
51 Brooklawn Dr 07950 973-682-2847
Michele Hoffman, prin. Fax 984-2980

St. Virgil S 200/PK-8
238 Speedwell Ave 07950 973-539-7267
Cathy Condon, prin. Fax 292-5157

Morristown, Morris, Pop. 18,851
Morris SD 4,500/K-12
31 Hazel St 07960 973-292-2300
Thomas Ficarra, supt. Fax 292-2057
www.morrisschooldistrict.org
Frelinghuysen MS 900/6-8
200 W Hanover Ave 07960 973-292-2200
Ethel Minchello, prin. Fax 292-2458
Hamilton ES 200/3-5
34 Mills St 07960 973-292-2190
Josephine Noone, prin. Fax 292-2194
Hillcrest ES 300/K-2
160 Hillcrest Ave 07960 973-292-2240
Kelly Harte, prin. Fax 292-2236
Jefferson ES 300/3-5
101 James St 07960 973-292-2090
Cristina Frazzano, prin. Fax 292-2069
Normandy Park ES 300/K-5
19A Normandy Pkwy 07960 973-889-7690
Joseph Schmidt, prin.
Sussex Avenue ES 300/3-5
125 Sussex Ave 07960 973-292-2250
Peter Frazzano, prin.
Woodland Avenue ES 300/K-2
15 Johnston Dr 07960 973-292-2230
David Gidich, prin.
Other Schools – See Morris Plains

Assumption of the BVM S 400/K-8
63 MacCulloch Ave 07960 973-538-0590
Sr. Merris Larkin, prin. Fax 984-3632
Cheder Lubavitch S 200/PK-8
PO Box 1996 07962 973-455-0168
Peck S 300/K-8
247 South St 07960 973-539-8660
John Kowalik, hdmstr. Fax 539-6894
Red Oaks S 200/PK-6
21 Cutler St 07960 973-539-7853
Marilyn Stewart, hdmstr. Fax 539-5182

Mountain Lakes, Morris, Pop. 4,336
Mountain Lakes SD 1,600/K-12
400 Boulevard Ste 3 07046 973-334-8280
Dr. John Kazmark, supt. Fax 334-2316
www.mtlakes.org
Briarcliff MS 300/6-8
93 Briarcliff Rd 07046 973-334-0342
Constance Sakala, prin. Fax 334-6857
Wildwood ES 500/K-5
51 Glen Rd 07046 973-334-3609
Robert Reid, prin. Fax 334-4905

Craig S 100/3-8
10 Tower Hill Rd 07046 973-334-4375
David Blanchard, hdmstr. Fax 334-2861
Wilson S 100/PK-8
271 Boulevard 07046 973-334-0181
Carolyn Borlo, hdmstr. Fax 334-1852

Mountainside, Union, Pop. 6,635
Mountainside SD 800/PK-8
1497 Woodacres Dr 07092 908-232-3232
Dr. Jeanette Baubles, admin. Fax 232-1743
www.mountainsideschools.org/
Beechwood S 300/PK-2
1497 Woodacres Dr 07092 908-301-9104
Dr. Jeanette Baubles, prin. Fax 301-1249
Deerfield S 500/3-8
302 Central Ave 07092 908-232-8828
Robert Phillips, prin. Fax 232-7338

Holy Trinity S, 304 Central Ave 07092 100/PK-K
Sr. Maureen Fichner, prin. 908-233-1899

Mount Arlington, Morris, Pop. 5,332
Mount Arlington SD 400/K-8
446 Howard Blvd 07856 973-398-6400
Jane Mullins Jameson, supt. Fax 398-3614
mtarlingtonschools.org
Decker ES 100/K-2
446 Howard Blvd 07856 973-398-6400
Stuart Mason, prin. Fax 398-3614
Mount Arlington MS 300/3-8
235 Howard Blvd 07856 973-398-4400
Stuart Mason, prin. Fax 398-5726

Mount Ephraim, Camden, Pop. 4,467
Mount Ephraim Borough SD 400/PK-8
125 S Black Horse Pike 08059 856-931-1634
Joseph Rafferty, supt. Fax 931-0202
mtephraimschools.org/
Bray ES 300/PK-4
225 W Kings Hwy 08059 856-931-7807
Kershaw MS 200/5-8
125 S Black Horse Pike 08059 856-931-1634

Mount Holly, Burlington, Pop. 10,639
Mount Holly Township SD 1,100/PK-8
330 Levis Dr 08060 609-267-7108
David Gentile, supt. Fax 702-9082
www.mtholly.k12.nj.us
Brainerd ES 300/PK-4
100 Wollner Dr 08060 609-267-3600
Carolyn McDonald, prin. Fax 702-0569
Folwell ES 300/PK-4
455 Jacksonville Rd 08060 609-267-0071
Joseph Convery, prin. Fax 267-0062
Holbein MS 500/5-8
333 Levis Dr 08060 609-267-7200
Roy Rakszawski, prin. Fax 702-9775

Sacred Heart S 400/PK-8
250 High St 08060 609-267-1728
Priscilla Vimislik, prin. Fax 267-4476

Mount Laurel, Burlington
Mount Laurel Township SD 4,300/K-8
330 Mount Laurel Rd 08054 856-235-3387
Dr. Antoinette Rath, supt. Fax 235-1837
mtlaurelschools.org
Countryside ES 300/K-4
115 Schoolhouse Ln 08054 856-234-2750
Robert Smith, prin. Fax 222-9755
Fleetwood ES 300/K-4
231 Fleetwood Ave 08054 856-235-3004
Michael Profico, prin. Fax 222-9756
Harrington MS 1,100/7-8
514 Mount Laurel Rd 08054 856-234-1610
Robert Mitchell, prin. Fax 222-9754
Hartford S 1,000/5-6
397 Hartford Rd 08054 856-231-5899
Steve Bollar, prin. Fax 222-1221
Hillside ES 400/K-4
1370 Hanesport Mt Laurel Rd 08054 856-235-1341
Mary Fitzgerald, prin. Fax 222-9757
Larchmont ES 400/K-4
301 Larchmont Blvd 08054 856-273-3700
Kelly Graber, prin. Fax 222-9759
Parkway ES 400/K-4
142 Ramblewood Pkwy 08054 856-235-3364
Donna Kinn, prin. Fax 222-9758
Springville ES 400/K-4
520 Hartford Rd 08054 856-231-4140
Dr. Gailen Mitchell, prin. Fax 231-4146

Heritage Christian Academy 100/PK-12
530 Union Mill Rd 08054 856-234-1145
Fax 222-9699

Mount Tabor, Morris
Parsippany-Troy Hills Township SD
Supt. — See Parsippany
Mt. Tabor ES 300/K-5
PO Box 509 07878 973-889-3361
John Anzul, prin. Fax 451-1958

Mullica Hill, Gloucester, Pop. 1,117
Clearview Regional HSD 2,300/7-12
420 Cedar Rd 08062 856-223-2765
John Horchak, supt. Fax 478-0409
www.clearviewregional.edu
Clearview Regional MS 900/7-8
595 Jefferson Rd 08062 856-223-2740
David Kelk, prin. Fax 223-9068

Harrison Township SD 1,400/K-6
120 N Main St 08062 856-478-2016
Dr. Patricia Hoey, supt. Fax 478-4825
www.harrisontwp.k12.nj.us
Harrison Township ES 800/K-3
120 N Main St 08062 856-478-2016
Mariann Edelmayer, prin. Fax 223-1672
Pleasant Valley IS 600/4-6
401 Cedar Rd 08062 856-223-5120
Andrew Davis, prin. Fax 223-2692

Friends S of Mullica Hill 200/PK-8
15 High St 08062 856-478-2908
Drew Smith, hdmstr. Fax 478-0263

National Park, Gloucester, Pop. 3,223
National Park Borough SD 300/PK-6
516 Lakehurst Ave 08063 856-845-6876
Ray Bider, supt. Fax 848-6710
www.npelem.com/
National Park ES 300/PK-6
516 Lakehurst Ave 08063 856-845-6876
Jim Conaway, prin. Fax 848-6710

Neptune, Monmouth, Pop. 5,062
Neptune CSD 400/K-8
210 W Sylvania Ave 07753 732-775-5319
Thomas Campbell, admin. Fax 775-4335
www.neptunecityschool.org/
Wilson S 400/K-8
210 W Sylvania Ave 07753 732-775-5319
Thomas Campbell, admin. Fax 775-4335

Neptune Township SD 4,800/PK-12
60 Neptune Blvd 07753 732-776-2000
David Mooij, supt. Fax 776-2003
www.neptune.k12.nj.us/
ECC 200/PK-PK
11 Memorial Dr 07753 732-776-2200
James Nulle, prin. Fax 897-0878
Gables ES 400/PK-5
1 Gables Ct 07753 732-776-2200
Sally Millaway, prin. Fax 776-2260
Green Grove ES 500/PK-5
909 Green Grove Rd 07753 732-776-2200
Benedict Yennella, prin. Fax 776-2257
Midtown Community ES 200/K-5
1150 Embury Ave 07753 732-776-2200
Jerard Terrell, prin. Fax 897-0213
Neptune MS 900/6-8
2300 Heck Ave 07753 732-776-2200
Mark Alfone, prin. Fax 776-2254
Shark River Hills ES 400/PK-5
312 Brighton Ave 07753 732-776-2200
Dennis Thompson, prin. Fax 776-2259
Summerfield ES 400/PK-5
1 Summerfield Ln 07753 732-776-2200
Dr. Arlene Rogo, prin. Fax 643-8695

Collingwood Park SDA S 50/K-8
474 Shark River Rd 07753 732-922-4286
Nadege Adam, prin. Fax 922-6662
Holy Innocents S 200/PK-8
3455 W Bangs Ave 07753 732-922-3141
Elizabeth Barrella, prin. Fax 922-6531

Neshanic Station, Somerset
Branchburg Township SD
Supt. — See Branchburg
Whiton ES 600/K-2
470 Whiton Rd 08853 908-371-0842
Rebecca Gensel, prin. Fax 369-1583

Netcong, Morris, Pop. 3,294
Netcong SD 300/PK-8
26 College Rd 07857 973-347-0020
Arthur DiBenedetto, supt. Fax 347-5864
www.netcongschool.org
Netcong S 300/PK-8
26 College Rd 07857 973-347-0020
Arthur DiBenedetto, prin. Fax 347-5864

St. Michael S 300/PK-8
10 Church St 07857 973-347-0039
Marianne Volonnino, prin. Fax 347-0054

Newark, Essex, Pop. 280,666
Newark SD 37,100/PK-12
2 Cedar St 07102 973-733-7333
Dr. Clifford Janey, supt. Fax 733-6834
www.nps.k12.nj.us/
Abington Avenue S 900/PK-8
209 Abington Ave 07107 973-268-5230
Dennis Torsiello, prin. Fax 497-5743
Alexander Annex ECC 100/PK-1
15 Boylan St 07106 973-374-2490
J. Blamo-Hawthorne, prin. Fax 374-2112
Alexander Street ES 400/1-6
43 Alexander St 07106 973-374-2390
J. Blamo-Hawthorne, prin. Fax 374-2222
Ann Street S 1,200/PK-8
30 Ann St 07105 973-465-4890
Linda Richardson, prin. Fax 465-4185
Avon Avenue S 500/K-8
219 Avon Ave 07108 973-733-6750
Denise Cooper, prin. Fax 733-6841
Belmont-Runyon ES 500/PK-4
1 Belmont Runyon Way 07108 973-733-6920
Dorothy Handfield, prin. Fax 424-4447
Bragaw Avenue S 300/K-8
103 Bragaw Ave 07112 973-705-3970
Tony Motley, prin. Fax 705-3973
Broadway ES 300/K-4
180 Oraton St 07104 973-268-5340
Alejandro Echevarria, prin. Fax 268-5358
Brown Academy 200/5-8
695 Bergen St 07108 973-733-6844
Kevin Guyton, prin. Fax 733-6887
Burnet Street S 400/PK-8
28 Burnet St 07102 973-733-7138
Kathy Duke-Jackson, prin. Fax 456-7013
Camden MS, 321 Bergen St 07103 400/5-8
Dr. Shirley Brewton, prin. 973-733-8351
Camden Street ES 300/PK-4
281 Camden St 07103 973-733-6994
Lavonne Pack, prin. Fax 733-8452
Carver S 700/PK-8
333 Clinton Pl 07112 973-705-3800
Winston Jackson, prin. Fax 705-3818
Chancellor Avenue Annex ES 200/K-2
255 Chancellor Ave 07112 973-705-3860
Eugene Brown, prin. Fax 705-3862
Chancellor Avenue MS 300/3-8
321 Chancellor Ave 07112 973-705-3870
Eugene Brown, prin. Fax 705-3003
Clemente ES 600/PK-4
257 Summer Ave 07104 973-268-5290
Yolanda Mendez, prin. Fax 483-5524
Cleveland S 200/PK-8
388 Bergen St 07103 973-733-6944
Zakiyya Razzaq, prin. Fax 733-7021
Clinton Avenue ECC 50/PK-PK
534 Clinton Ave 07108 973-733-6970
Dorothy Handfield, prin. Fax 733-7984
Dayton Street S 300/PK-8
226 Dayton St 07114 973-733-7004
Ronald Karsen, prin. Fax 733-7020
Eighteenth Avenue S 200/PK-8
229 18th Ave 07108 973-733-6824
Barbara Ervin, prin. Fax 733-8780
Elliott Street @ Good Counsel 1-2
284 1st Ave W 07107 973-412-1241
Eva Ortiz, prin.
Elliott Street Annex 100/PK-K
243 Woodside Ave 07104 973-268-5368
Eva Ortiz, prin.
Fifteenth Avenue S 300/K-8
557 15th Ave 07103 973-733-6924
Malcolm Outlaw, prin. Fax 733-8934
First Avenue S 900/K-8
214 1st Ave W 07107 973-268-5240
Anthony Orsini, prin. Fax 268-5333
Flagg S 600/K-8
150 3rd St 07107 973-268-5190
Roy Wilson, prin. Fax 268-5197
Fourteenth Avenue ES 200/K-4
186 14th Ave 07103 973-733-6940
Alyson Barillarri, prin. Fax 733-8675
Franklin ES 500/K-4
42 Park Ave 07104 973-268-5250
Susan Taylor, prin. Fax 483-5482
Hawkins Street S 500/PK-8
8 Hawkins St 07105 973-465-4920
Joseph Randeiro, prin. Fax 465-4222
Hawthorne Avenue S 300/K-8
428 Hawthorne Ave 07112 973-705-3960
LaShawn Gibson-Burney, prin. Fax 705-3962
Hernandez S 700/PK-8
345 Broadway 07104 973-481-5004
Juan Ruiz, prin. Fax 497-5703
Horton S 800/K-8
291 N 7th St 07107 973-268-5260
Kimberly Wright-White, prin. Fax 268-5261
Ivy Hill ES, 107 Ivy St 07106 400/K-7
Keith Barton, prin. 973-351-2121
King S 500/K-8
108 S 9th St 07107 973-733-7368
Anita Ziyad, prin. Fax 733-8678
Lafayette Street S 800/PK-8
205 Lafayette St 07105 973-465-4860
Maria Merlo, prin. Fax 465-4863
Lincoln ES 500/PK-7
87 Richelieu Ter 07106 973-374-2290
James Montemurro, prin. Fax 374-2223
Madison ES 500/PK-5
823 S 16th St 07108 973-374-2980
Jennifer Carlisle-Peters, prin. Fax 374-2853
Maple Annex ES 200/K-2
200 Lyons Ave 07112 973-705-3850
Daneen Washington, prin.
Maple Avenue S 500/K-8
33 Maple Ave 07112 973-705-3850
Daneen Washington, prin. Fax 705-3013
Marin MS 600/5-8
663 Broadway 07104 973-268-5330
Sylvia Esteves, prin. Fax 268-5972
McKinley S 700/PK-8
1 Colonnade Pl 07104 973-268-5270
Carolyn Granato, prin. Fax 481-5339
Miller Street S 500/PK-8
41 Miller St 07114 973-733-6815
Shakirah Miller, prin. Fax 424-4439
Mt. Vernon S 1,000/PK-8
142 Mount Vernon Pl 07106 973-374-2090
Bertha Dyer, prin. Fax 374-2292
Newton Street S 400/PK-8
150 Newton St 07103 973-733-6848
James Carlo, prin. Fax 733-8334
Oliver Street S 800/PK-8
104 Oliver St 07105 973-465-4870
Mariana Golden, prin. Fax 465-4873
Peshine Avenue S 700/PK-8
433 Peshine Ave 07112 973-705-3890
Wanda Brooks-Long, prin. Fax 705-3898
Quitman Street S 400/PK-8
21 Quitman St 07103 973-733-6947
Jacquelynn D. Hartsfield, prin. Fax 733-6636
Ridge Street S 800/K-8
735 Ridge St 07104 973-268-5210
Emil Garruto, prin. Fax 268-5283
Roseville Avenue ES 200/K-4
70 Roseville Ave 07107 973-268-5312
Rose Serra, prin. Fax 268-5993
South Seventeenth Street S 400/PK-8
619 S 17th St 07103 973-374-2570
Clarence Allen, prin. Fax 374-2345
South Street ES 200/K-5
151 South St 07114 973-465-4880
Karen George-Gray, prin. Fax 465-4024
Speedway Avenue ES 200/K-4
26 Speedway Ave 07106 973-374-2740
Gerald Samuels, prin. Fax 374-2152
Spencer S 500/PK-8
66 Muhammad Ali Ave 07108 973-733-6931
Joseph Brown, prin. Fax 424-4371
Sussex Avenue S 500/PK-8
307 Sussex Ave 07107 973-268-5200
Joann Gilmore, prin. Fax 268-5282
Thirteenth Avenue S 500/PK-8
359 13th Ave 07103 973-733-7045
Orville Harris, prin. Fax 733-7926
Tubman ES 300/PK-6
504 S 10th St 07103 973-733-6934
Deborah Terrell, prin. Fax 733-8628
Vailsburg MS 100/8-8
107 Ivy St 07106 973-351-2256
Wilson Avenue S 800/K-8
19 Wilson Ave 07105 973-465-4910
Margarita Hernandez, prin. Fax 465-4912
Other Schools – See Belleville

Alpha & Omega Christian S 50/PK-12
4 Fleming Ave 07105 973-465-5333
Rev. Jose Torres, dir. Fax 465-5335
Bethel Christian Academy 200/K-12
580 Mount Prospect Ave 07104 973-484-6646
Lisa Pastori, prin. Fax 484-5328
Calvary Christian S 100/PK-8
17 Lyons Ave 07112 973-923-4222
Rhonda Davis, prin. Fax 923-5177
Ironbound Catholic Academy 300/PK-8
366 E Kinney St 07105 973-589-0108
Lorraine Novak, prin. Fax 589-0239

Link Community S 100/7-8
120 Livingston St 07103 973-642-0529
Marnie McKoy, hdmstr. Fax 642-1978
Newark Boys Chorus S 100/4-8
1016 Broad St 07102 973-621-8900
Lawrence Emery, hdmstr. Fax 621-1343
New Testament Church S 50/K-12
511 Orange St 07107 973-268-1310
Mollie Haynes, prin.
Queen of Angels S 200/PK-8
44 Irvine Turner Blvd 07103 973-642-1531
Everlyn Hay, prin. Fax 622-0472
Sacred Heart S 300/PK-8
24 Hazelwood Ave 07106 973-372-4441
Sr. Gloria Doria, prin. Fax 372-3571
St. Francis Xavier S 200/PK-8
594 N 7th St 07107 973-482-9410
Sr. Clare Ricciardelli, prin. Fax 482-2466
St. Mary S 200/K-8
180 William St 07103 973-286-3870
Sr. Teresa Shaw, prin. Fax 286-3873
St. Michael S 600/K-8
27 Crittenden St 07104 973-482-7400
Linda Cerino, prin. Fax 482-1833
St. Philips Academy 300/K-8
342 Central Ave 07103 973-624-0644
Miguel Brito, hdmstr. Fax 624-8355
St. Rose of Lima S 200/K-8
540 Orange St 07107 973-481-5582
Arthur Wilson, prin. Fax 481-3398

New Brunswick, Middlesex, Pop. 50,156
New Brunswick SD 6,600/PK-12
PO Box 2683 08903 732-745-5300
Richard Kaplan, supt. Fax 745-5459
www.nbps.k12.nj.us
Lincoln S 700/PK-8
66 Bartlett St 08901 732-745-5300
Susan McGinty, prin. Fax 937-7574
Livingston S 500/K-8
206 Delavan St 08901 732-745-5300
Kathryn Schneekloth, prin. Fax 937-7575
Lord Stirling ES 500/K-5
101 Redmond St 08901 732-745-5300
Luis Hernandez, prin. Fax 937-7576
McKinley Community S 600/K-8
35 Van Dyke Ave 08901 732-745-5300
Raymond Ivey, prin. Fax 937-7577
New Brunswick MS 800/6-8
30 Van Dyke Ave 08901 732-745-5300
Fred Brown, prin. Fax 565-7621
Redshaw ES 500/PK-5
40 Van Dyke Ave 08901 732-745-5300
Kathy Antoine-Smith, prin. Fax 745-5343
Robeson Community ES 300/PK-5
30 Van Dyke Ave 08901 732-745-5300
Denise Dover, prin. Fax 937-7570
Roosevelt S 1,000/K-8
83 Livingston Ave 08901 732-745-5300
Jorge Diaz, prin. Fax 937-7562
Wilson S 400/PK-8
133 Tunison Rd 08901 732-745-5300
Jeremiah Clifford, prin. Fax 937-7579

SS. Mary and Peter Catholic S 100/K-8
167 Somerset St 08901 732-545-1473
Frances Comiskey, prin. Fax 545-2508

New Egypt, Ocean, Pop. 2,327
Plumsted Township SD 1,800/PK-12
117 Evergreen Rd 08533 609-758-6800
Dr. Mark DeMareo, supt. Fax 758-6808
www.newegypt.us
New Egypt MS 400/6-8
115 Evergreen Rd 08533 609-758-6800
Andrea Caldes, prin. Fax 758-5538
New Egypt PS 300/PK-1
131 Evergreen Rd 08533 609-758-6800
Toni Ferry, prin. Fax 758-0912
Woehr ES 600/2-5
44 N Main St 08533 609-758-6800
Robert Burkhardt, prin. Fax 758-6868

Newfield, Gloucester, Pop. 1,661
Buena Regional SD
Supt. — See Buena
Edgarton Memorial ES 200/K-5
212 Catawba Ave 08344 856-697-1141
Donald Weisenstein, prin. Fax 697-1659

Franklin Township SD
Supt. — See Franklinville
Main Road ES 500/3-6
1452 Main Rd 08344 856-697-0220
Richard Dantinne, prin. Fax 629-1486

Notre Dame Regional S - Newfield 200/K-8
108 Church St 08344 856-697-0155
Dr. Mary Alimenti, prin. Fax 697-8540

New Gretna, Burlington
Bass River Township SD 100/K-6
PO Box 304 08224 609-296-4230
Lawrence Mathis, supt. Fax 296-4953
www.bassriver-nj.org/school/
Bass River Township ES 100/K-6
PO Box 304 08224 609-296-4230
Lawrence Mathis, supt. Fax 296-4953

New Milford, Bergen, Pop. 16,318
New Milford SD 2,000/K-12
145 Madison Ave 07646 201-261-2952
Nicholas Brown, supt. Fax 261-8018
www.newmilfordschools.org
Berkley Street ES 400/K-5
812 Berkley St 07646 201-262-0191
Patricia Aufiero, prin. Fax 967-8947
Gibbs ES 500/K-5
195 Sutton Pl 07646 201-261-0939
Scott Davies, prin. Fax 967-8952
Owens MS 500/6-8
470 Marion Ave 07646 201-265-8661
Whitney Perro, prin. Fax 265-5680

Hovnanian S 200/PK-8
817 River Rd 07646 201-967-5940
Anahid Garmiryan, prin. Fax 967-0249
Solomon Schecter Day S 500/PK-8
275 Mckinley Ave 07646 201-262-9898
Ruth Gafni, hdmstr. Fax 262-3026
Transfiguration Academy - Upper 100/5-8
1092 Carnation Dr 07646 201-836-7074
Salvatore Tralongo, prin. Fax 836-4475

New Monmouth, Monmouth
Middletown Township SD
Supt. — See Middletown
Harmony ES, 100 Murphy Rd 07748 500/K-5
Patricia Corridon, prin. 732-671-2111

St. Mary S 700/PK-8
538 Church St 07748 732-671-0129
William Smith, prin. Fax 671-2653

Newport, Cumberland
Downe Township SD 200/PK-8
220 Main St 08345 856-447-3878
Dina Elliott, supt. Fax 447-5130
Downe Township S 200/PK-8
220 Main St 08345 856-447-4673
Dina Elliott, prin. Fax 447-3005

New Providence, Union, Pop. 11,905
New Providence SD 2,200/K-12
356 Elkwood Ave 07974 908-464-9050
David Miceli Ed.D., supt. Fax 464-9041
www.npsd.k12.nj.us
New Providence MS 300/7-8
35 Pioneer Dr 07974 908-464-9161
Gina Hansen, prin. Fax 464-5927
Roberts ES 600/K-6
80 Jones Dr 07974 908-464-4707
Dr. Nell Sanders, prin. Fax 464-4144
Salt Brook ES 600/K-6
40 Maple St 07974 908-464-7100
Jean Maier, prin. Fax 464-0786

Academy of Our Lady of Peace 200/PK-8
99 South St 07974 908-464-8657
Thomas Berrios, prin. Fax 464-3377
St. Andrew's S 200/PK-K
419 South St 07974 908-464-4878
Mary Donohue, dir. Fax 464-2439

Newton, Sussex, Pop. 8,416
Andover Regional SD 600/PK-8
707 Limecrest Rd 07860 973-383-3746
Bernard Baggs, supt. Fax 579-3972
www.andoverregional.org
Burd S 300/PK-4
219 Newton Sparta Rd 07860 973-940-1234
Albert Muccilli, prin. Fax 383-3778
Long Pond S 300/5-8
707 Limecrest Rd 07860 973-940-1234
T. Jon Sinclair, prin. Fax 579-2690

Fredon Township SD 300/K-6
459 State Route 94 S 07860 973-383-4151
Sal Constantino, supt. Fax 383-3644
www.fredon.org
Fredon Township ES 300/K-6
459 State Route 94 S 07860 973-383-4151
Sal Constantino, prin. Fax 383-3644

Hampton Township SD 400/K-6
1 School Rd 07860 973-383-5300
Everett Burns, supt. Fax 383-3835
www.mckeown.org
McKeown ES 400/K-6
1 School Rd 07860 973-383-5300
Fax 383-3835

Newton SD 1,600/PK-12
57 Trinity St 07860 973-383-1900
William King, supt. Fax 383-5378
www.newtonnj.org
Halsted Street MS 300/6-8
59 Halsted St 07860 973-383-7440
Martin Fleming, prin. Fax 383-7432
Merriam Avenue ES 500/PK-5
81 Merriam Ave 07860 973-383-7202
Steve Rivlin, prin. Fax 383-7276

Camp Auxillium Learning Center 200/PK-K
14 Old Swartswood Rd 07860 973-383-2621
Sr. Karen Dunn, prin. Fax 383-3214
Northwest Christian S 200/PK-8
92 County Road 519 07860 973-383-9713
Joseph Cottrell, prin. Fax 383-6141
St. Joseph Regional S 200/K-8
20 Jefferson St 07860 973-383-2909
Joann Higgs, prin. Fax 383-6353

New Vernon, Morris
Harding Township SD 300/K-8
PO Box 248 07976 973-267-6398
Timothy Purnell, supt. Fax 267-7133
www.hardingtwp.org
Harding Township S 300/K-8
PO Box 248 07976 973-267-6398
Dee Klikier, prin. Fax 292-1318

North Arlington, Bergen, Pop. 15,179
North Arlington SD 1,500/PK-12
222 Ridge Rd 07031 201-991-6800
Dr. Oliver Stringham, supt. Fax 991-1656
www.narlington.k12.nj.us
Jefferson ES 300/PK-5
100 Prospect Ave 07031 201-991-6800
Lawrence McKeown, prin. Fax 955-5254
North Arlington MS 300/6-8
45 Beech St 07031 201-991-6800
Daniel DiGuglielmo, prin. Fax 246-0703
Roosevelt ES, 4 Webster St 07031 200/PK-5
Claire Greene, prin. 201-991-6800
Washington ES 200/PK-5
175 Albert St 07031 201-991-6800
John Delaney, prin. Fax 246-0135

Queen of Peace S 500/PK-8
21 Church Pl 07031 201-998-8222
Terri Suchocki, prin. Fax 997-7930

North Bergen, Hudson, Pop. 59,000
North Bergen SD 6,800/K-12
7317 Kennedy Blvd 07047 201-295-2706
Robert Dandorph, supt.
www.northbergen.k12.nj.us/
Franklin S, 5211 Columbia Ave 07047 600/K-8
Peter Clark, prin. 201-974-7007
Fulton S, 7407 Hudson Ave 07047 1,100/K-8
Patrick Capotorto, prin. 201-295-2900
Kennedy S, 1210 11th St 07047 500/K-8
Michael Guasconi, prin. 201-974-7000
Lincoln S, 1206 63rd St 07047 1,000/K-8
Arlene McGowan, prin. 201-295-2850
Mann S, 1215 83rd St 07047 1,000/K-8
Jorge Prado, prin. 201-295-2880
McKinley S, 3110 Liberty Ave 07047 400/K-8
Joanne Harrington, prin. 201-974-7020

North Hudson Academy 50/1-12
PO Box 390 07047 201-865-9577

North Brunswick, Middlesex, Pop. 37,400
North Brunswick Township SD 5,300/K-12
PO Box 6016 08902 732-289-3030
Dr. Brian Zychowski, supt. Fax 297-8567
www.nbtschools.org
Adams ES 500/K-5
1450 Redmond St 08902 732-289-3100
Dr. Barbara Tylka, prin. Fax 249-4521
Judd ES 600/K-5
1601 Roosevelt Ave 08902 732-289-3200
Barbara Gibbons, prin. Fax 297-0036
Linwood MS 1,200/6-8
25 Linwood Pl 08902 732-289-3600
J. Peter Clark, prin. Fax 247-7033
Livingston Park ES 600/K-5
1128 Livingston Ave 08902 732-289-3300
Dr. Peter Bowman, prin. Fax 249-5283
Parsons ES 600/K-5
899 Hollywood St 08902 732-289-3400
Bruce Rothenberg, prin. Fax 435-1709

South Brunswick Township SD 8,600/K-12
231 Black Horse Ln 08902 732-297-7800
Gary P. McCartney Ed.D., supt. Fax 297-8456
www.sbschools.org
Other Schools – See Dayton, Kendall Park, Monmouth Junction

North Caldwell, Essex, Pop. 7,284
North Caldwell SD 600/K-6
132 Gould Ave 07006 973-228-6439
Dr. Linda Freda, supt. Fax 228-4581
www.ncboe.org/
Gould S 300/4-6
132 Gould Ave 07006 973-226-2782
Chris Checchetto, prin. Fax 226-5234
Other Schools – See Caldwell

West Essex Regional SD 1,600/7-12
65 W Greenbrook Rd 07006 973-582-1600
Dr. Janice Dime, supt. Fax 228-0559
www.westex.org
West Essex MS 600/7-8
65 W Greenbrook Rd 07006 973-228-1200
David Montgomery, prin. Fax 228-5852

Northfield, Atlantic, Pop. 8,025
Northfield CSD 900/K-8
2000 New Rd 08225 609-407-4000
Richard Stepura Ed.D., supt. Fax 646-0608
northfield.groupfusion.net
Northfield Community ES 500/K-4
2000 New Rd 08225 609-407-4005
Janice Fipp Ed.D., prin. Fax 645-3252
Northfield Community MS 400/5-8
2000 New Rd 08225 609-407-4008
Maria Caiafa, prin. Fax 641-2646

North Haledon, Passaic, Pop. 9,073
North Haledon SD 600/K-8
515 High Mountain Rd 07508 973-427-1220
Donna Cardiello, supt. Fax 427-4357
www.nhschools.net
High Mountain MS 300/5-8
515 High Mountain Rd 07508 973-427-1220
Donna Cardiello, prin. Fax 427-7685
Memorial ES 400/K-4
201 Squaw Brook Rd 07508 973-427-8993
Matthew Wilson, prin. Fax 427-4357

North Plainfield, Somerset, Pop. 21,608
North Plainfield Borough SD 3,100/K-12
33 Mountain Ave 07060 908-769-6060
Dr. Marilyn Birnbaum, supt. Fax 755-5490
www.nplainfield.org

East End ES 400/K-4
170 Oneida Ave 07060 908-769-6070
Kathleen Herrmann, prin. Fax 668-5536
Somerset IS, 303 Somerset St 07060 500/5-6
Reginald Sainte-Rose, prin. 908-769-6080
Stony Brook ES 200/K-4
269 Grove St 07060 908-769-6063
Catherine Kobylarz, prin. Fax 668-5535
West End ES 500/K-4
447 Greenbrook Rd 07063 908-769-6083
Beth Sobel, prin. Fax 668-5538

Sundance S 400/PK-4
401 Greenbrook Rd 07063 908-561-5055
Jeffrey Tobey, prin. Fax 791-0549

Northvale, Bergen, Pop. 4,564
Northvale SD 500/K-8
441 Tappan Rd 07647 201-768-8484
Sylvan Hershey, supt. Fax 768-4948
www.northvaleschools.org/
Hale MS 300/4-8
441 Tappan Rd 07647 201-768-8484
Michael Pinajian, prin. Fax 768-4948
Jefferson ES 200/K-3
441 Tappan Rd 07647 201-768-8484
Michael Pinajian, prin. Fax 768-4948

North Wildwood, Cape May, Pop. 4,778
North Wildwood CSD 300/K-8
1201 Atlantic Ave 08260 609-522-6885
Michael BucciALIA, supt. Fax 522-2308
mmace.capemayschools.com
Mace S 300/K-8
1201 Atlantic Ave 08260 609-522-1454
Michael Bucciaglia, prin. Fax 522-2308

Norwood, Bergen, Pop. 6,249
Norwood SD 600/K-8
177 Summit St 07648 201-768-6363
Dr. Andrew Rose, supt. Fax 768-4916
www.nvnet.org/k8/norwood/index.html
Norwood S 600/K-8
177 Summit St 07648 201-768-6363
Betty Johnson, prin. Fax 768-4916

Holy Family S 200/PK-8
200 Summit St 07648 201-768-1605
Patricia Bliss, prin. Fax 768-0796

Nutley, Essex, Pop. 27,400
Nutley SD 3,900/K-12
315 Franklin Ave 07110 973-661-8798
Joseph Zarra, supt. Fax 320-8476
www.nutleyschools.org
Lincoln ES 400/K-6
301 Harrison St 07110 973-661-8883
Lorraine Restel, prin. Fax 661-4392
Radcliffe ES 400/K-6
379 Bloomfield Ave 07110 973-661-8820
Michael Kearney, prin. Fax 661-4395
Spring Garden ES 400/K-6
59 S Spring Garden Ave 07110 973-661-8983
Rosemary Clerico, prin. Fax 661-5138
Walker MS 600/7-8
325 Franklin Ave 07110 973-661-8871
John Calicchio, prin. Fax 661-3775
Washington ES 400/K-6
155 Washington Ave 07110 973-661-8888
Douglas Jones, prin. Fax 661-1369
Yantacaw ES 500/K-6
20 Yantacaw Pl 07110 973-661-8892
David Sorensen, prin. Fax 661-5289

Abundant Life Academy 400/PK-12
390 Washington Ave 07110 973-667-9700
Suzanne Bruno, prin. Fax 667-1278
Good Shepherd Academy 200/K-8
24 Brookline Ave 07110 973-667-2049
Sr. Domenica Troina, prin. Fax 661-9259

Oakhurst, Monmouth, Pop. 4,130
Ocean Township SD 4,100/K-12
163 Monmouth Rd 07755 732-531-5600
Thomas Pagano, supt. Fax 531-3874
www.ocean.k12.nj.us
Ocean Township ES 400/K-4
555 Dow Ave 07755 732-531-5690
Doreen Ryan, prin. Fax 531-3682
Other Schools – See Ocean, Wanamassa

Oakland, Bergen, Pop. 13,645
Oakland SD 1,700/K-8
315 Ramapo Valley Rd 07436 201-337-6156
Dr. Richard Heflich, supt. Fax 405-1237
www.oaklandschoolsnj.org/
Dogwood Hill ES 300/K-5
25 Dogwood Dr 07436 201-337-5822
Glenn Clark, prin. Fax 337-3268
Heights ES 400/K-5
114 Seminole Ave 07436 201-337-4147
Barbara Ciambra, prin. Fax 337-5694
Manito ES 400/K-5
111 Manito Ave 07436 201-337-6106
Adam Silverstein, prin. Fax 337-3571
Valley MS 600/6-8
71 Oak St 07436 201-337-8185
Dr. Christopher Lane, prin. Fax 337-7089

Berman Day S 100/PK-8
45 Spruce St 07436 201-337-1111
Rabbi Ellen Bernhardt, hdmstr. Fax 337-7795

Oaklyn, Camden, Pop. 4,116
Haddon Township SD
Supt. — See Westmont
Jennings ES 100/PK-5
100 E Cedar Ave 08107 856-869-7720
Charles Warfield, prin. Fax 869-7722

Oaklyn Borough SD 50/PK-9
156 Kendall Blvd 08107 856-858-0335
Tommie Stringer, supt. Fax 869-3474
www.oaklyn.k12.nj.us
Oaklyn ES 50/K-6
156 Kendall Blvd 08107 856-858-0335
James Sanders, prin. Fax 858-1623
Oaklyn S 50/PK-9
156 Kendall Blvd 08107 856-858-0335
James Sanders, prin. Fax 858-1623

Oak Ridge, Passaic
Jefferson Township SD
Supt. — See Lake Hopatcong
Cozy Lake ES 300/1-2
205 Cozy Lake Rd 07438 973-697-4777
Timothy Plotts, prin. Fax 697-3569
Jefferson Township MS 800/6-8
1000 Weldon Rd 07438 973-697-1980
Jeanne Howe, prin. Fax 697-1348
Milton K 100/K-K
52 School House Rd 07438 973-697-4742
Timothy Plotts, prin. Fax 697-8623
White Rock IS 400/3-5
2 Francine Pl 07438 973-697-2414
Michael Valenti, prin. Fax 697-2049

West Milford Township SD
Supt. — See West Milford
Paradise Knoll ES 300/K-6
103 Paradise Rd 07438 973-697-7142
Stephen Wisniewski, prin. Fax 697-9444

Ocean, Monmouth, Pop. 26,700
Ocean Township SD
Supt. — See Oakhurst
Ocean Township IS 1,300/5-8
1200 W Park Ave 07712 732-531-5630
Larry Kostula, prin. Fax 493-1891
Wayside ES, 733 Bowne Rd 07712 600/K-4
David Enderly, prin. 732-531-5710

Deal Yeshiva 300/K-12
1515 Logan Rd 07712 732-663-1717
Rabbi Isaac Dwek, dean Fax 663-1700
Hillel Yeshiva S 500/PK-8
PO Box 2288 07712 732-493-9300
Dr. Ruth Katz, hdmstr. Fax 493-8930

Ocean City, Cape May, Pop. 15,330
Ocean City SD 2,100/K-12
501 Atlantic Ave Ste 1 08226 609-399-5150
Dr. Kathleen Taylor, supt. Fax 399-4656
www.ocean.city.k12.nj.us
Ocean City IS 400/4-8
1801 Bay Ave 08226 609-399-5611
Dr. Pamela Vaughan, prin. Fax 398-7089
Ocean City PS 300/K-3
550 West Ave 08226 609-399-3191
Dr. Joanne Walls, prin. Fax 399-8257

Ocean Gate, Ocean, Pop. 2,109
Ocean Gate SD 100/PK-6
PO Box 478 08740 732-269-3023
Frank Vanalesti, supt. Fax 269-9777
www.oceangateschool.net
Ocean Gate ES 100/PK-6
PO Box 478 08740 732-269-3023
Frank Vanalesti, prin. Fax 269-9777

Oceanport, Monmouth, Pop. 5,780
Oceanport Borough SD 700/K-8
29 Wolf Hill Ave 07757 732-544-8588
Andrew Orefice, supt. Fax 544-0386
www.oceanport.k12.nj.us
Maple Place MS 300/5-8
2 Maple Pl 07757 732-229-0267
Dr. John Amato, prin. Fax 229-0961
Wolf Hill ES 300/K-4
29 Wolfhill Ave 07757 732-542-0683
Renee Bonin, prin. Fax 544-0386

Ogdensburg, Sussex, Pop. 2,631
Ogdensburg Borough SD 300/K-8
100 Main St 07439 973-827-7127
John Petrelli, supt. Fax 827-0134
Ogdensburg S 300/K-8
100 Main St 07439 973-827-7126
John Petrelli, prin. Fax 827-0134

Old Bridge, Middlesex, Pop. 22,151
Old Bridge Township SD
Supt. — See Matawan
Carpenter ES 300/K-5
1 Par Ave 08857 732-360-4452
John Phillips, prin. Fax 360-2964
Grissom ES 200/K-5
1 Sims Ave 08857 732-360-4481
Joseph Sgalia, prin. Fax 360-0725
McDivitt ES 500/K-5
1 Manny Martin Way 08857 732-360-4512
Laurie Coletti, prin. Fax 721-5706
Miller S 400/K-5
2 Old Matawan Rd 08857 732-360-4589
Eileen Vogel, prin. Fax 698-0448
Salk MS 1,200/6-8
155 W Greystone Rd 08857 732-360-4519
David Cittadino, prin. Fax 251-1690
Sandburg MS 1,300/6-8
3439 Highway 516 08857 732-360-0505
Kenneth Popovich, prin. Fax 360-9676
Schirra ES 400/K-5
1 Awn St 08857 732-360-4495
Colleen Montuori, prin. Fax 360-0736
Shepard ES 300/K-5
33 Bushnell Rd 08857 732-360-4499
Dr. Kathleen Hoeker, prin. Fax 679-5112
Southwood ES 400/K-5
64 Southwood Dr 08857 732-360-4539
Raymond Payton, prin. Fax 257-2356
Voorhees ES 400/K-5
11 Liberty St 08857 732-360-4544
Cecilia Skove, prin. Fax 251-8549

Calvary Christian S 200/PK-8
123 White Oak Ln 08857 732-479-0700
Eric Morris, prin. Fax 679-1948
Good Shepherd Lutheran S 200/PK-K
3139 Highway 516 08857 732-679-8887
Fax 679-0125
St. Ambrose S 400/PK-8
81 Throckmorton Ln 08857 732-679-4700
Joseph Norris, prin. Fax 679-6062
St. Thomas the Apostle S 400/PK-8
333 State Route 18 08857 732-251-4812
Thomasina Wyatt, prin. Fax 251-5315

Old Tappan, Bergen, Pop. 5,903
Old Tappan SD 900/K-8
277 Old Tappan Rd 07675 201-664-1421
William Ward, supt. Fax 664-4418
DeMarest ES 400/K-4
1 School St 07675 201-664-7176
Don Duin, prin. Fax 664-7167
DeWolf MS 400/5-8
275 Old Tappan Rd 07675 201-664-1475
Dennis Rossi, prin. Fax 664-8101

Oradell, Bergen, Pop. 8,005
Oradell SD 800/K-6
350 Prospect Ave 07649 201-261-1180
Dr. Jeffrey Mohre, supt. Fax 261-1167
www.oradell.k12.nj.us
Oradell ES 800/K-6
350 Prospect Ave 07649 201-261-1180
W. Scott Ryan, prin. Fax 261-1167

St. Joseph S 500/PK-8
305 Elm St 07649 201-261-2388
Colette Vail, prin. Fax 261-0830

Orange, Essex, Pop. 33,300
Orange Township SD 4,400/K-12
451 Lincoln Ave 07050 973-677-4015
Dr. Judith Kronin, supt. Fax 677-0486
orange.schoolwires.com/orange/site/default.asp
Central ES 300/K-6
33 Cleveland St 07050 973-677-4110
Debby Lucky, prin. Fax 677-1838
Cleveland Street ES 300/K-6
355 Cleveland St 07050 973-677-4100
Denise White, prin. Fax 676-8492
Forest Street ES 200/K-6
651 Forest St 07050 973-677-4120
Vancisca Cooke, prin. Fax 676-5387
Heywood Avenue ES 400/K-6
421 Heywood Ave 07050 973-677-4105
Faith Alcantara, prin. Fax 672-2107
Lincoln Avenue ES 500/K-6
216 Lincoln Ave 07050 973-677-4130
Amanda Stafford, prin. Fax 673-6669
Main Street S 500/K-8
369 Main St 07050 973-677-4515
Amod Field, prin. Fax 675-0925
Oakwood Avenue ES 300/K-6
135 Oakwood Ave 07050 973-677-4095
Kalisha Neain, prin. Fax 674-8015
Orange MS 500/7-8
400 Central Ave 07050 973-677-4135
Dr. Judith Kronin, prin. Fax 677-2439
Park Avenue ES 300/K-6
231 Park Ave 07050 973-677-4124
Dr. Myron Hackett, prin. Fax 678-1291

St. John S 200/PK-8
455 White St 07050 973-674-8951
Sr. Kieran Chidi Nduagbo, prin. Fax 674-6126

Oxford, Warren, Pop. 1,767
Oxford Township SD 300/K-8
17 Kent St 07863 908-453-4101
Bob Magnuson, admin. Fax 453-0022
www.warrennet.org/oxford
Oxford Central S 300/K-8
17 Kent St 07863 908-453-4101
Bob Magnuson, admin. Fax 453-0022

Palisades Park, Bergen, Pop. 18,857
Palisades Park SD 1,500/K-12
270 1st St 07650 201-947-3560
Dr. Mark Hayes, supt. Fax 947-4079
Lindbergh ES 700/2-7
401 Glen Ave 07650 201-947-3556
Jean Colosso, prin. Fax 947-2721
Smith ECC 200/K-1
271 2nd St 07650 201-947-2761

Notre Dame Interparochial S 200/PK-8
312 1st St 07650 201-947-5262
Rita Miragliotta, prin. Fax 947-8319

Palmyra, Burlington, Pop. 7,641
Palmyra Borough SD 1,000/K-12
301 Delaware Ave 08065 856-786-2963
Dr. Richard Perry, supt. Fax 829-9638
www.palmyra.k12.nj.us
Charles Street ES 400/K-6
100 W Charles St 08065 856-829-3601
Jeanne Barber, prin. Fax 303-0481

Paramus, Bergen, Pop. 26,545
Paramus SD 4,100/K-12
145 Spring Valley Rd 07652 201-261-7800
James Montesano Ed.D., supt. Fax 261-5861
www.paramus.k12.nj.us
East Brook MS 600/5-8
190 Spring Valley Rd 07652 201-261-7800
Kevin Brentnall, prin. Fax 262-1541
Memorial ES 300/K-4
203 E Midland Ave 07652 201-261-7800
Oscar Diaz, prin. Fax 262-5619
Midland ES 300/K-4
245 W Midland Ave 07652 201-261-7800
Cynthia Hulse, prin. Fax 262-1541
Parkway ES 300/K-4
145 E Ridgewood Ave 07652 201-261-7800
Mary Anne Evangelist Ph.D., prin. Fax 262-8214
Ridge Ranch ES 400/K-4
345 Lockwood Dr 07652 201-261-7800
Jeanine Nostrame, prin. Fax 262-2998
Stony Lane ES 200/K-4
110 W Ridgewood Ave 07652 201-261-7800
Angelo Casillo, prin. Fax 445-8971
West Brook MS 700/5-8
550 Roosevelt Blvd 07652 201-261-7800
Joan Broe, prin. Fax 652-0376

Visitation Academy 300/PK-8
222 N Farview Ave 07652 201-262-6067
Sr. Philomena McCartney, prin. Fax 261-4613
Yavneh Academy 700/PK-8
155 N Farview Ave 07652 201-262-8494
Rabbi Jonathan Knapp, dean Fax 262-0463

Park Ridge, Bergen, Pop. 8,959
Park Ridge SD 1,300/K-12
2 Park Ave 07656 201-573-6000
Dr. Patricia Johnson, supt. Fax 391-6511
www.parkridge.k12.nj.us
East Brook ES 300/K-6
167 Sibbald Dr 07656 201-930-4888
Sheldon Silver, prin. Fax 930-1650
West Ridge ES 400/K-6
18 S 1st St 07656 201-930-4898
Christine McCaffery, prin. Fax 573-8658

Our Lady of Mercy S 400/PK-8
25 Fremont Ave 07656 201-391-3838
Laraine Meehan, prin. Fax 391-3080

Parlin, Middlesex
Old Bridge Township SD
Supt. — See Matawan
Madison Park ES 300/K-5
33 Harvard Rd 08859 732-360-4485
Dr. Kimberley Giles, prin. Fax 721-4924

Sayreville SD
Supt. — See South Amboy
Arleth ES 500/K-3
3198 Washington Rd 08859 732-525-5244
Timothy Byrne, prin. Fax 525-5554
Eisenhower ES 400/K-3
601 Ernston Rd 08859 732-525-5229
William Skowronski, prin. Fax 525-5234
Samsel Upper ES 800/4-5
298 Ernston Rd 08859 732-316-4055
Edward Aguiles, prin. Fax 316-4096
Sayreville MS 1,300/6-8
800 Washington Rd 08859 732-525-5288
Donna Jakubik, prin. Fax 727-5621
Truman ES 400/K-3
1 Taft Pl 08859 732-525-5214
Linda Coffey, prin. Fax 727-5563

Parsippany, Morris, Pop. 51,000
Parsippany-Troy Hills Township SD 6,900/PK-12
PO Box 52 07054 973-263-7250
LeRoy Seitz Ed.D., supt. Fax 263-7230
www.pthsd.k12.nj.us/
Brooklawn MS 800/6-8
250 Beachwood Rd 07054 973-428-7551
Eileen Hoehne, prin. Fax 781-0309
Central MS 800/6-8
1620 US Highway 46 07054 973-263-7125
Jeffrey Rutzky, prin. Fax 402-1579
Eastlake ES 300/K-5
40 Eba Rd 07054 973-428-7583
Mark Gray, prin. Fax 428-3352
Lake Parsippany ES 300/K-5
225 Kingston Rd 07054 973-428-7572
Denis Mulroony, prin. Fax 781-0307
Northvail ES 400/K-5
10 Eileen Ct 07054 973-263-7070
Jeff Martens, prin. Fax 316-1086
Rockaway Meadow ES 300/K-5
160 Edwards Rd 07054 973-263-7308
Angelina Finnegan, prin. Fax 402-1478
Troy Hills ES 300/K-5
509 S Beverwyck Rd 07054 973-428-7588
Renee Brandler, prin. Fax 781-0308
Other Schools – See Boonton, Lake Hiawatha, Morris Plains, Mount Tabor

All Saints Academy 200/PK-8
189 Baldwin Rd 07054 973-334-4704
Judith Berg, prin. Fax 334-0622
Parsippany Christian S 200/PK-12
PO Box 5365 07054 973-539-7012
Rev. Philip Thibault, prin. Fax 539-2527
St. Elizabeth S 200/PK-K
499 Park Rd 07054 973-540-0721
Fax 540-9186

Passaic, Passaic, Pop. 68,338
Passaic CSD 11,500/PK-12
PO Box 388 07055 973-470-5500
Dr. Robert Holster, supt. Fax 470-8984
www.passaic-city.k12.nj.us
Capuana K 15 200/K-K
362 Broadway 07055 973-815-8563
Thomas Focacci, prin. Fax 815-8568
Cruise Memorial ES 11 1,000/K-5
390 Gregory Ave 07055 973-470-5511
Kyra Aycart, prin. Fax 470-5134
Drago ES 3 900/PK-6
155 Van Houten Ave 07055 973-470-5503
Talma Addes, prin. Fax 470-5127
Gero ES 9 500/2-6
140 1st St 07055 973-470-5509
Isabel Leon, prin. Fax 470-5132
Grant ES 7 400/PK-2
181 Myrtle Ave 07055 973-470-5507
Pat Ramsay, prin. Fax 470-5130
Jefferson ES 1 600/PK-6
390 Van Houten Ave 07055 973-470-5501
Thomas Focacci, prin. Fax 470-5125
King ES 6 1,000/PK-6
85 Hamilton Ave 07055 973-470-5506
Celinda Barreto, prin. Fax 470-5129
Learning Center 100/3-6
20 Wall St 07055 973-470-5498
Rafael Fraguela, prin. Fax 815-2765
Lincoln MS 1,500/7-8
291 Lafayette Ave 07055 973-470-5504
John Scozzaro, prin. Fax 470-5128
Passaic City ES 5 200/4-6
168 Monroe St 07055 973-591-6747
Salvatore Puzzo, prin. Fax 591-6751
Passaic City IS 14 200/6-6
266 Harrison St 07055 973-815-8887
Manuel Fuentes, prin. Fax 815-8892
Passaic City K 16 500/PK-K
657 Main Ave 07055 973-815-8516
Lisa Wozny, prin. Fax 574-2145
Passaic City Preschool 17 300/PK-PK
95 Dayton Ave 07055 973-591-8544
Maria Kenney, prin. Fax 591-8545
Passaic City Preschool 18 100/PK-PK
158 Passaic St 07055 973-591-6957
Gwen Sanford, prin. Fax 591-5221
Passaic City PS 2 200/K-2
48 Bergen St 07055 973-470-5578
Luis Lobelo, prin. Fax 470-5126
Pulaski ES 8 400/K-2
100 4th St 07055 973-470-5508
Mark Spindel, prin. Fax 470-8828
Roosevelt ES 10 600/PK-4
266 Harrison St 07055 973-470-5510
Dr. Gloria Vargas, prin. Fax 470-5133

Collegiate S 100/PK-12
22 Kent Ct 07055 973-777-1714
Paula Grassie, hdmstr. Fax 777-3255
Our Lady of Mt. Carmel S 300/PK-8
7 Saint Francis Way 07055 973-473-8183
Sr. Clare Conforti, prin. Fax 473-0937
Passaic/Clifton Cheder/Bais Yaakov PK-4
151 Lafayette Ave 07055 973-472-0011
St. Anthony of Padua S - Passaic Cath S 200/PK-8
40 Tulip St 07055 973-773-0970
Sr. Joselle Ratka, prin. Fax 779-6864
St. Nicholas Ukranian S 100/PK-8
223 President St 07055 973-779-0249
Ann Roman, prin. Fax 779-6309
Yeshiva Beit Hillel Academy 300/PK-8
270 Passaic Ave 07055 973-777-0735
Yeshiva Ktana of Passaic Boys Division 500/K-8
1 Main Ave 07055 973-916-1555
Yeshiva Ktana of Passaic Girls Division 700/PK-8
181 Pennington Ave 07055 973-365-0100

Paterson, Passaic, Pop. 149,843
Paterson SD 22,500/PK-12
33 Church St 07505 973-321-1000
Dr. Dennis Clancy, supt. Fax 321-0470
www.paterson.k12.nj.us
Academy of Performing Arts 5-8
45 Smith St 07505 973-321-0570
Cora Quince, admin. Fax 321-0577
B.U.I.L.D. Academy 6-8
202 Union Ave 07502 973-321-1000
Rosalie Bespalko, prin. Fax 321-0587
Clemente ES 300/1-4
434 Rosa Parks Blvd 07501 973-321-0340
Lourdes Rodriguez, prin. Fax 321-0347
Dale Avenue ES 300/PK-1
21 Dale Ave 07505 973-321-0410
Christine Johnson, prin. Fax 321-0417
Early Learning Center K-K
660 14th Ave 07504 973-321-0660
Nancy Forsberg, admin. Fax 321-0667
Hamilton Academy 300/K-8
11-27 16th Ave 07501 973-321-0320
Virginia Galizia, prin. Fax 321-0327
Kilpatrick ES 400/K-5
295 Ellison St 07501 973-321-0330
Richard Sanducci, prin. Fax 321-0337
King S 1,000/K-8
851 E 28th St 07513 973-321-0300
Muriel Garcia, prin. Fax 321-0307
New Roberto Clemente S K-8
482 Market St 07501 973-321-0240
JoAnne Riviello, prin. Fax 321-0247
Paterson City S 1 300/PK-6
589 11th Ave 07514 973-321-0490
Marlene Toomey, prin. Fax 321-0496
Paterson City S 2 600/PK-8
22 Passaic St 07501 973-321-0020
Felisa VanLiew, prin. Fax 321-0027
Paterson City S 3 500/K-8
448 Main St 07501 973-321-0030
Grisell Hernandez, prin. Fax 321-0037
Paterson City S 4 400/5-8
55 Clinton St 07522 973-321-0040
David Cozart, prin. Fax 321-0047
Paterson City S 5 1,100/1-8
430 Totowa Ave 07502 973-321-0050
Ramiro Borja, prin. Fax 321-0057
Paterson City S 6 500/K-8
137 Carroll St 07501 973-321-0060
Derrick Hoff, prin. Fax 321-0067
Paterson City S 7 200/5-8
106 Ramsey St 07501 973-321-0070
Christine Damasceno, prin. Fax 321-0077
Paterson City S 8 500/K-8
35 Chadwick St 07503 973-321-0080
Aubrey Johnson, prin. Fax 321-0087
Paterson City S 9 1,200/K-8
9 Getty Ave 07503 973-321-0090
Linda Crescione, prin. Fax 321-0097
Paterson City S 10 700/PK-8
48 Mercer St 07524 973-321-0100
Dorothy Douge, prin. Fax 321-0107
Paterson City S 11 300/1-8
350 Market St 07501 973-321-0110
Paula Santana, prin. Fax 321-0117
Paterson City S 12 600/PK-8
121 N 2nd St 07522 973-321-0120
Hector Montes, prin. Fax 321-0127
Paterson City S 13 800/K-8
690 E 23rd St 07504 973-321-0130
Hillburn Sparrow, prin. Fax 321-0137
Paterson City S 14 200/K-4
522 Union Ave 07522 973-321-0140
Michelle James, prin. Fax 321-0147
Paterson City S 15 900/K-8
98 Oak St 07501 973-321-0150
Sham Bacchus, prin. Fax 321-0157
Paterson City S 17 200/1-4
112 N 5th St 07522 973-321-0170
Carlos Ortiz, prin. Fax 321-0177
Paterson City S 18 1,200/K-8
51 E 18th St 07524 973-321-0180
Natalie Heard-Hackett, prin. Fax 321-0187
Paterson City S 19 400/K-4
31 James St 07502 973-321-0190
Michael Osofsky, prin. Fax 321-0197
Paterson City S 20 500/K-8
500 E 37th St 07504 973-321-0200
Courtney Glover, prin. Fax 321-0207
Paterson City S 21 700/K-8
322 10th Ave 07514 973-321-0210
Frank Puglise, prin. Fax 321-0217
Paterson City S 25 700/K-8
287 Trenton Ave 07503 973-321-0250
Dr. Sandra Mickens, prin. Fax 321-0257
Paterson City S 26 600/K-8
1 E 32nd St 07514 973-321-0260
Jennifer Crewes-Reynolds, prin. Fax 321-0267
Paterson City S 27 800/K-8
250 Richmond Ave 07502 973-321-0270
Boblyn Ranger-Dobbs, prin. Fax 321-0277
Paterson City S 28 400/K-4
200 Presidential Blvd 07522 973-321-0280
Christopher Pringle, prin. Fax 321-0287
Paterson City S 29 300/K-4
88 Danforth Ave 07501 973-321-0290
Maria Santa, prin. Fax 321-0297
Urban Leadership Academy 200/1-5
144 Beech St 07501 973-321-2520
George Featherson, prin. Fax 321-2527
Weir S 200/1-8
152 College Blvd 07505 973-321-0750
Grace Giglio, prin. Fax 321-0757

Al-Huda S 100/K-12
154 Ellison St 07505 973-742-7474
Blessed Sacrament S 200/PK-8
277 6th Ave 07524 973-278-8787
Sr. Noreen Holly, prin. Fax 278-6436
LaGarde Sr Academy 100/PK-8
535 Martin Luther Kings Way 07514 973-742-9119
Fred LaGarde, supt. Fax 742-9122
Madison Avenue Baptist Academy 200/K-12
900 Madison Ave 07501 973-279-5800
Brandon Black, prin. Fax 684-6289
St. Gerard Majella S 200/PK-8
10 Carrelton Dr 07522 973-595-5640
Sr. Joann Pompa, prin. Fax 595-5475
St. Mary S 300/PK-8
95 Sherman Ave 07502 973-956-1542
Kathleen Fields, prin. Fax 956-1759
St. Therese S 300/PK-8
765 14th Ave 07504 973-278-4135
Sr. Maryann Jacobs, prin. Fax 278-3228
Treader Christian S 100/K-8
1 Market St 07501 973-345-9830
Mona Timms, admin. Fax 345-6668

Paulsboro, Gloucester, Pop. 6,096
Paulsboro SD 1,300/PK-12
662 N Delaware St 08066 856-423-5515
Dr. Frank Scambia, supt. Fax 423-4602
www.paulsboro.k12.nj.us/
Billingsport ES 400/PK-2
441 Nassau Ave 08066 856-423-2226
Phillip Neff, prin. Fax 423-8912
Loudenslager ES 300/3-6
100 Baird Ave 08066 856-423-2228
Mildred Williams, prin. Fax 423-8914

Pedricktown, Salem
Oldmans Township SD 200/K-8
10 Freed Rd 08067 856-299-4240
Stephen Combs, admin. Fax 299-8182

Oldmans Township S 200/K-8
10 Freed Rd 08067 856-299-4240
David Lindenmuth, prin. Fax 299-8182

Pemberton, Burlington, Pop. 1,323
Pemberton Township SD 4,600/PK-12
PO Box 228 08068 609-893-8141
Dr. Michael Gorman, supt. Fax 894-0933
www.pemberton.k12.nj.us
Busansky ES 200/K-5
16 Scrapetown Rd 08068 609-893-8141
Eldrean Attaway, prin. Fax 894-0545
Emmons ES 300/PK-4
14 Scrapetown Rd 08068 609-893-8141
J. Ronald Beebe, prin. Fax 894-0544
Fort MS 700/7-8
301 Fort Dix Rd 08068 609-893-8141
Mary Hutchinson, prin. Fax 894-9287
Newcomb ES 400/4-6
300 Fort Dix Rd 08068 609-893-8141
Frank Miller, prin. Fax 726-1597
Other Schools – See Browns Mills, Fort Dix

Pennington, Mercer, Pop. 2,696
Hopewell Valley Regional SD 4,000/K-12
425 S Main St 08534 609-737-4000
Dr. Tom Smith, supt. Fax 737-1418
www.hvrsd.org/
Stony Brook ES 500/K-5
20 Stephenson Rd 08534 609-737-4000
Steve Wilfing, prin. Fax 730-3888
Timberlane MS 900/6-8
51 Timberlane Dr 08534 609-737-4000
Tony Suozzo, prin. Fax 737-2718
Toll Gate Grammar S 300/K-5
275 S Main St 08534 609-737-4000
Daniel Umstead, prin. Fax 737-7348
Other Schools – See Hopewell, Titusville

Pennsauken, Camden, Pop. 35,900
Pennsauken Township SD 4,900/PK-12
1695 Hylton Rd 08110 856-662-8505
James Chapman Ed.D., supt. Fax 663-5865
www.pennsauken.net
Baldwin Preschool 100/PK-PK
3901 Sharon Ter 08110 856-662-8464
Andrea Rivera, dir. Fax 665-4134
Burling ES 100/K-4
3600 Harris Ave 08110 856-662-1923
William Snyder, prin. Fax 662-5420
Carson ES 200/K-4
4150 Garfield Ave 08109 856-662-5751
Andrea Rivera, prin. Fax 486-7992
Fine ES 200/PK-4
3800 Gladwyn Ave 08109 856-662-8568
Rosalyn Lawrence, prin. Fax 317-0363
Franklin ES 400/PK-4
7201 Irving Ave 08109 856-662-6455
Landrus Lewis, prin. Fax 662-8469
Longfellow ES 200/K-4
5700 Forrest Ave 08110 856-662-9037
William Snyder, prin. Fax 317-0366
Pennsauken IS 700/5-6
8125 Park Ave 08109 856-662-8501
Dr. Anne Morris, prin. Fax 662-5387
Phifer MS 800/7-8
8201 Park Ave 08109 856-662-8500
Curt Wrzeszczinski, prin. Fax 486-1422
Roosevelt ES 200/K-4
5526 Wisteria Ave 08109 856-662-8141
Rosalyn Lawrence, prin. Fax 317-0365
Other Schools – See Delair

Camden Forward S 100/K-8
3700 Rudderow St 08110 856-382-1857
Denise Baker, prin. Fax 661-1954
JDT Christian Academy 50/K-12
3600 Earle St 08110 856-910-2815
Fax 910-2815
Martin Luther Christian S 200/PK-8
4106 Terrace Ave 08109 856-665-0231
Lisa Steele, prin. Fax 665-5312
St. Cecilia S 200/PK-8
4851 Camden Ave 08110 856-662-0149
Ernest Benson, prin. Fax 662-7460
St. Stephen Regional S 300/PK-8
6300 Browning Rd 08109 856-662-5935
Patricia Higgins, prin. Fax 662-6128

Penns Grove, Salem, Pop. 4,824
Penns Grove-Carneys Point Regional SD 2,300/PK-12
100 Iona Ave 08069 856-299-4250
Joseph A. Massare Ed.D., supt. Fax 299-5226
www.pennsgrove.k12.nj.us
Carleton ES 300/4-5
251 E Maple Ave 08069 856-299-1706
Emma Shockley, prin. Fax 299-1545
Penns Grove MS 500/6-8
351 E Maple Ave 08069 856-299-0576
Jean Spinelli, prin. Fax 299-4378
Other Schools – See Carneys Point

Pennsville, Salem, Pop. 12,218
Pennsville Township SD 2,000/K-12
30 Church St 08070 856-540-6200
Dr. Mark Jones, supt. Fax 678-7565
www.pennsville.k12.nj.us
Central Park ES 300/K-5
43 Oliver Ave 08070 856-540-6260
Edmund Lytle, prin. Fax 678-4728
Penn Beach ES 400/K-5
96 Kansas Rd 08070 856-540-6250
Dr. Lori Moore, prin. Fax 540-6217
Pennsville MS 500/6-8
4 William Penn Ave 08070 856-540-6240
Sheila Burris, prin. Fax 678-2908
Valley Park ES 300/K-5
63 Mahoney Rd 08070 856-540-6255
Bobbie-Ann Jordan, prin. Fax 540-6218

Park Bible Academy 100/PK-12
104 Sparks Ave 08070 856-678-9464

Pequannock, Morris, Pop. 12,844
Pequannock Township SD
Supt. — See Pompton Plains
Gerace ES 300/K-5
59 Boulevard 07440 973-305-5615
Dr. Gina Verrone-Coffaro, prin. Fax 305-5831

Holy Spirit S 200/PK-8
330 Newark Pompton Tpke 07440 973-835-5680
Sr. Marie Antonelli, prin. Fax 835-1757

Perth Amboy, Middlesex, Pop. 48,797
Perth Amboy SD 8,000/PK-12
178 Barracks St 08861 732-376-6200
John Rodecker, supt. Fax 826-1644
www.perthamboy.k12.nj.us/
Ceres ES 600/K-4
445 State St 08861 732-376-6020
Dr. Myrna Garcia, prin. Fax 376-6025
Cruz ECC 700/PK-PK
581 Cortlandt St 08861 732-376-6250
Susan Roque, prin. Fax 376-6255
Flynn ES 700/K-4
850 Chamberlain Ave 08861 732-376-6080
John Cilia, prin. Fax 376-6087
McGinnis MS 700/7-8
271 State St 08861 732-376-6040
Ana Marie Mascenik, prin. Fax 376-6047
Patten ES 700/K-4
500 Charles St 08861 732-376-6050
Joyce DeFeo, prin. Fax 376-6057
Richardson ES 600/K-4
318 Stockton St 08861 732-376-6010
Helen Horan, prin. Fax 376-6016
St. Mary's ECC 300/PK-PK
351 Mechanic St 08861 732-324-9860
Dr. Gerarda Mast, prin. Fax 324-8236
Shull IS 700/5-6
380 Hall Ave 08861 732-376-6060
Lorraine Morgan, prin. Fax 376-6067
Wilentz ES 800/K-4
51 1st St 08861 732-376-6070
Roland Jenkins, prin. Fax 376-6077

Assumption Catholic S 100/PK-8
380 Meredith St 08861 732-826-8721
Michael Szpyhulsky, prin. Fax 826-5013
Perth Amboy Catholic PS 200/PK-3
613 Carlock Ave 08861 732-826-5747
Sr. Beverly Policastro, prin. Fax 826-6096
Perth Amboy Catholic Upper S 200/4-8
500 State St 08861 732-826-1598
Sr. Mary Rebecca Piatek, prin. Fax 826-7063

Petersburg, See Woodbine
Upper Township SD 1,400/K-8
525 Perry Rd 08270 609-628-3513
Vincent Palmieri, supt. Fax 628-2002
upperschools.org/
Upper Township MS 600/6-8
525 Perry Rd 08270 609-628-3500
Ken Barth, prin. Fax 628-3506
Other Schools – See Marmora

Parkway South Christian S 50/K-8
18 Sunset Dr 08270 609-628-3252

Phillipsburg, Warren, Pop. 14,920
Harmony Township SD 300/K-8
2551 Belvidere Rd 08865 908-859-1001
Jason Kornegay, supt. Fax 859-2277
www.warrennet.org/harmonyschool/
Harmony Township S 300/K-8
2551 Belvidere Rd 08865 908-859-1001
Jason Kornegay, prin. Fax 859-2277

Lopatcong Township SD 900/PK-8
263 State Route 57 08865 908-859-0800
Vicki Pede, supt. Fax 213-1339
www.lopatcongschool.org/
Lopatcong ES 500/PK-4
263 State Route 57 08865 908-859-0800
Matthew Eagleburger, prin. Fax 213-1339
Lopatcong MS 400/5-8
321 Stonehenge Dr 08865 908-213-2955
Ms. Rosemary Kowalchuk, prin. Fax 213-1339

Phillipsburg SD 3,700/PK-12
445 Marshall St 08865 908-454-3400
Mark Miller, supt. Fax 454-1746
www.pburgsd.net/
Andover-Morris ES 200/3-5
712 S Main St 08865 908-454-2476
John Consentino, prin. Fax 213-2542
Barber ES 200/1-2
50 Sargent Ave 08865 908-213-2560
Raffaele LaForgia, prin. Fax 213-2408
Freeman ES 200/1-2
120 Filmore St 08865 908-454-2263
Cathy Olson, prin. Fax 213-2553
Green Street ES 300/3-5
1000 Green St 08865 908-213-2585
John Finken, prin. Fax 213-2552
Phillipsburg ECC 500/PK-K
459 Center St 08865 908-213-2700
Judith Bonos, prin. Fax 213-2821
Phillipsburg MS 600/6-8
525 Warren St 08865 908-454-5577
Dr. John Milone, prin. Fax 213-2546

Pohatcong Township SD 400/K-8
240 County Road 519 08865 908-859-8155
Diane Mandry, supt. Fax 859-8067
www.warrennet.org/pohatcong/
Pohatcong Township S 400/K-8
240 County Road 519 08865 908-859-8155
Dan Patton, prin. Fax 859-8067

Phillipsburg Christian Academy 100/PK-8
300 Cromwell St 08865 908-859-6464
Rev. Douglas Batchelder, admin. Fax 213-0619
SS. Philip & James S 300/PK-8
137 Roseberry St 08865 908-859-1244
Judith Francisco, prin. Fax 859-1202

Pine Beach, Ocean, Pop. 2,025
Toms River Regional SD
Supt. — See Toms River
Pine Beach ES 400/K-5
101 Pennsylvania Ave 08741 732-505-5870
Tricia Moran, prin. Fax 286-2132

Pine Brook, Morris
Montville Township SD 4,100/K-12
328 Changebridge Rd 07058 973-808-8580
Dr. Gary Bowen, supt. Fax 331-1307
www.montville.net
Hilldale ES 400/K-5
123 Konner Ave 07058 973-808-2040
Marianne Dispenziere, prin. Fax 882-9123
Woodmont ES 300/K-5
39 Woodmont Rd 07058 973-808-2030
Fax 808-8361
Other Schools – See Montville, Towaco

Pine Hill, Camden, Pop. 11,305
Pine Hill Borough SD 2,000/PK-12
1003 Turnerville Rd 08021 856-783-6900
Dr. Kenneth Koczur, supt. Fax 783-2955
www.pinehill.k12.nj.us
Bean ES 300/PK-5
70 E 3rd Ave 08021 856-783-5300
Daniel Schuster, prin. Fax 741-0377
Glenn ES 400/PK-5
1005 Turnerville Rd 08021 856-783-4100
James Vacca, prin. Fax 741-0347
Pine Hill MS 400/6-8
1100 Turnerville Rd 08021 856-210-0200
Kate Klemick, prin. Fax 210-0195

Piscataway, Middlesex, Pop. 48,900
Piscataway Township SD 6,600/K-12
PO Box 1332 08855 732-572-2289
Robert Copeland, supt. Fax 777-1361
www.piscatawayschools.org/
Arbor IS 500/4-5
1717 Lester Pl 08854 732-752-8652
Susan Sposato Chalfin, prin. Fax 752-8102
Conackamack MS 500/6-8
5205 Witherspoon St 08854 732-699-1577
Dr. Suzanne Westberg, prin. Fax 699-0118
Eisenhower ES 500/K-3
360 Stelton Rd 08854 732-752-1801
Mylo Wright, prin. Fax 752-7670
Grandview ES 500/K-3
130 N Randolphville Rd 08854 732-752-2501
Celeste Gagliardi, prin. Fax 752-8101
King IS 500/4-5
5205 Ludlow St 08854 732-699-1563
Shirley Eyler, prin. Fax 699-1677
Knollwood ES 500/K-3
333 Willow Ave 08854 732-885-1528
Patricia McFall, prin. Fax 885-5831
Quibbletown MS 500/6-8
99 Academy St 08854 732-752-0444
Deidre Ortiz, prin. Fax 752-5798
Randolphville ES 500/K-3
1 Suttie Ave 08854 732-699-1573
Perry Stio, prin. Fax 699-1985
Schor MS 500/6-8
243 N Randolphville Rd 08854 732-752-4457
Richard Hueston, prin. Fax 424-9445

An-Noor Academy 300/PK-12
120 Ethel Rd W Ste A 08854 732-287-1530
Ahmad Ansari, prin. Fax 287-1564
Lake Nelson SDA S 100/K-8
555 S Randolphville Rd 08854 732-981-0626
Elisa Maragoto, prin. Fax 981-0770
Our Lady of Fatima S 200/PK-8
499 New Market Rd 08854 732-968-5017
Joan Simon, prin. Fax 968-9259
Timothy Christian S 600/K-12
2008 Ethel Rd 08854 732-985-0300
Michael Keller, supt. Fax 985-8008
Yeshiva Shaarei Tzion Boys Division 100/1-8
71 Ethel Rd W 08854 732-777-0029
Yeshiva Shaarei Tzion Girls Division 200/PK-8
51 Park Ave 08854 732-235-0042

Pitman, Gloucester, Pop. 9,251
Pitman SD 1,500/K-12
420 Hudson Ave 08071 856-589-2145
Thomas Shulte, supt. Fax 582-5465
www.pitman.k12.nj.us
Elwood Kindle ES 200/K-5
211 Washington Ave 08071 856-589-2628
Frances Harper, prin.
Pitman Memorial ES 300/K-5
400 Hudson Ave 08071 856-589-2526
Thomas Agnew, prin.
Pitman MS, 138 E Holly Ave 08071 400/6-8
Eileen Salmon, prin. 856-589-0636
Walls ES, 320 Grant Ave 08071 200/K-5
Chris Morris, prin. 856-589-1316

Bright Beginnings West S 100/PK-K
536 Lambs Rd 08071 856-256-1166
Cindy Delia, dir. Fax 256-1572

Pittsgrove, Salem
Pittsgrove Township SD 1,800/PK-12
1076 Almond Rd 08318 856-358-3094
Henry Bermann, supt. Fax 358-6020
www.pittsgrove.org
Norma K 200/PK-K
873 Gershal Ave 08318 856-358-6904
Patricia Gaburo, prin. Fax 691-2285
Olivet ES 500/1-4
235 Sheep Pen Rd 08318 856-358-2081
Patricia Gaburo, prin. Fax 358-0231
Pittsgrove Township MS 600/5-8
1082 Almond Rd 08318 856-358-8529
Priscilla Vanderhoff, prin. Fax 358-2686

Pittstown, Hunterdon
Alexandria Township SD 600/K-8
557 County Road 513 08867 908-996-6811
Dr. Matthew Jennings, supt. Fax 996-7029
www.alexandriaschools.org
Alexandria MS 400/4-8
557 County Road 513 08867 908-996-6811
David Pawlowski, prin. Fax 996-7963
Wilson ES 300/K-3
525 County Road 513 08867 908-996-6812
Sandra Kacedon, prin. Fax 996-3163

Plainfield, Union, Pop. 47,642
Plainfield SD 6,200/PK-12
504 Madison Ave 07060 908-731-4335
Steve Gallon, supt. Fax 731-4336
www.plainfieldnjk12.org
Barlow ES 300/K-5
2 Farragut Rd 07062 908-731-4300
Caryn Cooper, prin. Fax 731-4294
Cedarbrook ES 400/K-5
1049 Central Ave 07060 908-731-4280
Frank Asante, prin. Fax 731-4277
Clinton ES 300/PK-5
1302 W 4th St 07063 908-731-4220
BJ BrownJohnson, prin. Fax 731-4222
Cook ES 200/K-5
739 Leland Ave 07062 908-731-4215
Dr. Christopher Lommerin, prin. Fax 731-4213
Emerson ES 300/K-5
305 Emerson Ave 07062 908-731-4205
Janet Grooms, prin. Fax 731-4206
Evergreen ES 400/K-5
1033 Evergreen Ave 07060 908-731-4260
Wilson Aponte, prin. Fax 731-4259
Hubbard MS 600/6-8
661 W 8th St 07060 908-731-4320
Gwynetta Joe, prin. Fax 731-4315
Jefferson ES 400/K-5
1200 Myrtle Ave 07063 908-731-4250
Christy Oliver, prin. Fax 731-4249
Maxson MS 800/6-8
920 E 7th St 07062 908-731-4310
Anthony Jenkins, prin. Fax 731-4306
Stillman ES 200/K-5
201 W 4th St 07060 908-731-4240
Dr. Phillip Williamson, prin. Fax 731-4239
Washington ES 400/K-5
427 Darrow Ave 07060 908-731-4230
Yvonne Breauxsaus, prin. Fax 731-4231
Woodland ES 200/PK-5
730 Central St 07062 908-731-4290
Gloria Williams, prin. Fax 731-4286

Koinonia Academy 300/K-12
1040 Plainfield Ave 07060 908-668-9002
Fax 668-9883
New Covenant Christian Academy 50/K-8
315 W 7th St 07060 908-756-3322
Stephanie DeGeneste, dir. Fax 756-3302
Star Bright Christian Learning Center 100/PK-2
145 Park Ave 07060 908-756-7927
Sylvia Bright, dir. Fax 756-7258

Plainsboro, Middlesex
West Windsor-Plainsboro Regional SD
Supt. — See Princeton Junction
Community MS 1,200/6-8
55 Grovers Mill Rd 08536 609-716-5300
Dr. Arthur Downs, prin. Fax 716-5333
Millstone River S 800/4-5
75 Grovers Mill Rd 08536 609-716-5500
Mary Ann Isaacs, prin. Fax 716-5544
Town Center ES 700/K-3
700 Wyndhurst Dr 08536 609-716-8330
Brian Stevens, prin.
Wicoff ES 400/K-3
506 Plainsboro Rd 08536 609-716-5450
Michael Welborn, prin. Fax 716-5462

Montessori Corner at Princeton Meadows 300/PK-6
666 Plainsboro Rd Bldg 2100 08536 609-799-6668
Eileen Spiewak, hdmstr. Fax 799-1775
Montessori Country Day S 100/PK-6
72 Grovers Mill Rd 08536 609-799-7990
Eileen Spiewak, hdmstr.

Pleasantville, Atlantic, Pop. 19,032
Pleasantville SD 3,300/PK-12
PO Box 960 08232 609-383-6800
Dr. Clarence Alston, supt. Fax 677-8122
www.pps-nj.us/pps/
Leeds Avenue ES 500/PK-5
100 W Leeds Ave 08232 609-383-6800
Daniel Smith, prin. Fax 383-1260
North Main Street ES 300/PK-5
215 N Main St 08232 609-383-6800
Ada Barlatt, prin. Fax 569-0182
Pleasantville MS 700/6-8
801 Mill Rd 08232 609-383-6800
Briggitte White, prin. Fax 677-0852
South Main Street ES 500/K-5
701 S Main St 08232 609-383-6800
Rosemay Clarke, prin. Fax 407-9125
Washington Avenue ES 400/PK-5
225 W Washington Ave 08232 609-383-6800
Effie Jenkins-Smith, prin. Fax 641-6865

Point Pleasant, Ocean, Pop. 19,861
Point Pleasant Borough SD 3,100/PK-12
2100 Panther Path 08742 732-701-1900
Vincent Smith, supt. Fax 892-8403
www.pointpleasant.k12.nj.us/
Bennett ES 800/K-5
2000 Riviera Pkwy 08742 732-701-1900
James Karaba, prin. Fax 892-0981
Memorial MS 800/6-8
808 Laura Herbert Dr 08742 732-701-1900
Robert Alfonse, prin. Fax 892-0984
Ocean Road ES 500/PK-5
Benedict St 08742 732-701-1900
Sheila Buck, prin. Fax 892-1056

Pt Pleas Bch, Ocean, Pop. 5,302
Point Pleasant Beach SD 900/K-12
299 Cooks Ln 08742 732-899-8840
Dr. John Ravally, supt. Fax 899-1730
ptbeach.com
Antrim S 500/K-8
401 Niblick St 08742 732-899-3737
Thomas O'Hara, prin. Fax 892-1081

St. Peter S 200/K-8
415 Atlantic Ave 08742 732-892-1260
Kathleen Berlino, prin. Fax 892-3488

Pompton Lakes, Passaic, Pop. 11,313
Pompton Lakes SD 1,800/K-12
237 Van Ave 07442 973-835-4334
Dr. Terrance Brennan, supt. Fax 835-1748
www.plps.org
Lakeside MS 400/6-8
316 Lakeside Ave 07442 973-835-2221
Dr. Paul Amoroso, prin. Fax 835-8088
Lenox ES 400/K-5
35 Lenox Ave 07442 973-839-3777
Vincent Iraggi, prin. Fax 839-0793
Lincoln ES 300/K-5
40 Mill St 07442 973-835-1910
Louis Shadiack, prin. Fax 835-2369

St. Mary S 300/PK-8
25 Pompton Ave 07442 973-835-2010
Sr. Mary Byrnes, prin. Fax 835-7529

Pompton Plains, Morris
Pequannock Township SD 2,400/K-12
538 Newark Pompton Tpke 07444 973-616-6040
William Trusheim Ed.D., supt. Fax 616-6043
www.pequannock.org
Hillview ES 400/K-5
206 Boulevard 07444 973-616-6080
Linda Thompson, prin. Fax 616-5997
North Boulevard ES 400/K-5
363 Boulevard 07444 973-616-6070
Jerome Cammarata, prin. Fax 616-5309
Pequannock Valley MS 600/6-8
493 Newark Pompton Tpke 07444 973-616-6050
Sue Schwartz, prin. Fax 616-8370
Other Schools – See Pequannock

Netherlands Reformed Christian S 200/PK-12
164 Jacksonville Rd 07444 973-628-7400
John Vanderbrink, prin. Fax 628-0461

Port Elizabeth, Cumberland
Maurice River Township SD 400/PK-8
PO Box 464 08348 856-825-7411
John Saporito, supt. Fax 825-1248
www.mrtschool.com
Maurice River Township S 400/PK-8
PO Box 464 08348 856-825-7411
John Saporito, prin. Fax 825-1248

Port Monmouth, Monmouth, Pop. 3,558
Middletown Township SD
Supt. — See Middletown
Port Monmouth ES, 202 Main St 07758 200/K-5
Dean Bisgrove, prin. 732-787-0441
Thorne MS, 70 Murphy Rd 07758 800/6-8
Alvaro Cores, prin. 732-787-1220

Port Murray, Warren
Mansfield Township SD 700/K-6
50 Port Murray Rd 07865 908-689-3212
Edward Kemp, supt. Fax 689-6576
www.warrennet.org/mansfield
Mansfield Township ES 700/K-6
50 Port Murray Rd 07865 908-689-3212
John Melitsky, prin. Fax 689-6576

Port Norris, Cumberland, Pop. 1,701
Commercial Township SD 700/PK-8
PO Box 650 08349 856-785-0840
Barry Ballard, supt. Fax 785-2354
www.commercial.k12.nj.us
Haleyville-Mauricetown ES 500/PK-5
PO Box 650 08349 856-785-0222
Jean Smith, prin. Fax 785-8120
Port Norris MS 200/6-8
PO Box 670 08349 856-785-1611
Peter Koza, prin. Fax 785-2556

Port Reading, Middlesex, Pop. 3,977
Woodbridge Township SD
Supt. — See Woodbridge
Port Reading ES 400/K-5
77 Turner St 07064 732-602-8409
John Bader, prin. Fax 541-0195

Port Republic, Atlantic, Pop. 1,194
Port Republic SD 100/K-8
137 Pomona Ave 08241 609-652-7377
Janet Wilbraham, supt. Fax 652-3664
www.port-republic.k12.nj.us/
Port Republic S 100/K-8
137 Pomona Ave 08241 609-652-7377
Janet Wilbraham, prin. Fax 652-3664

Princeton, Mercer, Pop. 13,495
Princeton Regional SD 3,700/K-12
25 Valley Rd 08540 609-806-4220
Judith Wilson, supt. Fax 806-4221
www.prs.k12.nj.us
Community Park ES 300/K-5
372 Witherspoon St 08542 609-806-4230
Sharon Goldman, prin. Fax 806-4231
Johnson Park ES 300/K-5
285 Rosedale Rd 08540 609-806-4240
Robert Ginsberg, prin. Fax 806-4241
Littlebrook ES 300/K-5
39 Magnolia Ln 08540 609-806-4250
Anna Kosek, prin. Fax 806-4251
Riverside ES 600/K-5
58 Riverside Dr 08540 609-806-4260
William Cirullo, prin. Fax 806-4261
Witherspoon MS 500/6-8
217 Walnut Ln 08540 609-806-4270
William Johnson, prin. Fax 806-4271

American Boychoir S 50/4-8
19 Lambert Dr 08540 609-924-5858
Robert Rund, pres. Fax 924-5812
Chapin S 300/PK-8
4101 Princeton Pike 08540 609-924-2449
Richard Johnson, prin. Fax 924-2364
Princeton Academy of the Sacred Heart 200/K-8
1128 Great Rd 08540 609-921-6499
Olen Kalkus, hdmstr. Fax 921-9198
Princeton Day S 900/PK-12
PO Box 75 08542 609-924-6700
Paul Stellato, hdmstr. Fax 924-8944
Princeton Friends S 100/PK-8
470 Quaker Rd 08540 609-683-1194
Jane Fremon, prin. Fax 252-0686
Princeton Montessori S 300/PK-8
487 Cherry Valley Rd 08540 609-924-4594
Marsha Stencel, hdmstr. Fax 924-2216
St. Paul S 400/K-8
218 Nassau St 08542 609-921-7587
Ryan Killeen, prin. Fax 921-0264
Stuart Country Day S 600/PK-12
1200 Stuart Rd 08540 609-921-2330
Ann Soos, prin. Fax 497-0784
Waldorf S of Princeton 200/PK-8
1062 Cherry Hill Rd 08540 609-466-1970
Nancy Lemmo, admin. Fax 333-9991

Princeton Junction, Mercer, Pop. 2,362
West Windsor-Plainsboro Regional SD 9,300/K-12
PO Box 505 08550 609-716-5000
Victoria Kniewel Ed.D., supt. Fax 716-5012
www.ww-p.org
Dutch Neck ES 700/K-3
392 Village Rd E 08550 609-716-5400
Scott Feder, prin. Fax 716-5409
Grover MS 1,200/6-8
10 Southfield Rd 08550 609-716-5250
Dennis Lepold, prin. Fax 716-5270
Hawk ES 800/K-3
303 Clarksville Rd 08550 609-716-5425
Denise Mengani, prin. Fax 716-5439
Village S 700/4-5
601 New Village Rd 08550 609-716-5200
Christine Capaci, prin. Fax 716-5206
Other Schools – See Plainsboro

Prospect Park, Passaic, Pop. 5,760
Prospect Park SD 800/PK-8
290 N 8th St 07508 973-720-1981
Dr. James Barriale, supt. Fax 720-1992
www.prospectparknj.com/
Prospect Park S 1 800/PK-8
94 Brown Ave 07508 973-790-7909
Allison Angermeyer, prin. Fax 790-3635

Al-Hikmah S 400/PK-6
278 N 8th St 07508 973-790-4700

Quakertown, Hunterdon
Franklin Township SD 400/K-8
PO Box 368 08868 908-735-7929
Dr. James Dwyer, supt. Fax 735-0368
www.ftschool.org/
Franklin Township S 400/K-8
PO Box 368 08868 908-735-7929
Dr. James Dwyer, prin. Fax 735-0368

Quinton, Salem
Quinton Township SD 300/PK-8
PO Box 365 08072 856-935-2379
Dr. Donna Agnew, supt. Fax 935-1978
quinton.nj.schoolwebpages.com
Quinton Township S 300/PK-8
PO Box 365 08072 856-935-2379
Stewart Potter, prin. Fax 935-1978

Rahway, Union, Pop. 27,563
Rahway SD 3,800/PK-12
1200 Kline Pl 07065 732-396-1020
Frank Buglione, supt. Fax 396-1391
www.rahway.net
Cleveland ES 300/PK-5
486 E Milton Ave 07065 732-396-1040
Alan Johnson, prin. Fax 396-2636

Franklin ES 600/PK-5
1809 Saint Georges Ave 07065 732-396-1050
Arina Robinson, prin. Fax 396-2638
Madison ES 300/PK-5
944 Madison Ave 07065 732-396-1070
Fran Gavin, prin. Fax 396-2641
Rahway MS 900/6-8
1200 Kline Pl 07065 732-396-1025
John Perillo, prin. Fax 396-2633
Roosevelt ES 600/PK-5
811 Saint Georges Ave 07065 732-396-1060
Rocco Collucci, prin. Fax 396-2643

Ramsey, Bergen, Pop. 14,558
Ramsey SD 3,000/K-12
266 E Main St 07446 201-785-2300
Dr. Roy Montesano, supt. Fax 934-6623
www.ramsey.k12.nj.us
Dater IS 500/4-5
35 School St 07446 201-785-2325
Michael Gratale, prin. Fax 785-2333
Hubbard ES 400/K-3
421 Wyckoff Ave 07446 201-785-2301
Molly Dinning, prin. Fax 785-2311
Smith MS 800/6-8
2 Monroe St 07446 201-785-2313
Dr. Richard Weiner, prin. Fax 785-2320
Tisdale ES 400/K-3
200 Island Ave 07446 201-785-2336
Dr. Susan Morton, prin. Fax 785-2344

St. Paul S 300/K-8
187 Wyckoff Ave 07446 201-327-1108
Gail Ritchie, prin. Fax 236-1318

Randolph, Morris, Pop. 19,974
Randolph Township SD 5,400/K-12
25 Schoolhouse Rd 07869 973-361-0808
Dr. Max Riley, supt. Fax 361-2405
www.rtnj.org
Center Grove ES 600/K-5
25 Schoolhouse Rd 07869 973-361-7835
Debbie Iosso, prin.
Fernbrook ES 500/K-5
206 Quaker Church Rd 07869 973-361-0660
Deborah Grefe, prin.
Ironia ES 600/K-5
303 Dover Chester Rd 07869 973-584-8588
Dr. Dennis Copeland, prin. Fax 927-5791
Randolph MS 1,300/6-8
507 Millbrook Ave 07869 973-366-8700
Joseph Miceli Ed.D., prin.
Shongum ES, 9 Arrow Pl 07869 600/K-5
April Lowe, prin. 973-895-2322

Hebrew Academy of Morris County 200/PK-8
146 Dover Chester Rd 07869 973-584-5530
Moshe Vaknin, hdmstr. Fax 584-0602

Raritan, Somerset, Pop. 6,391
Bridgewater-Raritan Regional SD
Supt. — See Bridgewater
Kennedy ES 500/K-4
255 Woodmere St 08869 908-231-1179
Joseph Walsh, prin. Fax 231-1050

St. Ann S 300/PK-8
29 2nd Ave 08869 908-725-7787
Sr. Gloria Caglioti, prin. Fax 541-9335

Red Bank, Monmouth, Pop. 11,876
Middletown Township SD
Supt. — See Middletown
Fairview ES, 230 Cooper Rd 07701 300/K-5
Matthew Kirkpatrick, prin. 732-747-3308
River Plaza ES 300/K-5
155 Hubbard Ave 07701 732-747-3679
Linda Pesce, prin.

Red Bank Borough SD 800/PK-8
76 Branch Ave 07701 732-758-1507
Laura Morana, supt. Fax 212-1356
www.rbb.k12.nj.us
Red Bank MS 400/4-8
101 Harding Rd 07701 732-758-1515
Terence Wilkins, prin. Fax 758-1518
Red Bank PS 500/PK-3
222 River St 07701 732-758-1530
Richard Cohen, prin. Fax 758-0363

St. James S 600/PK-8
30 Peters Pl 07701 732-741-3363
Janet Dolan, prin. Fax 933-4960

Ridgefield, Bergen, Pop. 11,014
Ridgefield SD 1,700/1-12
555 Chestnut St 07657 201-945-9236
Dr. Richard Brockel, supt. Fax 945-7830
www.ridgefieldschools.com
Bergen Boulevard ES 200/1-2
635 Bergen Blvd 07657 201-943-5974
Gary Behan, prin. Fax 943-8397
Slocum/Skewes ES 800/3-8
650 Prospect Ave 07657 201-943-5974
Janet Seabold, prin. Fax 941-7967

Ridgefield Park, Bergen, Pop. 12,746
Ridgefield Park SD 2,000/K-12
712 Lincoln Ave 07660 201-641-0800
Dr. John Richardson, supt. Fax 641-2203
www.rpps.net
Grant ES 200/K-6
104 Henry St 07660 201-641-0441
Angela Bender, prin. Fax 440-9579
Lincoln ES 300/K-6
712 Lincoln Ave 07660 201-994-1830
James Donohue, prin. Fax 994-1626

Roosevelt ES 400/K-6
508 Teaneck Rd 07660 201-440-0808
Michael Alberque, prin. Fax 440-9573

St. Francis of Assisi S 300/PK-8
110 Mt Vernon St 07660 201-641-9159
Sr. Patricia Meidhof, prin. Fax 641-4091

Ridgewood, Bergen, Pop. 24,790
Ridgewood Village SD 5,500/K-12
49 Cottage Pl 07450 201-670-2700
Dr. Daniel Fishbein, supt. Fax 670-2668
www.ridgewood.k12.nj.us
Franklin MS 600/6-8
335 N Van Dien Ave 07450 201-670-2780
Anthony Orsini, prin.
Hawes ES, 531 Stevens Ave 07450 400/K-5
Kathi Rodger-Sachs, prin. 201-670-2720
Orchard ES, 230 Demarest St 07450 300/K-5
Dr. Robert Muller, prin. 201-670-2730
Ridge ES 500/K-5
325 W Ridgewood Ave 07450 201-670-2740
Jean Schoenlank, prin.
Somerville ES 500/K-5
45 S Pleasant Ave 07450 201-670-2750
Dr. Monica Browne, prin. Fax 670-3381
Travell ES, 340 Bogert Ave 07450 400/K-5
Margy Leininger, prin. 201-670-2760
Washington MS 700/6-8
155 Washington Pl 07450 201-670-2790
Katie Kashmanian, prin.
Willard ES, 601 Morningside Rd 07450 500/K-5
Marianne Williams, prin. 201-670-2770

Ringoes, Hunterdon
East Amwell Township SD 500/PK-8
PO Box 680 08551 908-782-6464
Edward Stoloski, supt. Fax 782-8529
www.eastamwell.org
East Amwell Township S 500/PK-8
PO Box 680 08551 908-782-6464
John Capuano, prin. Fax 782-8529

Flemington-Raritan Regional SD
Supt. — See Flemington
Copper Hill ES 500/K-4
100 Everitt Rd 08551 908-284-7660
Kevin McPeek, prin. Fax 284-7671

Ringwood, Passaic, Pop. 12,809
Ringwood SD 1,400/K-8
121 Carletondale Rd 07456 973-962-7028
Dr. Patrick Martin, supt. Fax 962-9211
www.ringwoodschools.org/
Cooper ES 300/K-3
54 Roger Ct 07456 973-835-5844
Michael Sutcliffe, prin. Fax 835-0986
Erskine ES 300/K-3
88 Erskine Rd 07456 973-962-7026
Nancy Dondero, prin. Fax 962-9186
Hewitt ES 300/4-5
266 Sloatsburg Rd 07456 973-962-7015
Timothy Johnson, prin. Fax 962-6963
Ryerson MS 500/6-8
130 Valley Rd 07456 973-962-7063
Paul Scutti, prin. Fax 962-6905

Ringwood Christian S 100/PK-8
30 Carletondale Rd 07456 973-962-4996
Donna Furrey Ed.D., admin. Fax 962-0365
St. Catherine of Bologna S 300/PK-8
112 Erskine Rd 07456 973-962-7131
Sr. Theresa Firenze, prin. Fax 962-0585

Riverdale, Morris, Pop. 2,635
Riverdale Borough SD 300/PK-8
52 Newark Pompton Tpke 07457 973-839-1300
Dr. Betty Ann Wyks, supt. Fax 839-8856
www.morris.k12.nj.us/riverdale
Riverdale S 300/PK-8
52 Newark Pompton Tpke 07457 973-839-1300
Keith Cortright, prin. Fax 839-8856

River Edge, Bergen, Pop. 10,911
River Dell Regional HSD 1,500/7-12
230 Woodland Ave 07661 201-599-7206
Patrick Fletcher, supt. Fax 261-3809
www.riverdell.org/
River Dell MS 500/7-8
230 Woodland Ave 07661 201-599-7250
Richard Freedman, prin. Fax 599-2202

River Edge SD 1,100/K-6
410 Bogert Rd 07661 201-261-3408
Erika Steinbauer, supt. Fax 261-0698
www.riveredgeschools.org
Cherry Hill ES 600/K-6
410 Bogert Rd 07661 201-261-3405
Denise Heitman, prin. Fax 986-1256
Roosevelt ES 500/K-6
711 Summit Ave 07661 201-261-1546
Anthony Vouvalides, prin. Fax 261-0798

St. Peter Academy 200/PK-8
431 5th Ave 07661 201-261-3468
Sr. Barbara Takacs, prin. Fax 261-4316
Yeshiva of North Jersey S 800/K-8
666 Kinderkamack Rd 07661 201-986-1414

Riverside, Burlington, Pop. 7,974
Riverside Township SD 1,400/PK-12
112 E Washington St 08075 856-461-1255
Robert Goldschmidt, supt. Fax 461-5168
www.riverside.k12.nj.us
Riverside ES 600/PK-5
112 E Washington St 08075 856-461-1255
Scott Shumway, prin. Fax 461-1674

Riverside MS 300/6-8
112 E Washington St 08075 856-461-1255
Robin Ehrich, prin. Fax 461-7277

Riverton, Burlington, Pop. 2,739
Riverton Borough SD 200/K-8
600 5th St 08077 856-829-0087
Mary Ellen Eck, supt. Fax 829-5317
www.riverton.k12.nj.us
Riverton S 200/K-8
600 5th St 08077 856-829-0087
Mary Ellen Eck, prin. Fax 829-5317

Orchard Friends S 50/K-8
405 Linden Ave 08077 856-786-1123
Kevin Cerula, hdmstr. Fax 786-0349

River Vale, Bergen, Pop. 9,410
River Vale SD 1,300/K-8
609 Westwood Ave 07675 201-358-4000
David Verducci Ph.D., supt. Fax 358-8319
www.rivervaleschools.com/
Holdrum MS 400/6-8
393 Rivervale Rd 07675 201-358-4016
Jayellen Jenkins, prin. Fax 358-8427
Roberge ES 400/K-5
617 Westwood Ave 07675 201-358-4006
James Tis, prin.
Woodside ES 500/K-5
801 Rivervale Rd 07675 201-358-4028
Allen Spatola, prin. Fax 358-8335

Robbinsville, Mercer
Robbinsville SD 2,100/K-12
155 Robbinsville Edinburg 08691 609-632-0910
Dr. John Szabo, supt. Fax 371-7964
www.robbinsville.k12.nj.us
Pond Road MS 1,000/4-8
150 Pond Rd 08691 609-632-0940
Paul Gizzo, prin. Fax 918-9011
Sharon ES 800/K-3
234 Sharon Rd 08691 609-632-0960
Janet Sinkewicz, prin. Fax 259-7506
Other Schools – See Windsor

Rochelle Park, Bergen, Pop. 5,587
Rochelle Park SD 500/PK-8
300 Rochelle Ave 07662 201-843-3120
Dr. C. Lauren Schoen, supt. Fax 843-7293
www.bergen.org/edpartners/midland
Midland S 1 500/PK-8
300 Rochelle Ave 07662 201-843-3120
Mark Mongon, prin. Fax 843-7293

Rockaway, Morris, Pop. 6,419
Rockaway Borough SD 600/K-8
103 E Main St 07866 973-625-8601
Emil Suarez, supt. Fax 625-7355
www.rockboro.org/
Jefferson MS, 95 E Main St 07866 300/5-8
Patrick Tierney, prin. 973-625-8603
Lincoln ES, 37 Keller Ave 07866 300/K-4
Phyllis Alpaugh, prin. 973-625-8602

Rockaway Township SD
Supt. — See Hibernia
Copeland MS 1,000/6-8
100 Lake Shore Dr 07866 973-627-2465
F. Scott Allshouse, prin. Fax 983-1843
Malone ES 400/K-5
524 Green Pond Rd 07866 973-627-7512
Stephen Gottlieb, prin. Fax 627-1729
Stony Brook ES 400/K-5
18 1/2 Stony Brook Rd 07866 973-627-2411
Dr. Margaret McCluskey, prin. Fax 627-1689

Sacred Heart S 200/PK-8
40 E Main St 07866 973-627-7689
Sr. Marie DiLorenzo, prin. Fax 627-2500
St. Cecilia S 300/PK-8
87 Halsey Ave 07866 973-627-6003
Sr. Marie Elise Briel, prin. Fax 627-5217

Roebling, Burlington
Florence Township SD
Supt. — See Florence
Roebling ES 500/K-3
1330 Hornberger Ave 08554 609-499-4640
David Connor, prin. Fax 499-4664

Roosevelt, Monmouth, Pop. 917
Roosevelt Borough SD 100/PK-6
PO Box 160 08555 609-448-2798
Shari Payson, supt. Fax 448-2681
www.rps1.org
Roosevelt ES 100/PK-6
PO Box 160 08555 609-448-2798
Shari Payson, prin. Fax 448-2681

Roseland, Essex, Pop. 5,402
Roseland SD 500/K-6
100 Passaic Ave 07068 973-226-1296
Richard Sierchio, supt. Fax 228-0407
www.lestercnoecker.org
Noecker ES 500/K-6
100 Passaic Ave 07068 973-226-7644
Doreen Schwarz, prin. Fax 226-3074

Roselle, Union, Pop. 21,265
Roselle Borough SD 2,700/K-12
710 Locust St 07203 908-298-2040
Dr. Elnardo Webster, supt. Fax 298-3353
www.roselleschools.org
Harrison ES 300/K-3
310 Harrison Ave 07203 908-298-2052
Lissette Gonzalez-Perez, prin. Fax 298-3371
Moore MS 400/4-5
720 Locust St 07203 908-298-2047
Alexis Osterhoudt, prin. Fax 298-3333

Polk ES 300/K-3
1100 Warren St 07203 908-298-2061
Andreea Harry, prin. Fax 298-3381
Washington ES 300/K-3
501 W 5th Ave 07203 908-298-2072
Dana Walker, prin. Fax 298-9450
Wilday MS 400/6-7
400 Brooklawn Ave 07203 908-298-2040
Reginald Mirthil, prin. Fax 298-2068

St. Joseph the Carpenter S 300/PK-8
140 E 3rd Ave 07203 908-245-6560
Maryellen Woodstock, prin. Fax 245-3342

Roselle Park, Union, Pop. 13,189
Roselle Park SD 1,800/K-12
510 Chestnut St 07204 908-245-1197
Patrick Spagnoletti, supt. Fax 245-1226
www.roselleparkschools.org
Finzio-Aldene ES 300/K-5
339 W Webster Ave 07204 908-245-1521
Virginia Gilcrest, prin. Fax 245-5168
Gordon ES 300/K-5
59 W Grant Ave 07204 908-245-2285
James Salvo, prin. Fax 245-4574
Roselle Park MS 300/6-7
57 W Grant Ave 07204 908-245-1634
Jeannine Grasso, prin. Fax 245-7491
Sherman ES 300/K-5
375 E Grant Ave 07204 908-245-1886
Mary Christensen, prin. Fax 245-4741

Rosenhayn, Cumberland, Pop. 1,053
Deerfield Township SD 300/K-8
PO Box 375 08352 856-451-6610
Edythe Austermuhl Ed.D., supt. Fax 451-6720
www.deerfield.k12.nj.us/
Deerfield Township S 300/K-8
PO Box 375 08352 856-451-6610
Edythe Austermuhl Ed.D., prin. Fax 451-6720

Rumson, Monmouth, Pop. 7,233
Rumson Borough SD 900/K-8
60 Forrest Ave 07760 732-842-4747
Roger Caruba, supt. Fax 842-4877
www.rumson.k12.nj.us
Deane-Porter ES 400/K-3
12 Black Point Rd 07760 732-842-0330
Richard Karas, prin.
Forrestdale MS, 60 Forrest Ave 07760 600/4-8
Jennifer Gibbons, prin. 732-842-0383

Holy Cross S 400/PK-8
40 Rumson Rd 07760 732-842-0348
Patricia Graham, prin. Fax 741-3134
Rumson Country Day S 400/PK-8
35 Bellevue Ave 07760 732-842-0527
Chad Small, hdmstr. Fax 758-6528

Runnemede, Camden, Pop. 8,520
Runnemede Borough SD 700/K-8
505 W 3rd Ave 08078 856-931-5365
Nancy Ward, supt. Fax 931-4446
Bingham ES, 100 Orchard Ave 08078 200/K-3
Marie Gallagher, prin. 856-939-3192
Downing ES, 100 E 3rd Ave 08078 200/K-3
Marie Gallagher, prin. 856-939-4036
Volz MS, 505 W 3rd Ave 08078 400/4-8
David Gentile, prin. 856-931-5353

St. Teresa Regional S 200/K-8
27 E Evesham Rd 08078 856-939-0333
Sr. Patricia Scanlon, prin. Fax 939-1204

Rutherford, Bergen, Pop. 17,967
Rutherford SD 2,400/K-12
176 Park Ave 07070 201-939-1717
Leslie O'Keefe, supt. Fax 939-6350
www.rutherfordschools.org
Lincoln ES 300/K-3
414 Montross Ave 07070 201-438-7675
Jeanna Velechko, prin. Fax 438-4915
Pierrepont S 500/4-8
70 E Pierrepont Ave 07070 201-438-7675
Margaret Vaccarino, prin. Fax 842-0452
Union S 500/4-8
359 Union Ave 07070 201-438-7675
Kenneth Polakowski, prin. Fax 804-8248
Washington ES 300/K-3
89 Wood St 07070 201-438-7675
William Mulcahy, prin. Fax 438-5386

St. Mary S 200/PK-8
72 Chestnut St 07070 201-933-8410
Elena Simmons, prin. Fax 531-9020
Yeshivas Mesillah 6-8
185 Montross Ave 07070 201-372-0020

Saddle Brook, Bergen, Pop. 13,296
Saddle Brook Township SD 1,500/K-12
355 Mayhill St 07663 201-843-2133
Dr. Harry Groveman, supt. Fax 843-8265
www.saddlebrookschools.org/
Franklin ES 300/K-6
95 Caldwell Ave 07663 201-843-8664
Salvatore Cusmano, prin. Fax 843-3231
Long Memorial ES 300/K-6
260 Floral Ln 07663 201-796-6250
Dorothy Gorman, prin. Fax 796-1671
Smith ES 300/K-6
230 Cambridge Ave 07663 201-796-6650
Caroline Gaynor, prin. Fax 796-0665

Saddle River, Bergen, Pop. 3,766
Saddle River SD 200/PK-5
97 E Allendale Rd 07458 201-327-0727
Dr. David Goldblatt, supt. Fax 327-0704
www.wandellschool.org

Wandell ES 200/PK-5
97 E Allendale Rd 07458 201-327-0727
Dr. David Goldblatt, prin. Fax 327-0704

Saddle River Day S 300/K-12
147 Chestnut Ridge Rd 07458 201-327-4050
Michael Eanes, hdmstr. Fax 327-6161

Salem, Salem, Pop. 5,812
Elsinboro Township SD 100/K-8
631 Salem Fort Elfsborg Rd 08079 856-935-3817
Constance McAllister, admin. Fax 935-6944
www.elsinboroschool.org
Elsinboro Township S 100/K-8
631 Salem Fort Elfsborg Rd 08079 856-935-3817
Constance McAllister, prin. Fax 935-6944

Lower Alloways Creek Township SD 200/PK-8
967 Main St 08079 856-935-2707
Fred Pratta, supt. Fax 935-9673
www.lac-k8.net/
Lower Alloways Creek S 200/PK-8
967 Main St 08079 856-935-2707
Fred Pratta, prin. Fax 935-9673

Mannington Township SD 200/PK-8
495 Route 45 08079 856-935-1078
Dr. Walter Uszenski, supt. Fax 935-3747
www.manningtonschool.org/
Mannington Township S 200/PK-8
495 Route 45 08079 856-935-1078
Dr. Walter Uszenski, prin. Fax 935-3747

Salem CSD 1,400/PK-12
205 Walnut St 08079 856-935-3800
Patrick Michel, supt. Fax 935-6977
www.salemnj.org
Fenwick ES 400/PK-2
183 Smith St 08079 856-935-4100
Carol Burke-Doherty, prin. Fax 935-1252
Salem MS 500/3-8
51 New Market St 08079 856-935-2700
John Mulhorn, prin. Fax 935-2284

Sayreville, Middlesex, Pop. 43,017
Sayreville SD
Supt. — See South Amboy
Wilson ES 300/K-3
65 Dane St 08872 732-525-5239
Georgia Baumann, prin. Fax 698-9529

Agapeland Childcare Center 100/PK-K
2707 Main St 08872 732-727-7999
Jaclyn Demola-Pitre, dir. Fax 727-5796
Our Lady of Victories S 200/PK-8
36 Main St 08872 732-254-1676
Rosalind Esemplare, prin. Fax 254-5066
St. Stanislaus Kostka S 200/PK-8
221 MacArthur Ave 08872 732-254-5819
Harriet Samim, prin. Fax 254-7220

Scotch Plains, Union, Pop. 21,160
Scotch Plains-Fanwood SD 5,200/PK-12
2280 Evergreen Ave 07076 908-232-6161
Dr. Margaret Hayes, supt. Fax 889-1769
www.spfk12.org
Brunner ES 400/PK-4
721 Westfield Rd 07076 908-889-2148
Jodi Frank, prin. Fax 889-4718
Coles ES 500/PK-4
16 Kevin Rd 07076 908-757-7555
Dr. Deborah Evans, prin. Fax 561-1840
Evergreen ES 400/PK-4
2280 Evergreen Ave 07076 908-889-5331
Colleen Haubert, prin. Fax 889-9332
McGinn ES 500/K-4
1100 Roosevelt Ave 07076 908-233-7950
Susan Kukucka, prin. Fax 233-6766
Park MS 700/5-8
580 Park Ave 07076 908-322-4445
Lisa Rebimbas, prin. Fax 561-5929
School One 400/K-4
563 Willow Ave 07076 908-322-7731
Jeffrey Grysko, prin. Fax 322-7142
Terrill MS 900/5-8
1301 Terrill Rd 07076 908-322-5215
Kevin Holloway, prin. Fax 322-6813

St. Bartholomew Academy 200/PK-8
2032 Westfield Ave 07076 908-322-4265
Sr. Elizabeth Calello, prin. Fax 322-7065

Seabrook, Cumberland, Pop. 1,457
Upper Deerfield Township SD 900/PK-8
1369 Highway 77 08302 856-455-2267
Dr. Philip Exley, supt. Fax 455-0419
Moore ES 200/4-5
1361 Highway 77 08302 856-455-2267
Mercedes Berrios, prin. Fax 451-8678
Seabrook ES 400/PK-3
1373 Highway 77 08302 856-455-2267
Morris Gaburo, prin. Fax 451-1930
Woodruff MS 300/6-8
1385 Highway 77 08302 856-455-2267
Dr. James Turner, prin. Fax 453-7077

Sea Girt, Monmouth, Pop. 2,069
Sea Girt Borough SD 200/K-8
451 Bell Pl 08750 732-449-3422
Stephen LaValva, supt. Fax 449-1204
www.seagirt.k12.nj.us
Sea Girt S 200/K-8
451 Bell Pl 08750 732-449-3422
Stephen LaValva, prin. Fax 449-1204

Wall Township SD
Supt. — See Wall
Old Mill ES 500/K-5
2119 Old Mill Rd 08750 732-556-2140
Eric Laughlin, prin. Fax 449-4260

Brookside S 200/PK-8
2135 Highway 35 08750 732-449-4747
John Quakenbush, dir. Fax 449-4547

Sea Isle City, Cape May, Pop. 2,968
Sea Isle City SD 100/PK-8
4501 Park Rd 08243 609-263-8461
Michael Schreiner Ed.D., supt. Fax 263-6142
www.seaisleschool.com
Sea Isle S 100/PK-8
4501 Park Rd 08243 609-263-8461
James Thompson, prin. Fax 263-6142

Seaside Heights, Ocean, Pop. 3,220
Seaside Heights Borough SD 200/PK-6
1200 Bay Blvd 08751 732-793-8485
Michael Ritacco, supt. Fax 793-5874
www.ssheights.k12.nj.us/
Boyd ES 200/PK-6
1200 Bay Blvd 08751 732-793-8485
Gemma MacCarrick Ed.D., prin. Fax 793-5874

Seaside Park, Ocean, Pop. 2,301
Seaside Park Borough SD 100/K-6
107 3rd Ave 08752 732-793-0177
Theresa Hamilton, supt. Fax 793-9028
www.seasideparkschool.com/
Seaside Park ES 100/K-6
313 SW Central Ave 08752 732-793-0177
Thomas Matthews, prin. Fax 793-9028

Secaucus, Hudson, Pop. 15,623
Secaucus SD 2,000/PK-12
PO Box 1496 07096 201-974-2004
Cynthia Randina, supt. Fax 974-1911
www.sboe.org
Clarendon ES 600/PK-6
685 5th St 07094 201-974-2012
Deidre Ertle, prin. Fax 974-0530
Huber Street ES 500/PK-6
1520 Paterson Plank Rd 07094 201-974-2055
Fred Ponti, prin. Fax 974-0626
Secaucus MS 300/7-8
11 Millridge Rd 07094 201-974-2025
Pasquale Cocucci, prin. Fax 974-0026

Immaculate Conception S 100/PK-8
760 Post Pl 07094 201-864-9346
Beverly Trotte, prin. Fax 864-0245

Sergeantsville, Hunterdon
Delaware Township SD 500/K-8
PO Box 1000 08557 609-397-3179
Dr. Richard Wiener, supt. Fax 397-0057
www.dtsk8.org
Delaware Township S 500/K-8
PO Box 1000 08557 609-397-3179
Patricia Ryan, prin. Fax 397-1485

Sewaren, Middlesex, Pop. 2,569
Woodbridge Township SD
Supt. — See Woodbridge
Jago ES 300/K-5
99 Central Ave 07077 732-602-8428
Robert Patten, prin. Fax 855-0826

Sewell, Gloucester
Deptford Township SD
Supt. — See Deptford
Monongahela MS 600/7-8
890 Bankbridge Rd 08080 856-415-9540
Brian Wert, prin. Fax 464-9284

Mantua Township SD 1,500/K-6
684 Main St 08080 856-468-2225
Steven Crispin, supt. Fax 468-5563
www.mantuaschools.com
Sewell ES 300/K-4
40 McAnally Dr 08080 856-468-0626
Daniel McKee, prin. Fax 468-7130
Other Schools – See Mantua

Washington Township SD 8,300/PK-12
206 E Holly Ave 08080 856-589-6644
Dr. Cheryl Simone, supt. Fax 582-1918
www.wtps.org
Bunker Hill MS 700/6-8
372 Pitman Downer Rd 08080 856-881-7007
Mark Ebner, prin. Fax 881-5414
Chestnut Ridge MS 700/6-8
641 Hurffville Crosskeys Rd 08080 856-582-3535
James Barnes, prin. Fax 589-0683
Grenloch Terrace ECC 500/PK-K
251 Woodbury Turnersville 08080 856-227-1303
Wendy Crawford, prin. Fax 227-8207
Hurffville ES 500/1-5
200 Hurffville Grenloch Rd 08080 856-589-7459
JoAnne Robertson, prin. Fax 589-6909
Orchard Valley MS 700/6-8
238 Pitman Downer Rd 08080 856-582-5353
Stephan Buono, prin. Fax 589-0197
Wedgwood ES 500/1-5
236 Hurffville Rd 08080 856-227-8110
Michael Landon, prin. Fax 227-8163
Other Schools – See Turnersville

Bethel Prep Classical Christian Academy 100/K-9
359 Chapel Heights Rd 08080 856-270-6022
Rev. Robert Barber, hdmstr. Fax 582-9228
Gloucester County Christian S 400/PK-12
151 Golf Club Rd 08080 856-589-1665
Donald Netz, prin. Fax 582-4989

Shamong Township, Burlington, Pop. 5,765
Shamong Township SD 900/K-8
295 Indian Mills Rd 08088 609-268-0120
Thomas Christensen, supt. Fax 268-1229
www.ims.k12.nj.us
Indian Mills ES 500/K-4
112 Indian Mills Rd 08088 609-268-0220
Nicole Moore, prin. Fax 268-9535
Indian Mills Memorial MS 400/5-8
295 Indian Mills Rd 08088 609-268-0440
Timothy Carroll, prin. Fax 268-1229

Ship Bottom, Ocean, Pop. 1,418
Long Beach Island SD
Supt. — See Surf City
Long Beach Island ES 100/3-6
1901 Central Ave 08008 609-494-8851
Frances Meyer, prin. Fax 494-8035

Short Hills, Essex
Millburn Township SD
Supt. — See Millburn
Deerfield ES 500/K-5
26 Troy Ln 07078 973-379-4843
Kelly Salazar, prin. Fax 912-4456
Glenwood ES 500/K-5
325 Taylor Rd S 07078 973-379-7576
David Jasin, prin. Fax 912-4497
Hartshorn ES 600/K-5
400 Hartshorn Dr 07078 973-379-7550
Ronald Castaldo, prin. Fax 912-5205

Far Brook S 200/PK-8
52 Great Hills Rd 07078 973-379-3442
Murray Lopdell-Lawrence, hdmstr. Fax 379-6740
St. Rose of Lima S 300/PK-8
52 Short Hills Ave 07078 973-379-3973
Judith Mautone, prin. Fax 379-3722
Winston S 100/1-8
100 East Ln 07078 973-379-4114
Pamela Bloom, hdmstr. Fax 379-3984

Shrewsbury, Monmouth, Pop. 3,742
Shrewsbury Borough SD 500/K-8
20 Obre Pl 07702 732-747-0882
Brent MacConnell, supt. Fax 747-7510
www.sbs.k12.nj.us
Shrewsbury S 500/K-8
20 Obre Pl 07702 732-747-0882
Brent MacConnell, prin. Fax 747-7510

Sicklerville, Camden
Gloucester Township SD
Supt. — See Blackwood
Erial ES 700/K-5
20 Essex Ave 08081 856-627-5415
Timothy Trow, prin. Fax 783-6003
Mullen MS 1,200/6-8
1400 Sicklerville Rd 08081 856-875-8777
Joanne Acerba, prin. Fax 875-0902

Winslow Township SD
Supt. — See Atco
Winslow Township ES 2 400/PK-2
125 1st Ave 08081 609-561-8450
Dr. Maureen Grippen, prin. Fax 704-1024
Winslow Township ES 3 500/PK-2
131 Sicklerville Rd 08081 856-728-1080
Monalisa Kalina, prin. Fax 875-5147
Winslow Township ES 4 500/PK-2
541 Kali Rd 08081 856-728-2440
Deborah Lupia, prin. Fax 875-5401
Winslow Township Upper ES 6 700/3-5
617 Sickler Ave 08081 856-875-4110
Dr. Robert Riccardi, prin. Fax 875-8052

Skillman, Somerset
Montgomery Township SD 5,200/K-12
1014 Route 601 08558 609-466-7601
Earl Kim, supt. Fax 466-0944
www.mtsd.k12.nj.us
Montgomery Lower MS 800/5-6
373 Burnt Hill Rd 08558 609-466-7604
Michael Richards, prin. Fax 874-4857
Montgomery Upper MS 800/7-8
375 Burnt Hill Rd 08558 609-466-7603
William Robbins, prin. Fax 874-7045
Orchard Hill ES 1,000/K-2
244 Orchard Rd 08558 609-466-7605
Thomas Barclay, prin. Fax 359-1126
Village ES 800/3-4
100 Main Blvd 08558 609-466-7606
Susan Lacy, prin. Fax 333-0280

Somerdale, Camden, Pop. 5,155
Somerdale Borough SD 500/PK-8
301 Grace St 08083 856-783-2933
Dr. Debra Bruner, supt. Fax 783-2607
www.somerdale-park.org
Somerdale Park S 500/PK-8
301 Grace St 08083 856-783-2933
Kristine Height, prin. Fax 783-2607

Somerset, Somerset, Pop. 22,070
Franklin Township SD 7,100/PK-12
1755 Amwell Rd 08873 732-873-2400
Edward Seto, supt. Fax 873-2132
www.franklinboe.org
Conerly Road ES 400/PK-4
35 Conerly Rd 08873 732-249-9362
Donna Silva-Burnett, prin. Fax 247-7076
Elizabeth Avenue ES 500/PK-4
363 Elizabeth Ave 08873 732-356-0113
Gloria Harzold, prin. Fax 271-2534
Franklin MS 1,000/7-8
415 Francis St 08873 732-249-6410
Roberta Mitchell, prin. Fax 246-0770
Hillcrest ES 400/PK-4
500 Franklin Blvd 08873 732-246-0170
Joan Harris, prin. Fax 247-8405
MacAfee Road ES 400/PK-4
53 MacAfee Rd 08873 732-249-9097
Gerald Rosen, prin. Fax 247-1408
Pine Grove Manor ES 400/PK-4
130 Highland Ave 08873 732-246-2424
Jennifer Whitner, prin. Fax 843-5572
Smith Upper ES 1,100/5-6
1649 Amwell Rd 08873 732-873-2800
William Grippo, prin. Fax 873-0451
Other Schools – See Franklin Park

Community Baptist Christian Academy 100/PK-2
211 Demott Ln 08873 732-246-9383
Terry Taylor, dir. Fax 246-1884
Rutgers Prep S 700/PK-12
1345 Easton Ave 08873 732-545-5600
Dr. Steven Loy, hdmstr. Fax 214-1819
St. Matthias S 600/PK-8
170 John F Kennedy Blvd 08873 732-828-1402
Dr. Anthony Ingenito, prin. Fax 846-3099

Somers Point, Atlantic, Pop. 11,701
Somers Point SD 1,100/PK-8
121 W New York Ave 08244 609-927-2053
Gerald Toscano, supt. Fax 927-7351
www.somersptschools.org/
Dawes Avenue ES 300/K-6
22 W Dawes Ave 08244 609-653-1027
Doreen Lee, prin. Fax 653-6143
Jordan Road S 700/K-8
129 Jordan Rd 08244 609-927-7161
Jeff Miller, prin. Fax 927-9648
New York Avenue S 50/PK-PK
121 W New York Ave 08244 609-653-1027
Susan Dugan, prin.

St. Joseph Regional S 400/K-8
11 Harbor Ln 08244 609-927-2228
Sr. Frances Kane, prin. Fax 927-7834

Somerville, Somerset, Pop. 12,478
Somerville Borough SD 2,100/K-12
51 W Cliff St 08876 908-218-4101
Dr. Carolyn Leary, supt. Fax 526-9668
www.somervillenjk12.org
Somerville MS, 51 W Cliff St 08876 400/6-8
Georgette Boulegeris, prin. 908-218-4107
Van Derveer ES, 51 Union Ave 08876 700/K-5
Susan Haynes, prin. 908-218-4105

Immaculate Conception S 500/PK-8
41 Mountain Ave 08876 908-725-6516
Sr. John Magdalen, prin. Fax 725-3172

South Amboy, Middlesex, Pop. 7,975
Sayreville SD 5,400/K-12
150 Lincoln St 08879 732-525-5203
Dr. Frank Alfano, supt. Fax 727-5769
www.sayrevillek12.net/
Other Schools – See Parlin, Sayreville

South Amboy SD 1,100/PK-12
240 John St 08879 732-525-2102
Robert Sheedy, supt. Fax 727-0730
www.saboe.k12.nj.us/
South Amboy ES 600/PK-6
249 John St 08879 732-525-2118
William Ciullo, prin. Fax 316-1588

Sacred Heart S 300/PK-8
PO Box 728 08879 732-721-0834
Sr. Marie Connolly, prin. Fax 316-0326

Southampton, Burlington
Southampton Township SD 800/K-8
177 Main St 08088 609-859-2256
Michael Harris, supt. Fax 859-1542
www.southampton.k12.nj.us
Southampton Township IS 2 300/3-5
100 Miss Mabel Dr 08088 609-859-2256
Jennifer Horner, prin. Fax 859-3048
Southampton Township MS 3 300/6-8
100 Warrior Way 08088 609-859-2256
Jennifer Horner, prin. Fax 801-0754
Southampton Township PS 1 200/K-2
26 Pleasant St 08088 609-859-2256
Sharon Danfield, prin. Fax 859-0142

South Bound Brook, Somerset, Pop. 4,505
South Bound Brook Borough SD 400/K-8
122 Elizabeth St 08880 732-356-0018
Dr. Carol Rosevear, supt. Fax 356-0621
www.rmschool.com
Morris S 400/K-8
122 Elizabeth St 08880 732-356-3018
Dennis Donahue, prin. Fax 356-0621

South Hackensack, Bergen
South Hackensack SD 200/PK-8
1 Dyer Ave 07606 201-440-2783
Dr. William DeFabiis, supt. Fax 440-9156
Memorial S 200/PK-8
1 Dyer Ave 07606 201-440-2783
Dr. William DeFabiis, prin. Fax 440-9156

South Orange, Essex, Pop. 16,390
South Orange-Maplewood SD
Supt. — See Maplewood
Marshall ES 400/K-2
262 Grove Rd 07079 973-378-7698
Angelica Allen, prin. Fax 378-5243
South Mountain ES 300/2-5
444 W South Orange Ave 07079 973-378-5216
Thomas Gibbons, prin. Fax 378-5620
South Mountain ES Annex 200/K-1
112 Glenview Rd 07079 973-378-2801
Thomas Gibbons, prin. Fax 378-2033
South Orange MS 700/6-8
70 N Ridgewood Rd 07079 973-378-2772
Kirk Smith, prin. Fax 378-2775

Our Lady of Sorrows S 200/PK-8
172 Academy St 07079 973-762-5169
Sr. Judith Blair, prin. Fax 378-9781

South Plainfield, Middlesex, Pop. 23,064
South Plainfield SD 3,700/K-12
125 Jackson Ave 07080 908-754-4620
Jose Negron Ed.D., supt. Fax 754-3960
www.spnet.k12.nj.us
Franklin ES 300/K-4
1000 Franklin Ave 07080 908-754-4620
Ellen Decker-Lorys, prin. Fax 754-8819
Grant ES 600/5-6
305 Cromwell Pl 07080 908-754-4620
Leo Whalen, prin. Fax 755-5895
Kennedy ES 300/K-4
2900 Norwood Ave 07080 908-754-4620
Kelly Richkus, prin. Fax 754-8659
Riley ES 300/K-4
100 Morris Ave 07080 908-754-4620
Al Czech, prin. Fax 754-8591
Roosevelt ES 400/K-4
135 Jackson Ave 07080 908-754-4620
Robert Diehl, prin. Fax 822-9375
South Plainfield MS 600/7-8
2201 Plainfield Ave 07080 908-754-4620
Steven Novak, prin. Fax 791-1152

Sacred Heart S 200/PK-8
1 Sacred Heart Dr 07080 908-756-0632
Sr. Mary Nadine Boyle, prin. Fax 756-2650

South River, Middlesex, Pop. 16,060
South River SD 2,000/K-12
15 Montgomery St 08882 732-613-4000
Ronald Grygo, supt. Fax 613-4756
www.srivernj.org
South River ES 500/K-K, 3-5
81 Johnson Pl 08882 732-613-4073
Wayne Sherman, prin. Fax 698-9269
South River MS 500/6-8
3 Montgomery St 08882 732-613-4073
Dr. Richard Sternberg, prin. Fax 698-9305
South River PS 500/K-2
22 David St 08882 732-613-4006
Dorothy Unkel, prin. Fax 613-4020

Sparta, Sussex, Pop. 15,157
Sparta Township SD 4,000/K-12
18 Mohawk Ave 07871 973-729-7886
Dr. J. Thomas Morton, supt. Fax 729-0576
www.sparta.org
Mohawk Avenue S 400/5-5
18 Mohawk Ave 07871 973-729-1289
Michael Gregory, prin. Fax 729-5574
Morgan ES 600/K-4
100 Stanhope Rd 07871 973-729-5770
Lorise Goeke Ed.D., prin. Fax 729-0245
Sparta Alpine ES 800/K-4
151 Andover Rd 07871 973-729-3107
Laura Trent, prin. Fax 729-0483
Sparta MS 1,000/6-8
350 Main St 07871 973-729-3151
Linda Nick, prin. Fax 729-0573

Brown Memorial S 500/PK-8
294 Sparta Ave 07871 973-729-9174
Dr. Catherine Duncan, prin. Fax 729-0318
Hilltop Country Day S 200/PK-8
32 Lafayette Rd 07871 973-729-5485
Joseph Stefani, hdmstr. Fax 729-9057

Spotswood, Middlesex, Pop. 8,237
Spotswood SD 1,700/PK-12
105 Summerhill Rd 08884 732-723-2236
John Krewer Ed.D., supt. Fax 251-7666
www.spotswood.k12.nj.us
Appleby ES 400/2-5
23 Vliet St 08884 732-723-2213
Karen Boyle, prin. Fax 251-7666
Schoenly ES 200/PK-1
80 Kane Ave 08884 732-723-2220
Jon Cochran, prin. Fax 251-7666
Spotswood Memorial MS 300/6-8
115 Summerhill Rd 08884 732-723-2227
Michael Mastroserio, prin. Fax 251-7666

Immaculate Conception S 600/PK-8
23 Manalapan Rd 08884 732-251-3090
Mary Hamm, prin. Fax 251-8270
United Academy, 208 Main St 08884 200/K-8

Springfield, Union, Pop. 13,420
Springfield SD 2,000/PK-12
PO Box 210 07081 973-376-1025
Michael Davino, supt. Fax 912-9229
www.springfieldschools.com
Caldwell ES 200/3-5
36 Caldwell Pl 07081 973-376-1025
David Rennie, prin. Fax 379-8372
Gaudineer MS 400/6-8
75 S Springfield Ave 07081 973-376-1025
Timothy Kielty, prin. Fax 376-3259
Sandmeier ES 200/3-5
666 S Springfield Ave 07081 973-376-1025
Michael Antolino, prin. Fax 379-8371
Walton ES 600/PK-2
601 Mountain Ave 07081 973-376-1025
Dr. Suzy Hung, prin. Fax 258-0753

Holy Cross Christian Nursery S & K 100/PK-K
639 Mountain Ave 07081 973-379-7160
Donna Hydock, dir. Fax 379-8887

St. James the Apostle S 200/PK-8
41 S Springfield Ave 07081 973-376-5194
Patricia Dolansky, prin. Fax 376-5228

Spring Lake, Monmouth, Pop. 3,506
Spring Lake Borough SD 300/PK-8
411 Tuttle Ave 07762 732-449-6380
Patricia Wright, supt. Fax 449-2058
www.hwmountz.k12.nj.us
Mountz S 300/PK-8
411 Tuttle Ave 07762 732-449-6380
Patricia Wright, prin. Fax 449-2058

St. Catharine S 500/K-8
301 2nd Ave 07762 732-449-4424
Sr. Margo Kavanaugh, prin. Fax 449-7876

Spring Lake Heights, Monmouth, Pop. 5,135
Spring Lake Heights Borough SD 400/K-8
1110 Highway 71 07762 732-449-6149
Ruth Ziznewski, supt. Fax 449-9429
www.slh.k12.nj.us
Spring Lake Heights S 400/K-8
1110 Highway 71 07762 732-449-6149
Ruth Ziznewski, prin. Fax 449-9492

Stanhope, Sussex, Pop. 3,701
Byram Township SD 1,100/K-8
12 Mansfield Dr 07874 973-347-6663
Dr. Gayle Strauss, supt. Fax 347-9001
www.byramschools.org
Byram IS 500/5-8
12 Mansfield Dr 07874 973-347-1019
Jack Leonard, prin. Fax 347-9001
Byram Lakes ES 600/K-4
11 Mansfield Dr 07874 973-347-1019
Dr. Thomas Podgurski, prin. Fax 691-7771

Stanhope Borough SD 400/K-8
24 Valley Rd 07874 973-347-0008
Arthur DiBenedetto, supt. Fax 347-8368
www.stanhopeschools.org/
Valley Road S 400/K-8
24 Valley Rd 07874 973-347-0008
Clifford Burns, prin. Fax 347-8368

Stewartsville, Warren
Greenwich Township SD 900/K-8
101 Wyndham Farm Blvd 08886 908-859-2022
Maria Eppolite, supt. Fax 859-4522
www.greenwichschool.org
Greenwich S 600/K-5
101 Wyndham Farm Blvd 08886 908-859-2022
Sarah Bilotti, prin. Fax 859-4522
Stewartsville MS 300/6-8
642 S Main St 08886 908-859-2023
Patricia Lantz, prin. Fax 859-1809

Stillwater, Sussex
Stillwater Township SD 400/K-6
PO Box 12 07875 973-383-6171
S. William Shelton, admin. Fax 383-7021
www.stillwaterschool.net
Stillwater Township ES 400/K-6
PO Box 12 07875 973-383-6171
Anna Memmelaar, prin. Fax 383-1895

Stirling, Morris
Long Hill Township SD
Supt. — See Gillette
Central MS 400/6-8
90 Central Ave 07980 908-647-2311
Richard Cimino, prin. Fax 647-0610

St. Vincent De Paul S 200/PK-8
249 Bebout Ave 07980 908-647-0421
Nora Didia, prin. Fax 647-3878

Stockton, Hunterdon, Pop. 560
Stockton Borough SD 50/K-6
19 S Main St 08559 609-397-2012
Suzanne Ivans, supt. Fax 397-2602
www.stocktonschool.us
Stockton ES 50/K-6
19 S Main St 08559 609-397-2012
Suzanne Ivans, prin. Fax 397-2602

Stone Harbor, Cape May, Pop. 1,062
Stone Harbor SD 100/K-8
275 93rd St 08247 609-368-4413
David Rauenzahn, supt. Fax 368-6545
Stone Harbor S 100/K-8
275 93rd St 08247 609-368-4413
David Rauanzahn, prin. Fax 368-6545

Stratford, Camden, Pop. 7,184
Stratford Borough SD 800/K-8
111 Warwick Rd 08084 856-783-2555
Albert Brown, supt. Fax 309-0304
www.stratford.k12.nj.us
Parkview ES 300/K-3
123 Parkview Rd 08084 856-783-2876
Michele D'Amore, prin. Fax 783-3468
Yellin MS 500/4-8
111 Warwick Rd 08084 856-783-1094
Thomas Attanasi, prin. Fax 309-0304

John Paul II Regional S 200/PK-8
55 Warwick Rd 08084 856-783-3088
Helen Persing, prin. Fax 783-9302
Stratford Classical Christian Academy 50/K-7
710 W Laurel Rd 08084 856-882-7222
Sidney Henriquez, admin. Fax 882-7226

Succasunna, Morris, Pop. 11,781
Roxbury Township SD 4,300/K-12
42 N Hillside Ave 07876 973-584-6867
Dr. Michael Rossi, supt. Fax 252-1434
www.roxbury.org
Eisenhower MS 700/7-8
47 Eyland Ave 07876 973-584-2973
Lee Nittel, prin. Fax 584-4529
Franklin ES 400/K-4
8 Meeker St 07876 973-584-5549
Mary Ann Boyd, prin. Fax 252-1151
Jefferson ES 500/K-4
35 Cornhollow Rd 07876 973-584-8955
Karen Carlson, prin. Fax 584-4380
Kennedy ES 300/K-4
24 Pleasant Hill Rd 07876 973-584-3938
Audrey Wallock, prin. Fax 584-8098
Lincoln/Roosevelt ES 600/5-6
34 N Hillside Ave 07876 973-584-4331
Jack Curtis, prin. Fax 584-4257
Other Schools – See Landing

American Christian S 100/PK-9
126 S Hillside Ave 07876 973-584-6616
Dr. Carol Midkiff, hdmstr. Fax 584-0686
St. Therese S 200/K-8
135 Main St 07876 973-584-0812
Sr. M. Elizabeth Davies, prin. Fax 584-2029

Summit, Union, Pop. 21,200
Summit CSD 3,600/PK-12
14 Beekman Ter 07901 908-918-2100
Dr. Nathan Parker, supt. Fax 273-3656
www.summit.k12.nj.us
Brayton ES 500/K-5
89 Tulip St 07901 908-273-1276
Dr. Cheryl Moretz, prin. Fax 918-2112
Franklin ES 400/K-5
136 Blackburn Rd 07901 908-277-2613
Dr. Sheila Cole, prin. Fax 918-2114
Jefferson ES 200/1-5
110 Ashwood Ave 07901 908-273-3807
Ron Poles, prin. Fax 918-2116
Jefferson Primary Center PK-K
110 Ashwood Ave 07901 908-918-2160
Felix Gil, prin. Fax 918-2133
Lincoln-Hubbard ES 400/K-5
52 Woodland Ave 07901 908-273-1333
Matthew Carlin, prin. Fax 918-2118
Summit MS 800/6-8
272 Morris Ave 07901 908-273-1190
Matthew Block, prin. Fax 273-8320
Washington ES 300/K-5
507 Morris Ave 07901 908-273-0817
Lauren Banker, prin. Fax 918-2120
Wilson Primary Center PK-K
14 Beekman Ter 07901 908-918-2175
Felix Gil, prin. Fax 918-2134

Kent Place S 600/PK-12
42 Norwood Ave 07901 908-273-0900
Susan Bosland, hdmstr. Fax 273-9390
Oak Knoll S of the Holy Child 600/K-12
44 Blackburn Rd 07901 908-522-8100
Timothy Saburn, hdmstr. Fax 277-1838
St. Theresa S 200/PK-K
306 Morris Ave 07901 908-277-6043
LeAnn Durner, prin. Fax 277-1770

Surf City, Ocean, Pop. 1,527
Long Beach Island SD 200/K-6
200 S Barnegat Ave 08008 609-494-2341
Robert Garguilo, supt. Fax 494-2921
www.lbischools.org
Jacobsen ES 100/K-2
200 S Barnegat Ave 08008 609-494-2341
Robert Garguilo, prin. Fax 494-2921
Other Schools – See Ship Bottom

Sussex, Sussex, Pop. 2,189
Sussex-Wantage Regional SD 1,600/K-8
27 Bank St 07461 973-875-3175
Dr. Edward Izbicki, supt. Fax 875-7175
www.swregional.org
Lawrence ES 500/K-2
31 Ryan Rd 07461 973-875-8820
Barbara Cimorelli, prin. Fax 875-8933
Sussex MS 500/6-8
10 Loomis Ave 07461 973-875-4138
Kristin Touw, prin. Fax 875-6790
Wantage ES 500/3-5
815 State Rt 23 07461 973-875-4589
Sharon Hosking, prin. Fax 875-2184

Sussex Christian S 200/PK-8
51 Unionville Ave 07461 973-875-5595
Patricia King, admin. Fax 875-5420

Swedesboro, Gloucester, Pop. 2,050
Swedesboro-Woolwich SD 1,000/PK-6
15 Fredrick Blvd 08085 856-241-1136
Richard Fisher, supt. Fax 467-7041
www.swedesboro-woolwich.com
Clifford S 300/PK-K
601 Auburn Ave 08085 856-241-1552
Karen Pszwaro, prin. Fax 241-9285
Hill ES 300/5-6
1815 Kings Hwy 08085 856-241-1552
Karen Pszwaro, prin. Fax 467-4016
Stratton S 400/PK-2
15 Fredrick Blvd 08085 856-241-1136
James Marchesani, prin. Fax 467-4379
Other Schools – See Woolwich

Tabernacle, Burlington
Tabernacle Township SD 900/K-8
132 New Rd 08088 609-268-0153
Bernice Blum-Bart, supt. Fax 268-1006
www.tabernacle.k12.nj.us
Olson MS 400/5-8
132 New Rd 08088 609-268-0153
Susan Grosser, prin. Fax 268-1006
Tabernacle ES 400/K-4
141 New Rd 08088 609-268-0150
Betty Jean Wissinger, prin. Fax 268-3233

Teaneck, Bergen, Pop. 39,500
Teaneck SD 4,000/PK-12
1 Merrison St 07666 201-833-5510
Linda Kuhran, supt. Fax 837-9468
www.teaneckschools.org/
Bryant K, 1 E Tryon Ave 07666 300/PK-K
Dr. Elise Bourne-Busby, prin. 201-833-5546
Franklin MS, 1315 Taft Rd 07666 600/5-8
Dr. Lennox Small, prin. 201-833-5451
Hawthorne ES, 201 Fycke Ln 07666 400/1-4
Vincent McHale, prin. 201-833-5540
Jefferson MS, 655 Teaneck Rd 07666 700/5-8
Antoine Green, prin. 201-833-5471
Lowell ES, 1025 Lincoln Pl 07666 400/1-4
Leslie Abrew, prin. 201-833-5550
Whittier ES 300/1-4
491 W Englewood Ave 07666 201-833-5535
Suzanna Kaplan, prin.

Mays SDA S 50/K-4
405 Englewood Ave 07666 201-837-6655

Tenafly, Bergen, Pop. 14,362
Tenafly SD 3,400/K-12
500 Tenafly Rd 07670 201-816-4500
Dr. Eugene Westlake, supt. Fax 816-4521
www.tenafly.k12.nj.us
Mackay ES 300/K-5
111 Jefferson Ave 07670 201-816-7700
John Fabbo, prin. Fax 568-7687
Maugham ES 400/K-5
111 Magnolia Ave 07670 201-816-7705
Dr. Tova Ben-Dov, prin. Fax 871-9641
Smith ES 300/K-5
101 Downey Dr 07670 201-816-7715
Neil Kaplicer, prin. Fax 568-7801
Stillman ES 400/K-5
75 Tenafly Rd 07670 201-816-7710
Barbara Laudicina, prin. Fax 568-7760
Tenafly MS 900/6-8
10 Sunset Ln 07670 201-816-4900
Lawrence Hughes, prin. Fax 569-0327

Our Lady of Mt. Carmel S 200/PK-8
10 County Rd 07670 201-567-6491
Sylvia Cosentino, prin. Fax 568-1402
Spring S 300/PK-8
67 N Summit St 07670 201-541-5780
Fax 541-5782

Three Bridges, Hunterdon
Readington Township SD
Supt. — See White House Station
Three Bridges ES 400/K-3
PO Box 443 08887 908-782-2141
Kristen Higgins, prin. Fax 782-4887

Tinton Falls, Monmouth, Pop. 17,274
Tinton Falls SD 1,500/K-8
658 Tinton Ave 07724 732-460-2400
John Russo, supt. Fax 542-1158
www.tfs.k12.nj.us
Atchison ES 700/K-3
961 Sycamore Ave 07724 732-542-2500
Mary Polese, prin. Fax 542-4905
Swimming River ES 300/4-5
220 Hance Ave 07724 732-460-2416
Dr. Marion Lamberti, prin. Fax 530-8684
Tinton Falls MS 500/6-8
674 Tinton Ave 07724 732-542-0775
David Hallman, prin. Fax 542-8723

Ranney S 800/PK-12
235 Hope Rd 07724 732-542-4777
Lawrence Sykoff Ed.D., hdmstr. Fax 544-1629

Titusville, Mercer
Hopewell Valley Regional SD
Supt. — See Pennington
Bear Tavern ES 500/K-5
1162 Bear Tavern Rd 08560 609-737-4000
Bruce Arcurio, prin. Fax 737-7351

Toms River, Ocean, Pop. 7,524
Toms River Regional SD 16,900/K-12
1144 Hooper Ave 08753 732-505-5510
Michael Ritacco, supt. Fax 505-9330
www.trschools.com
Cedar Grove ES 800/K-5
179 Cedar Grove Rd 08753 732-505-5830
Jeffrey Ryan, prin. Fax 914-1350
Citta ES 700/K-5
2050 Route 9 08755 732-818-8550
Greg Guito, prin. Fax 240-0156
East Dover ES 700/K-5
725 Vaughn Ave 08753 732-505-5840
Linda Downing, prin. Fax 270-4757
Hooper Avenue ES 800/K-5
1571 Hooper Ave 08753 732-505-5850
Theodore Schelmay, prin. Fax 914-1253
North Dover ES 700/K-5
1759 New Hampshire Ave 08755 732-505-5860
Edward Keller, prin. Fax 914-9706
Silver Bay ES 700/K-5
100 Silver Bay Rd 08753 732-505-5880
Michael DeVita, prin. Fax 255-0649
South Toms River ES 300/K-5
419 Dover Rd 08757 732-505-5890
Eileen Matus, prin. Fax 914-1861
Toms River IS East 1,500/6-8
1519 Hooper Ave 08753 732-505-5777
Bryan Madigan, prin. Fax 286-1290

Toms River IS North 1,300/6-8
150 Intermediate North Way 08753 732-505-5800
Lynn Fronzak, prin. Fax 286-1291
Walnut Street ES 800/K-5
60 Walnut St 08753 732-505-5900
Kevin Smith, prin. Fax 914-9724
Washington Street ES 400/K-5
500 W Earl Ct 08753 732-505-5910
Jill MacIntosh, prin. Fax 914-9715
West Dover ES 400/K-5
50 Blue Jay Dr 08755 732-505-5920
Michael Pallen, prin. Fax 914-2174
Other Schools – See Beachwood, Pine Beach

Ambassador Christian Academy 100/PK-8
700 Main St 08753 732-341-0860
Christina Hutchings, admin. Fax 349-0731
Grace and Peace Academy 200/PK-8
1563 Old Freehold Rd 08755 732-286-1761
Thomas Hoffman, admin. Fax 286-3036
St. Joseph S 800/K-8
711 Hooper Ave 08753 732-349-2355
Michele Williams, prin. Fax 349-1064

Totowa, Passaic, Pop. 10,592
Totowa SD 1,000/K-8
10 Crews St 07512 973-956-0010
Vincent Varcadipane, supt. Fax 956-9859
www.totowa.k12.nj.us
Memorial ES 300/K-2
294 Totowa Rd 07512 973-942-0010
Patricia Lindsley, prin. Fax 904-1082
Washington Park MS 700/3-8
10 Crews St 07512 973-956-0010
John Vanderberg, prin. Fax 389-2270

Academy of St. Francis of Assisi 200/PK-8
400 Totowa Rd 07512 973-956-8824
Carol LaSalle, prin. Fax 956-8824

Towaco, Morris
Montville Township SD
Supt. — See Pine Brook
Cedar Hill ES 400/K-5
46 Pine Brook Rd 07082 973-331-7130
Dr. Michael Raj, prin. Fax 331-9356

Trenton, Mercer, Pop. 84,639
Trenton SD 11,200/PK-12
108 N Clinton Ave 08609 609-656-4900
Rodney Lofton, supt. Fax 989-2682
www.trenton.k12.nj.us
Cadwalader ES 200/PK-5
501 Edgewood Ave 08618 609-656-4660
Jeannette Harris, prin. Fax 278-3066
Dunn MS 600/6-8
401 Dayton St 08610 609-656-4700
Helene Feldman, prin. Fax 989-9693
Franklin ES 400/K-5
200 William St 08610 609-656-4720
Mark Maurice, prin. Fax 278-1758
Grant S 400/PK-8
159 N Clinton Ave 08609 609-656-4730
Christopher DeJesus, prin. Fax 989-2919
Gregory S 500/PK-8
500 Rutherford Ave 08618 609-656-4740
Marzene Bennett, prin. Fax 989-2905
Harrison ES 200/K-5
461 Genesee St 08611 609-656-4750
Hariette Bass, prin. Fax 989-2910
Hedgepeth-Williams S 800/PK-8
301 Gladstone Ave 08629 609-656-4810
Dr. Rosario Casiano, prin. Fax 656-6060
Hill S 600/PK-8
1010 E State St 08609 609-656-4980
Addie Daniels-Lane, prin. Fax 989-2915
Jefferson ES 200/PK-5
1 Whittlesey Rd 08618 609-656-4790
Valerie Butler, prin. Fax 989-2922
Kilmer S 600/PK-8
1300 Stuyvesant Ave 08618 609-656-4800
Deborah Green, prin. Fax 989-2737
Monument S 300/PK-8
145 Pennington Ave 08618 609-656-4820
Bernadette Trapp, prin. Fax 989-2926
Mott S 400/PK-8
45 Stokely Ave 08611 609-656-4830
Dr. Heather Jackson, prin. Fax 989-2900
Munoz-Rivera S 500/PK-8
400 N Montgomery St 08618 609-656-4840
Joseph Marazzo, prin. Fax 989-2921
Parker ES 600/PK-5
800 S Warren St 08611 609-656-4880
Willie Solomon, prin. Fax 989-2901
Robbins Annex S K-8
520 Chestnut Ave 08611 609-989-2662
Edna Margolin, prin. Fax 989-2752
Robbins ES 500/K-3
283 Tyler St 08609 609-656-4910
Judy Steele, prin. Fax 989-2918
Stokes ES 300/K-5
915 Parkside Ave 08618 609-656-4930
Harriet Murray, prin. Fax 989-2907
Washington ES 300/PK-5
331 Emory Ave 08611 609-656-4960
Gloria Tunstall, prin. Fax 989-2911
Wilson ES 400/PK-5
175 Girard Ave 08638 609-656-4970
Gwendolyn Jennings, prin. Fax 989-2913

Incarnation - St. James S 200/K-8
1555 Pennington Rd 08618 609-882-3228
Sr. Patricia O'Donnell, prin. Fax 637-0460
Morris Private S 100/PK-8
3332 S Broad St 08610 609-585-7223
St. Raphael S 200/K-8
151 Gropp Ave 08610 609-585-7733
Timothy Lynch, prin. Fax 581-8436

Tuckerton, Ocean, Pop. 3,780
Tuckerton Borough SD 300/PK-6
PO Box 217 08087 609-294-2858
Dr. Robert Gray, supt. Fax 294-1480
www.tuckerton.k12.nj.us
Tuckerton ES 300/PK-6
PO Box 217 08087 609-296-2858
Dr. Rebecca Overholt, prin. Fax 296-1480

Turnersville, Gloucester, Pop. 3,843
Washington Township SD
Supt. — See Sewell
Bells ES 500/1-5
227 Greentree Rd 08012 856-589-8441
Dominick Renzi, prin. Fax 589-6607
Birches ES 500/1-5
416 Westminster Blvd 08012 856-232-1290
Annette Miller, prin. Fax 232-7963
Jefferson ES 400/1-5
95 Altair Dr 08012 856-589-8248
Jeff Pollock, prin. Fax 589-6919
Whitman ES 600/1-5
827 Whitman School Rd 08012 856-227-1103
Vincent Cardile, prin. Fax 227-0965

Apostles Ark S 50/PK-K
4401 Route 42 08012 856-629-4228

Union, Union, Pop. 55,000
Township of Union SD 7,700/PK-12
2369 Morris Ave 07083 908-851-6420
Dr. Theodore Jakubowski, supt. Fax 851-6421
www.twpunionschools.org
Battle Hill ES 400/PK-4
2600 Killian Pl 07083 908-851-6480
Michelle Warren, prin. Fax 851-4687
Burnet MS 1,000/6-8
1000 Caldwell Ave 07083 908-851-6490
Raymond Salvatore, prin. Fax 687-2645
Caldwell ES 600/PK-4
1120 Commerce Ave 07083 908-206-6100
Dr. Anthony Lentine, prin. Fax 206-9282
Connecticut Farms ES 500/PK-4
875 Stuyvesant Ave 07083 908-851-6470
Annie Waller-Moses, prin. Fax 687-7332
Franklin ES 500/PK-4
1500 Lindy Ter 07083 908-851-6450
Corey Lowery, prin. Fax 810-0710
Kawameeh MS 700/6-8
490 David Ter 07083 908-851-6570
Harold Bell, prin. Fax 687-5741
Livingston ES 400/PK-4
960 Midland Blvd 07083 908-851-6440
Kathryn DiGiovanni, prin. Fax 810-0417
Washington ES 600/PK-4
301 Washington Ave 07083 908-851-6460
Mark Hoyt, prin. Fax 810-1012
Other Schools – See Vauxhall

Holy Spirit S 200/PK-8
970 Suburban Rd 07083 908-687-8415
Barbara Prescott, prin. Fax 687-3996
St. Michael S 400/PK-8
1212 Kelly St 07083 908-688-1063
Antoinette Telle, prin. Fax 687-7927

Union Beach, Monmouth, Pop. 6,659
Union Beach Borough SD 800/PK-8
1207 Florence Ave 07735 732-264-5405
Arthur Waltz Ed.D., supt. Fax 264-6109
www.unionbeachschools.org/ubsd
Memorial S 800/PK-8
221 Morningside Ave 07735 732-264-5400
Joseph Annibale, prin. Fax 264-0964

Union City, Hudson, Pop. 65,128
Union City SD, 3912 32nd St 07087 9,200/PK-12
Stanley Sanger, supt. 201-348-5852
www.union-city-nj.org/modules/AMS/
Edison S 1,200/PK-8
507 West St 07087 201-348-5965
Alexandria Conti, prin. Fax 348-4306
Eugenio Maria de Hostos ECC PK-PK
2200 Kennedy Blvd 07087 201-271-2310
Adriana Birne, prin.
Gilmore ES 400/K-5
815 17th St 07087 201-348-5930
Rolanda Cabana, prin. Fax 271-1032
Hudson ES 400/K-5
167 19th St 07087 201-348-5920
Fran Levy, prin. Fax 866-7259
Jefferson ES 300/PK-4
3400 Palisade Ave 07087 201-348-5960
Karen Wilson, prin. Fax 601-2396
Marti MS 500/6-8
1800 Summit Ave 07087 201-348-5400
Geraldine Perez, prin. Fax 348-5405
Roosevelt S 900/PK-8
4507 Hudson Ave 07087 201-348-5971
Joseph Polinik, prin. Fax 348-3331
Veteran's Memorial ES 400/K-5
1401 Central Ave 07087 201-348-2737
Lois Corrigan, prin. Fax 583-0656
Washington S 800/PK-8
3905 New York Ave 07087 201-348-5954
Robert Wendelken, prin. Fax 348-1602
Waters S 1,200/PK-8
2800 Summit Ave 07087 201-348-5925
Bruce Naszento, prin. Fax 866-6598
Other Schools – See Weehawken

Bnos Sanz S 100/PK-8
3300 New York Ave 07087 201-867-2264
Mesivta Sanz Hudson County S 300/K-12
3400 New York Ave 07087 201-867-8690
Miftaahul Uloom S 300/PK-12
501 15th St 07087 201-223-9920
Mother Seton Interparochial S 200/PK-8
1501 New York Ave 07087 201-863-8433
Mary McElraine, prin. Fax 863-8145
St. Augustine S 300/PK-8
3920 New York Ave 07087 201-865-5319
Sr. Roberta O'Hea, prin. Fax 865-2567
St. Francis Academy 300/PK-8
1601 Central Ave 07087 201-863-4112
Deborah Savage, prin. Fax 601-5905

Upper Saddle River, Bergen, Pop. 8,509
Upper Saddle River SD 1,300/K-8
395 W Saddle River Rd 07458 201-961-6502
Dr. Monica Browne, supt. Fax 934-4923
www.usronline.org
Bogert ES 400/3-5
391 W Saddle River Rd 07458 201-961-6350
David Kaplan, prin. Fax 825-9101
Cavallini MS 500/6-8
392 W Saddle River Rd 07458 201-961-6400
Gene Solomon Ed.D., prin. Fax 236-9662
Reynolds ES 400/K-2
391 W Saddle River Rd 07458 201-961-6300
Joanne Vernon, prin. Fax 236-8432

Vauxhall, Union
Township of Union SD
Supt. — See Union
Central Five-Jefferson MS 500/5-5
155 Hilton Ave 07088 908-851-6560
Thomas Tsirikos, prin. Fax 687-8464

Ventnor City, Atlantic, Pop. 12,737
Ventnor City SD 900/PK-8
400 N Lafayette Ave 08406 609-487-7918
Carmine Bonanni, supt. Fax 822-0150
www.vecc.atlnet.org
Ventnor ES 600/PK-5
400 N Lafayette Ave 08406 609-487-7900
Eileen Johnson, prin. Fax 822-5840
Ventnor MS 300/6-8
400 N Lafayette Ave 08406 609-487-7900
Robert Baker, prin. Fax 823-4036

Holy Family Regional S 100/PK-8
30 S Portland Ave 08406 609-822-2234
Sr. Lydia Etter, prin. Fax 822-7941

Vernon, Sussex
Vernon Township SD 4,800/K-12
PO Box 99 07462 973-764-2900
Anthony Macerino, supt. Fax 764-0033
www.vtsd.com
Cedar Mountain PS 400/2-4
PO Box 420 07462 973-764-2890
Maureen McCall, prin. Fax 764-3294
Glen Meadow MS 800/7-8
PO Box 516 07462 973-764-8981
Carol Nelson Ed.D., prin. Fax 764-3295
Lounsberry Hollow MS 700/5-6
PO Box 219 07462 973-764-8745
Stewart Stumper, prin. Fax 764-0101
Rolling Hills PS 500/2-4
PO Box 769 07462 973-764-2784
Philip Schmidt, prin. Fax 764-3284
Walnut Ridge PS 600/K-1
PO Box 190 07462 973-764-2801
Pauline Anderson, prin. Fax 764-0066

Verona, Essex, Pop. 13,597
Verona SD 2,000/K-12
121 Fairview Ave 07044 973-239-2100
Charles Sampson, supt. Fax 571-6779
www.veronaschools.org
Brookdale Avenue ES 100/K-4
14 Brookdale Ct 07044 973-239-4250
Richard Rampolla, prin. Fax 239-4277
Brown ES 200/K-4
125 Grove Ave 07044 973-239-5241
Anthony Lanzo, prin. Fax 571-9889
Forest Avenue ES 200/K-4
118 Forest Ave 07044 973-239-2422
Thomas Valente, prin. Fax 857-2506
Laning Avenue ES 200/K-4
18 Lanning Rd 07044 973-239-5590
Frank Albano, prin. Fax 857-1720
Whitehorne MS 600/5-8
600 Bloomfield Ave 07044 973-239-1300
Yvette McNeal, prin. Fax 857-1611

Our Lady of the Lake S 200/PK-8
22 Lakeside Ave 07044 973-239-1160
Sr. Mary Sullivan, prin. Fax 239-6496

Villas, Cape May, Pop. 8,136
Lower Township ESD
Supt. — See Cape May
Douglas Veterans Memorial S 400/PK-K
2600 Bayshore Rd Ste 3 08251 609-884-9430
Shelleymarie Magan, prin. Fax 886-0515

Vineland, Cumberland, Pop. 58,164
Vineland CSD 8,900/PK-12
625 E Plum St 08360 856-794-6700
Charles Ottinger, supt. Fax 794-9464
www.vineland.org/vps.html
Barse ES 400/K-5
240 S Orchard Rd 08360 856-794-6940
Nedd Johnson, prin. Fax 507-8743
Dallago Preschool PK-PK
240 S 6th St 08360 856-641-8502
Nancee Bleistine, prin. Fax 362-8978
D'Ippolito ES 500/PK-5
1578 N Valley Ave 08360 856-794-6934
Gail Curcio, prin. Fax 507-8757

Durand ES 500/K-5
371 W Forest Grove Rd 08360 856-794-6929
Dale Horner, prin. Fax 507-8745
Johnstone ES 400/K-5
165 S Brewster Rd 08361 856-794-6967
Dr. Louise Karwowski, prin. Fax 507-8746
Landis MS 500/6-8
61 W Landis Ave 08360 856-794-6925
Donald Kohaut, prin. Fax 507-8763
Leuchter Preschool Ctr 200/PK-PK
519 N West Ave 08360 856-794-6922
Nancee Bleistine, prin. Fax 507-8738
Mennies ES 600/K-5
361 E Grant Ave 08360 856-794-6957
Lisa Arena, prin. Fax 507-8742
Oak & Main K 100/K-K
1654 E Oak Rd 08361 856-794-6956
Amy Kimmel, lead tchr. Fax 507-1864
Petway ES 500/K-5
1115 S Lincoln Ave 08361 856-362-8855
Jennifer Frederico, prin. Fax 362-6981
Rossi IS 400/6-8
2572 Palermo Ave 08361 856-794-6961
Lawrence Ricci, prin. Fax 507-8786
Sabater ES K-5
301 S East Blvd 08360 856-641-8502
Monica Dannenberger, prin. Fax 362-8979
Veterans Memorial MS 500/6-8
424 S Main Rd 08360 856-794-6918
Rusty Phillips, prin. Fax 507-8759
Wallace MS 500/6-8
688 N Mill Rd 08360 856-362-8887
Belinda Hall, prin. Fax 362-8980
Winslow ES 500/K-5
1335 Magnolia Rd 08361 856-794-6973
Maria Gallagher, prin. Fax 507-8739

Bishop Schad Regional S 400/K-8
922 E Landis Ave 08360 856-691-4490
Patrice DeMartino, prin. Fax 691-5579
Cumberland Christian S 500/PK-12
1100 W Sherman Ave 08360 856-696-1600
Wayne Baker, hdmstr. Fax 696-0631
Ellison S 100/PK-8
1017 S Spring Rd 08361 856-691-1734
Karen Springer, hdmstr. Fax 794-8361
St. Marys Regional S 300/PK-8
735 Union Rd 08360 856-692-8537
Sr. Margaret Curcio, prin. Fax 692-5034
Vineland Regional Adventist S K-8
PO Box 2239 08362 856-691-9393

Voorhees, Camden, Pop. 24,559
Voorhees Township SD 3,300/PK-8
329 Route 73 08043 856-751-8446
Raymond Brosel, supt. Fax 751-3666
www.voorhees.k12.nj.us/
Hamilton ES 500/K-5
23 Northgate Dr 08043 856-767-4888
Kristine diCoio, prin. Fax 753-2894
Kresson ES 500/PK-5
1 School Ln 08043 856-424-1816
Barbara Dunleavy, prin. Fax 424-2728
Osage ES 600/K-5
112 Somerdale Rd 08043 856-428-2990
Diane Young, prin. Fax 427-0296
Signal Hill ES 500/PK-5
33 Signal Hill Dr 08043 856-767-6749
Sheila Ferreri, prin. Fax 767-6221
Voorhees MS 1,200/6-8
1000 Holly Oak Dr 08043 856-795-2025
Charles Ronkin, prin. Fax 795-4611

Kellman Brown Academy 200/PK-8
1007 Laurel Oak Rd 08043 856-679-2929
Gail Cohen, dir.

Waldwick, Bergen, Pop. 9,650
Waldwick SD 1,600/PK-12
155 Summit Ave 07463 201-445-3131
Dr. Robert Penna, supt. Fax 445-0584
www.waldwick.k12.nj.us/
Crescent ES 400/PK-5
165 Crescent Ave 07463 201-445-0690
Karen Mulroe, prin. Fax 445-6955
Traphagen ES 400/K-5
153 Summit Ave 07463 201-445-0730
Robert Sileo, prin. Fax 445-7196
Waldwick MS 400/6-8
155 Wyckoff Ave 07463 201-652-9000
Michael Meyers, prin. Fax 652-5053

Village S for Children 300/PK-8
100 W Prospect St 07463 201-445-6160
Marilyn Larkin, dir. Fax 445-7686
Waldwick SDA S 100/PK-12
70 Wyckoff Ave 07463 201-652-6078
Wayne Edwards, prin. Fax 652-4652

Wall, Monmouth, Pop. 5,201
Wall Township SD 4,300/PK-12
PO Box 1199 07719 732-556-2000
Dr. James Habel, supt. Fax 556-2101
www.wall.k12.nj.us/
Central ES 600/K-5
PO Box 1199 07719 732-556-2540
Greg Storts, prin. Fax 556-2551
Wall IS 1,100/6-8
PO Box 1199 07719 732-556-2500
Rosaleen Sirchio, prin. Fax 556-2535
Wall PS, PO Box 1199 07719 100/PK-PK
Sharon Cox, prin. 732-556-2114
West Belmar ES 200/K-5
PO Box 1199 07719 732-556-2560
Anthony Abeal, prin. Fax 556-2571
Other Schools – See Allenwood, Sea Girt

Wallington, Bergen, Pop. 11,491
Wallington SD 1,100/K-12
30 Pine St 07057 973-777-4421
Dr. Frank Cocchiola, supt. Fax 614-9391
www.wboe.org
Gavlak ES 400/K-6
106 King St 07057 973-777-4420
Nancy Giambrone, prin. Fax 574-9517
Jefferson ES 200/K-3
30 Pine St 07057 973-777-4420
John Markey, prin. Fax 614-9391

Most Sacred Heart of Jesus S 200/PK-8
6 Bond St 07057 973-777-4817
Sr. Lisa Disabatino, prin. Fax 778-7750

Wanamassa, Monmouth, Pop. 4,530
Ocean Township SD
Supt. — See Oakhurst
Wanamassa ES 300/K-4
901 Bendermere Ave 07712 732-531-5700
Justine Salvo, prin. Fax 531-3720

Wanaque, Passaic, Pop. 10,616
Wanaque SD
Supt. — See Haskell
Wanaque S 600/K-8
1 1st St 07465 973-839-6990
Judith Young, prin. Fax 839-0843

Waretown, Ocean, Pop. 1,283
Ocean Township SD 500/PK-6
64 Railroad Ave 08758 609-693-3329
Donald Bochicchio, supt. Fax 693-5833
www.otsdk6.org
Priff ES 200/4-6
139 Wells Mill Rd 08758 609-693-0360
Annjanette Youngblood, prin. Fax 693-6972
Waretown ES 300/PK-3
64 Railroad Ave 08758 609-693-3131
Diana MacKenzie, prin. Fax 242-2190

Warren, Somerset
Warren Township SD 2,200/K-8
213 Mount Horeb Rd 07059 732-753-5300
Dr. James Crisfield, supt. Fax 560-8801
www.warrentboe.org
Central ES 400/K-5
109 Mount Bethel Rd 07059 908-757-3058
MaryLou Cebula, prin. Fax 757-3930
Mt. Horeb ES 400/K-5
80 Mount Horeb Rd 07059 732-356-3313
William Kimmick, prin. Fax 356-3753
Tomaso ES 400/K-5
46 Washington Valley Rd 07059 732-302-0541
Kathy Bond, prin. Fax 302-9140
Warren MS 700/6-8
100 Old Stirling Rd 07059 908-753-5300
Robert Comba, prin. Fax 753-4789
Woodland ES 300/K-5
114 Stirling Rd 07059 908-604-4999
Chic Hansen, prin. Fax 604-6633

Washington, Warren, Pop. 6,876
Franklin Township SD 400/PK-6
52 Asbury Broadway Rd 07882 908-689-2958
Paul Rinaldi, supt. Fax 689-1786
www.franklinschool.org
Franklin Township ES 400/PK-6
52 Asbury Broadway Rd 07882 908-689-2958
Paul Rinaldi, prin. Fax 689-1786

Warren Hills Regional HSD 2,100/7-12
89 Bowerstown Rd 07882 908-689-3143
Peter Merluzzi, supt. Fax 689-4814
www.warrenhills.org
Warren Hills Regional MS 700/7-8
64 Carlton Ave 07882 908-689-0750
Jack Paulus, prin. Fax 689-3663

Washington Borough SD 500/PK-6
300 W Stewart St 07882 908-689-0241
Lance Rozsa, supt. Fax 689-8269
www.warrennet.org/washingtonboro
Taylor Street ES 200/PK-2
16 Taylor St 07882 908-689-0091
Jacqueline Nassry, prin. Fax 689-8273
Washington Memorial ES 300/3-6
300 W Stewart St 07882 908-689-0241
Lance Rozsa, prin. Fax 689-8269

Washington Township SD 600/K-6
16 Castle St 07882 908-689-1119
Roger Jinks, supt. Fax 689-3748
www.washingtontownshipschools.org/
Brass Castle ES 300/K-K, 4-6
16 Castle St 07882 908-689-1188
Valerie Mattes, prin. Fax 689-2356
Port Colden ES 300/1-3
30 Port Colden Rd 07882 908-689-0681
Kelly Mason, prin. Fax 689-8584

Good Shepherd Christian Academy 200/PK-8
490 State Route 57 W 07882 908-835-1399
Cindy Weaver, admin. Fax 835-1398

Washington Township, Bergen, Pop. 9,245
Westwood Regional SD 2,600/K-12
701 Ridgewood Rd 07676 201-664-0880
Geoffrey Zoeller Ed.D., supt. Fax 664-7642
www.wwrsd.org/
George ES 300/K-4
1 Palm St 07676 201-664-3033
Patricia Eckel, prin. Fax 722-0670
Washington ES 300/K-4
1 School St 07676 201-664-6440
Rachelle Parker Ed.D., prin. Fax 722-0793
Other Schools – See Westwood

Watchung, Somerset, Pop. 6,170
Watchung Borough SD 700/K-8
1 Dr Parenty Way 07069 908-755-8121
Dr. Mary Louise Malyska, supt. Fax 755-6946
www.watchungschools.com
Bayberry ES 400/K-4
113 Bayberry Ln 07069 908-755-8184
Mary Nunn, prin. Fax 755-0366
Valley View MS 300/5-8
50 Valley View Rd 07069 908-755-4422
Charles Miller, prin. Fax 755-4035

Waterford Works, Camden
Waterford Township SD 900/K-6
1106 Old White Horse Pike 08089 856-767-0331
Gary Dentino, supt. Fax 768-8086
www.wtsd.org
Waterford ES 400/4-6
1106 Old White Horse Pike 08089 856-767-8293
Fred Hair, prin. Fax 768-8086
Other Schools – See Atco

Wayne, Passaic, Pop. 55,000
Wayne Township SD 8,500/K-12
50 Nellis Dr 07470 973-633-3000
Dr. John Sico, supt. Fax 628-8058
www.wayneschools.com
Carter ES 300/K-5
531 Alps Rd 07470 973-633-3145
Kenneth Kaplan, prin. Fax 694-4370
Dey ES 400/K-5
55 Webster Dr 07470 973-633-3155
Dr. Laura Russomano, prin. Fax 633-6916
Fallon ES 400/K-5
51 Clifford Dr 07470 973-633-3125
Ethan Maayan, prin. Fax 633-0601
Kennedy ES 400/K-5
1310 Ratzer Rd 07470 973-633-3160
Richard Erck, prin. Fax 942-1711
Lafayette ES 400/K-5
100 Laauwe Ave 07470 973-633-3165
Stella Cosmas, prin. Fax 942-1457
Packanack ES 500/K-5
190 Oakwood Dr 07470 973-633-3170
Fax 872-1215
Pines Lake ES 500/K-5
511 Pines Lake Dr E 07470 973-633-3175
Pamela Longo, prin. Fax 839-7885
Ryerson ES 300/K-5
30 McClelland Ave 07470 973-633-3180
Marianela Martin, prin. Fax 633-2595
Schuyler-Colfax MS 800/6-8
1500 Hamburg Tpke 07470 973-633-3130
Fax 633-3195
Terhune ES 400/K-5
40 Geoffrey Way 07470 973-633-3150
Marion McGrath, prin. Fax 831-7450
Washington MS 600/6-8
68 Lenox Rd 07470 973-633-3140
MaryJane Tierney, prin. Fax 633-7590
Wayne MS 700/6-8
201 Garside Ave 07470 973-389-2120
Diane Pandolfi, prin. Fax 389-2130

Apple Montessori of Wayne 300/PK-6
25 Nevins Rd 07470 973-696-9750
Fax 696-9010
Calvary Christian Academy 100/PK-8
1111 Preakness Ave 07470 973-694-3584
Alexandra Woody, prin. Fax 694-7785
Immaculate Heart of Mary S 200/PK-8
580 Ratzer Rd 07470 973-694-1225
MaryAnn Oesterle, prin. Fax 872-9043
Our Lady of Consolation S 200/PK-8
1799 Hamburg Tpke 07470 973-839-2323
Cassie DeBow, prin. Fax 616-5379

Weehawken, Hudson, Pop. 12,385
Union City SD
Supt. — See Union City
Wilson S 300/K-8
80 Hauxhurst Ave 07086 201-348-2701
Ronald Treanor, prin. Fax 348-2703

Weehawken Township SD 1,200/PK-12
53 Liberty Pl 07086 201-422-6130
Kevin McLellan, supt.
www.weehawken.k12.nj.us
Roosevelt ES, 1 Louisa Pl 07086 300/3-6
Anthony D'Angelo, prin. 201-422-6140
Webster ES, 2700 Palisade Ave 07086 300/PK-2
Anthony Colasurdo, prin. 201-422-6150

Wenonah, Gloucester, Pop. 2,332
Deptford Township SD
Supt. — See Deptford
Oak Valley ES 300/2-6
525 College Blvd 08090 856-415-9218
John Schilling, prin. Fax 464-1794
Pine Acres ECC 200/PK-1
720 Purdue Ave 08090 856-464-1260
Scott MacDonald, prin. Fax 464-1788

Wenonah SD 200/K-6
200 N Clinton Ave 08090 856-468-6000
Frank Vogel, supt. Fax 468-9674
www.wenonahschool.org/
Wenonah ES 200/K-6
200 N Clinton Ave 08090 856-468-6000
Frank Vogel, prin. Fax 468-9674

Westampton, Burlington, Pop. 60,004
Westampton Township SD 900/K-8
710 Rancocas Rd 08060 609-267-2053
Dr. Kenneth Hamilton, supt. Fax 267-2760
www.westamptonschools.org
Holly Hills ES 500/K-4
500 Ogden Dr 08060 609-267-8565
Rachel Feldman, prin. Fax 702-9744

Westampton MS 500/5-8
700 Rancocas Rd 08060 609-267-2722
Anne Lipsett, prin. Fax 702-9017

Friends Academy of Westampton 200/PK-8
315 Bridge St 08060 609-267-8198
Constance Beetle, hdmstr. Fax 267-8178

West Berlin, Camden, Pop. 3,000
Berlin Township SD 600/PK-8
225 Grove Ave 08091 856-767-9480
Brian Betze, supt. Fax 767-8235
www.btwpschools.org/berlin
Eisenhower MS 200/5-8
235 Grove Ave 08091 856-767-0203
Leslie Koller, prin. Fax 767-7992
Kennedy Memorial ES 300/PK-4
228 Mount Vernon Ave 08091 856-767-9164
Marilyn Bright, prin. Fax 768-9066

West Caldwell, Essex, Pop. 10,422
Caldwell-West Caldwell SD 2,600/K-12
104 Gray St 07006 973-228-6979
Daniel Gerardi, supt. Fax 228-8716
www.cwcboe.org/
Washington ES 400/K-5
201 Central Ave 07006 973-228-8941
Barbara Adams, prin.
Wilson ES, Orton Rd 07006 200/K-5
Scott Keena, prin. 973-228-7173
Other Schools – See Caldwell

West Cape May, Cape May, Pop. 1,038
West Cape May SD 50/K-6
301 Moore St 08204 609-884-4614
William Flynn, admin. Fax 884-0932
wcm.capemayschools.com/
West Cape May ES 50/K-6
301 Moore St 08204 609-884-4614
William Flynn, admin. Fax 884-0932

West Collingswood, See Collingswood
Collingswood Borough SD
Supt. — See Collingswood
Sharp ES 100/K-6
400 Comly Ave 08107 856-962-5707
Stella Nwanguma, prin. Fax 962-5724

West Creek, Ocean
Eagleswood Township SD 100/K-6
PO Box 355 08092 609-597-3663
Deborah Snyder, supt. Fax 978-0949
www.eagleswood.org
Eagleswood Township ES 100/K-6
PO Box 355 08092 609-597-3663
Deborah Snyder, prin. Fax 978-0949

West Deptford, Gloucester, Pop. 19,380
West Deptford Township SD 3,200/K-12
675 Grove Rd 08066 856-848-4300
Edward Wasilewski, supt. Fax 845-5743
www.wdeptford.k12.nj.us/
Green-Fields ES 600/K-4
15 Hill Ln, 856-845-7929
Jonathan Cohen, prin. Fax 384-6505
Oakview ES 300/K-4
350 Dubois Ave, 856-845-1856
Sally Cohill, prin. Fax 845-3241
Red Bank ES 300/K-4
192 Philadelphia Ave, 856-845-2727
Karry Corbitt, prin. Fax 251-1927
West Deptford MS 1,000/5-8
675 Grove Rd 08066 856-848-1200
Brian Gismondi, prin. Fax 848-2325

Westfield, Union, Pop. 29,918
Westfield SD 5,900/PK-12
302 Elm St 07090 908-789-4420
Margaret Dolan, supt. Fax 789-4192
www.westfieldnjk12.org
Edison IS 700/6-8
800 Rahway Ave 07090 908-789-4470
Cheryl O'Brien, prin. Fax 789-1506
Franklin ES 600/K-5
700 Prospect St 07090 908-789-4590
Eileen Cambria, prin. Fax 789-0263
Jefferson ES 500/K-5
1200 Boulevard 07090 908-789-4490
Jeanette Munoz, prin. Fax 789-0939
Lincoln ECC PK-K
728 Westfield Ave 07090 908-789-4455
Audrey Zavetz, prin. Fax 232-1734
McKinley ES 300/K-5
500 1st St 07090 908-789-4555
Claudia Andreski, prin. Fax 789-6116
Roosevelt IS 700/6-8
301 Clark St 07090 908-789-4560
Stewart Carey, prin. Fax 789-4193
Tamaques ES 500/K-5
641 Willow Grove Rd 07090 908-789-4580
Michael Cullen, prin. Fax 789-2566
Washington ES 300/K-5
900 Saint Marks Ave 07090 908-789-4600
Andrew Perry, prin. Fax 789-2597
Wilson ES 600/K-5
301 Linden Ave 07090 908-789-4605
Joseph Malanga, prin. Fax 789-2890

Holy Trinity S 300/1-8
336 1st St 07090 908-233-0484
Sr. Maureen Fichner, prin. Fax 233-6204
Redeemer Lutheran S 100/PK-6
229 Cowperthwaite Pl 07090 908-232-1592
Joy Wagenblast, prin. Fax 317-9301
St. Pauls Day S 300/PK-K
414 E Broad St 07090 908-233-5417
Fax 232-9723

West Long Branch, Monmouth, Pop. 8,286
West Long Branch SD 800/K-8
135 Locust Ave 07764 732-222-5900
Karen Wood, supt. Fax 222-9325
www.wlbschools.com
Antonides MS 500/4-8
135 Locust Ave 07764 732-222-5080
James Erhardt, prin. Fax 222-8154
McElmon ES 300/K-3
20 Parker Rd 07764 732-222-6500
Maureen O'Reilly, prin. Fax 483-0845

Colonial Christian Academy 50/3-8
197 Locust Ave 07764 732-222-5683
Jonathan Yagid, prin. Fax 831-0353
Deal Yeshiva 300/K-12
200 Wall St 07764 732-229-1717
St. Jerome S 300/PK-8
250 Wall St 07764 732-222-8686
Sr. Angelina Pelliccia, prin. Fax 263-0343

West Milford, Passaic, Pop. 26,600
West Milford Township SD 4,200/PK-12
46 Highlander Dr 07480 973-697-1700
Bernice Colefield, supt. Fax 697-8351
www.wmtps.org
Apshawa ES 300/K-6
140 High Crest Dr 07480 973-838-6515
Jeanne Apryasz, prin. Fax 838-6896
Macopin MS 700/7-8
70 Highlander Dr 07480 973-697-5691
Raymond Johnson, prin. Fax 697-0301
Maple Road ES 300/K-6
36 Maple Rd 07480 973-697-3606
Faith Delaney, prin. Fax 208-0257
Marshall Hill ES 400/K-6
210 Marshall Hill Rd 07480 973-728-3430
Michael McCormick, prin. Fax 728-1444
Westbrook ES 500/PK-6
55 Nosenzo Pond Rd 07480 973-697-5700
Joan Oberer, prin. Fax 208-0136
Other Schools – See Hewitt, Oak Ridge

Westmont, Camden, Pop. 5,500
Haddon Township SD 2,100/PK-12
500 Rhoads Ave 08108 856-869-7700
Mark Raivetz, supt. Fax 854-7792
www.haddon.k12.nj.us
Edison ES, 205 Melrose Ave 08108 100/PK-5
Eileen Smith, prin. 856-869-7715
Rohrer MS, 101 MacArthur Blvd 08108 400/6-8
Kevin Rooney, prin. 856-869-7770
Strawbridge ES 300/K-5
307 Strawbridge Ave 08108 856-869-7735
Eileen Smith, prin.
Other Schools – See Haddonfield, Oaklyn

West New York, Hudson, Pop. 46,667
West New York SD 6,900/PK-12
6028 Broadway 07093 201-553-4000
Dr. Robert VanZanten, supt. Fax 865-2725
www.wnyschools.net
Bain ES 600/PK-6
6200 Broadway 07093 201-553-4095
Sixto Cardenas, prin. Fax 758-0366
Early Childhood S 1,000/PK-PK
5204 Hudson Ave 07093 201-553-4035
Marilyn Duran, prin. Fax 330-2945
Public S 1 900/K-6
6129 Madison St 07093 201-553-4025
Clara Brito Herrera, prin. Fax 861-7392
Public S 2 400/PK-6
317 66th St 07093 201-553-4040
Patrick Gagliardi, prin. Fax 865-6828
Public S 3 400/PK-6
5401 Polk St 07093 201-553-4055
Claire Warnock, prin. Fax 758-0366
Public S 4 400/PK-6
317 66th St 07093 201-553-4200
Bernard Abbadessa, prin. Fax 861-5681
Public S 5 700/K-6
5401 Hudson Ave 07093 201-553-4080
Israel Rodriguez, prin. Fax 330-7828
West New York MS 800/7-8
201 57th St 07093 201-563-4160
Tony Ferrainolo, prin. Fax 863-6698

Our Lady of Libera S 200/PK-8
5800 Kennedy Blvd 07093 201-864-5557
Ann Maria Castaneda, prin. Fax 601-3156
St. Joseph of the Palisades S 300/PK-8
6408 Palisade Ave 07093 201-861-3227
Eileen Donovan-Ferrando, prin. Fax 861-5744
San Pablo Lutheran S 50/PK-K
5106 Palisade Ave 07093 201-348-0713
Mercedes Lopez, prin. Fax 348-0713

West Orange, Essex, Pop. 45,500
West Orange SD 5,900/K-12
179 Eagle Rock Ave 07052 973-669-5400
Jerry Tarnoff, supt. Fax 669-1432
schools.woboe.org/Pages/Default.aspx
Edison MS 400/6-8
75 William St 07052 973-669-5360
Xavier Fitzgerald, prin. Fax 243-9802
Gregory ES 400/K-5
301 Gregory Ave 07052 973-669-5397
John Nittolo, prin. Fax 243-0251
Hazel Avenue ES 300/K-5
45 Hazel Ave 07052 973-669-5448
Marguerite DeCarlo, prin. Fax 243-0696
Liberty MS 500/6-8
1 Kelly Dr 07052 973-243-2007
John Vogler, prin. Fax 243-2743
Mt. Pleasant ES 400/K-5
9 Manger Rd 07052 973-669-5480
Michael Schiavo, prin. Fax 669-5496
Pleasantdale ES 300/K-5
555 Pleasant Valley Way 07052 973-669-5452
John Halak, prin. Fax 669-5455
Redwood ES 500/K-5
75 Redwood Ave 07052 973-669-5457
Barbara Kivlon, prin. Fax 324-9224
Roosevelt MS 400/6-8
36 Gilbert Pl 07052 973-669-5373
Frank Corrado, prin. Fax 243-9807
St. Cloud ES 300/K-5
71 Sheridan Ave 07052 973-669-5393
Dr. Joseph Bruno, prin. Fax 325-1685
Washington ES 400/K-5
289 Main St 07052 973-669-5385
Marie DeMaio, prin. Fax 669-5462

Blessed Pope John XXIII Academy 200/PK-8
8 Saint Cloud Pl 07052 973-731-3503
Lynda Wright, prin. Fax 669-0385
Solomon Schecter Day S 300/PK-5
122 Gregory Ave 07052 973-602-3700
Joyce Raynor Ph.D., hdmstr. Fax 669-8689

West Paterson, Passaic, Pop. 11,245
West Paterson SD 700/K-8
853 McBride Ave 07424 973-317-7710
Scott Rixford, supt. Fax 317-7773
wpschools.org
Gilmore ES 100/3-4
1075 McBride Ave 07424 973-317-7740
Margaret Odoksta, prin. Fax 317-7743
Memorial MS 400/5-8
15 Memorial Dr 07424 973-317-7750
Charles Silverstein, prin. Fax 317-7753
Olbon ES 200/K-2
50 Lincoln Ln 07424 973-317-7730
Linda Dewey, prin. Fax 317-7733

Westville, Gloucester, Pop. 4,466
Deptford Township SD
Supt. — See Deptford
Shady Lane ES 400/K-6
130 Peach St 08093 856-384-6046
Jackie Scerbo, prin. Fax 845-3459

Westville SD 300/PK-6
101 Birch Ave 08093 856-456-0235
Shannon Whalen, supt. Fax 456-0484
www.westvillesd.com
Parkview ES 300/PK-6
101 Birch Ave 08093 856-456-0235
Renee Egan, prin. Fax 456-0484

Holy Trinity Regional S 300/K-8
1215 Delsea Dr 08093 856-848-6826
Patricia Mancuso, prin. Fax 251-0344

Westwood, Bergen, Pop. 10,994
Westwood Regional SD
Supt. — See Washington Township
Berkeley Avenue ES 200/K-4
47 Berkeley Ave 07675 201-664-7760
Michael Fiorello, prin. Fax 664-1168
Brookside Upper ES 400/5-6
20 Lake Dr 07675 201-664-9000
Rory McCourt, prin. Fax 722-0661
Ketler ES 300/K-4
23 3rd Ave 07675 201-664-5560
Lisa Shifrin, prin. Fax 722-0704

Zion Lutheran S 200/PK-8
64 1st Ave 07675 201-664-8060
Fax 664-7092

Wharton, Morris, Pop. 6,222
Jefferson Township SD
Supt. — See Lake Hopatcong
Stanlick ES 400/3-5
155 E Shawnee Trl 07885 973-663-0520
Kelly Cooke, prin. Fax 663-7854

Rockaway Township SD
Supt. — See Hibernia
Dwyer ES 300/K-5
665 Mount Hope Rd 07885 973-361-7450
Michael McGovern, prin. Fax 361-8751

Wharton Borough SD 600/K-8
137 E Central Ave 07885 973-361-2592
Richard Bitondo, supt. Fax 895-2187
www.wbps.org/
Duffy ES 400/K-5
137 E Central Ave 07885 973-361-2506
Pamela Blalock, prin. Fax 361-4917
MacKinnon MS 200/6-8
137 E Central Ave 07885 973-361-1253
Christopher Herdman, prin. Fax 361-4805

Whippany, Morris
Hanover Township SD 1,500/K-8
61 Highland Ave 07981 973-515-2404
Scott Pepper, supt. Fax 540-1023
www.hanovertwpschools.com/
Bee Meadow ES 400/K-5
120 Reynolds Ave 07981 973-515-2419
John Leister, prin. Fax 515-7528
Memorial JHS 500/6-8
61 Highland Ave 07981 973-515-2427
Michael Wasko, prin. Fax 515-2481
Salem Drive ES 300/K-5
29 Salem Dr N 07981 973-515-2440
Rob Camean, prin. Fax 515-5097
Other Schools – See Morris Plains

Our Lady of Mercy S 100/PK-5
90 Whippany Rd 07981 973-887-2611
Elizabeth Ventola, prin. Fax 887-6629

White House Station, Hunterdon, Pop. 1,287
Readington Township SD 2,200/K-8
PO Box 807 08889 908-534-2195
Jordan Schiff Ed.D., supt. Fax 534-9551
www.readington.k12.nj.us
Holland Brook ES 500/4-5
PO Box 1500 08889 908-823-0454
Alfonzo Llano, prin. Fax 823-0464
Readington MS 800/6-8
PO Box 700 08889 908-534-2113
Catherine Hollinger, prin. Fax 534-6802
Whitehouse ES 500/K-3
PO Box 157 08889 908-534-4411
Ann DeRosa, prin. Fax 534-9157
Other Schools – See Three Bridges

Whiting, Ocean
Manchester Township SD 3,100/K-12
121 Route 539 08759 732-350-5900
David Trethaway, supt. Fax 350-0436
www.manchestertwp.org
Whiting ES 300/K-5
412 Manchester Blvd 08759 732-350-4994
Marjorie Stevens, prin. Fax 350-4476
Other Schools – See Manchester

Wildwood, Cape May, Pop. 5,291
Wildwood CSD 800/PK-12
4300 Pacific Ave 08260 609-522-4157
Dennis Anderson, supt. Fax 523-8161
www.edline.net/pages/Wildwood_PSD
Glenwood Avenue ES 400/PK-5
2900 New York Ave 08260 609-522-1630
John Kummings, prin. Fax 729-5243
Wildwood MS 100/6-8
4300 Pacific Ave 08260 609-522-7922
Dr. Gladys Lauriello, prin. Fax 522-7914

Wildwood Crest SD 300/K-8
9100 Pacific Ave 08260 609-729-3760
Dennis Anderson, supt. Fax 522-0732
Crest Memorial S 300/K-8
9100 Pacific Ave 08260 609-729-3760
Fax 729-0732

St. Ann Regional S 200/K-8
2901 New Jersey Ave 08260 609-522-2704
Sr. Sheila Murphy, prin. Fax 522-5329

Williamstown, Gloucester, Pop. 10,891
Buena Regional SD
Supt. — See Buena
Collings Lake ES 300/K-5
620 Cains Mill Rd 08094 856-885-4994
Daniel Benedetto, prin. Fax 561-5646

Monroe Township SD 5,700/K-12
75 E Academy St 08094 856-629-6400
Vincent Tarantino, supt. Fax 262-2499
www.monroetwp.k12.nj.us
Holly Glen ES 600/K-4
900 N Main St 08094 856-728-8706
Thomas Myers, prin. Fax 262-4732
Oak Knoll ES 500/K-4
23 Bodine Ave 08094 856-728-3944
Bruce Sheppard, prin. Fax 728-6791
Radix ES 600/K-4
363 Radix Rd 08094 856-728-8650
Raymond Dinovi, prin. Fax 262-7491
Whitehall ES 400/K-4
161 Whitehall Rd 08094 856-728-8782
Marcia Pietroski, prin. Fax 262-7923
Williamstown MS 1,800/5-8
561 Clayton Rd 08094 856-629-7444
Charles Folker, prin. Fax 875-6757

St. Mary S 500/K-8
32 Carroll Ave 08094 856-629-6190
Judith McBride, prin. Fax 728-1437
Victory Christian S 200/PK-12
PO Box 806 08094 856-629-4300

Willingboro, Burlington, Pop. 32,400
Willingboro Township SD 4,700/PK-12
440 Beverly Rancocas Rd 08046 609-835-8600
Dr. Roy Dawson, supt. Fax 835-3880
www.willingboroschools.org/
Garfield East ES 400/PK-4
150 Evergreen Dr 08046 609-835-8990
Cheryl Davis-Smith, prin. Fax 835-8999
Hawthorne ES 400/PK-4
84 Hampshire Ln 08046 609-835-8960
Nadine Tribbett, prin. Fax 835-8969
James ES 400/PK-4
41 Pinetree Ln 08046 609-835-8940
JoAnn Berkley, prin. Fax 835-8929
Levitt MS 900/7-8
50 Salem Rd 08046 609-835-8900
Theodore Boler, prin. Fax 835-3974
Memorial Upper ES 800/5-6
451 Van Sciver Pkwy 08046 609-835-8700
Keith Ellerbe, prin. Fax 835-1457
Stuart ES 400/PK-4
70 Sunset Rd 08046 609-835-3881
Douglas Austin, prin. Fax 835-3889

Twin Hills ES 400/PK-4
110 Twin Hill Dr 08046 609-835-8980
Barbara Doneghy, prin. Fax 835-8989

Pope John Paul II S 200/K-8
11 S Sunset Rd 08046 609-877-2144
Catherine Zagola, prin. Fax 877-3153

Windsor, Mercer
Robbinsville SD
Supt. — See Robbinsville
Windsor K K-K
16 School Dr 08561 609-371-0859
Janet Sinkewicz, prin. Fax 448-2352

Winfield Park, Union, Pop. 1,576
Winfield Township SD 100/PK-8
7 1/2 Gulfstream Ave 07036 908-486-7410
Alice D'Ambola, supt. Fax 486-4571
www.winfieldschool.org
Winfield Township S 100/PK-8
7 1/2 Gulfstream Ave 07036 908-486-7410
Alice D'Ambola, prin. Fax 486-4571

Woodbine, Cape May, Pop. 2,569
Woodbine SD 200/PK-8
801 Webster St 08270 609-861-5174
Lynda Anderson-Towns, supt. Fax 861-0723
woodbine.capemayschools.com/
Woodbine S 200/PK-8
801 Webster St 08270 609-861-5174
Lynda Anderson-Towns, prin. Fax 861-0723

Woodbridge, Middlesex, Pop. 17,434
Woodbridge Township SD 13,000/K-12
PO Box 428 07095 732-602-8550
Dr. John Crowe, supt. Fax 750-3493
www.woodbridge.k12.nj.us
Mawbey Street ES 300/K-5
275 Mawbey St 07095 732-602-8401
Geraldine Rinaldo, prin. Fax 855-7654
Ross Street ES 400/K-5
110 Ross St 07095 732-602-8511
Sharon Strack, prin. Fax 855-0597
Woodbridge MS 500/6-8
525 Barron Ave 07095 732-602-8690
James Sullivan, prin. Fax 855-0326
Other Schools – See Avenel, Colonia, Fords, Iselin, Metuchen, Port Reading, Sewaren

---

St. James S 300/PK-8
341 Amboy Ave 07095 732-634-2090
Mary Erath, prin. Fax 634-4390

Woodbury, Gloucester, Pop. 10,435
Woodbury SD 1,500/PK-12
25 N Broad St 08096 856-853-0123
Joseph Jones, supt. Fax 853-0704
www.woodburysch.com
Evergreen Avenue ES 300/PK-5
160 N Evergreen Ave 08096 856-853-0125
Tonya Breland, prin. Fax 853-2867
Walnut Street ES 100/K-5
60 Walnut St 08096 856-853-0126
Dr. Jeffrey Adams, prin. Fax 384-1040
West End Memorial ES 300/K-5
215 Queen St 08096 856-853-0124
Vincent Myers, prin. Fax 853-2667

Woodbury Heights, Gloucester, Pop. 3,022
Woodbury Heights SD 200/K-6
100 Academy Ave 08097 856-848-2610
Dr. Janie Haines, admin. Fax 848-8739
www.woodburyhtselem.com/
Woodbury Heights ES 200/K-6
100 Academy Ave 08097 856-848-2610
Janie Haines, prin. Fax 848-8739

St. Margaret Regional S 500/PK-8
773 3rd St 08097 856-845-5200
Sr. Michele DeGregorio, prin. Fax 845-2405

Woodcliff Lake, Bergen, Pop. 5,887
Woodcliff Lake SD 900/PK-8
134 Woodcliff Ave 07677 201-930-5600
Peter Lisi, supt. Fax 930-0488
www.woodcliff-lake.com
Dorchester ES 600/PK-5
100 Dorchester Rd 07677 201-930-5600
John Fierro, prin. Fax 930-0488
Woodcliff MS 300/6-8
134 Woodcliff Ave 07677 201-930-5600
Lauren Barbelet, prin. Fax 391-7932

Woodlynne, Camden, Pop. 2,745
Woodlynne Borough SD 400/PK-8
131 Elm Ave 08107 856-962-8822
Patricia Doloughty Ed.D., supt. Fax 962-0191
www.woodlynne.k12.nj.us
Woodlynne S 400/PK-8
131 Elm Ave 08107 856-962-8822
Patricia Gunning, prin. Fax 962-0191

Wood Ridge, Bergen, Pop. 7,607
Wood-Ridge SD 1,100/K-12
89 Hackensack St 07075 201-933-6777
Elaine Giugliano, supt. Fax 804-9204
www.wood-ridgeschools.org

Doyle ES 500/K-5
250 Wood Ridge Ave 07075 201-933-0440
Joseph Fulco, prin. Fax 939-6049
Ostrovsky MS 200/6-8
540 Windsor Rd 07075 201-939-2103
Robert Recchione, prin. Fax 939-0259

Assumption S 200/PK-8
151 1st St 07075 201-933-0239
Dr. Aileen Gianelli, prin. Fax 438-6408

Woodstown, Salem, Pop. 3,312
Woodstown-Pilesgrove Regional SD 1,600/PK-12
135 East Ave 08098 856-769-0144
James Kerfoot, supt. Fax 769-4549
www.woodstown.org
Shoemaker ES 500/PK-4
207 E Millbrooke Ave 08098 856-769-0144
Diane Cioffi, prin. Fax 769-9388
Woodstown MS 400/5-8
15 Lincoln Ave 08098 856-769-0144
John Fargnoli, prin. Fax 769-3872

Woolwich, Gloucester
Kingsway Regional SD 2,000/7-12
213 Kings Hwy 08085 856-467-4600
Ave Altersitz, supt. Fax 467-5382
www.kingsway.k12.nj.us
Kingsway Regional MS 600/7-8
203 Kings Hwy 08085 856-467-3300
Troy Walton, prin. Fax 467-2703

Swedesboro-Woolwich SD
Supt. — See Swedesboro
Harker ES 3-5
1771 Oldmans Creek Rd 08085 856-241-1552
Robert Titus, prin. Fax 241-2365

Wrightstown, Burlington, Pop. 746
New Hanover Township SD 100/K-8
122 Fort Dix St 08562 609-723-2139
Terri Sackett, supt. Fax 723-6694
www.newhanover.k12.nj.us
New Hanover Twp. S 100/K-8
122 Fort Dix St 08562 609-723-2139
Terri Sackett, prin. Fax 723-6694

North Hanover Township SD 1,000/K-6
331 Monmouth Rd 08562 609-738-2600
Richard Carson Ed.D., supt. Fax 738-2659
nhanover.com
Lamb ES 200/1-4
46 Schoolhouse Rd 08562 609-738-2630
Lynn Misek Ed.D., prin. Fax 738-4993
North Hanover Township Upper ES 200/5-6
351 Monmouth Rd 08562 609-738-2622
Paul Murdaco, prin. Fax 738-2658
Other Schools – See Mc Guire AFB

Kings Academy 100/PK-8
131 E Main St 08562 609-723-8216
Lorna Hassel, prin. Fax 724-9311

Wyckoff, Bergen, Pop. 15,372
Wyckoff Township SD 2,400/K-8
241 Morse Ave 07481 201-848-5700
Dr. Janet Razze, supt. Fax 848-5695
www.wyckoffps.org/
Coolidge ES 400/K-5
420 Grandview Ave 07481 201-848-5710
Robert Famularo, prin. Fax 848-5719
Eisenhower MS 800/6-8
344 Calvin Ct 07481 201-848-5750
Richard Kuder, prin. Fax 848-5682
Lincoln ES 400/K-5
325 Mason Ave 07481 201-848-5720
Dr. Mary Orr, prin. Fax 848-1607
Sicomac ES 400/K-5
356 Sicomac Ave 07481 201-848-5730
Debra Kirsch, prin. Fax 848-5739
Washington ES 400/K-5
270 Woodland Ave 07481 201-848-5740
Scott Blake, prin. Fax 848-0630

Eastern Christian MS 200/5-8
518 Sicomac Ave 07481 201-891-3663
Richard VanYperen, prin. Fax 847-0902
St. Elizabeth S 300/PK-8
Greenwood Ave 07481 201-891-1481
Constance McCue, prin. Fax 891-8669
Wyckoff Christian S 200/PK-K
485 Wyckoff Ave 07481 201-891-7140
Rose Barrett, dir. Fax 891-6119

Yardville, Mercer, Pop. 9,248
Hamilton Township SD
Supt. — See Hamilton
Yardville Heights ES 300/K-5
3880 S Broad St 08620 609-631-4171
Barbara Antonelli, prin. Fax 631-4141

Zarephath, Somerset

Somerset Christian Academy 100/PK-8
595 Weston Canal Rd 08890 732-356-3488
Mary Martin, prin. Fax 868-0386

NEW MEXICO

NEW MEXICO PUBLIC EDUCATION DEPARTMENT
300 Don Gaspar Ave, Santa Fe 87501-2786
Telephone 505-827-5800
Fax 505-827-6696
Website http://www.sde.state.nm.us

Secretary of Education Veronica Garcia

NEW MEXICO BOARD OF EDUCATION
300 Don Gaspar Ave, Santa Fe 87501-2786

Chairperson Carolyn Shearman

REGIONAL EDUCATION COOPS (REC) & REGIONAL CENTER COOPS (RCC)

Central REC 5
Nina Tafoya, dir. 505-889-3412
PO Box 37440, Albuquerque 87176 Fax 889-3422
www.crecnm.org/
High Plains REC 3
Stephen Aguirre, dir. 575-445-7090
101 N 2nd St, Raton 87740 Fax 445-7663
hprec.com
Northeast REC 4
Mary Schutz, dir. 505-426-2085
PO Box 927, Las Vegas 87701 Fax 454-1473
www.rec4.com
Pecos Valley REC 8
Lena Trujillo-Chavez, dir. 575-748-6100
PO Box 155, Artesia 88211 Fax 748-6160
www.pvrec8.com/
REC 2
Dr. Kris Baca, dir. 575-638-5491
PO Box 230, Gallina 87017 Fax 638-0131
REC 6
Patti Harrelson, dir. 575-562-4455
1500 S Avenue K, Portales 88130 Fax 562-4460
www.rec6.net
REC 7
Belinda Morris, dir. 575-393-0755
315 E Clinton St, Hobbs 88240 Fax 393-0249
REC 9
Cathy Jones, dir. 575-257-2368
1400 Sudderth Dr, Ruidoso 88345 Fax 257-2141
www.recixnm.org/
Southwest REC 10
Bruce Hegwer, dir., PO Box 4075 575-894-7589
Truth or Consequences 87901 Fax 894-7584
www.swrecnm.org

PUBLIC, PRIVATE AND CATHOLIC ELEMENTARY SCHOOLS

Abiquiu, Rio Arriba
Espanola SD
Supt. — See Espanola
Abiquiu ES 100/K-6
PO Box 727 87510 505-685-4457
David Maestas, prin. Fax 685-4644

Alamogordo, Otero, Pop. 36,245
Alamogordo SD 6,400/PK-12
PO Box 650 88311 575-812-6000
Michael Harris, supt. Fax 812-6003
aps4kids.org
Buena Vista ES 300/K-5
PO Box 650 88311 575-812-5100
Michelle Korbakes, prin. Fax 812-5103
Chaparral MS 800/6-8
PO Box 650 88311 575-812-6300
Cheryl Kullman, prin. Fax 812-6303
Heights ES 300/K-5
PO Box 650 88311 575-812-5200
Gerald Wheeler, prin. Fax 812-5203
Mountain View MS 500/6-8
PO Box 650 88311 575-812-6400
Mike Farley, prin. Fax 812-6403
North ES 400/PK-5
PO Box 650 88311 575-812-5400
Nicole Henderson, prin. Fax 812-5403
Oregon ES 300/K-5
PO Box 650 88311 575-812-5600
Bertha Garza, prin. Fax 812-5603
Sacramento ES 300/K-5
PO Box 650 88311 575-812-5700
Teresa Valenzuela, prin. Fax 812-5703
Sierra ES 300/K-5
PO Box 650 88311 575-812-5800
Paul Sena, prin. Fax 812-5803
Yucca ES 500/K-5
PO Box 650 88311 575-812-5900
Adrianne Salas, prin. Fax 812-5903
Other Schools – See High Rolls Mountain Park, Holloman AFB, La Luz

---

Fr. James B Hay S 100/PK-8
1000 8th St 88310 575-437-7821
Linda Pickett, prin. Fax 443-6129
Legacy Christian Academy 100/K-12
1206 Greenwood Ln 88310 575-434-0352
Diane Baker, admin. Fax 434-0352

Albuquerque, Bernalillo, Pop. 494,236
Albuquerque SD 86,700/PK-12
PO Box 25704 87125 505-880-3700
Linda Sink, supt. Fax 872-8855
ww2.aps.edu
Acoma ES 300/K-5
11800 Princess Jeanne NE 87112 505-291-6866
Joni Hagemeyer, prin. Fax 299-3625
Adams MS 900/6-8
5401 Glenrio Rd NW 87105 505-831-0400
Renee Salazar, prin. Fax 836-7760
Adobe Acres ES 900/PK-5
1724 Camino Del Valle SW 87105 505-877-4799
Sam Candelaria, prin. Fax 873-8533
Alameda ES 400/K-5
412 Alameda Blvd NW 87114 505-898-0070
Beverly Moya, prin. Fax 898-7430
Alamosa ES 700/PK-5
6500 Sunset Gardens Rd SW 87121 505-836-0288
Florence Goldberg, prin. Fax 831-5643
Alvarado ES 400/K-5
1100 Solar Rd NW 87107 505-344-4412
Leon Bartels, prin. Fax 761-8405
Apache ES 400/PK-5
12800 Copper Ave NE 87123 505-292-7735
Stephanie Fascitelli, prin. Fax 296-2669
Armijo ES 400/K-5
1440 Gatewood Ave SW 87105 505-877-2920
Dolores Vigil-Frank, prin. Fax 877-5613
Arroyo Del Oso ES 400/PK-5
6504 Harper Dr NE 87109 505-821-9393
Joyce Newman, prin. Fax 821-9060
Atrisco ES 300/PK-5
1201 Atrisco Dr SW 87105 505-877-2772
Linda Corona, prin. Fax 873-8542
Baker ES 500/K-5
12015 Tivoli Ave NE Ste B 87111 505-298-7486
Denise Brigman, prin. Fax 299-1495
Bandelier ES 600/K-6
3309 Pershing Ave SE 87106 505-255-8744
Glenda Armstrong, prin. Fax 260-2035
Barcelona ES 600/K-8
2311 Barcelona Rd SW 87105 505-877-0400
Rose White, prin. Fax 873-8531
Bel-Air ES 400/PK-5
4725 Candelaria Rd NE 87110 505-888-4511
Carla Cano, prin. Fax 880-3950
Bellhaven ES 400/K-5
8701 Princess Jeanne Ave NE 87112 505-298-7489
Nedda Hamilton, prin. Fax 291-6871
Binford ES 900/K-5
1400 Corriz Dr SW 87121 505-836-0623
Cecelia Sanchez, prin. Fax 836-7734
Carson ES 800/PK-8
1921 Byron St SW 87105 505-877-2724
Fax 877-1191
Carter MS 1,200/6-8
8901 Bluewater Rd NW 87121 505-833-7540
Rita Martinez, prin. Fax 833-7559
Chamiza ES 700/K-5
5401 Homestead Cir NW 87120 505-897-5174
Deborah Henwood, prin. Fax 897-5176
Chaparral ES 800/PK-5
6325 Milne Rd NW 87120 505-831-3301
Blair Kaufman, prin. Fax 831-6314
Chavez ES 800/PK-5
7500 Barstow St NE 87109 505-821-1810
Kathy Alexander, prin. Fax 857-0171
Chavez ES 400/K-5
2700 Mountain Rd NW 87104 505-764-2008
Loretta Huerta, prin. Fax 764-2010
Chelwood ES 500/K-5
12701 Constitution Ave NE 87112 505-296-5655
Dr. Alan Holmquist, prin. Fax 291-6872
Cleveland MS 700/6-8
6910 Natalie Ave NE 87110 505-881-9227
Susan Labarge, prin. Fax 881-9441
Cochiti ES 300/K-5
3100 San Isidro St NW 87107 505-345-1432
Bernice Herrera, prin. Fax 761-8406
Collet Park ES 400/PK-5
2100 Morris St NE 87112 505-298-3010
Manuel Alzaga, prin. Fax 291-6868
Comanche ES 400/K-5
3505 Pennsylvania St NE 87110 505-884-5275
Rena Highland, prin. Fax 880-3988
Desert Ridge MS 1,100/6-8
8400 Barstow St NE 87122 505-857-9282
Todd Resch, prin. Fax 857-0201
Double Eagle ES 500/K-5
8901 Lowell Dr NE 87122 505-857-0187
Troy Hughes, prin. Fax 857-0188
Duranes ES 300/K-6
2436 Zickert Rd NW 87104 505-764-2017
Gabe Garcia, prin. Fax 764-2019
East San Jose ES 600/K-5
415 Thaxton Ave SE 87102 505-764-2005
Steve Tognoni, prin. Fax 764-2007
Eisenhower MS 900/6-8
11001 Camero Ave NE 87111 505-292-2530
Debra Hamilton, prin. Fax 291-6884
Emerson ES 500/K-5
620 Georgia St SE 87108 505-255-9091
Jacque Costales, prin. Fax 260-2036
Eubank ES 400/K-5
9717 Indian School Rd NE 87112 505-299-4483
Karin Butchart, prin. Fax 298-3088
Field ES 400/PK-5
700 Edith Blvd SE 87102 505-764-2014
James Lujan, prin. Fax 764-2016
Garfield MS 400/6-8
3501 6th St NW 87107 505-344-1647
Rhonda Sandoval, prin. Fax 344-6562
Gonzales ES 400/K-5
900 Atlantic Ave SW 87102 505-764-2020
Dora Ortiz, prin. Fax 243-5440
Gonzales ES 1,200/K-5
554 90th St SW 87121 505-831-6214
Michael Carrillo, prin. Fax 831-3036
Governor Bent ES 600/K-5
5700 Hendrix Rd NE 87110 505-881-9797
Patricia Willis, prin. Fax 881-8885
Grant MS 800/6-8
1111 Easterday Dr NE 87112 505-299-2113
Ed Briggs, prin. Fax 291-6881
Griegos ES 300/K-5
4040 San Isidro St NW 87107 505-345-3661
Thomas Graham, prin. Fax 344-2565
Harrison MS 800/6-8
3912 Isleta Blvd SW 87105 505-877-1279
Christine Eisenberg, prin. Fax 877-6797
Hawthorne ES 500/PK-5
420 General Somervell St NE 87123 505-299-0796
Debbie Montoya, prin. Fax 291-6836
Hayes MS 500/6-8
1100 Texas St NE 87110 505-265-7741
Stephanie Williams, prin. Fax 260-6108
Hodgin ES 600/PK-5
3801 Morningside Dr NE 87110 505-881-9855
Mickey Kortsch, prin. Fax 881-0706
Hoover MS 700/6-8
12015 Tivoli Ave NE Ste A 87111 505-298-6896
Wayne Knight, prin. Fax 291-6880
Hughes ES 700/K-5
5701 Mojave St NW 87120 505-897-3080
Jami Jacobson, prin. Fax 898-2894
Humphrey ES 500/PK-5
9801 Academy Hills Dr NE 87111 505-821-4981
Paula Miller, prin. Fax 857-0185

Inez ES 500/PK-5
1700 Pennsylvania St NE 87110 505-299-9010
Alexis Kern, prin. Fax 299-5311
Jackson ES 500/K-5
4720 Cairo Dr NE 87111 505-296-9536
Jack Vermillion, prin. Fax 292-2346
Jackson MS 700/6-8
10600 Indian School Rd NE 87112 505-299-7377
Ann Piper, prin. Fax 291-6887
Jefferson MS 800/6-8
712 Girard Blvd NE 87106 505-255-8691
Michael McNamara, prin. Fax 268-2334
Johnson MS 1,000/6-8
6811 Taylor Ranch Rd NW 87120 505-898-1492
Marcie Johnson, prin. Fax 898-7150
Kennedy MS 500/6-8
721 Tomasita St NE 87123 505-298-6701
Ruby Ethridge, prin. Fax 291-6879
Kirtland ES 300/K-5
3530 Gibson Blvd SE 87116 505-255-3131
Peter Espinosa, prin. Fax 255-1255
La Luz ES 400/PK-5
225 Griegos Rd NW 87107 505-761-8415
Linda Duran, prin. Fax 344-2890
La Mesa ES 700/PK-5
7500 Copper Ave NE 87108 505-262-1581
Monica Tapia, prin. Fax 260-2033
Lavaland ES 600/PK-5
501 57th St NW 87105 505-836-4911
V. Webb Jaramillo, prin. Fax 833-1332
Longfellow ES 400/K-5
400 Edith Blvd NE 87102 505-764-2024
Ninfa Agnello-Harrington, prin. Fax 766-5243
Los Padillas ES 500/K-6
2525 Los Padillas Rd SW 87105 505-877-0108
Sara Keeney, prin. Fax 873-8527
Los Ranchos ES 400/K-5
7609 4th St NW 87107 505-898-0794
Christine Lopez, prin. Fax 898-2080
Lowell ES 400/PK-5
1700 Sunshine Ter SE 87106 505-764-2011
Renee Gallegos, prin. Fax 764-2013
MacArthur ES 300/PK-5
1100 Douglas MacArthur NW 87107 505-344-1482
Fax 344-3927
Madison MS 800/6-8
3501 Moon St NE 87111 505-299-4735
Sean Joyce, prin. Fax 323-9512
Manzano Mesa ES 700/K-5
801 Elizabeth St SE 87123 505-292-6707
Audie Brown, prin. Fax 292-6719
Marmon ES 800/K-5
6401 Iliff Rd NW 87120 505-831-5400
Maria Barraza-Martinez, prin. Fax 833-1565
Matheson Park ES 300/K-5
10809 Lexington Ave NE 87112 505-299-5087
Stephen Maresca, prin. Fax 298-4302
McCollum ES 400/PK-5
10900 San Jacinto Ave NE 87112 505-298-5009
Letha Oman, prin. Fax 298-3840
McKinley MS 700/6-8
4500 Comanche Rd NE 87110 505-881-9390
Fax 880-3968
Mission Avenue ES 400/PK-5
725 Mission Ave NE 87107 505-344-5269
Stephen Pino, prin. Fax 761-8413
Mitchell ES 400/K-5
10121 Comanche Rd NE 87111 505-299-1937
Deborah Garrison, prin. Fax 296-0012
Monroe MS 1,400/6-8
6100 Paradise Blvd NW 87114 505-897-0101
Vernon Martinez, prin. Fax 897-2371
Monte Vista ES 500/K-5
3211 Monte Vista Blvd NE 87106 505-268-3520
Leith Page, prin. Fax 255-4680
Montezuma ES 500/K-5
3100 Indian School Rd NE 87106 505-260-2040
Deborah Detorie, prin. Fax 268-7731
Mountain View ES 300/K-5
5317 2nd St SW 87105 505-877-3800
Richard Ulibarri, prin. Fax 873-8511
Navajo ES 600/K-5
2936 Hughes Rd SW 87105 505-873-8512
Tracy Herrera, prin. Fax 873-8513
North Star ES K-5
9301 Ventura St NE 87122 505-856-6578
Diane Kerschen, prin. Fax 856-7486
O'Keefe ES 600/K-5
11701 San Victorio Ave NE 87111 505-293-4259
Janis Keene, prin. Fax 293-4586
Onate ES 300/PK-5
12415 Brntwod Hills Blvd NE 87112 505-291-6819
Theresa Fullerton, prin. Fax 275-0648
Osuna ES 400/K-5
4715 Moon St NE 87111 505-296-4811
Rebecca Robertson, prin. Fax 291-6840
Painted Sky ES 1,000/K-5
8101 Gavin Dr NW 87120 505-836-7763
Pat Woodard Ph.D., prin. Fax 836-7765
Pajarito ES 600/K-8
2701 Don Felipe Rd SW 87105 505-877-9718
Gene Saavedra, prin. Fax 873-8539
Petroglyph ES 800/PK-5
5100 Marna Lynn Ave NW 87114 505-898-0923
George Jackson, prin. Fax 898-0949
Polk MS 400/6-8
2220 Raymac Rd SW 87105 505-877-6444
Eva Vigil, prin. Fax 877-1618
Pyle MS 700/6-8
1820 Valdora Rd SW 87105 505-877-3770
Agnes Cordoba, prin. Fax 873-8540
Rey ES 900/PK-5
1215 Cerrillos Rd SW 87121 505-836-7738
Judith Touloumis, prin. Fax 831-4401
Ross ES 500/K-5
6700 Palomas Ave NE 87109 505-821-0185
Sara Sanchez, prin. Fax 821-8688

Sandia Base ES 500/K-6
21001 Wyoming Blvd SE 87116 505-268-4356
Marcella Jones, prin. Fax 260-2028
Seven Bar ES 800/K-5
4501 Seven Bar Loop Rd NW 87114 505-899-2797
Nancy Lacher, prin. Fax 899-4376
Sierra Vista ES 800/K-5
10220 Paseo Del Norte NW 87114 505-898-0272
Gionna Jaramillo, prin. Fax 898-1796
Sombra Del Monte ES 400/PK-5
9110 Shoshone Rd NE 87111 505-291-6842
Donna Key, prin. Fax 292-8237
Taylor MS 600/6-8
8200 Guadalupe Trl NW 87114 505-898-3666
Nancy Romero, prin. Fax 897-5165
Tomasita ES 400/K-5
701 Tomasita St NE 87123 505-291-6844
Deborah Vehar, prin. Fax 275-0224
Truman MS 1,100/6-8
9400 Benavides Rd SW 87121 505-836-3030
Judith Martin-Tafoya, prin. Fax 836-7745
Twain ES 300/PK-5
6316 Constitution Ave NE 87110 505-255-8337
Glenn Wilcox, prin. Fax 268-3220
Valle Vista ES 500/PK-5
1700 Mae Ave SW 87105 505-836-7739
Teresa Archuleta, prin. Fax 831-2222
Van Buren MS 600/6-8
700 Louisiana Blvd SE 87108 505-268-3833
Mary Cade, prin. Fax 260-6104
Ventana Ranch ES 1,300/K-5
6801 Ventana Village Rd NW 87114 505-890-7375
Lynn McMahan, prin. Fax 890-4124
Wallace ES 300/K-5
513 6th St NW 87102 505-848-9409
Jo Peters, prin. Fax 848-9411
Washington MS 600/6-8
1101 Park Ave SW 87102 505-764-2000
Cynthia Challberg-Hale, prin. Fax 764-2022
Whittier ES 400/K-5
1110 Quincy St SE 87108 505-255-2008
Cindy Bazner, prin. Fax 260-2026
Wilson MS 500/6-8
1138 Cardenas Dr SE 87108 505-268-3961
Connie Hansen, prin. Fax 260-2000
Zia ES 400/PK-5
440 Jefferson St NE 87108 505-260-2020
Gregory McMann, prin. Fax 255-1014
Zuni ES 500/K-5
6300 Claremont Ave NE 87110 505-881-8313
Debbie Elder, prin. Fax 889-8621
Other Schools – See Corrales, Kirtland AFB, Los Ranchos, Sandia Park, Tijeras

---

Albuquerque Christian S 400/PK-8
7201B Montgomery Blvd NE 87109 505-872-0777
Shaun Adams, prin. Fax 830-3889
Calvary Christian Academy 200/PK-12
1404 Lead Ave SE 87106 505-842-8681
George Cowan, hdmstr. Fax 842-8746
Christ Lutheran S 200/PK-8
7701 Candelaria Rd NE 87110 505-884-3876
Mark Van Soosten, prin. Fax 888-0655
Crestview SDA S 50/PK-8
6000 Ouray Rd NW 87120 505-836-0536
Cross of Hope Lutheran S 100/K-5
6104 Taylor Ranch Rd NW 87120 505-897-1832
Anna Ulibarri, prin. Fax 897-9455
Eastern Hills Christian Academy 300/PK-8
3100 Morris St NE 87111 505-294-3373
Dee Hutson, admin. Fax 298-8564
Escuela del Sol Montessori 200/PK-6
1114 7th St NW 87102 505-242-3033
Friedje Van Gils, prin. Fax 317-4752
Evangel Christian Academy 300/PK-12
4501 Montgomery Blvd NE 87109 505-883-4674
Nick Olona M.A., prin. Fax 883-1229
Heights Adventist S 50/1-8
PO Box 14528 87191 505-292-0913
Holy Ghost S 200/PK-8
6201 Ross Ave SE 87108 505-256-1563
Noreen Copeland, prin. Fax 262-9635
Hope Christian S 1,400/PK-12
8005 Louisiana Blvd NE 87109 505-822-8868
Kelly McEachran, hdmstr. Fax 822-8260
Immanuel Lutheran S 200/K-8
300 Gold Ave SE 87102 505-243-2589
R. Charlie Pflieger, prin.
Manzano Day S 500/PK-5
1801 Central Ave NW 87104 505-243-6659
Neal Piltch, hdmstr. Fax 243-4711
Nativity of Blessed Virgin Mary S 50/PK-K
9502 4th St NW 87114 505-897-6501
Nancy Suedkamp, prin. Fax 898-0496
New Life Baptist Academy 200/PK-12
6900 Los Volcanes Rd NW 87121 505-352-2628
Lillie Allen, prin. Fax 352-2684
Our Lady of Fatima S 200/K-8
4020 Lomas Blvd NE 87110 505-255-6391
Tim Whalen, prin. Fax 268-0680
Our Lady of the Annunciation S 400/PK-8
2610 Utah St NE 87110 505-299-6783
Cindy Shields, prin. Fax 299-2182
Our Lady of the Assumption S 200/PK-8
815 Guaymas Pl NE 87108 505-256-3167
Robert Kaiser, prin. Fax 256-3131
Queen of Heaven S 200/K-8
5303 Phoenix Ave NE 87110 505-881-2484
Richard Dodson, prin. Fax 837-1123
St. Charles Borromeo S 400/K-8
1801 Hazeldine Ave SE 87106 505-243-5788
Barbara Rossow-Deming, prin. Fax 764-8842
St. Mary S 600/PK-8
224 7th St NW 87102 505-243-5470
Sr. Marianella Domenici, prin. Fax 242-4837

St. Therese S 100/PK-8
311 Shropshire Ave NW 87107 505-344-4479
Roman Garcia, prin. Fax 344-4486
San Felipe Del Neri S 200/PK-8
2000 Lomas Blvd NW 87104 505-242-2411
Nancy Suedkamp, prin. Fax 242-7355
Shepherd Lutheran S 50/K-8
3900 Wyoming Blvd NE 87111 505-292-6622
Paul Schultz, prin. Fax 323-6766
Solomon Schechter Day S of Albuquerque 100/K-5
5520 Wyoming Blvd NE Ste A 87109 505-232-2325
Kathryn Weil Ph.D., prin. Fax 232-3422
Sunset Mesa S 400/PK-5
3020 Morris St NE 87111 505-298-7626
Alan Mask, dir. Fax 298-6132
Temple Baptist Academy 200/PK-12
1621 Arizona St NE 87110 505-262-0969
Monty Wyss, admin. Fax 262-0996
Valley Christian Academy 100/PK-6
2850 Gun Club Rd SW 87105 505-877-5510
David Morgan, prin. Fax 877-3208
Victory Christian S 100/K-12
220 El Pueblo Rd NW 87114 505-898-3060
Glenn Frey, admin. Fax 898-6690
Western Heights Christian S 100/PK-5
6415 Sage Rd SW 87121 505-247-2079
Brenda Franklin, prin. Fax 247-2079

Alcalde, Rio Arriba, Pop. 308
Espanola SD
Supt. — See Espanola
Alcalde ES 200/K-6
PO Box 219 87511 505-852-4253
Leroy Martinez, prin. Fax 852-2523

Algodones, Sandoval
Bernalillo SD
Supt. — See Bernalillo
Algodones ES 100/PK-5
1399 Highway 313 87001 505-867-2803
Laura Greenleaf, prin. Fax 867-7853

Animas, Hidalgo
Animas SD 300/PK-12
PO Box 85 88020 575-548-2299
Jerry Birdwell, supt. Fax 548-2388
www.animask12.net
Animas ES 100/PK-4
PO Box 110 88020 575-548-2297
Jerry Birdwell, prin. Fax 548-2388
Animas MS 100/5-8
PO Box 110 88020 575-548-2296
Jerry Birdwell, prin. Fax 548-2388

Anthony, Dona Ana, Pop. 5,160
Gadsden ISD
Supt. — See Sunland Park
Anthony ES 700/PK-6
PO Box 2631 88021 575-882-4561
Graciela Marquez, prin. Fax 882-4696
Berino ES 700/PK-6
92 Shrode Rd 88021 575-882-2242
Reyes Valtierra, prin. Fax 882-7249
Gadsden MS 1,000/7-8
1301 Washington St 88021 575-882-2372
Dr. David Garcia, prin. Fax 882-5227
Loma Linda ES 500/K-6
1451 Donaldson Ave 88021 575-882-6000
Charlene Bonham, prin. Fax 882-4718

Anton Chico, Guadalupe
Santa Rosa Consolidated SD
Supt. — See Santa Rosa
Anton Chico MS 50/6-8
PO Box 169 87711 575-427-6038
Ted Hern, prin. Fax 427-4246
Marquez ES 50/K-5
PO Box 169 87711 575-427-6038
Ted Hern, prin. Fax 427-4246

Arrey, Sierra
Truth or Consequences Municipal SD
Supt. — See Truth or Consequences
Arrey ES 200/PK-5
PO Box 336 87930 575-267-4778
Susan Taylor, prin. Fax 267-5865

Arroyo Seco, Taos
Taos Municipal SD
Supt. — See Taos
Arroyo Del Norte ES 200/K-5
405 Hondo Seco Rd 87514 575-737-6175
Lucille Jaramillo, prin. Fax 737-6176

Artesia, Eddy, Pop. 10,481
Artesia SD 3,600/PK-12
1106 W Quay Ave 88210 575-746-3585
Mike Phipps, supt. Fax 746-6232
www.bulldogs.org
Artesia IS 500/6-7
1100 W Bullock Ave 88210 575-746-2766
John Ross Null, prin. Fax 746-4097
Central ES, 405 S 6th St 88210 100/1-5
Tammy Davis, prin. 575-746-4811
Grand Heights ECC 400/PK-K
2302 W Grand Ave 88210 575-746-6282
Lisa Robinson, prin.
Hermosa ES 400/1-5
601 W Hermosa Dr 88210 575-746-3812
Paula Menefee, prin.
Roselawn ES 200/1-5
600 N Roselawn Ave 88210 575-746-2812
Tina Perez, prin.
Yeso ES, 1812 W Centre Ave 88210 400/1-5
Danny Parker, prin. 575-748-2755
Yucca ES, 1106 W Quay Ave 88210 300/1-5
Sylvia Flores, prin. 575-746-3711
Other Schools – See Hope

Aztec, San Juan, Pop. 7,084
Aztec Municipal SD — 3,100/PK-12
1118 W Aztec Blvd 87410 — 505-334-9474
Dr. Linda Paul, supt. — Fax 334-9861
www.aztecschools.com
Koogler MS — 700/6-8
455 N Light Plant Rd 87410 — 505-334-6102
Rick Espinoza, prin. — Fax 599-4385
McCoy Avenue ES — 500/PK-3
901 McCoy Ave 87410 — 505-334-6831
Cynthia Sosaya, prin. — Fax 599-4384
Park Avenue ES — 400/4-5
507 S Park Ave 87410 — 505-334-9469
Tania Prokop, prin. — Fax 599-4336
Rippey ES — 400/PK-3
401 Rio Pecos Rd 87410 — 505-334-2621
Judy Englehart, prin. — Fax 599-4391

Bayard, Grant, Pop. 2,397
Cobre Consolidated SD — 1,400/PK-12
PO Box 1000 88023 — 575-537-4010
Dane Kennon, supt. — Fax 537-5455
www.cobre.k12.nm.us
Bayard ES — 200/K-6
PO Box 1040 88023 — 575-537-4040
Duane Springer, prin. — Fax 537-3335
Snell MS — 200/7-8
PO Box 729 88023 — 575-537-4030
Jeff Gorum, prin. — Fax 537-3358
Other Schools – See Central, Hurley, San Lorenzo

Belen, Valencia, Pop. 7,121
Belen Consolidated SD — 4,800/PK-12
520 N Main St 87002 — 505-966-1000
Dr. Patricia Rael, supt. — Fax 966-1005
belen.schoolfusion.us
Belen MS — 700/7-8
520 N Main St 87002 — 505-966-1600
Buddy Dillow, prin. — Fax 966-1650
Central ES, 520 N Main St 87002 — 300/4-6
Sonia Lawson, prin. — 505-966-1200
Chavez ES — 400/PK-6
520 N Main St 87002 — 505-966-1800
Armando Reyes, prin. — Fax 966-1850
Jaramillo ES — 400/PK-3
520 N Main St 87002 — 505-966-2000
Julie Benavidez, prin. — Fax 966-2050
La Merced ES — 600/K-6
520 N Main St 87002 — 505-966-2100
John Caldarera, prin. — Fax 966-2150
La Promesa ES — 200/PK-6
520 N Main St 87002 — 505-966-2400
Diane Vallejos, prin. — Fax 966-2450
Rio Grande ES — 300/PK-6
520 N Main St 87002 — 505-966-2200
Dolores Gabaldon, prin. — Fax 966-2250
Sanchez ES — 400/PK-6
520 N Main St 87002 — 505-966-1900
Jennifer Brown, prin. — Fax 966-1950

Calvary Chapel Academy — 50/K-6
19381 Highway 314 87002 — 505-864-6611
Johnny Sanchez, prin. — Fax 864-1364
St. Mary S — 200/PK-8
Church and Tenth St 87002 — 505-864-0484
Dr. Gayle Fortna, prin. — Fax 864-2414

Bernalillo, Sandoval, Pop. 6,938
Bernalillo SD — 3,100/PK-12
224 N Camino Del Pueblo 87004 — 505-867-2317
Barbara Vigil-Lowder, supt. — Fax 867-7850
www.bernalillo-schools.org/
Bernalillo MS — 500/6-8
485 Camino don Tomas 87004 — 505-867-3309
Donna Miles, prin. — Fax 867-7819
Carroll ES — 400/3-5
301 Calle Del Escuela 87004 — 505-867-3366
Keith Cowan, prin. — Fax 867-7851
Roosevelt ES — 500/PK-2
842 Camino don Tomas 87004 — 505-867-5472
Ruth Cerutti, prin. — Fax 867-7872
Other Schools – See Algodones, Pena Blanca, Placitas, Santo Domingo Pueblo

Bloomfield, San Juan, Pop. 7,442
Bloomfield SD — 3,000/PK-12
325 N Bergin Ln 87413 — 505-632-3316
Randy Allison, supt. — Fax 632-4371
www.bsin.k12.nm.us
Blanco ES — 300/PK-6
7313 Highway 64 87413 — 505-634-3900
Fax 634-3902
Bloomfield ECC — 100/PK-PK
310 LaJara St 87413 — 505-634-3883
Deb Latta, prin. — Fax 634-3856
Central PS — 700/1-3
310 W Sycamore Ave 87413 — 505-634-3603
Karen Smith, prin. — Fax 634-3675
Mesa Alta JHS — 500/7-8
329 N Bergin Ln 87413 — 505-632-4350
Robert Ford, prin. — Fax 634-3835
Naaba Ani ES — 600/4-6
1201 N 1st St 87413 — 505-634-3500
Allan Bassing, prin. — Fax 634-3584

Bluewater, Cibola
Grants-Cibola County SD
Supt. — See Grants
Bluewater ES — 100/K-6
General Delivery 87005 — 505-285-2695
Sergio Castanon, prin. — Fax 285-2698

Bosque Farms, Valencia, Pop. 3,969
Los Lunas SD
Supt. — See Los Lunas
Bosque Farms ES — 400/PK-5
1390 W Bosque Loop 87068 — 505-869-2646
Ron Hendrix, prin. — Fax 869-5146

Capitan, Lincoln, Pop. 1,500
Capitan Municipal SD — 600/PK-12
PO Box 278 88316 — 575-354-8500
Shirley Crawford, supt. — Fax 354-8505
www.capitan.k12.nm.us
Capitan ES — 300/PK-5
PO Box 278 88316 — 575-354-8501
Tootsie Monroe, prin. — Fax 354-8506
Capitan MS — 100/6-8
PO Box 278 88316 — 575-354-8502
Teresa Burns, prin. — Fax 354-8507

Carlsbad, Eddy, Pop. 25,300
Carlsbad Municipal SD — 5,700/K-12
408 N Canyon St 88220 — 575-234-3300
Sheri Williams, supt. — Fax 234-3367
www.carlsbad.k12.nm.us
Alta Vista MS — 600/6-8
408 N Canyon St 88220 — 575-234-3316
Claudia Krause-Johnson, prin. — Fax 234-3478
Craft ES — 200/1-5
408 N Canyon St 88220 — 575-234-3304
Merci Montoya, prin. — Fax 234-3492
Early Childhood Education Center — 500/K-K
408 N Canyon St 88220 — 575-234-3303
Misti Fernandez, prin. — Fax 234-3445
Eddy ES — 200/1-5
408 N Canyon St 88220 — 575-234-3305
Sandra Nunley, prin. — Fax 234-3511
Hillcrest ES — 200/1-5
408 N Canyon St 88220 — 575-234-3308
Janey Lynn, prin. — Fax 234-3522
Leyva MS — 800/6-8
408 N Canyon St 88220 — 575-234-3318
LaQuita Wheeler, prin. — Fax 234-3452
Monterrey ES — 300/1-5
408 N Canyon St 88220 — 575-234-3309
Therese Rodriguez, prin. — Fax 234-3531
Pate ES — 100/1-5
408 N Canyon St 88220 — 575-234-3310
Bernita Smith-Payne, prin. — Fax 234-3543
Puckett ES — 200/1-5
408 N Canyon St 88220 — 575-234-3311
Deborah Beard, prin. — Fax 234-3552
Riverside ES — 300/1-5
408 N Canyon St 88220 — 575-234-3312
Edith Bryant, prin. — Fax 234-3561
Smith ES — 200/1-5
408 N Canyon St 88220 — 575-234-3314
Ernie Garcia, prin. — Fax 234-3581
Sunset ES — 400/1-5
408 N Canyon St 88220 — 575-234-3315
Lee White, prin. — Fax 234-3593

St. Edward S — 50/K-5
805 Walter St 88220 — 575-885-4620
David Gomez, prin. — Fax 885-7706

Carrizozo, Lincoln, Pop. 1,063
Carrizozo Municipal SD — 200/PK-12
PO Box 99 88301 — 575-648-2348
Robert Cobos, supt. — Fax 648-2216
www.cmsgrizzlies.org/
Carrizozo ES — 100/PK-4
PO Box 99 88301 — 575-648-2346
Jerrett Perry, prin. — Fax 648-3255
Carrizozo MS — 100/5-8
PO Box 99 88301 — 575-648-2346
Jerrett Perry, prin. — Fax 648-3255

Cedar Crest, Bernalillo

Prince of Peace Lutheran S — 100/PK-8
12121 State Highway 14 N 87008 — 505-281-6833
Alan Geuder, prin. — Fax 281-3918

Central, Grant, Pop. 2,054
Cobre Consolidated SD
Supt. — See Bayard
Central ES — 300/PK-6
PO Box 315 88026 — 575-537-4050
Johnny Benavidez, prin. — Fax 537-5382

Chama, Rio Arriba, Pop. 1,173
Chama Valley ISD
Supt. — See Tierra Amarilla
Chama ES — 100/PK-5
PO Box 337 87520 — 575-756-2146
Larkin Vigil, prin. — Fax 756-2538
Chama MS — 50/6-8
PO Box 337 87520 — 575-756-2161
Larkin Vigil, prin. — Fax 756-2538

Chaparral, Dona Ana, Pop. 2,962
Gadsden ISD
Supt. — See Sunland Park
Chaparral ES — 800/PK-6
300 E Lisa Dr, — 575-824-4722
Brenda Ballard, prin. — Fax 824-4034
Chaparral MS — 300/7-8
290 E Lisa Dr, — 575-824-4847
Marti Muela, prin. — Fax 824-4045
Desert Trail ES — 600/K-6
310 E Lisa Dr, — 575-824-6500
Pat Martinez, prin. — Fax 824-3390
Sunrise ES — 500/K-6
1000 S County Line Dr, — 575-824-0060
Cecilia Doran, prin. — Fax 824-3136

Chimayo, Rio Arriba, Pop. 2,789
Espanola SD
Supt. — See Espanola
Chimayo ES — 200/K-6
PO Box 219 87522 — 505-351-4207
Wilfredo Aguilar, prin. — Fax 351-2475

Church Rock, McKinley
Gallup-McKinley County SD
Supt. — See Gallup
Church Rock ES — 300/PK-5
PO Box 40 87311 — 505-488-5273
Gary Schuster, prin. — Fax 721-1499

Cimarron, Colfax, Pop. 877
Cimarron Municipal SD — 400/K-12
125 N Collison Ave 87714 — 575-376-2445
James Gallegos, supt. — Fax 376-2442
cimarronschools.org/
Cimarron ES — 100/K-4
125 N Collison Ave 87714 — 575-376-2512
Penny Coppedge, prin. — Fax 376-2217
Cimarron MS — 100/5-8
125 N Collison Ave 87714 — 575-376-2512
Penny Coppedge, prin. — Fax 376-2217
Other Schools – See Eagle Nest

Clayton, Union, Pop. 2,186
Clayton Municipal SD — 500/PK-12
323 S 5th St 88415 — 575-374-9611
Jack Wiley, supt. — Fax 374-9881
www.claytonschools.us/
Alvis ES — 200/PK-4
323 S 5th St 88415 — 575-374-2321
Claudia Montoya, prin. — Fax 374-9881
Clayton JHS — 100/7-8
323 S 5th St 88415 — 575-374-9543
Terrell Jones, prin. — Fax 374-9469
Kiser ES — 100/5-6
323 S 5th St 88415 — 575-374-2741
Stacy Diller, prin. — Fax 374-9881

Cliff, Grant
Silver Consolidated SD
Supt. — See Silver City
Cliff ES — 100/K-6
PO Box 9 88028 — 575-535-2050
Clayton Ellwanger, prin. — Fax 535-2054

Cloudcroft, Otero, Pop. 764
Cloudcroft Municipal SD — 400/PK-12
PO Box 198 88317 — 575-682-2361
Tommy Hancock, supt. — Fax 682-2921
www.cmsbears.org
Cloudcroft S — 200/PK-8
PO Box 198 88317 — 575-682-3336
Fred Wright, prin. — Fax 682-2776

Clovis, Curry, Pop. 33,357
Clovis Municipal SD — 7,600/PK-12
PO Box 19000 88102 — 575-769-4300
Dr. Rhonda Seidenwurm, supt. — Fax 769-4334
www.clovis-schools.org/
Arts Academy at Bella Vista — 400/K-6
2900 Cesar Chavez Dr 88101 — 575-769-4435
Shelly Norris, prin. — Fax 769-4437
Barry ES — 300/K-6
3401 N Thornton St 88101 — 575-769-4430
Carrie Bunce, prin. — Fax 769-4433
Bickley ES — 400/K-6
500 W 14th St 88101 — 575-769-4450
Todd Morris, prin. — Fax 769-4826
Cameo ES — 400/PK-6
1500 Cameo St 88101 — 575-769-4440
Tony Igo, prin. — Fax 769-4444
Highland ES — 400/K-6
100 E Plains Ave 88101 — 575-769-4445
Matthew Trujillo, prin. — Fax 769-4449
La Casita ES — 500/K-6
400 N Davis St 88101 — 575-769-4455
Henry Montano, prin. — Fax 769-4454
Lockwood ES — 400/K-6
400 Lockwood Dr 88101 — 575-769-4465
Adan Estrada, prin. — Fax 769-4467
Marshall MS — 300/7-8
100 Commerce Way 88101 — 575-769-4410
Jay Brady, prin. — Fax 769-4413
Mesa ES — 500/K-6
4801 N Norris St 88101 — 575-769-4470
Jan Cox, prin. — Fax 769-4472
Parkview ES — 400/K-6
1121 Maple St 88101 — 575-769-4475
Joe Parks, prin. — Fax 769-4478
Ranchvale ES — 200/K-6
1606 SR 311 88101 — 575-985-2277
Suzanne Brockmeier, prin. — Fax 985-2618
Sandia ES — 400/K-6
2801 Lore St 88101 — 575-769-4480
Matthew Vetterly, prin. — Fax 769-4482
Yucca MS — 500/7-8
1500 Sycamore St 88101 — 575-769-4420
Alan Dropps, prin. — Fax 769-4421
Zia ES — 400/K-6
2400 N Norris St 88101 — 575-769-4485
Jarilyn Butler, prin. — Fax 769-4487

Clovis Christian S — 300/PK-12
PO Box 608 88102 — 575-763-5311
Steven Schultze, supt. — Fax 763-4469

Columbus, Luna, Pop. 1,841
Deming SD
Supt. — See Deming
Columbus ES — 500/K-6
PO Box 210 88029 — 575-531-2710
Hector Madrid, prin. — Fax 531-2303

Cordova, Rio Arriba
Espanola SD
Supt. — See Espanola
Mountain View ES — 100/K-6
PO Box 39 87523 — 505-351-4480
Grace Martinez, lead tchr. — Fax 351-2401

Corona, Lincoln, Pop. 170
Corona Municipal SD — 100/PK-12
PO Box 258 88318 — 575-849-1911
Travis Lightfoot, supt. — Fax 849-2026
www.cpscardinals.org

Corona ES 50/PK-6
PO Box 258 88318 575-849-1711
Rick Cogdill, prin. Fax 849-2026

Corrales, Sandoval, Pop. 7,638
Albuquerque SD
Supt. — See Albuquerque
Corrales ES 600/K-5
200 Target Rd 87048 505-792-7400
Deanne Golleher, prin. Fax 897-5167

Cottonwood Montessori S 200/PK-5
3896 Corrales Rd 87048 505-897-8375
Patricia Nickerson, prin. Fax 890-1533
Sandia View S 100/K-8
24 Academy Dr 87048 505-897-4805

Costilla, Taos
Questa ISD
Supt. — See Questa
Rio Costilla ES 50/K-6
PO Box 99 87524 575-586-0089
Diana Sanchez, prin. Fax 586-2154

Coyote, Rio Arriba
Jemez Mountain SD
Supt. — See Gallina
Coyote ES 50/K-5
PO Box 100 87012 575-638-5422
Vicky Abreu, prin. Fax 638-5355

Crownpoint, McKinley, Pop. 2,108
Gallup-McKinley County SD
Supt. — See Gallup
Crownpoint ES 300/PK-6
PO Box 709 87313 505-786-5323
Jackie Gilman, prin. Fax 721-1599
Crownpoint MS 200/6-8
PO Box 1318 87313 505-786-5663
John Bryant, prin. Fax 721-5499

Cuba, Sandoval, Pop. 616
Cuba ISD 700/PK-12
PO Box 70 87013 575-289-3211
Victor Velarde, supt. Fax 289-3314
cuba.k12.nm.us/
Cuba ES 200/PK-5
PO Box 70 87013 575-289-3211
Bill Hamm, prin. Fax 289-3314
Cuba MS 100/6-8
PO Box 70 87013 575-289-3211
Ed Painter, prin. Fax 289-3314

Jemez Mountain SD
Supt. — See Gallina
Lybrook S 100/K-8
US Highway 550 Box 9935 87013 575-568-4491
Jacqueline Mangham, prin. Fax 568-9413

Immaculate Conception S 50/PK-5
PO Box 218 87013 575-289-3749
Richard Barncord, prin. Fax 289-0031

Cubero, Cibola
Grants-Cibola County SD
Supt. — See Grants
Cubero ES 200/K-6
PO Box 8128 87014 505-285-2706
Guy Archambeau, prin. Fax 285-2709

Datil, Catron
Quemado ISD
Supt. — See Quemado
Datil ES 50/K-6
PO Box 200 87821 575-772-5574
Mona Bassett, prin. Fax 772-5575

Deming, Luna, Pop. 14,876
Deming SD 3,500/PK-12
1001 S Diamond Ave 88030 575-546-8841
Harvielee Moore, supt. Fax 546-8517
www.demingps.org
Bataan ES 500/K-5
2200 Highway 418 SW 88030 575-544-0900
Debbie Robertson, prin. Fax 544-0829
Bell ES, 1000 E Maple St 88030 100/K-5
Marlene Padron, prin. 575-546-9712
Chaparral ES 500/K-5
1400 E Holly St 88030 575-546-2047
Denise Wilkin, prin. Fax 546-6062
Deming IS 400/6-6
500 W Ash St 88030 575-546-6560
Denise Ruttle, prin. Fax 544-3656
Memorial ES 300/K-5
1000 S 10th St 88030 575-546-2502
Frank Milo, prin. Fax 546-6013
My Little S 100/PK-PK
905 S Zinc St 88030 575-546-6899
Beth Boggs, prin. Fax 546-6786
Red Mountain MS 7-8
2100 Highway 418 SW 88030 575-546-0668
Robin Parnell, prin. Fax 546-9263
Torres ES K-5
1910 8th St NW 88030 575-544-2723
Vicki Chavez, prin. Fax 544-2726
Other Schools – See Columbus

Des Moines, Union, Pop. 154
Des Moines Municipal SD 100/K-12
PO Box 38 88418 575-278-2611
Garrett Bosarge, supt. Fax 278-2617
Des Moines ES 100/K-6
PO Box 38 88418 575-278-2611
Ray Churchman, prin. Fax 278-2617

Dexter, Chaves, Pop. 1,230
Dexter Consolidated SD 1,100/PK-12
PO Box 159 88230 575-734-5420
Patricia Parsons, supt. Fax 734-6813
www.dexterdemons.org
Dexter ES 500/PK-5
PO Box 159 88230 575-734-5420
Nancy Corn, prin. Fax 734-5424
Dexter MS 300/6-8
PO Box 159 88230 575-734-5420
Lesa Dodd, prin. Fax 734-6811

Dixon, Rio Arriba
Espanola SD
Supt. — See Espanola
Dixon ES 100/K-6
PO Box 40 87527 505-579-4325
Kiva Moulton-Duckworth, lead tchr. Fax 579-4049

Dora, Roosevelt, Pop. 127
Dora Consolidated SD 200/PK-12
PO Box 327 88115 575-477-2216
Steve Barron, supt. Fax 477-2464
www.doraschools.com
Dora ES 100/PK-6
PO Box 327 88115 575-477-2211
David Bass, prin. Fax 477-2464

Dulce, Rio Arriba, Pop. 2,438
Dulce ISD 600/K-12
PO Box 547 87528 575-759-3225
Dr. Ralph Friedly, supt. Fax 759-3533
www.dulceschools.com/
Dulce ES 300/K-5
PO Box 590 87528 575-759-2925
Barbara Ashcraft, prin. Fax 759-2992
Dulce MS 200/6-8
PO Box 547 87528 575-759-3646
Pam Siders, prin. Fax 759-1349

Eagle Nest, Colfax, Pop. 292
Cimarron Municipal SD
Supt. — See Cimarron
Eagle Nest ES 100/K-4
PO Box 287 87718 575-377-6991
Lee Mills, prin. Fax 377-3646
Eagle Nest MS 100/5-8
PO Box 287 87718 575-377-6991
Lee Mills, prin. Fax 377-3646

Edgewood, Santa Fe, Pop. 1,791
Moriarty-Edgewood SD
Supt. — See Moriarty
Edgewood ES 400/PK-6
Highway 66 87015 505-832-5741
Teresa Salazar, prin. Fax 281-8384
Route 66 ES 400/K-6
805 Barton Rd 87015 505-832-5760
Selia Gomez, prin. Fax 281-0980
South Mountain ES 300/K-6
577 State Road 344 87015 505-832-5700
Josh McCleave, prin. Fax 286-8017

Edgewood Christian S 100/K-8
PO Box 949 87015 505-281-5091
Christine Hackett, prin. Fax 286-8344

Elida, Roosevelt, Pop. 178
Elida Municipal SD 100/K-12
PO Box 8 88116 575-274-6211
Jack Burch, supt. Fax 274-6213
www.elidaschools.net/
Elida ES 100/K-6
PO Box 8 88116 575-274-6211
Jim Daugherty, prin. Fax 274-6213

El Rito, Rio Arriba
Mesa Vista Consolidated SD 500/K-12
PO Box 6 87530 575-581-4504
Robert Archuleta, supt. Fax 581-4613
www.mesavista.org
El Rito ES 100/K-6
PO Box 267 87530 575-581-4723
Benjamin Trujillo, prin. Fax 581-4403
Other Schools – See Ojo Caliente

Espanola, Rio Arriba, Pop. 9,655
Espanola SD 3,700/PK-12
714 Calle Don Diego 87532 505-753-2254
Dr. David Cockerham, supt. Fax 753-2321
www.k12espanola.org
Los Ninos K 200/PK-K
323 N Coronado Ave 87532 505-753-6819
Felix Gonzales, prin. Fax 753-3477
Rodriguez ES 400/1-6
420 N Cordova Ave 87532 505-753-2256
Maxine Abeyta, prin. Fax 753-2257
Salazar ES 400/PK-6
PO Box 3219 87533 505-753-2391
Ruby Montoya, prin. Fax 753-0510
Sombrillo ES 300/1-6
County Rd 106 Ste 20C 87532 505-753-3213
Myra Maestas, prin. Fax 747-3772
Vigil MS 300/7-8
1260 Industrial Park Rd 87532 505-753-1348
Lewis Johnson, prin. Fax 747-3083
Other Schools – See Abiquiu, Alcalde, Chimayo, Cordova, Dixon, Hernandez, San Juan Pueblo, Velarde

---

McCurdy S 300/PK-12
261 S Mccurdy Rd 87532 505-753-7221
Rev. Daniel Garcia, supt. Fax 753-7830

Estancia, Torrance, Pop. 1,552
Estancia Municipal SD 900/PK-12
PO Box 68 87016 505-384-2001
Carolyn Allen-Renteria, supt. Fax 384-2015
www.estancia.k12.nm.us
Estancia ES 100/PK-1
PO Box 68 87016 505-384-2005
Lane Widner, prin. Fax 384-2015
Estancia MS 100/7-8
PO Box 68 87016 505-384-2003
Shauna Branch, prin. Fax 384-2015
Estancia Upper ES 300/3-6
PO Box 68 87016 505-384-2004
Lane Widner, prin. Fax 384-2015
Van Stone ES 50/2-2
PO Box 68 87016 505-384-2005
Lane Widner, prin. Fax 384-2015

Liberty Ranch Christian S 50/PK-12
Blue Grass Rd 87016 505-384-2530
Edward Bragg, prin. Fax 384-2530

Eunice, Lea, Pop. 2,602
Eunice SD 600/PK-12
PO Box 129 88231 575-394-2524
Dwain Haynes, supt. Fax 394-3006
www.eunice.org/
Caton MS 100/6-8
PO Box 129 88231 575-394-3338
Dwain Haynes, prin. Fax 394-3661
Jordan ES 300/PK-5
PO Box 129 88231 575-394-2440
Ricardo Rendon, prin. Fax 394-2086

Farmington, San Juan, Pop. 43,161
Farmington Municipal SD 10,000/PK-12
PO Box 5850 87499 505-324-9840
Janel Ryan, supt. Fax 599-8806
www.fms.k12.nm.us/home_body.html
Animas ES 400/K-5
1612 Hutton Ave 87402 505-599-8601
Marilee Dexel, prin. Fax 599-8632
Apache ES 400/PK-5
700 W Apache St 87401 505-599-8602
Debbie Braff, prin. Fax 599-8635
Bluffview ES 500/K-5
1204 Camino Real 87401 505-599-8603
Jay Gardenhire, prin. Fax 599-8696
Country Club ES 500/K-5
5300 Foothills Dr 87402 505-599-8604
Koleen Martinez, prin. Fax 599-8645
Esperanza ES 600/PK-5
4501 Wildflower Dr 87401 505-599-8676
Jeff Treat, prin. Fax 599-8679
Heights MS 700/6-8
3700 College Blvd 87402 505-599-8611
Janet Hunter, prin. Fax 599-8673
Hermosa MS 500/6-8
1500 E 25th St 87401 505-599-8612
Bob Rank, prin. Fax 599-8681
Ladera Del Norte ES 600/K-5
308 E 35th St 87401 505-599-8605
Gary Jackson, prin. Fax 599-8649
McCormick ES 400/K-5
701 McCormick School Rd 87401 505-599-8606
Lyn White, prin. Fax 599-8653
McKinley ES 500/K-5
1201 N Butler Ave 87401 505-599-8607
Julie Ellison, prin. Fax 599-8657
Mesa Verde ES 500/K-5
3801 College Blvd 87402 505-599-8608
Cindy Sosaya, prin. Fax 599-8661
Mesa View MS 500/6-8
4451 Wildflower Dr 87401 505-599-8622
Kim Salazar, prin. Fax 599-8646
Northeast ES 400/K-5
1400 E 23rd St 87401 505-599-8609
Joe Parks, prin. Fax 599-8664
Tibbetts MS 500/6-8
312 E Apache St 87401 505-599-8613
Karen Brown, prin. Fax 599-8675

Emmanuel Baptist Academy 200/PK-8
211 W 20th St 87401 505-325-0090
Emanuel Weigand, prin. Fax 325-2090
La Vida Mission S 50/K-8
PO Box 3308 87499 505-786-5539
Warren Breadenkamp, admin. Fax 786-7650
Pinion Hills Christian S 50/K-9
5509 Sagebrush Dr 87402 505-325-5875
Carol Rowe, prin. Fax 325-4867
Sacred Heart S 100/PK-5
404 N Allen Ave 87401 505-325-7152
Orla Lybrook, prin. Fax 325-6157

Floyd, Roosevelt, Pop. 76
Floyd Municipal SD 300/PK-12
PO Box 65 88118 575-478-2211
Paul Benoit, supt. Fax 478-2811
www.floydbroncos.com/
Floyd ES 100/PK-4
PO Box 65 88118 575-478-2211
Damon Terry, prin. Fax 478-2811
Floyd MS 100/5-8
PO Box 65 88118 575-478-2211
Chris Duncan, prin. Fax 478-2811

Fort Sumner, DeBaca, Pop. 1,060
Fort Sumner Municipal SD 300/PK-12
PO Box 387 88119 575-355-7734
Patricia Miller, supt. Fax 355-7716
www.ftsumnerk12.com/
Fort Sumner ES 200/PK-5
PO Box 387 88119 575-355-7766
Scott McMath, prin. Fax 355-7716
Fort Sumner MS 100/6-8
PO Box 387 88119 575-355-2231
Doreen Winn, prin. Fax 355-7663

Fruitland, San Juan
Central Consolidated SD 22
Supt. — See Shiprock
Ojo Amarillo ES 400/PK-6
PO Box 768 87416 505-598-5271
Ann Kluth-Clark, prin. Fax 598-6324

Gallina, Rio Arriba
Jemez Mountain SD 300/K-12
PO Box 230 87017 575-638-5419
Adan Delgado, supt. Fax 638-5571
www.jmsk12.com/
Gallina ES 50/K-5
PO Box 230 87017 575-638-5649
Vicky Abreu, prin. Fax 638-5571
Other Schools – See Coyote, Cuba

Gallup, McKinley, Pop. 19,378
Gallup-McKinley County SD 11,700/PK-12
PO Box 1318 87305 505-722-1000
Ray Arsenault, supt. Fax 721-1199
www.gmcs.k12.nm.us/
Chief Manuelito MS 6-8
1325 Rico St 87301 505-721-5600
Daniel Smith, prin. Fax 721-5699
de Onate ES 300/K-5
505 E Vega Ave 87301 505-721-3300
Rachael Rodriguez, prin. Fax 721-3399
Gallup MS 700/6-7
1001 S Grandview Dr 87301 505-721-2700
Peggy Taylor, prin. Fax 721-2799
Indian Hills ES 400/PK-5
3604 Ciniza Dr 87301 505-721-2900
Ronald Donkersloot, prin. Fax 721-2999
Jefferson ES 200/PK-5
300 Mollica Dr 87301 505-721-3000
Kim Orr, prin. Fax 721-3099
Kennedy MS 500/6-7
600 S Boardman Ave 87301 505-721-3100
Sammy Orr, prin. Fax 721-3199
Lincoln ES 300/PK-5
801 W Hill Ave 87301 505-721-3400
Diana White, prin. Fax 721-3499
Red Rock ES 300/PK-5
1305 Redrock Dr 87301 505-721-3900
John Hartog, prin. Fax 721-1399
Rocky View ES 300/K-5
345 Basileo Dr 87301 505-721-4000
Carol Sanches, prin. Fax 721-4099
Roosevelt ES 200/K-5
400 E Logan Ave 87301 505-721-4100
Richard Ferguson, prin. Fax 721-4199
Stagecoach ES 300/PK-5
725 Freedom Dr 87301 505-721-4300
Estela Carrillo, prin. Fax 721-4399
Tobe Turpen ES 400/PK-5
3310 Manuelito Dr 87301 505-721-5000
Debra Moya, prin. Fax 721-5099
Twin Lakes ES 200/PK-5
HC 30 Box 40 87301 505-735-2211
Mark Chandler, prin. Fax 735-2460
Washington ES 300/PK-5
700 W Wilson Ave 87301 505-863-3111
Tamara Allison, prin. Fax 863-5228
Other Schools – See Church Rock, Crownpoint, Navajo, Ramah, Thoreau, Tohatchi, Vanderwagen, Yatahey

---

Gallup Catholic S 200/PK-8
514 Park Ave 87301 505-863-6652
Thomas Rogozinski, prin. Fax 726-8142
Gallup Christian S 50/PK-12
PO Box 578 87305 505-722-2007
Jim Christian, prin. Fax 863-5530
Hilltop Christian S 200/PK-8
02A Deerfield Rd 87301 505-371-5726
Marti Grant, admin. Fax 371-5773
St. Francis of Assisi S 100/PK-5
215 W Wilson Ave 87301 505-863-3145
Mary Frank, prin. Fax 863-8150

Garfield, Dona Ana
Hatch Valley SD
Supt. — See Hatch
Garfield ES 200/K-5
8820 Highway 187 87936 575-267-8280
Richard Marquez, prin. Fax 267-8282

Glenwood, Catron
Reserve ISD
Supt. — See Reserve
Glenwood ES 50/K-6
PO Box 98 88039 575-539-2341
Cindy Shellhorn, prin. Fax 539-2341

Grady, Curry, Pop. 97
Grady Municipal SD 100/PK-12
PO Box 71 88120 575-357-2192
Joel Shirley, supt. Fax 357-2000
www.gradyschool.com/
Grady ES 100/PK-5
PO Box 71 88120 575-357-2192
Darrel Bollinger, prin. Fax 357-2000
Grady MS 50/6-8
PO Box 71 88120 575-357-2192
Darrel Bollinger, prin. Fax 357-2000

Grants, Cibola, Pop. 9,043
Grants-Cibola County SD 3,600/PK-12
PO Box 8 87020 505-285-2600
Kilino Marquez, supt. Fax 285-2628
www.gccs.cc/
Los Alamitos MS 500/7-8
1100 Mount Taylor Ave 87020 505-285-2683
Joan Gilmore, prin. Fax 285-2692
Mesa View ES 400/PK-6
400 Washington Ave 87020 505-285-2716
Mike O'Connell, prin. Fax 285-2725
Mt. Taylor ES 500/K-6
1670 Del Norte Blvd 87020 505-285-2740
Benny Gallegos, prin. Fax 285-2747
Other Schools – See Bluewater, Cubero, Milan, San Rafael, Seboyeta

---

St. Teresa of Avila S 100/PK-8
PO Box 729 87020 505-287-2261
Maria Mirabal, prin. Fax 285-4350

Hagerman, Chaves, Pop. 1,162
Hagerman Municipal SD 500/PK-12
PO Box B 88232 575-752-3254
Steven Starkey, supt. Fax 752-3255
bobcat.net
Hagerman ES 200/PK-5
PO Box B 88232 575-752-3279
Mark Lovas, prin. Fax 752-0207
Hagerman MS 100/6-8
PO Box B 88232 575-752-3283
Michael Chavez, prin. Fax 752-0241

Hatch, Dona Ana, Pop. 1,654
Hatch Valley SD 1,400/K-12
PO Box 790 87937 575-267-8200
William Coker, supt. Fax 267-8210
www.hatch.k12.nm.us/
Hatch Valley ES 200/K-2
PO Box 790 87937 575-267-8270
Manuela Kiehne, prin. Fax 267-8275
Hatch Valley MS 300/6-8
PO Box 790 87937 575-267-8252
Pauline Staski, prin. Fax 267-8255
Rio Grande ES 200/3-5
PO Box 790 87937 575-267-8260
Sally Mendez, prin. Fax 267-8265
Other Schools – See Garfield

Hernandez, Rio Arriba
Espanola SD
Supt. — See Espanola
Hernandez ES 87532 300/K-6
Benjamin Gurule, prin. 505-753-4008
Fax 753-8381

High Rolls Mountain Park, Otero
Alamogordo SD
Supt. — See Alamogordo
High Rolls Mountain Park ES 50/K-5
23 Karr Canyon Rd 88325 575-812-5275
Gerald Wheeler, prin. Fax 812-5278

Hobbs, Lea, Pop. 29,006
Hobbs Municipal SD 7,800/PK-12
PO Box 1030 88241 575-433-0100
Cliff Burch, supt. Fax 433-0140
www.hobbsschools.net
Broadmoor ES 300/K-6
1500 N Houston St 88240 575-433-1500
Karen Loving, prin. Fax 433-1520
College Lane ES 400/K-6
2000 W College Ln 88242 575-433-2600
Deanna Batista, prin. Fax 433-2628
Coronado ES 400/K-6
2600 N Brazos Ave 88240 575-433-2300
Kevin Black, prin. Fax 433-2327
Edison ES 300/K-6
501 E Gypsy St 88240 575-433-1600
Michael Hunt, prin. Fax 433-1626
Highland JHS 600/7-8
2500 N Jefferson St 88240 575-433-1200
John Notaro, prin. Fax 433-1203
Houston JHS 600/7-8
300 N Houston St 88240 575-433-1300
Jeff Cearley, prin. Fax 433-1304
Jefferson ES 300/K-6
1200 W Park St 88240 575-433-1700
Dixie Vegil, prin. Fax 433-1727
Mills ES 400/K-6
200 W Copper Ave 88240 575-433-2400
Gail Bryant, prin. Fax 433-2428
Rogers ES 400/K-6
300 E Clinton St 88240 575-433-2200
Amy Magness, prin. Fax 433-2229
Sanger ES 300/K-6
2020 N Adobe Dr 88240 575-433-1800
Nancy Havink, prin. Fax 433-1828
Southern Heights ES 400/K-6
101 E Texas St 88240 575-433-1900
Patricia Duran, prin. Fax 433-1938
Stone ES 400/K-6
1015 W Calle Sur St 88240 575-433-2500
Dawni Nelson, prin. Fax 433-2527
Taylor ES 400/K-6
1700 E Yeso Dr 88240 575-433-2000
Sandi Segars, prin. Fax 433-2032
Washington Center 200/PK-K
1200 E Humble St 88240 575-433-2100
LaToshia Thomas, prin. Fax 433-2120

St. Helena S 100/K-6
105 E Saint Anne Pl 88240 575-392-5405
Sheila Fuentes, prin. Fax 392-0128

Holloman AFB, Otero, Pop. 5,891
Alamogordo SD
Supt. — See Alamogordo
Holloman IS 200/3-5
580 Arnold Ave 88330 575-812-6150
Jerry Lott, prin. Fax 812-6153
Holloman MS 100/6-8
381 1st St Bldg 768 88330 575-812-6200
Maria Showalter, prin. Fax 812-6203
Holloman PS 300/PK-2
750 Arnold Ave 88330 575-812-6100
Jerry Lott, prin. Fax 812-6103

Hondo, Lincoln
Hondo Valley SD 100/PK-12
PO Box 55 88336 575-653-4411
Andrea Nieto, supt. Fax 653-4414
www.hondoeagles.org
Hondo ES 100/PK-6
PO Box 55 88336 575-653-4411
Andrea Nieto, prin. Fax 653-4414

Hope, Chaves, Pop. 106
Artesia SD
Supt. — See Artesia
Penasco S 50/K-8
12 Dunken Rte 88250 575-687-3360
Joel Pate, prin. Fax 687-2479

House, Quay, Pop. 64
House Municipal SD 100/K-12
PO Box 673 88121 575-279-7353
Donna McGee, supt. Fax 279-6201
www.houseschools.net
House ES 50/K-6
PO Box 673 88121 575-279-7353
Donna McGee, prin. Fax 279-6201

Hurley, Grant, Pop. 1,378
Cobre Consolidated SD
Supt. — See Bayard
Hurley ES 200/K-6
PO Box 39 88043 575-537-4060
Iris Wilson, prin. Fax 537-3300

Jal, Lea, Pop. 2,021
Jal SD 400/PK-12
PO Box 1386 88252 575-395-2101
Rick Ferguson, supt. Fax 395-2146
www.jalnm.org/
Jal ES 200/PK-6
PO Box 1386 88252 575-395-2840
Ron Verschueren, prin. Fax 395-2419

Jemez Pueblo, Sandoval, Pop. 1,301
Jemez Valley SD 300/PK-12
8501 Highway 4 87024 575-834-7391
David Atencio, supt. Fax 834-7394
www.jvps.org
Jemez Valley ES 100/PK-5
8501 Highway 4 87024 575-834-7393
Brad Parker, prin. Fax 834-7130
Jemez Valley MS 100/6-8
8501 Highway 4 87024 575-834-7393
Brad Parker, prin. Fax 834-7130

Kirtland, San Juan, Pop. 3,552
Central Consolidated SD 22
Supt. — See Shiprock
Bond ES 400/PK-3
5 Rd 6575 87417 505-598-5178
Raul Sanchez, prin. Fax 598-9507
Kirtland ES 500/PK-6
30 Rd 6446 87417 505-598-5893
Don Hornbecker, prin. Fax 598-5894
Kirtland MS 500/7-8
538 Rd 6100 87417 505-598-6114
Randy Mason, prin. Fax 598-9497
Wilson IS 200/4-6
40 Road 6580 87417 505-598-6285
Steve Carlson, prin. Fax 598-9495

Kirtland AFB, Bernalillo
Albuquerque SD
Supt. — See Albuquerque
Wherry ES 500/PK-5
Bldg 25000 87116 505-268-2434
Kathy Harper, prin. Fax 260-2025

Lake Arthur, Chaves, Pop. 432
Lake Arthur Municipal SD 200/PK-12
PO Box 98 88253 575-365-2001
Michael Grossman, supt. Fax 365-2002
www.la-panthers.org/
Lake Arthur ES 100/PK-5
PO Box 98 88253 575-365-2001
Dale Ballard, prin. Fax 365-2002
Lake Arthur MS 50/6-8
PO Box 98 88253 575-365-2001
Dale Ballard, prin. Fax 365-2002

La Luz, Otero, Pop. 1,625
Alamogordo SD
Supt. — See Alamogordo
La Luz ES 300/K-5
99 Alamo St 88337 575-812-5300
Victor Gonzales, prin. Fax 812-5303

Las Cruces, Dona Ana, Pop. 82,671
Las Cruces SD 23,000/PK-12
505 S Main St Ste 249 88001 575-527-5807
Stan Rounds, supt. Fax 527-5972
www.lcps.k12.nm.us
Alameda ES 500/K-5
505 S Main St Ste 249 88001 575-527-9486
Bobbie Grace, prin. Fax 527-9472
Camino Real MS 1,100/6-8
505 S Main St Ste 249 88001 575-527-6030
Ralph Ramos, prin. Fax 527-6031
Central ES 200/PK-5
505 S Main St Ste 249 88001 575-527-9496
Eloisa Solis, prin. Fax 527-9713
Chavez ES 600/K-2
505 S Main St Ste 249 88001 575-527-6022
Carmen Gallegos-Marrujo, prin. Fax 527-6036
Columbia ES 500/K-5
505 S Main St Ste 249 88001 575-527-1561
Judith Tanner, prin. Fax 527-5621
Conlee ES 500/K-5
505 S Main St Ste 249 88001 575-527-9656
Jennifer Terrazas, prin. Fax 527-9664
Desert Hills ES 600/PK-5
505 S Main St Ste 249 88001 575-527-9619
Vince Rivera, prin. Fax 527-9785
Dona Ana ES 400/PK-5
505 S Main St Ste 249 88001 575-527-9506
Irene Gomez, prin. Fax 527-9716
East Picacho ES 500/K-5
505 S Main St Ste 249 88001 575-527-9516
Diane Patterson, prin. Fax 527-9717
Fairacres ES 300/K-5
505 S Main St Ste 249 88001 575-527-9606
Kathy Norris, prin. Fax 527-9612

Hermosa Heights ES 500/PK-5
505 S Main St Ste 249 88001 575-527-9530
Cynthia Risner-Schiller, prin. Fax 527-9528
Highland ES 700/PK-5
505 S Main St Ste 249 88001 575-527-9636
Theresa Jaramillo-Jones, prin. Fax 527-9711
Hillrise ES 500/K-5
505 S Main St Ste 249 88001 575-527-9666
Julieta Marta, prin. Fax 527-9668
Jornada ES 500/K-5
505 S Main St Ste 249 88001 575-527-9536
Arsenio Romero, prin. Fax 527-9762
Loma Heights ES 400/PK-5
505 S Main St Ste 249 88001 575-527-9546
Rudy Leos, prin. Fax 527-9553
Lynn MS 800/6-8
505 S Main St Ste 249 88001 575-527-9445
Kathie Davis, prin. Fax 527-9454
MacArthur ES 400/PK-5
505 S Main St Ste 249 88001 575-527-9556
Terry Stuart, prin. Fax 527-6029
Picacho MS 800/6-8
505 S Main St Ste 249 88001 575-527-9455
Michael Montoya, prin. Fax 527-9459
Sierra MS 900/6-8
505 S Main St Ste 249 88001 575-527-9640
Brenda Lewis, prin. Fax 527-9768
Sonoma ES PK-5
505 S Main St Ste 249 88001 575-541-7320
Wendi Hammond, prin. Fax 541-7321
Sunrise ES 500/3-5
505 S Main St Ste 249 88001 575-527-9626
Brian Peterson, prin. Fax 527-9633
Tombaugh ES 700/PK-5
505 S Main St Ste 249 88001 575-527-9575
Cindy Baker, prin. Fax 527-9546
University Hills ES 400/PK-5
505 S Main St Ste 249 88001 575-527-9649
Judy Foster, prin. Fax 527-9450
Valley View ES 500/PK-5
505 S Main St Ste 249 88001 575-527-9586
Sharon Robinson, prin. Fax 527-9731
Vista MS 900/6-8
505 S Main St Ste 249 88001 575-527-9465
Dan Davis, prin. Fax 527-9470
Washington ES 300/PK-5
505 S Main St Ste 249 88001 575-527-9595
Teresa Romano, prin. Fax 527-9520
Zia MS 900/6-8
505 S Main St Ste 249 88001 575-527-9475
Jed Hendee, prin. Fax 527-9479
Other Schools – See Mesilla, Mesilla Park, White Sands

College Heights K 100/K-K
1210 Wofford Dr 88001 575-522-6922
Cyndy Moon, dir. Fax 522-6392
Las Cruces Catholic S 200/PK-8
1331 N Miranda St 88005 575-526-2517
Dr. Karen Trujillo, prin. Fax 524-0544
Mesilla Valley Christian S 500/K-12
3850 Stern Dr 88001 575-525-8515
Ivan Stubbs, supt. Fax 526-2713
Mission Lutheran S 100/PK-5
2752 N Roadrunner Pkwy 88011 575-532-5489
Ruth Staffeldt, dir. Fax 522-5345

Las Vegas, San Miguel, Pop. 14,020
Las Vegas City SD 2,100/PK-12
901 Douglas Ave 87701 505-454-5700
Dr. Pete Campos, supt. Fax 454-6965
cybercardinal.com/
ECC 100/K-K
901 Douglas Ave 87701 505-425-9205
Lee Ette Quintana, prin. Fax 425-6856
Henry ES 200/PK-5
901 Douglas Ave 87701 505-454-5730
Aylene Griego, prin. Fax 426-0324
Legion Park ES 200/K-5
901 Douglas Ave 87701 505-454-5760
Jane Chavez, prin. Fax 425-6250
Los Ninos ES 200/K-5
901 Douglas Ave 87701 505-454-5720
Casimiro Floyd Chavez, prin. Fax 426-0322
Memorial MS 500/6-8
901 Douglas Ave 87701 505-454-5710
Sandra Madrid, prin. Fax 426-0303
Sena ES 100/K-5
901 Douglas Ave 87701 505-425-6043
Lee Ette Quintana, prin. Fax 425-2631
Sierra Vista ES 200/1-5
901 Douglas Ave 87701 505-454-5740
Manuel Lucero, prin. Fax 426-0321

West Las Vegas SD 1,700/K-12
179 Bridge St 87701 505-426-2300
James Abreu, supt. Fax 426-2332
www.wlvs.k12.nm.us/
Armijo ES 200/K-1
179 Bridge St 87701 505-426-2661
Margarita Larranaga, prin. Fax 426-2662
Martinez ES 200/2-5
179 Bridge St 87701 505-426-2861
Martha Johnsen, prin. Fax 426-2862
Serna ES 200/2-5
179 Bridge St 87701 505-426-2621
Margarita Larranaga, prin. Fax 426-2622
Union ES 100/2-5
179 Bridge St 87701 505-426-2701
Delbert Saavedra, prin. Fax 426-2702
West Las Vegas MS 300/6-8
179 Bridge St 87701 505-426-2541
Steve Sandoval, prin. Fax 426-2542
Other Schools – See Ribera

La Union, Dona Ana
Gadsden ISD
Supt. — See Sunland Park
La Union ES 300/K-6
875 Mercantil Ave 88021 575-874-3592
Cissy Andreas, prin. Fax 874-8335

Logan, Quay, Pop. 986
Logan Municipal SD 200/PK-12
PO Box 67 88426 575-487-2252
Doug Hulce, supt. Fax 487-9479
logan.echalk.com
Logan ES 100/PK-5
PO Box 67 88426 575-487-2252
Gary Miller, prin. Fax 487-9479
Logan MS 100/6-8
PO Box 67 88426 575-487-2252
Gary Miller, prin. Fax 487-9479

Lordsburg, Hidalgo, Pop. 2,815
Lordsburg Municipal SD 700/PK-12
PO Box 430 88045 575-542-9361
Jim Barentine, supt. Fax 542-9364
www.lmsed.org
Central ES 100/5-6
207 High St 88045 575-542-9222
Kris Baca, prin. Fax 542-9223
Dugan-Tarango MS 100/7-8
1352 Hardin St 88045 575-542-9806
David Lackey, prin. Fax 542-9811
Southside ES 100/3-4
200 E 9th St 88045 575-542-9473
Kris Baca, prin. Fax 542-9489
Traylor ES 200/PK-2
500 Ownby St 88045 575-542-3252
Alicemary Pelayo, prin. Fax 542-3239

Los Alamos, Los Alamos, Pop. 11,455
Los Alamos SD 3,600/PK-12
PO Box 90 87544 505-663-2222
Eugene Schmidt, supt. Fax 661-6300
www.laschools.net
Aspen ES 300/K-6
2182 33rd St 87544 505-663-2275
Kathryn Vandenkieboom, prin. Fax 662-4398
Barranca Mesa ES 400/PK-6
57 Loma Del Escolar St 87544 505-663-2730
Paula Dean, prin. Fax 662-6645
Los Alamos MS 600/7-8
2101 Hawk Dr 87544 505-663-2375
Donna Grim, prin. Fax 662-4270
Mountain ES 400/K-6
2280 North Rd 87544 505-663-2325
Gerry Washburn, prin. Fax 662-4368
Other Schools – See White Rock

Ponderosa Montessori S 100/PK-3
304 Rover Blvd 87544 505-672-9211
Joan Ellard, admin. Fax 672-9218

Los Lunas, Valencia, Pop. 11,338
Los Lunas SD 8,600/PK-12
PO Box 1300 87031 505-866-8231
Walter Gibson, supt. Fax 865-7766
www.llschools.net/
Desert View ES 500/PK-6
PO Box 1300 87031 505-866-2488
Jeannie Moore, prin. Fax 866-2485
Fernandez IS 400/5-6
PO Box 1300 87031 505-865-1044
Cindy Carter, prin. Fax 866-2156
Gabaldon IS 500/5-6
PO Box 1300 87031 505-866-0456
Sharon Tregembo, prin. Fax 866-2166
Gallegos ES 700/PK-4
PO Box 1300 87031 505-865-6223
Mildred Chavez, prin. Fax 866-2159
Los Lunas ES 500/PK-4
PO Box 1300 87031 505-865-9313
Therese Sanchez, prin. Fax 866-2151
Los Lunas MS 800/7-8
PO Box 1300 87031 505-865-7273
Russell Hague, prin. Fax 865-9742
Manzano Vista MS 600/7-8
PO Box 1300 87031 505-865-1750
David Yates, prin. Fax 866-8921
Parish ES 500/PK-4
PO Box 1300 87031 505-865-9652
Angela Griego, prin. Fax 865-7364
Tome ES 500/PK-6
PO Box 1300 87031 505-865-1102
Felipe Armijo, prin. Fax 865-8995
Valencia ES 400/PK-4
PO Box 1300 87031 505-865-3017
Jim Snell, prin. Fax 866-2169
Other Schools – See Bosque Farms, Peralta

Christ the King S 50/K-12
PO Box 907 87031 505-865-9226
Rev. Alan R. Coleman, prin. Fax 865-9226

Los Ranchos, Bernalillo
Albuquerque SD
Supt. — See Albuquerque
Taft MS 600/6-8
620 Schulte Rd NW, 505-344-4389
Jimmie Lueder, prin. Fax 761-8440

Loving, Eddy, Pop. 1,313
Loving Municipal SD 600/PK-12
PO Box 98 88256 575-745-2000
David Chavez, supt. Fax 745-2002
www.lovingschools.com
Loving ES 300/PK-5
PO Box 98 88256 575-745-2070
Mark Barela, prin. Fax 745-2072
Loving MS 100/6-8
PO Box 98 88256 575-745-2050
Jesse Fuentes, prin. Fax 745-2052

Lovington, Lea, Pop. 9,603
Lovington Municipal SD 3,000/PK-12
18 W Washington Ave 88260 575-739-2200
Steven O'Quinn, supt. Fax 739-2205
lovington.nm.schoolwebpages.com
Alexander ES 200/2-2
1400 S 6th St 88260 575-739-2580
Doug Choate, prin. Fax 739-2584
Jefferson ES 200/3-3
300 W Jefferson Ave 88260 575-739-2540
Ivan DeAnda, prin. Fax 739-2584
Lea ES 200/1-1
1202 W Birch Ave 88260 575-739-2625
Pam Quinones, prin. Fax 739-2631
Llano K 500/PK-K
1000 S 1st St 88260 575-739-2670
Barbara Sims, prin. Fax 739-2672
Sixth Grade Academy 400/6-6
500 W Jefferson Ave 88260 575-739-2330
Robert De La Cruz, prin. Fax 739-2330
Taylor MS 200/7-8
700 S 11th St 88260 575-739-2435
Darin Manes, prin. Fax 739-2438
Yarbro ES 400/4-5
700 W Jefferson Ave 88260 575-739-2490
Irene Livingston, prin. Fax 739-2493

Lumberton, Rio Arriba

St. Francis S 100/K-8
HC 71 Box 26 87528 575-759-3252
Leonard Meyer, prin. Fax 759-3844

Magdalena, Socorro, Pop. 877
Magdalena Municipal SD 500/PK-12
PO Box 24 87825 575-854-2241
Mike Chambers, supt. Fax 854-2531
www.magdalena.k12.nm.us
Magdalena ES 200/PK-5
PO Box 629 87825 575-854-2241
Kitty Martin, prin. Fax 854-2531
Magdalena MS 100/6-8
PO Box 629 87825 575-854-2241
Regina Lane, prin. Fax 854-2531

Maxwell, Colfax, Pop. 262
Maxwell Municipal SD 100/PK-12
PO Box 275 87728 575-375-2371
Dr. Alan Aufderheide, supt. Fax 375-2375
www.maxwellp12.com/
Maxwell ES 50/PK-6
PO Box 275 87728 575-375-2371
Thomas Lewis, prin. Fax 375-2375
Maxwell MS 50/7-8
PO Box 275 87728 575-375-2371
Thomas Lewis, prin. Fax 375-2375

Melrose, Curry, Pop. 728
Melrose SD 200/PK-12
PO Box 275 88124 575-253-4269
Dr. Ronald Windom, supt. Fax 253-4291
www.melroseschools.org
Melrose ES 100/PK-6
PO Box 275 88124 575-253-4266
Miles Mitchell, prin. Fax 253-4291

Mesilla, Dona Ana, Pop. 2,205
Las Cruces SD
Supt. — See Las Cruces
Mesilla ES 300/K-5
2363 Calle del Sur 88046 575-527-9566
Barbara Bencomo, prin. Fax 527-9756

Mesilla Park, See Las Cruces
Las Cruces SD
Supt. — See Las Cruces
Mesilla Park ES 500/K-5
955 W Union Ave 88047 575-527-9615
Lillian Duran, prin. Fax 527-9728

Mesquite, Dona Ana
Gadsden ISD
Supt. — See Sunland Park
Mesquite ES 500/PK-6
PO Box 320 88048 575-233-3925
Jacob Montano, prin. Fax 233-0905

Milan, Cibola, Pop. 2,524
Grants-Cibola County SD
Supt. — See Grants
Milan ES 500/PK-6
404 Sand 87021 505-285-2727
Edwina Trujillo, prin. Fax 285-2731

Mora, Mora
Mora ISD 600/K-12
PO Box 179 87732 575-387-3101
Phillip Tapia, supt. Fax 387-3111
Garcia MS 100/6-8
PO Box 687 87732 575-387-3128
Loretto Griego, prin. Fax 387-3126
Holman S, PO Box 140 87732 50/K-K
Ray Maestas, prin. 575-387-2727
Mora ES 200/1-5
PO Box 140 87732 575-387-3133
Ray Maestas, prin. Fax 387-3131

Moriarty, Torrance, Pop. 1,808
Moriarty-Edgewood SD 3,800/PK-12
PO Box 2000 87035 505-832-4471
Dr. Karen Couch, supt. Fax 832-4472
www.moriarty.k12.nm.us
Edgewood MS 400/7-8
PO Box 2000 87035 505-832-5880
Barbara Gradner, prin. Fax 281-7210
Moriarty ES 500/PK-6
PO Box 2000 87035 505-832-4927
Robert Adams, prin. Fax 832-2474
Moriarty MS 300/7-8
PO Box 2000 87035 505-832-6200
Dawn Tinsley, prin. Fax 832-5919

Mountainview ES 400/PK-6
PO Box 2000 87035 505-832-6827
Laura Moffitt, prin. Fax 832-6009
Other Schools – See Edgewood

Mosquero, Harding, Pop. 95
Mosquero Municipal SD 50/K-12
PO Box 258 87733 575-673-2271
Bill Ward, supt. Fax 673-2305
Mosquero ES 50/K-6
PO Box 258 87733 575-673-2271
Bill Ward, prin. Fax 673-2305

Mountainair, Torrance, Pop. 1,078
Mountainair SD 300/PK-12
PO Box 456 87036 505-847-2333
Jay Mortensen, supt. Fax 847-2843
Mountainair ES 200/PK-5
PO Box 456 87036 505-847-2231
Yvonne Zenga, prin. Fax 847-2843

Navajo, McKinley, Pop. 1,985
Gallup-McKinley County SD
Supt. — See Gallup
Navajo ES 300/PK-6
PO Box 1012 87328 505-777-2381
Margaret Hotchkiss, prin. Fax 777-2380
Navajo MS 200/6-8
PO Box 1287 87328 505-777-2390
Pauletta White, prin. Fax 777-2375

Newcomb, San Juan, Pop. 388
Central Consolidated SD 22
Supt. — See Shiprock
Newcomb ES 300/PK-5
PO Box 7917 87455 505-696-3434
Abena McNeely, prin. Fax 696-3430
Newcomb MS 200/6-8
PO Box 7973 87455 505-696-3417
Leland Roundy, prin. Fax 696-3487

Ojo Caliente, Taos
Mesa Vista Consolidated SD
Supt. — See El Rito
Mesa Vista MS 100/7-8
PO Box 50 87549 575-583-2275
Janette Archuleta, prin. Fax 583-9133
Ojo Caliente ES 100/K-6
PO Box 369 87549 575-583-2316
Rick Romero, prin. Fax 583-2105

Pecos, San Miguel, Pop. 1,407
Pecos ISD 800/PK-12
PO Box 368 87552 505-757-4700
Roy Herrera, supt. Fax 757-8721
www.pecos.k12.nm.us/
Pecos ES 400/PK-5
PO Box 368 87552 505-757-4770
Dennis Paluszcyk, prin. Fax 757-2165
Pecos MS 200/6-8
PO Box 368 87552 505-757-4620
Dan Padilla, prin. Fax 757-2561

Pena Blanca, Sandoval, Pop. 300
Bernalillo SD
Supt. — See Bernalillo
Cochiti S 100/K-8
800 Quail Hill Trl 87041 505-867-5547
Michael Weinberg, prin. Fax 867-7846

Penasco, Taos, Pop. 648
Penasco ISD 600/K-12
PO Box 520 87553 575-587-2230
Ernesto Valdez, supt. Fax 587-2513
Penasco ES 300/K-6
PO Box 520 87553 575-587-2395
Melissa Sandoval, prin. Fax 587-1845
Penasco MS 100/7-8
PO Box 520 87553 575-587-2503
Phyllis Martinez, prin. Fax 587-9910

Peralta, Valencia, Pop. 3,182
Los Lunas SD
Supt. — See Los Lunas
Peralta ES 400/PK-5
3645 State Highway 47 87042 505-869-2679
Elena Trodden, prin. Fax 869-5428

Placitas, Sandoval, Pop. 1,611
Bernalillo SD
Supt. — See Bernalillo
Placitas ES 200/K-5
PO Box 730 87043 505-867-2488
Dan MacEachen, prin. Fax 867-7812

Polvadera, Socorro
Socorro Consolidated SD
Supt. — See Socorro
Midway ES, 9 Midway Rd 87828 100/K-5
Linda Perdue, prin. 575-835-1098

Portales, Roosevelt, Pop. 11,295
Portales Municipal SD 2,800/PK-12
501 S Abilene Ave 88130 575-356-7000
Randy Fowler, supt. Fax 356-4377
www.portalesschools.com
Brown ECC 300/PK-K
520 W 5th St 88130 575-356-7075
Becky Flen, prin. Fax 356-4839
James ES 500/2-3
701 W 18th St 88130 575-359-3675
Mark Gormley, prin. Fax 356-4852
Lindsey ES 200/6-6
1216 W Ivy St 88130 575-356-7060
Rick Segovia, prin. Fax 356-4461
Portales JHS 400/7-8
700 E 3rd St 88130 575-356-7045
Steve Harris, prin. Fax 359-0826
Steiner ES 200/1-1
525 S Chicago Ave 88130 575-359-3690
Sharon Epps, prin. Fax 356-5461

Valencia ES 400/4-5
1415 S Globe Ave 88130 575-356-7090
Michael Terry, prin. Fax 356-2846

Quemado, Catron
Quemado ISD 200/K-12
PO Box 128 87829 575-773-4700
Bill Green, supt. Fax 773-4717
www.quemadoschools.org
Quemado ES 100/K-6
PO Box 128 87829 575-773-4645
Valerie Brea, prin. Fax 773-4717
Other Schools – See Datil

Questa, Taos, Pop. 1,913
Questa ISD 400/K-12
PO Box 440 87556 575-586-0421
Eric Martinez, supt. Fax 586-0531
www.questa.k12.nm.us
Alta Vista ES 100/K-3
PO Box 829 87556 575-586-0541
Fax 586-2061
Alta Vista IS 100/4-6
PO Box 829 87556 575-586-0032
Fax 586-2061
Questa JHS 100/7-8
PO Box 529 87556 575-586-1604
Kevin Hubka, prin. Fax 586-2282
Other Schools – See Costilla

Ramah, McKinley
Gallup-McKinley County SD
Supt. — See Gallup
Ramah ES 200/K-6
PO Box 869 87321 505-783-4219
Ann Walker, prin. Fax 783-4378

Ranchos de Taos, Taos, Pop. 1,779
Taos Municipal SD
Supt. — See Taos
Ranchos De Taos ES 400/PK-5
200 Sanders Ln 87557 575-737-6150
Robert Trujillo, prin. Fax 737-6151

Raton, Colfax, Pop. 6,944
Raton SD 1,400/PK-12
PO Box 940 87740 575-445-9111
David Willden, supt. Fax 445-5641
www.ratonschools.org
Columbian ES 200/2-3
700 N 2nd St 87740 575-445-9851
Pam Hunnicutt, prin. Fax 445-4187
Kearny ES 200/4-5
800 S 3rd St 87740 575-445-3871
Randy Hestand, prin. Fax 445-0944
Longfellow ES 300/PK-1
700 E 4th St 87740 575-445-9261
Andy Ortiz, prin. Fax 445-5306
Raton MS 300/6-8
500 S 3rd St 87740 575-445-9881
Olga Neurauter, prin. Fax 445-3682

Rehoboth, McKinley

Rehoboth Christian S 200/K-12
PO Box 41 87322 505-863-4412
Ron Polinder, supt. Fax 863-2185

Reserve, Catron, Pop. 338
Reserve ISD 200/PK-12
PO Box 350 87830 575-533-6241
Loren Cushman, supt. Fax 533-6647
www.reserve.k12.nm.us/
Reserve ES 100/PK-6
PO Box 350 87830 575-533-6243
Cindy Shellhorn, prin. Fax 533-6647
Other Schools – See Glenwood

Ribera, San Miguel
West Las Vegas SD
Supt. — See Las Vegas
Valley ES 100/K-5
PO Box 519 87560 505-426-2581
Becky Gallegos, prin. Fax 426-2582
Valley MS 100/6-8
PO Box 519 87560 505-426-2581
Becky Gallegos, prin. Fax 426-2582

Rio Rancho, Sandoval, Pop. 66,599
Rio Rancho SD 12,700/PK-12
500 Laser Dr NE 87124 505-896-0667
Dr. V. Sue Cleveland, supt. Fax 896-0662
www.rrps.net
Cielo Azul ES PK-5
1550 34th Ave NE, 505-338-2320
Patricia Cruz, prin. Fax 896-0302
Colinas del Norte ES 1,000/PK-5
1001 23rd Ave NE, 505-896-3378
Laura Moore, prin. Fax 896-3387
Cordova ES PK-5
1500 Veranda Rd SE 87124 505-994-0229
Cathy Gaarden, prin. Fax 994-2684
Eagle Ridge MS 700/6-8
800 Fruta Rd NE 87124 505-892-6630
Debbie Morrell, prin. Fax 892-6909
Enchanted Hills ES 800/PK-5
5400 Obregon Rd NE, 505-891-8526
Cathy Baehr, prin. Fax 892-9809
King ES 900/PK-5
1301 27th St SE 87124 505-892-2575
Marilee Bryant, prin. Fax 892-9862
Lincoln MS 800/6-8
2287 Lema Rd SE 87124 505-892-1100
Myra Roosevelt, prin. Fax 892-9728
Mountain View MS 600/6-8
4101 Montreal Loop NE, 505-867-0711
Kathy Pinkel, prin. Fax 867-7901
Puesta Del Sol ES 800/PK-5
450 Southern Blvd SE 87124 505-994-3305
G. Bryan Garcia, prin. Fax 994-3316

Rio Rancho ES 800/PK-5
4601 Pepe Ortiz Rd SE 87124 505-892-0220
Barbara Bruce, prin. Fax 892-5724
Rio Rancho MS 1,200/6-8
1600 40th St NE, 505-891-5335
Lisa Dobson, prin. Fax 891-1180
Sandia Vista ES PK-5
6800 Franklin NE, 505-338-2526
Lavonna Archuleta, prin. Fax 771-0956
Shining Stars Preschool 300/PK-PK
4477 9th Ave NE 87124 505-892-7735
Suzanne Harper, prin. Fax 896-6166
Stapleton ES 900/PK-5
3100 8th Ave NE 87124 505-891-8473
Linda Sanasac, prin. Fax 891-8498
Vista Grande ES 900/PK-5
7001 Chayote Rd NE, 505-771-2366
Trent Heffner, prin. Fax 771-2369

St. Thomas Aquinas S 400/K-8
1100 Hood Rd SE 87124 505-892-3221
Sr. Anne Louise Abascal, prin. Fax 892-3350

Roswell, Chaves, Pop. 45,199
Roswell ISD 9,300/PK-12
PO Box 1437 88202 575-627-2500
Michael Gottlieb, supt. Fax 627-2512
www.risd.k12.nm.us
Berrendo ES 400/K-5
505 W Pine Lodge Rd 88201 575-627-2875
Curt Tarter, prin. Fax 625-8292
Berrendo MS 600/6-8
800 Marion Richards Rd 88201 575-627-2775
Laura Herrera, prin. Fax 625-8248
Del Norte ES 400/PK-5
2701 N Garden Ave 88201 575-637-3325
Billy Carlyle, prin. Fax 625-8227
East Grand Plains ES 200/K-5
3773 E Grand Plains Rd 88203 575-637-3350
Fermin Velasquez, prin. Fax 625-8195
El Capitan ES 400/K-5
2807 W Bland St 88203 575-637-3400
Mona Kirk-Vogel, prin. Fax 625-8243
Lopez ES 300/K-5
1208 E Bland St 88203 575-637-3500
Jennifer Bolanos, prin. Fax 625-8282
Mesa MS 400/6-8
1601 E Bland St 88203 575-627-2800
Ruben Bolanos, prin. Fax 625-8263
Military Heights ES 400/K-5
1900 N Michigan Ave 88201 575-637-3425
Scott Schoen, prin. Fax 625-8272
Missouri Avenue ES 300/K-5
700 S Missouri Ave 88203 575-637-3450
Glenda Moore, prin. Fax 625-8222
Monterrey ES 400/K-5
910 W Gayle St 88203 575-637-3475
Joan Accardi, prin. Fax 625-8302
Mountain View MS 400/6-8
312 E Mountain View Rd 88203 575-627-2825
Glenda Grant, prin. Fax 625-8260
Parkview Preschool 300/PK-K
1700 W Alameda St 88203 575-637-3525
Virginia Eudy, prin.
Pecos ES 300/K-5
600 E Hobbs St 88203 575-637-3550
Dr. Barbara Ryan, prin. Fax 625-8293
Sierra MS 600/6-8
615 S Sycamore Ave 88203 575-627-2850
Josie Turner, prin. Fax 625-8283
Sunset ES 300/K-5
25 W Martin St 88203 575-637-3575
Hilda Sanchez, prin. Fax 625-8278
Valley View ES 400/K-5
1400 S Washington Ave 88203 575-637-3600
Dixie Johnson, prin. Fax 625-8297
Washington Avenue ES 400/K-5
408 N Washington Ave 88201 575-637-3625
Ron Tidmore, prin. Fax 625-8249

All Saints Catholic S 100/PK-1
2808 N Kentucky Ave 88201 575-627-5744
Louis Mestas, prin. Fax 622-6845
Gateway Christian S 300/PK-12
PO Box 1642 88202 575-622-9710
Rick Rapp, admin. Fax 622-9739
Immanuel Lutheran S K-7
1405 N Sycamore Ave 88201 575-622-2853
Rev. Daniel Praeuner, prin. Fax 622-3723
Valley Christian Academy 200/1-12
505 N Sycamore Ave 88201 575-627-1500
Gregg Ammons, prin. Fax 627-1501

Roy, Harding, Pop. 239
Roy Municipal SD 100/PK-12
PO Box 430 87743 575-485-2242
Richard Hazen, supt. Fax 485-2497
Roy ES 50/PK-6
PO Box 430 87743 575-485-2242
Richard Hazen, prin. Fax 485-2497

Ruidoso, Lincoln, Pop. 8,812
Ruidoso Municipal SD 2,000/PK-12
200 Horton Cir 575-257-4051
BeaEtta Harris Ed.D., supt. Fax 257-4150
www.ruidososchools.org/
Nob Hill ECC 200/PK-K
200 Horton Cir 88345 575-257-9041
Michelle Perry, prin. Fax 257-3689
Ruidoso MS 400/6-8
200 Horton Cir 88345 575-257-7324
George Heaton, prin. Fax 257-3946
Sierra Vista PS 400/1-2
200 Horton Cir 88345 575-258-4943
Dave Bishop, prin. Fax 258-1300
White Mountain ES 300/3-5
200 Horton Cir 88345 575-258-4220
Ron Elkin, prin. Fax 258-5578

Sierra Blanca Christian Academy 50/PK-6
PO Box 2349 88355 575-630-0144
James Robbins, prin. Fax 257-3510

San Antonio, Socorro
Socorro Consolidated SD
Supt. — See Socorro
San Antonio ES, PO Box 277 87832 50/K-5
John Dennis, prin. 575-835-1758

Sandia Park, Bernalillo
Albuquerque SD
Supt. — See Albuquerque
San Antonito ES 300/K-5
12555 State Highway 14 N 87047 505-281-3931
Jane Lujan, prin. Fax 281-5864

San Fidel, Cibola

St. Joseph S 100/PK-8
PO Box 370 87049 505-552-6362
David Jiron, prin. Fax 552-6362

San Jon, Quay, Pop. 274
San Jon Municipal SD 100/PK-12
PO Box 5 88434 575-576-2466
Gary Salazar, supt. Fax 576-2772
www.sanjonschools.com/
San Jon ES 50/PK-5
PO Box 5 88434 575-576-2466
DeLoyce Smith, prin. Fax 576-2772
San Jon MS 50/6-8
PO Box 5 88434 575-576-2466
DeLoyce Smith, prin. Fax 576-2772

San Juan Pueblo, Rio Arriba
Espanola SD
Supt. — See Espanola
San Juan ES 400/K-6
PO Box 1029 87566 505-852-4225
Ruben Salazar, prin. Fax 852-4975

San Lorenzo, Grant
Cobre Consolidated SD
Supt. — See Bayard
San Lorenzo ES 100/K-6
HC 71 Box 1500 88041 575-536-9348
Gena Vega, prin. Fax 536-9490

San Miguel, Dona Ana
Gadsden ISD
Supt. — See Sunland Park
North Valley ES K-6
PO Box C 88058 575-233-1092
Wilfred Trujillo, prin. Fax 233-3772

San Rafael, Cibola
Grants-Cibola County SD
Supt. — See Grants
San Rafael ES 100/K-6
General Delivery 87051 505-285-2750
Sergio Castanon, prin. Fax 285-2753

Santa Cruz, Santa Fe, Pop. 2,504

Holy Cross S 200/PK-6
PO Box 1260 87567 505-753-4644
Lorraine Madrid Sanchez, prin. Fax 753-7401

Santa Fe, Santa Fe, Pop. 70,631
Pojoaque Valley SD 2,000/PK-12
PO Box 3468 87501 505-455-2282
Toni Nolan-Trujillo, supt. Fax 455-7152
pvs.k12.nm.us/
Pojoaque Valley IS 300/5-6
PO Box 3468 87501 505-455-2910
Juliana Lujan, prin. Fax 455-3003
Pojoaque Valley MS 400/7-8
PO Box 3468 87501 505-455-2238
Eileen Chavez, prin. Fax 455-3392
Roybal ES 700/PK-4
PO Box 3468 87501 505-455-7603
Diane Delgado, prin. Fax 455-3940

Santa Fe SD 11,800/PK-12
610 Alta Vista St 87505 505-467-2000
Bobbie Gutierrez, supt. Fax 995-3300
www.sfps.info
Acequia Madre ES 200/K-6
700 Acequia Madre 87505 505-467-4000
Bill Beacham, prin. Fax 995-3320
Agua Fria ES 500/PK-6
3160 Agua Fria St 87507 505-467-1300
Dr. Suzanne Jacquez-Gorman, prin. Fax 995-3323
Alvord ES 100/K-6
551 Alarid St 87501 505-467-4200
Fax 995-3312
Atalaya ES 200/K-6
721 Camino Cabra 87505 505-467-4400
Andrea Hamilton, prin. Fax 995-3313
Capshaw MS 500/7-8
351 W Zia Rd 87505 505-467-4300
Sue Lujan, prin. Fax 989-5439
Chaparral ES 400/K-6
2451 Avenida Chaparral 87505 505-467-1400
Theresa Ulibarri, prin. Fax 995-3324
Chavez ES 600/K-5
6251 Jaguar Dr 87507 505-467-3200
Felicia Sen, prin. Fax 995-3373
De Vargas MS 500/7-8
1720 Llano St 87505 505-467-3300
Barbara Lange, prin. Fax 995-3307
El Dorado S 500/PK-8
2 Avenida Torreon 87508 505-467-4900
Yann Lussiez, prin. Fax 466-8277
Gilbert ES 300/K-6
450 La Madera St 87501 505-467-4700
Kristy Janda, prin. Fax 995-3314
Gonzales S 400/K-8
851 W Alameda St 87501 505-467-3100
Michael Lee, prin. Fax 995-3315
Kaune ES 200/PK-6
1409 Monterey Dr 87505 505-467-2700
Danny Pena, prin. Fax 995-3316
Kearny ES 400/K-6
901 Avenida De Las Campana 87507 505-467-1800
Karen Webb, prin. Fax 995-3325
Larragoite ES 200/K-6
1604 Agua Fria St 87505 505-467-3700
Ellen Perez, prin. Fax 995-3317
Martinez ES 400/K-6
401 W San Mateo Rd 87505 505-467-3800
Nancy Olivares, prin. Fax 995-3318
Nava ES 200/K-6
2655 Siringo Rd 87505 505-467-1200
Anita Cisneros, prin. Fax 995-3326
Nye Bilingual ECC PK-PK
3200 Calle Po Ae Pi 87507 505-467-3000
Christina Jirsa, prin. Fax 989-5465
Ortiz MS 500/6-8
4164 S Meadows Rd 87507 505-467-2300
Denine Mares, prin. Fax 989-5597
Pinon ES 700/K-6
2921 Camino De Los Caballos 87507 505-467-1600
Janis DeVoti, prin. Fax 995-3327
Ramirez Thomas ES 500/K-5
3200 Calle Po Ae Pi 87507 505-467-3000
Robin Nobel, prin. Fax 989-5465
Salazar ES 400/K-6
1231 Apache Ave 87505 505-467-3900
Margo Shirley, prin. Fax 995-3319
Sweeney ES 600/K-5
501 Airport Rd 87507 505-467-1500
Matthew Martinez, prin. Fax 995-3328
Wood-Gormley ES 400/K-6
141 E Booth St 87505 505-467-4800
Dr. Linda Besett, prin. Fax 995-3322
Other Schools – See Tesuque

Christian Life Academy 100/K-12
121 Siringo Rd 87505 505-984-1001
Jennifer Sanchez, prin. Fax 988-4781
Mission Viejo Christian Academy 200/PK-8
4601 Mission Bnd 87507 505-474-8080
Bernadette Shanaberger, prin. Fax 474-8082
Rio Grande S 200/PK-6
715 Camino Cabra 87505 505-983-1621
Jay Underwood, hdmstr. Fax 986-0012
Sante Fe S for the Arts & Sciences 100/PK-8
5912 Jaguar Dr 87507 505-438-8585
Rayna Dineen, prin. Fax 438-6236
Sante Fe Waldorf S 200/PK-12
26 Puesta Del Sol 87508 505-992-0556
Barbara Booth, admin. Fax 992-0568
Santo Nino Regional S 400/PK-6
23 College Dr 87508 505-424-1766
Sr. Theresa Vaisa, prin. Fax 473-1441

Santa Rosa, Guadalupe, Pop. 2,509
Santa Rosa Consolidated SD 700/PK-12
344 S 4th St 88435 575-472-3171
Dan Flores, supt. Fax 472-5609
Santa Rosa ES 200/PK-5
658 S 5th St 88435 575-472-3172
Lee Vega, prin. Fax 472-5638
Santa Rosa MS 100/6-8
116 Camino de Vida 88435 575-472-3633
Joseph Salas, prin. Fax 472-0663
Other Schools – See Anton Chico

Santa Teresa, Dona Ana, Pop. 900
Gadsden ISD
Supt. — See Sunland Park
Santa Teresa ES 500/K-6
201 Comerciantes Blvd 88008 575-589-3445
Ralph Yturralde, prin. Fax 589-3429
Santa Teresa MS 700/7-8
4800 McNutt Rd 88008 575-874-7200
Rosa Lovelace, prin. Fax 589-2780

Santo Domingo Pueblo, Sandoval, Pop. 2,866
Bernalillo SD
Supt. — See Bernalillo
Santo Domingo ES 300/K-5
PO Box 459 87052 505-867-4441
Susan Neddeau, prin. Fax 867-7862
Santo Domingo MS 100/6-8
PO Box 459 87052 505-867-4441
Fax 867-7862

Seboyeta, Cibola
Grants-Cibola County SD
Supt. — See Grants
Seboyeta ES 50/K-6
HC 77 Box 43 87014 505-285-2760
Penny Utley, lead tchr. Fax 285-2765

Sheep Springs, San Juan, Pop. 30
Central Consolidated SD 22
Supt. — See Shiprock
Naschitti ES 100/K-6
PO Box F 87364 505-732-4204
Mamie Becenti, prin. Fax 732-4203

Shiprock, San Juan, Pop. 7,687
Central Consolidated SD 22 6,600/PK-12
PO Box 1199 87420 505-368-4984
Gregg Epperson, supt. Fax 368-5232
www.centralschools.org/
Mesa ES 200/4-6
PO Box 1803 87420 505-368-4529
Pandora Mike, prin. Fax 368-5765
Natanni Nez ES 300/PK-3
PO Box 3658 87420 505-368-4687
Roselyn Begay, prin. Fax 368-4690
Nizhoni ES 300/PK-3
PO Box 1968 87420 505-368-4565
Wynora Bekis, prin. Fax 368-4814
Stokely IS 300/4-6
PO Box 3568 87420 505-368-5109
Sharon Jenson, prin. Fax 368-5158
Tse' Bit'ai MS 400/7-8
PO Box 1703 87420 505-368-4741
Don Levinski, prin. Fax 368-5105
Other Schools – See Fruitland, Kirtland, Newcomb, Sheep Springs

Silver City, Grant, Pop. 9,999
Silver Consolidated SD 3,100/PK-12
2810 N Swan St 88061 575-956-2000
Dick Pool, supt. Fax 956-2039
www.silverschools.org/
Barrios ES 300/K-5
1625 Little Walnut Rd 88061 575-956-2120
Tom Schnalzer, prin. Fax 956-2134
La Plata MS 700/6-8
3500 N Silver St 88061 575-956-2060
Frank Quarrell, prin. Fax 956-2098
Schmitt ES 500/PK-5
4042 Highway 90 S 88061 575-956-2170
Gus Benakis, prin. Fax 956-2182
Sixth Street ES 200/K-5
405 W 6th St 88061 575-956-2150
Alan Ramirez, prin. Fax 956-2169
Stout ES 400/PK-5
2601 N Silver St 88061 575-956-2100
Joan Collins-Garcia, prin. Fax 956-2119
Other Schools – See Cliff

Guadalupe Montessori S 100/PK-6
1731 N Alabama St 88061 575-388-3343
Carey Walker, prin. Fax 538-8757

Socorro, Socorro, Pop. 8,621
Socorro Consolidated SD 1,700/K-12
PO Box 1157 87801 575-835-0300
Dr. Cheryl Wilson, supt. Fax 835-1682
www.socorro.k12.nm.us/
Parkview ES 400/K-3
107 Francisco De Avando St 87801 575-835-1086
Kim Ortiz, prin. Fax 835-2962
Sarracino MS 400/6-8
PO Box X 87801 575-835-0283
Jean Walker, prin. Fax 835-0360
Zimmerly ES 200/4-5
511 El Camino Real St 87801 575-835-1436
Rey Carrejo, prin.
Other Schools – See Polvadera, San Antonio

Springer, Colfax, Pop. 1,224
Springer Municipal SD 200/K-12
PO Box 308 87747 575-483-3432
Zita Rae Lopez, supt. Fax 483-2387
www.springerschools.org
Forrester ES 50/K-2
PO Box 308 87747 575-483-3485
Darice Balizan, prin. Fax 483-5012
Miranda JHS 100/6-8
PO Box 308 87747 575-483-3485
Darice Balizan, prin. Fax 483-5012
Wilferth IS 50/3-5
PO Box 308 87747 575-483-3485
Darice Balizan, prin. Fax 483-5012

Sunland Park, Dona Ana, Pop. 14,089
Gadsden ISD 13,300/PK-12
4950 McNutt Rd 88008 575-882-6200
Cynthia Nava, supt. Fax 882-6229
www.gisd.k12.nm.us
Desert View ES 500/K-6
PO Box 450 88063 575-589-1180
Fernando Carrasco, prin. Fax 589-2212
Riverside ES 600/K-6
4085 McNutt Rd 88063 575-589-1663
Vicente Sanchez, prin. Fax 874-3611
Sunland Park ES 400/PK-6
305 Alto Vista Dr 88063 575-589-1114
Linda Perez, prin. Fax 874-9442
Other Schools – See Anthony, Chaparral, La Union, Mesquite, San Miguel, Santa Teresa, Vado

Taos, Taos, Pop. 5,126
Taos Municipal SD 2,900/PK-12
213 Paseo Del Canon E 87571 575-758-5202
Roberto Gonzales, supt. Fax 758-5298
www.taosschools.org/
Garcia ES 700/PK-5
305 Don Fernando St 87571 575-737-6070
Nadine Vigil, prin. Fax 737-6091
Taos MS 600/6-8
235 Paseo Del Canon E 87571 575-737-6000
Alfred Cordova, prin. Fax 737-6001
Other Schools – See Arroyo Seco, Ranchos de Taos

Yaxche S 100/PK-8
4100 NDCBU 87571 575-751-4419
Dmitri Ross Calvert M.A., hdmstr. Fax 751-9896

Tatum, Lea, Pop. 693
Tatum Municipal SD 300/PK-12
PO Box 685 88267 575-398-4455
Buddly Little, supt. Fax 398-8220
www.tatumschools.org/
Tatum ES 200/PK-6
PO Box 685 88267 575-398-4191
Marisela Lain, prin. Fax 398-8220

Tesuque, Santa Fe, Pop. 1,490
Santa Fe SD
Supt. — See Santa Fe
Tesuque ES 100/K-6
PO Box 440 87574 505-467-4100
Carlos Alarid, prin. Fax 989-5523

Texico, Curry, Pop. 1,060
Texico Municipal SD 500/PK-12
PO Box 237 88135 575-482-3801
Dr. R. L. Richards, supt. Fax 482-3650
www.texicoschools.com
Texico ES 200/PK-5
PO Box 237 88135 575-482-3492
Rick Stanley, prin. Fax 482-3650
Texico MS 100/6-8
PO Box 237 88135 575-482-9520
Wayne Anderson, prin. Fax 482-3650

Thoreau, McKinley
Gallup-McKinley County SD
Supt. — See Gallup
Thoreau ES 300/PK-5
PO Box 839 87323 505-862-7425
Yvonne Crooker, prin. Fax 862-7426
Thoreau MS 300/6-8
PO Box 787 87323 505-862-7463
Alberta Nozie, prin. Fax 862-7464

St. Bonaventure S 200/PK-8
PO Box 909 87323 505-862-7465
Sr. Natalie Bussiere, prin. Fax 862-7029

Tierra Amarilla, Rio Arriba
Chama Valley ISD 400/PK-12
PO Box 10 87575 575-588-7285
Manuel Valdez, supt. Fax 588-7860
www.chamaschools.com/
Tierra Amarilla ES 100/K-5
PO Box 66 87575 575-588-7294
Dr. Rebecca Truelove, prin. Fax 588-7360
Other Schools – See Chama

Tijeras, Bernalillo, Pop. 499
Albuquerque SD
Supt. — See Albuquerque
Montoya ES 400/PK-5
24 Public School Rd 87059 505-281-0880
Venesee Mildren, prin. Fax 281-1905
Roosevelt MS 500/6-8
11799 State Highway 337 87059 505-281-3316
Lee Roy Martinez, prin. Fax 281-5120

East Mountain Christian Academy 100/PK-12
PO Box 1779 87059 505-286-1482
Dede Ferguson, prin. Fax 286-7609
Holy Child S, PO Box 130 87059 1-8
Nancy Fitzpatrick, prin. 505-281-2297

Tohatchi, McKinley, Pop. 661
Gallup-McKinley County SD
Supt. — See Gallup
Tohatchi ES 200/PK-5
PO Box 31 87325 505-733-2297
Venisa Holly, prin. Fax 271-4799
Tohatchi MS 200/6-8
PO Box 322 87325 505-733-2555
Tammy Somers, prin. Fax 733-2556

Truth or Consequences, Sierra, Pop. 7,071
Truth or Consequences Municipal SD 1,500/PK-12
180 N Date St 87901 575-894-8150
Tom Burris, supt. Fax 894-7532
www.torc.k12.nm.us
Sierra ES 200/4-5
1500 N Silver St 87901 575-894-8360
Angela Rael, dean Fax 894-8080
Truth or Consequences ES 400/PK-3
1500 N Silver St 87901 575-894-8370
Hank Hopkins, prin. Fax 894-5503
Truth or Consequences MS 300/6-8
1802 Pershing St 87901 575-894-8380
Brenda Doil, prin. Fax 894-0606
Other Schools – See Arrey

AppleTree Education Center 100/PK-12
1300 S Broadway St 87901 575-894-5646
Rebecca Dow, dir. Fax 894-0132

Tucumcari, Quay, Pop. 5,335
Tucumcari SD 1,100/PK-12
PO Box 1046 88401 575-461-3910
Aaron McKinney, supt. Fax 461-3554
www.gorattlers.org
Tucumcari ES, 1701 S 9th St 88401 500/PK-5
Teresa Stephenson, prin. 575-461-8460
Tucumcari MS, 914 S 5th St 88401 200/6-8
Roberta Segura, prin. 575-461-2310

Tularosa, Otero, Pop. 2,858
Tularosa Municipal SD 900/K-12
504 1st St 88352 575-585-8800
Brenda Vigil, supt. Fax 585-4439
www.tularosa.k12.nm.us
Tularosa ES 200/K-2
504 1st St 88352 575-585-8801
Melva Gimbel, prin. Fax 585-2332
Tularosa IS 200/3-6
504 1st St 88352 575-585-8802
Ray Gonzalez, prin. Fax 585-2345
Tularosa MS 200/7-8
504 1st St 88352 575-585-8803
Diane Baker, prin. Fax 585-4739

Vado, Dona Ana
Gadsden ISD
Supt. — See Sunland Park
Vado ES 500/K-6
330 Holguin Rd 88072 575-233-2861
Lucia Servin, prin. Fax 233-3400

Vanderwagen, McKinley
Gallup-McKinley County SD
Supt. — See Gallup
Skeet ES 200/PK-5
PO Box 128 87326 505-778-5571
Mary Washburn, prin. Fax 778-5572

Vaughn, Guadalupe, Pop. 469
Vaughn Municipal SD 100/PK-12
PO Box 489 88353 575-584-2283
Lorena Garcia, supt. Fax 584-2355
www.vaughn.k12.nm.us/
Vaughn ES 100/PK-6
PO Box 489 88353 575-584-2676
Michael Foster, prin. Fax 584-2355

Velarde, Rio Arriba
Espanola SD
Supt. — See Espanola
Velarde ES 200/K-6
PO Box 310 87582 505-852-4331
Roberto Archuleta, prin. Fax 852-2993

Wagon Mound, Mora, Pop. 352
Wagon Mound SD 200/K-12
PO Box 158 87752 575-666-3000
Albert Martinez, supt. Fax 666-9001
www.wm.k12.nm.us
Wagon Mound ES 50/K-6
PO Box 158 87752 575-666-3004
Sheryl McNellis, prin. Fax 666-9002

White Rock, Los Alamos, Pop. 6,192
Los Alamos SD
Supt. — See Los Alamos
Chamisa ES 300/K-6
301 Meadow Ln, Los Alamos NM 87544
505-663-2470
Cindy Montoya, prin. Fax 672-0170
Pinon ES 400/PK-6
90 Grand Canyon Dr, Los Alamos NM 87544
505-663-2680
Megan Lee, prin. Fax 672-1999

White Sands, Dona Ana, Pop. 2,616
Las Cruces SD
Supt. — See Las Cruces
White Sands ES 200/PK-5
1 Viking St 88002 575-674-1241
Gabriel Jacquez, prin. Fax 674-1515
White Sands MS 100/6-8
1 Viking St 88002 575-674-1241
Gabriel Jacquez, prin. Fax 674-1515

Yatahey, McKinley
Gallup-McKinley County SD
Supt. — See Gallup
Chee Dodge ES 400/PK-5
PO Box 4039 87375 505-863-9379
Edie Morris, prin. Fax 863-9370

Zuni, McKinley, Pop. 5,857
Zuni SD 1,300/K-12
PO Box A 87327 505-782-5511
Dr. Kaye Peery, supt. Fax 782-5505
www.zpsd.org
A:shiwi ES 200/K-5
PO Box 310 87327 505-782-4443
Karen Freedle, prin. Fax 782-2600
Dowa Yalanne ES 300/K-5
PO Box D 87327 505-782-4441
Caroline Ukestine, prin. Fax 782-5879
Zuni MS 200/6-8
PO Box E 87327 505-782-5561
Susan Montoya, prin. Fax 782-5563

St. Anthony S 100/PK-8
PO Box 486 87327 505-782-4596
Nenita Mosqueda, prin. Fax 782-2013
Zuni Christian Mission S 100/K-8
PO Box 445 87327 505-782-4546
Kathleen Bosscher, prin. Fax 782-4546

NEW YORK

NEW YORK EDUCATION DEPARTMENT
89 Washington Ave, Albany 12234-1000
Telephone 518-474-3852
Fax 518-473-4909
Website http://www.nysed.gov

Commissioner of Education David Steiner

NEW YORK BOARD OF REGENTS
Washington Ave, Albany 12234-0001

Chancellor Merryl Tisch

BOARDS OF COOPERATIVE EDUCATIONAL SERVICES (BOCES)

Broome-Tioga BOCES
Allen Buyck, supt. 607-766-3802
435 Glenwood Rd Fax 763-3215
Binghamton 13905
www.btboces.org/

Capital Region BOCES
Charles Dedrick, supt. 518-862-4900
1031 Watervliet Shaker Rd Fax 862-4903
Albany 12205
www.capregboces.org

Cattaraugus/Allegany/Erie/Wy BOCES
Dr. Robert Olczak, supt. 585-376-8246
1825 Windfall Rd, Olean 14760 Fax 376-8452
caew-boces.wnyric.org/

Cayuga/Onondaga BOCES
William Speck, supt. 315-253-0361
1879 W Genesee Street Rd Fax 252-6493
Auburn 13021
cayboces.org

Champlain Valley Educational Services
Craig King, supt. 518-561-0100
PO Box 455, Plattsburgh 12901 Fax 562-1471
www.cves.org/

Delaware/Chenango/Mdsn/Otsg BOCES
Bill Tammaro, supt. 607-335-1233
6678 County Road 32 Fax 334-9848
Norwich 13815
www.dcmoboces.com

Dutchess BOCES
Dr. John Pennoyer, supt. 845-486-4800
5 Boces Rd, Poughkeepsie 12601 Fax 486-4981
www.dcboces.org

Eastern Suffolk BOCES
Edward Zero, supt. 631-289-2200
201 N Service Rd Fax 289-2381
Patchogue 11772
www.esboces.org/

Erie 1 BOCES
Donald Ogilvie, supt. 716-821-7002
355 Harlem Rd Fax 821-7242
West Seneca 14224
www.erie1boces.org

Erie 2-Chautauqua-Cattaraugus BOCES
Robert Guiffreda, supt. 716-549-4454
8685 Erie Rd, Angola 14006 Fax 549-1758

Franklin-Essex-Hamilton BOCES
Stephen Shafer, supt. 518-483-6420
PO Box 28, Malone 12953 Fax 483-2178
www.fehb.org/

Genesee Valley BOCES
Dr. Michael Glover, supt. 585-344-7903
80 Munson St, Le Roy 14482 Fax 658-7910
www.gvboces.org

Greater Southern Tier BOCES
Anthony Micha, supt. 607-962-3175
9579 Vocational Dr Fax 962-1579
Painted Post 14870
www.gstboces.org/index.cfm

Hamilton-Fulton-Montgomery BOCES
Dr. Geoffrey Davis, supt. 518-736-4300
2755 State Highway 67 Fax 762-4724
Johnstown 12095
www.hfmboces.org/indexmap.html

Herkimer-Fulton-Hamilton-Otsego BOCES
Sandra Simpson, supt. 315-867-2023
352 Gros Blvd, Herkimer 13350 Fax 867-2002
www.herkimer-boces.org

Jeffrsn-Lws-Hmltn-Hrkmr-Oneida BOCES
Jack Boak, supt. 315-779-7012
20104 State Route 3 Fax 785-8300
Watertown 13601
www.boces.com/

Madison-Oneida BOCES
Jacklin Starks, supt. 315-361-5500
PO Box 168, Verona 13478 Fax 361-5595
www.moboces.org

Monroe 1 BOCES
Daniel White, supt. 585-383-2200
41 OConnor Rd, Fairport 14450 Fax 383-6404
www.monroe.edu/

Monroe 2 - Orleans BOCES
Dr. Michael O'Laughlin, supt. 585-352-2400
3599 Big Ridge Rd Fax 352-2442
Spencerport 14559
www.monroe2boces.org

Nassau BOCES
Edward Zero, supt. 516-396-2200
PO Box 9195, Garden City 11530 Fax 997-8742
www.nassauboces.org

Oneida-Herkimer-Madison BOCES
Howard Mettelman, supt. 315-793-8561
PO Box 70, New Hartford 13413 Fax 793-8541
www.oneida-boces.org/

Onondaga-Cortland-Madison BOCES
Dr. Jessica Cohen, supt. 315-433-2602
PO Box 4754, Syracuse 13221 Fax 437-4816
www.ocmboces.org/

Orange-Ulster BOCES
Dr. John Pennoyer, supt. 845-291-0100
53 Gibson Rd, Goshen 10924 Fax 291-0118
www.ouboces.org/

Orleans-Niagara BOCES
Dr. Clark Godshall, supt. 800-836-7510
4232 Shelby Basin Rd Fax 798-1317
Medina 14103
www.onboces.org

Oswego BOCES
Dr. Joseph Camerino, supt. 315-963-4222
179 County Route 64 Fax 963-7131
Mexico 13114
www.oswegoboces.org/

Otsego-Northern Catskills BOCES
Dr. Geoff Davis, supt. 607-652-1209
159 W Main St, Stamford 12167 Fax 652-1215
www.oncboces.org

Putnam Northern Westchester BOCES
Dr. James T. Langlois, supt. 914-248-2302
200 BOCES Dr Fax 248-2308
Yorktown Heights 10598
www.pnwboces.org

Questar III BOCES
James Baldwin, supt. 518-477-8771
10 Empire State Blvd Fax 477-9833
Castleton on Hudson 12033
www.questar.org/

Rockland BOCES
Dr. James Langlois, supt. 845-627-4701
65 Parrott Rd, West Nyack 10994 Fax 624-1764
www.rocklandboces.org/

St. Lawrence-Lewis BOCES
Jack Boak, supt. 315-386-4504
139 State Street Rd, Canton 13617 Fax 386-3395
www.sllboces.org/

Southern Westchester BOCES
Dr. Robert Monson, supt. 914-937-3820
17 Berkley Dr, Rye Brook 10573 Fax 937-7850
www.swboces.org/

Sullivan County BOCES
Anthony Micha, supt. 845-295-4015
6 Wierk Ave, Liberty 12754 Fax 292-8694
www.scboces.com

Tompkins-Seneca-Tioga BOCES
Dr. Ellen A. O'Donnell, supt. 607-257-1551
555 Warren Rd, Ithaca 14850 Fax 257-2825
www.tstboces.org/

Ulster BOCES
Martin Ruglis, supt. 845-255-3040
175 State Route 32 N Fax 255-7942
New Paltz 12561
www.ulsterboces.org/

Washington-Srtg-Warren-Hmltn-Essex BOCES
Dr. John Stoothoff, supt. 518-746-3310
1153 Burgoyne Ave Ste 2 Fax 746-3309
Fort Edward 12828
wswheboces.org/

Wayne-Finger Lakes BOCES
Dr. Joseph Marinelli, supt. 315-332-7284
131 Drumlin Ct, Newark 14513 Fax 332-7425
www.wflboces.org/wflboces/index.cfm

Western Suffolk BOCES
Edward Zero, supt. 631-549-4900
507 Deer Park Rd, Dix Hills 11746 Fax 423-1821
www.wsboces.org/

PUBLIC, PRIVATE AND CATHOLIC ELEMENTARY SCHOOLS

Accord, Ulster
Rondout Valley Central SD 2,600/K-12
PO Box 9 12404 845-687-2400
Eileen Camasso, supt. Fax 687-9577
www.rondout.k12.ny.us
Rondout Valley MS 800/5-8
PO Box 9 12404 845-687-2400
Raymond Palmer, prin. Fax 687-8980
Other Schools – See Cottekill, Kerhonkson, Stone Ridge

Adams, Jefferson, Pop. 1,663
South Jefferson Central SD
Supt. — See Adams Center
Clarke MS 500/6-8
11060 US Route 11 13605 315-232-4531
Tom O'Brien, prin. Fax 232-4620

Adams Center, Jefferson, Pop. 1,675
South Jefferson Central SD 2,000/K-12
13180 US Route 11 13606 315-583-6104
Jamie Moesel, supt. Fax 583-6381
www.spartanpride.org
Wilson ES 500/K-5
13180 US Route 11 13606 315-583-5418
Rebecca Stone, prin. Fax 583-6381
Other Schools – See Adams, Mannsville

Addison, Steuben, Pop. 1,765
Addison Central SD 1,200/PK-12
1 Colwell St 14801 607-359-2244
Betsy Stiker, supt. Fax 359-2246
www.addisoncsd.org/
Tuscarora ES 600/PK-6
7 Cleveland Dr 14801 607-359-2261
Deborah Flint, prin. Fax 359-3443
Other Schools – See Cameron Mills

Afton, Chenango, Pop. 831
Afton Central SD 700/K-12
PO Box 5 13730 607-639-8229
Elizabeth Briggs, supt. Fax 639-1801
www.afton.stier.org
Afton ES 300/K-5
PO Box 5 13730 607-639-8234
Kimberly Werth, prin. Fax 639-8257

Akron, Erie, Pop. 3,067
Akron Central SD 1,700/PK-12
47 Bloomingdale Ave 14001 716-542-5010
Robin Zymroz, supt. Fax 542-5018
www.akronschools.org
Akron ES 700/PK-5
47 Bloomingdale Ave 14001 716-542-5050
Todd Esposito, prin. Fax 542-5018
Akron MS 400/6-8
47 Bloomingdale Ave 14001 716-542-5040
Anthony Panella, prin. Fax 542-5018

Albany, Albany, Pop. 93,523
Albany CSD 8,200/PK-12
1 Academy Park 12207 518-475-6000
Dr. Raymond Colucciello, supt. Fax 475-6009
www.albanyschools.org

Albany S of Humanities 500/PK-6
108 Whitehall Rd 12209 518-462-7258
Rosalyn Wallace, prin. Fax 462-7265
Arbor Hill ES 400/PK-6
141 Western Ave 12203 518-462-7166
Rosalind Gaines-Harrell, prin. Fax 462-7164
Delaware Community S 300/PK-5
43 Bertha St 12209 518-475-6750
Tom Giglio, prin. Fax 475-6754
Eagle Point ES 200/PK-5
1044 Western Ave 12203 518-475-6825
Kendra Chaires, prin. Fax 475-6827
Giffen Memorial ES 500/PK-6
274 S Pearl St 12202 518-462-7177
Maxine Fantroy-Ford, prin. Fax 462-7134
Hackett MS 500/6-8
45 Delaware Ave 12202 518-462-7186
Fax 462-7161
Montessori Magnet ES 300/PK-5
65 Tremont St 12205 518-475-6675
Ken Lein, prin. Fax 475-6677
Myers MS 600/6-8
100 Elbel Ct 12209 518-475-6425
Kimberly Wilkins, prin. Fax 475-6427
New Scotland ES 400/K-5
369 New Scotland Ave 12208 518-475-6775
Gregory Jones, prin. Fax 475-6777
North Albany Academy 400/PK-8
570 N Pearl St 12204 518-475-6800
Dale Getto, prin. Fax 475-6802
O'Brien Academy of Science/Tech. 500/PK-6
100 Delaware Ave 12202 518-462-7262
Timothy Fowler, prin. Fax 462-7152
Pine Hills ES 300/K-5
41 N Allen St 12203 518-475-6725
Vibetta Sanders, prin. Fax 475-6729
Schuyler Achievement Academy 300/PK-5
676 Clinton Ave 12206 518-475-6700
Dorinda Davis, prin. Fax 475-6702
Sheridan Preparatory Academy 300/PK-5
400 Sheridan Ave 12206 518-475-6850
Cecily Wilson, prin. Fax 463-0799

Guilderland Central SD
Supt. — See Guilderland
Westmere ES 500/K-5
6270 Johnston Rd 12203 518-456-3771
Beth Bini, prin. Fax 464-6443

South Colonie Central SD 5,600/K-12
102 Loralee Dr 12205 518-869-3576
Jonathan Buhner, supt. Fax 869-6517
www.southcolonieschools.org
Forest Park ES 300/K-4
100 Forest Dr 12205 518-869-3006
Patrick Gunner, prin. Fax 869-5891
Lisha Kill MS 800/5-8
68 Waterman Ave 12205 518-456-2306
Joseph Guardino, prin. Fax 452-8165
Roessleville ES 300/K-4
100 California Ave 12205 518-459-2157
Fax 459-0268
Saddlewood ES 300/K-4
100 Loralee Dr 12205 518-456-2608
Ernest Casile, prin. Fax 862-0271
Sand Creek MS 1,000/5-8
329 Sand Creek Rd 12205 518-459-1333
David Perry, prin. Fax 459-1404
Shaker Road ES 300/K-4
512 Albany Shaker Rd 12211 518-458-1440
William Dollard, prin. Fax 459-1283
Veeder ES 500/K-4
25 Veeder Dr 12205 518-869-4661
Kathleen Gottschalk, prin. Fax 869-4495

Academy of the Holy Names 200/PK-8
1065 New Scotland Rd 12208 518-438-6553
Maureen Ferris, prin. Fax 438-7368
Albany Academies East Campus 400/PK-12
140 Academy Rd 12208 518-429-2300
Dr. Richard Barter, hdmstr. Fax 463-5096
Albany Academies West Campus 400/PK-12
135 Academy Rd 12208 518-429-2300
Dr. Richard Barter, hdmstr. Fax 427-7016
Bet Shraga Hebrew Academy 100/K-8
54 Sand Creek Rd 12205 518-482-0464
Rami Strosberg, dir. Fax 482-0129
Blessed Sacrament S 200/PK-8
605 Central Ave 12206 518-438-5854
Sr. Patricia Lynch, prin. Fax 438-1532
Christ the King S 200/PK-8
20 Sumpter Ave Ste 1 12203 518-456-5400
Judy Smith, prin. Fax 456-4696
Doane Stuart S 300/PK-12
799 S Pearl St 12202 518-465-5222
Dr. Richard Enemark, hdmstr. Fax 465-5230
Holy Cross S 200/PK-8
10 Rosemont St 12203 518-438-0066
Sr. Mary Ellen Owens, prin. Fax 438-0066
Maimonides Hebrew Day S 100/PK-12
404 Partridge St 12208 518-453-9363
Marcia Rosenfield, prin. Fax 453-9362
St. Casimir Regional S 100/PK-8
309 Sheridan Ave 12206 518-434-4264
James Leveskas, prin. Fax 434-3511
St. Catherine of Siena S 300/PK-8
35 Hurst Ave 12208 518-489-3111
Theresa Ewell, prin. Fax 489-5865
St. Matthew Lutheran S 100/PK-K
75 Whitehall Rd 12209 518-463-6495
Gail Macintosh, dir. Fax 463-9417
St. Teresa of Avila S 200/PK-8
8 Hollywood Ave 12208 518-482-3736
Sr. Patricia Houlihan, prin. Fax 482-3745

Albertson, Nassau, Pop. 5,166
Herricks UFD
Supt. — See New Hyde Park
Herricks MS 1,000/6-8
7 Hilldale Dr 11507 516-305-8600
Joseph Leccese, prin. Fax 248-3281
Searingtown ES 600/K-5
106 Beverly Dr 11507 516-305-8950
Elizabeth Guercin, prin. Fax 248-3281

Mineola UFD
Supt. — See Mineola
Meadow Drive ES 200/PK-5
25 Meadow Dr 11507 516-237-2400
Patricia Molloy, prin. Fax 484-2785

Albion, Orleans, Pop. 5,766
Albion Central SD 2,500/PK-12
324 East Ave 14411 585-589-2050
Dr. Ada Grabowski, supt. Fax 589-2059
www.albionk12.org/
Bergerson MS, 254 East Ave 14411 600/6-8
Daniel Monacelli, prin. 585-589-2020
Sodoma ES, 324 East Ave 14411 1,100/PK-5
James Wood, prin. 585-589-2030

Alden, Erie, Pop. 2,613
Alden Central SD 1,900/K-12
13190 Park St 14004 716-937-9116
Lynn Fusco Ph.D., supt. Fax 937-7132
www.aldenschools.org
Alden IS 400/3-5
1648 Crittenden Rd 14004 716-937-9116
Thomas Lyons, prin. Fax 937-3376
Alden MS 400/6-8
13250 Park St 14004 716-937-9116
Adam Stoltman, prin. Fax 937-3563
Alden PS at Townline 400/K-2
11197 Broadway St 14004 716-937-9116
Melanie Monacelli, prin. Fax 937-9839

St. John the Baptist S 100/PK-8
2028 Sandridge Rd 14004 585-937-9483
Marilynn Camp, prin. Fax 937-9794

Alexander, Genesee, Pop. 497
Alexander Central SD 1,000/K-12
3314 Buffalo St 14005 585-591-1551
Kathleen Maerten, supt. Fax 591-2257
www.alexandercsd.org
Alexander ES 400/K-5
3314 Buffalo St 14005 585-591-1551
Matthew Stroud, prin. Fax 591-4713

Alexandria Bay, Jefferson, Pop. 1,100
Alexandria Central SD 700/PK-12
34 Bolton Ave 13607 315-482-9971
Robert Wagoner, supt. Fax 482-9973
www.alexandriacentral.org
Alexandria Central ES 300/PK-6
34 Bolton Ave 13607 315-482-9971
Rebecca Mulford, prin. Fax 482-9973

Allegany, Cattaraugus, Pop. 1,831
Allegany-Limestone Central SD 1,400/PK-12
3131 Five Mile Rd 14706 585-375-6600
Diane Munro, supt.
www.alli.wnyric.org
Allegany ES, 120 Maple Ave 14706 500/PK-5
Cyndy Christopher, prin. 585-375-6600
Allegany-Limestone MS 300/6-8
3131 Five Mile Rd 14706 585-375-6600
Timothy McMullen, prin. Fax 375-6630
Other Schools – See Limestone

Almond, Allegany, Pop. 446
Alfred-Almond Central SD 700/K-12
6795 State Route 21 14804 607-276-2981
Richard Nicol, supt. Fax 276-6304
www.aacs.wnyric.org
Alfred-Almond ES 300/K-6
6795 State Route 21 14804 607-276-2171
Tracie Preston, prin. Fax 276-6304

Altamont, Albany, Pop. 1,720
Guilderland Central SD
Supt. — See Guilderland
Altamont ES 300/K-5
PO Box 648 12009 518-861-8528
Peter Brabant, prin. Fax 861-5189

Altmar, Oswego, Pop. 358
Altmar-Parish-Williamstown Central SD
Supt. — See Parish
Altmar ES 200/K-4
52 Pulaski St 13302 315-625-5260
Gerry Hudson, prin. Fax 298-7731

Amagansett, Suffolk
Amagansett UFD 100/PK-6
PO Box 7062 11930 631-267-3572
Eleanor Tritt, supt. Fax 267-7504
www.amagansettschool.org
Amagansett ES 100/PK-6
PO Box 7062 11930 631-267-3572
Eleanor Tritt, prin. Fax 267-7504

Amenia, Dutchess, Pop. 1,057
Webutuck Central SD 400/PK-12
PO Box 405 12501 845-373-4100
Fax 373-4102
www.webutuckschools.org/
Brooks IS, PO Box 405 12501 4-6
Kathleen McEnroe, prin. 845-373-4100
Webutuck ES 100/K-3
PO Box 400 12501 845-373-4122
Kathleen McEnroe, prin. Fax 373-4125
Other Schools – See Millerton

Kildonan S 100/2-12
425 Morse Hill Rd 12501 845-373-8111
Ronald Wilson, hdmstr. Fax 373-9793

Amherst, Erie, Pop. 45,800
Amherst Central SD 3,000/K-12
55 Kings Hwy 14226 716-362-3000
Laura Chabe, supt. Fax 836-2537
amherstschools.org
Amherst MS 700/6-8
55 Kings Hwy 14226 716-362-7100
Diane Klein, prin. Fax 836-0193
Smallwood Drive ES 700/K-5
300 Smallwood Dr 14226 716-362-2100
Lydia Brenner, prin. Fax 839-3578
Windermere Boulevard ES 600/K-5
291 Windermere Blvd 14226 716-362-4100
Daniel Lewis, prin. Fax 838-3764

Sweet Home Central SD 3,800/PK-12
1901 Sweet Home Rd 14228 716-250-1402
Geoffrey Hicks, supt. Fax 250-1374
www.sweethomeschools.com
Heritage Heights ES 300/PK-5
2545 Sweet Home Rd 14228 716-250-1525
Scott Wolf, prin. Fax 250-1531
Maplemere ES 500/K-5
236 E Maplemere Rd 14221 716-250-1550
Ann Laudisio, prin. Fax 250-1555
Sweet Home MS 900/6-8
4150 Maple Rd 14226 716-250-1450
Gregory Smorol, prin. Fax 250-1490
Willow Ridge ES 400/K-5
480 Willow Ridge Dr 14228 716-250-1575
David Lovering, prin. Fax 250-1585
Other Schools – See Tonawanda

Christ the King S 300/PK-8
2 Lamarck Dr 14226 716-839-0473
Jo Ann Mikulec, prin. Fax 568-8198
Jewish Heritage Day S 50/PK-8
411 John James Audubon Pkwy 14228
716-568-0226
Rabbi S. Shanowitz, prin. Fax 568-0226
Kadimah S 100/PK-8
1085 Eggert Rd 14226 716-836-6903
Joel Weiss, hdmstr. Fax 837-7322
St. Leo the Great S 200/PK-8
903 Sweet Home Rd 14226 716-832-6340
Carolyn Kraus, prin. Fax 835-8997

Amityville, Suffolk, Pop. 9,477
Amityville UFD 2,800/PK-12
150 Park Ave 11701 631-598-6507
Dr. John Williams, supt. Fax 691-4108
www.amityvilleufsd.org/
Miles MS 600/6-8
501 Broadway 11701 631-789-6200
Mark Pitterson, prin. Fax 789-1655
Northeast K 300/PK-K
420 Albany Ave 11701 631-789-6230
Pauline Collins, prin. Fax 789-6225
Northwest ES 400/1-2
450 County Line Rd 11701 631-789-6240
Stacey Fischer, prin. Fax 691-6235
Park Avenue ES, 140 Park Ave 11701 600/3-5
Betsy Gorman, prin. 631-691-2874

Bethesda S 100/PK-8
PO Box 781 11701 631-842-3321
St. Martin of Tours S 400/PK-8
41 Union Ave 11701 631-264-7166
Kathleen Razzetti, prin. Fax 264-0136

Amsterdam, Montgomery, Pop. 17,749
Broadalbin-Perth Central SD
Supt. — See Broadalbin
Broadalbin-Perth IS 400/4-6
1870 County Highway 107 12010 518-954-2750
Susan Casper, prin. Fax 954-2759
Broadalbin-Perth MS 300/7-8
1870 County Highway 107 12010 518-954-2700
Wayne Bell, prin. Fax 954-2709

Greater Amsterdam SD 3,700/K-12
11 Liberty St 12010 518-843-5217
Thomas Perillo, supt. Fax 842-0012
www.gasd.org
Barkley ES 300/K-5
66 Destefano Pl 12010 518-843-1850
Richard Capel, prin. Fax 843-6183
Curie ES 500/K-5
9 Brice St 12010 518-843-2871
Mary Mathey, prin. Fax 843-6290
Lynch MS 900/6-8
55 Brandt Pl 12010 518-843-3716
John Penman, prin. Fax 843-6287
McNulty ES 400/K-5
60 Brandt Pl 12010 518-843-4773
Barbara Petersen, prin. Fax 843-5475
Tecler ES 500/K-5
210 Northern Blvd 12010 518-843-4805
Terry Dewey, prin. Fax 843-6184

St. Mary's Institute S 300/PK-8
10 Kopernick Rd 12010 518-842-4100
Giovanni Virgiglio, prin. Fax 842-0217

Andes, Delaware, Pop. 278
Andes Central SD 100/K-12
PO Box 248 13731 845-676-3167
John Bernhardt, supt. Fax 676-3181
www.andescentralschool.org
Andes Central S 100/K-12
PO Box 248 13731 845-676-3166
Pat Norton-White, prin. Fax 676-3181

Andover, Allegany, Pop. 1,037
Andover Central SD 400/PK-12
PO Box G 14806 607-478-8491
William Berg, supt. Fax 478-8833
www.andovercsd.org/

Andover S 400/PK-12
PO Box G 14806 607-478-8491
Brian Gerbracht, prin. Fax 478-8833

Angola, Erie, Pop. 2,194
Evans-Brant Central SD (Lake Shore) 3,000/K-12
959 Beach Rd 14006 716-926-2201
Jeffrey Rabey, supt. Fax 549-6407
www.lakeshore.wnyric.org
Hoag ES 200/K-5
42 Sunset Blvd 14006 716-549-2306
Paula Eastman, prin. Fax 549-4391
Lake Shore Central MS 700/6-8
8855 Erie Rd 14006 716-549-2302
Erich Reidell, prin. Fax 549-4374
Schmidt ES 200/K-5
9455 Lake Shore Rd 14006 716-549-2303
Jennifer Makowski, prin. Fax 549-4428
Waugh ES 300/K-5
100 High St 14006 716-549-2305
David Patronik, prin. Fax 549-2380
Other Schools – See Brant, Derby

Antwerp, Jefferson, Pop. 730
Indian River Central SD
Supt. — See Philadelphia
Antwerp PS 200/K-3
PO Box 10 13608 315-659-8386
Allan O'Brien, prin. Fax 659-8944

Apalachin, Tioga, Pop. 1,208
Owego-Apalachin Central SD
Supt. — See Owego
Apalachin ES 400/K-5
405 Pennsylvania Ave 13732 607-687-6289
Joseph Dicosimo, prin. Fax 625-5811

Vestal Central SD
Supt. — See Vestal
Tioga Hills ES 400/K-5
48 Glann Rd 13732 607-757-2366
Kent Maslin, prin. Fax 757-2344

Aquebogue, Suffolk, Pop. 2,060
Riverhead Central SD
Supt. — See Riverhead
Aquebogue ES 400/K-4
PO Box 1200 11931 631-369-6780
Philip Kent, prin. Fax 369-0543

Our Redeemer Lutheran S of Aqueboque 100/PK-6
PO Box 960 11931 631-722-4000
Fax 722-3993

Arcade, Wyoming, Pop. 1,951
Yorkshire-Pioneer Central SD
Supt. — See Yorkshire
Arcade ES 500/K-4
PO Box 9 14009 585-492-9423
Kevin Munro, prin. Fax 492-9433

Ardsley, Westchester, Pop. 4,815
Ardsley UFD 2,200/K-12
500 Farm Rd 10502 914-693-6300
Dr. Charles Khoury, supt. Fax 693-8340
www.ardsleyschools.org
Ardsley MS 700/5-8
700 Ashford Ave 10502 914-693-7564
Amy Watkins, prin. Fax 693-7896
Concord Road ES 800/K-4
2 Concord Rd 10502 914-693-7510
Layne Hudes, prin. Fax 693-8720

Argyle, Washington, Pop. 287
Argyle Central SD 700/K-6
5023 State Route 40 12809 518-638-8243
Jan Jehring, supt. Fax 638-6373
www.argylecsd.org
Argyle Central ES 300/K-6
5023 State Route 40 12809 518-638-8243
Jan Jehring, prin. Fax 638-6373

Arkport, Steuben, Pop. 828
Arkport Central SD 600/K-12
35 East Ave 14807 607-295-7471
William Locke, supt. Fax 295-7473
www.stev.net
Arkport Central S 600/K-12
35 East Ave 14807 607-295-9823
Brennan Fahey, prin. Fax 295-7473

Armonk, Westchester, Pop. 2,745
Byram Hills Central SD 2,800/K-12
10 Tripp Ln Ste 1 10504 914-273-4082
Dr. Jacquelyn Taylor, supt. Fax 273-2516
www.byramhills.org
Coman Hill ES 700/K-2
558 Bedford Rd Ste 1 10504 914-273-4183
Carol Fisher, prin. Fax 273-3257
Crittenden MS 600/6-8
10 MacDonald Ave 10504 914-273-4250
Dr. H. Evan Powderly, prin. Fax 273-4618
Wampus ES 700/3-5
41 Wampus Ave Ste 1 10504 914-273-4190
Barbara Topiol, prin. Fax 273-3608

Montessori Children's Room 100/PK-K
67 Old Route 22 10504 914-273-3291
Marina Anandappa, prin. Fax 273-3936

Arverne, See New York
NYC Department of Education
Supt. — See New York
Maple Academy PK-8
365 Beach 56th St 11692 718-945-3300
Angela Logan, prin. Fax 945-3303
Public S 42 700/K-8
488 Beach 66th St 11692 718-634-7914
Riva Madden, prin. Fax 474-7591

Astoria, See New York
NYC Department of Education
Supt. — See New York
IS 10 800/6-8
4511 31st Ave 11103 718-278-7054
Clemente Lopes, prin. Fax 274-1578
IS 235 200/6-8
3014 30th St 11102 718-932-5876
Carmen Rivera, prin. Fax 932-5990
Public S 234 700/PK-5
3015 29th St 11102 718-932-5650
Thea Pallos, prin. Fax 932-5398

Immaculate Conception S 200/K-8
2163 29th St 11105 718-728-1969
Eileen Harnischfeger, prin. Fax 728-3374
Queens Lutheran S 100/1-8
3120 21st Ave 11105 718-721-4313
Bettye Lee, prin. Fax 721-7662
St. Demetrios Greek American S 600/PK-12
3003 30th Dr 11102 718-728-1754
Anastasios Koularmanis, prin. Fax 726-3482
St. Francis of Assisi S 300/PK-8
2118 46th St 11105 718-726-9405
Barbara McArdle, prin. Fax 721-2577
St. Joseph S 500/PK-8
2846 44th St 11103 718-728-0724
Luke Nawrocki, prin. Fax 728-6142

Athens, Greene, Pop. 1,733
Coxsackie-Athens Central SD
Supt. — See Coxsackie
Arthur ES 200/K-4
51 3rd St 12015 518-731-1750
Paul Snyder, prin. Fax 731-1765

Attica, Wyoming, Pop. 2,496
Attica Central SD 1,700/K-12
3338 E Main Street Rd 14011 585-591-0400
Bryce Thompson, supt. Fax 591-2681
www.atticacsd.org
Attica ES 400/K-4
31 Prospect St 14011 585-591-0400
Kelly Bissell, prin. Fax 591-4497
Attica JHS 500/5-8
3338 E Main Street Rd 14011 585-591-0400
Kenneth Hammel, prin. Fax 591-4496
Other Schools – See Varysburg

Auburn, Cayuga, Pop. 27,941
Auburn CSD 4,800/K-12
78 Thornton Ave 13021 315-255-8800
J.D. Pabis, supt. Fax 253-6068
district.auburn.cnyric.org
Casey Park ES 400/K-5
101 Pulaski St 13021 315-255-8760
Phyllis Price, prin. Fax 255-5910
East MS 600/6-8
191 Franklin St 13021 315-255-8480
David Oliver, prin. Fax 255-5910
Genesee Street ES 400/K-5
242 Genesee St 13021 315-255-8640
Ronald Gorney, prin. Fax 255-5910
Herman Avenue ES 500/K-5
2 N Herman Ave 13021 315-255-8680
Cynthia Lattimore, prin. Fax 255-5910
Owasco ES 400/K-5
66 Letchworth St 13021 315-255-8720
Miguelina Cuevas-Post, prin. Fax 255-5910
Seward ES 400/K-5
52 Metcalf Dr 13021 315-255-8600
JoAnn Wixson, prin. Fax 255-5910
West MS 500/6-8
217 Genesee St 13021 315-255-8540
Deborah Carey, prin. Fax 255-8559

St. Joseph S 200/PK-8
89 E Genesee St 13021 315-253-8327
Kathleen Coye, prin. Fax 253-2401
SS. Peter & Paul S 100/K-8
134 Washington St 13021 315-252-5567
Sr. Kathleen Hutsko, prin. Fax 252-7469

Aurora, Cayuga, Pop. 659
Southern Cayuga Central SD 900/K-12
2384 State Route 34B 13026 315-364-7211
Mary Worth, supt. Fax 364-7863
www.southerncayuga.org
Howland ES 300/K-4
2892 State Route 34B 13026 315-364-7621
Mary Lou Cronin, prin. Fax 364-7546
Southern Cayuga MS 300/5-8
2384 State Route 34B 13026 315-364-7098
Patricia Reilley, prin. Fax 364-7590

Au Sable Forks, Clinton
Au Sable Valley Central SD
Supt. — See Clintonville
Au Sable Forks ES 200/K-6
28 Church Ln 12912 518-647-5503
Dean Lincoln, prin. Fax 647-8471

Holy Name S 100/PK-6
5 Pleasant St 12912 518-647-8444
Jean Pulsifer, prin. Fax 647-5394

Averill Park, Rensselaer, Pop. 1,656
Averill Park Central SD 3,400/K-12
8439 Miller Hill Rd 12018 518-674-7050
Josephine Moccia Ed.D., supt. Fax 674-3802
www.averillpark.k12.ny.us/
Algonquin MS 800/6-8
333 NY Highway 351 12018 518-674-7100
James Franchini, prin. Fax 674-0671
Sand Lake/Miller Hill ES 500/K-5
8439 Miller Hill Rd 12018 518-674-7075
Denis Sibson, prin. Fax 674-7096
Other Schools – See Poestenkill, Troy, West Sand Lake

Avoca, Steuben, Pop. 986
Avoca Central SD 600/K-12
PO Box G 14809 607-566-2221
Richard Yochem, supt. Fax 566-2398
www.avocacsd.org/
Avoca Central S 600/K-12
PO Box G 14809 607-566-2221
Matthew Pfleegor, prin. Fax 566-8384

Avon, Livingston, Pop. 2,972
Avon Central SD 1,000/K-12
191 Clinton St 14414 585-226-2455
Bruce Amey, supt. Fax 226-8202
www.avoncsd.org
Avon Central PS 300/K-4
161 Clinton St 14414 585-226-2455
Robert Lupisella, prin. Fax 226-8202
Avon MS 300/5-8
191 Clinton St 14414 585-226-2455
Jennifer Miller, prin. Fax 226-8202

St. Agnes S 100/PK-6
60 Park Pl 14414 585-226-8500
Dr. Gerald Benjamin, prin. Fax 226-8500

Babylon, Suffolk, Pop. 12,659
Babylon UFD 1,900/K-12
50 Railroad Ave 11702 631-893-7925
Ellen Best-Laimit, supt. Fax 893-7935
www.babylonschools.org
Babylon ES 400/K-2
171 Ralph Ave 11702 631-893-7960
Dana Spincola, prin. Fax 893-7967
Babylon Memorial Grade S 600/3-6
169 Park Ave 11702 631-893-7980
Eric Freidman, prin. Fax 893-7990

Babylon Christian S 100/PK-5
79 E Main St 11702 631-422-4340
Fax 422-7416
South Bay Jr Academy of SDA 50/1-8
150 Fire Island Ave 11702 631-321-0857

Bainbridge, Chenango, Pop. 1,354
Bainbridge-Guilford Central SD 1,000/K-12
18 Juliand St 13733 607-967-6321
Karl Brown, supt. Fax 967-4231
www.bgcsd.org
Bainbridge-Guilford MS 200/6-8
18 Juliand St 13733 607-967-6300
Victoria Gullo, prin. Fax 967-4231
Greenlawn ES 300/2-5
43 Greenlawn Ave 13733 607-967-6327
Michele Shirkey, prin. Fax 967-3080
Other Schools – See Guilford

Baldwin, Nassau, Pop. 22,719
Baldwin UFD 5,200/K-12
960 Hastings St 11510 516-377-9271
Dr. James Mapes, supt. Fax 377-9421
www.baldwinschools.org/
Baldwin MS 1,300/6-8
3211 Schreiber Pl 11510 516-377-9321
James Brown, prin. Fax 377-9432
Brookside ES 200/K-5
940 Stanton Ave 11510 516-377-9318
Ivy Sherman, prin. Fax 377-9425
Lenox ES 300/K-5
551 Lenox Rd 11510 516-377-9344
Bernice Acevedo, prin. Fax 377-9426
Meadow ES 600/K-5
880 Jackson St 11510 516-377-9348
Joan Flatley, prin. Fax 377-9427
Milburn ES 200/K-5
2501 Milburn Ave 11510 516-377-9358
Mark Gray, prin. Fax 377-9428
Plaza ES 500/K-5
501 Seaman Ave 11510 516-377-9361
Charlene Maniscalco, prin. Fax 377-9429
Shubert ES 200/K-5
835 De Mott Ave 11510 516-377-9366
Echele May, prin. Fax 377-9430
Steele ES 200/K-5
860 Church St 11510 516-377-9368
Lori Presti, prin. Fax 377-9431

St. Christopher S 400/K-8
15 Pershing Blvd 11510 516-223-4404
Anne Lederer, prin. Fax 223-1409

Baldwinsville, Onondaga, Pop. 7,149
Baldwinsville Central SD 6,000/K-12
29 E Oneida St 13027 315-638-6043
Jeanne Dangle, supt. Fax 638-6041
www.bville.org
Elden ES 500/K-5
29 E Oneida St 13027 315-638-6118
Anthony Cardamone, prin. Fax 635-3950
McNamara ES 600/K-5
7344 Obrien Rd 13027 315-638-6130
Jane Nadolski, prin. Fax 638-5049
Palmer ES 500/K-5
7864 Hicks Rd 13027 315-638-6127
Steven Frey, prin. Fax 638-3970
Ray IS 1,000/6-7
7650 Van Buren Rd 13027 315-638-6106
Geoffrey Morton, prin. Fax 638-6041
Reynolds ES 400/K-5
222 Deerwood Dr 13027 315-638-6124
Olivia Cambs, prin. Fax 638-6169
Van Buren ES 500/K-5
14 Ford St 13027 315-638-6121
Theresa Bick, prin. Fax 635-3970

St. Mary's S 200/PK-6
49 Syracuse St 13027 315-635-3977
Debra Brillante, prin. Fax 635-8137

Ballston Lake, Saratoga
Burnt Hills-Ballston Lake Central SD
Supt. — See Scotia
Charlton Heights ES 500/K-5
170 Stage Rd 12019 518-399-9141
Tim Sinnenberg, prin. Fax 399-0227
Stevens ES 500/K-5
25 Lakehill Rd 12019 518-399-9141
Ralph Rothacker, prin. Fax 399-0343

Shenendehowa Central SD
Supt. — See Clifton Park
Chango ES 600/K-5
100 Chango Dr 12019 518-881-0520
Karin Skarka, prin. Fax 899-5971

Ballston Spa, Saratoga, Pop. 5,574
Ballston Spa Central SD 4,400/K-12
70 Malta Ave 12020 518-884-7195
Joseph Dragone Ph.D., supt. Fax 885-3201
www.bscsd.org
Ballston Spa MS 1,100/6-8
210 Ballston Ave 12020 518-884-7200
Michael Selkis, prin. Fax 884-7234
Malta Avenue ES 400/K-5
70 Malta Ave 12020 518-884-7250
Sharon D'Agostino, prin. Fax 884-7258
Milton Terrace North ES K-5
200 Wood Rd 12020 518-884-7210
Kathleen Chaucer, prin. Fax 884-7219
Milton Terrace South ES 900/K-5
100 Wood Rd 12020 518-884-7270
Jeffrey Palmer, prin. Fax 884-7268
Wood Road ES 600/K-5
300 Wood Rd 12020 518-884-7290
David Blanchard, prin. Fax 884-7286

St. Mary's S 200/PK-5
40 Thompson St 12020 518-885-7300
Sr. Jeanne Marie Gocha, prin. Fax 885-7378
Spa Christian S 100/PK-6
206 Greenfield Ave 12020 518-885-0508
Laureen Slater, admin. Fax 885-0508

Bardonia, Rockland, Pop. 4,487
Clarkstown Central SD
Supt. — See New City
Bardonia ES 500/K-5
31 Bardonia Rd 10954 845-624-3970
Christine Conway, prin. Fax 627-7633

Barker, Niagara, Pop. 557
Barker Central SD 1,100/PK-12
1628 Quaker Rd 14012 716-795-3832
Roger Klatt, supt. Fax 795-3394
barkercsd.net
Barker MS 300/5-8
1628 Quaker Rd 14012 716-795-3203
Barbara Converso, prin. Fax 795-9437
Pratt ES 400/PK-4
1628 Quaker Rd 14012 716-795-3237
Deborah Sinnott, prin. Fax 795-9330

Batavia, Genesee, Pop. 15,661
Batavia CSD 2,300/K-12
PO Box 677 14021 585-343-2480
Margaret Puzio, supt. Fax 344-8204
www.bataviacsd.org
Batavia MS 500/6-8
96 Ross St 14020 585-343-2480
Sandra Griffin, prin. Fax 344-8626
Jackson ES 300/K-5
411 S Jackson St 14020 585-343-2480
Shawn Clark, prin. Fax 344-8621
Kennedy ES 300/K-5
166 Vine St 14020 585-343-2480
Paul Kesler, prin. Fax 344-8617
Morris ES 300/K-5
80 Union St 14020 585-343-2480
Diane Bonarigo, prin. Fax 344-8607

St. Joseph S 300/PK-8
2 Summit St 14020 585-343-6154
Karen Green, prin. Fax 343-8911
St. Paul Lutheran S 50/PK-5
31 Washington Ave 14020 585-343-0488
Ann Werk, prin. Fax 344-0470

Bath, Steuben, Pop. 5,589
Bath Central SD 1,900/PK-12
25 Ellas Ave 14810 607-776-3301
Marion Tunney, supt. Fax 776-5021
www.bathcsd.org
Haverling MS 500/6-8
25 Ellas Ave 14810 607-776-4110
Michael Siebert, prin. Fax 776-5625
Lyon ES 200/4-5
25 Ellas Ave 14810 607-776-2170
Susan Graham, prin. Fax 776-1470
Wightman PS 500/PK-3
216 Maple Hts 14810 607-776-4123
Tracey Marchionda, prin. Fax 776-4124

Bayport, Suffolk, Pop. 7,702
Bayport-Blue Point UFD 2,500/K-12
189 Academy St 11705 631-472-7860
Anthony Annunziato Ed.D., supt. Fax 472-7873
www.bbpschools.org/
Academy Street ES 500/K-5
150 Academy St 11705 631-472-7850
Kerry Vann, prin. Fax 472-7858
Sylvan Avenue ES 400/K-5
600 Sylvan Ave 11705 631-472-7840
Alane Dugan, prin. Fax 472-7857
Young MS 600/6-8
602 Sylvan Ave 11705 631-472-7820
Susan Haske, prin. Fax 472-7849
Other Schools – See Blue Point

Bay Shore, Suffolk, Pop. 21,279
Bay Shore UFD 5,600/K-12
75 Perkal St 11706 631-968-1115
Evelyn Holman Ph.D., supt. Fax 968-1129
www.bayshore.k12.ny.us
Bay Shore MS 1,300/6-8
393 Brook Ave 11706 631-968-1208
LaQuita Outlaw, prin. Fax 968-2342
Brook Avenue ES 400/K-2
45 Brook Ave 11706 631-968-1130
Regina Vorwald, prin. Fax 968-2439
Clarkson ES 500/K-2
1415 E 3rd Ave 11706 631-968-1204
Leticia Garcia, prin. Fax 968-2461
Fifth Avenue ES 400/K-2
217 5th Ave 11706 631-968-1139
Frank Fallon, prin. Fax 968-2463
Gardiner Manor ES 600/3-5
125 Wohseepee Dr 11706 631-968-1149
Carlton Brown, prin. Fax 968-2487
South Country ES 500/3-5
885 Hampshire Rd 11706 631-968-1249
Johnna Grasso, prin. Fax 968-2499

Brentwood UFD
Supt. — See Brentwood
Hemlock Park ES 600/1-5
19 Hemlock Dr 11706 631-434-2451
Laura Alicastro, prin. Fax 434-2191
Oak Park ES 600/1-5
775 Wisconsin Ave 11706 631-434-2255
Irma Colon, prin. Fax 434-2183
Southwest ES 1,000/PK-5
1095 Joselson Ave 11706 631-434-2261
Marilyn Friend-Ituarte, prin. Fax 434-2196
West MS 800/6-8
2030 Udall Rd 11706 631-434-2371
Adrienne Ratuszny, prin. Fax 242-3992

St. Patrick S 400/PK-8
Montauk Hwy 11706 631-665-0569
Roseann Petruccio, prin. Fax 968-6007
St. Peter's By-The-Sea Episcopal Day S 200/PK-8
500 S Country Rd 11706 631-666-0908
Dr. John Caruso, hdmstr. Fax 666-7106

Bayside, See New York
NYC Department of Education
Supt. — See New York
MS 158 1,100/6-8
4635 Oceania St 11361 718-423-8100
Marie Nappi, prin. Fax 423-8135
Bell Academy 6-8
1825 212th St 11360 718-428-0587
Cheryl Quatrano, prin. Fax 428-0237
Public S 31 600/PK-5
21145 46th Rd 11361 718-423-8288
Terri Graybow, prin. Fax 423-8303
Public S 41 400/K-5
21443 35th Ave 11361 718-423-8333
Sari Latto, prin. Fax 423-8362
Public S 130 300/K-3
20001 42nd Ave 11361 718-357-6606
Michelle Contratti, prin. Fax 428-5927
Public S 159 500/PK-5
20501 33rd Ave 11361 718-423-8553
Marlene Zucker, prin. Fax 423-8583
Public S 169 300/PK-5
1825 212th St 11360 718-428-6160
Annette Kunin, prin. Fax 224-1013

Lutheran S of Flushing & Bayside 100/PK-8
3601 Bell Blvd 11361 718-225-5502
Pia Haselbach, prin. Fax 225-7446
Our Lady of the Blessed Sacrament S 300/PK-8
3445 202nd St 11361 718-229-4434
Joan Kane, prin. Fax 229-5820
Sacred Heart S 500/PK-8
21601 38th Ave 11361 718-631-4804
Dennis Farrell, prin. Fax 631-5738

Bayville, Nassau, Pop. 7,123
Locust Valley Central SD
Supt. — See Locust Valley
Bayville ES 500/K-5
50 Mountain Ave 11709 516-624-3300
Scott McElhiney, prin. Fax 624-6841

Beacon, Dutchess, Pop. 14,836
Beacon CSD 3,500/PK-12
10 Education Dr 12508 845-838-6900
Dr. Fern Aefsky, supt. Fax 838-6905
www.beaconcityk12.org/
Forrestal ES 400/PK-5
125 Liberty St 12508 845-838-6900
Steve Borrello, prin. Fax 838-0792
Rombout MS 800/6-8
84 Matteawan Rd 12508 845-838-6900
Brian Archer, prin. Fax 231-0474
Sargent ES 300/K-5
29 Education Dr 12508 845-838-6900
Tarkan Ceng, prin. Fax 838-6978
South Avenue ES 400/K-5
60 South Ave 12508 845-838-6900
Ophelia Richards, prin. Fax 838-6922
Other Schools – See Fishkill

Alpha and Omega S 50/PK-4
333 Fishkill Ave 12508 845-838-3333
Joanne Farwell, dir. Fax 838-3333

Beaver Falls, Lewis
Beaver River Central SD 900/K-12
PO Box 179 13305 315-346-1211
Leueen Smithling, supt. Fax 346-6775
www.brcsd.org/
Beaver River ES 400/K-5
PO Box 179 13305 315-346-1211
Kimberly Lyman-Wright, prin. Fax 346-6775

Bedford, Westchester, Pop. 1,828
Bedford Central SD 4,300/K-12
632 S Bedford Rd 10506 914-241-6000
Dr. Jere Hochman, supt. Fax 241-6004
www.bcsdny.org
Bedford Village ES 500/K-5
45 Court St 10506 914-234-4178
Karen Eldon, prin. Fax 234-6071
Fox Lane MS 1,000/6-8
S Bedford Rd 10506 914-241-6126
Anne Marie Berardi, prin. Fax 241-6129
Other Schools – See Bedford Hills, Mount Kisco, Pound Ridge

St. Patrick S 100/PK-8
483 Old Post Rd 10506 914-234-7914
Dr. Elizabeth Frangella, prin. Fax 234-0773

Bedford Hills, Westchester, Pop. 3,200
Bedford Central SD
Supt. — See Bedford
Bedford Hills ES 300/K-5
123 Babbitt Rd 10507 914-666-2708
Zbynek Gold, prin. Fax 666-3510
West Patent ES 300/K-5
80 W Patent Rd 10507 914-666-2190
Vera Berezowsky, prin. Fax 666-3819

Belfast, Allegany
Belfast Central SD 400/PK-12
1 King St 14711 585-365-9940
Judy May, supt. Fax 365-2648
www.belfast.wnyric.org
Belfast Central S 400/PK-12
1 King St 14711 585-365-8285
Jennifer Amos, prin. Fax 365-2648

Belle Harbor, Queens

St. Francis De Sales S 600/PK-8
219 Beach 129th St, 718-634-2775
Sr. Patricia Chelius, prin. Fax 634-6673
Yeshiva of Belle Harbor 100/PK-5
13401 Rockaway Beach Blvd, 718-474-0045

Bellerose, Queens, Pop. 1,153
NYC Department of Education
Supt. — See New York
Public S 133 500/PK-5
24805 86th Ave 11426 718-831-4016
Shelley Steppel, prin. Fax 831-4020
Public S 186 300/PK-5
25212 72nd Ave 11426 718-831-4021
Dolores Troy-Quinn, prin. Fax 831-4029
Public S 208 700/K-8
7430 Commonwealth Blvd 11426 718-468-6420
James Philemy, prin. Fax 468-5054
Public S 266 600/PK-8
7410 Commonwealth Blvd 11426 718-479-3920
Nicole Scott, prin. Fax 479-2482

St. Gregory the Great S 400/K-8
24444 87th Ave 11426 718-343-5053
Joann Aldorisio, prin. Fax 347-1142
Yeshiva Har Torah 400/PK-8
25010 Grand Central Pkwy 11426 718-343-2533
Rabbi Gary Menchel, prin. Fax 631-2513

Belleville, Jefferson
Belleville Henderson Central SD 600/PK-12
PO Box 158 13611 315-846-5411
Rick Moore, supt. Fax 846-5826
www.bhpanthers.org
Belleville Henderson Central S 600/PK-12
PO Box 158 13611 315-846-5121
Scott Storey, prin. Fax 846-5826

Bellmore, Nassau, Pop. 16,438
Bellmore UFD 1,200/PK-6
580 Winthrop Ave 11710 516-679-2909
Joseph Famularo Ed.D., supt. Fax 679-3027
www.bellmoreschools.org
Reinhard ECC 500/PK-2
2750 S Saint Marks Ave 11710 516-679-2930
Clifford Molinelli, prin. Fax 679-2936
Shore Road IS 400/5-6
2801 Shore Rd 11710 516-679-2950
Christine Augusto, prin. Fax 679-5637
Winthrop Avenue PS 300/3-4
580 Winthrop Ave 11710 516-679-2919
Sally Curto, prin. Fax 679-5643

Bellmore-Merrick Central HSD
Supt. — See North Merrick
Grand Avenue MS 1,100/7-8
2301 Grand Ave 11710 516-992-1100
Lewis Serra, prin. Fax 679-5068

St. Elizabeth Ann Seton S 300/PK-8
2341 Washington Ave 11710 516-785-5709
Leeann Graziose, prin. Fax 785-4468

Bellport, Suffolk, Pop. 2,359
South Country Central SD
Supt. — See East Patchogue
Bellport MS 1,000/6-8
35 Kreamer St 11713 631-730-1657
Fax 286-4460
Kreamer Street ES 400/K-3
37 Kreamer St 11713 631-730-1651
Sean Clark, prin. Fax 776-0903
Long IS 700/4-5
599 Brookhaven Ave 11713 631-730-1726
Gary Dabrusky, prin. Fax 286-4412

Belmont, Allegany, Pop. 912
Genesee Valley Central SD 700/PK-12
1 Jaguar Dr 14813 585-268-7900
Ralph Wilson, supt. Fax 268-7990
Genesee Valley ES 300/PK-4
1 Jaguar Dr 14813 585-268-7900
Mia Warner, prin. Fax 268-7932
Genesee Valley MS 200/5-8
1 Jaguar Dr 14813 585-268-7900
Brian Edmister, prin. Fax 268-7992

Bemus Point, Chautauqua, Pop. 338
Bemus Point Central SD 800/K-12
PO Box 468 14712 716-386-2375
Albert D'Attilio, supt. Fax 386-2376
www.bemusptcsd.org
Bemus ES 400/K-6
PO Box 468 14712 716-386-3795
P. Sawyer, prin. Fax 386-4293

Bergen, Genesee, Pop. 1,195
Byron-Bergen Central SD 1,200/K-12
6917 W Bergen Rd 14416 585-494-1220
Dr. Gregory Geer, supt. Fax 494-2613
www.bbcs.k12.ny.us
Byron-Bergen ES 400/K-4
6917 W Bergen Rd 14416 585-494-1220
NancyJean Osborn, prin. Fax 494-2433
Byron-Bergen MS 300/5-8
6917 W Bergen Rd 14416 585-494-1220
Daniel Bedette, prin. Fax 494-2613

Berlin, Rensselaer
Berlin Central SD 1,000/PK-12
PO Box 259 12022 518-658-2690
Charlotte Gregory, supt. Fax 658-3822
www.berlincentral.org/
Berlin ES 200/PK-5
PO Box 259 12022 518-658-2127
Michelle Colvin, prin. Fax 658-3822
Other Schools – See Cropseyville, Stephentown

Berne, Albany
Berne-Knox-Westerlo Central SD 1,100/K-12
1738 Helderberg Trl 12023 518-872-1293
Steven Schrade, supt. Fax 872-0341
www.bkwcsd.k12.ny.us/
Berne ES 400/K-5
1738 Helderberg Trl 12023 518-872-2030
Brian Corey, prin. Fax 872-2031

Bethpage, Nassau, Pop. 15,761
Bethpage UFD 3,000/K-12
10 Cherry Ave 11714 516-644-4000
Dr. Richard Marsh, supt. Fax 931-8783
www.bethpagecommunity.com/Schools/
Campagne ES 400/K-5
601 Plainview Rd 11714 516-644-4400
Angelita Cintado, prin. Fax 827-5486
Central Boulevard ES 500/K-5
60 Central Blvd 11714 516-644-4300
Steven Furrey, prin. Fax 827-3178
Kennedy MS 700/6-8
500 Broadway 11714 516-644-4200
Kerri McCarthy, prin. Fax 937-0540
Other Schools – See Plainview

Plainedge UFD
Supt. — See North Massapequa
Plainedge MS 800/6-8
200 Stewart Ave 11714 516-992-7650
Anthony DeRiso Ed.D., prin. Fax 992-7645
West ES 600/K-5
499 Boundary Ave 11714 516-992-7500
Carol Muscarella, prin. Fax 992-7505

Big Flats, Chemung, Pop. 2,658
Horseheads Central SD
Supt. — See Horseheads
Big Flats ES 300/K-4
543 Maple St 14814 607-739-6373
Fax 795-2555

Binghamton, Broome, Pop. 45,492
Binghamton CSD 6,000/PK-12
PO Box 2126 13902 607-762-8100
Peggy Wozniak, supt. Fax 762-8112
www.binghamtonschools.org
Coolidge ES 400/K-5
261 Robinson St 13904 607-762-8290
David Constantine, prin. Fax 762-8396
East MS 600/6-8
167 E Frederick St 13904 607-762-8300
Michael O'Branski, prin. Fax 762-8398
Franklin ES 500/PK-5
262 Conklin Ave 13903 607-762-8340
Noreen Dolan, prin. Fax 762-8393
Jefferson ES 300/K-5
151 Helen St 13905 607-763-8430
E. Timothy O'Hare, prin. Fax 763-8436
Mac Arthur ES 500/PK-5
1123 Vestal Ave 13903 607-762-8180
Maria McIver, prin. Fax 762-8397
Mann ES 400/K-5
30 College St 13905 607-762-8270
Peter Stewart, prin. Fax 762-8394
Roosevelt ES 400/PK-5
9 Ogden St 13901 607-762-8280
David Chilson, prin. Fax 762-8395
West MS 700/6-8
W Middle Ave 13905 607-763-8400
Michael Holly, prin. Fax 763-8429
Wilson ES 400/K-5
287 Prospect St 13905 607-763-8440
Barb McLean, prin. Fax 763-8448

Chenango Forks Central SD 1,800/PK-12
1 Gordon Dr 13901 607-648-7543
Robert Bundy Ed.D., supt. Fax 648-7560
www.cforks.org
Chenango Forks MS 400/6-8
1 Gordon Dr 13901 607-648-7576
William Burke, prin. Fax 648-7560
Harshaw PS 400/PK-2
6 Patch Rd 13901 607-648-7580
Fax 648-7560
Kenyon IS 300/3-5
6 Patch Rd 13901 607-648-7520
Bernie McDermott, prin. Fax 648-7560

Chenango Valley Central SD 1,900/PK-12
221 Chenango Bridge Rd 13901 607-779-4710
Dr. Thomas Douglas, supt. Fax 779-8610
www.cvcsd.stier.org/
Chenango Bridge IS 400/4-6
221 Chenango Bridge Rd 13901 607-648-9135
Tamara Ivan, prin. Fax 648-8959
Chenango Valley MS 300/7-8
221 Chenango Bridge Rd 13901 607-779-4755
David Gill, prin. Fax 779-4784
Port Dickinson ES 600/PK-3
221 Chenango Bridge Rd 13901 607-779-4736
James Pritchard, prin. Fax 779-7830

Susquehanna Valley Central SD
Supt. — See Conklin
Brookside ES 500/K-5
3849 Saddlemire Rd 13903 607-669-4105
Joanne Simpson, prin. Fax 669-4811

St. John the Evangelist S 200/PK-8
9 Livingston St 13903 607-723-0703
Mary Ellen Kelly, prin. Fax 772-6210
St. Thomas Aquinas S 200/PK-3
3 Aquinas St 13905 607-797-6528
Suzanne Miller, prin. Fax 797-6541

Black River, Jefferson, Pop. 1,327
Carthage Central SD
Supt. — See Carthage
Black River ES 400/K-5
160 Leray St 13612 315-773-5911
Staci Kline, prin. Fax 773-3747

Blasdell, Erie, Pop. 2,578
Frontier Central SD
Supt. — See Hamburg
Blasdell ES 500/K-5
3780 S Park Ave 14219 716-926-1750
Linda Dansa, prin. Fax 823-6153

Blauvelt, Rockland, Pop. 4,838
South Orangetown Central SD 3,400/K-12
160 Van Wyck Rd 10913 845-680-1050
Dr. Ken Mitchell, supt. Fax 680-1900
www.socsd.org
Cottage Lane ES 600/4-5
120 Cottage Ln 10913 845-680-1500
Michael Fiorentino, prin. Fax 680-1940
South Orangetown MS 800/6-8
160 Van Wyck Rd 10913 845-680-1100
Dr. William Lee, prin. Fax 680-1905
Other Schools – See Piermont, Tappan

Bloomfield, Ontario, Pop. 1,325
Bloomfield Central SD 1,100/K-12
1 Oakmount Ave 14469 585-657-6121
Michael Midey, supt. Fax 657-6060
www.bloomfieldcsd.org
Bloomfield ES 500/K-5
PO Box 220 14469 585-657-6121
Mary Sue Bennett, prin. Fax 657-6926
Bloomfield MS 300/6-8
PO Box 250 14469 585-657-6121
Steven Lysenko, coord. Fax 657-4771

Bloomingdale, Essex
Saranac Lake Central SD
Supt. — See Saranac Lake
Bloomingdale ES 200/K-5
93 Main St 12913 518-891-3198
Patrick Hogan, prin. Fax 891-4675

Blossvale, Oneida, Pop. 300
Camden Central SD
Supt. — See Camden
Mc Connellsville ES 200/K-5
8564 State Route 13 13308 315-245-3412
Craig Ferretti, prin. Fax 245-4193

Blue Point, Suffolk, Pop. 4,230
Bayport-Blue Point UFD
Supt. — See Bayport
Blue Point ES 300/K-5
212 Blue Point Ave 11715 631-472-6100
Diana Ketcham, prin. Fax 472-6110

Bohemia, Suffolk, Pop. 9,556
Connetquot Central SD 7,100/K-12
780 Ocean Ave 11716 631-244-2215
Dr. Alan Groveman, supt. Fax 589-0683
www.connetquot.k12.ny.us/
Bosti ES 500/K-5
50 Bourne Blvd 11716 631-244-2291
Barbara Lightstone, prin. Fax 244-2290
Pearl ES 300/K-5
1070 Smithtown Ave 11716 631-244-2301
Susan White, prin. Fax 244-2282
Sycamore Avenue ES 400/K-5
745 Sycamore Ave 11716 631-244-2261
Stuart Pollak, prin. Fax 244-2260
Other Schools – See Oakdale, Ronkonkoma

Boiceville, Ulster
Onteora Central SD 1,900/K-12
PO Box 300 12412 845-657-6383
Dr. Leslie Ford, supt. Fax 657-9687
onteora.schoolwires.com/
Bennett ES 300/K-6
4166 State Route 28 12412 845-657-2354
Gabriel Buono, prin. Fax 657-8504
Onteora MS 300/7-8
4166 State Route 28 12412 845-657-2373
Andrew Davenport, prin. Fax 657-7763
Other Schools – See Phoenicia, Woodstock

Bolivar, Allegany, Pop. 1,139
Bolivar-Richburg Central SD 900/PK-12
100 School St 14715 585-928-2561
Joseph Decerbo, supt. Fax 928-2411
www.brcs.wnyric.org
Bolivar-Richburg Pre K 100/PK-PK
422 Main St 14715 585-928-1919
Jennifer Sorochin, dir. Fax 928-2159
Other Schools – See Richburg

Bolton Landing, Warren
Bolton Central SD 300/K-12
PO Box 120 12814 518-644-2400
Raymond Ciccarelli, supt. Fax 644-2124
www.boltoncsd.org
Bolton Central S 300/K-12
PO Box 120 12814 518-644-2400
Damian Switzer, prin. Fax 644-2124

Boonville, Oneida, Pop. 2,095
Adirondack Central SD 1,400/K-12
110 Ford St 13309 315-942-9200
Frederick Morgan, supt. Fax 942-5522
www.adirondackcsd.org
Adirondack MS 300/6-8
8181 State Route 294 13309 315-942-9202
Patricia Thomas, prin. Fax 942-9211
Boonville ES 400/K-5
110 Ford St 13309 315-942-9220
Marie McDonald, prin. Fax 942-6162
Other Schools – See Forestport, West Leyden

Bradford, Schuyler
Bradford Central SD 300/K-12
2820 State Route 226 14815 607-583-4616
Wendy Field, supt. Fax 583-4013
www.bradfordcsd.org/bcs/site/default.asp
Bradford Central S 300/K-12
2820 State Route 226 14815 607-583-4616
Kelly Houck, prin. Fax 583-4013

Brant, Erie
Evans-Brant Central SD (Lake Shore)
Supt. — See Angola
Brant ES 100/K-5
PO Box 247 14027 716-549-2304
Susan Ciminelli, prin. Fax 549-4439

Brasher Falls, Saint Lawrence, Pop. 1,271
Brasher Falls Central SD 1,000/PK-12
PO Box 307 13613 315-389-5131
Stephen Putman, supt. Fax 389-5245
bfcsd.org
St. Lawrence Central ES 400/PK-4
PO Box 307 13613 315-389-5131
Lisa Grenville, prin. Fax 389-4651
St. Lawrence Central MS 300/5-8
PO Box 307 13613 315-389-5131
Christoper Rose, prin. Fax 389-4185

Brentwood, Suffolk, Pop. 55,000
Brentwood UFD 15,800/PK-12
52 3rd Ave 11717 631-434-2323
Donna Jones, supt. Fax 273-6575
www.bufsd.org/
Cannon Southeast ES 600/1-5
1 Melody Ln 11717 631-434-2265
Lisa Calderaro, prin. Fax 434-2186
East K 600/PK-K
50 Timberline Dr 11717 631-434-2525
Michele Rogers, prin. Fax 434-2186
East MS 900/6-8
70 Hilltop Dr 11717 631-434-2473
Kyrie Siegel, prin. Fax 434-2171
Laurel Park ES 500/1-5
48 Swan Ln 11717 631-434-2464
Eric Snell, prin. Fax 434-2190
Loretta Park ES 700/1-5
77 Stahley St 11717 631-434-2246
Dr. Marian Nasta, prin. Fax 434-2189
Northeast ES 900/1-5
2 Devon Rd 11717 631-434-2435
Kevin McWhirter, prin. Fax 434-2188
North ES 700/1-5
50 W White St 11717 631-434-2275
Patrick Morris, prin. Fax 434-2181
North MS 1,000/6-8
350 Wicks Rd 11717 631-434-2356
Mae Lane, prin. Fax 952-9249
Pine Park K 600/K-K
1 Mur Pl 11717 631-434-2251
Ann Weishahn, prin. Fax 434-2168
South MS 900/6-8
785 Candlewood Rd 11717 631-434-2341
Richard Loeschner, prin. Fax 434-2560
Twin Pines ES 800/1-5
2 Mur Pl 11717 631-434-2457
Robert McCarthy, prin. Fax 434-2187
Other Schools – See Bay Shore

Academy of St. Joseph 400/PK-12
1725 Brentwood Rd 11717 631-273-2406
Sr. Kerry Handal, prin. Fax 273-6184

Brewerton, Onondaga, Pop. 2,954
Central Square Central SD
Supt. — See Central Square

Brewerton ES 500/K-5
9530 Brewerton Rd 13029 315-668-4201
Linda Goeway, prin. Fax 668-8175

Brewster, Putnam, Pop. 2,158
Brewster Central SD 3,600/K-12
30 Farm To Market Rd 10509 845-279-8000
Dr. Jane Sandbank, supt. Fax 279-3510
www.brewsterschools.org
Garden Street ES 400/K-3
20 Garden St 10509 845-279-5091
Eileen McGuire, prin. Fax 279-2808
Kennedy ES 500/K-3
31 Foggintown Rd 10509 845-279-2087
Robin Young, prin. Fax 279-7638
Starr IS 500/4-5
20 Farm to Market Rd 10509 845-279-4018
Frank Zamperlin, prin. Fax 279-8154
Wells MS 900/6-8
570 Route 312 10509 845-279-3702
JoAnne Januzzi, prin. Fax 279-7634

Melrose S 100/PK-8
120 Federal Hill Rd 10509 845-279-2406
Diane Cikoski, hdmstr. Fax 279-3878

Briarcliff Manor, Westchester, Pop. 7,938
Briarcliff Manor UFD 1,800/K-12
45 Ingham Rd 10510 914-941-8880
Dr. Frances Wills, supt. Fax 941-2177
www.briarcliffschools.org
Briarcliff MS 400/6-8
444 Pleasantville Rd 10510 914-769-6343
Susan Howard, prin. Fax 769-6375
Todd ES 700/K-5
45 Ingham Rd 10510 914-941-8300
Debra Cagliostro, prin. Fax 941-2603

St. Theresa S 200/PK-8
300 Dalmeny Rd 10510 914-762-1050
Sally Powers, prin. Fax 941-9483

Bridgehampton, Suffolk, Pop. 1,997
Bridgehampton UFD 100/PK-12
PO Box 3021 11932 631-537-0271
Dr. Dianne Youngblood, supt. Fax 537-9038
www.bridgehampton.k12.ny.us/
Bridgehampton S 100/PK-12
PO Box 3021 11932 631-537-0271
John Pryor, prin. Fax 537-0443

Ross S 100/PK-4
PO Box 604 11932 631-537-1240
Michele Claeys, hdmstr. Fax 537-5183

Bridgeport, Madison, Pop. 2,107
Chittenango Central SD
Supt. — See Chittenango
Bridgeport ES 300/K-5
9076 North Rd 13030 315-633-9611
Mary Farber, prin. Fax 633-5606

Broadalbin, Fulton, Pop. 1,407
Broadalbin-Perth Central SD 1,900/K-12
20 Pine St 12025 518-954-2500
Stephen Tomlinson, supt. Fax 954-2509
www.bpcsd.org
Broadalbin-Perth PS 500/K-3
100 Bridge St 12025 518-954-2650
Theresa LaFountain, prin. Fax 954-2659
Other Schools – See Amsterdam

Broad Channel, See New York
NYC Department of Education
Supt. — See New York
Public S 47 200/PK-8
9 Power Rd 11693 718-634-7167
Janet Donohue, prin. Fax 945-5394

Brockport, Monroe, Pop. 8,134
Brockport Central SD 4,200/K-12
40 Allen St 14420 585-637-1810
Garry Stone, supt. Fax 637-0165
brockport.k12.ny.us
Barclay ES 500/2-3
40 Allen St 14420 585-637-1840
Rhonda Steffen, prin. Fax 637-1845
Ginther ES 500/K-1
40 Allen St 14420 585-637-1830
Rosemary Custer, prin. Fax 637-1835
Hill ES 600/4-5
40 Allen St 14420 585-637-1850
Sean Bruno, prin. Fax 637-1855
Oliver MS 1,000/6-8
40 Allen St 14420 585-637-1860
Melody Martinez-Davis, prin. Fax 637-1869

Christ Community Church S 50/K-8
36 Coleman Creek Rd 14420 585-637-3979
Cheryl Ann Seddio, prin. Fax 637-0071

Brocton, Chautauqua, Pop. 1,487
Brocton Central SD 700/K-12
138 W Main St 14716 716-792-2173
John Skahill, supt. Fax 792-9965
www.broctoncsd.org
Brocton ES 300/K-5
138 W Main St 14716 716-792-2100
Brenda Peters, prin. Fax 792-2260

Bronx, See New York
NYC Department of Education
Supt. — See New York
Academy of Applied Math & Technology 300/6-8
345 Brook Ave 10454 718-292-3883
Rose-Marie Mills, prin. Fax 292-4473
Academy of Public Relations 200/6-8
778 Forest Ave 10456 718-665-8866
Amy Andino, prin. Fax 401-0051
Accion Academy 200/6-8
1825 Prospect Ave 10457 718-294-0514
Adrian Manuel, prin. Fax 294-3869
Ampark Neighborhood S 100/K-3
3990 Hillman Ave 10463 718-548-3451
Elizabeth Lopez-Towey, prin.
Aspire Preparatory S 300/6-8
2441 Wallace Ave 10467 718-231-6592
Steven Cobb, prin. Fax 231-6591
Bronx Dance Academy 300/6-8
3617 Bainbridge Ave 10467 718-515-0410
Sandra Sanchez, prin. Fax 515-0345
ES for Math Science and Technology 300/K-5
125 E 181st St 10453 718-933-8061
Avon Connell-Cowell, prin. Fax 933-8157
Bronx Green MS 300/6-8
2441 Wallace Ave 10467 718-325-6593
Emily Becker, prin. Fax 325-3625
IS 117 1,000/6-8
1865 Morris Ave 10453 718-583-7750
Delise Jones, prin. Fax 583-7658
IS 129 400/6-8
2055 Mapes Ave 10460 718-933-5976
Yvette Beasley, prin. Fax 933-8132
IS 181 500/6-8
800 Baychester Ave 10475 718-904-5600
Christopher Warnock, prin. Fax 904-5620
IS 190 200/6-8
1550 Crotona Park E 10460 718-620-9423
Diana Santiago, prin. Fax 620-9927
IS 206 400/5-8
2280 Aqueduct Ave 10468 718-584-1570
David Neering, prin. Fax 584-7928
IS 219 500/6-8
3630 3rd Ave 10456 718-681-7093
Dominic Cipollone, prin. Fax 681-7324
IS 224 400/6-8
345 Brook Ave 10454 718-665-9804
Charles Johnson, prin. Fax 665-0078
IS 228 - Jonas Bronck Academy 100/6-8
4525 Manhattan College Pkwy 10471 718-884-6773
Donalda Chumney, prin. Fax 884-6775
IS 229 300/5-8
275 Harlem River Park Brg 10453 718-583-6266
Dr. Ezra Matthias, prin. Fax 583-6325
IS 232 500/6-8
1700 Macombs Rd 10453 718-583-7007
Neifi Acosta, prin. Fax 583-4864
IS 254 400/6-8
2452 Washington Ave 10458 718-220-8700
Wilfred Heymans, prin. Fax 220-4881
IS 303 300/6-8
1700 Macombs Rd 10453 718-583-5466
Patricia Bentley, prin. Fax 583-2463
IS 318 400/6-8
1919 Prospect Ave 10457 718-294-8504
Maria Lopez, prin. Fax 901-0778
IS 339 800/6-8
1600 Webster Ave 10457 718-583-6767
Jason Levy, prin. Fax 583-0281
JHS 22 700/5-8
270 E 167th St 10456 718-681-6850
Linda Rosenbury, prin. Fax 681-6895
JHS 45 1,100/6-8
2502 Lorillard Pl 10458 718-584-1660
Anna Maria Giordano, prin. Fax 584-7968
JHS 80 700/6-8
149 E Mosholu Pkwy N 10467 718-405-6300
Lovey Mazique-Rivera, prin. Fax 405-6324
JHS 98 400/5-8
1619 Boston Rd 10460 718-589-8200
Claralee Irobunda, prin. Fax 589-8179
JHS 118 1,100/6-8
577 E 179th St 10457 718-584-2330
Elizabeth Lawrence, prin. Fax 584-7763
JHS 123 500/6-8
1025 Morrison Ave 10472 718-328-2105
Virginia Connelly, prin. Fax 328-8561
JHS 125 700/6-8
1111 Pugsley Ave 10472 718-822-5186
Hilda Bairan, prin. Fax 239-3121
JHS 127 700/5-8
1560 Purdy St 10462 718-892-8600
Harry Sherman, prin. Fax 892-8300
JHS 131 1,100/5-8
885 Bolton Ave 10473 718-991-7490
Ed Leotta, prin. Fax 328-6705
JHS 142 900/6-8
3750 Baychester Ave 10466 718-231-0100
Casimiro Cibelli, prin. Fax 231-3046
JHS 144 1,000/6-8
2545 Gunther Ave 10469 718-379-7400
Katina Lotakis, prin. Fax 320-7135
JHS 145 500/5-8
1000 Teller Ave 10456 718-681-7219
Robert Hannibal, prin. Fax 681-6913
JHS 151 300/6-8
250 E 156th St 10451 718-292-0260
John Piazza, prin. Fax 292-5704
JHS 162 900/6-8
600 Saint Anns Ave 10455 718-292-0880
Maryann Manzolillo, prin. Fax 292-5735
JHS 166 900/5-8
250 E 164th St 10456 718-681-6334
Lauren Reiss-Meredith, prin. Fax 537-6043
Bronx Little S PK-5
1827 Archer St 10460 718-792-2650
Janice Gordon, prin. Fax 792-4149
Bronx Mathematics Preparatory S 100/6-8
456 White Plains Rd 10473 718-542-5063
Mark Clarke, prin. Fax 542-5236
MS 101 400/6-8
2750 Lafayette Ave 10465 718-829-6372
Kim Hampton-Hewitt, prin. Fax 829-6594
MS 180 700/6-8
700 Baychester Ave 10475 718-904-5650
Frank Uzzo, prin. Fax 904-5655
MS 203 500/6-8
339 Morris Ave 10451 718-292-1052
William Hewlett, prin. Fax 292-5765
MS 223 400/6-8
360 E 145th St 10454 718-292-8627
Ramon Gonzalez, prin. Fax 292-7435
MS 273 200/6-8
2111 Crotona Ave 10457 718-561-1617
Deborah Cimini, prin. Fax 561-2184
MS 301 400/6-8
890 Cauldwell Ave 10456 718-585-2950
Benjamin Basile, prin. Fax 401-2567
MS 302 800/6-8
681 Kelly St 10455 718-292-6070
Angel Rodriguez, prin. Fax 401-2958
MS 327 200/6-8
580 Crotona Park S 10456 718-861-0852
Manuel Ramirez, prin. Fax 993-2990
MS 331 500/6-8
40 W Tremont Ave 10453 718-583-4146
John Barnes, prin. Fax 583-4292
MS 366 100/6-8
650 Hollywood Ave 10465 718-822-0126
Cameron Berube, prin. Fax 822-1049
MS 371 300/6-8
650 Hollywood Ave 10465 718-823-6042
Jennifer Joynt, prin. Fax 823-6347
MS 390 500/5-8
1930 Andrews Ave 10453 718-901-1024
Robert Mercedes, prin. Fax 583-5556
MS 391 700/6-8
2225 Webster Ave 10457 718-584-0980
Pedro Santana, prin. Fax 294-7208
MS 399 700/6-8
120 E 184th St 10468 718-584-0350
Angelo Ledda, prin. Fax 584-0730
Bronx Writing Academy 500/6-8
270 E 167th St 10456 718-293-9048
Nick Marinacci, prin. Fax 293-9748
Business S for Entrepreneurial Studies 300/6-8
977 Fox St 10459 718-991-8489
Domingo Martinez, prin. Fax 378-3352
Cornerstone Academy for Social Action 300/PK-6
3441 Steenwick Ave 10475 718-794-6160
Malissa Mootoo, prin. Fax 794-6170
Emolior Academy 100/6-8
1330 Bristow St 10459 718-589-3126
Derick Spaulding, prin. Fax 589-3903
Entrada Academy 100/6-8
977 Fox St 10459 718-378-1649
Socorro Diaz, prin. Fax 378-4707
Forward School of Creative Writing 200/6-8
3710 Barnes Ave 10467 718-652-0519
Adrienne Phifer, prin. Fax 652-0428
Hamer MS 300/6-8
1001 Jennings St 10460 718-860-2707
Lorraine Chanon, prin. Fax 860-3212
Hunts Point S 400/6-8
730 Bryant Ave 10474 718-328-1972
John Hughes, prin. Fax 328-7330
KAPPA 300/5-8
3630 3rd Ave 10456 718-590-5455
Sheri Warren, prin. Fax 681-4266
KAPPA III S 200/6-8
2055 Mapes Ave 10460 718-561-3580
Elisa Alvarez, prin. Fax 561-3719
Mott Hall III 300/6-8
450 Saint Pauls Pl 10456 718-992-9506
Jorisis Stupart, prin. Fax 681-6905
Mott Hall V 100/6-7
2055 Mapes Ave 10460 718-295-4105
Peter Oroszlany, prin. Fax 295-4014
New Millenium Business Academy 300/6-8
1000 Teller Ave 10456 718-588-8308
Dorald Bastian, prin. Fax 681-6913
New School 1 at Public S 60 400/PK-3
888 Rev James A Polite Ave 10459 718-860-3313
Sylvia Sanchez, prin. Fax 842-8734
New School 2 at Public S 60 200/4-5
888 Rev James A Polite Ave 10459 718-860-3401
Erik Wright, prin. Fax 860-4290
New S for Leadership and Journalism 700/6-8
120 W 231st St 10463 718-601-2869
Dolores Peterson, prin. Fax 601-2867
Performance S 600/PK-5
750 Concourse Vlg W 10451 718-292-5070
Scott Parker, prin. Fax 292-5071
Public S 1 600/PK-5
335 E 152nd St 10451 718-292-9191
Jorge Perdomo, prin. Fax 292-2227
Public S 2 200/K-5
1260 Franklin Ave 10456 718-620-0724
Alexei Nichols, prin. Fax 620-1292
Public S 3 400/PK-8
2100 La Fontaine Ave 10457 718-584-1899
Denise Brown, prin. Fax 584-3590
Public S 4 400/K-8
1701 Fulton Ave 10457 718-583-6655
Vincent Resto, prin. Fax 583-6668
Public S 5 600/PK-5
564 Jackson Ave 10455 718-292-2683
Mary Padilla, prin. Fax 292-2495
Public S 6 700/PK-5
1000 E Tremont Ave 10460 718-542-7676
Darlene McWhales, prin. Fax 589-7278
Public S 7 600/K-5
3201 Kingsbridge Ave 10463 718-796-8695
Renee Cloutier, prin. Fax 796-7204
Public S 8 1,100/K-5
3010 Briggs Ave 10458 718-584-3043
Rosa Peralta, prin. Fax 584-7376
Public S 9 700/PK-5
230 E 183rd St 10458 718-584-3291
Denise Eggleston, prin. Fax 584-7579
Public S 11 700/K-4
1257 Ogden Ave 10452 718-681-7553
Elizabeth Hachar, prin. Fax 681-7711

Public S 14 500/K-5
3041 Bruckner Blvd 10461 718-822-5341
Jason Kovac, prin. Fax 239-6386

Public S 15 500/K-8
2195 Andrews Ave 10453 718-563-0473
Eddice Griffin, prin. Fax 563-1568

Public S 16 600/PK-5
4550 Carpenter Ave 10470 718-324-1262
Yvonne Williams, prin. Fax 324-8370

Public S 18 500/PK-5
502 Morris Ave 10451 718-292-2868
Jeanene Breeden, prin. Fax 292-2862

Public S 19 500/K-8
4318 Katonah Ave 10470 718-324-1924
Timothy Sullivan, prin. Fax 994-9132

Public S 20 1,100/PK-8
3050 Webster Ave 10467 718-515-9370
Carol Carlsen, prin. Fax 515-9378

Public S 21 700/K-5
715 E 225th St 10466 718-652-3903
Joyce Coleman, prin. Fax 231-2556

Public S 23 500/PK-2
2151 Washington Ave 10457 718-584-3992
Carolyn Jones, prin. Fax 584-7252

Public S 24 600/K-5
660 W 236th St 10463 718-796-8845
Philip Scharper, prin. Fax 796-7243

Public S 25 500/PK-8
811 E 149th St 10455 718-292-2995
Carmen Toledo, prin. Fax 292-2997

Public S 28 700/PK-5
1861 Anthony Ave 10457 718-583-6444
Marie Barresi, prin. Fax 583-6537

Public S 29 700/PK-8
758 Courtlandt Ave 10451 718-292-3785
Fax 292-3784

Public S 30 600/PK-5
510 E 141st St 10454 718-292-8817
Roxanne Marks, prin. Fax 292-3962

Public S 31 800/PK-8
250 E 156th St 10451 718-292-4397
Liza Diaz, prin. Fax 292-4399

Public S 32 800/K-5
690 E 183rd St 10458 718-584-3645
Esther Schwartz, prin. Fax 584-7927

Public S 33 1,000/PK-5
2424 Jerome Ave 10468 718-584-3926
Lynette Santos, prin. Fax 584-7004

Public S 35 700/K-4
261 E 163rd St 10451 718-681-7214
Graciela Navarro, prin. Fax 681-7264

Public S 36 600/PK-5
1070 Castle Hill Ave 10472 718-822-5345
Nilda Rivera, prin. Fax 239-6390

Public S 37 500/K-8
360 W 230th St 10463 718-796-0360
Kenneth Petriccione, prin. Fax 796-0054

Public S 41 800/K-5
3352 Olinville Ave 10467 718-652-3461
Erika Tobia, prin. Fax 231-2668

Public S 42 400/PK-5
1537 Washington Ave 10457 718-583-7366
Camille Wallin, prin. Fax 583-7345

Public S 43 500/PK-5
165 Brown Pl 10454 718-292-4502
Giovanna Delucchi, prin. Fax 292-4504

Public S 44 300/PK-5
1825 Prospect Ave 10457 718-583-2360
Mildred Jones, prin. Fax 901-4068

Public S 46 1,100/K-5
279 E 196th St 10458 718-584-4450
Jennifer Alexander-Ade, prin. Fax 584-7402

Public S 47 1,100/K-5
1794 E 172nd St 10472 718-824-0950
Thomas Guarnieri, prin. Fax 904-1166

Public S 48 900/PK-5
1290 Spofford Ave 10474 718-589-4312
Roxanne Cardona, prin. Fax 842-6993

Public S 49 600/PK-5
383 E 139th St 10454 718-292-4623
Laura Galloway, prin. Fax 292-4568

Public S 50 500/PK-5
1550 Vyse Ave 10460 718-542-2650
Francisco Cruz, prin. Fax 589-7284

Public S 51 200/K-5
3200 Jerome Ave 10468 718-584-8772
Paul Smith, prin. Fax 584-8935

Public S 53 1,300/PK-5
360 E 168th St 10456 718-681-7276
Collin Wolfe, prin. Fax 681-7298

Public S 54 400/K-5
2703 Webster Ave 10458 718-584-4203
Maribelle Pardo, prin. Fax 584-4326

Public S 55 600/PK-5
450 Saint Pauls Pl 10456 718-681-6227
Luis Torres, prin. Fax 681-6247

Public S 56 500/K-5
341 E 207th St 10467 718-405-6330
Priscilla Sheeran, prin. Fax 405-6341

Public S 57 400/PK-5
2111 Crotona Ave 10457 718-367-9446
Edsel Philip, prin. Fax 584-1937

Public S 58 400/K-6
459 E 176th St 10457 718-583-6866
Velma Gunn, prin. Fax 583-6895

Public S 59 500/PK-5
2185 Bathgate Ave 10457 718-584-4730
Christine McHugh, prin. Fax 584-7518

Public S 61 400/PK-5
1550 Crotona Park E 10460 718-542-7230
Patricia Quigley, prin. Fax 589-7361

Public S 62 700/PK-5
660 Fox St 10455 718-585-1617
Lisa Manfredonia, prin. Fax 292-6327

Public S 63 400/PK-5
1260 Franklin Ave 10456 718-589-3058
Reinaldo Diaz-Lens, prin. Fax 589-4917

Public S 64 900/K-5
1425 Walton Ave 10452 718-681-8088
Beverley Harrigan, prin. Fax 537-6015

Public S 65 400/PK-5
677 E 141st St 10454 718-292-4628
TaShon McKeithan, prin. Fax 292-4695

Public S 66 500/PK-5
1001 Jennings St 10460 718-542-2974
Tom DeGrazia, prin. Fax 589-7375

Public S 67 600/PK-5
2024 Mohegan Ave 10460 718-589-8090
Emily Grimball, prin. Fax 589-7399

Public S 68 700/PK-5
4011 Monticello Ave 10466 718-324-2854
Cheryl Coles, prin. Fax 324-3852

Public S 69 400/PK-5
560 Thieriot Ave 10473 718-378-4736
Alan Cohen, prin. Fax 328-0925

Public S 70 1,400/K-5
1691 Weeks Ave 10457 718-583-6000
Kerry Castellano, prin. Fax 583-6006

Public S 71 1,300/PK-8
3040 Roberts Ave 10461 718-822-5351
Lance Cooper, prin. Fax 239-3111

Public S 72 800/PK-5
2951 Dewey Ave 10465 718-822-5311
Margarita Colon, prin. Fax 828-4459

Public S 73 800/PK-5
1020 Anderson Ave 10452 718-681-6776
Jean Mirbil, prin. Fax 681-6749

Public S 75 600/PK-5
984 Faile St 10459 718-860-1630
Marines Arrieta-Cruz, prin. Fax 860-4480

Public S 76 1,000/K-5
900 Adee Ave 10469 718-882-8865
Louise Sedotto, prin. Fax 882-8870

Public S 78 700/K-5
1400 Needham Ave 10469 718-652-1244
Claudina Skerritt, prin. Fax 231-2756

Public S 79 1,000/PK-5
125 E 181st St 10453 718-584-4810
Pamela Edwards, prin. Fax 584-7481

Public S 81 700/K-5
5550 Riverdale Ave 10471 718-796-8965
Melodie Mashel, prin. Fax 796-7242

Public S 83 1,400/K-8
950 Rhinelander Ave 10462 718-863-1993
Benjamin Soccodato, prin. Fax 863-5525

Public S 85 1,000/K-5
2400 Marion Ave 10458 718-584-5275
Ted Husted, prin. Fax 584-7765

Public S 86 1,500/PK-6
2756 Reservoir Ave 10468 718-584-5585
Sheldon Benardo, prin. Fax 584-7027

Public S 87 500/K-5
1935 Bussing Ave 10466 718-324-5188
Donna Anaman, prin. Fax 325-1148

Public S 88 300/K-3
1340 Sheridan Ave 10456 718-681-6220
Melinda Hyer, prin. Fax 681-6224

Public S 89 1,200/PK-8
980 Mace Ave 10469 718-653-0835
Ronald Rivera, prin. Fax 231-2863

Public S 90 1,200/K-4
1116 Sheridan Ave 10456 718-681-7023
Patricia West, prin. Fax 681-6966

Public S 91 700/K-5
2200 Aqueduct Ave E 10453 718-584-5805
Rosemary Prati, prin. Fax 584-7495

Public S 92 500/PK-5
700 E 179th St 10457 718-731-7900
Anthony Warn, prin. Fax 294-1561

Public S 93 400/PK-5
1535 Story Ave 10473 718-842-2655
Donald Mattson, prin. Fax 328-5506

Public S 94 1,000/K-5
3530 Kings College Pl 10467 718-405-6345
Diane DaProcida, prin. Fax 405-6358

Public S 95 1,200/K-8
3961 Hillman Ave 10463 718-796-9200
Serge Davis, prin. Fax 796-7330

Public S 96 900/K-5
650 Waring Ave 10467 718-652-4959
Marta Garcia, prin. Fax 231-2889

Public S 97 600/PK-5
1375 Mace Ave 10469 718-655-4446
Kathleen Bornkamp, prin. Fax 655-6063

Public S 100 600/PK-5
800 Taylor Ave 10473 718-842-1461
Chad Altman, prin. Fax 328-5520

Public S 102 1,100/PK-5
1827 Archer St 10460 718-792-4003
Tanyua Trezevantte, prin. Fax 409-2626

Public S 103 1,100/K-5
4125 Carpenter Ave 10466 718-655-0261
Alice Brown, prin. Fax 654-7930

Public S 105 1,400/K-5
725 Brady Ave 10462 718-824-7350
Christopher Eustace, prin. Fax 828-4531

Public S 106 900/PK-5
2120 Saint Raymonds Ave 10462 718-892-1006
Eugenia Montalvo, prin. Fax 823-8008

Public S 107 500/PK-5
1695 Seward Ave 10473 718-860-2596
Melba Parks, prin. Fax 328-5799

Public S 108 500/K-5
1166 Neill Ave 10461 718-863-9829
Charles Sperrazza, prin. Fax 828-1712

Public S 109 700/PK-5
1771 Popham Ave 10453 718-583-8878
Amanda Blatter, prin. Fax 583-7618

Public S 110 400/PK-5
580 Crotona Park S 10456 718-861-0759
Daisy Perez, prin. Fax 861-2750

Public S 111 500/PK-5
3740 Baychester Ave 10466 718-881-2418
Julia Rivers-Jones, prin. Fax 405-5927

Public S 112 600/PK-5
1925 Schieffelin Ave 10466 718-654-6377
Susan Barnes, prin. Fax 654-7931

Public S 114 800/K-4
1155 Cromwell Ave 10452 718-681-7507
Olivia Webber, prin. Fax 681-7519

Public S 119 700/PK-5
1075 Pugsley Ave 10472 718-822-5198
Lydia Bassett Tyner, prin. Fax 239-3112

Public S 121 700/PK-5
2750 Throop Ave 10469 718-654-2055
Rachel Donnelly, prin. Fax 519-2613

Public S 126 700/PK-6
175 W 166th St 10452 718-681-6120
Nadine Kee-Foster, prin. Fax 681-6131

Public S 130 600/PK-5
750 Prospect Ave 10455 718-665-0962
Lourdes Velazquez, prin. Fax 292-0417

Public S 132 500/PK-5
1245 Washington Ave 10456 718-681-6455
Anissa Chalmers, prin. Fax 681-6466

Public S 134 600/PK-5
1330 Bristow St 10459 718-328-3351
Kenneth Thomas, prin. Fax 589-7581

Public S 138 700/PK-5
2060 Lafayette Ave 10473 718-822-5325
Lorraine Carol-Dawkins, prin. Fax 239-3114

Public S 140 500/PK-5
916 Eagle Ave 10456 718-585-1205
Paul Cannon, prin. Fax 292-1349

Public S 146 400/PK-5
968 Cauldwell Ave 10456 718-378-9664
Janet Sanderson-Brown, prin. Fax 328-5858

Public S 150 600/PK-5
920 E 167th St 10459 718-328-7729
Edwin Irizarry, prin. Fax 589-7590

Public S 152 800/PK-5
1007 Evergreen Ave 10472 718-589-4560
Frances Lynch, prin. Fax 328-5867

Public S 153 500/K-5
650 Baychester Ave 10475 718-904-5550
Veronica Goka, prin. Fax 904-5564

Public S 154 500/PK-5
333 E 135th St 10454 718-292-4742
Linda Irizarry, prin. Fax 292-4721

Public S 157 500/PK-5
757 Cauldwell Ave 10456 718-292-5255
Ramona Duran, prin. Fax 292-5258

Public S 159 200/K-5
2315 Washington Ave 10458 718-584-6140
Luis Liz, prin. Fax 584-7794

Public S 160 400/K-5
4140 Hutchinson River Pkwy 10475 718-379-5951
Lori Baker, prin. Fax 320-0392

Public S 161 400/PK-5
628 Tinton Ave 10455 718-292-5478
Pablo Lasalle, prin. Fax 292-5476

Public S 163 700/K-5
2075 Webster Ave 10457 718-584-3045
Dilsia Martinez, prin. Fax 584-3276

Public S 170 300/K-2
1598 Townsend Ave 10452 718-583-0662
Nancy Ramos, prin. Fax 583-0685

Public S 175 400/K-8
200 City Island Ave 10464 718-885-1093
Amy Lipzon, prin. Fax 885-2315

Public S 178 400/K-5
850 Baychester Ave 10475 718-904-5570
Evelyn Fulton, prin. Fax 904-5575

Public S 179 400/PK-5
468 E 140th St 10454 718-292-2237
Sherry Williams, prin. Fax 292-3623

Public S 182 900/PK-5
601 Stickball Blvd 10473 718-828-6607
Anne O'Grady, prin. Fax 409-8152

Public S 194 1,200/K-8
1301 Zerega Ave 10462 718-892-5270
Elmer Myers, prin. Fax 892-2495

Public S 195 300/2-5
1250 Ward Ave 10472 718-861-4461
Andrew Kavanagh, prin. Fax 861-7935

Public S 196 300/2-5
1250 Ward Ave 10472 718-328-7187
Lizzette Rivera, prin. Fax 861-8401

Public S 197 600/PK-1
1250 Ward Ave 10472 718-842-2111
Grace Formica, prin. Fax 589-7473

Public S 198 400/PK-5
1180 Tinton Ave 10456 718-842-5656
Judy Hunt-Hutchings, prin. Fax 589-7680

Public S 199X 700/PK-5
1449 Shakespeare Ave 10452 718-681-7172
Lilia Navarrete, prin. Fax 681-7176

Public S 204 400/K-5
108 W 174th St 10453 718-583-6636
Marcy Glattstein, prin. Fax 583-6394

Public S 205 900/K-5
2475 Southern Blvd 10458 718-584-6390
Maria Pietrosanti, prin. Fax 584-7941

Public S 207 400/PK-2
3030 Godwin Ter 10463 718-796-9645
Maria Rosado, prin. Fax 796-7206

Public S 209 200/PK-2
317 E 183rd St 10458 718-364-0085
Anne Keagan, prin. Fax 364-9548

Public S 211 600/PK-8
1919 Prospect Ave 10457 718-901-0436
Betty Gonzalez-Soto, prin. Fax 901-4681

Public S 212 500/PK-8
800 Home St 10456 718-617-0662
Yohan Lim, prin. Fax 991-3732

Public S 214 700/PK-8
1970 W Farms Rd 10460 718-589-6728
David Cintron, prin. Fax 328-7762

Public S 218 900/K-8
1220 Gerard Ave 10452 718-410-7230
Leticia Rosario, prin. Fax 410-8933

Public S 226 400/PK-4
1950 Sedgwick Ave 10453 718-583-5560
Gloria Darden, prin. Fax 583-5557
Public S 230 400/K-4
275 Harlem River Park Brg 10453 718-583-6116
Rowena Penn-Jackson, prin. Fax 583-6222
Public S 236 400/PK-2
499 E 175th St 10457 718-583-7510
Beverly Ellis, prin. Fax 583-7512
Public S 246 700/K-6
2641 Grand Concourse 10468 718-584-6764
Beverly Miller, prin. Fax 584-7005
Public S 277 500/PK-5
519 Saint Anns Ave 10455 718-292-3594
Cheryl Tyler, prin. Fax 292-3630
Public S 279 1,000/K-8
2100 Walton Ave 10453 718-584-6004
James Waslawski, prin. Fax 584-7220
Public S 280 700/K-8
3202 Steuben Ave 10467 718-405-6360
James Weeks, prin. Fax 405-6329
Public S 291 500/K-4
2195 Andrews Ave 10453 718-563-0776
Carlos Velez, prin. Fax 563-1499
Public S 300 600/PK-5
2050 Prospect Ave 10457 718-584-6310
Venessa Singleton, prin. Fax 220-1370
Public S 304 400/PK-5
2750 Lafayette Ave 10465 718-822-5307
Joseph Nobile, prin. Fax 904-0956
Public S 306 600/K-5
40 W Tremont Ave 10453 718-583-5355
Cynthia Riley, prin. Fax 583-5885
Public S 307 200/PK-5
124 Eames Pl 10468 718-601-2632
Luisa Fuentes, prin. Fax 796-7490
Public S 310 700/PK-5
260 W Kingsbridge Rd 10463 718-796-9434
Elizabeth Cardona, prin. Fax 796-9528
Public S 315 200/K-8
2246 Jerome Ave 10453 718-584-7441
E. Cardona-Bernardinelli, prin. Fax 584-7433
Public S 340 500/PK-6
25 W 195th St 10468 718-220-1830
Nelly Maldonado, prin. Fax 220-1866
Public S 360 500/PK-6
2880 Kingsbridge Ter 10463 718-548-1511
Nancy Rodriguez Lewis, prin. Fax 548-1536
Public S 396 300/PK-4
1930 Andrews Ave 10453 718-294-0862
Lawrence Wright, prin. Fax 583-5556
Public S 691 PK-5
1300 Boynton Ave 10472 718-860-8181
Janice Gordon, prin. Fax 842-1932
School for Environmental Citizenship 100/PK-5
125 E 181st St 10453 718-563-3292
Heather Dawe, prin. Fax 563-3453
School for Inquiry & Social Justice 300/6-8
1025 Morrison Ave 10472 718-860-4181
Andrea Cyprys, prin. Fax 860-4163
School of Performing Arts 300/6-8
977 Fox St 10459 718-589-4844
Seth Litt, prin. Fax 589-7998
South Bronx Academy for Applied Media 200/6-8
778 Forest Ave 10456 718-401-0059
Roshone Ault, prin. Fax 401-0577
Urban Assembly S Wildlife Conservation 100/6-8
2441 Wallace Ave 10467 718-654-2065
Mark Ossenheimer, prin. Fax 654-4018
Urban Science Academy 400/5-8
1000 Teller Ave 10456 718-588-8221
Patrick Kelly, prin. Fax 588-8263
Young Leaders ES 300/PK-5
468 E 140th St 10454 718-292-7391
Karen Collins, prin. Fax 292-8535
Young Scholars Academy 400/6-8
3710 Barnes Ave 10467 718-325-5834
Vaughn Thompson, prin. Fax 325-5676

Beth Jacob-Beth Miriam S 50/PK-8
1242 Pinchot Pl 10461 718-892-8830
Blessed Sacrament S 300/PK-8
1160 Beach Ave 10472 718-892-0433
Grace Chemi, prin. Fax 892-3777
Bronx-Manhattan SDA S 200/K-8
1440 Plimpton Ave 10452 718-588-7598
Marlene Romeo, prin. Fax 588-1052
Christ the King S 600/K-8
1345 Grand Concourse 10452 718-538-5959
Lenora Yzaguirre, prin. Fax 538-6369
Ethical Culture Fieldston S 300/PK-5
3901 Fieldston Rd 10471 718-329-7310
George Burns, prin. Fax 329-7304
Faith Christian Academy 100/PK-8
1137 E 223rd St 10466 718-881-0185
Donna Taylor, prin. Fax 881-1085
Greek American S 200/PK-8
3573 Bruckner Blvd 10461 718-823-2393
Holy Cross S 300/PK-8
1846 Randall Ave 10473 718-842-4492
Fax 842-4052
Holy Family S 500/PK-8
2169 Blackrock Ave 10472 718-863-7280
Fax 931-8690
Holy Rosary S 600/PK-8
1500 Arnow Ave 10469 718-652-1838
Mary Ann Fusco, prin. Fax 515-9872
Holy Spirit S 300/PK-8
1960 Univ Blvd 10453 718-583-1570
Grace Lucie, prin. Fax 583-3378
Hudson S 100/PK-8
1122 Forest Ave 10456 718-328-3322
Immaculate Conception S 500/PK-8
378 E 151st St 10455 718-585-4843
Sr. Patrice Owens, prin. Fax 585-6846
Immaculate Conception S 600/PK-8
760 E Gun Hill Rd 10467 718-547-3346
Sr. Leticia Aviles, prin. Fax 547-5505
Kinneret Day S 200/PK-8
2600 Netherland Ave 10463 718-548-0900
Fax 548-0901
Mann S 500/K-5
4440 Tibbett Ave 10471 718-432-3300
Dr. Thomas Kelly, hdmstr. Fax 601-0949
Mt. St. Michael Academy 100/6-8
4300 Murdock Ave 10466 718-515-6400
Lillian Dippolito, prin. Fax 994-7729
Nativity of Our Blessed Lady S 300/PK-8
3893 Dyre Ave 10466 718-324-2188
Ralph Carbonaro, prin. Fax 324-1128
New Covenant Christian S 200/PK-5
1497 Needham Ave 10469 718-519-8884
Dr. Joseph Alexander, supt. Fax 519-8691
Our Lady of Angels S 300/K-8
2865 Claflin Ave 10468 718-549-3503
Sr. Mary Cleary, prin. Fax 549-4002
Our Lady of Grace S 400/PK-8
3981 Bronxwood Ave 10466 718-547-9918
Daphne Lewis, prin. Fax 547-7602
Our Lady of Mercy S 300/PK-8
2512 Marion Ave 10458 718-367-0237
Margaret Knoesel, prin. Fax 367-0529
Our Lady of Mt. Carmel S 200/PK-8
2465 Bathgate Ave 10458 718-295-6080
Susan Cotronei, prin. Fax 329-1269
Our Lady of Refuge S 300/PK-8
2708 Briggs Ave 10458 718-367-3081
Marivel Colon, prin. Fax 367-0741
Our Lady of the Assumption S 400/PK-8
1617 Parkview Ave 10461 718-829-1706
Barbara Kavanagh, prin. Fax 931-2693
Our Saviour Lutheran S 400/PK-12
1734 Williamsbridge Rd 10461 718-409-3877
Fax 409-3877
Regent S 200/K-6
719 E 216th St 10467 718-653-2900
Fax 653-1166
Riverdale Country S - River Campus PK-5
1 Spaulding Ln 10471 718-549-7780
Dominic Randolph, hdmstr.
Sacred Heart S 800/PK-8
95 W 168th St 10452 718-293-4288
Kevin Smith, prin. Fax 293-4886
Sacred Heart S 200/PK-8
1651 Zerega Ave 10462 718-863-5047
Sr. Judith Musco, prin. Fax 828-1946
St. Angela Merici S 500/PK-8
266 E 163rd St 10451 718-293-3365
Sr. Lourdes Mercado, prin. Fax 293-6617
St. Ann S 300/PK-8
3511 Bainbridge Ave 10467 718-655-3449
Lucia DiJusto, prin. Fax 547-4020
St. Anselm S 500/PK-8
685 Tinton Ave 10455 718-993-9464
Teresa Lopes, prin. Fax 292-3496
St. Anthony/St. Frances S 200/PK-8
4520 Matilda Ave 10470 718-324-5104
Christopher D'Armiento, prin. Fax 324-6354
St. Anthony S 200/K-8
1776 Mansion St 10460 718-892-1244
Frances Acosta, prin. Fax 892-4656
St. Athanasius S 300/PK-8
830 Southern Blvd 10459 718-542-5161
Marianne Kraft, prin. Fax 542-7584
St. Augustine S 200/PK-8
1176 Franklin Ave 10456 718-542-3633
Cathryn Trapp, prin. Fax 542-7871
St. Barnabas S 500/PK-8
413 E 241st St 10470 718-324-1088
Ann Zagaglia, prin. Fax 324-2397
St. Benedict S 300/K-8
1016 Edison Ave 10465 718-829-9557
Carol Arbolino, prin. Fax 319-1898
St. Brendan S 400/PK-8
268 E 207th St 10467 718-653-2292
Patricia Gatti, prin. Fax 653-3234
St. Clare of Assisi S 500/PK-8
1911 Hone Ave 10461 718-892-4080
Janice Desmond, prin. Fax 239-1007
St. Dominic S 400/PK-8
1684 White Plains Rd 10462 718-829-4837
Sr. Josefa Marie Curcio, prin. Fax 792-6912
St. Frances De Chantal S 400/PK-8
2962 Harding Ave 10465 718-892-5359
Debra Trigani, prin. Fax 892-6937
St. Francis of Assisi S 300/PK-8
4300 Baychester Ave 10466 718-994-4650
Dr. Patrick Taharally, prin. Fax 994-6990
St. Francis Xavier S 500/PK-8
1711 Haight Ave 10461 718-863-0531
Angela Deegan, prin. Fax 319-1152
St. Gabriel S 200/PK-8
590 W 235th St 10463 718-548-0444
Deborah Pitula, prin. Fax 796-2638
St. Helena S 600/PK-8
2050 Benedict Ave 10462 718-892-3234
Richard Meller, prin. Fax 892-3924
St. Ignatius Academy 100/5-8
740 Manida St 10474 718-861-9084
Dr. Jennifer Gallagher, prin. Fax 861-9096
St. Jerome S 300/PK-8
222 Alexander Ave 10454 718-292-4920
Rocco Martz, prin. Fax 292-3111
St. John Chrysostom S 500/PK-8
1144 Hoe Ave 10459 718-328-7226
Sr. Mary Mooney, prin. Fax 378-5368
St. John S 300/PK-8
3143 Kingsbridge Ave 10463 718-548-0255
Ray Vitiello, prin. Fax 548-0864
St. John Vianney Cure of Ars S 300/PK-8
2141 Seward Ave 10473 718-892-4400
Alberto Vazquez, prin. Fax 931-0865
St. Joseph S 500/PK-8
1946 Bathgate Ave 10457 718-583-9432
Janine Hughes, prin. Fax 299-0780
St. Lucy S 400/PK-8
830 Mace Ave 10467 718-882-2203
Jane Stefanini, prin. Fax 547-8351
St. Luke S 300/PK-8
608 E 139th St 10454 718-585-0380
Sr. Patricia Howell, prin. Fax 585-0380
St. Margaret Mary S 400/PK-8
121 E 177th St 10453 718-731-5905
Sr. Ann Bivona, prin. Fax 731-8924
St. Margaret of Cortona S 200/PK-8
452 W 260th St 10471 718-549-8580
Sr. Kathleen Gerritse, prin. Fax 884-3298
St. Martin of Tours S 200/K-8
695 E 182nd St 10457 718-733-0347
Sr. Nora McArt, prin. Fax 733-5142
St. Mary S 300/PK-8
3956 Carpenter Ave 10466 718-547-0500
Veronica Walsh, prin. Fax 547-0532
St. Mary Star of the Sea S 200/PK-8
580 Minnieford Ave 10464 718-885-1527
Sr. James Kavanagh, prin. Fax 885-1552
St. Nicholas of Tolentine S 400/K-8
2336 Andrews Ave 10468 718-364-5110
Estelle Moffa, prin. Fax 561-3964
St. Philip Neri S 500/PK-8
3031 Grand Concourse 10468 718-365-8806
Thomas Celestino, prin. Fax 365-1482
St. Pius V S 200/PK-8
413 E 144th St 10454 718-665-5075
Violeta Domingo, prin. Fax 665-2987
St. Raymond S 700/PK-8
2380 E Tremont Ave 10462 718-597-3232
Sr. Patricia Brito, prin. Fax 892-4449
St. Simon Stock S 300/K-8
2195 Valentine Ave 10457 718-367-0453
A. Ceparano, prin. Fax 733-1441
St. Theresa S 400/PK-8
2872 Saint Theresa Ave 10461 718-792-3688
Josephine Fanelli, prin. Fax 892-9441
St. Thomas Aquinas S 300/PK-8
1909 Daly Ave 10460 718-893-7600
John Burke, prin. Fax 378-5531
Santa Maria S 300/PK-8
1510 Zerega Ave 10462 718-823-3636
Sr. Ellen O'Connor, prin. Fax 823-7008
SS. Peter & Paul S 200/PK-8
838 Brook Ave 10451 718-665-2056
Sr. Michelle McKeon, prin. Fax 665-2725
SS. Philip & James S 300/PK-8
1160 E 213th St 10469 718-882-4576
Catherine Lavelle, prin. Fax 653-6167
Villa Maria Academy 500/PK-8
3335 Country Club Rd 10465 718-824-3260
Sr. Theresa Barton, prin. Fax 239-0432
Visitation S 200/K-8
171 W 239th St 10463 718-543-2250
Sr. Rosemarie Connell, prin. Fax 543-3665

Bronxville, Westchester, Pop. 6,455

Bronxville UFD 1,500/K-12
177 Pondfield Rd 10708 914-395-0500
David Quattrone, supt. Fax 961-2364
www.bronxville.k12.ny.us
Bronxville ES 700/K-5
177 Pondfield Rd 10708 914-395-0500
Thomas Wilson, prin. Fax 337-6827
Bronxville MS 400/6-8
177 Pondfield Rd 10708 914-395-0500
Dr. Barry Richelsoph, prin. Fax 771-6223

Chapel Lutheran S 400/PK-8
172 White Plains Rd 10708 914-337-3202
James Dhyne, prin. Fax 771-9711
St. Joseph S 200/K-8
30 Meadow Ave 10708 914-337-0261
Nancy Langehennig, prin. Fax 395-1192

Brookfield, Madison

Brookfield Central SD 200/K-12
PO Box 60 13314 315-899-3323
Sherri Morris-Schiebel, supt. Fax 899-8902
www.brookfieldcsd.org
Brookfield Central S 200/K-12
PO Box 60 13314 315-899-3323
Sherri Morris-Schiebel, prin. Fax 899-8902

Brookhaven, Suffolk, Pop. 3,118

South Country Central SD
Supt. — See East Patchogue
Brookhaven ES 800/PK-3
101 Fireplace Neck Rd 11719 631-730-1700
Lisa Greiner, prin. Fax 286-6210

Brooklyn, See New York

NYC Department of Education
Supt. — See New York
Brighter Choice Community S 100/PK-5
280 Hart St 11206 718-574-2378
Fabayo Mcintosh, prin. Fax 443-0639
Brooklyn Brownstone S 100/K-5
272 MacDonough St 11233 718-573-2307
Nakia Haskins, prin. Fax 573-2434
IS 30 300/6-8
415 Ovington Ave 11209 718-491-5684
Danielle DiMango-Maringo, prin. Fax 491-0071
IS 35 300/6-8
272 MacDonough St 11233 718-574-2345
Jackie Charles-Marcus, prin. Fax 452-1273
IS 68 1,000/6-8
956 E 82nd St 11236 718-241-4800
Alex Fralin, prin. Fax 241-5582
IS 98 1,000/6-8
1401 Emmons Ave 11235 718-891-9005
Marian Nagler, prin. Fax 891-3865

IS 136 400/6-8
4004 4th Ave 11232 718-965-3333
Eric Sackler, prin. Fax 965-9567

IS 171 900/5-8
528 Ridgewood Ave 11208 718-647-0111
Yolanda Fustanio, prin. Fax 827-5834

IS 187 1,000/6-8
1171 65th St 11219 718-236-3394
Justin Berman, prin. Fax 236-3638

IS 211 700/6-8
1001 E 100th St 11236 718-251-4411
Buffie Simmons-Peart, prin. Fax 241-2503

IS 228 1,100/6-8
228 Avenue S 11223 718-375-7635
Dominick D'Angelo, prin. Fax 998-4013

IS 239 1,200/6-8
2401 Neptune Ave 11224 718-266-0814
Carol Moore, prin. Fax 266-1693

IS 240 1,500/6-8
2500 Nostrand Ave 11210 718-253-3700
Elena O'Sullivan, prin. Fax 253-0356

IS 252 200/7-8
1084 Lenox Rd 11212 718-342-1144
Mendis Brown, prin. Fax 485-8117

IS 281 1,200/6-8
8787 24th Ave 11214 718-996-6706
Stephen Rosenblum, prin. Fax 996-4186

IS 285 1,000/6-8
5909 Beverley Rd 11203 718-451-2200
Frederick Underwood, prin. Fax 451-0229

IS 303 900/6-8
501 West Ave 11224 718-996-0100
Gary Ingrassia, prin. Fax 996-3785

IS 311 200/6-8
590 Sheffield Ave 11207 718-272-8371
Gail Gaines, prin. Fax 272-8372

IS 318 1,300/6-8
101 Walton St 11206 718-782-0589
Fortunato Rubino, prin. Fax 384-7715

IS 340 300/6-8
227 Sterling Pl 11238 718-857-5516
Jean Williams, prin. Fax 230-5479

IS 347 500/6-8
35 Starr St 11221 718-821-4248
John Barbella, prin. Fax 821-1332

IS 349 500/6-8
35 Starr St 11221 718-418-6389
Rogelis Parris, prin. Fax 418-6146

IS 364 400/6-8
1426 Freeport Loop 11239 718-642-3007
Dale Kelly, prin. Fax 642-8516

IS 381 400/6-8
1599 E 22nd St 11210 718-252-0058
Mary Harrington, prin. Fax 252-0035

IS 392 300/5-8
104 Sutter Ave 11212 718-498-2491
Shirley Wheeler, prin. Fax 346-2804

JHS 14 700/6-8
2424 Batchelder St 11235 718-743-0220
Anne Tully, prin. Fax 769-8632

JHS 49 300/7-8
223 Graham Ave 11206 718-387-7697
Claytisha Walden, prin. Fax 302-2318

JHS 50 700/6-8
183 S 3rd St 11211 718-387-4184
Denise Jamison, prin. Fax 302-2320

JHS 57 300/6-8
125 Stuyvesant Ave 11221 718-574-2357
Celeste Douglas, prin. Fax 453-0577

JHS 62 1,000/6-8
700 Cortelyou Rd 11218 718-941-5450
Barry Kevorkian, prin. Fax 693-7433

JHS 78 1,100/6-8
1420 E 68th St 11234 718-763-4701
Phyllis Marino, prin. Fax 251-3439

JHS 88 900/6-8
544 7th Ave 11215 718-788-4482
Ailene Altman-Mitchell, prin. Fax 768-0213

JHS 117 300/7-8
300 Willoughby Ave 11205 718-230-5400
Alander Hasty, prin. Fax 622-3570

JHS 126 600/6-8
424 Leonard St 11222 718-782-2527
Rosemary Ochoa, prin. Fax 302-2319

JHS 162 700/6-8
1390 Willoughby Ave 11237 718-821-4860
Barbara DeMartino, prin. Fax 821-1728

JHS 166 600/6-8
800 Van Siclen Ave 11207 718-649-0765
Maria Ortega, prin. Fax 927-2172

JHS 201 1,700/6-8
8010 12th Ave 11228 718-833-9363
Madeleine Brennan, prin. Fax 836-1786

JHS 218 900/6-8
370 Fountain Ave 11208 718-647-9050
Joseph Costa, prin. Fax 827-5839

JHS 220 1,300/6-8
4812 9th Ave 11220 718-633-8200
Loretta Witek, prin. Fax 871-7466

JHS 223 600/6-8
4200 16th Ave 11204 718-438-0155
Gertrude Adduci, prin. Fax 871-7477

JHS 227 1,200/6-8
6500 16th Ave 11204 718-256-8218
Brenda Champion, prin. Fax 234-6204

JHS 234 1,700/6-8
1875 E 17th St 11229 718-645-1334
Susan Schaeffer, prin. Fax 645-7759

JHS 258 300/7-8
141 Macon St 11216 718-398-3764
Stanley Walker, prin. Fax 857-3422

JHS 259 1,300/6-8
7301 Fort Hamilton Pkwy 11228 718-833-1000
Janice Geary, prin. Fax 833-3419

JHS 278 1,100/6-8
1925 Stuart St 11229 718-375-3523
Debra Garofalo, prin. Fax 998-7324

JHS 291 800/6-8
231 Palmetto St 11221 718-574-0361
Sean Walsh, prin. Fax 574-1360

JHS 292 800/6-8
301 Vermont St 11207 718-498-6562
Everett Hughes, prin. Fax 345-3327

JHS 296 700/6-8
125 Covert St 11207 718-574-0288
Maria Barreto, prin. Fax 574-1368

JHS 302 1,000/6-8
350 Linwood St 11208 718-647-9500
Lisa Linder, prin. Fax 827-3294

JHS 383 1,000/5-8
1300 Greene Ave 11237 718-574-0390
Barbara Sanders, prin. Fax 574-1366

MS 51 900/6-8
350 5th Ave 11215 718-369-7603
Lenore Berner, prin. Fax 499-4948

MS 55 100/8-8
2021 Bergen St 11233 718-495-7736
Alma Summors, prin. Fax 270-8725

MS 61 900/6-8
400 Empire Blvd 11225 718-774-1002
Rhonda Taylor, prin. Fax 467-4335

MS 113 800/6-8
300 Adelphi St 11205 718-834-6734
Khalek Kirkland, prin. Fax 596-2802

MS 246 900/6-8
72 Veronica Pl 11226 718-282-5230
Bently Warrington, prin. Fax 284-6429

MS 266 200/6-8
62 Park Pl 11217 718-857-2291
Michele Robinson, prin. Fax 857-2347

MS 267 400/6-8
800 Gates Ave 11221 718-574-2319
Patricia King, prin. Fax 574-2320

MS 385 300/6-8
125 Stuyvesant Ave 11221 718-602-3271
Glyn Marryshow, prin. Fax 602-3274

MS 447 500/6-8
345 Dean St 11217 718-330-9328
Lisa Gioe-Cordi, prin. Fax 330-0944

MS 534 200/6-8
787 Lafayette Ave 11221 718-574-6032
William Cooper, prin. Fax 602-2357

MS 571 300/6-8
80 Underhill Ave 11238 718-638-1740
Santosha Troutman, prin. Fax 638-0295

MS 577 300/6-8
208 N 5th St 11211 718-486-6773
Maria Masullo, prin. Fax 486-6771

MS 581 100/6-7
905 Winthrop St 11203 718-773-3059
David Manning, prin. Fax 773-3827

MS 582 200/6-8
207 Bushwick Ave 11206 718-456-8218
Brian Walsh, prin. Fax 456-8220

MS 584 300/6-8
130 Rochester Ave 11213 718-604-1380
Gilleyan Hargrove, prin. Fax 604-3784

MS 598 100/6-7
905 Winthrop St 11203 718-773-7343
Jameela Horton-Ball, prin. Fax 773-7946

MS for Academic and Social Excellence 100/6-7
1224 Park Pl 11213 718-774-0105
Kathleen Clarke-Glover, prin. Fax 774-0298

MS for the Arts 400/6-8
790 E New York Ave 11203 718-773-3343
Susan Hobson-Ransom, prin. Fax 773-4168

Douglass Academy VIII MS 100/6-8
1400 Pennsylvania Ave 11239 718-642-4305
Yolanda Martin, prin. Fax 642-4537

Ebbets Field MS 500/6-8
46 McKeever Pl 11225 718-941-5097
Margaret Baker, prin. Fax 284-7973

Edmonds Learning Center II 100/6-8
430 Howard Ave 11233 718-467-0306
Herbert Daughtry, prin. Fax 953-0682

James ES of Science 400/PK-5
76 Riverdale Ave 11212 718-498-0952
Margaret Mcauley, prin. Fax 495-1134

James MS of Science 200/6-8
76 Riverdale Ave 11212 718-498-5276
Willis Perry, prin. Fax 498-5361

KAPPA VII 100/6-8
300 Willoughby Ave 11205 718-230-3273
Rosa Smith-Norman, prin. Fax 230-0173

KAPPA V S, 985 Rockaway Ave 11212 200/6-8
Dellie Edwards, prin. 718-922-4690

Middle School for Art and Philosophy 100/6-8
1084 Lenox Rd 11212 718-342-7563
Andrew Buck, prin. Fax 342-8131

Mott Hall IV MS 200/6-8
1137 Herkimer St 11233 718-485-5240
Lajuan White, prin.

New Horizons S 100/6-8
317 Hoyt St 11231 718-330-9227
Mary Lou Aranyos, dir. Fax 330-9251

New Voices S of Academic & Creative Arts 400/6-8
330 18th St 11215 718-965-0390
Frank Giordano, prin. Fax 965-0603

Public S 1 1,000/PK-5
309 47th St 11220 718-567-7661
Zaida Vega, prin. Fax 567-9771

Public S 3 600/PK-5
50 Jefferson Ave 11216 718-622-2960
Kristina Beecher, prin. Fax 623-3193

Public S 5 400/PK-5
820 Hancock St 11233 718-574-2333
Lena Gates, prin. Fax 574-3925

Public S 6 600/K-5
43 Snyder Ave 11226 718-856-6560
Ellen Carlisle, prin. Fax 856-7493

Public S 7 900/PK-4
858 Jamaica Ave 11208 718-647-3600
Nydia Acevedo, prin. Fax 827-4004

Public S 8 400/PK-5
37 Hicks St 11201 718-834-6740
Seth Phillips, prin. Fax 834-7690

Public S 9 500/PK-5
80 Underhill Ave 11238 718-638-3260
Sandra D'Avilar, prin. Fax 622-2961

Public S 10 500/PK-5
511 7th Ave 11215 718-965-1190
Laura Scott, prin. Fax 369-1736

Public S 11 500/PK-5
419 Waverly Ave 11238 718-638-2661
Alonta Wrighton, prin. Fax 622-3028

Public S 12 400/PK-8
430 Howard Ave 11233 718-953-4569
Nyree Dixon, prin. Fax 953-4428

Public S 13 600/PK-5
557 Pennsylvania Ave 11207 718-498-3717
Barbara Ashby, prin. Fax 345-2396

Public S 15 300/PK-5
71 Sullivan St 11231 718-330-9280
Peggy Wyns-Madison, prin. Fax 596-2576

Public S 16 400/PK-5
157 Wilson St 11211 718-782-5352
Virginia Berrios, prin. Fax 486-8447

Public S 17 400/PK-5
208 N 5th St 11211 718-387-2929
Dr. Robert Marchi, prin. Fax 302-2311

Public S 18 300/PK-5
101 Maujer St 11206 718-387-3241
Karen Ford, prin. Fax 599-7744

Public S 19 500/1-5
325 S 3rd St 11211 718-387-7820
Maria Witherspoon, prin. Fax 782-2446

Public S 20 400/PK-5
225 Adelphi St 11205 718-834-6744
Sean Keaton, prin. Fax 243-0712

Public S 21 700/PK-5
180 Chauncey St 11233 718-493-9681
Harold Anderson, prin. Fax 953-3980

Public S 22 500/PK-5
433 Saint Marks Ave 11238 718-857-4503
Carlen Padmore, prin. Fax 857-4464

Public S 23 300/PK-5
545 Willoughby Ave 11206 718-387-0375
Sharon Meade, prin. Fax 302-2312

Public S 24 700/PK-5
427 38th St 11232 718-832-9366
Christina Fuentes, prin. Fax 832-9360

Public S 25 400/PK-5
787 Lafayette Ave 11221 718-574-2336
Anita Coley, prin. Fax 455-5838

Public S 26 400/PK-5
1014 Lafayette Ave 11221 718-919-5707
Michele Ashley, prin. Fax 574-2803

Public S 27 400/PK-10
27 Huntington St 11231 718-330-9285
Sarah Belcher-Barnes, prin. Fax 596-4889

Public S 28 200/PK-5
1001 Herkimer St 11233 718-467-2865
Sadie Silver, prin. Fax 953-4189

Public S 29 700/PK-5
425 Henry St 11201 718-330-9277
Melanie Raneri-Woods, prin. Fax 596-1887

Public S 31 600/PK-5
75 Meserole Ave 11222 718-383-8998
Mary Scarlato, prin. Fax 383-5652

Public S 32 200/PK-5
317 Hoyt St 11231 718-330-9295
Deborah Florio, prin. Fax 797-4362

Public S 34 500/PK-5
131 Norman Ave 11222 718-389-5842
Alicia Winnicki, prin. Fax 389-0356

Public S 38 400/PK-5
450 Pacific St 11217 718-330-9305
Yolanda Ramirez, prin. Fax 802-9542

Public S 39 400/PK-5
417 6th Ave 11215 718-330-9310
Anita DePaz, prin. Fax 832-2010

Public S 40 300/PK-5
265 Ralph Ave 11233 718-574-2353
Leonie Hibbert, prin. Fax 453-0686

Public S 41 800/PK-8
411 Thatford Ave 11212 718-495-7732
Theresa Siegel, prin. Fax 346-2141

Public S 44 600/PK-5
432 Monroe St 11221 718-834-6939
Valerie Taylor, prin. Fax 574-8501

Public S 45 700/PK-5
84 Schaefer St 11207 718-574-0235
Tracy Lott-Davis, prin. Fax 574-1043

Public S 46 400/PK-5
100 Clermont Ave 11205 718-834-7694
Karyn Nicholson, prin. Fax 243-0726

Public S 48 600/PK-5
6015 18th Ave 11204 718-232-3873
Diane Picucci, prin. Fax 232-3451

Public S 52 700/PK-5
2675 E 29th St 11235 718-648-0882
Ilene Altschul, prin. Fax 648-4636

Public S 54 300/PK-5
195 Sandford St 11205 718-834-6752
Lorna Khan, prin. Fax 852-8129

Public S 56 300/PK-5
170 Gates Ave 11238 718-857-3149
Deborah Clark-Johnson, prin. Fax 783-7379

Public S 58 400/PK-5
330 Smith St 11231 718-330-9322
Giselle McGee, prin. Fax 596-2969

Public S 59 500/PK-5
211 Throop Ave 11206 718-443-3600
Dawn Best, prin. Fax 574-6634

Public S 65 500/K-5
158 Richmond St 11208 718-277-4821
Daysi Garcia, prin. Fax 827-4132

Public S 66 600/PK-8
845 E 96th St 11236 718-922-3505
Joel Rubenfeld, prin. Fax 922-3105

Public S 67 300/PK-5
51 Saint Edwards St 11205 718-834-6756
Corinne Seabrook, prin. Fax 834-6719

Public S 69 700/K-5
6302 9th Ave 11220 718-833-6710
Jaynemarie Capetanakis, prin. Fax 833-9781

Public S 72 700/PK-7
605 Shepherd Ave 11208 718-345-4100
Gena Lipscomb, prin. Fax 927-2160

Public S 73 500/PK-8
251 MacDougal St 11233 718-573-0288
Joelle McKen, prin. Fax 455-1835

Public S 75 600/PK-5
95 Grove St 11221 718-574-0244
Christopher Tricarico, prin. Fax 574-1051

Public S 81 400/PK-5
990 Dekalb Ave 11221 718-574-2365
Cheryl Ault, prin. Fax 919-9872

Public S 84 500/PK-5
250 Berry St 11211 718-384-8063
Stefanie Greco, prin. Fax 302-2313

Public S 86 500/K-5
220 Irving Ave 11237 718-574-0252
Mabel Sarduy, prin. Fax 919-1839

Public S 89 200/K-8
350 Linwood St 11208 718-277-5044
Irene Leon, prin. Fax 277-5051

Public S 90 500/PK-5
2840 W 12th St 11224 718-266-8090
Madelene Chan, prin. Fax 266-7018

Public S 91 600/PK-5
532 Albany Ave 11203 718-756-0243
Solomon Long, prin. Fax 221-1316

Public S 92 800/PK-5
601 Parkside Ave 11226 718-462-2087
Diana Rahmann, prin. Fax 284-8289

Public S 93 500/PK-5
31 New York Ave 11216 718-604-7363
Yvonne Knight, prin. Fax 771-1369

Public S 94 1,100/K-5
5010 6th Ave 11220 718-435-6034
Jeanette Caban, prin. Fax 871-6251

Public S 95 900/PK-8
345 Van Sicklen St 11223 718-449-5050
Carolyn Teles-Manich, prin. Fax 449-3047

Public S 97 800/PK-5
1855 Stillwell Ave 11223 718-372-7393
Kristine Mustillo, prin. Fax 372-3842

Public S 99 800/PK-8
1120 E 10th St 11230 718-338-9201
Gregory Pirraglia, prin. Fax 951-0418

Public S 100 700/PK-5
2951 W 3rd St 11224 718-266-9477
Katherine Moloney, prin. Fax 266-7112

Public S 101 800/PK-5
2360 Benson Ave 11214 718-372-0221
Greg Korrol, prin. Fax 372-1873

Public S 102 1,000/K-5
211 72nd St 11209 718-748-7404
Theresa Dovi, prin. Fax 836-9265

Public S 104 1,300/K-8
9115 5th Ave 11209 718-836-4630
Marie Dibella, prin. Fax 836-9412

Public S 105 1,200/PK-5
1031 59th St 11219 718-438-3230
Johanna Castronovo, prin. Fax 853-9633

Public S 106 600/PK-5
1314 Putnam Ave 11221 718-574-0261
Robert Flores, prin. Fax 574-1054

Public S 107 500/PK-5
1301 8th Ave 11215 718-330-9340
Cynthia Holton, prin. Fax 965-6479

Public S 108 1,000/K-5
200 Linwood St 11208 718-277-7010
Constance Hahn, prin. Fax 827-4137

Public S 109 700/K-8
1001 E 45th St 11203 718-693-3426
Denise Talley, prin. Fax 693-3072

Public S 110 400/PK-5
124 Monitor St 11222 718-383-7600
Anna Amato, prin. Fax 383-5053

Public S 112 500/K-5
7115 15th Ave 11228 718-232-0685
Louise Verdemare, prin. Fax 232-3609

Public S 114 900/PK-5
1077 Remsen Ave 11236 718-257-4428
Maria Pena-Herrera, prin. Fax 649-5216

Public S 115 1,200/PK-5
1500 E 92nd St 11236 718-241-1000
Mitchell Pinsky, prin. Fax 209-1714

Public S 116 400/K-5
515 Knickerbocker Ave 11237 718-821-4623
Anna Santiago, prin. Fax 821-0363

Public S 119 500/2-5
3829 Avenue K 11210 718-377-7696
Lisa Fernandez, prin. Fax 338-0694

Public S 120 400/PK-5
18 Beaver St 11206 718-455-1000
Liza Caraballo, prin. Fax 574-6637

Public S 121 200/PK-8
5301 20th Ave 11204 718-377-8845
Lillian Catalano, prin. Fax 252-4075

Public S 123 1,000/K-5
100 Irving Ave 11237 718-821-4810
Veronica Greene, prin. Fax 821-0858

Public S 124 300/PK-5
515 4th Ave 11215 718-788-0246
Annabelle Martinez, prin. Fax 965-9558

Public S 127 400/K-5
7805 7th Ave 11228 718-833-2323
Pauline Frank, prin. Fax 836-9427

Public S 128 300/PK-5
2075 84th St 11214 718-373-5900
Marcia Robins, prin. Fax 266-6254

Public S 130 500/PK-5
70 Ocean Pkwy 11218 718-686-1940
Maria Nunziata, prin. Fax 854-9756

Public S 131 900/PK-5
4305 Fort Hamilton Pkwy 11219 718-686-1457
Ruth Quiles, prin. Fax 853-5952

Public S 132 600/PK-5
320 Manhattan Ave 11211 718-599-7301
Beth Ceffalia, prin. Fax 599-7417

Public S 133 200/PK-5
375 Butler St 11217 718-857-4810
Heather Foster-Mann, prin. Fax 622-3264

Public S 134 400/PK-5
4001 18th Ave 11218 718-436-7200
Debra Ramsaran, prin. Fax 854-4115

Public S 135 800/PK-5
684 Linden Blvd 11203 718-693-4363
Penny Grinage, prin. Fax 941-0847

Public S 137 400/PK-8
121 Saratoga Ave 11233 718-453-2926
Loria Tucker, prin. Fax 453-5363

Public S 138 900/PK-8
760 Prospect Pl 11216 718-467-0800
Marie Chauvet-Monchik, prin. Fax 953-3422

Public S 139 1,000/PK-5
330 Rugby Rd 11226 718-282-5254
Mary McDonald, prin. Fax 940-1205

Public S 145 1,000/PK-5
100 Noll St 11206 718-821-4823
Marilyn Torres, prin. Fax 417-3453

Public S 146 500/PK-5
610 Henry St 11231 718-923-4750
Anna Allanbrook, prin. Fax 923-4780

Public S 147 300/PK-5
325 Bushwick Ave 11206 718-497-0326
Julia Drake, prin. Fax 628-4988

Public S 149 700/PK-5
700 Sutter Ave 11207 718-385-8666
Enid Silvera, prin. Fax 345-8118

Public S 150 500/PK-10
364 Sackman St 11212 718-495-7746
Sharon Wallace, prin. Fax 922-3785

Public S 151 500/PK-5
763 Knickerbocker Ave 11207 718-821-4800
Jeanette Sosa, prin. Fax 821-0166

Public S 152 700/K-5
725 E 23rd St 11210 718-434-5222
Dr. Rhonda Farkas, prin. Fax 859-5965

Public S 153 500/PK-5
1970 Homecrest Ave 11229 718-375-4484
Carl Santamaria, prin. Fax 375-4439

Public S 154 400/PK-5
1625 11th Ave 11215 718-768-0057
Samuel Ortiz, prin. Fax 832-2573

Public S 155 600/PK-8
1355 Herkimer St 11233 718-495-7751
Nelly Cortes, prin. Fax 345-9064

Public S 156 900/PK-5
104 Sutter Ave 11212 718-498-2811
Beverly Logan, prin. Fax 346-2804

Public S 157 300/PK-5
850 Kent Ave 11205 718-622-9285
Maribel Torres, prin. Fax 398-4155

Public S 158 500/PK-5
400 Ashford St 11207 718-277-6116
Audrey Wilson, prin. Fax 827-4300

Public S 159 900/K-5
2781 Pitkin Ave 11208 718-277-4828
Monica Duncan, prin. Fax 827-4531

Public S 160 800/PK-5
5105 Fort Hamilton Pkwy 11219 718-438-0337
Margaret Russo, prin. Fax 871-7920

Public S 161 1,000/K-8
330 Crown St 11225 718-756-3100
Deborah Barrett, prin. Fax 953-3605

Public S 163 400/PK-5
1664 Benson Ave 11214 718-236-9003
Maryann Wasmuth, prin. Fax 259-3042

Public S 164 400/PK-5
4211 14th Ave 11219 718-854-4100
Margaret Choy-Shan, prin. Fax 853-9306

Public S 165 600/PK-8
76 Lott Ave 11212 718-495-7759
Fran Ellers, prin. Fax 345-8255

Public S 167 500/PK-5
1025 Eastern Pkwy 11213 718-774-2640
Joan Palmer, prin. Fax 953-1954

Public S 169 1,000/K-5
4305 7th Ave 11232 718-853-3224
Josephine Santiago, prin. Fax 633-9621

Public S 170 700/K-5
7109 6th Ave 11209 718-748-0333
Suzanne Gray, prin. Fax 921-6351

Public S 172 500/PK-5
825 4th Ave 11232 718-965-4200
Jack Spatola, prin. Fax 965-2468

Public S 174 500/PK-8
574 Dumont Ave 11207 718-342-3625
Ingrid Mason, prin. Fax 342-7562

Public S 176 1,000/K-5
1225 69th St 11219 718-236-7755
Elizabeth Culkin, prin. Fax 331-9188

Public S 177 800/PK-5
346 Avenue P 11204 718-375-9506
Shoshana Singer, prin. Fax 375-4450

Public S 178 600/PK-8
2163 Dean St 11233 718-495-7768
Joseph Henry, prin. Fax 495-2304

Public S 179 900/PK-5
202 Avenue C 11218 718-438-4010
Valerie Joseph, prin. Fax 871-7484

Public S 180 600/PK-8
5601 16th Ave 11204 718-851-8070
Gary Williams, prin. Fax 853-9308

Public S 181 1,100/PK-8
1023 New York Ave 11203 718-462-5298
Dr. Lowell Coleman, prin. Fax 284-5053

Public S 184 500/PK-8
273 Newport St 11212 718-495-7775
Maryanne Devivio, prin. Fax 385-4655

Public S 185 800/K-5
8601 Ridge Blvd 11209 718-745-6610
Kenneth Llinas, prin. Fax 836-9631

Public S 186 700/PK-5
7601 19th Ave 11214 718-236-7071
Bayan Cadotte, prin. Fax 331-9181

Public S 188 600/PK-5
3314 Neptune Ave 11224 718-266-6380
Fred Tudda, prin. Fax 266-7103

Public S 189 1,100/K-8
1100 E New York Ave 11212 718-756-0210
Berthe Faustin, prin. Fax 604-1865

Public S 190 300/PK-5
590 Sheffield Ave 11207 718-346-8780
Stephaun Hill, prin. Fax 345-8765

Public S 191 300/PK-5
1600 Park Pl 11233 718-756-1206
Elsi Capolongo, prin. Fax 756-5417

Public S 192 300/PK-6
4715 18th Ave 11204 718-633-3061
Liset Isaac, prin. Fax 871-8721

Public S 193 800/PK-5
2515 Avenue L 11210 718-338-9011
Frank Cimino, prin. Fax 338-9074

Public S 194 400/PK-5
3117 Avenue W 11229 718-648-8804
Mary Zissler-Lynch, prin. Fax 934-0244

Public S 195 400/PK-5
131 Irwin St 11235 718-648-9102
Arthur Forman, prin. Fax 934-0625

Public S 196 300/PK-5
207 Bushwick Ave 11206 718-497-0139
Janine Colon, prin. Fax 628-5134

Public S 197 400/PK-5
1599 E 22nd St 11210 718-377-7890
Rosemarie Nicoletti, prin. Fax 377-7505

Public S 198 700/PK-5
4105 Farragut Rd 11210 718-282-4920
Joy-Ann Morgan, prin. Fax 940-0821

Public S 199 500/PK-5
1100 Elm Ave 11230 718-339-1422
Rosalia Bacarella, prin. Fax 336-5562

Public S 200 1,200/K-5
1940 Benson Ave 11214 718-236-5466
Javier Muniz, prin. Fax 232-3428

Public S 202 1,000/PK-8
982 Hegeman Ave 11208 718-649-7880
Pauline Smyth, prin. Fax 927-2173

Public S 203 800/PK-5
5101 Avenue M 11234 718-241-8488
Lisa Esposito, prin. Fax 209-9641

Public S 204 900/PK-5
8101 15th Ave 11228 718-236-2906
Marie Reilly, prin. Fax 232-9265

Public S 205 800/PK-5
6701 20th Ave 11204 718-236-2380
Beth Grater, prin. Fax 331-7299

Public S 206 1,200/PK-8
2200 Gravesend Neck Rd 11229 718-743-5598
Dierdre Keys, prin. Fax 332-4986

Public S 207 800/PK-7
4011 Fillmore Ave 11234 718-645-8667
Mary Bosco, prin. Fax 645-8139

Public S 208 600/PK-5
4801 Avenue D 11203 718-629-1670
Kristy Parris, prin. Fax 451-0185

Public S 209 600/PK-8
2609 E 7th St 11235 718-743-1954
Frances Locurcio, prin. Fax 743-6361

Public S 212 500/PK-5
87 Bay 49th St 11214 718-266-4841
Josephine Marsella, prin. Fax 266-7080

Public S 213 500/PK-5
580 Hegeman Ave 11207 718-257-4034
Joan Webson, prin. Fax 272-3446

Public S 214 1,000/PK-5
2944 Pitkin Ave 11208 718-647-1740
Patricia Tubridy, prin. Fax 827-5838

Public S 215 600/PK-5
415 Avenue S 11223 718-339-2464
Antonella Bove, prin. Fax 998-7235

Public S 216 400/PK-5
350 Avenue X 11223 718-645-2862
Celia Kaplinsky, prin. Fax 645-2610

Public S 217 1,100/PK-5
1100 Newkirk Ave 11230 718-434-6960
Franca Conti, prin. Fax 434-8170

Public S 219 900/PK-5
1060 Clarkson Ave 11212 718-342-0493
Winsome Smith, prin. Fax 345-3065

Public S 221 600/PK-5
791 Empire Blvd 11213 718-756-0122
Clara Moodie-Kirkland, prin. Fax 953-2657

Public S 222 800/PK-5
3301 Quentin Rd 11234 718-998-4298
Louise Blake, prin. Fax 339-2107

Public S 224 800/PK-6
755 Wortman Ave 11208 718-235-3600
George Andrews, prin. Fax 827-5840

Public S 225 900/PK-8
1075 Ocean View Ave 11235 718-743-9793
Joseph Montebello, prin. Fax 743-7096

Public S 226 700/PK-8
6006 23rd Ave 11204 718-256-1118
Sherry Tannenbaum, prin. Fax 256-0384

Public S 229 600/K-5
1400 Benson Ave 11228 718-236-5447
James Harrigan, prin. Fax 331-8173

Public S 230 1,100/PK-5
1 Albemarle Rd 11218 718-437-6135
Sharon Fiden, prin. Fax 871-2624

Public S 233 700/PK-5
9301 Avenue B 11236 718-346-8103
Denean Stephens-Spellman, prin. Fax 345-3078

Public S 235 1,400/PK-8
525 Lenox Rd 11203 718-773-4869
Lisa Solitario, prin. Fax 773-0048

Public S 236 600/PK-5
6302 Avenue U 11234 718-444-6969
Mary Barton, prin. Fax 241-6630

Public S 238 300/PK-5
1633 E 8th St 11223 718-339-4355
Harla Musoff-Weiss, prin. Fax 998-4351

Public S 241 600/PK-5
976 President St 11225 718-636-4725
Philip Dominique, prin. Fax 230-5468

Public S 243 400/PK-5
1580 Dean St 11213 718-953-1658
Karen Glover, prin. Fax 778-0492

Public S 244 900/PK-5
5404 Tilden Ave 11203 718-346-6240
Grace Alesia, prin. Fax 345-3083

Public S 245 200/PK-5
249 E 17th St 11226 718-284-2330
Pat Kannen-Gieser, prin. Fax 856-0646

Public S 247 600/PK-5
7000 21st Ave 11204 718-236-4205
Christopher Ogno, prin. Fax 331-8563

Public S 249 700/PK-3
18 Marlborough Rd 11226 718-282-8828
Elisa Brown, prin. Fax 284-5146

Public S 250 900/PK-5
108 Montrose Ave 11206 718-384-0889
Nora Barnes, prin. Fax 302-2314

Public S 251 600/PK-5
1037 E 54th St 11234 718-251-4110
Steven Boyer, prin. Fax 241-3200

Public S 253 600/PK-5
601 Ocean View Ave 11235 718-332-3331
Lisa Speroni, prin. Fax 743-7194

Public S 254 600/PK-5
1801 Avenue Y 11235 718-743-0890
Linda Alhonote, prin. Fax 332-4477

Public S 255 600/PK-5
1866 E 17th St 11229 718-376-8494
Linda Singer, prin. Fax 627-0626

Public S 256 400/PK-5
114 Kosciuszko St 11216 718-857-9820
Sharyn Hemphill, prin. Fax 783-7384

Public S 257 500/PK-5
60 Cook St 11206 718-384-7128
Brian Devale, prin. Fax 387-8115

Public S 260 400/PK-6
875 Williams Ave 11207 718-649-9216
Pierre Raymond, prin. Fax 927-2215

Public S 261 700/PK-5
314 Pacific St 11201 718-330-9275
Zipporiah Mills, prin. Fax 875-9503

Public S 262 300/PK-5
500 Macon St 11233 718-453-0780
Joeletha Ferguson, prin. Fax 453-0679

Public S 268 600/PK-5
133 E 53rd St 11203 718-773-5332
Mosezetta Overby, prin. Fax 493-7448

Public S 269 500/3-5
1957 Nostrand Ave 11210 718-941-2800
Phyllis Corbin, prin. Fax 940-3098

Public S 270 300/PK-5
241 Emerson Pl 11205 718-622-2443
Mitra Lutchman, prin. Fax 622-3370

Public S 272 700/PK-5
10124 Seaview Ave 11236 718-241-1300
Dakota Keyes, prin. Fax 241-5549

Public S 273 500/K-5
923 Jerome St 11207 718-649-5739
Melissa Avery, prin. Fax 927-2230

Public S 274 800/PK-5
800 Bushwick Ave 11221 718-574-0273
Maritza Jones, prin. Fax 574-1059

Public S 276 900/PK-5
1070 E 83rd St 11236 718-241-5757
Jonathan Straughn, prin. Fax 241-5560

Public S 277 400/PK-5
2529 Gerritsen Ave 11229 718-743-6689
Jeanne Fish, prin. Fax 368-0920

Public S 279 700/PK-5
1070 E 104th St 11236 718-444-4316
Lorenzo Chambers, prin. Fax 241-5581

Public S 282 700/PK-5
180 6th Ave 11217 718-622-1626
Magalie Alexis, prin. Fax 622-3471

Public S 284 700/PK-8
220 Watkins St 11212 718-495-7791
Shenean Lindsay, prin. Fax 495-7839

Public S 287 200/PK-5
50 Navy St 11201 718-834-4745
Michele Rawlins, prin. Fax 834-6766

Public S 288 500/PK-8
2950 W 25th St 11224 718-449-8000
Joelene Kinard, prin. Fax 449-7682

Public S 289 700/PK-5
900 Saint Marks Ave 11213 718-493-3824
Dennis Jeffers, prin. Fax 467-3735

Public S 290 600/K-5
135 Schenck Ave 11207 718-647-1113
Willena George, prin. Fax 827-5842

Public S 295 400/PK-5
330 18th St 11215 718-965-0390
Deanna Marco, prin. Fax 965-0603

Public S 297 400/PK-5
700 Park Ave 11206 718-388-4581
Maureen Garrity, prin. Fax 302-2315

Public S 298 600/PK-8
85 Watkins St 11212 718-495-7793
Yvonne Graham, prin. Fax 566-8770

Public S 299 400/PK-5
88 Woodbine St 11221 718-574-0301
Wilma Kirk, prin. Fax 574-1080

Public S 305 400/PK-5
344 Monroe St 11216 718-789-3962
Dr. Julia Mortley, prin. Fax 622-3474

Public S 306 600/PK-8
970 Vermont St 11207 718-649-3155
Lawrence Burroughs, prin. Fax 927-2243

Public S 307 300/PK-5
209 York St 11201 718-834-4748
Roberta Davenport, prin. Fax 855-4181

Public S 308 800/PK-8
616 Quincy St 11221 718-574-2373
Renara Clement, prin. Fax 453-0663

Public S 309 400/PK-5
794 Monroe St 11221 718-574-2381
Rebecca Fonville, prin. Fax 453-0643

Public S 312 800/PK-5
7103 Avenue T 11234 718-763-4015
Linda Beal-Benigno, prin. Fax 531-2796

Public S 315 800/PK-5
2310 Glenwood Rd 11210 718-421-9560
Beverly Ffolkes-Bryant, prin. Fax 421-9561

Public S 316 300/PK-5
750 Classon Ave 11238 718-638-4043
Elif Gure, prin. Fax 230-5366

Public S 319 200/PK-1
360 Keap St 11211 718-388-1588
Aleyda Zamora-Martinez, prin. Fax 302-2316

Public S 321 1,200/PK-5
180 7th Ave 11215 718-499-2412
Elizabeth Phillips, prin. Fax 965-9605

Public S 323 500/PK-8
210 Chester St 11212 718-495-7781
Linda Harris, prin. Fax 346-4614

Public S 326 300/PK-1
1800 Utica Ave 11234 718-241-4828
Colleen Ducey, prin. Fax 763-5567

Public S 327 700/PK-8
111 Bristol St 11212 718-495-7801
Dr. Stephen Appea, prin. Fax 495-7828

Public S 328 700/PK-8
330 Alabama Ave 11207 718-345-9393
Douglas Avila, prin. Fax 345-6566

Public S 329 600/PK-5
2929 W 30th St 11224 718-996-3800
Selema Dawson, prin. Fax 265-1525

Public S 332 500/PK-8
51 Christopher Ave 11212 718-495-7805
Deborah Pierce, prin. Fax 495-7708

Public S 335 400/PK-5
130 Rochester Ave 11213 718-493-7736
Laverne Nimmons, prin. Fax 953-4697

Public S 345 700/PK-5
111 Berriman St 11208 718-647-8387
Wanda Holt, prin. Fax 827-5884

Public S 346 700/PK-5
1400 Pennsylvania Ave 11239 718-642-3000
Kevin Caifa, prin. Fax 642-8498

Public S 361 600/PK-2
3109 Newkirk Ave 11226 718-856-0600
Dianne Martin, prin. Fax 856-0300

Public S 375 500/PK-5
46 McKeever Pl 11225 718-693-6655
Marion Wilson, prin. Fax 284-6433

Public S 376 500/K-5
194 Harman St 11237 718-573-0781
Brenda Perez, prin. Fax 573-0769

Public S 377 800/PK-8
200 Woodbine St 11221 718-574-0325
Dominic Zagami, prin. Fax 574-1082

Public S 380 400/PK-5
370 Marcy Ave 11206 718-388-0607
Josephine Viars, prin. Fax 599-3231

Public S 384 600/PK-8
242 Cooper St 11207 718-574-0382
Brunhilda Ortiz, prin. Fax 574-1364

Public S 394 700/PK-8
188 Rochester Ave 11213 718-756-3164
Claudette Murray, prin. Fax 756-3177

Public S 397 400/K-5
490 Fenimore St 11203 718-774-5200
Nancy Colon, prin. Fax 953-4856

Public S 398 400/PK-5
60 E 94th St 11212 718-774-4466
Diane Danay-Cavan, prin. Fax 467-4018

Public S 399 400/K-5
2707 Albemarle Rd 11226 718-693-3023
Marion Brown, prin. Fax 940-0702

Public S 503 800/PK-5
330 59th St 11220 718-439-5962
Bernadette Fitzgerald, prin. Fax 439-0948

Public S 506, 330 59th St 11220 700/PK-5
Elizabeth Waters, prin. 718-492-0087

Satellite East 200/6-8
344 Monroe St 11216 718-789-4251
Kim McPherson, prin. Fax 789-4823

Satellite III S 300/6-8
170 Gates Ave 11238 718-789-5835
Kenyatte Reid, prin. Fax 789-5814

Satellite West MS 300/6-8
209 York St 11201 718-834-6774
Suzanne Joseph, prin. Fax 834-2979

School of Integrated Learning 200/6-8
1224 Park Pl 11213 718-774-0362
Monique Campbell, prin. Fax 774-0521

Stroud MS 50/6-8
750 Classon Ave 11238 718-638-3067
Claudette Essor, prin. Fax 638-3515

Sunset Park Prep MS 400/6-8
4004 4th Ave 11232 718-965-3331
Lola Padin, prin. Fax 965-3330

Urban Assembly Acad of Arts and Letters 200/6-7
225 Adelphi St 11205 718-222-1605
Allison Gaines-Pell, prin. Fax 852-6020

Young Scholars Academy 200/K-5
280 Hart St 11206 718-453-4081
Danika Lacroix, prin. Fax 453-7843

Adelphi Academy 100/PK-12
8515 Ridge Blvd 11209 718-238-3308
Dr. Roy Blash, pres. Fax 238-2894

Ahi Ezer Yeshiva 300/PK-8
2433 Ocean Pkwy 11235 718-648-6100

Al-Noor S 700/PK-12
675 4th Ave 11232 718-768-7181
Nidal Abuasi, prin. Fax 768-7088

America Come Back to God Christian Acad 100/PK-8
822 Dumont Ave 11207 718-240-9828
Dr. Cynthia Furrs-Gilmore, prin. Fax 270-9766

Arista Prep S 100/K-8
275 Kingston Ave 11213 718-493-9292
Fax 493-0376

Bais Brocha Stolin Karlin 600/PK-12
4314 10th Ave 11219 718-853-1222

Bais Esther S 300/PK-12
1353 50th St 11219 718-436-1234

Bais Isaac Zvi 100/PK-1
1019 46th St 11219 718-854-7777

Bais Rochel S 50/1-8
227 Marcy Ave 11211 718-963-9294

Bais Rochel S of Boro Park 3,000/K-12
5301 14th Ave 11219 718-438-7822

Bais Sarah Girls S 800/PK-12
6101 16th Ave 11204 718-871-7571

Bais Tziporah S 400/PK-12
1449 39th St 11218 718-436-8336

Bais Yaakov Academy 900/PK-12
1213 Elm Ave 11230 718-339-4747

Bais Yaakov Adas Yereim 300/PK-12
563 Bedford Ave 11211 718-302-7500

Bais Yaakov Adas Yereim 300/PK-12
1169 43rd St 11219 718-435-5111

Bais Yaakov D'Chassidei Gur 300/K-8
1975 51st St 11204 718-338-5600

Bais Yaakov of 18th Avenue S 300/PK-8
4419 18th Ave 11204 718-633-6050

Bais Yaakov of Bensonhurst 50/PK-7
2025 67th St 11204 718-940-1075

Bais Yaakov of Brooklyn/Midwood 100/PK-8
3609 13th Ave 11218 718-435-1166

Bais Yitzchak S 300/K-10
1413 45th St 11219 718-633-4802
Philip Gross, prin. Fax 633-1063

Barkai Yeshivah 300/PK-8
5302 21st Ave 11204 718-998-7473
Fax 758-3551

Bas Melech S for Girls 100/PK-5
4421 15th Ave 11219 718-677-7999

Battalion Christian Academy 200/PK-5
661 Linden Blvd 11203 718-774-5447

Bay Ridge Christian Academy 100/PK-8
6324 7th Ave 11220 718-238-0958
Judy Vega, prin. Fax 921-4005

Be'er Hagolah Institute 600/K-12
671 Louisiana Ave 11239 718-642-6800
Pearl Kaufman, dir. Fax 642-4740

Beikvei Hatzoin S 200/PK-12
31 Division Ave 11211 718-486-6363

Beis Chaya Mushka 200/PK-12
350 Troy Ave 11213 718-756-0770

Belz Girls S 900/PK-12
600 McDonald Ave 11218 718-871-0500

Berkeley Carroll S 300/PK-4
701 Carroll St 11215 718-789-6060
Robert Vitalo, hdmstr. Fax 638-4993

Beth Chana S 300/1-12
712 Bedford Ave 11206 718-935-1845

Beth Chana S 50/PK-1
204 Keap St 11211 718-388-5491

Bethel S 50/PK-8
457 Grand Ave 11238 718-789-1259
Edward Jackson, prin. Fax 399-7404

Beth Jacob of Boro Park 1,700/PK-8
PO Box 199036 11219 718-436-7300

Beth Jacob S 800/PK-12
85 Parkville Ave 11230 718-633-6555

Beth Rivka Girls S 900/K-8
470 Lefferts Ave 11225 718-735-0770
Chavie Altein, prin. Fax 735-4712

Bet Yaakov Ateret Torah S 200/PK-8
2166 Coney Island Ave 11223 718-732-7770

Big Apple Academy 1,000/PK-8
2937 86th St 11223 718-333-0300
Fax 333-1311

Blessed Sacrament S 300/PK-8
187 Euclid Ave 11208 718-235-4863
Marylou Celmer, prin. Fax 235-1132

Bnei Shimon Yisroel of Sopron 300/PK-9
215 Hewes St 11211 718-855-4092

Bnos Margulia Viznitz 200/PK-8
1824 53rd St 11204 718-234-2050

Bnos Menachem S for Girls 400/PK-12
739 E New York Ave 11203 718-493-1100

Bnos Spinka 200/PK-3
127 Wallabout St 11206 718-254-8006

Bnos Yaakov Educational Center 600/1-12
62 Harrison Ave 11211 718-387-7905

Bnos Yaakov Educational Kindervelt 50/PK-PK
274 Keap St 11211 718-387-6880

Bnos Yaakov of Boro Park 900/PK-12
1402 40th St 11218 718-851-0316

Bnos Yisroel S 300/K-8
1629 E 15th St 11229 718-339-4229
Rabbi Boruch Barnetsky, hdmstr. Fax 645-3175

Bnos Yisroel Viznitz S 600/PK-12
12 Franklin Ave 11211 718-330-0222

Bnos Zion of Bobov PK-8
4024 New Utrecht Ave 11219 718-438-0060

Bnos Zion of Bobov 1,400/PK-12
5000 14th Ave 11219 718-438-3080

Bobover Yeshiva Bnei Zion 1,200/K-8
4206 15th Ave 11219 718-851-4000

Bobover Yeshiva Bnei Zion S 50/6-8
1533 48th St 11219 718-435-8033

Brooklyn Amity S 200/K-12
1501 Hendrickson St 11234 718-891-6100
Fax 891-6841

Brooklyn Friends S 600/PK-12
375 Pearl St 11201 718-852-1029
Michael Nill, hdmstr. Fax 643-4868

Brooklyn Heights Montessori S 200/PK-8
185 Court St 11201 718-858-5100
Dane Peters, hdmstr. Fax 858-0500
Brooklyn Jesuit Prep S 200/5-8
560 Sterling Pl 11238 718-638-5884
Emily Seelaus, prin. Fax 228-6324
Brooklyn S 50/PK-3
126 Saint Felix St 11217 718-783-3270
Brooklyn SDA S 100/PK-8
1260 Ocean Ave 11230 718-859-1313
Laura Mayne, prin. Fax 859-8105
Brooklyn Temple S 100/PK-8
3 Lewis Ave 11206 718-574-0907
Cheder S 400/PK-8
129 Elmwood Ave 11230 718-252-6333
Christian Heritage Academy 300/PK-12
1100 E 42nd St 11210 718-377-9406
Rev. Albert Delmadge, hdmstr. Fax 338-9870
Churn Christian Academy 100/PK-8
1052 Greene Ave 11221 718-919-6887
CYCLE Education Center 100/PK-5
2412 Church Ave 11226 718-462-2222
East Midwood Hebrew Day S 100/PK-8
1256 E 21st St 11210 718-253-1555
Alese Gingold, hdmstr. Fax 338-3934
Ebenezer Prep S 300/PK-8
5464 Kings Hwy 11203 718-629-4231
Epiphany Lutheran S 300/PK-8
721 Lincoln Pl 11216 718-773-7200
Robert Gahagen, hdmstr. Fax 773-1244
Ericson S 200/PK-8
1037 72nd St 11228 718-748-9023
Christine Hauge, prin. Fax 748-0473
Excelsior S 200/K-8
418 E 45th St 11203 718-693-5500
Fantis Parochial S 100/PK-8
195 State St 11201 718-624-0501
Dr. Alice Farkouh, prin. Fax 624-6868
Flatbush Academy 200/PK-8
2520 Church Ave 11226 718-282-1710
Vincent Tannacore, prin. Fax 287-6446
Flatbush SDA S 200/PK-8
5810 Snyder Ave 11203 718-385-7800
Followers of Jesus S 50/1-12
3065 Atlantic Ave 11208 718-235-5493
James Gochnauer, prin. Fax 484-1477
Gan Yisroel S 200/PK-K
3909 15th Ave 11218 718-853-9853
Gan Yisroel S PK-5
13 Church Ave 11218 718-435-0101
Brocha Retek, prin. Fax 853-0902
Gan Yisroel S 100/1-5
1581 52nd St 11219 718-436-9130
Good Shepherd S 400/PK-8
1943 Brown St 11229 718-339-2745
Anthony Paparelli, prin. Fax 645-4513
Grayson Christian Academy 200/PK-6
1237 Eastern Pkwy 11213 718-774-4924
Great Oak S 100/K-8
4718 Farragut Rd 11203 718-346-4934
Jasmin Hoyt, prin. Fax 346-0339
Hanson Place SDA S 200/PK-8
38 Lafayette Ave 11217 718-625-3030
Raymond Dixon, prin. Fax 625-1727
Hebron SDA Bilingual Union S 200/PK-8
920 Park Pl 11213 718-778-5124
Lude Lamour-Michel, prin. Fax 493-6303
Holy Name of Jesus S 200/PK-8
241 Prospect Park W 11215 718-768-7629
Joan Caccamo, prin. Fax 768-3007
Immaculate Heart of Mary S 200/PK-8
3002 Fort Hamilton Pkwy 11218 718-438-7373
Maureen Rooney, prin. Fax 853-5994
Kaloidis Parochial S 200/PK-8
8502 Ridge Blvd 11209 718-836-8096
Lev Bais Yaakov S 300/K-8
2710 Avenue X 11235 718-332-6000
Lubavitcher S Chabad 200/PK-12
841 Ocean Pkwy 11230 718-859-7600
Lubavitcher Yeshiva S 400/K-8
570 Crown St 11213 718-774-4131
Luria Academy of Brooklyn 50/PK-8
535 Dean St Ste 12 11217 718-398-3290
Dina Lipkind, prin.
Lutheran S of Bay Ridge 200/PK-8
440 Ovington Ave 11209 718-748-9502
Lorraine Tuccillo, prin. Fax 748-0818
Madrasa Al Islamiya S 200/PK-8
5224 3rd Ave 11220 718-567-3334
Belquis Defendini, coord. Fax 567-7383
Magen David Yeshivah 1,900/PK-8
2130 McDonald Ave 11223 718-236-5905
Fax 954-3315
Mary Queen of Heaven S 300/PK-8
1326 E 57th St 11234 718-763-2360
Sr. Mary Murphy, prin. Fax 763-7540
Masores Bais Yaakov S 700/PK-12
1395 Ocean Ave 11230 718-692-2424
Me'orot Beit Yaakov S 200/PK-10
1123 Avenue N 11230 718-627-8758
Midwood Academy 200/K-8
1340 E 29th St 11210 718-377-1800
Elena Heimbach, prin. Fax 377-6374
Mikdash Melech S 100/PK-4
1326 Ocean Pkwy 11230 718-627-0687
Mirrer Yeshiva Educational Institute 500/PK-8
1791 Ocean Pkwy 11223 718-375-4321
Maita Rosenblum, admin. Fax 375-6501
Mosdos Bnos Frima 300/PK-10
1377 42nd St 11219 718-972-7666
Mosdos Chasidei Square 300/K-12
1373 43rd St 11219 718-436-2550
Most Precious Blood S 200/K-8
133 27th Ave 11214 718-373-7343
Sr. Elenora Athonappa, prin. Fax 373-5887
Mt. Moriah Christian Academy 100/PK-6
1149 Eastern Pkwy 11213 718-953-4364
Dr. Jerry West, prin. Fax 953-4527

Murray Christian Academy 100/PK-8
760 Dekalb Ave 11216 718-384-1577
Alfonzo Forrest, admin. Fax 384-3379
Nefesh Academy 200/PK-12
1750 E 18th St 11229 718-627-4463
Sandra Newhouse, prin. Fax 645-8755
Nesivos Bais Yaakov 100/PK-4
1021 45th St 11219 718-972-0804
New Grace Education Center 300/PK-8
650 Livonia Ave 11207 718-498-7175
Fax 498-1656
New Hope Christian Academy 200/PK-8
257 Bay Ridge Ave 11220 718-921-3737
New Vistas Academy 300/PK-12
3321 Glenwood Rd 11210 718-421-1786
Fax 421-1786
Northside Catholic Academy - Mt. Carmel 100/6-8
10 Withers St 11211 718-782-1110
Valerie Graziano, prin. Fax 782-1110
Northside Catholic Academy - St. Vincent 100/PK-5
180 N 7th St 11211 718-384-3496
Valerie Graziano, prin. Fax 384-6937
Of The Risen Christ Lutheran S 50/PK-5
250 Blake Ave 11212 718-498-3651
Nellie Hanley, admin. Fax 498-7786
Oholei Torah - Oholei Menachem 1,100/PK-8
667 Eastern Pkwy 11213 718-778-3340
Our Lady of Angels S 200/PK-8
337 74th St 11209 718-238-5045
Rosemarie McGoldrick, prin. Fax 748-9775
Our Lady of Grace S 300/PK-8
385 Avenue W 11223 718-375-2081
Joan McMaster, prin. Fax 376-7685
Our Lady of Guadalupe S 500/PK-8
1518 73rd St 11228 718-331-2070
Diana Meringolo, prin. Fax 236-5587
Our Lady of Perpetual Help S 300/PK-8
5902 6th Ave 11220 718-439-8067
Anne Stefano, prin. Fax 439-8081
Our Lady of Trust School at Holy Family 200/PK-8
9719 Flatlands Ave 11236 718-257-2954
Robert Hughes, prin. Fax 257-3043
Our Lady of Trust School at OLO Miracles 200/PK-8
744 E 87th St 11236 718-649-0271
Robert Hughes, prin. Fax 272-0442
Our Lady of Trust School at Saint Jude 300/PK-8
1696 Canarsie Rd 11236 718-241-6633
Robert Hughes, prin. Fax 531-9655
Packer Collegiate Institute 900/PK-12
170 Joralemon St 11201 718-250-0200
Dr. Bruce Dennis, hdmstr. Fax 875-1363
Phyl's Academy 400/PK-5
3520 Tilden Ave 11203 718-469-9400
Abenna Frempong-Boadu, prin. Fax 284-1438
Poly Prep Country Day S 200/PK-4
50 Prospect Park W 11215 718-768-1103
David Harman, hdmstr. Fax 768-1687
Prospect Park Yeshiva 500/1-8
1784 E 17th St 11229 718-376-4446
Prospect Park Yeshiva ECC 200/PK-K
1784 E 17th St 11229 718-376-5959
Queen of All Saints S 300/K-8
300 Vanderbilt Ave 11205 718-857-3114
Theresa Desposito, prin. Fax 857-0632
St. Agatha S 200/PK-8
736 48th St 11220 718-435-3137
Eilleen Bubbico, prin. Fax 437-7505
St. Ann's S 1,100/PK-12
129 Pierrepont St 11201 718-522-1660
Dr. Larry Weiss, hdmstr. Fax 522-2599
St. Anselm S 500/PK-8
365 83rd St 11209 718-745-7643
Linda Addonisio, prin. Fax 745-0086
St. Athanasius S 300/PK-8
6120 Bay Pkwy 11204 718-236-4791
Lorraine Garone-Tesoro, prin. Fax 621-1423
St. Bernadette S 400/PK-8
1313 83rd St 11228 718-236-1560
Sr. Joan DiRienzo, prin. Fax 236-3364
St. Bernard S 300/PK-8
2030 E 69th St 11234 718-241-6040
Kathleen Buscemi, prin. Fax 241-7258
St. Brigid S 200/PK-8
438 Grove St 11237 718-821-1477
Sheila Smith-Gonzalez, prin. Fax 821-1079
St. Catherine of Genoa S 300/PK-8
870 Albany Ave 11203 718-284-1050
Kathleen Trainor, prin. Fax 284-3461
St. Edmund S 300/PK-8
1902 Avenue T 11229 718-648-9229
Jean McEvoy, prin. Fax 743-6402
St. Elizabeth Seton S 200/PK-8
751 Knickerbocker Ave 11221 718-386-4050
Louise McNamara, prin. Fax 386-1565
St. Ephrem S 400/PK-8
7415 Fort Hamilton Pkwy 11228 718-833-1440
Anna Marie Bartone, prin. Fax 833-1440
St. Frances Cabrini 300/PK-8
181 Suydam St 11221 718-386-9277
Maria Crifasi, prin. Fax 386-9064
St. Francis of Assisi S 400/K-8
400 Lincoln Rd 11225 718-778-3700
Sr. Theresa Scanlon, prin. Fax 778-7877
St. Francis Xavier S 300/K-8
763 President St 11215 718-857-2559
Sr. Kathleen Sullivan, prin. Fax 857-5391
St. Gregory the Great S 300/PK-8
991 Saint Johns Pl 11213 718-774-3330
Rudolph Cyrus-Charles, prin. Fax 774-3332
St. Jerome S 300/PK-8
465 E 29th St 11226 718-462-0211
Marie Jean-Louis, prin. Fax 462-1828
St. John Evangelist Lutheran S 50/PK-8
195 Maujer St 11206 718-963-3074
Carolyn Hupe, prin. Fax 963-3074
St. John the Baptist S 300/K-8
82 Lewis Ave 11206 718-453-1000
Bruno Marchan, prin. Fax 453-1000

St. Mark S 300/PK-8
1346 President St 11213 718-756-6602
William Macatee Ed.D., prin. Fax 467-4655
St. Mark S 300/PK-8
2602 E 19th St 11235 718-332-9304
Carol Donnelly, prin. Fax 891-9677
St. Mary Mother of Jesus S / St. Frances 200/PK-8
8401 23rd Ave 11214 718-372-0025
Vincent Bellafiore Ed.D., prin. Fax 265-6498
St. Michael S 300/PK-8
237 Jerome St 11207 718-277-6766
Sr. Margaret Merritt, prin. Fax 348-0513
St. Nicholas S 200/PK-8
287 Powers St 11211 718-388-7992
Sr. Joan Losson, prin. Fax 388-7543
St. Patrick S 200/PK-8
401 97th St 11209 718-833-0124
Andrea D'Emic, prin. Fax 238-6480
St. Peter's Lutheran S 100/PK-1
105 Highland Pl 11208 718-647-1014
Fax 647-9260
St. Rita S 500/PK-8
260 Shepherd Ave 11208 718-647-6040
William Geasor, prin. Fax 647-5298
St. Saviour S 400/PK-8
701 8th Ave 11215 718-768-8000
James Flanagan, prin. Fax 768-4872
St. Stanislaus Kostka S 300/PK-8
10 Newell St 11222 718-383-1970
Sr. Dorothea Jurkowski, prin. Fax 383-1711
St. Sylvester S 300/PK-8
396 Grant Ave 11208 718-235-4729
Ana Maria Ricciardi, prin. Fax 235-6976
St. Therese of Lisieux S 300/PK-8
4410 Avenue D 11203 718-629-9330
Sr. Paulette Pollina, prin. Fax 629-6854
St. Vincent Ferrer S 300/PK-8
1603 Brooklyn Ave 11210 718-859-3505
Mary Agresto, prin. Fax 859-9545
Senesh Community S 100/K-8
342 Smith St 11231 718-858-8663
Nicole Nash, prin. Fax 858-7190
Shalsheles Bais Yaakov S 100/K-10
1681 42nd St 11204 718-436-1122
Shulamith S for Girls 200/1-5
1277 E 14th St 11230 718-338-4000
Shulamis Goldberg, prin. Fax 258-9626
SS. Joseph and Dominic Academy 200/PK-8
140 Montrose Ave 11206 718-384-1101
Evette Ngadi, prin. Fax 384-6567
Talmud Torah Bnei Zion D'Bobov PK-PK
1362 49th St 11219 718-851-3937
Talmud Torah Bnei Zion D'Bobov 1-9
1320 43rd St 11219 718-431-9595
Talmud Torah D'Rabinu Yoel S 1,100/K-6
5411 Fort Hamilton Pkwy 11219 718-854-2476
Talmud Torah Imrei Chaim 600/PK-12
1824 53rd St 11204 718-234-2000
Talmud Torah Tiferes Bunim Munkacs 100/PK-8
5202 13th Ave 11219 718-436-6868
Talmud Torah Toldos Yakov Yosef 200/K-8
105 Heyward St 11206 718-852-0502
Tomer Dvora S 700/1-8
4500 9th Ave 11220 718-853-9400
United Talmudical Academy 2,800/K-12
82 Lee Ave 11211 718-963-9260
United Talmudical Academy 50/PK-1
82 Lee Ave 11211 718-963-9284
United Talmudical Academy 50/1-5
82 Lee Ave 11211 718-963-9560
United Talmudical Academy 1,200/PK-6
5411 Fort Hamilton Pkwy 11219 718-438-7822
Visitation Academy 200/PK-8
8902 Ridge Blvd 11209 718-680-9452
Arlene Figaro, prin. Fax 680-4441
Williston Academy 100/PK-5
1 Jefferson St 11206 718-398-0304
Windmill Montessori S 100/PK-8
1317 Avenue T 11229 718-375-4277
Liza Herzberg, prin. Fax 375-6701
Yeshiva Ahaba Ve Ahava 100/PK-8
2001 E 7th St 11223 718-376-3140
Rabbi Jacob Israel, prin. Fax 376-6097
Yeshiva Ahavas Torah 200/K-8
2961 Nostrand Ave 11229 718-339-9656
Yeshiva Ahavas Yisroel 600/K-12
2 Lee Ave 11211 718-388-0848
Yeshiva & Mesivta of Brooklyn 200/PK-8
1200 Ocean Pkwy 11230 718-252-9500
Yeshiva & Mesivta Torah Temimah 700/PK-12
555 Ocean Pkwy 11218 718-853-8500
Yeshiva Ateres Yisroel 200/PK-8
8101 Avenue K 11236 718-763-6777
Rena Shalmone, prin. Fax 763-1798
Yeshiva Bais Yitzchok D'Spinka 500/PK-12
575 Bedford Ave 11211 718-387-4597
Yeshiva Beth Hillel D'Krasna 400/K-9
1364 42nd St 11219 718-438-3535
Yeshiva Beth Hillel of Williamsburg 300/K-9
35 Hewes St 11211 718-802-9567
Yeshiva Chasdei Torah 200/K-8
54 Avenue O 11204 718-677-1630
Yeshiva Chatzar Hakodesh Sanz 700/PK-9
4511 14th Ave 11219 718-436-1248
Yeshiva Darchai Menachem 50/4-9
823 Eastern Pkwy 11213 718-953-2919
Rabbi Chaim Perl, admin. Fax 666-2919
Yeshiva Derech HaTorah 300/PK-10
2810 Nostrand Ave 11229 718-258-4441
Yeshivah of Crown Heights 300/PK-8
6363 Avenue U 11234 718-444-5800
Shirley Rothberg, prin. Fax 444-5851
Yeshivah of Flatbush 1,300/PK-8
919 E 10th St 11230 718-377-4466
Fax 377-0135
Yeshivah Ohel Moshe 100/PK-8
7914 Bay Pkwy 11214 718-236-4003
Shifra Stone, prin. Fax 236-4923

Yeshiva Imrei Yoseph Spinka 200/K-8
PO Box 439 11219 718-851-1600
Yeshiva Kehilath Yaakov 700/PK-10
183 Wilson St Ste 136 11211 718-486-7934
Yeshiva Kehilath Yaakov 50/K-2
206 Wilson St 11211 718-486-8760
Yeshiva Ketana of Bensonhurst 200/PK-10
2025 67th St 11204 718-236-4100
Rabbi Osher Levovitz, admin. Fax 236-1909
Yeshiva Machzikei Hadas Belz 900/PK-12
1601 42nd St 11204 718-436-4445
Yeshiva Mesivta Arugath Habosem 400/K-12
40 Lynch St 11206 718-237-4500
Yeshiva Mesivta Karlin Stolin 500/PK-12
1818 54th St 11204 718-232-7800
Yeshiva Mesivta Rabbi Shlomo Kluger 300/K-12
1876 50th St 11204 718-236-1171
Yeshiva Mesivta Tiferes Yisroel S 700/K-12
1271 E 35th St 11210 718-258-9006
Yeshiva Mesivta Torah Vodaath 400/K-12
425 E 9th St 11218 718-941-8000
Chaim Schilit, prin. Fax 693-5282
Yeshiva of Brooklyn-Girls 700/PK-12
1470 Ocean Pkwy 11230 718-376-3775
Yeshiva of Kings Bay 300/PK-8
2611 Avenue Z 11235 718-646-8500
Yeshiva of Manhattan Beach 200/PK-8
60 W End Ave 11235 718-743-5511
Yeshiva Ohel Sarah PK-1
1968 Ocean Ave 11230 718-513-1931
Yeshiva Ohr Shraga Veretzky 300/PK-8
1102 Avenue L 11230 718-252-7777
Risa Glatzer, prin. Fax 252-7797
Yeshiva Rabbi Chaim Berlin 600/PK-8
1310 Avenue I 11230 718-377-5800
Yeshiva R'tzahd S 400/5-8
8700 Avenue K 11236 718-444-5996
Yeshiva Ruach Chaim 100/PK-8
2294 Nostrand Ave 11210 718-253-1611
Yeshivas Boyan Tiferes Mordechai Shlomo 400/PK-12
1205 44th St 11219 718-435-6060
Yeshiva Sharei Hayosher S 50/PK-PK
PO Box 190295 11219 718-376-4555
Yeshivat Ateret Torah 1,400/PK-12
901 Quentin Rd 11223 718-375-7100
Yeshiva Tiferes Elimelech 500/PK-8
1650 56th St 11204 718-438-1177
Yeshivat Ohel Torah 100/PK-8
1760 53rd St 11204 718-431-0915
Yeshivat Ohr Hatorah PK-1
2959 Avenue Y 11235 718-252-8308
Yeshiva Toras Emes Kamenitz 500/PK-12
1904 Avenue N 11230 718-375-0900
Yeshivat Shaare Torah Boys S 100/PK-12
1202 Avenue P 11229 718-645-1216
Yeshivat Shaare Torah Girls 200/1-8
222 Ocean Pkwy 11218 718-437-6120
Shelia Feinstein, prin. Fax 437-6119
Yeshiva Tzemach Tzadik Viznitz 200/PK-8
186 Ross St 11211 718-782-6383
Yeshiva Yagdil Torah 200/PK-8
5110 18th Ave 11204 718-871-9100
Yeshiva Yesode Hatorah 200/K-9
620 Bedford Ave 11211 718-802-1613
Rabbi Samuel Felberbaum, prin. Fax 852-4364
Yeshiva Yesode Hatorah Adas Yereim 300/PK-9
505 Bedford Ave 11211 718-302-7500
Yeshiva Yesode Hatorah Adas Yereim 300/PK-8
1350 50th St 11219 718-851-6462
Youngblood Academy 100/PK-8
818 Schenck Ave 11207 718-257-3900
Fax 272-1714

Brownville, Jefferson, Pop. 1,047
General Brown Central SD
Supt. — See Dexter
Brownville/Glen Park ES 500/K-6
PO Box 10 13615 315-788-5100
Joseph O'Donnell, prin. Fax 788-6976

Brushton, Franklin, Pop. 471
Brushton-Moira Central SD 800/K-12
758 County Route 7 12916 518-529-8948
Robin Jones, supt. Fax 529-6062
www.bmcsd.org
Brushton ES 400/K-6
758 County Route 7 12916 518-529-7324
Cynthia Lauzon, prin. Fax 529-6644

Buchanan, Westchester, Pop. 2,249
Hendrick Hudson Central SD
Supt. — See Montrose
Buchanan-Verplanck ES 300/K-5
160 Westchester Ave 10511 914-257-5400
Lynda Hall, prin. Fax 257-5401

Buffalo, Erie, Pop. 279,745
Buffalo CSD 33,800/PK-12
713 City Hall 14202 716-816-3500
James Williams Ed.D., supt. Fax 851-3535
www.buffaloschools.org/
Drew Science Magnet S 200/7-8
1 N Meadow Dr 14214 716-816-4440
Delcene West, prin. Fax 838-7422
Public MS 66 400/5-8
780 Parkside Ave 14216 716-816-3440
Sabatino Cimato, prin. Fax 838-7448
Public MS 79 700/5-8
225 Lawn Ave 14207 716-816-4040
Michael O'Brien, prin. Fax 871-6115
Public MS 97 400/5-8
1405 Sycamore St 14211 716-816-4460
Brigette Gillespie, prin. Fax 897-8162
Public S 3 700/PK-8
255 Porter Ave 14201 716-816-3120
Silvia Baines, prin. Fax 888-7004
Public S 6 700/PK-8
414 S Division St 14204 716-816-3767
Debra Sevillian-Poles, prin. Fax 851-3770
Public S 11 400/PK-4
100 Poplar Ave 14211 716-816-3140
Janet Barnes, prin. Fax 897-8005
Public S 17 600/PK-4
1045 W Delavan Ave 14209 716-816-3150
Debra Washington, prin. Fax 888-7023
Public S 18 300/PK-4
118 Hampshire St 14213 716-816-3160
Valarie Kent, prin. Fax 888-7036
Public S 19 500/PK-8
97 W Delavan Ave 14213 716-816-3180
Sixto Indalecio, prin. Fax 888-7042
Public S 27 500/PK-8
1515 S Park Ave 14220 716-816-4770
Margaret Boorady, prin. Fax 828-4947
Public S 30 PK-8
21 Lowell Pl 14213 716-816-3220
Fax 888-2032
Public S 31 700/PK-8
212 Stanton St 14212 716-816-3780
Fax 851-3787
Public S 32 500/PK-8
120 Minnesota Ave 14214 716-816-3410
Judith Fix, prin. Fax 888-7010
Public S 33 400/PK-8
157 Elk St 14210 716-816-4783
Kathleen Marion, prin. Fax 828-4786
Public S 36 300/PK-2
10 Days Park 14201 716-816-3210
Wanda Schoenfeld, prin. Fax 888-7048
Public S 37 700/PK-8
295 Carlton St 14204 716-816-3800
Deana Stevenson, prin. Fax 851-3796
Public S 39 800/PK-8
487 High St 14211 716-816-3240
Elzie Fisher, prin. Fax 888-7010
Public S 43 500/PK-8
156 Newburgh Ave 14211 716-816-3470
David Hills, prin. Fax 816-3850
Public S 45 900/PK-8
425 S Park Ave 14204 716-816-3760
Colleen Carota, prin. Fax 888-7074
Public S 53 500/PK-8
329 Roehrer Ave 14208 716-816-3330
Fax 888-7099
Public S 54 500/PK-4
2358 Main St 14214 716-816-3340
Elizabeth Martina, prin. Fax 838-7403
Public S 59 500/2-6
1 Martin Luther King Park 14211 716-816-3370
Delcene West, prin. Fax 897-8049
Public S 61 400/PK-4
453 Leroy Ave 14215 716-816-3400
Laura Harris, prin. Fax 838-7436
Public S 64 500/PK-4
874 Amherst St 14216 716-816-3420
Michael Gruber, prin. Fax 871-6021
Public S 65 400/PK-4
249 Skillen St 14207 716-816-3430
Cynthia Mathews, prin. Fax 871-6031
Public S 67 500/PK-8
911 Abbott Rd 14220 716-816-4922
Carmela Botticello, prin. Fax 828-4925
Public S 69 300/PK-8
1725 Clinton St 14206 716-816-4794
Elaine Vandi, prin. Fax 828-4947
Public S 72 600/PK-8
71 Lorraine Ave 14220 716-816-4809
David Mauricio, prin. Fax 828-4811
Public S 74 400/PK-8
126 Donaldson Rd 14208 716-816-3490
Tracie Lewis, prin. Fax 888-7109
Public S 76 400/3-8
370 Normal Ave 14213 716-816-3848
Donna Jackson, prin. Fax 851-3853
Public S 78 300/PK-6
345 Olympic Ave 14215 716-816-4020
Fax 838-7469
Public S 80 600/PK-8
600 Highgate Ave 14215 716-816-4050
Gayle Irving-White, prin. Fax 838-7475
Public S 81 700/PK-8
140 Tacoma Ave 14216 716-816-4060
Robert Clemens, prin. Fax 871-6041
Public S 82 500/PK-4
230 Easton Ave 14215 716-816-4070
Denise Segars-McPhatter, prin. Fax 897-8073
Public S 89 800/PK-8
106 Appenheimer Ave 14214 716-816-4110
Mary Jo Conrad, prin. Fax 897-8093
Public S 90 300/PK-1
50 A St 14211 716-816-4120
Jean Polino, prin. Fax 897-8105
Public S 91 700/PK-8
340 Fougeron St 14211 716-816-4140
Cassandra Harrington, prin. Fax 897-8117
Public S 93 1,100/PK-8
430 Southside Pkwy 14210 716-816-4818
Theresa Schuta, prin. Fax 828-4820
Public S 94 600/PK-8
489 Hertel Ave 14207 716-816-4150
Sharon Ruffin-Brown, prin. Fax 871-6071
Public S 95 900/PK-8
95 4th St 14202 716-816-3900
Linda Brancantella, prin. Fax 851-3861
Public S 96 800/PK-8
1300 Elmwood Ave 14222 716-878-6412
Nora Trincanati, prin. Fax 888-7129
Public S 99 800/PK-4
1095 Jefferson Ave 14208 716-816-4180
Dawn Dinatale, prin. Fax 888-2012

Cheektowaga Central SD
Supt. — See Cheektowaga
Pine Hill PS 400/PK-1
1635 E Delavan Ave 14215 716-686-3680
Alison Caputy, prin. Fax 892-0634

Cheektowago-Sloan UFD 1,600/PK-12
166 Halstead Ave 14212 716-891-6402
James Mazgajewski, supt. Fax 891-6435
www.sloanschools.org
Other Schools – See Cheektowaga, Sloan

Kenmore-Tonawanda UFSD 8,400/K-12
1500 Colvin Blvd 14223 716-874-8400
Mark Mondanaro, supt. Fax 874-8624
www.kenton.k12.ny.us/
Franklin ES 500/K-5
500 Parkhurst Blvd 14223 716-874-8415
Pat Kosis, prin. Fax 874-8520
Franklin MS 600/6-8
540 Parkhurst Blvd 14223 716-874-8404
Douglas Smith, prin. Fax 874-8480
Hoover ES 600/K-5
199 Thorncliff Rd 14223 716-874-8414
Frances Paskowitz, prin. Fax 874-8460
Hoover MS 700/6-8
249 Thorncliff Rd 14223 716-874-8405
Christian Cornwell, prin. Fax 874-8470
Jefferson ES 300/K-5
250 Athens Blvd 14223 716-874-8418
Karen Wegst, prin. Fax 874-8438
Lindbergh ES 500/K-5
184 Irving Ter 14223 716-874-8410
Michael Muscarella, prin. Fax 874-8570
Other Schools – See Kenmore, Tonawanda

Ambrose Catholic Academy 300/PK-8
260 Okell St 14220 716-824-6360
Laura Kazmierczak, prin. Fax 826-5899
Catholic Academy of West Buffalo 200/PK-8
1069 Delaware Ave 14209 716-885-6111
Sr. Gail Glenn, prin. Fax 885-6452
Catholic Central S - St. Augustine\Boys 100/5-8
21 Davidson Ave 14215 716-836-5188
Fr. James Joyce, dir. Fax 836-5189
Catholic Central S - St. Monica\Girls 100/5-8
1955 Genesee St 14211 716-852-6854
Fr. James Joyce, prin. Fax 852-8410
Elmwood Franklin S 400/PK-8
104 New Amsterdam Ave 14216 716-877-5035
Anthony Featherston, hdmstr. Fax 877-9680
Nardin Academy 300/1-8
135 Cleveland Ave 14222 716-881-6262
Margaret Ables, prin. Fax 881-4681
Nardin Montessori S 200/PK-3
700 W Ferry St 14222 716-881-6565
Kristin Whitlock, dir. Fax 886-5931
Nazareth Lutheran S 50/PK-8
265 Skillen St 14207 716-876-7709
Fax 876-7709
Notre Dame Academy 300/PK-8
1125 Abbott Rd 14220 716-824-0726
Kimberly Suminski, prin. Fax 825-7685
Our Lady of Black Rock S 100/K-8
16 Peter St 14207 716-873-7497
Julie Watroba, prin. Fax 447-9926
St. Joseph S - University Heights 200/PK-8
3275 Main St 14214 716-835-7395
Sr. Fredrica Polanski, prin. Fax 833-6550
St. Margaret S 200/PK-8
1395 Hertel Ave 14216 716-876-8885
Toni Marie DiLeo, prin. Fax 876-7553
St. Mark S 300/K-8
399 Woodward Ave 14214 716-836-1191
Sr. Jeanne Eberle, prin. Fax 836-0391
SS. Columba & Brigid Montessori S 100/PK-1
75 Hickory St 14204 716-842-6213
Sr. Diane Bernbeck, prin. Fax 842-1454
Torah Temimah S of Buffalo PK-3
500 Starin Ave 14216 716-862-8089
Trinity Catholic Academy 200/PK-8
16 Hayden St 14210 716-822-4546
Delores Oakes, prin. Fax 822-2576

Burnt Hills, Saratoga
Burnt Hills-Ballston Lake Central SD
Supt. — See Scotia
O'Rourke MS 900/6-8
173 Lake Hill Rd 12027 518-399-9141
Donald Germain, prin. Fax 384-2588

Burt, Niagara
Newfane Central SD
Supt. — See Newfane
Newfane ECC 200/PK-K
6048 Godfrey Rd 14028 716-778-6352
Peter Young, prin. Fax 778-6860

Cairo, Greene, Pop. 1,273
Cairo-Durham Central SD 1,700/K-12
PO Box 780 12413 518-622-8534
Sally Sharkey, supt. Fax 622-9566
www.cairodurham.org/content/
Cairo-Durham MS 400/6-8
PO Box 1139 12413 518-622-0490
Kerry Overbaugh, prin. Fax 622-0493
Cairo ES 500/K-5
PO Box 780 12413 518-622-3231
Scott Richards, prin. Fax 622-9060
Other Schools – See Durham

Calcium, Jefferson, Pop. 2,465
Indian River Central SD
Supt. — See Philadelphia
Calcium PS 300/K-3
25440 Indian River Dr 13616 315-629-1100
Wanda Reardon, prin. Fax 629-5254

Caledonia, Livingston, Pop. 2,223
Caledonia-Mumford Central SD 1,100/K-12
99 North St 14423 585-538-3400
David Dinolfo, supt. Fax 538-3450
www.cal-mum.org

Caledonia-Mumford ES 400/K-5
99 North St 14423 585-538-3481
James Wolinsky, prin. Fax 538-3460
Caledonia-Mumford MS 300/6-8
99 North St 14423 585-538-3482
Robert Molisani, prin. Fax 538-3430

Calverton, Suffolk, Pop. 4,759
Riverhead Central SD
Supt. — See Riverhead
Riley Avenue PS 600/K-4
374 Riley Ave 11933 631-369-6804
David Enos, prin. Fax 369-6807

Cambria Heights, See New York
NYC Department of Education
Supt. — See New York
Public S 147 800/PK-8
21801 116th Ave 11411 718-528-2420
Ann Cohen, prin. Fax 723-7819
Public S 176 600/PK-5
12045 235th St 11411 718-525-4057
Arlene Bartlett, prin. Fax 276-3458

Cambria Center for Gifted Children 300/PK-5
23310 Linden Blvd 11411 718-341-1991
Cheder at the Ohel 50/PK-8
22420 Francis Lewis Blvd 11411 718-528-8989
Sacred Heart S 300/PK-8
11550 221st St 11411 718-527-0123
Yvonne Russell-Smith, prin. Fax 527-1204
Word Christian Academy 100/K-8
23001 Linden Blvd 11411 718-276-0300
Bridget Fontanelle, prin. Fax 978-9673

Cambridge, Washington, Pop. 1,875
Cambridge Central SD 1,100/K-12
58 S Park St 12816 518-677-2653
Dan Severson, supt. Fax 677-3889
www.cambridgecsd.org
Cambridge ES 500/K-6
24 S Park St 12816 518-677-8527
Vincent Delucia, prin. Fax 677-3031

Camden, Oneida, Pop. 2,288
Camden Central SD 2,400/K-12
51 3rd St 13316 315-245-4075
Richard Keville, supt. Fax 245-1622
www.camdenschools.org/
Camden ES 400/K-5
1 Oswego St 13316 315-245-2616
N. Pulizzi, prin. Fax 245-4194
Camden MS 400/6-8
32 Union St 13316 315-245-0080
Mary Barker, prin. Fax 245-0083
Other Schools – See Blossvale, North Bay, Taberg

Cameron Mills, Steuben
Addison Central SD
Supt. — See Addison
Valley ES 100/PK-4
6786 County Route 119 14820 607-359-2261
Deborah Flint, prin. Fax 359-3443

Camillus, Onondaga, Pop. 1,211
West Genesee Central SD 5,100/K-12
300 Sanderson Dr 13031 315-487-4562
Christopher Brown, supt. Fax 487-2999
www.westgenesee.org
Camillus MS 600/6-8
5525 Ike Dixon Rd 13031 315-672-3159
Robert Honcharski, prin. Fax 672-3309
East Hill ES, 401 Blackmore Rd 13031 500/K-5
Donna Zeolla Ph.D., prin. 315-487-4648
Split Rock ES 500/K-5
4151 Split Rock Rd 13031 315-487-4656
Theresa Williams, prin. Fax 488-2250
Stonehedge ES - Blue 900/K-5
400 Sanderson Dr 13031 315-487-4633
Lori Keevil, prin. Fax 487-4599
Stonehedge ES - Gold K-5
400 Sanderson Dr 13031 315-487-4631
Beth Lozier, prin. Fax 487-4599
West Genesee MS 700/6-8
500 Sanderson Dr 13031 315-487-4615
Earl Sanderson, prin. Fax 487-4618
Other Schools – See Syracuse

Campbell, Steuben
Campbell-Savona Central SD 1,100/K-12
8455 County Route 125 14821 607-527-9800
Lynn Lyndes, supt. Fax 527-8363
www.campbellsavona.wnyric.org
Other Schools – See Savona

Canajoharie, Montgomery, Pop. 2,191
Canajoharie Central SD 1,100/PK-12
136 Scholastic Way 13317 518-673-6302
Richard Rose, supt. Fax 673-3177
www.canajoharieschools.org
Canajoharie MS 300/6-8
25 School District Rd 13317 518-673-6320
Thomas Sincavage, prin. Fax 673-5557
East Hill ES 500/PK-5
25 School District Rd 13317 518-673-6310
Virginia Nyahay, prin. Fax 673-3887

Canandaigua, Ontario, Pop. 11,391
Canandaigua CSD 4,000/K-12
143 N Pearl St 14424 585-396-3700
Donald Raw, supt. Fax 396-7306
www.canandaiguaschools.org/
Canandaigua ES 900/3-5
90 W Gibson St 14424 585-396-3900
Mark Lavner, prin. Fax 396-3909
Canandaigua MS 900/6-8
215 Granger St 14424 585-396-3850
Ralph Undercoffler, prin. Fax 396-3863
Canandaigua PS 800/K-2
96 W Gibson St 14424 585-396-3930
Jeff Linn, prin. Fax 396-3938

St. Mary S 200/PK-8
16 Gibson St 14424 585-394-4300
Ann Marie Deutsch, prin. Fax 394-3954

Canaseraga, Allegany, Pop. 574
Canaseraga Central SD 300/K-12
PO Box 230 14822 607-545-6421
Marie Blum, supt. Fax 545-6265
www.ccsdny.org/
Canaseraga S 300/K-12
PO Box 230 14822 607-545-6421
James Anderson, prin. Fax 545-6265

Canastota, Madison, Pop. 4,429
Canastota Central SD 1,600/K-12
120 Roberts St 13032 315-697-2025
Frederick Bragan, supt. Fax 697-6368
www.canastotacsd.org
Peterboro Street ES 200/K-1
220 N Peterboro St 13032 315-697-2027
Jennifer Carnahan, prin. Fax 697-6368
Roberts Street MS 400/4-6
120 Roberts St 13032 315-697-2029
Tracy Mosher, prin. Fax 697-6368
South Side ES 200/2-3
200 High St 13032 315-697-6372
Jennifer Carnahan, prin. Fax 697-6368

Candor, Tioga, Pop. 830
Candor Central SD 900/K-12
PO Box 145 13743 607-659-5010
Jeffrey Kisloski, supt. Fax 659-7112
candor.org
Candor ES 400/K-6
PO Box 145 13743 607-659-3935
Kim Nichols, prin. Fax 659-4688

Canisteo, Steuben, Pop. 2,281
Canisteo-Greenwood Central SD 800/PK-12
84 Greenwood St 14823 607-698-4225
Jeffrey Matteson, supt. Fax 698-2833
www.cg.wnyric.org
Canisteo-Greenwood ES 300/PK-4
120 Greenwood St 14823 607-698-4225
Colleen Brownell, prin. Fax 698-2345
Other Schools – See Greenwood

Canton, Saint Lawrence, Pop. 6,060
Canton Central SD 1,400/PK-12
99 State St 13617 315-386-8561
William Gregory, supt. Fax 386-1323
www.ccsdk12.org/
Banford ES 500/PK-3
99 State St 13617 315-386-8561
Richard Tomlinson, prin. Fax 386-1323
McKenney MS 500/4-8
99 State St 13617 315-386-8561
Jennifer Rurak, prin. Fax 386-1323

St. Mary S 100/PK-6
2 Powers St 13617 315-386-3572
Marianne Jadlos, prin. Fax 386-8870

Cape Vincent, Jefferson, Pop. 780
Thousand Islands Central SD
Supt. — See Clayton
Cape Vincent ES 100/K-5
PO Box 282 13618 315-686-5594
Tiffany Squires, prin. Fax 654-4599

Carle Place, Nassau, Pop. 5,107
Carle Place UFD 1,400/K-12
168 Cherry Ln 11514 516-622-6442
W. Michael Mahoney, supt. Fax 622-6447
www.cps.k12.ny.us
Cherry Lane ES 300/K-2
475 Roslyn Ave 11514 516-622-6400
Marilyn Manfredi, prin. Fax 622-6513
Rushmore Avenue S 400/3-6
251 Rushmore Ave 11514 516-622-6400
Susan Folkson, prin. Fax 622-6588

Carmel, Putnam, Pop. 4,800
Carmel Central SD
Supt. — See Patterson
Fischer MS 1,500/5-8
281 Fair St 10512 845-228-2300
William Manfredonia, prin. Fax 228-2304
Kent ES 600/K-4
1091 Route 52 10512 845-225-5029
Joseph Keenan, prin. Fax 225-1849
Kent PS 500/K-4
1065 Route 52 10512 845-225-5025
Joan Pinkerton, prin. Fax 228-4824

St. James the Apostle S 200/PK-8
12 Gleneida Ave 10512 845-225-9365
Valerie Crocco, prin. Fax 228-2859

Caroga Lake, Fulton
Wheelerville UFD 200/K-8
PO Box 756 12032 518-835-2171
David Carr, supt. Fax 835-3551
www.wufselementary.k12.ny.us/
Wheelerville S 200/K-8
PO Box 756 12032 518-835-2171
David Carr, prin. Fax 835-3551

Carthage, Jefferson, Pop. 3,790
Carthage Central SD 3,000/K-12
25059 County Route 197 13619 315-493-5000
Joseph Caranzaro, supt. Fax 493-5069
www.carthagecsd.org
Carthage ES 400/K-5
900 Beaver Ln 13619 315-493-1570
Jennifer Vail, prin. Fax 493-6028
Carthage MS 700/6-8
21986 Cole Rd 13619 315-493-5020
Andrea Miller, prin. Fax 493-5029
West Carthage ES 500/K-6
21568 Cole Rd 13619 315-493-2400
Judy Duppert, prin. Fax 493-6536
Other Schools – See Black River

Augustinian Academy 200/PK-8
317 West St 13619 315-493-1301
Sr. Annunciata Collins, prin. Fax 493-0632

Cassadaga, Chautauqua, Pop. 649
Cassadaga Valley Central SD
Supt. — See Sinclairville
Cassadaga ES 300/PK-5
175 Maple Ave 14718 716-595-3070
Roberta Traks, prin. Fax 595-2481

Castleton on Hudson, Rensselaer, Pop. 1,525
East Greenbush Central SD
Supt. — See East Greenbush
Green Meadow ES 400/K-5
234 Schuurman Rd 12033 518-477-6422
Mary Wagner, prin. Fax 479-7954

Schodack Central SD 1,100/K-12
1216 Maple Hill Rd 12033 518-732-2297
Douglas Hamlin, supt. Fax 732-7710
www.schodack.k12.ny.us/
Castleton ES 300/K-4
80 Scott Ave 12033 518-732-7755
Jason Chevrier, prin. Fax 732-0495
Maple Hill MS 400/5-8
1477 S Schodack Rd 12033 518-732-7736
Michael Bennett, prin. Fax 732-0493

Cato, Cayuga, Pop. 592
Cato-Meridian Central SD 1,100/PK-12
2851 State Route 370 13033 315-626-3439
Deborah Bobo, supt. Fax 626-2888
www.catomeridian.org/
Cato-Meridian ES 400/PK-4
2851 State Route 370 13033 315-626-3320
Robert Wren, prin. Fax 626-2293
Cato-Meridian MS 300/5-8
2851 State Route 370 13033 315-626-3319
Sean Gleason, prin. Fax 626-2888

Catskill, Greene, Pop. 4,367
Catskill Central SD 1,800/K-12
343 W Main St 12414 518-943-4696
Kathleen Farrell Ph.D., supt. Fax 943-7116
www.catskillcsd.org
Catskill ES 900/K-6
770 Embought Rd 12414 518-943-0574
Dawn Scannapieco, prin. Fax 943-5396
Catskill MS 300/7-8
345 W Main St 12414 518-943-5665
Marielena Davis, prin. Fax 943-3001

Cattaraugus, Cattaraugus, Pop. 1,029
Cattaraugus-Little Valley Central SD
Supt. — See Little Valley
Cattaraugus ES 300/PK-5
25 N Franklin St 14719 716-257-3436
June Karassik, prin. Fax 257-5237
Cattaraugus-Little Valley MS 300/6-8
25 N Franklin St 14719 716-257-3483
Anthony Giannicchi, prin. Fax 257-5108

Cayuga, Cayuga, Pop. 494
Union Springs Central SD
Supt. — See Union Springs
Cayuga ES 300/K-3
255 Wheat St 13034 315-889-4170
Sheila LaDouce, prin. Fax 889-4175

Cazenovia, Madison, Pop. 2,698
Cazenovia Central SD 1,800/K-12
31 Emory Ave 13035 315-655-1317
Robert Dubik, supt. Fax 655-1375
www.caz.cnyric.org
Burton Street ES 600/K-4
37 Burton St 13035 315-655-1325
Mary Ann Macintosh, prin. Fax 655-1353
Cazenovia MS 400/5-7
31 Emory Ave 13035 315-655-1324
Jean Regan, prin. Fax 655-1305

Cedarhurst, Nassau, Pop. 6,082
Lawrence UFD
Supt. — See Lawrence
Public S 5 300/1-5
305 Cedarhurst Ave 11516 516-295-6500
Melissa Krieger, prin. Fax 295-6509

Centereach, Suffolk, Pop. 27,400
Middle Country Central SD 10,700/PK-12
8 43rd St 11720 631-285-8005
Dr. Roberta Gerold, supt. Fax 738-2719
www.middlecountry.k12.ny.us/
Dawnwood MS 1,000/6-8
10 43rd St 11720 631-285-8200
Linda Peyser, prin. Fax 285-8201
Holbrook Road ES 400/K-5
170 Holbrook Rd 11720 631-285-8560
Dr. Craig Unkenholz, prin. Fax 285-8561
Jericho ES 500/1-5
34 N Coleman Rd 11720 631-285-8600
Claudine DiMuzio, prin. Fax 285-8601
North Coleman Road ES 400/1-5
197 N Coleman Rd 11720 631-285-8660
Michael Febbraro, prin. Fax 285-8661
Oxhead Road ES 400/1-5
144 Oxhead Rd 11720 631-285-8700
Corinne Seeh, prin. Fax 285-8701
Selden MS 1,100/6-8
22 Jefferson Ave 11720 631-285-8400
Barbara Phillipson, prin. Fax 285-8401

Unity Drive Pre-K/K Center 600/PK-K
11 Unity Dr 11720 631-285-8760
Dr. Alise Guarnaschelli, prin. Fax 285-8761
Other Schools – See Lake Grove, Selden

Our Savior New American S 300/PK-12
140 Mark Tree Rd 11720 631-588-2757
Dolores Reade, prin. Fax 588-2617

Center Moriches, Suffolk, Pop. 5,987
Center Moriches UFD 1,500/K-12
529 Main St 11934 631-878-0052
Dr. Donald James, supt. Fax 878-4326
www.cmschools.org
Center Moriches MS 300/6-8
311 Frowein Rd 11934 631-878-2519
Patricia Cunningham, prin. Fax 878-0362
Huey ES 700/K-5
511 Main St 11934 631-878-0052
Ricardo Soto, prin. Fax 878-0238

Burket Christian S 200/PK-12
34 Oak St 11934 631-878-1727
Dominick Scibetta, admin. Fax 878-8968
Our Lady Queen of Apostles S 200/PK-8
2 Saint Johns Pl 11934 631-878-1033
Sr. Helen Charlebois, prin. Fax 878-1059

Centerport, Suffolk, Pop. 5,333
Harborfields Central SD
Supt. — See Greenlawn
Washington Drive PS 800/K-2
95 Washington Dr 11721 631-754-5592
Maureen Kelly, prin. Fax 754-3346

Love of Learning Montessori S 100/PK-6
105 Prospect Rd 11721 631-754-4109
Sheldon Thompson, prin. Fax 754-4109

Central Islip, Suffolk, Pop. 33,400
Central Islip UFD 6,200/PK-12
50 Wheeler Rd 11722 631-348-5001
Dr. Craig Carr, supt. Fax 348-0366
www.centralislip.k12.ny.us
Central Islip ECC 600/PK-K
50 Wheeler Rd 11722 631-348-5139
Fax 348-5184
Cordello Avenue ES 400/1-4
51 Cordello Ave 11722 631-348-4191
Sharon Dungee, prin. Fax 348-7712
Mulligan IS 900/5-6
1 Broadway Ave 11722 631-348-5042
Brenda Jackson, prin. Fax 348-5164
Mulvey ES 500/1-4
44 E Cherry St 11722 631-348-5053
Catherine Vereline, prin. Fax 348-1532
O'Neill ES 400/1-4
545 Clayton St 11722 631-348-5061
Kristine LoCascio, prin. Fax 348-5162
Reed MS 1,000/7-8
200 Half Mile Rd 11722 631-348-5066
Christopher Brown, prin. Fax 348-5159
Other Schools – See Islandia

Our Lady of Providence S 300/PK-8
82 Carleton Ave 11722 631-234-6324
JoAnn DiNardo, prin. Fax 234-6360

Central Square, Oswego, Pop. 1,658
Central Square Central SD 4,800/K-12
642 S Main St 13036 315-668-4220
Carolyn Costello, supt. Fax 676-4437
www.centralsquareschools.org/
Central Square IS 400/3-5
68 School Dr Unit 1 13036 315-668-4229
Concetta Galvan, prin. Fax 668-4348
Central Square MS 1,200/6-8
248 US Route 11 13036 315-668-4216
Paul Schoeneck, prin. Fax 668-8410
Hastings-Mallory ES 300/K-5
93 Barker Rd 13036 315-668-4252
Larry Wink, prin. Fax 668-4299
Hawk PS 400/K-2
74 School Dr 13036 315-668-4310
Tiffany Squires, prin. Fax 668-4356
Other Schools – See Brewerton, Cleveland, Constantia

Central Valley, Orange, Pop. 1,929
Monroe-Woodbury Central SD 7,500/K-12
278 Route 32 10917 845-460-6200
Joseph DiLorenzo, supt. Fax 460-6080
www.mw.k12.ny.us
Central Valley ES 700/2-5
45 Route 32 10917 845-460-6700
Eric Hassler, prin. Fax 460-6047
Monroe-Woodbury MS 1,800/6-8
199 Dunderberg Rd 10917 845-460-6400
Elsie Rodriguez, prin. Fax 460-6044
Smith Clove ES 700/K-1
21 Smith Clove Rd 10917 845-460-6300
Debra Turnquist, prin. Fax 460-6043
Other Schools – See Harriman, Monroe

Champlain, Clinton, Pop. 1,159
Northeastern Clinton Central SD 1,600/K-12
103 State Route 276 12919 518-298-8242
Peter Turner, supt. Fax 298-4293
www.nccscougars.org/
Northeastern Clinton MS 400/6-8
103 State Route 276 12919 518-298-8681
Thomas Brandell, prin. Fax 298-4293
Other Schools – See Mooers, Rouses Point

St. Mary's Academy 100/PK-6
1129 State Route 9 12919 518-298-3372
Sr. Marie Codata Kelly, prin. Fax 298-3886

Chappaqua, Westchester, Pop. 6,400
Chappaqua Central SD 4,200/K-12
PO Box 21 10514 914-238-7200
David Fleishman, supt. Fax 238-7218
www.ccsd.ws
Bell MS 600/5-8
50 Senter St 10514 914-238-6170
Martin Fitzgerald, prin. Fax 238-2085
Grafflin ES 500/K-4
650 King St 10514 914-238-5560
Michael Kirsch, prin. Fax 238-3285
Roaring Brook ES 500/K-4
530 Quaker Rd 10514 914-238-6156
Eric Byrne, prin. Fax 238-4716
Seven Bridges MS 600/5-8
PO Box 22 10514 914-666-7330
Martha Zornow, prin. Fax 666-7306
Westorchard ES 500/K-4
25 Granite Rd 10514 914-238-6250
James Skoog, prin. Fax 238-6885

Chateaugay, Franklin, Pop. 786
Chateaugay Central SD 600/K-12
PO Box 904 12920 518-497-6420
Dale Breault, supt. Fax 497-3170
www.chateaugay.org/
Chateaugay ES 300/K-6
PO Box 904 12920 518-497-6290
Loretta Fowler, prin. Fax 497-3170

Chatham, Columbia, Pop. 1,761
Chatham Central SD 1,400/K-12
50 Woodbridge Ave 12037 518-392-1501
Lee Bordick, supt. Fax 392-2413
www.chathamcentralschools.com/
Chatham MS 500/5-8
50 Woodbridge Ave 12037 518-392-1560
Gordon Fitting, prin. Fax 392-1559
Dardess ES 400/K-4
50 Woodbridge Ave 12037 518-392-2255
Charlotte Frye, prin. Fax 392-2795

Chaumont, Jefferson, Pop. 606
Lyme Central SD 400/K-12
PO Box 219 13622 315-649-2417
Karen Donahue, supt. Fax 649-2663
www.lymecsd.org
Lyme Central S 400/K-12
PO Box 219 13622 315-649-2417
Patricia Gibbons, prin. Fax 649-2663

Chazy, Clinton
Chazy Central UFD 600/K-12
609 Miner Farm Rd 12921 518-846-7135
Kevin Mulligan, supt. Fax 846-8322
www.chazy.org
Chazy Central Rural ES 300/K-6
609 Miner Farm Rd 12921 518-846-7212
Thomas Tregan, prin. Fax 846-8515

Cheektowaga, Erie, Pop. 79,200
Cheektowaga Central SD 2,500/PK-12
3600 Union Rd 14225 716-686-3606
Delia Bonenberger, supt. Fax 681-5232
www.cheektowagacentral.org
Cheektowaga Central MS 500/6-8
3600 Union Rd 14225 716-686-3660
Brian Bridges, prin. Fax 686-3669
Union East ES 700/2-5
3550 Union Rd 14225 716-686-3620
Katherine Rudewicz, prin. Fax 686-3666
Other Schools – See Buffalo

Cheektowaga-Maryvale UFD 2,300/K-12
1050 Maryvale Dr 14225 716-631-7407
Robert Zimmerman, supt. Fax 635-4699
www.maryvale.wnyric.org
Maryvale IS 500/3-5
1050 Maryvale Dr 14225 716-631-7423
Michael Viscome, prin. Fax 631-4858
Maryvale MS 600/6-8
1050 Maryvale Dr 14225 716-631-7425
Jeffrey Barthelme, prin. Fax 631-7499
Maryvale PS 500/K-2
1 Nagel Dr 14225 716-685-5800
Deborah Ziolkowski, prin. Fax 651-0031

Cheektowago-Sloan UFD
Supt. — See Buffalo
Kennedy MS 400/6-8
305 Cayuga Creek Rd 14227 716-897-7300
David Peters, prin. Fax 891-6430
Roosevelt ES 400/PK-2
2495 William St 14206 716-891-6423
Thomas Slaiman, prin. Fax 891-6435

Cleveland Hill UFD 1,100/PK-12
105 Mapleview Rd 14225 716-836-7200
Gordon Salisbury, supt. Fax 836-0675
www.clevehill.wnyric.org/
Cleveland Hill ES 600/PK-5
105 Mapleview Rd 14225 716-836-7200
Patrick McCabe, prin. Fax 836-0675

Mary Queen of Angels S 300/PK-8
170 Rosewood Ter 14225 716-895-6280
Sr. Diane Szylkowski, prin. Fax 895-6359

Chemung, Chemung
Waverly Central SD
Supt. — See Waverly
Chemung ES 100/K-5
71 North St 14825 607-529-3221
Dave Mastrantuono, prin. Fax 565-4997

Cherry Valley, Otsego, Pop. 561
Cherry Valley-Springfield Central SD 600/PK-12
PO Box 485 13320 607-264-9332
Robert Miller, supt. Fax 264-9023
www.cvscs.org

Cherry Valley-Springfield ES 300/PK-6
PO Box 485 13320 607-264-3257
Barry Gould, prin. Fax 264-3458

Chester, Orange, Pop. 3,604
Chester UFD 1,000/K-12
64 Hambletonian Ave 10918 845-469-5052
Helen Livingston, supt. Fax 469-2377
chesterufsd.org
Chester ES 400/K-5
2 Herbert Dr 10918 845-469-2178
Cindy Walsh, prin. Fax 469-2794

Chestertown, Warren
North Warren Central SD 600/PK-12
6110 State Route 8 12817 518-494-3015
Joseph Murphy, supt. Fax 494-2929
www.northwarren.k12.ny.us
North Warren Central S 600/PK-12
6110 State Route 8 12817 518-494-3015
Theresa Andrew, prin. Fax 494-2929

Chestnut Ridge, Rockland, Pop. 7,843
East Ramapo Central SD
Supt. — See Spring Valley
Chestnut Ridge MS 500/7-8
892 Chestnut Ridge Rd 10977 845-577-6300
Maria Vergez, prin. Fax 426-1063
Eldorado IS 400/4-6
5 Eldorado Dr 10977 845-577-6150
Margo Spielberg, prin. Fax 426-0850
Fleetwood ES 500/K-3
22 Fleetwood Ave 10977 845-577-6170
Patricia Simmons, prin. Fax 426-1807

Green Meadow Waldorf S 400/PK-12
307 Hungry Hollow Rd 10977 845-356-2514
Kay Hoffman, admin. Fax 356-2921

Chittenango, Madison, Pop. 4,901
Chittenango Central SD 2,400/K-12
1732 Fyler Rd 13037 315-687-2669
Thomas Marzeski, supt. Fax 687-9830
www.chittenangoschools.org
Bolivar Road ES 400/3-5
6983 Bolivar Rd 13037 315-687-2684
Arnold Merola, prin. Fax 687-2683
Chittenango MS 600/6-8
1732 Fyler Rd 13037 315-687-2648
Linda LLewellyn, prin. Fax 687-5482
Lake Street ES 300/K-2
127 Lake St 13037 315-687-2660
Jason Clark, prin. Fax 687-7828
Other Schools – See Bridgeport

Churchville, Monroe, Pop. 1,901
Churchville-Chili Central SD 3,300/K-12
139 Fairbanks Rd 14428 585-293-1800
Dr. Pamela Kissel, supt. Fax 293-1013
www.cccsd.org
Churchville-Chili MS 600/5-8
139 Fairbanks Rd 14428 585-293-4541
Giulio Bosco, prin. Fax 293-4516
Churchville ES 400/K-4
36 W Buffalo St 14428 585-293-2022
David Johnson, prin. Fax 293-4504
Fairbanks Road ES 500/K-4
175 Fairbanks Rd 14428 585-293-4543
Todd Yunker, prin. Fax 293-4510
Other Schools – See Rochester

Cicero, Onondaga
North Syracuse Central SD
Supt. — See North Syracuse
Cicero ES 700/K-4
5979 State Route 31 13039 315-218-2500
Kathleen Wheeler, prin. Fax 218-2585
Gillette Road MS 1,300/5-7
6150 S Bay Rd 13039 315-218-3000
Audrey Gangloff, prin. Fax 218-3085
Lakeshore Road ES 600/K-4
7180 Lakeshore Rd 13039 315-218-2600
John Cole, prin. Fax 218-2685

Cincinnatus, Cortland
Cincinnatus Central SD 600/K-12
2809 Cincinnatus Rd 13040 607-863-4069
Steven Hubbard, supt. Fax 863-4109
www.cc.cnyric.org/
Cincinnatus ES 200/K-4
2809 Cincinnatus Rd 13040 607-863-3200
Mary Wright, prin. Fax 863-4559
Cincinnatus MS 200/5-8
2809 Cincinnatus Rd 13040 607-863-3200
Joseph Mack, prin. Fax 863-4559

Circleville, Orange, Pop. 1,350
Pine Bush Central SD
Supt. — See Pine Bush
Circleville ES 600/K-5
PO Box 43 10919 845-744-2031
Ellen Helt, prin. Fax 361-2136
Circleville MS 600/6-8
PO Box 143 10919 845-744-2031
Ralph LaRocca, prin. Fax 361-3811
Pakanasink ES 500/K-5
PO Box 148 10919 845-744-2031
Donna Geidel, prin. Fax 361-3816

Clarence, Erie
Clarence Central SD 5,100/K-12
9625 Main St 14031 716-407-9100
Thomas Coseo Ed.D., supt. Fax 407-9126
www.clarenceschools.org
Clarence MS 1,200/6-8
10150 Greiner Rd 14031 716-407-9200
Jeff White, prin. Fax 407-9229
Ledgeview ES 600/K-5
5150 Old Goodrich Rd 14031 716-407-9275
Keith Kuwik, prin. Fax 407-9279

Other Schools – See Clarence Center, Williamsville

Clarence Center, Erie, Pop. 1,376
Clarence Central SD
Supt. — See Clarence
Clarence Center ES 600/K-5
9600 Clarence Center Rd 14032 716-407-9150
Neil Burns, prin. Fax 407-9157

Clarksville, Albany
Bethlehem Central SD
Supt. — See Delmar
Clarksville ES 300/K-5
58 Verda Ln 12041 518-768-2318
Dorothy McDonald, prin. Fax 475-0352

Clayton, Jefferson, Pop. 1,866
Thousand Islands Central SD 1,200/K-12
PO Box 1000 13624 315-686-5594
Dr. John Slattery, supt. Fax 686-5511
www.1000islandsschools.org
Guardino ES 400/K-5
600 High St 13624 315-686-5578
Joyce Clark, prin. Fax 686-2874
Thousand Islands MS 300/6-8
PO Box 1000 13624 315-686-5594
Debra Percy, prin. Fax 654-5038
Other Schools – See Cape Vincent

Cleveland, Oswego, Pop. 750
Central Square Central SD
Supt. — See Central Square
Cleveland ES 200/K-5
140 Bridge St 13042 315-668-4213
Michael Eiffe, prin. Fax 675-3018

Clifton Park, Saratoga
Shenendehowa Central SD 9,600/K-12
5 Chelsea Pl 12065 518-881-0600
L. Oliver Robinson, supt. Fax 371-9393
www.shenet.org/
Acadia MS 800/6-8
970 Route 146 Ste 54 12065 518-881-0450
Jonathan Burns, prin. Fax 371-3981
Arongen ES 800/K-5
489 Clifton Park Ctr Rd 12065 518-881-0510
Dr. Richard McDonald, prin. Fax 371-8177
Gowana MS 800/6-8
970 Route 146 Ste 55 12065 518-881-0460
Jill Bush, prin. Fax 383-1490
Karigon ES 600/K-5
970 Route 146 Ste 50 12065 518-881-0530
Gregory Wing, prin. Fax 383-1176
Koda MS 700/6-8
970 Route 146 Ste 59 12065 518-881-0470
Bruce Ballan, prin. Fax 383-1532
Okte ES 600/K-5
1581 Crescent Rd 12065 518-881-0540
Deborah Price, prin. Fax 383-1964
Orenda ES 600/K-5
970 Route 146 Ste 51 12065 518-881-0550
Dr. Ann Frantti, prin. Fax 383-1219
Shatekon ES, 35 Maxwell Dr 12065 K-5
Elizabeth Wood, prin. 518-881-0580
Skano ES 600/K-5
970 Route 146 Ste 52 12065 518-881-0560
Mary Fitzgerald, prin. Fax 383-1260
Tesago ES 700/K-5
970 Route 146 Ste 53 12065 518-881-0570
Gregory Pace, prin. Fax 383-1486
Other Schools – See Ballston Lake

Clifton Springs, Ontario, Pop. 2,195
Phelps-Clifton Springs Central SD 1,900/K-12
1490 State Route 488 14432 315-548-6420
Michael Ford, supt. Fax 548-6429
www.midlakes.org
Midlakes IS 400/3-5
1510 State Route 488 14432 315-548-6900
Janice Driscoll, prin. Fax 548-6909
Midlakes MS 500/6-8
1550 State Route 488 14432 315-548-6600
Jamie Farr, prin. Fax 548-6619
Midlakes PS 400/K-2
1500 State Route 488 14432 315-548-6700
Karen Cameron, prin. Fax 548-6709

Climax, Greene

Grapeville Christian S 100/K-12
2416 County Route 26 12042 518-966-5037
Nicole Orsino, prin. Fax 966-4265

Clinton, Oneida, Pop. 1,918
Clinton Central SD 1,500/K-12
75 Chenango Ave 13323 315-557-2253
Dr. Marie Wiles, supt. Fax 853-8727
www.ccs.edu
Clinton ES 500/K-5
75 Chenango Ave 13323 315-557-2255
Steven Marcus, prin. Fax 557-2331
Clinton MS 400/6-8
75 Chenango Ave 13323 315-557-2260
Matthew Reilly, prin. Fax 853-8727

Clinton Corners, Dutchess

Upton Lake Christian S 100/K-12
PO Box 63 12514 845-266-3497
Dietlind Hoiem, admin. Fax 266-3828

Clintonville, Clinton
Au Sable Valley Central SD 1,300/K-12
1273 Route 9N 12924 518-834-2845
Paul Savage, supt. Fax 834-2843
www.avcs.org
Au Sable Valley MS 300/7-8
1490 Route 9N 12924 518-834-2800
Philip Mero, prin. Fax 834-2847
Other Schools – See Au Sable Forks, Keeseville

Clyde, Wayne, Pop. 2,181
Clyde-Savannah Central SD 1,000/K-12
215 Glasgow St 14433 315-902-3000
Marilyn Barr, supt. Fax 923-2560
www.clydesavannah.org/
Clyde ES 300/K-4
212 E Dezeng St 14433 315-902-3100
William Schmidt, prin. Fax 923-2560
Other Schools – See Savannah

Clymer, Chautauqua
Clymer Central SD 400/K-12
8672 E Main St 14724 716-355-4444
Scott Smith, supt. Fax 355-2200
www.clymer.wnyric.org/
Clymer Central S 400/K-12
8672 E Main St 14724 716-355-4444
Edward Bailey, prin. Fax 355-4467

Cobleskill, Schoharie, Pop. 4,706
Cobleskill-Richmondville Central SD 2,000/K-12
155 Washington Ave 12043 518-234-4032
Lynn Macan, supt. Fax 234-7721
www.crcs.k12.ny.us/
Golding IS 200/4-5
177 Golding Dr 12043 518-234-3533
Bonnie Tryon, prin. Fax 234-1018
Golding MS 500/6-8
193 Golding Dr 12043 518-234-8368
Scott McDonald, prin. Fax 234-1018
Ryder ES 300/K-3
143 Golding Dr 12043 518-234-2585
Jean Schultz, prin. Fax 234-1018
Other Schools – See Richmondville

Coeymans, Albany
Ravena-Coeymans-Selkirk Central SD
Supt. — See Selkirk
Coeymans ES 500/K-5
66 Church St 12045 518-756-5200
Elizabeth Smith, prin. Fax 756-9162

Cohocton, Steuben, Pop. 833
Wayland-Cohocton Central SD
Supt. — See Wayland
Cohocton ES 200/PK-4
30 Park Ave 14826 585-384-5234
Cindy Flowers, prin. Fax 384-5677

Cohoes, Albany, Pop. 15,085
Cohoes CSD 2,100/K-12
7 Bevan St 12047 518-237-0100
Robert Libby, supt. Fax 237-2912
www.cohoes.org/
Cohoes MS 500/6-8
7 Bevan St 12047 518-237-4131
Mark Perry, prin. Fax 237-2253
Harmony Hill ES 400/K-5
120 Madelon K Hickey Way 12047 518-233-1900
Kitty Summers, prin. Fax 237-1964
Lansing ES 400/K-5
26 James St 12047 518-237-5044
Clifford Bird, prin. Fax 237-1879
Van Schaick Island ES 100/K-5
150 Continental Ave 12047 518-237-2828
Jacqueline DeChiaro, prin. Fax 237-3597

North Colonie Central SD
Supt. — See Latham
Boght Hills ES 500/K-6
38 Dunsbach Ferry Rd 12047 518-785-0222
Kimberly Greiner, prin. Fax 785-8801

Colden, Erie
Springville-Griffith Inst. Central SD
Supt. — See Springville
Colden ES 200/K-5
8263 Boston Colden Rd 14033 716-941-5218
Fax 941-9252

Cold Spring, Putnam, Pop. 2,009
Haldane Central SD 700/K-12
15 Craigside Dr 10516 845-265-9254
Dr. Mark Villanti, supt. Fax 265-9213
www.haldaneschool.org/
Haldane S 400/K-8
15 Craigside Dr 10516 845-265-9254
Maggie Davis, prin. Fax 265-2674

Cold Spring Harbor, Suffolk, Pop. 4,789
Cold Spring Harbor Central SD 2,100/K-12
75 Goose Hill Rd 11724 631-367-8800
Judith Wilansky Ed.D., supt. Fax 367-3108
www.csh.k12.ny.us
Goose Hill PS 300/K-1
75 Goose Hill Rd 11724 631-367-5941
Lydia Bellino, prin. Fax 367-2157
Other Schools – See Huntington, Syosset

College Point, See New York
NYC Department of Education
Supt. — See New York
Public S 29 500/PK-5
12510 23rd Ave 11356 718-886-5111
Jamie Adams, prin. Fax 461-6812
Public S 129 800/PK-5
12802 7th Ave 11356 718-353-3150
Marilyn Alesi, prin. Fax 321-2476

St. Fidelis S 200/PK-8
12406 14th Ave 11356 718-539-2628
Br. Robert Russo, prin. Fax 888-1524
St. John Lutheran S 50/PK-8
12307 22nd Ave 11356 718-463-4790
Fax 463-4795

Colonie, Albany, Pop. 8,236

Our Savior's Lutheran S 200/PK-8
63 Mountain View Ave 12205 518-459-2273
Cheryl Pangburn, prin. Fax 459-1330

Colton, Saint Lawrence
Colton-Pierrepont Central SD 400/PK-12
4921 State Highway 56 13625 315-262-2100
Martin Bregg, supt. Fax 262-2644
www.cpcs.k12.ny.us
Colton-Pierrepont ES 200/PK-6
4921 State Highway 56 13625 315-262-2100
Julie Welch, prin. Fax 262-2644

Commack, Suffolk, Pop. 36,400
Commack UFD
Supt. — See East Northport
Burr IS, 235 Burr Rd 11725 1,000/3-5
Charles Heppeler, prin. 631-858-3636
Commack MS 1,800/6-8
700 Vanderbilt Pkwy 11725 631-858-3500
Pamela Travis-Moore, prin.
Indian Hollow ES 400/K-2
151 Kings Park Rd 11725 631-858-3590
Judy Pace, prin.
Mandracchia/Sawmill IS 800/3-5
103 New Hwy 11725 631-858-3650
Michelle Tancredi, prin.
North Ridge ES 500/K-2
300 Townline Rd 11725 631-912-2190
Katherine Rihm, prin.
Wood Park ES, 35 New Hwy 11725 400/K-2
Michelle Collison, prin. 631-858-3680

Holy Family S 300/PK-8
PO Box 729 11725 631-543-0202
Constance Jenkins, prin. Fax 543-2818

Congers, Rockland, Pop. 8,003
Clarkstown Central SD
Supt. — See New City
Congers ES 300/K-5
9 Lake Rd 10920 845-268-5010
Martha Ryan, prin. Fax 268-0140
Lakewood ES 400/K-5
77 Lakeland Ave 10920 845-268-5760
Dr. Joan Taylor, prin. Fax 268-1902

Rockland Country Day S 200/PK-12
34 Kings Hwy 10920 845-268-6802
Dr. Lee Hancock, hdmstr. Fax 268-4644

Conklin, Broome
Susquehanna Valley Central SD 2,000/K-12
PO Box 200 13748 607-775-0170
Gerardo Tagliaferri, supt. Fax 775-4575
www.svsabers.org/
Donnelly ES 400/K-5
1168 Conklin Rd 13748 607-775-0176
Margo Undercoffer, prin. Fax 775-9313
Stank MS 500/6-8
1040 Conklin Rd 13748 607-775-0303
Roland Doig, prin. Fax 775-9142
Other Schools – See Binghamton

Constableville, Lewis, Pop. 285
South Lewis Central SD
Supt. — See Turin
Constableville ES 100/K-5
PO Box 356 13325 315-348-2600
Kristy McGrath, prin. Fax 348-2510

Constantia, Oswego, Pop. 1,140
Central Square Central SD
Supt. — See Central Square
Cole ES 300/K-5
1683 State Route 49 13044 315-668-4207
Brent Bowden, prin. Fax 623-7209

Cooperstown, Otsego, Pop. 1,938
Cooperstown Central SD 1,000/K-12
39 Linden Ave 13326 607-547-5364
Mary Jo McPhail, supt. Fax 547-5100
www.cooperstowncs.org/
Cooperstown ES 400/K-5
21 Walnut St 13326 607-547-9976
Teresa Gorman, prin. Fax 547-4427
Cooperstown MS 300/6-8
39 Linden Ave 13326 607-547-5512
Michael Cring, prin. Fax 547-5100

Copenhagen, Lewis, Pop. 812
Copenhagen Central SD 600/K-12
PO Box 30 13626 315-688-4411
Mary-Margaret Zehr, supt. Fax 688-2001
www.ccsknights.org/
Copenhagen Central S 600/K-12
PO Box 30 13626 315-688-4411
Nadine O'Shaughnessy, prin. Fax 688-2001

Copiague, Suffolk, Pop. 20,769
Copiague UFD 4,400/K-12
2650 Great Neck Rd 11726 631-842-4015
Charles Leunig, supt. Fax 841-4614
www.copiague.k12.ny.us/
Copiague MS 1,000/6-8
2650 Great Neck Rd 11726 631-842-4011
Andrew Lagnado, prin. Fax 841-4630
Deauville Gardens ES 800/K-5
100 Deauville Blvd 11726 631-842-4012
Robert Donnellan, prin. Fax 841-4656
Great Neck Road ES 400/K-5
1400 Great Neck Rd 11726 631-842-4013
Joseph Agosta, prin. Fax 842-4676
Wiley ES 700/K-5
365 Scudder Ave 11726 631-842-4014
Michael Kelly, prin. Fax 841-4670

Coram, Suffolk, Pop. 36,000
Longwood Central SD
Supt. — See Middle Island
Coram ES 1,000/K-4
61 Mount Sinai Coram Rd 11727 631-698-0077
Roni Robbins, prin. Fax 698-0807

Corfu, Genesee, Pop. 763
Pembroke Central SD 1,300/PK-12
PO Box 308 14036 585-599-4525
Gary Mix, supt. Fax 762-9993
www.pembroke.k12.ny.us
Pembroke IS 300/3-6
58 Alleghany Rd 14036 585-599-4531
Matthew Calderon, prin. Fax 762-9993
Other Schools – See East Pembroke

Corinth, Saratoga, Pop. 2,472
Corinth Central SD 1,300/K-12
105 Oak St 12822 518-654-2601
Dr. Daniel Starr, supt. Fax 654-6266
www.corinthcsd.com/
Corinth ES 500/K-4
105 Oak St 12822 518-654-2960
Susan Kazilas, prin. Fax 654-6235
Corinth MS 400/5-8
105 Oak St 12822 518-654-9005
Gregory Kreis, prin. Fax 654-6266

Corning, Steuben, Pop. 10,551
Corning CSD
Supt. — See Painted Post
Carder ES 500/K-5
289 State St 14830 607-962-2454
Dan Davis, prin. Fax 654-2829
Corning Free Academy MS 600/6-8
11 W 3rd St 14830 607-936-3788
Richard Kimble, prin. Fax 654-2809
Gregg ES 200/K-5
164 Flint Ave 14830 607-962-1514
Ann Collins, prin. Fax 654-2815
Northside Blodgett MS 600/6-8
143 Princeton Ave 14830 607-936-3791
Jeffrey Marchionda, prin. Fax 654-2798
Phillips ES 200/K-5
120 Corning Blvd 14830 607-962-4631
Siobhan Alexander, prin. Fax 654-2838
Severn ES 400/K-5
36 McMahon Ave 14830 607-962-6844
John Whaley, prin. Fax 654-2869
Winfield Street ES 200/K-5
193 Winfield St 14830 607-962-6706
Thomas Tunney, prin. Fax 654-2848

All Saints Academy 200/PK-8
158 State St 14830 607-936-9234
Rose Ann Ewanyk, prin. Fax 936-1797
Corning Christian Academy 200/PK-12
11 Aisne St 14830 607-962-4220
Ross Perry, admin. Fax 962-4410

Cornwall, Orange, Pop. 11,270
Cornwall Central SD
Supt. — See Cornwall on Hudson
Cornwall Central MS 1,000/5-8
122 Main St 12518 845-534-8009
Diana Musich, prin. Fax 534-7809
Cornwall ES 500/K-4
99 Lee Rd 12518 845-534-8009
Donna Hannon, prin. Fax 534-0569
Willow Avenue ES 300/K-4
67 Willow Ave 12518 845-534-8009
Greg Schmalz, prin. Fax 534-7708

Cornwall on Hudson, Orange, Pop. 3,110
Cornwall Central SD 3,200/K-12
24 Idlewild Ave 12520 845-534-8009
Timothy Rehm, supt. Fax 534-4231
www.cornwallschools.com/
Cornwall on Hudson ES 200/K-4
234 Hudson St 12520 845-534-8009
Kenneth Schmidt, prin. Fax 534-7599
Other Schools – See Cornwall

St. Thomas of Canterbury S 200/K-8
336 Hudson St 12520 845-534-2019
Agnus Malekaas, prin. Fax 534-2483

Corona, See New York
NYC Department of Education
Supt. — See New York
IS 61 1,900/6-8
9850 50th Ave 11368 718-760-3233
Joseph Lisa, prin. Fax 760-5220
Pioneer Academy 200/PK-5
4020 100th St 11368 718-779-5068
Cecilia Jackson, prin. Fax 779-5109
Public S 14 1,100/K-5
10701 Otis Ave 11368 718-699-6071
Dr. Rosemary Sklar, prin. Fax 699-3224
Public S 16 1,200/K-5
4115 104th St 11368 718-505-0140
Elaine Iodice, prin. Fax 505-0141
Public S 19 1,900/K-5
9802 Roosevelt Ave 11368 718-424-5859
Genie Calibar, prin. Fax 672-3136
Public S 28 400/PK-2
10910 47th Ave 11368 718-271-4971
Elizabeth Lutkowski, prin. Fax 271-2576
Public S 92 700/PK-5
9901 34th Ave 11368 718-533-1013
Pasquale Baratta, prin. Fax 533-1083
Public S 143 1,200/K-5
3474 113th St 11368 718-429-5700
Sheila Gorski, prin. Fax 478-8306

Mt. Olivet Christian S 50/PK-1
3327 97th St 11368 718-478-0780
Alice Williams, dir. Fax 478-6815
Our Lady of Sorrows S 300/PK-8
3534 105th St 11368 718-426-5517
Sr. Katherine Hanrahan, prin. Fax 651-5585
St. Leo S 400/PK-8
10419 49th Ave 11368 718-592-7050
Maureen Blaine, prin. Fax 592-0787

Cortland, Cortland, Pop. 18,522
Cortland CSD 2,800/K-12
1 Valley View Dr 13045 607-758-4100
Laurence Spring, supt. Fax 758-4128
www.cortlandschools.org
Barry ES, 20 Raymond Ave 13045 400/K-6
Lydia Rosero, prin. 607-758-4150
Parker ES, 89 Madison St 13045 300/K-6
Kevin Yard, prin. 607-758-4160
Randall ES 300/K-6
31 Randall St 13045 607-758-4170
Clifford Kostuk, prin. Fax 758-4179
Smith ES, 33 Wheeler Ave 13045 300/K-6
Angela Wanish, prin. 607-758-4180
Virgil ES, 1208 Church St 13045 100/K-6
Lynn New, prin. 607-758-4130

Cortland Christian Academy 100/PK-12
15 West Rd 13045 607-756-5838
Craig Miller, admin. Fax 756-7716
St. Mary's S 300/PK-6
61 N Main St 13045 607-756-5614
Susan McInvale, prin. Fax 756-9968

Cortlandt Manor, See Peekskill
Hendrick Hudson Central SD
Supt. — See Montrose
Blue Mountain MS 700/6-8
7 Furnace Woods Rd 10567 914-257-5700
John Owens, prin. Fax 257-5701
Furnace Woods ES 400/K-5
239 Watch Hill Rd 10567 914-257-5600
Dr. Helene Kane, prin. Fax 257-5601

St. Columbanus S 200/PK-8
122 Oregon Rd 10567 914-739-1200
Frank Disanza, prin. Fax 739-1109

Cottekill, Ulster
Rondout Valley Central SD
Supt. — See Accord
Rosendale ES 300/K-4
1915 Lucas Ave 12419 845-687-7607
Patricia Robbins, prin. Fax 687-9563

Coxsackie, Greene, Pop. 2,853
Coxsackie-Athens Central SD 1,600/K-12
24 Sunset Blvd 12051 518-731-1710
Dr. Earle Gregory, supt. Fax 731-1729
www.coxsackie-athens.org
Coxsackie-Athens MS 500/5-8
24 Sunset Blvd 12051 518-731-1850
Joseph Posillico, prin. Fax 731-1859
Coxsackie ES 300/K-4
24 Sunset Blvd 12051 518-731-1770
Noreen Carroll, prin. Fax 731-1785
Other Schools – See Athens

Craryville, Columbia
Taconic Hills Central SD 1,700/K-12
73 County Route 11A 12521 518-325-0300
Mark Sposato Ed.D., supt. Fax 325-3557
www.taconichills.k12.ny.us/
Taconic Hills ES 600/K-4
73 County Route 11A 12521 518-325-0370
John Gulisane, prin. Fax 325-9053
Taconic Hills MS 500/5-8
73 County Route 11A 12521 518-325-0420
Neil Howard, prin. Fax 325-9051

Crompond, Westchester
Lakeland Central SD
Supt. — See Shrub Oak
Lincoln-Titus ES 500/K-5
10 Lincoln Ave 10517 914-528-2519
Elizabeth McGowan, prin. Fax 528-1471

Cropseyville, Rensselaer
Berlin Central SD
Supt. — See Berlin
Grafton ES 100/K-3
13 Babcock Rd 12052 518-279-1771
Pat O'Grady, prin. Fax 279-0920

Cross River, Westchester
Katonah-Lewisboro UFD
Supt. — See South Salem
Jay MS 1,000/6-8
40 N Salem Rd 10518 914-763-7500
Rich Leprine, prin. Fax 763-7665

Croton Falls, Westchester

St. Joseph S 200/PK-8
PO Box 719 10519 914-277-3783
Hugh Keenan, prin. Fax 277-3238

Croton on Hudson, Westchester, Pop. 7,134
Croton-Harmon UFD 1,600/K-12
10 Gerstein St 10520 914-271-4793
Edward Fuhrman, supt. Fax 271-8685
www.croton-harmonschooldistrict.org
Tompkins ES 700/K-5
8 Gerstein St 10520 914-271-5184
Kelly Maloney, prin. Fax 271-5337
Van Cortlandt MS 400/6-8
3 Glen Pl 10520 914-271-2191
Dr. Barbara Ulm, prin. Fax 271-6618

Holy Name of Mary Montessori S K-8
110 Grand St 10520 914-271-5182
Jeanne Gagnon, dir. Fax 271-6841

Crown Point, Essex
Crown Point Central SD 300/K-12
PO Box 35 12928 518-597-4200
Shari Brannock, supt. Fax 597-4121
cpcsteam.org/
Crown Point Central S 300/K-12
PO Box 35 12928 518-597-3285
Agatha Mace, prin. Fax 597-4121

Cuba, Allegany, Pop. 1,586
Cuba-Rushford Central SD 1,000/K-12
5476 Route 305 14727 585-968-2650
Kevin Shanley, supt. Fax 968-2651
www.crcs.wnyric.org/
Cuba ES 300/K-5
15 Elm St 14727 585-968-1760
Kevin Erickson, prin. Fax 968-3181
Cuba-Rushford MS 200/6-8
5476 Route 305 14727 585-968-2650
Carlos Gildemeister, prin. Fax 968-2651
Other Schools – See Rushford

Cuddebackville, Orange
Port Jervis CSD
Supt. — See Port Jervis
Hamilton Bicentennial ES 600/K-6
929 US Route 209 12729 845-754-8314
Sharon Dickstein, prin. Fax 754-7355

Cutchogue, Suffolk, Pop. 2,627
Mattituck-Cutchogue UFD 1,500/1-12
385 Depot Ln 11935 631-298-4242
James McKenna, supt. Fax 298-8573
www.mufsd.com/cms/
Mattituck-Cutchogue ES 700/1-6
34900 Main Rd 11935 631-734-6049
Anne Smith, prin. Fax 734-4299

Our Lady of Mercy S 200/PK-6
PO Box 970 11935 631-734-5166
Lorraine Del Genio, prin. Fax 734-4266

Dalton, Livingston
Keshequa Central SD
Supt. — See Nunda
Keshequa ES 400/K-5
1716 Church St 14836 585-476-2234
Ami Hunt, prin. Fax 476-5606

Dannemora, Clinton, Pop. 4,108
Saranac Central SD 1,700/K-12
32 Emmons St 12929 518-565-5600
Kenneth Cringle, supt. Fax 565-5617
www.saranac.org
Other Schools – See Morrisonville, Saranac

Dansville, Livingston, Pop. 4,640
Dansville Central SD 1,600/K-12
284 Main St 14437 585-335-4000
Matthew McGarrity, supt. Fax 335-4002
www.dansvillecsd.org
Dansville MS 400/6-8
31 Clara Barton St 14437 585-335-4020
Amy Schiavi, prin. Fax 335-4021
Dansville PS 300/K-2
284 Main St 14437 585-335-4040
Christopher Lynch, prin. Fax 335-8181
Hyde ES 400/3-5
280 Main St 14437 585-335-4030
Jeremy Palotti, prin. Fax 335-4056

Davenport, Delaware
Charlotte Valley Central SD 400/K-12
15611 State Highway 23 13750 607-278-5511
Mark Dupra, supt. Fax 278-5900
www.charlottevalleycs.org
Charlotte Valley S 400/K-12
15611 State Highway 23 13750 607-278-5511
Edgar Whaley, prin. Fax 278-5900

Deerfield, Oneida
Whitesboro Central SD
Supt. — See Yorkville
Deerfield ES 400/K-5
115 Schoolhouse Rd 13502 315-266-3410
Kelli McGowan, prin. Fax 797-7145

Deer Park, Suffolk, Pop. 28,300
Deer Park UFD 4,500/PK-12
1881 Deer Park Ave 11729 631-274-4000
Elizabeth Marino, supt. Fax 242-6762
www.deerparkschools.org/
Adams ES 500/K-2
172 Old Country Rd 11729 631-274-4400
Kelly Diamond, prin. Fax 242-6762
Frost MS 1,000/6-8
450 Half Hollow Rd 11729 631-274-4200
Eliana Levey, prin. Fax 242-0035
Kennedy IS 1,000/3-5
101 Lake Ave 11729 631-274-4300
Susan Bonner, prin. Fax 242-8934
Lincoln S 200/PK-PK
300 Park Ave 11729 631-274-4350
Fax 242-6424
Moore ES 400/K-2
239 Central Ave 11729 631-274-4450
Alicia Konecny, prin. Fax 242-6762

SS. Cyril & Methodius S 300/PK-8
105 Half Hollow Rd 11729 631-667-6229
Dr. Victor Lana, prin. Fax 667-0093

De Kalb Junction, Saint Lawrence
Hermon-DeKalb Central SD 400/PK-12
709 E DeKalb Rd 13630 315-347-3442
Ann Adams, supt. Fax 347-3817
www.hdcsk12.org
Hermon-DeKalb Central S 400/PK-12
709 E DeKalb Rd 13630 315-347-3442
Mark White, prin. Fax 347-3817

Delanson, Schenectady, Pop. 404
Duanesburg Central SD 1,000/K-12
133 School Rd 12053 518-895-2279
Christine Crowley, supt. Fax 895-2626
www.duanesburg.org/

Duanesburg ES 400/K-5
165 Chadwick Rd 12053 518-895-2580
Erica Ryan, prin. Fax 895-2957

Delevan, Cattaraugus, Pop. 1,047
Yorkshire-Pioneer Central SD
Supt. — See Yorkshire
Delevan ES 400/K-4
PO Box 217 14042 585-492-9463
Jeannene Wagner, prin. Fax 492-9477

Delhi, Delaware, Pop. 2,720
Delhi Central SD 900/K-12
2 Sheldon Dr 13753 607-746-1300
John Mulholland, supt. Fax 746-6028
www.delhischools.org
Delhi ES 300/K-5
2 Sheldon Dr 13753 607-746-2105
Julie Maney, prin. Fax 746-6223
Delhi MS 200/6-8
2 Sheldon Dr 13753 607-746-1282
Judith Byam, prin. Fax 746-1210

Delmar, Albany, Pop. 8,360
Bethlehem Central SD 5,200/K-12
90 Adams Pl 12054 518-439-7098
Leslie Loomis, supt. Fax 475-0352
bcsd.k12.ny.us
Bethlehem Central MS 1,200/6-8
332 Kenwood Ave 12054 518-439-7460
Jody Monroe, prin. Fax 475-0092
Eagle ES, 27 Van Dyke Rd 12054 K-5
Dianna Reagan, prin. 518-694-8825
Elsmere ES 300/K-5
247 Delaware Ave 12054 518-439-4996
Katherine Kloss, prin. Fax 439-7546
Hamagrael ES 500/K-5
1 McGuffey Ln 12054 518-439-4905
Dave Ksanznak, prin. Fax 475-9659
Slingerland ES 700/K-5
25 Union Ave 12054 518-439-7681
Heidi Bonacquist, prin. Fax 475-1931
Other Schools – See Clarksville, Glenmont

St. Thomas the Apostle S 200/PK-8
42 Adams Pl 12054 518-439-5573
Thomas Kane, prin. Fax 439-0108

Depew, Erie, Pop. 15,798
Depew UFD 2,200/K-12
591 Terrace Blvd 14043 716-686-2253
Kimberly Mueller, supt. Fax 686-2269
www.depewschools.org/
Cayuga Heights ES 800/K-4
1780 Como Park Blvd 14043 716-686-2451
Robert Puchalski, prin. Fax 686-2459
Depew MS 700/5-8
5201 Transit Rd 14043 716-686-2440
Joseph D'Amato, prin. Fax 686-2410

Lancaster Central SD
Supt. — See Lancaster
Sciole ES 400/K-3
86 Alys Dr E 14043 716-686-3285
Margaret Hopkins, prin. Fax 686-3309

Our Lady of the Blessed Sacrament S 200/K-8
20 French Rd 14043 716-685-2544
Sr. Mary Krawczyk, prin. Fax 685-9103

Deposit, Delaware, Pop. 1,636
Deposit Central SD 700/K-12
171 2nd St 13754 607-467-5380
Bonnie Hauber, supt. Fax 467-5535
www.depositcsd.org/
Deposit ES 300/K-5
171 2nd St 13754 607-467-2198
Denise Cook, prin. Fax 467-4495
Deposit MS 100/6-8
171 2nd St 13754 607-467-2197
Barbara Phillips, prin. Fax 467-5504

Derby, Erie
Evans-Brant Central SD (Lake Shore)
Supt. — See Angola
Highland ES 400/K-5
6745 Erie Rd 14047 716-549-4397
Dawn Mirand, prin. Fax 947-9269

DeRuyter, Madison, Pop. 518
De Ruyter Central SD 300/PK-12
711 Railroad St 13052 315-852-3410
Charles Walters, supt. Fax 852-9600
www.deruytercentral.org/
De Ruyter Central S 300/PK-12
711 Railroad St 13052 315-852-3400
David Hubman, prin. Fax 852-9600

De Witt, Onondaga, Pop. 8,244
Jamesville-DeWitt Central SD 2,900/K-12
PO Box 606 13214 315-445-8304
Alice Kendrick, supt. Fax 445-8477
www.jamesvilledewitt.org
De Witt ES 300/K-4
201 Jamesville Rd 13214 315-445-8370
Erica Miller, prin. Fax 445-2274
Other Schools – See Jamesville

Holy Cross S 200/K-6
4112 E Genesee St 13214 315-446-4890
David Wheeler, prin. Fax 446-4799
Manlius Pebble Hill S 600/PK-12
5300 Jamesville Rd 13214 315-446-2452
Baxter Ball, prin. Fax 446-2620
Syracuse Hebrew S 100/K-6
5655 Thompson Rd 13214 315-446-1900

Dexter, Jefferson, Pop. 1,138
General Brown Central SD 1,600/K-12
PO Box 500 13634 315-639-5100
Stephan Vigliotti, supt. Fax 639-6916
www.gblions.org
Dexter ES 300/K-6
415 E Grove St 13634 315-639-5100
Michael Lennox, prin. Fax 639-6845
Other Schools – See Brownville

Dix Hills, Suffolk, Pop. 26,100
Commack UFD
Supt. — See East Northport
Rolling Hills ES 300/K-2
25 McCulloch Dr 11746 631-858-3570
Janet Studley, prin.

Half Hollow Hills Central SD 10,100/K-12
525 Half Hollow Rd 11746 631-592-3000
Dr. Sheldon Karnilow, supt. Fax 592-3900
www.hhh.k12.ny.us
Candlewood MS 1,000/6-8
1200 Carlls Straight Path 11746 631-592-3300
Andrew Greene, prin. Fax 592-3921
Chestnut Hill ES 700/K-5
600 S Service Rd 11746 631-592-3500
Linda Rudes, prin. Fax 592-3911
Forest Park ES 600/K-5
30 Deforest Rd 11746 631-592-3550
Ross Diener, prin. Fax 592-3914
Otsego ES 700/K-5
55 Otsego Ave 11746 631-592-3600
Sharon Stepankewich, prin. Fax 592-3915
Paumanok ES 800/K-5
1 Seaman Neck Rd 11746 631-592-3650
Kendra Cooper, prin. Fax 592-3916
Signal Hill ES 700/K-5
670 Caledonia Rd 11746 631-592-3700
Deborah Ostrosky, prin. Fax 592-3917
Vanderbilt ES 700/K-5
350 Deer Park Rd 11746 631-592-3800
Martin Boettcher, prin. Fax 592-3918
Other Schools – See Melville

Upper Room Christian S 300/PK-12
722 Deer Park Rd 11746 631-242-5359
Gregory Eck, prin. Fax 242-5418

Dobbs Ferry, Westchester, Pop. 11,070
Dobbs Ferry UFD 1,400/K-12
505 Broadway 10522 914-693-1506
Debra Kaplan, supt. Fax 693-1787
www.dfsd.org
Dobbs Ferry MS 300/6-8
505 Broadway 10522 914-693-7640
Patrick Mussolini, prin. Fax 693-5229
Springhurst ES 700/K-5
175 Walgrove Ave 10522 914-693-1503
Douglas Berry, prin. Fax 693-3188

Greenburgh Eleven UFD 300/K-12
PO Box 501 10522 914-693-8500
Sandra Mallah, supt. Fax 693-4029
Greenburgh Eleven S 100/K-8
PO Box 501 10522 914-693-8500
JoAnn Murphy, prin. Fax 693-4029

Dolgeville, Herkimer, Pop. 2,095
Dolgeville Central SD 800/PK-12
38 Slawson St 13329 315-429-3155
Theodore Kawryga, supt. Fax 429-8473
www.dolgeville.org
Dolgeville Central ES 400/PK-4
38 Slawson St 13329 315-429-3155
Susan Butler, prin. Fax 429-9328
Dolgeville Central MS 100/5-8
38 Slawson St 13329 315-429-3155
Melissa Hoskey, prin. Fax 429-8473

Douglaston, See New York
NYC Department of Education
Supt. — See New York
Public S 98 300/K-5
4020 235th St 11363 718-423-8535
Sheila Huggins, prin. Fax 423-8550

St. Anastasia S 200/PK-8
4511 245th St 11362 718-631-3153
Lucy Mihulka, prin. Fax 631-3945

Dover Plains, Dutchess, Pop. 1,847
Dover UFD 1,700/K-12
2368 Route 22 12522 845-832-4500
Dr. Craig Onofry, supt. Fax 832-4511
www.doverschools.org
Dover ES 300/3-5
9 School St 12522 845-877-4700
Herman Harmelink, prin. Fax 877-3460
Dover MS 400/6-8
2368 Route 22 12522 845-832-4521
Donna Basting, prin. Fax 832-3924
Other Schools – See Wingdale

Downsville, Delaware
Downsville Central SD 300/K-12
PO Box J 13755 607-363-2100
James Abrams, supt. Fax 363-2105
www.dcseagles.org
Downsville Central S 300/K-12
PO Box J 13755 607-363-2111
Timothy McNamara, prin. Fax 363-2105

Dryden, Tompkins, Pop. 1,833
Dryden Central SD 1,600/K-12
PO Box 88 13053 607-844-8694
Sandra Sherwood, supt. Fax 844-4733
www.dryden.k12.ny.us
Dryden ES K-2
PO Box 88 13053 607-844-8694
David Thon, prin. Fax 844-4641
Dryden IS 400/3-5
PO Box 88 13053 607-844-8694
David Thon, prin. Fax 844-4641
Dryden MS 400/6-8
PO Box 88 13053 607-844-8694
Lawrence Hinkle, prin. Fax 844-5174
Other Schools – See Freeville, Mc Lean

Dundee, Yates, Pop. 1,645
Dundee Central SD 900/K-12
55 Water St 14837 607-243-5533
Nancy Zimar, supt. Fax 243-7912
www.dundeecs.org
Dundee ES 500/K-6
55 Water St 14837 607-243-5535
Kathy Ring, prin. Fax 243-7912

Dunkirk, Chautauqua, Pop. 12,493
Dunkirk CSD 2,100/K-12
620 Marauder Dr 14048 716-366-9300
Gary Cerne, supt. Fax 366-9399
www.dunkirkcsd.org
Dunkirk MS 500/6-8
525 Eagle St 14048 716-366-9380
David Boyda, prin. Fax 366-9357
Public S 3 200/K-5
742 Lamphere St 14048 716-366-9330
Daniel Genovese, prin. Fax 366-0565
Public S 4 200/K-5
752 Central Ave 14048 716-366-9340
Joelle Vanegas, prin. Fax 366-0548
Public S 5 200/K-5
117 Brigham Rd 14048 716-366-9350
Roxanne Michalak, prin. Fax 366-9355
Public S 7 300/K-5
348 Lake Shore Dr E 14048 716-366-9370
Elaine Hayes, prin. Fax 366-9426

Northern Chautauqua Catholic S 200/PK-8
336 Washington Ave 14048 716-366-0630
Kathy Moser, prin. Fax 366-5101

Durham, Greene
Cairo-Durham Central SD
Supt. — See Cairo
Durham ES 200/K-5
PO Box 53 12422 518-239-8412
Kristen Reno, prin. Fax 239-5925

Durhamville, Oneida
Oneida CSD
Supt. — See Oneida
Durhamville ES 300/K-6
5462 Main St 13054 315-363-8065
Margaret Visalli, prin. Fax 366-0615

East Amherst, Erie
Williamsville Central SD 10,700/K-12
PO Box 5000 14051 716-626-8000
Dr. Howard Smith, supt. Fax 626-8089
www.williamsvillek12.org
Casey MS 800/5-8
105 Casey Rd 14051 716-626-8585
Francis McGreevy, prin. Fax 626-8562
Dodge ES 600/K-4
1900 Dodge Rd 14051 716-626-9820
Lynn Fritzinger, prin. Fax 626-9849
Transit MS 1,000/5-8
8730 Transit Rd 14051 716-626-8701
Jill Pellis, prin. Fax 626-8796
Other Schools – See Williamsville

East Aurora, Erie, Pop. 6,418
East Aurora UFD 1,600/K-12
430 Main St 14052 716-687-2302
James Bodziak, supt. Fax 652-8581
eastauroraschools.org/
East Aurora MS 500/5-8
430 Main St 14052 716-687-2453
Mark Mambretti, prin. Fax 652-8581
Parkdale ES 400/K-4
141 Girard Ave 14052 716-687-2352
Colleen Klimchuck, prin. Fax 687-2350

Iroquois Central SD
Supt. — See Elma
Wales PS 200/K-3
4650 Woodchuck Rd 14052 716-652-3000
Kimberly Oar, prin. Fax 995-2340

Immaculate Conception S 200/K-8
510 Oakwood Ave 14052 585-652-5855
Karen Adamski, prin. Fax 805-0192

Eastchester, Westchester, Pop. 18,537
Eastchester UFD 2,900/K-12
580 White Plains Rd 10709 914-793-6130
Dr. Marilyn Terranova, supt. Fax 793-9006
www2.lhric.org/eastchester/
Eastchester MS 700/6-8
550 White Plains Rd 10709 914-793-6130
Dr. Walter Moran, prin. Fax 793-1699
Hutchinson ES 500/2-5
60 Mill Rd 10709 914-793-6130
Theresa Cherry, prin. Fax 793-9006
Waverly PS 500/K-1
45 Hall Ave 10709 914-793-6130
Dr. Jeffrey Melendez, prin. Fax 793-9006
Other Schools – See Scarsdale

Tuckahoe UFD
Supt. — See Tuckahoe
Cottle ES 500/K-5
2 Siwanoy Blvd 10709 914-337-5376
Anthony DiCarlo, prin. Fax 337-5334
Tuckahoe MS 200/6-8
65 Siwanoy Blvd 10709 914-337-5376
Carl Albano, prin. Fax 337-5236

East Elmhurst, See New York
NYC Department of Education
Supt. — See New York
IS 227 1,300/5-8
3202 Junction Blvd 11369 718-335-7500
Renee David, prin. Fax 779-7186
Public S 127 1,000/PK-8
9801 25th Ave 11369 718-446-4700
Avita Sanavria, prin. Fax 397-7645
Public S 148 1,100/PK-5
8902 32nd Ave 11369 718-898-8181
Andrew Paccione, prin. Fax 476-2992
Public S 228 300/PK-2
3265 93rd St 11369 718-899-5799
Olga Guzman, prin. Fax 899-7323

St. Gabriel S 300/PK-8
2625 97th St 11369 718-426-7170
Br. Edward Shields, prin. Fax 426-1714

East Greenbush, Rensselaer, Pop. 3,784
East Greenbush Central SD 4,500/K-12
29 Englewood Ave 12061 518-477-2755
Angela Guptill Ph.D., supt. Fax 477-4833
www.egcsd.org
Genet ES 400/K-5
29 Englewood Ave 12061 518-477-2735
Ana Yeomans, prin. Fax 477-4466
Goff MS 1,000/6-8
35 Gilligan Rd 12061 518-477-2731
Brian Reeve, prin. Fax 477-2667
Other Schools – See Castleton on Hudson, Nassau, Rensselaer, Troy

Holy Spirit S 300/PK-8
54 Highland Dr 12061 518-477-5739
Roger Rooney, prin. Fax 477-5743

East Hampton, Suffolk, Pop. 1,357
East Hampton UFD 1,900/PK-12
231 Pantigo Rd 11937 631-329-4100
Dr. Raymond Gualtieri, supt. Fax 324-0109
www.ehufsd.org
East Hampton MS 400/5-8
76 Newtown Ln 11937 631-329-4116
Dr. Thomas Lamorgese, prin. Fax 329-4187
Marshall ES 400/PK-4
3 Gingerbread Ln 11937 631-329-4156
Jennifer Tarbet, prin. Fax 329-4157

Springs UFD 600/PK-8
48 School St 11937 631-324-0144
Thomas Quinn, supt. Fax 324-0269
www.springs.k12.ny.us
Springs S 600/PK-8
48 School St 11937 631-324-0144
Eric Casale, prin. Fax 324-0269

Stella Maris ECC PK-PK
44 Meadow Way 11937 631-329-3934
Jane Peters, prin.

East Islip, Suffolk, Pop. 14,325
East Islip UFD
Supt. — See Islip Terrace
Kennedy ES 500/1-5
94 Woodland Dr 11730 631-581-1608
Aileen O'Connor, prin. Fax 581-1354
Timber Point ES 500/1-5
180 Timberpoint Rd 11730 631-581-1887
Margaret Harper, prin. Fax 581-4078

St. Mary S 500/PK-8
16 Harrison Ave 11730 631-581-4266
Biagio Arpino, prin. Fax 581-7509

East Meadow, Nassau, Pop. 37,600
East Meadow UFD
Supt. — See Westbury
Barnum Woods ES 800/K-5
500 May Ln 11554 516-564-6500
Gregory Bottari, prin. Fax 564-6507
McVey ES 700/K-5
2201 Devon St 11554 516-228-5300
Dr. Rita Meyerowitz, prin. Fax 228-5317
Meadowbrook ES 500/K-5
241 Old Westbury Rd 11554 516-520-4400
Susan Hyde, prin. Fax 520-4403
Parkway ES 500/K-5
465 Bellmore Rd 11554 516-679-3500
Louis Panzica, prin. Fax 679-3507
Woodland MS 1,200/6-8
690 Wenwood Dr 11554 516-564-6523
James Lethbridge, prin. Fax 564-6519

East Moriches, Suffolk, Pop. 4,021
East Moriches UFD 800/K-8
9 Adelaide Ave 11940 631-878-0162
Dr. Charles Russo, supt. Fax 878-0186
www.eastmoriches.k12.ny.us
East Moriches ES 400/K-4
523 Montauk Hwy 11940 631-878-0162
Dr. Charles Russo, prin. Fax 878-1097
East Moriches MS 400/5-8
9 Adelaide Ave 11940 631-878-0162
Robert McIntyre, prin. Fax 874-0096

East Northport, Suffolk, Pop. 20,411
Commack UFD 7,600/K-12
480 Clay Pitts Rd 11731 631-912-2000
Dr. James Feltman, supt. Fax 266-2406
www.commack.k12.ny.us
Other Schools – See Commack, Dix Hills

Northport-East Northport UFD
Supt. — See Northport
Bellerose ES 500/K-5
253 Bellerose Ave 11731 631-262-6800
Barbara Falotico, prin. Fax 262-6805
Dickinson Avenue ES 400/K-5
120 Dickinson Ave 11731 631-262-6810
Anne Whooley, prin. Fax 262-6815
East Northport MS 700/6-8
1075 5th Ave 11731 631-262-6770
Joanne Kroon, prin. Fax 262-6773
Fifth Avenue ES 600/K-5
1157 5th Ave 11731 631-262-6820
Joan Baltman, prin. Fax 262-6825
Pulaski Road ES 400/K-5
623 9th Ave 11731 631-262-6850
Jeffrey Haubrich, prin. Fax 262-6855

Jewish Academy 100/PK-2
178 Cedar Rd 11731 631-368-2600
Michele Rosenberg, dir. Fax 368-2384
St. Paul's Lutheran S 300/PK-5
106 Vernon Valley Rd 11731 631-754-4424
Irene Mazur, prin. Fax 754-4427
Trinity Regional S 500/K-8
1025 5th Ave 11731 631-261-5130
Jeanne Morcone, prin. Fax 266-5345

East Norwich, Nassau, Pop. 2,698
Oyster Bay-East Norwich Central SD
Supt. — See Oyster Bay
Vernon S 500/3-6
880 Oyster Bay Rd 11732 516-624-6562
Nancy Gaiman, prin. Fax 624-6522

East Patchogue, Suffolk, Pop. 20,195
South Country Central SD 4,600/PK-12
189 N Dunton Ave 11772 631-730-1510
Raymond Walsh, supt. Fax 286-6394
www.southcountry.org/
Critz ES 400/K-3
185 N Dunton Ave 11772 631-730-1675
Kathleen Munisteri, prin. Fax 286-5518
Other Schools – See Bellport, Brookhaven

East Pembroke, Genesee
Pembroke Central SD
Supt. — See Corfu
Pembroke PS 300/PK-2
PO Box 190 14056 585-762-8713
Jeffrey Evoy, prin. Fax 762-9993

Eastport, Suffolk
Eastport-South Manor Central SD
Supt. — See Manorville
Eastport ES 1,100/K-6
390 Montauk Hwy 11941 631-325-0800
Susan Kenny, prin. Fax 325-1066

East Quogue, Suffolk, Pop. 4,372
East Quogue UFD 400/K-6
6 Central Ave 11942 631-653-5210
Les Black, supt. Fax 653-3752
www.eastquogue.k12.ny.us
East Quogue ES 400/K-6
6 Central Ave 11942 631-653-5210
Robert Long, prin. Fax 653-8644

East Rochester, Monroe, Pop. 6,366
East Rochester UFD 1,200/PK-12
222 Woodbine Ave 14445 585-248-6302
Howard Maffucci, supt. Fax 586-3254
www.erschools.org
East Rochester ES 700/PK-6
400 Woodbine Ave 14445 585-248-6311
Harold Leve, prin. Fax 248-6318

Trinity Montessori S 50/PK-6
501 Garfield St 14445 585-586-1044
Lorraine Scarafile, admin. Fax 586-1821

East Rockaway, Nassau, Pop. 10,263
East Rockaway UFD 1,200/K-12
443 Ocean Ave 11518 516-887-8300
Dr. Roseanne Melucci, supt. Fax 887-8308
www.eastrockawayschools.org
Centre Avenue ES 300/K-6
55 Centre Ave 11518 516-887-8300
Timothy Silk, prin. Fax 599-5727
Rhame Avenue ES 300/K-6
100 Rhame Ave 11518 516-887-8300
Laura Guggino, prin. Fax 887-8332

Lynbrook UFD
Supt. — See Lynbrook
Waverly Park ES 300/1-5
320 Waverly Ave 11518 516-887-6590
Lucille McAssey, prin. Fax 887-8262

St. Raymond S 400/PK-8
263 Atlantic Ave 11518 516-593-9010
Sr. Ruthanne Gypalo, prin. Fax 593-0986

East Setauket, See Setauket
Three Village Central SD 7,900/K-12
PO Box 9050 11733 631-730-4000
Donald Webster Ed.D., supt.
www.threevillagecsd.org
Arrowhead ES 800/K-6
62 Arrowhead Ln 11733 631-730-4100
Marisa Redden, prin. Fax 730-4104
Minnesauke ES 800/K-6
21 High Gate Dr 11733 631-730-4200
Paula Bienia, prin. Fax 730-4202
Other Schools – See Setauket, Stony Brook

Laurel Hill S 400/PK-8
201 Old Town Rd 11733 631-751-1154
Robert Stark, hdmstr. Fax 751-2421

East Syracuse, Onondaga, Pop. 3,076
East Syracuse-Minoa Central SD 3,600/PK-12
407 Fremont Rd 13057 315-434-3012
Dr. Donna DeSiato, supt. Fax 434-3020
www.esmschools.org
East Syracuse ES 300/K-5
230 Kinne St 13057 315-434-3850
Patricia Charboneau, prin. Fax 434-3855
Fremont ES 300/K-5
115 W Richmond Rd 13057 315-434-3480
Janice Ahlsen, prin. Fax 434-3490
Park Hill Preschool 200/PK-PK
303 Roby Ave 13057 315-434-3800
Carol Feldmeier, prin. Fax 434-3820
Pine Grove MS 800/6-8
6318 Fremont Rd 13057 315-434-3050
Kelly Sajnog, prin. Fax 434-3070
Woodland ES 400/K-5
6316 Fremont Rd 13057 315-434-3440
Lee Carulli, prin. Fax 434-3450
Other Schools – See Minoa

Abundant Life Academy 100/PK-6
7000 All Nations Blvd 13057 315-463-7300
Rev. Harry Patterson, admin. Fax 463-7343
St. Daniel / St. Matthew's Academy 200/PK-6
214 Kinne St 13057 315-437-1339
Joseph Celentano, prin. Fax 437-1330

East Williston, Nassau, Pop. 2,514
East Williston UFD
Supt. — See Old Westbury
North Side ES 700/K-4
110 E Williston Ave 11596 516-333-6860
James Bloomgarden, prin.

Eden, Erie, Pop. 3,088
Eden Central SD 1,800/PK-12
3150 Schoolview Rd 14057 716-992-3629
Ronald Buggs, supt. Fax 992-3682
www.edencsd.org/
Eden ES 500/3-6
8289 N Main St 14057 716-992-3610
Richard Schaefer, prin. Fax 992-3658
Preiss PS 400/PK-2
3000 Schoolview Rd 14057 716-992-3638
Loran Carter, prin. Fax 992-3631

Edinburg, Fulton
Edinburg Common SD 100/PK-6
4 Johnson Rd 12134 518-863-8412
Randy Teetz, supt. Fax 863-2564
www.edinburgcs.org/
Edinburg Common ES 100/PK-6
4 Johnson Rd 12134 518-863-8412
Randy Teetz, prin. Fax 863-2564

Edmeston, Otsego
Edmeston Central SD 500/K-12
11 North St 13335 607-965-8931
David Rowley, supt. Fax 965-8942
edmestoncentralschool.net
Edmeston Central S 500/K-12
11 North St 13335 607-965-8931
Martha Winsor, prin. Fax 965-8942

Eggertsville, Erie

St. Benedict S 200/K-8
3980 Main St 14226 716-835-2518
Kerri Nowak, prin. Fax 834-4932

Elba, Genesee, Pop. 667
Elba Central SD 500/K-12
PO Box 370 14058 585-757-9967
Joan Cole, supt. Fax 757-2713
www.elbacsd.org
Elba ES 300/K-6
PO Box 370 14058 585-757-9967
Jason Smith, prin. Fax 757-2979

Elbridge, Onondaga, Pop. 1,074
Jordan-Elbridge Central SD 1,600/K-12
130 E Main St 13060 315-689-8500
Marilyn Dominick, supt. Fax 689-0084
www.jecsd.org
Elbridge ES 300/K-2
PO Box 170 13060 315-689-8540
John Borne, prin. Fax 689-3320
Other Schools – See Jordan

Eldred, Sullivan
Eldred Central SD 700/K-12
PO Box 249 12732 845-456-1100
Berneice Brownell, supt. Fax 557-3672
www.eldred.k12.ny.us/
Other Schools – See Glen Spey

Elizabethtown, Essex
Elizabethtown-Lewis Central SD 400/K-12
PO Box 158 12932 518-873-6371
Gail Else, supt. Fax 873-9552
elcsd.org
Elizabethtown-Lewis Central S 400/K-12
PO Box 158 12932 518-873-6371
Kenneth Hughes, prin. Fax 873-9552

Ellenburg Depot, Clinton
Northern Adirondack Central SD 1,000/K-12
PO Box 164 12935 518-594-7060
Laura Marlow, supt. Fax 594-7255
www.nacs1.org/
North Adirondack ES 400/K-5
PO Box 164 12935 518-594-3986
Lisa Silver, prin. Fax 594-7255

Ellenville, Ulster, Pop. 3,954
Ellenville Central SD 1,700/K-12
28 Maple Ave 12428 845-647-0100
Lisa Wiles, supt. Fax 647-0105
www.ecs.k12.ny.us

Ellenville ES 600/K-4
28 Maple Ave 12428 845-647-0131
Holly Eikszta, prin. Fax 647-7090
Ellenville MS 500/5-8
28 Maple Ave 12428 845-647-0126
Debra Clinton, prin. Fax 647-0230

Ellicottville, Cattaraugus, Pop. 538
Ellicottville Central SD 600/K-12
5873 Route 219 S 14731 716-699-2368
Mark Ward, supt. Fax 699-6017
www.ellicottvillecentral.com/
Ellicottville ES 200/K-5
5873 Route 219 S 14731 716-699-2318
Connie Pound, prin. Fax 699-5635

Elma, Erie
Iroquois Central SD 2,800/K-12
PO Box 32 14059 716-652-3000
Neil Rochelle, supt. Fax 652-9305
www.iroquoiscsd.org
Elma PS 300/K-3
PO Box 32 14059 716-995-2320
Darcy Walker, prin. Fax 995-2321
Iroquois IS 400/4-5
PO Box 32 14059 716-652-3000
Amy Stanfield, prin. Fax 995-2346
Iroquois MS 700/6-8
PO Box 32 14059 716-652-3000
Ann Marie Spitzer, prin. Fax 995-2335
Other Schools – See East Aurora, Marilla

Annunciation S 100/PK-8
7580 Clinton St 14059 716-681-1327
Sr. Marilyn Dudek, prin. Fax 685-6380

Elmhurst, See New York
NYC Department of Education
Supt. — See New York
IS 5 1,400/6-8
5040 Jacobus St 11373 718-205-6788
Debra Van Nostrandt, prin. Fax 429-6518
51st Avenue Academy 4-5
7605 51st Ave 11373 718-429-5287
Digna Erstejn, prin. Fax 429-7344
Public S 7 1,100/K-3
8055 Cornish Ave 11373 718-446-2726
Sara Tucci, prin. Fax 397-7916
Public S 13 1,300/K-5
5501 94th St 11373 718-271-1021
Dr. Yvonne Angelastro, prin. Fax 699-3008
Public S 89 1,600/K-5
8528 Britton Ave 11373 718-898-2230
Casper Cacioppo, prin. Fax 672-3066
Public S 102 800/PK-6
5524 Van Horn St 11373 718-446-3308
Anthony Pisacano, prin. Fax 672-3101

Jewish Institute of Queens 600/PK-12
6005 Woodhaven Blvd 11373 718-426-9369
Fax 446-2071
St. Adalbert S 500/PK-8
5217 83rd St 11373 718-424-2376
Sr. Kathleen Maciej, prin. Fax 898-7852
St. Bartholomew S 300/PK-8
4415 Judge St 11373 718-446-7575
J. Boursiquot-Charles, prin. Fax 446-7743

Elmira, Chemung, Pop. 29,928
Elmira CSD 6,900/PK-12
951 Hoffman St 14905 607-735-3000
Dr. Joseph Hochreiter, supt. Fax 735-3009
www.elmiracityschools.com
Beecher ES 400/PK-5
310 Sullivan St 14901 607-735-3500
Michael Lanning, prin. Fax 735-3509
Broadway ES 400/PK-5
1000 Broadway St 14904 607-735-3600
Rebecca Kiley, prin. Fax 735-3609
Broadway MS 800/6-8
1000 Broadway St 14904 607-735-3300
Brian LeBaron, prin. Fax 735-3309
Coburn ES 500/PK-5
216 Mount Zoar St 14904 607-735-3650
Jason Johnston, prin. Fax 735-3659
Davis MS 700/6-8
610 Lake St 14901 607-735-3400
Derek Almy, prin. Fax 735-3409
Diven ES 500/PK-5
1115 Hall St 14901 607-735-3700
Pam Davis-Webb, prin. Fax 735-3709
Fassett ES PK-5
309 W Thurston St 14901 607-735-3900
Brad Pollack, prin. Fax 735-3909
Hendy Avenue ES 500/PK-5
110 Hendy Ave 14905 607-735-3750
Madge Larrimore, prin. Fax 735-3759
Riverside ES 400/PK-5
409 Riverside Ave 14904 607-735-3850
Carrie Rollins, prin. Fax 735-3859
Other Schools – See Pine City

Chemung Valley Montessori S 200/PK-8
23 Winters Rd 14903 607-562-8754
George Conway, hdmstr. Fax 562-3655
Holy Family IS 100/4-6
301 Demarest Pkwy 14905 607-734-0841
Brenda Lisi, prin. Fax 732-6638
Holy Family JHS 100/7-8
1010 Davis St 14901 607-734-0336
Elizabeth Berliner, prin. Fax 734-4977
Holy Family PS 200/PK-3
421 Fulton St 14904 607-732-3588
Bernadette McClelland, prin. Fax 732-1850

Elmira Heights, Chemung, Pop. 4,011
Elmira Heights Central SD 1,100/K-12
2083 College Ave 14903 607-734-7114
Mary Beth Fiore, supt. Fax 734-7134
www.heightsschools.com
Cohen ES 500/K-5
100 Robinwood Ave 14903 607-734-7132
Kathy Plumley, prin. Fax 734-9574
Cohen MS 300/6-8
100 Robinwood Ave 14903 607-734-5078
Jeff Lawrence, prin. Fax 734-9382

Elmont, Nassau, Pop. 33,600
Elmont UFD 3,800/PK-6
135 Elmont Rd 11003 516-326-5500
Al Harper, supt. Fax 326-5574
www.elmontschools.org
Carlson ES 800/K-6
235 Belmont Blvd 11003 516-326-5570
Kenneth Rosner, prin. Fax 326-0349
Covert Avenue ES 700/K-6
144 Covert Ave 11003 516-326-5560
Margaret Pleta, prin. Fax 326-0547
Dutch Broadway ES 900/K-6
1880 Dutch Broadway 11003 516-326-5550
Walter Aksionoff, prin. Fax 326-0519
Elmont Preschool PK-PK
1735 Hempstead Tpke 11003 516-326-5580
Stephanie Muller, prin. Fax 326-6127
Gotham Avenue ES 600/K-6
181 Gotham Ave 11003 516-326-5540
Marshall Zucker, prin. Fax 326-0563
Other Schools – See Stewart Manor, Valley Stream

Elmsford, Westchester, Pop. 4,727
Elmsford UFD 1,000/PK-12
98 S Goodwin Ave 10523 914-592-6632
Dr. Barbara Peters, supt. Fax 592-2181
www.elmsd.org
Dixson PS 200/PK-1
22 S Hillside Ave 10523 914-592-2092
Wayne Harders, prin. Fax 592-5439
Grady ES 300/2-6
45 Cobb Ln 10523 914-592-8962
Wayne Harders, prin. Fax 592-5439

Our Lady of Mt. Carmel S 200/PK-8
59 E Main St 10523 914-592-7575
Sr. Mary Healey, prin. Fax 345-1591

Elwood, Suffolk, Pop. 10,916
Elwood UFD
Supt. — See Greenlawn
Elwood MS 700/6-8
478 Elwood Rd 11731 631-266-5420
David Klecher, prin. Fax 266-3987
Harley Avenue PS 600/K-2
30 Harley Ave 11731 631-266-5445
Dr. Virginia Cancroft, prin. Fax 266-3985

Endicott, Broome, Pop. 12,639
Union-Endicott Central SD 4,300/K-12
1100 E Main St 13760 607-757-2111
Dr. Suzanne McLeod, supt. Fax 757-2809
www.uetigers.stier.org
Johnson ES 400/K-5
715 Paden St 13760 607-757-2137
Michelle Robinson, prin. Fax 757-2878
Johnson ES 700/K-5
999 Taft Ave 13760 607-757-2143
Jim Fountaine, prin. Fax 658-7119
McGuinness IS 300/4-6
1301 Union Center Maine Hwy 13760 607-757-2131
Tim Lowie, prin. Fax 757-2127
Snapp MS 900/6-8
101 S Loder Ave 13760 607-757-2156
Ann Marie Foley, prin. Fax 658-7117
Watson ES 300/K-5
263 Ridgefield Rd 13760 607-757-2152
Deborah Fletcher, prin. Fax 757-2864
West PS 300/K-3
1201 Union Center Maine Hwy 13760 607-757-2149
Victoria Wychock, prin. Fax 757-2867

Our Lady of Sorrows-Seton Campus S 200/PK-8
1112 Broad St 13760 607-748-7423
Jo Ann Rowan, prin. Fax 484-9576
St. Joseph S 200/PK-8
210 N Jackson Ave 13760 607-748-8631
Angela Tierno, prin. Fax 748-8621

Endwell, Broome, Pop. 12,602
Maine-Endwell Central SD 2,600/K-12
712 Farm To Market Rd 13760 607-754-1400
Joseph Stoner, supt. Fax 754-1650
www.me.stier.org//main.html
Brink ES 700/K-5
3618 Briar Ln 13760 607-786-8244
Darlene Darrow, prin. Fax 786-8213
Maine-Endwell MS 600/6-8
1119 Farm To Market Rd 13760 607-786-8271
Richard Otis, prin. Fax 786-5137
Other Schools – See Maine

Evans Mills, Jefferson, Pop. 624
Indian River Central SD
Supt. — See Philadelphia
Evans Mills PS 400/K-3
8442 S Main St 13637 315-629-4331
Pamela Knight, prin. Fax 629-5257

Fabius, Onondaga, Pop. 344
Fabius-Pompey Central SD 900/K-12
1211 Mill St 13063 315-683-5301
Timothy Ryan, supt. Fax 683-5827
www.fabiuspompey.org
Fabius-Pompey ES 400/K-5
7800 Main St 13063 315-683-5857
Andrea Nardozzi, prin. Fax 683-5680

Fairport, Monroe, Pop. 5,576
Fairport Central SD 7,100/K-12
38 W Church St 14450 585-421-2004
Jon Hunter, supt. Fax 421-3421
www.fairport.org
Brooks Hill ES 800/K-5
181 Hulburt Rd 14450 585-421-2170
Margaret Cardona, prin. Fax 421-2173
Brown MS 900/6-8
665 Ayrault Rd 14450 585-421-2065
David Dunn, prin. Fax 421-2136
Dudley ES 700/K-2
211 Hamilton Rd 14450 585-421-2155
Karen Fingar, prin. Fax 421-2328
Jefferson Avenue ES 800/K-5
303 Jefferson Ave 14450 585-421-2185
Richard Greene, prin. Fax 377-3320
Northside IS 800/3-5
181 Hamilton Rd 14450 585-421-2140
Carolyn Shea, prin. Fax 421-2162
Perrin MS 800/6-8
85 Potter Pl 14450 585-421-2080
Brett Provenzano, prin. Fax 421-2097

Falconer, Chautauqua, Pop. 2,419
Falconer Central SD 900/PK-12
2 East Ave N 14733 716-665-6624
Jane Fosberg, supt. Fax 665-9265
www.falconerschools.org
Fenner ES 300/3-5
2 East Ave N 14733 716-665-6627
Larry Spangenburg, prin. Fax 665-6668
Other Schools – See Kennedy

Fallsburg, Sullivan
Fallsburg Central SD 1,500/PK-12
PO Box 124 12733 845-434-5884
Ivan Katz, supt. Fax 434-8346
www.fallsburgcsd.net/
Cosor ES 800/PK-6
PO Box 123 12733 845-434-4110
Martin Tawil, prin. Fax 434-0871

Fallsburg Cheder S 200/PK-8
PO Box 400 12733 845-434-5240

Farmingdale, Nassau, Pop. 8,668
Farmingdale UFD 6,200/K-12
50 Van Cott Ave 11735 516-752-6510
John Lorentz, supt.
www.farmingdaleschools.org
Howitt MS 1,500/6-8
70 Van Cott Ave 11735 516-752-6519
Luis Pena, prin. Fax 752-2004
Northside ES 500/K-5
55 Powell Pl 11735 516-752-6575
Elizabeth Garavuso, prin. Fax 752-7026
Saltzman East Memorial ES 600/K-5
25 Mill Ln 11735 631-752-6565
Eve Dieringer, prin. Fax 752-7038
Woodward Parkway ES 900/K-5
95 Woodward Pkwy 11735 516-752-6560
Carol Anselmo, prin. Fax 752-7018
Other Schools – See North Massapequa

New Jerusalem Christian Academy 50/1-12
816 Main St 11735 516-249-0955
Alan Brandenburg, prin. Fax 249-0955
St. John Baptist De La Salle S 300/PK-8
50 Cherry St 11735 516-694-3610
Christine Bendish, prin. Fax 694-7296

Farmingville, Suffolk, Pop. 14,842
Sachem Central SD
Supt. — See Holbrook
Lynwood Avenue ES 500/K-5
50 Lynwood Ave 11738 631-696-8652
Danielle DeLorenzo, prin. Fax 736-9478
Tecumseh ES 500/K-5
179 Granny Rd 11738 631-696-8660
Laura Amato, prin. Fax 736-9479

Faith Academy 200/PK-12
1070 Portion Rd 11738 631-732-7088
Karen Warren, admin. Fax 696-2799

Far Rockaway, See New York
NYC Department of Education
Supt. — See New York
MS 53 700/6-8
1045 Nameoke St 11691 718-471-6900
Claude Monereau, prin. Fax 471-6955
Knowledge & Power Preparatory Academy VI 200/6-8
821 Bay 25th St 11691 718-471-6934
Peter Dalton, prin. Fax 471-6938
Public S 43 1,300/PK-8
160 Beach 29th St 11691 718-327-5860
John Quattrocchi, prin. Fax 327-6925
Public S 104 500/PK-6
2601 Mott Ave 11691 718-327-1910
Katie Grady, prin. Fax 337-2146
Public S 105 800/PK-8
420 Beach 51st St 11691 718-474-8615
Laurie Shapiro, prin. Fax 474-8841
Public S 106 400/PK-5
180 Beach 35th St 11691 718-327-5828
Marcella Sills, prin. Fax 327-5956
Public S 197 500/PK-6
825 Hicksville Rd 11691 718-327-1083
Jean Mckeon, prin. Fax 327-3518
Public S 215 500/PK-5
535 Briar Pl 11691 718-327-7928
Susan Hofmann, prin. Fax 327-7804
Public S 253 400/PK-5
1307 Central Ave 11691 718-327-0895
Robin Johnson, prin. Fax 327-3964

Bnos Bais Yaakov of Far Rockaway 500/PK-8
PO Box 900418 11690 718-337-6000
Clarke JHS, Beach 112th St 11694 7-8
Ann Cordes, prin. 718-449-9413
St. Camillus S 200/K-8
185 Beach 99th St 11694 718-634-5260
Sr. Agnes White, prin. Fax 634-8353
St. Mary Star of the Sea S 200/K-8
595 Beach 19th St 11691 718-327-2242
Angela Brucia, prin. Fax 327-0797
St. Rose of Lima S 400/PK-8
154 Beach 84th St 11693 718-474-7079
Theresa Andersen, prin. Fax 634-0524
Talmud Torah Siach Yitzchok S 200/PK-8
1513 Central Ave 11691 718-327-6247
Torah Academy for Girls 800/PK-8
444 Beach 6th St 11691 718-471-8444
Yeshiva Darchei Torah S 1,000/PK-8
1214 Heyson Rd 11691 718-868-2300
Rabbi Yehuda Harbater, dir. Fax 868-4450

Fayetteville, Onondaga, Pop. 4,171
Fayetteville-Manlius Central SD
Supt. — See Manlius
Fayetteville ES 500/K-4
704 S Manlius St 13066 315-692-1600
Nancy Smith, prin. Fax 692-1055
Mott Road ES 500/K-4
7173 Mott Rd 13066 315-692-1700
Lynnette Bonner, prin. Fax 692-1054
Wellwood MS 800/5-8
700 S Manlius St 13066 315-692-1300
John Almonte, prin. Fax 692-1049

Immaculate Conception S 300/PK-6
400 Salt Springs St 13066 315-637-3961
Sally Lisi, prin. Fax 637-2672

Fillmore, Allegany, Pop. 450
Fillmore Central SD 700/K-12
PO Box 177 14735 585-567-2251
Martin Cox, supt. Fax 567-2541
www.fillmorecsd.org/fillmorecsd/site/default.asp
Fillmore Central S 700/K-12
PO Box 177 14735 585-567-2289
Kyle Faulkner, prin. Fax 567-2541

Fishers Island, Suffolk
Fishers Island UFD 100/PK-12
PO Box A 06390 631-788-7444
Margaret McKenna, supt. Fax 788-5562
www.fischool.com
Fishers Island Central S 100/PK-12
PO Box A 06390 631-788-7444
Margaret McKenna, prin. Fax 788-5562

Fishkill, Dutchess, Pop. 1,749
Beacon CSD
Supt. — See Beacon
Glenham ES 400/K-5
20 Chase Dr 12524 845-838-6900
Dawn Condello, prin. Fax 838-6976

Wappingers Central SD
Supt. — See Wappingers Falls
Brinckerhoff ES 600/K-5
16 Wedgewood Rd 12524 845-897-6800
Ursula Platz, prin. Fax 897-6802
Fishkill ES 500/K-5
20 Church St 12524 845-897-6780
Andy McNally, prin. Fax 897-6788

St. Mary S 300/K-8
106 Jackson St 12524 845-896-9561
Ellen Anderson, prin. Fax 896-8477

Fleetwood, See Mount Vernon

Milestone S 100/PK-4
70 Broad St W 10552 914-667-3478
Angela Freeman, admin. Fax 667-2259

Floral Park, Nassau, Pop. 15,737
Floral Park-Bellrose UFD 1,600/PK-6
1 Poppy Pl 11001 516-327-9300
Dr. Lynn Pombonyo, supt. Fax 327-9304
www.floralpark.k12.ny.us
Childs ES 700/PK-6
10 Elizabeth St 11001 516-327-9317
Pamela Orleman Fine, prin. Fax 327-9304
Floral Park-Bellerose ES 900/PK-6
2 Larch Ave 11001 516-327-9307
Dr. Thomas Piro, prin. Fax 327-9304

NYC Department of Education
Supt. — See New York
MS 172 1,000/6-8
8114 257th St 11004 718-831-4000
Jeffrey Slivko, prin. Fax 831-4008
Public S 115 400/PK-5
8051 261st St 11004 718-831-4010
James Ambrose, prin. Fax 831-4014
Public S 191 400/PK-5
8515 258th St 11001 718-831-4032
Michael Ranieri, prin. Fax 831-4036

Our Lady of the Snows S 500/PK-8
7933 258th St 11004 718-343-1346
Sr. Roberta Oberle, prin. Fax 343-7303
Our Lady of Victory S 500/PK-8
2 Bellmore St 11001 516-352-4466
Margaret Augello, prin. Fax 352-2998

Florida, Orange, Pop. 2,781
Florida UFD 800/K-12
PO Box 757 10921 845-651-3095
Douglas Burnside, supt. Fax 651-6801
www.floridaufsd.org
Golden Hill ES 400/K-5
PO Box 757 10921 845-651-4407
Ronald Depace, prin. Fax 651-7460

Flushing, See New York
NYC Department of Education
Supt. — See New York
IS 25 800/6-8
3465 192nd St 11358 718-961-3480
Joseph Catone, prin. Fax 358-1563
IS 237 800/6-8
4621 Colden St 11355 718-353-6464
Judith Freidman, prin. Fax 460-6427
IS 250 100/6-8
15840 76th Rd 11366 718-591-9000
Marc Rosenberg, prin. Fax 591-2340
JHS 185 700/6-8
14726 25th Dr 11354 718-445-3232
Valerie Sawinski, prin. Fax 359-5352
JHS 189 600/6-8
14480 Barclay Ave 11355 718-359-6676
Cindy Diaz-Burgos, prin. Fax 358-0155
JHS 216 1,200/6-8
6420 175th St 11365 718-358-2005
Reginald Landeau, prin. Fax 358-2070
Public S 20 1,400/PK-6
14230 Barclay Ave 11355 718-359-0321
Victoria Hart, prin. Fax 358-0762
Public S 21 900/PK-5
14736 26th Ave 11354 718-445-8833
Debra Buszko, prin. Fax 358-0891
Public S 22 600/PK-5
15301 Sanford Ave 11355 718-762-4141
Priscilla Milito, prin. Fax 358-1260
Public S 24 600/PK-5
14111 Holly Ave 11355 718-359-2288
Lori Golan, prin. Fax 460-3251
Public S 26 600/PK-5
19502 69th Ave 11365 718-464-4505
Dr. Dina Koski, prin. Fax 464-4644
Public S 32 500/PK-5
17111 35th Ave 11358 718-463-3747
Betsey Malesardi, prin. Fax 358-1622
Public S 107 900/PK-5
16702 45th Ave 11358 718-762-5995
James Phair, prin. Fax 461-4989
Public S 120 800/PK-5
5801 136th St 11355 718-359-3390
Joan Monroe, prin. Fax 460-4513
Public S 154 600/PK-5
7502 162nd St 11366 718-591-1500
Danielle Giunta, prin. Fax 591-8751
Public S 163 400/PK-5
15901 59th Ave 11365 718-353-2514
Lucius Young, prin. Fax 460-4244
Public S 164 600/PK-8
13801 77th Ave 11367 718-544-1083
Anne Alfonso, prin. Fax 544-2042
Public S 165 500/PK-5
7035 150th St 11367 718-263-4004
Raquel Demillio, prin. Fax 793-9812
Public S 173 800/PK-5
17410 67th Ave 11365 718-358-2243
Molly Wang, prin. Fax 358-2989
Public S 200 400/PK-8
7010 164th St 11365 718-969-7780
Denize Brewer, prin. Fax 380-2615
Public S 201 300/PK-5
6511 155th St 11367 718-359-0620
Brett Gallini, prin. Fax 321-2081
Public S 214 400/PK-5
3115 140th St 11354 718-461-4055
Wendy Goldberg, prin. Fax 460-6841
Public S 219 500/PK-8
14439 Gravett Rd 11367 718-793-2130
Meredith Deckler, prin. Fax 793-1039
Public S 242 300/K-3
2966 137th St 11354 718-445-2902
Patricia Costa, prin. Fax 939-7751
Public S 499 PK-8
14820 Reeves Ave 11367 718-461-7462
Vivacca Lamourt, prin. Fax 461-7244
The Active Learning ES 100/PK-3
13720 Franklin Ave 11355 718-445-5730
Ivan Tolentino, prin. Fax 445-5856

Flushing Christian S 100/K-8
4154 Murray St 11355 718-445-3533
Karen Blatt, dir. Fax 445-7546
Full Gospel Christian S 200/PK-7
13030 31st Ave 11354 718-461-4409
Holy Family S 300/PK-8
7415 175th St 11366 718-969-2124
Mary Scheer, prin. Fax 380-2183
Mary's Nativity S 200/PK-8
14628 Jasmine Ave 11355 718-359-1800
Anne-Marie Baumis, prin. Fax 327-2242
St. Andrew Avellino S 400/PK-8
3550 158th St 11358 718-359-7887
Debora Hanna, prin. Fax 359-2295
St. Ann S 200/K-8
14245 58th Rd 11355 718-463-1238
Robert DiNardo, prin. Fax 539-6678
St. Kevin S 300/PK-8
4550 195th St 11358 718-357-8110
Sue Roye, prin. Fax 357-2519
St. Mel S 500/PK-8
15424 26th Ave 11354 718-539-8211
Diane Competello, prin. Fax 539-6563
St. Michael S 200/PK-8
13658 41st Ave 11355 718-961-0246
Maureen Rogone, prin. Fax 961-1403
Solomon Schechter S of Queens 400/PK-8
7616 Parsons Blvd 11366 718-591-9800
Martin Mayerson, hdmstr. Fax 591-3946

Spyropoulos S 500/K-8
4315 196th St 11358 718-357-5583
Athena Kromidas, prin. Fax 428-3051
Yeshiva Ketana of Queens 400/PK-8
7815 Parsons Blvd 11366 718-969-1000
Yeshiva of Central Queens 800/PK-8
14737 70th Rd 11367 718-793-8500

Fonda, Montgomery, Pop. 779
Fonda-Fultonville Central SD 1,500/K-12
PO Box 1501 12068 518-853-4415
James Hoffman, supt. Fax 853-4461
www.fondafultonvilleschools.org
Fonda-Fultonville ES 500/K-4
PO Box 1501 12068 518-853-3332
Alicia Henry, prin. Fax 853-1455
Fonda-Fultonville MS 500/5-8
PO Box 1501 12068 518-853-4747
Elizabeth Donovan, prin. Fax 853-4461

Forest Hills, See New York
NYC Department of Education
Supt. — See New York
Academy for Excellence through the Arts 100/PK-3
10855 69th Ave 11375 718-459-1358
Barbara Leto, prin.
Public S 101 600/PK-6
2 Russell Pl 11375 718-268-7231
Ronnie Feder, prin. Fax 575-3571
Public S 144 600/PK-6
9302 69th Ave 11375 718-268-2775
Reba Schneider, prin. Fax 575-3734
Public S 196 600/K-5
7125 113th St 11375 718-263-9770
Mary Hughes, prin. Fax 575-3934
Public S 220 400/PK-5
6210 108th St 11375 718-592-3030
Josette Pizarro, prin. Fax 271-7642

Bnos Malka Academy 200/PK-8
7102 113th St 11375 718-268-2667
Forest Hills Montessori S 100/PK-6
6704 Austin St 11375 718-275-0173
Sunila Tejpaul, dir. Fax 275-0176
Hebrew Academy of West Queens 100/K-8
7502 113th St 11375 718-847-1462
Kew-Forest S 300/K-12
11917 Union Tpke 11375 718-268-4667
Peter Lewis, hdmstr. Fax 268-9121
Our Lady of Mercy S 400/PK-8
7025 Kessel St 11375 718-793-2086
Linda Dougherty, prin. Fax 897-2144
Our Lady Queen of Martyrs S 300/PK-8
7255 Austin St 11375 718-263-2622
Anne Zuschlag, prin. Fax 263-0063
Sha'arei Zion Ohel Bracha - Boys 300/PK-8
7524 Grand Central Pkwy 11375 718-268-3444
Sha'arei Zion Ohel Bracha - Girls 50/PK-5
7524 Grand Central Pkwy 11375 718-897-6771
Yeshiva Tifereth Moshe Dov Revel 200/PK-3
7102 113th St 11375 718-544-5400

Forestport, Oneida
Adirondack Central SD
Supt. — See Boonville
Forestport ES 100/K-5
10275 State Route 28 13338 315-392-2700
Dr. Elizabeth Lemieux, prin. Fax 392-2707

Forestville, Chautauqua, Pop. 733
Forestville Central SD 600/K-12
12 Water St 14062 716-965-2742
John O'Connor, supt. Fax 965-2117
www.forestville.com
Forestville ES 300/K-5
12 Water St 14062 716-965-2742
Daniel Grande, prin. Fax 965-2117

Fort Ann, Washington, Pop. 469
Fort Ann Central SD 600/K-12
1 Catherine St 12827 518-639-5594
Maureen VanBuren, supt. Fax 639-8911
www.fortannschool.org/
Fort Ann S 600/K-12
1 Catherine St 12827 518-639-5594
Dan Ward, prin. Fax 639-8911

Fort Covington, Franklin
Salmon River Central SD 1,600/PK-12
637 County Route 1 12937 518-358-6610
Jane Collins, supt. Fax 358-3492
www.srk12.org/
Salmon River ES 400/PK-6
637 County Route 1 12937 518-358-6670
Kevin Walbridge, prin. Fax 358-3492
Other Schools – See Hogansburg

Fort Edward, Washington, Pop. 3,120
Fort Edward UFD 500/PK-12
220 Broadway 12828 518-747-4594
Jeffery Ziegler, supt. Fax 747-4289
www.fortedward.org
Fort Edward S 500/PK-12
220 Broadway 12828 518-747-4529
John Godfrey, prin. Fax 747-4289

Fort Montgomery, Orange, Pop. 1,450
Highland Falls Ft. Montgomery Central SD 1,200/PK-12
21 Morgan Farm Rd 10922 845-446-9575
Debra Jackson, supt. Fax 446-3321
www.hffmcsd.org/
Fort Montgomery ES 200/K-2
895 Route 9W 10922 845-446-1008
Dr. Maureen Lamb, prin. Fax 446-6608
Other Schools – See Highland Falls

Fort Plain, Montgomery, Pop. 2,211
Fort Plain Central SD 900/PK-12
25 High St 13339 518-993-4000
Douglas Burton, supt. Fax 993-3393
www.fortplain.org
Hoag ES 500/PK-6
25 High St 13339 518-993-4000
Linda Tharp, prin. Fax 993-4501

Frankfort, Herkimer, Pop. 2,452
Frankfort-Schuyler Central SD 800/K-12
605 Palmer St 13340 315-894-5083
Robert Reina, supt. Fax 895-7011
www.frankfort-schuyler.org
Reese Road ES 300/K-5
610 Reese Rd 13340 315-895-7491
Joyce Dayton, prin. Fax 895-4102
West Frankfort ES 300/K-5
160 School Ln 13340 315-735-8336
Frank Saraceno, prin. Fax 735-9231

Franklin, Delaware, Pop. 384
Franklin Central SD 300/PK-12
PO Box 888 13775 607-829-3551
Gordon Daniels, supt. Fax 829-2101
www.franklincsd.org
Franklin Central S 300/PK-12
PO Box 888 13775 607-829-3551
Jason Thomson, prin. Fax 829-2101

Franklin Square, Nassau, Pop. 29,500
Franklin Square UFD 1,800/K-6
760 Washington St 11010 516-505-6975
Dr. Anthony Pecorale, supt. Fax 505-6972
www.franklinsquare.k12.ny.us
John Street ES 400/K-6
560 Nassau Blvd 11010 516-505-6955
Ceil Candreva, prin. Fax 505-6988
Polk Street ES 700/K-6
960 Polk Ave 11010 516-326-3785
Elizabeth Hunt, prin. Fax 326-3794
Washington Street ES 700/K-6
760 Washington St 11010 516-505-6995
Valerie Mazzone, prin. Fax 505-6991

Valley Stream 13 UFD
Supt. — See Valley Stream
Willow Road ES 500/K-6
880 Catalpa Dr 11010 516-568-6640
Stephanie Capozzoli, prin. Fax 292-2095

St. Catherine of Siena S 300/PK-8
990 Holzheimer St 11010 516-437-2733
Cecelia Rando, prin. Fax 437-6073

Franklinville, Cattaraugus, Pop. 1,778
Franklinville Central SD 800/K-12
31 N Main St 14737 716-676-8029
Dennis Johnson, supt. Fax 676-3779
www.franklinville.wnyric.org
Franklinville ES 400/K-6
32 N Main St 14737 716-676-8020
Jennifer Cappelletti, prin. Fax 676-2797

Fredonia, Chautauqua, Pop. 10,735
Fredonia Central SD 1,800/PK-12
425 E Main St 14063 716-679-1581
Paul DiFonzo, supt. Fax 679-1555
www.fredonia.wnyric.org
Fredonia ES 300/3-5
425 E Main St 14063 716-679-1581
James Detwiler, prin. Fax 679-9043
Fredonia MS 400/6-8
425 E Main St 14063 716-679-1581
Andrew Ludwig, prin. Fax 672-2686
Wheelock PS 400/PK-2
425 E Main St 14063 716-679-1581
Danielle Grimm, prin. Fax 672-4802

Freeport, Nassau, Pop. 43,519
Freeport UFD 6,400/PK-12
235 N Ocean Ave 11520 516-867-5200
Dr. Eric Eversley, supt. Fax 623-4759
www.freeportschools.org
Archer St ES Language Arts Math & Tech 500/1-4
255 Archer St 11520 516-867-5250
Paula Lein, prin. Fax 379-6577
Atkinson ES 1,000/5-6
58 W Seaman Ave 11520 516-867-5270
Linda Carter, prin. Fax 379-7678
Bayview Avenue ES 500/1-4
325 W Merrick Rd 11520 516-867-5255
Odette Wills, prin. Fax 379-6906
Columbus Ave S 500/PK-K
150 N Columbus Ave 11520 516-867-5240
Peggy Miller, prin. Fax 379-6793
Dodd MS 1,000/7-8
25 Pine St 11520 516-867-5280
John O'Mard, prin. Fax 379-6794
Giblyn ES 500/1-4
450 S Ocean Ave 11520 516-867-5260
Amanda Villalba, prin. Fax 379-6887
New Visions Museum ES 400/1-4
80 Raynor St 11520 516-867-5390
Renee Crump, prin. Fax 867-0392

De LaSalle S 50/5-8
87 Pine St 11520 516-379-8660
Kathleen Boniello, prin. Fax 379-8806
Freeport Christian Academy 200/PK-8
50 N Main St 11520 516-546-2020
Tito Mattei, hdmstr. Fax 546-8394

Freeville, Tompkins, Pop. 507
Dryden Central SD
Supt. — See Dryden
Freeville ES 100/K-2
43 Main St 13068 607-844-9251
Audrey Ryan, prin. Fax 844-3826

Covenant Love Community S 50/K-8
1768 Dryden Rd 13068 607-347-4413
Pamela Bateman, prin. Fax 347-4466

Fresh Meadows, See New York
NYC Department of Education
Supt. — See New York
Queens S of Inquiry 200/6-8
15840 76th Rd 11366 718-380-6929
Elizabeth Ophals, prin. Fax 380-6809

Frewsburg, Chautauqua, Pop. 1,817
Frewsburg Central SD 900/PK-12
PO Box 690 14738 716-569-9241
Stephen Vanstrom, supt. Fax 569-4681
frewsburg.wnyric.org
Jackson ES 400/PK-6
PO Box 690 14738 716-569-5630
Anne Ray, prin. Fax 569-5682

Friendship, Allegany, Pop. 1,423
Friendship Central SD 400/PK-12
46 W Main St 14739 585-973-3534
Maureen Donahue, supt. Fax 973-2023
www.friendship.wnyric.org/
Friendship Central S 400/PK-12
46 W Main St 14739 585-973-3311
Donald Putnam, prin. Fax 973-2023

Fulton, Oswego, Pop. 11,525
Fulton CSD 3,700/K-12
167 S 4th St 13069 315-593-5510
William Lynch, supt. Fax 598-6351
www.fulton.cnyric.org/
Fairgrieve ES 600/K-6
716 Academy St 13069 315-593-5550
Jean Ciesla, prin. Fax 593-5561
Fulton JHS 600/7-8
129 Curtis St 13069 315-593-5440
Donna Parkhurst, prin. Fax 593-5459
Granby ES 500/K-6
400 W 7th St N 13069 315-593-5480
Heather Perry, prin. Fax 598-2835
Lanigan ES 500/K-6
59 Bakeman St 13069 315-593-5470
Dan Johnson, prin. Fax 593-5479
Volney ES 400/K-6
2592 State Route 3 13069 315-593-5570
Jeff Hendrickson, prin. Fax 593-5579

Mexico Central SD
Supt. — See Mexico
Palermo ES 200/K-4
1638 County Route 45 13069 315-963-8400
Margaret Scorzelli, prin. Fax 598-5070

Dexterville SDA S 50/1-8
785 County Route 3 13069 315-593-8674

Gainesville, Wyoming, Pop. 292
Letchworth Central SD 1,100/K-12
5550 School Rd 14066 585-493-5450
Joseph Backer, supt. Fax 493-2762
www.letchworth.k12.ny.us/
Letchworth ES 400/K-4
5550 School Rd 14066 585-493-2581
William Bean, prin. Fax 493-2762
Letchworth MS 400/5-8
5550 School Rd 14066 585-493-2592
Paula Roberts-Mighells, prin. Fax 493-2762

Galway, Saratoga, Pop. 213
Galway Central SD 1,100/K-12
5317 Sacandaga Rd 12074 518-882-1033
Clifford Moses, supt.
www.galwaycsd.org/
Galway MS 200/7-8
5317 Sacandaga Rd 12074 518-882-5047
Paul Berry, prin. Fax 882-5850
Henry ES 500/K-6
5317 Sacandaga Rd 12074 518-882-1291
Norman Griffin, prin. Fax 882-5250

Garden City, Nassau, Pop. 21,697
Garden City UFD 4,300/K-12
56 Cathedral Ave 11530 516-478-1000
Dr. Robert Feirsen, supt. Fax 294-5631
www.gardencity.k12.ny.us
Garden City MS 1,100/6-8
98 Cherry Valley Ave 11530 516-478-3000
Peter Osroff, prin. Fax 294-0732
Hemlock ES 200/K-1
78 Bayberry Ave 11530 516-478-1600
Audrey Bellovin, prin. Fax 747-4767
Homestead ES 300/K-1
2 Homestead Ave 11530 516-478-1700
Suzanne Viscovich, prin. Fax 616-0906
Locust ES 200/K-1
220 Boylston St 11530 516-478-1800
Jean Ricotta, prin. Fax 747-4586
Stewart ES 600/2-5
501 Stewart Ave 11530 516-478-1400
Linda Norton, prin. Fax 294-5781
Stratford Avenue ES 700/2-5
97 Stratford Ave 11530 516-478-1500
Diane Hopkins, prin. Fax 294-9061

St. Anne S 500/PK-8
25 Dartmouth St 11530 516-352-1205
Dr. William O'Sullivan, prin. Fax 352-5969
St. Joseph S 300/PK-8
450 Franklin Ave 11530 516-747-2730
Dr. Eileen Kilbride, prin. Fax 747-2854
Waldorf S of Garden City 400/PK-12
225 Cambridge Ave 11530 516-742-3434
Susan Braun, admin. Fax 742-3457

Garnerville, See West Haverstraw
North Rockland Central SD 7,900/PK-12
65 Chapel St 10923 845-942-3000
Ileann Eckert, supt. Fax 942-3002
www.nrcsd.org
North Garnerville ES 300/PK-4
63 Chapel St 10923 845-942-3120
Mary Esposito, prin. Fax 942-3014
Other Schools – See Haverstraw, Stony Point, Thiells, West Haverstraw

---

St. Gregory Barbarigo S 200/PK-8
29 Cinder Rd 10923 845-947-1330
Cathleen Cassel, prin. Fax 947-4392

Garrison, Putnam
Garrison UFD 300/K-8
PO Box 193 10524 845-424-3689
Gloria Colucci, supt. Fax 424-4733
www.gufs.org
Garrison Union Free S 300/K-8
PO Box 193 10524 845-424-3689
Stephanie Impellittiere, prin. Fax 424-4733

Gasport, Niagara, Pop. 1,336
Royalton-Hartland Central SD
Supt. — See Middleport
Royalton-Hartland ES 600/K-4
4500 Orchard Pl 14067 716-772-2616
Andrew Auer, prin. Fax 772-2227

Geneseo, Livingston, Pop. 7,809
Geneseo Central SD 1,000/K-12
4050 Avon Rd 14454 585-243-3450
Timothy Hayes, supt. Fax 243-9481
geneseocsd.org/
Geneseo ES 400/K-5
4050 Avon Rd 14454 585-243-3450
Mark Linton, prin. Fax 243-9481

Genesee Country Christian S 100/PK-6
4120 Long Point Rd 14454 585-243-9580
Susan Teitsworth, admin. Fax 243-5604

Geneva, Ontario, Pop. 13,509
Geneva CSD 2,400/K-12
649 Exchange St 14456 315-781-0400
Dr. Robert Young, supt. Fax 781-4193
www.genevacsd.org
Geneva MS 600/6-8
101 Carter Rd 14456 315-781-0404
Carmine Calabria, prin. Fax 781-0694
North Street ES 500/K-5
400 W North St 14456 315-781-0489
Nina McCarthy, prin. Fax 781-4195
West Street ES 500/K-5
30 West St 14456 315-781-0406
Arlene McDermott, prin. Fax 781-0599

Maxwell Christian S K-8
3550 Number 9 Rd 14456 585-526-7131
SS. Francis De Sales & Stephen S 200/PK-8
17 Elmwood Ave 14456 315-789-1828
Elaine Morrow, prin. Fax 789-9179

Georgetown, Madison
Otselic Valley Central SD
Supt. — See South Otselic
Otselic Valley ES 200/K-6
PO Box 190 13072 315-837-4407
Nancy Gallaher, prin. Fax 837-4775

Germantown, Columbia
Germantown Central SD 700/K-12
123 Main St 12526 518-537-6280
Patrick Gabriel, supt. Fax 537-6283
www.germantowncsd.org
Germantown Central ES 300/K-6
123 Main St 12526 518-537-6281
Sue Brown, prin. Fax 537-6893

Ghent, Columbia

Hawthorne Valley S 300/PK-12
330 County Route 21C 12075 518-672-7092
Caroline Geisler, admin. Fax 672-0181

Gilbertsville, Otsego, Pop. 351
Gilbertsville-Mount Upton Central SD 500/K-12
693 State Highway 51 13776 607-783-2207
Glenn Hamilton, supt. Fax 783-2254
www.gmucsd.org/
Gilbertsville-Mount Upton ES 200/K-6
693 State Highway 51 13776 607-783-2207
Karen Volpi, prin. Fax 783-2254

Gilboa, Schoharie
Gilboa-Conesville Central SD 400/K-12
132 Wyckoff Rd 12076 607-588-7541
Dr. Darlene McDonough, supt. Fax 588-6820
www.gilboa-conesville.k12.ny.us/
Gilboa-Conesville Central S 400/K-12
132 Wyckoff Rd 12076 607-588-7555
Ben Badurina, prin. Fax 588-6820

Glasco, Ulster, Pop. 1,538
Saugerties Central SD
Supt. — See Saugerties
Riccardi ES 400/K-6
70 Plenty 12432 845-247-6870
Michael Miller, prin. Fax 246-2582

Glen Cove, Nassau, Pop. 26,633
Glen Cove CSD 2,900/PK-12
150 Dosoris Ln 11542 516-801-7010
Dr. Laurence Aronstein, supt. Fax 801-7019
www.glencove.k12.ny.us
Connolly ES 300/3-5
1 Ridge Dr 11542 516-801-7310
Rosemarie Sekelsky, prin. Fax 801-7319

Deasy ES 400/PK-2
2 Dosoris Ln 11542 516-801-7110
Julio Delgado, prin. Fax 801-7119
Finley MS 600/6-8
1 Forest Ave 11542 516-801-7510
Anael Alston, prin. Fax 801-7519
Gribbin ES 300/K-2
100 Seaman Rd 11542 516-801-7210
Francine Santoro, prin. Fax 801-7219
Landing ES 300/3-5
60 McLoughlin St 11542 516-801-7410
Dr. Michael Israel, prin. Fax 801-7419

All Saints S 400/PK-8
12 Pearsall Ave 11542 516-676-0762
James Thompson, prin. Fax 676-0660

Glendale, See New York
NYC Department of Education
Supt. — See New York
IS 119 1,000/6-8
7401 78th Ave 11385 718-326-8261
Dr. Jeanne Fagan, prin. Fax 456-9523
Public S 91 700/K-5
6810 Central Ave 11385 718-821-6880
Ken Lombardi, prin. Fax 386-0216
Public S 113 500/K-5
8721 79th Ave 11385 718-847-0724
Anthony Pranzo, prin. Fax 805-0737

Redeemer Lutheran S 200/PK-8
6926 Cooper Ave 11385 718-821-6670
Fax 366-0338
Sacred Heart S 300/PK-8
8405 78th Ave 11385 718-456-6636
Joanne Gangi, prin. Fax 456-0286
St. John Evangelical Lutheran S 200/PK-8
8824 Myrtle Ave 11385 718-441-2120
C. Barbara Chin-Sinn, prin. Fax 805-4735
St. Pancras S 300/PK-8
6820 Myrtle Ave 11385 718-821-6721
Philip Ciani, prin. Fax 418-8991

Glenfield, Lewis
South Lewis Central SD
Supt. — See Turin
Glenfield ES 200/K-5
PO Box 66 13343 315-348-2620
Martha Jones, prin. Fax 348-2510

Glen Head, Nassau, Pop. 4,488
North Shore Central SD
Supt. — See Sea Cliff
Glen Head ES 500/K-5
7 School St 11545 516-277-7700
Lori Nimmo, prin. Fax 277-7701
Glenwood Landing ES 500/K-5
60 Cody Ave 11545 516-277-7600
Bridget Finder, prin. Fax 277-7601
North Shore MS 700/6-8
505 Glen Cove Ave 11545 516-277-7300
Marc Ferris, prin. Fax 277-7301

Glenmont, Albany
Bethlehem Central SD
Supt. — See Delmar
Glenmont ES 500/K-5
328 Route 9W 12077 518-463-1154
Laura Heffernan, prin. Fax 432-5209

Glens Falls, Warren, Pop. 14,108
Glens Falls CSD 2,400/K-12
15 Quade St 12801 518-792-1212
Thomas McGowan, supt. Fax 792-1538
www.gfsd.org
Big Cross Street ES 200/K-5
15 Big Cross St 12801 518-792-2619
Debbie Hall, prin. Fax 792-2668
Glens Falls MS 600/6-8
20 Quade St 12801 518-793-3418
Christopher Reed, prin. Fax 793-4888
Jackson Heights ES 200/K-5
24 Jackson Ave 12801 518-792-1071
Paul Berkheimer, prin. Fax 798-6501
Kensington Road ES 200/K-5
43 Kensington Rd 12801 518-793-5151
Jennifer Hayes, prin. Fax 793-5404
Sanford Street ES 200/K-5
10 Sanford St 12801 518-793-5653
Patrick Dee, prin. Fax 793-5770

Glens Falls Common SD 100/K-6
120 Lawrence St 12801 518-792-3231
Ella Collins, supt. Fax 792-2557
abewing.nycap.rr.com
Wing ES 100/K-6
120 Lawrence St 12801 518-792-3231
Ella Collins, prin. Fax 792-2557

SS. Mary/Alphonsus Regional Catholic S 300/PK-8
10-12 Church St 12801 518-792-3178
Kathryn Mahoney Fowler, prin. Fax 792-6056

Glen Spey, Sullivan
Eldred Central SD
Supt. — See Eldred
MacKenzie ES 300/K-6
PO Box 249 12737 845-456-1100
Kathryn Ryan, prin. Fax 557-8579

Homestead S 200/PK-3
428 Hollow Rd 12737 845-856-6359
Peter Comstock, prin. Fax 858-4145

Gloversville, Fulton, Pop. 15,283
Gloversville CSD 3,200/PK-12
PO Box 593 12078 518-775-5700
Robert DeLilli, supt. Fax 725-8793
www.gloversvilleschools.org
Boulevard ES 600/PK-5
56 East Blvd 12078 518-775-5740
Tom Komp, prin. Fax 725-9216
Gloversville MS 700/6-8
234 Lincoln St 12078 518-775-5720
James Christopher, prin. Fax 773-9865
Kingsborough ES 300/K-5
24 W 11th Ave 12078 518-775-5730
Jane Parsons, prin. Fax 773-7357
McNab ES 300/2-5
230 W Fulton St 12078 518-775-5760
Mike Ponticello, prin. Fax 725-6754
Meco ES 100/PK-1
140 County Highway 101 12078 518-775-5770
Mike Ponticello, prin. Fax 725-0724
Park Terrace ES 300/PK-5
50 Bloomingdale Ave 12078 518-775-5750
Stephen Pavone, prin. Fax 725-7156

Goldens Bridge, Westchester, Pop. 1,589
Katonah-Lewisboro UFD
Supt. — See South Salem
Increase Miller ES 400/K-5
186 Waccabuc Rd 10526 914-763-7100
Kerry Sullivan, prin. Fax 763-7173

Gorham, Ontario
Marcus Whitman Central SD
Supt. — See Rushville
Gorham ES 300/K-5
PO Box 217 14461 585-526-6351
Paul Lahue, prin. Fax 526-4435

Goshen, Orange, Pop. 5,437
Goshen Central SD 2,900/K-12
227 Main St 10924 845-615-6720
Daniel Connor, supt. Fax 615-6725
www.goshenschoolsny.org
Goshen IS 600/3-5
13 McNally St 10924 845-615-6500
Mary Ann Knight, prin. Fax 615-6505
Hooker MS 700/6-8
41 Lincoln Ave 10924 845-615-6300
Colleen Kane, prin. Fax 615-6310
Scotchtown Avenue ES 700/K-2
120 Scotchtown Ave 10924 845-615-6600
Daria Murphy, prin. Fax 615-6610

Goshen Christian S 100/PK-9
43 Route 17A 10924 845-294-6365
David Landdeck, prin. Fax 294-0668
St. John S 200/1-8
77 Murray Ave 10924 845-294-6434
Sr. Barbara Werner, prin. Fax 294-7303

Gouverneur, Saint Lawrence, Pop. 4,127
Gouverneur Central SD 1,800/K-12
133 E Barney St 13642 315-287-4870
Christine LaRose, supt. Fax 287-4736
gcs.neric.org/newweb/
East Side ES 400/K-6
111 Gleason St 13642 315-287-2260
Victoria Day, prin. Fax 287-2410
Fowler ES 100/K-5
3845 State Highway 58 13642 315-287-1949
Fax 287-2350
Gouverneur MS 300/6-8
113 E Barney St 13642 315-287-1903
Lauren French, prin. Fax 287-2666
West Side ES 200/K-5
25 Wilson St 13642 315-287-3200
Janine Manley, prin. Fax 287-7222

St. James S 100/PK-6
20 S Gordon St 13642 315-287-0130
Bridgette La Pierre, prin. Fax 287-0054

Gowanda, Cattaraugus, Pop. 2,716
Gowanda Central SD 1,500/PK-12
10674 Prospect St 14070 716-532-3325
Charles Rinaldi, supt. Fax 995-2156
www.gowcsd.com
Gowanda ES 500/PK-4
10674 Prospect St 14070 716-532-3325
Janice Stokes, prin. Fax 532-0287
Gowanda MS 500/5-8
10674 Prospect St 14070 716-532-3325
David Smith, prin. Fax 995-2127

St. Joseph S 100/PK-8
71 E Main St 14070 716-532-2520
Patrick Brady, prin. Fax 532-4172

Grahamsville, Sullivan
Tri-Valley Central SD 1,200/PK-12
34 Moore Hill Rd 12740 845-985-2296
Thomas Palmer, supt. Fax 985-0310
tvcs.k12.ny.us
Tri-Valley ES 400/PK-4
34 Moore Hill Rd 12740 845-985-2278
Dr. Linda Widomski, prin. Fax 985-0046
Tri-Valley MS 400/5-8
34 Moore Hill Rd 12740 845-985-2296
Mary Killian, prin. Fax 985-7261

Grand Island, Erie
Grand Island Central SD 3,200/K-12
1100 Ransom Rd 14072 716-773-8800
Robert Christmann, supt. Fax 773-8843
www.grandisland-cs.k12.ny.us
Connor MS 700/6-8
1100 Ransom Rd 14072 716-773-8830
Bruce Benson, prin. Fax 773-8983
Huth Road ES 500/2-5
1773 Huth Rd 14072 716-773-8850
Kerri Nowak, prin. Fax 773-8984
Kaegebein ES 500/2-5
1690 Love Rd 14072 716-773-8840
Mary Haggerty, prin. Fax 773-8991
Sidway ES 400/K-1
2451 Baseline Rd 14072 716-773-8870
Denise Dunbar, prin. Fax 773-8985

St. Stephen S 200/PK-8
2080 Baseline Rd 14072 716-773-4347
Donna Ende, prin. Fax 773-1438

Granville, Washington, Pop. 2,623
Granville Central SD 1,400/K-12
58 Quaker St 12832 518-642-1051
Daniel Teplesky, supt. Fax 642-2491
www.granvillecsd.org
Granville ES 400/3-6
61 Quaker St 12832 518-642-9357
Diane Dumas, prin. Fax 642-0770
Other Schools – See Middle Granville

Great Neck, Nassau, Pop. 9,605
Great Neck UFD 6,200/PK-12
345 Lakeville Rd 11020 516-441-4001
Dr. Thomas Dolan, supt. Fax 441-4994
www.greatneck.k12.ny.us
Baker ES 500/K-5
69 Baker Hill Rd 11023 516-441-4100
Sharon Fougner, prin. Fax 441-4190
Great Neck South MS 900/6-8
349 Lakeville Rd 11020 516-441-4600
Dr. James Welsch, prin. Fax 441-4690
Kennedy ES 500/K-5
1A Grassfield Rd 11024 516-441-4200
Dr. Sue Kincaid, prin. Fax 441-4290
Lakeville ES 800/K-5
4727 Jayson Ave 11020 516-441-4300
Barbara Raber, prin. Fax 441-4316
Saddle Rock ES 500/K-5
10 Hawthorne Ln 11023 516-441-4400
Eric Nezowitz, prin. Fax 441-4993
Sherman Great Neck North MS 600/6-8
77 Polo Rd 11023 516-441-4500
Denise Desmond-Nolan, prin. Fax 441-4594
Other Schools – See New Hyde Park

Long Island Hebrew Academy 100/PK-4
122 Cutter Mill Rd 11021 516-466-3656
North Shore Hebrew Academy 500/PK-5
16 Cherry Ln 11024 516-487-8687
Yeshayahu Greenfeld, dean Fax 487-8721
North Shore Hebrew Academy 200/6-8
26 Old Mill Rd 11023 516-487-9163

Greene, Chenango, Pop. 1,690
Greene Central SD 1,300/K-12
40 S Canal St 13778 607-656-4161
Jonathan Retz, supt. Fax 656-9362
www.greenecsd.org
Greene IS 300/3-5
105 Elementary Ln 13778 607-656-9891
Bryan Ayres, prin. Fax 656-8092
Greene MS 300/6-8
40 S Canal St 13778 607-656-4161
Judy Gorton, prin. Fax 656-4520
Greene PS 300/K-2
127 Elementary Ln 13778 607-656-5174
Carole Stanbro, prin. Fax 656-4044

Greenfield Center, Saratoga
Saratoga Springs CSD
Supt. — See Saratoga Springs
Greenfield Center ES 400/K-5
3180 Route 9N 12833 518-893-7402
Michael Hewitt, prin. Fax 893-7408

Green Island, Albany, Pop. 2,572
Green Island UFD 300/K-12
171 Hudson Ave 12183 518-273-1422
John McKinney, supt. Fax 270-0818
www.greenisland.org
Heatly S 300/K-12
171 Hudson Ave 12183 518-273-1422
Erin Peteani, prin. Fax 270-0818

Greenlawn, Suffolk, Pop. 13,208
Elwood UFD 2,600/K-12
100 Kenneth Ave 11740 631-266-5402
David Cenerelli, supt. Fax 266-3834
www.elwood.k12.ny.us
Other Schools – See Elwood, Huntington

Harborfields Central SD 3,700/K-12
2 Oldfield Rd 11740 631-754-5320
Frank Carasiti, supt. Fax 261-0068
www.harborfieldscsd.net
Lahey ES 900/3-5
625 Pulaski Rd 11740 631-754-5400
Florence Tuzzi, prin. Fax 754-5412
Oldfield MS 900/6-8
2 Oldfield Rd 11740 631-754-5310
Joanne Giordano, prin. Fax 754-2677
Other Schools – See Centerport

Greenport, Suffolk, Pop. 2,079
Greenport UFD 700/K-12
720 Front St 11944 631-477-1950
Michael Comanda, supt. Fax 477-2164
www.gufsd.org/
Greenport ES 300/K-6
720 Front St 11944 631-477-1950
Paul Read, prin. Fax 477-2164

Greenvale, Nassau
Roslyn UFD
Supt. — See Roslyn
Harbor Hill ES 600/1-5
3 Glen Cove Rd 11548 516-801-5401
Mary Liguori, prin. Fax 801-5408

Greenville, Greene, Pop. 9,528
Greenville Central SD 1,400/K-12
4982 State Route 81 12083 518-966-5070
Cheryl Dudley, supt.
www.greenville.k12.ny.us
Ellis ES, 11219 State Route 32 12083 600/K-5
Peter Mahan, prin. 518-966-5070
Greenville MS 300/6-8
4976 State Route 81 12083 518-966-5070
Brian Reeve, prin.

Greenwich, Washington, Pop. 1,886
Greenwich Central SD 1,100/K-12
10 Gray Ave 12834 518-692-9542
Matthias Donnelly, supt. Fax 692-9547
www.greenwichcsd.org/
Greenwich ES 600/K-6
10 Gray Ave 12834 518-692-9542
Benjamin Pisani, prin. Fax 692-7658

Greenwood, Steuben
Canisteo-Greenwood Central SD
Supt. — See Canisteo
Canisteo-Greenwood MS 200/5-8
PO Box 936 14839 607-225-4292
Nick Rossio, prin. Fax 225-4944

Greenwood Lake, Orange, Pop. 3,461
Greenwood Lake UFD
Supt. — See Monroe
Greenwood Lake ES 300/K-4
PO Box 8 10925 845-477-2411
Natasha Shea, prin. Fax 477-3180

Groton, Tompkins, Pop. 2,432
Groton Central SD 1,000/K-12
PO Box 99 13073 607-898-5301
Dr. Brenda Myers, supt. Fax 898-4647
www.grotoncs.org
Groton ES 500/K-5
516 Elm St 13073 607-898-5853
Timothy Heller, prin. Fax 898-5886
Groton MS 300/6-8
400 Peru Rd 13073 607-898-5803
Connie Filzen, prin. Fax 898-5824

Guilderland, Albany
Guilderland Central SD 5,400/K-12
6076 State Farm Rd 12084 518-456-6200
John McGuire, supt. Fax 456-1152
www.guilderlandschools.org/
Farnsworth MS 1,400/6-8
6072 State Farm Rd 12084 518-456-6010
Mary Summermatter, prin. Fax 456-3747
Guilderland ES 500/K-5
2225 Western Ave 12084 518-869-0293
Allan Lockwood, prin. Fax 464-6458
Other Schools – See Albany, Altamont, Schenectady

Guilford, Chenango
Bainbridge-Guilford Central SD
Supt. — See Bainbridge
Guilford ES 100/K-1
138 School St 13780 607-895-6700
Richard Howard, prin. Fax 895-6713

Hamburg, Erie, Pop. 9,637
Frontier Central SD 5,400/K-12
5120 Orchard Ave 14075 716-926-1711
Ronald DeCarli, supt. Fax 926-1776
www.frontier.wnyric.org
Big Tree ES 700/K-5
4460 Bay View Rd 14075 716-926-1740
Joanne Saniewski, prin. Fax 646-2111
Cloverbank ES 600/K-5
2761 Cloverbank Rd 14075 716-926-1760
Fax 627-7959
Frontier MS 1,300/6-8
2751 Amsdell Rd 14075 716-926-1730
M. Kerry Courtney, prin. Fax 646-2207
Other Schools – See Blasdell, Lake View

Hamburg Central SD 4,100/PK-12
5305 Abbott Rd 14075 716-646-3220
Dr. Mark Crawford, supt. Fax 646-3209
www.hamburgschools.org/
Armor ES 400/K-5
5301 Abbott Rd 14075 716-646-3350
Leslie Bennett, prin. Fax 646-3368
Boston Valley ES 300/K-5
7476 Back Creek Rd 14075 716-646-3240
Paul Pietrantone, prin. Fax 646-3244
Charlotte Avenue ES 400/PK-5
301 Charlotte Ave 14075 716-646-3370
Trena Mooar, prin. Fax 646-6396
Hamburg MS 900/6-8
360 Division St 14075 716-646-3250
Geoffrey Grace, prin. Fax 646-6380
Union Pleasant Avenue ES 700/K-5
150 Pleasant Ave 14075 716-646-3280
Jacqueline Peffer, prin. Fax 646-3237

St. Mary of the Lake S 200/PK-8
S4737 Lake Shore Rd 14075 716-627-7700
Kristine Hider, prin. Fax 627-1255
SS. Peter & Paul S 300/PK-8
68 E Main St 14075 716-649-7030
Jenny Bainbridge, prin. Fax 649-5218

Hamilton, Madison, Pop. 3,550
Hamilton Central SD 600/K-12
47 W Kendrick Ave 13346 315-824-3721
Diana Bowers, supt. Fax 824-3745
www.hamiltoncentral.org/
Hamilton ES 300/K-5
47 W Kendrick Ave 13346 315-824-3736
Kevin Ellis, prin. Fax 824-3745

Hammond, Saint Lawrence, Pop. 294
Hammond Central SD 300/PK-12
PO Box 185 13646 315-324-5931
Douglas McQueer, supt. Fax 324-6057
hammond.sllboces.org/
Hammond Central S 300/PK-12
PO Box 185 13646 315-324-5931
Douglas McQueer, prin. Fax 324-6057

Hammondsport, Steuben, Pop. 707
Hammondsport Central SD 600/K-12
PO Box 368 14840 607-569-5200
Kyle Bower, supt. Fax 569-5212
www.hammondsportcsd.org
Curtiss Memorial ES 300/K-6
8272 Main Street Ext 14840 607-569-5236
James McCormick, prin. Fax 569-5225

Hampton Bays, Suffolk, Pop. 7,893
Hampton Bays UFD 1,500/K-12
86 Argonne Rd E 11946 631-723-2100
Joanne Loewenthal, supt. Fax 723-2109
www.hbschools.us
Hampton Bays ES 700/K-4
72 Ponquogue Ave 11946 631-723-2121
Marc Meyer, prin. Fax 723-2840
Hampton Bays MS 300/5-8
70 Ponquogue Ave 11946 631-723-4700
Lois Clemensen, prin. Fax 723-4900

Our Lady of the Hamptons ECC PK-PK
31 E Montauk Hwy 11946 631-728-9461
Sr. Kathryn Schlueter, prin. Fax 723-3740

Hancock, Delaware, Pop. 1,139
Hancock Central SD 500/PK-12
67 Education Ln 13783 607-637-1301
Terrance Dougherty, supt. Fax 637-2512
hancock.stier.org
Hancock ES 200/PK-4
206 Wildcat Dr 13783 607-637-1217
Jason Hans, prin. Fax 637-2512

Hannibal, Oswego, Pop. 527
Hannibal Central SD 1,600/K-12
928 Cayuga St 13074 315-564-7900
Michael DiFabio, supt. Fax 564-7263
www.hannibalcsd.org/
Fairley ES 600/K-4
953 Auburn St 13074 315-564-7945
Roseann Schoonmaker, prin. Fax 564-7105
Kenney MS 500/5-8
846 Cayuga St 13074 315-564-7955
Patrick Keefe, prin. Fax 564-7509

Harpursville, Broome
Harpursville Central SD 900/PK-12
PO Box 147 13787 607-693-8101
Kathleen Wood, supt. Fax 693-1480
www.hcs.stier.org/
Harpursville MS 200/5-8
PO Box 147 13787 607-693-8110
Joshua Quick, prin. Fax 693-1480
Olmsted ES 400/PK-4
PO Box 147 13787 607-693-8115
Gregory Jones, prin. Fax 693-1480

Harriman, Orange, Pop. 2,284
Monroe-Woodbury Central SD
Supt. — See Central Valley
Sapphire ES 400/K-1
159 Harriman Heights Rd 10926 845-460-6500
Charlene Kelemen, prin. Fax 460-6045

Harrison, Westchester, Pop. 25,827
Harrison Central SD 3,500/K-12
50 Union Ave 10528 914-835-3300
Louis Wool, supt. Fax 835-5893
www.harrisoncsd.org
Harrison Avenue ES 500/K-5
480 Harrison Ave 10528 914-630-3002
Alice Pratt, prin. Fax 835-4311
Klein MS 800/6-8
50 Union Ave 10528 914-630-3033
Scott Fried, prin. Fax 777-1346
Parsons Memorial ES 400/K-5
200 Halstead Ave 10528 914-630-3222
Robert Torp, prin. Fax 835-4657
Other Schools – See Purchase, West Harrison

St. Gregory the Great S PK-PK
94 Broadway 10528 914-835-1278
Maria Gaudelli, prin. Fax 835-2070

Harrisville, Lewis, Pop. 612
Harrisville Central SD 400/K-12
14371 Pirate Ln 13648 315-543-2707
Rolf Waters, supt. Fax 543-2360
www.hcsk12.org/
Harrisville ES 200/K-5
14371 Pirate Ln 13648 315-543-2707
Rolf Waters, prin. Fax 543-2360

Hartford, Washington
Hartford Central SD 600/PK-12
4704 State Route 149 12838 518-632-5931
Thomas Abraham, supt. Fax 632-5231
www.hartfordcsd.org
Hartford Central ES 300/PK-5
4704 State Route 149 12838 518-632-5222
Bethellen Mannix, prin. Fax 632-5231

Hartsdale, Westchester, Pop. 9,587
Greenburgh Central SD 7 1,800/PK-12
475 W Hartsdale Ave 10530 914-761-6000
Ronald Smalls, supt. Fax 761-6075
www.greenburgh.k12.ny.us
Early Childhood Program 200/PK-PK
475 W Hartsdale Ave 10530 914-949-2745
Dawn Male, dir. Fax 949-1548
Highview ES 200/2-3
200 N Central Ave 10530 914-946-6946
Gary Mastrangelo, prin. Fax 946-0397
Woodland MS 200/7-8
475 W Hartsdale Ave 10530 914-761-6052
Michael Chambless, prin. Fax 686-0445
Other Schools – See White Plains

Sacred Heart S 200/PK-8
59 Wilson St 10530 914-946-7242
Virginia Salamone, prin. Fax 946-7323

Hastings on Hudson, Westchester, Pop. 8,021
Greenburgh-Graham UFD 400/1-12
1 S Broadway 10706 914-478-1106
Amy Goodman, supt. Fax 478-0904
www.greenburghgraham.org/
Ziccolella S 200/1-8
1 S Broadway 10706 914-478-8004
Donald Griggs, prin. Fax 478-8028

Hastings-on-Hudson UFD 1,600/K-12
27 Farragut Ave 10706 914-478-6200
Robert Shaps, supt. Fax 478-6209
www.hastings.k12.ny.us
Farragut MS 500/5-8
27 Farragut Ave 10706 914-478-6230
Gail Kipper, prin. Fax 478-6314
Hillside ES 600/K-4
120 Lefurgy Ave 10706 914-478-6270
William Huppuch, prin. Fax 478-6279

Hauppauge, Suffolk, Pop. 19,750
Hauppauge UFD 4,100/K-12
PO Box 6006 11788 631-265-3630
Patricia Sullivan-Kriss, supt. Fax 265-3649
www.hauppauge.k12.ny.us
Bretton Woods ES 700/K-5
PO Box 6006 11788 631-582-6633
Matthew Giordano, prin. Fax 582-1136
Hauppauge MS 900/6-8
PO Box 6006 11788 631-265-3630
Maryann Fletcher, prin. Fax 265-9546
Other Schools – See Smithtown

Haverstraw, Rockland, Pop. 10,487
North Rockland Central SD
Supt. — See Garnerville
Haverstraw MS 500/5-7
16 Grant St 10927 845-942-3400
Avis Shelby, prin. Fax 942-3403
Neary ES 500/PK-2
20 George St 10927 845-942-3450
Miguelina Lopez, prin. Fax 942-3476

St. Peter S 200/PK-8
21 Ridge St 10927 845-429-5311
Margaret Hamilton, prin. Fax 429-5140

Hawthorne, Westchester, Pop. 4,764
Mount Pleasant Central SD
Supt. — See Thornwood
Hawthorne ES 300/K-1
225 Memorial Dr 10532 914-769-8536
Ethel Zai-Fiorello, prin. Fax 769-8527

Holy Rosary S 100/PK-8
180 Bradhurst Ave 10532 914-769-0030
Carolyn Slattery, prin. Fax 769-2768

Hempstead, Nassau, Pop. 52,829
Hempstead UFD 6,000/PK-12
185 Peninsula Blvd 11550 516-292-7111
Dr. Joseph Laria, supt. Fax 292-9471
www.hempsteadschools.org/
Franklin ES 700/1-5
335 S Franklin St 11550 516-292-7111
John Moore, prin. Fax 292-7008
Fulton ES 500/1-5
40 Fulton Ave 11550 516-292-7111
Regina Robinson, prin. Fax 489-6492
Hempstead ECC 300/K-K
436 Front St 11550 516-292-7111
Richard Brown, prin. Fax 489-5701
Hempstead Pre-K PK-PK
120 Greenwich St 11550 516-292-7113
Carolyn Townes-Richards, prin. Fax 292-1460
Jackson Annex ES 400/1-3
380 Jackson St 11550 516-292-7111
Arthur Spitzli, prin. Fax 564-3040
Jackson ES 400/3-5
451 Jackson St 11550 516-292-7111
Rodney Gilmore, prin. Fax 292-0933
Ludlum ES 400/1-5
176 William St 11550 516-292-7111
Jean Bligen, prin. Fax 489-1107
Marshall K 200/K-K
15 E Marshall St 11550 516-292-7111
Sheryl McBeth, prin. Fax 292-1433
Schultz MS 1,300/6-8
70 Greenwich St 11550 516-292-7111
Clarence Williams, prin. Fax 483-2549

Uniondale UFD
Supt. — See Uniondale
Lawrence Road MS 800/6-8
50 Lawrence Rd 11550 516-918-1500
Dexter Hodge, prin. Fax 565-5023

Crescent S 200/PK-9
130 Front St 11550 516-292-1787
Epiphany Early Childhood Learning Center 50/PK-K
35 Fulton Ave 11550 516-481-9344
Fax 487-7744

Henrietta, Monroe
Rush-Henrietta Central SD 5,700/K-12
2034 Lehigh Station Rd 14467 585-359-5012
Dr. J. Kenneth Graham, supt. Fax 359-5045
www.rhnet.org
Roth MS 800/6-8
4000 E Henrietta Rd 14467 585-359-5108
Denise Zeh, prin. Fax 359-5164
Sherman ES 500/K-5
50 Authors Ave 14467 585-359-5498
Jeffrey Pollard, prin. Fax 359-5493
Winslow ES 500/K-5
755 Pinnacle Rd 14467 585-359-5098
Andrea Hyatt, prin. Fax 359-5073
Other Schools – See Rochester, Rush, West Henrietta

Herkimer, Herkimer, Pop. 7,264
Herkimer Central SD 1,200/K-12
801 W German St 13350 315-866-2230
Carol Zygo, supt.
www.herkimercsd.org/
Herkimer ES 600/K-6
255 Gros Blvd 13350 315-866-8562
Kathleen Carney, prin. Fax 866-8568

St. Francis De Sales Regional S 100/PK-6
220 Henry St 13350 315-866-4831
Sr. Rosalie Kelley, prin. Fax 866-9043

Heuvelton, Saint Lawrence, Pop. 777
Heuvelton Central SD 600/K-12
PO Box 375 13654 315-344-2414
Susan Todd, supt. Fax 344-2349
www.heuvelton.k12.ny.us/
Heuvelton Central S 600/K-12
PO Box 375 13654 315-344-2414
Michael Warden, prin. Fax 344-2349

Hewlett, Nassau, Pop. 6,620
Hewlett-Woodmere UFD
Supt. — See Woodmere
Franklin ECC 500/PK-1
1180 Henrietta Pl 11557 516-374-8157
Bonnie Epstein, prin. Fax 374-4690
Hewlett ES 500/2-5
1570 Broadway 11557 516-374-8086
Sandra Pensak, prin. Fax 374-8182
Woodmere MS 800/6-8
1170 Peninsula Blvd 11557 516-374-8068
Richard Berkowitz, prin. Fax 374-4571

Hebrew Academy of Long Beach ECC 200/PK-K
291 Meadowview Ave 11557 516-374-7195
Dr. Shmuel Klammer, prin. Fax 374-9054
Yeshiva Toras Chaim at South Shore 400/PK-8
1170 William St 11557 516-374-7363
Rabbi Chanina Herzberg, prin. Fax 374-2024

Hicksville, Nassau, Pop. 41,400
Hicksville UFD 5,400/PK-12
200 Division Ave 11801 516-733-6600
Maureen Bright, supt. Fax 733-6584
www.hicksvillepublicschools.com
Burns Avenue ES 300/K-5
40 Burns Ave 11801 516-733-6541
Michael Dunn, prin. Fax 733-6694
Dutch Lane ES 400/PK-5
50 Stewart Ave 11801 516-733-6544
Susan Strauss, prin. Fax 733-3520
East Street ES 400/K-5
50 East St 11801 516-733-3531
Jean-Marie Serra, prin. Fax 733-3533
Fork Lane ES 300/K-5
4 Fork Ln 11801 516-733-6551
Christopher Scardino, prin. Fax 733-3521
Hicksville MS 1,300/6-8
215 Jerusalem Ave 11801 516-733-6521
Fax 733-6528
Lee Avenue ES 400/K-5
1 7th St 11801 516-733-6554
Fax 733-3522
Old Country Road ES 300/K-5
49 Rhodes Ln 11801 516-733-6559
Anthony Lubrano, prin. Fax 733-3523
Woodland Avenue ES 400/K-5
85 Ketcham Rd 11801 516-733-6566
Mary Hance, prin. Fax 733-3524

Holy Family S 500/PK-8
17 Fordham Ave 11801 516-938-3846
Vincent Albrecht, prin. Fax 938-5041
Our Lady of Mercy S 500/PK-8
520 S Oyster Bay Rd 11801 516-433-7040
Sr. Mary Deegan, prin. Fax 433-8286
St. Ignatius Loyola S 300/PK-8
30 E Cherry St 11801 516-931-0831
Sr. Mary Ann Noonan, prin. Fax 933-6528
Trinity Lutheran S 500/PK-8
40 W Nicholai St 11801 516-931-2211
Lawrence Puccio, prin. Fax 931-6345

Highland, Ulster, Pop. 4,492
Highland Central SD 1,900/K-12
320 Pancake Hollow Rd 12528 845-691-1012
Vic Liviccori, supt. Fax 691-1039
www.highland-k12.org/
Highland ES 800/K-5
16 Lockhart Ln 12528 845-691-1072
Joel Freer, prin. Fax 691-1073
Highland MS 400/6-8
71 Main St 12528 845-691-1081
Jo Burruby, prin. Fax 691-1083

St. Augustine S 200/PK-8
35 Phillips Ave 12528 845-691-2338
Patricia O'Connor, prin. Fax 691-2338

Highland Falls, Orange, Pop. 3,761
Highland Falls Ft. Montgomery Central SD
Supt. — See Fort Montgomery
Highland Falls ES 100/PK-PK, 3-
PO Box 287 10928 845-446-5898
Christine Armstrong, prin. Fax 446-6603
Highland Falls MS 300/5-8
PO Box 287 10928 845-446-4761
Ellen Connors, prin. Fax 446-0858

Sacred Heart of Jesus S 200/PK-8
7 Cozzens Ave 10928 845-446-2674
Donna Sutton, prin. Fax 446-3713

Highland Mills, Orange, Pop. 2,576

Thevenet Montessori S 100/PK-3
21 Bethany Dr 10930 845-928-6981
Sr. Norene Costa, prin. Fax 928-3179

Hillburn, Rockland, Pop. 890
Ramapo Central SD 4,700/K-12
45 Mountain Ave 10931 845-357-7783
Robert MacNaughton Ph.D., supt. Fax 357-5707
www.ramapocentral.org
Other Schools – See Sloatsburg, Suffern

Hilton, Monroe, Pop. 5,957
Hilton Central SD 4,500/K-12
225 West Ave 14468 585-392-1000
David Dimbleby, supt. Fax 392-1038
www.hilton.k12.ny.us
Northwood ES 900/K-6
433 N Greece Rd 14468 585-392-1000
Kirk Ashton, prin. Fax 392-1026
Quest ES 400/K-6
225 West Ave 14468 585-392-1000
Karen Spillman, prin. Fax 392-1033
Village ES 1,000/K-6
100 School Ln 14468 585-392-1000
Tracie Czebatol, prin. Fax 392-1012
Williams MS 700/7-8
200 School Ln 14468 585-392-1000
Carol Stehm, prin. Fax 392-1054

St. Paul Lutheran S 100/PK-8
158 East Ave 14468 585-392-4000
Clifford Hummel, prin. Fax 392-4001

Hinsdale, Cattaraugus
Hinsdale Central SD 400/K-12
3701 Main St 14743 716-557-2227
Judi McCarthy, supt. Fax 557-2259
www.hinsdalebobcats.org/hinsdale
Hinsdale Central S 400/K-12
3701 Main St 14743 716-557-2227
Laurie Edmonston, prin. Fax 557-2259

Hogansburg, Franklin
Salmon River Central SD
Supt. — See Fort Covington
St. Regis Mohawk ES 500/PK-6
385 Church St 13655 518-358-2763
Sharlee Thomas, prin. Fax 358-9275

Holbrook, Suffolk, Pop. 27,900
Sachem Central SD 15,400/K-12
245 Union Ave 11741 631-471-1336
Robert Parry, supt. Fax 471-1341
www.sachem.edu
Grundy Avenue ES 500/K-5
950 Grundy Ave 11741 631-471-1820
Dominique Kawas, prin. Fax 467-3867
Merrimac ES 500/K-5
1090 Broadway Ave 11741 631-244-5670
Maribeth Olsen, prin. Fax 563-3369
Nokomis ES 600/K-5
151 Holbrook Rd 11741 631-471-1840
Gloria Flynn, prin. Fax 467-3894
Seneca MS 800/6-8
850 Main St 11741 631-471-1850
Gemma Salvia, prin. Fax 471-1849
Other Schools – See Farmingville, Holtsville, Lake Grove, Lake Ronkonkoma

Holland, Erie, Pop. 1,288
Holland Central SD 1,200/K-12
103 Canada St 14080 716-537-8222
Garry Stone, supt. Fax 537-2453
www.holland.wnyric.org/
Brumsted ES 400/K-4
173 Canada St 14080 716-537-8255
Jeffrey Mochrie, prin. Fax 537-8252
Holland MS 400/5-8
11720 Partridge Rd 14080 716-537-8277
Eric Lawton, prin. Fax 537-2669

Holland Patent, Oneida, Pop. 459
Holland Patent Central SD 1,700/K-12
9601 Main St 13354 315-865-7221
Kathleen Davis, supt. Fax 865-4057
www.hpschools.org/
Floyd ES 400/K-5
9601 Main St 13354 315-865-5721
Kristin Casab, prin. Fax 865-7284
Holland Patent ES 300/K-5
9601 Main St 13354 315-865-8151
Allen Hyde, prin. Fax 865-7265
Holland Patent MS 400/6-8
9601 Main St 13354 315-865-8152
Charles Pratt, prin. Fax 865-7243

Holley, Orleans, Pop. 1,750
Holley Central SD 1,200/K-12
3800 N Main Street Rd 14470 585-638-6316
Robert D'Angelo, supt. Fax 638-7409
www.holleycsd.org
Holley ES 600/K-6
3800 N Main Street Rd 14470 585-638-6318
William Ottman, prin. Fax 638-0602

Sandy Creek Christian S 50/K-8
16858 Ridge Rd 14470 585-638-8271

Hollis, See New York
NYC Department of Education
Supt. — See New York
IS 238 1,400/6-8
8815 182nd St 11423 718-297-9821
Joseph Gates, prin. Fax 658-5288
Public S 35 600/PK-5
19102 90th Ave 11423 718-465-6820
Mark Dempsey, prin. Fax 217-4314

Holy Trinity Community S 100/PK-8
9020 191st St 11423 718-465-3739
Sharon Garrett, prin. Fax 465-3429
St. Gerard Majella S 200/PK-8
188th and 91st Ave 11423 718-468-1166
Sue Roye, prin. Fax 465-5634

Holtsville, Suffolk, Pop. 14,972
Sachem Central SD
Supt. — See Holbrook
Chippewa ES 600/K-5
31 Morris Ave 11742 631-696-8640
Patricia Pontius, prin. Fax 696-8645
Sagamore MS 900/6-8
57 Division St 11742 631-696-8600
Steve Siciliano, prin. Fax 696-8620
Sequoya MS 1,000/6-8
750 Waverly Ave 11742 631-207-7100
Frank Panasci, prin. Fax 207-7115
Tamarac ES 700/K-5
50 Spence Ave 11742 631-244-5680
Cheryl Scheidet, prin. Fax 244-5685
Waverly Avenue ES 700/K-5
1111 Waverly Ave 11742 631-654-8690
Susan Greiner, prin. Fax 475-3970

Homer, Cortland, Pop. 3,303
Homer Central SD 2,200/K-12
PO Box 500 13077 607-749-7241
Douglas Larison, supt. Fax 749-2312
www.homercentral.org
Homer ES 400/K-2
7 Park Pl 13077 607-749-1250
Ruth King, prin. Fax 749-1261
Homer IS 600/3-6
58 Clinton St 13077 607-749-1240
Stephanie Falls, prin. Fax 749-1238
Homer JHS 400/7-8
58 Clinton St 13077 607-749-1230
Tom Turck, prin. Fax 749-1238
Other Schools – See Truxton

Honeoye, Ontario
Honeoye Central SD 700/K-12
PO Box 170 14471 585-229-4125
David Bills, supt. Fax 229-5633
www.honeoye.org
Honeoye ES 400/K-5
PO Box 170 14471 585-229-5171
Michael Bastian, prin. Fax 229-4187

Honeoye Falls, Monroe, Pop. 2,571
Honeoye Falls-Lima Central SD 2,600/K-12
20 Church St 14472 585-624-7000
Dr. Michelle Kavanaugh, supt. Fax 624-7003
www.hflcsd.org/
Honeoye Falls-Lima MS 700/6-8
619 Quaker Meeting House Rd 14472 585-624-7100
Shawn Williams, prin. Fax 624-7121
Manor IS 700/2-5
147 East St 14472 585-624-7160
Daniel McCarthy, prin. Fax 624-3722
Other Schools – See Lima

Hoosick Falls, Rensselaer, Pop. 3,350
Hoosick Falls Central SD 1,300/K-12
PO Box 192 12090 518-686-7012
Kenneth Facin, supt. Fax 686-9060
www.hoosickfallscsd.org/
Hoosick Falls ES 700/K-6
PO Box 192 12090 518-686-9492
Patrick Dailey, prin. Fax 686-9060

St. Mary's Academy 100/PK-8
4 Parsons Ave 12090 518-686-4314
Rebecca Martin, prin. Fax 686-5957

Hopewell Junction, Dutchess, Pop. 1,786
Wappingers Central SD
Supt. — See Wappingers Falls
Gayhead ES, 15 Entry Rd 12533 1,000/K-5
Jose Olavarria, prin. 845-227-1756

St. Aloysius Happy House Learning Center PK-PK
PO Box 98 12533 845-226-5671
Gloria Castro, dir. Fax 226-5671
SS. Dennis & Columba S 500/1-8
PO Box 368 12533 845-227-7777
Sr. Anne Young, prin. Fax 226-8470

Hornell, Steuben, Pop. 8,762
Hornell CSD 1,800/K-12
25 Pearl St 14843 607-324-1302
George Kiley, supt. Fax 324-4060
www.hornell.wnyric.org
Bryant ES 200/K-2
173 Terry St 14843 607-324-2171
Barbara Kramer, prin. Fax 324-5588
Hornell IS 500/3-6
71 Buffalo St 14843 607-324-1304
Colleen Argentieri, prin. Fax 324-4060

North Hornell ES 300/K-2
Avondale Avenue 14843 607-324-0014
Barbara Kramer, prin. Fax 324-4060

St. Ann S 100/PK-8
27 Erie Ave 14843 607-324-0733
Sr. Dolores Ann Stein, prin. Fax 324-0985

Horseheads, Chemung, Pop. 6,366
Horseheads Central SD 4,200/K-12
1 Raider Ln 14845 607-739-5601
Ralph Marino, supt. Fax 739-5832
www.horseheadsdistrict.org
Center Street ES 300/K-4
812 Center St 14845 607-795-2580
Patricia Sotero, prin. Fax 795-2585
Gardner Road ES 400/K-4
541 Gardner Rd 14845 607-739-6347
Mary Ann Suggs, prin. Fax 795-2545
Horseheads IS 600/5-6
952 Sing Sing Rd 14845 607-739-6366
Bobbi Brock, prin. Fax 795-2495
Horseheads MS 700/7-8
950 Sing Sing Rd 14845 607-739-6356
Fax 795-2525
Ridge Road ES 400/K-4
112 Ridge Rd 14845 607-739-6351
Anne Marie Bailey, prin. Fax 795-2485
Other Schools – See Big Flats

St. Mary Our Mother S 100/PK-6
811 Westlake St 14845 607-739-9157
Marilyn Zinn, prin. Fax 739-2532

Howard Beach, See New York
NYC Department of Education
Supt. — See New York
Public S 146 400/PK-7
9801 159th Ave 11414 718-843-4880
Mary Reilly, prin. Fax 641-0901
Public S 207 700/PK-8
15915 88th St 11414 718-848-2700
Linda Spadaro, prin. Fax 848-4226
Public S 232 600/K-8
15323 83rd St 11414 718-848-9247
Lisa Josephson, prin. Fax 738-8505

Our Lady of Grace S 200/K-8
15820 101st St 11414 718-848-7440
Barbara Kavanagh, prin. Fax 641-3464
St. Helen S 300/PK-8
8309 157th Ave 11414 718-835-4155
Peter Doran, prin. Fax 738-0580

Hudson, Columbia, Pop. 7,145
Hudson CSD 2,000/K-12
215 Harry Howard Ave 12534 518-828-4360
David Paciencia, supt. Fax 697-8777
www.hudsoncityschooldistrict.com/
Edwards ES 400/K-2
360 State St 12534 518-828-9493
Carol Gans, prin. Fax 697-8516
Greenport ES 300/3-4
158 Union Tpke 12534 518-828-4305
Thomas Baumgartner, prin. Fax 697-8522
Hudson MS 700/5-8
102 Harry Howard Ave 12534 518-828-4650
Ryan Groat, prin. Fax 697-8434

Hudson Falls, Washington, Pop. 6,864
Hudson Falls Central SD 2,300/K-12
PO Box 710 12839 518-747-2121
Mark Doody, supt. Fax 747-0951
www.hfcsd.org
Hudson Falls IS 300/4-5
135 Maple St 12839 518-747-2121
Robert Cook, prin. Fax 747-2774
Hudson Falls MS 600/6-8
131 Notre Dame St 12839 518-747-2121
Todd Gonyeau, prin. Fax 746-2790
Hudson Falls PS 500/1-3
47 Vaughn Rd 12839 518-747-2121
Janet Gallant, prin. Fax 747-3502
Murphy K 200/K-K
2 Clark St 12839 518-747-2121
Janet Gallant, prin. Fax 747-3853

Kingsbury Junior Academy 50/1-8
PO Box 185 12839 518-747-4424
Fax 746-1750

Hunter, Greene, Pop. 494
Hunter-Tannersville Central SD
Supt. — See Tannersville
Hunter ES 300/PK-6
7794 Main St 12442 518-263-4256
Melinda McCool, prin. Fax 263-4086

Huntington, Suffolk, Pop. 18,243
Cold Spring Harbor Central SD
Supt. — See Cold Spring Harbor
Lloyd Harbor ES 500/2-6
7 School Ln 11743 631-421-3700
Valerie Massimo, prin. Fax 421-4229

Elwood UFD
Supt. — See Greenlawn
Boyd IS 600/3-5
286 Cuba Hill Rd 11743 631-266-5430
Sharon McCabe, prin. Fax 266-6265

Huntington UFD
Supt. — See Huntington Station
Finley JHS 600/7-8
20 Greenlawn Rd 11743 631-673-2020
John Amato, prin. Fax 425-4746
Flower Hill PS 300/K-3
98 Flower Hill Rd 11743 631-673-2050
Marlon Small, prin. Fax 425-6255
Jefferson PS 400/K-3
253 Oakwood Rd 11743 631-673-2070
Margaret Evers, prin. Fax 425-6257
Southdown PS 400/K-3
125 Browns Rd 11743 631-673-2080
Michelle Marino, prin. Fax 425-6258
Woodhull IS 500/4-6
140 Woodhull Rd 11743 631-673-2030
Dr. Kenneth Card, prin. Fax 425-4718

South Huntington UFD
Supt. — See Huntington Station
Oakwood PS 700/K-2
264 W 22nd St 11743 631-425-5500
Eileen Kerrigan, prin. Fax 425-5479

St. Patrick S 800/PK-8
360 Main St 11743 631-385-3311
Sr. Maureen McDade, prin. Fax 673-4609

Huntington Station, Suffolk, Pop. 30,200
Huntington UFD 4,200/K-12
50 Tower St 11746 631-673-2038
John Finello, supt. Fax 423-3447
www.hufsd.edu/
Huntington IS 500/4-6
115 Lowndes Ave 11746 631-673-2060
Mary Stokkers, prin. Fax 425-6256
Washington PS 300/K-3
78 Whitson Rd 11746 631-673-2090
Marsha Neville, prin. Fax 425-6259
Other Schools – See Huntington

South Huntington UFD 5,500/K-12
60 Weston St 11746 631-425-5300
Thomas Shea Ed.D., supt. Fax 425-5362
www.shufsd.org
Countrywood PS 700/K-2
499 Old Country Rd 11746 631-425-5470
Karen Siegel, prin. Fax 425-5415
Maplewood IS 700/3-5
19 School Ln 11746 631-425-5336
Vito D'Elia, prin. Fax 425-5555
Stimson MS 900/7-8
401 Oakwood Rd 11746 631-425-5432
Faye Robins, prin. Fax 425-5449
Wood 6th Grade Center 6-6
23 Harding Pl 11746 631-425-5511
Roberta Lewis, prin. Fax 425-5469
Other Schools – See Huntington, Melville

Long Island S for the Gifted 300/PK-9
165 Pidgeon Hill Rd 11746 631-423-3557
Carol Yilmaz, dir. Fax 423-4368

Hurley, Ulster, Pop. 4,644
Kingston CSD
Supt. — See Kingston
Myer ES 300/K-5
Millbrook Ave 12443 845-331-6905
Andrea Lambeth-Smith, prin. Fax 331-1520

Hyde Park, Dutchess, Pop. 21,230
Hyde Park Central SD 4,400/K-12
PO Box 2033 12538 845-229-4000
Carole Pickering, supt. Fax 229-4056
www.hydeparkschools.org
Haviland MS 1,100/6-8
PO Box 721 12538 845-229-4030
Matt Latvis, prin. Fax 229-2475
Hyde Park ES 300/K-5
4327 Albany Post Rd 12538 845-229-4050
Kate Blossom, prin. Fax 229-2933
Netherwood ES 500/K-5
648 Netherwood Rd 12538 845-229-4055
Richard Wert, prin. Fax 229-2797
North Park ES 400/K-5
PO Box 722 12538 845-229-4040
Lisa Hecht, prin. Fax 229-5655
Smith ES 300/K-5
16 Smith Ct 12538 845-229-4060
Rachel Turner, prin. Fax 229-2828
Other Schools – See Poughkeepsie

Regina Coeli S 200/PK-8
4337 Albany Post Rd 12538 845-229-8589
Eileen Kerins, prin. Fax 229-1388

Ilion, Herkimer, Pop. 8,330
Ilion Central SD 1,800/PK-12
PO Box 480 13357 315-894-9934
Fax 894-2716
www.ilioncsd.org/
Barringer Road ES 500/K-6
326 Barringer Rd 13357 315-894-8420
Frances Lapaglia, prin. Fax 894-0153
Remington ES 500/PK-6
77 E North St 13357 315-895-7720
Jeremy Rich, prin. Fax 894-2488

Indian Lake, Hamilton
Indian Lake Central SD 200/K-12
28 W Main St 12842 518-648-5024
Mark Brand, supt. Fax 648-6346
ilcsd.org
Indian Lake Central S 200/K-12
28 W Main St 12842 518-648-5024
David Snide, prin. Fax 648-6346

Inlet, Hamilton
Inlet Common SD, PO Box 207 13360 50/PK-6
Donald Gooley, supt. 315-369-3222
Inlet ES 50/PK-6
PO Box 207 13360 315-357-3305
Sandra Knoblock, prin. Fax 357-2177

Interlaken, Seneca, Pop. 670
South Seneca Central SD
Supt. — See Ovid
South Seneca ES 400/PK-6
8326 State Route 96 14847 607-869-9636
Margarete Couture, prin. Fax 532-8540

Inwood, Nassau, Pop. 7,767
Lawrence UFD
Supt. — See Lawrence
Public K 4 300/PK-K
87 Wanser Ave 11096 516-295-6400
Ann Pederson, prin. Fax 295-6416
Public S 2 400/1-5
1 Donahue Ave 11096 516-295-6200
Cynthia Lee, prin. Fax 239-6603

Irvington, Westchester, Pop. 6,615
Irvington UFD 2,000/K-12
40 N Broadway 10533 914-591-8501
Dr. Kathleen Matusiak, supt. Fax 591-9781
www.irvingtonschools.org
Dows Lane ES 500/K-3
6 Dows Ln 10533 914-591-6012
Renay Sadis, prin. Fax 591-6863
Irvington MS 500/6-8
40 N Broadway 10533 914-591-9494
Joe Witazek, prin. Fax 591-8535
Main Street IS 300/4-5
101 Main St 10533 914-591-1961
Raina Kor, prin. Fax 591-6863

Immaculate Conception S 200/PK-8
16 N Broadway Ste 1 10533 914-591-9330
Victor Presto, prin. Fax 591-8639

Islandia, Suffolk, Pop. 3,125
Central Islip UFD
Supt. — See Central Islip
Morrow ES 600/1-4
299 Sycamore Ln 11749 631-348-5037
Lawrence Nagy, prin. Fax 348-5163

Island Park, Nassau, Pop. 4,741
Island Park UFD 700/K-8
150 Trafalgar Blvd 11558 516-431-8100
Dr. Rosmarie Bovino, supt. Fax 431-7550
www.ips.k12.ny.us
Hegarty ES 400/K-4
99 Radcliffe Rd 11558 516-431-4740
Jacob Russum, prin. Fax 431-7550
Island Park/Lincoln Orens MS 300/5-8
150 Trafalgar Blvd 11558 516-431-7194
Dr. Thalia Vendetti, prin. Fax 431-7550

Islip, Suffolk, Pop. 18,924
Islip UFD 3,500/K-12
215 Main St 11751 631-859-2200
Susan Schnebel, supt. Fax 859-2224
www.islipufsd.org/
Commack Road ES 600/2-5
300 Commack Rd 11751 631-859-2321
Jeannette Feminella, prin. Fax 859-2332
Islip MS 800/6-8
211 Main St 11751 631-859-2274
Timothy Martin, prin. Fax 859-2277
Sherwood ES 400/2-5
301 Smith Ave 11751 631-859-2340
Vincent Veglia, prin. Fax 859-2346
Wing ES 400/K-1
1 Winganhauppauge Rd 11751 631-859-2350
Diane Druckman, prin. Fax 859-2356

Islip Terrace, Suffolk, Pop. 5,530
East Islip UFD 5,200/PK-12
1 Craig B Gariepy Ave 11752 631-224-2000
Wendell Chu, supt. Fax 581-1617
www.eischools.org
Connetquot ES 400/1-5
1 Merrick St 11752 631-581-1778
Dr. Lisa Belz, prin. Fax 581-5315
East Islip ECC 500/PK-K
1 Craig B Gariepy Ave 11752 631-224-2070
Michael Saidens, prin. Fax 581-0894
East Islip MS 1,300/6-8
100 Redmen St 11752 631-224-2170
Mark Bernard, prin. Fax 859-3745
Kinney ES 400/1-5
1 Spur Dr S 11752 631-581-1862
Danielle Naccarato, prin. Fax 581-0969
Other Schools – See East Islip

Ithaca, Tompkins, Pop. 29,766
Ithaca CSD 5,500/PK-12
400 Lake St 14850 607-274-2101
Dr. Judith Pastel, supt. Fax 274-2271
www.icsd.k12.ny.us
Belle Sherman ES 300/PK-5
501 Mitchell St 14850 607-274-2206
Sloan Sherridan-Thomas, prin. Fax 272-4059
Boynton MS 600/6-8
1601 N Cayuga St 14850 607-274-2241
Jason Trumble, prin. Fax 274-2357
Cayuga Heights ES 300/K-5
110 E Upland Rd 14850 607-257-8557
Patrick Jensen, prin. Fax 257-8142
De Witt MS 500/6-8
560 Warren Rd 14850 607-257-3222
Ronald Acerra, prin. Fax 266-3502
Enfield ES 200/PK-5
20 Enfield Main Rd 14850 607-274-2221
Michael Simons, prin. Fax 274-6810
Fall Creek ES 200/PK-5
202 King St 14850 607-274-2214
Karen Keller, prin. Fax 274-2339
Martin ES 300/PK-5
302 W Buffalo St 14850 607-274-2209
Denise Gomber, prin. Fax 274-2196
Northeast ES 400/K-5
425 Winthrop Dr 14850 607-257-2121
Jeffrey Tomasik, prin. Fax 257-8157

South Hill ES 400/PK-5
520 Hudson St 14850 607-274-2129
Rae Covey, prin. Fax 274-2379
Other Schools – See Slaterville Springs

Clune Montessori S 200/PK-8
120 E King Rd 14850 607-277-7335
Andrea Riddle, prin. Fax 277-0251
Immaculate Conception S 100/PK-8
320 W Buffalo St 14850 607-273-2707
Diana Oravec, prin. Fax 272-8456
Ithaca Children's S K-8
339 Turkey Hill Rd 14850 607-273-5184
Ithaca Montessori S 100/PK-1
12 Ascot Pl 14850 607-266-0788
Kristin Campagnolo, prin. Fax 266-0887

Jackson Heights, See New York
NYC Department of Education
Supt. — See New York
IS 145 1,900/6-8
3334 80th St 11372 718-457-1242
Delores Beckham, prin. Fax 335-0601
IS 230 900/6-8
7310 34th Ave 11372 718-335-7648
Sharon Terry, prin. Fax 335-7513
Public S 2 600/K-5
7510 21st Ave, East Elmhurst NY 11370 718-728-1459
Joseph Taddeo, prin. Fax 274-4332
Public S 69 1,100/PK-5
7702 37th Ave 11372 718-424-7700
Martha Vazquez, prin. Fax 458-6567
Public S 149 1,000/K-5
9311 34th Ave 11372 718-898-3630
Marlene Gonzalez, prin. Fax 476-1976
Public S 212 700/K-5
3425 82nd St 11372 718-898-6973
Carin Ellis, prin. Fax 898-7068
Public S 222 300/PK-2
8615 37th Ave 11372 718-429-2563
Yvonne Marrero, prin. Fax 429-3484

Blessed Sacrament S 200/PK-8
3420 94th St 11372 718-446-4449
Barbara Kingston, prin. Fax 446-5366
Garden S 400/PK-12
3316 79th St 11372 718-335-6363
Dr. Richard Marotta, hdmstr. Fax 565-1169
Our Lady of Fatima S 600/K-8
2538 80th St, East Elmhurst NY 11370 718-429-7031
Cassie Zelic, prin. Fax 899-2811
St. Joan of Arc S 500/PK-8
3527 82nd St 11372 718-639-9020
Linda Kelly, prin. Fax 639-5428

Jamaica, See New York
NYC Department of Education
Supt. — See New York
JHS 8 900/6-8
10835 167th St 11433 718-739-6883
John Murphy, prin. Fax 526-2727
JHS 72 800/6-8
13325 Guy R Brewer Blvd 11434 718-723-6200
Chrystal Taylor-Brown, prin. Fax 527-1675
JHS 217 1,200/6-8
8505 144th St 11435 718-657-1120
Patrick Burns, prin. Fax 291-3668
Public S 30 500/PK-5
12610 Bedell St 11434 718-276-8785
Dwayne Crowder, prin. Fax 949-0029
Public S 37 500/PK-6
17937 137th Ave 11434 718-528-5399
Beverly Mitchell, prin. Fax 949-0887
Public S 40 500/PK-6
10920 Union Hall St 11433 718-526-1906
Alison Branker, prin. Fax 526-1209
Public S 48 400/PK-5
15502 108th Ave 11433 718-739-4463
Patricia Mitchell, prin. Fax 297-0087
Public S 50 800/PK-6
14326 101st Ave 11435 718-526-5336
Maureen Lore, prin. Fax 526-7261
Public S 52 600/PK-6
17837 146th Ter 11434 718-528-2238
Linda Pough, prin. Fax 276-2854
Public S 55 700/PK-6
13110 97th Ave 11419 718-849-3845
Ralph Honore, prin. Fax 847-5473
Public S 80 500/K-5
17105 137th Ave 11434 718-528-7070
Paulette Glenn, prin. Fax 949-0963
Public S 82 500/PK-5
8802 144th St 11435 718-526-4139
Angela Boykin, prin. Fax 297-0290
Public S 86 900/3-6
8741 Parsons Blvd 11432 718-291-6264
Karen Zuvic, prin. Fax 297-0298
Public S 95 1,200/K-5
17901 90th Ave 11432 718-739-0007
Dolores Reid-Barker, prin. Fax 658-5271
Public S 116 800/PK-8
10725 Wren Pl 11433 718-526-4884
Barbara Fuller, prin. Fax 658-5663
Public S 117 1,100/PK-6
8515 143rd St 11435 718-526-4780
Harvey Katz, prin. Fax 297-1796
Public S 118 600/PK-5
19020 109th Rd 11412 718-465-5538
Adele Armstrong, prin. Fax 264-9178
Public S 131 600/K-5
17045 84th Ave 11432 718-739-4229
Randolph Ford, prin. Fax 658-5690
Public S 140 700/PK-6
11600 166th St 11434 718-657-4760
Elaine Brittenum, prin. Fax 526-1051
Public S 160 700/PK-6
10959 Inwood St 11435 718-526-5523
Jermaine Garden, prin. Fax 526-8191
Public S 178 400/PK-8
18910 Radnor Rd 11423 718-464-5763
Jennifer Ambert, prin. Fax 464-5766
Public S 182 900/PK-2
9036 150th St 11435 718-291-8500
Andrew Topol, prin. Fax 297-0182
Public S 223 600/PK-5
12520 Sutphin Blvd 11434 718-322-9012
Deborah Otto, prin. Fax 925-9020
Public S 268 500/K-8
9207 175th St 11433 718-206-3240
Lissa Stewart, admin. Fax 206-2938
York Early College Academy 6-8
13325 Guy R Brewer Blvd 11434 718-978-1127
Deborah Burnett, prin. Fax 978-1994

Al-Iman S 200/PK-12
8989 Van Wyck Expy 11435 718-297-6520
Sr. Iman Dakmak-Rakka, prin. Fax 658-5530
Allen Christian S 600/PK-8
17110 Linden Blvd 11434 718-657-1676
Linda Morant, dir. Fax 291-7751
Divine Mercy Academy 100/6-8
9001 101st Ave 11416 718-845-3188
Sr. Frances Wystepeck, prin. Fax 835-9447
Ideal Montessori S 200/PK-8
8741 165th St 11432 718-523-6237
Immaculate Conception S 500/PK-8
17914 Dalny Rd 11432 718-739-5933
Dori Breen, prin. Fax 523-7436
Jamaica Day S of St. Demetrios 100/PK-8
8435 152nd St 11432 718-526-2622
Dr. George Melikokis, prin. Fax 526-1680
Jamaica SDA S 100/K-8
8828 163rd St 11432 718-297-3491
Our Saviour Lutheran Preschool 100/PK-PK
9004 175th St 11432 718-739-7452
Natalie Charles, dir. Fax 739-3964
St. Nicholas of Tolentine S 300/PK-8
8022 Parsons Blvd 11432 718-380-1900
Anne Badalamenti, prin. Fax 591-6977
U N International S 200/K-8
17353 Croydon Rd 11432 718-658-6166
Dr. Judith Honor, prin. Fax 658-5742

Jamestown, Chautauqua, Pop. 30,381
Jamestown CSD 4,800/PK-12
197 Martin Rd 14701 716-483-4420
Daniel Kathman, supt. Fax 483-4421
www.jamestown.wnyric.org
Bush ES 200/K-4
150 Pardee Ave 14701 716-483-4401
Tina Sandstrom, prin. Fax 483-7100
Fletcher ES 400/K-4
301 Cole Ave 14701 716-483-4404
Michael Mansfield, prin. Fax 483-4210
Jefferson MS 400/5-8
195 Martin Rd 14701 716-483-4411
Carm Proctor, prin. Fax 483-4273
Lincoln ES 300/K-4
301 Front St 14701 716-483-4412
Felix Muzza, prin. Fax 483-4435
Love ES 300/PK-4
50 E 8th St 14701 716-483-4405
Renee Hartling, prin. Fax 483-4291
Persell MS 500/5-8
375 Baker St 14701 716-483-4406
Philip Cammarata, prin. Fax 483-4417
Ring ES 400/K-4
333 Buffalo St 14701 716-483-4407
Connie Foster, prin. Fax 483-4232
Rogers ES 300/PK-4
41 Hebner St 14701 716-483-4408
Chris Tracey, prin. Fax 483-4237
Washington MS 500/5-8
159 Buffalo St 14701 716-483-4413
Melissa Emerson, prin. Fax 483-4268

Southwestern Central SD 1,600/K-12
600 Hunt Rd 14701 716-484-1136
Daniel George, supt. Fax 488-1139
swcs.wnyric.org/
Southwestern ES 700/K-5
600 Hunt Rd 14701 716-664-1881
William Caldwell, prin. Fax 487-3170
Southwestern MS 400/6-8
600 Hunt Rd 14701 716-664-6270
Gregory Paterniti, prin. Fax 487-0855

Bethel Baptist Christian Academy 100/K-12
200 Hunt Rd 14701 716-484-7420
Clarence Lee, admin. Fax 484-0087
Holy Family S 100/PK-8
1135 N Main St 14701 716-483-3245
Samuel Pellerito, prin. Fax 483-3245
Jamestown S 50/1-8
130 McDaniel Ave 14701 716-484-2065

Jamesville, Onondaga
Jamesville-DeWitt Central SD
Supt. — See De Witt
Jamesville-DeWitt MS 900/5-8
6280 Randall Rd 13078 315-445-8360
Peter Smith, prin. Fax 445-8421
Jamesville ES 300/K-4
6409 E Seneca Tpke 13078 315-445-8460
Mary Sylvester, prin. Fax 445-8444
Tecumseh ES 400/K-4
901 Nottingham Rd Ste 1 13078 315-445-8320
Jill Zerrillo, prin. Fax 445-9872

Jasper, Steuben
Jasper-Troupsburg Central SD 700/PK-12
PO Box 81 14855 607-792-3675
Chad Groff, supt. Fax 792-3749
www.jt.wnyric.org/
Other Schools – See Troupsburg

Jefferson, Schoharie
Jefferson Central SD 300/K-12
1332 State Route 10 12093 607-652-7821
Carl Mummenthey, supt. Fax 652-7806
www.jeffersoncs.org
Jefferson Central S 300/K-12
1332 State Route 10 12093 607-652-7821
Carl Mummenthey, prin. Fax 652-7806

Jeffersonville, Sullivan, Pop. 412
Sullivan West Central SD 1,400/K-12
PO Box 308 12748 845-482-4610
Kenneth Hilton, supt. Fax 482-3022
www.swcsd.org/
Sullivan West ES 700/K-6
PO Box 308 12748 845-482-4610
Rebecca Green, prin. Fax 482-4720

Jericho, Nassau, Pop. 13,141
Jericho UFD 3,200/K-12
99 Old Cedar Swamp Rd 11753 516-203-3600
Henry Grishman, supt. Fax 933-2047
www.jerichoschools.org
Cantiague ES 400/K-5
678 Cantiague Rock Rd 11753 516-203-3650
Antony Sinanis, prin. Fax 681-0341
Jackson ES 500/K-5
58 Maytime Dr 11753 516-203-3640
Berardino D'Aquila, prin. Fax 681-2891
Jericho MS 800/6-8
99 Old Cedar Swamp Rd 11753 516-203-3620
Donald Gately, prin. Fax 681-8984
Seaman ES 400/K-5
137 Leahy St 11753 516-203-3630
Adam Winnick, prin. Fax 681-9493

Solomon Schecter Day S of Nassau Co. 200/K-5
1 Barbara Ln 11753 516-935-1441
Dr. Cindy Dolgin, prin. Fax 935-8280

Johnson City, Broome, Pop. 14,955
Johnson City Central SD 2,600/K-12
666 Reynolds Rd 13790 607-763-1230
Mary Kay Frys, supt. Fax 729-2767
www.jcschools.com
Johnson City IS 600/3-5
601 Columbia Dr 13790 607-763-1254
Daniel Erickson, prin. Fax 763-1272
Johnson City MS 600/6-8
601 Columbia Dr 13790 607-763-1240
Margaret Kucko, prin. Fax 763-1297
Johnson City PS 600/K-2
601 Columbia Dr 13790 607-763-1243
Gail Holleran, prin. Fax 763-1280

St. James MS 100/4-8
143 Main St 13790 607-797-5444
George Clancy, prin. Fax 797-6794

Johnstown, Fulton, Pop. 8,572
Johnstown CSD 1,900/PK-12
1 Sirbill Cir Ste 101 12095 518-762-4611
Katherine Sullivan, supt. Fax 762-6379
www.johnstownschools.org/
Glebe Street ES 300/K-6
502 Glebe St 12095 518-762-3714
William Crankshaw, prin. Fax 762-3756
Jansen Avenue ES 200/K-6
305 Jansen Ave 12095 518-762-9119
Colleen Lester, prin. Fax 762-1239
Knox JHS 300/7-8
400 S Perry St 12095 518-762-3711
Steven Drescher, prin. Fax 762-2775
Pleasant Avenue ES 300/K-6
235 Pleasant Ave 12095 518-762-8610
David Blanchard, prin. Fax 762-1217
Warren Street ES 300/PK-6
110 Warren St 12095 518-762-3715
Anne Christiano, prin. Fax 762-8805

Jordan, Onondaga, Pop. 1,346
Jordan-Elbridge Central SD
Supt. — See Elbridge
Jordan-Elbridge MS 400/6-8
PO Box 1150 13080 315-689-8520
David Shafer, prin. Fax 689-6524
Ramsdell ES 300/3-5
PO Box 903 13080 315-689-8530
Eric Varney, prin. Fax 689-5243

Katonah, Westchester
Katonah-Lewisboro UFD
Supt. — See South Salem
Katonah ES 500/K-5
106 Huntville Rd 10536 914-763-7700
Jonathan Kaplan, prin. Fax 763-7789

Keene Valley, Essex
Keene Central SD 200/K-12
PO Box 67 12943 518-576-4555
Cynthia Ford-Johnston, supt. Fax 576-4599
keenecentralschool.org
Keene Central S 200/K-12
PO Box 67 12943 518-576-4555
Cynthia Ford-Johnston, prin. Fax 576-4599

Keeseville, Clinton, Pop. 1,796
Au Sable Valley Central SD
Supt. — See Clintonville
Keeseville ES 400/K-6
1825 Route 22 12944 518-834-2839
Kevin Hulbert, prin. Fax 834-2857

Kendall, Orleans
Kendall Central SD — 1,000/K-12
1932 Kendall Rd 14476 — 585-659-2741
Julie Christensen, supt. — Fax 659-8903
www.kendallschools.org
Kendall ES — 400/K-6
1932 Kendall Rd 14476 — 585-659-8317
Scott Wright, prin. — Fax 659-2952

Kenmore, Erie, Pop. 15,555
Kenmore-Tonawanda UFSD
Supt. — See Buffalo
Kenmore MS — 700/6-8
155 Delaware Rd 14217 — 716-874-8403
Elaine Thomas, prin. — Fax 874-8650
Roosevelt ES — 400/K-5
283 Washington Ave 14217 — 716-874-8409
Bernadine Moldoch, prin. — Fax 874-8490

St. Andrew's Country Day S — 400/PK-8
1545 Sheridan Dr 14217 — 716-877-0422
Dennis Welka, prin. — Fax 877-3973
St. John the Baptist S — 300/PK-8
1085 Englewood Ave 14223 — 716-877-6401
Cynthia Jacobs, prin. — Fax 877-9139
St. Paul S — 300/PK-8
47 Victoria Blvd 14217 — 716-877-6308
Christopher Meagher, prin. — Fax 877-3874

Kennedy, Chautauqua
Falconer Central SD
Supt. — See Falconer
Temple ES — 300/PK-2
3470 Cemetery St 14747 — 716-267-3255
Terry English, prin. — Fax 267-9420

Kerhonkson, Ulster, Pop. 1,629
Rondout Valley Central SD
Supt. — See Accord
Kerhonkson ES — 300/K-4
30 Academy St 12446 — 845-626-2451
Alan Baker, prin. — Fax 626-5767

Kew Gardens, See New York
NYC Department of Education
Supt. — See New York
Public S 99 — 700/K-6
8237 Kew Gardens Rd 11415 — 718-544-4343
Paulette Foglio, prin. — Fax 544-5992

Bais Yaakov Academy for Girls — 600/PK-8
12450 Metropolitan Ave 11415 — 718-847-5352
Yeshiva Tifereth Moshe Dov Revel Center — 200/4-8
8306 Abingdon Rd 11415 — 718-846-7300

Kiamesha Lake, Sullivan

Hebrew Day S — 100/PK-8
PO Box 239 12751 — 845-794-7890
Rabbi Menachem Fruchter, prin. — Fax 794-0859

Kinderhook, Columbia, Pop. 1,320
Kinderhook Central SD
Supt. — See Valatie
Van Buren ES — 200/3-5
25 Broad St 12106 — 518-758-7569
John Stickles, prin. — Fax 758-9808

Kings Park, Suffolk, Pop. 17,773
Kings Park Central SD — 4,200/K-12
180 Lawrence Rd 11754 — 631-269-3310
Dr. Susan Agruso, supt. — Fax 269-0750
www.kpcsd.org/
Parkview ES — 600/K-3
23 Roundtree Dr 11754 — 631-269-3770
Jeanne Devine, prin. — Fax 361-6590
RJO IS — 700/4-5
99 Old Dock Rd 11754 — 631-269-3798
Rudy Massimo, prin. — Fax 269-3203
Rogers MS — 1,000/6-8
97 Old Dock Rd 11754 — 631-269-3369
John Craig, prin. — Fax 269-3282
Other Schools – See Northport

Kingston, Ulster, Pop. 23,067
Kingston CSD — 7,400/PK-12
61 Crown St 12401 — 845-339-3000
Gerard Gretzinger, supt. — Fax 339-2249
www.kingstoncityschools.org/
Bailey MS — 1,000/6-8
Merilina Ave Ext 12401 — 845-338-6390
Julie Linton, prin. — Fax 338-6312
Chambers ES — 400/K-5
945 Morton Blvd 12401 — 845-336-5995
Stacia Felicello, prin. — Fax 336-5616
Edson ES — 400/K-5
116 Merilina Ave 12401 — 845-338-6990
Joellen Gibbons, prin. — Fax 331-9034
Finn ES — 200/PK-5
94 Marys Ave 12401 — 845-338-6370
Anthony Erena, prin. — Fax 331-0863
Kennedy ES — 200/K-5
107 Gross St 12401 — 845-331-3174
Clark Waters, prin. — Fax 331-2477
Meagher ES — 300/K-5
21 Wynkoop Pl 12401 — 845-338-8660
Brian Martin, prin. — Fax 338-5693
Washington ES — 400/PK-5
67 Wall St 12401 — 845-338-1978
Valerie Hannum, prin. — Fax 338-3041
Zena ES — 200/K-5
1700 Sawkill Rd 12401 — 845-679-8160
Therese Higgins, prin. — Fax 679-6494
Other Schools – See Hurley, Lake Katrine, Port Ewen, Ulster Park

Good Shepherd Christian S — 100/PK-8
83 E Chester St 12401 — 845-339-4488
Kiya Cordeau, prin. — Fax 331-5206
Kingston Catholic S — 200/PK-8
159 Broadway 12401 — 845-331-9318
Jill Albert, prin. — Fax 331-2674
St. Joseph S — 200/PK-8
235 Wall St 12401 — 845-339-4390
Rita Kunkel, prin. — Fax 339-7994

Kirkwood, Broome
Windsor Central SD
Supt. — See Windsor
Bell ES — 300/K-5
15 Golden St 13795 — 607-775-2730
Frances Kennedy, prin. — Fax 775-4834

Lackawanna, Erie, Pop. 18,175
Lackawanna CSD — 2,000/PK-12
245 S Shore Blvd 14218 — 716-827-6767
Frederick Wille, supt. — Fax 827-6710
www.lackawannaschools.org
Lackawanna MS — 300/7-8
550 Martin Rd 14218 — 716-827-6704
Michael Jakubowski, prin. — Fax 827-6784
Martin Road ES — 500/3-6
135 Martin Rd 14218 — 716-827-6734
Jared Taft, prin. — Fax 827-6715
Truman ES — 500/PK-2
15 Inner Dr 14218 — 716-827-6741
Maureen Fernandez, prin. — Fax 827-6779

Our Lady of Victory S — 300/PK-8
2760 S Park Ave 14218 — 716-828-9434
Sr. Ellen O'Keefe, prin. — Fax 828-9383

La Fargeville, Jefferson
La Fargeville Central SD — 600/K-12
PO Box 138 13656 — 315-658-2241
Susan Whitney, supt. — Fax 658-4223
www.lafargevillecsd.org
La Fargeville Central ES — 300/K-6
PO Box 138 13656 — 315-658-2241
Anita James, prin. — Fax 658-4223

La Fayette, Onondaga
La Fayette Central SD — 900/K-12
5955 US Route 20 13084 — 315-677-9728
Peter Tighe, supt. — Fax 677-3372
www.lafayetteschools.com
Grimshaw ES — 400/K-6
5957 US Route 20 13084 — 315-677-3152
Dona McIntyre, prin. — Fax 677-3154
Other Schools – See Nedrow

Lagrangeville, Dutchess
Arlington Central SD
Supt. — See Poughkeepsie
Lagrange ES — 500/K-5
144 Todd Hill Rd 12540 — 845-227-1793
JoAnne Mahar, prin. — Fax 227-1821
Lagrange MS — 900/6-8
110 Stringham Rd 12540 — 845-486-4880
Eric Schetter, prin. — Fax 486-8863
Union Vale MS — 1,000/6-8
1657 E Noxon Rd 12540 — 845-223-8600
Steven Kerins, prin. — Fax 223-8610
Vail Farm ES — 700/K-5
1659 E Noxon Rd 12540 — 845-223-8030
Michael Kessler, prin. — Fax 227-1940

Nurtury Montessori S of LaGrange — 100/PK-4
1515 Route 55 12540 — 845-223-7414
Cathy Billone, dir. — Fax 223-7417

Lake George, Warren, Pop. 991
Lake George Central SD — 1,100/K-12
381 Canada St 12845 — 518-668-5456
Mary Cahill, supt. — Fax 668-2285
www.lkgeorge.org
Lake George ES — 500/K-6
69 Sun Valley Dr 12845 — 518-668-5714
James Conway, prin. — Fax 668-5876

Lake Grove, Suffolk, Pop. 10,670
Middle Country Central SD
Supt. — See Centereach
Auer Memorial ES — 500/1-5
17 Wing St 11755 — 631-285-8500
Kenneth Gutmann, prin. — Fax 285-8501

Sachem Central SD
Supt. — See Holbrook
Cayuga ES — 600/K-5
865 Hawkins Ave 11755 — 631-471-1800
Matthew Wells, prin. — Fax 467-2486
Wenonah ES — 600/K-5
251 Hudson Ave 11755 — 631-471-1880
Christine DiPaola, prin. — Fax 471-1886

Maimonides Day S — 50/PK-6
821 Hawkins Ave 11755 — 631-585-0521
Goldie Baumgarten, prin. — Fax 585-0570

Lake Katrine, Ulster, Pop. 1,998
Kingston CSD
Supt. — See Kingston
Crosby ES — 300/K-5
767 Neighborhood Rd 12449 — 845-382-2633
John Voerg, prin. — Fax 382-2668
Miller MS — 800/6-8
65 Fording Place Rd 12449 — 845-382-2960
Jo Burruby, prin. — Fax 382-6069

Lake Luzerne, Warren, Pop. 2,042
Hadley-Luzerne Central SD — 900/K-12
27 Ben Rosa Park Rd 12846 — 518-696-2112
Irwin Sussman, supt. — Fax 696-5402
www.hlcs.org
Hadley-Luzerne ES — 200/K-2
273 Lake Ave 12846 — 518-696-2112
Steve Danna, prin. — Fax 696-6110
Townsend MS — 400/3-8
27 Hyland Dr 12846 — 518-696-2378
Patrick Cronin, prin. — Fax 696-2485

Lake Placid, Essex, Pop. 2,757
Lake Placid Central SD — 800/K-12
50 Cummings Rd 12946 — 518-523-2475
James Donnelly, supt. — Fax 523-4971
www.edline.net/pages/Lake_Placid_CSD
Lake Placid ES — 300/K-5
318 Old Military Rd 12946 — 518-523-3640
Richard Retrosi, prin. — Fax 523-4314

North Country S — 100/4-9
PO Box 187 12946 — 518-523-9329
David Hochschartner, hdmstr. — Fax 523-4858
St. Agnes S — 100/PK-5
2322 Saranac Ave 12946 — 518-523-3771
Anne Bayruns, prin. — Fax 523-2203

Lake Ronkonkoma, Suffolk, Pop. 18,997
Sachem Central SD
Supt. — See Holbrook
Gatelot Avenue ES — 600/K-5
65 Gatelot Ave 11779 — 631-471-1810
Denise Kleinman, prin. — Fax 467-2459
Hiawatha ES — 600/K-5
97 Patchogue Holbrook Rd 11779 — 631-471-1830
Anthony Mauro, prin. — Fax 467-3861
Samoset MS — 900/6-8
51 School St 11779 — 631-471-1700
Mary Cavanaugh, prin. — Fax 471-1706

St. Joseph S — 200/PK-8
25 Church St 11779 — 631-588-4760
Leona Arpino, prin. — Fax 588-0543

Lake View, Erie
Frontier Central SD
Supt. — See Hamburg
Pinehurst ES — 600/K-5
6050 Fairway Ct 14085 — 716-926-1770
Larry Leaven, prin. — Fax 627-3132

Southtowns Catholic S — 300/PK-8
PO Box 86 14085 — 716-627-5011
Judith MacDonald, prin. — Fax 627-5335

Lancaster, Erie, Pop. 11,490
Lancaster Central SD — 6,200/K-12
177 Central Ave 14086 — 716-686-3201
Edward Myszka, supt. — Fax 686-3350
lancasterschools.org
Central Avenue ES — 200/K-3
149 Central Ave 14086 — 716-686-3230
Patricia Comeford-Haley, prin. — Fax 686-3302
Como Park ES — 300/K-3
1985 Como Park Blvd 14086 — 716-686-3235
Mary Marcinelli, prin. — Fax 686-3303
Court Street ES — 400/K-3
91 Court St 14086 — 716-686-3240
Deborah Bojanowski, prin. — Fax 686-3284
Hillview ES — 400/K-3
11 Pleasant View Dr 14086 — 716-686-3280
Kathleen Knauth, prin. — Fax 686-3307
Lancaster MS — 1,000/7-8
148 Aurora St 14086 — 716-686-3220
Peter Kruszynski, prin. — Fax 686-3223
William Street ES — 1,400/4-6
5201 William St 14086 — 716-686-3800
Jacqueline Bull, prin. — Fax 686-3822
Other Schools – See Depew

Buffalo Suburban Christian Academy — 50/K-8
5580 Genesee St 14086 — 716-684-2943
Our Lady of Pompeii S — 200/PK-8
129 Laverack Ave 14086 — 716-684-4664
Harlean Nehrbass, prin. — Fax 684-4699
St. Mary S — 400/PK-8
2 Saint Marys Hl 14086 — 716-683-2112
Jane Driscoll, prin. — Fax 683-2134

Lansing, Tompkins, Pop. 3,417
Lansing Central SD — 1,300/K-12
284 Ridge Rd 14882 — 607-533-4294
Dr. Stephen Grimm, supt. — Fax 533-3602
www.lansingschools.org
Buckley ES — 400/K-4
284 Ridge Rd 14882 — 607-533-4183
Chris Pettograsso, prin. — Fax 533-4684
Lansing MS — 400/5-8
6 Ludlowville Rd 14882 — 607-533-4271
James Thomas, prin. — Fax 533-3543

Larchmont, Westchester, Pop. 6,487
Mamaroneck UFD
Supt. — See Mamaroneck
Central ES — 500/K-5
1100 Palmer Ave 10538 — 914-220-3400
Carol Houseknecht, prin. — Fax 220-3415
Chatsworth Avenue ES — 600/K-5
34 Chatsworth Ave 10538 — 914-220-3500
Gail Boyle, prin. — Fax 220-3515
Hommocks MS — 1,200/6-8
10 Hommocks Rd 10538 — 914-220-3300
Dr. Seth Weitzman, prin. — Fax 220-3315
Murray Avenue ES — 700/K-5
250 Murray Ave 10538 — 914-220-3700
Jennifer Monaco, prin. — Fax 220-3715

French-American S of NY — 800/PK-12
111 Larchmont Ave 10538 — 914-250-0000
Robert M. Leonhardt, hdmstr. — Fax 834-1284
SS. John & Paul S — 300/K-8
280 Weaver St Ste 2 10538 — 914-834-6332
Anne Menno, prin. — Fax 834-7493

Latham, Albany, Pop. 10,131
North Colonie Central SD 5,700/K-12
91 Fiddlers Ln 12110 518-785-8591
Randy Ehrenberg, supt. Fax 785-8502
www.northcolonie.org
Blue Creek ES 500/K-6
100 Clinton Rd 12110 518-785-7451
Annette Trapini, prin. Fax 785-3273
Forts Ferry ES 500/K-6
95 Forts Ferry Rd 12110 518-785-9203
Candace Lobdell, prin. Fax 783-8874
Latham Ridge ES 400/K-6
6 Mercer Ave 12110 518-785-3211
James Martin, prin. Fax 783-8875
Shaker JHS 900/7-8
475 Watervliet Shaker Rd 12110 518-785-1341
Russell Moore, prin. Fax 783-8877
Other Schools – See Cohoes, Loudonville, Watervliet

St. Ambrose S 200/PK-8
347 Old Loudon Rd 12110 518-785-6453
Sr. James Marie Carras, prin. Fax 785-8370

Laurelton, See New York
NYC Department of Education
Supt. — See New York
IS 231 900/7-8
14500 Springfield Blvd 11413 718-276-5140
Emmanuel Lubin, prin. Fax 276-2259

Linden SDA S 100/1-8
13701 228th St 11413 718-527-6868
George Coke, prin. Fax 527-6650

Laurens, Otsego, Pop. 263
Laurens Central SD 400/K-12
PO Box 301 13796 607-432-2050
Romona Wenck, supt. Fax 432-4388
laurenscs.org
Laurens Central S 400/K-12
PO Box 301 13796 607-432-2050
Bill Dorritie, prin. Fax 432-4388

Lawrence, Nassau, Pop. 6,501
Lawrence UFD 2,800/PK-12
PO Box 477 11559 516-295-7030
Dr. John Fitzsimons, supt. Fax 239-7164
www.lawrence.org/
Lawrence MS 700/6-8
195 Broadway 11559 516-295-7000
George Akst, prin. Fax 295-7196
Other Schools – See Cedarhurst, Inwood

Brandeis S 300/PK-8
25 Frost Ln 11559 516-371-4747
Dr. Mildred David, hdmstr. Fax 371-1572
Hebrew Academy of Five Towns & Rockaway 700/PK-5
33 Washington Ave 11559 516-569-3043
Joy Hammer, prin. Fax 569-3014
Hebrew Academy of Five Towns MS 300/6-8
44 Frost Ln 11559 516-569-6352
Rabbi Dovid Kupchik, prin. Fax 569-6457

Le Roy, Genesee, Pop. 4,290
Le Roy Central SD 1,400/K-12
2 Trigon Park 14482 585-768-8133
Cindy Herzog, supt. Fax 768-8929
www.leroycsd.org
Wolcott Street ES 700/K-6
2 Trigon Park 14482 585-768-7115
Casey Kosiorek, prin. Fax 768-8929

Holy Family S 100/K-8
44 Lake St 14482 585-768-7390
Kevin Robertson, prin. Fax 768-6680

Levittown, Nassau, Pop. 53,000
Island Trees UFD 2,700/K-12
74 Farmedge Rd 11756 516-520-2100
James Parla, supt. Fax 520-2113
www.islandtrees.org
Island Trees Memorial MS 900/5-8
45 Wantagh Ave 11756 516-520-2157
Roger Bloom, prin. Fax 520-2168
Sparke ES 300/K-4
100 Robin Pl 11756 516-520-2126
Penny Fisher, prin. Fax 520-0987
Stokes ES 600/K-4
101 Owl Pl 11756 516-520-2103
Lisa Newman, prin. Fax 520-0984

Levittown UFD 7,800/K-12
150 Abbey Ln 11756 516-520-8300
Herman Sirois, supt. Fax 520-8314
www.levittownschools.com
Abbey Lane ES 600/K-5
239 Gardiners Ave 11756 516-520-8495
Joann Wallace, prin. Fax 520-8494
Gardiners Avenue ES 600/K-5
610 Gardiners Ave 11756 516-520-8485
Susan Hendler, prin. Fax 520-8490
Northside ES 500/K-5
35 Pelican Rd 11756 516-520-8395
Keith Squillacioti, prin. Fax 520-8394
Salk MS 1,100/6-8
3359 N Jerusalem Rd 11756 516-520-8470
John Zampaglione, prin. Fax 520-8479
Summit Lane ES 500/K-5
4 Summit Ln 11756 516-520-8385
Sally Evans, prin. Fax 520-8390
Wisdom Lane MS 900/6-8
120 Center Ln 11756 516-520-8370
Dr. Robert Tymann, prin. Fax 520-8380
Other Schools – See Seaford, Wantagh

Maria Montessori S 100/PK-8
5 N Village Grn 11756 516-520-0301
Carolyn Larcy, admin. Fax 520-2935

Lewiston, Niagara, Pop. 2,687
Niagara-Wheatfield Central SD
Supt. — See Niagara Falls
Tuscarora Indian S 100/PK-5
2015 Mount Hope Rd 14092 716-298-8320
Elizabeth Carr, prin. Fax 297-5070

Sacred Heart Villa S 50/PK-5
5269 Lewiston Rd 14092 716-285-9257
Sr. Elizabeth Domin, prin. Fax 284-8273
St. Peter S 200/PK-8
140 N 6th St 14092 716-754-4470
Kami Halgash, prin. Fax 754-0167

Liberty, Sullivan, Pop. 3,923
Liberty Central SD 1,700/PK-12
115 Buckley St 12754 845-292-6990
Michael Vanyo, supt. Fax 292-1164
www.libertyk12.org
Liberty ES 600/PK-4
201 N Main St 12754 845-292-5400
Jeri Finnegan, prin. Fax 295-9201
Liberty MS 500/5-8
145 Buckley St 12754 845-292-5400
Mary Greynolds, prin. Fax 292-5691

Light and Life Christian S 100/PK-8
2535 State Route 52 12754 845-292-4360
Cheryl Hendrickson, admin. Fax 292-4360
St. Peter S 100/PK-8
121 Lincoln Pl 12754 845-292-7270
Maureen Stiene, prin. Fax 292-2891

Lido Beach, Nassau, Pop. 2,786
Long Beach CSD 4,200/PK-12
235 Lido Blvd 11561 516-897-2104
Dr. Robert Greenberg, supt. Fax 897-2107
www.lbeach.org
Blackheath Preschool 200/PK-PK
322 Blackheath Rd 11561 516-897-2081
Christine Zawatson, prin. Fax 897-2128
East ES 300/K-5
456 Neptune Blvd 11561 516-897-2184
Ronni Reimel, prin. Fax 897-2291
Lido ES 500/K-5
237 Lido Blvd 11561 516-897-2140
Brenda Young, prin. Fax 771-3783
Lindell Boulevard ES 500/K-5
601 Lindell Blvd 11561 516-897-2198
Karen Sauter, prin. Fax 897-2288
Long Beach MS 900/6-8
239 Lido Blvd 11561 516-897-2166
Audrey Goropeuschek, prin. Fax 897-2145
Other Schools – See Long Beach

Lima, Livingston, Pop. 2,425
Honeoye Falls-Lima Central SD
Supt. — See Honeoye Falls
Lima ES 300/K-1
7342 College St 14485 585-624-7140
Jeanine Lupisella, prin. Fax 624-7003

Lima Christian S 200/K-12
1574 Rochester St 14485 585-624-3841
Ralph Dewey, prin. Fax 624-8293

Limestone, Cattaraugus, Pop. 403
Allegany-Limestone Central SD
Supt. — See Allegany
Limestone ES 100/K-5
PO Box 8 14753 716-925-8873
Dave Taylor, prin. Fax 925-7287

Lincolndale, Westchester
Somers Central SD
Supt. — See Somers
Primrose ES 800/K-2
PO Box 630 10540 914-248-8888
Richard Fisher, prin. Fax 248-5384

Lindenhurst, Suffolk, Pop. 28,248
Lindenhurst UFD 7,200/K-12
PO Box 621 11757 631-226-6441
Richard Nathan, supt. Fax 226-6865
www.lindenhurstschools.org
Albany Avenue ES 500/K-5
180 Albany Ave 11757 631-226-6400
Frank Grotschel, prin. Fax 226-6500
Alleghany Avenue ES 400/K-5
250 S Alleghany Ave 11757 631-226-6404
Laura Newman, prin. Fax 226-6407
Bower ES 300/K-5
315 W Montauk Hwy 11757 631-226-6409
Donna Smawley, prin. Fax 226-5240
Daniel Street ES 600/K-5
289 Daniel St 11757 631-226-6413
Frank Picozzi, prin. Fax 226-6417
Harding Avenue ES 300/K-5
2 Harding Ave 11757 631-226-6420
Brian Chamberlin, prin. Fax 226-6422
Lindenhurst MS 1,800/6-8
350 S Wellwood Ave 11757 631-226-6521
Frank Naccarato, prin. Fax 226-6554
Rall ES 600/K-5
761 Wellwood Ave 11757 631-226-6433
Patricia Castine, prin. Fax 226-6487
West Gates Avenue ES 400/K-5
175 W Gates Ave 11757 631-226-6437
Lisa Omeis, prin. Fax 226-6428

Our Lady of Perpetual Help S 400/PK-8
240 S Wellwood Ave 11757 631-226-0208
Cammy Lubrano, prin. Fax 226-4221

Lisbon, Saint Lawrence
Lisbon Central SD 500/PK-12
6866 County Route 10 13658 315-393-4951
Erin Woods, supt. Fax 393-7666
lisboncs.schoolwires.com
Lisbon Central S 500/PK-12
6866 County Route 10 13658 315-393-4951
Eric Burke, prin. Fax 393-7666

Little Falls, Herkimer, Pop. 5,026
Little Falls CSD 1,100/K-12
15 Petrie St 13365 315-823-1470
Louis Patrei, supt. Fax 823-0321
www.lfcsd.org
Benton Hall Academy 500/K-5
1 Ward Sq 13365 315-823-1400
Anna Spagnolo, prin. Fax 823-4407
Little Falls MS 300/6-8
1 High School Rd 13365 315-823-4300
Bart Tooley, prin. Fax 823-3920

Little Neck, See New York
NYC Department of Education
Supt. — See New York
JHS 67 900/6-8
5160 Marathon Pkwy 11362 718-423-8138
Zoi McGrath, prin. Fax 423-8281
Public S 94 400/K-5
4177 Little Neck Pkwy 11363 718-423-8491
JoAnn Barbeosch, prin. Fax 423-8531
Public S 221 600/PK-5
5740 Marathon Pkwy 11362 718-423-8825
Sheelia Twomey, prin. Fax 423-8841

Little Valley, Cattaraugus, Pop. 1,090
Cattaraugus-Little Valley Central SD 1,100/PK-12
207 Rock City St 14755 716-938-9155
Sylvia Root, supt. Fax 938-6576
www.cattlv.wnyric.org/
Little Valley ES 200/PK-5
207 Rock City St 14755 716-938-9155
Carrie Yohe, prin. Fax 938-6576
Other Schools – See Cattaraugus

Liverpool, Onondaga, Pop. 2,415
Liverpool Central SD 7,300/PK-12
195 Blackberry Rd 13090 315-622-7125
Janice Matousek, supt. Fax 622-7124
www.liverpool.k12.ny.us
Chestnut Hill ES 300/K-6
200 Saslon Park Dr 13088 315-453-0242
Martha O'Leary, prin. Fax 453-0283
Chestnut Hill MS 300/7-8
204 Saslon Park Dr 13088 315-453-0245
Peter Ianzito, prin. Fax 453-0278
Donlin Drive ES 500/PK-6
299 Donlin Dr 13088 315-453-0249
John Sardella, prin. Fax 453-0253
Elmcrest ES 400/K-6
350 Woodspath Rd 13090 315-453-1252
Daphne Valentine, prin. Fax 453-1258
Liverpool ES 300/PK-6
910 2nd St 13088 315-453-0254
William Mugridge, prin. Fax 453-0286
Liverpool MS 500/7-8
700 7th St 13088 315-453-0258
Joseph Mussi, prin. Fax 453-0281
Long Branch ES 400/K-6
4035 Long Branch Rd 13090 315-453-0261
Robert McCrone, prin. Fax 453-0269
Morgan Road ES 500/K-6
7795 Wetzel Rd 13090 315-453-1268
Mary Schiltz, prin. Fax 453-0275
Perry ES 400/K-6
7053 Buckley Rd 13088 315-453-0272
Margo Ross, prin. Fax 453-0281
Soule Road ES 500/K-6
8338 Soule Rd 13090 315-453-1280
Jeanne Brown, prin. Fax 453-1286
Soule Road MS 400/7-8
8340 Soule Rd 13090 315-453-1283
Robert Sheitz, prin. Fax 453-1286
Wetzel Road ES 400/K-6
4246 Wetzel Rd 13090 315-453-1291
Brenda Zavaski, prin. Fax 453-1263
Willow Field ES 500/K-6
3900 State Route 31 13090 315-453-1196
Henry Quattrini, prin. Fax 453-1255

Livingston Manor, Sullivan, Pop. 1,482
Livingston Manor Central SD 600/PK-12
PO Box 947 12758 845-439-4400
Deborah Fox, supt. Fax 439-4717
lmcs.k12.ny.us
Livingston Manor ES 300/PK-6
PO Box 947 12758 845-439-4400
Sandra Johnson, prin. Fax 439-4717

Livonia, Livingston, Pop. 1,527
Livonia Central SD 2,000/PK-12
PO Box E 14487 585-346-4000
Scott Bischoping, supt. Fax 346-6145
www.livoniacsd.org
Livonia IS 500/4-6
PO Box E 14487 585-346-4030
Deborah Haefele, prin. Fax 346-4068
Livonia JHS 300/7-8
PO Box E 14487 585-346-4050
Charles D'Imperio, prin. Fax 346-6835
Livonia PS 500/PK-3
PO Box E 14487 585-346-4020
MaryLou Bircher, prin. Fax 346-4082

Lockport, Niagara, Pop. 21,271
Lockport CSD 5,100/PK-12
130 Beattie Ave 14094 716-478-4800
Terry Carbone, supt. Fax 478-4863
www.lockport.k12.ny.us

Belknap MS 600/6-8
491 High St 14094 716-478-4550
Gary Wilson, prin. Fax 478-4535
Clinton ES 200/K-5
85 N Adam St 14094 716-478-4600
Amy Moeller, prin. Fax 478-4615
Hunt ES 300/K-5
50 Rogers Ave 14094 716-478-4650
Christopher Arnold, prin. Fax 478-4654
Kelley ES 300/K-5
610 E High St 14094 716-478-4670
Marianne Currie-Hall, prin. Fax 478-4685
Merritt ES 300/PK-5
389 Green St 14094 716-478-4725
Michael Sobieraski, prin. Fax 478-4730
North Park MS 600/6-8
160 Passaic Ave 14094 716-478-4700
James Snyder, prin. Fax 478-4705
Pound ES 200/K-5
51 High St 14094 716-478-4750
Roberta Donovan, prin. Fax 478-4755
Southard ES 500/K-5
6385 Locust Street Ext 14094 716-478-4770
Ryan Schoenfeld, prin. Fax 478-4775
Upson ES 500/PK-5
28 Harding Ave 14094 716-478-4400
Jennifer Gilson, prin. Fax 439-6857

Starpoint Central SD 2,800/K-12
4363 Mapleton Rd 14094 716-210-2352
Dr. C. Douglas Whelan, supt.
www.starpointcsd.org/
Fricano PS, 4363 Mapleton Rd 14094 500/K-2
Bonnie Calamita, prin. 716-210-2100
Starpoint IS, 4363 Mapleton Rd 14094 600/3-5
Dr. Douglas Regan, prin. 716-210-2150
Starpoint MS 700/6-8
4363 Mapleton Rd 14094 716-210-2200
James Bryer, prin.

Christian Academy of Western New York 100/PK-12
120 Main St 14094 716-433-1652
Patricia Poeller, admin. Fax 478-7979
Desales Catholic S 500/PK-8
6914 Chestnut Ridge Rd 14094 716-433-6422
Michael Powers, prin. Fax 434-4002
St. Peter Ev. Lutheran S - North Ridge 50/PK-8
4169 Church Rd 14094 716-433-9013
Kathleen Nagel, prin. Fax 433-9012

Locust Valley, Nassau, Pop. 3,963
Locust Valley Central SD 2,300/K-12
22 Horse Hollow Rd 11560 516-674-6390
Anna Hunderfund, supt. Fax 674-0138
www.lvcsd.k12.ny.us/
Locust Valley ES 600/K-5
119 Ryefield Rd 11560 516-674-6400
Sophia Gary, prin. Fax 674-3482
Locust Valley MS 500/6-8
99 Horse Hollow Rd 11560 516-674-6370
John Christie, prin. Fax 674-3795
Other Schools – See Bayville

Friends Academy 700/PK-12
270 Duck Pond Rd 11560 516-676-0393
William Morris, hdmstr. Fax 393-4276
Portledge S 400/PK-12
355 Duck Pond Rd 11560 516-750-3100
Steven Hahn, hdmstr. Fax 671-2039

Long Beach, Nassau, Pop. 35,336
Long Beach CSD
Supt. — See Lido Beach
West ES 400/K-5
91 Maryland Ave 11561 516-897-2215
Sandra Schneider, prin. Fax 897-2290

Hebrew Academy Long Beach 800/1-8
530 W Broadway 11561 516-432-8285
Richard Hagler, prin. Fax 432-0077
Long Beach Catholic S 500/PK-8
735 W Broadway 11561 516-432-8900
Veronica Danca, prin. Fax 432-3841
Montessori S of Long Beach 50/PK-4
111 Delaware Ave 11561 516-897-3031
Priscilla Carreon, prin. Fax 897-3031

Long Island City, See New York
NYC Department of Education
Supt. — See New York
IS 126 600/6-8
3151 21st St 11106 718-274-8316
Alexander Angueira, prin. Fax 278-6512
IS 141 1,000/6-8
3711 21st Ave 11105 718-278-6403
Miranda Pavlou, prin. Fax 278-2884
IS 204 900/6-8
3641 28th St 11106 718-937-1463
Yvonne Leimsider, prin. Fax 937-7964
Public S 17 700/PK-5
2837 29th St 11102 718-278-1220
Cynthia Dickman, prin. Fax 278-8257
Public S 70 1,100/PK-5
3045 42nd St 11103 718-728-4646
Donna Geller, prin. Fax 728-5817
Public S 76 600/PK-5
3636 10th St 11106 718-361-7464
Mary Schafenberg, prin. Fax 361-8014
Public S 78 200/PK-5
4809 Center Blvd 11109 718-392-5402
Luis Pavone, prin. Fax 392-5434
Public S 84 300/PK-6
2245 41st St 11105 718-278-1915
John Buffa, prin. Fax 932-4649
Public S 85 400/PK-5
2370 31st St 11105 718-278-3630
Ann Gordon-Chang, prin. Fax 278-8312
Public S 111 400/PK-7
3715 13th St 11101 718-786-2073
Randy Seabrook, prin. Fax 729-7102
Public S 112 500/K-5
2505 37th Ave 11101 718-784-5250
Rafael Campos, prin. Fax 784-5681
Public S 122 1,300/PK-8
2121 Ditmars Blvd 11105 718-721-6410
Pamela Sabel, prin. Fax 726-0016
Public S 150 1,100/PK-6
4001 43rd Ave 11104 718-784-2252
Carmen Parache, prin. Fax 729-7823
Public S 166 1,100/PK-5
3309 35th Ave 11106 718-786-6703
Janet Farrell, prin. Fax 729-7443
Public S 171 700/PK-5
1414 29th Ave 11102 718-932-0909
Ann Bussel, prin. Fax 932-6749
Public S 199 1,000/K-4
3920 48th Ave 11104 718-784-3431
Anthony Inzerillo, prin. Fax 786-1375
Young Womens Leadership S 6-8
2315 Newtown Ave 11102 718-267-2839
Laura Mitchell, prin. Fax 728-0218

Evangel Christian S 400/PK-12
3921 Crescent St 11101 718-937-9600
Rev. Robert Johansson, hdmstr. Fax 937-1613
Most Precious Blood S 500/PK-8
3252 37th St 11103 718-278-4081
Barbara DeMaio, prin. Fax 278-3089
St. Raphael S 300/PK-8
4825 37th St 11101 718-784-0482
Sr. Maureen Ahlemeyer, prin. Fax 482-0214

Long Lake, Hamilton
Long Lake Central SD 100/PK-12
PO Box 217 12847 518-624-2147
Kevin Crampton, supt. Fax 624-3896
www.longlakecsd.org/
Long Lake Central S 100/PK-12
PO Box 217 12847 518-624-2147
Kevin Crampton, prin. Fax 624-3896

Loudonville, Albany, Pop. 10,822
North Colonie Central SD
Supt. — See Latham
Loudonville ES 300/K-6
349 Osborne Rd 12211 518-434-1960
Kerry Flynn, prin. Fax 434-0739
Southgate ES 400/K-6
30 Southgate Rd 12211 518-785-6607
Jerri Lynne Dedrick, prin. Fax 783-8878

Loudonville Christian S 300/PK-12
374 Loudon Rd 12211 518-434-6051
Valyn Anderson, hdmstr. Fax 935-2258
St. Gregory's S 200/PK-8
121 Old Niskayuna Rd 12211 518-785-6621
Francis Foley, hdmstr. Fax 782-1364
St. Pius X S 600/PK-8
75 Upper Loudon Rd 12211 518-465-4539
Dennis Mullaly, prin. Fax 465-4895

Lowville, Lewis, Pop. 3,250
Lowville Central SD 1,400/K-12
7668 N State St 13367 315-376-9000
Kenneth McAuliffe, supt. Fax 376-1933
www.lacs-ny.org
Lowville ES 700/K-5
7668 N State St 13367 315-376-9005
Cheryl Steckly, prin. Fax 376-1933
Lowville MS 300/6-8
7668 N State St 13367 315-376-9010
Scott Exford, prin. Fax 376-9011

Lynbrook, Nassau, Pop. 19,640
Lynbrook UFD 3,100/K-12
111 Atlantic Ave 11563 516-887-0253
Dr. Santo Barbarino, supt. Fax 887-3263
www.lynbrook.k12.ny.us
Atlantic Avenue K 200/K-K
111 Atlantic Ave 11563 516-887-8065
Ellen Postman, prin. Fax 887-8264
Lynbrook North MS 300/6-8
529 Merrick Rd 11563 516-887-0282
Sean Fallon, prin. Fax 887-0286
Lynbrook South MS 500/6-8
333 Union Ave 11563 516-887-0266
Margaret Ronai Ed.D., prin. Fax 887-0268
Marion Street ES 400/1-5
100 Marion St 11563 516-887-0295
Barbara Moore, prin. Fax 887-3350
West End ES 400/1-5
30 Clark Ave 11563 516-887-0288
Alison Puliatte, prin. Fax 887-8269
Other Schools – See East Rockaway

Malverne UFD
Supt. — See Malverne
Davison Avenue ES 300/K-4
49 Davison Ave 11563 516-887-6462
Edward Tallon, prin. Fax 887-6468

Our Lady of Peace S 300/PK-8
21 Fowler Ave 11563 516-593-4884
Sr. Mary Dowden, prin. Fax 593-9861

Lyndonville, Orleans, Pop. 847
Lyndonville Central SD 600/K-12
PO Box 540 14098 585-765-3101
Barbara Deane-Williams, supt. Fax 765-2106
www.lyndonvillecsd.org/
Lyndonville ES 300/K-6
PO Box 540 14098 585-765-3122
Patrick Whipple, prin. Fax 765-2106

Lyons, Wayne, Pop. 3,553
Lyons Central SD 800/K-12
10 Clyde Rd 14489 315-946-2200
Richard Amundson, supt. Fax 946-2205
www.lyonscsd.org
Lyons ES 500/K-6
98 William St 14489 315-946-2200
Mark Clark, prin. Fax 946-2254

Macedon, Wayne, Pop. 1,531
Gananda Central SD
Supt. — See Walworth
Gananda / Mann ES 500/K-5
PO Box 609 14502 315-986-3521
Kim Ernstberger, prin. Fax 986-3506

Palmyra-Macedon Central SD
Supt. — See Palmyra
Palmyra-Macedon IS 200/3-5
4 West St 14502 315-986-4474
Chip Dolce, prin. Fax 986-8223

Mc Graw, Cortland, Pop. 1,032
Mc Graw Central SD 600/K-12
PO Box 556 13101 607-836-3636
Maria Fragnoli-Ryan, supt. Fax 836-3635
www.mcgrawschools.org
Mc Graw ES 300/K-6
PO Box 556 13101 607-836-3650
Beth Carsello, prin. Fax 836-3609

Mc Lean, Tompkins
Dryden Central SD
Supt. — See Dryden
Cassavant ES 100/K-2
36 School St 13102 607-838-3522
Audrey Ryan, prin. Fax 838-8907

Madison, Madison, Pop. 312
Madison Central SD 500/K-12
7303 State Route 20 13402 315-893-1878
Cynthia DeDominick, supt. Fax 893-7111
www.madisoncentralny.org
Madison Central S 500/K-12
7303 State Route 20 13402 315-893-1878
Christopher Harper, prin. Fax 893-7111

Madrid, Saint Lawrence
Madrid-Waddington Central SD 700/K-12
PO Box 67 13660 315-322-5746
Lynn Roy, supt. Fax 322-4462
www.mwcsk12.org
Madrid-Waddington ES 300/K-5
PO Box 67 13660 315-322-5634
Molly Pressey, prin. Fax 322-0030

Mahopac, Putnam, Pop. 7,755
Mahopac Central SD 5,300/K-12
179 E Lake Blvd 10541 845-628-3415
Thomas Manko, supt. Fax 628-5502
www.mahopac.k12.ny.us
Austin Road ES 700/1-5
390 Austin Rd 10541 845-628-1346
Robert Meyer, prin. Fax 628-5521
Fulmar Road ES 600/1-5
55 Fulmar Rd 10541 845-628-0440
Gary Chadwick, prin. Fax 628-5714
Lakeview ES 600/1-5
112 Lakeview Dr 10541 845-628-3331
Jennifer Pontillo, prin. Fax 628-5849
Mahopac Falls K 300/K-K
100 Myrtle Ave 10541 845-621-0656
Kathleen Lowell, prin. Fax 628-4819
Mahopac MS 1,300/6-8
425 Baldwin Place Rd 10541 845-621-1330
Ira Gurkin, prin. Fax 628-5847

St. John the Evangelist S 200/PK-8
239 E Lake Blvd 10541 845-628-6464
Paul Henshaw, prin. Fax 628-6469

Mahopac Falls, Putnam

Hudson Valley Christian Academy 50/PK-6
PO Box 135 10542 845-628-2775
Martha Burton, prin. Fax 621-9135

Maine, Broome
Maine-Endwell Central SD
Supt. — See Endwell
Maine Memorial ES 500/K-5
PO Box 218 13802 607-862-3263
Nikki Berkowitz, prin. Fax 862-3323

Malone, Franklin, Pop. 5,929
Malone Central SD 2,500/PK-12
PO Box 847 12953 518-483-7800
Wayne Walbridge, supt. Fax 483-3071
malone.k12.ny.us/
Davis ES 600/PK-2
179 Webster St 12953 518-483-7802
Lisa Dupree, prin. Fax 483-6390
Flanders ES 200/3-5
524 E Main St 12953 518-483-7803
Mary Seymour, prin. Fax 483-9491
Malone MS 600/6-8
15 Francis St 12953 518-483-7801
Robert Stewart, prin. Fax 483-9497
St. Josephs ES 300/3-5
99 Elm St 12953 518-483-7806
Keely Dunshee, prin. Fax 483-3071

Holy Family S 200/PK-8
12 Homestead Park 12953 518-483-4443
Anne Marie Wiseman, prin. Fax 481-6762

Malverne, Nassau, Pop. 8,832
Malverne UFD 1,700/K-12
301 Wicks Ln 11565 516-887-6405
Dr. James Hunderfund, supt. Fax 596-2910
www.malverne.k12.ny.us
Downing ES 300/K-4
55 Lindner Pl 11565 516-887-6469
Margaret McDaid, prin. Fax 887-8620
Herber MS 500/5-8
75 Ocean Ave 11565 516-887-6444
Steven Gilhuley, prin. Fax 596-0525
Other Schools – See Lynbrook

Grace Lutheran S 300/PK-6
400 Hempstead Ave 11565 516-599-6557
Wanda Walters, prin. Fax 599-6151
Our Lady of Lourdes S 300/PK-8
76 Park Blvd 11565 516-599-7328
John McQuillan, prin. Fax 599-3813

Mamaroneck, Westchester, Pop. 18,350
Mamaroneck UFD 5,000/PK-12
1000 W Boston Post Rd 10543 914-220-3000
Dr. Paul Fried, supt. Fax 220-3010
www.mamkschools.org
Mamaroneck Avenue ES 600/PK-5
850 Mamaroneck Ave 10543 914-220-3600
Carrie Amon, prin. Fax 220-3615
Other Schools – See Larchmont

Rye Neck UFD 1,400/K-12
310 Hornidge Rd 10543 914-777-5200
Dr. Peter Mustich, supt. Fax 777-5201
www.ryeneck.k12.ny.us/
Bellows ES 300/2-4
200 Carroll Ave 10543 914-777-5200
Margaret Longabucco, prin. Fax 777-4601
Rye Neck MS 400/5-8
300 Hornidge Rd 10543 914-777-5200
Eric Lutinski, prin. Fax 777-4701
Warren ES 200/K-1
1310 Harrison Ave 10543 914-777-5200
Joan Babcock, prin. Fax 777-4201

Little Flower Nursery S PK-PK
310 E Boston Post Rd 10543 914-777-1281
Leila Marie Badran, prin. Fax 698-5274
Westchester Day S 400/PK-8
856 Orienta Ave 10543 914-698-8900
Rachel Goldman, dir. Fax 777-2145

Manhasset, Nassau, Pop. 7,718
Manhasset UFD 2,900/K-12
200 Memorial Pl 11030 516-267-7700
Charles Cardillo, supt. Fax 627-1618
www.manhasset.k12.ny.us
Manhasset MS 500/7-8
200 Memorial Pl 11030 516-267-7500
Dean Schlanger, prin. Fax 627-8157
Munsey Park ES 900/K-6
1 Hunt Ln 11030 516-267-7400
Jean Kendall, prin. Fax 869-8244
Shelter Rock ES 800/K-6
27 Shelter Rock Rd 11030 516-267-7450
Robert Geczik, prin. Fax 365-3937

Our Lady of Grace Montessori S 200/PK-3
29 Shelter Rock Rd 11030 516-365-9832
Sr. Kelly Quinn, prin. Fax 365-9329
St. Mary S 500/PK-8
1340 Northern Blvd 11030 516-627-0184
Dr. Celeste Checchia, prin. Fax 627-3795

Manlius, Onondaga, Pop. 4,695
Fayetteville-Manlius Central SD 4,700/K-12
8199 E Seneca Tpke 13104 315-692-1200
Corliss Kaiser, supt. Fax 692-1227
www.fmschools.org
Eagle Hill MS 800/5-8
4645 Enders Rd 13104 315-692-1400
Maureen McCrystal, prin. Fax 692-1046
Enders Road ES 600/K-4
4725 Enders Rd 13104 315-692-1500
Deborah Capri, prin. Fax 692-1053
Other Schools – See Fayetteville

Mannsville, Jefferson, Pop. 410
South Jefferson Central SD
Supt. — See Adams Center
Mannsville Manor ES 400/K-5
423 N Main St 13661 315-465-4281
Ron Perry, prin. Fax 465-4088

Manorville, Suffolk, Pop. 6,198
Eastport-South Manor Central SD 3,900/K-12
149 Dayton Ave 11949 631-874-6720
Mark Nocero, supt. Fax 878-6308
www.esmonline.org
Dayton Avenue S 600/3-6
151 Dayton Ave 11949 631-878-4441
Barbara Lassen, prin. Fax 878-6404
South Street ES 400/K-2
130 South St 11949 631-878-4900
Robin Barbera, prin. Fax 878-4954
Other Schools – See Eastport

Marathon, Cortland, Pop. 1,034
Marathon Central SD 900/K-12
PO Box 339 13803 607-849-3251
Timothy Turecek, supt. Fax 849-3305
www.marathonschools.org/
Appleby ES 400/K-6
PO Box 339 13803 607-849-3281
Shelley Warnow, prin. Fax 849-3305

Marcellus, Onondaga, Pop. 1,793
Marcellus Central SD 2,100/K-12
2 Reed Pkwy 13108 315-673-0201
Dr. Craig Tice, supt. Fax 673-1727
marcellusschools.org
Driver MS 800/4-8
2 Reed Pkwy 13108 315-673-0219
Michael Dardaris, prin. Fax 673-1727
Heffernan ES 600/K-3
2 Learners Ldg 13108 315-673-0282
Gary Bissaillon, prin. Fax 673-1117

Marcy, Oneida, Pop. 8,685
Whitesboro Central SD
Supt. — See Yorkville
Marcy ES 300/K-5
9479 Maynard Dr 13403 315-266-3420
Laurie Fitzgerald, prin. Fax 735-3358

Margaretville, Delaware, Pop. 653
Margaretville Central SD 500/K-12
PO Box 319 12455 845-586-2647
Anthony Albanese, supt. Fax 586-2949
www.margaretvillecs.org
Margaretville Central S 500/K-12
PO Box 319 12455 845-586-2647
Linda Taylor, prin. Fax 586-2949

Marilla, Erie
Iroquois Central SD
Supt. — See Elma
Marilla PS 200/K-3
11683 Bullis Rd 14102 716-652-3000
Regina Becker, prin. Fax 995-2330

Marion, Wayne
Marion Central SD 1,100/K-12
4034 Warner Rd 14505 315-926-2300
Kathryn Wegman, supt. Fax 926-5797
www.marioncs.org/
Marion ES 500/K-6
3863 N Main St 14505 315-926-4256
Michele Murdock, prin. Fax 926-3115

Marlboro, Ulster, Pop. 2,200
Marlboro Central SD 2,100/K-12
50 Cross Rd 12542 845-236-5802
Raymond Castellani, supt. Fax 236-5817
www.marlboroschools.org
Marlboro ES 200/K-2
1380 Route 9W 12542 845-236-5830
Scott Brown, prin. Fax 236-5834
Marlboro IS 400/3-5
1380 Route 9W 12542 845-236-1636
Marie Toombs, prin. Fax 236-1639
Marlboro MS 500/6-8
1375 Route 9W 12542 845-236-5842
Roseanne Collins-Judon, prin. Fax 236-3634
Other Schools – See Milton, Newburgh

Maspeth, See New York
NYC Department of Education
Supt. — See New York
IS 73 1,600/6-8
7002 54th Ave 11378 718-639-3817
Patricia Reynolds, prin. Fax 429-5162
Public S 58 800/PK-6
7250 Grand Ave 11378 718-533-6712
Adelina Tripoli, prin. Fax 533-6794
Public S 153 1,300/PK-6
6002 60th Ln 11378 718-821-7850
Susan Bauer, prin. Fax 386-7392

St. Stanislaus Kostka S 200/PK-8
6117 Grand Ave 11378 718-326-1585
Sr. Rose Torma, prin. Fax 326-1745

Massapequa, Nassau, Pop. 22,018
Massapequa UFD 8,200/K-12
4925 Merrick Rd 11758 516-797-6600
Charles Sulc, supt. Fax 797-6072
www.msd.k12.ny.us
Berner MS 1,400/7-8
50 Carman Mill Rd 11758 516-797-6080
Stephen Scarallo, prin. Fax 797-6638
Fairfield ES 800/K-6
330 Massapequa Ave 11758 516-797-6030
Jason Esposito, prin. Fax 797-6658
Lockhart ES 500/K-6
199 Pittsburgh Ave 11758 516-797-6050
Lori Dano, prin. Fax 797-6660
Unqua ES 700/K-6
350 Unqua Rd 11758 516-797-6060
Diana Haanraadts, prin. Fax 797-6662
Other Schools – See Massapequa Park

Plainedge UFD
Supt. — See North Massapequa
Schwarting ES 600/K-5
1 Flower Rd 11758 516-992-7400
Beth McCoy, prin. Fax 992-7405

Grace Day S 400/PK-8
23 Cedar Shore Dr 11758 516-798-1122
Laurance Anderson, hdmstr. Fax 799-0711
Montessori Children's S 200/PK-K
98 Jerusalem Ave 11758 516-541-6365
Diane Beatty, dir. Fax 565-1904
St. Rose of Lima S 500/PK-8
4704 Merrick Rd 11758 516-541-1546
Sr. Kathleen Gallina, prin. Fax 797-0351

Massapequa Park, Nassau, Pop. 17,270
Massapequa UFD
Supt. — See Massapequa
Birch Lane ES 1,000/K-6
41 Birch Ln 11762 516-797-6010
Joyce Becker, prin. Fax 797-6643

East Lake ES 700/K-6
154 Eastlake Ave 11762 516-797-6020
Thomas McKillop, prin. Fax 797-6649
McKenna ES 600/K-6
210 Spruce St 11762 516-797-6040
Jean Castelli, prin. Fax 797-6641

Our Lady of Lourdes S 200/PK-8
379 Linden St 11762 516-798-7926
Robert Lanzisera, prin. Fax 798-8159

Massena, Saint Lawrence, Pop. 10,859
Massena Central SD 2,800/K-12
84 Nightengale Ave 13662 315-764-3700
Roger Clough, supt. Fax 764-3701
www.mcs.k12.ny.us
Jefferson ES 500/K-6
84 Nightengale Ave 13662 315-764-3730
Duane Richards, prin. Fax 764-3739
Leary JHS 500/7-8
84 Nightengale Ave 13662 315-764-3720
Jesse Coburn, prin. Fax 764-3723
Madison ES 400/K-6
84 Nightengale Ave 13662 315-764-3740
Shannon Jordan, prin. Fax 764-3743
Nightengale ES 400/K-6
84 Nightengale Ave 13662 315-764-3750
Michele Meyers, prin. Fax 764-3753

Trinity Catholic S 300/PK-6
188 Main St 13662 315-769-5911
Joan Rufa, prin. Fax 769-1185

Mastic Beach, Suffolk, Pop. 10,293
William Floyd UFD 9,900/K-12
240 Mastic Beach Rd 11951 631-874-1100
Dr. Paul Casciano, supt. Fax 281-3047
www.wfsd.k12.ny.us
Paca MS 1,100/6-8
338 Blanco Dr 11951 631-874-1414
Barbara Butler, prin. Fax 874-1561
Tangier Smith ES 800/K-5
336 Blanco Dr 11951 631-874-1342
Tom Harrison, prin. Fax 874-1416
Other Schools – See Moriches, Shirley

Mattydale, Onondaga, Pop. 6,418

St. Margaret S 300/PK-6
201 Roxboro Rd 13211 315-455-5791
Suzanne Donze, prin. Fax 455-1250

Maybrook, Orange, Pop. 4,068
Valley Central SD
Supt. — See Montgomery
Maybrook ES 300/K-5
120 Broadway 12543 845-457-2400
Anne Sussdorff, prin. Fax 427-5132

Mayfield, Fulton, Pop. 800
Mayfield Central SD 1,100/PK-12
27 School St 12117 518-661-8207
Paul Williamsen, supt. Fax 661-7666
www.mayfieldk12.com/
Mayfield ES 600/PK-6
80 N Main St 12117 518-661-8251
Nicholas Criscone, prin. Fax 661-6590

Mayville, Chautauqua, Pop. 1,721
Chautauqua Lake SD 900/PK-12
100 N Erie St 14757 716-753-5808
Benjamin Spitzer, supt. Fax 753-5813
www.clake.org
Chautauqua Lake ES 400/PK-5
100 N Erie St 14757 716-753-5842
Ela Ames, prin. Fax 753-5850
Chautauqua Lake MS 200/6-8
100 N Erie St 14757 716-753-5872
Rosemary Andrews, prin. Fax 753-5876

Mechanicville, Saratoga, Pop. 4,997
Mechanicville CSD 1,300/K-12
25 Kniskern Ave 12118 518-664-5727
Michael McCarthy, supt. Fax 514-2101
www.mechanicville.org/
Mechanicville ES 600/K-5
25 Kniskern Ave 12118 518-664-7336
Stephen Marra, prin. Fax 514-2119
Mechanicville MS 300/6-8
25 Kniskern Ave 12118 518-664-6303
Kevin Duffy, prin. Fax 514-2104

Medford, Suffolk, Pop. 21,274
Patchogue-Medford UFD
Supt. — See Patchogue
Eagle ES, 1000 Wave Ave 11763 600/K-5
Neil Katz, prin. 631-687-8150
Tremont ES, 143 Tremont Ave 11763 600/K-5
Joey Cohen, prin. 631-687-8700

Medina, Orleans, Pop. 6,235
Medina Central SD 1,900/PK-12
1 Mustang Dr 14103 585-798-2700
Neal Miller, supt. Fax 798-5676
www.medinacsd.org
Oak Orchard ES 400/3-5
335 W Oak Orchard St 14103 585-798-2350
Cathy Joynt, prin. Fax 798-2352
Towne ES 400/PK-2
181 Bates Rd 14103 585-798-4011
Daniel Doctor, prin. Fax 798-5907
Wise MS 400/6-8
1016 Gwinn St 14103 585-798-2100
Elaine Wendt, prin. Fax 798-1062

Orleans County Christian S 50/K-12
PO Box 349 14103 585-798-2992
Linda Strickland, admin. Fax 798-3766

Melville, Suffolk, Pop. 12,586
Half Hollow Hills Central SD
Supt. — See Dix Hills
Sunquam ES 700/K-5
515 Sweet Hollow Rd 11747 631-592-3750
Karen Littell, prin. Fax 592-3920
West Hollow MS 1,400/6-8
250 Old East Neck Rd 11747 631-592-3400
Milton Strong, prin. Fax 592-3922

South Huntington UFD
Supt. — See Huntington Station
Birchwood IS 600/3-5
121 Wolf Hill Rd 11747 631-425-5460
Anthony Ciccarelli, prin. Fax 425-5391

Trinity Regional S 100/PK-PK
175 Wolf Hill Rd 11747 631-549-7450
Jeanne Morcone, prin.
West Hills Montessori at Crestwood 200/PK-6
313 Round Swamp Rd 11747 631-367-8060
Perla Wassel, dir.

Menands, Albany, Pop. 3,825
Menands UFD 200/K-8
19 Wards Ln 12204 518-465-4561
Kathy Meany, supt. Fax 465-4572
www.menandsschool.nycap.rr.com
Menands S 200/K-8
19 Wards Ln 12204 518-465-4561
Kathy Meany, prin. Fax 465-4572

Merrick, Nassau, Pop. 23,042
Bellmore-Merrick Central HSD
Supt. — See North Merrick
Merrick Avenue MS 1,000/7-8
1870 Merrick Ave 11566 516-992-1200
Caryn Blum, prin. Fax 867-6391

Merrick UFD 1,900/K-6
21 Babylon Rd 11566 516-992-7200
Dr. Ranier Melucci, supt. Fax 378-3904
www.merrick-k6.org
Birch ES 600/K-6
2400 Central Pkwy 11566 516-992-7249
Eric Arlin, prin. Fax 546-1723
Chatterton ES 500/K-6
108 Merrick Ave 11566 516-992-7269
Cindy Davidowitz, prin. Fax 546-1718
Levy Lakeside ES 700/K-6
21 Babylon Rd 11566 516-992-7230
Miriam Hanan, prin. Fax 546-6592

Grace Christian Academy 100/K-12
36 Smith St 11566 516-379-2223
Richard Jensen, hdmstr. Fax 771-8063
Progressive S of Long Island 100/K-8
1425 Merrick Ave 11566 516-868-6835
Fax 868-7033
South Shore Montessori S 50/PK-6
2323 Merrick Ave 11566 516-379-3138
Bernardita Reed, prin.

Mexico, Oswego, Pop. 1,560
Mexico Central SD 2,500/K-12
40 Academy St 13114 315-963-8400
Nelson Bauersfeld, supt. Fax 963-3325
www.mexico.cnyric.org
Mexico ES 400/K-4
26 Academy St 13114 315-963-8400
Robert Briggs, prin. Fax 963-8992
Mexico MS 700/5-8
16 Fravor Rd 13114 315-963-8400
Kim Holliday, prin. Fax 963-3848
Other Schools – See Fulton, New Haven

Middleburgh, Schoharie, Pop. 1,554
Middleburgh Central SD 900/PK-12
PO Box 606 12122 518-827-3600
Michele Weaver, supt. Fax 827-6632
www.middleburgh.k12.ny.us
Middleburgh ES 400/PK-5
PO Box 850 12122 518-827-3600
Amy Lennon, prin. Fax 827-5321
Middleburgh MS 200/6-8
PO Box 400 12122 518-827-3600
Maura Green, prin. Fax 827-9533

St. Mark's Christian S 50/K-8
326 Main St 12122 518-827-5318
Lori Lower, contact

Middle Granville, Washington
Granville Central SD
Supt. — See Granville
Tanner PS 200/K-2
PO Box 200 12849 518-642-9460
Kristie Gijanto, prin. Fax 642-9594

Middle Island, Suffolk, Pop. 7,848
Longwood Central SD 9,300/K-12
35 Yaphank Middle Island Rd 11953 631-345-2172
Dr. Allan Gerstenlauer, supt. Fax 345-2166
www.longwood.k12.ny.us
Longwood JHS 1,500/7-8
198 Longwood Rd 11953 631-345-2701
Levi McIntyre, prin. Fax 345-9281
Longwood MS 1,300/5-6
41 Yaphank Middle Island Rd 11953 631-345-2735
Lisa Mato, prin. Fax 345-9296
West Middle Island ES 800/K-4
30 Swezey Ln 11953 631-345-2160
Wynstelle Nicholson, prin. Fax 345-2193
Other Schools – See Coram, Ridge, Yaphank

Middleport, Niagara, Pop. 1,826
Royalton-Hartland Central SD 1,600/K-12
54 State St 14105 716-735-3031
Paul Bona, supt. Fax 735-3660
www.royhart.org/
Royalton-Hartland MS 500/5-8
78 State St 14105 716-735-3722
John Fisgus, prin. Fax 735-0047
Other Schools – See Gasport

Middletown, Orange, Pop. 26,067
Middletown CSD 6,800/PK-12
223 Wisner Ave 10940 845-326-1193
Dr. Kenneth Eastwood, supt. Fax 326-1215
www.middletowncityschools.org/
Chorley PS 600/K-1
50 Roosevelt Ave 10940 845-341-5241
Frederick Griffin, prin. Fax 342-1925
Maple Hill ES 1,300/2-5
491 County Highway 78 10940 845-326-1741
Eileen Casey, prin. Fax 326-1795
Mechanicstown ES 900/PK-PK, 2-
435 E Main St 10940 845-341-5260
Sue Short, prin. Fax 343-2104
Monhagen MS 800/6-8
555 County Highway 78 10940 845-346-4800
Tracey Sorrentino, prin. Fax 346-4868
Truman Moon PS 400/K-1
53 Bedford Ave 10940 845-326-1770
Donna Napolitano, prin. Fax 326-1788
Twin Towers MS 700/6-8
112 Grand Ave 10940 845-341-5400
Gordon Dean, prin. Fax 343-4515

Harmony Christian S 300/PK-12
1790 Route 211 E 10941 845-692-5353
Kevin Barry, admin. Fax 692-7140
Middletown SDA Christian S 50/PK-8
70 Highland Ave 10940 845-343-3775
Our Lady of Mt. Carmel S 200/PK-8
205 Wawayanda Ave 10940 845-343-8836
Karen DeCrosta, prin. Fax 342-1404
St. Joseph S 200/PK-8
113 Cottage St 10940 845-343-3139
Richard Jackson, prin. Fax 346-4647

Middle Village, See New York
NYC Department of Education
Supt. — See New York
Public S 49 500/K-5
7915 Penelope Ave 11379 718-326-2111
Anthony Lombardi, prin. Fax 894-3026
Public S 87 500/PK-8
6754 80th St 11379 718-326-8243
Caryn Michaeli, prin. Fax 894-3797
Public S 128 400/K-5
6926 65th Dr 11379 718-894-8385
John Lavelle, prin. Fax 894-7327

Our Lady of Hope S 600/PK-8
6121 71st St 11379 718-458-3535
Sr. Jean Redigan, prin. Fax 458-9031
St. Margaret S 500/PK-8
6610 80th St 11379 718-326-0922
Sr. Rena Perrone, prin. Fax 326-3308

Milford, Otsego, Pop. 485
Milford Central SD 500/K-12
PO Box 237 13807 607-286-3341
Peter Livshin, supt. Fax 286-7879
Milford Central S 500/K-12
PO Box 237 13807 607-286-3349
Michael Miller, prin. Fax 286-7879

Millbrook, Dutchess, Pop. 1,559
Millbrook Central SD 1,100/K-12
PO Box AA 12545 845-677-4200
Dr. R. Lloyd Jaeger, supt. Fax 677-4206
www.millbrookcsd.org/
Alden Place ES 300/3-5
PO Box AA 12545 845-677-4220
Thomas Libka, prin. Fax 677-4213
Elm Drive ES 200/K-2
PO Box AA 12545 845-677-4225
Karen Fitzgerald, prin. Fax 677-4224
Millbrook MS 300/6-8
PO Box AA 12545 845-677-4210
Brian Fried, prin. Fax 677-6913

Dutchess Day S 200/PK-8
415 Route 343 12545 845-677-5014
John Cissel, hdmstr. Fax 677-6722
St. Joseph S 200/PK-8
PO Box 587 12545 845-677-3670
Rosalie Fegan, prin. Fax 677-8365

Miller Place, Suffolk, Pop. 9,315
Miller Place UFD 3,200/K-12
275 Route 25A Unit 43 11764 631-474-2700
Dr. Grace Brindley, supt. Fax 474-0686
www.millerplace.k12.ny.us
Muller PS 700/K-2
65 Lower Rocky Point Rd 11764 631-474-2715
Karen Reichert, prin. Fax 474-4738
North Country Road MS 800/6-8
191 N Country Rd 11764 631-474-2710
Matthew Clark, prin. Fax 474-5178
Sound Beach ES 700/3-5
197 N Country Rd 11764 631-474-2719
Catherine Pugliese, prin. Fax 474-2497

Millerton, Dutchess, Pop. 931
Webutuck Central SD
Supt. — See Amenia
Millerton S 50/PK-PK
4833 S Elm Ave 12546 518-789-4671
Kathleen McEnroe, prin. Fax 789-8046

Milton, Ulster, Pop. 3,032
Marlboro Central SD
Supt. — See Marlboro
Milton ES 100/K-2
PO Box 813 12547 845-795-2730
Patricia Walsh, prin. Fax 795-2153

Mineola, Nassau, Pop. 18,978
Mineola UFD 2,700/PK-12
121 Jackson Ave 11501 516-237-2001
Dr. Lorenzo Licopoli, supt. Fax 739-4783
www.mineola.k12.ny.us
Hampton Street ES 200/PK-5
10 Hampton St 11501 516-237-2200
Dr. SueCaryl Fleischmann, prin. Fax 739-4068
Jackson Avenue ES 400/PK-5
300 Jackson Ave 11501 516-237-2300
Matthew Gaven, prin. Fax 741-2308
Mineola MS 600/6-8
200 Emory Rd 11501 516-237-2500
Mark Barth, prin. Fax 739-4129
Willis Avenue S 300/PK-K
121 Jackson Ave 11501 516-237-2900
Deborah Shaw, prin.
Other Schools – See Albertson, Williston Park

Corpus Christi S 200/PK-8
120 Searing Ave 11501 516-746-2966
Susan Anaischik, prin. Fax 739-3363

Minetto, Oswego, Pop. 1,252
Oswego CSD
Supt. — See Oswego
Minetto ES 400/K-6
PO Box 189 13115 315-341-2600
Rosann Bayne, prin. Fax 341-2960

Minoa, Onondaga, Pop. 3,255
East Syracuse-Minoa Central SD
Supt. — See East Syracuse
Minoa ES 400/K-5
501 N Main St 13116 315-434-3420
Mary Ward, prin. Fax 434-3430

Mohawk, Herkimer, Pop. 2,569
Mohawk Central SD 900/K-12
28 Grove St 13407 315-867-2904
Joyce Caputo, supt. Fax 867-2918
www.mohawk.k12.ny.us
Fisher ES 500/K-6
10 Fisher Ave 13407 315-866-4851
Colleen Vetere, prin. Fax 866-0055

Mohegan Lake, Westchester, Pop. 3,600
Lakeland Central SD
Supt. — See Shrub Oak
Van Cortlandtville ES 600/K-5
3100 E Main St 10547 914-528-1354
Jacqueline Lewis, prin. Fax 528-1376
Washington ES 500/K-5
3634 Lexington Ave 10547 914-528-2021
Tracy Norman, prin. Fax 528-2134

Monroe, Orange, Pop. 8,127
Greenwood Lake UFD 600/K-8
1247 Lakes Rd 10950 845-477-7395
Harvey Hillburgh, supt. Fax 477-7398
gwl.ouboces.org/
Greenwood Lake MS 300/5-8
1247 Lakes Rd 10950 845-986-8624
Michael Gillespie, prin. Fax 782-2004
Other Schools – See Greenwood Lake

Kiryas Joel Village UFSD 200/PK-12
PO Box 398, 845-782-2300
Joel Petlin, supt. Fax 782-4176
Kiryas Joel Village S 200/PK-12
PO Box 398, 845-782-7510
Susan Gartenberg, prin. Fax 782-5849

Monroe-Woodbury Central SD
Supt. — See Central Valley
North Main Street ES 600/2-5
212 N Main St 10950 845-460-6800
Matthew Kravatz, prin. Fax 460-6048
Pine Tree ES 900/2-5
156 Pine Tree Rd 10950 845-460-6900
Gale Katenkamp, prin. Fax 460-6049

Sacred Heart S 200/PK-8
26 Still Rd 10950 845-783-0365
Catharine Muenkel, prin. Fax 782-0354
St. Paul Christian Education Center 200/PK-1
21 Still Rd 10950 845-783-1068
Ramona Adams, dir. Fax 783-7593
UTA of Kiryas Joel 2,600/K-12
PO Box 477, 845-783-5800
Rabbi Baruch Weinberger, prin. Fax 782-1922

Monsey, Rockland, Pop. 13,986
East Ramapo Central SD
Supt. — See Spring Valley
Elmwood IS 300/4-6
43 Robert Pitt Dr 10952 845-577-6160
Dr. Nancy Kavanagh, prin. Fax 426-0852
Grandview ES 400/K-3
151 Grandview Ave 10952 845-577-6260
Patricia Smith, prin. Fax 362-0646
Margetts ES 500/K-3
25 Margetts Rd 10952 845-577-6190
Eileen McGuire, prin. Fax 426-0958

Ateres Bais Yaakov 300/PK-12
236 Cherry Ln 10952 845-368-2200
Bais Malka Girls S of Belz 400/PK-12
PO Box 977 10952 845-371-0500
Bais Mikroh 400/K-8
221 Viola Rd 10952 845-425-4880
Rabbi G. Bodenheimer, dean Fax 425-1062

Bais Shifra Miriam S 300/K-12
PO Box 682 10952 845-356-0061
Bais Trany 50/PK-2
PO Box 870 10952 845-371-6900
Beth Rochel School for Girls 100/K-12
145 Saddle River Rd 10952 845-352-5000
Rabbi Jacob Przewozman, admin. Fax 352-6571
Bnos Yisroel Girls S of Viznitz 50/1-12
1 School Ter 10952 845-731-3700
Bnos Yisroel Girls S of Viznitz 50/PK-1
20 Ashel Ln 10952 845-731-3777
Cheder Ateres Tzvi 100/K-7
230 Viola Rd 10952 845-425-5656
Schreiber Hebrew Academy 300/PK-8
70 Highview Rd 10952 845-357-1515
Josh Friedman, dir. Fax 357-6872
Yeshiva Beth David S 600/K-12
PO Box 136 10952 845-352-3100
Yeshiva Derech Emes 200/PK-8
133 Route 59 10952 845-426-2130
David Rosenberg, prin. Fax 426-0771
Yeshiva Eitz Chaim 50/PK-1
13 Ashel Ln Apt 2B 10952 845-425-3623
Yeshiva of Spring Valley 1,500/PK-8
230 Maple Ave 10952 845-356-1400
Yeshiva Viznitz 2,500/PK-12
PO Box 446 10952 845-356-1010

Montauk, Suffolk, Pop. 3,001
Montauk UFD 300/K-8
50 S Dorset Dr 11954 631-668-2474
J. Philip Perna, supt. Fax 668-1107
www.montaukschool.org
Montauk S 300/K-8
50 S Dorset Dr 11954 631-668-2474
J. Philip Perna, prin. Fax 668-1107

Montgomery, Orange, Pop. 4,238
Valley Central SD 5,100/K-12
944 State Route 17K 12549 845-457-2400
Richard Hooley Ed.D., supt. Fax 457-4319
www.vcsd.k12.ny.us
Berea ES 400/K-5
946 State Route 17K 12549 845-457-2400
Hope Stuart, prin. Fax 457-4442
Montgomery ES 600/K-5
141 Union St 12549 845-457-2400
Marianne Serratore, prin. Fax 457-9120
Valley Central MS 1,200/6-8
1189 State Route 17K 12549 845-457-2400
Ned Hayes, prin. Fax 457-4311
Other Schools – See Maybrook, Newburgh, Walden

Monticello, Sullivan, Pop. 6,649
Monticello Central SD 3,400/K-12
237 Forestburgh Rd 12701 845-794-7700
Dr. Patrick Michel, supt. Fax 794-7710
www.monticelloschools.net
Cooke ES 500/K-2
69 Richardson Ave 12701 845-794-8830
Sandra Johnson-Fields, prin. Fax 794-8854
Kaiser MS 800/6-8
45 Breakey Ave 12701 845-796-3058
Deborah Wood, prin. Fax 796-3099
Rutherford ES 500/3-5
26 Patricia Pl 12701 845-794-4240
Kimberly Patterson, prin. Fax 794-5137
Other Schools – See White Lake, Wurtsboro

Montour Falls, Schuyler, Pop. 1,781
Odessa-Montour Central SD
Supt. — See Odessa
Cate ES 200/K-2
262 Canal St 14865 607-535-7267
Gregory Conlon, prin. Fax 535-7802

Montrose, Westchester
Hendrick Hudson Central SD 2,800/K-12
61 Trolley Rd 10548 914-257-5112
Dr. Daniel McCann, supt. Fax 257-5121
www.henhudschools.org/
Lindsey ES 400/K-5
57 Trolley Rd 10548 914-257-5500
Donna Torrisi, prin. Fax 257-5501
Other Schools – See Buchanan, Cortlandt Manor

Mooers, Clinton, Pop. 419
Northeastern Clinton Central SD
Supt. — See Champlain
Mooers ES 300/K-5
16 School St 12958 518-236-7373
Dennis Rasco, prin. Fax 298-4293

Moravia, Cayuga, Pop. 1,326
Moravia Central SD 1,100/K-12
PO Box 1189 13118 315-497-2670
William Tammaro, supt. Fax 497-2260
www.moraviaschool.org/
Fillmore ES 600/K-6
PO Box 1188 13118 315-497-2670
Howard Seamans, prin. Fax 497-3961

Moriches, Suffolk
William Floyd UFD
Supt. — See Mastic Beach
Floyd MS 1,200/6-8
630 Moriches Middle Island 11955 631-874-5500
Carolyn Schick, prin. Fax 874-5508
Moriches ES 900/K-5
16 Louis Ave 11955 631-874-1398
Eileen Filippone, prin. Fax 874-1890

Morris, Otsego, Pop. 561
Morris Central SD 400/PK-12
PO Box 40 13808 607-263-6100
Michael Virgil, supt. Fax 263-2483
morriscs.org
Morris Central S 400/PK-12
PO Box 40 13808 607-263-6100
Leone Schermerhorn, prin. Fax 263-2483

Morrisonville, Clinton, Pop. 1,742
Saranac Central SD
Supt. — See Dannemora
Morrisonville ES 300/K-6
47 Sand Rd 12962 518-565-5980
Brad Ott, prin. Fax 565-5972

Morristown, Saint Lawrence, Pop. 441
Morristown Central SD 400/K-12
PO Box 217 13664 315-375-8814
Beverly Ouderkirk, supt. Fax 375-8604
mcsd.schoolfusion.us/
Morristown Central S 400/K-12
PO Box 217 13664 315-375-8814
Ruth Lincoln, prin. Fax 375-8604

Morrisville, Madison, Pop. 2,304
Morrisville-Eaton Central SD 900/K-12
PO Box 990 13408 315-684-9300
Michael Drahos, supt. Fax 684-9399
www.m-ecs.org
Andrews ES 400/K-6
PO Box 990 13408 315-684-9288
Debra Dushko, prin. Fax 684-7252

Mount Kisco, Westchester, Pop. 10,331
Bedford Central SD
Supt. — See Bedford
Mount Kisco ES 500/K-5
47 W Hyatt Ave 10549 914-666-2677
Susan Ostrofsky, prin. Fax 666-8245

Rippowam Cisqua S 300/PK-4
325 W Patent Rd 10549 914-244-1200
Eileen F. Lambert, hdmstr. Fax 244-1234
Talmud Torah Bais Yechiel-Nitra 200/K-9
PO Box 241 10549 914-666-2929
Reuven Lefkowitz, prin. Fax 242-0368

Mount Morris, Livingston, Pop. 2,978
Mount Morris Central SD 600/K-12
30 Bonadonna Ave 14510 585-658-2568
Renee Garrett, supt. Fax 658-4814
www.mt-morris.k12.ny.us
Mount Morris ES 300/K-6
30 Bonadonna Ave 14510 585-658-2019
Michael Murray, prin. Fax 658-4814

Mount Sinai, Suffolk, Pop. 8,023
Mount Sinai UFD 2,600/K-12
150 N Country Rd 11766 631-870-2550
Dr. Anthony Bonasera, supt. Fax 473-0905
www.mtsinai.k12.ny.us
Mount Sinai ES 900/K-4
150 N Country Rd 11766 631-820-2600
Dr. John Gentilcore, prin. Fax 928-3860
Mount Sinai MS 800/5-8
150 N Country Rd 11766 631-870-2700
Robert Grable, prin. Fax 928-3129

Mount Vernon, Westchester, Pop. 67,924
Mount Vernon CSD 9,400/PK-12
165 N Columbus Ave 10553 914-665-5000
Dr. Welton Sawyer, supt. Fax 665-6077
www.mtvernoncsd.org/education
Columbus ES at Franko 600/K-6
455 N High St 10552 914-358-2701
Peter Ragaglia, prin. Fax 665-0481
Davis MS 900/7-8
350 Gramatan Ave 10552 914-665-5120
Murdisia Orr, prin. Fax 665-5128
Graham ES 500/K-6
421 E 5th St 10553 914-665-5080
Natasha Hunter-McGregor, prin. Fax 665-5073
Grimes ES 500/K-6
58 S 10th Ave 10550 914-665-5020
Frances Lightsy, prin. Fax 665-5016
Hamilton ES 500/K-6
20 Oak St 10550 914-358-2434
Diaquino DeFreitas, prin. Fax 665-5052
Holmes ES 500/PK-6
195 N Columbus Ave 10553 914-665-5110
Louis Cioffi, prin. Fax 665-5116
Lincoln ES 700/K-6
170 E Lincoln Ave 10552 914-665-5030
George Albano, prin. Fax 665-5378
Longfellow ES 400/K-6
625 S 4th Ave 10550 914-665-5100
Lynette Harris, prin. Fax 665-5096
Longfellow MS 600/7-8
624 S 3rd Ave 10550 914-665-5151
Brodrick Spencer, prin. Fax 665-5152
Parker ES 400/K-6
461 S 6th Ave 10550 914-665-5040
Patricia Meed, prin. Fax 665-5353
Pennington ES 400/K-6
20 Fairway St 10552 914-665-5105
Danielle Marrow, prin. Fax 665-5107
Traphagen ES 300/K-6
72 Lexington Ave 10552 914-358-2447
Joe Jordano, prin. Fax 665-5062
Williams ES 500/K-6
9 Union Ln 10553 914-665-5070
Ernest Gregg, prin. Fax 665-5237

Emmanuel Children's Mission S 200/PK-6
32 S 5th Ave 10550 914-668-5006
Fortress Christian Academy 50/K-12
51 N 10th Ave 10550 914-699-9039
Rev. Dennis Karaman, admin. Fax 699-6819
Our Lady of Victory S 300/PK-8
38 N 5th Ave 10550 914-667-4063
Denise Rigano, prin. Fax 665-3135
Sacred Heart S for Arts 300/PK-8
71 Sharpe Blvd 10550 914-667-1734
Gabriel De Jesus, prin. Fax 667-1497
SS. Peter & Paul S 200/PK-8
125 E Birch St 10552 914-664-1321
Catherine Ryall, prin. Fax 664-2951

Munnsville, Madison, Pop. 426
Stockbridge Valley Central SD 500/K-12
PO Box 732 13409 315-495-4400
Chuck Chafee, supt. Fax 495-4492
www.stockbridgevalley.org
Stockbridge Valley Central S 500/K-12
PO Box 732 13409 315-495-4550
Mary Anne Iritz, prin. Fax 495-4492

Nanuet, Rockland, Pop. 14,065
Nanuet UFD 2,300/K-12
101 Church St 10954 845-627-9888
Dr. Mark McNeill, supt. Fax 624-5338
nanunet.lhric.org/
Barr MS 700/5-8
143 Church St 10954 845-627-4040
Roger Guccione, prin. Fax 624-3138
Highview ES 300/3-4
24 Highview Ave 10954 845-627-3460
Barbara Auriemma, prin. Fax 627-0340
Miller ES 500/K-2
50 Blauvelt Rd Ste 1 10954 845-627-4860
Elizabeth Smith, prin. Fax 624-1534

St. Anthony S 200/PK-8
34 W Nyack Rd 10954 845-623-2311
Joanne Fratello, prin. Fax 623-0055

Naples, Ontario, Pop. 1,050
Naples Central SD 900/K-12
136 N Main St 14512 585-374-7900
Kimberle Ward, supt. Fax 374-5859
www.naples.k12.ny.us
Naples ES 400/K-6
2 Academy St 14512 585-374-7952
Alan Moore, prin. Fax 374-7955

Nassau, Rensselaer, Pop. 1,132
East Greenbush Central SD
Supt. — See East Greenbush
Sutherland ES 300/K-5
PO Box 429 12123 518-766-3888
John Alvey, prin. Fax 766-9548

Nedrow, Onondaga, Pop. 2,700
La Fayette Central SD
Supt. — See La Fayette
Onondaga Nation S 100/K-8
RR 1 Box 270 13120 315-469-6991
Diane Ellsworth, prin. Fax 469-0994

Onondaga Central SD 1,000/PK-12
4466 S Onondaga Rd 13120 315-492-1701
Joseph Rotella, supt. Fax 492-4650
www.ocs.cnyric.org
Rockwell ES 200/PK-2
208 Rockwell Rd 13120 315-469-6926
Margaret Hart, prin. Fax 469-7732
Wheeler IS 300/3-6
4543 S Onondaga Rd 13120 315-492-1746
Steve Winschel, prin. Fax 492-4433

Nesconset, Suffolk, Pop. 10,712
Smithtown Central SD
Supt. — See Smithtown
Great Hollow MS 1,000/6-8
150 Southern Blvd 11767 631-382-2800
Daniel Goitia, prin. Fax 382-2807
Nesconset ES 300/K-5
29 Gibbs Pond Rd 11767 631-382-4400
Janine Lavery, prin. Fax 382-4406
Tackan ES 600/K-5
99 Midwood Ave 11767 631-382-2670
Allyn Leeds, prin. Fax 382-2676

Newark, Wayne, Pop. 9,411
Newark Central SD 2,400/PK-12
100 E Miller St Ste 5 14513 315-332-3217
Henry Hann, supt. Fax 332-3523
newarkcsd.schoolwires.com
Kelley ES 500/3-5
316 W Miller St 14513 315-332-3326
M. Chris Mizro, prin. Fax 332-3624
Lincoln ES 200/PK-2
1014 N Main St 14513 315-332-3342
Donna Buck, prin. Fax 332-3604
Newark MS 600/6-8
701 Peirson Ave 14513 315-332-3295
Mark Miller, prin. Fax 332-3584
Perkins ES 300/PK-2
439 W Maple Ave 14513 315-332-3315
Susan Achille, prin. Fax 332-3614

St. Michael S 100/PK-8
320 S Main St 14513 315-331-2297
Pauline DeCann, prin. Fax 331-2299

Newark Valley, Tioga, Pop. 1,038
Newark Valley Central SD 1,300/K-12
PO Box 547 13811 607-642-3221
Mary Ellen Grant, supt. Fax 642-8821
www.nvcs.stier.org/
Hall PS 400/K-3
86 Whig St 13811 607-642-3340
Robert Rodgers, prin. Fax 642-5004
Newark Valley MS 400/4-7
88 Whig St 13811 607-642-5524
Sheila Bertoni, prin. Fax 642-8175

New Berlin, Chenango, Pop. 1,123
Unadilla Valley Central SD 1,000/PK-12
PO Box F 13411 607-847-7500
Robert Mackey, supt. Fax 847-6924
www.uvstorm.org
Unadilla Valley ES 400/PK-5
PO Box F 13411 607-847-7500
Stephen Bradley, admin. Fax 847-9988
Unadilla Valley MS 200/6-8
PO Box F 13411 607-847-7500
Lee Supensky, prin. Fax 847-8045

Newburgh, Orange, Pop. 28,548
Marlboro Central SD
Supt. — See Marlboro
Middle Hope ES 100/K-2
13 Overlook Dr 12550 845-565-9620
Stephen Walker, prin. Fax 565-1320

Newburgh Enlarged CSD 11,600/PK-12
124 Grand St 12550 845-563-3500
Dr. Annette Saturnelli, supt. Fax 563-3501
www.newburghschools.org/newburgh/newburgh.cfm
Balmville ES 300/K-6
5144 Route 9W 12550 845-563-8550
Carla Sigelbaum, prin. Fax 563-8554
Fostertown E.T.C. Magnet ES 600/K-6
364 Fostertown Rd 12550 845-568-6425
Maritza Ramos, prin. Fax 568-6430
GAMS Tech Magnet ES 1,000/K-6
300 Gidney Ave 12550 845-563-8450
Elsa Kortright-Torres, prin. Fax 563-8459
Gardnertown Fundamental Magnet ES 700/K-6
6 Plattekill Tpke 12550 845-568-6400
Gail Thomas-Wilson, prin. Fax 568-6408
Horizons-on-the-Hudson Magnet ES 500/K-6
137 Montgomery St 12550 845-563-3725
Lisa Buon, prin. Fax 563-3730
Meadow Hill Global Explortns Magnet ES 1,000/K-8
124 Meadow Hill Rd 12550 845-568-6600
Barbara Weiss, prin. Fax 568-6609
Pre-Kindergarten Center at Renwick St PK-PK
245 Renwick St 12550 845-568-6650
Arthur Mamazza, admin. Fax 568-6653
Pre-Kindergarten Center at Washington St 300/PK-PK
191 Washington St 12550 845-563-8575
Joan Goudy-Crosson, prin. Fax 563-8585
West Street ES 100/K-3
39 West St 12550 845-563-8500
Lillian Torres, prin. Fax 563-8509
Other Schools – See New Windsor

Valley Central SD
Supt. — See Montgomery
East Coldenham ES 300/K-5
286 Route 17K 12550 845-457-2400
Mark Ray, prin. Fax 564-1554

Bishop Dunn Memorial S 300/PK-8
50 Gidney Ave 12550 845-569-3494
James DelViscio, prin. Fax 569-3303
Cronin Presentation Academy 50/5-6
120 South St 12550 845-567-0708
Sr. Ylianna Hernandez, prin. Fax 567-0709
Leptondale Christian Academy 200/PK-8
1771 Route 300 12550 845-564-2860
Gary Heotzler, prin. Fax 566-9185
Sacred Heart/St. Francis S 200/K-8
24 S Robinson Ave 12550 845-561-1433
Marylyn White, prin. Fax 561-4383
San Miguel Academy 50/5-5
241 Liberty St 12550 845-561-2822
Sr. Lois Dee, prin. Fax 561-0312

New City, Rockland, Pop. 34,100
Clarkstown Central SD 9,400/K-12
62 Old Middletown Rd 10956 845-639-6419
Dr. Margaret Keller-Cogan, supt. Fax 639-6488
www.ccsd.edu
Laurel Plains ES 400/K-5
14 Teakwood Dr 10956 845-639-6350
Carol Pilla, prin. Fax 639-4206
Link ES 500/K-5
55 Red Hill Rd 10956 845-639-6370
Francine Cuccia, prin. Fax 638-1615
Little Tor ES 300/K-5
56 Gregory St 10956 845-639-6365
Mi Jung An, prin. Fax 638-0807
New City ES 400/K-5
60 Crestwood Dr 10956 845-639-6360
Debra Forman, prin. Fax 638-0504
Woodglen ES 500/K-5
121 Phillips Hill Rd 10956 845-639-6355
Lisa Maher, prin. Fax 639-6017
Other Schools – See Bardonia, Congers, West Nyack

East Ramapo Central SD
Supt. — See Spring Valley
Hillcrest IS 400/4-6
32 Addison Boyce Dr 10956 845-577-6180
Jennifer Wilmoth, prin. Fax 426-0946
Summit Park ES 500/K-3
925 Route 45 10956 845-577-6290
Kim Hewlett, prin. Fax 362-0920

Cornerstone Christian S 100/K-6
384 New Hempstead Rd 10956 845-634-7977
Linda D'Amato, admin. Fax 634-1885
Gittelman Hebrew Day S 300/PK-8
360 New Hempstead Rd 10956 845-634-5200
Nadine Alperin, prin. Fax 634-5392
Hebrew Academy 100/PK-8
315 N Main St 10956 845-634-0951
St. Augustine S 200/K-8
114 S Main St 10956 845-634-7060
Katharine Murphy, prin. Fax 634-8725

Newcomb, Essex
Newcomb Central SD 100/PK-12
PO Box 418 12852 518-582-3341
Clark Hults, supt. Fax 582-2163
www.newcombcsd.org
Newcomb Central S 100/PK-12
PO Box 418 12852 518-582-3341
Clark Hults, prin. Fax 582-2163

Newfane, Niagara, Pop. 3,001
Newfane Central SD 2,000/PK-12
6273 Charlotteville Rd 14108 716-778-6850
Gary Pogorzelski, supt. Fax 778-6852
www.newfane.wnyric.org
Newfane ES 400/1-3
2909 Transit Rd 14108 716-778-6376
Kathleen Nagle, prin. Fax 778-6377
Newfane IS 300/4-5
6175 East Ave 14108 716-778-6469
Thomas Adams, prin. Fax 778-6454
Newfane MS 500/6-8
2700 Transit Rd 14108 716-778-6452
Thomas Adams, prin. Fax 778-6460
Other Schools – See Burt

Newfield, Tompkins
Newfield Central SD 1,000/PK-12
247 Main St 14867 607-564-9955
William Hurley, supt. Fax 564-0055
www.newfieldschools.org
Newfield ES 400/PK-5
247 Main St 14867 607-564-9955
Vicky Volpicelli, prin. Fax 564-0055
Newfield MS 200/6-8
247 Main St 14867 607-564-9955
Catherine Griggs, prin. Fax 564-3403

New Hartford, Oneida, Pop. 1,843
New Hartford Central SD 2,700/K-12
33 Oxford Rd 13413 315-624-1218
Daniel Gilligan, supt. Fax 724-8940
www.newhartfordschools.org
Hughes ES 500/K-6
340 Higby Rd 13413 315-738-9350
Mark Dunn, prin. Fax 724-1899
Myles ES 400/K-6
100 Clinton Rd 13413 315-738-9600
Cindy Langone, prin. Fax 724-2653
Oxford Road ES 500/K-6
33 Oxford Rd 13413 315-738-9220
Maureen Futscher, prin. Fax 735-1873

New Haven, Oswego, Pop. 2,778
Mexico Central SD
Supt. — See Mexico
New Haven ES 200/K-4
4320 State Route 104 13121 315-963-8400
Catherine Carros, prin. Fax 963-8813

New Hyde Park, Nassau, Pop. 9,472
Great Neck UFD
Supt. — See Great Neck
Parkville S 100/PK-K
10 Campbell St 11040 516-441-4350
Debra Shalom, prin. Fax 441-4367

Herricks UFD 4,100/K-12
999 Herricks Rd 11040 516-305-8901
Dr. John Bierwirth, supt. Fax 248-3108
www.herricks.org/
Denton Avenue ES 500/K-5
1050 Denton Ave 11040 516-305-8400
Mary Haley, prin. Fax 248-3281
Other Schools – See Albertson, Williston Park

New Hyde Park-Garden City Park UFD 1,600/K-6
1950 Hillside Ave 11040 516-352-6257
Robert Katulak, supt. Fax 352-6282
nhp-gcp.org
Garden City Park ES 300/K-6
51 Central Ave 11040 516-746-3025
James Svendsen, prin. Fax 873-6368
Hillside ES 500/K-6
150 Maple Dr W 11040 516-354-3666
Karen Olynk, prin. Fax 352-6081
Manor Oaks/Bowie ES 400/K-6
1950 Hillside Ave 11040 516-352-2227
Diane Weiss, prin. Fax 616-1959
New Hyde Park Road ES 500/K-6
300 New Hyde Park Rd 11040 516-354-1205
Margaret Marenghi, prin. Fax 352-6059

Notre Dame S 400/PK-8
25 Mayfair Rd 11040 516-354-5618
Margaret Moss, prin. Fax 354-5373

New Lebanon, Columbia
New Lebanon Central SD 600/K-12
14665 State Route 22 12125 518-794-9016
Karen McGraw, supt. Fax 766-5574
www.newlebanoncsd.org
Howard ES 300/K-6
1478 State Route 20 12125 518-794-8554
Daniel Packard, prin. Fax 766-2220

New Paltz, Ulster, Pop. 6,765
New Paltz Central SD 2,300/K-12
196 Main St 12561 845-256-4020
Maria Rice, supt. Fax 256-4025
www.newpaltz.k12.ny.us
Duzine ES 500/K-2
196 Main St 12561 845-256-4350
Debra Hogencamp, prin. Fax 256-4359
Lenape ES 500/3-5
196 Main St 12561 845-256-4300
Stephanie Giammatteo, prin. Fax 256-4309
New Paltz MS 500/6-8
196 Main St 12561 845-256-4200
Richard Wiesenthal, prin. Fax 256-4209

Mountain Laurel Waldorf S 100/PK-8
PO Box 939 12561 845-255-0033
Judy Jaeckel, admin. Fax 255-0597

Newport, Herkimer, Pop. 619
West Canada Valley Central SD 900/K-12
PO Box 360 13416 315-845-6800
Kenneth Slentz, supt. Fax 845-8652
www.westcanada.org/
West Canada Valley ES 400/K-6
PO Box 360 13416 315-845-6801
Ann Maher, prin. Fax 845-8652

New Rochelle, Westchester, Pop. 72,967
New Rochelle CSD 10,400/PK-12
515 North Ave 10801 914-576-4300
Richard Organisciak, supt. Fax 632-4144
www.nred.org
Barnard ECC 600/PK-2
129 Barnard Rd 10801 914-576-4386
Patricia Lambert, prin. Fax 576-4625
Columbus ES 800/K-5
275 Washington Ave 10801 914-576-4401
Dr. Yigal Joseph, prin. Fax 576-4628
Davis ES 600/K-5
80 Iselin Dr 10804 914-576-4420
William Harrell, prin. Fax 576-4225
Jefferson ES 500/K-5
131 Weyman Ave 10805 914-576-4430
Cynthia Slotkin, prin. Fax 576-4631
Leonard MS 1,200/6-8
25 Gerada Ln 10804 914-576-4339
William Evans, prin. Fax 576-4784
Trinity ES 800/K-5
180 Pelham Rd 10805 914-576-4440
Richard McMahon, prin. Fax 576-4266
Ward ES 1,100/K-5
311 Broadfield Rd 10804 914-576-4450
Kenneth Regan, prin. Fax 576-4263
Webster ES 500/K-5
95 Glenmore Dr 10801 914-576-4460
Joseph Williams, prin. Fax 576-4479
Young MS 1,100/6-8
270 Centre Ave 10805 914-576-4360
Anthony Bongo, prin. Fax 632-2738

Holy Name of Jesus S 200/PK-8
70 Petersville Rd 10801 914-576-6672
Albert D'Angelo, prin. Fax 576-6676
Hudson Country Montessori S 200/PK-6
340 Quaker Ridge Rd 10804 914-636-6202
Mark Meyer, dir. Fax 636-5139
Iona Grammar S 200/PK-8
173 Stratton Rd 10804 914-633-7744
Peter Borchetta, prin. Fax 235-6338
New Testament Church S 50/K-12
138 Mayflower Ave 10801 914-766-1766
Mary Zachariah, admin. Fax 932-2572
Thornton-Donovan S 200/K-12
100 Overlook Cir 10804 914-632-8836
Douglas Fleming, hdmstr. Fax 576-7936
Westchester Area S 100/PK-8
456 Webster Ave 10801 914-235-5799

New Square, Rockland, Pop. 6,332

Avir Yaakov Girl's S 1,200/K-12
15 N Roosevelt Ave 10977 845-354-0874

New Suffolk, Suffolk
New Suffolk Common SD 50/PK-6
PO Box 111 11956 631-734-6940
Robert Feger, supt. Fax 734-6940
New Suffolk ES 50/PK-6
PO Box 111 11956 631-734-6940
Nicole Valentine-Knoll, lead tchr. Fax 734-6940

New Windsor, Orange, Pop. 8,898
Newburgh Enlarged CSD
Supt. — See Newburgh
Heritage JHS Stewart Campus 7-7
1001 1st St 12553 845-568-6550
Gail Tummarello, prin. Fax 568-6556
New Windsor ES 500/K-6
175 Quassaick Ave 12553 845-563-3700
Dr. Roberto Calderin, prin. Fax 563-3709
Temple Hill Academy 1,100/K-8
525 Union Ave 12553 845-568-6450
Joyce Mucci, prin. Fax 568-6470
Vails Gate High Tech Magnet ES 600/K-6
400 Old Forge Hill Rd 12553 845-563-7900
Melinda Lamarche, prin. Fax 563-7909

Washingtonville Central SD
Supt. — See Washingtonville
Little Britain ES 600/K-5
1160 Little Britain Rd 12553 845-497-4000
Barbara Quinn, prin. Fax 496-2303

St. Joseph S 200/K-8
148 Windsor Hwy 12553 845-565-5110
Sr. Lucy Povilonis, prin. Fax 565-6321

New York, New York, Pop. 8,143,197
NYC Department of Education 917,100/PK-12
52 Chambers St 10007 718-935-2000
Joel Klein, chnclr.
www.nycenet.edu
Academy of Collaborative Education 200/6-8
222 W 134th St 10030 212-694-8750
Rashaunda Shaw, prin.
American Sign Language S 200/PK-6
225 E 23rd St 10010 917-326-6609
Rebecca Marshall, prin.
Baker S 300/PK-8
317 E 67th St, 212-717-8809
Laura Garcia, prin. Fax 717-8807
Bilingual Bicultural ES 400/K-5
219 E 109th St 10029 212-860-6031
Andrea Hernandez, prin. Fax 860-4536
Central Park East S I 200/PK-5
1573 Madison Ave 10029 212-860-5821
Julie Zuckerman, prin. Fax 860-6017
Central Park East S II 200/PK-5
19 E 103rd St 10029 212-860-5992
Naomi Smith, prin. Fax 410-6041
Earth S 300/PK-5
600 E 6th St 10009 212-477-1735
Alison Hazut, prin. Fax 477-2396

Esperanza Preparatory Academy 100/6-8
240 E 109th St 10029 212-722-6507
Alex Estrella, prin. Fax 722-6717
Greenwich Village MS 200/6-8
490 Hudson St 10014 212-691-7384
Kelly McGuire, prin. Fax 691-9489
Hamilton Heights ES 200/K-5
508 W 153rd St 10031 212-281-1947
Alva Buxenbaum, prin. Fax 281-7168
Harbor Heights MS 200/6-8
549 Audubon Ave 10040 212-927-1841
Monica Klehr, prin.
KAPPA II S 200/6-8
144 E 128th St 10035 212-828-6892
Sean Dunning, prin. Fax 828-6896
KAPPA IV S 300/6-8
6 Edgecombe Ave 10030 212-690-4963
Briony Carr, prin. Fax 690-5047
Marshall Academy Lower S 100/K-6
276 W 151st St 10039 212-368-8731
Sean Davenport, prin. Fax 368-8641
Mosaic Preparatory Academy 300/PK-6
141 E 111th St 10029 212-722-3109
Lisette Caesar, prin. Fax 722-3167
Mott Hall II 300/6-8
234 W 109th St 10025 212-678-2960
Ana De Los Santos, prin. Fax 222-0560
New Explorations Sci Tech/Math S 900/K-12
111 Columbia St 10002 212-677-5190
Olga Livanis, prin. Fax 260-8124
Newton JHS for Science Math Tech 400/6-8
280 Pleasant Ave 10029 212-860-6006
Lisa Nelson, prin. Fax 987-4197
IS 195 800/6-8
625 W 133rd St 10027 212-690-5848
Rosarie Jean, prin. Fax 690-5999
IS 223 400/4-8
71111 Convent Ave 10027 212-281-5028
Cynthia Arndt, prin. Fax 491-3451
IS 286 200/6-8
509 W 129th St 10027 212-690-5972
Qadir Dixon, prin. Fax 694-4124
IS 289 300/6-8
201 Warren St 10282 212-571-9268
Ellen Foote, prin. Fax 587-6610
IS 528 300/6-8
180 Wadsworth Ave 10033 212-740-4900
Norma Perez, prin. Fax 781-7302
JHS 13 400/6-8
1573 Madison Ave 10029 212-860-8935
Jacob Michelman, prin. Fax 860-5933
JHS 44 500/6-8
100 W 77th St 10024 212-441-1163
Liza Ortiz, prin. Fax 501-0912
JHS 45 600/6-8
2351 1st Ave 10035 212-860-5838
Maria Aviles, prin. Fax 860-5837
JHS 52 1,000/5-8
650 Academy St 10034 212-567-9162
Aileen Feliberty, prin. Fax 942-4952
JHS 54 900/6-8
103 W 107th St 10025 212-678-2861
Dr. Elana Elster, prin. Fax 316-0883
JHS 104 1,000/6-8
330 E 21st St 10010 212-674-4545
Rosemarie Gaetani, prin. Fax 477-2205
JHS 117 500/6-8
240 E 109th St 10029 212-860-5872
Ralph Martinez, prin. Fax 876-3782
JHS 143 1,100/6-8
511 W 182nd St 10033 212-927-7739
Ourania Pappas, prin. Fax 781-5539
JHS 167 1,200/6-8
220 E 76th St 10021 212-535-8610
Jennifer Rehn, prin. Fax 472-9385
MS 114 300/6-8
1458 York Ave, 212-439-6278
David Getz, prin. Fax 717-5606
MS 131 800/6-8
100 Hester St 10002 212-219-1204
Phyllis Tam, prin. Fax 925-6386
MS 224 200/6-8
410 E 100th St 10029 212-860-6047
Lillian Sarro, prin. Fax 410-0678
MS 243 200/5-8
270 W 70th St 10023 212-799-1477
Elaine Schwartz, prin. Fax 579-9728
MS 245 200/6-8
100 W 77th St 10024 212-441-0873
Henry Zymeck, prin. Fax 678-5908
MS 246 200/6-8
234 W 109th St 10025 212-678-5850
Gary Isinger, prin. Fax 678-4275
MS 247 200/6-8
32 W 92nd St 10025 212-799-2653
Claudia Aguirre, prin. Fax 579-2407
MS 250 200/6-8
735 W End Ave 10025 212-866-6313
Jeanne Rotunda, dir. Fax 678-5295
MS 255 400/6-8
320 E 20th St 10003 212-614-8785
Rhonda Perry, prin. Fax 614-0095
MS 256 100/6-8
154 W 93rd St 10025 212-222-2857
Kenneth Peterson, prin. Fax 531-0586
MS 258 200/6-8
154 W 93rd St 10025 212-678-5888
John Curry, prin. Fax 961-1613
MS 260 200/6-8
320 W 21st St 10011 212-255-8860
Jeanne Fraino, prin. Fax 807-0421
MS 319 400/6-8
21 Jumel Pl 10032 212-923-3827
Ysidro Abreu, prin. Fax 923-3676
MS 321 300/6-8
21 Jumel Pl 10032 212-923-5129
Pamela Glover, prin. Fax 923-5180

MS 322 500/6-8
4600 Broadway 10040 212-304-0853
Erica Zigelman, prin. Fax 567-3016
MS 324 400/6-8
21 Jumel Pl 10032 212-923-4057
Janet Heller, prin. Fax 923-4626
MS 326 500/6-8
401 W 164th St 10032 917-521-1875
Sharon Weissbrot, prin. Fax 521-1750
MS 328 600/6-8
401 W 164th St 10032 917-521-2508
Jorge Estrella, prin. Fax 521-7797
MS 332 200/6-8
220 Henry St 10002 212-267-5701
Laura Peynado, prin. Fax 267-5703
MS 345 - CASTLE 300/6-8
220 Henry St 10002 212-227-0762
Mauriciere Degovia, prin. Fax 577-9785
Powell MS for Law & Social Justice 400/7-8
509 W 129th St 10027 212-690-5977
Winston Riley, prin. Fax 690-5980
Public S 1 600/PK-5
8 Henry St 10038 212-267-4133
Amy Hom, prin. Fax 267-4469
Public S 2 700/PK-5
122 Henry St 10002 212-964-0350
Brett Gustafson, prin. Fax 608-4080
Public S 3 500/PK-5
490 Hudson St 10014 212-691-1183
Lisa Siegman, prin. Fax 675-5306
Public S 4 700/PK-5
500 W 160th St 10032 212-928-0739
Delois White, prin. Fax 928-2532
Public S 5 900/K-5
3703 10th Ave 10034 212-567-8109
Wanda Soto, prin. Fax 567-6526
Public S 6 700/K-5
45 E 81st St 10028 212-737-9774
Lauren Fontana, prin. Fax 772-8669
Public S 7 400/PK-8
160 E 120th St 10035 212-860-5827
Racquel Jones, prin. Fax 860-6070
Public S 8 600/K-5
465 W 167th St 10032 212-928-4364
Rafaela Landin, prin. Fax 928-4072
Public S 9 500/PK-5
100 W 84th St 10024 212-678-2812
Diane Brady, prin. Fax 280-6223
Public S 11 400/PK-5
320 W 21st St 10011 212-929-1743
Robert Bender, prin. Fax 989-7816
Public S 15 200/PK-5
333 E 4th St 10009 212-228-8730
Thomas Staebell, prin. Fax 477-0931
Public S 18 400/K-8
4124 9th Ave 10034 212-567-4353
Aurea Porrata-Doria, prin. Fax 304-1423
Public S 19 300/PK-5
185 1st Ave 10003 212-533-5340
Ivan Kushner, prin. Fax 673-1477
Public S 20 600/PK-5
166 Essex St 10002 212-254-9577
James Lee, prin. Fax 254-3526
Public S 28 1,200/PK-5
475 W 155th St 10032 212-690-3014
Elsa Nunez, prin. Fax 368-5978
Public S 30 300/PK-6
144 E 128th St 10035 212-876-1825
Karen Melendez-Hutt, prin. Fax 876-4034
Public S 33 300/PK-5
281 9th Ave 10001 212-244-6426
Linore Lindy, prin. Fax 629-6893
Public S 34 400/PK-8
730 E 12th St 10009 212-228-4433
Joyce Stallings-Harte, prin. Fax 353-1973
Public S 36 500/PK-2
123 Morningside Dr 10027 212-690-5807
Cynthia Mullins-Simmons, prin. Fax 690-5811
Public S 38 300/PK-5
232 E 103rd St 10029 212-860-5882
Norma Caraballo, prin. Fax 860-6093
Public S 40 500/PK-5
320 E 20th St 10003 212-475-5500
Susan Felder, prin. Fax 533-5388
Public S 41 700/PK-5
116 W 11th St 10011 212-675-2756
Kelly Shannon, prin. Fax 924-0910
Public S 42 700/PK-5
71 Hester St 10002 212-226-8410
Rosa O'Day, prin. Fax 431-7384
Public S 46 800/PK-6
2987 8th Ave 10039 212-690-5911
George Young, prin. Fax 690-5913
Public S 48 600/PK-5
4360 Broadway 10033 917-521-3800
Tracy Walsh, prin. Fax 521-3805
Public S 50 500/K-8
433 E 100th St 10029 212-860-5976
Rebekah Mitchell, prin. Fax 860-6071
Public S 51 300/PK-5
520 W 45th St 10036 212-757-3067
Nancy Sing-Bock, prin. Fax 582-8661
Public S 57 600/PK-8
176 E 115th St 10029 212-860-5812
Israel Soto, prin. Fax 860-6072
Public S 59 400/PK-5
213 E 63rd St, 212-888-7870
Adele Schroeter, prin. Fax 888-7872
Public S 63 200/PK-5
121 E 3rd St 10009 212-674-3180
Darlene Despeignes, prin. Fax 420-9018
Public S 64 300/PK-5
600 E 6th St 10009 212-673-6510
Marlon Hosang, prin. Fax 477-2369
Public S 72 500/PK-5
131 E 104th St 10029 212-860-5831
Loren Bohlen, prin. Fax 860-6094

Public S 75 800/K-5
735 W End Ave 10025 212-866-5400
Robert O'Brien, prin. Fax 678-2878
Public S 76 400/PK-5
220 W 121st St 10027 212-678-2865
Charles DeBerry, prin. Fax 678-2867
Public S 77 300/K-5
1700 3rd Ave 10128 212-427-2798
Renay Sadis, prin. Fax 423-0634
Public S 83 400/PK-5
219 E 109th St 10029 212-860-5847
Frances Castillo, prin. Fax 860-6073
Public S 84 400/PK-5
32 W 92nd St 10025 212-799-2534
Robin Sundick, prin. Fax 501-9071
Public S 87 900/PK-6
160 W 78th St 10024 212-678-2826
Jacqui Getz, prin. Fax 678-5886
Public S 89 500/PK-5
201 Warren St 10282 212-571-5659
Veronica Najjar, prin. Fax 571-0739
Public S 92 300/PK-5
222 W 134th St 10030 212-690-5915
Rosa Davila, prin. Fax 690-5920
Public S 96 600/PK-8
216 E 120th St 10035 212-860-5851
Claudia Hamilton, prin. Fax 860-6074
Public S 98 600/PK-4
512 W 212th St 10034 212-927-7870
Maritza Rodriguez, prin. Fax 569-1827
Public S 102 300/PK-5
315 E 113th St 10029 212-860-5834
Sandra Gittens, prin. Fax 860-6076
Public S 108 600/PK-8
1615 Madison Ave 10029 212-860-5803
Lourdes Arroyo, prin. Fax 860-6095
Public S 110 400/PK-5
285 Delancey St 10002 212-674-2690
Karen Feuer, prin. Fax 475-5835
Public S 111 500/PK-8
440 W 53rd St 10019 212-582-7420
Irma Medina, prin. Fax 245-7236
Public S 112 300/PK-2
535 E 119th St 10035 212-860-5868
Eileen Reiter, prin. Fax 860-6077
Public S 115 900/K-6
586 W 177th St 10033 212-927-9233
Sara Carvajal, prin. Fax 795-4051
Public S 116 700/PK-5
210 E 33rd St 10016 212-685-4366
Jane Hsu, prin. Fax 696-1009
Public S 123 600/PK-6
301 W 140th St 10030 212-690-5925
Dr. Beverly Lewis, prin. Fax 690-5930
Public S 124 1,000/PK-5
40 Division St 10002 212-966-7237
Alice Hom, prin. Fax 219-3069
Public S 125 400/K-6
425 W 123rd St 10027 212-666-6400
Claudette Lustin, prin. Fax 749-1291
Public S 126 600/PK-8
80 Catherine St 10038 212-962-2188
Kerry Decker, prin. Fax 349-7342
Public S 128 800/PK-5
560 W 169th St 10032 212-927-0607
Rosa Arredondo, prin. Fax 781-8002
Public S 129 500/PK-6
425 W 130th St 10027 212-690-5932
Odelphia Pierre, prin. Fax 690-5934
Public S 130 1,100/PK-5
143 Baxter St 10013 212-226-8072
Lily Woo, prin. Fax 431-5524
Public S 132 900/K-5
185 Wadsworth Ave 10033 212-927-7857
Xiomara Nova, prin. Fax 568-8163
Public S 133 300/PK-6
2121 5th Ave 10037 212-690-5936
Pamela Craig, prin. Fax 690-5939
Public S 134 300/PK-5
293 E Broadway 10002 212-673-4470
Loretta Caputo, prin. Fax 475-6142
Public S 137 200/PK-5
293 E Broadway 10002 212-602-2143
Melissa Rodriguez, prin. Fax 602-2146
Public S 140 400/PK-8
123 Ridge St 10002 212-677-4680
Esteban Barrientos, prin. Fax 677-3907
Public S 142 400/PK-5
100 Attorney St 10002 212-598-3800
Rhonda Levy, prin. Fax 598-3810
Public S 145 500/PK-5
150 W 105th St 10025 212-678-2857
Ivelisse Alvarez, prin. Fax 222-4610
Public S 146 400/PK-5
421 E 106th St 10029 212-860-5877
Mona Silfen, prin. Fax 860-6078
Public S 149 400/K-8
41 W 117th St 10026 646-672-9020
Shaniquia Dixon, prin. Fax 672-9302
Public S 150 200/PK-5
334 Greenwich St 10013 212-732-4392
Maggie Siena, prin. Fax 766-5895
Public S 152 1,100/PK-5
93 Nagle Ave 10040 212-567-5456
Julie Pietri, prin. Fax 942-6319
Public S 153 1,000/PK-5
1750 Amsterdam Ave 10031 212-927-8611
Karen Bailey, prin. Fax 234-4616
Public S 154 400/PK-5
250 W 127th St 10027 212-864-2400
Elizabeth Jarrett, prin. Fax 864-3933
Public S 155 400/PK-5
319 E 117th St 10035 212-860-5885
Lillian Ortiz, prin. Fax 828-3587
Public S 158 700/PK-5
1458 York Ave, 212-744-6562
Darryl Alhadeff, prin. Fax 772-8424

Public S 161 800/PK-6
499 W 133rd St 10027 212-690-5945
Barbara Freeman, prin. Fax 507-0524
Public S 163 600/PK-5
163 W 97th St 10025 212-678-2854
Dr. Virginia Pepe, prin. Fax 678-2856
Public S 165 600/PK-5
234 W 109th St 10025 212-678-2873
Pedro De La Cruz, prin. Fax 222-6700
Public S 166 600/PK-5
132 W 89th St 10024 212-678-2829
Debbie Hand, prin. Fax 579-4542
Public S 171 600/PK-8
19 E 103rd St 10029 212-860-5801
Dimitres Pantelides, prin. Fax 860-6079
Public S 173 800/PK-5
306 Fort Washington Ave 10033 212-927-7850
Dawn Boursiquot, prin. Fax 740-0905
Public S 175 400/PK-5
175 W 134th St 10030 212-283-0426
Cheryl McClendon, prin. Fax 286-6319
Public S 178 300/PK-2
12 Ellwood St 10040 212-569-0327
Dierdre Budd, prin. Fax 569-0389
Public S 180 500/PK-8
370 W 120th St 10027 212-678-2849
Dr. Peter McFarlane, prin. Fax 665-1572
Public S 183 500/K-5
419 E 66th St, 212-734-7719
Mary Sacco, prin. Fax 861-8314
Public S 184 600/PK-8
327 Cherry St 10002 212-602-9700
Ling Ling Chou, prin. Fax 602-9710
Public S 185 300/PK-2
20 W 112th St 10026 212-534-7490
Norma Genao, prin. Fax 831-8613
Public S 187 400/PK-4
349 Cabrini Blvd 10040 212-927-8218
Cynthia Chory, prin. Fax 795-9119
Public S 188 400/PK-8
442 E Houston St 10002 212-677-5710
Dr. Barbara Slatin, prin. Fax 228-3007
Public S 189 1,100/PK-5
2580 Amsterdam Ave 10040 212-927-8303
Theresa Luger, prin. Fax 928-7733
Public S 191 300/PK-5
210 W 61st St 10023 212-757-4343
Sandra Perez, prin. Fax 757-1022
Public S 192 500/PK-6
500 W 138th St 10031 212-281-8395
Elizabeth Pacheco, prin. Fax 862-7129
Public S 194 300/K-5
244 W 144th St 10030 212-690-5954
Charyn Cleary, prin. Fax 862-5743
Public S 197 500/PK-6
2230 5th Ave 10037 212-690-5960
Renardo Wright, prin. Fax 690-5959
Public S 198 500/PK-5
1700 3rd Ave 10128 212-289-3702
Sharon Jeffrey-Roebuck, prin. Fax 410-1731
Public S 199 600/K-5
270 W 70th St 10023 212-799-1033
Katy Rosen, prin. Fax 799-1179
Public S 200 800/PK-6
2589 7th Ave 10039 212-491-6636
Renee Belton, prin. Fax 491-6925
Public S 206 200/3-5
508 E 120th St 10035 212-860-5809
Myrna Rodriguez, prin. Fax 860-6080
Public S 208 200/3-5
21 W 111th St 10026 212-534-9580
Susan Green, prin. Fax 534-8227
Public S 210 300/PK-8
501 W 152nd St 10031 212-283-0012
Evelyn Linares, prin. Fax 283-0017
Public S 212 300/K-5
328 W 48th St 10036 212-247-0208
Dean Ketchum, prin. Fax 757-4933
Public S 217 400/PK-8
645 Main St 10044 212-980-0294
Mandana Beckman, prin. Fax 980-1192
Public S 234 700/K-5
292 Greenwich St 10007 212-233-6034
Lisa Ripperger, prin. Fax 374-1719
Public S 241 400/PK-8
240 W 113th St 10026 212-678-2898
Diana Diaz, prin. Fax 678-2975
Public S 242 300/K-5
134 W 122nd St 10027 212-678-2908
Denise Gomez, prin. Fax 678-2927
Public S 278 400/K-8
421 W 219th St 10034 212-942-3440
Maureen Guido, prin. Fax 942-8177
Public S 290 600/K-5
311 E 82nd St 10028 212-734-7127
Sharon Hill, prin. Fax 772-8879
Public S 311 400/K-8
4862 Broadway 10034 212-544-8021
Miriam Pedraja, prin. Fax 569-7765
Public S 314 1,500/K-5
4862 Broadway 10034 212-544-0614
Tomasz Grabski, prin. Fax 544-2678
Public S 315 200/PK-5
610 E 12th St 10009 212-982-0682
Robin Williams, prin. Fax 260-4012
Public S 325 400/K-6
500 W 138th St 10031 212-234-1335
Gary Cruz, prin. Fax 234-2022
Public S 333 600/K-8
154 W 93rd St 10025 212-222-1450
Susan Rappaport, prin. Fax 222-1828
Public S 334 500/K-8
100 W 84th St 10024 212-595-7193
Brian Coulet, prin. Fax 496-2854
Public S 361 300/PK-5
610 E 12th St 10009 212-614-9531
Maria Velez-Clarke, prin. Fax 614-9462
Public S 363 Neighborhood S 300/PK-5
121 E 3rd St 10009 212-387-0195
Milo Novello, prin. Fax 387-0198
Public S 366 100/K-5
93 Nagle Ave 10040 212-942-1450
Crystal Felix, prin. Fax 942-2740
Renaissance School of the Arts 100/6-8
410 E 100th St 10029 212-369-1564
Tammy Pate-Spears, prin. Fax 369-1693
School for Global Leaders 100/6-8
145 Stanton St 10002 212-260-5375
Carry Chan, prin. Fax 260-7386
TAG Young Scholars 500/K-8
240 E 109th St 10029 212-860-6003
Janette Cesar, prin. Fax 831-1842
Technology Arts & Sciences Studio 200/6-8
185 1st Ave 10003 212-982-1836
George Morgan, prin. Fax 982-0528
Tompkins Square MS 300/6-8
600 E 6th St 10009 212-995-1430
Sonhando Estwick, prin. Fax 979-1341
Washington Hts. Expeditionary Learning S 200/6-8
511 W 182nd St 10033 212-781-0524
Brett Kimmel, prin. Fax 781-0742
Other Schools – See Arverne, Astoria, Bayside, Bellerose, Broad Channel, Bronx, Brooklyn, Cambria Heights, College Point, Corona, Douglaston, East Elmhurst, Elmhurst, Far Rockaway, Floral Park, Flushing, Forest Hills, Fresh Meadows, Glendale, Hollis, Howard Beach, Jackson Heights, Jamaica, Kew Gardens, Laurelton, Little Neck, Long Island City, Maspeth, Middle Village, Oakland Gardens, Ozone Park, Queens Village, Rego Park, Richmond Hill, Ridgewood, Rockaway Beach, Rockaway Park, Rosedale, Saint Albans, South Ozone Park, Springfield Gardens, Staten Island, Whitestone, Wood Haven, Woodside

---

Academy of St. Joseph PK-8
111 Washington Pl 10014 212-243-5420
Angela Coombs, prin. Fax 414-4526
Allen-Stevenson S 400/K-9
132 E 78th St, 212-288-6710
David Trower, hdmstr. Fax 288-6802
All Saints S 300/PK-8
52 E 130th St 10037 212-534-0558
Anthony Georges, prin. Fax 831-6343
Annunciation S 200/PK-8
461 W 131st St 10027 212-281-7174
David Smithers, prin. Fax 281-1732
Ascension S 300/PK-8
220 W 108th St 10025 212-222-5161
Fr. Sean McCaughley, prin. Fax 280-4690
Bank Street S for Children 400/PK-8
610 W 112th St 10025 212-875-4420
Susan Kluver, dean Fax 875-4454
Beth Jacob S 100/K-8
142 Broome St 10002 212-473-4500
Birch Wathen Lenox S 500/K-12
210 E 77th St, 212-861-0404
Frank Carnabuci, prin. Fax 879-5309
Blessed Sacrament S 300/PK-8
147 W 70th St 10023 212-724-7561
Imelda Engel, prin. Fax 724-0735
Brearley S 700/K-12
610 E 83rd St 10028 212-744-8582
Dr. Stephanie Hull, hdmstr. Fax 472-8020
Brick Church S 200/PK-K
62 E 92nd St 10128 212-289-5683
Lydia Spinelli Ed.D., dir. Fax 289-5372
Browning S 400/K-12
52 E 62nd St, 212-838-6280
Stephen Clement, hdmstr. Fax 355-5602
Buckley S 400/K-9
113 E 73rd St 10021 212-535-8787
Gregory O'Melia, hdmstr. Fax 472-0583
Caedmon S 200/PK-5
416 E 80th St, 212-879-2296
Dr. Greg Blackburn, hdmstr. Fax 879-0627
Calhoun Lower S 200/PK-1
160 W 74th St 10023 212-497-6550
Steve Nelson, hdmstr. Fax 721-5247
Calhoun S 500/2-12
433 W End Ave 10024 212-497-6500
Steven Nelson, hdmstr. Fax 497-6530
Cathedral S 300/K-8
1047 Amsterdam Ave 10025 212-316-7500
Marsha Nelson, hdmstr. Fax 316-7558
Chapin S 600/K-12
100 E End Ave 10028 212-744-2335
Patricia Hayot, hdmstr. Fax 535-8138
Churchill S and Center 400/K-12
301 E 29th St 10016 212-722-0610
Robert Siebert, hdmstr. Fax 722-1387
City & Country S 200/PK-8
146 W 13th St 10011 212-242-7802
Kate Turley, prin. Fax 242-7996
Collegiate S 600/K-12
260 W 78th St 10024 212-812-8500
Lee Levison, hdmstr. Fax 812-8524
Columbia Grammar & Prep S 1,100/PK-12
5 W 93rd St 10025 212-749-6200
Richard Soghoian, hdmstr. Fax 865-4278
Connelly Center for Education 100/5-8
220 E 4th St 10009 212-982-2287
Kimberly Morcate, prin. Fax 984-0547
Convent of the Sacred Heart S 700/PK-12
1 E 91st St 10128 212-722-4745
Joseph Ciancaglini, hdmstr. Fax 996-1784
Corlears S 100/PK-4
324 W 15th St 10011 212-741-2800
Thya Merz, hdmstr. Fax 807-1550
Corpus Christi S 200/PK-8
535 W 121st St 10027 212-662-9344
Dorothy Valla, prin. Fax 662-2725
Dalton S 1,300/K-12
108 E 89th St 10128 212-423-5200
Ellen Stein, hdmstr. Fax 423-5259
De La Salle Academy 100/6-8
202 W 97th St 10025 212-316-5840
Br. Brian Carty, hdmstr. Fax 316-5998
Dwight S 500/K-12
291 Central Park W 10024 212-724-6360
Stephen Spahn, chncllr. Fax 874-4232
Epiphany S 500/PK-8
234 E 22nd St 10010 212-473-4128
James Hayes, prin. Fax 473-4392
Ethical Culture S 400/PK-5
33 Central Park W 10023 212-712-6220
Ann Vershbow, prin. Fax 712-8444
Family S 900/PK-6
323 E 47th St 10017 212-688-5950
Lesley Haberman, prin. Fax 980-2475
Friends Seminary S 700/K-12
222 E 16th St 10003 212-979-5030
Robert Lauder, prin. Fax 979-5034
Geneva S of Manhattan 100/PK-8
PO Box 1533 10101 212-754-9988
Anthony Wilson, hdmstr. Fax 754-9987
Good Shepherd S 200/PK-8
620 Isham St 10034 212-567-5800
Matthew Gaynord, prin. Fax 567-5839
Grace Church S 400/PK-8
86 4th Ave 10003 212-475-5609
George Davison, hdmstr. Fax 475-5015
Guardian Angel S 200/PK-8
193 10th Ave 10011 212-989-8280
Maureen McElduff, prin. Fax 352-1467
Harlem Academy 1-5
1330 5th Ave 10026 212-348-2600
Vincent Dotoli, hdmstr. Fax 348-3500
Harlem International Community S 50/PK-12
2116 Adam Clayton Powell Jr 10027 212-222-7798
Ms. Wallie Simpson, prin. Fax 222-7798
Heschel MS 100/6-8
314 W 91st St 10024 212-595-7817
Lori Skopp, prin. Fax 595-6281
Heschel S 800/PK-5
270 W 89th St 10024 212-595-7087
Dina Bray, prin. Fax 595-7252
Hewitt S 500/K-12
45 E 75th St 10021 212-288-1919
Linda MacMurray Gibbs, hdmstr. Fax 472-7531
Holy Cross S 300/PK-8
332 W 43rd St 10036 212-246-0923
Sr. Mary Dixon, prin. Fax 246-4324
Holy Name of Jesus S 500/PK-8
202 W 97th St 10025 212-749-1240
Br. Richard Grieco, prin. Fax 663-1939
Hunter College Campus S 300/K-12
71 E 94th St 10128 212-860-1267
Randy Collins, dir. Fax 289-2209
Immaculate Conception S 300/PK-8
419 E 13th St 10009 212-475-2590
Donna Vincent, prin. Fax 777-2818
Incarnation S 600/K-8
570 W 175th St 10033 212-795-1030
Patricia O'Keefe, prin. Fax 795-1564
La Scuola D'Italia Gueglealmo Marconi S 200/PK-12
12 E 96th St 10128 212-369-3290
Fax 369-1164
LREI Little Red School House 400/PK-12
272 Avenue of the Americas 10014 212-477-5316
Philip Kassen, dir. Fax 677-9159
Lycee Francais De New York 1,300/PK-12
505 E 75th St 10021 212-369-1400
Yves Theze, prin. Fax 439-4210
Lyceum Kennedy S 200/PK-11
225 E 43rd St 10017 212-681-1877
Yves Rivaud, hdmstr. Fax 681-1922
Manhattan Christian Academy 300/PK-8
401 W 205th St 10034 212-567-5521
Dr. Richard Bonifas, prin. Fax 567-2815
Manhattan Country S 200/PK-8
7 E 96th St 10128 212-348-0952
Michele Sola, prin. Fax 348-1621
Manhattan Day S 400/PK-8
310 W 75th St 10023 212-376-6800
Rabbi Mordechai Besser, prin. Fax 376-6389
Mann K 50/PK-K
55 E 90th St 10128 212-369-4600
Dr. Thomas Kelly, hdmstr. Fax 722-1157
Marymount S 600/PK-12
1026 5th Ave 10028 212-744-4486
Concepcion Alvar, hdmstr. Fax 744-0163
Mesivta Tifereth Jerusalem S 200/PK-12
145 E Broadway 10002 212-964-2830
Metropolitan Montessori S 200/PK-6
325 W 85th St 10024 212-579-5525
Mary Gaines, hdmstr. Fax 579-5526
Mt. Carmel-Holy Rosary S 300/PK-8
371 Pleasant Ave 10035 212-876-7555
Suzanne Kaszynski, prin. Fax 876-0152
Nativity Mission MS 50/6-8
204 Forsyth St 10002 212-477-2472
Nicholas Romero, prin. Fax 473-0538
Nightingale-Bamford S 600/K-12
20 E 92nd St 10128 212-289-5020
Dorothy Hutcheson, hdmstr. Fax 876-1045
Our Lady of Lourdes S 200/PK-8
468 W 143rd St 10031 212-926-5820
Cathy Hufnagel, prin. Fax 491-6034
Our Lady of Pompeii S 300/PK-8
240 Bleecker St 10014 212-242-4147
Sr. Maureen Flynn, prin. Fax 691-2361
Our Lady of Sorrows S 200/PK-8
219 Stanton St 10002 212-473-0320
Mary George, prin. Fax 420-0285
Our Lady Queen of Angels S 300/PK-8
232 E 113th St 10029 212-722-9277
Joanne Walsh, prin. Fax 987-8837

Our Lady Queen of Martyrs S 400/PK-8
71 Arden St 10040 212-567-3190
Andrew Woods, prin. Fax 304-8587
Philosophy Day S 100/PK-5
12 E 79th St, 212-744-7300
William Fox, hdmstr. Fax 744-5876
Ramaz Lower S 400/PK-4
125 E 85th St 10028 212-774-8010
Judith Fagin, hdmstr. Fax 774-8039
Ramaz MS 200/5-8
114 E 85th St 10028 212-774-8040
Judith Fagin, hdmstr. Fax 774-8061
Resurrection Episcopal Day S 100/PK-K
119 E 74th St 10021 212-535-9666
Laurie Boone Hogen, admin. Fax 535-3191
Rodeph Sholom Day S 700/PK-8
10 W 84th St 10024 212-362-8769
Paul Druzinsky, hdmstr. Fax 362-8069
Sacred Heart of Jesus S 200/PK-8
456 W 52nd St 10019 212-246-4784
Noelle Beale, prin. Fax 707-8382
St. Aloysius S 300/PK-8
223 W 132nd St 10027 212-283-0921
Richard Burke, prin. Fax 234-4198
St. Ann S 300/PK-8
314 E 110th St 10029 212-722-1295
Sr. Josephine Cioffi, prin. Fax 722-8267
St. Bernard's S 400/K-9
4 E 98th St 10029 212-289-2878
Stuart Johnson, hdmstr. Fax 410-6628
St. Brigid S 100/PK-8
185 E 7th St 10009 212-677-5210
Suzanne Katusin, prin. Fax 260-2262
St. Charles Borromeo S 300/K-8
214 W 142nd St 10030 212-368-6666
Sr. Marianne Poole, prin. Fax 281-1323
St. David's S 400/PK-8
12 E 89th St 10128 212-369-0058
Dr. David O'Halloran, hdmstr. Fax 722-6127
St. Elizabeth S 400/PK-8
612 W 187th St 10033 212-568-7291
Sr. Noreen Nolan, prin. Fax 928-2515
St. George S 100/K-8
215 E 6th St 10003 212-473-3130
Sr. Theodosia Lukiw, prin. Fax 534-0819
St. Gregory the Great S 200/PK-8
138 W 90th St 10024 212-362-5410
Donna Gabella, prin. Fax 362-5026
St. Hilda's & St. Hugh's 400/PK-8
619 W 114th St 10025 212-932-1980
Virginia Connor, hdmstr. Fax 531-0102
St. Ignatius Loyola S 500/K-8
48 E 84th St 10028 212-861-3820
Mary Larkin, prin. Fax 879-8248
St. James S 200/PK-8
37 Saint James Pl 10038 212-267-9289
Ann Marie McGoldrick, prin. Fax 227-0065
St. Joseph of the Holy Family S 200/PK-8
168 Morningside Ave 10027 212-662-1736
Agnes Sayaman, prin. Fax 662-1490
St. Joseph of Yorkville S 300/PK-8
420 E 87th St 10128 212-289-3057
Theresa Bernero, prin. Fax 289-7239
St. Joseph S 200/PK-8
1 Monroe St 10002 212-233-5152
Sr. Deborah Lopez, prin. Fax 267-4357
St. Jude S 300/PK-8
433 W 204th St 10034 212-569-3400
Michael Deegan, prin. Fax 304-4479
St. Luke's S 200/PK-8
487 Hudson St 10014 212-924-5960
Bart Baldwin, hdmstr. Fax 924-1352
St. Mark the Evangelist S 200/PK-8
55 W 138th St 10037 212-283-4848
Sr. Catherine Hagan, prin. Fax 926-0419
St. Patrick Old Cathedral S 200/PK-8
233 Mott St 10012 212-226-3984
Maureen Burgio, prin. Fax 226-4469
St. Paul S 300/PK-8
114 E 118th St 10035 212-534-0619
Charles Celauro, prin. Fax 534-3990
St. Rose of Lima S 300/PK-8
517 W 164th St 10032 212-927-1619
Bernedette Lopez, prin. Fax 927-0648
St. Spyridon Parochial S 200/PK-8
120 Wadsworth Ave 10033 212-795-6870
Fr. George Passias, prin. Fax 795-6871
St. Stephen of Hungary S 200/PK-8
408 E 82nd St 10028 212-288-1989
Adele Kosinski, prin. Fax 517-5877
St. Thomas Choir S 50/3-8
202 W 58th St 10019 212-247-3311
Rev. Charles Wallace, hdmstr. Fax 247-3393
Schneier Park East S 300/PK-8
164 E 68th St, 212-737-7330
Barbara Etra, prin. Fax 639-1568
Solomon Schechter S of Manhattan 200/K-8
50 E 87th St 10128 212-427-9500
Dr. Steven Lorch, hdmstr. Fax 427-5300
Spence S 700/K-12
22 E 91st St 10128 212-289-5940
Ellanor Brizendine, hdmstr. Fax 860-2652
Steiner S 200/PK-6
15 E 79th St, 212-535-2130
Josh Eisen, admin. Fax 744-4497
Town S 400/PK-8
540 E 76th St 10021 212-288-4383
Christopher Marblo, hdmstr. Fax 988-5846
Transfiguration K 200/PK-K
10 Confucius Plz 10002 212-431-8769
Emily Eng-Tran, admin. Fax 431-8917
Transfiguration S 300/1-8
29 Mott St 10013 212-962-5265
Dr. Patrick Taharally, prin. Fax 964-8965
Trevor Day S 400/PK-5
4 E 90th St 10128 212-426-3300
Pamela Clarke, hdmstr. Fax 426-3337

Trinity S 900/K-12
139 W 91st St 10024 212-873-1650
Henry Moses, hdmstr. Fax 799-3417
U.N. International S 1,400/K-12
2450 FDR Dr 10010 212-684-7400
Dr. Kenneth Wrye, dir. Fax 684-1382
Village Community S 300/K-8
272 W 10th St 10014 212-691-5146
Eve Kleger, dir. Fax 691-9767
West Side Montessori S 200/PK-K
309 W 92nd St 10025 212-662-8000
Mimi Basso, prin. Fax 662-8323
Yeshiva Ketana of Manhattan 100/PK-8
346 W 89th St 10024 212-769-1790
Yeshiva Rabbi S.R. Hirsch 400/PK-12
91 Bennett Ave 10033 212-568-6200

New York Mills, Oneida, Pop. 3,146
New York Mills UFD 600/K-12
1 Marauder Blvd 13417 315-768-8127
Kathy Houghton, supt. Fax 768-3521
www.newyorkmills.org
New York Mills ES 300/K-6
1 Marauder Blvd 13417 315-768-8129
Rene Wilson, prin. Fax 768-3521

Niagara Falls, Niagara, Pop. 52,866
Niagara Falls CSD 6,100/PK-12
630 66th St 14304 716-286-4205
Cynthia Bianco, supt. Fax 286-4283
www.nfschools.net/
Abate ES 600/K-6
1625 Lockport St 14305 716-278-7960
Diane Coty, prin. Fax 284-0184
Cataract ES K-6
6431 Girard Ave 14304 716-278-9120
Maria Chille-Zafuto, prin. Fax 278-9122
Gaskill Preparatory S 500/7-8
910 Hyde Park Blvd 14301 716-278-5820
Joseph Colburn, prin. Fax 278-5829
Hyde Park ES 400/K-6
1620 Hyde Park Blvd 14305 716-278-7980
Larry Martinez, prin. Fax 278-7988
Kalfas Magnet ES 400/PK-6
1880 Beech Ave 14305 716-278-9180
Marie Catherine, prin. Fax 278-9173
La Salle Preparatory S 400/7-8
7436 Buffalo Ave 14304 716-278-5880
Richard Carella, prin. Fax 283-2494
Mann ES 400/K-6
1330 95th St 14304 716-278-7940
Mary Kerins, prin. Fax 298-5192
Maple Avenue ES 300/K-6
952 Maple Ave 14305 716-278-9140
Tina Smeal, prin. Fax 285-8880
Niagara Street ES 500/K-6
2513 Niagara St 14303 716-278-5860
Paulette Pierce, prin. Fax 284-2980
Seventy Ninth Street ES 300/K-6
551 79th St 14304 716-278-7900
Harriet Fogan, prin. Fax 278-7901

Niagara-Wheatfield Central SD 4,100/PK-12
6700 Schultz St 14304 716-215-3003
Dr. Carl Militello, supt. Fax 215-3039
www.nwcsd.k12.ny.us
Colonial Village ES 500/K-5
1456 Saunders Settlement Rd 14305 716-215-3270
Timothy Carter, prin. Fax 215-3290
Other Schools – See Lewiston, North Tonawanda, Sanborn

Holy Ghost Lutheran S 100/PK-8
6630 Luther St 14304 716-731-3030
Kevin Gundell, prin. Fax 731-9449
Our Lady of Mt. Carmel S 100/PK-5
2499 Independence Ave 14301 716-282-0645
Jeannine Fortunate, prin. Fax 282-7681
Prince of Peace S 200/PK-5
1055 N Military Rd 14304 716-283-1455
Christopher Hope, prin. Fax 283-1355
St. Dominic Savio MS 200/6-8
504 66th St 14304 716-215-1461
Rose Mary Buscaglia, prin. Fax 215-1465

Nichols, Tioga, Pop. 554
Tioga Central SD
Supt. — See Tioga Center
Nichols ES 100/K-4
PO Box 199 13812 607-699-7458
Kathleen Keene, prin. Fax 699-7204

North Babylon, Suffolk, Pop. 18,081
North Babylon UFD 5,000/K-12
5 Jardine Pl 11703 631-321-3226
Dr. Robert Aloise, supt. Fax 321-3295
www.northbabylonschools.net/
Deluca ES 400/K-5
223 Phelps Ln 11703 631-321-3270
Norann McManus, prin. Fax 321-3331
Moses MS 1,200/6-8
250 Phelps Ln 11703 631-321-3251
Kathleen Hartnett, prin. Fax 587-2619
Parliament Place ES 500/K-5
80 Parliament Pl 11703 631-243-4420
Drew Olsen, prin. Fax 254-2318
Vedder ES 400/K-5
794 Deer Park Ave 11703 631-321-3265
Kerry Larke, prin. Fax 587-2480
Woods Road ES 400/K-5
110 Woods Rd 11703 631-243-4400
Steven Golub, prin. Fax 243-5492
Other Schools – See West Babylon

North Baldwin, See Baldwin
Uniondale UFD
Supt. — See Uniondale

Grand Avenue ES 300/K-5
711 School Dr 11510 516-918-2100
Juanita Bryant-Bell, prin. Fax 483-4345

North Bay, Oneida
Camden Central SD
Supt. — See Camden
North Bay Area ES 200/K-5
2050 State Route 49 13123 315-245-2640
Fax 245-4191

North Bellmore, Nassau, Pop. 19,707
North Bellmore UFD 2,400/K-6
2616 Martin Ave 11710 516-992-3000
Arnold Goldstein, supt. Fax 992-3020
www.northbellmoreschools.org
Dinkelmeyer ES 400/K-6
2100 Waltoffer Ave 11710 516-992-3000
Faith Skelos, prin. Fax 992-3054
Gunther ES 300/K-6
2600 Regent Pl 11710 516-992-3000
Marie Testa, prin. Fax 992-3114
Martin Avenue ES 400/K-6
2616 Martin Ave 11710 516-992-3000
Mark Wiener, prin. Fax 992-3164
Newbridge Road ES 400/K-6
1601 Newbridge Rd 11710 516-992-3000
Marilyn Hirschfield, prin. Fax 992-3214
Saw Mill Road ES 500/K-6
2801 Sawmill Rd 11710 516-992-3000
Fran Bennett, prin. Fax 992-3324
Other Schools – See North Merrick

North Collins, Erie, Pop. 1,033
North Collins Central SD 700/K-12
2045 School St 14111 716-337-0101
Benjamin Halsey, supt. Fax 337-3457
www.northcollins.com
North Collins ES 300/K-6
10469 Bantle Rd 14111 716-337-0166
John Cataldo, prin. Fax 337-0598

North Creek, Warren
Johnsburg Central SD 400/K-12
PO Box 380 12853 518-251-2814
Michael Markwica, supt. Fax 251-2562
Johnsburg Central S 400/K-12
PO Box 380 12853 518-251-3504
Nadine Allard, prin. Fax 251-2562

North Massapequa, Nassau, Pop. 19,365
Farmingdale UFD
Supt. — See Farmingdale
Albany Avenue ES 700/K-5
101 N Albany Ave 11758 516-752-6570
Joseph Valentine, prin. Fax 752-7039

Plainedge UFD 3,500/K-12
241 Wyngate Dr 11758 516-992-7455
Christine P'Simer, supt. Fax 992-7446
www.plainedgeschools.org
Eastplain ES 500/K-5
301 N Delaware Ave 11758 516-992-7600
Emily O'Brien, prin. Fax 992-7605
Other Schools – See Bethpage, Massapequa

North Merrick, Nassau, Pop. 12,113
Bellmore-Merrick Central HSD 6,100/7-12
1260 Meadowbrook Rd 11566 516-992-1000
Dr. Henry Kiernan, supt. Fax 623-0151
www.bellmore-merrick.k12.ny.us
Other Schools – See Bellmore, Merrick

North Bellmore UFD
Supt. — See North Bellmore
Park Avenue ES 300/K-6
1599 Park Ave 11566 516-992-3000
Eileen Speidel, prin. Fax 992-3274

North Merrick UFD 1,300/K-6
1057 Merrick Ave 11566 516-292-3694
David Feller, supt. Fax 292-3097
Camp Avenue ES 500/K-6
1712 Merrick Ave 11566 516-379-3732
Ronald Reinken, prin. Fax 292-3097
Fayette ES 300/K-6
1057 Merrick Ave 11566 516-489-3090
Howard Merims, prin. Fax 292-3097
Old Mill Road ES 500/K-6
1775 Old Mill Rd 11566 516-379-0945
Laura Leudesdorff, prin. Fax 379-1695

Sacred Heart S 200/PK-8
730 Merrick Ave 11566 516-378-5797
Kerry Kahn, prin. Fax 378-5797

Northport, Suffolk, Pop. 7,587
Kings Park Central SD
Supt. — See Kings Park
Ft. Salonga ES 600/K-3
39 Sunken Meadow Rd 11768 631-269-3364
Arlene Mullin, prin. Fax 269-2190

Northport-East Northport UFD 6,600/K-12
PO Box 210 11768 631-262-6604
Marylou McDermott, supt. Fax 262-6607
northport.k12.ny.us
Northport MS 900/6-8
11 Middleville Rd 11768 631-262-6750
Timothy Hoss, prin. Fax 262-6793
Norwood Avenue ES 500/K-5
25 Norwood Rd 11768 631-262-6830
Michael Genovese, prin. Fax 262-6835
Ocean Avenue ES 500/K-5
100 Ocean Ave 11768 631-262-6840
Sabina Larkin, prin. Fax 262-6845
Other Schools – See East Northport

Trinity Regional S 100/PK-PK
364 Main St 11768 631-261-8520
Jeanne Morcone, prin. Fax 261-8560

North Rose, Wayne
North Rose-Wolcott Central SD
Supt. — See Wolcott
North Rose ES 300/3-5
10456 Salter Rd 14516 315-587-4005
Neil Thompson, prin. Fax 587-2432

North Salem, Westchester
North Salem Central SD 1,400/K-12
230 June Rd 10560 914-669-5414
Dr. Kenneth Freeston, supt. Fax 669-8753
northsalem.k12.ny.us
Pequenakonck ES 600/K-5
173 June Rd 10560 914-669-5317
Roberta Reiner, prin. Fax 669-4326

North Syracuse, Onondaga, Pop. 6,726
North Syracuse Central SD 10,300/PK-12
5355 W Taft Rd 13212 315-218-2151
Jerome Melvin, supt. Fax 218-2185
www.nscsd.org
Allen Road ES 500/K-4
803 Allen Rd 13212 315-218-2300
David Lunden, prin. Fax 218-2385
Bear Road ES 700/K-4
5590 Bear Rd 13212 315-218-2400
Irene Thames, prin. Fax 218-2485
Main Street Preschool 300/PK-PK
205 S Main St 13212 315-218-2200
Kathleen Esposito, prin. Fax 218-2285
Smith Road ES 600/K-4
5959 Smith Rd 13212 315-218-2800
Donna Fountain, prin. Fax 218-2885
Other Schools – See Cicero, Syracuse

St. Rose of Lima S 400/PK-6
411 S Main St 13212 315-458-6036
Sr. Catherine Laboure, prin. Fax 458-6038

North Tonawanda, Niagara, Pop. 32,072
Niagara-Wheatfield Central SD
Supt. — See Niagara Falls
Errick Road ES 600/K-5
6839 Errick Rd 14120 716-215-3240
Nora O'Bryan, prin. Fax 215-3260

North Tonawanda CSD 4,400/PK-12
175 Humphrey St 14120 716-807-3599
Vincent Vecchiarella, supt. Fax 807-3525
Drake ES 400/K-6
380 Drake Dr 14120 716-807-3725
Janet Matyevich, prin. Fax 807-3726
Gilmore ES 300/K-6
789 Gilmore Ave 14120 716-807-3750
Patrick Holesko, prin. Fax 807-3751
Grant S 100/PK-PK
35 Grant St 14120 716-807-3775
Fax 807-3776
Meadow ES 400/K-6
455 Meadow Dr 14120 716-807-3825
Patricia Adler, prin. Fax 807-3835
North Tonawanda MS 700/7-8
1500 Vanderbilt Ave 14120 716-807-3700
Wendy Richards, prin. Fax 807-3701
Ohio ES 500/K-6
625 Ohio St 14120 716-807-3800
Karen Cuddy-Miller, prin. Fax 807-3801
Spruce ES 500/K-6
195 Spruce St 14120 716-807-3850
Richard Jetter, prin. Fax 807-3858

North Tonawanda Catholic S 100/PK-8
75 Keil St 14120 716-693-2828
Martha Eadie, prin. Fax 693-0169
St. John Lutheran S 100/PK-8
6950 Ward Rd 14120 716-693-9677
Herbert Meissner, prin. Fax 693-2686
St. Matthew Lutheran S 200/PK-8
875 Eggert Dr 14120 716-692-1811
Toni Ricchiazzi, prin. Fax 692-0242
St. Paul Lutheran S 50/PK-PK
453 Old Falls Blvd 14120 716-692-3255
Linda Gerlach, dir. Fax 692-3643

Northville, Fulton, Pop. 1,159
Northville Central SD 500/PK-12
PO Box 608 12134 518-863-7000
Kathy Dougherty, supt. Fax 863-7011
northvillecsd.k12.ny.us
Northville ES 200/PK-5
PO Box 608 12134 518-863-7000
Barbara Sperry, prin. Fax 863-7011

North White Plains, See White Plains
Valhalla UFD
Supt. — See Valhalla
Virginia Road ES 400/K-2
86 Virginia Rd 10603 914-683-5035
Ada Parker, prin. Fax 683-5291

Norwich, Chenango, Pop. 7,233
Norwich CSD 1,900/PK-12
19 Eaton Ave Ste 500 13815 607-334-1600
Gerard O'Sullivan, supt. Fax 336-8652
www.norwichcityschooldistrict.com/
Browne IS 300/3-5
19 Eaton Ave Ste 500 13815 607-334-1600
Heather Collier, prin. Fax 334-6201
Gibson PS 500/PK-2
19 Eaton Ave Ste 500 13815 607-334-1600
Dara Lewis, prin. Fax 334-4193
Norwich MS 300/6-8
19 Eaton Ave Ste 500 13815 607-334-1600
Lisa Schuchman, prin. Fax 334-6210

Holy Family S 100/PK-6
17 Prospect St 13815 607-337-2207
Eugene Chilion, prin. Fax 337-2210

Norwood, Saint Lawrence, Pop. 1,627
Norwood-Norfolk Central SD 1,100/K-12
PO Box 194 13668 315-353-9951
Elizabeth Kirnie, supt. Fax 353-2467
www.nncsk12.org/
Norwood-Norfolk ES 400/K-4
PO Box 202 13668 315-353-6674
Joanne Bigwarfe, prin. Fax 353-2408
Norwood-Norfolk MS 300/5-8
PO Box 194 13668 315-353-6674
Jon Sovay, prin.

Nunda, Livingston, Pop. 1,280
Keshequa Central SD 900/K-12
PO Box 517 14517 585-468-2541
Marilyn Capawan, supt. Fax 468-3814
www.keshequa.org
Keshequa MS 200/6-8
PO Box 517 14517 585-468-2541
Mark Mattle, prin. Fax 468-3814
Other Schools – See Dalton

Nyack, Rockland, Pop. 6,676
Nyack UFD 2,900/K-12
13A Dickinson Ave 10960 845-353-7015
Dr. Valencia Douglas, supt. Fax 353-0508
www.nyackschools.com
Nyack MS 600/6-8
98 S Highland Ave 10960 845-353-7200
Nicole Saieva, prin. Fax 353-0506
Other Schools – See Upper Nyack, Valley Cottage

Oakdale, Suffolk, Pop. 7,875
Connetquot Central SD
Supt. — See Bohemia
Idle Hour ES 400/K-5
334 Idle Hour Blvd 11769 631-244-2306
Denise Toscano, prin. Fax 244-2305
Oakdale-Bohemia Road MS 900/6-8
60 Oakdale Bohemia Rd 11769 631-244-2268
Susanne Bailey, prin. Fax 563-6167

Oakfield, Genesee, Pop. 1,721
Oakfield-Alabama Central SD 1,000/K-12
7001 Lewiston Rd 14125 585-948-5211
Christopher Todd, supt. Fax 948-9362
www.oahornets.org
Oakfield-Alabama ES 400/K-5
7001 Lewiston Rd 14125 585-948-5211
Mark Alexander, prin. Fax 948-9362

Oakland Gardens, See New York
NYC Department of Education
Supt. — See New York
JHS 74 1,000/6-8
6115 Oceania St 11364 718-631-6800
Andrea Dapolito, prin. Fax 631-6899
Public S 46 300/K-5
6445 218th St 11364 718-423-8395
Marsha Goldberg, prin. Fax 423-8472
Public S 162 700/K-5
20102 53rd Ave 11364 718-423-8621
Dena Poulos, prin. Fax 423-8647
Public S 188 400/K-5
21812 Hartland Ave 11364 718-464-5768
Janet Caraisco, prin. Fax 464-5771
Public S 203 700/PK-5
5311 Springfield Blvd 11364 718-423-8652
Carol Nussbaum, prin. Fax 423-8713
Public S 205 300/PK-5
7525 Bell Blvd 11364 718-464-5773
Karen Scott-Piazza, prin. Fax 464-5875
Public S 213 400/PK-5
23102 67th Ave 11364 718-423-8747
Bruce Baronoff, prin. Fax 423-8805

St. Robert Bellarmine S 200/PK-8
5610 214th St 11364 718-225-8795
Angela Fazio, prin. Fax 423-5612

Ocean Beach, Suffolk, Pop. 146
Fire Island UFD 50/PK-6
PO Box 428 11770 631-583-5626
Loretta Ferraro, supt. Fax 583-5167
www.fi.k12.ny.us
Woodhull ES 50/PK-6
PO Box 428 11770 631-583-5626
Loretta Ferraro, prin. Fax 583-5167

Oceanside, Nassau, Pop. 32,800
Oceanside UFD 6,200/PK-12
145 Merle Ave 11572 516-678-1215
Dr. Herb Brown, supt. Fax 678-7503
www.oceansideschools.org
Fulton Ave ES 500/1-6
3252 Fulton Ave 11572 516-678-8503
Ronald Schoen, prin. Fax 678-6591
North Oceanside Rd ES 500/1-6
2440 Oceanside Rd 11572 516-678-7585
Diane Provvido, prin. Fax 678-6597
Oaks ES 500/1-6
2852 Fortesque Ave 11572 516-678-7564
Dr. Jill Derosa, prin. Fax 678-6568
Oceanside MS 1,000/7-8
186 Alice Ave 11572 516-678-8518
Allison Glickman-Rogers, prin. Fax 594-2365
Public K 6 400/PK-K
25 Castleton Ct 11572 516-594-2345
Rhonda Gelbwasser, prin. Fax 678-7347
Public S 9E 400/1-6
170 Beatrice Ave 11572 516-678-8510
Dr. Karen Siris, prin. Fax 678-7336
Smith ES 500/1-6
2745 Terrell Ave 11572 516-678-7557
Thomas Capone, prin. Fax 678-6513
South Oceanside Road ES 300/1-6
3210 Oceanside Rd 11572 516-678-7581
Joanna Kletter, prin. Fax 678-6583

Odessa, Schuyler, Pop. 608
Odessa-Montour Central SD 800/K-12
PO Box 430 14869 607-594-3341
James Frame, supt. Fax 594-3976
www.omschools.org
Hanlon ES 200/3-5
PO Box 430 14869 607-594-3341
Tim Young, prin. Fax 594-3976
Other Schools – See Montour Falls

Ogdensburg, Saint Lawrence, Pop. 11,422
Ogdensburg CSD 1,700/K-12
1100 State St 13669 315-393-0900
Timothy Vernsey, supt. Fax 393-2767
www.ogdensburgk12.org/
Kennedy ES 300/3-6
900 Park St 13669 315-393-4264
Susan Jacobs, prin. Fax 394-0480
Lincoln ES 200/K-2
1515 Knox St 13669 315-393-7836
Paula Scott, prin. Fax 393-7652
Madill ES 300/K-6
800 Jefferson Ave 13669 315-393-7729
Debora Hannan, prin. Fax 393-0419
Sherman ES 100/K-2
615 Franklin St 13669 315-393-6271
Paula Scott, prin. Fax 393-6049

St. Marguerite D'Youville Academy 100/PK-6
315 Gates St 13669 315-393-0165
Celina Burns, prin. Fax 394-0499

Old Bethpage, Nassau, Pop. 5,610
Plainview-Old Bethpage Central SD
Supt. — See Plainview
Old Bethpage ES 400/1-4
1191 Round Swamp Rd 11804 516-756-3200
Suzanne Gray, prin. Fax 756-3204

Old Brookville, Nassau, Pop. 2,244

Green Vale S 500/PK-9
250 Valentines Ln 11545 516-621-2420
Stephen Watters, hdmstr. Fax 621-1317

Old Forge, Herkimer
Town of Webb UFD 300/K-12
PO Box 38 13420 315-369-3222
Donald Gooley, supt. Fax 369-6216
www.towschool.org
Town of Webb S 300/K-12
PO Box 38 13420 315-369-3222
Rex Germer, dean Fax 369-6216

Old Westbury, Nassau, Pop. 5,035
East Williston UFD 1,900/K-12
11 Bacon Rd 11568 516-333-1630
Dr. Lorna Lewis, supt. Fax 333-1937
www.ewsdonline.org/
Other Schools – See East Williston, Roslyn Heights

Westbury UFD 4,100/PK-12
2 Hitchcock Ln 11568 516-874-1829
Dr. Constance Clark-Snead, supt. Fax 876-5187
www.westburyschools.org
Other Schools – See Westbury

Holy Child Academy 200/PK-8
25 Store Hill Rd 11568 516-626-9300
Michael O'Donoghue, prin. Fax 626-7914
Whispering Pines SDA S 100/PK-8
211 Jericho Tpke 11568 516-997-5177
Regina Gray, prin. Fax 997-2138

Olean, Cattaraugus, Pop. 14,799
Olean CSD 2,400/PK-12
410 W Sullivan St 14760 716-375-8018
Colleen Taggerty, supt. Fax 375-8047
www.oleanschools.org
Boardmanville ES 300/PK-5
622 Main St 14760 716-375-8900
John White, prin. Fax 375-8910
East View ES 400/PK-5
690 E Spring St 14760 716-375-8920
David Olson, prin. Fax 375-8929
Norton ES 200/PK-5
411 W Henley St 14760 716-375-8940
Linda Nottingham, prin. Fax 375-8950
Olean MS 500/6-8
401 Wayne St 14760 716-375-8060
Gerald Trietley, prin. Fax 375-8070
Washington West ES 300/PK-5
1626 Washington St 14760 716-375-8960
Joel Whitcher, prin. Fax 375-8970

Southern Tier Catholic S 100/PK-8
205 W Henley St 14760 585-372-2891
Daniel McCarthy, prin. Fax 373-1175

Olmstedville, Essex
Minerva Central SD 100/K-12
PO Box 39 12857 518-251-2000
Timothy Farrell, supt. Fax 251-2395
www.minervasd.org/
Minerva Central S 100/K-12
PO Box 39 12857 518-251-2000
Heidi Kelly, prin. Fax 251-2395

Oneida, Madison, Pop. 10,923
Oneida CSD 2,400/K-12
PO Box 327 13421 315-363-2550
Ronald Spadafora, supt. Fax 363-6728
www.oneidacsd.org/
North Broad Street ES 200/K-6
230 N Broad St 13421 315-363-3650
William Simmons, prin. Fax 366-0617
Oneida Castle ES 100/K-6
10 Castle St 13421 315-363-5910
Rhonda Rueger, prin. Fax 366-0621

Prior ES 300/K-6
205 East Ave 13421 315-363-2190
Moira Yardley, prin. Fax 366-0616
Seneca Street ES 300/K-6
436 Seneca St 13421 315-363-3930
Theresa McCann, prin. Fax 363-0618
Other Schools – See Durhamville, Wampsville

St. Patrick S 100/K-6
354 Elizabeth St 13421 315-363-3620
Peg Brown, prin. Fax 363-5075

Oneonta, Otsego, Pop. 13,206
Oneonta CSD 2,100/PK-12
189 Main St 13820 607-433-8200
Michael Shea, supt. Fax 433-8290
oneontacsd.org
Center Street ES 200/K-6
31 Center St 13820 607-433-8271
John Cook, prin. Fax 433-8206
Greater Plains ES 300/PK-6
60 W End Ave 13820 607-433-8272
Timothy Gracy, prin. Fax 433-8207
Oneonta MS 300/7-8
130 East St 13820 607-433-8262
Kevin Johnson, prin. Fax 433-8203
Riverside ES 200/K-6
39 House St 13820 607-433-8273
Melinda Murdock, prin. Fax 433-8210
Valleyview ES 300/K-6
40 Valleyview St 13820 607-433-8252
Walter Baskin, prin. Fax 433-8211

Lighthouse Christian Academy 50/K-12
12 Grove St 13820 607-432-2031
Jacqueline Yarborough, admin. Fax 432-3403
Oneonta Community Christian S 100/PK-12
158 River St 13820 607-432-0383
Jane Cook, admin. Fax 436-9137
St. Mary's S 100/PK-6
5588 State Highway 7 13820 607-432-1450
Patricia Bliss, prin. Fax 432-1656

Ontario Center, Wayne
Wayne Central SD 2,600/K-12
PO Box 155 14520 315-524-1001
Michael Havens, supt. Fax 524-1049
www.wayne.k12.ny.us
Armstrong MS 600/6-8
PO Box 155 14520 315-524-1080
Robert Armocida, prin. Fax 524-1119
Ontario ES 400/3-5
PO Box 155 14520 315-524-1130
Michael Pullen, prin. Fax 524-1149
Ontario PS 300/K-2
PO Box 155 14520 315-524-1150
Robert LaRuche, prin. Fax 524-1169
Other Schools – See Walworth

Orchard Park, Erie, Pop. 3,147
Orchard Park Central SD 5,200/K-12
3330 Baker Rd 14127 716-209-6222
Joan Thomas, supt. Fax 209-6353
www.opschools.org
Eggert Road ES 700/K-5
3580 Eggert Rd 14127 716-209-6215
Lisa Krueger, prin. Fax 209-6371
Ellicott Road ES 700/K-5
5180 Ellicott Rd 14127 716-209-6278
Terry Spicola, prin. Fax 209-6203
Orchard Park MS 1,200/6-8
60 S Lincoln Ave 14127 716-209-6227
Jennifer Curci, prin. Fax 209-6338
South Davis ES 400/K-5
51 S Davis St 14127 716-209-6246
Christine Rassow, prin. Fax 209-8195
Windom ES 500/K-5
3870 Sheldon Rd 14127 716-209-6279
Wendy Gloss, prin. Fax 209-6490

Nativity of Our Lord S 300/PK-8
4414 S Buffalo St 14127 716-662-7572
Ruth Frost, prin. Fax 662-3483
Our Lady of the Sacred Heart S 200/PK-8
3144 Abbott Rd 14127 716-824-8208
Christopher Gardon, prin. Fax 824-8779
St. Bernadette S 200/PK-8
5890 S Abbott Rd 14127 716-649-3369
Sr. Diane Swanson, prin. Fax 649-3963
St. John Vianney S 200/PK-8
2950 Southwestern Blvd 14127 716-674-9232
Teresa Siuta, prin. Fax 674-9248

Orient, Suffolk
Oysterponds UFD 100/K-6
23405 Main Rd 11957 631-323-2410
Dr. Stuart Rachlin, supt. Fax 323-3713
www.oysterponds.k12.ny.us
Oysterponds ES 100/K-6
23405 Main Rd 11957 631-323-2410
Dr. Stuart Rachlin, prin. Fax 323-3713

Oriskany, Oneida, Pop. 1,423
Oriskany Central SD 700/K-12
PO Box 539 13424 315-768-2058
Michael Deuel, supt. Fax 768-1733
Walbran ES 400/K-6
PO Box 539 13424 315-768-2149
Jason Evangelist, prin. Fax 768-4485

Ossining, Westchester, Pop. 23,547
Ossining UFD 3,300/PK-12
190 Croton Ave 10562 914-941-7700
Dr. Phyllis Glassman, supt. Fax 941-2794
ossiningufsd.org
Brookside S 300/1-2
30 Ryder Rd 10562 914-762-5780
Ann Dealy, prin. Fax 941-4674
Claremont S 300/3-4
30 Claremont Rd 10562 914-762-5830
Felix Flores, prin. Fax 941-4964
Dorner MS 800/6-8
90 Van Cortlandt Ave 10562 914-762-5740
Regina Cellio, prin. Fax 762-5246
Park ECC 300/PK-K
22 Edward St 10562 914-762-5850
Ziola Tazi, prin. Fax 941-4335
Roosevelt S 300/5-5
190 Croton Ave 10562 914-941-7700
Elizabeth Wallinger, prin. Fax 941-7291

St. Ann S 200/PK-8
16 Elizabeth St 10562 914-941-0312
Jayson Bock, prin. Fax 941-3514
St. Augustine S 500/PK-8
301 Eagle Park 10562 914-941-3849
Sr. Mary Donoghue, prin. Fax 941-4342

Oswego, Oswego, Pop. 17,705
Oswego CSD 4,500/K-12
120 E 1st St Ste 1 13126 315-341-2001
William Crist, supt. Fax 341-2910
www.oswego.org
Fitzhugh Park ES 400/K-6
195 E Bridge St 13126 315-341-2400
Donna Simmons, prin. Fax 341-2940
Kingsford Park ES 400/K-6
275 W 5th St 13126 315-341-2500
Mary Volkomer, prin. Fax 341-2950
Leighton ES 400/K-6
1 Buccaneer Blvd 13126 315-341-2700
Julie Burger, prin. Fax 341-2970
Oswego MS 700/7-8
100 Mark Fitzgibbons Dr 13126 315-341-2300
Bonnie Finnerty, prin. Fax 341-2390
Riley ES 400/K-6
269 E 8th St 13126 315-341-2800
Dr. Randy Richards, prin. Fax 341-2980
Other Schools – See Minetto

Oswego Community Christian S 100/PK-12
400 E Albany St 13126 315-342-9322
Fax 342-0268
Trinity Catholic S 200/PK-6
115 E 5th St 13126 315-343-6700
David Friedlander, prin. Fax 342-9471

Otego, Otsego, Pop. 1,007
Otego-Unadilla Central SD 900/K-12
2641 State Highway 7 13825 607-988-5038
Charles Molloy, supt. Fax 988-1039
unatego.org
Otego ES 200/K-5
353 Main St 13825 607-988-6700
Timothy Ryan, prin. Fax 988-1012
Unatego MS 6-8
2641 State Highway 7 13825 607-988-5036
Bill Diamond, prin. Fax 988-5058
Other Schools – See Unadilla

Otisville, Orange, Pop. 1,060
Minisink Valley Central SD
Supt. — See Slate Hill
Otisville ES 400/K-5
2525 Mt Hope Rd 10963 845-355-5850
Alice Reh, prin. Fax 355-5853

Ovid, Seneca, Pop. 609
South Seneca Central SD 900/PK-12
7263 Main St 14521 607-869-9636
Janie Nusser, supt. Fax 532-8540
www.southseneca.com/
South Seneca MS 100/7-8
7263 Main St 14521 607-869-9636
Robert Fitzsimmons, prin. Fax 532-8540
Other Schools – See Interlaken

Owego, Tioga, Pop. 3,794
Owego-Apalachin Central SD 2,300/K-12
36 Talcott St 13827 607-687-6224
Dr. William Russell, supt. Fax 687-6313
www.oacsd.org
Owego-Apalachin MS 500/6-8
3 Sheldon Guile Blvd 13827 607-687-6248
Jill Clark, prin. Fax 687-6259
Owego ES 500/K-5
1 Christa Mcauliffe Dr 13827 607-687-6261
Laurie McKeveny, prin. Fax 687-6268
Other Schools – See Apalachin

St. Patrick S 100/PK-5
309 Front St 13827 607-687-1770
Linda Biggs, prin. Fax 687-4305
Zion Lutheran S 50/PK-5
3917 Waverly Rd 13827 607-687-6376
Janet Pawlak, prin. Fax 687-6376

Oxford, Chenango, Pop. 1,571
Oxford Academy & Central SD 900/K-12
PO Box 192 13830 607-843-2025
Randall Squier, supt. Fax 843-3241
www.oxac.org
Oxford Academy MS 300/5-8
PO Box 192 13830 607-843-2025
Kathleen Hansen, prin. Fax 843-3241
Oxford Academy PS 300/K-4
PO Box 192 13830 607-843-2025
Timothy McDonald, prin. Fax 843-7030

Oyster Bay, Nassau, Pop. 6,687
Oyster Bay-East Norwich Central SD 1,700/PK-12
1 McCouns Ln 11771 516-624-6505
Dr. Phyllis Harrington, supt. Fax 624-6520
obenschools.org
Roosevelt ES 400/PK-2
150 W Main St 11771 516-624-6572
Gina Faust, prin. Fax 624-6591
Other Schools – See East Norwich

East Woods S 300/PK-9
31 Yellow Cote Rd 11771 516-922-4400
Nathaniel Peirce Ed.D., hdmstr. Fax 922-2589
St. Dominic S 200/PK-8
35 School St 11771 516-922-4233
Sr. Mary Slavinskas, prin. Fax 624-7613

Ozone Park, See New York
NYC Department of Education
Supt. — See New York
JHS 202 1,100/6-8
13830 Lafayette St 11417 718-848-0001
William Fitzgerald, prin. Fax 848-8082
JHS 210 2,000/6-8
9311 101st Ave 11416 718-845-5942
Rosalyn Allman-Manning, prin. Fax 845-4037
MS 137 1,800/6-8
10915 98th St 11417 718-659-0471
Laura Mastrogiovanni, prin. Fax 659-4594
Public S 63 1,200/K-5
9015 Sutter Ave 11417 718-845-7560
Deidra Graulich, prin. Fax 845-7269
Public S 64 700/K-5
8201 101st Ave 11416 718-845-8290
Laura Kaiser, prin. Fax 848-0052
Public S 65 500/K-5
10322 99th St 11417 718-323-1685
Rafael Morales, prin. Fax 323-1785

Divine Mercy Academy 200/PK-5
10160 92nd St 11416 718-845-3074
Sr. Francis Wystepek, prin. Fax 845-5068
St. Elizabeth S 300/PK-8
9401 85th St 11416 718-641-6990
William Ferguson, prin. Fax 296-1140
St. Mary Gate of Heaven S 500/K-8
10406 101st Ave 11416 718-846-0689
Patrick Scannell, prin. Fax 846-1059

Painted Post, Steuben, Pop. 1,805
Corning CSD 5,700/PK-12
165 Charles St 14870 607-936-3704
Michael Ginalski, supt. Fax 654-2735
www.corningareaschools.com
Erwin Valley ES 400/K-5
16 Beartown Rd 14870 607-936-6514
Kate Merrill, prin. Fax 654-2878
Lindley-Presho ES 100/K-5
9183 Presho School Rd 14870 607-523-7252
Betsy Fogelsonger, prin. Fax 654-2888
Pierce ECC 200/PK-PK
3805 Meads Creek Rd 14870 607-962-6083
Jennifer Batzing, admin. Fax 654-2898
Smith ES 300/K-5
3414 Stanton St 14870 607-936-4156
Kerry Elsasser, prin. Fax 654-2859
Other Schools – See Corning

Palmyra, Wayne, Pop. 3,429
Palmyra-Macedon Central SD 1,600/K-12
151 Hyde Pkwy 14522 315-597-3401
Robert Ike, supt. Fax 597-3898
www.palmaccsd.org
Palmyra-Macedon MS 500/6-8
163 Hyde Pkwy 14522 315-597-3450
Darcy Smith, prin. Fax 597-3460
Palmyra-Macedon PS 200/K-2
120 Canandaigua St 14522 315-597-3475
Fax 597-6903
Other Schools – See Macedon

East Palmyra Christian S 100/PK-8
2023 E Palmyra Port Gibson 14522 315-597-4400
Keith Vanderzwan, prin. Fax 597-9717

Panama, Chautauqua, Pop. 471
Panama Central SD 300/K-12
41 North St 14767 716-782-2455
Carol Hay, supt. Fax 782-4281
www.pancent.org
Panama Central S 300/K-12
41 North St 14767 716-782-2455
Bert Lictus, prin. Fax 782-4281

Parish, Oswego, Pop. 496
Altmar-Parish-Williamstown Central SD 1,300/K-12
PO Box 97 13131 315-625-5251
Deborah Haab, supt. Fax 625-7952
www.apw.cnyric.org
Altmar-Parish-Williamstown MS 300/5-8
640 County Route 22 13131 315-625-5200
Rose Darby, prin. Fax 625-4937
Parish ES 200/K-4
25 Union St 13131 315-625-7911
Michael McAuliff, prin. Fax 625-4429
Other Schools – See Altmar

Parishville, Saint Lawrence
Parishville-Hopkinton Central SD 500/K-12
PO Box 187 13672 315-265-4642
Thomas Burns, supt. Fax 268-1309
phcs.neric.org
Parishville-Hopkinton ES 200/K-6
PO Box 187 13672 315-265-4642
Pamela Claus, prin. Fax 268-1309

Patchogue, Suffolk, Pop. 11,901
Patchogue-Medford UFD 8,000/PK-12
241 S Ocean Ave 11772 631-687-6380
Michael Mostow, supt.
pat-med.k12.ny.us
Barton ES, 199 Barton Ave 11772 700/PK-5
Judith Soltner, prin. 631-687-6900
Bay ES 400/K-5
114 Bay Ave 11772 631-687-6950
Dr. Peter Nicolino, prin. Fax 758-1126

Canaan ES, 59 Fry Blvd 11772 — 600/K-5
Robert Epstein, prin. — 631-687-8100
Medford ES, 281 Medford Ave 11772 — 600/K-5
Fran Lizewski, prin. — 631-687-8300
River ES, 46 River Ave 11772 — 300/K-5
Karen Malone, prin. — 631-687-8350
Other Schools – See Medford

Emanuel Lutheran S — 200/PK-8
179 E Main St 11772 — 631-758-2250
Lori Joerz, prin. — Fax 758-2418
Holy Angels S — 400/K-8
Division St 11772 — 631-475-0422
Maria Martinez, prin. — Fax 475-2036

Patterson, Putnam
Carmel Central SD — 4,800/K-12
PO Box 296 12563 — 845-878-2094
James Ryan Ed.D., supt. — Fax 878-2566
www.ccsd.k12.ny.us
Paterson ES — 600/K-4
100 South St 12563 — 845-878-3211
Linda Rossetti, prin. — Fax 878-3964
Other Schools – See Carmel

Pattersonville, Schenectady
Schalmont Central SD
Supt. — See Schenectady
Mariaville ES — 100/K-5
9210 Mariaville Rd 12137 — 518-864-5411
Brian Hunt, prin. — Fax 864-5522

Pavilion, Genesee
Pavilion Central SD — 900/K-12
7014 Big Tree Rd 14525 — 585-584-3115
Edward Orman, supt. — Fax 584-3421
www.pavilioncsd.org
Bunce ES — 300/K-5
7071 York Rd 14525 — 585-584-3011
Barbara Partell, prin. — Fax 584-3421

Pawling, Dutchess, Pop. 2,313
Pawling Central SD — 1,400/K-12
32 Holiday Hills Ln 12564 — 845-855-4600
Joseph Sciortino, supt. — Fax 855-4659
www.pawlingschools.org
Pawling ES — 600/K-4
7 Haight St 12564 — 845-855-4630
Matthew Herz, prin. — Fax 855-4636
Pawling MS — 400/5-8
80 Wagner Dr 12564 — 845-855-4653
Allan Lipsky, prin. — Fax 855-4134

Mizzentop Day S — 200/PK-8
64 E Main St 12564 — 845-855-7338
Steve Cash, prin. — Fax 855-1239

Pearl River, Rockland, Pop. 15,314
Pearl River UFD — 2,600/K-12
275 E Central Ave 10965 — 845-620-3900
Dr. Frank Auriemma, supt. — Fax 620-3927
www.pearlriver.org
Evans Park ES — 300/K-4
40 Marion Pl 10965 — 845-620-3950
Peggy Lynch, prin. — Fax 620-7570
Franklin Avenue ES — 300/K-4
48 Franklin Ave 10965 — 845-620-3965
Carla Silberstein, prin. — Fax 620-3981
Lincoln Ave ES — 300/K-4
115 Lincoln Ave 10965 — 845-620-3850
Fred Weitz, prin. — Fax 620-3975
Pearl River MS — 600/5-7
520 Gilbert Ave 10965 — 845-620-3870
Maria Paese, prin. — Fax 620-3894

Pearl River SDA S — 50/PK-8
210 N Middletown Rd 10965 — 845-735-8603
St. Margaret S — 200/PK-8
34 N Magnolia St 10965 — 845-735-2855
Carolyn Slattery, prin. — Fax 735-0131

Peekskill, Westchester, Pop. 24,044
Peekskill CSD — 2,900/PK-12
1031 Elm St 10566 — 914-737-3300
Judith Johnson, supt. — Fax 737-3912
www.peekskillcsd.org
Hillcrest ES — 400/4-5
99 Horton Dr 10566 — 914-739-2284
Joseph Mosey, prin. — Fax 737-9053
Oakside ES — 400/2-3
200 Decatur Ave 10566 — 914-737-1591
Mary Foster, prin. — Fax 737-1530
Peekskill MS — 400/6-8
212 Ringgold St 10566 — 914-737-4542
David Fine, prin. — Fax 737-3253
Woodside ES — 400/PK-1
980 Depew St 10566 — 914-739-0093
Staci Woodley, prin. — Fax 737-9039

Our Lady of the Assumption S — 300/PK-K, 2-8
920 1st St 10566 — 914-737-0680
Sr. M. Ann Michael, prin. — Fax 737-1322

Pelham, Westchester, Pop. 6,364
Pelham UFD — 2,700/K-12
18 Franklin Pl 10803 — 914-738-3434
Dr. Dennis Lauro, supt. — Fax 738-7223
www.pelhamschools.org
Colonial ES — 300/K-5
315 Highbrook Ave 10803 — 914-738-2680
Dr. Janet Rothstein, prin. — Fax 738-8187
Hutchinson ES — 400/K-5
301 Third Ave 10803 — 914-738-3640
Carla Tarazi, prin. — Fax 738-8198
Pelham MS — 600/6-8
28 Franklin Pl 10803 — 914-738-8190
Joseph Longobardi, prin. — Fax 738-8132

Prospect Hill ES — 300/K-5
1000 Washington Ave 10803 — 914-738-6690
Dr. Richard Limato, prin. — Fax 738-8258
Siwanoy ES — 300/K-5
489 Siwanoy Pl 10803 — 914-738-7650
Susan Gilbert, prin. — Fax 738-8199

Our Lady of Perpetual Help S — 200/PK-8
575 Fowler Ave 10803 — 914-738-5158
Susan Cotronei, prin. — Fax 738-8974

Penfield, Monroe, Pop. 30,219
Penfield Central SD — 4,800/K-12
PO Box 900 14526 — 585-249-5700
John Carlevatti, supt. — Fax 248-8412
www.penfield.edu
Bay Trail MS — 1,200/6-8
1760 Scribner Rd 14526 — 585-249-6450
Winton Buddington, prin. — Fax 248-0735
Cobbles ES — 500/K-5
140 Gebhardt Rd 14526 — 585-249-6500
Donald Bavis, prin. — Fax 248-2108
Harris Hill ES — 500/K-5
2126 Penfield Rd 14526 — 585-249-6600
Marc Nelson, prin. — Fax 377-9485
Scribner Road ES — 500/K-5
1750 Scribner Rd 14526 — 585-249-6400
Dr. Mark Miele, prin. — Fax 248-9176
Other Schools – See Rochester

St. Joseph S — 400/PK-6
39 Gebhardt Rd 14526 — 585-586-6968
Sr. Christina Luczynski, prin. — Fax 586-4619

Penn Yan, Yates, Pop. 5,170
Penn Yan Central SD — 1,900/PK-12
1 School Dr 14527 — 315-536-3371
Ann Orman, supt. — Fax 536-0068
www.pycsd.org
Penn Yan ES — 800/PK-5
3 School Dr 14527 — 315-536-3346
Ed Bronson, prin. — Fax 536-7162
Penn Yan MS — 500/6-8
515 Liberty St 14527 — 315-536-3366
David Pullen, prin. — Fax 536-7769

St. Michael S — 100/PK-5
214 Keuka St 14527 — 315-536-6112
Dr. James Tette, prin. — Fax 536-6112

Perry, Wyoming, Pop. 3,792
Perry Central SD — 1,000/PK-12
33 Watkins Ave 14530 — 585-237-0270
Edward Stores, supt. — Fax 237-6172
www.perry.k12.ny.us
Perry ES — 400/PK-4
50 Olin Ave 14530 — 585-237-0270
Stephen Haynes, prin. — Fax 237-3483
Perry MS — 300/5-8
50 Olin Ave 14530 — 585-237-0270
Katherine Waite, prin. — Fax 237-3483

Peru, Clinton, Pop. 1,565
Peru Central SD — 2,100/K-12
PO Box 68 12972 — 518-643-6000
A. Paul Scott, supt. — Fax 643-2043
www.peru.com
Peru IS — 500/3-5
PO Box 68 12972 — 518-643-6200
Scott Storms, prin. — Fax 643-6212
Peru MS — 500/6-8
PO Box 68 12972 — 518-643-6300
Cheryl Felt, prin. — Fax 643-6313
Peru PS — 500/K-2
PO Box 68 12972 — 518-643-6100
Chris Angevine, prin. — Fax 643-6126

Philadelphia, Jefferson, Pop. 1,560
Indian River Central SD — 3,500/K-12
32735 County Route 29 Ste B 13673 — 315-642-3441
James Kettrick, supt. — Fax 642-3738
www.ircsd.org/
Indian River IS — 500/4-5
32430 US Route 11 13673 — 315-642-0405
Lana Taylor, prin.
Indian River MS — 800/6-8
32735 County Route 29 13673 — 315-642-0125
Nancy Taylor-Schmitt, prin. — Fax 642-0802
Philadelphia PS — 200/K-3
3 Sand St 13673 — 315-642-3432
Michael Bashaw, prin. — Fax 642-5650
Other Schools – See Antwerp, Calcium, Evans Mills, Theresa

Phoenicia, Ulster
Onteora Central SD
Supt. — See Boiceville
Phoenicia ES — 200/K-6
PO Box 599 12464 — 845-688-5580
Linda Sella, prin. — Fax 688-2324

Phoenix, Oswego, Pop. 2,198
Phoenix Central SD — 2,300/K-12
116 Volney St 13135 — 315-695-1555
Rita Racette, supt. — Fax 695-1201
www.phoenix.k12.ny.us
Dillon MS — 500/6-8
116 Volney St 13135 — 315-695-1521
Susan Anderson, prin. — Fax 695-1523
Maroun ES — 1,000/K-5
11 Elm St 13135 — 315-695-1561
Mary Stanton, prin. — Fax 695-1528

Piermont, Rockland, Pop. 2,598
South Orangetown Central SD
Supt. — See Blauvelt
Tappan Zee ES — 500/2-3
561 Route 9W 10968 — 845-680-1400
Mark Soss, prin. — Fax 680-1930

Pine Bush, Orange, Pop. 1,445
Pine Bush Central SD — 6,100/K-12
PO Box 700 12566 — 845-744-2031
Philip Steinberg, supt. — Fax 744-6189
www.pinebushschools.org
Crispell MS — 800/6-8
PO Box 780 12566 — 845-744-2031
John Boyle, prin. — Fax 744-2261
Pine Bush ES — 800/K-5
PO Box 899 12566 — 845-744-2031
Steven Fisch, prin. — Fax 744-8092
Russell ES — 700/K-5
PO Box 730 12566 — 845-744-2031
Lisa Burnside, prin. — Fax 744-3308
Other Schools – See Circleville

AEF Chapel Field S — 200/K-12
211 Fleury Rd 12566 — 845-778-1881
Fax 778-5841

Pine City, Chemung
Elmira CSD
Supt. — See Elmira
Pine City ES — 400/PK-5
1551 Pennsylvania Ave 14871 — 607-735-3800
Rhonda Baran, prin. — Fax 735-3809

Pine Island, Orange
Warwick Valley Central SD
Supt. — See Warwick
Pine Island ES — 200/K-5
20 Schoolhouse Rd 10969 — 845-987-3190
Jane Hamburger, prin. — Fax 258-1914

Pine Plains, Dutchess, Pop. 1,312
Pine Plains Central SD — 1,200/K-12
2829 Church St 12567 — 518-398-7181
Linda Kaumeyer, supt. — Fax 398-6592
www.pineplainsschools.org
Smith ES — 300/K-5
41 Academy St 12567 — 518-398-3000
Richard Azoff, prin. — Fax 398-6592
Stissing Mountain MS — 300/6-8
2829 Church St 12567 — 518-398-7181
Robert Hess, prin. — Fax 398-6592
Other Schools – See Stanfordville

Piseco, Hamilton
Piseco Common SD — 50/PK-6
PO Box 7 12139 — 518-548-7555
Peter Hallock, supt. — Fax 548-5310
Piseco ES — 50/PK-6
PO Box 7 12139 — 518-548-7555
Peter Hallock, prin. — Fax 548-5310

Pittsford, Monroe, Pop. 1,352
Pittsford Central SD — 5,300/K-12
42 W Jefferson Rd 14534 — 585-267-1000
Mary Alice Price, supt. — Fax 267-1088
www.pittsfordschools.org
Barker Road MS — 700/6-8
75 Barker Rd 14534 — 585-267-1800
Michael Pero, prin. — Fax 385-5960
Calkins Road MS — 6-8
1899 Calkins Rd 14534 — 585-267-1900
Scott Reinhart, prin. — Fax 264-0053
Jefferson Road ES — 400/K-5
15 School Ln 14534 — 585-267-1300
Carole Schwab, prin. — Fax 385-6426
Mendon Center ES — 800/K-5
110 Mendon Center Rd 14534 — 585-267-1400
Melanie Ward, prin. — Fax 218-1430
Park Road ES — 500/K-5
50 Park Rd 14534 — 585-267-1500
Debbie Rose, prin. — Fax 385-6356
Thornell Road ES — 500/K-5
431 Thornell Rd 14534 — 585-267-1700
Michael Doughty, prin. — Fax 385-2099
Other Schools – See Rochester

St. Louis S — 400/PK-6
11 Rand Pl 14534 — 585-586-5200
Kathleen Carroll, prin. — Fax 586-4561

Plainview, Nassau, Pop. 25,600
Bethpage UFD
Supt. — See Bethpage
Kramer ES — 300/K-5
1 Kramer Ln 11803 — 516-644-4500
Frank Cicione, prin. — Fax 933-9819

Plainview-Old Bethpage Central SD — 5,100/K-12
106 Washington Ave 11803 — 516-937-6301
Gerard Dempsey, supt. — Fax 937-6303
www.pob.k12.ny.us/
Mattlin MS — 800/5-8
100 Washington Ave 11803 — 516-937-6393
Dean Mittleman, prin. — Fax 937-6431
Parkway ES — 300/1-4
300 Manetto Hill Rd 11803 — 516-349-4778
Ronelle Hershkowitz, prin. — Fax 349-4780
Pasadena ES — 400/1-4
3 Richard Ct 11803 — 516-937-2785
Paulette Miller, prin. — Fax 937-7291
Plainview-Old Bethpage K — 400/K-K
33 Bedford Rd 11803 — 516-937-6356
Francine Leiboff, prin. — Fax 937-6347
Plainview-Old Bethpage MS — 800/5-8
121 Central Park Rd 11803 — 516-349-4750
John McNamara, prin. — Fax 349-4777
Stratford Road ES — 400/1-4
33 Bedford Rd 11803 — 516-937-6333
Alison Clark, prin. — Fax 937-6347
Other Schools – See Old Bethpage

Syosset Central SD
Supt. — See Syosset
Baylis ES, 580 Woodbury Rd 11803 — 400/K-5
Dr. Sharyn Goodman, prin. — 516-364-5798

Good Shepherd Lutheran K 100/PK-K
99 Central Park Rd 11803 516-349-1966
Judy Hinsch, dir. Fax 349-8434
Hebrew Academy of Nassau County 200/PK-6
25 Country Dr 11803 516-681-5922
Rabbi Kalman Fogel, prin. Fax 681-8351

Plattekill, Ulster
Wallkill Central SD
Supt. — See Wallkill
Plattekill ES 600/K-6
Route 32 12568 845-895-7250
Lou Pietrogallo, prin. Fax 564-5103

Plattsburgh, Clinton, Pop. 19,181
Beekmantown Central SD
Supt. — See West Chazy
Beekmantown ES 500/PK-5
6944 Route 22 12901 518-563-8035
Sandra Gardner, prin. Fax 563-8087
Beekmantown MS 500/6-8
6944 Route 22 12901 518-563-8690
Sue Coonrod, prin. Fax 563-8691
Cumberland Head ES 500/PK-5
1187 Cumberland Head Rd 12901 518-563-8321
Diane Fox, prin. Fax 563-8343

Plattsburgh CSD 2,000/PK-12
49 Broad St 12901 518-957-6002
James Short, supt. Fax 561-6605
www.plattscsd.org/
Bailey Avenue ES 200/K-2
50 Bailey Ave 12901 518-563-2410
Diane Thompson, prin. Fax 566-7663
Momot ES 500/PK-5
60 Monty St 12901 518-563-1140
Mary Lamberti, prin. Fax 566-7739
Oak Street IS 200/3-5
108 Oak St 12901 518-563-4950
Carrie Zales, prin. Fax 561-5828
Stafford MS 400/6-8
15 Broad St 12901 518-563-6800
Patricia Amo, prin. Fax 563-8520

New Life Christian Academy 50/K-10
164 Prospect Ave 12901 518-563-2842
Rev. James Miller, admin. Fax 563-8331
Seton Academy 200/PK-6
23 St Charles St 12901 518-825-7386
Sr. Helen Hermann, prin. Fax 563-4553

Pleasant Valley, Dutchess, Pop. 1,688
Arlington Central SD
Supt. — See Poughkeepsie
Traver Road PS 400/K-2
801 Traver Rd 12569 845-486-4300
Micah Brown, prin. Fax 635-4316
West Road/D'Aquanni IS 400/3-5
181 West Rd 12569 845-635-4310
Heather Ogborn, prin. Fax 635-4317

Pleasantville, Westchester, Pop. 7,130
Pleasantville UFD 1,800/K-12
60 Romer Ave 10570 914-741-1400
Dr. Donald Antonecchia, supt. Fax 741-1499
www.pleasantvilleschools.com
Bedford Road PS 700/K-4
289 Bedford Rd 10570 914-741-1440
Margaret Galotti, prin. Fax 741-1468
Pleasantville MS 500/5-8
40 Romer Ave 10570 914-741-1450
Vivian Ossowski, prin. Fax 741-1476

Poestenkill, Rensselaer, Pop. 1,000
Averill Park Central SD
Supt. — See Averill Park
Poestenkill ES 400/K-5
1 School Rd 12140 518-674-7125
Peter DeWitt, prin. Fax 286-1971

Poland, Herkimer, Pop. 449
Poland Central SD 800/PK-12
74 Cold Brook St 13431 315-826-0203
Laura Dutton, supt. Fax 826-7516
www.polandcs.org
Poland ES 400/PK-6
74 Cold Brook St 13431 315-826-7000
John Banek, prin. Fax 826-7516

Pomona, Rockland, Pop. 2,945

Bais Yaakov Chofetz Chaim of Pomona 400/PK-8
PO Box 704 10970 845-362-3166

Port Byron, Cayuga, Pop. 1,268
Port Byron Central SD 800/K-12
30 Maple Ave 13140 315-776-5728
Neil O'Brien, supt. Fax 776-4050
portbyron.cnyric.org/
Gates ES 400/K-6
30 Maple Ave 13140 315-776-5731
Mitchell Toleson, prin. Fax 776-4050

Port Chester, Westchester, Pop. 27,886
Port Chester-Rye UFD
Supt. — See Rye Brook
Edison ES 400/K-5
132 Rectory St 10573 914-934-7980
Dr. Eileen Santiago, prin. Fax 934-7879
Kennedy ES 600/K-5
40 Olivia St 10573 914-934-7990
Louis Cuglietto, prin. Fax 939-6625
King Street ES 400/K-5
697 King St 10573 914-934-7995
Dolores Obuch, prin. Fax 939-9351
Park Avenue ES 400/K-5
75 Park Ave 10573 914-934-7895
Rosa Taylor, prin. Fax 939-9243
Port Chester MS 800/6-8
113 Bowman Ave 10573 914-934-7930
Carmen Macchia, prin. Fax 934-7886

Corpus Christi S 200/PK-8
135 S Regent St 10573 914-937-4407
Sr. Agatha Cosentino, prin. Fax 937-6904
Holy Rosary S 200/PK-8
21 Central Ave 10573 914-939-1021
MaryEve Norelli, prin. Fax 939-7127

Port Ewen, Ulster, Pop. 3,444
Kingston CSD
Supt. — See Kingston
Graves ES 300/K-5
345 Mountain View Ave 12466 845-338-1945
Errin Parese, prin. Fax 338-3049

Port Henry, Essex, Pop. 1,089
Moriah Central SD 800/PK-12
39 Viking Ln 12974 518-546-3301
William Larrow, supt. Fax 546-7895
www.moriahk12.org/
Moriah ES 400/PK-6
39 Viking Ln 12974 518-546-3301
Valerie Stahl, prin. Fax 546-7895

Port Jefferson, Suffolk, Pop. 7,935
Port Jefferson UFD 1,300/PK-12
550 Scraggy Hill Rd 11777 631-476-4404
Dr. Max Riley, supt. Fax 476-4409
www.portjeff.k12.ny.us
Port Jefferson MS 300/6-8
350 Old Post Rd 11777 631-474-4440
Roseann Cirnigliaro, prin. Fax 476-4430
Spear ES 700/PK-5
500 Scraggy Hill Rd 11777 631-476-4420
Lynn Burke, prin. Fax 476-4419

Our Lady of Wisdom S 200/K-8
114 Myrtle Ave 11777 631-473-1211
Dorothy Onysko, prin. Fax 473-1064

Port Jefferson Station, See Port Jefferson
Comsewogue SD 4,100/K-12
290 Norwood Ave 11776 631-474-8105
Dr. Shelley Saffer, supt. Fax 474-3568
www.comsewogue.k12.ny.us
Boyle Road ES 500/K-5
424 Boyle Rd 11776 631-474-8140
Jennifer Polychronakos, prin. Fax 474-8498
Clinton Avenue ES 400/K-5
140 Clinton Ave 11776 631-474-8150
Toni Bifalco, prin. Fax 474-8499
Kennedy MS 1,000/6-8
200 Jayne Blvd 11776 631-474-8160
Michael Fama, prin. Fax 474-8176
Norwood Avenue ES 300/K-5
290 Norwood Ave 11776 631-474-8130
Leah Anesta, prin. Fax 474-3568
Terryville Road ES 500/K-5
401 Terryville Rd 11776 631-474-2834
April Victor, prin. Fax 474-2846

North Shore Christian S 200/PK-8
324 Jayne Blvd 11776 631-473-2222
Paul Peterson, prin. Fax 474-2816

Port Jervis, Orange, Pop. 9,202
Port Jervis CSD 3,200/K-12
9 Thompson St 12771 845-858-3175
John Xanthis, supt. Fax 856-1885
www.pjschools.org/
Kuhl ES 1,000/K-6
10 Route 209 12771 845-858-3135
John Solimando, prin. Fax 858-2894
Port Jervis MS 500/7-8
118 E Main St 12771 845-858-3148
Cynthia Benedict, prin. Fax 858-2893
Other Schools – See Cuddebackville

Port Leyden, Lewis, Pop. 624
South Lewis Central SD
Supt. — See Turin
Port Leyden ES 200/K-5
PO Box 68 13433 315-348-2660
Kristy McGrath, prin. Fax 348-2570

Portville, Cattaraugus, Pop. 994
Portville Central SD 900/K-12
500 Elm St 14770 585-933-7141
Thomas Simon Ph.D., supt. Fax 933-7161
www.portville.wnyric.org/
Portville ES 500/K-6
500 Elm St 14770 585-933-6001
Charles Hild, prin. Fax 933-7161

Port Washington, Nassau, Pop. 15,387
Port Washington UFD 4,900/K-12
100 Campus Dr 11050 516-767-5000
Dr. Geoffrey Gordon, supt. Fax 767-5007
www.portnet.k12.ny.us
Daly ES 400/K-5
36 Rockwood Ave 11050 516-767-5200
Elaine Ajello, prin. Fax 767-5207
Guggenheim ES 500/K-5
38 Poplar Pl 11050 516-767-5250
Barbara Giebel, prin. Fax 767-5257
Manorhaven ES 400/K-5
12 Morewood Oaks 11050 516-767-5300
Bonni Cohen, prin. Fax 767-5303
Sousa ES 500/K-5
101 Sands Point Rd 11050 516-767-5350
Dr. David Meoli, prin. Fax 767-5356
South Salem ES 400/K-5
10 Newbury Rd 11050 516-767-5400
Christopher Shields, prin. Fax 767-5407
Weber MS 1,100/6-8
Port Washington Blvd 11050 516-767-5500
Marilyn Rodahan, prin. Fax 767-5507

St. Peter of Alcantara S 300/PK-8
1321 Port Washington Blvd 11050 516-944-3772
Sean O'Connell, prin. Fax 767-8075
Schwartz Torah Academy 100/PK-8
80 Shore Rd 11050 516-767-8672
Robyn Mandor, hdmstr. Fax 767-8673

Potsdam, Saint Lawrence, Pop. 9,705
Potsdam Central SD 1,400/PK-12
29 Leroy St 13676 315-265-2000
Patrick Brady, supt. Fax 265-2048
www.potsdam.k12.ny.us
Kingston MS 400/5-8
29 Leroy St 13676 315-265-2000
James Cruikshank, prin. Fax 265-8103
Lawrence Avenue ES 500/PK-4
29 Leroy St 13676 315-265-2000
Larry Jenne, prin. Fax 265-5458

Poughkeepsie, Dutchess, Pop. 30,355
Arlington Central SD 10,300/K-12
696 Dutchess Tpke Ste J 12603 845-486-4460
Frank Pepe, supt. Fax 486-4457
www.arlingtonschools.org
Arlington MS 600/6-8
601 Dutchess Tpke 12603 845-486-4480
Brendan Lyons, prin. Fax 486-4446
May ES 500/K-5
25 Raymond Ave 12603 845-486-4960
Emily Gorton, prin. Fax 486-4777
Noxon Road ES 400/K-5
4 Old Noxon Rd 12603 845-486-4950
Linda Roy, prin. Fax 486-4774
Overlook ES 400/K-2
11 Mapleview Rd 12603 845-486-4970
Brady Fister, prin. Fax 486-7792
Titusville IS 500/3-5
128 Meadow Ln 12603 845-486-4470
Daniel Shornstein, prin. Fax 486-4475
Other Schools – See Lagrangeville, Pleasant Valley, Poughquag

Hyde Park Central SD
Supt. — See Hyde Park
Violet Avenue ES 400/K-5
191 Violet Ave 12601 845-486-4499
Aviva Kafka, prin. Fax 486-7796

Poughkeepsie CSD 4,400/K-12
11 College Ave 12603 845-451-4900
Dr. Laval Wilson, supt. Fax 451-4955
www.poughkeepsieschools.org/
Clinton ES 400/K-5
100 Montgomery St 12601 845-451-4600
Nadine Jackson-Ivey, prin. Fax 451-4614
Columbus ES 300/K-5
18 S Perry St 12601 845-451-4630
Thomas Hartford, prin. Fax 451-4655
Krieger ES 500/K-5
265 Hooker Ave 12603 845-451-4660
Sam Letterii, prin. Fax 451-4672
Morse Young Child Magnet ES 400/K-2
101 Mansion St 12601 845-451-4690
Ronel Cook, prin. Fax 451-4711
Poughkeepsie MS 900/6-8
55 College Ave 12603 845-451-4800
Edgar Glascott, prin. Fax 451-4836
Smith ES 200/3-5
372 Church St 12601 845-471-4720
Nadine Straughn, prin. Fax 451-4741
Warring Magnet Academy of Sci & Tech ES 400/K-5
283 Mansion St 12601 845-451-4750
Lisa Thompson, prin. Fax 451-4769

Spackenkill UFD 1,800/K-12
15 Croft Rd 12603 845-463-7800
Dr. Lois Powell, supt. Fax 463-7804
www.dcboces.org/sufsd/
Hagan ES 500/K-5
42 Hagan Dr 12603 845-463-7840
Eileen Sicina, prin. Fax 463-7804
Nassau ES 200/K-5
7 Nassau Rd 12601 845-463-7843
Barbara.Craft-Reiss, prin. Fax 462-1109
Todd MS 400/6-8
11 Croft Rd 12603 845-463-7830
Steven Malkischer, prin. Fax 462-1109

Wappingers Central SD
Supt. — See Wappingers Falls
Kinry Road ES 500/4-6
58 Kinry Rd 12603 845-463-7322
John Farrell, prin. Fax 463-7327
Oak Grove ES 500/K-5
40 Kerr Rd 12601 845-298-5280
Angelina Alvarez-Rooney, prin. Fax 298-5270
Vassar Road ES 400/K-3
174 Vassar Rd 12603 845-463-7860
Frank Annis, prin. Fax 463-7859

Faith Christian Academy 200/PK-9
254 Spackenkill Rd 12603 845-462-0266
Wendy Wright, admin. Fax 462-1561
Holy Trinity S 200/PK-8
20 Springside Ave 12603 845-471-0520
Mary Ann McGivney, prin. Fax 471-0309
Poughkeepsie Day S 400/PK-12
260 Boardman Rd 12603 845-462-7600
Josie Holford, hdmstr. Fax 462-7603
Poughkeepsie SDA S 50/PK-8
71 Mitchell Ave 12603 845-454-1781
Andrea Hanson, prin. Fax 790-5223
St. Martin DePorres S 300/PK-8
122 Cedar Valley Rd 12603 845-452-4428
Kathy Leahy, prin. Fax 473-4223

St. Peter S — 100/PK-8
12 Father Cody Dr 12601 — 845-452-8580
Susan Roach, prin. — Fax 454-1674
Tabernacle Christian Academy — 200/K-12
155 Academy St 12601 — 845-454-2792
Timothy Hostetter, prin. — Fax 483-0926

Poughquag, Dutchess
Arlington Central SD
Supt. — See Poughkeepsie
Beekman ES — 600/K-5
201 Lime Ridge Rd 12570 — 845-227-1834
Duane Ragucci, prin. — Fax 227-1822

Pound Ridge, Westchester
Bedford Central SD
Supt. — See Bedford
Pound Ridge ES — 400/K-5
7 Pound Ridge Rd 10576 — 914-764-8133
Peter Politi, prin. — Fax 764-4009

Prattsburgh, Steuben
Prattsburg Central SD — 500/PK-12
1 Academy St 14873 — 607-522-3795
Jeffrey Black, supt. — Fax 522-6221
Prattsburg Central S — 500/PK-12
1 Academy St 14873 — 607-522-3795
Jeffrey Black, prin. — Fax 522-6221

Pulaski, Oswego, Pop. 2,345
Pulaski Central SD — 1,200/K-12
2 Hinman Rd 13142 — 315-298-5188
Dr. Marshall Marshall, supt. — Fax 298-4390
www.pacs.cnyric.org
Sharp ES — 600/K-6
2 Hinman Rd 13142 — 315-298-2412
Jean Lynch, prin. — Fax 298-7464

Providence Christian S — 50/K-8
5353 US Route 11 13142 — 315-387-3057
Richard Van Dyke, pres.

Purchase, See Harrison
Harrison Central SD
Supt. — See Harrison
Purchase ES — 500/K-5
2995 Purchase St 10577 — 914-630-3172
Robert Kalman, prin. — Fax 946-0286

Putnam Station, Washington
Putnam Central SD — 50/PK-6
126 County Route 2 12861 — 518-547-8266
Matthew Boucher, supt. — Fax 547-8266
putnamcs.neric.org/
Putnam Central ES — 50/PK-6
126 County Route 2 12861 — 518-547-8266
Matthew Boucher, prin. — Fax 547-8266

Putnam Valley, Putnam
Putnam Valley Central SD — 1,900/K-12
146 Peekskill Hollow Rd 10579 — 845-528-8143
Marc Space, supt. — Fax 528-0274
www.putnamvalleyschools.org
Putnam Valley ES — 700/K-4
171 Oscawana Lake Rd 10579 — 845-528-8092
Jamie Edelman, prin. — Fax 528-8171
Putnam Valley MS — 600/5-8
142 Peekskill Hollow Rd 10579 — 845-528-8101
Edward Hallisey, prin. — Fax 528-8145

Queensbury, Warren
Queensbury UFD — 3,900/K-12
429 Aviation Rd 12804 — 518-824-5600
Douglas Huntley, supt. — Fax 793-4476
www.queensburyschool.org/
Barton IS — 600/4-5
425 Aviation Rd 12804 — 518-824-2609
Kyle Gannon, prin. — Fax 824-2681
Queensbury ES — 1,100/K-3
431 Aviation Rd 12804 — 518-824-1604
Patrick Pomerville, prin. — Fax 824-1680
Queensbury MS — 900/6-8
455 Aviation Rd 12804 — 518-824-3610
Douglas Silvernell, prin. — Fax 824-3682

Queens Village, See New York
NYC Department of Education
Supt. — See New York
Public S 18 — 500/PK-5
8635 235th Ct 11427 — 718-464-4167
Kathleen Peknic, prin. — Fax 464-4273
Public S 33 — 1,100/K-5
9137 222nd St 11428 — 718-465-6283
Erich Wagner, prin. — Fax 464-7588
Public S 34 — 500/PK-5
10412 Springfield Blvd 11429 — 718-465-6818
Pauline Shakespeare, prin. — Fax 464-9073
Public S 135 — 1,200/K-5
20711 89th Ave 11427 — 718-464-2119
George Hadjoglou, prin. — Fax 464-8448
Public S 295 — PK-8
22214 Jamaica Ave 11428 — 718-464-1433
Angela Thompson, prin.
IS 109 — 1,500/6-8
21310 92nd Ave 11428 — 718-465-0651
Miatheresa Alexander, prin. — Fax 264-1246

Grace Lutheran S — 100/K-8
10005 Springfield Blvd 11429 — 718-465-1010
Dr. LuJuanna Butts, prin. — Fax 465-9069
Incarnation S — 300/K-8
8915 Francis Lewis Blvd 11427 — 718-465-5066
Sati Marchan, prin. — Fax 464-4128
Our Lady of Lourdes S — 400/PK-8
9280 220th St 11428 — 718-464-1480
Sr. Josephine Barbiere, prin. — Fax 740-4091
SS. Joachim & Anne S — 500/PK-8
21819 105th Ave 11429 — 718-465-2230
Linda Freebes, prin. — Fax 468-5698

Quogue, Suffolk, Pop. 1,116
Quogue UFD — 100/PK-6
PO Box 957 11959 — 631-653-4285
Richard Benson, supt. — Fax 996-4600
www.quogueschool.com
Quogue ES — 100/PK-6
PO Box 957 11959 — 631-653-4285
Richard Benson, prin. — Fax 996-4600

Randolph, Cattaraugus, Pop. 1,266
Randolph Central SD — 1,000/PK-12
18 Main St 14772 — 716-358-7005
Kimberly Moritz, supt. — Fax 358-7072
www.randolphcsd.org/
Chapman ES — 400/PK-4
22 Main St 14772 — 716-358-7030
Jerry Mottern, prin. — Fax 358-7060
Randolph MS — 300/5-8
22 Main St 14772 — 716-358-7028
William Caldwell, prin. — Fax 358-7060

Ransomville, Niagara, Pop. 1,542
Wilson Central SD
Supt. — See Wilson
Stevenson ES — 300/K-5
3745 Ransomville Rd 14131 — 716-751-9341
Michael Cancilla, prin. — Fax 791-8043

Raquette Lake, Hamilton
Raquette Lake UFD — K-6
PO Box 10 13436 — 315-354-4733
Peter Hallock, supt. — Fax 354-4144
Raquette Lake ES — K-6
PO Box 10 13436 — 315-354-4733
Peter Hallock, prin. — Fax 354-4144

Ravena, Albany, Pop. 3,323
Ravena-Coeymans-Selkirk Central SD
Supt. — See Selkirk
Ravena-Coeymans-Selkirk MS — 500/5-8
2025 US Route 9W 12143 — 518-756-5200
Pam Black, prin. — Fax 756-1988

Red Creek, Wayne, Pop. 503
Red Creek Central SD — 1,000/K-12
PO Box 190 13143 — 315-754-2010
David Sholes, supt. — Fax 754-8169
www.rccsd.org
Cuyler ES — 400/K-5
PO Box 190 13143 — 315-754-2100
Lynda Sereno, prin. — Fax 754-2192
Red Creek MS — 200/6-8
PO Box 190 13143 — 315-754-2070
Randall Lawrence, prin. — Fax 754-2077

Red Hook, Dutchess, Pop. 1,825
Red Hook Central SD — 2,300/K-12
7401 S Broadway 12571 — 845-758-2241
Paul Finch Ed.D., supt. — Fax 758-3366
www.redhookcentralschools.org/
Linden Avenue MS — 600/6-8
65 W Market St 12571 — 845-758-2241
Steven Chaikin, prin. — Fax 758-0688
Mill Road ES — 500/K-2
9 Mill Rd 12571 — 845-758-2241
Donna Gaynor, prin. — Fax 758-0385
Mill Road IS — 500/3-5
9 Mill Rd 12571 — 845-758-2241
Brian Boyd, prin. — Fax 758-0289

Rego Park, See New York
NYC Department of Education
Supt. — See New York
Public S 139 — 700/K-6
9306 63rd Dr 11374 — 718-459-1044
Monica Powers-Meade, prin. — Fax 997-8639
Public S 174 — 500/PK-6
6510 Dieterle Cres 11374 — 718-897-7006
Karin Kelly, prin. — Fax 897-7254
Public S 175 — 600/PK-5
6435 102nd St 11374 — 718-897-8600
Linda Green, prin. — Fax 997-8644
Public S 206 — 600/PK-5
6121 97th Pl 11374 — 718-592-0300
Nicholas Bologna, prin. — Fax 271-7011

Our Lady of the Angelus S — 200/PK-8
9805 63rd Dr 11374 — 718-896-7220
Joan Armstrong, prin. — Fax 896-5723
Our Saviour Lutheran S — 100/PK-8
6433 Woodhaven Blvd 11374 — 718-897-4343
Debra Niebling, prin. — Fax 830-9275
Resurrection-Ascension S — 300/PK-8
8525 61st Rd 11374 — 718-426-4963
JoAnn Heppt, prin. — Fax 426-0940

Remsen, Oneida, Pop. 522
Remsen Central SD — 500/K-12
PO Box 406 13438 — 315-831-3797
Ann Turner, supt. — Fax 831-2172
www.remsencsd.org/
Remsen ES — 200/K-6
PO Box 406 13438 — 315-831-3797
Ann Turner, prin. — Fax 831-2172

Remsenburg, Suffolk, Pop. 1,851
Remsenburg-Speonk UFD — 200/K-6
PO Box 900 11960 — 631-325-0203
Dr. Katherine Salomone, supt. — Fax 325-8439
www.rsufsd.org
Remsenburg-Speonk ES — 200/K-6
PO Box 900 11960 — 631-325-0203
Dr. Katherine Salomone, prin. — Fax 325-8439

Rensselaer, Rensselaer, Pop. 7,859
East Greenbush Central SD
Supt. — See East Greenbush
Red Mill ES — 400/K-5
225 McCullough Pl 12144 — 518-449-2475
John Caporta, prin. — Fax 449-2480

North Greenbush Common SD — 50/K-2
476 N Greenbush Rd 12144 — 518-283-6748
Joseph Padalino, supt.
Other Schools – See Troy

Rensselaer CSD — 1,100/PK-12
25 Van Rensselaer Dr 12144 — 518-465-7509
Gordon Reynolds, supt. — Fax 436-0479
www.rcsd.k12.ny.us
Rensselaer MS — 200/6-8
25 Van Rensselaer Dr 12144 — 518-436-8561
Karen Urbanski, prin. — Fax 436-8566
Van Rensselaer ES — 500/PK-5
25 Van Rensselaer Dr 12144 — 518-436-4618
Sally Shields, prin. — Fax 436-4692

Woodland Hill Montessori S — 200/PK-8
100 Montessori Pl 12144 — 518-283-5400
Susan Kambrich, hdmstr. — Fax 283-4861

Retsof, Livingston
York Central SD — 700/K-12
PO Box 102 14539 — 585-243-1730
Thomas Manko, supt. — Fax 243-5269
www.yorkcsd.org/
York Central ES — 300/K-5
PO Box 102 14539 — 585-243-1730
Tracie Czebatol, prin. — Fax 243-5269

Rexford, Saratoga
Niskayuna Central SD
Supt. — See Schenectady
Glencliff ES — 300/K-5
961 Riverview Rd 12148 — 518-399-2323
Frances Reinl, prin. — Fax 399-4072

Rhinebeck, Dutchess, Pop. 3,126
Rhinebeck Central SD — 1,200/K-12
PO Box 351 12572 — 845-871-5520
Joseph Phelan, supt. — Fax 876-4276
www.rhinebeckcsd.org/
Bulkeley MS — 300/6-8
PO Box 351 12572 — 845-871-5500
John Kemnitzer, prin. — Fax 871-5553
Livingston ES — 500/K-5
PO Box 351 12572 — 845-871-5570
Brett King, prin. — Fax 876-4174

Richburg, Allegany, Pop. 437
Bolivar-Richburg Central SD
Supt. — See Bolivar
Bolivar-Richburg ES — 400/K-5
PO Box 158 14774 — 585-928-1380
Michael Schott, prin. — Fax 928-2362

Richfield Springs, Otsego, Pop. 1,194
Richfield Springs Central SD — 600/K-12
PO Box 631 13439 — 315-858-0610
Robert Barraco, supt. — Fax 858-2440
www.richfieldcsd.org
Richfield Springs Central S — 600/K-12
PO Box 631 13439 — 315-858-0610
Penny Harrington, prin. — Fax 858-2440

Richmond Hill, See New York
NYC Department of Education
Supt. — See New York
Public S 51 — 300/PK-1
8745 117th St 11418 — 718-850-0738
Magdaly St. Just, prin. — Fax 850-0830
Public S 54 — 500/K-5
8602 127th St 11418 — 718-849-0962
Diane Jones, prin. — Fax 847-4629
Public S 56 — 400/2-5
8610 114th St 11418 — 718-441-4448
Ann Leiter, prin. — Fax 805-1538
Public S 62 — 900/K-5
9725 108th St, S Richmond Hl NY 11419 — 718-849-0992
Angela O'Dowd, prin. — Fax 850-5521
Public S 66 — 400/K-5
8511 102nd St 11418 — 718-849-0184
Phyllis Leinwand, prin. — Fax 846-6889
Public S 90 — 800/PK-5
8650 109th St 11418 — 718-847-3370
Adrienne Ubertini, prin. — Fax 847-2965
Public S 161 — 800/PK-6
10133 124th St, S Richmond Hl NY 11419 — 718-441-5493
Jill Hoder, prin. — Fax 441-6202
Public S 254 — 400/PK-5
8440 101st St 11418 — 718-846-1840
Naomi Drouillard, prin. — Fax 846-7404

Holy Child Jesus S — 400/PK-8
11102 86th Ave 11418 — 718-849-3988
Martin Abruzzo, prin. — Fax 850-2842
St. Benedict Joseph Labre S — 200/PK-8
9425 117th St, S Richmond Hl NY 11419 — 718-441-6674
Mary Mazzella, prin. — Fax 441-4367
Yeshivat Ohr Haiim S — 300/PK-8
8606 135th St 11418 — 718-658-7066

Richmondville, Schoharie, Pop. 798
Cobleskill-Richmondville Central SD
Supt. — See Cobleskill
Radez ES — 400/K-5
319 Main St 12149 — 518-294-6621
Brian Dineen, prin. — Fax 234-3165

Ridge, Suffolk, Pop. 11,734
Longwood Central SD
Supt. — See Middle Island
Ridge ES — 800/K-4
105 Ridge Rd 11961 — 631-345-2765
Janine Rozycki, prin. — Fax 345-9289

Ridgewood, See New York
NYC Department of Education
Supt. — See New York
Learners and Leaders S 100/PK-3
384 Seneca Ave 11385
Lynn Botfeld, prin.
Public S 68 800/PK-5
5909 Saint Felix Ave 11385 718-821-7246
Ann Marie Snadecky, prin. Fax 497-8945
Public S 71 900/K-5
6285 Forest Ave 11385 718-821-7772
Walkydia Olivella, prin. Fax 386-7088
Public S 81 1,100/K-5
559 Cypress Ave 11385 718-821-9800
Genevieve Ventura, prin. Fax 386-7203
Public S 88 900/PK-5
6085 Catalpa Ave 11385 718-821-8121
Linda China, prin. Fax 386-7214
Public S 239 800/PK-5
1715 Weirfield St 11385 718-381-4009
Robin Connolly, prin. Fax 381-0592
IS 77 1,200/6-8
976 Seneca Ave 11385 718-366-7120
Joseph Miller, prin. Fax 456-9512
IS 93 1,300/6-8
6656 Forest Ave 11385 718-821-4882
Edward Santos, prin. Fax 456-9521

Notre Dame Catholic Academy of Ridgewood 300/PK-8
61st St and Bleecker St 11385 718-821-2221
Fax 821-1058
St. Aloysius S 200/K-8
360 Seneca Ave 11385 718-821-7384
Virginia Daly, prin. Fax 821-6854
St. Matthias S 400/PK-8
5825 Catalpa Ave 11385 718-381-8003
Barbara Wehnes, prin. Fax 381-3519

Ripley, Chautauqua, Pop. 1,189
Ripley Central SD 400/PK-12
PO Box 688 14775 716-736-6201
John Hogan, supt. Fax 736-6226
www.ripleycsd.wnyric.org
Ripley Central S 400/PK-12
PO Box 688 14775 716-736-2631
Susan Hammond, prin. Fax 736-6226

Riverdale, See New York

Salanter Akiba Riverdale Academy 800/PK-8
655 W 254th St 10471 718-548-1717
Rabbi Binyamin Krauss, prin. Fax 601-0082

Riverhead, Suffolk, Pop. 8,814
Riverhead Central SD 4,600/K-12
700 Osborn Ave 11901 631-369-6700
Diane Scricca, supt. Fax 369-6816
www.riverhead.net
Phillips Avenue PS 500/K-4
141 Phillips Ave 11901 631-369-6787
Thomas Payton, prin. Fax 369-6833
Pulaski Street MS 700/5-6
300 Pulaski St 11901 631-369-6794
David Densieski, prin. Fax 369-7795
Riverhead MS 700/7-8
600 Harrison Ave 11901 631-369-6759
Andrea Pekar, prin. Fax 369-6829
Roanoke Avenue PS 300/K-4
549 Roanoke Ave 11901 631-369-6813
Debra Rodgers, prin. Fax 369-6830
Other Schools – See Aquebogue, Calverton

St. Isidore S 300/PK-8
515 Marcy Ave 11901 631-727-1650
Sr. Linda Chichi, prin. Fax 727-3945

Rochester, Monroe, Pop. 211,091
Brighton Central SD 3,500/K-12
2035 Monroe Ave 14618 585-242-5080
Harv Peris, supt. Fax 242-5164
www.bcsd.org
Council Rock PS 700/K-2
600 Grosvenor Rd 14610 585-242-5170
Janet Gibbons, prin. Fax 242-5186
French Road ES 800/3-5
488 French Rd 14618 585-242-7526
Tom Hall, prin. Fax 242-5156
Twelve Corners MS 900/6-8
2643 Elmwood Ave 14618 585-242-5100
Rob Thomas, prin. Fax 242-2540

Churchville-Chili Central SD
Supt. — See Churchville
Chestnut Ridge ES 600/K-4
3560 Chili Ave 14624 585-889-2188
Karen Jensen, prin. Fax 293-4512

East Irondequoit Central SD 3,500/K-12
600 Pardee Rd 14609 585-339-1210
Susan Allen, supt. Fax 339-1219
www.eicsd.k12.ny.us/
Durand-Eastman IS 400/3-5
95 Point Pleasant Rd 14622 585-339-1350
Lori Ann Roe, prin. Fax 339-1359
East Irondequoit MS 900/6-8
155 Densmore Rd 14609 585-339-1400
Deborah Decker, prin. Fax 339-1409
Green ES 400/K-2
800 Brown Rd 14622 585-339-1310
Joanne Zito, prin. Fax 339-1319
Helendale Road PS 300/K-2
220 Helendale Rd 14609 585-339-1330
Eric Daniels, prin. Fax 339-1339
Laurelton/Pardee IS 300/3-5
600 Pardee Rd 14609 585-339-1370
Bruce Gorman, prin. Fax 339-1379

Gates-Chili Central SD 4,700/K-12
3 Spartan Way 14624 585-247-5050
Mark Davey, supt. Fax 340-5569
www.gateschili.org
Armstrong ES 500/K-5
3273 Lyell Rd 14606 585-247-3190
LeRoy Greer, prin. Fax 340-5550
Brasser ES 300/K-5
1000 Coldwater Rd 14624 585-247-1880
Timothy Young, prin. Fax 340-5577
Disney ES 500/K-5
175 Coldwater Rd 14624 585-247-3151
Brian Brooks, prin. Fax 340-5567
Gates-Chili MS 1,300/6-8
2 Spartan Way 14624 585-247-5050
Gerard Iuppa, prin. Fax 340-5532
Paul Road ES 400/K-5
571 Paul Rd 14624 585-247-2144
Peter Hens, prin. Fax 340-5571

Greece Central SD 13,300/PK-12
750 Maiden Ln 14615 585-621-1000
Steven Achramovitch, supt. Fax 581-8203
www.greece.k12.ny.us
Apollo MS 900/6-8
750 Maiden Ln 14615 585-966-5200
Linda Pickering, prin. Fax 966-5239
Arcadia MS 900/6-8
130 Island Cottage Rd 14612 585-966-3300
Karen D'Angelo, prin. Fax 966-3339
Athena MS 1,000/6-8
800 Long Pond Rd 14612 585-966-4200
John Rivers, prin. Fax 966-4239
Autumn Lane ES 500/PK-2
2089 Maiden Ln 14626 585-966-4700
Tasha Potter, prin. Fax 966-4739
Buckman Heights ES 300/3-5
500 Buckman Rd 14615 585-966-5900
Valerie Burke, prin. Fax 966-5939
Craig Hill ES 400/3-5
320 W Craig Hill Dr 14626 585-966-4500
Melissa Pacelli, prin. Fax 966-4539
English Village ES 500/PK-2
800 Tait Ave 14616 585-966-3800
Kathy Zodarecky, prin. Fax 966-3839
Holmes Road ES 400/PK-2
300 Holmes Rd 14626 585-966-4900
Charlene Frye, prin. Fax 966-4939
Kirk Road ES 300/3-5
299 Kirk Rd 14612 585-966-4300
Caroline Critchlow, prin. Fax 966-4339
Lakeshore ES 400/PK-2
1200 Latta Rd 14612 585-966-3900
Douglas Pacelli, prin. Fax 966-3939
Longridge ES 800/PK-5
190 Longridge Ave 14616 585-966-5800
Susan Streicher, prin. Fax 966-5839
Paddy Hill ES 400/PK-2
1801 Latta Rd 14612 585-966-3700
Kathleen Graupman, prin. Fax 966-3739
Parkland-Brookside ES 300/PK-2
1010 English Rd 14616 585-966-3600
Lisa Johnson, prin. Fax 966-3639
Parkland-Brookside ES 300/3-5
1144 Long Pond Rd 14626 585-966-4800
Elizabeth Bentley, prin. Fax 966-4839
Pine Brook ES 600/K-5
2300 English Rd 14616 585-966-4600
Elizabeth Boily, prin. Fax 966-4639
West Ridge ES 400/K-5
200 Alcott Rd 14626 585-966-4400
Dr. Mark Balsamo, prin. Fax 966-4439

Penfield Central SD
Supt. — See Penfield
Indian Landing ES 500/K-5
702 Landing Rd N 14625 585-249-6900
Terri Connell, prin. Fax 387-9276

Pittsford Central SD
Supt. — See Pittsford
Allen Creek ES 400/K-5
3188 East Ave 14618 585-267-1200
Michael Biondi, prin. Fax 381-9217

Rochester CSD 30,300/PK-12
131 W Broad St 14614 585-262-8100
Jean-Claude Brizard, supt. Fax 262-5151
www.rcsdk12.org/
Brown Pre-Kindergarten Center PK-PK
595 Upper Falls Blvd 14605 585-288-2410
Rose Urzetta, prin. Fax 654-1089
Public S 1 300/PK-6
85 Hillside Ave 14610 585-473-1533
Kimberly Harris-Pappin, prin. Fax 256-8993
Public S 2 300/PK-6
190 Reynolds St 14608 585-235-2820
Najmah Abdulmateen, prin. Fax 464-6174
Public S 3 700/K-9
85 Adams St 14608 585-454-3525
Connie Wehner, prin. Fax 262-8938
Public S 4 400/K-6
198 Dr Samuel Mccree Way 14611 585-235-7848
Karon Jackson, prin. Fax 464-6194
Public S 5 500/K-6
555 Plymouth Ave N 14608 585-325-2255
Joanne Wideman, prin. Fax 262-8959
Public S 6 300/K-6
595 Upper Falls Blvd 14605 585-546-7780
Miriam Miranda-Jurado, prin. Fax 262-8961
Public S 7 600/PK-6
31 Bryan St 14613 585-254-3110
Wakili Moore, prin. Fax 277-0104
Public S 8 600/PK-6
1180 Saint Paul St 14621 585-262-8888
Jacqueline Cox-Cooper, prin. Fax 262-8990
Public S 9 700/PK-6
485 Clinton Ave N 14605 585-325-7828
Sharon Jackson, prin. Fax 262-8962

Public S 12 700/K-6
999 South Ave 14620 585-461-3280
Michele Liguori-Alampi, prin. Fax 256-8987
Public S 14 400/PK-6
200 University Ave 14605 585-325-6738
Camaron Clyburn, prin. Fax 262-8963
Public S 15 300/K-6
494 Averill Ave 14607 585-262-8830
Patricia Townsend, prin. Fax 262-8834
Public S 16 500/PK-6
321 Post Ave 14619 585-235-1272
Sylvia Cooksey, prin. Fax 464-6188
Public S 17 500/PK-6
158 Orchard St 14611 585-436-2560
Patricia Jones, prin. Fax 464-6100
Public S 19 300/PK-6
465 Seward St 14608 585-328-7454
Anne Brown Scott, prin. Fax 464-6195
Public S 20 300/PK-6
54 Oakman St 14605 585-325-2920
D'Onnarae Johnson, prin. Fax 262-8885
Public S 22 500/PK-6
27 Zimbrich St 14621 585-467-7160
T'Hani Pantoja, prin. Fax 336-5573
Public S 23 300/PK-6
170 Barrington St 14607 585-473-5099
Marlene Blocker, prin. Fax 256-8994
Public S 25 300/PK-6
965 Goodman St N 14609 585-288-3654
Deborah Lazio, prin. Fax 654-1074
Public S 28 600/K-6
450 Humboldt St 14610 585-482-4836
Susan Ladd, prin. Fax 324-2103
Public S 29 400/PK-6
88 Kirkland Rd 14611 585-328-8228
Clinton Strickland, prin. Fax 464-6196
Public S 30 400/K-6
36 Otis St 14606 585-254-3836
Petrina Johnson, prin. Fax 277-0105
Public S 33 1,100/PK-6
690 Saint Paul St 14605 585-482-9290
Larry Ellison, prin. Fax 654-1077
Public S 34 400/K-6
530 Lexington Ave 14613 585-458-3210
Debra Ramsperger, prin. Fax 277-0106
Public S 35 500/K-6
194 Field St 14620 585-271-4583
Robert Kuter, prin. Fax 473-7131
Public S 36 400/PK-6
85 Saint Jacob St 14621 585-342-7270
Paul Montanarello, prin. Fax 336-5574
Public S 39 600/PK-6
145 Midland Ave 14621 585-467-8816
Kevin Klein, prin. Fax 336-5575
Public S 41 600/PK-6
279 Ridge Rd W 14615 585-254-4472
RoShon Bradley, prin. Fax 277-0107
Public S 42 500/PK-6
3330 Lake Ave 14612 585-663-4330
Richard Derose, prin. Fax 621-0276
Public S 43 600/K-6
1305 Lyell Ave 14606 585-458-4200
Anne McAndrew, prin. Fax 277-0102
Public S 44 300/PK-6
820 Chili Ave 14611 585-328-5272
Diana Hernandez, prin. Fax 464-6197
Public S 45 700/PK-6
1445 Clifford Ave 14621 585-325-6945
Shirley Green, prin. Fax 262-8037
Public S 46 400/K-6
250 Newcastle Rd 14610 585-288-8008
Sharon Delly, prin. Fax 654-1078
Public S 50 600/K-6
301 Seneca Ave 14621 585-266-0331
Tim Mains, prin. Fax 336-5576
Public S 52 400/PK-6
100 Farmington Rd 14609 585-482-9614
Denise Rainey, prin. Fax 654-1079
Public S 53 200/PK-6
950 Norton St 14621 585-325-0935
Donna Gattelaro-Andersen, prin. Fax 324-3709
Public S 54 200/K-6
311 Flower City Park 14615 585-254-2080
Lessie Hamilton-Rose, prin.
Public S 57 200/PK-2
15 Costar St 14608 585-277-0190
Cheryl Moss, prin. Fax 277-0108
Public S 58 300/K-6
200 University Ave 14605 585-325-6170
Elizabeth Miller, prin. Fax 262-8964
Rochester Community S K-9
85 Adams St 14608 585-454-3525
Connie Wehner, prin. Fax 262-8938
School Without Walls Foundation Academy 7-8
111 Clinton Ave N 14604 585-324-3111
Idonia Owens, prin.

Rush-Henrietta Central SD
Supt. — See Henrietta
Crane ES 500/K-5
85 Shell Edge Dr 14623 585-359-5408
Nick DiPonzio, prin. Fax 359-5403
Fyle ES 400/K-5
133 Vollmer Pkwy 14623 585-359-5438
Gina Diesenberg, prin. Fax 359-5433

West Irondequoit Central SD 3,900/K-12
321 List Ave 14617 585-342-5500
Jeffrey Crane, supt. Fax 266-1556
www.westirondequoit.org
Briarwood ES 100/K-3
215 Briarwood Dr 14617 585-336-1610
Kathleen Bush, prin. Fax 336-1611
Brookview ES 200/K-3
300 Brookview Dr 14617 585-336-1630
Michelle Cramer, prin. Fax 336-1631

Colebrook ES 200/K-3
210 Colebrook Dr 14617 585-336-1600
Kathleen Bush, prin. Fax 336-1601
Dake MS 700/7-8
350 Cooper Rd 14617 585-342-2140
Timothy Terranova, prin. Fax 336-3034
Iroquois MS 400/4-6
150 Colebrook Dr 14617 585-342-3450
Charles Miller, prin. Fax 336-3042
Listwood ES 200/K-3
325 List Ave 14617 585-336-1640
Bridget Harris, prin. Fax 336-1641
Rogers MS 500/4-6
219 Northfield Rd 14617 585-342-1330
James Brennan, prin. Fax 336-3097
Seneca ES 200/K-3
4143 Saint Paul Blvd 14617 585-336-1620
Michelle Cramer, prin. Fax 336-1621
Southlawn ES 300/K-3
455 Rawlinson Rd 14617 585-266-5070
Bridget Harris, prin. Fax 336-3042

Allendale Columbia S 400/PK-12
519 Allens Creek Rd 14618 585-381-4560
Charles Hertrick, hdmstr. Fax 383-1191
Bay Knoll S 50/PK-8
2639 E Ridge Rd 14622 585-467-2722
Cynthia Kowski, admin. Fax 544-4340
Cathedral S at Holy Rosary 100/PK-6
420 Lexington Ave 14613 585-254-8180
Kathleen Dougherty, prin. Fax 254-4604
Christ the King S 200/PK-6
445 Kings Hwy S 14617 585-467-8730
Colleen D'Hondt, prin. Fax 467-5392
Cobblestone S 100/K-8
10 Prince St 14607 585-271-4548
Paula Wooters, dir. Fax 271-3501
Derech HaTorah 100/K-8
125 Kings Hwy S 14617 585-266-2920
Lea Goldstein, prin. Fax 486-1089
Greece Christian S 200/K-8
750 Long Pond Rd 14612 585-723-1165
Dr. Herbert Parker, prin. Fax 723-8241
Harley S 500/PK-12
1981 Clover St 14618 585-442-1770
Dr. Timothy Cottrell, hdmstr. Fax 442-5758
Mother of Sorrows S 200/K-8
1777 Latta Rd 14612 585-663-1100
Samuel Zalacca, prin. Fax 663-5552
Nazareth Hall ES 200/PK-5
180 Raines Park 14613 585-458-3786
Diana Duell, dir. Fax 458-8941
Nazareth Hall MS 200/6-8
1001 Lake Ave 14613 585-647-8716
Sr. Elizabeth Snyder, dir. Fax 254-5468
North Baptist Christian S 100/PK-6
2052 Saint Paul St 14621 585-338-7810
Judson Stuart, prin. Fax 467-8662
Northside Christian Academy 50/PK-12
PO Box 67173 14617 585-266-3140
Northstar Christian Academy 300/PK-12
332 Spencerport Rd 14606 585-429-5530
Rob Johnson, prin. Fax 429-7913
Pinnacle Lutheran S 100/PK-K
250 Pinnacle Rd 14623 585-334-6500
Fax 334-6022
Rochester Christian S 200/PK-8
260 Embury Rd 14625 585-671-4910
John DeMaster, prin. Fax 671-3676
Rochester SDA Junior Academy 100/PK-12
309 Jefferson Ave 14611 585-436-5915
St. John Neumann S 100/PK-6
31 Empire Blvd 14609 585-288-0580
Marie Arcuri, prin. Fax 288-2612
St. Lawrence S 200/PK-6
1000 N Greece Rd 14626 585-225-3870
Joseph Holleran, prin. Fax 225-1336
St. Pius X S 200/PK-6
3000 Chili Ave 14624 585-247-5650
Stephen Oberst, prin. Fax 247-7409
Seton Catholic S 400/PK-6
165 Rhinecliff Dr 14618 585-473-6604
Sr. Kathleen Lurz, prin. Fax 473-3347
Siena Catholic Academy 400/7-8
2617 East Ave 14610 585-381-1220
Timothy Leahy, prin. Fax 381-1223

Rockaway Beach, See New York
NYC Department of Education
Supt. — See New York
Public S 114 800/PK-8
13401 Cronston Ave, Rockaway Park NY 11694
718-634-3382
Stephen Grill, prin. Fax 945-4510
Public S 183 600/PK-8
245 Beach 79th St 11693 718-634-9459
Renee Peart, prin. Fax 634-9458

Rockaway Park, See New York
NYC Department of Education
Supt. — See New York
Public S 225 600/PK-8
190 Beach 110th St 11694 718-945-5218
Matthew Melchiorre, prin. Fax 474-8176

Rockville Centre, Nassau, Pop. 24,237
Rockville Centre UFD 3,600/K-12
128 Shepherd St 11570 516-255-8957
Dr. William Johnson, supt. Fax 255-8810
www.rvcschools.org
Hewitt ES 500/K-5
446 Demott Ave 11570 516-255-8913
Elizabeth Pryke, prin. Fax 763-1817
Riverside ES 200/K-5
110 Riverside Dr 11570 516-255-8902
Patricia Bock, prin. Fax 763-1812
South Side MS 800/6-8
67 Hillside Ave 11570 516-255-8976
Shelagh McGinn, prin. Fax 763-0914
Watson ES 200/K-5
277 N Centre Ave 11570 516-255-8904
Joan Waldman, prin. Fax 763-1808
Wilson ES 400/K-5
25 Buckingham Rd 11570 516-255-8910
Thomas Ricupero, prin. Fax 763-1806
Other Schools – See South Hempstead

St. Agnes Cathedral S 900/K-8
70 Clinton Ave 11570 516-678-5550
Sr. Kathleen Carlin, prin. Fax 678-0437

Rocky Point, Suffolk, Pop. 8,596
Rocky Point UFD 3,500/K-12
170 Route 25A 11778 631-744-1600
Dr. Carla D'ambrosio, supt. Fax 744-0817
www.rockypointschools.org
Carasiti ES 800/K-2
90 Rocky Point Yaphank Rd 11778 631-744-1601
Scott O'Brien, prin. Fax 209-0617
Edgar IS 800/3-5
525 Route 25A 11778 631-744-1602
Carol Tvelia, prin. Fax 744-4898
Rocky Point MS 800/6-8
76 Rocky Point Yaphank Rd 11778 631-744-1603
Fax 886-0000

Rome, Oneida, Pop. 34,344
Rome CSD 5,700/PK-12
112 E Thomas St 13440 315-338-6521
Jeffrey Simons, supt. Fax 334-6526
www.romecsd.org/
Bellamy ES 300/K-4
7118 Brennon Ave 13440 315-338-5260
Nancy Opperman, prin. Fax 338-7472
Clough ES 200/K-4
409 Bell Rd S 13440 315-338-5280
Fax 338-7482
Denti ES 600/PK-4
1001 Ruby St 13440 315-338-5360
Sherry Lubey, prin. Fax 334-7528
Ft. Stanwix ES 200/K-4
110 W Linden St 13440 315-338-5380
Susan Getnick, prin. Fax 338-7599
Gansevoort ES 300/K-4
758 W Liberty St 13440 315-334-5180
Karen Miller, prin. Fax 334-7352
Joy ES 200/K-4
8194 Bielby Rd 13440 315-334-1260
Andria Lacey, prin. Fax 334-7362
Ridge Mills ES 200/K-4
7841 Ridge Mills Rd 13440 315-334-1280
Sheila Spencer, prin. Fax 334-7382
Staley Upper ES 800/5-6
620 E Bloomfield St 13440 315-338-5300
Fax 338-5306
Stokes ES 200/K-4
9095 Turin Rd 13440 315-334-1220
Judith Mullin, prin. Fax 334-7399
Strough MS 800/7-8
801 Laurel St 13440 315-338-5200
Riccardo Ripa, prin. Fax 334-7465

Mohawk Valley SDA S 50/K-8
6739 Sutliff Rd 13440 315-336-2918
Rome Catholic S 400/PK-12
800 Cypress St 13440 315-336-6190
Barbara Jacques, prin. Fax 336-6194

Romulus, Seneca
Romulus Central SD 500/PK-12
5705 State Route 96 14541 866-810-0345
Michael Hoose, supt. Fax 869-5961
www.rcs.k12.ny.us
Romulus Central ES 300/PK-6
5705 State Route 96 14541 866-810-0345
Lynn Rhone, prin. Fax 869-5961

Ronkonkoma, Suffolk, Pop. 20,391
Connetquot Central SD
Supt. — See Bohemia
Cherokee Street ES 700/K-5
130 Cherokee St 11779 631-467-6027
Bridgette Wilson, prin. Fax 467-6166
Duffield ES 400/K-5
600 1st St 11779 631-467-6010
Lisa Farrell, prin. Fax 467-6326
Ronkonkoma MS 800/6-8
501 Peconic St 11779 631-467-6000
Charles Morea, prin. Fax 467-6003
Slocum ES 400/K-5
2460 Sycamore Ave 11779 631-467-6040
Sandy Rubin, prin. Fax 467-6446

Roosevelt, Nassau, Pop. 15,030
Roosevelt UFD 2,800/PK-12
240 Denton Pl 11575 516-345-7000
Robert Harris, supt. Fax 379-0178
www.rooseveltufsd.com/
Bauer Avenue Pre-Kindergarten Center 100/PK-PK
1 Rose Ave 11575 516-345-7659
Janie West-Mays, prin. Fax 345-7690
Byas ES 400/K-6
60 Underhill Ave 11575 516-345-7500
Lillian Watson, prin. Fax 867-4189
Centennial Avenue ES 700/K-6
140 W Centennial Ave 11575 516-345-7400
Patricia Charthern, prin. Fax 345-7502
Roosevelt MS 400/7-8
335 E Clinton Ave 11575 516-345-7700
Dr. Robert Tucker, prin. Fax 345-7791
Washington Rose ES 400/K-6
1 Rose Ave 11575 516-345-7600
Perletter Wright, prin. Fax 345-7690

Roscoe, Sullivan
Roscoe Central SD 300/PK-12
6 Academy St 12776 607-498-4126
Carmine Giangreco, supt. Fax 498-5609
www.roscoe.k12.ny.us
Roscoe Central S 300/PK-12
6 Academy St 12776 607-498-4126
Scott Haberli, prin. Fax 498-5609

Rosedale, See New York
NYC Department of Education
Supt. — See New York
Public S 38 400/K-6
13521 241st St 11422 718-528-2276
Cassandra Hundley, prin. Fax 712-1598
Public S 138 900/PK-8
25111 Weller Ave 11422 718-528-9053
Nichele Manning-Andrews, prin. Fax 723-5670
Public S 195 600/PK-6
25350 149th Ave 11422 718-723-0313
Beryl Bailey, prin. Fax 723-7826
Public S 270 600/K-8
23315 Merrick Blvd 11422 718-341-8280
Eleanor Andrew, prin. Fax 341-5589

St. Clare S 400/PK-8
13725 Brookville Blvd 11422 718-528-7174
Mary Rafferty-Basile, prin. Fax 528-4389

Roslyn, Nassau, Pop. 2,879
Roslyn UFD 3,400/PK-12
PO Box 367 11576 516-801-5001
Dr. Dan Brenner, supt. Fax 801-5008
www.roslynschools.org
Other Schools – See Greenvale, Roslyn Heights

Buckley Country Day S 300/PK-8
2 I U Willets Rd 11576 516-627-1910
Dr. Jean-Marc Juhel, prin. Fax 627-8627

Roslyn Heights, Nassau, Pop. 6,405
East Williston UFD
Supt. — See Old Westbury
Willets Road MS 500/5-7
455 I U Willets Rd 11577 516-333-8797
Stephen Kimmel, prin.

Roslyn UFD
Supt. — See Roslyn
East Hills ES 500/2-5
400 Round Hill Rd 11577 516-801-5301
Allison Brown, prin. Fax 801-5308
Heights S 400/PK-1
240 Willow St 11577 516-801-5501
Regina Colardi, prin. Fax 801-5508
Roslyn MS 800/6-8
PO Box 9006 11577 516-801-5201
Jack Palmadesso, prin. Fax 801-5208

Rotterdam Junction, Schenectady
Schalmont Central SD
Supt. — See Schenectady
Woestina ES 100/K-5
1292 Main St 12150 518-887-5600
Shari Lontrato, prin. Fax 887-2297

Rouses Point, Clinton, Pop. 2,400
Northeastern Clinton Central SD
Supt. — See Champlain
Rouses Point ES 200/K-5
80 Maple St 12979 518-297-7211
Robin Garrand, prin. Fax 298-4293

Roxbury, Delaware
Roxbury Central SD 300/K-12
53729 State Highway 30 12474 607-326-4151
Thomas O'Brien, supt. Fax 326-4154
www.roxburycs.org
Roxbury Central S 300/K-12
53729 State Highway 30 12474 607-326-4151
Eric Windover, prin. Fax 326-4154

Rush, Monroe
Rush-Henrietta Central SD
Supt. — See Henrietta
Leary ES 500/K-5
5509 E Henrietta Rd 14543 585-359-5468
Jennifer Tomalty, prin. Fax 359-5463

Rushford, Allegany
Cuba-Rushford Central SD
Supt. — See Cuba
Rushford ES 100/K-5
PO Box 310 14777 585-437-2217
Gregory Hardy, prin. Fax 437-2093

Rushville, Ontario, Pop. 634
Marcus Whitman Central SD 1,500/K-12
4100 Baldwin Rd 14544 585-554-4848
Michael Chirco, supt. Fax 554-4882
www.mwcsd.org/
Middlesex Valley ES 300/K-5
149 State Route 245 14544 585-554-3115
Susan Wissick, prin. Fax 554-6172
Whitman MS 400/6-8
4100 Baldwin Rd 14544 585-554-6442
Clayton Cole, prin. Fax 554-3414
Other Schools – See Gorham

Russell, Saint Lawrence
Edwards-Knox Central SD 600/K-12
PO Box 630 13684 315-562-8326
Suzanne Kelly, supt. Fax 562-2477
www.ekcsk12.org
Edwards-Knox ES 300/K-6
PO Box 630 13684 315-562-3284
Ronald Burke, prin. Fax 562-2477

Rye, Westchester, Pop. 14,992
Rye CSD 2,900/K-12
411 Theodore Fremd Ave 10580 914-967-6100
Dr. Edward Shine, supt. Fax 967-6957
www.ryeschools.org/
Midland ES 600/K-5
312 Midland Ave 10580 914-967-6100
Dr. Angela Grille, prin. Fax 921-6848
Milton ES 300/K-5
12 Hewlett St 10580 914-967-6100
Dr. JoAnne Nardone, prin. Fax 921-0487
Osborn ES 600/K-5
10 Osborn Rd 10580 914-967-6100
Clarita Zeppie, prin. Fax 921-3842
Rye MS 700/6-8
3 Parsons St 10580 914-967-6100
Dr. Ann Edwards, prin. Fax 921-6189

Resurrection S 600/PK-8
116 Milton Rd 10580 914-967-1218
Harold Nielson, prin. Fax 925-3511
Rye Country Day S 900/PK-12
Cedar St 10580 914-967-1417
Scott Nelson, hdmstr. Fax 967-1418

Rye Brook, Westchester, Pop. 9,471
Blind Brook-Rye UFD 1,500/K-12
390 N Ridge St 10573 914-937-3600
William Stark, supt. Fax 937-5871
blindbrook.org
Blind Brook MS, 840 King St 10573 300/6-8
Karen Bronson, prin. 914-937-3600
Ponterio Ridge Street ES 800/K-5
390 N Ridge St 10573 914-937-3600
Joseph Rodriguez, prin. Fax 937-1265

Port Chester-Rye UFD 3,600/K-12
113 Bowman Ave 10573 914-934-7901
Dr. Donald Carlisle, supt. Fax 934-0727
www.portchesterschools.org/
Other Schools – See Port Chester

Sackets Harbor, Jefferson, Pop. 1,418
Sackets Harbor Central SD 500/K-12
PO Box 290 13685 315-646-3575
Frederick Hall, supt. Fax 646-1038
www.sacketsharborschool.org
Sackets Harbor Central S 500/K-12
PO Box 290 13685 315-646-3575
Jennifer Gaffney, prin. Fax 646-1038

Sagaponack, Suffolk
Sagaponack Common SD 50/1-4
PO Box 1500 11962 631-537-0651
Fax 537-2342
www.sagaponackschool.com/
Sagaponack ES 50/1-4
PO Box 1500 11962 631-537-0651
Diana McGinniss, lead tchr. Fax 537-2342

Sag Harbor, Suffolk, Pop. 2,368
Sag Harbor UFD 900/K-12
200 Jermain Ave 11963 631-725-5300
Dr. John Gratto, supt. Fax 725-5307
www.sagharborschools.org
Sag Harbor ES 400/K-5
68 Hampton St 11963 631-725-5301
Joan Frisicano, prin. Fax 725-5331

Stella Maris S 200/PK-8
135 Division St 11963 631-725-2525
Jane Peters, prin. Fax 725-0568

Saint Albans, See New York
NYC Department of Education
Supt. — See New York
Public S 36 400/K-5
18701 Foch Blvd 11412 718-528-1862
Lynn Staton, prin. Fax 723-6928
Public S 134 400/PK-5
20302 109th Ave 11412 718-464-5544
Cheryl Marmon-Halm, prin. Fax 464-7779
Public S 136 700/PK-5
20115 115th Ave 11412 718-465-2286
Tanya Walker, prin. Fax 464-0040
IS 192 600/6-8
10989 204th St 11412 718-479-5540
Harriett Diaz, prin. Fax 217-4645

St. Albans Deliverance Christian Academy 50/PK-8
20512 Hollis Ave 11412 718-468-6060
Claudia Johnson, admin. Fax 465-7176
St. Catherine of Sienna S 400/K-8
11834 Riverton St 11412 718-528-1857
Sr. Barbara Kradick, prin. Fax 949-8739

Saint James, Suffolk, Pop. 12,703
Smithtown Central SD
Supt. — See Smithtown
Mills Pond ES 500/K-5
246 Moriches Rd 11780 631-382-4300
Arlene Wild, prin. Fax 382-4304
Nesaquake MS 900/6-8
479 Edgewood Ave 11780 631-382-5100
Kevin Simmons, prin. Fax 382-5107
Saint James ES 500/K-5
580 Lake Ave 11780 631-382-4450
Mary Grace Lynch, prin. Fax 382-4456

Harbor Country Day S 200/PK-8
17 Three Sisters Rd 11780 631-584-5555
Christopher Pryor, hdmstr. Fax 862-7664
SS. Philip & James S 400/PK-8
359 Clinton Ave 11780 631-584-7896
Anthony Giordano, prin. Fax 584-3258

Saint Johnsville, Montgomery, Pop. 1,650
Oppenheim-Ephratah Central SD 400/PK-12
6486 State Highway 29 13452 518-568-2014
Dan Russom, supt. Fax 568-2941
oecs.k12.ny.us
Oppenheim-Ephratah Central S 400/PK-12
6486 State Highway 29 13452 518-568-2014
C. Fatta, prin. Fax 568-2941

Saint Johnsville Central SD 500/PK-12
61 Monroe St 13452 518-568-7023
Christine Battisti, supt. Fax 568-5407
sjcsd.org
Robbins ES 300/PK-6
61 Monroe St 13452 518-568-7023
Laura Campione, prin. Fax 568-5407

Saint Regis Falls, Franklin
Saint Regis Falls Central SD 300/PK-12
PO Box 309 12980 518-856-9421
Patricia Dovi, supt. Fax 856-0142
www.fehb.org/stregis.htm
Saint Regis Falls S 300/PK-12
PO Box 309 12980 518-856-9421
Marc Czadzeck, prin. Fax 856-0142

Salamanca, Cattaraugus, Pop. 5,851
Salamanca CSD 1,400/K-12
79 River St 14779 716-945-2403
Douglas Hay, supt. Fax 945-3964
www.salamancany.org/
Prospect ES 300/K-2
300 Prospect Ave 14779 716-945-5170
Jean Pascarella, prin. Fax 945-2374
Salamanca MS 300/6-8
50 Iroquois Dr 14779 716-945-2405
Laurence Whitcomb, prin. Fax 945-5738
Seneca ES 300/3-5
25 Center St 14779 716-945-5140
Charles Crist, prin. Fax 945-3567

Salem, Washington, Pop. 911
Salem Central SD 700/K-12
PO Box 517 12865 518-854-7855
Charles Kremer, supt. Fax 854-3957
salemcsd.org/
Salem ES 300/K-6
PO Box 517 12865 518-854-9505
Kerri Zappala, prin. Fax 854-3957

Sanborn, Niagara
Niagara-Wheatfield Central SD
Supt. — See Niagara Falls
Town MS 900/6-8
2292 Saunders Settlement Rd 14132 716-215-3150
Dr. Laura Palka, prin. Fax 215-3160
West Street ES 400/K-5
5700 West St 14132 716-215-3200
Theron Mong, prin. Fax 215-3216

St. Peter's Lutheran S 100/PK-8
6168 Walmore Rd 14132 716-731-4422
William Bullwinkle, prin. Fax 731-1439

Sandy Creek, Oswego, Pop. 771
Sandy Creek Central SD 1,000/PK-12
PO Box 248 13145 315-387-3445
Stewart Amell, supt. Fax 387-2196
www.sccs.cnyric.org/
Sandy Creek ES 400/PK-5
PO Box 248 13145 315-387-3445
Sue Ann Archibee, prin. Fax 387-2196
Sandy Creek MS 300/6-8
PO Box 248 13145 315-387-3445
Joanne Shelmidine, prin. Fax 387-2196

Saranac, Clinton
Saranac Central SD
Supt. — See Dannemora
Saranac ES 400/K-6
PO Box 8 12981 518-565-5900
Marguerite Tamer, prin. Fax 565-5890
Saranac JHS 300/7-8
PO Box 8 12981 518-565-5700
James Gratto, prin. Fax 565-5706

Saranac Lake, Franklin, Pop. 4,923
Saranac Lake Central SD 1,500/PK-12
79 Canaras Ave 12983 518-891-5460
Gerald Goldman, supt. Fax 891-5140
slcsd.ny.schoolwebpages.com
Lake Colby S 50/PK-K
79 Canaras Ave 12983 518-891-3350
Patrick Hogan, prin. Fax 891-4601
Petrova ES 300/K-5
79 Canaras Ave 12983 518-891-4221
Joshua Dann, prin. Fax 891-6548
Petrova MS 400/6-8
79 Canaras Ave 12983 518-891-4221
Patricia Kenyon, prin. Fax 891-6615
Other Schools – See Bloomingdale

St. Bernard S 100/PK-5
63 River St 12983 518-891-2830
Anne Bayruns, prin. Fax 891-4619

Saratoga Springs, Saratoga, Pop. 28,036
Saratoga Springs CSD 6,900/K-12
3 Blue Streak Blvd 12866 518-583-4709
Janice White, supt. Fax 584-6624
www.saratogaschools.org
Caroline Street ES 500/K-5
310 Caroline St 12866 518-584-7612
Dan O'Rourke, prin. Fax 583-3696
Division Street ES 400/K-5
220 Division St 12866 518-583-4794
Dr. Greer Miller, prin. Fax 583-4722
Geyser Road ES 400/K-5
61 Geyser Rd 12866 518-584-7699
Melodye Eldeen, prin. Fax 583-4733

Lake Avenue ES 400/K-5
126 Lake Ave 12866 518-584-3678
Dr. Barbara Messier, prin. Fax 583-4778
Maple Ave MS 1,600/6-8
515 Maple Ave 12866 518-587-4551
Stuart Byrne, prin. Fax 587-5759
Nolan ES 900/K-5
221 Jones Rd 12866 518-584-7383
Kevin Froats, prin. Fax 583-4726
Other Schools – See Greenfield Center

St. Clement Regional Catholic S 300/PK-5
231 Lake Ave 12866 518-584-7350
Jane Kromm, prin. Fax 587-2623
Waldorf S of Saratoga Springs 300/PK-12
122 Regent St 12866 518-587-7643
Katherine Scharff, admin. Fax 581-1466

Saugerties, Ulster, Pop. 3,930
Saugerties Central SD 3,300/K-12
PO Box A 12477 845-247-6550
Seth Turner, supt. Fax 246-8364
www.saugerties.k12.ny.us
Cahill ES 400/K-6
PO Box A 12477 845-247-6800
Susan Gies, prin. Fax 246-4302
Morse ES 400/K-6
PO Box A 12477 845-247-6960
Donald Dieckmann, prin. Fax 246-4184
Mount Marion ES 400/K-6
PO Box A 12477 845-247-6920
Lawrence Mautone, prin. Fax 246-4103
Saugerties JHS 600/7-8
PO Box A 12477 845-247-6560
Thomas Averill, prin. Fax 246-4322
Other Schools – See Glasco

St. Mary of the Snow S 100/PK-8
25 Cedar St 12477 845-246-6381
Christine Molinelli, prin. Fax 246-4996
Woodstock Day S 200/PK-12
1430 Glasco Tpke 12477 845-246-3744
Jim Handlin, hdmstr. Fax 246-0053

Sauquoit, Oneida
Sauquoit Valley Central SD 1,200/K-12
2601 Oneida St 13456 315-839-6311
Deborah Flack, supt. Fax 839-5352
www.svcsd.org
Sauquoit Valley ES 500/K-5
2601 Oneida St 13456 315-839-6339
Kim Newton, prin. Fax 839-6366
Sauquoit Valley MS 300/6-8
2601 Oneida St 13456 315-839-6371
Ron Wheelock, prin. Fax 839-6390

Savannah, Wayne
Clyde-Savannah Central SD
Supt. — See Clyde
Savannah ES, PO Box 218 13146 100/5-6
Belinda Crowe, prin. 315-902-3200

Savona, Steuben, Pop. 798
Campbell-Savona Central SD
Supt. — See Campbell
Campbell-Savona ES 500/K-6
64 E Lamoka Ave 14879 607-527-9800
Joseph McKenna, prin. Fax 583-4283

Sayville, Suffolk, Pop. 16,550
Sayville UFD 3,500/K-12
99 Greeley Ave 11782 631-244-6510
Dr. Rosemary Jones, supt. Fax 244-6504
www.sayville.k12.ny.us
Lincoln Avenue ES 500/K-5
440 Lincoln Ave 11782 631-244-6725
Michele Gunther, prin. Fax 244-6507
Sayville MS 900/6-8
291 Johnson Ave 11782 631-244-6650
Dr. Walter Schartner, prin. Fax 244-6655
Sunrise Drive ES 500/K-5
320 Sunrise Dr 11782 631-244-6750
Rose Castello, prin. Fax 244-6509
Other Schools – See West Sayville

Prince of Peace S 200/PK-8
200 W Main St 11782 631-589-3426
Jane Harrigan, prin. Fax 589-4523

Scarsdale, Westchester, Pop. 17,763
Eastchester UFD
Supt. — See Eastchester
Greenvale ES 500/2-5
1 Gabriel Resicgno Dr 10583 914-793-6130
Theresa Sullivan, prin. Fax 793-9006

Edgemont UFD 1,900/K-12
300 White Oak Ln 10583 914-472-7768
Nancy Taddiken, supt. Fax 472-6846
www.edgemont.org/
Greenville ES 500/K-6
100 Glendale Rd 10583 914-472-7760
Dr. Marc Heller, prin. Fax 472-6232
Seely Place ES 500/K-6
51 Seely Pl 10583 914-472-8040
Dr. Edward Kennedy, prin. Fax 472-7252

Scarsdale UFD 4,700/K-12
2 Brewster Rd Ste 2 10583 914-721-2412
Michael McGill, supt. Fax 722-2822
www.scarsdaleschools.k12.ny.us
Edgewood ES 400/K-5
1 Roosevelt Pl 10583 914-721-2700
Scott Houseknecht, prin. Fax 721-2717
Fox Meadow ES 500/K-5
59 Brewster Rd 10583 914-721-2720
Duncan Wilson, prin. Fax 721-2730

Greenacres ES 400/K-5
41 Huntington Rd 10583 914-721-2740
Gerry Young, prin. Fax 721-2755
Heathcote ES 400/K-5
26 Palmer Ave 10583 914-721-2760
Maria Stile, prin. Fax 721-2777
Quaker Ridge ES 500/K-5
125 Weaver St 10583 914-721-2780
Robyn Lane, prin. Fax 721-2784
Scarsdale MS 1,100/6-8
134 Mamaroneck Rd 10583 914-721-2600
Michael McDermott, prin. Fax 721-2655

Yonkers CSD
Supt. — See Yonkers
Pulaski S 500/PK-8
150 Kings Cross 10583 914-377-8575
Brian Curtis, prin. Fax 722-7697

Immaculate Heart of Mary S 200/PK-8
201 Boulevard 10583 914-723-5608
Patricia Gatti, prin. Fax 723-8004
Our Lady of Fatima S 200/PK-8
963 Scarsdale Rd 10583 914-723-0460
Janice Arcaro, prin. Fax 723-0460

Schaghticoke, Rensselaer, Pop. 675
Hoosic Valley Central SD 1,300/K-12
2 Pleasant Ave 12154 518-753-4450
Douglas Kelley, supt. Fax 753-7665
www.hoosicvalley.k12.ny.us/
Hoosic Valley ES 400/K-4
22 Pleasant Ave 12154 518-753-4491
Mark Foti, prin. Fax 753-7576
Hoosic Valley MS 400/5-8
1548 State Route 67 12154 518-753-4432
Amy Goodell, prin. Fax 753-7491

Schenectady, Schenectady, Pop. 61,280
Guilderland Central SD
Supt. — See Guilderland
Lynnwood ES 400/K-5
8 Regina Dr 12303 518-355-7930
James Dillon, prin. Fax 356-3087
Pine Bush ES 500/K-5
3437 Carman Rd 12303 518-357-2770
Christopher Sanita, prin. Fax 356-3172

Mohonasen Central SD 3,400/K-12
2072 Curry Rd 12303 518-356-8200
Kathleen Spring, supt. Fax 356-8247
www.mohonasen.org
Bradt PS 600/K-2
2719 Hamburg St 12303 518-356-8400
Diane McIver, prin. Fax 356-8404
Draper MS 800/6-8
2070 Curry Rd 12303 518-356-8350
Debra Male, prin. Fax 356-8359
Pinewood IS 800/3-5
901 Kings Rd 12303 518-356-8430
Michele Hunter, prin. Fax 356-8434

Niskayuna Central SD 4,300/K-12
1239 Van Antwerp Rd 12309 518-377-4666
Dr. Kevin Baughman, supt. Fax 377-4074
www.nisk.k12.ny.us
Birchwood ES 300/K-5
897 Birchwood Ln 12309 518-785-3445
Debra Berndt, prin. Fax 785-3776
Craig ES 400/K-5
2566 Balltown Rd 12309 518-377-0156
William Anders, prin. Fax 377-1075
Hillside ES 300/K-5
1100 Cornelius Ave 12309 518-377-1856
Dr. Shireen Yadegari, prin. Fax 377-1099
Iroquois MS 600/6-8
2495 Rosendale Rd 12309 518-377-2233
Vicki Wyld, prin. Fax 377-2219
Rosendale ES 400/K-5
2455 Rosendale Rd 12309 518-377-3123
Lauren Gemmell, prin. Fax 377-1098
Van Antwerp MS 400/6-8
2253 Story Ave 12309 518-370-1243
Luke Rakoczy, prin. Fax 370-4610
Other Schools – See Rexford

Schalmont Central SD 2,000/K-12
401 Duanesburg Rd 12306 518-355-9200
Dr. Valerie Kelsey, supt. Fax 355-9203
www.schalmont.org
Jefferson ES 600/K-5
100 Princetown Rd 12306 518-355-1342
Joby Gifford, prin. Fax 355-1346
Schalmont MS 500/6-8
2 Sabre Dr 12306 518-355-6110
Michael Kondratowicz, prin. Fax 355-5329
Other Schools – See Pattersonville, Rotterdam Junction

Schenectady CSD 9,200/PK-12
108 Education Dr 12303 518-370-8100
Eric Ely, supt. Fax 370-8173
www.schenectady.k12.ny.us
Blodgett ES PK-6
520 Bradt St 12306 518-881-3950
Nancy Fontaine, prin. Fax 881-3951
Central Park International Magnet S 600/K-8
421 Elm St 12304 518-370-8250
Tonya Federico, prin. Fax 881-3602
Elmer Avenue ES 500/PK-6
90 Elmer Ave 12308 518-370-8310
Sean Inglee, prin. Fax 881-3762
Fulton ECC PK-PK
408 Eleanor St 12306 518-881-3980
Susan Gorman, prin. Fax 881-3982
Hamilton ES 500/PK-6
1091 Webster St 12303 518-881-3720
Robert Flanders, prin. Fax 881-3722
Howe ECC PK-K
1065 Baker Ave 12309 518-370-8295
Mariann Bellai, admin. Fax 881-3542

Keane ES K-6
1252 Albany St 12304 518-881-3960
John Sardos, prin. Fax 881-3961
King Magnet S 400/PK-8
918 Stanley St 12307 518-370-8360
Comfort Sarfoh, prin. Fax 370-8363
Lincoln ES 400/PK-6
2 Robinson St 12304 518-370-8355
Pedro Roman, prin. Fax 395-3576
Mont Pleasant MS 800/6-8
1121 Forest Rd 12303 518-370-8160
Nicola DiLeva, prin. Fax 881-3562
Oneida MS 600/6-8
1629 Oneida St 12308 518-370-8260
Karmen McEvoy, prin. Fax 370-8267
Paige ES 400/K-6
104 Elliott Ave 12304 518-370-8300
Patricia Paser, prin. Fax 881-3522
Pleasant Valley ES 400/K-5
1097 Forest Rd 12303 518-881-3640
Joseph DiCaprio, prin. Fax 881-3642
Roosevelt ES PK-6
570 Lansing St 12303 518-881-3970
Constance DuVerney, prin. Fax 881-3971
Van Corlaer ES 500/K-6
2310 Guilderland Ave 12306 518-370-8270
Michelle VanDerLinden, prin. Fax 881-3742
Woodlawn ES 400/PK-6
3311 Wells Ave 12304 518-370-8280
Barbara Coffey, prin. Fax 370-8283
Yates Arts-In-Education Magnet S 300/K-6
725 Salina St 12308 518-370-8320
Valarie Scott, prin. Fax 881-3862
Zoller ES 500/K-6
1880 Lancaster St 12308 518-370-8290
Patricia Doyle, prin. Fax 370-8291

Brown S 300/PK-8
150 Corlaer Ave 12304 518-370-0366
John Barry, hdmstr. Fax 370-1514
St. Helen S 200/PK-5
1801 Union St 12309 518-382-8225
Sr. Anne Marie Glenn, prin. Fax 374-8522
St. John the Evangelist S 200/PK-5
806 Union St 12308 518-393-5331
Marie Keenan, prin. Fax 374-4663
St. Madeleine Sophie S 200/PK-6
3510 Carman Rd 12303 518-355-3080
Teresa Kovarovic, prin. Fax 355-3106

Schenevus, Otsego, Pop. 529
Schenevus Central SD 400/K-12
159 Main St 12155 607-638-5530
Lynda Bookhard, supt. Fax 638-5600
www.schenevuscs.org/
Schenevus Central S 400/K-12
159 Main St 12155 607-638-5881
Tom Jennings, prin. Fax 638-5600

Schoharie, Schoharie, Pop. 988
Schoharie Central SD 1,000/K-12
PO Box 430 12157 518-295-6600
Brian Sherman, supt. Fax 295-8178
www.schoharie.k12.ny.us
Schoharie ES 500/K-6
PO Box 430 12157 518-295-6652
Maryellen Gillis, prin. Fax 295-9506

Schroon Lake, Essex
Schroon Lake Central SD 300/K-12
PO Box 338 12870 518-532-7164
Michael Bonnewell, supt. Fax 532-0284
www.schroonschool.org
Schroon Lake Central S 300/K-12
PO Box 338 12870 518-532-7164
Michael Bonnewell, prin. Fax 532-0284

Schuylerville, Saratoga, Pop. 1,389
Schuylerville Central SD 1,800/K-12
14 Spring St 12871 518-695-3255
Dr. Leon Reed, supt. Fax 695-6491
www.schuylervilleschools.org
Schuylerville ES 1,000/K-6
14 Spring St 12871 518-695-3255
Michael Mugits, prin. Fax 695-6405

Scio, Allegany
Scio Central SD 400/PK-12
3968 Washington St 14880 585-593-5076
Michael McArdle, supt. Fax 593-3468
scio.schooltools.us/
Scio Central S 400/PK-12
3968 Washington St 14880 585-593-5510
Matthew Hopkins, prin. Fax 593-0653

Scotia, Schenectady, Pop. 7,958
Burnt Hills-Ballston Lake Central SD 3,500/K-12
50 Cypress Dr Ste 4 12302 518-399-9141
Jim Schultz, supt. Fax 399-1882
www.bhbl.org
Pashley ES 500/K-5
30 Pashley Rd 12302 518-399-9141
Jill Bonacio, prin. Fax 399-0534
Other Schools – See Ballston Lake, Burnt Hills

Scotia-Glenville Central SD 2,900/K-12
900 Preddice Pkwy 12302 518-382-1215
Susan Swartz, supt. Fax 382-1222
www.scotiaglenvilleschools.org/
Glendaal ES 300/K-5
774 Sacandaga Rd 12302 518-382-1202
Thomas Eagan, prin. Fax 382-1203
Glen-Worden ES 300/K-5
30 Worden Rd 12302 518-346-0469
James Dunham, prin. Fax 346-0855
Lincoln ES 300/K-5
40 Albion St 12302 518-382-1297
Ann Comley, prin. Fax 382-1298

Sacandaga ES 300/K-5
300 Wren St 12302 518-382-1282
John Tobiassen, prin. Fax 386-4311
Scotia-Glenville MS 700/6-8
10 Prestige Pkwy 12302 518-382-1263
Sharyll Keller, prin. Fax 382-1263

Schenectady Christian S 300/K-12
36-38 Sacandaga Rd 12302 518-370-4272
John Bishop, hdmstr. Fax 370-4778

Scottsville, Monroe, Pop. 2,071
Wheatland-Chili Central SD 800/K-12
13 Beckwith Ave 14546 585-889-6246
Thomas Gallagher, supt. Fax 889-6284
www.wheatland.k12.ny.us
Connor ES, 13 Beckwith Ave 14546 300/K-5
Diane Kannel, prin. 585-889-6298

Sea Cliff, Nassau, Pop. 4,996
North Shore Central SD 2,900/K-12
112 Franklin Ave 11579 516-277-7800
Edward Melnick, supt. Fax 277-7801
www.northshoreschools.org/
Sea Cliff ES 400/K-5
280 Carpenter Ave 11579 516-277-7500
Adam Frankel, prin. Fax 277-7501
Other Schools – See Glen Head

Seaford, Nassau, Pop. 15,597
Levittown UFD
Supt. — See Levittown
East Broadway ES 700/K-5
751 Seamans Neck Rd 11783 516-520-5180
Jeanmarie Wink, prin. Fax 785-5186

Seaford UFD 2,600/K-12
1600 Washington Ave 11783 516-592-4000
Thomas Markle, supt.
www.seaford.k12.ny.us/
Seafood Harbor ES 600/K-5
3500 Bayview St 11783 516-592-4100
Donna Delucia-Troisi, prin.
Seaford Manor ES 500/K-5
1590 Washington Ave 11783 516-592-4050
John Striffolino, prin.
Seaford MS, 3940 Sunset Ave 11783 700/6-8
RoseAnne Careri, prin. 516-592-4200

Maria Regina S 500/PK-8
4045 Jerusalem Ave 11783 516-541-1229
Denise Seck, prin. Fax 541-1235
St. William the Abbot S 600/PK-8
2001 Jackson Ave 11783 516-785-6784
Anna Guardino, prin. Fax 785-2752

Selden, Suffolk, Pop. 20,608
Middle Country Central SD
Supt. — See Centereach
Bicycle Path Pre-K/K Center 500/PK-K
27 N Bicycle Path 11784 631-285-8800
Glenn Rogers, prin. Fax 285-8801
Hawkins Path ES 400/1-5
485 Hawkins Rd 11784 631-285-8530
Dr. Michael Dantona, prin. Fax 285-8531
New Lane Memorial ES 1,000/1-5
15 New Ln 11784 631-285-8900
Diane Trupia, prin. Fax 285-8901
Stagecoach ES 400/1-5
205 Dare Rd 11784 631-285-8730
Joseph Elsasser, prin. Fax 285-8731

Selkirk, Albany
Ravena-Coeymans-Selkirk Central SD 2,200/PK-12
26 Thatcher St 12158 518-756-5200
Vicki Wright, supt. Fax 767-2644
www.rcscsd.org
Becker ES 500/PK-5
1146 US Route 9W 12158 518-756-5200
Claudia Verga, prin. Fax 767-2512
Other Schools – See Coeymans, Ravena

Seneca Falls, Seneca, Pop. 6,837
Seneca Falls Central SD 1,400/K-12
PO Box 268 13148 315-568-5500
Robert McKeveny, supt. Fax 712-0535
www.sfcs.k12.ny.us/
Knight ES 300/K-2
98 Clinton St 13148 315-568-5500
Michele Van Coppenolle, prin. Fax 712-0527
Seneca Falls MS 300/6-8
95 Troy St 13148 315-568-5500
Kevin Rhinehart, prin. Fax 712-0524
Stanton ES 300/3-5
38 Garden St 13148 315-568-5500
Andrew Doell, prin. Fax 712-0526

Finger Lakes Christian S 100/PK-12
2291 State Route 89 13148 315-568-2216
Scott VanKirk, admin. Fax 568-6638

Setauket, Suffolk, Pop. 13,634
Three Village Central SD
Supt. — See East Setauket
Nassakeag ES 800/K-6
490 Pond Path 11733 631-730-4400
Gail Casciano, prin. Fax 730-4403
Setauket ES 800/K-6
134 Main St 11733 631-730-4600
Anne Rullan, prin. Fax 730-4604

Sharon Springs, Schoharie, Pop. 540
Sharon Springs Central SD 400/K-12
PO Box 218 13459 518-284-2266
Patterson Green, supt. Fax 284-9033
www.sharonsprings.org/
Sharon Springs Central S 400/K-12
PO Box 218 13459 518-284-2267
Patterson Green, prin. Fax 284-9075

Shelter Island, Suffolk, Pop. 1,193
Shelter Island UFD 300/K-12
PO Box 2015 11964 631-749-0302
Sharon Clifford, supt. Fax 749-1262
www.shelterisland.k12.ny.us
Shelter Island Central S 300/K-12
PO Box 2015 11964 631-749-0302
Sharon Clifford, prin. Fax 749-1262

Sherburne, Chenango, Pop. 1,446
Sherburne-Earlville Central SD 1,600/K-12
15 School St 13460 607-674-7300
Gayle Hellert, supt. Fax 674-9742
secsd.org
Sherburne-Earlville ES 600/K-5
15 School St 13460 607-674-7336
John Douchinsky, prin. Fax 674-9742
Sherburne-Earlville MS 400/6-8
13 School St 13460 607-674-7350
Nenette Greeno, prin. Fax 674-7392

Sherman, Chautauqua, Pop. 679
Sherman Central SD 500/K-12
PO Box 950 14781 716-761-6121
Thomas Schmidt, supt. Fax 761-6119
www.sherman.wnyric.org
Sherman ES 300/K-6
PO Box 950 14781 716-761-6121
Kaine Kelly, prin. Fax 761-6119

Sherrill, Oneida, Pop. 3,164
Vernon-Verona-Sherrill Central SD
Supt. — See Verona
McAllister ES 400/PK-6
217 Kinsley St 13461 315-363-3080
James Rozwod, prin. Fax 361-4783

Shirley, Suffolk, Pop. 22,936
William Floyd UFD
Supt. — See Mastic Beach
Floyd ES 800/K-5
111 Lexington Rd 11967 631-874-1257
Keith Fasciana, prin. Fax 874-1637
Hobart ES 900/K-5
230 Van Buren St 11967 631-874-1296
James Westcott, prin. Fax 874-1618
Woodhull ES 800/K-5
6 Francis Landau Pl 11967 631-874-1302
Monica Corona, prin. Fax 874-1804

Shoreham, Suffolk, Pop. 423
Shoreham-Wading River Central SD 2,800/K-12
250B Route 25A 11786 631-821-8100
Harriet Copel Ed.D., supt. Fax 929-3001
www.swrcsd.org
Briarcliff PS 300/K-1
18 Tower Hill Rd 11786 631-821-8200
Jane Ruthkowski, prin. Fax 821-8206
Miller Avenue ES 500/2-5
3 Miller Ave 11786 631-821-8232
Lou Parrinello, prin. Fax 821-8249
Prodell MS 700/6-8
100 Randall Rd 11786 631-821-8212
Linda Anthony, prin. Fax 821-8275
Other Schools – See Wading River

Shortsville, Ontario, Pop. 1,298
Manchester-Shortsville Central SD 900/K-12
1506 State Route 21 14548 585-289-3964
Robert Leiby, supt. Fax 289-6660
www.redjacket.org
Red Jacket ES 400/K-5
1506 State Route 21 14548 585-289-9647
James Falanga, prin. Fax 289-4499
Red Jacket MS 200/6-8
1506 State Route 21 14548 585-289-3967
Charlene Harvey, prin. Fax 289-8715

Shrub Oak, Westchester
Lakeland Central SD 6,300/K-12
1086 E Main St 10588 914-245-1700
Kenneth Connolly, supt. Fax 245-7817
www.lakelandschools.org
Other Schools – See Crompond, Mohegan Lake, Yorktown Heights

St. Elizabeth Ann Seton S 400/PK-8
1375 E Main St 10588 914-528-3563
Sr. Gabriel Obraz, prin. Fax 528-0341

Sidney, Delaware, Pop. 3,905
Sidney Central SD 1,200/K-12
95 W Main St 13838 607-563-2135
Sandra Cooper, supt. Fax 563-2386
www.sidneycsd.org
Sidney ES 500/K-5
15 Pearl St E 13838 607-563-2135
Corey Green, prin. Fax 563-9257
Sidney MS 300/6-8
13 Pearl St E 13838 607-563-2135
James Walters, prin. Fax 563-7242

Silver Creek, Chautauqua, Pop. 2,863
Silver Creek Central SD 1,100/K-12
1 Dickinson St 14136 716-934-2603
David O'Rourke, supt. Fax 934-2103
www.silvercreek.wnyric.org/
Silver Creek ES 500/K-5
1 Dickinson St 14136 716-934-2603
Lynne Gowan, prin. Fax 934-2173
Silver Creek MS 300/6-8
1 Dickinson St 14136 716-934-2603
Patricia Krenzer, prin. Fax 934-2103

Sinclairville, Chautauqua, Pop. 635
Cassadaga Valley Central SD 1,300/PK-12
PO Box 540 14782 716-962-5155
John Brown, supt. Fax 962-5976
cvweb.wnyric.org/
Sinclairville ES 300/PK-5
PO Box 540 14782 716-962-5195
John Kwietniewski, prin. Fax 962-5468
Other Schools – See Cassadaga

Skaneateles, Onondaga, Pop. 2,589
Skaneateles Central SD 1,700/K-12
49 E Elizabeth St 13152 315-291-2221
Philip D'Angelo, supt. Fax 685-0347
www.skanschools.org/
Skaneateles MS 400/6-8
35 East St 13152 315-291-2241
Timothy Chiavara, prin. Fax 291-2267
State Street IS 400/3-5
72 State St 13152 315-291-2261
Stephen Widrick, prin. Fax 291-2256
Waterman ES 400/K-2
55 East St 13152 315-291-2351
Marianne Young, prin. Fax 291-2302

Slate Hill, Orange
Minisink Valley Central SD 4,600/K-12
PO Box 217 10973 845-355-5110
Dr. Martha Murray, supt. Fax 355-5119
www.minisink.com
Minisink Valley ES 700/K-2
PO Box 217 10973 845-355-5270
Paul Dombal, prin. Fax 355-5147
Minisink Valley IS 900/3-5
PO Box 217 10973 845-355-5250
Joyce Memmelaar, prin. Fax 355-5252
Minisink Valley MS 1,100/6-8
PO Box 217 10973 845-355-5200
Michael Giardina, prin. Fax 355-5205
Other Schools – See Otisville

Slaterville Springs, Tompkins
Ithaca CSD
Supt. — See Ithaca
Caroline ES 300/K-5
2439 Slaterville Rd 14881 607-539-7155
Alaine Troisi, prin. Fax 539-6966

Sleepy Hollow, Westchester, Pop. 9,977
Pocantico Hills Central SD 400/PK-8
599 Bedford Rd 10591 914-631-2440
Dr. Fred Smith, supt. Fax 631-3280
www.pocanticohills.org
Pocantico Hills Central S 400/PK-8
599 Bedford Rd 10591 914-631-2440
Stanley Steele, prin. Fax 631-3280

Tarrytown UFD 3,000/PK-12
200 N Broadway 10591 914-631-9404
Dr. Howard Smith, supt. Fax 332-6283
www.tufsd.org
Morse ES 400/2-3
30 Pocantico St 10591 914-631-4144
Meghan Fitzgerald, prin. Fax 332-4267
Sleepy Hollow MS 800/7-8
210 N Broadway 10591 914-332-6275
Elizabeth Lopez, prin. Fax 332-6219
Other Schools – See Tarrytown

St. Teresa Montessori S PK-PK
113 DePeyster St 10591 914-631-1831
Sr. Mary Anne Maceda, prin. Fax 366-6459

Sloan, Erie, Pop. 3,576
Cheektowago-Sloan UFD
Supt. — See Buffalo
Wilson ES 300/3-5
166 Halstead Ave 14212 716-891-6418
Andrea Galenski, prin. Fax 891-6435

Sloatsburg, Rockland, Pop. 3,092
Ramapo Central SD
Supt. — See Hillburn
Sloatsburg ES 300/K-5
11 2nd St 10974 845-753-2720
Eric Baird, prin. Fax 753-6636

Smithtown, Suffolk, Pop. 27,100
Hauppauge UFD
Supt. — See Hauppauge
Forest Brook ES, Lilac Ln 11787 500/K-5
Christopher Michael, prin. 631-265-3265
Pines ES 700/K-5
22 Holly Dr 11787 631-543-8700
Michele Rothfeld, prin. Fax 543-3632

Smithtown Central SD 10,700/K-12
26 New York Ave 11787 631-382-2006
Edward Ehmann, supt. Fax 382-2010
www.smithtown.k12.ny.us
Accompsett ES 900/K-5
1 Lincoln St 11787 631-382-4150
Jeanne Kull-Minarik, prin. Fax 382-4157
Accompsett MS 800/6-8
660 Meadow Rd 11787 631-382-2300
John Nocero, prin. Fax 382-2307
Branch Brook ES 400/K-5
15 Ridgeley Rd 11787 631-382-4200
Irene Westrack, prin. Fax 382-4204
Dogwood ES 500/K-5
50 Dogwood Dr 11787 631-382-4250
Renee Carpenter, prin. Fax 382-4256
Mt. Pleasant ES 600/K-5
33 Plaisted Ave 11787 631-382-4350
Julie McGahan, prin. Fax 382-4356
Smithtown ES 600/K-5
51 Lawrence Ave 11787 631-382-4500
Paul Graf, prin. Fax 382-4507
Other Schools – See Nesconset, Saint James

Ivy League S 200/PK-6
211 Brooksite Dr 11787 631-265-4177
Linda Kaplan, prin. Fax 265-4698
St. Patrick S 500/PK-8
284 E Main St 11787 631-724-0285
Eileen Sadicario, prin. Fax 265-4841
Smithtown Christian S 600/PK-12
1 Higbie Dr 11787 631-265-3334
Nancy Bambino, prin. Fax 265-1079

Snyder, Erie

Park S of Buffalo 200/PK-12
4625 Harlem Rd 14226 716-839-1242
Chris Lauricella, prin. Fax 839-2014

Sodus, Wayne, Pop. 1,673
Sodus Central SD 1,200/PK-12
PO Box 220 14551 315-483-5201
Susan Kay Salvaggio, supt. Fax 483-4755
www.soduscsd.org
Sodus IS 300/4-6
PO Box 220 14551 315-483-5221
Alan Autovino, prin. Fax 483-5291
Sodus MS 200/7-8
PO Box 220 14551 315-483-5214
Darleen Contario, prin. Fax 483-6168
Sodus PS 400/PK-3
PO Box 220 14551 315-483-5226
Julie Miranda, prin. Fax 483-5292

Solvay, Onondaga, Pop. 6,606
Solvay UFD 1,700/K-12
103 3rd St 13209 315-468-1111
J. Francis Manning, supt. Fax 468-2755
www.solvayschools.org
Solvay ES 400/K-3
701 Woods Rd 13209 315-488-5422
Paula Kopp, prin. Fax 484-1417
Other Schools – See Syracuse

Somers, Westchester
Somers Central SD 3,400/K-12
334 Route 202 10589 914-277-2400
Dr. Joanne Marien, supt. Fax 248-7886
www.somers.k12.ny.us/
Somers IS 800/3-5
240 Route 202 10589 914-277-4344
John Griffiths, prin. Fax 277-3168
Somers MS 800/6-8
250 Route 202 10589 914-277-3399
Geraldine Paige, prin. Fax 277-2236
Other Schools – See Lincolndale

Southampton, Suffolk, Pop. 4,109
Southampton UFD 1,700/PK-12
70 Leland Ln 11968 631-591-4510
Dr. J. Richard Boyes, supt. Fax 591-4528
www.southampton.k12.ny.us
Southampton ES 500/K-4
30 Pine St 11968 631-591-4800
Bertha Richard, prin. Fax 283-6891
Southampton IS 500/5-8
70 Leland Ln 11968 631-591-4700
Timothy Frazier, prin. Fax 283-6899
Southampton Pre-Kindergarten 100/PK-PK
2 S Main St 11968 631-287-3306
Donna Denon, prin. Fax 287-1455

Tuckahoe Common SD 300/PK-8
468 Magee St 11968 631-283-3550
Linda Rozzi, supt. Fax 283-3469
www.tuckahoe.k12.ny.us
Tuckahoe S 300/PK-8
468 Magee St 11968 631-283-3550
Linda Rozzi, prin. Fax 283-3469

Our Lady of the Hamptons S 400/PK-8
160 N Main St 11968 631-283-9140
Sr. Kathryn Schlueter, prin. Fax 287-3958

South Dayton, Chautauqua, Pop. 637
Pine Valley Central SD 700/K-12
7755 Route 83 14138 716-988-3293
Pete Morgante, supt. Fax 988-3139
www.pval.org/
Pine Valley ES 300/K-6
7755 Route 83 14138 716-988-3291
Scott Burdick, prin. Fax 988-3864

South Glens Falls, Saratoga, Pop. 3,445
South Glens Falls Central SD 3,400/PK-12
6 Bluebird Rd 12803 518-793-9617
Dr. James McCarthy, supt. Fax 761-0723
www.sgfallssd.org/
Harrison Avenue ES 400/K-5
76 Harrison Ave 12803 518-793-9048
Joseph Palmer, prin. Fax 793-9095
Moreau ES 300/K-5
76 Bluebird Rd 12803 518-793-9644
Robert Lemieux, prin. Fax 793-9561
Tanglewood ES 500/K-5
60 Tanglewood Dr 12803 518-793-5631
Andrew Hills, prin. Fax 793-9241
Winch MS 800/6-8
99 Hudson St 12803 518-792-5891
Mark Fish, prin. Fax 793-9505
Other Schools – See Wilton

South Hempstead, Nassau, Pop. 3,014
Rockville Centre UFD
Supt. — See Rockville Centre
Covert ES 300/K-5
379 Willow St 11550 516-255-8916
Darren Raymar, prin. Fax 538-3165

South Kortright, Delaware
South Kortright Central SD 300/K-12
PO Box 113 13842 607-538-9111
Benjamin Berliner, supt. Fax 538-9205
www.skcs.org

South Kortright Central S 300/K-12
PO Box 113 13842 607-538-9111
John Bonhotal, prin. Fax 538-9205

Southold, Suffolk, Pop. 5,192
Southold UFD 1,000/K-12
PO Box 470 11971 631-765-5400
David Gamberg, supt. Fax 765-5086
www.southoldufsd.net/
Southold ES 500/K-6
PO Box 470 11971 631-765-5208
Ellen Waldron-O'Neill, prin. Fax 765-6893

South Otselic, Chenango
Otselic Valley Central SD 400/K-12
PO Box 161 13155 315-653-7591
Larry Thomas, supt. Fax 653-7500
www.ovcs.org/
Other Schools – See Georgetown

South Ozone Park, See New York
NYC Department of Education
Supt. — See New York
Public S 45 400/PK-6
12628 150th St, Jamaica NY 11436 718-529-1885
Evelyn Terrell, prin. Fax 322-8287
Public S 96 300/PK-6
13001 Rockaway Blvd 11420 718-529-2547
Joyce Walker, prin. Fax 659-0113
Public S 100 1,100/K-5
11111 118th St 11420 718-843-8390
Michelle Betancourt, prin. Fax 641-2474
Public S 108 1,300/PK-5
10810 109th Ave 11420 718-641-4956
Marie Biondollilo, prin. Fax 323-5379
Public S 121 1,000/PK-6
12610 109th Ave 11420 718-738-5126
Henry Somers, prin. Fax 843-5584
Public S 123 600/PK-5
14501 119th Ave, Jamaica NY 11436 718-529-4300
Cynthia Sumay-Eaton, prin. Fax 529-4290
Public S 124 1,100/PK-8
12915 150th Ave 11420 718-529-2580
Valarie Lewis, prin. Fax 322-4039
Public S 155 600/PK-5
13002 115th Ave 11420 718-529-0767
Dorothy Morris, prin. Fax 529-0773
JHS 226 1,600/6-8
12110 Rockaway Blvd 11420 718-843-2260
Sonia Nieves, prin. Fax 835-6317

Al-Ihsan Academy 400/PK-12
PO Box 200215 11420 718-322-3154
Refeek Mohamed, prin. Fax 322-7069
Our Lady of Perpetual Help S 600/PK-8
11110 115th St 11420 718-843-4184
Ms. Frances DeLuca, prin. Fax 843-6838
St. Anthony of Padua S 300/K-8
12518 Rockaway Blvd 11420 718-641-0212
Jerry Sgambati, prin. Fax 641-8079
St. Teresa of Avila S 300/K-8
10955 128th St 11420 718-641-1316
Loretta Rybacki, prin. Fax 843-0769

South Salem, Westchester
Katonah-Lewisboro UFD 4,000/K-12
1 Shady Ln 10590 914-763-7000
Dr. Robert Roelle, supt. Fax 763-7033
www.klschools.org/home.aspx
Lewisboro ES 500/K-5
79 Bouton Rd 10590 914-763-7800
Cristy Harris, prin. Fax 763-7871
Meadow Pond ES 400/K-5
185 Smith Ridge Rd 10590 914-763-7900
Carolann Castellone, prin. Fax 763-7986
Other Schools – See Cross River, Goldens Bridge, Katonah

Speculator, Hamilton, Pop. 335
Lake Pleasant Central SD 100/PK-9
PO Box 140 12164 518-548-7571
Ernest Virgil, supt. Fax 548-3230
lpschool.com
Lake Pleasant S 100/PK-9
PO Box 140 12164 518-548-7571
Ernest Virgil, prin. Fax 548-3230

Spencer, Tioga, Pop. 709
Spencer-Van Etten Central SD 1,100/PK-12
PO Box 307 14883 607-589-7100
Steven Schoonmaker, supt. Fax 589-3010
www.svecsd.org/
Spencer-Van Etten MS 300/5-8
1 Center St 14883 607-589-7120
Marcia Bishop, prin. Fax 589-3020
Other Schools – See Van Etten

North Spencer Christian Academy 100/PK-9
721 Ithaca Rd 14883 607-589-6366
Lori Bell, admin. Fax 589-6366

Spencerport, Monroe, Pop. 3,519
Spencerport Central SD 4,200/K-12
71 Lyell Ave 14559 585-349-5000
Bonnie Seaburn, supt. Fax 349-5011
www.spencerportschools.org
Bernabi ES 400/K-5
1 Bernabi Rd 14559 585-349-5400
Andrea Campo, prin. Fax 349-5466
Canal View ES 400/K-5
1 Ranger Rd 14559 585-349-5700
Michael Tenebruso, prin. Fax 349-5766
Cosgrove MS 1,000/6-8
2749 Spencerport Rd 14559 585-349-5300
Ned Dale, prin. Fax 349-5346
Munn ES 400/K-5
2333 Manitou Rd 14559 585-349-5500
Michael Canny, prin. Fax 349-5566

Taylor ES 500/K-5
399 Ogden Parma Town Line 14559 585-349-5600
Monica Macaluso, prin. Fax 349-5666

Spring Brook, Erie

St. Vincent De Paul S 200/K-8
PO Box 290 14140 585-652-8697
Lisa Ann Meegan, prin. Fax 652-7485

Springfield Gardens, See New York
NYC Department of Education
Supt. — See New York
Public S 15 400/K-5
12115 Lucas St 11413 718-525-1670
Antonio K'Tori, prin. Fax 723-7613
Public S 132 400/PK-5
13215 218th St 11413 718-528-5734
Alicia Davis, prin. Fax 723-6931
Public S 156 700/K-8
22902 137th Ave 11413 718-528-9173
Noreen Little, prin. Fax 723-7720
Public S 181 500/PK-6
14815 230th St 11413 718-528-5807
Andrea Belcher, prin. Fax 723-7825
Public S 251 400/K-3
14451 Arthur St 11413 718-276-2745
Edna Lonckey, prin. Fax 723-7822
IS 59 900/6-8
13255 Ridgedale St 11413 718-527-3501
Carleton Gordon, prin. Fax 276-1364

Spring Valley, Rockland, Pop. 25,355
East Ramapo Central SD 7,900/PK-12
105 S Madison Ave 10977 845-577-6000
Dr. Ira Oustatcher, supt. Fax 577-6168
www.eram.k12.ny.us
ECC, 465 Viola Rd 10977 100/PK-K
Laura Mungin, coord.
Hempstead ES 500/K-6
80 Brick Church Rd 10977 845-577-6270
Maureen Barnett, prin. Fax 362-0627
Other Schools – See Chestnut Ridge, Monsey, New City, Suffern

---

Bas Mikroh Girls S 300/PK-8
381 Viola Rd 10977 845-352-5296
Bnos Esther Pupa 300/PK-11
246 N Main St 10977 845-425-6905
Sarah Nueberger, prin. Fax 371-1237
Cong Machzikei Hadas of Beltz S 300/K-8
3 N Cole Ave 10977 845-425-0909
Talmud Torah Khal Adas Yereim 300/K-8
33 Union Rd 10977 845-425-5678
United Talmudical Academy 1,100/K-12
89 S Main St 10977 845-425-0392
Yeshiva Avir Yaakov 3,300/PK-12
PO Box 840 10977 845-362-6600
Yeshiva Bais Hachinuch 100/3-8
50A S Main St 10977 845-354-3805
Rabbi Naftoli Eisgrau, prin. Fax 354-3806
Yeshiva Degel Hatorah 200/K-12
111 Maple Ave 10977 845-356-4610
Yeshiva Machzikei Hadas Belz 300/K-8
3 N Cole Ave 10977 845-425-0909
Yeshiva Tzoin Yosef-Pupa 300/PK-12
15 Widman Ct 10977 845-371-1220
J. Kohn, prin. Fax 371-1237

Springville, Erie, Pop. 4,311
Springville-Griffith Inst. Central SD 2,200/K-12
307 Newman St 14141 716-592-3230
Vicki Wright, supt. Fax 592-3209
www.springvillegi.wnyric.org
Griffith Institute MS 500/6-8
267 Newman St 14141 716-592-3270
John Baronich, prin. Fax 592-0746
Springville ES 700/K-5
283 North St 14141 716-592-3260
Scott Tellgren, prin. Fax 592-0747
Other Schools – See Colden

St. Aloysius Regional S 100/PK-8
186 Franklin St 14141 716-592-7002
Bonnie Renzi, prin. Fax 592-7002

Stamford, Delaware, Pop. 1,269
Stamford Central SD 400/K-12
1 River St 12167 607-652-7301
Gregory Sanik, supt. Fax 652-3446
stamfordcs.org/
Stamford Central S 400/K-12
1 River St 12167 607-652-7301
Gregory Sanik, prin. Fax 652-3446

Stanfordville, Dutchess
Pine Plains Central SD
Supt. — See Pine Plains
Cold Spring ES 200/K-5
358 Homan Rd 12581 845-868-7451
James Glynn, prin. Fax 868-1105

Star Lake, Saint Lawrence, Pop. 1,092
Clifton-Fine Central SD 300/PK-12
11 Hall Ave 13690 315-848-3333
Dr. Paul Alioto, supt. Fax 848-3350
www.cfeagles.org
Clifton-Fine ES 200/PK-6
11 Hall Ave 13690 315-848-3333
Susan Shene, prin. Fax 848-3350

Staten Island, See New York
NYC Department of Education
Supt. — See New York
Marsh Ave S for Expeditionary Learning 100/6-8
Marsh Ave and Essex Dr 10314 718-370-6850
Jessica Jenkins-Milona, prin. Fax 370-6860

Public S 1 500/PK-5
58 Summit St 10307 718-984-0960
Diane Gordin, prin. Fax 984-3389
Public S 3 700/PK-5
80 S Goff Ave 10309 718-984-1021
Donna Gioello, prin. Fax 984-3628
Public S 4 700/PK-5
200 Nedra Pl 10312 718-984-1197
Marc Harris, prin. Fax 984-2324
Public S 5 200/K-5
348 Deisius St 10312 718-984-2233
Katherine Corso, prin. Fax 984-4761
Public S 6 800/PK-5
555 Page Ave 10307 718-356-4789
Erminia Claudio, prin. Fax 356-8491
Public S 8 400/PK-5
100 Lindenwood Rd 10308 718-356-2800
Lisa Esposito, prin. Fax 356-2065
Public S 11 200/PK-5
50 Jefferson St 10304 718-979-1030
Erica Mattera, prin. Fax 979-0259
Public S 13 700/PK-5
191 Vermont Ave 10305 718-447-1462
Constance Montijo, prin. Fax 447-8681
Public S 14 600/PK-5
100 Tompkins Ave 10304 718-727-0985
Nancy Hargett, prin. Fax 727-6351
Public S 16 900/PK-5
80 Monroe Ave 10301 718-447-0124
Vincenza Gallassio, prin. Fax 447-5398
Public S 18 400/PK-5
221 Broadway 10310 718-442-0216
Donna Luisi, prin. Fax 720-1558
Public S 19 600/PK-5
780 Post Ave 10310 718-442-3860
Mary Petrone, prin. Fax 815-2862
Public S 20 400/PK-5
161 Park Ave 10302 718-442-4110
Marie Munoz, prin. Fax 815-2228
Public S 21 500/PK-5
168 Hooker Pl 10302 718-442-1520
Gina Moreno, prin. Fax 815-3149
Public S 22 1,100/PK-5
1860 Forest Ave 10303 718-442-2219
Melissa Donath, prin. Fax 815-3104
Public S 23 500/PK-5
30 Natick St 10306 718-351-1155
Mark Bronstein, prin. Fax 667-4958
Public S 26 200/K-5
4108 Victory Blvd 10314 718-698-1530
Joanne Mecane, prin. Fax 982-9798
Public S 29 500/PK-5
1581 Victory Blvd 10314 718-442-2891
Linda Manfredi, prin. Fax 815-3712
Public S 30 800/K-5
200 Wardwell Ave 10314 718-442-0462
Denise Spina, prin. Fax 442-4265
Public S 31 400/PK-5
55 Layton Ave 10301 718-273-3500
Patricia Covington, prin. Fax 815-4826
Public S 32 900/PK-5
32 Elverton Ave 10308 718-984-1688
Nancy Spataro, prin. Fax 227-5736
Public S 35 300/K-5
60 Foote Ave 10301 718-442-3037
Melissa Garofalo, prin. Fax 815-4855
Public S 36 900/PK-5
255 Ionia Ave 10312 718-984-1422
Barbara Bellafatto, prin. Fax 227-6354
Public S 38 400/PK-5
421 Lincoln Ave 10306 718-351-1225
Everlidys Robles, prin. Fax 979-2487
Public S 39 500/PK-5
71 Sand Ln 10305 718-447-4543
Robert Corso, prin. Fax 447-0500
Public S 41 600/PK-5
216 Clawson St 10306 718-351-6777
Elise Feldman, prin. Fax 667-8200
Public S 42 900/PK-5
380 Genesee Ave 10312 718-984-3800
Brian Sharkey, prin. Fax 227-6358
Public S 44 700/PK-5
80 Maple Pkwy 10303 718-442-0433
Joseph Miller, prin. Fax 442-2323
Public S 45 900/PK-5
58 Lawrence Ave 10310 718-442-6123
Teresa Caccavale, prin. Fax 442-4141
Public S 46 300/PK-5
41 Reid Ave 10305 718-987-5155
Andrea Maffeo, prin. Fax 987-1703
Public S 48 400/PK-5
1055 Targee St 10304 718-447-8323
Jacqueline Mammolito, prin. Fax 815-3956
Public S 50 500/PK-5
200 Adelaide Ave 10306 718-987-0396
Sharon Fine, prin. Fax 987-1925
Public S 52 500/PK-5
450 Buel Ave 10305 718-351-5454
Evelyn Mastroianni, prin. Fax 667-8900
Public S 53 600/PK-5
330 Durant Ave 10308 718-987-8020
Annette Esposito, prin. Fax 987-3675
Public S 54 800/PK-5
1060 Willowbrook Rd 10314 718-698-0600
Anna Castley, prin. Fax 698-1736
Public S 55 600/PK-5
54 Osborne St 10312 718-356-2211
Kathleen Schultz, prin. Fax 356-0114
Public S 56 700/PK-5
250 Kramer Ave 10309 718-605-1189
Dean Scali, prin. Fax 605-1195
Public S 57 500/PK-5
140 Palma Dr 10304 718-447-1191
Sandra Barnes, prin. Fax 720-0747
Public S 58 700/PK-5
77 Marsh Ave 10314 718-761-2155
Roseann Mezzacappa, prin. Fax 761-7384

Public S 60 800/PK-5
55 Merrill Ave 10314 718-761-3325
Bonnie Ferretti, prin. Fax 983-8534
Public S 65 100/PK-3
98 Grant St 10301 718-981-5034
Sophie Scarmadella, prin. Fax 981-6109
Public S 69 700/K-5
144 Keating Pl 10314 718-698-6661
Doreen Murphy, prin. Fax 698-1903
Public S 80 1,200/K-12
715 Ocean Ter 10301 718-815-0186
Joanne Buckheit, prin. Fax 815-9638
IS 2 900/6-8
333 Midland Ave 10306 718-987-5336
Adrienne Stallone, prin. Fax 987-6937
IS 7 1,100/6-8
1270 Huguenot Ave 10312 718-356-2314
Dr. Nora Derosa-Karby, prin. Fax 967-0809
IS 24 1,500/6-8
225 Cleveland Ave 10308 718-356-4200
Rosemarie O'Neill, prin. Fax 356-5834
IS 27 800/6-8
11 Clove Lake Pl 10310 718-981-8800
Tracey Kornish, prin. Fax 815-4677
IS 34 1,100/6-8
528 Academy Ave 10307 718-984-0772
Jeffrey Preston, prin. Fax 227-4074
IS 49 900/6-8
101 Warren St 10304 718-727-6040
Linda Hill, prin. Fax 876-8207
IS 51 1,100/6-8
20 Houston St 10302 718-981-0502
Emma Della Rocca, prin. Fax 815-3957
IS 61 1,200/6-8
445 Castleton Ave 10301 718-727-8481
Richard Gallo, prin. Fax 447-2112
IS 72 1,700/6-8
33 Ferndale Ave 10314 718-698-5757
Peter Macellari, prin. Fax 761-5928
IS 75 1,300/6-8
455 Huguenot Ave 10312 718-356-0130
Mark Cannizzaro, prin. Fax 984-5302

Academy of St. Dorothy S 300/PK-8
1305 Hylan Blvd 10305 718-351-0939
Sr. Sharon McCarthy, prin. Fax 351-0661
Blessed Sacrament S 600/PK-8
830 Delafield Ave 10310 718-442-3090
Linda Magnusson, prin. Fax 442-9654
El-Bethel Christian Academy 100/PK-8
900 Jewett Ave 10314 718-981-1721
Camille Andrews, admin. Fax 727-1799
Eltingville Lutheran S 200/PK-8
300 Genesee Ave 10312 718-356-7811
Janet Scheiper, prin. Fax 967-8892
Gateway Academy 200/PK-8
200 Boscombe Ave 10309 718-966-8695
JoAnn Asciutto, prin. Fax 948-2241
Holy Rosary S 600/PK-8
100 Jerome Ave 10305 718-447-1195
Diane Murphy, prin. Fax 815-5862
Immaculate Conception S 200/PK-8
104 Gordon St 10304 718-447-7018
Kathleen Curatolo, prin. Fax 447-4365
Jewish Foundation S of Staten Island 400/PK-8
400 Caswell Ave 10314 718-983-6042
Fax 370-2591
New Dorp Christian Academy 200/PK-8
259 Rose Ave 10306 718-351-4442
Dr. Anthony Luciano, prin. Fax 351-1765
Notre Dame Academy 300/PK-8
78 Howard Ave 10301 718-273-9096
Sr. Rosemary Galligan, prin. Fax 442-6919
Oakdale Academy 100/PK-1
2734 Victory Blvd 10314 718-494-4448
Fax 494-1827
Oakdale Academy 200/2-5
366 Oakdale St 10312 718-948-4220
Our Lady Help of Christians S 300/PK-8
23 Summit St 10307 718-984-1360
Mary Chiapperino, prin. Fax 966-9356
Our Lady of Good Counsel S 300/PK-8
42 Austin Pl 10304 718-447-7260
Frances Santangelo, prin. Fax 815-7262
Our Lady of Mt. Carmel St. Benedicta S 300/PK-8
285 Clove Rd 10310 718-981-5131
Jeannine Roland, prin. Fax 981-0027
Our Lady Queen of Peace S 500/PK-8
22 Steele Ave 10306 718-351-0370
Theresa Signorile, prin. Fax 351-0950
Our Lady Star of the Sea S 900/PK-8
5411 Amboy Rd 10312 718-984-5750
Irma Cummings, prin. Fax 984-1346
Rabbi Jacob Joseph S for Boys 200/PK-8
3495 Richmond Rd 10306 718-979-6333
Rabbi Jacob Joseph S for Girls 200/PK-8
400 Caswell Ave 10314 718-982-8745
Sacred Heart S 400/PK-8
301 N Burgher Ave 10310 718-442-0347
Cynthia Reimer, prin. Fax 442-6978
St. Adalbert S 400/PK-8
355 Morningstar Rd 10303 718-442-2020
Diane Hesterhagen, prin. Fax 447-2012
St. Ann S 300/K-8
125 Cromwell Ave 10304 718-351-4343
Michael Mazzella, prin. Fax 980-4731
St. Charles S 700/PK-8
200 Penn Ave 10306 718-987-0200
Nancy Bushman, prin. Fax 987-0200
St. Christopher S 200/PK-8
15 Lisbon Pl 10306 718-351-0902
Catherine Falabella, prin. Fax 351-0975
St. Clare S 600/K-8
151 Lindenwood Rd 10308 718-984-7091
Josephine Rossicone, prin. Fax 227-5052
St. John's Lutheran S 200/PK-8
663 Manor Rd 10314 718-761-1858
Rosemary Palisay, prin. Fax 761-4962
St. John Villa Academy 300/PK-8
57 Cleveland Pl 10305 718-447-2668
Sr. Lucita Bacat, prin. Fax 447-2079
St. Joseph Hill Academy 600/PK-8
850 Hylan Blvd 10305 718-981-1187
Dorothy Zissler, prin. Fax 448-7016
St. Joseph S 200/PK-8
139 Saint Marys Ave 10305 718-447-7686
Linda Bilotti, prin. Fax 447-7687
St. Margaret Mary S 200/K-8
1128 Olympia Blvd 10306 718-351-4778
Rita Vallebuona, prin. Fax 351-3786
St. Mary S 200/PK-8
1124 Bay St 10305 718-447-1842
Virginia Savarese, prin. Fax 447-0986
St. Patrick S 500/K-8
3560 Richmond Rd 10306 718-979-8815
Sr. Mary Ferro, prin. Fax 979-4984
St. Peter S 300/PK-8
300 Richmond Ter 10301 718-447-1796
Lisa Moudatsos, prin. Fax 447-4240
St. Rita S 400/PK-8
30 Wellbrook Ave 10314 718-761-2504
Barbara Logan, prin. Fax 761-0014
St. Roch S 200/K-8
465 Villa Ave 10302 718-448-2424
Sr. Mary Lardieri, prin. Fax 556-1467
St. Sylvester S 200/PK-8
884 Targee St 10304 718-442-4938
Donald Kramer, prin. Fax 442-8177
St. Teresa S 400/PK-8
1632 Victory Blvd 10314 718-448-9650
Catherine Dempsey, prin. Fax 447-6426
SS. Joseph & Thomas S 300/PK-8
50 Maguire Ave 10309 718-356-3344
Joann Gaal, prin. Fax 227-9531
Staten Island Academy 400/PK-12
715 Todt Hill Rd 10304 718-987-8100
Diane Hulse, hdmstr. Fax 979-7641
Trinity Lutheran S 200/PK-8
309 Saint Pauls Ave 10304 718-447-4600
Vernell Davis, prin. Fax 815-6619

Stella Niagara, Niagara

Stella Niagara Education Park 100/K-8
4421 Lower River Rd 14144 716-754-4314
Sr. Margaret Sullivan, prin. Fax 754-2964

Stephentown, Rensselaer
Berlin Central SD
Supt. — See Berlin
Stephentown ES 100/K-3
473 Route 43 12168 518-733-5454
Eileen Leffler, prin. Fax 733-6995

Stewart Manor, Nassau, Pop. 1,900
Elmont UFD
Supt. — See Elmont
Stewart Manor ES 300/K-6
38 Stewart Ave 11530 516-326-5530
Hope Kranidis, prin. Fax 326-0548

Stillwater, Saratoga, Pop. 1,706
Stillwater Central SD 1,300/K-12
334 Hudson Ave 12170 518-373-6100
Stan Maziejka, supt. Fax 664-9134
www.scsd.org/
Stillwater ES 500/K-4
334 Hudson Ave 12170 518-373-6100
John Goralski, prin. Fax 664-1805
Stillwater MS 400/5-8
334 Hudson Ave 12170 518-373-6100
Pattie Morris, prin. Fax 664-1832

Stone Ridge, Ulster
Rondout Valley Central SD
Supt. — See Accord
Marbletown ES 300/K-4
12 Pine Bush Rd 12484 845-687-0284
William Cafiero, prin. Fax 687-7691

High Meadow S 100/PK-8
PO Box 552 12484 845-687-4855
Suzanne Borris, dir. Fax 687-5151

Stony Brook, Suffolk, Pop. 13,726
Three Village Central SD
Supt. — See East Setauket
Mount ES 900/K-6
50 Dean Ln 11790 631-730-4300
Nathalie Lilavois, prin. Fax 730-4309

North Shore Montessori S 200/PK-K
218 Christian Ave 11790 631-689-8273
Crystal Benenati, dir. Fax 941-3889

Stony Point, Rockland, Pop. 10,587
North Rockland Central SD
Supt. — See Garnerville
Farley MS 500/5-7
140 Route 210 10980 845-942-3200
Kris Felicello, prin. Fax 942-3207
Stony Point ES 600/K-4
7 Gurnee Dr 10980 845-942-3140
Diane Bane, prin. Fax 942-3083

Children of Mary Kindergarten PK-K
174 Filors Ln 10980 845-947-3183
Kathleen Sweeney, dir. Fax 947-3183

Suffern, Rockland, Pop. 10,897
East Ramapo Central SD
Supt. — See Spring Valley
Lime Kiln IS 400/4-6
35 Lime Kiln Rd 10901 845-577-6280
Lori Lowe-Stokes, prin. Fax 362-3570
Pomona MS 800/7-8
101 Pomona Rd 10901 845-577-6200
Dr. Brenda Shannon, prin. Fax 577-6245

Ramapo Central SD
Supt. — See Hillburn
Cherry Lane ES 500/K-5
1 Heather Dr 10901 845-357-3988
David Leach, prin. Fax 357-2191
Connor ES 400/K-5
13 Cypress Rd 10901 845-357-2858
Mary DiPersio, prin. Fax 357-8657
Montebello Road ES 400/K-5
52 Montebello Rd 10901 845-357-4466
Michele Cohen Ph.D., prin. Fax 368-4161
Suffern JHS 1,100/6-8
80 Hemion Rd 10901 845-357-7400
Brian Fox, prin. Fax 357-4563
Viola ES 500/K-5
557 Haverstraw Rd 10901 845-357-8315
Christine Druss, prin. Fax 357-2230

Sacred Heart S 300/PK-8
60 Washington Ave 10901 845-357-1684
Karen Wizeman, prin. Fax 357-0318
Yeshiva Darchei Noam 300/PK-8
257 Grandview Ave 10901 845-352-7100

Swormville, Erie

St. Mary S 300/PK-8
6919 Transit Rd 14051 716-689-8424
Sr. Sheila Burke, prin. Fax 689-8424

Syosset, Nassau, Pop. 18,967
Cold Spring Harbor Central SD
Supt. — See Cold Spring Harbor
West Side ES 300/2-6
1597 Laurel Hollow Rd 11791 516-692-7900
Lynn Herschlein, prin. Fax 692-4845

Syosset Central SD 6,700/K-12
99 Pell Ln 11791 516-364-5600
Dr. Carole Hankin, supt. Fax 921-5616
www.syosset.k12.ny.us
Berry Hill ES 500/K-5
181 Cold Spring Rd 11791 516-364-5790
Joanne Mannion, prin.
Robbins Lane ES 500/K-5
157 Robbins Ln 11791 516-364-5804
Julia Schnurman, prin. Fax 942-3892
South Grove ES, 60 Colony Ln 11791 400/K-5
Theresa Scrocco, prin. 516-364-5810
South Woods MS 800/6-8
99 Pell Ln 11791 516-364-5621
Michelle Burget, prin. Fax 921-5616
Thompson MS 900/6-8
98 Ann Dr 11791 516-364-5760
James Kassebaum, prin. Fax 921-5616
Village ES 400/K-5
90 Convent Rd 11791 516-364-5817
Jeffery Kasper, prin. Fax 921-5616
Willits ES 300/K-5
99 Nana Pl 11791 516-364-5829
Mary Tabone, prin. Fax 921-5616
Other Schools – See Plainview, Woodbury

St. Edward Confessor S 300/PK-8
2 Teibrook Ave 11791 516-921-7767
Anne Schaefer, prin. Fax 496-0001

Syracuse, Onondaga, Pop. 141,683
Lyncourt UFD 300/K-8
2707 Court St 13208 315-455-7571
Michael Schiedo, supt. Fax 455-7573
lyncourt.cnyric.org/
Lyncourt S 300/K-8
2709 Court St 13208 315-455-7571
James Austin, prin. Fax 455-7573

North Syracuse Central SD
Supt. — See North Syracuse
Roxboro Road ES 600/K-4
200 Bernard St 13211 315-218-2700
Jacquelyn Grace-Rasheed, prin. Fax 218-2785
Roxboro Road MS 1,000/5-7
300 Bernard St 13211 315-218-3300
Steven Wolf, prin. Fax 218-3385

Solvay UFD
Supt. — See Solvay
Solvay MS 600/4-8
299 Bury Dr 13209 315-487-7061
James Werbeck, prin. Fax 484-1444

Syracuse CSD 19,800/K-12
725 Harrison St 13210 315-435-4161
Daniel Lowengard, supt. Fax 435-4015
www.syracusecityschools.com/
Bellevue ES 400/K-5
530 Stolp Ave 13207 315-435-4520
Joanne Harlow, prin. Fax 435-6207
Bellevue MS Academy 200/6-8
1607 S Geddes St 13207 315-435-4480
Corliss Herr, prin. Fax 435-6232
Blodgett S 600/K-8
312 Oswego St 13204 315-435-4386
Melissa Evans, prin. Fax 435-4539
Clary Magnet MS 400/6-8
100 Amidon Dr 13205 315-435-4411
Pamela Odom-Cain, prin. Fax 435-5832
Danforth Magnet MS 600/6-8
309 W Brighton Ave 13205 315-435-4535
Patricia Clark, prin. Fax 435-6208

Delaware ES 500/K-5
900 S Geddes St 13204 315-435-4540
Amy Fazio Evans, prin. Fax 435-4544
Elmwood ES 400/K-5
1728 South Ave 13207 315-435-4545
Marcia Haynes, prin. Fax 435-6210
Expeditionary Learning S 6-8
4942 S Salina St 13205 315-435-6416
Kevin Burns, prin.
Franklin Magnet ES 700/K-5
428 S Alvord St 13208 315-435-4550
Ann Sherwood, prin. Fax 435-6211
Frazer S 800/K-8
741 Park Ave 13204 315-435-4555
Robert DiFlorio, prin. Fax 435-4820
Grant MS 700/6-8
2400 Grant Blvd 13208 315-435-4433
Andrew Rudd, prin. Fax 435-4856
Hughes Magnet ES 400/K-6
345 Jamesville Ave 13210 315-435-4404
Iverna Minor, prin. Fax 435-6552
Huntington S 900/K-8
400 Sunnycrest Rd 13206 315-435-4565
Marc Parrillo, prin. Fax 435-6206
Hyde ES 500/K-6
450 Durston Ave 13203 315-435-4570
Octavia Wilcox, prin. Fax 435-6212
King Magnet ES 500/K-5
416 E Raynor Ave 13202 315-435-4580
Patricia Floyd-Echols, prin. Fax 435-6213
LeMoyne ES 400/K-5
1528 Lemoyne Ave 13208 315-435-4590
Lynne Kelly, prin. Fax 435-4591
Levy S 500/K-8
157 Fellows Ave 13210 315-435-4444
Margaret Wilson, prin. Fax 435-4443
Lincoln MS 500/6-8
1613 James St 13203 315-435-4450
Dean DeSantis, prin. Fax 435-4455
McKinley-Brighton Magnet ES 400/K-5
141 W Newell St 13205 315-435-4605
Rosa Clark, prin. Fax 435-4603
Meachem ES 400/K-5
171 Spaulding Ave 13205 315-435-4610
Adrienne Spencer, prin. Fax 435-6216
Porter Magnet ES 500/K-6
512 Emerson Ave 13204 315-435-4625
Milagros Escalera, prin. Fax 435-4897
Roberts S 700/K-8
715 Glenwood Ave 13207 315-435-4635
Janet Kimatian, prin. Fax 435-6217
Seymour Magnet ES 400/K-5
108 Shonnard St 13204 315-435-4645
Marie Lostumbo, prin. Fax 435-4646
Smith S 600/K-8
1106 Lancaster Ave 13210 315-435-4650
Daryl Hall, prin. Fax 435-6219
Smith S 700/K-8
1130 Salt Springs Rd 13224 315-435-4490
Sharon Birnkrant, prin. Fax 435-6220
Van Duyn ES 300/K-5
401 Loomis Ave 13207 315-435-4660
Claudia Stockard, prin. Fax 435-6221
Webster ES 500/K-5
500 Wadsworth St 13208 315-435-4670
Paula DiGirolamo, prin. Fax 435-4021
Weeks ES 600/K-5
710 Hawley Ave 13203 315-435-4097
Dare Dutter, prin. Fax 435-6222

West Genesee Central SD
Supt. — See Camillus
Onondaga Road ES 300/K-5
703 S Onondaga Rd 13219 315-487-4653
Deborah Geiss, prin. Fax 487-2999

Westhill Central SD 2,000/K-12
400 Walberta Rd 13219 315-426-3218
Stephen Bocciolatt, supt. Fax 488-6411
www.westhillschools.org/
Cherry Road ES 300/3-4
201 Cherry Rd 13219 315-426-3300
Sarah Vanliew, prin. Fax 468-0623
Onondaga Hill MS 600/5-8
4860 Onondaga Rd 13215 315-426-3400
Douglas Hutson, prin. Fax 492-0156
Walberta Park PS 400/K-2
400 Walberta Rd 13219 315-426-3200
Maureen Mulderig, prin. Fax 484-9056

Bishop's Academy at Holy Family 300/PK-6
130 Chapel Dr 13219 315-487-8515
Helen Chajka, prin. Fax 487-8515
Bishop's Academy at Most Holy Rosary S 200/PK-6
1031 Bellevue Ave 13207 315-476-6035
Melanie Carroll, prin. Fax 476-0219
Bishop's Academy at St. Charles 200/PK-6
200 W High Ter 13219 315-488-7631
Sr. Donna Driscoll, prin. Fax 488-0617
Blessed Sacrament S 300/PK-6
3129 James St 13206 315-463-1261
Andrea Polcaro, prin. Fax 463-0253
Cathedral Academy at Pompei 100/PK-6
923 N McBride St 13208 315-422-8548
Charles LaBarbera, prin. Fax 472-0754
Faith Heritage S 500/PK-12
3740 Midland Ave 13205 315-469-7777
Jeff Shaver, dir. Fax 492-7440
Living Word Academy 200/PK-12
6101 Court Street Rd 13206 315-437-6744
Philip Mastroleo, prin. Fax 437-6766
Montessori S of Syracuse 200/PK-6
155 Waldorf Pkwy 13224 315-449-9033
Parkview Junior Academy 50/PK-8
412 S Avery Ave 13219 315-468-0117

Taberg, Oneida
Camden Central SD
Supt. — See Camden
Annsville Area ES 200/K-5
9374 Main St 13471 315-334-8030
Patricia Fallon, prin. Fax 334-8032

Tannersville, Greene, Pop. 446
Hunter-Tannersville Central SD 500/PK-12
PO Box 1018 12485 518-589-5400
Patrick Sweeney, supt. Fax 589-5403
www.htcsd.org/
Other Schools – See Hunter

Tappan, Rockland, Pop. 6,867
South Orangetown Central SD
Supt. — See Blauvelt
Schaefer ES 500/K-1
140 Lester Dr 10983 845-680-1300
Nora Polansky, prin. Fax 680-1920

Tarrytown, Westchester, Pop. 11,346
Tarrytown UFD
Supt. — See Sleepy Hollow
Irving IS 600/4-6
103 S Broadway 10591 914-631-4442
Bill Greene, prin. Fax 332-4266
Paulding ES 200/1-1
154 N Broadway 10591 914-631-5526
Marilyn Mercado-Belvin, prin. Fax 332-6283
Tappan Hill K 300/PK-K
50 Ichabod Ln 10591 914-631-9252
Michele Milliam, prin. Fax 332-4268

Hackley S 800/K-12
293 Benedict Ave 10591 914-631-0128
Walter Johnson, hdmstr. Fax 366-2636
Transfiguration S 200/PK-8
40 Prospect Ave 10591 914-631-3737
Audrey Woods, prin. Fax 631-6640

Theresa, Jefferson, Pop. 824
Indian River Central SD
Supt. — See Philadelphia
Theresa PS 100/K-3
125 Bridge St 13691 315-628-4432
Fax 628-5890

Thiells, Rockland, Pop. 5,204
North Rockland Central SD
Supt. — See Garnerville
Thiells ES 800/PK-4
78 Rosman Rd 10984 845-942-3160
Stephanie Viola, prin. Fax 429-4419
Willow Grove MS 700/5-7
153 Storrs Rd 10984 845-942-8000
Michael Roth, prin. Fax 942-8009

Thornwood, Westchester, Pop. 7,025
Mount Pleasant Central SD 1,700/K-12
825 Westlake Dr 10594 914-769-5500
Susan Guiney, supt. Fax 769-3733
www.mtplcsd.org
Columbus ES 300/2-4
580 Columbus Ave 10594 914-769-8538
Michael Cunzio, prin. Fax 769-8512
Westlake MS 500/5-8
825 Westlake Dr 10594 914-769-8540
Jerry Schulman, prin. Fax 769-8550
Other Schools – See Hawthorne

Ticonderoga, Essex, Pop. 2,726
Ticonderoga Central SD 1,000/K-12
5 Calkins Pl 12883 518-585-6674
John McDonald, supt. Fax 585-9158
www.ticonderogak12.org
Ticonderoga ES 400/K-5
116 Alexandria Ave 12883 518-585-7437
Anne Dreimiller, prin. Fax 585-9065
Ticonderoga MS 200/6-8
116 Alexandria Ave 12883 518-585-7442
Bruce Tubbs, prin. Fax 585-2716

St. Mary S 100/K-8
64 Amherst Ave 12883 518-585-7433
Sr. Sharon Dalton, prin. Fax 585-7505

Tioga Center, Tioga
Tioga Central SD 1,100/K-12
PO Box 241 13845 607-687-8000
Patrick Dougherty, supt. Fax 687-8007
www.tiogacentral.org/
Tioga ES 300/K-4
PO Box 241 13845 607-687-8002
Robert James, prin. Fax 687-6945
Tioga MS 300/5-8
PO Box 241 13845 607-687-8004
Cynthia Bennett, prin. Fax 687-6910
Other Schools – See Nichols

Tonawanda, Erie, Pop. 15,335
Kenmore-Tonawanda UFSD
Supt. — See Buffalo
Edison ES 500/K-5
236 Grayton Rd 14150 716-874-8416
Mary Pauly, prin. Fax 874-8526
Hamilton ES 400/K-5
44 Westfall Dr 14150 716-874-8419
Michael Huff, prin. Fax 874-8550
Holmes ES 300/K-5
365 Dupont Ave 14150 716-874-8423
Lisa Cross, prin. Fax 874-8560

Sweet Home Central SD
Supt. — See Amherst
Glendale ES 400/K-5
101 Glendale Dr 14150 716-250-1500
Joyce Brace, prin. Fax 250-1510

Tonawanda CSD 1,600/PK-12
100 Hinds St 14150 716-694-7784
Dr. Whitney Vantine, supt. Fax 695-8738
www.tonawandacsd.org
Fletcher ES 50/4-5
555 Fletcher St 14150 716-694-7694
John McKenna, prin. Fax 694-3449
Mullen ES 200/PK-3
130 Syracuse St 14150 716-694-6805
Susan D'Angelo, prin. Fax 694-5897
Riverview ES 200/PK-3
55 Taylor Dr 14150 716-694-7697
Claudia Panaro, prin. Fax 694-7172
Tonawanda MS 500/6-8
600 Fletcher St 14150 716-694-7660
James Newton, prin. Fax 743-8839

St. Amelia S 500/PK-8
2999 Eggert Rd 14150 716-836-2230
James Mule, prin. Fax 832-9700
St. Christopher S 600/PK-8
2660 Niagara Falls Blvd 14150 716-693-5604
Elizabeth Philage, prin. Fax 693-5127
St. Francis of Assisi S 200/PK-8
70 Adam St 14150 716-692-7886
Mary Balistreri, prin. Fax 693-2025

Troupsburg, Steuben
Jasper-Troupsburg Central SD
Supt. — See Jasper
Jasper-Troupsburg ES 400/PK-6
PO Box 98 14885 607-525-6301
John Cain, prin. Fax 525-6309

Troy, Rensselaer, Pop. 48,310
Averill Park Central SD
Supt. — See Averill Park
Washington ES 100/K-5
344 Menemsha Ln 12180 518-674-7150
Barbara Goldstein, prin. Fax 283-3908

Brunswick Central SD 1,400/K-12
3992 State Highway 2 12180 518-279-4600
Louis McIntosh, supt. Fax 279-4588
www.brittonkill.k12.ny.us
Tamarac ES 600/K-5
3992 State Highway 2 12180 518-279-4600
Karen Lederman, prin. Fax 279-0612

East Greenbush Central SD
Supt. — See East Greenbush
Bell Top ES 400/K-5
39 Reynolds Rd 12180 518-283-0727
James McHugh, prin. Fax 283-1184

Lansingburgh Central SD 2,500/K-12
576 5th Ave 12182 518-233-6850
George Goodwin, supt. Fax 235-7436
www.lansingburgh.org
Knickerbacker MS 600/6-8
320 7th Ave 12182 518-233-6811
Shaun Paolino, prin. Fax 238-2518
Rensselaer Park ES 600/K-5
70 110th St 12182 518-233-6823
Marcella Fushs, prin. Fax 238-1708
Turnpike ES 600/K-5
55 New Turnpike Rd 12182 518-233-6822
Dawne Steenrod, prin. Fax 235-3593

North Greenbush Common SD
Supt. — See Rensselaer
Little Red School House 50/K-2
49 N Greenbush Rd 12180 518-283-6748
Joseph Padalino, prin.

Troy CSD 4,300/PK-12
2920 5th Ave 12180 518-328-5052
Fadhilika Atiba-Weza, supt. Fax 271-5229
www.troy.k12.ny.us/
Carroll Hill ES 300/PK-6
112 Delaware Ave 12180 518-328-5701
Casey Parker, prin. Fax 274-4587
Doyle MS 700/7-8
1976 Burdett Ave 12180 518-328-5301
Jennifer Span, prin. Fax 271-8160
Public S 2 300/PK-6
470 10th St 12180 518-328-5601
Linda Martin, prin. Fax 271-5205
Public S 12 500/PK-6
475 1st St 12180 518-328-5201
Tracy Ford, prin. Fax 271-5206
Public S 14 500/PK-6
1700 Tibbits Ave 12180 518-328-5801
Karen Cloutier, prin. Fax 274-0371
Public S 16 300/K-6
40 Collins Ave 12180 518-328-5101
Jeanna Kukulka, prin. Fax 274-4585
Public S 18 300/K-6
417 Hoosick St 12180 518-328-5501
Cynthia Kilgallon, prin. Fax 274-4374

Oakwood Christian S 200/PK-12
260 Oakwood Ave 12182 518-271-0526
Rev. James DuJack, hdmstr. Fax 270-1659
Our Lady of Victory S 100/PK-6
451 Marshland Ct 12180 518-274-6202
Karen Snyder, prin. Fax 271-8680
Sacred Heart S 200/PK-6
310 Spring Ave 12180 518-274-3655
Susan Holland, prin. Fax 274-8720
St. Augustine's S 100/PK-6
525 4th Ave 12182 518-235-7287
James Clement, prin. Fax 235-7287

Trumansburg, Tompkins, Pop. 1,588
Trumansburg Central SD 1,300/K-12
100 Whig St 14886 607-387-7551
Paula Hurley, supt. Fax 387-2807
www.tburg.k12.ny.us

Doig MS 400/5-8
100 Whig St 14886 607-387-7551
Michael Hayden, prin. Fax 387-2807
Trumansburg ES 400/K-4
100 Whig St Bldg 2 14886 607-387-7551
Jean Wiggins, prin. Fax 387-2807

Truxton, Cortland
Homer Central SD
Supt. — See Homer
Hartnett ES 100/K-6
Academy St 13158 607-842-6216
Michael Falls, prin. Fax 842-6878

Tuckahoe, Westchester, Pop. 6,256
Tuckahoe UFD 1,000/K-12
29 Elm St 10707 914-337-6600
Michael Yazurlo Ed.D., supt. Fax 337-3072
www.tuckahoeschools.org/
Other Schools – See Eastchester

Annunciation S 600/K-8
465 Westchester Ave 10707 914-337-8760
Sr. Anne Massell, prin. Fax 337-8878
Immaculate Conception S 400/PK-8
53 Winter Hill Rd 10707 914-961-3785
Maureen Harten, prin. Fax 961-6054

Tully, Onondaga, Pop. 891
Tully Central SD 1,200/K-12
PO Box 628 13159 315-696-6204
Kraig Pritts, supt. Fax 883-1343
www.tullyschools.org/
Tully ES 600/K-6
PO Box 628 13159 315-696-6213
Kimberly O'Brien, prin. Fax 696-6220

Tupper Lake, Franklin, Pop. 3,856
Tupper Lake Central SD 1,000/K-12
294 Hosley Ave 12986 518-359-3371
Seth McGowan, supt. Fax 359-7862
www.tupperlakecsd.net/
Quinn ES 500/K-6
294 Hosley Ave 12986 518-359-2981
Carolyn Merrihew, prin. Fax 359-3415

Turin, Lewis, Pop. 246
South Lewis Central SD 1,100/K-12
PO Box 10 13473 315-348-2500
Douglas Premo, supt. Fax 348-2510
www.southlewis.org
South Lewis MS 300/6-8
PO Box 70 13473 315-348-2570
Philomena Goss, prin. Fax 348-2510
Other Schools – See Constableville, Glenfield, Port Leyden

Tuxedo Park, Orange, Pop. 732
Tuxedo UFD 700/K-12
PO Box 2002 10987 845-351-4799
Joseph Zanetti, supt. Fax 351-5296
tuxedoschooldistrict.com
Mason S 300/K-8
PO Box 2002 10987 845-351-4797
Barbara Geoghan, prin. Fax 351-3402

Tuxedo Park S 200/PK-9
Mountain Farm Rd 10987 845-351-4737
James Burger, hdmstr. Fax 351-4219

Ulster Park, Ulster
Kingston CSD
Supt. — See Kingston
Devine ES 200/K-5
1372 Old Post Rd 12487 845-658-8342
William Krupp, prin. Fax 658-3811

Unadilla, Otsego, Pop. 1,070
Otego-Unadilla Central SD
Supt. — See Otego
Unadilla ES 300/K-5
265 Main St 13849 607-369-6200
Gary Guidici, prin. Fax 369-6222

Uniondale, Nassau, Pop. 20,328
Uniondale UFD 6,100/K-12
933 Goodrich St 11553 516-560-8824
William Lloyd Ph.D., supt. Fax 292-2659
www.uniondale.k12.ny.us
California Avenue ES 800/K-5
236 California Ave 11553 516-918-1850
Jennifer Bumford, prin. Fax 505-9763
Northern Parkway ES 700/K-5
440 Northern Pkwy 11553 516-918-1700
Dr. Brenda Williams-Jackson, prin. Fax 481-0541
Smith Street ES 500/K-5
780 Smith St 11553 516-918-2000
Lynnda Nadien, prin. Fax 486-2441
Turtle Hook MS 700/6-8
975 Jerusalem Ave 11553 516-918-1300
Dr. Ann Marie Ginsberg, prin. Fax 505-2533
Walnut Street ES 500/K-5
1270 Walnut St 11553 516-918-2200
Linda Friedman, prin. Fax 485-9724
Other Schools – See Hempstead, North Baldwin

Pat-Kam S & ECC 100/PK-5
705 Nassau Rd 11553 516-486-7887
Ronald Clahar, prin. Fax 486-7905
St. Martin DePorres S 400/PK-8
530 Hempstead Blvd 11553 516-481-3303
John Holian, prin. Fax 483-4138

Union Springs, Cayuga, Pop. 1,069
Union Springs Central SD 1,000/K-12
239 Cayuga St 13160 315-889-4101
Linda Rice, supt. Fax 889-4108
www.uscsd.info/
Smith ES 200/4-6
26 Homer St 13160 315-889-7102
Karen Burcroff, prin. Fax 889-4165
Union Springs MS 100/7-8
239 Cayuga St 13160 315-889-4112
Thomas Eldridge, prin. Fax 889-4108
Other Schools – See Cayuga

Frontenac S 50/K-8
963 Spring Street Rd 13160 315-889-5094

Upper Nyack, Rockland, Pop. 1,873
Nyack UFD
Supt. — See Nyack
Upper Nyack ES 400/K-5
336 N Broadway 10960 845-353-7260
Dr. Anne Roberts, prin. Fax 353-7262

Utica, Oneida, Pop. 59,336
Utica CSD 8,800/K-12
1115 Mohawk St 13501 315-792-2222
Marilyn Skermont, supt. Fax 792-2200
www.uticaschools.org
Albany ES 400/K-5
1151 Albany St 13501 315-792-2150
Tania Kalavazoff, prin. Fax 792-2151
Columbus ES 700/K-5
930 Armory Dr 13501 315-792-2011
Dona Dawes, prin. Fax 792-2014
Donovan MS 1,000/6-8
1701 Noyes St 13502 315-792-2007
Richard Ambruso, prin. Fax 792-2077
Herkimer ES 500/K-5
420 Keyes Rd 13502 315-792-2160
Elaine Galime, prin. Fax 792-2034
Hughes ES 400/K-5
24 Prospect St 13501 315-792-2165
Joanne Russo, prin. Fax 792-2271
Jefferson ES 500/K-5
190 Booth St 13502 315-792-2163
Elizabeth Paul, prin. Fax 732-5902
Jones ES 400/K-5
2630 Remington Rd 13501 315-792-2171
Allaine Hartnett, prin. Fax 792-2154
Kennedy MS 1,000/6-8
500 Deerfield Dr E 13502 315-792-2086
Dolores Chainey, prin. Fax 792-2084
Kernan ES 600/K-5
929 York St 13502 315-792-2185
Henry Frasca, prin. Fax 792-2187
King ES 200/K-5
211 Square St 13501 315-792-2175
Mark DeSalvo, prin. Fax 792-0051
Watson Williams ES 400/K-5
107 Elmwood Pl 13501 315-792-2167
Cheryl Beckett-Minor, prin. Fax 792-1133

Notre Dame ES 300/PK-6
11 Barton Ave 13502 315-732-4374
Judith Hauck, prin. Fax 738-9720

Valatie, Columbia, Pop. 1,910
Kinderhook Central SD 2,100/K-12
PO Box 820 12184 518-758-7575
James Dexter, supt. Fax 758-7579
Crane MS 600/6-8
PO Box 820 12184 518-758-7676
Tim Farley, prin. Fax 758-1405
Crane PS 400/K-2
PO Box 820 12184 518-758-6931
Melissa Murray, prin. Fax 758-2199
Glynn ES 200/3-5
PO Box 820 12184 518-758-7559
John Stickles, prin. Fax 758-2251
Other Schools – See Kinderhook

Valhalla, Westchester, Pop. 6,200
Valhalla UFD 1,500/K-12
316 Columbus Ave 10595 914-683-5040
Dr. Diane Ramos-Kelly, supt. Fax 683-5075
www.valhallaufsd.com
Kensico S 400/3-5
320 Columbus Ave 10595 914-683-5030
Sal Miele, prin. Fax 683-5304
Valhalla MS 300/6-8
300 Columbus Ave 10595 914-683-5011
Steven Garcia, prin. Fax 683-5003
Other Schools – See North White Plains

Holy Name of Jesus S 100/PK-8
2 Broadway 10595 914-948-1744
Antonella Corso, prin. Fax 948-1749

Valley Cottage, Rockland, Pop. 9,007
Nyack UFD
Supt. — See Nyack
Liberty ES 500/K-5
142 Lake Rd 10989 845-353-7240
Ellen Rechenberger, prin. Fax 353-7243
Valley Cottage ES 400/K-5
26 Lake Rd 10989 845-353-7280
Andrea Coddett, prin. Fax 353-7287

St. Paul S 300/PK-8
365 Kings Hwy 10989 845-268-6506
Sr. Stephen Miick, prin. Fax 268-1809

Valley Stream, Nassau, Pop. 35,799
Elmont UFD
Supt. — See Elmont
Alden Terrace ES 500/K-6
1835 N Central Ave 11580 516-285-8310
Amy Buchanan, prin. Fax 285-8610
Hewlett-Woodmere UFD
Supt. — See Woodmere
Ogden ES 400/2-5
875 Longview Ave 11581 516-374-8091
Joan Birringer-Haig, prin. Fax 374-4643
Valley Stream 13 UFD 2,200/K-6
585 N Corona Ave 11580 516-568-6100
Dr. Elizabeth Lison, supt. Fax 825-2537
www.valleystream13.com
Dever ES 500/K-6
585 N Corona Ave 11580 516-568-6120
Darren Gruen, prin. Fax 568-6115
Howell Road ES 600/K-6
1475 Howell Rd 11580 516-568-6130
Frank Huplosky, prin. Fax 568-6107
Wheeler Avenue ES 600/1-6
1 Wheeler Ave W 11580 516-568-6140
Christine Zerillo, prin. Fax 568-0061
Other Schools – See Franklin Square
Valley Stream 24 UFD 1,100/K-6
75 Horton Ave 11581 516-256-0153
Edward Fale, supt. Fax 256-0163
www.valleystreamdistrict24.org/
Brooklyn Avenue ES 300/K-6
24 Brooklyn Ave 11581 516-256-0165
Dr. Scott Comis, prin. Fax 256-0169
Buck ES 300/K-6
75 Horton Ave 11581 516-256-0160
Mark Onorato, prin. Fax 256-0157
Carbonaro ES 400/K-6
50 Hungry Harbor Rd 11581 516-791-5456
Lisa Conte Ed.D., prin. Fax 791-4573
Valley Stream 30 UFD 1,400/K-6
175 N Central Ave 11580 516-285-9881
Dr. Elaine Kanas, supt. Fax 285-9839
www.valleystream30.com
Clearstream Avenue ES 500/K-6
60 Clearstream Ave 11580 516-872-4333
Fax 872-1205
Forest Road ES 300/K-6
16 Forest Rd 11581 516-791-6134
Theresa Scrocco, prin. Fax 792-2931
Shaw Avenue ES 700/K-6
99 Shaw Ave 11580 516-872-4320
Angela Hudson, prin. Fax 568-2436

Blessed Sacrament S 200/PK-8
50 Rose Ave 11580 516-825-7334
Mary Earvolino, prin. Fax 825-4376
Holy Name of Mary S 400/PK-8
90 S Grove St 11580 516-825-4009
JoAnn Vitiello, prin. Fax 825-2710
Valley Stream Christian Academy 100/K-12
12 E Fairview Ave 11580 516-823-0022
Leslie Fowley, admin. Fax 823-0228
Yeshiva Ketana of Long Island 300/PK-8
31 Doughty Blvd 11581 516-791-2800

Van Etten, Chemung, Pop. 564
Spencer-Van Etten Central SD
Supt. — See Spencer
Spencer-Van Etten ES 400/PK-4
PO Box 98 14889 607-589-7110
Melissa Jewell, prin. Fax 589-3017

Van Hornesville, Herkimer
Van Hornesville-Owen D. Young Central SD 200/K-12
PO Box 125 13475 315-858-0729
Virginia Keegan, supt. Fax 858-2019
Young Central S 200/K-12
PO Box 125 13475 315-858-0729
Fax 858-2019

Varysburg, Wyoming
Attica Central SD
Supt. — See Attica
Sheldon ES 100/K-4
2588 School St 14167 585-591-0400
Karen Tomidy, prin. Fax 535-0110

Vernon, Oneida, Pop. 1,171
Vernon-Verona-Sherrill Central SD
Supt. — See Verona
Wettel ES 400/PK-6
PO Box 990 13476 315-829-3615
Vincent Pompo, prin. Fax 829-4326

Verona, Oneida
Vernon-Verona-Sherrill Central SD 2,300/PK-12
PO Box 128 13478 315-829-2520
Norman Reed, supt. Fax 829-4949
www.vvscentralschools.org/
George ES 400/PK-6
PO Box 108 13478 315-363-2580
Stephen Orcutt, prin. Fax 361-5895
Vernon-Verona-Sherrill MS 400/7-8
PO Box 128 13478 315-829-2520
James Kramer, prin. Fax 829-5966
Other Schools – See Sherrill, Vernon

Vestal, Broome, Pop. 5,000
Vestal Central SD 4,000/K-12
201 Main St Ste 6 13850 607-757-2241
Mark Capobianco, supt. Fax 757-2227
www.vestal.k12.ny.us/
African Road ES 300/K-5
600 S Benita Blvd 13850 607-757-2311
Joanne Mitchell, prin. Fax 757-2705
Clayton Avenue ES 400/K-5
209 Clayton Ave 13850 607-757-2271
Jeffrey DeAngelo, prin. Fax 757-2372
Glenwood ES 400/K-5
337 Jones Rd 13850 607-757-2391
Fax 757-2233
Vestal Hills ES 300/K-5
709 Country Club Rd 13850 607-757-2357
Therese Mastro, prin. Fax 757-2347

Vestal MS 1,000/6-8
600 S Benita Blvd 13850 607-757-2331
Ann Marie Loose, prin. Fax 757-2229
Other Schools – See Apalachin

Hillel Academy 50/PK-8
4737 Deerfield Pl 13850 607-722-9274
Ross Corners Christian Academy 200/PK-12
2101 Owego Rd 13850 607-748-3301
Donald Prue, admin. Fax 748-3301

Victor, Ontario, Pop. 2,547
Victor Central SD 3,900/PK-12
953 High St 14564 585-924-3252
Dawn Santiago-Marullo, supt. Fax 742-7090
www.victorschools.org
Victor Early Childhood Ed Center 400/PK-K
953 High St 14564 585-924-3252
Dorothy DiAngelo, prin. Fax 742-7033
Victor IS 900/4-6
953 High St 14564 585-924-3252
Mary Szlosek, prin. Fax 924-7016
Victor JHS 600/7-8
953 High St 14564 585-924-3252
Carl Christensen, prin. Fax 924-9535
Victor PS 900/K-3
953 High St 14564 585-924-3252
Danielle Dehm, prin. Fax 924-4497

Voorheesville, Albany, Pop. 2,782
Voorheesville Central SD 1,300/K-12
432 New Salem Rd 12186 518-765-3313
Raymond Colucciello Ed.D., supt. Fax 765-2751
vcsd.neric.org/
Voorheesville ES 500/K-5
129 Maple Ave 12186 518-765-2382
Edward Diegel, prin. Fax 765-3842

Wading River, Suffolk, Pop. 5,317
Shoreham-Wading River Central SD
Supt. — See Shoreham
Wading River ES 400/1-5
1900 Wading River Manor Rd 11792 631-821-8254
Steven Donohue, prin. Fax 821-8256

Wainscott, Suffolk
Wainscott Common SD 50/K-3
PO Box 79 11975 631-537-1080
Dr. Dominic Annacone, supt. Fax 537-6977
www.wainscottschool.com/
Wainscott Common S 50/K-3
PO Box 79 11975 631-537-1080
Julie Medler, lead tchr. Fax 537-6977

Walden, Orange, Pop. 6,755
Valley Central SD
Supt. — See Montgomery
Walden ES 600/K-5
75 Orchard St 12586 845-457-2400
Veronica Casillo, prin. Fax 778-7110

Most Precious Blood S 100/PK-8
180 Ulster Ave 12586 845-778-3028
Sr. Margaret Strychalski, prin. Fax 778-3785

Wallkill, Ulster, Pop. 2,125
Wallkill Central SD 3,700/K-12
PO Box 310 12589 845-895-7100
William Hecht, supt. Fax 895-3630
www.wallkillcsd.k12.ny.us
Borden MS 600/7-8
PO Box 310 12589 845-895-7175
Yvonne Herrington, prin. Fax 895-8036
Leptondale ES 600/K-6
PO Box 310 12589 845-895-7200
Richard Kelly, prin. Fax 564-8098
Ostrander ES 600/K-6
PO Box 310 12589 845-895-7225
Maureen Dart, prin. Fax 895-8043
Other Schools – See Plattekill

Walton, Delaware, Pop. 2,951
Walton Central SD 1,100/K-12
47-49 Stockton Ave 13856 607-865-4116
Thomas Austin, supt. Fax 865-8568
www.waltoncsd.stier.org/
Townsend ES 500/K-5
42 North St 13856 607-865-4116
Michael Snider, prin. Fax 865-8568
Walton MS 300/6-8
47-49 Stockton Ave 13856 607-865-4116
Michael MacDonald, prin. Fax 865-8568

Walworth, Wayne
Gananda Central SD 1,200/K-12
1500 Dayspring Rdg 14568 315-986-3521
Shawn VanScoy Ed.D., supt. Fax 986-2003
www.gananda.org
Gananda MS 300/6-8
1500 Dayspring Rdg 14568 315-986-3521
Matthew Mahoney, prin. Fax 986-2003
Other Schools – See Macedon

Wayne Central SD
Supt. — See Ontario Center
Freewill ES 400/K-5
4320 Canandaigua Rd 14568 315-524-1170
Jona Wright, prin. Fax 524-1199

Wampsville, Madison, Pop. 569
Oneida CSD
Supt. — See Oneida
Shortell MS 400/7-8
PO Box 716 13163 315-363-1050
Robin Price, prin. Fax 366-0622

Wantagh, Nassau, Pop. 18,567
Levittown UFD
Supt. — See Levittown
Lee Road ES 300/K-5
901 Lee Rd 11793 516-783-5190
Anthony Goss, prin. Fax 783-5194

Wantagh UFD 3,700/K-12
3301 Beltagh Ave 11793 516-781-8000
Lydia Begley, supt. Fax 781-6076
www.wantaghschools.org
Forest Lake ES 500/K-5
3100 Beltagh Ave 11793 516-679-6470
Maureen Goldberg, prin. Fax 679-6478
Mandalay ES 400/K-5
2667 Bayview Ave 11793 516-679-6390
Lynne D'Agostino, prin. Fax 679-6484
Wantagh ES 900/K-5
1765 Beech St 11793 516-679-6480
Dr. Donald Sternberg, prin. Fax 679-6365
Wantagh MS 900/6-8
3299 Beltagh Ave 11793 516-679-6350
Dr. Jeannette Stern, prin. Fax 679-6311

Maplewood S 200/PK-K
2166 Wantagh Ave 11793 516-221-2121
Joseph Holden, dir. Fax 221-9303

Wappingers Falls, Dutchess, Pop. 5,085
Wappingers Central SD 12,500/K-12
167 Myers Corners Rd 12590 845-298-5000
Richard Powell, supt. Fax 298-5041
www.wappingersschools.org
Evans ES 300/K-5
747 Old Route 9 N 12590 845-298-5240
Rick Dominick, prin. Fax 298-5232
Fishkill Plains ES 600/K-5
17 Lake Walton Rd 12590 845-227-1770
Sylvia Epstein, prin. Fax 227-1747
Myers Corners ES 900/K-6
156 Myers Corners Rd 12590 845-298-5260
Gail Wehmann, prin. Fax 298-5258
Sheafe Road ES 500/K-5
287 Sheafe Rd 12590 845-298-5290
Franco Miele, prin. Fax 298-5282
Van Wyck JHS 1,500/6-8
10 Hillside Lake Rd 12590 845-227-1700
Steve Shuchat, prin. Fax 227-1748
Wappingers Falls JHS 1,000/7-8
30 Major MacDonald Way 12590 845-298-5200
Vince DiGrandi, prin. Fax 298-5156
Other Schools – See Fishkill, Hopewell Junction, Poughkeepsie

---

St. Mary S 200/K-8
2 Convent Ave 12590 845-297-7500
Mary Ellen Larose, prin. Fax 297-0886

Warrensburg, Warren, Pop. 3,204
Warrensburg Central SD 900/K-12
103 Schroon River Rd 12885 518-623-2861
Timothy Lawson, supt. Fax 623-2436
www.wcsd.org/
Warrensburg ES 500/K-6
1 James St 12885 518-623-9747
Amy Langworthy, prin. Fax 623-3336

Warsaw, Wyoming, Pop. 3,701
Warsaw Central SD 1,000/K-12
153 W Buffalo St 14569 585-786-8000
Kevin McGowan, supt. Fax 786-8008
www.warsaw.k12.ny.us/
Warsaw ES 500/K-5
153 W Buffalo St 14569 585-786-8000
Stephen Saxton, prin. Fax 786-2537

Warwick, Orange, Pop. 6,571
Warwick Valley Central SD 4,500/K-12
PO Box 595 10990 845-987-3000
Dr. Frank Greenhall, supt. Fax 987-1147
www.warwickvalleyschools.com
Kings ES 500/K-5
PO Box 595 10990 845-987-3150
Sandra Wood, prin. Fax 986-3314
Park Avenue ES 500/K-5
PO Box 595 10990 845-987-3170
Kathleen Affigne, prin. Fax 988-5893
Sanfordville ES 600/K-5
PO Box 595 10990 845-987-3300
Roger Longfield, prin. Fax 987-7287
Warwick Valley MS 1,100/6-8
PO Box 595 10990 845-987-3100
John Kolesar, prin. Fax 986-6942
Other Schools – See Pine Island

Calvary Christian Academy 100/PK-8
5 Wisner Rd 10990 845-986-5437
Melissa Penney, prin. Fax 986-2706
SS. Stephen & Edward S 300/PK-8
75 Sanfordville Rd 10990 845-986-3533
Mary Lou Moccia, prin. Fax 987-7023

Washingtonville, Orange, Pop. 6,236
Washingtonville Central SD 4,800/K-12
52 W Main St 10992 845-497-4000
Roberta Greene, supt. Fax 496-2330
www.ws.k12.ny.us
Round Hill ES 700/K-5
1314 Route 208 10992 845-497-4000
Steven Kiel, prin. Fax 496-6945
Taft ES 700/K-5
20 Toleman Rd 10992 845-497-4000
Richard Quattrocchi, prin. Fax 496-8980
Washingtonville MS 1,200/6-8
38 W Main St 10992 845-497-4000
Maureen Peterson, prin. Fax 496-2099
Other Schools – See New Windsor

Waterford, Saratoga, Pop. 2,182
Waterford-Halfmoon UFD 600/K-12
125 Middletown Rd 12188 518-237-0800
Timothy Lange, supt. Fax 237-7335
www.whufsd.org
Waterford-Halfmoon ES 300/K-6
125 Middletown Rd 12188 518-237-0800
Joseph Siracuse, prin. Fax 237-7083

St. Mary's S 300/PK-8
12 6th St 12188 518-237-0652
Mary Rushkoski, prin. Fax 233-0898

Waterloo, Seneca, Pop. 5,134
Waterloo Central SD 1,900/K-12
109 Washington St 13165 315-539-1500
Terry MacNabb, supt. Fax 539-1504
www.waterloocsd.org/
La Fayette IS 400/3-5
71 Inslee St 13165 315-539-1530
Sally Covert, prin. Fax 539-1529
Main Street ES K-5
202 W Main St 13165 315-539-5600
Wendy Doyle, prin. Fax 539-1548
Skoi-Yase ES 400/K-2
65 Fayette St 13165 315-539-1520
Elizabeth Springer, prin. Fax 539-1504
Waterloo MS 500/6-8
65 Center St 13165 315-539-1540
Michael Ferrara, prin. Fax 539-1504

Watertown, Jefferson, Pop. 27,220
Watertown CSD 4,500/K-12
1351 Washington St 13601 315-785-3700
Terry Fralick, supt. Fax 785-6855
www.watertowncsd.org
Case MS 700/7-8
1237 Washington St 13601 315-785-3870
Donald Whitney, prin. Fax 785-3731
Knickerbocker ES 500/K-4
739 Knickerbocker Dr 13601 315-785-3740
Chad Fairchild, prin. Fax 779-5654
North ES 700/K-4
171 E Hoard St 13601 315-785-3750
Irene Wilson, prin. Fax 785-3752
Ohio Street ES 500/K-4
1537 Ohio St 13601 315-785-3755
Elizabeth Stever, prin. Fax 785-9742
Sherman ES 400/K-4
836 Sherman St 13601 315-785-3760
Margaret Drappo, prin. Fax 785-0152
Starbuck ES K-4
430 E Hoard St 13601 315-785-3765
Mark Taylor, prin. Fax 785-0919
Wiley IS 600/5-6
1351 Washington St 13601 315-785-3780
Patricia LaBarr, prin. Fax 785-3764

Faith Fellowship Christian S 100/PK-12
131 Moore Ave 13601 315-782-9342
Fax 786-0309
Immaculate Heart S 400/PK-6
122 Winthrop St 13601 315-788-7011
Gail Baker Graham, prin. Fax 788-7011

Waterville, Oneida, Pop. 1,682
Waterville Central SD 900/K-12
381 Madison St 13480 315-841-3900
Gary Lonczak, supt. Fax 841-3939
www.watervilleschools.org/
Memorial Park ES 400/K-5
145 E Bacon St 13480 315-841-3700
Matthew St. Peter, prin. Fax 841-3718

Watervliet, Albany, Pop. 9,889
North Colonie Central SD
Supt. — See Latham
Maplewood ES 100/K-6
32 Cohoes Rd 12189 518-273-1512
Jerome Steele, prin. Fax 273-0269

Watervliet CSD 1,300/K-12
1245 Hillside Dr 12189 518-629-3200
Paul Padalino, supt. Fax 629-3265
vliet.neric.org/
Watervliet ES 700/K-6
2557 10th Ave 12189 518-629-3400
Theresa O'Brien, prin. Fax 629-3250

St. Brigid's Regional S 200/PK-8
700 5th Ave 12189 518-273-3321
Ralph Provenza, prin. Fax 273-9355

Watkins Glen, Schuyler, Pop. 2,099
Watkins Glen Central SD 1,300/K-12
303 12th St 14891 607-535-3219
Thomas Phillips, supt. Fax 535-4629
www.watkinsglenschools.org/
Watkins Glen ES 500/K-4
612 S Decatur St 14891 607-535-3250
Rodney Weeden, prin. Fax 535-7012
Watkins Glen MS 400/5-8
200 10th St 14891 607-535-3230
Kristine Somerville, prin. Fax 535-4532

Waverly, Tioga, Pop. 4,493
Waverly Central SD 1,800/K-12
15 Frederick St 14892 607-565-2841
Michael McMahon, supt. Fax 565-4997
www.waverlyschools.com/
Elm Street ES 500/K-6
145 Elm St 14892 607-565-8186
Anne Bernard, prin. Fax 565-4997
Lincoln Street ES 300/K-6
45 Lincoln St 14892 607-565-8176
John McGuire, prin. Fax 565-4997
Waverly MS 300/7-8
1 Frederick St 14892 607-565-3410
Diane Tymoski, prin. Fax 565-4997

Other Schools – See Chemung

Wayland, Steuben, Pop. 1,842
Wayland-Cohocton Central SD 1,800/PK-12
2350 State Route 63 14572 585-728-2211
Michael Wetherbee, supt. Fax 728-3566
www.wccsk12.org
Wayland-Cohocton MS 500/5-8
2350 State Route 63 14572 585-728-2551
Eileen Feinman, prin. Fax 728-3556
Wayland ES 400/PK-4
2350 State Route 63 14572 585-728-3547
Todd Campbell, prin. Fax 728-3566
Other Schools – See Cohocton

Webster, Monroe, Pop. 5,089
Webster Central SD 8,700/K-12
119 South Ave 14580 585-265-3600
Adele Bovard, supt. Fax 265-6561
www.websterschools.org
Dewitt Road ES 500/K-5
722 Dewitt Rd 14580 585-671-0710
Jan Barrett, prin. Fax 671-4366
Klem Road North ES 500/K-5
1015 Klem Rd 14580 585-872-1770
Steven La Monica, prin. Fax 872-2763
Klem Road South ES 500/K-5
1025 Klem Rd 14580 585-872-1320
Mary Ann Krog, prin. Fax 872-2067
Plank Road North ES 500/K-5
705 Plank Rd 14580 585-671-8858
David Peter, prin. Fax 787-9009
Plank Road South ES 500/K-5
715 Plank Rd 14580 585-671-3190
Mike Davis, prin.
Schlegel Road ES 500/K-5
1548 Schlegel Rd 14580 585-265-2500
Theresa Pulos, prin. Fax 265-0716
Spry MS 1,000/6-8
119 South Ave 14580 585-265-6500
David Swinson, prin. Fax 265-6512
State Road ES 500/K-5
1401 State Rd 14580 585-872-4200
Carmen Gumina, prin. Fax 872-5834
Willink MS 1,000/6-8
900 Publishers Pkwy 14580 585-670-1030
Ted Binion, prin. Fax 671-1978

St. Rita S 400/PK-6
1008 Maple Dr 14580 585-671-3132
Sr. Katherine Ann Rappl, prin. Fax 671-4562
Webster Christian S 200/PK-12
675 Holt Rd 14580 585-872-5150
Keith Bell, admin. Fax 872-5932
Webster Montessori S 100/K-3
1310 Five Mile Line Rd 14580 585-347-0055
Gary Goodwin, dir. Fax 347-0057

Weedsport, Cayuga, Pop. 1,970
Weedsport Central SD 900/K-12
2821 E Brutus Street Rd 13166 315-834-6637
Shaun O'Connor, supt.
Weedsport ES 400/K-5
8954 Jackson St 13166 315-834-6685
Tim Cowan, prin. Fax 834-8693

Wells, Hamilton
Wells Central SD 200/PK-12
PO Box 300 12190 518-924-6000
Gavin Murdoch, supt. Fax 924-9246
Wells S 200/PK-12
PO Box 300 12190 518-924-6000
Gavin Murdoch, prin. Fax 924-9246

Wellsville, Allegany, Pop. 4,773
Wellsville Central SD 1,300/K-12
126 W State St 14895 585-596-2170
Byron Chandler Ed.D., supt. Fax 596-2177
www.wellsville.wnyric.org
Wellsville ES 600/K-5
50 School St 14895 585-596-2122
Tyke Tenney, prin. Fax 596-2120
Wellsville MS 300/6-8
126 W State St 14895 585-596-2144
Mary Ellen O'Connell, prin. Fax 596-2142

Immaculate Conception S 200/PK-8
24 Maple Ave 14895 585-593-5840
Charles Cutler, prin. Fax 593-5846

West Babylon, Suffolk, Pop. 43,700
North Babylon UFD
Supt. — See North Babylon
Belmont ES 400/K-5
108 Barnum St 11704 631-321-3259
Valerie Jackson, prin. Fax 376-0278

West Babylon UFD 4,700/K-12
10 Farmingdale Rd 11704 631-321-3142
Anthony Cacciola, supt. Fax 661-5166
www.westbabylon.k12.ny.us
Forest Avenue ES 400/K-5
200 Forest Ave 11704 631-321-3067
Christine Tona, prin. Fax 321-3100
Kennedy ES 500/K-5
175 Brookvale Ave 11704 631-321-3053
Gregg Cunningham, prin. Fax 321-3101
Santapogue ES 400/K-5
1130 Herzel Blvd 11704 631-321-3125
Eleanor Levy, prin. Fax 321-3127
South Bay ES 400/K-5
160 Great East Neck Rd 11704 631-321-3145
JoAnn Scott, prin. Fax 321-3111
Tooker Avenue ES 400/K-5
855 Tooker Ave 11704 631-321-3136
Dr. Joseph Hickey, prin. Fax 321-6749
West Babylon JHS 1,100/6-8
200 Old Farmingdale Rd 11704 631-321-3084
Scott Payne, prin. Fax 321-3079

Westbury, Nassau, Pop. 14,691
East Meadow UFD 7,800/K-12
718 The Plain Rd 11590 516-478-5776
Leon Campo, supt.
www.eastmeadow.k12.ny.us
Bowling Green ES 700/K-5
2340 Stewart Ave 11590 516-876-7480
Maria Ciarametaro, prin. Fax 876-7489
Clarke MS 700/6-8
740 Edgewood Dr 11590 516-876-7401
Stacey Breslin, prin. Fax 876-7407
Other Schools – See East Meadow

Westbury UFD
Supt. — See Old Westbury
Drexel Avenue ES 400/3-5
161 Drexel Ave 11590 516-876-5030
Dr. Wanda Toledo, prin. Fax 876-5032
Dryden Street S 600/PK-K
545 Dryden St 11590 516-876-5039
Dale Telmer, prin. Fax 876-5172
Park Ave ES 600/1-2
100 Park Ave 11590 516-876-5109
Gloria Dingwall, prin. Fax 876-5190
Powells Lane ES 400/3-5
603 Powells Ln 11590 516-876-5125
Claudia Germain, prin. Fax 876-5160
Westbury MS 900/6-8
455 Rockland St 11590 516-876-5082
Dennis Hinson, prin. Fax 876-5141

St. Brigid/Our Lady of Hope S 300/PK-8
101 Maple Ave 11590 516-333-0580
Paul Clagnaz, prin. Fax 333-0590
Westbury Friends S 100/PK-5
550 Post Ave 11590 516-333-3178
Geraldine Faivre, dir. Fax 333-1353

West Chazy, Clinton
Beekmantown Central SD 2,200/PK-12
37 Eagle Way 12992 518-563-8250
Scott Amo, supt. Fax 563-8132
www.bcsdk12.org
Other Schools – See Plattsburgh

Westerlo, Albany, Pop. 1,880

Helderberg Christian S 50/K-7
PO Box 164 12193 518-797-3977
Jacqueline Packham, admin. Fax 797-3977

West Falls, Erie

Aurora Waldorf S 200/PK-8
525 W Falls Rd 14170 716-655-2029
Fax 655-3265

Westfield, Chautauqua, Pop. 3,464
Westfield Central SD 800/K-12
203 E Main St 14787 716-326-2151
Mark Sissel, supt. Fax 326-2195
www.wacs.wnyric.org/
Westfield ES 300/K-5
203 E Main St 14787 716-326-2180
Suzette Benson, prin. Fax 326-2157
Westfield MS 200/6-8
203 E Main St 14787 716-326-2151
Lawrence Studd, prin. Fax 326-2157

Westhampton Beach, Suffolk, Pop. 1,957
Westhampton Beach UFD 1,800/K-12
340 Mill Rd 11978 631-288-3800
Lynn Schwartz, supt. Fax 288-8351
www.westhamptonbeach.k12.ny.us
Westhampton Beach ES 400/K-5
379 Mill Rd 11978 631-288-3800
Ron Masera, prin. Fax 288-5784
Westhampton Beach MS 400/6-8
340 Mill Rd 11978 631-288-3800
Charisse Miller, prin. Fax 288-5496

West Harrison, Westchester
Harrison Central SD
Supt. — See Harrison
Preston ES 300/K-5
50 Taylor Ave 10604 914-630-3152
Jeremy Barker, prin. Fax 761-7166

St. Anthony of Padua S 200/PK-8
45 Gainsborg Ave E 10604 914-949-6986
Sr. Mary Kellogg, prin. Fax 328-1981

West Haverstraw, Rockland, Pop. 10,259
North Rockland Central SD
Supt. — See Garnerville
West Haverstraw ES 700/PK-4
71 Blauvelt Ave 10993 845-942-3180
Peter DiBernardi, prin. Fax 942-3084

West Hempstead, Nassau, Pop. 17,689
West Hempstead UFD 2,300/K-12
252 Chestnut St 11552 516-390-3107
John Hogan, supt. Fax 489-1776
www.westhempstead.k12.ny.us
Chestnut Street S 100/K-K
252 Chestnut St 11552 516-390-3150
Daniel Rehman, prin. Fax 390-3152
Cornwell Avenue ES 300/1-5
250 Cornwell Ave 11552 516-390-3140
Anthony Cali, prin. Fax 489-0365
Washington ES 400/1-5
347 William St 11552 516-390-3130
Theresa Ganley, prin. Fax 489-0068
West Hempstead MS 500/6-8
450 Nassau Blvd 11552 516-390-3160
Joseph Cirnigliaro, prin. Fax 489-8946

HANC - Samuel & Eliz Bass Golding Schl 300/K-6
609 Hempstead Ave 11552 516-485-7786
Rabbi Benjamin Yasgur, prin. Fax 485-0422
St. Thomas the Apostle S 500/PK-8
12 Westminster Rd 11552 516-481-9310
Christina Teisch, prin. Fax 481-8769

West Henrietta, Monroe
Rush-Henrietta Central SD
Supt. — See Henrietta
Burger MS 500/6-8
639 Erie Station Rd 14586 585-359-5308
Shaun Nelms, prin. Fax 359-5333

West Islip, Suffolk, Pop. 29,000
West Islip UFD 5,700/K-12
100 Sherman Ave 11795 631-893-3200
Beth Virginia Blau Ed.D., supt. Fax 893-3212
www.wi.k12.ny.us/
Bayview ES 400/K-5
165 Snedecor Ave 11795 631-893-3330
Rhonda Pratt, prin. Fax 893-3335
Beach Street MS 700/6-8
17 Beach St 11795 631-893-3310
Andrew O'Farrell, prin. Fax 893-3318
Bellew ES 400/K-5
25 Higbie Ln 11795 631-893-3340
Daniel Hunter, prin. Fax 893-3346
Kirdahy ES 400/K-5
339 Snedecor Ave 11795 631-893-3390
John Mullins, prin. Fax 893-3395
Manetuck ES 500/K-5
800 Van Buren Ave 11795 631-893-3350
Mary Anderson, prin. Fax 893-3356
Oquenock ES 300/K-5
425 Spruce Ave 11795 631-893-3360
Dawn Morrison, prin. Fax 893-3367
Udall Road MS 800/6-8
900 Udall Rd 11795 631-893-3290
Daniel Marquardt, prin. Fax 893-3301
Westbrook ES 400/K-5
350 Higbie Ln 11795 631-893-3370
Jack Maniscalco, prin. Fax 893-3373

Our Lady of Lourdes S 300/PK-8
44 Toomey Rd 11795 631-587-7200
Louise Krol, prin. Fax 587-4531

West Leyden, Lewis
Adirondack Central SD
Supt. — See Boonville
West Leyden ES 200/K-5
PO Box 304 13489 315-942-9280
Maria Faelacaro Smith, prin. Fax 942-9212

Westmoreland, Oneida
Westmoreland Central SD 900/K-12
5176 State Route 233 13490 315-557-2614
Rocco Migliori, supt. Fax 853-4602
www.westmorelandschool.org
Westmoreland ES 300/K-4
5176 State Route 233 13490 315-557-2626
Joann Ottman, prin. Fax 853-6597
Westmoreland MS 300/5-8
5176 State Route 233 13490 315-557-2618
Brian Kavanagh, prin. Fax 853-4602

West Nyack, Rockland, Pop. 3,437
Clarkstown Central SD
Supt. — See New City
Festa MS 2,200/6-8
30 Parrott Rd 10994 845-639-6339
Dianne Basso, prin. Fax 634-5874
Strawtown ES 400/K-5
413 Strawtown Rd 10994 845-353-4480
Jacqueline Sinatra, prin. Fax 348-0118
West Nyack ES 300/K-5
661 W Nyack Rd 10994 845-353-4990
Ide Seide, prin. Fax 348-0115

Westport, Essex, Pop. 524
Westport Central SD 300/K-12
PO Box 408 12993 518-962-8244
Karen Tromblee, supt. Fax 962-4571
www.westportcs.org
Westport Central S 300/K-12
PO Box 408 12993 518-962-8244
Karen Tromblee, prin. Fax 962-4571

West Sand Lake, Rensselaer, Pop. 2,251
Averill Park Central SD
Supt. — See Averill Park
West Sand Lake ES 500/K-5
24 Meeler Rd 12196 518-674-7175
Laura Canny, prin. Fax 674-3225

West Sayville, Suffolk, Pop. 4,680
Sayville UFD
Supt. — See Sayville
Cherry Avenue ES 400/K-5
155 Cherry Ave 11796 631-244-6700
John Stimmel, prin. Fax 244-6506

West Sayville Christian S 100/K-8
37 Rollstone Ave 11796 631-589-2180
Joseph Klass, prin. Fax 589-2143

West Seneca, Erie, Pop. 45,600
West Seneca Central SD 7,500/K-12
1397 Orchard Park Rd 14224 716-677-3101
Jean Kovach, supt. Fax 677-3104
www.wscschools.org/
Allendale ES 500/K-6
1399 Orchard Park Rd 14224 716-677-3660
Margaret Bochert, prin. Fax 675-3104
Clinton Street ES 500/K-6
4100 Clinton St 14224 716-677-3620
Christine Angrisano, prin. Fax 674-7821

East ES 500/K-6
1415 Center Rd 14224 716-677-3560
Deborah Staszak, prin. Fax 674-1506
East MS 500/7-8
1445 Center Rd 14224 716-677-3530
Monica Witman, prin. Fax 674-1046
Northwood ES 600/K-6
250 Northwood Ave 14224 716-677-3640
Catherine Huber, prin. Fax 674-3505
Potters Road ES 600/K-6
675 Potters Rd 14224 716-677-3600
Holly Quinn, prin. Fax 822-0579
West ES 700/K-6
1397 Orchard Park Rd 14224 716-677-3250
Rachel Badger, prin. Fax 677-3123
West MS 700/7-8
395 Center Rd 14224 716-677-3500
Brian Graham, prin. Fax 675-6134
Winchester ES 300/K-6
650 Harlem Rd 14224 716-677-3580
Kathleen Brachmann, prin. Fax 822-2670

Fourteen Holy Helpers S 300/PK-8
1339 Indian Church Rd 14224 716-674-1670
Joseph Duttweiler, prin. Fax 675-4864
Queen of Heaven S 300/PK-8
839 Mill Rd 14224 716-674-5206
Barbara Ryan, prin. Fax 674-2793
Trinity Lutheran S 100/PK-8
146 Reserve Rd 14224 716-674-5353
Fax 674-4910
West Seneca Christian S 200/PK-12
511 Union Rd 14224 716-674-1820
Dr. Orlando Buria, admin. Fax 674-4894

West Valley, Cattaraugus
West Valley Central SD 400/PK-12
PO Box 290 14171 716-942-3293
Hillary Bowen, supt. Fax 942-3440
www.wvalley.wnyric.org
West Valley Central S 400/PK-12
PO Box 290 14171 716-942-3293
Hillary Bowen, prin. Fax 942-3440

West Winfield, Herkimer, Pop. 843
Mount Markham CSD 1,300/K-12
500 Fairground Rd 13491 315-822-6161
Casey Barduhn, supt. Fax 822-6162
www.mmcsd.org
Mount Markham ES 400/K-4
500 Fairground Rd 13491 315-822-6326
Carol Dumka, prin. Fax 822-3436
Mount Markham MS 400/5-8
500 Fairground Rd 13491 315-822-6361
Dawn Yerkie, prin. Fax 822-6125

Whitehall, Washington, Pop. 2,648
Whitehall Central SD 900/K-12
87 Buckley Rd 12887 518-499-1772
James Watson, supt. Fax 499-1759
railroaders.net/
Whitehall ES 400/K-6
99 Buckley Rd 12887 518-499-0330
David St. Germain, prin. Fax 499-1752

White Lake, Sullivan
Monticello Central SD
Supt. — See Monticello
Duggan ES 200/K-5
3460 State Route 55 12786 845-583-5390
Patti Sonnenschein, prin. Fax 583-5436

White Plains, Westchester, Pop. 56,733
Greenburgh Central SD 7
Supt. — See Hartsdale
Bailey S 400/4-6
33 Hillside Ave S 10607 914-948-8107
Marguerite Clarkson, prin. Fax 948-2934
Jackson ES 300/K-1
Saratoga Rd 10607 914-948-2992
Patricia Simone, prin. Fax 681-9038

White Plains CSD 6,700/K-12
5 Homeside Ln 10605 914-422-2019
Timothy Connors, supt. Fax 422-2024
www.wpcsd.k12.ny.us
Church Street ES 600/K-5
295 Church St 10603 914-422-2400
Michael DeChance, prin. Fax 422-2409
Mamaroneck Avenue ES 600/K-5
7 Nosband Ave 10605 914-422-2286
Gail Epstein, prin. Fax 422-2109
Post Road ES 500/K-5
175 W Post Rd 10606 914-422-2320
Laura Havis, prin. Fax 422-2097
Ridgeway ES 600/K-5
225 Ridgeway 10605 914-422-2081
Evette Avila, prin. Fax 422-2366
Washington ES 700/K-5
100 Orchard St 10604 914-422-2380
Dr. Terri Klemm, prin. Fax 422-2108
White Plains MS - Eastview Campus 6-8
350 Main St 10601 914-422-2223
Joseph Cloherty, prin. Fax 422-2222
White Plains MS - Highlands Campus 1,500/6-8
128 Grandview Ave 10605 914-422-2092
Diana Knight, prin. Fax 422-2273

German S 400/K-12
50 Partridge Rd 10605 914-948-6513
Wolfgang Dietrich, hdmstr. Fax 948-6529
Good Counsel Academy 200/PK-8
52 N Broadway 10603 914-761-4423
Sr. Mary Arenholz, prin. Fax 997-4195
Our Lady of Sorrows S 200/1-8
888 Mamaroneck Ave 10605 914-761-0124
Sr. Marie Cecile Larizza, prin. Fax 761-0176

Solomon Schechter S of Westchester 400/K-5
30 Dellwood Rd 10605 914-948-3111
Dr. Elliot Spiegel, hdmstr. Fax 948-4356
Windward S 200/1-4
13 Windward Ave 10605 914-949-6968
Dr. John Russell, hdmstr. Fax 949-8220

Whitesboro, Oneida, Pop. 3,854
Whitesboro Central SD
Supt. — See Yorkville
Harts Hill ES 400/K-5
8551 Clark Mills Rd 13492 315-266-3430
Lisa Anderson, prin. Fax 768-9855
Parkway MS 300/6-6
65 Oriskany Blvd 13492 315-266-3175
Christopher Staats, prin. Fax 768-9882
Westmoreland Road ES 400/K-5
8596 Westmoreland Rd 13492 315-266-3440
Dave Russo, prin. Fax 768-9789
Whitesboro MS 600/7-8
75 Oriskany Blvd 13492 315-266-3100
Christopher Staats, prin. Fax 768-9770

Whitestone, See New York
NYC Department of Education
Supt. — See New York
Public S 79 800/PK-5
14727 15th Dr 11357 718-746-0396
Paula Marron, prin. Fax 746-3103
Public S 184 400/PK-5
16315 21st Ave 11357 718-352-7800
Dora Pantelis, prin. Fax 352-0311
Public S 193 500/PK-5
15220 11th Ave 11357 718-767-8810
Joyce Bush, prin. Fax 746-7617
Public S 209 500/PK-5
1610 Utopia Pkwy 11357 718-352-3939
Mary McDonnell, prin. Fax 352-0367
JHS 194 700/6-8
15460 17th Ave 11357 718-746-0818
Anne Marie Iannizzi, prin. Fax 746-7618

Holy Trinity S 300/PK-8
1445 143rd St 11357 718-746-1479
Eleanor Menna, prin. Fax 746-4793
St. Luke S 400/PK-8
1601 150th Pl 11357 718-746-3833
Barbara Reiter, prin. Fax 747-2101

Whitesville, Allegany
Whitesville Central SD 300/K-12
692 Main St 14897 607-356-3301
Douglas Wyant, supt. Fax 356-3598
www.whitesville.wnyric.org
Whitesville Central S 300/K-12
692 Main St 14897 607-356-3301
Tina Wilson, prin. Fax 356-3598

Whitney Point, Broome, Pop. 939
Whitney Point Central SD 1,400/PK-12
PO Box 249 13862 607-692-8202
Mary Hibbard, supt. Fax 692-4434
www.wpcsd.org
Adams PS 500/PK-3
PO Box 249 13862 607-692-8241
JoAnne Knapp, prin. Fax 692-8297
Whitney Point MS 400/4-8
PO Box 249 13862 607-692-8232
Dan Sweeney, prin. Fax 692-8283

Williamson, Wayne
Williamson Central SD 1,200/K-12
PO Box 900 14589 315-589-9661
Maria Ehresman, supt. Fax 589-7611
www.williamsoncentral.org
Williamson ES 400/K-4
PO Box 900 14589 315-589-9668
Anne Ressler, prin. Fax 589-8315
Williamson MS 400/5-8
PO Box 900 14589 315-589-9665
John Fulmer, prin. Fax 589-8314

Williamsville, Erie, Pop. 5,315
Clarence Central SD
Supt. — See Clarence
Harris Hill ES 500/K-5
4260 Harris Hill Rd 14221 716-407-9175
Susan Corrie, prin. Fax 407-9182
Sheridan Hill ES 500/K-5
4560 Boncrest Dr E 14221 716-407-9250
Dr. Michael Codd, prin. Fax 407-9258

Williamsville Central SD
Supt. — See East Amherst
Country Parkway ES 600/K-4
35 Hollybrook Dr 14221 716-626-9860
Larry Militello, prin. Fax 626-9879
Forest ES 600/K-4
250 N Forest Rd 14221 716-626-9800
Shirlee Paveljack, prin. Fax 626-9819
Heim ES 700/K-4
155 Heim Rd 14221 716-626-8686
Patricia Langton, prin. Fax 626-8679
Heim MS 600/5-8
175 Heim Rd 14221 716-626-8600
Valerie Keipper, prin. Fax 626-8626
Maple ES 700/K-4
1500 Maple Rd 14221 716-626-8801
Mary Mallon, prin. Fax 626-8808
Maple West ES 600/K-4
851 Maple Rd 14221 716-626-8840
Charles Galluzzo, prin. Fax 626-8859
Mill MS 900/5-8
505 Mill St 14221 716-626-8300
Michael Calandra, prin. Fax 626-8326

Christian Central Academy 400/K-12
39 Academy St 14221 716-634-4821
Nurline Lawrence, hdmstr. Fax 634-5851

Nativity of BVM S 200/PK-8
8550 Main St 14221 716-633-7441
Cherie Ansuini, prin. Fax 632-7898
St. Gregory the Great S 600/K-8
250 Saint Gregory Ct 14221 716-688-5323
Patricia Freund, prin. Fax 688-6629
SS. Peter & Paul S 500/PK-8
5480 Main St 14221 716-632-6146
Marianne Maines, prin. Fax 626-0971

Williston Park, Nassau, Pop. 7,113
Herricks UFD
Supt. — See New Hyde Park
Center Street ES 600/K-5
240 Center St 11596 516-305-8300
Edward Bellomo, prin. Fax 248-3281

Mineola UFD
Supt. — See Mineola
Cross Street ES 200/PK-5
6 Cross St 11596 516-237-2100
Devra Small, prin. Fax 739-4772

St. Aidan S 200/PK-8
510 Willis Ave 11596 516-746-6585
Eileen Oliver, prin. Fax 746-3086

Willsboro, Essex
Willsboro Central SD 400/PK-12
PO Box 180 12996 518-963-4456
Stephen Broadwell, supt. Fax 963-7577
www.willsborocsd.org/
Willsboro Central S 400/PK-12
PO Box 180 12996 518-963-4456
Stephen Broadwell, prin. Fax 963-7577

Wilson, Niagara, Pop. 1,167
Wilson Central SD 1,400/K-12
PO Box 648 14172 716-751-9341
Dr. Michael Wendt, supt. Fax 751-6556
www.wilson.wnyric.org/
Marks ES 400/K-5
PO Box 648 14172 716-751-9341
John Diodate, prin. Fax 751-1269
Wilson MS 300/6-8
PO Box 648 14172 716-751-9341
Peter Rademacher, prin. Fax 751-9597
Other Schools – See Ransomville

Wilton, Saratoga
South Glens Falls Central SD
Supt. — See South Glens Falls
Ballard ES 400/PK-5
300 Ballard Rd 12831 518-587-0600
Rosemary Porteus, prin. Fax 587-2248

Windham, Greene
Windham-Ashland-Jewett Central SD 500/K-12
PO Box 429 12496 518-734-3400
John Wiktorko, supt. Fax 734-6050
www.wajcs.org/
Windham-Ashland Central S 500/K-12
PO Box 429 12496 518-734-3400
Anne Rode, prin. Fax 734-6050

Windsor, Broome, Pop. 872
Windsor Central SD 1,800/K-12
215 Main St 13865 607-655-8216
Jason Andrews, supt. Fax 655-3553
www.windsor-csd.org
Palmer ES 200/K-5
213 Main St 13865 607-655-8247
Jamie Bernard, prin. Fax 655-3760
Weeks ES 300/K-5
440 Foley Rd 13865 607-775-3226
Lisa Milano, prin. Fax 775-4835
Windsor MS 500/6-8
213 Main St 13865 607-655-8247
Scott Beattie, prin. Fax 655-3760
Other Schools – See Kirkwood

Wingdale, Dutchess
Dover UFD
Supt. — See Dover Plains
Wingdale ES 400/K-2
6413 Route 55 12594 845-832-4530
Catherine Alvarez, prin. Fax 832-3974

Wolcott, Wayne, Pop. 1,664
North Rose-Wolcott Central SD 1,500/K-12
11669 Salter Colvin Rd 14590 315-594-3141
Lucinda Miner, supt. Fax 594-2352
www.nrwcs.org/
Hendrick ES 300/K-2
5751 New Hartford St 14590 315-594-3132
Linda Haensch, prin. Fax 594-3137
North Rose-Wolcott MS 400/6-8
5957 New Hartford St 14590 315-594-3130
Michele Sullivan, prin. Fax 594-3120
Other Schools – See North Rose

Woodbury, Nassau, Pop. 8,008
Syosset Central SD
Supt. — See Syosset
Whitman ES, 482 Woodbury Rd 11797 400/K-5
Patricia Varrone, prin. 516-364-5823

Wood Haven, See New York
NYC Department of Education
Supt. — See New York
New York City Academy for Discovery 100/PK-5
9516 89th Ave, 718-441-2165
Jennifer Flandro, prin. Fax 441-5923
Public S 60 1,100/PK-5
9102 88th Ave, 718-441-5046
Frank Desario, prin. Fax 805-1487
Public S 97 700/PK-5
8552 85th St, 718-849-4870
Maureen Ingram, prin. Fax 849-5356

St. Thomas Apostle S 300/PK-8
8749 87th St, 718-847-3904
Cathleen Quinn, prin. Fax 847-3513

Woodmere, Nassau, Pop. 15,578
Hewlett-Woodmere UFD 3,200/PK-12
1 Johnson Pl 11598 516-374-8100
Les Omotani, supt. Fax 374-8101
www.hewlett-woodmere.net
Other Schools – See Hewlett, Valley Stream

Bnot Shulamith of Long Island 400/K-8
140 Irving Pl 11598 516-295-1745
Joyce Yarmak, prin. Fax 295-3613
Lawrence Woodmere Academy 400/PK-12
336 Woodmere Blvd 11598 516-374-9000
Alan Bernstein, hdmstr. Fax 374-4707

Woodside, See New York
NYC Department of Education
Supt. — See New York
Public S 11 1,200/K-6
5425 Skillman Ave 11377 718-779-2090
Anna Efkarpides, prin. Fax 458-6362
Public S 12 1,200/K-5
4200 72nd St 11377 718-424-5905
Patricia Perry, prin. Fax 424-0207
Public S 151 600/PK-5
5005 31st Ave 11377 718-728-2676
Jason Gouldner, prin. Fax 545-2028
Public S 152 1,200/PK-6
3352 62nd St 11377 718-429-3141
Vincent Vitolo, prin. Fax 779-7532
Public S 229 1,100/PK-6
6725 51st Rd 11377 718-446-2120
Dr. Sibylle Ajwani, prin. Fax 672-3117
IS 125 1,600/5-8
4602 47th Ave 11377 718-937-0320
Judy Mittler, prin. Fax 361-2451

Corpus Christi S 200/PK-8
3129 60th St 11377 718-721-2484
Linda Parisi, prin. Fax 721-4579
Jackson Heights SDA S 100/K-8
7225 Woodside Ave 11377 718-426-5729
Fax 426-0079
Rainbow Christian Preschool 100/PK-PK
7201 43rd Ave 11377 718-335-3361
Cleide Willik Capelozza, dir. Fax 505-0985
Razi S 400/PK-12
5511 Queens Blvd 11377 718-779-0711
Dr. Ghassan Elcheikhali, prin. Fax 779-0103
St. Sebastian S 500/PK-8
3976 58th St 11377 718-429-1982
JoAnn Dolan, prin. Fax 446-7225

Woodstock, Ulster, Pop. 1,870
Onteora Central SD
Supt. — See Boiceville
Woodstock ES 300/K-6
8 W Hurley Rd 12498 845-679-2316
Barbara Schnell, prin. Fax 679-1207

Worcester, Otsego
Worcester Central SD 400/K-12
198 Main St 12197 607-397-8785
Gary Kuch, supt. Fax 397-8464
www.worcestercs.org
Worcester Central S 400/K-12
198 Main St 12197 607-397-8785
Dr. Ann Cole, prin. Fax 397-9454

Wurtsboro, Sullivan, Pop. 1,263
Monticello Central SD
Supt. — See Monticello
Chase ES 300/K-5
28 Pennsylvania Ave 12790 845-888-2471
Susan Gottlieb, prin. Fax 888-2029

Wyandanch, Suffolk, Pop. 8,950
Wyandanch UFD 1,900/PK-12
1445 Straight Path 11798 631-491-1012
Dr. Mary Jones, supt. Fax 253-0522
www.wyandanch.k12.ny.us/
Hardiman ES 600/PK-2
792 Mount Ave 11798 631-491-5640
Delores Jenkins, prin. Fax 491-1480
King ES 400/3-5
792 Mount Ave 11798 631-491-1041
Dr. Darlene White, prin. Fax 491-3237
Olive MS 400/6-8
140 Garden City Ave 11798 631-491-1047
Gina Talbert, prin. Fax 491-1917

Wynantskill, Rensselaer, Pop. 3,329
Wynantskill UFD 400/K-8
PO Box 345 12198 518-283-4679
Christine Hamill, supt. Fax 283-3799
www.wynantskillufsd.org
Gardner-Dickinson S 400/K-8
PO Box 345 12198 518-283-4600
Jack Lynskey, prin. Fax 283-3684

St. Jude the Apostle S 200/PK-6
42 Dana Ave 12198 518-283-0333
Cathleen Carney, prin. Fax 283-0475

Wyoming, Wyoming, Pop. 493
Wyoming Central SD 200/K-8
PO Box 244 14591 585-495-6222
Sandra Duckworth, supt. Fax 495-6341
www.wyoming.k12.ny.us
Wyoming Central S 200/K-8
PO Box 244 14591 585-495-6222
Sandra Duckworth, prin. Fax 495-6341

Yaphank, Suffolk, Pop. 4,637
Longwood Central SD
Supt. — See Middle Island
Walters ES 900/K-4
15 Everett Dr 11980 631-345-2758
Linda Cornigans, prin. Fax 345-2849

Yonkers, Westchester, Pop. 196,425
Yonkers CSD 21,900/PK-12
1 Larkin Ctr 10701 914-376-8000
Bernard Pierorazio, supt. Fax 376-8062
www.yonkerspublicschools.org
Cedar Place ES 400/PK-5
20 Cedar Pl 10705 914-376-8969
Magdaline Delany, prin. Fax 376-8972
de Hostos Micro ES 300/PK-5
75 Morris St 10705 914-376-8430
Elda Perez-Mejia, prin. Fax 376-8432
Dichiaro ES 400/PK-5
373 Bronxville Rd 10708 914-376-8566
Patricia Langan, prin. Fax 376-8567
Dodson S 900/PK-8
105 Avondale Rd 10710 914-376-8159
Dr. Jennifer Schulman, prin. Fax 337-5207
Emerson MS 700/6-8
160 Bolmer Ave 10703 914-376-8300
Robert Riccuiti, prin. Fax 376-8499
Family S 32 500/PK-8
1 Montclair Rd 10710 914-376-8595
Dr. Edward Beglane, prin. Fax 376-8597
Fermi Performing Arts S 900/PK-8
27 Poplar St 10701 914-376-8460
Miriam Digneo, prin. Fax 376-8468
Foxfire ES 400/PK-5
1061 N Broadway 10701 914-376-8563
Dr. Catherine Mayus, prin. Fax 376-8578
Gibran ES 200/PK-5
18 Rosedale Rd 10710 914-376-8580
Dr. Christopher Macaluso, prin. Fax 376-8583
King Computer Magnet ES 500/PK-6
135 Locust Hill Ave 10701 914-376-8470
Leslie Grant, prin. Fax 376-8472
Montessori ES 27 300/PK-6
132 Valentine Ln 10705 914-376-8455
Dr. Florence Taylor, prin. Fax 376-8457
Montessori ES 31 300/PK-6
7 Ravenswood Rd 10710 914-376-8623
Sharon Banks-Williams, prin. Fax 376-8626
Museum ES 25 500/PK-5
579 Warburton Ave 10701 914-376-8450
Denise German, prin. Fax 376-8452
Paideia ES 24 300/PK-5
50 Colin St 10701 914-376-8640
Ellen O'Brien-Scully, prin. Fax 376-8642
Paideia S 15 500/PK-8
175 Westchester Ave 10707 914-376-8645
Leslie Hamilton, prin. Fax 376-8630
Pearls Hawthorne S 1,100/PK-8
350 Hawthorne Ave 10705 914-376-8250
Marjorie Brown-Anfelouss, prin. Fax 376-8257
Public S 5 400/PK-8
118 Lockwood Ave 10701 914-376-8320
Dr. Geraldine Pisacreta, prin. Fax 376-8322
Public S 9 400/PK-5
53 Fairview St 10703 914-376-8325
Dr. Eric Mayus, prin. Fax 376-8327
Public S 13 500/PK-5
195 McLean Ave 10705 914-376-8335
Dr. Fred Hernandez, prin. Fax 377-9189
Public S 16 300/PK-5
759 N Broadway 10701 914-376-8340
Cynthia Eisner, prin. Fax 376-8342
Public S 17 300/PK-5
745 Midland Ave 10704 914-376-8345
Rita Morehead, prin. Fax 376-8347
Public S 21 400/PK-5
100 Lee Ave 10705 914-376-8435
Timo Hughes, prin. Fax 375-3907
Public S 22 400/PK-5
1408 Nepperhan Ave 10703 914-376-8440
Dr. Marvin Feldberg, prin. Fax 376-8442
Public S 23 300/PK-8
56 Van Cortlandt Pk Ave 10701 914-376-8445
Christine Montero, prin. Fax 376-8448
Public S 29 500/PK-8
47 Croydon Rd 10710 914-376-8585
Carol Blakney, prin. Fax 961-1287
Public S 30 400/PK-5
30 Nevada Pl 10708 914-376-8590
Kim Davis, prin. Fax 376-8592
Scholastic Academy 500/PK-8
77 Park Hill Ave 10701 914-376-8420
Taren Washington, prin. Fax 376-8423
Siragusa ES 400/PK-5
60 Crescent Pl 10704 914-376-8570
Ada Petrone, prin. Fax 776-2845
Yonkers MS 800/6-8
150 Rockland Ave 10705 914-376-8200
Anthony Cioffi, prin. Fax 376-8245
Yonkers Montessori Academy 700/PK-PK, 1-
160 Woodlawn Ave 10704 914-376-8540
Eileen Rivera-Shapiro, prin. Fax 376-8552
Other Schools – See Scarsdale

Christ the King S 200/PK-8
750 N Broadway 10701 914-476-1711
Dorothy Williams, prin. Fax 423-4101
Oakview Preparatory S of SDA 200/PK-8
29 Chestnut St 10701 914-423-7369
Jean Imbert, prin. Fax 423-0813
Sacred Heart S 300/PK-8
34 Convent Ave 10703 914-963-5318
Tatiana Ferraro, prin. Fax 965-4510
St. Ann S 200/PK-8
40 Brewster Ave 10701 914-965-4333
Lisa Lanni, prin. Fax 965-1778
St. Anthony S 200/PK-8
1395 Nepperhan Ave 10703 914-476-8489
Elizabeth Carney, prin. Fax 965-7939
St. Bartholomew S 200/PK-8
278 Saw Mill River Rd 10701 914-476-7949
Mark Valentinetti, prin. Fax 476-7957
St. Casimir S 200/PK-8
259 Nepperhan Ave 10701 914-965-2730
Helen DiNoia, prin. Fax 965-3347
St. Eugene S 400/PK-8
707 Tuckahoe Rd 10710 914-779-2956
Dolores Sullivan, prin. Fax 779-7668
St. John the Baptist S 300/PK-8
670 Yonkers Ave 10704 914-965-2356
Sr. Maryalice Reamer, prin. Fax 375-1115
St. Mark Lutheran S 100/PK-8
7 Saint Marks Pl 10704 914-237-4944
Tom Schnetzer, prin. Fax 237-1346
St. Mary S 200/PK-8
15 Saint Marys St 10701 914-965-7048
Patricia Raczy, prin. Fax 423-2826
St. Paul the Apostle S 300/PK-8
77 Lee Ave 10705 914-965-2165
Grace Mallardi, prin. Fax 965-5792
St. Peter S 200/PK-8
204 Hawthorne Ave 10705 914-963-2314
Dana Spicer, prin. Fax 966-8822
Stein Yeshiva of Lincoln Park 100/PK-8
287 Central Park Ave 10704 914-965-7082
Rabbi Joseph Cherns, prin. Fax 965-1902
Yonkers Christian Academy 200/PK-8
229 N Broadway 10701 914-963-0507
Ruth Narvaez, prin. Fax 966-1538

Yorkshire, Cattaraugus, Pop. 1,340
Yorkshire-Pioneer Central SD 2,600/K-12
PO Box 579 14173 585-492-9300
Jeffrey Bowen Ed.D., supt. Fax 492-9360
www.pioneerschools.org/
Pioneer MS 800/5-8
PO Box 619 14173 585-492-9375
Ravo Root, prin. Fax 492-9372
Other Schools – See Arcade, Delevan

Yorktown Heights, Westchester, Pop. 7,690
Lakeland Central SD
Supt. — See Shrub Oak
Franklin ES 700/K-5
3477 Kamhi Dr 10598 914-245-7444
Patricia McIlvenny, prin. Fax 245-7668
Jefferson ES 500/K-5
3636 Gomer St 10598 914-245-4802
Karen Gagliardi, prin. Fax 245-0511
Lakeland-Copper Beech MS 1,400/6-8
3401 Old Yorktown Rd 10598 914-245-1885
Jean Miccio, prin. Fax 245-1259

Yorktown Central SD 4,100/K-12
2725 Crompond Rd 10598 914-243-8000
Dr. Ralph Napolitano, supt. Fax 243-8003
www.yorktowncsd.org/
Brookside IS 500/3-5
2285 Broad St 10598 914-243-8130
Kenneth Levy, prin. Fax 243-0017
Crompond IS 400/3-5
2901 Manor St 10598 914-243-8140
Lisa O'Shea, prin. Fax 243-0018
French Hill ES 400/K-2
2051 Baldwin Rd 10598 914-243-8090
John Wells, prin. Fax 243-8099
Mohansic ES 400/K-2
704 Locksley Rd 10598 914-243-8160
Susan Berry, prin. Fax 243-0019
Strang MS 1,000/6-8
2701 Crompond Rd 10598 914-243-8100
Linda Grimm, prin. Fax 243-0016

Our Montessori S 200/PK-6
PO Box 72 10598 914-962-9466
Betty Hengst, dir. Fax 962-9470
St. Patrick S 300/PK-8
117 Moseman Rd 10598 914-962-2211
Nan Gollogly, prin. Fax 243-4814

Yorkville, Oneida, Pop. 2,613
Whitesboro Central SD 3,700/K-12
PO Box 304 13495 315-266-3300
David Langone, supt. Fax 768-9730
www.wboro.org
Other Schools – See Deerfield, Marcy, Whitesboro

Youngstown, Niagara, Pop. 1,901
Lewiston-Porter Central SD 2,300/K-12
4061 Creek Rd 14174 716-286-7266
Chris Roser, supt. Fax 754-2755
lew-port.com
Lewiston-Porter IS 500/3-5
4061 Creek Rd 14174 716-286-7253
Tamara Larson, prin. Fax 286-7854
Lewiston-Porter MS 600/6-8
4061 Creek Rd 14174 716-286-7201
Vincent Dell'Oso, prin. Fax 286-7204
Lewiston-Porter PS 500/K-2
4061 Creek Rd 14174 716-286-7220
Margaret Beach, prin. Fax 286-7855

NORTH CAROLINA

NORTH CAROLINA DEPT. PUBLIC INSTRUCTION
301 N Wilmington St, Raleigh 27601-1058
Telephone 919-807-3300
Fax 919-807-3445
Website http://www.dpi.state.nc.us

Superintendent of Public Instruction June Atkinson

NORTH CAROLINA BOARD OF EDUCATION
301 N Wilmington St, Raleigh 27601-1058

Chairperson William Harrison

PUBLIC, PRIVATE AND CATHOLIC ELEMENTARY SCHOOLS

Aberdeen, Moore, Pop. 4,794
Moore County SD
Supt. — See Carthage
Aberdeen ES 300/3-5
503 N Sandhills Blvd 28315 910-944-1124
Debbie Warren, prin. Fax 944-3597
Aberdeen PS 300/K-2
310 Keyser St 28315 910-944-1523
Sloan Browning, prin. Fax 944-3171
Southern MS 700/6-8
717 Johnson St 28315 910-693-1550
Mike Metcalf, prin. Fax 693-1544

Advance, Davie
Davie County SD
Supt. — See Mocksville
Ellis MS 6-8
144 William Ellis Dr 27006 336-998-2007
Larry Bridgewater, prin. Fax 998-6249
Shady Grove ES 700/K-5
3179 Cornatzer Rd 27006 336-998-4719
Maureen Gildein, prin. Fax 998-7024

Ahoskie, Hertford, Pop. 4,324
Hertford County SD
Supt. — See Winton
Ahoskie ES 500/4-6
200 Talmage Ave N 27910 252-332-2588
Stan Warren, prin. Fax 332-2017
Bearfield PS 900/PK-3
145 Hertford County High Rd 27910 252-209-6140
Julie Shields, prin. Fax 209-6148

Ahoskie Christian S 200/K-12
500 Kiwanis St 27910 252-332-2764
Ridgecroft S 300/PK-12
PO Box 1008 27910 252-332-2964
Elton Winslow, prin. Fax 332-7586

Albemarle, Stanly, Pop. 15,325
Stanly County SD 9,700/PK-12
1000 N 1st St Ste 4 28001 704-983-5151
Dr. Samuel DePaul, supt. Fax 982-3618
www.scs.k12.nc.us
Albemarle MS 500/6-8
1811 Badin Rd 28001 704-982-5480
Todd Thorpe, prin. Fax 983-2600
Central ES 300/K-5
206 N 3rd St 28001 704-982-3213
Melissa Smith, prin. Fax 982-9131
East Albemarle ES 300/K-5
1813 E Main St 28001 704-982-5113
Steve Coats, prin. Fax 982-3463
Endy S 400/K-8
27670 Betty Rd 28001 704-982-5193
Jessie Morton, prin. Fax 982-4059
Millingport S 200/K-8
24198 NC 73 Hwy 28001 704-982-2261
Julie McSwain, prin. Fax 983-1642
North Albemarle ES 300/PK-5
1121 Austin St 28001 704-982-2614
Donna Staats, prin. Fax 982-2616
Other Schools – See Badin, Locust, New London, Norwood, Oakboro, Richfield, Stanfield

---

Park Ridge Christian S 200/K-8
312 Park Ridge Rd 28001 704-982-9798
Starr Wagoner, prin.

Albertson, Duplin
Duplin County SD
Supt. — See Kenansville
Grady S 900/PK-8
2627 N NC 11 903 Hwy 28508 252-568-3487
Douglas Hill, prin. Fax 568-6238

Andrews, Cherokee, Pop. 1,703
Cherokee County SD
Supt. — See Murphy
Andrews ES 400/PK-5
205 Walnut St 28901 828-321-4415
Judy Vickers, prin. Fax 321-0401
Andrews MS 200/6-8
2750 Business 19 28901 828-321-5762
DavAnn Hubbard, prin. Fax 321-2009

Angier, Harnett, Pop. 4,107
Harnett County SD
Supt. — See Lillington
Angier ES 300/4-5
130 E Mciver St 27501 919-639-2635
Sharon Patterson, prin. Fax 639-9583
Harnett Central MS 1,100/6-8
2529 Harnett Central Rd 27501 919-639-6000
Chris Mace, prin. Fax 639-9617
North Harnett PS 600/K-3
282 N Harnett School Rd 27501 919-639-4480
Monica Thompson, prin. Fax 639-7064

Johnston County SD
Supt. — See Smithfield
McGee's Crossroads ES 800/PK-5
10330 NC 50 Hwy N 27501 919-894-7161
Terry Weakley, prin. Fax 894-1960

Apex, Wake, Pop. 28,551
Wake County SD
Supt. — See Raleigh
Apex ES 600/K-5
700 Tingen Rd 27502 919-387-2150
Dr. Laurel Crissman, prin. Fax 387-2152
Apex MS 1,200/6-8
400 E Moore St 27502 919-387-2181
Timothy Locklair, prin. Fax 387-2203
Baucom ES 900/K-5
400 Hunter St 27502 919-387-2168
Ve-Lecia Council, prin. Fax 387-2170
Laurel Park ES K-5
2450 Laura Duncan Rd, 919-290-2333
Gail Turner, prin. Fax 290-2334
Lufkin Road MS 1,100/6-8
1002 Lufkin Rd, 919-387-4465
Frank Graham, prin. Fax 363-1095
Middle Creek ES 1,000/K-5
110 Middle Creek Park Ave, 919-773-9555
Charles Miller, prin. Fax 773-9568
Olive Chapel Road ES 900/K-5
1751 Olive Chapel Rd 27502 919-387-4440
Melissa Burns, prin. Fax 387-4447
Salem ES 800/K-5
6116 Old Jenks Rd, 919-363-2865
Savon Willard, prin. Fax 363-2973
Salem MS 1,000/6-8
6150 Old Jenks Rd, 919-363-1870
Herbert Ellzey, prin. Fax 363-1876
West Lake ES 1,100/PK-5
4500 W Lake Rd, 919-662-2300
Mary Warren, prin. Fax 662-2313
West Lake MS 1,300/6-8
4600 W Lake Rd, 919-662-2900
Dr. Gregory Decker, prin. Fax 662-2906

St. Andrew's ECC 100/PK-PK
3008 Old Raleigh Rd 27502 919-387-8656
Ann Graf, dir. Fax 362-5778
St. Mary Magdalene S 500/PK-8
625 Magdala Pl 27502 919-657-4800
Robert Cadran, prin. Fax 657-4805

Archdale, Randolph, Pop. 9,428
Randolph County SD
Supt. — See Asheboro
Archdale ES 400/K-5
207 Trindale Rd 27263 336-431-9121
Lynn Smith, prin. Fax 431-5943
Lawrence ES 500/K-5
6068 Suits Rd 27263 336-861-8100
Aaron Woody, prin. Fax 861-8101
Trindale ES 400/K-5
400 Balfour Dr 27263 336-434-1516
Dr. Terry Burgin, prin. Fax 434-2508

Mount Calvary Christian S 100/K-12
6551 Weant Rd 27263 336-434-6800

Arden, Buncombe
Buncombe County SD
Supt. — See Asheville
Avery's Creek ES 700/K-5
15 Park South Rd 28704 828-654-1810
Malorie McGinnis, prin. Fax 654-9801
Glen Arden ES 700/K-5
50 Pinehurst Cir 28704 828-654-1800
Linda Bradley, prin. Fax 654-1801
Valley Springs MS 800/6-8
224 Long Shoals Rd 28704 828-654-1785
Eddie Burchfield, prin. Fax 654-1789

Ash, Brunswick
Brunswick County SD
Supt. — See Bolivia
Monroe ES 500/PK-5
250 Pea Landing Rd NW 28420 910-287-4014
Patricia Rourk, prin. Fax 287-4027
Waccamaw S 600/K-8
5901 Waccamaw School Rd NW 28420 910-287-6437
Beverly Marlowe, prin. Fax 287-5123

Asheboro, Randolph, Pop. 23,639
Asheboro CSD 4,500/PK-12
PO Box 1103 27204 336-625-5104
Dr. Diane Frost, supt. Fax 625-9238
www.asheboro.k12.nc.us
Balfour ES 500/K-5
2097 N Asheboro School Rd 27203 336-672-0322
Janet Means, prin. Fax 672-0328
Lindley Park ES 400/PK-5
312 Cliff Rd 27203 336-625-6226
Robin Harris, prin. Fax 629-5895
Loflin ES 400/PK-5
405 S Park St 27203 336-625-1685
Candace Call, prin. Fax 625-1688
McCrary ES 500/K-5
400 Ross St 27203 336-629-1817
Julie Brady, prin. Fax 629-1327
North Asheboro MS 500/6-8
1861 N Asheboro School Rd 27203 336-672-1900
Leigh Jones, prin. Fax 672-6267
South Asheboro MS 600/6-8
523 W Walker Ave 27203 336-629-4141
Carol Grant, prin. Fax 629-3761
Teachey ES 400/PK-5
294 Newbern Ave 27205 336-625-4163
Susan Vanderburg, prin. Fax 629-6178

Randolph County SD 19,000/K-12
2222 S Fayetteville St 27205 336-318-6100
Donald Andrews, supt. Fax 318-6155
www.randolph.k12.nc.us
Farmer ES 400/K-5
3557 Grange Hall Rd 27205 336-857-3400
Brian Toth, prin. Fax 857-3409
Southmont ES 700/K-5
2497 Southmont Dr 27205 336-625-1558
Sherri Hall, prin. Fax 625-5693
Southwestern Randolph MS 700/6-8
1509 Hopewell Friends Rd 27205 336-381-3900
Holly Embree, prin. Fax 381-3905
Tabernacle ES 500/K-5
4901 Tabernacle School Rd 27205 336-629-3533
Jack Blanchard, prin. Fax 629-4463
Other Schools – See Archdale, Franklinville, Liberty, Ramseur, Randleman, Seagrove, Sophia, Trinity

---

Fayetteville Street Christian S 200/K-12
151 W Pritchard St 27203 336-629-1383
David Jeffreys, admin. Fax 629-0067
Neighbors Grove Christian Academy 100/K-9
1928 N Fayetteville St 27203 336-672-1147
Kris Leroy, admin. Fax 672-5500

Asheville, Buncombe, Pop. 72,231
Asheville CSD 3,600/PK-12
85 Mountain St 28801 828-350-7000
Allen Johnson, supt. Fax 255-5131
www.asheville.k12.nc.us
Asheville City Preschool PK-PK
441 Haywood Rd 28806 828-255-5423
Debra Preneta, dir. Fax 251-4913
Asheville MS 600/6-8
197 S French Broad Ave 28801 828-350-6200
Mary Sullivan, prin. Fax 255-5311

Claxton ES 400/K-5
241 Merrimon Ave 28801 828-350-6500
Dr. Ayesha McArthur, prin. Fax 255-5239
Dickson ES 400/K-5
125 Hill St 28801 828-350-6800
Alida Woods, prin. Fax 255-5589
Fletcher ES 300/K-5
60 Ridgelawn Rd 28806 828-350-6400
Dr. Cheryl Witherspoon, prin. Fax 255-5070
Jones ES 400/K-5
544 Kimberly Ave 28804 828-350-6700
Marsha Lipe, prin. Fax 251-4914
Vance ES 300/K-5
98 Sulphur Springs Rd 28806 828-350-6600
Cynthia Sellinger, prin. Fax 251-4952

Buncombe County SD 25,600/K-12
175 Bingham Rd 28806 828-255-5921
Tony Baldwin, supt. Fax 255-5923
www.buncombe.k12.nc.us/
Bell ES 300/K-5
90 Maple Springs Rd 28805 828-298-3789
Carleene Finger, prin. Fax 299-0685
Emma ES 500/K-5
37 Brickyard Rd 28806 828-232-4272
Deborah DeVane, prin. Fax 232-4275
Erwin MS 1,100/6-8
20 Erwin Hills Rd 28806 828-232-4264
Gayland Welborn, prin. Fax 232-5407
Estes ES 800/K-5
275 Overlook Rd 28803 828-654-1795
John Barbour, prin. Fax 654-1798
Haw Creek ES 500/K-5
21 Trinity Chapel Rd 28805 828-298-4022
Marcia Perry, prin. Fax 299-8117
Johnston ES 300/K-5
230 Johnston Blvd 28806 828-232-4291
Gardner Bridges, prin. Fax 252-7653
Oakley ES 500/K-5
753 Fairview Rd 28803 828-274-7515
Brian Chandler, prin. Fax 274-1721
Reynolds MS 600/6-8
2 Rocket Dr 28803 828-298-7484
Robbie Adell, prin. Fax 298-7503
Sand Hill-Venable ES 700/K-5
154 Sand Hill School Rd 28806 828-670-5028
Diane McEntire, prin. Fax 670-5034
West Buncombe ES 700/K-5
175 Erwin Hills Rd 28806 828-232-4282
Carmen Murray, prin. Fax 232-1316
Woodfin ES 200/K-5
108 Elk Mountain Rd 28804 828-232-4287
Cynthia Porter, prin. Fax 232-4288
Other Schools – See Arden, Barnardsville, Black Mountain, Candler, Fairview, Fletcher, Leicester, Swannanoa, Weaverville

---

Asheville Catholic S 200/PK-8
12 Culvern St 28804 828-252-7896
Donna Gilson, prin. Fax 252-5708
Carolina Christian S 200/PK-12
48 Woodland Hills Rd 28804 828-658-8964
Dema Barishnikov, admin. Fax 658-8965
Carolina Day S 600/PK-12
1345 Hendersonville Rd 28803 828-274-0757
Dr. Beverly Sgro, hdmstr. Fax 274-0756
Emmanuel Lutheran S 200/PK-8
51 Wilburn Pl 28806 828-281-8182
Luke Schmelzle, prin. Fax 254-3940
Nazarene Christian S 50/K-8
385 Hazel Mill Rd 28806 828-252-9713
Peggy Neighbors, admin. Fax 253-6946
North Asheville Christian S 200/PK-12
20 Reynolds Mountain Blvd 28804 828-645-8053
Susie Hepler, admin. Fax 645-2973
Temple Baptist S 200/PK-12
985 1/2 Patton Ave 28806 828-252-3712
William Spence, prin. Fax 254-5119

Atlantic, Carteret
Carteret County SD
Supt. — See Beaufort
Atlantic S 200/PK-8
PO Box 98 28511 252-225-3961
Chris Yeomans, prin. Fax 225-1077

Aulander, Bertie, Pop. 893
Bertie County SD
Supt. — See Windsor
Aulander ES 200/PK-5
PO Box 310 27805 252-345-3211
Elaine White, prin. Fax 345-0066

Aurora, Beaufort, Pop. 581
Beaufort County SD
Supt. — See Washington
Snowden S 200/PK-8
6921 NC Highway 306 S 27806 252-322-5351
Virginia Simmons, prin. Fax 322-4372

Autryville, Sampson, Pop. 205
Sampson County SD
Supt. — See Clinton
Clement ES 400/PK-5
3220 Maxwell Rd 28318 910-567-2112
Linda Williams, prin. Fax 567-5910

Ayden, Pitt, Pop. 4,798
Pitt County SD
Supt. — See Greenville
Ayden ES 600/PK-5
187 3rd St 28513 252-746-2121
Gail Haney, prin. Fax 746-6470
Ayden MS 400/6-8
192 3rd St 28513 252-746-3672
Seth Brown, prin. Fax 746-9923

Badin, Stanly, Pop. 1,250
Stanly County SD
Supt. — See Albemarle
Badin S 400/K-8
PO Box 308 28009 704-422-3660
Anne Faulkenberry, prin. Fax 422-3513

Bahama, Durham
Durham County SD
Supt. — See Durham
Mangum ES 400/K-5
9008 Quail Roost Rd 27503 919-560-3948
Gwendolyn Johnson, prin. Fax 560-2204

Bailey, Nash, Pop. 675
Nash-Rocky Mount SD
Supt. — See Nashville
Bailey ES 700/PK-5
PO Box 39 27807 252-451-2892
Georgia Dixon, prin. Fax 235-6028

Bakersville, Mitchell, Pop. 353
Mitchell County SD 2,200/K-12
72 Ledger School Rd 28705 828-766-2220
Dr. Brock Womble, supt. Fax 766-2221
central.mitchell.k12.nc.us
Bowman MS 200/5-8
PO Box 46 28705 828-688-2752
Angela Burleson, prin. Fax 688-6002
Buladean S 100/K-8
12190 N 226 Hwy 28705 828-688-2324
Rick McCourry, prin. Fax 688-1184
Gouge ES 200/K-4
134 Laurel St 28705 828-688-2141
Colby Calhoun, prin. Fax 688-9344
Other Schools – See Green Mountain, Spruce Pine

Banner Elk, Avery, Pop. 958
Avery County SD
Supt. — See Newland
Banner Elk ES 200/PK-5
PO Box 218 28604 828-898-5575
Ken Townsend, prin. Fax 898-6036

High Country Christian S 50/1-8
1551 Tynecastle Hwy 28604 828-898-3677
Eulita Heisey, prin.

Barco, Currituck
Currituck County SD
Supt. — See Currituck
Central ES 300/PK-5
504 Shortcut Rd 27917 252-453-0010
Rhonda James-Davis, prin. Fax 453-0011
Currituck County MS 500/6-8
4263 Caratoke Hwy 27917 252-453-2171
Bill Wicks, prin. Fax 453-0019

Barnardsville, Buncombe
Buncombe County SD
Supt. — See Asheville
Barnardsville ES 200/K-4
20 Hillcrest Dr 28709 828-626-2290
Steve Chandler, prin. Fax 626-3750

Bath, Beaufort, Pop. 272
Beaufort County SD
Supt. — See Washington
Bath S 600/K-8
110 S King St 27808 252-923-3251
Pamela Hodges, prin. Fax 923-0202

Battleboro, Edgecombe, Pop. 559
Edgecombe County SD
Supt. — See Tarboro
Coker-Wimberly ES 400/PK-5
1619 NC Highway 97 W 27809 252-823-4446
Lisa Howell, prin. Fax 641-5704
Phillips MS 200/6-8
4371 Battleboro Leggett Rd 27809 252-446-2031
William Etheridge, prin. Fax 446-1629

Nash-Rocky Mount SD
Supt. — See Nashville
Hubbard ES 600/K-5
7921 Red Oak Battleboro Rd 27809 252-446-5135
Robin May, prin. Fax 985-4326
Red Oak MS 1,000/6-8
3170 Red Oak Battleboro Rd 27809 252-451-5500
Connie Bobbitt, prin. Fax 451-5510

Bayboro, Pamlico, Pop. 716
Pamlico County SD 1,600/PK-12
507 Anderson Dr 28515 252-745-4171
Dr. James Coon, supt. Fax 745-4172
www.pamlico.k12.nc.us
Anderson ES 300/3-5
PO Box 417 28515 252-745-4611
Sherry Meador, prin. Fax 745-5021
Pamlico County MS 300/6-8
15526 NC Highway 55 28515 252-745-4061
Henry Rice, prin. Fax 745-5583
Pamlico County PS 400/PK-2
323 Neals Creek Rd 28515 252-745-3404
Linda Ollison, prin. Fax 745-3118

Beaufort, Carteret, Pop. 4,119
Carteret County SD 8,300/PK-12
107 Safrit Dr 28516 252-728-4583
Brad Sneeden, supt. Fax 728-3028
www.carteretcountyschools.org
Beaufort ES 500/PK-5
110 Carraway Dr 28516 252-728-3316
Vicki Fritz, prin. Fax 728-2753
Beaufort MS 200/6-8
100 Carraway Dr 28516 252-728-4520
Becky Misner, prin. Fax 728-3392
Other Schools – See Atlantic, Cape Carteret, Harkers Island, Morehead City, Newport, Smyrna

Belhaven, Beaufort, Pop. 1,965

Pungo Christian Academy 200/PK-12
983 W Main St 27810 252-943-2678
Marcy Morgan, prin. Fax 943-3292

Belmont, Gaston, Pop. 8,779
Gaston County SD
Supt. — See Gastonia
Belmont Central ES 600/2-5
310 Eagle Rd 28012 704-825-8479
Sara Moore, prin. Fax 825-8080
Belmont MS 700/6-8
110 N Central Ave 28012 704-825-9619
Mark Schultz, prin. Fax 825-6951
Catawba Heights ES 300/PK-5
101 Ivey St 28012 704-827-3221
Phyllis Whitworth, prin. Fax 827-2419
North Belmont ES 400/PK-5
210 School St 28012 704-827-4043
Chris Germain, prin. Fax 827-0423
Page ES 300/PK-1
215 Ewing Dr 28012 704-825-2614
Mark Fisher, prin. Fax 825-4883

Bennett, Chatham
Chatham County SD
Supt. — See Pittsboro
Bennett S 200/K-8
PO Box 107 27208 336-581-3586
Dorthy Ritter-Phillips, prin. Fax 581-4054

Benson, Johnston, Pop. 3,282
Johnston County SD
Supt. — See Smithfield
Benson ES 500/PK-4
2040 NC Highway 50 N 27504 919-894-4233
Betty Bennett, prin. Fax 894-7133
Benson MS 400/5-8
1600 N Wall St 27504 919-894-3889
Sheila Singleton, prin. Fax 894-1551
McGee's Crossroads MS 700/6-8
13353 NC Highway 210 27504 919-894-6003
Barretta Haynes, prin. Fax 894-6007
Meadow S 600/K-8
7507 NC Highway 50 S 27504 919-894-4226
Rodney Peterson, prin. Fax 894-1804

Bessemer City, Gaston, Pop. 5,319
Gaston County SD
Supt. — See Gastonia
Bessemer City Central ES 500/2-5
PO Box 794 28016 704-629-2206
Darcy Hay, prin. Fax 629-6320
Bessemer City MS 600/6-8
525 Ed Wilson Rd 28016 704-629-3281
Rebecca Wilson, prin. Fax 629-4501
Bessemer City PS 200/K-1
1320 N 12th St 28016 704-629-4181
Todd Dellinger, prin. Fax 629-6119
Tryon ES 500/PK-5
2620 Tryon Courthouse Rd 28016 704-629-2942
Terry Usery, prin. Fax 629-5967

Bethel, Pitt, Pop. 1,689
Pitt County SD
Supt. — See Greenville
Bethel S 300/PK-8
210 E Washington St 27812 252-825-3801
Betty Tolar, prin. Fax 825-1203

Beulaville, Duplin, Pop. 1,098
Duplin County SD
Supt. — See Kenansville
Beulaville S 900/PK-8
138 Lyman Rd 28518 910-298-3171
Michelle Thigpen, prin. Fax 298-3342

Biscoe, Montgomery, Pop. 1,715
Montgomery County SD
Supt. — See Troy
East MS 500/6-8
1834 US Highway 220 Alt S 27209 910-428-3278
Vivacious Crews, prin. Fax 428-1279
Green Ridge ES K-5
129 McCaskill Rd 27209 910-576-6511
Donna Kennedy, prin.

Black Creek, Wilson, Pop. 706
Wilson County SD
Supt. — See Wilson
Woodard ES 300/K-5
PO Box 26 27813 252-399-7940
Kelly Andrews, prin. Fax 399-7898

Black Mountain, Buncombe, Pop. 7,650
Buncombe County SD
Supt. — See Asheville
Black Mountain ES 200/4-5
100 Flat Creek Rd 28711 828-669-5217
Norman Bossert, prin. Fax 669-5529
Black Mountain PS 500/K-3
301 E State St 28711 828-669-2645
Jerry Green, prin. Fax 669-1616

Bladenboro, Bladen, Pop. 1,713
Bladen County SD
Supt. — See Elizabethtown
Bladenboro MS 400/5-8
910 S Main St 28320 910-863-3232
Wilbert Stokes, prin. Fax 863-4683
Bladenboro PS 500/PK-4
PO Box 820 28320 910-863-3387
Deborah Guyton, prin. Fax 863-3358

Blowing Rock, Watauga, Pop. 1,424
Watauga County SD
Supt. — See Boone
Blowing Rock S 400/K-8
PO Box 228 28605 828-295-3204
Patrick Sukow, prin. Fax 295-4977

Bolivia, Brunswick, Pop. 168
Brunswick County SD — 11,700/PK-12
35 Referendum Dr NE 28422 — 910-253-2900
Dr. Katie McGee, supt. — Fax 253-2983
www.bcswan.net
Bolivia ES — 700/PK-5
4036 Business 17 E 28422 — 910-253-6516
David Cupolo, prin. — Fax 253-8162
Williamson ES — 600/K-5
1020 Zion Hill Rd SE 28422 — 910-754-8660
Caryl Fullwood, prin. — Fax 754-8661
Other Schools – See Ash, Leland, Shallotte, Southport, Supply

Bonlee, Chatham
Chatham County SD
Supt. — See Pittsboro
Bonlee S — 400/K-8
PO Box 168 27213 — 919-837-5316
Daniel Haithcox, prin. — Fax 837-5583

Boomer, Wilkes
Wilkes County SD
Supt. — See North Wilkesboro
Boomer-Ferguson ES — 200/PK-5
556 Boomer Frgson School Rd 28606 — 336-921-3015
Sharon Shoupe, prin. — Fax 921-4290

Boone, Watauga, Pop. 13,192
Watauga County SD — 4,000/PK-12
PO Box 1790 28607 — 828-264-7190
Dr. Marty Hemric, supt. — Fax 264-7196
www.watauga.k12.nc.us
Green Valley S — 400/PK-8
189 Big Hill Rd 28607 — 828-264-3606
Phillip Griffin, prin. — Fax 264-8108
Hardin Park S — 100/PK-8
361 Jefferson Rd 28607 — 828-264-8481
Mary Smalling, prin. — Fax 265-3609
Parkway S — 600/PK-8
160 Parkway School Dr 28607 — 828-264-3032
Doug Falkner, prin. — Fax 264-7999
Other Schools – See Blowing Rock, Sugar Grove, Vilas, Zionville

Boonville, Yadkin, Pop. 1,113
Yadkin County SD
Supt. — See Yadkinville
Boonville ES — 400/PK-6
232 E Main St 27011 — 336-367-7021
David Brown, prin. — Fax 367-5172
Starmount MS — 7-8
2626 Longtown Rd 27011 — 336-468-6833
Rick Swaim, prin. — Fax 468-6838

Bostic, Rutherford, Pop. 327
Rutherford County SD
Supt. — See Forest City
East Rutherford MS — 700/6-8
259 E Church St 28018 — 828-245-4836
Brad Teague, prin. — Fax 245-1491
Sunshine ES — 300/K-5
231 Toney Rd 28018 — 828-245-0658
Neil Higgins, prin. — Fax 248-2407

Brevard, Transylvania, Pop. 6,643
Transylvania County SD — 3,800/K-12
225 Rosenwald Ln 28712 — 828-884-6173
Jeffrey McDaris, supt. — Fax 884-9524
www.transylvania.k12.nc.us
Brevard ES — 500/K-5
601 Greenville Hwy 28712 — 828-884-2001
Tammy Bellefeuill, prin. — Fax 884-3304
Brevard MS — 600/6-8
400 Fisher Rd 28712 — 828-884-2091
David Williams, prin. — Fax 883-3150
Pisgah Forest ES — 600/K-5
1076 Ecusta Rd 28712 — 828-877-4481
Mike Bailey, prin. — Fax 884-2551
Other Schools – See Lake Toxaway, Rosman

Broadway, Lee, Pop. 1,102
Lee County SD
Supt. — See Sanford
Broadway ES — 600/K-5
307 S Main St 27505 — 919-258-3828
Clara Ephriam, prin. — Fax 258-6954

Browns Summit, Guilford
Guilford County SD
Supt. — See Greensboro
Brown Summit MS — 200/6-8
4720 E NC Highway 150 27214 — 336-656-0432
Deborah Mott, prin. — Fax 656-0439
Monticello-Brown Summit ES — 800/PK-5
5006 E NC Highway 150 27214 — 336-656-4010
Dr. Benita Lawrence, prin. — Fax 656-4616

Bryson City, Swain, Pop. 1,361
Swain County SD — 1,700/K-12
PO Box 2340 28713 — 828-488-3129
Bob Marr, supt. — Fax 488-8510
www.swain.k12.nc.us
Swain County East ES — 300/K-5
4747 Ela Rd 28713 — 828-488-0939
Shirley Grant, prin. — Fax 488-6635
Swain County MS — 400/6-8
135 Arlington Ave 28713 — 828-488-3480
Mark Sale, prin. — Fax 488-0949
Swain County West ES — 400/K-5
4142 Highway 19 W 28713 — 828-488-2119
Michael Treadway, prin. — Fax 488-0797

Buies Creek, Harnett, Pop. 2,085
Harnett County SD
Supt. — See Lillington
Buies Creek ES — 300/K-5
PO Box 68 27506 — 910-893-3505
Alice Cobb, prin. — Fax 893-6979

Bunn, Franklin, Pop. 391
Franklin County SD
Supt. — See Louisburg
Bunn ES — 700/K-5
PO Box 143 27508 — 919-496-4015
Jewel Eason, prin. — Fax 496-0301
Bunn MS — 700/6-8
4742 NC 39 Hwy S 27508 — 919-496-7700
Roosevelt Alston, prin. — Fax 496-1404

Bunnlevel, Harnett
Harnett County SD
Supt. — See Lillington
Anderson Creek PS — 600/K-2
914 Anderson Creek Sch Rd 28323 — 910-893-4523
Leanne O'Quinn, prin. — Fax 893-6752
South Harnett ES — 600/3-5
8335 NC Highway 210 S 28323 — 910-893-9153
Clara Clinton, prin. — Fax 893-5726

Burgaw, Pender, Pop. 3,756
Pender County SD — 7,800/PK-12
925 Penderlea Hwy 28425 — 910-259-2187
Allison Sholar, supt. — Fax 259-0133
www.pendercountyschools.net/
Burgaw ES — 600/PK-5
400 N Wright St 28425 — 910-259-0145
Cindy Faulk, prin. — Fax 259-0148
Burgaw MS — 300/6-8
500 S Wright St 28425 — 910-259-0149
M.D. Coleman, prin. — Fax 259-0150
Malpass Corner ES — 600/PK-5
4992 Malpass Corner Rd 28425 — 910-283-5889
Stephen Buchanan, prin. — Fax 283-5868
West Pender MS — 200/6-8
10750 NC Highway 53 W 28425 — 910-283-5626
June Robbins, prin. — Fax 283-9537
Other Schools – See Hampstead, Rocky Point, Willard

Burlington, Alamance, Pop. 47,592
Alamance-Burlington SD — 22,700/PK-12
1712 Vaughn Rd 27217 — 336-570-6060
Randy Bridges Ed.D., supt. — Fax 570-6218
www.abss.k12.nc.us
Andrews ES — 600/PK-5
2630 Buckingham Rd 27217 — 336-570-6170
Martha Brown-Caulder, prin. — Fax 570-6201
Broadview MS — 700/6-8
2229 Broadview Dr 27217 — 336-570-6195
Nakia Hardy, prin. — Fax 570-6202
Eastlawn ES — 600/PK-5
502 N Graham Hopedale Rd 27217 — 336-570-6180
Sabre Robinson, prin. — Fax 570-6204
Grove Park ES — 600/PK-5
141 Trail One 27215 — 336-570-6115
Jennifer Reed, prin. — Fax 570-6205
Highland ES — K-5
3720 Bonnar Bridge Rd 27215 — 336-538-8700
Nan Wooten, prin. — Fax 538-8705
Hillcrest ES — 700/PK-5
1714 W Davis St 27215 — 336-570-6120
Robin Woody, prin. — Fax 570-6206
Holt ES — 700/K-5
4751 S NC Highway 62 27215 — 336-570-6420
Darrell Thomas, prin. — Fax 570-6429
Newlin ES — 600/PK-5
316 Carden St 27215 — 336-570-6125
Dr. Erica Vernold-Miller, prin. — Fax 570-6207
Pleasant Grove ES — 300/PK-5
2847 Pleasant Grove Un Sch 27217 — 336-421-3701
Devon Carson, prin. — Fax 421-9844
Smith ES — 600/K-5
2235 Delaney Dr 27215 — 336-570-6140
Wendy Gooch, prin. — Fax 570-6209
Turrentine MS — 900/6-8
1710 Edgewood Ave 27215 — 336-570-6150
Dr. John Swajkoski, prin. — Fax 570-6210
Other Schools – See Elon, Graham, Haw River, Mebane, Snow Camp

---

Blessed Sacrament S — 300/PK-8
515 Hillcrest Ave 27215 — 336-570-0019
Fax 570-9623
Burlington Christian Academy — 500/PK-12
621 E 6th St 27215 — 336-227-0288
Michael Brown, admin. — Fax 570-1314
Burlington Day S — 200/K-8
1615 Greenwood Ter 27215 — 336-228-0296
Stephen Switzer, hdmstr. — Fax 226-6249

Burnsville, Yancey, Pop. 1,628
Yancey County SD — 2,500/K-12
PO Box 190 28714 — 828-682-6101
Dr. Thomas Little, supt. — Fax 682-7110
www.yanceync.net
Bald Creek ES — 200/K-5
100 Bald Creek School Rd 28714 — 828-682-2535
Sherry Robinson, prin. — Fax 682-3575
Bee Log ES — 100/K-5
55 Bee Log Rd 28714 — 828-682-3271
Andrea Allen, prin. — Fax 682-3790
Burnsville ES — 400/K-5
395 Burnsville School Rd 28714 — 828-682-4515
Shane Cassida, prin. — Fax 682-3566
Cane River MS — 300/6-8
1128 Cane River School Rd 28714 — 828-682-2202
Alton Robinson, prin. — Fax 682-3754
East Yancey MS — 400/6-8
285 Georges Fork Rd 28714 — 828-682-2281
Rick Tipton, prin. — Fax 682-3513
South Toe ES — 100/K-5
139 S Toe School Rd 28714 — 828-675-4321
Doris Deyton, prin. — Fax 675-0098
Other Schools – See Green Mountain, Micaville

Butner, Granville, Pop. 4,679
Granville County SD
Supt. — See Oxford
Butner-Stem ES — 500/PK-5
201 E D St 27509 — 919-575-6947
Gus Gillespie, prin. — Fax 528-6130
Butner-Stem MS — 500/6-8
501 E D St 27509 — 919-575-9429
Calvin Timberlake, prin. — Fax 575-5894

Buxton, Dare
Dare County SD
Supt. — See Nags Head
Cape Hatteras ES — 300/PK-5
PO Box 989 27920 — 252-995-6196
Ray Gray, prin. — Fax 995-3950

Camden, Camden
Camden County SD — 1,700/PK-12
174 NC Highway 343 N 27921 — 252-335-0831
Ron Melchiorre, supt. — Fax 331-2300
www.camden.k12.nc.us
Camden IS — 300/4-6
123 Noblitt Dr 27921 — 252-335-7808
Parrish Griffin, prin. — Fax 335-4327
Camden MS — 300/7-8
248 Scotland Rd 27921 — 252-338-3349
Jean Gray, prin. — Fax 331-2253
Grandy PS — 600/PK-3
175 NC Highway 343 N 27921 — 252-331-4838
Becky Phelps, prin. — Fax 338-5443

Cameron, Moore, Pop. 157
Harnett County SD
Supt. — See Lillington
Johnsonville ES — 400/K-5
18495 NC Highway 27 W 28326 — 919-499-4912
Belvia Williams, prin. — Fax 499-1402

Moore County SD
Supt. — See Carthage
Cameron ES — 200/K-5
2636 NC Highway 24 27 28326 — 910-245-7814
Priscilla Riley, prin. — Fax 245-2760
New Century MS — 900/6-8
1577 Union Church Rd 28326 — 910-947-1301
Cindy Holland, prin. — Fax 947-1227

Candler, Buncombe
Buncombe County SD
Supt. — See Asheville
Candler ES — 600/K-5
121 Candler School Rd 28715 — 828-670-5018
Jackie Byerly, prin. — Fax 667-2439
Enka MS — 1,000/6-8
390 Asbury Rd 28715 — 828-670-5010
Pam Fourtenbary, prin. — Fax 670-5015
Hominy Valley ES — 500/K-5
450 Enka Lake Rd 28715 — 828-665-0619
Angie Jackson, prin. — Fax 667-3770
Pisgah ES — 300/K-5
1495 Pisgah Hwy 28715 — 828-670-5023
Jay Dale, prin. — Fax 667-9357

Asheville-Pisgah S — 100/PK-8
90 Academy Dr 28715 — 828-667-3255
Harry Janetzko, prin. — Fax 667-8465

Candor, Montgomery, Pop. 829
Montgomery County SD
Supt. — See Troy
Candor ES — 700/PK-5
414 S Main St 27229 — 910-974-4582
Donnie Lynthacum, prin. — Fax 974-4315

Canton, Haywood, Pop. 4,002
Haywood County SD
Supt. — See Waynesville
Bethel ES — 500/K-5
4700 Old River Rd 28716 — 828-646-3448
Jill Barker, prin. — Fax 646-3470
Canton MS — 600/6-8
60 Penland St 28716 — 828-646-3467
Greg Bailey, prin. — Fax 646-3478
Meadowbrook ES — 300/K-5
85 Morning Star Rd 28716 — 828-646-3445
Travis Collins, prin. — Fax 648-8506
North Canton ES — 400/K-5
60 Thompson St 28716 — 828-646-3444
Josh Morgan, prin. — Fax 648-6668

Cape Carteret, Carteret, Pop. 1,400
Carteret County SD
Supt. — See Beaufort
White Oak ES — 600/K-5
555 WB McLean Dr 28584 — 252-393-3990
Roxann Everett, prin. — Fax 393-2773

Carolina Beach, New Hanover, Pop. 5,388
New Hanover County SD
Supt. — See Wilmington
Carolina Beach ES — 600/K-5
400 S 4th St 28428 — 910-458-4340
Cynthia Wartel, prin. — Fax 458-0459

Carrboro, Orange, Pop. 16,425
Chapel Hill-Carrboro CSD
Supt. — See Chapel Hill
Carrboro ES — 500/PK-5
400 Shelton St 27510 — 919-968-3652
Emily Bivins, prin. — Fax 969-2476

Carthage, Moore, Pop. 1,935
Moore County SD — 12,300/K-12
PO Box 1180 28327 — 910-947-2976
Susan Purser Ed.D., supt. — Fax 947-3011
www.mcs.k12.nc.us/
Carthage ES — 400/K-5
312 Rockingham St 28327 — 910-947-2781
Rose Cooper, prin. — Fax 947-5670
Sandhills Farm Life ES — 500/K-5
2201 Farm Life School Rd 28327 — 910-949-2501
Nora McNeill, prin. — Fax 949-2927

Other Schools – See Aberdeen, Cameron, Highfalls, Pinehurst, Robbins, Seagrove, Southern Pines, Vass, West End

Cary, Wake, Pop. 106,439

Wake County SD
Supt. — See Raleigh

Adams ES 800/K-5
805 Cary Towne Blvd 27511 919-460-3431
Douglas Hooper, prin. Fax 460-3439

Briarcliff ES 500/K-5
1220 Pond St 27511 919-460-3443
Joy Gorman, prin. Fax 460-3420

Carpenter ES 500/K-5
2100 Morrisville Pkwy 27519 919-462-6780
Vickie Brown, prin. Fax 462-6809

Cary ES 600/PK-5
400 Kildaire Farm Rd 27511 919-460-3455
Rodney Stanton, prin. Fax 460-3550

Davis Drive ES 1,000/K-5
2151 Davis Dr 27519 919-387-2130
Patricia Andrews, prin. Fax 387-2132

Davis Drive MS 1,100/6-8
2101 Davis Dr 27519 919-387-3033
Dr. Tina Hoots, prin. Fax 387-3039

East Cary MS 6-8
1111 SE Maynard Rd 27511 919-466-4377
Dixie Frazier, prin. Fax 466-4388

Farmington Woods ES 800/K-5
1413 Hampton Valley Rd 27511 919-460-3469
Frances Venezia, prin. Fax 460-3423

Green Hope ES 900/K-5
2700 Louis Stephens Rd 27519 919-388-5270
Lisa Spalding, prin. Fax 388-5294

Highcroft ES 900/K-5
5415 Highcroft Dr 27519 919-460-3527
Jane Ann Hughes, prin. Fax 463-8626

Kingswood ES 400/K-5
200 E Johnson St 27513 919-460-3481
Sherry Schliesser, prin. Fax 460-3387

Mills Park ES K-5
509 Mills Park Dr 27519 919-466-1466
Michael Regan, prin. Fax 466-1478

Northwoods ES 600/PK-5
8850 Chapel Hill Rd 27513 919-460-3491
Mary Swan, prin. Fax 460-3493

Penny Road ES 700/K-5
10900 Penny Rd 27518 919-387-2136
Mark Barbar, prin. Fax 387-4403

Reedy Creek ES 600/K-5
940 Reedy Creek Rd 27513 919-380-3660
Hilton Evans, prin. Fax 380-3678

Reedy Creek MS 800/6-8
930 Reedy Creek Rd 27513 919-460-3504
Lawrence Jackson, prin. Fax 460-3391

Turner Creek ES 800/K-5
6801 Turner Creek Rd 27519 919-363-1391
Jan Hargrove, prin. Fax 290-2011

Weatherstone ES 800/PK-5
1000 Olde Weatherstone Way 27513 919-380-6988
Robin Wahl, prin. Fax 380-6967

West Cary MS 1,100/6-8
1000 Evans Rd 27513 919-460-3528
Wanza Cole, prin. Fax 460-3540

Cary Christian S 800/K-12
1330 Old Apex Rd 27513 919-303-2560
Larry Stephenson, admin. Fax 367-7558

Heartwood Montessori S 100/K-9
112 Byrum St 27511 919-465-2113

Resurrection Lutheran S 100/K-8
100 W Lochmere Dr 27518 919-851-7270
Tom Kolb, prin. Fax 851-6411

St. Michaels ECC 200/PK-K
804 High House Rd 27513 919-468-6110
Marianna Toscano, dir. Fax 468-6130

St. Michael the Archangel S 500/PK-8
810 High House Rd 27513 919-468-6150
Sarah Wannemuehler, prin. Fax 468-6160

Casar, Cleveland, Pop. 311

Cleveland County SD
Supt. — See Shelby

Casar ES of the Arts 400/PK-5
PO Box 128 28020 704-538-9982
Eric Lamanna, prin. Fax 538-5601

Cashiers, Jackson

Jackson County SD
Supt. — See Sylva

Blue Ridge S 200/PK-6
95 Bobcat Dr 28717 828-743-2646
Theresa Winburn, prin. Fax 743-5320

Castle Hayne, New Hanover, Pop. 1,182

New Hanover County SD
Supt. — See Wilmington

Castle Hayne ES K-5
4416 Holly Shelter Rd 28429 910-602-4970
Margaret Dickens, prin.

Catawba, Catawba, Pop. 739

Catawba County SD
Supt. — See Newton

Catawba ES 300/PK-6
5415 Hudson Chapel Rd 28609 828-241-3131
Vermel Moore, prin. Fax 241-2332

Cerro Gordo, Columbus, Pop. 240

Columbus County SD
Supt. — See Whiteville

Cerro Gordo S 300/PK-8
PO Box 9 28430 910-654-4250
Tanya Head, prin. Fax 654-6155

Chadbourn, Columbus, Pop. 2,105

Columbus County SD
Supt. — See Whiteville

Chadbourn ES 400/PK-5
409 E 3rd Ave 28431 910-654-3825
Deanna Shuman, prin. Fax 654-5366

Chadbourn MS 200/6-8
801 W Smith St 28431 910-654-4300
Georgia Spaulding, prin. Fax 654-6809

Chapel Hill, Orange, Pop. 49,543

Chapel Hill-Carrboro CSD 11,100/PK-12
750 S Merritt Mill Rd 27516 919-967-8211
Dr. Neil Pedersen, supt. Fax 933-4560
www.chccs.k12.nc.us

Ephesus Road ES 400/K-5
1495 Ephesus Church Rd 27517 919-929-8715
Phil Holmes, prin. Fax 969-2366

Estes Hills ES 500/K-5
500 N Estes Dr 27514 919-942-4753
Cheryl Carnahan, prin. Fax 969-2475

Glenwood ES 500/PK-5
2 Prestwick Rd 27517 919-968-3473
Minnie Goins, prin. Fax 969-2387

Graham ES 600/K-5
101 Smith Level Rd 27516 919-942-6491
Sheila Burnette, prin. Fax 942-5405

Grey Culbreth MS 600/6-8
225 Culbreth Rd 27516 919-929-7161
Susan Wells, prin. Fax 969-2412

McDougle ES 600/PK-5
890 Old Fayetteville Rd 27516 919-969-2435
Amanda Hartness, prin. Fax 969-2454

McDougle MS 600/6-8
900 Old Fayetteville Rd 27516 919-933-1556
Debra Scott, prin. Fax 969-2433

Morris Grove ES K-5
215 Eubanks Rd 27516 919-918-4800
Amy Rickard, prin. Fax 969-2592

Phillips MS 600/6-8
606 N Estes Dr 27514 919-929-2188
Cicily McCrimmon, prin. Fax 969-2477

Rashkis ES 600/K-5
601 Meadowmont Ln 27517 919-918-2160
Deshera Mack, prin. Fax 918-7085

Scroggs ES 700/PK-5
501 Kildaire Rd 27516 919-918-7165
Grace Repass, prin. Fax 918-7173

Seawell ES 600/PK-5
9115 Seawell School Rd 27516 919-967-4343
Marny Ruben, prin. Fax 969-2404

Smith MS 700/6-8
9201 Seawell School Rd 27516 919-918-2145
Valerie Reinhardt, prin. Fax 918-2079

Other Schools – See Carrboro

Chatham County SD
Supt. — See Pittsboro

North Chatham S 700/K-8
3380 Lystra Rd 27517 919-967-3094
Charles Aiken, prin. Fax 968-6216

Orange County SD
Supt. — See Hillsborough

New Hope ES 500/K-5
1900 New Hope Church Rd 27514 919-942-9696
Kathy Rumley, prin. Fax 942-2493

Emerson Waldorf S 300/PK-12
6211 New Jericho Rd 27516 919-967-1858
Joanne Andruscavage, admin. Fax 967-2732

St. Thomas More S 500/PK-8
920 Carmichael St 27514 919-929-1546
Sr. Catherine Fee, prin. Fax 929-1783

Charlotte, Mecklenburg, Pop. 610,949

Charlotte/Mecklenburg County SD 129,300/PK-12
PO Box 30035 28230 980-343-3000
Dr. Peter Gorman, supt. Fax 343-3647
www.cms.k12.nc.us/

Albemarle Road ES 800/K-5
7800 Riding Trail Rd 28212 980-343-6414
Stan Fraizer, prin. Fax 343-6503

Albemarle Road MS 800/6-8
6900 Democracy Dr 28212 980-343-6420
Thomas Lamb, prin. Fax 343-6501

Alexander ES 1,000/K-5
7910 Neal Rd 28262 980-343-5268
Thelma Smith, prin. Fax 343-5190

Allenbrook ES 400/K-5
1430 Allenbrook Dr 28208 980-343-6004
LaWanda Williams, prin. Fax 343-6115

Ashley Park ES 300/K-5
2401 Belfast Dr 28208 980-343-6018
Dr. Jennifer Smith, prin. Fax 343-6120

Ballantyne ES K-5
15425 Scholastic Dr 28277 980-343-0413
Sharon Damare, prin. Fax 343-1828

Barringer Academic Center 700/PK-5
1546 Walton Rd 28208 980-343-5533
Catherine Fellows, prin. Fax 343-5603

Berryhill ES 300/K-5
10501 Windy Grove Rd 28278 980-343-6100
Paul Pratt, prin. Fax 343-6146

Beverly Woods ES 800/K-5
6001 Quail Hollow Rd 28210 980-343-3627
Caroline Horne, prin. Fax 343-3733

Billingsville ES 400/K-5
124 Skyland Ave 28205 980-343-5520
Byron Campbell, prin. Fax 343-5583

Bishop Spaugh Community Academy 600/6-8
1901 Herbert Spaugh Ln 28208 980-343-6025
Tyrone McDonal, prin. Fax 343-6124

Briarwood ES 500/K-5
1001 Wilann Dr 28215 980-343-6475
Brenda Steadman, prin. Fax 343-6525

Bruns Avenue ES 400/K-5
501 S Bruns Ave 28208 980-343-5495
Steve Hall, prin. Fax 343-5598

Byers ES 400/K-5
1415 Hamilton St 28206 980-343-6940
Terri Edmunds-Heard, prin. Fax 343-6943

Carmel MS 1,000/6-8
5001 Camilla Dr 28226 980-343-6705
Mark Angerer, prin. Fax 343-6749

Chantilly Montessori S 100/PK-5
701 Briar Creek Rd 28205 980-343-0692
Dr. Leslie McCarley, prin. Fax 343-0694

Clear Creek ES 500/K-5
13501 Albemarle Rd 28227 980-343-6922
Dr. Dale Ritchie, prin. Fax 343-6156

Cochrane MS 600/6-8
6200 Starhaven Dr 28215 980-343-6460
Valarie Williams, prin. Fax 343-6521

Collinswood Language Academy 500/K-5
4000 Applegate Rd 28209 980-343-5820
Maria Petrea, prin. Fax 343-5850

Community House MS 1,200/6-8
9500 Community House Rd 28277 980-343-0689
Jamie Brooks, prin. Fax 343-0691

Cotswold ES 500/K-5
300 Greenwich Rd 28211 980-343-6720
Denise Hearne, prin. Fax 343-6739

Coulwood MS 1,200/6-8
500 Kentberry Dr 28214 980-343-6090
Robert Folk, prin. Fax 343-6142

Croft Community S K-5
4911 Hucks Rd 28269 980-343-0371
Kathleen Elling, prin. Fax 343-1793

David Cox Road ES 1,200/K-5
4215 David Cox Rd 28269 980-343-6540
Chuck Nusinov, prin. Fax 343-6566

Devonshire ES 500/K-5
6500 Barrington Dr 28215 980-343-6445
Suzanne Gimenez, prin. Fax 343-6519

Dilworth ES 400/K-5
405 E Park Ave 28203 980-343-5485
Cynthia King, prin. Fax 343-5587

Double Oaks Pre-Kindergarten PK-PK
1326 Woodward Ave 28206 980-343-5052
Cheryl Merritt, prin. Fax 343-5350

Druid Hills ES 400/K-5
2801 Lucena St 28206 980-343-5515
Priscilla Graham, prin. Fax 343-5581

Eastover ES 500/PK-5
500 Cherokee Rd 28207 980-343-5505
Vanessa Ashford, prin. Fax 343-5524

Eastway MS 900/6-8
1501 Norland Rd 28205 980-343-6410
Anne Brinkley, prin. Fax 343-6406

Elizabeth Traditional Classical ES 500/K-5
1601 Park Dr 28204 980-343-5475
Susan Spencer-Smith, prin. Fax 343-5474

Elon Park ES K-5
11425 Ardrey Kell Rd 28277 980-343-1440
Steve Drye, prin. Fax 343-1439

Endhaven ES 800/K-4
6815 Endhaven Ln 28277 980-343-5436
Beverly Newsome, prin. Fax 343-5437

First Ward ES 500/K-5
715 N Caldwell St 28202 980-343-5427
April Butler, prin. Fax 343-5555

Graham MS 1,000/6-8
1800 Runnymede Ln 28211 980-343-5810
William Leach, prin. Fax 343-5868

Greenway Park ES 700/K-5
8301 Monroe Rd 28212 980-343-5060
Valerie Gray, prin. Fax 343-5064

Grier Academy 800/K-5
8330 Grier Rd 28215 980-343-5671
Celia Brandon-Phelan, prin. Fax 343-5394

Gunn ES 800/K-5
7400 Harrisburg Rd 28215 980-343-6477
Ivey Gill, prin. Fax 343-6527

Hawk Ridge ES 1,400/K-5
9201 Bryant Farms Rd 28277 980-343-5927
Kathleen Fox, prin. Fax 343-5933

Hickory Grove ES 900/K-5
6709 Pence Rd 28215 980-343-6464
Billie Gentry, prin. Fax 343-6517

Hidden Valley ES 600/K-5
5100 Snow White Ln 28213 980-343-6810
Sarika Pride, prin. Fax 343-6798

Highland Creek ES 900/K-5
7242 Highland Creek Pkwy 28269 980-343-1065
Dr. Ann Nivens, prin. Fax 343-1066

Highland Mill Montessori S 200/PK-5
3201 Clemson Ave 28205 980-343-5525
Maria Ropic, prin. Fax 343-5589

Highland Renaissance Academy 600/K-5
125 W Craighead Rd 28206 980-343-5511
Natalie Lowe, prin. Fax 343-5579

Hornets Nest ES 900/PK-5
6700 Beatties Ford Rd 28216 980-343-6110
Vickie Hicks, prin. Fax 343-6148

Huntingtowne Farms ES 500/PK-5
2520 Huntingtowne Farms Ln 28210 980-343-3625
Pamela Frederick, prin. Fax 343-3731

Idlewild ES 700/K-5
7101 Idlewild Rd 28212 980-343-6411
Jane Collins, prin. Fax 343-6499

Irwin Avenue Open ES 500/PK-5
329 N Irwin Ave 28202 980-343-5480
Judy Fahl, prin. Fax 343-5574

James Pre-K Center PK-PK
2414 Lester St 28208 980-343-5550
Susie A. Johnson, prin. Fax 343-5605

Kennedy MS 600/6-8
4000 Gallant Ln 28273 980-343-5540
Alicia McCree Springs, prin. Fax 343-5412

King MS 900/6-8
500 Bilmark Ave 28213 980-343-0698
Dr. Mark Robertson, prin. Fax 343-0700

Lake Wylie ES 1,000/K-5
13620 Erwin Rd 28273 980-343-3680
Acquanetta Edmond, prin. Fax 343-3719

Lansdowne ES 600/K-5
6400 Prett Ct 28270 980-343-6733
Mary Jo Koenig, prin. Fax 343-6747
Lincoln Heights ES 400/K-5
1900 Newcastle St 28216 980-343-6067
Fax 343-3749
Mallard Creek ES 1,000/K-5
9801 Mallard Creek Rd 28262 980-343-3980
Alison Hiltz, prin. Fax 343-3984
Martin MS 1,300/6-8
7800 IBM Dr 28262 980-343-5382
Anna Renfro, prin. Fax 343-5135
McAlpine ES 800/K-5
9100 Carswell Ln 28277 980-343-3750
Tonya Kales, prin. Fax 343-3759
McClintock MS 800/6-8
2101 Rama Rd 28212 980-343-6425
Pamela Espinosa, prin. Fax 343-6509
McKee Road ES 900/K-5
4101 McKee Rd 28270 980-343-3970
Lane Price, prin. Fax 343-3976
Merry Oaks International Academy 600/K-5
3508 Draper Ave 28205 980-343-6422
Philip Steffes, prin. Fax 343-6505
Montclaire ES 500/K-5
5801 Farmbrook Dr 28210 980-343-3635
Leah Davis, prin. Fax 343-3737
Morehead ES 700/K-5
7810 Neal Rd 28262 980-343-5775
Crystal Agurs, prin. Fax 343-5781
Mountain Island ES 1,300/K-5
7905 Pleasant Grove Rd 28216 980-343-6948
Jeff Ruppenthal, prin. Fax 343-6954
Myers Park Traditional ES 700/K-5
2132 Radcliffe Ave 28207 980-343-5522
Paul Bonner, prin. Fax 343-5518
Nations Ford ES 500/K-5
8300 Nations Ford Rd 28217 980-343-5838
Gifford Lockley, prin. Fax 343-5870
Newell ES 800/K-5
8601 Old Concord Rd 28213 980-343-6820
Diana Evans, prin. Fax 343-6792
Northridge MS 800/6-8
7601 the Plz 28215 980-343-5015
Jamal Crawford, prin. Fax 343-5174
Oakdale ES 600/K-5
1825 Oakdale Rd 28216 980-343-6076
Charles H. Bohlen, prin. Fax 343-6134
Oakhurst ES 500/K-5
4511 Monroe Rd 28205 980-343-6482
Cheryl Turner, prin. Fax 343-6507
Oaklawn Language Academy 300/K-5
1810 Oaklawn Ave 28216 980-343-0400
Patricia Garcia, prin. Fax 343-0410
Olde Providence ES 800/K-5
3800 Rea Rd 28226 980-343-3755
Rachel McKenzie, prin. Fax 343-3722
Park Road Montessori S 400/PK-5
3701 Haven Dr 28209 980-343-5830
Anna Moraglia, prin. Fax 343-5858
Paw Creek ES 900/K-5
1300 Cathey Rd 28214 980-343-6088
Sharon Harris, prin. Fax 343-6140
Pawtuckett ES 500/K-5
8701 Moores Chapel Rd 28214 980-343-6085
Lisa Moss Pratt, prin. Fax 343-6138
Piedmont Open MS 1,000/6-8
1241 E 10th St 28204 980-343-5435
Deirdta Gardner, prin. Fax 343-5557
Pinewood ES 400/K-5
805 Seneca Pl 28210 980-343-5825
Trish Sexton, prin. Fax 343-5852
Piney Grove ES 800/K-5
8801 Eaglewind Dr 28212 980-343-6470
Halina Robertson, prin. Fax 343-6523
Plaza Road Pre-Kindergarten PK-PK
1000 Anderson St 28205 980-343-5535
Valerie Todd, prin. Fax 343-5599
Polo Ridge ES K-5
11830 Tom Short Rd 28277 980-343-0749
Patricia Riska, prin. Fax 343-0758
Providence Spring ES 900/K-5
10045 Providence Church Ln 28277 980-343-6935
Diane Adams, prin. Fax 343-6939
Quail Hollow MS 1,100/6-8
2901 Smithfield Church Rd 28210 980-343-3620
Tara Sullivan, prin. Fax 343-3622
Rama Road ES 600/K-5
1035 Rama Rd 28211 980-343-6730
Brian Bambauer, prin. Fax 343-6745
Randolph MS 900/6-8
4400 Water Oak Rd 28211 980-343-6700
Jackie Menser, prin. Fax 343-6741
Ranson MS 1,100/6-8
5850 Statesville Rd 28269 980-343-6800
Nancy Hicks, prin. Fax 343-6796
Reedy Creek ES 800/K-5
10801 Plaza Rd Ext 28215 980-343-6480
Dr. Lisa Cantrell, prin. Fax 343-6529
Reid Park ES 500/PK-5
4108 W Tyvola Rd 28208 980-343-5035
Mary Sturge, prin. Fax 343-3826
Robinson MS 1,100/6-8
5925 Ballantyne Commons Pky 28277 980-343-6944
Tracey Harrill, prin. Fax 343-6947
Sedgefield ES 500/K-5
715 Hartford Ave 28209 980-343-5826
Lenora Shipp, prin. Fax 343-5856
Sedgefield MS 500/6-8
2700 Dorchester Pl 28209 980-343-5840
Darius Adamson, prin. Fax 343-5862
Selwyn ES 600/K-5
2840 Colony Rd 28211 980-343-5835
Linda Mintz, prin. Fax 343-5864
Shamrock Gardens ES 400/K-5
3301 Country Club Dr 28205 980-343-6440
Duane Wilson, prin. Fax 343-6513

Sharon ES 600/K-5
4330 Foxcroft Rd 28211 980-343-6725
Catherine Phelan, prin. Fax 343-6743
Smithfield ES 900/K-5
3200 Smithfield Church Rd 28210 980-343-6550
C. Allison Harris, prin. Fax 343-6555
Smith Language Academy 1,000/K-8
1600 Tyvola Rd 28210 980-343-5815
Ynez Olshausen, prin. Fax 343-5854
South Charlotte MS 1,000/6-8
8040 Strawberry Ln 28277 980-343-3670
V. Christine Waggoner, prin. Fax 343-3725
Southwest MS 1,100/6-8
13624 Steele Creek Rd 28273 980-343-5006
Valerie Williams, prin. Fax 343-3239
Starmount Pre-K PK-PK
1600 Brookdale Ave 28210 980-343-3630
Selestine Young-Crowder, prin. Fax 343-3735
Statesville Road ES 500/K-5
5833 Milhaven Ln 28269 980-343-6815
Ronnie Scott, prin. Fax 343-6794
Steele Creek ES 1,100/K-5
4100 Gallant Ln 28273 980-343-3810
Gina O'Hare, prin. Fax 343-3814
Thomasboro ES 400/K-5
538 Bradford Dr 28208 980-343-6000
Vickie Patterson, prin. Fax 343-6017
Tryon Hills Pre-Kindergarten PK-PK
2600 Grimes St 28206 980-343-5510
Bonnie Schmidt, prin. Fax 343-5577
Tuckaseegee ES 700/K-5
2028 Little Rock Rd 28214 980-343-6055
Marilyn T. Osborne, prin. Fax 343-6128
University Meadows ES 1,200/K-5
1600 Pavilion Blvd 28262 980-343-3685
Dawn Parker, prin. Fax 343-3728
University Park Creative Arts ES 500/K-5
2400 Hildebrand St 28216 980-343-5178
Janice Davidson, prin. Fax 343-5182
Villa Heights Academic Center 300/K-5
800 Everett Pl 28205 980-343-3666
James Aiken, prin. Fax 343-3668
Westerly Hills ES 300/K-5
4420 Denver Ave 28208 980-343-6021
Kendra March, prin. Fax 343-6122
Whitewater Academy K-5
1340 Belmeade Dr 28214 980-343-0003
Sheila Gorham, prin. Fax 343-1773
Williams MS 600/6-8
2400 Carmine St 28206 980-343-5544
Dr. Ronald Dixon, prin. Fax 343-5601
Wilson MS 800/6-8
7020 Tuckaseegee Rd 28214 980-343-6070
Eric Ward, prin. Fax 343-6129
Winding Springs ES 500/K-5
6601 Horace Mann Rd 28269 980-343-5140
Myrna Meehan, prin. Fax 343-5144
Windsor Park ES 700/K-5
3910 Sudbury Rd 28205 980-343-6405
Kevin Woods, prin. Fax 343-6495
Winget Park ES 800/K-5
12235 Winget Rd 28278 980-343-1063
Carol Barbour, prin. Fax 343-1062
Winterfield ES 600/K-5
3100 Winterfield Pl 28205 980-343-6400
Jacqueline Blackwell, prin. Fax 343-6493
Other Schools – See Cornelius, Davidson, Huntersville, Matthews, Mint Hill, Pineville

---

Adventist Christian Academy 100/PK-12
4601 Emory Ln 28211 704-366-4351
Fax 367-1872
Anami Montessori S 100/PK-6
2901 Archdale Dr 28210 704-556-0042
Joan Horlbeck, dir. Fax 556-0127
Back Creek Christian Academy 200/PK-8
1827 Back Creek Church Rd 28213 704-549-4101
Janet Ballard, prin. Fax 548-1152
Berean Junior Academy 100/K-8
3748 Beatties Ford Rd 28216 704-391-7800
Branch Christian Academy 100/K-8
9100 Olmsted Dr 28262 704-717-8264
Teresa Fetch, admin. Fax 717-8266
British American S 100/PK-8
7000 Endhaven Ln 28277 704-341-3236
Adam Stevens, prin.
Charlotte Christian S 1,100/PK-12
7301 Sardis Rd 28270 704-366-5657
Dr. Leo Orsino, hdmstr. Fax 366-5678
Charlotte Country Day S 1,600/PK-12
1440 Carmel Rd 28226 704-943-4500
Margaret Gragg, hdmstr. Fax 943-4577
Charlotte Islamic Academy 200/K-12
4301 Shamrock Dr 28215 704-537-1772
Charlotte Jewish Day S 100/K-8
PO Box 79180 28271 704-366-4558
Mariasha Groner, prin. Fax 364-0443
Charlotte Latin S 1,400/PK-12
9502 Providence Rd 28277 704-846-1100
Arch McIntosh, hdmstr. Fax 846-1712
Charlotte Preparatory S 400/PK-8
212 Boyce Rd 28211 704-366-5994
Maura Leahy-Tucker, hdmstr. Fax 366-0221
Christ Church K 200/PK-K
1412 Providence Rd 28207 704-333-5818
Fax 333-4573
Countryside Montessori S 200/PK-K
4755 Prosperity Church Rd 28269 704-503-6000
Debbie Haugh, hdmstr. Fax 548-0088
Countryside Montessori S 200/1-8
9026 Mallard Creek Rd 28262 704-549-4253
Lynne Erickson, admin. Fax 548-0088
Dore Academy 100/K-12
1727 Providence Rd 28207 704-365-5490
Roberta Smith, hdmstr. Fax 365-5087

Fletcher S 200/K-12
8500 Sardis Rd 28270 704-365-4658
Margaret Sigmon, hdmstr. Fax 364-2978
Friends S of Charlotte 50/K-4
7001 Wallace Rd Ste 400 28212 704-567-9445
David Kern, hdmstr. Fax 567-9870
Garr Christian Academy 100/K-10
7700 Wallace Rd 28212 704-568-7700
Randy Briscoe, admin. Fax 537-0568
Greater Charlotte Christian Academy 100/K-10
4620 E WT Harris Blvd 28215 704-531-9230
Hickory Grove Baptist Christian S 1,100/K-12
6050 Hickory Grove Rd 28215 704-531-4008
Henry Ward, admin. Fax 531-4082
Holy Trinity Catholic MS 900/6-8
3100 Park Rd 28209 704-527-7822
Kevin Parks, prin. Fax 525-7288
Northside Christian Academy 900/PK-12
333 Jeremiah Blvd 28262 704-596-4074
Joel Woodcock, hdmstr. Fax 921-1384
Omni Montessori Center 200/PK-9
9536 Blakeney Heath Rd 28277 704-541-1326
Lauren Marlis, prin. Fax 541-1603
Our Lady of Assumption S 100/PK-5
4225 Shamrock Dr 28215 704-531-0067
Allana Ramkissoon, prin. Fax 531-7633
Palisades Episcopal S 50/K-5
13120 Grand Palisades Pkwy 28278 704-583-1825
Kerin Smith-Hughes, hdmstr. Fax 583-1885
Providence Christian S 200/K-8
4906 Providence Rd 28226 704-364-0824
Kathleen Tatro, admin. Fax 364-7538
Providence Day S 1,500/PK-12
5800 Sardis Rd 28270 704-887-7041
Jack Creeden, hdmstr. Fax 887-7042
Resurrection Christian S 100/PK-12
2940 Commonwealth Ave 28205 704-334-9898
Janet Atwell, prin. Fax 347-0811
St. Ann S 200/K-5
600 Hillside Ave 28209 704-525-4938
Peggy Mazzola, prin. Fax 525-2640
St. Gabriel S 600/K-5
3028 Providence Rd 28211 704-366-2409
Sharon Broxterman, prin. Fax 362-5063
St. Matthew S 700/K-5
11525 Elm Ln 28277 704-544-2070
Kevin O'Herron, prin. Fax 544-2184
St. Patrick S 300/K-5
1125 Buchanan St 28203 704-333-3174
Debbie Mixer, prin. Fax 333-3178
Trinity Episcopal S 400/K-8
750 E 9th St 28202 704-358-8101
Dr. Louis Oats, hdmstr. Fax 358-9908
United Faith Christian Academy 300/PK-12
8617 Providence Rd 28277 704-541-1742
Dr. Joseph Siragusa, hdmstr. Fax 540-7926
Victory Christian Center S 400/PK-12
1501 Carrier Dr 28216 704-391-7339
Michael Pratt, prin. Fax 391-0494

Cherryville, Gaston, Pop. 5,455
Gaston County SD
Supt. — See Gastonia
Beam IS 300/4-5
401 E 1st St 28021 704-435-8330
Emily Smallwood, prin. Fax 435-6056
Chavis MS 500/6-8
103 S Chavis Dr 28021 704-435-6045
James Montgomery, prin. Fax 435-6168
Cherryville ES 500/K-3
700 E Academy St 28021 704-435-6800
Lonnia Beam, prin. Fax 435-9611

China Grove, Rowan, Pop. 3,714
Rowan-Salisbury County SD
Supt. — See Salisbury
Bostian ES 500/K-5
4245 Old Beatty Ford Rd 28023 704-857-2322
Lisa Sigmon, prin. Fax 857-8800
China Grove ES 700/K-5
514 S Franklin St 28023 704-857-7708
Jenny Kennerly, prin. Fax 857-7710
China Grove MS 600/6-8
1013 N Main St 28023 704-857-7038
James Davis, prin. Fax 857-6650
Enochville ES 400/K-5
925 N Enochville Ave 28023 704-933-2534
Barry Haywood, prin. Fax 933-6253
Millbridge ES 500/K-5
155 Ed Deal Rd 28023 704-855-5591
David Miller, prin. Fax 855-5597

Chinquapin, Duplin
Duplin County SD
Supt. — See Kenansville
Chinquapin S 600/PK-8
3894 S NC 50 Hwy 28521 910-285-3476
Pamela Jenkins, prin. Fax 285-6879

Chocowinity, Beaufort, Pop. 731
Beaufort County SD
Supt. — See Washington
Chocowinity MS 500/5-8
3831 US Highway 17 S 27817 252-946-6191
Renee Boyd, prin. Fax 975-3812
Chocowinity PS 600/PK-4
606 Gray Rd 27817 252-946-3881
John Conway, prin. Fax 946-4869

Claremont, Catawba, Pop. 1,104
Catawba County SD
Supt. — See Newton
Claremont ES 500/PK-6
3384 E Main St 28610 828-459-7921
Chris Gibbs, prin. Fax 459-1734
Mill Creek MS 500/7-8
1041 Shiloh Rd 28610 828-241-2711
Rob Rucker, prin. Fax 241-2743

Oxford ES 600/PK-6
5915 Oxford School Rd 28610 828-459-7220
Kelly Nicholson, prin. Fax 459-1122
River Bend MS 600/7-8
4670 Oxford School Rd 28610 828-241-2754
Donna Heavner, prin. Fax 241-2820

Clarkton, Bladen, Pop. 702
Bladen County SD
Supt. — See Elizabethtown
Clarkton MS of Discovery 300/6-8
PO Box 127 28433 910-647-6531
Michelle Mena, prin. Fax 647-6671
Washington ES 300/PK-5
66 Booker T Washington Rd 28433 910-647-4161
Clarissa Kelly, prin. Fax 647-0960

Clayton, Johnston, Pop. 12,943
Johnston County SD
Supt. — See Smithfield
Clayton MS 700/6-8
490 Guy Rd 27520 919-553-5811
Eddie Price, prin. Fax 553-6978
Cleveland ES 700/PK-5
10225 Cleveland Rd 27520 919-550-2700
Linda Edmundson, prin. Fax 553-2920
Cooper ES 500/K-5
849 Mial St 27520 919-553-0256
Julie Jaillall, prin. Fax 553-0723
East Clayton ES 1,000/PK-5
2075 NC Highway 42 E, 919-550-5311
Patty Whittington, prin. Fax 550-5266
Powhatan ES PK-5
3145 Vinson Rd, 919-553-3259
Nancy Nettles, prin. Fax 553-6349
River Dell ES 700/PK-5
12100 Buffalo Rd, 919-553-1977
Bridgette Spaulding, prin. Fax 553-1774
Riverwood ES 700/PK-5
108 Athletic Club Blvd, 919-359-6300
Frank Knott, prin. Fax 359-6301
Riverwood MS 1,100/6-8
204 Athletic Club Blvd, 919-359-2769
Phillip Lee, prin. Fax 359-1519
West Clayton ES 1,000/K-5
1012 S Lombard St 27520 919-553-7113
Bruce Bunn, prin. Fax 553-0930

Clemmons, Forsyth, Pop. 16,430
Winston-Salem/Forsyth SD
Supt. — See Winston Salem
Clemmons ES 800/K-5
6200 Bingham Ave 27012 336-712-4444
Dr. Ron Montaquila, prin. Fax 712-4420
Southwest ES 900/K-5
1631 SW School Rd 27012 336-712-4422
Michael Hayes, prin. Fax 712-4425

Montessori S of Winston-Salem 200/PK-5
6050 Holder Rd 27012 336-766-5550
Angela Manning, hdmstr. Fax 766-5547

Cleveland, Rowan, Pop. 823
Iredell-Statesville SD
Supt. — See Statesville
Cool Spring ES 500/PK-5
1969 Mocksville Hwy 27013 704-873-4949
Judy Hix, prin. Fax 873-2661

Rowan-Salisbury County SD
Supt. — See Salisbury
Cleveland ES 300/K-5
107 School St 27013 704-278-2131
Rebecca Kepley-Lee, prin. Fax 278-2507

Clearview Christian Academy 100/PK-12
200 Clearview Dr 27013 704-278-0420
Lori Jarvis, dir. Fax 278-0480

Cliffside, Rutherford
Rutherford County SD
Supt. — See Forest City
Cliffside ES 500/K-5
PO Box 338 28024 828-657-6004
Jason Byrd, prin. Fax 657-6067

Clinton, Sampson, Pop. 8,768
Clinton CSD 2,400/PK-12
606 College St 28328 910-592-3132
Gene Hales Ed.D., supt. Fax 592-2011
www.clinton.k12.nc.us
Butler Avenue ES 200/2-3
301 W Butler Ave 28328 910-592-2629
Mary Nell Darden, prin. Fax 592-2183
Kerr ES 700/PK-1
112 Kimbrough Rd 28328 910-592-3066
Vivian Maynor, prin. Fax 592-0404
Sampson MS 700/6-8
1201 W Elizabeth St 28328 910-592-3327
Vanessa Brown, prin. Fax 592-6185
Sunset Avenue ES 4-5
505 Sunset Ave 28328 910-592-5623
Greg Dirks, prin. Fax 592-2292

Sampson County SD 8,200/PK-12
PO Box 439 28329 910-592-1401
Dr. Ethan Lenker, supt. Fax 590-2445
www.sampson.k12.nc.us/
Union ES 700/PK-3
10400 Taylors Bridge Hwy 28328 910-532-2104
Lou Anna Moore, prin. Fax 532-4434
Union IS 300/4-5
1190 Edmond Matthis Rd 28328 910-592-2287
Jim Workman, prin. Fax 592-7382
Union MS 500/6-8
455 River Rd 28328 910-592-4547
O.C. Holland, prin. Fax 592-4211
Other Schools – See Autryville, Dunn, Faison, Newton Grove, Roseboro, Salemburg

Clyde, Haywood, Pop. 1,357
Haywood County SD
Supt. — See Waynesville
Clyde ES 500/K-5
4182 Old Clyde Rd 28721 828-627-2206
Jeff Haney, prin. Fax 627-1471
Riverbend ES 300/K-5
71 Learning Ln 28721 828-627-6565
Greg Parker, prin. Fax 627-3269

Haywood Christian Academy 100/PK-12
1400 Old Clyde Rd 28721 828-627-0229
Blake Stanbery, hdmstr. Fax 880-8447

Coats, Harnett, Pop. 2,028
Harnett County SD
Supt. — See Lillington
Coats ES 700/K-5
585 Brick Mill Rd 27521 910-897-8353
Sandy Howard, prin. Fax 897-4737

Colerain, Bertie, Pop. 213
Bertie County SD
Supt. — See Windsor
Colerain ES 300/PK-5
PO Box 188 27924 252-356-4714
Fannie Williams, prin. Fax 356-4522

Colfax, Guilford
Guilford County SD
Supt. — See Greensboro
Colfax ES 1,000/PK-5
9112 W Market St 27235 336-275-4332
Michelle Thigpen, prin. Fax 993-0172

Collettsville, Caldwell
Caldwell County SD
Supt. — See Lenoir
Collettsville S 400/K-8
PO Box 46 28611 828-754-6913
Jason Krider, prin. Fax 758-5800

Columbia, Tyrrell, Pop. 784
Tyrrell County SD 600/PK-12
PO Box 328 27925 252-796-1121
Dr. Michael Dunsmore, supt. Fax 796-1492
www.tyrrell.k12.nc.us
Columbia MS 100/6-8
PO Box 839 27925 252-796-0369
Jana Rawls, prin. Fax 796-3639
Tyrrell ES 300/PK-5
486 Elementary School Rd 27925 252-796-3881
Sheila Cumiskey, prin. Fax 796-0544

Columbus, Polk, Pop. 994
Polk County SD 2,600/PK-12
PO Box 638 28722 828-894-3051
William Miller, supt. Fax 894-8153
www.polk.k12.nc.us
Other Schools – See Mill Spring, Saluda, Tryon

Comfort, Jones
Jones County SD
Supt. — See Trenton
Comfort ES 200/PK-6
PO Box 188 28522 910-324-4249
Dawn Peluso, prin. Fax 324-6729

Concord, Cabarrus, Pop. 61,092
Cabarrus County SD 26,000/PK-12
PO Box 388 28026 704-786-6191
Dr. Barry Shepherd, supt. Fax 786-6141
www.cabarrus.k12.nc.us
Allen ES 500/K-5
3801 US Highway 601 S 28025 704-788-2182
Hilda Batts, prin. Fax 782-0645
Beverly Hills ES 400/K-5
87 Palaside Dr NE 28025 704-782-0115
Phyllis Phifer, prin. Fax 782-0954
Coltrane-Webb ES 600/PK-5
61 Spring St NW 28025 704-782-5912
Paige Moore, prin. Fax 784-1965
Concord MS 1,000/6-8
1500 Gold Rush Dr 28025 704-786-4121
James Carroll, prin. Fax 782-8632
Cox Mill ES 1,300/K-5
1450 Cox Mill Rd 28027 704-795-6519
Phil Hull, prin. Fax 795-1011
Fries MS 900/6-8
133 Stonecrest Cir SW 28027 704-788-4140
Kecia Coln, prin. Fax 784-2086
Furr ES K-5
2725 Clover Rd NW 28027 704-788-4300
Greg Liddle, prin. Fax 795-9332
Griffin MS 1,400/6-8
7650 Griffins Gate Dr SW 28025 704-455-4700
Dr. Jim Williams, prin. Fax 455-4780
Harris Road MS 1,200/6-8
1251 Patriot Plantation Blv 28027 704-782-2002
Susan Cline, prin. Fax 262-4298
Irvin ES 800/PK-5
1400 Gold Rush Dr 28025 704-782-8864
Judi Mullis, prin. Fax 795-4376
Long Preschool Center/Head Start PK-PK
310 Kerr St NW 28025 704-782-5712
Alicianna Smith-Ward, dir. Fax 784-2346
McAllister ES 300/K-5
541 Sunnyside Dr SE 28025 704-788-3165
Alison Moore, prin. Fax 782-1539
Northwest Cabarrus MS 900/6-8
5140 NW Cabarrus Dr 28027 704-788-4135
Tim Farrar, prin. Fax 784-2649
Odell ES 1,000/K-5
1215 Moss Farms Rd NW 28027 704-782-0601
Lynne Marsh, prin. Fax 782-2057
Pitts School Road ES 900/K-5
720 Pitts School Rd SW 28027 704-788-3430
Chuck Borders, prin. Fax 788-3452

Rocky River ES 900/K-5
5454 Rocky River Rd 28025 704-795-4505
Terri Chaney, prin. Fax 795-4555
Weddington Hills ES 1,000/K-5
4401 Weddington Rd NW 28027 704-795-9385
Janet Joyner Smith, prin. Fax 795-9388
Winecoff ES 1,100/K-5
375 Winecoff School Rd 28027 704-782-4322
Michael Kelly, prin. Fax 784-8512
Wolf Meadow ES 700/K-5
150 Wolfmeadow Dr SW 28027 704-786-9173
Dr. Pat Smith, prin. Fax 782-7011
Other Schools – See Harrisburg, Kannapolis, Midland, Mount Pleasant

---

Cannon S 900/PK-12
5801 Poplar Tent Rd 28027 704-786-8171
Matthew Gossage, hdmstr. Fax 788-7779
Covenant Classical S 200/PK-12
3200 Patrick Henry Dr NW 28027 704-792-1854
Corie Crouch, hdmstr. Fax 792-2102
First Assembly Christian S 800/PK-12
154 Warren C Coleman Blvd N 28027 704-792-4750
Frank Cantadore, hdmstr. Fax 793-4784

Connellys Springs, Burke, Pop. 1,494
Burke County SD
Supt. — See Morganton
East Burke MS 800/6-8
3519 Miller Bridge Rd 28612 828-397-7446
Randy Sain, prin. Fax 397-1086
Hildebrand ES 500/PK-5
8078 George Hldebran Sch Rd 28612 828-879-9595
Phil Smith, prin. Fax 879-1184
Icard ES 300/PK-5
3087 Icard School Rd 28612 828-397-3491
Mike Holden, prin. Fax 397-7296

Conover, Catawba, Pop. 7,093
Catawba County SD
Supt. — See Newton
Lyle Creek ES 700/K-6
1845 Edgewater Dr NW 28613 828-464-0299
Sharon Harwood, prin. Fax 464-3397
St. Stephens ES 800/K-6
684 30th St NE 28613 828-256-2570
Donna Sigmon, prin. Fax 256-5641

Newton-Conover CSD
Supt. — See Newton
Shuford ES 500/PK-5
810 Hunsucker Dr NE 28613 828-464-1973
Patrick Nelson, prin. Fax 464-1405

Christian Family Academy 200/K-12
4639 County Home Rd 28613 828-256-8474
David Gruver, prin. Fax 256-8474
Concordia Christian S 300/PK-8
215 5th Ave SE 28613 828-464-3011
William Unverfehrt, prin. Fax 464-9899
Tri-City Christian S 200/PK-12
PO Box 1690 28613 828-465-0475
Bob Templeton, admin. Fax 466-3749

Conway, Northampton, Pop. 704
Northampton County SD
Supt. — See Jackson
Conway MS 400/5-8
400 E Main St 27820 252-585-0312
Barbara Drummond, prin. Fax 585-0335

Cooleemee, Davie, Pop. 957
Davie County SD
Supt. — See Mocksville
Cooleemee ES 500/K-5
PO Box 128 27014 336-284-2581
Carol Cozart, prin. Fax 284-6618

Cordova, Richmond
Richmond County SD
Supt. — See Hamlet
Cordova ES 300/PK-5
PO Box 149 28330 910-997-9805
Willette Surgeon, prin. Fax 997-9857

Cornelius, Mecklenburg, Pop. 18,870
Charlotte/Mecklenburg County SD
Supt. — See Charlotte
Bailey MS 1,100/6-8
11900 Bailey Rd 28031 980-343-1068
Jennifer Dean, prin. Fax 343-1069
Cornelius ES 900/K-5
21126 Catawba Ave 28031 980-343-3905
Barry Burford, prin. Fax 343-3907
Washam ES 700/K-5
9611 Westmoreland Rd 28031 980-343-1071
Raymond Giovanelli, prin. Fax 343-1072

Grace Covenant Academy 100/PK-7
17301 Statesville Rd 28031 704-892-5601
Kim Goodwin, dir. Fax 892-7206
Phoenix Montessori Academy 100/PK-10
17609 Old Statesville Rd 28031 704-892-7536
India Adams, prin. Fax 892-8481

Cove City, Craven, Pop. 409
Craven County SD
Supt. — See New Bern
Smith ES 600/K-5
150 Koonce Town Rd 28523 252-514-6466
Debbie Kirkman, prin. Fax 514-6469

Cramerton, Gaston, Pop. 3,005
Gaston County SD
Supt. — See Gastonia
Cramerton MS 900/6-8
601 Cramer Mountain Rd 28032 704-824-2907
Cristi Bostic, prin. Fax 824-0228

Cramerton Christian Academy 400/K-12
426 Woodlawn Ave 28032 704-824-2840
Kyle Brown, prin. Fax 824-9642

Creedmoor, Granville, Pop. 3,155
Granville County SD
Supt. — See Oxford
Creedmoor ES 600/PK-5
305 E Wilton Ave 27522 919-528-2313
Chris Elliott, prin. Fax 528-9523
Hawley MS 600/6-8
2173 Brassfield Rd 27522 919-528-0091
Frank Wiggins, prin. Fax 528-0051
Mt. Energy ES 600/PK-5
2652 NC Highway 56 27522 919-529-0586
Diane Garrison, prin. Fax 529-0238

Christian Faith Center Academy 100/K-12
PO Box 510 27522 919-528-1581
Gloria McKain, prin. Fax 528-4380

Creswell, Washington, Pop. 267
Washington County SD
Supt. — See Plymouth
Creswell ES 200/PK-6
PO Box 327 27928 252-797-7474
Robert Moore, prin. Fax 797-7343

Crossnore, Avery, Pop. 237
Avery County SD
Supt. — See Newland
Crossnore ES 300/PK-5
PO Box 566 28616 828-737-7204
Brenda Reese, prin. Fax 737-7209

Cullowhee, Jackson, Pop. 4,029
Jackson County SD
Supt. — See Sylva
Cullowhee Valley S 700/PK-8
240 Wisdom Dr 28723 828-293-5667
Nathan Frizzell, prin. Fax 293-5845

Currituck, Currituck
Currituck County SD 4,400/PK-12
2958 Caratoke Hwy 27929 252-232-2223
Dr. Meghan Doyle, supt. Fax 232-3655
www.currituck.k12.nc.us
Other Schools – See Barco, Jarvisburg, Knotts Island, Moyock, Poplar Branch, Shawboro

Dallas, Gaston, Pop. 3,411
Gaston County SD
Supt. — See Gastonia
Carr ES 600/PK-5
301 W Carpenter St 28034 704-922-3636
Susan Hutton, prin. Fax 922-7992
Costner ES 600/PK-5
PO Box 980 28034 704-922-3522
Matt Crain, prin. Fax 922-7503
Friday MS 600/6-8
1221 Ratchford Dr 28034 704-922-5297
Jessica McGee, prin. Fax 922-9841

Tabernacle Christian Academy 200/K-12
2128 Dallas Cherryville Hwy 28034 704-922-9143
Patricia Hedrick, prin. Fax 922-9988

Dana, Henderson
Henderson County SD
Supt. — See Hendersonville
Dana ES 600/K-5
PO Box 37 28724 828-685-7743
Kelly Schofield, prin. Fax 685-4004

Danbury, Stokes, Pop. 108
Stokes County SD 7,400/PK-12
PO Box 50 27016 336-593-8146
Dr. Stewart Hobbs, supt. Fax 593-2041
www.stokes.k12.nc.us
Other Schools – See Germanton, King, Lawsonville, Pine Hall, Pinnacle, Sandy Ridge, Walnut Cove, Westfield

Davidson, Mecklenburg, Pop. 8,581
Charlotte/Mecklenburg County SD
Supt. — See Charlotte
Davidson ES 1,000/K-5
635 South St 28036 980-343-3900
Celeste Spears-Ellis, prin. Fax 343-3909
Davidson International Baccalaureate MS 200/6-8
PO Box 369 28036 980-343-5185
Dr. Jo Karney, prin. Fax 343-5187

Davidson Day S 300/PK-12
750 Jetton St 28036 704-237-5200
Bonnie Cotter, prin. Fax 896-5535
Woodlawn S 100/2-11
PO Box 549 28036 704-895-8653
Angela McKenzie, prin. Fax 895-8634

Delco, Columbus
Columbus County SD
Supt. — See Whiteville
Acme-Delco MS 200/6-8
PO Box 40 28436 910-655-3200
Miriam Davis, prin. Fax 655-6865

Denton, Davidson, Pop. 1,472
Davidson County SD
Supt. — See Lexington
Denton ES 500/PK-5
305 W Salisbury St 27239 336-242-5708
Marie Casiday, prin. Fax 242-5713
South Davidson MS 400/6-8
14954 S NC Highway 109 27239 336-242-5705
Loretta Fulbright, prin. Fax 242-5707

Denver, Lincoln
Lincoln County SD
Supt. — See Lincolnton
Catawba Springs ES 500/K-5
206 N Little Egypt Rd 28037 704-736-1895
Kristi Smith, prin. Fax 736-1893
North Lincoln MS 700/6-8
1503 Amity Church Rd 28037 704-736-0262
Rhonda Hager, prin. Fax 736-9812
Rock Springs ES 600/K-5
3633 N Highway 16 28037 704-483-2281
Rhonda Harrill, prin. Fax 483-1633
St. James ES 500/K-5
1774 Saint James Church Rd 28037 704-736-1958
E. Larry Shouse, prin. Fax 736-1947

Dobson, Surry, Pop. 1,508
Surry County SD 8,700/PK-12
PO Box 364 27017 336-386-8211
Dr. Ashley Hinson, supt. Fax 386-4279
www.surry.k12.nc.us/
Central MS 700/6-8
PO Box 768 27017 336-386-4018
Janet Atkins, prin. Fax 386-4371
Copeland ES 500/PK-5
948 Copeland School Rd 27017 336-374-2572
Denny Barr, prin. Fax 374-4700
Dobson ES 700/PK-5
PO Box 248 27017 336-386-8913
Jan Varney, prin. Fax 386-4347
Other Schools – See Lowgap, Mount Airy, Pilot Mountain, Pinnacle, State Road

Drexel, Burke, Pop. 1,894
Burke County SD
Supt. — See Morganton
Drexel PS 300/PK-2
PO Box 2387 28619 828-437-3160
Jeannie Snipes, prin. Fax 437-1227
Hallyburton ES 300/3-5
PO Box 3238 28619 828-437-4184
Ross Rumbaugh, prin. Fax 437-0655

Dublin, Bladen, Pop. 250
Bladen County SD
Supt. — See Elizabethtown
Dublin ES 300/PK-4
PO Box 307 28332 910-862-2202
Victoria Nance, prin. Fax 862-5329

Dudley, Wayne
Wayne County SD
Supt. — See Goldsboro
Brogden MS 600/5-8
3761 US Hwy 117 South Alt 28333 919-705-6010
Karen Wellington, prin. Fax 705-6000
Brogden PS 700/K-4
2253 Old Mount Olive Hwy 28333 919-705-6020
Wendy Hooks, prin. Fax 731-5956

Dunn, Harnett, Pop. 9,889
Harnett County SD
Supt. — See Lillington
Coats-Erwin MS 700/6-8
2833 NC Highway 55 E 28334 910-230-0300
Whit Bradham, prin. Fax 230-0306
Dunn MS 300/6-8
1301 Meadow Lark Rd 28334 910-892-1017
Stan Williams, prin. Fax 892-7923
Harnett PS 700/K-3
800 W Harnett St 28334 910-892-0126
Sabrina Hendley, prin. Fax 892-5561
Wayne Avenue ES 300/4-5
910 W Harnett St 28334 910-892-1059
Hugh Bradham, prin. Fax 892-2257

Sampson County SD
Supt. — See Clinton
Midway ES 400/PK-5
1500 Midway Elementary Rd 28334 910-567-2244
Gaynor Hammond, prin. Fax 567-2999
Midway MS 600/6-8
1115 Roberts Grove Rd 28334 910-567-5879
Joan Jones, prin. Fax 567-5131
Plain View ES 400/K-5
4140 Plain View Hwy 28334 910-891-4354
Dr. Henry Stumpf, prin. Fax 891-4868

Durham, Durham, Pop. 204,845
Durham County SD 31,600/PK-12
PO Box 30002 27702 919-560-2000
Dr. Carl Harris, supt. Fax 560-2422
www.dpsnc.net
Bethesda ES 700/K-5
2009 S Miami Blvd 27703 919-560-3904
Doris Walker, prin. Fax 560-3482
Brogden MS 800/6-8
1001 Leon St 27704 919-560-3906
Alexis Spann, prin. Fax 560-3957
Burton ES 300/K-5
1500 Mathison St 27701 919-560-3908
Takeisha Ford, prin. Fax 560-2087
Carrington MS 1,200/6-8
227 Milton Rd 27712 919-560-3916
Julie Spencer, prin. Fax 560-3522
Chewning MS 800/6-8
5001 Red Mill Rd 27704 919-560-3914
Everette Johnson, prin. Fax 477-9189
Club Boulevard ES 500/K-5
400 W Club Blvd 27704 919-560-3918
Micah Copeland, prin. Fax 560-2525
Creekside ES 700/K-5
5321 Ephesus Church Rd 27707 919-560-3919
Letisha Judd, prin. Fax 560-2355
Easley ES 600/K-5
302 Lebanon Cir 27712 919-560-3913
Timothy Gibson, prin. Fax 560-3523
Eastway ES 500/K-5
610 N Alston Ave 27701 919-560-3910
Star Sampson, prin. Fax 560-3421
Eno Valley ES 700/K-5
117 Milton Rd 27712 919-560-3915
Tonya Williams, prin. Fax 560-3922
Fayetteville Street ES 300/K-5
2905 Fayetteville St 27707 919-560-3944
Rodriguez Teal, prin. Fax 560-3489
Forest View ES 600/K-5
3007 Mount Sinai Rd 27705 919-560-3932
Lisa Napp, prin. Fax 560-3735
Githens MS 1,000/6-8
4800 Old Chapel Hill Rd 27707 919-560-3966
Emmett Tilley, prin. Fax 560-3454
Glenn ES 700/PK-5
2415 E Geer St 27704 919-560-3920
Reginald Davis, prin. Fax 560-2101
Harris ES 300/K-5
1520 Cooper St 27703 919-560-3967
Barbara Parker, prin. Fax 560-3951
Hillandale ES 700/K-5
2730 Hillandale Rd 27705 919-560-3924
Sandra Bates, prin. Fax 560-3644
Holt ES 600/K-5
4019 Holt School Rd 27704 919-560-3928
George Koop, prin. Fax 560-3759
Hope Valley ES 800/K-5
3005 Dixon Rd 27707 919-560-3980
Nancy Jirtle, prin. Fax 560-2616
Lakewood ES 300/K-5
2520 Vesson Ave 27707 919-560-3939
Cornelius Redfearn, prin. Fax 560-2398
Little River ES 700/K-5
2315 Snow Hill Rd 27712 919-560-3940
Thomas Seckler, prin. Fax 560-3427
Lowes Grove MS 700/6-8
4418 S Alston Ave 27713 919-560-3946
Kathleen Kirkpatrick, prin. Fax 560-2102
Merrick-Moore ES 600/K-5
2325 Cheek Rd 27704 919-560-3952
Gregory McKnight, prin. Fax 560-2128
Morehead Montessori S 200/PK-5
909 Cobb St 27707 919-560-3954
Cory Hogans, prin. Fax 560-2527
Neal MS 800/6-8
201 Baptist Rd 27704 919-560-3955
Myron Wilson, prin. Fax 560-3451
Oak Grove ES 1,000/K-5
3810 Wake Forest Rd 27703 919-560-3960
Andrea Carroll, prin. Fax 596-4145
Parkwood ES 700/K-5
5207 Revere Rd 27713 919-560-3962
Fax 560-3768
Pearson ES 500/PK-5
3501 Fayetteville St 27707 919-560-3988
Sandy Chambers, prin. Fax 560-2661
Pearson MS 6-8
600 E Umstead St 27701 919-560-2208
Valerie Griffin-Puryear, prin. Fax 560-3834
Pearsontown ES 800/K-5
4915 Barbee Rd 27713 919-560-3964
Therman Flowers, prin. Fax 560-2103
Powe ES 400/PK-5
913 9th St 27705 919-560-3963
Jeanne Bishop, prin. Fax 560-2315
Rogers-Herr MS 600/6-8
911 W Cornwallis Rd 27707 919-560-3970
Drew Sawyer, prin. Fax 560-2439
Shepard MS 400/6-8
2401 Dakota St 27707 919-560-3938
James Ingram, prin. Fax 560-3945
Smith ES 300/PK-5
2410 E Main St 27703 919-560-3900
Cassandra Fogg, prin. Fax 560-3909
Southwest ES 700/K-5
2320 Cook Rd 27713 919-560-3972
Ari Cohen, prin. Fax 544-1112
Spaulding ES 200/PK-5
1531 S Roxboro St 27707 919-560-3974
Vandi Kelley, prin. Fax 560-3882
Spring Valley ES K-5
2051 N Durham Pkwy 27703 919-560-2890
Sylvia Bittle, prin. Fax 560-2648
Watts ES 300/K-5
700 Watts St 27701 919-560-3947
Patti Crum, prin. Fax 560-3949
Other Schools – See Bahama

Bethesda Christian Academy 200/K-8
1914 S Miami Blvd 27703 919-598-0190
Tony Manning, admin. Fax 596-3760
Carolina Friends S 500/PK-12
4809 Friends School Rd 27705 919-383-6602
Mike Hanas, prin. Fax 383-6009
Cresset Christian Academy 200/PK-12
3707 Garrett Rd 27707 919-489-2655
Gail Murphy, admin. Fax 493-8102
Duke S for Children 500/PK-8
3716 Erwin Rd 27705 919-493-2642
Dave Michelman, hdmstr. Fax 286-7196
Durham Academy 1,100/PK-12
3601 Ridge Rd 27705 919-493-5787
Edward Costello, hdmstr. Fax 489-4893
Fellowship Baptist Academy 100/K-12
515 Southerland St 27703 919-596-9331
Paul Moolenaar, prin.
Five Oaks Adventist Christian S 50/PK-8
4124 Farrington Rd 27707 919-493-5555
Bobbi Zeismer, prin. Fax 493-5555
Gorman Christian Academy 200/PK-8
3311 E Geer St 27704 919-688-2567
Terry Chambers, prin. Fax 688-6948
Hill Center 200/K-12
3200 Pickett Rd 27705 919-489-7464
Sharon Maskel Ed.D., prin. Fax 489-7466
Immaculata Catholic S 400/PK-8
721 Burch Ave 27701 919-682-5847
Rob Gasparello, prin. Fax 956-7073
Liberty Christian S 300/K-12
3864 Guess Rd 27705 919-471-5522
Dr. Jack Cox, admin. Fax 620-6870

Montessori Children's House of Durham 100/PK-6
2400 University Dr 27707 919-489-9045
Happy Sayre-McCord, hdmstr. Fax 590-2673
Montessori Community S 300/PK-8
4512 Pope Rd 27707 919-493-8541
Dave Carman, prin. Fax 493-8165
Mt. Zion Christian Academy 200/K-12
3519 Fayetteville St 27707 919-688-4245
Peggy McIlwain, prin. Fax 688-2201
Triangle Day S 200/K-8
4911 Neal Rd 27705 919-383-8800
Mason Goss, hdmstr. Fax 383-7157
Trinity S of Durham & Chapel Hill 400/PK-12
4011 Pickett Rd 27705 919-402-8262
Dr. Peter Denton, hdmstr. Fax 402-0762

East Bend, Yadkin, Pop. 666
Yadkin County SD
Supt. — See Yadkinville
East Bend ES 400/PK-6
205 School St 27018 336-699-3989
Kelly Byrd-Johnson, prin. Fax 699-2607
Fall Creek ES 300/PK-6
2720 Smithtown Rd 27018 336-699-8257
Angie Choplin, prin. Fax 699-2136
Forbush ES 300/PK-6
1400 Bloomtown Rd 27018 336-699-8447
Douglas Sheek, prin. Fax 699-2793
Forbush MS 7-8
1431 Falcon Rd 27018 336-961-6360
Kelly Mabe, prin. Fax 961-6370

East Flat Rock, Henderson, Pop. 3,218
Henderson County SD
Supt. — See Hendersonville
Flat Rock MS 800/6-8
191 Preston Ln 28726 828-697-4775
Scott Rhodes, prin. Fax 698-6124
Hillandale ES 400/K-5
40 Preston Ln 28726 828-697-4782
Denise Holland, prin. Fax 697-4661

Eden, Rockingham, Pop. 15,679
Rockingham County SD 13,900/PK-12
511 Harrington Hwy 27288 336-627-2600
Dr. Rodney Shotwell, supt. Fax 627-2660
www.rock.k12.nc.us
Central ES 100/K-5
435 E Stadium Dr 27288 336-623-8378
Janet King, prin. Fax 623-8405
Douglass ES 500/PK-5
1130 Center Church Rd 27288 336-623-6521
Gary Pyrtle, prin. Fax 627-0348
Draper ES 300/PK-5
1719 E Stadium Dr 27288 336-635-6541
Tammy Heath, prin. Fax 635-3203
Holmes MS 900/6-8
211 N Pierce St 27288 336-623-9791
Mavis Dillon, prin. Fax 627-0075
Leaksville-Spray ES 500/PK-5
415 Highland Dr 27288 336-627-7068
Cindy Corcoran, prin. Fax 627-8823
Other Schools – See Madison, Reidsville, Ruffin, Stoneville

Edenton, Chowan, Pop. 5,001
Edenton/Chowan County SD 2,600/PK-12
PO Box 206 27932 252-482-4436
Allan Smith, supt. Fax 482-7309
www.edenton-chowan.net
Walker ES 500/3-5
125 Sandy Ridge Rd 27932 252-221-4151
Sheila Evans, prin. Fax 221-4386
White Oak ES 700/PK-2
111 Sandy Ridge Rd 27932 252-221-4078
Amy Steinert, prin. Fax 221-4552
Other Schools – See Tyner

Efland, Orange
Orange County SD
Supt. — See Hillsborough
Efland Cheeks ES 400/K-5
4401 Fuller Rd 27243 919-563-5112
Lisa Napp, prin. Fax 563-3137
Gravelly Hill MS 300/6-8
4819 W Ten Rd 27243 919-732-8126
Jason Johnson, prin. Fax 245-4055

Elizabeth City, Pasquotank, Pop. 18,456
Elizabeth City/Pasquotank County SD 6,300/PK-12
1200 Halstead Blvd 27909 252-335-2981
Linwood Williams, supt. Fax 335-0974
www.ecpps.k12.nc.us
Central ES 400/PK-5
1059 US Highway 17 S 27909 252-335-4305
Terrell Jones, prin. Fax 337-6601
Elizabeth City MS 700/6-8
1066 Northside Rd 27909 252-335-2974
Cynthia Morris, prin. Fax 335-1751
Moore ES 500/PK-5
606 Roanoke Ave 27909 252-338-5000
Lindsey James, prin. Fax 338-6554
Northside ES 600/PK-5
1062 Northside Rd 27909 252-335-2033
Glenn Harris, prin. Fax 331-1322
Pasquotank ES 400/PK-5
1407 Peartree Rd 27909 252-335-4205
Dottie Anderson, prin. Fax 335-4966
River Road MS 700/6-8
1701 River Rd 27909 252-333-1454
Carolyn Jennings, prin. Fax 331-1339
Sawyer ES 500/PK-5
1007 Park St 27909 252-338-1012
Thomas Hill, prin. Fax 338-2388
Sheep-Harney ES 400/PK-5
200 W Elizabeth St 27909 252-335-4303
Andrea Adams, prin. Fax 335-4738
Weeksville ES 300/PK-5
1170 Salem Church Rd 27909 252-330-2606
Walter Jolly, prin. Fax 330-5700

Albemarle S 200/K-12
1210 US Highway 17 S 27909 252-338-0883
Elaine Pritchard, prin. Fax 338-1222
Elizabeth City SDA S 1-8
1117 US Highway 17 S 27909 252-335-0343
Victory Christian S 200/PK-12
684 Old Hertford Hwy 27909 252-264-2011

Elizabethtown, Bladen, Pop. 3,844
Bladen County SD 5,800/PK-12
PO Box 37 28337 910-862-4136
Dr. Kenneth Dinkins, supt. Fax 862-4277
bladencounty.nc.schoolwebpages.com
Bladen Lakes ES 400/PK-4
9554 Johnsontown Rd 28337 910-588-4606
Jose Rodriquez, prin. Fax 588-4316
Elizabethtown MS 500/5-8
PO Box 639 28337 910-862-4071
Linda Baldwin, prin. Fax 862-7426
Elizabethtown PS 600/PK-4
PO Box 2649 28337 910-862-3380
Kent Allen, prin. Fax 862-7465
Other Schools – See Bladenboro, Clarkton, Dublin, Riegelwood, Tar Heel

Elkin, Surry, Pop. 4,315
Elkin CSD 1,200/PK-12
202 W Spring St 28621 336-835-3135
Dr. Randy Bledsoe, supt. Fax 835-3376
www.elkincityschools.com
Elkin ES 600/PK-6
135 Old Virginia Rd 28621 336-835-2756
Tom Caton, prin. Fax 835-6042
Elkin MS 200/7-8
300 Elk Spur St 28621 336-835-3175
Pam Colbert, prin. Fax 835-1427

Wilkes County SD
Supt. — See North Wilkesboro
Eller ES 300/K-5
1288 CB Eller School Rd 28621 336-835-5640
Carrie Allen, prin. Fax 526-2220

Elk Park, Avery, Pop. 448
Avery County SD
Supt. — See Newland
Beech Mountain S 100/K-8
60 Flat Springs Rd 28622 828-898-4343
Frank Taylor, prin. Fax 898-8318
Cranberry MS 200/6-8
PO Box 38 28622 828-733-2932
Kim Davis, prin. Fax 733-6863
Freedom Trail ES 300/PK-5
PO Box 38 28622 828-733-4744
Ruth Shirley, prin. Fax 733-6863

Ellenboro, Rutherford, Pop. 476
Rutherford County SD
Supt. — See Forest City
Ellenboro ES 600/K-5
PO Box 1419 28040 828-453-8185
Bill Bass, prin. Fax 453-0231

Ellerbe, Richmond, Pop. 993
Richmond County SD
Supt. — See Hamlet
Ellerbe MS 200/6-8
128 W Ballard St 28338 910-652-3231
Melvin Ingram, prin. Fax 652-3106
Mineral Springs ES 300/PK-5
1426 Greenlake Rd 28338 910-652-2931
Terri Brown, prin. Fax 652-7750

Elm City, Wilson, Pop. 1,381
Nash-Rocky Mount SD
Supt. — See Nashville
Coopers ES 700/PK-5
6833 S NC Highway 58 27822 252-937-5612
Jill Sutton, prin. Fax 937-5648

Wilson County SD
Supt. — See Wilson
Elm City ES 400/K-5
5544 Lake Wilson Rd 27822 252-236-4574
Debora Ray, prin. Fax 236-3666
Elm City MS 500/6-8
215 Church St E 27822 252-236-4148
Eddie Doll, prin. Fax 236-3754
Gardners ES 300/K-5
5404 NC Highway 42 E 27822 252-399-7920
Michael Kennedy, prin. Fax 399-7895

Elon, Alamance, Pop. 7,100
Alamance-Burlington SD
Supt. — See Burlington
Altamahaw Ossipee ES 600/K-5
2832 N NC Highway 87 27244 336-538-6030
Donna King, prin. Fax 538-6032
Elon ES 800/K-5
510 E Haggard Ave 27244 336-538-6000
Amy Harper-Wallace, prin. Fax 538-6003
Western MS 800/6-8
2100 Eldon Dr 27244 336-538-6010
Dr. Lizzie Alston, prin. Fax 538-6012

Enfield, Halifax, Pop. 2,302
Halifax County SD
Supt. — See Halifax
Enfield MS 200/6-8
PO Box 128 27823 252-445-5502
Linda Bulluck, prin. Fax 445-3600
Inborden ES 400/PK-5
13587 NC Highway 481 27823 252-445-3525
Bettie Archibald, prin. Fax 445-3885
Pittman ES 300/PK-5
25041 NC Highway 561 27823 252-445-5268
Edna Williams, prin. Fax 445-2511

Ennice, Alleghany
Alleghany County SD
Supt. — See Sparta
Glade Creek S 200/PK-8
32 Glade Creek School Rd 28623 336-657-3388
Janice Linker, prin. Fax 657-3435

Erwin, Harnett, Pop. 4,792
Harnett County SD
Supt. — See Lillington
Erwin ES 300/3-5
301 S 10th St 28339 910-897-7178
Donna Thurman, prin. Fax 897-3460
Gentry PS 300/K-2
114 Porter Dr 28339 910-897-5711
Fax 897-4543

Cape Fear Christian Academy 300/PK-12
138 Erwin Chapel Rd 28339 910-897-5423
Thomas Scarborough, hdmstr. Fax 897-2150

Etowah, Henderson, Pop. 1,997
Henderson County SD
Supt. — See Hendersonville
Etowah ES 600/K-5
320 Etowah School Rd 28729 828-891-6560
Michael Thorpe, prin. Fax 891-6579

Evergreen, Columbus
Columbus County SD
Supt. — See Whiteville
Evergreen S 400/PK-8
7211 Old Highway 74 28438 910-654-3502
Emmett Lay, prin. Fax 654-4207

Fairmont, Robeson, Pop. 2,618
Robeson County SD
Supt. — See Lumberton
Fairgrove MS 300/4-8
1953 Fairgrove Rd 28340 910-628-8290
Ruth Harding, prin. Fax 628-6181
Fairmont MS 400/5-8
402 Iona St 28340 910-628-4363
Avery Brooks, prin. Fax 628-0335
Green Grove ES 300/PK-3
1850 School Rd 28340 910-628-7433
Cazzie McClamb, prin. Fax 628-8715
Rosenwald ES 700/PK-4
301 Martin Luther King Dr 28340 910-628-9786
Dr. Effie McGill, prin. Fax 628-4361

Fairview, Buncombe, Pop. 4,493
Buncombe County SD
Supt. — See Asheville
Fairview ES 800/K-5
1355 Charlotte Hwy 28730 828-628-2732
Chad Upton, prin. Fax 628-4950

Faison, Sampson, Pop. 770
Sampson County SD
Supt. — See Clinton
Hargrove ES 400/K-5
7725 Faison Hwy 28341 910-533-3444
Jennifer Daughtry, prin. Fax 533-2121

Faith, Rowan, Pop. 702
Rowan-Salisbury County SD
Supt. — See Salisbury
Faith ES 500/PK-5
PO Box 161 28041 704-279-3195
Jacqueline Maloney, prin. Fax 279-2469

Fallston, Cleveland, Pop. 610
Cleveland County SD
Supt. — See Shelby
Fallston ES 600/PK-5
PO Box 39 28042 704-538-7341
Mary Frye, prin. Fax 538-5347

Farmville, Pitt, Pop. 4,546
Pitt County SD
Supt. — See Greenville
Bundy ES 400/3-5
3994 Grimmersburg St 27828 252-753-2013
Valerie Galberth, prin. Fax 753-2812
Farmville MS 600/6-8
3914 Grimmersburg St 27828 252-753-2116
Mary Carter, prin. Fax 753-7995
Sugg ES 400/PK-2
3992 Grimmersburg St 27828 252-753-2671
Valerie Galberth, prin. Fax 753-7997

Fayetteville, Cumberland, Pop. 129,928
Cumberland County SD 52,900/PK-12
PO Box 2357 28302 910-678-2300
William Harrison Ed.D., supt. Fax 678-2339
www.ccs.k12.nc.us
Abbott MS 1,000/6-8
590 Winding Creek Rd 28305 910-323-2201
Myra Holloway, prin. Fax 485-0841
Alderman Road ES 700/PK-5
2860 Alderman Rd 28306 910-321-0398
Cal Violette, prin. Fax 321-0744
Armstrong ES 400/K-5
3395 Dunn Rd, 910-483-2425
Rhonda McNatt, prin. Fax 483-1842
Ashley ES 300/3-5
810 Trainer Dr 28304 910-484-4156
Barbara West, prin. Fax 484-3175
Auman ES 600/K-5
6882 Raeford Rd 28304 910-868-8153
Melody Boyd, prin. Fax 868-0712
Berrien ES 200/PK-5
800 North St 28301 910-483-8288
Charla Weber-Trogdon, prin. Fax 483-3634
Brentwood ES 600/K-5
1115 Bingham Dr 28304 910-864-5310
Karen Roberts, prin. Fax 864-2266
Byrd MS 700/7-8
1616 Ireland Dr 28304 910-483-3101
Vanessa Alford, prin. Fax 483-3741
Cashwell ES 800/PK-5
2970 Legion Rd 28306 910-424-2312
Cathy Tearry, prin. Fax 423-9673

Chesnutt MS 700/6-8
2121 Skibo Rd 28314 910-867-9147
Tom Hatch, prin. Fax 868-3695
Cliffdale ES 700/K-5
6450 Cliffdale Rd 28314 910-864-3442
Melanie Hamblin, prin. Fax 867-2940
College Lakes ES 400/PK-5
4963 Rosehill Rd 28311 910-488-6650
Sheldon Harvey, prin. Fax 630-0221
Coon ES 300/PK-5
905 Hope Mills Rd 28304 910-425-6141
Ella McRae, prin. Fax 425-0878
Cumberland Mills ES 600/PK-5
2576 Hope Mills Rd 28306 910-424-4536
Lenora Locklear, prin. Fax 423-6359
Cumberland Road ES 400/PK-5
2700 Cumberland Rd 28306 910-485-7171
Sandra Barefoot, prin. Fax 484-5616
Easom ES 200/K-1
1610 Westlawn Ave 28305 910-484-0194
Connie Graham, prin. Fax 484-4486
Eastover Central ES 400/K-5
5174 Dunn Rd, 910-483-8997
Ronnie Parker, prin. Fax 483-6177
Ferguson-Easley ES 400/K-5
1857 Seabrook Rd 28301 910-483-4883
Mellotta Hill, prin. Fax 483-0324
Glendale Acres ES 300/K-2
2915 Skycrest Dr 28304 910-484-9031
Donna Vann, prin. Fax 486-8750
Griffin MS 1,300/6-8
5551 Fisher Rd 28304 910-424-7678
Mike Magnum, prin. Fax 424-7602
Hall ES 600/K-5
526 Andrews Rd 28311 910-822-5100
Kimberly Robertson, prin. Fax 822-8413
Hefner ES 900/K-5
7059 Calamar Dr 28314 910-860-7058
Brenda Bethea, prin. Fax 860-7062
Honeycutt ES 900/K-5
4665 Lakewood Dr 28306 910-426-2020
Lori Bostrom-Mueller, prin. Fax 426-2024
Ireland Drive MS 300/6-6
1606 Ireland Dr 28304 910-483-4037
Shanessa Fenner, prin. Fax 483-4885
Jeralds MS 600/6-8
2517 Ramsey St 28301 910-822-2570
Shirley Gamble, prin. Fax 822-1534
Jones ES 200/PK-5
225 B St 28301 910-483-5434
Rudy Tatum, prin. Fax 485-6347
Lake Rim ES 700/K-5
1455 Hoke Loop Rd 28314 910-867-1133
Renee Jackson, prin. Fax 867-0819
Lewis Chapel MS 900/6-8
2150 Skibo Rd 28314 910-864-1407
Kevin Coleman, prin. Fax 864-8298
Long Hill ES 500/2-5
6490 Ramsey St 28311 910-488-0012
Donna Albaugh, prin. Fax 488-0014
Martin ES 600/PK-5
430 N Reilly Rd 28303 910-864-4843
Crystal Brown, prin. Fax 867-3777
McArthur ES 500/PK-5
3809 Village Dr 28304 910-424-2206
Lola Williams, prin. Fax 426-0756
Miller ES 700/K-5
1361 Rim Rd 28314 910-868-2800
Tonya Page, prin. Fax 867-1960
Montclair ES 500/PK-5
555 Glensford Dr 28314 910-868-5124
Sylvia Schmidt, prin. Fax 868-5125
Morganton Road ES 600/K-5
102 Bonanza Dr 28303 910-867-4137
Charlotte McLaurin, prin. Fax 867-1030
Owen ES 400/PK-5
4533 Raeford Rd 28304 910-425-6163
Felix Keyes, prin. Fax 425-6165
Pine Forest MS 800/6-8
6901 Ramsey St 28311 910-488-2711
Dan Krumanocker, prin. Fax 630-2357
Ponderosa ES 400/PK-5
311 Bonanza Dr 28303 910-864-0148
Maria Pierce-Ford, prin. Fax 867-8902
Seabrook ES 400/PK-5
4619 NC Highway 210 S, 910-323-2930
Donna Parnell, prin. Fax 486-8872
Seventy-First Classical MS 500/6-8
6830 Raeford Rd 28304 910-864-0092
Scott Pope, prin. Fax 487-8547
Sherwood Park ES 600/PK-5
2115 Hope Mills Rd 28304 910-424-4797
Dr. Don Cahill, prin. Fax 424-2087
Souders ES 400/PK-5
128 Hillview Ave 28301 910-488-6705
Tammy Holland, prin. Fax 630-2010
Stoney Point ES 900/K-5
7411 Rockfish Rd 28306 910-424-3945
Susan McCray, prin. Fax 424-6924
Sunnyside ES 300/PK-5
3876 Sunnyside School Rd, 910-483-4319
Dawn Collins, prin. Fax 483-5711
Vanstory Hills ES 500/2-5
400 Foxhall Rd 28303 910-483-0809
Betty Musselwhite, prin. Fax 483-6679
Warrenwood ES 500/PK-5
4618 Rosehill Rd 28311 910-488-6609
Ann-Marie Palmer, prin. Fax 488-1722
Westarea ES 500/PK-5
941 Country Club Dr 28301 910-488-1705
Allie Hill, prin. Fax 488-9484
Westover MS 800/6-8
275 Bonanza Dr 28303 910-864-0813
Myron Williams, prin. Fax 864-7906
Wilkins ES 300/PK-5
1429 Skibo Rd 28303 910-864-5438
Dennis Monroe, prin. Fax 868-1777

Williams MS 1,200/6-8
4464 Clinton Rd, 910-483-8222
Donna Hancock, prin. Fax 483-4831
Willis ES 300/PK-5
1412 Belvedere Ave 28305 910-484-9064
Margaret Raymes, prin. Fax 484-9065
Other Schools – See Hope Mills, Linden, Roseboro, Spring Lake, Stedman, Wade

---

Abney Chapel Christian S 50/K-8
PO Box 9803 28311 910-488-7525
Bal-Perazim Christian Academy 100/PK-12
4921 Bragg Blvd 28303 910-487-4220
Morris Braxton, pres. Fax 864-3451
Berean Baptist Academy 300/PK-12
518 Glensford Dr 28314 910-868-2511
Donald Adams, prin. Fax 868-1550
Cornerstone Christian Academy 200/PK-12
3000 Scotty Hill Rd 28303 910-867-1166
Greg DeBruler, prin. Fax 867-2166
Fayetteville Academy 400/PK-12
3200 Cliffdale Rd 28303 910-868-5131
Richard Cameron, hdmstr. Fax 868-7351
Fayetteville Adventist Christian S 50/K-12
PO Box 64397 28306 910-484-6091
Fayetteville Christian S 600/PK-12
1422 Ireland Dr 28304 910-483-3905
Tammi Peters, admin. Fax 483-6966
Harvest Preparatory Academy 100/K-6
PO Box 2391 28302 910-433-3036
E.B. Herman, admin. Fax 433-2364
Liberty Christian Academy 300/PK-12
6548 Rockfish Rd 28306 910-424-1205
Fax 424-8049
Montessori S of Fayetteville 50/PK-4
PO Box 40138 28309 910-323-4183
Bianca Jones, prin. Fax 323-4183
Northwood Temple Academy 400/PK-12
4200 Ramsey St 28311 910-822-7711
Dr. J.C. Basnight, supt. Fax 488-7299
St. Ann S 100/K-8
365 N Cool Spring St 28301 910-483-3902
N. Rene Corders, prin. Fax 483-3195
St. Patrick S 300/PK-8
1620 Marlborough Rd 28304 910-323-1865
Thomas Manion, prin. Fax 484-1573
Trinity Christian S 200/K-12
3727 Rosehill Rd 28311 910-488-6779
Dennis Vandevender, prin. Fax 488-2729
Village Christian Academy 900/K-12
908 S McPherson Church Rd 28303 910-483-5500
Jeremy Cowin, supt. Fax 483-5335

Ferguson, Wilkes
Wilkes County SD
Supt. — See North Wilkesboro
Mt. Pleasant ES 300/PK-5
532 Champion Mt Pleasant Rd 28624 336-973-3780
Susan Blackburn, prin. Fax 973-7099

Flat Rock, Henderson, Pop. 2,750
Henderson County SD
Supt. — See Hendersonville
Upward ES 600/K-5
45 Education Dr 28731 828-697-4764
Rebecca Poplin, prin. Fax 698-6131

Fletcher, Henderson, Pop. 4,522
Buncombe County SD
Supt. — See Asheville
Cane Creek MS 800/6-8
570 Lower Brush Creek Rd 28732 828-628-0824
Amy Rhoney, prin. Fax 628-9833

Henderson County SD
Supt. — See Hendersonville
Fletcher ES 600/K-5
500 Howard Gap Rd 28732 828-684-0580
Christine Smith, prin. Fax 687-1217

Gilmer S 100/K-8
PO Box 5338 28732 828-684-8221
Veritas Christian Academy 300/PK-12
17 Cane Creek Rd 28732 828-681-0546
Kay Belknap, hdmstr. Fax 681-0547

Forest City, Rutherford, Pop. 7,273
Rutherford County SD 9,800/K-12
382 W Main St 28043 828-245-0252
Dr. John Kinlaw, supt. Fax 245-4151
www2.rcsnc.org
Chase MS 700/6-8
840 Chase High Rd 28043 828-247-1044
Joey Glenn, prin. Fax 247-0551
Forest City - Dunbar ES 500/K-5
286 Learning Pkwy 28043 828-245-4978
Sally Blanton, prin. Fax 245-4444
Harris ES 600/K-5
3330 US Highway 221 S 28043 828-248-2354
Don Ingle, prin. Fax 248-9471
Hunt ES 500/K-5
100 Forrest W Hunt Dr 28043 828-245-2161
Brad Richardson, prin. Fax 248-3286
Mt. Vernon-Ruth ES 300/K-5
2785 Hudlow Rd 28043 828-287-4792
Sheila Hutchins, prin. Fax 287-5253
Other Schools – See Bostic, Cliffside, Ellenboro, Rutherfordton, Spindale

---

Master's Academy 100/PK-8
120 School Dr 28043 828-245-7203
George Allen, admin. Fax 247-0403

Four Oaks, Johnston, Pop. 1,765
Johnston County SD
Supt. — See Smithfield
Four Oaks ES 1,000/K-5
180 W Hatcher St 27524 919-963-2166
David Pearce, prin. Fax 963-3851
Four Oaks MS 500/6-8
1475 Boyette Rd 27524 919-963-4022
Lisa Edwards, prin. Fax 963-4123

Franklin, Macon, Pop. 3,611
Macon County SD 4,300/K-12
PO Box 1029 28744 828-524-3314
Dan Brigman, supt. Fax 524-5938
www.macon.k12.nc.us
Cartoogechaye ES 400/K-5
3295 Old Murphy Rd 28734 828-524-2845
Jan Gann, prin. Fax 369-3263
Cowee ES 100/3-5
51 Cowee School Dr 28734 828-524-2938
William Brooks, prin. Fax 369-8403
Cullasaja ES 200/K-5
145 River Rd 28734 828-524-2744
Gary Brown, prin. Fax 524-0294
East Franklin ES 400/K-5
100 Watauga St 28734 828-524-3216
Terry Bradley, prin. Fax 369-6779
Iotla ES 100/K-2
1166 Iotla Church Rd 28734 828-524-2552
Karen Norton, prin. Fax 524-0459
Macon MS 900/6-8
1345 Wells Grove Rd 28734 828-524-3766
Scot Maslin, prin. Fax 349-3900
South Macon ES 500/K-5
855 Addington Bridge Rd 28734 828-369-0796
Tolly Bowles, prin. Fax 369-0947
Other Schools – See Highlands, Topton

Trimont Christian Academy 200/PK-12
98 Promise Ln 28734 828-369-6756
Robert Ricotta, admin. Fax 524-0622

Franklinton, Franklin, Pop. 1,899
Franklin County SD
Supt. — See Louisburg
Franklinton ES 600/K-5
431 S Hillsborough St 27525 919-494-2479
Carol Davis, prin. Fax 494-7115

Granville County SD
Supt. — See Oxford
Wilton ES 500/PK-5
2555 NC Highway 96 27525 919-528-0033
Jennifer Carraway, prin. Fax 528-9852

Franklinville, Randolph, Pop. 1,300
Randolph County SD
Supt. — See Asheboro
Franklinville ES 500/K-5
PO Box 258 27248 336-824-2306
Kebbler Williams, prin. Fax 824-1427
Grays Chapel ES 600/K-5
5322 NC Highway 22 N 27248 336-824-8620
Yvonne Gilmer, prin. Fax 824-3992

Fremont, Wayne, Pop. 1,441
Wayne County SD
Supt. — See Goldsboro
Fremont STARS ES 200/K-5
PO Box 428 27830 919-242-3410
Sheila Wolfe, prin. Fax 242-3359
Norwayne MS 1,000/6-8
1394 Norwayne School Rd 27830 919-242-3414
Mario Re, prin. Fax 242-3418

Fuquay Varina, Wake, Pop. 6,525
Wake County SD
Supt. — See Raleigh
Ballentine ES 800/K-5
1651 McLaurin Ln 27526 919-557-1120
Kimberly Short, prin. Fax 557-1144
Fuquay-Varina ES 900/K-5
6600 Johnson Pond Rd 27526 919-557-2566
Franklin Creech, prin. Fax 557-2548
Fuquay-Varina MS 1,000/6-8
109 N Ennis St 27526 919-557-2727
William Holley, prin. Fax 557-2732
Lincoln Heights ES 600/K-5
307 Bridge St 27526 919-557-2587
Milinda Demchak-Crawford, prin. Fax 557-2769

Hilltop Christian S 200/K-12
10212 Fayetteville Rd 27526 919-552-5612
Fax 552-3189

Garner, Wake, Pop. 22,364
Johnston County SD
Supt. — See Smithfield
Cleveland MS 800/6-8
2323 Cornwallis Rd 27529 919-553-7500
Kathleen McLamb, prin. Fax 553-7798
Polenta ES 800/PK-5
105 Josephine Rd 27529 919-989-6039
Deborah Johnson, prin. Fax 989-6272
West View ES 800/K-5
11755 Cleveland Rd 27529 919-661-6184
Brian Vetrano, prin. Fax 661-6192

Wake County SD
Supt. — See Raleigh
Aversboro ES 600/PK-5
1605 Aversboro Rd 27529 919-662-2325
Paul Domenico, prin. Fax 662-2329
Creech Road ES 500/K-5
450 Creech Rd 27529 919-662-2359
Jennifer Benkovitz, prin. Fax 662-2372
East Garner ES K-5
5545 Jones Sausage Rd 27529 919-773-7411
James Overman, prin. Fax 773-7415
East Garner MS 1,100/6-8
6301 Jones Sausage Rd 27529 919-662-2339
Cathy Williams, prin. Fax 662-2357

North Garner MS 900/6-8
720 Powell Dr 27529 919-662-2434
John Wall, prin. Fax 662-5637
Rand Road ES 800/PK-5
300 Arbor Greene Dr 27529 919-662-2275
Rhonda Jones, prin. Fax 662-2432
Timber Drive ES 900/K-5
1601 Timber Dr 27529 919-773-9500
Kendra Culberson, prin. Fax 773-9507
Vandora Springs ES 600/PK-5
1300 Vandora Springs Rd 27529 919-662-2486
Troy Peuler, prin. Fax 662-5626

Lord of Life S 100/PK-1
2100 Buffaloe Rd 27529 919-772-5444
Deborah LaVine, dir.
St. Mary Child Development Center 100/PK-PK
1008 Vandora Springs Rd 27529 919-772-0009
Karen Williams, dir. Fax 772-5534

Gaston, Northampton, Pop. 936
Northampton County SD
Supt. — See Jackson
Gaston ES 200/2-6
PO Box J 27832 252-537-2520
Martha Paige, prin. Fax 535-5692
Squire ES 400/PK-1
PO Box G 27832 252-537-2877
Clarence Hicks, prin. Fax 537-8706

Gastonia, Gaston, Pop. 68,964
Gaston County SD 32,700/PK-12
PO Box 1397 28053 704-866-6100
L. Reeves McGlohon, supt. Fax 866-6321
www.gaston.k12.nc.us/
Beam ES 700/PK-5
200 Davis Park Rd 28052 704-866-6618
Marcia Hunter, prin. Fax 866-6320
Bess ES 700/K-5
4340 Beaty Rd 28056 704-866-6075
Laura Dixon, prin. Fax 866-6102
Brookside ES 700/PK-5
1950 Rhyne Carter Rd 28054 704-866-6283
Jerry Bostic, prin. Fax 866-6294
Chapel Grove ES 600/K-5
5201 Lewis Rd 28052 704-866-6077
Roxann Saunders, prin. Fax 861-1204
Forest Heights ES 500/PK-5
1 Learning Pl 28052 704-866-6079
Mike Grimmer, prin. Fax 866-6304
Gardner Park ES 600/K-5
738 Armstrong Park Rd 28054 704-866-6082
Shay Matthews, prin. Fax 854-3096
Grier MS 800/6-8
1622 E Garrison Blvd 28054 704-866-6086
Joey Clinton, prin. Fax 866-6116
Hawks Nest IS 4-5
3430 Robinwood Rd 28054 704-886-6100
Alisha Carr, prin.
Lingerfeldt ES 400/PK-5
1601 Madison St 28052 704-866-6094
Torben Ross, prin. Fax 861-2497
New Hope ES 500/PK-5
137 Stowe Rd 28056 704-824-1617
Allen Lewis, prin. Fax 824-4715
Pleasant Ridge ES 300/PK-5
937 Miller St 28052 704-866-6096
Louise Lomick, prin. Fax 866-6097
Rhyne ES 400/PK-5
1900 W Davidson Ave 28052 704-866-6098
Joey Hopper, prin. Fax 861-2495
Robinson ES 600/K-5
3122 Union Rd 28056 704-866-6607
Johnny Biles, prin. Fax 866-6314
Sadler ES 500/PK-5
3950 W Franklin Blvd 28052 704-862-5895
Rebekah Duncan, prin. Fax 862-5899
Sherwood ES 600/PK-5
1744 Dixon Rd 28054 704-866-6609
Leigh Smith, prin. Fax 866-6617
Southwest MS 800/6-8
1 Roadrunner Dr 28052 704-866-6290
Glynis Brooks, prin. Fax 866-6293
Woodhill ES 400/PK-5
1027 Woodhill Dr 28054 704-866-6295
Jacob Barr, prin. Fax 866-6170
York-Chester MS 500/6-8
601 S Clay St 28052 704-866-6297
Cindy White, prin. Fax 866-6319
Other Schools – See Belmont, Bessemer City, Cherryville, Cramerton, Dallas, Lowell, Mc Adenville, Mount Holly, Stanley

---

First Assembly Christian Academy 100/PK-8
PO Box 12367 28052 704-853-1777
Fax 853-2972
First Wesleyan Christian S 300/PK-8
208A S Church St 28054 704-865-9823
John Wilfong, admin. Fax 852-4219
Gaston Christian S 900/PK-12
1625 Lowell Bethesda Rd 28056 704-349-5020
Daniel Patton, hdmstr. Fax 349-5029
Gaston Day S 400/PK-12
2001 Gaston Day School Rd 28056 704-864-7744
Dr. Richard Rankin, prin. Fax 865-3813
Hope Lutheran S 100/PK-6
2502 Gleneagles Dr 28056 704-868-0003
Marsha Howe, prin. Fax 868-0003
St. Michael S 200/PK-8
704 Saint Michaels Ln 28052 704-865-4382
Joseph Puceta, prin. Fax 864-5108

Gates, Gates
Gates County SD
Supt. — See Gatesville
Buckland ES 300/PK-5
PO Box 68 27937 252-357-1611
Charles Gregory, prin. Fax 357-1106

Gatesville, Gates, Pop. 297
Gates County SD 2,100/PK-12
PO Box 125 27938 252-357-1113
Dr. Zenobia Smallwood, supt. Fax 357-0207
coserver.gates.k12.nc.us/
Central MS 500/6-8
362 US Highway 158 W 27938 252-357-0470
Earl Norfleet, prin. Fax 357-1319
Gatesville ES 300/PK-5
709 Main St 27938 252-357-0613
Sallie Ryan, prin. Fax 357-2809
Other Schools – See Gates, Sunbury

Germanton, Stokes, Pop. 220
Stokes County SD
Supt. — See Danbury
Germanton ES 200/PK-5
6085 NC 8 Hwy S 27019 336-591-4021
Karen Boles, prin. Fax 591-7013

Gibson, Scotland, Pop. 576
Scotland County SD
Supt. — See Laurinburg
Pate Gardner ES 200/PK-5
14241 Oil Mill Rd 28343 910-268-4480
Vicki Kirby, prin. Fax 268-2543

Gibsonville, Guilford, Pop. 4,569
Guilford County SD
Supt. — See Greensboro
Eastern MS 900/6-8
435 Peeden Dr 27249 336-697-3199
Michael Ferrell, prin. Fax 449-0728
Gibsonville ES 400/PK-5
401 E Joyner St 27249 336-449-4214
Cathy Batts, prin. Fax 449-6745

Gold Hill, Rowan
Rowan-Salisbury County SD
Supt. — See Salisbury
Morgan ES 500/PK-5
3860 Liberty Rd 28071 704-636-0169
Susan Sigmon, prin. Fax 633-8689

Goldsboro, Wayne, Pop. 38,670
Wayne County SD 19,400/K-12
PO Box 1797 27533 919-731-5900
Dr. Steven Taylor, supt. Fax 705-6199
www.waynecountyschools.org
Carver Heights ES 300/K-4
411 Bunche Dr 27530 919-731-7222
Carole Battle, prin. Fax 731-4503
Dillard MS 400/7-8
1101 Devereaux St 27530 919-580-9360
Sylvester Townsend, prin. Fax 736-1121
Eastern Wayne ES 800/K-5
1271 E New Hope Rd 27534 919-751-7130
Beverly Smith, prin. Fax 751-7146
Eastern Wayne MS 600/6-8
3518 Central Heights Rd 27534 919-751-7110
Catherine Eubanks, prin. Fax 751-7114
Goldsboro IS 400/5-6
801 Lionel St 27530 919-731-5940
Cortrina Smith, prin. Fax 731-5945
Grantham S 900/K-8
174 Grantham School Rd 27530 919-689-5000
Lisa Tart, prin. Fax 689-5004
Greenwood MS 600/5-8
3209 E Ash St 27534 919-751-7100
Rolanda Best, prin. Fax 751-7201
Meadow Lane ES 800/K-4
3500 E Ash St 27534 919-751-7150
Celia James, prin. Fax 751-7108
North Drive ES 500/K-4
1108 North Dr 27534 919-731-5950
Carol Artis, prin. Fax 705-6029
Rosewood ES 700/K-5
126 Charlie Braswell Rd 27530 919-705-6040
Richard Sauls, prin. Fax 705-6003
Rosewood MS 500/6-8
541 NC 581 Hwy S 27530 919-736-5050
Susie Shepherd, prin. Fax 736-5055
School Street ES 200/K-4
415 S Virginia St 27530 919-731-5960
Dan McPhail, prin. Fax 731-5963
Spring Creek ES 900/K-5
1050 Saint John Church Rd 27534 919-751-7155
Charles Ivey, prin. Fax 751-7165
Tommys Road ES 600/K-5
1150 Tommys Rd 27534 919-736-5040
Patsy Faison, prin. Fax 736-5039
Other Schools – See Dudley, Fremont, Mount Olive, Pikeville

Faith Christian Academy 400/PK-12
1200 W Grantham St 27530 919-734-8701
Walter Sloan, prin. Fax 734-9658
St. Mary S 200/PK-8
1601 Edgerton St 27530 919-735-1931
Lynn Magoon, prin. Fax 735-1917
Summit Christian Academy 100/PK-8
3016 Summit Rd 27534 919-759-2002
Cindy King, admin. Fax 759-0050
Wayne Christian S 500/PK-12
1201 Patetown Rd 27530 919-735-5605
Lynn Mooring, admin. Fax 735-5229
Wayne Country Day S 50/PK-12
480 Country Day Rd 27530 919-736-1045
Todd Anderson, prin. Fax 583-9493
Wayne Montessori S 100/PK-4
PO Box 10646 27532 919-778-0022
Ann Cox, prin. Fax 735-0123

Goldston, Chatham, Pop. 353
Chatham County SD
Supt. — See Pittsboro
Waters S 300/K-8
PO Box 99 27252 919-898-2259
Beverly Browne, prin. Fax 898-4160

Graham, Alamance, Pop. 13,952
Alamance-Burlington SD
Supt. — See Burlington
Graham MS 700/6-8
311 E Pine St 27253 336-570-6460
Teresa Faucette, prin. Fax 570-6464
Jordan ES 500/K-5
5827 Church Rd 27253 336-376-3673
Mariah Vignali, prin. Fax 376-6243
North Graham ES 400/PK-5
1025 Trollinger Rd 27253 336-578-2272
Greg Holland, prin. Fax 578-8335
Southern MS 800/6-8
771 Southern High School Rd 27253 336-570-6500
Heather Ward, prin. Fax 570-6504
South Graham ES 600/PK-5
320 Ivey Rd 27253 336-570-6520
Elizabeth Price, prin. Fax 570-6521
Wilson ES 600/PK-5
2518 S NC Highway 54 27253 336-578-1366
Cynthia McKee, prin. Fax 578-8092

Alamance Christian S 300/K-12
PO Box 838 27253 336-578-0318
Mike Loflin, prin. Fax 578-7200

Granite Falls, Caldwell, Pop. 4,573
Caldwell County SD
Supt. — See Lenoir
Baton ES 500/K-5
1400 Baton School Rd 28630 828-728-9531
Katie Justice, prin. Fax 728-7548
Dudley Shoals ES 500/K-5
1500 Dudley Shoals Rd 28630 828-396-3457
Andy Berry, prin. Fax 396-3461
Granite Falls ES 700/K-5
60 N Highland Ave 28630 828-396-2222
Andrew Miller, prin. Fax 396-7796
Granite Falls MS 700/6-8
90 N Main St 28630 828-396-2341
Brian Suddreth, prin. Fax 396-7072
Sawmills ES 500/K-5
4436 Sawmills School Rd 28630 828-396-2610
Robin DiBernardi, prin. Fax 396-2232

Granite Quarry, Rowan, Pop. 2,232
Rowan-Salisbury County SD
Supt. — See Salisbury
Granite Quarry ES 400/K-5
PO Box 279 28072 704-279-2154
Vickie Booker, prin. Fax 279-4625

Green Mountain, Yancey
Mitchell County SD
Supt. — See Bakersville
Tipton Hill S 100/K-8
4256 NC Highway 197 28740 828-688-4853
Mark Hughes, prin. Fax 688-4853

Yancy County SD
Supt. — See Burnsville
Clearmont ES 100/K-5
1175 Clearmont School Rd 28740 828-682-2337
Angie Anglin, prin. Fax 682-3656

Greensboro, Guilford, Pop. 231,962
Guilford County SD 70,800/PK-12
PO Box 880 27402 336-370-8100
Dr. Terry Grier, supt. Fax 370-8299
www.gcsnc.com/
Academy at Lincoln 700/4-8
1016 Lincoln St 27401 336-370-3471
Rodney Boone, prin. Fax 370-3480
Alamance ES 900/PK-5
3600 Williams Dairy Rd 27406 336-697-3177
Pam Early, prin. Fax 697-3175
Alderman ES 400/PK-5
4211 Chateau Dr 27407 336-294-7320
Sadiyah Abdullah, prin. Fax 294-7330
Allen MS 800/6-8
1108 Glendale Dr 27406 336-294-7325
Jamal Woods, prin. Fax 294-7315
Archer ES 400/PK-5
2610 Four Seasons Blvd 27407 336-294-7335
Patrice Brown, prin. Fax 294-7359
Aycock MS 700/6-8
811 Cypress St 27405 336-370-8110
Valerie Akins, prin. Fax 370-8044
Bessemer ES 500/PK-5
918 Huffine Mill Rd 27405 336-375-2585
Carolyn Haley, prin. Fax 375-2588
Bluford ES 400/K-5
1901 Tuscaloosa St 27401 336-370-8120
Stephanie Boykin, prin. Fax 370-8124
Brightwood ES 800/PK-5
2001 Brightwood School Rd 27405 336-375-2565
Melinda Mayhew, prin. Fax 375-2570
Brooks Global ES 400/K-5
1215 Westover Ter 27408 336-370-8228
Charles Foust, prin. Fax 370-8173
Claxton ES 600/K-5
3720 Pinetop Rd 27410 336-545-2010
Anessa Burgman, prin. Fax 545-2025
Cone ES 500/PK-5
2501 N Church St 27405 336-375-2595
Felicia R. McKinnon, prin. Fax 375-2597
Erwin Montessori ES 300/PK-5
3012 E Bessemer Ave 27405 336-370-8151
Deborah Parker, prin. Fax 574-3855
Falkener ES 600/PK-5
3931 Naco Rd 27401 336-370-8150
Edwina Monroe, prin. Fax 370-8025
Foust ES 300/PK-5
2610 Floyd St 27406 336-370-8155
Tamilyn Washington, prin. Fax 370-8057
Frazier ES 400/PK-5
4215 Galway Dr 27406 336-294-7340
Laverne Bass, prin. Fax 294-7364

Gillespie Park ES 300/PK-5
1900 Martin Luther King Dr 27406 336-370-8640
Gail Brady, prin. Fax 574-1608
Greene ES 500/K-5
1501 Benjamin Pkwy 27408 336-545-2015
George Boschini, prin. Fax 545-2037
Guilford ES 400/PK-5
920 Stage Coach Trl 27410 336-316-5844
Eunice Isley, prin. Fax 316-5840
Guilford MS 900/4-8
401 College Rd 27410 336-316-5833
Cynthia Kremer, prin. Fax 316-5837
Hairston MS 600/6-8
3911 Naco Rd 27401 336-378-8280
Dr. Teresa Daye, prin. Fax 370-8153
Hampton Academy 400/PK-5
2301 Trade St 27401 336-370-8220
David Jarmon, prin. Fax 370-8192
Hunter ES 500/PK-5
1305 Merritt Dr 27407 336-294-7345
Judith Thompson, prin. Fax 294-7379
Irving Park ES 700/PK-5
1310 Sunset Dr 27408 336-370-8225
Melissa Nixon, prin. Fax 370-8105
Jackson MS 500/6-8
2200 Ontario St 27403 336-294-7350
Rodney Wilds, prin. Fax 294-7316
Jefferson ES 800/PK-5
1400 New Garden Rd 27410 336-316-5870
Tanya W. Feagins, prin. Fax 316-5878
Jones ES 700/PK-5
502 South St 27406 336-370-8230
Bea Jones, prin. Fax 370-8034
Joyner ES 400/K-5
3300 Normandy Rd 27408 336-545-2020
Trina Bethea, prin. Fax 545-2029
Kernodle MS 1,000/6-8
3600 Drawbridge Pkwy 27410 336-545-3717
Laine William, prin. Fax 545-3714
Kiser MS 900/6-8
716 Benjamin Pkwy 27408 336-370-8240
Sharon McCants, prin. Fax 370-8248
Lindley ES 400/PK-5
2700 Camden Rd 27403 336-294-7360
Merrie Conaway, prin. Fax 294-7363
Mendenhall MS 1,000/6-8
205 Willoughby Blvd 27408 336-545-2000
Julie Olson, prin. Fax 545-2004
Morehead ES 500/K-5
4630 Tower Rd 27410 336-294-7370
Darcy Kemp, prin. Fax 294-7368
Murphey Traditional Academy 400/PK-5
2306 Ontario St 27403 336-294-7380
Richard Thomae, prin. Fax 294-7450
Northern ES K-5
3801 NC Highway 150 E 27455 336-643-4032
Teresa Richardson, prin. Fax 643-4043
Northern MS 200/6-8
616 Simpson Calhoun Rd 27455 336-605-3342
Sam Misher, prin. Fax 643-8435
Northwest Guilford MS 1,100/6-8
5300 NW School Rd 27409 336-605-3333
Dr. William Stewart, prin. Fax 605-3325
Pearce ES K-5
2006 Pleasant Ridge Rd 27410 336-605-5480
Pam Misher, prin. Fax 605-5488
Peck ES 400/PK-5
1601 W Florida St 27403 336-370-8235
Francine Mallory, prin. Fax 370-8237
Peeler Open ES 400/K-5
2200 Randall St 27401 336-370-8270
Marshall Matson, prin. Fax 370-8039
Pilot ES 900/PK-5
4701 Chimney Springs Dr 27407 336-316-5820
Max Pope, prin. Fax 316-5818
Rankin ES 700/PK-5
3301 Summit Ave 27405 336-375-2545
Geraldine Cox, prin. Fax 375-2542
Reedy Fork ES PK-5
4571 Reedy Fork Pkwy 27405 336-656-3723
Denise Schroeder, prin. Fax 656-3488
Sedgefield ES 400/PK-5
2905 Groometown Rd 27407 336-316-5858
Michele Meley, prin. Fax 316-5855
Southeast Guilford MS 1,000/6-8
4825 Woody Mill Rd 27406 336-674-4280
Karen Burress, prin. Fax 674-4276
Southern ES 300/PK-5
5720 Drake Rd 27406 336-674-4325
John Lawrence, prin. Fax 674-4330
Southern MS 700/6-8
5747 Drake Rd 27406 336-674-4266
Kevin Wheat, prin. Fax 674-4278
Sternberger ES 400/PK-5
518 N Holden Rd 27410 336-294-7390
Jill Hall, prin. Fax 294-7394
Sumner ES 600/PK-5
1915 Harris Dr 27406 336-316-5888
Brian Clarida, prin. Fax 316-5880
Vandalia ES 300/PK-5
407 E Vandalia Rd 27406 336-370-8275
Keisha McMillan, prin. Fax 370-8053
Washington Montessori S 200/PK-5
1110 E Washington St 27401 336-370-8290
Sharon Jacobs, prin. Fax 370-8963
Wharton ES 1,000/PK-5
5813 Lake Brandt Rd 27455 336-545-3700
Valerie Bridges, prin. Fax 545-3703
Wiley ES 300/PK-5
600 W Terrell St 27406 336-370-8295
LaToy Kennedy, prin. Fax 370-8040
Other Schools – See Browns Summit, Colfax, Gibsonville, High Point, Jamestown, Liberty, Mc Leansville, Oak Ridge, Pleasant Garden, Sedalia, Stokesdale, Summerfield

---

B'nai Shalom Day S 100/PK-8
804A Winview Dr 27410 336-855-5091
Judy Groner, hdmstr. Fax 855-1018
Caldwell Academy 700/K-12
2900 Horse Pen Creek Rd 27410 336-665-1161
Mark Guthrie, hdmstr. Fax 665-1178
Canterbury S 400/K-8
5400 Old Lake Jeanette Rd 27455 336-288-2007
Burns Jones, hdmstr. Fax 288-1933
Covenant Christian Day S 100/PK-8
1414 Cliffwood Dr 27406 336-370-1222
Vicki Beale, prin. Fax 274-9717
Greensboro Day S 900/PK-12
5401 Lawndale Dr 27455 336-288-8590
Mark Hale, hdmstr. Fax 282-2905
Greensboro Montessori S 300/PK-8
2856 Horse Pen Creek Rd 27410 336-668-0119
Frank Brainard, prin. Fax 665-9531
Guilford Day S 100/1-12
3310 Horse Pen Creek Rd 27410 336-282-7044
Laura Mlatac, hdmstr. Fax 282-2048
New Garden Friends S 300/PK-12
1128 New Garden Rd 27410 336-299-0964
Marty Goldstein, prin. Fax 292-0347
Our Lady of Grace S 400/PK-8
2205 W Market St 27403 336-275-1522
Gary Gelo, prin. Fax 279-8824
St. Pius X S 500/K-8
2200 N Elm St 27408 336-273-9865
Anne Knapke, prin. Fax 273-0199
Shining Light Academy 200/K-12
4530 W Wendover Ave 27409 336-299-9688
Chuck Russ, prin. Fax 299-6126
Smith SDA Academy 50/K-8
1802 E Market St 27401 336-273-0054
Vandalia Christian S 700/PK-12
3919 Pleasant Garden Rd 27406 336-379-8380
Mark Weatherford, admin. Fax 379-8671

Greenville, Pitt, Pop. 69,517
Pitt County SD 22,400/PK-12
1717 W 5th St 27834 252-830-4200
Dr. Beverly Reep, supt. Fax 830-4239
www.pitt.k12.nc.us/
Aycock MS 700/6-8
1325 Red Banks Rd 27858 252-756-4181
Julie Cary, prin. Fax 756-2408
Belvoir ES 500/PK-5
2568 NC Highway 33 W 27834 252-752-6365
Sandra Morris, prin. Fax 752-5008
Chicod S 900/K-8
7557 NC Highway 43 S 27858 252-746-6742
Glenn Joyner, prin. Fax 746-4751
Eastern ES 500/K-5
1700 Cedar Ln 27858 252-758-4813
Nicole Smith, prin. Fax 758-7508
Elmhurst ES 400/PK-5
1815 W Berkley Rd 27858 252-756-0180
Donna Gillam, prin. Fax 756-0513
Eppes MS 600/6-8
1100 S Elm St 27858 252-757-2160
Charlie Langley, prin. Fax 757-2163
Falkland ES 500/K-5
503 NC Highway 121 27834 252-752-7820
Dennis Teel, prin. Fax 752-3017
Hope MS 500/6-8
2995 Mills Rd 27858 252-355-7071
Pat Clark, prin. Fax 355-6055
Northwest ES 500/PK-5
1471 Holland Rd 27834 252-752-6329
Roscoe Locke, prin. Fax 752-6906
Pactolus S 600/PK-8
3405 Yankee Hall Rd 27834 252-752-6941
Joseph Nelson, prin. Fax 758-5817
Saulter ES 200/PK-5
1019 Fleming St 27834 252-758-4621
Fredonia Stewart, prin. Fax 758-5893
South Greenville ES 500/PK-5
811 Howell St 27834 252-756-7004
Lavette Ford, prin. Fax 756-3285
Third Street Center PK-PK
600 W 3rd St 27834 252-752-3227
Judy Beckert-Jones, prin. Fax 758-1429
Wahl-Coates ES 500/PK-5
2200 E 5th St 27858 252-752-2514
Will Sanderson, prin. Fax 758-6205
Wellcome MS 500/6-8
3101 N Memorial Dr 27834 252-752-5938
Jeff Theus, prin. Fax 752-1685
Wintergreen IS 700/3-5
4720 County Home Rd 27858 252-355-2411
Dawn Singleton, prin. Fax 355-0284
Wintergreen PS 700/PK-2
4710 County Home Rd 27858 252-353-5270
Dawn Singleton, prin. Fax 353-5275
Other Schools – See Ayden, Bethel, Farmville, Grifton, Grimesland, Stokes, Winterville

---

Greenville Christian Academy 400/K-12
1621 Greenville Blvd SW 27834 252-756-0939
Paul Aynes, prin.
Greenville Montessori S 100/PK-6
139 Winding Branches Dr, 252-355-6268
Lesley Byrne-Steedly, prin.
Oakwood S 300/PK-12
4000 MacGregor Downs Rd 27834 252-931-0760
Robert Peterson, hdmstr. Fax 931-0964
St. Peter S 500/K-8
2606 E 5th St 27858 252-752-3529
Fax 752-7604
Trinity Christian S 400/PK-12
3111 Golden Rd 27858 252-758-0037
Denise Mills, admin. Fax 758-0767

Grifton, Lenoir, Pop. 2,066
Pitt County SD
Supt. — See Greenville
Grifton S 500/PK-8
PO Box 219 28530 252-524-5141
Ronda Sortino, prin. Fax 524-4505

Grimesland, Pitt, Pop. 423
Pitt County SD
Supt. — See Greenville
Whitfield S 600/PK-8
PO Box 129 27837 252-752-6614
Gloria Snead, prin. Fax 752-7484

Grover, Cleveland, Pop. 693
Cleveland County SD
Supt. — See Shelby
Grover ES 400/PK-4
206 Carolina Ave 28073 704-734-5643
Janet Anthony, prin. Fax 734-5616

Halifax, Halifax, Pop. 325
Halifax County SD 4,200/PK-12
PO Box 468 27839 252-583-5111
Geraldine Middleton, supt. Fax 583-1474
www.halifax.k12.nc.us/
Other Schools – See Enfield, Hollister, Littleton, Roanoke Rapids, Scotland Neck

Weldon CSD
Supt. — See Weldon
Weldon MS 200/6-8
4489 US Highway 301 27839 252-536-2571
Raymond Barnes, prin. Fax 536-3485

Hallsboro, Columbus
Columbus County SD
Supt. — See Whiteville
Hallsboro-Artesia ES 500/PK-5
1337 Giles Byrd Rd 28442 910-646-3510
Josephine Graham, prin. Fax 646-3571
Hallsboro MS 300/6-8
PO Box 248 28442 910-646-4192
Michael Mobley, prin. Fax 646-5072

Hamilton, Martin, Pop. 493
Martin County SD
Supt. — See Williamston
Andrews ES 200/PK-5
PO Box 250 27840 252-798-5631
Deborah Horton, prin. Fax 798-2726

Hamlet, Richmond, Pop. 5,824
Richmond County SD 6,400/PK-12
PO Box 1259 28345 910-582-5860
Dr. George Norris, supt. Fax 582-7921
www.richmond.k12.nc.us
Fairview Heights ES 500/PK-5
104 Hamilton St 28345 910-582-7900
Keith McKenzie, prin. Fax 582-7901
Hamlet MS 400/6-8
1406 Mcdonald Ave 28345 910-582-7903
Jim Butler, prin. Fax 582-5730
Monroe Avenue ES 400/PK-5
400 Monroe Ave 28345 910-582-7907
Alva Ezzell, prin. Fax 582-7913
Other Schools – See Cordova, Ellerbe, Rockingham

Second Baptist Church Day S 100/K-4
518 4th St 28345 910-205-0055

Hampstead, Pender
Pender County SD
Supt. — See Burgaw
North Topsail ES 600/K-5
1310 Sloop Point Loop Rd 28443 910-270-0694
Peter Wildeboer, prin. Fax 270-9533
South Topsail ES 700/K-5
997 Hoover Rd 28443 910-270-2756
AnnaMaria Romero-Lehrer, prin. Fax 270-4056
Topsail MS 700/6-8
17385 US Highway 17 N 28443 910-270-2612
James Klingensmith, prin. Fax 270-3190

Life Christian Academy 50/K-12
15965B US Highway 17 N 28443 910-270-9558
Dr. Christina Gray, supt. Fax 270-9556

Hamptonville, Yadkin
Yadkin County SD
Supt. — See Yadkinville
West Yadkin ES 600/PK-6
4432 W Old US 421 Hwy 27020 336-468-2526
Charles Conner, prin. Fax 468-1178

Harkers Island, Carteret, Pop. 1,759
Carteret County SD
Supt. — See Beaufort
Harkers Island S 200/K-8
1163 Island Rd 28531 252-728-3755
April Lilley, prin. Fax 728-6399

Harmony, Iredell, Pop. 592
Iredell-Statesville SD
Supt. — See Statesville
Harmony ES 500/K-5
139 Harmony School Rd 28634 704-546-2643
Bill Long, prin. Fax 546-3074

Harrells, Sampson, Pop. 209

Harrells Christian Academy 500/K-12
PO Box 88 28444 910-532-4575
Dr. Ronald Montgomery, prin. Fax 532-2958

Harrisburg, Cabarrus, Pop. 5,145
Cabarrus County SD
Supt. — See Concord
Harrisburg ES 1,000/K-5
3900 Stallings Rd 28075 704-455-5118
Martha McCall, prin. Fax 455-5414

Havelock, Craven, Pop. 21,827
Craven County SD
Supt. — See New Bern
Barden ES 400/PK-5
200 Cedar Dr 28532 252-444-5100
Joan Bjork, prin. Fax 444-5103
Bell ES 500/K-5
804 Fontana Blvd 28532 252-444-5133
Paul Gainey, prin. Fax 444-5136
Edwards ES 600/K-5
200 Education Ln 28532 252-444-5140
Kathleen Leffler, prin. Fax 444-5145
Gurganus ES 500/K-5
535 US Highway 70 W 28532 252-444-5150
C. Pat Williams, prin. Fax 444-5154
Havelock ES 400/K-5
201 Cunningham Blvd 28532 252-444-5106
Renate Lee, prin. Fax 444-5109
Havelock MS 500/6-8
102 High School Dr 28532 252-444-5125
Tabari Wallace, prin. Fax 444-5129
Tucker Creek MS 600/6-8
200 Sermons Rd 28532 252-444-7200
Angie Franks, prin. Fax 444-7206

Annunciation S 200/PK-8
246 E Main St 28532 252-447-3137
June Pietras, prin. Fax 447-3138

Haw River, Alamance, Pop. 1,981
Alamance-Burlington SD
Supt. — See Burlington
Haw River ES 500/K-5
701 E Main St 27258 336-578-0177
Jeffrey Rachlin, prin. Fax 578-8336

Hayesville, Clay, Pop. 469
Clay County SD 1,400/PK-12
PO Box 178 28904 828-389-8513
Douglas Penland, supt. Fax 389-3437
www.clayschools.org/
Hayesville ES 600/PK-4
72 Elementary Dr 28904 828-389-8586
Tommy Hollingsworth, prin. Fax 389-3243
Hayesville MS 400/5-8
135 School Dr 28904 828-389-9924
Mickey Noe, prin. Fax 389-1706

Hays, Wilkes, Pop. 1,522
Wilkes County SD
Supt. — See North Wilkesboro
Mountain View ES 700/PK-5
PO Box 390 28635 336-696-5512
Debbie Love, prin. Fax 696-7216

Henderson, Vance, Pop. 16,213
Vance County SD 8,200/PK-12
PO Box 7001 27536 252-492-2127
Dr. Norman Shearin, supt. Fax 438-6119
www.vcs.k12.nc.us
Aycock ES 500/PK-5
305 Carey Chapel Rd 27537 252-492-1516
Laura Rigsbee, prin. Fax 492-7038
Carver ES 200/PK-5
987 Carver School Rd 27537 252-438-6955
Harold Thompson, prin. Fax 438-7323
Clark Street ES 200/PK-5
212 N Clark St 27536 252-438-8415
John Hargrove, prin. Fax 438-6193
Dabney ES 600/PK-5
150 Lanning Rd 27537 252-438-6918
Michael Putney, prin. Fax 438-2604
Eaton-Johnson MS 900/6-8
500 N Beckford Dr 27536 252-438-5017
Dr. Larry Webb, prin. Fax 738-0250
Henderson MS 900/6-8
219 Charles St 27536 252-492-0054
Victor Fenner, prin. Fax 430-8588
New Hope ES 200/PK-5
10199 NC 39 Hwy N 27537 252-438-6549
Carolyn Harris, prin. Fax 438-7389
Pinkston Street ES 400/PK-5
855 Adams St 27536 252-438-3441
Dr. Beverly Joseph, prin. Fax 438-5524
Rollins ES 500/PK-5
1600 S Garnett Street Ext 27536 252-438-2189
Dean Thomas, prin. Fax 438-2180
Yancey ES 400/PK-5
311 Hawkins Dr 27536 252-438-8336
Kimberly Simms, prin. Fax 438-2541
Other Schools – See Kittrell, Middleburg

Crossroads Christian S 400/PK-12
PO Box 249 27536 252-431-1333
Jeanae Wheeler, hdmstr. Fax 431-0333
Kerr-Vance Academy 400/PK-12
700 Vance Academy Rd 27537 252-492-0018
Paul Villatico, hdmstr. Fax 438-4652
Victory Baptist S 100/K-12
PO Box 592 27536 252-492-6079

Hendersonville, Henderson, Pop. 11,396
Henderson County SD 12,900/K-12
414 4th Ave W 28739 828-697-4733
Stephen Page Ed.D., supt. Fax 697-5541
www.henderson.k12.nc.us
Apple Valley MS 800/6-8
43 Fruitland Rd 28792 828-697-4545
Marcie Wilson, prin. Fax 698-6119
Atkinson ES 400/K-5
2510 Old Kanuga Rd 28739 828-697-4755
Kimberly Deaton, prin. Fax 698-6120
Clear Creek ES 700/K-5
737 N Clear Creek Rd 28792 828-697-4760
Audrey Reneau, prin. Fax 698-6121
Drysdale ES 400/K-5
834 N Main St 28792 828-697-5568
Kelly Walker, prin. Fax 698-6122
Edneyville ES 600/K-5
2875 Pace Rd 28792 828-685-7600
Chad Auten, prin. Fax 685-4006
Hendersonville ES 400/K-5
1039 Randall Cir 28791 828-697-4752
Shannon Marlowe, prin. Fax 698-6125
Hendersonville MS 500/6-8
825 N Whitted St 28791 828-697-4800
Jenny Moreno, prin. Fax 698-6127
Rugby MS 800/6-8
3345 Haywood Rd 28791 828-891-6566
Bill Reedy, prin. Fax 891-6589
Sugarloaf ES K-5
2270 Sugarloaf Rd 28792 828-697-4600
Kevin Weis, prin. Fax 697-4632
Other Schools – See Dana, East Flat Rock, Etowah, Flat Rock, Fletcher, Mills River

Hendersonville Christian S 100/K-12
708 Old Spartanburg Hwy 28792 828-692-0556
Gregory Mosely, hdmstr. Fax 692-0557
Immaculata S 200/PK-8
711 Buncombe St 28791 828-693-3277
Carole Breerwood, prin. Fax 696-3677

Hertford, Perquimans, Pop. 2,104
Perquimans County SD 1,800/PK-12
PO Box 337 27944 252-426-5741
Dwayne Stallings, supt. Fax 426-4913
www.pcs.k12.nc.us
Hertford ES 400/3-5
PO Box 397 27944 252-426-7166
Dianne Meiggs, prin. Fax 426-7293
Other Schools – See Winfall

Hickory, Catawba, Pop. 40,232
Burke County SD
Supt. — See Morganton
Childers ES 500/PK-5
1183 Cape Hickory Rd 28601 828-324-1340
Shane Mace, prin. Fax 324-1390

Catawba County SD
Supt. — See Newton
Arndt MS 700/7-8
3350 34th Street Dr NE 28601 828-256-9545
David Fonseca, prin. Fax 256-6748
Campbell ES 800/K-6
2121 35th Avenue Dr NE 28601 828-256-2769
Scottie Houston, prin. Fax 256-2846
Mountain View ES 800/PK-6
5911 Dwayne Starnes Rd 28602 828-294-2020
Jessica Minton-Cable, prin. Fax 294-3239
Murray ES 500/K-6
3901 Section House Rd 28601 828-256-2196
Chip Cathey, prin. Fax 256-2197
Snow Creek ES K-6
3238 Snow Creek Rd NE 28601 828-449-1076
Walter Zahler, prin. Fax 256-2187

Hickory CSD 4,600/PK-12
432 4th Ave SW 28602 828-322-2855
Dr. Ric Vandett, supt. Fax 322-1834
www.hickoryschools.net
Grandview MS 500/6-8
451 Catawba Valley Blvd 28602 828-328-2289
Dr. Vanessa Howerton, prin. Fax 328-2992
Jenkins ES 500/PK-5
3750 N Center St 28601 828-327-3491
Stephanie Feller, prin. Fax 327-3590
Longview ES 300/PK-5
2430 2nd Ave SW 28602 828-327-2070
John Black, prin. Fax 324-8892
Northview MS 500/6-8
302 28th Ave NE 28601 828-327-6300
Pamela Helms, prin. Fax 327-6367
Oakwood ES 400/PK-5
366 4th St NW 28601 828-322-1340
Jeff Hodakowski, prin. Fax 322-4980
Southwest ES 400/PK-5
1580 32nd St SW 28602 828-324-8884
Sherry Willis, prin. Fax 345-6226
Viewmont ES 600/PK-5
21 16th Ave NW 28601 828-324-7049
Judy Jolly, prin. Fax 327-4619

Hickory Christian Academy 300/K-12
PO Box 5203 28603 828-324-5405
Tracy Robinson, hdmstr. Fax 324-4353
Johnston SDA S 50/1-8
174 23rd St NW 28601 828-327-4005
St. Stephen Lutheran S 300/PK-8
2304 Springs Rd NE 28601 828-256-2166
Jonathan Guelzow, prin. Fax 256-7994
Tabernacle Christian S 200/PK-12
1225 29th Avenue Dr NE 28601 828-324-9936
Dr. Gordon Fenlason, prin. Fax 324-8921

Hiddenite, Alexander
Alexander County SD
Supt. — See Taylorsville
East Alexander MS 700/6-8
1285 White Plains Rd 28636 828-632-7565
Sheila Jenkins, prin. Fax 632-4508
Hiddenite ES 600/K-5
374 Sulphur Springs Rd 28636 828-632-2503
Alisha Cloer, prin. Fax 635-0656

Highfalls, Moore
Moore County SD
Supt. — See Carthage
Highfalls S 300/K-8
PO Box 206 27259 910-464-3600
Seth Powers, prin. Fax 464-5404

Highlands, Macon, Pop. 941
Macon County SD
Supt. — See Franklin
Highlands S 400/K-12
PO Box 940 28741 828-526-2147
Brian Jetter, prin. Fax 526-0615

High Point, Guilford, Pop. 95,086
Guilford County SD
Supt. — See Greensboro
Fairview ES 600/PK-5
608 Fairview St 27260 336-819-2890
Rhonda Copeland, prin. Fax 819-2892
Ferndale MS 600/6-8
701 Ferndale Blvd 27262 336-819-2855
Mark Harris, prin. Fax 885-2854
Florence ES 700/PK-5
7605 Florence School Dr 27265 336-819-2120
James McNeil, prin. Fax 454-5579
Jay ES 500/PK-5
1311 E Springfield Rd 27263 336-434-8490
Dawn Spencer, prin. Fax 431-6555
Johnson Street Global Studies 400/K-8
1601 Johnson St 27262 336-819-2900
Vernon Trent, prin. Fax 819-2899
Kirkman Park ES 200/PK-5
1101 N Centennial St 27262 336-819-2905
Naquita McCormick, prin. Fax 889-6218
Montlieu Math and Science Academy 500/PK-5
1105 Montlieu Ave 27262 336-819-2910
Rochelle Bailey, prin. Fax 819-2915
Northwood ES 500/PK-5
818 W Lexington Ave 27262 336-819-2920
Scott Winslow, prin. Fax 819-2921
Oak Hill ES 400/PK-5
320 Wrightenberry St 27260 336-819-2925
Sara Roberts, prin. Fax 819-2931
Oak View ES 600/PK-5
614 Oakview Rd 27265 336-819-2935
Heather Bare, prin. Fax 869-6856
Parkview ES 500/PK-5
506 Henry Pl 27260 336-819-2945
Bryan Johnson, prin. Fax 819-2943
Shadybrook ES 600/PK-5
503 Shady Brook Rd 27265 336-819-2950
Dennis Foster, prin. Fax 869-1575
Southwest ES 900/K-5
4372 SW School Rd 27265 336-819-2992
Susan Allen, prin. Fax 454-8372
Southwest Guilford MS 1,100/6-8
4368 Barrow Rd 27265 336-819-2985
Beverly Wilson, prin. Fax 454-4015
Triangle Lake Montessori ES 500/PK-5
2401 Triangle Lake Rd 27260 336-819-2883
Cheri Keels, prin. Fax 819-2754
Union Hill ES 400/PK-5
1201 E Fairfield Rd 27263 336-819-2130
Dean LaVere, prin. Fax 882-7162
Welborn MS 600/6-8
1710 McGuinn Dr 27265 336-819-2880
Lori Bolds, prin. Fax 819-2878

Baldwin's Chapel SDA S 50/K-8
1202 Leonard Ave 27260 336-889-7930
Beatrice Banks, prin. Fax 889-3212
Hayworth Christian S 200/PK-12
PO Box 5448 27262 336-882-3126
Ed Kingdon, admin. Fax 882-9157
High Point Christian Academy 800/PK-12
800 Phillips Ave 27262 336-841-8702
Richard Hardee, hdmstr. Fax 841-8850
High Point Friends S 100/K-8
800 Quaker Ln Ste A 27262 336-886-5516
David Girardi, prin. Fax 886-7420
Immaculate Heart of Mary S 200/K-8
605 Barbee St 27262 336-887-2613
Wanda Garrett, prin. Fax 884-1849
Tri-City Junior Academy 100/PK-12
8000 Clinard Farms Rd 27265 336-665-9822
Clint Sutton, prin. Fax 665-9834
Wesleyan Christian Academy 1,000/PK-12
1917 N Centennial St 27262 336-884-3333
Joel Farlow, admin. Fax 884-8232
Westchester Country Day S 400/K-12
2045 N Old Greensboro Rd 27265 336-869-2128
Charles Hamblet, hdmstr. Fax 869-6685

Hildebran, Burke, Pop. 1,840
Burke County SD
Supt. — See Morganton
Hildebran ES 400/PK-5
703 US Highway 70 W 28637 828-397-3181
Wendi Barber, prin. Fax 397-5330

Hillsborough, Orange, Pop. 5,382
Orange County SD 6,900/K-12
200 E King St 27278 919-732-8126
Patrick Rhodes, supt. Fax 732-8120
www.orange.k12.nc.us
Brown ES 500/K-5
1100 New Grdy Brown Schl Rd 27278 919-732-6138
Sherron Leplin, prin. Fax 644-2800
Cameron Park ES 500/K-5
240 Saint Marys Rd 27278 919-732-9326
Terry Rogers, prin. Fax 732-9736
Central ES 300/K-5
154 Hayes St 27278 919-732-3622
Clara Daniels, prin. Fax 732-2352
Hillsborough ES 400/K-5
402 N Nash St 27278 919-732-6137
Martinette Horner, prin. Fax 732-7791
Pathways ES 400/K-5
431 Strouds Creek Rd 27278 919-732-9136
Connie Brimmer, prin. Fax 732-9142
Stanback MS 600/6-8
3700 NC Highway 86 S 27278 919-644-3200
Gloria Jones, prin. Fax 644-3226
Stanford MS 700/6-8
308 Orange High School Rd 27278 919-732-6121
Anne Purcell, prin. Fax 732-6910
Other Schools – See Chapel Hill, Efland

Pinewoods Montessori S 100/PK-6
109 Millstone Dr 27278 919-644-2090
Jennifer Sewell, admin.

Hobgood, Halifax, Pop. 389

Hobgood Academy 200/K-12
201 S Beech St 27843 252-826-4116
William Whitehurst, hdmstr. Fax 826-2265

Hollister, Halifax
Halifax County SD
Supt. — See Halifax
Hollister ES 200/PK-5
37432 NC Highway 561 27844 252-586-4344
Allen Sledge, prin. Fax 586-6124

Holly Ridge, Onslow, Pop. 761
Onslow County SD
Supt. — See Jacksonville
Dixon ES 800/PK-5
130 Betty Dixon Rd 28445 910-327-2104
Peggy Kelley, prin. Fax 327-3336
Dixon MS 500/6-8
200 Dixon School Rd 28445 910-347-2738
Jay Strope, prin. Fax 347-4399

Holly Springs, Wake, Pop. 15,228
Wake County SD
Supt. — See Raleigh
Holly Grove ES 500/K-5
1451 Avent Ferry Rd 27540 919-577-1700
Wiladean Thomas, prin. Fax 577-1706
Holly Ridge ES 700/K-5
900 Holly Springs Rd 27540 919-577-1300
Pamela Peters, prin. Fax 577-1311
Holly Ridge MS 1,300/6-8
950 Holly Springs Rd 27540 919-577-1335
Brian Pittman, prin. Fax 577-1379
Holly Springs ES 800/K-5
401 Holly Springs Rd 27540 919-557-2660
Windell Harris, prin. Fax 557-2666

New S Montessori Center 100/PK-6
5617 Sunset Lake Rd 27540 919-303-3636
Jonathan Schroer, hdmstr. Fax 303-3636
Southern Wake Montessori 100/PK-10
5108 Old Powell Rd 27540 919-577-0081
Betsy Lovejoy, prin. Fax 577-0074

Hope Mills, Cumberland, Pop. 12,782
Cumberland County SD
Supt. — See Fayetteville
Baldwin ES 600/K-5
4441 Legion Rd 28348 910-424-0145
Rhonda Hill, prin. Fax 424-7359
Collier ES 600/PK-5
3522 Sturbridge Dr 28348 910-424-7200
Gwen Hedgepeth, prin. Fax 424-1684
Galberry Farm ES 1,000/K-5
8019 Byerly Dr 28348 910-424-1490
Jane Barnes, prin. Fax 424-1173
Grays Creek MS 600/6-8
2964 School Rd 28348 910-483-4124
Sara Whitaker, prin. Fax 483-5296
Hope Mills MS 800/6-8
4975 Cameron Rd 28348 910-425-5106
Patsy Ray, prin. Fax 423-5887
Rockfish ES 800/K-5
5763 Rockfish Rd 28348 910-424-5313
Donna Mims, prin. Fax 424-5338
South View MS 900/6-8
4100 Elk Rd 28348 910-424-3131
Garda Tatum, prin. Fax 424-2402

Hot Springs, Madison, Pop. 642
Madison County SD
Supt. — See Marshall
Hot Springs ES 100/K-5
63 N Serpentine Ave 28743 828-622-3292
Lisa Snelson, prin. Fax 622-3685

Hubert, Onslow
Onslow County SD
Supt. — See Jacksonville
Sand Ridge ES 600/K-5
868 Sandridge Rd 28539 910-326-5199
Harold Jurewicz, prin. Fax 326-5622

Hudson, Caldwell, Pop. 3,061
Caldwell County SD
Supt. — See Lenoir
Hudson ES 800/K-5
200 Roy E Coffey Dr 28638 828-728-3712
Robyn Stella, prin. Fax 728-8353
Hudson MS 800/6-8
291 Pine Mountain Rd 28638 828-728-4281
Bill Griffin, prin. Fax 726-8157

Harris Chapel Christian Academy 100/K-12
1444 Cajah Mountain Rd 28638 828-728-3721
Heritage Christian S 200/K-12
239 Mount Herman Rd 28638 828-726-0055

Huntersville, Mecklenburg, Pop. 36,377
Charlotte/Mecklenburg County SD
Supt. — See Charlotte
Alexander MS 1,700/6-8
12201 Hambright Rd 28078 980-343-3830
Joanna Smith, prin. Fax 343-3851
Barnette ES K-5
13659 Beatties Ford Rd 28078 980-343-0372
Jacquelyn Touchton, prin. Fax 343-1171
Blythe ES 900/K-5
12202 Hambright Rd 28078 980-343-5770
Bill Shapcott, prin. Fax 343-5766
Bradley MS 1,000/6-8
13345 Beatties Ford Rd 28078 980-343-5750
Carol Owen, prin. Fax 343-5743
Huntersville ES 800/K-5
200 Gilead Rd 28078 980-343-3835
Deborah Mangieri, prin. Fax 343-3849
Long Creek ES 700/K-5
9213 Beatties Ford Rd 28078 980-343-6095
Chad Thomas, prin. Fax 343-6144
Torrence Creek ES 1,200/K-5
14550 Ranson Rd 28078 980-343-0695
Fax 343-0697

Lake Norman Christian Academy 100/K-8
PO Box 1552 28070 704-987-9811
Mary Morgan, admin. Fax 987-9814
St. Mark S 700/K-8
14750 Stumptown Rd 28078 704-766-5000
Debbie Butler, prin. Fax 875-6377
SouthLake Christian Academy 800/K-12
13901 Hagers Ferry Rd 28078 704-949-2200
C. Wayne Parker, hdmstr. Fax 949-2203

Hurdle Mills, Person
Person County SD
Supt. — See Roxboro
Oak Lane ES 300/K-5
2076 Jim Morton Rd 27541 336-364-2204
Rick Chambers, prin. Fax 364-1036

Indian Trail, Union, Pop. 16,473
Union County SD
Supt. — See Monroe
Hemby Bridge ES 900/K-5
6701 Indian Trail Fairview 28079 704-882-1191
Casey Ball, prin. Fax 882-1192
Indian Trail ES 800/PK-5
200 Education St 28079 704-821-7614
Sherry Richardson, prin. Fax 821-7712
Poplin ES K-5
Poplin Rd 28079 704-296-0320
Stephanie McManus, prin. Fax 882-4853
Porter Ridge ES 900/K-5
2843 Ridge Rd 28079 704-289-1965
Wanda Stegall, prin. Fax 289-6523
Porter Ridge MS 1,300/6-8
2827 Ridge Rd 28079 704-225-7555
Timothy Conner, prin. Fax 226-9844
Sun Valley MS 1,200/6-8
1409 Wesley Chapel Rd 28079 704-296-3009
Blaire Traywick, prin. Fax 296-3045

Central Academy at Lake Park 100/K-12
3624 Lake Park Rd 28079 704-882-6267
Carrie Neller, admin. Fax 882-4651
Metrolina Christian Academy 1,000/PK-12
PO Box 1460 28079 704-882-3375
Rick Calloway, hdmstr. Fax 882-0631

Iron Station, Lincoln
Lincoln County SD
Supt. — See Lincolnton
East Lincoln MS 600/6-8
4137 Highway 73 28080 704-732-0761
Marty Helton, prin. Fax 732-4456
Iron Station ES 500/PK-5
4207 E Highway 27 28080 704-736-4292
Bobby Harkey, prin. Fax 735-8336

Jackson, Northampton, Pop. 672
Northampton County SD 3,000/PK-12
PO Box 158 27845 252-534-1371
Dr. Eric Bracy, supt. Fax 534-4631
www.northampton.k12.nc.us/
Central ES 200/PK-4
9742 NC Highway 305 27845 252-534-3381
Mary Harrell-Sessoms, prin. Fax 534-6591
Other Schools – See Conway, Gaston, Pendleton

Jacksonville, Onslow, Pop. 62,628
Onslow County SD 23,200/PK-12
PO Box 99 28541 910-455-2211
Dr. Kathy Spencer, supt. Fax 455-1965
onslowcounty.schoolinsites.com
Bell Fork ES 400/PK-5
500 Bell Fork Rd 28540 910-347-4459
Dr. Gregory Williams, prin. Fax 347-6555
Blue Creek ES 700/PK-5
1260 Burgaw Hwy 28540 910-347-1717
Glenn Reed, prin. Fax 347-0095
Carolina Forest ES 600/K-5
141 Carolina Forest Blvd 28546 910-346-1778
Helen Gross, prin. Fax 347-2108
Erwin ES 400/PK-5
323 New River Dr 28540 910-347-1261
Lori Howard, prin. Fax 989-2034
Hunters Creek ES 800/PK-5
95 Hunters Trl 28546 910-353-4443
Mary Dyer, prin. Fax 353-4425
Hunters Creek MS 900/6-8
85 Hunters Trl 28546 910-353-2147
Tim Foster, prin. Fax 353-7939
Jacksonville Commons ES 700/PK-5
1121 Commons Dr N 28546 910-347-1056
Mark Bulris, prin. Fax 347-2007
Jacksonville Commons MS 700/6-8
315 Commons Dr S 28546 910-346-6888
Gail Pylant, prin. Fax 938-1682
Meadow View ES K-5
1026 Fire Tower Rd 28540 910-478-3522
Vickie Brown, prin. Fax 478-3422
Morton ES 500/PK-5
485 Old 30 Rd 28546 910-353-0930
Chris Barnes, prin. Fax 353-0103
New Bridge MS 500/6-8
401 New Bridge St 28540 910-346-5144
Brent Anderson, prin. Fax 346-5402
Northwoods ES 400/PK-5
617 Henderson Dr 28540 910-347-2808
Elbert Garvey, prin. Fax 347-2939
Northwoods Park MS 700/6-8
904 Sioux Dr 28540 910-347-1202
Dennie Fidalgo, prin. Fax 347-0713
Parkwood ES 600/PK-5
2900 Northwoods Dr 28540 910-347-6711
Jane Dennis, prin. Fax 347-2745
Southwest ES 900/PK-5
2601 Burgaw Hwy 28540 910-347-0900
Gail Normanly, prin. Fax 347-0909
Southwest MS 600/6-8
3000 Furia Dr 28540 910-455-1105
Lisa Brewer, prin. Fax 455-4082
Summersill ES 800/PK-5
250 Summersill School Rd 28540 910-455-2672
Linda Kopec, prin. Fax 455-2129
Thompson ECC PK-PK
440 College St 28540 910-346-6222
Claire Pfeffer, dir. Fax 346-6636
Other Schools – See Holly Ridge, Hubert, Maysville, Richlands, Swansboro

---

Infant of Prague Catholic S 200/PK-8
501 Bordeaux St 28540 910-353-1300
Myra Marks, prin. Fax 455-0270
Jacksonville Christian Academy 200/K-12
919 Gum Branch Rd 28540 910-347-2358
Living Water Christian S 200/K-12
3980 Gum Branch Rd 28540 910-938-7017
Barbara Koebbe, prin. Fax 938-7025
St. Annes Parish Day S 200/PK-3
711 Henderson Dr 28540 910-347-0755
Fax 347-5051

Jamestown, Guilford, Pop. 2,997
Guilford County SD
Supt. — See Greensboro
Jamestown ES 500/PK-5
108 Potter Dr 27282 336-819-2110
Kimberly Fleming, prin. Fax 454-6588
Jamestown MS 1,200/6-8
4401 Vickery Chapel Rd N 27282 336-819-2100
Denise Richmond, prin. Fax 454-6734
Millis Road ES 500/PK-5
4310 Millis Rd 27282 336-819-2125
Russell Harper, prin. Fax 819-2127

Jamesville, Martin, Pop. 478
Martin County SD
Supt. — See Williamston
Jamesville ES 300/PK-6
PO Box 190 27846 252-792-8304
Jim Lammert, prin. Fax 809-4813

Jarvisburg, Currituck
Currituck County SD
Supt. — See Currituck
Jarvisburg ES 200/K-5
110 Jarvisburg Rd 27947 252-491-2050
Sharon Forbes, prin. Fax 491-2085

Jefferson, Ashe, Pop. 1,366
Ashe County SD 3,400/PK-12
PO Box 604 28640 336-246-7175
Dr. Travis Reeves, supt. Fax 246-7609
www.ashe.k12.nc.us/
Mountain View ES 700/PK-6
2789 US Highway 221 N 28640 336-982-4200
Kim Ball, prin. Fax 982-4203
Other Schools – See Warrensville, West Jefferson

Jonesville, Yadkin, Pop. 2,276
Yadkin County SD
Supt. — See Yadkinville
Jonesville ES 400/PK-6
101 Cedarbrook Rd 28642 336-835-3201
Junior Luffman, prin. Fax 835-1882

Kannapolis, Cabarrus, Pop. 39,041
Cabarrus County SD
Supt. — See Concord
Boger ES K-5
5150 Dovefield Ln 28081 704-788-1600
Cathy Hyatt, prin. Fax 794-6232
Royal Oaks ES 400/K-5
608 Dakota St 28083 704-932-4111
Rick Seaford, prin. Fax 932-2350

Kannapolis CSD 4,800/K-12
100 Denver St 28083 704-938-1131
Jo Anne Byerly, supt. Fax 933-6370
www.kannapolis.k12.nc.us
Forest Park ES 600/K-4
1333 Forest Park Dr 28083 704-932-8121
Melia Neale, prin. Fax 932-4889
Jackson Park ES 500/K-4
1400 Jackson St 28083 704-933-2831
Walter Graham, prin. Fax 932-1677
Kannapolis IS 700/5-6
525 E C St 28083 704-932-4161
Rob Knuschke, prin. Fax 938-4010
Kannapolis MS 700/7-8
1445 Oakwood Ave 28081 704-932-4102
Daron Buckwell, prin. Fax 932-4104
Shady Brook ES 300/K-4
903 Rogers Lake Rd 28081 704-933-2434
Rachel Zaionz, prin. Fax 933-9571
Wilson ES 300/K-4
1401 Pine St 28081 704-932-8656
Todd Parker, prin. Fax 933-7798
Wilson ES 400/K-4
800 N Walnut St 28081 704-933-2935
David Fleischmann, prin. Fax 932-5502

North Kannapolis Christian Academy 50/PK-K
312 Locust St 28081 704-932-6138
Frances Roberson, dir. Fax 933-5983

Kenansville, Duplin, Pop. 881
Duplin County SD 9,000/PK-12
PO Box 128 28349 910-296-1521
Dr. Wiley Doby, supt. Fax 296-1396
www.duplinschools.net
Kenansville ES 400/PK-5
PO Box 98 28349 910-296-1647
Keith Williams, prin. Fax 296-0022
Smith MS 300/6-8
PO Box 369 28349 910-296-0309
Kenneth Houston, prin. Fax 296-0086
Other Schools – See Albertson, Beulaville, Chinquapin, Mount Olive, Rose Hill, Wallace, Warsaw

Kenly, Johnston, Pop. 1,830
Johnston County SD
Supt. — See Smithfield
Glendale-Kenly ES 600/PK-5
PO Box 279 27542 919-284-2821
Tandra Batchelor-Mapp, prin. Fax 284-5087

Kernersville, Forsyth, Pop. 21,361
Winston-Salem/Forsyth SD
Supt. — See Winston Salem
Cash ES 800/K-5
4700 Old Hollow Rd 27284 336-996-3321
Judy Jones, prin. Fax 996-2809
East Forsyth MS 800/6-8
810 Bagley Rd 27284 336-703-6765
Dossie Poteat, prin. Fax 607-8531
Kernersville ES 900/K-5
512 W Mountain St 27284 336-996-1080
David Fitzpatrick, prin. Fax 996-8664
Kernersville MS 700/6-8
110 Brown Rd 27284 336-996-5566
Deborah Brooks, prin. Fax 996-1966
Piney Grove ES 800/K-5
1500 Piney Grove Rd 27284 336-993-0372
Sandy Sikes, prin. Fax 993-9429
Sedge Garden ES 1,100/K-5
475 Sedge Garden Rd 27284 336-771-4545
Gaye Weatherman, prin. Fax 771-4784
Southeast MS 900/6-8
1200 Old Salem Rd 27284 336-996-5848
Debbie Blanton-Warren, prin. Fax 996-0148
Union Cross ES 1,100/K-5
4300 High Point Rd 27284 336-769-9031
Michael Land, prin. Fax 769-3311

Brookside Montessori S 50/PK-6
736 Piney Grove Rd 27284 336-996-5351
Marjorie Carson, prin. Fax 996-6940
First Christian Academy 200/PK-12
1130 N Main St 27284 336-996-1660
Bryan Ross, admin. Fax 996-6511
Fountain of Life Lutheran S 50/PK-PK
323 Hopkins Rd 27284 336-993-9628
Debbie Travis, dir. Fax 993-0941

Kill Devil Hills, Dare, Pop. 6,550
Dare County SD
Supt. — See Nags Head
First Flight ES 400/PK-5
107 Veterans Dr 27948 252-441-1111
Margie Parker, prin. Fax 441-5832
First Flight MS 200/6-8
109 Veterans Dr 27948 252-441-8888
John Donlan, prin. Fax 441-7694

King, Stokes, Pop. 6,353
Stokes County SD
Supt. — See Danbury
Chestnut Grove MS 800/6-8
2185 Chestnut Grove Rd 27021 336-983-2106
David Hicks, prin. Fax 983-2725
King ES 600/PK-5
152 E School St 27021 336-983-5824
Shannon Boles, prin. Fax 985-0432
Mt. Olive ES 800/K-5
2145 Chestnut Grove Rd 27021 336-983-4351
Amy Nail, prin. Fax 983-9428

Calvary Christian S 200/K-12
748 Spainhour Rd 27021 336-983-3743
Sid Main, prin. Fax 983-8426

Kings Mountain, Cleveland, Pop. 10,862
Cleveland County SD
Supt. — See Shelby
Bethware ES 500/PK-4
115 Bethware Dr 28086 704-734-5623
Valerie Boyd, prin. Fax 734-5606
East ES 200/K-4
600 Cleveland Ave 28086 704-734-5633
Jennifer Wampler, prin. Fax 734-5617
Kings Mountain IS 600/5-6
227 Kings Mountain Blvd 28086 704-734-5658
Henry Gilmore, prin. Fax 734-5682
Kings Mountain MS 800/7-8
1000 Phifer Rd 28086 704-734-5667
Aaron Allen, prin. Fax 734-5615
North ES 200/PK-4
900 Ramseur St 28086 704-734-5663
Lynda Stewart, prin. Fax 734-5607
West ES 300/PK-4
500 W Mountain St 28086 704-734-5693
Brian Hunnell, prin. Fax 734-5618

Kinston, Lenoir, Pop. 22,851
Lenoir County SD 9,500/PK-12
PO Box 729 28502 252-527-1109
Terry Cline Ed.D., supt. Fax 527-6884
www.lenoir.k12.nc.us
Banks ES 500/K-5
2148 Falling Creek Rd 28504 252-527-9470
Cynthia Faulkner, prin. Fax 522-9714
Bynum ES 200/K-5
100 Bynum Blvd 28501 252-527-4166
Robert Dotson, prin. Fax 527-6010
Contentnea-Savannah S 500/K-8
3400 Ferrell Rd 28501 252-527-8591
Kay Blizzard, prin. Fax 527-9014
Moss Hill ES 500/K-5
6040 NC Highway 55 W 28504 252-569-5071
Donna Grady, prin. Fax 569-1405
Northwest ES 600/K-5
1701 Old Well Rd 28504 252-527-5143
Tina Letchworth, prin. Fax 527-9375
Rochelle MS 600/6-8
301 N Rochelle Blvd 28501 252-527-4290
Nicholas Harvey, prin. Fax 527-6498
Southeast ES 300/PK-5
201 McDaniels St 28501 252-527-4210
Felicia Solomon, prin. Fax 527-5965
Southwood ES 400/K-5
1245 NC Highway 58 S 28504 252-527-9081
Jerry Walton, prin. Fax 527-6417
Teachers Memorial ES 500/PK-5
500 Marcella Dr 28501 252-527-0225
Mildred Dunn, prin. Fax 527-3040
Woodington MS 700/6-8
4939 US Highway 258 S 28504 252-527-9570
Diane Heath, prin. Fax 527-3883
Other Schools – See La Grange, Pink Hill

Arendell Parrott Academy 700/PK-12
PO Box 1297 28503 252-522-4222
Dr. Ike Southerland, hdmstr. Fax 522-0672
Bethel Christian Academy 300/K-12
1936 Banks School Rd 28504 252-522-4636
Robert Spruill, prin. Fax 523-7290

Kipling, Harnett
Harnett County SD
Supt. — See Lillington
LaFayette ES 700/K-5
PO Box 129 27543 919-552-4353
Sonya Yates, prin. Fax 557-3066

Kittrell, Vance, Pop. 148
Vance County SD
Supt. — See Henderson
Vance ES 500/PK-5
4800 Raleigh Rd 27544 252-438-8492
Anne Garrison, prin. Fax 431-0570

Kitty Hawk, Dare, Pop. 3,358
Dare County SD
Supt. — See Nags Head
Kitty Hawk ES 500/K-5
16 S Dogwood Trl 27949 252-261-2313
Gregory Florence, prin. Fax 261-3400

Knightdale, Wake, Pop. 6,319
Wake County SD
Supt. — See Raleigh
Forestville Road ES 600/K-5
100 Lawson Ridge Rd 27545 919-266-8487
Dianne Pridgen, prin. Fax 266-8494
Hodge Road ES 700/K-5
2128 Mingo Bluff Blvd 27545 919-266-8599
Debra Pearce, prin. Fax 266-8558
Knightdale ES 700/PK-5
109 Ridge St 27545 919-266-8540
Linda Roberson, prin. Fax 266-8582
Lockhart ES 800/K-5
1320 N Smithfield Rd 27545 919-266-8525
Martha Lewis Martin, prin. Fax 266-8537

Knotts Island, Currituck
Currituck County SD
Supt. — See Currituck
Knotts Island ES 100/K-6
PO Box 40 27950 252-429-3327
Rick Hopkins, prin. Fax 429-3172

La Grange, Lenoir, Pop. 2,804
Lenoir County SD
Supt. — See Kinston
Frink MS 600/6-8
102 Martin Luther King Jr 28551 252-566-3326
Teresa George, prin. Fax 566-4027
La Grange ES 600/PK-5
402 W Railroad St 28551 252-566-4036
Kristie Brennan, prin. Fax 566-9055

Lake Toxaway, Transylvania
Transylvania County SD
Supt. — See Brevard
Henderson ES 200/K-5
11839 Rosman Hwy 28747 828-862-4463
Tony Meachum, prin. Fax 862-4621

Landis, Rowan, Pop. 3,064
Rowan-Salisbury County SD
Supt. — See Salisbury
Corriher-Lipe MS 600/6-8
214 W Rice St 28088 704-857-7946
Dr. Beverly S. Pugh, prin. Fax 855-2670
Landis ES 600/PK-5
801 W Ryder Ave 28088 704-857-3111
Mariann Haywood, prin. Fax 857-3131

Lasker, Northampton, Pop. 99

Northeast Academy 200/PK-12
210 Church St 27845 252-539-2461
Russell Leake, hdmstr. Fax 539-3919

Laurel Hill, Scotland
Scotland County SD
Supt. — See Laurinburg
Carver MS 500/6-8
18601 Fieldcrest Rd 28351 910-462-4669
Anne McLean, prin. Fax 462-4674
Laurel Hill ES 500/PK-5
11340 Old Wire Rd 28351 910-462-2111
Cindy Goodman, prin. Fax 462-3502
Scotland Accelerated Academy 200/PK-3
8901 Malloy Ave 28351 910-462-3601
Steve Wilson, prin. Fax 462-3760

Laurinburg, Scotland, Pop. 15,810
Scotland County SD 6,500/PK-12
322 S Main St 28352 910-276-1138
Dr. Shirley Prince, supt. Fax 277-4310
www.scsnc.org
Covington Street ES 400/PK-5
615 W Covington St 28352 910-277-4312
Sandra Wilcher, prin. Fax 277-4315
Johnson ES 400/PK-5
815 McGirts Bridge Rd 28352 910-277-4308
Emma McNeil-Stone, prin. Fax 277-4314
North Laurinburg ES 300/PK-5
831 N Gill St 28352 910-277-4336
Melody Snead, prin. Fax 277-4317
Shaw ES 200/4-5
18700 Old Wire Rd 28352 910-276-0611
Jack Davern, prin. Fax 266-8352
South Scotland ES 500/PK-5
17200 Barnes Bridge Rd 28352 910-277-4356
Pat Gates, prin. Fax 276-4154
Spring Hill MS 500/6-8
22801 Airbase Rd 28352 910-369-0590
Beth Ammons, prin. Fax 369-0595
Sycamore Lane MS 600/6-8
2100 Sycamore Ln 28352 910-277-4350
Rick Singletary, prin. Fax 277-4321
Washington Park ES 400/PK-5
1225 S Caledonia Rd 28352 910-277-4364
Harriet Jackson, prin. Fax 277-4349
Other Schools – See Gibson, Laurel Hill, Wagram

Scotland Christian Academy 300/K-12
10300 McColl Rd 28352 910-276-7722
Phillip Cline, hdmstr. Fax 277-2735

Lawndale, Cleveland, Pop. 636
Cleveland County SD
Supt. — See Shelby
Burns MS 1,000/6-8
215 Shady Grove Rd 28090 704-538-3126
Jeff Benfield, prin. Fax 538-3944

Lawsonville, Stokes
Stokes County SD
Supt. — See Danbury
Lawsonville ES 300/PK-5
4611 NC 8 Hwy N 27022 336-593-8284
Greg Ottaway, prin. Fax 593-2290
Piney Grove MS 400/6-8
3415 Piney Grove Church Rd 27022 336-593-4000
Roger Tucker, prin. Fax 593-4003

Leicester, Buncombe
Buncombe County SD
Supt. — See Asheville
Leicester ES 600/K-5
31 Gilbert Rd 28748 828-683-2341
Melanie Collins, prin. Fax 683-9179

Leland, Brunswick, Pop. 4,440
Brunswick County SD
Supt. — See Bolivia
Belville ES 800/K-5
575 River Rd SE 28451 910-371-0601
Tracey Coston, prin. Fax 371-0063
Leland MS 700/6-8
927 Old Fayetteville Rd NE 28451 910-371-3030
Patricia Underwood, prin. Fax 371-0647
Lincoln ES 700/PK-5
1664 Lincoln Rd NE 28451 910-371-3597
Retha Rusk, prin. Fax 371-6149

Leland Christian Academy 100/PK-6
517 Village Rd NE 28451 910-371-0688
Dwight Jenkins, prin. Fax 371-0688

Lenoir, Caldwell, Pop. 17,912
Caldwell County SD 13,000/PK-12
1914 Hickory Blvd SW 28645 828-728-8407
Dr. Steve Stone, supt. Fax 728-0012
www.caa.k12.nc.us
Davenport ES 500/K-5
901 College Ave SW 28645 828-754-6941
Julia Curry, prin. Fax 758-5034
Gamewell ES 600/K-5
2904 Morganton Blvd SW 28645 828-758-1193
Pat Pennington, prin. Fax 754-3503
Gamewell MS 500/6-8
3210 Gamewell School Rd 28645 828-754-6204
Keith Hindman, prin. Fax 754-6278
Kings Creek S 200/K-8
3680 Wilkesboro Blvd 28645 828-754-6039
Milland Bradley, prin. Fax 754-9477
Lenoir MS 500/6-8
332 Greenhaven Dr NW 28645 828-758-2500
Dr. Pete Yount, prin. Fax 758-1570
Lower Creek ES 400/K-5
630 Lower Creek Dr NE 28645 828-754-4022
Debbie Indicott, prin. Fax 754-8758
Oak Hill S 200/K-8
4603 Oakhill School Rd 28645 828-754-6128
Dr. Phyllis Blair, prin. Fax 758-1884
Valmead Basic ES 200/K-5
111 Elizabeth St NW 28645 828-754-9612
Lisa Vaughn, prin. Fax 758-4936
West Lenoir ES 300/K-5
125 Maple Dr NW 28645 828-754-5161
Felicia Simmons, prin. Fax 758-4738
Whitnel Four Seasons ES 400/PK-5
116 Hibriten Dr SW 28645 828-728-6423
Annette Swanson, prin. Fax 728-2204
Other Schools – See Collettsville, Granite Falls, Hudson, Patterson

Lewiston Woodville, Bertie, Pop. 598
Bertie County SD
Supt. — See Windsor
West Bertie ES 400/PK-5
PO Box 279 27849 252-344-7621
Wayne Mayo, prin. Fax 344-2828

Lewisville, Forsyth, Pop. 9,547
Winston-Salem/Forsyth SD
Supt. — See Winston Salem
Lewisville ES 600/K-5
150 Lucy Ln 27023 336-945-5355
Debbie Hampton, prin. Fax 945-3915

Forsyth Country Day S 1,000/PK-12
PO Box 549 27023 336-945-3151
Henry Battle, prin. Fax 945-2907

Lexington, Davidson, Pop. 20,398
Davidson County SD 20,500/PK-12
PO Box 2057 27293 336-249-8182
Dr. Fred Mock, supt. Fax 249-1062
www.davidson.k12.nc.us
Central Davidson MS 800/6-8
2591 NC Highway 47 27292 336-357-2310
Chris Johnston, prin. Fax 357-5965
Churchland ES 600/PK-5
7571 S NC Highway 150 27295 336-242-5690
Tammy Bush, prin. Fax 242-5691
Davis-Townsend ES 600/PK-5
975 Heath Church Rd 27292 336-249-9880
Steven Reynolds, prin. Fax 249-8565
Midway ES 600/PK-5
318 Midway School Rd 27295 336-764-0064
Lisa Nelson, prin. Fax 764-2313
North Davidson MS 1,200/6-8
333 Critcher Dr 27295 336-731-2331
Dr. Denise Hedrick, prin. Fax 731-2328
Northwest ES 600/K-5
400 NW Elementary Rd 27295 336-764-0360
Angelia Kiger, prin. Fax 764-3398
Reeds ES 700/K-5
791 S NC Highway 150 27295 336-242-5620
Julie Hamilton, prin. Fax 242-5621
Silver Valley ES 300/K-5
11161 E Old US Highway 64 27292 336-472-1576
Kim Loflin, prin. Fax 472-3250
Southwood ES 1,100/K-5
5850 NC Highway 8 27292 336-357-2777
Deana Coley, prin. Fax 357-5227
Tyro ES K-5
450 Cow Palace Rd 27295 336-242-5760
Kim Dixon, prin. Fax 242-5761
Tyro MS 600/6-8
2946 Michael Rd 27295 336-853-7795
Harry Mock, prin. Fax 853-7357
Welcome ES 700/PK-5
5701 Old US Highway 52 27295 336-731-3361
Diana Thomas-Louya, prin. Fax 731-2799
Other Schools – See Denton, Thomasville, Winston Salem

Lexington CSD 3,200/PK-12
1010 Fair St 27292 336-242-1527
Richard Kriesky, supt. Fax 249-3206
lexcs.org
England IS 500/4-5
111 Cornelia St 27292 336-242-1552
Emy Calderone, prin. Fax 242-1252
Lexington MS 700/6-8
100 E Hemstead St 27292 336-242-1557
Patti Kroh, prin. Fax 242-1372
Pickett PS 400/PK-3
200 Biesecker Rd 27295 336-242-1546
Gina Spencer, prin. Fax 249-3969
Southwest ES 400/PK-3
434 Central Ave 27292 336-242-1548
Sharolyn Harry-Clark, prin. Fax 249-7684

Sheets Memorial Christian S 300/PK-12
307 Holt St 27292 336-249-4224
Dan Hightower, admin. Fax 249-6985
Union Grove Christian S 300/K-12
2295 Union Grove Rd 27295 336-764-3105
Pete Steinhaus, prin. Fax 764-8657

Liberty, Randolph, Pop. 2,712
Guilford County SD
Supt. — See Greensboro
Greene ES 400/K-5
2717 NC Highway 62 E 27298 336-685-5000
Angella Hauser, prin. Fax 685-5006

Randolph County SD
Supt. — See Asheboro
Liberty ES 500/K-5
206 N Fayetteville St 27298 336-622-2253
Jennifer Williams, prin. Fax 622-2255
Northeastern Randolph MS 500/6-8
3493 Ramseur Julian Rd 27298 336-622-5808
Kristen Miller, prin. Fax 622-5868

Lilesville, Anson, Pop. 440
Anson County SD
Supt. — See Wadesboro
Lilesville ES 300/K-6
121 Camden St 28091 704-848-4975
Marty Godwin, prin. Fax 848-4205

Lillington, Harnett, Pop. 3,162
Harnett County SD 17,900/K-12
PO Box 1029 27546 910-893-8151
Dan Honeycutt, supt. Fax 893-4279
www.harnett.k12.nc.us/
Boone Trail ES 600/K-5
8500 Old US 421 27546 910-893-4013
Brookie Ferguson, prin. Fax 893-6865
Lillington-Shawtown ES 600/K-5
855 Old US 421 27546 910-893-3483
Linda Stewart, prin. Fax 893-8243
Western Harnett MS 1,000/6-8
11135 NC 27 W 27546 919-499-4497
Linwood Smith, prin. Fax 499-1788
Other Schools – See Angier, Buies Creek, Bunnlevel, Cameron, Coats, Dunn, Erwin, Kipling, Olivia, Sanford, Spring Lake

Lincolnton, Lincoln, Pop. 10,393
Lincoln County SD 11,800/PK-12
PO Box 400 28093 704-732-2261
David Martin, supt. Fax 736-4321
www.lincoln.k12.nc.us
Battleground ES 400/K-3
201 Jeb Seagle Dr 28092 704-735-3146
Diana Carpenter, prin. Fax 736-4262
Childers ES 400/K-5
2595 Rock Dam Rd 28092 704-736-9610
Heath Belcher, prin. Fax 736-9612
Kiser IS 400/4-5
301 Jeb Seagle Dr 28092 704-736-1626
Anita Robinson, prin. Fax 736-1628
Lincolnton MS 700/6-8
2361 Startown Rd 28092 704-735-1120
Scott Carpenter, prin. Fax 732-6811
Love Memorial ES 400/PK-5
1463 Love Memorial School R 28092 704-735-5649
Diand Canipe, prin. Fax 736-4265
Lowder ES 300/K-3
350 Kennedy Dr 28092 704-735-2741
Donald Welch, prin. Fax 736-4267
Massey ES 300/PK-3
130 Newbold St 28092 704-735-2322
Kirby Oldham, prin. Fax 732-0968
Pumpkin Center IS 3-5
3980 King Wilkinson Rd 28092 704-736-1504
Isabelle Wadsworth, prin. Fax 736-1177
Pumpkin Center PS 300/K-2
3970 King Wilkinson Rd 28092 704-736-1394
Dr. Mitch Eisner, prin. Fax 736-4914
West Lincoln MS 700/6-8
260 Shoal Rd 28092 704-276-1760
John Robinson, prin. Fax 276-2293
Other Schools – See Denver, Iron Station, Vale

Linden, Cumberland, Pop. 126
Cumberland County SD
Supt. — See Fayetteville
Raleigh Road ES 200/PK-1
8330 Ramsey St 28356 910-488-0850
Lisa Troutman, prin. Fax 822-5663

Littleton, Halifax, Pop. 662
Halifax County SD
Supt. — See Halifax
Aurelian Springs ES 400/PK-5
10536 NC Highway 48 27850 252-586-4944
Carla Amason, prin. Fax 586-2701

Locust, Stanly, Pop. 2,526
Stanly County SD
Supt. — See Albemarle
Locust S 300/K-8
103 School Rd 28097 704-888-5921
Theresa Troutman, prin. Fax 888-6631
Ridgecrest S 300/K-8
24791 Millingport Rd 28097 704-485-3825
Amy Blake, prin. Fax 485-2515
Running Creek S 400/K-8
339 Running Creek Church Rd 28097 704-485-8030
Damon Rhodes, prin. Fax 485-8060

Carolina Christian S 200/PK-9
PO Box 399 28097 704-888-4332
Adam Thomas, hdmstr. Fax 888-4492

Louisburg, Franklin, Pop. 3,356
Franklin County SD 8,300/K-12
53 W River Rd 27549 919-496-2600
Dr. Eddie Ingram, supt. Fax 496-2104
www.fcschools.net
Best ES 500/K-5
4011 NC 56 Hwy E 27549 919-853-2347
Debbie Ayscue, prin. Fax 853-6759
Laurel Mill ES 300/K-5
730 Laurel Mill Rd 27549 919-853-3577
Genie Faulkner, prin. Fax 853-3579
Louisburg ES 500/K-5
50 Stone Southerland Rd 27549 919-496-3676
William Harris, prin. Fax 496-2460
Royal ES 600/K-5
308 Flat Rock Church Rd 27549 919-496-7377
Shawnee Perry-Manley, prin. Fax 496-7343
Terrell Lane MS 600/6-8
101 Terrell Ln 27549 919-496-1855
Novella Brown, prin. Fax 496-1370
Other Schools – See Bunn, Franklinton, Youngsville

Lowell, Gaston, Pop. 2,671
Gaston County SD
Supt. — See Gastonia
Holbrook MS 800/6-8
418 S Church St 28098 704-824-2381
Chad Carper, prin. Fax 824-4529
Lowell ES 600/K-5
1500 Power Dr 28098 704-824-2264
Juanita Knight, prin. Fax 824-7427

Lowgap, Surry
Surry County SD
Supt. — See Dobson
Cedar Ridge ES 500/PK-5
734 Flippin Rd 27024 336-352-4320
Sharon Hardy, prin. Fax 352-4347

Lucama, Wilson, Pop. 865
Wilson County SD
Supt. — See Wilson
Lucama ES 500/K-5
6260 Blalock Rd 27851 252-239-1257
John Joyner, prin. Fax 239-1943
Springfield MS 500/6-8
5551 Wiggins Mill Rd 27851 252-239-1347
Ronald Barringer, prin. Fax 239-1686

Lumber Bridge, Robeson, Pop. 119
Hoke County SD
Supt. — See Raeford
Sandy Grove ES 700/PK-5
8452 N Old Wire Rd 28357 910-875-6008
Tonya Caulder, prin. Fax 875-8498

Lumberton, Robeson, Pop. 21,591
Robeson County SD 24,300/PK-12
PO Box 2909 28359 910-671-6000
Dr. Johnny Hunt, supt. Fax 671-6024
www.robeson.k12.nc.us
Carroll MS 600/5-6
300 Bailey Rd 28358 910-671-6098
Tina Coleman, prin. Fax 671-6033
Deep Branch ES 500/PK-6
4045 Deep Branch Rd 28360 910-738-2514
Elvera Locklear, prin. Fax 738-6811
East Robeson PS 700/PK-3
4840 7th Street Rd 28358 910-671-6055
Barbara McQueen, prin. Fax 738-6639
Hargrave ES 300/PK-4
100 Hargrave St 28358 910-671-6060
Shelia Gasque, prin. Fax 671-4388
Knuckles ES 300/PK-4
1520 Martin Luther King Jr 28358 910-671-6020
Karen Brooks-Floyd, prin. Fax 671-4380
Littlefield MS 800/4-8
9674 NC Highway 41 N 28358 910-671-6065
Wesley Floyd, prin. Fax 671-6068
Long Branch ES 500/PK-4
10218 NC Highway 72 E 28358 910-739-3864
Dr. Penny Britt, prin. Fax 739-8710
Lumberton JHS 700/7-8
82 Marion Rd 28358 910-735-2108
Gary Patrick, prin. Fax 671-4350
Magnolia S 800/PK-8
10928 US Highway 301 N 28360 910-671-6070
Robert Locklear, prin. Fax 738-4182
Piney Grove ES 700/PK-6
1680 Piney Grove Rd 28360 910-671-6025
Jill Hathaway, prin. Fax 671-6010
Rowland-Norment ES 600/PK-4
701 Godwin Ave 28358 910-671-6030
Laura Owens-Dif, prin. Fax 671-4390
Shining Stars Preschool PK-PK
430 Caton Rd 28360 910-671-4343
Mary Schultz, prin. Fax 671-4345
Tanglewood ES 500/K-4
400 W 29th St 28358 910-671-6035
Jones Culbreth, prin. Fax 671-6036
West Lumberton ES 200/PK-4
451 School St 28358 910-671-6045
Dr. Juanita Clark, prin. Fax 671-6046
Other Schools – See Fairmont, Maxton, Orrum, Parkton, Pembroke, Red Springs, Rowland, Saint Pauls, Shannon

---

Antioch Christian Academy 200/K-12
5071 Old Whiteville Rd 28358 910-735-1011
James Coleman, prin. Fax 737-6301

Mc Adenville, Gaston, Pop. 846
Gaston County SD
Supt. — See Gastonia
Mc Adenville ES 200/PK-5
PO Box 129 28101 704-824-2236
James Ramere, prin. Fax 824-8192

Mc Leansville, Guilford, Pop. 1,154
Guilford County SD
Supt. — See Greensboro
Madison ES 600/K-5
3600 Hines Chapel Rd 27301 336-375-2555
Judy Robbins, prin. Fax 375-2560
McLeansville ES 400/PK-5
5315 Frieden Church Rd 27301 336-698-0144
Beverly Tucker, prin. Fax 698-0266
Northeast Guilford MS 1,000/6-8
6720 Mcleansville Rd 27301 336-375-2525
Johncarlos Miller, prin. Fax 375-2534

Madison, Rockingham, Pop. 2,239
Rockingham County SD
Supt. — See Eden
Dillard ES 500/PK-5
810 Cure Dr 27025 336-548-2472
Angela Martin, prin. Fax 548-6442
Huntsville ES 500/PK-5
2020 Sardis Church Rd 27025 336-427-3266
Judy Coleman, prin. Fax 427-4089
New Vision S of Math Science Technology 300/K-5
705 Ayersville Rd 27025 336-548-4780
Kay Frey, prin. Fax 548-4779
Western Rockingham MS 800/6-8
915 Ayersville Rd 27025 336-548-2168
George Murphy, prin. Fax 548-1799

Maiden, Catawba, Pop. 3,264
Catawba County SD
Supt. — See Newton
Maiden ES 600/K-6
201 N Main Ave 28650 828-428-8769
Lori Reed, prin. Fax 428-4374
Maiden MS 400/7-8
518 N C Ave 28650 828-428-2326
Nan VanHoy, prin. Fax 428-5389
Tuttle ES 400/K-6
2872 Water Plant Rd 28650 828-428-3080
DeAnna Finger, prin. Fax 428-0675

Lincoln Catawba Christian Academy 100/PK-12
935 Island Ford Rd 28650 828-428-8857
Dr. Clyde Smith, hdmstr. Fax 428-9639

Manteo, Dare, Pop. 1,301
Dare County SD
Supt. — See Nags Head
Manteo ES 600/PK-5
701 US Highway 64 and 264 27954 252-473-2742
Mary Anne Wetzel, prin. Fax 473-2496
Manteo MS 400/6-8
1000 US Highway 64 and 264 27954 252-473-5549
Terry McGinnis, prin. Fax 473-2612

Marble, Cherokee
Cherokee County SD
Supt. — See Murphy
Marble ES 200/PK-5
PO Box 70 28905 828-837-5485
Ron Ledford, prin. Fax 837-5364

Marion, McDowell, Pop. 5,013
McDowell County SD 6,500/K-12
334 S Main St 28752 828-652-4535
Dr. Ira Trollinger, supt. Fax 659-2238
www.mcdowell.k12.nc.us/
Eastfield ES 300/K-6
170 Eastfield School Rd 28752 828-652-3730
Susan Pool, prin. Fax 652-4191
Glenwood ES 500/K-6
1545 Old US 221 S 28752 828-738-4220
Lynn McNeilly, prin. Fax 738-3828
Marion ES 500/K-6
209 Robert St 28752 828-652-2141
Elaine Seals, prin. Fax 652-7301
North Cove ES 300/K-6
401 American Thread Rd 28752 828-756-4342
Desarae Kirkpatrick, prin. Fax 756-7316
Pleasant Gardens ES 500/K-6
100 John Roach Dr 28752 828-724-4422
Vicki Webb, prin. Fax 724-4217
West Marion ES 500/K-6
820 Marler Rd 28752 828-738-3353
Natalie Gouge, prin. Fax 738-3592
Other Schools – See Nebo, Old Fort

Marion Christian Academy 100/PK-12
PO Box 1045 28752 828-652-2033
Lincoln Walters, admin. Fax 652-1856
New Manna Christian S 100/K-12
PO Box 1085 28752 828-652-7729
Anthony Shirley, prin. Fax 652-7729

Marshall, Madison, Pop. 837
Madison County SD 2,600/K-12
5738 US Highway 25/70 28753 828-649-9276
Ronald Wilcox Ed.D., supt. Fax 649-9334
www.madison.k12.nc.us
Brush Creek ES 400/K-5
265 Upper Brush Creek Rd 28753 828-649-1547
Keith Ray, prin. Fax 649-1528
Laurel ES 100/K-5
4100 Highway 212 28753 828-656-2223
Charles Cutshall, prin. Fax 656-2308
Madison MS 600/6-8
95 Upper Brush Creek Rd 28753 828-649-2269
Dr. Barbara Tipton, prin. Fax 649-9015
Other Schools – See Hot Springs, Mars Hill

Mars Hill, Madison, Pop. 1,834
Madison County SD
Supt. — See Marshall
Mars Hill ES 600/K-5
200 School House Ln 28754 828-689-2922
Christiaan Ramsey, prin. Fax 689-5536

Marshville, Union, Pop. 2,820
Union County SD
Supt. — See Monroe
East Union MS 800/6-8
6010 W Marshville Blvd 28103 704-290-1540
Kevin Plue, prin. Fax 624-9302
Marshville ES 600/PK-5
515 N Elm St 28103 704-624-2133
Tina Miller, prin. Fax 624-6946
New Salem ES 300/K-5
6106 Highway 205 28103 704-385-9430
Neil Hawkins, prin. Fax 385-8205

Marvin, Union, Pop. 1,358
Union County SD
Supt. — See Monroe
Marvin ES 1,000/K-5
9700 Marvin School Rd, 704-843-5399
Dr. Jay Jones, prin. Fax 843-6911

Matthews, Mecklenburg, Pop. 25,306
Charlotte/Mecklenburg County SD
Supt. — See Charlotte
Crestdale MS 1,000/6-8
940 Sam Newell Rd 28105 980-343-5755
Avery Mitchell, prin. Fax 343-5761
Crown Point ES 800/K-5
3335 Sam Newell Rd 28105 980-343-6535
Mark Anderson, prin. Fax 343-6539
Elizabeth Lane ES 1,000/K-5
121 Elizabeth Ln 28105 980-343-5700
Diane Burnham, prin. Fax 343-5704
Matthews ES 1,100/K-5
200 Mcdowell St 28105 980-343-3940
Dan Witt, prin. Fax 343-3944
Mint Hill MS 1,300/6-8
11501 Idlewild Rd 28105 980-343-5439
Denise Watts, prin. Fax 343-5442

Union County SD
Supt. — See Monroe
Antioch ES 800/K-5
3101 Antioch Church Rd 28104 704-841-2505
Ken Hoover, prin. Fax 841-2578
Weddington ES 700/K-5
3927 Twelve Mile Creek Rd 28104 704-849-7238
Brenda Kasell, prin. Fax 849-2238
Weddington MS 1,600/6-8
5903 Deal Rd 28104 704-814-9772
Steven Wray, prin. Fax 814-9775

Arborbrook Christian Academy 100/K-12
4823 Waxhaw Indian Trail Rd 28104 704-821-9952
Naomi Heidorn, prin.
Bible Baptist Christian S 200/PK-12
2724 Margaret Wallace Rd 28105 704-535-1694
David King, prin. Fax 536-1289
Carmel Christian S 400/K-8
1145 Pineville Matthews Rd 28105 704-849-9723
J. Van Wade, hdmstr. Fax 847-9908
Covenant Day S 800/K-12
800 Fullwood Rd 28105 704-847-2385
Dr. Marni Halvorson, hdmstr. Fax 708-6137

Maxton, Robeson, Pop. 2,629
Robeson County SD
Supt. — See Lumberton
Dean ES 400/PK-4
202 S Hooper St 28364 910-844-5982
Jestine Wade, prin. Fax 844-9419
Oxendine ES 400/PK-6
5599 Oxendine School Rd 28364 910-843-4243
Bobby Oxendine, prin. Fax 843-9144
Prospect S 900/PK-8
4024 Missouri Rd 28364 910-521-4766
Johnathan Blue, prin. Fax 521-8638
Townsend MS 200/5-8
105 W Carolina St 28364 910-844-5086
Eric Sanders, prin. Fax 844-4292

Maysville, Onslow, Pop. 990
Jones County SD
Supt. — See Trenton
Maysville ES 200/PK-6
814 6th St 28555 910-743-3631
Joanne Stone, prin. Fax 743-2319

Onslow County SD
Supt. — See Jacksonville
Silverdale ES 500/PK-5
841 Smith Rd 28555 910-326-5146
Mary McAllister, prin. Fax 326-5976

Mebane, Alamance, Pop. 8,945
Alamance-Burlington SD
Supt. — See Burlington
Garrett ES 700/PK-5
3224 Old Hillsborough Rd 27302 919-563-2088
Steve Achey, prin. Fax 304-5384
Hawfields MS 600/6-8
1951 S NC Highway 119 27302 919-563-5303
Amy Walker, prin. Fax 563-1351
South Mebane ES 500/K-5
600 S Third St 27302 919-563-6905
Rebecca Royal, prin. Fax 563-4616
Woodlawn MS 600/6-8
3970 Mebane Rogers Rd 27302 919-563-3222
Diane Hill, prin. Fax 563-6807
Yoder ES 400/PK-5
301 N Charles St 27302 919-563-3722
Louise Butler, prin. Fax 563-9079

Caswell County SD
Supt. — See Yanceyville
South ES 400/PK-5
8925 NC Highway 86 S 27302 336-694-1212
M. Reagan, prin. Fax 694-1249

Merry Hill, Bertie

Lawrence Academy 300/PK-12
PO Box 70 27957 252-482-4748
Ed McFarlane, hdmstr. Fax 482-2215

Micaville, Yancey
Yancy County SD
Supt. — See Burnsville
Micaville ES 200/K-5
PO Box 122 28755 828-675-4161
Michele Laws, prin. Fax 675-0370

Micro, Johnston, Pop. 502
Johnston County SD
Supt. — See Smithfield
North Johnston MS 600/6-8
PO Box 69 27555 919-284-3374
Jarvis Ellis, prin. Fax 284-3399

Middleburg, Vance, Pop. 164
Vance County SD
Supt. — See Henderson
Young ES 300/PK-5
PO Box 160 27556 252-438-6423
Dr. Adrienne Morton, prin. Fax 433-0215

Middlesex, Nash, Pop. 851
Nash-Rocky Mount SD
Supt. — See Nashville
Middlesex ES 400/PK-5
13081 W Hanes Ave 27557 252-462-2815
Samantha Gillespie, prin. Fax 235-5216

Midland, Cabarrus, Pop. 2,834
Cabarrus County SD
Supt. — See Concord
Bethel ES 700/K-5
2425 Midland Rd 28107 704-888-5811
Kristi Williford, prin. Fax 888-1550

Millers Creek, Wilkes, Pop. 1,787
Wilkes County SD
Supt. — See North Wilkesboro
Millers Creek ES 900/PK-5
4320 N NC Highway 16 28651 336-667-2379
Michelle Shepherd, prin. Fax 667-2937

Millers Creek Christian S 100/PK-12
PO Box 559 28651 336-838-2517
April Huffman, admin. Fax 838-2546

Mill Spring, Polk
Polk County SD
Supt. — See Columbus
Polk Central ES 400/PK-5
2141 Highway 9 S 28756 828-894-8233
Dottie Kinlaw, prin. Fax 894-3916
Polk County MS 600/6-8
321 Wolverine Trl 28756 828-894-2215
Hank Utz, prin. Fax 894-0191
Sunny View ES 200/PK-5
86 Sunny View School Rd 28756 828-625-4530
Fax 625-8409

Mills River, Henderson
Henderson County SD
Supt. — See Hendersonville
Marlow ES 500/K-5
1985 Butler Bridge Rd, 828-654-3225
Jan King, prin. Fax 687-1214
Mills River ES 500/K-5
94 School House Rd, 828-891-6563
Jeff Treadway, prin. Fax 891-6584

Mint Hill, Mecklenburg, Pop. 17,871
Charlotte/Mecklenburg County SD
Supt. — See Charlotte
Bain ES 1,000/K-5
11524 Bain School Rd 28227 980-343-6915
Mike Drye, prin. Fax 343-6150
Lebanon Road ES 700/K-5
7300 Lebanon Rd 28227 980-343-3640
Guyla Vardell, prin. Fax 343-3717
Northeast MS 1,100/6-8
5960 Brickstone Dr 28227 980-343-6920
David Switzer, prin. Fax 343-3264

Mocksville, Davie, Pop. 4,464
Davie County SD 6,500/PK-12
220 Cherry St 27028 336-751-5921
Dr. Robert Landry, supt. Fax 751-9013
www.davie.k12.nc.us
Cornatzer ES 400/K-5
552 Cornatzer Rd 27028 336-940-5097
Dr. Cinde Rinn, prin. Fax 940-5647
Davie ES 400/PK-5
3437 US Highway 601 N 27028 336-492-5421
Rex Allen, prin. Fax 492-2699
Mocksville ES 600/K-5
295 Cemetery St 27028 336-751-2740
Lynne Marrs, prin. Fax 751-4883
North Davie MS 800/6-8
497 Farmington Rd 27028 336-998-5555
Jennifer Custer, prin. Fax 998-7233
Pinebrook ES 500/K-5
477 Pinebrook School Rd 27028 336-998-3868
Joy Morrison, prin. Fax 940-5663
South Davie MS 800/6-8
700 Hardison St 27028 336-751-5941
Dr. Danny Cartner, prin. Fax 751-5656
Other Schools – See Advance, Cooleemee

Moncure, Chatham
Chatham County SD
Supt. — See Pittsboro
Moncure S 200/K-8
PO Box 260 27559 919-542-3725
Dr. Justin Bartholomew, prin. Fax 542-2035

Monroe, Union, Pop. 29,987
Union County SD 35,900/PK-12
400 N Church St 28112 704-296-0766
Dr. Ed Davis, supt. Fax 282-2171
www.ucps.k12.nc.us
Benton Heights ES 700/PK-5
1200 Concord Ave 28110 704-296-3100
Mike Harvey, prin. Fax 296-3106
Bickett Education Center PK-PK
501 Lancaster Ave 28112 704-289-7497
Fo Roldan, admin. Fax 295-3066
Bickett ES 700/K-5
830 M L King Blvd S 28112 704-283-8520
Theresa Benson, prin. Fax 225-9543
East ES 500/PK-5
515 Elizabeth Ave 28112 704-296-3110
Karen Anderson, prin. Fax 296-3112
Fairview ES 600/K-5
110 Clontz Rd 28110 704-753-2800
Kelly Thomas, prin. Fax 753-2804
Monroe MS 800/6-8
601 E Sunset Dr 28112 704-296-3120
Montrio Belton, prin. Fax 296-3122
Parkwood MS 1,000/6-8
3219 Parkwood School Rd 28112 704-764-2910
Kimberly Chinnis, prin. Fax 764-2914
Piedmont MS 800/6-8
2816 Sikes Mill Rd 28110 704-753-2840
Anne Radke, prin. Fax 753-2846
Prospect ES 600/K-5
3005 Ruben Rd 28112 704-764-2920
Jannie Bankston, prin. Fax 764-2923
Rock Rest ES 400/PK-5
814 Old Pageland Monroe Rd 28112 704-290-1513
Wendy Graveley, prin. Fax 283-6528
Rocky River ES 900/PK-5
500 N Rocky River Rd 28110 704-290-1523
Scott Broome, prin. Fax 292-1395

Sardis ES 900/PK-5
4416 Sardis Church Rd 28110 704-882-4303
Margaret Proctor, prin. Fax 882-4305
Shiloh ES 1,200/PK-5
5210 Rogers Rd 28110 704-296-3035
Mike Henderson, prin. Fax 296-3039
Sun Valley ES PK-5
5200 Rogers Rd 28110 704-290-1559
Patrice Parker, prin. Fax 282-8234
Unionville ES 800/K-5
4511 Unionville Rd 28110 704-296-3055
Sharyn Von Cannon, prin. Fax 296-3057
Wesley Chapel ES 1,100/K-5
110 S Potter Rd 28110 704-296-3081
Rosanne Bateman, prin. Fax 296-3080
Other Schools – See Indian Trail, Marshville, Marvin, Matthews, Stallings, Waxhaw, Wingate

First Assembly Christian S 100/K-12
2500 Arnold Dr 28110 704-283-2739
Tabernacle Christian S 100/K-12
2900 Walkup Ave 28110 704-283-4395

Mooresville, Iredell, Pop. 20,488
Iredell-Statesville SD
Supt. — See Statesville
Brawley MS 1,000/6-8
664 Brawley School Rd 28117 704-664-4430
Jimmie Dancy, prin. Fax 664-9846
Lake Norman ES 700/K-5
255 Oak Tree Rd 28117 704-662-8261
Boen Nutting, prin. Fax 662-8264
Lakeshore ES 700/K-5
252 Lakeshore Dr 28117 704-660-5970
Pam Aman, prin. Fax 660-7809
Lakeshore MS 700/6-8
244 Lakeshore School Dr 28117 704-799-0187
Jim Gaghan, prin. Fax 663-6431
Mount Mourne ES 600/PK-5
1431 Mecklenburg Hwy 28115 704-892-4711
Brian Foster, prin. Fax 892-3804
Shepherd ES 500/K-5
1748 Charlotte Hwy 28115 704-664-2582
Karen Morning-Cain, prin. Fax 660-1642
Woodland Heights ES 900/K-5
288 Forest Lake Blvd 28117 704-663-1370
Ethan Todd, prin. Fax 663-1383

Mooresville CSD 5,000/PK-12
305 N Main St 28115 704-658-2530
Dr. Mark Edwards, supt. Fax 663-3005
www.mgsd.k12.nc.us
East Mooresville IS 700/4-6
1711 Landis Hwy 28115 704-658-2700
Tom Miller, prin. Fax 799-2580
Mooresville IS 600/4-6
1438 Coddle Creek Rd 28115 704-658-2680
Julie Morrow, prin. Fax 799-2965
Mooresville MS 800/7-8
233 Kistler Farm Rd 28115 704-658-2720
Rick Reynolds, prin. Fax 664-5101
Park View ES 600/PK-3
217 W McNeely Ave 28115 704-658-2550
Dr. Crystal Hill, prin. Fax 664-7935
Rocky River ES PK-3
483 Rocky River Rd 28115 704-658-2740
Felicia Burgess, prin.
South ES 700/PK-3
839 S Magnolia St 28115 704-658-2650
Debbie Marsh, prin. Fax 664-5103

Harbor Christian Academy 50/K-1
433 Williamson Rd 28117 704-663-2254
Bill Heard, prin.
Mooresville Christian Academy 100/K-12
PO Box 114 28115 704-663-4690
Janet Moore, prin. Fax 663-0272
St. Mark Lutheran K 100/PK-K
454 Fieldstone Rd 28115 704-664-2009

Moravian Falls, Wilkes, Pop. 1,736
Wilkes County SD
Supt. — See North Wilkesboro
Central Wilkes MS 800/6-8
3541 S NC Highway 16 28654 336-667-7453
Jodi Weatherman, prin. Fax 667-5825
Moravian Falls ES 300/PK-5
PO Box 818 28654 336-838-4077
Ramona Hemric, prin. Fax 838-8450

Morehead City, Carteret, Pop. 8,847
Carteret County SD
Supt. — See Beaufort
Morehead City ES at Camp Glenn 300/4-5
3316 Arendell St 28557 252-726-1131
Dr. Rita Mullins, prin. Fax 726-5896
Morehead City MS 500/6-8
400 Barbour Rd 28557 252-726-1126
Suzanne Kreuser, prin. Fax 726-4980
Morehead City PS 700/PK-3
4409 Country Club Rd 28557 252-247-2448
Greg Guthrie, prin. Fax 247-3127

St. Egbert S 100/K-5
1705 Evans St 28557 252-726-3418
Lesley Ferguson, prin. Fax 727-0150

Morganton, Burke, Pop. 17,041
Burke County SD 14,400/PK-12
PO Box 989 28680 828-439-4312
Rick Sherrill, supt. Fax 439-4314
www.burke.k12.nc.us
Chesterfield ES 300/PK-5
2142 Pax Hill Rd 28655 828-437-3026
Darryl Corley, prin. Fax 433-4806
Forest Hill ES 400/PK-5
304 Ann St 28655 828-437-5906
Deborah Kendall, prin. Fax 430-9323
Glen Alpine ES 600/PK-5
302 London St 28655 828-584-0661
Leicha San Miguel, prin. Fax 584-6669
Hillcrest ES 200/PK-5
201 Tennessee St 28655 828-437-4258
Shanda McFarlin, prin. Fax 437-6311
Johnson MS 600/6-8
701 Lenoir Rd 28655 828-430-7340
Todd Sudderth, prin. Fax 430-4801
Liberty MS 600/6-8
529 Enola Rd 28655 828-437-1330
Angela Williams, prin. Fax 432-2124
Mountain View ES 300/PK-5
106 Alphabet Ln 28655 828-437-1584
Jennifer Hawkins, prin. Fax 437-3879
Mull ES 400/PK-5
1140 Old NC 18 28655 828-437-5785
Jill King, prin. Fax 437-8325
Oak Hill ES 500/PK-5
2363 NC 181 28655 828-433-1533
Kathy Amos, prin. Fax 430-9356
Salem ES 600/PK-5
1329 Salem Rd 28655 828-437-5901
Jan Crump, prin. Fax 437-8419
Table Rock MS 700/6-8
1581 NC 126 28655 828-437-5212
Sharon Colaw, prin. Fax 439-5702
Young ES 500/PK-5
325 Conley Rd 28655 828-584-0632
Larry Putnam, prin. Fax 584-1463
Other Schools – See Connellys Springs, Drexel, Hickory, Hildebran, Rutherford College, Valdese

Morganton Christian Academy 100/PK-12
201 Believers Way 28655 828-437-1897
Dan Qurollo, prin. Fax 439-8948
Silver Creek Adventist S 50/K-8
2195 Jamestown Rd 28655 828-584-3010
Wanda Beck, prin.

Morrisville, Wake, Pop. 12,192
Wake County SD
Supt. — See Raleigh
Cedar Fork ES 600/K-5
1050 Town Hall Dr 27560 919-388-5240
Kathleen Marynak, prin. Fax 462-6824
Morrisville ES 700/K-5
1519 Morrisville Pkwy 27560 919-460-3400
Robin Swaim, prin. Fax 460-3410

Morven, Anson, Pop. 563
Anson County SD
Supt. — See Wadesboro
Morven ES 300/PK-6
6715 US Highway 52 S 28119 704-851-9306
Marilynn Bennett, prin. Fax 851-9308

Mount Airy, Surry, Pop. 8,454
Mt. Airy CSD 1,800/PK-12
130 Rawley Ave 27030 336-786-8355
Darrin Hartness, supt. Fax 786-7553
www.mtairy.k12.nc.us
Jones ES 400/3-5
2170 Riverside Dr 27030 336-786-4131
Chad Beasley, prin. Fax 719-2339
Mount Airy MS 400/6-8
249 Hamburg St 27030 336-789-9021
Joey Hearl, prin. Fax 789-6074
Tharrington ES 400/PK-2
315 Culbert St 27030 336-789-9046
Lydia Lovell, prin. Fax 789-6068

Surry County SD
Supt. — See Dobson
Flat Rock ES 400/PK-5
1539 E Pine St 27030 336-786-2910
Diane Beane, prin. Fax 786-5058
Franklin ES 600/PK-5
519 S Franklin Rd 27030 336-786-2459
Terry Marcum, prin. Fax 786-2835
Gentry MS 400/6-8
1915 W Pine St 27030 336-786-4155
Tom Hemmings, prin. Fax 786-6863
Meadowview MS 400/6-8
1282 Mckinney Rd 27030 336-789-0276
Angela Carson, prin. Fax 789-0449
White Plains ES 400/PK-5
710 Cadle Ford Rd 27030 336-320-3434
Sandra Scott, prin. Fax 320-3090

White Plains Christian S 100/K-12
609 Old Highway 601 27030 336-786-9585

Mount Gilead, Montgomery, Pop. 1,387
Montgomery County SD
Supt. — See Troy
Mount Gilead ES 400/K-5
PO Box 308 27306 910-439-5411
Charles Delforge, prin. Fax 439-1074
West MS 500/6-8
129 NC Highway 109 S 27306 910-572-9378
Wayne Talley, prin. Fax 572-2114

Mount Holly, Gaston, Pop. 9,676
Gaston County SD
Supt. — See Gastonia
Mount Holly MS 700/6-8
124 S Hawthorne St 28120 704-827-4811
Judy Moore, prin. Fax 822-1049
Pinewood ES 600/PK-5
1925 N Main St 28120 704-827-2236
Kristin Kiser, prin. Fax 822-0227
Rankin ES 700/PK-5
301 W Central Ave 28120 704-827-7266
Ronald Foulk, prin. Fax 827-9116

Mount Olive, Wayne, Pop. 4,442
Duplin County SD
Supt. — See Kenansville
North Duplin ES 600/PK-6
157 N Duplin School Rd 28365 919-658-2931
Ben Sautler, prin. Fax 658-2983

Wayne County SD
Supt. — See Goldsboro
Carver ES 700/K-5
400 Old 7 Springs Rd 28365 919-658-7330
Debbie Ogburn, prin. Fax 658-7326
Mount Olive MS 300/6-8
309 Wooten St 28365 919-658-7320
Gail Sasser, prin. Fax 658-7325

Mount Pleasant, Cabarrus, Pop. 1,429
Cabarrus County SD
Supt. — See Concord
Mount Pleasant ES 900/K-5
8555 North Dr 28124 704-436-6534
Corey Cochran, prin. Fax 436-2710
Mount Pleasant MS 700/6-8
8325 Highway 49 N 28124 704-436-9302
Sam Treadaway, prin. Fax 436-6112

Mount Ulla, Rowan
Rowan-Salisbury County SD
Supt. — See Salisbury
Mount Ulla ES 300/K-5
13155 NC Highway 801 28125 704-278-2750
Lea Anne Thomas, prin. Fax 278-1901

Moyock, Currituck
Currituck County SD
Supt. — See Currituck
Moyock ES 500/K-5
255 Tulls Creek Rd 27958 252-435-6521
Whitney Bisbing, prin. Fax 435-6351
Moyock MS 500/6-8
216 Survey Rd 27958 252-435-2566
Virginia Arrington, prin. Fax 435-2576

Murfreesboro, Hertford, Pop. 2,221
Hertford County SD
Supt. — See Winton
Hertford County MS 600/7-8
1850 NC Highway 11 27855 252-398-4091
Carson Watford, prin. Fax 398-5570
Riverview ES 600/PK-6
236 US Highway 158 Bus 27855 252-398-4862
Patty Hardy, prin. Fax 398-3600

Murphy, Cherokee, Pop. 1,565
Cherokee County SD 3,800/PK-12
911 Andrews Rd 28906 828-837-2722
Dr. Stephen Lane, supt. Fax 837-5799
www.cherokee.k12.nc.us
Hiwassee Dam Union S 200/PK-8
337 Blue Eagle Cir 28906 828-644-5115
Tom Graham, prin. Fax 644-9463
Martins Creek S 300/PK-8
1459 Tobe Stalcup Rd 28906 828-837-2831
Arnold Mathews, prin. Fax 837-0023
Murphy ES 500/PK-5
315 Valley River Ave 28906 828-837-2424
Cynthia Bean, prin. Fax 837-3887
Murphy MS 300/6-8
65 Middle School Dr 28906 828-837-0160
Barry McClure, prin. Fax 837-5814
Peachtree ES 200/PK-5
30 Upper Peachtree Rd 28906 828-837-2479
Kim Gibson, prin. Fax 837-6494
Ranger S 400/PK-8
101 Hardy Truett Rd 28906 828-644-5111
Michael Penninger, prin. Fax 644-9828
Other Schools – See Andrews, Marble

Murphy Adventist Christian S 50/PK-12
PO Box 620 28906 828-837-5857
Joan Bilbo, prin. Fax 835-9300

Nags Head, Dare, Pop. 3,076
Dare County SD 4,500/PK-12
PO Box 1508 27959 252-480-8888
Dr. Sue Burgess, supt. Fax 480-8889
www.dare.k12.nc.us
Nags Head ES 500/PK-5
3100 S Wrightsville Ave 27959 252-480-8880
Adrienne Palma, prin. Fax 480-8881
Other Schools – See Buxton, Kill Devil Hills, Kitty Hawk, Manteo

Nashville, Nash, Pop. 4,477
Nash-Rocky Mount SD 17,300/PK-12
930 Eastern Ave 27856 252-459-5220
Richard McMahon, supt. Fax 459-6403
www.nrms.k12.nc.us
Cedar Grove ES 300/PK-5
8967 Cedar Grove School Rd 27856 252-462-2830
Jerry Smith, prin. Fax 459-5347
Nash Central MS 700/6-8
1638 S 1st St 27856 252-459-5292
Lorenza Morgan, prin. Fax 459-5297
Nashville ES 800/PK-5
209 E Virginia Ave 27856 252-459-1195
Beth Lucas, prin. Fax 459-1135
Other Schools – See Bailey, Battleboro, Elm City, Middlesex, Red Oak, Rocky Mount, Spring Hope, Whitakers

Nebo, McDowell
McDowell County SD
Supt. — See Marion
Nebo ES 600/K-6
254 Nebo School Rd 28761 828-652-4737
Joyce Poplin, prin. Fax 652-8404

New Bern, Craven, Pop. 24,106
Craven County SD 14,700/PK-12
3600 Trent Rd 28562 252-514-6300
Larry Moser, supt. Fax 514-6351
www.craven.k12.nc.us

Bangert ES 500/K-5
3712 Canterbury Rd 28562 252-514-6415
Kim Sarver, prin. Fax 514-6418
Barber ES 400/PK-5
1700 Cobb St 28560 252-514-6460
Herman Greene, prin. Fax 514-6464
Bridgeton ES 500/K-5
230 Branch Canal Rd 28560 252-514-6425
Renee Whitford, prin. Fax 514-6428
Brinson Memorial ES 1,000/K-5
319 Neuse Forrest Ave 28560 252-514-6431
Todd Bradley, prin. Fax 514-6434
Creekside ES K-5
2790 Landscape Dr 28562 252-514-4360
Karen Wood, prin. Fax 514-4365
Fields MS 600/6-8
2000 Dr M L King Jr Blvd 28560 252-514-6438
Thomasine Hassell, prin. Fax 514-6443
MacDonald MS 800/6-8
3127 Elizabeth Ave 28562 252-514-6450
Deborah Langhans, prin. Fax 514-6456
Oaks Road ES 500/K-5
2811 Oaks Rd 28560 252-514-6475
Sudie Way, prin. Fax 514-6478
Quinn ES 500/PK-5
4275 Dr ML King Jr Blvd 28562 252-514-6420
Curtis Gatlin, prin. Fax 514-6423
Trent Park ES 400/K-5
2500 Educational Dr 28562 252-514-6481
Cheryl Wilson, prin. Fax 514-6485
West Craven MS 900/6-8
515 NW Crvn Mddle School Rd 28562 252-514-6488
Renee Franklin, prin. Fax 514-6491
Other Schools – See Cove City, Havelock, Vanceboro

Ruths Chapel Christian S 600/K-12
2709 Oaks Rd 28560 252-638-1297
Sherry Myers, prin. Fax 638-5770
St. Paul Education Center 200/PK-8
3007 Country Club Rd 28562 252-633-0100
Monette Mahoney, prin. Fax 633-4457

Newland, Avery, Pop. 686
Avery County SD 2,400/PK-12
PO Box 1360 28657 828-733-6006
Dr. Keith Eades, supt. Fax 733-8943
www.averyschools.net
Avery County MS 300/6-8
102 Old Montezuma Rd 28657 828-733-0145
David Wright, prin. Fax 733-3506
Newland ES 300/PK-5
PO Box 160 28657 828-733-4911
Tammy Beach, prin. Fax 733-1402
Riverside ES 200/PK-5
8020 S US 19E Hwy 28657 828-765-9414
Ricky Ward, prin. Fax 765-0922
Other Schools – See Banner Elk, Crossnore, Elk Park

New London, Stanly, Pop. 320
Stanly County SD
Supt. — See Albemarle
Kendall Valley S 500/K-8
36605 Old Salisbury Rd 28127 704-983-5200
Rhonda Gainey, prin. Fax 983-5215
New London Choice MS 300/6-8
215 N Main St 28127 704-463-7962
Sandra Carter, prin. Fax 463-5340

Christ the King Christian Academy 100/K-12
PO Box 279 28127 704-463-7285
Rev. John Kahl, prin. Fax 463-7285

Newport, Carteret, Pop. 3,840
Carteret County SD
Supt. — See Beaufort
Bogue Sound ES 400/K-5
3323 Highway 24 28570 252-393-1279
Terrie Beeson, prin. Fax 393-1379
Broad Creek MS 500/6-8
2382 Highway 24 28570 252-247-3135
Cathy Tomon, prin. Fax 247-5114
Newport ES 800/PK-5
219 Chatham St 28570 252-223-4201
Fax 223-4107
Newport MS 500/6-8
500 E Chatham St 28570 252-223-3482
Bud Lanning, prin. Fax 223-4914

Gramercy Christian S 200/K-12
8170 Highway 70 28570 252-223-4384
Vicki Bishop, hdmstr. Fax 223-5199

Newton, Catawba, Pop. 13,016
Catawba County SD 17,200/PK-12
PO Box 1010 28658 828-464-8333
Tim Markley, supt. Fax 464-0925
www.catawbaschools.net/
Balls Creek ES 600/PK-6
2620 Balls Creek Rd 28658 828-464-4766
Lisa Thompson, prin. Fax 464-5396
Blackburn ES 700/K-6
4377 W NC 10 Hwy 28658 704-462-1344
Brian Hefner, prin. Fax 462-4496
Jacobs Fork MS 600/7-8
3431 Plateau Rd 28658 704-462-1827
Jeff Isenhour, prin. Fax 462-1600
Startown ES 700/PK-6
4119 Startown Rd 28658 828-464-1257
Barbara Bell, prin. Fax 465-6568
Other Schools – See Catawba, Claremont, Conover, Hickory, Maiden, Sherrills Ford, Vale

Newton-Conover CSD 2,900/PK-12
605 N Ashe Ave 28658 828-464-3191
Dr. Barry Redmond, supt. Fax 466-0063
www.nccs.k12.nc.us
Newton-Conover MS 700/6-8
221 W 26th St 28658 828-464-4221
Jimmy Elliott, prin. Fax 464-5238
South Newton ES 400/PK-5
306 W I St 28658 828-464-4061
Shelly Cornwell, prin. Fax 464-7528
Thornton ES 400/PK-5
301 W 18th St 28658 828-464-2631
Tammy Brown, prin. Fax 464-5891
Other Schools – See Conover

Newton Grove, Sampson, Pop. 623
Sampson County SD
Supt. — See Clinton
Hobbton ES 500/PK-5
12361 Hobbton Hwy 28366 910-594-0392
Rhonda Spell, prin. Fax 594-1610
Hobbton MS 400/6-8
12081 Hobbton Hwy 28366 910-594-1420
Kevin Hunter, prin. Fax 594-0049

Norlina, Warren, Pop. 1,060
Warren County SD
Supt. — See Warrenton
Northside ES 400/K-5
164 Elementary Ave 27563 252-456-2656
Jamar Perry, prin. Fax 456-2043

Norlina Christian S 100/PK-12
PO Box 757 27563 252-456-3385
Abidan Shah, admin. Fax 456-3354

North Wilkesboro, Wilkes, Pop. 4,204
Wilkes County SD 10,300/PK-12
613 Cherry St 28659 336-667-1121
Dr. Stephen Laws, supt. Fax 667-0871
www.wilkes.k12.nc.us
Mulberry ES 500/PK-5
190 Mulberry School Rd 28659 336-670-2825
Rebecca Mastin, prin. Fax 670-9783
North Wilkesboro ES 300/PK-5
200 Flint Hill Rd 28659 336-838-2872
Jeffery Johnson, prin. Fax 667-6863
North Wilkes MS 600/6-8
2776 Yellow Banks Rd 28659 336-696-2724
Westly Wood, prin. Fax 696-4183
Wright ES 500/PK-5
200 CC Wright School Rd 28659 336-838-5513
Lisa Joies, prin. Fax 667-6099
Other Schools – See Boomer, Elkin, Ferguson, Hays, Millers Creek, Moravian Falls, Roaring River, Ronda, Traphill, Wilkesboro

Montessori Learning Center of Wilkes 50/PK-K
601 Boston Ave 28659 336-667-4356
Sharon Clem, prin. Fax 667-4356

Norwood, Stanly, Pop. 2,160
Stanly County SD
Supt. — See Albemarle
Aquadale ES 300/K-5
11707 NC 138 Hwy 28128 704-474-3212
Robert Patterson, prin. Fax 474-7209
Norwood ES 500/PK-5
PO Box 636 28128 704-474-3126
Chuck Isenhour, prin. Fax 474-5226
South Stanly MS 400/6-8
12492 Cottonville Rd 28128 704-474-5355
Daniel Goodman, prin. Fax 474-5579

Oakboro, Stanly, Pop. 1,180
Stanly County SD
Supt. — See Albemarle
Oakboro S 400/K-8
1244 N Main St 28129 704-485-3541
Debbie Oliver, prin. Fax 485-8422

Oak Ridge, Guilford, Pop. 4,196
Guilford County SD
Supt. — See Greensboro
Oak Ridge ES 800/PK-5
2050 Oak Ridge Rd 27310 336-643-8410
Ann Kraft, prin. Fax 643-8415

Ocracoke, Hyde
Hyde County SD
Supt. — See Swanquarter
Ocracoke S 100/K-12
PO Box 189 27960 252-928-3251
George Ortman, prin. Fax 928-5380

Old Fort, McDowell, Pop. 968
McDowell County SD
Supt. — See Marion
Old Fort ES 500/K-6
128 Mauney Ave 28762 828-668-7646
Charles Gaffigan, prin. Fax 668-4939

Olin, Iredell
Iredell-Statesville SD
Supt. — See Statesville
North Iredell MS 700/6-8
2467 Jennings Rd 28660 704-876-4802
Kelly Cooper, prin. Fax 876-6190

Olivia, Harnett
Harnett County SD
Supt. — See Lillington
Benhaven ES 600/K-5
PO Box 9 28368 919-499-4811
Brian Graham, prin. Fax 499-1401

Orrum, Robeson, Pop. 81
Robeson County SD
Supt. — See Lumberton
Orrum MS 400/5-8
PO Box 129 28369 910-628-6285
Chris Burton, prin. Fax 628-8408

Oxford, Granville, Pop. 8,530
Granville County SD 8,200/PK-12
101 Delacroix St 27565 919-693-4613
Timothy Farley, supt. Fax 693-7391
eclipse.gcs.k12.nc.us/
Credle ES 500/PK-5
223 College St 27565 919-693-9191
Tonya Thomas, prin. Fax 603-0047
Northern Granville MS 800/6-8
3144 Webb School Rd 27565 919-693-1483
Daniel Callaghan, prin. Fax 693-1716
Potter MS 200/6-8
200 Taylor St 27565 919-693-3914
Beth Cook, prin. Fax 693-2896
Toler-Oak Hill ES 200/PK-5
8176 NC Highway 96 27565 919-693-8935
Michael Allen, prin. Fax 693-4040
West Oxford ES 400/PK-5
412 Ivey Day Rd 27565 919-693-9161
Melody Wilson, prin. Fax 693-9163
Other Schools – See Butner, Creedmoor, Franklinton, Stovall

Pantego, Beaufort, Pop. 170

Terra Ceia Christian S 200/K-12
4428 Christian School Rd 27860 252-943-2485
Ken Leys, prin. Fax 943-2139

Parkton, Robeson, Pop. 432
Robeson County SD
Supt. — See Lumberton
Parkton S 600/PK-8
PO Box 189 28371 910-858-3951
Melinda Sellers, prin. Fax 858-0009

Patterson, Caldwell
Caldwell County SD
Supt. — See Lenoir
Happy Valley S 400/K-8
PO Box 130 28661 828-754-3496
Andy Puhl, prin. Fax 758-1044

Peachland, Anson, Pop. 537
Anson County SD
Supt. — See Wadesboro
Peachland-Polkton ES 500/K-6
9633 US Highway 74 W 28133 704-272-8061
Craig Wright, prin. Fax 272-9278

Pembroke, Robeson, Pop. 2,693
Robeson County SD
Supt. — See Lumberton
Pembroke ES 800/PK-5
PO Box 878 28372 910-521-4204
Tona Jacobs, prin. Fax 521-3510
Pembroke MS 700/6-8
PO Box 1148 28372 910-522-5013
Chris Clark, prin. Fax 522-1562
Shining Stars Preschool PK-PK
818 W 3rd St 28372 910-521-0559
Mary Schultz, prin. Fax 521-1784
Union Chapel ES 600/PK-6
4271 Union Chapel Rd 28372 910-521-4456
Virginia Emanuel, prin. Fax 521-4991

Pendleton, Northampton
Northampton County SD
Supt. — See Jackson
Hare ES 400/PK-4
479 Willis Hare Rd 27862 252-585-1900
Barbara Stephenson, prin. Fax 585-1616

Pfafftown, Forsyth
Winston-Salem/Forsyth SD
Supt. — See Winston Salem
Vienna ES 600/K-5
1975 Chickasha Dr 27040 336-945-5163
Patrick Mitze, prin. Fax 945-9506

Pikeville, Wayne, Pop. 709
Wayne County SD
Supt. — See Goldsboro
Northeast ES 700/K-5
4665 NC Highway 111 N 27863 919-705-6030
Gail Richards, prin. Fax 731-5957
Northwest ES 900/K-5
1769 Pikeville Princeton Hw 27863 919-242-3419
Theresa Cox, prin. Fax 242-3714

Pilot Mountain, Surry, Pop. 1,277
Surry County SD
Supt. — See Dobson
Pilot Mountain MS 500/6-8
202 Friends St 27041 336-368-2641
Neil Atkins, prin. Fax 368-3935
Westfield ES 600/PK-5
273 Jessup Grove Church Rd 27041 336-351-2745
Tracey Lewis, prin. Fax 351-4467

Pine Hall, Stokes
Stokes County SD
Supt. — See Danbury
Pine Hall ES 200/PK-5
1400 Pine Hall Rd 27042 336-427-3689
Amy Musten, prin. Fax 427-4944

Pinehurst, Moore, Pop. 11,437
Moore County SD
Supt. — See Carthage
Academy Heights ES 300/K-5
PO Box 579 28370 910-295-5610
Dale Buie, prin. Fax 295-8338
Pinehurst ES 700/K-5
PO Box 729 28370 910-295-6969
Sara Bigley, prin. Fax 295-1027

Sacred Heart ECC 50/PK-PK
PO Box 5174 28374 910-295-3514
Jan Gatti, dir. Fax 255-0299

Pine Level, Johnston, Pop. 1,450
Johnston County SD
Supt. — See Smithfield
Micro-Pine Level ES 500/K-5
PO Box 69 27568 919-965-3323
Angie Jacobs, prin. Fax 965-6723

Pinetops, Edgecombe, Pop. 1,320
Edgecombe County SD
Supt. — See Tarboro
Carver ES 600/PK-5
PO Box 48 27864 252-827-2116
William Ellis, prin. Fax 827-2814
South Edgecombe MS 400/6-8
230 Pinetops Crisp Rd 27864 252-827-5083
William Grady, prin. Fax 827-2811

Pinetown, Beaufort
Beaufort County SD
Supt. — See Washington
Northeast S 700/PK-8
21000 US Highway 264 E 27865 252-943-6545
Charles Clark, prin. Fax 943-9160

Pineville, Mecklenburg, Pop. 3,650
Charlotte/Mecklenburg County SD
Supt. — See Charlotte
Pineville ES 700/K-5
210 Lowry St 28134 980-343-3920
Brian Doerer, prin. Fax 343-3925
Sterling Paideia Academy 600/K-5
9601 China Grove Church Rd 28134 980-343-3636
Nancy Guzman, prin. Fax 343-3743

Piney Creek, Alleghany
Alleghany County SD
Supt. — See Sparta
Piney Creek S 200/PK-8
559 Piney Creek School Rd 28663 336-359-2988
Mike Edwards, prin. Fax 359-8246

Pink Hill, Lenoir, Pop. 541
Lenoir County SD
Supt. — See Kinston
Pink Hill ES 500/K-5
2666 HC Turner Rd 28572 252-568-4176
Tina Hinson, prin. Fax 568-6144

Pinnacle, Stokes
Stokes County SD
Supt. — See Danbury
Pinnacle ES 300/PK-5
1095 Surry Line Rd 27043 336-368-2990
Robin Layman, prin. Fax 368-5107

Surry County SD
Supt. — See Dobson
Shoals ES 400/K-5
1800 Shoals Rd 27043 336-325-2518
Eric Riggs, prin. Fax 325-2143

Pittsboro, Chatham, Pop. 2,452
Chatham County SD 7,600/PK-12
PO Box 128 27312 919-542-3626
Robert Logan, supt. Fax 542-1380
www.chatham.k12.nc.us
Harrison S 700/K-8
2655 Hamlet Chapel Rd 27312 919-967-9925
Janice Frazier, prin. Fax 967-5844
Horton MS 300/5-8
PO Box 639 27312 919-542-2303
Mattie Smith, prin. Fax 542-7099
Pittsboro ES 500/K-4
375 Pittsboro School Rd 27312 919-542-3987
Dale Minge, prin. Fax 542-1146
Other Schools – See Bennett, Bonlee, Chapel Hill, Goldston, Moncure, Siler City

Pleasant Garden, Guilford, Pop. 4,911
Guilford County SD
Supt. — See Greensboro
Pleasant Garden ES 600/PK-5
4833 Pleasant Garden Rd 27313 336-674-4321
Sarah Matthews, prin. Fax 674-4320

Plymouth, Washington, Pop. 3,964
Washington County SD 2,200/PK-12
802 Washington St 27962 252-793-5171
Julius Walker, supt. Fax 793-5062
www.washingtonco.k12.nc.us/
Pines ES 700/PK-4
3177 US Highway 64 E 27962 252-793-1137
Robert Ricketson, prin. Fax 793-1105
Other Schools – See Creswell, Roper

Pollocksville, Jones, Pop. 263
Jones County SD
Supt. — See Trenton
Pollocksville ES 200/PK-6
300 Trent St 28573 252-224-8071
Jeannie Smith, prin. Fax 224-0290

Poplar Branch, Currituck
Currituck County SD
Supt. — See Currituck
Griggs ES 500/K-5
261 Poplar Branch Rd 27965 252-453-2700
Sharon Lewis, prin. Fax 453-2132

Princeton, Johnston, Pop. 1,200
Johnston County SD
Supt. — See Smithfield
Princeton ES 700/K-5
650 Holts Pond Rd 27569 919-936-0755
Kim Wellons, prin. Fax 936-0750

Princeville, Edgecombe, Pop. 1,670
Edgecombe County SD
Supt. — See Tarboro
Princeville Montessori ES 400/PK-5
306 Walston St 27886 252-823-4718
Amy Marshall-Brown, prin. Fax 641-5702

Providence, Caswell
Caswell County SD
Supt. — See Yanceyville
North ES 500/PK-5
10390 NC Highway 86 N 27315 336-388-2222
Tina Clayton, prin. Fax 388-5522

Raeford, Hoke, Pop. 3,594
Hoke County SD 7,400/PK-12
PO Box 370 28376 910-875-4106
Dr. Freddie Williamson, supt. Fax 875-3362
www.hcs.k12.nc.us
East Hoke MS 900/6-8
4702 Fayetteville Rd 28376 910-875-5048
Erica Fortenberry, prin. Fax 875-9307
McLauchlin ES 400/PK-5
326 N Main St 28376 910-875-8721
Mike Modlin, prin. Fax 904-6868
Rockfish Hoke ES 600/PK-5
6251 Rockfish Rd 28376 910-875-9343
Debbie Dowless, prin. Fax 875-3761
Scurlock ES 600/PK-5
775 Rockfish Rd 28376 910-875-4182
Dawn Ramsuer, prin. Fax 875-0292
Steed ES K-5
800 Phillipi Church Rd 28376 910-875-1125
Kimberly Gray, prin. Fax 875-2274
Upchurch ES 800/PK-5
730 Turnpike Rd 28376 910-875-1574
Betty Brum, prin. Fax 904-0624
West Hoke ES 500/PK-5
6050 Turnpike Rd 28376 910-875-2584
Jackie Samuels, prin. Fax 875-7312
West Hoke MS 800/6-8
200 NC Highway 211 28376 910-875-3411
John Teal, prin. Fax 875-0332
Other Schools – See Lumber Bridge, Red Springs

Raleigh, Wake, Pop. 341,530
Wake County SD 126,700/PK-12
PO Box 28041 27611 919-850-1600
Dr. Del Burns, supt. Fax 850-1819
www.wcpss.net
Baileywick Road ES 600/K-5
9425 Baileywick Rd 27615 919-518-0090
Kathy Hartenstine, prin. Fax 518-0101
Barwell Road ES K-5
3925 Barwell Rd 27610 919-661-5405
Dr. Annice Williams, prin. Fax 662-2111
Brassfield ES 700/K-5
2001 Brassfield Rd 27614 919-870-4080
Pamela Kinsey-Barker, prin. Fax 676-5022
Brentwood ES 500/K-5
3426 Ingram Dr 27604 919-850-8720
Pamela Johnson, prin. Fax 850-8728
Brier Creek ES 500/K-5
9801 Brier Creek Pkwy 27617 919-484-4747
Isobel Harris, prin. Fax 484-4724
Brooks ES 500/K-5
700 Northbrook Dr 27609 919-881-1350
Felecia Locklear, prin. Fax 881-1349
Bugg ES 500/PK-5
825 Cooper Rd 27610 919-250-4750
Mary Page, prin. Fax 250-4753
Carnage MS 1,100/6-8
1425 Carnage Dr 27610 919-856-7600
Delores Fogg, prin. Fax 856-7619
Carroll MS 600/6-8
4520 Six Forks Rd 27609 919-881-1370
Mary Rich, prin. Fax 881-5016
Centennial MS 600/6-8
1900 Main Campus Dr 27606 919-233-4217
Edye Bryant, prin. Fax 233-4268
Combs ES 800/K-5
2001 Lorimer Rd 27606 919-233-4300
Muriel Summers, prin. Fax 233-4042
Conn ES 600/PK-5
1220 Brookside Dr 27604 919-856-7637
Diann Kearney, prin. Fax 856-7643
Daniels MS 1,000/6-8
2816 Oberlin Rd 27608 919-881-4860
Stephen Mares, prin. Fax 881-1418
Dillard Drive ES 700/K-5
5018 Dillard Dr 27606 919-233-4200
Sylvia Wilkins, prin. Fax 854-1631
Dillard Drive MS 1,000/6-8
5200 Dillard Dr 27606 919-233-4228
Teresa Abron, prin. Fax 854-1615
Douglas ES 500/K-5
600 Ortega Rd 27609 919-881-4894
Donna Spivey, prin. Fax 881-4896
Durant Road ES 1,000/PK-5
9901 Durant Rd 27614 919-870-4220
Teresa Winstead, prin. Fax 870-4218
Durant Road MS 1,100/6-8
10401 Durant Rd 27614 919-870-4098
Robert E. Smith, prin. Fax 518-0021
East Millbrook MS 1,100/6-8
3801 Spring Forest Rd 27616 919-850-8755
Larry Livengood, prin. Fax 850-8770
East Wake MS 900/6-8
2700 Old Milburnie Rd 27604 919-266-8500
Bradford Shackelford, prin. Fax 266-8506
Forest Pines ES 500/PK-5
11455 Forest Pines Dr 27614 919-562-6262
Freda Cole, prin. Fax 562-6260
Fox Road ES 800/K-5
7101 Fox Rd 27616 919-850-8845
Melanie J. Rhoads, prin. Fax 850-8854
Fuller ES 600/K-5
806 Calloway Dr 27610 919-856-7625
Christopher Scott, prin. Fax 856-7633
Green ES 600/K-5
5307 Six Forks Rd 27609 919-881-1390
Shelly Watson, prin. Fax 881-1398
Harris Creek ES 900/K-5
3829 Forestville Rd 27616 919-217-5100
Vicki Perry, prin. Fax 217-3273
Hilburn Drive ES 800/K-5
7100 Hilburn Dr 27613 919-571-6800
Gregory Ford, prin. Fax 571-6804
Hunter ES 800/K-5
1018 E Davie St 27601 919-856-7676
David Schwenker, prin. Fax 856-7680
Jeffreys Grove ES 600/PK-5
6119 Creedmoor Rd 27612 919-881-4910
Jacob Bryant, prin. Fax 881-4911
Joyner ES 500/PK-5
2300 Lowden St 27608 919-856-7650
Christopher Knott, prin. Fax 856-7661
Lacy ES 700/K-5
1820 Ridge Rd 27607 919-881-4920
Dr. Marcia Alford, prin. Fax 881-1434
Lead Mine ES 600/K-5
8301 Old Lead Mine Rd 27615 919-870-4120
Gary Baird, prin. Fax 870-4122
Leesville Road ES 900/K-5
8401 Leesville Rd 27613 919-870-4200
Cecilia Chapman, prin. Fax 870-4188
Leesville Road MS 1,300/6-8
8405 Leesville Rd 27613 919-870-4141
Patti Hamler, prin. Fax 870-4166
Ligon MS 1,100/6-8
706 E Lenoir St 27601 919-856-7929
Scott Lyons, prin. Fax 856-3745
Lynn Road ES 500/K-5
1601 Lynn Rd 27612 919-870-4074
Eloise Sheats, prin. Fax 870-4094
Martin MS 1,000/6-8
1701 Ridge Rd 27607 919-881-4970
Wade Martin, prin. Fax 881-1416
Millbrook ES 700/PK-5
1520 E Millbrook Rd 27609 919-850-8700
Paula Trantham, prin. Fax 850-8709
Moore Square MS 500/6-8
301 S Person St 27601 919-664-5737
David Kershner, prin. Fax 856-8194
North Forest Pines Drive ES K-5
11501 Forest Pines Dr 27614 919-570-2220
Christopher McCabe, prin. Fax 570-2219
North Ridge ES 800/K-5
7120 Harps Mill Rd 27615 919-870-4100
Terri Allen, prin. Fax 870-4051
Oak Grove ES 900/K-5
10401 Penny Rd 27606 919-387-4490
Beth Jarman, prin. Fax 387-4496
Olds ES 300/K-5
204 Dixie Trl 27607 919-856-7699
Dr. Mary Wheeler, prin. Fax 856-2989
Partnership ES 300/K-5
601 Devereux St 27605 919-856-8200
Mark Kenjarski, prin. Fax 856-8234
Pleasant Union ES 700/K-5
1900 Plsant Union Church Rd 27614 919-870-4230
Kevin Biles, prin. Fax 870-4229
Poe ES 400/PK-5
400 Peyton St 27610 919-250-4777
Sally Reynolds, prin. Fax 250-4774
Powell ES 500/K-5
1130 Marlborough Rd 27610 919-856-7737
James Sposato, prin. Fax 856-7749
River Bend ES 500/K-5
6710 Perry Creek Rd 27616 919-431-8010
Dr. Lois Hart, prin. Fax 431-8047
River Oaks MS 50/6-8
4700 New Bern Ave 27610 919-231-5600
Carolyn Younce, prin. Fax 231-5607
Root ES 500/K-5
3202 Northhampton St 27609 919-881-4940
James Mack, prin. Fax 881-1427
Smith ES 500/PK-5
10225 Chambers Rd 27603 919-662-2458
Christopher Lassiter, prin. Fax 662-2948
Stough ES 500/K-5
4210 Edwards Mill Rd 27612 919-881-4950
Cynthia Keech, prin. Fax 881-1422
Swift Creek ES 500/K-5
5601 Tryon Rd 27606 919-233-4320
James Argent, prin. Fax 233-4344
Sycamore Creek ES K-5
10921 Leesville Rd 27613 919-841-4333
Kristen Faircloth, prin. Fax 841-4337
Underwood ES 500/K-5
1614 Glenwood Ave 27608 919-856-7663
Jacqueline Jordan, prin. Fax 856-7981
Vance ES 500/K-5
8808 Old Stage Rd 27603 919-662-2472
Donald Rose, prin. Fax 662-2498
Wakefield ES 1,100/K-5
2400 Wakefield Pines Dr 27614 919-562-3555
Sylvia Faulk, prin. Fax 562-3553
Wakefield MS 1,300/6-8
2300 Wakefield Pines Dr 27614 919-562-3500
Tripp Crayton, prin. Fax 562-3527
Washington ES 600/PK-5
1000 Fayetteville St 27601 919-856-7960
Peggy Beasley-Rodger, prin. Fax 856-7985
West Millbrook MS 1,100/6-8
8115 Strickland Rd 27615 919-870-4050
Anthony Muttillo, prin. Fax 870-4064
Wilburn ES 1,000/K-5
3707 Marsh Creek Rd 27604 919-850-8738
Jennifer Carnes, prin. Fax 850-8780
Wildwood Forest ES 700/K-5
8401 Wildwood Forest Dr 27616 919-713-0600
Gretta Dula, prin. Fax 713-0615
Wiley ES 400/K-5
301 Saint Marys St 27605 919-856-7723
Erin Kershner, prin. Fax 856-2956

Yates Mill ES 600/K-5
5993 Yates Mill Pond Rd 27606 919-233-4244
Dr. Lynn Williams, prin. Fax 233-4241
York ES 600/K-5
5201 Brookhaven Dr 27612 919-881-4960
Sandra Barefoot, prin. Fax 881-1338
Other Schools – See Apex, Cary, Fuquay Varina, Garner, Holly Springs, Knightdale, Morrisville, Rolesville, Wake Forest, Wendell, Willow Spring, Zebulon

---

Adventist Christian Academy of Raleigh 50/K-9
4805 Dillard Dr 27606 919-233-1300
Wanda Williams, prin. Fax 233-1305
Al-Iman S 200/K-8
3020 Ligon St 27607 919-821-1699
Mussarut Jabeen, prin. Fax 821-2988
Body of Christ Christian Academy 50/K-4
4501 Spring Forest Rd 27616 919-872-3622
Edward Davis, admin. Fax 872-7661
Cathedral S 300/PK-8
204 Hillsborough St 27603 919-832-4711
Donna Moss, prin. Fax 832-8329
Fletcher Academy 100/1-12
400 Cedarview Ct 27609 919-782-5082
Junell Blaylock, prin. Fax 782-5980
Franciscan S 700/K-8
10000 Saint Francis Dr 27613 919-847-8205
Jennifer Bigelow, prin. Fax 847-9558
Friendship Christian S 300/PK-12
5510 Falls of Neuse Rd 27609 919-872-2133
Fax 872-7451
Gethsemane SDA Church S 50/K-8
2523 Sanderford Rd 27610 919-833-1844
GRACE Christian S 300/PK-6
801 Buck Jones Rd 27606 919-783-6618
Kathie Thompson, prin. Fax 783-0856
Hillel Day S 50/PK-PK
7400 Falls of Neuse Rd 27615 919-846-2449
Elie Estrin, dir. Fax 847-3142
Montessori S of Raleigh 500/PK-9
7005 Lead Mine Rd 27615 919-848-1545
Meg Thomas, hdmstr. Fax 848-9611
Neuse Baptist Christian S 200/K-12
8700 Capital Blvd 27616 919-876-0990
Fax 876-3168
North Raleigh Christian Academy 1,200/K-12
7300 Perry Creek Rd 27616 919-573-7900
Dr. S.L. Sherrill, supt. Fax 573-7901
Our Lady of Lourdes S 500/K-8
2710 Overbrook Dr 27608 919-861-4610
Robert Scripko, prin. Fax 861-4620
Raleigh Christian Academy 500/PK-12
2110 Trawick Rd 27604 919-872-2215
Dwight Ausley, admin. Fax 861-1000
Raleigh S 300/K-5
1141 Raleigh School Dr 27607 919-546-0788
Harriet Lasher, hdmstr. Fax 546-9045
Ravenscroft S 1,200/PK-12
7409 Falls of Neuse Rd 27615 919-847-0900
Doreen Kelly, hdmstr. Fax 846-2371
Rejoice Academy 100/K-12
3510 Edwards Mill Rd 27612 919-848-8585
Dr. Sue Romano, admin. Fax 848-0189
St. David's S 500/K-12
3400 White Oak Rd 27609 919-782-3331
Kevin Lockerbie, hdmstr. Fax 571-3330
St. Francis of Assisi ECC 200/PK-PK
11401 Leesville Rd 27613 919-847-8205
Nancy Bourke, dir. Fax 870-1790
St. Joseph Roman Catholic Preschool 50/PK-PK
2817 Poole Rd 27610 919-231-4545
Marjorie Shaughnessy, dir. Fax 231-9884
St. Raphael Catholic S 500/K-8
5815 Falls of Neuse Rd 27609 919-865-5750
Barry Thomas, prin. Fax 865-5751
St. Raphael ECC 200/PK-PK
5801 Falls of Neuse Rd 27609 919-865-5717
Carrie Griffith, dir. Fax 865-5701
St. Timothy's S 500/K-8
PO Box 17787 27619 919-787-3011
Michael Bailey, prin. Fax 787-1131
Trinity Academy of Raleigh 300/K-12
10224 Baileywick Rd 27613 919-786-0114
Dr. Robert Littlejohn, prin. Fax 786-0621
Upper Room Christian Academy 500/PK-8
3330 Idlewood Village Dr 27610 919-829-6250
Melany Alexander, admin. Fax 829-6193
Wake Christian Academy 1,000/K-12
5500 Wake Academy Dr 27603 919-772-6264
Mike Woods, admin. Fax 779-0948
Word of God Christian Academy 200/PK-12
PO Box 14408 27620 919-834-8200
Anesha Pittman, prin. Fax 899-3640

Ramseur, Randolph, Pop. 1,704
Randolph County SD
Supt. — See Asheboro
Coleridge ES 400/K-5
4528 NC Hwy 22 S 27316 336-879-3348
Billy Tanner, prin. Fax 879-4199
Ramseur ES 500/K-5
6755 Jordan Rd 27316 336-824-4106
Tammie Abernethy, prin. Fax 824-7174
Southeastern Randolph MS 600/6-8
5302 Foushee Rd 27316 336-824-6700
Stephanie Bridges, prin. Fax 824-6705

Faith Christian S 300/PK-12
5449 Brookhaven Rd 27316 336-824-4156
William Hohneisen, prin. Fax 824-1012

Randleman, Randolph, Pop. 3,653
Randolph County SD
Supt. — See Asheboro
Level Cross ES 600/K-5
5417 Old Greensboro Rd 27317 336-495-5915
Laurie Sypole, prin. Fax 495-6216
Randleman ES 800/K-5
100 Swaim St 27317 336-495-1322
Melanie Curtis, prin. Fax 495-6447
Randleman MS 900/6-8
800 High Point St 27317 336-498-2606
Dennis Hamilton, prin. Fax 498-8015

Red Oak, Nash, Pop. 2,820
Nash-Rocky Mount SD
Supt. — See Nashville
Red Oak ES 300/K-2
PO Box 70 27868 252-462-2496
Rossie Williams, prin. Fax 937-2746

Red Springs, Robeson, Pop. 3,484
Hoke County SD
Supt. — See Raeford
Hawk Eye ES 500/PK-5
4321 Old Maxton Rd 28377 910-875-2470
Teres Anderson, prin. Fax 875-1702

Robeson County SD
Supt. — See Lumberton
Peterson ES 600/PK-4
102 Phillips Ave 28377 910-843-4125
Kristen Stone, prin. Fax 843-2414
Red Springs MS 600/5-8
302 W 2nd Ave 28377 910-843-3883
Vivian Tyndall, prin. Fax 843-3765

Macdonald Academy 200/PK-12
200 N College St 28377 910-843-4995
Paschal Stewart, hdmstr. Fax 843-8102

Reidsville, Rockingham, Pop. 14,778
Caswell County SD
Supt. — See Yanceyville
Stoney Creek ES 200/K-5
1803 Stoney Creek School Rd 27320 336-694-6222
Fernandez Johnson, prin. Fax 694-5840

Rockingham County SD
Supt. — See Eden
Bethany ES 500/PK-5
271 Bethany Rd 27320 336-951-2710
Duane Hensley, prin. Fax 951-3788
Lawsonville Avenue ES 300/PK-5
212 Lawsonville Ave 27320 336-349-5524
Barbara Brown, prin. Fax 349-3321
Monroeton ES 500/PK-5
8081 US 158 27320 336-634-3280
Robin Finberg, prin. Fax 634-3043
Moss Street ES 100/K-5
419 Moss St 27320 336-349-5370
Vickie McKinney, prin. Fax 342-3145
Reidsville MS 800/6-8
1903 S Park Dr 27320 336-342-4726
Charles Perkins, prin. Fax 342-9434
Rockingham County MS 900/6-8
182 High School Rd 27320 336-616-0073
Steve Hall, prin. Fax 616-0870
South End ES 300/PK-5
1307 S Park Dr 27320 336-349-6085
Tiffany Perkins, prin. Fax 349-5119
Wentworth ES 500/PK-5
8806 NC Highway 87 27320 336-634-3250
Debbie Smith, prin. Fax 342-9380
Williamsburg ES 500/PK-5
2830 NC Highway 87 27320 336-349-4632
Erselle Young, prin. Fax 342-2699

Community Baptist S 200/K-12
509 Triangle Rd 27320 336-342-5991
Celeste Bailey, prin. Fax 342-7180

Richfield, Stanly, Pop. 514
Stanly County SD
Supt. — See Albemarle
Richfield S 300/PK-8
120 Morgan St 28137 704-463-7712
Brian Barrett, prin. Fax 463-1174

Richlands, Onslow, Pop. 827
Onslow County SD
Supt. — See Jacksonville
Richlands ES 700/3-5
PO Box 67 28574 910-324-4142
Tammie Hudspeth, prin. Fax 324-4879
Richlands PS 800/K-2
7444 Richlands Hwy 28574 910-324-3139
Allene Batchelor, prin. Fax 324-7801
Trexler MS 700/6-8
PO Box 188 28574 910-324-4414
Lynn Jackson, prin. Fax 324-3963

Riegelwood, Columbus
Bladen County SD
Supt. — See Elizabethtown
East Arcadia S 200/PK-8
21451 NC Highway 87 E 28456 910-669-2390
Margaret Moore, prin. Fax 669-2692

Columbus County SD
Supt. — See Whiteville
Acme-Delco ES 300/PK-5
PO Box 704 28456 910-655-2957
Janet Hedrick, prin. Fax 655-6890

Roanoke Rapids, Halifax, Pop. 16,458
Halifax County SD
Supt. — See Halifax
Davie MS 400/6-8
4391 US Highway 158 27870 252-519-0300
Dennis Carrington, prin. Fax 519-0222
Everetts ES 300/PK-5
458 Everetts School Rd 27870 252-537-5484
Vivian Branch, prin. Fax 537-8402
Roanoke Rapids CSD 2,900/PK-12
536 Hamilton St 27870 252-519-7100
Dennis Sawyer, supt. Fax 535-5919
www.rrgsd.org
Belmont ES 700/PK-5
1517 Bolling Rd 27870 252-519-7500
Loret Riddick, prin. Fax 537-0166
Chaloner MS 600/6-8
2100 Virginia Ave 27870 252-519-7600
Jimmy Kearney, prin. Fax 537-9947
Manning ES 700/PK-5
1102 Barrett St 27870 252-519-7400
Andy Kennedy, prin. Fax 537-4366

Halifax Academy 600/PK-12
1400 Three Bridges Rd 27870 252-537-8527
Glenn Wiggs, hdmstr. Fax 308-0555

Roaring River, Wilkes
Wilkes County SD
Supt. — See North Wilkesboro
Roaring River ES 200/K-5
283 White Plains Rd 28669 336-696-4628
Craig Tidline, prin. Fax 696-7839

Robbins, Moore, Pop. 1,217
Moore County SD
Supt. — See Carthage
Elise MS 200/6-8
PO Box 850 27325 910-948-2421
Brenda Cassady, prin. Fax 948-4112
Robbins ES 500/K-5
PO Box 189 27325 910-948-2411
Heather Seawell, prin. Fax 948-3264

Robbinsville, Graham, Pop. 736
Graham County SD 1,200/PK-12
52 Moose Branch Rd 28771 828-479-3413
Clark Carringer, supt. Fax 479-7950
www.gcsk12.com
Robbinsville ES 700/PK-6
54 Moose Branch Rd 28771 828-479-3453
Shane Laughter, prin. Fax 479-6290
Robbinsville MS 200/7-8
301 Sweetwater Rd 28771 828-479-8488
Robert Moody, prin. Fax 479-6847

Robersonville, Martin, Pop. 1,637
Martin County SD
Supt. — See Williamston
East End ES 400/PK-5
1121 3rd Street Ext 27871 252-795-4775
Harry Respass, prin. Fax 795-4220
Roanoke MS 300/6-8
21230 NC Highway 903 27871 252-795-3910
Jan Wagner, prin. Fax 795-3890

Rockingham, Richmond, Pop. 9,220
Richmond County SD
Supt. — See Hamlet
Ashley Chapel ES 200/4-6
377 Mizpah Rd 28379 910-997-9797
Wendy Jordan, prin. Fax 997-8170
Bell ES 600/PK-5
442 Hawthorne Ave 28379 910-997-9834
Bobbie Sue Ormsby, prin. Fax 997-9848
Rockingham MS 500/6-8
415 Wall St 28379 910-997-9827
Shirley Fuller, prin. Fax 997-9859
Rohanen MS 200/6-8
252 School St 28379 910-997-9839
Pamela Francisco, prin. Fax 997-8172
Rohanen PS 300/PK-3
102 6th St 28379 910-997-9824
Wendy Jordan, prin. Fax 997-9832
Washington Street ES 400/PK-5
566 E Washington Street Ext 28379 910-997-9836
Marsha Porter, prin. Fax 895-0208
West Rockingham ES 300/PK-5
271 W US Highway 74 28379 910-997-9802
William Kelley, prin. Fax 997-9803

Temple Christian S 200/K-12
165 Airport Rd 28379 910-997-3179

Rockwell, Rowan, Pop. 1,982
Rowan-Salisbury County SD
Supt. — See Salisbury
Rockwell ES 800/K-5
114 Link St 28138 704-279-3145
Laura Kerr, prin. Fax 279-8657

Grace Academy 50/K-5
6725 Highway 152 E 28138 704-279-6683
Daryl Bolden, admin. Fax 279-6192
Rockwell Christian S 200/K-12
PO Box 609 28138 704-279-8854
Ken Prater, admin. Fax 279-1442

Rocky Mount, Edgecombe, Pop. 56,626
Edgecombe County SD
Supt. — See Tarboro
Bulluck ES 600/PK-5
3090 Bulluck School Rd 27801 252-985-3456
Charlene Pittman, prin. Fax 442-2370
West Edgecombe MS 400/6-8
6301 Nobles Mill Pond Rd 27801 252-446-2030
Laverne Daniels, prin. Fax 446-1592

Nash-Rocky Mount SD
Supt. — See Nashville
Baskerville ES 400/K-5
1100 Stokes St 27801 252-451-2880
Ann Mitchell, prin. Fax 977-0714
Benvenue ES 800/K-5
2700 Nicodemus Mile 27804 252-462-2835
Kay Bolt, prin. Fax 937-5650

Braswell ES 200/PK-5
224 S Pearl St 27804 252-451-2875
Quintin Mangano, prin. Fax 985-4336
Edwards MS 900/6-8
720 Edwards St 27803 252-977-3328
Beezie Whitaker, prin. Fax 446-5527
Englewood ES 300/3-5
101 S Englewood Dr 27804 252-462-2501
Connie Luper, prin. Fax 937-5652
Fairview ECC 100/PK-PK
720 N Fairview Rd 27801 252-985-4337
Denise Warner Ed.D., prin. Fax 985-4342
Johnson ES 500/K-5
600 N Fairview Rd 27801 252-451-2895
Prudence Boseman, prin. Fax 446-5703
Parker MS 600/6-8
1500 E Virginia St 27801 252-977-3486
Charles Davis, prin. Fax 446-5756
Pope ES 300/K-5
226 Coleman Ave 27801 252-451-2885
Sheila Wallace, prin. Fax 985-2765
Williford ES 500/K-5
801 Williford St 27803 252-446-5113
Sandra Farmer, prin. Fax 985-4331
Winstead Avenue ES 300/K-2
991 S Winstead Ave 27803 252-462-2845
Larry Catalano, prin. Fax 451-5540

Faith Christian S 300/K-12
PO Box 8165 27804 252-443-1700
Edward Bunn, hdmstr. Fax 443-2456
Falls Road Baptist Church S 200/PK-12
113 Trevathan St 27804 252-977-2401
Jonathan Wright, prin. Fax 977-3493
Our Lady of Perpetual Help S 100/PK-5
315 Hammond St 27804 252-972-1971
Connie Urbanski, prin. Fax 972-7831
Rocky Mount Academy 400/PK-12
1313 Avondale Ave 27803 252-443-4126
Thomas Stevens, hdmstr. Fax 937-7922

Rocky Point, Pender
Pender County SD
Supt. — See Burgaw
Cape Fear ES 400/3-5
1882 NC Highway 133 28457 910-602-3767
Stephanie Willis, prin. Fax 602-7828
Cape Fear MS 400/6-8
1886 NC Highway 133 28457 910-602-3334
Edith Skipper, prin. Fax 602-3036
Rocky Point PS 400/K-2
255 Rocky Point Elementary 28457 910-675-2309
Donna Redinger, prin. Fax 675-8730

Rolesville, Wake, Pop. 1,238
Wake County SD
Supt. — See Raleigh
Rolesville ES 600/PK-5
307 S Main St 27571 919-554-8686
Shane Barham, prin. Fax 554-8601
Sanford Creek ES K-5
701 Granite Falls Blvd 27571 919-570-2100
Jamee Lynch, prin. Fax 570-2168

Ronda, Wilkes, Pop. 467
Wilkes County SD
Supt. — See North Wilkesboro
East Wilkes MS 400/6-8
2202 Macedonia Church Rd 28670 336-928-9800
Chris Jones, prin. Fax 957-8734
Ronda-Clingman ES 300/PK-5
316 Ronda Clingman School 28670 336-957-8210
Sandra Burchette, prin. Fax 984-3201

Roper, Washington, Pop. 588
Washington County SD
Supt. — See Plymouth
Washington County Union MS 600/5-8
PO Box 309 27970 252-793-2835
Earnell Purington, prin. Fax 793-4411

Roseboro, Sampson, Pop. 1,297
Cumberland County SD
Supt. — See Fayetteville
Beaver Dam ES 100/PK-5
12059 NC Highway 210 S 28382 910-531-3378
Jeanna Daniels, prin. Fax 531-4353

Sampson County SD
Supt. — See Clinton
Perry ES 400/PK-5
PO Box 829 28382 910-525-4204
Donald Boykin, prin. Fax 525-4345
Roseboro-Salemburg MS 400/6-8
PO Box 976 28382 910-525-4764
Lisa Reynolds, prin. Fax 525-3471

Rose Hill, Duplin, Pop. 1,377
Duplin County SD
Supt. — See Kenansville
Charity MS 500/6-8
PO Box 70 28458 910-289-3323
Janice Wynn, prin. Fax 289-2064
Rose Hill-Magnolia ES 700/PK-5
PO Box 340 28458 910-289-3667
Felicia Brown, prin. Fax 289-3378

Rosman, Transylvania, Pop. 483
Transylvania County SD
Supt. — See Brevard
Rosman ES 400/K-5
PO Box 578 28772 828-862-4431
Donna Raspa, prin. Fax 862-4281
Rosman MS 300/6-8
749 Pickens Hwy 28772 828-862-4286
Greg Carter, prin. Fax 885-8222

Rowland, Robeson, Pop. 1,148
Robeson County SD
Supt. — See Lumberton
Rowland MS 200/6-8
408 W Chapel St 28383 910-422-3983
Larry Brooks, prin. Fax 422-8369
Southside/Ashpole ES 400/PK-5
607 S Martin Luther King Jr 28383 910-422-3791
Dacia Bullard, prin. Fax 422-3105
Union ES 500/PK-6
2547 NC Highway 710 S 28383 910-521-4272
Darlene Cummings, prin. Fax 521-0167

Roxboro, Person, Pop. 8,755
Person County SD 5,700/PK-12
304 S Morgan St Ste 25 27573 336-599-2191
Larry Cartner Ed.D., supt. Fax 599-2194
www.person.k12.nc.us
Bradsher Preschool Center PK-PK
404 S Morgan St 27573 336-599-7585
Amy Seate, dir. Fax 599-3484
North ES 300/K-5
260 Henderson Rd 27573 336-599-7262
Marionette Jeffers, prin. Fax 599-0128
North End ES 300/K-5
378 Mill Creek Rd, 336-599-3313
Chrystal Brooks, prin. Fax 597-8700
Northern MS 600/6-8
1935 Carver Dr, 336-599-6344
Darkarai Bryant, prin. Fax 598-9207
South ES 400/K-5
1333 Hurdle Mills Rd 27573 336-599-7133
Michael Ziemba, prin. Fax 597-4611
Southern MS 700/6-8
209 Southern Middle School 27573 336-599-6995
John McCain, prin. Fax 503-0587
Stories Creek ES 400/K-5
133 Stories Creek School Rd, 336-503-8071
Veronica Clay, prin. Fax 503-8083
Other Schools – See Hurdle Mills, Semora, Timberlake

Roxboro Christian Academy 100/K-12
PO Box 1357 27573 336-599-0208
Wallace Cowan, prin.

Ruffin, Rockingham
Rockingham County SD
Supt. — See Eden
Lincoln ES 400/PK-5
2660 Oregon Hill Rd 27326 336-939-2435
Linda Bass, prin. Fax 939-7779

Rural Hall, Forsyth, Pop. 2,577
Winston-Salem/Forsyth SD
Supt. — See Winston Salem
Rural Hall ES 600/K-5
275 College St 27045 336-969-9376
Frank Holcumb, prin. Fax 969-5994

Rutherford College, Burke, Pop. 1,283
Burke County SD
Supt. — See Morganton
Rutherford College ES 300/PK-5
PO Box 247 28671 828-879-8870
Becky Roach, prin. Fax 879-9470

Rutherfordton, Rutherford, Pop. 4,099
Rutherford County SD
Supt. — See Forest City
Pinnacle ES 500/K-5
1204 Painters Gap Rd 28139 828-287-3440
LaRonda Whiteside, prin. Fax 287-0950
R-S MS 800/6-8
545 Charlotte Rd 28139 828-286-4461
John McSwain, prin. Fax 286-4882
Rutherfordton ES 400/K-5
134 Maple St 28139 828-287-3778
Linda Edgerton, prin. Fax 286-0346

Trinity S 200/PK-8
299 Deter St 28139 828-286-3900
Lewis Freeman, hdmstr. Fax 286-3816

Saint Pauls, Robeson, Pop. 2,235
Robeson County SD
Supt. — See Lumberton
Saint Pauls ES 900/PK-5
222 Martin Luther King Rd 28384 910-865-4103
Deena Revels, prin. Fax 865-3951
Saint Pauls MS 500/6-8
526 W Shaw St 28384 910-865-4070
Barbara Thompson, prin. Fax 865-1599

Salemburg, Sampson, Pop. 480
Sampson County SD
Supt. — See Clinton
Salemburg ES 600/K-5
PO Box 9 28385 910-525-5547
Gerald Johnson, prin. Fax 525-4002

Salisbury, Rowan, Pop. 27,563
Rowan-Salisbury County SD 19,600/PK-12
PO Box 2349 28145 704-636-7500
Dr. Judy Grissom, supt. Fax 630-6129
www.rss.k12.nc.us
Dole ES 600/PK-5
465 Choate Rd 28146 704-639-3046
James Griffin, prin. Fax 639-3073
Erwin MS 900/6-8
170 Saint Luke Church Rd 28146 704-279-7265
Ray Whitaker, prin. Fax 279-7954
Hurley ES 600/PK-5
625 Hurley School Rd 28147 704-639-3038
Kim Walton, prin. Fax 639-3111
Isenberg ES 500/PK-5
2800 Jake Alexander Blvd N 28147 704-639-3009
Nathan Currie, prin. Fax 639-3113
Knollwood ES 600/K-5
3075 Shue Rd 28147 704-857-3400
Shonda Hairston, prin. Fax 855-1703
Knox MS 600/6-8
1625 W Park Rd 28144 704-633-2922
Brian MorganeEl, prin. Fax 638-3538
Koontz ES K-5
685 E Ritchie Rd 28146 704-216-0273
Ricky Dunlap, prin. Fax 216-0294
Overton ES 400/PK-5
1825 W Park Rd 28144 704-639-3000
Betty Tunks, prin. Fax 638-3534
Southeast MS 700/6-8
1570 Peeler Rd 28146 704-638-5561
Louis Kraft, prin. Fax 638-5719
West Rowan MS 700/6-8
5925 Statesville Blvd 28147 704-633-4775
Nancy Barkemeyer, prin. Fax 633-3157
Other Schools – See China Grove, Cleveland, Faith, Gold Hill, Granite Quarry, Landis, Mount Ulla, Rockwell, Spencer, Woodleaf

---

North Hills Christian S 200/PK-12
2970 W Innes St 28144 704-636-3005
Matthew Mitchell, hdmstr. Fax 636-3597
Sacred Heart S 200/K-8
385 Lumen Christi Ln 28147 704-633-2841
Sr. Anastacia Pagulayan, prin. Fax 633-6033
St. Johns Child Development Center 50/PK-PK
300 W Innes St 28144 704-636-6756
Fax 636-6845
Salisbury Academy 100/K-8
2210 Jake Alexander Blvd N 28147 704-636-3002
Diane Fisher, hdmstr. Fax 636-0778
Salisbury SDA S 50/PK-8
305 Rudolph Rd 28146 704-633-1282
Jan Hefner, prin. Fax 210-8307

Saluda, Polk, Pop. 579
Polk County SD
Supt. — See Columbus
Saluda ES 200/PK-5
PO Box 127 28773 828-749-5571
Ronette Dill, prin. Fax 749-1106

Sandy Ridge, Stokes
Stokes County SD
Supt. — See Danbury
Sandy Ridge ES 200/K-5
1070 Amos Town Rd 27046 336-871-2400
Rich Pekar, prin. Fax 871-8415

Sanford, Lee, Pop. 26,710
Harnett County SD
Supt. — See Lillington
Highlands ES 1,100/K-5
1915 Buffalo Lake Rd 27332 919-499-2200
Terry Blalock, prin. Fax 499-2524

Lee County SD 9,400/K-12
PO Box 1010 27331 919-774-6226
Jeffrey Moss Ed.D., supt. Fax 776-0443
www.lee.k12.nc.us
Bullock ES 600/K-5
1410 McNeill Rd 27330 919-718-0160
Pam Sutton, prin. Fax 708-7347
Deep River ES 600/K-5
4000 Deep River Rd 27330 919-776-2722
Dianne Straub, prin. Fax 776-0737
East Lee MS 1,000/6-8
1337 Broadway Rd 27332 919-776-8441
Dr. Tom Harvley-Felder, prin. Fax 774-7451
Edwards ES 600/K-5
3115 Cemetery Rd 27332 919-774-3733
Bonnie Almond, prin. Fax 776-8689
Greenwood ES 600/K-5
1127 Greenwood Rd 27332 919-776-0506
George Raley, prin. Fax 776-5574
Ingram Jr. ES 700/K-5
3309 Wicker St 27330 919-774-3772
Gary Moore, prin. Fax 774-7090
San Lee MS 6-8
2309 Tramway Rd 27332 919-708-7227
Kenna Wilson, prin. Fax 718-2875
Tramway ES 600/K-5
360 Center Church Rd 27330 919-718-0170
Anne Beal, prin. Fax 774-1325
West Lee MS 1,100/6-8
3301 Wicker St 27330 919-775-7351
Stella Farrow, prin. Fax 776-3694
Other Schools – See Broadway

Grace Christian S 300/K-12
2601 Jefferson Davis Hwy 27332 919-774-4415
William Carver, admin. Fax 718-6777
Lee Christian S 400/PK-12
3220 Keller Andrews Rd 27330 919-708-5115
Dr. Stephen Coble, prin. Fax 708-6933

Scotland Neck, Halifax, Pop. 2,240
Halifax County SD
Supt. — See Halifax
Dawson ES 200/PK-5
6878 Old 125 Rd 27874 252-826-4905
Sharon Arrington, prin. Fax 826-5155
Scotland Neck PS 200/PK-2
901 Jr High School Rd 27874 252-826-4413
Bonnie Johnson, prin. Fax 826-4309

Seagrove, Randolph, Pop. 253
Moore County SD
Supt. — See Carthage
Westmoore S 400/K-8
2159 S NC Highway 705 27341 910-464-3401
Bruce Williams, prin. Fax 464-5293

Randolph County SD
Supt. — See Asheboro
Seagrove ES 500/K-5
528 Old Plank Rd 27341 336-873-7321
Lisa Thompson, prin. Fax 873-8745

Sedalia, Guilford, Pop. 645
Guilford County SD
Supt. — See Greensboro
Sedalia ES 400/K-5
6120 Burlington Rd 27342 336-449-4711
Lance Stokes, prin. Fax 449-6523

Selma, Johnston, Pop. 6,646
Johnston County SD
Supt. — See Smithfield
Selma ES 900/PK-4
311 W Richardson St 27576 919-965-3361
Janice Jett, prin. Fax 965-0639
Selma MS 600/5-8
1533 US Highway 301 N 27576 919-965-2555
Jennifer Moore, prin. Fax 202-0116

Semora, Person
Person County SD
Supt. — See Roxboro
Woodland ES 200/K-5
7391 Semora Rd 27343 336-599-7442
Kelly Gentry, prin. Fax 599-8730

Shallotte, Brunswick, Pop. 1,588
Brunswick County SD
Supt. — See Bolivia
Shallotte MS 900/6-8
225 Village Rd SW 28470 910-754-6882
Paul Price, prin. Fax 754-3108
Union ES 600/K-5
180 Union School Rd NW 28470 910-579-3591
Vickie Smith, prin. Fax 579-5542

Southeastern Christian Academy 100/PK-8
PO Box 2328 28459 910-754-2389
Elaina Tartt, prin. Fax 754-4895

Shannon, Robeson
Robeson County SD
Supt. — See Lumberton
Rex-Rennert ES 400/PK-5
11780 Rennert Rd 28386 910-843-5298
Katie Brewer, prin. Fax 843-8533

Shawboro, Currituck
Currituck County SD
Supt. — See Currituck
Shawboro ES 200/K-5
370 Shawboro Rd 27973 252-232-2237
Terrie Godfrey, prin. Fax 232-2287

Shelby, Cleveland, Pop. 21,263
Cleveland County SD 17,600/PK-12
130 S Post Rd Ste 2 28152 704-476-8000
Dr. Bruce Boyles, supt. Fax 476-8300
www.clevelandcountyschools.org
Boiling Springs ES 700/PK-5
1522 Patrick Ave 28152 704-434-2772
June Lail, prin. Fax 434-5286
Crest MS of Technology 1,100/6-8
315 Beaver Dam Church Rd 28152 704-482-0343
Amy Jones, prin. Fax 487-0378
Elizabeth ES 600/K-5
220 S Post Rd 28152 704-487-9940
Brenda Shackleford, prin. Fax 480-0856
Graham ES 200/PK-3
1100 Blanton St 28150 704-487-6161
Bob Luckadoo, prin. Fax 487-2868
Jefferson ES 400/PK-3
1166 Wyke Rd 28150 704-487-5431
Paula Peeler, prin. Fax 487-2880
Love ES 300/PK-3
309 James Love School Rd 28152 704-487-4541
Pam Merritt, prin. Fax 487-2882
Marion IS 400/4-5
410 Forest Hill Dr 28150 704-487-5931
Jane Blake, prin. Fax 487-2861
Shelby MS 800/6-8
400 W Marion St 28150 704-482-6331
Tim Quattlebaum, prin. Fax 487-2889
Springmore ES 700/K-5
616 Mcbrayer Homestead Rd 28152 704-434-7371
Gloria Sherman, prin. Fax 434-2216
Township Three ES 800/PK-5
526 Davis Rd 28152 704-487-7809
Tropzie McCluney, prin. Fax 487-0460
Union ES 600/PK-5
1440 Union Church Rd 28150 704-481-8001
Sandy McNeely, prin. Fax 481-1940
Washington Math & Science ES 500/PK-5
1907 Stony Point Rd 28150 704-435-9521
Coleman Hunt, prin. Fax 435-5777
Other Schools – See Casar, Fallston, Grover, Kings Mountain, Lawndale

Sherrills Ford, Catawba, Pop. 3,185
Catawba County SD
Supt. — See Newton
Sherrills Ford ES 700/K-6
8103 Sherrills Ford Rd 28673 828-478-2662
Shelly Black, prin. Fax 478-5927

Siler City, Chatham, Pop. 8,079
Chatham County SD
Supt. — See Pittsboro
Chatham MS 500/5-8
2025 S 2nd Avenue Ext 27344 919-663-2414
Tracy Fowler, prin. Fax 663-2871
Cross ES K-5
234 Cross School Rd 27344 919-742-4279
Dr. Julie Vandiver, prin. Fax 742-5266
Siler City ES 800/PK-5
671 Ellington Rd 27344 919-663-2032
Angie Brady-Andrew, prin. Fax 742-5591
Silk Hope S 500/K-8
7945 Silk Hope Gum Springs 27344 919-742-3911
Chad Morgan, prin. Fax 742-5032

Smithfield, Johnston, Pop. 11,970
Johnston County SD 29,200/PK-12
PO Box 1336 27577 919-934-6031
Edward Croom Ed.D., supt. Fax 934-6035
www.johnston.k12.nc.us
Smithfield MS 900/6-8
1455 Buffalo Rd 27577 919-934-4696
Anne Meredith, prin. Fax 934-7552
South Smithfield ES 500/PK-5
201 W Sanders St 27577 919-934-8979
Carla Taylor, prin. Fax 934-1739
West Smithfield ES 500/K-5
2665 Galilee Rd 27577 919-989-6418
Chad Jewett, prin. Fax 989-3470
Other Schools – See Angier, Benson, Clayton, Four Oaks, Garner, Kenly, Micro, Pine Level, Princeton, Selma, Wendell, Willow Spring, Wilsons Mills, Zebulon

---

Adventist Bilingual S of Smithfield 1-8
121 Packing Plant Rd 27577 919-934-8313
Johnston Christian Academy 200/PK-12
PO Box 1599 27577 919-934-1248
John Floyd, prin. Fax 934-1289

Smyrna, Carteret
Carteret County SD
Supt. — See Beaufort
Smyrna S 300/PK-8
174 Marshallberg Rd 28579 252-729-2301
Lillie Miller, prin. Fax 729-1015

Snow Camp, Alamance
Alamance-Burlington SD
Supt. — See Burlington
Sylvan ES 300/K-5
7718 Sylvan Rd 27349 336-376-3350
Whitney Oakley, prin. Fax 376-3318

Snow Hill, Greene, Pop. 1,442
Greene County SD 3,400/PK-12
301 Kingold Blvd 28580 252-747-3425
Patrick Miller, supt. Fax 747-5942
www.gcsedu.org/
Greene County MS 700/6-8
485 Middle School Rd 28580 252-747-8191
Gregory Monroe, prin. Fax 747-8696
Snow Hill PS 1,000/PK-2
502 SE 2nd St 28580 252-747-8113
Brenda Hagen, prin. Fax 747-4656
West Greene ES 800/3-5
303 Kingold Blvd 28580 252-747-3955
Debbie Daniell, prin. Fax 747-7591

Sophia, Randolph
Randolph County SD
Supt. — See Asheboro
New Market ES 500/K-5
6096 US Highway 311 27350 336-495-3340
Kim Leake, prin. Fax 495-3343

Southern Pines, Moore, Pop. 11,881
Moore County SD
Supt. — See Carthage
Southern Pines ES 400/3-6
255 S May St 28387 910-692-2357
Marcy Cooper, prin. Fax 693-1745
Southern Pines PS 400/K-2
1250 W New York Ave 28387 910-692-8659
Mary Harrison, prin. Fax 692-8259

Calvary Christian S 200/K-12
400 S Bennett St 28387 910-692-8311
Fax 692-1992
Episcopal Day S 200/PK-5
340 E Massachusetts Ave 28387 910-692-3492
Jay St. John, hdmstr. Fax 692-7914
O'Neal S 400/PK-12
PO Box 290 28388 910-692-6920
John Neiswender, hdmstr. Fax 692-6930
Pope John Paul II S 100/PK-6
PO Box 29 28388 910-692-6241
Rick Kruska, prin. Fax 692-4964

Southport, Brunswick, Pop. 2,725
Brunswick County SD
Supt. — See Bolivia
South Brunswick MS 900/6-8
100 Cougar Rd 28461 910-845-2771
David Kulp, prin. Fax 845-8972
Southport ES 600/K-5
701 W 9th St 28461 910-457-6036
Randy Horne, prin. Fax 457-6042

Southport Christian S 200/PK-5
8070 River Rd 28461 910-457-5060
Lisa Kjome, prin. Fax 457-5017

Sparta, Alleghany, Pop. 1,797
Alleghany County SD 1,700/PK-12
85 Peachtree St 28675 336-372-4345
Dr. Jeff Cox, supt. Fax 372-4204
www.alleghany.k12.nc.us
Sparta S 800/PK-8
450 N Main St 28675 336-372-8546
Christopher Barnes, prin. Fax 372-8732
Other Schools – See Ennice, Piney Creek

Spencer, Rowan, Pop. 3,345
Rowan-Salisbury County SD
Supt. — See Salisbury
North Rowan ES 500/PK-5
600 Charles St 28159 704-639-3042
Rick Hampton, prin. Fax 639-3080
North Rowan MS 600/6-8
512 Charles St 28159 704-639-3018
Darrell McDowell, prin. Fax 639-3099

Spindale, Rutherford, Pop. 3,921
Rutherford County SD
Supt. — See Forest City
Spindale ES 500/K-5
201 N Oak St 28160 828-286-2861
Angel King, prin. Fax 287-1026

Spring Hope, Nash, Pop. 1,272
Nash-Rocky Mount SD
Supt. — See Nashville
Southern Nash MS 1,100/6-8
5301 S NC Highway 581 27882 252-478-4807
Carina Bissette, prin. Fax 478-4861
Spring Hope ES 600/PK-5
PO Box 10 27882 252-478-4835
Bebe Wall, prin. Fax 478-4859

Spring Lake, Cumberland, Pop. 8,197
Cumberland County SD
Supt. — See Fayetteville
Black ES 300/K-5
125 S 3rd St 28390 910-497-7147
Brenda Minor, prin. Fax 497-3817
Brown ES 600/PK-5
2522 Andrews Church Rd 28390 910-497-1258
Annette Evans, prin. Fax 497-0882
Manchester ES 300/K-5
611 Spring Ave 28390 910-436-2151
Jenny Price, prin. Fax 436-6034
Spring Lake MS 500/6-8
612 Spring Ave 28390 910-497-1175
James Ellerbe, prin. Fax 497-3467

Harnett County SD
Supt. — See Lillington
Overhills MS 900/6-8
2711 Ray Rd 28390 910-436-0009
Fax 436-0948

Spruce Pine, Mitchell, Pop. 1,998
Mitchell County SD
Supt. — See Bakersville
Deyton ES 300/3-5
308 Harris St 28777 828-765-2504
Gary Moore, prin. Fax 765-0052
Greenlee PS 300/K-2
2206 Carters Ridge Rd 28777 828-766-9562
Alan English, prin. Fax 766-9566
Harris MS 300/6-8
121 Harris St 28777 828-765-2321
Jack Brooks, prin. Fax 765-1595

Altapass Christian S 50/K-12
50 Altapass Trl 28777 828-765-0660

Stallings, Union, Pop. 3,854
Union County SD
Supt. — See Monroe
Stallings ES K-5
3501 Stallings Rd 28104 704-290-1558
Bill Breckenridge, prin. Fax 893-0825

Stanfield, Stanly, Pop. 1,110
Stanly County SD
Supt. — See Albemarle
Stanfield S 500/PK-8
PO Box 250 28163 704-888-5261
Kim Page, prin. Fax 888-5194

Stanley, Gaston, Pop. 3,094
Gaston County SD
Supt. — See Gastonia
Kiser ES 300/3-5
311 E College St 28164 704-263-4121
Lynn Shaffer, prin. Fax 263-9372
Springfield PS 500/PK-2
900 S Main St 28164 704-263-4091
Beth Germain, prin. Fax 263-1890
Stanley MS 500/6-8
317 Hovis Rd 28164 704-263-2941
Staci Bradley, prin. Fax 263-0993

Stantonsburg, Wilson, Pop. 712
Wilson County SD
Supt. — See Wilson
Stantonsburg ES 300/K-5
PO Box 160 27883 252-238-3639
Vernita Smith, prin. Fax 238-2290

Star, Montgomery, Pop. 810
Montgomery County SD
Supt. — See Troy
Star-Biscoe ES 600/PK-5
302 S Main St 27356 910-428-4333
Vance Thomas, prin. Fax 428-1439

State Road, Surry
Surry County SD
Supt. — See Dobson
Mountain Park ES 200/PK-5
505 Mountain Park Rd 28676 336-874-3933
Alison York, prin. Fax 874-7963

Statesville, Iredell, Pop. 24,875
Iredell-Statesville SD 20,500/PK-12
PO Box 911 28687 704-872-8931
Dr. Terry Holliday, supt. Fax 871-2834
www.iss.k12.nc.us
Central ES 400/PK-5
4083 Wilkesboro Hwy 28625 704-876-0746
Diana Eller, prin. Fax 876-6226
East Iredell ES 500/2-5
400 E Elementary Rd 28625 704-872-9541
Phyllis Pegram, prin. Fax 872-1085
East Iredell MS 700/6-8
590 Chestnut Grove Rd 28625 704-872-4666
Dr. Katherine Stillerman, prin. Fax 873-6602
Ebenezer ES 200/3-5
134 Ebenezer Rd 28625 704-876-4145
Sheila Alston, prin. Fax 876-0803

Henkel ES 600/K-5
1503 Old Mountain Rd 28677 704-873-7333
Steve Sheets, prin. Fax 871-0153
Mills ES 300/PK-2
1410 Pearl St 28677 704-873-8498
Stacy Williams, prin. Fax 872-3755
Northview ES 300/PK-2
625 N Carolina Ave 28677 704-873-7354
Wayne Harwell, prin. Fax 873-6149
Pressly ES 300/K-1
222 Knox St 28677 704-872-7606
Fax 838-0839
Scotts ES 400/K-5
4743 Taylorsville Hwy 28625 704-585-6526
Gene May, prin. Fax 585-6971
Sharon ES 300/K-5
880 Sharon School Rd 28625 704-872-3401
Beverly Roberts, prin. Fax 924-9963
Statesville MS 600/6-8
321 Clegg St 28677 704-872-2135
Roberta Ellis, prin. Fax 871-9279
Third Creek ES 600/K-5
361 E Barkley Rd 28677 704-873-3002
Amy Rhyne, prin. Fax 871-0755
West Iredell MS 800/6-8
303 Watermelon Rd 28625 704-873-2887
Michael Sherrill, prin. Fax 881-0582
Other Schools – See Cleveland, Harmony, Mooresville, Olin, Troutman, Union Grove

---

Crossroads Adventist S 50/1-8
2429 E Broad St 28625 704-878-2070
Crossroads Christian S 100/K-12
PO Box 2102 28687 704-871-1515
Anne Wooten, admin.
Southview Christian S 100/K-12
625 Wallace Springs Rd 28677 704-872-9554
Statesville Christian S 400/PK-12
1210 Museum Rd 28625 704-873-9511
Dent Miller, dir. Fax 873-0841
Statesville Montessori S 200/PK-8
1012 Harmony Dr 28677 704-873-1092
Stacey Crosswhite, dir. Fax 873-1093

Stedman, Cumberland, Pop. 651
Cumberland County SD
Supt. — See Fayetteville
Stedman ES 300/2-5
7370 Clinton Rd 28391 910-483-3886
Anne McFadyen, prin. Fax 483-0519
Stedman PS 200/PK-1
155 E 1st St 28391 910-484-6954
Deborah Faircloth, prin. Fax 484-1604

Stokes, Pitt
Pitt County SD
Supt. — See Greenville
Stokes S 300/PK-8
2683 NC Highway 903 N 27884 252-752-6907
Jennifer Poplin, prin. Fax 752-2956

Stokesdale, Guilford, Pop. 3,524
Guilford County SD
Supt. — See Greensboro
Stokesdale ES 500/PK-5
8025 US Highway 158 27357 336-643-8420
Amy Koonce, prin. Fax 643-8425

Oak Level Baptist Academy 100/K-12
1569 Oak Level Church Rd 27357 336-643-9288
Clay Walker, prin. Fax 643-9284

Stoneville, Rockingham, Pop. 988
Rockingham County SD
Supt. — See Eden
Stoneville ES 400/PK-5
PO Box 7 27048 336-573-4000
Debbie Claybrook, prin. Fax 573-4002

Stone-Eden Christian S 100/K-12
PO Box 505 27048 336-573-3335
Laurie Young, prin. Fax 573-3335

Stony Point, Alexander, Pop. 1,286
Alexander County SD
Supt. — See Taylorsville
Stony Point ES 300/K-5
311 Stony Point School Rd 28678 704-585-6981
Elizabeth Curry, prin. Fax 585-6812

Stovall, Granville, Pop. 387
Granville County SD
Supt. — See Oxford
Stovall-Shaw ES 400/PK-5
PO Box 38 27582 919-693-3478
Kathy Twisdale, prin. Fax 693-4959

Sugar Grove, Watauga
Watauga County SD
Supt. — See Boone
Bethel S 100/PK-8
138 Bethel School Rd 28679 828-297-2240
Randy Bentley, prin. Fax 297-5182
Valle Crucis S 400/K-8
2998 Broadstone Rd 28679 828-963-4712
Wayne Eberle, prin. Fax 963-8185

Summerfield, Guilford, Pop. 7,228
Guilford County SD
Supt. — See Greensboro
Summerfield ES 800/K-5
7515 Trainer Dr 27358 336-643-8444
Jill Walsh, prin. Fax 643-8447

Sunbury, Gates
Gates County SD
Supt. — See Gatesville
Cooper ES 300/K-5
PO Box 58 27979 252-465-4091
Susan Ward, prin. Fax 465-4238

Supply, Brunswick
Brunswick County SD
Supt. — See Bolivia
Cedar Grove MS 6-8
750 Grove Trl SW 28462 910-846-3400
Rhonda Benton, prin. Fax 846-3401
Supply ES 700/PK-5
51 Benton Rd SE 28462 910-754-7644
Dr. Dwight Willis, prin. Fax 754-3112

Swannanoa, Buncombe, Pop. 3,538
Buncombe County SD
Supt. — See Asheville
Owen MS 700/6-8
730 Old US 70 Hwy 28778 828-686-7739
Vicky Matthews, prin. Fax 686-7938
Williams ES 500/K-5
161 Bee Tree Rd 28778 828-686-3856
Patricia Morgan, prin. Fax 686-3075

Asheville Christian Academy 600/PK-12
PO Box 1089 28778 828-581-2200
William George, hdmstr. Fax 581-2218

Swanquarter, Hyde
Hyde County SD 700/PK-12
PO Box 217 27885 252-926-3281
Gregory Todd, supt. Fax 926-3083
www.hyde.k12.nc.us/
Mattamuskeet ES 200/PK-5
60 Juniper Bay Rd 27885 252-926-0240
Jeremiah Jackson, prin. Fax 926-0243
Mattamuskeet MS 100/6-8
20400 US Highway 264 27885 252-926-0015
Chris Weikart, prin. Fax 926-0016
Other Schools – See Ocracoke

Swansboro, Onslow, Pop. 1,338
Onslow County SD
Supt. — See Jacksonville
Queens Creek ES 600/K-5
159 Queens Creek Rd 28584 910-326-5115
Elaine Justice, prin. Fax 326-5235
Swansboro ES 500/PK-5
118 School Rd 28584 910-326-1501
Lisa Rice, prin. Fax 326-6170
Swansboro MS 800/6-8
1240 W Corbett Ave 28584 910-326-3601
Darin Cloninger, prin. Fax 326-5848

Sylva, Jackson, Pop. 2,398
Jackson County SD 3,600/PK-12
398 Hospital Rd 28779 828-586-2311
Sue Nations, supt. Fax 586-5450
www.jcps.k12.nc.us
Fairview S 800/PK-8
251 Big Orange Way 28779 828-586-2819
Carolyn Pannell, prin. Fax 586-3462
Scotts Creek S 500/PK-8
516 Parris Branch Rd 28779 828-631-2740
Dr. Wanda Fernandez, prin. Fax 631-2478
Other Schools – See Cashiers, Cullowhee, Whittier

Tabor City, Columbus, Pop. 2,629
Columbus County SD
Supt. — See Whiteville
Guideway S 300/PK-8
11570 Swamp Fox Hwy E 28463 910-653-2723
Jonathan Williams, prin. Fax 653-3744
Tabor City ES 600/PK-5
203 Stake Rd 28463 910-653-3618
Debra Hammond, prin. Fax 653-4274
Tabor City MS 200/6-8
701 W 6th St 28463 910-653-3637
Kent Lovett, prin. Fax 653-2093

Tarboro, Edgecombe, Pop. 10,600
Edgecombe County SD 6,900/PK-12
PO Box 7128 27886 252-641-2600
Dr. Craig Witherspoon, supt. Fax 641-5714
www.ecps.us/
Martin MS 500/7-8
400 E Johnston St 27886 252-641-5710
Marc Whichard, prin. Fax 641-5713
Pattillo A+ S 500/4-6
501 East Ave 27886 252-823-3812
Sylvia Cobb, prin. Fax 641-5706
Stocks ES 700/PK-3
400 W Hope Lodge St 27886 252-823-2632
Russell Johnson, prin. Fax 823-7834
Other Schools – See Battleboro, Pinetops, Princeville, Rocky Mount

Tar Heel, Bladen, Pop. 69
Bladen County SD
Supt. — See Elizabethtown
Plain View ES 200/PK-4
1963 Chicken Foot Rd 28392 910-862-2371
Dennis Rigans, prin. Fax 862-4899
Tar Heel MS 400/5-8
PO Box 128 28392 910-862-2475
Susan Inman, prin. Fax 872-5599

Taylorsville, Alexander, Pop. 1,855
Alexander County SD 5,700/PK-12
700 Liledoun Rd 28681 828-632-7001
Jack Hoke, supt. Fax 632-8862
www.alexander.k12.nc.us
Bethlehem ES 500/K-5
7900 NC Highway 127 28681 828-495-8198
Jennifer Hefner, prin. Fax 495-2580
Ellendale ES 400/PK-5
175 Ellendale Park Ln 28681 828-632-4866
Jessica Stout, prin. Fax 632-4912
Sugar Loaf ES 300/K-5
3600 NC Highway 16 N 28681 828-632-2192
Cary Cash, prin. Fax 635-1742
Taylorsville ES 300/K-5
100 7th St SW 28681 828-632-3072
Susan Campbell, prin. Fax 632-0276
West Alexander MS 700/6-8
85 Bulldog Ln 28681 828-495-4611
Susan Gantt, prin. Fax 495-3527
Wittenburg ES 400/K-5
7300 Church Rd 28681 828-632-2395
Mary Brown, prin. Fax 635-0405
Other Schools – See Hiddenite, Stony Point

Thomasville, Davidson, Pop. 25,872
Davidson County SD
Supt. — See Lexington
Brier Creek ES 400/K-5
175 Watford Rd 27360 336-474-8200
Dr. Susan Allen, prin. Fax 474-8201
Brown MS 800/6-8
1140 Kendall Mill Rd 27360 336-475-8845
Randy Holmes, prin. Fax 475-3842
Fair Grove ES 700/PK-5
217 Cedar Lodge Rd 27360 336-472-7020
Audrey Wagner, prin. Fax 472-3462
Hasty ES 500/K-5
325 Hasty School Rd 27360 336-475-1924
Jane Withers, prin. Fax 475-3723
Ledford MS 900/6-8
3954 N NC Highway 109 27360 336-476-4816
J. Evan Myers, prin. Fax 476-1479
Pilot ES 500/PK-5
145 Pilot School Rd 27360 336-472-7965
Sandra Everhart, prin. Fax 472-3323

Thomasville CSD 2,600/K-12
400 Turner St 27360 336-474-4200
Keith Tobin, supt. Fax 475-0356
www.tcs.k12.nc.us
Liberty Drive ES 600/3-5
401 Liberty Dr 27360 336-474-4186
Jeanne Croft, prin. Fax 472-3723
Thomasville MS 600/6-8
400 Unity St 27360 336-474-4120
Georgia Marshall, prin. Fax 472-5081
Thomasville PS 600/K-2
915 E Sunrise Ave 27360 336-474-4160
Paula Gaylord, prin. Fax 472-5020

Carolina Christian Academy 100/K-12
367 Academy Dr 27360 336-472-8950
Daniel Lee, prin. Fax 472-8920

Timberlake, Person
Person County SD
Supt. — See Roxboro
Helena ES 700/K-5
355 Helena Moriah Rd 27583 336-364-7715
Dr. Kay Allen, prin. Fax 364-2501

Tobaccoville, Forsyth, Pop. 2,429
Winston-Salem/Forsyth SD
Supt. — See Winston Salem
Old Richmond ES 600/K-5
6315 Tobaccoville Rd 27050 336-924-2451
Kathryn Fariss, prin. Fax 924-2442

Topton, Macon
Macon County SD
Supt. — See Franklin
Nantahala S 100/K-12
213 Winding Stairs Rd 28781 828-321-4388
Chris Baldwin, prin. Fax 321-4834

Traphill, Wilkes
Wilkes County SD
Supt. — See North Wilkesboro
Traphill ES 200/PK-5
PO Box 6 28685 336-957-2379
John Parsons, prin. Fax 957-4032

Trenton, Jones, Pop. 253
Jones County SD 1,400/PK-12
320 W Jones St 28585 252-448-2531
Michael Bracy, supt. Fax 448-1394
www.jonesnc.net
Jones MS 200/7-8
190 Old New Bern Rd 28585 252-448-3956
Michael White, prin. Fax 448-1044
Trenton ES 300/PK-6
188 Elementary School Ln 28585 252-448-3441
Margaret Williams, prin. Fax 448-1449
Other Schools – See Comfort, Maysville, Pollocksville

Trinity, Randolph, Pop. 6,915
Randolph County SD
Supt. — See Asheboro
Archdale-Trinity MS 800/7-8
PO Box 232 27370 336-431-2589
Andrea Haynes, prin. Fax 431-1809
Braxton Craven IS 400/6-6
7037 NC Highway 62 27370 336-431-4078
Dana Albright-Johnson, prin. Fax 431-0145
Hopewell ES 600/K-5
6294 Welborn Rd 27370 336-861-2030
Sharon Harper, prin. Fax 861-7040
Trinity ES 500/K-5
5457 Braxton Craven Rd 27370 336-431-1027
Susan Huneycutt, prin. Fax 431-9088
Uwharrie MS 400/6-8
1463 Pleasant Union Rd 27370 336-241-3900
Linda Johnson, prin. Fax 241-3904

Troutman, Iredell, Pop. 1,706
Iredell-Statesville SD
Supt. — See Statesville
Troutman ES 800/K-5
220 S Main St 28166 704-528-4526
Kim Cressman, prin. Fax 528-0988

Troutman MS 400/6-8
PO Box 807 28166 704-528-5137
Jeff James, prin. Fax 528-4006

Troy, Montgomery, Pop. 3,269
Montgomery County SD 4,600/PK-12
PO Box 427 27371 910-576-6511
Dr. Donna Cox Peters, supt. Fax 576-2044
www.montgomery.k12.nc.us
Page Street ES 300/3-5
897 Page St 27371 910-576-1307
Emilie Simeon, prin. Fax 576-1310
Troy ES 400/PK-2
310 N Russell St 27371 910-576-3651
Emilie Simeon, prin. Fax 572-2082
Other Schools – See Biscoe, Candor, Mount Gilead, Star

Wescare Christian Academy 100/K-10
1368 NC Highway 134 N 27371 910-572-2270
Phill Phillips, admin. Fax 572-2257

Tryon, Polk, Pop. 1,752
Polk County SD
Supt. — See Columbus
Tryon ES 500/PK-5
100 School Pl 28782 828-859-6584
Walker Williams, prin. Fax 859-6170

Tryon SDA S, 2820 Lynn Rd 28782 50/1-8
Norma Collson, prin. 828-859-6889

Tyner, Chowan
Edenton/Chowan County SD
Supt. — See Edenton
Chowan MS 600/6-8
2845 Virginia Rd 27980 252-221-4131
Tanya Turner, prin. Fax 221-8033

Union Grove, Iredell
Iredell-Statesville SD
Supt. — See Statesville
Union Grove ES 300/K-5
1314 Sloans Mill Rd 28689 704-539-4354
Julia Stikeleather, prin. Fax 539-5500

Valdese, Burke, Pop. 4,530
Burke County SD
Supt. — See Morganton
Heritage MS 700/6-8
1951 Enon Rd 28690 828-874-0731
Doug Rhoney, prin. Fax 879-6330
Valdese ES 400/K-5
298 Praley St NW 28690 828-874-0704
Bob Acord, prin. Fax 874-1571

Vale, Lincoln
Catawba County SD
Supt. — See Newton
Banoak ES 400/K-6
7651 W NC 10 Hwy 28168 704-462-2849
Dyanne Sherrill, prin. Fax 462-4125

Lincoln County SD
Supt. — See Lincolnton
North Brook ES 400/K-5
642 Highway 274 28168 704-276-2479
Rusty Saine, prin. Fax 276-3378
Union ES 300/K-5
4875 Reepsville Rd 28168 704-276-1493
Chris Kolasinski, prin. Fax 276-3072

Vanceboro, Craven, Pop. 846
Craven County SD
Supt. — See New Bern
Vanceboro-Farm Life ES 600/PK-5
PO Box 879 28586 252-244-3215
Judy Fussell, prin. Fax 244-3219

Vass, Moore, Pop. 770
Moore County SD
Supt. — See Carthage
Vass-Lakeview ES 600/K-5
141 James St 28394 910-245-3444
Donna McClary, prin. Fax 245-1301

Vaughan, Warren
Warren County SD
Supt. — See Warrenton
Vaughan ES 200/K-5
PO Box 199 27586 252-586-4739
Noel Robertson, prin. Fax 586-7350

Vilas, Watauga
Watauga County SD
Supt. — See Boone
Cove Creek S 300/PK-8
930 Vanderpool Rd 28692 828-297-2781
Tom Trexler, prin. Fax 297-1311

Wade, Cumberland, Pop. 502
Cumberland County SD
Supt. — See Fayetteville
District 7 ES 300/PK-5
5721 Smithfield Rd 28395 910-483-0001
Renee Collins, prin. Fax 483-6047

Wadesboro, Anson, Pop. 5,263
Anson County SD 4,200/PK-12
320 Camden Rd 28170 704-694-4417
Dr. Gregory Firn, supt. Fax 694-7470
www.ansonschools.org/
Anson MS 700/7-8
832 US Highway 52 N 28170 704-694-3945
Howard McLean, prin. Fax 694-5209
Ansonville ES 300/PK-6
9104 US Highway 52 N 28170 704-826-8337
Randy High, prin. Fax 926-6136
Wadesboro ES 300/4-6
321 Camden Rd 28170 704-694-9383
Mary Ratliff, prin. Fax 694-5816

Wadesboro PS 400/K-3
1542 US Highway 52 S 28170 704-694-4423
Elizabeth Ammons, prin. Fax 695-1490
Other Schools – See Lilesville, Morven, Peachland

Wagram, Scotland, Pop. 789
Scotland County SD
Supt. — See Laurinburg
Wagram PS 400/PK-3
24081 Main St 28396 910-369-2252
Jamie Synan, prin. Fax 369-2438

Wake Forest, Wake, Pop. 20,126
Wake County SD
Supt. — See Raleigh
Heritage ES 1,000/K-5
3500 Rogers Rd 27587 919-562-6000
George Risinger, prin. Fax 562-6006
Heritage MS 1,300/6-8
3500 Rogers Rd 27587 919-562-6204
Dhedra Cross, prin. Fax 562-6227
Jones Dairy ES 1,000/K-5
1100 Jones Dairy Rd 27587 919-562-6181
Mike Chappell, prin. Fax 562-6186
Wake Forest ES 700/K-5
136 W Sycamore Ave 27587 919-554-8655
Denise Tillery, prin. Fax 554-8660
Wake Forest-Rolesville MS 1,100/6-8
1800 S Main St 27587 919-554-8440
Elaine Hanzer, prin. Fax 554-8435

St. Catherine of Siena Catholic S 200/PK-8
520 W Holding Ave 27587 919-556-7613
Marcy Henehan, prin. Fax 570-0071
St. Catherine of Sienna ECC 100/PK-PK
520 W Holding Ave 27587 919-556-4104
Jane Haga, prin. Fax 570-0071

Walkertown, Forsyth, Pop. 4,294
Winston-Salem/Forsyth SD
Supt. — See Winston Salem
Middle Fork ES 600/K-5
3125 Williston Rd 27051 336-727-2995
Donald Hampton, prin. Fax 727-2942
Walkertown ES 800/PK-5
2971 Main St 27051 336-595-2311
Dr. Neil Raymer, prin. Fax 595-3964
Walkertown MS 600/6-8
3175 Ruxton Dr 27051 336-595-2161
Piper Hendrix, prin. Fax 595-3423

Wallace, Duplin, Pop. 3,531
Duplin County SD
Supt. — See Kenansville
Wallace ES 800/PK-5
4266 S NC Highway 11 28466 910-285-7183
Susan Sellers, prin. Fax 285-4340

Walnut Cove, Stokes, Pop. 1,571
Stokes County SD
Supt. — See Danbury
London ES 300/PK-5
609 School St 27052 336-591-7204
Brett Denney, prin. Fax 591-7032
Southeastern Stokes MS 500/6-8
1044 N Main St 27052 336-591-4371
Doug Rose, prin. Fax 591-8164
Walnut Cove ES 300/PK-5
1211 Walnut Cove School Rd 27052 336-591-4408
James Kirkpatrick, prin. Fax 591-8068

Warrensville, Ashe
Ashe County SD
Supt. — See Jefferson
Ashe County MS 500/7-8
PO Box 259 28693 336-384-3591
W. Bobby Ashley, prin. Fax 384-2112
Blue Ridge ES 500/PK-6
PO Box 229 28693 336-384-4500
Rick Powers, prin. Fax 384-4512

Warrenton, Warren, Pop. 770
Warren County SD 2,800/K-12
PO Box 110 27589 252-257-3184
Dr. Ray Spain, supt. Fax 257-5357
www.wcsk12.org
Boyd ES 400/K-5
203 Cousin Lucys Ln 27589 252-257-3695
Canecca Davis, prin. Fax 257-0163
South Warren ES 200/K-5
216 Shocco Springs Rd 27589 252-257-4606
Dr. Tony Cozart, prin. Fax 257-7123
Warren County MS 700/6-8
118 Campus Dr 27589 252-257-3751
Angela Richardson, prin. Fax 257-4532
Other Schools – See Norlina, Vaughan

Warsaw, Duplin, Pop. 3,092
Duplin County SD
Supt. — See Kenansville
Warsaw ES 600/PK-5
158 Lanefield Rd 28398 910-293-3121
Daren Tyndall, prin. Fax 293-4096
Warsaw MS 200/6-8
738 W College St 28398 910-293-7997
Leon Kea, prin. Fax 293-7397

Washington, Beaufort, Pop. 9,841
Beaufort County SD 7,200/PK-12
4103 Market Street Ext 27889 252-946-6593
Dr. Jeffrey Moss, supt. Fax 946-3255
www.beaufort.k12.nc.us
Eastern ES 700/PK-1
947 Hudnell St 27889 252-946-1611
Patrick Abele, prin. Fax 974-1228
Jones MS 700/6-8
4105 Market Street Ext 27889 252-946-0874
Donna Moore, prin. Fax 946-7604

Small ES 500/4-5
4103 N Market Street Ext 27889 252-946-3941
Lisa Tate, prin. Fax 946-0260
Tayloe ES 500/2-3
910 Tarboro St 27889 252-946-3350
Marion Carson, prin. Fax 974-7712
Other Schools – See Aurora, Bath, Chocowinity, Pinetown

Waxhaw, Union, Pop. 3,207
Union County SD
Supt. — See Monroe
Cuthbertson MS 6-8
1520 Cuthbertson Rd 28173 704-296-0107
Laurel Healy, prin. Fax 243-1673
Kensington ES 500/K-5
8701 Kensington Dr 28173 704-290-1500
Rachel Clarke, prin. Fax 243-3821
Marvin Ridge MS 800/6-8
2831 Crane Rd 28173 704-290-1510
Dr. Tom Bulla, prin. Fax 243-0153
New Town ES K-5
1100 Waxhaw Indian Trail S 28173 704-290-1525
Priscilla Davis, prin. Fax 843-8422
Rea View ES K-5
320 Reid Dairy Rd 28173 704-290-1524
Donna Cook, prin. Fax 845-1653
Sandy Ridge ES 1,000/K-5
10101 Waxhaw Manor Dr 28173 704-290-1505
Tom Childers, prin. Fax 243-3812
Waxhaw ES 700/K-5
1101 Old Providence Rd 28173 704-290-1590
Cheryl Lawrence, prin. Fax 843-4259
Western Union ES 600/PK-5
4111 Western Union School 28173 704-843-2153
Rita Webb, prin. Fax 843-9019

Waynesville, Haywood, Pop. 9,386
Haywood County SD 7,900/K-12
1230 N Main St 28786 828-456-2400
Anne Garrett, supt. Fax 456-2438
www.haywood.k12.nc.us
Bethel MS 300/6-8
730 Sonoma Rd 28786 828-646-3442
Jan Nesbitt, prin. Fax 648-6259
Central ES 300/K-5
62 Joy Ln 28786 828-456-2405
Trevor Putnam, prin. Fax 456-2453
Hazelwood ES 500/K-5
1111 Plott Creek Rd 28786 828-456-2406
Sherri Arrington, prin. Fax 456-5438
Jonathan Valley ES 400/K-5
410 Hall Dr 28785 828-926-3207
Nancy Beeker, prin. Fax 926-2678
Junaluska ES 500/K-5
2238 Asheville Rd 28786 828-456-2407
Merita Noland, prin. Fax 456-2446
Waynesville MS 1,000/6-8
495 Brown Ave 28786 828-456-2403
Keith Roden, prin. Fax 452-7905
Other Schools – See Canton, Clyde

Weaverville, Buncombe, Pop. 2,508
Buncombe County SD
Supt. — See Asheville
North Buncombe ES 700/K-4
251 Flat Creek Church Rd 28787 828-645-6054
Andy Peoples, prin. Fax 658-3059
North Buncombe MS 600/7-8
51 N Buncombe School Rd 28787 828-645-7944
Vicki Biggers, prin. Fax 645-2509
North Windy Ridge S 600/5-6
20 Doan Rd 28787 828-658-1892
Debbie McDermott, prin. Fax 658-1983
Weaverville ES 300/2-4
129 S Main St 28787 828-645-3127
Brent Wise, prin. Fax 645-5129
Weaverville PS 300/K-1
39 S Main Street Ext 28787 828-645-4275
Kay Southern, prin. Fax 658-0121

Weldon, Halifax, Pop. 1,315
Weldon CSD 1,100/PK-12
301 Mulberry St 27890 252-536-4821
Dr. Elie Bracy, supt. Fax 536-3062
www.weldoncityschools.k12.nc.us
Weldon ES 500/PK-5
805 Washington Ave 27890 252-536-4815
Willa Johnson-Wall, prin. Fax 536-3633
Other Schools – See Halifax

Wendell, Wake, Pop. 4,516
Johnston County SD
Supt. — See Smithfield
Archer Lodge MS 6-8
740 Wendell Rd 27591 919-553-0714
Paula Coates, prin. Fax 553-8540

Wake County SD
Supt. — See Raleigh
Carver ES 600/K-5
291 Liles Dean Rd 27591 919-365-2680
Allison Baker, prin. Fax 365-2622
Wendell ES 600/K-5
3355 Wendell Blvd 27591 919-365-2660
Winston Pierce, prin. Fax 365-2666
Wendell MS 6-8
3409 NC Highway 97 27591 919-365-1667
Mary Castleberry, prin. Fax 365-1686

West End, Moore
Moore County SD
Supt. — See Carthage
West End ES 600/K-5
PO Box 290 27376 910-673-6691
Johnnye Waller, prin. Fax 673-7640
West Pine MS 800/6-8
144 Archie Rd 27376 910-673-1464
Dr. Candace Turk, prin. Fax 673-1272

Westfield, Surry
Stokes County SD
Supt. — See Danbury
Francisco ES 100/PK-5
7165 NC Highway 89 W 27053 336-351-2453
Nichole Rose, prin. Fax 351-2562
Reynolds ES 200/K-5
1585 NC Highway 66 N 27053 336-351-2480
Pamela Holt, prin. Fax 351-6130

West Jefferson, Ashe, Pop. 1,082
Ashe County SD
Supt. — See Jefferson
Westwood ES 700/PK-6
4083 US Highway 221 S 28694 336-877-2921
John Gregory, prin. Fax 877-2932

Whitakers, Nash, Pop. 773
Nash-Rocky Mount SD
Supt. — See Nashville
Swift Creek Magnet S 100/PK-PK, 3-
2420 Swift Creek School Rd 27891 252-462-2840
Amy Thornton, prin. Fax 937-1817

Whiteville, Columbus, Pop. 5,212
Columbus County SD 6,900/PK-12
PO Box 729 28472 910-642-5168
Dr. Dan Strickland, supt. Fax 640-1010
www.columbus.k12.nc.us/
Nakina MS 6-8
12489 New Britton Hwy E 28472 910-642-8301
Richard Gore, prin. Fax 642-6097
Old Dock S 400/PK-8
12489 New Britton Hwy E 28472 910-642-2084
Cassandra Cartrette, prin. Fax 642-7872
Williams Township S 700/PK-8
10400 James B White Hwy S 28472 910-653-3791
Jeffrey Spivey, prin. Fax 653-6459
Other Schools – See Cerro Gordo, Chadbourn, Delco, Evergreen, Hallsboro, Riegelwood, Tabor City

Whiteville CSD 2,600/PK-12
PO Box 609 28472 910-642-4116
Randy Shaver, supt. Fax 642-0564
www.whiteville.k12.nc.us
Central MS 500/6-8
310 S Mrtn Lthr King Jr Ave 28472 910-642-3546
Fred Hill, prin. Fax 642-7484
Edgewood ES 600/3-5
317 E Calhoun St 28472 910-642-3121
Thomas McLam, prin. Fax 642-2284
Whiteville PS 700/PK-2
805 Barbcrest Ave 28472 910-642-4119
Lynn Spaulding, prin. Fax 642-4506

Carolina Adventist Academy 50/K-8
3710 James B White Hwy S 28472 910-640-0855
Karen Taylor, prin. Fax 640-1062
Columbus Christian Academy 200/K-12
115 W Calhoun St 28472 910-642-6196
Debra Edwards, prin. Fax 642-3066
Waccamaw Academy 200/K-12
PO Box 507 28472 910-642-7530
Dennis Williamson, hdmstr. Fax 642-6938

Whittier, Jackson
Jackson County SD
Supt. — See Sylva
Smokey Mountain S 400/PK-8
884 US 441 N 28789 828-497-5535
Elizabeth Younce, prin. Fax 497-4907

Wilkesboro, Wilkes, Pop. 3,204
Wilkes County SD
Supt. — See North Wilkesboro
West Wilkes MS 600/6-8
1677 N NC Highway 16 28697 336-973-1700
Dion Stocks, prin. Fax 973-7423
Wilkesboro ES 400/K-5
1248 School St 28697 336-838-4261
Mike Dancy, prin. Fax 667-8611

Willard, Pender
Pender County SD
Supt. — See Burgaw
Penderlea S 500/K-8
82 Penderlea School Rd 28478 910-285-2761
Thomas Byrne, prin. Fax 285-2990

Williamston, Martin, Pop. 5,650
Martin County SD 4,300/PK-12
300 N Watts St 27892 252-792-1575
Dr. Thomas Daly, supt. Fax 792-1965
martin.nc.schoolwebpages.com/
Hayes ES 400/3-5
201 Andrews St 27892 252-792-3678
Susan Peele, prin. Fax 792-5510
Rodgers ES 400/K-6
2277 Rodgers School Rd 27892 252-792-3834
Janet Kallen, prin. Fax 809-4900
Williamston MS 400/6-8
600 N Smithwick St 27892 252-792-1111
Serena Paschal, prin. Fax 792-6644
Williamston PS 500/PK-2
400 West Blvd 27892 252-792-3253
Patricia Moore, prin. Fax 792-7470
Other Schools – See Hamilton, Jamesville, Robersonville

Willow Spring, Wake
Johnston County SD
Supt. — See Smithfield
Dixon Road ES 500/K-5
835 Dixon Rd 27592 919-894-7771
Dawn Alligood, prin. Fax 894-3642

Wake County SD
Supt. — See Raleigh
Willow Springs ES 900/K-5
6800 Dwight Rowland Rd 27592 919-557-2770
Camille Miller, prin. Fax 557-2953

Wilmington, New Hanover, Pop. 95,476
New Hanover County SD 23,500/PK-12
6410 Carolina Beach Rd 28412 910-763-5431
Dr. Alfred Lerch, supt. Fax 254-4479
www.nhcs.net
Alderman ES 400/K-5
2025 Independence Blvd 28403 910-350-2031
Mark Tracy, prin. Fax 350-2035
Anderson ES K-5
455 Halyburton Memorial Pky 28412 910-798-3311
Vicki Hayes, prin. Fax 798-3358
Bellamy ES 500/K-5
70 Sanders Rd 28412 910-350-2039
Dr. Bennie Bryant, prin. Fax 350-2036
Blair ES 600/K-5
6510 Market St 28405 910-350-2045
Barbara Stock, prin. Fax 350-2049
Bradley Creek ES 400/K-5
6211 Greenville Loop Rd 28409 910-350-2051
Sherry Pinto, prin. Fax 350-2053
Codington ES 500/K-5
4321 Carolina Beach Rd 28412 910-790-2236
Budd Dingwall, prin. Fax 790-2238
College Park ES 400/K-5
5001 Oriole Dr 28403 910-350-2058
Maria Greene, prin. Fax 350-2162
Eaton ES 600/K-5
6701 Gordon Rd 28411 910-397-1544
Heather Byers, prin. Fax 397-1546
Forest Hills ES 400/K-5
602 Colonial Dr 28403 910-251-6190
Michael Cobb, prin. Fax 251-6054
Freeman S of Engineering 400/K-5
2601 Princess Place Dr 28405 910-251-6011
Elizabeth Miars, prin. Fax 251-6013
Gregory S of Science-Math & Technology 600/K-5
1106 Ann St 28401 910-251-6185
Dawn Vickers, prin. Fax 251-6023
Holly Tree ES 500/K-5
3020 Web Trce 28409 910-790-2250
Laura Holliday, prin. Fax 790-2252
Howe Preschool PK-PK
1020 Meares St 28401 910-251-6195
Patricia Waddell, prin. Fax 251-6040
Lake Forest Academy 50/K-5
1806 S 15th St 28401 910-772-2515
Kristin Jackson, prin. Fax 772-2516
Murray MS 900/6-8
655 Halyburton Memorial Pky 28412 910-790-2363
Patrick McCarty, prin. Fax 790-2351
Murrayville ES 700/K-5
225 Mabee Way 28411 910-790-5067
Dr. Julie Duclos, prin. Fax 790-5068
Myrtle Grove MS 900/6-8
901 Piner Rd 28409 910-350-2100
Robin Meiers, prin. Fax 350-2104
New Hanover County Schools Pre - K Ctr PK-PK
4905 S College Rd 28412 910-815-6940
Tim Dominowski, prin. Fax 815-6943
Noble MS 800/6-8
6520 Market St 28405 910-350-2112
Wade Smith, prin. Fax 350-2109
Ogden ES 400/K-5
3637 Middle Sound Loop Rd 28411 910-686-6464
Tammy Bruestle, prin. Fax 686-2096
Parsley ES 700/K-5
3518 Masonboro Loop Rd 28409 910-790-2355
Robin Hamilton, prin. Fax 790-2362
Pine Valley ES 700/K-5
440 John S Mosby Dr 28412 910-350-2121
Rebecca Higgins-Opgrand, prin. Fax 350-2116
Roe Preschool PK-PK
2875 Worth Dr 28412 910-350-2127
Ed Adams, prin. Fax 350-2169
Roland-Grise MS 800/6-8
4412 Lake Ave 28403 910-350-2136
Will Hatch, prin. Fax 350-2133
Snipes Academy of Arts & Design 400/K-5
1100 McRae St 28401 910-251-6175
Allison Ward, prin. Fax 815-6974
Sunset Park ES 400/K-5
613 Alabama Ave 28401 910-815-6948
LaChawn Smith, prin. Fax 815-6901
Trask MS 800/6-8
2900 N College Rd 28405 910-350-2142
Sharon Dousharm, prin. Fax 350-2144
Virgo MS 400/6-8
813 Nixon St 28401 910-251-6150
Megan Silvey, prin. Fax 251-6055
Williams ES 500/K-5
801 Silver Lake Rd 28412 910-350-2150
Terilyn Stone, prin. Fax 350-2168
Williston MS 900/6-8
401 S 10th St 28401 910-815-6906
MaryPaul Beall, prin. Fax 815-6904
Winter Park ES 300/K-5
2045 MacMillan Ave 28403 910-350-2159
Lynn Fulton, prin. Fax 350-2155
Wrightsboro ES 600/K-5
2716 Castle Hayne Rd 28401 910-815-6909
Boni Hall, prin. Fax 815-6915
Other Schools – See Carolina Beach, Castle Hayne, Wrightsville Beach

---

Calvary Christian S 100/PK-8
423 N 23rd St 28405 910-343-1565
Nick Smith, prin. Fax 762-5847
Cape Fear Academy 700/PK-12
3900 S College Rd 28412 910-791-0287
John Meehl, hdmstr. Fax 791-0290
Children's Schoolhouse/Montessori 100/PK-1
612 S College Rd 28403 910-799-1531
Lucy Hieronymus, dir.
Ephesus Junior Academy 50/1-8
1002 Castle St 28401 910-762-9989
Joyce Dyson, prin. Fax 762-5422
Friends S of Wilmington 200/PK-8
350 Peiffer Ave 28409 910-792-1811
Ethan Williamson, hdmstr. Fax 792-9274
Myrtle Grove Christian S 400/PK-8
806 Piner Rd 28409 910-392-2067
Stacey Miller, admin. Fax 792-0016
St. Mark Catholic S 300/K-7
1013 Eastwood Rd 28403 910-392-0720
Peggy DiFulvio, prin. Fax 392-6777
St. Mark Montessori Preschool 50/PK-PK
1011 Eastwood Rd 28403 910-392-0720
Cindy Antonelli, dir. Fax 392-6777
St. Mary S 200/K-8
217 S 4th St 28401 910-762-5491
Joyce Price, prin. Fax 762-9664
Wilmington Christian Academy 700/PK-12
1401 N College Rd 28405 910-791-4248
Barren Nobles, admin. Fax 791-4276
Wilmington SDA S 50/1-8
2833 Market St 28403 910-762-4224

Wilson, Wilson, Pop. 46,967
Wilson County SD 12,500/PK-12
PO Box 2048 27894 252-399-7700
Dr. Larry Price, supt. Fax 399-7743
www.wilson.k12.nc.us/
Barnes ES 400/PK-5
1913 Martin Luther King Jr 27893 252-399-7875
Beverly Woodard, prin. Fax 399-7833
Darden MS 400/6-8
1665 Lipscomb Rd E 27893 252-206-4973
Charles Chestnut, prin. Fax 206-1508
Forest Hills MS 600/6-8
1210 Forest Hills Rd NW 27896 252-399-7913
Jerry Simmons, prin. Fax 399-7894
Hearne ES 400/K-5
300 W Gold St 27893 252-399-7925
Melissa Dancy-Smith, prin. Fax 399-7896
New Hope ES 700/K-5
4826 Packhouse Rd 27896 252-399-7950
Eddie Hicks, prin. Fax 399-7899
Rock Ridge ES 600/K-5
6605 Rock Ridge School Rd 27893 252-399-7955
Beverly Boyette, prin. Fax 399-7995
Speight MS 500/6-8
5514 Old Stantonsburg Rd, 252-238-3983
Sarah Ellington, prin. Fax 238-2104
Toisnot MS 500/6-8
1301 Corbett Ave N 27893 252-399-7973
Craig Harris, prin. Fax 399-7749
Vick ES 400/K-5
504 Carroll St N 27893 252-399-7886
Denise Taylor, prin. Fax 399-7873
Vinson-Bynum ES 700/K-5
1601 Tarboro St SW 27893 252-399-7981
Suzette Miller, prin. Fax 399-7758
Wells ES 600/K-5
1400 Grove St N 27893 252-399-7986
James Davis, prin. Fax 399-7771
Winstead ES 500/PK-5
1713 Downing St SW 27893 252-399-7990
Cynthia Dawes, prin. Fax 399-7772
Other Schools – See Black Creek, Elm City, Lucama, Stantonsburg

---

Community Christian S 200/PK-12
5160 Packhouse Rd 27896 252-399-1376
Paula Webb, admin. Fax 243-6973
Greenfield S 300/PK-12
PO Box 3525 27895 252-237-8046
Janet Beaman, hdmstr. Fax 237-1825
Mount Hebron Adventist Christian S 50/1-8
PO Box 1701 27894 252-237-5026
St. Therese Catholic S 100/PK-5
700 Nash St NE 27893 252-237-5342
Fax 237-2042
Wilson Christian Academy 400/K-12
PO Box 3818 27895 252-237-8064
Dwight Vanderboegh, admin. Fax 234-9164

Wilsons Mills, Johnston
Johnston County SD
Supt. — See Smithfield
Wilsons Mills ES 700/K-5
4654 Wilsons Mills Rd 27593 919-934-2978
Tamara Barbour, prin. Fax 934-5640

Windsor, Bertie, Pop. 2,231
Bertie County SD 2,900/PK-12
PO Box 10 27983 252-794-3173
Dr. Sidney Zullinger, supt. Fax 794-9727
www.bertie.k12.nc.us
Bertie MS 500/6-8
652 US Highway 13 N 27983 252-794-2143
Sandra Hardy, prin. Fax 794-4024
Windsor ES 500/PK-5
104 Cooper Hill Rd 27983 252-794-5221
Renee Duckenfield, prin. Fax 794-5218
Other Schools – See Aulander, Colerain, Lewiston Woodville

Bethel Assembly Christian Academy 200/PK-12
105 Askewville Bryant St 27983 252-794-4034
Chris Howerton, prin. Fax 794-3733

Winfall, Perquimans, Pop. 567
Perquimans County SD
Supt. — See Hertford
Perquimans Central ES 400/PK-2
PO Box 129 27985 252-426-5332
Sylvia Johnson, prin. Fax 426-5480
Perquimans County MS 400/6-8
PO Box 39 27985 252-426-7355
Jamie Liverman, prin. Fax 426-1424

Wingate, Union, Pop. 2,866
Union County SD
Supt. — See Monroe

Union ES 500/PK-5
5320 White Store Rd 28174 704-624-5400
Cynthia Croffut, prin. Fax 624-5406
Wingate ES 800/PK-5
301 Bivens St 28174 704-233-4045
Kristy Thomas, prin. Fax 233-9415

Winston Salem, Forsyth, Pop. 188,934
Davidson County SD
Supt. — See Lexington
Friedberg ES 500/K-5
1131 Friedberg Church Rd 27127 336-764-2059
Amy Hyatt, prin. Fax 775-4722
Friendship ES 400/K-5
1490 Friendship Ledford Rd 27107 336-231-8744
Debbie Dawson, prin. Fax 231-8746
Wallburg ES 900/PK-5
205 Motsinger Rd 27107 336-769-2921
Donna Stafford, prin. Fax 769-0967

Winston-Salem/Forsyth SD 49,900/PK-12
PO Box 2513 27102 336-727-2816
Dr. Donald Martin, supt. Fax 727-8404
wsfcs.k12.nc.us
Ashley ES 500/PK-5
1647 NE Ashley School Cir 27105 336-727-2343
Brenda Butler, prin. Fax 727-2344
Bolton ES 700/PK-5
1250 Bolton St 27103 336-774-4626
Doreen Sorensen, prin. Fax 774-4618
Brunson ES 500/K-5
155 N Hawthorne Rd 27104 336-727-2856
Jeff Faullin, prin. Fax 748-3233
Clemmons MS 1,200/6-8
3785 Fraternity Church Rd 27127 336-774-4677
Sandra Hunter, prin. Fax 774-4678
Cook ES 200/PK-5
920 W 11th St 27105 336-727-2784
Ted Burcaw, prin. Fax 727-8458
Diggs ES 300/PK-5
950 Mock St 27127 336-727-2424
Vera Wright, prin. Fax 748-3151
Downtown ES 300/PK-5
601 N Cherry St 27101 336-727-2914
Janet Atkinson, prin. Fax 748-3361
Easton ES 600/PK-5
734 E Clemmonsville Cir 27107 336-771-4520
Steve Flora, prin. Fax 771-4733
Forest Park ES 500/PK-5
2019 Milford St 27107 336-771-4530
Sandra Gilmer, prin. Fax 771-4726
Gibson ES 800/K-5
2020 Walker Rd 27106 336-922-6612
Ron Davis, prin. Fax 922-7335
Griffith ES 700/K-5
1385 W Clemmonsville Rd 27127 336-771-4544
Carolyn F. Fair-Parker, prin. Fax 771-4735
Hall-Woodward ES 700/PK-5
125 Nicholson Rd 27107 336-771-4555
Essie McKoy, prin. Fax 771-4727
Hanes MS 600/6-8
2900 Indiana Ave 27105 336-727-2252
Joe Childers, prin. Fax 727-3207
Hill MS 400/6-8
2200 Tryon St 27107 336-771-4515
Becky Hodges, prin. Fax 771-4519
Ibraham ES 400/PK-5
5036 Old Walkertown Rd 27105 336-661-4850
Lee Koch, prin. Fax 661-4852
Jefferson ES 700/K-5
4000 Jefferson School Ln 27106 336-923-2110
Nora Baker, prin. Fax 923-2111
Jefferson MS 1,100/6-8
3500 Sally Kirk Rd 27106 336-774-4630
Frank Martin, prin. Fax 774-4635
Kimberley Park ES 300/PK-5
1701 Cherry St 27105 336-727-2116
Amy Baker, prin. Fax 727-8245
Konnoak ES 600/K-5
3200 Renon Rd 27127 336-771-4567
Jay Jones, prin. Fax 771-4565
Latham ES 300/PK-5
986 Hutton St 27101 336-727-2310
Celena Clark, prin. Fax 727-2073
Meadowlark ES 700/K-5
401 Meadowlark Dr 27106 336-924-3434
Dr. Ann Aust, prin. Fax 924-8419
Meadowlark MS 1,200/6-8
301 Meadowlark Dr 27106 336-922-1730
Loretta Rowland-Kitley, prin. Fax 922-1745
Mineral Springs ES 700/K-5
4527 Ogburn Ave 27105 336-661-4860
Constance Hash, prin. Fax 661-4865
Mineral Springs MS 500/6-8
4559 Ogburn Ave 27105 336-661-4870
Randy Fulton, prin. Fax 661-4857
Moore ES 600/K-5
451 Knollwood St 27103 336-727-2860
Amanda Wooten, prin. Fax 748-3233
North Hills ES 400/PK-5
340 Alspaugh Dr 27105 336-661-4940
Nathaniel Barber, prin. Fax 661-4943
Northwest MS 900/6-8
5501 Murray Rd 27106 336-924-5126
Sharon Richardson, prin. Fax 924-5128
Old Town ES 700/PK-5
3930 Reynolda Rd 27106 336-924-2915
Vicki Stevens, prin. Fax 924-5610
Petree ES 400/PK-5
3815 Old Greensboro Rd 27101 336-748-3454
Sheila Burlock, prin. Fax 748-3455
Philo MS 500/6-8
410 Haverhill St 27127 336-771-4570
Mark Hairston, prin. Fax 771-4578
Sherwood Forest ES 500/K-5
1055 Yorkshire Rd 27106 336-774-4646
Dan Gallimore, prin. Fax 774-4693
South Fork ES 500/PK-5
4332 Country Club Rd 27104 336-774-4664
Tricia Spencer, prin. Fax 774-4666
Speas ES 300/PK-5
2000 Polo Rd 27106 336-774-4699
Kent Reichert, prin. Fax 774-4697
Ward ES 900/K-5
3775 Fraternity Church Rd 27127 336-774-4676
Dr. Wendy Johnson, prin. Fax 774-4687
Whitaker ES 500/PK-5
2600 Buena Vista Rd 27104 336-727-2244
Brenda Herman, prin. Fax 727-2303
Wiley MS 700/6-8
1400 W Northwest Blvd 27104 336-727-2378
Ed Weiss, prin. Fax 727-8412
Other Schools – See Clemmons, Kernersville, Lewisville, Pfafftown, Rural Hall, Tobaccoville, Walkertown

Calvary Baptist Day S 700/PK-12
5000 Country Club Rd 27104 336-765-5546
Roger Wiles, hdmstr. Fax 714-5577
Ephesus Junior Academy 50/K-8
1225 N Cleveland Ave 27101 336-779-4541
Joy Campbell, prin. Fax 724-3046
First Assembly Christian S 300/K-8
3730 University Pkwy 27106 336-759-7762
Annette Burrow, prin. Fax 896-7667
Gospel Light Christian S 500/PK-12
4940 Gospel Light Church Rd 27101 336-722-6100
Delores Yokely, prin. Fax 722-9640
Our Lady of Mercy S 300/K-8
1730 Link Rd 27103 336-722-7204
Sr. Geri Rogers, prin. Fax 725-2294
Redeemer S 200/K-8
1046 Miller St 27103 336-724-9460
Billy Creech, prin. Fax 724-9555
St. John's Lutheran S 200/PK-8
2415 Silas Creek Pkwy 27103 336-725-1651
Fax 725-1603
St. Leo S 300/PK-8
333 Springdale Ave 27104 336-748-8252
Georgette Schraeder, prin. Fax 748-9005
Salem Baptist Christian S 300/PK-12
429 S Broad St 27101 336-725-6113
Martha Drake, admin. Fax 725-8455
Summit S 600/PK-9
2100 Reynolda Rd 27106 336-722-2777
Michael Ebeling, prin. Fax 724-0099
Woodland Baptist Christian S 200/PK-12
3665 N Patterson Ave 27105 336-767-6176
Steve Holley, admin. Fax 767-9116

Winterville, Pitt, Pop. 4,688
Pitt County SD
Supt. — See Greenville
Cox MS 1,000/6-8
2657 Church St 28590 252-756-3105
Tracy Cole-Williams, prin. Fax 756-1081
Creekside ES 800/PK-5
431 Forlines Rd 28590 252-353-5253
Carla Frinsko, prin. Fax 353-8107
Ridgewood ES PK-5
3601 S Bend Rd 28590 252-355-7879
Cheryl Olmsted, prin. Fax 755-3349
Robinson ES 1,000/PK-5
2439 Railroad St 28590 252-756-3707
Tiffany Vincent, prin. Fax 756-5072

Brookhaven SDA S 50/K-8
4658 Reedy Branch Rd 28590 252-756-5777
James Morgan, prin.
Christ Covenant S 200/K-8
4889 Old Tar Rd 28590 252-756-3002
Steve Elliott, hdmstr. Fax 756-4072

Winton, Hertford, Pop. 920
Hertford County SD 3,600/PK-12
PO Box 158 27986 252-358-1761
Dr. Michael Basham, supt. Fax 358-4745
www.hertford.k12.nc.us
Other Schools – See Ahoskie, Murfreesboro

Woodleaf, Rowan
Rowan-Salisbury County SD
Supt. — See Salisbury
Woodleaf ES 400/K-5
PO Box 10 27054 704-278-2203
Susan Herrington, prin. Fax 278-2204

Wrightsville Beach, New Hanover, Pop. 2,567
New Hanover County SD
Supt. — See Wilmington
Wrightsville Beach ES 200/K-5
220 Coral Dr 28480 910-256-3171
Pansy Rumley, prin. Fax 256-4386

Yadkinville, Yadkin, Pop. 2,867
Yadkin County SD 5,300/PK-12
121 Washington St 27055 336-679-2051
James Benfield, supt. Fax 679-4013
www.yadkin.k12.nc.us
Courtney ES 300/PK-6
2529 Courtney Huntsville Rd 27055 336-463-5510
Diana Jones, prin. Fax 463-2883
Yadkinville ES 700/PK-6
305 N State St 27055 336-679-8921
Dr. James Sheek, prin. Fax 679-2909
Other Schools – See Boonville, East Bend, Hamptonville, Jonesville

Yanceyville, Caswell, Pop. 2,147
Caswell County SD 3,400/PK-12
PO Box 160 27379 336-694-4116
Douglas Barker, supt. Fax 694-5154
www.caswell.k12.nc.us/
Dillard MS 800/6-8
PO Box 310 27379 336-694-4941
Frank Scott, prin. Fax 694-6353
Oakwood ES 500/PK-5
PO Box 640 27379 336-694-4221
Jerome Wilson, prin. Fax 694-4376
Other Schools – See Mebane, Providence, Reidsville

Youngsville, Franklin, Pop. 712
Franklin County SD
Supt. — See Louisburg
Cedar Creek MS 700/6-8
2228 Cedar Creek Rd 27596 919-554-4848
Brooke Wheeler, prin. Fax 570-5143
Long Mill ES K-5
1753 Long Mill Rd 27596 919-554-0667
Kim Ferrell, prin. Fax 554-1765
Youngsville ES 700/K-5
125 US 1A Hwy 27596 919-556-5250
Richard Smith, prin. Fax 556-3962

Zebulon, Wake, Pop. 4,218
Johnston County SD
Supt. — See Smithfield
Corinth Holder S 700/PK-8
3976 NC Highway 231 27597 919-365-7560
Amy Renfrow, prin. Fax 365-7717

Wake County SD
Supt. — See Raleigh
Wakelon ES 400/K-5
8921 Pippin Rd 27597 919-404-3844
Tammie Sexton, prin. Fax 404-3766
Zebulon ES 500/PK-5
700 Proctor St 27597 919-404-3680
Marion Evans, prin. Fax 404-3676
Zebulon MS 1,000/6-8
1000 Shepard School Rd 27597 919-404-3630
Dalphine Perry, prin. Fax 404-3651

Heritage Christian Academy 100/K-12
615 Mack Todd Rd 27597 919-269-6915

Zionville, Watauga
Watauga County SD
Supt. — See Boone
Mabel S 200/PK-8
404 Mabel School Rd 28698 828-297-2512
Mark Hagaman, prin. Fax 297-4109

NORTH DAKOTA

NORTH DAKOTA DEPT. OF PUBLIC INSTRUCTION
600 E Boulevard Ave, Bismarck 58505
Telephone 701-328-2260
Fax 701-328-2461
Website http://www.dpi.state.nd.us

Superintendent of Public Instruction Wayne Sanstead

NORTH DAKOTA BOARD OF EDUCATION
600 E Boulevard Ave, Bismarck 58505

COUNTY SUPERINTENDENTS OF SCHOOLS

Adams County Office of Education
Patricia Carroll, supt. 701-567-4363
PO Box 589, Hettinger 58639 Fax 567-2910
Barnes County Office of Education
Edward McGough, supt. 701-845-8500
230 4th St NW Rm 203 Fax 845-8548
Valley City 58072
Benson County Office of Education
Jean Olson, supt. 701-473-5370
PO Box 347, Minnewaukan 58351 Fax 473-5571
www.tradecorridor.com/minnewaukan/
Billings County Office of Education
Virginia Bares, supt. 701-623-4366
PO Box 334, Medora 58645 Fax 623-4896
Bottineau County Office of Education
Dwane Getzlaff, supt. 701-228-2815
314 5th St W Ste 8A Fax 228-3658
Bottineau 58318
www.tradecorridor.com/bottineaucounty/index.html
Bowman County Office of Education
Lois Anderson, supt. 701-523-3478
PO Box 380, Bowman 58623 Fax 523-3428
Burke County Office of Education
Teri Baumann, supt. 701-377-2861
PO Box 310, Bowbells 58721 Fax 377-2020
Burleigh County Office of Education
Karen Kautzmann, supt. 701-667-3315
210 2nd Ave NW, Mandan 58554 Fax 667-3348
www.co.burleigh.nd.us
Cass County Office of Education
Mike Montplaisir, supt. 701-241-5601
PO Box 2806, Fargo 58108 Fax 241-5728
www.co.cass.nd.us
Cavalier County Office of Education
Dawn Roppel, supt. 701-256-2229
901 3rd St Ste 11, Langdon 58249 Fax 256-2546
Dickey County Office of Education
Tom Strand, supt. 701-349-3249
PO Box 148, Ellendale 58436 Fax 349-4639
Divide County Office of Education
Donald Nielsen, supt. 701-965-6313
PO Box G, Crosby 58730 Fax 965-6004
Dunn County Office of Education
Reinhard Hauck, supt. 701-573-4448
PO Box 105, Manning 58642 Fax 573-4444
Eddy County Office of Education
Joan Schaefer, supt. 701-947-5615
524 Central Ave Ste 301 Fax 947-2279
New Rockford 58356
Emmons County Office of Education
Shawna Paul, supt. 701-254-4486
PO Box 338, Linton 58552 Fax 254-4322
Foster County Office of Education
Roger Schlotman, supt. 701-652-2441
PO Box 80, Carrington 58421 Fax 652-2173
Golden Valley County Office of Education
Virginia Bares, supt. 701-872-4543
PO Box 35, Beach 58621 Fax 872-4383
www.beachnd.com
Grand Forks County Office of Education
David Godfread, supt. 701-795-2777
500 Stanford Rd Fax 795-2770
Grand Forks 58203
Grant County Office of Education
Judy Zins, supt. 701-622-3238
PO Box 279, Carson 58529 Fax 622-3717
Griggs County Office of Education
Ardis Oettle, supt. 701-797-2411
PO Box 340, Cooperstown 58425 Fax 797-3587
www.cooperstownnd.com
Hettinger County Office of Education
Sheila Steiner, supt. 701-824-2500
336 Pacific Ave, Mott 58646 Fax 824-2717
ndaco.org
Kidder County Office of Education
Michelle Keily, supt. 701-475-2632
PO Box 66, Steele 58482 Fax 475-2202
www.ndaco.org
La Moure County Office of Education
Margaret Witt, supt. 701-883-5301
PO Box 128, La Moure 58458 Fax 883-5304
Logan County Office of Education
Gary Schumacher, supt. 701-754-2756
301 Broadway, Napoleon 58561 Fax 754-2270
McHenry County Office of Education
Maxine Rognlien, supt. 701-537-5642
PO Box 147, Towner 58788 Fax 537-5969
McIntosh County Office of Education
Coreen Schumacher, supt. 701-288-3346
PO Box 290, Ashley 58413 Fax 288-3671
McKenzie County Office of Education
Carol Kieson, supt. 701-444-3456
PO Box 503, Watford City 58854 Fax 444-4113
www.4eyes.net
McLean County Office of Education
Lori Foss, supt. 701-462-8541
PO Box 1108, Washburn 58577 Fax 462-3542
www.tradecorridor.com/mcleancounty/
Mercer County Office of Education
Gontran Langowski, supt. 701-873-7692
1021 Arthur St, Stanton 58571 Fax 873-5890
Morton County Office of Education
Karen Kautzmann, supt. 701-667-3315
210 2nd Ave NW, Mandan 58554 Fax 667-3348
www.co.morton.nd.us/
Mountrail County Office of Education
Karen Eliason, supt. 701-628-2145
PO Box 69, Stanley 58784 Fax 628-3975
Nelson County Office of Education
Sharon Young, supt. 701-247-2472
210 B Ave W, Lakota 58344 Fax 247-2943
Oliver County Office of Education
Barbara Fleming, supt. 701-794-8721
PO Box 188, Center 58530 Fax 794-3476
Pembina County Office of Education
Dorothy L. Robinson, supt. 701-265-4336
301 Dakota St W Unit 6 Fax 265-4876
Cavalier 58220
Pierce County Office of Education
Karin Fursather, supt. 701-776-5225
240 2nd St SE Ste 7, Rugby 58368 Fax 776-5707
Ramsey County Office of Education
Lisa Diseth, supt. 701-662-7062
524 4th Ave NE, Devils Lake 58301 Fax 662-7049
Ransom County Office of Education
Suzanne Anderson, supt. 701-683-5823
PO Box 112, Lisbon 58054 Fax 683-5827
Renville County Office of Education
Marvin Madsen, supt. 701-756-6389
PO Box 68, Mohall 58761 Fax 756-6391
Richland County Office of Education
Harris Bailey, supt. 701-642-7700
418 2nd Ave N Ofc 15 Fax 642-7701
Wahpeton 58075
Rolette County Office of Education
Dwane Getzlaff, supt. 701-477-5265
PO Box 939, Rolla 58367 Fax 477-6339
www.tradecorridor.com/rolettecounty
Sargent County Office of Education
Sherry Hosford, supt. 701-724-6241
PO Box 177, Forman 58032 Fax 724-6244
Sheridan County Office of Education
Tracy Laib, supt. 701-363-2205
PO Box 636, Mc Clusky 58463 Fax 363-2953
www.ndaco.org
Sioux County Office of Education
Barb Hettich, supt. 701-854-3481
PO Box L, Fort Yates 58538 Fax 854-3854
Slope County Office of Education
Kathy Walser, supt. 701-879-6277
PO Box MM, Amidon 58620 Fax 879-6278
Stark County Office of Education
Alice Schultz, supt. 701-456-7630
PO Box 130, Dickinson 58602 Fax 456-7634
Steele County Office of Education
Linda Leadbetter, supt. 701-524-2110
PO Box 275, Finley 58230 Fax 524-1715
Stutsman County Office of Education
Noel Johnson, supt. 701-252-9035
511 2nd Ave SE, Jamestown 58401 Fax 251-1603
Towner County Office of Education
Wayne Lingen, supt. 701-968-4346
PO Box 603, Cando 58324 Fax 968-4342
Traill County Office of Education
Rebecca Braaten, supt. 701-636-4458
PO Box 429, Hillsboro 58045 Fax 636-0429
Walsh County Office of Education
Sharon Kinsala, supt. 701-352-2851
600 Cooper Ave, Grafton 58237 Fax 352-3340
Ward County Office of Education
Jodi Johnson, supt. 701-857-6495
PO Box 5005, Minot 58702 Fax 857-6424
Wells County Office of Education
Janelle Rudel, supt. 701-547-3221
PO Box 408, Fessenden 58438 Fax 547-3719
Williams County Office of Education
Grant Archer, supt. 701-577-4580
PO Box 2047, Williston 58802 Fax 577-4579

PUBLIC, PRIVATE AND CATHOLIC ELEMENTARY SCHOOLS

Abercrombie, Richland, Pop. 290
Richland SD 44
Supt. — See Colfax
Richland ES 200/K-6
PO Box 139 58001 701-553-8321
Cindy Erbes, prin. Fax 553-8520

Adams, Walsh, Pop. 188
Adams SD 128 100/K-6
PO Box 76 58210 701-944-2745
Jim Larson, supt. Fax 944-2700
Adams ES 100/K-6
PO Box 76 58210 701-944-2745
Barbara Kendall, prin. Fax 944-2700

Alexander, McKenzie, Pop. 213
Alexander SD 2 50/K-12
PO Box 66 58831 701-828-3335
Murray Kline, supt. Fax 828-3134
www.alexander.k12.nd.us/
Alexander ES 50/K-6
PO Box 66 58831 701-828-3334
Michelle Simonson, prin. Fax 828-3134

Amidon, Slope, Pop. 24
Central Elementary SD 32 50/K-8
106 Court Ave 58620 701-879-6353
Fax 879-6278
Amidon S 50/K-8
106 Court Ave 58620 701-879-6231
Autumn Criswell, prin. Fax 879-6278

Anamoose, McHenry, Pop. 264
Anamoose SD 14 100/K-6
706 3rd St W 58710 701-465-3258
Steven Heim, supt. Fax 465-3259
www.anamoose.k12.nd.us
Anamoose ES 50/K-6
706 3rd St W 58710 701-465-3258
Deborah Reinowski, prin. Fax 465-3259

Ashley, McIntosh, Pop. 783
Ashley SD 9 100/K-12
703 W Main St 58413 701-288-3456
Les Dale, supt. Fax 288-3457
www.ashley.k12.nd.us/
Ashley ES 100/K-6
703 W Main St 58413 701-288-3456
Les Dale, prin. Fax 288-3457

Baldwin, Burleigh
Baldwin SD 29 50/K-8
PO Box 154 58521 701-255-4363
Fax 255-2148
www.baldwin.k12.nd.us/index.htm
Baldwin S 50/K-8
PO Box 154 58521 701-255-4363
Tania Schroeder, prin. Fax 255-2148

Beach, Golden Valley, Pop. 1,000
Beach SD 3 300/K-12
PO Box 368 58621 701-872-4161
Larry Helvik, supt. Fax 872-3801
www.beach.k12.nd.us
Lincoln ES 100/K-6
PO Box 639 58621 701-872-4253
David Wegner, prin. Fax 872-3805

Belcourt, Rolette, Pop. 2,458
Belcourt SD 7 1,600/K-12
PO Box 440 58316 701-477-6471
Roman Marcellais, supt. Fax 477-6470
www.belcourt.k12.nd.us/
Turtle Mountain Community ES 700/K-5
PO Box 440 58316 701-477-6471
David Gourneau, prin. Fax 477-8006
Turtle Mountain Community MS 400/6-8
PO Box 440 58316 701-477-6471
Louis Dauphinais, prin. Fax 477-3973

St. Ann S 50/PK-5
PO Box 2020 58316 701-477-5601
Angie Zaccardelli, prin. Fax 477-0602

Belfield, Stark, Pop. 820
Belfield SD 13 200/K-12
PO Box 97 58622 701-575-4275
Darrel Remington, supt. Fax 575-8533
www.belfield.k12.nd.us/
Belfield ES, PO Box 97 58622 100/K-6
Louise Lorge, prin. 701-575-4275

Billings County SD 1
Supt. — See Medora
Prairie S 50/K-8
12793 20th St 58622 701-623-4363
Denise Soehren, prin. Fax 575-4110

Berthold, Ward, Pop. 442
Lewis and Clark SD 161 400/PK-12
PO Box 185 58718 701-453-3484
Brian Nelson, supt. Fax 453-3488
www.lewisandclark.k12.nd.us/
Berthold S 200/PK-8
PO Box 185 58718 701-453-3484
Melissa Lahti, prin. Fax 453-3488
Other Schools – See Plaza, Ryder

Beulah, Mercer, Pop. 3,036
Beulah SD 27 700/K-12
204 5th St NW 58523 701-873-2261
Robert Lech, supt. Fax 873-5273
www.beulah.k12.nd.us
Beulah ES 200/K-4
200 7th St NW 58523 701-873-2298
Mitch Lunde, prin. Fax 873-2842
Beulah MS 200/5-8
1700 Central Ave N 58523 701-873-4325
Gail Wold, prin. Fax 873-2844

Binford, Griggs, Pop. 178
Midkota SD 7 100/K-12
PO Box 38 58416 701-676-2511
Kerwin Borgen, supt. Fax 676-2510
www.midkota.k12.nd.us
Midkota ES 100/K-6
PO Box 38 58416 701-676-2511
Jeanne Hoyt, prin. Fax 676-2510

Bismarck, Burleigh, Pop. 57,377
Apple Creek SD 39 100/K-6
2000 93rd St SE 58504 701-223-7349
Fax 223-1991
Apple Creek ES 100/K-6
2000 93rd St SE 58504 701-223-7349
Charlotte Knittel, prin. Fax 223-1991

Bismarck SD 1 10,800/PK-12
806 N Washington St 58501 701-355-3000
Dr. Paul Johnson, supt. Fax 355-3001
www.bismarckschools.org
Bismarck ECC 100/PK-PK
1227 Park Ave 58504 701-221-3490
Michelle Hougen, prin. Fax 221-3493
Centennial ES 500/K-6
2800 Ithica Dr 58503 701-221-3735
Jason Hornbacher, prin. Fax 221-3736
Grimsrud ES 300/K-6
716 W Saint Benedict Dr 58501 701-221-3401
Connie Herman, prin. Fax 221-3403
Highland Acres ES 100/K-6
1200 Prairie Dr 58501 701-221-3405
Terry Kuester, prin. Fax 221-3407
Miller ES 500/K-6
1989 N 20th St 58501 701-221-3410
John Alstad, prin. Fax 221-3412
Moses ES 400/K-6
1312 Columbia Dr 58504 701-221-3415
Lynn Wolf, prin. Fax 221-3423
Murphy ES 700/K-6
611 N 31st St 58501 701-221-3424
Angela Durbin, prin. Fax 221-3426
Myhre ES 400/K-6
919 S 12th St 58504 701-221-3430
Dr. Jean Hall, prin. Fax 221-3432
Northridge ES 700/K-6
1727 N 3rd St 58501 701-221-3435
Bobby Olson, prin. Fax 221-3440
Pioneer ES 300/K-6
1400 Braman Ave 58501 701-221-3445
Teresa Delorme, prin. Fax 221-3447
Prairie Rose ES 200/K-6
2200 Oahe Bnd 58504 701-221-3795
Michele Svihovec, prin. Fax 221-3797
Riverside ES 100/K-6
406 S Anderson St 58504 701-221-3455
Willie Nelson, prin. Fax 221-3457
Roosevelt ES 100/K-6
613 W Avenue B 58501 701-221-3460
Cindy Wilcox, prin. Fax 221-3462
Saxvik ES 300/K-6
523 N 21st St 58501 701-221-3465
Maynard Gunderson, prin. Fax 221-3467
Solheim ES 500/K-6
325 Munich Dr 58504 701-221-3495
Jim Jeske, prin. Fax 221-3497
Will-Moore ES 300/K-6
400 E Avenue E 58501 701-221-3470
Joyce Hinman, prin. Fax 221-3711

Manning SD 45 50/K-8
10500 Highway 1804 S 58504 701-223-0082
Manning S 50/K-8
10500 Highway 1804 S 58504 701-223-0082
Rachael Steffen, prin.

Naughton SD 25 50/K-8
9101 123rd Ave NE 58503 701-258-6299
Fax 673-3349
Naughton S 50/K-8
9101 123rd Ave NE 58503 701-673-3119
Kristine Polsfut, prin. Fax 673-3349

Brentwood SDA S 50/1-8
9111 Wentworth Dr 58503 701-258-1579
Joyce Freese, prin.
Cathedral of the Holy Spirit S 300/K-8
508 Raymond St 58501 701-223-5484
Leann Binde, prin. Fax 223-5485
Martin Luther S 200/PK-8
413 E Avenue D 58501 701-224-9070
Kristi Voeller, prin. Fax 250-9487
St. Anne S 200/PK-8
1315 N 13th St 58501 701-223-3373
Cori Hilzendeger, prin. Fax 250-9214
St. Marys S 200/PK-8
807 E Thayer Ave 58501 701-223-0225
Tom Hesford, prin. Fax 250-9918
Shiloh Christian S 400/PK-12
1915 Shiloh Dr 58503 701-221-2104
Ross Reinhiller, admin. Fax 224-8221

Bottineau, Bottineau, Pop. 2,157
Bottineau SD 1 700/K-12
301 Brander St 58318 701-228-2266
Jason Kersten, supt. Fax 228-2021
www.bottineau.k12.nd.us/
Bottineau ES 300/K-6
301 Brander St 58318 701-228-3718
Michael Forsberg, prin. Fax 228-2021

Bowbells, Burke, Pop. 361
Bowbells SD 14 100/K-12
PO Box 279 58721 701-377-2396
Brent Johnston, supt. Fax 377-2399
www.bowbells.k12.nd.us
Bowbells ES 50/K-6
PO Box 279 58721 701-377-2396
Brent Johnston, prin. Fax 377-2399

Bowman, Bowman, Pop. 1,513
Bowman County SD 1 400/K-12
PO Box H 58623 701-523-3283
Tony Duletski, supt. Fax 523-3849
www.bowman.k12.nd.us
Bowman S 200/K-8
PO Box H 58623 701-523-3358
Elizabeth Peterson, prin. Fax 523-3849
Other Schools – See Rhame

Buchanan, Stutsman, Pop. 73
Pingree-Buchanan SD 10
Supt. — See Pingree
Pingree Buchanan ES 100/K-7
PO Box 99 58420 701-252-4653
Terrie Neys, prin. Fax 252-4660

Buffalo, Cass, Pop. 192
Maple Valley SD 4
Supt. — See Tower City
West ES 100/K-6
PO Box 165 58011 701-633-5183
Patricia Johnson, prin. Fax 633-5193

Burlington, Ward, Pop. 1,016
United SD 7
Supt. — See Des Lacs
Burlington Des Lacs S 400/PK-8
PO Box 158 58722 701-839-7135
Norma Klein, prin. Fax 838-1573

Buxton, Traill, Pop. 348
Central Valley SD 3 100/K-12
1556 Highway 81 NE 58218 701-847-2220
Marcia Hall, supt. Fax 847-2407
www.centralvalley.k12.nd.us/
Central Valley S 100/K-12
1556 Highway 81 NE 58218 701-847-2220
Jeremy Brandt, prin. Fax 847-2407

Cando, Towner, Pop. 1,172
North Star SD 100/K-12
PO Box 489 58324 701-968-4416
Mark Lindahl, supt. Fax 968-4418
www.northstar.k12.nd.us//index.html
North Star S 100/K-12
PO Box 489 58324 701-968-4416
Kathleen Lalum, prin. Fax 968-4418

Cannon Ball, Sioux, Pop. 702
Solen SD 3
Supt. — See Solen
Cannon Ball S 100/PK-8
PO Box 218 58528 701-854-3341
Wayne Fox, prin. Fax 854-3342

Carrington, Foster, Pop. 2,148
Carrington SD 49 600/PK-12
PO Box 48 58421 701-652-3136
Brian Duchscherer, supt. Fax 652-1243
www.carrington.k12.nd.us/
Carrington ES 300/PK-6
232 9th Ave N 58421 701-652-2739
Juanita Short, prin. Fax 652-2740

Prairie View SDA S 50/1-8
17 3rd St SE 58421 701-652-2261

Carson, Grant, Pop. 284
Roosevelt SD 18 100/K-8
PO Box 197 58529 701-622-3263
Martin Schock, supt. Fax 622-3236
www.roosevelt.k12.nd.us/
Roosevelt S 100/K-8
PO Box 197 58529 701-622-3263
Keith Anderson, prin. Fax 622-3236

Cartwright, McKenzie
Horse Creek SD 32 50/K-8
1812 Horse Creek Rd 58838 701-481-1373
Fax 481-1373
Horse Creek S 50/K-8
1812 Horse Creek Rd 58838 701-481-1373
Laura Enerson, prin. Fax 481-1373

Casselton, Cass, Pop. 1,920
Central Cass SD 17 800/K-12
802 5th St N 58012 701-347-5352
Michael Severson, supt. Fax 347-5354
www.central-cass.k12.nd.us/
Central Cass ES 300/K-5
802 5th St N 58012 701-347-5353
Christopher Bastian, prin. Fax 347-5354
Central Cass MS 200/6-8
802 5th St N 58012 701-347-5352
Pete Pogatshnik, prin. Fax 347-5354

Cavalier, Pembina, Pop. 1,443
Cavalier SD 6 400/K-12
PO Box 410 58220 701-265-8417
Francis Schill, supt. Fax 265-8106
cavalier.nd.schoolwebpages.com/
Cavalier S 300/K-8
PO Box 410 58220 701-265-8417
Jolyn Greenwood, prin. Fax 265-8106

Center, Oliver, Pop. 593
Center-Stanton SD 1 200/K-12
PO Box 248 58530 701-794-8778
Royal Lyson, supt. Fax 794-3659
www.center.k12.nd.us/
Center S 100/K-6
PO Box 248 58530 701-794-8731
Kathleen Bullinger, prin. Fax 794-3659

Colfax, Richland, Pop. 91
Richland SD 44 300/K-12
PO Box 49 58018 701-372-3713
Wayne Ulven, supt. Fax 372-3718
www.richland.k12.nd.us
Other Schools – See Abercrombie

Cooperstown, Griggs, Pop. 945
Griggs County Central SD 18 300/K-12
1207 Foster Ave NE 58425 701-797-3114
Wade Faul, supt. Fax 797-3130
www.griggs-co.k12.nd.us/
Griggs County Central ES 200/K-6
1207 Foster Ave NE 58425 701-797-3114
Audrey Faul, prin. Fax 797-3130

Crosby, Divide, Pop. 1,017
Divide County SD 1 200/K-12
PO Box G 58730 701-965-6313
Donald Nielsen, supt. Fax 965-6004
www.divide-co.k12.nd.us/
Divide County ES 100/K-6
PO Box G 58730 701-965-6324
Sherry Lalum, prin. Fax 965-6004

Crystal, Pembina, Pop. 160
Valley SD 12
Supt. — See Hoople
Valley S 100/PK-8
PO Box 129 58222 701-657-2163
Gary Jackson, prin. Fax 657-2150

Davenport, Cass, Pop. 246
Kindred SD 2
Supt. — See Kindred
Davenport ES 100/K-1
PO Box 97 58021 701-428-3388
Ron Zehren, prin. Fax 428-3736

Des Lacs, Ward, Pop. 193
United SD 7 600/PK-12
PO Box 117 58733 701-725-4334
Clarke Ranum, supt. Fax 725-4375
www.united.k12.nd.us/
Other Schools – See Burlington

Devils Lake, Ramsey, Pop. 6,816
Devils Lake SD 1 1,800/PK-12
1601 College Dr N 58301 701-662-7640
Steven Swiontek, supt. Fax 662-7646
www.dlschools.org/
Central MS 600/5-8
325 7th St NE 58301 701-662-7664
Joshua Johnson, prin. Fax 662-7649
Minnie H ES 100/K-4
210 College Dr S 58301 701-662-7670
Kimberly Krogfoss, prin. Fax 662-7677
Prairie View ES 300/K-4
200 12th Ave NE 58301 701-662-7626
Lynn Goodwill, prin. Fax 662-7629

Sweetwater ES 200/PK-4
1304 2nd Ave NE 58301 701-662-7630
Debra Follman, prin. Fax 662-7637

St. Joseph S 200/PK-6
824 10th Ave NE 58301 701-662-5016
Thomas Burckhard, prin. Fax 662-5017

Dickinson, Stark, Pop. 15,666
Dickinson SD 1 2,500/PK-12
PO Box 1057 58602 701-456-0002
Douglas Sullivan, supt. Fax 456-0035
www.dickinson.k12.nd.us
Berg ES 50/6-6
PO Box 1057 58602 701-456-0010
Tammy Praus, prin. Fax 456-0039
ECC 50/PK-PK
PO Box 1057 58602 701-227-3010
Sharon Hansen, dir. Fax 225-1968
Hagen JHS 400/7-8
PO Box 1057 58602 701-456-0020
Perry Braunagel, prin. Fax 456-0044
Heart River ES 200/K-6
PO Box 1057 58602 701-456-0012
Sherry Libis, prin. Fax 456-0005
Jefferson ES 300/K-6
PO Box 1057 58602 701-456-0013
Rebecca Meduna, prin. Fax 456-0025
Lincoln ES 300/K-6
PO Box 1057 58602 701-456-0014
Del Quigley, prin. Fax 456-0029
Roosevelt ES 300/K-6
PO Box 1057 58602 701-456-0015
Henry Mack, prin. Fax 456-0001

Hope Christian Academy 50/PK-8
2891 5th Ave W 58601 701-225-3919
Ron Dazell, admin. Fax 227-1464
Trinity East ES 100/K-6
515 3rd St E 58601 701-225-9463
Peggy Mayer, prin. Fax 225-0474
Trinity West ES 200/PK-6
145 3rd Ave W 58601 701-225-8094
Peggy Mayer, prin. Fax 225-8831

Drake, McHenry, Pop. 287
Drake SD 57 100/K-6
PO Box 256 58736 701-465-3732
Steven Heim, supt. Fax 465-3634
drake.nd.schoolwebpages.com
Drake ES 100/K-6
PO Box 256 58736 701-465-3732
Marvin Goplen, prin. Fax 465-3634

Drayton, Pembina, Pop. 852
Drayton SD 19 100/K-12
108 S 5th St 58225 701-454-3324
Hy Schlieve, supt. Fax 454-3485
Drayton ES 100/K-6
108 S 5th St 58225 701-454-3324
Gregory Pollestad, prin. Fax 454-3485

Dunseith, Rolette, Pop. 748
Dunseith SD 1 400/K-12
PO Box 789 58329 701-244-0480
Lanelia DeCoteau, supt. Fax 244-5129
www.dunseith.k12.nd.us/
Dunseith ES 200/K-6
PO Box 789 58329 701-244-5792
Rebecca Bless, prin. Fax 244-5183

Edgeley, LaMoure, Pop. 578
Edgeley SD 3 200/K-12
PO Box 37 58433 701-493-2292
Richard Diegel, supt. Fax 493-2411
www.edgeley.k12.nd.us/
Edgeley ES 100/K-6
PO Box 37 58433 701-493-2292
Tyler Hanson, prin. Fax 493-2411
Willow Bank Colony S 50/K-8
PO Box 37 58433 701-493-2292
Tyler Hanson, prin. Fax 493-2411

Edinburg, Walsh, Pop. 233
Edinburg SD 106 100/K-12
PO Box 6 58227 701-993-8312
Andrew Currie, supt. Fax 993-8313
www.edinburg.k12.nd.us/
Edinburg ES 100/K-6
PO Box 6 58227 701-993-8312
Karen Kertz, prin. Fax 993-8313

Elgin, Grant, Pop. 600
Elgin - New Leipzig SD 49 200/K-12
PO Box 70 58533 701-584-2374
Martin Schock, supt. Fax 584-3018
www.elgin.k12.nd.us
Elgin / New Leipzig ES 100/K-4
PO Box 70 58533 701-584-2374
Roxann Tietz, prin. Fax 584-3018

Ellendale, Dickey, Pop. 1,500
Ellendale SD 40 400/K-12
PO Box 400 58436 701-349-3232
Jeff Fastnacht, supt. Fax 349-3447
www.ellendale.k12.nd.us
Ellendale ES 200/K-6
PO Box 400 58436 701-349-3232
Anna Sell, prin. Fax 349-3447
Other Schools – See Fullerton

Emerado, Grand Forks, Pop. 483
Emerado SD 127 100/K-8
PO Box 69 58228 701-594-5125
Fax 594-8180
www.emerado.k12.nd.us/
Emerado S 100/K-8
PO Box 69 58228 701-594-5125
Brandon Lunak, prin. Fax 594-8180

Enderlin, Ransom, Pop. 1,055
Enderlin SD 24 300/K-12
410 Bluff St 58027 701-437-2240
Patrick Feist, supt. Fax 437-2242
www.enderlin.k12.nd.us/
Enderlin ES 100/K-6
410 Bluff St 58027 701-437-2240
Brian Midthun, prin. Fax 437-2242

Fairmount, Richland, Pop. 386
Fairmount SD 18 100/K-12
PO Box 228 58030 701-474-5469
Ron Stahlecker, supt. Fax 474-5862
www.fairmount.k12.nd.us/
Fairmount ES 100/K-6
PO Box 228 58030 701-474-5469
Blake Dahlberg, prin. Fax 474-5862

Fargo, Cass, Pop. 90,672
Fargo SD 1 9,800/PK-12
415 4th St N 58102 701-446-1000
Rick Buresh, supt. Fax 446-1200
www.fargo.k12.nd.us/
Barton ES 200/3-5
1417 6th St S 58103 701-446-4400
Dana Carlson, prin. Fax 446-4499
Bennett ES 600/K-5
2000 58th Ave S 58104 701-446-4000
Vicky Stormoe, prin. Fax 446-4099
Centennial ES 600/K-5
4201 25th St S 58104 701-446-4300
Jeff Reznecheck, prin. Fax 446-4399
Discovery MS 800/6-8
1717 40th Ave S 58104 701-446-3300
Linda Davis, prin. Fax 446-3599
Eagles ECC 100/PK-PK
3502 University Dr S 58104 701-446-3900
Barb Swegarden, prin. Fax 446-3999
Eielson MS 500/6-8
1601 13th Ave S 58103 701-446-1700
Brad Larson, prin. Fax 446-1799
Franklin MS 800/6-8
1420 8th St N 58102 701-446-3600
John Nelson, prin. Fax 446-3899
Hawthorne ES 200/K-2
555 8th Ave S 58103 701-446-4500
Dana Carlson, prin. Fax 446-4599
Jefferson ES 400/K-5
1701 4th Ave S 58103 701-446-4700
Brad Franklin, prin. Fax 446-4799
Kennedy ES 500/K-5
4401 42nd St S 58104 701-446-4200
Maggie Mitzel, prin. Fax 446-4299
Lewis & Clark ES 400/K-5
1729 16th St S 58103 701-446-4800
Tricia Erickson, prin. Fax 446-4899
Lincoln ES 500/K-5
2120 9th St S 58103 701-446-4900
Manix Zepeda, prin. Fax 446-4999
Longfellow ES 400/K-5
20 29th Ave NE 58102 701-446-5000
Robert Rohla, prin. Fax 446-5099
Madison ES 200/K-5
1040 29th St N 58102 701-446-5100
Chris Triggs, prin. Fax 446-5199
Mann ES 100/K-2
1025 3rd St N 58102 701-446-4600
Kim Colwell, prin. Fax 446-4699
McKinley ES 200/K-5
2930 8th St N 58102 701-446-5200
Dawn Streifel, prin. Fax 446-5299
Roosevelt ES 100/3-5
1026 10th St N 58102 701-446-5300
Kim Colwell, prin. Fax 446-5399
Washington ES 300/K-5
1725 Broadway N 58102 701-446-5400
Linda McKibben, prin. Fax 446-5499

West Fargo SD 6
Supt. — See West Fargo
Osgood K Center PK-K
5550 44th Ave S 58104 701-356-2190
Darren Sheldon, prin. Fax 356-2199

Dakota Montessori S 200/PK-6
1134 Westrac Dr S 58103 701-235-9184
Julia Jones, prin. Fax 235-6303
Grace Lutheran S 100/PK-8
1025 14th Ave S 58103 701-232-7747
Jean Syverson, prin. Fax 237-0618
Holy Spirit S 200/PK-5
1441 8th St N 58102 701-232-4087
Jason Kotrba, prin. Fax 232-8240
Nativity S 400/PK-5
1825 11th St S 58103 701-232-7461
Cindy Hutchins, prin. Fax 298-8981
Oak Grove Lutheran S 200/PK-5
2720 32nd Ave S 58103 701-893-3073
Kim Forness, prin. Fax 893-3076
Sullivan MS 300/6-8
5600 25th St S 58104 701-893-3200
Darrin Roach, prin. Fax 893-3277

Fessenden, Wells, Pop. 547
Fessenden-Bowdon SD 25 200/K-12
PO Box 67 58438 701-547-3296
Terry Olschlager, dir. Fax 547-3125
www.fessenden-bowdon.k12.nd.us/
Fessenden-Bowdon S 100/K-8
PO Box 67 58438 701-547-3296
Jon Bertsch, prin. Fax 547-3125

Finley, Steele, Pop. 447
Finley-Sharon SD 19 200/K-12
PO Box 448 58230 701-524-2420
Merlin H. Dahl, supt. Fax 524-2588
www.finley.k12.nd.us/
Finely-Sharon ES 100/K-6
PO Box 448 58230 701-524-2420
Virgil Babinski, prin. Fax 524-2588

Flasher, Morton, Pop. 272
Flasher SD 39 200/K-12
PO Box 267 58535 701-597-3355
John Barry, supt. Fax 597-3781
www.flasher.k12.nd.us/
Flasher ES 100/K-6
PO Box 267 58535 701-597-3555
Janet Ripplinger, prin. Fax 597-3781

Forbes, Dickey, Pop. 62
Leola SD 44-2
Supt. — See Leola, SD
Spring Creek Colony S 50/K-8
36562 102nd St 58439 605-439-3143
Jamie Hermann, prin. Fax 439-3206

Fordville, Walsh, Pop. 246
Fordville-Lankin SD 5 100/K-12
PO Box 127 58231 701-229-3297
Michael O'Brien, supt. Fax 229-3231
www.fordville-lankin.k12.nd.us/
Fordville Lankin S 50/K-6
PO Box 127 58231 701-229-3297
Karen O'Neil, prin. Fax 229-3231

Forman, Sargent, Pop. 476
Sargent Central SD 6 300/K-12
575 5th St SW 58032 701-724-3205
Michael Campbell, supt. Fax 724-3559
www.sargent.k12.nd.us
Sargent Central ES 100/K-6
575 5th St SW 58032 701-724-3205
Terry Buringrud, prin. Fax 724-3559

Fort Ransom, Ransom, Pop. 101
Fort Ransom SD 6 50/K-6
135 Mill Rd 58033 701-973-2591
Steven Johnson, supt. Fax 973-2491
Fort Ransom ES 50/K-6
135 Mill Rd 58033 701-973-2591
Elinor Meckle, prin. Fax 973-2491

Fort Yates, Sioux, Pop. 236
Fort Yates SD 4 200/6-8
9189 Highway 24 58538 701-854-2142
Dr. Harold Larson, supt. Fax 854-2145
www.fort-yates.k12.nd.us/
Fort Yates MS 200/6-8
9189 Highway 24 58538 701-854-3819
Tomi Kuntz, prin. Fax 854-7467

St. Bernards Mission S 100/1-6
PO Box 394 58538 701-854-7413
Sr. Richarde Wolf, prin. Fax 854-3474

Fullerton, Dickey, Pop. 80
Ellendale SD 40
Supt. — See Ellendale
Maple River S 50/K-8
9262 93rd Ave SE 58441 701-349-3232
Anna Sell, prin. Fax 349-3447

Gackle, Logan, Pop. 298
Gackle-Streeter SD 56 100/K-12
PO Box 375 58442 701-485-3692
Norman Fries, supt. Fax 485-3620
www.gacklestreeter.k12.nd.us/
Gackle-Streeter ES 50/K-6
PO Box 375 58442 701-485-3692
Carol Entzminger, prin. Fax 485-3620

Garrison, McLean, Pop. 1,216
Garrison SD 51 300/PK-12
PO Box 249 58540 701-463-2818
Steve Brannan, supt. Fax 463-2067
www.garrison.k12.nd.us/
Callies ES 200/PK-6
PO Box 369 58540 701-463-2213
Michelle Fuller, prin. Fax 463-2214

Glenburn, Renville, Pop. 338
Glenburn SD 26 100/K-12
PO Box 138 58740 701-362-7426
David Wisthoff, supt. Fax 362-7349
www.glenburn.k12.nd.us/
Glenburn S 100/K-12
PO Box 138 58740 701-362-7426
Patrick Dean, prin. Fax 362-7349

Lynch Immanuel Lutheran S 100/PK-1
18301 Highway 83 N 58740 701-727-4994
Rev. Thomas Eaves, prin. Fax 362-7755

Glen Ullin, Morton, Pop. 829
Glen Ullin SD 48 200/K-12
PO Box 548 58631 701-348-3590
Kyle Christensen, supt. Fax 348-3084
www.glen-ullin.k12.nd.us
Glen Ullin ES 100/K-6
PO Box 548 58631 701-348-3590
Kris Nelson, prin. Fax 348-3084

Golva, Golden Valley, Pop. 95
Lone Tree SD 6 50/K-8
PO Box 170 58632 701-872-3674
Fax 872-3004
Golva S 50/K-8
PO Box 170 58632 701-872-3674
Julie Zook, prin. Fax 872-3004

Goodrich, Sheridan, Pop. 133
Goodrich SD 16 50/K-12
PO Box 159 58444 701-884-2469
Rodney Scherbenske, supt. Fax 884-2496
Goodrich ES 50/K-6
PO Box 159 58444 701-884-2469
Julie Bender, prin. Fax 884-2496

Grafton, Walsh, Pop. 4,248
Grafton SD 3 900/K-12
1548 School Rd 58237 701-352-1930
Jack Maus, supt. Fax 352-1943
www.grafton.k12.nd.us/
Century ES 300/K-4
830 W 15th St 58237 701-352-1739
Nancy Burke, prin. Fax 352-0163
Grafton Central MS 300/5-8
725 Griggs Ave 58237 701-352-1469
Dennis Hammer, prin. Fax 352-1120

Grand Forks, Grand Forks, Pop. 49,792
Grand Forks SD 1 7,200/PK-12
PO Box 6000 58206 701-746-2200
Larry Nybladh, supt. Fax 772-7739
www.gfschools.org
Century ES 500/PK-5
3351 17th Ave S 58201 701-746-2440
Cindy Cochran, prin. Fax 787-4079
Franklin ES 300/K-5
1016 S 20th St 58201 701-746-2250
Beth Randklev, prin. Fax 746-2255
Kelly ES 500/K-5
3000 Cherry St 58201 701-746-2265
Mike LaMoine, prin. Fax 746-2266
Lake Agassiz ES 300/PK-5
605 Stanford Rd 58203 701-746-2275
George Whalen, prin. Fax 746-2274
Lewis & Clark ES 200/K-5
1100 13th Ave S 58201 701-746-2285
Scott Johnson, prin. Fax 746-2288
Phoenix ES 200/K-5
351 4th Ave S 58201 701-746-2240
Darryl Tunseth, prin. Fax 746-2244
Schroeder MS 500/6-8
800 32nd Ave S 58201 701-746-2330
Ken Schill, prin. Fax 746-2332
South MS 600/6-8
1999 47th Ave S 58201 701-746-2345
Nancy Dutot, prin. Fax 746-2355
Valley MS 400/6-8
2100 5th Ave N 58203 701-746-2360
Kevin Ohnstad, prin. Fax 746-2363
Viking ES 300/K-5
809 22nd Ave S 58201 701-746-2300
Roanne Malm, prin. Fax 746-2303
West ES 300/K-5
615 N 25th St 58203 701-746-2310
Ali Parkinson, prin. Fax 746-2454
Wilder ES 100/K-5
1009 N 3rd St 58203 701-746-2320
Gail Kalenze, prin. Fax 746-2322
Winship ES 100/K-5
1412 5th Ave N 58203 701-746-2325
Gail Kalenze, prin. Fax 746-2374
Other Schools – See Grand Forks AFB

Holy Family S 100/PK-6
1001 17th Ave S 58201 701-775-9886
Charles Scherr, prin. Fax 775-0221
St. Michael S 100/PK-6
504 5th Ave N 58203 701-772-1822
Gerri Lorenz, prin. Fax 772-0211

Grand Forks AFB, Grand Forks, Pop. 9,343
Grand Forks SD 1
Supt. — See Grand Forks
Eielson ES 300/PK-3
1238 Louisiana St 58204 701-787-5000
Angie Jonasson, prin. Fax 787-5053
Twining S 200/4-8
1422 Louisiana St 58204 701-787-5100
Barry Lentz, prin. Fax 787-5143

Granville, McHenry, Pop. 255
TGU SD 60
Supt. — See Towner
TGU Granville ES 100/K-6
210 6th St SW 58741 701-728-6641
Tonya Hunskor, prin. Fax 728-6386

Grenora, Williams, Pop. 194
Grenora SD 99 100/K-12
PO Box 38 58845 701-694-2711
Shannon Faller, supt. Fax 694-2717
www.grenora.k12.nd.us/
Grenora ES 50/K-6
PO Box 38 58845 701-694-2711
Troy Walters, prin. Fax 694-2717

Gwinner, Sargent, Pop. 709
North Sargent SD 3 200/K-12
PO Box 289 58040 701-678-2492
Harlan Heinrich, supt. Fax 678-2311
www.northsargent.k12.nd.us
North Sargent ES 100/K-6
PO Box 289 58040 701-678-2492
Michael Sorlie, prin. Fax 678-2311

Hague, Emmons, Pop. 82
Bakker SD 10 50/PK-8
880 96th St SE 58542 701-336-7667
Fax 336-4600
Bakker S 50/PK-8
880 96th St SE 58542 701-336-7284
Joy Dykema, prin. Fax 336-4600

Halliday, Dunn, Pop. 215
Halliday SD 19 50/K-12
PO Box 188 58636 701-938-4391
Dale Gilje, supt. Fax 938-4373
www.halliday.k12.nd.us/
Halliday ES 50/K-6
PO Box 188 58636 701-938-4391
Ronald Biberdorf, prin. Fax 938-4373

Hankinson, Richland, Pop. 1,011
Hankinson SD 8 300/K-12
PO Box 220 58041 701-242-7516
Jess Smith, supt. Fax 242-7434
www.hankinson.k12.nd.us/
Hankinson ES 200/K-6
PO Box 220 58041 701-242-8336
Anne Biewer, prin. Fax 242-7434

Harvey, Wells, Pop. 1,759
Harvey SD 38 400/K-12
811 Burke Ave 58341 701-324-4692
Daniel Stutlien, supt. Fax 324-4414
www.harvey.k12.nd.us/
Harvey S 300/K-8
811 Burke Ave 58341 701-324-2265
Gayle Lee, prin. Fax 324-4414

Harwood, Cass, Pop. 638
West Fargo SD 6
Supt. — See West Fargo
Harwood ES 100/1-5
110 Freedland Dr 58042 701-356-2040
Jerry Barnum, prin. Fax 356-2049

Hatton, Traill, Pop. 684
Hatton SD 7 200/K-12
PO Box 200 58240 701-543-3455
Kevin Rogers, supt. Fax 543-3459
www.hatton.k12.nd.us/
Hatton ES 100/K-6
PO Box 200 58240 701-543-3455
Chad Omdahl, prin. Fax 543-3459

Hazelton, Emmons, Pop. 210
Hazelton-Moffit-Braddock SD 6 100/K-12
PO Box 209 58544 701-782-6231
Brandt Dick, supt. Fax 782-6245
www.hmb.k12.nd.us/
Hazelton-Moffit-Braddock ES 100/K-6
PO Box 209 58544 701-782-4226
Dianne Kalberer, prin. Fax 782-6245

Hazen, Mercer, Pop. 2,356
Hazen SD 3 700/PK-12
PO Box 487 58545 701-748-2345
Michael Ness, supt. Fax 748-2342
www.hazen.k12.nd.us
Hazen ES 300/PK-5
PO Box 487 58545 701-748-6120
Gontran Langowski, prin. Fax 748-6647
Hazen MS 100/6-8
PO Box 487 58545 701-748-6649
Bradley Foss, prin. Fax 748-6650

Hebron, Morton, Pop. 754
Hebron SD 13 200/K-12
PO Box Q 58638 701-878-4442
Robert Osland, supt. Fax 878-4345
www.hebron.k12.nd.us/
Hebron ES 100/K-6
PO Box Q 58638 701-878-4442
Kristen Nelson, prin. Fax 878-4345

Hettinger, Adams, Pop. 1,231
Hettinger SD 13 300/K-12
PO Box 1188 58639 701-567-5315
Brian Christopherson, supt. Fax 567-5094
www.hettinger.k12.nd.us
Hettinger ES 100/K-6
PO Box 1188 58639 701-567-4501
Lyn Hendry, prin. Fax 567-5094

Hillsboro, Traill, Pop. 1,529
Hillsboro SD 9 400/K-12
PO Box 579 58045 701-636-4360
Mike Bitz, supt. Fax 636-4362
www.hillsboro.k12.nd.us/
Hillsboro ES 200/K-6
PO Box 579 58045 701-636-4711
Paula Pederson, prin. Fax 636-4712

Hoople, Walsh, Pop. 270
Valley SD 12 200/PK-12
PO Box 150 58243 701-894-6226
John Oistad, supt. Fax 894-6146
Other Schools – See Crystal

Horace, Cass, Pop. 1,069
West Fargo SD 6
Supt. — See West Fargo
Horace ES 200/1-5
110 3rd Ave N 58047 701-356-2080
Jerry Barnum, prin. Fax 356-2089

Hunter, Cass, Pop. 307
Northern Cass SD 97 400/K-12
16021 18th St SE 58048 701-874-2322
Allen Burgad, supt. Fax 874-2422
www.northerncass.k12.nd.us
Northern Cass ES 200/K-6
16021 18th St SE 58048 701-874-2322
Shelly Swanson, prin. Fax 874-2422

Hurdsfield, Wells, Pop. 83
Pleasant Valley SD 35 50/K-8
PO Box 165 58451 701-962-3322
Julie Hartman, admin. Fax 962-3872
Hurdsfield ES 50/K-8
PO Box 165 58451 701-962-3322
Julie Hartman, prin. Fax 962-3872

Inkster, Grand Forks, Pop. 97
Midway SD 128 200/K-12
3202 33rd Ave NE 58244 701-869-2432
Roger Abbe, supt. Fax 869-2688
midway.nd.schoolwebpages.com
Midway ES 100/K-5
3202 33rd Ave NE 58244 701-869-2432
Nancy Brueckner, prin. Fax 869-2688
Midway MS 100/6-8
3202 33rd Ave NE 58244 701-869-2432
Nancy Brueckner, prin. Fax 869-2688

Jamestown, Stutsman, Pop. 14,826
Jamestown SD 1 2,200/PK-12
PO Box 269 58402 701-252-1950
Robert Toso, supt. Fax 251-2011
www.jamestown.k12.nd.us
Gussner ES 200/K-5
PO Box 269 58402 701-252-0867
Peter Carvell, prin. Fax 251-2011
Jamestown MS 600/6-8
PO Box 269 58402 701-252-0317
Joseph Hegland, prin. Fax 252-3310
L'Amour ES 100/K-5
PO Box 269 58402 701-251-2102
Vikki Coombs, prin. Fax 251-2011
Lincoln ES 200/PK-5
PO Box 269 58402 701-252-3846
Sherry Schmidt, prin. Fax 251-2011
Roosevelt ES 200/K-5
PO Box 269 58402 701-252-1679
Patricia Smith, prin. Fax 251-2011
Washington ES 100/PK-5
PO Box 269 58402 701-252-0468
David Saxberg, prin. Fax 251-2011

Hillcrest SDA S 50/1-8
116 15th Ave NE 58401 701-252-5409
Carol Toay, prin.
St. Johns Academy 200/PK-6
215 5th St SE 58401 701-252-3397
Charles Stastny, prin. Fax 252-4453

Kenmare, Ward, Pop. 1,098
Kenmare SD 28 300/K-12
PO Box 667 58746 701-385-4996
Duane Mueller, supt. Fax 385-4390
www.kenmare.k12.nd.us/
Kenmare ES 100/K-6
PO Box 667 58746 701-385-4688
Duane Mueller, prin. Fax 385-4390

Kensal, Stutsman, Pop. 153
Kensal SD 19 50/K-12
803 1st Ave 58455 701-435-2484
Tom Tracy, supt. Fax 435-2486
www.kensal.k12.nd.us/
Kensal ES 50/K-6
803 1st Ave 58455 701-435-2484
Tom Tracy, prin. Fax 435-2486

Killdeer, Dunn, Pop. 683
Killdeer SD 16 400/K-12
PO Box 579 58640 701-764-5877
Gary Wilz, supt. Fax 764-5648
www.killdeer.k12.nd.us
Killdeer ES 200/K-6
PO Box 579 58640 701-764-5877
Peggy Wagner, prin. Fax 764-5648

Kindred, Cass, Pop. 574
Kindred SD 2 700/K-12
55 1st Ave S 58051 701-428-3177
Steve Hall, supt. Fax 428-3149
www.kindred.k12.nd.us/
Kindred ES 300/2-6
55 1st Ave S 58051 701-428-3177
Ron Zehren, prin. Fax 428-3149
Other Schools – See Davenport

Kulm, LaMoure, Pop. 391
Kulm SD 7 100/K-12
PO Box G 58456 701-647-2303
Thomas Nitschke, supt. Fax 647-2304
www.kulm.k12.nd.us/
Kulm ES 100/K-6
PO Box G 58456 701-647-2303
Pat Rutschke, prin. Fax 647-2304

Lakota, Nelson, Pop. 754
Lakota SD 66 200/K-12
PO Box 388 58344 701-247-2992
Joe Harder, supt. Fax 247-2910
www.lakota.k12.nd.us
Lakota ES 100/K-6
PO Box 388 58344 701-247-2955
Jason Wiberg, prin. Fax 247-2995

La Moure, LaMoure, Pop. 892
La Moure SD 8 300/K-12
PO Box 656 58458 701-883-5396
Mitch Carlson, supt. Fax 883-5144
www.lamoure.k12.nd.us/
La Moure Colony S 50/K-8
PO Box 656 58458 701-883-5397
Denise Musland, prin. Fax 883-5144
La Moure ES 100/K-6
PO Box 656 58458 701-883-5397
Denise Musland, prin. Fax 883-5144

Langdon, Cavalier, Pop. 1,863
Langdon Area SD 23 400/PK-12
715 14th Ave 58249 701-256-5291
Rich Rogers, supt. Fax 256-2606
lhs.utma.com/
Langdon Area ES 200/PK-6
721 11th Ave 58249 701-256-3270
Mitch Jorgensen, prin. Fax 256-3291

St. Alphonsus S 100/PK-8
209 10th Ave 58249 701-256-2354
Sr. Anne Frawley, prin. Fax 256-2358

Larimore, Grand Forks, Pop. 1,325
Larimore SD 44 500/PK-12
PO Box 769 58251 701-343-2366
Roger Abbe, supt. Fax 343-2908
www.larimore.k12.nd.us/

Larimore ES 200/PK-6
PO Box 769 58251 701-343-2249
Leslie Wiegandt, prin. Fax 343-2463

Leeds, Benson, Pop. 452
Leeds SD 6 200/K-12
PO Box 189 58346 701-466-2461
Joel Braaten, supt. Fax 466-2422
Leeds ES 100/K-6
PO Box 189 58346 701-466-2461
Carol Braaten, prin. Fax 466-2422

Lidgerwood, Richland, Pop. 746
Lidgerwood SD 28 200/K-12
PO Box 468 58053 701-538-7341
Tony Grubb, supt. Fax 538-4483
www.lidgerwood.k12.nd.us/
Lidgerwood ES 100/K-6
PO Box 468 58053 701-538-7341
Wayne Hinrichs, prin. Fax 538-4483

Lignite, Burke, Pop. 158
Burke Central SD 36 100/K-12
PO Box 91 58752 701-933-2821
Mike Klabo, supt. Fax 933-2823
Burke Central ES 50/K-6
PO Box 91 58752 701-933-2821
Mike Klabo, prin. Fax 933-2823

Linton, Emmons, Pop. 1,158
Linton SD 36 300/K-12
PO Box 970 58552 701-254-4138
Alan Bjornson, supt. Fax 254-4313
www.linton.k12.nd.us
Linton ES 100/K-5
PO Box 970 58552 701-254-4173
Brian Flyberg, prin. Fax 254-0159
Linton MS 100/6-8
PO Box 970 58552 701-254-4173
Brian Flyberg, prin. Fax 254-0159

Lisbon, Ransom, Pop. 2,237
Lisbon SD 19 600/K-12
PO Box 593 58054 701-683-4106
Steven Johnson, supt. Fax 683-4414
www.lisbon.k12.nd.us/
Lisbon ES 200/K-4
PO Box 593 58054 701-683-4107
Elinor Meckle, prin. Fax 683-4111
Lisbon MS 200/5-8
PO Box 593 58054 701-683-4108
Elinor Meckle, prin. Fax 683-4111

Litchville, Barnes, Pop. 175
Litchville-Marion SD 46
Supt. — See Marion
Litchville-Marion ES 100/K-6
PO Box 25 58461 701-762-4234
Chad Lueck, prin. Fax 762-4233

Mc Clusky, Sheridan, Pop. 428
Mc Clusky SD 19 100/K-12
PO Box 499 58463 701-363-2470
Gaillord Peltier, supt. Fax 363-2239
mcclusky.nd.schoolwebpages.com/
Mc Clusky ES 50/K-6
PO Box 499 58463 701-363-2647
Daniel Klemisch, prin. Fax 363-2239

Mc Ville, Nelson, Pop. 501
Dakota Prairie SD 1
Supt. — See Petersburg
Dakota Prairie ES 100/K-6
PO Box 337, 701-322-4771
Cindy Bjornstad, prin. Fax 322-5128

Maddock, Benson, Pop. 483
Maddock SD 9 200/K-12
PO Box 398 58348 701-438-2531
Kimberly Anderson, supt. Fax 438-2620
Maddock S 100/K-8
PO Box 398 58348 701-438-2531
Penelope Leier, prin. Fax 438-2620

Mandan, Morton, Pop. 17,225
Mandan SD 1 2,900/PK-12
309 Collins Ave 58554 701-663-9531
Wilfred Volesky, supt. Fax 663-0328
www.mandan.k12.nd.us
Custer ES 100/PK-5
205 8th Ave NE 58554 701-663-5798
Susan Atkinson, prin. Fax 663-6139
Fort Lincoln ES 400/PK-5
2007 8th Ave SE 58554 701-663-0922
Jean Schafer, prin. Fax 663-4058
Great Plains 6th Grade Academy 6-6
406 4th St NW 58554 701-751-1107
Ryan Leingang, prin. Fax 751-2067
Lewis & Clark ES 400/K-5
600 14th St NW 58554 701-663-7551
Owen Stockdill, prin. Fax 663-0770
Mandan MS 500/7-8
2901 12th Ave NW 58554 701-663-7491
Harlan Haak, prin. Fax 667-0984
Roosevelt ES 300/K-5
305 10th Ave NW 58554 701-663-5796
Robert Klemisch, prin. Fax 663-6045
Stark ES 200/K-5
405 8th Ave SW 58554 701-663-7514
Dave Steckler, prin. Fax 663-0670

Sweet Briar SD 17 50/K-8
4060 County Road 83 58554 701-663-2720
Fax 667-3315
Sweet Briar S 50/K-8
4060 County Road 83 58554 701-663-7453
Sherilyn Johnson, prin. Fax 667-3315

Christ the King S 100/PK-8
1100 3rd St NW 58554 701-663-6200
Catherine Berg, prin. Fax 667-1730

St. Joseph S 100/PK-6
410 Collins Ave 58554 701-663-9563
Valerie Vogel, prin. Fax 663-0183

Mandaree, McKenzie, Pop. 367
Mandaree SD 36 200/K-12
PO Box 488 58757 701-759-3311
Gerald Gourneau, supt. Fax 759-3493
www.mandaree.k12.nd.us/
Mandaree ES 100/K-6
PO Box 488 58757 701-759-3311
Wade Northrop, prin. Fax 759-3493

Manvel, Grand Forks, Pop. 341
Manvel SD 125 100/K-8
801 Oldham Ave 58256 701-696-2212
Fax 696-8217
www.manvel.k12.nd.us
Manvel S 100/K-8
801 Oldham Ave 58256 701-696-2212
Richard Ray, prin. Fax 696-8217

Mapleton, Cass, Pop. 611
Mapleton SD 7 100/K-6
PO Box 39 58059 701-282-3833
Timothy Jacobson, supt. Fax 282-3855
www.mapleton.k12.nd.us
Mapleton ES 100/K-6
PO Box 39 58059 701-282-3833
Timothy Jacobson, prin. Fax 282-3855

Marion, LaMoure, Pop. 131
Litchville-Marion SD 46 200/K-12
PO Box 159 58466 701-669-2262
Steven Larson, supt. Fax 669-2316
www.litchville-marion.k12.nd.us/
Other Schools – See Litchville

Marmarth, Slope, Pop. 125
Marmarth SD 12 50/K-8
PO Box 70 58643 701-279-6991
Fax 879-6278
Marmarth S 50/K-8
PO Box 70 58643 701-279-5521
Jedd Susag, prin. Fax 879-6278

Max, McLean, Pop. 262
Max SD 50 100/K-12
PO Box 297 58759 701-679-2685
Jim Blomberg, supt. Fax 679-2245
www.max.k12.nd.us/
Max ES 100/K-6
PO Box 297 58759 701-679-2685
Susan Plesuk, prin. Fax 679-2245

Mayville, Traill, Pop. 1,931
May-Port CG SD 14 600/K-12
900 Main St W 58257 701-788-2281
Michael Bradner, supt. Fax 788-2959
www.mayportcg.com/
Boe ES 200/K-5
20 2nd St NW 58257 701-788-2116
Jeffrey Houdek, prin. Fax 788-9115
Mayville-Portland CG MS 100/6-8
900 Main St W 58257 701-788-2281
Jeffrey Houdek, prin. Fax 788-2959

Medina, Stutsman, Pop. 310
Medina SD 3 100/PK-12
PO Box 547 58467 701-486-3121
Tom Rettig, supt. Fax 486-3138
www.medina.k12.nd.us/
Medina S 100/PK-8
PO Box 547 58467 701-486-3121
Joni Zink, prin. Fax 486-3138

Medora, Billings, Pop. 94
Billings County SD 1 50/K-8
PO Box 307 58645 701-623-4363
Fax 623-4941
www.billingscounty.k12.nd.us
Demores S 50/K-8
PO Box 307 58645 701-623-4363
Denise Soehren, prin. Fax 623-4941
Other Schools – See Belfield

Menoken, Burleigh
Menoken SD 33 50/1-8
PO Box D 58558 701-673-3175
Fax 673-3075
www.menoken.k12.nd.us/
Menoken S 50/1-8
PO Box D 58558 701-673-3175
Amanda Zabel, prin. Fax 673-3075

Milnor, Sargent, Pop. 676
Milnor SD 2 300/K-12
PO Box 369 58060 701-427-5237
Diann Aberle, supt. Fax 427-5304
www.milnor.k12.nd.us/
Milnor ES 100/K-6
PO Box 369 58060 701-427-5237
Diann Aberle, prin. Fax 427-5304
Sundale Colony S 50/K-8
PO Box 369 58060 701-427-5237
Diann Aberle, prin. Fax 427-5304

Minnewaukan, Benson, Pop. 307
Minnewaukan SD 5 200/K-12
PO Box 348 58351 701-473-5306
Myron Jury, supt. Fax 473-5420
www.minnewaukan.k12.nd.us/
Minnewaukan ES 100/K-6
PO Box 348 58351 701-473-5306
Jean Callahan, prin. Fax 473-5420

Minot, Ward, Pop. 34,984
Eureka SD 19 50/1-6
6621 Highway 83 N 58703 701-838-7190
Eureka ES, 6621 Highway 83 N 58703 50/1-6
Janice Gietzen, prin. 701-838-7356

Minot SD 1 6,600/PK-12
215 2nd St SE 58701 701-857-4422
Dr. David Looysen, supt. Fax 857-4432
www.minot.k12.nd.us/
Bel Air ES 300/K-5
501 25th St NW 58703 701-857-4590
Michael Fogarty, prin. Fax 857-8762
Bell ES 100/K-6
5901 Highway 52 S 58701 701-420-1880
Richard Solberg, prin. Fax 838-7048
Dakota ES 500/PK-6
101 Eagle Way 58704 701-727-3310
Kathryn Lenertz, prin. Fax 727-3318
Edison ES 400/K-5
701 17th Ave SW 58701 701-857-4595
Joy Walker, prin. Fax 857-8752
Hill MS 600/6-8
1000 6th St SW 58701 701-857-4477
Cindy Mau, prin. Fax 857-4479
Lewis and Clark ES 300/PK-5
2215 8th St NW 58703 701-857-4665
Brian Wolf, prin. Fax 857-8757
Lincoln ES 200/K-5
1 7th St SW 58701 701-857-4605
Pat Slotsve, prin. Fax 857-8754
Longfellow ES 200/K-5
600 16th St NW 58703 701-857-4610
Tracey Lawson, prin. Fax 857-8755
McKinley ES 100/PK-5
5 5th Ave NE 58703 701-857-4615
Pat Slotsve, prin. Fax 857-8756
Memorial MS 100/7-8
1 Rocket Rd 58704 701-727-3300
Tom Holtz, prin. Fax 727-3303
North Plains ES 200/PK-6
101 C St 58704 701-727-3320
Wayne Strand, prin. Fax 727-3328
Perkett ES 200/PK-5
2000 5th Ave SW 58701 701-857-4680
Ed Sehn, prin. Fax 857-8758
Ramstad MS 500/6-8
501 Lincoln Ave 58703 701-857-4466
Jim Tschetter, prin. Fax 857-4464
Roosevelt ES 100/K-5
715 8th St NE 58703 701-857-4685
Ed Sehn, prin. Fax 857-8759
Sunnyside ES 300/K-5
1000 5th Ave SE 58701 701-857-4690
Cindy Cook, prin. Fax 857-8760
Washington ES 200/K-5
600 17th Ave SE 58701 701-857-4695
Ione Sautner, prin. Fax 857-8761

Nedrose SD 4 200/K-8
6900 Highway 2 E 58701 701-838-5552
Fax 852-6971
Nedrose S 200/K-8
6900 Highway 2 E 58701 701-838-5552
Charles Miller, prin. Fax 852-6971

South Prairie SD 70 100/PK-8
100 177th Ave SW 58701 701-722-3537
Fax 722-3280
southprairie.nd.schoolwebpages.com/
South Prairie S 100/PK-8
100 177th Ave SW 58701 701-722-3537
Delwyn Groninger, prin. Fax 722-3280

Little Flower S 100/PK-2
800 University Ave W 58703 701-839-5882
Gary Volk, prin. Fax 839-8567
Our Redeemer's Christian S 300/PK-12
700 16th Ave SE 58701 701-839-0772
Julie Smesrud, admin. Fax 858-0994
St. Leos S 100/PK-5
208 1st St SE 58701 701-838-2597
Gary Volk, prin. Fax 838-2597

Minto, Walsh, Pop. 626
Minto SD 20 200/K-12
PO Box 377 58261 701-248-3479
Harold Mach, supt. Fax 248-3001
www.minto.k12.nd.us/
Minto ES 100/K-6
PO Box 377 58261 701-248-3400
Jane Misialek, prin. Fax 248-3001

Mohall, Renville, Pop. 754
Mohall-Lansford-Sherwood SD 1 300/PK-12
PO Box 187 58761 701-756-6660
Kelly Taylor, supt. Fax 756-6549
www.mohall.k12.nd.us/
Mohall ES 100/K-6
PO Box 187 58761 701-756-6660
Robby Voigt, prin. Fax 756-6549
Other Schools – See Sherwood

Montpelier, Stutsman, Pop. 95
Montpelier SD 14 100/K-12
PO Box 10 58472 701-489-3348
Lynn Krueger, supt. Fax 489-3349
www.montpelier.k12.nd.us
Montpelier ES 50/K-6
PO Box 10 58472 701-489-3348
Mary Steele, prin. Fax 489-3349

Mott, Hettinger, Pop. 718
Mott-Regent SD 1 200/K-12
205 Dakota Ave 58646 701-824-2249
Myron Schweitzer, supt. Fax 824-2249
mott.nd.schoolwebpages.com/
Mott / Regent ES at Mott 100/K-4
205 Dakota Ave 58646 701-824-2247
Deb Bohn, prin. Fax 824-2249
Other Schools – See Regent

Munich, Cavalier, Pop. 235
Munich SD 19 100/K-12
PO Box 39 58352 701-682-5321
Kevin Baumgarn, supt. Fax 682-5323
www.munich.k12.nd.us/
Munich ES 50/K-6
PO Box 39 58352 701-682-5321
Kevin Baumgarn, prin. Fax 682-5323

Napoleon, Logan, Pop. 750
Napoleon SD 2 200/K-12
PO Box 69 58561 701-754-2244
Elroy Burkle, supt. Fax 754-2233
www.napoleon.k12.nd.us/
Napoleon ES 100/K-6
PO Box 69 58561 701-754-2244
Elroy Burkle, prin. Fax 754-2233

Neche, Pembina, Pop. 424
North Border SD 100
Supt. — See Pembina
Neche ES 100/K-6
PO Box 50 58265 701-886-7604
Paul Hagness, prin. Fax 886-7552

Newburg, Bottineau, Pop. 84
Newburg - United SD 54 100/K-12
PO Box 427 58762 701-272-6151
Jason Kertsen, supt. Fax 272-6117
www.newburg.k12.nd.us/
Newburg United ES 50/K-6
PO Box 427 58762 701-272-6151
Nina Sattler, prin. Fax 272-6117

New England, Hettinger, Pop. 543
New England SD 9 200/K-12
PO Box 307 58647 701-579-4160
Kelly Rasch, supt. Fax 579-4462
www.new-england.k12.nd.us
New England ES 100/K-6
PO Box 307 58647 701-579-4160
Kelly Rasch, prin. Fax 579-4462

New Rockford, Eddy, Pop. 1,372
New Rockford-Sheyenne SD 2 400/K-12
437 1st Ave N 58356 701-947-5036
Kurt Eddy, supt. Fax 947-2195
www.newrockford.k12.nd.us/
New Rockford-Sheyenne ES 200/K-6
437 1st Ave N 58356 701-947-5036
Shirley Lindstrom, prin. Fax 947-2195

New Salem, Morton, Pop. 890
New Salem SD 7 300/PK-12
PO Box 378 58563 701-843-7846
Fax 843-7011
www.newsalem.k12.nd.us/
Prairie View ES 200/PK-6
PO Box 29 58563 701-843-7711
Deborah Vining, prin. Fax 843-8493

New Town, Mountrail, Pop. 1,415
New Town SD 1 700/PK-12
PO Box 700 58763 701-627-3650
Marc Bluestone, supt. Fax 627-3689
www.new-town.k12.nd.us/
Loe ES 300/PK-5
PO Box 700 58763 701-627-3718
Carolyn Bluestone, prin. Fax 627-4100
New Town MS 200/6-8
PO Box 700 58763 701-627-3660
John Gartner, prin. Fax 627-3689

Northwood, Grand Forks, Pop. 884
Northwood SD 129 300/K-12
300 35th St 58267 701-587-5221
Kevin Coles, supt. Fax 587-5423
www.northwood.k12.nd.us
Northwood ES 200/K-6
300 35th St 58267 701-587-5221
Shari Bilden, prin. Fax 587-5423

Oakes, Dickey, Pop. 1,848
Oakes SD 41 500/PK-12
804 Main Ave 58474 701-742-3234
Arthur Conklin, supt. Fax 742-2812
www.oakes.k12.nd.us
Oakes ES 300/PK-6
804 Main Ave 58474 701-742-3204
Gary Fitzgerald, prin. Fax 742-2812

Oberon, Benson, Pop. 82
Oberon SD 16 50/K-8
PO Box 2 58357 701-798-2231
Renae Kennedy, supt. Fax 798-2091
Oberon S 50/K-8
PO Box 2 58357 701-798-2231
Kenneth Ploium, prin. Fax 798-2091

Oriska, Barnes, Pop. 119
Maple Valley SD 4
Supt. — See Tower City
Oriska ES 100/K-6
PO Box 337 58063 701-845-2846
Patricia Johnson, prin. Fax 845-5830

Page, Cass, Pop. 206
Page SD 80 100/PK-6
PO Box 26 58064 701-668-2520
Jeffrey Watts, supt. Fax 668-2292
Page ES 100/PK-6
PO Box 26 58064 701-668-2520
Lucas Soine, prin. Fax 668-2292

Park River, Walsh, Pop. 1,438
Park River SD 78 400/K-12
PO Box 240 58270 701-284-7164
Kirk Ham, supt. Fax 284-7936
www.parkriver.k12.nd.us/
Park River ES 200/K-6
PO Box 240 58270 701-284-6550
Brenda Nilson, prin. Fax 284-7936

Parshall, Mountrail, Pop. 1,027
Parshall SD 3 300/PK-12
PO Box 158 58770 701-862-3129
Stephen Cascaden, supt. Fax 862-3801
Parshall ES 200/PK-6
PO Box 69 58770 701-862-3417
Brenda Herland, prin. Fax 862-3419

Pembina, Pembina, Pop. 599
North Border SD 100 500/K-12
155 S 3rd St 58271 701-825-6261
Wade Defoe, supt. Fax 825-6645
Pembina MS 50/7-8
PO Box 409 58271 701-825-6261
Jeff Carpenter, prin. Fax 825-6645
Other Schools – See Neche, Walhalla

Petersburg, Nelson, Pop. 179
Dakota Prairie SD 1 300/K-12
PO Box 37 58272 701-345-8233
Janet Edlund, supt. Fax 345-8251
www.dakotaprairie.k12.nd.us/
Other Schools – See Mc Ville

Pingree, Stutsman, Pop. 61
Pingree-Buchanan SD 10 200/K-12
111 Lincoln Ave 58476 701-252-5563
Jeremiah Olson, supt. Fax 252-2245
www.pingree.k12.nd.us/
Other Schools – See Buchanan

Plaza, Mountrail, Pop. 158
Lewis and Clark SD 161
Supt. — See Berthold
Plaza ES 50/PK-6
PO Box 38 58771 701-497-3734
Brian Nelson, prin. Fax 497-3401

Powers Lake, Burke, Pop. 273
Powers Lake SD 27 100/K-12
PO Box 346 58773 701-464-5432
Ruth Ann Larshus, supt. Fax 464-5435
www.powerslake.k12.nd.us/
Powers Lake ES 50/K-6
PO Box 346 58773 701-464-5431
Betty Ledene, prin. Fax 464-5435

Ray, Williams, Pop. 525
Nesson SD 2 200/K-12
PO Box 564 58849 701-568-3301
Daniel Anderson, supt. Fax 568-3302
www.ray.k12.nd.us
Ray ES 100/K-6
PO Box 564 58849 701-568-3301
Stacy Murschel, prin. Fax 568-3302

Regent, Hettinger, Pop. 182
Mott-Regent SD 1
Supt. — See Mott
Mott/Regent MS at Regent 100/5-8
PO Box 219 58650 701-824-2249
Deb Bohn, prin. Fax 563-4315

Rhame, Bowman, Pop. 176
Bowman County SD 1
Supt. — See Bowman
Rhame S 50/K-6
PO Box 250 58651 701-279-5523
Elizabeth Peterson, prin. Fax 279-5750

Richardton, Stark, Pop. 581
Richardton-Taylor SD 34 300/K-12
PO Box 289 58652 701-974-2111
Brent Bautz, supt. Fax 974-2161
www.richardton-taylor.k12.nd.us
Other Schools – See Taylor

Robinson, Kidder, Pop. 64
Robinson SD 14 50/K-6
PO Box 38 58478 701-392-8542
Fax 392-8543
Robinson ES 50/K-6
PO Box 38 58478 701-392-8542
Sheila Zerr, prin. Fax 392-8543

Rocklake, Towner, Pop. 167
North Central SD 28 100/K-12
PO Box 188 58365 701-266-5539
Dean Ralston, supt. Fax 266-5533
www.rocklake.k12.nd.us/
North Central ES 50/K-6
PO Box 188 58365 701-266-5539
Vicki Held, prin. Fax 266-5533

Rogers, Barnes, Pop. 58
Barnes County North SD 7 300/K-12
10860 20 1/2 St SE 58479 701-646-6202
Doug Jacobson, supt. Fax 646-6566
www.barnescountynorth.k12.nd.us/
North Central ES 100/K-6
10860 20 1/2 St SE 58479 701-646-6202
Daren Christianson, prin. Fax 646-6566
Other Schools – See Spiritwood, Wimbledon

Rolette, Rolette, Pop. 540
Rolette SD 29 200/K-12
PO Box 97 58366 701-246-3595
Larry Zavada, supt. Fax 246-3452
www.rolettepublicschools.com
Rolette ES 100/K-6
PO Box 97 58366 701-246-3595
Wade Sherwin, prin. Fax 246-3452

Rolla, Rolette, Pop. 1,442
Mt. Pleasant SD 4 300/PK-12
201 5th St NE 58367 701-477-3151
Brian Palmer, supt. Fax 477-5001
www.rolla.k12.nd.us
Mt. Pleasant ES 100/PK-6
201 5th St NE 58367 701-477-3151
JoHanna Dunlop, prin. Fax 477-5001

Rugby, Pierce, Pop. 2,688
Rugby SD 5 500/PK-12
1123 S Main Ave 58368 701-776-5201
Jeffery Lind, supt. Fax 776-5091
www.rugby.k12.nd.us/
Rugby Ely ES 200/PK-6
207 2nd St SW 58368 701-776-5757
Jason Gullickson, prin. Fax 776-5759

Little Flower S 100/PK-6
306 3rd Ave SE 58368 701-776-6258
Bruce Ganarelli, prin. Fax 776-6740

Ryder, Ward, Pop. 84
Lewis and Clark SD 161
Supt. — See Berthold
North Shore ES 50/K-6
PO Box 40 58779 701-758-2416
Brian Nelson, prin. Fax 758-2418

Saint Anthony, Morton
Little Heart SD 4 50/K-8
PO Box 35 58566 701-445-7387
Fax 445-7331
Little Heart S 50/K-8
PO Box 35 58566 701-445-7387
Carlene Bahm, prin. Fax 445-7331

Saint John, Rolette, Pop. 357
Saint John SD 3 300/K-12
PO Box 200 58369 701-477-5651
Donald Davis, supt. Fax 477-8195
www.stjohn.k12.nd.us
Saint John S 200/K-8
PO Box 200 58369 701-477-5651
Paul Frydenlund, prin. Fax 477-8195

Saint Thomas, Pembina, Pop. 424
Saint Thomas SD 43 100/K-12
PO Box 150 58276 701-257-6424
Larry Durand, supt. Fax 257-6461
www.stthomas.k12.nd.us
Saint Thomas ES 100/K-6
PO Box 150 58276 701-257-6424
James Hanson, prin. Fax 257-6461

Sawyer, Ward, Pop. 348
Sawyer SD 16 100/K-12
PO Box 167 58781 701-624-5167
Daniel Larson, supt. Fax 624-5482
www.sawyer.k12.nd.us/
Sawyer ES 100/K-6
PO Box 167 58781 701-624-5167
Shonda Mertz, prin. Fax 624-5482

Scranton, Bowman, Pop. 286
Scranton SD 33 200/K-12
PO Box 126 58653 701-275-8897
John Pretzer, supt. Fax 275-6221
www.scrantonpublicschool.homestead.com/
Scranton ES 100/K-6
PO Box 126 58653 701-275-8266
Kelly Pierce, prin. Fax 275-6221

Selfridge, Sioux, Pop. 220
Selfridge SD 8 50/K-12
PO Box 45 58568 701-422-3353
James Gross, supt. Fax 422-3348
Selfridge ES 50/K-6
PO Box 45 58568 701-422-3353
Kristi Miller, prin. Fax 422-3348

Sherwood, Renville, Pop. 230
Mohall-Lansford-Sherwood SD 1
Supt. — See Mohall
Sherwood ES 50/PK-6
PO Box 9 58782 701-459-2214
Robby Voigt, prin. Fax 459-2749

Solen, Sioux, Pop. 89
Solen SD 3 100/PK-12
PO Box 128 58570 701-445-3331
Judy Zins, supt. Fax 445-3323
Other Schools – See Cannon Ball

South Heart, Stark, Pop. 296
South Heart SD 9 200/K-12
PO Box 159 58655 701-677-5671
Riley Mattson, supt. Fax 677-5616
www.southheart.k12.nd.us/
South Heart ES 100/K-6
PO Box 159 58655 701-677-5671
Riley Mattson, prin. Fax 677-5616

Spiritwood, Stutsman
Barnes County North SD 7
Supt. — See Rogers
Spiritwood ES 50/K-6
PO Box 37 58481 701-252-0193
Daren Christianson, prin. Fax 252-9703

Stanley, Mountrail, Pop. 1,222
Stanley SD 2 400/K-12
PO Box 10 58784 701-628-3811
Kelly Koppinger, supt. Fax 628-3358
www.stanley.k12.nd.us/
Stanley ES 200/K-6
PO Box 10 58784 701-628-2422
Mark Morgan, prin. Fax 628-2279

Starkweather, Ramsey, Pop. 147
Starkweather SD 44 100/K-12
PO Box 45 58377 701-292-4381
Kevin Baumgarn, supt. Fax 292-5714
www.starkweather.k12.nd.us/
Starkweather ES 50/K-6
PO Box 45 58377 701-292-4381
Karen Lindenberg, prin. Fax 292-5714

Steele, Kidder, Pop. 694
Kidder County SD 1 400/K-12
PO Box 380 58482 701-475-2243
Ken Miller, supt. Fax 475-2737
Steele-Dawson ES 100/K-6
PO Box 380 58482 701-475-2243
Kay Mayer, prin. Fax 475-2737
Other Schools – See Tappen

Sterling, Burleigh
Sterling SD 35 50/K-8
PO Box 68 58572 701-387-4413
Fax 387-4415
Sterling S 50/K-8
PO Box 68 58572 701-387-4413
Dave Torbert, prin. Fax 387-4415

Strasburg, Emmons, Pop. 491
Strasburg SD 15 200/K-12
PO Box 308 58573 701-336-2667
James Eiseman, supt. Fax 336-7490
www.strasburg.k12.nd.us/
Strasburg ES 100/K-6
PO Box 308 58573 701-336-2667
Daren Kurle, prin. Fax 336-7490

Surrey, Ward, Pop. 870
Surrey SD 41 300/PK-12
PO Box 40 58785 701-839-8867
Kevin Klassen, supt. Fax 838-8822
www.surreyschool.com/
Surrey ES 200/PK-6
PO Box 40 58785 701-838-3282
Debbie Hansen, prin. Fax 838-1262

Tappen, Kidder, Pop. 188
Kidder County SD 1
Supt. — See Steele
Tappen S 100/K-8
PO Box 127 58487 701-327-4256
Shelly Mann, prin. Fax 327-4255

Taylor, Stark, Pop. 143
Richardton-Taylor SD 34
Supt. — See Richardton
Taylor Richardton ES 100/K-6
PO Box 157 58656 701-974-3585
Janine Olson, prin. Fax 974-3520

Thompson, Grand Forks, Pop. 962
Thompson SD 61 400/K-12
PO Box 269 58278 701-599-2765
Jerry Bartholomay, supt. Fax 599-2819
www.thompson.k12.nd.us
Thompson ES 200/K-6
PO Box 269 58278 701-599-2765
John Maus, prin. Fax 599-2819

Tioga, Williams, Pop. 1,090
Tioga SD 15 200/K-12
PO Box 69 58852 701-664-2333
D'Wayne Johnston, supt. Fax 664-4441
www.tioga.k12.nd.us
Central ES 100/K-6
PO Box 69 58852 701-664-3441
Tim Schaffer, prin. Fax 664-4441

Tower City, Cass, Pop. 240
Maple Valley SD 4 300/K-12
PO Box 168 58071 701-749-2570
Roger Mulvaney, supt. Fax 749-2313
www.maple-valley.k12.nd.us/
Other Schools – See Buffalo, Oriska

Towner, McHenry, Pop. 516
TGU SD 60 300/K-12
PO Box 270 58788 701-537-5414
Debby Marshall, supt. Fax 537-5413
TGU Towner S 100/K-8
PO Box 270 58788 701-537-5414
Wade Schock, prin. Fax 537-5413
Other Schools – See Granville

Turtle Lake, McLean, Pop. 527
Turtle Lake - Mercer SD 72 200/K-12
PO Box 160 58575 701-448-2365
Gaillord Peltier, supt. Fax 448-2368
www.tlm.k12.nd.us/
Turtle Lake Mercer ES 100/K-6
PO Box 160 58575 701-448-2365
Katie Heger, prin. Fax 448-2368

Underwood, McLean, Pop. 739
Underwood SD 8 200/K-12
PO Box 100 58576 701-442-3201
Dale Ekstrom, supt. Fax 442-3704
www.underwood.k12.nd.us/
Underwood ES 100/K-6
PO Box 100 58576 701-442-3274
Barbara Robinson, prin. Fax 442-3704

Valley City, Barnes, Pop. 6,439
Valley City SD 2 1,100/PK-12
460 Central Ave N 58072 701-845-0483
Dean Koppelman, supt. Fax 845-4109
www.valley-city.k12.nd.us
Jefferson ES 300/PK-3
1150 Central Ave N 58072 701-845-0622
Troy Miller, prin. Fax 845-5497
Valley City JHS 200/7-8
460 Central Ave N 58072 701-845-0483
Al Cruchet, prin. Fax 845-2762
Washington ES 200/4-6
510 8th Ave SW 58072 701-845-0849
Wayne Denault, prin. Fax 845-3560

St. Catherine S 100/PK-6
540 3rd Ave NE 58072 701-845-1453
Ralph Dyrness, prin. Fax 845-0556

Velva, McHenry, Pop. 966
Velva SD 1 400/K-12
PO Box 179 58790 701-338-2022
Steven Dick, supt. Fax 338-2023
velva.nd.schoolwebpages.com/
Velva ES 200/K-6
PO Box 179 58790 701-338-2022
Nancy Dockter, prin. Fax 338-2023

Wahpeton, Richland, Pop. 8,220
Wahpeton SD 37 1,300/PK-12
1505 11th St N 58075 701-642-6741
Michael Connell, supt. Fax 642-4908
www.wahpeton.k12.nd.us
Central ES 400/1-5
212 3rd Ave N 58075 701-642-8328
Steve Hockert, prin. Fax 642-2420
Wahpeton MS 300/6-8
1209 Loy Ave 58075 701-642-6687
Beverly Jacobson, prin. Fax 642-5622
Zimmerman ES 100/PK-1
508 9th St N 58075 701-642-3050
Steve Hockert, prin. Fax 642-5499

St. John S 100/PK-6
122 2nd St N 58075 701-642-6116
Renee Langenwalter, prin. Fax 642-9134

Walhalla, Pembina, Pop. 982
North Border SD 100
Supt. — See Pembina
Walhalla S 200/K-8
PO Box 558 58282 701-549-3751
Shon Horgan, prin. Fax 549-3753

Warwick, Benson, Pop. 76
Warwick SD 29 200/K-12
PO Box 7 58381 701-294-2561
Charles Guthrie, supt. Fax 294-2626
www.warwick.k12.nd.us
Warwick ES 100/K-6
PO Box 7 58381 701-294-2561
Steve Jacobson, prin. Fax 294-2626

Washburn, McLean, Pop. 1,264
Washburn SD 4 300/K-12
PO Box 280 58577 701-462-3228
Brad Rinas, supt. Fax 462-3561
www.washburn.k12.nd.us
Washburn ES 200/K-6
PO Box 280 58577 701-462-3261
Holly Becker, prin. Fax 462-3561

Watford City, McKenzie, Pop. 1,357
McKenzie County SD 1 500/K-12
PO Box 589 58854 701-444-3626
Steven Holen, supt. Fax 444-6345
Watford City ES 200/K-6
PO Box 589 58854 701-444-2985
Sherry Lervick, prin. Fax 444-2986

West Fargo, Cass, Pop. 19,487
West Fargo SD 6 6,400/PK-12
207 Main Ave W 58078 701-356-2000
Dana Wallace, supt. Fax 356-2009
www.west-fargo.k12.nd.us
Aurora ES 400/1-5
3420 9th St W 58078 701-356-2130
Carol Zent, prin. Fax 356-2139
Berger ES 400/1-5
631 4th Ave E 58078 701-356-2010
Dennis Howitz, prin. Fax 356-2019
Cheney MS 1,400/6-8
825 17th Ave E 58078 701-356-2090
Don Lennon, prin. Fax 356-2099
Eastwood ES 500/1-5
500 10th Ave E 58078 701-356-2030
Jeffrey Johnson, prin. Fax 356-2039
Lodoen K Center 500/PK-K
330 3rd Ave E 58078 701-356-2020
Betty Hanson, prin. Fax 356-2029
South ES 500/1-5
117 6th Ave W 58078 701-356-2100
Loren Kersting, prin. Fax 356-2109
Westside ES 600/1-5
945 7th Ave W 58078 701-356-2110
Beth Slette, prin. Fax 356-2119
Other Schools – See Fargo, Harwood, Horace

Westhope, Bottineau, Pop. 492
Westhope SD 17 100/K-12
395 Main St 58793 701-245-6444
Robert Thom, supt. Fax 245-6418
www.westhope.k12.nd.us/
Westhope ES 100/K-6
395 Main St 58793 701-245-6444
Terri Greenwood, prin. Fax 245-6418

Williston, Williams, Pop. 12,193
New SD 8 100/K-8
1201 9th Ave NW Ste 102 58801 701-572-6359
Gregory McNary, supt. Fax 572-9311
Garden Valley MS 50/7-8
1201 9th Ave NW Ste 102 58801 701-572-6359
Gregory McNary, prin. Fax 826-4531
Round Prairie ES 50/K-6
1201 9th Ave NW Ste 102 58801 701-572-6359
Gregory McNary, prin. Fax 875-4344
Stoney Creek ES 100/K-6
1201 9th Ave NW Ste 102 58801 701-572-6359
Gregory McNary, prin. Fax 572-2731

Williston SD 1 2,100/K-12
PO Box 1407 58802 701-572-1580
Larry Klundt, supt. Fax 572-3547
www.williston.k12.nd.us
Hagan ES 300/K-6
PO Box 1407 58802 701-572-4960
Darla Ratzak, prin. Fax 572-3147
Lewis & Clark ES 200/K-6
PO Box 1407 58802 701-572-6331
Terry Quintas, prin. Fax 572-0171
Rickard ES 300/K-6
PO Box 1407 58802 701-572-5412
Keith Leintz, prin. Fax 572-0347
Wilkinson ES 200/K-6
PO Box 1407 58802 701-572-6532
Pam Lambert, prin. Fax 572-0384
Williston MS 400/7-8
PO Box 1407 58802 701-572-5618
Marcia Armogost, prin. Fax 774-3109

St. Josephs S 100/K-6
124 6th St W 58801 701-572-6384
Peter Lingen, contact Fax 774-0998
Trinity Christian S 200/PK-12
2419 9th Ave W 58801 701-774-9056
Doug Black, admin. Fax 774-3158

Wilton, McLean, Pop. 745
Montefiore SD 1 200/K-12
PO Box 249 58579 701-734-6559
Craig Johnson, supt. Fax 734-6944
www.wilton.k12.nd.us
Wilton ES 100/K-6
PO Box 249 58579 701-734-6331
Craig Johnson, prin. Fax 734-6944

Wimbledon, Barnes, Pop. 216
Barnes County North SD 7
Supt. — See Rogers
Wimbledon Courtney ES 100/K-6
PO Box 255 58492 701-435-2494
Joshua Johnson, prin. Fax 435-2365

Wing, Burleigh, Pop. 117
Wing SD 28 100/K-12
PO Box 130 58494 701-943-2310
Bradley Webster, supt. Fax 943-2318
www.wing.k12.nd.us/
Wing ES 100/K-6
PO Box 130 58494 701-943-2319
Julie Hein, prin. Fax 943-2318

Wishek, McIntosh, Pop. 1,000
Wishek SD 19 200/K-12
PO Box 247 58495 701-452-2892
Terrence Erholtz, supt. Fax 452-4273
www.wishek.k12.nd.us
Wishek ES 100/K-6
PO Box 247 58495 701-452-2892
Terrence Erholtz, prin. Fax 452-4273

Wolford, Pierce, Pop. 47
Wolford SD 1 50/K-12
PO Box 478 58385 701-583-2387
Larry Zavada, supt. Fax 583-2519
www.wolford.k12.nd.us/
Wolford ES 50/K-6
PO Box 478 58385 701-583-2387
Fax 583-2519

Wyndmere, Richland, Pop. 503
Wyndmere SD 42 200/K-12
PO Box 190 58081 701-439-2287
Rick Jacobson, supt. Fax 439-2804
Wyndmere ES 100/K-6
PO Box 190 58081 701-439-2287
David Hanson, prin. Fax 439-2804

Zeeland, McIntosh, Pop. 127
Zeeland SD 4 100/K-12
PO Box 2 58581 701-423-5429
Corbley Ogren, supt. Fax 423-5465
www.zeeland.k12.nd.us/
Zeeland ES 50/K-6
PO Box 2 58581 701-423-5634
Ladean Hettich, prin. Fax 423-5465

OHIO

OHIO DEPARTMENT OF EDUCATION
25 S Front St, Columbus 43215-4183
Telephone 877-644-6338
Website http://www.ode.state.oh.us

Superintendent of Public Instruction Deborah Delisle

OHIO BOARD OF EDUCATION
25 S Front St, Columbus 43215-4176

President Deborah Cain

EDUCATIONAL SERVICE CENTERS (ESC)

Allen County ESC
Brian Rockhold, supt. 419-222-1836
1920 Slabtown Rd, Lima 45801 Fax 224-0718
www.noacsc.org/allen/ac/

Ashtabula County ESC
John Rubesich, supt. 440-576-9023
PO Box 186, Jefferson 44047 Fax 576-3065

Athens-Meigs Counties ESC
John Costanzo, supt. 740-593-8001
507 Richland Ave Ste 108 Fax 593-5968
Athens 45701

Auglaize County ESC
Patrick Niekamp, supt. 419-738-3422
1045 Dearbaugh Ave Ste 2 Fax 738-1267
Wapakoneta 45895
www.auglaizeesc.k12.oh.us/

Belmont County ESC
Michael Crawford, supt. 740-695-9773
101 N Market St Fax 695-2177
Saint Clairsville 43950
www.belmontcountyesc.k12.oh.us/

Brown County ESC
James Frazier, supt. 937-378-6118
325 W State St, Georgetown 45121 Fax 378-4286
brown.k12.oh.us

Butler County ESC
Daniel Hare, supt. 513-887-3710
1910 Fairgrove Ave Ste B Fax 887-3709
Hamilton 45011
www.bcesc.org

Clark County ESC
Stacia Smith, supt., 25 W Pleasant St 937-325-7671
Springfield 45506 Fax 325-9915
www.clarkesc.k12.oh.us/

Clermont County ESC
Glenn Alexander, supt. 513-735-8300
2400 Clermont Center Dr Fax 735-8371
Batavia 45103
www.clermontcountyschools.org

Columbiana County ESC
Anna Vaughn, supt. 330-424-9591
38720 Saltwell Rd, Lisbon 44432 Fax 424-9481
www.ccesc.k12.oh.us/

Cuyahoga County ESC
Harry Eastridge, supt. 216-524-3000
5811 Canal Rd, Valley View 44125 Fax 524-3683
www.cuyahoga.k12.oh.us/

Darke County ESC
Michael Gray, supt. 937-548-4915
5279 Education Dr Fax 548-8920
Greenville 45331
www.darke.k12.oh.us

Delaware-Union Counties ESC
Dr. Marie Ward, supt. 740-548-7880
4565 Columbus Pike Fax 548-4465
Delaware 43015
www.duesc.org/

ESC of Central Ohio
Bart Anderson, supt. 614-445-3750
2080 Citygate Dr, Columbus 43219 Fax 445-3767
www.fcesc.org/

Fairfield County ESC
J. Larry Miller, supt. 740-653-3193
995 Liberty Dr, Lancaster 43130 Fax 653-4053

Gallia-Vinton Counties ESC
Denise Shockley, supt. 740-245-0593
PO Box 178, Rio Grande 45674 Fax 245-0596

Geauga County ESC
Matthew Galemmo, supt. 440-279-1700
470 Center St Bldg 2 Fax 286-7106
Chardon 44024
www.gcesc.k12.oh.us/

Greene County ESC
Terry Thomas, supt., 360 E Enon Rd 937-767-1303
Yellow Springs 45387 Fax 767-1025
www.greene.esc.org

Hamilton County ESC
David Distel, supt. 513-674-4200
11083 Hamilton Ave Fax 742-8339
Cincinnati 45231
www.hcesc.org/

Hancock County ESC
Larry Busdeker, supt. 419-422-7525
7746 County Road 140 Fax 422-8766
Findlay 45840

Hardin County ESC
Ronald Pepple, supt. 419-674-2288
1211 W Lima St Ste A Fax 675-3309
Kenton 43326
www.hardinesc.org

Jefferson County ESC
Joyce Howell, supt. 740-283-3347
2023 Sunset Blvd Fax 283-2709
Steubenville 43952
www.jcesc.k12.oh.us/

Knox County ESC
David Southward, supt. 740-393-6767
308 Martinsburg Rd Fax 393-6812
Mount Vernon 43050
www.treca.org/schools/knoxesc/ppp.html

Lake County ESC
Dr. Linda Williams, supt. 440-350-2563
30 S Park Pl Ste 320 Fax 350-2566
Painesville 44077
www.lcesc.k12.oh.us/

Lawrence County ESC
Harold Shafer, supt. 740-532-4223
111 S 4th St, Ironton 45638 Fax 532-7226

Licking County ESC
Dr. Nelson McCray, supt. 740-349-6084
675 Price Rd NE, Newark 43055 Fax 349-6107
www.lcesc.org/

Logan County ESC
Joyce Roberts, supt. 937-599-5195
121 S Opera St Fax 599-1959
Bellefontaine 43311
www.loganesc.k12.oh.us/

Lorain County ESC
Thomas Rockwell, supt. 440-324-5777
1885 Lake Ave, Elyria 44035 Fax 324-7355

Lucas County ESC
Sandra Frisch, supt. 419-245-4150
2275 Collingwood Blvd Fax 245-4186
Toledo 43620
www.lucas.k12.oh.us/

Madison-Champaign Counties ESC
Dr. Daniel Kaffenbarger, supt. 937-484-1557
1512 S US Highway 68 Ste J Fax 484-1571
Urbana 43078
www.mccesc.k12.oh.us/

Mahoning County ESC
Richard Denaman, supt. 330-965-7828
100 DeBartolo Pl Ste 220 Fax 965-7902
Youngstown 44512
www.mcesc.k12.oh.us

Medina County ESC
William J. Koran, supt. 330-723-6393
124 W Washington St Fax 723-0573
Medina 44256
www.medina-esc.k12.oh.us

Mercer County ESC
Andrew Smith, supt. 419-586-6628
441 E Market St, Celina 45822 Fax 586-3377
www.noacsc.org/mercer/mc/

Miami County ESC
John Decker, supt. 937-339-5100
2000 W Stanfield Rd, Troy 45373 Fax 339-3256
www.miami.k12.oh.us/

Mid-Ohio ESC
Michael Cline, supt. 419-774-5520
890 W 4th St, Ontario Fax 774-5523
www.moesc.k12.oh.us/

Montgomery County ESC
Frank DePalma, supt. 937-225-4598
200 S Keowee St, Dayton 45402 Fax 496-7426
www.montgomery.k12.oh.us

Muskingum Valley ESC
Richard Murray, supt. 740-452-4518
205 N 7th St, Zanesville 43701 Fax 455-6702
www.mvesc.k12.oh.us/

North Central Ohio ESC
James Lahoski, supt. 419-447-2927
65 Saint Francis Ave, Tiffin 44883 Fax 447-2825
www.ncoesc.esu.k12.oh.us/

North Point ESC
William Lally, supt. 419-625-6274
2900 Columbus Ave Fax 627-1104
Sandusky 44870
www.npesc.org

Northwest Ohio ESC
Darren Jenkins, supt. 419-335-1070
PO Box 552, Wauseon 43567 Fax 335-5464
www.nwoesc.k12.oh.us/

Ohio Valley ESC
Steven Mumma, supt. 740-439-3558
128 E 8th St, Cambridge 43725 Fax 439-0012

Perry-Hocking Counties ESC
Dale Dickson, supt., 1605 Airport Rd 740-342-3502
New Lexington 43764 Fax 342-1961

Pickaway County ESC
Tyrus Ankrom, supt. 740-474-7529
2050 Stoneridge Dr Fax 474-7251
Circleville 43113
pickawayesc.org/

Portage County ESC
Dewey Chapman, supt. 330-297-1436
326 E Main St, Ravenna 44266 Fax 297-1113
www.portagenet.sparcc.org/

Preble County ESC
Kevin Turner, supt. 937-456-1187
597 Hillcrest Dr, Eaton 45320 Fax 456-3253
www.preble.k12.oh.us/

Putnam County ESC
Dr. Jan Osborn, supt. 419-523-5951
124 Putnam Pkwy, Ottawa 45875 Fax 523-6126
putnam.noacsc.org/

Ross-Pike Counties ESC
Philip Satterfield, supt. 740-702-3120
475 Western Ave Ste E Fax 702-3123
Chillicothe 45601
gsn.k12.oh.us/RossCO/

Shelby County ESC
Heather Neer, supt. 937-498-1354
129 E Court St, Sidney 45365 Fax 498-4850
www.scesc.k12.oh.us

South Central Ohio ESC
Lowell Howard, supt. 740-354-7761
411 Court St Rm 105 Fax 353-1882
Portsmouth 45662
www.scoesc.k12.oh.us/

Southern Ohio ESC
Robert Dalton, supt. 937-382-6921
3321 Airborne Rd Fax 383-3171
Wilmington 45177
www.cfhesd.k12.oh.us/

Stark County ESC
Larry Morgan, supt. 330-492-8136
2100 38th St NW, Canton 44709 Fax 492-6381
www.stark.k12.oh.us/

Summit County ESC
Linda Fuline, supt. 330-945-5600
420 Washington Ave Ste 200 Fax 945-6222
Cuyahoga Falls 44221
www.cybersummit.org/

Tri-County ESC
Eugene Linton, supt. 330-345-6771
741 Winkler Dr, Wooster 44691 Fax 345-7622
www.youresc.k12.oh.us/

Trumbull County ESC
Vicki Giovangnoli Ed.D., supt. 330-505-2800
6000 Youngstown Warren Rd Fax 505-2814
Niles 44446
www.trumbull.k12.oh.us/

Tuscarawas-Carroll-Harrison Counties ESC
Kevin Spears, supt., 834 E High Ave 330-308-9939
New Philadelphia 44663 Fax 308-0964
www.tchesc.k12.oh.us/

Warren County ESC
John Lazares, supt. 513-695-2900
320 E Silver St, Lebanon 45036 Fax 695-2961
www.warren.k12.oh.us/

Western Buckeye ESC
John Basinger, supt. 419-399-4711
PO Box 176, Paulding 45879 Fax 399-3346
www.noacsc.org/vanwert/wb/

Wood County ESC
Douglas Garman, supt. 419-354-9010
1867 N Research Dr Fax 354-1146
Bowling Green 43402
www.wood.k12.oh.us/

PUBLIC, PRIVATE AND CATHOLIC ELEMENTARY SCHOOLS

Aberdeen, Brown, Pop. 1,670
Ripley-Union-Lewis-Huntington Local SD
Supt. — See Ripley
Ripley-Union-Lewis-Huntington MS 400/5-8
2300 Rains Eitel Rd 45101 937-795-8001
Michael Kennedy, prin. Fax 795-8035

Ada, Hardin, Pop. 5,847
Ada EVD 900/K-12
725 W North Ave 45810 419-634-6421
Dr. Suzanne Darmer, supt. Fax 634-0311
www.ada.k12.oh.us
Ada ES 500/K-6
725 W North Ave 45810 419-634-2341
Robin VanBuskirk, prin. Fax 634-3948

Adamsville, Muskingum, Pop. 132
Tri-Valley Local SD
Supt. — See Dresden
Adamsville ES 300/K-6
7950 East St 43802 740-796-2153
Heather Welch, prin. Fax 796-4781

Adena, Jefferson, Pop. 776
Buckeye Local SD
Supt. — See Dillonvale
Buckeye West ES 300/PK-5
243 N Mill St 43901 740-546-3413
Melissa Runnion, prin. Fax 546-3815

Akron, Summit, Pop. 210,795
Akron CSD 25,400/K-12
70 N Broadway St 44308 330-761-1661
David James, supt. Fax 761-3225
www.akronschools.com
Arnold Community Learning Center 500/K-5
450 Vernon Odom Blvd 44307 330-376-0153
Lamonica Davis, prin. Fax 376-7765
Barber ES 300/K-5
366 Beaver St 44306 330-794-4152
Dr. Jennie Naidu, prin. Fax 761-1753
Barrett ES 300/K-5
888 Jonathan Ave 44306 330-773-1227
Suzette Smith, prin. Fax 773-1012
Bettes ES 200/K-5
1333 Betana Ave 44310 330-761-1655
Marla Knabel, prin. Fax 761-1654
Betty Jane Community Learning Center 500/K-5
444 Darrow Rd 44305 330-794-4117
Teresa Kossuth, prin. Fax 794-6970
Case ES 400/K-5
1393 Westvale Ave 44313 330-873-3350
Sharon Hill, prin. Fax 873-3326
Crouse ES 200/K-5
1000 Diagonal Rd 44320 330-761-1625
Angela Harper-Brooks, prin. Fax 761-1629
Erie Island ES 200/K-5
1532 Peckham St 44320 330-873-3355
Johnnette Curry, prin. Fax 873-3362
Essex ES 300/K-5
1160 Winhurst Dr 44313 330-873-3365
Mae Walker, prin. Fax 873-3364
Findley ES 300/K-5
225 E Tallmadge Ave 44310 330-761-1635
Charles Jones, prin. Fax 761-1713
Firestone Park ES 500/K-5
1479 Girard St 44301 330-773-1308
Michael Kossuth, prin. Fax 773-1025
Forest Hill Community Learning Center 300/K-5
850 Damon St 44310 330-761-1645
Jennifer Lucas, prin. Fax 761-3175
Glover ES 500/K-5
935 Hammel St 44306 330-773-1245
Rebecca Cacioppo, prin. Fax 773-1065
Goodrich MS 600/6-8
700 Lafollette St 44306 330-773-6689
Jo Anne Orlando, prin. Fax 773-7807
Goodyear MS 600/6-8
49 N Martha Ave 44305 330-794-4135
Rochelle Brown-Hall, prin. Fax 794-4142
Harris ES 400/K-5
959 Dayton St 44310 330-761-1315
Martin Shaw, prin. Fax 761-1313
Hatton ES 500/K-5
1933 Baker Ave 44312 330-794-4179
Gregory Blondheim, prin. Fax 794-4187
Hill Community Learning Center 200/K-5
1060 E Archwood Ave 44306 330-773-1129
Joan Thompson, prin. Fax 773-7308
Hyre MS 800/6-8
2443 Wedgewood Dr 44312 330-794-4144
Cynthia Wilhite, prin. Fax 794-4143
Innes Seventh/Eighth Grade Academy 500/7-8
1413 Manchester Rd 44314 330-848-5210
James McCoy, prin. Fax 848-3637
Innes Sixth Grade Academy 6-6
2228 11th St SW 44314 330-848-5224
James McCoy, prin. Fax 848-5228
Jennings Community Learning Center 600/6-8
227 E Tallmadge Ave 44310 330-761-2002
Nicki Embly, prin. Fax 761-2611
Kent MS 700/6-8
1445 Hammel St 44306 330-773-7631
Ronald Stuecher, prin. Fax 773-6442
King ES 300/K-5
805 Memorial Pkwy 44303 330-873-3375
Mary Dean, prin. Fax 873-3380
Lawndale ES 200/K-5
2330 25th St SW 44314 330-848-5237
J. Craig Wendt, prin. Fax 848-5263
Leggett ES 300/K-5
619 Sumner St 44311 330-761-1735
Philomena Vincente, prin. Fax 761-1739
Lincoln ES 400/K-5
175 W Crosier St 44311 330-761-1745
Cherry Gore, prin. Fax 761-1743
Litchfield MS 700/6-8
1540 Fairfax Rd 44313 330-873-3330
Michelle Marquess-Kearns, prin. Fax 873-3337
Mason Community Learning Center 300/K-5
700 E Exchange St 44306 330-761-2237
Stephanie Churn, prin. Fax 761-3309
McEbright ES 300/K-5
349 Cole Ave 44301 330-773-1186
David Brown, prin. Fax 773-1176
Miller South S for Visual & Perform Arts 500/4-8
1055 East Ave 44307 330-761-1765
Kathy Maddex, prin. Fax 761-1764
Perkins MS 600/6-8
630 Mull Ave 44313 330-873-3340
Felisha Cheatem, prin. Fax 873-3347
Pfeiffer ES 200/K-5
2081 9th St SW 44314 330-848-5244
Debra Michalec, prin. Fax 848-5249
Portage Path ES 400/K-5
400 W Market St 44303 330-761-2795
Kimberly Wilson, prin. Fax 761-2793
Rankin ES 300/K-5
415 Storer Ave 44320 330-761-3235
Megan Mannion, prin. Fax 761-3233
Resnik Community Learning Center K-5
65 N Meadowcroft Dr 44313 330-873-3370
Toan Dang-Nguyen, prin. Fax 873-3325
Riedinger MS 500/6-8
77 W Thornton St 44311 330-761-1345
Traci Buckner, prin. Fax 761-1349
Rimer Community Learning Center 200/K-5
1875 Glenmount Ave 44301 330-848-5250
Nancy Ritch, prin. Fax 773-1288
Ritzman Community Learning Center 300/K-5
629 Canton Rd 44312 330-794-4195
Larry Bender, prin. Fax 761-1514
Robinson Community Learning Center 300/K-5
1156 4th Ave 44306 330-761-2785
Linda Green, prin. Fax 761-5566
Salem Community Learning Center 300/K-5
1222 W Waterloo Rd 44314 330-848-5231
Elaine Marcius, prin. Fax 848-5213
Schumacher Academy 300/K-5
1031 Greenwood Ave 44320 330-873-3386
Constance Willliams, prin. Fax 873-3390
Seiberling ES 600/K-5
400 Brittain Rd 44305 330-794-4204
Karen Gregick, prin. Fax 794-4211
Smith ES 200/K-5
941 Chester Ave 44314 330-848-5255
Theresa Fennell, prin. Fax 848-5261
Stewart ES 200/K-5
1191 Vernon Odom Blvd 44307 330-873-3396
George Whitfield, prin. Fax 873-3392
Voris Community Learning Center 300/K-5
1885 Glenmount Ave 44301 330-773-6926
Kathleen Koehler, prin. Fax 773-8073
Windemere ES 400/K-5
400 Darrow Rd 44305 330-794-4214
Patricia Durkin, prin. Fax 794-4169

Copley-Fairlawn CSD
Supt. — See Copley
Herberich PS 300/K-4
2645 Smith Rd 44333 330-664-4991
Kathleen Ashcroft, prin. Fax 664-4989

Coventry Local SD 1,800/PK-12
3257 Cormany Rd 44319 330-644-8489
Russell Chaboudy, supt. Fax 644-0159
www.coventryschools.org/
Erwine MS 600/5-7
1135 Portage Lakes Dr 44319 330-644-2281
Tina Norris, prin. Fax 644-1142
Lakeview ES 100/3-4
2910 S Main St 44319 330-644-5817
Donald Schenz, prin. Fax 644-1207
Turkeyfoot ES 100/PK-2
530 W Turkeyfoot Lake Rd 44319 330-644-8469
Timothy Bryan, prin. Fax 644-1215

Manchester Local SD 1,500/K-12
6075 Manchester Rd 44319 330-882-6926
Sam Reynolds, supt. Fax 882-0013
www.panthercountry.org/
Manchester MS 500/5-8
760 W Nimisila Rd 44319 330-882-3812
James Miller, prin. Fax 882-2013
Nolley ES 500/K-4
6285 Renninger Rd 44319 330-882-4133
Dennis Archey, prin. Fax 882-2001

Revere Local SD
Supt. — See Richfield
Bath ES 400/4-5
1246 N Clvland Massillon Rd 44333 330-666-4155
Frederick Tomei, prin. Fax 666-3058

Springfield Local SD 2,300/K-12
2960 Sanitarium Rd 44312 330-798-1111
William Stauffer, supt. Fax 798-1161
www.springfieldspartans.org/
Roosevelt ES 200/K-3
3110 Farmdale Rd 44312 330-798-1006
Lucille Brown, prin. Fax 798-1166
Schrop ES 400/4-6
2215 Pickle Rd 44312 330-798-1007
Lisa Vardon, prin. Fax 798-1167
Spring Hill JHS 500/7-8
660 Lessig Ave 44312 330-798-1003
Jennifer Ganzer, prin. Fax 798-1163
Young ES 200/K-3
3258 Nidover Dr 44312 330-798-1008
John Morris, prin. Fax 798-1168

Arlington Christian Academy 100/K-8
539 S Arlington St 44306 330-785-9116
Dr. Diana Swoope, prin. Fax 785-9361
Chapel Hill Christian S Green Campus 200/PK-6
946 E Turkeyfoot Lake Rd 44312 330-896-0852
Greg McAbee, supt. Fax 896-9918
Emmanuel Christian Academy 100/PK-8
1650 Diagonal Rd 44320 330-836-7182
Rena Suber, prin. Fax 836-7274
Lippman Jewish Community Day S 100/K-8
750 White Pond Dr 44320 330-836-0419
Ruthellen Fein, prin. Fax 869-2514
Mogadore Christian Academy 100/K-12
3603 Carper Ave 44312 330-628-8482
Dennis Calaway, prin. Fax 628-2677
North Akron Catholic S 200/K-8
1570 Creighton Ave 44310 330-633-1383
Christine Lackney, prin. Fax 633-4512
Our Lady of the Elms JHS 50/7-8
1375 W Exchange St 44313 330-867-0880
Lisa Massello, prin. Fax 864-6488
Our Lady of the Elms S 200/PK-6
1290 W Market St 44313 330-864-7210
Marie Reichart, prin. Fax 867-1262
St. Anthony of Padua S 200/PK-8
80 E York St 44310 330-253-6918
Sr. Elizabeth Szilvasi, prin. Fax 376-6163
St. Francis De Sales S 300/K-8
4009 Manchester Rd 44319 330-644-0638
Carol Trifonoff, prin. Fax 644-2663
St. Hilary S 700/K-8
645 Moorfield Rd 44333 330-867-8720
Dr. Patricia Nugent, prin. Fax 867-5081
St. Mary S 200/K-8
750 S Main St 44311 330-253-1233
David Csank, prin. Fax 253-1472
St. Matthew S 300/K-8
2580 Benton Ave 44312 330-784-1711
Diane Kee, prin. Fax 733-1004
St. Paul S 200/PK-8
1580 Brown St 44301 330-724-1253
Rosemary Capotasto, prin. Fax 724-1127
St. Sebastian S 400/PK-8
352 Elmdale Ave 44320 330-836-9107
Howard Scheetz, prin. Fax 836-7690
St. Vincent De Paul S 200/PK-8
17 S Maple St 44303 330-762-5912
James Tawney, prin. Fax 535-2515

Albany, Athens, Pop. 815
Alexander Local SD 1,700/PK-12
6091 Ayers Rd 45710 740-698-8831
Robert Bray, supt. Fax 698-2038
www.alexanderschools.org/
Alexander ES 800/PK-5
6105 School Rd 45710 740-698-8831
Nedra Zirkle, prin. Fax 698-2137
Alexander MS 400/6-8
6115 School Rd 45710 740-698-8831
Kara Wingett, prin. Fax 698-8833

Alexandria, Licking, Pop. 252
Northridge Local SD
Supt. — See Johnstown
Northridge PS 200/K-3
PO Box 68 43001 740-924-2691
Andra Kisner, prin. Fax 924-6013

Alliance, Stark, Pop. 22,801
Alliance CSD 3,100/K-12
200 Glamorgan St 44601 330-821-2100
Peter Basil, supt. Fax 821-0202
www.aviators.stark.k12.oh.us/
Alliance MS 700/6-8
3205 S Union Ave 44601 330-829-2254
Kenneth Faye, prin. Fax 823-0872
Northside ES 400/K-5
701 Johnson Ave 44601 330-829-2269
Lori Grimaldi, prin. Fax 823-0761
Parkway ES 300/K-5
1490 Parkway Blvd 44601 330-829-2264
Kathie Mathie, prin. Fax 829-0559
Rockhill ES 400/K-5
2400 S Rockhill Ave 44601 330-829-2260
Susan Koulianos, prin. Fax 829-8829
South Lincoln ES 300/K-5
285 W Oxford St 44601 330-829-2266
Sheila Billheimer, prin. Fax 823-8106

Marlington Local SD 2,600/K-12
10320 Moulin Ave NE 44601 330-823-7458
James Nicodemo, supt. Fax 823-7759
www.dukes.stark.k12.oh.us/
Lexington ES 400/K-5
12333 Atwater Ave NE 44601 330-823-7570
David Rogers, prin. Fax 829-1980
Marlington MS 600/6-8
10325 Moulin Ave NE 44601 330-823-7566
Dan Swisher, prin. Fax 823-7594
Washington ES 300/K-5
5786 Beechwood Ave 44601 330-823-7586
Steve Viscounte, prin. Fax 823-7465
Other Schools – See Louisville

West Branch Local SD
Supt. — See Beloit
Knox ES 300/K-5
2900 Knox School Rd 44601 330-938-1122
John Airhart, prin. Fax 938-1121

Regina Coeli / St. Joseph S 200/PK-8
733 Fernwood Blvd 44601 330-823-9239
Claire Valentino, prin. Fax 823-1877

Amanda, Fairfield, Pop. 722
Amanda-Clearcreek Local SD 1,700/K-12
328 E Main St 43102 740-969-7250
Michael Johnsen, supt. Fax 969-7620
www.amanda.k12.oh.us
Amanda-Clearcreek ES 400/3-5
328 E Main St 43102 740-969-7253
Angela Harrison, prin. Fax 969-7729
Amanda-Clearcreek MS 400/6-8
328 E Main St 43102 740-969-7252
Kenneth Dille, prin. Fax 969-7638
Amanda-Clearcreek Primary ES 300/K-2
414 N School St 43102 740-969-7254
James Dick, prin. Fax 969-7729

Amelia, Clermont, Pop. 3,481
West Clermont Local SD
Supt. — See Cincinnati
Amelia ES 700/K-5
5 E Main St 45102 513-943-3800
Stephanie Walker, prin. Fax 943-3642
Holly Hill ES 400/K-5
3520 State Route 132 45102 513-943-8900
Nancy Parks, prin. Fax 797-5604

St. Bernadette S 200/PK-8
1453 Locust Lake Rd 45102 513-753-4744
Thomas Salerno, prin. Fax 753-9018

Amesville, Athens, Pop. 189
Federal Hocking Local SD
Supt. — See Stewart
Amesville ES 300/PK-5
PO Box 189 45711 740-448-2501
Kimberly Chadwell, prin. Fax 448-3500

Amherst, Lorain, Pop. 11,872
Amherst EVD 4,300/PK-12
185 Forest St 44001 440-988-4406
Steven Sayers, supt. Fax 988-4413
www.amherst.k12.oh.us
Amherst JHS 700/7-8
548 Milan Ave 44001 440-988-0324
Michael Diamond, prin. Fax 988-0328
Harris ES 300/4-4
393 S Lake St 44001 440-984-2496
Rhonda Neuhoff, prin. Fax 985-1278
Nord MS 700/5-6
501 Lincoln St 44001 440-988-4441
Todd Stuart, prin. Fax 988-2371
Powers ES 600/2-3
401 Washington St 44001 440-988-8670
Paula Roth, prin. Fax 988-8674
Shupe ES 600/PK-1
600 Shupe Ave 44001 440-988-4090
Deborah Waller, prin. Fax 988-7086

St. Joseph S 300/PK-8
175 Saint Joseph Dr 44001 440-988-4244
Karen Casper-Linn, prin. Fax 988-5249

Andover, Ashtabula, Pop. 1,247
Pymatuning Valley Local SD 1,200/K-12
PO Box 1180 44003 440-293-6488
Dr. John Rose, supt. Fax 293-7654
www.pvschools.k12.oh.us/
Pymatuning Valley MS 400/4-8
PO Box 1180 44003 440-293-6981
Andrew Kuthy, prin. Fax 293-7237
Pymatuning Valley PS 400/K-3
PO Box 1180 44003 440-293-6206
Erin Pierce, prin. Fax 293-5152

Anna, Shelby, Pop. 1,442
Anna Local SD 1,300/K-12
PO Box 169 45302 937-394-2011
Andrew Bixler, supt. Fax 394-7658
www.anna.k12.oh.us
Anna ES 600/K-5
PO Box 169 45302 937-394-2011
John Holtzapple, prin. Fax 394-3119
Anna MS 400/6-8
PO Box 169 45302 937-394-2011
Matthew Meyer, prin. Fax 394-7658

Ansonia, Darke, Pop. 1,115
Ansonia Local SD 700/K-12
PO Box 279 45303 937-337-4000
James Atchley, supt. Fax 337-9520
www.ansonia.k12.oh.us/
Ansonia ES 300/K-6
PO Box 279 45303 937-337-5141
Marla Threewits, prin. Fax 337-9520
Ansonia MS 100/7-8
PO Box 279 45303 937-337-5591
Stephen Garman, prin. Fax 337-9520

Antwerp, Paulding, Pop. 1,649
Antwerp Local SD 500/K-12
303 S Harrmann Rd 45813 419-258-5421
Mark Hartman, supt. Fax 258-4041
www.noacsc.org/paulding/aw/
Antwerp Local ES 300/K-5
303 S Harrmann Rd 45813 419-258-5421
Travis Lichty, prin. Fax 258-4041
Antwerp Local MS 6-8
303 S Harrmann Rd 45813 419-258-5420
Stephen Arnold, prin. Fax 258-4041

Apple Creek, Wayne, Pop. 983
Southeast Local SD 1,700/PK-12
9048 Dover Rd 44606 330-698-3001
Dr. Michael Shreffler, supt. Fax 698-5000
www.southeast.k12.oh.us
Apple Creek ES 400/PK-6
173 W Main St 44606 330-698-3111
Larry Tausch, prin. Fax 698-2922
Lea MS 200/7-8
9130 Dover Rd 44606 330-698-3151
Patti Arnold, prin. Fax 698-1922
Other Schools – See Fredericksburg, Holmesville, Mount Eaton

Arcadia, Hancock, Pop. 596
Arcadia Local SD 500/K-12
19033 State Route 12 44804 419-894-6431
Laurie Walles, supt. Fax 894-6970
www.noacsc.org/hancock/ad/
Arcadia ES 300/K-6
19033 State Route 12 44804 419-894-6431
David Golden, prin. Fax 894-6970

Arcanum, Darke, Pop. 2,032
Arcanum Butler Local SD 1,000/PK-12
2 Weisenbarger Ct 45304 937-692-5174
Joe Scholler, supt. Fax 692-5959
www.arcanum-butler.k12.oh.us
Arcanum ES 500/PK-5
310 N Main St 45304 937-692-5176
John Stephens, prin. Fax 692-5959
Butler MS 200/6-8
1481 State Route 127 45304 937-678-6571
Kirby Tipple, prin. Fax 678-6581

Franklin Monroe Local SD
Supt. — See Pitsburg
Franklin Monroe ES 400/K-6
8982 Hogpath Rd 45304 937-548-5588
Jill Holland Beiser, prin. Fax 548-3486

Archbold, Fulton, Pop. 4,505
Archbold Area Local SD 1,300/K-12
600 Lafayette St 43502 419-446-2728
David Deskins, supt. Fax 445-8536
www.archbold.k12.oh.us
Archbold ES 500/K-4
500 Lafayette St 43502 419-446-2727
Dorothy Lambert, prin. Fax 446-4627
Archbold MS 400/5-8
306 Stryker St 43502 419-446-2726
Mike Pressler, prin. Fax 445-8402

Arlington, Hancock, Pop. 1,293
Arlington Local SD 600/K-12
PO Box 260 45814 419-365-5121
Kevin Haught, supt. Fax 365-1282
www.noacsc.org/hancock/ag
Arlington Local ES 300/K-6
PO Box 260 45814 419-365-5121
Chelsea Bodnarik, prin. Fax 365-1282

Ashland, Ashland, Pop. 21,550
Ashland CSD 3,600/K-12
PO Box 160 44805 419-289-1117
Mark Robinson, supt. Fax 289-9534
www.ashlandcityschools.org/
Ashland MS 500/7-8
345 Cottage St 44805 419-289-7966
Mike Heimann, prin. Fax 289-2303
Edison ES 500/K-6
1202 Masters Ave 44805 419-289-7965
Cheryl Boyles, prin. Fax 281-3947
Lincoln ES 200/K-6
30 W 11th St 44805 419-289-3790
Stephen McDonnell, prin. Fax 281-4138
Montgomery ES 400/K-6
725 US Highway 250 E 44805 419-289-7967
Julie Petruna, prin. Fax 281-4233
Osborn ES 300/K-6
544 E Main St 44805 419-289-7964
Timothy Channel, prin. Fax 289-8563
Taft ES 500/K-6
825 Smith Rd 44805 419-289-7969
Tim Keller, prin. Fax 281-4516

Crestview Local SD 1,300/K-12
1575 State Route 96 44805 419-895-1700
William Seder, supt. Fax 895-1733
www.crestview-richland.k12.oh.us
Crestview ES 400/K-3
1575 State Route 96 44805 419-895-1700
Tamara Webb, prin. Fax 895-1733
Crestview MS 500/4-8
1575 State Route 96 44805 419-895-1700
John McNeely, prin. Fax 895-1733

Mapleton Local SD 1,000/K-12
635 County Road 801 44805 419-945-2188
John Marks, supt. Fax 945-8133
www.mapleton.k12.oh.us/
Mapleton ES 400/K-5
2 Mountie Dr 44805 419-945-2188
LuAnn Kunisch, prin. Fax 945-8199
Mapleton MS 200/6-8
1 Mountie Dr 44805 419-945-2188
Rick Mullins, prin. Fax 945-8166

Ashland Christian S 200/PK-8
1144 W Main St 44805 419-289-6617
Bessann Carr, admin. Fax 281-1425
St. Edward S 200/K-8
433 Cottage St 44805 419-289-7456
Suellen Valentine, prin. Fax 289-9474

Ashley, Delaware, Pop. 1,285
Buckeye Valley Local SD
Supt. — See Delaware
Buckeye Valley East ES 400/K-5
522 E High St 43003 740-363-2253
Teresa Goins, prin. Fax 747-3510

Ashtabula, Ashtabula, Pop. 20,321
Ashtabula Area CSD 3,600/K-12
PO Box 290 44005 440-993-2500
Joseph Donatone, supt. Fax 993-2626
www.aacs.net
Jefferson ES 300/K-3
2630 W 13th St 44004 440-993-2569
Rosemary Bernato, prin. Fax 993-2568
Lakeside IS, 401 W 44th St 44004 600/4-6
Valerie Harper, prin.
Lakeside JHS 700/7-8
6620 Sanborn Rd 44004 440-993-2618
Kathleen Reichert, prin. Fax 992-2647
McKinsey ES 200/K-3
1113 Bunker Hill Rd 44004 440-993-2606
Rebecca Evanson, prin. Fax 998-6079
Plymouth ES 200/K-6
1002 Plymouth Rd 44004 440-993-2613
James Cantela, prin. Fax 993-2612
Saybrook ES 400/K-6
7911 Depot Rd 44004 440-993-2597
James Beitel, prin. Fax 993-3450
State Road ES 100/K-3
4200 State Rd 44004 440-993-2610
Janie Carey, prin. Fax 998-1619

Buckeye Local SD 2,100/K-12
3436 Edgewood Dr 44004 440-998-4411
Nancy Williams, supt. Fax 992-8369
www.buckeyeschools.info/
Braden JHS 400/7-8
3436 Edgewood Dr 44004 440-998-0550
Bill Billington, prin.
Ridgeview ES, 3456 Liberty St 44004 400/K-6
Mary Balmford, prin. 440-997-7321
Other Schools – See Kingsville, North Kingsville

Christian Faith Academy 50/K-6
PO Box 692 44005 440-998-6630
Jeffrey Dreger, prin.
SS. John & Paul S 200/K-6
2150 Columbus Ave 44004 440-997-5821
Thomas Thornton, prin. Fax 998-0514

Ashville, Pickaway, Pop. 3,252
Teays Valley Local SD 3,600/K-12
385 Circleville Ave 43103 740-983-4111
Jeff Sheets, supt. Fax 983-4158
www.tvsd.us/
Ashville ES 500/K-5
90 Walnut St 43103 740-983-2921
Gary Wilcoxon, prin. Fax 983-5073
Teays Valley MS 800/6-8
383 Circleville Ave 43103 740-983-4074
Mike Kauffeld, prin. Fax 983-5037
Walnut ES 500/K-5
7150 Ashville Fairfield Rd 43103 740-983-2324
David Schiff, prin. Fax 983-5049
Other Schools – See Commercial Point

Athens, Athens, Pop. 20,918
Athens CSD
Supt. — See The Plains
Athens MS 400/7-8
51 W State St 45701 740-593-7107
Paul Grippa, prin. Fax 594-6506
East ES, 3 Wallace Dr 45701 300/K-6
Denny Boger, prin. 740-593-6901
Morrison ES 400/K-6
793 W Union St 45701 740-593-5445
John Gordon, prin. Fax 594-5362
West ES, 41 Central Ave 45701 300/K-6
Joan Linscott, prin. 740-593-6866

Attica, Seneca, Pop. 925
Seneca East Local SD 600/K-12
13343 E US Highway 224 44807 419-426-7041
Michael Wank, supt. Fax 426-5514
www.seneca-east.k12.oh.us/
Seneca East ES 300/K-6
PO Box 462 44807 419-426-3344
Bradley Powers, prin. Fax 426-5400

Atwater, Portage
Waterloo Local SD 1,400/K-12
1464 Industry Rd 44201 330-947-2664
Robert Wolf, supt. Fax 947-2847
www.viking.portage.k12.oh.us
Waterloo ES 600/K-5
1464 Industry Rd 44201 330-947-2153
Tracy Early, prin. Fax 947-3331
Waterloo MS 400/6-8
1464 Industry Rd 44201 330-947-0033
Paul Woodard, prin. Fax 947-4073

Aurora, Portage, Pop. 14,353
Aurora CSD 2,800/PK-12
102 E Garfield Rd 44202 330-954-2228
Russell Bennett, supt. Fax 562-4892
www.aurora-schools.org
Craddock ES 400/1-2
105 Hurd Rd 44202 330-562-3175
Patricia Minrovic, prin. Fax 562-4892
Harmon MS 700/6-8
130 Aurora Hudson Rd 44202 330-562-3375
Mark Abramovich, prin. Fax 562-4796
Leighton ES 700/3-5
121 Aurora Hudson Rd 44202 330-562-2209
Gregory Pollock, prin. Fax 562-2265
Miller ES PK-K
646 S Chillicothe Rd 44202 330-562-6199
Patricia Minrovic, prin. Fax 954-2272

Valley Christian Academy 300/K-8
1037 East Blvd 44202 330-562-8191
Connie Eide, prin. Fax 562-9257

Austinburg, Ashtabula
Geneva CSD
Supt. — See Geneva
Austinburg ES 300/K-6
3030 State Route 307 44010 440-466-4831
Kaye Haskins, prin. Fax 275-3195

Austintown, Mahoning, Pop. 31,500

St. Joseph & Immaculate Heart of Mary S 200/PK-8
4470 Norquest Blvd 44515 330-799-1944
John Rozzo, prin. Fax 799-0151

Avon, Lorain, Pop. 15,741
Avon Local SD 3,100/K-12
35573 Detroit Rd 44011 440-937-4680
Jim Reitenbach, supt. Fax 937-4688
www.avon.k12.oh.us
Avon East ES 600/1-2
3100 Nagel Rd 44011 440-937-5565
Sherry Szczepanski, prin. Fax 937-5525
Avon Heritage North ES 500/5-6
35575 Detroit Rd 44011 440-937-9660
Brent Betts, prin. Fax 937-9620
Avon Heritage South ES 500/3-4
35600 Bentley Dr 44011 440-937-3055
Jason Call, prin. Fax 937-3054
Avon MS 500/7-8
3075 Stoney Ridge Rd 44011 440-934-3800
Craig Koehler, prin. Fax 934-3803
Avon Village PS 300/K-K
36600 Detroit Rd 44011 440-934-5124
Yolanda Little, prin. Fax 934-5147

Holy Trinity S 500/PK-8
2610 Nagel Rd 44011 440-937-6420
Sr. Mary Groh, prin. Fax 937-1029
St. Mary S 200/K-8
2680 Stoney Ridge Rd 44011 440-934-6246
John Stipek, prin. Fax 934-6250

Avon Lake, Lorain, Pop. 20,608
Avon Lake CSD 3,500/K-12
175 Avon Belden Rd 44012 440-933-6210
Robert Scott, supt. Fax 933-6711
www.avonlakecityschools.org
Eastview ES 300/K-4
230 Lear Rd 44012 440-933-6283
Michael Matthews, prin. Fax 930-7012
Erieview ES 300/K-4
32630 Electric Blvd 44012 440-933-6282
Carl Bosworth, prin. Fax 933-6381
Learwood MS 500/7-8
340 Lear Rd 44012 440-933-8142
Jane Ramsay, prin. Fax 933-8406
Redwood ES 400/K-4
32967 Redwood Blvd 44012 440-933-5145
James Flanigan, prin. Fax 933-6230
Troy IS 500/5-6
237 Belmar Blvd 44012 440-933-2701
Mary O'Dee, prin. Fax 930-7005
Westview ES 200/K-4
155 Moore Rd 44012 440-933-8131
Paul Holland, prin. Fax 933-7025

St. Joseph S 300/1-8
32929 Lake Rd 44012 440-933-6233
Patricia Vaccaro, prin. Fax 933-2463

Bainbridge, Ross, Pop. 1,048
Paint Valley Local SD 1,200/K-12
7454 US Highway 50 W 45612 740-634-2826
Gary Uhrig, supt. Fax 634-2890
gsn.k12.oh.us/PaintValley/index.htm
Paint Valley ES 500/K-5
7454 US Highway 50 W 45612 740-634-3454
Brent Taylor, prin. Fax 634-3459
Paint Valley MS 300/6-8
7454 US Highway 50 W 45612 740-634-3512
Heather Bowles, prin. Fax 634-3459

Baltic, Holmes, Pop. 748
Garaway Local SD
Supt. — See Sugarcreek
Baltic ES 200/K-6
PO Box 266 43804 330-897-7261
Casey Travis, prin. Fax 897-3201

Baltimore, Fairfield, Pop. 2,919
Liberty Union-Thurston Local SD 1,400/K-12
621 W Washington St 43105 740-862-4171
Paul Mathews, supt. Fax 862-2015
www.libertyunion.org
Liberty Union ES 500/K-4
1000 S Main St 43105 740-862-4143
Kelli Brownfield, prin. Fax 862-0253
Liberty Union MS 400/5-8
600 W Washington St 43105 740-862-4126
Henry Gavarkavich, prin. Fax 862-2015

Barberton, Summit, Pop. 27,192
Barberton CSD 4,100/K-12
479 Norton Ave 44203 330-753-1025
John Hall, supt. Fax 848-0884
www.barbertonschools.org
Highland MS 400/6-8
1152 Belleview Ave 44203 330-848-4243
Tara Reis, prin. Fax 848-4221
Johnson ES 300/K-5
1340 Auburn Ave 44203 330-848-4246
Amy Meredith, prin. Fax 825-2351
Light MS 500/6-8
292 Robinson Ave 44203 330-848-4236
Justin Gates, prin. Fax 848-1272
Memorial ES 400/K-5
291 W Summit St 44203 330-848-4230
Deidre Parsons, prin. Fax 848-1667
Portage ES 400/K-5
800 Wooster Rd N 44203 330-848-4241
Amy Wilson, prin. Fax 848-5535
Santrock ES 400/K-5
88 19th St NW 44203 330-848-4229
Ken Lasky, prin. Fax 825-0278
Woodford ES 400/K-5
315 E State St 44203 330-848-4232
Kimberly Buehler, prin. Fax 848-1790

St. Augustine S 300/PK-8
195 7th St NW 44203 330-753-6435
Timothy Albrecht, prin. Fax 753-4095

Barnesville, Belmont, Pop. 4,149
Barnesville EVD 1,200/K-12
210 W Church St 43713 740-425-3615
Randy Lucas, supt. Fax 425-5000
www.barnesville.k12.oh.us/
Barnesville ES 400/K-4
210 W Church St 43713 740-425-3639
Angela Hannahs, prin. Fax 425-1136
Barnesville MS 300/5-8
970 Shamrock Dr 43713 740-425-3116
Julie Erwin, prin. Fax 425-9204

Barnesville Independent S 100/PK-8
998 Shamrock Dr 43713 740-425-3420
Jita Kay Knox, prin. Fax 425-2728

Bascom, Seneca
Hopewell-Loudon Local SD 900/K-12
PO Box 400 44809 419-937-2216
Geoffrey Palmer, supt. Fax 937-2516
www.hlschool.org/
Hopewell-Loudon Local ES 400/K-6
PO Box 400 44809 419-937-2804
Scott Hall, prin. Fax 937-2516

Batavia, Clermont, Pop. 1,669
Batavia Local SD 2,000/K-12
800 Bauer Ave 45103 513-732-2343
Barbara Bradley, supt. Fax 732-3221
www.bataviaschools.org
Batavia ES 800/K-4
215 Broadway St 45103 513-732-0780
Renee Munro, prin. Fax 732-1863
Batavia MS 600/5-8
800 Bauer Ave 45103 513-732-9534
Karyn Strong, prin. Fax 732-3696

Clermont Northeastern Local SD 1,800/PK-12
2792 US Highway 50 45103 513-625-5478
Neil Leist, supt. Fax 625-6080
www.cneschools.org
Clermont Northeastern ECC 200/PK-K
2792 US Highway 50 45103 513-625-5478
Wayne Johnson, dean Fax 625-6080
Clermont Northeastern MS 600/5-8
5347 Hutchinson Rd 45103 513-625-7075
Heather Powell, prin. Fax 625-3325
Other Schools – See Owensville

West Clermont Local SD
Supt. — See Cincinnati
Amelia MS 1,000/6-8
1341 Clough Pike 45103 513-947-7500
David Mack, prin. Fax 753-7851
Willowville ES 500/K-5
4529 Schoolhouse Rd 45103 513-943-6800
Denise Nicholas, prin. Fax 752-9181

Bath, Summit
Revere Local SD
Supt. — See Richfield
Revere MS 700/6-8
PO Box 339 44210 330-666-4155
Joe Niemantsverdriet, prin. Fax 659-3795

Old Trail S 500/PK-8
2315 Ira Rd 44210 330-666-1118
John Farber, hdmstr. Fax 666-2187

Bay Village, Cuyahoga, Pop. 15,236
Bay Village CSD 2,500/K-12
377 Dover Center Rd 44140 440-617-7300
Clinton Keener, supt. Fax 617-7301
www.bayvillageschools.com
Bay MS 800/5-8
27725 Wolf Rd 44140 440-617-7600
Sean McAndrews, prin. Fax 617-7601
Normandy ES 500/K-2
26920 Normandy Rd 44140 440-617-7350
James McGlamery, prin. Fax 617-7351
Westerly ES 400/3-4
30301 Wolf Rd 44140 440-617-7550
Josie Caputo, prin. Fax 617-7551

St. Raphael S 800/K-8
525 Dover Center Rd 44140 440-871-6760
Ann Miller, prin. Fax 871-1358

Beachwood, Cuyahoga, Pop. 11,535
Beachwood CSD 1,300/PK-12
24601 Fairmount Blvd 44122 216-464-2600
Dr. Richard Markwardt, supt. Fax 292-2340
www.beachwoodschools.org/
Beachwood MS 300/6-8
2860 Richmond Rd 44122 216-831-0355
Linda LoGalbo, prin. Fax 831-1891
Bryden ES 200/K-2
25501 Bryden Rd 44122 216-831-3933
Christi Bernetich, prin. Fax 292-2375
Fairmount Preschool 50/PK-PK
24601 Fairmount Blvd 44122 216-292-2344
Jane Mayers, dir. Fax 292-4174
Hilltop ES 200/3-5
24524 Hilltop Dr 44122 216-831-7144
Michael Molnar, prin. Fax 292-4236

Agnon S 400/PK-8
26500 Shaker Blvd 44122 216-464-4055
Jerry Isaak Shapiro, prin. Fax 464-3229

Beallsville, Monroe, Pop. 422
Switzerland of Ohio Local SD
Supt. — See Woodsfield
Beallsville ES 200/K-6
PO Box 262 43716 740-926-1300
Dave Summers, prin. Fax 926-2487

Beaver, Pike, Pop. 466
Eastern Local SD 800/K-12
1170 Tile Mill Rd 45613 740-226-4851
Dr. Charles Shreve, supt. Fax 226-1331
www.ep.k12.oh.us
Eastern IS 200/3-5
1170 Tile Mill Rd 45613 740-226-6402
Pamala Brown, prin. Fax 226-6122
Eastern MS 200/6-8
1170 Tile Mill Rd 45613 740-226-1544
Steven Kempf, prin. Fax 226-6322
Eastern PS 200/K-2
1170 Tile Mill Rd 45613 740-226-6402
Pamala Brown, prin. Fax 226-6122

Beavercreek, Greene, Pop. 39,655
Beavercreek CSD 7,700/PK-12
3040 Kemp Rd 45431 937-426-1522
Mark North, supt. Fax 429-7517
www.beavercreek.k12.oh.us/
Ankeney MS 900/6-8
4085 Shakertown Rd 45430 937-429-7567
Nick Verhoff, prin. Fax 429-2566
Fairbrook ES 600/K-5
260 N Fairfield Rd 45430 937-429-7616
Deron Schwieterman, prin. Fax 429-7687
Ferguson MS 900/6-8
2680 Dayton Xenia Rd 45434 937-429-7577
Brad Wolgast, prin. Fax 429-7686
Main ES 900/K-5
2942 Dayton Xenia Rd 45434 937-429-7588
Tom Dvorak, prin. Fax 429-7688
Parkwood ES 500/PK-5
1791 Wilene Dr 45432 937-429-7604
Ann-Olivia Westbeld, prin. Fax 429-7684
Shaw ES 700/K-5
3560 Kemp Rd 45431 937-429-7610
Dena Doolin, prin. Fax 429-2542
Valley ES 500/K-5
3601 Jonathon Dr 45434 937-429-7597
Lisa Walk, prin. Fax 429-7691

Discovery House Montessori S 100/PK-6
4114 Mapleview Dr 45432 937-427-1550
Ardyce Powell, dir. Fax 427-4317
St. Luke S 500/K-8
1442 N Fairfield Rd 45432 937-426-8551
Leslie Vondrell, prin. Fax 426-6435

Bedford, Cuyahoga, Pop. 13,571
Bedford CSD 3,300/PK-12
475 Northfield Rd 44146 440-439-1500
Martha Motsco, supt. Fax 439-4850
www.bedford.k12.oh.us
Carylwood IS 300/4-6
1387 Caryl Dr 44146 440-439-4509
Lea Travis, prin. Fax 439-0365
Central PS 400/K-3
799 Washington St 44146 440-439-4225
Terry Lipford, prin. Fax 439-4361
Glendale ES 400/PK-3
400 W Glendale St 44146 440-439-4227
Nora Beach, prin. Fax 439-3487
Other Schools – See Bedford Heights

Holy Spirit Academy 200/K-8
370 Center Rd 44146 440-232-1531
Sharon Vejdovec, prin. Fax 232-1534

Bedford Heights, Cuyahoga, Pop. 10,855
Bedford CSD
Supt. — See Bedford
Columbus IS 300/4-6
23600 Columbus Rd 44146 440-786-3322
Iwanda Huggins, prin. Fax 439-0495
Heskett MS 700/7-8
5771 Perkins Rd 44146 440-439-4450
Virginia Golden, prin. Fax 786-3572

Bellaire, Belmont, Pop. 4,738
Bellaire Local SD 1,500/K-12
340 34th St 43906 740-676-1826
John Stinoski, supt. Fax 671-6002
www.bellaire.k12.oh.us
Bellaire ES 500/K-4
53299 Pike St 43906 740-676-1272
Charles Tucker, prin. Fax 676-2334
Bellaire MS 500/5-8
54555 Neffs Bellaire Rd 43906 740-676-1635
John Foley, prin. Fax 676-3014

St. John Central S 200/PK-8
350 37th St 43906 740-676-2620
Joe De Genova, prin. Fax 676-8502

Bellbrook, Greene, Pop. 6,960
Sugarcreek Local SD 2,600/PK-12
60 E South St 45305 937-848-6251
Keith St. Pierre, supt. Fax 848-5018
www.sugarcreek.k12.oh.us
Bellbrook MS 600/6-8
3600 Feedwire Rd 45305 937-848-2141
Jenness Sigman, prin. Fax 848-2152
Bell Creek ES 400/3-5
3777 Upper Bellbrook Rd 45305 937-848-3757
Mike Baldridge, prin. Fax 848-5078
Bell ES 600/PK-2
4122 N Linda Dr 45305 937-848-7831
Ginger Keeton, prin. Fax 848-5007

Bellefontaine, Logan, Pop. 13,009
Bellefontaine CSD 2,200/K-12
820 Ludlow Rd 43311 937-593-9060
Beth Harman, supt. Fax 599-1346
www.bellefontaine.k12.oh.us/
Bellefontaine MS 600/6-8
509 N Park St 43311 937-593-9010
Vincent Spirko, prin. Fax 593-9030
Northeastern ES 300/K-3
600 E Brown Ave 43311 937-599-4431
Krista Adelsberger, prin. Fax 599-3262
Southeastern ES 300/K-3
613 Hamilton St 43311 937-599-4331
Patricia Martz, prin. Fax 599-3362
Western ES 100/4-5
1130 W Sandusky Ave 43311 937-592-5646
Shanel Henry, prin. Fax 599-3327

Benjamin Logan Local SD 2,000/K-12
4740 County Road 26 43311 937-593-9211
Stanley Mounts, supt. Fax 599-4059
www.benlogan.k12.oh.us
Logan ES 700/K-4
4560 County Road 26 43311 937-592-4838
Shari Rice, prin. Fax 592-4063
Logan MS 600/5-8
4626 County Road 26 43311 937-599-2386
James Cox, prin. Fax 599-4062

Calvary Christian S 100/PK-8
1140 Rush Ave 43311 937-599-6847
Rev. Larry Czerniak, admin. Fax 599-4879

Bellevue, Huron, Pop. 8,029
Bellevue CSD 1,500/PK-12
125 North St 44811 419-484-5000
William Martin, supt. Fax 483-0723
www.bellevueschools.org
Bellevue MS 300/6-8
215 North St 44811 419-484-5060
John Redd, prin. Fax 484-5096
Ridge ES 50/2-2
126 Ridge Rd 44811 419-484-5030
Jerrold Garman, prin. Fax 484-5103
Shumaker ES, 1035 Castalia St 44811 100/PK-1
Jerrold Garman, prin. 419-484-5040
Other Schools – See Clyde

Immaculate Conception S 300/PK-8
304 E Main St 44811 419-483-6066
Kathleen Bolen, prin. Fax 483-2736

Bellville, Richland, Pop. 1,754
Clear Fork Valley Local SD 1,900/K-12
92 Hines Ave 44813 419-886-3855
Daniel Freund, supt. Fax 886-2237
www.clearfork.k12.oh.us
Bellville ES 500/K-5
195 School St 44813 419-886-3244
Mike Byrns, prin. Fax 886-3851
Clear Fork MS 500/6-8
987 State Route 97 E 44813 419-886-3111
Steve Bloir, prin. Fax 886-4749
Other Schools – See Butler

Belmont, Belmont, Pop. 518
Union Local SD
Supt. — See Morristown
Union Local ES 600/K-5
66699 Belmont Morristown Rd 43718 740-782-1384
Scott Bowling, prin. Fax 782-0181
Union Local MS 400/6-8
66859 Belmont Morristown Rd 43718 740-782-1388
Jamie Yonak, prin. Fax 782-1474

Beloit, Mahoning, Pop. 1,016
West Branch Local SD 2,500/K-12
14277 S Main St 44609 330-938-9324
Dr. Scott Weingart, supt. Fax 938-6815
www.westbranch.k12.oh.us/
Beloit ES 300/K-5
14409 Beloit Snodes Rd 44609 330-938-4300
Roger Kitzmiller, prin. Fax 938-4301
West Branch MS 600/6-8
14409 Beloit Snodes Rd 44609 330-938-4300
Matthew Manley, prin. Fax 938-4301
Other Schools – See Alliance, Salem

Belpre, Washington, Pop. 6,560
Belpre CSD 700/K-12
2014 Washington Blvd 45714 740-423-9511
Harry Fleming, supt. Fax 423-3050
www.belpre.k12.oh.us
Belpre ES 300/K-6
2000 Rockland Ave 45714 740-423-3010
Bernie Boice, prin. Fax 423-3012

Berea, Cuyahoga, Pop. 18,242
Berea CSD 6,900/K-12
390 Fair St 44017 440-243-6000
Derran Wimer, supt. Fax 234-2309
www.berea.k12.oh.us
Parknoll ES 300/K-5
499 Nobottom Rd 44017 440-243-3855
Ben Hodge, prin. Fax 891-3767
Riveredge ES 200/K-5
224 Emerson Ave 44017 440-234-0900
Tom Kelley, prin. Fax 891-3768
Roehm MS 700/6-8
7220 Pleasant Ave 44017 440-234-1326
Jason Niedermeyer, prin. Fax 891-3764
Smith ES 200/K-5
535 Wyleswood Dr 44017 440-234-2797
Theresa Grimm, prin. Fax 891-3769
Other Schools – See Brook Park, Middleburg Heights

Academy of St. Adalbert 100/PK-8
56 Adelbert St 44017 440-234-5529
John Gregory, prin. Fax 234-2881

St. Mary S 500/PK-8
265 Baker St 44017 440-243-4555
Mary Whelan, prin. Fax 243-6214

Bergholz, Jefferson, Pop. 753
Edison Local SD
Supt. — See Hammondsville
Gregg ES 300/PK-4
212 County Road 75A 43908 740-768-2100
Fatima Smuck, prin. Fax 768-2616
Springfield MS 300/5-8
4569 County Road 75 43908 740-768-2420
Edward Chanoski, prin. Fax 768-2403

Berlin, Holmes
East Holmes Local SD 1,800/K-12
PO Box 182 44610 330-893-2610
Joe Wengerd, supt. Fax 893-2838
www.eastholmes.k12.oh.us
Berlin ES 400/K-6
PO Box 310 44610 330-893-2817
Darren Blochlinger, prin. Fax 893-3503
Chestnut Ridge S 300/K-8
PO Box 232 44610 330-893-2413
J.T. Luneborg, prin. Fax 893-2827
Other Schools – See Charm, Mount Hope, Walnut Creek, Winesburg

Berlin Center, Mahoning
Western Reserve Local SD 800/K-12
13850 W Akron Canfield Rd 44401 330-547-4100
Charles Swindler, supt. Fax 547-9302
www.westernreserve.k12.oh.us
Western Reserve MS 200/5-8
15904 W Akron Canfield Rd 44401 330-547-0814
Deborah Farelli, prin. Fax 547-9302
Other Schools – See Ellsworth

Berlin Heights, Erie, Pop. 658
Berlin-Milan Local SD
Supt. — See Milan
Berlin ES 300/PK-6
20 Center St 44814 419-588-2079
Diane Miller, prin. Fax 588-3212
Berlin-Milan MS 300/7-8
20 Center St 44814 419-588-2078
Matthew Ehrhardt, prin. Fax 588-3212

Bethel, Clermont, Pop. 2,590
Bethel-Tate Local SD 2,000/K-12
675 W Plane St 45106 513-734-2271
James Smith, supt. Fax 734-4792
www.betheltate.org
Bethel-Tate MS 500/6-8
649 W Plane St 45106 513-734-2271
Steve Gill, prin. Fax 734-0888
Bick PS 400/K-2
101 Fossyl Dr 45106 513-734-2271
Matthew Wagner, prin. Fax 734-0444
Hill IS 400/3-5
150 Fossyl Dr 45106 513-734-2271
Kay Nau, prin. Fax 734-3013

Bettsville, Seneca, Pop. 761
Bettsville Local SD 100/K-12
PO Box 6 44815 419-986-5166
Paul Orshoski, supt. Fax 986-6039
www.bettsville.k12.oh.us/
Bettsville S 100/K-12
PO Box 6 44815 419-986-5166
Paul Orshoski, prin. Fax 986-6039

Beverly, Washington, Pop. 1,272
Fort Frye Local SD 1,200/K-12
PO Box 1149 45715 740-984-2497
Dr. Dora Jean Bumgarner, supt. Fax 984-8784
www.fortfrye.k12.oh.us/
Beverly-Center ES 200/K-6
PO Box 1028 45715 740-984-2371
Laura Warren, prin. Fax 984-8167
Other Schools – See Lowell, Lower Salem

Bexley, Franklin, Pop. 12,322
Bexley CSD 2,200/K-12
348 S Cassingham Rd 43209 614-231-7611
Michael Johnson, supt. Fax 231-8448
www.bexleyschools.org
Bexley MS 400/7-8
300 S Cassingham Rd 43209 614-237-4277
Harley Williams, prin. Fax 338-2090
Cassingham ES 400/K-6
250 S Cassingham Rd 43209 614-237-4266
Barb Heisel, prin. Fax 338-2092
Maryland ES 300/K-6
2754 Maryland Ave 43209 614-237-3280
Jon Hood, prin. Fax 338-2080
Montrose ES 400/K-6
2555 E Main St 43209 614-237-4226
Quint Gage, prin. Fax 338-2088

Bidwell, Gallia
Gallia County Local SD
Supt. — See Gallipolis
River Valley MS 100/6-8
8779 State Route 160 45614 740-446-8399
David Moore, prin. Fax 441-3038

Blacklick, Franklin
Gahanna-Jefferson CSD
Supt. — See Gahanna
Blacklick ES 500/K-5
6540 Havens Corners Rd 43004 614-759-5100
Robin Schmidt, prin. Fax 759-5110

Licking Heights Local SD
Supt. — See Pataskala
Licking Heights West ES 600/K-1
1490 Climbing Fig Dr 43004 614-864-9089
Laura Hill, prin. Fax 501-4672

Grace Christian S 300/K-8
7510 E Broad St 43004 614-861-0724
Cynthia Phillips, admin. Fax 863-8509

Bladensburg, Knox
East Knox Local SD
Supt. — See Howard
East Knox ES 400/K-4
25821 New Guilford Rd 43005 740-599-7000
Steve Rose, prin. Fax 668-9100

Blanchester, Clinton, Pop. 4,348
Blanchester Local SD 1,800/PK-12
951 Cherry St 45107 937-783-3523
Brian Ruckel, supt. Fax 783-2990
www.blanchester.k12.oh.us/
Blanchester IS, 955 Cherry St 45107 300/4-5
Beverly Carroll, prin. 937-783-2040
Blanchester MS 400/6-8
955 Cherry St 45107 937-783-3642
Joel King, prin. Fax 783-3477
Putman ES 600/PK-3
327 E Baldwin St 45107 937-783-2681
Christine Branson, prin. Fax 783-5192

Bloomdale, Wood, Pop. 709
Elmwood Local SD 1,200/K-12
7650 Jerry City Rd 44817 419-655-2583
Steven Pritts, supt. Fax 655-3995
www.elmwood.k12.oh.us
Elmwood ES 400/K-4
7650 Jerry City Rd 44817 419-655-2583
Michelle Tuite, prin. Fax 655-2153
Elmwood MS 400/5-8
7650 Jerry City Rd 44817 419-655-2583
Jesse Steiner, prin. Fax 655-2153

Bloomingburg, Fayette, Pop. 850
Miami Trace Local SD
Supt. — See Washington Court House
Miami Trace MS 400/6-8
103 Main St 43106 740-437-7344
Jeff Conroy, prin. Fax 437-6061

Bloomingdale, Jefferson, Pop. 214
Indian Creek Local SD
Supt. — See Wintersville
Wayne ES 200/K-6
5926 County Road 22A 43910 740-944-1751
Cecilia Fritz, prin. Fax 944-1377

Bloomville, Seneca, Pop. 1,012
Buckeye Central Local SD
Supt. — See New Washington
Buckeye North ES 100/K-6
69 S Marion St 44818 419-983-2061
Evadyne Troyer, prin. Fax 983-4016

Bluffton, Allen, Pop. 4,013
Bluffton EVD 1,100/K-12
102 S Jackson St 45817 419-358-5901
Gregory Denecker, supt. Fax 358-4871
www.bluffton.noacsc.org/
Bluffton ES 500/K-5
102 S Jackson St 45817 419-358-7951
Timothy Closson, prin. Fax 358-4871
Bluffton MS 300/6-8
116 S Jackson St 45817 419-358-7961
Dean Giesige, prin. Fax 358-4871

Boardman, Mahoning, Pop. 37,100

St. Charles S 500/K-8
7325 Westview Dr 44512 330-758-6689
Mary Welsh, prin. Fax 758-7404
St. Luke S 200/PK-8
5225 South Ave 44512 330-782-4060
Catherine Wigley, prin. Fax 782-4842

Bolivar, Tuscarawas, Pop. 900
Tuscarawas Valley Local SD
Supt. — See Zoarville
Tuscarawas Valley IS 300/2-4
216 Park Ave NW 44612 330-874-3234
Diana Flickinger, prin. Fax 859-8875

Botkins, Shelby, Pop. 1,181
Botkins Local SD 300/K-12
PO Box 550 45306 937-693-4241
Connie Schneider, supt. Fax 693-2557
www.botkins.k12.oh.us
Botkins S 300/K-12
PO Box 550 45306 937-693-4241
Jeff McPheron, prin. Fax 693-2557

Bowerston, Harrison, Pop. 424
Conotton Valley Union Local SD
Supt. — See Sherrodsville
Bowerston ES 200/K-6
600 Main St 44695 740-269-2141
Michael Wright, prin. Fax 269-1492

Bowling Green, Wood, Pop. 29,793
Bowling Green CSD 3,100/K-12
140 S Grove St 43402 419-352-3576
Hugh Caumartin, supt. Fax 352-1701
www.bgcs.k12.oh.us
Bowling Green JHS 500/7-8
215 W Wooster St 43402 419-354-0200
Lee Vincent, prin. Fax 353-1958
Conneaut ES 500/K-6
542 Haskins Rd 43402 419-354-0300
Lorraine Flick, prin. Fax 352-6661
Crim ES 300/K-6
1020 Scott Hamilton Ave 43402 419-354-0400
Martha Fether, prin. Fax 352-7675
Kenwood ES 500/K-6
710 Kenwood Ave 43402 419-354-0500
Gary Keller, prin. Fax 352-8261

Ridge ES 200/K-6
225 Ridge St 43402 419-354-0800
Dan Sheperd, prin. Fax 352-9415
Other Schools – See Custar

Bowling Green Christian Academy 100/K-9
1165 Haskins Rd 43402 419-354-2422
Wendie Cuckler, prin. Fax 354-0232

Montessori S Bowling Green 100/K-6
515 Sand Ridge Rd 43402 419-352-4203
Tammy Thompson, admin. Fax 353-1914

St. Aloysius S 200/PK-8
PO Box 485 43402 419-352-8614
Mary Williams, prin. Fax 352-4738

Bradford, Darke, Pop. 1,891

Bradford EVD 600/K-12
760 Railroad Ave 45308 937-448-2770
Jeff Patrick, supt. Fax 448-2493
www.bradford.k12.oh.us/

Bradford ES 300/K-5
740 Railroad Ave 45308 937-448-2811
John Virgint, prin. Fax 448-2742

Bradner, Wood, Pop. 1,159

Lakota Local SD
Supt. — See Risingsun

Lakota West ES 200/K-1
218 E Lightner St 43406 419-288-3053
Joshua Matz, prin. Fax 288-3316

Brecksville, Cuyahoga, Pop. 13,250

Brecksville-Broadview Heights CSD 4,600/K-12
6638 Mill Rd 44141 440-740-4010
Thomas Diringer Ed.D., supt. Fax 740-4014
www.bbhcsd.org

Central ES 700/4-5
27 Public Sq 44141 440-740-4100
Beverly Chambers, prin. Fax 740-4104

Chippewa ES 400/K-3
8611 Wiese Rd 44141 440-740-4200
Christopher Hartland, prin. Fax 740-4204

Highland Drive ES 400/K-3
9457 Highland Dr 44141 440-740-4300
Eva O'Mara, prin. Fax 740-4304

Hilton ES 400/K-3
6812 Mill Rd 44141 440-740-4600
David Martin, prin. Fax 740-4604
Other Schools – See Broadview Heights

South Suburban Montessori S 100/PK-8
4450 Oakes Rd Bldg 6 44141 440-526-1966
Amy Mackie-Barr, prin. Fax 526-6026

Bremen, Fairfield, Pop. 1,251

Fairfield Union Local SD
Supt. — See Rushville

Bremen ES 400/K-4
210 Strayer Ave 43107 740-569-4135
Frederick Burns, prin. Fax 569-9605

Brice, Franklin, Pop. 80

Brice Christian Academy 200/K-6
PO Box 370 43109 614-866-6789
Catherine Wells, admin. Fax 861-4217

Bridgeport, Belmont, Pop. 2,107

Bridgeport EVD 600/K-12
55781 National Rd 43912 740-635-1713
Gerald Narcisi, supt. Fax 635-6003
www.bevs.k12.oh.us/

Bridgeport ES 100/K-4
55707 Industrial Dr 43912 740-635-2565
Kamaron Sabinski, prin. Fax 635-6006

Bridgeport MS 200/5-8
55707 Industrial Dr 43912 740-635-0853
Rob Zitzelsberger, prin. Fax 635-6003

St. Joseph Central S 100/PK-8
55505 National Rd 43912 740-635-3313
Daniel Delande, prin. Fax 635-0707

Brilliant, Jefferson, Pop. 1,604

Buckeye Local SD
Supt. — See Dillonvale

Buckeye North ES 300/PK-5
1004 3rd St 43913 740-598-4589
Susan Nolan, prin. Fax 598-3909

Buckeye North MS 200/6-8
1004 3rd St 43913 740-598-4540
Sharon Wallace, prin. Fax 598-4154

Bristolville, Trumbull

Bristol Local SD 800/K-12
PO Box 260 44402 330-889-3882
Dr. Marty Santillo, supt. Fax 889-2529
www.bristol.k12.oh.us

Bristol ES 400/K-6
PO Box 260 44402 330-889-2700
Christopher Dray, prin. Fax 889-2529

Broadview Heights, Cuyahoga, Pop. 17,505

Brecksville-Broadview Heights CSD
Supt. — See Brecksville

Brecksville-Broadview Heights MS 1,200/6-8
6376 Mill Rd 44147 440-740-4400
Patrick Farrell, prin. Fax 740-4404

North Royalton CSD
Supt. — See North Royalton

Lil Bears Preschool & K 300/PK-K
9543 Broadview Rd Ste 15-18 44147 440-582-9140
Julie Bogden, prin. Fax 582-9039

Assumption Academy 300/PK-8
9183 Broadview Rd 44147 440-526-4877
Donna Sejba, prin. Fax 526-3752

Lawrence S 300/1-12
1551 E Wallings Rd 44147 440-526-0003
Lou Salza, hdmstr. Fax 526-0595

Brookfield, Trumbull

Brookfield Local SD 1,300/K-12
PO Box 209 44403 330-448-4930
Steve Stohla, supt. Fax 448-5026
www.brookfield.k12.oh.us/

Brookfield MS 500/4-8
PO Box 209 44403 330-448-3003
Sherri Baxter, prin. Fax 448-5028

Brooklyn, Cuyahoga, Pop. 10,901

Brooklyn CSD 1,500/K-12
9200 Biddulph Rd 44144 216-485-8110
Cynthia Walker, supt. Fax 485-8118
www.brooklyn.k12.oh.us/

Brooklyn MS 400/6-8
9200 Biddulph Rd 44144 216-485-8126
Ted Caleris, prin. Fax 485-8118

Brookridge ES 300/3-5
4500 Ridge Rd 44144 216-485-8177
Brent Monnin, prin. Fax 485-8120

Roadoan ES 300/K-2
4525 Roadoan Rd 44144 216-485-8173
Colleen Longville, prin. Fax 485-8140

St. Thomas More S 400/PK-8
4180 N Amber Dr 44144 216-749-1660
Jennifer Francis, prin. Fax 398-4265

Brook Park, Cuyahoga, Pop. 20,059

Berea CSD
Supt. — See Berea

Brookpark Memorial ES 600/K-5
16900 Holland Rd 44142 216-433-1350
Michael Kostyack, prin. Fax 676-2073

Brookview ES 500/K-5
14105 Snow Rd 44142 216-676-4334
Susan Humphrey, prin. Fax 676-2074

Ford MS 1,000/6-8
17001 Holland Rd 44142 216-433-1133
Michael Pelegrino, prin. Fax 676-2072

Brookville, Montgomery, Pop. 5,317

Brookville Local SD 1,600/K-12
325 Simmons Ave 45309 937-833-2181
Timothy Hopkins, supt. Fax 833-2787
www.brookville.k12.oh.us/

Brookville IS 600/4-8
2 Blue Pride Dr 45309 937-833-6731
Rebecca Hagan, prin. Fax 833-6756

Westbrook ES 400/K-3
75 June Pl 45309 937-833-6796
Constance Gilhooly, prin. Fax 833-5354

Brunswick, Medina, Pop. 35,159

Brunswick CSD 7,500/K-12
3643 Center Rd 44212 330-225-7731
Michael Mayell, supt. Fax 273-0507
www.bcsoh.org

Applewood ES 400/K-5
3891 Applewood Dr 44212 330-225-7731
Mike Kis, prin. Fax 273-0508

Brunswick Memorial ES 500/K-5
3845 Magnolia Dr 44212 330-225-7731
Judith Galo, prin. Fax 273-0513

Crestview ES 400/K-5
300 W 130th St 44212 330-225-7731
Dennis Haft, prin. Fax 273-0446

Edwards MS 500/6-8
1497 Pearl Rd 44212 330-225-7731
Kent Morgan, prin. Fax 273-0519

Hickory Ridge ES 400/K-5
4628 Hickory Ridge Ave 44212 330-225-7731
Mary Anne Melvin, prin. Fax 273-0510

Huntington ES 500/K-5
1931 Huntington Cir 44212 330-225-7731
Keith Merrill, prin. Fax 273-0389

Kidder ES 500/K-5
3650 Grafton Rd 44212 330-225-7731
Mark Mabry, prin. Fax 273-0512

Towslee ES 500/K-5
3555 Center Rd 44212 330-225-7731
Lisa Mayle, prin. Fax 273-0516

Visintainer MS 600/6-8
1459 Pearl Rd 44212 330-225-7731
Carol Yost, prin. Fax 273-0400

Willetts MS 700/6-8
1045 Hadcock Rd 44212 330-225-7731
Mike Hodson, prin. Fax 273-0222

St. Ambrose S 500/K-8
923 Pearl Rd 44212 330-225-2116
Christine Bopp, prin. Fax 225-5425

St. Mark Lutheran S 200/PK-8
1330 N Carpenter Rd 44212 330-225-4395
Sharon Wallace, prin. Fax 225-4380

Bryan, Williams, Pop. 8,360

Bryan CSD 2,200/PK-12
1350 Fountain Grove Dr 43506 419-636-6973
Diana Savage, supt. Fax 633-6280
www.bryan.k12.oh.us

Bryan MS 800/4-8
1301 Center St 43506 419-636-6766
Beth Hollabaugh, prin. Fax 633-6282

Lincoln ES 300/2-3
301 E Butler St 43506 419-636-6931
Mark Miller, prin. Fax 633-6283

Washington ES 400/PK-1
510 Avenue A 43506 419-636-5034
Ron Rittichier, prin. Fax 633-6284

Fountain City Christian S 100/K-12
PO Box 150 43506 419-636-2333
James Garrett, admin. Fax 636-2888

St. Patrick S 200/PK-8
610 S Portland St 43506 419-636-3592
Lisa Cinadr, prin. Fax 636-5054

Bucyrus, Crawford, Pop. 12,885

Bucyrus CSD 1,500/PK-12
117 E Mansfield St 44820 419-562-4045
Dr. Todd Nichols, supt. Fax 562-3990
www.bucyrus.k12.oh.us

Bucyrus ES 600/PK-5
245 Woodlawn Ave 44820 419-562-6089
Robin Showers, prin. Fax 563-9658

Bucyrus MS 300/6-8
455 Redmen Way 44820 419-562-0003
Fax 562-1773

Wynford Local SD 1,200/K-12
3288 Holmes Center Rd 44820 419-562-7828
Steve Mohr, supt. Fax 562-7825
www.wynford.k12.oh.us

Wynford ES 600/K-6
3300 Holmes Center Rd 44820 419-562-4619
Mark Murphy, prin. Fax 563-2905

Holy Trinity S 100/PK-8
740 Tiffin St 44820 419-562-2741
Mary Radke, prin. Fax 562-7659

Burbank, Wayne, Pop. 274

North Central Local SD
Supt. — See Creston

Burbank ES 200/K-4
PO Box 148 44214 330-624-2962
Andrew Froelich, prin. Fax 435-4633

Burgoon, Sandusky, Pop. 199

Lakota Local SD
Supt. — See Risingsun

Lakota East ES 100/5-6
1582 State Route 590 S 43407 419-334-9591
Norman Elchert, prin. Fax 334-9041

Burton, Geauga, Pop. 1,446

Berkshire Local SD 1,200/K-12
PO Box 364 44021 440-834-4123
Douglas DeLong, supt. Fax 834-2058
www.berkshire.k12.oh.us

Burton ES 400/K-6
PO Box 406 44021 440-834-4616
Cynthia Ducca, prin. Fax 834-8361

Troy ES 200/1-6
17791 Claridon Troy Rd 44021 440-834-8962
Gina Symsek, prin. Fax 834-1805

Agape Christian Academy 100/PK-7
14220 Claridon Troy Rd 44021 440-834-8022
Susan Gifford, pres. Fax 834-4931

Butler, Richland, Pop. 908

Clear Fork Valley Local SD
Supt. — See Bellville

Butler ES 300/K-5
125 College St 44822 419-883-3451
Roger Knight, prin. Fax 883-3395

Byesville, Guernsey, Pop. 2,597

Rolling Hills Local SD
Supt. — See Cambridge

Brook ES 400/K-5
58601 Marietta Rd 43723 740-685-2526
W. Gail Thomas, prin. Fax 685-5230

Byesville ES 300/K-5
212 E Main Ave 43723 740-685-2523
Patricia Landenberger, prin. Fax 685-5410

Meadowbrook MS 500/6-8
58607 Marietta Rd 43723 740-685-2561
Larry Touvell, prin. Fax 685-2628

Cadiz, Harrison, Pop. 3,396

Harrison Hills CSD
Supt. — See Hopedale

Harrison Westgate ES 200/K-3
730 Peppard Ave 43907 740-942-7450
John Alleman, prin. Fax 942-7454

Caldwell, Noble, Pop. 1,911

Caldwell EVD 900/K-12
516 Fairground St 43724 740-732-5637
William Brelsford, supt. Fax 732-7303
www.caldwell.k12.oh.us/

Caldwell S 600/K-8
44350 Fairground Rd 43724 740-732-4614
J. Morris, prin.

Caledonia, Marion, Pop. 556

River Valley Local SD 1,900/K-12
197 Brocklesby Rd 43314 740-725-5400
Thomas Shade, supt. Fax 725-5499
www.rivervalley.k12.oh.us

Liberty ES 400/K-5
1932 Whetstone River Rd N 43314 740-725-5600
Jonathan Langhals, prin. Fax 725-5699

River Valley MS 400/6-8
4334 Marion Mount Gilead Rd 43314 740-725-5700
Donald Gliebe, prin. Fax 725-5799
Other Schools – See Marion

Cambridge, Guernsey, Pop. 11,562

Cambridge CSD 2,500/K-12
6111 Fairdale Dr 43725 740-439-5021
Dennis Dettra, supt. Fax 439-3796
www.cambridge.k12.oh.us/

Cambridge MS 600/6-8
1400 Deerpath Dr 43725 740-435-1140
Donald Vogt, prin. Fax 435-1141

Central ES 400/K-5
1115 Clairmont Ave 43725 740-439-7547
Leslie Leppla, prin. Fax 439-7590

North ES 500/K-5
1451 Deerpath Dr 43725 740-435-1180
Heath Hayes, prin. Fax 435-1181

South ES 300/K-5
518 S 8th St 43725 740-439-7592
Linda Halterman, prin. Fax 439-7641

East Muskingum Local SD
Supt. — See New Concord
Pike ES 100/K-2
4533 Peters Creek Rd 43725 740-439-1645
David Adams, prin. Fax 432-3201

Rolling Hills Local SD 2,000/K-12
60851 Southgate Rd 43725 740-432-5370
Tom Perkins, supt. Fax 435-8312
www.omeresa.net/Schools/Meadowbrook/
Other Schools – See Byesville, Senecaville

St. Benedict S 100/K-8
220 N 7th St 43725 740-432-6751
Sr. Theresa Feldkamp, prin. Fax 432-4511

Camden, Preble, Pop. 2,264
Preble Shawnee Local SD 1,200/K-12
124 Bloomfield St 45311 937-452-3323
Dale Robertson, supt. Fax 452-3926
www.preble-shawnee.k12.oh.us
Camden ES 400/K-3
120 Bloomfield St 45311 937-452-1204
Rodney Shockey, prin. Fax 343-4636
Other Schools – See West Elkton

Campbell, Mahoning, Pop. 8,888
Campbell CSD 1,400/K-12
280 6th St 44405 330-799-8777
Thomas Robey, supt. Fax 799-0875
www.campbell.k12.oh.us
Campbell ES 500/K-4
2002 Community Cir 44405 330-799-5211
Robert Walls, prin. Fax 799-8272
Campbell MS 400/5-8
2002 Community Cir 44405 330-799-0054
Marcia Ruse, prin. Fax 799-8259

St. Joseph the Provider S 100/K-8
633 Porter Ave 44405 330-755-4747
Cheryl Jablonski, prin. Fax 755-4799

Canal Fulton, Stark, Pop. 5,054
Northwest Local SD 2,500/K-12
8614 Erie Ave N 44614 330-854-2291
William Stetler, supt. Fax 854-3591
www.northwest.sparcc.org/
Northwest ES 500/K-2
8436 Erie Ave N 44614 330-854-5405
James Lariccia, prin. Fax 854-5809
Northwest IS 400/5-6
8540 Erie Ave N 44614 330-854-4537
Jay Baughman, prin. Fax 854-7170
Northwest MS 400/7-8
8614 Erie Ave N 44614 330-854-3303
Robert Venables, prin. Fax 854-5883
Stinson ES 300/3-4
8454 Erie Ave N 44614 330-854-4646
Lori Mariani, prin. Fax 854-7136

SS. Philip & James S 200/PK-8
532 High St NE 44614 330-854-2823
Patricia Vacucci, prin. Fax 854-1109

Canal Winchester, Franklin, Pop. 5,652
Canal Winchester Local SD 2,800/K-12
100 Washington St 43110 614-837-4533
Kimberley Miller-Smith, supt. Fax 833-2165
www.canalwin.k12.oh.us
Canal Winchester MS 500/6-8
7155 Parkview Dr 43110 614-833-2151
Cassandra Miller, prin. Fax 833-2173
Indian Trail ES 800/K-2
6767 Gender Rd 43110 614-833-2154
Beverly Downing, prin. Fax 833-2167
Winchester Trail ES 500/3-5
6865 Gender Rd 43110 614-833-2150
Bill Whitlatch, prin. Fax 833-2161

Harvest Preparatory S 600/PK-12
4595 Gender Rd 43110 614-382-1111
Norbert Tate, prin. Fax 834-1276

Canfield, Mahoning, Pop. 7,153
Canfield Local SD 3,100/K-12
100 Wadsworth St 44406 330-533-3303
Dante Zambrini, supt. Fax 533-6827
canfield.access-k12.org
Campbell ES 500/K-4
300 Moreland Dr 44406 330-533-5959
Kent Polen, prin. Fax 702-7061
Canfield Village MS 1,000/5-8
42 Wadsworth St 44406 330-533-4019
Ronald Infante, prin. Fax 702-7064
Hilltop ES 500/K-4
400 Hilltop Blvd 44406 330-533-9806
Cathy Mowry, prin. Fax 702-7051

Canton, Stark, Pop. 79,478
Canton CSD 10,300/PK-12
305 McKinley Ave NW 44707 330-438-2500
Michele Evans-Gardell Ph.D., supt. Fax 455-0682
www.ccsdistrict.org
Allen ES 400/PK-6
1326 Sherrick Rd SE 44707 330-453-2782
Dan Lowmiller, prin. Fax 580-3008
Arts Academy at Summit 400/K-8
1100 10th St NW 44703 330-452-6537
Tom Piccari, prin. Fax 580-3190
Belden ES 400/PK-6
2115 Georgetown Rd NE 44704 330-453-6902
Mallory Floyd, prin. Fax 588-2128
Cedar ES 500/PK-6
2823 9th St SW 44710 330-453-0065
Carol Herring, prin. Fax 580-3165
Clarendon ES 400/PK-6
412 Clarendon Ave NW 44708 330-453-7681
Nicole Herberghs, prin. Fax 588-2130
Compton Learning Center 200/K-6
401 14th St SE 44707 330-456-1189
Sylvera Greene, prin. Fax 580-2404
Crenshaw MS 400/6-8
2525 19th St NE 44705 330-454-7717
Edward Rehfus, prin. Fax 588-2120
Deuber ES 300/K-6
815 Dueber Ave SW 44706 330-580-3517
Christen Sedmock, prin. Fax 580-3517
ECC 100/PK-K
1350 Cherry Ave NE 44714 330-580-3008
Sylvera Greene Ph.D., prin. Fax 580-3008
Fairmount ES 300/K-6
2701 Coventry Blvd NE 44705 330-456-3167
Beverly Ciricosta, prin. Fax 588-2151
Gibbs ES 300/PK-6
1320 Gibbs Ave NE 44705 330-456-1521
Cynthia Viscounte, prin. Fax 580-3164
Harter ES 400/K-5
317 Raff Rd NW 44708 330-456-1001
Brian Wycuff, prin. Fax 588-2132
Hartford MS 300/6-8
1824 3rd St SE 44707 330-453-6012
Sandy Womack, prin. Fax 453-5096
Lehman MS 700/6-8
1400 Broad Ave NW 44708 330-456-1963
Diane Mizer, prin. Fax 456-8121
Mason ES 200/K-5
316 30th St NW 44709 330-588-2156
Barbara Maceyak, prin. Fax 580-3038
McGregor ES 300/PK-6
2339 17th St SW 44706 330-452-7069
Victor Johnson, prin. Fax 588-2133
Schreiber ES 300/PK-6
1503 Woodland Ave NW 44703 330-452-1672
Clifford Reynolds, prin. Fax 580-3031
Stone ES 300/PK-5
2100 Rowland Ave NE 44714 330-452-6521
Robert Vero, prin. Fax 452-6858
Worley ES 400/K-5
1340 23rd St NW 44709 330-452-5748
Ann Bartley, prin. Fax 588-2150
Youtz ES 400/K-6
1901 Midway Ave NE 44705 330-452-7601
Chet Lenartowicz, prin. Fax 588-2159
Other Schools – See North Canton

Canton Local SD 2,200/PK-12
4526 Ridge Ave SE 44707 330-484-8010
Teresa Purses, supt. Fax 484-8032
www.cantonlocal.org
Faircrest Memorial MS 500/6-8
616 Faircrest St SW 44706 330-484-8015
Timothy Welker, prin. Fax 484-8033
McDannel ES 200/K-1
210 38th St SE 44707 330-484-8030
DaNita Berry, prin. Fax 484-8031
Prairie College Preschool 50/PK-PK
3021 Prairie College St SW 44706 330-484-8025
Danita Berry, prin. Fax 484-8026
Walker ES 500/2-5
3525 Sandy Ave SE 44707 330-484-8020
Christopher Noll, prin. Fax 484-8134

Jackson Local SD
Supt. — See Massillon
Lake Cable ES 600/K-5
5335 Villa Padova Dr NW 44718 330-494-8171
Kathleen Clark, prin. Fax 494-3040

Perry Local SD
Supt. — See Massillon
Knapp ES 400/PK-5
5151 Oakcliff St SW 44706 330-478-6174
Linnea Gallagher-Olbon, prin. Fax 477-4542
Reedurban ES 300/PK-5
1221 Perry Dr SW 44710 330-478-6150
Cynthia Wagner, prin. Fax 476-6152
Whipple Heights ES 400/K-5
4800 12th St NW 44708 330-478-6177
David Guertal, prin. Fax 478-6179

Plain Local SD 6,200/K-12
901 44th St NW 44709 330-492-3500
Christopher Smith, supt. Fax 493-5542
www.plainlocal.org/
Avondale ES 300/1-5
3933 Eaton Rd NW 44708 330-491-3720
Scott Esporite, prin. Fax 491-3721
Barr ES 300/1-5
2000 47th St NE 44705 330-491-3730
Michael Milford, prin. Fax 491-3731
Frazer ES 300/1-5
3900 Frazer Ave NW 44709 330-491-3740
Beth Kline, prin. Fax 491-3741
Glenwood MS 700/6-8
1015 44th St NW 44709 330-491-3780
Leigh Kummer, prin. Fax 491-3781
Little Eagle Kindergarten at Day 200/K-K
3101 38th St NW 44718 330-491-3710
Erick Hendrickson, prin. Fax 491-3711
Oakwood MS 800/6-8
2300 Schneider St NE 44721 330-491-3790
Brian Matthews, prin. Fax 491-3791
Taft ES 400/1-5
3829 Guilford Ave NW 44718 330-491-3760
Cassandra Sponseller, prin. Fax 491-3761
Warstler ES 400/1-5
2500 Schneider St NE 44721 330-491-3770
Jody Ditcher, prin. Fax 491-3771
Other Schools – See North Canton

Canton Country Day S 200/PK-8
3000 Demington Ave NW 44718 330-453-8279
Pamela Shaw, hdmstr. Fax 453-6038
Heritage Christian S 300/PK-12
2107 6th St SW 44706 330-452-8271
Howard Pizor, prin. Fax 452-0672
Holy Cross Lutheran S 100/PK-K
7707 Market Ave N 44721 330-494-6478
Marjorie James, prin. Fax 499-2319
Our Lady of Peace S 200/K-8
1001 39th St NW 44709 330-492-0622
Donna Mertes, prin. Fax 492-0959
St. Joan of Arc S 400/PK-8
120 Bordner Ave SW 44710 330-477-2972
Mary Fiala, prin. Fax 478-2606
St. Joseph S 200/PK-8
126 Columbus Ave NW 44708 330-454-9787
Joellen Esber, prin. Fax 454-9866
St. Michael S 400/K-8
3431 Saint Michaels Blvd NW 44718 330-492-2657
Sally Roden, prin. Fax 492-9618
St. Peter S 200/PK-8
702 Cleveland Ave NW 44702 330-452-0125
Rita Kingsbury, prin. Fax 453-8083
Stark County Christian Academy 50/K-2
2651 Market Ave N 44714 330-454-3737
Ellie Burfield, prin. Fax 454-3371

Cardington, Morrow, Pop. 1,992
Cardington-Lincoln Local SD 1,300/K-12
121 Nichols St 43315 419-864-3691
Patrick Drouhard, supt. Fax 864-0946
www.cardington.k12.oh.us/
Cardington IS 300/4-6
3700 County Road 168 43315 419-864-3152
Brian Petrie, prin. Fax 864-3143
Cardington-Lincoln ES 400/K-3
121 Nichols St 43315 419-864-6692
Scott Hardwick, prin. Fax 864-8701
Cardington-Lincoln JHS 200/7-8
349 Chesterville Ave 43315 419-864-0609
Barry Dutt, admin. Fax 864-3168

Carey, Wyandot, Pop. 3,868
Carey EVD 900/K-12
357 E South St 43316 419-396-7922
Mark Vehre, supt. Fax 396-3158
careyevs.schoolwires.com/
Crawford ES 400/K-6
357 E South St 43316 419-396-6767
Tammy Wagner, prin. Fax 396-3158

Our Lady of Consolation S 100/1-8
401 Clay St 43316 419-396-6166
Jean Schott, prin. Fax 396-3355

Carlisle, Warren, Pop. 5,688
Carlisle Local SD 1,800/K-12
724 Fairview Dr 45005 937-746-0710
Michael Griffith, supt. Fax 746-0438
www.carlisle-local.k12.oh.us
Brown ES 400/K-2
310 Jamaica Rd 45005 937-746-7610
Allyson Couch, prin. Fax 746-0511
Chamberlain MS 400/6-8
720 Fairview Dr 45005 937-746-3227
Mike Milner, prin. Fax 746-0519
Grigsby IS 400/3-5
100 Jamaica Rd 45005 937-746-8969
David Starkey, prin. Fax 746-0512

Carroll, Fairfield, Pop. 474
Bloom-Carroll Local SD 1,600/K-12
PO Box 338 43112 614-837-6560
Roger Mace, supt. Fax 756-4221
www.bloom-carroll.k12.oh.us
Bloom-Carroll MS 400/6-8
PO Box 338 43112 740-756-9231
Mark Fenik, prin. Fax 756-7466
Carroll ES 400/K-5
PO Box 338 43112 740-756-4326
Mathew Dill, prin. Fax 756-7551
Other Schools – See Lithopolis

Carrollton, Carroll, Pop. 3,297
Carrollton EVD 2,500/PK-12
252 3rd St NE 44615 330-627-2181
Palmer Fogler, supt. Fax 627-2182
www.carrollton.k12.oh.us
Augusta ES 100/PK-5
3117 Aurora Rd NE 44615 330-627-2442
Christina Hull, prin. Fax 627-2442
Bell-Herron MS 500/6-8
252 3rd St NE 44615 330-627-7188
Tricia Green, prin. Fax 627-8429
Carrollton ES 700/PK-5
252 3rd St NE 44615 330-627-4592
Edward Darnley, prin. Fax 627-8433
Other Schools – See Dellroy

Casstown, Miami, Pop. 326
Miami East Local SD 1,300/K-12
3825 N State Route 589 45312 937-335-7505
Dr. Todd Rappold, supt. Fax 335-6309
www.miamieast.k12.oh.us
Miami East ES 600/K-5
4025 N State Route 589 45312 937-335-5439
Wes Welbaum, prin. Fax 332-9488
Miami East JHS 300/6-8
4025 N State Route 589 45312 937-335-5439
Allen Mack, prin. Fax 332-7927

Castalia, Erie, Pop. 906
Margaretta Local SD 1,100/K-12
305 S Washington St 44824 419-684-5322
Edward Kurt, supt. Fax 684-9003
www.margaretta.k12.oh.us/
Margaretta ES 400/K-6
5906 Bogart Rd W 44824 419-684-5357
Lynn Hurd, prin. Fax 684-6001

Firelands Christian Academy 100/K-8
3809 Maple Ave 44824 419-684-8642
Rusty Yost, pres. Fax 684-5378

Cedarville, Greene, Pop. 4,037
Cedar Cliff Local SD 600/K-12
PO Box 45 45314 937-766-6000
David Baits, supt. Fax 766-4717
www.cedarcliffschools.org
Cedarville ES 300/K-5
PO Box 45 45314 937-766-3811
Eric Snead, prin. Fax 766-5211

Celina, Mercer, Pop. 10,348
Celina CSD 2,900/K-12
585 E Livingston St 45822 419-586-8300
Matt Miller, supt. Fax 586-7046
www.celinaschools.org
Celina IS 400/5-6
227 Portland St 45822 419-586-8300
Sally Tatham, prin. Fax 584-0353
Celina MS 400/7-8
615 Holly St 45822 419-586-8300
Ann Esselstein, prin. Fax 586-9166
East ES 600/K-4
615 E Wayne St 45822 419-586-8300
Michelle Duncan, prin. Fax 584-0215
West ES 300/K-4
1225 W Logan St 45822 419-586-8300
Susan Aukerman, prin. Fax 586-6541

Immaculate Conception S 200/PK-6
200 W Wayne St 45822 419-586-2379
Kathryn Mescher, prin. Fax 586-6649

Centerburg, Knox, Pop. 1,483
Centerburg Local SD 1,200/K-12
119 S Preston St 43011 740-625-6346
Dorothy Holden, supt. Fax 625-9939
www.centerburgschools.org/
Centerburg ES 500/K-5
207 S Preston St 43011 740-625-6488
Charles Davis, prin. Fax 625-5894
Centerburg MS 300/6-8
3782 Columbus Rd 43011 740-625-6055
Mike Hebenthal, prin. Fax 625-5799

Centerville, Montgomery, Pop. 23,162
Centerville CSD 8,300/K-12
111 Virginia Ave 45458 937-433-8841
Tom Henderson, supt. Fax 438-6057
www.centerville.k12.oh.us
Centerville PS Village North 600/K-1
6450 Marshall Rd 45459 937-438-6062
Mindy Cline, prin. Fax 438-6076
Centerville PS Village South 700/K-1
8388 Paragon Rd 45458 937-312-1273
Stephanie Owens, prin. Fax 312-1274
Cline ES 500/2-5
99 Virginia Ave 45458 937-435-1315
Susan Duffy, prin. Fax 435-3893
Magsig MS 600/6-8
192 W Franklin St 45459 937-433-0965
S. Westendorf-Wozniak, prin. Fax 433-5256
Stingley ES 400/2-5
95 Linden Dr 45459 937-434-1054
Diana Keller, prin. Fax 438-6049
Tower Heights MS 600/6-8
195 N Johanna Dr 45459 937-434-0383
Clint Freese, prin. Fax 434-3033
Weller ES 500/2-5
9600 Sheehan Rd 45458 937-885-3273
Theresa Gum, prin. Fax 885-5092
Other Schools – See Dayton

Springboro Community CSD
Supt. — See Springboro
Five Points ES East 400/1-5
650 E Lytle 5 Points Rd 45458 937-748-6090
Tammy Stritenberger, prin. Fax 748-6068
Five Points ES West 300/1-5
650 E Lytle 5 Points Rd 45458 937-748-6090
Vic Johantges, prin. Fax 748-6069

Incarnation S 900/PK-8
45 Williamsburg Ln 45459 937-433-1051
Dr. Cheryl Reichel, prin. Fax 433-9796
Spring Valley Academy 300/K-12
1461 E Spring Valley Pike 45458 937-433-0790
Jeff Bovee, prin. Fax 433-0914

Chagrin Falls, Cuyahoga, Pop. 3,808
Chagrin Falls EVD 2,000/PK-12
400 E Washington St 44022 440-247-4363
Stephen Thompson, supt. Fax 247-5883
www.mychagrin.net/public/default.aspx
Chagrin Falls IS 400/4-6
77 E Washington St 44022 440-893-7690
Charles Murphy, prin. Fax 893-7694
Chagrin Falls MS 300/7-8
342 E Washington St 44022 440-247-4746
Lisa Bontempo, prin. Fax 247-4855
Gurney ES 600/PK-3
1155 Bell Rd 44022 440-893-4030
Rachel Jones, prin. Fax 338-4272

Kenston Local SD 3,200/K-12
17419 Snyder Rd 44023 440-543-9677
Robert Lee, supt. Fax 543-8634
www.kenstonlocal.com
Gardiner Early Learning Center 200/K-K
9421 Bainbridge Rd 44023 440-543-2822
Marilyn Kahle, prin. Fax 543-3070
Kenston IS 500/4-5
17419 Snyder Rd 44023 440-543-9722
Jack Dicello, prin. Fax 543-3159

Kenston MS 800/6-8
17425 Snyder Rd 44023 440-543-8241
Patricia Brockway, prin. Fax 543-4851
Timmons ES 700/1-3
9595 Washington St 44023 440-543-9380
Kathleen Poe, prin. Fax 543-9163

St. Joan of Arc S 200/K-8
498 E Washington St 44022 440-247-6530
Shelley DiBacco, prin. Fax 247-2045
Solon Montessori S - Bainbridge 100/K-6
17892 Chillicothe Rd 44023 440-543-9135
Nelunika Rajapakse, prin.

Chardon, Geauga, Pop. 5,280
Chardon Local SD 3,300/K-12
428 North St 44024 440-285-4052
Joseph Bergant, supt. Fax 285-7229
www.chardon.k12.oh.us
Chardon MS 800/6-8
424 North St 44024 440-285-4062
Steven Kofol, prin. Fax 286-0461
Hambden ES 300/K-5
13871 Gar Hwy 44024 440-286-7503
David Rogaliner, prin. Fax 286-0507
Maple ES 300/K-5
308 Maple Ave 44024 440-285-4065
Kathleen Sawyer, prin. Fax 286-0469
Munson ES 400/K-5
12687 Bass Lake Rd 44024 440-286-5901
Louise Henry, prin. Fax 286-3460
Park ES 300/K-5
111 Goodrich Ct 44024 440-285-4067
Rhonda Garrett, prin. Fax 286-0515

Notre Dame Preschool 100/PK-PK
13000 Auburn Rd 44024 440-286-7101
Sr. Margaret Friel, prin. Fax 286-9364
Notre Dame S 500/PK-8
13000 Auburn Rd 44024 440-279-1127
Barbara Doering, prin. Fax 286-1235
St. Mary S 400/PK-8
401 North St 44024 440-286-3590
Sr. Sandra Nativio, prin. Fax 285-2818

Charm, Holmes
East Holmes Local SD
Supt. — See Berlin
Charm ES, PO Box 159 44617 100/K-1
Jon Wilson, prin. 330-893-2300
Flat Ridge S, PO Box 159 44617 100/2-4
Jon Wilson, prin. 330-893-3156
Wise MS, PO Box 159 44617 100/5-8
Jon Wilson, prin. 330-893-2505

Chatfield, Crawford, Pop. 207
Buckeye Central Local SD
Supt. — See New Washington
Buckeye West ES 100/K-6
PO Box 187 44825 419-988-2431
Evadyne Troyer, prin. Fax 492-2039

Chauncey, Athens, Pop. 1,105
Athens CSD
Supt. — See The Plains
Chauncey ES, PO Box 225 45719 200/K-6
Margaret Williams, prin. 740-797-4588

Chesapeake, Lawrence, Pop. 879
Chesapeake Union EVD 1,400/K-12
10183 County Road 1 45619 740-867-3135
Dr. Scott Howard, supt. Fax 867-3136
www.peake.k12.oh.us
Chesapeake ES 600/K-4
11359 County Road 1 45619 740-867-3448
Kim Wells, prin. Fax 867-3136
Chesapeake MS 500/5-8
10335 County Road 1 45619 740-867-3972
Benjamin Coleman, prin. Fax 867-1120

Chesterland, Geauga, Pop. 2,078
West Geauga Local SD 2,400/K-12
8615 Cedar Rd 44026 440-729-5900
Anthony Podojil, supt. Fax 729-5939
www.westg.org/
Lindsey ES 500/K-5
11844 Caves Rd 44026 440-729-5980
Kenneth Bernacki, prin. Fax 729-5989
West Geauga MS 600/6-8
8611 Cedar Rd 44026 440-729-5940
James Kish, prin. Fax 729-5909
Other Schools – See Novelty

St. Anselm S 300/PK-8
13013 Chillicothe Rd 44026 440-729-7806
Joan Agresta, prin. Fax 729-3524

Chesterville, Morrow, Pop. 201
Highland Local SD
Supt. — See Marengo
Highland North ES 100/K-5
PO Box 7 43317 419-768-2631
Debra Knechtly, prin. Fax 768-4046

Chillicothe, Ross, Pop. 22,081
Chillicothe CSD 2,900/K-12
235 Cherry St 45601 740-775-4250
Roger Crago, supt. Fax 775-4270
www.chillicothe.k12.oh.us
Allen ES 300/K-5
174 Plyleys Ln 45601 740-774-1119
Jane Caine, prin. Fax 774-9460
Chillicothe MS 600/6-8
381 Yoctangee Pkwy 45601 740-773-2241
Diane Neal, prin. Fax 774-9482
Mt. Logan ES 400/K-5
841 E Main St 45601 740-773-2638
Matt Thornsberry, prin. Fax 774-9480

Tiffin ES 300/K-5
145 S Bridge St 45601 740-774-2123
Charles Kolb, prin. Fax 774-9465
Worthington ES 300/K-5
450 Allen Ave 45601 740-774-3307
Lawrence Butler, prin. Fax 774-9466

Huntington Local SD 1,300/K-12
188 Huntsman Rd 45601 740-663-5892
Jerry Mowery, supt. Fax 663-6078
www.hunt.k12.oh.us/
Huntington ES 600/K-5
188 Huntsman Rd 45601 740-663-2191
Denise Hulbert, prin. Fax 663-4584
Huntington MS 300/6-8
188 Huntsman Rd 45601 740-663-6079
Alice Kellough, prin. Fax 663-6080

Southeastern Local SD 1,300/K-12
2003 Lancaster Rd 45601 740-774-2003
Brian Justice, supt. Fax 774-1687
www.sepanthers.k12.oh.us/
Southeastern ES 500/K-4
2003 Lancaster Rd 45601 740-774-2003
Zachary Pfeifer, prin. Fax 774-1673
Southeastern MS 400/5-8
2003 Lancaster Rd 45601 740-774-2003
David Shea, prin. Fax 774-1684

Union-Scioto Local SD 2,000/K-12
1565 Egypt Pike 45601 740-773-4102
Dwight Garrett, supt. Fax 775-2852
www.unioto.k12.oh.us
Unioto ES 1,100/K-6
138 Sandusky Rd 45601 740-773-4103
Karen Mercer, prin. Fax 775-4074
Unioto JHS 300/7-8
160 Moundsville Rd 45601 740-773-5211
Ron Lovely, prin. Fax 772-2974

Zane Trace Local SD 1,600/K-12
946 State Route 180 45601 740-775-1355
Carolyn Everidge, supt. Fax 773-0249
gsn.k12.oh.us/zanetrace/index.html
Zane Trace ES 600/K-4
946 State Route 180 45601 740-775-1304
Gary Stump, prin. Fax 775-1301
Zane Trace MS 500/5-8
946 State Route 180 45601 740-773-9854
Bret Mavis, prin. Fax 773-9998

Bishop Flaget S 100/PK-8
570 Parsons Ave 45601 740-774-2970
Laura Corcoran, prin. Fax 774-2998
Ross County Christian Academy 50/PK-7
2215 Egypt Pike 45601 740-772-4532
Jake Grooms, hdmstr.

Cincinnati, Hamilton, Pop. 308,728
Cincinnati CSD, PO Box 5381 45201 32,700/PK-12
Mary Ronan, supt. 513-363-0000
www.cps-k12.org
Academy Multilingual Immersion Studies 600/PK-8
7001 Reading Rd 45237 513-363-1800
Sherwin Ealy, prin. Fax 363-1820
Academy World Languages S 600/PK-8
2030 Fairfax Ave 45207 513-363-7800
Jacquelyn Rowedder, prin. Fax 363-7820
Bond Hill Academy 400/PK-8
1510 California Ave 45237 513-363-7900
Thomas Boggs, prin. Fax 363-7920
Carson S 500/PK-8
4323 Glenway Ave 45205 513-363-9800
Ruthenia Jackson, prin. Fax 363-9820
Chase S 600/PK-8
1710 Bruce Ave 45223 513-363-1300
Therman Sampson, prin. Fax 363-1320
Cheviot S 600/PK-8
4040 Harrison Ave 45211 513-363-1400
Maria Bonavita, prin. Fax 363-1420
College Hill Fundamental Academy 500/PK-6
1402 W North Bend Rd 45224 513-363-1600
Barbara Gordon, prin. Fax 363-1620
Covedale ES 400/K-6
5130 Sidney Rd 45238 513-363-1700
Greg Hook, prin. Fax 363-1720
Dater Montessori S 700/PK-6
1700 Grand Ave 45214 513-363-0900
Beth Schnell, prin. Fax 363-0920
Douglass S 400/PK-8
2627 Park Ave 45206 513-363-1900
Renee Rashad, prin. Fax 363-1920
Fairview-Clifton German Language School 600/K-6
3689 Clifton Ave 45220 513-363-2100
Karen Mulligan, prin. Fax 363-2120
Hartwell S 400/PK-8
125 W North Bend Rd 45216 513-363-2300
Cheryl Jones, prin. Fax 363-2320
Hays-Porter S 200/PK-8
1030 Cutter St 45203 513-363-1000
Nedria McClain, prin. Fax 363-1020
Hoffman-Parham S 300/PK-8
3060 Durrell Ave 45207 513-363-2700
Stacey Hill-Simmons, prin. Fax 363-2720
Kilgour ES 500/K-6
1339 Herschel Ave 45208 513-363-3000
Angela Cook, prin. Fax 363-3020
Midway S 600/PK-8
3156 Glenmore Ave 45211 513-363-3500
Cathy Lutts, prin. Fax 363-3520
Mt. Airy S 500/PK-8
5730 Colerain Ave 45239 513-363-3700
Nicole Davis, prin. Fax 363-3720
Mt. Washington S 400/PK-8
1730 Mears Ave 45230 513-363-3800
Debra Klein, prin. Fax 363-3820
North Avondale Montessori S 600/PK-6
876 Glenwood Ave 45229 513-363-3900
Carmen Hull, prin. Fax 363-3920

Oyler S 800/PK-12
2121 Hatmaker St 45204 513-363-4100
Craig Hockenberry, prin. Fax 363-4120
Parker S 500/PK-8
3500 Lumford Pl 45213 513-363-2900
Kimberly Mack, prin. Fax 363-2920
Pleasant Hill Academy 600/PK-8
1350 W North Bend Rd 45224 513-363-4300
Cherese Campbell-Clark, prin. Fax 363-4320
Pleasant Ridge Montessori S 400/PK-8
5945 Montgomery Rd 45213 513-363-4400
Maria Lagdameo, prin. Fax 363-4420
Price Academy 600/PK-8
1228 Considine Ave 45204 513-363-6000
Alesia Smith, prin. Fax 363-6020
Quebec Heights S 400/PK-8
1655 Ross Ave 45205 513-363-4500
Janice Pitts, prin. Fax 363-4520
Riverview East Academy 500/PK-12
3555 Kellogg Ave 45226 513-363-3400
Eugene Smith, prin. Fax 363-3420
Roberts Paideia Academy 700/PK-8
1702 Grand Ave 45214 513-363-4600
Vera Brooks, prin. Fax 363-4620
Rockdale Academy 500/PK-8
335 Rockdale Ave 45229 513-363-4700
Cheron Reid, prin. Fax 363-4720
Roll Hill Academy 600/PK-8
2411 Baltimore Ave 45225 513-363-4000
Vicki Graves-Hill, prin. Fax 363-4020
Roselawn-Condon S 500/PK-8
7735 Greenland Pl 45237 513-363-4800
Randal Yunker, prin. Fax 363-4820
Rothenberg Preparatory Academy 300/PK-8
2120 Vine St 45202 513-363-5700
Thomas Miller, prin. Fax 363-5720
Sands Montessori ES 700/PK-6
6421 Corbly Rd 45230 513-363-5000
Rita Swegman, prin. Fax 363-5020
Sayler Park S 400/PK-8
6700 Home City Ave 45233 513-363-5100
Gary Vale, prin. Fax 363-5120
Schiel Arts Enrichment PS 400/K-3
2821 Vine St 45219 513-363-5200
Roger Lewis, prin. Fax 363-5220
Silverton Paideia Academy 400/PK-6
6829 Stewart Rd 45236 513-363-5400
Tomasine Dendy, prin. Fax 363-5420
South Avondale S 300/PK-8
636 Prospect Pl 45229 513-363-5500
Sammy Yates, prin. Fax 363-5520
Taft S 200/PK-8
270 Southern Ave 45219 513-363-5600
Donna Fields, prin. Fax 363-5620
Taylor Academy 300/PK-8
1930 Fricke Rd 45225 513-363-3600
Sean McCauley, prin. Fax 363-3620
Westwood S 400/PK-8
2601 Westwood Northern Blvd 45211 513-363-5900
Bruce Breiner, prin. Fax 363-5920
Winton Hills Academy 500/PK-8
5300 Winneste Ave 45232 513-363-6300
Christina Russo, prin. Fax 363-6320
Winton Montessori S 400/PK-6
4750 Winton Rd 45232 513-363-6200
Whitney Simmons, prin. Fax 363-6220
Woodford Paideia Academy 600/PK-6
6065 Red Bank Rd 45213 513-363-6400
Cindi Menefield, prin. Fax 363-6420

Deer Park Community CSD 1,200/K-12
4131 Matson Ave 45236 513-891-0222
Kimberlee Gray, supt. Fax 891-2930
www.deerparkcityschools.org
Amity IS 300/4-6
4320 E Galbraith Rd 45236 513-891-5995
Debbie Farley, prin. Fax 891-3508
Holmes ES 200/K-3
8688 Donna Ln 45236 513-891-6662
Amy Byrne, prin. Fax 891-3519

Finneytown Local SD 1,500/K-12
8916 Fontainebleau Ter 45231 513-728-3700
Randall Parsons, supt. Fax 931-0986
www.finneytown.org
Brent ES 300/K-2
8791 Brent Dr 45231 513-728-3720
Marianne Tranter, prin. Fax 728-7243
Whitaker ES 200/3-6
7400 Winton Rd 45224 513-728-3737
Stephanie Kessling, prin. Fax 728-3725

Forest Hills Local SD 7,600/K-12
7550 Forest Rd 45255 513-231-3600
John Patzwald Ph.D., supt. Fax 231-3830
www.foresthills.edu
Ayer ES 700/K-6
8471 Forest Rd 45255 513-474-3811
Dr. Shirley Curtis, prin. Fax 474-7228
Maddux ES 700/K-6
943 Rosetree Ln 45230 513-231-0780
Steve Troehler, prin. Fax 231-5308
Mercer ES 700/K-6
2600 Bartels Rd 45244 513-232-7000
Scott Gates, prin. Fax 232-3156
Nagel MS 1,200/7-8
1500 Nagel Rd 45255 513-474-5407
Natasha Adams, prin. Fax 474-5584
Sherwood ES 600/K-6
7080 Grantham Way 45230 513-231-7565
Dan Hamilton, prin. Fax 231-3666
Summit ES 500/K-6
8400 Northport Dr 45255 513-474-2270
Kathy Marx, prin. Fax 474-1525
Wilson ES 700/K-6
2465 Little Dry Run Rd 45244 513-231-3240
Dr. Ann Roberts, prin. Fax 231-3202

Indian Hill EVD 2,300/K-12
6855 Drake Rd 45243 513-272-4500
Jane Knudson Ed.D., supt. Fax 272-4512
www.ih.k12.oh.us
Indian Hill ES 500/3-5
6100 Drake Rd 45243 513-272-4703
Melissa Stewart, prin. Fax 272-4708
Indian Hill MS 600/6-8
6845 Drake Rd 45243 513-272-4642
Kim Miller, prin. Fax 272-4690
Indian Hill PS 400/K-2
6207 Drake Rd 45243 513-272-4754
Sandra Harte, prin. Fax 272-4759

Lakota Local SD
Supt. — See Liberty Twp
Shawnee Early Childhood S 200/PK-1
9394 Sterling Dr 45241 513-779-3014
Ronda Reimer, prin. Fax 779-3494

Lockland Local SD 600/K-12
210 N Cooper Ave 45215 513-563-5000
Donna Hubbard, supt. Fax 563-9611
www.locklandschools.org
Other Schools – See Lockland

Madeira CSD 1,600/PK-12
7465 Loannes Dr 45243 513-985-6070
Stephen Kramer, supt. Fax 985-6072
www.madeiracityschools.org
Madeira ES 600/PK-4
7840 Thomas Dr 45243 513-985-6080
Sallie Weisgerber, prin. Fax 985-6082
Madeira MS 500/5-8
6612 Miami Ave 45243 513-561-5555
Robert Kramer, prin. Fax 272-4145

Mariemont CSD 1,700/K-12
6743 Chestnut St 45227 513-272-7500
Paul Imhoff, supt. Fax 527-3436
www.mariemontschools.org
Fairfax ES 200/K-6
3847 Southern Ave 45227 513-272-7800
Lance Hollander, prin. Fax 527-3424
Mariemont ES 400/K-6
6750 Wooster Pike 45227 513-272-7400
Steve Brokamp, prin. Fax 527-3411
Mariemont JHS 300/7-8
6743 Chestnut St 45227 513-272-7300
Keith Koehne, prin. Fax 527-3432
Other Schools – See Terrace Park

Mt. Healthy CSD 3,300/PK-12
7615 Harrison Ave 45231 513-729-0077
David Horine, supt. Fax 728-4692
www.mthcs.org/
Duvall ES 400/K-6
1411 Compton Rd 45231 513-728-4683
Eugene Blalock, prin. Fax 521-0796
Frost ES 300/K-6
2065 Mistyhill Dr 45240 513-742-6004
Mark Walden, prin. Fax 728-4691
Greener ES 400/K-6
2400 Adams Rd 45231 513-742-6008
Jennifer Moody, prin. Fax 728-4691
Hoop ES 400/K-6
1738 Compton Rd 45231 513-522-6430
Beth Hendricks, prin. Fax 728-4691
Mt. Healthy JHS 300/7-8
1917 Miles Rd 45231 513-742-0666
Joseph Porter, prin. Fax 742-2797
New Burlington ES 400/K-6
10268 Burlington Rd 45231 513-742-6012
Robert Kelly, prin. Fax 728-4691
Ralph Center 100/PK-PK
1310 Adams Rd 45231 513-728-4685
Susan Heitner, admin. Fax 522-3010

New Richmond EVD
Supt. — See New Richmond
Locust Corner ES 400/K-6
3431 Locust Corner Rd 45245 513-752-1432
Juliann Renner, prin. Fax 752-0611

North College Hill CSD 1,600/PK-12
1498 W Galbraith Rd 45231 513-728-4770
Gary Gellert, supt. Fax 728-4774
www.nchcityschools.org
Becker ES 300/PK-6
6525 Simpson Ave 45239 513-728-4779
Joanna Sears, prin. Fax 728-4782
Clovernook ES 400/K-6
1500 W Galbraith Rd 45231 513-728-4775
Sheri Johnson, prin. Fax 728-4777
Goodman ES 100/PK-3
1731 Goodman Ave 45239 513-728-2610
Joanna Sears, prin. Fax 728-2613

Northwest Local SD 9,400/PK-12
3240 Banning Rd 45239 513-923-1000
Richard Glatfelter, supt. Fax 923-3644
www.nwlsd.org
Bevis ES 500/K-5
10133 Pottinger Rd 45251 513-825-3102
Collin Climer, prin. Fax 825-3084
Colerain ES 700/K-5
4850 Poole Rd 45251 513-385-8740
Denny Nagel, prin. Fax 385-8770
Colerain MS 700/6-8
4700 Poole Rd 45251 513-385-8490
Chris Shisler, prin. Fax 385-6685
Houston Early Learning Center PK-PK
3308 Compton Rd 45251 513-385-8000
Barb Hill, admin. Fax 385-8090
Monfort Heights ES 700/PK-5
3711 W Fork Rd 45247 513-389-1570
Deborah Estabrook, prin. Fax 389-1572
Pleasant Run ES 200/3-5
11765 Hamilton Ave 45231 513-825-7070
Joan Farabee, prin. Fax 825-1076

Pleasant Run MS 900/6-8
11770 Pippin Rd 45231 513-851-2400
David Maine, prin. Fax 851-7071
Struble ES 400/K-5
2760 Jonrose Ave 45239 513-522-2700
Sue Caron, prin. Fax 522-0347
Taylor ES 300/K-5
3173 Springdale Rd 45251 513-825-3000
Becky Karlak, prin. Fax 825-2983
Weigel ES 500/K-5
3242 Banning Rd 45239 513-923-4040
Holly Coombs, prin. Fax 923-3644
Welch ES 200/PK-2
12084 Deerhorn Dr 45240 513-742-1240
Fax 742-8632
White Oak MS 800/6-8
3130 Jessup Rd 45239 513-741-4300
Jamie Birdsong, prin. Fax 741-0717

Oak Hills Local SD 8,000/K-12
6325 Rapid Run Rd 45233 513-574-3200
Harry Kemen, supt. Fax 598-2947
www.oakhills.k12.oh.us
Bridgetown MS 500/6-8
3900 Race Rd 45211 513-574-3511
Tim Cybulski, prin. Fax 574-6689
Delhi MS 600/6-8
5280 Foley Rd 45238 513-922-8400
Daniel Beckenhaupt, prin. Fax 922-8472
Delshire ES 500/K-5
4402 Glenhaven Rd 45238 513-471-1766
Jeffrey Hunt, prin. Fax 471-1767
Dulles ES 800/K-5
6481 Bridgetown Rd 45248 513-574-3443
John Stoddard, prin. Fax 574-3182
Harrison ES 1,000/K-5
585 Neeb Rd 45233 513-922-1485
Deborah Haffey, prin. Fax 922-3330
Oakdale ES 700/K-5
3850 Virginia Ct 45248 513-574-1100
Sandra Bauman, prin. Fax 574-5116
Rapid Run MS 600/6-8
6345 Rapid Run Rd 45233 513-467-0300
Robert Sehlhorst, prin. Fax 467-0333
Springmyer ES 400/K-5
4179 Ebenezer Rd 45248 513-574-1205
Thomas Melvin, prin. Fax 574-1206

Princeton CSD 5,600/PK-12
25 W Sharon Rd 45246 513-864-1000
Dr. William Pack, supt. Fax 864-1008
www.princeton.k12.oh.us
Evendale ES 200/PK-5
3940 Glendale Milford Rd 45241 513-864-1200
Robin Wiley, prin. Fax 864-1291
Glendale ES 200/K-5
930 Congress Ave 45246 513-864-1300
Julie Ayers, prin. Fax 864-1391
Heritage Hill ES 300/PK-5
11961 Chesterdale Rd 45246 513-864-1400
Tianay Amat-Outlaw, prin. Fax 864-1491
Lincoln Heights ES 400/PK-5
1113 Adams St 45215 513-864-2400
Mary Goodwin-Corbin, prin. Fax 864-2491
Princeton Community MS 1,200/6-8
11157 Chester Rd 45246 513-552-8500
Kimberly Pence, prin. Fax 552-8511
Sharonville ES 400/PK-5
11150 Maple St 45241 513-864-2600
Edward Theroux, prin. Fax 864-2691
Springdale ES 500/PK-5
350 W Kemper Rd 45246 513-864-2700
Kelly Wilham, prin. Fax 864-2791
Stewart ES 400/PK-5
11850 Conrey Rd 45249 513-864-2800
David Schmitz, prin. Fax 864-2891
Woodlawn ES 300/PK-5
31 Riddle Rd 45215 513-864-2900
Sherry Myers, prin. Fax 864-2991

Sycamore Community CSD 5,500/K-12
4881 Cooper Rd 45242 513-686-1700
Dr. Adrienne James, supt. Fax 791-4873
www.sycamoreschools.org
Blue Ash ES 500/K-4
9541 Plainfield Rd 45236 513-686-1710
Marianne Sweetwood, prin. Fax 792-0305
Greene IS 900/5-6
5200 Aldine Dr 45242 513-686-1750
Philip Hackett, prin. Fax 792-6172
Maple Dale ES 400/K-4
6100 Hagewa Dr 45242 513-686-1720
Ron Brooks, prin. Fax 792-6112
Montgomery ES 500/K-4
9609 Montgomery Rd 45242 513-686-1730
Linda Overbeck, prin. Fax 792-6131
Sycamore JHS 900/7-8
5757 Cooper Rd 45242 513-686-1760
Karen Naber, prin. Fax 891-3162
Other Schools – See Loveland

Three Rivers Local SD
Supt. — See Cleves
Miami Heights ES 400/PK-1
7670 Bridgetown Rd 45248 513-467-3210
Donald Larrick, prin. Fax 467-0474

West Clermont Local SD 9,000/K-12
4350 Aicholtz Rd 45245 513-943-5000
Gary Brooks, supt. Fax 752-6158
www.westcler.k12.oh.us
Brantner Lane ES 400/K-5
609 Brantner Ln 45244 513-943-6400
Cindy Leazer, prin. Fax 528-0179
Clough Pike ES 500/K-5
808 Clough Pike 45245 513-943-6700
Patrick Crahan, prin. Fax 752-7347

Glen Este MS 1,000/6-8
4342 Glen Este Wthmsvlle Rd 45245 513-947-7700
Kevin Thacker, prin. Fax 753-3462
Merwin ES 700/K-5
1040 Gaskins Rd 45245 513-947-7800
Jacqueline Hospelhorn, prin. Fax 752-5629
Summerside ES 600/K-5
4639 Vermona Dr 45245 513-947-7900
Linda Austin, prin. Fax 528-3520
Withamsville-Tobasco ES 500/K-5
733 Ohio Pike 45245 513-943-6900
Tonya Schmidt, prin. Fax 752-6571
Other Schools – See Amelia, Batavia

Winton Woods CSD 2,500/PK-12
1215 W Kemper Rd 45240 513-619-2300
Camille Nasbe, supt. Fax 619-2309
www.wintonwoods.org
Winton Woods ES 100/3-4
1501 Kingsbury Dr 45240 513-619-2490
Steven Denny, prin. Fax 619-2497
Winton Woods IS 100/5-6
825 Waycross Rd 45240 513-619-2450
Tonya West-Wright, prin. Fax 619-2451
Winton Woods MS 700/7-8
147 Farragut Rd 45218 513-619-2240
Dwight Campbell, prin. Fax 619-2452
Winton Woods North PS 200/PK-2
73 Junefield Ave 45218 513-619-2390
Claire Crook, prin. Fax 619-2398
Winton Woods South PS 200/K-2
825 Lakeridge Dr 45231 513-619-2470
Linda Giuliano, prin. Fax 619-2479

Aldersgate Christian Academy 100/K-12
1810 Young St 45202 513-721-7944
William Marshall, prin. Fax 721-3971
All Saints S 500/K-8
8939 Montgomery Rd 45236 513-792-4732
Mary Stratford, prin. Fax 792-7990
Annunciation S 100/K-8
3545 Clifton Ave 45220 513-221-1230
Cindy Hardesty, prin. Fax 281-8009
Beautiful Savior Lutheran S 100/K-8
11981 Pippin Rd 45231 513-825-2290
Daniel Markgraf, prin. Fax 825-2172
Bethany S 300/K-8
555 Albion Ave 45246 513-771-7462
Cheryl Pez, hdmstr. Fax 771-2292
Cardinal Pacelli S 400/PK-8
927 Ellison Ave 45226 513-321-1048
Kimberly A. Roy, prin. Fax 533-6113
Central Baptist Academy 200/K-12
7645 Winton Rd 45224 513-521-5481
Richard Voiles, admin. Fax 521-5481
Central Montessori Academy 100/PK-6
1904 Springdale Rd 45231 513-742-5800
Laura Saylor, prin. Fax 742-5870
Cincinnati Country Day S 1,400/PK-12
6905 Given Rd 45243 513-561-4278
Dr. Robert Macrae, hdmstr. Fax 527-7600
Cincinnati Hebrew Day S 200/PK-8
2222 Losantiville Ave 45237 513-351-7777
Rabbi Y. Kernerman, prin. Fax 351-7794
Cincinnati Hills Christian Academy 500/5-8
11300 Snider Rd 45249 513-247-0900
Randy Brunk, hdmstr. Fax 247-9362
Cincinnati Hills Chrstn Acad - Armleder 200/PK-8
140 W 9th St 45202 513-721-2422
Susan Miller, prin. Fax 721-3300
Cincinnati Hills Chrstn Acad - Lindner 500/K-4
11312 Snider Rd 45249 513-247-0900
Randy Brunk, hdmstr. Fax 247-0125
Cincinnati Junior Academy 100/K-10
3798 Clifton Ave 45220 513-751-1255
Sherry Herdman, prin. Fax 751-1224
Cincinnati Waldorf S 200/PK-8
5555 Little Flower Ave 45239 513-541-0220
Christine Masur, dir. Fax 541-3586
Concordia Lutheran S 50/PK-PK
1133 Clifton Hills Ave 45220 513-502-2761
Corryville Catholic S 200/PK-8
108 Calhoun St 45219 513-281-4856
Sr. Marie Smith, prin. Fax 281-6497
Eden Grove Academy 100/PK-8
6277 Collegevue Pl 45224 513-542-0643
Ed Myers, prin. Fax 681-3450
Guardian Angels S 600/K-8
6539 Beechmont Ave 45230 513-624-3141
William Kenney, prin. Fax 624-3150
Heaven's Treasures Academy 100/PK-2
3308 Springdale Rd 45251 513-245-2901
Donna Mears, admin. Fax 245-2902
Holy Family S 200/K-8
3001 Price Ave 45205 513-921-8483
Sr. Brenda Busch, prin. Fax 921-2460
Immaculate Heart of Mary S 700/1-8
7800 Beechmont Ave 45255 513-388-4086
Mary Hedger, prin. Fax 388-4097
John Paul II S 600/K-8
9375 Winton Rd 45231 513-521-0860
Sharon Willmes, prin. Fax 728-3110
Mercy Montessori Center 300/PK-8
2335 Grandview Ave 45206 513-475-6700
Patricia Normile, prin. Fax 475-6755
Miami Valley Christian Academy 400/PK-12
6830 School St 45244 513-272-6822
Matthew Long, hdmstr. Fax 272-3711
Nativity of Our Lord S 400/K-8
5936 Ridge Ave 45213 513-458-6767
Robert Herring, prin. Fax 458-6761
New S 100/PK-6
3 Burton Woods Ln 45229 513-281-7999
Eric Dustman, prin. Fax 281-7996
Our Lady of Grace S 300/K-8
2940 W Galbraith Rd 45239 513-931-3070
Mike Johnson, prin. Fax 931-3707
Our Lady of Lourdes S 400/K-8
5835 Glenway Ave 45238 513-347-2660
Karen Rusche, prin. Fax 347-2663
Our Lady of Victory S 600/K-8
808 Neeb Rd 45233 513-347-2072
Kathleen Kane, prin. Fax 922-5476
Our Lady of Visitation S 900/1-8
3180 South Rd 45248 513-347-2222
Terry Chapman, prin. Fax 347-2225
Prince of Peace S 100/K-8
6000 Murray Ave 45227 513-271-8288
Joan Tessarolo, prin. Fax 272-1740
Queen of Angels Montessori S 200/PK-8
4460 Berwick St 45227 513-271-4171
Daniel Teller, prin. Fax 271-4680
Resurrection of Our Lord Academy 200/K-8
1740 Iliff Ave 45205 513-471-6600
Kathleen Sparks, prin. Fax 471-2610
Rockwern Academy 100/K-8
8401 Montgomery Rd 45236 513-984-3770
Susan Moore, prin.
St. Aloysius Gonzaga S 300/K-8
4390 Bridgetown Rd 45211 513-574-4035
James Leisring, prin. Fax 574-5421
St. Aloysius on the Ohio S 100/PK-8
6207 Portage St 45233 513-941-7831
Ed Jung, prin. Fax 941-5418
St. Antoninus S 500/K-8
5425 Julmar Dr 45238 513-922-2500
Jack Corey, prin. Fax 922-5519
St. Bernard S 200/K-8
7115 Springdale Rd 45247 513-353-4224
Leanora Roach, prin. Fax 353-3958
St. Boniface S 200/K-8
4305 Pitts Ave 45223 513-541-5122
Sr. Ann Gorman, prin. Fax 541-3939
St. Catherine of Siena S 200/K-8
3324 Wunder Ave 45211 513-481-7683
Mary Bernier, prin. Fax 481-9438
St. Cecilia S 200/K-8
4115 Taylor Ave 45209 513-533-6060
Lori Heffner, prin. Fax 533-6068
St. Dominic S 600/K-8
371 Pedretti Ave 45238 513-251-1276
Aloysius H. Grote, prin. Fax 251-6428
St. Francis De Sales S 200/K-8
1602 Madison Rd Unit 1 45206 513-961-1953
Dr. William Shula, prin. Fax 961-2900
St. Francis Seraph S 100/K-8
14 E Liberty St 45202 513-721-7778
Wanda Hill, prin. Fax 721-5445
St. Gabriel Consolidated S 400/K-8
18 W Sharon Rd 45246 513-771-5220
Joe Epplin, prin. Fax 771-5133
St. Gertrude S 400/PK-8
6543 Miami Ave 45243 513-561-8020
Sr. Mary Maksim, prin. Fax 561-7184
St. Ignatius Loyola S 900/K-8
5222 N Bend Rd Ste 1 45247 513-389-3242
Tim Reilly, prin. Fax 389-3255
St. James of the Valley S 200/K-8
411 Springfield Pike Ste 1 45215 513-821-9054
Marianne Rosemond, prin. Fax 821-9556
St. James the Greater S 900/K-8
6111 Cheviot Rd 45247 513-741-5333
Donna Beebe, prin. Fax 741-5312
St. John the Baptist S 500/PK-8
5375 Dry Ridge Rd 45252 513-385-7970
Richard Harrman, prin. Fax 699-6964
St. Joseph S 200/K-8
745 Ezzard Charles Dr 45203 513-381-2126
Dionne Thompson, prin. Fax 381-6513
St. Jude S 500/K-8
5940 Bridgetown Rd 45248 513-598-2100
Bob Huber, prin. Fax 598-2118
St. Lawrence S 300/PK-8
1020 Carson Ave 45205 513-921-4996
Alma Lee Joesting, prin. Fax 921-5108
St. Martin of Tours S 200/K-8
3729 Harding Ave 45211 513-661-7609
Pat Dieckman, prin. Fax 661-8102
St. Mary S 500/K-8
2845 Erie Ave 45208 513-321-0703
Suzanne McBrayer, prin. Fax 533-5517
St. Nicholas Academy 300/PK-8
7131 Plainfield Rd 45236 513-686-2727
Gerry Myers, prin. Fax 686-2729
St. Teresa of Avila S 400/K-8
1194 Rulison Ave 45238 513-471-4530
William Cavanaugh, prin. Fax 471-1254
St. Ursula Villa S 400/PK-8
3660 Vineyard Pl 45226 513-871-7218
Sally Hicks, prin. Fax 871-0082
St. Veronica S 500/K-8
4475 Mount Carmel Tobasco 45244 513-528-0442
Paul McLaughlin, prin. Fax 528-0513
St. Vincent Ferrer S 200/K-8
7754 Montgomery Rd 45236 513-791-6320
Stephen Zinser, prin. Fax 791-3332
St. Vivian S 400/PK-8
885 Denier Pl 45224 513-522-6858
Jean M. Margello, prin. Fax 728-4336
St. William S 200/PK-8
4125 Saint Williams Ave 45205 513-471-2989
Catie Blum, prin. Fax 471-8226
Seven Hills S 1,100/PK-12
5400 Red Bank Rd 45227 513-271-9027
Christopher Garten, hdmstr. Fax 271-2471
Summit Country Day S 1,100/PK-12
2161 Grandin Rd 45208 513-871-4700
Jerry Jellig, hdmstr. Fax 871-6558
Xavier University Montessori Lab S 50/PK-4
3800 Victory Pkwy Dept 84 45207 513-745-3424
Gina Lofquist, prin. Fax 745-4378

Circleville, Pickaway, Pop. 13,559
Circleville CSD 2,400/K-12
388 Clark Dr 43113 740-474-4340
Sam Lucas, supt. Fax 474-6600
www.circlevillecityschools.org/
Atwater ES 400/1-2
870 Atwater Ave 43113 740-474-4706
Sue Haley, prin. Fax 477-6680
Court ES 400/4-5
1250 S Court St 43113 740-474-2495
Karen Bullock, prin. Fax 474-2495
Everts MS 600/6-8
520 S Court St 43113 740-474-2345
Kevin Fox, prin. Fax 477-6384
Mound Street K 200/K-K
424 E Mound St 43113 740-474-3940
Robert McFerin, prin. Fax 474-3897
Nicholas Drive ES 200/3-3
410 Nicholas Dr 43113 740-474-7311
Tom Patterson, prin. Fax 477-8742

Logan Elm Local SD 2,300/K-12
9579 Tarlton Rd 43113 740-474-7501
Jan Broughton, supt. Fax 477-6525
www.loganelmschools.com/
McDowell-Exchange JHS 400/7-8
9579 Tarlton Rd 43113 740-474-7538
Keitha Lane, prin. Fax 474-8539
Pickaway ES 300/K-6
28158 Kingston Pike 43113 740-474-3877
James Wolfe, prin. Fax 477-1324
Washington ES 200/K-6
7990 Stoutsville Pike 43113 740-474-2851
Sandy Elsea, prin. Fax 474-7693
Other Schools – See Kingston, Laurelville

New Hope Christian S 300/PK-8
2264 Walnut Creek Pike 43113 740-477-6427
Michael Fluhart, admin. Fax 420-3910
Trinity Lutheran Christian Preschool & K 100/PK-K
135 E Mound St 43113 740-474-9870
Nancy Harrow, dir. Fax 474-4268

Clarksville, Clinton, Pop. 498
Clinton-Massie Local SD 1,900/K-12
2556 Lebanon Rd 45113 937-289-2471
Ronald Rudduck, supt. Fax 289-3313
www.clinton-massie.k12.oh.us
Clinton-Massie ES 800/K-5
2556 Lebanon Rd 45113 937-289-2515
Mark Wilkie, prin. Fax 289-3608
Clinton-Massie MS 500/6-8
2556 Lebanon Rd 45113 937-289-2932
Greg Grove, prin. Fax 289-8100

Clayton, Montgomery, Pop. 13,194
Northmont CSD
Supt. — See Englewood
Northmont MS 1,000/7-8
4810 National Rd 45315 937-832-6500
David Weekley, prin. Fax 832-6501

Salem Christian Academy 200/K-6
PO Box 309 45315 937-836-9910
Timothy Kegley, prin. Fax 836-7630

Cleveland, Cuyahoga, Pop. 452,208
Cleveland Municipal SD 54,000/PK-12
1380 E 6th St 44114 216-574-8000
Dr. Eugene Sanders, supt. Fax 574-8193
www.cmsdnet.net
Agassiz S 300/K-8
3595 Bosworth Rd 44111 216-251-7747
Christine Hericks, prin. Fax 251-4735
Alcott ES 200/K-5
10308 Baltic Rd 44102 216-631-3151
Eileen Stull, prin. Fax 631-3309
Almira S 500/K-8
3380 W 98th St 44102 216-631-0714
Gretchen Liggens, prin. Fax 634-2429
Audubon S 600/K-8
3055 Mrtn Luther King Jr Dr 44104 216-421-3132
George Henderson, prin. Fax 421-7694
Baker S of Arts 700/K-8
3690 W 159th St 44111 216-252-2131
Juliane Fouse-Shepard, prin. Fax 476-6829
Bell S 500/PK-8
11815 Larchmere Blvd 44120 216-229-6966
Amy Peck, prin. Fax 795-0446
Bethune S 400/K-8
11815 Moulton Ave 44106 216-231-0100
Ann Strohmeyer, prin. Fax 231-0110
Bolton S 300/PK-8
9803 Quebec Ave 44106 216-231-2585
Branka Vinski, prin. Fax 795-2948
Booker Montessori S 600/PK-8
2121 W 67th St 44102 216-961-1753
Kathy Baker, prin. Fax 634-8702
Brooklawn S 300/K-8
11801 Worthington Ave 44111 216-476-6810
Sylvia Whitt, prin. Fax 476-6680
Bryant S 500/K-8
3121 Oak Park Ave 44109 216-351-6343
Melissa Watts, prin. Fax 749-8139
Buckeye-Woodland S 300/K-8
9511 Buckeye Rd 44104 216-231-2661
Dakota Williams, prin. Fax 421-7160
Buhrer S @ Kentucky 400/PK-8
3805 Terrett Ave 44113 216-631-3310
Sandra Velazquez, prin. Fax 634-2177
Carver S 500/K-8
5393 Quincy Ave 44104 216-391-2916
Cheryl Elder-Taylor, prin. Fax 391-5041
Case S 600/PK-8
4050 Superior Ave 44103 216-431-4390
Temujin Taylor, prin. Fax 431-4375

Clark S 600/K-8
5550 Clark Ave 44102 216-631-2760
Amanda Rodriguez, prin. Fax 634-2217
Clement S 300/PK-3
14311 Woodworth Rd 44112 216-541-7543
Damon Loretz, prin. Fax 541-7562
Cleveland S of the Arts - Dike Campus 300/PK-6
2501 E 61st St 44104 216-361-0708
Andrew Koonce, prin. Fax 431-8710
Denison S 700/K-8
3799 W 33rd St 44109 216-741-2916
Leslie Rotatori-Tranter, prin. Fax 778-6578
DeSauze S 400/K-8
4747 E 176th St 44128 216-587-2133
Margaret Bates-Moore, prin. Fax 662-2072
Dickens S 400/K-8
3552 E 131st St 44120 216-921-8558
Bessie Durr, prin. Fax 921-2546
Dunbar S 400/PK-8
2200 W 28th St 44113 216-281-7224
Darlene Thaxton, prin. Fax 634-8724
East Clark S @ Margaret Spellacy 400/K-8
655 E 162nd St 44110 216-531-2872
Clifford Hayes, prin. Fax 531-2874
Eliot S 300/K-8
15700 Lotus Dr 44128 216-752-0100
Nell Byrd, prin. Fax 295-3570
Empire Computech S 400/K-8
9113 Parmelee Ave 44108 216-268-6350
Valerie Flowers, prin. Fax 268-6353
Forest Hill Parkway Academy 400/K-8
450 E 112th St 44108 216-268-6138
Stella Antwine, prin. Fax 681-3810
Franklin S 800/PK-8
1905 Spring Rd 44109 216-749-8580
Kim Cantwell, prin. Fax 778-6575
Fullerton S 400/K-8
5920 Fullerton Ave 44105 216-341-2393
Rita Smith-Rogers, prin. Fax 441-8049
Fulton S 400/K-8
3291 E 140th St 44120 216-921-6177
Chantelle Lewis, prin. Fax 295-2613
Gallagher S 800/K-8
6601 Franklin Blvd 44102 216-961-0057
Jennifer Rhone, prin. Fax 634-2353
Gibbons-Nottingham S 200/K-8
1401 Larchmont Rd 44110 216-383-4555
Shalom Norton, prin. Fax 383-4556
Giddings S 400/PK-8
2250 E 71st St 44103 216-431-1298
Gerard Leslie, prin. Fax 431-4380
Gracemount S 600/K-8
16200 Glendale Ave 44128 216-921-8833
Katrina Hicks, prin. Fax 295-2615
Grdina S 600/PK-8
3050 E 77th St 44104 216-641-7477
Marwa Ibrahim, prin. Fax 641-2009
Hale S 400/K-8
3588 Mrtn Luther King Jr Dr 44105 216-641-4485
Joelle McIntosh, prin. Fax 441-8033
Hart S 500/K-8
3901 E 74th St 44105 216-341-0874
Joyce Cummings, prin. Fax 441-8083
Henry S @ Stephen Howe 400/K-8
1000 Lakeview Rd 44108 216-851-6600
Charlene Williams, prin. Fax 541-7075
Iowa-Maple S 500/PK-8
12510 Maple Ave 44108 216-451-6630
Stacy Lambert-Johnson, prin. Fax 541-7669
Jamison Computech S 600/K-8
13905 Harvard Ave 44105 216-295-0655
Dr. Rashid Shabazz, prin. Fax 295-2678
Jones S 300/K-8
3575 W 130th St 44111 216-889-4071
Joshua Gunvalsen, prin. Fax 889-4075
Lake S 400/PK-8
815 Linn Dr 44108 216-541-5727
Jason Greathouse, prin. Fax 541-8144
Landis S 400/K-8
10118 Hampden Ave 44108 216-421-2115
Sandra Brinson, prin. Fax 421-7100
Longfellow S 300/PK-8
650 E 140th St 44110 216-451-5732
Sean Patton, prin. Fax 268-6150
MacArthur ES 200/PK-3
4401 Valleyside Rd 44135 216-267-5969
Toni Miller, prin. Fax 433-7466
Marin S 800/K-8
1701 Castle Ave 44113 216-241-7440
Jamie Lawrence, prin. Fax 241-4958
Marion-Sterling S 500/PK-8
3033 Central Ave 44115 216-621-0612
Sondra Powers, prin. Fax 694-4746
Martin S 400/K-8
8200 Brookline Ave 44103 216-229-2025
Kimberly Huckaby, prin. Fax 229-2052
McKinley S 400/K-8
3349 W 125th St 44111 216-251-4175
Sydney Scott, prin. Fax 476-6847
Memorial S 500/PK-8
410 E 152nd St 44110 216-692-4180
Lori Rondo, prin. Fax 692-4181
Miles Park S 500/K-8
4090 E 93rd St 44105 216-641-3993
Francie Watson, prin. Fax 641-3991
Miles S 400/K-8
11918 Miles Ave 44105 216-641-2019
Robert Early, prin. Fax 441-8050
Mooney S 500/K-8
3213 Montclair Ave 44109 216-741-1183
Maureen Berg, prin. Fax 741-8722
Morgan S 400/PK-8
1440 E 92nd St 44106 216-983-8300
Margretta Curtis, prin. Fax 983-8301
Mound S 400/K-8
5405 Mound Ave 44105 216-341-2671
Brenda Turner, prin. Fax 441-8082

Orchard S 600/PK-8
4200 Bailey Ave 44113 216-631-1854
Mary Anne Knapp, prin. Fax 634-2143
Perry S 400/PK-8
18400 Schenely Ave 44119 216-481-7528
Victoria Mousty, prin. Fax 383-5163
Raper S 500/PK-8
1601 E 85th St 44106 216-421-1922
Sylvia Aziz, prin. Fax 795-2936
Revere S 500/PK-8
10706 Sandusky Ave 44105 216-341-2172
Joyce Hunter, prin. Fax 641-2077
Rickoff S 600/PK-8
3500 E 147th St 44120 216-767-2100
Dr. Robert Moore, prin. Fax 767-2101
Riverside S 500/K-8
14601 Montrose Ave 44111 216-476-6800
Charles Byrd, prin. Fax 688-3603
Rockefeller Fundamental Academy 300/K-8
5901 Whittier Ave 44103 216-881-7887
Edna Connally, prin. Fax 432-4500
Roosevelt Academy 300/PK-8
800 Linn Dr 44108 216-268-8100
Samuel Vawters, prin. Fax 268-6954
Roth S 400/K-8
12523 Woodside Ave 44108 216-761-6528
Conrad Hamlet, prin. Fax 541-7128
Scranton S 600/K-8
1991 Barber Ave 44113 216-621-2165
Mary Maul, prin. Fax 363-5034
Seltzer S 600/K-8
1468 W 98th St 44102 216-631-0678
Judith Kean, prin. Fax 634-8733
Stevenson S 300/K-8
3938 Jo Ann Dr 44122 216-751-3443
Jacqueline Schuenaman, prin. Fax 751-2060
Stokes Academy 500/K-8
2225 E 40th St 44103 216-431-4410
Donna Baynes, prin. Fax 432-4607
Sunbeam S 200/K-8
11731 Mount Overlook Ave 44120 216-231-0961
Melanie Sinks, prin. Fax 795-8095
Tremont Montessori 500/PK-8
2409 W 10th St 44113 216-621-2082
Heather Grant, prin. Fax 621-2066
Union S 300/K-8
6701 Union Ave 44105 216-341-2360
Sophia Karnavas, prin. Fax 441-8068
Valley View S - Boys Leadership Academy 100/PK-2
17200 Valleyview Ave 44135 216-251-3876
Dr. Terrance Menefee, prin. Fax 889-4093
Wade Park S @ Harry Davis 300/PK-8
10700 Churchill Ave 44106 216-361-0580
Audrey Staton-Thompson, prin. Fax 361-7113
Walton S 700/K-8
3409 Walton Ave 44113 216-961-1649
Serena Houston-Edwards, prin. Fax 634-8790
Ward S 400/PK-8
4315 W 140th St 44135 216-634-2714
Neil Murphy, prin. Fax 631-2835
Warner S - Girls Leadership Academy 400/PK-2
8315 Jeffries Ave 44105 216-206-4620
Lesley Jones Sessler, prin. Fax 206-4621
Watterson-Lake S 600/K-8
1422 W 74th St 44102 216-961-0154
Serena Houston-Edwards, prin. Fax 634-2231
Waverly S 400/K-8
1810 W 54th St 44102 216-634-2121
Eleanore Parker, prin. Fax 634-8746
Westropp S 600/PK-8
19101 Puritas Ave 44135 216-267-3706
Christine Shaefer, prin. Fax 267-5940
White S 400/K-8
1000 E 92nd St 44108 216-451-7013
Dessie Sanders, prin. Fax 451-4692
Willow S 300/K-8
5004 Glazier Ave 44127 216-883-6118
Angela Powers, prin. Fax 429-3294
Woodland Hills S 400/K-8
9201 Crane Ave 44105 216-641-2062
Suszanne Hawthorne-Clay, prin. Fax 441-8037
Wright S 600/PK-8
11005 Parkhurst Dr 44111 216-476-4200
Michael Murawski, prin. Fax 476-4206

Orange CSD 2,400/PK-12
32000 Chagrin Blvd 44124 216-831-8600
Nancy Wingenbach, supt. Fax 831-8029
www.orangeschools.org
Brady MS 500/6-8
32000 Chagrin Blvd 44124 216-831-8600
Brian Frank, prin. Fax 839-1335
Moreland Hills ES 1,000/PK-5
32000 Chagrin Blvd 44124 216-831-8600
Marc Haag, prin. Fax 831-4298

Academy of St. Bartholomew 400/PK-8
14875 Bagley Rd 44130 440-845-6660
Elizabeth Palascak, prin. Fax 845-6672
Archbishop Lyke ES 200/K-4
18230 Harvard Ave 44128 216-991-9644
Mary Pat Hable, prin. Fax 991-9470
Birchwood S 100/1-8
4370 W 140th St 44135 216-251-2321
Charles Debelak, dir. Fax 251-2787
Holy Name S 200/K-8
8328 Broadway Ave 44105 216-341-0084
Penny Lins, prin. Fax 341-1122
Immaculate Conception S 200/K-8
4129 Superior Ave 44103 216-361-1883
Rosemary DiPietro, prin. Fax 881-4274
Luther Memorial Lutheran S 100/PK-8
8607 Sauer Ave 44102 216-631-3640
Peggy Schauer, prin. Fax 631-4073
Metro Catholic S 600/PK-8
1910 W 54th St 44102 216-281-4044
Sr. Ann Maline, prin. Fax 634-2853

Montessori S at Holy Rosary 100/K-8
12009 Mayfield Rd 44106 216-421-0700
Tina Schneider, prin. Fax 421-2310
Our Lady of Angels S 400/K-8
3644 Rocky River Dr 44111 216-251-6841
Kathleen Lynch, prin. Fax 251-7831
Our Lady of Good Counsel S 200/PK-8
4419 Pearl Rd 44109 216-741-3685
Kimberly Browning, prin. Fax 741-5534
Our Lady of Mt. Carmel West S 300/PK-8
1355 W 70th St 44102 216-281-7146
Sr. Rosario Vega, prin. Fax 281-7001
Our Lady of Peace S 200/K-8
12406 Buckingham Ave 44120 216-795-7161
William DiBacco, prin. Fax 795-7370
Ramah Junior Academy 100/K-9
4770 Lee Rd 44128 216-581-2626
Mary Conwell, prin. Fax 581-4128
St. Adalbert S 200/PK-8
2345 E 83rd St 44104 216-881-6250
Paula Mattis, prin. Fax 881-9030
St. Francis S 200/K-8
7206 Myron Ave 44103 216-361-4858
Sr. Karen Somerville, prin. Fax 361-1673
St. Ignatius S 400/K-8
10205 Lorain Ave 44111 216-671-0535
Margaret Ricksecker, prin. Fax 671-0536
St. Jerome S 200/K-8
15100 Lake Shore Blvd 44110 216-486-3587
Mark Dudek, prin. Fax 486-4288
St. John Lutheran S 100/K-8
1027 E 176th St 44119 216-531-8204
Gregory Kita, prin. Fax 531-8204
St. John Nepomucene S 200/K-8
3777 Independence Rd 44105 216-341-1347
Roswitha Wunker, prin. Fax 341-4466
St. Joseph-Collinwood Preschool 50/PK-PK
14405 Saint Clair Ave 44110 216-681-4007
Sr. Barbara Eppich, prin. Fax 451-8832
St. Joseph Collinwood S 200/K-8
14405 Saint Clair Ave 44110 216-451-2143
Sandria Dixon, prin. Fax 451-8832
St. Leo the Great S 300/PK-8
4900 Broadview Rd 44109 216-661-2120
Diane Weiss, prin. Fax 661-7125
St. Mark Lutheran S 100/K-8
4464 Pearl Rd 44109 216-749-3545
Winnie Rathbun, prin. Fax 749-4270
St. Mark S 400/K-8
15724 Montrose Ave 44111 216-521-4115
Dr. Marilyn Kurnath, prin. Fax 221-8664
St. Mary Byzantine S 200/PK-8
4600 State Rd 44109 216-749-7980
Rita Basalla, prin. Fax 749-7775
St. Mary S - Collinwood 200/K-8
716 E 156th St 44110 216-451-1717
Luis Pla, prin. Fax 451-4425
St. Mel S 200/K-8
14440 Triskett Rd 44111 216-941-6879
Thomas McFadden, prin. Fax 941-1005
St. Rocco S 200/K-8
3205 Fulton Rd 44109 216-961-8557
Sr. Judith Wulk, prin. Fax 961-1112
St. Stanislaus S 300/K-8
6615 Forman Ave 44105 216-883-3307
Deborah Martin, prin. Fax 883-0514
St.Thomas Aquinas S 200/K-8
9101 Superior Ave 44106 216-421-4668
Sr. Michelle Kelly, prin. Fax 721-8444
St. Vincent De Paul S 200/K-8
13442 Lorain Ave 44111 216-251-3932
Sr. Caroline Kocur, prin. Fax 251-0455
SS. Agatha & Aloysius S 200/K-8
640 Lakeview Rd 44108 216-451-2050
Sr. Sandra Sabo, prin. Fax 451-1601
Urban Community S 500/PK-8
4909 Lorain Ave 44102 216-939-8330
Pam Delly, prin. Fax 939-8324
Villa Montessori Center 50/PK-K
5620 Broadway Ave 44127 216-641-4770
Sr. Marie Veres, prin. Fax 641-4771
Westpark Catholic Academy 300/K-8
17720 Puritas Ave 44135 216-671-4314
Anne Marie Rajnicek, prin. Fax 671-5277
West Park Lutheran S 100/K-8
4260 Rocky River Dr 44135 216-941-2770
Nancy Clark, prin. Fax 941-3035

Cleveland Heights, Cuyahoga, Pop. 48,029
Cleveland Hts - University Hts CSD
Supt. — See University Heights
Boulevard ES 300/K-5
1749 Lee Rd 44118 216-371-7140
Lawrence Swoope, prin. Fax 397-5955
Canterbury ES 400/K-5
2530 Canterbury Rd 44118 216-371-7470
Kevin Harrell, prin. Fax 397-5956
Fairfax ES 400/K-5
3150 Fairfax Rd 44118 216-371-7480
Jacky Brown, prin. Fax 397-5958
Monticello MS 500/6-8
3665 Monticello Blvd 44121 216-371-6520
Sheldon Smith, prin. Fax 397-5967
Noble ES 400/K-5
1293 Ardoon St 44121 216-371-6535
Julie Beers, prin. Fax 397-5960
Oxford ES 400/K-5
939 Quilliams Rd 44121 216-371-6525
Stacy Stuhldreher, prin. Fax 397-5961
Roxboro ES 300/K-5
2405 Roxboro Rd 44106 216-371-7115
Tara Keller, prin. Fax 397-5962
Roxboro MS 600/6-8
2400 Roxboro Rd 44106 216-371-7440
Brian Sharosky, prin. Fax 397-3857

Hebrew Academy of Cleveland 700/PK-12
1860 S Taylor Rd 44118 216-321-5838
Rabbi Simcha Dessler, dir. Fax 932-4597
Mosdos Ohr HaTorah S - Boys 400/PK-12
1508 Warrensville Center Rd 44121 216-382-6248
Shmuel Berkovicz, prin. Fax 382-4585
Mosdos Ohr HaTorah S - Girls 200/PK-12
1700 S Taylor Rd 44118 216-321-1547
Ruffing Montessori S 300/PK-8
3380 Fairmount Blvd 44118 216-321-7571
Gordon Maas, hdmstr. Fax 321-7568
St. Ann S 300/K-8
2160 Stillman Rd 44118 216-932-4177
Meg Cosgriff, prin. Fax 932-7439

Cleves, Hamilton, Pop. 2,574
Three Rivers Local SD 2,000/PK-12
92 Cleves Ave 45002 513-941-6400
Rhonda Bohannon, supt. Fax 941-1102
www.threeriversschools.org
Three Rivers MS 600/5-8
8575 Bridgetown Rd 45002 513-467-3500
Thomas Huber, prin. Fax 467-1238
Young ES 400/2-4
401 N Miami Ave 45002 513-467-3225
Tom Bailey, prin. Fax 467-0925
Other Schools – See Cincinnati

Clinton, Summit, Pop. 1,395
Norton CSD
Supt. — See Norton
Grill ES 200/PK-4
6125 Kungle Rd 44216 330-825-2677
Roger Plaster, prin. Fax 706-1027

Clyde, Sandusky, Pop. 6,143
Bellevue CSD
Supt. — See Bellevue
York ES 200/3-5
2314 US Highway 20 E 43410 419-484-5050
Luana Coppus, prin.

Clyde-Green Springs EVD 2,400/K-12
106 S Main St 43410 419-547-0588
Todd Helms, supt. Fax 547-8644
www.clyde.k12.oh.us
McPherson MS 400/7-8
201 Spring St 43410 419-547-9150
Jon Detwiler, prin. Fax 547-9173
South Main ES 400/K-4
821 S Main St 43410 419-547-9868
Rod McMaster, prin. Fax 547-8644
Vine Street ES 300/K-4
521 Vine St 43410 419-547-9816
Peggy Stickney, prin. Fax 547-8644
Other Schools – See Green Springs

St. Mary S 100/K-8
615 Vine St 43410 419-547-9687
Kathy Holcomb, prin. Fax 547-9687

Coal Grove, Lawrence, Pop. 2,081
Dawson-Bryant Local SD 1,300/K-12
222 Lane St 45638 740-532-6451
Dennis DeCamp, supt. Fax 533-6019
db.k12.oh.us
Dawson-Bryant MS 300/6-8
1 Hornet Ln 45638 740-532-1664
Ellen Adkins, prin. Fax 533-6003
Other Schools – See Ironton

Coldwater, Mercer, Pop. 4,438
Coldwater EVD 1,500/K-12
310 N 2nd St 45828 419-678-2611
Richard Seas, supt. Fax 678-3100
cw.noacsc.org
Coldwater ES 500/K-4
310 N 2nd St 45828 419-678-2613
Wade Spencer, prin. Fax 678-3100
Coldwater MS 400/5-8
310 N 2nd St 45828 419-678-3331
Jerry Kanney, prin. Fax 678-3100

College Corner, Preble, Pop. 424
College Corner Local SD 100/PK-5
230 Ramsey St 45003 765-732-3183
Michael Raymond, supt. Fax 732-3574
College Corner Union ES 100/PK-5
230 Ramsey St 45003 765-732-3183
Fax 732-3574

Collins, Huron
Western Reserve Local SD 1,300/K-12
3765 State Route 20 44826 419-660-8508
Mark Gagyi, supt. Fax 660-8429
www.western-reserve.org
Western Reserve ES 700/K-6
3851 State Route 20 44826 419-660-9824
Mary Lynn Mahoney, prin. Fax 660-8566
Western Reserve MS 200/7-8
3841 State Route 20 44826 419-668-1924
Lisa Border, prin.

Columbiana, Columbiana, Pop. 5,807
Columbiana EVD 1,000/PK-12
700 Columbiana Waterford Rd 44408 330-482-5352
Ronald Iarussi, supt. Fax 482-5361
www.columbiana.k12.oh.us
Dixon ES 400/PK-3
333 N Middle St 44408 330-482-5355
Kimberly Sharshan, prin. Fax 482-5358
South Side MS 300/4-8
720 Columbiana Waterford Rd 44408 330-482-5354
David Cappuzzello, prin. Fax 482-6332

Crestview Local SD 1,200/K-12
44100 Crestview Rd Ste A 44408 330-482-5526
John Dilling, supt. Fax 482-5367
www.crestviewlocal.k12.oh.us/
Crestview ES 400/K-4
3407 Middleton Rd 44408 330-482-5370
Marian Dangerfield, prin. Fax 482-5373
Crestview MS 300/5-8
44100 Crestview Rd Ste C 44408 330-482-4648
David MacKay, prin. Fax 482-5374

Heartland Christian S 300/PK-12
28 Pittsburgh St 44408 330-482-2331
Dallas Lehman, admin. Fax 482-2413

Columbia Station, Lorain
Columbia Local SD 1,200/K-12
25796 Royalton Rd 44028 440-236-5008
John Kuhn, supt. Fax 236-8817
www.columbia.k12.oh.us/
Columbia MS 400/5-8
13646 W River Rd 44028 440-236-5741
James Cottom, prin. Fax 236-9274
Copopa ES 400/K-4
14168 W River Rd 44028 440-236-5020
Vince Ketterer, prin. Fax 236-1220

Columbus, Franklin, Pop. 730,657
Columbus CSD 54,100/PK-12
270 E State St 43215 614-365-5000
Gene Harris, supt. Fax 365-5689
www.columbus.k12.oh.us/
Africentric Early College ES 400/K-5
300 E Livingston Ave 43215 614-365-6517
Andre Jones, prin. Fax 365-6520
Alpine ES 500/K-5
1590 Alpine Dr 43229 614-365-5359
Cheryl Lumpkin, prin. Fax 365-5358
Arlington Park ES 300/K-5
2400 Mock Rd 43219 614-365-5453
April Knight, prin. Fax 365-8656
Avalon ES 500/K-5
5220 Avalon Ave 43229 614-365-5361
Sandee Donald, prin. Fax 365-8221
Avondale ES 300/K-5
1486 Watkins Rd 43207 614-365-6091
Kathleen Lensenmayer, prin. Fax 365-6093
Beery MS 400/6-8
2740 Lockbourne Rd 43207 614-365-5414
Edmund Baker, prin. Fax 365-5412
Berwick Alternative ES 400/PK-6
2655 Scottwood Rd 43209 614-365-6140
Walter Jeffreys, prin. Fax 365-6142
Binns ES 200/K-5
1080 Binns Blvd 43204 614-365-5911
Barbara Edwards, prin. Fax 365-5910
Broadleigh ES 300/K-5
3039 Maryland Ave 43209 614-365-6144
Charlotte Rudd, prin. Fax 365-6143
Buckeye MS 600/6-8
2950 Parsons Ave 43207 614-365-5417
Marianne Minshall, prin. Fax 365-5895
Burroughs ES 400/K-5
3220 Groveport Rd 43207 614-365-5423
Steven Holland, prin. Fax 365-5425
Cassady Alternative ES 400/K-5
2500 N Cassady Ave 43219 614-365-5456
Nakita Smoot, prin. Fax 365-8700
Cedarwood Alternative ES 400/K-5
775 Bartfield Dr 43207 614-365-5421
Breanna Shea Reed, prin. Fax 365-5420
Champion MS 300/6-8
284 N 22nd St 43203 614-365-6082
William Anderson, prin. Fax 365-6080
Clinton ES 300/K-5
10 Clinton Heights Ave 43202 614-365-6532
Kathy R. Leffler, prin. Fax 365-6530
Clinton MS 500/6-8
3940 Karl Rd 43224 614-365-5996
Patricia Dubose, prin. Fax 365-5999
Columbus Spanish Immersion Academy 400/K-8
2155 Fenton St 43224 614-365-8129
Carmen Graff, prin. Fax 365-8130
Como ES 400/K-5
2989 Reis Ave 43224 614-365-6013
Christopher Brady, prin. Fax 365-6011
Cranbrook ES 300/K-5
908 Bricker Blvd 43221 614-365-5497
Cynthia Ball, prin. Fax 365-5496
Dana Avenue ES 400/K-5
300 Dana Ave 43223 614-365-5925
David Kindinger, prin. Fax 365-5927
Deshler ES 300/K-5
1234 E Deshler Ave 43206 614-365-5518
Deborah Copeland, prin. Fax 365-6631
Devonshire Alternative ES 500/K-5
6286 Ambleside Dr 43229 614-365-5335
Patricia Price, prin. Fax 365-8094
Dominion MS 600/6-8
330 E Dominion Blvd 43214 614-365-6020
Dorothy Flanagan, prin. Fax 365-6018
Douglas Alternative ES 300/K-5
43 S Douglass St 43205 614-365-6087
Stanley Embry, prin. Fax 365-6452
Duxberry Park Alternative ES 300/K-5
1779 E Maynard Ave 43219 614-365-6023
Deborah Carter, prin. Fax 365-6022
Eakin ES 300/K-5
3774 Eakin Rd 43228 614-365-5928
Donna Latif, prin. Fax 365-5930
East Columbus ES 300/K-5
3100 E 7th Ave 43219 614-365-6147
Shawyna McFadden, prin. Fax 365-6146
Eastgate ES K-6
1925 Stratford Way 43219 614-365-6132
Carol Wheat, prin. Fax 365-6131

Easthaven ES 300/K-5
2360 Garnet Pl 43232 614-365-6149
Melanie McGue, prin. Fax 365-6721
East Linden ES 200/K-5
2505 Brentnell Ave 43211 614-365-5459
Angela Sweeney, prin. Fax 365-5458
Eastmoor MS 500/6-8
3450 Medway Ave 43213 614-365-6166
Sherri Edwards, prin. Fax 365-6164
Ecole Kenwood S 300/K-8
3770 Shattuck Ave 43220 614-365-5502
Elvina Palma, prin. Fax 365-5504
Fair Alternative ES 300/K-5
1395 Fair Ave 43205 614-365-6107
Christine DeLauter, prin. Fax 365-6106
Fairmoor ES 500/K-5
3281 Mayfair Park Pl 43213 614-365-6169
Maria Malik, prin. Fax 365-6171
Fairwood Alternative ES 500/K-5
726 Fairwood Ave 43205 614-365-6111
Cynthia Moore, prin. Fax 365-6110
Fifth Avenue Alternative ES 200/K-5
1300 Forsythe Ave 43201 614-365-5564
Lisa Adams, prin. Fax 365-5562
Forest Park ES 400/K-5
5535 Sandalwood Blvd 43229 614-365-5337
Rhonna McKibbin, prin. Fax 365-8219
Gables ES 300/K-5
1680 Becket Ave 43235 614-365-5499
Jill Lausch, prin. Fax 365-6451
Georgian Heights Alternative ES 400/K-5
784 Georgian Dr 43228 614-365-5931
Rhonda Peeples, prin. Fax 365-6885
Hamilton STEM Academy 400/PK-6
2047 Hamilton Ave 43211 614-365-5568
Timothy Buckley, prin. Fax 365-5570
Heyl ES 300/K-5
760 Reinhard Ave 43206 614-365-5521
Donna Onesto, prin. Fax 365-5520
Highland ES 400/K-5
40 S Highland Ave 43223 614-365-5935
Jaime Taylor, prin. Fax 365-8726
Hilltonia MS 600/6-8
2345 W Mound St 43204 614-365-5937
Donna LeBeau, prin. Fax 365-8015
Huy ES 200/K-5
1965 Gladstone Ave 43211 614-365-5565
Leslie Charlemagne, prin. Fax 365-5567
Indianola Informal ES 400/K-8
100 W 4th Ave 43201 614-365-5579
Kathryn Moser, prin. Fax 365-8324
Indianola MS 600/6-8
420 E 19th Ave 43201 614-365-5575
Colon Lewis, prin. Fax 365-5577
Indian Springs ES 400/K-5
50 E Henderson Rd 43214 614-365-6032
James Eslinger, prin. Fax 365-6031
Innis ES 300/K-5
3399 Kohr Blvd 43224 614-365-5462
Linda Cameron, prin. Fax 365-5461
Johnson Park MS 500/6-8
1130 S Waverly St 43227 614-365-6501
Charmaine W. Tinker, prin. Fax 365-8698
Leawood ES 200/K-5
1677 S Hamilton Rd 43227 614-365-6504
Annette Tooman, prin. Fax 365-6506
Liberty ES 400/K-5
2949 Whitlow Rd 43232 614-365-6482
Cheryl Jones, prin. Fax 365-5698
Lincoln Park ES 300/K-5
579 E Markison Ave 43207 614-365-5524
Eric Secrest, prin. Fax 365-5523
Lindbergh ES 300/K-5
2541 Lindbergh Dr 43223 614-365-6727
Jennifer Quesenberry, prin. Fax 365-5598
Linden ES 600/PK-6
2626 Cleveland Ave 43211 614-365-6537
Janet Hinds, prin. Fax 365-6536
Livingston ES 200/K-5
825 E Livingston Ave 43205 614-365-6513
Melinda Dixon, prin. Fax 365-6515
Maize Road ES 400/K-5
4360 Maize Rd 43224 614-365-6040
Ranea Williams, prin. Fax 365-6039
Maybury ES 400/K-5
2633 Maybury Rd 43232 614-365-5381
Kristen L. Whiting, prin. Fax 365-8505
Medina MS 500/6-8
1425 Huy Rd 43224 614-365-6050
Michelle Myles, prin. Fax 365-8136
Moler ES 200/K-5
1560 Moler Rd 43207 614-365-5529
Barbara Blake, prin. Fax 365-5531
North Linden ES 300/K-5
1718 E Cooke Rd 43224 614-365-6055
Lenelle E. Taylor, prin. Fax 365-6054
Northtowne ES 200/K-5
4767 Northtowne Blvd 43229 614-365-5488
Ronda Welch, prin. Fax 365-5487
Oakland Park Alternative ES 300/K-5
3392 Atwood Ter 43224 614-365-6058
Mary Allen, prin. Fax 365-6057
Oakmont ES 300/K-5
5666 Oakmont Dr 43232 614-365-5385
Amber Hatcher, prin. Fax 365-5384
Ohio Avenue ES 300/K-5
505 S Ohio Ave 43205 614-365-6130
Jill Bender, prin. Fax 365-6128
Olde Orchard Alternative ES 500/K-5
800 McNaughten Rd 43213 614-365-5388
Leslie Williams, prin. Fax 365-5387
Parkmoor ES 300/K-5
1711 Penworth Dr 43229 614-365-5349
Stacy Macarthy, prin. Fax 365-5348
Parsons ES 500/K-5
3231 Lee Ellen Pl 43207 614-365-5099
Candace Nespeca, prin. Fax 365-5115

Ridgeview MS 500/6-8
4241 Rudy Rd 43214 614-365-5506
Sharee Wells, prin. Fax 365-5505
Salem ES 300/K-5
1040 Garvey Rd 43229 614-365-5351
Gail Buick, prin. Fax 365-5353
Scottwood ES 300/K-5
3392 Scottwood Rd 43227 614-365-6507
Maria Stockard, prin. Fax 365-6509
Shady Lane ES 300/K-5
1444 Shady Lane Rd 43227 614-365-5391
Linda Willis, prin. Fax 365-5390
Sherwood MS 400/6-8
1400 Shady Lane Rd 43227 614-365-5393
Ray Caruthers, prin. Fax 365-8351
Siebert ES 300/K-5
385 Reinhard Ave 43206 614-365-6613
Debra Archie-Wilkerson, prin. Fax 365-6612
South Mifflin ES 300/PK-6
2365 Middlehurst Dr 43219 614-365-6135
Andrew Smith, prin. Fax 365-6134
Southmoor MS 400/6-8
1201 Moler Rd 43207 614-365-5550
Theresa Pettis, prin. Fax 365-6637
Southwood ES 400/K-5
280 Reeb Ave 43207 614-365-5533
Carla Gale, prin. Fax 365-5532
Starling MS 400/6-8
120 S Central Ave 43222 614-365-5945
Mark Hayward, prin. Fax 365-5942
Stewart Alternative ES 300/K-5
40 Stewart Ave 43206 614-365-5556
Kimberly Jones, prin. Fax 365-6704
Sullivant ES 200/K-5
791 Griggs Ave 43223 614-365-6524
Lisa Stamos, prin. Fax 365-6522
Trevitt ES 200/K-5
519 Trevitt St 43203 614-365-6137
Wendell Edwards, prin. Fax 365-6139
Valley Forge ES 300/K-5
1321 Urban Dr 43229 614-365-5648
Stephanie Bland, prin. Fax 365-5779
Valleyview ES 400/K-5
2989 Valleyview Dr 43204 614-365-6312
DeWayne Davis, prin. Fax 365-6768
Watkins ES 300/K-5
1520 Watkins Rd 43207 614-365-6411
Tom Revou, prin. Fax 365-6415
Wedgewood MS 600/6-8
3800 Briggs Rd 43228 614-365-5947
Stephen Hoffman, prin. Fax 365-5950
Weinland Park ES 300/K-5
211 E 7th Ave 43201 614-365-5321
Monica Gant, prin. Fax 365-5431
West Broad Street ES 500/K-5
2744 W Broad St 43204 614-365-5964
Pete Kurty, prin. Fax 365-5966
Westgate Alternative ES 400/K-5
3080 Wicklow Rd 43204 614-365-5971
Levonda J. Kreitzburg, prin. Fax 365-5149
Westmoor MS 500/6-8
3001 Valleyview Dr 43204 614-365-5974
William Doermann, prin. Fax 365-6705
West Mound ES 300/K-5
2051 W Mound St 43223 614-365-5968
Karla Case, prin. Fax 365-6937
Windsor Alternative Academy 400/PK-6
1219 E 12th Ave 43211 614-365-5906
Christopher Scott, prin. Fax 365-6939
Winterset ES 300/K-5
4776 Winterset Dr 43220 614-365-5510
Theresa Tracy, prin. Fax 365-5509
Woodcrest ES 400/K-5
5321 E Livingston Ave 43232 614-365-6747
Lindsey Kubli, prin. Fax 365-6751
Woodward Park MS 900/6-8
5151 Karl Rd 43229 614-365-5354
Timothy Donahue, prin. Fax 365-5357
Yorktown MS 600/6-8
5600 E Livingston Ave 43232 614-365-5408
Pamela Smith, prin. Fax 365-5411

Dublin CSD
Supt. — See Dublin
Wright ES 400/K-5
2335 W Case Rd 43235 614-538-0464
Ron Widman, prin. Fax 761-5874

Grandview Heights CSD 1,000/K-12
1587 W 3rd Ave 43212 614-481-3600
Edward O'Reilly, supt. Fax 481-3648
www.grandviewschools.org/
Edison Intermediate MS 200/4-8
1240 Oakland Ave 43212 614-481-3630
Robert Baeslack, prin.
Stevenson ES, 1065 Oxley Rd 43212 300/K-3
Brian Bowser, prin. 614-481-3640

Groveport Madison Local SD
Supt. — See Groveport
Asbury ES 400/K-5
5127 Harbor Blvd 43232 614-833-2000
James Sullivan, prin. Fax 833-2004
Dunloe ES 400/K-5
3200 Dunloe Rd 43232 614-833-2008
Emily Jane Curry, prin. Fax 833-2007
Groveport Madison MS North 500/6-7
5474 Sedalia Dr 43232 614-837-5508
David Lanning, prin. Fax 833-2033
Madison ES 400/K-5
4600 Madison School Dr 43232 614-833-2011
Cyndi Toledo, prin. Fax 836-4683
Sedalia ES 400/K-5
5400 Sedalia Dr 43232 614-833-2014
Dorethia Copas, prin. Fax 833-2017

Hamilton Local SD 2,500/PK-12
775 Rathmell Rd 43207 614-491-8044
Christopher Lester, supt. Fax 491-8323
www.hamilton-local.k12.oh.us
Other Schools – See Lockbourne

Hilliard CSD
Supt. — See Hilliard
Hilliard Horizon ES 600/K-5
6000 Renner Rd 43228 614-851-2180
Britanie Risner, prin. Fax 851-2184

South-Western CSD
Supt. — See Grove City
East Franklin ES 300/K-4
1955 Richmond Rd 43223 614-801-8100
Michele Harkins, prin. Fax 801-8111
Finland ES 400/K-4
1835 Finland Ave 43223 614-801-8125
Kenneth Pease, prin. Fax 801-8128
Finland MS 700/7-8
1825 Finland Ave 43223 614-801-3600
Paul Smathers, prin. Fax 278-6334
Franklin Woods IS 700/5-6
1831 Finland Ave 43223 614-801-8600
Garilee Ogden, prin. Fax 801-8601
Harmon ES 500/K-4
2090 Frank Rd 43223 614-801-8150
Michael Wang, prin. Fax 801-8166
North Franklin ES 300/K-4
1122 N Hague Ave 43204 614-801-8275
Elaine Lawless, prin. Fax 801-8282
Norton MS 500/7-8
215 Norton Rd 43228 614-801-3700
Scott Cunningham, prin. Fax 870-5528
Prairie Lincoln ES 500/K-4
4900 Amesbury Way 43228 614-801-8300
James LeVally, prin. Fax 801-8313
Prairie Norton ES 600/PK-4
117 Norton Rd 43228 614-801-8450
Michael Gosztyla, prin. Fax 801-8461
Stiles ES 600/PK-4
4700 Stiles Ave 43228 614-801-8375
Drenda Kemp, prin. Fax 801-8386
West Franklin ES 500/K-4
3501 Briggs Rd 43204 614-801-8400
Dawn Lauridsen, prin. Fax 801-8411

Westerville CSD
Supt. — See Westerville
Hawthorne ES 700/K-5
5001 Farview Dr 43231 614-797-7130
Frederick Tombaugh, prin. Fax 797-7131

Worthington CSD
Supt. — See Worthington
Bluffsview ES 400/K-6
7111 Linworth Rd 43235 614-883-2700
Cindy Fox, prin. Fax 883-2710
Brookside ES 300/K-6
6700 Mcvey Blvd 43235 614-883-2750
Frederick Monroe, prin. Fax 883-2760
Granby ES 400/K-6
1490 Hard Rd 43235 614-883-2900
Linda Dawson, prin. Fax 883-2910
McCord MS 300/7-8
1500 Hard Rd 43235 614-883-3550
Michael Kuri, prin. Fax 883-3560
Worthington Hills ES 400/K-6
1221 Candlewood Dr 43235 614-883-3400
Tamu Gibbs, prin. Fax 883-3410

All Saints Academy 300/PK-8
2855 E Livingston Ave 43209 614-231-3391
Barb Cooper, prin. Fax 338-2170
Calumet Christian S 300/PK-8
2774 Calumet St 43202 614-261-8136
David Glover, prin. Fax 261-9086
Central Ohio Christian S 100/K-7
4581 Cleveland Ave 43231 614-410-5861
Raymond Sweet, prin. Fax 360-1037
Clintonville Academy 200/PK-8
3916 Indianola Ave 43214 614-267-4799
Sarah Lindsay, prin. Fax 267-1723
Columbus Adventist Academy 100/K-8
3650B Sunbury Rd 43219 614-471-2083
Brenda Arthurs, prin. Fax 471-5035
Columbus Montessori Education Center 200/PK-8
979 S James Rd 43227 614-231-3790
Ann Timm, prin. Fax 231-3780
Columbus School for Girls 700/PK-12
56 S Columbia Ave 43209 614-252-0781
Diane Cooper, hdmstr. Fax 252-0571
Columbus Torah Academy 200/K-12
181 Noe Bixby Rd 43213 614-864-0299
Rabbi Zvi Kahn, hdmstr. Fax 864-2119
Friend Christian Academy 50/K-5
428 E Main St 43215 614-221-1518
Eleanor Young, admin. Fax 221-8470
Holy Spirit S 300/PK-8
4382 Duchene Ln 43213 614-861-0475
Linda Saelzler, prin. Fax 861-8608
Immaculate Conception S 500/K-8
366 E North Broadway St 43214 614-267-6579
John Grossman, prin. Fax 267-2549
Liberty Christian Academy 500/PK-12
4938 Beatrice Dr 43227 614-864-5332
LaVonne McIlrath, admin. Fax 864-5381
Marburn Academy 100/K-12
1860 Walden Dr 43229 614-433-0822
Earl Oremus, hdmstr. Fax 433-0812
Our Lady of Bethlehem S 200/PK-3
4567 Olentangy River Rd 43214 614-451-6631
Lori Dulin, prin. Fax 451-3706
Our Lady of Peace S 200/K-8
40 E Dominion Blvd 43214 614-267-4535
Carol Folian, prin. Fax 267-2333

St. Agatha S 300/K-8
1880 Northam Rd 43221 614-488-9000
Joan Mastell, prin. Fax 488-5783
St. Andrew S 500/PK-8
4081 Reed Rd 43220 614-451-1626
Joel Wichtman, prin. Fax 451-0272
St. Anthony S 200/K-8
1300 Urban Dr 43229 614-888-4268
Chris Iaconis, prin. Fax 888-4435
St. Catharine S 300/PK-8
2865 Fair Ave 43209 614-235-1396
Janet Weisner, prin. Fax 235-9708
St. Cecilia S 300/PK-8
440 Norton Rd 43228 614-878-3555
Marge Moretti, prin. Fax 878-6852
St. James the Less S 300/K-8
1628 Oakland Park Ave 43224 614-268-3311
Yvonne Schwab, prin. Fax 268-1808
St. Joseph Montessori S 300/PK-8
933 Hamlet St 43201 614-291-8601
Fax 291-7411
St. Mary Magdalene S 300/PK-8
2940 Parkside Rd 43204 614-279-9935
Rocco Fumi, prin. Fax 279-9575
St. Mary S 200/PK-8
700 S 3rd St 43206 614-444-8994
Sr. Regina Snyder, prin. Fax 449-2853
St. Matthias S 300/K-8
1566 Ferris Rd 43224 614-268-3030
Dan Kinley, prin. Fax 268-4681
St. Paul Lutheran S 100/K-8
322 Stewart Ave 43206 614-444-4216
Philip Glende, prin. Fax 444-4216
St. Timothy S 300/K-8
1070 Thomas Ln 43220 614-451-1405
George Mosholder, prin. Fax 451-3108
Sonshine Christian Academy 100/PK-8
3400 Kohr Blvd 43224 614-498-0082
Sandra Jackson, prin. Fax 475-1108
Southeast Christian Academy 50/PK-5
1500 Barnett Rd 43227 614-231-0051
Mary West, admin. Fax 236-0506
Tree of Life Christian S - Indianola 100/PK-5
2141 Indianola Ave 43201 614-299-4906
Beverly Bosworth, prin. Fax 299-3047
Trinity S 200/PK-8
1381 Ida Ave 43212 614-488-7650
Jeffery Grimmett, prin. Fax 488-7885
Wellington S 600/PK-12
3650 Reed Rd 43220 614-457-7883
Rob Brisk, hdmstr. Fax 442-3286
Worthington Christian - Westview ES 300/1-5
50 Westview Ave 43214 614-431-8240
James Parrish, prin. Fax 438-5581
Xenos Christian S 200/K-5
1390 Community Park Dr 43229 614-823-6540
Carole Bucklew, prin.

Columbus Grove, Putnam, Pop. 2,178
Columbus Grove Local SD 900/K-12
201 W Cross St 45830 419-659-2639
Robert Jennell, supt. Fax 659-5134
Columbus Grove ES 300/K-4
201 W Cross St 45830 419-659-2631
James Kincaid, prin. Fax 659-5134
Columbus Grove MS 300/5-8
201 W Cross St 45830 419-659-2631
James Kincaid, prin. Fax 659-5134

St. Anthony of Padua S 200/1-8
520 W Sycamore St 45830 419-659-2103
Lois Karhoff, prin. Fax 659-4194

Commercial Point, Pickaway, Pop. 824
Teays Valley Local SD
Supt. — See Ashville
Scioto ES 600/K-5
PO Box 327 43116 740-983-3221
Robin Halley, prin. Fax 983-5088

Conesville, Coshocton, Pop. 376
River View Local SD
Supt. — See Warsaw
Conesville ES 300/K-6
199 State St 43811 740-829-2334
Joel Moore, prin. Fax 829-2856

Conneaut, Ashtabula, Pop. 12,648
Conneaut Area CSD 2,400/K-12
400 Mill St Ste B 44030 440-593-7200
Kent Houston, supt. Fax 593-6253
www.cacsk12.org
Conneaut MS 600/6-8
230 Gateway Ave 44030 440-593-7240
Linda Bernay, prin. Fax 593-6289
Gateway ES 500/3-5
229 Gateway Ave 44030 440-593-7280
James Lutes, prin. Fax 593-6038
Lakeshore PS 500/K-2
755 Chestnut St 44030 440-593-7250
Ruth Farr, prin. Fax 599-7149

Continental, Putnam, Pop. 1,188
Continental Local SD 600/K-12
5211 State Route 634 45831 419-596-3671
Gary Jones, supt. Fax 596-3861
cn2.noacsc.org
Continental ES 300/K-5
5211 State Route 634 45831 419-596-3860
Brian Gerdeman, prin. Fax 596-2652
Continental MS 100/6-8
5211 State Route 634 45831 419-596-3871
Joel Mengerink, prin. Fax 596-2651

Convoy, Van Wert, Pop. 1,065
Crestview Local SD 1,000/K-12
531 E Tully St 45832 419-749-9100
Mike Estes, supt. Fax 749-4235
www.crestviewknights.com/

Crestview ES 500/K-6
531 E Tully St 45832 419-749-9100
Kathy Mollenkopf, prin. Fax 749-2026

Coolville, Athens, Pop. 546
Federal Hocking Local SD
Supt. — See Stewart
Coolville ES 300/PK-5
PO Box 490 45723 740-667-3121
Shirley Sayre, prin. Fax 667-6183

Copley, Summit, Pop. 11,130
Copley-Fairlawn CSD 3,400/K-12
3797 Ridgewood Rd 44321 330-664-4800
Roger Saurer, supt. Fax 664-4811
www.copley-fairlawn.org
Arrowhead PS 400/K-4
1600 Raleigh Blvd 44321 330-664-4885
Andrew LaBadie, prin. Fax 664-4927
Copley-Fairlawn MS 1,100/5-8
1531 S Cleveland Massillon 44321 330-664-4875
William Kerrigan, prin. Fax 664-4912
Other Schools – See Akron, Fairlawn

Spring Garden Waldorf S 200/PK-8
1791 Jacoby Rd 44321 330-666-0574
Steven Tabeling, prin. Fax 666-9210

Corning, Perry, Pop. 616
Southern Local SD 600/K-12
10397 State Route 155 SE 43730 740-394-2402
Greg Holbert, supt. Fax 394-2083
www.spsd.k12.oh.us
Millcreek ES 300/K-6
10397 State Route 155 SE 43730 740-394-2734
Mary Lou Wycinski, prin. Fax 394-2083

Cortland, Trumbull, Pop. 6,640
Lakeview Local SD 2,100/K-12
300 Hillman Dr 44410 330-637-8741
Robert Wilson, supt. Fax 638-1060
www.lakeviewlocal.org
Cortland ES 500/3-5
264 Park Ave 44410 330-637-2871
Scott Taylor, prin. Fax 638-0872
Lakeview MS 500/6-8
640 Wakefield Dr 44410 330-637-4360
Nancy Krygowski, prin. Fax 638-1060
Other Schools – See Warren

Maplewood Local SD 1,000/K-12
2414 Greenville Rd 44410 330-637-7506
Perry Nicholas, supt. Fax 637-6616
www.maplewood.k12.oh.us/
Maplewood MS 300/5-8
4174 Greenville Rd 44410 330-924-2431
Elizabeth Goerig, prin. Fax 924-5151
Other Schools – See North Bloomfield

Mathews Local SD
Supt. — See Vienna
Currie ES, 3306 Ridge Rd 44410 200/K-2
Michael King, prin. 330-637-2976

Coshocton, Coshocton, Pop. 11,632
Coshocton CSD 1,700/K-12
1207 Cambridge Rd 43812 740-622-1901
David Hire, supt. Fax 623-5803
www.coshoctonredskins.com/
Central ES 400/K-6
724 Walnut St 43812 740-622-5514
Grant Fauver, prin. Fax 623-0620
Lincoln ES 300/K-6
801 Cambridge Rd 43812 740-622-9726
Francie Berg, prin. Fax 623-0731
South Lawn ES 100/K-6
753 S Lawn Ave 43812 740-622-3239
Todd Johnson, prin. Fax 623-0726

River View Local SD
Supt. — See Warsaw
Keene ES 300/K-6
27052 County Road 1 43812 740-622-5884
Jerry Olinger, prin. Fax 622-5458

Coshocton Christian S 50/K-12
23891 Airport Rd 43812 740-622-5052
Wesley Courser, prin. Fax 622-9244
Sacred Heart S 100/PK-6
39 Burt Ave 43812 740-622-3728
Mary Stenner, prin. Fax 622-9151

Covington, Miami, Pop. 2,575
Covington EVD 900/K-12
25 N Grant St 45318 937-473-2249
Randy Earl, supt. Fax 473-3730
www.covington.k12.oh.us
Covington ES 400/K-5
707 Chestnut St 45318 937-473-2252
Linda Gephart, prin. Fax 473-3685
Covington MS 200/6-8
25 N Grant St 45318 937-473-2833
David Larson, prin. Fax 473-8189

Crestline, Crawford, Pop. 4,964
Colonel Crawford Local SD
Supt. — See North Robinson
Crawford ES, 5444 Crestline Rd 44827 200/PK-5
Ruthann Noblet, prin. 419-562-5753
Crawford IS, 5444 Crestline Rd 44827 200/6-8
Kevin Ruth, prin. 419-562-7529

Crestline EVD 700/K-12
PO Box 350 44827 419-683-3647
Dave Heflinger, supt. Fax 683-2330
www.crestline.k12.oh.us
Crestline North ES 200/K-3
401 Heiser Ct 44827 419-683-3647
Carole Neighbor, prin. Fax 683-4984

Crestline Southeast S 200/4-6
300 E Arnold St 44827 419-683-3647
Carole Neighbor, prin. Fax 683-4030

St. Joseph S 100/K-8
333 N Thoman St 44827 419-683-1284
Carolyn Price, prin. Fax 683-8957

Creston, Wayne, Pop. 2,140
North Central Local SD 1,400/K-12
350 S Main St 44217 330-435-6382
Larry Acker, supt. Fax 435-4633
www.northcentral.k12.oh.us/
Creston MS 400/5-8
PO Box 4443 44217 330-435-4255
Karen O'Hare, prin. Fax 435-4633
Other Schools – See Burbank, Sterling

Cridersville, Allen, Pop. 1,796
Wapakoneta CSD
Supt. — See Wapakoneta
Cridersville ES 300/K-4
300 E Main St 45806 419-645-3000
David Tester, prin. Fax 645-3003

Crooksville, Perry, Pop. 2,485
Crooksville EVD 1,200/K-12
4065 School Dr 43731 740-982-7040
Jeff Childers, supt. Fax 982-3551
www.crooksville.k12.oh.us/
Crooksville ES 500/K-5
12400 Tunnel Hill Rd 43731 740-982-7010
John Toeller, prin. Fax 982-5087
Crooksville MS 300/6-8
12400 Tunnel Hill Rd 43731 740-982-7010
Alea Barker, prin. Fax 982-5087

Crown City, Gallia, Pop. 434
Gallia County Local SD
Supt. — See Gallipolis
Hannan Trace S 400/K-8
9345 State Route 218 45623 740-256-6468
Edie Bostic, prin. Fax 256-1803

Curtice, Lucas
Genoa Area Local SD
Supt. — See Genoa
Allen ES 400/3-5
4865 N Genoa Clay Center Rd 43412 419-855-7795
Brenda Murphy, prin. Fax 855-4957

Oregon CSD
Supt. — See Oregon
Jerusalem ES 400/K-5
535 S Yondota Rd 43412 419-836-6111
Jennifer Conkle, prin. Fax 836-1501

Custar, Wood, Pop. 207
Bowling Green CSD
Supt. — See Bowling Green
Milton ES 100/K-6
22550 Mermill Rd 43511 419-353-1249
George Offenburg, prin. Fax 353-9027

St. Louis S 50/PK-6
22776 Defiance Pike 43511 419-669-2878
Richelle Piercefield, prin. Fax 669-2878

Cuyahoga Falls, Summit, Pop. 50,494
Cuyahoga Falls CSD 5,200/K-12
PO Box 396 44222 330-926-3800
Dr. Edwin Holland, supt. Fax 920-1074
www.cfalls.summit.k12.oh.us
Bolich MS 700/6-8
2630 13th St 44223 330-926-3801
Chris McBurney, prin. Fax 920-3737
Dewitt ES 500/K-5
425 Falls Ave 44221 330-926-3802
Renee Schoonover, prin. Fax 916-6016
Lincoln ES 500/K-5
3131 Bailey Rd 44221 330-926-3803
Rose Heintz, prin. Fax 916-6024
Preston ES 300/K-5
800 Tallmadge Rd 44221 330-926-3805
John Haubert, prin. Fax 916-6027
Price ES 400/K-5
2610 Delmore St 44221 330-926-3806
Dyanne Schoterman, prin. Fax 929-3171
Richardson ES 400/K-5
2226 23rd St 44223 330-926-3807
Frank Margida, prin. Fax 916-6022
Roberts MS 500/6-8
3333 Charles St 44221 330-926-3809
Sean Wolanin, prin. Fax 920-3748
Other Schools – See Silver Lake

Woodridge Local SD
Supt. — See Peninsula
Woodridge PS 400/K-2
3313 Northampton Rd 44223 330-928-1223
Karen Sykes, prin. Fax 928-2050

Chapel Hill Christian S North Campus 500/PK-6
1090 Howe Ave 44221 330-929-1901
Greg McAbee, supt. Fax 929-1737
Immaculate Heart of Mary S 400/K-8
2859 Lillis Dr 44223 330-923-1220
Robert Hardesty, prin. Fax 929-4373
Redeemer Christian S 200/PK-8
2141 5th St 44221 330-923-1280
Travis Grulke, prin. Fax 923-4517
St. Joseph S 400/K-8
1909 3rd St 44221 330-928-2151
Robert Kochanski, prin. Fax 928-3139
Summit Christian S 100/PK-8
2800 13th St 44223 330-762-3382
Melanie Kemp, admin. Fax 926-9058

Cuyahoga Heights, Cuyahoga, Pop. 559
Cuyahoga Heights Local SD 900/PK-12
4820 E 71st St 44125 216-429-5700
Peter Guerrera, supt. Fax 341-3737
www.cuyhts.org/
Cuyahoga Heights ES 400/PK-5
4880 E 71st St 44125 216-429-5880
Andrew Picciano, prin. Fax 429-5883
Cuyahoga Heights MS 200/6-8
4840 E 71st St 44125 216-429-5757
Tom Burton, prin. Fax 429-5735

Dalton, Wayne, Pop. 1,582
Dalton Local SD 800/K-12
PO Box 514 44618 330-828-2267
Scott Beatty, supt. Fax 828-2800
www.dalton.k12.oh.us
Dalton ES 200/3-5
PO Box 514 44618 330-828-2707
Robert Neading, prin. Fax 828-2802
Dalton IS 200/6-8
PO Box 514 44618 330-828-2405
Broc Bidlack, prin. Fax 828-2801
Other Schools – See Kidron

Danville, Knox, Pop. 1,096
Danville Local SD 700/K-12
PO Box 30 43014 740-599-6116
Dan Harper, supt. Fax 599-5417
www.danville.k12.oh.us/
Danville ES 400/K-6
PO Box 30 43014 740-599-6116
Lynn Shoemaker, prin. Fax 599-5904
Danville MS 100/7-8
PO Box 30 43014 740-599-6116
Linda Rex, prin. Fax 599-5904

Darbydale, Franklin
South-Western CSD
Supt. — See Grove City
Darbydale ES 200/PK-4
7000 State Route 665 43123 614-801-8050
Beverlee Powers, prin. Fax 801-8060

Dayton, Montgomery, Pop. 158,873
Centerville CSD
Supt. — See Centerville
Driscoll ES 300/2-5
5767 Marshall Rd 45429 937-434-0562
Sherley Kurtz, prin. Fax 434-0393
Hole ES 300/2-5
180 W Whipp Rd 45459 937-434-0725
Jeremy Miller, prin. Fax 434-0557
Normandy ES 400/2-5
401 Normandy Ridge Rd 45459 937-434-0917
Rebecca O'Neil, prin. Fax 434-0953
Watts MS 700/6-8
7056 McEwen Rd 45459 937-434-0370
Brian Miller, prin. Fax 434-2907

Dayton CSD 15,100/PK-12
115 S Ludlow St 45402 937-542-3000
Percy Mack Ph.D., supt. Fax 542-3188
www.dps.k12.oh.us
Adams Earley Academy for Girls 200/K-3
450 Shoup Mill Rd 45415 937-542-5840
Peggy Burks, prin. Fax 542-5841
Belle Haven S 500/PK-8
4401 Free Pike 45416 937-542-4220
Wyetta Hayden, prin. Fax 542-4221
Carlson ES 400/PK-6
807 S Gettysburg Ave 45408 937-542-4290
Georchia Higgins, prin. Fax 542-4291
Cleveland S 400/PK-8
1102 Pursell Ave 45420 937-542-4340
Arlana Daniel, prin. Fax 542-4341
Dayton Boys Prep Academy 100/PK-3
2400 Hoover Ave 45402 937-542-5340
Horace Lovelace, prin. Fax 542-5341
Eastmont Park S 600/PK-8
1480 Edendale Rd 45432 937-542-4490
Albert Jordan, prin. Fax 542-4491
Edison ES 400/PK-7
2408 Philadelphia Dr 45406 937-542-4540
Antoinette Adkins, prin. Fax 542-4541
Fairview ES 400/PK-6
1305 W Fairview Ave 45406 937-542-4590
Charles Davis, prin. Fax 542-4591
Fairview MS 300/8-8
2408 Philadelphia Dr 45406 937-542-6050
Anthony Graham, prin. Fax 542-6051
Franklin Montessori ES 400/PK-6
2617 E 5th St 45403 937-542-4640
Holli Gover, prin. Fax 542-4641
Kemp S 400/PK-8
1923 Gondert Ave 45403 937-542-5090
Lisa Minor, prin. Fax 542-5091
Kiser S 500/PK-8
1401 Leo St 45404 937-542-6130
James Fowler, prin. Fax 542-6131
Loos ES 400/PK-6
45 Wampler Ave 45405 937-542-5190
Marcia Jones, prin. Fax 542-5191
Mann ES 300/PK-6
715 Krebs Ave 45419 937-542-4890
Theolanda Harewood, prin. Fax 542-4919
Meadowdale S 600/PK-8
4448 Thompson Dr 45416 937-542-5390
Jalma Fields, prin. Fax 542-5391
Parks S 500/PK-8
3705 Lori Sue Ave 45406 937-542-4390
Mitzi Sanders, prin. Fax 542-4391
Patterson-Kennedy S 800/PK-8
258 Wyoming St 45409 937-542-5490
Marilyn Croker, prin. Fax 542-5491
Preschool Academy at Jackson 300/PK-K
329 Abbey Ave 45417 937-542-4740
Margo Gaillard-Barnes, prin. Fax 542-4741

Valerie S 400/PK-8
4020 Bradwood Dr 45405 937-542-5690
Delores Evans, prin. Fax 542-5691
Van Cleve S 400/PK-8
132 Alaska St 45404 937-542-5740
Hindy Gruber, prin. Fax 542-5740
Wogaman S 500/PK-8
920 McArthur Ave 45408 937-542-5890
Saundra Collie, prin. Fax 542-5891
World of Wonder MS 4-7
2826 Campus Dr 45406 937-542-3650
Cleaster Jackson Ed.D., prin. Fax 542-3673
World of Wonder PS 200/K-3
2826 Campus Dr 45406 937-542-3600
Cleaster Jackson Ed.D., prin. Fax 542-3601
Wright ES 500/PK-6
200 S Wright Ave 45403 937-542-5940
Tracey Mallory, prin. Fax 542-5941
Wright MS 600/7-8
1361 Huffman Ave 45403 937-542-6380
Shawna Welch, prin. Fax 542-6381

Jefferson Township Local SD 700/K-12
2625 S Union Rd 45418 937-835-5682
Dr. Richard Gates, supt. Fax 835-5955
www.jeffersontwp.k12.oh.us/
Blairwood ES 300/K-6
1241 Blairwood Ave 45418 937-263-3504
Hella Scott, prin. Fax 263-6496

Mad River Local SD 3,700/K-12
801 Old Harshman Rd 45431 937-259-6606
Michael Eaglowski, supt. Fax 259-6607
www.madriverschools.org
Beverly Gardens ES 400/K-4
5555 Enright Ave 45431 937-259-6620
Cristal Fields, prin. Fax 259-6614
Brantwood ES 300/K-4
4350 Schwinn Dr 45404 937-237-4270
Chad Wyen, prin. Fax 237-4277
Mad River MS 600/7-8
1801 Harshman Rd 45424 937-237-4265
Donald Kuntz, prin. Fax 237-4273
Saville ES 400/K-4
5800 Burkhardt Rd 45431 937-259-6625
Steven Kandel, prin. Fax 259-6648
Spinning Hills MS 500/5-6
5001 Eastman Ave 45432 937-259-6635
Mark Henderson, prin. Fax 259-6644
Stevenson ES 400/K-4
805 Old Harshman Rd 45431 937-259-6630
Debra Root, prin. Fax 259-6628

Miamisburg CSD
Supt. — See Miamisburg
Bauer ES 600/K-5
6951 Springboro Pike 45449 937-434-9191
Kelly Lee Marker, prin. Fax 434-8879

Northmont CSD
Supt. — See Englewood
Northwood ES 500/K-6
6200 Noranda Dr 45415 937-832-6240
Robert Best, prin. Fax 832-6241

Northridge Local SD 1,700/K-12
2011 Timber Ln 45414 937-278-5885
Tod Perez, supt. Fax 276-8351
www.northridgeschools.org/
Dennis MS 400/6-8
5120 N Dixie Dr 45414 937-274-2135
Timothy Whitestone, prin. Fax 276-8354
Kennedy ES 300/1-5
2655 Wagoner Ford Rd 45414 937-275-6833
Jennifer Schmidlapp, prin. Fax 276-8357
Morrison ES 300/1-5
2235 Arthur Ave 45414 937-276-8341
Derrick Thomas, prin. Fax 276-8343
Timberlane Learning Center 200/K-K
2131 Timber Ln 45414 937-278-0689
Heather Koehl, prin. Fax 278-4029

Oakwood CSD 2,200/K-12
20 Rubicon Rd 45409 937-297-5332
Mary Jo Scalzo Ph.D., supt. Fax 297-5345
www.oakwood.k12.oh.us
Harman ES 500/1-6
735 Harman Ave 45419 937-297-5338
Allyson Couch, prin. Fax 297-1514
Lange S 100/K-K
219 W Dorothy Ln 45429 937-299-8730
Kathleen Bartalo, prin. Fax 299-8734
Oakwood JHS 400/7-8
1200 Far Hills Ave 45419 937-297-5328
Dan Weckstein, prin. Fax 297-7807
Smith ES 500/1-6
1701 Shafor Blvd 45419 937-297-5335
Nance Bradds, prin. Fax 297-1841

Trotwood-Madison CSD
Supt. — See Trotwood
Trotwood-Madison MS 500/6-8
4420 N Union Rd 45426 937-854-0017
Gerry Griffith, prin. Fax 854-8433
Westbrooke Village ES 200/2-5
6500 Westford Rd 45426 937-854-3196
Tyrone Nadir, prin. Fax 854-8704

Vandalia-Butler CSD
Supt. — See Vandalia
Murlin Heights ES 400/K-4
8515 N Dixie Dr 45414 937-415-3900
Connie Strehle, prin. Fax 415-3941
Smith MS 500/5-8
3625 Little York Rd 45414 937-415-7000
Shannon White, prin. Fax 415-7051

West Carrollton CSD
Supt. — See West Carrollton
Holliday ES 400/1-5
4100 S Dixie Dr 45439 937-859-5121
Chris Price, prin. Fax 643-5460
Nicholas ES 200/1-5
3846 Vance Rd 45439 937-859-5121
Melissa Theis, prin. Fax 859-2765

Bishop Leibold Consolidated S East 500/K-8
6666 Springboro Pike 45449 937-434-9343
Paul Beyerle, prin. Fax 436-3048
East Dayton Christian S 300/K-12
999 Spinning Rd 45431 937-252-5400
Melony Marciniak, prin. Fax 258-4099
Gloria Dei Montessori S 100/PK-6
615 Shiloh Dr 45415 937-274-7195
Christina Allen, prin. Fax 274-7195
Hillel Academy of Dayton 50/K-8
100 E Woodbury Dr 45415 937-277-8966
Thomas Tudor, hdmstr. Fax 276-5686
Holy Angels S 300/PK-8
223 L St 45409 937-229-5959
Rob Fortener, prin. Fax 229-5960
Lutheran S of Dayton 100/PK-2
PO Box 68 45401 937-224-1939
Theresa Ankenman, dir. Fax 224-7111
Mary Queen of Peace S 600/PK-8
200 Homewood Ave 45405 937-228-3091
Kathleen Driesen, prin. Fax 449-2440
Mary Queen of Peace S 200/K-8
138 Gramont Ave 45417 937-268-6391
Debra Johnson, prin. Fax 268-9775
Miami Valley S 500/PK-12
5151 Denise Dr 45429 937-434-4444
Peter Benedict, hdmstr. Fax 434-1033
Montessori Children's Center 100/PK-6
4369 Valley St 45424 937-236-6805
Mary vanLoveren, prin.
Our Lady of the Immaculate Conception S 200/K-8
2268 S Smithville Rd 45420 937-253-8831
Karyn Hecker, prin. Fax 253-8832
Our Lady of the Rosary S 200/K-8
40 Notre Dame Ave 45404 937-222-7231
Gregg Marino, prin. Fax 222-7393
Precious Blood S 300/PK-8
4870 Denlinger Rd 45426 937-277-2291
Dan Mecoli, prin. Fax 277-2217
St. Anthony S 200/PK-8
1824 Saint Charles Ave 45410 937-253-6251
David Bogle, prin. Fax 253-1541
St. Helen S 400/K-8
5086 Burkhardt Rd 45431 937-256-1761
Barbara Markus, prin. Fax 254-4614
St. Rita S 300/K-8
251 Erdiel Dr 45415 937-277-8978
Veronica Murphy, prin. Fax 277-8979

Defiance, Defiance, Pop. 16,150
Ayersville Local SD 900/K-12
28046 Watson Rd 43512 419-395-1111
Tod Hug, supt. Fax 395-9990
www.ayersville.k12.oh.us
Ayersville ES 300/K-4
28046 Watson Rd 43512 419-395-1111
Ronald Zachrich, prin. Fax 395-9990
Ayersville MS 300/5-8
28046 Watson Rd 43512 419-395-1111
Keith Ruhe, prin. Fax 395-9990

Defiance CSD 1,200/K-12
629 Arabella St 43512 419-782-0070
Michael Struble, supt. Fax 782-4395
www.defiancecityschools.org
Defiance ES, 400 Carter Rd 43512 K-5
Sheri Steyer, prin. 419-785-2260
Defiance JHS 400/6-8
629 Arabella St 43512 419-782-0050
Kelly Davis, prin. Fax 782-0060

Northeastern Local SD 1,200/K-12
5921 Domersville Rd 43512 419-497-3461
James Roach, supt. Fax 497-3401
www.tinora.k12.oh.us
Noble ES 200/K-1
10553 Haller St 43512 419-782-7941
Dennis Wright, prin. Fax 784-3788
Tinora ES 400/2-6
5751 Domersville Rd 43512 419-497-1022
Larry Acocks, prin. Fax 497-1024
Tinora JHS 200/7-8
5921 Domersville Rd 43512 419-497-2361
G. Kent Adams, prin. Fax 497-3401

Defiance Catholic S - St. John Campus 100/PK-2
800 5th St 43512 419-782-2136
Sandy Herman, prin. Fax 784-5410
Defiance Catholic S - St. Mary Campus 100/3-6
702 Washington Ave 43512 419-782-2751
Sandy Herman, prin. Fax 782-8835
St. John Lutheran S 200/PK-8
635 Wayne Ave 43512 419-782-6166
Deb Kane, prin. Fax 782-0954

De Graff, Logan, Pop. 1,174
Riverside Local SD 800/K-12
2096 County Road 24 S 43318 937-585-5981
Bernie Pachmayer, supt. Fax 585-4599
www.riverside.k12.oh.us
Riverside ES 500/K-6
2096 County Road 24 S 43318 937-585-5981
Tim Walls, prin. Fax 585-4599

Delaware, Delaware, Pop. 31,322
Buckeye Valley Local SD 2,300/K-12
679 Coover Rd 43015 740-369-8735
John Schiller, supt. Fax 363-7654
www.buckeyevalley.k12.oh.us
Buckeye Valley MS 500/6-8
683 Coover Rd 43015 740-363-6626
Andrew Miller, prin. Fax 363-4483
Other Schools – See Ashley, Ostrander, Radnor

Delaware CSD 4,600/K-12
248 N Washington St 43015 740-833-1100
Dr. Mary Anne Ashworth, supt. Fax 833-1149
www.dcs.k12.oh.us
Carlisle ES 500/K-4
746 State Route 37 W 43015 740-833-1450
Steven Andrews, prin. Fax 833-1499
Conger ES 400/K-4
10 Channing St 43015 740-833-1300
Jerry Stewart, prin. Fax 833-1349
Dempsey MS 700/7-8
599 Pennsylvania Ave 43015 740-833-1800
Andrew Hatton, prin. Fax 833-1899
Schultz ES 400/K-4
499 Applegate Ln 43015 740-833-1400
Susann Sparks, prin. Fax 833-1449
Smith ES 400/K-4
355 N Liberty St 43015 740-833-1350
Rochelle Thompson, prin. Fax 833-1399
Willis IS 700/5-6
74 W William St 43015 740-833-1700
Heidi Kegley, prin. Fax 833-1799
Woodward ES 300/K-4
200 S Washington St 43015 740-833-1600
Paula Jorge, prin. Fax 833-1649

Delaware Christian S 300/K-12
45 Belle Ave 43015 740-363-8425
Gordon McDonald, admin. Fax 203-2117
Grace Community S 50/K-5
PO Box 358 43015 740-363-5800
Phil Mears, admin. Fax 363-5800
St. Mary S 400/PK-8
66 E William St 43015 740-362-8961
Becky Piela, prin. Fax 362-3733

Dellroy, Carroll, Pop. 295
Carrollton EVD
Supt. — See Carrollton
Dellroy ES 200/K-5
34 Main St 44620 330-735-2850
Patricia Lamielle, prin. Fax 735-3202

Delphos, Allen, Pop. 6,820
Delphos CSD 1,100/K-12
234 N Jefferson St 45833 419-692-2509
Jeff Price, supt. Fax 692-2653
www.noacsc.org/allen/dl/
Franklin ES 400/K-5
310 E 4th St 45833 419-692-8766
Tim Larimore, prin. Fax 692-2766
Jefferson MS 200/6-8
227 N Jefferson St 45833 419-695-2523
Terry Moreo, prin. Fax 692-2302
Landeck ES 100/1-6
14750 Landeck Rd 45833 419-695-3185
Mark Fuerst, prin. Fax 695-3185

St. John S 600/K-8
110 N Pierce St 45833 419-692-8561
Theresa Kemmann, prin. Fax 692-8561

Delta, Fulton, Pop. 2,927
Pike-Delta-York Local SD 1,300/K-12
504 Fernwood St 43515 419-822-3391
Robin Rayfield, supt. Fax 822-4478
www.pdy.k12.oh.us
Delta ES 400/K-5
419 Fernwood St 43515 419-822-5630
Jay LeFevre, prin. Fax 822-4478
Pike-Delta-York MS 300/6-8
1101 Panther Pride Dr 43515 419-822-9118
Dennis Ford, prin. Fax 822-8490

Dennison, Tuscarawas, Pop. 2,927
Claymont CSD 2,200/PK-12
201 N 3rd St 44621 740-922-5478
Ryan Delaney, supt. Fax 922-7325
www.claymont.k12.oh.us
Claymont IS 300/5-6
220 N 3rd St 44621 740-922-1901
Jodie Miles, prin. Fax 922-6302
Northside Preschool PK-PK
215 N 3rd St 44621 740-922-5888
Avalene Neininger, prin. Fax 922-6722
Park ES 100/K-4
200 Jewett Ave 44621 740-922-2930
Richard Page, prin. Fax 922-7425
Other Schools – See Uhrichsville

Immaculate Conception S 100/PK-8
100 Sherman St 44621 740-922-3539
John Zucal, prin. Fax 922-2486

Deshler, Henry, Pop. 1,849
Patrick Henry Local SD
Supt. — See Hamler
Deshler ES 200/K-2
221 E Maple St 43516 419-278-1611
Sue Hammer, prin. Fax 278-0955

Diamond, Portage
Southeast Local SD
Supt. — See Ravenna
Southeast MS 500/6-8
8540 Tallmadge Rd 44412 330-654-5842
James Ries, prin. Fax 654-9110

Dillonvale, Jefferson, Pop. 750
Buckeye Local SD 2,400/PK-12
6899 State Route 150 43917 740-769-7395
Mark Miller, supt. Fax 769-2361
www.omeresa.net/schools/buckeye/

Other Schools – See Adena, Brilliant, Rayland, Tiltonsville, Yorkville

Dola, Hardin
Hardin Northern Local SD 500/K-12
11589 State Route 81 45835 419-759-2331
Larry Claypool, supt. Fax 759-2581
www.hn.k12.oh.us/
Hardin Northern ES 200/K-6
11589 State Route 81 45835 419-759-3158
Misha Boyer, prin. Fax 759-2581

Donnelsville, Clark, Pop. 289
Tecumseh Local SD
Supt. — See New Carlisle
Donnelsville ES 300/PK-5
PO Box 130 45319 937-845-4540
Karyl Strader, prin. Fax 845-4504

Dover, Tuscarawas, Pop. 12,516
Dover CSD 2,500/K-12
219 W 6th St 44622 330-364-1906
Robert Hamm, supt. Fax 343-7070
www.dover.k12.oh.us/
Dover Avenue ES 300/K-5
125 W 13th St 44622 330-364-7117
Renee Sattler, prin. Fax 343-7636
Dover MS 600/6-8
2131 N Wooster Ave 44622 330-364-7121
Ronald Bond, prin. Fax 364-7127
East ES 500/K-5
325 Betscher Ave 44622 330-364-7114
Jerry Compton, prin. Fax 343-8526
South ES 400/K-5
280 E Shafer Ave 44622 330-364-7111
Tracie Murphy, prin. Fax 343-3976

Tuscarawas Central Catholic ES 200/PK-6
600 N Tuscarawas Ave 44622 330-343-9134
Theresa Layton, prin. Fax 364-6509

Doylestown, Wayne, Pop. 2,851
Chippewa Local SD 1,500/K-12
56 N Portage St 44230 330-658-6368
Doug Shamp, supt. Fax 658-5842
www.chippewa.k12.oh.us
Chippewa MS 400/5-8
257 High St 44230 330-658-2214
Sandy Stebly, prin. Fax 658-5842
Harvey ES 500/K-4
165 Brooklyn Ave 44230 330-658-2522
Ronna Haer, prin. Fax 658-4255

SS. Peter & Paul S 100/K-8
169 W Clinton St 44230 330-658-2804
Katherine Yaussy, prin. Fax 658-2287

Dresden, Muskingum, Pop. 1,427
Tri-Valley Local SD 2,800/K-12
36 E Muskingum Ave 43821 740-754-1572
Mark Neal, supt. Fax 754-6400
www.tvschools.org
Dresden ES 400/K-6
1318 Main St 43821 740-754-4001
Linda Huston, prin. Fax 754-6405
Tri-Valley MS 500/7-8
1358 Main St 43821 740-754-3531
Jennifer Penczarski, prin. Fax 754-1879
Other Schools – See Adamsville, Frazeysburg, Nashport

Dublin, Franklin, Pop. 34,964
Dublin CSD 13,100/K-12
7030 Coffman Rd 43017 614-764-5913
Dr. David Axner, supt. Fax 761-5899
www.dublinschools.net
Bailey ES 500/K-5
4900 Brandonway Dr 43017 614-717-6611
William Sternberg, prin. Fax 717-6610
Davis MS 800/6-8
2400 Sutter Pkwy 43016 614-761-5820
David Nosker, prin. Fax 761-5893
Deer Run ES 400/K-5
8815 Manley Rd 43017 614-764-5932
Lorraine Rubadue, prin. Fax 718-8759
Glacier Ridge ES 400/K-5
7175 Glacier Ridge Blvd 43017 614-733-0012
Karen Szymusiak, prin. Fax 718-8791
Griffith Thomas ES 500/K-5
4671 Tuttle Rd 43017 614-764-5970
Jennifer Davis, prin. Fax 718-8879
Grizzell MS 800/6-8
8705 Avery Rd 43017 614-798-3569
Thomas Jones, prin. Fax 761-6514
Indian Run ES 600/K-5
80 W Bridge St 43017 614-764-5928
Janet Rinefierd, prin. Fax 764-5998
Karrer MS 800/6-8
7245 Tullymore Dr 43016 614-873-0459
Rick Weininger, prin. Fax 718-8505
Olde Sawmill ES 400/K-5
2485 Olde Sawmill Blvd 43016 614-764-5936
Tyler Wolfe, prin. Fax 764-5988
Pinney ES 700/K-5
9989 Concord Rd 43017 614-798-3570
Troy Ehrsam, prin. Fax 718-8961
Riverside ES 400/K-5
3260 Riverside Green Dr 43017 614-764-5940
Connie Stitzlein, prin. Fax 764-5987
Scottish Corners ES 600/K-5
5950 Sells Mill Dr 43017 614-764-5963
Mitch Emmons, prin. Fax 761-5814
Sells MS 800/6-8
150 W Bridge St 43017 614-764-5919
Rich Baird, prin. Fax 764-5923
Wyandot ES 500/K-5
5620 Dublinshire Dr 43017 614-761-5840
John Pfieffer, prin. Fax 718-8929
Other Schools – See Columbus, Powell

Hilliard CSD
Supt. — See Hilliard
Washington ES 300/K-5
5675 Eiterman Rd 43016 614-921-6200
Jennifer Lowery, prin. Fax 921-6201

St. Brigid of Kildare S 600/PK-8
7175 Avery Rd 43017 614-718-5825
Kathleen O'Reilly, prin. Fax 718-5831
Tree of Life Christian S - Dublin 200/PK-5
2900 Martin Rd 43017 614-792-2671
Lydia Seevers, prin. Fax 889-6501

Duncan Falls, Muskingum
Franklin Local SD 2,200/K-12
PO Box 428 43734 740-674-5203
David Branch, supt. Fax 674-5214
www.franklin-local.k12.oh.us
Duncan Falls ES 800/K-5
397 Oak St 43734 740-674-5211
Steven Rice, prin. Fax 674-5216
Other Schools – See Philo, Roseville

Dundee, Tuscarawas
Garaway Local SD
Supt. — See Sugarcreek
Dundee ES 200/K-6
PO Box 146 44624 330-852-2022
Larry Compton, prin. Fax 852-9952

East Canton, Stark, Pop. 1,619
Osnaburg Local SD 900/K-12
310 Browning Ct N 44730 330-488-1609
Jeffrey Talbert, supt. Fax 488-4001
ecweb.sparcc.org
East Canton ES 200/K-3
137 Liberty St W 44730 330-488-0392
Melanie Davis, prin. Fax 488-4014
East Canton MS 300/4-8
310 Browning Ct N 44730 330-488-0229
Erica Knowles, prin. Fax 488-4001

East Cleveland, Cuyahoga, Pop. 25,708
East Cleveland CSD 3,500/K-12
15305 Terrace Rd 44112 216-268-6570
Myrna Loy Corley, supt. Fax 268-6676
www.east-cleveland.k12.oh.us
Caledonia ES 300/K-6
914 Caledonia Ave 44112 216-268-6690
Vernillis Chambers, prin. Fax 268-6676
Chambers S 700/K-6
14305 Shaw Ave 44112 216-268-6640
Phyliss Banks-Cook, prin. Fax 268-6676
Heritage MS, 14410 Terrace Rd 44112 300/7-8
Beverly Bright-Lloyd, prin. 216-268-6610
Mayfair ES 300/K-6
13916 Mayfair Ave 44112 216-268-6651
Hiawatha Shivers, prin. Fax 268-6496
Prospect ES 300/K-6
1843 Stanwood Rd 44112 216-268-6630
Charles McCants, prin. Fax 268-6676
Superior ES 300/K-6
1865 Garfield Rd 44112 216-268-6670
Paula Elder, prin. Fax 268-6676

Eastlake, Lake, Pop. 19,795
Willoughby-Eastlake CSD
Supt. — See Willoughby
Eastlake MS 500/6-8
35972 Lake Shore Blvd 44095 440-942-5696
Michael Chokshi, prin. Fax 918-8973
Jefferson ES 500/K-5
35980 Lake Shore Blvd 44095 440-942-7244
Barrie Alves, prin. Fax 954-3550
Longfellow ES 400/K-5
35200 Stevens Blvd 44095 440-975-3720
Dr. Ruth Ann Plate, prin. Fax 269-3022
Washington ES 600/K-5
503 Vegas Dr 44095 440-975-3710
Betty Stevens, prin. Fax 975-3761

St. Mary Magdalene-St. Justin Martyr S 300/PK-8
35741 Stevens Blvd 44095 440-946-5414
Sr. Mary Quinlan, prin. Fax 946-2074

East Liverpool, Columbiana, Pop. 12,396
Beaver Local SD
Supt. — See Lisbon
Calcutta ES 400/K-4
15482 State Route 170 43920 330-386-8709
Tessa Trainer, prin. Fax 386-0879

East Liverpool CSD 2,400/K-12
500 Maryland St 43920 330-385-7132
Ken Halbert, supt. Fax 382-7673
www.elcsd.k12.oh.us
East Liverpool MS 600/6-8
810 W 8th St 43920 330-386-8765
Randy Taylor, prin. Fax 382-7670
La Croft ES 400/K-4
1417 Etruria St 43920 330-386-8774
Linda Lindsey, prin. Fax 382-1867
North ES 400/K-4
90 Maine Blvd 43920 330-386-8772
Amy Mabbott, prin. Fax 386-4228
Westgate ES 200/5-5
810 W 8th St 43920 330-386-8768
Randy Taylor, prin. Fax 382-7670

American Spirit Academy 200/PK-12
46682 Florence St 43920 330-385-5588
Jeff Nutter, supt. Fax 385-1267
St. Aloysius S 100/PK-8
335 W 5th St 43920 330-385-5963
Virginia Lopata, prin. Fax 385-6455

East Palestine, Columbiana, Pop. 4,805
East Palestine CSD 1,400/PK-12
200 W North Ave 44413 330-426-4191
Thomas Inchak, supt. Fax 426-9592
www.epschools.k12.oh.us/
East Palestine ES 600/PK-5
195 W Grant St 44413 330-426-3638
Jeffrey Richardson, prin.
East Palestine MS 300/6-8
320 W Grant St 44413 330-426-9451
Lynn Campbell, prin.

East Rochester, Columbiana
Minerva Local SD
Supt. — See Minerva
West ES 200/K-5
24604 US Route 30 44625 330-894-2311
Gary Chaddock, prin. Fax 894-2967

Eaton, Preble, Pop. 8,242
Eaton Community SD 2,300/K-12
307 N Cherry St 45320 937-456-1107
Bradley Neavin, supt. Fax 472-1057
www.eatoncommunityschools.org/
Bruce ES 500/3-5
201 E Saint Clair St 45320 937-456-3875
Marty Tucker, prin. Fax 472-2092
Eaton MS 500/6-8
311 N Cherry St 45320 937-456-2286
Kern Carpenter, prin. Fax 456-2022
Hollingsworth East ES 500/K-2
506 Aukerman St 45320 937-456-5173
Pam Friesel, prin. Fax 456-4656

Edgerton, Williams, Pop. 2,015
Edgerton Local SD 700/PK-12
324 N Michigan Ave 43517 419-298-2112
J. Richard Gieringer, supt. Fax 298-2281
www.edgerton.k12.oh.us/
Edgerton ES 300/PK-6
324 N Michigan Ave 43517 419-298-2332
Andrew Morr, prin. Fax 298-3466

St. Mary S 100/1-6
PO Box 309 43517 419-298-2531
Julie Taylor, prin. Fax 298-3123

Edon, Williams, Pop. 863
Edon-Northwest Local SD 600/K-12
802 W Indiana St 43518 419-272-3213
Bruce Brown, supt. Fax 272-2240
www.edon.k12.oh.us/
Edon ES 200/K-6
802 W Indiana St 43518 419-272-3213
Bonnie Troyer, prin. Fax 272-2240
Edon MS 100/7-8
802 W Indiana St 43518 419-272-3213
Chad Bassett, prin. Fax 272-2240

Elida, Allen, Pop. 1,894
Elida Local SD 2,500/K-12
4380 Sunnydale St 45807 419-331-4155
Don Diglia, supt. Fax 331-1656
home.elida.k12.oh.us/
Elida ES 900/1-5
300 Pioneer Rd 45807 419-331-7901
Bruce Sommers, prin. Fax 331-2706
Elida MS 600/6-8
4500 Sunnydale St 45807 419-331-2505
Herbert Purton, prin. Fax 331-6822
Other Schools – See Gomer

Ellsworth, Mahoning
Western Reserve Local SD
Supt. — See Berlin Center
Western Reserve-Ellsworth ES 300/K-4
PO Box 88 44416 330-547-0817
Peter Morabito, prin. Fax 547-9302

Elmwood Place, Hamilton, Pop. 2,439
St. Bernard-Elmwood Place CSD
Supt. — See Saint Bernard
Elmwood Place ES 300/PK-6
400 Maple St, 513-482-7115
Lisa Pfalzgraf, prin. Fax 641-5502

Elyria, Lorain, Pop. 56,061
Elyria CSD 6,900/K-12
42101 Griswold Rd 44035 440-284-8000
Paul Rigda, supt. Fax 284-0678
www.elyriaschools.org
Crestwood ES 400/K-6
42331 Griswold Rd 44035 440-284-8002
Sherri Parent, prin.
Eastern Heights JHS 400/7-8
528 Garford Ave 44035 440-284-8015
Kimberly Benetto, prin. Fax 323-0827
Ely ES 400/K-6
312 Gulf Rd 44035 440-284-8005
Dr. Jack Dibee, prin. Fax 284-8148
Erie ES 300/K-6
333 Naples Dr 44035 440-284-8006
Tim Brown, prin. Fax 284-8151
Franklin ES 300/K-6
446 11th St 44035 440-284-8007
Kimberly Conley, prin. Fax 284-8371
Kindergarten Village 300/K-K
42101 Griswold Rd 44035 440-284-8000
Rita Tomsic, prin. Fax 284-8162
McKinley ES 400/K-6
620 E River St 44035 440-284-8009
Lonnie Hall, prin. Fax 284-8382
Northwood JHS 400/7-8
700 Gulf Rd 44035 440-284-8016
Jamill Wiley, prin. Fax 284-1546
Oakwood ES 400/K-6
925 Spruce St 44035 440-284-8010
Aretha Dixon, prin. Fax 284-8181

Prospect ES 300/K-6
1410 Prospect St 44035 440-284-8011
Charles Sanfilippo, prin. Fax 284-8051
Roosevelt ES 400/K-6
6121 W River Rd S 44035 440-284-8012
Elaine Carlin, prin. Fax 284-8189
Westwood JHS 400/7-8
42350 Adelbert St 44035 440-284-8017
Ramona Mendak, prin. Fax 284-1055
Windsor ES 400/K-6
264 Windsor Dr 44035 440-284-8014
Richard Ackerman, prin. Fax 284-8199

Elyria Christian Academy 50/K-8
9652 Murray Ridge Rd 44035 440-284-1516
Renee Truax, prin. Fax 284-1516
First Baptist Christian S 200/PK-12
11400 Lagrange Rd 44035 440-458-5185
Brenda Milam, prin. Fax 458-8717
Open Door Christian S 600/PK-12
8287 W Ridge Rd 44035 440-322-6386
Darrell Dunckel, prin. Fax 284-6033
St. Jude S 500/PK-8
594 Poplar St 44035 440-366-1681
Rozann Swanson, prin. Fax 366-5238
St. Mary S 200/PK-8
237 4th St 44035 440-322-2808
Sheila Mannix, prin. Fax 322-1423

Englewood, Montgomery, Pop. 12,727
Northmont CSD 5,800/K-12
4001 Old Salem Rd 45322 937-832-5000
Douglas Lantz, supt. Fax 832-5001
www.northmontschools.com/
Edgington ES 500/K-6
515 N Main St 45322 937-832-6750
Patrick Masters, prin. Fax 832-6751
Englewood ES 400/K-6
702 Albert St 45322 937-832-5900
Beth Wyandt, prin. Fax 832-5901
Englewood Hills ES 400/1-6
508 Durst Dr 45322 937-832-5950
Monica Richardson, prin. Fax 832-5951
Northmoor ES 600/K-6
4421 Old Salem Rd 45322 937-832-6800
Rachael Phillips, prin. Fax 832-6801
Other Schools – See Clayton, Dayton, Union

Enon, Clark, Pop. 2,581
Greenon Local SD 2,000/K-12
500 S Xenia Dr 45323 937-864-1202
Lori Lytle, supt. Fax 864-2470
www.greenon.k12.oh.us
Enon ES 400/K-4
120 S Xenia Dr 45323 937-864-7361
Scott Howell, prin. Fax 864-6014
Indian Valley MS 700/5-8
510 S Xenia Dr 45323 937-864-7348
Richard Quisenberry, prin. Fax 864-6009
Other Schools – See Springfield

Euclid, Cuyahoga, Pop. 49,619
Euclid CSD 6,400/K-12
651 E 222nd St 44123 216-261-2900
Dr. Joffrey Jones, supt. Fax 261-3120
www.euclid.k12.oh.us
Euclid Central MS 800/6-8
20701 Euclid Ave 44117 216-797-5300
Mike Mennel, prin. Fax 797-5333
Forest Park MS 700/6-8
27000 Elinore Ave 44132 216-797-4700
Charlie Smialek, prin. Fax 797-4710
Glenbrook ES 300/K-5
23500 Glenbrook Blvd 44117 216-797-4500
Charita Buchanan, prin. Fax 797-4515
Indian Hills ES 200/K-5
1941 Sagamore Dr 44117 216-732-2600
Linda Knight, prin. Fax 732-2605
Jefferson Magnet S 400/K-5
1455 E 260th St 44132 216-797-4450
Jevonne Smith, prin. Fax 797-4445
Lincoln ES 400/K-5
280 E 206th St 44123 216-797-4250
Mary Thomas, prin. Fax 797-4255
Memorial Park ES 400/K-5
22800 Fox Ave 44123 216-732-2700
Ken Ferlito, prin. Fax 732-2705
Roosevelt ES 400/K-5
551 E 200th St 44119 216-797-4810
Kathy Keaveney, prin. Fax 797-4848
Upson ES 600/K-5
490 E 260th St 44132 216-797-7525
Andrea Celico, prin. Fax 797-7525

Holy Cross S 400/K-8
175 E 200th St 44119 216-481-6824
Patricia Patterson, prin. Fax 481-9841
St. Felicitas S 400/PK-8
140 Richmond Rd 44143 216-261-1240
Martha Dodd, prin. Fax 261-5843
St. William S 300/PK-8
351 E 260th St 44132 216-731-3060
Susan Pohly, prin. Fax 731-0300

Fairborn, Greene, Pop. 31,650
Fairborn CSD 4,600/PK-12
306 E Whittier Ave 45324 937-878-3961
Dave Scarberry, supt. Fax 879-8180
www.fairborn.k12.oh.us
Baker MS 1,000/6-8
200 Lincoln Dr 45324 937-878-4681
Joe Mitchell, prin. Fax 879-8193
Fairborn IS 600/4-5
25 Dellwood Dr 45324 937-878-3969
Sue Brackenhoff, prin. Fax 879-8191
Fairborn PS 1,500/PK-3
4 W Dayton Yellow Springs 45324 937-878-8668
Nancy McMahan, prin. Fax 879-8181

Bethlehem Lutheran S 100/PK-8
1240 S Maple Ave 45324 937-878-7050
Margaret Geilenfeldt, prin. Fax 878-8794

Fairfield, Butler, Pop. 42,294
Fairfield CSD 9,900/K-12
211 Donald Dr 45014 513-829-6300
Catherine Milligan, supt. Fax 829-0148
www.fairfieldcityschools.com
Fairfield Central ES 600/1-4
5058 Dixie Hwy 45014 513-829-7979
Richard Wood, prin. Fax 829-7830
Fairfield IS 1,500/5-6
255 Donald Dr 45014 513-829-4504
Roger Martin, prin. Fax 829-7447
Fairfield K 700/K-K
4641 Bach Ln 45014 513-829-3900
Kim Wotring, prin. Fax 829-4993
Fairfield MS 1,500/7-8
1111 Nilles Rd 45014 513-829-4433
Katie Pospisil, prin. Fax 829-6480
Fairfield South ES 500/1-4
5460 Bibury Rd 45014 513-829-3078
Leslie Laney, prin. Fax 829-8350
Fairfield West ES 600/1-4
4700 River Rd 45014 513-868-3021
Dan Jeffers, prin. Fax 868-3624
Other Schools – See Hamilton

Cincinnati Christian Schools - ES Campus 300/PK-6
7350 Dixie Hwy 45014 513-874-8500
Dan Bragg, supt. Fax 874-9718
Sacred Heart S 400/1-8
400 Nilles Rd 45014 513-858-4215
Joseph Nagle, prin. Fax 858-4218

Fairlawn, Summit, Pop. 7,202
Copley-Fairlawn CSD
Supt. — See Copley
Ft. Island PS 500/K-4
496 Trunko Rd 44333 330-664-4890
Robert Whitaker, prin. Fax 664-4921

Fairport Harbor, Lake, Pop. 3,223
Fairport Harbor EVD 500/K-12
329 Vine St 44077 440-354-5400
Domenic Paolo, supt. Fax 354-1724
www.fairport.k12.oh.us/home.htm
McKinley ES 200/K-5
602 Plum St 44077 440-354-4982
Edward Dombroski, prin. Fax 354-4012

Fairview Park, Cuyahoga, Pop. 16,528
Fairview Park CSD 1,700/PK-12
21620 Mastick Rd 44126 440-331-5500
Brion Deitsch, supt. Fax 356-3545
www2.fairviewparkschools.org
Fairview Park Early Education Ctr 50/PK-PK
21620 Mastick Rd 44126 440-356-3515
Jeff Hicks, prin.
Gilles-Sweet ES 800/K-6
4320 W 220th St 44126 440-356-3525
Barbara Schutte, prin. Fax 356-3701
Mayer MS 300/7-8
21200 Campus Dr 44126 440-356-3510
Thomas Kairis, prin. Fax 895-2191

Messiah Lutheran S 200/K-8
4401 W 215th St 44126 440-331-6553
Kyle Chuhran, prin. Fax 331-1604
St. Angela Merici S 500/PK-8
20830 Lorain Rd 44126 440-333-2126
Denise Modic-Urban, prin. Fax 333-8480

Farmersville, Montgomery, Pop. 964
Valley View Local SD
Supt. — See Germantown
Farmersville ES 400/K-5
202 Jackson St 45325 937-696-2591
Todd Kozarec, prin. Fax 696-1007

Fayette, Fulton, Pop. 1,326
Gorham Fayette Local SD 300/K-12
400 E Gamble Rd 43521 419-237-2573
Russ Griggs, supt. Fax 237-3125
www.gorham-fayette.k12.oh.us
Gorham Fayette ES 100/K-6
400 E Gamble Rd 43521 419-237-2114
LuAnn Boyer, prin. Fax 237-3125

Fayetteville, Brown, Pop. 390
Fayetteville-Perry Local SD 1,000/PK-12
551 S Apple St 45118 513-875-2423
Roy Hill, supt. Fax 875-2703
www.fp.k12.oh.us
Fayetteville-Perry ES 400/PK-5
601 S Apple St 45118 513-875-2083
Gregory Barlow, prin. Fax 875-4511
Fayetteville-Perry MS 200/6-8
521 S Apple St 45118 513-875-2829
David Tatman, prin. Fax 875-4200

Felicity, Clermont, Pop. 915
Felicity-Franklin Local SD 1,200/PK-12
PO Box 839 45120 513-876-2113
Glenn Moore, supt. Fax 876-2519
www.felicityfranklinschools.org/
Felicity-Franklin Local ES 500/PK-4
PO Box 839 45120 513-876-2113
Jennifer Keller, prin. Fax 876-2051
Felicity-Franklin Local MS 400/5-8
PO Box 839 45120 513-876-2113
Sabrina Armstrong, prin. Fax 876-2519

Findlay, Hancock, Pop. 39,118
Findlay CSD 6,500/K-12
1219 W Main Cross St # 101 45840 419-425-8212
Dr. Dean Wittwer, supt. Fax 425-8203
www.findlaycityschools.org
Bigelow Hill ES 300/3-5
300 Hillcrest Ave 45840 419-425-8317
Pam Hamlin, prin. Fax 427-5456
Central MS 500/6-8
200 W Main Cross St 45840 419-425-8257
Richard Steiner, prin. Fax 427-5453
Chamberlin Hill ES 200/3-5
600 W Yates Ave 45840 419-425-8328
Susan McGonnell, prin. Fax 427-5457
Donnell MS 500/6-8
301 Baldwin Ave 45840 419-425-8370
Donald Williams, prin. Fax 427-5454
Glenwood MS 400/6-8
1715 N Main St 45840 419-425-8373
David Alvarado, prin. Fax 427-5455
Jacobs ES 300/K-2
600 Jacobs Ave 45840 419-425-8299
Nicholas Say, prin. Fax 427-5458
Jefferson ES 300/K-2
204 Fairlawn Pl 45840 419-425-8298
T. Michael Wallace, prin. Fax 427-5459
Lincoln ES 400/K-5
200 W Lincoln St 45840 419-425-8310
Barbara Peterson, prin. Fax 427-5460
Northview ES 300/K-2
133 Lexington Ave 45840 419-425-8290
Rosemary Lugabihl, prin. Fax 427-5462
Vance ES 400/3-5
610 Bristol Dr 45840 419-425-8332
David Barnhill, prin. Fax 427-5465
Washington ES 200/3-5
1100 Broad Ave 45840 419-425-8291
Andrea King, prin. Fax 427-5463
Whittier ES 400/K-2
733 Wyandot St 45840 419-425-8358
Susan Chesebro, prin. Fax 427-5464

Liberty-Benton Local SD 1,300/K-12
9190 County Road 9 45840 419-422-8526
Jim Kanable, supt. Fax 422-5108
www.noacsc.org/hancock/lb/
Liberty-Benton ES 600/K-5
9050 W State Route 12 45840 419-422-9161
Brian Burkett, prin. Fax 422-5108
Liberty Benton MS 300/6-8
9050 W State Route 12 45840 419-422-9166
Bruce Otley, prin. Fax 420-9237

Faith Academy of Findlay 100/PK-12
701 Adams St 45840 419-421-0590
Kevin Foreman, admin. Fax 423-7540
St. Michael S 600/PK-8
723 Sutton Pl 45840 419-422-2512
Anne Brehm, prin. Fax 423-2720

Fort Jennings, Putnam, Pop. 431
Jennings Local SD 400/K-12
PO Box 98 45844 419-286-2238
Frank Sukup, supt. Fax 286-2240
jennings.noacsc.org/
Fort Jennings ES 200/K-6
PO Box 187 45844 419-286-2762
Kathleen Verhoff, prin. Fax 286-2240

Fort Loramie, Shelby, Pop. 1,459
Fort Loramie Local SD 800/K-12
PO Box 26 45845 937-295-3931
Daniel Holland, supt. Fax 295-2758
www.loramie.k12.oh.us/
Fort Loramie ES 400/K-6
PO Box 34 45845 937-295-2931
Scott Rodeheffer, prin. Fax 295-2758

Fort Recovery, Mercer, Pop. 1,323
Fort Recovery Local SD 1,100/PK-12
PO Box 604 45846 419-375-4139
David Riel, supt. Fax 375-1058
www.noacsc.org/mercer/fr/
Fort Recovery ES 500/PK-5
865 Sharpsburg Rd 45846 419-375-2768
Michelle Vaughn, prin. Fax 375-1126
Fort Recovery MS 300/6-8
865 Sharpsburg Rd 45846 419-375-2815
Ted Shuttleworth, prin. Fax 375-1126

Fostoria, Seneca, Pop. 13,395
Fostoria CSD 2,000/PK-12
500 Parkway Dr 44830 419-435-8163
Dr. Cynthia Lemmerman, supt. Fax 436-4109
www.fostoria.k12.oh.us/
Field ES 300/2-3
127 W 6th St 44830 419-436-4125
Jennifer Losey, prin. Fax 436-4159
Fostoria MS 500/6-8
1202 H L Ford Dr 44830 419-436-4120
Diana Weasner, prin. Fax 436-4169
Longfellow ES 400/PK-1
619 Sandusky St 44830 419-436-4135
Melissa Depinet, prin. Fax 436-4155
Riley ES 300/4-5
1326 Walnut St 44830 419-436-4145
Tera Matz, prin. Fax 436-4158

Lakota Local SD
Supt. — See Risingsun
Lakota JHS 200/7-8
8351 W County Road 28 44830 419-435-2497
Norman Elchert, prin. Fax 435-9401

St. Wendelin S 200/PK-8
300 N Wood St 44830 419-435-1809
Cathy Krupp, prin. Fax 435-7826

Fowler, Trumbull
Mathews Local SD
Supt. — See Vienna
Neal MS, PO Box 179 44418 200/6-8
George Garrett, prin. 330-637-3066

Frankfort, Ross, Pop. 1,040
Adena Local SD 1,300/K-12
3367 County Road 550 45628 740-998-4633
David Warne, supt. Fax 998-4632
adena.k12.oh.us/
Adena ES 600/K-5
3367 County Road 550 45628 740-998-5293
Lee Snyder, prin. Fax 998-2359
Adena MS 300/6-8
3367 County Road 550 45628 740-998-2313
Richard Clark, prin. Fax 998-2317

Franklin, Warren, Pop. 12,410
Franklin CSD 2,500/K-12
150 E 6th St 45005 937-746-1699
Arnol Elam, supt. Fax 743-4135
www.franklin-city.k12.oh.us
Bennett ECC, 150 E 6th St 45005 K-K
Tim Crowe, prin. 937-743-5290
Franklin JHS 500/7-8
136 E 6th St 45005 937-743-8630
James Martin, prin. Fax 743-8637
Gerke ES 300/1-6
312 Sherman Dr 45005 937-743-8650
Steven Greenwood, prin. Fax 743-8652
Hunter ES 300/1-6
4418 State Route 122 45005 937-743-8655
Robyn Donisi, prin. Fax 743-8657
Pennyroyal ES 200/1-6
4203 Pennyroyal Rd 45005 937-743-8660
Thomas Pecor, prin. Fax 743-8662
Schenck ES 200/1-6
350 Arlington Dr 45005 937-743-8665
Tim Crowe, prin. Fax 743-8667
Wayne ES 200/1-6
16 Farm Ave 45005 937-743-8640
Dana Miller, prin. Fax 743-4134

Middletown Christian S 500/PK-12
3011 Union Rd 45005 513-423-4542
Mark Spradling, supt. Fax 261-6841

Franklin Furnace, Scioto, Pop. 1,212
Green Local SD 600/K-12
4070 Gallia Pike 45629 740-354-9221
Ronald Lindsey, supt. Fax 355-8975
www.green.k12.oh.us
Green ES 200/3-6
46 Braunlin Rd 45629 740-354-9290
Jodi Armstrong, prin. Fax 354-9904
Green PS 200/K-2
535 Jr Furnace Powellsville 45629 740-354-9551
Jodi Armstrong, prin. Fax 355-8779

Frazeysburg, Muskingum, Pop. 1,298
Tri-Valley Local SD
Supt. — See Dresden
Frazeysburg ES 300/K-6
120 E 3rd St 43822 740-828-2781
Rebecca Norris, prin. Fax 828-9227

Fredericksburg, Wayne, Pop. 483
Southeast Local SD
Supt. — See Apple Creek
Fredericksburg S 200/K-8
PO Box 249 44627 330-695-2741
Patty Weber, prin. Fax 695-2116

Fredericktown, Knox, Pop. 2,526
Fredericktown Local SD 700/K-12
117 Columbus Rd 43019 740-694-2956
James Peterson, supt. Fax 694-0956
www.fredericktownschools.com
Fredericktown ES 400/K-5
111 Stadium Dr 43019 740-694-2781
Emily Funston, prin. Fax 694-1294

Freeport, Harrison, Pop. 409
Harrison Hills CSD
Supt. — See Hopedale
Harrison Lakeland ES 100/PK-6
77520 Freeport Tipp Rd 43973 740-942-7400
John Alleman, prin. Fax 942-7403

Antrim Mennonite S 50/1-12
20360 Cadiz Rd 43973 740-489-5161
Titus Lapp, prin.

Fremont, Sandusky, Pop. 17,049
Fremont CSD 4,100/K-12
1220 Cedar St Ste A 43420 419-332-6454
Dr. Traci McCaudy, supt. Fax 334-5454
www.fremont.k12.oh.us
Atkinson ES 300/K-6
1100 Delaware Ave 43420 419-332-5361
Diana McNulty, prin. Fax 334-6749
Croghan ES 300/K-6
1110 Chestnut St 43420 419-332-1511
Shanita Aaron, prin. Fax 332-4314
Fremont MS 700/7-8
501 Croghan St 43420 419-332-5569
Anthony Walker, prin. Fax 334-5494
Hayes ES 300/K-6
916 Hayes Ave 43420 419-332-6371
Laurel Selvey, prin. Fax 334-6761
Lutz ES 300/K-6
1929 Buckland Ave 43420 419-332-0091
Christyl Erickson, prin. Fax 334-5499
Otis ES 400/K-6
718 N Brush St 43420 419-332-8964
Denice Hirt, prin. Fax 334-6788
Stamm ES 400/K-6
1038 Miller St 43420 419-332-5538
Fax 334-6746
Other Schools – See Lindsey

Sacred Heart S 300/K-8
500 Smith Rd 43420 419-332-7102
Katie Mellor, prin. Fax 332-1542
St. Ann S 100/PK-8
1011 W State St 43420 419-332-2461
Judy Hall, prin. Fax 332-2461
St. Joseph S 300/PK-8
716 Croghan St 43420 419-332-5161
Christine Oravats, prin. Fax 332-7299

Gahanna, Franklin, Pop. 33,077
Gahanna-Jefferson CSD 7,000/K-12
160 S Hamilton Rd 43230 614-471-7065
Gregg Morris, supt. Fax 478-5568
www.gahannaschools.org
Chapelfield ES 300/K-5
280 Chapelfield Rd 43230 614-478-5575
Scott Schmidt, prin. Fax 337-3755
Gahanna MS East 500/6-8
730 Clotts Rd 43230 614-478-5550
Brad Barboza, prin. Fax 478-5544
Gahanna MS South 600/6-8
349 Shady Spring Dr 43230 614-337-3730
Angie Adrean, prin. Fax 337-3734
Gahanna MS West 600/6-8
350 N Stygler Rd 43230 614-478-5570
Brett Harmon, prin. Fax 337-3771
Goshen Lane ES 400/K-5
370 Goshen Ln 43230 614-478-5580
Chad Reynolds, prin. Fax 337-3757
High Point ES 500/K-5
700 Venetian Way 43230 614-478-5545
Kathleen Erhard, prin. Fax 337-3762
Jefferson ES 500/K-5
136 Carpenter Rd 43230 614-478-5560
Robin Frentzel, prin. Fax 337-3766
Lincoln ES 400/K-5
515 Havens Corners Rd 43230 614-478-5555
Kristen Groves, prin. Fax 337-3750
Royal Manor ES 300/K-5
299 Empire Dr 43230 614-478-5585
Rick Oxley, prin. Fax 413-5589
Other Schools – See Blacklick

Columbus Academy 1,000/PK-12
PO Box 30745 43230 614-475-2311
John Mackenzie, hdmstr. Fax 475-0396
Gahanna Christian Academy 500/PK-12
817 N Hamilton Rd 43230 614-471-9270
Ruth Bischoff, supt. Fax 471-9201
St. Matthew S 600/K-8
795 Havens Corners Rd 43230 614-471-4930
Carole Marsh, prin. Fax 471-1673
Shepherd Christian S 100/PK-5
425 S Hamilton Rd 43230 614-471-0859
Rev. Gerri Nugent, prin. Fax 471-3466

Galena, Delaware, Pop. 505
Big Walnut Local SD 2,700/K-12
PO Box 218 43021 740-965-2706
Steve Mazzi, supt. Fax 965-4688
www.bigwalnut.k12.oh.us/
Hylen Souders ES 400/K-5
4121 Miller Paul Rd 43021 740-965-3200
Joe Jude, prin. Fax 965-3986
Other Schools – See Sunbury

Olentangy Local SD
Supt. — See Lewis Center
Johnnycake Corners ES 500/PK-5
6783 Falling Meadows Dr 43021 740-657-5650
Cynthia Deangelis, prin. Fax 657-5699
Walnut Creek ES 700/K-5
5600 Grand Oak Blvd 43021 740-657-4750
Michelle Seitz, prin. Fax 657-4799

Galion, Crawford, Pop. 11,449
Galion CSD 1,700/PK-12
470 Portland Way N 44833 419-468-3432
Dr. Kathleen Jenney, supt. Fax 468-4333
www.galion-city.k12.oh.us/
Galion IS 300/3-5
476 Portland Way N 44833 419-468-3676
Cindy Parrott, prin. Fax 468-5781
Galion MS 500/6-8
474 Portland Way N 44833 419-468-3134
Andrew Johnson, prin. Fax 468-7868
Galion PS 300/PK-2
478 Portland Way N 44833 419-468-4010
Cindy Voss, prin. Fax 468-7182

Northmor Local SD 1,300/K-12
5247 County Road 29 44833 419-946-8861
Brent Winand, supt. Fax 947-6255
www.northmor.k12.oh.us
Other Schools – See Iberia, Shauck

St. Joseph S 100/PK-8
138 N Liberty St 44833 419-468-5436
Robert Lavengood, prin. Fax 468-3611

Gallipolis, Gallia, Pop. 4,212
Gallia County Local SD 2,100/K-12
230 Shawnee Ln 45631 740-446-7917
Dr. Charla Evans, supt. Fax 446-3187
gallialocal.org
Addaville ES 200/K-4
1333 Brick School Rd 45631 740-367-7283
Silas Johnson, prin. Fax 367-5004
Other Schools – See Bidwell, Crown City, Patriot, Vinton

Gallipolis CSD 2,300/K-12
61 State St 45631 740-446-3211
Jack Payton, supt. Fax 446-6433
gallipoliscityschools.k12.oh.us
Gallia Academy MS 400/7-8
340 4th Ave 45631 740-446-3214
Brent Saunders, prin.
Green ES 400/K-6
113 Centenary Church Rd 45631 740-446-3236
Brett Wilson, prin. Fax 446-0482
Washington ES 600/K-6
450 4th Ave 45631 740-446-3213
James Pope, prin. Fax 446-0355
Other Schools – See Rio Grande

Ohio Valley Christian S 100/K-12
455 3rd Ave 45631 740-446-0374
Patrick O'Donnell, admin. Fax 446-8593

Galloway, Franklin
South-Western CSD
Supt. — See Grove City
Alton Hall ES 600/K-4
1000 Alton Rd 43119 614-801-8000
Tim Barton, prin. Fax 801-8003
Darby Woods ES 700/K-4
255 Westwoods Blvd 43119 614-801-8075
Debbie Willoughby Reed, prin. Fax 801-8090
Galloway Ridge IS 700/5-6
122 Galloway Rd 43119 614-801-8850
Mimi Padovan, prin. Fax 801-8851

Cypress Christian S 400/K-8
PO Box 590 43119 614-870-1181
Bruce Barkhurst, admin. Fax 878-5866

Gambier, Knox, Pop. 2,050
Mt. Vernon CSD
Supt. — See Mount Vernon
Wiggin Street ES 200/K-5
PO Box 352 43022 740-427-4262
Lynn Riggenbach, prin. Fax 427-3926

Garfield Heights, Cuyahoga, Pop. 29,042
Garfield Heights CSD 4,100/K-12
5640 Briarcliff Dr 44125 216-475-8100
Jeanne Sternad, supt. Fax 475-1824
www.garfieldheightscityschools.com/
Elmwood ES 500/K-3
5275 Turney Rd 44125 216-475-8110
Jody Saxton, prin. Fax 475-8371
Foster ES 600/K-3
12801 Bangor Ave 44125 216-475-8123
Sandy Powers, prin. Fax 475-8080
Garfield Heights MS 1,000/6-8
12000 Mapleleaf Dr 44125 216-475-8105
Keith Ahearn, prin. Fax 475-8146
Maple Leaf IS 600/4-5
5764 Turney Rd 44125 216-662-3800
Thomas Matthews, prin. Fax 662-9949

Archbishop Lyke MS 200/5-8
4351 E 131st St 44105 216-581-3517
Margarete Smith, prin. Fax 581-6204
John Paul II Academy 200/PK-8
10608 Penfield Ave 44125 216-581-3080
Sr. Helene Skrzyniarz, prin. Fax 581-3031
St. Monica S 400/K-8
13633 Rockside Rd 44125 216-662-9380
Ruth Downey, prin. Fax 662-3137

Garrettsville, Portage, Pop. 2,222
James A. Garfield Local SD 1,600/K-12
10235 State Route 88 44231 330-527-4336
Charles Klamer, supt. Fax 527-5941
garfield.sparcc.org/
Garfield ES 600/K-4
10207 State Route 88 44231 330-527-2184
Keri Dornack, prin. Fax 527-3015
Garfield IS 200/5-6
8233 Park Ave 44231 330-527-7436
Donald Long, prin. Fax 527-0087
Garfield MS 200/7-8
10231 State Route 88 44231 330-527-2151
Tom Sullivan, prin. Fax 527-2601

Gates Mills, Cuyahoga, Pop. 2,370
Mayfield CSD
Supt. — See Mayfield Heights
Gates Mills ES 100/K-5
7639 Colvin Rd 44040 440-995-7500
Spencer Wiersma, prin. Fax 995-7505

Gilmour Academy Lower S 200/PK-6
34001 Cedar Rd 44040 440-473-8160
Dr. Monica Veto, prin. Fax 473-8157
Gilmour Academy MS 100/7-8
34001 Cedar Rd 44040 440-473-8111
Yvonne Saunders, prin. Fax 473-8112
St. Francis of Assisi S 500/PK-8
6850 Mayfield Rd 44040 440-442-7450
Adrienne Publicover, prin. Fax 446-1132

Geneva, Ashtabula, Pop. 6,478
Geneva CSD 2,800/K-12
135 S Eagle St 44041 440-466-4831
Mary Zappitelli, supt. Fax 466-0908
www.genevaschools.org/
Cork ES 300/K-6
341 State Route 534 S 44041 440-466-4831
Melissa Doherty, prin. Fax 466-0715
Geneva ES 300/K-6
119 S Eagle St 44041 440-466-4831
Steve Candela, prin. Fax 466-0824
Geneva JHS 500/7-8
839 Sherman St 44041 440-466-4831
Richard Belconis, prin. Fax 466-5692
Spencer ES 500/K-6
4641 N Ridge Rd E 44041 440-466-4831
Michael Penzenik, prin. Fax 466-0592
Other Schools – See Austinburg

Assumption S 100/K-6
30 Lockwood St 44041 440-466-2104
Cheryl Woodward, prin. Fax 466-7769

Genoa, Ottawa, Pop. 2,351
Genoa Area Local SD 1,600/K-12
2810 N Genoa Clay Center Rd 43430 419-855-7741
Dennis Mock, supt. Fax 855-4030
www.genoaschools.com
Brunner ES 300/K-2
1224 West St 43430 419-855-8373
Brenda Murphy, prin. Fax 855-9027
Genoa Area MS 400/6-8
2950 N Genoa Clay Center Rd 43430 419-855-7781
Kevin Katafias, prin. Fax 855-7784
Other Schools – See Curtice

Georgetown, Brown, Pop. 3,720
Georgetown EVD 1,100/K-12
1043 Mount Orab Pike 45121 937-378-3730
Tony Dunn, supt. Fax 378-2219
www.gtown.k12.oh.us/
Georgetown ES 600/K-6
935 Mount Orab Pike 45121 937-378-6235
Rebecca Honaker, prin. Fax 378-3560

Germantown, Montgomery, Pop. 5,157
Valley View Local SD 2,000/PK-12
64 Comstock St 45327 937-855-6581
Sherry Parr, supt. Fax 855-7156
www.valleyview.k12.oh.us
Germantown ES 500/PK-5
110 Comstock St 45327 937-855-6571
Bill Lauson, prin. Fax 855-6283
Valley View MS 500/6-8
64 Comstock St 45327 937-855-4203
Harold Bowman, prin. Fax 855-7156
Other Schools – See Farmersville

Germantown Christian S 100/PK-12
9440 Eby Rd 45327 937-855-7334
Patricia Proctor, prin. Fax 855-7746

Gibsonburg, Sandusky, Pop. 2,460
Gibsonburg EVD 1,300/PK-12
301 S Sunset Ave 43431 419-637-2479
Thomas Peiffer, supt. Fax 637-3029
www.gibsonburg.k12.oh.us/
Gibsonburg MS 300/6-8
740 S Main St 43431 419-637-7954
Danny Kissell, prin. Fax 637-2046
Hilfiker ES 600/PK-5
301 S Sunset Ave 43431 419-637-7249
Meri Skilliter, prin. Fax 637-2478

Girard, Trumbull, Pop. 10,490
Girard CSD 1,700/K-12
704 E Prospect St 44420 330-545-2596
Joseph Jeswald, supt. Fax 545-2597
www.girardcityschools.org/
Girard IS 400/4-6
702 E Prospect St 44420 330-545-5219
David Leo, prin. Fax 545-2597
Girard JHS 300/7-8
31 N Ward Ave 44420 330-545-5431
Louise Mason, prin. Fax 545-5440
Prospect ES 500/K-3
700 E Prospect St 44420 330-545-3854
Debra Gratz, prin. Fax 545-2597

St. Rose S 300/K-8
61 E Main St 44420 330-545-1163
Linda Borton, prin. Fax 545-1584

Glandorf, Putnam, Pop. 952
Ottawa-Glandorf Local SD
Supt. — See Ottawa
Glandorf S 500/K-8
PO Box 129 45848 419-538-6880
Scott Ketner, prin. Fax 538-6115

Glenford, Perry, Pop. 198
Northern Local SD
Supt. — See Thornville
Glenford ES 300/K-5
PO Box 70 43739 740-659-2209
Angie Gussler, prin. Fax 659-2228

Glouster, Athens, Pop. 2,029
Trimble Local SD 900/K-12
1 Tomcat Dr 45732 740-767-4444
Cindy Johnston, supt. Fax 767-4901
trimble.k12.oh.us/
Trimble ES 400/K-4
18500 Jacksonville Rd 45732 740-767-2810
Mary Mitchell, prin. Fax 767-9523
Trimble MS 300/5-8
18500 Jacksonville Rd 45732 740-767-2810
Curtis Martin, prin. Fax 767-9523

Gnadenhutten, Tuscarawas, Pop. 1,294
Indian Valley Local SD 1,600/K-12
PO Box 171 44629 740-254-4334
Roger Bond, supt. Fax 254-9271
www.ivschools.org/
Other Schools – See Midvale, Port Washington, Tuscarawas

Gomer, Allen
Elida Local SD
Supt. — See Elida
Elida K 200/K-K
4040 W Lincoln Hwy 45809 419-642-3181
Bob Kiracofe, prin. Fax 642-3238

Goshen, Clermont
Goshen Local SD 2,500/K-12
6694 Goshen Rd 45122 513-722-2222
Charlene Thomas, supt. Fax 722-3767
www.goshenlocalschools.org
Goshen MS 500/6-8
6692 Goshen Rd 45122 513-722-2226
Troy Smith, prin. Fax 722-2246
Marr/Cook ES 600/K-2
6696 Goshen Rd 45122 513-722-2224
Teresa Rohrkemper, prin. Fax 722-2244
Spaulding ES 600/3-5
6755 Linton Rd 45122 513-722-2225
Darrell Edwards, prin. Fax 722-2245

Grafton, Lorain, Pop. 5,855
Midview Local SD 2,800/K-12
1010 Vivian Dr 44044 440-926-3737
John Kuhn, supt. Fax 926-2675
www.midviewk12.org
Midview East IS 200/5-6
13070 Durkee Rd 44044 440-748-1851
Charles Laubacher, prin. Fax 748-7016
Midview MS 600/7-8
37999 Capel Rd 44044 440-748-2122
Scott Goggin, prin. Fax 748-0131
Midview North ES 400/K-4
13070 Durkee Rd 44044 440-748-6869
Audrey Fountain, prin. Fax 748-7056
Midview West ES 400/K-4
13070 Durkee Rd 44044 440-748-2305
Patricia Hamilton, prin. Fax 748-4032

Grand Rapids, Wood, Pop. 998
Otsego Local SD
Supt. — See Tontogany
Grand Rapids ES 200/PK-5
17595 Bridge St 43522 419-832-4765
Harold Bower, prin. Fax 832-2803

Granville, Licking, Pop. 5,281
Granville EVD 2,400/K-12
PO Box 417 43023 740-587-8101
Scot Prebles, supt. Fax 587-8191
www.granville.k12.oh.us/
Granville ES 700/K-3
310 N Granger St 43023 740-587-8102
Todd Rogers, prin. Fax 587-2374
Granville IS 600/4-6
2025 Burg St 43023 740-587-8103
Gayle Burris, prin. Fax 587-1138
Granville MS 400/7-8
210 New Burg St 43023 740-587-8104
Lisa Sealover-Ormond, prin. Fax 587-8194

Granville Christian Academy 200/K-12
1820 Newark Granville Rd 43023 740-587-4423
Nancy Warner, prin. Fax 587-1266
Welsh Hills S 100/PK-8
2610 Newark Granville Rd 43023 740-522-2020
Gina Reeves, hdmstr. Fax 522-1500

Graysville, Monroe, Pop. 112
Switzerland of Ohio Local SD
Supt. — See Woodsfield
Skyvue S 300/K-8
33329 Hartshorn Ridge Rd 45734 740-567-3312
Neil Ritchie, prin. Fax 567-3498

Graytown, Ottawa
Benton Carroll Salem Local SD
Supt. — See Oak Harbor
Graytown ES 100/K-5
1661 N Walker St 43432 419-862-2082
Mary Ann Widmer, prin. Fax 862-3642

Green, Summit, Pop. 23,463
Green Local SD 3,600/PK-12
PO Box 218 44232 330-896-7500
Wade Lucas, supt. Fax 896-7580
www.greenlocalschools.org
Kleckner ES 600/3-4
PO Box 218 44232 330-896-7515
Judith Elfrink, prin. Fax 896-7529
Other Schools – See Uniontown

Green Camp, Marion, Pop. 323
Elgin Local SD
Supt. — See Marion
Elgin JHS 300/7-8
PO Box 214 43322 740-528-2320
Michelle Kaffenbarger, prin. Fax 528-2618

Greenfield, Highland, Pop. 5,146
Greenfield EVD 2,300/PK-12
200 N 5th St 45123 937-981-2152
Terrence Fouch, supt. Fax 981-4395
greenfield.k12.oh.us
Greenfield ES 400/K-4
200 N 5th St 45123 937-981-3241
Bob Schumm, prin. Fax 981-2521
Greenfield MS 500/5-8
200 N 5th St 45123 937-981-2197
Howard Zody, prin. Fax 981-0417
Rainsboro ES 300/K-5
12916 Barretts Mill Rd 45123 937-365-1271
James Taylor, prin. Fax 365-2006
Other Schools – See South Salem

Green Springs, Sandusky, Pop. 1,235
Clyde-Green Springs EVD
Supt. — See Clyde
Green Springs ES 600/K-6
420 N Broadway St 44836 419-639-2902
Laura Kagy, prin. Fax 547-8108

Greenville, Darke, Pop. 13,166
Greenville CSD 1,900/K-12
215 W 4th St 45331 937-548-3185
Susan Riegle, supt. Fax 548-6943
www.greenville.k12.oh.us
Greenville IS 100/3-4
301 E 5th St 45331 937-548-2815
Jeanna Zumbrink, prin. Fax 548-8125
Greenville JHS 500/7-8
131 Central Ave 45331 937-548-3202
Carl Brown, prin. Fax 548-3315
Greenville MS 100/5-6
701 Wayne Ave 45331 937-548-3525
Chris Scholl, prin. Fax 548-2155
Greenville PS 200/K-2
7550 State Route 118 45331 937-548-1013
Krista Stump, prin. Fax 548-2175

St. Mary S 200/PK-8
238 W 3rd St 45331 937-548-2345
Carol Hertel, prin. Fax 548-0878

Greenwich, Huron, Pop. 1,549
South Central Local SD 900/K-12
3305 Greenwich Angling Rd 44837 419-752-3815
Ben Chaffee, supt. Fax 752-0182
www.south-central.org
South Central S 600/K-8
3291 Greenwich Angling Rd 44837 419-752-0011
Terry Goodsite, prin. Fax 752-8705

Grove City, Franklin, Pop. 30,892
South-Western CSD 20,800/PK-12
3805 Marlane Dr 43123 614-801-3000
Dr. Bill Wise, supt. Fax 871-2781
www.swcs.us
Brookpark MS 600/7-8
2803 Southwest Blvd 43123 614-801-3500
Bob Rains, prin. Fax 871-6512
Buckeye Woods ES 800/K-4
2525 Holton Rd 43123 614-801-8025
Jan Wilson, prin. Fax 801-8045
Hayes IS 400/5-6
4436 Haughn Rd 43123 614-801-6200
Kevin Laffin, prin. Fax 801-6201
Highland Park ES 500/K-4
2600 Cameron St 43123 614-801-8200
Lynn Saxton, prin. Fax 801-8212
Holt Crossing IS 700/5-6
2706 Holt Rd 43123 614-801-8700
Linda Kuhn, prin. Fax 801-8701
Jackson MS 600/7-8
2271 Holton Rd 43123 614-801-3800
Dr. Erik Shuey, prin. Fax 801-3818
Monterey ES 400/K-4
2584 Dennis Ln 43123 614-801-8250
Jane Ferry, prin. Fax 801-8259
Park Street IS 700/5-6
3205 Park St 43123 614-801-8800
Ed Gwazdauskas, prin. Fax 801-8801
Pleasant View MS 900/7-8
7255 Kropp Rd 43123 614-801-3900
Thom Gamertsfelder, prin. Fax 870-5530
Richard Avenue ES 500/K-4
3646 Richard Ave 43123 614-801-8325
Catherine Moore, prin. Fax 801-8336
Sommer ES 600/K-4
3055 Kingston Ave 43123 614-801-8350
Elaine Clay-McLaughlin, prin. Fax 871-6599
Other Schools – See Columbus, Darbydale, Galloway

Beautiful Savior Lutheran S 100/K-8
2213 White Rd 43123 614-875-1147
David Knittel, prin. Fax 875-9637
Grove City Christian S 700/K-12
4750 Hoover Rd 43123 614-875-3000
Joyce Schneider, admin. Fax 875-8933
Our Lady of Perpetual Help S 500/PK-8
3752 Broadway 43123 614-875-6779
Susan Donovan, prin. Fax 539-5719

Groveport, Franklin, Pop. 4,753
Groveport Madison Local SD 5,900/K-12
5940 Clyde Moore Dr 43125 614-492-2520
Scott McKenzie, supt. Fax 492-2533
www.gocruisers.org
Glendening ES 500/K-5
4200 Glendenning Dr 43125 614-836-4972
Curt Brogan, prin. Fax 836-4974
Groveport ES 500/K-5
715 Main St 43125 614-836-4975
Mary Schroeder, prin. Fax 836-4680
Groveport Madison JHS 500/8-8
751 Main St 43125 614-836-4957
Lea Ann Yoakum, prin. Fax 836-4999
Groveport Madison MS South 500/6-7
4400 Glendenning Dr 43125 614-836-4953
Bill Young, prin. Fax 836-4956
Other Schools – See Columbus

Madison Christian S 500/PK-12
3565 Bixby Rd 43125 614-497-3456
Debbie Ostrander, admin. Fax 497-3057

Grover Hill, Paulding, Pop. 382
Wayne Trace Local SD
Supt. — See Haviland
Grover Hill ES 300/PK-6
PO Box 125 45849 419-587-3414
Alan Lautzenheiser, prin. Fax 587-3415

Hamden, Vinton, Pop. 940
Vinton County Local SD
Supt. — See Mc Arthur
South ES 200/PK-5
38234 State Route 93 45634 740-384-2731
Saundra Allman, prin. Fax 384-4001

Hamersville, Brown, Pop. 530
Western Brown Local SD
Supt. — See Mount Orab
Hamersville S 700/K-8
PO Box 205 45130 937-379-1144
Peggy McKinney, prin. Fax 379-1676

Hamilton, Butler, Pop. 61,943
Edgewood CSD
Supt. — See Trenton

Edgewood MS 900/6-8
3440 Busenbark Rd 45011 513-867-7430
Tim Spinner, prin. Fax 867-7571

Fairfield CSD
Supt. — See Fairfield
Fairfield East ES 700/1-4
6711 Morris Rd 45011 513-737-5000
Paige Gillespie, prin. Fax 737-5225
Fairfield North ES 600/1-4
6116 Morris Rd 45011 513-868-0070
Diane Stacy, prin. Fax 868-3621

Hamilton CSD 8,700/K-12
PO Box 627 45012 513-887-5000
Janet Baker, supt. Fax 868-4473
www.hamiltoncityschools.com/
Adams ES 500/K-6
450 S F St 45013 513-887-5065
Pam Rowe, prin. Fax 887-5068
Buchanan ES 300/K-6
263 Hancock Ave 45011 513-887-5070
Suelee Litman, prin. Fax 887-5072
Cleveland ES 400/K-6
900 Brookwood Ave 45013 513-887-5075
Terri Fitton, prin. Fax 887-5078
Fillmore ES 700/K-6
1125 Main St 45013 513-887-5085
Rex Bucheit, prin. Fax 887-4712
Garfield MS 700/7-8
250 N Fair Ave 45011 513-887-5035
Patricia Blake, prin. Fax 887-4700
Grant ES 200/K-6
415 Campbell Dr 45011 513-887-5100
Suelee Litman, prin. Fax 887-5103
Harrison ES 400/K-6
250 Knightsbridge Dr 45011 513-887-5105
Susan Schnell, prin. Fax 887-5107
Hayes ES 300/K-6
901 Hoadley Ave 45015 513-887-5110
Chad Konkle, prin. Fax 887-5113
Jefferson ES 400/K-6
526 S 8th St 45011 513-887-5120
Mary Anne Hughes, prin. Fax 887-5123
Lincoln ES 500/K-6
701 N E St 45013 513-887-5130
Sandra Bussell, prin. Fax 887-5133
Madison ES 300/K-6
250 N 9th St 45011 513-887-5140
Deborah Alf, prin. Fax 887-4701
Monroe ES 300/K-6
951 Carriage Hill Ln 45013 513-887-5150
Kathy Wagonfield, prin. Fax 887-5152
Pierce ES 400/K-6
2890 Freeman Ave 45015 513-887-5160
David Bowling, prin. Fax 887-5162
Van Buren ES 400/K-6
2231 Lincoln Ave 45011 513-887-5165
Joan Schumacher, prin. Fax 887-5168
Wilson MS 600/7-8
714 Eaton Ave 45013 513-887-5170
Sheryl Burk, prin. Fax 887-5186

Lakota Local SD
Supt. — See Liberty Twp
Heritage ES 600/2-6
5052 Hamilton Mason Rd 45011 513-863-7060
Marco Pangallo, prin. Fax 887-5483

New Miami Local SD 800/K-12
600 Seven Mile Ave 45011 513-863-0833
Melissa Kircher, supt. Fax 863-0497
www.new-miami.k12.oh.us
New Miami ES 400/K-6
606 Seven Mile Ave 45011 513-896-7153
Rhonda Parker, prin. Fax 896-9313
New Miami MS 100/7-8
600 Seven Mile Ave 45011 513-863-4917
Robert Fischer, prin.

Ross Local SD 2,900/PK-12
3371 Hamilton Cleves Rd 45013 513-863-1253
Todd Yohey, supt. Fax 863-6250
www.rosd.k12.oh.us
Elda ES 700/K-4
3980 Hamilton Cleves Rd 45013 513-738-1972
Deborah Johnsen, prin. Fax 738-0163
Morgan ES 500/PK-5
3427 Chapel Rd 45013 513-738-1986
Tom Perry, prin. Fax 738-4887
Ross MS 800/5-8
3425 Hamilton Cleves Rd 45013 513-863-1251
Christopher Saylor, prin. Fax 863-0066

Ham-Mid SDA S 50/K-8
3570 Hamilton Middletown Rd 45011 513-868-9101
Immanuel Lutheran S 100/PK-8
1285 Main St 45013 513-895-9212
Michael Mayo, prin. Fax 863-2502
Queen of Peace S 300/PK-8
2550 Millville Ave 45013 513-863-8705
Bernadette Zimmerman, prin. Fax 863-4310
St. Ann S 200/K-8
3064 Pleasant Ave 45015 513-863-0604
Donna Weber, prin. Fax 863-2017
St. Joseph Consolidated S 200/K-8
925 S 2nd St 45011 513-863-8758
William Hicks, prin. Fax 863-5772
St. Peter in Chains S 200/K-8
451 Ridgelawn Ave 45013 513-863-0685
Charlotte Sharon, prin. Fax 863-1859

Hamler, Henry, Pop. 678
Patrick Henry Local SD 1,100/K-12
6900 State Route 18 43524 419-274-5451
Susan Miko, supt. Fax 274-1641
www.patrickhenry.k12.oh.us/
Henry MS 300/5-8
E050 County Road 7 43524 419-274-3431
Jennifer Ripke, prin. Fax 274-1890
Other Schools – See Deshler, Malinta

Hammondsville, Jefferson
Edison Local SD 2,000/PK-12
14890 State Route 213 43930 330-532-3199
David Quattrochi, supt. Fax 532-2860
www.edisonlocal.k12.oh.us/
Stanton MS 400/5-8
14890 State Route 213 43930 330-532-1594
Scott Hiemstra, prin. Fax 532-1594
Other Schools – See Bergholz, Steubenville

Hannibal, Monroe
Switzerland of Ohio Local SD
Supt. — See Woodsfield
Hannibal S 200/K-8
PO Box 56 43931 740-483-1624
Micah Fuchs, prin. Fax 483-1630

Hanoverton, Columbiana, Pop. 385
United Local SD 1,400/K-12
8143 State Route 9 44423 330-223-1521
Thomas Davis, supt. Fax 223-2363
www.united.k12.oh.us/
United ES 700/K-6
8143 State Route 9 44423 330-223-8001
Ruthann Rinto, prin. Fax 223-2363

Harrison, Hamilton, Pop. 7,821
Southwest Local SD 3,600/K-12
230 S Elm St 45030 513-367-4139
Chris Brown, supt. Fax 367-2287
www.southwestschools.org
Crosby ES 300/K-6
8382 New Haven Rd 45030 513-738-1717
Laura Meyers, prin. Fax 738-1718
Harrison ES 600/K-6
600 E Broadway St 45030 513-367-4161
Stephanie Tillman, prin.
Harrison MS 600/7-8
9830 West Rd 45030 513-367-4831
John Hamstra, prin. Fax 367-0370
Whitewater Valley ES 500/K-6
10800 Campbell Rd 45030 513-367-5577
Daniel Rouster, prin. Fax 367-5594
Other Schools – See Hooven, Miamitown

Christ Centered S 50/PK-12
220 Sunset Ave 45030 513-367-4564
Jerry Goodbar, admin. Fax 367-7981
Harrison Christian S 100/PK-6
949 Harrison Ave 45030 513-367-6100
John Hembree, prin. Fax 367-7280
St. John the Baptist S 300/K-8
508 Park Ave 45030 513-367-6826
Carey Owens, prin. Fax 367-6864

Harrod, Allen, Pop. 482
Allen East Local SD 700/K-12
9105 Harding Hwy 45850 419-648-3333
Michael Richards, supt. Fax 648-5282
www.noacsc.org/allen/ae
Allen East ES 300/K-6
9105 Harding Hwy 45850 419-648-3333
Larry Altenburger, prin. Fax 648-5282

Hartville, Stark, Pop. 2,389
Lake Local SD
Supt. — See Uniontown
Hartville ES 500/K-3
245 Belle St SW 44632 330-877-4278
Gary Kandel, prin. Fax 877-4758
Lake ES 600/4-5
225 Lincoln St SW 44632 330-877-4276
Donna Bruner, prin. Fax 877-4738
Lake MS 800/6-8
12001 Market Ave N 44632 330-877-4290
Jeffrey Durbin, prin. Fax 877-1384

Lake Center Christian S 600/K-12
12893 Kaufman Ave NW 44632 330-877-2049
Matthew McMullen, supt. Fax 877-2040

Haskins, Wood, Pop. 637
Otsego Local SD
Supt. — See Tontogany
Haskins ES 300/PK-5
405 N Findlay Rd 43525 419-823-1591
Anita Kuhlman, prin. Fax 823-1116

Haviland, Paulding, Pop. 171
Wayne Trace Local SD 1,100/PK-12
4915 US Route 127 45851 419-263-2415
Brian Gerber, supt. Fax 263-2377
www.noacsc.org/paulding/wt/
Other Schools – See Grover Hill, Payne

Hayesville, Ashland, Pop. 348
Hillsdale Local SD
Supt. — See Jeromesville
Hillsdale ES 400/K-4
W Main St 44838 419-368-4364
Mike Shambre, prin. Fax 368-3701

Heath, Licking, Pop. 8,888
Heath CSD 1,700/K-12
107 Lancaster Dr 43056 740-522-2816
Tom Forman, supt. Fax 522-4697
www.heath.k12.oh.us/
Garfield ES 400/K-2
680 S 30th St 43056 740-522-4810
Valerie Bailey, prin. Fax 522-8830
Heath MS 400/6-8
310 Licking View Dr 43056 740-788-3200
Timothy Winland, prin. Fax 788-3209
Stevenson ES 400/3-5
152 Cynthia St 43056 740-522-8442
Penny Coleman, prin. Fax 522-6241

Newark SDA S 50/K-8
701 Linnville Rd 43056 740-323-1531
Harriet Snyder, prin. Fax 323-1531

Hebron, Licking, Pop. 2,149
Lakewood Local SD 1,800/K-12
PO Box 70 43025 740-928-5878
Jay Gault, supt. Fax 928-3152
www.lakewoodlocal.k12.oh.us/
Hebron ES 300/K-2
PO Box 70 43025 740-928-2661
Marilyn Fox, prin. Fax 928-7510
Jackson IS 300/3-5
PO Box 70 43025 740-928-1915
Patti Pickering, prin. Fax 928-3756
Lakewood MS 500/6-8
PO Box 70 43025 740-928-8330
Jim Riley, prin. Fax 928-5627

Hicksville, Defiance, Pop. 3,533
Hicksville EVD 1,000/K-12
958 E High St 43526 419-542-7665
Kevin Miller, supt. Fax 542-8534
www.hicksvilleschools.org/
Hicksville ES 500/K-6
958 E High St 43526 419-542-7475
Keith Countryman, prin. Fax 542-8711

Highland Heights, Cuyahoga, Pop. 8,621
Mayfield CSD
Supt. — See Mayfield Heights
Millridge ES 500/K-5
962 Millridge Rd 44143 440-995-7250
Mary Myers, prin. Fax 995-7255

St. Paschal Baylon S 500/PK-8
5360 Wilson Mills Rd 44143 440-442-6766
John Bednar, prin. Fax 446-9037

Hilliard, Franklin, Pop. 26,656
Hilliard CSD 15,000/PK-12
5323 Cemetery Rd 43026 614-771-4273
Dale McVey, supt. Fax 777-2424
www.hilliard.k12.oh.us
Avery ES 500/K-5
4388 Avery Rd 43026 614-771-2250
Kathy Curtis, prin. Fax 529-7407
Beacon ES 500/K-5
3600 Lacon Rd 43026 614-771-2256
Jane Leach, prin. Fax 529-7430
Britton ES 400/K-5
4501 Britton Pkwy 43026 614-771-2275
Rob Spicer, prin. Fax 771-2816
Brown ES 500/K-5
2494 Walker Rd 43026 614-771-2270
Brian Blum, prin. Fax 771-2817
Darby Creek ES 700/K-5
6305 Pinefield Dr 43026 614-850-1020
Vicky Clark, prin. Fax 850-1016
Darby ES 600/K-5
2730 Alton Darby Creek Rd 43026 614-334-1400
Barbara Orr, prin. Fax 334-1411
Hilliard City Preschool PK-PK
2874 Alton Darby Creek Rd 43026 614-334-1404
Sharon Balduf, prin. Fax 334-1410
Hilliard Crossing ES 600/K-5
3340 Hilliard Rome Rd 43026 614-777-2202
Cindi Montgomery, prin. Fax 777-2416
Hilliard Heritage MS 800/7-8
5670 Scioto Darby Rd 43026 614-771-2800
Suzanne McCoy, prin. Fax 771-2808
Hilliard Memorial MS 800/7-8
5600 Scioto Darby Rd 43026 614-334-3057
Doug Lowery, prin. Fax 334-3058
Hilliard Station Sixth Grade S 600/6-6
3859 Main St 43026 614-777-2426
Bruce Stephanic, prin. Fax 529-7402
Hilliard Weaver MS 800/7-8
4600 Avery Rd 43026 614-529-7424
Craig Vroom, prin. Fax 529-7425
Hoffman Trails ES 600/K-5
4301 Hoffman Farms Dr 43026 614-334-0505
Shelli Miller, prin. Fax 334-0504
Norwich ES 600/K-5
4454 Davidson Rd 43026 614-777-2418
Karen Lehrer, prin. Fax 777-2422
Reason ES 500/K-5
4790 Cemetery Rd 43026 614-771-2253
Greg Hennes, prin. Fax 529-7429
Ridgewood ES 500/K-5
4237 Dublin Rd 43026 614-771-2262
Tamar Campbell-Sauer, prin. Fax 771-2819
Scioto Darby ES 500/K-5
5380 Scioto Darby Rd 43026 614-771-2259
Kayla Pinnick, prin. Fax 771-2820
Tharp Sixth Grade S 500/6-6
4681 Leap Rd 43026 614-334-1600
Cori Kindl, prin. Fax 334-1600
Other Schools – See Columbus, Dublin

St. Brendan S 500/K-8
4475 Dublin Rd 43026 614-876-6132
Mary Lang, prin. Fax 529-8929
Sunrise Academy 300/K-12
5657 Scioto Darby Rd 43026 614-527-0465
Leah Mohiuddin, dir. Fax 527-4265

Hillsboro, Highland, Pop. 6,677
Bright Local SD
Supt. — See Mowrystown
Bright ES 400/PK-6
6100 Fair Ridge Rd 45133 937-927-7010
Michael Roades, prin. Fax 927-7015

Hillsboro CSD 2,000/PK-12
338 W Main St 45133 937-393-3475
Art Reiber, supt. Fax 393-5841
www.hcs-k12.org/
Hillsboro ECC 100/PK-1
500 US Highway 62 45133 937-393-3132
Kathy Hoop, prin. Fax 393-3077
Hillsboro IS 50/4-5
500 US Highway 62 45133 937-393-3132
Lew Ewry, prin. Fax 393-3077
Hillsboro MS 600/6-8
550 US Highway 62 45133 937-393-9877
Chris Burrows, prin. Fax 393-5843
Hillsboro PS 400/2-3
500 US Highway 62 45133 937-393-3132
Jacob Zink, prin. Fax 393-3077

Highland County Christian S 100/K-6
265 W Walnut St 45133 937-393-9090
Connie Sears, prin. Fax 393-4963
St. Mary S 100/PK-6
212 S High St 45133 937-840-9932
Kevin Bararras, prin. Fax 840-9932

Hinckley, Medina
Highland Local SD
Supt. — See Medina
Hinckley ES 500/PK-5
1586 Center Rd 44233 330-239-1901
Stacie Rastok, prin. Fax 278-2727

Holgate, Henry, Pop. 1,165
Holgate Local SD 500/K-12
801 Joe E Brown Ave 43527 419-264-5141
Anthony Meinerding, supt. Fax 264-1965
www.holgate.k12.oh.us/
Holgate ES 200/K-5
801 Joe E Brown Ave 43527 419-264-5231
Jim George, prin. Fax 264-1965

Holland, Lucas, Pop. 1,326
Springfield Local SD 3,900/K-12
6900 Hall St 43528 419-867-5600
Kathryn Hott, supt. Fax 867-5700
www.springfieldlocalschools.net
Crissey ES 400/K-5
9220 Geiser Rd 43528 419-867-5677
Cheri Copeland-Shull, prin. Fax 867-5739
Holland ES 500/K-5
7001 Madison Ave 43528 419-867-5655
Gerald Devol, prin. Fax 867-5738
Holloway ES 400/K-5
6611 Pilliod Rd 43528 419-867-5703
William Renwand, prin. Fax 867-5707
Springfield MS 900/6-8
7001 Madison Ave 43528 419-867-5644
Matt Geha, prin. Fax 867-5732
Other Schools – See Toledo

Holmesville, Holmes, Pop. 416
Southeast Local SD
Supt. — See Apple Creek
Holmesville ES 100/K-6
PO Box 8 44633 330-279-2341
Holly Lawver, prin. Fax 279-2023

Hooven, Hamilton
Southwest Local SD
Supt. — See Harrison
Hooven ES, PO Box 127 45033 100/K-6
David Kelly, prin. 513-353-2620

Hopedale, Harrison, Pop. 994
Harrison Hills CSD 2,100/PK-12
PO Box 356 43976 740-942-7800
Jim Drexler, supt. Fax 942-7808
www.harrisonhills.k12.oh.us/
Harrison Hopedale ES 300/PK-6
PO Box 307 43976 740-942-7550
Clara Joyce, prin. Fax 942-7554
Other Schools – See Cadiz, Freeport, Jewett, Scio

Hopewell, Muskingum
West Muskingum Local SD
Supt. — See Zanesville
Hopewell ES 400/K-5
11100 West Pike 43746 740-787-2449
Kathy Robbins, prin. Fax 787-2548

Houston, Shelby
Hardin-Houston Local SD 900/K-12
5300 Houston Rd 45333 937-295-3010
John Scheu, supt. Fax 295-3737
www.houston.k12.oh.us
Other Schools – See Sidney

Howard, Knox
East Knox Local SD 1,000/K-12
23201 Coshocton Rd 43028 740-599-7493
John Marschhausen, supt. Fax 599-5863
www.ekschools.com
East Knox MS 200/5-8
23081 Coshocton Rd 43028 740-599-7000
Hub Reed, prin. Fax 599-6397
Other Schools – See Bladensburg

Hoytville, Wood, Pop. 296
Mc Comb Local SD
Supt. — See Mc Comb
Mc Comb Local MS 200/6-8
PO Box 157 43529 419-278-8194
Jeremy Herr, lead tchr. Fax 278-7166

Hubbard, Trumbull, Pop. 8,006
Hubbard EVD 2,200/K-12
150 Hall Ave 44425 330-534-1921
Richard Buchenic, supt. Fax 534-0522
www.hubbard.k12.oh.us/
Reed MS 700/5-8
150 Hall Ave 44425 330-534-1129
Jon Young, prin. Fax 534-0522

Roosevelt ES 700/K-4
110 Orchard Ave 44425 330-534-1981
Raymond Soloman, prin. Fax 534-1926

St. Patrick S 200/K-8
38 E Water St 44425 330-534-2509
Cynthia Lacko, prin. Fax 534-0305

Huber Heights, Montgomery, Pop. 38,089
Huber Heights CSD 6,500/K-12
5954 Longford Rd 45424 937-237-6300
William Kirby, supt. Fax 237-6307
www.huberheightscityschools.org/
Kitty Hawk ES 300/K-5
5758 Harshmanville Rd 45424 937-237-6392
Rebecca Molfenter, prin.
Lamendola ES, 5363 Tilbury Rd 45424 500/K-5
Delores Pugh, prin. 937-237-6370
Menlo Park ES 400/K-5
5701 Rosebury Dr 45424 937-237-6355
Robert Pohlmeyer, prin.
Monticello ES, 6523 Alter Rd 45424 400/K-5
Gary Doll, prin. 937-237-6360
Rushmore ES 400/K-5
7701 Berchman Dr 45424 937-237-6365
Tamara Granata, prin.
Studebaker MS 800/6-8
5950 Longford Rd 45424 937-237-6345
Tom Heid, prin.
Titus ES, 7450 Taylorsville Rd 45424 300/K-5
William Anderson, prin. 937-237-6375
Valley Forge ES 400/K-5
7191 Troy Manor Rd 45424 937-237-6380
Matthew Housh, prin.
Weisenborn MS 800/6-8
6061 Troy Pike 45424 937-237-6350
Kathy Leary, prin.

St. Peter S 600/PK-8
6185 Chambersburg Rd 45424 937-233-8710
Feliza Poling, prin. Fax 237-3974

Hudson, Summit, Pop. 23,084
Hudson CSD 5,100/PK-12
2400 Hudson Aurora Rd 44236 330-653-1200
Steven Farnsworth, supt. Fax 653-1474
www.hudson.edu
East Woods IS 800/4-5
120 N Hayden Pkwy 44236 330-653-1256
Ted Embacher, prin. Fax 653-1269
Ellsworth Hill PS 200/PK-PK, 2-
7750 Stow Rd 44236 330-653-1236
Lisa Hunt, prin. Fax 653-1236
Evamere ES 600/K-1
76 N Hayden Pkwy 44236 330-653-1226
Andrew Wilson, prin. Fax 653-1234
Hudson MS 1,300/6-8
77 N Oviatt St 44236 330-653-1316
Charles DiLauro, prin. Fax 653-1368
McDowell PS 400/3-3
280 N Hayden Pkwy 44236 330-653-1246
Mark Leventhal, prin. Fax 653-1238

Hudson Montessori S 300/PK-8
7545 Darrow Rd 44236 330-650-0424
Julia Brown, hdmstr.
Seton Catholic S 300/K-8
6923 Stow Rd 44236 330-342-4200
Harry Selner, prin. Fax 342-4276

Huron, Erie, Pop. 7,581
Huron CSD 1,300/PK-12
712 Cleveland Rd E 44839 419-433-3911
Fred Fox, supt. Fax 433-7095
www.huron-city.k12.oh.us/
McCormick JHS 200/7-8
325 Ohio St 44839 419-433-1234
Chad Carter, prin. Fax 433-8427
Shawnee ES 300/PK-2
712 Cleveland Rd E 44839 419-433-1234
Satanta Vonthron, prin. Fax 433-7095
Woodlands ES 200/3-6
1810 Maple Ave 44839 419-433-1234
Mark Doughty, prin. Fax 433-9619

Firelands Montessori Academy 100/PK-8
329 Ohio St 44839 419-433-6181
Trevah Harvey, prin. Fax 433-8199
St. Peter S 200/K-8
429 Huron St 44839 419-433-4640
Linda Smith, prin. Fax 433-2118

Iberia, Morrow
Northmor Local SD
Supt. — See Galion
Iberia ES 300/K-6
PO Box 87 43325 419-947-1900
Rebecca Oliver, prin. Fax 946-2397

Independence, Cuyahoga, Pop. 6,869
Independence Local SD 1,100/PK-12
7733 Stone Rd 44131 216-642-5850
David Laurenzi, supt. Fax 642-3482
www.independence.k12.oh.us
Independence MS 400/5-8
6111 Archwood Rd 44131 216-642-5865
Carl Smilan, prin. Fax 520-7002
Independence PS 400/PK-4
7600 Hillside Rd 44131 216-642-5870
Judith Schulz, prin. Fax 642-1318

St. Michael S 400/PK-8
6906 Chestnut Rd 44131 216-524-6405
Michelle Nowakowski, prin. Fax 524-7538

Ironton, Lawrence, Pop. 11,417
Dawson-Bryant Local SD
Supt. — See Coal Grove

Dawson-Bryant ES 600/K-5
4503 State Route 243 45638 740-532-6898
Eric Holmes, prin. Fax 534-5582

Ironton CSD 800/K-12
105 S 5th St 45638 740-532-4133
Dean Nance, supt. Fax 532-2314
www.tigertown.com
Ironton ES 200/K-5
302 Delaware St 45638 740-532-4054
Kim Brown, prin. Fax 533-6041
Ironton MS 100/6-8
302 Delaware St 45638 740-532-9458
Toben Schreck, prin. Fax 532-0091

Rock Hill Local SD 1,800/K-12
2325 County Road 26 Unit A 45638 740-532-7030
Lloyd Evans, supt. Fax 532-2092
rockhill.org/
Rock Hill ES 800/K-5
2676 County Road 26 45638 740-532-7016
Fred Evans, prin. Fax 532-7020
Rock Hill MS 400/6-8
2171 County Road 26 45638 740-532-7026
Wes Hairston, prin. Fax 532-7028

St. Lawrence S 100/K-6
305 N 7th St 45638 740-532-5052
James Mains, prin. Fax 532-5082

Jackson, Jackson, Pop. 6,240
Jackson CSD 2,700/K-12
450 Vaughn St 45640 740-286-6442
Phil Howard, supt. Fax 286-6445
www.jcs.k12.oh.us
Jackson MS 600/6-8
21 Tropic St 45640 740-286-7586
Mark Broermann, prin. Fax 286-8637
Jackson Northview ES 200/K-5
11507 Chillicothe Pike 45640 740-286-2390
Scott Lowe, prin. Fax 286-7845
Jackson Southview ES 500/K-5
13842 State Route 93 45640 740-286-1831
Phillip Kuhn, prin. Fax 286-7834
Jackson Westview ES 500/K-5
16349 Beaver Pike 45640 740-286-2790
Deborah Biggs, prin. Fax 286-7831

Jackson Center, Shelby, Pop. 1,459
Jackson Center Local SD 400/PK-12
PO Box 849 45334 937-596-6053
Jerry Harmon, supt. Fax 596-6490
www.jackson-center.k12.oh.us
Jackson Center ES 200/PK-3
PO Box 849 45334 937-596-6053
Ginger Heuker, prin. Fax 596-6490

Jamestown, Greene, Pop. 1,854
Greeneview Local SD 1,500/K-12
4 S Charleston Rd 45335 937-675-2728
Fax 675-6807
www.greeneview.k12.oh.us
Greeneview IS 600/4-8
53 N Limestone St 45335 937-675-9391
Harold Farley, prin. Fax 675-6866
Greeneview PS 400/K-3
51 N Limestone St 45335 937-675-6867
William Hayes, prin. Fax 675-2438

Jefferson, Ashtabula, Pop. 3,514
Jefferson Area Local SD 2,100/K-12
45 E Satin St 44047 440-576-9180
Douglas Hladek, supt. Fax 576-9876
www.jefferson.k12.oh.us/
Jefferson ES 800/K-6
204 W Mulberry St 44047 440-576-2646
Todd Tulino, prin. Fax 576-9876
Other Schools – See Rock Creek

Jenera, Hancock, Pop. 228

Trinity Evangelical S 100/K-8
PO Box 25 45841 419-326-4685
William Hinz, prin. Fax 326-9001

Jeromesville, Ashland, Pop. 485
Hillsdale Local SD 1,100/K-12
485 Township Road 1902 44840 419-368-8231
Joel Roscoe, supt. Fax 368-7504
www.hillsdale.k12.oh.us/
Hillsdale MS 300/5-8
PO Box 57 44840 419-368-4911
Tom Gaus, prin. Fax 368-3613
Other Schools – See Hayesville

Jewett, Harrison, Pop. 795
Harrison Hills CSD
Supt. — See Hopedale
Harrison Jewett ES 400/PK-6
PO Box 336 43986 740-942-7500
G. Edward Kovacik, prin. Fax 942-7504

Johnstown, Licking, Pop. 3,883
Johnstown-Monroe Local SD 1,600/K-12
441 S Main St 43031 740-967-6846
Damien Bawn, supt. Fax 967-1106
www.johnstown.k12.oh.us/
Adams MS 400/6-8
80 W Maple St 43031 740-967-8766
Debbie Seibel, prin. Fax 967-0051
Oregon ES 400/1-3
125 N Oregon St 43031 740-967-5461
Linda Brobeck, prin. Fax 967-4108
Searfoss ES 400/K-K, 4-5
85 W Douglas St 43031 740-967-5456
Janet Smith, prin. Fax 967-1142

Northridge Local SD 1,000/K-12
6097 Johnstown Utica Rd 43031 740-967-6631
John Shepard, supt. Fax 967-5022
northridge.k12.oh.us
Northridge IS 4-5
6066 Johnstown Utica Rd 43031 740-967-1401
Robin Elliott, prin. Fax 967-2140
Northridge MS 400/6-8
6066 Johnstown Utica Rd 43031 740-967-6671
Amy Anderson, prin. Fax 967-7083
Other Schools – See Alexandria

Junction City, Perry, Pop. 858
New Lexington CSD
Supt. — See New Lexington
Junction City ES 400/K-5
PO Box 248 43748 740-987-3751
Janie Halaiko, prin. Fax 987-3752

Kalida, Putnam, Pop. 1,124
Kalida Local SD 600/K-12
PO Box 269 45853 419-532-3534
Don Horstman, supt. Fax 532-2277
www.kalida.k12.oh.us
Kalida ES 300/K-5
PO Box 358 45853 419-532-3845
Karl Lammers, prin. Fax 532-3541

Kelleys Island, Erie, Pop. 384
Kelleys Island Local SD 50/K-12
PO Box 349 43438 419-746-2730
Phil Thiede, supt. Fax 746-2271
www.kelleys.k12.oh.us/
Kelleys Island S 50/K-12
PO Box 349 43438 419-746-2730
Phil Thiede, prin. Fax 746-2271

Kent, Portage, Pop. 28,135
Field Local SD
Supt. — See Mogadore
Brimfield ES 500/K-5
4170 State Route 43 44240 330-673-8581
Pam Way, prin. Fax 677-2514

Kent CSD 3,800/PK-12
321 N Depeyster St 44240 330-673-6515
Joseph Giancola, supt. Fax 677-6166
www.kent.k12.oh.us/
Davey ES 500/PK-5
196 N Prospect St 44240 330-673-6703
Linda Walker, prin. Fax 677-6190
Franklin ES 300/K-5
6662 State Route 43 44240 330-673-6704
Todd Poole, prin. Fax 677-6194
Holden ES 200/K-5
132 W School St 44240 330-673-6737
Julie Troman, prin. Fax 677-6192
Longcoy ES 300/K-5
1069 Elno Ave 44240 330-673-6772
Janice Swan, prin. Fax 677-6198
Stanton MS 800/6-8
1175 Hudson Rd 44240 330-673-6693
Thomas Larkin, prin. Fax 673-1561
Walls ES 300/K-5
900 Doramor St 44240 330-673-6862
Sandra Goodrich, prin. Fax 677-6196

St. Patrick S 300/K-8
127 Portage St 44240 330-673-7232
John Mazan, prin. Fax 678-6612

Kenton, Hardin, Pop. 8,169
Kenton CSD 2,100/PK-12
222 W Carrol St 43326 419-673-0775
Doug Roberts, supt. Fax 673-3180
www.kentoncityschools.org/
Eastcrest ES 100/1-5
409 Madison St 43326 419-675-9101
Lucinda Quinn, prin. Fax 673-7102
Espy ES 200/K-5
520 S Detroit St 43326 419-673-1162
Michael Blechinger, prin. Fax 673-0885
Hardin Central ES 300/1-5
1000 E Columbus St 43326 419-673-7248
Ann Brien, prin. Fax 673-8928
Kenton MS 500/6-8
300 Oriental St 43326 419-673-1237
Steven Ickes, prin. Fax 673-1626
Northwood ES 100/1-5
530 Gilmore St 43326 419-673-9291
Ann Quinn, prin. Fax 675-3376
Westview S 200/PK-K
401 Scott Ave 43326 419-673-4294
Angela Butterman, prin. Fax 675-3350

Kettering, Montgomery, Pop. 55,481
Kettering CSD 7,500/K-12
3750 Far Hills Ave 45429 937-499-1400
Robert Mengerink, supt. Fax 499-1519
www.ketteringschools.org/
Beavertown ES 400/K-5
2700 Wilmington Pike 45419 937-499-1740
Michael Kozarec, prin. Fax 499-1779
Greenmont ES 300/K-5
1 E Wren Cir 45420 937-499-1850
Timothy Johnson, prin. Fax 499-1859
Indian Riffle ES 400/K-5
3090 Glengarry Dr 45420 937-499-1720
Debbie Beiter, prin. Fax 499-1739
Kennedy ES 500/K-5
5030 Polen Dr 45440 937-499-1830
George Caras, prin. Fax 499-1839
Kettering MS 1,000/6-8
3000 Glengarry Dr 45420 937-499-1550
James Justice, prin. Fax 499-1598
Oakview ES 400/K-5
4001 Ackerman Blvd 45429 937-499-1870
Margaret Engelhardt, prin. Fax 499-1885
Orchard Park ES 300/K-5
600 E Dorothy Ln 45419 937-499-1910
David Timpone, prin. Fax 499-1929
Prass ES 300/K-5
2601 Parklawn Dr 45440 937-499-1780
Richard Bowden, prin. Fax 499-1799
Southdale ES 500/K-5
1200 W Dorothy Ln 45409 937-499-1890
Deborah Mears, prin. Fax 499-1909
Van Buren JHS 700/6-8
3775 Shroyer Rd 45429 937-499-1800
Matthew Rugh, prin. Fax 499-1820
Other Schools – See Moraine

Ascension S 400/K-8
2001 Woodman Dr 45420 937-254-5411
Brent Devitt, prin. Fax 254-1150
Montessori Center of South Dayton 100/K-3
2900 Acosta St 45420 937-293-8986
Toby Meikner, prin. Fax 293-8996
St. Albert the Great S 500/PK-8
104 W Dorothy Ln 45429 937-293-9452
Mike Kirry, prin. Fax 293-7525
St. Charles Borromeo S 500/K-8
4600 Ackerman Blvd 45429 937-434-4933
Fran Moore, prin. Fax 434-6692

Kidron, Wayne
Dalton Local SD
Supt. — See Dalton
Kidron ES 100/K-2
PO Box 227 44636 330-857-2781
Pam Domer, prin. Fax 857-4026

Killbuck, Holmes, Pop. 899
West Holmes Local SD
Supt. — See Millersburg
Killbuck ES 300/K-5
299 School St 44637 330-276-2891
David Wade, prin. Fax 276-1382

Kings Mills, Warren
Kings Local SD 3,800/K-12
PO Box 910 45034 513-398-8050
Valerie Browning, supt. Fax 229-7590
www.kingslocal.k12.oh.us
Burns ES 600/K-4
8471 Columbia Rd 45034 513-398-8050
Cheryl Montag, prin. Fax 683-8367
Columbia ES 600/5-6
8263 Columbia Rd 45034 513-398-8050
Gerald Gasper, prin. Fax 459-2961
Kings JHS 600/7-8
5620 Columbia Rd 45034 513-398-8050
James Acton, prin. Fax 459-2951
Kings Mills ES 500/K-4
1780 King Ave 45034 513-398-8050
Peggy Phillips, prin. Fax 398-4863
Other Schools – See Maineville

Kingston, Ross, Pop. 1,037
Logan Elm Local SD
Supt. — See Circleville
Saltcreek ES 300/K-6
13190 State Route 56 45644 740-332-4212
Marsha Waidelich, prin. Fax 332-1751

Kingsville, Ashtabula
Buckeye Local SD
Supt. — See Ashtabula
Kingsville ES 300/K-6
PO Box 17 44048 440-224-0281
Nicholas Orlando, prin. Fax 224-2452

Kinsman, Trumbull
Joseph Badger Local SD 1,100/K-12
7119 State Route 7 44428 330-876-2800
David Bair, supt. Fax 876-2811
www.joseph-badger.k12.oh.us/
Badger ES 400/K-4
7119 State Route 7 44428 330-876-2860
Mary Williams, prin. Fax 876-2861
Badger MS 300/5-8
7119 State Route 7 44428 330-876-2840
Robert Moon, prin. Fax 876-2841

Kirkersville, Licking, Pop. 528
Southwest Licking Local SD
Supt. — See Pataskala
Kirkersville ES 400/1-5
PO Box 401 43033 740-927-7281
Nicole Jiran, prin. Fax 927-4720

Kirtland, Lake, Pop. 7,251
Kirtland Local SD 1,200/K-12
9252 Chillicothe Rd 44094 440-256-3311
Stan Lipinski, supt. Fax 256-3831
www.kirtland.k12.oh.us
Kirtland ES 500/K-5
9140 Chillicothe Rd 44094 440-256-3344
Patrick Willis, prin. Fax 256-1045
Kirtland MS 300/6-8
9152 Chillicothe Rd 44094 440-256-3358
Lynn Campbell, prin. Fax 256-3928

Peaceful Children Montessori S 100/PK-8
8100 Eagle Rd 44094 440-256-1976
Jennifer Massiello, prin. Fax 256-4370

La Grange, Lorain, Pop. 1,551
Keystone Local SD 1,800/K-12
PO Box 65, 440-355-5131
Dr. Gary Friedt, supt. Fax 355-6052
www.keystonelocalschools.org/
Keystone ES 600/K-4
PO Box 65, 440-355-5134
Ryan Coleman, prin. Fax 355-6676
Keystone MS 600/5-8
PO Box 65, 440-355-5133
Timothy Jenkins, prin. Fax 355-6678

Lakeside, Ottawa
Danbury Local SD 600/K-12
9451 E Harbor Rd 43440 419-798-5185
Daniel Parent, supt. Fax 798-2260
www.danbury.k12.oh.us
Danbury ES 300/K-6
9451 E Harbor Rd 43440 419-798-4081
Ross Klima, prin. Fax 798-2261

Lakeville, Holmes
West Holmes Local SD
Supt. — See Millersburg
Lakeville ES 200/3-5
PO Box 68 44638 419-827-2006
Sheila Hanna, prin. Fax 827-2352

Lakewood, Cuyahoga, Pop. 53,244
Lakewood CSD 5,800/K-12
1470 Warren Rd 44107 216-529-4092
Dr. P. Joseph Madak, supt. Fax 228-8327
www.lakewoodcityschools.org/
Emerson ES 700/K-5
13439 Clifton Blvd 44107 216-529-4254
Margaret Seibel, prin. Fax 529-4309
Garfield MS 700/6-8
13114 Detroit Ave 44107 216-529-4241
Mark Walter, prin. Fax 529-4301
Grant ES 400/K-5
1470 Victoria Ave 44107 216-529-4217
Mark Gleichauf, prin. Fax 529-4302
Harding MS 500/6-8
16601 Madison Ave 44107 216-529-4261
Keith Ahern, prin. Fax 529-4708
Harrison ES 100/K-5
2080 Quail St 44107 216-529-4230
Philis Muth, prin. Fax 529-4303
Hayes ES 200/K-5
16401 Delaware Ave 44107 216-529-4228
Robert Curtin, prin. Fax 529-4304
Lincoln ES 400/K-5
15615 Clifton Blvd 44107 216-529-4232
Noreen Hazen, prin. Fax 529-4305
Mann ES 300/K-5
1215 W Clifton Blvd 44107 216-529-4257
Dr. Kathleen McGorray, prin. Fax 529-4307
Roosevelt ES 300/K-5
14237 Athens Ave 44107 216-529-4224
Eileen Griffiths, prin. Fax 529-4308

Holy Family Learning Center 50/PK-PK
14808 Lake Ave 44107 216-521-4352
Sr. Kathleen Ogrin, prin. Fax 521-0515
Lakewood Catholic Academy 600/PK-8
14808 Lake Ave 44107 216-521-0559
Maureen Arbeznik, prin. Fax 521-0515
Lakewood Lutheran S 100/PK-8
1419 Lakeland Ave 44107 216-221-6941
Gary Dittmar, prin. Fax 226-4082
SS. Cyril & Methodius S 200/K-8
1639 Alameda Ave 44107 216-221-9409
William Bistak, prin. Fax 221-8516

Lancaster, Fairfield, Pop. 36,063
Fairfield Union Local SD
Supt. — See Rushville
Fairfield Union JHS 300/7-8
6401 Cincinnati Zanesville 43130 740-536-7846
Dale Ferbrache, prin. Fax 536-7911

Lancaster CSD 5,800/K-12
345 E Mulberry St 43130 740-687-7300
Denise Callihan, supt. Fax 687-7303
www.lancaster.k12.oh.us
Cedar Heights ES 400/K-5
1515 Cedar Hill Rd 43130 740-687-7334
Jeromey Sheets, prin. Fax 687-7203
East ES 400/K-5
751 E Wheeling St 43130 740-687-7338
Nathan Hale, prin. Fax 687-7207
Ewing JHS 600/6-8
825 E Fair Ave 43130 740-687-7347
Steve Poston, prin. Fax 687-3446
Medill ES 300/K-5
1151 James Rd 43130 740-687-7352
Sandra Svoboda, prin. Fax 687-7205
Sanderson ES 300/K-5
1450 Marietta Rd NE 43130 740-687-7354
Carol Spires, prin. Fax 687-7206
Sherman JHS 700/6-8
701 Union St 43130 740-687-7344
Fax 687-3443
South ES 300/K-5
220 E Walnut St 43130 740-687-7340
Robin Cathers, prin. Fax 687-7208
Tallmadge ES 300/K-5
611 Lewis Ave 43130 740-687-7336
Brian Lawson, prin. Fax 687-7204
Tarhe ES 400/K-5
425 Whittier Dr N 43130 740-687-7330
Dustin Knight, prin. Fax 687-7201
West ES 400/K-5
625 Garfield Ave 43130 740-687-7332
Terri Garrett, prin. Fax 687-7202

Fairfield Christian Academy 700/PK-12
1965 N Columbus St 43130 740-654-2889
Kenneth Beck, supt. Fax 654-7689
Faith Academy 100/PK-4
2610 W Fair Ave 43130 740-653-1358
Amy Gulling, admin. Fax 653-3713
Lancaster SDA S 50/K-8
2640 Lncaster Thrnvll Rd NE 43130 740-687-1741
Al Schone, prin.
Redeemer Lutheran S 300/PK-K
1400 Concordia Dr 43130 740-653-9727
Rebecca Daubenmire, prin. Fax 653-1778

St. Bernadette S 200/PK-5
1325 Wheeling Rd NE 43130 740-654-3137
Pamela Eltringham, prin. Fax 654-1602
St. Mary S 500/K-8
309 E Chestnut St 43130 740-654-1632
Carlton Rider, prin. Fax 654-0877

La Rue, Marion, Pop. 735
Elgin Local SD
Supt. — See Marion
Elgin West ES 400/K-6
350 N High St 43332 740-499-3277
Harlan Needham, prin. Fax 499-3610

Latham, Pike
Western Local SD 800/K-12
PO Box 130 45646 740-493-3113
Terry Leeth, supt. Fax 493-2065
www.westernlocalschools.com/
Western ES 500/K-6
PO Box 129 45646 740-493-2881
Beth Alexander, prin. Fax 493-1059

Laurelville, Hocking, Pop. 555
Logan Elm Local SD
Supt. — See Circleville
Laurelville ES 400/K-6
16138 Pike St 43135 740-332-2021
Vicki Scott, prin. Fax 332-1401

Leavittsburg, Trumbull
LaBrae Local SD 1,600/K-12
1001 N Leavitt Rd 44430 330-898-0800
Patrick Guliano, supt. Fax 898-6112
www.labrae.k12.oh.us/
Bascom ES 400/K-2
1015 N Leavitt Rd 44430 330-898-0800
Walter Carpenter, prin. Fax 898-1448
LaBrae IS 400/3-5
1001 N Leavitt Rd 44430 330-898-0800
Milajean Harkabus, prin. Fax 898-7808
LaBrae MS 400/6-8
1001 N Leavitt Rd 44430 330-898-0800
Martin Kelly, prin. Fax 898-7808

Lebanon, Warren, Pop. 19,978
Lebanon CSD 5,300/K-12
700 Holbrook Ave 45036 513-934-5770
Mark North, supt. Fax 932-5906
www.lebanon.k12.oh.us
Berry IS 800/5-6
23 Oakwood Ave 45036 513-934-5700
Mark Graler, prin. Fax 228-1944
Bowman PS 800/1-2
825 Hart Rd 45036 513-934-5800
Dr. Gregg Tracy, prin. Fax 934-2466
Donovan ES 800/3-4
401 Justice Dr 45036 513-934-5400
Clifton Franz, prin. Fax 934-2467
Lebanon JHS 800/7-8
160 Miller Rd 45036 513-934-5300
Ian Frank, prin. Fax 932-9436
Wright ECC 400/K-K
600 S East St 45036 513-934-5460
Kelley Lacey, prin. Fax 934-2412

Lebanon Christian S 400/PK-8
1436 Deerfield Rd 45036 513-932-5590
Rick Milligan, admin. Fax 934-5698
St. Francis De Sales S 200/K-8
20 DeSales Ave Ste A 45036 513-932-6501
Regina Seubert, prin. Fax 932-9919

Leesburg, Highland, Pop. 1,341
Fairfield Local SD 900/K-12
11611 State Route 771 45135 937-780-2221
William Garrett, supt. Fax 780-6900
www.fairfield-highland.k12.oh.us
Fairfield ES 400/K-4
11611 State Route 771 45135 937-780-2988
Carl McCrory, prin. Fax 780-2841
Fairfield MS 300/5-8
11611 State Route 771 45135 937-780-2977
Michael Daye, prin. Fax 780-2841

Lees Creek, Clinton
East Clinton Local SD 1,500/K-12
97 College St 45138 937-584-2461
Gary West, supt. Fax 584-2817
www.east-clinton.k12.oh.us
East Clinton MS 400/6-8
PO Box 19 45138 937-584-9267
Jana Huff-Daye, prin. Fax 584-9558
Other Schools – See New Vienna, Sabina

Leetonia, Columbiana, Pop. 2,043
Leetonia EVD 700/K-12
450 Walnut St 44431 330-427-6594
Robert Mehno, supt. Fax 427-1136
www.leetonia.k12.oh.us
Leetonia ES 300/K-4
450 Walnut St 44431 330-427-6129
Judith Dargay, prin. Fax 427-2549
Leetonia MS 100/5-6
450 Walnut St 44431 330-427-2444
Judith Dargay, prin. Fax 427-2549

Leipsic, Putnam, Pop. 2,232
Leipsic Local SD 700/K-12
232 Oak St 45856 419-943-2165
Alice Dewar, supt. Fax 943-4331
www.lp.noacsc.org
Leipsic ES 300/K-6
232 Oak St 45856 419-943-2163
Richard Bryan, prin. Fax 943-2185

St. Mary S 200/K-8
129 Saint Marys St 45856 419-943-2801
Sr. Mary Ellen Schroeder, prin. Fax 943-2801

Lewisburg, Preble, Pop. 1,784
Tri-County North Local SD 1,100/K-12
PO Box 40 45338 937-962-2671
William Derringer, supt. Fax 962-4731
tricounty.oh.schoolwebpages.com/
Tri-County North ES 400/K-4
PO Box 219 45338 937-962-2673
Dennis Dyer, prin. Fax 962-4731
Tri-County North MS 300/5-8
PO Box 699 45338 937-962-2631
Joseph Finkbine, prin. Fax 833-4860

Lewis Center, Delaware, Pop. 300
Olentangy Local SD 14,500/PK-12
814 Shanahan Rd Ste 100 43035 740-657-4050
Dr. Wade Lucas, supt. Fax 657-4099
www.olentangy.k12.oh.us
Alum Creek ES 600/K-5
2515 Parklawn Dr 43035 740-657-4600
Stephen Sargent, prin. Fax 657-4649
Arrowhead ES 700/PK-5
2385 Hollenback Rd 43035 740-657-4650
Nadine Ross, prin. Fax 657-4699
Glen Oak ES 600/PK-5
7300 Blue Holly Dr 43035 740-657-5500
Susan Staum, prin. Fax 657-5549
Oak Creek ES 600/K-5
1256 Westwood Dr 43035 740-657-4700
Julie Lather, prin. Fax 657-4749
Olentangy Meadows ES 600/K-5
8950 Emerald Hill Dr 43035 740-657-5550
Jennifer Denny, prin. Fax 657-5599
Olentangy Orange MS 900/6-8
2680 E Orange Rd 43035 740-657-5300
Brian Lidle, prin. Fax 657-5399
Olentangy Shanahan MS 900/6-8
814 Shanahan Rd 43035 740-657-4300
Penny Stires, prin. Fax 657-4398
Other Schools – See Galena, Powell

Polaris Christian Academy 100/K-8
2150 E Powell Rd 43035 614-431-6888
Nanci Griffith, prin. Fax 431-0137

Lewistown, Logan
Indian Lake Local SD 1,400/K-12
6210 State Route 235 N 43333 937-686-8601
Dr. William McGlothlin, supt. Fax 686-8421
www.indianlake.k12.oh.us
Indian Lake ES 100/K-4
8770 County Road 91 43333 937-686-7323
Diane Gillespie, prin. Fax 686-0049
Indian Lake MS 600/5-8
8920 County Road 91 43333 937-686-8833
Misha Boyer, prin. Fax 686-8993

Lexington, Richland, Pop. 4,224
Lexington Local SD 2,700/K-12
103 Clever Ln 44904 419-884-2132
James Ziegelhofer, supt. Fax 884-3129
www.lexington.k12.oh.us
Central ES 400/K-4
124 Frederick St 44904 419-884-1308
Kathleen Dinkel, prin. Fax 884-6154
Eastern ES 500/4-6
155 Castor Rd 44904 419-884-3610
Jacque Daup, prin. Fax 884-2987
Lexington JHS 500/7-8
90 Frederick St 44904 419-884-2112
William Ferguson, prin. Fax 884-0134
Western ES 300/K-3
385 W Main St 44904 419-884-2765
Claudia Ruihley, prin. Fax 884-2221

Grace Christian S 100/PK-8
215 W Main St 44904 419-884-1780
Lois Barrett, prin. Fax 884-9612

Liberty Center, Henry, Pop. 1,117
Liberty Center Local SD 1,200/K-12
PO Box 434 43532 419-533-5011
Jack Loudin, supt. Fax 533-5036
www.libertycenter.k12.oh.us/
Liberty Center ES 400/K-4
PO Box 434 43532 419-533-2604
Stephen Seagrave, prin. Fax 533-5036
Liberty Center MS 400/5-8
PO Box 434 43532 419-533-0020
Fax 533-5036

Liberty Twp, Butler
Lakota Local SD 16,400/PK-12
5572 Princeton Rd 45011 513-874-5505
Michael Taylor, supt. Fax 644-1167
www.lakotaonline.com
Cherokee ES 800/2-6
5345 Kyles Station Rd 45011 513-755-8200
Jennifer Forren, prin. Fax 755-6838
Lakota Plains JHS 700/7-8
5500 Princeton Rd 45011 513-644-1130
Michael Holbrook, prin. Fax 644-1135
Liberty ES 100/K-1
6040 Princeton Rd 45011 513-777-6194
Debi LaFrankie, prin. Fax 755-5972
VanGordon ES 700/2-6
6475 Lesourdsville 45011 513-644-1150
Clayton Ash, prin. Fax 644-1160
Other Schools – See Cincinnati, Hamilton, Middletown, West Chester

Lima, Allen, Pop. 38,608
Bath Local SD 2,000/K-12
2650 Bible Rd 45801 419-221-0807
William Lodermeier, supt. Fax 221-0983
www.bathwildcats.org
Bath ES 700/K-4
2501 Slabtown Rd 45801 419-221-1837
Christopher Renner, prin. Fax 221-3937
Bath MS 600/5-8
2700 Bible Rd 45801 419-221-1839
Bradley Clark, prin. Fax 221-2431

Lima CSD 4,800/K-12
515 Calumet Ave 45804 419-996-3400
Karel Oxley, supt. Fax 996-3401
www.limacityschools.org
Freedom ES 300/K-4
575 Calumet Ave 45804 419-996-3380
Julie Stewart, prin. Fax 996-3381
Heritage ES 600/K-4
816 College Ave 45805 419-996-3390
Kevin Fraley, prin. Fax 996-3391
Independence ES 500/K-4
615 Tremont Ave 45801 419-996-3330
Chad Fallis, prin. Fax 996-3331
Liberty ES 300/K-4
338 W Kibby St 45804 419-996-3320
Chandra Nuveman, prin. Fax 996-3321
Lima North MS 500/5-8
1135 N West St 45801 419-996-3100
Mark Vaughn, prin. Fax 996-3101
Lima South MS 400/5-8
755 Saint Johns Ave 45804 419-996-3190
Jean Snyder, prin. Fax 996-3191
Lima West MS 500/5-8
503 N Cable Rd 45805 419-996-3150
Rise Light, prin. Fax 996-3151
Unity ES 300/K-4
925 E 3rd St 45804 419-996-3300
Tricia Winkler, prin. Fax 996-3301

Perry Local SD 800/K-12
2770 E Breese Rd 45806 419-221-2770
Omer Schroeder, supt. Fax 221-2773
www.noacsc.org/allen/pe/index.htm
Perry ES 500/K-6
2770 E Breese Rd 45806 419-221-2771
Kelly Schooler, prin. Fax 221-2773

Shawnee Local SD 2,700/K-12
3255 Zurmehly Rd 45806 419-998-8031
Paul Nardini, supt. Fax 998-8050
www.limashawnee.com
Elmwood ES 600/K-2
4295 Shawnee Rd 45806 419-998-8090
Daniel Vermillion, prin. Fax 998-8110
Maplewood ES 400/3-4
1670 Wonderlick Rd 45805 419-998-8076
James Cypher, prin. Fax 998-8085
Shawnee MS 800/5-8
3235 Zurmehly Rd 45806 419-998-8057
Tony Cox, prin. Fax 222-6572

Liberty Christian S 50/PK-12
801 Bellefontaine Ave 45801 419-229-6266
Nadine Wagner, admin. Fax 229-6266
Lima SDA S 50/K-8
1976 Spencerville Rd 45805 419-227-6385
Elizabeth Hancock, prin.
St. Charles S 500/PK-8
2175 W Elm St 45805 419-222-2536
Thomas Huffman, prin. Fax 222-8720
St. Gerard S 200/PK-8
1311 N Main St 45801 419-222-0431
Mary Camp, prin. Fax 224-6580
St. Rose of Lima S 100/K-8
523 N West St 45801 419-223-6361
Patricia Shanahan, prin. Fax 222-2032
Temple Christian S 200/K-12
982 Brower Rd 45801 419-227-1644
Dr. Kenneth Grunden, supt. Fax 227-6635

Lindsey, Sandusky, Pop. 485
Fremont CSD
Supt. — See Fremont
Washington ES 100/K-6
109 W Lincoln St 43442 419-665-2327
Dwayne Arnold, prin. Fax 665-2241

Lisbon, Columbiana, Pop. 3,082
Beaver Local SD 2,400/K-12
13093 State Route 7 44432 330-385-6831
Dr. Sandra DiBacco, supt. Fax 386-8711
www.beaver.k12.oh.us/
Beaver Local MS 800/5-8
13052 State Route 7 44432 330-386-8707
Thomas Sapp, prin. Fax 382-0317
West Point ES 200/K-4
13360 W Point Rd 44432 330-385-6406
Elizabeth Scott, prin. Fax 385-6407
Other Schools – See East Liverpool, Rogers

Lisbon EVD 1,100/K-12
317 N Market St 44432 330-424-7714
Donald Thompson, supt. Fax 424-0135
www.lisbon.k12.oh.us/
McKinley ES 500/K-5
441 E Chestnut St 44432 330-424-9869
Helen Otto, prin. Fax 424-7750

Lithopolis, Fairfield, Pop. 785
Bloom-Carroll Local SD
Supt. — See Carroll
Bloom ES 300/K-5
PO Box 208 43136 614-837-4044
Vicky Pease, prin. Fax 837-8144

Little Hocking, Washington
Warren Local SD
Supt. — See Vincent
Little Hocking S 400/K-8
95 Federal Rd 45742 740-989-2000
Thomas Ellsworth, prin. Fax 989-2585

Lockbourne, Franklin, Pop. 267
Hamilton Local SD
Supt. — See Columbus

Hamilton ES 500/PK-3
5050 Parsons Ave 43137 614-491-1086
Ann Marie Carley, prin. Fax 492-1499
Hamilton IS 700/4-6
5132 Parsons Ave 43137 614-492-1047
James Meade, prin. Fax 492-1059
Hamilton MS 500/7-8
5150 Parsons Ave 43137 614-491-3468
James Miller, prin. Fax 491-0260

Lockland, Hamilton, Pop. 3,393
Lockland Local SD
Supt. — See Cincinnati
Lockland ES 300/K-6
200 N Cooper Ave 45215 513-563-5000
Michele Kipp, prin. Fax 563-9611
Lockland Local MS 6-8
249 W Forrer St 45215 513-563-5000
John Eckert, prin.

Lodi, Medina, Pop. 3,287
Cloverleaf Local SD 3,300/PK-12
8525 Friendsville Rd 44254 330-948-2500
Daryl Kubilus, supt. Fax 948-1034
www.cls.k12.oh.us
Lodi ES 600/PK-2
301 Mill St 44254 330-948-2286
Karen Martin, prin. Fax 948-7050
Other Schools – See Seville, Westfield Center

Logan, Hocking, Pop. 7,090
Logan-Hocking Local SD 4,000/PK-12
2019 E Front St 43138 740-385-8517
Stephen Stirn, supt. Fax 385-3683
www.loganhocking.k12.oh.us
Central IS 200/4-5
680 W Hunter St 43138 740-385-3092
Andrew Potter, prin. Fax 385-5629
Central PS 300/PK-3
501 E Main St 43138 740-385-4083
Courtney Spatar, prin. Fax 385-5588
Chieftain ES 400/K-5
28296 Chieftain Dr 43138 740-385-1171
Sharon Elder, prin. Fax 380-6684
Green ES 400/K-5
15663 State Route 595 43138 740-385-7789
Rob Ramage, prin. Fax 385-5321
Hocking Hills ES 300/K-5
19197 State Route 664 S 43138 740-385-7071
Colleen Hockman, prin. Fax 380-6695
Logan-Hocking MS 900/6-8
1 Middleschool Dr 43138 740-385-8764
Myles Kiphen, prin. Fax 385-9547
Other Schools – See Union Furnace

Logan Christian S 100/PK-6
650 Walhonding Ave 43138 740-385-5360
Lou Ann Jones, prin. Fax 385-5360
St. John S 100/PK-6
321 N Market St 43138 740-385-2767
Erin Schornack, prin. Fax 385-9727

London, Madison, Pop. 9,396
Jonathan Alder Local SD
Supt. — See Plain City
Monroe ES 300/PK-4
5000 State Route 38 NW 43140 614-873-8503
John Lanka, prin. Fax 873-0685

London CSD 1,800/PK-12
60 S Walnut St 43140 740-852-5700
Steven Allen, supt. Fax 852-7360
www.london.k12.oh.us/
London ES 800/PK-5
380 Elm St 43140 740-845-3272
Carol Daniels, prin. Fax 845-3281
London MS 6th Grade 6-6
20 S Walnut St 43140 740-852-5700
Darren Fillman, prin. Fax 845-2870
London MS 300/7-8
60 S Walnut St 43140 740-852-5700
Darren Fillman, prin. Fax 845-2869

Madison-Plains Local SD 1,400/K-12
55 Linson Rd 43140 740-852-3712
Bernie Hall, supt. Fax 852-5895
www.mplsd.org/
Madison-Plains MS 400/6-8
9940 State Route 38 SW 43140 740-852-1707
Jeffrey Beane, prin. Fax 852-6351
Madison Rural ES 200/K-5
375 Old Xenia Rd SE 43140 740-852-2806
Linda Nier, prin. Fax 852-2124
Other Schools – See Mount Sterling, Sedalia

St. Patrick S 200/PK-8
226 Elm St 43140 740-852-0161
Jacob Froning Ph.D., prin. Fax 852-0602

Lorain, Lorain, Pop. 67,820
Clearview Local SD 1,600/K-12
4700 Broadway 44052 440-233-5412
Rick Buckosh, supt. Fax 233-6034
www.clearview.k12.oh.us/
Durling MS 500/5-8
100 N Ridge Rd W 44053 440-233-6869
Jerome Davis, prin. Fax 233-6204
Vincent ES 600/K-4
2303 N Ridge Rd E 44055 440-233-7113
Virginia Fitch, prin. Fax 233-7114

Lorain CSD 6,600/PK-12
2350 Pole Ave 44052 440-233-2271
Dr. Cheryl Atkinson, supt. Fax 282-9151
www.lorainschools.org
Garfield ES 300/K-5
200 W 31st St 44055 440-246-1114
Carol Zacovic, prin. Fax 246-1121
Irving ES 300/K-6
1110 W 4th St 44052 440-244-3171
Leila Flores, prin. Fax 244-0038
Jacinto ES 400/K-6
2515 Marshall Ave 44052 440-960-5800
Iris Morales, prin. Fax 960-5810
Lakeview ES 500/PK-6
1953 W 11th St 44052 440-245-6315
Dr. Heather Kantola, prin. Fax 245-4251
Larkmoor ES 400/K-6
1201 Nebraska Ave 44052 440-288-3203
David Hall, prin. Fax 288-5017
Longfellow MS 400/6-8
305 Louisiana Ave 44052 440-288-1025
Tom Roth, prin. Fax 288-1116
Lowell ES 500/K-6
3200 Clinton Ave 44055 440-277-8157
Kathryn Lantz, prin. Fax 277-0152
Masson ES, 1800 W 40th St 44053 200/PK-2
Marcy Smith, prin. 440-282-5412
Morrison ES 300/3-5
1830 W 40th St 44053 440-960-7008
Fatima Kurianowicz, prin. Fax 960-7015
Palm ES, 3330 Palm Ave 44055 300/K-6
Pam Szegedy, prin. 440-240-1439
Rice ES 400/3-5
4500 Tacoma Ave 44055 440-240-1220
Alexis Hayden, prin. Fax 240-1221
Washington ES 400/K-5
1025 W 23rd St 44052 440-246-2187
Michelle Spotts, prin. Fax 246-4920
Whittier MS 500/6-8
3201 Seneca Ave 44055 440-277-7261
Aliceson Humphries, prin. Fax 277-5566
Wilson MS 600/6-8
602 Washington Ave 44052 440-246-1020
Sam Newsome, prin. Fax 246-0180

Sheffield-Sheffield Lake CSD
Supt. — See Sheffield Lake
Sheffield MS 500/6-8
1919 Harris Rd 44054 440-949-4228
Michael Cook, prin. Fax 949-4204

St. Anthony of Padua S 200/PK-8
1339 E Erie Ave 44052 440-288-2155
Daniel Humphrey, prin. Fax 288-2159
St. Peter S 400/PK-8
3601 Oberlin Ave 44053 440-282-9909
Emily Fabanich, prin. Fax 282-9320

Lore City, Guernsey, Pop. 305
East Guernsey Local SD
Supt. — See Old Washington
Buckeye Trail ES 500/K-5
65553 Wintergreen Rd 43755 740-489-5100
Marcia Lucas, prin. Fax 489-9049
Buckeye Trail MS 300/6-8
65553 Wintergreen Rd 43755 740-489-5100
Lonnie Caudill, prin. Fax 489-9049

Loudonville, Ashland, Pop. 2,982
Loudonville-Perrysville EVD 1,300/K-12
210 E Main St 44842 419-994-3912
John Miller, supt. Fax 994-3912
www.lpschools.k12.oh.us
Budd ES 300/4-6
210 E Main St 44842 419-994-3327
Steve Orchard, prin. Fax 994-7003
McMullen ES 400/K-3
224 E Bustle St 44842 419-994-3913
Sally Warbel, prin. Fax 994-5116
Other Schools – See Perrysville

Louisville, Stark, Pop. 9,367
Louisville CSD 3,300/K-12
504 E Main St 44641 330-875-1666
David Redd, supt. Fax 875-7603
www.leopard.sparcc.org
Fairhope ES 300/K-5
4001 Addison Ave 44641 330-875-2776
Michele Shaffer, prin. Fax 875-7612
Louisville ES 500/K-5
1025 Washington Ave 44641 330-875-1177
Lee Smith, prin. Fax 875-7608
Louisville MS 800/6-8
1300 S Chapel St 44641 330-875-5597
Jason Rimmele, prin. Fax 875-7620
North Nimishillen ES 400/K-5
7337 Easton St 44641 330-875-2661
Jason Orin, prin. Fax 875-7614
Pleasant Grove ES 300/K-5
9955 Louisville St 44641 330-875-2530
Thomas McAlister, prin. Fax 275-7610

Marlington Local SD
Supt. — See Alliance
Marlboro ES 300/K-5
8131 Edison St 44641 330-935-2469
Cyndee Farrell, prin. Fax 935-2155

Good Shepherd S 50/1-12
8700 Edison St 44641 330-935-0623
Rev. Gary Spencer, admin. Fax 935-0433
St. Louis S 100/K-8
214 N Chapel St 44641 330-875-1467
Sr. Carole Von Buelow, prin. Fax 875-2511

Loveland, Hamilton, Pop. 11,219
Loveland CSD 4,600/PK-12
757 S Lebanon Rd 45140 513-683-5600
Kevin Boys Ed.D., supt. Fax 683-5697
www.lovelandschools.org/
Loveland ECC 500/PK-K
6740 Loveland Miamiville Rd 45140 513-683-4200
Kyle Bush, prin. Fax 677-7960
Loveland ES 700/3-4
600 Loveland Madeira Rd 45140 513-683-4333
Douglas Savage, prin. Fax 677-7932
Loveland IS 700/5-6
757 S Lebanon Rd 45140 513-774-7000
Chad Hilliker, prin. Fax 677-7978
Loveland MS 700/7-8
801 S Lebanon Rd 45140 513-683-3100
Erica Kramer, prin. Fax 677-7986
Loveland PS 600/1-2
550 Loveland Madeira Rd 45140 513-683-3101
Douglas Savage, prin. Fax 677-7922

Milford EVD
Supt. — See Milford
McCormick ES 600/K-6
751 Loveland Miamiville Rd 45140 513-575-0190
Donald Baker, prin. Fax 575-4019

Sycamore Community CSD
Supt. — See Cincinnati
Symmes ES 400/K-4
11820 Enyart Rd 45140 513-686-1740
Anne Van Kirk, prin. Fax 677-7861

Childrens Meeting House Montessori S 200/PK-6
927 OBannonville Rd 45140 513-683-4757
Karen Kissell, prin. Fax 697-4191
St. Columban S 700/K-8
896 Oakland Rd 45140 513-683-7903
Joann Rhoten, prin. Fax 683-7904
St. Margaret of York S 700/K-8
9495 Columbia Rd 45140 513-683-9793
Nancy Shula, prin. Fax 683-7101

Lowell, Washington, Pop. 602
Fort Frye Local SD
Supt. — See Beverly
Lowell ES 200/K-6
305 Market St 45744 740-896-2523
Patrick Taylor, prin. Fax 896-3425

Lowellville, Mahoning, Pop. 1,200
Lowellville Local SD 700/K-12
52 Rocket Pl 44436 330-536-6318
Rocco Nero, supt. Fax 536-8221
www.lowellville.k12.oh.us/
North Side ES 300/K-6
52 Rocket Pl 44436 330-536-8426
Samuel Ramunno, prin. Fax 536-8468

Lower Salem, Washington, Pop. 104
Fort Frye Local SD
Supt. — See Beverly
Salem-Liberty ES 200/K-6
10930 State Route 821 45745 740-585-2252
Patrick Taylor, prin. Fax 585-2252

Lucas, Richland, Pop. 608
Lucas Local SD 600/K-12
84 Lucas North Rd 44843 419-892-2338
Steven Dickerson, supt. Fax 892-1138
www.lucascubs.org
Lucas ES 300/K-5
84 Lucas North Rd 44843 419-892-2338
Tom Barcroft, prin. Fax 892-1138
Lucas Heritage MS 100/6-7
80 Lucas North Rd 44843 419-892-2338
Tom Barcroft, prin. Fax 892-1138

Lucasville, Scioto, Pop. 1,575
Valley Local SD 1,200/K-12
1821 State Route 728 45648 740-259-3115
Eugene Thomas, supt. Fax 259-2314
www.valleyls.org/district/index.php
Valley ES 400/K-4
1821A State Route 728 45648 740-259-2611
Paul Alderfer, prin. Fax 259-3822
Valley MS, 393 Indian Dr 45648 400/5-8
Lisa Harley, prin. 740-259-2651

Luckey, Wood, Pop. 988
Eastwood Local SD
Supt. — See Pemberville
Luckey ES 200/K-5
524 Krotzer Ave 43443 419-833-2821
Joe Morgan, prin. Fax 833-2660

Lynchburg, Highland, Pop. 1,432
Lynchburg-Clay Local SD 1,300/K-12
PO Box 515 45142 937-364-2338
Gregory Hawk, supt. Fax 364-2339
www.lynchclay.k12.oh.us
Lynchburg-Clay ES 600/K-5
6760 State Route 134 45142 937-364-9119
Joni Minton, prin. Fax 364-8119
Lynchburg-Clay MS 300/6-8
8250 State Route 134 45142 937-364-2811
Eric Magee, prin. Fax 364-2159

Lyndhurst, Cuyahoga, Pop. 14,450
South Euclid-Lyndhurst CSD 3,700/K-12
5044 Mayfield Rd 44124 216-691-2000
William Zelei, supt. Fax 691-2033
www.sel.k12.oh.us
Memorial JHS 700/7-8
1250 Professor Rd 44124 216-691-2140
Lori Sandel, prin. Fax 691-2159
Sunview ES 200/K-3
5520 Meadow Wood Blvd 44124 216-691-2225
Diane Wieland, prin. Fax 691-2226
Other Schools – See South Euclid

Hawken S 500/PK-8
5000 Clubside Rd 44124 440-423-4446
D. Scott Looney, hdmstr. Fax 423-2123
St. Clare S 200/PK-8
5655 Mayfield Rd 44124 440-449-4242
Frank Przybojewski, prin. Fax 449-1497

Mc Arthur, Vinton, Pop. 1,645
Vinton County Local SD 2,200/PK-12
307 W High St 45651 740-596-5218
John Simmons, supt. Fax 596-3142

Central ES 400/PK-5
507 Jefferson Ave 45651 740-596-4386
Terri Snider-Boring, prin. Fax 596-4027
Vinton County MS 400/6-8
63780 Locker Plant Rd 45651 740-596-5243
Dee Caudill, prin. Fax 596-3815
West ES 400/PK-5
57750 US Highway 50 45651 740-596-5236
Rick Brooks, prin. Fax 596-5237
Other Schools – See Hamden

Mc Comb, Hancock, Pop. 1,632
Mc Comb Local SD 700/K-12
PO Box 877 45858 419-293-3979
Michael Lamb, supt. Fax 293-2412
www.noacsc.org/hancock/mb
Mc Comb Local ES 300/K-5
PO Box 877 45858 419-293-3286
Teresa Kozarec, prin. Fax 293-2412
Other Schools – See Hoytville

Mc Connelsville, Morgan, Pop. 1,829
Morgan Local SD 2,200/K-12
PO Box 509 43756 740-962-2782
Lori Snyder-Lowe, supt. Fax 962-4931
www.mlsd.k12.oh.us/
East ES 300/K-6
4265 N State Route 376 NW 43756 740-962-3361
Susan Troutner, prin. Fax 962-6804
Morgan JHS 300/7-8
820 Junior Raider Dr 43756 740-962-2833
Timothy Hopkins, prin. Fax 962-3389
Other Schools – See Malta, Stockport

Mc Dermott, Scioto
Northwest Local SD 1,700/K-12
800 Mohawk Dr 45652 740-259-5558
Norman Crabtree, supt. Fax 259-3476
www.northwest.k12.oh.us
Northwest ES 800/K-5
4738 Henley Deemer Rd 45652 740-259-2250
Brian Martin, prin. Fax 259-5442
Northwest MS 400/6-8
692 Mohawk Dr 45652 740-259-2528
Gregory Tipton, prin. Fax 259-5731

Mc Donald, Trumbull, Pop. 3,501
McDonald Local SD 900/K-12
600 Iowa Ave 44437 330-530-8051
Michael Wasser, supt. Fax 530-7041
www.mcdonald.k12.oh.us
Roosevelt ES 500/K-6
410 W 7th St 44437 330-530-8051
Anthony Russo, prin. Fax 530-7033

Macedonia, Summit, Pop. 10,314
Nordonia Hills CSD
Supt. — See Northfield
Ledgeview ES 600/K-4
9130 Shepard Rd 44056 330-467-0583
Donna Bambic, prin. Fax 468-4647

Mc Guffey, Hardin, Pop. 572
Upper Scioto Valley Local SD 800/K-12
PO Box 305 45859 419-757-3231
Rick Rolston Ed.D., supt. Fax 757-0135
usv.k12.oh.us/
Upper Scioto Valley ES 300/K-5
PO Box 305 45859 419-757-3231
Melanie Nixon, prin. Fax 757-0135
Upper Scioto Valley MS 200/6-8
PO Box 305 45859 419-757-3231
Craig Hurley, prin. Fax 757-0135

Madison, Lake, Pop. 3,070
Madison Local SD 3,500/K-12
6741 N Ridge Rd 44057 440-428-2166
Dr. Roger Goudy, supt. Fax 946-6472
www.madisonschools.net/
Kimball ES 500/K-5
94 River St 44057 440-428-5121
David DeLong, prin. Fax 428-8438
Madison MS 800/6-8
1941 Red Bird Rd 44057 440-428-1196
Thomas Brady, prin. Fax 428-9389
North Madison ES 500/K-5
6735 N Ridge Rd 44057 440-428-2155
Sally Rogus, prin. Fax 428-9382
Red Bird ES 500/K-5
1956 Red Bird Rd 44057 440-428-2151
DeWayne Nicholes, prin. Fax 428-9384

Magnolia, Stark, Pop. 935
Sandy Valley Local SD 700/K-12
5362 State Route 183 NE 44643 330-866-3339
David Janofa, supt. Fax 866-5238
cardweb.stark.k12.oh.us/
Sandy Valley ES K-5
5018 State Route 183 NE 44643 330-866-9225
Mark Yocum, prin. Fax 866-2572

Maineville, Warren, Pop. 1,011
Kings Local SD
Supt. — See Kings Mills
South Lebanon ES 400/K-4
50 Ridgeview Ln 45039 513-398-8050
Randy Willis, prin. Fax 494-1469

Little Miami Local SD
Supt. — See Morrow
Hamilton-Maineville ES 500/1-3
373 E Foster Maineville Rd 45039 513-899-4760
Regina Morgan, prin. Fax 683-3879
Little Miami IS, 7247 Zoar Rd 45039 300/3-5
Rom Turner, prin. 513-899-2264

Malinta, Henry, Pop. 286
Patrick Henry Local SD
Supt. — See Hamler
Malinta-Grelton ES 100/3-4
PO Box 87 43535 419-256-7222
Larry Long, prin. Fax 256-6582

Malta, Morgan, Pop. 680
Morgan Local SD
Supt. — See Mc Connelsville
West ES 400/K-6
9675 State Route 37 43758 740-342-4873
Sherry Poling, prin. Fax 342-7326

Malvern, Carroll, Pop. 1,229
Brown Local SD 700/K-12
401 W Main St 44644 330-863-1170
Connie Griffin, supt. Fax 863-1172
www.hornet.sparcc.org
Malvern ES 300/K-5
401 W Main St 44644 330-863-1355
Matthew Rodriguez, prin. Fax 863-1915
Malvern MS 200/6-8
401 W Main St 44644 330-863-1355
Jane Swinderman, prin. Fax 863-1915

Manchester, Adams, Pop. 2,082
Manchester Local SD 800/K-12
130 Wayne Frye Dr 45144 937-549-4777
Robert Ralstin, supt. Fax 549-4744
www.manchester.k12.oh.us/
Manchester ES 500/K-6
130 Wayne Frye Dr 45144 937-549-4777
William Nichols, prin. Fax 549-3554

Mansfield, Richland, Pop. 50,615
Madison Local SD 2,900/PK-12
1379 Grace St 44905 419-589-2600
Lee Kaple, supt. Fax 589-3653
www.mlsd.net/
Eastview ES 400/K-6
1262 Eastview Dr 44905 419-589-7335
Tim Rupert, prin. Fax 589-3031
Madison JHS 500/7-8
690 Ashland Rd 44905 419-522-0471
Scott Kullman, prin. Fax 522-1463
Madison South ES 600/PK-6
700 S Illinois Ave 44907 419-522-4319
Michael Marshall, prin. Fax 526-2911
Mifflin ES 400/K-6
441 Reed Rd 44903 419-589-6517
Martin Breitinger, prin. Fax 589-6659
Wooster Heights ES 300/K-6
1419 Grace St 44905 419-589-5963
Amy Parr, prin. Fax 589-5963

Mansfield CSD 3,000/PK-12
PO Box 1448 44901 419-525-6400
Dr. Lloyd Martin, supt. Fax 525-6415
www.tygerpride.com
Brinkerhoff IS 100/4-6
240 Euclid Ave 44903 419-525-6321
Barbara Gerhardt, prin. Fax 525-6386
Hedges IS 50/4-6
176 Hedges St 44902 419-525-6317
Gregory Bob, prin. Fax 525-6316
Malabar MS 400/7-8
205 W Cook Rd 44907 419-525-6374
Stacey Cooper, prin. Fax 525-6376
Newman ES 200/PK-3
457 Central Ave 44905 419-525-6315
Alicia Hinson, prin. Fax 525-6314
Prospect ES 200/PK-3
485 Gilbert Ave 44907 419-525-6313
Robert Singleton, prin. Fax 525-6312
Raemelton ES PK-3
856 W Cook Rd 44907 419-525-6378
Jody Nash, prin. Fax 525-6322
Sherman ES 300/PK-3
1138 Springmill St 44906 419-525-6337
Andrea Moyer, prin. Fax 525-6340
Springmill IS 100/4-6
1200 Nestor Dr 44906 419-525-6307
Lisa Brown, prin. Fax 525-6306
Woodland ES 200/PK-3
460 Davis Rd 44907 419-525-6325
Stephen Rizzo, prin. Fax 525-6392

Discovery S 200/PK-8
855 Millsboro Rd 44903 419-756-8880
Lisa Cook, prin. Fax 756-7479
Mansfield Christian S 600/PK-12
500 Logan Rd 44907 419-756-5651
Dr. Cy Smith, supt. Fax 756-7470
Mansfield SDA S 50/K-8
1040 W Cook Rd 44906 419-756-9947
Dallas Melashenko, prin.
St. Mary S 200/PK-8
1630 Ashland Rd 44905 419-589-2114
Roger Harraman, prin. Fax 589-7085
St. Peter S 400/PK-8
63 S Mulberry St 44902 419-524-3351
Jim Smith, prin. Fax 524-3366
Temple Christian S 200/K-12
752 Stewart Rd N 44905 419-589-9707
Dave Cook, prin. Fax 589-7213

Mantua, Portage, Pop. 1,026
Crestwood Local SD 2,500/K-12
4565 W Prospect St 44255 330-274-8511
Joseph Iacano, supt. Fax 274-3710
www.crestwood.sparcc.org/
Crestwood IS 500/3-5
11260 Bowen Rd 44255 330-422-3103
Patricia Dimaso, prin. Fax 274-3825
Crestwood MS 600/6-8
10880 John Edward Dr 44255 330-274-2249
Andrew Hill, prin. Fax 274-3705
Crestwood PS 400/K-2
11256 Bowen Rd 44255 330-422-3104
Thomas Rauber, prin. Fax 274-3824

St. Joseph S 100/K-8
11045 Saint Joseph Blvd 44255 330-274-2268
Beth Frank, prin. Fax 274-2269

Maple Heights, Cuyahoga, Pop. 24,739
Maple Heights CSD 3,700/PK-12
14605 Granger Rd 44137 216-587-6100
Dr. Charles Keenan, supt. Fax 518-2674
www.mapleschools.com/
Dunham ES 300/PK-PK, 6-
5965 Dunham Rd 44137 216-587-6125
Zelina Pames, prin. Fax 587-6497
Milkovich MS 700/7-8
5460 West Blvd 44137 216-587-3200
Tracy Williams, prin. Fax 587-6166
Raymond ES 500/K-1
18500 Raymond St 44137 216-587-6135
Tara Scott, prin. Fax 518-2685
Rockside ES 500/2-3
5740 Lawn Ave 44137 216-587-6140
Alicia Lenczewski, prin. Fax 475-1660
Stafford ES 500/4-5
19800 Stafford Ave 44137 216-587-6145
Susan Harvey, prin. Fax 587-6148

St. Martin of Tours S 100/K-8
14600 Turney Rd 44137 216-475-3633
James King, prin. Fax 475-2484

Marengo, Morrow, Pop. 314
Highland Local SD 1,800/K-12
6506 State Route 229 43334 419-768-2206
Timothy Hilborn, supt. Fax 768-3115
www.highland.k12.oh.us/
Highland West ES 300/K-5
19 West St 43334 419-253-2371
Shawn Winkelfoos, prin. Fax 253-3691
Other Schools – See Chesterville, Sparta

Maria Stein, Mercer
Marion Local SD 900/K-12
7956 State Route 119 45860 419-925-4294
Carl Metzger, supt. Fax 925-0212
marionlocal.k12.oh.us/
Marion S 600/K-8
7956 State Route 119 45860 419-925-4595
Karen Post, prin. Fax 925-5199

Marietta, Washington, Pop. 14,270
Frontier Local SD
Supt. — See New Matamoras
Lawrence S 100/K-8
14800 State Route 26 45750 740-473-2635
William Creighton, prin. Fax 473-2669

Marietta CSD 3,000/K-12
111 Academy Dr 45750 740-374-6500
Herb Young, supt. Fax 374-6506
mariettacityschools.k12.oh.us
Harmar ES 300/K-5
100 Fort Sq 45750 740-374-6510
Cheryl Cook, prin. Fax 376-2465
Marietta MS 700/6-8
242 N 7th St 45750 740-374-6530
William Hampton, prin. Fax 374-6531
Phillips ES 400/K-5
300 Pike St 45750 740-374-6514
Stephen Arnold, prin. Fax 374-6515
Putnam ES 300/K-5
598 Masonic Park Rd 45750 740-374-6516
Joseph Finley, prin. Fax 374-6517
Washington ES 400/K-5
401 Washington St 45750 740-374-6520
D. Scott Kratche, prin. Fax 374-6521

Warren Local SD
Supt. — See Vincent
Warren S 500/K-8
16855 State Route 550 45750 740-373-4937
Shirley Cox, prin. Fax 373-5909

St. John S 100/PK-8
17654 State Route 676 45750 740-896-2697
Jane Hofbauer, prin. Fax 896-2555
St. Mary S 200/PK-8
320 Marion St 45750 740-374-8181
Rita Angel, prin. Fax 374-8602

Marion, Marion, Pop. 36,494
Elgin Local SD 1,600/K-12
4616 Larue Prospect Rd W 43302 740-382-1101
Doug Ute, supt. Fax 382-1672
www.elgin.k12.oh.us
Other Schools – See Green Camp, La Rue, Prospect

Marion CSD 4,900/K-12
910 E Church St 43302 740-387-3300
Dr. James Barney, supt. Fax 223-4400
www.marioncityschools.org/
Garfield ES 300/K-5
1170 Brookside Rd 43302 740-223-4444
Jeff Berringer, prin. Fax 223-4485
Grant MS 1,100/6-8
420 Presidential Dr 43302 740-223-4900
Les Ryle, prin. Fax 223-4820
Harrison ES 300/K-5
625 Brightwood Dr 43302 740-223-4999
Marianne Bailey, prin. Fax 223-4990
Hayes ES 300/K-5
750 Silver St 43302 740-223-4950
William Glenn, prin. Fax 223-4960
McKinley ES 400/K-5
925 Chatfield Rd 43302 740-223-4600
Fredrick Saull, prin. Fax 223-4574
Taft ES 500/K-5
1000 Robinson St 43302 740-223-4500
Sean Smith, prin. Fax 223-4499

Washington ES 400/K-5
400 Pennsylvania Ave 43302 740-223-3883
Dave Hamrick, prin. Fax 223-3726

Pleasant Local SD 1,400/K-12
1107 Owens Rd W 43302 740-389-4476
Steve Larcomb, supt. Fax 389-6985
www.pleasant.treca.org/index.html
Pleasant ES 600/K-5
1105 Owens Rd W 43302 740-389-4815
Shelly Dason, prin. Fax 389-5063
Pleasant MS 400/6-8
3507 Smeltzer Rd 43302 740-389-5167
Lane Warner, prin. Fax 389-5111

River Valley Local SD
Supt. — See Caledonia
Heritage ES 500/K-5
720 Columbus Sandusky Rd S 43302 740-725-5500
Craig Lautenschleger, prin. Fax 725-5599

St. Mary S 200/PK-6
274 N Prospect St 43302 740-382-1607
Bob Rush, prin. Fax 382-6577

Marshallville, Wayne, Pop. 817
Green Local SD
Supt. — See Smithville
Marshallville ES 200/K-4
5 Chestnut St 44645 330-855-2471
Laurie Parrish-Storm, prin. Fax 855-2949

Martins Ferry, Belmont, Pop. 6,860
Martins Ferry CSD 1,200/K-12
5001 Ayers Lime Stone Rd 43935 740-633-1732
Nick Stankovich, supt. Fax 633-5666
www.mfcsd.k12.oh.us
Ayers ES 200/K-4
5002 Ayers Lime Stone Rd 43935 740-635-2444
Sue Ferrelli, prin. Fax 635-3108
Martins Ferry MS 300/5-7
5000 Ayers Lime Stone Rd 43935 740-633-9741
Mike Delatore, prin. Fax 635-6107

Martins Ferry Christian S 100/K-7
710 S Zane Hwy 43935 740-633-0199
Becky Hill, admin. Fax 633-0974
St. Mary Central S 100/PK-8
24 N 4th St 43935 740-633-5424
Mary Nichelson, prin. Fax 633-5462

Marysville, Union, Pop. 17,483
Marysville EVD 5,200/K-12
1000 Edgewood Dr 43040 937-644-8105
Larry Zimmerman, supt. Fax 644-1849
www.marysville.k12.oh.us
Bunsold MS 800/7-8
14198 State Route 4 43040 937-642-1721
Kathy McKinniss, prin. Fax 642-2170
Creekview IS 800/5-6
2000 Creekview Dr 43040 937-642-1154
Tim Kannally, prin. Fax 642-3749
Edgewood ES 500/K-4
203 Grove St 43040 937-642-7801
Colene Thomas, prin. Fax 642-1854
Mill Valley ES 500/K-4
633 Mill Wood Blvd 43040 937-642-3822
Greg Casto, prin. Fax 642-5526
Navin ES 500/K-4
16265 County Home Rd 43040 937-578-0138
Leanne Katterheinrich, prin. Fax 578-0198
Northwood ES 300/K-4
1000 Edgewood Dr 43040 937-644-8106
Melissa Hackett, prin. Fax 644-8251
Other Schools – See Raymond

Christian Academy 50/K-12
1003 N Maple St 43040 937-644-0911
Donna Moceri, prin. Fax 644-0911
St. John Lutheran S 200/K-8
12809 State Route 736 43040 937-644-5540
Royce Hartmann, prin. Fax 644-1086
Trinity Lutheran S 300/PK-6
220 S Walnut St 43040 937-642-1726
Cathy McNabb, prin. Fax 642-1875

Mason, Warren, Pop. 28,847
Mason CSD 10,400/PK-12
211 N East St 45040 513-398-0474
Kevin Bright, supt. Fax 398-4554
www.masonohioschools.com
Mason ECC 1,900/PK-1
4631 Hickory Woods Ln 45040 513-398-3741
Mike Zimmermann, prin. Fax 398-2169
Mason Heights ES 800/2-3
200 Northcrest Dr 45040 513-398-8866
Eric Messer, prin. Fax 398-9472
Mason IS Campus 2,500/4-6
6307 S Mason Montgomery Rd 45040 513-459-2850
Greg Sears, prin. Fax 459-2874
Mason MS 1,500/7-8
6370 S Mason Montgomery Rd 45040 513-398-9035
Tonya McCall, prin. Fax 459-0904
Western Row ES 900/2-3
755 Western Row Rd 45040 513-398-5821
Joe Norton, prin. Fax 398-1072

King of Kings Lutheran S 200/PK-K
3621 Socialville Foster Rd 45040 513-398-6089
Gilbert Schepmann, dir. Fax 459-9896
Liberty Bible Academy 200/PK-8
4900 Old Irwin Simpson Rd 45040 513-754-1234
Christine Hackler, prin. Fax 754-1237
Mars Hill Academy 200/K-12
4230 Aero Dr 45040 513-770-3223
Roger Wismer, hdmstr. Fax 770-3443

Montessori Academy of Cincinnati 300/PK-8
8293 Duke Blvd 45040 513-398-7773
Patricia Elder, prin. Fax 398-1031
Royalmont Academy 100/K-8
723 Western Row Rd 45040 513-754-0555
Antonio Ferraro, prin.
St. Susanna S 600/1-8
500 Reading Rd 45040 513-398-3821
Kevan Hartmann, prin. Fax 398-1657

Massillon, Stark, Pop. 32,150
Jackson Local SD 5,800/K-12
7984 Fulton Dr NW 44646 330-830-8000
Cheryl Haschak, supt. Fax 830-8008
jackson.stark.k12.oh.us
Amherst ES 500/K-5
8750 Jane St NW 44646 330-830-8024
Elaine Ferguson, prin. Fax 830-8071
Jackson Memorial MS 1,300/6-8
7355 Mudbrook Rd NW 44646 330-830-8034
Monica Myers, prin. Fax 830-8068
Sauder ES 700/K-5
7503 Mudbrook Rd NW 44646 330-830-8028
Cynthia Brown, prin. Fax 830-8032
Strausser ES 800/K-5
8646 Strausser St NW 44646 330-830-8056
Anna Minor, prin. Fax 834-4656
Other Schools – See Canton

Massillon CSD 4,300/K-12
207 Oak Ave SE 44646 330-830-1810
John McGrath, supt. Fax 830-0953
www.massillon.sparcc.org
Bowers ES 200/K-4
1041 32nd St NW 44647 330-830-1847
Julie Brokaw, prin. Fax 830-6422
Emerson ES 200/K-4
724 Walnut Rd SW 44647 330-830-1845
Toni Contini, prin. Fax 830-6484
Franklin ES 300/K-4
1237 16th St SE 44646 330-830-1820
Mike Medure, prin. Fax 830-6532
Gorrell ES 300/K-4
2420 Schuler Ave NW 44647 330-830-1837
Kathy Harper, prin. Fax 830-6533
Massillon MS 1,300/5-8
250 29th St NW 44647 330-830-3902
Gary McPherson, prin. Fax 830-3952
Smith ES 200/K-4
930 17th St NE 44646 330-830-1828
Lori Kiefer-Davila, prin. Fax 830-6537
Whittier ES 400/K-4
1212 10th St NE 44646 330-830-1826
Matthew Plybon, prin. Fax 830-6592

Perry Local SD 4,900/PK-12
4201 13th St SW 44646 330-477-8121
John Richard, supt. Fax 478-6184
perrynet.stark.k12.oh.us
Genoa ES 400/K-5
519 Genoa Ave SW 44646 330-478-6171
Diane Kittelberger, prin. Fax 478-6173
Pfeiffer MS 700/6-7
4315 13th St SW 44646 330-478-6163
Amanda Gardinsky, prin. Fax 478-6800
Watson ES 300/K-5
515 Marion Ave NW 44646 330-832-8100
Donna Bishop, prin. Fax 832-1427
Other Schools – See Canton, Navarre

Tuslaw Local SD 1,500/K-12
1835 Manchester Ave NW 44647 330-837-7813
Alan Osler, supt. Fax 837-7804
www.tuslaw.sparcc.org/
Beech Grove ES 300/K-2
1548 Manchester Ave NW 44647 330-837-7809
Carol Carlin, prin. Fax 837-7810
Tuslaw MS 700/3-8
1723 Manchester Ave NW 44647 330-837-7807
Renee Magnacca, prin. Fax 837-6015

Massillon Christian S 100/K-12
965 Overlook Ave SW 44647 330-833-1039
Carol Crowley, prin. Fax 830-5981
St. Barbara S 100/PK-8
2809 Lincoln Way NW 44647 330-833-9510
Robert Otte, prin. Fax 833-3297
St. Mary S 300/PK-8
640 1st St NE 44646 330-832-9355
Donna Shadle, prin. Fax 832-9030

Maumee, Lucas, Pop. 14,285
Maumee CSD 2,900/K-12
716 Askin St 43537 419-893-3200
Gregory Smith, supt. Fax 891-5387
www.maumee.k12.oh.us
Fairfield ES 300/K-5
1313 Eastfield Dr 43537 419-893-9821
Joe Taylor, prin. Fax 891-5377
Fort Miami ES 300/K-5
2501 River Rd 43537 419-893-2201
Dwight Fertig, prin. Fax 891-5380
Gateway MS 700/6-8
900 Gibbs St 43537 419-893-3386
Christopher Conroy, prin. Fax 893-2263
Union ES 200/K-5
102 E Broadway St 43537 419-893-2221
Lydia Maxfield, prin. Fax 891-5379
Wayne Trail ES 300/K-5
1147 7th St 43537 419-893-2851
Jim Wilson, prin. Fax 891-5378

St. Joseph S 200/K-8
112 W Broadway St 43537 419-893-3304
Gary Rettig, prin. Fax 891-6969

Mayfield, Cuyahoga, Pop. 3,242
Mayfield CSD
Supt. — See Mayfield Heights

Center ES 400/K-5
6625 Wilson Mills Rd 44143 440-995-7400
Sonia Brule, prin. Fax 995-7405

Mayfield Heights, Cuyahoga, Pop. 18,380
Mayfield CSD 4,400/K-12
1101 SOM Center RD 44124 440-995-6800
Phillip Price Ph.D., supt. Fax 995-7205
www.mayfield.k12.oh.us
Lander ES 400/K-4
1714 Lander Rd 44124 440-995-7350
Tammi Bender, prin. Fax 995-7355
Mayfield MS 700/5-7
1123 SOM Center Rd 44124 440-995-7800
Paul Destino, prin. Fax 995-7805
Other Schools – See Gates Mills, Highland Heights, Mayfield

Mechanicsburg, Champaign, Pop. 1,716
Mechanicsburg EVD 900/K-12
60 High St 43044 937-834-2453
Dr. Bobby Moore, supt. Fax 834-3954
www.mechanicsburg.k12.oh.us
Wilson ES 500/K-6
60 High St 43044 937-834-2453
Ronald Widman, prin. Fax 834-3954

Medina, Medina, Pop. 26,461
Buckeye Local SD 2,300/PK-12
3044 Columbia Rd 44256 330-722-8257
Dennis Honkala, supt. Fax 722-5793
www.buckeye.k12.oh.us
Buckeye JHS 400/7-8
3024 Columbia Rd 44256 330-725-0118
Roger Cramer, prin. Fax 722-8257
Liverpool ES 600/PK-6
3140 Columbia Rd 44256 330-483-3803
Larry Taylor, prin. Fax 722-8257
York ES 600/K-6
3180 Columbia Rd 44256 330-725-0164
Dawn Hartwell, prin. Fax 722-8257

Highland Local SD 3,200/PK-12
3880 Ridge Rd 44256 330-239-1901
Catherine Aukerman, supt. Fax 239-2456
www.highlandschools.org
Granger ES 500/PK-5
3940 Ridge Rd 44256 330-239-1901
Linda Collins, prin. Fax 239-7379
Highland MS 800/6-8
3880 Ridge Rd 44256 330-239-1901
John Deuber, prin. Fax 239-2487
Sharon ES 500/PK-5
6335 Ridge Rd 44256 330-239-1901
Constance Marzullo, prin. Fax 239-2597
Other Schools – See Hinckley

Medina CSD 7,800/PK-12
140 W Washington St 44256 330-636-3010
Randy Stepp, supt. Fax 764-3501
www.mcsoh.org
Blake ES 700/K-5
4704 Lexington Ridge Dr 44256 330-636-3900
Kathleen Wetta, prin. Fax 764-3569
Canavan ES 800/K-5
825 Lawrence St 44256 330-636-4000
Brian Condit, prin. Fax 725-9379
Claggett MS 700/6-8
420 E Union St 44256 330-636-3600
Craig Komar, prin. Fax 725-9349
Fenn ES 600/K-5
320 N Spring Grove St 44256 330-636-4100
David Knight, prin. Fax 725-9397
Garfield ES 600/K-5
234 S Broadway St 44256 330-636-4200
Karen McGinty, prin. Fax 725-9396
Heritage ES 500/K-5
833 Guilford Blvd 44256 330-636-4400
Julie Burke, prin. Fax 725-9394
Northrop ES 200/PK-5
950 E Reagan Pkwy 44256 330-636-4600
Stephen Heidorf, prin. Fax 722-2098
Root MS 1,000/6-8
333 W Sturbridge Dr 44256 330-636-3500
Chad Wise, prin. Fax 764-1471
Waite ES 200/K-5
4765 Cobblestone Park Dr 44256 330-636-4500
Cindy Komar, prin. Fax 722-8010

Medina Christian Academy 100/PK-8
3646 Medina Rd 44256 330-725-3227
William Taylor, prin. Fax 725-7762
St. Francis Xavier S 500/K-8
612 E Washington St 44256 330-725-3345
Sr. Sandra Bevec, prin. Fax 721-8626

Medway, Clark
Tecumseh Local SD
Supt. — See New Carlisle
Medway ES 300/PK-5
116 Middle St 45341 937-845-4475
Chad Miller, prin. Fax 845-4463

Mentor, Lake, Pop. 51,485
Mentor EVD 7,500/K-12
6451 Center St 44060 440-255-4444
Dr. Jacqueline Hoynes, supt. Fax 255-4622
www.mentorschools.org
Bellflower ES 400/K-5
6655 Reynolds Rd 44060 440-255-4212
Bobbi Ingraham, prin. Fax 255-1602
Brentmoor ES 300/K-5
7671 Johnnycake Ridge Rd 44060 440-255-7813
Timothy Tatko, prin. Fax 974-5272
Fairfax ES 300/K-5
6465 Curtiss Ct 44060 440-255-7223
Dr. Stephen Heller, prin. Fax 974-5294
Garfield ES 400/K-5
7090 Hopkins Rd 44060 440-255-6609
Ken Buckley, prin. Fax 974-5283

Headlands ES 200/K-5
5028 Forest Rd 44060 440-257-5951
Janice Price, prin. Fax 257-8766
Hopkins ES 500/K-5
7565 Hopkins Rd 44060 440-255-6179
Linda Elegante, prin. Fax 974-5419
Lake ES 300/K-5
7625 Pinehurst Dr 44060 440-257-5953
Michael Lynch, prin. Fax 257-8773
Memorial MS 500/6-8
8979 Mentor Ave 44060 440-974-2250
Patrick McKenrick, prin. Fax 974-2259
Morton ES 300/K-5
9292 Jordan Dr 44060 440-257-5954
Christine Bergant, prin. Fax 257-8799
Orchard Hollow ES 400/K-5
8700 Hendricks Rd 44060 440-257-5955
Karen Trunk, prin. Fax 257-8779
Rice ES 300/K-5
7640 Lakeshore Blvd 44060 440-257-5957
Rosemarie Rogers, prin. Fax 257-8770
Ridge MS 300/6-8
7860 Johnnycake Ridge Rd 44060 440-974-5400
Megan Kinsey, prin. Fax 974-5285
Shore MS 600/6-8
5670 Hopkins Rd 44060 440-257-8750
Douglas Baker, prin. Fax 257-8761

St. Gabriel S 700/PK-8
9935 Johnnycake Ridge Rd 44060 440-352-6169
Donna Becka, prin. Fax 639-0143
St. Mary of the Assumption S 600/PK-8
8540 Mentor Ave 44060 440-255-9781
Candice Konicki, prin. Fax 974-8107

Metamora, Fulton, Pop. 607
Evergreen Local SD 1,300/K-12
14544 County Road 6 43540 419-644-3521
James Wyse, supt. Fax 644-6070
www.evergreen.k12.oh.us
Evergreen ES 500/K-5
14844 County Road 6 43540 419-644-9221
Scott Lockwood, prin. Fax 644-9226
Evergreen MS 300/6-8
14544 County Road 6 43540 419-644-2331
Thomas Shafer, prin. Fax 644-9203

Miamisburg, Montgomery, Pop. 19,796
Miamisburg CSD 5,600/PK-12
540 Park Ave 45342 937-866-3381
Dr. Dallas Jackson, supt. Fax 865-5250
www.miamisburgcityschools.org
Bear ES 200/K-5
545 School St 45342 937-866-4691
Amy Dobson, prin. Fax 866-4065
Kinder ES 200/K-5
536 E Central Ave 45342 937-866-4461
Dale Geyer, prin. Fax 866-4070
Maddux-Lang PS PK-K
4010 Crains Run Rd 45342 937-847-2766
Susan Woods, prin.
Medlar View ES 700/K-5
4400 Medlar Rd 45342 937-865-5257
Susan Woods, prin. Fax 865-5295
Mound ES 400/K-5
1108 Range Ave 45342 937-866-4641
Barry Coleman, prin. Fax 866-6767
Neff Building ES 400/6-6
29 S 6th St 45342 937-866-5919
Erin Wheat, prin. Fax 865-5278
Twain ES 400/K-5
822 N 9th St 45342 937-866-2581
Jill Patrick, prin. Fax 866-4085
Wantz MS 800/7-8
117 S 7th St 45342 937-866-3431
Erin Wheat, prin. Fax 866-6891
Other Schools – See Dayton

Bishop Leibold Consolidated S West 600/K-8
24 S 3rd St 45342 937-866-3021
Paul Beyerle, prin. Fax 866-5680
Dayton Christian S 1,500/PK-12
9391 Washington Church Rd 45342 937-291-7201
Lee Reno, supt. Fax 291-7202
Miamisburg Christian Academy 50/K-12
8500 S Union Rd 45342 937-866-6226
Charles Maqsud, prin. Fax 866-0112

Miamitown, Hamilton
Southwest Local SD
Supt. — See Harrison
Miamitown ES 200/K-6
6578 State Route 128 45041 513-353-1416
Carter Cordes, prin. Fax 353-9026

Middleburg Heights, Cuyahoga, Pop. 15,437
Berea CSD
Supt. — See Berea
Big Creek ES 800/K-5
7247 Big Creek Pkwy 44130 440-243-0600
John Brzozowski, prin. Fax 891-3765

Middlefield, Geauga, Pop. 2,411
Bloomfield-Mespo Local SD
Supt. — See North Bloomfield
Mesopotamia ES 200/K-5
4466 Kinsman Rd 44062 440-693-4125
Russell McQuaide, prin. Fax 693-4656

Cardinal Local SD 1,400/K-12
PO Box 188 44062 440-632-0261
Paul Yocum, supt. Fax 632-5886
www.cardinal.k12.oh.us
Cardinal IS 200/4-5
PO Box 188 44062 440-632-6376
Lynne Muzik, prin. Fax 632-9674
Cardinal MS 300/6-8
PO Box 879 44062 440-632-0263
James Millet, prin. Fax 632-0294
Jordak ES 500/K-3
PO Box 188 44062 440-632-0262
Alanna Hruska, prin. Fax 632-5192

Middleport, Meigs, Pop. 2,517
Meigs Local SD
Supt. — See Pomeroy
Meigs IS 400/3-5
36871 State Route 124 45760 740-742-2666
Rusty Bookman, prin. Fax 742-2825
Meigs PS 500/K-2
36871 State Route 124 45760 740-742-3000
Kristin Acree, prin. Fax 742-2651

Mid Valley Christian S 100/PK-10
500 N 2nd Ave 45760 740-992-2962
Brenda Barnhart, admin. Fax 992-6556

Middletown, Butler, Pop. 51,472
Lakota Local SD
Supt. — See Liberty Twp
Independence ES 700/2-6
7480 Princeton Rd 45044 513-755-8300
Greg Finke, prin. Fax 755-6941
Liberty JHS 700/7-8
7055 Dutchland Blvd 45044 513-777-4420
Gabriel Lofton, prin. Fax 777-7950
Woodland ES 700/2-6
6923 Dutchland Blvd 45044 513-779-7775
Linda French, prin. Fax 779-7389
Wyandot Early Childhood S 900/K-1
7667 Summerlin Blvd 45044 513-759-8100
Elizabeth Spurlock, prin. Fax 759-8105

Madison Local SD 1,600/K-12
1324 Middletown Eaton Rd 45042 513-420-4750
Charles Philpot, supt. Fax 420-4781
www.madisonmohawks.org/
Madison IS 500/3-6
1368 Middletown Eaton Rd 45042 513-420-4766
Mat Gray, prin. Fax 420-4990
Madison PS 400/K-2
1380 Middletown Eaton Rd 45042 513-420-4755
Mike Chaney, prin. Fax 420-4915

Middletown CSD 6,800/PK-12
1515 Girard Ave 45044 513-423-0781
Dr. Steve Price, supt. Fax 420-4579
www.middletowncityschools.com
Amanda ES 500/PK-5
1300 Oxford State Rd 45044 513-420-4542
Beth Prince, prin. Fax 420-4632
Central Academy 300/K-7
4601 Sophie Ave 45042 513-420-4537
Dr. Dianne Suiter, prin. Fax 420-4589
Creekview ES 500/PK-5
4800 Timber Trail Dr 45044 513-420-4544
Derrick Bobbitt, prin. Fax 420-4587
Highview ES 500/K-5
106 S Highview Rd 45044 513-420-4566
Joy Stokes, prin. Fax 420-4647
Mayfield ES 400/K-5
3325 Burbank Ave 45044 513-420-4549
Marla Marsh, prin. Fax 420-4551
Miller Ridge ES 300/K-5
4704 Miller Rd 45042 513-420-4559
Michael Lolli, prin. Fax 420-4560
Parks ES 500/PK-5
1210 S Verity Pkwy 45044 513-420-4552
Kee Edwards, prin. Fax 420-4553
Vail MS 900/6-8
1415 Girard Ave 45044 513-420-4528
Michael Valenti, prin. Fax 420-4527
Verity MS 600/6-8
1900 Johns Rd 45044 513-420-4635
Greg Williams, prin. Fax 420-4615
Wildwood ES 600/PK-5
3300 Wildwood Rd 45042 513-420-4564
James Thomas, prin. Fax 420-4627

John XXIII Consolidated S 500/K-8
3806 Manchester Rd 45042 513-424-1196
Brenda Neu, prin. Fax 420-8480
Mother Teresa S 400/K-8
6085 Jackie Dr 45044 513-779-6585
Sr. Anne Schulz, prin. Fax 779-6468

Midvale, Tuscarawas, Pop. 594
Indian Valley Local SD
Supt. — See Gnadenhutten
Midvale ES 400/K-5
PO Box 337 44653 330-339-1191
G. Ira Wentworth, prin. Fax 339-1194

Milan, Erie, Pop. 1,381
Berlin-Milan Local SD 1,600/PK-12
140 S Main St 44846 419-499-4272
David Snook, supt. Fax 499-4859
www.berlin-milan.org
Milan ES 500/PK-6
140 S Main St 44846 419-499-2471
David Hermes, prin. Fax 499-4859
Other Schools – See Berlin Heights

Milford, Clermont, Pop. 6,325
Milford EVD 6,600/PK-12
777 Garfield Ave 45150 513-831-1314
Dr. Robert Farrell, supt. Fax 831-3208
www.milfordschools.org
Meadowview ES 600/K-6
5556 Mount Zion Rd 45150 513-831-9170
Robert Dunn, prin. Fax 831-9340
Milford JHS 1,000/7-8
5735 Pleasant Hill Rd 45150 513-831-1900
Kelli Ellison, prin. Fax 248-3451
Milford Preschool 100/PK-PK
1039 State Route 28 45150 513-831-9690
Jennie Berkley, dir. Fax 831-8764
Mulberry ES 700/K-6
5950 Buckwheat Rd 45150 513-722-3588
Gary Schulte, prin. Fax 722-4584
Pattison ES 700/K-6
5330 S Milford Rd 45150 513-831-6570
Gregg Curless, prin. Fax 831-9693
Seipelt ES 500/K-6
5684 Cromley Dr 45150 513-831-9460
Missy Borger, prin. Fax 248-5443
Smith ES 500/K-6
1052 Jer Les St 45150 513-575-1643
Dr. Jill Chin, prin. Fax 575-2835
Other Schools – See Loveland

St. Andrew/St. Elizabeth Ann Seton S 300/K-4
5900 Buckwheat Rd 45150 513-575-0093
Jerry Sasson, prin. Fax 575-1078
St. Andrew/St. Elizabeth Ann Seton S 200/5-8
555 Main St 45150 513-831-5277
Jerry Sasson, prin. Fax 831-8436
St. Mark's Lutheran S 100/PK-7
5849 Buckwheat Rd 45150 513-575-3354
Robert Reisenbichler, prin. Fax 575-2472

Milford Center, Union, Pop. 684
Fairbanks Local SD 1,000/K-12
11158 State Route 38 43045 937-349-3731
Bob Humble, supt. Fax 349-8885
www.fairbanks.k12.oh.us/
Fairbanks ES 300/K-4
11140 State Route 38 43045 937-349-2381
Mark Lotycz, prin. Fax 349-2471
Fairbanks MS 300/5-8
11158 State Route 38 43045 937-349-6841
Patricia Lucas, prin. Fax 349-2013

St. Paul Lutheran S 100/PK-7
7960 State Route 38 43045 937-349-5939
Lois Vollrath, prin. Fax 349-5939

Millbury, Wood, Pop. 1,156
Lake Local SD 1,600/K-12
28090 Lemoyne Rd 43447 419-661-6690
Jim Witt, supt. Fax 661-6678
www.lakelocal.k12.oh.us
Lake ES 500/2-5
28150 Lemoyne Rd 43447 419-661-6680
Christie McPherson, prin. Fax 661-6683
Lake JHS 400/6-8
28100 Lemoyne Rd 43447 419-661-6660
Lee Herman, prin. Fax 661-6664
Other Schools – See Walbridge

Miller City, Putnam, Pop. 130
Miller City-New Cleveland Local SD 500/K-12
PO Box 38 45864 419-876-3172
William Kreinbrink, supt. Fax 876-3849
web.ml.noacsc.org/
Miller City-New Cleveland ES 200/K-5
PO Box 38 45864 419-876-3174
Cathy Burgei, prin. Fax 876-2020
Miller City-New Cleveland MS 100/6-8
PO Box 38 45864 419-876-3174
Kevin McGlaughlin, prin. Fax 876-2020

Millersburg, Holmes, Pop. 3,582
West Holmes Local SD 2,800/K-12
28 W Jackson St 44654 330-674-3546
Kristie Pipes-Perone, supt. Fax 674-1177
www.westholmes.k12.oh.us
Clark ES 100/K-5
1390 State Route 83 44654 330-674-7936
Renee Woods, prin. Fax 674-3246
Millersburg ES 400/K-5
430 E Jackson St 44654 330-674-5681
Tim Wigton, prin. Fax 674-2506
West Holmes MS 600/6-8
10901 State Route 39 44654 330-674-4761
Jeff Woods, prin. Fax 674-2311
Other Schools – See Killbuck, Lakeville, Nashville

Millersport, Fairfield, Pop. 967
Walnut Township Local SD 700/K-12
11850 Lancaster St 43046 740-467-2802
Ronald Thornton, supt. Fax 467-3494
www.walnuttsd.org
Millersport ES 400/K-6
11850 Lancaster St 43046 740-467-2216
Cheryl Thomson, prin. Fax 467-3494

Mineral City, Tuscarawas, Pop. 855
Tuscarawas Valley Local SD
Supt. — See Zoarville
Tuscarawas Valley PS 100/PK-1
PO Box 428 44656 330-859-2461
Mary Beth Markley, prin. Fax 859-8885

Mineral Ridge, Trumbull, Pop. 3,928
Weathersfield Local SD 1,000/K-12
3750 Main St 44440 330-652-0287
Michael Hanshaw, supt. Fax 544-7476
www.weathersfield.k12.oh.us/
Mineral Ridge MS 300/5-8
3750 Main St 44440 330-652-2120
Bill Koppel, prin. Fax 544-7476
Seaborn ES 400/K-4
3800 Niles Carver Rd 44440 330-652-9695
Cynthia Mulgrew, prin. Fax 544-7482

Minerva, Stark, Pop. 3,976
Minerva Local SD 2,200/K-12
303 Latzer Ave 44657 330-868-4332
Douglas Marrah Ed.D., supt. Fax 868-4731
lion.stark.k12.oh.us/
Day ES 700/K-5
130 Bonnieview Ave 44657 330-868-4011
Michelle Nervo, prin. Fax 868-3681

Minerva MS 600/6-8
600 E Line St 44657 330-868-4497
Richard Mikes, prin. Fax 868-3144
Other Schools – See East Rochester

Minerva Area Christian S 100/K-9
300 W Lincoln Way 44657 330-868-5728
Joseph Ellis, admin. Fax 868-5834

Minford, Scioto
Minford Local SD 1,600/K-12
PO Box 204 45653 740-820-3896
Mark Wilcheck, supt. Fax 820-3334
www.minfordfalcons.net/
Minford MS 600/4-8
PO Box 204 45653 740-820-2181
Kevin Lloyd, prin. Fax 820-2191
Minford PS 500/K-3
PO Box 204 45653 740-820-2287
Dennis Evans, prin. Fax 820-2466

Mingo Junction, Jefferson, Pop. 3,426
Indian Creek Local SD
Supt. — See Wintersville
Hills ES 400/K-6
707 Wilson Ave 43938 740-283-2479
Clyde DiAngelo, prin. Fax 283-2286
Indian Creek JHS 300/7-8
110 Steuben St 43938 740-266-2916
John Belt, prin. Fax 535-9100

Jefferson County Christian S 200/PK-12
2501 Commercial Ave 43938 740-535-1337
Diane Hutchison, prin.

Minster, Auglaize, Pop. 2,820
Minster Local SD 900/K-12
100 E 7th St 45865 419-628-3397
Gayl Ray, supt. Fax 628-2495
www.minster.k12.oh.us
Minster ES 200/K-3
86 N Hanover St 45865 419-628-2214
Brenda Boeke, prin. Fax 628-2601
Minster MS 300/4-8
50 E 7th St 45865 419-628-4174
Brenda Boeke, prin. Fax 628-2482

Mogadore, Summit, Pop. 3,966
Field Local SD 2,200/K-12
2900 State Route 43 44260 330-673-2659
David Brobeck, supt. Fax 673-0270
www.fieldlocalschools.org
Field MS 500/6-8
1379 Saxe Rd 44260 330-673-4176
Susan Blake, prin. Fax 673-0942
Other Schools – See Kent, Suffield

Mogadore Local SD 800/K-12
1 S Cleveland Ave 44260 330-628-9946
Terry Byers, supt. Fax 628-6661
www.mogadore.net
Somers ES 500/K-6
3600 Herbert St 44260 330-628-9947
Jerry Wolf, prin. Fax 628-6662

St. Joseph S 100/K-8
2617 Waterloo Rd Ste 1 44260 330-628-9555
Dorenda Demyan, prin. Fax 628-9942

Monclova, Lucas
Anthony Wayne Local SD
Supt. — See Whitehouse
Monclova ES 600/K-4
8035 Monclova Rd 43542 419-865-9408
Vicky Griggs, prin. Fax 865-1397

Monclova Christian Academy 200/K-12
PO Box 15 43542 419-866-7630
Neil Black, prin. Fax 868-1062

Monroe, Butler, Pop. 10,410
Monroe Local SD 2,100/PK-12
231 Macready Ave 45050 513-539-2536
Dr. Elizabeth Lolli, supt. Fax 539-2648
www.monroelocalschools.com/
Monroe ES 600/3-6
230 Yankee Rd 45050 513-539-8101
Patti Shull, prin. Fax 539-8151
Monroe JHS 300/7-8
210 Yankee Rd 45050 513-539-8471
Lisa Hodits, prin. Fax 539-8474
Monroe PS 500/PK-2
225 Macready Ave 45050 513-360-0700
Jody Long, prin. Fax 360-0720

Monroeville, Huron, Pop. 1,396
Monroeville Local SD 700/K-12
101 West St 44847 419-465-2610
David Stubblebine, supt. Fax 465-4263
www.monroeville.k12.oh.us
Monroeville ES 300/K-6
101 West St 44847 419-465-2533
William Butler, prin. Fax 465-4263

Willard CSD
Supt. — See Willard
Greenfield ES 100/1-6
2634 State Route 162 44847 419-935-4001
Neil Lydy, prin.

St. Joseph S 200/PK-8
79 Chapel St 44847 419-465-2625
James Francis, prin. Fax 465-2170

Montpelier, Williams, Pop. 4,135
Montpelier EVD 1,100/K-12
PO Box 193 43543 419-485-6700
Jamison Grime, supt. Fax 485-3676
www.montpelier-k12.org/
Montpelier ES 400/K-3
PO Box 193 43543 419-485-6700
Connie Graham, prin. Fax 485-6700
Montpelier MS 400/4-8
PO Box 193 43543 419-485-6700
Randy Stuckey, prin. Fax 485-6700

Moraine, Montgomery, Pop. 6,702
Kettering CSD
Supt. — See Kettering
Moraine Meadows ES 200/K-5
2600 Holman St 45439 937-499-1530
James Rhoades, prin. Fax 499-1537

Morral, Marion, Pop. 385
Ridgedale Local SD 900/PK-12
3103 Hillman Ford Rd 43337 740-382-6065
Robert Britton, supt. Fax 383-6538
www.ridgedale.k12.oh.us/
Ridgedale ES 400/PK-5
3105 Hillman Ford Rd 43337 740-382-6065
Bill Stoner, prin. Fax 383-2020

Morristown, Belmont, Pop. 302
Union Local SD 1,500/K-12
PO Box 300 43759 740-782-1978
H. Kirk Glasgow, supt. Fax 695-5066
www.union-local.k12.oh.us
Other Schools – See Belmont

Morrow, Warren, Pop. 1,500
Little Miami Local SD 2,100/K-12
5819 Morrow Rossburg Rd 45152 513-899-2264
Daniel Bennett, supt. Fax 899-3244
www.littlemiamischools.com
Little Miami JHS 300/6-7
5290 Morrow Cozaddale Rd 45152 513-899-2264
Tom Turner, prin.
Salem ES K-2
605 Welch Rd 45152 513-899-5275
Scott Counts, prin. Fax 899-2891
Other Schools – See Maineville

Mount Blanchard, Hancock, Pop. 461
Riverdale Local SD 800/K-12
20613 State Route 37 45867 419-694-4994
Eric Hoffman, supt. Fax 694-6465
www.riverdale.k12.oh.us
Riverdale ES 200/K-5
20613 State Route 37 45867 419-694-2211
Dr. Julie Spade, prin. Fax 694-8005
Riverdale MS 200/6-8
20613 State Route 37 45867 419-694-2211
Terry Huffman, prin. Fax 694-5008

Mount Eaton, Wayne, Pop. 244
Southeast Local SD
Supt. — See Apple Creek
Mount Eaton S 200/K-8
PO Box 268 44659 330-359-5519
Rhoda Mast, prin. Fax 857-3703

Mount Gilead, Morrow, Pop. 3,547
Mt. Gilead EVD 1,300/K-12
145 1/2 N Cherry St 43338 419-946-1646
Robert Alexander, supt. Fax 946-3651
www.treca.org/schools/mtg/
Mount Gilead MS 300/6-8
145 N Cherry St 43338 419-947-9517
Rick Nabors, prin. Fax 947-9518
Park Avenue ES 600/K-5
335 W Park Ave 43338 419-946-5736
Diana Keplinger, prin. Fax 946-2336

Gilead Christian S North Campus 200/PK-6
220 S Main St 43338 419-947-5739
Connie Olmstead, prin. Fax 947-5010

Mount Hope, Holmes
East Holmes Local SD
Supt. — See Berlin
Mount Hope S 200/K-8
PO Box 128 44660 330-674-0418
Daniel McKey, prin. Fax 674-4647

Mount Orab, Brown, Pop. 2,909
Western Brown Local SD 3,300/K-12
524 W Main St 45154 937-444-2044
Jeffrey Royalty, supt. Fax 444-4303
www.wb.k12.oh.us/
Mount Orab ES 900/K-4
474 W Main St 45154 937-444-2528
David McDonough, prin. Fax 444-4183
Mount Orab MS 700/5-8
472 W Main St 45154 937-444-2529
Marty Paeltz, prin. Fax 444-4268
Other Schools – See Hamersville

Mount Sterling, Madison, Pop. 1,840
Madison-Plains Local SD
Supt. — See London
Mount Sterling ES 200/K-5
94 W Main St 43143 740-869-2107
Lori Carnevale, prin. Fax 869-4813

Mount Vernon, Knox, Pop. 16,000
Mt. Vernon CSD 4,200/PK-12
300 Newark Rd 43050 740-397-7422
Steve Short, supt. Fax 397-4174
www.mt-vernon.k12.oh.us
Columbia ES 200/K-5
150 Columbus Rd 43050 740-393-5975
Pam Rose, prin. Fax 393-5976
East ES 300/K-5
714 E Vine St 43050 740-393-5985
Eric Brown, prin. Fax 393-5987
Emmett ES 300/K-5
108 Mansfield Ave 43050 740-393-5950
Margy Arck, prin. Fax 393-5953
Mount Vernon MS 1,000/6-8
298 Martinsburg Rd 43050 740-392-6867
William White, prin. Fax 392-3369
Pleasant Street ES 500/PK-5
305 E Pleasant St 43050 740-393-5990
Karen Boylan, prin. Fax 393-3175
Twin Oak ES 400/K-5
8888 Martinsburg Rd 43050 740-393-5970
Suzanne Miller, prin. Fax 397-2598
Other Schools – See Gambier

Christian Star Academy 50/PK-12
7 E Sugar St 43050 740-393-0251
Suzanne Feasel, admin. Fax 393-0067
Mount Vernon SDA S 50/K-8
221 Sychar Rd 43050 740-393-7060
Kim Myers, prin. Fax 393-7060
St. Vincent de Paul S 200/PK-8
206 E Chestnut St 43050 740-393-3611
Martha Downs, prin. Fax 393-0236

Mount Victory, Hardin, Pop. 605
Ridgemont Local SD 600/PK-12
330 Taylor St W 43340 937-354-2441
Bruce Gast, supt. Fax 354-2194
www.ridgemontschools.org/
Ridgemont ES 400/PK-6
310 Taylor St W 43340 937-354-2141
R. Harlan Needham, prin. Fax 354-5099

Mowrystown, Highland, Pop. 392
Bright Local SD 700/PK-12
PO Box 299 45155 937-442-3114
Dee Wright, supt. Fax 442-6655
www.bright.k12.oh.us/
Other Schools – See Hillsboro

Munroe Falls, Summit, Pop. 5,300
Stow-Munroe Falls CSD
Supt. — See Stow
Kimpton MS 900/7-8
380 N River Rd 44262 330-689-5288
Robert Knisely, prin. Fax 686-4718
Riverview ES 300/K-4
240 N River Rd 44262 330-689-5310
Brenda Harriss, prin. Fax 686-4713

Napoleon, Henry, Pop. 9,169
Napoleon Area CSD 1,600/K-12
701 Briarheath Ave Ste 108 43545 419-599-7015
Dr. Al Haschak, supt. Fax 599-7035
www.napoleon.k12.oh.us/
Brillhart ES 100/K-1
201 Rohrs Ave 43545 419-592-2521
Karen Bachman, prin. Fax 592-1487
Central ES 100/4-5
315 W Main St 43545 419-599-1851
Adam Niese, prin. Fax 599-1463
Napoleon MS 400/6-8
303 W Main St 43545 419-592-6991
Tony Borton, prin. Fax 599-7638
West ES 100/2-3
700 Clairmont Ave 43545 419-592-4641
Fax 592-0045

St. Augustine S 100/K-8
722 Monroe St 43545 419-592-3641
Nancy Ann Schroeder, prin. Fax 592-6316
St. John Lutheran S 100/PK-8
16035 County Road U 43545 419-598-8702
Mary Rettig, prin. Fax 598-8518
St. Paul Lutheran S 200/K-8
1075 Glenwood Ave 43545 419-592-5536
Steven Wentzel, prin. Fax 592-0652

Nashport, Muskingum
Tri-Valley Local SD
Supt. — See Dresden
Nashport ES 300/K-6
3775 Creamery Rd 43830 740-452-3977
Fritzi Gibson, prin. Fax 452-7101

Nashville, Holmes, Pop. 186
West Holmes Local SD
Supt. — See Millersburg
Nashville ES 200/K-2
PO Box 400 44661 330-378-2111
Brian Zimmerly, prin. Fax 378-2323

Navarre, Stark, Pop. 1,431
Fairless Local SD 1,200/K-12
11885 Navarre Rd SW 44662 330-767-3577
Mona Fair, supt. Fax 767-3298
www.falcon.stark.k12.oh.us/
Fairless ES 200/K-5
12000 Navarre Rd SW 44662 330-767-3913
Julie Kerby, prin. Fax 767-4398
Fairless MS 300/6-8
11836 Navarre Rd SW 44662 330-767-4293
Theodore George, prin. Fax 767-3807

Perry Local SD
Supt. — See Massillon
Lohr ES 300/K-5
5300 Richville Dr SW 44662 330-484-3924
Michael Griffith, prin. Fax 484-4987

Nelsonville, Athens, Pop. 5,444
Nelsonville-York CSD 1,300/PK-12
2 Buckeye Dr 45764 740-753-4441
Ted Bayat, supt. Fax 753-1968
www.nelsonvilleyork.k12.oh.us/
Nelsonville-York ES 700/PK-5
2 Buckeye Dr 45764 740-753-4441
Teresa Dearth, prin. Fax 753-1968
Nelsonville-York MS 200/6-8
14455 Kimberley Rd 45764 740-753-4441
Joseph Malesick, prin. Fax 753-1087

Nelsonville Christian Academy 50/K-12
PO Box 90 45764 740-753-4002
Linda Edwards, admin.

New Albany, Franklin, Pop. 5,827
New Albany - Plain Local SD 3,700/K-12
55 N High St 43054 614-855-2040
Dr. Steve Castle, supt. Fax 855-2043
www.new-albany.k12.oh.us
New Albany ES 600/2-3
87 N High St 43054 614-413-8600
Robin Ryan, prin. Fax 413-8601
New Albany IS 600/4-5
87 N High St 43054 614-413-8600
Chris Briggs, prin. Fax 413-8601
New Albany MS 900/6-8
6600 E Dublin Granville Rd 43054 614-413-8500
Andrew Culp, prin. Fax 413-8501
New Albany PS 700/K-1
5101 Swickard Woods Blvd 43054 614-413-8700
Deloris McCafferty, prin. Fax 413-8701

Columbus Jewish Day S 100/K-5
79 N High St 43054 614-939-5311
Rabbi Mitchell Levine, prin. Fax 939-5312

Newark, Licking, Pop. 47,301
Licking Valley Local SD 1,500/K-12
1379 Licking Valley Rd 43055 740-763-3525
David Hile, supt. Fax 763-0471
www.lickingvalley.k12.oh.us/
Licking Valley ES 300/K-5
1510 Licking Valley Rd 43055 740-763-3525
Todd Carmer, prin.
Licking Valley MS 500/6-8
1379 Licking Valley Rd 43055 740-763-3396
Scott Beery, prin. Fax 763-2612

Newark CSD 5,900/K-12
85 E Main St 43055 740-670-7000
Douglas Ute, supt. Fax 670-7009
www.newarkcityschools.org
Carson ES 500/K-5
549 E Main St 43055 740-670-7305
Sara Brlas, prin. Fax 670-7309
Cherry Valley ES 400/K-5
1040 W Main St 43055 740-670-7330
Mindy Vaughn, prin. Fax 670-7339
Clem ES 400/K-5
621 Mount Vernon Rd 43055 740-349-2350
Lynda Nabors, prin. Fax 328-2353
Franklin ES 300/K-5
112 W Main St 43055 740-670-7340
Stephen Stahley, prin. Fax 670-7349
Heritage MS 400/6-8
471 E Main St 43055 740-345-4440
Tom Suriano, prin. Fax 328-2042
Hillview ES 400/K-5
1927 Horns Hill Rd 43055 740-670-7315
Barbara Quackenbush, prin. Fax 670-7319
Legend ES 500/K-5
1075 Evans Blvd 43055 740-670-7100
Ellen Cooper, prin. Fax 670-7109
Liberty MS 500/6-8
1055 Evans Blvd 43055 740-670-7325
Diane Henry, prin. Fax 670-7329
McGuffey ES 400/K-5
112 W Main St 43055 740-349-2382
Martha Harmon, prin. Fax 328-2172
Wilson MS 400/6-8
805 W Church St 43055 740-670-7120
John Davis, prin. Fax 670-7129

North Fork Local SD
Supt. — See Utica
Newton ES 500/K-6
6645 Mount Vernon Rd 43055 740-745-5982
Michele Gorius, prin. Fax 745-5524

Blessed Sacrament S 200/K-8
394 E Main St 43055 740-345-4125
Mary Packham, prin. Fax 345-6168
Excel Academy 100/K-12
116 W Church St 43055 740-323-1102
Marlene Jacob, prin. Fax 349-5834
St. Francis De Sales S 400/K-8
38 Granville St 43055 740-345-4049
Dr. Cheryl Spain, prin. Fax 345-9768

New Boston, Scioto, Pop. 2,189
New Boston Local SD 400/PK-12
522 Glenwood Ave 45662 740-456-4626
Mike Staggs, supt. Fax 456-5252
www.newboston.k12.oh.us
Oak IS, 824 Harrisonville Ave 45662 100/3-6
Diane Chamberlin, prin. 740-456-5225
Stanton PS, 3800 Stanton Ave 45662 100/PK-2
Diane Chamberlin, prin. 740-456-4637

New Bremen, Auglaize, Pop. 2,993
New Bremen Local SD 900/K-12
901 E Monroe St 45869 419-629-8606
Ann Harvey, supt. Fax 629-2443
www.bremen.k12.oh.us
New Bremen S 600/K-8
202 S Walnut St 45869 419-629-2373
Karen Smith, prin. Fax 629-3244

Newbury, Geauga
Newbury Local SD 800/K-12
14775 Auburn Rd 44065 440-564-5501
Richard Wagner, supt. Fax 564-9460
newbury.k12.oh.us
Newbury ES 400/K-6
14775 Auburn Rd 44065 440-564-2282
Janis Gingerich, prin. Fax 564-9690

St. Helen S 300/PK-8
12060 Kinsman Rd 44065 440-564-7125
Sr. Christin Alfieri, prin. Fax 564-7969

New Carlisle, Clark, Pop. 5,639
Tecumseh Local SD 3,100/PK-12
9760 W National Rd 45344 937-845-3576
Jim Gay, supt. Fax 845-4453
www.tecumseh.k12.oh.us
New Carlisle ES 500/PK-5
1203 Kennison Ave 45344 937-845-4480
Sharon Powers, prin. Fax 845-4482
Park Layne ES 400/K-5
12355 Dille Rd 45344 937-845-4470
Greg Baker, prin. Fax 845-4458
Tecumseh MS 400/6-8
10000 W National Rd 45344 937-845-4465
Brad Martin, prin. Fax 845-4484
Other Schools – See Donnelsville, Medway

Newcomerstown, Tuscarawas, Pop. 3,952
Newcomerstown EVD 1,200/K-12
702 S River St 43832 740-498-8373
Jeffrey Staggs, supt. Fax 498-8375
www.nctschools.org/
Newcomerstown East ES 100/K-1
137 S College St 43832 740-498-6601
Kathy Reid, prin. Fax 498-4997
Newcomerstown MS 300/6-8
325 W State St 43832 740-498-8151
Jason Peoples, prin. Fax 498-4991
Newcomerstown West ES 400/2-5
517 Beaver St 43832 740-498-4151
Patrick Cadle, prin. Fax 498-4998

New Concord, Muskingum, Pop. 2,660
East Muskingum Local SD 2,100/K-12
13505 John Glenn School Rd 43762 740-826-7655
Jim Heagen, supt. Fax 826-7194
www.east-muskingum.k12.oh.us
East Muskingum MS 500/6-8
13120 John Glenn School Rd 43762 740-826-7631
Robert Baier, prin. Fax 826-4392
Miller IS 500/3-5
13125 John Glenn School Rd 43762 740-826-2271
Sandra Scholl, prin. Fax 826-7443
New Concord ES 200/K-2
4 Stormont St 43762 740-826-4453
Ann Troendly, prin. Fax 826-1332
Other Schools – See Cambridge, Zanesville

New Haven, Huron
Willard CSD
Supt. — See Willard
New Haven ES 200/K-6
PO Box 176 44850 419-933-8822
James Sellers, prin. Fax 933-2481

New Knoxville, Auglaize, Pop. 915
New Knoxville Local SD 400/K-12
PO Box 476 45871 419-753-2431
Kim Waterman, supt. Fax 753-2333
www.nk.k12.oh.us
New Knoxville ES 300/K-6
PO Box 476 45871 419-753-2431
Julie Willoughby, prin. Fax 753-2333

New Lebanon, Montgomery, Pop. 4,208
New Lebanon Local SD 1,200/K-12
320 S Fuls Rd 45345 937-687-1301
Dr. Barbara Curry, supt. Fax 687-7321
www.newlebanon.k12.oh.us/
Dixie ES 500/K-4
1150 W Main St 45345 937-687-3511
Dr. Charles Wilkins, prin. Fax 687-3579
Dixie MS 400/5-8
200 S Fuls Rd 45345 937-687-3508
Thomas Sarver, prin. Fax 687-7705

New Lexington, Perry, Pop. 4,632
New Lexington CSD 1,900/K-12
101 3rd Ave 43764 740-342-4133
Dr. Larry Rentschler, supt. Fax 342-6051
www.nlcs.k12.oh.us/
New Lexington ES 400/K-5
2550 Panther Dr NE 43764 740-342-2556
Karen Robinson, prin. Fax 342-7755
New Lexington MS 400/6-8
2549 Panther Dr NE 43764 740-342-4128
Tonya Cline, prin. Fax 342-6071
Other Schools – See Junction City

St. Rose of Lima S 100/K-8
119 W Water St 43764 740-342-3043
Roxanne Demeter, prin. Fax 342-1082

New London, Huron, Pop. 2,668
New London Local SD 1,200/PK-12
2 Wildcat Dr 44851 419-929-8433
Carol Girton, supt. Fax 929-4108
www.newlondon.k12.oh.us/
New London ES 500/K-5
1 Wildcat Dr 44851 419-929-8117
Laura Dowdell, prin. Fax 929-9512
New London MS 300/6-8
1 Wildcat Dr 44851 419-929-5409
Dennis Gable, prin. Fax 929-9513
New London Preschool 100/PK-PK
3 Wildcat Dr 44851 419-929-8191
Liz Ohm, lead tchr.

New Madison, Darke, Pop. 780
Tri-Village Local SD 800/K-12
PO Box 31 45346 937-996-6261
Anthony Thomas, supt. Fax 996-5537
www.tri-village.k12.oh.us
Tri-Village ES 400/K-6
PO Box 31 45346 937-996-1511
Josh Sagester, prin. Fax 996-0307

New Matamoras, Washington, Pop. 1,019
Frontier Local SD 900/K-12
44870 State Route 7 45767 740-865-3473
Troy Thacker, supt. Fax 865-2010
www.flsd.k12.oh.us/
Matamoras S 200/K-8
PO Box 339 45767 740-865-3422
William Wotring, prin. Fax 865-3423
Other Schools – See Marietta, Newport

New Middletown, Mahoning, Pop. 1,620
Springfield Local SD 1,200/K-12
PO Box 549 44442 330-542-2929
Debra Mettee, supt. Fax 542-9453
www.springfield.k12.oh.us
Springfield ES 400/K-4
10580 Main St 44442 330-542-3722
Thomas Yazvac, prin. Fax 542-2488
Springfield IS 400/5-8
11333 Yngstwn Pittsburgh Rd 44442 330-542-3624
David Malone, prin. Fax 542-2159

New Paris, Preble, Pop. 1,546
National Trail Local SD 1,100/K-12
6940 Oxford Gettysburg Rd 45347 937-437-3333
Clinton Moore, supt. Fax 437-7865
www.nationaltrail.k12.oh.us/
National Trail ES 400/K-4
6940 Oxford Gettysburg Rd 45347 937-437-3333
Ed Eales, prin. Fax 437-7306
National Trail MS 400/5-8
6940 Oxford Gettysburg Rd 45347 937-437-3333
Mark Wiseman, prin. Fax 437-7306

New Philadelphia, Tuscarawas, Pop. 17,430
New Philadelphia CSD 3,000/K-12
248 Front Ave SW 44663 330-364-0600
Richard Varrati, supt. Fax 364-9310
www.npschools.org
Central ES 300/K-5
145 Ray Ave NW 44663 330-364-0700
Laura Mariol, prin. Fax 364-0611
East ES 300/K-5
470 Fair Ave NE 44663 330-364-0715
Laurie Hall, prin. Fax 364-0611
South ES 300/K-5
132 Providence Ave SW 44663 330-364-0725
Jacklyn Triplett, prin. Fax 364-0611
Welty MS 700/6-8
315 4th St NW 44663 330-364-0645
Sallie Stroup, prin. Fax 364-0611
West ES 300/K-5
232 Tuscarawas Ave NW 44663 330-364-0755
Christina Ziga-Budd, prin. Fax 364-0611
York ES 200/K-5
938 Stonecreek Rd SW 44663 330-364-0770
Donna Edwards, prin. Fax 364-0611

Indian Hills Christian S 100/PK-6
878 Commercial Ave SW 44663 330-339-1041
Mark Aksterowicz, admin. Fax 339-2095

Newport, Washington
Frontier Local SD
Supt. — See New Matamoras
Newport S 200/K-8
100 Harrison St 45768 740-473-2667
Greg Morus, prin. Fax 473-2963

New Richmond, Clermont, Pop. 2,463
New Richmond EVD 2,500/K-12
212 Market St 45157 513-553-2616
Thomas Durbin, supt. Fax 553-6431
www.nrschools.org
Monroe ES 500/K-6
2117 Laurel Lindale Rd 45157 513-553-3183
Mark Bailey, prin. Fax 553-6033
New Richmond ES 500/K-6
1141 Bethel New Richmond Rd 45157513-553-3181
Gary Combs, prin. Fax 553-2604
New Richmond MS 400/7-8
1135 Bethel New Richmond Rd 45157513-553-3161
Adam Bird, prin. Fax 553-6412
Other Schools – See Cincinnati

New Riegel, Seneca, Pop. 218
New Riegel Local SD 400/K-12
44 N Perry St 44853 419-595-2265
Elaine Nye, supt. Fax 595-2901
www.new-riegel.k12.oh.us
New Riegel ES 200/K-6
44 N Perry St 44853 419-595-2265
David Rombach, prin. Fax 595-2901

Newton Falls, Trumbull, Pop. 4,833
Newton Falls EVD 1,200/K-12
909 1/2 Milton Blvd 44444 330-872-5445
David Wilson, supt. Fax 872-3351
www.newton-falls.k12.oh.us/
Newton Falls ES 300/K-2
909 Milton Blvd 44444 330-872-5225
Ron Purnell, prin. Fax 872-0228
Newton Falls MS 400/3-6
905 Milton Blvd 44444 330-872-0695
Marilyn Liber, prin. Fax 872-8327

SS. Mary & Joseph S 200/PK-8
709 Milton Blvd 44444 330-872-7676
Sr. Carole Suhar, prin. Fax 872-1013

New Vienna, Clinton, Pop. 1,380
East Clinton Local SD
Supt. — See Lees Creek
New Vienna ES 300/K-5
301 E Church St 45159 937-987-2448
Jason Jones, prin. Fax 987-2485

New Washington, Crawford, Pop. 960
Buckeye Central Local SD 700/K-12
306 S Kibler St 44854 419-492-2864
Ronald Cirata, supt. Fax 492-2039
www.buckeye-central.k12.oh.us
Other Schools – See Bloomville, Chatfield, Tiro

St. Bernard S 100/K-8
320 W Mansfield St 44854 419-492-2693
Ben Lash, prin. Fax 492-2604

Niles, Trumbull, Pop. 20,016
Niles CSD 2,900/K-12
100 West St 44446 330-652-2509
Rocco Adduci, supt. Fax 652-3522
www.nilescityschools.org/
Bonham ES 300/K-5
120 E Margaret Ave 44446 330-652-6970
Gerome Gentile, prin. Fax 505-2191
Jackson ES 200/K-5
522 Emma St 44446 330-652-4711
John Vross, prin. Fax 544-5501
Lincoln ES 300/K-5
960 Frederick St 44446 330-652-9410
Joanna Gatta, prin. Fax 544-1629
Niles MS 700/6-8
411 Brown St 44446 330-652-5656
John Yuhasz, prin. Fax 652-9158
Washington ES 500/K-5
805 Hartzell Ave 44446 330-652-3939
Linda Ruggles, prin. Fax 652-4511

St. Stephen S 200/PK-8
45 S Chestnut Ave 44446 330-652-5511
Paula Ekis, prin. Fax 652-4264
Victory Christian S 100/K-12
2053 Pleasant Valley Rd 44446 330-539-9827
Rhonda Buie, prin. Fax 539-9828

North Baltimore, Wood, Pop. 3,343
North Baltimore Local SD 800/K-12
201 S Main St 45872 419-257-3531
Kyle Clark, supt. Fax 257-2008
www.northbaltimoreschools.org/
North Baltimore MS 100/7-8
124 S 2nd St 45872 419-257-3464
Jason Kozina, prin. Fax 257-3601
Powell ES 400/K-6
500 N Main St 45872 419-257-2124
Marlene North, prin. Fax 257-3044

North Bloomfield, Trumbull
Bloomfield-Mespo Local SD 300/K-12
2077 Park West Rd 44450 440-685-4710
Lewis Strohm, supt. Fax 685-4751
www.bloomfield.k12.oh.us
Other Schools – See Middlefield

Maplewood Local SD
Supt. — See Cortland
Maplewood ES 400/K-4
1699 Kinsman Rd NE 44450 330-583-2321
Kevin O'Connell, prin. Fax 583-3321

North Canton, Stark, Pop. 16,780
Canton CSD
Supt. — See Canton
Portage Montessori S 200/K-8
239 Portage St NW 44720 330-966-1912
Fax 966-0737

North Canton CSD 5,000/PK-12
525 7th St NE 44720 330-497-5600
Michael Gallina, supt. Fax 497-5618
www.northcanton.sparcc.org/~nccs/
Clearmount ES 300/1-5
150 Clearmount Ave SE 44720 330-497-5640
Barbara Jones, prin. Fax 966-0801
Evans ECC 400/PK-K
301 Portage St NW 44720 330-497-5608
David Stein, prin. Fax 966-0703
Greentown ES 500/1-5
3330 State St NW 44720 330-497-5645
Marjorie McDougal, prin. Fax 966-1603
North Canton MS 1,100/6-8
605 Fair Oaks Ave SW 44720 330-497-5635
John Stanley, prin. Fax 497-5659
Northwood ES 500/1-5
1500 School Ave NE 44720 330-497-5650
Benny Griffiths, prin. Fax 966-1503
Orchard Hill ES 300/1-5
1305 Jonathan Ave SW 44720 330-497-5655
Mary Juersivich, prin. Fax 966-1701

Plain Local SD
Supt. — See Canton
Little Eagle Kindergarten Plain Center 200/K-K
1000 55th St NE, Canton OH 44721 330-491-3715
Marlene Digiacinto, prin. Fax 491-3716
Middlebranch ES 400/1-5
7500 Middlebranch Ave NE, Canton OH 44721
330-491-3750
Gerald Mohn, prin. Fax 491-3751

Fieldcrest Montessori S 100/PK-8
1346 Easthill St SE 44720 330-966-2222
Scarlet Rue, hdmstr. Fax 966-1601
St. Paul S 400/K-8
303 S Main St 44720 330-494-0223
Jackie Zufall, prin. Fax 494-3226

North Eaton, Lorain

Christian Community S 200/K-12
35716 Royalton Rd 44044 440-748-6224
Richard Willis, hdmstr. Fax 748-1007

Northfield, Summit, Pop. 3,722
Nordonia Hills CSD 4,000/K-12
9370 Olde 8 Rd 44067 330-467-0580
J. Wayne Blankenship, supt. Fax 468-0152
www.nordonia.summit.k12.oh.us
Eaton ES 600/5-6
115 Ledge Rd 44067 330-467-0582
Christopher Woofter, prin. Fax 468-5218
Nordonia MS 600/7-8
73 Leonard Ave 44067 330-467-0584
Dave Wilson, prin. Fax 468-6719
Northfield ES 400/K-4
9370 Olde 8 Rd 44067 330-467-2010
Dr. Karen Muffley, prin. Fax 468-5216
Rushwood ES 400/K-4
8200 Rushwood Ln 44067 330-467-0581
Jaqueline O'Connor, prin. Fax 468-4631
Other Schools – See Macedonia

Northfield Baptist Christian S 100/PK-6
311 W Aurora Rd 44067 330-467-8918
Terry Mencarini, admin. Fax 467-4248
St. Barnabas S 800/PK-8
9200 Olde 8 Rd 44067 330-467-7921
Beverly Tabacco, prin. Fax 468-1926

North Jackson, Mahoning
Jackson-Milton Local SD 900/K-12
14110 Mahoning Ave 44451 330-538-3232
Kirk Baker, supt. Fax 538-2259
www.jacksonmilton.k12.oh.us/
Jackson-Milton ES 400/K-5
14110 Mahoning Ave 44451 330-538-2257
Joseph Diloreto, prin. Fax 538-2259
Jackson-Milton MS 200/6-8
10748 Mahoning Ave 44451 330-538-3308
David Vega, prin. Fax 538-0821

North Kingsville, Ashtabula, Pop. 2,638
Buckeye Local SD
Supt. — See Ashtabula
North Kingsville ES 200/K-6
PO Box 249 44068 440-224-0905
Ken Veon, prin.

North Lewisburg, Union, Pop. 1,590
Triad Local SD 1,100/K-12
7920 Brush Lake Rd 43060 937-826-4961
Craig Meredith, supt. Fax 826-3281
www.triad.k12.oh.us
Triad ES 400/K-4
7920 Brush Lake Rd 43060 937-826-3102
Lee Claypool, prin. Fax 826-0111
Triad MS 300/5-8
7941 Brush Lake Rd 43060 937-826-3071
Duane Caudill, prin. Fax 826-1000

North Lima, Mahoning
South Range Local SD 1,300/K-12
11836 South Ave 44452 330-549-5226
Dennis Dunham, supt. Fax 549-4740
www.southrange.k12.oh.us/
South Range ES 400/K-3
11836 South Ave 44452 330-549-5578
Steven Matos, prin. Fax 549-3430
Other Schools – See Salem

North Olmsted, Cuyahoga, Pop. 32,653
North Olmsted CSD 4,600/PK-12
27425 Butternut Ridge Rd 44070 440-779-3549
Dr. Cheryl Dubsky, supt. Fax 779-3505
www.northolmstedschools.org/
Birch PS 400/K-3
24100 Palm Dr 44070 440-779-3570
Frank Samerigo, prin. Fax 779-3521
Butternut PS 300/K-3
26669 Butternut Ridge Rd 44070 440-779-3523
Chris Sumpter, prin. Fax 779-3615
Chestnut IS 300/4-6
30395 Lorain Rd 44070 440-779-3641
Scott Moore, prin. Fax 779-3645
Forest PS 300/K-3
28963 Tudor Dr 44070 440-779-3526
Brent Monnin, prin. Fax 779-3529
Maple IS 300/4-6
24101 Maple Ridge Rd 44070 440-779-3533
Thomas Dreilling, prin. Fax 779-3617
North Olmsted MS 700/7-8
27351 Butternut Ridge Rd 44070 440-779-8501
Kurt Gabram, prin. Fax 779-8510
Pine S 400/PK-PK, 4-
4267 Dover Center Rd 44070 440-779-3536
Terese D'Amico, prin. Fax 779-3618
Spruce PS 200/K-3
28590 Windsor Dr 44070 440-779-3541
Dan Mohar, prin. Fax 779-3542

Ascension Lutheran ECC 100/PK-K
28081 Lorain Rd 44070 440-777-6365
Fax 777-1609
Hearts for Jesus Christ Christian S 300/K-12
23420 Lorain Rd Ste 206 44070 440-552-6952
Deborah Brown, admin.
St. Brendan S 200/PK-8
4242 Brendan Ln 44070 440-777-8433
Julie Onacila, prin. Fax 779-7997
St. Richard S 400/PK-8
26855 Lorain Rd 44070 440-777-2922
Michael Cappabianca, prin. Fax 777-7374

North Ridgeville, Lorain, Pop. 26,108
North Ridgeville CSD 3,800/K-12
5490 Mills Creek Ln 44039 440-327-4444
Craig Phillips, supt. Fax 327-9774
www.nrcs.k12.oh.us
Lear North ES 300/1-1
5580 Lear Nagle Rd 44039 440-353-1178
Bill Greene, prin. Fax 353-1172
Liberty ES 500/2-5
5700 Jaycox Rd 44039 440-327-6767
Linda Lapp, prin. Fax 353-3683
North Ridgeville Education Center 300/K-K
5490 Mills Creek Ln 44039 440-353-1100
Andrea Vance, prin. Fax 327-1824
North Ridgeville MS 800/6-8
35895 Center Ridge Rd 44039 440-353-1180
John Komperda, prin. Fax 353-1144
Wilcox ES 600/2-5
34580 Bainbridge Rd 44039 440-327-2220
Mark Millar, prin. Fax 353-3682

Lake Ridge Academy 400/K-12
37501 Center Ridge Rd 44039 440-327-1175
Carol Klimas, pres. Fax 353-0324
St. Peter S 300/K-8
35749 Center Ridge Rd 44039 440-327-3212
Sr. Patricia Vovk, prin. Fax 327-6843

North Robinson, Crawford, Pop. 203
Colonel Crawford Local SD 800/PK-12
PO Box 7 44856 419-562-4666
Ted Bruner, supt. Fax 562-3304
www.colonel-crawford.k12.oh.us/
Other Schools – See Crestline

North Royalton, Cuyahoga, Pop. 29,538
North Royalton CSD 4,700/PK-12
6579 Royalton Rd 44133 440-237-8800
Edward Vittardi, supt. Fax 582-7336
www.northroyaltonsd.org
Albion ES 400/1-4
9360 Albion Rd 44133 440-582-9060
Melissa Vojta, prin. Fax 582-7237
North Royalton MS 1,400/5-8
14709 Ridge Rd 44133 440-582-9120
Kirk Pavelich, prin. Fax 582-7229
Royal View ES 400/1-4
13220 Ridge Rd 44133 440-582-9080
Andrea Lasko, prin. Fax 582-7254
Valley Vista ES 400/1-4
4049 Wallings Rd 44133 440-582-9101
Elizabeth O'Donnell, prin. Fax 582-7239
Other Schools – See Broadview Heights

Royal Redeemer Lutheran S 300/PK-8
11680 Royalton Rd 44133 440-237-7988
Krista Nagy, prin. Fax 237-7713
St. Albert the Great S 800/K-8
6667 Wallings Rd 44133 440-237-1032
Tom Brownfield, prin. Fax 237-3308

North Star, Darke, Pop. 209
Versailles EVD
Supt. — See Versailles
North Star ES 100/K-5
PO Box 159 45350 419-336-7371
Brenda Braun, prin. Fax 336-7371

Northwood, Wood, Pop. 5,499
Northwood Local SD 700/K-12
600 Lemoyne Rd 43619 419-691-3888
Gregory Clark, supt. Fax 697-2470
www.northwood.k12.oh.us
Lark ES 100/K-1
331 W Andrus Rd 43619 419-666-5110
Christie McPherson, prin. Fax 666-9756
Northwood MS 200/5-8
500 Lemoyne Rd 43619 419-691-4621
Jason Kozina, prin. Fax 697-2479
Olney ES 100/2-4
512 Lemoyne Rd 43619 419-691-2601
Christie McPherson, prin. Fax 697-2473

Norton, Summit, Pop. 11,563
Norton CSD 2,400/PK-12
4128 Cleveland Massillon Rd 44203 330-825-0863
David Dunn, supt. Fax 825-0929
www.norton.k12.oh.us
Norton Cornerstone ES 200/K-4
4138 Cleveland Massillon Rd 44203 330-825-3828
Julie Gulley, prin. Fax 825-3817
Norton MS 800/5-8
3390 Cleveland Massillon Rd 44203 330-825-5607
Joyce Gerber, prin. Fax 825-1461
Norton PS 400/K-4
3163 Greenwich Rd 44203 330-825-5133
Eric Morris, prin. Fax 825-0794
Other Schools – See Clinton

Norwalk, Huron, Pop. 16,505
Norwalk CSD 3,100/K-12
134 Benedict Ave 44857 419-668-2779
Dennis Doughty, supt. Fax 663-3302
www.norwalk-city.k12.oh.us
League ES 300/K-4
16 E League St 44857 419-668-2450
Corey Ream, prin. Fax 668-6794
Main Street S 500/5-6
80 E Main St 44857 419-660-1957
Ken Moore, prin. Fax 668-0354
Maplehurst ES 500/K-4
195 Saint Marys St 44857 419-668-6035
Jacqueline Davis, prin. Fax 668-5895
Norwalk MS 500/7-8
64 Christie Ave 44857 419-668-8370
James Hagemeyer, prin. Fax 668-6622
Pleasant ES 400/K-4
16 S Pleasant St 44857 419-668-4134
Janice Smith, prin. Fax 668-4964

Norwalk Catholic S - Early Childhood Ctr 50/PK-K
77 State St 44857 419-668-8480
Cindy McLaughlin, dir. Fax 668-3269
Norwalk Catholic S - St. Paul Campus 500/PK-8
31 Milan Ave 44857 419-668-6091
Valerie French, prin. Fax 668-5584

Norwood, Hamilton, Pop. 19,997
Norwood CSD 2,400/K-12
2132 Williams Ave Ste 1 45212 513-924-2500
Steve Collier, supt. Fax 396-6420
www.norwoodschools.org
Allison Street ES 400/K-6
4300 Allison St 45212 513-924-2650
Bob Schnur, prin. Fax 396-5512
Norwood MS 400/7-8
2060 Sherman Ave 45212 513-924-2700
Kathy Sabo, prin. Fax 396-5537
Norwood View ES 400/K-6
5328 Carthage Ave 45212 513-924-2610
Sue Cash, prin. Fax 396-5527
Sharpsburg ES 300/K-6
4400 Smith Rd 45212 513-924-2600
Lori Riehle, prin. Fax 396-5528
Williams Avenue ES 200/K-6
2132 Williams Ave Ste 2 45212 513-924-2520
Tom Kitchen, prin. Fax 396-5593

Cornerstone Christian Academy 50/PK-9
PO Box 12824 45212 513-351-7900
Phyllis Wilson, dir. Fax 351-7900

Novelty, Geauga
West Geauga Local SD
Supt. — See Chesterland
Westwood ES 400/K-5
13738 Caves Rd 44072 440-729-5990
Denise Brewster, prin. Fax 729-5924

Oak Harbor, Ottawa, Pop. 2,816
Benton Carroll Salem Local SD 2,000/K-12
11685 W State Route 163 43449 419-898-6210
Diane Kershaw, supt. Fax 898-4303
www.bcs.k12.oh.us/
Carroll ES 100/K-5
3536 N State Route 19 43449 419-898-6215
Judy Peters, prin. Fax 898-1703
Oak Harbor MS 500/6-8
315 N Church St 43449 419-898-6217
Marie Wittman, prin. Fax 898-1613
Waters ES 400/K-5
220 E Ottawa St 43449 419-898-6219
Karen Gruber, prin. Fax 898-1412
Other Schools – See Graytown, Rocky Ridge

St. Boniface S 100/K-5
215 W Oak St 43449 419-898-1340
Millie Greggila, prin. Fax 898-4193

Oak Hill, Jackson, Pop. 1,656
Oak Hill Union Local SD 1,300/K-12
205 Western Ave 45656 740-682-7595
Carl McCrory, supt. Fax 682-6998
www.oakhill.k12.oh.us
Oak Hill ES 600/K-5
401 Evans St 45656 740-682-7096
Deborah Canter, prin. Fax 682-7065

Oakwood, Paulding, Pop. 8,749
Paulding EVD
Supt. — See Paulding
Oakwood ES 300/PK-6
PO Box 37 45873 419-594-3346
Jennifer Manz, prin. Fax 594-3929

Oberlin, Lorain, Pop. 8,280
Firelands Local SD 2,100/K-12
11970 Vermilion Rd 44074 440-965-5821
Gregory Ring, supt. Fax 965-5990
www.firelandsschools.org/
Firelands ES 700/K-4
10779 Vermilion Rd 44074 440-965-5381
Richard Killen, prin. Fax 965-8849
Other Schools – See South Amherst

Oberlin CSD 1,100/K-12
153 N Main St 44074 440-774-1458
Geoffrey Andrews, supt. Fax 774-4492
www.oberlin.k12.oh.us
Eastwood ES 200/K-2
198 E College St 44074 440-775-3473
Brian Carter, prin. Fax 774-7209
Langston MS 300/6-8
150 N Pleasant St 44074 440-775-7961
John Crecelius, prin. Fax 776-4520
Prospect ES 200/3-5
36 S Prospect St 44074 440-774-4421
James Eibel, prin. Fax 775-2609

Old Fort, Seneca
Old Fort Local SD 500/K-12
PO Box 64 44861 419-992-4291
Laura Keller, supt. Fax 992-4269
www.old-fort.k12.oh.us/
Old Fort ES 200/K-6
PO Box 64 44861 419-992-1024
Tim Harbal, prin. Fax 992-4293

Old Washington, Guernsey, Pop. 267
East Guernsey Local SD 1,300/K-12
PO Box 128 43768 740-489-5190
Richard Hall, supt. Fax 489-9813
www.eguernsey.k12.oh.us
Other Schools – See Lore City

Olmsted Falls, Cuyahoga, Pop. 8,437
Olmsted Falls CSD 3,600/K-12
PO Box 38010 44138 440-427-6000
Dr. Todd Hoadley, supt. Fax 427-6010
www.ofcs.k12.oh.us/
Falls-Lenox PS 1,100/K-3
26450 Bagley Rd 44138 440-427-6400
Neil Roseberry, prin. Fax 427-6410
Fitch IS 500/4-5
7105 Fitch Rd 44138 440-427-6500
Don Svec, prin. Fax 427-6510
Olmsted Falls MS 800/6-8
27045 Bagley Rd 44138 440-427-6200
Mark Kurz, prin. Fax 427-6210

St. Mary of the Falls S 200/PK-8
8262 Columbia Rd 44138 440-235-4580
Sandra Isabella, prin. Fax 235-6833

Ontario, Richland, Pop. 5,350
Ontario Local SD 1,800/PK-12
457 Shelby Ontario Rd, 419-747-4311
Daryl Hall, supt. Fax 747-6859
www.ontarioschools.org
Ontario MS 400/6-8
447 Shelby Ontario Rd, 419-529-5507
Monty Perry, prin. Fax 529-7058
Stingel IS 400/3-5
416 Shelby Ontario Rd, 419-529-7021
Mike Ream, prin. Fax 529-5037
Stingel PS 400/PK-2
426 Shelby Ontario Rd, 419-529-4955
George Fisk, prin. Fax 529-2392

Orange Village, See Cleveland

Bethlehem Christian Academy 100/PK-8
27250 Emery Rd 44128 216-292-4685
Christine Warner, hdmstr. Fax 360-9995

Oregon, Lucas, Pop. 19,175
Lucas County ESC
Supt. — See Toledo
Shuer Center S 100/K-12
4955 Seaman Rd 43616 419-698-1501
Fax 245-4186

Oregon CSD 3,900/K-12
5721 Seaman Rd 43616 419-693-0661
Mike Zalar, supt. Fax 698-6016
www.oregon.k12.oh.us
Coy ES 400/K-5
3604 Pickle Rd 43616 419-693-0624
Dawn Henry, prin. Fax 698-6018
Eisenhower MS 400/6-8
331 N North Curtice Rd 43618 419-836-8498
Jeff Thompson, prin. Fax 836-2005
Fassett MS 500/6-8
3025 Starr Ave 43616 419-693-0455
Dean Ensey, prin. Fax 698-6048
Starr ES 600/K-5
3230 Starr Ave 43616 419-693-0589
Amy Molnar, prin. Fax 698-6019
Wynn ES 300/K-5
5224 Bayshore Rd 43618 419-698-8003
Tim Holcombe, prin. Fax 698-6020
Other Schools – See Curtice

Orrville, Wayne, Pop. 8,485
Orrville CSD 1,500/K-12
815 N Ella St 44667 330-682-4651
James Ritchie, supt. Fax 682-0073
www.orrville.k12.oh.us
Maple Street ES 400/K-2
215 Maple St 44667 330-682-1761
Beverly Waseman, prin. Fax 682-2143
North ES 300/3-4
217 E Church St 44667 330-682-1851
Jennifer Gravatt, prin. Fax 683-2521
Orrville MS 300/5-8
801 Mineral Springs St 44667 330-682-1791
David Sovacool, prin. Fax 682-2743

Kingsway Christian S 300/K-12
11138 Old Lincoln Way E 44667 330-683-0012
Hollings Belcher, admin. Fax 683-0017

Orwell, Ashtabula, Pop. 1,515
Grand Valley Local SD 1,400/K-12
111 W Grand Valley Ave 44076 440-437-6260
William Nye, supt. Fax 437-1025
www.grand-valley.k12.oh.us
Grand Valley ES 500/K-4
111 W Grand Valley Ave 44076 440-437-6260
Ellen Winer, prin. Fax 437-2050
Grand Valley MS 500/5-8
111 W Grand Valley Ave 44076 440-437-6260
Lowell Moodt, prin. Fax 437-6156

Ostrander, Delaware, Pop. 527
Buckeye Valley Local SD
Supt. — See Delaware
Buckeye Valley West ES 400/K-5
61 N 3rd St 43061 740-666-2731
Mary Schroeder, prin. Fax 666-2221

Ottawa, Putnam, Pop. 4,479
Ottawa-Glandorf Local SD 1,600/K-12
630 Glendale Ave 45875 419-523-5261
Kevin Brinkman, supt. Fax 523-5978
og.noacsc.org/
Ottawa S 500/K-8
751 E 4th St 45875 419-523-4290
Denise Phillips, prin. Fax 523-6032
Other Schools – See Glandorf

SS. Peter & Paul S 300/1-8
320 N Locust St 45875 419-523-3697
William Kuhlman, prin.

Ottoville, Putnam, Pop. 864
Ottoville Local SD 600/K-12
PO Box 248 45876 419-453-3356
Scott Mangas, supt. Fax 453-3367
www.ottovilleschools.org
Ottoville ES 200/K-6
PO Box 248 45876 419-453-3357
Scott Mangas, prin. Fax 453-3367

Owensville, Clermont, Pop. 830
Clermont Northeastern Local SD
Supt. — See Batavia
Clermont Northeastern ES 500/1-4
PO Box 86 45160 513-732-0661
Chris Smith, prin. Fax 732-0285

St. Louis S 200/K-8
PO Box 85 45160 513-732-0636
Margaret Hunsberger, prin. Fax 732-1748

Oxford, Butler, Pop. 22,123
Talawanda CSD 3,000/PK-12
131 W Chestnut St 45056 513-273-3333
Dr. Philip Cagwin, supt. Fax 273-3113
www.talawanda.org
Bogan ES 400/PK-5
5200 Hamilton Richmond Rd 45056 513-273-3400
Deanna Lancaster, prin. Fax 273-3405
Kramer ES 400/PK-5
400 W Sycamore St 45056 513-273-3500
Candace McIntosh, prin. Fax 273-3505
Marshall ES 400/PK-5
3260 Oxford Millville Rd 45056 513-273-3600
Chad Hinton, prin. Fax 273-3606
Talawanda MS 700/6-8
4030 Oxford Reily Rd 45056 513-273-3300
Sharon Lytle, prin. Fax 273-3303

Painesville, Lake, Pop. 17,789
Painesville City Local SD 2,100/PK-12
58 Jefferson St 44077 440-392-5060
Michael Hanlon Ph.D., supt. Fax 392-5089
www.painesville-city.k12.oh.us
Chestnut ES 600/K-5
341 Chestnut St 44077 440-392-5350
Marilynn Leahy, prin. Fax 392-5359
Elm Street ES K-5
585 Elm St 44077 440-392-5520
Joelle Magyar, prin. Fax 392-5529
Heritage MS 6-8
135 Cedarbrook Dr 44077 440-392-5250
Denise Ward, prin. Fax 392-5259
Maple ES 300/K-5
560 W Jackson St 44077 440-392-5440
Dan Sebring, prin. Fax 392-5449
Red Raider Preschool 400/PK-PK
350 Cedarbrook Dr 44077 440-392-5610
Hannah Fairbanks, dir.

Riverside Local SD 4,700/K-12
585 Riverside Dr 44077 440-352-0668
James Kalis, supt. Fax 639-1959
www.painesville-township.k12.oh.us
Buckeye ES 300/K-5
175 Buckeye Rd 44077 440-352-2191
Eric Kujala, prin. Fax 352-1087
Hadden ES 300/K-5
1800 Mentor Ave 44077 440-354-4414
Michelle Walker, prin. Fax 354-8246
Hale Road ES 400/K-5
56 Hale Rd 44077 440-352-2300
Jack Miley, prin. Fax 352-0665
LaMuth MS 800/6-7
6700 Auburn Rd 44077 440-354-4394
Chris Rateno, prin. Fax 354-8218
Leroy ES 300/K-5
13613 Painesville Warren Rd 44077 440-358-8750
Heidi Stark, prin. Fax 254-0503
Madison Avenue ES 400/K-5
845 Madison Ave 44077 440-357-6171
Melissa Mlakar, prin. Fax 357-5690
Melridge ES 400/K-5
6689 Melridge Dr 44077 440-352-3854
Timothy St. Clair, prin. Fax 352-2076

Hershey Montessori 200/PK-8
10229 Prouty Rd 44077 440-357-0918
Laurie Ewert-Krocker, prin. Fax 357-9096
Our Shepherd Lutheran S 200/K-8
508 Mentor Ave 44077 440-357-7776
John Lelle, prin. Fax 358-1149

Pandora, Putnam, Pop. 1,214
Pandora-Gilboa Local SD 600/K-12
410 Rocket Rdg 45877 419-384-3227
Dale Lewellen, supt. Fax 384-3230
www.pg.noacsc.org
Pandora-Gilboa ES 200/K-4
410 Rocket Rdg 45877 419-384-3225
Todd Schmutz, prin. Fax 384-3230
Pandora-Gilboa MS 200/5-8
410 Rocket Rdg 45877 419-384-3225
Todd Schmutz, prin. Fax 384-3230

Parma, Cuyahoga, Pop. 81,469
Parma CSD 12,500/PK-12
5311 Longwood Ave 44134 440-842-5300
Dr. Sarah Zatik, supt. Fax 885-2452
www.parmacityschools.org/
Dentzler ES 400/K-6
3600 Dentzler Rd 44134 440-885-2430
Dr. Gayle Clapp, prin. Fax 885-3704
Greenbriar MS 800/7-8
11810 Huffman Rd 44130 440-885-2368
Frank Spisak, prin. Fax 885-8353
Green Valley ES 400/K-6
2401 W Pleasant Valley Rd 44134 440-885-2431
Dr. E.J. Mahoney, prin. Fax 885-3705
Hammarskjold ES 300/K-6
4040 Tamarack Dr 44134 440-885-2383
Rick Ruth, prin. Fax 885-3703
Hanna ES 400/K-6
11212 Snow Rd 44130 440-885-3712
Jacqueline Marconi, prin. Fax 885-2358
Muir ES 600/K-6
5531 W 24th St 44134 440-885-2424
Denver Daniel, prin. Fax 885-2472

Parkview Preschool 300/PK-PK
5210 Loya Pkwy 44134 440-885-2455
Fax 885-3718
Pleasant Valley ES 500/K-6
9906 W Pleasant Valley Rd 44130 440-885-2380
Susan Rueger, prin. Fax 885-8664
Renwood ES 300/K-6
8020 Deerfield Dr 44129 440-885-2338
Lillian Scafidi, prin. Fax 885-3716
Ridge-Brook ES 400/K-6
7915 Manhattan Ave 44129 440-885-2350
Regina Ohlrogge, prin. Fax 885-3717
Shiloh MS 700/7-8
2303 Grantwood Dr 44134 440-885-8485
Phyllis Spears, prin. Fax 885-8486
State Road ES 400/K-6
6121 State Rd 44134 440-885-2334
Jill Zidow, prin. Fax 885-3719
Thoreau Park ES 700/K-6
5401 W 54th St 44129 440-885-2351
Karen Hronek, prin. Fax 885-2460
Other Schools – See Parma Heights, Seven Hills

Bethany Christian S 200/K-6
6195 Broadview Rd 44134 216-661-6600
Allen Lindsay, prin. Fax 661-2095
Bethany Lutheran S 400/PK-8
6041 Ridge Rd 44129 440-884-1010
Kenneth Boerger, prin. Fax 884-9834
Bethel Christian Academy 200/PK-8
12901 W Pleasant Valley Rd 44130 440-842-8575
Nancy Roenn, prin. Fax 842-3226
Holy Family S 300/PK-8
7367 York Rd 44130 440-842-7785
Mary Ann Murnyack, prin. Fax 842-3634
St. Anthony of Padua S 400/K-8
6800 State Rd 44134 440-845-3444
Sr. Roberta Goebel, prin. Fax 884-4548
St. Bridget S 200/PK-8
5620 Hauserman Rd 44130 440-886-1468
Karen Lamson, prin. Fax 886-5121
St. Charles Borromeo S 600/PK-8
7107 Wilber Ave 44129 440-886-5546
Eileen Updegrove, prin. Fax 886-1163
St. Columbkille S 500/PK-8
6740 Broadview Rd 44134 216-524-4816
Rita Klement, prin. Fax 524-4153
St. Francis De Sales S 200/K-8
3421 Snow Rd 44134 440-884-2340
Anne Sweeney, prin. Fax 884-8211

Parma Heights, Cuyahoga, Pop. 20,657
Parma CSD
Supt. — See Parma
Parma Park ES 400/K-6
6800 Commonwealth Blvd 44130 440-885-2390
Jodie Hausmann, prin. Fax 885-3707
Pearl Road ES 400/K-6
6125 Pearl Rd 44130 440-885-2342
Patrick Yarman, prin. Fax 885-3708

Incarnate Word Academy 500/K-8
6618 Pearl Rd 44130 440-842-6818
Martha Jacobs, prin. Fax 888-1377
Parma Heights Christian Academy 200/K-6
8971 W Ridgewood Dr 44130 440-845-8668
David Griffey, admin. Fax 886-5748

Pataskala, Licking, Pop. 12,624
Licking Heights Local SD 2,700/K-12
6539 Summit Rd SW 43062 740-927-6926
Dr. Thomas Tucker, supt. Fax 927-9043
www.licking-heights.k12.oh.us/
Licking Heights Central MS 600/6-8
6565 Summit Rd SW 43062 740-927-3365
Brian Wilkenson, prin. Fax 927-5845
Licking Heights North ES 300/4-5
6507 Summit Rd SW 43062 740-927-3268
Kimberly Henderson, prin. Fax 927-5736
Licking Heights South ES 600/2-4
6623 Summit Rd SW 43062 740-964-1674
James Kennedy, prin. Fax 964-1625
Other Schools – See Blacklick

Southwest Licking Local SD 3,700/K-12
927 South St Unit A 43062 740-927-3941
Forest Yocum, supt. Fax 927-4648
www.swl.k12.oh.us
Etna ES 600/1-5
8500 Columbia Rd SW 43062 740-927-5906
Paula Englert, prin. Fax 964-0129
Pataskala ES 500/1-5
395 S High St 43062 740-927-3861
Denise Staffilino, prin. Fax 927-7259
Southwest Licking K 300/K-K
927 South St Unit B 43062 740-927-1130
Dana Letts, prin. Fax 927-6506
Watkins MS 900/6-8
8808 Watkins Rd SW 43062 740-927-5767
G. Chris Kyre, prin. Fax 927-2337
Other Schools – See Kirkersville

Liberty Christian Academy - East Campus 100/PK-12
10447 Refugee Rd SW 43062 740-964-2211
LaVonne McIlrath, admin. Fax 964-2311

Patriot, Gallia
Gallia County Local SD
Supt. — See Gallipolis
Southwestern S 300/K-8
4834 State Route 325 45658 740-379-2532
Larry Carter, prin. Fax 379-2000

Paulding, Paulding, Pop. 3,430
Paulding EVD 1,700/PK-12
405 N Water St 45879 419-399-4656
Patricia Ross, supt. Fax 399-2404
www.pauldingschools.org/
Paulding ES 500/PK-5
405 N Water St 45879 419-399-4656
Martin Miller, prin. Fax 399-2404
Paulding MS 300/6-8
405 N Water St 45879 419-399-4656
David Stallkamp, prin. Fax 399-2404
Other Schools – See Oakwood

Payne, Paulding, Pop. 1,149
Wayne Trace Local SD
Supt. — See Haviland
Payne ES 300/PK-6
501 W Townline St 45880 419-263-2512
Sarah Deatrick, prin. Fax 263-1313

Divine Mercy Catholic S 100/PK-6
PO Box 98 45880 419-263-2114
Cathy Schoenauer, prin. Fax 263-2114

Peebles, Adams, Pop. 1,845
Adams County/Ohio Valley Local SD
Supt. — See West Union
Peebles ES 600/K-6
1 Simmons Ave 45660 937-587-2611
Ann Charles, prin. Fax 587-5240

Pemberton, Shelby
Fairlawn Local SD
Supt. — See Sidney
Fairlawn ES 300/K-5
PO Box 24A 45353 937-492-1654
Eric Barr, prin. Fax 492-5326

Pemberville, Wood, Pop. 1,351
Eastwood Local SD 1,700/K-12
4800 Sugar Ridge Rd 43450 419-833-6411
Brent Welker, supt. Fax 833-4915
www.eastwood.k12.oh.us/
Eastwood MS 500/6-8
4800 Sugar Ridge Rd 43450 419-833-6011
John Obrock, prin. Fax 833-7454
Pemberville ES 300/K-5
120 W College Ave 43450 419-287-3200
Thomas Lingenfelder, prin. Fax 287-4245
Webster ES 200/K-5
17345 State Route 199 43450 419-833-5751
Thomas Lingenfelder, prin. Fax 833-5917
Other Schools – See Luckey

Peninsula, Summit, Pop. 664
Woodridge Local SD 1,900/K-12
4411 Quick Rd 44264 330-928-9074
Dr. Jeffrey Graham, supt. Fax 928-1542
www.woodridge.k12.oh.us/
Woodridge IS 400/3-5
1930 Bronson St 44264 330-657-2351
Betsy Gorrell, prin. Fax 657-2353
Woodridge MS 500/6-8
4451 Quick Rd 44264 330-928-7420
Linda Ocepek, prin. Fax 928-5645
Other Schools – See Cuyahoga Falls

Pepper Pike, Cuyahoga, Pop. 5,794

Gross Schechter Day S 300/PK-8
27601 Fairmount Blvd 44124 216-763-1400
Rabbi Jim Rogozen, prin. Fax 763-1106
Ratner S 200/PK-8
27575 Shaker Blvd 44124 216-464-0033
Sam Chestnut, dir. Fax 464-0031

Perry, Lake, Pop. 1,267
Perry Local SD 1,900/K-12
4325 Manchester Rd 44081 440-259-3881
Michael Sawyers, supt. Fax 259-3607
www.perry-lake.k12.oh.us
Perry ES 700/K-4
1 Learning Ln 44081 440-259-2781
Michele Pulling, prin. Fax 259-9649
Perry MS 600/5-8
2 Learning Ln 44081 440-259-3026
Scott Hunt, prin. Fax 259-5149

Perrysburg, Wood, Pop. 16,980
Perrysburg EVD 4,400/K-12
140 E Indiana Ave 43551 419-874-9131
Thomas Hosler, supt. Fax 872-8820
www.perrysburg.k12.oh.us
Fort Meigs ES 500/K-5
26431 Fort Meigs Rd 43551 419-872-8822
Scott Best, prin. Fax 872-8825
Frank ES 400/K-5
401 W South Boundary St 43551 419-874-8721
Brent Swartzmiller, prin. Fax 874-1808
Perrysburg JHS 1,100/6-8
550 E South Boundary St 43551 419-874-9193
Dale Wiltse, prin. Fax 872-8812
Toth ES 400/K-5
200 E 7th St 43551 419-874-3123
Dr. M. Beth Christoff, prin. Fax 872-8828
Woodland ES 500/K-5
27979 White Rd 43551 419-874-8736
Daniel Creps, prin. Fax 874-2964

Rossford EVD
Supt. — See Rossford
Glenwood ES 400/K-6
8950 Avenue Rd 43551 419-666-8130
William Buzzell, prin. Fax 661-2848

St. Rose S 400/PK-8
217 E Front St 43551 419-874-5631
Barbara Jenks, prin. Fax 874-1002

Perrysville, Ashland, Pop. 822
Loudonville-Perrysville EVD
Supt. — See Loudonville
Perrysville JHS 200/7-8
PO Box 426 44864 419-938-7193
John Lance, prin. Fax 938-3304

Pettisville, Fulton
Pettisville Local SD 600/K-12
PO Box 53001 43553 419-446-2705
Stephen Switzer, supt. Fax 445-2992
blackbirds.pettisville.k12.oh.us/
Pettisville ES 300/K-6
PO Box 53001 43553 419-446-2705
Jason Waldvogel, prin. Fax 445-2992

Philo, Muskingum, Pop. 769
Franklin Local SD
Supt. — See Duncan Falls
Philo JHS 400/6-8
PO Box 178 43771 740-674-5210
Tony Sines, prin. Fax 674-5217

Pickerington, Fairfield, Pop. 15,878
Pickerington Local SD 10,000/K-12
777 Long Rd 43147 614-833-2110
Dr. Karen Mantia, supt. Fax 833-2143
www.pickerington.k12.oh.us
Diley MS 700/5-6
750 Preston Trails Dr 43147 614-833-3630
Mark Jones, prin. Fax 833-3640
Fairfield ES 800/K-4
13000 Coventry Ave 43147 614-866-1225
Ruth Stickel, prin. Fax 866-1302
Harmon MS 900/5-6
12410 Harmon Rd 43147 614-751-3570
Gary Morrow, prin. Fax 751-3580
Heritage ES 700/K-4
100 N East St 43147 614-833-6385
David Toopes, prin. Fax 833-6415
Pickerington ES 700/K-4
775 Long Rd 43147 614-833-2115
Jane Vazquez, prin. Fax 833-3054
Pickerington Lakeview JHS 900/7-8
12445 Ault Rd 43147 614-830-2200
Jeff Clark, prin. Fax 834-3267
Pickerington Ridgeview JHS 800/7-8
130 Hill Rd S 43147 614-833-2100
Charles Byers, prin. Fax 833-2127
Violet ES 700/K-4
8855 Education Dr 43147 614-833-2130
Kristi Motsch, prin. Fax 833-3060
Other Schools – See Reynoldsburg

Piketon, Pike, Pop. 1,973
Scioto Valley Local SD 1,700/K-12
PO Box 600 45661 740-289-4456
Dr. Todd Burkitt, supt. Fax 289-3065
www.piketon.k12.oh.us/
Jasper ES 500/K-3
3185 Jasper Rd 45661 740-289-2425
James Roberts, prin. Fax 289-4437
Zahn's MS 300/4-6
2379 Schuster Rd 45661 740-289-2871
Wayne Bloomfield, prin. Fax 289-2291

Miracle City Academy 50/PK-12
204 Commercial Blvd 45661 740-289-2787
Malcolm Cisco, prin. Fax 289-2013

Pioneer, Williams, Pop. 1,428
North Central Local SD 700/PK-12
400 E Baubice St 43554 419-737-2392
Kenneth Boyer, supt. Fax 737-3361
www.ncschool.k12.oh.us/
North Central ES 400/PK-6
400 E Baubice St 43554 419-737-2293
Erik Belcher, prin. Fax 737-3361

Piqua, Miami, Pop. 20,883
Piqua CSD 3,800/K-12
719 E Ash St 45356 937-773-4321
Richard Hanes, supt. Fax 778-4518
portal2.piqua.org/
Bennett IS 300/4-6
625 S Main St 45356 937-773-0386
Dan Hake, prin. Fax 778-2986
Favorite Hill PS 300/1-3
950 South St 45356 937-773-4678
Melinda Gearhardt, prin. Fax 778-2991
High Street PS 300/1-3
1249 W High St 45356 937-773-3567
Rick Fry, prin. Fax 778-2992
Nicklin Learning Center 300/K-K
818 Nicklin Ave 45356 937-773-4742
Teresa Anderson, prin. Fax 778-2993
Piqua JHS 600/7-8
1 Tomahawk Trl 45356 937-778-2997
Jeff Clark, prin. Fax 773-3574
Springcreek PS 300/1-3
145 E US Route 36 45356 937-773-6540
Molly Hay, prin. Fax 778-2995
Washington IS 300/4-6
800 N Sunset Dr 45356 937-773-8472
Loretta Henderson, prin. Fax 778-2996
Wilder IS 300/4-6
1120 Nicklin Ave 45356 937-773-2017
Curtis Montgomery, prin. Fax 778-2988

Piqua Catholic S 100/K-3
218 S Downing St 45356 937-773-3876
Anthony Frierott, prin. Fax 773-5875
Piqua Catholic S - North 200/4-8
503 W North St 45356 937-773-1564
Anthony Frierott, prin. Fax 773-0380
Piqua SDA S 50/1-8
4020 W State Route 185 45356 937-778-0223
Mark Mirek, prin.

Pitsburg, Darke, Pop. 393
Franklin Monroe Local SD 800/K-12
PO Box 78 45358 937-692-8637
David Gray, supt. Fax 692-6547
www.franklin-monroe.k12.oh.us/
Other Schools – See Arcanum

Plain City, Madison, Pop. 3,462
Jonathan Alder Local SD 2,000/PK-12
9200 US Highway 42 S 43064 614-873-5621
Douglas Carpenter Ph.D., supt. Fax 873-8462
www.alder.k12.oh.us
Alder JHS 300/7-8
6440 Kilbury Huber Rd 43064 614-873-4635
Jud Ross, prin. Fax 873-0845
Canaan MS 300/5-6
7055 US Highway 42 S 43064 614-733-3975
Chris Piper, prin. Fax 733-3972
Plain City ES 500/PK-4
340 W Main St 43064 614-873-4608
Kelly Hicks, prin. Fax 873-2559
Other Schools – See London

Pleasant Hill, Miami, Pop. 1,140
Newton Local SD 500/K-12
PO Box 803 45359 937-676-3271
Pat McBride, supt. Fax 676-2054
www.newton.k12.oh.us/
Newton ES 300/K-6
PO Box 803 45359 937-676-8355
Danielle Davis, prin. Fax 676-2054

Pleasant Plain, Warren, Pop. 164

Village Christian S 200/PK-12
PO Box 48 45162 513-877-2143
Chuck Chapman, admin. Fax 877-2102

Pleasantville, Fairfield, Pop. 856
Fairfield Union Local SD
Supt. — See Rushville
Pleasantville ES 400/K-4
225 Lincoln Ave 43148 740-468-2181
Rebecca Parrott, prin. Fax 468-3539

Plymouth, Huron, Pop. 1,860
Plymouth-Shiloh Local SD 1,000/K-12
365 Sandusky St 44865 419-687-4733
James Metcalf, supt. Fax 687-1541
plymouth.schoolwires.com/plymouth/site/
Plymouth PS 200/K-1
400 Trux St 44865 419-896-3721
Susan Gray, admin. Fax 896-2937
Shiloh ES 200/2-5
420 Trux St 44865 419-896-2691
Susan Gray, prin. Fax 896-2937
Shiloh MS 200/6-8
400 Trux St 44865 419-687-4061
Bradley Turson, prin. Fax 887-8175

Poland, Mahoning, Pop. 2,750
Poland Local SD 2,400/K-12
3199 Dobbins Rd 44514 330-757-7000
Robert Zorn, supt. Fax 757-2390
www.polandbulldogs.com/
Dobbins ES 200/K-4
3030 Dobbins Rd 44514 330-757-7011
Cheryl Borovitcky, prin. Fax 757-2390
McKinley ES 400/5-6
7 Elm St 44514 330-757-7015
Edward Kempers, prin. Fax 757-2390
North ES 200/K-4
361 Johnston Pl 44514 330-757-7008
Michael Masucci, prin. Fax 757-2390
Poland MS 400/7-8
47 College St 44514 330-757-7003
Mark Covell, prin. Fax 757-2390
Poland Union ES 300/K-4
30 Riverside Dr 44514 330-757-7014
Carmella Smallhoover, prin. Fax 757-2390

Holy Family S 300/K-8
2731 Center Rd 44514 330-757-3713
Christine Kijowski, prin. Fax 757-7648

Pomeroy, Meigs, Pop. 1,999
Meigs Local SD 2,000/K-12
41765 Pomeroy Pike 45769 740-992-2153
William Buckley, supt. Fax 992-7814
www.meigslocalschools.org/
Meigs MS 500/6-8
42353 Charles Chancey Dr 45769 740-992-3058
Mary Hawk, prin. Fax 992-6952
Other Schools – See Middleport

Port Clinton, Ottawa, Pop. 6,336
Port Clinton CSD 1,200/K-12
431 Portage Dr 43452 419-732-2102
Patrick Adkins, supt. Fax 734-4527
www.port-clinton.k12.oh.us
Bataan Memorial ES 100/K-2
525 W 6th St 43452 419-734-2815
Kendra Van Doren, prin. Fax 734-2682
Jefferson ES 100/3-5
430 Jefferson St 43452 419-734-3931
Gary Steyer, prin. Fax 734-3705
Port Clinton MS 300/6-8
110 E 4th St 43452 419-734-4448
Robert Nobles, prin. Fax 734-4440

Immaculate Conception S 200/PK-6
109 W 4th St 43452 419-734-3315
Sr. Rosemary Hug, prin. Fax 734-6172

Portsmouth, Scioto, Pop. 20,101
Clay Local SD 600/K-12
44 Clay High St 45662 740-354-6645
Anthony Mantell, supt. Fax 354-5746
clay.k12.oh.us/
Rosemount ES 200/K-3
4484 Rose Valley Rd 45662 740-353-0428
Tony Piguet, prin. Fax 354-3822
Rubyville ES 100/4-6
3019 Maple Benner Rd 45662 740-353-0272
Tony Piguet, prin. Fax 353-6620

Portsmouth CSD 2,100/K-12
923 Findlay St 45662 740-354-5663
Donald Armstrong, supt. Fax 354-8872
www.portsmouthtrojans.org
East Portsmouth ES 200/K-6
5929 Harding Ave 45662 740-776-6444
Kristi Toppins, prin. Fax 776-6296
Portsmouth ES 1,000/K-6
514 Union St 45662 740-353-6719
Charles Kemp, prin. Fax 353-1778

Notre Dame S 300/PK-6
1401 Gallia St 45662 740-353-8610
Kay Kern, prin. Fax 353-6769

Port Washington, Tuscarawas, Pop. 567
Indian Valley Local SD
Supt. — See Gnadenhutten
Port Washington ES 400/K-5
PO Box 8 43837 740-498-8389
James Kennedy, prin. Fax 498-6312

Powell, Delaware, Pop. 10,504
Dublin CSD
Supt. — See Dublin
Chapman ES 500/K-5
8450 Sawmill Rd 43065 614-761-5864
Dr. Robyn Floyd, prin. Fax 761-5867

Olentangy Local SD
Supt. — See Lewis Center
Indian Springs ES 700/K-5
3828 Home Rd 43065 740-657-4950
Chris Heuser, prin. Fax 657-4999
Liberty Tree ES 600/PK-5
6877 Sawmill Pkwy 43065 740-657-5600
Teresa Caton, prin. Fax 657-5649
Olentangy Hyatts MS 600/6-8
6885 Sawmill Pkwy 43065 740-657-5400
Kathy McFarland, prin. Fax 657-5499
Olentangy Liberty MS 1,000/6-8
7940 Liberty Rd N 43065 740-657-4400
Gena Williams, prin. Fax 657-4499
Scioto Ridge ES 600/K-5
8715 Big Bear Ave 43065 740-657-4800
Julie Nolan, prin. Fax 657-4849
Tyler Run ES 700/K-5
580 Salisbury Dr 43065 740-657-4900
Jennifer Mazza, prin. Fax 657-4949
Wyandot Run ES 800/PK-5
2800 Carriage Rd 43065 740-657-4850
Laurie Feehan, prin. Fax 657-4899

Worthington CSD
Supt. — See Worthington
Liberty ES 500/K-6
8081 Saddle Run 43065 614-883-2950
Jim Baker, prin. Fax 883-2960

Village Academy 500/PK-12
284 S Liberty St 43065 614-841-0050
Susan Lasley, dir. Fax 841-0501
Worthington Christian - Powell S 50/K-3
7600 Liberty Rd N 43065 740-881-6212
Troy McIntosh, prin. Fax 881-6719

Powhatan Point, Belmont, Pop. 1,703
Switzerland of Ohio Local SD
Supt. — See Woodsfield
Powhatan Point S 300/K-8
125 2nd St 43942 740-795-5665
Curtis Wisvari, prin. Fax 795-5830

Proctorville, Lawrence, Pop. 629
Fairland Local SD 1,800/K-12
228 Private Drive 10010 45669 740-886-3100
Jerry McConnell, supt. Fax 886-7253
fairland.k12.oh.us/
Fairland East ES 400/K-2
10732 State Route 7 45669 740-886-3120
Margaret Keeney, prin. Fax 886-7630
Fairland MS 400/6-8
7875 County Road 107 45669 740-886-3200
Michael Whitley, prin. Fax 886-5125
Fairland West ES 400/3-5
110 Township Road 1125 45669 740-886-3150
Mary Cooper-Johnson, prin. Fax 886-5259

Prospect, Marion, Pop. 1,142
Elgin Local SD
Supt. — See Marion
Elgin South ES 400/K-6
200 N East St 43342 740-494-2677
Jennifer Adams, prin. Fax 494-2991

Put in Bay, Ottawa, Pop. 135
Put-in-Bay Local SD 100/K-12
PO Box 659 43456 419-285-3614
Steven Poe, supt. Fax 285-2137
www.put-in-bay.k12.oh.us
Put-in-Bay ES 50/K-6
PO Box 659 43456 419-285-3614
Steven Poe, prin. Fax 285-2137

Racine, Meigs, Pop. 757
Southern Local SD 700/K-12
920 Elm St 45771 740-949-2669
Tony Deem, supt. Fax 949-3309
www.southernlocalmeigs.org/
Southern ES 300/K-4
906 Elm St 45771 740-949-4222
Scott Wolfe, prin. Fax 949-1101
Southern MS 200/5-8
920 Elm St 45771 740-949-4222
Kent Wolfe, prin. Fax 949-1101

Radnor, Delaware
Buckeye Valley Local SD
Supt. — See Delaware

Buckeye Valley North ES 300/K-5
4230 State Route 203 43066 740-363-6695
Barry Lyons, prin. Fax 595-3441

Ravenna, Portage, Pop. 11,510
Ravenna CSD 2,600/K-12
507 E Main St 44266 330-296-9679
Dr. Tim Calfee, supt. Fax 297-4158
www.ravenna.portage.k12.oh.us
Brown MS 500/6-8
228 S Scranton St 44266 330-296-3849
Judy Paydock, prin. Fax 297-4146
Carlin ES 200/1-5
531 Washington Ave 44266 330-296-6622
Robert Mittiga, prin. Fax 297-4144
Tappan ES 200/1-5
310 Bennett Ave 44266 330-296-6721
Ben Ribelin, prin. Fax 297-4145
West Main ES 300/1-5
639 W Main St 44266 330-296-6522
Deborah Grant, prin. Fax 297-4149
West Park S 300/K-K
1071 Jones St 44266 330-297-1744
Donna Sell, prin. Fax 297-4167
Willyard ES 300/1-5
680 Summit Rd 44266 330-296-6481
Diana Kentner, prin. Fax 297-4151

Southeast Local SD 1,700/K-12
8245 Tallmadge Rd 44266 330-654-5841
Tom Harrison, supt. Fax 654-9110
se-web.portage.k12.oh.us/
Southeast Campus PS 100/K-2
8301 Tallmadge Rd 44266 330-654-5841
David Ulbricht, prin. Fax 654-9110
Southeast IS 400/3-5
8301 Tallmadge Rd 44266 330-654-5841
Abbey Bolton, prin. Fax 654-9110
Other Schools – See Diamond

Rawson, Hancock, Pop. 462
Cory-Rawson Local SD 500/K-12
3930 County Road 26 45881 419-963-3415
Jay Arbaugh, supt. Fax 963-4400
cory-rawson.k12.oh.us
Cory-Rawson ES 200/K-6
220 S Main St 45881 419-963-2121
Ann Spuller, prin. Fax 963-4400

Rayland, Jefferson, Pop. 412
Buckeye Local SD
Supt. — See Dillonvale
Buckeye Northwest ES 200/PK-5
680 Hill St 43943 740-733-7700
Ken Bonnell, prin. Fax 733-7125

Raymond, Union
Marysville EVD
Supt. — See Marysville
Raymond ES 300/K-4
21511 Main St 43067 937-246-2861
Donna Ball, prin. Fax 246-2801

Reading, Hamilton, Pop. 10,320
Reading Community CSD 1,400/K-12
1301 Bonnell St 45215 513-554-1800
L. Scott Inskeep, supt. Fax 483-6754
www.readingschools.org
Central Community ES 300/K-6
1301 Bonnell St 45215 513-554-1001
Connie Garafalo, prin. Fax 483-6754
Hilltop Community ES 400/K-6
2236 Bolser Dr 45215 513-733-4322
Robert Longworth, prin. Fax 483-6772

Our Lady of the Sacred Heart S 300/K-8
170 Siebenthaler Ave 45215 513-733-5225
JoAnne Fischesser, prin. Fax 733-0186
SS. Peter & Paul S 200/K-8
231 Clark Rd 45215 513-761-7772
Glenda Donnelly, prin.

Reedsville, Meigs
Eastern Local SD 800/K-12
50008 State Route 681 45772 740-667-6079
Rick Edwards, supt. Fax 667-3978
el.k12.oh.us/
Eastern S 600/K-8
38850 State Route 7 45772 740-985-3304
Jody Howard, prin. Fax 985-4318

Reynoldsburg, Franklin, Pop. 33,059
Pickerington Local SD
Supt. — See Pickerington
Tussing ES 800/K-4
7117 Tussing Rd 43068 614-759-3400
Jeannette Henson, prin. Fax 759-3404

Reynoldsburg CSD 7,300/K-12
7244 E Main St 43068 614-501-1020
Stephen Dackin, supt. Fax 501-1050
www.reyn.org/
Ashton MS 500/5-6
1482 Jackson St 43068 614-367-1530
Tina Thomas-Manning, prin. Fax 367-1549
Baldwin Road JHS 1,100/7-8
2300 Baldwin Pl 43068 614-367-1600
Terrance Hubbard, prin. Fax 367-1625
French Run ES 400/K-4
1200 Epworth Ave 43068 614-367-1950
Jana Alig, prin. Fax 367-1958
Graham Road ES 200/K-4
1555 Graham Rd 43068 614-367-1980
Mary Ann Burns, prin. Fax 367-1984
Mills ES 400/K-4
6826 Retton Rd 43068 614-367-2160
Craig Seckel, prin. Fax 367-2168
Rose Hill ES 400/K-4
760 Rosehill Rd 43068 614-367-2390
Theodore Frissora, prin. Fax 575-5868

Slate Ridge ES 500/K-4
10466 Taylor Rd SW 43068 614-501-5500
Karen Hand, prin. Fax 501-5520
Taylor Road ES 500/K-4
8200 Taylor Rd SW 43068 614-367-2930
Darrell Propst, prin. Fax 367-2933
Waggoner Road JHS 600/7-8
360 Waggoner Rd 43068 614-501-5700
Tyrone Olverson, prin. Fax 501-5700
Waggoner Road MS 500/5-6
340 Waggoner Rd 43068 614-501-5600
Valerie Maher, prin. Fax 501-5622

New Life S of Excellence 50/K-12
PO Box 461 43068 614-501-8363
Lee Hutcheson, prin. Fax 501-8363
St. Pius X S 600/PK-8
1061 Waggoner Rd 43068 614-866-6050
Kathy DeMatteo, prin. Fax 866-6187

Richfield, Summit, Pop. 3,553
Revere Local SD 2,800/K-12
3496 Everett Rd 44286 330-666-4155
Randy Boroff, supt. Fax 659-3127
www.revere.k12.oh.us
Hillcrest ES 700/K-3
3080 Revere Rd 44286 330-659-6111
Katie Kowza, prin. Fax 659-6701
Other Schools – See Akron, Bath

Richmond Heights, Cuyahoga, Pop. 10,521
Richmond Heights Local SD 900/PK-12
447 Richmond Rd 44143 216-692-8485
Jim Herrholtz, supt. Fax 692-2820
www.richmond-heights.k12.oh.us
Richmond Heights ES 500/PK-6
447 Richmond Rd 44143 216-692-0099
Pam Barovian, prin. Fax 692-8499

Richmond Heights Christian S 100/K-6
25595 Chardon Rd 44143 216-261-0901
Rev. Richard Youngstrom, prin. Fax 261-7088

Richwood, Union, Pop. 2,132
North Union Local SD 1,500/K-12
12920 State Route 739 43344 740-943-2509
Rick Smith, supt. Fax 943-2534
www.n-union.k12.oh.us
North Union ES 700/K-5
420 Grove St 43344 740-943-3113
Lisa Wolfe, prin. Fax 943-1010
North Union MS 400/6-8
16 Norris St 43344 740-943-2369
Diana Martin, prin. Fax 943-9279

Rio Grande, Gallia, Pop. 875
Gallipolis CSD
Supt. — See Gallipolis
Rio Grande ES 300/K-6
PO Box 197 45674 740-245-5333
Rick Bowman, prin. Fax 245-9235

Ripley, Brown, Pop. 1,813
Ripley-Union-Lewis-Huntington Local SD 1,300/K-12
120 Main St 45167 937-392-4396
Charles Birkholtz, supt. Fax 392-7003
www.rulh.k12.oh.us
Ripley-Union-Lewis-Huntington ES 400/K-4
502 S 2nd St 45167 937-392-1141
Jane Massie, prin. Fax 392-7027
Other Schools – See Aberdeen

St. Michael S 100/PK-8
300 Market St 45167 937-392-4202
Sr. Carol Ann Mause, prin. Fax 392-4248

Risingsun, Wood, Pop. 607
Lakota Local SD 1,100/PK-12
PO Box 5 43457 419-457-2911
Rebecca Heimlich, supt. Fax 457-0535
www.lakota-sandusky.k12.oh.us
Lakota Central ES 200/PK-K, 2-4
PO Box 5 43457 419-457-2441
Joshua Matz, prin. Fax 457-0535
Other Schools – See Bradner, Burgoon, Fostoria

Risingsun Community Christian S 50/K-6
238 State Route 23 43457 419-457-3325
Linda Carpenter, dir. Fax 457-4285

Rittman, Wayne, Pop. 6,311
Rittman EVD 1,100/K-12
75 N Main St 44270 330-927-7400
James Ritchie, supt. Fax 927-7405
www.rittman.k12.oh.us/
Rittman ES 500/K-5
131 N Metzger Ave 44270 330-927-7460
Elizabeth McNicholas, prin. Fax 927-7465
Rittman MS 200/6-7
75 N Main St 44270 330-927-7100
Stephen Breckner, prin. Fax 927-7105

Eastern Road Christian Academy 50/K-12
2600 Eastern Rd 44270 330-925-5437
Faron Cole, prin. Fax 927-0448

Rock Creek, Ashtabula, Pop. 572
Jefferson Area Local SD
Supt. — See Jefferson
Rock Creek ES 300/K-6
3134 N Main St 44084 440-563-3820
Larry Meloro, prin. Fax 576-9876

Rockford, Mercer, Pop. 1,118
Parkway Local SD 900/K-12
400 Buckeye St 45882 419-363-3045
Gregory Puthoff, supt. Fax 363-2595
www.parkwayschools.org/
Parkway ES 200/K-5
400 Buckeye St 45882 419-363-3045
Mark Esselstein, prin. Fax 363-2598
Parkway MS 300/6-8
400 Buckeye St 45882 419-363-3045
Steve Baumgartner, prin. Fax 363-2597

Rocky Ridge, Ottawa, Pop. 394
Benton Carroll Salem Local SD
Supt. — See Oak Harbor
Rocky Ridge ES 100/K-5
1098 N West St 43458 419-898-6218
Mary Ann Widmer, prin. Fax 898-1530

Rocky River, Cuyahoga, Pop. 19,681
Rocky River CSD 2,700/K-12
21600 Center Ridge Rd 44116 440-333-6000
Michael Shoaf, supt. Fax 356-6014
www.rrcs.org
Goldwood PS 600/K-2
21600 Center Ridge Rd 44116 440-356-6720
Marianne Winemiller, prin. Fax 356-6044
Kensington IS 600/3-5
20140 Lake Rd 44116 440-356-6770
Todd Murphy, prin. Fax 356-6040
Rocky River MS 600/6-8
1631 Lakeview Ave 44116 440-356-6870
David Root, prin. Fax 356-6881

Ruffing Montessori S 300/K-8
1285 Orchard Park Dr 44116 440-333-2250
John McNamara, prin. Fax 333-2540
St. Christopher S 500/K-8
1610 Lakeview Ave 44116 440-331-3075
Joyce Needham, prin. Fax 331-0674
St. Thomas Lutheran S 100/PK-8
21211 Detroit Rd 44116 440-331-4426
Cathie Lucarelli, prin. Fax 331-2681

Rogers, Columbiana, Pop. 260
Beaver Local SD
Supt. — See Lisbon
Rogers ES 200/K-4
8059 Sprucevale Rd 44455 330-385-6401
Elizabeth Scott, prin. Fax 385-6402

Rootstown, Portage
Rootstown Local SD 1,300/K-12
4140 State Route 44 44272 330-325-9911
Andrew Hawkins, supt. Fax 325-4105
rootstown.sparcc.org
Rootstown ES 600/K-5
4140 State Route 44 44272 330-325-7971
Michael Capitena, prin. Fax 325-2683
Rootstown MS 300/6-8
4140 State Route 44 44272 330-325-9956
Neal Beans, prin. Fax 325-8505

Roseville, Perry, Pop. 1,922
Franklin Local SD
Supt. — See Duncan Falls
Roseville ES 200/K-3
35 Elm St 43777 740-697-7216
Shannon McLendon, prin. Fax 697-7216
Roseville MS 100/4-6
76 W Athens Rd 43777 740-697-7317
Shannon McLendon, prin. Fax 697-7186

Rossford, Wood, Pop. 6,387
Rossford EVD 1,900/K-12
601 Superior St 43460 419-666-2010
Susan Lang, supt. Fax 661-2856
www.rossfordschools.org/
Eagle Point ES 300/K-6
203 Eagle Point Rd 43460 419-666-1174
Jeff Taylor, prin. Fax 662-3050
Indian Hills ES 300/K-6
401 Glenwood Rd 43460 419-666-0140
Holly Schmidbauer, prin. Fax 661-5432
Rossford JHS 300/7-8
651 Superior St 43460 419-666-5254
Lester Pierson, prin. Fax 661-2890
Other Schools – See Perrysburg

All Saints S 200/PK-8
630 Lime City Rd 43460 419-661-2070
Theresa Richardson, prin. Fax 661-2077

Rushville, Fairfield, Pop. 273
Fairfield Union Local SD 2,100/K-12
7698 Main St 43150 740-536-7384
James Herd, supt. Fax 536-9132
www.fairfield-union.k12.oh.us/
Rushville MS 300/5-6
8155 Rushville Rd NE 43150 740-536-7321
Michael Meyers, prin. Fax 536-9206
Other Schools – See Bremen, Lancaster, Pleasantville

Russellville, Brown, Pop. 464
Eastern Local SD
Supt. — See Sardinia
Russellville ES 400/K-5
239 W Main St 45168 937-377-4771
Susan Paeltz, prin. Fax 377-9110

Russia, Shelby, Pop. 611
Russia Local SD 500/K-12
100 School St 45363 937-295-3454
Michael Moore, supt. Fax 526-9519
www.russia.k12.oh.us
Russia ES 300/K-6
100 School St 45363 937-295-3454
Steven Rose, prin. Fax 526-9519

Sabina, Clinton, Pop. 2,831
East Clinton Local SD
Supt. — See Lees Creek
Sabina ES 400/K-5
246 W Washington St 45169 937-584-5421
Teresa Barton, prin. Fax 584-5232

Saint Bernard, Hamilton, Pop. 4,640
St. Bernard-Elmwood Place CSD 1,000/PK-12
105 Washington Ave 45217 513-482-7121
Dr. Mimi Webb, supt. Fax 641-0066
stbernard.hccanet.org/
Saint Bernard ES 300/K-6
4515 Tower Ave 45217 513-482-7110
David Query, prin. Fax 641-0278
Other Schools – See Elmwood Place

St. Clement S 200/PK-8
4534 Vine St 45217 513-641-2137
Cathy Stover, prin. Fax 242-6036

Saint Clairsville, Belmont, Pop. 5,025
St. Clairsville-Richland CSD 1,600/K-12
108 Woodrow Ave 43950 740-695-1624
Walter Skaggs, supt. Fax 695-1627
www.stcs.k12.oh.us/
St. Clairsville ES 700/K-5
120 Norris St 43950 740-695-0783
Kathy Garrison, prin. Fax 695-2753
St. Clairsville MS 400/6-8
104 Woodrow Ave 43950 740-695-1591
Diane Thompson, prin. Fax 695-2317

New Covenant Academy 100/PK-8
67885 Friends Church Rd 43950 740-695-2005
Patricia Weeks, admin. Fax 699-0562
St. Mary S 200/PK-8
226 W Main St 43950 740-695-3189
Nannette Kennedy, prin. Fax 695-3851

Saint Henry, Mercer, Pop. 2,301
St. Henry Consolidated Local SD 1,100/K-12
391 E Columbus St 45883 419-678-4834
Rodney Moorman, supt. Fax 678-1724
www.noacsc.org/mercer/sh/
Saint Henry ES 400/K-4
251 E Columbus St 45883 419-678-4834
Sandra Stammen, prin. Fax 678-2544
Saint Henry MS 300/5-8
381 E Columbus St 45883 419-678-4834
Julie Garke, prin. Fax 678-1724

Saint Marys, Auglaize, Pop. 8,276
St. Mary's CSD 2,400/K-12
101 W South St 45885 419-394-4312
Mary Riepenhoff, supt. Fax 394-5638
sm.k12.oh.us/
East ES 600/K-6
650 Armstrong St 45885 419-394-2616
Sue Sherman, prin. Fax 394-1149
McBroom MS 300/7-8
210 S Front St 45885 419-394-2112
Ken Neff, prin. Fax 394-3022
West ES 500/1-6
1301 W High St 45885 419-394-2016
Lisa Elson, prin. Fax 394-1881

Grand Lake Christian S 100/PK-12
1001 Holly St Ste A 45885 419-300-9001
Teresa Howell, prin.
Holy Rosary S 100/PK-8
128 S Pine St 45885 419-394-5291
Lora Krugh, prin. Fax 394-6585

Saint Paris, Champaign, Pop. 1,984
Graham Local SD 1,800/PK-12
370 E Main St 43072 937-663-4123
James Zerkle, supt. Fax 663-4670
www.graham.k12.oh.us
Graham ES 500/PK-5
9464 US Highway 36 43072 937-663-4449
Valerie Robb, prin. Fax 663-0257
Graham MS 600/6-8
9644 US Highway 36 43072 937-663-5339
Jacob Conley, prin. Fax 663-4674

Salem, Columbiana, Pop. 12,005
Salem CSD 2,200/K-12
1226 E State St 44460 330-332-0316
Tom Bratten, supt. Fax 332-8936
www.salem.k12.oh.us
Buckeye ES 500/K-2
1200 Buckeye Ave 44460 330-332-8917
Dennis Niederhiser, prin. Fax 332-2137
Reilly ES 300/3-4
491 Reilly Ave 44460 330-332-8921
Lori Thayer, prin. Fax 332-2138
Salem JHS 400/7-8
1200 E 6th St 44460 330-332-8914
Sean Kirkland, prin. Fax 332-8923
Southeast ES 300/5-6
2200 Merle Rd 44460 330-332-8925
Lisa Whitacre, prin. Fax 332-8953

South Range Local SD
Supt. — See North Lima
South Range MS 500/4-8
7600 W South Range Rd 44460 330-533-3335
Albert Toth, prin. Fax 533-7593

West Branch Local SD
Supt. — See Beloit
Damascus ES 400/K-5
14405 Pricetown Rd 44460 330-938-4500
Matthew Bowen, prin. Fax 938-4501

St. Paul S 100/K-6
925 E State St 44460 330-337-3451
Patricia Bauman, prin. Fax 337-3607
Salem Wesleyan Academy 100/PK-12
1095 Newgarden Ave 44460 330-332-4819
Dan Forrider, prin. Fax 332-4819

Salineville, Columbiana, Pop. 1,363
Southern Local SD 900/K-12
38095 State Route 39 43945 330-679-2343
James Herring, supt. Fax 679-0193
www.southern.k12.oh.us
Southern Local ES 500/K-6
38095E State Route 39 43945 330-679-0281
Tom Cunningham, prin. Fax 679-3005

Sandusky, Erie, Pop. 26,666
Perkins Local SD 2,100/K-12
1210 E Bogart Rd 44870 419-625-0484
James Gunner, supt. Fax 621-2052
www.perkins.k12.oh.us
Furry ES 400/K-2
310 Douglas Dr 44870 419-625-4352
Ryan Coleman, prin. Fax 625-6211
Meadowlawn ES 500/2-5
1313 E Strub Rd 44870 419-625-0214
Jude Andres, prin. Fax 625-6459
Perkins MS 500/6-8
3700 South Ave 44870 419-625-0132
Dean Janitzki, prin. Fax 625-0523

Sandusky CSD 3,500/PK-12
407 Decatur St 44870 419-626-6940
William Pahl, supt. Fax 621-2784
www.scs-k12.net
Adams JHS 300/7-8
318 Columbus Ave 44870 419-621-2810
Robert Toney, prin. Fax 621-2849
Hancock ES 300/K-6
2314 Hancock St 44870 419-627-8501
Kathy Pace-Sanders, prin. Fax 621-2854
Jackson ES 300/PK-3
314 W Madison St 44870 419-621-2818
Linda Wohl, prin. Fax 621-2824
Mills ES 300/K-6
1918 Mills St 44870 419-627-8195
Jude Andres, prin. Fax 621-2855
Ontario ES 400/K-6
924 Ontario St 44870 419-627-8544
Jill Wasiniak, prin. Fax 621-2852
Osborne ES 300/K-6
920 W Osborne St 44870 419-627-8610
Rebecca Muratori, prin. Fax 626-9435
Venice Heights ES 400/K-6
4501 Venice Heights Blvd 44870 419-627-8613
Donna Brown, prin. Fax 621-2850

Sandusky Central Catholic S Holy Angels 50/PK-K
1603 W Jefferson St 44870 419-626-3075
Sally Dwight, dir. Fax 625-5183
Sandusky Central Cath S - St. Mary ES K-3
530 Decatur St 44870 419-626-1648
Sandusky Ctrl Cath S - SS. Peter/Paul S 200/K-3
514 Jackson St 44870 419-625-1017
Rita Dominick, prin.

Sarahsville, Noble, Pop. 195
Noble Local SD 1,200/K-12
20977 Zep Rd E 43779 740-732-2084
Daniel Doyle, supt. Fax 732-7669
www.gozeps.org/
Shenandoah S 800/K-8
20977 Zep Rd E 43779 740-732-5661
Sandra Goff, prin.

Sardinia, Brown, Pop. 901
Eastern Local SD 1,400/K-12
PO Box 500 45171 937-378-3981
Alan Simmons, supt. Fax 695-9046
www.eb.k12.oh.us
Eastern JHS 200/6-8
PO Box 25 45171 937-378-6720
Rob Beucler, prin. Fax 695-1299
Sardinia ES 300/K-6
PO Box 67 45171 937-446-2250
Michael Bick, prin. Fax 446-3518
Other Schools – See Russellville

Sardis, Monroe
Switzerland of Ohio Local SD
Supt. — See Woodsfield
Sardis S 200/K-8
PO Box 305 43946 740-483-1421
Micah Fuchs, prin. Fax 483-9037

Scio, Harrison, Pop. 781
Harrison Hills CSD
Supt. — See Hopedale
Harrison JHS 300/7-8
322 W Main St 43988 740-942-7600
Sandra Leggett, prin. Fax 942-7605

Seaman, Adams, Pop. 1,084
Adams County/Ohio Valley Local SD
Supt. — See West Union
North Adams ES 700/K-6
355 Broadway St 45679 937-386-2516
Robin Lucas, prin. Fax 386-2032

Sebring, Mahoning, Pop. 4,706
Sebring Local SD 700/K-12
510 N 14th St 44672 330-938-6165
Howard Friend, supt. Fax 938-4701
www.sebring.k12.oh.us/
Miller ES 300/K-6
506 W Virginia Ave 44672 330-938-2025
Vito Weeda, prin. Fax 938-4703

Sedalia, Madison, Pop. 316
Madison-Plains Local SD
Supt. — See London
Midway ES 200/K-5
13880 Main St SW 43151 740-874-3310
Madeline Holt, lead tchr. Fax 874-3104

Senecaville, Guernsey, Pop. 454
Rolling Hills Local SD
Supt. — See Cambridge
Secrest ES 200/K-5
58860 Wintergreen Rd 43780 740-685-2504
James Bakos, prin. Fax 685-6220

Seven Hills, Cuyahoga, Pop. 12,041
Parma CSD
Supt. — See Parma
Glenn ES 400/K-6
1300 E Dartmoor Ave 44131 440-885-2420
Ava Yeager, prin. Fax 887-4888
Hillside MS 500/7-8
1 Educational Park Dr 44131 440-885-2373
Jeff Cook, prin. Fax 885-8448

Seven Mile, Butler, Pop. 727
Edgewood CSD
Supt. — See Trenton
Seven Mile ES 400/1-5
200 W Ritter St 45062 513-726-6234
Alesia Beckett, prin. Fax 726-6239

Seville, Medina, Pop. 2,462
Cloverleaf Local SD
Supt. — See Lodi
Cloverleaf MS 600/7-8
7500 Buffham Rd 44273 330-948-2500
Sean Osborne, prin. Fax 721-3619
Seville ES 500/3-4
24 E Main St 44273 330-769-3407
Robert Falkenberg, prin. Fax 769-0091

Shadyside, Belmont, Pop. 3,562
Shadyside Local SD 900/PK-12
3890 Lincoln Ave 43947 740-676-3121
Terry Brinker, supt. Fax 676-6616
www.shadyside.k12.oh.us
Jefferson Avenue ES 300/PK-3
4895 Jefferson Ave 43947 740-676-9669
Cynthia Caldwell, prin. Fax 671-5002
Leona Avenue MS 200/4-6
3795 Leona Ave 43947 740-676-9220
Susan Fox, prin. Fax 676-6616

Shaker Heights, Cuyahoga, Pop. 27,723
Shaker Heights CSD 5,500/K-12
15600 Parkland Dr 44120 216-295-1400
Mark Freeman, supt. Fax 295-4340
www.shaker.org
Boulevard ES 400/K-4
14900 Drexmore Rd 44120 216-295-4020
Colleen Longo, prin. Fax 295-4019
Fernway ES 300/K-4
17420 Fernway Rd 44120 216-295-4040
Christopher Hayward, prin. Fax 295-4036
Lomond ES 500/K-4
17917 Lomond Blvd 44122 216-295-4050
Sue Alig, prin. Fax 295-4016
Mercer ES 400/K-4
23325 Wimbledon Rd 44122 216-295-4070
Lindsay Florence, prin. Fax 295-4017
Onaway ES 400/K-4
3115 Woodbury Rd 44120 216-295-4080
Lynn Cowen, prin. Fax 295-4018
Shaker Heights MS 900/7-8
20600 Shaker Blvd 44122 216-295-4100
Randall Yates, prin. Fax 295-4129
Woodbury MS 800/5-6
15400 S Woodland Rd 44120 216-295-4150
Barbara Whitaker, prin. Fax 295-4032

Hathaway Brown S 300/PK-12
19600 N Park Blvd 44122 216-932-4214
William Christ, hdmstr. Fax 371-1501
Laurel S 600/PK-12
1 Lyman Cir 44122 216-464-1441
Ann Klotz, hdmstr. Fax 464-8483
St. Dominic S 200/PK-8
3455 Norwood Rd 44122 216-561-4400
Kathleen Cherney, prin. Fax 561-1573
University S 500/K-8
20701 Brantley Rd 44122 216-321-8260
Stephen Murray, hdmstr. Fax 321-4074

Sharonville, Hamilton, Pop. 13,079

St. Michael S 400/K-8
11136 Oak St 45241 513-554-3555
Josephine Farrell, prin. Fax 554-3551

Shauck, Morrow
Northmor Local SD
Supt. — See Galion
Johnsville ES 300/K-6
PO Box 213 43349 419-362-2161
Debra Ruhl, prin. Fax 362-8135

Shawnee Hills, Delaware, Pop. 536

Natural Learning Montessori Academy 100/PK-11
9345 Dublin Rd 43065 614-889-0811
Mary Trickett, dir. Fax 793-0676

Sheffield Lake, Lorain, Pop. 9,157
Sheffield-Sheffield Lake CSD 1,800/K-12
1824 Harris Rd 44054 440-949-6181
Will Folger, supt. Fax 949-4204
www.sheffield.k12.oh.us
Barr ES 100/4-4
2180 Lake Breeze Rd 44054 440-949-4233
Susan Enos, prin. Fax 949-4204
Forestlawn ES 100/5-5
3975 Forestlawn Ave 44054 440-949-4238
Susan Enos, prin. Fax 949-4204
Knollwood ES 200/K-1
4975 Oster Rd 44054 440-949-4234
Laureen Roemer, prin. Fax 949-4204
Tennyson ES 300/2-3
555 Kenilworth Ave 44054 440-949-4236
Gretchen Loper, prin. Fax 949-4204
Other Schools – See Lorain

Shelby, Richland, Pop. 9,471
Shelby CSD 2,300/K-12
25 High School Ave 44875 419-342-3520
Bryan Neff, supt. Fax 347-3586
www.shelbyk12.org
Auburn ES 500/K-4
109 Auburn Ave 44875 419-342-5456
Kelly Kuhn, prin. Fax 342-3032
Central ES 300/4-6
25 High School Ave 44875 419-347-1018
Anne Bender, prin. Fax 347-3586
Dowds ES 400/K-4
18 Seneca Dr 44875 419-342-4641
Paul Walker, prin. Fax 342-2825
Shelby MS 400/7-8
16 Park Ave 44875 419-347-5451
Tim Tarvin, prin. Fax 347-2095

Sacred Heart S 100/PK-8
5754 State Route 61 S 44875 419-683-1697
Lisa Myers, prin. Fax 342-2797
St. Mary S 100/PK-6
26 West St 44875 419-342-2626
Sally Dunbar, prin. Fax 347-2763

Sherrodsville, Carroll, Pop. 317
Conotton Valley Union Local SD 600/K-12
PO Box 187 44675 740-269-2000
Jeff Bleininger, supt. Fax 269-7901
www.conottonvalley.k12.oh.us
Sherrodsville ES 100/K-6
PO Box 218 44675 740-269-7772
Michael Wright, prin. Fax 269-4803
Other Schools – See Bowerston

Sherwood, Defiance, Pop. 807
Central Local SD 1,200/K-12
6289 US Highway 127 43556 419-658-2808
David Bagley, supt. Fax 658-4010
www.centrallocal.k12.oh.us/default.htm
Fairview ES 500/K-5
14060 Blosser Rd 43556 419-658-2511
Collene Hill, prin. Fax 658-2302
Fairview MS 300/6-8
6289 US Highway 127 43556 419-658-2331
Robert Lloyd, prin. Fax 658-4010

Shreve, Wayne, Pop. 1,516
Triway Local SD
Supt. — See Wooster
Shreve ES 500/K-6
598 N Market St 44676 330-567-2837
Joseph Edinger, prin. Fax 567-9107

Sidney, Shelby, Pop. 20,188
Fairlawn Local SD 600/K-12
18800 Johnston Rd 45365 937-492-1974
Steve Mascho, supt. Fax 492-8613
www.fairlawn.k12.oh.us
Other Schools – See Pemberton

Hardin-Houston Local SD
Supt. — See Houston
Hardin ES 500/K-6
10207 State Route 47 W 45365 937-492-2196
Rick Norviel, prin. Fax 492-6170

Sidney CSD 3,700/K-12
750 S 4th Ave 45365 937-497-2200
Pat O'Donnell, supt. Fax 497-2211
www.sidney.k12.oh.us
Central ES 100/K-3
102 N Miami Ave 45365 937-497-2258
Hugh Aukerman, prin. Fax 497-2257
Emerson ES 400/K-3
901 Campbell Rd 45365 937-497-2261
Dee Mullins, prin. Fax 497-2262
Longfellow ES 300/K-3
1250 Park St 45365 937-497-2264
Ken Miller, prin. Fax 497-2263
Northwood MS 500/4-5
1152 Saint Marys Rd 45365 937-497-2231
Greg Johnson, prin. Fax 497-2232
Sidney MS 900/6-8
980 Fair Rd 45365 937-497-2225
John Stekli, prin. Fax 497-2204
Whittier ES 300/K-3
425 Belmont St 45365 937-497-2275
Keith Helmlinger, prin. Fax 497-2276

Christian Academy S 200/K-12
2151 W Russell Rd 45365 937-492-7556
Mary Smith, supt. Fax 492-5399
Holy Angels S 300/K-8
120 E Water St 45365 937-492-9293
Dr. Halver Belcher, prin. Fax 492-8578

Silver Lake, Summit, Pop. 3,159
Cuyahoga Falls CSD
Supt. — See Cuyahoga Falls
Silver Lake ES 200/K-5
2970 Overlook Rd 44224 330-926-3811
Ellen McClure, prin. Fax 916-6023

Smithville, Wayne, Pop. 1,312
Green Local SD 1,300/K-12
PO Box 438 44677 330-669-3921
Larry Brown, supt. Fax 669-2121
www.green-local.k12.oh.us/
Greene MS 400/5-8
PO Box 367 44677 330-669-2751
Jason Demassimo, prin. Fax 669-2121
Smithville ES 300/K-4
PO Box 176 44677 330-669-3501
Laurie Parrish-Storm, prin. Fax 669-2121
Other Schools – See Marshallville

Solon, Cuyahoga, Pop. 22,335
Solon CSD 5,400/PK-12
33800 Inwood Dr 44139 440-248-1600
Joseph Regano, supt. Fax 248-7665
www.solonschools.org
Arthur Road ES 600/PK-4
33425 Arthur Rd 44139 440-349-6210
Mariann Moeschberger, prin. Fax 349-8018
Lewis ES 400/K-4
32345 Cannon Rd 44139 440-349-6225
Fred Bolden, prin. Fax 349-8012
Orchard MS 800/5-6
6800 Som Center Rd 44139 440-349-6215
Michael Acomb, prin. Fax 349-8054
Parkside ES 500/K-4
6845 Som Center Rd 44139 440-349-2175
Martha Keeney, prin. Fax 349-8055
Roxbury ES 400/K-4
6795 Solon Blvd 44139 440-349-6220
Carla Rodenbucher, prin. Fax 349-8048
Solon MS 900/7-8
6835 Som Center Rd 44139 440-349-3848
Eugenia Robinson-Green, prin. Fax 349-8034

St. Rita S 500/PK-8
33200 Baldwin Rd 44139 440-248-1350
Mary Peterlin, prin. Fax 248-9442

Somerset, Perry, Pop. 1,577
Northern Local SD
Supt. — See Thornville
Somerset ES 300/K-5
100 High St 43783 740-743-1454
Larry Saunders, prin. Fax 743-3324

Holy Trinity S 100/K-8
225 S Columbus St 43783 740-743-1324
Joan Miller, prin. Fax 743-1324

South Amherst, Lorain, Pop. 1,800
Firelands Local SD
Supt. — See Oberlin
South Amherst MS 600/5-8
152 W Main St 44001 440-986-7021
Tony Reaser, prin. Fax 986-7022

South Charleston, Clark, Pop. 1,821
Southeastern Local SD 800/K-12
PO Box Z 45368 937-462-8388
John Abdella, supt. Fax 462-7915
www.sels.us
Miami View ES 300/K-4
230 Clifton Rd 45368 937-462-8364
Marvin Dalton, prin. Fax 462-7914
Miami View MS 300/5-8
230 Clifton Rd 45368 937-462-8364
Marvin Dalton, prin. Fax 462-7914

South Euclid, Cuyahoga, Pop. 22,210
South Euclid-Lyndhurst CSD
Supt. — See Lyndhurst
Adrian ES 200/K-3
1071 Homestead Rd 44121 216-691-2170
Mark Woodby, prin. Fax 691-2295
Greenview Upper ES 600/4-6
1825 S Green Rd 44121 216-691-2245
Reginald Holland, prin. Fax 691-3482
Rowland ES 300/K-3
4300 Bayard Rd 44121 216-691-2200
Maleeka Bussey, prin. Fax 691-2206

St. Gregory the Great S 700/PK-8
4478 Rushton Rd 44121 216-381-0363
Peter Wilson, prin. Fax 381-7561
St. John Lutheran S 100/PK-8
4386 Mayfield Rd 44121 216-381-8595
Barbara Knight, prin. Fax 381-1564

Southington, Trumbull
Southington Local SD 700/K-12
4432 State Route 305 44470 330-898-7480
Frank Danso, supt. Fax 898-4828
www.southington.k12.oh.us/
Southington ES 300/K-4
4432 State Route 305 44470 330-898-7480
Fax 898-4828
Southington MS 200/5-8
4432 State Route 305 44470 330-898-1781
Fax 898-4828

South Point, Lawrence, Pop. 3,922
South Point Local SD 1,900/K-12
203 Park Ave 45680 740-377-4315
Ken Cook, supt. Fax 377-9735
www.southpoint.k12.oh.us
Burlington ES 300/K-5
8781 County Road 1 45680 740-894-4230
Henrietta Kitchen, prin.
South Point ES 600/K-5
501 Washington St Ste 2 45680 740-377-2756
Chris Mathes, prin.
South Point MS, 201 Park Ave 45680 400/6-8
T.J. Howard, prin. 740-377-4343

South Salem, Ross, Pop. 218
Greenfield EVD
Supt. — See Greenfield
Buckskin ES 400/PK-5
PO Box 69 45681 937-981-2673
Mike Shumate, prin. Fax 981-1924

South Vienna, Clark, Pop. 504
Northeastern Local SD
Supt. — See Springfield
South Vienna ES 600/K-5
140 W Main St 45369 937-568-4038
Todd Justice, prin. Fax 568-4988
South Vienna MS 400/6-8
140 W Main St 45369 937-568-4765
Ted Williams, prin. Fax 568-4988

South Webster, Scioto, Pop. 751
Bloom-Vernon Local SD 1,000/K-12
PO Box 237 45682 740-778-2281
Rick Carrington, supt. Fax 778-2526
www.bv.k12.oh.us/
Bloom-Vernon ES 500/K-6
PO Box 479 45682 740-778-2339
Scott Holstein, prin. Fax 778-7600

Sparta, Morrow, Pop. 202
Highland Local SD
Supt. — See Marengo
Highland Central ES 400/K-5
PO Box 69 43350 419-768-3040
Mark Lambka, prin. Fax 768-2127
Highland MS 400/6-8
PO Box 68 43350 419-768-2781
Rob Terrill, prin. Fax 768-2742

Spencerville, Allen, Pop. 2,209
Spencerville Local SD 1,000/K-12
600 School St 45887 419-647-4111
Joel Hatfield, supt. Fax 647-6498
www.spencervillebearcats.com
Spencerville ES 300/K-4
2500 Wisher Dr 45887 419-647-4113
Ted Savidge, prin. Fax 647-5124
Spencerville MS 300/5-8
2500 Wisher Dr 45887 419-647-4112
Dennis Fuge, prin. Fax 647-5124

Springboro, Warren, Pop. 16,403
Springboro Community CSD 4,300/K-12
1685 S Main St 45066 937-748-3960
David Baker Ph.D., supt. Fax 748-3956
www.springboro.org
Clearcreek ES 200/K-K
750 S Main St 45066 937-748-3958
Sarah Lord, prin. Fax 748-3980
Dennis ES East 400/1-5
1695 S Main St 45066 937-748-6070
Fax 748-6067
Dennis ES West 500/1-5
1695 S Main St 45066 937-748-6075
Sandy Wray, prin. Fax 748-6077
Springboro IS 400/6-6
705 S Main St 45066 937-748-4113
Bruce Lewis, prin. Fax 748-8498
Springboro JHS 700/7-8
1605 S Main St 45066 937-748-3953
Andrea Cook, prin. Fax 748-3964
Other Schools – See Centerville

Springfield, Clark, Pop. 63,302
Clark-Shawnee Local SD 2,500/K-12
3680 Selma Rd 45502 937-328-5378
Debbie Finkes, supt. Fax 328-5379
www.clark-shawnee.k12.oh.us/
Clark-Shawnee K Village 200/K-K
3825 Old Clifton Rd 45502 937-328-2200
Sara Suver, prin. Fax 328-2202
Possum S 600/1-8
2589 S Yellow Springs St 45506 937-328-5383
Scott Heintz, prin. Fax 328-5390
Reid S 600/1-8
3640 E High St 45505 937-328-5380
Pamela Young, prin. Fax 328-5392
Rockway S 300/1-8
3500 W National Rd 45504 937-328-5385
Brad Silvus, prin. Fax 328-5399

Greenon Local SD
Supt. — See Enon
Hustead ES 300/K-4
3600 Hustead Rd 45502 937-328-5360
Jack Hillard, prin. Fax 328-0805

Northeastern Local SD 3,800/K-12
1414 Bowman Rd 45502 937-325-7615
Richard Broderick, supt. Fax 328-6592
www.northeastern.k12.oh.us
Northridge ES 500/K-5
4445 Ridgewood Rd E 45503 937-342-4627
Steven Linson, prin. Fax 342-4631
Northridge MS 500/6-8
4445 Ridgewood Rd E 45503 937-399-2852
Michelle Heims, prin. Fax 342-4631
Rolling Hills ES 600/K-5
2613 Moorefield Rd 45502 937-399-2250
Shawn Blazer, prin. Fax 399-3454
Other Schools – See South Vienna

Northwestern Local SD 1,900/K-12
5610 Troy Rd 45502 937-964-1318
Anthony Orr, supt. Fax 964-6019
www.northwestern.k12.oh.us
Northwestern ES 700/K-4
5780 Troy Rd 45502 937-964-1351
Cynthia Pierson, prin. Fax 964-6008
Northwestern MS 600/5-8
5610 Troy Rd 45502 937-964-1391
Cheryl Leedy, prin. Fax 964-6003

Springfield CSD 7,000/K-12
1500 W Jefferson St 45506 937-505-2800
David Estrop Ph.D., supt. Fax 328-6855
www.spr.k12.oh.us/
Fulton ES 300/K-5
631 S Yellow Springs St 45506 937-505-4150
Sherry Cross, prin. Fax 322-5246
Hayward MS 400/6-8
1700 Clifton Ave 45505 937-505-4190
Susie Samuels, prin. Fax 323-9812
Kenton ES 400/K-5
731 E Home Rd 45503 937-505-4210
Cristina Sanchez, prin. Fax 342-8528
Kenwood Heights ES 400/K-5
1421 Nagley St 45505 937-505-4220
Jan Taylor, prin. Fax 324-9721
Lagonda ES 400/K-5
800 E McCreight Ave 45503 937-505-4240
Cynthia Dillard, prin. Fax 342-8954
Lincoln ES 400/K-5
1500 Tibbetts Ave 45505 937-505-4260
Michael Wilson, prin. Fax 342-8684
Mann ES 400/K-5
521 Mount Joy St 45505 937-505-4280
Cathie Scott, prin. Fax 323-7646
Perrin Woods ES 400/K-5
431 W John St 45506 937-505-4310
Nena Dorsey, prin. Fax 322-7576
Roosevelt MS 500/6-8
721 E Home Rd 45503 937-505-4370
Monte Brigham, prin. Fax 342-0280
Schaefer MS 500/6-8
147 S Fostoria Ave 45505 937-505-4390
Fax 325-8974
Snowhill ES 400/K-5
531 W Harding Rd 45504 937-505-4410
Rita Lane, prin. Fax 399-2585
Snyder Park ES 400/K-5
1600 Maiden Ln 45504 937-505-4430
Linda Newsome, prin. Fax 324-2246
Warder Park - Wayne ES 400/K-5
2820 Hillside Ave 45503 937-505-4450
Roy Swanson, prin. Fax 323-7924

Catholic Central ES Lagonda Campus 100/K-6
800 Lagonda Ave 45503 937-324-4551
Mary Callahan, prin. Fax 327-4070
Catholic Central ES Limestone Campus 100/PK-6
1817 N Limestone St 45503 937-399-5451
Mary Callahan, prin. Fax 342-0042
Emmanuel Christian Academy 400/K-12
2177 Emmanuel Way 45502 937-390-3777
Robert Elliott, dir. Fax 390-0966
Maiden Lane Edu-Care Center 50/PK-3
1201 Maiden Ln 45504 937-325-6528
Roberta Gates, prin. Fax 322-4853
Nightingale Montessori S 100/PK-12
1106 E High St 45505 937-324-0336
Nancy Schwab, prin. Fax 398-0086
Risen Christ Lutheran S 50/PK-5
41 E Possum Rd 45502 937-323-3688
Rebecca Reid, prin. Fax 323-3746
Springfield Christian S 100/PK-8
311 W High St 45506 937-325-3113
Judy Loy, prin. Fax 325-9302
Twin Oaks SDA S 50/1-8
151 S Bird Rd 45505 937-323-7660
Wee Leong, prin.

Sterling, Wayne
North Central Local SD
Supt. — See Creston
Sterling ES 300/K-4
13323 Kauffman Ave 44276 330-939-2341
David Dreher, prin. Fax 435-4633

Steubenville, Jefferson, Pop. 19,314
Edison Local SD
Supt. — See Hammondsville
Pleasant Hill ES 200/PK-4
129 School St 43952 740-282-2578
Dana Snider, prin. Fax 282-4652

Steubenville CSD 1,700/PK-12
PO Box 189 43952 740-283-3767
Richard Ranallo, supt. Fax 283-8930
www.steubenville.k12.oh.us/
East Garfield ES PK-5
936 N 5th St 43952 740-282-5112
Marjorie Radakovich, prin. Fax 283-8935
Harding MS 500/6-8
2002 Sunset Blvd 43952 740-282-3481
Rob Rembold, prin. Fax 283-8949
McKinley ES 100/PK-5
W Adams St 43952 740-283-3211
Fax 283-8943
Wells Academy 200/K-5
420 N 4th St 43952 740-282-1651
Melinda Young, prin. Fax 283-8945
West Pugliese ES 300/K-5
3800 Schenley Ave 43952 740-264-1590
Joseph Nocera, prin. Fax 264-2190

Bishop John King Mussio Central JHS 7-8
320 Westview Ave Ste 2 43952 740-346-0028
Theresa Danaher, admin. Fax 346-0070
Bishop John King Mussio Central S 300/PK-8
100 Etta Ave 43952 740-264-2550
Theresa DiPiero, prin. Fax 266-2843
Bishop John King Mussio Central S 200/PK-8
625 Lovers Ln 43953 740-264-3651
Victoria Nurczyk, admin. Fax 264-4277

Stewart, Athens
Federal Hocking Local SD 1,200/PK-12
PO Box 117 45778 740-662-6691
James Patsey, supt. Fax 662-5065
www.federalhocking.k12.oh.us
Federal Hocking MS 300/6-8
8461 State Route 144 45778 740-662-6691
Dr. George Wood, prin. Fax 662-5065
Other Schools – See Amesville, Coolville

Stockport, Morgan, Pop. 551
Morgan Local SD
Supt. — See Mc Connelsville
South ES 400/K-6
3555 State Route 792 43787 740-559-2377
Janet Sukoski, prin. Fax 559-2864

Stow, Summit, Pop. 34,404
Stow-Munroe Falls CSD 5,900/PK-12
4350 Allen Rd 44224 330-689-5445
Dr. Russell Jones, supt. Fax 688-1629
www.smfcsd.org
Echo Hills ES 400/K-4
4405 Stow Rd 44224 330-689-5450
Susan Martucci, prin. Fax 686-3129
Fishcreek ES 400/K-4
5080 Fishcreek Rd 44224 330-689-5460
Jim Saxer, prin. Fax 686-3126
Highland ES 400/K-4
1843 Graham Rd 44224 330-689-5330
Meghan Graziano, prin. Fax 686-4711
Indian Trail ES 400/PK-4
3512 Kent Rd 44224 330-689-5320
John Lacoste, prin. Fax 686-4716
Lakeview IS 900/5-6
1819 Graham Rd 44224 330-689-5250
Kim Lockhart, prin. Fax 686-4708
Woodland ES 300/K-4
2908 Graham Rd 44224 330-689-5470
Debra Milford, prin. Fax 686-4712
Other Schools – See Munroe Falls

Cornerstone Community S 100/K-6
4510 Stow Rd 44224 330-686-8900
Karen Chivers, prin. Fax 686-8224
Holy Family S 700/PK-8
3163 Kent Rd 44224 330-688-3816
Sharon Fournier, prin. Fax 688-3474

Strasburg, Tuscarawas, Pop. 2,607
Strasburg-Franklin Local SD 700/K-12
140 N Bodmer Ave 44680 330-878-5571
Gene Feucht, supt. Fax 878-7900
www.strasburg.k12.oh.us/
Strasburg-Franklin ES 400/K-6
140 N Bodmer Ave 44680 330-878-6503
Laurel Dorsey, prin. Fax 878-5983

Streetsboro, Portage, Pop. 14,210
Streetsboro CSD 2,100/K-12
9000 Kirby Ln 44241 330-626-4900
Linda Keller, supt. Fax 626-8102
www.streetsboroschools.com
Campus ES 300/2-3
8955 Kirby Ln 44241 330-626-4907
David Kish, prin. Fax 626-8106
Defer IS 500/4-6
1895 Annalane Dr 44241 330-422-2480
Lisa Shannon, prin. Fax 626-4192
Streetsboro MS 400/7-8
1951 Annalane Dr 44241 330-626-4905
Steve Hatch, prin. Fax 626-8104
Wait PS 300/K-1
899 Frost Rd 44241 330-422-2400
Jon Natko, prin. Fax 650-5795

Strongsville, Cuyahoga, Pop. 43,949
Strongsville CSD 7,200/PK-12
13200 Pearl Rd 44136 440-572-7010
Jefferey Lampert, supt. Fax 572-7041
strongnet.org
Albion MS 600/7-8
11109 Webster Rd 44136 440-572-7070
David Riley, prin. Fax 572-7079
Allen ES 600/K-6
16400 Park Lane Dr 44136 440-572-7130
R. Todd Clifford, prin. Fax 572-7136
Center MS 600/7-8
13200 Pearl Rd 44136 440-572-7090
Cameron Ryba, prin. Fax 572-7094
Chapman ES 400/K-6
13883 Drake Rd 44136 440-572-7140
Andy Trujillo, prin. Fax 572-7146
Drake ES 400/K-6
20566 Albion Rd 44149 440-572-7150
Glen Stacho, prin. Fax 572-7155
Kinsner ES 500/K-6
19091 Waterford Pkwy 44149 440-572-7120
Ervin Reed, prin. Fax 572-7125
Muraski ES 500/K-6
20270 Royalton Rd 44149 440-572-7160
Justina Peters, prin. Fax 572-7165
Strongsville Early Learning Preschool PK-PK
19543 Lunn Rd 44149 440-572-7046
Bethany Britt, admin. Fax 846-3227
Surrarrer ES 400/K-6
9306 Priem Rd 44149 440-572-7170
Kesh Boodheshwar, prin. Fax 572-7175
Whitney ES 400/K-6
13548 Whitney Rd 44136 440-572-7180
Kathleen Urmston, prin. Fax 572-7185
Zellers ES 300/K-6
18199 Cook Ave 44136 440-572-7190
Susan Harb, prin. Fax 572-7195

SS. Joseph & John S 700/K-8
12580 Pearl Rd 44136 440-238-4877
Darlene Thomas, prin. Fax 238-8745

Struthers, Mahoning, Pop. 11,240
Struthers CSD 2,100/K-12
99 Euclid Ave 44471 330-750-1061
Robert Rostan, supt. Fax 750-5516
www.struthers.k12.oh.us/
Struthers ES 700/K-4
520 9th St 44471 330-750-1065
Pete Pirone, prin. Fax 750-1489
Struthers MS 700/5-8
800 5th St 44471 330-750-1064
Sandy Mislevy-Kelty, prin. Fax 755-4749

St. Nicholas S 200/K-8
762 5th St 44471 330-755-2128
Elizabeth McCullough, prin. Fax 755-9949

Stryker, Williams, Pop. 1,391
Stryker Local SD 500/K-12
400 S Defiance St 43557 419-682-6961
Nathaniel Johnson, supt. Fax 682-2646
www.stryker.k12.oh.us
Stryker ES 200/K-6
400 S Defiance St 43557 419-682-2841
Denise Meyer, prin. Fax 682-3508

Suffield, Portage
Field Local SD
Supt. — See Mogadore
Suffield ES 400/K-5
1128 Waterloo Rd 44260 330-628-3430
Shawn Bookman, prin. Fax 628-9160

Sugarcreek, Tuscarawas, Pop. 2,159
Garaway Local SD 1,300/K-12
146 Dover Rd NW 44681 330-852-2421
Darryl Jones, supt. Fax 852-2991
www.garaway.k12.oh.us/
Garaway MS 200/7-8
146 Dover Rd NW 44681 330-852-3418
Kelly Luneborg, prin. Fax 852-3213
Miller Avenue ES 200/K-6
840 Miller Ave SW 44681 330-852-2441
Larry Compton, prin. Fax 852-7702
Ragersville ES 200/K-6
2405 Ragersville Rd SW 44681 330-897-5021
Casey Travis, prin. Fax 897-9941
Other Schools – See Baltic, Dundee

Sugar Grove, Fairfield, Pop. 443
Berne Union Local SD 1,000/K-12
PO Box 187 43155 740-746-8341
Richard Spindler, supt. Fax 746-9824
www.berne-union.k12.oh.us
Berne Union ES 300/K-4
PO Box 187 43155 740-746-9668
Steven Templin, prin. Fax 746-9824
Berne Union MS 300/5-8
PO Box 187 43155 740-746-9738
Sara Hayes, prin. Fax 746-9824

Sullivan, Ashland
Black River Local SD 1,700/PK-12
257A County Road 40 44880 419-736-3300
Janice Wyckoff, supt. Fax 736-3308
www.blackriver.k12.oh.us/
Black River ES 800/PK-5
257 County Road 40 44880 419-736-2161
Pamela Oberholtzer, prin. Fax 736-3309
Black River MS 400/6-8
257 County Road 40 44880 419-736-3304
Cathy Aviles, prin. Fax 736-3309

Sunbury, Delaware, Pop. 3,225
Big Walnut Local SD
Supt. — See Galena
Big Walnut ES 500/K-5
940 S Old 3C Rd 43074 740-965-3902
Peggy McMurry, prin. Fax 965-3168
Big Walnut MS 700/6-8
105 Baughman St 43074 740-965-3006
Angela Pollock, prin. Fax 965-6471
Harrison Street ES 300/K-5
70 Harrison St 43074 740-965-2291
Lynn Kaszynski, prin. Fax 965-9909

Swanton, Fulton, Pop. 3,557
Swanton Local SD 1,400/K-12
108 N Main St 43558 419-826-7085
Paulette Baz, supt. Fax 825-1197
www.swanton.k12.oh.us
Crestwood ES 300/K-2
111 Crestwood Dr 43558 419-826-8991
Angela Lutz, prin. Fax 826-8646
Park ES 300/3-5
101 Elton Pkwy 43558 419-826-3766
Jane Myers, prin. Fax 826-2965
Swanton MS 300/6-8
206 Cherry St 43558 419-826-4016
Ben Ohlemacher, prin. Fax 826-5176

Holy Trinity S 100/PK-8
2639 US Highway 20 43558 419-644-3971
Linda Justen, prin. Fax 644-5018
St. Richard S 100/PK-8
333 Brookside Dr 43558 419-826-5041
Sr. Bernarda Breidenbach, prin. Fax 826-7256

Sycamore, Wyandot, Pop. 894
Mohawk Local SD 500/K-12
605 State Highway 231 44882 419-927-2414
Sam Martin, supt. Fax 927-2393
www.mohawk.k12.oh.us/
Mohawk ES 200/K-6
605 State Highway 231 44882 419-927-2595
Carl Long, prin. Fax 927-6139

Sylvania, Lucas, Pop. 19,069
Sylvania CSD 7,700/K-12
PO Box 608 43560 419-824-8500
Bradley Rieger, supt. Fax 824-8503
www.sylvania.k12.oh.us
Arbor Hills JHS 600/6-8
5334 Whiteford Rd 43560 419-824-8640
Rose Gaiffe, prin. Fax 824-8659
Highland ES 600/K-5
7720 Erie St 43560 419-824-8611
Deb Serdar, prin. Fax 824-8635
Hill View ES 400/K-5
5424 Whiteford Rd 43560 419-824-8612
Adam Fineske, prin. Fax 824-8639
Maplewood ES 400/K-5
6769 Maplewood Ave 43560 419-824-8613
Edward Eding, prin. Fax 824-8649
McCord JHS 600/6-8
4304 N Mccord Rd 43560 419-824-8650
Jeff Robbins, prin. Fax 824-8619
Sylvan ES 300/K-5
4830 Wickford Dr E 43560 419-824-8615
John Duwve, prin. Fax 824-8665
Timberstone JHS 600/6-8
9000 Sylvania Ave 43560 419-824-8680
Jane Spurgeon, prin. Fax 824-8690
Other Schools – See Toledo

St. Joseph S 800/K-8
5411 Main St 43560 419-882-6670
Sally Koppinger, prin. Fax 885-1990
Sylvania Franciscan Academy 300/PK-8
5335 Silica Dr 43560 419-885-3273
Martha Hartman, prin. Fax 882-5653
Toledo Islamic Academy 100/K-12
5225 Alexis Rd 43560 419-882-3339
Aalaa Eldeib, prin. Fax 882-3334

Tallmadge, Summit, Pop. 17,408
Tallmadge CSD 2,700/K-12
486 East Ave 44278 330-633-3291
Jeffrey Ferguson, supt. Fax 633-5331
www.tallmadge.k12.oh.us/index.htm
Dunbar ES 400/2-3
731 Dunbar Rd 44278 330-633-4515
Archie Beaton, prin. Fax 630-5981
Munroe ES 400/4-5
230 N Munroe Rd 44278 330-633-5427
Shelley Monachino, prin. Fax 630-5983
Overdale ES 300/K-1
90 W Overdale Dr 44278 330-630-5987
John Ross, prin. Fax 630-5990
Tallmadge MS 700/6-8
484 East Ave 44278 330-633-4994
Gregory Misch, prin. Fax 630-5984

Fact Academy 50/PK-6
PO Box 123 44278 330-633-9049
Teresa Hymes, prin. Fax 630-1792

Terrace Park, Hamilton, Pop. 2,136
Mariemont CSD
Supt. — See Cincinnati
Terrace Park ES 300/K-6
723 Elm Ave 45174 513-272-7700
Linda Lee, prin. Fax 831-1249

The Plains, Athens, Pop. 2,644
Athens CSD 2,800/K-12
25 S Plains Rd 45780 740-797-4544
Carl Martin, supt. Fax 797-2486
athenscity.k12.oh.us/
The Plains ES 400/K-6
90 Connett Rd 45780 740-797-4572
Kacey Cottrill, prin. Fax 797-3450
Other Schools – See Athens, Chauncey

Thompson, Geauga
Ledgemont Local SD 700/K-12
16200 Burrows Rd 44086 440-298-3341
John Marshall, supt. Fax 298-3342
www.ledgemont.k12.oh.us
Ledgemont S 500/K-8
16200 Burrows Rd 44086 440-298-3366
John Marshall, prin. Fax 298-3342

Thornville, Perry, Pop. 1,034
Northern Local SD 2,300/K-12
8700 Sheridan Dr 43076 740-743-1303
Jack Porter, supt. Fax 743-3301
www.nlsd.k12.oh.us
Sheridan MS 600/6-8
8660 Sheridan Dr 43076 740-743-1315
Casey Coffey, prin. Fax 743-3319
Thornville ES 300/K-5
PO Box 246 43076 740-246-6636
James Burden, prin. Fax 246-5399
Other Schools – See Glenford, Somerset

Tiffin, Seneca, Pop. 17,438
Tiffin CSD 2,900/K-12
244 S Monroe St 44883 419-447-2515
Donald Coletta, supt. Fax 448-5202
www.tiffin.k12.oh.us
Clinton ES 200/K-5
2036 E Township Road 122 44883 419-447-8727
Mike Newlove, prin. Fax 448-5225
Krout ES 400/K-5
20 Glenn St 44883 419-447-2652
Rebecca Osborne, prin. Fax 448-5223
Lincoln ES 200/K-5
124 Ohio Ave 44883 419-447-8674
Douglas Hartenstein, prin. Fax 448-5221
Noble ES 300/K-5
130 Minerva St 44883 419-447-1566
Michael Steyer, prin. Fax 448-5219
Tiffin MS 600/6-8
103 Shepherd Dr 44883 419-447-3358
Robert Boes, prin. Fax 448-5250
Washington ES 300/K-5
151 Elmer St 44883 419-447-1072
Candace Wingert, prin. Fax 448-5217

Calvert Catholic Schools - St. Joseph 400/PK-8
357 S Washington St 44883 419-447-5790
Patricia Haley, prin. Fax 447-7580
Calvert Schools - St. Mary Campus 300/PK-3
75 S Sandusky St 44883 419-447-5202
Patricia Haley, prin. Fax 447-0142

Tiltonsville, Jefferson, Pop. 1,244
Buckeye Local SD
Supt. — See Dillonvale
Buckeye Southwest MS 300/6-8
100 Walden Ave 43963 740-859-2357
George Bell, prin. Fax 859-2660

Tipp City, Miami, Pop. 9,357
Bethel Local SD 900/K-12
7490 State Route 201 45371 937-845-9414
Robert Hoover, supt. Fax 845-5007
www.bethel.k12.oh.us
Bethel ES 500/K-6
7490 State Route 201 45371 937-845-9439
Jodi Petty, prin. Fax 845-5007
Bethel JHS 200/7-8
7490 State Route 201 45371 937-845-9430
Fax 845-5007

Tipp City EVD 2,700/K-12
90 S Tippecanoe Dr 45371 937-667-8444
John Kronour Ph.D., supt. Fax 667-6886
www.tippcityschools.com/
Ball IS 400/4-5
575 N Hyatt St 45371 937-667-8454
Gary Pfister, prin. Fax 667-0874
Broadway ES 400/K-3
223 W Broadway St 45371 937-667-6216
Galen Gingerich, prin. Fax 669-9405
Coppock ES 400/K-3
525 N Hyatt St 45371 937-667-2275
Richard Brownlee, prin. Fax 669-5508
Tippecanoe MS 600/6-8
555 N Hyatt St 45371 937-667-8454
Greg Southers, prin. Fax 667-0874

Little Lighthouse Preschool 50/PK-K
1427 W Main St 45371 937-667-6215
Teresa Kinnison, admin. Fax 667-8712

Tiro, Crawford, Pop. 267
Buckeye Central Local SD
Supt. — See New Washington
Buckeye East ES 100/K-6
PO Box 98 44887 419-342-3721
Fax 492-2039

Toledo, Lucas, Pop. 301,285
Lucas County ESC 300/
2275 Collingwood Blvd 43620 419-245-4150
Sandra Frisch, supt. Fax 245-4186
www.lucas.k12.oh.us/
Collingwood S 100/K-12
2275 Collingwood Blvd 43620 419-245-4150
Fax 246-3076
Other Schools – See Oregon, Waterville

Ottawa Hills Local SD 1,000/K-12
3600 Indian Rd 43606 419-536-6371
Cathleen Heidelberg, supt. Fax 534-5380
www.ohschools.k12.oh.us
Ottawa Hills ES 500/K-6
3602 Indian Rd 43606 419-536-8329
Kevin Herman, prin. Fax 536-6932

Springfield Local SD
Supt. — See Holland
Dorr Street ES 500/K-5
1205 King Rd 43617 419-867-5666
Kenneth Newbury, prin. Fax 867-5734

Sylvania CSD
Supt. — See Sylvania
Central ES 600/K-5
7460 W Central Ave 43617 419-824-8610
Toni Gerber, prin. Fax 824-8606
Stranahan ES 400/K-5
3840 N Holland Sylvania Rd 43615 419-824-8614
Robert Biglin, prin. Fax 824-8665
Whiteford ES 400/K-5
4708 Whiteford Rd 43623 419-824-8616
Michael Bader, prin. Fax 824-8697

Toledo CSD 27,100/PK-12
420 E Manhattan Blvd 43608 419-671-8200
John Foley, supt. Fax 671-8425
www.tps.org
Arlington ES 500/K-6
707 Woodsdale Ave 43609 419-671-2550
Lori Reffert, prin. Fax 671-2595
Beverly ES 300/K-6
4022 Rugby Dr 43614 419-389-5036
Linda Meyers, prin. Fax 389-5056
Birmingham ES 300/K-6
355 Dearborn Ave 43605 419-691-4545
Barbara Guthrie, prin. Fax 691-2494
Burroughs ES 400/K-6
2420 South Ave 43609 419-671-2350
Thomas DeMarco, prin. Fax 671-2395
Byrnedale MS 600/7-8
3645 Glendale Ave 43614 419-671-2200
Karen Schultz-Gray, prin. Fax 671-2260
Chase ES 200/K-6
600 Bassett St 43611 419-671-6650
Fax 671-6695
Cherry Preschool PK-PK
4801 290th St 43611 419-729-3293
Trent Leedy, prin. Fax 729-8597
Crossgates ES 400/K-6
3901 Shadylawn Dr 43614 419-385-4571
Dennis Delucia, prin. Fax 385-3689
DeVeaux MS 900/6-8
2626 W Sylvania Ave 43613 419-475-4213
Chad Henderly, prin. Fax 473-2123
East Broadway MS 700/7-8
1755 E Broadway St 43605 419-671-7200
Paul Gibbs, prin. Fax 671-7260
East Side Central ES 500/K-6
815 Navarre Ave 43605 419-691-4510
Elaine Burton, prin. Fax 691-2567
Edgewater ES 200/K-6
5549 Edgewater Dr 43611 419-726-2254
Stacey Scharf, prin. Fax 729-8596
Elmhurst ES 400/K-6
4530 Elmhurst Rd 43613 419-475-3701
Betsey Murry, prin. Fax 479-3157
Garfield ES 400/K-6
1103 N Ravine Pkwy 43605 419-671-7550
James Lang, prin. Fax 671-7595
Glendale-Feilbach ES 400/K-6
2317 Cass Rd 43614 419-385-0621
Pam Knox, prin. Fax 385-2204
Glenwood ES 500/K-5
2860 Glenwood Ave 43610 419-244-4647
Sandra Ellis, prin. Fax 249-8278
Grove Patterson Academy 300/K-8
3301 Upton Ave 43613 419-671-3350
Gretchen Bueter, prin. Fax 671-3395
Harvard ES 400/K-6
1949 Glendale Ave 43614 419-382-2112
Deborah Washington, prin. Fax 385-3903
Hawkins ES 400/K-5
5550 W Bancroft St 43615 419-671-1550
Ann Baker, prin. Fax 671-1595
Jones MS 200/6-8
430 Nebraska Ave 43604 419-671-5400
Pamela King, prin. Fax 671-5460
Keyser ES 500/K-6
3900 Hill Ave 43607 419-671-1450
Lawrence Foos, prin. Fax 671-1495
King ES K-5
1300 Forest Ave 43607 419-671-4550
Chad Kolebuck, prin. Fax 671-4595
LaGrange ES 400/K-6
1001 N Erie St 43604 419-243-4556
Gary Forquer, prin. Fax 249-8280
Larchmont ES 300/K-6
1515 Slater St 43612 419-671-3650
Jeffrey Hanthorn, prin. Fax 671-3695
Leverette MS 500/7-8
445 E Manhattan Blvd 43608 419-671-6200
Steve Riddle, prin. Fax 671-6262
Lincoln Academy for Boys 200/K-6
514 Palmwood Ave 43604 419-244-5823
Teresa Quinn, prin. Fax 249-8281
Longfellow ES 700/K-6
4112 Jackman Rd 43612 419-478-7765
Suzanne Joseph, prin. Fax 470-6559
Marshall ES 300/K-5
415 Colburn St 43609 419-241-4725
Bulista Kimbraugh, prin. Fax 249-8282
McKinley ES 400/K-5
1901 W Central Ave 43606 419-472-3755
John Korenowsky, prin. Fax 473-2105
McTigue MS 500/6-8
5555 Nebraska Ave 43615 419-671-1200
Robert Yenrick, prin. Fax 671-1260
Navarre ES 400/K-6
800 Kingston Ave 43605 419-671-7600
Katherine Taylor, prin. Fax 671-7645
Oakdale ES 500/K-6
1620 E Broadway St 43605 419-671-7350
Tracy Knighten, prin. Fax 671-7395
Old Orchard ES 300/K-5
2402 Cheltenham Rd 43606 419-536-1261
Jennifer Spoores, prin. Fax 578-4974
Old West End Academy 300/K-8
3131 Cambridge St 43610 419-242-1050
Tiffani Conner, prin. Fax 242-1041
Ottawa River ES 300/K-6
4747 290th St 43611 419-671-6350
Trent Leedy, prin. Fax 671-6395
Parks ES 300/K-6
3350 Cherry St 43608 419-671-4350
Diane McGee, prin. Fax 671-4395
Pickett ES 400/K-5
1144 Blum St 43607 419-243-1114
Susan Koester, prin. Fax 249-8284
Raymer ES 500/K-6
550 Raymer Blvd 43605 419-671-7650
Sandra Goodwin, prin. Fax 671-7695
Reynolds ES 500/K-6
5000 Norwich Rd 43615 419-671-1500
Sue Finck, prin. Fax 671-1545
Riverside ES 600/K-6
1111 E Manhattan Blvd 43608 419-726-1412
Todd Deem, prin. Fax 729-8825
Robinson MS 500/6-8
1075 Horace St 43606 419-671-4200
Deborah Rivers, prin. Fax 671-4260
Sherman ES 700/K-6
817 Sherman St 43608 419-243-1224
Anthony Bronaugh, prin. Fax 249-8285
Spring ES 600/K-5
730 Spring St 43608 419-671-6600
Janice Richardson, prin. Fax 671-6645
Stewart Academy for Girls 300/K-7
707 Avondale Ave 43604 419-671-5350
William Keaton, prin. Fax 671-5395
Walbridge ES 400/K-5
1040 Newbury St 43609 419-243-4020
Teri Sherwood, prin. Fax 249-8287
Washington Preschool & K 100/PK-K
514 Palmwood Ave 43604 419-244-2701
Keith Scott, lead tchr. Fax 244-8359
Westfield ES 400/K-5
617 Western Ave 43609 419-241-8527
Marsha Jackisch, prin. Fax 249-8290
Whittier ES 700/K-6
4221 Walker Ave 43612 419-476-0400
Laurie Cranston, prin. Fax 470-6558

Washington Local SD 6,800/PK-12
3505 W Lincolnshire Blvd 43606 419-473-8220
Patrick Hickey, supt. Fax 473-8200
www.washloc.k12.oh.us
Greenwood ES 400/K-6
760 Northlawn Dr 43612 419-473-8263
William Colon, prin. Fax 473-8264
Hiawatha ES 300/K-6
3020 Photos Dr 43613 419-473-8268
Lynita Bigelow, prin. Fax 473-8269
Jackman ES 400/K-6
2010 Northover Rd 43613 419-473-8274
Kristine Martin, prin. Fax 473-8275
Jefferson JHS 500/7-7
5530 Whitmer Dr 43613 419-473-8482
Albert Bernhardt, prin. Fax 473-8393
McGregor ES 300/K-6
3535 McGregor Ln 43623 419-473-8279
Jeremy Bauer, prin. Fax 473-8280
Meadowvale ES 500/K-6
2755 Edgebrook Dr 43613 419-473-8284
Amy Franco, prin. Fax 473-8285
Monac ES 400/K-6
3845 Clawson Ave 43623 419-473-8289
William Magginis, prin. Fax 473-8290
Shoreland ES 500/K-6
5650 Suder Ave 43611 419-473-8294
Scott Scharf, prin. Fax 473-8295
Trilby ES 300/PK-6
5720 Secor Rd 43623 419-473-8299
Linda Culp, prin. Fax 473-8300
Washington JHS 500/8-8
5700 Whitmer Dr 43613 419-473-8449
David Ibarra, prin. Fax 473-8340
Wernert ES 400/PK-6
5050 Douglas Rd 43613 419-473-8218
Dr. Carol Rosiak, prin. Fax 473-8219

Blessed Sacrament S 300/PK-8
2216 Castlewood Dr 43613 419-472-1121
Kathy White, prin. Fax 472-1679
CCMT-Queen of Apostles S 100/K-8
235 Courtland Ave 43609 419-241-7829
Sr. Mary Haynes, prin. Fax 241-4180
CCMT-Rosary Cathedral S 200/PK-8
2535 Collingwood Blvd 43610 419-243-4396
Paul Conrad, prin. Fax 243-6049
Christ the King S 600/PK-8
4100 Harvest Ln 43623 419-475-0909
Karen Malcom, prin. Fax 475-4050
Emmanuel Christian S 500/PK-12
4607 W Laskey Rd 43623 419-885-3558
Robert Flamm, admin. Fax 885-3558
Gesu S 400/PK-8
2045 Parkside Blvd 43607 419-536-5634
Beth Janke, prin. Fax 531-8932
Harvest Lane Christian Academy 50/K-8
5132 Harvest Ln 43623 419-474-6989
Irene Tipping, prin. Fax 473-0849
Little Flower of Jesus S 200/PK-8
1620 Olimphia Rd 43615 419-536-1194
Carol Huss, prin. Fax 531-5140
Maumee Valley Country Day S 500/PK-12
1715 S Reynolds Rd 43614 419-381-1313
Gary Boehm, hdmstr. Fax 381-9941
Notre Dame Junior Academy 7-8
3535 Sylvania Ave 43623 419-475-9359
Nichole Flores, prin.
Our Lady of Lourdes S 200/K-8
6145 Hill Ave 43615 419-866-0736
Carol Farnsworth, prin. Fax 866-1351
Our Lady of Perpetual Help S 400/PK-8
2255 Central Grv 43614 419-382-5696
Lori Anderson, prin. Fax 382-7360
Regina Coeli S 400/PK-8
600 Regina Pkwy 43612 419-476-0920
Barbara Lane, prin. Fax 476-6792
Sacred Heart of Jesus S 200/K-8
824 6th St 43605 419-691-0869
Sr. Nancy Vance, prin. Fax 691-7720
St. Catherine of Siena S 300/PK-8
1155 Corbin Rd 43612 419-478-9900
Sr. Carol Smith, prin. Fax 478-9434
St. Clement S 200/PK-8
3020 Tremainsville Rd 43613 419-474-9657
Patti Irons, prin. Fax 479-3215
St. Joan of Arc S 500/K-8
5950 Heatherdowns Blvd 43614 419-866-6177
Sandi Shinaberry, prin. Fax 866-4107
St. John's Jesuit Academy 100/7-8
5901 Airport Hwy 43615 419-865-5743
Christopher Knight, prin. Fax 861-5002
St. John the Baptist S 200/K-8
2729 124th St 43611 419-726-7761
Tom Gladieux, prin. Fax 726-1031
St. Patrick of Heatherdowns S 600/PK-8
4201 Heatherdowns Blvd 43614 419-381-1775
Eric Wagener, prin. Fax 381-2727
St. Pius X S 200/PK-8
2950 Ilger Ave 43606 419-535-7688
Debora O'Shea, prin. Fax 535-7829
St. Thomas Aquinas S 200/K-8
1430 Idaho St 43605 419-691-4328
Joanne Allan, prin. Fax 691-4365
Toledo Christian S 800/PK-12
2303 Brookford Dr 43614 419-389-8700
James Ellinger, supt. Fax 389-8704
Toledo Junior Academy 50/K-9
4909 W Sylvania Ave 43623 419-841-0082
Kells Hall, prin. Fax 843-5494
Trinity Lutheran S 200/PK-8
4560 Glendale Ave 43614 419-385-2301
Christine Spohn, prin. Fax 385-2636
West Side Montessori Center 100/4-8
7115 W Bancroft St 43615 419-843-5703
Lynn Fisher, prin.
Westside Montessori - McCord Campus 300/PK-3
2105 N McCord Rd 43615 419-866-1931
Lynn Fisher, prin. Fax 866-4310
Zion Lutheran S 50/K-8
630 Cuthbert Rd 43607 419-531-1507
Luke Scherschel, prin. Fax 531-1507

Tontogany, Wood, Pop. 371
Otsego Local SD 1,400/PK-12
PO Box 290 43565 419-823-4381
James Garber, supt. Fax 823-3035
www.otsegoknights.org
Otsego JHS 300/6-8
PO Box 290 43565 419-823-4381
Priscilla Pixler, prin. Fax 823-1703
Other Schools – See Grand Rapids, Haskins

Toronto, Jefferson, Pop. 5,402
Toronto CSD 500/PK-12
1307 Dennis Way 43964 740-537-2456
Fred Burns, supt. Fax 537-1102
www.torontocityschools.k12.oh.us
Dennis ES, 1305 Dennis Way 43964 100/PK-2
Patricia Quinn, prin. 740-537-2172
Karaffa MS, 1307 Dennis Way 43964 100/3-6
Maureen Taggart, prin. 740-537-2471

St. Francis S 100/PK-6
601 Loretta Ave 43964 740-537-2151
Marian Barker, prin. Fax 537-9380

Trenton, Butler, Pop. 10,488
Edgewood CSD 3,900/PK-12
3500 Busenbark Rd 45067 513-863-4692
Larry Knapp, supt. Fax 867-7421
www.edgewoodschools.com/index.cfm
Babeck ES 500/1-5
100 Maple Ave 45067 513-988-0111
Jeff Banks, prin. Fax 988-5756
Bloomfield ES 1,000/PK-5
300 N Miami St 45067 513-988-6385
Steve Miller, prin. Fax 988-5253
Other Schools – See Hamilton, Seven Mile

Trotwood, Montgomery, Pop. 26,608
Trotwood-Madison CSD 2,200/K-12
444 S Broadway St 45426 937-854-3050
Dr. Lowell Draffen, supt. Fax 854-3057
www.trotwood.k12.oh.us/
Madison Park ES 2-5
301 S Broadway 45426 937-854-4456
Deborah Smith, prin. Fax 854-4493
Trotwood-Madison Early Learning Center 400/K-1
4400 N Union Rd 45426 937-854-4511
Jeffery Hall, prin. Fax 854-4624
Other Schools – See Dayton

Troy, Miami, Pop. 22,343
Troy CSD 4,600/K-12
500 N Market St 45373 937-332-6700
Tom Dunn, supt. Fax 332-6771
www.troy.k12.oh.us
Concord ES 600/K-5
3145 State Route 718 45373 937-332-6730
Linda Lamb, prin. Fax 332-3840
Cookson ES 400/K-5
921 Mystic Ln 45373 937-332-6740
David Foltz, prin. Fax 332-3980
Forest ES 300/K-5
413 E Canal St 45373 937-332-6746
Alan Zunke, prin. Fax 332-3976
Heywood ES 300/K-5
260 S Ridge Ave 45373 937-332-6750
Maurice Sadler, prin. Fax 332-3891
Hook ES 300/K-5
729 Trade Sq W 45373 937-332-6760
Penny Johnson, prin. Fax 332-3911
Kyle ES 200/K-5
501 S Plum St 45373 937-332-6770
Kimbe Lange, prin. Fax 335-9585
Troy JHS 700/7-8
556 Adams St 45373 937-332-6720
Chad Mason, prin. Fax 332-3812
Van Cleve 6th Grade S 300/6-6
617 E Main St 45373 937-332-6780
Paul Keller, prin. Fax 332-3951

Miami Montessori S 50/PK-6
86 Troy Town Dr 45373 937-339-0025
Paulyne Holten-Sinder, prin. Fax 339-0055
St. Patrick S 200/PK-6
420 E Water St 45373 937-339-3705
Robert Barrett, prin. Fax 339-1158
Troy Christian S 300/K-6
1586 McKaig Rd 45373 937-339-5692
Sue Meckstroth, prin. Fax 335-6258

Tuscarawas, Tuscarawas, Pop. 986
Indian Valley Local SD
Supt. — See Gnadenhutten
Indian Valley MS 200/6-8
PO Box 356 44682 740-922-4226
Eric Jurkovic, prin. Fax 922-2493

Twinsburg, Summit, Pop. 17,380
Twinsburg CSD 4,200/PK-12
11136 Ravenna Rd 44087 330-486-2000
Steve Marlow, supt. Fax 425-7216
twinsburg.k12.oh.us
Bissell ES 600/2-3
1811 Glenwood Dr 44087 330-486-2100
Sharon Sanders, prin. Fax 963-8333
Chamberlin MS 700/7-8
10270 Ravenna Rd 44087 330-486-2281
Belinda Scott, prin. Fax 963-8313
Dodge IS 1,000/4-6
10225 Ravenna Rd 44087 330-486-2200
Barbara Werstler, prin. Fax 963-8323
Wilcox PS 700/PK-1
9198 Darrow Rd 44087 330-486-2030
Judith Latin, prin. Fax 963-8332

Uhrichsville, Tuscarawas, Pop. 5,647
Claymont CSD
Supt. — See Dennison
Claymont JHS 300/7-8
215 E 6th St 44683 740-922-5241
Scott Golec, prin. Fax 922-7330
Eastport Avenue ES 300/K-4
1200 Eastport Ave 44683 740-922-4641
Elizabeth Johnson, prin. Fax 922-7428
Trenton Avenue ES 300/K-4
320 Trenton Ave 44683 740-922-5641
Troy Page, prin. Fax 922-7427

Rush Christian S 50/K-8
4617 Watson Creek Rd SE 44683 740-254-9091
Ethel Moore, prin. Fax 254-9091

Union, Montgomery, Pop. 5,920
Northmont CSD
Supt. — See Englewood
Union ES 400/K-6
418 W Martindale Rd 45322 937-832-6700
Kevin Grone, prin. Fax 832-6701

Union City, Darke, Pop. 1,701
Mississinawa Valley Local SD 700/K-12
1469 State Road 47 E 45390 937-968-5656
Lisa Wendel, supt. Fax 968-6731
www.mississinawa.k12.oh.us
Mississinawa Valley ES 400/K-6
10480 Staudt Rd 45390 937-968-4464
Stephanie Klingshirn, prin. Fax 968-6731

Union Furnace, Hocking
Logan-Hocking Local SD
Supt. — See Logan
Union Furnace ES 300/PK-5
PO Box 172 43158 740-380-6881
Lisa Frasure, prin. Fax 380-6831

Uniontown, Stark, Pop. 3,074
Green Local SD
Supt. — See Green
Green IS 600/5-6
1737 Steese Rd 44685 330-896-7700
Mark Booth, prin. Fax 896-7725
Green MS 700/7-8
1711 Steese Rd 44685 330-896-7710
Jeffrey Miller, prin. Fax 896-7760
Green PS 1-2
2300 Graybill Rd 44685 330-899-8700
Kathy Nolan, prin. Fax 899-8799
Greenwood Early Learning Center 300/PK-K
2250 Graybill Rd 44685 330-896-7474
Rebecca Wolfe, prin. Fax 896-7492

Lake Local SD 3,600/K-12
11936 King Church Ave NW 44685 330-877-9383
Jeff Wendorf, supt. Fax 877-4754
lake.stark.k12.oh.us/
Uniontown ES 500/K-3
13244 Cleveland Ave NW 44685 330-877-4298
Phillip Burns, prin. Fax 699-3101
Other Schools – See Hartville

Mayfair Christian S 50/K-8
2350 Graybill Rd 44685 330-896-3184
Leona Bange, prin. Fax 896-0703

University Heights, Cuyahoga, Pop. 13,242
Cleveland Hts - University Hts CSD 6,000/PK-12
2155 Miramar Blvd 44118 216-371-7171
Christine Fowler-Mack, supt. Fax 397-3698
www.chuh.org
Gearity Professional Development S 300/PK-5
2323 Wrenford Rd 44118 216-371-6515
Sherry Miller, prin. Fax 397-5959
Wiley MS 400/6-8
2181 Miramar Blvd 44118 216-371-7270
Kelli Cogan, prin. Fax 397-5968
Other Schools – See Cleveland Heights

Fuchs Mizrachi S 400/PK-12
2301 Fenwick Rd 44118 216-932-0220
Rabbi Pinchos Hecht, hdmstr. Fax 932-0345
Gesu S 800/PK-8
2450 Miramar Blvd 44118 216-932-0620
Sr. Linda Martin, prin. Fax 932-8326

Upper Arlington, Franklin, Pop. 31,550
Upper Arlington CSD 5,200/K-12
1950 N Mallway Dr 43221 614-487-5000
Jeffrey Weaver Ph.D., supt. Fax 487-5012
www.uaschools.org
Barrington Road ES 700/K-5
1780 Barrington Rd 43221 614-487-5180
Pam Yoder, prin. Fax 487-5189
Greensview ES 400/K-5
4301 Greensview Dr 43220 614-487-5050
Jason Wulf, prin. Fax 487-5190
Hastings MS 600/6-8
1850 Hastings Ln 43220 614-487-5100
Beverly Von Zielonka, prin. Fax 487-5116
Jones MS 700/6-8
2100 Arlington Ave 43221 614-487-5080
Matt Petersen, prin. Fax 487-5307
Tremont ES 500/K-5
2900 Tremont Rd 43221 614-487-5170
Tom Bates, prin. Fax 487-5746
Windermere ES 400/K-5
4101 Windermere Rd 43220 614-487-5060
Steve Scarpitti, prin. Fax 487-5378

Upper Sandusky, Wyandot, Pop. 6,455
Upper Sandusky EVD 1,700/K-12
800 N Sandusky Ave Ste A 43351 419-294-2307
Kenneth Doseck, supt. Fax 294-6891
www.uppersandusky.k12.oh.us
East ES 100/K-5
401 N 3rd St 43351 419-294-2396
Michael Courtad, prin. Fax 294-6895
South ES 100/K-5
444 S 8th St 43351 419-294-2304
Laurie Vent, prin. Fax 294-6892
Union ES 300/K-3
390 W Walker St 43351 419-294-5721
Laurie Vent, prin. Fax 294-2586
Union MS 600/4-8
390 W Walker St 43351 419-294-5721
James Wheeler, prin. Fax 294-2586

St. Peter S 100/K-6
310 N 8th St 43351 419-294-1395
Mary Alice Harbour, prin. Fax 209-0295

Urbana, Champaign, Pop. 11,561
Urbana CSD 2,300/K-12
711 Wood St 43078 937-653-1402
Charles Thiel, supt. Fax 652-3845
www.urbana.k12.oh.us
East ES 300/3-4
630 Washington Ave 43078 937-653-1453
Brenda Riley, prin. Fax 652-3845
Local IS 400/5-6
2468 State Route 54 43078 937-484-1457
Joanne Petty, prin. Fax 652-3845
North ES 300/K-2
626 N Russell St 43078 937-653-1445
Tom Topolewski, prin. Fax 653-1447
South ES 300/K-2
725 S Main St 43078 937-653-1449
Linda Locke, prin. Fax 652-0233
Urbana JHS 400/7-8
500 Washington Ave 43078 937-653-1439
Fax 658-1487

Johnny Appleseed Montessori Center 50/PK-4
PO Box 189 43078 937-653-8146
Sarah Goldstein, dir.

Utica, Licking, Pop. 2,109
North Fork Local SD 1,900/K-12
PO Box 497 43080 740-892-3666
Scott Hartley, supt. Fax 892-2937
www.northfork.k12.oh.us
Utica ES 500/K-6
PO Box 956 43080 740-892-2551
Sharon Greene, prin. Fax 892-2138
Utica JHS 300/7-8
PO Box 647 43080 740-892-2691
Greg Sampson, prin. Fax 892-2203
Other Schools – See Newark

Van Buren, Hancock, Pop. 304
Van Buren Local SD 1,000/K-12
217 S Main St 45889 419-299-3578
Timothy Myers, supt. Fax 299-3668
www.vbschools.net
Van Buren ES 400/K-5
301 S Main St 45889 419-299-3416
Richard Lehman, prin. Fax 299-3566
Van Buren MS 200/6-8
217 S Main St 45889 419-299-3385
Jason Clark, prin. Fax 299-3340

Vandalia, Montgomery, Pop. 14,298
Vandalia-Butler CSD 3,500/K-12
306 S Dixie Dr 45377 937-415-6400
Dr. Christy Donnelly, supt. Fax 415-6429
www.vandaliabutlerschools.org
Demmitt ES 400/K-4
1010 E National Rd 45377 937-415-6500
Daniel Dodds, prin. Fax 415-6538
Helke ES 400/K-4
611 Randler Ave 45377 937-415-3000
Cheryl Stidham, prin. Fax 415-3031
Morton MS 500/5-8
231 W National Rd 45377 937-415-6600
Russ Garman, prin. Fax 415-6648
Other Schools – See Dayton

St. Christopher S 400/K-8
405 E National Rd 45377 937-898-5104
Sr. Patricia Kremer, prin. Fax 454-4790

Vanlue, Hancock, Pop. 360
Vanlue Local SD 300/K-12
PO Box 250 45890 419-387-7724
Rodney Russell, supt. Fax 387-7722
www.noacsc.org/hancock/vl/
Vanlue ES 100/K-6
PO Box 250 45890 419-387-7724
Scott Hall, prin. Fax 387-7722

Van Wert, Van Wert, Pop. 10,435
Lincolnview Local SD 1,000/K-12
15945 Middle Point Rd 45891 419-968-2226
Doug Fries, supt. Fax 968-2227
www.noacsc.org/vanwert/lv/main.html
Lincolnview ES 500/K-6
15945 Middle Point Rd 45891 419-968-2351
William Kelly, prin. Fax 968-2227

Van Wert CSD 2,000/K-12
205 W Crawford St 45891 419-238-0648
Ken Amstutz, supt. Fax 238-3974
www.vanwertcougars.net
Franklin ES 200/K-4
305 Frothingham St 45891 419-238-1761
Beth Runnion, prin. Fax 238-5055
Goedde ES 100/5-5
205 W Crawford St 45891 419-238-5976
Mark Bagley, prin. Fax 238-3974
Jefferson ES 200/K-4
1120 Buckeye Dr 45891 419-238-6540
Kevin Gehres, prin. Fax 238-5058
Van Wert MS 500/6-8
305 W Crawford St 45891 419-238-0727
Mark Bagley, prin. Fax 238-7166

Washington ES 200/K-4
839 Prospect Ave 45891 419-238-0384
William Wisher, prin. Fax 238-2137

St. Mary of the Assumption S 100/K-6
611 Jennings Rd 45891 419-238-5186
Janice Schimmoeller, prin. Fax 238-5842

Vermilion, Erie, Pop. 11,000
Vermilion Local SD 2,400/K-12
1230 Beechview Dr 44089 440-204-1700
Philip Pempin, supt. Fax 204-1771
vermilionschools.org
Sailorway MS 600/6-8
5355 Sailorway Dr 44089 440-204-1700
Heidi Riddle, prin. Fax 204-1757
South Street ES 500/K-2
5735 South St 44089 440-204-1700
Tina Swinehart, prin. Fax 204-1766
Vermilion IS 500/3-5
935 Decatur St 44089 440-204-1700
Bonnie Meyer, prin. Fax 204-1747

St. Mary S 100/K-6
5450 Ohio St 44089 440-967-7911
Barbara Bialko, prin. Fax 967-8287

Versailles, Darke, Pop. 2,539
Versailles EVD 1,400/K-12
PO Box 313 45380 937-526-4773
David Vail, supt. Fax 526-5745
www.versailles.k12.oh.us
Versailles ES 400/K-4
PO Box 313 45380 937-526-4681
Brenda Braun, prin. Fax 526-3480
Versailles MS 200/5-6
PO Box 313 45380 937-526-4426
Jeanne Osterfeld, prin. Fax 526-3085
Other Schools – See North Star

Vienna, Trumbull, Pop. 1,067
Mathews Local SD 900/K-12
4434 Warren Sharon Rd Ste B 44473 330-394-1800
Lee Seiple, supt. Fax 394-1930
www.mathews.k12.oh.us
Baker ES, 4095 Sheridan Dr 44473 200/3-5
Michael King, prin. 330-539-5042
Other Schools – See Cortland, Fowler

Vincent, Washington
Warren Local SD 2,500/K-12
220 Sweetapple Rd 45784 740-678-2366
Thomas Gibbs, supt. Fax 678-8275
www.warrenlocal.k12.oh.us/
Barlow-Vincent S 700/K-8
70 Warrior Dr 45784 740-678-2395
Stephanie Starcher, prin. Fax 678-0118
Other Schools – See Little Hocking, Marietta

Vinton, Gallia, Pop. 343
Gallia County Local SD
Supt. — See Gallipolis
Vinton S 200/K-8
123 Keystone Rd 45686 740-388-8261
Mark Carlisle, prin. Fax 388-4000

Wadsworth, Medina, Pop. 19,951
Wadsworth CSD 4,800/PK-12
360 College St 44281 330-336-3571
Dale Fortner, supt. Fax 335-1313
www.wadsworth.k12.oh.us/
Central IS 700/5-6
151 Main St 44281 330-335-1480
Paula Canterbury, prin. Fax 335-1484
Franklin ES 300/K-4
200 Takacs Dr 44281 330-335-1470
Roger Havens, prin. Fax 335-1468
Isham Memorial ES 500/K-4
348 College St 44281 330-335-1440
Nance Watts, prin. Fax 335-1330
Lincoln ES 300/PK-4
280 N Lyman St 44281 330-335-1460
Steve Brady, prin. Fax 335-1462
Overlook ES 200/K-4
524 Broad St 44281 330-335-1420
Erin Simpson, prin. Fax 335-1425
Valley View ES 400/K-4
160 W Good Ave 44281 330-335-1430
Paula Trenta, prin. Fax 335-1428
Wadsworth MS 700/7-8
150 Silvercreek Rd 44281 330-335-1410
Roger Wright, prin. Fax 336-3820

Northside Christian Academy 50/K-2
7615 Ridge Rd 44281 330-336-3979
Wendy Turocy, dir. Fax 334-7729
Reimer Road Baptist Christian S 100/PK-12
1055 Reimer Rd 44281 330-334-1480
Christy Varga, prin. Fax 336-3064
Sacred Heart Jesus S 300/K-8
110 Humbolt Ave 44281 330-334-6272
Tracy Arnone, prin. Fax 334-3236

Wakeman, Huron, Pop. 964

Clarksfield SDA S 50/1-8
5001 Zen Rd 44889 419-929-7833
Irwin Hoover, prin.

Walbridge, Wood, Pop. 3,096
Lake Local SD
Supt. — See Millbury
Walbridge ES 200/K-1
200 E Union St 43465 419-661-6520
Dolores Swineford, prin. Fax 661-6521

St. Jerome S 200/PK-8
300 Earl St 43465 419-666-9763
Gerald Schoen, prin. Fax 661-2285

Walnut Creek, Holmes
East Holmes Local SD
Supt. — See Berlin
Walnut Creek ES, PO Box 145 44687 200/K-6
Ken Miller, prin. 330-893-2213

Walton Hills, Cuyahoga, Pop. 2,347

New Covenant Christian Academy 100/K-6
7166 Dunham Rd 44146 440-439-6220
Fax 439-6257

Wapakoneta, Auglaize, Pop. 9,602
Wapakoneta CSD 3,100/K-12
1102 Gardenia Dr 45895 419-739-2900
Keith Horner, supt. Fax 739-2918
www.wapak.org/
Centennial ES 400/K-2
700 S Water St 45895 419-739-5000
Wesley Newland, prin. Fax 739-5033
Northridge ES 400/2-4
900 N Blackhoof St 45895 419-739-5050
Mark Selvaggio, prin. Fax 739-5051
Wapakoneta MS 700/5-7
400 W Harrison St 45895 419-739-5100
Ray Payne, prin. Fax 739-5165
Other Schools – See Cridersville

St. Joseph S 100/PK-8
1101 Lincoln Hwy 45895 419-738-3311
Ronald Fahncke, prin. Fax 738-7706

Warren, Trumbull, Pop. 45,796
Champion Local SD 1,700/K-12
5759 Mahoning Ave NW 44483 330-847-2330
Pamela Hood, supt. Fax 847-2336
www.champion.k12.oh.us
Champion Central ES 600/K-4
5759 Mahoning Ave NW 44483 330-847-2315
Cheryl Kirk, prin. Fax 847-2336
Champion MS 500/5-8
5435 Kuszmaul Ave NW 44483 330-847-2340
Mary Rose Walker, prin. Fax 847-3624

Howland Local SD 3,200/K-12
8200 South St SE 44484 330-856-8200
John Sheets, supt. Fax 856-8214
www.howlandschools.com
Howland Glen ES 300/K-2
8000 Bridle Ln NE 44484 330-856-8275
Gary Gawdyda, prin. Fax 856-8289
Howland MS 800/6-8
8100 South St SE 44484 330-856-8250
Kevin Spicher, prin. Fax 856-2157
Howland Springs ES 300/K-2
9500 Howland Springs Rd SE 44484 330-856-8280
Erin Pierce, prin. Fax 856-2475
Mines ES 400/3-5
850 Howland Wilson Rd NE 44484 330-856-8270
Karen Coleman, prin. Fax 856-8288
North Road ES 300/3-5
863 North Rd SE 44484 330-856-8265
Carl Clark, prin. Fax 856-8287

Lakeview Local SD
Supt. — See Cortland
Bazetta ES 500/K-2
2755 Bazetta Rd NE 44481 330-372-2145
Dennis Chupak, prin. Fax 372-6727

Lordstown Local SD 500/K-12
1824 Salt Springs Rd W 44481 330-824-2534
William Pfahler, supt. Fax 824-2847
www.lordstown.k12.oh.us/
Lordstown ES 300/K-6
1776 Salt Springs Rd 44481 330-824-2572
Laura Parise, prin. Fax 824-2568

Warren CSD 2,600/K-12
261 Monroe St NW 44483 330-841-2321
Dr. Kathryn Hellweg, supt. Fax 841-2434
www.warrenschools.k12.oh.us
Jefferson S 200/K-8
903 5th St SW 44485 330-841-2401
Steve Chiaro, prin. Fax 841-2399
Lincoln S 300/K-8
2253 Atlantic St NE 44483 330-373-4500
Jeffrey DeJulia, prin. Fax 373-4510
McGuffey S 400/K-8
Tod Ave NW 44485 330-841-2345
Linda Reigelman, prin. Fax 373-6065
Willard Avenue S K-8
2020 Willard Ave SE 44484 330-841-2255
Ed Ashcroft, prin. Fax 841-2328

Blessed Sacrament S 300/PK-6
3000 Reeves Rd NE 44483 330-372-2375
Theresa Dixon, prin. Fax 372-2465
St. Pius X S 100/PK-6
1461 Moncrest Dr NW 44485 330-399-5411
Mary Jo Dugan, prin. Fax 399-7364

Warrensville Heights, Cuyahoga, Pop. 14,223
Warrensville Heights CSD 2,500/K-12
4500 Warrensville Center Rd 44128 216-295-7710
Elaine Davis, supt. Fax 921-5902
www.warrensville.k12.oh.us
Dewey ES 300/K-4
23401 Emery Rd 44128 216-295-7790
Veda Giles, prin. Fax 921-5813
Eastwood ES 200/K-4
4050 Eastwood Ln 44122 216-295-7740
Felicia Woods-Wallace, prin. Fax 921-6463
Randallwood MS 400/5-6
21865 Clarkwood Pkwy 44128 216-831-7270
Katrinka Dean, prin. Fax 921-5922
Warrensville Heights MS 400/7-8
4285 Warrensville Center Rd 44128 216-752-4050
Lori Crum-Glenn, prin. Fax 752-5813
Westwood ES 300/K-4
19000 Garden Blvd 44128 216-752-1232
Kelley Dudley, prin. Fax 921-6557

Warsaw, Coshocton, Pop. 787
River View Local SD 2,400/K-12
26496 State Route 60 43844 740-824-3521
Kyle Kanuckel, supt. Fax 824-3760
www.river-view.k12.oh.us
River View JHS 400/7-8
26546 State Route 60 43844 740-824-3523
Sharon Tatro, prin. Fax 824-5241
Union ES 300/K-6
19781 State Route 79 43844 740-327-2351
Vicki Johnson, prin. Fax 327-2012
Warsaw ES 300/K-6
PO Box 97 43844 740-824-3727
Frank Polen, prin. Fax 824-4267
Other Schools – See Conesville, Coshocton

Washington Court House, Fayette, Pop. 13,471
Miami Trace Local SD 1,300/K-12
1400 US Highway 22 NW 43160 740-335-3010
Daniel Roberts, supt. Fax 335-5675
miamitrace.k12.oh.us
Miami Trace ES K-5
3836 State Route 41 NW 43160 740-333-2400
Julie Reisinger, prin. Fax 333-2300
Other Schools – See Bloomingburg

Washington Court House CSD 2,300/K-12
306 Highland Ave 43160 740-335-6620
Keith Brown, supt. Fax 335-1245
www.washingtonch.k12.oh.us
Belle Aire ES 400/1-5
1120 High St 43160 740-335-1810
Terrance Feick, prin. Fax 335-6432
Cherry Hill ES 100/1-5
720 W Oakland Ave 43160 740-335-3370
Craig Maddux, prin. Fax 335-2897
Eastside ES 300/1-5
506 S Elm St 43160 740-335-2301
Robert Runnels, prin. Fax 333-3613
Rose Avenue ES 100/1-5
412 Rose Ave 43160 740-335-1390
Craig Maddux, prin. Fax 333-3605
Sunnyside K 200/K-K
721 S Fayette St 43160 740-333-3612
Beth Justice, prin. Fax 333-3628
Washington MS 500/6-8
318 N North St 43160 740-335-0291
Steve Ross, prin. Fax 333-3606

Waterford, Washington
Wolf Creek Local SD 700/K-12
PO Box 67 45786 740-984-2373
Robert Caldwell, supt. Fax 984-4420
www.wolfcreek.k12.oh.us
Waterford S 400/K-8
PO Box 45 45786 740-984-2342
John Hoff, prin. Fax 984-4608

Waterville, Lucas, Pop. 5,189
Anthony Wayne Local SD
Supt. — See Whitehouse
Waterville ES 500/K-4
457 Sycamore Ln 43566 419-878-2436
Deb Thomas, prin. Fax 878-4312

Lucas County ESC
Supt. — See Toledo
Waterville Center S 100/K-12
1 S River Rd 43566 419-787-6320
Fax 245-4186

Wauseon, Fulton, Pop. 7,311
Wauseon EVD 2,100/K-12
126 S Fulton St 43567 419-335-6616
Marc Robinson, supt. Fax 335-3978
www.wauseon.k12.oh.us
Burr Road MS 500/6-8
717 Burr Rd 43567 419-335-2701
William Friess, prin. Fax 335-0089
Elm Street ES 500/3-5
440 E Elm St 43567 419-335-6581
David Burkholder, prin. Fax 335-0045
Leggett Street PS 400/K-2
940 E Leggett St 43567 419-335-4000
Troy Armstrong, prin. Fax 335-4003

Waverly, Pike, Pop. 5,086
Waverly CSD 2,100/K-12
1 Tiger Dr 45690 740-947-4770
Cheryl Francis, supt. Fax 947-4483
www.waverly.k12.oh.us
Waverly IS 500/3-5
5 Tiger Dr 45690 740-947-5173
Andrew Seddelmeyer, prin. Fax 947-0301
Waverly JHS 500/6-8
3 Tiger Dr 45690 740-947-4527
Bill Hoover, prin. Fax 947-8047
Waverly PS 500/K-2
7 Tiger Dr 45690 740-947-2813
Melissa Marquez, prin. Fax 947-8284

Pike Christian Academy 200/PK-9
400 Clough St 45690 740-947-5700
Gayle Kramer, prin. Fax 947-9500

Waynesburg, Stark, Pop. 983

St. James S 200/PK-6
400 W Lisbon St 44688 330-866-9556
Kathleen Untch, prin. Fax 866-1750

Waynesfield, Auglaize, Pop. 819
Waynesfield-Goshen Local SD 600/K-12
500 N Westminster St 45896 419-568-2391
Joanne Kerekes, supt. Fax 568-8024
www.wgschools.org
Waynesfield-Goshen ES 300/K-5
500 N Westminster St 45896 419-568-4451
Timothy Pence, prin. Fax 568-8024

Waynesville, Warren, Pop. 2,980
Wayne Local SD 1,500/K-12
659 Dayton Rd 45068 513-897-6971
Patrick Dubbs, supt. Fax 897-9605
www.wayne-local.k12.oh.us
Waynesville ES 600/K-5
659 Dayton Rd 45068 513-897-2761
Jean Hartman, prin. Fax 897-9605
Waynesville MS 400/6-8
723 Dayton Rd 45068 513-897-4706
Thomas Olson, prin. Fax 897-9605

Wellington, Lorain, Pop. 4,648
Wellington EVD 1,600/K-12
201 S Main St 44090 440-647-4286
Francis Scruci, supt. Fax 647-4806
www.wellington.k12.oh.us
McCormick MS 600/4-8
201 S Main St 44090 440-647-2342
Tom Durham, prin. Fax 647-7310
Westwood ES 500/K-3
305 Union St 44090 440-647-3636
Sheila Buckeye, prin. Fax 647-1089

Wellston, Jackson, Pop. 6,025
Wellston CSD 1,700/PK-12
1 E Broadway St 45692 740-384-2152
Eric Meredith, supt. Fax 384-3948
www.wcs.k12.oh.us
Bundy ES 500/PK-2
525 W 7th St 45692 740-384-6245
Ruth Spatar, prin. Fax 384-4683
Wellston IS 400/3-5
225 Golden Rocket Dr 45692 740-384-2060
Dana Stevison, prin. Fax 384-9801
Wellston MS 400/6-8
227 Golden Rocket Dr 45692 740-384-2251
Megan Aubrey, prin. Fax 384-9801

SS. Peter & Paul S 100/PK-8
229 S New York Ave 45692 740-384-6354
Jeff Plummer, prin. Fax 384-2945

Wellsville, Columbiana, Pop. 4,034
Wellsville Local SD 1,000/K-12
929 Center St 43968 330-532-2643
Richard Bereschik, supt. Fax 532-6204
www.wellsville.k12.oh.us
Daw MS, 929 Center St 43968 400/4-8
David Buzzard, prin. 330-532-1372
Garfield ES 300/K-3
1600 Lincoln Ave 43968 330-532-3301
Lisa Ferguson, prin. Fax 532-1108

West Alexandria, Preble, Pop. 1,343
Twin Valley Community Local SD 1,100/K-12
100 Education Dr 45381 937-839-4688
Vernon Rosenbeck, supt. Fax 839-4898
www.tvs.k12.oh.us
Twin Valley South ES 500/K-5
100 Education Dr 45381 937-839-4315
Patti Precht, prin. Fax 839-4898
Twin Valley South MS 300/6-8
100 Education Dr 45381 937-839-4165
Eva Howard, prin. Fax 839-4898

West Carrollton, Montgomery, Pop. 14,072
West Carrollton CSD 3,800/PK-12
430 E Pease Ave 45449 937-859-5121
Rusty Clifford, supt. Fax 859-2766
www.westcarrolltonschools.com
Russell ES 400/1-5
123 Elementary Dr 45449 937-859-5121
Tony Mennett, prin. Fax 865-5720
Schnell ES 500/1-5
5995 Student St 45449 937-859-5121
Barbara Gardecki, prin. Fax 859-2775
Shade ECC 400/PK-K
510 E Pease Ave 45449 937-859-5121
Kimberly Hall-Alt, prin. Fax 859-2768
West Carrollton MS 900/6-8
424 E Main St 45449 937-859-5121
John Runzo, prin. Fax 859-2780
Other Schools – See Dayton

West Chester, Butler
Lakota Local SD
Supt. — See Liberty Twp
Adena ES 500/2-6
9316 Minuteman Way 45069 513-777-0100
Ericka Simmons, prin. Fax 777-3475
Creekside Early Childhood S 1,100/K-1
5070 Tylersville Rd 45069 513-874-0175
Todd Petrey, prin. Fax 682-4213
Endeavor ES 600/2-6
4400 Smith Rd 45069 513-759-8300
Tim Weber, prin. Fax 759-8301
Freedom ES 600/2-6
6035 Beckett Ridge Blvd 45069 513-777-9787
Sabrina Hubert, prin. Fax 777-6014
Hopewell ES 700/2-6
8300 Cox Rd 45069 513-777-6128
Denise Hayes, prin. Fax 777-3805
Hopewell JHS 700/7-8
8200 Cox Rd 45069 513-777-2258
David Pike, prin. Fax 777-1908
Lakota Ridge JHS 700/7-8
6199 Beckett Ridge Blvd 45069 513-777-0552
Andre Gendreau, prin. Fax 777-0919
Union ES 500/2-6
7670 Lesourdsville W Chestr 45069 513-777-2201
Robert Winterberger, prin. Fax 777-3603

West Elkton, Preble, Pop. 179
Preble Shawnee Local SD
Supt. — See Camden
West Elkton ES 300/4-6
PO Box 97 45070 937-787-4102
Kipling Powell, prin. Fax 787-3453

Westerville, Franklin, Pop. 34,722
Westerville CSD 14,100/K-12
336 S Otterbein Ave 43081 614-797-5700
Dr. James Good, supt. Fax 797-5701
www.westerville.k12.oh.us
Alcott ES 700/K-5
7117 Mount Royal Ave 43082 614-797-7350
Robert Hoffman, prin. Fax 797-7351
Annehurst ES 400/K-5
925 W Main St 43081 614-797-7000
Howard Baum, prin. Fax 797-7001
Blendon MS 600/6-8
223 S Otterbein Ave 43081 614-797-6400
David Baker, prin. Fax 797-6401
Central College ES 100/1-5
825 S Sunbury Rd 43081 614-797-7030
Steve Petercsak, prin. Fax 797-7031
Cherrington ES 300/K-5
522 Cherrington Rd 43081 614-797-7050
Andrew Heck, prin. Fax 797-7051
Emerson ES 200/1-5
44 N Vine St 43081 614-797-7080
Vicki Jarrell, prin. Fax 797-7081
Fouse ES 700/K-5
5800 S Old 3C Hwy 43082 614-797-7400
Brian Orrenmaa, prin. Fax 797-7401
Frost ES 300/K-5
270 N Spring Rd 43082 614-797-7280
Sara Berka, prin. Fax 797-7281
Genoa MS 900/6-8
5948 S Old 3C Hwy 43082 614-797-6500
Barry Ackerman, prin. Fax 797-6501
Hanby ES 300/1-5
56 S State St 43081 614-797-7100
Janet Fedorenko, prin. Fax 797-7101
Heritage MS 900/6-8
390 N Spring Rd 43082 614-797-6600
Felicia Harper, prin. Fax 797-6601
Huber Ridge ES 500/K-5
5757 Buenos Aires Blvd 43081 614-797-7150
Barb Wallace, prin. Fax 797-7151
Longfellow ES 100/1-5
120 Hiawatha Ave 43081 614-797-7180
Steve Petercsak, prin. Fax 797-7181
McVay ES 500/K-5
270 S Hempstead Rd 43081 614-797-7230
Suzanne Kile, prin. Fax 797-7231
Pointview ES 300/K-5
720 Pointview Dr 43081 614-797-7250
Jeanne Roth, prin. Fax 797-7251
Twain ES 400/K-5
799 E Walnut St 43081 614-797-7200
Scott Ebbrecht, prin. Fax 797-7201
Walnut Springs MS 1,000/6-8
888 E Walnut St 43081 614-797-6700
Matt Lutz, prin. Fax 797-6701
Whittier ES 300/K-5
130 E Walnut St 43081 614-797-7300
Kimberly Woosley, prin. Fax 797-7301
Wilder ES 500/K-5
6375 Goldfinch Dr 43081 614-797-7330
Rebecca Yanni, prin. Fax 797-7331
Other Schools – See Columbus

Worthington CSD
Supt. — See Worthington
Worthington Park ES 400/K-6
500 Park Rd 43081 614-883-3450
Joy Tremmel, prin. Fax 883-3460

Central College Christian Academy 200/K-5
975 S Sunbury Rd 43081 614-794-8146
Robert Kimball, dir. Fax 794-8146
Eastwood SDA Junior Academy 50/K-8
6350 S Sunbury Rd 43081 614-794-6350
J. Carlos, prin. Fax 794-6352
Genoa Christian Academy 300/PK-8
7562 Lewis Center Rd 43082 740-965-5433
Terri Foltz, supt. Fax 965-8214
St. Paul S 900/K-8
61 Moss Rd 43082 614-882-2710
Kathleen Norris Ph.D., prin. Fax 882-5998
Worthington Christian K 200/PK-K
8225 Worthington Galena Rd 43081 614-431-8228
Tim Adams, dir. Fax 431-8206
Worthington Christian MS 200/6-8
8225 Worthington Galena Rd 43081 614-431-8230
Richard Dray, prin. Fax 431-8216

Westfield Center, Medina, Pop. 1,151
Cloverleaf Local SD
Supt. — See Lodi
Westfield ES 500/5-6
PO Box 5003 44251 330-887-5619
James Carpenter, prin. Fax 887-1049

West Jefferson, Madison, Pop. 4,287
Jefferson Local SD 1,300/PK-12
906 W Main St 43162 614-879-7654
William Mullett, supt. Fax 879-5376
www.west-jefferson.k12.oh.us
Norwood ES 600/PK-5
899 Norwood Dr 43162 614-879-7642
Gary Bell, prin. Fax 879-5377
West Jefferson MS 300/6-8
2 Roughrider Dr 43162 614-879-8345
Debbie Omen, prin. Fax 879-5399

West Lafayette, Coshocton, Pop. 2,535
Ridgewood Local SD 1,100/PK-12
301 S Oak St 43845 740-545-6354
Rick Raach, supt. Fax 545-6336
www.ridgewood.k12.oh.us
Ridgewood ES 300/PK-3
225 W Union Ave 43845 740-545-5312
Brian Rentsch, prin. Fax 545-7015
Ridgewood MS 200/4-7
517 S Oak St 43845 740-545-6335
Mike Masloski, prin. Fax 545-5300

Westlake, Cuyahoga, Pop. 31,331
Westlake CSD 4,000/K-12
27200 Hilliard Blvd 44145 440-871-7300
Daniel Keenan, supt. Fax 871-6034
www.wlake.org/
Bassett ES 400/K-4
2155 Bassett Rd 44145 440-835-6330
Tim Rickard, prin. Fax 899-7409
Burneson MS 700/7-8
2240 Dover Center Rd 44145 440-835-6340
G. Newman, prin. Fax 835-5987
Dover ES 400/K-4
2300 Dover Center Rd 44145 440-835-6322
Timothy Barrett, prin. Fax 899-7407
Hilliard ES 300/K-4
24365 Hilliard Blvd 44145 440-835-6343
Mary Flanagan, prin. Fax 835-5698
Holly Lane ES 300/K-4
3057 Holly Ln 44145 440-835-6332
Marilyn Verdone, prin. Fax 734-4312
Parkside IS 600/5-6
24525 Hilliard Blvd 44145 440-835-6325
Mark Bregar, prin. Fax 835-5798

Montessori Children's S 100/PK-3
28370 Bassett Rd 44145 440-871-8773
Barbara Kincaid, dir. Fax 871-1799
St. Bernadette S 500/K-8
2300 Clague Rd 44145 440-734-7717
Helen Bykowski, prin. Fax 734-9198
St. Paul Lutheran S 300/PK-8
27981 Detroit Rd 44145 440-835-3051
Dale Lehrke, prin. Fax 835-8216
Westside Christian Academy 100/K-8
23096 Center Ridge Rd 44145 440-331-1300
Kathy Mack, prin. Fax 331-1301

West Liberty, Champaign, Pop. 1,760
West Liberty-Salem Local SD 1,200/K-12
7208 US Highway 68 N 43357 937-465-1075
Fax 465-1095
www.wlstigers.org/
West Liberty-Salem ES 500/K-5
7208 US Highway 68 N 43357 937-465-0060
Aaron Hollar, prin. Fax 465-1095

West Milton, Miami, Pop. 4,684
Milton-Union EVD 1,700/K-12
112 S Spring St 45383 937-884-7910
Dr. Virginia Rammel, supt. Fax 884-7911
www.milton-union.k12.oh.us
Milton-Union ES 700/K-5
43 Wright Rd 45383 937-884-7920
Jarrod Brumbaugh, prin. Fax 884-7921
Milton-Union MS 400/6-8
146 S Spring St 45383 937-884-7930
Laurie Grube, prin. Fax 884-7931

West Portsmouth, Scioto, Pop. 3,551
Washington-Nile Local SD 1,600/K-12
15332 US Highway 52 45663 740-858-1111
Patricia Ciraso, supt. Fax 858-1110
www.west.k12.oh.us
Portsmouth West ES 800/K-5
15332 US Highway 52 Unit A 45663 740-858-1116
William Platzer, prin. Fax 858-1118
Portsmouth West MS 400/6-8
1420 13th St 45663 740-858-6668
Christopher Jordan, prin. Fax 858-4101

West Salem, Wayne, Pop. 1,488
Northwestern Local SD 1,500/K-12
7571 N Elyria Rd 44287 419-846-3151
Jeffrey Layton, supt. Fax 846-3361
www.northwestern-wayne.k12.oh.us
Northwestern ES 700/K-5
7334 N Elyria Rd 44287 419-846-3519
Julie McCumber, prin. Fax 846-3584
Northwestern MS 300/6-8
7569 N Elyria Rd 44287 419-846-3974
Scott Smith, prin. Fax 846-3750

West Union, Adams, Pop. 3,108
Adams County/Ohio Valley Local SD 4,100/K-12
141 Lloyd Rd 45693 937-544-5586
Charles Kimble, supt. Fax 544-3720
www.ohiovalley.k12.oh.us
West Union ES 800/K-6
201 W South St 45693 937-544-2951
Linda Naylor, prin. Fax 544-7380
Other Schools – See Peebles, Seaman

Adams County Christian S 100/K-12
187 Willow Dr 45693 937-544-5502
Shirley Lewis, admin. Fax 544-5503

West Unity, Williams, Pop. 1,803
Millcreek-West Unity Local SD 800/K-12
113 S Defiance St 43570 419-924-2365
Deb Piotrowski, supt. Fax 924-2367
www.hilltop.k12.oh.us
Hilltop ES 400/K-6
113 S Defiance St 43570 419-924-2368
Charles Johnston, prin. Fax 924-2367

Wheelersburg, Scioto, Pop. 5,113
Wheelersburg Local SD 1,400/PK-12
PO Box 340 45694 740-574-8484
Mark Knapp, supt. Fax 574-6134
www.burg.k12.oh.us
Wheelersburg ES 500/PK-3
800 Pirate Dr 45694 740-574-8130
Angela Holmes, prin. Fax 574-9201
Wheelersburg MS 400/4-8
800 Pirate Dr 45694 740-574-2515
Amber Fannin, prin. Fax 574-9201

Whitehall, Franklin, Pop. 18,052
Whitehall CSD 2,700/K-12
625 S Yearling Rd 43213 614-417-5000
Judyth Dobbert-Meloy, supt. Fax 417-5023
www.whitehall.k12.oh.us
Beechwood ES 500/K-5
455 Beechwood Rd 43213 614-417-5300
Chad Lape, prin. Fax 417-5304
Etna Road ES 400/K-5
4531 Etna Rd 43213 614-417-5400
Suellen Fitzwater, prin. Fax 417-5410
Kae Avenue ES 400/K-5
4738 Kae Ave 43213 614-417-5600
Berta Johnson, prin. Fax 417-5607
Rosemore MS 700/6-8
4735 Kae Ave 43213 614-417-5200
Mark Trace, prin. Fax 417-5212

Whitehouse, Lucas, Pop. 3,303
Anthony Wayne Local SD 4,400/K-12
PO Box 2487 43571 419-877-5377
John Granger, supt. Fax 877-9352
www.anthonywayneschools.org
Fallen Timbers MS 700/5-6
6119 Finzel Rd 43571 419-877-0601
Gary Gardner, prin. Fax 877-4907
Wayne JHS 700/7-8
6035 Finzel Rd 43571 419-877-5342
Kevin Pfefferle, prin. Fax 877-4908
Whitehouse ES 600/K-4
6510 N Texas St 43571 419-877-0543
Brad Rhodes, prin. Fax 877-4905
Other Schools – See Monclova, Waterville

Lial S 200/PK-7
5700 Davis Rd 43571 419-877-5167
Sr. Patricia McClain, prin. Fax 877-9385

Wickliffe, Lake, Pop. 13,205
Wickliffe CSD 1,500/K-12
2221 Rockefeller Rd 44092 440-943-6900
Kathleen Cintavey, supt. Fax 943-7738
www.wickliffe-city.k12.oh.us
Wickliffe ES 500/K-4
1821 Lincoln Rd 44092 440-943-0320
Gregory Bonamase, prin. Fax 943-7738
Wickliffe MS 500/5-8
29240 Euclid Ave 44092 440-943-3220
A. William Kermavner, prin. Fax 943-7755

All Saints of St. John Vianney S 300/PK-8
28702 Euclid Ave 44092 440-943-1395
Rosemary Wilson, prin. Fax 943-4468
Our Lady of Mt. Carmel S 300/PK-8
29840 Euclid Ave 44092 440-585-0800
Rose Witmer, prin. Fax 585-9391

Willard, Huron, Pop. 6,818
Willard CSD 2,200/PK-12
PO Box 150 44890 419-935-1541
Dennis Doughty, supt. Fax 935-8491
www.willard.k12.oh.us
Central ES, 206 W Pearl St 44890 500/PK-4
Sandra Sutherland, prin. 419-935-5341
Richmond ES 100/K-6
3565 Section Line Road 30 S 44890 419-935-1311
James Sellers, prin.
Willard MS, 949 S Main St 44890 500/5-8
Mike Eicher, prin. 419-933-8312
Other Schools – See Monroeville, New Haven

Celeryville Christian S 100/K-8
4200 Broadway Rd 44890 419-935-3633
Sue Smith, prin. Fax 933-6030
St. Francis Xavier S 100/K-6
25 W Perry St 44890 419-935-4744
Donna McDowell, prin. Fax 933-6000

Williamsburg, Clermont, Pop. 2,332
Williamsburg Local SD 1,000/K-12
549 W Main St Ste A 45176 513-724-3077
Jeffery Weir, supt. Fax 724-1504
www.burgschools.org
Williamsburg ES 500/K-5
839 Spring St 45176 513-724-2241
Jane Croswell, prin. Fax 724-3902

Williamsport, Pickaway, Pop. 1,020
Westfall Local SD 1,700/K-12
19463 Pherson Pike 43164 740-986-3671
Randall Cotner, supt. Fax 986-8375
gsn.k12.oh.us/westfall/default.htm
Westfall ES 800/K-5
9391 State Route 56 43164 740-986-4008
Janice Gearhart, prin. Fax 986-4018
Westfall MS 400/6-8
19545 Pherson Pike 43164 740-986-2941
Kathy Payne, prin. Fax 986-8882

Willoughby, Lake, Pop. 22,336
Willoughby-Eastlake CSD 8,800/K-12
37047 Ridge Rd 44094 440-946-5000
Dr. Keith Miller, supt. Fax 946-4671
www.willoughby-eastlake.k12.oh.us
Edison ES 600/K-5
5288 Karen Isle Dr 44094 440-942-2099
Brian Patrick, prin. Fax 975-3837
Grant ES 500/K-5
38281 Hurricane Dr 44094 440-942-5944
Susan Kahl, prin. Fax 918-8980
McKinley ES 300/K-5
1200 Lost Nation Rd 44094 440-942-1525
Pamela Sosler, prin. Fax 975-3762
Willoughby MS 900/4-8
36901 Ridge Rd 44094 440-975-3600
Lawrence Keller, prin. Fax 975-3618
Other Schools – See Eastlake, Willowick

Andrews Osborne Academy 100/PK-12
38588 Mentor Ave 44094 440-942-3600
Charles Roman, hdmstr. Fax 942-3660
Immaculate Conception S 300/K-8
37940 Euclid Ave 44094 440-942-2121
Kathy Hrutkay, prin. Fax 942-6766
Willo-Hill Christian S 100/PK-6
4200 State Route 306 44094 440-951-5391
Carol Sperry, prin. Fax 951-5434

Willoughby Hills, Lake, Pop. 8,459

Cornerstone Christian Academy 400/K-12
2846 SOM Center Rd, 440-943-9260
Daniel Buell Ph.D., hdmstr. Fax 943-9262

Willowick, Lake, Pop. 14,004
Willoughby-Eastlake CSD
Supt. — See Willoughby
Royalview ES 900/K-5
31500 Royalview Dr 44095 440-944-3130
Tamee Tucker, prin. Fax 943-9965
Willowick MS 600/6-8
31500 Royalview Dr 44095 440-943-2950
Loretta Rodman, prin. Fax 943-9964

Willow Wood, Lawrence
Symmes Valley Local SD 900/K-12
14778 State Route 141 45696 740-643-2451
Thomas Ben, supt. Fax 643-1219
www.symmesvalley.k12.oh.us
Symmes Valley S 600/K-8
14860 State Route 141 45696 740-643-0022
Bob Harris, prin. Fax 643-0033

Wilmington, Clinton, Pop. 12,474
Wilmington CSD 3,300/K-12
341 S Nelson Ave 45177 937-382-1641
Ronald Sexton, supt. Fax 382-1645
www.wilmingtoncityschool.com
Denver Place ES 700/K-5
291 Lorish Ave 45177 937-382-2380
Natalie Harmeling, prin. Fax 383-2711
East End ES 300/K-5
769 Rombach Ave 45177 937-382-2443
Linda Mead, prin. Fax 382-2872
Holmes ES 700/K-5
1350 W Truesdell St 45177 937-382-2750
Carrie Zeigler, prin. Fax 382-2881
O'Borror MS 700/6-8
275 Thorne Ave 45177 937-382-7556
Matthew Freeman, prin. Fax 382-3295

Wilmington Christian Academy 50/K-8
PO Box 801 45177 937-383-1319
Brian Tubbs, prin. Fax 383-1319

Windham, Portage, Pop. 2,749
Windham EVD 900/PK-12
9530 Bauer Ave 44288 330-326-2711
Carol Kropinak, supt. Fax 326-2134
www.edline.net/pages/windham_evsd
Thomas ES 400/PK-5
9032 Maple Grove Rd 44288 330-326-9800
Joanne Brookover, prin. Fax 326-9810
Windham JHS 200/6-8
9530 Bauer Ave 44288 330-326-3490
Carol Kropinak, prin. Fax 326-3713

Winesburg, Holmes
East Holmes Local SD
Supt. — See Berlin
Winesburg ES, PO Box 207 44690 200/K-6
Dan McKey, prin. 330-359-5059

Wintersville, Jefferson, Pop. 3,889
Indian Creek Local SD 2,200/PK-12
587 Bantam Ridge Rd 43953 740-264-3502
Jene Watkins, supt. Fax 266-2915
www.indian-creek.k12.oh.us
Wintersville ES 200/PK-K
587 Bantam Ridge Rd 43953 740-264-1691
Toni Dondzilla, prin. Fax 264-0623
Wintersville ES 500/1-6
100 Park Dr 43953 740-264-1691
Toni Dondzilla, prin. Fax 264-1112
Other Schools – See Bloomingdale, Mingo Junction

Withamsville, Clermont, Pop. 2,834

St. Thomas More S 300/K-8
788 Ohio Pike 45245 513-753-2540
Margaret Fischer, prin. Fax 753-2554

Woodsfield, Monroe, Pop. 2,501
Switzerland of Ohio Local SD 2,600/K-12
304 Mill St 43793 740-472-5801
Larry Elliott, supt. Fax 472-5806
www.swissohio.k12.oh.us
Woodsfield S 500/K-8
118 N Paul St 43793 740-472-0953
Kathryn Anderson, prin. Fax 472-1646
Other Schools – See Beallsville, Graysville, Hannibal, Powhatan Point, Sardis

---

St. Sylvester S 100/PK-8
119 Wayne St 43793 740-472-0321
Jill Schumacher, prin. Fax 472-1994

Woodville, Sandusky, Pop. 2,003
Woodmore Local SD 1,200/K-12
115 Water St 43469 419-849-2381
Jane Garling, supt. Fax 849-2396
www.woodmore.k12.oh.us/
Woodmore ES 600/K-6
708 W Main St 43469 419-849-2382
Joe Wank, prin. Fax 849-2132

Solomon Lutheran S 100/PK-6
305 W Main St 43469 419-849-3600
Natalie Schiets, admin. Fax 849-2260

Wooster, Wayne, Pop. 25,668
Triway Local SD 2,000/K-12
3205 Shreve Rd 44691 330-264-9491
David Rice, supt. Fax 262-3955
www.tccsa.net/dp/trwy
Franklin Township ES 100/K-6
2060 E Moreland Rd 44691 330-264-2378
Claudia Stupi, prin. Fax 263-7057
Triway JHS 300/7-8
3145 Shreve Rd 44691 330-264-2114
Mitchell Caraway, prin. Fax 264-6025
Wooster Township ES 400/K-6
1071 Dover Rd 44691 330-264-6252
Jeff Wright, prin. Fax 263-7078
Other Schools – See Shreve

Wooster CSD 3,900/K-12
144 N Market St 44691 330-264-0869
Michael Tefs, supt. Fax 262-3407
www.wooster.k12.oh.us
Cornerstone ES 300/K-6
101 W Bowman St 44691 330-262-9666
Sharon Ferguson, prin. Fax 262-7611
Edgewood MS 600/7-8
2695 Graustark Path 44691 330-345-6475
Richard Leone, prin. Fax 345-8237
Kean ES 300/K-6
432 Oldman Rd 44691 330-345-6634
Peg Butler, prin. Fax 345-7845
Lincoln Way ES 300/K-6
905 Pittsburg Ave 44691 330-262-9646
Michael Mann, prin. Fax 262-4547
Melrose ES 400/K-6
1641 Sunset Ln 44691 330-345-6434
Dean Frank, prin. Fax 345-7868
Parkview ES 300/K-6
773 Parkview Dr 44691 330-262-3821
Julie Frankl, prin. Fax 262-4655
Wayne ES 300/K-6
1700 E Smthville Western Rd 44691 330-345-6474
Jim Carpenter, prin. Fax 345-7952

Montessori S of Wooster 100/PK-6
1859 Burbank Rd 44691 330-264-5222
Pamela Matsos, prin.
St. Mary S 200/PK-8
515 Beall Ave 44691 330-262-8671
Richard Carestia, prin. Fax 262-0967
Wooster Christian S 200/PK-8
4599 Burbank Rd 44691 330-345-6436
Gary Rogers, admin. Fax 345-4330

Worthington, Franklin, Pop. 13,202
Worthington CSD 9,300/K-12
200 E Wilson Bridge Rd 43085 614-883-3000
Melissa Conrath, supt. Fax 883-3010
www.worthington.k12.oh.us
Colonial Hills ES 300/K-6
5800 Greenwich St 43085 614-883-2800
Henk DeRee, prin. Fax 883-2810
Evening Street ES 500/K-6
885 Evening St 43085 614-883-2850
Mary Rykowsky, prin. Fax 883-2860
Kilbourne MS 400/7-8
50 E Dublin Granville Rd 43085 614-883-3500
Pamela VanHorn, prin. Fax 883-3510
Perry MS 400/7-8
2341 Snouffer Rd 43085 614-883-3600
Jeff Maddox, prin. Fax 883-3610
Slate Hill ES 400/K-6
7625 Alta View Blvd 43085 614-883-3200
Daniel Girard, prin. Fax 883-3210
Wilson Hill ES 500/K-6
6500 Northland Rd 43085 614-883-3300
Patricia Reeder, prin. Fax 883-3310
Worthington Estates ES 500/K-6
6760 Rieber St 43085 614-883-3350
Dan Williams, prin. Fax 883-3360
Worthingway MS 400/7-8
6625 Guyer St 43085 614-883-3650
Santha Stall, prin. Fax 883-3660
Other Schools – See Columbus, Powell, Westerville

St. Michael S 600/K-8
64 E Selby Blvd 43085 614-885-3149
Christine Armbrust, prin. Fax 885-1249
Worthington Adventist Academy 100/K-8
870 Griswold St 43085 614-885-9525
Bradley Booth, prin. Fax 885-9501

Wyoming, Hamilton, Pop. 7,719
Wyoming CSD 2,000/K-12
420 Springfield Pike 45215 513-772-2343
Dr. Gail Kist-Kline, supt. Fax 672-3355
www.wyomingcityschools.org
Elm Avenue ES 200/K-4
134 Elm Ave 45215 513-761-6767
Robert Carovillano, prin. Fax 761-0153
Hilltop ES 200/K-4
425 Oliver Rd 45215 513-761-7575
Robert Carovillano, prin. Fax 761-5922
Vermont Avenue ES 200/K-4
33 Vermont Ave 45215 513-761-5275
Robert Carovillano, prin. Fax 761-3180

Wyoming MS 600/5-8
17 Wyoming Ave 45215 513-761-7248
Mario Basora, prin. Fax 761-7319

Xenia, Greene, Pop. 23,600
Xenia Community CSD 5,000/K-12
578 E Market St 45385 937-376-2961
Jeffrey Lewis Ed.D., supt. Fax 372-4701
www.xenia.k12.oh.us
Arrowood ES 200/K-5
1694 Pawnee Dr 45385 937-372-9208
Judith Roby, prin. Fax 374-4412
Central MS 600/6-8
425 Edison Blvd 45385 937-372-7635
Mike Earley, prin. Fax 374-4410
Cox ES 400/K-5
506 Dayton Ave 45385 937-372-9201
Lisa Peterson, prin. Fax 374-4723
Kenton ES 400/K-5
1087 W 2nd St 45385 937-372-9251
Travis Yost, prin. Fax 374-4402
McKinley ES 400/K-5
819 Colorado Dr 45385 937-372-1251
Garry Hawes, prin. Fax 374-4406
Shawnee ES 300/K-5
92 E Ankeney Mill Rd 45385 937-372-5323
Karen Miller, prin. Fax 374-4404
Spring Hill ES 200/K-5
860 Ormsby Dr 45385 937-372-6461
Tracy Weissmann, prin. Fax 374-4230
Tecumseh ES 300/K-5
1058 Old Springfield Pike 45385 937-372-3321
Carla Long, prin. Fax 374-4398
Warner MS 600/6-8
600 Buckskin Trl 45385 937-376-9488
Dr. Peg McAtee, prin. Fax 374-4228

St. Brigid S 300/PK-8
312 Fairground Rd 45385 937-372-3222
Janell Klippel, prin. Fax 374-3622
Xenia Christian ES 200/K-6
1101 Wesley Ave 45385 937-352-1640
Natalie Demana, prin. Fax 352-1641
Xenia Nazarene Christian S 200/K-12
1204 W 2nd St 45385 937-372-4362
Harold Horton, prin. Fax 372-1074

Yellow Springs, Greene, Pop. 3,665
Yellow Springs EVD 700/K-12
201 S Walnut St 45387 937-767-7381
Norman Glismann, supt. Fax 767-6604
www.yellow-springs.k12.oh.us/
Mills Lawn ES 300/K-6
200 S Walnut St 45387 937-767-7217
Christine Hatton, prin. Fax 767-6602

Yorkville, Jefferson, Pop. 1,189
Buckeye Local SD
Supt. — See Dillonvale
Buckeye South ES 300/PK-5
209 Market St 43971 740-859-2800
Gus Hanson, prin. Fax 859-4004

Youngstown, Mahoning, Pop. 82,837
Austintown Local SD 3,700/K-12
700 S Raccoon Rd 44515 330-797-3900
Vincent Colauca, supt. Fax 792-8625
www.austintown.k12.oh.us
Austintown MS 600/6-8
800 S Raccoon Rd 44515 330-797-3900
Daniel Bokesch, prin. Fax 797-3965
Lloyd ES 300/K-3
5705 Norquest Blvd 44515 330-797-3900
Thomas Lenton, prin. Fax 797-3935
Lynn-Kirk ES 300/K-3
4211 Evelyn Rd 44511 330-797-3900
Anthony Russo, prin. Fax 797-3947
Ohl IS 200/4-5
255 Idaho Rd 44515 330-797-3900
Dennis Rice, prin. Fax 797-3964
Watson ES 300/K-3
215 Idaho Rd 44515 330-797-3900
James Carchedi, prin. Fax 799-0530

Woodside ES 300/K-3
4105 Elmwood Ave 44515 330-797-3900
Carole Sutton, prin. Fax 797-3950

Boardman Local SD 4,800/K-12
7410 Market St 44512 330-726-3404
Frank Lazzeri, supt. Fax 726-3432
www.boardman.k12.oh.us
Center MS 800/5-8
7410 Market St 44512 330-726-3400
Randall Ebie, prin. Fax 726-3431
Glenwood MS 700/5-8
7635 Glenwood Ave 44512 330-726-3414
Anthony Alvino, prin. Fax 758-8067
Market Street ES 400/K-4
5555 Market St 44512 330-782-3743
James Stitt, prin. Fax 782-1063
Robinwood Lane ES 400/K-4
835 Indianola Rd 44512 330-782-3164
Donald Robinson, prin. Fax 782-2405
Stadium Drive ES 400/K-4
111 Stadium Dr 44512 330-726-3428
James Goske, prin. Fax 726-0496
West Boulevard ES 500/K-4
6125 West Blvd 44512 330-726-3427
Alphonse Cervello, prin. Fax 726-0397

Liberty Local SD 1,800/K-12
4115 Shady Rd 44505 330-759-0807
Mark Lucas, supt. Fax 759-1209
www.liberty.k12.oh.us
Blott ES 600/K-4
4003 Shady Rd 44505 330-759-1053
Jason Menz, prin. Fax 759-9151
Guy MS 500/5-8
4115 Shady Rd 44505 330-759-1733
Margaret Dolwick, prin. Fax 759-4507

Youngstown CSD 6,000/K-12
PO Box 550 44501 330-744-6900
Wendy Webb Ed.D., supt. Fax 743-1557
www.youngstown.k12.oh.us/
Alpha: S of Excellence for Boys 200/7-8
2546 Hillman St 44507 330-744-7535
Jerome Harrell, prin. Fax 480-1906
Berry MS 500/5-8
940 Bryn Mawr Ave 44505 330-744-8845
Deborah DiFrancesco, prin. Fax 480-1910
Bunn ES 200/K-6
1825 Sequoya Dr 44514 330-744-8963
Maria Pappas, prin. Fax 744-8586
Harding ES 400/K-5
1903 Cordova Ave 44504 330-744-7517
Diane Guarnieri, prin. Fax 744-8589
Hayes MS 300/6-8
1616 Ford Ave 44504 330-744-7602
Dorothy Davis, prin. Fax 480-1905
King ES 300/K-4
2724 Mariner Ave 44505 330-744-7823
Catherine Dorbish, prin. Fax 480-1907
Kirkmere ES 300/K-6
2851 Kirk Rd 44511 330-744-7725
Beverly Schumann, prin. Fax 744-8593
McGuffey ES 600/K-6
310 S Schenley Ave 44509 330-744-7999
Rachael Smith, prin. Fax 744-8796
Taft ES 400/K-6
730 E Avondale Ave 44502 330-744-7973
Deborah Hagg, prin. Fax 744-8595
Volney Rogers JHS 500/7-8
134 N Hazelwood Ave 44509 330-744-7996
Marilyn Mastronardi, prin. Fax 480-1908
Williamson ES 400/K-6
58 Williamson Ave 44507 330-744-7155
Wanda Clark, prin. Fax 480-1902

St. Christine S 500/PK-8
3125 S Schenley Ave 44511 330-792-4544
Doreen DeMarco, prin. Fax 792-6888
Willow Creek Learning Center 100/PK-8
1322 W Western Reserve Rd 44514 330-758-6871
Lynn Rabosky, dir. Fax 758-6871

Youngstown Christian S 500/PK-12
4401 Southern Blvd 44512 330-788-8088
Gary Johnston, prin. Fax 788-2875
Zion Christian S 50/K-K
3300 Canfield Rd 44511 330-792-4066
Shana Prince, prin.

Zanesville, Muskingum, Pop. 25,253
East Muskingum Local SD
Supt. — See New Concord
Perry ES 100/K-2
6975 East Pike 43701 740-872-3436
David Adams, prin. Fax 872-3372

Maysville Local SD 2,100/K-12
PO Box 1818 43702 740-453-0754
Monte Bainter, supt. Fax 455-4081
maysvillelsd.schoolwires.com/
Maysville ES, 3850 Panther Dr 43701 1,000/K-5
Dustan Henderson, prin. 740-454-4490
Maysville MS 500/6-8
3725 Panther Dr 43701 740-454-7982
Joseph Daniels, prin. Fax 452-9921

West Muskingum Local SD 1,900/K-12
4880 West Pike 43701 740-455-4052
Sharon Smith, supt. Fax 455-4063
www.westm.k12.oh.us
Falls ES 500/K-5
200 Kimes Rd 43701 740-455-4058
Elizabeth Carpenter, prin. Fax 455-2592
West Muskingum MS 400/6-8
100 Kimes Rd 43701 740-455-4055
Jim Spisak, prin. Fax 455-9717
Other Schools – See Hopewell

Zanesville CSD 3,700/PK-12
160 N 4th St 43701 740-454-9751
Terry Martin, supt. Fax 455-4325
www.zanesville.k12.oh.us
Cleveland MS 400/6-8
968 Pine St 43701 740-453-0636
Ronald Denton, prin. Fax 450-1335
McIntire/Munson ES 300/K-5
1275 Roosevelt Ave 43701 740-453-2851
Jeffrey Moore, prin. Fax 452-1292
National Road ES 400/K-5
3505 East Pike 43701 740-450-1538
Paul Thompson, prin. Fax 450-1544
Putnam Preschool 100/PK-K
920 Moxahala Ave 43701 740-452-8441
Vicky French, dir. Fax 455-4343
Roosevelt MS 500/6-8
1429 Blue Ave 43701 740-452-0711
James Lear, prin. Fax 450-1408
Westview ES 400/K-5
2256 Dresden Rd 43701 740-453-7558
Steven Foreman, prin. Fax 453-7027
Wilson ES 400/K-5
1063 Superior St 43701 740-453-0575
Michelle Jordan, prin. Fax 455-4333

Bishop Fenwick ES 200/1-5
139 N 5th St 43701 740-454-9731
Mary Walsh, prin. Fax 454-8775
Bishop Fenwick S 200/PK-K, 6-8
1030 E Main St 43701 740-453-2637
Mary Walsh, prin. Fax 454-0653
Muskingum Christian Academy 100/K-12
PO Box 1445 43702 740-454-7116
Craig Naugle, prin. Fax 454-7174
Zanesville SDA S, 824 Taylor St 43701 50/K-8
Clare Hoover, prin. 740-453-6050

Zoarville, Tuscarawas
Tuscarawas Valley Local SD 1,400/PK-12
2637 Tusky Valley Rd NE 44656 330-859-2213
Mark Murphy, supt. Fax 859-2706
www.tuskyvalley.k12.oh.us
Tuscarawas Valley MS 500/5-8
2633 Tusky Valley Rd NE 44656 330-859-2427
Timothy McCrate, prin. Fax 859-8845
Other Schools – See Bolivar, Mineral City

OKLAHOMA

OKLAHOMA DEPARTMENT OF EDUCATION
2500 N Lincoln Blvd Rm 112, Oklahoma City 73105-4503
Telephone 405-521-3301
Fax 405-521-6205
Website http://www.sde.state.ok.us

Superintendent of Public Instruction Sandy Garrett

OKLAHOMA BOARD OF EDUCATION
2500 N Lincoln Blvd Rm 112, Oklahoma City 73105-4596

Chairperson Sandy Garrett

INTERLOCAL COOPERATIVES (IC)

Atoka-Coal Counties IC
Kris Hall, dir. 580-889-2664
PO Box 1231, Atoka 74525 Fax 889-6302
Cherokee County IC
Sheryl Lynn Rountree, dir. 918-456-1064
15481 N Jarvis Rd Fax 456-1041
Tahlequah 74464
Choctaw Nation IC
Shari Williams, dir. 580-931-0691
PO Box 602, Durant 74702 Fax 931-0683

Five Star IC
Nancy Anderson, dir. 918-225-5600
1405 E Moses St, Cushing 74023 Fax 225-3026
www.fsilc.k12.ok.us
Garfield County IC
Joel Quinn, dir. 580-233-3071
PO Box 56, Pond Creek 73766 Fax 233-3072
Osage County IC
Jacque Canady, dir. 918-885-2667
207 E Main St, Hominy 74035 Fax 885-6742
www.ocic.k12.ok.us/

Pooled Investment IC
Keith Ballard, pres. 405-528-3571
2801 N Lincoln Blvd Fax 528-5695
Oklahoma City 73105
Seminole County IC
Dr. Audie Woodard, dir. 405-382-6121
630 Golf Rd, Seminole 74868 Fax 382-5254
Southeastern Oklahoma IC
Rita Shaw Burke, dir. 580-286-3344
103 NE AVE A, Idabel 74745 Fax 286-5598
Tri-County IC
Ty Harman, dir. 580-673-2310
PO Box 217, Fox 73435 Fax 673-2309

PUBLIC, PRIVATE AND CATHOLIC ELEMENTARY SCHOOLS

Achille, Bryan, Pop. 520
Achille ISD 400/PK-12
PO Box 280 74720 580-283-3775
Dr. Charles Caughern, supt. Fax 283-3787
www.achilleisd.org
Achille S, PO Box 280 74720 200/PK-8
Pamela Reynolds, prin. 580-283-3002
Other Schools – See Hendrix

Ada, Pontotoc, Pop. 15,999
Ada ISD 2,700/PK-12
PO Box 1359 74821 580-310-7200
Pat Harrison, supt. Fax 310-7206
www.adapss.com/
Glenwood K 400/PK-K
825 W 10th St 74820 580-310-7283
Rita Cloar, prin. Fax 310-7284
Hayes ES 400/1-2
500 S Mississippi Ave 74820 580-310-7294
Patricia Stewart, prin. Fax 310-7295
Washington ES 300/3-4
600 S Oak Ave 74820 580-310-7303
Lisa Fulton, prin. Fax 310-7304
Willard IS 400/5-6
817 E 9th St 74820 580-310-7250
Kevin Mann, prin. Fax 310-7252

Byng ISD 1,700/PK-12
500 S New Bethel Blvd 74820 580-436-3020
Todd Crabtree, supt. Fax 436-3052
www.byngschools.com
Byng ES 200/4-6
500 S New Bethel Blvd 74820 580-310-6720
Dennis Kymes, prin. Fax 310-6721
Francis ES 200/PK-3
18461 County Road 1480 74820 580-332-4114
Robert Gregory, prin. Fax 436-6021
Homer ES 600/PK-5
1400 N Monte Vista St 74820 580-332-4303
Jana Davis, prin. Fax 436-3566

Latta ISD 700/PK-12
13925 County Road 1560 74820 580-332-2092
Cliff Johnson, supt. Fax 332-3116
www.latta.k12.ok.us/
Latta ES 400/PK-6
13925 County Road 1560 74820 580-332-7669
Phillip Shivers, prin.

Pickett-Center SD 100/PK-8
9660 State Highway 19 74820 580-332-7800
Daniel Pittman, supt. Fax 332-9460
Pickett-Center S 100/PK-8
9660 State Highway 19 74820 580-332-7800
Daniel Pittman, prin. Fax 332-9460

Vanoss ISD 500/PK-12
4665 County Road 1555 74820 580-759-2251
Janet Blocker, supt. Fax 759-3080
www.vanoss.k12.ok.us
Vanoss S 300/PK-8
4665 County Road 1555 74820 580-759-2623
Kathy Wellington, prin. Fax 759-3080

Adair, Mayes, Pop. 708
Adair ISD 900/PK-12
PO Box 197 74330 918-785-2424
Tom Linihan, supt. Fax 785-2491
adairschools.org
Adair MS 200/6-8
PO Box 197 74330 918-785-2425
Brad Rogers, prin. Fax 785-2491

Hughes ES 500/PK-5
PO Box 197 74330 918-785-2438
Cynthia Briggs, prin. Fax 785-2491

Afton, Ottawa, Pop. 1,106
Afton ISD 500/PK-12
PO Box 100 74331 918-257-8303
Randy Gardner, supt. Fax 257-4846
www.aftonschools.net/
Afton S 300/PK-8
PO Box 100 74331 918-257-8304
Lyle Crane, prin. Fax 257-4846

Cleora SD 100/K-8
451358 E 295 Rd 74331 918-256-6401
Tim Carson, supt. Fax 256-2128
cleora.net
Cleora S 100/K-8
451358 E 295 Rd 74331 918-256-6401
Tim Carson, prin. Fax 256-2128

Agra, Lincoln, Pop. 358
Agra ISD 400/PK-12
PO Box 279 74824 918-375-2262
Wesley McFarland, supt. Fax 375-2263
www.agra.k12.ok.us/
Agra S 300/PK-8
PO Box 279 74824 918-375-2261
Candace Stine, prin. Fax 375-2263

Albion, Pushmataha, Pop. 143
Albion SD 100/K-8
PO Box 100 74521 918-563-4331
Jim Hibdon, supt. Fax 563-4330
Albion S 100/K-8
PO Box 100 74521 918-563-4331
Jim Hibdon, prin. Fax 563-4330

Alex, Grady, Pop. 657
Alex ISD 300/K-12
PO Box 188 73002 405-785-2605
Norvel Heston, supt. Fax 785-2914
www.alex.k12.ok.us/
Alex ES 200/K-6
PO Box 188 73002 405-785-2217
Chris Sparks, prin. Fax 785-2302

Aline, Alfalfa, Pop. 197
Aline-Cleo ISD 200/PK-12
PO Box 49 73716 580-463-2255
Dwayne Noble, supt. Fax 463-2256
www.alinecleo.k12.ok.us
Other Schools – See Cleo Springs

Allen, Pontotoc, Pop. 957
Allen ISD 400/PK-12
PO Box 430 74825 580-857-2417
David Lassiter, supt. Fax 857-2636
www.allen.k12.ok.us/
Allen S 300/PK-8
PO Box 430 74825 580-857-2419
Mary Sappenfield, prin. Fax 857-2636

Altus, Jackson, Pop. 19,899
Altus ISD 4,000/PK-12
PO Box 558 73522 580-481-2100
Bob Drury, supt. Fax 481-2129
www.altusschools.k12.ok.us
Altus IS 600/5-6
PO Box 558 73522 580-481-2155
Robert Bowers, prin. Fax 481-2596
Altus JHS 600/7-8
PO Box 558 73522 580-481-2173
Roe Worbes, prin. Fax 481-2547

Rivers ES 400/PK-4
PO Box 558 73522 580-481-2183
Robbie Holder, prin. Fax 481-2124
Rogers ES 300/PK-4
PO Box 558 73522 580-481-2151
Jay Richeson, prin. Fax 481-2539
Roosevelt ES 300/PK-4
PO Box 558 73522 580-481-2185
Randy Ford, prin. Fax 477-7617
Sunset ES 400/PK-4
PO Box 558 73522 580-481-2180
Mark Whitlock, prin. Fax 481-2534
Washington ES 400/PK-4
PO Box 558 73522 580-481-2133
Renee Long, prin. Fax 481-2542

Navajo ISD 300/K-12
15695 S County Road 210 73521 580-482-7742
Gary Montgomery, supt. Fax 482-7749
www.navajo.k12.ok.us
Navajo ES 200/K-6
15695 S County Road 210 73521 580-482-7742
Glenn Hasty, prin. Fax 482-7749

Altus Christian Academy 100/PK-5
PO Box 393 73522 580-477-2511
Dr. Dana Darby, prin. Fax 477-2511

Alva, Woods, Pop. 4,900
Alva ISD 900/PK-12
418 Flynn St 73717 580-327-4823
Don Rader, supt. Fax 327-2965
www.alvaschools.com
Alva MS 200/6-8
800 Flynn St 73717 580-327-0608
Terry Conder, prin. Fax 327-4255
Lincoln ES 100/4-5
1540 Davis St 73717 580-327-3008
Greg Lyon, prin. Fax 327-3008
Longfellow ES 100/2-3
19 Barnes Ave 73717 580-327-3327
Steve Shiever, prin. Fax 327-4527
Washington ES 200/PK-1
701 Barnes Ave 73717 580-327-3518
Tracie Leeper, prin. Fax 327-6040

Amber, Grady, Pop. 522
Amber-Pocasset ISD 500/PK-12
PO Box 38 73004 405-224-5768
Jack Jerman, supt. Fax 224-5115
Amber-Pocasset ES 200/PK-6
PO Box 38 73004 405-459-6544
Hope Deaton, prin. Fax 459-9164

Anadarko, Caddo, Pop. 6,584
Anadarko ISD 1,900/PK-12
1400 S Mission St 73005 405-247-6605
Tom Cantrell, supt. Fax 247-6819
Anadarko MS 500/6-8
900 W College St 73005 405-247-6671
Doug Hall, prin. Fax 247-3666
East ES 300/2-3
107 SE 5th St 73005 405-247-2496
Roger Harris, prin. Fax 247-4133
Mission ES 400/PK-5
1200 S Mission St 73005 405-247-6607
Beverly Kenedy, prin. Fax 247-4142
Sunset ES 300/K-1
408 SW 7th St 73005 405-247-2503
Mary Jane Walzer, prin. Fax 247-2504

Antlers, Pushmataha, Pop. 2,508
Antlers ISD 1,000/K-12
PO Box 627 74523 580-298-5504
Mark Virden, supt. Fax 298-4006
www.antlers.k12.ok.us
Brantley ES 300/K-2
PO Box 627 74523 580-298-3108
Aletha Burrage, prin. Fax 298-4002
Obuch MS 200/6-8
PO Box 627 74523 580-298-3308
Pam Matthews, prin. Fax 298-4012
Vegher IS 200/3-5
PO Box 627 74523 580-298-3540
Aletha Burrage, prin. Fax 298-4004

Apache, Caddo, Pop. 1,597
Boone-Apache ISD 600/PK-12
PO Box 354 73006 580-588-3369
Joe Hulsey, supt. Fax 588-3400
www.apache.k12.ok.us/
Apache ES 300/PK-6
PO Box 354 73006 580-588-3577
Sheryl Rexach, prin. Fax 588-2030
Apache MS, PO Box 354 73006 100/7-8
Jayne Ivy, prin. 580-588-2122

Arapaho, Custer, Pop. 709
Arapaho ISD 300/PK-12
PO Box 160 73620 580-323-3261
Bob Haggard, supt. Fax 323-5886
www.arapaho.k12.ok.us/
Arapaho S 200/PK-8
PO Box 160 73620 580-323-7264
Brad Southell, prin. Fax 323-3469

Ardmore, Carter, Pop. 24,280
Ardmore ISD 3,100/PK-12
PO Box 1709 73402 580-223-2483
Dr. Ruth Ann Carr, supt. Fax 226-2472
www.ardmoreschools.org
Ardmore MS 600/6-8
PO Box 1709 73402 580-223-2475
Ron Beach, prin. Fax 221-3060
Evans ES 400/1-5
PO Box 1709 73402 580-223-2472
Kristie Jessop, prin. Fax 221-3020
Franklin ES 200/1-5
PO Box 1709 73402 580-223-2473
Chris McMurry, prin. Fax 221-3021
Jefferson ES 200/1-5
PO Box 1709 73402 580-223-2474
Carolyn McElroy, prin. Fax 221-3022
Lincoln ES 300/1-5
PO Box 1709 73402 580-223-2477
Jill Day, prin. Fax 221-3023
Rogers ES 500/PK-K
PO Box 1709 73402 580-223-2482
Cynthia Hunter, prin. Fax 224-9864

Dickson ISD 1,000/PK-12
4762 State Highway 199 73401 580-223-9557
Sherry Howe, supt. Fax 223-3624
www.dickson.k12.ok.us
Dickson JHS 200/6-8
4762 State Highway 199 73401 580-223-2700
Brad Jones, prin. Fax 223-3972
Dickson Lower ES 300/PK-2
4762 State Highway 199 73401 580-223-9509
Shannon Muck, prin. Fax 223-3543
Dickson Upper ES 200/3-5
4762 State Highway 199 73401 580-223-1443
Dama McKennell, prin. Fax 223-6347

Lone Grove ISD
Supt. — See Lone Grove
Lone Grove MS 300/6-8
6362 Meridian Rd 73401 580-657-3132
Ted Clardy, prin. Fax 657-2691

Plainview ISD 1,400/PK-12
1140 S Plainview Rd 73401 580-223-6319
Steve Merlyn, supt. Fax 490-3190
www.plainview.k12.ok.us/
Plainview IS 300/3-5
1140 S Plainview Rd 73401 580-223-6437
Lisa Hartman, prin. Fax 490-3193
Plainview MS 300/6-8
1140 S Plainview Rd 73401 580-223-6502
Julie Altom, prin. Fax 490-3192
Plainview PS 400/PK-2
1140 S Plainview Rd 73401 580-223-5757
Lisa Moore, prin. Fax 490-3194

Ardmore Adventist Academy 50/1-12
154 Beaver Academy Rd 73401 580-223-4948
Stephen Dennis, admin.
Oak Hall Episcopal S 100/PK-8
PO Box 1807 73402 580-226-2341
Laura Gallagher, hdmstr. Fax 226-8141

Arkoma, LeFlore, Pop. 2,191
Arkoma ISD 400/PK-12
PO Box 349 74901 918-875-3351
Katie Blagg, supt. Fax 875-3780
www.arkoma.k12.ok.us/
Singleton S 300/PK-8
PO Box 349 74901 918-875-3835
Shelly Harmon, prin. Fax 875-3780

Arnett, Ellis, Pop. 497
Arnett ISD 200/PK-12
PO Box 317 73832 580-885-7811
Tim Puett, supt. Fax 885-7922
www.arnett.k12.ok.us/
Arnett S 100/PK-8
PO Box 317 73832 580-885-7285
Scot Friesen, prin. Fax 885-7922

Asher, Pottawatomie, Pop. 434
Asher ISD, PO Box 168 74826 200/PK-12
Terry Grissom, supt. 405-784-2332
www.asher.k12.ok.us
Asher S, PO Box 168 74826 200/PK-8
Jamie Chambers, prin. 405-784-2331

Atoka, Atoka, Pop. 3,044
Atoka ISD 900/PK-12
PO Box 720 74525 580-889-6611
Mark McPherson, supt. Fax 889-2513
atoka.org
Atoka ES 400/PK-5
PO Box 720 74525 580-889-3553
Mary Rains, prin. Fax 889-4050
McCall MS 100/6-8
PO Box 720 74525 580-889-5640
Lane Jackson, prin. Fax 889-4064

Farris SD 100/PK-8
900 S Old Farris Rd 74525 580-889-5542
Wes Watson, supt. Fax 889-7742
www.farris.k12.ok.us/
Farris S 100/PK-8
900 S Old Farris Rd 74525 580-889-5542
Wes Watson, prin. Fax 889-7742

Harmony SD 200/PK-8
490 S Bentley Rd 74525 580-889-3687
Mark Thomas, supt. Fax 889-4631
Harmony S 200/PK-8
490 S Bentley Rd 74525 580-889-3687
Mark Thomas, prin. Fax 889-4631

Tushka ISD 400/PK-12
204 S Pecan St 74525 580-889-7355
Bill Pingleton, supt. Fax 889-6144
Tushka S 300/PK-8
204 S Pecan St 74525 580-889-7355
Thomas Walker, prin. Fax 889-6144

Avant, Osage, Pop. 361
Avant SD 100/K-8
PO Box 9 74001 918-263-2135
Richard Harris, supt. Fax 263-2143
www.avant.k12.ok.us/
Avant S 100/K-8
PO Box 9 74001 918-263-2135
Richard Harris, prin. Fax 263-2143

Balko, Beaver
Balko ISD, RR 1 Box 37 73931 100/PK-12
Larry Mills, supt. 580-646-3385
Balko S, RR 1 Box 37 73931 100/PK-8
Braden Naylor, prin. 580-646-3385

Barnsdall, Osage, Pop. 1,280
Barnsdall ISD 500/PK-12
PO Box 629 74002 918-847-2271
Rick Loggins, supt. Fax 847-3029
www.barnsdall.k12.ok.us/
Barnsdall ES, PO Box 629 74002 200/PK-6
Regiena Henderson, prin. 918-847-2731

Bartlesville, Washington, Pop. 34,734
Bartlesville ISD 5,600/PK-12
PO Box 1357 74005 918-336-8600
Dr. Gary Quinn, supt. Fax 337-3643
www.bps-ok.org
Central MS 700/6-8
408 E 9th St 74003 918-336-9302
LaDonna Chancellor, prin. Fax 337-6270
Hoover ES 400/PK-5
512 SE Madison Blvd 74006 918-333-9337
Rene Beisley, prin. Fax 335-6337
Kane ES 400/PK-5
801 E 13th St 74003 918-337-3711
Beth Cook, prin. Fax 337-6221
Madison MS 600/6-8
500 S Madison Blvd 74006 918-333-3176
Lexie Radebaugh, prin. Fax 335-6377
Oak Park ES 200/PK-5
200 Forrest Park Rd 74003 918-336-4655
Dr. Bobbi Sexson, prin. Fax 337-6216
Phillips ES 300/PK-5
1500 S Rogers Ave 74003 918-336-9479
Ken Copeland, prin. Fax 337-6251
Ranch Heights ES 300/PK-5
5100 David Dr 74006 918-333-3810
David Mueller, prin. Fax 335-6318
Rogers ECC PK-K
4620 E Frank Phillips Blvd 74006 918-336-4544
Tammie Krause, prin. Fax 335-1392
Wayside ES 400/K-5
3000 Wayside Dr 74006 918-333-8000
Richard Dennis, prin. Fax 335-6315
Wilson ES 300/PK-5
245 N Spruce Ave 74006 918-335-1177
Sandra Kent, prin. Fax 335-6313

Osage Hills SD 200/PK-8
225 County Road 2706 74003 918-336-6804
Jeannie O'Daniel, supt. Fax 336-4238
www.osagehills.k12.ok.us
Osage Hills S 200/PK-8
225 County Road 2706 74003 918-336-6804
Lance Miller, prin. Fax 336-4238

American Christian S of Bartlesville 100/PK-12
396980 W 2400 Rd 74006 918-331-0500
Danny Reich, hdmstr. Fax 331-0501
St. John Catholic S 100/PK-8
121 W 8th St 74003 918-336-0603
Jane Sears, prin. Fax 336-0624
Wesleyan Christian S 200/PK-12
1780 Silver Lake Rd 74006 918-333-8631
Mark Listen, admin. Fax 333-8632

Battiest, McCurtain
Battiest ISD 200/PK-12
PO Box 199 74722 580-241-7810
Lendall Martin, supt. Fax 241-7847
www.battiest.k12.ok.us/
Battiest S 200/PK-8
PO Box 199 74722 580-241-5499
Dixie Harder, prin. Fax 241-5499

Beaver, Beaver, Pop. 1,414
Beaver ISD 400/PK-12
PO Box 580 73932 580-625-3444
Scott Kinsey, supt. Fax 625-3690
Beaver S 300/PK-8
PO Box 580 73932 580-625-3444
Read Cates, prin. Fax 625-3690

Beggs, Okmulgee, Pop. 1,375
Beggs ISD 1,100/PK-12
1201 W 9th St 74421 918-267-3628
Marsha Norman, supt. Fax 267-3635
www.beggs.k12.ok.us
Beggs ES 500/PK-4
1201 W 9th St 74421 918-267-3620
Sue Spahn, prin. Fax 267-3629
Beggs MS 300/5-8
1201 W 9th St 74421 918-267-4916
Cindy Swearingen, prin. Fax 267-4779

Bennington, Bryan, Pop. 296
Bennington ISD 200/K-12
729 N Perry St 74723 580-847-2737
James Parrish, supt. Fax 847-2787
www.benningtonisd.org/
Bennington S 200/K-8
729 N Perry St 74723 580-847-2310
Mary Knight, prin. Fax 847-2787

Bethany, Oklahoma, Pop. 19,786
Bethany ISD 1,500/PK-12
6721 NW 42nd St 73008 405-789-3801
Dr. Kent Shellenberger, supt. Fax 499-4606
www.bethanyschools.com/
Bethany MS 400/6-8
6721 NW 42nd St 73008 405-787-3240
Chad Broughton, prin. Fax 499-4606
Harris ES 700/PK-5
6721 NW 42nd St 73008 405-789-6673
Tim Haws, prin. Fax 499-4625

Putnam City ISD
Supt. — See Oklahoma City
Apollo ES 400/PK-5
1901 N Peniel Ave 73008 405-787-6636
Barbara Crump, prin. Fax 491-7528
Lake Park ES 300/K-5
8221 NW 30th St 73008 405-789-7068
John Lunn, prin. Fax 491-7590
Overholser ES 400/PK-5
7900 NW 36th St 73008 405-789-7913
Lee Ann Teasley, prin. Fax 491-7586
Western Oaks ES 600/PK-5
7210 NW 23rd St 73008 405-789-1711
Drew Eichelberger, prin. Fax 491-7578
Western Oaks MS 600/6-8
7210 NW 23rd St 73008 405-789-4434
Patricia Balenseifen, prin. Fax 491-7616

Billings, Noble, Pop. 562
Billings ISD 100/PK-12
PO Box 39 74630 580-725-3271
Susan Ellis, supt. Fax 725-3278
www.billings.k12.ok.us
Billings S, PO Box 39 74630 100/PK-8
Susan Ellis, prin. 580-725-3213

Binger, Caddo, Pop. 708
Binger-Oney ISD 300/K-12
PO Box 280 73009 405-656-2304
Kevin Sims, supt. Fax 656-2267
www.binger-oney.k12.ok.us/
Binger-Oney S 200/K-8
PO Box 280 73009 405-656-2304
Lisa King, prin. Fax 656-2267

Bixby, Tulsa, Pop. 18,600
Bixby ISD 4,300/PK-12
109 N Armstrong St 74008 918-366-2200
Dr. Kyle Wood, supt. Fax 366-4241
www.bixbyps.org
Bixby MS 700/7-8
109 N Armstrong St 74008 918-366-2201
Sean Spellecy, prin. Fax 366-2337
Bixby North ES 1,000/PK-4
109 N Armstrong St 74008 918-366-2690
Phil Streets, prin. Fax 366-2684
Brassfield 5th - 6th Center 600/5-6
109 N Armstrong St 74008 918-366-2248
Erin Jones, prin. Fax 366-2263
Central ES 800/PK-4
109 N Armstrong St 74008 918-366-2282
Lydia Wilson, prin. Fax 366-2332
North 5th - 6th Center 5-6
109 N Armstrong St 74008 918-366-2669
Kelly Taliaferro, prin. Fax 366-1899

Blackwell, Kay, Pop. 7,297
Blackwell ISD 1,500/PK-12
201 E Blackwell Ave 74631 580-363-2570
Lesa Ward, supt. Fax 363-5513
www.blackwell.k12.ok.us/
Blackwell MS 300/6-8
1041 S 1st St 74631 580-363-2100
Jaylene Soulek, prin. Fax 363-7010
Huston Center ES 200/4-5
304 Vinnedge Ave 74631 580-363-0118
Janet Langdon, prin. Fax 363-7014
Northside ES PK-PK
720 W Doolin Ave 74631 580-363-2713
Krista Perkins, prin. Fax 363-1082
Parkside Center ES 300/K-1
502 E College Ave 74631 580-363-4175
Krista Perkins, prin. Fax 363-2162
Washington ES 200/2-3
723 W College Ave 74631 580-363-3197
Billie DeBoard, prin. Fax 363-7013

Blair, Jackson, Pop. 823
Blair ISD 300/PK-12
PO Box 428 73526 580-563-2632
Jimmy Smith, supt. Fax 563-9166
www.blairschool.org
Blair S 200/PK-8
PO Box 428 73526 580-563-2235
Sue Von Tungeln, prin. Fax 563-9166

Blanchard, McClain, Pop. 3,678
Blanchard ISD 1,500/PK-12
400 N Harrison Ave 73010 405-485-3391
Dr. Jim Beckham, supt. Fax 485-2985
www.blanchard.k12.ok.us/
Blanchard ES 500/PK-3
400 N Harrison Ave 73010 405-485-3394
Donna Edge, prin. Fax 485-9116
Blanchard IS 200/4-5
400 N Harrison Ave 73010 405-485-3391
Alan Schinnerer, prin.

Blanchard MS — 300/6-8
400 N Harrison Ave 73010 — 405-485-3393
Larry McVay, prin. — Fax 485-9103

Bridge Creek ISD — 1,200/PK-12
2209 E Sooner Rd 73010 — 405-387-4880
Randy Davenport, supt. — Fax 387-4882
www.bridgecreek.k12.ok.us/
Bridge Creek ES — 600/PK-5
2209 E Sooner Rd 73010 — 405-387-3681
Kay Norman, prin.
Bridge Creek MS — 300/6-8
2209 E Sooner Rd 73010 — 405-387-9681
David Morrow, prin.

Middleberg SD — 200/PK-8
2130 County Road 1317 73010 — 405-485-3612
Dena Stewart, supt. — Fax 485-3204
www.middleberg.k12.ok.us
Middleberg S — 200/PK-8
2130 County Road 1317 73010 — 405-485-3612
Dena Stewart, prin. — Fax 485-3204

Bluejacket, Craig, Pop. 285
Bluejacket ISD — 200/PK-12
PO Box 29 74333 — 918-784-2365
Almeda Carroll, supt. — Fax 784-2130
www.bluejacket.k12.ok.us
Bluejacket ES — 100/PK-5
PO Box 29 74333 — 918-784-2266
Amy Rogers, prin. — Fax 784-2130
Bluejacket MS, PO Box 29 74333 — 50/6-8
Shellie Baker, prin. — 918-784-2133

Boise City, Cimarron, Pop. 1,322
Boise City ISD — 300/PK-12
PO Box 1116 73933 — 580-544-3110
Dan Faulkner, supt. — Fax 544-2972
www.boisecity.k12.ok.us/
Boise City S — 200/PK-8
PO Box 1117 73933 — 580-544-3161
Brad Hurley, prin. — Fax 544-2146

Bokchito, Bryan, Pop. 570
Rock Creek ISD — 500/PK-12
200 E Steakley St 74726 — 580-295-3137
Preston Burns, supt. — Fax 295-3762
www.rockcreekisd.net
Other Schools – See Durant

Bokoshe, LeFlore, Pop. 462
Bokoshe ISD — 300/PK-12
PO Box 158 74930 — 918-969-2491
Dennis Shoup, supt. — Fax 969-2493
www.bokoshe.k12.ok.us
Bokoshe ES, PO Box 158 74930 — 100/PK-6
Jeremy Dyer, prin. — 918-969-2636

Boley, Okfuskee, Pop. 1,102
Boley SD — 50/PK-8
PO Box 248 74829 — 918-667-3324
Gretana Gonzales, supt. — Fax 667-3476
Boley S — 50/PK-8
PO Box 248 74829 — 918-667-3324
Gretana Gonzales, prin. — Fax 667-3476

Boswell, Choctaw, Pop. 701
Boswell ISD — 400/PK-12
PO Box 839 74727 — 580-566-2558
Gerald Stegall, supt. — Fax 566-2265
www.boswellschools.org/
Boswell ES — 200/PK-6
PO Box 839 74727 — 580-566-2655
Keith Edge, prin. — Fax 566-2265
Boswell MS — 50/7-8
PO Box 839 74727 — 580-566-2785
Keith Edge, prin. — Fax 566-2265

Bowlegs, Seminole, Pop. 371
Bowlegs ISD — 300/PK-12
PO Box 88 74830 — 405-398-4172
Bobbette Hamilton, supt. — Fax 398-4175
www.bowlegs.k12.ok.us
Bowlegs S — 200/PK-8
PO Box 88 74830 — 405-398-4322
Tommy Eaton, prin. — Fax 398-4327

Bowring, Osage
Bowring SD — 100/PK-8
PO Box 570, — 918-336-6892
Nicole Hinkle, supt. — Fax 336-1348
www.bowringps.k12.ok.us/
Bowring S — 100/PK-8
PO Box 668, — 918-336-6892
Nicole Hinkle, prin. — Fax 336-1348

Boynton, Muskogee, Pop. 278
Boynton-Moton ISD — 100/PK-12
115 S Cardinal Ave 74422 — 918-472-7330
James Christian, supt. — Fax 472-7410
www.bmps.k12.ok.us
Boynton-Moton S — 100/PK-8
115 S Cardinal Ave 74422 — 918-472-7330
DeShawn McCrary, prin. — Fax 472-7410

Braggs, Muskogee, Pop. 307
Braggs ISD — 200/PK-12
PO Box 59 74423 — 918-487-5265
Lucky McCrary, supt. — Fax 487-7171
www.braggs.k12.ok.us
Braggs S — 200/PK-8
PO Box 59 74423 — 918-487-5265
Rick Grimes, prin. — Fax 487-7171

Braman, Kay, Pop. 239
Braman ISD — 100/K-12
PO Box 130 74632 — 580-385-2191
Dr. John Sheridan, supt. — Fax 385-2193
Braman S — 100/K-8
PO Box 130 74632 — 580-385-2191
Dr. John Sheridan, prin. — Fax 385-2193

Bristow, Creek, Pop. 4,397
Bristow ISD — 1,700/PK-12
420 N Main St 74010 — 918-367-5555
Dr. Jeanene Barnett, supt. — Fax 367-5848
www.bristow.k12.ok.us
Bristow MS — 400/6-8
420 N Main St 74010 — 918-367-3551
Brian Lomenick, prin. — Fax 367-1362

Collins ES — 300/3-5
420 N Main St 74010 — 918-367-5551
Vicki Groom, prin. — Fax 367-9177
Edison ES — 500/PK-2
420 N Main St 74010 — 918-367-5521
Kim Stewart, prin. — Fax 367-5081

Bristow Adventist Academy — 50/1-8
PO Box 1074 74010 — 918-367-6782
Annette Park, lead tchr. — Fax 367-6992

Broken Arrow, Tulsa, Pop. 86,228
Broken Arrow ISD — 14,700/PK-12
601 S Main St 74012 — 918-259-4300
Dr. Gary Gerber, supt. — Fax 258-0399
www.baschools.org/
Arrowhead ES — 500/PK-5
915 W Norman St 74012 — 918-259-4390
Janice Blankenship, prin. — Fax 251-8183
Arrow Springs ES — 400/K-5
101 W Twin Oaks St 74011 — 918-259-4380
Karla Dyess, prin. — Fax 451-1640
Centennial MS — 800/6-8
225 E Omaha St 74012 — 918-259-4340
Amy Fichtner, prin. — Fax 251-8347
Childers MS — 600/6-8
301 E Tucson St 74011 — 918-259-4350
Elizabeth Burns, prin. — Fax 451-5465
Country Lane ES — 400/PK-3
301 E Omaha St 74012 — 918-259-4400
Jamie Milligan, prin. — Fax 259-4403
4th & 5th Grade Center — 4-5
251 E Omaha St 74012 — 918-449-5600
Sue Katterhenry, prin.
Haskell MS — 900/6-8
412 S 9th St 74012 — 918-259-4360
Phil Tucker, prin. — Fax 251-8685
Indian Springs ES — 500/PK-5
8800 S Fawnwood Ct 74011 — 918-259-4410
Larry Smith, prin. — Fax 455-1731
Leisure Park ES — 500/K-5
4300 S Juniper Pl 74011 — 918-259-4420
Ron Rieff, prin. — Fax 451-3386
Liberty ES — 600/PK-3
4300 S 209th East Ave 74014 — 918-259-4470
Karyne Gates, prin. — Fax 355-0095
Oak Crest ES — 500/PK-5
405 E Richmond St 74012 — 918-259-4450
Heather Adams, prin. — Fax 251-8553
Oliver MS — 800/6-8
3100 W New Orleans St 74011 — 918-259-4590
Tom Sorrells, prin. — Fax 250-8185
Park Lane ES — 600/K-5
7700 S Shelby Ln 74014 — 918-259-4460
Jean Brassfield, prin. — Fax 357-2378
Rhoades ES — 500/K-5
320 E Midway St 74012 — 918-259-4440
Sherri Kindley, prin. — Fax 258-4265
Sequoyah MS — 500/6-8
2701 S Elm Pl 74012 — 918-259-4370
Heidi McAnulty, prin. — Fax 451-2167
Spring Creek ES — 500/PK-5
6801 S 3rd St 74011 — 918-259-4480
Dorothy Pickney, prin. — Fax 455-9160
Vandever ES — 400/K-5
2200 S Lions Ave 74012 — 918-259-4490
Vicki Beckwith, prin. — Fax 455-0980
Westwood ES — 400/K-5
1712 N 18th St 74012 — 918-259-4500
Terry Carner, prin. — Fax 355-1174
Wolf Creek ES — 600/K-5
3000 W New Orleans St 74011 — 918-259-4510
Ron Beckwith, prin. — Fax 250-6769
Wood ES — 500/PK-5
1600 W Quincy St 74012 — 918-259-4430
Barbara Jones, prin. — Fax 258-0596

Union ISD
Supt. — See Tulsa
Andersen ES — 500/PK-5
1200 S Willow Ave 74012 — 918-357-4328
Larry Williams, prin. — Fax 357-8299
McAuliffe ES — 600/PK-5
6515 S Garnett Rd 74012 — 918-357-4336
Rita Martin, prin. — Fax 357-6599
Moore ES — 600/PK-5
800 N Butternut Pl 74012 — 918-357-4337
Sandi Calvin, prin. — Fax 357-6996
Peters ES — 600/PK-5
2900 W College St 74012 — 918-357-4338
Jennifer Randall, prin. — Fax 357-6799
Union Eighth Grade Center — 1,100/8-8
6501 S Garnett Rd 74012 — 918-357-4325
Marla Robinson, prin. — Fax 357-7899

All Saints Catholic S — 300/PK-8
299 S 9th St 74012 — 918-251-3000
Anne Scalet, prin. — Fax 258-9879
Grace Christian S — 300/PK-12
9610 S Garnett Rd 74012 — 918-249-9100
Dr. Ken Stewart, supt. — Fax 317-5156
Immanuel Christian Academy — 100/K-8
400 N Aspen Ave 74012 — 918-251-5422
Katherine McGrew, hdmstr. — Fax 251-8365
Summit Christian Academy — 400/K-12
200 E Broadway St 74012 — 918-251-1997
Dan Giddens, admin. — Fax 251-2831

Broken Bow, McCurtain, Pop. 4,170
Broken Bow ISD — 1,800/PK-12
108 W 5th St 74728 — 580-584-3306
Carolyn Davis, supt. — Fax 584-9482
www.bbisd.org
Bennett ES — 300/3-5
108 W 5th St 74728 — 580-584-6440
Charles Hubbard, prin. — Fax 584-9576
Dierks ES — 500/PK-2
108 W 5th St 74728 — 580-584-2765
Terry Stricker, prin. — Fax 584-5640
Rector Johnson MS — 300/6-8
108 W 5th St 74728 — 580-584-9603
David Williams, prin. — Fax 584-2549

Glover SD — 100/K-8
RR 3 Box 385 74728 — 580-420-3232
Mike Converse, supt. — Fax 420-3226
Glover S — 100/K-8
RR 3 Box 385 74728 — 580-420-3232
Mike Converse, prin. — Fax 420-3226

Holly Creek SD — 200/PK-8
RR 2 Box 260 74728 — 580-420-6961
Harvey Brumley, supt. — Fax 420-7022
www.hollycreek.org/
Holly Creek S — 200/PK-8
RR 2 Box 260 74728 — 580-420-6968
Linda Warren, prin. — Fax 420-7022

Lukfata SD — 300/PK-8
RR 2 Box 649 74728 — 580-584-6834
Forrest Mulkey, supt. — Fax 584-9473
Lukfata S — 300/PK-8
RR 2 Box 649 74728 — 580-584-6834
Kurt Neal, prin. — Fax 584-9473

Buffalo, Harper, Pop. 1,102
Buffalo ISD — 100/K-12
PO Box 130 73834 — 580-735-2419
Barry Nault, supt. — Fax 735-2619
www.buffalo.k12.ok.us
Buffalo S — 100/K-12
PO Box 130 73834 — 580-735-2448
Sarah Yauk, prin. — Fax 735-2619

Bunch, Adair
Cave Springs ISD — 200/PK-12
PO Box 200 74931 — 918-775-2364
Steve Adair, supt. — Fax 776-2052
www.cavesprings.k12.ok.us
Cave Springs S, PO Box 200 74931 — 100/PK-8
Darlene Adair, prin. — 918-776-2050

Greasy SD — 100/PK-8
RR 1 Box 1589 74931 — 918-696-7768
David Eads, supt. — Fax 696-7240
Greasy S — 100/PK-8
RR 1 Box 1589 74931 — 918-696-7768
David Eads, prin. — Fax 696-7240

Burlington, Alfalfa, Pop. 146
Burlington ISD — 100/PK-12
PO Box 17 73722 — 580-431-2501
Glen Elliott, supt. — Fax 431-2237
www.burlingtonschool.com/
Burlington S — 100/PK-8
PO Box 17 73722 — 580-431-2222
Joe Feely, prin. — Fax 431-2237

Burneyville, Love
Turner ISD — 300/PK-12
PO Box 159 73430 — 580-276-1307
Donald Simmons, supt. — Fax 276-2006
www.turnerisd.org
Turner S — 200/PK-8
PO Box 159 73430 — 580-276-2707
Jamie Roberts, prin. — Fax 276-1306

Burns Flat, Washita, Pop. 1,731
Burns Flat-Dill City ISD — 700/PK-12
PO Box 129 73624 — 580-562-4844
Ron Hughes, supt. — Fax 562-4847
Rogers S, PO Box 449 73624 — 500/PK-8
Jamie Matuszewski, prin. — 580-562-4851

Byars, McClain, Pop. 286
Byars SD — 100/PK-8
45218 110th St 74831 — 405-783-4366
Terry Selman, supt. — Fax 783-4237
Byars S — 100/PK-8
45218 110th St 74831 — 405-783-4366
Terry Selman, prin. — Fax 783-4237

Cache, Comanche, Pop. 2,406
Cache ISD — 1,500/PK-12
100 Buffalo Cir 73527 — 580-429-3266
Randy Batt, supt. — Fax 429-3271
www.cache.k12.ok.us
Cache IS, 201 W H Ave 73527 — 400/3-5
Jeremy Hogan, prin. — 580-429-8536
Cache MS, 201 W H Ave 73527 — 400/6-8
Debbie Hoffman, prin. — 580-429-8489
Cache PS, 201 W H Ave 73527 — 300/PK-2
C. Langley, prin. — 580-429-3542

Caddo, Bryan, Pop. 965
Caddo ISD — 500/PK-12
PO Box 128 74729 — 580-367-2208
Richard Thomas, supt. — Fax 367-2837
www.caddoisd.org
Caddo S, PO Box 128 74729 — 300/PK-8
Don Tidwell, prin. — 580-367-2515

Calera, Bryan, Pop. 1,784
Calera ISD — 600/PK-12
PO Box 386 74730 — 580-434-5700
Aaron Newcomb, supt. — Fax 434-5800
www.caleraisd.k12.ok.us
Calera S, PO Box 386 74730 — 500/PK-8
Don Joines, prin. — 580-434-5603

Calumet, Canadian, Pop. 534
Calumet ISD — 300/PK-12
PO Box 10 73014 — 405-893-2222
Keith Weldon, supt. — Fax 893-8019
Calumet ES — 100/PK-6
PO Box 10 73014 — 405-893-2222
Michael Higgins, prin. — Fax 893-8019
Calumet JHS — 50/7-8
PO Box 10 73014 — 405-893-2222
Jimmie Smith, prin. — Fax 893-8019

Maple SD — 100/PK-8
904 S Maple Rd 73014 — 405-262-5647
Arthur Eccard, supt. — Fax 262-5651
www.maple.k12.ok.us
Maple S — 100/PK-8
904 S Maple Rd 73014 — 405-262-5647
Arthur Eccard, prin. — Fax 262-5651

Calvin, Hughes, Pop. 269
Calvin ISD 200/PK-12
PO Box 127 74531 405-645-2411
Jon Tuck, supt. Fax 645-2384
www.calvin.k12.ok.us
Calvin S 100/PK-8
PO Box 127 74531 405-645-2411
Joanna Tuck, prin. Fax 645-2384

Cameron, LeFlore, Pop. 320
Cameron ISD 500/PK-12
PO Box 190 74932 918-654-3225
Carolyn White, supt. Fax 654-7387
www.cameron.k12.ok.us/
Cameron S 300/PK-8
PO Box 190 74932 918-654-3412
Doug Dodd, prin. Fax 654-7387

Canadian, Pittsburg, Pop. 243
Canadian ISD 400/PK-12
PO Box 168 74425 918-339-7251
Rodney Karch, supt. Fax 339-2393
Canadian S 300/PK-8
PO Box 168 74425 918-339-7253
Kristi Lockey, prin. Fax 339-2393

Caney, Atoka, Pop. 208
Caney ISD 300/PK-12
PO Box 60 74533 580-889-1996
Tommy Johnson, supt. Fax 889-5033
www.caneyisd.org/
Caney S 200/PK-8
PO Box 60 74533 580-889-6966
Brenda Whitmire, prin. Fax 889-2008

Canton, Blaine, Pop. 602
Canton ISD 400/PK-12
PO Box 639 73724 580-886-3516
Gayle Hajny, supt. Fax 886-3501
www.canton.k12.ok.us
Canton S, PO Box 639 73724 300/PK-8
Shelia Gilchrist, prin. 580-886-2251

Canute, Washita, Pop. 528
Canute ISD 200/PK-12
PO Box 490 73626 580-472-3295
Mike Maddox, supt. Fax 472-3187
Canute S 200/PK-8
PO Box 490 73626 580-472-3922
Nancy Cook, prin. Fax 472-3187

Carnegie, Caddo, Pop. 1,603
Carnegie ISD 500/K-12
315 S Carnegie St 73015 580-654-1470
Donny Darrow, supt. Fax 654-1644
www.carnegieschools.com
Carnegie ES 300/K-5
315 S Carnegie St 73015 580-654-1945
Lori Graham, prin. Fax 654-1807
Carnegie JHS 100/6-8
315 S Carnegie St 73015 580-654-1766
Jane Nix, dean Fax 654-2281

Carney, Lincoln, Pop. 644
Carney ISD 200/PK-12
PO Box 240 74832 405-865-2344
Dewayne Osborn, supt. Fax 865-2345
www.carney.k12.ok.us/
Carney S, PO Box 240 74832 100/PK-8
Connie Helfenbein, prin. 405-865-2290

Cashion, Logan, Pop. 716
Cashion ISD 500/K-12
101 N Euclid Ave 73016 405-433-2741
Todd Garrison, supt. Fax 433-2646
www.cashion.k12.ok.us/
Cashion S 300/K-8
101 N Euclid Ave 73016 405-433-2614
Ashley Hoggatt, prin. Fax 433-2646

Catoosa, Rogers, Pop. 6,440
Catoosa SD 2,300/PK-12
2000 S Cherokee St 74015 918-266-8603
Rick Kibbe, supt. Fax 266-1525
Cherokee ES 300/4-5
2000 S Cherokee St 74015 918-266-8630
Kristi Surface, prin. Fax 266-1478
Paul Learning Center 400/PK-1
2000 S Cherokee St 74015 918-266-8643
Keri Sitton, prin. Fax 266-0606
Sam ES 300/2-3
2000 S Cherokee St 74015 918-266-8637
Cindy Flanary, prin. Fax 266-1479
Wells MS 500/6-8
2000 S Cherokee St 74015 918-266-8623
Della Parrish, prin. Fax 266-1282

Cement, Caddo, Pop. 530
Cement ISD 300/PK-12
PO Box 60 73017 405-489-3216
Raymond Cole, supt. Fax 489-3219
www.cement.k12.ok.us
Cement S 200/PK-8
PO Box 60 73017 405-489-3217
Raymond Cole, prin. Fax 489-3219

Chandler, Lincoln, Pop. 2,859
Chandler ISD 1,100/PK-12
901 S CHS 74834 405-258-1450
Don Gray, supt. Fax 258-2657
www.chandler.k12.ok.us/
East Side ES 300/PK-2
901 S CHS 74834 405-258-1872
Lisa Hart, prin. Fax 240-5717
Park Road Upper ES 300/3-6
901 S CHS 74834 405-258-1828
Melody Howard, prin. Fax 258-1163

Chattanooga, Comanche, Pop. 431
Chattanooga ISD 300/PK-12
PO Box 129 73528 580-597-3347
Jerry Brown, supt. Fax 597-3344
www.chatty.k12.ok.us/
Chattanooga S, PO Box 129 73528 200/PK-8
Christy Fisher, prin. 580-597-6638

Checotah, McIntosh, Pop. 3,533
Checotah ISD 1,300/PK-12
PO Box 289 74426 918-473-5610
Robert Bible, supt. Fax 473-1020
www.checotah.k12.ok.us/
Checotah IS 200/3-5
PO Box 289 74426 918-473-2384
Pam Keeter, prin. Fax 473-1437
Checotah MS 300/6-8
PO Box 289 74426 918-473-5912
Jason Donathan, prin. Fax 473-1020
Marshall ES 400/PK-2
PO Box 289 74426 918-473-5832
Jann Ledbetter, prin. Fax 473-6654

Chelsea, Rogers, Pop. 2,262
Chelsea ISD 1,100/PK-12
206 E 4th St 74016 918-789-2528
Rich McSpadden, supt. Fax 789-3271
Chelsea JHS, 206 E 4th St 74016 200/7-8
Howard Hill, prin. 918-789-2521
Goad IS, 206 E 4th St 74016 200/4-6
Gayle Hendrickson, prin. 918-789-2521
McIntosh ES, 206 E 4th St 74016 400/PK-3
Zenda Willcut, prin. 918-789-2565

Cherokee, Alfalfa, Pop. 1,485
Cherokee ISD 300/PK-12
PO Box 325 73728 580-596-3391
Terry Chapman, supt. Fax 596-2217
Cherokee S, PO Box 325 73728 200/PK-8
Terry Chapman, prin. 580-596-3277

Cheyenne, Roger Mills, Pop. 733
Cheyenne ISD 300/PK-12
PO Box 650 73628 580-497-2666
Rick Garrison, supt. Fax 497-3373
www.cheyenne.k12.ok.us
Cheyenne S 200/PK-8
PO Box 650 73628 580-497-2486
Terrell Scroggins, prin. Fax 497-3373

Chickasha, Grady, Pop. 16,849
Chickasha ISD 2,600/PK-12
900 W Choctaw Ave 73018 405-222-6500
Jim Glaze, supt. Fax 222-6590
chickasha.ok.schoolwebpages.com
Chickasha MS 500/6-8
900 W Choctaw Ave 73018 405-222-6530
Debra Reynolds, prin. Fax 222-6594
Grand Avenue ES 400/1-5
900 W Choctaw Ave 73018 405-222-6524
Kathy Wenzel, prin. Fax 222-6565
Lincoln ES 200/1-5
900 W Choctaw Ave 73018 405-222-6522
Alton Rawlins, prin. Fax 222-6580
Southwest ES 300/1-5
900 W Choctaw Ave 73018 405-222-6540
Tressia Meeks, prin. Fax 222-6567
Wallace ECC 400/PK-K
900 W Choctaw Ave 73018 405-222-6544
Thomas Jeffries, prin. Fax 222-6582

Friend SD 200/PK-8
1307 County Road 1350 73018 405-224-3822
Dale Smith, supt. Fax 222-5416
www.friend.k12.ok.us/
Friend S 200/PK-8
1307 County Road 1350 73018 405-224-3822
Fax 222-5416

Pioneer SD 300/PK-8
3686 State Highway 92 73018 405-224-2700
Jackie Grass, supt. Fax 224-2755
Pioneer S 300/PK-8
3686 State Highway 92 73018 405-224-2700
Jackie Grass, prin. Fax 224-2755

Choctaw, Oklahoma, Pop. 10,529
Choctaw-Nicoma Park ISD 3,900/PK-12
12880 NE 10th St 73020 405-769-4859
Dr. Jim McCharen, supt. Fax 769-9821
www.cnpschools.org
Choctaw ES 300/PK-5
14663 NE 3rd St 73020 405-390-2225
Cheryl Lidia, prin. Fax 390-3101
Choctaw MS 400/6-8
14667 NE 3rd St 73020 405-390-2207
JeanAnn Gaona, prin. Fax 390-4439
Griffith IS 300/3-5
1861 S Indian Meridian 73020 405-390-2153
Kelli Hosford, prin. Fax 390-4429
Indian Meridian ES 500/PK-2
1865 S Indian Meridian 73020 405-390-8585
Karri Doughty, prin. Fax 390-2218
Nicoma Park IS 300/3-5
1318 Hickman Ave 73020 405-769-4693
Misti Tye, prin. Fax 769-6271
Nicoma Park MS 300/6-8
1321 Hickman Ave 73020 405-769-3106
David Reid, prin. Fax 769-9355
Westfall ES 400/PK-5
13239 NE 10th St 73020 405-769-3078
Brenda Stanley, prin. Fax 769-4365
Other Schools – See Nicoma Park

Chouteau, Mayes, Pop. 1,992
Chouteau-Mazie ISD 800/PK-12
PO Box 969 74337 918-476-8336
Dr. Lisa Horn, supt. Fax 476-8538
www.chouteauwildcats.com/
Chouteau ES 3-5
PO Box 969 74337 918-476-8336
Steve Boone, prin. Fax 476-8303
Chouteau-Mazie ECC 200/PK-2
PO Box 969 74337 918-476-6551
Cheryl McCartney, prin.
Chouteau-Mazie MS 200/6-8
PO Box 969 74337 918-476-8336
Charles Arnall, prin. Fax 476-8306
Mazie S 100/PK-8
PO Box 969 74337 918-476-5389
Dennis Stutzman, prin. Fax 476-4833

Claremore, Rogers, Pop. 17,161
Claremore ISD 4,100/PK-12
310 N Weenonah Ave 74017 918-699-7300
J. Michael McClaren, supt. Fax 341-8447
www.claremore.k12.ok.us
Central Upper ES 600/5-6
101 W 11th St 74017 918-341-7744
Kari Forest, prin. Fax 343-6333
Claremont ES 700/PK-4
318 E 7th St 74017 918-341-0273
Kellye Shuck, prin. Fax 343-6334
Rogers JHS 600/7-8
1915 N Florence Ave 74017 918-341-7411
Terry Adams, prin. Fax 343-6332
Roosa ES 300/PK-4
2001 N Sioux Ave 74017 918-341-5242
Fax 343-6337
Westside ES 700/PK-4
2600 Holly Rd 74017 918-699-7301
Lou Robertson, prin. Fax 343-6338

Justus-Tiawah SD 100/PK-8
14902 E School Rd, 918-341-3626
David Garroutte, supt. Fax 341-4920
www.justus.k12.ok.us
Justus-Tiawah ES PK-2
14902 E School Rd, 918-341-3626
Patricia Lehman, prin. Fax 341-4920
Justus-Tiawah MS North Campus 100/7-8
15011 E 523 Rd, 918-341-1252
David Garroutte, prin. Fax 341-4920
Justus-Tiawah MS South Campus 3-6
15011 E 523 Rd, 918-341-1252
Mark Ricks, prin. Fax 341-4920

Sequoyah ISD 1,400/PK-12
16441 S 4180 Rd 74017 918-341-5472
Terry Saul, supt. Fax 341-5764
www.sequoyaheagles.net
Sequoyah Lower ES 400/PK-3
16441 S 4180 Rd 74017 918-341-6111
Lisa Trent, prin. Fax 343-8108
Sequoyah Upper ES 300/4-6
16441 S 4180 Rd 74017 918-343-8106
Troy Steidley, prin. Fax 343-8108

Verdigris ISD 1,200/PK-12
8104 E 540 Rd, 918-266-7227
Michael Payne, supt. Fax 266-3910
vps.k12.ok.us
Verdigris ES 500/PK-4
26505 S 4110 Rd, 918-266-6333
Jim Anderson, prin. Fax 266-4569
Verdigris MS 300/5-8
8104 E 540 Rd, 918-266-6343
Denton Holland, prin. Fax 266-1554

Claremore Christian S 200/PK-12
1055 W Blue Starr Dr 74017 918-341-1805
Ryan Mullins, prin. Fax 341-1011
Legacy Christian S 100/PK-6
107 E Will Rogers Blvd 74017 918-342-1450
Pam Flood, admin. Fax 342-1477

Clayton, Pushmataha, Pop. 724
Clayton ISD 300/PK-12
PO Box 190 74536 918-569-4492
Jim Dominick, supt. Fax 569-7757
www.clayton.k12.ok.us
Crain ES 100/PK-4
PO Box 190 74536 918-569-4158
Patricia Glenn, prin. Fax 569-7656
Crain MS 100/5-8
PO Box 190 74536 918-569-4345
Lyndon Howze, prin. Fax 569-7757

Cleo Springs, Major, Pop. 311
Aline-Cleo ISD
Supt. — See Aline
Aline-Cleo Springs S 100/PK-8
PO Box 38 73729 580-438-2330
Jim Patton, prin. Fax 438-2330

Cleveland, Pawnee, Pop. 3,247
Cleveland ISD 1,700/PK-12
600 N Gilbert Ave 74020 918-358-2210
John Weaver, supt. Fax 358-3071
www.clevelandtigers.com/
Cleveland IS 400/3-5
705 N Swan Dr 74020 918-358-2210
Mark Williams, prin. Fax 358-2550
Cleveland MS 400/6-8
322 N Gilbert Ave 74020 918-358-2210
Noel Nation, prin. Fax 358-2534
Cleveland PS 400/K-2
300 N Gilbert Ave 74020 918-358-2210
Randy Mobley, prin. Fax 358-2532
ECC PK-PK
900 W Delaware St 74020 918-358-2210
Ada White, prin. Fax 358-5705

Clinton, Custer, Pop. 8,363
Clinton ISD 1,900/PK-12
PO Box 729 73601 580-323-1800
Jason Sternberger, supt. Fax 323-1804
www.clintonokschools.org/
Clinton MS 300/7-8
PO Box 729 73601 580-323-4228
Peggy Constien, prin. Fax 323-3896
Nance ES 500/PK-1
PO Box 729 73601 580-323-0260
Janalyn Taylor, prin. Fax 323-8672
Southwest ES 400/2-4
PO Box 729 73601 580-323-1290
Pauleta Hunter, prin. Fax 323-3769
Washington ES 300/5-6
PO Box 729 73601 580-323-0311
Beth Richert, prin. Fax 323-2618

Western Oklahoma Christian S 100/PK-6
2901 Beverly Ln 73601 580-323-9150
Joanie Quiring, prin. Fax 323-9150

Coalgate, Coal, Pop. 1,889
Coalgate ISD 600/PK-12
PO Box 368 74538 580-927-2351
Jim Girten, supt. Fax 927-2694
www.coalgateschools.org
Byrd MS 100/7-8
PO Box 368 74538 580-927-3560
Phillip Wilkinson, prin. Fax 927-4031
Emerson ES 300/PK-6
PO Box 368 74538 580-927-2350
Tena Houser, prin. Fax 927-3537

Cottonwood SD 200/PK-8
PO Box 347 74538 580-927-2937
Teri Brecheen, supt. Fax 927-2938
www.cottonwood.k12.ok.us/
Cottonwood S 200/PK-8
PO Box 347 74538 580-927-3907
John Daniel, prin. Fax 927-2938

Colbert, Bryan, Pop. 1,094
Colbert ISD 800/PK-12
PO Box 310 74733 580-296-2624
Jarvis Dobbs, supt. Fax 296-2088
www.colbert.k12.ok.us/
Colbert MS, PO Box 310 74733 100/7-8
Andy Goodson, prin. 580-296-2590
East Ward ES, PO Box 310 74733 200/4-6
Kenneth Taylor, prin. 580-296-2198
West Ward ES, PO Box 310 74733 300/PK-3
Gerald Thompson, prin. 580-296-2625

Colcord, Delaware, Pop. 851
Colcord ISD 400/PK-12
433 S Larmon 74338 918-326-4116
J.D. Parkerson, supt. Fax 326-4471
Colcord ES PK-5
433 S Larmon 74338 918-326-4117
Cheryl Snell, prin. Fax 326-4511
Colcord MS 200/6-8
433 S Larmon 74338 918-326-4852
Robert Hampton, prin. Fax 326-4468

Moseley SD 300/PK-8
7904 Moseley Rd 74338 918-422-5927
Holly Davis, supt. Fax 422-5971
www.moseleyschool.com/
Moseley S 300/PK-8
7904 Moseley Rd 74338 918-422-5927
Charlene Carter, prin. Fax 422-5971

Coleman, Johnston
Coleman ISD 200/PK-12
PO Box 188 73432 580-937-4418
Rick Webb, supt. Fax 937-4866
Coleman S 100/PK-8
PO Box 188 73432 580-937-4418
Rick Webb, prin. Fax 937-4866

Collinsville, Tulsa, Pop. 4,325
Collinsville ISD 2,000/PK-12
1119 W Broadway St 74021 918-371-2386
Pat Herald, supt. Fax 371-4285
www.collinsville.k12.ok.us/
Collinsville MS 500/6-8
1415 W Center St 74021 918-371-2541
Kelly Hamlin, prin. Fax 371-1302
ECC PK-K
12936 N 129th East Ave 74021 918-371-6870
Janice Pollard, prin. Fax 371-4773
Herald ES 500/3-5
12818 N 129th East Ave 74021 918-371-4173
Rachel Chronister, prin. Fax 371-3832
Wilson ES 400/1-2
402 N 17th St 74021 918-371-3144
Cheryl Hunt, prin. Fax 371-4811

Comanche, Stephens, Pop. 1,516
Comanche ISD 1,100/K-12
1030 Ash Ave 73529 580-439-2900
Terry Davidson, supt. Fax 439-2907
www.comanche.k12.ok.us
Comanche ES 500/K-5
1030 Ash Ave 73529 580-439-2911
Janice Vernon, prin. Fax 439-2947
Comanche MS 200/6-8
1030 Ash Ave 73529 580-439-2922
Brent Crow, prin. Fax 439-2979

Grandview SD 200/PK-8
RR 1 Box 105 73529 580-439-2467
Gary Wade, supt. Fax 439-5589
www.grandviewschool.k12.ok.us
Grandview S 200/PK-8
RR 1 Box 105 73529 580-439-2467
Gary Wade, prin. Fax 439-5589

Commerce, Ottawa, Pop. 2,573
Commerce ISD 900/PK-12
217 Commerce St 74339 918-675-4316
Jim Haynes, supt. Fax 675-4464
www.commercetigers.net
Alexander ES 500/PK-5
601 6th St 74339 918-675-4336
Kevin Wade, prin. Fax 675-5056
Commerce MS 200/6-8
500 Commerce St 74339 918-675-4101
Herb Logan, prin. Fax 675-5353

Copan, Washington, Pop. 809
Copan ISD 300/PK-12
PO Box 429 74022 918-532-4490
Steve Stanley, supt. Fax 532-4568
www.copan.k12.ok.us/
Copan S, PO Box 429 74022 200/PK-8
Tammy Shepherd, prin. 918-532-4344

Cordell, Washita, Pop. 2,809
Cordell ISD 700/PK-12
PO Box 290 73632 580-832-3420
Brad Overton, supt. Fax 832-4108
www.cordell.k12.ok.us
Cordell ES, PO Box 510 73632 400/PK-6
Alan Hull, prin. 580-832-3220

Corn, Washita, Pop. 578
Washita Heights ISD 200/PK-12
PO Box 8 73024 580-343-2228
Steve Richert, supt. Fax 343-2259
www.whchiefs.k12.ok.us/
Washita Heights S 100/PK-8
PO Box 8 73024 580-343-2298
Steve Richert, prin. Fax 343-2218

Council Hill, Muskogee, Pop. 131
Midway ISD 300/PK-12
PO Box 127 74428 918-474-3434
Don Ford, supt. Fax 474-3636
Other Schools – See Hitchita

Covington, Garfield, Pop. 542
Covington-Douglas ISD 300/PK-12
PO Box 9 73730 580-864-7481
Darren Sharp, supt. Fax 864-7644
www.c-d.k12.ok.us
Covington-Douglas S 200/PK-8
PO Box 9 73730 580-864-7849
Brian Smith, prin. Fax 864-7644

Coweta, Wagoner, Pop. 8,352
Coweta ISD 2,900/PK-12
PO Box 550 74429 918-486-6506
Jeff Holmes, supt. Fax 486-4167
www.cowetaps.com/
Central ES 400/PK-4
PO Box 550 74429 918-486-2130
Sherri Cook, prin. Fax 486-7810
Coweta IS 500/5-6
PO Box 550 74429 918-486-2186
Carolyn Rowe, prin. Fax 486-4404
Coweta JHS 500/7-8
PO Box 550 74429 918-486-2127
Mike Lingo, prin. Fax 486-7307
Northwest ES 400/PK-4
PO Box 550 74429 918-486-6559
Richard Lock, prin. Fax 279-1168
Southside ES 500/PK-4
PO Box 550 74429 918-279-0480
Doug Flanary, prin. Fax 279-1223

Coyle, Logan, Pop. 360
Coyle ISD 400/PK-12
PO Box 287 73027 405-466-2242
Robert Hightower, supt. Fax 466-2448
www.coyle.k12.ok.us
Coyle S 300/PK-8
PO Box 287 73027 405-466-2242
Gary Larman, prin. Fax 466-2448

Crescent, Logan, Pop. 1,336
Crescent ISD 700/PK-12
PO Box 719 73028 405-969-3738
Steve Shiever, supt. Fax 969-2003
www.crescentok.com/
Crescent ES 300/PK-5
PO Box 719 73028 405-969-3666
Jim Childers, prin. Fax 969-2835
Crescent JHS 100/6-8
PO Box 719 73028 405-969-2190
Wayne Owens, prin. Fax 969-2003

Cromwell, Seminole, Pop. 264
Butner ISD 300/PK-12
PO Box 157 74837 405-944-5530
Mike Bryan, supt. Fax 944-5746
Butner S 200/PK-8
PO Box 157 74837 405-944-5545
Jason Price, prin. Fax 944-5475

Crowder, Pittsburg, Pop. 440
Crowder ISD 400/PK-12
PO Box B 74430 918-334-3203
David Jones, supt. Fax 334-3295
Crowder S, PO Box B 74430 300/PK-8
Anna Cecil, prin. 918-334-3205

Cushing, Payne, Pop. 8,267
Cushing ISD 1,900/PK-12
PO Box 1609 74023 918-225-3425
Koln Knight, supt. Fax 225-5256
Cushing MS, 316 N Steele Ave 74023 400/6-8
Pat Elder, prin. 918-225-1311
Deep Rock ES 100/K-5
2601 N Linwood Ave 74023 918-225-4497
Teresa Shaffer, prin. Fax 225-4538
Harmony ES 300/K-5
1601 S Harmony Rd 74023 918-225-4697
Nancy Dowell, prin. Fax 225-2864
Harrison ES 100/K-5
610 S Noble Ave 74023 918-225-4433
Martha Cackler, prin. Fax 225-4434
Sunnyside ES 300/K-5
1919 S Kings Hwy 74023 918-225-1635
Gary Toland, prin. Fax 225-2906
Wilson S 100/PK-PK
1140 E Cherry St 74023 918-225-4683
Sally Wright, prin. Fax 225-6097

Oak Grove SD 200/PK-8
8409 E 9th St 74023 918-352-2889
Koln Knight, supt. Fax 352-4187
Oak Grove S 200/PK-8
8409 E 9th St 74023 918-352-2889
Koln Knight, prin. Fax 352-4187

Cyril, Caddo, Pop. 1,169
Cyril ISD 400/PK-12
PO Box 449 73029 580-464-2419
Jim Conger, supt. Fax 464-2445
Cyril S 300/PK-8
PO Box 449 73029 580-464-2437
Joyce Clift, prin. Fax 464-3703

Dale, Pottawatomie, Pop. 100
Dale ISD 600/PK-12
300 Smith Ave 74851 405-964-5558
Charles Dickinson, supt. Fax 964-5559
www.dale.k12.ok.us
Dale MS, 300 Smith Ave 74851 100/6-8
Benny Burnett, prin. 405-964-2799
Jackson ES 400/PK-5
300 Smith Ave 74851 405-964-5514
Scott Dennis, prin. Fax 964-5519

Davenport, Lincoln, Pop. 886
Davenport ISD 400/PK-12
PO Box 849 74026 918-377-2277
John Greenfield, supt. Fax 377-2553
www.davenport.k12.ok.us/
Davenport S 300/PK-8
PO Box 849 74026 918-377-2279
Paula Sporleder, prin. Fax 377-2339

Davidson, Tillman, Pop. 345
Davidson ISD 100/PK-12
PO Box 338 73530 580-568-2423
Phillip Ratcliff, supt. Fax 568-2423
www.davidson.k12.ok.us/
Davidson S 100/PK-8
PO Box 338 73530 580-568-2511
Jill Gable, prin. Fax 568-2423

Davis, Murray, Pop. 2,648
Davis ISD 900/PK-12
400 E Atlanta Ave 73030 580-369-2386
Monte Thompson, supt. Fax 369-3507
www.davis.k12.ok.us/
Davis ES 400/PK-4
400 E Atlanta Ave 73030 580-369-5544
Jim Clemons, prin. Fax 369-3983
Davis MS 300/5-8
400 E Atlanta Ave 73030 580-369-5565
Sheri Knight, prin. Fax 369-3289

Deer Creek, Grant, Pop. 137
Deer Creek-Lamont ISD
Supt. — See Lamont
Deer Creek-Lamont S 100/PK-8
PO Box 10 74636 580-267-3241
Barbara Regier, prin.

Del City, Oklahoma, Pop. 21,945
Midwest City-Del City ISD
Supt. — See Midwest City
Del City ES 400/PK-5
2400 Epperly Dr 73115 405-671-8640
Ruth Kizer, prin. Fax 671-8642
Del Crest MS 400/6-8
4731 Judy Dr 73115 405-671-8615
Shana Perry, prin. Fax 671-8618
Epperly Heights ES 600/PK-5
3805 Del Rd 73115 405-671-8650
Kevin Hill, prin. Fax 671-8652
Kerr MS 400/6-8
2300 Linda Ln 73115 405-671-8625
Rob Cherry, prin. Fax 671-8626
Townsend ES 500/PK-5
4000 Epperly Dr 73115 405-671-8680
Jeff Holland, prin. Fax 671-8682

Christian Heritage Academy 700/PK-12
4400 SE 27th St 73115 405-672-1787
Josh Bullard, hdmstr. Fax 672-1839
Destiny Christian S 500/PK-12
3801 SE 29th St 73115 405-677-6000
Jim Howard, admin. Fax 677-6066

Depew, Creek, Pop. 569
Depew ISD 400/PK-12
PO Box 257 74028 918-324-5466
Bruce Terronez, supt. Fax 324-5336
Depew S 200/PK-8
PO Box 257 74028 918-324-5368
Tony Martin, prin. Fax 324-5336

Gypsy SD 100/PK-8
30899 S 417th West Ave 74028 918-324-5365
Michael Clemmer, supt. Fax 324-5003
Gypsy S 100/PK-8
30899 S 417th West Ave 74028 918-324-5365
Michael Clemmer, prin. Fax 324-5003

Dewar, Okmulgee, Pop. 908
Dewar ISD 200/PK-12
PO Box 790 74431 918-652-9625
Todd Been, supt. Fax 652-3096
www.dewar.k12.ok.us/
Dewar ES PK-5
PO Box 790 74431 918-652-2184
Mickey Howk, prin. Fax 652-3096
Dewar MS 100/6-8
PO Box 790 74431 918-652-9625
Kate McDonald, prin. Fax 652-3096

Dewey, Washington, Pop. 3,288
Dewey ISD 1,100/PK-12
1 Bulldogger Rd 74029 918-534-2241
Paul Smith, supt. Fax 534-0149
www.dewey.k12.ok.us
Dewey ES, 1 Bulldogger Rd 74029 500/PK-5
Jerry Moore, prin. 918-534-3800
Dewey MS, 1 Bulldogger Rd 74029 200/6-8
Leta Moreland, prin. 918-534-0111

Dibble, McClain, Pop. 295
Dibble ISD 500/PK-12
PO Box 9 73031 405-344-6375
Chad Clanton, supt. Fax 344-6977
www.dibble.k12.ok.us
Dibble ES, PO Box 9 73031 PK-5
Darlene Hayhurst, prin. 405-344-6868
Dibble MS 300/6-8
PO Box 9 73031 405-344-6380
Jerime Parker, prin. Fax 344-7275

Dover, Kingfisher, Pop. 367
Dover ISD 200/PK-12
PO Box 195 73734 405-828-4206
Floyd Kirk, supt. Fax 828-7150
www.dover.k12.ok.us
Dover S 200/PK-12
PO Box 195 73734 405-828-4205
Richard Reed, prin. Fax 828-8019

Drummond, Garfield, Pop. 386
Drummond ISD 200/PK-12
PO Box 240 73735 580-493-2216
Mike Woods, supt. Fax 493-2273
www.drummond.k12.ok.us/
Drummond S, PO Box 240 73735 200/PK-8
Greg Kokojan, prin. 580-493-2271

Drumright, Creek, Pop. 2,877
Drumright ISD 700/PK-12
301 S Pennsylvania Ave 74030 918-352-2492
H.T. Gee, supt. Fax 352-4430
www.drumright.k12.ok.us/
Bradley ES 300/PK-5
508 S Skinner Ave 74030 918-352-9519
Leon Hiett, prin. Fax 352-4608
Edison MS 100/6-8
300 E Pine St 74030 918-352-2318
Kevin Bilyeu, prin. Fax 352-4033

Olive ISD 400/PK-12
9352 S 436th West Ave 74030 918-352-9567
Loren Tackett, supt. Fax 352-4379
www.olive.k12.ok.us/
Olive S, 9352 S 436th West Ave 74030 300/PK-8
Karen Wood, prin. 918-352-9569

Duke, Jackson, Pop. 392
Duke ISD 200/PK-12
PO Box 160 73532 580-679-3014
Kevin Cansler, supt. Fax 679-3017
www.dukeschools.com/
Duke S, PO Box 160 73532 100/PK-8
Darrel Humphries, prin. 580-679-3311

Duncan, Stephens, Pop. 22,306
Duncan ISD 3,700/PK-12
PO Box 1548 73534 580-255-0686
Dr. Sherry Labyer, supt. Fax 252-2453
www.duncanpublicschools.org
Duncan MS 800/6-8
PO Box 1548 73534 580-470-8106
Mike Toone, prin. Fax 470-8743
Emerson ES 400/K-5
PO Box 1548 73534 580-255-7146
Eva Spaulding, prin. Fax 252-5413
Mann ES 400/K-5
PO Box 1548 73534 580-255-6530
Marlon Gay, prin. Fax 255-3673
Plato ES 300/K-5
PO Box 1548 73534 580-255-6167
John Millirons, prin. Fax 255-3672
Rogers Preschool Center 200/PK-PK
PO Box 1548 73534 580-255-9012
Mona Evans, prin. Fax 255-1074
Twain ES 200/K-5
PO Box 1548 73534 580-255-1324
Dr. JoAnn Pierce, prin. Fax 255-3819
Wilson ES 400/K-5
PO Box 1548 73534 580-255-8107
Bud Conway, prin. Fax 255-3893

Empire ISD 600/PK-12
9450 W Cherokee Rd 73533 580-252-5392
Jim Motes, supt. Fax 252-4231
www.empireschools.org
Empire S, 9450 W Cherokee Rd 73533 400/PK-8
Josh Skiles, prin. 580-255-4150

Durant, Bryan, Pop. 14,795
Durant ISD 3,200/PK-12
PO Box 1160 74702 580-924-1276
Jason Simeroth Ph.D., supt. Fax 924-6019
www.durantisd.org
Durant IS 700/4-6
1314 Waco St 74701 580-924-1397
Tod Harrison, prin. Fax 920-7940
Durant MS 500/7-8
410 N 6th Ave 74701 580-924-1321
Kenny Chaffin, prin. Fax 924-8278
Irving ES 600/PK-3
812 W Locust St 74701 580-924-3805
Katy Pruitt, prin. Fax 920-4939
Lee ES 200/PK-3
824 W Louisiana St 74701 580-924-3628
Mike Dills, prin. Fax 920-4931
Northwest Heights ES 500/PK-3
1715 W University Blvd 74701 580-924-5595
Cindy Newell, prin. Fax 924-4748

Rock Creek ISD
Supt. — See Bokchito
Rock Creek S 300/PK-8
23072 US Highway 70 74701 580-924-9601
Bill Neyman, prin. Fax 924-1012

Silo ISD 700/PK-12
122 W Bourne St 74701 580-924-7003
Bill Caruthers, supt. Fax 920-7988
www.siloisd.org
Silo ES 400/PK-5
122 W Bourne St 74701 580-924-7001
Don Oller, prin. Fax 924-5771
Silo JHS 100/6-8
122 W Bourne St 74701 580-924-7000
Mike Palmer, prin. Fax 920-7983

Victory Life Academy 200/K-12
3412 W University Blvd 74701 580-920-0850
Mark Ackerson, prin. Fax 920-9923

Dustin, Hughes, Pop. 445
Dustin ISD 100/PK-12
PO Box 390660 74839 918-656-3230
Dr. Ron Ledford, supt. Fax 656-3242
www.dustin.k12.ok.us/
Dustin S 100/PK-8
PO Box 390660 74839 918-656-3239
Lee Northcutt, prin. Fax 656-3242

Eagletown, McCurtain
Eagletown ISD 200/PK-12
PO Box 38 74734 580-835-2242
Kent Hendon, supt. Fax 835-7420
www.eagletownisd.org
Eagletown S 200/PK-7
PO Box 38 74734 580-835-2241
Greg Holt, prin. Fax 835-7420

Earlsboro, Pottawatomie, Pop. 657
Earlsboro ISD 200/K-12
PO Box 10 74840 405-997-5616
Terry Brown, supt. Fax 997-3181
Earlsboro S 100/K-8
PO Box 10 74840 405-997-5312
Dianne Parris, prin. Fax 997-3181

Edmond, Oklahoma, Pop. 74,881
Deer Creek ISD 2,300/PK-12
20701 N MacArthur Blvd, 405-348-6100
Rebecca Wilkinson, supt. Fax 348-3049
www.deercreekschools.org/
Deer Creek ES 400/K-5
4704 NW 164th St 73013 405-348-9100
Bettina Kates, prin. Fax 359-3164
Deer Creek MS 700/6-8
21175 N MacArthur Blvd, 405-348-4830
Tracy Skinner, prin. Fax 359-3163
Grove Valley ES K-5
3500 NW 192nd St, 405-359-3195
Debbie Straughn, prin.
Prairie Vale ES 500/K-5
22522 N Pennsylvania Ave, 405-359-3170
Michelle Anderson, prin. Fax 359-1819
Rose Union ES PK-5
5100 NW 220th St, 405-359-3188
Stacy Edwards, prin. Fax 359-3191

Edmond ISD 19,100/PK-12
1001 W Danforth Rd 73003 405-340-2800
Dr. David Goin, supt. Fax 340-2835
www.edmondschools.net/
Centennial ES PK-PK, 1-
4400 N Coltrane Rd 73034 405-340-2275
Jesseele Miller, prin. Fax 340-2255
Central MS 800/6-8
500 E 9th St 73034 405-340-2890
Tara Fair, prin. Fax 340-3961
Cheyenne MS 900/6-8
1271 W Covell Rd 73003 405-330-7380
Susie Schinnerer, prin. Fax 330-7397
Chisholm ES 700/PK-5
2300 E 33rd St 73013 405-340-2950
Joann Graham, prin. Fax 330-3352
Cimarron MS 700/6-8
3701 S Bryant Ave 73013 405-340-2935
Andy North, prin. Fax 330-3398
Clegern ES 300/K-5
601 S Jackson St 73034 405-340-2955
Bill Powell, prin. Fax 330-3345
Cross Timbers ES 900/PK-5
4800 N Kelly Ave, 405-340-2200
Cathey Bugg, prin. Fax 330-3355
Debo ES 800/PK-5
16060 N May Ave 73013 405-340-2270
Beth Tollefson, prin. Fax 330-3357
Dougherty ES 300/PK-5
19 N Boulevard St 73034 405-340-2985
Paula Stafford, prin. Fax 330-3346
Freeman ES 500/PK-5
501 W Hurd St 73003 405-340-2965
Brenda McDonald, prin. Fax 330-3347
Haskell ES 800/PK-5
1701 NW 150th St 73013 405-340-2945
Angela Mills, prin. Fax 330-3354
Howell ECC PK-PK
45 E 12th St 73034 405-340-2960
Bill Powell, prin. Fax 330-3344
Irving ES 800/PK-5
18101 N Western Ave, 405-340-2210
Robert Evans, prin. Fax 330-3356
Northern Hills ES 800/PK-5
901 E Wayne St 73034 405-340-2975
Nellie Sizemore, prin. Fax 330-3348
Risner ES 600/PK-5
2801 S Rankin St 73013 405-340-2984
Paula Carlile, prin. Fax 330-3349
Rogers ES 700/PK-5
1215 E 9th St 73034 405-340-2995
Dr. Sheron House, prin. Fax 330-3351
Ross ES 1,000/PK-5
1901 Thomas Dr 73003 405-340-2970
Ruthie Riggs, prin. Fax 330-3353
Sequoyah MS 1,000/6-8
1125 E Danforth Rd 73034 405-340-2900
Angela Mills, prin. Fax 340-2909
Summit MS 800/6-8
1703 NW 150th St 73013 405-340-2920
Desarae Witmer, prin. Fax 340-2933
Sunset ES 700/PK-5
400 W 8th St 73003 405-340-2990
Dr. Barbara Siano, prin. Fax 330-3350
West Field ES PK-PK, 1-
17601 N Pennsylvania Ave, 405-340-2285
Cara Jernigan, prin. Fax 330-7364

Oakdale SD 400/PK-8
10901 N Sooner Rd 73013 405-771-3373
Kim Lanier, supt. Fax 771-3378
www.oakdale.org
Oakdale S 400/PK-8
10901 N Sooner Rd 73013 405-771-3373
Susan Honeycutt, prin. Fax 771-3378

Oklahoma Christian S 800/PK-12
PO Box 509 73083 405-341-2265
Dallas Caldwell, hdmstr. Fax 344-4710
St. Elizabeth Ann Seton S 500/PK-8
PO Box 510 73083 405-348-5364
Angie Howard, prin. Fax 340-9627
St. Mary's Episcopal S 200/PK-5
505 E Covell Rd 73034 405-341-9541
Nancy Hetherington, prin. Fax 285-4126

Eldorado, Jackson, Pop. 498
Eldorado ISD 100/PK-12
PO Box J 73537 580-633-2219
Mark Baumann, supt. Fax 633-2316
www.eldorado.k12.ok.us/
Eldorado S 100/PK-8
PO Box J 73537 580-633-2219
Pam Charlson, prin. Fax 633-2316

Elgin, Comanche, Pop. 1,278
Elgin ISD 1,500/PK-12
PO Box 369 73538 580-492-3663
Tom Crimmins, supt. Fax 492-4084
www.elgin.k12.ok.us/
Elgin ES 600/PK-4
PO Box 369 73538 580-492-3680
Doug Garland, prin. Fax 492-3698
Elgin MS 400/5-8
PO Box 369 73538 580-492-3655
Sammy Jackson, prin. Fax 492-3658

Elk City, Beckham, Pop. 10,743
Elk City ISD 2,000/PK-12
222 W Broadway Ave 73644 580-225-0175
Galeard Roper, supt. Fax 225-8644
www.elkcityschools.com/
Elk City MS 100/7-7
222 W Broadway Ave 73644 580-225-5043
Rick McNeil, prin. Fax 225-5043
Fairview ES 300/3-4
222 W Broadway Ave 73644 580-225-2590
Jimi O'Hara, prin. Fax 225-8812
Grandview ES 300/5-6
222 W Broadway Ave 73644 580-225-2687
Jamey Cook, prin. Fax 225-2687
Northeast ES 400/1-2
222 W Broadway Ave 73644 580-225-0194
Susan Eastton, prin. Fax 225-0194
Pioneer K 400/PK-K
222 W Broadway Ave 73644 580-225-7722
Jim Richardson, prin. Fax 225-7722

Merritt ISD 500/PK-12
19693 E 1130 Rd 73644 580-225-5460
Gary Higgins, supt. Fax 225-5469
Merritt S 400/PK-8
19693 E 1130 Rd 73644 580-225-5460
Roger Woodson, prin. Fax 225-5469

Elmore City, Garvin, Pop. 763
Elmore City-Pernell ISD 500/PK-12
100 N Muse Ave 73433 580-788-2566
Jim Smith, supt. Fax 788-4665
www.ecphs.k12.ok.us
Elmore City-Pernell S 400/PK-8
100 N Muse Ave 73433 580-788-2869
Dena York, prin. Fax 788-2860

El Reno, Canadian, Pop. 16,097
Banner SD 200/PK-8
2455 N Banner Rd 73036 405-262-0598
Larry York, supt. Fax 262-0628
Banner S 200/PK-8
2455 N Banner Rd 73036 405-262-0598
Larry York, prin. Fax 262-0628

Darlington SD 200/PK-8
4408 N Highway 81 73036 405-262-0137
Jim Shelton, supt. Fax 262-3215
www.darlington.k12.ok.us
Darlington S 200/PK-8
4408 N Highway 81 73036 405-262-0137
Jim Shelton, prin. Fax 262-3215

El Reno ISD 2,500/PK-12
PO Box 580 73036 405-262-1703
Ranet Tippens, supt. Fax 262-8620
www.elreno.k12.ok.us
Hillcrest ES 400/PK-5
PO Box 580 73036 405-262-2396
Jennifer Posey, prin. Fax 262-3265
Lincoln ES 300/PK-5
PO Box 580 73036 405-262-1941
Roger Roblyer, prin. Fax 262-8479
Roblyer MS 300/6-7
PO Box 580 73036 405-262-2700
Jason Pennington, prin. Fax 262-8449
Webster ES 100/K-5
PO Box 580 73036 405-262-1943
Lynn Zucksworth, prin. Fax 262-8400
Witcher ES 400/PK-5
PO Box 580 73036 405-262-5592
Julie Huber, prin. Fax 262-8439

Riverside SD 100/PK-8
4800 Foreman Rd E 73036 405-262-2907
Dr. Jeff Goure, supt. Fax 262-2925
Riverside S 100/PK-8
4800 Foreman Rd E 73036 405-262-2907
Dr. Jeff Goure, prin. Fax 262-2925

Sacred Heart S 100/PK-6
210 S Evans Ave 73036 405-262-2284
Shannon Statton, prin. Fax 262-3818

Enid, Garfield, Pop. 46,416
Chisholm ISD 800/PK-12
300 Colorado Ave 73701 580-237-5512
Roydon Tilley, supt. Fax 234-5334
www.chisholm.k12.ok.us
Chisholm ES 400/PK-5
300 Colorado Ave 73701 580-237-5645
Darla Smith, prin. Fax 234-5334
Chisholm MS 200/6-8
4202 W Carrier Rd 73703 580-234-0234
Shane Dent, prin. Fax 234-0343

Enid ISD 5,400/PK-12
500 S Independence St 73701 580-234-5270
Shawn Hime, supt. Fax 249-3565
www.enidpublicschools.org/
Adams ES 300/PK-5
2200 E Randolph Ave 73701 580-234-5959
Beverly James, prin. Fax 249-3594
Coolidge ES 500/PK-5
1515 E Ash Ave 73701 580-237-2775
Clark Koepping, prin. Fax 249-3595
Eisenhower ES 100/PK-5
1301 W Fox Dr 73703 580-234-5954
Polly Maxwell, prin. Fax 249-3596
Emerson MS 300/6-8
700 W Elm Ave 73701 580-237-3017
Kimberly Jones, prin. Fax 249-3587
Garfield ES 300/PK-5
900 E Broadway Ave 73701 580-234-5950
Kathy Edson, prin. Fax 249-3597
Glenwood ES 500/PK-5
824 N Oakwood Rd 73703 580-237-1466
James Rainey, prin. Fax 249-3598
Hayes ES 300/PK-5
2102 Beverly Dr 73703 580-234-5937
Jane Johnson, prin. Fax 242-6177
Hoover ES 300/PK-5
2800 W Maine Ave 73703 580-237-5029
Karen Heizer, prin. Fax 242-5970
Longfellow MS 200/6-8
900 E Broadway Ave 73701 580-234-7022
Ron Few, prin. Fax 249-3586
McKinley ES 300/PK-5
1701 W Broadway Ave 73703 580-234-5958
Jan Robinson, prin. Fax 249-3591
Monroe ES 400/PK-5
400 W Cottonwood Ave 73701 580-237-5225
Kay Kiner, prin. Fax 249-3592
Taft ES 300/PK-5
1002 Sequoyah Dr 73703 580-234-5957
Dr. Ann Reding, prin. Fax 249-3593
Waller MS 400/6-8
2604 W Randolph Ave 73703 580-234-5931
John Garvie, prin. Fax 249-3585

Pioneer-Pleasant Vale ISD
Supt. — See Waukomis
Pioneer-Pleasant Vale ES 300/PK-6
6020 E Willow Rd 73701 580-234-9628
Larry Coonrod, prin.

Emmanuel Christian S 200/PK-6
2505 W Owen K Garriott Rd 73703 580-237-0032
Dr. John Stam, hdmstr. Fax 237-0662
St. Joseph S 100/PK-6
PO Box 3527 73702 580-242-4449
Wade Laffey, prin. Fax 242-3541
St. Paul Lutheran S 50/K-6
1626 E Broadway Ave 73701 580-234-6646
Lisa Brainard, prin. Fax 234-6692

Erick, Beckham, Pop. 1,045
Erick ISD 200/PK-12
PO Box 9 73645 580-526-3476
Phil Compton, supt. Fax 526-3308
Erick S, PO Box 9 73645 200/PK-8
Jamey Chittum, prin. 580-526-3203

Eufaula, McIntosh, Pop. 2,789
Eufaula ISD 1,200/K-12
PO Box 609 74432 918-689-2152
Dan Edwards, supt. Fax 689-1080
www.eufaula.k12.ok.us/
Eufaula ES 500/K-5
PO Box 609 74432 918-689-2682
Victor Salcedo, prin. Fax 689-1067
Eufaula MS 300/6-8
PO Box 609 74432 918-689-2711
Chris Whelan, prin. Fax 689-2874

Stidham SD 100/PK-8
HC 64 Box 2110 74432 918-689-5241
Bart Banfield, supt. Fax 689-9163
Stidham S 100/PK-8
HC 64 Box 2110 74432 918-689-5241
Bart Banfield, prin. Fax 689-9163

Fairfax, Osage, Pop. 1,505
Woodland SD 400/PK-12
100 N 6th St 74637 918-642-3297
Kevin Hime, supt. Fax 642-5754
www.woodland.k12.ok.us/
Woodland ES 200/PK-4
100 N 6th St 74637 918-642-3295
Claudette Mashburn, prin. Fax 642-3280
Other Schools – See Ralston

Fairland, Ottawa, Pop. 1,012
Fairland ISD 600/PK-12
202 W Washington Ave 74343 918-676-3811
Mark Alexander, supt. Fax 676-3594
www.fairlandowls.com
Fairland S 400/PK-8
202 W Washington Ave 74343 918-676-3224
Angie Wade, prin.

Fairview, Major, Pop. 2,629
Fairview ISD 700/PK-12
408 E Broadway 73737 580-227-2531
Rocky Burchfield, supt. Fax 227-2642
www.fairviewhigh.com
Chamberlain MS 100/6-8
1000 E Elm St 73737 580-227-2555
Mark Van Meter, prin. Fax 227-2642
Cornelsen ES 300/PK-5
1200 E Elm St 73737 580-227-2561
Richard Beck, prin. Fax 227-2642

Fanshawe, LeFlore, Pop. 394
Fanshawe SD 100/PK-8
PO Box 100 74935 918-659-2341
C. Lynn Bullard, supt. Fax 659-2275
Fanshawe S 100/PK-8
PO Box 100 74935 918-659-2341
C. Lynn Bullard, prin. Fax 659-2275

Fargo, Ellis, Pop. 318
Fargo ISD 200/PK-12
PO Box 200 73840 580-698-2298
Jeff Thompson, supt. Fax 698-8019
www.fargo.k12.ok.us
Fargo S 200/PK-8
PO Box 200 73840 580-698-2298
Pamela Myers, prin. Fax 698-8019

Felt, Cimarron
Felt ISD 100/PK-12
PO Box 47 73937 580-426-2220
Barbalee Blair, supt. Fax 426-2799
www.felt.k12.ok.us
Felt S 100/PK-8
PO Box 47 73937 580-426-2220
Barbalee Blair, prin. Fax 426-2799

Fittstown, Pontotoc
Stonewall ISD
Supt. — See Stonewall
McLish MS 74842 100/PK-PK, 5-
Jack Wofford, prin. 580-777-2221
Fax 777-2222

Fletcher, Comanche, Pop. 1,038
Fletcher ISD 500/PK-12
PO Box 489 73541 580-549-6027
Kathryn Turner, supt. Fax 549-6016
www.fletcherschools.org/
Fletcher ES 200/PK-6
PO Box 489 73541 580-549-6020
Sandra Fehring, prin. Fax 549-6016

Forgan, Beaver, Pop. 493
Forgan ISD 200/PK-12
PO Box 406 73938 580-487-3366
Travis Smalts, supt. Fax 487-3368
www.forgan.k12.ok.us
Forgan S 100/PK-8
PO Box 406 73938 580-487-3366
Todd Kerr, prin. Fax 487-3368

Fort Cobb, Caddo, Pop. 651
Fort Cobb-Broxton ISD 400/PK-12
PO Box 130 73038 405-643-2336
Dennis Klugh, supt. Fax 643-2547
Fort Cobb-Broxton ES 200/PK-5
PO Box 130 73038 405-643-2334
James Biddy, prin.
Fort Cobb-Broxton MS 100/6-8
PO Box 130 73038 405-643-2820
James Biddy, prin.

Fort Gibson, Muskogee, Pop. 4,252
Fort Gibson ISD 1,900/PK-12
500 Ross Ave 74434 918-478-2474
Derald Glover, supt. Fax 478-8533
www.ftgibson.k12.ok.us
Fort Gibson Early Learning Center 500/PK-2
500 Ross Ave 74434 918-478-4841
Phyllis Kindle, prin. Fax 478-6411
Fort Gibson IS 400/3-5
500 Ross Ave 74434 918-478-2465
Sherry Rybolt, prin. Fax 478-6401
Fort Gibson MS 400/6-8
500 Ross Ave 74434 918-478-2471
Gregory Phares, prin. Fax 478-6412

Fort Sill, Comanche, Pop. 12,107
Lawton ISD
Supt. — See Lawton
Geronimo Road ES 500/PK-5
5727 Geronimo Rd 73503 580-248-7004
Harold McCann, prin. Fax 585-6458

Fort Supply, Woodward, Pop. 328
Fort Supply ISD 100/PK-12
PO Box 160 73841 580-766-2611
Pat Howell, supt. Fax 766-8019
www.fortsupply.k12.ok.us/
Fort Supply S 100/PK-8
PO Box 160 73841 580-766-2611
Pat Howell, prin. Fax 766-8019

Fort Towson, Choctaw, Pop. 611
Fort Towson ISD 400/PK-12
PO Box 39 74735 580-873-2712
Doug Evans, supt. Fax 873-1053
www.forttowson.k12.ok.us/
Fort Towson S 300/PK-8
PO Box 39 74735 580-873-2780
Tammy Neese, prin. Fax 873-2712

Fox, Carter
Fox ISD 300/PK-12
PO Box 248 73435 580-673-2081
Brent Phelps, supt. Fax 673-2389
www.foxps.k12.ok.us
Fox S 200/PK-8
PO Box 248 73435 580-673-2083
Mark Williams, prin. Fax 673-2389

Foyil, Rogers, Pop. 266
Foyil ISD 600/PK-12
PO Box 49 74031 918-341-1113
Pat Gougler, supt. Fax 341-1223
www.foyil.k12.ok.us
Foyil ES 400/PK-6
PO Box 49 74031 918-342-3310
Lisa Rader, prin. Fax 341-1223

Frederick, Tillman, Pop. 4,195
Frederick ISD 1,000/PK-12
PO Box 370 73542 580-335-5516
Tony O'Brien, supt. Fax 335-2324
www.frederickbombers.net
Frederick ES 500/PK-5
PO Box 310 73542 580-335-3513
Joel Read, prin. Fax 335-5088
Frederick MS 200/6-8
PO Box 490 73542 580-335-2014
Randy Biggs, prin. Fax 335-2763

Freedom, Woods, Pop. 262
Freedom ISD 100/PK-12
PO Box 5 73842 580-621-3271
Craig McVay, supt. Fax 621-3699
www.freedom.k12.ok.us
Freedom S 50/PK-8
PO Box 5 73842 580-621-3271
Craig McVay, prin. Fax 621-3699

Gage, Ellis, Pop. 408
Gage ISD 100/K-12
PO Box 60 73843 580-923-7666
Doug Taylor, supt. Fax 923-7907
www.gage.k12.ok.us/
Gage ES 100/K-6
PO Box 60 73843 580-923-7909
Darci Lingle, prin. Fax 923-7907

Gans, Sequoyah, Pop. 214
Gans ISD 400/PK-12
PO Box 70 74936 918-775-2236
Brenda Taylor, supt. Fax 775-5145
www.gans.k12.ok.us
Gans S 300/PK-8
PO Box 70 74936 918-775-2236
Larry Calloway, prin. Fax 775-5145

Garber, Garfield, Pop. 802
Garber ISD 300/PK-12
PO Box 539 73738 580-863-2220
Jim Lamer, supt. Fax 863-2259
www.garber.k12.ok.us/
Garber S, PO Box 539 73738 200/PK-8
Dusty Torrey, prin. 580-863-2232

Garvin, McCurtain, Pop. 222
Forest Grove SD 100/PK-8
PO Box 60 74736 580-286-3961
John Smith, supt. Fax 286-3961
www.forestgroveps.org/school/
Forest Grove S 100/PK-8
PO Box 60 74736 580-286-3961
John Smith, prin. Fax 286-3961

Geary, Blaine, Pop. 1,290
Geary ISD 400/PK-12
PO Box 188 73040 405-884-2989
Dr. Jeff Maddox, supt. Fax 884-2099
www.geary.k12.ok.us
Geary ES 200/PK-6
PO Box 188 73040 405-884-2442
Michael Cottongim, prin. Fax 884-2983

Geronimo, Comanche, Pop. 950
Geronimo ISD 300/PK-12
PO Box 99 73543 580-355-3801
Danny McCuiston, supt. Fax 357-8307
www.geronimo.k12.ok.us
Geronimo S 200/PK-8
PO Box 99 73543 580-353-3160
Amy Latimer, prin. Fax 355-9670

Glencoe, Payne, Pop. 562
Glencoe ISD 300/PK-12
201 E Lone Chimney Rd 74032 580-669-2261
John Lazenby, supt. Fax 669-2961
www.glencoe.k12.ok.us
Glencoe S 200/PK-8
201 E Lone Chimney Rd 74032 580-669-2254
Robert Crow, prin. Fax 669-2254

Glenpool, Tulsa, Pop. 8,960
Glenpool ISD 2,400/PK-12
PO Box 1149 74033 918-322-9500
Kathy Coley, supt. Fax 322-1529
www.glenpool.k12.ok.us
Glenpool ES 1,200/PK-5
PO Box 1149 74033 918-322-9801
Mary Champion, prin. Fax 322-9116
Glenpool MS 500/6-8
PO Box 1149 74033 918-322-9500
Danna Garland, prin. Fax 322-9333

Goodwell, Texas, Pop. 1,129
Goodwell ISD 200/PK-12
PO Box 580 73939 580-349-2271
Freida Burgess, supt. Fax 349-2531
www.gpseagles.org
Goodwell S 100/PK-8
PO Box 580 73939 580-349-2271
Steve Moore, prin. Fax 349-2531

Yarbrough ISD 100/PK-12
RR 1 Box 31 73939 580-545-3327
Jim Wiggin, supt. Fax 545-3392
www.yarbrough.k12.ok.us/
Yarbrough S 100/PK-8
RR 1 Box 31 73939 580-545-3327
Cliff Benson, prin. Fax 545-3392

Gore, Sequoyah, Pop. 907
Gore ISD 600/K-12
PO Box 580 74435 918-489-5587
Keith Kincade, supt. Fax 489-5664
www.gore.k12.ok.us/
Gore ES 200/K-5
PO Box 580 74435 918-489-5638
Richard Moseley, prin. Fax 489-2465
Gore MS 100/6-8
PO Box 580 74435 918-487-5587
Keith Kincade, prin. Fax 489-5664

Gracemont, Caddo, Pop. 336
Gracemont ISD 100/PK-8
PO Box 5 73042 405-966-2236
Robert Miller, supt. Fax 966-2395
www.gracemont.k12.ok.us
Gracemont S 100/PK-8
PO Box 5 73042 405-966-2551
Roberta Fullbright, prin. Fax 966-2100

Grandfield, Tillman, Pop. 1,007
Grandfield ISD 300/PK-12
PO Box 639 73546 580-479-5237
Ed Turlington, supt. Fax 479-3381
www.grandfield.k12.ok.us/
Grandfield S 200/PK-8
PO Box 639 73546 580-479-3288
Ben Bernard, prin. Fax 479-3381

Granite, Greer, Pop. 1,797
Granite ISD 300/PK-12
PO Box 98 73547 580-535-2104
Rick Beene, supt. Fax 535-2106
www.granite.k12.ok.us
Granite S 200/PK-8
PO Box 98 73547 580-535-2104
Skeeter Sampler, prin. Fax 535-2106

Grant, Choctaw
Grant SD 100/K-8
PO Box 159 74738 580-326-8315
Buck Hammers, supt. Fax 326-9236
Grant S 100/K-8
PO Box 159 74738 580-326-8315
Buck Hammers, prin. Fax 326-9236

Grove, Delaware, Pop. 5,752
Grove ISD 2,300/PK-12
PO Box 450789 74345 918-786-3003
Tom Steen, supt. Fax 786-9365
www.ridgerunners.net
Grove ECC 300/PK-K
PO Box 450789 74345 918-786-6127
Julie Bloss, prin. Fax 787-2004
Grove IS 300/4-5
PO Box 450789 74345 918-786-2297
Shelly Barnes, prin. Fax 786-5321
Grove MS 500/6-8
PO Box 450789 74345 918-786-2209
Pat Dodson, prin. Fax 786-6454
Grove PS 500/1-3
PO Box 450789 74345 918-786-5573
Sandy Harper, prin. Fax 787-5207

Guthrie, Logan, Pop. 10,800
Guthrie ISD 3,000/PK-12
802 E Vilas Ave 73044 405-282-8900
Terry Simpson, supt. Fax 282-5904
www.guthrie.k12.ok.us
Central ES 1-1
321 E Noble Ave 73044 405-282-0352
Karen Watkins, prin. Fax 282-9988
Cotteral ES 400/PK-K
2001 W Noble Ave 73044 405-282-5928
Kathryn McGee, prin. Fax 282-5322
Fogarty ES 500/2-3
902 N Wentz St 73044 405-282-5932
Ben Hardin, prin. Fax 282-6511
Guthrie JHS 500/7-8
705 E Oklahoma Ave 73044 405-282-5936
Tim Rawls, prin. Fax 282-3598

Guthrie Upper ES 700/4-6
702 N Crooks Dr 73044 405-282-5924
Susan Davison, prin. Fax 282-5946

St. Marys S 200/PK-8
502 E Warner Ave 73044 405-282-2071
Sheila Whalen-Guthrie, prin. Fax 282-2924

Guymon, Texas, Pop. 10,643
Guymon ISD 1,800/PK-12
PO Box 1307 73942 580-338-4340
Doug Melton, supt. Fax 338-3812
www.guymontigers.com
Academy ES 100/3-4
PO Box 1307 73942 580-338-4370
Bill Smith, prin. Fax 338-3812
Carrier ES 50/PK-PK
PO Box 1307 73942 580-338-4380
Loire Aubrey, prin. Fax 338-3812
Central JHS 400/7-8
PO Box 1307 73942 580-338-4360
Michelle Bryson, prin. Fax 338-3812
Long ES 100/K-2
PO Box 1307 73942 580-338-4370
Casey Hall, prin. Fax 338-3812
Northeast ES 100/K-2
PO Box 1307 73942 580-338-4380
Casey Hall, prin. Fax 338-3812
North Park IS 300/5-6
PO Box 1307 73942 580-338-4390
Howard Barton, prin. Fax 338-3812
Prairie ES K-2
PO Box 1307 73942 580-338-4380
Loire Aubrey, prin. Fax 338-3812
Salyer ES 100/K-2
PO Box 1307 73942 580-338-4380
Loire Aubrey, prin. Fax 338-3812

Straight SD 50/K-6
RR 1 Box 89 73942 580-652-2232
Laura Hill, supt. Fax 652-3299
www.straight.k12.ok.us/
Straight ES 50/K-6
RR 1 Box 89 73942 580-652-2232
Laura Hill, prin. Fax 652-3299

Haileyville, Pittsburg, Pop. 899
Haileyville ISD 500/PK-12
PO Box 29 74546 918-297-2626
Jim Caughern, supt. Fax 297-7136
haileyville.ok.schoolwebpages.com
Haileyville S 300/PK-8
PO Box 29 74546 918-297-2733
Dennis Ford, prin. Fax 297-3004

Hammon, Roger Mills, Pop. 454
Hammon ISD 200/PK-12
PO Box 279 73650 580-473-2221
Randy Ann Stickney, supt. Fax 473-2464
www.hammon.k12.ok.us/
Hammon S 100/PK-8
PO Box 279 73650 580-473-2289
Jeff Morton, prin. Fax 473-2464

Hanna, McIntosh, Pop. 135
Hanna ISD 100/PK-12
PO Box 10 74845 918-657-2523
Patricia Berry, supt. Fax 657-2424
Hanna S, PO Box 10 74845 100/PK-8
Deborah Fogle, prin. 918-657-2527

Hardesty, Texas, Pop. 277
Hardesty ISD 100/PK-12
PO Box 129 73944 580-888-4258
Wade Stafford, supt. Fax 888-4560
www.hardesty.k12.ok.us
Hardesty S 100/PK-8
PO Box 129 73944 580-888-4258
Beverly Richardson, prin. Fax 888-4560

Harrah, Oklahoma, Pop. 4,939
Harrah ISD 2,300/PK-12
20670 Walker St 73045 405-454-6244
Dr. Dean Hughes, supt. Fax 454-0022
www.harrahschools.com
Babb ES 300/4-5
20901 NE 10th St 73045 405-454-6213
Glendia Warren, prin. Fax 454-6844
Harrah MS 300/6-7
20665 Walker St 73045 405-454-2406
Zane Casey, prin. Fax 454-6841
Reynolds ES 300/2-3
755 Harrison St 73045 405-454-6201
Cheryl Hessman, prin. Fax 454-6843
Smith ES 400/PK-1
20227 NE 10th St 73045 405-454-3638
Doug Parker, prin. Fax 454-3698

Hartshorne, Pittsburg, Pop. 2,073
Hartshorne ISD 700/PK-12
520 S 5th St 74547 918-297-2534
Mark Ichord, supt. Fax 297-2698
www.hartshorne.k12.ok.us
Hartshorne ES 300/PK-6
821 Arapahoe Ave 74547 918-297-2345
Brian Akins, prin. Fax 297-2074

Haskell, Muskogee, Pop. 1,776
Haskell ISD 900/PK-12
PO Box 278 74436 918-482-5221
Dr. Landon Berry, supt. Fax 482-3346
www.haskell.k12.ok.us
Beavers MS 200/6-8
PO Box 278 74436 918-482-5221
Michael Broyles, prin. Fax 482-3346
White ES 500/PK-5
PO Box 278 74436 918-482-1402
Danny Harris, prin. Fax 482-3711

Haworth, McCurtain, Pop. 351
Haworth ISD 600/PK-12
HC 73 Box 1 74740 580-245-1406
Ted Brewer, supt. Fax 245-2265
www.haworth.k12.ok.us
Haworth ES 300/PK-6
HC 73 Box 1 74740 580-245-1472
Wynema Wright, prin. Fax 245-4912

Haywood, Pittsburg
Haywood SD 100/PK-8
HC 75 Box 3 74501 918-423-6265
Chad Graham, supt. Fax 423-8063
Haywood S 100/PK-8
HC 75 Box 3 74501 918-423-6265
Roger Smith, prin. Fax 423-8063

Healdton, Carter, Pop. 2,777
Healdton ISD 600/PK-12
PO Box 490 73438 580-229-0566
Don Lewis, supt. Fax 229-1522
Healdton ES 300/PK-5
PO Box 490 73438 580-229-1201
Kay Watson, prin. Fax 229-1481
Healdton MS 100/6-8
PO Box 490 73438 580-229-0303
Jason Midkiff, prin. Fax 229-1475

Heavener, LeFlore, Pop. 3,246
Heavener ISD 1,000/PK-12
PO Box 698 74937 918-653-7223
Edward Wilson, supt. Fax 653-7843
www.heavener.k12.ok.us
Heavener S, PO Box 698 74937 700/PK-8
Diane Cox, prin. 918-653-4313

Helena, Alfalfa, Pop. 1,392
Timberlake ISD 300/PK-12
PO Box 287 73741 580-852-3307
Brent Rousey, supt. Fax 852-8019
www.tlake.k12.ok.us
Other Schools – See Jet

Hendrix, Bryan, Pop. 79
Achille ISD
Supt. — See Achille
Yuba S 100/PK-8
101 Yuba Ln 74741 580-285-2100
Sharon Dunham, prin. Fax 285-2111

Hennessey, Kingfisher, Pop. 2,050
Hennessey ISD 800/PK-12
604 E Oklahoma St 73742 405-853-4321
Joe McCulley, supt. Fax 853-4439
www.hps.k12.ok.us
Hennessey Lower ES 400/PK-4
130 N Mitchell Rd 73742 405-853-4305
Gabrielle Ogle, prin. Fax 853-6106
Hennessey MS 200/5-8
120 N Mitchell Rd 73742 405-853-4303
David Garner, prin. Fax 853-4848

Henryetta, Okmulgee, Pop. 6,110
Henryetta ISD 1,300/PK-12
1801 W Troy Aikman Dr 74437 918-652-6523
Billy Green, supt. Fax 652-6510
www.henryetta.k12.ok.us
Henryetta ES 600/PK-5
1800 W Division St 74437 918-652-6587
Morris Dodge, prin. Fax 652-6598
Henryetta MS 300/6-8
1700 W Troy Aikman Dr 74437 918-652-6578
Brad Wion, prin. Fax 652-6506

Ryal SD 100/PK-8
RR 2 Box 427 74437 918-652-7461
Jerry Hurst, supt. Fax 652-7635
www.ryal.k12.ok.us/
Ryal S 100/PK-8
RR 2 Box 427 74437 918-652-7461
Jerry Hurst, prin. Fax 652-7635

Wilson ISD 300/PK-12
8867 Chestnut Rd 74437 918-652-3374
Rick Hatfield, supt. Fax 652-8140
www.wpstigers.k12.ok.us
Wilson S 200/PK-8
8867 Chestnut Rd 74437 918-652-3375
Rick Hatfield, prin. Fax 652-8140

Hillsdale, Garfield, Pop. 97

Hillsdale Christian S 100/PK-6
PO Box 8 73743 580-635-2211
James Hoffsommer, admin. Fax 635-2392

Hinton, Caddo, Pop. 2,183
Hinton ISD 600/PK-12
PO Box 1036 73047 405-542-3257
Chuck Hood, supt. Fax 542-3286
www.hinton.k12.ok.us
Hinton ES 300/PK-5
PO Box 1036 73047 405-542-3295
Patrick Duffy, prin. Fax 542-3286
Hinton MS 100/6-8
PO Box 1036 73047 405-542-3235
Robert Friesen, prin. Fax 542-3286

Hitchita, McIntosh, Pop. 112
Midway ISD
Supt. — See Council Hill
Midway S 200/PK-8
PO Box 98 74438 918-466-3303
Nathan Meaders, prin. Fax 466-3337

Hobart, Kiowa, Pop. 3,805
Hobart ISD 800/PK-12
PO Box 899 73651 580-726-5691
Roger Hill, supt. Fax 726-2855
www.hobart.k12.ok.us
Hobart ES, PO Box 899 73651 400/PK-5
Angie Winkler, prin. 580-726-5665
Hobart MS, PO Box 899 73651 200/6-8
Misty Reents, prin. 580-726-5615

Hodgen, LeFlore
Hodgen SD 300/PK-8
PO Box 69 74939 918-653-4476
Eddie Glenn, supt. Fax 653-2525
www.hodgen.k12.ok.us
Hodgen S 300/PK-8
PO Box 69 74939 918-653-4476
Ward Brown, prin. Fax 653-2525

Holdenville, Hughes, Pop. 5,538
Holdenville ISD 1,000/PK-12
210 Grimes Ave 74848 405-379-5483
Steve Butcher, supt. Fax 379-5874
www.holdenville.k12.ok.us
Reed ES 400/PK-3
210 Grimes Ave 74848 405-379-6618
Jean Alexander, prin. Fax 379-8100
Thomas ES 200/4-8
210 Grimes Ave 74848 405-379-6661
Mark Turner, prin. Fax 379-8118

Moss ISD 300/PK-12
8087 E 134 Rd 74848 405-379-7251
John Long, supt. Fax 379-2333
www.mossps.k12.ok.us/
Moss S 200/PK-8
8087 E 134 Rd 74848 405-379-7251
Tina Cartwright, prin. Fax 379-2333

Hollis, Harmon, Pop. 2,087
Hollis ISD 500/PK-12
PO Box 193 73550 580-688-3450
Wilmer Cooper, supt. Fax 688-2532
www.hollis.k12.ok.us
Hollis ES, PO Box 193 73550 300/PK-5
Amy Estes, prin. 580-688-3616
Hollis MS, PO Box 193 73550 100/6-8
Marty Webb, prin. 580-688-2707

Hominy, Osage, Pop. 3,733
Hominy ISD 600/PK-12
200 S Pettit Ave 74035 918-885-6511
Russell Hull, supt. Fax 885-2538
www.hominy.k12.ok.us/
Hominy MS, 200 S Pettit Ave 74035 100/7-8
Pat Drummond, prin. 918-885-6253
Mann ES, 200 S Pettit Ave 74035 300/PK-6
Mark Williams, prin. 918-885-6255

Hooker, Texas, Pop. 1,721
Hooker ISD 500/PK-12
PO Box 247 73945 580-652-2162
Billy Terry, supt. Fax 652-3118
Hooker S, PO Box 247 73945 400/PK-8
Pat Atkins, prin. 580-652-2463

Howe, LeFlore, Pop. 715
Howe ISD 500/PK-12
PO Box 259 74940 918-658-3666
Scott Parks, supt. Fax 658-2233
www.howeschools.org
Howe S 300/PK-8
PO Box 259 74940 918-658-3508
Sandra Cross, prin. Fax 658-2233

Hugo, Choctaw, Pop. 5,521
Goodland SD 100/PK-8
1218 N 4200 Rd 74743 580-326-8036
Steve Allred, supt. Fax 326-8026
Goodland S 100/PK-8
1218 N 4200 Rd 74743 580-326-8036
Steve Allred, prin. Fax 326-8026

Hugo ISD 1,100/K-12
208 N 2nd St 74743 580-326-6483
Tony Daugherty, supt. Fax 326-2480
www.hugoschools.com/
Hugo ES 400/K-3
208 N 2nd St 74743 580-326-8373
Nancy Welch, prin. Fax 326-6312
Hugo IS 100/4-5
208 N 2nd St 74743 580-326-8371
Tommy Cummings, prin. Fax 326-0213
Hugo MS 200/6-8
208 N 2nd St 74743 580-326-3365
Darnell Shanklin, prin. Fax 326-7352

Goodland Academy 100/K-12
1216 N 4200 Rd 74743 580-326-7568
David Dearinger, hdmstr. Fax 326-5556

Hulbert, Cherokee, Pop. 533
Hulbert ISD 500/PK-12
PO Box 188 74441 918-772-2501
Wayne Ryals, supt. Fax 772-2766
www.hulbertriders.com
Hulbert ES 300/PK-6
PO Box 188 74441 918-772-2861
Cole Purget, prin. Fax 772-1274

Norwood SD 200/PK-8
7966 W 790 Rd 74441 918-478-3092
Diana Garnatz, supt. Fax 478-3833
norwood.k12.ok.us
Norwood S 200/PK-8
7966 W 790 Rd 74441 918-478-3092
Diana Garnatz, prin. Fax 478-3833

Shady Grove SD 200/PK-8
11042 W Shady Grove Rd 74441 918-772-2511
Fred Ferguson, supt. Fax 772-2430
Shady Grove S 200/PK-8
11042 W Shady Grove Rd 74441 918-772-2511
Deborah Ferguson, prin. Fax 772-2430

Hydro, Caddo, Pop. 1,045
Hydro-Eakly ISD 500/PK-12
529 E 6th St 73048 405-663-2774
Bill Derryberry, supt. Fax 663-2139
www.hydroeakly.k12.ok.us/
Hydro-Eakly ES 200/PK-5
529 E 6th St 73048 405-663-2619
Denise Wieland, prin. Fax 663-2449
Hydro-Eakly MS 100/6-8
529 E 6th St 73048 405-663-2246
Kim Hale, prin. Fax 663-2139

Idabel, McCurtain, Pop. 6,916
Denison SD 300/PK-8
RR 4 Box 230 74745 580-286-3319
Bill Austin, supt. Fax 286-5743
Denison S 300/PK-8
RR 4 Box 230 74745 580-286-3319
Bill Austin, prin. Fax 286-5743

Idabel ISD 1,500/PK-12
200 NE Ave C 74745 580-286-7639
James Sharpe, supt. Fax 286-5585
www.idabelps.org
Central ES 300/3-5
206 SE Ave F 74745 580-286-5346
Laura Bullock, prin. Fax 286-3430

George K — 200/PK-K
3 NE 7th St 74745 — 580-286-2347
Curtis Fuller, prin. — Fax 286-2061
Idabel MS — 300/6-8
100 NE Ave D 74745 — 580-286-6558
Rebecca Brock, prin. — Fax 286-8272
Idabel PS — 200/1-2
1212 E Tyler Dr 74745 — 580-286-4400
Tammy Blackard, prin. — Fax 286-4443

Indiahoma, Comanche, Pop. 360
Indiahoma ISD — 200/PK-12
PO Box 8 73552 — 580-246-3448
Deanna Voegeli, supt. — Fax 246-3372
www.indiahoma.k12.ok.us
Indiahoma S — 100/PK-8
PO Box 8 73552 — 580-246-3202
James Todd, prin. — Fax 246-3372

Indianola, Pittsburg, Pop. 193
Indianola ISD — 300/PK-12
PO Box 119 74442 — 918-823-4231
Angela Weaver, supt. — Fax 823-4234
Indianola S, PO Box 119 74442 — 200/PK-8
Gina Barlow, prin. — 918-823-4244

Inola, Rogers, Pop. 1,725
Inola ISD — 1,300/PK-12
PO Box 1149 74036 — 918-543-2255
Dr. Kent Holbrook, supt. — Fax 543-8754
www.inola.k12.ok.us
Inola ES — 500/PK-4
PO Box 909 74036 — 918-543-2271
Kyle Ford, prin. — Fax 543-6866
Inola MS — 400/5-8
PO Box 819 74036 — 918-543-2434
Jeff Unrau, prin. — Fax 543-6268

Jay, Delaware, Pop. 2,840
Jay ISD — 1,700/PK-12
PO Box 630 74346 — 918-253-4293
Charles Thomas, supt. — Fax 253-8970
www.jay.k12.ok.us
Jay ES — 600/PK-3
PO Box 630 74346 — 918-253-4413
Marvin Stockton, prin. — Fax 253-4391
Jay MS — 300/7-8
PO Box 630 74346 — 918-253-8510
Shane Carroll, prin. — Fax 253-3342
Jay Upper ES, PO Box 630 74346 — 300/4-6
Shane Carroll, prin. — 918-253-3535

Jenks, Tulsa, Pop. 13,095
Jenks ISD — 9,600/PK-12
205 E B St 74037 — 918-299-4411
Dr. Kirby Lehman, supt. — Fax 299-9197
jenksps.org
East ES — 1,600/PK-4
205 E B St 74037 — 918-299-4411
Susan Oare, prin. — Fax 298-6628
West IS — 500/5-6
205 E B St 74037 — 918-299-4415
Michelle Sumner, prin. — Fax 298-0355
Other Schools – See Tulsa

Jennings, Pawnee, Pop. 382
Jennings SD — 200/K-8
523 N Oak St 74038 — 918-757-2536
Chris Ballenger, supt. — Fax 757-2338
www.jennings.k12.ok.us
Jennings S — 200/K-8
523 N Oak St 74038 — 918-757-2536
Derrick Meador, prin. — Fax 757-2338

Jet, Alfalfa, Pop. 216
Timberlake ISD
Supt. — See Helena
Timberlake S — 200/PK-8
PO Box 188 73749 — 580-626-4411
Brent Rousey, prin. — Fax 626-4414

Jones, Oklahoma, Pop. 2,611
Jones ISD — 1,000/PK-12
412 SW 3rd St 73049 — 405-399-9215
Mike Steele, supt. — Fax 399-9212
www.joneshs.k12.ok.us
Jones ES — 500/PK-5
13145 Montana St 73049 — 405-399-9118
Cindy Harrison, prin. — Fax 399-2897
Jones MS — 200/6-8
16011 E Wilshire Blvd 73049 — 405-399-9114
Pam Lucas, prin. — Fax 399-6101

Kansas, Delaware, Pop. 709
Kansas ISD — 1,000/PK-12
PO Box 196 74347 — 918-868-2562
Jim Burgess, supt. — Fax 868-3103
Kansas ES — 500/PK-5
PO Box 196 74347 — 918-868-2427
Gina Glass, prin. — Fax 868-5587
Kansas JHS — 200/6-8
PO Box 196 74347 — 918-868-5308
Bryon Arnold, prin. — Fax 868-5582

Kellyville, Creek, Pop. 918
Kellyville ISD — 1,300/PK-12
PO Box 99 74039 — 918-247-6133
Joe Pierce, supt. — Fax 247-6120
www.kellyvilleschools.org/
Kellyville ES, PO Box 99 74039 — 300/4-6
Mark Dolezal, prin. — 918-247-2257
Kellyville MS, PO Box 99 74039 — 200/7-8
John Castillo, prin. — 918-247-6134
Kellyville PS, PO Box 99 74039 — 400/PK-3
Jane Longan, prin. — 918-247-6300

Keota, Haskell, Pop. 530
Keota ISD — 400/PK-12
110 NE 6th St 74941 — 918-966-3950
Rita Echelle, supt. — Fax 966-3247
www.keota.k12.ok.us
Keota S — 300/PK-8
110 NE 6th St 74941 — 918-966-3141
Butch Booth, prin. — Fax 966-3247

Ketchum, Mayes, Pop. 293
Ketchum ISD — 700/PK-12
PO Box 720 74349 — 918-782-5091
Rick Pool, supt. — Fax 782-9018
www.ketchumwarriors.com
Ketchum ES — 300/PK-5
PO Box 720 74349 — 918-782-9543
Leslie Janis, prin. — Fax 782-9018
Ketchum MS — 100/6-8
PO Box 720 74349 — 918-782-3242
Joe Gramlich, prin. — Fax 782-3016

Keyes, Cimarron, Pop. 367
Keyes ISD — 100/PK-12
PO Box 47 73947 — 580-546-7231
Jim Washburn, supt. — Fax 546-7338
www.keyes.k12.ok.us
Keyes S — 100/PK-8
PO Box 47 73947 — 580-546-7231
Jim Washburn, prin. — Fax 546-7338

Kiefer, Creek, Pop. 1,313
Kiefer ISD — 400/PK-12
4600 W 151st St S 74041 — 918-321-3421
Mary Murrell, supt. — Fax 321-5216
www.kiefer.k12.ok.us/
Kiefer ES, 4600 W 151st St S 74041 — 200/PK-6
Brent Weaver, prin. — 918-321-5444
Rongey MS, 4600 W 151st St S 74041 — 50/7-8
Gayla Johnson, prin. — 918-321-3421

Kildare, Kay, Pop. 90
Kildare SD — 100/PK-6
1265 Church St, Ponca City OK 74604 — 580-362-2811
A.J. Ledwig, supt. — Fax 362-3342
www.kildare.k12.ok.us/
Kildare ES — 100/PK-6
1265 Church St, Ponca City OK 74604 — 580-362-2811
A.J. Ledwig, prin. — Fax 362-3342

Kingfisher, Kingfisher, Pop. 4,501
Kingfisher ISD — 1,200/PK-12
PO Box 29 73750 — 405-375-4194
Don Scales, supt. — Fax 375-5565
www.kingfisher.k12.ok.us
Gilmour ES — 500/PK-4
1400 S Oak St 73750 — 405-375-4080
Jim Hines, prin. — Fax 375-4456
Kingfisher MS — 300/5-8
601 S 13th St 73750 — 405-375-6607
Andy Evans, prin. — Fax 375-6410

SS. Peter & Paul S — 100/PK-8
315 S Main St 73750 — 405-375-4616
Kimberly Kroener, prin. — Fax 375-5296

Kingston, Marshall, Pop. 1,526
Kingston ISD — 1,100/PK-12
PO Box 370 73439 — 580-564-9033
Jay McAdams, supt. — Fax 564-9516
www.kingston.k12.ok.us
Kingston ES — 500/PK-5
PO Box 550 73439 — 580-564-2993
David Gill, prin. — Fax 564-0903
Kingston MS — 200/6-8
PO Box 370 73439 — 580-564-2996
Ron Slawson, prin. — Fax 564-0902

Kinta, Haskell, Pop. 250
Kinta ISD — 200/PK-12
PO Box 219 74552 — 918-768-3338
Patricia Deville, supt. — Fax 768-3221
Kinta S, PO Box 219 74552 — 100/PK-8
Patricia Deville, prin. — 918-768-3338

Kiowa, Pittsburg, Pop. 701
Kiowa ISD — 300/PK-12
PO Box 6 74553 — 918-432-5631
Michael W. Kellogg, supt. — Fax 432-5683
www.kiowa.k12.ok.us
Kiowa S, PO Box 6 74553 — 200/PK-8
Garry Rind, prin. — 918-432-5822

Konawa, Seminole, Pop. 1,434
Konawa ISD — 700/PK-12
701 W South St 74849 — 580-925-3244
Dr. Don Sjoberg, supt. — Fax 925-2146
www.konawa.k12.ok.us
Konawa ES — 400/PK-5
701 W South St 74849 — 580-925-3118
Andrea Sealock, prin. — Fax 925-2146
Konawa JHS — 200/6-8
701 W South St 74849 — 580-925-3221
Larry Marlow, prin. — Fax 925-2146

Krebs, Pittsburg, Pop. 2,120
Krebs SD — 400/PK-8
PO Box 67 74554 — 918-426-4700
Lawrence Scarpitti, supt. — Fax 423-2909
www.krebs.k12.ok.us
Krebs S — 400/PK-8
PO Box 67 74554 — 918-426-4700
Paula Meadows, prin. — Fax 423-2909

Kremlin, Garfield, Pop. 230
Kremlin-Hillsdale ISD — 300/PK-12
PO Box 198 73753 — 580-874-2284
Steve Hoffsommer, supt. — Fax 874-4488
www.kremlin.k12.ok.us/
Kremlin-Hillsdale S — 200/PK-8
PO Box 198 73753 — 580-874-2283
Steve Hoffsummer, prin.

Lahoma, Garfield, Pop. 562
Cimarron ISD — 300/PK-12
PO Box 8 73754 — 580-796-2204
Steve Walker, supt. — Fax 796-2350
www.cimarron.k12.ok.us
Cimarron S — 200/PK-8
PO Box 8 73754 — 580-796-2205
Steve Walker, prin. — Fax 796-2350

Lamont, Grant, Pop. 436
Deer Creek-Lamont ISD — 200/PK-12
PO Box 10 74643 — 580-388-4335
David Zachary, supt. — Fax 388-4341
www.dcla.k12.ok.us/
Other Schools – See Deer Creek

Lane, Atoka
Lane SD — 200/PK-8
PO Box 39 74555 — 580-889-2743
Roland Smith, supt. — Fax 889-9157
lane.ok.schoolwebpages.com
Lane S — 200/PK-8
PO Box 39 74555 — 580-889-2743
Roland Smith, prin. — Fax 889-9157

Laverne, Harper, Pop. 1,016
Laverne ISD — 500/PK-12
PO Box 40 73848 — 580-921-3362
Ed Thomas, supt. — Fax 921-3636
www.laverne.k12.ok.us
Laverne S — 300/PK-8
PO Box 40 73848 — 580-921-5025
Tim Allen, prin. — Fax 921-3636

Lawton, Comanche, Pop. 90,234
Bishop SD — 400/PK-6
2204 SW Bishop Rd 73505 — 580-353-4870
Howard Hampton, supt. — Fax 353-4879
www.bishop.k12.ok.us/
Bishop ES — 400/PK-6
2204 SW Bishop Rd 73505 — 580-353-4870
Howard Hampton, prin. — Fax 353-4879

Flower Mound SD — 300/PK-8
2805 SE Flower Mound Rd 73501 — 580-353-4088
Diana Jackson, supt. — Fax 353-5742
www.flowermound.k12.ok.us
Flower Mound S — 300/PK-8
2805 SE Flower Mound Rd 73501 — 580-353-4088
Diana Jackson, prin. — Fax 353-5742

Lawton ISD — 15,600/PK-12
PO Box 1009 73502 — 580-357-6900
Barry Beauchamp, supt. — Fax 585-6319
www.lawtonps.org
Adams ES — 200/K-5
3501 NW Ferris Ave 73505 — 580-353-7983
Tamara Horschler, prin. — Fax 585-4670
Almor West ES — 300/K-5
6902 SW Delta Ave 73505 — 580-536-6006
Lisa Carson, prin. — Fax 536-2547
Beginnings Academy — 300/PK-PK
501 NW Woodridge Dr 73507 — 580-355-4755
Rhonda Weber, prin. — Fax 585-4604
Bish ES — 400/K-5
5611 NW Alan A Dale Ln 73505 — 580-248-2244
Tamie Barrett, prin. — Fax 585-6482
Brockland ES — 300/K-5
6205 NW Ferris Ave 73505 — 580-536-6948
Susan McCann, prin. — Fax 536-0015
Carriage Hills ES — 400/PK-5
215 SE Warwick Way 73501 — 580-248-6161
Larry Stormer, prin. — Fax 585-4672
Central MS — 600/6-8
1201 NW Fort Sill Blvd 73507 — 580-355-8544
Teresa Jackson, prin. — Fax 585-6452
Cleveland ES — 200/K-5
1202 SW 27th St 73505 — 580-353-8861
Jamie Polk, prin. — Fax 585-4632
Country Club Heights ES — 200/K-5
714 SW 45th St 73505 — 580-355-5733
Kerry Malakosky, prin. — Fax 585-4614
Crosby Park ES — 300/K-5
1602 NW Horton Blvd 73505 — 580-353-7107
Resa Harvick, prin. — Fax 585-6493
Douglass ES — 200/K-5
102 E Gore Blvd 73501 — 580-355-2214
Ora Fitzgerald, prin. — Fax 585-4674
Edison ES — 400/K-5
5801 NW Columbia Ave 73505 — 580-536-4223
Vic Stoll, prin. — Fax 536-0858
Eisenhower ES — 200/K-5
315 SW 52nd St 73505 — 580-355-4599
Sylvia Moore, prin. — Fax 585-4603
Eisenhower MS — 700/6-8
5702 W Gore Blvd 73505 — 580-353-1040
Rick Owens, prin. — Fax 585-6436
Henry ES — 500/K-5
1401 NW Bessie Ave 73507 — 580-355-2617
Bill Ingram, prin. — Fax 585-6383
Howell ES — 200/K-5
2402 SW E Ave 73505 — 580-353-6699
Sherry Havron, prin. — Fax 585-4638
Jackson ES — 200/K-5
2102 NW Lindy Ave 73505 — 580-585-6380
Brenda Breeze, prin. — Fax 585-4680
Learning Tree Academy — 400/PK-PK
1908 NW 38th St 73505 — 580-355-6197
Traci Newell, prin. — Fax 585-4684
Lincoln ES — 200/K-5
601 SW Park Ave 73501 — 580-355-4799
Robbie Gillis, prin. — Fax 585-4608
MacArthur MS — 900/6-8
510 NE 45th St 73507 — 580-353-5111
Mark Mattingly, prin. — Fax 585-6435
Park Lane ES — 200/K-5
4912 SE Avalon Ave 73501 — 580-355-5811
Calvin Prince, prin. — Fax 585-4697
Pioneer Park ES — 400/K-5
3005 NE Angus Pl 73507 — 580-355-5844
Sally Greenlee, prin. — Fax 585-4626
Ridgecrest ES — 400/K-5
1614 NW 47th St 73505 — 580-355-6033
Jackie Herbert, prin. — Fax 585-4693
Sheridan Road ES — 400/PK-5
6500 Sheridan Rd 73503 — 580-357-8833
Mikel Ford, prin. — Fax 585-4671
Sullivan Village ES — 400/PK-5
3802 SE Elmhurst Ln 73501 — 580-355-0800
Jeanie Alldredge, prin. — Fax 585-4681
Swinney ES — 200/K-5
1431 NW 23rd St 73505 — 580-353-7899
Kathleen Dering, prin. — Fax 585-4683
Tomlinson MS — 600/6-8
702 NW Homestead Dr 73505 — 580-585-6416
Laura Puccino, prin. — Fax 585-6451
Washington ES — 200/PK-5
805 NW Columbia Ave 73507 — 580-353-6299
David Dehaven, prin. — Fax 585-4675
Whittier ES — 300/K-5
1115 NW Laird Ave 73507 — 580-355-5238
Brenda Hatch, prin. — Fax 585-4687

Wilson ES 200/K-5
102 NW 17th St 73507 580-355-1448
Phil Smith, prin. Fax 585-4690
Woodland Hills ES 400/K-5
405 NW Woodland Dr 73505 580-536-7991
Cheryl Adams, prin. Fax 536-1496
Other Schools – See Fort Sill

Lawton Christian S 500/PK-12
1 NW Crusader Dr 73505 580-536-6885
Dr. Michael Leaming, supt. Fax 536-5242
St. Mary S 100/PK-8
611 SW A Ave 73501 580-355-5288
Paolo Dulcamara, prin. Fax 355-4336
Trinity Christian Academy 100/PK-10
902 SW A Ave 73501 580-250-1900
Darrell Nightingale, prin. Fax 250-1932

Leedey, Dewey, Pop. 333
Leedey ISD 200/PK-12
PO Box 67 73654 580-488-3424
Rusty Puffinbarger, supt. Fax 488-3428
Leedey S, PO Box 67 73654 100/PK-8
Darren Danielson, prin. 580-488-3377

Le Flore, LeFlore, Pop. 172
LeFlore ISD 200/PK-12
PO Box 147, 918-753-2345
Dennis Hensley, supt. Fax 753-2604
www.lefloreps.k12.ok.us/
LeFlore S 200/PK-8
PO Box 147, 918-753-2345
Cory Wood, prin. Fax 753-2604

Lexington, Cleveland, Pop. 2,079
Lexington ISD 1,000/PK-12
420 NE 4th St 73051 405-527-7236
Denny Prince, supt. Fax 527-9517
www.lexington.k12.ok.us/
Lexington ES 500/PK-4
420 NE 4th St 73051 405-527-7236
Steve Blair, prin. Fax 527-9517
Lexington IS 100/5-6
420 NE 4th St 73051 405-527-7236
Steve Blair, prin. Fax 527-9517

Lindsay, Garvin, Pop. 2,890
Lindsay ISD 1,200/PK-12
800 W Creek St 73052 405-756-3131
Doyle Greteman, supt. Fax 756-8819
www.lindsay.k12.ok.us
Lindsay ES, 800 W Creek St 73052 600/PK-5
Dan Chapman, prin. 405-756-3134
Lindsay MS, 800 W Creek St 73052 200/6-8
Bob Ashley, prin. 405-756-3133

Locust Grove, Mayes, Pop. 1,576
Locust Grove ISD 1,500/PK-12
PO Box 399 74352 918-479-5243
David Cash, supt. Fax 479-6468
www.lg.k12.ok.us
Early Learning Center 300/PK-1
PO Box 399 74352 918-479-5233
Shane Holman, prin. Fax 479-6995
Locust Grove MS 300/6-8
PO Box 399 74352 918-479-5244
Charles Coleman, prin. Fax 479-2930
Locust Grove Upper ES 300/2-5
PO Box 399 74352 918-479-5234
Roy Flanary, prin. Fax 479-5277

Lone Grove, Carter, Pop. 5,075
Lone Grove ISD 1,600/PK-12
PO Box 1330 73443 580-657-3131
Gary Scott, supt. Fax 657-4355
www.lonegrove.k12.ok.us/
Lone Grove IS 400/3-5
PO Box 1330 73443 580-657-3720
Meri Jayne Miller, prin. Fax 657-3486
Lone Grove PS 500/PK-2
PO Box 1330 73443 580-657-4367
Tonya Finnerty, prin. Fax 657-2837
Other Schools – See Ardmore

Lone Wolf, Kiowa, Pop. 474
Lone Wolf ISD 100/PK-12
PO Box 158 73655 580-846-9091
James Sutherland, supt. Fax 846-5266
Lone Wolf S 100/PK-8
PO Box 158 73655 580-846-9091
Larry Terry, prin. Fax 846-5266

Lookeba, Caddo, Pop. 132
Lookeba-Sickles ISD 300/PK-12
RR 1 Box 34 73053 405-457-6623
Dennis Byrd, supt. Fax 457-6619
Lookeba-Sickles S, RR 1 Box 1 73053 200/PK-8
Mike Davis, prin. 405-457-6300

Loyal, Kingfisher, Pop. 83
Lomega ISD
Supt. — See Omega
Lomega S 100/PK-8
RR 1 Box 1 73756 405-729-4251
Steve Mendell, prin. Fax 729-4252

Luther, Oklahoma, Pop. 1,083
Luther ISD 800/PK-12
PO Box 430 73054 405-277-3233
W.B. Wilson, supt. Fax 277-3498
lutherlions.org
Luther ES 300/PK-4
PO Box 430 73054 405-277-3545
Paul Blessington, prin. Fax 277-3877
Luther MS 300/5-8
PO Box 430 73054 405-277-3264
Barry Gunn, prin. Fax 277-3877

Mc Alester, Pittsburg, Pop. 17,566
Frink-Chambers SD 400/PK-8
4610 Frink Rd, 918-423-2434
Ron Joslin, supt. Fax 423-4687
www.frink.k12.ok.us
Frink-Chambers S 400/PK-8
4610 Frink Rd, 918-423-2434
Susan Berry, prin. Fax 423-4687

McAlester ISD 2,800/PK-12
PO Box 1027, 918-423-4771
Tim Condict, supt. Fax 423-8166
www.mcalester.k12.ok.us/
Doyle ES 100/1-4
PO Box 1027, 918-423-0588
Deborah Forest, prin. Fax 423-8104
Emerson ES 300/1-4
PO Box 1027, 918-423-6465
Brenda LoPresto, prin. Fax 423-8151
Gay ECC 100/PK-K
PO Box 1027, 918-423-6229
Vanessa Cummings, prin. Fax 423-8201
Jefferson ECC, PO Box 1027, 100/PK-PK
Karla Brock, prin. 918-423-5963
Parker IS 300/5-6
PO Box 1027, 918-423-4647
Cindy Kemp, prin. Fax 423-8871
Puterbaugh MS 400/7-8
PO Box 1027, 918-423-5445
Paula Meadows, prin. Fax 423-7021
Rogers ES 400/1-4
PO Box 1027, 918-423-4542
Stacie Fryer, prin. Fax 423-8114
Washington ECC 100/PK-K
PO Box 1027, 918-423-0265
Shannon Scherman, prin. Fax 423-8112

Tannehill SD 200/PK-8
RR 1 Box 75, 918-423-6393
William Skimbo, supt. Fax 423-3068
www.tannehill.k12.ok.us
Tannehill S 200/PK-8
RR 1 Box 75, 918-423-6393
Bruce Douglas, prin. Fax 423-3068

McAlester Christian Academy K-12
1700 S Main St, 918-423-2230
Sean Ward, admin. Fax 423-7002

Mc Curtain, Haskell, Pop. 474
Mc Curtain ISD 300/PK-12
PO Box 189, 918-945-7237
Dart Drummonds, supt. Fax 945-7064
www.mccurtain.k12.ok.us/
Mc Curtain S 200/PK-8
PO Box 189, 918-945-7236
Fax 945-7384

Mc Loud, Pottawatomie, Pop. 2,821
Mc Loud ISD 1,700/K-12
PO Box 240, 405-964-3314
Ronnie Renfrow, supt. Fax 964-2801
www.mcloudschools.us/
Mc Loud ES 900/K-6
PO Box 690, 405-964-3315
Sandra Phillips, prin. Fax 964-2494
Mc Loud JHS 300/7-8
PO Box 730, 405-964-3312
Doug Van Scoyoc, prin. Fax 964-7530

White Rock SD 100/PK-8
RR 2 Box 325, 405-964-3428
Phillip Caffey, supt. Fax 964-3427
White Rock S 100/PK-8
RR 2 Box 325, 405-964-3428
Phillip Caffey, prin. Fax 964-3427

Macomb, Pottawatomie, Pop. 63
Macomb ISD 400/PK-12
36591 Highway 59B 74852 405-598-3892
Doran Smith, supt. Fax 598-8041
www.macomb.k12.ok.us/
Macomb S 300/PK-8
36591 Highway 59B 74852 405-598-2716
Brett Byrum, prin. Fax 598-6529

Madill, Marshall, Pop. 3,688
Madill ISD 1,200/K-12
601 W McArthur St 73446 580-795-3303
Jon Dotson, supt. Fax 795-3210
www.madillok.com
Madill ECC 300/K-1
707 S 12th Ave 73446 580-795-6934
Lynda McDaniel, prin. Fax 795-6939
Madill ES 2-5
701 W Tishomingo St 73446 580-795-3680
James Shipp, prin. Fax 795-3035
Madill MS 400/6-8
601 W McArthur St 73446 580-795-7373
Steve Wilburn, prin. Fax 795-6930

Mangum, Greer, Pop. 2,745
Mangum ISD 700/PK-12
400 N Pennsylvania Ave 73554 580-782-3371
Mike Southall, supt. Fax 782-2313
www.mangum.k12.ok.us/
Edison ES 300/PK-4
201 W Madison St 73554 580-782-2703
Roger Ford, prin. Fax 782-7908
Mangum MS 100/5-6
401 N Oklahoma Ave 73554 580-782-5912
Barbara Gahagan, prin. Fax 782-5914

Mannford, Creek, Pop. 2,758
Mannford ISD 1,500/K-12
136 Evans Ave 74044 918-865-4062
Dr. Emet Callaway, supt. Fax 865-3405
www.mannford.k12.ok.us
Mannford ES 400/K-3
219 Evans Ave 74044 918-865-4334
Robbie Dorsey, prin. Fax 865-2890
Mannford MS 300/6-8
100 Green Valley Rd 74044 918-865-4680
Kelly Spradlin, prin. Fax 865-2862
Mannford Upper ES 200/4-5
100 Green Valley Rd 74044 918-865-3092
Charlotte Parker, prin. Fax 865-6963

Mannsville, Johnston, Pop. 561
Mannsville SD 100/PK-8
PO Box 68 73447 580-371-2892
Robin Hatton, supt. Fax 371-2892
Mannsville S 100/PK-8
PO Box 68 73447 580-371-2892
Robin Hatton, prin. Fax 371-2892

Marble City, Sequoyah, Pop. 249
Marble CSD 200/PK-8
PO Box 10 74945 918-775-2135
Bill London, supt. Fax 775-3019
Marble City S 200/PK-8
PO Box 10 74945 918-775-2135
Bill London, prin. Fax 775-3019

Marietta, Love, Pop. 2,526
Greenville SD 100/PK-8
RR 1 Box 440 73448 580-276-2968
Michelle Taylor, supt. Fax 276-4605
Greenville S 100/PK-8
RR 1 Box 440 73448 580-276-2968
Michelle Taylor, prin. Fax 276-4605

Marietta ISD 900/PK-12
PO Box 289 73448 580-276-9444
James Howard, supt. Fax 276-4037
www.marietta.k12.ok.us
Marietta ES 500/PK-5
PO Box 289 73448 580-276-2455
Ken Chaney, prin. Fax 276-4489
Marietta MS 200/6-8
PO Box 289 73448 580-276-3886
Jeff Dooley, prin. Fax 276-1203

Marlow, Stephens, Pop. 4,531
Bray-Doyle ISD 500/PK-12
1205 S Brooks Rd 73055 580-658-5076
R. Kevin McKinley, supt. Fax 658-5888
Bray-Doyle S 300/PK-8
1205 S Brooks Rd 73055 580-658-5070
Carrie Garrett, prin.

Central High ISD 400/PK-12
RR 3 Box 249 73055 580-658-6858
Bennie Newton, supt. Fax 658-8010
www.centralhighpublicschools.com/
Central S 300/PK-8
RR 3 Box 249 73055 580-658-2970
Leann Johnson, prin. Fax 658-8005

Marlow ISD 1,300/PK-12
PO Box 73 73055 580-658-2719
George Coffman, supt. Fax 658-6455
www.marlow.k12.ok.us
Marlow ES 700/PK-5
PO Box 73 73055 580-658-1541
Kim Kizarr, prin. Fax 658-1540
Marlow MS 300/6-8
PO Box 73 73055 580-658-2619
Kirk Harris, prin. Fax 658-1169

Mason, Okfuskee
Mason ISD 200/PK-12
RR 1 Box 143B 74859 918-623-0231
John Cope, supt. Fax 623-0884
www.mason.k12.ok.us/
Mason S 200/PK-8
RR 1 Box 143B 74859 918-623-2218
Richard Williams, prin. Fax 623-3020

Maud, Pottawatomie, Pop. 1,159
Maud ISD 300/PK-12
PO Box 130 74854 405-374-2416
Gary Parris, supt. Fax 374-2628
www.maud.k12.ok.us
Maud S 200/PK-8
PO Box 130 74854 405-374-2421
Dawna Reynolds, prin. Fax 374-1109

Maysville, Garvin, Pop. 1,296
Maysville ISD 500/PK-12
600 1st St 73057 888-806-5220
William Martin, supt. Fax 867-4864
Maysville S 300/PK-8
600 1st St 73057 888-806-5440
Jeanna Bearden, prin. Fax 867-4046

Medford, Grant, Pop. 1,072
Medford ISD 300/PK-12
301 N Main St 73759 580-395-2392
Mickey Geurkink, supt. Fax 395-2391
www.medford.k12.ok.us/
Medford S 200/PK-8
301 N Main St 73759 580-395-2392
Jay Edelen, prin. Fax 395-2391

Meeker, Lincoln, Pop. 989
Meeker ISD 900/PK-12
214 E Carl Hubbell Blvd 74855 405-279-3511
Rita Palmer, supt. Fax 279-2765
www.meeker.k12.ok.us/
Meeker ES, 400 S Culver St 74855 400/PK-5
Candace Duncan, prin. 405-279-3811
Meeker MS 200/6-8
214 E Carl Hubbell Blvd 74855 405-279-2414
Mike Hill, prin.

Miami, Ottawa, Pop. 13,565
Miami ISD 2,400/K-12
26 N Main St 74354 918-542-8455
William Stephens, supt. Fax 542-1236
www.miami.k12.ok.us
Nichols ES 300/K-5
504 14th Ave NW 74354 918-542-3309
Melony King, prin. Fax 540-7004
Rockdale ES 100/K-5
2116 Rockdale Blvd 74354 918-542-6697
Robyn Barnes, prin. Fax 540-7013
Rogers MS 500/6-8
504 Goodrich Blvd 74354 918-542-5588
David Pendergraft, prin. Fax 542-4400
Roosevelt ES 200/K-5
129 G St NE 74354 918-542-5576
Frank Hecksher, prin. Fax 540-7002
Washington ES 200/K-5
1930 B St NE 74354 918-542-3394
Vicki Lewis, prin. Fax 540-7005
Wilson ES 200/K-5
308 G St NW 74354 918-542-8419
Cindy Machado, prin. Fax 540-7011

Mt. Olive Lutheran S 100/PK-5
2337 N Main St 74354 918-540-3456
Linda Oleman, admin. Fax 540-3456

Midwest City, Oklahoma, Pop. 54,890
Midwest City-Del City ISD 12,400/PK-12
7217 SE 15th St 73110 405-737-4461
William Scoggan M.Ed., supt. Fax 739-1615
www.mid-del.net
Albert MS 600/6-8
2515 S Post Rd 73130 405-739-1761
Joyce Honey, prin. Fax 739-1780
Bailey ES 400/PK-5
3301 Sunvalley Dr 73110 405-739-1656
Linda Laakman, prin. Fax 739-1658
Country Estates ES 300/PK-5
1609 Felix Pl 73110 405-739-1661
Patrice Tucker, prin. Fax 739-1663
East Side ES 400/PK-5
600 N Key Blvd 73110 405-739-1666
Rod Boyer, prin. Fax 739-1655
Jarman MS 300/6-8
5 W McArthur Dr 73110 405-739-1771
Jason Galloway, prin. Fax 739-1773
Monroney MS 400/6-8
7400 E Reno Ave 73110 405-739-1786
Chris Reynolds, prin. Fax 739-1789
Ridgecrest ES 400/PK-5
137 W Ridgewood Dr 73110 405-739-1671
Mike Stiglets, prin. Fax 739-1670
Soldier Creek ES 700/PK-5
9021 SE 15th St 73130 405-739-1676
Neal Johnson, prin. Fax 739-1679
Sooner-Rose ES 400/PK-5
5601 SE 15th St 73110 405-739-1681
LouAnn LeClair, prin. Fax 739-1684
Steed ES 500/PK-5
2118 Flannery Dr 73110 405-739-1686
Dayna Hamilton, prin. Fax 739-1688
Traub ES 300/PK-5
6500 SE 15th St 73110 405-739-1633
Rondall Jones, prin. Fax 739-1795
Other Schools – See Del City, Oklahoma City

Good Shepherd Lutheran S 100/PK-8
700 N Air Depot Blvd 73110 405-732-0070
Jeff Klade, admin. Fax 732-3977
St. Philip Neri S 200/PK-8
1121 Felix Pl 73110 405-737-4496
Mary Dresel, prin. Fax 732-7823

Milburn, Johnston, Pop. 301
Milburn ISD 200/PK-12
PO Box 429 73450 580-443-5522
Jon Holmes, supt. Fax 443-5303
www.milburn.k12.ok.us
Milburn S 100/PK-8
PO Box 429 73450 580-443-5322
Kathy Hays, prin. Fax 443-5303

Milfay, Creek
Milfay SD 100/PK-8
PO Box 219 74046 918-968-2802
Paul Allee, supt. Fax 968-0073
Milfay S 100/PK-8
PO Box 219 74046 918-968-2802
Paul Allee, prin. Fax 968-0073

Mill Creek, Johnston, Pop. 329
Mill Creek ISD 100/PK-12
PO Box 118 74856 580-384-5514
Lorinda Chancellor, supt. Fax 384-3920
www.millcreek.k12.ok.us
Mill Creek S 100/PK-8
PO Box 118 74856 580-384-5505
Chris Grimm, prin. Fax 384-3920

Minco, Grady, Pop. 1,767
Minco ISD 500/PK-12
PO Box 428 73059 405-352-4867
Richard Brownen, supt. Fax 352-4006
www.minco.k12.ok.us
Minco ES, PO Box 428 73059 300/PK-5
Stephen Carroll, prin. 405-352-4324
Minco MS 100/6-8
PO Box 428 73059 405-352-4377
Troy Wittrock, prin. Fax 352-4006

Moffett, Sequoyah, Pop. 178
Moffett SD 300/PK-8
PO Box 180 74946 918-875-3668
John Gordon, supt. Fax 875-3201
Moffett S 300/PK-8
PO Box 180 74946 918-875-3668
John Gordon, prin. Fax 875-3201

Monroe, LeFlore
Monroe SD 100/PK-8
PO Box 10 74947 918-658-3516
Dr. Paul Rainwater, supt. Fax 658-3347
Monroe S 100/PK-8
PO Box 10 74947 918-658-3516
Dr. Paul Rainwater, prin. Fax 658-3347

Moore, Cleveland, Pop. 47,697
Moore ISD 22,300/PK-12
1500 SE 4th St 73160 405-735-4200
Deborah Arato, supt. Fax 735-4392
www.mooreschools.com/
Apple Creek ES 500/PK-6
1101 SE 14th St 73160 405-735-4100
Shelley Jaques-McMillin, prin. Fax 793-3253
Broadmoore ES 600/K-6
3401 S Broadway St 73160 405-735-4120
Kathy Massey, prin. Fax 799-7554
Central ES 600/PK-6
123 NW 2nd St 73160 405-735-4340
Jackie Legg, prin. Fax 793-3289
Houchin ES 500/PK-6
3200 Webster St 73160 405-735-4190
Jason Perez, prin. Fax 912-5608
Kelly ES 500/PK-6
1900 N Janeway Ave 73160 405-735-4400
Kay Engle, prin. Fax 793-3238
Northmoor ES 400/PK-6
211 NE 19th St 73160 405-735-4420
Ben Randall, prin. Fax 912-5514
Plaza Towers ES 600/PK-6
852 SW 11th St 73160 405-735-4430
David Moore, prin. Fax 793-3232
Santa Fe ES 500/PK-6
501 N Santa Fe Ave 73160 405-735-4450
Mike Messerli, prin. Fax 895-6581
Sky Ranch ES 500/K-6
9501 S Western Ave, Oklahoma City OK 73139
405-735-4460
Karie Hill, prin. Fax 692-5653
Southgate-Rippetoe ES 700/PK-6
500 N Norman Ave 73160 405-735-4480
Dena Taylor, prin. Fax 793-3227
Winding Creek ES 600/K-6
1401 NE 12th St 73160 405-735-4510
Kevin McElroy, prin. Fax 793-3273
Other Schools – See Oklahoma City

St. John Lutheran S 100/PK-6
1032 NW 12th St 73160 405-794-8686
Maria Stockstill, admin. Fax 794-1579
Southwest Christian Academy 200/PK-12
1005 SW 4th St Ste A 73160 405-794-9000
Glen Sims, pres. Fax 794-7558

Mooreland, Woodward, Pop. 1,221
Mooreland ISD 500/PK-12
PO Box 75 73852 580-994-5388
Terry Kellner, supt. Fax 994-5900
www.mooreland.k12.ok.us
Mooreland S 300/PK-8
PO Box 75 73852 580-994-5520
Mickey Gregory, prin. Fax 994-5522

Morris, Okmulgee, Pop. 1,326
Morris ISD 1,100/PK-12
PO Box 80 74445 918-733-9072
James Lyons, supt. Fax 733-4205
www.morris.k12.ok.us/
Morris ES 400/PK-5
PO Box 80 74445 918-733-4219
Ronald Martin, prin. Fax 733-9215
Morris MS 200/6-8
PO Box 80 74445 918-733-4551
Greg Large, prin. Fax 733-4618

Morrison, Noble, Pop. 625
Morrison ISD 500/PK-12
PO Box 176 73061 580-724-3341
Jay Vernon, supt. Fax 724-3004
www.morrison.k12.ok.us
Morrison ES, PO Box 176 73061 300/PK-8
Linda Rieman, prin. 580-724-3620

Mounds, Creek, Pop. 1,278
Liberty ISD 600/PK-12
2727 E 201st St S 74047 918-366-8496
Donna Campo, supt. Fax 366-8497
www.liberty.k12.ok.us
Liberty S, 2727 E 201st St S 74047 400/PK-8
Cheryl Debolt, prin. 918-366-8311

Mounds ISD 500/PK-12
PO Box 189 74047 918-827-6100
Gary Lundy, supt. Fax 827-3704
www.mounds.k12.ok.us/
Mounds ES 300/PK-4
PO Box 189 74047 918-827-6897
Yvette Britt, prin. Fax 827-6897
Mounds MS 5-8
PO Box 189 74047 918-827-6300
Kelly Berry, prin. Fax 827-3703

Mountain View, Kiowa, Pop. 830
Mountain View-Gotebo ISD 300/PK-12
RR 2 Box 88 73062 580-347-2211
Paula Squires, supt. Fax 347-2869
Mountain View-Gotebo S 200/PK-8
RR 2 Box 88 73062 580-347-2214
Karen Mason, prin.

Moyers, Pushmataha
Moyers ISD 100/K-12
PO Box 88 74557 580-298-5549
Donna Dudley, supt. Fax 298-2022
www.moyers.k12.ok.us/
Moyers S 100/K-8
PO Box 88 74557 580-298-5547
Donna Dudley, prin. Fax 298-2022

Muldrow, Sequoyah, Pop. 3,168
Belfonte SD 100/PK-8
475751 State Highway 101 74948 918-427-3522
Paul Pinkerton, supt. Fax 427-1288
Belfonte S 100/PK-8
475751 State Highway 101 74948 918-427-3522
Paul Pinkerton, prin. Fax 427-1288

Liberty SD 300/PK-8
476490 E 1060 Rd 74948 918-427-3808
Jeff Ransom, supt. Fax 427-4961
Liberty S 300/PK-8
476490 E 1060 Rd 74948 918-427-3808
Jeff Ransom, prin. Fax 427-4961

Muldrow ISD 1,800/PK-12
PO Box 660 74948 918-427-7406
Roger Sharp, supt. Fax 427-6088
www.muldrow.k12.ok.us
Muldrow ES 700/PK-4
PO Box 550 74948 918-427-3316
Stephen Michael, prin. Fax 427-1033
Muldrow MS 500/5-8
PO Box 660 74948 918-427-5421
Montea Wight, prin. Fax 427-1034

Mulhall, Logan, Pop. 256
Mulhall-Orlando ISD
Supt. — See Orlando
Mulhall-Orlando S 200/PK-8
215 S Lewis St 73063 405-649-2000
Mat Luse, prin. Fax 649-2020

Muskogee, Muskogee, Pop. 39,766
Hilldale ISD 1,800/PK-12
500 E Smith Ferry Rd 74403 918-683-0273
D. B. Merrill, supt. Fax 683-8725
www.hilldale.k12.ok.us
Hilldale Lower ES 500/PK-2
3301 Grandview Park Blvd 74403 918-683-9167
Faye Garrison, prin. Fax 683-9204
Hilldale MS 400/6-8
400 E Smith Ferry Rd 74403 918-683-0763
Darren Riddle, prin. Fax 683-0766
Hilldale Upper ES 400/3-5
315 E Peak Blvd 74403 918-683-1101
Faye Garrison, prin. Fax 683-0556

Muskogee ISD 6,300/PK-12
202 W Broadway St 74401 918-684-3700
Michael Garde, supt. Fax 684-3827
www.mpsi20.org
Cherokee ES 300/K-6
2400 Estelle Ave 74401 918-684-3890
Daphne Cotton, prin. Fax 684-3891
Creek ES 400/K-6
200 S Country Club Rd 74403 918-684-3880
Rick Hoos, prin. Fax 684-3881
Franklin Science Academy 400/K-8
300 Virgil Matthews Dr 74401 918-684-3870
Peggy Jones, prin. Fax 684-3871
Goetz ES 400/K-6
2412 Haskell Blvd 74403 918-684-3810
Malinda Lindsey, prin. Fax 684-3811
Grant-Foreman ES 400/K-6
800 S Bacone St 74403 918-684-3860
Kerry Hillmon, prin. Fax 684-3861
Harris-Jobe ES 200/K-6
2809 N Country Club Rd 74403 918-684-3850
Kim Fleak, prin. Fax 684-3851
Irving ES 400/K-6
1100 N J St 74403 918-684-3840
P. David Shouse, prin. Fax 684-3841
Muskogee 7th & 8th Grade Center 700/7-8
402 N S St 74403 918-684-3775
Debra Barger, prin. Fax 684-3776
Muskogee ECC 400/PK-PK
901 Emporia St 74401 918-684-3770
Debra Horsechief, prin. Fax 684-3771
Pershing ES 300/K-6
301 N 54th St 74401 918-684-3830
Vickie Albin, prin. Fax 684-3831
Sadler Arts Academy 300/K-8
800 Altamont St 74401 918-684-3820
Maudye Winget, prin. Fax 684-3821
Whittier ES 300/K-6
1705 E Cincinnati Ave 74403 918-684-3800
Ed Wallace, prin. Fax 684-3801

St. Joseph Catholic S 100/PK-8
323 N Virginia St 74403 918-683-1291
Sandy Brewer, prin. Fax 682-5374

Mustang, Canadian, Pop. 15,887
Mustang ISD 7,900/PK-12
906 S Heights Dr 73064 405-376-2461
Bonnie Lightfoot, supt. Fax 376-7803
www.mustangps.org
Lakehoma ES 800/K-5
906 S Heights Dr 73064 405-376-2409
Shawna Carter, prin. Fax 376-7348
Mustang Centennial ES K-5
906 S Heights Dr 73064 405-256-6466
Neil Womack, prin. Fax 256-6661
Mustang Education Center 300/PK-PK
906 S Heights Dr 73064 405-376-7322
Michael Ossenkop, prin. Fax 376-9079
Mustang ES 700/K-5
906 S Heights Dr 73064 405-376-2491
Laquita Semmler, prin. Fax 376-7338
Mustang MS 900/6-8
906 S Heights Dr 73064 405-376-2448
Linda Wilkes, prin. Fax 376-7373
Mustang North MS 800/6-8
906 S Heights Dr 73064 405-324-2236
Dan Allen, prin. Fax 324-2258
Other Schools – See Yukon

Christ Lutheran S 50/PK-K
501 N Clear Springs Rd 73064 405-376-4235
Mabel Mailand, coord. Fax 376-3118

Mutual, Woodward, Pop. 78
Sharon-Mutual ISD 300/PK-12
RR 1 Box 290 73853 580-989-3210
Emma Sidders, supt. Fax 989-3241
www.smps.k12.ok.us
Other Schools – See Sharon

Nashoba, Pushmataha
Nashoba SD 100/PK-8
PO Box 17 74558 918-755-4343
Marcia Wright, supt. Fax 755-4418
www.nashoba.k12.ok.us/
Nashoba S 100/PK-8
PO Box 17 74558 918-755-4343
Marcia Wright, prin. Fax 755-4418

Newcastle, McClain, Pop. 6,303
Newcastle ISD 1,400/PK-12
101 N Main St 73065 405-387-2890
Robert Everett, supt. Fax 387-3482
www.newcastle.k12.ok.us
Newcastle ES 700/PK-5
410 NW 10th St 73065 405-387-5188
Mark Park, prin. Fax 387-4890
Newcastle MS 300/6-8
418 NW 10th St 73065 405-387-3139
Joey Billington, prin. Fax 387-5563

Newkirk, Kay, Pop. 2,162
Newkirk ISD 700/PK-12
PO Box 91 74647 580-362-2388
Carl Barnes, supt. Fax 362-3413
www.newkirk.k12.ok.us
Newkirk ES, PO Box 288 74647 300/PK-4
Pam Hunter, prin. 580-362-2279
Newkirk MS 200/5-8
PO Box 485 74647 580-362-2516
Jim Wiersig, prin. Fax 362-1150

Peckham SD 100/PK-8
7175 W School St 74647 580-362-2633
Gary Young, supt. Fax 362-3970
Peckham S 100/PK-8
7175 W School St 74647 580-362-2633
Gary Young, prin. Fax 362-3970

Nicoma Park, Oklahoma, Pop. 2,388
Choctaw-Nicoma Park ISD
Supt. — See Choctaw

Nicoma Park ES 300/PK-2
PO Box 947 73066 405-769-2445
Dorothy Shetley, prin. Fax 769-5067

Ninnekah, Grady, Pop. 1,046
Ninnekah ISD 500/PK-12
PO Box 275 73067 405-224-4092
Todd Bunch, supt. Fax 224-4096
www.ninnekah.ok.nph.schoolinsites.com/
Ninnekah ES 300/PK-6
PO Box 275 73067 405-222-0420
Steve Callen, prin. Fax 222-3371
Ninnekah JHS 100/7-8
PO Box 275 73067 405-224-4299
David Pitts, prin. Fax 224-4665

Noble, Cleveland, Pop. 5,518
Noble ISD 2,900/PK-12
PO Box 499 73068 405-872-3452
Greg Kasbaum, supt. Fax 872-3271
www.nobleps.com
Daily ES 600/PK-1
300 S 5th St 73068 405-872-3406
Kathy Hallmark, prin. Fax 872-7699
Hubbard ES 400/2-3
1104 E Maguire Rd 73068 405-872-9201
Nathan Gray, prin. Fax 872-7680
Inge MS 600/6-8
1201 N 8th St 73068 405-872-3495
Steve Barrett, prin. Fax 872-8670
Pioneer IS 400/4-5
611 Ash St 73068 405-872-3472
Karen Canfield, prin. Fax 872-9135

Norman, Cleveland, Pop. 101,719
Little Axe ISD 1,300/PK-12
2000 168th Ave NE 73026 405-329-7691
Barry Damrill, supt. Fax 579-2929
littleaxe.k12.ok.us
Little Axe ES 600/PK-5
2000 168th Ave NE 73026 405-447-0913
Sandra Staton, prin. Fax 579-2976
Little Axe MS 300/6-8
2000 168th Ave NE 73026 405-329-2156
Dalton Griffin, prin. Fax 579-2937

Norman ISD 13,100/PK-12
131 S Flood Ave 73069 405-364-1339
Dr. Joseph Siano, supt. Fax 366-5851
www.norman.k12.ok.us
Adams ES 500/PK-5
817 Denison Dr 73069 405-366-5972
Linda Baxter, prin. Fax 366-5975
Alcott MS 600/6-8
1919 W Boyd St 73069 405-366-5845
Dana Morris, prin. Fax 447-6572
Cleveland ES 500/PK-5
500 N Sherry Ave 73069 405-366-5875
Ty Bell, prin. Fax 366-5877
Eisenhower ES 500/PK-5
1415 Fairlawn Dr 73071 405-366-5879
Susan Powell, prin. Fax 573-3503
Irving MS 600/6-8
125 Vicksburg Ave 73071 405-366-5941
Jerry Privett, prin. Fax 366-5944
Jackson ES 400/PK-5
520 Wylie Rd 73069 405-366-5884
Dr. Craig Stevens, prin. Fax 447-6563
Jefferson ES 400/PK-5
250 N Cockrel Ave 73071 405-366-5889
Dr. Kathy Taber, prin. Fax 366-5892
Kennedy ES 400/PK-5
621 Sunrise St 73071 405-366-5894
Chris Crelia, prin. Fax 366-5896
Lakeview ES 200/PK-5
3310 108th Ave NE 73026 405-366-5899
Paula Palermo, prin. Fax 366-5901
Lincoln ES 300/PK-5
915 Classen Blvd 73071 405-366-5904
Kathy Crabtree, prin. Fax 366-5906
Longfellow MS 600/6-8
215 N Ponca Ave 73071 405-366-5948
Darien Moore, prin. Fax 366-5952
Madison ES 500/PK-5
500 James Dr 73072 405-366-5910
Pam Charlson, prin. Fax 366-5912
McKinley ES 300/PK-5
728 S Flood Ave 73069 405-366-5914
Terry Hopper, prin. Fax 366-5916
Monroe ES 400/PK-5
1601 McGee Dr 73072 405-366-5927
Gracie Branch, prin. Fax 366-5930
Roosevelt ES 500/PK-5
4250 W Tecumseh Rd 73072 405-447-6581
Beth Spears, prin. Fax 447-6583
Truman ES 700/PK-5
600 Parkside Rd 73072 405-366-5980
Kristie Eselin, prin. Fax 366-5988
Washington ES 600/PK-5
600 48th Ave SE 73026 405-366-5984
Dr. Linda Parsons, prin. Fax 366-5960
Whittier MS 900/6-8
2000 W Brooks St 73069 405-366-5956
Holly Swanson, prin. Fax 447-6562
Wilson ES 200/PK-5
800 N Peters Ave 73069 405-366-5932
Cherrie Birden, prin. Fax 366-5934

Robin Hill SD 200/PK-8
4801 E Franklin Rd 73026 405-321-4186
James Martin, supt. Fax 321-5179
www.robinhill.k12.ok.us
Robin Hill S 200/PK-8
4801 E Franklin Rd 73026 405-321-4186
James Martin, prin. Fax 321-5179

All Saints S 400/PK-8
4001 36th Ave NW 73072 405-447-4600
Leslie Schmitt, prin. Fax 447-7227
Blue Eagle Christian Academy 50/PK-12
2404 Classen Blvd 73071 405-364-7200
Bertha Symes, admin.
Children's House of Norman Inc 100/PK-K
606 S Santa Fe Ave 73069 405-321-1275
Susan Jones Jensen, prin.
Community Christian S 700/PK-12
3002 Broce Dr 73072 405-329-2500
Barbara Ohsfeldt, admin. Fax 329-3510

Trinity Lutheran S 50/PK-6
603 Classen Blvd 73071 405-329-1503
Christine Lee, prin. Fax 928-2686

Nowata, Nowata, Pop. 4,034
Nowata ISD 1,100/PK-12
707 W Osage Ave 74048 918-273-3425
Fred Bailey, supt. Fax 273-2105
www.nowataps.k12.ok.us/
Moore ES 500/PK-5
707 W Osage Ave 74048 918-273-0771
Michelle Miller, prin. Fax 273-2105
Nowata MS 300/6-8
707 W Osage Ave 74048 918-273-1346
Kathy Berry, prin. Fax 273-2105

Oaks, Delaware, Pop. 422
Oaks-Mission ISD 300/PK-12
PO Box 160 74359 918-868-2183
Wyman Thompson, supt. Fax 868-2707
Oaks-Mission S 200/PK-8
PO Box 160 74359 918-868-2455
Barbara Tucker, prin. Fax 868-5013

Oilton, Creek, Pop. 1,143
Oilton ISD 300/PK-12
PO Box 130 74052 918-862-3954
Matt Posey, supt. Fax 862-3955
Kennedy S 200/PK-8
PO Box 130 74052 918-862-3215
Scott Woodson, prin. Fax 862-3763

Okarche, Kingfisher, Pop. 1,158
Okarche ISD 300/PK-12
PO Box 276 73762 405-263-7300
Robert Barnett, supt. Fax 263-7515
www.okarche.k12.ok.us/
Okarche ES 100/PK-6
PO Box 276 73762 405-263-4447
Traci Fuller, prin. Fax 263-7515

Holy Trinity S 100/PK-8
PO Box 485 73762 405-263-4422
Tammy Jacobs, prin. Fax 263-9753
St. John Lutheran S 50/PK-PK
201 S 5th St 73762 405-263-4488
Jeff Klade, admin. Fax 263-7565

Okay, Wagoner, Pop. 593
Okay ISD 500/PK-12
PO Box 830 74446 918-682-2548
Mickey Igert, supt. Fax 683-8331
www.okayschool.k12.ok.us/
Okay S 300/PK-8
PO Box 830 74446 918-682-7961
Mike Lasater, prin. Fax 682-6532

Okeene, Blaine, Pop. 1,210
Okeene ISD 300/K-12
PO Box 409 73763 580-822-3268
Ron Pittman, supt. Fax 822-4123
www.okeene.k12.ok.us
Okeene ES 100/K-6
PO Box 409 73763 580-822-3425
Jeff Wardlaw, prin. Fax 822-4769

Okemah, Okfuskee, Pop. 2,970
Bearden SD 100/PK-8
RR 2 Box 52A 74859 918-623-0156
Leon McVeigh, supt. Fax 623-0156
www.bearden.k12.ok.us
Bearden S 100/PK-8
RR 2 Box 52A 74859 918-623-0156
Danielle Deere, prin. Fax 623-0156

Okemah ISD 800/PK-12
107 W Date St 74859 918-623-1874
Tom Condict, supt. Fax 623-1203
www.okemah.k12.ok.us
Oakes ES 300/PK-3
101 N 16th St 74859 918-623-1744
MaryAnn Tinsley, prin. Fax 623-2465
Okemah MS 200/4-8
107 W Date St 74859 918-623-0212
Tony Dean, prin. Fax 623-9151

Oklahoma City, Oklahoma, Pop. 531,324
Crooked Oak ISD 1,100/PK-12
1901 SE 15th St 73129 405-677-5252
Kathy Draper, supt. Fax 670-8070
www.crookedoak.org/
Central Oak ES 300/2-5
1901 SE 15th St 73129 405-677-5211
Kim Templeman, prin.
Crooked Oak MS 200/6-8
1901 SE 15th St 73129 405-677-5133
Richard Wallace, prin.
West Oak Park ES 300/PK-1
1901 SE 15th St 73129 405-677-6212
Kim Templeman, prin.

Crutcho SD 200/PK-8
2401 N Air Depot Blvd 73141 405-427-3771
Teresa McAfee, supt. Fax 427-3816
www.crutchoesd.org
Crutcho S 200/PK-8
2401 N Air Depot Blvd 73141 405-427-3771
Yolanda Alexander, prin. Fax 427-3816

Midwest City-Del City ISD
Supt. — See Midwest City
Barnes ES 400/PK-5
10551 SE 59th St 73150 405-739-1651
Vicki Vetter, prin. Fax 739-1653
Highland Park ES 500/PK-5
5301 S Dimple Dr 73135 405-671-8660
Dr. Donna Cloud, prin. Fax 671-8661
Parkview ES 600/PK-5
5701 Mackelman Dr 73135 405-671-8670
Bryan Kalsu, prin. Fax 671-8672
Pleasant Hill ES 100/PK-5
4346 NE 36th St 73121 405-427-6551
Nathan Boylan, prin. Fax 427-6552
Schwartz ES 300/PK-5
12001 SE 104th St 73165 405-794-4703
Johnny Thompson, prin. Fax 794-2178
Tinker ES 500/PK-5
4500 Tinker Rd 73135 405-739-1630
Carroll Asseo, prin. Fax 739-1635

Millwood ISD 1,000/PK-12
6724 N Martin Luther King 73111 405-478-1336
Dr. Gloria Griffin, supt. Fax 478-4698
www.millwood.k12.ok.us
Millwood Arts Academy 4-8
6700 N Martin Luther King 73111 405-478-0630
Christine Harrison, prin.
Millwood S 800/PK-8
6710 N Martin Luther King 73111 405-475-1004
Michael Prior, prin.

Moore ISD
Supt. — See Moore
Bonds ES 600/PK-6
14025 S May Ave 73170 405-735-4500
Michelle McNear, prin. Fax 692-6260
Briarwood ES 600/K-6
14901 S Hudson Ave 73170 405-735-4110
Dr. Loretta Autry, prin. Fax 793-3283
Bryant ES 600/K-6
9400 S Bryant Ave 73160 405-735-4130
Jo Clark, prin. Fax 793-2737
Earlywine ES 500/PK-6
12800 S May Ave 73170 405-735-4150
Chris Bolen, prin. Fax 692-5659
Eastlake ES 500/K-6
1301 SW 134th St 73170 405-735-4160
Johnny Bailey, prin. Fax 692-5763
Fairview ES 600/PK-6
2431 SW 89th St 73159 405-735-4170
Shannon Thompson, prin. Fax 682-5521
Fisher ES 500/K-6
11800 Southwood Dr 73170 405-735-4180
Becky Jackson, prin. Fax 692-5673
Kingsgate ES 500/PK-6
1400 Kingsgate Rd 73159 405-735-4410
Dan Neugent, prin. Fax 692-5643
Red Oak ES 500/PK-6
11224 S Pennsylvania Ave 73170 405-735-4440
Peggy Matlock, prin. Fax 692-5678
Sooner ES 600/K-6
5420 SE 89th St 73135 405-735-4470
Jamie Chuculate, prin. Fax 672-6498

Oklahoma City ISD 34,300/PK-12
900 N Klein Ave 73106 405-587-0000
Karl Springer, supt. Fax 587-0443
www.okcps.org/
Adams ES 600/PK-6
3416 SW 37th St 73119 405-685-5811
Dorothy Violett, prin. Fax 686-4013
Arthur ES 500/PK-5
5100 S Independence Ave 73119 405-685-9553
Barbara Hess, prin. Fax 686-4018
Belle Isle Enterprise MS 400/6-8
5904 N Villa Ave 73112 405-843-0888
Lynn Kellert, prin. Fax 841-3127
Bodine ES 600/PK-5
5301 S Bryant Ave 73129 405-231-2000
John Pundsack, prin. Fax 672-6274
Britton ES 300/PK-5
1215 NW 95th St 73114 405-751-2245
Kim Zachery, prin. Fax 752-6813
Buchanan ES 400/PK-5
4126 NW 18th St 73107 405-942-2049
Scott Kaufman, prin. Fax 945-1135
Capitol Hill ES 1,000/PK-6
2717 S Robinson Ave 73109 405-235-3531
Laura Morris, prin. Fax 231-2040
Cleveland ES 300/PK-5
2725 NW 23rd St 73107 405-945-1150
Max Miller, prin. Fax 945-1153
Columbus Enterprise ES 700/PK-6
2402 S Pennsylvania Ave 73108 405-632-3012
Phil Cunningham, prin. Fax 636-5033
Coolidge ES 600/PK-5
5212 S Villa Ave 73119 405-685-2777
Dr. Sue Greenfield, prin. Fax 686-4023
Dunbar ES 200/PK-6
1432 NE 7th St 73117 405-235-5326
Leota Bettes, prin. Fax 231-2019
Edgemere ES 200/PK-6
3200 N Walker Ave 73118 405-524-2941
Dennis Gentry, prin. Fax 556-5027
Edwards ES 100/PK-6
1123 NE Grand Blvd 73117 405-427-3800
Dr. Earline Peterson, prin. Fax 425-4617
Eisenhower ES 400/PK-5
2401 NW 115th Ter 73120 405-841-3111
Angela Houston, prin. Fax 478-3646
Field ES 600/PK-5
1515 N Klein Ave 73106 405-524-6625
Dr. Wilbur House, prin. Fax 556-5017
Fillmore ES 700/PK-5
5200 S Blackwelder Ave 73119 405-634-1878
Susan Martin, prin. Fax 636-5037
Gatewood ES 200/PK-5
1821 NW 21st St 73106 405-524-4008
Melissa Lawson, prin. Fax 556-5021
Hawthorne ES 400/PK-5
2300 NW 15th St 73107 405-524-5644
Randy Brewer, prin. Fax 556-5029
Hayes ES 400/PK-6
6900 S Byers Ave 73149 405-632-0752
Marionette Gibson, prin. Fax 636-5043
Heronville ES 600/PK-5
1240 SW 29th St 73109 405-634-7957
Cynthia Barchue, prin. Fax 636-5048
Hillcrest ES 500/PK-5
6421 S Miller Blvd 73159 405-685-2660
Betsy Davidson, prin. Fax 686-4028
Jackson MS 600/6-8
2601 S Villa Ave 73108 405-634-6357
Steve Johnson, prin. Fax 636-5078
Jefferson MS 900/6-8
6800 S Blackwelder Ave 73159 405-632-2341
Gloria Torres, prin. Fax 636-5084
Johnson ES 200/PK-5
1810 Sheffield Rd 73120 405-843-6216
Karen Simpkins, prin. Fax 841-3114
Kaiser ES 300/PK-5
3101 Lyon Blvd 73112 405-943-3571
Pam Mustain, prin. Fax 945-1137
King ES 400/PK-6
1201 NE 48th St 73111 405-587-4000
Dr. Norma Simpson, prin. Fax 587-4090

Lee ES 600/PK-5
424 SW 29th St 73109 405-634-5685
Fred Pahlke, prin. Fax 636-5053
Linwood ES 300/PK-5
3416 NW 17th St 73107 405-943-5623
Susan Combs, prin. Fax 945-1139
Madison ES 200/PK-5
3117 N Independence Ave 73112 405-943-1257
Lesla Tilley, prin. Fax 945-1116
Mann ES 300/PK-5
1105 NW 45th St 73118 405-587-3500
Dr. Judy Jones, prin. Fax 587-3505
Monroe ES 400/PK-5
4810 N Linn Ave 73112 405-942-4479
Chuck Tompkins, prin. Fax 945-1140
Moon Acad of Mass Media & Tech 300/PK-6
1901 NE 13th St 73117 405-427-8391
Ycedra Daughty, prin. Fax 425-4643
Nichols Hills ES 400/K-5
1301 W Wilshire Blvd 73116 405-841-3160
Carol Berry, prin. Fax 841-3163
North Highland Math & Science Academy 300/PK-5
8400 N Robinson Ave 73114 405-843-7957
Gloria Anderson, prin. Fax 841-3119
Oakridge ES 200/PK-5
4200 Leonhardt Dr 73115 405-231-2095
Susan Robertson, prin. Fax 672-6551
Parks ES 300/PK-5
1501 NE 30th St 73111 405-425-4670
Ricki Kelley, prin. Fax 425-4673
Parmelee ES 700/K-5
6700 S Hudson Ave 73139 405-632-6773
Jan Parks, prin. Fax 636-5064
Pierce ES 200/PK-5
2701 S Tulsa Ave 73108 405-685-1988
Jenny Vesper, prin. Fax 686-4033
Prairie Queen ES 600/PK-5
6609 S Blackwelder Ave 73159 405-681-2944
Jacqueline Horton, prin. Fax 686-4038
Putnam Heights ES 300/PK-5
1601 NW 36th St 73118 405-524-3049
Oliver Stripling, prin. Fax 556-5037
Quail Creek ES 400/PK-5
11700 Thorn Ridge Rd 73120 405-751-3231
Dr. Janice Matthews, prin. Fax 752-6817
Rancho Village ES 200/PK-5
1401 Johnston Dr 73119 405-634-1303
Gay Littlepage, prin. Fax 636-5049
Ridgeview ES 400/PK-5
10010 Ridgeview Dr 73120 405-587-6800
Natalie Johnson, prin. Fax 587-6805
Rockwood ES 500/PK-5
3101 SW 24th St 73108 405-685-5444
Gilbert Oliver, prin. Fax 686-4043
Roosevelt MS 800/6-8
3233 SW 44th St 73119 405-685-7795
Marilyn Vrooman, prin. Fax 686-4059
Sequoyah ES 400/PK-5
2400 NW 36th St 73112 405-946-2266
Montie Koehn, prin. Fax 945-1145
Shidler ES 300/PK-5
1415 S Byers Ave 73129 405-632-1070
Cathy Eyherabide, prin. Fax 636-5085
Southern Hills ES 400/PK-5
7800 S Kentucky Ave 73159 405-681-5433
Alice Loftin, prin. Fax 686-4047
Stand Watie ES 400/PK-5
3517 S Linn Ave 73119 405-681-2266
Rick Brown, prin. Fax 686-4052
Stonegate ES 500/PK-5
2525 NW 112th St 73120 405-751-3663
Carol Perry, prin. Fax 752-6828
Taft MS 900/6-8
2901 NW 23rd St 73107 405-946-1431
Lisa Johnson, prin. Fax 945-1126
Telstar ES 300/PK-5
9521 NE 16th St 73130 405-587-8900
Patricia Hunt, prin. Fax 587-8905
Twain ES 200/PK-5
2451 W Main St 73107 405-232-3724
Sandy Phillips, prin. Fax 231-2026
Van Buren ES 500/PK-5
2700 SW 40th St 73119 405-686-4080
Veleasha Stewart, prin. Fax 686-4083
Webster MS 700/6-8
6708 S Santa Fe Ave 73139 405-632-6653
Donna Lay, prin. Fax 636-5096
West Nichols Hills ES 400/PK-5
8400 Greystone Ave 73120 405-843-4218
John Addison, prin. Fax 841-3124
Westwood ES 300/PK-5
1701 Exchange Ave 73108 405-235-8810
Dr. Jan Borelli, prin. Fax 231-2060
Wheeler Community Learning Center 400/PK-6
501 SE 25th St 73129 405-587-7001
Sharon Creager, prin. Fax 587-7098
Willow Brook ES 500/PK-5
8105 NE 10th St 73110 405-771-2100
Arthur Houston, prin. Fax 741-6431
Wilson ES 300/PK-5
2215 N Walker Ave 73103 405-524-1140
Beverly Story, prin. Fax 556-5042
Other Schools – See Spencer

Putnam City ISD 18,600/PK-12
5401 NW 40th St 73122 405-495-5200
Paul Hurst, supt. Fax 495-8648
www.putnamcityschools.org
Capps MS 800/6-8
4020 N Grove Ave 73122 405-787-3660
Christie Baker, prin. Fax 491-7536
Cooper MS 800/6-8
8001 River Bend Blvd 73132 405-720-9887
Jennifer DeSouza, prin. Fax 728-5632
Coronado Heights ES 500/PK-5
5911 N Sapulpa Ave 73112 405-942-8593
Bart Daniel, prin. Fax 948-9014
Dennis ES 500/K-5
11800 James L Dennis Dr 73162 405-722-6510
Vivi Grigsby, prin. Fax 728-5613
Downs ES 600/PK-5
7501 W Hefner Rd 73162 405-721-4431
Dr. Nona Burling, prin. Fax 728-5625
Harvest Hills ES 400/K-5
8201 NW 104th St 73162 405-721-2013
Mickey Wilson, prin. Fax 728-5637
Hefner MS 1,100/6-8
8400 N MacArthur Blvd 73132 405-721-2411
Lise Finley, prin. Fax 728-5645
Hilldale ES 600/PK-5
4801 NW 16th St 73127 405-942-8600
Lynn Johnson, prin. Fax 948-9009
Kirkland ES 300/PK-5
6020 N Independence Ave 73112 405-842-1491
Bill Pierce, prin. Fax 842-5156
Mayfield MS 600/6-8
1600 N Purdue Ave 73127 405-947-8693
Dr. Dick Balenseifen, prin. Fax 948-9000
Northridge ES 600/K-5
8502 NW 82nd St 73132 405-722-5560
Randy Rader, prin. Fax 728-5649
Post ES 600/PK-5
6920 W Britton Rd 73132 405-721-8123
Stephanie Treadway, prin. Fax 728-5622
Rogers ES 400/K-5
8201 NW 122nd St 73142 405-722-9797
Pam Miller, prin. Fax 728-5636
Rollingwood ES 500/PK-5
6301 N Ann Arbor Ave 73122 405-721-3644
Debbie Hamilton, prin. Fax 728-5616
Tulakes ES 500/PK-5
6600 Galaxie Dr 73132 405-721-4360
Lee Roland, prin. Fax 728-5618
Windsor Hills ES 600/PK-5
2909 N Ann Arbor Ave 73127 405-942-8673
Renita White, prin. Fax 948-9006
Other Schools – See Bethany, Warr Acres

Western Heights ISD 3,300/PK-12
8401 SW 44th St 73179 405-350-3410
Joe Kitchens, supt. Fax 745-6322
www.westernheights.k12.ok.us
Council Grove ES 400/PK-5
7721 Melrose Ln 73127 405-350-3465
Phylis Hadley, prin. Fax 495-6620
Glenn ES 600/PK-5
6501 S Land Ave 73159 405-350-3480
Archie Scott, prin. Fax 681-8632
Greenvale ES 400/PK-5
901 Greenvale Rd 73127 405-350-3470
Diane Klein, prin. Fax 787-6539
Western Heights MS 700/6-8
8435 SW 44th St 73179 405-350-3455
Jennifer Colvin, prin. Fax 745-6341
Winds West ES 500/PK-5
8300 SW 37th St 73179 405-350-3475
Melissa Yarbrough, prin. Fax 745-2580

Antioch Christian Academy 100/K-8
3616 SW 119th St 73170 405-691-8012
Annette Schrag, prin. Fax 691-2697
Bishop John Carroll S 200/PK-8
1100 NW 32nd St 73118 405-525-0956
Connie Diotte, prin. Fax 523-3053
Casady S 900/PK-12
PO Box 20390 73156 405-749-3100
Christopher Bright, hdmstr. Fax 749-3214
Central SDA S 50/K-9
4747 NW 63rd St 73132 405-722-9703
Sueli Menezes, admin. Fax 722-9703
Christ the King S 400/PK-8
1905 Elmhurst Ave 73120 405-843-3909
Karen Carter, prin. Fax 843-6519
Crossings Christian S 400/PK-12
14400 N Portland Ave 73134 405-842-8495
Al King, hdmstr. Fax 767-1520
Gethsemane Lutheran S 50/PK-8
8811 W Wilshire Blvd 73132 405-721-1167
Daniel Johnson, prin. Fax 721-1167
Heritage Hall S 900/PK-12
1800 NW 122nd St 73120 405-749-3001
Guy Bramble, hdmstr. Fax 751-7372
Life Christian Academy 200/PK-12
6801 S Anderson Rd 73150 405-737-4902
Rodney Burchett, admin. Fax 869-9151
Messiah Lutheran S 100/PK-6
3600 NW Expressway 73112 405-946-0462
Sharla Lindley, admin. Fax 946-0682
Parkview Adventist Academy 100/K-10
4201 N Martin Luther King 73111 405-427-6525
Karen Murcia, admin. Fax 427-1154
Rosary S 200/PK-8
1910 NW 19th St 73106 405-525-9272
Karen Lynn, prin. Fax 525-5643
Sacred Heart S 200/PK-8
2700 S Shartel Ave 73109 405-634-5673
Joana Camacho, prin. Fax 634-7011
St. Charles Borromeo S 200/PK-8
5000 N Grove Ave 73122 405-789-0224
Joseph Sine, prin. Fax 789-3583
St. Eugene S 400/PK-8
PO Box 20930 73156 405-751-0067
Suzette Williams, prin. Fax 302-4254
St. James S 200/PK-8
1224 SW 41st St 73109 405-636-6810
Deborah Taber, prin. Fax 636-6818
St. John Christian Heritage Academy 100/PK-7
5700 N Kelley Ave 73111 405-478-8607
Dr. Betty Mason, prin. Fax 418-0043
Victory Academy 100/PK-12
1630 SW 74th St 73159 405-688-8000
Julie Moore, dir. Fax 686-0888
Villa Teresa-Moore K 100/PK-K
13501 S Western Ave 73170 405-691-7737
Ann Grover, dir. Fax 691-7981
Villa Teresa S 200/PK-4
1216 Classen Dr 73103 405-232-4286
Veronica Higgins, prin. Fax 552-2658
Westminister S 500/PK-8
600 NW 44th St 73118 405-524-0631
Robert Vernon, hdmstr. Fax 528-4412

Okmulgee, Okmulgee, Pop. 12,854
Okmulgee ISD 1,800/PK-12
PO Box 1346 74447 918-758-2000
Paul McGee, supt. Fax 758-2088
www.okmulgee.k12.ok.us
Okmulgee ES 400/3-5
1614 E 9th St 74447 918-758-2020
Carolyn Cope, prin. Fax 758-2090
Okmulgee MS 400/6-8
1421 Martin Luther King Dr 74447 918-758-2050
John Whitfield, prin. Fax 758-2095
Okmulgee PS 600/PK-2
1003 N Okmulgee Ave 74447 918-758-2030
James Clifford, prin. Fax 758-2093

Twin Hills SD 300/PK-8
7255 Twin Hills Rd 74447 918-733-2531
Robert Pinkston, supt. Fax 733-2861
Twin Hills S 300/PK-8
7255 Twin Hills Rd 74447 918-733-2531
Robert Pinkston, prin. Fax 733-2861

Oktaha, Muskogee, Pop. 334
Oktaha ISD 700/PK-12
PO Box 9 74450 918-687-7556
Jerry Needham, supt. Fax 687-0074
Oktaha S, PO Box 9 74450 500/PK-8
Tom Owens, prin. 918-682-5665

Olustee, Jackson, Pop. 645
Olustee ISD 200/PK-12
PO Box 70 73560 580-648-2243
Roger Allen, supt. Fax 648-2501
www.olustee.k12.ok.us
Olustee S 100/PK-8
PO Box 70 73560 580-648-2243
H. Mitchell, prin. Fax 648-2501

Omega, Kingfisher
Lomega ISD 200/PK-12
RR 1 Box 46 73764 405-729-4215
Steve Mendell, supt. Fax 729-4666
www.lomega.k12.ok.us
Other Schools – See Loyal

Oologah, Rogers, Pop. 1,121
Oologah-Talala ISD 1,700/K-12
PO Box 189 74053 918-443-6000
Rick Thomas, supt. Fax 443-9088
www.oologah.k12.ok.us
Oologah Lower ES 300/K-2
PO Box 189 74053 918-443-6141
Gina Metcalf, prin. Fax 443-8200
Oologah MS 400/6-8
PO Box 189 74053 918-443-6151
Kenneth Kinzer, prin. Fax 443-2875
Oologah Upper ES 400/3-5
PO Box 189 74053 918-443-6041
Mark Williams, prin. Fax 443-2672

Optima, Texas, Pop. 269
Optima SD 100/K-6
RR 1 Box 188 73945 580-338-6712
Rex Hale, supt. Fax 338-6721
Optima ES 100/K-6
RR 1 Box 188 73945 580-338-6712
Rex Hale, prin. Fax 338-6721

Orlando, Logan, Pop. 215
Mulhall-Orlando ISD 200/PK-12
PO Box 8 73073 580-455-2211
Mat Luse, supt. Fax 455-8019
www.mulhall-orlando.k12.ok.us
Other Schools – See Mulhall

Owasso, Tulsa, Pop. 23,771
Owasso ISD 8,100/K-12
1501 N Ash St 74055 918-272-5367
Dr. Clark Ogilvie, supt. Fax 272-8111
www.owasso.k12.ok.us
Ator ES 500/K-5
1501 N Ash St 74055 918-272-2204
Dianna Bishline, prin. Fax 272-2205
Bailey ES 600/K-5
1501 N Ash St 74055 918-272-5399
Mary Morris, prin. Fax 272-8437
Barnes ES 500/K-5
1501 N Ash St 74055 918-272-1153
David Riggs, prin. Fax 272-1154
Hodson ES 600/K-5
1501 N Ash St 74055 918-272-8160
Joy Hughes, prin. Fax 272-8081
Mills ES 500/K-5
1501 N Ash St 74055 918-272-2288
Brenda Casey, prin. Fax 272-8406
Northeast ES 400/K-5
1501 N Ash St 74055 918-272-0015
Michelle Aston, prin. Fax 272-0017
Owasso Eighth Grade Center 700/8-8
1501 N Ash St 74055 918-272-6274
Deirdre Hodge, prin. Fax 272-5562
Owasso Seventh Grade Center 600/7-7
1501 N Ash St 74055 918-272-1183
Bob Coke, prin. Fax 272-8050
Owasso Sixth Grade Center 700/6-6
1501 N Ash St 74055 918-274-3020
Kira Kelsey, prin. Fax 272-3024
Smith ES 500/K-5
1501 N Ash St 74055 918-272-5162
Ron Hughes, prin. Fax 272-5189

Rejoice Christian S 800/PK-12
12200 E 86th St N 74055 918-516-0050
Dr. Craig Shaw, supt. Fax 516-0299

Paden, Okfuskee, Pop. 430
Paden ISD 300/PK-12
PO Box 370 74860 405-932-5053
Jeremy Ramsey, supt. Fax 932-4132
www.paden.k12.ok.us/
Paden S 200/PK-8
PO Box 370 74860 405-932-4499

Panama, LeFlore, Pop. 1,396
Panama ISD 800/PK-12
PO Box 1680 74951 918-963-2217
Dr. Geary Brown, supt. Fax 963-4860
Panama ES 400/PK-5
PO Box 1680 74951 918-963-2218
Dearl Tobey, prin. Fax 963-4866
Panama MS 200/6-8
PO Box 1680 74951 918-963-2213
Grant Ralls, prin. Fax 963-2463

Panola, Latimer
Panola ISD 300/PK-12
PO Box 6 74559 918-465-3298
Alan Lumpkins, supt. Fax 465-3656
www.panola.k12.ok.us/

Panola S — 200/PK-8
PO Box 6 74559 — 918-465-0011
Brad Corcoran, prin. — Fax 465-3656

Paoli, Garvin, Pop. 654
Paoli ISD — 300/PK-12
PO Box 278 73074 — 405-484-7336
Rick Worden, supt. — Fax 484-7268
www.paoli.k12.ok.us/
Paoli S — 200/PK-8
PO Box 278 73074 — 405-484-7231
Paula Tooman, prin. — Fax 484-7268

Park Hill, Cherokee
Keys ISD — 900/PK-12
26622 S 520 Rd 74451 — 918-458-1835
Jerry Hood, supt. — Fax 456-1656
www.keys.k12.ok.us
Keys S — 500/PK-8
19061 E 840 Rd 74451 — 918-456-4501
George Kellner, prin. — Fax 456-7559

Pauls Valley, Garvin, Pop. 6,178
Pauls Valley ISD — 1,300/PK-12
PO Box 780 73075 — 405-238-6453
Bobby Russell, supt. — Fax 238-9178
www.paulsvalley.k12.ok.us
Jackson ES — 300/1-3
PO Box 780 73075 — 405-238-2312
Elaine Kennedy, prin. — Fax 238-1225
Jefferson Early Learning Center — 200/PK-K
PO Box 780 73075 — 405-238-6413
Jeanie Menefee, prin. — Fax 238-9370
Lee ES — 200/4-6
PO Box 780 73075 — 405-238-7336
Kristin Holt, prin. — Fax 238-1227

Whitebead SD — 400/PK-8
RR 3 Box 214 73075 — 405-238-3021
Mary Smith, supt. — Fax 238-6258
Whitebead S — 400/PK-8
RR 3 Box 214 73075 — 405-238-3021
Mary Smith, prin. — Fax 238-6258

Pawhuska, Osage, Pop. 3,533
Pawhuska ISD — 1,000/PK-12
1801 McKenzie Rd 74056 — 918-287-1281
Ben West, supt. — Fax 287-4461
pawhuska.k12.ok.us
Indian Camp ES — 200/4-6
2005 N Boundary St 74056 — 918-287-1977
Les Potter, prin. — Fax 287-1163
Pawhuska ES — 300/PK-3
1700 Lynn Ave 74056 — 918-287-1267
Beverly Moore, prin. — Fax 287-1244
Pawhuska JHS — 200/7-8
615 E 15th St 74056 — 918-287-1264
Jon Culver, prin. — Fax 287-2062

Pawnee, Pawnee, Pop. 2,204
Pawnee ISD — 800/PK-12
615 Denver St 74058 — 918-762-3676
Ned Williams, supt. — Fax 762-2704
www.pawnee-ps.k12.ok.us/
Pawnee ES, 602 Forest St 74058 — 300/PK-5
Rhonda Kuhn, prin. — 918-762-3618
Pawnee MS, 605 Denver St 74058 — 200/6-8
David Tanner, prin. — 918-762-3055

Peggs, Cherokee
Peggs SD — 200/PK-8
PO Box 119 74452 — 918-598-3412
Dr. R. John Cox, supt. — Fax 598-3833
Peggs S — 200/PK-8
PO Box 119 74452 — 918-598-3412
Dr. R. John Cox, prin. — Fax 598-3833

Perkins, Payne, Pop. 2,186
Perkins-Tryon ISD — 1,300/PK-12
PO Box 549 74059 — 405-547-5703
James Ramsey, supt. — Fax 547-2020
www.p-t.k12.ok.us
Perkins-Tryon ES — 500/PK-3
PO Box 549 74059 — 405-547-5741
Bobby Simma, prin. — Fax 547-5744
Perkins-Tryon IS — 300/4-6
PO Box 549 74059 — 405-547-5713
Milton Davis, prin. — Fax 547-2020

Perry, Noble, Pop. 5,105
Perry ISD — 700/PK-12
900 Fir St 73077 — 580-336-4511
Tim Smith, supt. — Fax 336-5185
www.perry.k12.ok.us/
Perry ES, 1207 Ivanhoe St 73077 — 500/PK-4
Ranay Roth, prin. — 580-336-4471
Perry MS, 1303 N 15th St 73077 — 200/5-7
Tom Betchan, prin. — 580-336-2577

Picher, Ottawa, Pop. 1,625
Picher-Cardin ISD — 100/PK-12
PO Box 280 74360 — 918-673-1714
Don Barr, supt. — Fax 673-1718
www.picher.k12.ok.us
Picher-Cardin S, PO Box 280 74360 — 100/PK-8
Kimberly Pace, prin. — 918-673-1783

Piedmont, Canadian, Pop. 4,685
Piedmont ISD — 2,200/PK-12
713 Piedmont Rd N 73078 — 405-373-2311
Mike Hyatt, supt. — Fax 373-0912
piedmont.k12.ok.us
Piedmont ES — 500/1-5
1011 Piedmont Rd N 73078 — 405-373-2353
Shari Zimmerman, prin. — Fax 373-5002
Piedmont MS — 400/6-8
823 2nd St NW 73078 — 405-373-1315
Terri Merveldt, prin. — Fax 373-5006
Piedmont PS — 200/PK-K
615 Edmond Rd NW 73078 — 405-373-4848
Lisa Campbell, prin. — Fax 373-3688
Other Schools – See Yukon

Pittsburg, Pittsburg, Pop. 283
Pittsburg ISD — 200/PK-12
PO Box 200 74560 — 918-432-5062
Tony Potts, supt. — Fax 432-5312
Pittsburg S, PO Box 200 74560 — 100/PK-8
Jimmy Harwood, prin. — 918-432-5513

Pocola, LeFlore, Pop. 4,373
Pocola ISD — 900/PK-12
PO Box 640 74902 — 918-436-2424
James Warden, supt. — Fax 436-2437
www.pocola.k12.ok.us
Pocola ES — 500/PK-5
PO Box 640 74902 — 918-436-2561
Kay Anderson, prin. — Fax 436-2488
Pocola MS, PO Box 640 74902 — 200/6-8
Mark McKenzie, prin. — 918-436-2091

Ponca City, Kay, Pop. 25,070
McCord SD — 200/PK-6
977 S McCord Rd 74604 — 580-765-8806
Boyd Braden, supt. — Fax 765-8552
McCord ES — 200/PK-6
977 S McCord Rd 74604 — 580-765-8806
Boyd Braden, prin. — Fax 765-8552

Ponca City ISD — 4,900/PK-12
111 W Grand Ave 74601 — 580-767-8000
David Pennington, supt. — Fax 767-8007
www.pcps.us
East MS — 400/8-8
612 E Grand Ave 74601 — 580-767-8010
Barbara Davis, prin. — Fax 762-5301
Garfield ES — PK-5
600 S 8th St 74601 — 580-767-8030
Dr. Lori Ryan-Elliott, prin. — Fax 767-9510
Liberty ES — 300/PK-5
505 W Liberty Ave 74601 — 580-767-8040
Meghan Eliason, prin. — Fax 767-8041
Lincoln ES — 500/PK-5
1501 W Grand Ave 74601 — 580-767-8050
Carla Fry, prin. — Fax 767-8051
Roosevelt ES — 300/PK-5
815 E Highland Ave 74601 — 580-767-8060
Ronda Merrifield, prin. — Fax 767-8062
Trout ES — 400/PK-5
2109 E Prospect Ave 74604 — 580-767-8070
Dawn Mills, prin. — Fax 767-8073
Union ES — 300/PK-5
2617 N Union St 74601 — 580-767-8035
Shelley Arrott, prin. — Fax 767-8038
West MS — 700/6-7
1401 W Grand Ave 74601 — 580-767-8020
Barbara Cusick, prin. — Fax 767-8094
Woodlands ES — 300/PK-5
2005 E Woodland Rd 74604 — 580-767-8025
Rebecca Krueger, prin. — Fax 767-9525

First Lutheran S — 300/PK-8
1104 N 4th St 74601 — 580-762-4243
Janet Goll, supt. — Fax 762-4243
Ponca City Christian Academy — 100/PK-6
901 Monument Rd Bldg 3 74604 — 580-765-6038
Ginger Henley, admin. — Fax 718-5108
St. Mary's S — 100/PK-8
415 S 7th St 74601 — 580-765-4387
Allyson Helm, prin. — Fax 765-1352

Pond Creek, Grant, Pop. 824
Pond Creek-Hunter ISD — 300/PK-12
PO Box 56 73766 — 580-532-4242
Joel Quinn, supt. — Fax 532-4965
www.pondcreek-hunter.k12.ok.us
Pond Creek-Hunter ES — 200/PK-6
PO Box 56 73766 — 580-532-4240
Steve Hendrix, prin. — Fax 532-4965

Porter, Wagoner, Pop. 581
Porter Consolidated ISD — 500/PK-12
PO Box 120 74454 — 918-483-2401
Mark Fenton, supt. — Fax 483-2310
www.porter.k12.ok.us
Porter Consolidated S — 400/PK-8
PO Box 120 74454 — 918-483-5231
Richard Cottle, prin. — Fax 483-2310

Porum, Muskogee, Pop. 733
Porum ISD — 500/PK-12
PO Box 189 74455 — 918-484-5121
Mark Calavan, supt. — Fax 484-2310
www.porum.k12.ok.us/
Porum S — 400/PK-8
PO Box 189 74455 — 918-484-5123
Teri McCullar, prin. — Fax 484-2310

Poteau, LeFlore, Pop. 8,152
Poteau ISD — 2,200/PK-12
100 Mockingbird Ln 74953 — 918-647-7700
Dr. Alice Smith, supt. — Fax 647-9357
www.poteau.k12.ok.us
Kidd MS — 500/6-8
100 Mockingbird Ln 74953 — 918-647-7741
Lorraine Caldwell, prin. — Fax 647-4286
Poteau PS — 700/PK-2
100 Mockingbird Ln 74953 — 918-647-7780
Kristie Smith, prin. — Fax 647-9143
Poteau Upper ES — 500/3-5
100 Mockingbird Ln 74953 — 918-647-7760
Linda Lee, prin. — Fax 647-1029

Prague, Lincoln, Pop. 2,124
Prague ISD — 1,000/K-12
3504 NBU 74864 — 405-567-4455
Rick Martin, supt. — Fax 567-3095
www.prague.k12.ok.us/
Prague ECC, 3504 NBU 74864 — 100/K-1
Judy Hightower, prin. — 405-567-2285
Prague ES — 300/2-5
3504 NBU 74864 — 405-567-2281
Jennifer Smith, prin. — Fax 567-8199
Prague MS — 200/6-8
3504 NBU 74864 — 405-567-2281
Jerry Martin, prin. — Fax 567-3095

Preston, Okmulgee
Preston ISD — 600/PK-12
PO Box 40 74456 — 918-756-3388
Mark Hudson, supt. — Fax 756-2122
www.preston.k12.ok.us/
Preston S — 400/PK-8
PO Box 40 74456 — 918-756-8470
Ida Nell Fox, prin. — Fax 756-2122

Prue, Osage, Pop. 438
Prue ISD — 400/PK-12
PO Box 130 74060 — 918-242-3351
Randy Cottrell, supt. — Fax 242-3392
www.prue.k12.ok.us/
Prue S — 300/PK-8
PO Box 130 74060 — 918-242-3385
Ginger James, prin. — Fax 242-3788

Pryor, Mayes, Pop. 8,921
Osage SD — 200/PK-8
PO Box 579 74362 — 918-825-2550
Larry Larmon, supt. — Fax 825-1433
Osage S — 200/PK-8
PO Box 579 74362 — 918-825-2550
Larry Larmon, prin. — Fax 825-1433

Pryor ISD — 2,500/PK-12
PO Box 548 74362 — 918-825-1255
Don Raleigh, supt. — Fax 825-3938
www.pryor.k12.ok.us
Jefferson ES — 300/K-6
PO Box 548 74362 — 918-825-1374
Tim Nutter, prin. — Fax 825-3966
Lincoln ES — 500/PK-6
PO Box 548 74362 — 918-825-0653
Theresa Sinor, prin. — Fax 825-3922
Roosevelt ES — 400/PK-6
PO Box 548 74362 — 918-825-3523
Brian Bradshaw, prin. — Fax 825-3970
Washington ES — 100/K-6
PO Box 548 74362 — 918-825-1364
Linda Tincher, prin. — Fax 825-3994

Bradford Christian S — 50/K-12
2320 NE 1st St 74361 — 918-825-7038
Amanda Rutherford, admin. — Fax 825-7037

Purcell, McClain, Pop. 5,858
Purcell ISD — 1,200/PK-12
919 N 9th Ave Ste 1 73080 — 405-527-2146
Dr. Tony Christian, supt. — Fax 527-6366
www.purcellps.k12.ok.us/
Purcell ES — 400/PK-2
809 N 9th Ave 73080 — 405-527-2146
Tammy Dillard, prin. — Fax 527-9676
Purcell IS — 100/3-4
919 1/2 N 9th Ave 73080 — 405-527-2146
Michelle Milner, prin. — Fax 527-3325
Purcell JHS — 200/7-8
201 Lester Ln 73080 — 405-527-6591
Bret Petty, prin. — Fax 527-6593
Purcell MS — 200/5-6
711 N 9th Ave 73080 — 405-527-2146
Tinas Swayze, prin. — Fax 527-4454

Quapaw, Ottawa, Pop. 975
Quapaw ISD — 700/PK-12
305 W 1st St 74363 — 918-674-2501
Dennis Earp, supt. — Fax 674-2721
Quapaw ES — 300/PK-5
305 W 1st St 74363 — 918-674-2236
James Dawson, prin. — Fax 674-2688
Quapaw MS — 200/6-8
305 W 1st St 74363 — 918-674-2496
Larry Radford, prin. — Fax 674-2721

Quinton, Pittsburg, Pop. 1,081
Quinton ISD — 500/PK-12
PO Box 670 74561 — 918-469-3100
Don Cox, supt. — Fax 469-3308
www.quinton.k12.ok.us/
Quinton S — 400/PK-8
PO Box 670 74561 — 918-469-3313
Linda Ballard, prin. — Fax 469-2710

Ralston, Pawnee, Pop. 360
Woodland SD
Supt. — See Fairfax
Woodland MS — 100/5-8
6th & McKinley 74650 — 918-738-4286
Bobby Rose, prin. — Fax 738-4287

Ramona, Washington, Pop. 574
Caney Valley ISD — 800/PK-12
PO Box 410 74061 — 918-536-2500
James Knox, supt. — Fax 536-2600
www.cvalley.k12.ok.us/
Caney Valley ES — 300/PK-5
401 W Main St 74061 — 918-535-2205
Nancy Collins, prin. — Fax 535-2764
Caney Valley MS, PO Box 410 74061 — 200/6-8
James Farrell, prin. — 918-536-2705

Randlett, Cotton, Pop. 518
Big Pasture ISD — 300/PK-12
PO Box 167 73562 — 580-281-3831
Ernest Copus, supt. — Fax 281-3299
Big Pasture S — 200/PK-8
PO Box 167 73562 — 580-281-3460
Diane Larson, prin. — Fax 281-3299

Rattan, Pushmataha, Pop. 242
Rattan ISD — 500/PK-12
PO Box 44 74562 — 580-587-2546
Bruce Lawless, supt. — Fax 587-4000
www.rattan.k12.ok.us
Rattan ES — 300/PK-6
PO Box 44 74562 — 580-587-2715
Cheryl Hedge, prin. — Fax 587-4001
Rattan JHS — 100/7-8
PO Box 44 74562 — 580-587-2715
Neil Birchfield, prin. — Fax 587-2476

Ravia, Johnston, Pop. 442
Ravia SD — 100/K-8
PO Box 299 73455 — 580-371-9163
David Duncan, supt. — Fax 371-3067
Ravia S — 100/K-8
PO Box 299 73455 — 580-371-9163
David Duncan, prin. — Fax 371-3067

Red Oak, Latimer, Pop. 572
Red Oak ISD — 200/PK-12
PO Box 310 74563 — 918-754-2426
Bryan Deatherage, supt. — Fax 754-2898
Red Oak S, PO Box 310 74563 — 100/PK-8
Jeremy Williams, prin. — 918-754-2426

Red Rock, Noble, Pop. 291
Frontier ISD — 400/PK-12
PO Box 130 74651 — 580-723-4361
Terri Taflinger, supt. — Fax 723-4516
www.frontierok.com
Frontier S — 300/PK-8
PO Box 130 74651 — 580-723-4582
Bob Weckstein, prin. — Fax 723-4516

Reydon, Roger Mills, Pop. 171
Reydon ISD — 100/PK-12
PO Box 10 73660 — 580-655-4375
Phil Drouhard, supt. — Fax 655-4622
Reydon S, PO Box 10 73660 — 100/PK-8
Jeff Kelly, prin. — 580-655-4376

Ringling, Jefferson, Pop. 1,082
Ringling ISD — 500/PK-12
PO Box 1010 73456 — 580-662-2385
James Miller, supt. — Fax 662-2683
www.ringling.k12.ok.us/
Ringling ES — 300/PK-6
PO Box 1010 73456 — 580-662-2388
Barry Benson, prin. — Fax 662-2683

Ringwood, Major, Pop. 419
Ringwood ISD — 400/PK-12
RR 2 Box 239 73768 — 580-883-2202
Ray Johnson, supt. — Fax 883-2220
www.ringwood.k12.ok.us/
Ringwood S — 300/PK-8
RR 2 Box 239 73768 — 580-883-2203
Jim Pearce, prin. — Fax 883-2220

Ripley, Payne, Pop. 426
Ripley ISD — 400/PK-12
PO Box 97 74062 — 918-372-4567
Dr. Kenny Beams, supt. — Fax 372-4608
www.ripley.k12.ok.us/
Ripley S — 300/PK-8
PO Box 97 74062 — 918-372-4570
Lisa Pitts, prin. — Fax 372-4608

Roff, Pontotoc, Pop. 724
Roff ISD — 300/PK-12
PO Box 157 74865 — 580-456-7663
Mike Martin, supt. — Fax 456-7245
www.roff.k12.ok.us
Roff S, PO Box 157 74865 — 200/PK-8
Tony Wellington, prin. — 580-456-7251

Roland, Sequoyah, Pop. 3,110
Roland ISD — 1,300/PK-12
300 Ranger Blvd 74954 — 918-427-4601
Paul Wood, supt. — Fax 427-1785
www.rolandschools.org
Roland ES — 700/PK-6
300 Ranger Blvd 74954 — 918-427-5993
Vickie Earnhart, prin. — Fax 427-3635

Rush Springs, Grady, Pop. 1,324
Rush Springs ISD — 600/PK-12
PO Box 308 73082 — 580-476-3929
Kathy Carroll, supt. — Fax 476-2018
www.rushsprings.k12.ok.us
Rush Springs ES — 300/PK-5
PO Box 308 73082 — 580-476-3172
Alan Perry, prin. — Fax 476-3777
Rush Springs MS — 100/6-8
PO Box 308 73082 — 580-476-3447
Shawn Haskins, prin. — Fax 476-2148

Ryan, Jefferson, Pop. 854
Ryan ISD — 300/PK-12
PO Box 369 73565 — 580-757-2308
Larry Ninman, supt. — Fax 757-2609
Ryan S, PO Box 369 73565 — 200/PK-8
Pete Maples, prin. — 580-757-2296

Salina, Mayes, Pop. 1,454
Kenwood SD — 100/K-8
48625 S 502 Rd 74365 — 918-434-5799
Dr. Kenneth Limore, supt. — Fax 434-5707
Kenwood S — 100/K-8
48625 S 502 Rd 74365 — 918-434-5799
Dr. Kenneth Limore, prin. — Fax 434-5707

Salina ISD — 800/PK-12
PO Box 98 74365 — 918-434-5091
Vol Woods, supt. — Fax 434-5346
www.salina.k12.ok.us
Salina ES — 400/PK-5
PO Box 98 74365 — 918-434-5300
Marie Holleyman, prin. — Fax 434-6051
Salina MS — 200/6-8
PO Box 98 74365 — 918-434-5311
Debbie Cox, prin. — Fax 434-5173

Wickliffe SD — 100/PK-8
11176 E 470 74365 — 918-434-5559
Rita Bradshaw, supt. — Fax 434-5515
www.wickliffeschoolok.com
Wickliffe S — 100/PK-8
11176 E 470 74365 — 918-434-5558
Rita Bradshaw, prin. — Fax 434-5515

Sallisaw, Sequoyah, Pop. 8,621
Brushy SD — 300/PK-8
RR 3 Box 231-8 74955 — 918-775-4458
Greg Reynolds, supt. — Fax 775-3638
Brushy S — 300/PK-8
RR 3 Box 231-8 74955 — 918-775-4458
Greg Reynolds, prin. — Fax 775-3638

Central ISD — 500/PK-12
RR 1 Box 36 74955 — 918-775-5525
Max Tanner, supt. — Fax 775-8557
centralps.k12.ok.us
Central S — 300/PK-8
RR 1 Box 36 74955 — 918-775-2216
Alfred Fullbright, prin. — Fax 775-5349

Sallisaw ISD — 2,100/PK-12
701 J T Stites Blvd 74955 — 918-775-5544
Ronald Wyrick, supt. — Fax 775-1257
Eastside ES — 400/3-5
1206 E Creek Ave 74955 — 918-775-9491
Gary Gunter, prin. — Fax 775-1277
Liberty ES — 600/PK-2
136 S Dogwood St 74955 — 918-775-4741
Randall Baker, prin. — Fax 775-1278
Spear MS, 211 S Main St 74955 — 500/6-8
Greg Cast, prin. — 918-775-3015

Sallisaw Christian S — 50/1-8
PO Box 793 74955 — 918-775-6481
Wilma Adams, admin.

Sand Springs, Tulsa, Pop. 17,667
Anderson SD — 300/PK-6
2195 Anderson Rd 74063 — 918-245-0289
Brent McKee, supt. — Fax 245-3931
www.anderson.k12.ok.us/
Anderson ES — 300/PK-6
2195 Anderson Rd 74063 — 918-245-0289
Brent McKee, prin. — Fax 245-3931

Keystone SD — 500/PK-8
23810 W Highway 51 74063 — 918-363-8711
Della Jones, supt. — Fax 363-8194
Keystone S — 500/PK-8
23810 W Highway 51 74063 — 918-363-8298
Craig Garner, prin. — Fax 363-8194

Sand Springs ISD — 5,300/PK-12
PO Box 970 74063 — 918-246-1400
Lloyd Snow, supt. — Fax 246-1401
www.sandites.org/
Angus Valley ES — 300/K-5
PO Box 970 74063 — 918-246-1520
Daylene Bowlin, prin. — Fax 246-1522
Boyd MS — 1,100/6-8
PO Box 970 74063 — 918-246-1535
Dr. Melissa Ellis, prin. — Fax 246-1544
Central ES — 500/K-2
PO Box 970 74063 — 918-246-1455
Jenny Chambers, prin. — Fax 246-1458
Garfield ES — 400/3-5
PO Box 970 74063 — 918-246-1462
Denis Clark, prin. — Fax 246-1465
Limestone ES — 300/K-5
PO Box 970 74063 — 918-246-1560
Lou Alice Pinkerton, prin. — Fax 246-1559
Pratt ES — 500/K-5
PO Box 970 74063 — 918-246-1550
James Roberts, prin. — Fax 246-1552
Sand Springs ECC — 200/PK-PK
PO Box 970 74063 — 918-246-1570
Teresa Ledbetter, prin. — Fax 246-1573

Sapulpa, Creek, Pop. 20,619
Lone Star SD — 800/PK-8
PO Box 1170 74067 — 918-224-0201
David Pritz, supt. — Fax 224-3927
www.lonestar.k12.ok.us/
Lone Star S — 800/PK-8
PO Box 1170 74067 — 918-224-0201
David Pritz, prin. — Fax 224-3927

Pretty Water SD — 200/PK-8
15223 W 81st St S 74066 — 918-224-4952
Jeff Taylor, supt. — Fax 224-4039
www.prettywater.k12.ok.us/
Pretty Water S — 200/PK-8
15223 W 81st St S 74066 — 918-224-4952
Jeff Taylor, prin. — Fax 224-4039

Sapulpa ISD — 4,100/PK-12
1 S Mission St 74066 — 918-224-3400
Dr. Mary Webb, supt. — Fax 227-3287
www.sapulpa.k12.ok.us
Freedom ES — 400/PK-5
9170 Freedom Ave 74066 — 918-227-7838
Nancy Turlington, prin. — Fax 227-7839
Jefferson Heights ES — 200/PK-5
1521 S Wickham Rd 74066 — 918-224-2028
Tom Walsh, prin. — Fax 224-0129
Liberty ES — 400/PK-5
631 N Brown St 74066 — 918-224-1492
Susan Gee, prin. — Fax 224-0134
Sapulpa MS — 600/6-7
1304 E Cleveland Ave 74066 — 918-224-8441
Kerry Gray, prin. — Fax 224-0184
Washington ES — 400/PK-5
511 E Lee Ave 74066 — 918-224-5521
Bobby Alfred, prin. — Fax 224-0041
Woodlawn ES — 300/K-5
1125 E Lincoln Ave 74066 — 918-224-6611
Ashley Hearn, prin. — Fax 224-0058

Eagle Point Christian Academy — 100/PK-12
602 S Mounds St 74066 — 918-227-2441
Jim Pryor, admin. — Fax 248-3117

Sasakwa, Seminole, Pop. 149
Sasakwa ISD — 200/PK-12
PO Box 323 74867 — 405-941-3213
Jim Mathews, supt. — Fax 941-3163
Sasakwa S — 200/PK-8
PO Box 323 74867 — 405-941-3591
Terry Byerly, prin. — Fax 941-3561

Savanna, Pittsburg, Pop. 744
Savanna ISD — 400/PK-12
PO Box 266 74565 — 918-548-3777
Mitch Tidwell, supt. — Fax 548-3836
www.savanna.k12.ok.us/
Savanna S — 200/PK-8
PO Box 266 74565 — 918-548-3864
Mark Inman, prin. — Fax 548-3914

Sayre, Beckham, Pop. 2,836
Sayre ISD — 700/PK-12
716 NE Highway 66 73662 — 580-928-5531
Todd Winn, supt. — Fax 928-5538
www.sayre.k12.ok.us
Sayre ES — 300/PK-5
716 NE Highway 66 73662 — 580-928-2013
Ronda Mendez, prin. — Fax 928-3936
Sayre MS — 100/6-8
716 NE Highway 66 73662 — 580-928-5578
Monica Brower, prin. — Fax 928-3045

Schulter, Okmulgee, Pop. 607
Schulter ISD — 200/PK-12
PO Box 203 74460 — 918-652-8219
Alfred Gaches, supt. — Fax 652-8474
Schulter S — 100/PK-8
PO Box 203 74460 — 918-652-8200
Denise Hensley, prin. — Fax 652-8474

Seiling, Dewey, Pop. 821
Seiling ISD — 300/PK-12
PO Box 780 73663 — 580-922-7383
Bob Bush, supt. — Fax 922-8019
www.seiling.k12.ok.us
Seiling ES — 200/PK-6
PO Box 780 73663 — 580-922-7381
Randy Seifried, prin. — Fax 922-8019

Seminole, Seminole, Pop. 6,913
Pleasant Grove SD — 100/PK-8
35231 EW 1235 74868 — 405-382-0454
Pamela Chesser, supt. — Fax 382-7454
Pleasant Grove S — 100/PK-8
35231 EW 1235 74868 — 405-382-0454
Pamela Chesser, prin. — Fax 382-7454

Seminole ISD — 1,700/PK-12
PO Box 1031 74818 — 405-382-5085
Jeff Pritchard, supt. — Fax 382-8281
www.sps.k12.ok.us
Lincoln Preschool — PK-PK
PO Box 1031 74818 — 405-382-1343
Dee Bennett, prin. — Fax 382-8656
Northwood ES — 300/4-6
PO Box 1031 74818 — 405-382-5800
Claudia Willis, prin. — Fax 382-8658
Seminole MS — 200/7-8
PO Box 1031 74818 — 405-382-5065
Michelle Sneed, prin. — Fax 382-8653
Smith ECC — K-K
PO Box 1031 74818 — 405-382-5962
Dee Bennett, prin. — Fax 382-5995
Wilson ES — 600/PK-3
PO Box 1031 74818 — 405-382-1431
Lisa Cobb, prin. — Fax 382-8657

Strother ISD — 300/PK-12
36085 EW 1140 74868 — 405-382-4014
Rick Ruckman, supt. — Fax 382-3339
Strother ES — 200/PK-5
36085 EW 1140 74868 — 405-382-6011
Rick Ruckman, prin. — Fax 382-8888

Varnum ISD — 300/PK-12
11929 NS 3550 74868 — 405-382-1448
Vic Woods, supt. — Fax 382-8618
Varnum S, 11929 NS 3550 74868 — 200/PK-8
Tina Judkins, prin. — 405-382-0812

Sentinel, Washita, Pop. 860
Sentinel ISD — 300/PK-12
PO Box 640 73664 — 580-393-2101
Hal Holt, supt. — Fax 393-2101
www.sentinel.k12.ok.us/
McMurray S — 200/PK-8
PO Box 640 73664 — 580-393-4997
Paula Combs, prin. — Fax 393-4334

Shady Point, LeFlore, Pop. 871
Shady Point SD — 100/PK-8
PO Box 1005 74956 — 918-963-2595
Sandy Thompson, supt. — Fax 963-2605
www.shadypoint.k12.ok.us
Shady Point S — 100/PK-8
PO Box 1005 74956 — 918-963-2595
Sandy Thompson, prin. — Fax 963-2605

Sharon, Woodward, Pop. 125
Sharon-Mutual ISD
Supt. — See Mutual
Sharon-Mutual S — 200/PK-8
PO Box 39 73857 — 580-866-3333
Dustie Shryock, prin. — Fax 866-3332

Shattuck, Ellis, Pop. 1,235
Shattuck ISD — 300/PK-12
PO Box 159 73858 — 580-938-2586
Randy Holley, supt. — Fax 938-8019
www.shattuck.k12.ok.us/
Shattuck ES — 200/PK-8
PO Box 159 73858 — 580-938-2222
Kasandra Nelson, prin. — Fax 938-8019

Shawnee, Pottawatomie, Pop. 29,824
Bethel ISD — 1,300/PK-12
36000 Clearpond Rd 74801 — 405-273-0385
David Glover, supt. — Fax 273-5056
www.bethel.k12.ok.us
Bethel ES — 700/PK-5
36000 Clearpond Rd 74801 — 405-273-7632
Larry Pendleton, prin. — Fax 273-5056
Bethel MS — 300/6-8
36000 Clearpond Rd 74801 — 405-273-5944
Gary Cartwright, prin. — Fax 273-5056

Grove SD — 400/K-8
2800 N Bryan Ave 74804 — 405-275-7435
Mickey Maynard, supt. — Fax 273-2541
www.grove.k12.ok.us
Grove S — 400/K-8
2800 N Bryan Ave 74804 — 405-275-7435
Sheril Payne, prin. — Fax 273-2541

North Rock Creek SD — 500/PK-8
42400 Garretts Lake Rd 74804 — 405-275-3473
Marc Moore, supt. — Fax 273-7368
North Rock Creek S — 500/PK-8
42400 Garretts Lake Rd 74804 — 405-275-3473
Denise Sims, prin. — Fax 273-7368

Pleasant Grove SD — 200/PK-8
1927 E Walnut St 74801 — 405-275-6092
Arlene Burton, supt. — Fax 275-6094
Pleasant Grove S — 200/PK-8
1927 E Walnut St 74801 — 405-275-6092
Arlene Burton, prin. — Fax 275-6094

Shawnee ISD 3,900/PK-12
326 N Union Ave 74801 405-273-0653
Marilyn Bradford, supt. Fax 273-6818
www.shawnee.k12.ok.us
Jefferson ES 400/1-5
800 N Louisa Ave 74801 405-273-1846
Vickie Penson, prin. Fax 878-1048
Mann ES 300/1-5
412 N Draper Ave 74801 405-273-1806
Susan Field, prin. Fax 273-1946
Rogers ES 400/1-5
2600 N Union Ave 74804 405-273-1519
John Wilson, prin. Fax 878-1041
Sequoyah ES 300/1-5
1401 E Independence St 74804 405-273-1878
Dr. Jesse Field, prin. Fax 273-1048
Shawnee ECC 500/PK-K
1831 N Airport Dr 74804 405-273-3388
Paul Pounds, prin. Fax 273-3389
Shawnee MS 800/6-8
4300 N Union Ave 74804 405-273-0403
Brent Houston, prin. Fax 275-9651

South Rock Creek SD 300/K-8
17800 S Rock Creek Rd 74801 405-273-6072
Ken Leone, supt. Fax 273-8926
South Rock Creek S 300/K-8
17800 S Rock Creek Rd 74801 405-273-6072
Brooks Malone, prin. Fax 273-8926

Family of Faith Christian S 100/K-12
PO Box 1442 74802 405-273-5331
Christopher Belyeu, admin. Fax 273-8535
Liberty Academy 200/PK-12
PO Box 1176 74802 405-273-3022
Lenore Matthews, admin. Fax 273-3029

Shidler, Osage, Pop. 520
Shidler ISD 200/PK-12
PO Box 85 74652 918-793-2021
John Herzig, supt. Fax 793-2061
www.shidler.k12.ok.us
Ward ES 100/PK-6
PO Box 85 74652 918-793-2051
Janice Finton, prin. Fax 793-2063

Skiatook, Tulsa, Pop. 6,290
Skiatook ISD 2,500/PK-12
355 S Osage St 74070 918-396-1792
Dr. Gary Johnson, supt. Fax 396-1799
www.skiatookschools.org
Marrs ES 700/PK-2
355 S Osage St 74070 918-396-2295
Joyce Jech, prin. Fax 396-1799
Newman MS 500/6-8
355 S Osage St 74070 918-396-2307
Steve Cantrell, prin. Fax 396-1799
Skiatook IS 500/3-5
355 S Osage St 74070 918-396-5745
Tim Buck, prin. Fax 396-1799

Smithville, McCurtain, Pop. 111
Smithville ISD 300/PK-12
PO Box 8 74957 580-244-3333
Delbert McBroom, supt. Fax 244-7214
www.smithville.k12.ok.us
Smithville ES 100/PK-5
PO Box 8 74957 580-244-7212
Stacy Nichols, prin. Fax 244-3651
Smithville MS, PO Box 8 74957 100/6-8
Stacy Nichols, prin. 580-244-7212

Snyder, Kiowa, Pop. 1,452
Snyder ISD 500/PK-12
PO Box 368 73566 580-569-2773
Robert Trammell, supt. Fax 569-4205
www.snyder.k12.ok.us
Snyder MS, PO Box 368 73566 200/4-8
Carol McPhail, prin. 580-569-2691
Snyder PS, PO Box 368 73566 200/PK-3
Ken McKee, prin. 580-569-2010

Soper, Choctaw, Pop. 300
Soper ISD 400/PK-12
PO Box 149 74759 580-345-2757
Olen Jestis, supt. Fax 345-2896
www.soperisd.org
Soper S 200/PK-8
PO Box 149 74759 580-345-2211
Tonya Scott, prin. Fax 345-2896

South Coffeyville, Nowata, Pop. 801
Oklahoma Union ISD 600/PK-12
RR 1 Box 377-7 74072 918-255-6550
Dr. Robert Jobe, supt. Fax 255-6817
www.okunion.k12.ok.us/
Oklahoma Union ES 300/PK-5
RR 1 Box 377-7 74072 918-255-6550
Brenda Taylor, prin. Fax 255-6817
Oklahoma Union MS 100/6-8
RR 1 Box 377-7 74072 918-255-6550
Lance Williams, prin. Fax 255-6817

South Coffeyville ISD 300/PK-12
PO Box 190 74072 918-255-6202
Colt Shaw, supt. Fax 255-6230
South Coffeyville S 200/PK-8
PO Box 190 74072 918-255-6087
Clem Haddox, prin. Fax 255-6115

Spavinaw, Mayes, Pop. 574
Spavinaw SD 100/PK-8
PO Box 108 74366 918-589-2228
Teresia Knott, supt. Fax 589-2476
www.spavinawok.net
Spavinaw S 100/PK-8
PO Box 108 74366 918-589-2228
Teresia Knott, prin. Fax 589-2476

Spencer, Oklahoma, Pop. 3,840
Oklahoma City ISD
Supt. — See Oklahoma City
Green Pastures ES 100/K-5
4300 N Post Rd 73084 405-769-4370
Harry Bryant, prin. Fax 769-9159
Parker ES 100/PK-5
12700 NE 42nd St 73084 405-769-3170
Margaret Carter, prin. Fax 769-9118
Rogers MS 500/6-8
4000 Spencer Rd 73084 405-771-3205
Michael Brown, prin. Fax 771-2114
Spencer ES 200/PK-5
8900 NE 50th St 73084 405-771-3246
Dr. Mary Coughlin, prin. Fax 771-2149

Spencer Road Christian S 50/PK-5
8515 NE 25th St 73084 405-769-7032
Shelly Paulk, admin. Fax 769-4173

Sperry, Tulsa, Pop. 1,017
Sperry ISD 1,100/PK-12
PO Box 610 74073 918-288-6258
Dr. Ryma Harchar, supt. Fax 288-7067
www.sperry.k12.ok.us
Sperry ES 500/PK-3
PO Box 610 74073 918-288-7213
Dr. Stephanie Holcomb, prin. Fax 288-7234
Sperry IS 4-5
PO Box 610 74073 918-288-7213
Richard Akin, prin. Fax 288-6608
Sperry MS 300/6-8
PO Box 610 74073 918-288-7213
Benny Ballard, prin. Fax 288-7231

Spiro, LeFlore, Pop. 2,287
Spiro ISD 900/K-12
600 W Broadway St 74959 918-962-2463
J. L. Williams, supt. Fax 962-2757
www.spiro.k12.ok.us/
Spiro ES, 600 W Broadway St 74959 K-2
Larry Greenwood, prin. 918-962-2413
Spiro MS, 600 W Broadway St 74959 300/6-8
Russell Thornton, prin. 918-962-2488
Spiro Upper ES 200/3-5
600 W Broadway St 74959 918-962-2414
Austin Morton, prin.

Springer, Carter, Pop. 592
Springer ISD 200/PK-12
PO Box 249 73458 580-653-2656
Rick Peters, supt. Fax 653-2666
www.springer.k12.ok.us/
Springer S, PO Box 249 73458 100/PK-8
Brenda Foster, prin. 580-653-2471

Sterling, Comanche, Pop. 748
Sterling ISD 400/PK-12
PO Box 158 73567 580-365-4307
Julie Poteete, supt. Fax 365-4705
www.sterling.k12.ok.us/
Sterling S, PO Box 158 73567 300/PK-8
Ross Ridge, prin. 580-365-4166

Stigler, Haskell, Pop. 2,821
Stigler ISD 1,200/PK-12
309 NW E St 74462 918-967-2805
Bill Self, supt. Fax 967-4550
www.stigler.k12.ok.us
Stigler ES 500/PK-4
309 NW E St 74462 918-967-8835
John McClain, prin. Fax 967-5124
Stigler MS 300/5-8
309 NW E St 74462 918-967-2521
Rick Prentice, prin. Fax 967-5125

Stillwater, Payne, Pop. 40,906
Stillwater ISD 5,400/PK-12
PO Box 879 74076 405-533-6300
Dr. Ann Caine, supt. Fax 743-6311
www.stillwater.k12.ok.us
Highland Park ES 400/PK-5
PO Box 879 74076 405-533-6350
Kurt Baze, prin. Fax 743-6354
Richmond ES 400/PK-5
PO Box 879 74076 405-533-6400
Darren Nelson, prin. Fax 743-6334
Rogers ES 400/PK-5
PO Box 879 74076 405-533-6380
Megan Matthews, prin. Fax 743-6329
Sangre Ridge ES 600/PK-5
PO Box 879 74076 405-533-6360
Andrea Rains, prin. Fax 743-6337
Skyline ES 400/PK-5
PO Box 879 74076 405-533-6390
Ryan Blake, prin. Fax 743-6388
Stillwater MS 700/6-7
PO Box 879 74076 405-533-6430
Steve Davis, prin. Fax 743-6324
Westwood ES 400/PK-5
PO Box 879 74076 405-533-6370
Jill Metzger, prin. Fax 743-6328

Sunnybrook Christian S 100/PK-12
421 E Richmond Rd 74075 405-377-3748
Dr. Matt Miles, admin. Fax 372-2505

Stilwell, Adair, Pop. 3,472
Bell SD 100/PK-8
PO Box 346 74960 918-696-7181
Nancy Thomas-Oosahwe, supt. Fax 696-2353
www.bell.k12.ok.us/
Bell S 100/PK-8
PO Box 346 74960 918-696-7181
Nancy Thomas-Oosahwe, prin. Fax 696-2353

Dahlonegah SD 100/PK-8
RR 1 Box 1795 74960 918-696-7807
Jeff Limore, supt. Fax 696-2192
www.dahlonegah.k12.ok.us/
Dahlonegah S 100/PK-8
RR 1 Box 1795 74960 918-696-7807
Jeff Limore, prin. Fax 696-2192

Maryetta SD 600/PK-8
RR 6 Box 2840 74960 918-696-2285
Lori Means, supt. Fax 696-6746
www.maryetta.k12.ok.us
Maryetta S 600/PK-8
RR 6 Box 2840 74960 918-696-2285
Rhonda Brown, prin. Fax 696-6746

Peavine SD 200/PK-8
PO Box 389 74960 918-696-7818
Michael Wolfe, supt. Fax 696-2199
Peavine S 200/PK-8
PO Box 389 74960 918-696-7818
Jeff Collyge, prin. Fax 696-2199

Rocky Mountain SD 200/PK-8
RR 1 Box 665 74960 918-696-7509
Terry Mays, supt. Fax 696-3654
www.rockymtn.k12.ok.us/
Rocky Mountain S 200/PK-8
RR 1 Box 665 74960 918-696-7509
Terry Mays, prin. Fax 696-3654

Stilwell ISD 1,500/PK-12
1801 W Locust St 74960 918-696-7001
Mary Fletcher, supt. Fax 696-2193
www.stilwellschools.org/
Stilwell ES 500/PK-4
10 S 6th St 74960 918-696-7656
Jerry Knight, prin. Fax 696-6040
Stilwell MS 300/5-8
12 N 7th St 74960 918-696-2685
Dan Eurich, prin. Fax 696-7761

Zion SD 300/PK-8
PO Box 347 74960 918-696-7866
Charles Benham, supt. Fax 696-6226
www.zionjets.com
Zion S 300/PK-8
PO Box 347 74960 918-696-7866
Joey O'Neal, prin. Fax 696-6226

Stonewall, Pontotoc, Pop. 471
Stonewall ISD 400/PK-12
600 Highschool 74871 580-265-4241
Kevin Flowers, supt. Fax 265-4536
stonewall.ok.schoolwebpages.com
Stonewall ES, 600 Highschool 74871 100/K-4
Larry Rayburn, prin. 580-265-4243
Other Schools – See Fittstown

Stratford, Garvin, Pop. 1,484
Stratford ISD 600/PK-12
PO Box 589 74872 580-759-3615
Brent Walden, supt. Fax 759-2669
www.stratfordisd.org
Stratford ES 300/PK-4
PO Box 589 74872 580-759-2382
Kathie Carter, prin. Fax 759-8914
Stratford JHS, PO Box 589 74872 200/5-8
Michael Blackburn, prin. 580-759-2381

Stringtown, Atoka, Pop. 412
Stringtown ISD 200/PK-12
PO Box 130 74569 580-346-7423
Richard Quaid, supt. Fax 346-7726
www.stringtown.k12.ok.us
Stringtown S 100/PK-8
PO Box 130 74569 580-346-7621
Gary McDonald, prin. Fax 346-7726

Stroud, Lincoln, Pop. 2,755
Stroud ISD 800/PK-12
212 W 7th St 74079 918-968-2541
Rick McDaniel, supt. Fax 968-2582
www.stroud.k12.ok.us
Parkview ES 400/PK-5
212 W 7th St 74079 918-968-4711
Brenda Gooch, prin. Fax 968-2622
Stroud MS 200/6-8
212 W 7th St 74079 918-968-2200
Marsha Thompson, prin. Fax 968-2391

Stuart, Hughes, Pop. 213
Stuart ISD 300/PK-12
8837 4th St 74570 918-546-2476
Bill San Millan, supt. Fax 546-2329
www.stuart.k12.ok.us/
Stuart S 200/PK-8
8837 4th St 74570 918-546-2627
Tracy Blasengame, prin. Fax 546-2329

Sulphur, Murray, Pop. 4,877
Sulphur ISD 1,400/PK-12
1021 W 9th St 73086 580-622-2061
Paula Crawford, supt. Fax 622-6789
www.sulphur.k12.ok.us
Sulphur ES 500/PK-3
1021 W 9th St 73086 580-622-3326
Cathryn Harmon, prin. Fax 622-2722
Sulphur IS 300/4-6
1021 W 9th St 73086 580-622-6161
Matt Holder, prin. Fax 622-4373
Sulphur JHS 200/7-8
1021 W 9th St 73086 580-622-4010
Tony Duck, prin. Fax 622-3900

Sweetwater, Roger Mills, Pop. 70
Sweetwater ISD 100/PK-12
11107 N Highway 30 73666 580-534-2272
Don Riley, supt. Fax 534-2273
www.sweetwater.k12.ok.us/
Sweetwater S 50/PK-8
11107 N Highway 30 73666 580-534-2272
Brenda Quinn, prin. Fax 534-2273

Swink, Choctaw
Swink SD 100/PK-8
PO Box 73 74761 580-873-2695
Mark Bush, supt. Fax 873-9493
www.swink.k12.ok.us
Swink S 100/PK-8
PO Box 73 74761 580-873-2695
Mark Bush, prin. Fax 873-9493

Tahlequah, Cherokee, Pop. 16,075
Briggs SD 500/PK-8
17210 S 569 Rd 74464 918-456-4221
Speedy Chaffin, supt. Fax 456-3228
Briggs S 500/PK-8
17210 S 569 Rd 74464 918-456-4221
George Ritzhaupt, prin. Fax 456-3228

Grand View SD 400/PK-8
15481 N Jarvis Rd 74464 918-456-5131
Marcus Crittenden, supt. Fax 456-1526
Grand View S 400/PK-8
15481 N Jarvis Rd 74464 918-456-5131
Allen Rule, prin. Fax 456-1526

Lowrey SD 100/PK-8
21132 E 640 Rd 74464 918-456-4053
J. Scott Trower, supt. Fax 458-0647
www.lowrey.k12.ok.us
Lowrey S 100/PK-8
21132 E 640 Rd 74464 918-456-4053
J. Scott Trower, prin. Fax 458-0647

Tahlequah ISD 3,100/PK-12
PO Box 517 74465 918-458-4100
Dr. Shannon Goodsell, supt. Fax 458-4103
www.tahlequah.k12.ok.us
Cherokee ES 500/PK-4
800 Goingsnake St 74464 918-458-4110
Kair Ridenhour, prin. Fax 458-4112
Greenwood ES 600/PK-4
400 E Ross St 74464 918-458-4120
Susan Van Zant, prin. Fax 458-4122
Sequoyah ES 300/PK-4
425 S College Ave 74464 918-458-4130
Tom Barlow, prin. Fax 458-4132
Tahlequah MS 400/5-8
871 Pendleton St 74464 918-458-4140
DeAnn Mashburn, prin. Fax 458-4142

Woodall SD 500/PK-8
14090 W 835 Rd 74464 918-458-5444
Stephen Haynes, supt. Fax 456-5015
Woodall S 500/PK-8
14090 W 835 Rd 74464 918-456-1581
Lance Crawley, prin. Fax 456-5015

Shiloh Christian S 50/K-8
1282 Amity Ln 74464 918-458-5041
Linda Richardson, admin. Fax 458-5041

Talihina, Latimer, Pop. 1,234
Buffalo Valley ISD 200/K-12
4384 SE Highway 63 74571 918-522-4426
Ira Harris, supt. Fax 522-4287
www.buffalovalley.k12.ok.us
Buffalo Valley S 100/K-8
4384 SE Highway 63 74571 918-522-4802
Debra Bray, prin. Fax 522-4287

Talihina ISD 600/PK-12
PO Box 38 74571 918-567-2259
Robert Perryman, supt. Fax 567-3507
www.talihina.k12.ok.us/
Talihina ES, PO Box 38 74571 300/PK-6
Cary Ammons, prin. 918-567-2238

Taloga, Dewey, Pop. 361
Taloga ISD 100/PK-12
PO Box 158 73667 580-328-5577
Ron Brown, supt. Fax 328-5237
www.taloga.k12.ok.us
Taloga S 100/PK-8
PO Box 158 73667 580-328-5586
Ron Brown, prin. Fax 328-5237

Tecumseh, Pottawatomie, Pop. 6,516
Tecumseh ISD 2,000/K-12
1301 E Highland St 74873 405-598-3739
Tom Wilsie, supt. Fax 598-2861
www.tecumseh.k12.ok.us
Barnard ES 300/1-2
315 E Locust St 74873 405-598-3169
Cindy Horn, prin. Fax 598-5520
Cross Timbers ES 400/3-5
1111 W Highland St 74873 405-598-3771
Vicki Brewer, prin. Fax 598-8717
Krouch K 200/K-K
723 W Park St 74873 405-598-2967
Don Warden, prin. Fax 598-1633
Tecumseh MS 400/6-8
315 W Park St 74873 405-598-3744
Jeff Pruitt, prin. Fax 598-1948

Temple, Cotton, Pop. 1,149
Temple ISD 200/PK-12
PO Box 400 73568 580-342-6230
David Brewer, supt. Fax 342-6463
www.temple.k12.ok.us/
Temple S 200/PK-8
PO Box 400 73568 580-342-6839
Darrell Reid, prin. Fax 342-6463

Terral, Jefferson, Pop. 359
Terral SD 100/PK-8
PO Box 340 73569 580-437-2244
Greg Fouse, supt. Fax 437-2246
Terral S 100/PK-8
PO Box 340 73569 580-437-2244
Charles White, prin. Fax 437-2246

Texhoma, Texas, Pop. 928
Plainview SD 50/PK-6
RR 1 Box 71 73949 580-543-6366
Ronald Murphey, supt. Fax 543-6367
Plainview ES 50/PK-6
RR 1 Box 71 73949 580-543-6366
Ronald Murphey, prin. Fax 543-6367

Texhoma ISD 200/5-12
PO Box 648 73949 580-423-7433
Eric Smith, supt. Fax 423-7096
www.texhoma61.net/
Texhoma S 100/5-8
PO Box 648 73949 580-423-7371
Johnny James, prin. Fax 423-7096

Thackerville, Love, Pop. 417
Thackerville ISD 300/PK-12
PO Box 377 73459 580-276-2630
David Herron, supt. Fax 276-2638
www.thackervilleschools.org
Thackerville S 200/PK-8
PO Box 377 73459 580-276-9655
Tonja Mayo, prin. Fax 276-2638

Thomas, Custer, Pop. 1,150
Thomas-Fay-Custer Unified ISD 400/PK-12
PO Box 190 73669 580-661-3527
Rob Royalty, supt. Fax 661-3589
Custer IS 100/4-6
PO Box 190 73669 580-593-2257
Jeanne Karns, prin. Fax 593-2276
Thomas ES 200/PK-3
PO Box 190 73669 580-661-3521
Jeanne Karns, prin. Fax 661-3589

Tipton, Tillman, Pop. 841
Tipton ISD 200/K-12
PO Box 340 73570 580-667-5268
Shane Boothe, supt. Fax 667-5267
www.tiptonps.k12.ok.us
Tipton ES 100/K-6
PO Box 340 73570 580-667-5268
Bob Ward, prin. Fax 667-5481
Tipton MS 7-8
PO Box 340 73570 580-667-5268
Tracy Kincannon, prin. Fax 667-5325

Tishomingo, Johnston, Pop. 3,136
Tishomingo ISD 900/PK-12
1300 E Main St 73460 580-371-9190
Ronald Hutchings, supt. Fax 371-3765
www.tishomingo.k12.ok.us/
Tishomingo ES, 1300 E Main St 73460 400/PK-5
Gary Webb, prin. 580-371-2548
Tishomingo MS, 1300 E Main St 73460 200/6-8
Larry Davis, prin. 580-371-3602

Tonkawa, Kay, Pop. 3,132
Tonkawa ISD 600/PK-12
500 E North Ave 74653 580-628-3597
Rod Reese, supt. Fax 628-5132
www.tonkawa.k12.ok.us/
Tonkawa ES 400/PK-5
501 N Public St 74653 580-628-2592
Lori Simpson, prin. Fax 628-7594

Tulsa, Tulsa, Pop. 382,457
Allen-Bowden SD 400/PK-8
7049 Frankoma Rd 74131 918-224-4440
Dr. Penny Haynes, supt. Fax 224-0617
www.allenbowden.k12.ok.us
Allen-Bowden S 400/PK-8
7049 Frankoma Rd 74131 918-224-4440
Carmen Walters, prin. Fax 224-0617

Berryhill ISD 1,000/PK-12
3128 S 63rd West Ave 74107 918-446-1966
Mike Campbell, supt. Fax 446-6370
www.berryhill.k12.ok.us
Berryhill North ES 4-6
3128 S 63rd West Ave 74107 918-446-0584
Debbie Garner, prin. Fax 446-0500
Berryhill South ES 400/PK-3
3128 S 63rd West Ave 74107 918-445-6041
Jan Warner, prin. Fax 445-6021

Jenks ISD
Supt. — See Jenks
East IS 900/5-6
3933 E 91st St 74137 918-299-4411
Jeff Wright, prin. Fax 298-6610
Jenks MS 1,500/7-8
3019 E 101st St 74137 918-299-4411
Rob Miller, prin. Fax 298-0652
Southeast ES 700/PK-4
10222 S Yale Ave 74137 918-299-4411
Dr. Marilyn Livingston, prin. Fax 298-6625
West ES 1,500/PK-4
1200 W 91st St 74132 918-299-4411
Suzanne Lair, prin. Fax 298-6636

Tulsa ISD 38,400/PK-12
PO Box 470208 74147 918-746-6800
Michael Zolkoski Ph.D., supt. Fax 746-6850
www.tulsaschools.org
Academy Central ES 400/PK-5
1789 W Seminole St 74127 918-833-8760
Ebony Johnson, prin. Fax 833-8775
Addams ES 200/PK-5
5323 S 65th West Ave 74107 918-746-8780
Sheila Armstrong, prin.
Alcott ES, 525 E 46th St N 74126 300/K-5
Julian Wilson, prin. 918-746-9660
Anderson ES, 1921 E 29th St N 74110 400/PK-5
Brenda Anderson, prin. 918-925-1300
Barnard ES 200/K-5
2324 E 17th St 74104 918-833-9420
Twyla Waterson, prin. Fax 833-9435
Bell ES, 6304 E Admiral Blvd 74115 500/PK-5
Mary Ann Patrick, prin. 918-833-8600
Bryant ES, 6201 E Virgin St 74115 300/K-5
Barbara Mayes, prin. 918-746-9300
Burroughs ES 300/PK-5
1924 N Cincinnati Ave 74106 918-833-8780
Tammy Briton, prin. Fax 833-8795
Byrd MS 700/6-8
7502 E 57th St 74145 918-833-9520
Garry Nichols, prin. Fax 833-9551
Carnegie ES 500/K-5
4309 E 56th St 74135 918-833-9440
Martha Raybourn, prin. Fax 833-9457
Carver MS 600/6-8
624 E Oklahoma Pl 74106 918-925-1420
Melissa Woolridge, prin. Fax 925-1450
Cherokee ES 300/PK-5
6001 N Peoria Ave 74126 918-833-8840
Jody Tell, prin. Fax 833-8846
Chouteau ES 300/PK-5
575 N 39th West Ave 74127 918-833-8800
Dr. Michael Burk, prin. Fax 833-8812
Cleveland MS 400/6-8
724 N Birmingham Ave 74110 918-746-9400
John Maxwell, prin. Fax 746-9426
Clinton ES 300/K-5
1740 N Harvard Ave 74115 918-746-9320
Tanya Davis, prin. Fax 746-9332
Clinton MS, 2224 W 41st St 74107 400/6-8
John Autry, prin. 918-746-8640
Columbus ES 300/K-5
10620 E 27th St 74129 918-925-1460
K. Jene Carpenter, prin. Fax 925-1466

Cooper ES 700/PK-5
1808 S 123rd East Ave 74128 918-746-9480
Barbara Penrose, prin. Fax 746-9497
Disney ES, 11702 E 25th St 74129 800/PK-5
Louis Galluzzi, prin. 918-925-1480
Edison Preparatory MS 900/6-8
2906 E 41st St 74105 918-746-8500
Stacey Vernon, prin.
Eisenhower International ES 300/K-5
2819 S New Haven Ave 74114 918-746-9100
Stacy Strow, prin. Fax 746-9103
Eliot ES, 1442 E 36th St 74105 500/K-5
Donna Redyke, prin. 918-746-8700
Emerson ES 300/K-5
909 N Boston Ave 74106 918-925-1320
Tammy States, prin. Fax 925-1333
Field ES, 2249 S Phoenix Ave 74107 300/PK-5
Cindy Hemm, prin. 918-746-8840
Foster MS, 12121 E 21st St 74129 600/6-8
Darin Schmidt, prin. 918-746-9500
Gilcrease IS 200/6-6
5550 N Cincinnati Ave 74126 918-746-9600
Jolly Meadows, prin. Fax 833-8918
Greeley ES 200/PK-5
105 E 63rd St N 74126 918-746-9680
Raye Nero, prin. Fax 746-9686
Grimes ES 300/K-5
3213 E 56th St 74105 918-746-8720
Belinda Baldwin, prin. Fax 746-8738
Grissom ES 400/PK-5
6646 S 73rd East Ave 74133 918-833-9460
Jennifer Gripado, prin.
Hamilton MS 500/6-8
2316 N Norwood Pl 74115 918-746-9440
Debra Wiggins, prin. Fax 746-9447
Hawthorne ES 400/PK-5
1105 E 33rd St N 74106 918-925-1340
Lynnette Dixon, prin. Fax 925-1354
Henry ES, 3820 E 41st St 74135 400/PK-5
Daniel DePalma, prin. 918-746-9160
Hoover ES 500/PK-5
2327 S Darlington Ave 74114 918-746-9120
Elaine Reusser, prin. Fax 746-9131
Houston ES 200/K-5
5402 N Cincinnati Ave 74126 918-746-9020
Vicki Smith, prin.
Jackson ES 300/PK-5
2137 N Pittsburg Ave 74115 918-746-9340
Tasha Johnson, prin.
Jones ES K-5
1515 S 71st East Ave 74112 918-746-9040
Howard Benyon, prin.
Kendall-Whittier ES 1,000/K-5
2601 E 5th Pl 74104 918-833-9900
Judy Feary, prin.
Kerr ES, 202 S 117th East Ave 74128 600/K-5
Scott Griffith, prin. 918-746-9580
Key ES 400/PK-5
5702 S Irvington Ave 74135 918-833-9480
Neal Pascoe, prin. Fax 833-9493
Lanier ES 300/PK-5
1727 S Harvard Ave 74112 918-833-9380
Robert Morris, prin. Fax 833-9393
Lee ES 500/PK-5
1920 S Cincinnati Ave 74119 918-833-9400
Cindy Taylor, prin. Fax 833-9415
Lewis & Clark MS 700/6-8
737 S Garnett Rd 74128 918-746-9540
Ginger Bunnell, prin.
Lindbergh ES 500/PK-5
931 S 89th East Ave 74112 918-833-8700
Deidre Prevett, prin.
MacArthur ES 400/K-5
2182 S 73rd East Ave 74129 918-746-9140
Howard Wyble, prin. Fax 746-9155
Madison MS 300/6-8
4132 W Cameron St 74127 918-833-8860
Ava Hicks, prin. Fax 833-8891
Marshall ES, 1142 E 56th St 74105 400/PK-5
Kayla Robinson, prin. 918-746-8740
Mayo Demonstration S 200/PK-5
2525 S 101st East Ave 74129 918-925-1500
Andy McKenzie, prin.
McClure ES, 1770 E 61st St 74136 400/PK-5
Susan Baston, prin. 918-746-8760
McKinley ES, 6703 E King St 74115 400/PK-5
Cassandra Funderburk, prin. 918-833-8720
Mitchell ES 500/PK-5
733 N 73rd East Ave 74115 918-833-8740
Joanne Fennell, prin. Fax 833-8757
Newcomer International S 200/K-5
10908 E 5th St 74128 918-746-6930
Consuela Franklin, prin.
Nimitz MS 400/6-8
3111 E 56th St 74105 918-746-8800
Earlene Gathright, prin. Fax 746-8826
Owen ES 400/PK-5
1132 N Vandalia Ave 74115 918-746-9230
Angie Teas, prin. Fax 746-9240
Park ES 200/PK-5
3205 W 39th St 74107 918-746-8860
Anita Schroeder, prin. Fax 746-8875
Peary ES 200/K-5
10818 E 17th St 74128 918-925-1520
Donna Ferrell, prin. Fax 925-1536
Penn ES 200/K-5
2138 E 48th St N 74130 918-833-8940
Phyllis Lovett, prin. Fax 833-8955
Phillips ES, 3613 S Hudson Ave 74135 300/PK-5
Stephen Skeie, prin. 918-746-9180
Remington ES 300/K-5
2524 W 53rd St 74107 918-746-8880
Shelly Holman, prin. Fax 746-8891
Robertson ES, 2721 W 50th St 74107 400/K-5
Jessica Haight, prin. 918-746-8900
Roosevelt ES 500/PK-5
1202 W Easton St 74127 918-833-8960
Diane Dross, prin.
Salk ES 500/PK-5
7625 E 58th St 74145 918-833-9500
Corsair Thurman, prin. Fax 833-9506
Sandburg ES, 18580 E 3rd St 74108 200/K-5
Barbara Burke, prin. 918-746-9640
Sequoyah ES, 3441 E Archer St 74115 400/PK-5
Doug Howard, prin. 918-746-9360
Skelly ES 600/K-5
2940 S 90th East Ave 74129 918-925-1540
Mike Howe, prin.

Springdale ES, 2510 E Pine St 74110 — 400/K-5
Bradley Eddy, prin. — 918-746-9380
Thoreau Demonstration Academy — 500/6-8
7370 E 71st St 74133 — 918-833-9700
Thomas Padalino, prin.
Tulsa ECC, 2703 N Yorktown Pl 74110 — 200/PK-PK
Chloe Brown, prin. — 918-925-1400
Twain ES — 400/PK-5
541 S 43rd West Ave 74127 — 918-833-8820
Dr. Diane Hensley, prin. — Fax 833-8823
Whitman ES — 300/K-5
3924 N Lansing Ave 74106 — 918-925-1380
Brenda Jeter, prin.
Whitney MS — 600/6-8
2177 S 67th East Ave 74129 — 918-746-9260
Derrick Schmidt, prin. — Fax 746-9291
Wilson MS — 700/6-8
1127 S Columbia Ave 74104 — 918-833-9340
Dr. Oliver Wallace, prin.
Wright ES, 1110 E 45th Pl 74105 — 400/PK-5
Martie McCain, prin. — 918-746-8920
Zarrow International S — 300/K-5
2714 S 90th East Ave 74129 — 918-925-1560
Robin Postier, prin.

Union ISD — 13,800/PK-12
8506 E 61st St 74133 — 918-357-4321
Cathy Burden, supt. — Fax 357-6019
www.unionps.org
Boevers ES — 400/PK-5
3433 S 133rd East Ave 74134 — 918-357-4329
Sherri Fair, prin. — Fax 357-8399
Briarglen ES — 600/PK-5
3303 S 121st East Ave 74146 — 918-357-4330
Tamra Bird, prin. — Fax 357-8499
Cedar Ridge ES — 500/PK-5
9817 S Mingo Rd 74133 — 918-357-4331
Ellen Crager, prin. — Fax 357-8600
Clark ES — 700/PK-5
3656 S 103rd East Ave 74146 — 918-357-4332
Theresa Kiger, prin. — Fax 357-8599
Darnaby ES — 500/PK-5
7625 E 87th St 74133 — 918-357-4333
Tom Carson, prin. — Fax 357-8799
Grove ES — 600/PK-5
10202 E 62nd St 74133 — 918-357-4334
Kim Berns, prin. — Fax 357-8899
Jarman ES — 600/PK-5
9015 E 79th St 74133 — 918-357-4335
Patti Pitcock, prin. — Fax 357-8999
Jefferson ES — PK-5
8418 S 107th East Ave 74133 — 918-357-4339
Kim Whiteley, prin. — Fax 357-6699
Parks ES — PK-5
13804 E 46th Pl 74134 — 918-357-2757
Karen Vance, prin. — Fax 357-6899
Six/Seventh Grade Center — 2,200/6-7
10100 E 61st St 74133 — 918-357-4326
Steve Pittman, prin. — Fax 357-8047
Other Schools – See Broken Arrow

Christ the Redeemer Lutheran S — 100/PK-PK
2550 E 71st St 74136 — 918-492-1416
Michele Ackerman, prin. — Fax 492-3524
Evangelistic Temple S — 200/K-12
1339 E 55th St 74105 — 918-743-5597
Randy Fulmer, supt. — Fax 747-3457
Holland Hall — 1,000/PK-12
5666 E 81st St 74137 — 918-481-1111
Mark Desjardins Ph.D., hdmstr. — Fax 481-1145
Holy Family Cathedral S — 100/PK-8
820 S Boulder Ave 74119 — 918-582-0422
Jay Luetkemeyer, prin. — Fax 582-9705
Lincoln Christian S — 700/K-12
1003 N 129th East Ave 74116 — 918-234-8863
Stan White, admin. — Fax 234-8864
Marquette Catholic S — 400/PK-8
1519 S Quincy Ave 74120 — 918-584-4631
Pete Theban, prin. — Fax 584-4847
Metro Christian Academy — 1,000/K-12
6363 S Trenton Ave 74136 — 918-745-9868
Tim Cameron, hdmstr. — Fax 747-8724
Mingo Valley Christian S — 300/PK-12
8720 E 61st St 74133 — 918-294-0404
Dennis Queen, prin. — Fax 294-0555
Mizel Jewish Community Day S — 50/PK-5
2021 E 71st St 74136 — 918-494-0953
Monte Cassino S — 900/PK-8
2206 S Lewis Ave 74114 — 918-742-3364
Sr. Mary Clare Buthod, dir. — Fax 742-5206
Roberts University eAcademy — 100/3-12
7777 S Lewis Ave 74171 — 800-678-5899
Gail Marten, admin. — Fax 493-8996
St. Catherine S — 100/PK-8
2515 W 46th St 74107 — 918-446-9756
Victoria Adams, prin. — Fax 447-3780
St. Pius X S — 400/PK-8
1717 S 75th East Ave 74112 — 918-627-5367
Matthew Vereecke, prin. — Fax 627-6179
San Miguel MS — 6-8
2434 E Admiral Blvd 74110 — 918-728-7337
Anne Edwards, pres. — Fax 592-2208
School of St. Mary — 300/PK-8
1365 E 49th Pl 74105 — 918-749-9361
Maureen Clements, prin. — Fax 712-9604
Solid Foundation Preparatory Academy — 100/PK-5
PO Box 481085 74148 — 918-794-7800
Jayme Broome, admin. — Fax 794-7801
Southpark Christian S — 100/PK-6
10811 E 41st St 74146 — 918-663-4141
Tracy Lewis, prin. — Fax 663-4687
SS. Peter & Paul Catholic S — 200/PK-8
1428 N 67th East Ave 74115 — 918-836-2165
Patrick Martin, prin. — Fax 836-2597
Tulsa Adventist Jr Academy — 100/K-10
900 S New Haven Ave 74112 — 918-834-1107
Roger Loewen, admin. — Fax 834-2151
Undercroft Montessori S — 200/PK-8
3745 S Hudson Ave 74135 — 918-622-2890
LeAnn Huxall, prin. — Fax 622-3203
Victory Christian S — 1,200/K-12
7700 S Lewis Ave 74136 — 918-491-7720
Dr. Dennis Demuth, supt. — Fax 491-7727
Wright Christian Academy — 300/PK-12
11391 E Admiral Pl 74116 — 918-438-0922
Jeff Brown, admin. — Fax 438-0700

Tupelo, Coal, Pop. 360
Tupelo ISD — 300/PK-12
PO Box 239 74572 — 580-845-2460
Tony Stevens, supt. — Fax 845-2565
www.tupelo.k12.ok.us
Tupelo S — 200/PK-8
PO Box 239 74572 — 580-845-2802
Jason Goostree, prin. — Fax 845-2565

Turpin, Beaver
Turpin ISD — 400/PK-12
PO Box 187 73950 — 580-778-3333
Glyndel Holland, supt. — Fax 778-3179
www.turpin.k12.ok.us
Turpin S, PO Box 187 73950 — 300/PK-8
Patricia Pulliam, prin. — 580-778-3331

Tuskahoma, Pushmataha
Tuskahoma SD — 100/PK-8
PO Box 100 74574 — 918-569-7737
Barry Simpson, supt. — Fax 569-4154
Tuskahoma S — 100/PK-8
PO Box 100 74574 — 918-569-7737
Barry Simpson, prin. — Fax 569-4154

Tuttle, Grady, Pop. 5,365
Tuttle ISD — 1,500/K-12
PO Box 780 73089 — 405-381-2605
Lee Coker, supt. — Fax 381-4008
www.tuttleschools.info/
Tuttle ES — 500/K-3
PO Box 780 73089 — 405-381-2486
Monique Blagowsky, prin. — Fax 381-5008
Tuttle IS — 200/4-5
PO Box 780 73089 — 405-381-2368
Cheryl Williams, prin. — Fax 381-5028
Tuttle MS — 400/6-8
PO Box 780 73089 — 405-381-2062
Scott Moore, prin. — Fax 381-4630

Twin Oaks, Delaware
Leach SD — 200/PK-8
PO Box 211 74368 — 918-868-2277
Bruce Davis, supt. — Fax 868-3501
Leach S — 200/PK-8
PO Box 211 74368 — 918-868-2277
Bruce Davis, prin. — Fax 868-3501

Tyrone, Texas, Pop. 857
Tyrone ISD — 200/PK-12
PO Box 168 73951 — 580-854-6298
Dave Easterday, supt. — Fax 854-6474
Tyrone S — 200/PK-8
PO Box 168 73951 — 580-854-6298
Steve Parks, prin. — Fax 854-6474

Union City, Canadian, Pop. 1,387
Union City ISD — 300/PK-12
PO Box 279 73090 — 405-483-3531
Todd Carel, supt. — Fax 483-5599
www.unioncity.k12.ok.us/
Union City S — 200/PK-8
PO Box 279 73090 — 405-483-5327
Kerri Griggs, prin. — Fax 483-5587

Valliant, McCurtain, Pop. 759
Valliant ISD — 1,000/PK-12
604 E Lucas St 74764 — 580-933-7232
Don Mullenix, supt. — Fax 933-7289
www.vpsd.org
Valliant ES — 400/PK-5
604 E Lucas St 74764 — 580-933-7248
Melvin Fenley, prin. — Fax 933-7249
Valliant MS — 200/6-8
604 E Lucas St 74764 — 580-933-4253
Dennis Robberson, prin. — Fax 933-4254

Velma, Stephens, Pop. 693
Velma-Alma ISD — 300/PK-12
PO Box 8 73491 — 580-444-3355
Jerry Garrett, supt. — Fax 444-2554
Velma-Alma S — 200/PK-8
PO Box 8 73491 — 580-444-3357
Raymond Rice, prin. — Fax 444-2554

Verden, Grady, Pop. 682
Verden ISD — 300/PK-12
PO Box 99 73092 — 405-453-7247
David Davidson, supt. — Fax 453-7246
www.verden.k12.ok.us/
Verden E — 200/PK-6
PO Box 99 73092 — 405-453-7104
Gayle Venable, prin. — Fax 453-7246

Vian, Sequoyah, Pop. 1,460
Vian ISD — 1,000/PK-12
PO Box 434 74962 — 918-773-5798
Lawrence Barnes, supt. — Fax 773-3051
www.vian.k12.ok.us/
Vian ES — 500/PK-5
PO Box 434 74962 — 918-773-5311
Arland Callison, prin. — Fax 773-3051
Vian MS — 200/6-8
PO Box 434 74962 — 918-773-8631
Dr. Carla Wortman, prin. — Fax 773-3051

Vici, Dewey, Pop. 647
Vici ISD — 300/PK-12
PO Box 60 73859 — 580-995-4744
Steven Peretto, supt. — Fax 995-3101
www.vicischools.k12.ok.us
Vici S — 200/PK-8
PO Box 60 73859 — 580-995-4252
Tonna Flanagan, prin. — Fax 995-3101

Vinita, Craig, Pop. 6,017
Vinita ISD — 1,700/PK-12
114 S Scraper St 74301 — 918-256-6778
James Palmer, supt. — Fax 256-5617
www.vinitahornets.com
Hall Halsell ES — 400/PK-2
402 W Clyde Ave 74301 — 918-256-6692
Cathy Williams, prin.
Rogers ES, 101 S Smith St 74301 — 400/3-5
Kelly Grimmett, prin. — 918-256-5350
Vinita MS, 226 N Miller St 74301 — 400/6-8
Mark Lippe, prin. — 918-256-2402

White Oak ISD — 200/PK-12
27355 S 4340 Rd 74301 — 918-256-4484
Mark Allgood, supt. — Fax 256-4486
White Oak S, 27355 S 4340 Rd 74301 — 100/PK-8
David Bowen, prin. — 918-256-4484

Ketchum Adventist Junior Academy — 50/K-10
35369 S Highway 82 74301 — 918-782-2986
Wes McWilliams, prin. — Fax 782-1567

Wagoner, Wagoner, Pop. 7,877
Wagoner ISD — 2,400/PK-12
PO Box 508 74477 — 918-485-4046
Sonny Bates, supt. — Fax 485-8710
www.wagonerps.org
Central IS — 300/4-5
202 N Casaver Ave 74467 — 918-485-9543
Kelli Dixon, prin. — Fax 485-9544
Ellington ES — 400/K-1
601 SE 6th St 74467 — 918-485-3692
Janet Dotson, prin. — Fax 485-5162
Lincoln S — 100/PK-PK
902 Martin Luther King Blvd 74467 — 918-485-7615
Janet Dotson, prin. — Fax 485-7616
Teague ES — 400/2-3
700 N Story Ave 74467 — 918-485-2212
Bill Teague, prin. — Fax 485-5206
Wagoner MS — 500/6-8
500 Bulldog Cir 74467 — 918-485-9541
Darrell Morgan, prin. — Fax 485-4149

Wainwright, Muskogee, Pop. 201
Wainwright SD — 100/PK-8
PO Box 189 74468 — 918-474-3484
Jim Ogden, supt. — Fax 474-3744
Wainwright S — 100/PK-8
PO Box 189 74468 — 918-474-3484
Jim Ogden, prin. — Fax 474-3744

Wakita, Grant, Pop. 396
Wakita ISD — 100/PK-12
PO Box 45 73771 — 580-594-2261
Mike Jones, supt. — Fax 594-2263
www.wakita.k12.ok.us
Wakita S — 100/PK-8
PO Box 45 73771 — 580-594-2262
Mike Jones, prin. — Fax 594-2263

Walters, Cotton, Pop. 2,610
Walters ISD — 700/PK-12
418 S Broadway St 73572 — 580-875-2568
Jimmie Dedmon, supt. — Fax 875-2831
blued.org
Walters ES, 418 S Broadway St 73572 — 300/PK-5
Howard Baggs, prin. — 580-875-3144
Walters MS, 418 S Broadway St 73572 — 100/6-8
Laurie Graham, prin. — 580-875-3214

Wanette, Pottawatomie, Pop. 418
Wanette ISD — 200/PK-12
PO Box 161 74878 — 405-383-2656
Rick Riggs, supt. — Fax 383-2449
www.wanette.k12.ok.us/
Wanette S — 100/PK-8
PO Box 161 74878 — 405-383-2222
LeGay Riggs, prin. — Fax 383-2185

Wapanucka, Johnston, Pop. 432
Wapanucka ISD — 200/PK-12
PO Box 188 73461 — 580-937-4466
Stanley Williams, supt. — Fax 937-4804
Wapanucka S, PO Box 188 73461 — 200/PK-8
Bill Vann, prin. — 580-937-4288

Warner, Muskogee, Pop. 1,443
Warner ISD — 700/PK-12
1012 5th Ave 74469 — 918-463-5171
Monte Madewell, supt. — Fax 463-2542
www.warner.k12.ok.us/
Warner S — 500/PK-8
1012 5th Ave 74469 — 918-463-2950
Brenda Bales, prin. — Fax 463-5936

Warr Acres, Oklahoma, Pop. 9,475
Putnam City ISD
Supt. — See Oklahoma City
Arbor Grove ES — 400/K-5
5430 NW 40th St 73122 — 405-789-4985
Dr. Diane Welker, prin. — Fax 491-7551
Central ES — 600/PK-5
5721 NW 39th St 73122 — 405-789-5696
Sherri Brown, prin. — Fax 491-7572

Washington, McClain, Pop. 530
Washington ISD — 900/PK-12
PO Box 98 73093 — 405-288-6190
A.J. Brewer, supt. — Fax 288-6214
www.washington.k12.ok.us/
Washington ES — 400/PK-5
PO Box 98 73093 — 405-288-2353
Rocky Clarke, prin. — Fax 288-6214
Washington MS — 200/6-8
PO Box 98 73093 — 405-288-2428
Stuart McPherson, prin. — Fax 288-6214

Watonga, Blaine, Pop. 5,588
Watonga ISD — 800/PK-12
PO Box 310 73772 — 580-623-7364
Dr. Craig Cummins, supt. — Fax 623-7370
www.watonga.k12.ok.us
Watonga ES — 400/PK-5
PO Box 640 73772 — 580-623-5248
Linda Gossett, prin. — Fax 623-5238
Watonga MS — 200/6-8
PO Box 310 73772 — 580-623-7361
Robin Roof, prin. — Fax 623-7371

Watson, McCurtain
Watson SD — 100/PK-8
PO Box 10 74963 — 580-244-3327
Frances Cavinder, supt. — Fax 244-3526
Watson S — 100/PK-8
PO Box 10 74963 — 580-244-3327
Larry Davis, prin. — Fax 244-3526

Watts, Adair, Pop. 328
Skelly SD — 100/PK-8
RR 1 Box 918 74964 — 918-723-5572
Paul Thompson, supt. — Fax 723-4516

Skelly S 100/PK-8
RR 1 Box 918 74964 918-723-5572
Paul Thompson, prin. Fax 723-4516

Watts ISD 400/PK-12
RR 2 Box 1 74964 918-422-5311
J. David Smith, supt. Fax 422-5556
www.wattsschool.com
Watts S, RR 2 Box 1 74964 300/PK-8
Kerry Husted, prin. 918-422-5131

Waukomis, Garfield, Pop. 1,201
Pioneer-Pleasant Vale ISD 500/PK-12
6520 E Wood Rd 73773 580-758-3282
Brent Koontz, supt. Fax 758-1541
www.ppv.k12.ok.us/
Pioneer-Pleasant Vale JHS 100/7-8
6520 E Wood Rd 73773 580-758-3282
Randy Schneider, prin.
Other Schools – See Enid

Waukomis ISD 300/PK-12
PO Box 729 73773 580-758-3247
Brad Goodwin, supt. Fax 758-3834
www.waukomis.k12.ok.us
Waukomis ES 200/PK-5
PO Box 729 73773 580-758-3264
Shawn Tennyson, prin. Fax 758-3078

Waurika, Jefferson, Pop. 1,857
Waurika ISD 400/PK-12
600 E Florida Ave 73573 580-228-3373
Roxie Terry, supt. Fax 228-3428
www.waurikaschools.org
Waurika ES 200/PK-5
600 Educational Ave 73573 580-228-3531
Cynthia Walker, prin. Fax 228-3428

Wayne, McClain, Pop. 727
Wayne ISD 500/PK-12
212 S Seifried St 73095 405-449-3646
David Powell, supt. Fax 449-7095
www.wayne.k12.ok.us
Wayne ES 200/PK-5
212 S Seifried St 73095 405-449-3305
Donna Soutee, prin. Fax 449-7095
Wayne MS 100/6-8
212 S Seifried St 73095 405-449-7047
Billy Lucas, prin. Fax 449-7095

Waynoka, Woods, Pop. 930
Waynoka ISD 200/PK-12
2134 Lincoln St 73860 580-824-6561
Dale Ross, supt. Fax 824-0656
www.waynoka.k12.ok.us/
Waynoka S, 2134 Lincoln St 73860 200/PK-8
Michael Meriwether, prin. 580-824-5151

Weatherford, Custer, Pop. 9,738
Weatherford ISD 1,800/PK-12
516 N Broadway St 73096 580-772-3327
Bill Seitter, supt. Fax 774-0821
www.wpsok.org
Burcham ES 400/PK-1
1401 N Lark St 73096 580-774-0812
Marla Pankratz, prin. Fax 774-1910
East ES 200/2-3
701 E Proctor Ave 73096 580-772-3533
Eddie Bennett, prin. Fax 774-1905
Weatherford MS 400/6-8
509 N Custer St 73096 580-772-2270
Tim Merchant, prin. Fax 774-1981
West ES 200/4-5
811 W Huber Ave 73096 580-772-2245
Charles Burr, prin. Fax 774-1903

Western Oklahoma Christian S 50/PK-2
1709 Lyle Rd 73096 580-774-8159
Joanie Quiring, prin.

Webbers Falls, Muskogee, Pop. 724
Webbers Falls ISD 300/PK-12
PO Box 300 74470 918-464-2580
Dudley Hume, supt. Fax 464-2313
www.webbersfalls.k12.ok.us/
Webbers Falls S 200/PK-8
PO Box 300 74470 918-464-2383
Judy Morton, prin. Fax 464-2313

Welch, Craig, Pop. 600
Welch ISD 400/PK-12
PO Box 189 74369 918-788-3319
Dr. Clark McKeon, supt. Fax 788-3734
welchwildcats.net
Welch ES 300/PK-6
PO Box 189 74369 918-788-3130
Kim Hall, prin. Fax 788-3322

Weleetka, Okfuskee, Pop. 954
Graham ISD 100/PK-12
RR 1 Box 91 74880 918-652-8935
Dusty Chancey, supt. Fax 652-2422
www.graham.k12.ok.us
Graham S 100/PK-8
RR 1 Box 91 74880 918-652-8935
Wanda Mankin, prin. Fax 652-2422

Weleetka ISD 500/PK-12
PO Box 278 74880 405-786-2442
Dan Parrish, supt. Fax 786-2625
www.weleetka.k12.ok.us
Spence Memorial ES 300/PK-6
PO Box 278 74880 405-786-2071
Kelly Bowen, prin. Fax 786-2625

Welling, Cherokee
Tenkiller SD 300/PK-8
26106 E 863 Rd 74471 918-457-5996
Randy Rountree, supt. Fax 457-5619
www.tenkiller.k12.ok.us/
Tenkiller S 300/PK-8
26106 E 863 Rd 74471 918-457-5996
Bryan Hix, prin. Fax 457-5619

Wellston, Lincoln, Pop. 826
Wellston ISD 700/PK-12
PO Box 60 74881 405-356-2534
Dwayne Danker, supt. Fax 356-2838
Wellston ES 300/PK-5
PO Box 60 74881 405-356-2256
Scott Roper, prin. Fax 356-4402
Wellston MS 200/6-8
PO Box 60 74881 405-356-2533
Mark Grubbs, prin. Fax 356-2838

Westville, Adair, Pop. 1,652
Westville ISD 800/PK-12
PO Box 410 74965 918-723-3181
Sherri Prentice, supt. Fax 723-3042
www.westville.k12.ok.us
Westville ES PK-2
PO Box 410 74965 918-723-4355
Ryan Swank, prin. Fax 723-3042
Westville IS 300/3-6
PO Box 410 74965 918-723-3351
Beth Glabas, prin. Fax 723-3042

Wetumka, Hughes, Pop. 1,420
Wetumka ISD 400/PK-12
416 S Tiger St 74883 405-452-5150
Michael Jaggars, supt. Fax 452-3052
www.wetumka.k12.ok.us/
Wetumka S 300/PK-8
416 S Tiger St 74883 405-452-3245
Amy Kent, prin. Fax 452-5809

Wewoka, Seminole, Pop. 3,437
Justice SD 200/PK-8
36507 EW 1310 74884 405-257-2962
William Harrison, supt. Fax 257-5514
www.justiceelem.k12.ok.us
Justice S 200/PK-8
36507 EW 1310 74884 405-257-2962
Chris Bryan, prin. Fax 257-5514

New Lima ISD 300/PK-12
116 Gross St 74884 405-257-5771
Gil Turpin, supt. Fax 257-2587
www.newlima.k12.ok.us
New Lima ES 200/PK-6
116 Gross St 74884 405-257-3948
Rebeccah Green, prin. Fax 257-9354

Wewoka ISD 700/PK-12
PO Box 870 74884 405-257-5475
Sam McElvany, supt. Fax 257-2303
www.wps.k12.ok.us/
Wewoka ES 300/PK-5
PO Box 870 74884 405-257-2341
Kellye Blankenship, prin. Fax 257-2303
Wewoka MS 100/6-8
PO Box 870 74884 405-257-2340
Darrell Brown, prin. Fax 257-2303

Whitefield, Haskell, Pop. 222
Whitefield SD 100/PK-8
PO Box 178 74472 918-967-8572
Brenda Edwards, supt. Fax 967-0007
www.whitefield.k12.ok.us
Whitefield S 100/PK-8
PO Box 178 74472 918-967-8572
Brenda Edwards, prin. Fax 967-0007

Whitesboro, LeFlore
Whitesboro ISD 200/PK-12
PO Box 150 74577 918-567-2556
Dr. John Turner, supt. Fax 567-2842
Whitesboro S, PO Box 150 74577 100/PK-8
Rocky Farris, prin. 918-567-3016

Wilburton, Latimer, Pop. 2,934
Wilburton ISD 900/PK-12
1201 W Blair Ave 74578 918-465-2100
Charles Enis, supt. Fax 465-3086
Wilburton ES, 1201 W Blair Ave 74578 500/PK-5
Jan Gilmore, prin. 918-465-2245
Wilburton JHS 200/6-8
1201 W Blair Ave 74578 918-465-2281
Tressa Taylor Moore, prin.

Wilson, Carter, Pop. 1,623
Wilson ISD 500/PK-12
1860 Hewitt Rd 73463 580-668-2306
Kevin Stinson, supt. Fax 668-2170
www.wilson.k12.ok.us/
Wilson S 300/PK-8
1860 Hewitt Rd 73463 580-668-2355
Denise Brunk, prin. Fax 668-2170

Zaneis SD 200/PK-8
30515 US Highway 70 73463 580-668-2955
Calvin Wade, supt. Fax 668-2955
Zaneis S 200/PK-8
30515 US Highway 70 73463 580-668-2955
Calvin Wade, prin. Fax 668-2955

Wister, LeFlore, Pop. 1,025
Wister ISD 600/PK-12
201 Logan St 74966 918-655-7381
Jerry Carpenter, supt. Fax 655-7402
www.wisterschools.org/
Wister S 400/PK-8
201 Logan St 74966 918-655-7481
Kay Garrett, prin. Fax 655-7402

Woodward, Woodward, Pop. 11,931
Woodward ISD 2,600/PK-12
PO Box 668 73802 580-256-6063
Dr. Vickie Williams, supt. Fax 256-4391
www.woodwardps.net
Cedar Heights ES 300/1-4
PO Box 668 73802 580-256-6521
Sharon Yeager, prin. Fax 571-6250
Highland Park ES 300/1-4
PO Box 668 73802 580-256-2500
Maggie Sander, prin. Fax 571-6251
Mann ES 300/1-4
PO Box 668 73802 580-256-2660
Petra Sullender, prin. Fax 571-6252
Woodward ECC 400/PK-K
PO Box 668 73802 580-256-2561
Debbie Jones, prin. Fax 571-3155
Woodward MS North 300/5-6
PO Box 668 73802 580-256-5357
Diana Ball, prin. Fax 571-3154
Woodward MS South 400/7-8
PO Box 668 73802 580-256-7901
Frank Harrington, prin. Fax 256-8014

Wright City, McCurtain, Pop. 814
Wright City ISD 500/PK-12
PO Box 329 74766 580-981-2824
David Hawkins, supt. Fax 981-2115
www.wcisd.org/
Wright City ES 300/PK-6
PO Box 329 74766 580-981-2248
Frank Partridge, prin. Fax 981-2304
Wright City JHS 100/7-8
PO Box 329 74766 580-981-2558
Bob Finley, prin. Fax 981-2329

Wyandotte, Ottawa, Pop. 359
Turkey Ford SD 100/PK-6
23900 S 670 Rd 74370 918-786-4902
Tamyra D. Larson, supt. Fax 787-5015
www.familyeducation.com/ok/turkey
Turkey Ford ES 100/PK-6
23900 S 670 Rd 74370 918-786-4902
Tamyra Larson, prin. Fax 787-5015

Wyandotte ISD 800/PK-12
PO Box 360 74370 918-678-2255
Duane Thomas, supt. Fax 678-2304
www.wyandotte.k12.ok.us
Wyandotte ES 400/PK-5
PO Box 360 74370 918-678-2299
Carla Lyons, prin. Fax 678-3907
Wyandotte MS 200/6-8
PO Box 360 74370 918-678-2222
Steve Buckingham, prin. Fax 678-3906

Wynnewood, Garvin, Pop. 2,314
Wynnewood ISD 700/PK-12
702 E Robert S Kerr Blvd 73098 405-665-2004
Bill Weldon, supt. Fax 665-5425
www.wynnewood.k12.ok.us/
Central ES 200/PK-4
702 E Robert S Kerr Blvd 73098 405-665-4371
Dennis Cain, prin.
Wynnewood MS 200/5-8
702 E Robert S Kerr Blvd 73098 405-665-4105
Mitzi Winters, prin.

Wynona, Osage, Pop. 535
Wynona ISD 200/PK-12
PO Box 700 74084 918-846-2467
Dixie Hurd, supt. Fax 846-2883
www.wynona.k12.ok.us
Wynona S 100/PK-8
PO Box 700 74084 918-846-2467
Joe Chandler, prin. Fax 846-2883

Yale, Payne, Pop. 1,254
Yale ISD 500/PK-12
315 E Chicago Ave 74085 918-387-2434
Mike Wilson, supt. Fax 387-2503
www.yale.k12.ok.us/
Yale ES 300/PK-6
800 N C St 74085 918-387-2428
Rodney Vollmer, prin. Fax 387-2847
Yale JHS 100/7-8
315 E Chicago Ave 74085 918-387-2118
Steve Shanks, prin. Fax 387-2503

Yukon, Canadian, Pop. 22,032
Mustang ISD
Supt. — See Mustang
Mustang Creek ES 800/K-5
10821 SW 15th Street 73099 405-324-4567
Meggan Wilson, prin. Fax 324-4562
Mustang Trails ES 600/K-5
12025 SW 15th Ter 73099 405-324-0016
Sondra Bivens, prin. Fax 324-4577
Mustang Valley ES 700/K-5
3100 S Morgan Rd 73099 405-324-2541
Pam McLaughlin, prin. Fax 324-4578

Piedmont ISD
Supt. — See Piedmont
Stone Ridge ES 600/PK-5
10000 W Memorial Rd 73099 405-373-4227
Margaret McNair, prin.

Yukon ISD 6,400/K-12
600 Maple St 73099 405-354-2587
Dr. Bill Denton, supt. Fax 354-4208
www.yukonps.com
Central ES 400/K-5
300 S 9th St 73099 405-354-2501
Carol Burton, prin. Fax 354-2502
Independence MS 700/6-8
500 E Vandament Ave 73099 405-354-5274
Tresa Smith, prin. Fax 354-0921
Lakeview MS 700/6-8
2700 N Mustang Rd 73099 405-350-2630
Janice McComas, prin. Fax 350-2632
Myers ES 300/K-5
1200 S 1st St 73099 405-354-5252
Robin Russell, prin. Fax 354-5253
Parkland ES 400/K-5
2201 S Cornwell Dr 73099 405-354-7786
Lance Haggard, prin. Fax 354-2327
Ranchwood ES 400/K-5
607 Annawood Dr 73099 405-354-6616
Kristin Kilpatrick, prin. Fax 354-4541
Shedeck ES 300/K-5
2100 S Holly Ave 73099 405-354-6601
Mark Park, prin. Fax 354-6602
Skyview ES 700/K-5
2800 N Mustang Rd 73099 405-354-4852
Cecil Bowles, prin. Fax 354-4853
Surrey Hills ES 300/K-5
10700 Hastings Ave 73099 405-373-1973
Carla Smith, prin. Fax 373-2021

St. John Nepomuk S 200/PK-8
600 Garth Brooks Blvd 73099 405-354-2509
Diane Floyd, prin. Fax 354-8192
Southwest Covenant S 200/PK-12
2250 N Mustang Rd 73099 405-354-0772
Ronald Yocum, hdmstr. Fax 350-2670

OREGON

OREGON DEPARTMENT OF EDUCATION
255 Capitol St NE, Salem 97310-0406
Telephone 503-947-5600
Fax 503-378-5156
Website http://www.ode.state.or.us

Superintendent of Public Instruction   Susan Castillo

OREGON BOARD OF EDUCATION
255 Capitol St NE, Salem 97310-0406

Chairperson   Duncan Wyse

EDUCATION SERVICE DISTRICTS (ESD)

Clackamas ESD
Milt Dennison, supt. 503-675-4000
13455 SE 97th Ave Fax 675-4200
Clackamas 97015
www.clackesd.k12.or.us

Columbia Gorge ESD
James Carnes Ed.D., supt. 541-298-5155
400 E Scenic Dr Ste 207 Fax 296-2965
The Dalles 97058
www.cgesd.k12.or.us/

Douglas ESD
Jonathan Hill, supt. 541-440-4777
1871 NE Stephens St Fax 440-4771
Roseburg 97470
www.douglasesd.k12.or.us

Grant ESD
Robert Waltenburg, supt. 541-575-1349
835 S Canyon Blvd Ste A Fax 575-3601
John Day 97845
www.grantesd.k12.or.us

Harney ESD
Dennis Mills, supt. 541-573-2426
PO Box 460, Burns 97720 Fax 573-1822
www.harneyesd.k12.or.us

High Desert ESD
Dennis Dempsey, supt. 541-693-5600
145 SE Salmon Ave Ste A Fax 693-5601
Redmond 97756
www.hdesd.org

Jefferson ESD
Kay Baker, supt. 541-475-2804
295 SE Buff St, Madras 97741 Fax 475-2827
www.jcesd.k12.or.us

Lake ESD
Judith May, supt. 541-947-3371
357 N L St, Lakeview 97630 Fax 947-3373
www.lakeesd.k12.or.us/

Lane ESD
Debbie Egan, supt. 541-461-8200
1200 Highway 99 N, Eugene 97402 Fax 461-8298
www.lane.k12.or.us

Linn-Benton-Lincoln ESD
Susan Waddell, supt. 541-812-2600
905 4th Ave SE, Albany 97321 Fax 926-6047
www.lblesd.k12.or.us

Malheur ESD
Tim Labrousse, supt. 541-473-3138
363 A St W, Vale 97918 Fax 473-3915
www.malesd.k12.or.us

Multnomah ESD
Ron Hitchcock, supt. 503-255-1841
PO Box 301039, Portland 97294 Fax 257-1525
www.mesd.k12.or.us

North Central ESD
Mike Carroll, supt. 541-384-2732
PO Box 637, Condon 97823 Fax 384-2752
www.ncesd.k12.or.us

Northwest Regional ESD
Jim Mabbott, supt. 503-614-1428
5825 NE Ray Cir, Hillsboro 97124 Fax 614-1440
www.nwresd.k12.or.us

Region 18 ESD
Edward Jensen, supt. 541-426-4997
107 SW 1st St Ste 105 Fax 426-3732
Enterprise 97828
www.r18esd.org/

South Coast ESD
George Woodruff, supt. 541-269-1611
1350 Teakwood Ave Fax 266-4040
Coos Bay 97420
www.scesd.k12.or.us

Southern Oregon ESD
Steve Boyarsky, supt. 541-776-8590
101 N Grape St, Medford 97501 Fax 779-2018
www.soesd.k12.or.us

Umatilla-Morrow ESD
Mark Mulvihill, supt. 541-276-6616
2001 SW Nye Ave Fax 276-4252
Pendleton 97801
www.umesd.k12.or.us

Union-Baker ESD
Michael Sowder, supt. 541-963-4106
10100 N McAlister Rd Fax 963-7256
La Grande 97850
www.ubesd.k12.or.us

Willamette ESD
Maureen Casey, supt. 503-588-5330
2611 Pringle Rd SE, Salem 97302 Fax 363-5787
www.wesd.org

PUBLIC, PRIVATE AND CATHOLIC ELEMENTARY SCHOOLS

Adel, Lake
Adel SD 21
Supt. — See Lakeview
Adel S, PO Box 117 97620 50/K-8
John Griffin, prin. 541-947-3371

Adrian, Malheur, Pop. 143
Adrian SD 61 300/K-12
PO Box 108 97901 541-372-2335
Gene Mills, supt. Fax 372-5380
www.adriansd.com
Adrian S 200/K-8
PO Box 108 97901 541-372-2337
Bill Ellsworth, prin. Fax 372-5380

Agness, Curry
Central Curry SD 1
Supt. — See Gold Beach
Agness S 50/K-8
PO Box 32 97406 541-247-7896
Helaine Truthstone, prin. Fax 247-9496

Albany, Linn, Pop. 44,797
Greater Albany SD 8J 8,800/K-12
718 7th Ave SW 97321 541-967-4501
Maria Delapoen, supt. Fax 967-4587
albany.k12.or.us
Calapooia MS 700/6-8
830 24th Ave SE, 541-967-4555
Pat Weidmann, prin. Fax 924-3702
Central ES 200/K-5
336 9th Ave SW 97321 541-967-4561
John Hunter, prin. Fax 924-3625
Clover Ridge ES 300/K-5
2953 Clover Ridge Rd NE, 541-967-4565
Jason Hoffert-Hay, prin. Fax 924-3707
Fairmount ES K-1
1005 NW Springhill Rd 97321 541-704-1021
Jay Thompson, prin. Fax 704-1140
Fir Grove PS 200/K-2
5355 NW Scenic Dr 97321 541-967-4570
Rich Sipe, prin. Fax 924-3714
Lafayette ES 400/K-5
3122 Madison St SE, 541-967-4575
Heather Huzefka, prin. Fax 924-3622
Liberty ES 400/K-5
2345 Liberty St SW 97321 541-967-4578
Janell Ediger, prin. Fax 924-3710
Memorial MS 700/6-8
1050 Queen Ave SW 97321 541-967-4537
Ken Gilbert, prin. Fax 924-3703
North Albany ES 200/2-5
815 NW Thornton Lake Dr 97321 541-967-4588
Jay Thompson, prin. Fax 924-3719
North Albany MS 600/6-8
1205 NW North Albany Rd 97321 541-967-4541
Jane Evans, prin. Fax 924-3704
Oak ES 300/K-5
3610 Oak St SE, 541-967-4591
Tonja Everest, prin. Fax 924-3708
Oak Grove IS 200/3-5
1500 NW Oak Grove Dr 97321 541-967-4596
Rich Sipe, prin. Fax 924-3715
Periwinkle ES 500/K-5
2196 21st Ave SE, 541-967-4600
Elisa Stephens, prin. Fax 924-3711
South Shore ES 400/K-5
910 Bain St SE, 541-967-4604
Judy Stoller, prin. Fax 924-3718
Sunrise ES 400/K-5
730 19th Ave SE, 541-967-4608
Lori Greenfield, prin. Fax 924-3726
Takena ES 200/K-5
1210 Takena St SW 97321 541-967-4613
John Hunter, prin. Fax 924-3717
Waverly ES 200/K-5
425 Columbus St SE 97321 541-967-4617
Frank Caropelo, prin. Fax 924-3620
Other Schools – See Tangent

Albany Christian S 200/PK-8
420 3rd Ave SE 97321 541-928-1110
Jason Platt, prin. Fax 791-1864
Fairview Christian S 100/K-12
35100 Goltra Rd SE, 541-928-4219
Ray Allen, prin. Fax 928-2140
Good Shepherd Lutheran Preschool 100/PK-K
1910 34th Ave SE, 541-926-0246
St. Mary's S 100/PK-8
815 Broadalbin St SW 97321 541-928-7474
Chris Meadows, prin. Fax 924-9342

Aloha, Washington, Pop. 43,600
Hillsboro SD 1J
Supt. — See Hillsboro
Butternut Creek ES 500/K-6
20395 SW Florence St 97007 503-844-1390
Enedelia Schofield, prin. Fax 591-7293

Faith Bible Christian S 300/PK-8
16860 SW Blanton St 97007 503-642-4112
Brad Wallace, prin. Fax 649-4470
Life Christian S 300/PK-12
5585 SW 209th Ave 97007 503-259-1329
Adam Kronberger, admin. Fax 649-5484

Alsea, Benton
Alsea SD 7J 200/K-12
PO Box B 97324 541-487-4305
Jason Larson, supt. Fax 487-4089
www.alsea.k12.or.us/
Alsea ES 100/K-6
PO Box B 97324 541-487-4305
Jason Larson, prin. Fax 487-4089

Amity, Yamhill, Pop. 1,463
Amity SD 4J 800/K-12
PO Box 138 97101 503-835-2171
Reg McShane, supt. Fax 835-5050
www.amity.k12.or.us
Amity ES 300/K-5
PO Box 138 97101 503-835-3751
Nanci Sheeran, prin. Fax 835-0411
Amity MS 200/6-8
PO Box 138 97101 503-835-0518
Dave Lund, prin. Fax 835-0418

Perrydale SD 21 200/K-12
7445 Perrydale Rd 97101 503-835-3184
Robin Stoutt, supt. Fax 835-0631
www.perrydale.k12.or.us
Perrydale ES K-5
7445 Perrydale Rd 97101 503-835-3184
Robin Stoutt, prin. Fax 835-0631

Applegate, Jackson
Three Rivers County SD
Supt. — See Grants Pass
Applegate S 100/K-8
14188 Highway 238 97530 541-846-6280
Stephanie Hart, prin. Fax 846-6055

Arlington, Gilliam, Pop. 490
Arlington SD 3 100/K-12
PO Box 10 97812 541-454-2632
Raymon Smith, supt. Fax 454-2137
www.honkernet.net
Arlington S 100/K-8
PO Box 10 97812 541-454-2727
Raymon Smith, prin. Fax 454-2335

Arock, Malheur
Arock SD 81 50/K-8
PO Box 131 97902 541-586-2325
Fax 586-2304
www.arock.k12.or.us
Jones S, PO Box 131 97902 50/K-8
Lisabeth Hassler, lead tchr. 541-586-2325

Ashland, Jackson, Pop. 20,829
Ashland SD 5 2,700/K-12
885 Siskiyou Blvd 97520 541-482-2811
Juli DiChiro, supt. Fax 482-2185
www.ashland.k12.or.us/
Ashland MS 600/6-8
100 Walker Ave 97520 541-482-1611
Steve Retzlaff, prin. Fax 482-8112
Bellview ES 300/K-5
1070 Tolman Creek Rd 97520 541-482-1310
Christine McCollom, prin. Fax 482-2591
Helman ES 300/K-5
705 Helman St 97520 541-482-5620
Susan Hollandsworth, prin. Fax 482-2560
Muir S K-8
100 Walker Ave 97520 541-482-8577
Michelle Zundel, prin. Fax 482-8112
Walker ES 300/K-5
364 Walker Ave 97520 541-482-1516
Patty Michiels, prin. Fax 482-2671

Pinehurst SD 94 50/K-8
15337 Highway 66 97520 541-482-1910
Fax 482-7956
pinehurst.k12.or.us
Pinehurst S 50/K-8
15337 Highway 66 97520 541-482-1910
Laurie Grupe, lead tchr. Fax 482-7956

Siskiyou S 200/1-8
631 Clay St 97520 541-482-8223
Catherine Razi, prin. Fax 488-9549

Ashwood, Jefferson
Ashwood SD 8 50/K-6
PO Box 2 97711 541-489-3433
Fax 489-3297
www.ashwood.k12.or.us
Ashwood ES, PO Box 2 97711 50/K-6
Penny Marston, lead tchr. 541-489-3297

Astoria, Clatsop, Pop. 9,784
Astoria SD 1 1,600/K-12
785 Alameda Ave 97103 503-325-6441
Craig Hoppes, supt. Fax 325-6524
www.astoria.k12.or.us/
Astor ES 300/K-2
3550 Franklin Ave 97103 503-325-6672
Travis Roe, prin. Fax 325-6335
Astoria MS 300/6-8
1100 Klaskanine Ave 97103 503-325-4331
Ron Alley, prin. Fax 325-3040
Lewis & Clark ES 300/3-5
92179 Lewis and Clark Rd 97103 503-325-2032
Brian Ploghoft, prin. Fax 325-2298

Knappa SD 4 500/K-12
41535 Old Highway 30 97103 503-458-6166
Rick Pass, supt. Fax 458-5466
www.knappasd.k12.or.us
Lahti S 300/K-8
41535 Old Highway 30 97103 503-458-6162
Lisa Darnold, prin. Fax 458-6979

Peace Learning Center 100/PK-PK
565 12th St 97103 – Lisa Berry, dir. 503-325-4041
Star of the Sea S 200/PK-8
1411 Grand Ave 97103 503-325-3771
Dr. Terry Campbell, prin. Fax 325-5413

Athena, Umatilla, Pop. 1,218
Athena-Weston SD 29RJ 600/K-12
375 S 5th St 97813 541-566-3551
Jerry Copeland, supt. Fax 566-9454
www.athwest.k12.or.us/
Athena ES 200/K-3
375 S 5th St 97813 541-566-3581
Jerry Copeland, prin. Fax 566-9454
Other Schools – See Weston

Aumsville, Marion, Pop. 3,202
Cascade SD 5
Supt. — See Turner
Aumsville ES 500/K-5
572 N 11th St 97325 503-749-8492
Jim Engles, prin. Fax 749-8327
Cascade Family and Child Development Ctr PK-PK
574 N 11th St 97325 503-749-8486
Linda Yoesel, dir. Fax 749-8480

Aurora, Marion, Pop. 879
North Marion SD 15 1,900/PK-12
20256 Grim Rd NE 97002 503-678-5835
Linda Reeves, supt. Fax 678-1473
www.nmarion.k12.or.us
North Marion IS 500/3-5
20237 Grim Rd NE 97002 503-678-7114
Julie Jackson, prin. Fax 678-7187
North Marion MS 500/6-8
20246 Grim Rd NE 97002 503-678-7118
Sharon Baum, prin. Fax 678-7185
North Marion PS 400/PK-2
20257 Grim Rd NE 97002 503-678-8500
Matthew Wilding, prin. Fax 678-8510

Baker City, Baker, Pop. 9,703
Baker SD 5J 1,300/K-12
2090 4th St 97814 541-524-2260
Don Ulrey, supt. Fax 524-2564
www.baker.k12.or.us
Baker MS 300/7-8
2320 Washington Ave 97814 541-524-2500
Minda Vaughan, prin. Fax 524-2563
Brooklyn PS 100/1-3
1350 Washington Ave 97814 541-524-2450
Troy Fisher, prin. Fax 524-2477
Keating ES 50/K-5
2090 4th St 97814 541-523-2377
Tony Fisher, prin. Fax 523-2377
South Baker IS 100/4-6
1285 3rd St 97814 541-524-2350
Betty Palmer, prin. Fax 524-2382
Other Schools – See Haines

Baker Valley SDA S 50/1-8
42171 Chico Rd 97814 541-523-4165
Gary Laabs, prin. Fax 523-4165

Bandon, Coos, Pop. 2,908
Bandon SD 54 800/K-12
455 9th St SW 97411 541-347-4411
Diane Buche, supt. Fax 347-3974
www.bandon.k12.or.us/
Harbor Lights MS 200/5-8
390 9th St SW 97411 541-347-4415
Gerald Prickett, prin. Fax 347-1280
Ocean Crest ES 200/K-4
1040 Allegheny Ave SW 97411 541-347-4416
Elizabeth Olive, prin. Fax 347-1898

Bandon Pacific Christian S 50/PK-8
PO Box 949 97411 541-347-4157
Tom Hutton, admin. Fax 347-4157

Banks, Washington, Pop. 1,562
Banks SD 13 1,200/K-12
450 S Main St 97106 503-324-8591
Marvin Ott, supt. Fax 324-6969
www.banks.k12.or.us
Banks ES 600/K-6
42350 NW Trellis Way 97106 503-324-2772
Bob Huston, prin. Fax 324-3333
Banks JHS 200/7-8
450 S Main St 97106 503-324-3111
Mark Everett, prin. Fax 324-7441

St. Francis of Assisi S 100/K-8
39085 NW Harrington Rd 97106 503-324-2182
Diane Ramsperger, prin. Fax 324-7032

Beaver, Tillamook
Nestucca Valley SD 101
Supt. — See Cloverdale
Nestucca Valley MS 100/6-8
PO Box 77 97108 503-398-5545
Ken Richwine, prin. Fax 398-5831

Beavercreek, Clackamas
Oregon City SD 62
Supt. — See Oregon City
Beavercreek ES 500/K-6
21944 S Yeoman Rd 97004 503-785-8350
Scott Curtis, prin. Fax 632-8264

Beaverton, Washington, Pop. 85,775
Beaverton SD 48J 37,500/K-12
16550 SW Merlo Rd 97006 503-591-8000
Jerome Colonna, supt. Fax 591-4175
www.beaverton.k12.or.us
Aloha-Huber Park S 900/K-8
5000 SW 173rd Ave 97007 503-259-6490
Scott Drue, prin. Fax 259-6487
Barnes ES 700/K-5
13730 SW Walker Rd 97005 503-672-3500
Susan Rodriguez, prin. Fax 672-3503
Beaver Acres ES 800/K-5
2125 SW 170th Ave 97006 503-259-3815
Stacy Geale, prin. Fax 259-3818
Bethany ES 500/K-5
3305 NW 174th Ave 97006 503-533-1810
John Engel, prin. Fax 533-1803
Carson MS 200/6-8
1600 NW 173rd Ave 97006 503-533-1890
Shirley Brock, prin. Fax 533-1898
Chehalem ES 500/K-5
15555 SW Davis Rd 97007 503-672-3515
Debbie Nicolai, prin. Fax 672-3518
Conestoga MS 1,100/6-8
12250 SW Conestoga Dr 97008 503-524-1345
Zan Hess, prin. Fax 524-1349
Cooper Mountain ES 500/K-5
7670 SW 170th Ave 97007 503-259-3830
Nicole Will, prin. Fax 259-3833
Elmonica ES 700/K-5
16950 SW Lisa Ct 97006 503-533-1815
Mike Mitchell, prin. Fax 533-1818
Fir Grove ES 500/K-5
6300 SW Wilson Ave 97008 503-672-3530
Jared Cordon, prin. Fax 672-3533
Five Oaks MS 1,100/6-8
1600 NW 173rd Ave 97006 503-533-1890
Shirley Brock, prin. Fax 533-1898
Greenway ES 400/K-5
9150 SW Downing Dr 97008 503-524-1300
Robert Matuszak, prin. Fax 524-1303
Hassell ES 500/K-5
18100 SW Bany Rd 97007 503-259-3845
Teresa Clemens-Brower, prin. Fax 259-3848
Hazeldale ES 600/K-5
20080 SW Farmington Rd 97007 503-259-3860
Glen Rutherford, prin. Fax 259-3863
Highland Park MS 900/6-8
7000 SW Wilson Ave 97008 503-672-3640
Allan Deckard, prin. Fax 672-3644

Hiteon ES 400/K-5
13800 SW Brockman St 97008 503-524-1315
Ginny Hansmann, prin. Fax 524-1318
Kinnaman ES 500/K-5
4205 SW 193rd Ave 97007 503-259-3875
Jan McCall, prin. Fax 259-3878
McKay ES 400/K-5
7485 SW Scholls Ferry Rd 97008 503-672-3545
Mary Jean Katz, prin. Fax 672-3548
McKinley ES 600/K-5
1500 NW 185th Ave 97006 503-533-1845
Susan McKinney, prin. Fax 533-1848
Meadow Park MS 1,000/6-8
14100 SW Downing St 97006 503-672-3660
Jill O'Neill, prin. Fax 672-3664
Mountain View MS 1,000/6-8
17500 SW Farmington Rd 97007 503-259-3890
Joann Hulquist, prin. Fax 259-3894
Oak Hills ES 600/K-5
2625 NW 153rd Ave 97006 503-533-1860
Cheryl Hagseth, prin. Fax 533-1863
Ryles ES 600/K-5
10250 SW Cormorant Dr 97007 503-524-1330
Ronald Porterfield, prin. Fax 524-1334
Scholls Heights ES 700/K-5
16400 SW Loon Dr 97007 503-524-1365
Joan Kern, prin. Fax 524-1368
Sexton Mountain ES 600/K-5
15645 SW Sexton Mountain Rd 97007 503-672-3560
Don Martin, prin. Fax 672-3563
Vose ES 600/K-5
11350 SW Denney Rd 97008 503-672-3590
Will Flores, prin. Fax 672-3593
Whitford MS 800/6-8
7935 SW Scholls Ferry Rd 97008 503-672-3680
Matt Casteel, prin. Fax 672-3684
Other Schools – See Portland

Hillsboro SD 1J
Supt. — See Hillsboro
Indian Hills ES 400/K-6
21260 SW Rock Rd 97006 503-844-1350
Steve Callaway, prin. Fax 642-9851
Reedville ES 300/K-6
2695 SW 209th Ave 97006 503-844-1570
Virginia Baez, prin. Fax 591-5874
Tobias ES 500/K-6
1065 SW 206th Ave 97006 503-844-1310
Tom Noesen, prin. Fax 848-2723

Holy Trinity S 200/K-8
13755 SW Walker Rd 97005 503-644-5748
Brenda Martinek, prin. Fax 643-4475
Pilgrim Lutheran S 200/PK-8
5650 SW Hall Blvd 97005 503-644-8697
Curtis Boeder, prin. Fax 644-8182
St. Cecilia S 200/K-8
12250 SW 5th St 97005 503-644-2619
Kathleen Harp, prin. Fax 646-4217
St. Stephens Academy 100/K-12
7275 SW Hall Blvd 97008 503-646-4617
John Breckenridge, prin. Fax 626-1522
Valley Catholic ES 400/K-6
4440 SW 148th Ave 97007 503-626-7781
Sue Friesen, prin. Fax 626-5731

Bend, Deschutes, Pop. 67,152
Bend-LaPine Administrative SD 1 15,100/K-12
520 NW Wall St 97701 541-383-6000
Ron Wilkinson, supt. Fax 383-6003
www.bend.k12.or.us
Amity Creek Magnet ES at Thompson 200/K-5
437 NW Wall St 97701 541-383-6195
Carol Hammett, admin. Fax 383-6199
Bear Creek ES 600/K-5
51 SE 13th St 97702 541-383-6120
Kathy Saterdahl, prin. Fax 383-6128
Buckingham ES 600/K-5
62560 Hamby Rd 97701 541-383-6135
Skip Offenhauser, prin. Fax 383-6454
Cascade MS 800/6-8
19619 Mountaineer Way 97702 541-383-6230
Michael Hecker, prin. Fax 383-6255
Elk Meadow ES 600/K-5
60880 Brookswood Blvd 97702 541-383-6420
Timothy Comfort, prin. Fax 383-6431
Ensworth ES 300/K-5
2150 NE Daggett Ln 97701 541-693-2200
Michael Hyder, prin. Fax 693-2210
High Desert MS 700/6-8
61111 SE 27th St 97702 541-383-6480
Gary DeFrang, prin. Fax 383-6499
High Lakes ES 800/K-5
2500 NW High Lakes Loop 97701 541-322-5200
Susan Heberlein, prin. Fax 322-5450
Highland Magnet ES at Kenwood 400/K-5
701 NW Newport Ave 97701 541-383-6220
Paul Dean, prin. Fax 383-6229
Jewell ES 700/K-5
20550 Murphy Rd 97702 541-383-6150
Bruce Reynolds, prin. Fax 383-6163
Juniper ES 500/K-5
1300 NE Norton Ave 97701 541-383-6165
Vicki Jenkins, prin. Fax 383-6177
Lava Ridge ES 700/K-5
20805 Cooley Rd 97701 541-383-6202
Gary Timms, prin. Fax 383-6217
Miller ES, 300 NW Crosby Dr 97701 K-5
Steve Hill, prin. 541-383-6195
Pilot Butte MS 600/6-8
1501 NE Neff Rd 97701 541-383-6260
Stephanie Bennett, prin. Fax 383-6286
Pine Ridge ES 400/K-5
19840 SW Hollygrape St 97702 541-388-5900
Kevin Gehrig, prin. Fax 388-5910
Ponderosa ES K-5
3790 NE Purcell Blvd 97701 541-323-4300
Teresa Hjeresen, prin.

Sky View MS 700/6-8
63555 18th St 97701 541-383-6479
D. Scott Edmondson, prin. Fax 322-5217
Westside Village Magnet S at Kingston 200/K-8
1101 NW 12th St 97701 541-383-6205
Wendy Winchel, admin. Fax 383-6206
Other Schools – See La Pine, Sunriver

Redmond SD 2J
Supt. — See Redmond
Tumalo Community S 500/K-8
19835 2nd St 97701 541-382-2853
Michelle Herron, prin. Fax 389-4197

Morning Star Christian S 200/PK-12
19741 Baker Rd 97702 541-382-5091
Gail Walker, admin. Fax 382-0268
St. Francis of Assisi S 300/PK-8
2450 NE 27th St 97701 541-382-4701
Fax 312-9111
Three Sisters Adventist Christian S 50/K-10
21155 Tumalo Rd 97701 541-389-2091
Chris Larson, prin. Fax 389-2091
Trinity Lutheran S 400/PK-12
2550 NE Butler Market Rd 97701 541-382-1850
Rev. Robert Luinstra, prin. Fax 382-1850
Waldorf S of Bend 100/PK-6
63175 O B Riley Rd 97701 541-330-8841
Paul Carlson, prin. Fax 322-9402

Blachly, Lane
Blachly SD 90 100/K-12
20264 Blachly Grange Rd 97412 541-925-3262
Steve Dickenson, supt. Fax 925-3062
www.blachly.k12.or.us/
Triangle Lake S 100/K-12
20264 Blachly Grange Rd 97412 541-925-3262
LeAnne Raze, prin. Fax 925-3062

Blodgett, Benton
Philomath SD 17J
Supt. — See Philomath
Blodgett ES 50/K-4
PO Box 27 97326 541-453-4101
Cindy Golston, prin. Fax 453-4389

Bly, Klamath
Klamath County SD
Supt. — See Klamath Falls
Gearhart ES 50/K-6
PO Box 47 97622 541-353-2363
Jim Libby, prin. Fax 353-2367

Boardman, Morrow, Pop. 3,051
Morrow SD 1
Supt. — See Lexington
Boardman ES 300/K-3
PO Box 529 97818 541-481-7383
Jaque Johnson, prin. Fax 481-2046
Windy River ES 200/4-6
500 Tatone St 97818 541-481-2526
Mark Jones, prin. Fax 481-3264

Bonanza, Klamath, Pop. 416
Klamath County SD
Supt. — See Klamath Falls
Bonanza S 200/K-12
PO Box 128 97623 541-545-6581
Jim Libby, prin. Fax 545-1719

Boring, Clackamas
Oregon Trail SD 46
Supt. — See Sandy
Boring MS 400/6-8
27801 SE Dee St 97009 503-668-9393
Tim Werner, prin. Fax 668-5291
Cottrell ES 100/K-5
36225 SE Proctor Rd 97009 503-668-5521
Kimberly Ball, prin. Fax 668-6250
Kelso ES 300/K-5
34651 SE Kelso Rd 97009 503-668-8020
Patrick Sanders, prin. Fax 668-0883
Naas ES 200/K-5
12240 SE School Ave 97009 503-668-4454
Kimberly Braunberger, prin. Fax 668-5428

Good Shepherd S 200/K-8
28986 SE Haley Rd 97009 503-663-5280
Greg Suminski, prin. Fax 663-7760
Hood View Junior Academy 100/PK-8
PO Box 128 97009 503-663-4568
Holley Bryant, prin. Fax 663-5110

Brookings, Curry, Pop. 6,297
Brookings-Harbor SD 17C 1,700/K-12
629 Easy St 97415 541-469-7443
John Garner, supt. Fax 469-6599
www.brookings.k12.or.us
Azalea MS 400/6-8
629 Easy St 97415 541-469-7427
Aaron Cooke, prin. Fax 469-7080
Kalmiopsis ES 700/K-5
629 Easy St 97415 541-469-7417
Brian Hodge, prin. Fax 469-0413

Brookings Harbor Christian S 100/PK-12
PO Box 5809 97415 541-469-6478
Christine Hudson, admin. Fax 412-7242

Brooks, Marion
Gervais SD 1
Supt. — See Gervais
Brooks ES 300/2-4
PO Box 9216 97305 503-393-6753
Dave James, prin. Fax 393-0316

Willamette Valley Christian S 200/PK-12
PO Box 9088 97305 503-393-5236
Gary Glassco, admin. Fax 485-8203

Brownsville, Linn, Pop. 1,517
Central Linn SD 552 700/K-12
331 E Blakely Ave 97327 541-466-3105
Edward Curtis, supt. Fax 466-3180
www.centrallinn.k12.or.us
Other Schools – See Halsey

Burns, Harney, Pop. 2,755
Harney County SD 3 1,000/K-12
550 N Court Ave 97720 541-573-6811
David Courtney, supt. Fax 573-7557
www.burnsschools.k12.or.us
Slater ES 400/K-5
800 N Fairview Ave 97720 541-573-7201
Gayle Mackey, prin. Fax 573-7272
Other Schools – See Hines

Suntex SD 10 50/K-8
693 W B St 97720 541-573-3229
Fax 573-3229

Other Schools – See Riley

Butte Falls, Jackson, Pop. 433
Butte Falls SD 91 200/K-12
PO Box 228 97522 541-865-3563
Tim Sweeney, supt. Fax 865-3217
www.buttefallsschools.org/
Butte Falls ES 100/K-7
PO Box 197 97522 541-865-3563
Tim Sweeney, prin. Fax 865-7731

Buxton, Washington

Banks Christian Academy 100/PK-12
22785 NW Fisher Rd 97109 503-324-4500
Odessa Falcon, prin. Fax 324-2126

Camp Sherman, Jefferson
Black Butte SD 41 50/K-8
PO Box 150 97730 541-595-6203
Fax 595-5016

Black Butte S 50/K-8
PO Box 150 97730 541-595-6203
Toni Coleman, lead tchr. Fax 595-5016

Canby, Clackamas, Pop. 14,989
Canby SD 86 5,000/K-12
1130 S Ivy St 97013 503-266-7861
Jeff Rose, supt. Fax 266-0022
www.canby.k12.or.us
Ackerman MS 400/6-8
350 SE 13th Ave 97013 503-263-7140
Joel Sebastian, prin. Fax 266-7489
Baker Prairie MS 500/6-8
1859 S Township Rd 97013 503-263-7170
Betty Rivinus, prin. Fax 263-7189
Eccles ES 400/K-5
562 NW 5th Ave 97013 503-263-7120
Jennifer Turner, prin. Fax 263-3225
Knight ES 400/K-5
501 N Grant St 97013 503-263-7100
Christine Taylor, prin. Fax 263-2459
Lee ES 400/K-5
1110 S Ivy St 97013 503-263-7150
Marilyn Wood, prin. Fax 263-7159
Trost ES 400/K-5
800 S Redwood St 97013 503-263-7130
Ricardo Marquez, prin. Fax 263-7139
Other Schools – See Hubbard, Oregon City

Cannon Beach, Clatsop, Pop. 1,700
Seaside SD 10
Supt. — See Seaside
Cannon Beach ES 100/K-5
PO Box 277 97110 503-436-2294
Rosemary Kemper-Riddock, prin. Fax 436-2203

Canyon City, Grant, Pop. 595
Grant SD 3 800/K-12
401 N Canyon City Blvd 97820 541-575-1280
Newell Cleaver, supt. Fax 575-0928
www.grantesd.k12.or.us
Humbolt ES 300/K-5
329 N Humbolt St 97820 541-575-0454
Kris Beal, prin. Fax 575-3609
Other Schools – See Mount Vernon, Seneca

Canyonville, Douglas, Pop. 1,397
South Umpqua SD 19
Supt. — See Myrtle Creek
Canyonville ES 100/K-5
PO Box 745 97417 541-839-4396
Tim Larkin, prin. Fax 839-6528

Canyonville SDA S 50/1-8
PO Box 1155 97417 541-839-4053

Carlton, Yamhill, Pop. 1,501
Yamhill-Carlton SD 1
Supt. — See Yamhill
Carlton S 300/K-6
420 S 3rd St 97111 503-852-7161
John Horne, prin. Fax 852-7364

Cascade Locks, Hood River, Pop. 1,109
Hood River County SD
Supt. — See Hood River
Cascade Locks S 200/K-12
PO Box 279 97014 541-374-8467
Ed Drew, prin. Fax 374-8446

Cave Junction, Josephine, Pop. 1,380
Three Rivers County SD
Supt. — See Grants Pass
Byrne MS 300/6-8
101 S Junction Ave 97523 541-592-2163
Damian Crowson, prin. Fax 592-4851
Evergreen ES 500/K-5
520 W River St 97523 541-592-3136
David Valenzuela, prin. Fax 592-3186

Madrone SDA S 50/1-8
4300 Holland Loop Rd 97523 541-592-3330

Central Point, Jackson, Pop. 15,672
Central Point SD 6 3,200/K-12
300 Ash St 97502 541-494-6200
Randal Gravon, supt. Fax 664-1637
www.district6.org
Central Point ES 500/K-5
450 S 4th St 97502 541-494-6500
Walt Davenport, prin. Fax 664-1147
Jewett ES 500/K-5
1001 Manzanita St 97502 541-494-6600
Scott Dippel, prin. Fax 664-5035
Richardson ES 500/K-5
200 W Pine St 97502 541-494-6700
Susan Dippel, prin. Fax 665-5881
Sams Valley ES 300/K-5
14235 Table Rock Rd 97502 541-494-6870
Christine Beck, prin. Fax 826-2469
Scenic MS 900/6-8
1955 Scenic Ave 97502 541-494-6400
Sheila Henson, prin. Fax 664-8534
Other Schools – See Gold Hill

Chiloquin, Klamath, Pop. 723
Klamath County SD
Supt. — See Klamath Falls
Chiloquin ES 300/K-6
PO Box 375 97624 541-783-2338
Cindy Moore, prin. Fax 783-2410

Christmas Valley, Lake

Solid Rock Christian S 50/K-12
PO Box 745 97641 541-576-2895
Dell Renee Wilson, prin. Fax 576-3554

Clackamas, Clackamas, Pop. 2,578
North Clackamas SD 12
Supt. — See Milwaukie
Clackamas ES 400/K-6
15301 SE 92nd Ave 97015 503-353-5380
Charles Foote, prin. Fax 353-5395
Oregon Trail ES 800/K-6
13895 SE 152nd Dr 97015 503-353-5540
Dean Long, prin. Fax 353-5555
Sunnyside ES 600/K-6
13401 SE 132nd Ave 97015 503-353-5620
Cathy Lehmann, prin. Fax 353-5635
Sunrise MS 1,200/7-8
14331 SE 132nd Ave 97015 503-353-5750
Elisabeth Guinn, prin. Fax 353-5765

Clatskanie, Columbia, Pop. 1,631
Clatskanie SD 6J 900/K-12
PO Box 678 97016 503-728-0587
Ed Serra, supt. Fax 728-0608
www.clat6j.k12.or.us/
Clatskanie ES 400/K-6
PO Box 327 97016 503-728-2191
Christine Collins, prin. Fax 728-2840

Cloverdale, Tillamook
Nestucca Valley SD 101 600/K-12
PO Box 99 97112 503-392-4892
Connie Kennedy, supt. Fax 392-9061
www.nestucca.k12.or.us
Nestucca Valley ES 200/K-5
36925 Highway 101 S 97112 503-392-3435
Nick Gelbard, prin. Fax 392-4948
Other Schools – See Beaver

Coburg, Lane, Pop. 999
Eugene SD 4J
Supt. — See Eugene
Coburg ES 200/K-5
91274 N Coburg Rd 97408 541-687-3408
Joane Butler, prin. Fax 334-4831

Colton, Clackamas
Colton SD 53 700/K-12
30429 S Grays Hill Rd 97017 503-824-3535
Linda Johnson, supt. Fax 824-3530
www.colton.k12.or.us
Colton ES 300/K-5
30439 S Grays Hill Rd 97017 503-824-3536
Susan Farley, prin. Fax 824-3538
Colton MS 200/6-8
21580 S Schieffer Rd 97017 503-824-2319
Beth Lund, prin. Fax 824-2309

Columbia City, Columbia, Pop. 1,797
Saint Helens SD 502
Supt. — See Saint Helens
Columbia City S 300/6-6
2000 2nd St 97018 503-366-7550
Lisa Rawlings, prin. Fax 366-3215

Condon, Gilliam, Pop. 708
Condon SD 25J 100/K-12
PO Box 615 97823 541-384-2581
Dick Allen, supt. Fax 384-2585
www.condon.k12.or.us
Condon S 100/K-8
PO Box 615 97823 541-384-2581
Tim Porter, prin. Fax 384-2585

Coos Bay, Coos, Pop. 15,823
Coos Bay SD 9 3,500/K-12
PO Box 509 97420 541-267-3104
Bob De La Vergne, supt. Fax 269-5366
www.coos-bay.k12.or.us
Blossom Gulch ES 500/K-4
PO Box 509 97420 541-267-1340
Jodi O'Mara, prin. Fax 267-7109
Bunker Hill ES 300/K-4
PO Box 509 97420 541-267-1350
Christine McCollom, prin. Fax 269-7649
Madison ES 400/K-4
PO Box 509 97420 541-888-1218
Arlene Roblan, prin. Fax 888-3064

Millicoma IS 500/5-6
PO Box 509 97420 541-267-1466
Travis Howard, prin. Fax 267-8225

Sunset MS 500/7-8
PO Box 509 97420 541-888-1242
Dale Inskeep, prin. Fax 888-9814

Christ Lutheran S 100/PK-8
1835 N 15th St 97420 541-267-3851
Tesa Robinson, prin. Fax 267-3331

Coquille, Coos, Pop. 4,254

Coquille SD 8 800/K-12
790 W 17th St 97423 541-396-2181
Diann Gillaspie, supt. Fax 396-5015
www.coquille.k12.or.us/

Coquille Valley S 200/4-8
1115 N Baxter St 97423 541-396-2914
Mark Nortness, prin. Fax 396-4543

Lincoln ES 300/K-3
1366 N Gould St 97423 541-396-2811
Julie Entz, prin. Fax 396-7351

United Valley Christian Academy 50/PK-8
1742 N Fir St 97423 541-396-6079
Lynn Potter, admin. Fax 824-0124

Corbett, Multnomah

Corbett SD 39 600/K-12
35800 Historic Columbia Riv 97019 503-695-3612
Robert Dunton, supt. Fax 695-3641
www.corbett.k12.or.us

Corbett ES 300/K-6
35800 Historic Columbia Riv 97019 503-695-3636
Randy Trani, prin. Fax 695-3641

Corbett MS 100/7-8
35800 Historic Columbia Riv 97019 503-695-3600
Randy Trani, prin. Fax 695-3641

Cornelius, Washington, Pop. 10,820

Forest Grove SD 15
Supt. — See Forest Grove

Cornelius ES 400/K-4
200 N 14th Ave 97113 503-359-2500
Perla Rodriquez, prin. Fax 359-2564

Echo Shaw ES 400/K-4
914 S Linden St 97113 503-359-2489
Rogelio Martinez, prin. Fax 359-2567

Hillsboro SD 1J
Supt. — See Hillsboro

Free Orchards ES K-6
2499 S Beech St 97113 503-844-1500
Patti Wiemer, prin. Fax 844-1140

Emmaus Christian S 200/PK-8
460 S Heather St 97113 503-357-4054
Timothy Welch, prin. Fax 992-0274

Forest Hills Lutheran S 200/K-8
4221 SW Golf Course Rd 97113 503-359-4853
Linda Hanson, prin. Fax 357-2213

Corvallis, Benton, Pop. 49,553

Corvallis SD 509J 6,800/K-12
PO Box 3509J 97339 541-757-5811
Dawn Tarzian, supt. Fax 757-5703
www.csd509j.net/

Adams ES 500/K-5
1615 SW 35th St 97333 541-757-5938
Patty Pearson, prin. Fax 757-4586

Cheldelin MS 600/6-8
987 NE Conifer Blvd 97330 541-757-5971
Lisa Harlan, prin. Fax 757-4596

Franklin S 400/K-8
750 NW 18th St 97330 541-757-5747
Gerry Kosanovic, prin. Fax 757-5766

Garfield ES 400/K-5
1205 NW Garfield Ave 97330 541-757-5941
Juan Baez, prin. Fax 757-4588

Hoover ES 400/K-5
3838 NW Walnut Blvd 97330 541-757-5958
Bryan Traylor, prin. Fax 757-4590

Jefferson ES 300/K-5
1825 NW 27th St 97330 541-757-5951
Denise Gorthy, prin. Fax 757-4592

Lincoln S 400/K-8
110 SE Alexander Ave 97333 541-757-5955
Oscar Moreno-Gilson, prin. Fax 757-4593

Mountain View ES 400/K-5
340 NE Granger Ave 97330 541-766-4760
Rosemary O'Neil, prin. Fax 766-4764

Pauling MS 700/6-8
1111 NW Cleveland Ave 97330 541-757-5961
James Wickman, prin. Fax 757-4598

Wilson ES 300/K-5
2701 NW Satinwood St 97330 541-757-5987
Jeff Brew, prin. Fax 757-4595

Corvallis Montessori S 100/PK-6
2730 NW Greeley Ave 97330 541-753-2513
Mark Berger, hdmstr. Fax 752-8176

Corvallis Waldorf S 100/PK-8
3855 NE Highway 20 97330 541-758-4674
Christine Wolf, admin. Fax 758-5091

Good Samaritan S 100/PK-2
333 NW 35th St 97330 541-758-1255
Jane Edson, dir. Fax 757-1537

Santiam Christian S 900/PK-12
7220 NE Arnold Ave 97330 541-745-5524
Stanton Baker, supt. Fax 745-6338

Zion Lutheran S 200/PK-8
2800 NW Tyler Ave 97330 541-753-7503
Jonathon Schultz, prin. Fax 754-8254

Cottage Grove, Lane, Pop. 8,724

South Lane SD 45J3 2,700/K-12
PO Box 218 97424 541-942-3381
Krista Parent, supt. Fax 942-8098
www.slane.k12.or.us/dsc

Bohemia ES 500/K-5
721 S R St 97424 541-942-3313
Jackie Lester, prin. Fax 767-5958

Delight Valley ES 100/K-5
79980 Delight Valley School 97424 541-942-5568
David Bascue, prin. Fax 767-3541

Harrison ES 400/K-5
1000 S 10th St 97424 541-942-3389
Ali Nice, prin. Fax 942-1316

Latham ES 100/K-5
32112 Latham Rd 97424 541-942-0147
Chad Hamilton, prin. Fax 767-2180

Lincoln MS 500/6-8
1565 S 4th St 97424 541-942-3316
Brian McCasline, prin. Fax 942-9801

London S 100/K-8
73288 London Rd 97424 541-942-0183
Laurie Klein, prin. Fax 942-8849

Other Schools – See Dorena

Cove, Union, Pop. 606

Cove SD 15 300/K-12
PO Box 68 97824 541-568-4424
Jeff Clark, supt. Fax 568-4251
www.cove.k12.or.us

Cove S 300/K-12
PO Box 68 97824 541-568-4424
Todd Shirley, prin. Fax 568-4251

Crane, Harney

Harney County SD 4 100/K-8
PO Box 828 97732 541-493-1923
Pat Sharp, supt. Fax 493-2331

Crane S 100/K-8
PO Box 828 97732 541-493-2641
Pat Sharp, prin. Fax 493-2051

Crawfordsville, Linn

Sweet Home SD 55
Supt. — See Sweet Home

Crawfordsville ES 100/K-6
PO Box 177 97336 541-367-7170
Elena Barton, prin. Fax 367-8906

Creswell, Lane, Pop. 4,632

Creswell SD 40 1,200/K-12
998 A St 97426 541-895-6000
Rick Stuber, supt. Fax 895-6019
www.creswell.k12.or.us

Creslane ES 600/K-5
996 A St 97426 541-895-6140
Jacque Robertson, prin. Fax 895-6199

Creswell MS 300/6-8
655 W Oregon Ave 97426 541-895-6090
Shirley Burrus, prin. Fax 895-6139

Creswell Christian S 100/K-8
PO Box 217 97426 541-895-4622
Rebecca Lake, admin. Fax 895-4622

Culver, Jefferson, Pop. 898

Culver SD 4 700/K-12
PO Box 228 97734 541-546-2541
Linda Florence, supt. Fax 546-7517
www.culver.k12.or.us/

Culver ES 300/K-5
PO Box 228 97734 541-546-6861
Stefanie Garber, prin. Fax 546-7522

Culver MS 100/6-8
PO Box 228 97734 541-546-3090
Alice Smith, prin. Fax 546-2137

Dallas, Polk, Pop. 14,001

Dallas SD 2 2,500/K-12
111 SW Ash St 97338 503-623-5594
Christy Perry, supt. Fax 623-5597
www.dallas.k12.or.us

LaCreole MS 700/6-8
701 SE Lacreole Dr 97338 503-623-6662
Steve Spencer, prin. Fax 623-8477

Lyle ES 300/K-3
185 SW Levens St 97338 503-623-8367
Todd Baughman, prin. Fax 623-2071

Oakdale Heights ES 300/K-3
1375 SW Maple St 97338 503-623-8316
Caleb Harris, prin. Fax 623-5165

Whitworth ES 200/4-5
1151 SE Miller Ave 97338 503-623-8351
Steve Martinelli, prin. Fax 623-6089

Faith Christian S 100/PK-8
2290 E Ellendale Ave 97338 503-623-6632
Al Perkins, admin. Fax 623-4563

Damascus, Clackamas, Pop. 9,454

Gresham-Barlow SD 10J
Supt. — See Gresham

Damascus MS 400/5-8
14151 SE 242nd Ave, 503-658-3171
Lori Walter, prin. Fax 658-6275

Deep Creek ES 300/K-4
15600 SE 232nd Dr, 503-658-3184
April Olson, prin. Fax 658-5635

Christ the Vine ECC 100/PK-K
18677 SE Highway 212, 503-658-5650
Leiloni Pfeifer, prin. Fax 658-3081

Damascus Christian S 300/K-12
14251 SE Rust Way, 503-658-4100
Timothy Oakley, admin. Fax 658-5827

Days Creek, Douglas

Douglas County SD 15 100/K-7
PO Box 10 97429 541-825-3296
Laurie Newton, supt. Fax 825-3052
days.or.schoolwebpages.com

Other Schools – See Tiller

Dayton, Yamhill, Pop. 2,206

Dayton SD 8 1,000/K-12
526 Ferry St 97114 503-864-2215
Janelle Beers, supt. Fax 864-3927
www.dayton.k12.or.us

Dayton ES 400/K-5
526 Ferry St 97114 503-864-2217
Laurel Woodworth, prin. Fax 864-3927

Dayton JHS 300/6-8
801 Ferry St 97114 503-864-2246
Jami Fluke, prin. Fax 864-3697

Dayville, Grant, Pop. 122

Dayville SD 16J 100/K-12
PO Box C 97825 541-987-2412
Debbie Gillespie, supt. Fax 987-2155

Dayville S 100/K-12
PO Box C 97825 541-987-2412
Debbie Gillespie, prin. Fax 987-2155

Dexter, Lane

Pleasant Hill SD 1
Supt. — See Pleasant Hill

Trent ES 300/K-4
37981 Wheeler Rd 97431 541-747-9232
Devery Stoneberg, prin. Fax 744-3345

Diamond, Harney

Diamond SD 7 50/K-8
40524 S Diamond Ln 97722 541-493-2464
Fax 493-2858

Diamond S 50/K-8
40524 S Diamond Ln 97722 541-493-2464
Crystal Franklin, lead tchr. Fax 493-2858

Dorena, Lane

South Lane SD 45J3
Supt. — See Cottage Grove

Dorena S 100/K-8
37141 Row River Rd 97434 541-946-1506
Jeremy Smith, prin. Fax 767-3516

Drain, Douglas, Pop. 1,039

North Douglas SD 22 400/K-12
PO Box 428 97435 541-836-2223
Dan Forbess, supt. Fax 836-7558
www.northdouglas.k12.or.us

North Douglas S 300/K-8
PO Box 338 97435 541-836-2213
Roger Vickery, prin. Fax 836-7034

Drewsey, Harney

Drewsey SD 13 50/K-8
PO Box 109 97904 541-493-2367
Fax 493-2401

Drewsey S 50/K-8
PO Box 109 97904 541-493-2367
Susan Gonzales, lead tchr. Fax 493-2401

Pine Creek SD 5
Supt. — See Hines

Pine Creek S 50/K-8
79654 Pine Creek Rd 97904 541-573-3229
Fax 573-3229

Dufur, Wasco, Pop. 582

Dufur SD 29 300/K-12
802 NE 5th St 97021 541-467-2509
Jack Henderson, supt. Fax 467-2589
www.dufur.k12.or.us

Dufur S 300/K-12
802 NE 5th St 97021 541-467-2509
Bert Wyatt, prin. Fax 467-2589

Dundee, Yamhill, Pop. 2,977

Newberg SD 29J
Supt. — See Newberg

Dundee ES 400/K-5
140 SW 5th St 97115 503-554-4850
Deborah Crueger, prin. Fax 538-0729

Eagle Creek, Clackamas

Estacada SD 108
Supt. — See Estacada

Eagle Creek ES 400/K-6
30391 SE Highway 211 97022 503-630-8621
Dan Draper, prin. Fax 630-8614

Eagle Point, Jackson, Pop. 7,496

Jackson County SD 9 4,200/K-12
PO Box 548 97524 541-830-1200
Cynda Rickert, supt. Fax 830-6200
www.eaglepnt.k12.or.us

Eagle Point MS 500/6-8
PO Box 218 97524 541-830-1250
Joni Parsons, prin. Fax 830-6086

Eagle Rock ES 400/K-5
1280 Barton Rd 97524 541-830-1275
Joni Parsons, prin. Fax 830-6195

Lake Creek Learning Center 100/K-5
391 Lake Creek Loop 97524 541-830-6319
Lisa Yamashita, prin. Fax 830-6353

Little Butte S 500/K-5
PO Box 549 97524 541-830-1225
Lynn Scott, prin. Fax 830-6150

Other Schools – See Shady Cove, Trail, White City

St. John Lutheran S 100/PK-5
PO Box 1049 97524 541-826-4334
Diane Gregg M.S., prin. Fax 830-1900

Shady Point SDA S 50/1-8
14611 Highway 62 97524 541-826-5821
Connie Allred, prin.

Echo, Umatilla, Pop. 691

Echo SD 5 300/K-12
600 E Gerone St 97826 541-376-8436
Rob Waite, supt. Fax 376-8473
www.echo.k12.or.us/

Echo S 300/K-12
600 E Gerone St 97826 541-376-8436
Norm Stewart, prin. Fax 376-8473

Elgin, Union, Pop. 1,642
Elgin SD 23 400/K-12
PO Box 68 97827 541-437-1211
Larry Christman, supt. Fax 437-1231
www.elgin.k12.or.us
Mayfield S 300/K-8
PO Box 35 97827 541-437-2321
Kristen Graber, prin. Fax 437-8212

Elkton, Douglas, Pop. 150
Elkton SD 34 200/PK-12
PO Box 390 97436 541-584-2228
Mike Hughes, supt. Fax 584-2227
www.elkton.k12.or.us/
Elkton S 100/PK-8
PO Box 390 97436 541-584-2228
Mike Hughes, prin. Fax 584-2113

Elmira, Lane
Fern Ridge SD 28J 1,500/K-12
88834 Territorial Rd 97437 541-935-2253
Ivan Hernandez, supt. Fax 935-8222
www.fernridge.k12.or.us
Elmira ES 300/K-5
88960 Territorial Rd 97437 541-935-8214
Meg Otto, prin. Fax 935-8243
Fern Ridge MS 400/6-8
88831 Territorial Rd 97437 541-935-8230
Doug Kartub, prin. Fax 935-8234
Other Schools – See Veneta

Enterprise, Wallowa, Pop. 1,800
Enterprise SD 21 400/K-12
201 SE 4th St 97828 541-426-3193
Brad Royse, supt. Fax 426-3504
www.enterprise.k12.or.us/
Enterprise ES 200/K-6
201 SE 4th St 97828 541-426-3812
Brad Royse, prin. Fax 426-4485

Troy SD 54 50/K-8
107 SW 1st St Ste 105 97828 541-426-4997
Edward Jensen, supt. Fax 426-3732
www.troy.k12.or.us
Troy S 50/K-8
66247 Redmond Grade Ln 97828 541-426-4997
Sherry Carman, lead tchr. Fax 828-7748

Enterprise SDA S 50/K-10
PO Box N 97828 541-426-8339

Estacada, Clackamas, Pop. 2,435
Estacada SD 108 2,200/K-12
255 NE 6th Ave 97023 503-630-6871
Howard Fetz, supt. Fax 630-8513
www.esd108.org/
Clackamas River ES 400/K-6
301 NE 2nd Ave 97023 503-630-8552
Nancy Torbert, prin. Fax 630-8577
Estacada JHS 400/7-8
500 NE Main St 97023 503-630-8516
Kevin Olds, prin. Fax 630-8693
River Mill ES 300/K-6
850 N Broadway St 97023 503-630-8517
Seth Johnson, prin. Fax 630-8676
Other Schools – See Eagle Creek

Eugene, Lane, Pop. 144,515
Bethel SD 52 5,800/K-12
4640 Barger Dr 97402 541-689-3280
Colt Gill, supt. Fax 689-0719
www.bethel.k12.or.us
Cascade MS 400/6-8
1525 Echo Hollow Rd 97402 541-689-0641
Glen Martz, prin. Fax 689-9622
Clear Lake ES 400/K-5
4646 Barger Dr 97402 541-689-0511
John Luhman, prin. Fax 689-5617
Danebo ES 300/K-5
1265 Candlelight Dr 97402 541-688-8735
Mari Ford, prin. Fax 607-8186
Fairfield ES 400/K-5
3455 Royal Ave 97402 541-689-3751
Marilyn Martin, prin. Fax 689-9956
Irving ES 400/K-5
3200 Hyacinth St 97404 541-688-2620
Greg James, prin. Fax 607-9706
Malabon ES 300/K-5
1380 Taney St 97402 541-461-6421
Maureen Spence, prin. Fax 607-9708
Meadow View S 700/K-8
1855 Legacy St 97402 541-607-9700
Brian Flick, prin. Fax 607-9702
Prairie Mountain S 700/K-8
5305 Royal Ave 97402 541-607-9849
Jennifer Haliski, prin. Fax 607-9856
Shasta MS 500/6-8
4656 Barger Dr 97402 541-688-9611
Bert Eliason, prin. Fax 689-9382

Crow-Applegate-Lorane SD 66 400/K-12
85955 Territorial Hwy 97402 541-935-2100
Dr. Don Anderson, supt. Fax 935-6107
www.cal.k12.or.us
Applegate ES 100/K-6
85955 Territorial Hwy 97402 541-935-2100
Kathi Holvey, prin. Fax 935-6107
Other Schools – See Lorane

Eugene SD 4J 16,900/K-12
200 N Monroe St 97402 541-687-3123
George Russell, supt. Fax 687-3691
www.4j.lane.edu
Adams ES 200/K-5
950 W 22nd Ave 97405 541-687-3475
Pamela Irvine, prin. Fax 334-4700
Arts and Technology Academy at Jefferson K-8
1650 W 22nd Ave 97405 541-687-3221
Jeff Johnson, prin. Fax 687-3675
Awbrey Park ES 500/K-5
158 Spring Creek Dr 97404 541-687-3443
Karen Hardin, prin. Fax 687-3600
Buena Vista Spanish Immersion ES 300/1-5
1500 Queens Way 97401 541-687-3368
B.J. Blake, prin. Fax 334-4892
Charlemagne at Fox Hollow ES 300/K-5
5055 Mahalo Dr 97405 541-687-3177
Martha Moultry, prin. Fax 334-4895
Chavez ES 400/K-5
1510 W 14th Ave 97402 541-687-4200
Denisa Taylor, prin. Fax 687-4210
Crest Drive ES 200/K-5
1155 Crest Dr 97405 541-687-3371
Joe Alsup, prin. Fax 334-4883
Edgewood ES 300/K-5
577 E 46th Ave 97405 541-687-3363
Larry Williams, prin. Fax 334-4715
Edison ES 300/K-5
1328 E 22nd Ave 97403 541-687-3284
Tom Maloney, prin. Fax 687-3487
Gilham ES 500/K-5
3307 Honeywood St 97408 541-687-3466
Gig Nelson, prin. Fax 334-4885
Harris ES 200/K-5
1150 E 29th Ave 97403 541-687-3286
Wally Bryant, prin. Fax 334-4723
Holt ES 600/K-5
770 Calvin St 97401 541-687-4100
Kevin Boling, prin. Fax 687-4141
Howard ES 300/K-5
700 Howard Ave 97404 541-687-3365
Kim Finch, prin. Fax 334-4836
Kelly MS 500/6-8
850 Howard Ave 97404 541-687-3224
Suzy Price, prin. Fax 687-3676
Kennedy MS 500/6-8
2200 Bailey Hill Rd 97405 541-687-3241
Charlie Smith, prin. Fax 687-3677
Madison MS 400/6-8
875 Wilkes Dr 97404 541-687-4300
Rick Gaultney, prin. Fax 687-4320
McCornack ES 400/K-5
1968 Brittany St 97405 541-687-3451
Tasha Katsuda, prin. Fax 334-4893
Meadowlark ES 200/K-5
1500 Queens Way 97401 541-687-3368
B.J. Blake, prin. Fax 334-4892
Monroe MS 600/6-8
2800 Bailey Ln 97401 541-687-3254
Peter Tromba, prin. Fax 687-3679
Parker ES 200/K-5
3875 Kincaid St 97405 541-687-3303
Scott Marsh, prin. Fax 687-3292
River Road/Camino del Rio ES 300/K-5
120 W Hilliard Ln 97404 541-687-3307
Paco Furlan, prin. Fax 334-4733
Roosevelt MS 700/6-8
680 E 24th Ave 97405 541-687-3227
Morley Hegstrom, prin. Fax 687-3680
Spencer Butte MS 500/6-8
500 E 43rd Ave 97405 541-687-3237
Cydney Vandercar, prin. Fax 687-3681
Spring Creek ES 400/K-5
560 Irvington Dr 97404 541-687-3313
Jane Carter, prin. Fax 687-3535
Twin Oaks ES 200/K-5
85916 Bailey Hill Rd 97405 541-687-3417
Larry Soberman, prin. Fax 334-4879
Willagillespie ES 300/K-5
1125 Willagillespie Rd 97401 541-687-3361
Stella Dadson, prin. Fax 687-3473
Young MS 600/6-8
2555 Gilham Rd 97408 541-687-5412
Sara Cramer, prin. Fax 687-5456
Other Schools – See Coburg

Springfield SD 19
Supt. — See Springfield
Goshen ES 100/K-5
34020 B St 97405 541-744-6422
Valerie King, prin. Fax 744-6424

Eugene Christian S 100/PK-8
4500 W Amazon Dr 97405 541-686-9145
Susan Baurer, admin. Fax 686-3190
Eugene Waldorf S 200/PK-8
1350 McLean Blvd 97405 541-683-6951
Fax 345-8774
Life Lutheran S 100/PK-8
710 E 17th Ave 97401 541-342-5433
Rev. Chris Curry, prin. Fax 342-2241
Oak Hill S 100/K-12
86397 Eldon Schafer Dr 97405 541-744-0954
Elliott Grey, hdmstr. Fax 741-6968
O'Hara Catholic S 400/PK-8
715 W 18th Ave 97402 541-485-5291
Dianne Bert, prin. Fax 484-9138
St. Paul S 300/PK-8
1201 Satre St 97401 541-344-1401
Kelli Braud, prin. Fax 344-2572
Williamette Christian S 300/PK-8
PO Box 22108 97402 541-686-8655
Joy Felt, admin. Fax 686-8747
Willow Creek Academy 50/PK-4
2370 Parliament St 97405 541-485-8488
Katherine Young, admin. Fax 343-2430

Fairview, Multnomah, Pop. 9,327
Reynolds SD 7 10,600/K-12
1204 NE 201st Ave 97024 503-661-7200
Robert Fisher, supt. Fax 667-6932
www.reynolds.k12.or.us
Fairview ES 400/K-5
225 Main St 97024 503-667-2954
Susan McKinney, prin. Fax 667-6343
Reynolds MS 1,000/6-8
1200 NE 201st Ave 97024 503-665-8166
Chris Russo, prin. Fax 667-6751
Salish Ponds ES 500/K-5
1210 NE 201st Ave 97024 503-492-7260
Ed Smith, prin. Fax 492-7260
Woodland ES 500/K-5
21607 NE Glisan St 97024 503-674-8188
Chris Greenhalgh, prin. Fax 674-8152
Other Schools – See Portland, Troutdale

Falls City, Polk, Pop. 1,014
Falls City SD 57 200/K-12
111 N Main St 97344 503-787-3521
Peter Tarzian, supt. Fax 787-1507
www.fallscityschools.org/
Falls City S 100/K-8
177 Prospect Ave 97344 503-787-3531
Aaron Hale, prin. Fax 787-3239

Fields, Harney
South Harney SD 33 50/K-8
23657 Fields Denio Rd 97710 541-495-2233
Fax 495-2247
Fields S 50/K-8
23657 Fields Denio Rd 97710 541-495-2233
Claudia Swan, lead tchr. Fax 495-2247

Finn Rock, Lane
McKenzie SD 68 200/K-12
51187 Blue River Dr, Vida OR 97488 541-822-3338
Dr. Sally Storm, supt. Fax 822-8014
www.mckenzie.k12.or.us
McKenzie ES 100/K-5
51187 Blue River Dr, Vida OR 97488 541-822-3315
Dr. Sally Storm, prin. Fax 822-8014

Florence, Lane, Pop. 7,841
Siuslaw SD 97J 1,500/K-12
2111 Oak St 97439 541-997-2651
George Winterscheid, supt. Fax 997-6748
www.siuslaw.k12.or.us
Siuslaw ES 600/K-5
2221 Oak St 97439 541-997-2514
Pam Vander Kley, prin. Fax 997-4163
Siuslaw MS 300/6-8
2525 Oak St 97439 541-997-8241
Lisa Petersen, prin. Fax 997-4161

Forest Grove, Washington, Pop. 19,689
Forest Grove SD 15 6,100/K-12
1728 Main St 97116 503-357-6171
Yvonne Curtis, supt. Fax 359-2520
www.fgsd.k12.or.us
Armstrong MS 900/7-8
1777 Mountain View Ln 97116 503-359-2465
Brandon Hundley, prin. Fax 359-2560
Clarke ES 400/K-4
2516 B St 97116 503-359-2478
Jerrie Matuszak, prin. Fax 359-2561
Dilley ES 300/K-4
4115 SW Dilley Rd 97116 503-359-2493
Naomi Montelongo, prin. Fax 359-2565
Fern Hill ES 300/K-4
4445 Heather St 97116 503-359-2550
David Dorman, prin. Fax 359-2570
Gale ES 300/K-4
3130 18th Ave 97116 503-359-2482
Melissa Carter, prin. Fax 359-2562
McCall Upper ES 900/5-6
1341 Pacific Ave 97116 503-359-2506
Chandra Wilson, prin. Fax 359-2566
Other Schools – See Cornelius, Gales Creek

Visitation S 100/K-8
4189 NW Visitation Rd 97116 503-357-6990
Ted Havens, prin. Fax 359-0819

Foster, Linn
Sweet Home SD 55
Supt. — See Sweet Home
Foster ES 300/K-6
PO Box 747 97345 541-367-7180
Glenna DeSouza, prin. Fax 367-8902

Frenchglen, Harney
Frenchglen SD 16 50/K-8
39235 Highway 205 97736 541-493-2404
Carolyn Koskela, supt. Fax 493-4660
Frenchglen S 50/K-8
39235 Highway 205 97736 541-493-2404
Carolyn Koskela, lead tchr. Fax 493-4660

Gales Creek, Washington
Forest Grove SD 15
Supt. — See Forest Grove
Gales Creek ES 100/K-4
9125 NW Sargent Rd 97117 503-359-2486
Naomi Montelongo, prin. Fax 359-2563

Garibaldi, Tillamook, Pop. 927
Neah-Kah-Nie SD 56
Supt. — See Rockaway
Garibaldi ES 100/K-5
PO Box 317 97118 503-322-0311
Carol Kearns, prin. Fax 322-2193

Gaston, Washington, Pop. 765
Gaston SD 511J 500/K-12
PO Box 68 97119 503-985-0210
David Beasley, supt. Fax 985-3366
www.gaston.k12.or.us
Gaston ES 300/K-6
PO Box 68 97119 503-985-7240
Lani Arakaki-Schadt, prin. Fax 985-7663

Laurelwood Adventist S 50/1-8
PO Box 39 97119 503-985-7289

Gates, Marion, Pop. 475
Santiam Canyon SD 129J
Supt. — See Mill City
Gates ES 200/K-4
PO Box 457 97346 503-897-2191
Jack Thompson, prin. Fax 897-3609

Gearhart, Clatsop, Pop. 1,077
Seaside SD 10
Supt. — See Seaside
Gearhart ES 300/K-5
1002 Pacific Way 97138 503-738-8348
Sande Brown, prin. Fax 738-8349

Gervais, Marion, Pop. 2,292
Gervais SD 1 1,100/K-12
PO Box 100 97026 503-792-3803
Rick Hensel, supt. Fax 792-3809
www.gervais.k12.or.us
Gervais MS 300/5-8
PO Box 176 97026 503-792-3803
Jon Zwemke, prin. Fax 792-3626
Other Schools – See Brooks, Salem

Sacred Heart S 100/K-8
PO Box 215 97026 503-792-4541
Lucy Shindler, prin. Fax 792-3826

Gilchrist, Klamath
Klamath County SD
Supt. — See Klamath Falls
Gilchrist S 200/K-12
PO Box 668 97737 541-433-2295
Kevin McDaniel, prin. Fax 433-2688

Gladstone, Clackamas, Pop. 12,117
Gladstone SD 115 2,200/K-12
17789 Webster Rd 97027 503-655-2777
Bob Stewart, supt. Fax 655-5201
www.gladstone.k12.or.us
Kraxberger MS 600/5-8
17777 Webster Rd 97027 503-655-3636
Joni Cesario, prin. Fax 650-2596
Wetten ES 700/K-4
250 E Exeter St 97027 503-656-6564
Kathy Hartlaub, prin. Fax 656-0917

Grace Christian S 200/PK-12
6460 Glen Echo Ave 97027 503-655-1702
Mardel Watterud, prin. Fax 655-1702
Rivergate Adventist S 200/PK-8
1505 Ohlson Rd 97027 503-656-0544
Ann Campbell, prin. Fax 656-5313

Glendale, Douglas, Pop. 897
Glendale SD 77 500/K-12
PO Box E 97442 541-832-2133
Lloyd Hartley, supt. Fax 832-3183
www.glendale.k12.or.us
Glendale ES 200/K-6
PO Box E 97442 541-832-2176
Lloyd Hartley, prin. Fax 832-2158

Glide, Douglas
Glide SD 12 800/PK-12
301 Glide Loop Dr 97443 541-496-3521
Don Schrader, supt. Fax 496-4300
www.glide.k12.or.us
Glide ES 300/K-6
1477 Glide Loop Dr 97443 541-496-3524
Jerry Halter, prin. Fax 496-4301
Glide MS 100/7-8
301 Glide Loop Dr 97443 541-496-3516
Ira Weir, prin. Fax 496-4302
Other Schools – See Idleyld Park

Gold Beach, Curry, Pop. 1,930
Central Curry SD 1 700/K-12
29516 Ellensburg Ave 97444 541-247-6648
Jeff Davis, supt. Fax 247-9717
www.ccsd.k12.or.us
Riley Creek S 400/K-8
94350 6th St 97444 541-247-6604
Tom Denning, prin. Fax 247-6484
Other Schools – See Agness

Gold Hill, Jackson, Pop. 1,062
Central Point SD 6
Supt. — See Central Point
Hanby MS 300/6-8
806 6th Ave 97525 541-494-6800
Rob Lewis, prin. Fax 855-1120
Patrick ES 300/K-5
1500 2nd Ave 97525 541-494-6840
Nanette Pergin, prin. Fax 664-7489

Grand Ronde, Polk
Willamina SD 30J
Supt. — See Willamina
Willamina MS at Grand Ronde 200/6-8
PO Box 7 97347 503-879-5210
Gus Forster, prin. Fax 879-5249

Grants Pass, Josephine, Pop. 28,882
Grants Pass SD 7 5,900/K-12
725 NE Dean Dr 97526 541-474-5700
Steve Iverson, supt. Fax 474-5705
www.grantspass.k12.or.us
Allen Dale ES 500/K-5
2320 Williams Hwy 97527 541-474-5760
Ryan Thompson, prin. Fax 474-5762
Highland ES 400/K-5
1845 NW Highland Ave 97526 541-474-5765
MaryBeth Munroe, prin. Fax 474-5767
Lincoln ES 500/K-5
1132 NE 10th St 97526 541-474-5770
Missy Fitzsimmons, prin. Fax 474-5718
North MS 700/6-8
1725 NW Highland Ave 97526 541-474-5740
Dan Smith, prin. Fax 474-5739
Parkside ES 300/K-5
735 SW Wagner Meadows Dr 97526 541-474-5777
Diane Mease, prin. Fax 474-9579
Redwood ES 500/K-5
3163 Leonard Rd 97527 541-474-5775
Patrice Davidson, prin. Fax 474-5768
Riverside ES 400/K-5
1200 SE Harvey Dr 97526 541-474-5780
Susan Zottola, prin. Fax 474-5782
South MS 700/6-8
350 W Harbeck Rd 97527 541-474-5750
Renee Cardiff, prin. Fax 474-9742

Three Rivers County SD 5,500/K-12
8550 New Hope Rd 97527 541-862-3111
Dan Huber-Kantola, supt. Fax 862-3119
www.threerivers.k12.or.us
Fleming MS 500/6-8
6001 Monument Dr 97526 541-476-8284
Greg Tardieu, prin. Fax 471-2458
Ft. Vannoy ES 300/K-5
5250 Upper River Rd 97526 541-479-4440
Kathie Hill, prin. Fax 471-2445
Fruitdale ES 300/K-5
1560 Hamilton Ln 97527 541-476-2276
Kelly Christensen, prin. Fax 471-2447
Jerome Prairie ES 200/K-5
2555 Walnut Ave 97527 541-476-2802
David Fuller, prin. Fax 471-2449
Lincoln Savage MS 400/6-8
8551 New Hope Rd 97527 541-862-2171
Brent Workley, prin. Fax 862-2713
Madrona ES 300/K-5
520 Detrick Dr 97527 541-476-6624
Lise Van Brunt, prin. Fax 471-2451
Manzanita ES 400/K-5
310 San Francisco St 97526 541-479-6433
Jessica Durrant, prin. Fax 471-2450
Other Schools – See Applegate, Cave Junction, Williams, Wolf Creek

Grants Pass SDA S 100/K-10
2250 NW Heidi Ln 97526 541-479-2293
Roger Knauff, prin. Fax 479-8412
New Hope Christian S 300/PK-12
5961 New Hope Rd 97527 541-476-4588
Terell Bowdoin, admin. Fax 474-7626
St. Anne S 100/PK-6
1131 NE 10th St 97526 541-479-1582
Jacqueline Henry, prin. Fax 479-1582
Vineyard Christian S 100/PK-12
275 Potts Way 97526 541-479-9649
Doug Thomas, prin. Fax 479-3506

Grass Valley, Sherman, Pop. 153
Sherman County SD
Supt. — See Wasco
South Sherman ES 100/K-6
PO Box 68 97029 541-333-2250
Nancy Kieling, prin. Fax 333-2388

Gresham, Multnomah, Pop. 96,072
Centennial SD 28J
Supt. — See Portland
Butler Creek ES 500/K-6
2789 SW Butler Rd 97080 503-762-6100
Sam Breyer, prin. Fax 762-6110
Pleasant Valley ES 500/K-6
17625 SE Foster Rd 97080 503-762-3209
Laurie Ernstrom, prin. Fax 762-3239

Gresham-Barlow SD 10J 12,000/K-12
1331 NW Eastman Pkwy 97030 503-618-2450
John Miner, supt. Fax 661-1589
www.gresham.k12.or.us
Clear Creek MS 700/6-8
219 NE 219th Ave 97030 503-492-6700
John Koch, prin. Fax 492-6707
East Gresham ES 500/K-5
900 SE 5th St 97080 503-661-6050
Tracy Klinger, prin. Fax 665-4131
East Orient ES 400/K-5
7431 SE 302nd Ave 97080 503-663-4818
Kathleen Copeland, prin. Fax 663-6008
Hall ES 500/K-5
2505 NE 23rd St 97030 503-661-6330
Carlynn Capps, prin. Fax 492-6728
Highland ES 600/K-5
295 NE 24th St 97030 503-665-7158
Terry Bothwell, prin. Fax 492-6755
Hogan Cedars ES 500/K-5
1770 SE Fleming Ave 97080 503-674-6100
Debra James, prin. Fax 674-6401
Hollydale ES 500/K-5
505 SW Birdsdale Dr 97080 503-661-6226
Elaine Luckenbaugh, prin. Fax 492-6718
Kelly Creek ES 500/K-5
2400 SE Baker Way 97080 503-663-7483
Robert Goerke, prin. Fax 663-7491
McCarty MS 700/6-8
1400 SE 5th St 97080 503-665-0148
Derek Garrison, prin. Fax 669-1892
North Gresham ES 500/K-5
1001 SE 217th Ave 97030 503-661-6415
Tom Klansnic, prin. Fax 666-4873
Powell Valley ES 500/K-5
4825 SE Powell Valley Rd 97080 503-661-1510
Rebecca Kadrmas, prin. Fax 492-6711
Russell MS 800/6-8
3625 SE Powell Valley Rd 97080 503-667-6900
Randy Bryant, prin. Fax 492-6708
West Gresham ES 400/K-5
330 W Powell Blvd 97030 503-661-0144
Anita Harris, prin. Fax 492-6735
West Orient MS 400/6-8
29805 SE Orient Dr 97080 503-663-3323
Tim Tutty, prin. Fax 663-2504
Other Schools – See Damascus

Eastside Christian S 100/PK-8
5001 W Powell Blvd 97030 503-661-7210
James Rhodes, admin. Fax 661-1083
Phonics Phactory 300/PK-8
PO Box 2128 97030 503-661-5632
Brian Mayer, admin. Fax 907-5827
Portland Adventist S 300/PK-8
3990 NW 1st St 97030 503-665-4102
Robert McDonald, prin. Fax 665-9486

Haines, Baker, Pop. 402
Baker SD 5J
Supt. — See Baker City
Haines ES 100/K-6
PO Box 306 97833 541-524-2400
Beth Bigelow, prin. Fax 524-2427

Halfway, Baker, Pop. 319
Pine Eagle SD 61 100/K-12
375 N Main St 97834 541-742-2811
Mike Corley, supt. Fax 742-2810
www.pineeagle.k12.or.us/
Pine Eagle S 100/K-8
375 N Main St 97834 541-742-2811
Mike Corley, prin. Fax 742-2422

Halsey, Linn, Pop. 745
Central Linn SD 552
Supt. — See Brownsville
Central Linn ES 400/K-6
239 W 2nd St 97348 541-369-2851
Angela Hansen, prin. Fax 369-3437

Happy Valley, Clackamas, Pop. 8,282
North Clackamas SD 12
Supt. — See Milwaukie
Happy Valley ES 800/K-6
13865 SE King Rd, 503-353-5420
Shelly Reggiani, prin. Fax 353-5435
Mt. Scott ES 500/K-6
11201 SE Stevens Rd, 503-353-5500
Jacque Shayne, prin. Fax 353-5515
Spring Mountain ES 600/K-6
11645 SE Masa Ln, 503-353-5600
Joel Stuart, prin. Fax 353-5615

Harper, Malheur
Harper SD 66 100/K-12
PO Box 800 97906 541-358-2473
Ron Talbot, supt. Fax 358-2488
www.harper.k12.or.us
Harper S 100/K-12
PO Box 800 97906 541-358-2473
Fax 358-2488

Harrisburg, Linn, Pop. 3,265
Harrisburg SD 7 900/K-12
PO Box 208 97446 541-995-6626
Ron Worrell, supt. Fax 995-3453
www.harrisburg.k12.or.us
Harrisburg ES 400/K-5
PO Box 247 97446 541-995-6544
Carol O'Connor, prin. Fax 995-6194
Harrisburg MS 200/6-8
PO Box 317 97446 541-995-6551
Darci Stuller, prin. Fax 995-5120

Harris S 100/PK-12
PO Box 347 97446 541-995-6444
Elton McMillan, supt. Fax 995-6444

Helix, Umatilla, Pop. 183
Helix SD 1 200/K-12
PO Box 398 97835 541-457-2175
Darrick Cope, supt. Fax 457-2481
www.helix.k12.or.us/
Helix S 200/K-12
PO Box 398 97835 541-457-2175
Darrick Cope, prin. Fax 457-2481

Heppner, Morrow, Pop. 1,438
Morrow SD 1
Supt. — See Lexington
Heppner ES 200/K-6
PO Box 367 97836 541-676-9128
Matt Combe, prin. Fax 676-5835

Hermiston, Umatilla, Pop. 14,657
Hermiston SD 8 4,800/K-12
502 W Standard Ave 97838 541-667-6000
Fred Maiocco, supt. Fax 667-6050
www.hermiston.k12.or.us
Desert View ES 400/K-5
1225 SW 9th St 97838 541-667-6900
Mike Scott, prin. Fax 667-6950
Highland Hills ES 400/K-5
450 SE 10th St 97838 541-667-6500
Niki Arnold-Smith, prin. Fax 667-6550
Larive MS 500/6-8
199 E Ridgeway Ave 97838 541-667-6200
Steve Carnes, prin. Fax 667-6250
Rocky Heights ES 500/K-5
650 W Standard Ave 97838 541-667-6600
B.J. Wilson, prin. Fax 667-6650
Sandstone MS 600/6-8
400 NE 10th St 97838 541-667-6300
Jon Mishra, prin. Fax 667-6350
Sunset ES 500/K-5
300 E Catherine Ave 97838 541-667-6700
Devin Grigg, prin. Fax 667-6750
West Park ES 500/K-5
555 SW 7th St 97838 541-667-6800
Shane Pratt, prin. Fax 667-6850

Hermiston Junior Academy 100/K-9
1300 NW Academy Ln 97838 541-567-8523

Hillsboro, Washington, Pop. 84,533
Hillsboro SD 1J 18,300/K-12
3083 NE 49th Pl 97124 503-844-1500
Mike Scott, supt. Fax 844-1540
www.hsd.k12.or.us
Brookwood ES 600/K-6
3960 SE Cedar St 97123 503-844-1715
Molly Siebert, prin. Fax 844-9547
Brown MS 900/7-8
1505 SW Cornelius Pass Rd 97123 503-844-1070
Don Brown, prin. Fax 693-1171
Eastwood ES 500/K-6
2100 NE Lincoln St 97124 503-844-1725
Monique Monahan, prin. Fax 844-6315

Evergreen MS 800/7-8
29850 NW Evergreen Rd 97124 503-844-1400
Ruben Degollado, prin. Fax 693-1706
Farmington View ES 200/K-6
8300 SW Hillsboro Hwy 97123 503-844-1735
William Tracy, prin. Fax 640-0364
Groner ES 200/K-6
23405 SW Scholls Ferry Rd 97123 503-844-1600
Bruce Bourget, prin. Fax 356-6279
Henry ES 600/K-6
1060 SE 24th Ave 97123 503-844-1690
Crystal Schmidt-Dipaola, prin. Fax 844-9702
Imlay ES 700/K-6
5900 SE Lois St 97123 503-844-1090
Kona Williams, prin. Fax 591-8439
Jackson ES 600/K-6
675 NE Estate Dr 97124 503-844-1670
Jon Pede, prin. Fax 844-9801
Ladd Acres ES 600/K-6
2425 SW Cornelius Pass Rd 97123 503-844-1300
David Cox, prin. Fax 649-4321
Lincoln Street ES K-6
801 NE Lincoln St 97124 503-844-1500
Toni Crummett, prin. Fax 844-1160
McKinney ES 500/K-6
535 NW Darnielle St 97124 503-844-1660
Celia Murray, prin. Fax 844-9901
Minter Bridge ES 400/K-6
1750 SE Jacquelin Dr 97123 503-844-1650
Dayle Spitzer Eder, prin. Fax 844-9607
Mooberry ES 500/K-6
1230 NE 10th Ave 97124 503-844-1640
Linda Bishop, prin. Fax 640-6935
Orenco ES 600/K-6
22550 NW Birch St 97124 503-844-1370
Tim Bishop, prin. Fax 648-5558
Patterson ES 700/K-6
261 NE Lenox St 97124 503-844-1380
Lauri Lewis, prin. Fax 648-4699
Poynter MS 800/7-8
1535 NE Grant St 97124 503-844-1580
Greg Timmons, prin. Fax 640-8965
Quatama ES K-6
6905 NE Campus Way 97124 503-844-1500
Janis Hill, prin. Fax 844-1180
Rosedale ES K-6
3963 W 229th Ave 97123 503-844-1200
Mike Donovan, prin. Fax 844-1202
South Meadows MS 7-8
4960 SE Davis Rd 97123 503-844-1220
Dave Parker, prin. Fax 844-1222
West Union ES 400/K-6
23870 NW West Union Rd 97124 503-844-1620
Grant Corliss, prin. Fax 647-2428
Witch Hazel ES 500/K-6
4950 SW Davis St 97123 503-844-1610
Kari Woyak, prin. Fax 681-2302
Other Schools – See Aloha, Beaverton, Cornelius, North Plains, Portland

---

Heritage Christian S 200/K-12
1679 SE Enterprise Cir 97123 503-640-1027
Todd Pfaff, hdmstr. Fax 846-0609
St. Matthew S 200/K-8
221 SE Walnut St 97123 503-648-2512
Jeannie Timoney, prin. Fax 648-4518
Swallowtail S 100/PK-8
PO Box 3753 97123 503-846-0336
Cecelia McClellan, dir. Fax 846-1626
Tualatin Valley Junior Academy 300/K-10
21975 SW Baseline Rd 97123 503-649-5518
Fax 642-7654

Hines, Harney, Pop. 1,493
Double O SD 28 50/K-8
PO Box 888 97738 541-493-2400
Double O S, PO Box 888 97738 50/K-8
W. Gordon Andrews, lead tchr. 541-493-2400

Harney County SD 3
Supt. — See Burns
Hines MS 200/6-8
PO Box 38 97738 541-573-6436
Gail Buermann, prin. Fax 573-7255

Pine Creek SD 5 50/K-8
PO Box 826 97738 541-573-3229
Fax 573-3229

Other Schools – See Drewsey

Hood River, Hood River, Pop. 6,480
Hood River County SD 3,700/K-12
1011 Eugene St 97031 541-386-2511
Dr. Pat Evenson-Brady, supt. Fax 387-5099
www.hoodriver.k12.or.us/
Hood River MS 400/6-8
1602 May St 97031 541-386-2114
Brent Emmons, prin. Fax 386-5070
May Street ES 400/K-5
911 May St 97031 541-386-2656
Susan Henness, prin. Fax 387-5068
Pine Grove ES 100/K-5
2405 Eastside Rd 97031 541-386-4919
Kelly Beard, prin. Fax 387-5041
Westside ES 300/K-5
3685 Belmont Dr 97031 541-386-1535
Dan Patton, prin. Fax 387-5059
Wy'East MS 400/6-8
3000 Wyeast Rd 97031 541-354-1548
Catherine Dalbey, prin. Fax 354-5120
Other Schools – See Cascade Locks, Mount Hood Parkdale, Odell

---

Horizon Christian S 200/PK-12
700 Pacific Ave 97031 541-387-3200
Ken Block, supt. Fax 387-3651
Mid-Columbia Adventist Academy 100/K-10
1100 22nd St 97031 541-386-3187
Peter Hardy, prin. Fax 386-5702

Hubbard, Clackamas, Pop. 2,545
Canby SD 86
Supt. — See Canby
Ninety-One S 500/K-8
5811 S Whiskey Hill Rd 97032 503-263-7110
Diane Hernandez, prin. Fax 263-7112

Huntington, Baker, Pop. 481
Huntington SD 16J 100/K-12
520 3rd St E 97907 541-869-2204
Brian Wolf, supt. Fax 869-2444
www.huntington.k12.or.us/
Huntington S 100/K-12
520 3rd St E 97907 541-869-2204
Brian Wolf, prin. Fax 869-2444

Idleyld Park, Douglas
Glide SD 12
Supt. — See Glide
Toketee Falls ES 50/PK-6
100 Toketee School Rd 97447 541-498-2490
Don Schrader, prin. Fax 496-0428

Imbler, Union, Pop. 282
Imbler SD 11 300/K-12
PO Box 164 97841 541-534-5331
Doug Hislop, supt. Fax 534-9650
www.imbler.k12.or.us
Imbler ES 200/K-6
PO Box 164 97841 541-534-2311
Mike Mills, prin. Fax 534-9650

Imnaha, Wallowa
Joseph SD 6
Supt. — See Joseph
Imnaha S 97842 50/K-8
Rhonda Shirley, prin. 541-577-3119

Independence, Polk, Pop. 8,193
Central SD 13J 2,600/K-12
1610 Monmouth St 97351 503-838-0030
Joseph Hunter, supt. Fax 838-0033
www.central.k12.or.us
Hill ES 300/K-5
750 S 5th St 97351 503-838-1828
Sharon Tebb, prin. Fax 838-6982
Independence ES 400/K-5
150 S 4th St 97351 503-838-1322
Steve Tillery, prin. Fax 838-6980
Talmadge MS 400/6-8
51 S 16th St 97351 503-838-1424
Perry LaBounty, prin. Fax 606-2436
Other Schools – See Monmouth

Irrigon, Morrow, Pop. 1,777
Morrow SD 1
Supt. — See Lexington
Houghton ES 300/K-4
1105 NE Main Ave 97844 541-922-3321
John Sebastian, prin. Fax 922-2949
Irrigon ES 100/5-6
490 SE Wyoming Ave 97844 541-922-2421
Joel Chavez, prin. Fax 922-5540

Jacksonville, Jackson, Pop. 2,230
Medford SD 549C
Supt. — See Medford
Jacksonville ES 400/K-6
655 Hueners Ln 97530 541-842-3790
Richard Snyder, prin. Fax 842-3155
Ruch S 200/K-8
156 Upper Applegate Rd 97530 541-842-3850
Terri Dahl, prin. Fax 842-3480

Jasper, Lane

Laurelwood Academy K-6
37466 Jasper Lowell Rd 97438 541-726-8340

Jefferson, Marion, Pop. 2,607
Jefferson SD 14J 900/K-12
1328 N 2nd St 97352 541-327-3337
Bob Wadlow, supt. Fax 327-2960
www.jefferson.k12.or.us
Jefferson ES 400/K-5
615 N 2nd St 97352 541-327-3337
Michael Knudson, prin. Fax 327-1216
Jefferson MS 200/6-8
1334 N 2nd St 97352 541-327-3337
Scott Linenberger, prin. Fax 327-7762

Jordan Valley, Malheur, Pop. 233
Jordan Valley SD 3 100/K-12
PO Box 99 97910 541-586-2213
Andree Scown, supt. Fax 586-2568
www.jordanvalley.k12.or.us/
Jordan Valley ES 50/K-6
PO Box 99 97910 541-586-2213
Andree Scown, prin. Fax 586-2568
Rockville S 50/K-8
PO Box 99 97910 541-339-3501
Andree Scown, prin. Fax 586-2213

Joseph, Wallowa, Pop. 1,005
Joseph SD 6 200/K-12
PO Box W 97846 541-432-7311
Rhonda Shirley, supt. Fax 432-1100
www.joseph.k12.or.us/
Joseph ES, PO Box W 97846 100/K-4
Rhonda Shirley, prin. 541-432-5361
Joseph MS 100/5-8
PO Box W 97846 541-432-7311
Sherri Kilgore, prin. Fax 432-1100
Other Schools – See Imnaha

Junction City, Lane, Pop. 5,369
Junction City SD 69 1,800/K-12
325 Maple St 97448 541-998-6311
Kathleen Rodden-Nord, supt. Fax 998-3926
www.junctioncity.k12.or.us
Laurel ES 500/K-4
1401 Laurel St 97448 541-998-2386
Amy Lesan, prin. Fax 998-8422

Oaklea MS 500/5-8
1515 Rose St 97448 541-998-3381
Tom Endersby, prin. Fax 998-3383
Territorial ES 100/K-5
92609 Territorial Hwy 97448 541-998-8371
Steve Jones, prin. Fax 998-4744

Juntura, Malheur
Juntura SD 12 50/K-8
PO Box 248 97911 541-277-3261
Bonnie Heinz, supt. Fax 277-3261
www.malesd.k12.or.us/Districts/Juntura/index.html
Juntura S 50/K-8
PO Box 248 97911 541-277-3261
Bonnie Heinz, lead tchr. Fax 277-3261

Keizer, Marion, Pop. 34,644
Salem-Keizer SD 24J
Supt. — See Salem
Claggett Creek MS 900/6-8
1810 Alder Dr NE 97303 503-399-3701
Peter Danner, prin. Fax 399-3708
Clear Lake ES 500/K-5
7425 Meadowglen St NE 97303 503-399-3138
Joe Grant, prin. Fax 391-4072
Cummings ES 400/K-5
613 Cummings Ln N 97303 503-399-3141
Lisa Sundseth, prin. Fax 391-4033
Forest Ridge ES 200/K-5
7905 June Reid Pl NE 97303 503-399-5548
Gary Etchemendy, prin. Fax 399-3469
Gubser ES 500/K-5
6610 14th Ave NE 97303 503-399-3275
Jesse Leonard, prin. Fax 319-4135
Keizer ES 500/K-5
5600 McClure St N 97303 503-399-3161
Tracy Moisan, prin. Fax 399-3435
Kennedy ES 500/K-5
4912 Noren Ave NE 97303 503-399-3163
Terry Gallagher, prin. Fax 399-3436
Weddle ES 500/K-5
1825 Alder Dr NE 97303 503-399-3604
Samantha Ragaisis, prin. Fax 362-7122
Whiteaker MS 800/6-8
1605 Lockhaven Dr NE 97303 503-399-3224
Laura Perez, prin. Fax 375-7872

Keno, Klamath
Klamath County SD
Supt. — See Klamath Falls
Keno ES 200/K-6
PO Box 180 97627 541-883-5055
Jennifer Hawkins, prin. Fax 883-5028

Klamath Falls, Klamath, Pop. 19,882
Klamath County SD 6,600/K-12
10501 Washburn Way 97603 541-883-5000
Greg Thede, supt. Fax 883-6677
www.kcsd.k12.or.us
Brixner JHS 400/7-8
4727 Homedale Rd 97603 541-883-5025
Polly Beam, prin. Fax 883-5019
Ferguson ES 500/K-6
2901 Homedale Rd 97603 541-883-5036
Linda Stastny, prin. Fax 885-3357
Henley ES 300/K-6
8205 Highway 39 97603 541-883-5038
Mike Kappas, prin. Fax 885-3356
Henley MS 500/7-8
7925 Highway 39 97603 541-883-5050
Steve Hamlin, prin. Fax 883-5012
Peterson ES 500/K-6
4856 Clinton Ave 97603 541-883-5058
Jim Smith, prin. Fax 883-6679
Shasta ES 600/K-6
1951 Madison St 97603 541-883-5060
Jim Houk, prin. Fax 850-3811
Stearns ES 300/K-6
3641 Crest St 97603 541-883-5063
Christie Gestvang, prin. Fax 883-4542
Other Schools – See Bly, Bonanza, Chiloquin, Gilchrist, Keno, Malin, Merrill

Klamath Falls CSD 2,900/K-12
1336 Avalon St 97603 541-883-4700
Cecelia Amuchastegui, supt. Fax 850-2766
www.kfalls.k12.or.us
Conger ES 300/K-6
1700 California Ave 97601 541-883-4772
Barbara Headden, prin. Fax 883-4752
Fairview ES 300/K-6
1017 Donald St 97601 541-883-4760
Tony Swan, prin. Fax 883-4773
Mills ES 500/K-6
520 E Main St 97601 541-883-4754
Bill Leary, prin. Fax 883-4775
Pelican ES 200/K-6
501 Mclean St 97601 541-883-4765
Fred Bartels, prin. Fax 883-4729
Ponderosa JHS 500/7-8
2554 Main St 97601 541-883-4740
Bob Vian, prin. Fax 885-4286
Roosevelt ES 300/K-6
1125 N Eldorado Ave 97601 541-883-4750
Ruth Krieger, prin. Fax 883-4728

Adventist Christian S 50/1-8
2499 Main St 97601 541-882-4151
Fax 882-4151
Hosanna Christian S 300/PK-12
5000 Hosanna Way 97603 541-882-7732
Jeff Mudrow, admin. Fax 882-6940
Little Lambs Lutheran S 50/PK-PK
1025 High St 97601 541-882-9552
Vicky Davis, prin. Fax 884-6868
Triad S 300/PK-12
4849 S 6th St 97603 541-885-7940
David Wehr, hdmstr. Fax 884-8725

Lafayette, Yamhill, Pop. 2,898
McMinnville SD 40
Supt. — See Mc Minnville
Wascher ES 400/K-5
PO Box 788 97127 503-565-5400
Kyra Donovan, prin. Fax 565-5406

La Grande, Union, Pop. 12,440
La Grande SD 1 1,900/K-12
1305 N Willow St 97850 541-663-3202
Larry Glaze, supt. Fax 663-3211
www.lagrande.k12.or.us
Central ES 400/1-5
402 K Ave 97850 541-663-3500
Bruce Kevan, prin. Fax 663-3502
Greenwood ES 300/1-5
2300 N Spruce St 97850 541-663-3580
Mike Gregory, prin. Fax 663-3582
Island City ES 200/1-5
10201 W 4th St 97850 541-663-3270
John Tolan, prin. Fax 663-3272
La Grande MS 400/6-8
1108 4th St 97850 541-663-3421
Kyle McKinney, prin. Fax 663-3422
Willow S, 1305 N Willow St 97850 K-K
Larry Glaze, prin. 541-663-3650

Grande Ronde Academy 100/PK-8
10702 S Walton Rd 97850 541-975-1147
Mike Kennedy, admin. Fax 963-3398
La Grande Adventist S 50/K-8
PO Box 1025 97850 541-963-6203
Ben Pflugrad, prin.

Lake Oswego, Clackamas, Pop. 36,502
Lake Oswego SD 7J 6,700/K-12
PO Box 70 97034 503-534-2000
William Korach, supt. Fax 534-2030
www.loswego.k12.or.us
Bryant ES 300/K-6
4750 Jean Rd 97035 503-534-2347
Dan Sterling, prin. Fax 534-2245
Forest Hills ES 400/K-6
1133 Andrews Rd 97034 503-534-2350
Gwen Hill, prin. Fax 534-2234
Hallinan ES 400/K-6
16800 Hawthorne Dr 97034 503-534-2353
Steve Mauritz, prin. Fax 534-2251
Lake Grove ES 500/K-6
15777 Boones Ferry Rd 97035 503-534-2357
Sara Deboy, prin. Fax 534-2388
Lake Oswego JHS 600/7-8
2500 Country Club Rd 97034 503-534-2335
Ann Gerson, prin. Fax 534-2341
Oak Creek ES 400/K-6
55 Kingsgate Rd 97035 503-534-2323
Michael Esping, prin. Fax 534-2257
Palisades ES 300/K-6
1500 Greentree Rd 97034 503-534-2345
Carol Whitten, prin. Fax 534-2255
River Grove ES 300/K-6
5850 Mcewan Rd 97035 503-534-2363
Nancy Verstegen, prin. Fax 534-2247
Uplands ES 400/K-6
2055 Wembley Park Rd 97034 503-534-2366
Karen Lachman, prin. Fax 534-2498
Waluga JHS 500/7-8
4700 Jean Rd 97035 503-534-2343
Jennifer Schiele, prin. Fax 534-2276
Westridge ES 300/K-6
3400 Royce Way 97034 503-534-2371
Scott Lane, prin. Fax 534-2373

Our Lady of the Lake S 200/K-8
716 A Ave 97034 503-636-2121
Joan Codd, prin. Fax 635-7760

Lakeview, Lake, Pop. 2,378
Adel SD 21 50/K-8
357 N L St 97630 541-947-5418
Fax 947-3373
Other Schools – See Adel

Lakeview SD 7 800/K-12
1341 S 1st St 97630 541-947-3347
Sean Gallagher, supt. Fax 947-3386
www.lakeview.k12.or.us/
Daly MS 100/7-8
220 S H St 97630 541-947-2257
Lane Stratton, prin. Fax 947-3506
Fremont/Hay ES 300/K-6
500 S I St 97630 541-947-2136
Will Cahill, prin. Fax 947-3535
Union ES 100/K-6
92398 Water Users Ln 97630 541-947-2553
Will Cahill, prin. Fax 947-2445

Langlois, Curry
Port Orford-Langlois SD 2CJ
Supt. — See Port Orford
Blanco S 100/K-8
48241 Highway 101 97450 541-348-2326
Ruby Price, prin. Fax 348-2246

La Pine, Deschutes
Bend-LaPine Administrative SD 1
Supt. — See Bend
La Pine ES 500/K-4
51615 Coach Rd 97739 541-536-2717
Tammy Doty, prin. Fax 536-5101
La Pine MS 500/5-8
PO Box 305 97739 541-536-5967
Patricia Yaeger, prin. Fax 536-5787

Lebanon, Linn, Pop. 13,834
Lebanon Community SD 9 4,100/K-12
485 S 5th St 97355 541-451-8511
Rob Hess, supt. Fax 451-8519
www.lebanon.k12.or.us
Cascades ES 300/K-5
2163 S 7th St 97355 541-451-8524
Susan Straight, prin. Fax 451-8439
Green Acres ES 400/K-5
700 S 10th St 97355 541-451-8534
Jan Zarate, prin. Fax 451-8429
Hamilton Creek S 300/K-8
32135 Berlin Rd 97355 541-451-8574
Dawn Baker, prin. Fax 451-8473
Lacomb S 200/K-8
34110 E Lacomb Rd 97355 541-451-8565
Jennifer Kelly, prin. Fax 451-8568
Pioneer S 500/K-8
500 N 5th St 97355 541-451-8487
Mark Finch, prin. Fax 451-8488
Riverview ES 500/K-5
1011 Mountain River Dr 97355 541-451-8451
Rynda Gregory, prin. Fax 451-8452
Seven Oak MS 600/6-8
550 Cascade Dr 97355 541-451-8416
Ed Sansom, prin. Fax 451-8431

Lexington, Morrow, Pop. 273
Morrow SD 1 2,300/K-12
PO Box 368 97839 541-989-8202
Mark Burrows, supt. Fax 989-8470
www.morrow.k12.or.us
Other Schools – See Boardman, Heppner, Irrigon

Lincoln City, Lincoln, Pop. 7,849
Lincoln County SD
Supt. — See Newport
Oceanlake ES 400/K-6
2420 NE 22nd St 97367 541-994-5296
Betsy Wilcox, prin. Fax 994-8102
Taft ES 400/K-6
4040 SE High School Dr 97367 541-996-2136
Dave Malcolm, prin. Fax 996-3999

Lincoln City SDA Junior Academy 100/1-12
2126 NE Surf Ave 97367 541-994-5181
Richard Worley, prin. Fax 994-9034

Long Creek, Grant, Pop. 202
Long Creek SD 17 50/PK-12
PO Box 429 97856 541-421-3896
Brian Gander, supt. Fax 421-3012
Long Creek S 50/PK-12
PO Box 429 97856 541-421-3896
Brian Gander, prin. Fax 421-3012

Lorane, Lane
Crow-Applegate-Lorane SD 66
Supt. — See Eugene
Lorane ES 100/K-6
PO Box 122 97451 541-942-3211
Kathi Holvey, prin. Fax 942-3287

Lowell, Lane, Pop. 923
Lowell SD 71 300/K-12
65 S Pioneer St 97452 541-937-8405
Aaron Brown, supt. Fax 937-2112
www.lowell.k12.or.us
Lundy ES 200/K-7
65 S Pioneer St 97452 541-937-2105
Christine Cox, prin. Fax 937-8709

Lyons, Linn, Pop. 1,083
North Santiam SD 29J
Supt. — See Stayton
Mari-Linn S 200/K-8
741 5th St 97358 503-859-2154
Paula Vawter, prin. Fax 859-2164

Mc Minnville, Yamhill, Pop. 23,136
McMinnville SD 40 6,000/K-12
1500 NE Baker St 97128 503-565-4000
Maryalice Russell, supt. Fax 565-4043
www.msd.k12.or.us
Buel ES K-5
1985 SE Davis St, 503-565-5500
Stephanie Legard, prin. Fax 565-5506
Columbus ES 500/K-5
1600 SW Fellows St, 503-565-4600
Kathi Fowler, prin. Fax 565-4606
Duniway MS 700/6-8
575 NW Michelbook Ln, 503-565-4400
Cathy Carnahan, prin. Fax 565-4414
Grandhaven ES 700/K-5
3200 NE Mcdonald Ln, 503-565-4700
Marjorie Johnson, prin. Fax 565-4706
Memorial ES 600/K-5
501 NW 14th St, 503-565-4800
Deborah Weiner, prin. Fax 565-4806
Newby ES 400/K-5
1125 NW 2nd St, 503-565-4900
Mark Hinthorn, prin. Fax 565-4943
Patton MS 800/6-8
1175 NE 19th St, 503-565-4500
Marty Palacios, prin. Fax 565-4515
Other Schools – See Lafayette

Bethel Christian S 200/PK-8
325 NW Baker Creek Rd, 503-472-6076
Joseph Ollis, admin. Fax 434-5543
Mc Minnville SDA S 50/K-8
1349 NW Elm St, 503-472-3336
June Graham, prin. Fax 474-9516
St. James S 200/PK-5
206 NE Kirby St, 503-472-2661
Kelly Cromwell, prin. Fax 472-4414
St. John Lutheran S 100/PK-5
2142 NE McDonald Ln, 503-472-9189
Char Kroemer, prin. Fax 472-6677
Trinity Learning Center 100/PK-K
125 SE Cowls St, 503-434-5695

Madras, Jefferson, Pop. 5,300
Jefferson County SD 509J 2,800/K-12
445 SE Buff St 97741 541-475-6192
Rick Molitor, supt. Fax 475-6856
www.whitebuffalos.net/
Big Muddy S, 445 SE Buff St 97741 50/K-8
Kathy Bishop, prin. 541-475-6192
Buff ES 300/K-5
375 SE Buff St 97741 541-475-2457
Marlys Alger, prin. Fax 325-5444
Jefferson County MS 700/6-8
1180 SE City View St 97741 541-475-7253
Ken Clark, prin. Fax 475-4825
Madras ES 300/K-5
215 SE 10th St 97741 541-475-3520
Darryl Smith, prin. Fax 475-9448
Other Schools – See Metolius, Warm Springs

Madras Christian S 50/K-8
66 SE H St 97741 541-475-7545

Malin, Klamath, Pop. 638
Klamath County SD
Supt. — See Klamath Falls
Malin ES 100/K-6
PO Box 25 97632 541-723-2261
Larita Ongman, prin. Fax 723-2184

Mapleton, Lane
Mapleton SD 32 200/K-12
10868 E Mapleton Rd 97453 541-268-4312
Kyle Tucker, supt. Fax 268-4632
www.mapleton.k12.or.us
Mapleton ES 100/K-6
10868 E Mapleton Rd 97453 541-268-4471
Brenda Moyer, prin. Fax 268-9919

Marcola, Lane
Marcola SD 79J 200/K-12
PO Box 820 97454 541-933-2512
W. Rolla Weber, supt. Fax 933-2338
www.marcola.k12.or.us
Marcola S 100/K-8
PO Box 820 97454 541-933-2411
W. Rolla Weber, prin. Fax 933-1428

Maupin, Wasco, Pop. 406
South Wasco County SD 1 200/K-12
PO Box 346 97037 541-395-2645
Dennis Hickey, supt. Fax 395-2679
www.swasco.net
Maupin ES 100/K-6
PO Box 346 97037 541-395-2665
Ryan Wraught, prin. Fax 395-2675

Medford, Jackson, Pop. 70,147
Medford SD 549C 11,800/K-12
500 Monroe St 97501 541-842-3636
Dr. Philip Long, supt. Fax 842-1087
www.medford.k12.or.us
Griffin Creek ES 600/K-6
2430 Griffin Creek Rd 97501 541-842-3740
Ginny Hicks, prin. Fax 842-1818
Hedrick MS 900/7-8
1501 E Jackson St 97504 541-842-3700
Paul Cataldo, prin. Fax 842-1548
Hoover ES 500/K-6
2323 Siskiyou Blvd 97504 541-842-3750
Phil Meager, prin. Fax 842-1874
Howard ES 500/K-6
286 Mace Rd 97501 541-842-3760
Sallie Johnson, prin. Fax 842-3010
Jackson ES 200/K-3
3070 Ross Ln 97502 541-842-3770
Tom Ettel, prin. Fax 842-3083
Jackson IS 4-6
320 W 2nd St 97501 541-842-3715
Tom Ettel, prin. Fax 842-1652
Jefferson ES 500/K-6
333 Holmes Ave 97501 541-842-3800
Thomas Sherwood, prin. Fax 842-3208
Kennedy ES 500/K-6
2860 N Keene Way Dr 97504 541-842-3810
Janis Shade, prin. Fax 842-3265
Lincoln ES 500/K-6
3101 McLoughlin Dr 97504 541-842-3730
Patricia Frazier, prin. Fax 842-1754
Lone Pine ES 500/K-6
3158 Lone Pine Rd 97504 541-842-3820
Kristi Anderson, prin. Fax 842-3319
McLoughlin MS 800/7-8
320 W 2nd St 97501 541-842-3720
Amy Tiger, prin. Fax 842-1652
Oak Grove ES 500/K-6
2838 W Main St 97501 541-842-3830
Julie Evans, prin. Fax 842-3375
Roosevelt ES 200/K-3
2323 Siskiyou Blvd 97504 541-842-3840
Anne Mitchell, prin. Fax 842-3430
Roosevelt IS 4-6
1501 E Jackson St 97504 541-842-3714
Anne Mitchell, prin. Fax 842-1548
Washington ES 400/K-6
610 S Peach St 97501 541-842-3860
Joe Frazier, prin. Fax 842-3520
Wilson ES 500/K-6
1400 Johnson St 97504 541-842-3870
Pam Zaklan, prin. Fax 842-3575
Other Schools – See Jacksonville

Phoenix-Talent SD 4
Supt. — See Phoenix
Orchard Hill ES 400/K-5
1011 La Loma Dr 97504 541-779-1766
Gerry Flock, prin. Fax 770-9037

Grace Christian S 700/PK-8
649 Crater Lake Ave 97504 541-772-1438
Ray Johnson, supt. Fax 858-7288

Harvest Baptist Christian S 100/PK-8
2001 S Columbus Ave 97501 541-773-6974
Bill Whittington, admin. Fax 773-4331
New Dimension Christian S 50/PK-8
1108 W Main St 97501 541-245-4136
Susan Warner, prin.
Rogue Valley Adventist Academy 100/K-12
3675 S Stage Rd 97501 541-773-2988
Fylvia Fowler Kline, prin. Fax 779-7575
Sacred Heart S 300/PK-8
431 S Ivy St 97501 541-772-4105
Shirley Gray, prin. Fax 732-0633

Merrill, Klamath, Pop. 897
Klamath County SD
Supt. — See Klamath Falls
Merrill ES 200/K-6
PO Box 468 97633 541-798-5723
Larita Ongman, prin. Fax 798-5814

Metolius, Jefferson, Pop. 739
Jefferson County SD 509J
Supt. — See Madras
Metolius ES 200/K-5
420 Butte Ave 97741 541-546-3104
Joshua Adams, prin. Fax 475-6421

Mill City, Linn, Pop. 1,593
Santiam Canyon SD 129J 600/K-12
PO Box 197 97360 503-897-2321
Brad Yates, supt. Fax 897-4004
www.santiam.k12.or.us
Mill City MS 200/5-8
PO Box 198 97360 503-897-2368
James Beck, prin. Fax 897-4034
Other Schools – See Gates

Milton Freewater, Umatilla, Pop. 5,886
Milton-Freewater USD 7 1,900/K-12
138 S Main St 97862 541-938-3551
Dr. Marilyn McBride, supt. Fax 938-6704
www.miltfree.k12.or.us
Central MS 400/6-8
306 SW 2nd Ave 97862 541-938-5504
Bruce Neil, prin. Fax 938-6615
Ferndale ES 300/K-5
53445 W Ferndale Rd 97862 541-938-5412
Jim Reger, prin. Fax 938-0503
Freewater ES 300/K-5
17 NW 8th Ave 97862 541-938-6611
Carrie Hendricks, prin. Fax 938-5337
Grove ES 400/K-5
129 SE 15th Ave 97862 541-938-3233
Jim Goodenough, prin. Fax 938-2100

Milton-Stateline SDA S 100/K-8
53565 W Crockett Rd 97862 541-938-7131
Leslie Briggs, prin. Fax 938-0236

Milwaukie, Clackamas, Pop. 20,810
North Clackamas SD 12 16,100/K-12
4444 SE Lake Rd 97222 503-353-6000
Ron Naso, supt. Fax 353-6007
www.nclack.k12.or.us
Alder Creek MS 700/7-8
13801 SE Webster Rd 97267 503-353-5700
Christine Garcia, prin. Fax 353-5715
Ardenwald ES 300/K-6
8950 SE 36th Ave 97222 503-353-5320
Sheila Shaw, prin. Fax 353-5335
Bilquist ES 500/K-6
15708 SE Webster Rd 97267 503-353-5340
Cam Kitchen, prin. Fax 353-5355
Campbell ES 300/K-6
11326 SE 47th Ave 97222 503-353-5360
Curtis Long, prin. Fax 353-5375
Concord ES 300/K-6
3811 SE Concord Rd 97267 503-353-5400
Jonni Lewis, prin. Fax 353-5415
El Puente ES 200/K-6
11250 SE 27th Ave 97222 503-353-5495
Molly Little, prin. Fax 653-3807
Lewelling ES 400/K-6
5325 SE Logus Rd 97222 503-353-5440
Liz Manspeaker, prin. Fax 353-5445
Linwood ES 300/K-6
11909 SE Linwood Ave 97222 503-353-5460
Kevin Spooner, prin. Fax 353-5475
Milwaukie ES 300/K-6
11250 SE 27th Ave 97222 503-353-5480
Molly Little, prin. Fax 653-3683
Oak Grove ES 600/K-6
2150 SE Torbank Rd 97222 503-353-5520
Tiffany Shireman, prin. Fax 353-5535
Riverside ES 300/K-6
16303 SE River Rd 97267 503-353-5560
Monique Singleton, prin. Fax 353-5575
Rowe MS 700/7-8
3606 SE Lake Rd 97222 503-353-5725
Larry Becker, prin. Fax 353-5740
Whitcomb ES 600/K-6
7400 SE Thompson Rd 97222 503-353-5660
Sidney Ong, prin. Fax 353-5675
Wichita ES 300/K-6
6031 SE King Rd 97222 503-353-5680
Mason Branstetter, prin. Fax 353-5695
Other Schools – See Clackamas, Happy Valley, Portland

Oregon City SD 62
Supt. — See Oregon City
Candy Lane ES 200/3-6
5901 SE Hull Ave 97267 503-785-8150
Pam Miller, prin. Fax 654-2693
Jennings Lodge ES 300/K-3
18521 SE River Rd 97267 503-785-8035
Pam Miller, prin. Fax 654-9240

Christ the King S 200/K-8
7414 SE Michael Dr 97222 503-785-2411
Michael Doran, prin. Fax 794-9607

Portland Waldorf S 400/PK-12
2300 SE Harrison St 97222 503-654-2200
Diane Rowley, admin. Fax 652-5162
St. John the Baptist S 200/K-8
10956 SE 25th Ave 97222 503-654-0200
Dr. Julie Vogel, prin. Fax 654-8419

Mist, Columbia
Vernonia SD 47J
Supt. — See Vernonia
Mist ES 50/K-5
69163 Highway 47 97016 503-755-2486
Aaron Miller, prin. Fax 755-2213

Mitchell, Wheeler, Pop. 158
Mitchell SD 55 100/K-12
PO Box 247 97750 541-462-3311
Susan Horton, supt. Fax 462-3849
www.mitchell.k12.or.us
Mitchell S 100/K-12
PO Box 247 97750 541-462-3311
Susan Horton, prin. Fax 462-3849

Molalla, Clackamas, Pop. 6,737
Molalla River SD 35 2,900/K-12
PO Box 188 97038 503-829-2359
Wayne Kostur, supt. Fax 829-5540
www.molallariv.k12.or.us
Maple Grove ES 100/K-5
39214 S Sawtell Rd 97038 503-829-8986
Mike Clarke, lead tchr. Fax 829-6337
Molalla ES 400/K-5
PO Box 206 97038 503-829-4333
Donna Carlson, prin. Fax 829-2614
Molalla River MS 700/6-8
PO Box 225 97038 503-829-6133
Robert Espenel, prin. Fax 829-5680
Rural Dell ES 200/K-5
10500 S Highway 211 97038 503-651-2128
Michael Nickless, prin. Fax 651-2127
Other Schools – See Mulino

Monmouth, Polk, Pop. 8,987
Central SD 13J
Supt. — See Independence
Ash Creek IS 200/K-5
1360 N 16th St 97361 503-606-9016
Barbara Welander, prin. Fax 606-3666
Monmouth ES 500/K-5
958 Church St E 97361 503-838-1433
Rich McFarland, prin. Fax 606-9797

Mid Valley Christian Academy 100/PK-12
1483 N 16th St 97361 503-838-2818
Ray Birch, admin.

Monroe, Benton, Pop. 581
Monroe SD 1J 400/K-12
365 N 5th St 97456 541-847-6292
Randall Crowson, supt. Fax 847-6290
www.monroe.k12.or.us/sd1j.htm
Monroe S 300/K-8
600 Dragon Dr 97456 541-847-5139
Brenda Goracke, prin. Fax 847-5128

Monument, Grant, Pop. 134
Monument SD 8 100/K-12
PO Box 127 97864 541-934-2646
Michael Reule, supt. Fax 934-2005
www.grantesd.k12.or.us/Monument/
Monument S 100/K-12
PO Box 127 97864 541-934-2646
Michael Reule, prin. Fax 934-2005

Mount Angel, Marion, Pop. 3,355
Mt. Angel SD 91 800/K-12
PO Box 1129 97362 503-845-2345
Robert Young, supt. Fax 845-2789
www.mtangel.k12.or.us
Mount Angel MS 200/6-8
460 E Marquam St 97362 503-845-6137
Kimberly Beddor, prin. Fax 845-2856
St. Mary's ES 400/K-5
590 E College St 97362 503-845-2547
Jennifer Christian, prin. Fax 845-9438

Silver Falls SD 4J
Supt. — See Silverton
Butte Creek S 300/K-8
37569 S Highway 213 97362 503-829-6803
Kevin Palmer, prin. Fax 829-8701
Monitor S 100/K-8
12465 Meridian Rd NE 97362 503-634-2421
Dustin Hoehne, prin. Fax 634-2486

Mount Hood Parkdale, Hood River, Pop. 250
Hood River County SD
Supt. — See Hood River
Parkdale ES 300/K-5
PO Box 69 97041 541-352-6255
Kim Vogel, prin. Fax 352-5207

Mount Vernon, Grant, Pop. 531
Grant SD 3
Supt. — See Canyon City
Mount Vernon MS 100/6-8
PO Box 648 97865 541-932-4733
Monty Nash, prin. Fax 932-4980

Mulino, Clackamas
Molalla River SD 35
Supt. — See Molalla
Clarkes ES 200/K-5
19100 S Windy City Rd 97042 503-632-3290
Michael Nickless, prin. Fax 632-5212
Mulino ES 300/K-5
PO Box 838 97042 503-829-6888
Alan Willey, prin. Fax 829-2037

Myrtle Creek, Douglas, Pop. 3,528
South Umpqua SD 19 1,700/K-12
558 Chadwick Ln 97457 541-863-3115
Beverly Parsons, supt. Fax 863-5212
www.susd.k12.or.us
Coffenberry MS 400/6-8
591 Rice St 97457 541-863-3104
Doug Park, prin. Fax 863-5187
Myrtle Creek ES 300/K-5
651 NE Division St 97457 541-863-3168
Darla Waite, prin. Fax 863-5185
Tri City ES 400/K-5
546 Chadwick Ln 97457 541-863-6887
Brody Guthrie, prin. Fax 863-5510
Other Schools – See Canyonville

Myrtle Point, Coos, Pop. 2,509
Myrtle Point SD 41 700/K-12
413 C St 97458 541-572-1224
Kent Klewitz, supt. Fax 572-5401
www.mpsd.k12.or.us/
Myrtle Crest ES 400/K-6
903 Myrtle Crest Ln 97458 541-572-1230
Ken Smith, prin. Fax 572-1907

Nehalem, Tillamook, Pop. 198
Neah-Kah-Nie SD 56
Supt. — See Rockaway
Nehalem ES 200/K-5
PO Box 190 97131 503-368-5185
Heidi Buckmaster, prin. Fax 368-7721

Newberg, Yamhill, Pop. 20,681
Newberg SD 29J 5,100/K-12
714 E 6th St 97132 503-554-5000
Dr. Paula Radich, supt. Fax 537-9474
www.newberg.k12.or.us
Antonia Crater ES 400/K-5
203 W Foothills Dr 97132 503-554-4650
Kevin Milner, prin. Fax 537-3251
Austin ES 400/K-5
2200 N Center St 97132 503-554-4550
Lesley Carsley, prin. Fax 538-4571
Chehalem Valley MS 700/6-8
403 W Foothills Dr 97132 503-554-4600
John Franco, prin. Fax 537-3239
Edwards ES 400/K-5
715 E 8th St 97132 503-554-5050
Sue Luthra, prin. Fax 537-3220
Mountain View MS 600/6-8
2015 N Emery Dr 97132 503-554-4500
Wayne Strong, prin. Fax 537-3337
Rush ES 500/K-5
1441 Deborah Rd 97132 503-554-4450
Shannon Stueckle, prin. Fax 554-1687
Young ES 200/K-5
17600 NE North Valley Rd 97132 503-554-4750
Kevin Purcell, prin. Fax 538-7269
Other Schools – See Dundee

Lewis Academy 200/PK-12
PO Box 3250 97132 503-538-0114
Dr. Wade Witherspoon, supt. Fax 538-4113
Open Bible Christian S 100/K-12
1605 N College St 97132 503-538-9833
John Lester, admin. Fax 538-4649

New Pine Creek, Lake
Modoc JUSD
Supt. — See Alturas, CA
State Line S 50/K-8
PO Box 99 97635 530-946-4127
Mike Martin, prin. Fax 946-4127

Newport, Lincoln, Pop. 9,833
Lincoln County SD 4,800/K-12
PO Box 1110 97365 541-265-9211
Tom Rinearson, supt. Fax 265-3231
www.lincoln.k12.or.us
Case ES 500/K-5
459 NE 12th St 97365 541-265-8598
Sharman Ensminger-Stapp, prin. Fax 574-2234
Newport MS 400/6-8
825 NE 7th St 97365 541-265-6601
Marsha Eckelman, prin. Fax 265-6493
Newton Magnet S 100/6-8
825 NE 7th St 97365 541-265-6601
Marsha Eckelman, prin.
Yaquina View ES 300/K-5
351 SE Harney St 97365 541-265-5351
Kristin Becker, prin. Fax 574-2224
Other Schools – See Lincoln City, Toledo, Waldport

North Bend, Coos, Pop. 9,843
North Bend SD 13 1,700/K-12
1913 Meade St 97459 541-756-2521
B.J. Hollensteiner, supt. Fax 756-1313
www.nbend.k12.or.us
Hillcrest ES 500/K-4
1100 Maine St 97459 541-756-8348
Bruce Martin, prin. Fax 751-7991
North Bay ES 200/K-5
93670 Viking Ln 97459 541-756-8351
Colleen Reeves, dean Fax 751-0501
North Bend MS 400/5-8
1500 16th St 97459 541-756-8341
Ralph Brooks, prin. Fax 756-6460

Gold Coast Christian S 50/K-8
1251 Clark St 97459 541-756-6307
Kingsview Christian S 100/PK-8
1850 Clark St 97459 541-756-1411
Rick Wetherell, admin. Fax 756-0105

North Plains, Washington, Pop. 1,775
Hillsboro SD 1J
Supt. — See Hillsboro
North Plains ES 300/K-6
PO Box 190 97133 503-844-1630
Fax 647-2290

North Powder, Union, Pop. 485
North Powder SD 8J 200/K-12
PO Box 10 97867 541-898-2244
Lance Dixon, supt. Fax 898-2046
www.npowder.k12.or.us
Powder Valley S 200/K-12
PO Box 10 97867 541-898-2244
Blake Jones, prin. Fax 898-2046

Nyssa, Malheur, Pop. 3,068
Nyssa SD 26 1,200/K-12
804 Adrian Blvd 97913 541-372-2275
Donald Grotting, supt. Fax 372-2204
www.nyssa.k12.or.us
Nyssa ES 600/K-5
809 Bower Ave 97913 541-372-3313
Darren Johnson, prin. Fax 372-5653
Nyssa MS 300/6-8
101 S 11th St 97913 541-372-3891
Jana Iverson, prin. Fax 372-3260

Oakland, Douglas, Pop. 973
Oakland SD 1 500/K-12
PO Box 390 97462 541-459-4341
Dan Forbess, supt. Fax 459-4120
www.oakland.k12.or.us
Lincoln MS 200/5-8
PO Box 420 97462 541-459-3407
Larry Watts, prin. Fax 459-9167
Oakland ES 200/K-4
PO Box 90 97462 541-459-2271
Julie Carson, prin. Fax 459-8998

Oakridge, Lane, Pop. 3,147
Oakridge SD 76 700/K-12
76499 Rose St 97463 541-782-2813
Donald Kordosky, supt. Fax 782-2982
www.oakridge.k12.or.us/
Oakridge ES 300/K-6
48119 E 1st St 97463 541-782-3226
Tamara Skordahl, prin. Fax 782-3122
Oakridge JHS 100/7-8
76486 Rose St 97463 541-782-2731
Donald Kordosky, prin. Fax 782-4647

Odell, Hood River
Hood River County SD
Supt. — See Hood River
Mid Valley ES 400/K-5
PO Box 188 97044 541-354-1691
Dennis McCauley, prin. Fax 354-5109

Ontario, Malheur, Pop. 11,125
Annex SD 29 50/K-8
402 Annex Rd 97914 541-262-3280
Fax 262-3578
Annex S 50/K-8
402 Annex Rd 97914 541-262-3280
Dan Beaubien, lead tchr. Fax 262-3578

Ontario SD 8C 2,800/K-12
195 SW 3rd Ave 97914 541-889-5374
Linda Florence, supt. Fax 889-8553
www.ontario.k12.or.us
Aiken ES 200/K-5
1297 W Idaho Ave 97914 541-889-5584
Julie Bainbridge, prin. Fax 889-4762
Alameda ES 300/K-5
1252 Alameda Dr 97914 541-889-5497
Nicole Albisu, prin. Fax 889-1993
Cairo ES 200/K-5
531 Highway 20 26 97914 541-889-5745
Steve Bishop, prin. Fax 889-5745
Ontario MS 700/6-8
573 SW 2nd Ave 97914 541-889-5377
Paul Erlebach, prin. Fax 881-0060
Pioneer ES 200/K-5
4744 Pioneer Rd 97914 541-262-3902
Steve Bishop, prin. Fax 262-3913
Roberts ES 400/K-5
590 NW 8th St 97914 541-889-5379
Frances Ramirez, prin. Fax 889-5370

St. Peter S 100/PK-6
98 SW 9th St 97914 541-889-7363
Roger Richmond, supt. Fax 889-2852
Treasure Valley Christian S 50/PK-8
386 N Verde Dr 97914 541-889-4662
Fran Renk, prin. Fax 889-9199

Oregon City, Clackamas, Pop. 30,221
Canby SD 86
Supt. — See Canby
Carus ES 400/K-6
14412 S Carus Rd 97045 503-632-3130
Noel Hygelund, prin. Fax 632-3148

Oregon City SD 62 7,800/K-12
PO Box 2110 97045 503-785-8000
Roger Rada, supt. Fax 657-2492
www.orecity.k12.or.us
Gaffney Lane ES 600/K-6
13521 Gaffney Ln 97045 503-785-8600
Javier Castaneda, prin. Fax 650-6688
Gardiner MS 600/7-8
180 Ethel St 97045 503-785-8200
Chris Mills, prin. Fax 650-5482
Holcomb ES 400/K-6
14625 Holcomb Blvd 97045 503-785-8100
Tim Graham, prin. Fax 657-4795
King ES 400/K-6
995 S End Rd 97045 503-785-8250
Kyle Laier, prin. Fax 657-2458
McLoughlin ES 600/K-6
19230 S End Rd 97045 503-785-8650
Carol Sanders, prin. Fax 657-2497
Mt. Pleasant ES 400/K-6
1232 Linn Ave 97045 503-785-8700
Carol Kemhus, prin. Fax 650-6690
Ogden MS 700/7-8
14133 Donovan Rd 97045 503-785-8300
John Olson, prin. Fax 657-2508
Park Place ES 300/K-6
16075 Front St 97045 503-785-8050
Gregory Cimmiyotti, prin. Fax 657-2479
Redland ES 500/K-6
18131 S Redland Rd 97045 503-785-8500
Cindy Fillis, prin. Fax 631-7645
Other Schools – See Beavercreek, Milwaukie

North Clackamas Christian S 200/PK-12
19575 Sebastian Way 97045 503-655-5961
Bruce Reinhardt, admin. Fax 655-4875
St. John the Apostle S 200/K-8
516 5th St 97045 503-742-8232
Machelle Nagel, prin. Fax 742-8239
Trinity Lutheran S 50/K-6
16000 S Henrici Rd 97045 503-632-5554
Kara Kaufman, prin. Fax 632-5546

Paulina, Crook
Crook County SD
Supt. — See Prineville
Paulina S 50/K-8
70050 SE Paulina City Rd 97751 541-477-3182
Penny LaFavor, prin. Fax 477-3512

Pendleton, Umatilla, Pop. 16,636
Pendleton SD 16 3,200/K-12
1207 SW Frazer Ave 97801 541-276-6711
Jim Keene, supt. Fax 278-3208
www.pendleton.k12.or.us
Lincoln PS, 107 NW 10th St 97801 200/K-2
Lori Hale, prin. 541-276-2351
McKay Creek ES 300/K-5
1539 SW 44th St 97801 541-966-3000
Laura Miltenberger, prin.
Sherwood Heights ES 400/K-5
3111 SW Marshall Ave 97801 541-276-1165
Jerry Archer, prin. Fax 966-3096
Sunridge MS 700/6-8
700 SW Runnion Ave 97801 541-276-4560
Jon Peterson, prin. Fax 276-4724
Washington ES 400/K-5
1205 SE Byers Ave 97801 541-276-2241
Rocky Penn, prin. Fax 966-3597
West Hills IS 200/3-5
1700 NW 15th Dr 97801 541-276-2543
Shelley Liscom, prin. Fax 966-3970

Harris Junior Academy 50/K-10
3121 SW Hailey Ave 97801 541-276-0615
Laurie Hosey, prin. Fax 276-3465
Mission Indian Adventist S 50/1-8
46576 Mission Rd 97801 541-276-6530
Bob Marcus, prin.

Philomath, Benton, Pop. 4,213
Philomath SD 17J 1,600/K-12
1620 Applegate St 97370 541-929-3169
Pete Tuana, supt. Fax 929-3991
www.philomath.k12.or.us
Clemens PS 200/K-1
535 S 19th St 97370 541-929-2082
George Winterscheid, prin. Fax 929-2536
Philomath ES 400/2-5
239 S 16th St 97370 541-929-3253
Cindy Golston, prin. Fax 929-3281
Philomath MS 400/6-8
2021 Chapel Dr 97370 541-929-3167
Steve Bell, prin. Fax 929-3180
Other Schools – See Blodgett

Phoenix, Jackson, Pop. 4,375
Phoenix-Talent SD 4 2,700/K-12
PO Box 698 97535 541-535-1517
Ben Bergreen, supt. Fax 535-3928
www.phoenix.k12.or.us
Phoenix ES 400/K-5
PO Box 727 97535 541-535-3353
Jeff Carpenter, prin. Fax 535-7533
Other Schools – See Medford, Talent

Pilot Rock, Umatilla, Pop. 1,525
Pilot Rock SD 2 400/K-12
PO Box BB 97868 541-443-8291
Gordon Munck, supt. Fax 443-8000
www.pilotrock.k12.or.us
Pilot Rock ES 200/K-6
PO Box A 97868 541-443-2838
Ryan Heinrich, prin. Fax 443-3550

Pleasant Hill, Lane
Pleasant Hill SD 1 900/K-12
36386 Highway 58 97455 541-746-9646
Tony Scurto, supt. Fax 746-2537
www.pleasanthill.k12.or.us/
Pleasant Hill MS 300/5-8
36386 Highway 58 97455 541-736-0400
Tony Scurto, prin. Fax 736-0446
Other Schools – See Dexter

Emerald Christian Academy 100/K-10
35582 Zephyr Way 97455 541-746-1708
Donald Bryan, prin. Fax 746-8353

Plush, Lake
Plush SD 18 50/K-8
PO Box 3 97637 541-947-3933
Plush S, PO Box 3 97637 50/K-8
LuAnn Anderson, lead tchr. 541-947-3933

Portland, Multnomah, Pop. 533,427
Beaverton SD 48J
Supt. — See Beaverton
Bonny Slope ES K-5
11775 NW McDaniel Rd 97229 503-672-3775
Kim Haskins, prin. Fax 672-3777
Cedar Mill ES 400/K-5
10265 NW Cornell Rd 97229 503-259-6685
Brian Horne, prin. Fax 259-6688
Cedar Park MS 800/6-8
11100 SW Park Way 97225 503-672-3620
Linda Hall, prin. Fax 672-3626
Findley ES 900/K-5
4155 NW Saltzman Rd 97229 503-533-1830
Kathleen Skidmore Dee, prin. Fax 533-1833
Montclair ES 300/K-5
7250 SW Vermont St 97223 503-259-7685
Verna Bailey, prin. Fax 259-7688
Raleigh Hills S 500/K-8
5225 SW Scholls Ferry Rd 97225 503-259-7385
John Peplinski, prin. Fax 259-7388
Raleigh Park ES 400/K-5
3670 SW 78th Ave 97225 503-259-7435
Barbara Millikan, prin. Fax 259-7438
Ridgewood ES 500/K-5
10100 SW Inglewood St 97225 503-259-7535
Scot Stockwell, prin. Fax 259-7538
Rock Creek ES 600/K-5
4125 NW 185th Ave 97229 503-533-1875
Arlene Hirsch, prin. Fax 533-1878
Springville S K-8
6655 NW Joss Ave 97229 503-533-1925
Cheryl Ames, prin. Fax 533-1927
Stoller MS 1,100/6-8
14141 NW Laidlaw Rd 97229 503-533-1910
Florence Richey, prin. Fax 533-1914
Terra Linda ES 500/K-6
1998 NW 143rd Ave 97229 503-672-3575
John Huelskamp, prin. Fax 672-3578
Walker ES 500/K-5
11940 SW Lynnfield Ln 97225 503-672-3605
Barbara Evans, prin. Fax 672-3608
West Tualatin View ES 400/K-5
8800 SW Leahy Rd 97225 503-259-7830
Kalay McNamee, prin. Fax 259-7833
Wismer ES 800/K-5
5477 NW Skycrest Pkwy 97229 503-533-1950
Joan McFadden, prin. Fax 533-1953

Centennial SD 28J 6,500/K-12
18135 SE Brooklyn St 97236 503-760-7990
Robert McKean, supt. Fax 762-3689
www.centennial.k12.or.us
Centennial MS 1,000/7-8
17650 SE Brooklyn St 97236 503-762-3206
Doug Cook, prin. Fax 762-3236
Lynch Meadows ES 500/K-6
18009 SE Brooklyn St 97236 503-762-3208
Laura Fendall, prin. Fax 762-3238
Lynch View ES 500/K-6
1546 SE 169th Pl 97233 503-762-3203
Lynn Blevens, prin. Fax 762-3243
Lynch Wood ES 600/K-6
3615 SE 174th Ave 97236 503-762-3204
Bjarne Kaer, prin. Fax 762-3244
Oliver IS 400/4-6
15840 SE Taylor St 97233 503-762-3207
Ben Egbers, prin. Fax 762-3237
Oliver PS 500/K-3
15811 SE Main St 97233 503-762-3205
Barbara Hicks, prin. Fax 762-3235
Other Schools – See Gresham

David Douglas SD 40 9,700/K-12
1500 SE 130th Ave 97233 503-252-2900
Barbara Rommel, supt. Fax 261-8208
www.ddouglas.k12.or.us
Boyles ES 500/K-5
10822 SE Bush St 97266 503-256-6554
Ericka Guynes, prin. Fax 261-8437
Cherry Park ES 500/K-5
1930 SE 104th Ave 97216 503-256-6501
Barbara Chester, prin. Fax 261-8428
Gilbert Heights ES 600/K-5
12839 SE Holgate Blvd 97236 503-256-6502
Kevin Fordney, prin. Fax 261-8454
Gilbert Park ES 600/K-5
13132 SE Ramona St 97236 503-256-6531
George Bryson, prin. Fax 261-8413
Light MS 800/6-8
10800 SE Washington St 97216 503-256-6511
Mark Gaulke, prin. Fax 261-8423
Lincoln Park ES 500/K-5
13200 SE Lincoln St 97233 503-256-6504
Linda Okazaki, prin. Fax 261-8444
Menlo Park ES 500/K-5
12900 NE Glisan St 97230 503-256-6506
Andy Long, prin. Fax 261-8449
Mill Park ES 500/K-5
1900 SE 117th Ave 97216 503-256-6507
Rolando Florez, prin. Fax 261-8418
North Powellhurst S K-K
1400 SE 135th Ave 97233 503-261-8470
Kate Barker, prin. Fax 261-0233
Ott MS 700/6-8
12500 SE Ramona St 97236 503-256-6510
James Johnston, prin. Fax 261-8403
Russell MS 800/6-8
3955 SE 112th Ave 97266 503-256-6519
Charlene Bassine, prin. Fax 761-7246
Ventura Park ES 500/K-5
145 SE 117th Ave 97216 503-256-6508
Susan Gerritz, prin. Fax 256-8439
West Powelhurst ES 500/K-5
2921 SE 116th Ave 97266 503-256-6509
Allen Browning, prin. Fax 261-8408

Hillsboro SD 1J
Supt. — See Hillsboro
Lenox ES 500/K-6
21200 NW Rock Creek Blvd 97229 503-844-1360
John Matsuo, prin. Fax 356-6289

North Clackamas SD 12
Supt. — See Milwaukie
Sojourner ES 200/K-6
1905 SE Oak Grove Blvd 97267 503-353-5580
Tricia George, dir. Fax 513-4026
View Acres ES 400/K-6
4828 SE View Acres Rd 97267 503-353-5640
David Frick-Wright, prin. Fax 353-5655

Parkrose SD 3 3,500/K-12
10636 NE Prescott St 97220 503-408-2100
Dr. Karen Fischer Gray, supt. Fax 408-2140
www.parkrose.k12.or.us
Parkrose MS 800/6-8
11800 NE Shaver St 97220 503-408-2700
Molly Davies, prin. Fax 408-2998
Prescott ES 400/K-5
10410 NE Prescott St 97220 503-408-2150
Michael Lopes, prin. Fax 408-2190
Russell Academy 400/K-5
2700 NE 127th Ave 97230 503-408-2750
Debbie Ebert, prin. Fax 408-2790
Sacramento ES 400/K-5
11400 NE Sacramento St 97220 503-408-2800
Stevie Blakely, prin. Fax 408-2840
Shaver ES 400/K-5
3701 NE 131st Pl 97230 503-408-2850
Cindy Bartman, prin. Fax 408-2890

Portland SD 1J 40,200/PK-12
PO Box 3107 97208 503-916-2000
Ed Schmitt, supt. Fax 916-3110
www.pps.k12.or.us/
Abernethy ES 400/K-5
2421 SE Orange Ave 97214 503-916-6190
Tamara Barron, prin. Fax 916-2600
Ainsworth ES 500/K-5
2425 SW Vista Ave 97201 503-916-6288
Liz Casson-Taylor, prin. Fax 916-2601
Alameda ES 700/PK-5
2732 NE Fremont St 97212 503-916-6036
Raddy Lurie, prin. Fax 916-2602
Arleta S 400/K-8
5109 SE 66th Ave 97206 503-916-6330
Lynn Ferguson, prin. Fax 916-2604
Astor S 300/K-8
5601 N Yale St 97203 503-916-6244
John Walden, prin. Fax 916-2605
Atkinson ES 500/K-5
5800 SE Division St 97206 503-916-6333
Chris Gutierrez, prin. Fax 916-2606
Beach S 400/PK-8
1710 N Humboldt St 97217 503-916-6236
Paige Fox, prin. Fax 916-2315
Beaumont MS 500/6-8
4043 NE Fremont St 97212 503-916-5610
Sherie Knutsen, prin. Fax 916-2609
Boise/Eliot ES 400/PK-8
620 N Fremont St 97227 503-916-6171
Molly Chun, prin. Fax 916-2611
Bridger S 400/K-8
7910 SE Market St 97215 503-916-6336
Tina Daily, prin. Fax 916-2612
Bridlemile ES 500/K-5
4300 SW 47th Dr 97221 503-916-6292
Tanya Ghattas, prin. Fax 916-2613
Buckman ES 500/K-5
320 SE 16th Ave 97214 503-916-6230
Claudia Mason, prin. Fax 916-2615
Capitol Hill ES 300/K-5
8401 SW 17th Ave 97219 503-916-6303
Pamela Wilson, prin. Fax 916-2616
Chapman ES 500/K-5
1445 NW 26th Ave 97210 503-916-6295
Scott Choate, prin. Fax 916-2617
Chief Joseph ES 400/PK-5
2409 N Saratoga St 97217 503-916-6255
Joe Galati, prin. Fax 916-2618
Clarendon-Portsmouth S 300/K-8
5103 N Willis Blvd 97203 503-916-5666
Antonio Lopez, prin. Fax 916-2663
Clark S 500/K-8
2225 SE 87th Ave 97216 503-916-5700
Chris Aanderud, prin. Fax 916-2610
Cleary S - Fernwood Campus 2-8
1915 NE 33rd Ave 97212 503-916-6480
Linda Kapranos, prin. Fax 916-2626
Cleary S - Hollyrood Campus 100/K-1
3560 NE Hollyrood Ct 97212 503-916-6766
Linda Kapranos, prin. Fax 916-2635
Creative Science S K-8
1231 SE 92nd Ave 97216 503-916-6431
Fax 916-2620
Creston S 300/K-8
4701 SE Bush St 97206 503-916-6340
Andy McKean, prin. Fax 916-2621
Duniway ES 400/K-5
7700 SE Reed College Pl 97202 503-916-6343
Tou Meksavanh, prin. Fax 916-2623
East Sylvan MS 300/6-6
1849 SW 58th Ave 97221 503-916-5560
Allison Couch, prin. Fax 916-5565
Faubion S 300/PK-8
3039 NE Rosa Parks Way 97211 503-916-5686
LaShawn Lee, prin. Fax 916-2625
Forest Park ES 500/K-5
9935 NW Durrett St 97229 503-916-5400
Kevin Crotchett, prin. Fax 916-2730
George MS 400/6-8
10000 N Burr Ave 97203 503-916-6262
Beth Madison, prin. Fax 916-2627
Glencoe ES 500/K-5
825 SE 51st Ave 97215 503-916-6207
Robi Osborn, prin. Fax 916-2628
Gray MS 500/6-8
5505 SW 23rd Ave, 503-916-5676
Larry Dashiell, prin. Fax 916-2629
Grout ES 300/K-5
3119 SE Holgate Blvd 97202 503-916-6209
Susan McElroy, prin. Fax 916-2632

Hayhurst ES 300/K-5
5037 SW Iowa St 97221 503-916-6300
Robin Morrison, prin. Fax 916-2633
Hosford International MS 500/6-8
2303 SE 28th Pl 97214 503-916-5640
Kevin Bacon, prin. Fax 916-2637
Humboldt S 200/PK-8
4915 N Gantenbein Ave 97217 503-916-5468
Jamilia Williams, prin. Fax 916-2638
Irvington S 500/K-8
1320 NE Brazee St 97212 503-916-6386
Cynthia MacLeod, prin. Fax 916-2639
Jackson MS 700/6-8
10625 SW 35th Ave 97219 503-916-5680
John Ferraro, prin. Fax 916-2640
John ES 500/K-5
7439 N Charleston Ave 97203 503-916-6266
Brenda Fox, prin. Fax 916-2641
Kelly ES 400/K-5
9030 SE Cooper St 97266 503-916-6350
Sharon Allen, prin. Fax 916-2644
King S 500/PK-8
4906 NE 6th Ave 97211 503-916-6456
LaDrena Rhodes, prin. Fax 916-2647
Lane MS 500/6-8
7200 SE 60th Ave 97206 503-916-6355
Karl Logan, prin. Fax 916-2648
Laurelhurst ES 600/K-5
840 NE 41st Ave 97232 503-916-6210
Dawn Corliss, prin. Fax 916-2649
Lee ES 400/K-6
2222 NE 92nd Ave 97220 503-916-6144
Sascha Perrins, prin. Fax 916-2650
Lent ES 400/K-6
5105 SE 97th Ave 97266 503-916-6322
Linda Ralley, prin. Fax 916-2651
Lewis ES 300/K-5
4401 SE Evergreen St 97206 503-916-6360
Tim Lauer, prin. Fax 916-2652
Llewellyn ES 300/K-5
6301 SE 14th Ave 97202 503-916-6216
Stephen Powell, prin. Fax 916-2653
Maplewood ES 300/K-5
7452 SW 52nd Ave 97219 503-916-6308
John Blanck, prin. Fax 916-2654
Markham ES 400/K-5
10531 SW Capitol Hwy 97219 503-916-5681
Sarah Lewins, prin. Fax 916-2655
Marysville S 400/K-8
7733 SE Raymond St 97206 503-916-6363
Lana Penley, prin. Fax 916-2656
Mt. Tabor MS 600/6-8
5800 SE Ash St 97215 503-916-5646
Van Troung, prin. Fax 916-2659
Ockley Green S 400/K-8
6031 N Montana Ave 97217 503-916-5660
Greg Jones, prin. Fax 916-2661
Odyssey S K-8
5037 SW Iowa St 97221 503-916-6300
Robin Morrison, prin. Fax 916-2633
Parks ES 400/K-5
8960 N Woolsey Ave 97203 503-916-6250
Tamala Newsome, prin. Fax 916-2607
Peninsula S 300/K-8
8125 N Emerald Ave 97217 503-916-6275
Carlos Galindo, prin. Fax 916-2662
Richmond Immersion ES 400/PK-5
2276 SE 41st Ave 97214 503-916-6220
Kathryn Anderson, prin. Fax 916-2665
Rieke S 300/K-7
1405 SW Vermont St 97219 503-916-5768
Charlene Russell, prin. Fax 916-2666
Rigler S 500/K-8
5401 NE Prescott St 97218 503-916-6451
Kristie Cunin, prin. Fax 916-2667
Roseway Heights S 500/K-8
7334 NE Siskiyou St 97213 503-916-5600
Mary Dingle, prin. Fax 916-2631
Sabin S 400/PK-8
4013 NE 18th Ave 97212 503-916-6181
Rich Schafer, prin. Fax 916-2669
Scott S 400/K-7
6700 NE Prescott St 97218 503-916-6369
Deanne Froehlich, prin. Fax 916-2671
Sellwood MS 500/6-8
8300 SE 15th Ave 97202 503-916-5656
Helen Nolen, prin. Fax 916-2672
Sitton ES 300/K-5
9930 N Smith St 97203 503-916-6277
Jane Fielding, prin. Fax 916-2673
Skyline S 200/K-8
11536 NW Skyline Blvd 97231 503-916-5212
Ben Keefer, prin. Fax 916-2765
Stephenson ES 300/K-5
2627 SW Stephenson St 97219 503-916-6318
Beth Shelby, prin. Fax 916-2675
Vernon S 400/PK-8
2044 NE Killingsworth St 97211 503-916-6415
Tina Acker, prin. Fax 916-2678
Vestal S 300/K-8
161 NE 82nd Ave 97220 503-916-6437
Susan Foxman, prin. Fax 916-2679
West Sylvan MS 600/7-8
8111 SW West Slope Dr 97225 503-916-5690
Allison Couch, prin. Fax 916-2681
Whitman ES 400/K-5
7326 SE Flavel St 97206 503-916-6370
Lori Clark, prin. Fax 916-2684
Winterhaven S 300/K-8
3830 SE 14th Ave 97202 503-916-6200
Rudy Rudolph, prin. Fax 916-2614
Woodlawn S 500/PK-8
7200 NE 11th Ave 97211 503-916-6282
Lemil Speed, prin. Fax 916-2686
Woodmere ES 400/K-5
7900 SE Duke St 97206 503-916-6373
Heather Hull, prin. Fax 916-2687

Woodstock ES 400/K-5
5601 SE 50th Ave 97206 503-916-6380
Mary Patterson, prin. Fax 916-2688

Reynolds SD 7
Supt. — See Fairview
Alder ES 500/K-5
17200 SE Alder St 97233 503-255-4673
Paz Ramos, prin. Fax 252-5989
Davis ES 500/K-5
19501 NE Davis St 97230 503-665-9193
Lisa Darnold, prin. Fax 667-6187
Glenfair ES 500/K-5
15300 NE Glisan St 97230 503-252-3479
Shane Bassett, prin. Fax 252-0159
Hartley ES 400/K-5
701 NE 185th Pl 97230 503-665-0134
Terri King, prin. Fax 667-6444
Lee MS 800/6-8
1121 NE 172nd Ave 97230 503-255-5686
Carla Sosanya, prin. Fax 252-0522
Scott ES 300/K-5
14700 NE Sacramento St 97230 503-255-2031
Kathy Nickoloff, prin. Fax 252-0492
Wilkes ES 500/K-5
17020 NE Wilkes Rd 97230 503-255-6133
Lisa Calcagno, prin. Fax 252-0339

Riverdale SD 51J 500/K-12
11733 SW Breyman Ave 97219 503-636-8611
Terry Hoagland, supt. Fax 635-6342
www.riverdale.k12.or.us
Riverdale Grade S 300/K-8
11733 SW Breyman Ave 97219 503-636-4511
Jeremiah Patterson, prin. Fax 635-7534

Scappoose SD 1J
Supt. — See Scappoose
Sauvie Island ES 100/K-6
14445 NW Charlton Rd 97231 503-621-3426
Chelsea Murphy, lead tchr. Fax 621-3384

Tigard-Tualatin SD 23J
Supt. — See Tigard
Metzger ES 600/K-5
10350 SW Lincoln St 97223 503-431-4600
Karen Twain, prin. Fax 431-4610
Tigard ES 600/K-5
12855 SW Grant Ave 97223 503-431-4400
Vanessa Bunker, prin. Fax 431-4410

All Saints S 500/PK-8
601 NE 39th Ave 97232 503-236-6205
Rose Rosinski, prin. Fax 236-0781
Archbishop Howard S 300/PK-8
5309 NE Alameda St 97213 503-281-1912
Karen Asbury, prin. Fax 281-0554
Ascension Early Childhood Education Ctr 100/PK-K
1440 SE 182nd Ave 97233 503-667-6750
Sue Wentela, dir. Fax 618-0810
Beautiful Savior Lutheran S 100/PK-K
9800 SE 92nd Ave, 503-788-7000
Fax 788-8468
Belmont Academy 50/K-2
3841 SE Belmont St 97214 503-232-8985
Cathedral S 200/K-8
110 NW 17th Ave 97209 503-275-9370
Dr. Diane Cronin, prin. Fax 275-9378
Catlin Gabel S 700/PK-12
8825 SW Barnes Rd 97225 503-297-1894
Dr. Lark Palma, prin. Fax 297-0139
Cedarwood S 200/PK-8
3030 SW 2nd Ave 97201 503-245-1477
Fax 245-5405
Childpeace Montessori S 200/PK-6
1516 NW Thurman St 97209 503-222-1197
Sue Pritzker, admin. Fax 222-1053
City Christian S 300/PK-12
9200 NE Fremont St 97220 503-252-5207
Fax 257-2221
Columbia Christian S 200/K-12
413 NE 91st Ave 97220 503-252-8577
Morgan Outlaw, prin. Fax 252-2108
Crossroads Christian S 200/PK-8
2505 NE 102nd Ave 97220 503-254-1431
Larry Whittlesey, prin. Fax 257-9284
Faithful Savior Community S 100/PK-8
PO Box 30957 97294 503-257-9409
Stephanie Thornton, prin. Fax 251-9409
Franciscan Montessori Earth S 200/PK-8
14750 SE Clinton St 97236 503-760-8220
Sr. Kathleen Cieslak, admin. Fax 760-8333
French American International S 400/PK-8
8500 NW Johnson St 97229 503-292-7776
Pam Dreisin, hdmstr. Fax 292-7444
Grace Lutheran S 100/K-8
2252 SE 92nd Ave 97216 503-777-8628
Mark Leitzke, prin. Fax 230-1354
Hilltop Christian S 100/PK-K
5700 SW Dosch Rd, 503-245-3183
Anna Busby, admin. Fax 892-5255
Holy Cross S 200/1-8
5202 N Bowdoin St 97203 503-289-3010
Sr. Ruth Frank, prin. Fax 286-5006
Holy Family S 300/PK-8
7425 SE 39th Ave 97202 503-774-8871
Christy Robinson, prin. Fax 774-8872
Holy Redeemer S 300/K-8
127 N Rosa Parks Way 97217 503-283-5197
Anna Raineri, prin. Fax 283-9479
International S 300/PK-5
025 SW Sherman St 97201 503-226-2496
Phil Sylla, hdmstr. Fax 525-0142
Madeleine S 200/K-8
3240 NE 23rd Ave 97212 503-288-9197
Susan Steele, prin. Fax 280-1196
Maimonodies Jewish Day S 50/PK-6
6612 SW Capitol Hwy, 503-977-7850

Montessori S of Alameda 100/PK-5
4210 NE Going St 97218 503-335-3321
Tammy Kennedy, prin. Fax 335-3321
Montessori S of Beaverton 200/PK-6
11065 NW Crystal Creek Ln 97229 503-439-1597
Leslie Logan, hdmstr. Fax 439-9159
Oregon Episcopal S 800/PK-12
6300 SW Nicol Rd 97223 503-246-7771
Matthew Hanly, hdmstr. Fax 293-1105
Portland Christian ES 400/PK-6
11845 SE Market St 97216 503-256-5455
Bill Buck, prin. Fax 253-2666
Portland Jewish Academy 300/PK-8
6651 SW Capitol Hwy 97219 503-244-0126
Patricia Schwartz, prin. Fax 452-7001
Portland Lutheran S 200/PK-12
740 SE 182nd Ave 97233 503-667-3199
Fax 667-4520
Prince of Peace Lutheran Preschool & K 300/PK-K
14175 NW Cornell Rd 97229 503-645-1211
Darlene Thauland, dir. Fax 531-2534
St. Agatha S 200/PK-8
7960 SE 15th Ave 97202 503-234-5500
Jeff Delegato, prin. Fax 232-7240
St. Andrew Nativity S 100/6-8
4925 NE 9th Ave 97211 503-335-9600
Rev. Jeff McDougall, prin. Fax 335-9494
St. Clare S 200/K-8
1807 SW Freeman St 97219 503-244-7600
Marilyn Isaac, prin. Fax 293-2076
St. Ignatius S 200/K-8
3330 SE 43rd Ave 97206 503-774-5533
John Matcovich, prin. Fax 788-1134
St. John Fisher S 200/K-8
7101 SW 46th Ave 97219 503-246-3234
Merrit Holub, prin. Fax 246-4117
St. Pius X S 300/K-8
1260 NW Saltzman Rd 97229 503-644-3244
Mary Thompson, prin. Fax 646-6568
St. Therese S 200/K-8
1260 NE 132nd Ave 97230 503-253-9400
Sr. Kathy Cordes, prin. Fax 253-9571
St. Thomas More S 200/K-8
3521 SW Patton Rd 97221 503-222-6105
Frank Murray, prin. Fax 227-5661
Serendipity Center 100/K-12
PO Box 33350 97292 503-761-7139
Chris Rust, prin. Fax 761-7917
Shining Star S of Oregon 100/PK-6
4317 NE Emerson St 97218 503-753-4459
Fax 281-0100
Sunstone Montessori S 100/1-6
4817 SW 53rd Ave 97221 503-892-6366
Cathy Newman, admin. Fax 244-0506
Trinity Lutheran S 200/PK-8
5520 NE Killingsworth St 97218 503-288-6403
James Riedl, prin. Fax 288-1095
Tucker-Maxon S 100/PK-5
2860 SE Holgate Blvd 97202 503-235-6551
Steven Noyce, dir. Fax 235-6973
West Hills Christian S 500/K-8
7945 SW Capitol Hill Rd 97219 503-245-6688
Benjamin Haskell, supt. Fax 245-4780

Port Orford, Curry, Pop. 1,180
Port Orford-Langlois SD 2CJ 300/K-12
PO Box 8 97465 541-348-2337
Ruby Price, supt. Fax 348-2228
www.2cj.com
Driftwood S 100/K-8
PO Box 8 97465 541-332-2712
Sean Wells, prin. Fax 332-0190
Other Schools – See Langlois

Powell Butte, Crook
Crook County SD
Supt. — See Prineville
Powell Butte ES 200/K-6
13650 SW Highway 126 97753 541-447-5094
D.C. Lundy, prin. Fax 548-7635

Powers, Coos, Pop. 754
Powers SD 31 100/K-12
PO Box 479 97466 541-439-2291
Matt Shorb, supt. Fax 439-2875
www.powers.k12.or.us
Powers ES 100/K-6
PO Box 479 97466 541-439-2281
Matt Shorb, prin. Fax 439-2875

Prairie City, Grant, Pop. 965
Prairie City SD 4 200/K-12
740 Overholt St 97869 541-820-3314
David Kerr, supt. Fax 820-4352
www.grantesd.k12.or.us
Prairie City S 200/K-12
740 Overholt St 97869 541-820-3314
David Kerr, prin. Fax 820-4352

Prineville, Crook, Pop. 8,908
Crook County SD 3,200/K-12
471 NE Ochoco Plaza Dr 97754 541-447-5664
Rich Shultz, supt. Fax 447-3645
www.crookcounty.k12.or.us
Crook County MS 700/6-8
100 NE Knowledge St 97754 541-447-6283
Rocky Miner, prin. Fax 447-3293
Crooked River ES 400/K-5
641 E 1st St 97754 541-447-6488
Cheri Rasmussen, prin. Fax 447-8395
Ochoco ES 400/K-5
440 NW Madras Hwy 97754 541-447-5211
Jan Boles, prin. Fax 447-8389
Sly ES 500/K-5
1400 SE 2nd St 97754 541-447-7675
Jim Bates, prin. Fax 447-3864
Other Schools – See Paulina, Powell Butte

Crook County Christian S 200/PK-12
839 S Main St 97754 541-416-0114
Sue Uptain-Gillham, prin. Fax 416-0330

Prospect, Jackson
Prospect SD 59 200/K-12
PO Box 40 97536 541-560-3653
Don Alexander, supt. Fax 560-3644
prospect.or.schoolwebpages.com/
Prospect S 200/K-12
PO Box 40 97536 541-560-3653
Wayne Gallagher, prin. Fax 560-3644

Rainier, Columbia, Pop. 1,816
Rainier SD 13 1,200/K-12
28168 Old Rainier Rd 97048 503-556-3777
R. Michael Carter, supt. Fax 556-3778
www.rainier.k12.or.us
Hudson Park ES 600/K-6
28176 Old Rainier Rd 97048 503-556-0196
Paul Coakley, prin. Fax 556-8212

Redmond, Deschutes, Pop. 19,771
Redmond SD 2J 6,500/K-12
145 SE Salmon Ave 97756 541-923-5437
Vickie Fleming, supt. Fax 923-5142
www.redmond.k12.or.us
Evergreen ES 400/K-5
437 SW 9th St 97756 541-923-4865
Carolyn Espinoza, prin. Fax 923-4861
Gregory MS 500/6-8
1220 NW Upas Ave 97756 541-526-6440
Mike McIntosh, prin. Fax 526-6441
Lynch ES 500/K-5
1314 SW Kalama Ave 97756 541-923-4876
John Hartford, prin. Fax 923-4875
McCall ES 500/K-5
1200 NW Upas Ave 97756 541-526-6400
Linda Seeberg, prin. Fax 526-6401
Obsidian MS 700/6-8
1335 SW Obsidian Ave 97756 541-923-4900
Joe Beck, prin. Fax 923-6509
Patrick ES 500/K-5
3001 SW Obsidian Ave 97756 541-923-4830
Kristen Allen, prin. Fax 923-4833
Tuck ES 500/K-5
209 NW 10th St 97756 541-923-4884
Dave Perdue, prin. Fax 923-4884
Other Schools – See Bend, Terrebonne

Central Christian S 200/PK-12
PO Box 639 97756 541-548-7803
Elisa Carlson, hdmstr. Fax 548-2801

Reedsport, Douglas, Pop. 4,361
Reedsport SD 105 700/K-12
100 Ranch Rd 97467 541-271-3656
Ike Launstein, supt. Fax 271-3658
www.reedsport.k12.or.us/
Highland ES 300/K-6
2605 Longwood Dr 97467 541-271-3616
Dave Tisler, prin. Fax 271-3618

Riddle, Douglas, Pop. 1,023
Riddle SD 70 400/K-12
PO Box 45 97469 541-874-3131
Dave Gianotti, supt. Fax 874-2345
Riddle ES, PO Box 45 97469 200/K-6
Kristi Reukauf, prin. 541-874-2226

Riley, Harney
Suntex SD 10
Supt. — See Burns
Suntex S 50/K-8
68178 Silver Creek Rd 97758 541-493-2500
Anne Clark, prin. Fax 493-2245

Rockaway, Tillamook, Pop. 1,074
Neah-Kah-Nie SD 56 700/K-12
PO Box 28 97136 503-355-2222
Jay Kosik, supt. Fax 355-3434
www.neahkahnie.k12.or.us
Neah-Kah-Nie MS 200/6-8
25111 Highway 101 N 97136 503-355-2990
Jim Severson, prin. Fax 355-8514
Other Schools – See Garibaldi, Nehalem

Rogue River, Jackson, Pop. 1,941
Rogue River SD 35 1,100/K-12
PO Box 1045 97537 541-582-3235
Harry Vanikiotis Ed.D., supt. Fax 582-1600
www.rogueriver.k12.or.us
Evans Valley ES 100/K-5
PO Box 1045 97537 541-582-3570
Jane McAlvage, prin. Fax 582-6006
Rogue River ES 300/K-5
PO Box 1045 97537 541-582-3234
Tom McCormick, prin. Fax 582-6007
Rogue River MS 300/6-8
PO Box 1045 97537 541-582-3233
Kathi Sue Summers, prin. Fax 582-6004

Christian Life S 100/PK-8
PO Box 1650 97537 541-582-5975
Mary Schaefer, prin. Fax 582-2656

Roseburg, Douglas, Pop. 20,727
Douglas County SD 4 6,400/K-12
1419 NW Valley View Dr, 541-440-4015
Larry Parsons, supt. Fax 440-4003
www.roseburg.k12.or.us
Eastwood ES 400/K-5
2550 SE Waldon Ave 97470 541-440-4181
Nicki Opp, prin. Fax 440-4182
Fir Grove ES 300/K-5
1360 W Harvard Ave, 541-440-4085
Jill Weber, prin. Fax 440-4086
Fremont MS 700/6-8
850 W Keady Ct, 541-440-4055
Keith Kronser, prin. Fax 440-4060
Fullerton IV ES 300/K-5
2560 W Bradford Ave, 541-440-4081
Mike Keizer, prin. Fax 440-4082
Green ES 400/K-5
4498 Carnes Rd, 541-440-4127
Kristen Garcia, prin. Fax 440-4017
Hucrest ES 400/K-5
1810 NW Kline St, 541-440-4188
Jeffery Plummer, prin. Fax 440-4191
Lane MS 800/6-8
2153 NE Vine St 97470 541-440-4104
Doug Freeman, prin. Fax 440-4100
Melrose ES 300/K-5
2960 Melrose Rd, 541-440-4077
Patricia McCracken, prin. Fax 440-4078
Rose ES 200/K-5
948 SE Roberts Ave 97470 541-440-4123
Tim Wilson, prin. Fax 440-4124
Sunnyslope ES 300/K-5
2230 Cannon Ave, 541-440-4193
Melissa Roberts, prin. Fax 679-9485
Other Schools – See Winchester

Winston-Dillard SD 116
Supt. — See Winston
Lookingglass ES 200/K-6
7421 Lookingglass Rd, 541-679-3006
Mike Narkiewicz, prin. Fax 784-2639

Roseburg Junior Academy 100/K-10
1653 NW Troost St, 541-673-5278
Thom Harder, prin. Fax 672-9785
St. Paul Lutheran S 100/PK-8
750 W Keady Ct, 541-673-7212
Fax 677-9561
Umpqua Valley Christian S 200/PK-12
359 Roberts Creek Rd, 541-679-4964
Doug Tharp, admin. Fax 679-1881

Saint Helens, Columbia, Pop. 11,209
Saint Helens SD 502 3,600/K-12
474 N 16th St 97051 503-397-3085
Patricia Adams, supt. Fax 397-1907
www.sthelens.k12.or.us
Lewis & Clark ES 900/3-5
111 S 9th St 97051 503-366-7603
Cathy Carson, prin. Fax 366-7656
McBride ES 800/K-2
2774 Columbia Blvd 97051 503-366-7700
Jerry Meadows, prin. Fax 366-7706
Saint Helens MS 500/7-8
354 N 15th St 97051 503-366-7300
Joanna Rau, prin. Fax 366-7306
Other Schools – See Columbia City

Saint Paul, Marion, Pop. 395
St. Paul SD 45 200/PK-12
20449 Main St NE 97137 503-633-2541
Bruce Shull, supt. Fax 633-2540
www.stpaul.k12.or.us
Saint Paul ES 100/PK-6
20449 Main St NE 97137 503-633-2691
Bruce Shull, prin. Fax 633-2540

St. Paul S 100/PK-8
PO Box 188 97137 503-633-4622
Charles Geis, prin. Fax 633-4624

Salem, Marion, Pop. 148,751
Gervais SD 1
Supt. — See Gervais
Eldriedge ES 200/K-1
10327 River Rd NE 97303 503-393-5977
Dave James, prin. Fax 390-9567

Salem-Keizer SD 24J 38,500/K-12
PO Box 12024 97309 503-399-3000
Sandy Husk, supt. Fax 399-5579
www.salkeiz.k12.or.us
Auburn ES 700/K-5
4612 Auburn Rd NE 97301 503-399-3128
Meera Kreitzer, prin. Fax 391-4110
Bethel ES 100/1-5
6580 State St, 503-399-3131
Grant Foster, prin. Fax 399-3452
Brush College ES 400/K-5
2623 Doaks Ferry Rd NW 97304 503-399-3132
Lance Cooley, prin. Fax 391-4077
Bush ES 300/K-5
410 14th St SE 97301 503-399-3134
Michelle Halter, prin. Fax 391-4021
Candalaria ES 300/K-5
935 Hansen Ave S 97302 503-399-3136
R. Clinton Gertenrich, prin. Fax 316-3525
Chapman Hill ES 500/K-5
1500 Doaks Ferry Rd NW 97304 503-399-3195
Nanette Willis, prin. Fax 375-7846
Crossler MS 800/6-8
1155 Davis Rd S 97306 503-399-3444
Jim Adams, prin. Fax 391-4005
Englewood ES 300/K-5
1132 19th St NE 97301 503-399-3143
Sharon Warren-Murrell, prin. Fax 391-4085
Eyre ES 600/K-5
4868 Buffalo Dr SE, 503-399-3311
Marc Morris, prin. Fax 391-4078
Four Corners ES 500/K-5
500 Elma Ave SE, 503-399-3145
Phil Decker, prin. Fax 391-4148
Fruitland ES 100/K-5
6425 Fruitland Rd NE, 503-399-3148
Grant Foster, prin. Fax 316-3526
Grant Community S 500/K-8
725 Market St NE 97301 503-399-3151
Jim Hicks, prin. Fax 399-5557
Hallman ES 400/K-5
4000 Deerhaven Dr NE 97301 503-399-3451
Steve Lush, prin. Fax 391-4063
Hammond ES 500/K-5
4900 Bayne St NE 97305 503-399-3454
Greg Cole, prin. Fax 584-5174

Harritt ES 600/K-5
2112 Linwood St NW 97304 503-399-3457
Bill Wittman, prin. Fax 399-2173
Hayesville ES 500/K-5
4545 Ward Dr NE 97305 503-399-3153
Suzanne Byers, prin. Fax 391-4076
Hazel Green ES 100/K-5
5774 Hazelgreen Rd NE 97305 503-399-3150
Manuel Palacio, prin. Fax 391-4091
Highland ES 300/K-5
530 Highland Ave NE 97301 503-399-3155
Olga Cobb, prin. Fax 391-4136
Hoover ES 600/K-5
1104 Savage Rd NE 97301 503-399-3157
Alan deMeurers, prin. Fax 375-7844
Houck MS 1,000/6-8
1155 Connecticut Ave SE, 503-399-3446
Susan Rieke-Smith, prin. Fax 391-4167
Judson MS 900/6-8
4512 Jones Rd SE 97302 503-399-3201
Lara Tiffin, prin. Fax 391-4041
Lake Labish ES 100/K-5
7495 Portland Rd NE 97305 503-399-3159
Manuel Palacio, prin. Fax 399-5565
Lamb ES 500/K-5
4930 Herrin Rd NE 97305 503-399-3477
Kerry Lohrman, prin. Fax 584-5079
Lee ES 400/K-5
5650 Venice St SE 97306 503-399-5570
Sara Casebeer, prin. Fax 399-3365
Leslie MS 900/6-8
3850 Pringle Rd SE 97302 503-399-3206
Steve Nelson, prin. Fax 399-3479
Liberty ES 300/K-5
4871 Liberty Rd S 97306 503-399-3165
Susan Smith, prin. Fax 391-4185
McKinley ES 300/K-5
466 McGilchrist St SE 97302 503-399-3167
Annie Morton, prin. Fax 316-3527
Middle Grove ES 200/K-5
4950 Silverton Rd NE 97305 503-399-3171
Monica Takata, prin. Fax 316-3572
Miller ES 400/K-5
1650 46th Pl SE, 503-399-3332
Mary Russell, prin. Fax 391-3318
Morningside ES 300/K-5
3513 12th St SE 97302 503-399-3173
Jennifer Neitzel, prin. Fax 316-3528
Myers ES 500/K-5
2160 Jewel St NW 97304 503-399-3175
Susan Adams, prin. Fax 391-4094
Parrish MS 700/6-8
802 Capitol St NE 97301 503-399-3210
Rob Schoepper, prin. Fax 391-4004
Pringle ES 500/K-5
5500 Reed Ln SE 97306 503-399-3178
Linda Dougherty, prin. Fax 316-3529
Richmond ES 300/K-5
466 Richmond Ave SE 97301 503-399-3180
Lizi Aguilar-Nelson, prin. Fax 316-3535
Rosedale ES 100/K-5
6974 Bates Rd S 97306 503-399-3186
Sue Hunt, prin. Fax 391-4010
Salem Heights ES 300/K-5
3495 Liberty Rd S 97302 503-399-3187
Mimi Pileggi, prin. Fax 391-4036
Schirle ES 500/K-5
4875 Justice Way S 97302 503-399-3277
Heidi Litchfield, prin. Fax 391-4087
Scott ES 600/K-5
4700 Arizona Ave NE 97305 503-399-3302
Dave Bertholf, prin. Fax 391-4030
Stephens MS 1,000/6-8
4962 Hayesville Dr NE 97305 503-399-3442
Neil Anderson, prin. Fax 391-4079
Sumpter ES 500/K-5
525 Rockwood St SE 97306 503-399-3337
Janet Prats, prin. Fax 391-4080
Swegle ES 500/K-5
4485 Market St NE 97301 503-399-3191
Corina Valencia-Chavez, prin. Fax 391-4138
Waldo MS 800/6-8
2805 Lansing Ave NE 97301 503-399-3215
Joe LaFountaine, prin. Fax 391-4070
Walker MS 1,100/6-8
1075 8th St NW 97304 503-399-3220
Tricia Nelson, prin. Fax 399-5540
Washington ES 400/K-5
3165 Lansing Ave NE 97301 503-399-3193
Linda St. Pierre, prin. Fax 391-4086
Wright ES 500/K-5
4060 Lone Oak Rd SE 97302 503-399-3198
Rachel Stucky, prin. Fax 391-4090
Yoshikai ES 500/K-5
4900 Jade St NE 97305 503-399-3438
Zan Payne, prin. Fax 391-4071
Other Schools – See Keizer

Silver Falls SD 4J
Supt. — See Silverton
Pratum S 100/K-8
8995 Sunnyview Rd NE 97305 503-362-8812
Mark Recker, prin. Fax 585-6889

Concordia Lutheran S 50/K-8
4663 Lancaster Dr NE 97305 503-393-7188
Vale Alley, prin. Fax 393-1057
Immanuel Lutheran S 100/K-8
510 Idylwood Dr SE 97302 503-371-5473
James Wendland, prin.
Livingstone Adventist Academy 300/K-12
5771 Fruitland Rd NE, 503-363-9408
Jon Dickerson, prin. Fax 363-5721
Queen of Peace S 100/K-6
PO Box 3696 97302 503-362-3443
Debilyn Janota, prin. Fax 589-9411
Riviera Christian S 100/PK-6
1650 Brush College Rd NW 97304 503-361-8779
Debbie Frost, admin. Fax 362-9670

St. John Lutheran S 50/PK-K
1350 Court St NE 97301 503-588-0171
Kelly Crabtree, prin. Fax 585-2801
St. Joseph S 100/K-6
373 Winter St NE 97301 503-581-2147
Mari Pat Brooks, prin. Fax 399-7045
St. Vincent DePaul S 100/PK-6
1015 Columbia St NE 97301 503-363-8457
Ruth Whitnah, prin. Fax 363-1516
Salem Academy 600/PK-12
942 Lancaster Dr NE 97301 503-378-1219
Dr. Ken Freisen, supt. Fax 375-3522
Salem Academy East ES 100/PK-5
942 Lancaster Dr NE 97301 503-399-7360
Sue Davenhill, dir. Fax 566-8747
Salem Academy West ES 200/PK-5
942 Lancaster Dr NE 97301 503-378-1221
Lois Gardner, prin. Fax 378-1407
Sonshine S 200/PK-5
395 Marion St NE 97301 503-375-5764
Wayne Bernard, admin. Fax 391-9272
Sunnyview Child Care Center 100/PK-K
3032 Sunnyview Rd NE 97301 503-364-3028

Sandy, Clackamas, Pop. 7,871
Oregon Trail SD 46 4,200/K-12
PO Box 547 97055 503-668-5541
Shelley Redinger, supt. Fax 668-7906
www.oregontrailschools.com
Cedar Ridge MS 400/6-8
17225 Smith Ave 97055 503-668-8067
Molly Knudsen, prin. Fax 668-3977
Firwood ES 400/K-5
42900 SE Trubel Rd 97055 503-668-8005
Scott Maltman, prin. Fax 668-3684
Sandy ES 400/K-5
38955 Pleasant Ave 97055 503-668-8065
James Phillips, prin. Fax 668-6246
Other Schools – See Boring, Welches

Scappoose, Columbia, Pop. 5,913
Scappoose SD 1J 2,200/K-12
33589 High School Way 97056 503-543-6374
Paul Peterson, supt. Fax 543-7011
www.scappoose.k12.or.us
Petersen ES 400/4-6
52181 SW EM Watts Rd 97056 503-543-7111
Kelly Powell, prin. Fax 543-7120
Scappoose MS 300/7-8
52265 Columbia River Hwy 97056 503-543-7163
Pam Reynolds, prin. Fax 543-7917
Watts ES 400/K-3
52000 SE 3rd Pl 97056 503-543-6372
Christine Stetzer, prin. Fax 543-6373
Other Schools – See Portland, Warren

Scappoose SDA S 100/K-8
PO Box 889 97056 503-543-6939
Steve McKeone, prin. Fax 543-6939

Scio, Linn, Pop. 704
Scio SD 95 700/K-12
38875 NW 1st Ave 97374 503-394-3261
Gary Tempel, supt. Fax 394-3920
www.scio.k12.or.us/
Centennial ES 300/K-5
38875 NW 1st Ave 97374 503-394-3265
Barbara Svensen, prin. Fax 394-3247
Scio MS 100/6-8
38875 NW 1st Ave 97374 503-394-3271
Kerry Lau, prin. Fax 394-4042

Scotts Mills, Marion, Pop. 316
Silver Falls SD 4J
Supt. — See Silverton
Scotts Mills S 100/K-8
PO Box 40 97375 503-873-4394
Marilyn Annen, prin. Fax 873-3324

Seaside, Clatsop, Pop. 6,116
Jewell SD 8 200/K-12
83874 Highway 103 97138 503-755-2451
Jerry Jones, supt. Fax 755-0616
www.jewell.k12.or.us/
Jewell S 200/K-12
83874 Highway 103 97138 503-755-2451
Jerry Jones, prin. Fax 755-0616

Seaside SD 10 1,600/K-12
1801 S Franklin St 97138 503-738-5591
Doug Dougherty, supt. Fax 738-3471
www.seaside.k12.or.us/
Broadway MS 400/6-8
1120 Broadway St 97138 503-738-6892
Doug Pease, prin. Fax 738-3900
Seaside Heights ES 300/K-5
2000 Spruce Dr 97138 503-738-5161
Dan Gaffney, prin. Fax 738-7303
Other Schools – See Cannon Beach, Gearhart

Faith Lutheran S 50/PK-PK
1115 Broadway St 97138 503-738-7223

Seneca, Grant, Pop. 198
Grant SD 3
Supt. — See Canyon City
Seneca S 100/K-8
PO Box 69 97873 541-542-2542
Adele Cerny, lead tchr. Fax 542-2115

Shady Cove, Jackson, Pop. 2,301
Jackson County SD 9
Supt. — See Eagle Point
Shady Cove S 200/4-8
PO Box 138 97539 541-878-1400
Tiffany O'Donnell, prin. Fax 830-6226

Sheridan, Yamhill, Pop. 5,570
Sheridan SD 48J 900/K-12
435 S Bridge St 97378 503-843-2433
A.J. Grauer, supt. Fax 843-3505
www.sheridan.k12.or.us
Faulconer-Chapman S 600/K-8
332 SW Cornwall St 97378 503-843-3732
Marta Hofenbredl, prin. Fax 843-3738

Delphian S 200/PK-12
20950 SW Rock Creek Rd 97378 503-843-3521
Rosemary Didear, hdmstr. Fax 843-4158
West Valley Academy 100/K-12
PO Box 127 97378 503-843-4123
Fax 843-2080

Sherwood, Washington, Pop. 15,398
Sherwood SD 88J 4,100/K-12
23295 SW Main St 97140 503-825-5000
Dan Jamison, supt. Fax 825-5001
www.sherwood.k12.or.us
Archer Glen ES 700/K-5
16155 SW Sunset Blvd 97140 503-825-5100
Jon Wollmuth, prin. Fax 825-5101
Edy Ridge ES K-5
21472 SW Copper Ter 97140 503-825-5700
Frank Luzaich, prin. Fax 525-5701
Hopkins ES 700/K-5
21920 SW Sherwood Blvd 97140 503-825-5200
Laura Shea, prin. Fax 825-5201
Laurel Ridge MS 6-8
21416 SW Copper Ter 97140 503-825-5800
Steve Emmert, prin. Fax 825-5801
Middleton ES 700/K-5
23505 SW Old Highway 99W 97140 503-825-5300
Tim Smith, prin. Fax 825-5301
Sherwood MS 1,000/6-8
21970 SW Sherwood Blvd 97140 503-825-5400
Gary Bennett, prin. Fax 825-5401

St. Francis S 200/K-8
15643 SW Oregon St 97140 503-625-0497
Michael Cantu, prin. Fax 625-5914
St. Paul Lutheran S 200/PK-5
17500 SW Cedarview Way 97140 503-625-6648
Axel Gruen, prin. Fax 625-8976

Silver Lake, Lake
North Lake SD 14 200/K-12
57566 Fort Rock Rd 97638 541-576-2121
Steve Staniak, supt. Fax 576-2705
www.nlake.k12.or.us/
North Lake S 200/K-12
57566 Fort Rock Rd 97638 541-576-2121
Steve Staniak, prin. Fax 576-2705

Silverton, Marion, Pop. 8,233
Silver Falls SD 4J 3,100/K-12
1456 Pine St 97381 503-873-5303
Craig Roessler, supt. Fax 873-2936
www.silverfalls.k12.or.us/
Central Howell S 100/K-8
8832 Silverton Rd NE 97381 503-873-4818
Linda Myers, prin. Fax 873-5909
Evergreen S 100/K-8
3727 Cascade Hwy NE 97381 503-873-4845
Dale Koger, prin. Fax 873-1495
Field ES 500/K-3
410 N Water St 97381 503-873-6341
Catherine Brosnan-Trepus, prin. Fax 873-8325
Frost ES 400/4-6
201 Westfield St 97381 503-873-5301
Beth Davisson, prin. Fax 873-8910
Silver Crest S 100/K-8
365 Loar Rd SE 97381 503-873-4428
Mark Recker, prin. Fax 873-8457
Twain MS 300/7-8
425 N Church St 97381 503-873-5317
Les Keele, prin. Fax 873-7108
Victor Point S 100/K-8
1175 Victor Point Rd SE 97381 503-873-4987
Linda Myers, prin. Fax 873-8048
Other Schools – See Mount Angel, Salem, Scotts Mills

Silverton Christian S 50/PK-8
PO Box 338 97381 503-873-5131
Jim Farmer, admin. Fax 873-6681

Sisters, Deschutes, Pop. 1,212
Sisters SD 6 1,500/K-12
525 E Cascade Ave 97759 541-549-8521
Elaine Drakulich, supt. Fax 549-8951
www.outlawnet.com/outlaw/ssd
Sisters ES 400/K-4
611 E Cascade Ave 97759 541-549-8981
Jan Silberman, prin. Fax 549-2093
Sisters MS 400/5-8
15200 McKenzie Rd 97759 541-549-2099
Kathy Miner, prin. Fax 549-2098

Sisters Christian S 100/PK-8
PO Box 1103 97759 541-549-4133
Peggy Miller, prin. Fax 549-1392

Spray, Wheeler, Pop. 130
Spray SD 1 100/K-12
PO Box 230 97874 541-468-2226
Mary Doherty, supt. Fax 468-2630
www.sprayschool.com
Spray S 100/K-12
PO Box 230 97874 541-468-2226
Mary Doherty, prin. Fax 468-2630

Springfield, Lane, Pop. 55,641
Springfield SD 19 10,200/K-12
525 Mill St 97477 541-747-3331
Nancy Golden, supt. Fax 726-3312
www.sps.lane.edu

Brattain ES 200/K-5
425 10th St 97477 541-744-6380
Jeff Butler, prin. Fax 744-6382
Briggs MS 500/6-8
2355 Yolanda Ave 97477 541-744-6350
Brooke Wagner, prin. Fax 744-6354
Camp Creek ES 100/K-5
37770 Upper Camp Creek Rd 97478 541-744-6425
Sheila Turner, prin. Fax 744-6427
Centennial ES 400/K-5
1315 Aspen St 97477 541-744-6383
Mike Donnelly, prin. Fax 744-6489
Douglas Gardens ES 400/K-5
3680 Jasper Rd 97478 541-744-6387
Dave Collins, prin. Fax 744-6390
Hamlin MS 400/6-8
326 Centennial Blvd 97477 541-744-6356
Mike Riplinger, prin. Fax 744-6360
Lee ES 400/K-5
755 Harlow Rd 97477 541-744-6391
Sarah Lewenberg, prin. Fax 744-6477
Maple ES 300/K-5
2109 J St 97477 541-744-6395
Jay Carter, prin. Fax 744-6398
Moffitt ES 300/K-5
1544 5th St 97477 541-744-6399
Bill Davis, prin. Fax 744-6432
Mohawk ES 100/K-5
91166 Sunderman Rd 97478 541-744-6428
Julie Collins, prin. Fax 744-6431
Mt. Vernon ES 500/K-5
935 Filbert Ln 97478 541-744-6403
Jim Keegan, prin. Fax 744-6405
Page ES 400/K-5
1300 Hayden Bridge Rd 97477 541-744-6407
Rosalynn Jaeger, prin. Fax 744-6410
Ridgeview ES 400/K-5
526 66th St 97478 541-744-6308
Jim Crist, prin. Fax 744-6311
Riverbend ES 400/K-5
320 51st St 97478 541-988-2511
Margot McDonnell, prin. Fax 988-2519
Springfield MS 300/6-8
1084 G St 97477 541-744-6362
Jeff Mather, prin. Fax 744-6366
Stewart MS 600/6-8
900 S 32nd St 97478 541-988-2520
Andy Dey, prin. Fax 988-2530
Thurston ES 400/K-5
7345 Thurston Rd 97478 541-744-6411
Shari Furtwangler, prin. Fax 744-6414
Thurston MS 500/6-8
6300 Thurston Rd 97478 541-744-6368
Carl Swan, prin. Fax 744-6372
Walterville S 200/K-8
40589 Mckenzie Hwy 97478 541-744-6415
Sheila Turner, prin. Fax 744-6417
Yolanda ES 400/K-5
2350 Yolanda Ave 97477 541-744-6418
Julie Collins, prin. Fax 744-6421
Other Schools – See Eugene

Stanfield, Umatilla, Pop. 1,979
Stanfield SD 61 600/K-12
1120 N Main St 97875 541-449-8766
Darce Driskel, supt. Fax 449-8768
www.stanfield.k12.or.us
Stanfield ES 300/K-6
1120 N Main St 97875 541-449-3305
Kevin Headings, prin. Fax 449-8772

Stayton, Marion, Pop. 7,184
North Santiam SD 29J 2,400/K-12
1155 N 3rd Ave 97383 503-769-6924
Dr. Jack Adams, supt. Fax 769-3578
www.nsantiam.k12.or.us
Stayton ES 500/K-3
875 N 3rd Ave 97383 503-769-2336
David Bolin, prin. Fax 769-1709
Stayton Intermediate MS 600/4-8
1021 Shaff Rd 97383 503-769-2198
Andy Gardner, prin. Fax 769-9524
Other Schools – See Lyons, Sublimity

St. Mary S 200/PK-8
1066 N 6th Ave 97383 503-769-2718
Richard Schindler, prin. Fax 769-0560
Stayton Christian S 100/PK-5
189 E Washington St 97383 503-769-7578
Richard Neely, prin. Fax 769-4396

Sublimity, Marion, Pop. 2,374
North Santiam SD 29J
Supt. — See Stayton
Sublimity S 400/K-8
PO Box 269 97385 503-769-2459
Jamie McCarty, prin. Fax 769-3383

Sunriver, Deschutes
Bend-LaPine Administrative SD 1
Supt. — See Bend
Three Rivers S 400/K-8
56900 Enterprise Dr 97707 541-593-3555
Gayle Vidal, prin. Fax 593-1945

Sutherlin, Douglas, Pop. 7,281
Sutherlin SD 130 1,500/K-12
531 E Central Ave 97479 541-459-2228
John Lahley, supt. Fax 459-2484
www.sutherlin.k12.or.us
Sutherlin East PS 400/K-3
323 E Third Ave 97479 541-459-2912
Ken Hart, prin. Fax 459-0898
Sutherlin MS 200/7-8
649 E Fourth Ave 97479 541-459-2668
Steve Perkins, prin. Fax 459-2047
Sutherlin West IS 300/4-6
531 N Comstock Ave 97479 541-459-3688
Robert Freeman, prin. Fax 459-5675

Sutherlin Adventist S 50/PK-6
841 W Central Ave 97479 541-459-9706
Fax 459-8970

Sweet Home, Linn, Pop. 8,389
Sweet Home SD 55 2,300/K-12
1920 Long St 97386 541-367-7126
Larry Horton, supt. Fax 367-7105
www.sweethome.k12.or.us
Hawthorne ES 300/K-6
3205 Long St 97386 541-367-7167
Ryan Beck, prin. Fax 367-8903
Holley ES 100/1-6
40336 Crawfordsville Dr 97386 541-367-7162
Tiffanie Lambert, prin. Fax 367-8904
Oak Heights ES 300/K-6
605 Elm St 97386 541-367-7165
Keith Winslow, prin. Fax 367-7192
Sweet Home JHS 400/7-8
880 22nd Ave 97386 541-367-7187
Hal Huschka, prin. Fax 367-7107
Other Schools – See Crawfordsville, Foster

East Linn Christian Academy 200/PK-6
28721 Liberty Rd 97386 541-367-2391
James Hill, prin. Fax 367-3801

Talent, Jackson, Pop. 6,018
Phoenix-Talent SD 4
Supt. — See Phoenix
Talent ES 500/K-5
PO Box 296 97540 541-535-1531
Aaron Santi, prin. Fax 535-1858
Talent MS 600/6-8
PO Box 359 97540 541-535-1552
Curt Shenk, prin. Fax 535-7532

Tangent, Linn, Pop. 968
Greater Albany SD 8J
Supt. — See Albany
Tangent ES 200/K-5
32100 Old Oak Dr 97389 541-967-4616
Ellen Carlson, prin. Fax 924-3716

Central Valley Christian S 100/PK-9
31630 Highway 34 97389 541-928-7820
Mike Meadows, prin. Fax 967-4410

Terrebonne, Deschutes, Pop. 1,143
Redmond SD 2J
Supt. — See Redmond
Terrebonne Community S 500/K-8
1199 B Ave 97760 541-923-4856
Rosann Stevenson, prin. Fax 923-4825

The Dalles, Wasco, Pop. 11,317
North Wasco County SD 21 2,800/K-12
3632 W 10th St 97058 541-506-3420
Candy Armstrong, supt. Fax 298-6018
www.nwasco.k12.or.us
Chenowith ES 400/K-5
922 Chenoweth Loop W 97058 541-506-3350
Matt Ihle, prin. Fax 296-1316
Dry Hollow ES 400/K-5
1314 E 19th St 97058 541-506-3370
Greg Bigelow, prin. Fax 298-6171
The Dalles MS 600/6-8
1100 E 12th St 97058 541-506-3380
Pat Consoliver, prin. Fax 298-1942
Wright ES 300/K-5
610 W 14th St 97058 541-506-3360
Theresa Peters, prin. Fax 298-6145

Covenant Christian Academy 100/PK-8
2630 E 18th St 97058 541-296-2952
Brett Hartley, admin. Fax 298-5553
St. Mary's Academy 200/PK-8
1112 Cherry Heights Rd 97058 541-296-6004
Mary Beth Thouvenel, prin. Fax 296-7858
The Dalles SDA S 50/1-8
3339 E 13th St 97058 541-296-2692
Bruce Schmidt, prin. Fax 296-4950

Tigard, Washington, Pop. 47,968
Tigard-Tualatin SD 23J 12,200/K-12
6960 SW Sandburg St 97223 503-431-4000
Rob Saxton, supt. Fax 431-4047
www.ttsd.k12.or.us
Deer Creek ES 600/K-5
16155 SW 131st Ave 97224 503-431-4450
Carole Biskar, prin. Fax 431-4460
Durham ES 500/K-5
7980 SW Durham Rd 97224 503-431-4500
Joyce Woods, prin. Fax 431-4510
Fowler MS 900/6-8
10865 SW Walnut St 97223 503-431-5000
Shelley Corry, prin. Fax 431-5010
Rider ES 500/K-5
14850 SW 132nd Ter 97224 503-431-4900
Darin Barnard, prin. Fax 431-4910
Templeton ES 600/K-5
9500 SW Murdock St 97224 503-431-4850
Todd Robson, prin. Fax 431-4860
Twality MS 900/6-8
14650 SW 97th Ave 97224 503-431-5200
Rick Patrick, prin. Fax 431-5210
Woodward ES 500/K-5
12325 SW Katherine St 97223 503-431-4700
Vickie Foiles, prin. Fax 431-4710
Other Schools – See Portland, Tualatin

Gaarde Christian S 200/PK-8
11265 SW Gaarde St 97224 503-639-5336
Kellie Hooper, admin. Fax 684-6492
St. Anthony S 500/PK-8
12645 SW Pacific Hwy 97223 503-639-4979
Jeananne Bloudek, prin. Fax 620-5117

Tillamook, Tillamook, Pop. 4,471
Tillamook SD 9 2,000/K-12
6825 Officer Row 97141 503-842-4414
Randy Schild, supt. Fax 842-6854
www.tillamook.k12.or.us
East ES 400/4-6
3905 Alder Ln 97141 503-842-7544
Greg English, prin. Fax 842-1246
Liberty ES 200/K-3
1700 9th St 97141 503-842-7501
Donna Minard, prin. Fax 842-1314
South Prairie ES 300/K-3
6855 S Prairie Rd 97141 503-842-8401
Kathy Gervasi, prin. Fax 842-1452
Tillamook JHS 300/7-8
3906 Alder Ln 97141 503-842-7531
Elroy Thompson, prin. Fax 842-1349

Pacific Christian S 50/1-6
2203 4th St 97141 503-842-4727
Harry Hewitt, prin. Fax 842-4727
Tillamook Adventist S 100/K-12
4300 12th St 97141 503-842-6533
Fax 842-6236

Tiller, Douglas
Douglas County SD 15
Supt. — See Days Creek
Tiller ES 100/K-7
PO Box 189 97484 541-825-3221
Laurie Newton, prin. Fax 825-3572

Toledo, Lincoln, Pop. 3,434
Lincoln County SD
Supt. — See Newport
Toledo ES 100/K-6
600 SE Sturdevant Rd 97391 541-336-5121
Pedra Berenson, prin. Fax 336-5407

Trail, Jackson
Jackson County SD 9
Supt. — See Eagle Point
Elk Trail ES 100/K-3
591 Elk Creek Rd 97541 541-878-1405
Tiffany O'Donnell, prin. Fax 830-6255

Troutdale, Multnomah, Pop. 14,898
Reynolds SD 7
Supt. — See Fairview
Morey MS 700/6-8
2801 SW Lucas Ave 97060 503-491-1935
Tony Mann, prin. Fax 491-0245
Sweetbriar ES 500/K-5
501 SE Sweetbriar Ln 97060 503-666-9441
Janice Hager, prin. Fax 667-6524
Troutdale ES 500/K-5
648 SE Harlow Ave 97060 503-665-4182
Stephen Johnson, prin. Fax 667-6657

Tualatin, Washington, Pop. 25,881
Tigard-Tualatin SD 23J
Supt. — See Tigard
Bridgeport ES 500/K-5
5505 SW Borland Rd 97062 503-431-4200
Jerry Nihill, prin. Fax 431-4210
Byrom ES 600/K-5
21800 SW 91st Ave 97062 503-431-4300
Rick Fraisse, prin. Fax 431-4310
Hazelbrook MS 1,000/6-8
11300 SW Hazelbrook Rd 97062 503-431-5100
Elizabeth Ryan, prin. Fax 431-5110
Tualatin ES 500/K-5
20405 SW 95th Ave 97062 503-431-4800
Johanna Cena, prin. Fax 431-4810

West Linn-Wilsonville SD 3J 8,100/K-12
22210 SW Stafford Rd 97062 503-673-7000
Roger Woehl, supt. Fax 673-7001
www.wlwv.k12.or.us
Other Schools – See West Linn, Wilsonville

Horizon Christian S 500/PK-12
PO Box 4190 97062 503-692-6385
Dr. Robert Tinnin, supt. Fax 691-9677
Stafford Academy 100/PK-5
21065 SW Stafford Rd 97062 503-638-8765
Dan Seale, admin. Fax 638-6316

Turner, Marion, Pop. 1,571
Cascade SD 5 2,200/PK-12
10226 Marion Rd SE 97392 503-749-8488
Darin Drill, supt. Fax 749-8321
www.cascade.k12.or.us
Cascade JHS 500/6-8
10226 Marion Rd SE 97392 503-749-8489
Leanne Deffenbaugh, prin. Fax 749-8323
Cloverdale ES 100/K-5
9666 Parrish Gap Rd SE 97392 503-749-8494
Arnie Lowder, prin. Fax 743-2189
Marion ES 100/K-5
6023 B St SE 97392 503-749-8495
Christy Wilkins, prin. Fax 769-6435
Turner ES 200/K-5
PO Box 129 97392 503-749-8491
Dan Petersen, prin. Fax 749-8326
Other Schools – See Aumsville

Willamette Christian S 200/PK-8
2707 Maranatha Ct SE 97392 503-391-9082
Jerry Huhn, prin. Fax 378-0507

Ukiah, Umatilla, Pop. 255
Ukiah SD 80R 50/K-12
PO Box 218 97880 541-427-3731
Dan Korber, supt. Fax 427-3730
www.ukiah.k12.or.us
Ukiah S 50/K-12
PO Box 218 97880 541-427-3731
Dan Korber, prin. Fax 427-3730

Umatilla, Umatilla, Pop. 6,306
Umatilla SD 6R 1,300/K-12
1001 6th St 97882 541-922-6500
Heidi Sipe, supt. Fax 922-6507
www.umatilla.k12.or.us/
Brownell MS 300/6-8
1460 7th St 97882 541-922-6625
Dianna Veleke, prin. Fax 922-6507
McNary Heights ES 600/K-5
120 Columbia Ave 97882 541-922-6650
Bob Lorence, prin. Fax 922-6599

Union, Union, Pop. 1,945
Union SD 5 500/K-12
PO Box K 97883 541-562-6115
Mike Wood, supt. Fax 562-8116
www.union.k12.or.us
Union ES 200/K-6
PO Box 868 97883 541-562-5278
Mike Wood, prin. Fax 562-9028

Unity, Baker, Pop. 124
Burnt River SD 30J 100/K-12
PO Box 8 97884 541-446-3466
Lorrie Andrews, supt. Fax 446-3581
Burnt River S 100/K-12
PO Box 8 97884 541-446-3336
Lorrie Andrews, prin. Fax 446-3581

Vale, Malheur, Pop. 1,926
Vale SD 84 900/K-12
403 E St W 97918 541-473-0201
Matthew Hawley, supt. Fax 473-3294
www.vale.k12.or.us
Vale ES 400/K-6
403 E St W 97918 541-473-3291
Darlene McConnell, prin. Fax 473-3294
Vale MS 100/7-8
403 E St W 97918 541-473-0241
Matt Cobb, prin. Fax 473-3293
Willowcreek S 100/K-8
2300 9th Ave W 97918 541-473-2345
Matt Cobb, prin. Fax 473-3620

Timberline SDA S 50/1-8
2582 10th Ave W 97918 541-473-9661
Fax 473-9661

Veneta, Lane, Pop. 3,477
Fern Ridge SD 28J
Supt. — See Elmira
Veneta ES 300/K-5
88131 Territorial Rd 97487 541-935-8225
Olivia Johnson, prin. Fax 935-8228

Countryside Christian S 50/1-8
88401 Huston Rd 97487 541-935-3017

Vernonia, Columbia, Pop. 2,287
Vernonia SD 47J 700/K-12
475 Bridge St 97064 503-429-5891
Kenneth Cox, supt. Fax 429-7742
www.vernonia.k12.or.us/
Vernonia MS 200/6-8
249 Bridge St 97064 503-429-0487
Brent McClain, prin. Fax 429-4731
Washington ES 300/K-5
199 Bridge St 97064 503-429-7941
Aaron Miller, prin. Fax 429-4539
Other Schools – See Mist

Vida, Lane

McKenzie River Christian S 50/K-12
PO Box I 97488 541-896-0554
Russ Conklin, admin. Fax 896-0554

Waldport, Lincoln, Pop. 2,094
Lincoln County SD
Supt. — See Newport
Crestview Heights S 400/K-8
PO Box 830 97394 541-563-3237
Mary Schaer, prin. Fax 563-2467

Wallowa, Wallowa, Pop. 824
Wallowa SD 12 200/K-12
PO Box 425 97885 541-886-2061
Bob Sisk, supt. Fax 886-7355
Wallowa ES 100/K-6
PO Box 425 97885 541-886-2061
Bob Sisk, prin. Fax 886-7355

Warm Springs, Jefferson, Pop. 2,287
Jefferson County SD 509J
Supt. — See Madras
Warm Springs ES 400/K-5
PO Box 1269 97761 541-553-1128
Dawn Smith, prin. Fax 553-6321

Warren, Columbia
Scappoose SD 1J
Supt. — See Scappoose
Warren ES 200/K-3
34555 Berg Rd 97053 503-397-2959
Mike Judah, prin. Fax 397-7860

Columbia County Christian S 50/K-6
56523 Columbia River Hwy 97053 503-366-9209
Rebecca Swatman, admin. Fax 397-7284

Warrenton, Clatsop, Pop. 4,310
Warrenton-Hammond SD 30 800/K-12
820 SW Cedar Ave 97146 503-861-2281
Craig Brewington, supt. Fax 861-2911
www.whsd.k12.or.us/
Warrenton S 600/K-8
820 SW Cedar Ave 97146 503-861-3376
Jan Schock, prin. Fax 861-2911

Pleasant View SDA S 50/1-8
91272 Highway 101 97146 503-861-1633

Wasco, Sherman, Pop. 341
Sherman County SD 300/K-12
PO Box 66 97065 541-442-5777
Ivan Ritchie, supt. Fax 442-5778
www.sherman.k12.or.us/District/
North Sherman ES 100/K-6
PO Box 66 97065 541-442-5533
Nancy Kieling, prin. Fax 442-5112
Other Schools – See Grass Valley

Welches, Clackamas
Oregon Trail SD 46
Supt. — See Sandy
Welches ES 300/K-5
24901 E Salmon River Rd 97067 503-622-3165
Michael McKinney, prin. Fax 622-4436
Welches MS 200/6-8
24903 E Salmon River Rd 97067 503-622-3166
Michael McKinney, prin. Fax 622-3398

West Linn, Clackamas, Pop. 25,094
West Linn-Wilsonville SD 3J
Supt. — See Tualatin
Athey Creek MS 600/6-8
2900 SW Borland Rd 97068 503-673-7400
Carol Egan, prin. Fax 638-8302
Bolton ES 300/K-5
5933 Holmes St 97068 503-673-7050
Holly Omlin-Ruback, prin. Fax 657-8711
Cedaroak Park ES 400/K-5
4515 Cedar Oak Dr 97068 503-673-7100
Carolyn Miller, prin. Fax 657-8722
Rosemont Ridge MS 700/6-8
20001 S Salamo Rd 97068 503-673-7550
Debi Briggs Crispin, prin. Fax 657-8720
Stafford ES 600/K-5
19875 SW Stafford Rd 97068 503-673-7150
Patrick Meigs, prin. Fax 638-5313
Sunset ES 500/K-5
2351 Oxford St 97068 503-673-7200
Kathy Ludwig, prin. Fax 657-8718
Willamette ES 600/K-5
1403 12th St 97068 503-673-7250
David Pryor, prin. Fax 655-3706

Weston, Umatilla, Pop. 714
Athena-Weston SD 29RJ
Supt. — See Athena
Weston MS 200/4-8
PO Box 158 97886 541-566-3548
Lori Mills, prin. Fax 566-2326

White City, Jackson, Pop. 5,891
Jackson County SD 9
Supt. — See Eagle Point
Mountain View ES 300/K-5
7837 Hale Way 97503 541-830-1360
Lisa Yamashita, prin. Fax 830-6353
White City ES 500/K-5
2830 Maple Ct 97503 541-830-1350
Ginny Walker, prin. Fax 830-6307
White Mountain MS 400/6-8
550 Wilson Way 97503 541-830-6315
Dan Johnson, prin. Fax 830-6751

Willamina, Yamhill, Pop. 1,874
Willamina SD 30J 900/K-12
324 SE Adams St 97396 503-876-1501
Gus Forster, supt. Fax 876-3610
www.willamina.k12.or.us
Willamina ES 400/K-5
1100 NE Oaken Hills Dr 97396 503-876-2374
Carrie Zimbrick, prin. Fax 876-4321
Other Schools – See Grand Ronde

West Valley Christian S 50/1-8
PO Box 38 97396 503-879-5812

Williams, Josephine
Three Rivers County SD
Supt. — See Grants Pass
Williams ES 100/K-5
20691 Williams Hwy 97544 541-846-7224
Michelle Sesock, prin. Fax 846-7225

Wilsonville, Clackamas, Pop. 16,075
West Linn-Wilsonville SD 3J
Supt. — See Tualatin
Boeckman Creek ES 600/K-5
PO Box 622 97070 503-673-7750
Charlotte Morris, prin. Fax 682-0738
Boones Ferry ES 800/K-5
PO Box 130 97070 503-673-7300
Michael Shay, prin. Fax 682-8761
Wood MS 700/6-8
PO Box 705 97070 503-673-7500
Barbara Soisson, prin. Fax 682-9109

Winchester, Douglas, Pop. 2,500
Douglas County SD 4
Supt. — See Roseburg
Winchester ES 400/K-5
PO Box 778 97495 541-440-4184
Curt Frye, prin. Fax 440-4187

Winston, Douglas, Pop. 4,764
Winston-Dillard SD 116 1,500/K-12
620 Elwood St 97496 541-679-3000
Duane Yecha, supt. Fax 679-4819
www.wdsd.org
Brockway ES 400/K-3
2520 Brockway Rd 97496 541-679-3037
Cathy Knapp, prin. Fax 679-3051
McGovern ES 300/4-6
600 Elwood St 97496 541-679-3003
Erika Pinkerton, prin. Fax 679-3027
Winston MS 200/7-8
330 Thompson Ave 97496 541-679-3002
David Welker, prin. Fax 679-3026
Other Schools – See Roseburg

Wolf Creek, Josephine
Three Rivers County SD
Supt. — See Grants Pass
Wolf Creek ES 100/K-5
PO Box 325 97497 541-866-2496
David Fuller, prin. Fax 866-2449

Woodburn, Marion, Pop. 21,736
Woodburn SD 103 3,500/K-12
965 N Boones Ferry Rd 97071 503-981-9555
Walt Blomberg, supt. Fax 981-8018
www.woodburn.k12.or.us
French Prairie MS 600/6-8
1025 N Boones Ferry Rd 97071 503-981-2650
Eric Swenson, prin. Fax 981-2724
Heritage ES 800/K-5
440 Parr Rd 97071 503-981-2850
Irene Novichihin, prin. Fax 981-2890
Lincoln ES 700/K-5
1041 N Boones Ferry Rd 97071 503-981-2660
Jennifer Crist, prin. Fax 981-2666
Muir ES 400/K-5
1800 W Hayes St 97071 503-981-2670
Sherrilyn Rawson, prin. Fax 981-2673
Valor MS 500/6-8
450 Parr Rd 97071 503-981-2750
Victor Vergara, prin. Fax 981-2790
Washington ES 600/K-5
777 E Lincoln St 97071 503-981-2680
Edward Tabet, prin. Fax 981-2720

Little Lambs Preschool 100/PK-K
1036 E Lincoln St 97071 503-981-1036
St. Luke S 200/K-8
529 Harrison St 97071 503-981-7441
David Guile, prin. Fax 982-4697

Yamhill, Yamhill, Pop. 823
Yamhill-Carlton SD 1 1,200/K-12
120 N Larch 97148 503-852-6980
Steve Chiovaro, supt. Fax 662-4931
www.ycsd.k12.or.us
Trask Mountain MS 200/7-8
310 E Main St 97148 503-852-7660
Gretchen Brunner, dean Fax 662-4079
Yamhill S 300/K-6
310 E Main St 97148 503-852-7660
Gretchen Brunner, prin. Fax 662-4079
Other Schools – See Carlton

Yoncalla, Douglas, Pop. 1,059
Yoncalla SD 32 300/K-12
PO Box 568 97499 541-849-2782
Marc Thielman, supt. Fax 849-2190
www.yoncalla.k12.or.us
Yoncalla S 200/K-8
PO Box 568 97499 541-849-2158
Jerry Fauci, prin. Fax 849-3162

PENNSYLVANIA

PENNSYLVANIA DEPARTMENT OF EDUCATION
333 Market St Fl 9, Harrisburg 17101-2215
Telephone 717-783-6788
Fax 717-787-7222
Website http://www.pde.psu.edu

Secretary of Education Gerald Zahorchak

PENNSYLVANIA BOARD OF EDUCATION
333 Market St Fl 10, Harrisburg 17101-2215

Chairperson Joseph Torsella

INTERMEDIATE UNITS (IU)

Allegheny IU 3
Dr. Donna Durno, dir. 412-394-5700
475 Waterfront Dr E Fax 394-5706
Homestead 15120
www.aiu3.net/

Appalachia IU 8
Dr. Michael Dillon, dir. 814-940-0223
4500 6th Ave, Altoona 16602 Fax 472-5033
www.iu08.org/

ARIN IU 28
Dr. Robert Coad, dir. 724-463-5300
2895 W Pike Rd, Indiana 15701 Fax 463-5315
www.arin.k12.pa.us

Beaver Valley IU 27
Thomas Zelesnik, dir. 724-774-7800
147 Poplar Dr, Monaca 15061 Fax 774-4751
www.bviu.org/bviu/site/default.asp

Berks County IU 14
Dr. Nancy Almon, dir. 610-987-2248
PO Box 16050, Reading 19612 Fax 987-8400
www.berksiu.org

Blast IU 17
Thomas Shivetts, dir. 570-323-8561
PO Box 3609, Williamsport 17701
www.iu17.org

Bucks County IU 22
Barry Galasso Ed.D., dir. 215-348-2940
705 N Shady Retreat Rd Fax 489-7874
Doylestown 18901
www.bciu.k12.pa.us

Capital Area IU 15
Amy Morton, dir. 717-732-8400
PO Box 489, Summerdale 17093 Fax 732-8421
www.caiu.org/caiu/site/default.asp

Carbon-Lehigh IU 21
Robert Keegan, dir. 610-769-4111
4210 Independence Dr Fax 769-1290
Schnecksville 18078
www.cliu.org

Central IU 10
Dr. Hugh Dwyer, dir. 814-342-0884
345 Link Rd, West Decatur 16878 Fax 342-5137
www.ciu10.com

Central Susquehanna IU 16
Dr. Robert Witten, dir. 570-523-1155
PO Box 213, Lewisburg 17837 Fax 524-7104
www.csiu.org/

Chester County IU 24
Dr. Joseph O'Brien, dir. 484-237-5000
455 Boot Rd, Downingtown 19335 Fax 237-5154
www.cciu.org/

IU 1
Dr. Lawrence O'Shea, dir. 724-938-3241
1 Intermediate Unit Dr Fax 938-8722
Coal Center 15423
www.iu1.k12.pa.us/

Colonial IU 20
Dr. Charlene Brennan, dir. 610-252-5550
6 Danforth Rd, Easton 18045 Fax 252-5740
www.ciu20.org

Delaware County IU 25
Dr. Barry Ersek, dir. 610-938-9000
200 Yale Ave, Morton 19070 Fax 565-1315
www.dciu.org/

Lancaster-Lebanon IU 13
Dr. Cynthia Burkhart, dir. 717-606-1600
1020 New Holland Ave
Lancaster 17601
www.iu13.k12.pa.us

Lincoln IU 12
Dr. Michael Thew, dir. 717-624-4616
PO Box 70, New Oxford 17350 Fax 624-6519
www.iu12.org

Luzerne IU 18
Michael Ostrowski, dir. 570-287-9681
PO Box 1649, Kingston 18704
www.liu18.org/

Midwestern IU 4
Cecilia Yauger, dir. 724-458-6700
453 Maple St, Grove City 16127 Fax 458-5083
www.miu4.k12.pa.us/

Montgomery County IU 23
Dr. Jerry Shiveley, dir. 610-539-8550
1605 W Main St Ste B Fax 539-5973
Norristown 19403
www.mciu.k12.pa.us

Northeastern Educational IU 19
Dr. Fred Rosetti, dir. 570-876-9200
1200 Line St, Archbald 18403 Fax 876-8660
www.neiu.org

Northwest Tri-County IU 5
Dr. Marjorie Wallace, dir. 814-734-5610
252 Waterford St, Edinboro 16412 Fax 734-5806
www.iu5.org/

Philadelphia IU 26
Dr. Arlene Ackerman, admin. 215-400-4000
440 N Broad St, Philadelphia 19130

Pittsburgh/Mt. Oliver IU 2
Mark Roosevelt, dir. 412-363-0851
515 N Highland Ave Fax 488-7271
Pittsburgh 15206

Riverview IU 6
Dr. William Kaufman, dir. 814-226-7103
270 Mayfield Rd, Clarion 16214 Fax 226-4850
www.riu6.org/

Schuylkill IU 29
Dr. Gerald Achenbach, dir. 570-544-9131
PO Box 130, Mar Lin 17951 Fax 544-6412
www.iu29.org/

Seneca Highlands IU 9
Mary Coif, dir. 814-887-5512
PO Box 1566, Smethport 16749 Fax 887-2157
www.iu9.org

Tuscarora IU 11
Richard Daubert, dir. 717-899-7143
2527 US Highway 522 S
Mc Veytown 17051
www.tiu.k12.pa.us/

Westmoreland IU 7
Dr. Luanne Matta, dir. 724-836-2460
102 Equity Dr, Greensburg 15601 Fax 836-1747
wiu.k12.pa.us/

PUBLIC, PRIVATE AND CATHOLIC ELEMENTARY SCHOOLS

Abington, Montgomery, Pop. 56,600
Abington SD 7,300/K-12
970 Highland Ave 19001 215-884-4700
Amy Sichel Ph.D., supt. Fax 881-2545
www.abington.k12.pa.us
Highland ES 400/K-6
1301 Edge Hill Rd 19001 215-884-1048
Marianne Kaemmer, prin. Fax 517-5039
Overlook ES 400/K-6
1750 Edge Hill Rd 19001 215-657-0857
Carla Greene, prin. Fax 884-3237
Other Schools – See Elkins Park, Glenside, Huntingdon Valley, Roslyn, Rydal, Willow Grove

Our Lady Help of Christians S 300/PK-8
1525 Elkins Ave 19001 215-887-3067
John Bellantoni, prin. Fax 887-3250

Adamstown, Lancaster, Pop. 1,301
Cocalico SD
Supt. — See Denver
Adamstown ES 400/K-5
PO Box 395 19501 717-484-1601
Nathan Van Deusen, prin. Fax 484-1613

Akron, Lancaster, Pop. 4,009
Ephrata Area SD
Supt. — See Ephrata
Akron ES 400/K-5
125 S 11th St 17501 717-859-0400
Mary Enrica Gerhart, prin. Fax 859-4589

Albion, Erie, Pop. 1,558
Northwestern SD 1,800/K-12
100 Harthan Way 16401 814-756-9400
Patrick Kelley, supt. Fax 756-9414
www.nwsd.org
Northwestern ES 500/K-5
10450 John Williams Ave 16401 814-756-9400
Terry Trimble, prin. Fax 756-9466
Northwestern MS 500/6-8
150 Harthan Way 16401 814-756-9400
Sandi Shaner, prin. Fax 756-9415
Other Schools – See East Springfield

Albrightsville, Carbon
Jim Thorpe Area SD
Supt. — See Jim Thorpe
Penn/Kidder S 700/K-8
2937 State Route 903 18210 570-722-1150
Brian Gasper, prin. Fax 722-0317

Alburtis, Lehigh, Pop. 2,203
East Penn SD
Supt. — See Emmaus
Alburtis ES, 222 W 3rd St 18011 500/1-5
Dr. Ronald Renaldi, prin. 610-965-1633

Aldan, Delaware, Pop. 4,294
William Penn SD
Supt. — See Lansdowne
Aldan ES 300/K-6
1 N Woodlawn Ave 19018 610-626-3410
Dr. Sherrell Mickens, prin. Fax 284-8059

Alexandria, Huntingdon, Pop. 382
Juniata Valley SD 800/K-12
PO Box 318 16611 814-669-9150
James Foster, supt. Fax 669-4492
www.jvsd.org/jv/site/default.asp
Juniata Valley ES 400/K-6
PO Box 318 16611 814-669-4422
David Christopher, prin. Fax 669-3413

Aliquippa, Beaver, Pop. 11,105
Aliquippa SD 1,300/K-12
100 Harding Ave 15001 724-857-7500
John Thomas, supt. Fax 857-3404
www.aliquippa.k12.pa.us
Aliquippa ES 500/K-4
800 21st St 15001 724-857-7550
Rachel Gray, prin. Fax 857-7569
Aliquippa MS 400/5-8
100 Harding Ave 15001 724-857-7565
Peter Carbone, prin. Fax 857-7568

Central Valley SD
Supt. — See Monaca
Center Grange PS 400/K-2
225 Center Grange Rd 15001 724-775-8201
Ronald Kitsko, prin. Fax 775-4303

Hopewell Area SD 2,500/K-12
2354 Brodhead Rd 15001 724-375-6691
Dr. Charles Reina, supt. Fax 375-0942
www.hopewell.k12.pa.us
Hopewell ES 300/K-4
3000 Kane Rd 15001 724-375-1111
Sandra Gladis, prin. Fax 375-4729
Hopewell JHS 900/5-8
2354 Brodhead Rd 15001 724-375-7765
Edward Katkich, prin. Fax 378-2594
Independence ES 200/K-4
103 School Rd 15001 724-375-3201
Patricia Simmons, prin. Fax 375-5141
Ross ES 200/K-4
1955 Maratta Rd 15001 724-375-2956
Sandra Gladis, prin. Fax 378-8555

Our Lady of Fatima S 200/PK-8
3005 Fatima Dr 15001 724-375-7565
Linda Liberatore, prin. Fax 375-0219
St. Francis Cabrini S 100/PK-PK
115 Trinity Dr 15001 724-774-4888
Gayle Piroli, prin. Fax 775-3848
St. Titus S 200/K-8
107 Sycamore St 15001 724-375-7940
Janet Escovitz, prin. Fax 375-8893

Allentown, Lehigh, Pop. 106,992
Allentown CSD 18,000/PK-12
PO Box 328 18105 484-765-4000
Karen Angello Ph.D., supt. Fax 765-4230
www.allentownsd.org/
Central ES 800/1-5
829 W Turner St 18102 484-765-4800
Michael Rodriguez, prin. Fax 765-4810
Cleveland ES 300/2-5
424 N 9th St 18102 484-765-4820
Robert Wheeler, prin. Fax 765-4830
Dodd ES 700/K-5
1944 S Church St 18104 484-765-4500
Dr. Tina Belardi, prin. Fax 765-4510
Harrison-Morton MS 800/6-8
137 N 2nd St 18101 484-765-5700
Burdette Chapel, prin. Fax 765-5715
Jackson ES 400/1-5
517 N 15th St 18102 484-765-4840
Marybeth Kornfeind, prin. Fax 765-4850
Jefferson ES 800/K-5
750 Saint John St 18103 484-765-4420
Nicolas Perez, prin. Fax 765-4430
Lehigh Parkway ES 200/1-5
1708 Coronado St 18103 484-765-4440
Betty Shankweiler, prin. Fax 765-4450
Lincoln ECC 500/PK-K
1402 W Walnut St 18102 484-765-5440
Elsie Pletz, prin. Fax 765-5450
McKinley ES 200/1-5
1124 W Turner St 18102 484-765-5460
Richard Kern, prin. Fax 765-5470
Midway Manor ECC 300/K-K
2020 E Pennsylvania St 18109 484-765-5680
Jeffrey Fries, prin. Fax 765-5690
Mosser ES 500/K-5
129 S Dauphin St 18109 484-765-5880
Peter Mayes, prin. Fax 765-5960
Muhlenberg ES 600/K-5
740 N 21st St 18104 484-765-4860
Phillip Turton, prin. Fax 765-4878
Raub MS 1,100/6-8
102 S Saint Cloud St 18104 484-765-5300
Susan Elliott, prin. Fax 765-5310
Ritter ES 500/1-5
740 Plymouth St 18109 484-765-5660
Melissa Marcks, prin. Fax 765-5901
Roosevelt ES 400/1-5
210 W Susquehanna St 18103 484-765-4460
Heather Bennett, prin. Fax 765-4470
Sheridan ES 700/1-5
521 N 2nd St 18102 484-765-4880
Michele Ryan, prin. Fax 765-4890
South Mountain MS 1,300/6-8
709 W Emaus Ave 18103 484-765-4300
Ralph Lovelidge, prin. Fax 765-4310
Trexler MS 1,100/6-8
851 N 15th St 18102 484-765-4600
Karen Gabryluk, prin. Fax 765-4610
Union Terrace ES 700/K-5
1939 W Union St 18104 484-765-5480
David Hahn, prin. Fax 765-5489
Washington ES 500/1-5
837 N 9th St 18102 484-765-4940
Donna Scholtis, prin. Fax 765-4955

Parkland SD 9,100/K-12
1210 Springhouse Rd 18104 610-351-5503
Dr. Louise Donohue, supt. Fax 351-5509
www.parklandsd.org
Cetronia ES 600/K-5
3635 Broadway 18104 610-351-5860
Diana Schantz, prin. Fax 351-5869
Kratzer ES 400/K-5
2200 Huckleberry Rd 18104 610-351-5820
Cheryl McCue, prin. Fax 351-5829
Parkway Manor ES 600/K-5
768 Parkway Rd 18104 610-351-5850
Scott Bartman, prin. Fax 351-5859
Springhouse MS 900/6-8
1200 Springhouse Rd 18104 610-351-5700
Michelle Minotti, prin. Fax 351-5748
Other Schools – See Breinigsville, Coplay, Orefield, Schnecksville

Salisbury Township SD 1,800/K-12
1140 Salisbury Rd 18103 610-797-2062
Mary Anne Wright, supt. Fax 791-9983
www.salisbury.k12.pa.us/
Truman ES 400/K-5
1400 Gaskill St 18103 610-791-2800
Barbara Samide, prin. Fax 797-9640
Western Salisbury ES 300/K-5
3201 Devonshire Rd 18103 610-797-1688
Fax 797-9641

Cathedral of St. Catharine of Siena S 300/K-8
210 N 18th St 18104 610-435-8981
Robin Fredericks, prin. Fax 437-7951
Grace Montessori S 100/PK-4
814 W Linden St 18101 610-435-4060
Priya Amin, dir. Fax 351-6276
Holy Spirit S 100/PK-8
510 Ridge Ave 18102 610-434-4044
Sr. Catherine Bones, prin. Fax 434-5458
Jewish Day S 100/K-8
2313 W Pennsylvania St 18104 610-437-0721
Lehigh Christian Academy 300/PK-8
1151 S Cedar Crest Blvd 18103 610-776-7301
Barbara Williams, prin. Fax 776-1417
Life Academy 200/K-8
855 N Maxwell St 18109 610-434-0703
Sandra Figueroa-Torres, prin. Fax 434-2505
Lutheran Academy 100/K-8
802 N 19th St 18104 610-841-4144
Christine Leonard, prin. Fax 841-4155
Our Lady Help of Christians S 200/K-8
934 Hanover Ave 18109 610-433-1592
Mary Vanya, prin. Fax 434-7123
Sacred Heart S 300/PK-8
325 N 4th St 18102 610-437-3031
James Krupka, prin. Fax 437-2724
St. Francis of Assisi S 200/PK-8
1035 W Washington St 18102 610-435-0364
Angela Tully, prin. Fax 435-2666
St. Paul S 100/K-8
219 W Susquehanna St 18103 610-797-5321
Janet Brogan, prin. Fax 791-5356
St. Thomas More S 600/K-8
1040 Flexer Ave 18103 610-432-0396
Dr. Carl Weber, prin. Fax 432-1395
Swain S 300/PK-8
1100 S 24th St 18103 610-433-4542
Todd Stansbery, prin. Fax 433-3844

Allenwood, Union
Montgomery Area SD
Supt. — See Montgomery
Elimsport ES 100/K-5
69 Petersburg Rd 17810 570-547-1796
Karen Snyder, prin. Fax 547-1908

Allison Park, Allegheny, Pop. 6,000
Hampton Township SD 3,100/K-12
4591 School Dr 15101 412-492-6302
Dr. John Hoover, supt. Fax 487-6898
www.ht-sd.org/
Central ES 500/K-5
4100 Middle Rd 15101 412-492-6320
Cathleen Cubelic, prin. Fax 486-1144
Hampton MS 800/6-8
4589 School Dr 15101 412-492-6356
Dr. Eric Stennett, prin. Fax 487-7544
Wyland ES 400/K-5
2284 Wyland Ave 15101 412-492-6345
Dr. Roberta Good, prin. Fax 486-6718
Other Schools – See Gibsonia

North Allegheny SD
Supt. — See Pittsburgh
Hosack ES 400/K-5
9275 Peebles Rd 15101 412-366-9664
Craig Slaubaugh, prin. Fax 366-9019

Shaler Area SD
Supt. — See Glenshaw
Burchfield PS 400/K-3
1500 Burchfield Rd 15101 412-492-1200
William Tomicek, prin. Fax 486-7631

Providence Heights Alpha S 200/K-8
9000 Babcock Blvd 15101 412-366-4455
Sr. Rochelle Holly, prin. Fax 635-6317
St. Ursula S 200/K-8
3937 Kirk Ave 15101 412-486-5511
Sr. Marie Fedor, prin. Fax 492-7295
Winchester Thurston S - North Hills 100/PK-5
4225 Middle Rd 15101 412-486-8341
Gary Niels, hdmstr. Fax 486-8378

Altoona, Blair, Pop. 47,176
Altoona Area SD 8,000/PK-12
1415 6th Ave 16602 814-946-8211
Dr. Dennis Murray, supt. Fax 946-8375
www.aasdcat.com/aasd/
Baker ES 300/K-6
108 W Ward Ave 16602 814-946-8388
Patrick Labriola, prin. Fax 946-8472
Ebner ES 400/K-6
910 Poland Ave 16601 814-946-8400
Sherry Wells, prin. Fax 946-8580
Irving ES 300/K-6
110 Cherry Ave 16601 814-946-8392
Sherry Buck, prin. Fax 946-8581
Juniata ES 500/K-6
418 N 8th Ave 16601 814-946-8394
Jill Daloisio, prin. Fax 946-8582
Juniata Gap ES 600/K-6
Juniata Gap Rd 16601 814-946-8401
Catherine Keefe, prin. Fax 946-8583
Logan ES 500/K-6
301 Sycamore St 16602 814-946-8370
Erik Dambeck, prin. Fax 946-8584
Penn-Lincoln ES 400/PK-6
411 12th St 16602 814-946-8396
Robert Duffett, prin. Fax 946-8585
Pleasant Valley ES 500/K-6
310 Cayuga Ave 16602 814-946-8397
Susan Richardella, prin. Fax 946-8399
Washington-Jefferson ES 400/PK-6
420 1st St 16602 814-946-8403
Dr. Bernard Joyce, prin. Fax 946-8586
Wright ES 300/K-6
1809 11th St 16601 814-946-8407
Richard Adams, prin. Fax 946-8409

Altoona Central Catholic S 100/PK-8
1400 4th Ave 16602 814-944-1250
Jeffrey Maucieri, prin. Fax 944-1252
Great Commission S 100/K-12
1100 6th Ave 16602 814-942-9710
Van Wiedemann, supt. Fax 942-7147
St. John the Evangelist S 100/PK-8
311 Lotz Ave 16602 814-943-4966
Cheryl Zuiker, prin. Fax 943-8832
St. Rose of Lima S 200/PK-8
5519 6th Ave 16602 814-942-7835
Patricia Ronan, prin. Fax 942-1095
Tender Love for Children S 100/PK-K
1401 12th Ave 16601 814-942-3816
Barbara Crago, dir.

Alverton, Westmoreland
Southmoreland SD
Supt. — See Scottdale
Southmoreland PS 100/K-1
PO Box C 15612 724-887-2027
Tim Scott, prin. Fax 887-2044

Ambler, Montgomery, Pop. 6,349
Hatboro-Horsham SD
Supt. — See Horsham
Limekiln-Simmons S 100/K-K
1125 Limekiln Pike 19002 215-420-5800
Karen Kanter, prin. Fax 420-5829

Wissahickon SD 4,500/K-12
601 Knight Rd 19002 215-619-8000
Dr. Stanley Durtan, supt. Fax 619-8002
wsdweb.org
Lower Gwynedd ES 500/K-5
571 Houston Rd 19002 215-619-8100
Larry Feeley, prin. Fax 619-8101
Mattison Avenue ES 100/K-3
131 Rosemary Ave 19002 215-619-8104
Nicole West, prin. Fax 619-8105
Shady Grove ES 500/K-5
351 W Skippack Pike 19002 215-619-8106
Elizabeth Bauer, prin. Fax 619-8107
Wissahickon MS 1,100/6-8
500 Houston Rd 19002 215-619-8110
Lynda Fields, prin. Fax 619-8111
Other Schools – See Blue Bell

SS. Anthony & Joseph S 200/PK-8
260 Forest Ave 19002 215-646-6150
Kathleen Dilts, prin. Fax 654-5254
Twin Spring Farm Day S 200/PK-6
1632 E Butler Pike 19002 215-646-2665
Lucia Hood, dir. Fax 646-4546

Ambridge, Beaver, Pop. 7,329
Ambridge Area SD 2,900/K-12
740 Park Rd 15003 724-266-2833
Dr. Erwin Weischedel, supt. Fax 266-3981
www.ambridge.k12.pa.us
Highland ES 600/K-6
1101 Highland Ave 15003 724-266-2833
Aphrodite Galitsis, prin. Fax 524-1299
Other Schools – See Baden, Freedom

Anita, Jefferson
Punxsutawney Area SD
Supt. — See Punxsutawney
Parkview ES, PO Box 285 15711 100/K-6
Travis Monroe, prin. 814-938-5120

Annville, Lebanon, Pop. 4,294
Annville-Cleona SD 1,600/K-12
520 S White Oak St 17003 717-867-7600
Marsha Zehner, supt. Fax 867-7610
www.acschools.org
Annville ES 300/4-6
205 S White Oak St 17003 717-867-7620
Nathan Rackley, prin. Fax 867-7624
North Annville ES 200/2-3
755 N State Route 934 17003 717-867-7660
Mary Dague, prin. Fax 867-7664
Other Schools – See Cleona

Northern Lebanon SD
Supt. — See Fredericksburg
East Hanover ES 200/K-6
1098 School House Rd 17003 717-865-3595
Renee Tobias, prin. Fax 865-0608

Apollo, Armstrong, Pop. 1,672
Apollo-Ridge SD 1,500/K-12
1825 State Route 56 15613 724-478-6000
Dr. Cheryl Griffith, supt. Fax 478-1149
www.apolloridge.com/
Other Schools – See Spring Church

Kiski Area SD
Supt. — See Leechburg
North Washington ES 100/K-2
4350 State Route 66 15613 724-727-3421
Pat Marchand, prin. Fax 727-2861
Washington ES 200/3-6
4728 State Route 66 15613 724-727-3426
Pat Marchand, prin. Fax 727-2966

Orchard Hills Christian Academy 50/K-12
385 Kings Rd 15613 724-478-3455
Sandra Cornell, prin. Fax 478-1174

Archbald, Lackawanna, Pop. 6,290
Valley View SD 2,600/K-12
1 Columbus Dr 18403 570-876-5080
Joseph Daley, supt. Fax 876-6365
www.valleyviewsd.org/
Valley View IS 600/3-5
3 Columbus Dr 18403 570-876-2263
James McKane, prin. Fax 803-0355
Valley View MS 600/6-8
1 Columbus Dr 18403 570-876-6461
Craig Sweeney, prin. Fax 803-0276
Other Schools – See Peckville

Ardmore, Montgomery, Pop. 12,646
Haverford Township SD
Supt. — See Havertown
Chestnutwold ES K-5
630 Lorraine Ave 19003 610-853-5900
Timothy Bickhart, prin. Fax 853-5979

Lower Merion SD 6,900/K-12
301 E Montgomery Ave 19003 610-645-1800
Dr. Christopher McGinley, supt. Fax 645-9772
www.lmsd.org
Other Schools – See Bala Cynwyd, Gladwyne, Merion Station, Narberth, Wynnewood

Ardsley, Montgomery

Queen of Peace S 200/K-8
835 N Hills Ave 19038 215-886-4782
Michael Patterson, prin. Fax 887-8328

Arendtsville, Adams, Pop. 893
Upper Adams SD
Supt. — See Biglerville
Arendtsville IS 200/4-6
PO Box 340 17303 717-677-4300
James Kerstetter, prin. Fax 677-6432

Armagh, Indiana, Pop. 125
United SD 1,300/K-12
10780 Route 56 Hwy E 15920 814-446-5618
Dr. Kathy Myers Wunder, supt. Fax 446-6615
www.unitedsd.net/
United ES 700/K-6
10775 Route 56 Hwy E 15920 814-446-5615
Patricia Berezansky, prin. Fax 446-4210

Armbrust, Westmoreland

Armbrust Wesleyan Christian Academy 100/PK-8
PO Box 115 15616 724-925-3830
Betty Sweitzer, prin. Fax 925-1862

Arnold, Westmoreland, Pop. 5,401
New Kensington-Arnold SD
Supt. — See New Kensington
Berkey ES 300/4-5
1739 Victoria Ave 15068 724-335-1713
Thomas Rocchi, prin. Fax 337-5552
Valley MS 500/6-8
1701 Alcoa Dr 15068 724-335-2511
Patrick Nee, prin. Fax 339-5532

Ashland, Schuylkill, Pop. 3,159
North Schuylkill SD 1,200/K-12
15 Academy Ln 17921 570-874-0466
Mark Semanchik, supt. Fax 874-3334
www.northschuylkill.net
North Schuylkill ES, 38 Line St 17921 K-6
Neall Jones, prin. 570-874-3661
Other Schools – See Ringtown

Aspinwall, Allegheny, Pop. 2,789

Christ the Divine Teacher Academy 200/PK-8
205 Brilliant Ave 15215 412-781-7927
John Marino, prin. Fax 781-0891

Aston, Delaware
Chichester SD 3,600/K-12
401 Cherry Tree Rd 19014 610-485-6881
Michael Golde, supt. Fax 485-3086
www.chichestersd.org
Hilltop ES 400/K-4
401 Cherry Tree Rd 19014 610-485-6746
Marjorie Mroz, prin. Fax 859-0606
Other Schools – See Boothwyn, Linwood, Marcus Hook

Penn-Delco SD 3,300/K-12
2821 Concord Rd 19014 610-497-6300
Dr. George Steinhoff, supt. Fax 497-1798
www.pdsd.org
Aston ES 400/K-5
900 Tryens Rd 19014 610-497-6300
Gary Bender, prin. Fax 558-7881
Northley MS 800/6-8
2801 Concord Rd 19014 610-497-6300
Pete Donaghy, prin. Fax 497-5737
Pennell ES 400/K-5
3300 Richard Rd 19014 610-497-6300
Shawn Dutkiewicz, prin. Fax 485-5557
Other Schools – See Brookhaven, Parkside

First Family Christian S 100/K-5
4150 Market St 19014 610-497-0700
Barbara Shergalis, admin. Fax 497-0785
St. Francis De Sales S 200/K-8
39 New Rd 19014 610-459-0799
Sr. Mary Farrell, prin. Fax 558-3058
St. Joseph S 200/PK-8
3265 Concord Rd 19014 610-494-0147
Ann Cook, prin. Fax 497-3383

Atglen, Chester, Pop. 1,350
Octorara Area SD 2,500/K-12
228 Highland Rd Ste 1 19310 610-593-8238
Dr. Thomas Newcome, supt. Fax 593-6425
www.octorara.k12.pa.us
Octorara Area ES 400/3-4
104 Highland Rd 19310 610-593-8238
Kelley Harmer, prin. Fax 593-8248
Octorara Area IS 200/5-6
221 Highland Rd 19310 610-593-8238
Christian Haller, prin. Fax 593-4611
Octorara Area MS 400/7-8
228 Highland Rd 19310 610-593-8238
Jonathan Propper, prin. Fax 593-5185
Octorara Primary Learning Center 600/K-2
87 Highland Rd 19310 610-593-8238
Lisa McNamara, prin. Fax 593-8365

West Fallowfield Christian S 200/K-8
PO Box 279 19310 610-593-5011
Elvin Kennel, prin. Fax 593-6041

Athens, Bradford, Pop. 3,301
Athens Area SD 2,400/K-12
204 Willow St 18810 570-888-7766
Douglas Ulkins, supt. Fax 888-3186
www.athensasd.k12.pa.us
Lynch - Bustin ES 600/K-5
253 Pennsylvania Ave 18810 570-888-7766
Christine Sullivan, prin. Fax 888-8675
Other Schools – See East Smithfield, Gillett, Ulster

Austin, Potter, Pop. 597
Austin Area SD 200/PK-12
138 Costello Ave 16720 814-647-8603
Matthew Hutcheson, supt. Fax 647-8869
www.austinsd.com
Austin Area ES 100/PK-6
138 Costello Ave 16720 814-647-8603
Kimberly Rees, prin. Fax 647-8869

Avella, Washington
Avella Area SD 700/K-12
1000 Avella Rd 15312 724-356-2218
Wayde Killmeyer, supt. Fax 356-2207
www.avella.k12.pa.us
Avella ES 400/K-6
1000 Avella Rd 15312 724-356-2294
Joel Kirsch, prin. Fax 356-7892

Avis, Clinton, Pop. 1,472

Walnut Street Christian S 200/PK-12
PO Box 616 17721 570-753-3400
Kathy Gottschall, prin. Fax 753-5728

Baden, Beaver, Pop. 4,172
Ambridge Area SD
Supt. — See Ambridge
State Street ES 300/K-6
600 Harmony Rd 15005 724-266-2833
Barry King, prin. Fax 869-1030

Mt. Gallitzin Academy 200/PK-8
1016 W State St 15005 724-869-2505
Sr. Christine Hill, prin. Fax 869-4932

Bainbridge, Lancaster
Elizabethtown Area SD
Supt. — See Elizabethtown
Bainbridge ES 300/K-5
PO Box 305 17502 717-426-4203
Lois Brewer, prin. Fax 426-0134

Bala Cynwyd, Montgomery, Pop. 8,000
Lower Merion SD
Supt. — See Ardmore
Bala-Cynwyd MS 800/6-8
510 Bryn Mawr Ave 19004 610-645-1480
Dr. Patricia Haupt, prin.
Belmont Hills ES, 200 School St 19004 400/K-5
Judy Vietri, prin. 610-645-1420
Cynwyd ES 500/K-5
101 W Levering Mill Rd 19004 610-645-1430
Connie DiMedio, prin.

French International S of Philadelphia 300/PK-8
150 Highland Ave 19004 610-667-1284
Pascale Davidson, hdmstr. Fax 667-1286

Bally, Berks, Pop. 1,102

St. Francis Academy 200/PK-8
668 Pine St 19503 610-845-7364
Thomas Murphy, prin. Fax 845-2223

Bangor, Northampton, Pop. 5,305
Bangor Area SD 3,600/K-12
123 Five Points Richmond Rd 18013 610-588-2163
John Reinhart, supt. Fax 599-7040
www.bangor.k12.pa.us
Bangor Area MS 600/7-8
401 Five Points Richmond Rd 18013 610-599-7012
Allison Tucker, prin. Fax 599-7045
Defranco ES 800/4-6
267 Five Points Richmond Rd 18013 610-599-7013
Roberta Walker, prin. Fax 599-7041
Five Points ES 800/K-3
363 Five Points Richmond Rd 18013 610-599-7015
Mario Lucrezi, prin. Fax 599-7042
Washington ES 200/K-4
381 Washington Blvd 18013 610-599-7014
Lynne Bustos, prin. Fax 599-7046

Barto, Berks
Boyertown Area SD
Supt. — See Boyertown
Washington ES 700/K-6
1406 Route 100 19504 610-754-9589
Christopher Iacobelli, prin.

Bath, Northampton, Pop. 2,768
Northampton Area SD
Supt. — See Northampton
Moore Township ES 600/K-6
2835 Mountain View Dr 18014 610-837-1859
Curtis Dimmick, prin. Fax 837-7239
Wolf ES 700/K-6
300 Allen St 18014 610-837-1833
Michael Monaghan, prin. Fax 837-7308

Sacred Heart S 200/PK-8
115 Washington St 18014 610-837-6391
Donna Blaszka, prin. Fax 837-2469

Beaver, Beaver, Pop. 4,550
Beaver Area SD 1,600/K-12
855 2nd St Ste 6 15009 724-774-4010
Dr. John Hansen, supt. Fax 774-8770
www.basd.k12.pa.us/
Beaver Area MS 300/7-8
Gypsy Glen Rd 15009 724-774-0253
Carrie Rowe, prin. Fax 774-3926

College Square ES 200/K-2
375 College Ave 15009 724-774-9126
Dennis Pittman, prin. Fax 774-1168
Dutch Ridge ES 400/3-6
2220 Dutch Ridge Rd 15009 724-774-1016
Steve Grossman, prin. Fax 774-1033

SS. Peter & Paul S 200/K-8
370 E End Ave 15009 724-774-4450
Judith Deelo, prin. Fax 774-5192

Beaver Falls, Beaver, Pop. 9,402
Big Beaver Falls Area SD 1,800/K-12
1503 8th Ave 15010 724-843-3470
Donna Nugent, supt. Fax 843-2360
www.tigerweb.org
Beaver Falls MS 400/6-8
1601 8th Ave 15010 724-846-5470
Thomas House, prin. Fax 846-2579
Central ES 400/K-5
805 15th St 15010 724-843-3420
Linda Edel, prin. Fax 843-5740
Other Schools – See Darlington

Blackhawk SD 2,700/K-12
500 Blackhawk Rd 15010 724-846-6600
Dr. Paul Kasunich, supt. Fax 846-2021
www.bsd.k12.pa.us
Blackhawk IS 600/3-5
635 Shenango Rd 15010 724-843-5050
Carol Sprinker, prin. Fax 843-9175
Highland MS 400/6-7
402 Shenango Rd 15010 724-843-1700
Nancy Bowman, prin. Fax 843-0934
Patterson ES 200/K-2
701 Darlington Rd 15010 724-843-1268
Jane Fucci, prin. Fax 846-8082
Other Schools – See Darlington

Beaver County Christian S 200/K-8
3601 Short St 15010 724-843-8331
Jeffrey Miller, prin. Fax 891-3315
Divine Mercy Academy 100/PK-8
609 10th St 15010 724-846-5955
Annie Raybuck, prin. Fax 846-1894

Beaver Springs, Snyder
Midd-West SD
Supt. — See Middleburg
West Snyder MS 300/5-8
645 Snyder Ave 17812 570-658-8144
David Harrison, prin. Fax 658-7287

Bechtelsville, Berks, Pop. 975

Brookeside Montessori S 100/PK-6
1075 Route 100 19505 610-473-0408
Robin John, prin. Fax 473-9142

Bedford, Bedford, Pop. 3,051
Bedford Area SD 2,300/K-12
330 E John St 15522 814-623-4295
Dr. Glenn Thompson, supt. Fax 623-4299
www.bedford.k12.pa.us
Bedford ES 800/K-5
3639 Business 220 15522 814-623-4221
Leslie Turkovich, prin. Fax 623-3989
Bedford MS 400/6-8
440 E Watson St 15522 814-623-4200
Fax 623-4214
Other Schools – See Hyndman

St. Thomas the Apostle S 100/PK-5
129 W Penn St 15522 814-623-8873
Joyce Wityk, prin. Fax 623-1208

Bellefonte, Centre, Pop. 6,161
Bellefonte Area SD 3,000/K-12
318 N Allegheny St 16823 814-355-4814
James T. Masullo, supt. Fax 353-5342
www.basd.net
Bellefonte Area MS 700/6-8
100 N School St 16823 814-355-5466
Karen Krisch, prin. Fax 353-5350
Bellefonte ES 400/K-5
100 W Linn St 16823 814-355-5519
Elaine Cutler, prin. Fax 353-5338
Benner ES 200/K-5
490 Buffalo Run Rd 16823 814-355-2812
Connie Puckett, prin. Fax 353-5339
Marion-Walker ES 300/K-5
100 School Dr 16823 814-357-2425
Sherry Yontosh, prin. Fax 357-2426
Other Schools – See Pleasant Gap

Centre County Christian Academy 100/PK-12
100 Hertzler Dr 16823 814-355-7805
Dr. Robert Baylor, admin. Fax 355-9395
St. John the Evangelist S 100/PK-5
116 E Bishop St 16823 814-355-7859
Pamela Vaiana, prin. Fax 355-2939

Belle Vernon, Fayette, Pop. 1,163
Belle Vernon Area SD 2,900/K-12
270 Crest Ave 15012 724-929-5262
Robert Nagy, supt. Fax 930-9460
www.bvasd.net/
Bellmar MS, 500 Perry Ave 15012 300/6-8
Stephen Russell, prin. 724-929-9030
Marion ES, 500 Perry Ave 15012 600/K-5
Dr. Keith McMonagle, prin. 724-929-7444
Rostraver ES, 300 Crest Ave 15012 600/K-5
Frederick Labutta, prin. 724-929-8883
Rostraver MS, 250 Crest Ave 15012 300/6-8
Dr. John Folmar, prin. 724-929-2993

St. Sebastian S 300/PK-8
815 Broad Ave 15012 724-929-5143
Steven Dorko, prin. Fax 929-3038

Belleville, Mifflin, Pop. 1,589
Mifflin County SD
Supt. — See Lewistown
Union Township ES 100/K-5
PO Box 978 17004 717-248-7154
Michael Lamarca, prin. Fax 935-5454

Belleville Mennonite S 200/PK-12
4105 Front Mountain Rd 17004 717-935-2184
R. Ann Kanagy, supt. Fax 935-5641

Bellevue, Allegheny, Pop. 8,231
Northgate SD
Supt. — See Pittsburgh
Bellevue ES 400/K-6
435 Lincoln Ave 15202 412-732-3300
John Primrose, prin. Fax 734-8047

Bellwood, Blair, Pop. 1,916
Bellwood-Antis SD 1,300/K-12
400 Martin St 16617 814-742-2271
G. Brian Toth, supt. Fax 742-9049
www.blwd.k12.pa.us
Bellwood-Antis MS 400/5-8
400 Martin St 16617 814-742-2273
Donald Wagner, prin. Fax 742-9817
Myers ES 500/K-4
220 Martin St 16617 814-742-2272
Terri Harpster, prin. Fax 742-9040

Bendersville, Adams, Pop. 603
Upper Adams SD
Supt. — See Biglerville
Bendersville IS 200/4-6
PO Box 447 17306 717-677-3300
Ann Wolfe, prin. Fax 677-9385

Bensalem, Bucks, Pop. 59,700
Bensalem Township SD 6,100/K-12
3000 Donallen Dr 19020 215-750-2800
Dr. James Lombardo, supt. Fax 359-0181
www.bensalemsd.org/
Belmont Hills ES 700/K-6
5000 Neshaminy Blvd 19020 215-750-2800
Marla Zeisler, prin. Fax 750-2887
Cornwells ES 500/K-6
2215 Hulmeville Rd 19020 215-750-2800
Shawn Mark, prin. Fax 245-3559
Faust ES 500/K-6
2901 Bellview Dr 19020 215-750-2800
Maribel Camps, prin. Fax 244-2973
Rush ES 400/K-6
3400 Hulmeville Rd 19020 215-750-2800
Dr. Mary Gentile, prin. Fax 244-2976
Shafer MS 500/7-8
3333 Hulmeville Rd 19020 215-750-2800
William Incollingo, prin. Fax 244-2964
Snyder MS 400/7-8
3330 Hulmeville Rd 19020 215-750-2800
Dr. Deborah McKay, prin. Fax 244-2851
Struble ES 500/K-6
4300 Bensalem Blvd 19020 215-750-2800
Lana Judy, prin. Fax 244-2803
Valley ES 400/K-6
3100 Donallen Dr 19020 215-750-2800
Mary Glaesser, prin. Fax 750-2880

Christian Life S 200/PK-K
3100 Galloway Rd 19020 215-752-2823
Joanna Ratz, dir. Fax 752-2607
Our Lady of Fatima S 200/PK-8
2915 Street Rd 19020 215-638-3256
Sr. Barbara Browne, prin. Fax 639-6424
St. Charles Borromeo S 300/PK-8
1704 Bristol Pike 19020 215-639-3456
Sr. Rita Marian Angelilli, prin. Fax 639-0496
St. Ephrem S 500/K-8
5340 Hulmeville Rd 19020 215-639-9488
Sr. Barbara Brahl, prin. Fax 639-0206

Bentleyville, Washington, Pop. 2,448
Bentworth SD 1,200/K-12
150 Bearcat Dr 15314 724-239-2861
Charles Baker, supt. Fax 239-2865
bentworth.org
Bentworth ES 600/K-6
100 Bearcat Dr 15314 724-239-3606
Susanne Macik, prin. Fax 239-3205
Other Schools – See Ellsworth

Benton, Columbia, Pop. 923
Benton Area SD 800/K-12
600 Green Acres Rd 17814 570-925-6651
Gary Powlus, supt. Fax 925-6973
www.bentonsd.k12.pa.us/
Appleman ES 400/K-6
600 Green Acres Rd 17814 570-925-6971
William Jones, prin. Fax 925-5405

Berlin, Somerset, Pop. 2,130
Berlin Brothersvalley SD 1,000/K-12
1025 Main St 15530 814-267-4621
Margie Zorn, supt. Fax 267-6060
www.bbsd.com/
Berlin Brothersvalley ES 400/K-4
1025 Main St 15530 814-267-4623
Pamela Webreck, prin. Fax 267-6060
Berlin Brothersvalley MS 300/5-8
1025 Main St 15530 814-267-6931
Martin Mudry, prin. Fax 267-6060

Bernville, Berks, Pop. 881
Tulpehocken Area SD 1,700/K-12
428 New Schaefferstown Rd 19506 610-488-9555
Fax 488-7914
www.tulpehocken.org
Penn Bernville ES 400/K-6
24 Shartlesville Rd 19506 610-488-6248
Bonnie Benfer, prin. Fax 488-1188
Other Schools – See Bethel

Berwick, Columbia, Pop. 10,352
Berwick Area SD 3,200/K-12
500 Line St 18603 570-759-6400
Wayne Brookhart, supt. Fax 759-6439
www.berwicksd.org
Berwick Area MS 900/6-8
1100 Evergreen Dr 18603 570-759-6400
Ralph Norce, prin. Fax 759-7978
Fourteenth Street ES 200/K-5
1401 N Market St 18603 570-759-6400
Sally DeFinnis, prin. Fax 759-6499
Orange Street ES 400/K-5
845 Orange St 18603 570-759-6400
Randy Peters, prin. Fax 759-2461
Salem ES 500/K-5
810 E 10th St 18603 570-759-6400
Robert Bulkley, prin. Fax 759-2784
Other Schools – See Nescopeck

Holy Family Consolidated S 100/PK-5
728 Washington St 18603 570-752-2021
Sr. Judith Tarozzi, prin. Fax 752-2914

Berwyn, See Devon
Tredyffrin-Easttown SD
Supt. — See Wayne
Hillside ES 500/K-4
507 Howellville Rd 19312 610-240-1500
Diane Cohle, prin. Fax 240-1510
Tredyffrin-Easttown MS 900/5-8
801 Conestoga Rd 19312 610-240-1200
Mark Cataldi, prin. Fax 240-1225

St. Monica S 200/PK-8
601 1st Ave 19312 610-644-8848
Diana Thompson, prin. Fax 695-8515
Tarleton S 100/PK-1
327 Waterloo Ave 19312 610-644-5623

Bessemer, Lawrence, Pop. 1,126
Mohawk Area SD 1,800/K-12
PO Box 25 16112 724-667-7723
Dr. Timothy McNamee, supt. Fax 667-0602
www.mohawk.k12.pa.us
Mohawk ES 800/K-6
PO Box 799 16112 724-667-7749
Patricia Monaco, prin. Fax 667-7235

Bethel, Berks
Tulpehocken Area SD
Supt. — See Bernville
Bethel ES 400/K-6
8390 Lancaster Ave 19507 717-933-4131
Cynthia Jenkins, prin. Fax 933-8485

Bethel Park, Allegheny, Pop. 32,313
Bethel Park SD 5,000/K-12
301 Church Rd 15102 412-854-8402
Dr. Thomas Knight, supt. Fax 854-8430
www.bpsd.org
Armstrong MS 800/5-6
5800 Murray Ave 15102 412-854-8751
Janet O'Rourke, prin. Fax 833-5029
Bethel Memorial ES 300/K-4
3301 S Park Rd 15102 412-854-8506
Eric Chalus, prin. Fax 833-5014
Franklin ES 400/K-4
5400 Florida Ave 15102 412-854-8741
Dr. Shirley Dickinson, prin. Fax 833-5016
Independence MS 800/7-8
2807 Bethel Church Rd 15102 412-854-8677
David Muench, prin. Fax 854-8732
Penn ES 200/K-4
110 Woodlet Ln 15102 412-854-8522
George Spalaris, prin. Fax 854-8411
Washington ES 300/K-4
515 Clifton Rd 15102 412-854-8546
Fred Pearson, prin. Fax 854-8435
Other Schools – See Pittsburgh

Hillcrest Christian Academy 300/PK-8
2500 Bethel Church Rd 15102 412-854-4040
Dr. Kenneth Barbour, prin. Fax 854-4051
St. Katharine Drexel S 100/PK-8
7001 Baptist Rd 15102 412-833-0223
Patricia Bibro, prin. Fax 347-0361
St. Valentine S 200/PK-8
2709 Mesta St 15102 412-835-3780
Anna Watt, prin. Fax 835-4417

Bethlehem, Northampton, Pop. 72,895
Bethlehem Area SD 15,200/K-12
1516 Sycamore St 18017 610-861-0500
Dr. Joseph Lewis, supt. Fax 807-5599
www.beth.k12.pa.us/
Broughal MS 600/6-8
125 W Packer Ave 18015 610-866-5041
Joseph Santoro, prin. Fax 807-5909
Buchanan ES 300/K-5
1621 Catasauqua Rd 18017 610-865-1766
Mary Tachovsky, prin. Fax 807-5503
Calypso ES 300/K-5
1021 Calypso Ave 18018 610-691-0152
Dr. Elizabeth Conard, prin. Fax 807-5565
Clearview ES 400/K-5
2121 Abington Rd 18018 610-868-5994
Mary Colon, prin. Fax 807-5525
Donegan ES 600/K-5
1210 E 4th St 18015 610-866-0031
Kathleen Quigney, prin. Fax 807-5524
East Hills MS 1,200/6-8
2005 Chester Rd 18017 610-867-0541
David Horvath, prin. Fax 807-5941
Fountain Hill ES 700/K-5
1330 Church St 18015 610-865-5881
Nathan Stannard, prin. Fax 807-5989
Hanover ES 300/K-5
3890 Jacksonville Rd 18017 610-691-3210
Michael Metarko, prin. Fax 807-5560

Jefferson ES 300/K-5
404 E North St 18018 610-691-1776
Karen Aulisio, prin. Fax 807-5981
Lincoln ES 400/K-5
1260 Gresham St 18017 610-866-8727
Benita Draper-Smith, prin. Fax 807-5545
Marvine ES 300/K-5
1425 Livingston St 18017 610-865-0012
Karen Gomez, prin. Fax 849-6558
Miller Heights ES 500/K-5
3605 Allen St 18020 610-868-6441
Deborah Roeder, prin. Fax 807-5549
Nitschmann MS 900/6-8
909 W Union Blvd 18018 610-866-5781
Jacqueline Santarasto, prin. Fax 866-1435
Northeast MS 800/6-8
1170 Fernwood St 18018 610-868-8581
Joseph Rahs, prin. Fax 807-5997
Packer ES 400/K-5
1650 Kenwood Dr 18017 610-865-0660
Carol Jacoby, prin. Fax 807-5540
Penn ES 200/K-5
1002 Main St 18018 610-694-0116
Lisa Lynch, prin. Fax 807-5532
Spring Garden ES 500/K-5
901 North Blvd 18017 610-868-6071
Eric Smith, prin. Fax 807-5931
Wolf ES 500/K-5
1920 Butztown Rd 18017 610-867-8191
Jodi Sponchiado, prin. Fax 867-6768
Other Schools – See Easton, Freemansburg

Southern Lehigh SD
Supt. — See Center Valley
Southern Lehigh IS 4-6
5438 Route 378 18015 610-282-3121
Mary Farris, prin. Fax 861-4040

Bethlehem Christian S Calvary Campus 100/5-8
111 Dewberry Ave 18017 610-865-9878
Tim Wilkins, supt. Fax 954-9504
Bethlehem Christian S Ebenezer Campus 200/K-4
3100 Hecktown Rd 18020 610-868-6020
Tim Wilkins, supt. Fax 868-6939
Covenant Christian Academy 50/K-8
1414 Pennsylvania Ave 18018 610-868-7302
Philip Miller, prin. Fax 866-0269
Holy Infancy S 200/PK-8
127 E 4th St 18015 610-868-2621
Sr. Joyce Valese, prin. Fax 868-5402
Moravian Academy - Lower S 300/PK-5
422 Heckewelder Pl 18018 610-868-8571
George King, hdmstr. Fax 868-9319
Moravian Academy MS 200/6-8
11 W Market St 18018 610-866-6677
George King, hdmstr. Fax 866-6337
Notre Dame of Bethlehem S 400/PK-8
1835 Catasauqua Rd 18018 610-866-2231
Kathy Maziarz, prin. Fax 866-4374
Our Lady of Perpetual Help S 300/K-8
3221 Santee Rd 18020 610-868-6570
Harry Reese, prin. Fax 868-7941
Sacred Heart S 200/K-8
1814 2nd St 18020 610-867-0221
John Schulte, prin. Fax 867-8351
St. Anne S 400/PK-8
375 Hickory St 18017 610-868-4182
Annette Filler, prin. Fax 868-8709
St. Michael the Archangel S 400/PK-8
4121 Old Bethlehem Pike 18015 610-965-4441
Carol Sonon, prin. Fax 865-2098
Seton Academy 300/PK-8
623 6th Ave 18018 610-867-9530
Joan West, prin. Fax 868-6784

Bigler, Clearfield
Clearfield Area SD
Supt. — See Clearfield
Bradford Township ES 200/K-4
50 Bigler Rd 16825 814-857-7607
Mary Sayers, prin. Fax 857-5215

Biglerville, Adams, Pop. 1,152
Upper Adams SD 1,600/K-12
PO Box 847 17307 717-677-7191
Eric Eshbach, supt. Fax 677-9807
www.uasd.k12.pa.us
Biglerville PS 400/K-3
3270 Biglerville Rd 17307 717-677-5200
Kathleen Ciolino, prin. Fax 677-0101
Upper Adams MS 300/7-8
161 N Main St 17307 717-677-7191
David Zinn, prin. Fax 677-0219
Other Schools – See Arendtsville, Bendersville

Bird in Hand, Lancaster

Weavertown Mennonite S 200/K-8
73 Orchard Rd 17505 717-768-3627

Birdsboro, Berks, Pop. 5,191
Daniel Boone Area SD 3,300/K-12
PO Box 490 19508 610-582-6140
Dr. Gary Otto, supt. Fax 582-0059
www.dboone.org
Birdsboro Elementary Center 500/1-5
400 W 2nd St 19508 610-582-6190
Marybeth Kiesel, prin. Fax 582-6169
Monocacy ES K-4
576 Monocacy Creek Rd 19508 610-385-6800
Melanie Hefter, prin. Fax 385-6810
Other Schools – See Douglassville

Twin Valley SD
Supt. — See Elverson
Robeson ES 400/K-4
801 White Bear Rd 19508 610-582-9580
Bill McKay, prin. Fax 582-9588

Berks Christian S 100/K-12
926 Philadelphia Ter 19508 610-582-1000
Frank Love, admin. Fax 404-0126

Blain, Perry, Pop. 246
West Perry SD
Supt. — See Elliottsburg
Blain ES 300/K-5
132 Blain Rd 17006 717-536-3219
Lucas Clouse, prin. Fax 536-3718

Blairsville, Indiana, Pop. 3,460
Blairsville-Saltsburg SD 2,000/K-12
102 School Ln 15717 724-459-5500
Joseph Marasti Ed.D., supt. Fax 459-9209
www.b-ssd.org
Blairsville ES 500/K-5
106 School Ln 15717 724-459-8883
Debra Shirley, prin. Fax 459-7985
Blairsville MS 300/6-8
104 School Ln 15717 724-459-8880
Joseph Baker, prin. Fax 459-0213
Other Schools – See Saltsburg

Blanchard, Centre
Keystone Central SD
Supt. — See Lock Haven
Liberty Curtin ES 300/K-5
PO Box 329 16826 570-962-2008
Steve Kreger, prin. Fax 962-3124

Blandon, Berks
Fleetwood Area SD
Supt. — See Fleetwood
Maier ES 500/K-4
355 Andrew Maier Blvd 19510 610-926-2502
Steve Schutt, prin. Fax 926-0923

Bloomsburg, Columbia, Pop. 12,915
Bloomsburg Area SD 1,700/K-12
728 E 5th St 17815 570-784-5000
Joseph Kelly, supt. Fax 387-8832
bloomsburgasd.schoolwires.com
Beaver-Main ES 100/K-5
245 Beaver Valley Rd 17815 570-784-0309
Michael Pawlik, prin. Fax 784-4308
Bloomsburg Area MS 400/6-8
1100 Railroad St 17815 570-784-9100
Lee Gump, prin. Fax 387-3491
Evans Memorial ES 300/K-5
59 Perry Ave 17815 570-784-3167
Michael Pawlik, prin. Fax 784-4314
Memorial ES 400/K-5
500 Market St 17815 570-784-7885
Ryan Moran, prin. Fax 784-4341

Central Columbia SD 2,100/K-12
4777 Old Berwick Rd 17815 570-784-2850
Harry Mathias, supt. Fax 387-0192
www.ccsd.cc
Central Columbia ES 700/K-4
4777 Old Berwick Rd 17815 570-784-6120
Helen Lewis, prin. Fax 784-2582
Central Columbia MS 700/5-8
4777 Old Berwick Rd 17815 570-784-2850
Chad Heintzelman, prin. Fax 784-4935

Columbia County Christian S 200/PK-12
123 Schoolhouse Rd 17815 570-784-2977
Charles Atkins, hdmstr. Fax 784-1755
St. Columba S 100/PK-8
40 E 3rd St 17815 570-784-5932
Mary Ann Venarchick, prin. Fax 387-1257

Blossburg, Tioga, Pop. 1,477
Southern Tioga SD 2,200/K-12
241 Main St 16912 570-638-2183
Joseph Kalata, supt. Fax 638-3512
www.southerntioga.org
Blossburg ES 300/K-6
133 Hannibal St 16912 570-638-2146
Albert Lindner, prin. Fax 638-2150
Other Schools – See Liberty, Mansfield

Blue Bell, Montgomery, Pop. 6,091
Wissahickon SD
Supt. — See Ambler
Blue Bell ES 400/K-5
801 Symphony Ln 19422 215-619-8102
Denise Fagan, prin. Fax 619-8103
Stony Creek ES 400/K-5
1721 Yost Rd 19422 215-619-8108
Dr. Joan Evans, prin. Fax 619-8109

Centre Square Montessori S 100/PK-K
1775 Skippack Pike 19422 610-275-1775
Patricia McNicholas, dir. Fax 272-6719
Oak Lane Day S 100/PK-6
137 Stenton Ave 19422 610-825-1055
Karl Welsh, hdmstr. Fax 825-9288
St. Helena S 400/K-8
1499 DeKalb Pike 19422 610-279-3345
Sr. Cathe Shoulberg, prin. Fax 279-3272

Bobtown, Greene, Pop. 1,100
Southeastern Greene SD
Supt. — See Greensboro
Bobtown ES 400/K-6
PO Box 58 15315 724-839-7241
Scott Sinn, prin. Fax 839-7575

Boiling Springs, Cumberland, Pop. 1,978
Cumberland Valley SD
Supt. — See Mechanicsburg
Monroe ES 300/K-5
1240 Boiling Springs Rd 17007 717-258-6208
William Creps, prin. Fax 258-8819

South Middleton SD 2,200/K-12
4 Forge Rd 17007 717-258-6484
Patricia Sanker Ed.D., supt. Fax 258-1214
www.bubblers.k12.pa.us
Iron Forge Educational Center 300/4-5
4 Forge Rd 17007 717-258-6484
Janet Adams, prin. Fax 243-3009
Yellow Breeches MS 500/6-8
4 Forge Rd 17007 717-258-6484
Frederick Withum, prin. Fax 258-0301
Other Schools – See Mount Holly Springs

Boothwyn, Delaware, Pop. 5,069
Chichester SD
Supt. — See Aston
Boothwyn ES 300/K-4
PO Box 2100 19061 610-485-4241
Kathleen Sherman, prin. Fax 494-1786
Chichester MS 1,100/5-8
PO Box 2100 19061 610-485-6881
Paula Husar, prin. Fax 494-3064

Boswell, Somerset, Pop. 1,290
North Star SD 900/K-12
1200 Morris Ave 15531 814-629-5631
Dennis Leyman, supt. Fax 629-6181
district.nscougars.com/
North Star Central ES 300/K-4
1215 Morris Ave 15531 814-629-5627
Dawn Maluchnick, prin. Fax 629-5295
Other Schools – See Stoystown

Boyertown, Berks, Pop. 3,946
Boyertown Area SD 7,000/K-12
911 Montgomery Ave 19512 610-367-6031
Dr. Harry Morgan, supt. Fax 369-7620
basd.netjunction.com
Boyertown ES, 641 E 2nd St 19512 700/K-6
Greg Miller, prin. 610-369-7462
Colebrookdale ES 300/K-6
1001 Montgomery Ave 19512 610-369-7427
Dr. Thomas Shugar, prin.
Earl ES, 22 School House Rd 19512 300/K-6
Dr. Craig Zerr, prin. 610-369-7504
Pine Forge ES, 8 Glendale Rd 19512 300/K-6
Melissa Woodard, prin. 610-323-7609
Other Schools – See Barto, Frederick, Gilbertsville

Brackenridge, Allegheny, Pop. 3,322
Highlands SD
Supt. — See Natrona Heights
Fairmount ES 200/K-5
1060 Atlantic Ave 15014 724-224-5880
Charles Mort, prin. Fax 224-2413

Braddock, Allegheny, Pop. 2,744
Woodland Hills SD
Supt. — See Pittsburgh
Fairless IS 400/4-6
531 Jones Ave 15104 412-271-1317
Dr. Deborah Vereen, prin. Fax 271-6657

Good Shepherd S 100/K-8
1025 Braddock Ave 15104 412-271-2492
Sr. Marie Novachek, prin. Fax 271-3248

Bradford, McKean, Pop. 8,651
Bradford Area SD 2,800/PK-12
PO Box 375 16701 814-362-3841
Sandra Romanowski, supt. Fax 362-2552
www.bradfordareaschools.org
Blaisdell ES 600/PK-2
265 Constitution Ave 16701 814-362-6834
David Jones, prin. Fax 362-7163
Fretz MS 700/6-8
140 Lorana Ave 16701 814-362-3500
Tina Slaven, prin. Fax 362-1812
School Street ES 500/3-5
76 School St 16701 814-368-3183
Sarah Tingley, prin. Fax 362-5232

Bradford Area Christian Academy 50/PK-6
23 Chambers St 16701 814-368-6800
Jim Machuga, prin. Fax 362-3585
Learning Center 100/PK-6
90 Jackson Ave 16701 814-368-6622
St. Bernard S 200/PK-8
450 W Washington St 16701 814-368-5302
Kimberly Mooney, prin. Fax 368-1464

Bradfordwoods, Allegheny, Pop. 1,097
North Allegheny SD
Supt. — See Pittsburgh
Bradford Woods ES 400/K-5
41 Forest Rd 15015 724-935-5081
Debra Somerhalder, prin. Fax 935-6076

Breezewood, Bedford
Everett Area SD
Supt. — See Everett
Breezewood ES 100/K-5
133 N Main St 15533 814-652-9114
James Droz, lead tchr. Fax 735-2495

Breinigsville, Lehigh
Parkland SD
Supt. — See Allentown
Fogelsville ES 600/K-5
312 S Route 100 18031 610-351-5800
Diane Neikam, prin. Fax 351-5809

Brentwood, Allegheny, Pop. 9,811
Brentwood Borough SD
Supt. — See Pittsburgh
Elroy Avenue ES 300/K-5
3129 Elroy Ave 15227 412-881-4484
Amy Burch, prin. Fax 881-9448

Bridgeport, Montgomery, Pop. 4,402
Upper Merion Area SD
Supt. — See King of Prussia
Bridgeport ES 300/K-4
900 Bush St 19405 610-205-3601
Alan Futrick, prin. Fax 205-3649

Bridgeville, Allegheny, Pop. 5,022
Chartiers Valley SD
Supt. — See Pittsburgh
Chartiers Valley MS 800/6-8
50 Thoms Run Rd 15017 412-429-2220
John Ackermann, prin. Fax 429-2226
Chartiers Valley PS 700/K-2
125 Thoms Run Rd 15017 412-429-3270
Kevin Kuhn, prin. Fax 429-7030

Holy Child S 200/PK-8
220 Station St 15017 412-221-4720
Sr. Barbara Quinn, prin. Fax 257-9742
Zion Lutheran S 100/PK-PK
3197 Washington Pike 15017 412-221-4776
Carole Davis, dir. Fax 220-9741

Bristol, Bucks, Pop. 9,810
Bristol Borough SD 1,300/PK-12
420 Buckley St 19007 215-781-1011
Dr. Broadus Davis, supt. Fax 781-1012
www.bbsd.org/
Bristol MS, 1801 Wilson Ave 19007 200/7-8
Thomas Shaffer, prin. 215-781-1034
Snyder-Girotti ES 700/PK-6
420 Buckley St 19007 215-781-1020
Rosemary Parmigiani, prin.

Bristol Township SD
Supt. — See Levittown
LaFayette ES 300/K-6
4201 Fayette Dr 19007 215-788-5400
James Moore, prin. Fax 788-8283
Roosevelt MS 400/7-8
1001 New Rodgers Rd 19007 215-788-0436
Ruth Geisel, prin. Fax 788-2629

St. Ann S 200/K-8
418 Jefferson Ave 19007 215-788-2030
Sr. Mary Donald, prin. Fax 788-2979
St. Mark S 200/K-8
1024 Radcliffe St 19007 215-785-0973
Angelina Clair, prin. Fax 781-0268

Brockway, Jefferson, Pop. 2,101
Brockway Area SD 1,100/K-12
40 North St 15824 814-265-8411
Stephen Zarlinski, supt. Fax 265-8498
www.brockway.k12.pa.us/
Brockway Area ES 600/K-6
40 North St 15824 814-265-8417
Amy Glasl, prin. Fax 265-8498

Brodheadsville, Monroe, Pop. 1,389
Pleasant Valley SD 6,800/K-12
1 School Ln 18322 570-402-1000
Dr. Douglas Arnold, supt. Fax 992-7275
www.pvbears.org/
Chestnuthill ES 200/K-4
Route 115 18322 570-402-1000
Joseph Kondisko, prin. Fax 992-5610
Other Schools – See Kresgeville, Kunkletown

Brogue, York
Red Lion Area SD
Supt. — See Red Lion
Clearview ES 300/K-6
2650 Delta Rd 17309 717-927-6791
Jayne LeGore, prin. Fax 927-6545

Brookhaven, Delaware, Pop. 7,849
Chester-Upland SD
Supt. — See Chester
Toby Farms S 500/PK-8
201 Bridgewater Rd 19015 610-447-3815
Patricia Sofia, prin. Fax 447-3991

Penn-Delco SD
Supt. — See Aston
Coebourn ES 300/K-5
1 Coeburn Blvd 19015 610-497-6300
Dr. Holly Acosta, prin. Fax 876-4938

Christian Academy 400/K-12
4301 Chandler Dr 19015 610-872-7600
Anita Gray, prin. Fax 876-2173
Our Lady of Charity S 200/PK-8
245 Upland Rd 19015 610-874-0410
Marie Anderson, prin. Fax 874-5879

Brookville, Jefferson, Pop. 4,077
Brookville Area SD 1,800/K-12
PO Box 479 15825 814-849-1100
Sandra Craft, supt. Fax 849-6842
Hickory Grove ES 500/3-6
PO Box 479 15825 814-849-1112
Edward Dombroski, prin. Fax 849-1115
Northside ES 100/K-K
PO Box 479 15825 814-849-1118
Robin Fillman, prin. Fax 849-1130
Pinecreek ES 200/1-2
PO Box 479 15825 814-849-1119
Robin Fillman, prin. Fax 849-1131

Broomall, Delaware, Pop. 10,930
Marple Newtown SD
Supt. — See Newtown Square
Loomis ES 300/K-5
369 N Central Blvd 19008 610-359-4350
Victoria Teti, prin. Fax 359-4373
Paxon Hollow MS 900/6-8
815 Paxon Hollow Rd 19008 610-359-4320
Stephen Subers Ed.D., prin. Fax 353-4061
Russell ES 400/K-5
2201 Sproul Rd 19008 610-359-4310
Dianne Smith, prin. Fax 359-4371

Worrall ES 300/K-5
2979 Pennview Ave 19008 610-359-4300
John Trezise Ed.D., prin. Fax 359-1680

St. Pius X S 400/PK-8
204 Lawrence Rd 19008 610-356-7222
Sr. Diane Licordare, prin. Fax 356-5380

Brownstown, Lancaster, Pop. 834
Conestoga Valley SD
Supt. — See Lancaster
Brownstown ES 400/K-6
PO Box 250 17508 717-656-6021
Kelly Cartwright, prin. Fax 656-9172

Brownsville, Fayette, Pop. 2,690
Brownsville Area SD 1,700/K-12
1025 Lewis St 15417 724-785-2021
Lawrence Golembiewski, supt. Fax 785-6988
www.basd.org
Brownsville MS 300/7-8
3 Falcon Dr 15417 724-785-2155
Vincent Nesser, prin. Fax 785-2502
Cox-Donahey ES 300/K-6
200 Thornton Rd 15417 724-785-9600
Connie Horka, prin. Fax 785-5614
Other Schools – See East Millsboro, New Salem

Bruin, Butler, Pop. 514
Karns City Area SD
Supt. — See Karns City
Bruin ES 200/K-6
139 School St 16022 724-753-2203
Gregg Paladina, prin. Fax 753-2567

Bryn Athyn, Montgomery, Pop. 1,354

Bryn Athyn Church S 300/K-8
PO Box 277 19009 215-947-4086
Donald Fitzpatrick, hdmstr. Fax 938-1871

Bryn Mawr, Montgomery, Pop. 3,271
Haverford Township SD
Supt. — See Havertown
Coopertown ES 400/K-5
800 Coopertown Rd 19010 610-853-5900
Angela Sorrentino, prin. Fax 853-5976

Radnor Township SD
Supt. — See Wayne
Ithan ES 500/K-5
695 Clyde Rd 19010 610-527-1357
Dr. Patricia Madeira, prin. Fax 527-0459

Baldwin S 600/PK-12
701 Montgomery Ave 19010 610-525-2700
Sally Powell, hdmstr. Fax 525-7534
Country Day S of the Sacred Heart 400/PK-12
480 S Bryn Mawr Ave 19010 610-527-3915
Sr. Matthew MacDonald Ph.D., hdmstr. Fax 527-0942
St. Aloysius Academy 200/K-8
401 S Bryn Mawr Ave 19010 610-525-1670
Sr. Carolyn Dimick, prin. Fax 525-5140
St. Thomas of Villanova PK-PK
1236 Montrose Ave 19010 610-525-7554
Mary Kurek, dir. Fax 525-6041
Shipley S 900/PK-12
814 Yarrow St 19010 610-525-4300
Steven Piltch, prin. Fax 525-5082
SS. Colman & Neumann S 200/K-8
372 Highland Ln 19010 610-525-3266
Catherine M. Blumstein, prin. Fax 525-6103

Buckingham, Bucks
Central Bucks SD
Supt. — See Doylestown
Buckingham ES 400/K-6
PO Box 158 18912 267-893-4200
Margaret Solitario, prin. Fax 893-5802

Burgettstown, Washington, Pop. 1,521
Burgettstown Area SD 1,600/K-12
100 Bavington Rd 15021 724-947-8136
Deborah Jackson, supt. Fax 947-8143
www.burgettstown.k12.pa.us
Burgettstown ES 800/K-5
100 Bavington Rd 15021 724-947-8150
Melissa Mankey, prin. Fax 947-8143

Tri State Christian Academy 100/PK-12
750 Steubenville Pike 15021 724-947-8722
William Wright, prin. Fax 947-0821

Butler, Butler, Pop. 14,521
Butler Area SD 8,100/K-12
110 Campus Ln 16001 724-287-8721
Dr. Edward Fink, supt. Fax 287-1802
www.butler.k12.pa.us
Brittain ES 400/K-6
338 N Washington St 16001 724-287-8721
Dale Markle, prin. Fax 282-1013
Broad Street ES 300/K-6
200 Broad St 16001 724-287-8721
Linda Peifer, prin. Fax 283-5434
Butler Area JHS 1,300/7-8
225 E North St 16001 724-287-8721
James Allen, prin. Fax 287-7847
Center Avenue ES 200/K-6
102 Lincoln Ave 16001 724-287-8721
Barbara Keiser, prin. Fax 287-0263
Center Township ES 700/K-6
950 Mercer Rd 16001 724-287-8721
Roger Snodgrass, prin. Fax 282-3503
McQuistion ES 500/K-6
210 Mechling Dr 16001 724-287-8721
Kirk Fox, prin. Fax 287-1119
Meridian ES 400/K-6
135 Sparks Ave 16001 724-287-8721
Tim Sisinni, prin. Fax 482-2518

Northwest ES 500/K-6
124 Staley Ave 16001 724-287-8721
Alvin Vavro, prin. Fax 287-2516
Oakland Township ES 300/K-6
545 Chicora Rd 16001 724-287-8721
William Chwalik, prin. Fax 287-0935
Summit Township ES 300/K-6
351 Brinker Rd 16002 724-287-8721
Jack Ratica, prin. Fax 287-2734
Other Schools – See Fenelton, Renfrew

Butler Catholic S 200/PK-8
515 E Locust St 16001 724-285-4276
Sr. John Ann Mulhern, prin. Fax 285-4896
First Baptist Christian S 100/PK-12
221 New Castle St 16001 724-287-1188
Fax 287-6934
Holy Sepulcher S 200/K-8
6515 Old Route 8 N 16002 724-586-5022
Jacqueline Delaney, prin. Fax 586-5073
Penn Christian Academy 200/PK-6
199 Airport Rd 16002 724-586-5200
Cindy Dodds, admin. Fax 586-2891
St. Wendelin S 100/PK-8
211 Saint Wendelin Rd 16002 724-285-4986
Robert Childs, prin. Fax 287-6253

Cabot, Butler

St. Luke Lutheran S 200/PK-8
330 Hannahstown Rd 16023 724-352-2221
Mark Wilt, prin. Fax 352-2355

Cairnbrook, Somerset
Shade-Central CSD 600/K-12
203 McGreagor Ave 15924 814-754-4648
John Krupper, supt. Fax 754-5848
www.shade.k12.pa.us
Cairnbrook ES 300/K-6
235 McGreagor Ave 15924 814-754-5021
John Krupper, prin. Fax 754-5848

Cambridge Springs, Crawford, Pop. 2,282
Penncrest SD
Supt. — See Saegertown
Cambridge Springs ES 500/K-6
130 Steele St 16403 814-398-4636
Patti Fiely, prin. Fax 398-4593

Camp Hill, Cumberland, Pop. 7,424
Camp Hill SD 1,200/K-12
2627 Chestnut St 17011 717-901-2400
Connie Kindler, supt. Fax 901-2421
www.camphillsd.k12.pa.us
Camp Hill MS 300/6-8
2401 Chestnut St 17011 717-901-2450
Daniel Roesch, prin. Fax 901-2573
Hoover ES 300/3-5
420 S 24th St 17011 717-901-2600
Sandra Fauser, prin. Fax 901-2461
Schaeffer ES 200/K-2
2900 Walnut St 17011 717-901-2550
Patricia Craig, prin. Fax 901-2594

East Pennsboro Area SD
Supt. — See Enola
West Creek Hills ES 500/K-4
400 Erford Rd 17011 717-732-0142
Debra McDonald, prin.

West Shore SD
Supt. — See Lewisberry
Allen MS, 4225 Gettysburg Rd 17011 500/6-8
Timothy Dorsey, prin. 717-901-9552
Highland ES, 1325 Carlisle Rd 17011 500/K-5
Joanna McIntyre, prin. 717-901-9860
Lower Allen ES 200/K-2
4100 Gettysburg Rd 17011 717-761-8415
Deborah Rundall, prin.

Good Shepherd S 300/K-8
3400 Market St 17011 717-737-7261
Patrick Bowe, admin. Fax 761-4673

Canonsburg, Washington, Pop. 8,810
Canon-McMillan SD 4,600/K-12
1 N Jefferson Ave 15317 724-746-2940
Dr. Helen McCracken, supt. Fax 746-9184
www.cmsd.k12.pa.us
Borland Manor ES 300/K-4
30 Giffin Dr 15317 724-745-2700
Grace Lani, prin. Fax 873-5190
Canonsburg MS 700/7-8
25 E College St 15317 724-745-9030
Mark Abbondanza, prin. Fax 873-5230
First Street ES 200/K-4
803 1st St 15317 724-745-3130
Dr. Dawn Nicolaus, prin. Fax 873-5229
Hills-Hendersonville ES 200/K-4
50 Mayview Rd 15317 724-745-8390
Dr. Dawn Nicolaus, prin. Fax 873-5226
North Strabane IS 300/5-6
20 Giffin Dr 15317 724-873-5252
Tom Theodore, prin. Fax 873-5216
South Central ES 400/K-4
230 S Central Ave 15317 724-745-4475
Michelle Tomicek, prin. Fax 873-5228
Other Schools – See Cecil, Eighty Four, Mc Donald, Muse

St. Patrick S 200/PK-8
200 Murdock St 15317 724-745-7977
Stanley Mozina, prin. Fax 746-9778

Canton, Bradford, Pop. 1,745
Canton Area SD 1,100/K-12
139 E Main St 17724 570-673-3191
W. Jeffrey Johnston, supt. Fax 673-3680
www.canton.k12.pa.us

Canton Area ES 600/K-6
141 E Union St 17724 570-673-5196
Diane Barrett, prin. Fax 673-7929

Carbondale, Lackawanna, Pop. 9,348
Carbondale Area SD 1,500/PK-12
101 Brooklyn St 18407 570-282-4660
Dominick Famularo, supt. Fax 282-6988
gateway.ca.k12.pa.us
Carbondale ES 700/PK-6
103 Brooklyn St 18407 570-282-5656
Paul Kaczmarcik, prin. Fax 282-3203

Sacred Heart S 200/PK-8
27 Farview St 18407 570-282-0340
Ellen Murphy, prin. Fax 281-3677

Carlisle, Cumberland, Pop. 18,108
Big Spring SD
Supt. — See Newville
Plainfield ES 300/K-5
7 Springview Rd, 717-243-5703
Krista Zeigler, prin. Fax 243-5036

Carlisle Area SD 4,900/K-12
623 W Penn St 17013 717-240-6800
Mary Kay Durham, supt. Fax 240-6898
www.carlisleschools.org
Bellaire ES 400/K-5
623 W Penn St 17013 717-240-6800
James Burgess, prin. Fax 241-0097
Crestview ES 500/K-5
623 W Penn St 17013 717-240-6800
Carole Holly, prin. Fax 241-0302
Hamilton ES 300/K-5
623 W Penn St 17013 717-240-6800
Monique Varner, prin. Fax 241-0079
Lamberton MS 600/6-8
623 W Penn St 17013 717-240-6800
Keith Colestock, prin. Fax 240-2066
Letort ES 200/K-5
623 W Penn St 17013 717-240-6800
Laura Shaffer, prin. Fax 240-7002
Mooreland ES 300/K-5
623 W Penn St 17013 717-240-6800
Kim Truckenmiller, prin. Fax 241-0308
North Dickinson ES 200/K-5
623 W Penn St 17013 717-240-6800
Jeffery Bell, prin. Fax 241-0077
Wilson MS 600/6-8
623 W Penn St 17013 717-240-6800
Colleen Friend, prin. Fax 240-2050
Other Schools – See Mount Holly Springs

Cumberland Valley SD
Supt. — See Mechanicsburg
Middlesex ES 400/K-5
250 N Middlesex Rd 17013 717-249-5586
Donald Snyder, prin. Fax 249-0251

Carlisle Christian Academy 100/K-12
1412 Holly Pike, 717-249-3692
Matthew Tuckey, admin. Fax 240-0644
Grace Baptist Christian S 100/K-8
777 W North St 17013 717-243-8820
Gene Drummond, hdmstr. Fax 249-0486
St. Patrick S 400/PK-8
87 Marsh Dr, 717-249-4826
Ricman Fly, prin. Fax 245-0522

Carmichaels, Greene, Pop. 525
Carmichaels Area SD 1,100/K-12
225 N Vine St 15320 724-966-5045
Craig Baily, supt. Fax 966-8793
www.carmarea.org/Carm_Web/MainIndex.htm
Carmichaels Area ES 600/K-6
225 N Vine St 15320 724-966-5045
Robyn Cole, prin. Fax 966-8789

Carnegie, Allegheny, Pop. 8,149
Carlynton SD 1,500/K-12
435 Kings Hwy 15106 412-429-8400
Dr. Michael Panza, supt. Fax 429-2502
www.carlynton.k12.pa.us
Carnegie ES 400/K-6
301 Franklin Ave 15106 412-429-2540
Christopher Very, prin. Fax 429-3253
Other Schools – See Crafton

Carrolltown, Cambria, Pop. 996
Cambria Heights SD
Supt. — See Patton
Cambria Heights ES 600/K-5
PO Box 510 15722 814-344-8506
Michael Strasser, prin. Fax 344-6274

St. Benedict S 200/PK-8
PO Box 596 15722 814-344-6512
Kathy Lamont, prin. Fax 344-8530

Cashtown, Adams
Gettysburg Area SD
Supt. — See Gettysburg
Franklin Township ES 300/K-3
PO Box 124 17310 717-334-6254
Steven Fehringer, prin. Fax 337-4432

Cassville, Huntingdon, Pop. 145
Southern Huntingdon County SD
Supt. — See Three Springs
Trough Creek Valley ES 100/K-5
18549 Cooks Rd 16623 814-448-3255
Cathie Brouse, prin. Fax 448-9489

Catasauqua, Lehigh, Pop. 6,553
Catasauqua Area SD 1,700/K-12
201 N 14th St 18032 610-264-5571
Robert Spengler, supt. Fax 264-5618
www.cattysd.org

Catasauqua MS 500/5-8
850 Pine St 18032 610-264-4341
Melissa Inselmann, prin. Fax 264-5458
Sheckler ES 600/K-4
201 N 14th St 18032 610-264-5601
Eric Dauberman, prin. Fax 264-5618

Catawissa, Columbia, Pop. 1,557
Southern Columbia Area SD 1,400/K-12
800 Southern Dr 17820 570-356-2331
Charles Reh, supt. Fax 356-2892
www.scasd.us/
Hartman ES 500/K-4
802 Southern Dr 17820 570-356-3250
Joseph Shirvinski, prin. Fax 356-7169
Southern Columbia MS 400/5-8
810 Southern Dr 17820 570-356-3400
Roger Nunkester, prin. Fax 356-2835

Cecil, Washington, Pop. 2,701
Canon-McMillan SD
Supt. — See Canonsburg
Cecil ES 200/K-4
36 Cecil Elementary Dr 15321 412-221-6808
Robert Kleinhans, prin. Fax 221-3323

Center Valley, Lehigh
Southern Lehigh SD 2,700/K-12
5775 Main St 18034 610-282-3121
Joseph Liberati, supt. Fax 282-0193
www.slsd.org
Hopewell ES 300/K-3
4625 W Hopewell Rd 18034 610-791-0200
Lori Limpar, prin. Fax 791-2444
Southern Lehigh MS 700/6-8
3715 Preston Ln 18034 610-282-3700
Dr. Edward Donahue, prin. Fax 282-2963
Other Schools – See Bethlehem, Coopersburg

Centre Hall, Centre, Pop. 1,080
Penns Valley Area SD
Supt. — See Spring Mills
Centre Hall-Potter ES 200/K-4
211 N Hoffer Ave 16828 814-364-1481
Carolyn Payne, prin. Fax 364-9631

Chadds Ford, Chester
Unionville-Chadds Ford SD
Supt. — See Kennett Square
Chadds Ford ES 300/K-5
3 Baltimore Pike 19317 610-388-1112
Mark Ransford, prin. Fax 388-8481
Hillendale ES 400/K-5
1850 Hillendale Rd 19317 610-388-1439
Steve Dissinger, prin. Fax 388-2266

St. Cornelius S 200/K-5
160 Ridge Rd 19317 610-459-8663
Sr. Barbara Thomas, prin. Fax 459-7728

Chalfont, Bucks, Pop. 4,198
Central Bucks SD
Supt. — See Doylestown
Butler ES 800/K-6
200 Brittany Dr 18914 267-893-4250
Joseph Brereton, prin. Fax 893-5803

Plumstead Christian S - Peace Valley 200/K-5
753 New Galena Rd 18914 215-822-0187
Dean Whiteway, hdmstr. Fax 822-5890
St. Jude S 400/PK-8
323 W Butler Ave 18914 215-822-9225
Sr. Elizabeth Marley, prin. Fax 822-0722

Chambersburg, Franklin, Pop. 17,961
Chambersburg Area SD 8,400/PK-12
435 Stanley Ave 17201 717-263-9281
Dr. Joseph Padasak, supt.
www.chambersburg.k12.pa.us
Buchanan ES 300/K-5
730 E Washington St 17201 717-261-3432
Andrew Nelson, prin. Fax 261-3492
Chambersburg Area MS 1,300/6-7
1151 E McKinley St 17201 717-261-3385
Kurt Widmann, prin. Fax 261-3401
Coldbrook ES 200/K-5
756 S Coldbrook Ave 17201 717-261-3434
Kirk Crouse, prin.
Falling Spring ES 300/K-5
1006 Falling Spring Rd, 717-261-3440
Dr. Paul Sick, prin. Fax 261-3493
Gordy ES, 401 Miller St 17201 100/K-5
Gladys Leon, prin. 717-261-3449
Grandview ES 200/K-5
5538 Cumberland Hwy, 717-261-3446
Reid Pletcher, prin. Fax 261-3497
Guilford Hills ES 300/K-5
2105 Lincoln Way E, 717-352-2124
Bonnie Huber, prin.
Hamilton Heights ES 500/K-5
1589 Johnson Rd, 717-267-4475
Cynthia Henry, prin.
King Street ES, 145 E King St 17201 100/1-5
Gladys Leon, prin. 717-261-3451
New Franklin ES 100/K-5
3584 Wayne Rd, 717-261-3454
Brian Mackey, prin.
Sharpe ES, 850 Broad St 17201 200/K-5
Trisha Thomas, lead tchr. 717-261-3463
South Hamilton ES 300/K-5
1019 Warm Spring Rd, 717-261-3449
Reid Pletcher, prin. Fax 261-3498
Stevens ES, 800 Hollywell Ave 17201 300/PK-5
Richard Bonitz, prin. 717-261-3470
Other Schools – See Fayetteville, Lurgan, Marion, Scotland

Corpus Christi S 300/PK-8
305 N 2nd St 17201 717-263-5036
Robert Dortenzo, prin. Fax 263-6079
Cumberland Valley Christian S 400/PK-12
600 Miller St 17201 717-264-3266
Rev. Carl McKee, prin. Fax 264-0416
Montessori Academy of Chambersburg 100/K-8
875 Ragged Edge Rd, 717-261-1110
John Krebs, prin. Fax 267-3626
Shalom Christian Academy 500/PK-12
126 Social Island Rd, 717-375-2223
Conrad Swartzentruber, admin. Fax 375-2224

Champion, Westmoreland

Champion Christian S 100/PK-12
2166 Indian Head Rd 15622 724-593-9200
Merle Skinner, dir. Fax 593-9210

Charleroi, Washington, Pop. 4,696
Charleroi Area SD 1,600/K-12
125 Fecsen Dr 15022 724-483-3509
Dr. Brad Ferko, supt. Fax 483-3776
www.charleroisd.org
Charleroi Area ES 700/K-5
75 Fecsen Dr 15022 724-483-5554
Joan Adams, prin. Fax 483-9367
Charleroi Area MS 400/6-8
100 Fecsen Dr 15022 724-483-3600
Mary Tickner, prin. Fax 489-9128

Cheltenham, Montgomery, Pop. 34,800
Cheltenham Township SD
Supt. — See Elkins Park
Cheltenham ES 400/K-4
7853 Front St 19012 215-635-7415
Mia Kim, prin. Fax 635-7548

Presentation BVM S 300/K-8
107 Old Soldiers Rd 19012 215-379-3798
Nancy Scharnikow, prin. Fax 379-4430

Cherryville, Northampton

Bethlehem Christian S 100/K-8
PO Box 1029 18035 610-767-7227
Tim Wilkins, supt. Fax 767-8137

Chester, Delaware, Pop. 37,058
Chester-Upland SD 3,700/PK-12
1720 Melrose Ave 19013 610-447-3600
Dr. Gregory Thornton, supt. Fax 447-3616
www.chesteruplandsd.org/
Chester Upland S of the Arts 200/PK-8
501 W 9th St 19013 610-447-3777
Janet Baldwin, prin.
Columbus S 800/PK-8
320 W 10th St 19013 610-447-3800
Sterling Garris, prin. Fax 447-3802
Stetser ES 300/PK-6
808 E 17th St 19013 610-447-3795
Tamika Ford, prin. Fax 447-3987
Other Schools – See Brookhaven, Upland

Douglass Christian S 100/K-3
700 Central Ave 19013 610-499-9030
Patricia Vallot, prin. Fax 872-8479
Drexel Neumann Academy 200/PK-8
1901 Potter St 19013 610-872-7358
Sr. Cathy McGowan, prin. Fax 872-7833

Chester Springs, Chester
Downingtown Area SD
Supt. — See Downingtown
Pickering Valley ES 600/K-5
121 Byers Rd 19425 610-458-5324
Joseph Fernandes, prin. Fax 458-8356

Owen J. Roberts SD
Supt. — See Pottstown
West Vincent ES K-6
2750 Conestoga Rd 19425 610-469-5108
Barbara Guy, prin.

Montgomery S 300/PK-8
1141 Kimberton Rd 19425 610-827-7222
Kevin Conklin, hdmstr. Fax 827-7639

Cheswick, Allegheny, Pop. 1,790
Allegheny Valley SD 1,200/K-12
300 Pearl Ave 15024 724-274-5300
Cheryl Griffith Ed.D., supt. Fax 274-8040
www.avsd.k12.pa.us
Acmetonia PS 300/K-3
300 Pearl Ave 15024 724-274-6500
Gregory Heavner, prin. Fax 274-2816
Other Schools – See Springdale

Cheswick Christian Academy 200/K-12
1407 Pittsburgh St 15024 724-274-4846
Fax 274-8300

Chicora, Butler, Pop. 1,004
Karns City Area SD
Supt. — See Karns City
Chicora ES 500/K-6
PO Box 241 16025 724-445-3680
James Zambelli, prin. Fax 445-2776

Chinchilla, Lackawanna
Abington Heights SD
Supt. — See Clarks Summit
South Abington ES 300/K-4
PO Box 163 18410 570-585-2100
Robert Bugno, prin. Fax 585-2112

Christiana, Lancaster, Pop. 1,091
Solanco SD
Supt. — See Quarryville
Bart-Colerain ES 300/K-5
1336 Noble Rd 17509 717-529-2181
Robert Dangler, prin. Fax 529-6879

Churchville, Bucks, Pop. 4,255
Council Rock SD
Supt. — See Newtown
Churchville ES 700/K-6
100 New Rd 18966 215-944-1700
Jill Kingston, prin. Fax 944-1797
Welch ES 700/K-6
750 New Rd 18966 215-944-1800
Michael Reid, prin. Fax 944-1896

Clairton, Allegheny, Pop. 8,081
Clairton CSD 900/K-12
502 Mitchell Ave 15025 412-233-7090
Dr. Lucille Abellonio, supt. Fax 233-4755
www.clairton.k12.pa.us/
Clairton ES 400/K-5
501 Waddell Ave 15025 412-233-6010
Maureen Dobson, prin. Fax 233-4982
Clairton MS 200/6-8
501 Waddell Ave 15025 412-233-9200
Deborah Marshall, prin. Fax 233-3243

Clarendon, Warren, Pop. 530
Warren County SD
Supt. — See North Warren
Allegheny Valley ES 100/K-5
100 N Main St 16313 814-723-4991
Deborah Dwyer, prin. Fax 726-7832

Clarion, Clarion, Pop. 5,507
Clarion Area SD 900/PK-12
221 Liberty St 16214 814-226-6110
Dr. George White, supt. Fax 226-9292
www.clarion-schools.com
Clarion Area ES 500/PK-6
800 Boundary St 16214 814-226-8118
Todd MacBeth, prin. Fax 226-4889

Immaculate Conception S 100/PK-8
729 Main St 16214 814-226-8433
Donna Gaydash, prin. Fax 226-4998

Clarks Green, Lackawanna, Pop. 1,572

Abington Christian Academy 50/PK-7
204 S Abington Rd 18411 570-586-5270
Jan Wells, admin. Fax 587-4648
Our Lady of Peace S 400/K-8
410 N Abington Rd 18411 570-587-4152
Jane Quinn, prin. Fax 586-5393

Clarks Summit, Lackawanna, Pop. 5,010
Abington Heights SD 3,600/K-12
200 E Grove St 18411 570-586-2511
Michael Mahon, supt. Fax 586-1756
www.ahsd.org
Abington Heights MS 1,100/5-8
1555 Newton Ransom Blvd 18411 570-586-1281
Edward Kairis, prin. Fax 586-6361
Clarks Summit ES 400/K-4
401 W Grove St 18411 570-585-7300
Mariellen Sluko, prin. Fax 585-7307
Newton-Ransom ES 300/K-4
1549 Newton Ransom Blvd 18411 570-585-8300
Robert Bugno, prin.
Other Schools – See Chinchilla, Waverly

St. Gregory ECC 50/PK-K
330 N Abington Rd 18411 570-587-4808
Msgr. John Louis, dir. Fax 586-4515
Summit Christian Academy 100/PK-12
232 Noble Rd 18411 570-586-3500
Tim Connor, admin. Fax 587-4840

Claysburg, Blair, Pop. 1,399
Claysburg-Kimmel SD 900/K-12
RR 1 Box 522 16625 814-239-5141
James O'Harrow, supt. Fax 239-5896
www.cksd.k12.pa.us
Claysburg-Kimmel ES 500/K-6
240 C K Elementary Dr 16625 814-239-5144
Mark Loucks, prin. Fax 239-8994

Claysville, Washington, Pop. 695
McGuffey SD 2,200/K-12
90 McGuffey Dr 15323 724-948-3731
Joseph Stefka, supt. Fax 948-3769
mcguffey.k12.pa.us
Claysville ES 600/K-5
PO Box 421 15323 724-663-7772
Tommy Bedillion, prin. Fax 663-4298
McGuffey MS 600/6-8
86 McGuffey Dr 15323 724-948-3323
Mark Bonus, prin. Fax 948-2413
Other Schools – See Washington

Clearfield, Clearfield, Pop. 6,339
Clearfield Area SD 2,700/K-12
PO Box 710 16830 814-765-5511
Dr. Richard Makin, supt. Fax 765-5515
www.clearfield.org
Centre ES 200/K-4
PO Box 710 16830 814-765-1761
Mary Sayers, prin. Fax 765-5999
Clearfield Area MS 800/5-8
PO Box 710 16830 814-765-5302
Fred Redden, prin. Fax 765-4604
Clearfield ES 400/K-4
700 High Level Rd 16830 814-762-8011
Jamie Quick, prin. Fax 762-8037
Other Schools – See Bigler, Frenchville

Clearfield Alliance Christian S 100/K-12
56 Alliance Rd 16830 814-765-0216
St. Francis S 200/PK-8
230 S 2nd St 16830 814-765-2618
Dr. Michael Spencer, prin. Fax 765-6704

Clearville, Bedford
Everett Area SD
Supt. — See Everett

Mann-Monroe ES 100/K-5
268 Rock Hill Church Rd 15535 814-652-9114
Paul Clark, lead tchr. Fax 784-5037

Cleona, Lebanon, Pop. 2,107
Annville-Cleona SD
Supt. — See Annville
Cleona ES 200/K-1
50 E Walnut St 17042 717-867-7640
Mary Dague, prin. Fax 867-7644

Clifton Heights, Delaware, Pop. 6,626
Upper Darby SD
Supt. — See Drexel Hill
Westbrook Park ES 400/K-5
199 Westbrook Dr 19018 610-626-9363
Marylisa Kostaneski, prin.

St. Mark's Christian S 100/PK-K
436 N Oak Ave 19018 610-626-6837
Kathleen Cosentino, prin.

Clymer, Indiana, Pop. 1,467
Penns Manor Area SD 1,000/K-12
6003 Route 553 Hwy 15728 724-254-2666
Thomas Kakabar, supt. Fax 254-3418
www.pennsmanor.org/
Penns Manor Area ES 500/K-6
6003 Route 553 Hwy 15728 724-254-2666
David Grimaldi, prin. Fax 254-3415

Coal Center, Washington, Pop. 130
California Area SD 1,000/K-12
11 Trojan Way Ste 100 15423 724-785-5800
Linda Mancini, supt.
www.calsd.org/calsd/site/default.asp
California Area ES 400/K-5
40 Trojan Way 15423 724-785-5800
Michael Sears, prin. Fax 785-5458
California Area MS 200/6-8
40 Trojan Way 15423 724-785-5800
Raymond Huffman, prin. Fax 785-5458

Coal Township, Northumberland, Pop. 9,922
Shamokin Area SD 2,600/PK-12
2000 W State St 17866 570-648-5752
James Zack, supt. Fax 648-2592
www.indians.k12.pa.us/
Shamokin Area ES 1,300/PK-6
3000 W State St 17866 570-648-5721
Mary Teresa Komara, prin.

Our Lady of Lourdes Regional S 400/K-12
2108 N Jackson St 17866 570-644-0375
Sr. Margaret McCullough, admin. Fax 644-7655

Coatesville, Chester, Pop. 11,495
Coatesville Area SD 6,800/K-12
545 E Lincoln Hwy 19320 610-466-2400
Richard Como, supt. Fax 383-1426
www.coatesville.k12.pa.us/
Friendship ES 400/K-5
296 Reeceville Rd 19320 610-383-3770
Jason Palaia, prin. Fax 383-3774
Kings Highway ES 500/K-5
841 W Kings Hwy 19320 610-383-3775
Stevan LeFever, prin. Fax 383-3779
North Brandywine MS 500/6-8
256 Reeceville Rd 19320 610-383-3745
Jeffrey Cupano, prin. Fax 383-3749
Rainbow ES 600/K-5
50 Country Club Rd 19320 610-383-3780
Clifford Maloney, prin. Fax 383-3784
Reeceville ES 400/K-5
248 Reeceville Rd 19320 610-383-3785
Anthony Buckwash, prin. Fax 383-3789
Scott MS 500/6-8
800 Olive St 19320 610-383-6946
Chamise Taylor, prin. Fax 383-7110
South Brandywine MS 600/6-8
600 Doe Run Rd 19320 610-383-3750
John Reid, prin. Fax 383-3754
Other Schools – See E Fallowfield, Thorndale

Cochranton, Crawford, Pop. 1,092
Crawford Central SD
Supt. — See Meadville
Cochranton ES 400/K-6
225 S Franklin St 16314 814-425-2105
Patricia Deardorff, prin. Fax 425-3761

Cochranville, Chester

Fox Friends S 50/PK-K
2009 Gap Newport Pike 19330 610-593-7122
Jennifer Eckert, hdmstr. Fax 593-5834

Cogan Station, Lycoming
Williamsport Area SD
Supt. — See Williamsport
Hepburn-Lycoming ES 400/K-5
355 State Route 973 E 17728 570-494-1112
Gary Gonsar, prin. Fax 494-0534

Collegeville, Montgomery, Pop. 5,055
Methacton SD
Supt. — See Eagleville
Arrowhead ES 400/K-5
232 Level Rd 19426 610-489-5000
Daniel Petino, prin. Fax 489-4350

Perkiomen Valley SD 5,500/K-12
3 Iron Bridge Dr 19426 610-489-8506
Dr. Clifford Rogers, supt. Fax 489-2974
www.pvsd.org
Evergreen ES 700/K-5
98 Kagey Rd 19426 610-409-9751
Kimberly Minor, prin. Fax 409-9756
Perkiomen Valley East MS 700/6-8
100 Kagey Rd 19426 610-409-8580
Seamus Clune, prin. Fax 409-0625
Perkiomen Valley South ES 700/K-5
200 E 3rd Ave 19426 610-489-2991
Michelle Cinciripino, prin. Fax 409-8754
Skippack ES 800/K-5
4081 Heckler Rd 19426 610-409-6060
Kimberly Boyd, prin. Fax 409-6099
Other Schools – See Schwenksville, Zieglerville

Spring-Ford Area SD 6,700/K-12
199 Bechtel Rd 19426 610-705-6000
Marsha Hurda Ed.D., supt. Fax 705-6245
www.spring-ford.net
Other Schools – See Limerick, Oaks, Royersford, Spring City

St. Eleanor S 500/K-8
701 Locust St 19426 610-489-9434
Molly Paulhamus, prin. Fax 489-6137
Valley Forge Baptist Academy 200/K-12
616 S Trappe Rd 19426 610-792-1884
Lois Rall, prin. Fax 948-6423

Collingdale, Delaware, Pop. 8,501
Southeast Delco SD
Supt. — See Folcroft
Harris S 700/1-8
501 Sharon Ave 19023 610-522-4370
Shawn McDougal, prin. Fax 586-7161

St. Joseph S 400/PK-8
502 Woodlawn Ave 19023 610-586-0356
Sr. Gerald Helene, prin. Fax 586-7710

Columbia, Lancaster, Pop. 10,092
Columbia Borough SD 1,400/K-12
200 N 5th St 17512 717-684-2283
Barry Clippinger, supt. Fax 681-2220
www.columbia.k12.pa.us
Park ES 500/K-6
50 S 6th St 17512 717-684-9780
Deb Wallace, prin. Fax 681-2619
Taylor ES 300/K-6
45 N 9th St 17512 717-684-4010
Andrew Graybill, prin. Fax 681-2408

Our Lady of the Angels PS 100/PK-3
215 Union St 17512 717-684-2433
Theresa Burg, prin. Fax 684-5039
Our Lady of the Angels S 100/4-8
404 Cherry St 17512 717-684-2664
Theresa Burg, prin.

Colwyn, Delaware, Pop. 2,394
William Penn SD
Supt. — See Lansdowne
Colwyn ES 200/K-6
211 Pine St 19023 610-957-5470
Rene Garner, prin. Fax 957-5485

Commodore, Indiana
Purchase Line SD, PO Box 374 15729 1,200/K-12
Dr. Richard Makin, supt. 724-254-4312
www.plsd.k12.pa.us/
Purchase Line South ES 500/K-6
PO Box 374 15729 724-254-4312
Carol Ayers, prin. Fax 254-3113
Other Schools – See Mahaffey

Conestoga, Lancaster
Penn Manor SD
Supt. — See Lancaster
Conestoga ES 300/K-6
100 Hill St 17516 717-872-9535
Daniel Martino, prin. Fax 872-9516

Confluence, Somerset, Pop. 793
Turkeyfoot Valley Area SD 400/K-12
172 Turkeyfoot Rd 15424 814-395-3621
Darlene Sherrard, supt. Fax 395-3366
www.turkeyfoot.k12.pa.us
Turkeyfoot Valley Area ES 200/K-6
172 Turkeyfoot Rd 15424 814-395-3623
Jeffrey Malaspino, dean Fax 395-3366

Conneaut Lake, Crawford, Pop. 676
Conneaut SD
Supt. — See Linesville
Conneaut Lake ES 500/K-6
630 Line St 16316 814-382-8191
Marcia deKramer, prin. Fax 382-4477

Conneautville, Crawford, Pop. 807
Conneaut SD
Supt. — See Linesville
Conneaut Valley ES 400/K-6
22361 Highway 18 16406 814-587-6326
Stephen Corsi, prin. Fax 587-2930

Connellsville, Fayette, Pop. 8,644
Connellsville Area SD 5,400/K-12
732 Rockridge Rd 15425 724-628-3300
James Duncan, supt. Fax 628-9002
www.casdfalcons.org
Bullskin Township ES 400/K-6
125 Pleasant Valley Rd 15425 724-628-6540
Kristen Porter, prin.
Connell ES, 700 Park St 15425 400/K-6
Geoffrey Snyder, prin. 724-628-8003
Connellsville Township ES 100/K-6
730 Rockridge Rd 15425 724-628-9299
Traci Kuhns, prin. Fax 626-1013
Dunbar Township ES 600/K-6
711 Ridge Blvd 15425 724-628-6330
Traci Kuhns, prin.
South Side ES 300/K-6
1135 Race St 15425 724-628-5682
Geoffrey Snyder, prin. Fax 628-0254
Other Schools – See Dunbar, Melcroft, Normalville

Conn Area Catholic S 100/PK-6
110 N Prospect St 15425 724-628-5090
Cecilia Solan, prin. Fax 628-1745

Conshohocken, Montgomery, Pop. 7,711
Colonial SD
Supt. — See Plymouth Meeting
Conshohocken ES 100/K-3
301 Harry St 19428 610-828-0362
Denise Marks, prin. Fax 828-4582
Ridge Park ES 300/K-3
200 Karrs Ln 19428 610-825-1083
Jason Bacani, prin. Fax 825-7983

Conshohocken Catholic PS 100/PK-K
130 W 5th Ave 19428 610-828-0755
Patricia Kaeser, prin. Fax 828-5191
Conshohocken Catholic S 100/1-8
205 Fayette St 19428 610-828-2007
Patricia Kaeser, prin. Fax 825-8796
Miquon S 100/PK-6
2025 Harts Ln 19428 610-828-1231
Julia Finney, prin. Fax 828-6149

Conway, Beaver, Pop. 2,191
Freedom Area SD
Supt. — See Freedom
Conway ES 200/K-4
801 1st Ave 15027 724-869-3081
Debra Baycura, prin. Fax 869-2951

Coopersburg, Lehigh, Pop. 2,570
Southern Lehigh SD
Supt. — See Center Valley
Liberty Bell ES 300/K-3
960 W Oxford St 18036 610-282-1850
Samuel Hafner, prin. Fax 282-3676
Lower Milford ES 200/K-3
7350 Elementary Rd 18036 610-965-4095
Carol Mickley, prin. Fax 965-8977

Cooperstown, Venango, Pop. 436
Oil City Area SD
Supt. — See Oil City
Oakland ES 100/K-5
2111 Creek Rd 16317 814-677-3015
Lynda Weller, prin. Fax 677-7515

Coplay, Lehigh, Pop. 3,371
Parkland SD
Supt. — See Allentown
Ironton ES 500/K-5
3135 Levans Rd 18037 610-351-5810
Lynette Smith, prin. Fax 351-5819

Coraopolis, Allegheny, Pop. 5,754
Cornell SD 500/K-12
1099 Maple Street Ext 15108 412-264-5010
Donna Belas, supt. Fax 264-1445
www.cornell.k12.pa.us
Cornell ES 300/K-6
1099 Maple Street Ext 15108 412-264-5010
Donna Belas, prin. Fax 264-4142

Montour SD
Supt. — See Mc Kees Rocks
Forest Grove ES 600/K-4
1 Forest Grove Rd 15108 412-264-6452
Dr. Eric Sparkenbaugh, prin. Fax 264-5130
Williams MS 500/5-8
Porters Hollow Rd 15108 412-771-8802
Dominic Salpeck, prin. Fax 771-3772

St. Joseph S 100/K-8
1313 5th Ave 15108 412-264-6141
Sr. Grace Spera, prin. Fax 264-1518
St. Malachy S 100/PK-8
343 Forest Grove Rd 15108 412-771-4545
Dr. Bruno Raso, prin. Fax 771-0922

Corry, Erie, Pop. 6,548
Corry Area SD 1,900/K-12
540 E Pleasant St 16407 814-664-4677
Dr. Brian Dougherty, supt. Fax 664-9645
www.corrysd.net
Columbus ES 200/K-6
100 W Main St 16407 814-665-9491
Dina Wadding, prin. Fax 663-0411
Conelway ES 200/K-6
18700 Conelway Rd 16407 814-665-9512
Sheri Yetzer, prin. Fax 664-7227
Corry ES K-6
423 Wayne St 16407 814-665-6341
Matthew Patterson, prin. Fax 663-4795
Corry MS 400/7-8
534 E Pleasant St 16407 814-665-8297
Gail Swank, prin. Fax 664-3650
Other Schools – See Spartansburg

Corry Alliance Academy 50/K-2
721 Hatch St 16407 814-664-8658
Dale Dorman, admin. Fax 665-8015
St. Thomas S 100/PK-8
229 W Washington St 16407 814-665-7375
Karen Beer, prin. Fax 664-4025

Coudersport, Potter, Pop. 2,551
Coudersport Area SD 900/K-12
698 Dwight St 16915 814-274-9480
Richard Toner, supt. Fax 274-7551
coudersport.schoolwires.com/
Coudersport Area ES 500/K-6
802 Vine St 16915 814-274-8500
Sherry Cowburn, prin. Fax 274-2235

Cowansville, Armstrong
Karns City Area SD
Supt. — See Karns City
Sugarcreek ES 300/K-6
1290 State Route 268 16218 724-545-2409
Gregg Paladina, prin. Fax 543-5853

Crafton, Allegheny, Pop. 6,289
Carlynton SD
Supt. — See Carnegie
Crafton ES 400/K-6
1874 Crafton Blvd 15205 412-922-7196
Jacie Maslyk, prin. Fax 922-7587

Cranberry Township, Butler
Seneca Valley SD
Supt. — See Harmony
Haine ES 800/K-4
1516 Haine School Rd 16066 724-776-1581
Kyra Bobak, prin. Fax 776-1481
Haine MS 600/5-6
1516 Haine School Rd 16066 724-776-1581
Steven Smith, prin. Fax 776-2213
Rowan ES 700/K-4
8051 Rowan Rd 16066 724-776-1518
John Giancola, prin. Fax 776-9574

St. Killian S 500/PK-8
7076 Franklin Rd 16066 724-625-1665
Kathleen Kudlac, prin. Fax 625-1922

Creekside, Indiana, Pop. 306
Marion Center Area SD
Supt. — See Marion Center
Creekside Washington ES K-4
181 Hudson Rd 15732 724-397-5561

Cresco, Monroe
Pocono Mountain SD
Supt. — See Swiftwater
Barrett Elementary Center 500/K-5
RR 2 Box 2402 18326 570-839-7121
Heidi Donohue, prin. Fax 595-2658

Monsignor McHugh S 400/PK-8
RR 1 Box 1780 18326 570-595-7463
Christopher Tigue, prin. Fax 595-9639

Cresson, Cambria, Pop. 1,538
Penn Cambria SD 1,400/PK-12
201 6th St 16630 814-886-8121
Mary Beth Whited, supt. Fax 886-4809
www.pcam.org
Penn Cambria Pre PS 100/PK-K
205 6th St 16630 814-886-8166
Cindy Pacifico, prin. Fax 886-4809
Other Schools – See Gallitzin, Lilly

All Saints Catholic S 200/PK-8
220 Powell Ave 16630 814-886-7942
Susan Glass, prin. Fax 886-7942

Cressona, Schuylkill, Pop. 1,563
Blue Mountain SD
Supt. — See Orwigsburg
Blue Mountain El Cressona ES 200/K-5
45 Wilder St 17929 570-385-5580
Heath Renninger, prin. Fax 385-7206

Croydon, Bucks, Pop. 9,967
Bristol Township SD
Supt. — See Levittown
Devine ES 400/K-6
1800 Keystone St 19021 215-788-7995
Cathy Karasakal, prin. Fax 781-1468
Maple Shade ES 300/K-6
2335 Prospect Ave 19021 215-788-0200
Margaret Deni, prin. Fax 781-1466

St. Thomas Aquinas S 200/K-8
130 Walnut Ave 19021 215-785-1130
Colleen Noone, prin. Fax 785-2564

Curwensville, Clearfield, Pop. 2,540
Curwensville Area SD 1,200/K-12
650 Beech St 16833 814-236-1101
Norman Hatten, supt. Fax 236-1103
www.curwensville.org/
Curwensville Area ES 500/K-6
650 Beech St 16833 814-236-1411
Susan Wingard, prin.
Other Schools – See Grampian

Dallas, Luzerne, Pop. 2,508
Dallas SD 2,800/K-12
PO Box 2000 18612 570-674-7221
Frank Galicki, supt. Fax 674-7295
www.dallassd.com/
Dallas ES 700/K-5
PO Box 2000 18612 570-674-7271
Tom Traver, prin. Fax 674-7267
Dallas MS 700/6-8
PO Box 2000 18612 570-674-7245
Thomas Duffy, prin. Fax 674-7219
Wycallis ES 400/K-5
PO Box 2000 18612 570-674-7283
Kathleen McCarthy, prin. Fax 674-7291

Gate of Heaven S 300/K-8
40 Machell Ave 18612 570-675-6566
Lucille Procopio, prin. Fax 674-0198

Dallastown, York, Pop. 4,080
Dallastown Area SD 5,900/K-12
700 New School Ln 17313 717-244-4021
Dr. Stewart Weinberg, supt. Fax 246-0597
www.dallastown.net/
Dallastown Area MS 1,500/6-8
700 New School Ln 17313 717-244-4021
Joshua Doll, prin. Fax 244-0350
Dallastown ES 200/K-5
105 S Charles St 17313 717-244-3785
Stephanie Ferree, prin. Fax 244-3090
Other Schools – See York

St. Joseph S 200/PK-6
271 E Main St 17313 717-244-9386
Margaret Snyder Ed.D., prin. Fax 244-9478

Dalmatia, Northumberland
Line Mountain SD
Supt. — See Herndon
Dalmatia ES 300/K-6
162 School Rd 17017 570-758-6243
Thea Tafner, prin. Fax 758-4769

Dalton, Lackawanna, Pop. 1,233
Tunkhannock Area SD
Supt. — See Tunkhannock
Mill City ES 200/K-4
RR 2 18414 570-378-2525
Ann Way, prin. Fax 378-3580

Damascus, Wayne
Wayne Highlands SD
Supt. — See Honesdale
Damascus Area S 400/K-8
174 High School Rd 18415 570-224-4114
Maralyn Nalesnik, prin. Fax 224-4997

Danville, Montour, Pop. 4,640
Danville Area SD 2,500/K-12
600 Walnut St 17821 570-271-3268
Susan Bickford, supt. Fax 275-7712
www.danville.k12.pa.us
Danville Area MS 600/6-8
120 Northumberland St 17821 570-271-3268
Cynthia Hutchinson, prin. Fax 275-1281
Danville ES 200/K-5
401 E Front St 17821 570-271-3268
Molly Nied, prin. Fax 271-3127
Liberty-Valley ES 400/K-5
175 Liberty Valley Rd 17821 570-271-3268
Daniel Rathfon, prin. Fax 275-5047
Mahoning-Cooper ES 200/K-5
1605 Bloom Rd 17821 570-271-3268
John Bickhart, prin. Fax 271-0531
Other Schools – See Riverside

St. Cyril K 100/PK-K
580 Railroad St 17821 570-275-1505
Sr. Donna Marie, prin. Fax 275-5997
St. Joseph S 100/1-8
511 Ferry St 17821 570-275-2435
Ronald Valania, prin. Fax 275-3947

Darby, Delaware, Pop. 10,046
William Penn SD
Supt. — See Lansdowne
Park Lane ES 400/K-6
1300 Park Ln 19023 610-534-4880
Dujuana Ambrose-Dessau, prin. Fax 534-4495
Penn Wood MS 500/7-8
121 Summit St 19023 610-586-1804
Brian Wilson, prin. Fax 586-7372
Walnut Street ES 500/K-6
224 S 6th St 19023 610-534-5660
Dr. Ivy Brown, prin. Fax 534-4412

Blessed Virgin Mary S 200/K-8
51 N MacDade Blvd 19023 610-586-0638
Sr. Virginia Paschall, prin. Fax 586-1582
Christ Haven Christian Academy 100/PK-6
521 Walnut St 19023 610-583-6011
Naomi Knight, admin. Fax 538-5772

Darlington, Beaver, Pop. 282
Big Beaver Falls Area SD
Supt. — See Beaver Falls
Big Beaver ES 300/K-5
588 Friendship Rd 16115 724-827-2828
Valarie Williams, prin. Fax 827-8453

Blackhawk SD
Supt. — See Beaver Falls
Northwestern ES 300/K-2
256 Elmwood Blvd 16115 724-827-2116
Jane Fucci, prin. Fax 827-8294

Dauphin, Dauphin, Pop. 725
Central Dauphin SD
Supt. — See Harrisburg
Middle Paxton ES 300/K-5
931 Peters Mountain Rd 17018 717-921-8951
Carol Lopez, prin. Fax 921-3366

Davidsville, Somerset, Pop. 1,167
Conemaugh Township Area SD 1,100/K-12
PO Box 407 15928 814-479-7575
Dr. Joseph DiBartola, supt. Fax 479-2620
www.ctasd.org
Other Schools – See Jerome, Johnstown

Dayton, Armstrong, Pop. 513
Armstrong SD
Supt. — See Ford City
Dayton ES, 175 E Grant Ave 16222 300/K-6
Paula Berry, prin. 814-257-8816

Defiance, Bedford
Tussey Mountain SD
Supt. — See Saxton
Defiance ES 100/K-6
PO Box 126 16633 814-928-4611
Kathy Lazor, prin. Fax 928-5136

Delta, York, Pop. 725
South Eastern SD
Supt. — See Fawn Grove
Delta-Peach Bottom ES 300/K-4
1081 Atom Rd 17314 717-456-5313
Stephen Hagenbuch, prin. Fax 456-6042

Denver, Lancaster, Pop. 3,646
Cocalico SD 3,600/PK-12
PO Box 800 17517 717-336-1413
Bruce Sensenig, supt. Fax 336-1415
www.cocalico.org/
Cocalico MS 900/6-8
PO Box 800 17517 717-336-1471
Stephen Melnyk, prin. Fax 336-1482
Denver ES 500/K-5
PO Box 800 17517 717-336-1501
Angela Marley, prin. Fax 336-1503
Other Schools – See Adamstown, Reamstown, Stevens

Eastern Lancaster County SD
Supt. — See New Holland
Brecknock ES 500/K-6
361 School Rd 17517 717-445-8600
Lynmarie Hilt, prin. Fax 445-8604

Gehmans Mennonite S 200/K-12
650 Gehman School Rd 17517 717-484-4222

Derry, Westmoreland, Pop. 2,869
Derry Area SD 2,600/K-12
982 N Chestnut Street Ext 15627 724-694-1401
Roberta McCahan, supt. Fax 694-1429
derryasd.schoolwires.com/derryasd/
Derry Area MS 600/6-8
994 N Chestnut Street Ext 15627 724-694-8231
Cheryl Walters, prin. Fax 694-0288
Grandview ES 800/K-5
188 Recreation Rd 15627 724-694-2400
Kristine Higgs, prin. Fax 694-1351
Other Schools – See Latrobe, New Derry

Devon, Chester, Pop. 5,019
Tredyffrin-Easttown SD
Supt. — See Wayne
Beaumont ES 400/K-4
575 Beaumont Rd 19333 610-240-1400
Dr. Stephanie Demming, prin. Fax 240-1410
Devon ES 400/K-4
400 S Fairfield Rd 19333 610-240-1450
Thomas Tobin, prin. Fax 240-1466

Dickson City, Lackawanna, Pop. 5,967

LaSalle Academy-Primary Campus 200/PK-8
1090 Carmalt St 18519 570-489-0061
Sr. Donna Cerminaro, prin. Fax 489-0157

Dillsburg, York, Pop. 2,321
Northern York County SD 3,100/K-12
149 S Baltimore St 17019 717-432-8691
Linda Lemmon, supt. Fax 432-1421
www.northernpolarbears.com
Dillsburg ES 400/K-5
202 S Chestnut St 17019 717-432-8691
Patricia Franko, prin. Fax 432-7580
Northern ES 300/K-5
657 S Baltimore St 17019 717-432-8691
Joyce Cal, prin. Fax 502-8707
Northern MS 800/6-8
655 S Baltimore St 17019 717-432-8691
Sylvia Murray, prin. Fax 432-5889
South Mountain ES 400/K-5
711 S Mountain Rd 17019 717-432-8691
Keith Yarger, prin. Fax 502-1472
Other Schools – See Wellsville

Dimock, Susquehanna
Elk Lake SD 1,500/K-12
PO Box 100 18816 570-278-1106
William Bush, supt. Fax 278-4838
www.elklakeschool.org
Elk Lake ES 700/K-6
PO Box 100 18816 570-278-1106
Charles Pirone, prin. Fax 278-4356

Dingmans Ferry, Pike
Delaware Valley SD
Supt. — See Milford
Dingman-Delaware ES 700/3-5
1355 Route 739 18328 570-296-3120
Thomas Smith, prin. Fax 296-3171
Dingman-Delaware MS 800/6-8
1365 Route 739 18328 570-296-3140
Joseph Caramanica, prin. Fax 296-3170
Dingman-Delaware PS 600/K-2
1375 Route 739 18328 570-296-3130
Victoria McNeeley, prin. Fax 296-3173

East Stroudsburg Area SD
Supt. — See East Stroudsburg
Bushkill ES 600/K-5
HC 12 Box 700 18328 570-588-4400
Richard Carty, prin. Fax 588-4406
Lehman IS 900/6-8
HC 12 Box 695 18328 570-588-4410
Robert Dilliplane, prin. Fax 588-4411

Donora, Washington, Pop. 5,420
Ringgold SD
Supt. — See New Eagle
Donora ES 400/K-5
401 Waddell Ave 15033 724-379-7600
Ross Ference, prin. Fax 379-7632

Madonna Regional S 200/PK-8
1 Park Mnr 15033 724-379-5977
Sharon Loughran Brown, prin. Fax 379-7633

Douglassville, Berks
Daniel Boone Area SD
Supt. — See Birdsboro
Amity Intermediate Center 700/2-5
200 Boone Dr 19518 610-689-6240
Marybeth Torchia, prin. Fax 689-6265
Boone Area MS 900/6-8
1845 Weavertown Rd 19518 610-689-6300
Thomas Hankel, prin. Fax 689-6306

Immaculate Conception Academy 200/K-8
903 Chestnut St 19518 610-404-8645
Christine Foley, prin. Fax 404-4890

Dover, York, Pop. 1,922
Dover Area SD 3,600/K-12
2 School Ln 17315 717-292-3671
Robert Krantz, supt. Fax 292-9659
www.dover.k12.pa.us
Dover Area ES 300/K-4
109 E Canal St 17315 717-292-3671
Steven Walker, prin. Fax 292-4645
Dover Area IS 600/7-8
4500 Intermediate Ave 17315 717-292-3671
Julie Sterner, prin. Fax 292-9849
Leib ES 500/K-4
2925 Oakland Rd 17315 717-292-3671
Troy Wiestling, prin. Fax 292-4828
North Salem ES 600/5-6
5161 N Salem Church Rd 17315 717-292-3671
William O'Donnell, prin. Fax 292-4388
Weigelstown ES 400/K-4
3205 Carlisle Rd 17315 717-292-3671
Davanna Rickard, prin. Fax 292-6390
Other Schools – See East Berlin

Downingtown, Chester, Pop. 7,858
Downingtown Area SD 11,600/K-12
126 Wallace Ave 19335 610-269-8460
Dr. Lawrence Mussoline, supt. Fax 873-1404
www.dasd.org
Beaver Creek ES 500/K-5
601 W Pennsylvania Ave 19335 610-269-2790
Dawn Lawless, prin. Fax 269-4572
Bradford Heights ES 500/K-5
1330 Romig Rd 19335 610-269-6021
Michael Solon, prin. Fax 518-0656
Brandywine-Wallace ES 600/K-5
435 Dilworth Rd 19335 610-269-2083
Norma Welsh, prin. Fax 269-2829
Downingtown MS 1,200/6-8
115 Rock Raymond Rd 19335 610-518-0685
Thomas Mulvey, prin. Fax 518-0685
East Ward ES 600/K-5
435 Washington Ave 19335 610-269-8282
Nancy Fuhrman, prin. Fax 873-3440
Lionville ES 600/K-5
526 W Uwchlan Ave 19335 610-363-6580
David Hemingway, prin. Fax 363-3065
Shamona Creek ES 700/K-5
501 Dorlan Mill Rd 19335 610-458-8703
Robert Reed, prin. Fax 458-9130
Uwchlan Hills ES 600/K-5
50 Peck Rd 19335 610-269-5656
Dave Davis, prin. Fax 269-6793
West Bradford ES 600/K-5
1475 Broadrun Rd 19335 610-384-9030
Robert Clegg, prin. Fax 466-0914
Other Schools – See Chester Springs, Exton, Glenmoore

Copeland Run Academy 100/PK-1
407 Lloyd Ave 19335 610-269-4423
Patricia Kirkner, dir.
St. Joseph S 600/K-8
340 Manor Ave 19335 610-269-8999
Sr. John Magdalen, prin. Fax 269-2252

Doylestown, Bucks, Pop. 8,225
Central Bucks SD 20,200/K-12
20 Weldon Dr 18901 267-893-2000
Dr. N. Robert Laws, supt. Fax 893-5800
www.cbsd.org
Cold Spring ES 1,000/K-6
4150 Durham Rd, 267-893-3800
Shawn Ortman, prin. Fax 340-2227
Doyle ES 500/K-6
260 N West St 18901 267-893-4300
Susan Salvesen, prin. Fax 893-5806
Gayman ES 600/K-6
4440 Point Pleasant Pike, 267-893-4350
Brian Finger, prin. Fax 348-4092
Groveland ES 1,100/K-6
1100 N Easton Rd, 267-893-4600
David Heineman, prin. Fax 893-5808
Kutz ES 500/K-6
1950 Turk Rd 18901 267-893-3900
JeanAnn Kahley, prin. Fax 340-9636
Linden ES 500/K-6
480 Linden Ave 18901 267-893-4400
Sue Klimpl, prin. Fax 348-4203
Other Schools – See Buckingham, Chalfont, Furlong, Jamison, New Britain, Warrington

Good Beginnings S 100/PK-K
311 W State St 18901 215-345-4210
Pam Whalen, dir. Fax 348-9054
Our Lady of Mt. Carmel S 400/K-8
225 E Ashland St 18901 215-348-5907
Elizabeth Barry, prin. Fax 348-5671

Dresher, Montgomery
Upper Dublin SD
Supt. — See Maple Glen
Jarrettown ES 500/K-5
1520 Limekiln Pike 19025 215-643-8951
Cheryl Arena Ed.D., prin. Fax 641-9133
Sandy Run MS 1,000/6-8
520 Twining Rd 19025 215-576-3280
Denise Falconi, prin. Fax 572-3886

New Horizons Montessori S 100/PK-6
1701 Jarrettown Rd 19025 215-542-0740
Laura Stulb, hdmstr. Fax 542-2381

Drexel Hill, Delaware, Pop. 29,300
Upper Darby SD 12,100/K-12
4611 Bond Ave 19026 610-789-7200
Louis DeVlieger, supt. Fax 789-8671
www.udsd.k12.pa.us
Aronimink ES, 4611 Bond Ave 19026 300/1-5
Jennifer Saksa, prin. 610-853-4510
Drexel Hill MS, 3001 State Rd 19026 1,300/6-8
Jonathan Ross, prin. 610-853-4580
Garrettford ES, 3830 Garrett Rd 19026 600/1-5
Wayne McAllister, prin. 610-626-9168
Hillcrest ES, 2601 Bond Ave 19026 600/K-5
Christopher Pugliese, prin. 610-853-4520
Kelly ES, 3400 Dennison Ave 19026 1-5
Tanya Glenn-Butler, prin. 610-638-1070
Upper Darby K, 3200 State Rd 19026 600/K-K
Patrice Scanlon, prin. 610-284-7992
Other Schools – See Clifton Heights, Glenolden, Primos Secane, Upper Darby

Holy Child Academy 200/PK-8
475 Shadeland Ave 19026 610-259-2712
Anita Coll, hdmstr. Fax 259-1862
St. Andrew S 300/PK-8
535 Mason Ave 19026 610-259-5145
Helen McLean, prin. Fax 284-6956
St. Bernadette S 400/PK-8
1015 Turner Ave 19026 610-449-6126
Sr. John Marie, prin. Fax 789-0890
St. Dorothy S 400/K-8
1225 Burmont Rd 19026 610-789-4100
Louise Sheehan, prin. Fax 536-3101

Drums, Luzerne
Hazleton Area SD
Supt. — See Hazleton
Drums S 800/K-8
85 S Old Turnpike Rd 18222 570-788-1991
Daniel Diehl, prin. Fax 788-3276

Du Bois, Clearfield, Pop. 8,117
Du Bois Area SD 4,300/K-12
500 Liberty Blvd 15801 814-371-2700
Timothy Deluccia, supt. Fax 371-2544
www.dasd.k12.pa.us
Du Bois Area MS 1,000/6-8
404 Liberty Blvd 15801 814-375-8770
Michael Newman, prin. Fax 375-8780
Highland Street ES 100/K-5
493 S Highland St 15801 814-371-4072
Kathleen Gintler, prin. Fax 371-5096
Juniata ES 400/K-5
248 Juniata St 15801 814-371-1090
Elizabeth Shindledecker, prin. Fax 371-5235
Oklahoma ES 400/K-5
1023 Chestnut Ave 15801 814-371-3660
Kathleen Ginther, prin. Fax 371-5360
Wasson Avenue ES 300/K-5
300 Wasson Ave 15801 814-371-6171
Shawna Grim, prin. Fax 371-8635
Other Schools – See Luthersburg, Penfield, Reynoldsville

Du Bois Central Catholic ES 300/PK-5
PO Box 567 15801 814-371-2570
Fax 371-1551
Du Bois Central Catholic MS 100/6-8
PO Box 567 15801 814-371-3060
Rev. Marc Stockton, prin. Fax 371-3215
DuBois Christian S 100/PK-12
197 Eastern Ave 15801 814-371-7395
Greg Reese, prin. Fax 371-7399

Duke Center, McKean
Otto-Eldred SD 800/K-12
143 Sweitzer Dr 16729 814-966-3214
Robert Falk, supt. Fax 966-3911
www.ottoeldred.org
Other Schools – See Eldred

Dunbar, Fayette, Pop. 1,172
Connellsville Area SD
Supt. — See Connellsville
Dunbar Borough ES 200/K-6
175 Pechin Rd 15431 724-626-1633
Kristen Porter, prin. Fax 626-2504

Duncannon, Perry, Pop. 1,496
Susquenita SD 2,100/K-12
1725 Schoolhouse Rd 17020 717-957-6000
Dr. Daniel Sheats, supt. Fax 957-2463
www.susq.k12.pa.us/
Susquenita ES 700/K-4
101 Susquenita Dr 17020 717-957-6000
Craig Funk, prin. Fax 957-3229
Susquenita MS 700/5-8
200 Susquenita Dr 17020 717-957-6000
William Quigley, prin. Fax 957-9334

Duncansville, Blair, Pop. 1,194
Hollidaysburg Area SD
Supt. — See Hollidaysburg
Allegheny ES 200/1-6
1160 Municipal Dr 16635 814-695-3561
Francine Endler, prin. Fax 695-6028
Foot of Ten ES 500/K-6
450 Foot of Ten Rd 16635 814-695-1941
Robert Gildea, prin. Fax 695-3753

Dunmore, Lackawanna, Pop. 13,968
Dunmore SD 1,700/K-12
300 W Warren St 18512 570-343-2110
Richard McDonald, supt. Fax 343-1458
www.dunmoreschooldistrict.net/
Dunmore ES 800/K-6
300 W Warren St 18512 570-347-6794
Matthew Quinn, prin. Fax 207-6765
Dunmore MS 300/7-8
300 W Warren St 18512 570-346-2043
Robert Gallela, prin. Fax 343-1458

St. Mary of Mt. Carmel S 200/PK-8
325 Chestnut St 18512 570-346-4429
Joseph Triano, prin. Fax 346-3016

Dupont, Luzerne, Pop. 2,626
Pittston Area SD
Supt. — See Pittston
Franklin K 200/K-K
611 Walnut St 18641 570-654-0503
Theresa Babonis, prin. Fax 655-8707

Duquesne, Allegheny, Pop. 6,875
Duquesne CSD 500/K-8
300 Kennedy Ave 15110 412-466-5300
Dr. Donna Durno, supt.
Duquesne S, 300 Kennedy Ave 15110 500/K-8
Dr. Vernon Tipton, prin. 412-466-0663

Duryea, Luzerne, Pop. 4,414

Holy Rosary S 200/PK-8
125 Stephenson St 18642 570-457-2553
Kathleen Gilmartin, prin. Fax 457-3537

Dushore, Sullivan, Pop. 613
Sullivan County SD 700/K-12
PO Box 346 18614 570-928-8194
Dr. Kathryn Gruber, supt. Fax 928-8196
www.sulcosd.k12.pa.us
Other Schools – See Laporte, Mildred

Eagleville, Montgomery, Pop. 3,637
Methacton SD 5,500/K-12
1001 Kriebel Mill Rd 19403 610-489-5000
Dr. Timothy Quinn, supt. Fax 489-5019
www.methacton.org
Arcola IS 1,300/6-8
4000 Eagleville Rd 19403 610-489-5000
Mary Anne DelCollo, prin. Fax 831-5317
Audubon ES 600/K-5
2765 Egypt Rd 19403 610-489-5000
Melissa Gorla, prin. Fax 489-5007
Eagleville ES 400/K-5
125 Summit Ave 19403 610-489-5000
Jason Sorgini, prin. Fax 831-5324
Woodland ES 400/K-5
2700 Woodland Ave 19403 610-489-5000
Zanthia Reddish, prin. Fax 831-5319
Other Schools – See Collegeville, Lansdale

East Berlin, York, Pop. 1,430
Dover Area SD
Supt. — See Dover
Kralltown ES 100/K-4
21 Creek Rd 17316 717-292-3671
David Depew, prin. Fax 432-0087

East Earl, Lancaster
Eastern Lancaster County SD
Supt. — See New Holland
Blue Ball ES 400/K-6
126 Ewell Rd 17519 717-354-1525
Curtis McCaskey, prin. Fax 354-1527

E Fallowfield, Chester
Coatesville Area SD
Supt. — See Coatesville
East Fallowfield ES 300/K-5
2254 Strasburg Rd 19320 610-383-3765
Dr. Marie Walker, prin. Fax 383-3769

East Greenville, Montgomery, Pop. 3,085
Upper Perkiomen SD
Supt. — See Pennsburg
Upper Perkiomen MS 800/6-8
510 Jefferson St 18041 215-679-6288
Duane Wickard, prin. Fax 679-3091

St. Philip Neri S 100/PK-8
26 E 6th St 18041 215-679-7481
Patricia Schleeweiss, prin. Fax 679-8370

East Lansdowne, Delaware, Pop. 2,517
William Penn SD
Supt. — See Lansdowne
East Lansdowne ES 300/K-6
401 Emerson Ave 19050 610-626-2415
Dr. Dawnee Watson-Bouie, prin. Fax 284-8060

St. Cyril of Alexandria S 200/K-8
716 Emerson Ave 19050 610-623-1113
Sr. Barbara Montague, prin. Fax 623-2427

East Millsboro, Fayette
Brownsville Area SD
Supt. — See Brownsville
Central ES 200/K-6
234 Arensburg Rd Ext 15433 724-785-6316
Susan Solomon, prin. Fax 785-4710

East Norriton, Montgomery, Pop. 13,324

Our Lady of Victory S 200/PK-8
351 E Johnson Hwy, 610-275-2990
Angela Ciccanti, prin. Fax 275-0470

Easton, Northampton, Pop. 26,267
Bethlehem Area SD
Supt. — See Bethlehem
Farmersville ES 600/K-5
7036 William Penn Hwy 18045 610-868-0471
Michele Fragnito, prin. Fax 807-5980

Easton Area SD 9,000/K-12
1801 Bushkill Dr 18040 610-250-2400
Susan McGinley, supt. Fax 923-8954
www.eastonsd.org
Cheston ES 500/K-4
723 Coal St 18042 610-250-2542
Tracy Piazza, prin. Fax 923-6046
Easton Area MS 1,300/5-6
990 Echo Trl 18040 610-250-2440
Charlene Symia, prin. Fax 250-2440
Easton Area MS 1,500/7-8
1010 Echo Trl 18040 610-250-2460
Angela DeVietro, prin. Fax 250-2613

Forks ES 500/K-4
1709 Richmond Rd 18040 610-250-2536
Michael McCauley, prin. Fax 923-8933
March ES 300/K-4
429 Reeder St 18042 610-250-2531
Judith Steinberg, prin. Fax 250-2458
Palmer ES 700/K-4
3050 Green Pond Rd 18045 610-250-2521
Meredith Naumann, prin. Fax 923-6955
Paxinosa ES 600/K-4
1221 Northampton St 18042 610-250-2551
David Hightower, prin. Fax 923-8934
Shawnee ES K-4
1315 Echo Trl 18040 610-250-2551
Josephine Galloway, prin. Fax 923-8934
Tracy ES 700/K-4
1243 Tatamy Rd 18045 610-250-2556
Robert Steckel, prin. Fax 250-2602

Wilson Area SD 2,200/K-12
2040 Washington Blvd 18042 484-373-6000
Douglas Wagner, supt. Fax 258-6421
www.wilsonareasd.org
Avona ES 200/K-5
2317 Front St 18042 484-373-6250
Kathleen Thomas, prin. Fax 258-9407
Lauer MS 500/6-8
2400 Firmstone St 18042 484-373-6110
Kevin Steidle, prin. Fax 258-4014
Williams Twp. ES 300/K-5
2660 Morgan Hill Rd 18042 484-373-6170
Dale Ann Brown, prin. Fax 258-8717
Wilson Borough ES 400/K-5
301 S 21st St 18042 484-373-6220
Anthony Tarsi, prin. Fax 258-9436

Easton Catholic S 100/K-8
841 Washington St 18042 610-252-1393
Frank Creazzo, prin. Fax 253-6184
Rock Christian Academy 50/PK-12
PO Box 636 18044 610-253-8161
Rev. Arlene Santos, admin. Fax 250-8794
St. Jane Frances deChantal S 500/PK-8
1900 Washington Blvd 18042 610-253-8442
Isabel Conlin, prin. Fax 253-2427

East Petersburg, Lancaster, Pop. 4,346
Hempfield SD
Supt. — See Landisville
East Petersburg ES 500/K-6
5700 Lemon St 17520 717-569-1211
Randa Rineer, prin. Fax 618-0998

East Prospect, York, Pop. 762
Eastern York SD
Supt. — See Wrightsville
Canadochly ES 400/K-5
PO Box 118 17317 717-252-3674
Mary Jo Moczulski, prin. Fax 252-5397

East Smithfield, Bradford
Athens Area SD
Supt. — See Athens
Child ES 100/K-5
PO Box 38 18817 570-596-4244
Andrew Latchford, prin. Fax 596-4141
SRU MS 300/6-7
PO Box 38 18817 570-596-3171
Donald Jones, prin. Fax 596-4141

East Springfield, Erie
Northwestern SD
Supt. — See Albion
Springfield ES 300/K-5
PO Box 248 16411 814-756-9400
Pamela Lenz, prin. Fax 922-3140

East Stroudsburg, Monroe, Pop. 10,621
East Stroudsburg Area SD 8,200/K-12
PO Box 298 18301 570-424-8500
Dr. Rachael Heath, supt. Fax 424-5646
www.esasd.net
East Stroudsburg ES 100/K-5
30 Independence Rd 18301 570-421-1905
Irene Livingston, prin. Fax 420-8310
Hill ES 600/K-5
151 E Broad St 18301 570-424-8073
Michelle Arnold, prin. Fax 476-0720
Lambert IS 1,100/6-8
2000 Milford Rd 18301 570-424-8430
Michael Catrillo, prin. Fax 476-0464
Middle Smithfield ES 800/K-5
5180 Milford Rd, 570-223-8082
David Baker, prin. Fax 223-2110
Resica ES 700/K-5
1 Gravel Ridge Rd, 570-223-6911
Gail Kulick, prin. Fax 223-2100
Smithfield ES 500/K-5
RR 5 Box 5210 18301 570-421-2841
John Burrus, prin. Fax 476-0488
Other Schools – See Dingmans Ferry

Notre Dame MS 200/5-8
60 Spangenburg Ave 18301 570-421-7883
Thomas McCloskey, prin. Fax 421-2366
Notre Dame S 400/PK-4
78 Ridgeway St 18301 570-421-3651
Sr. Mary Alice Kane, prin. Fax 422-6935
St. Paul's Lutheran S 50/PK-PK
RR 2 Box 2157 18301 570-223-7700
John Harding, prin. Fax 223-7700

Ebensburg, Cambria, Pop. 2,938
Central Cambria SD 1,900/K-12
208 Schoolhouse Rd 15931 814-472-8870
Dr. Susan Makosy, supt. Fax 472-9695
www.cchs.k12.pa.us/
Cambria ES 500/K-5
212 Schoolhouse Rd 15931 814-472-8432
Dr. Ronald Rufrano, prin. Fax 472-8674
Central Cambria MS 400/6-8
205 W Highland Ave 15931 814-472-6505
Kimberly McDermott, prin. Fax 472-4187
Other Schools – See Johnstown

Holy Name S 200/PK-8
215 W Horner St 15931 814-472-8817
Joan Meintel, prin. Fax 471-0500

Eddystone, Delaware, Pop. 2,381
Ridley SD
Supt. — See Folsom
Eddystone ES 200/K-5
1410 E 9th St 19022 610-534-1900
Dr. Joseph Wallen, prin. Fax 874-4321

Edinboro, Erie, Pop. 6,737
General McLane SD 2,300/K-12
11771 Edinboro Rd 16412 814-273-1033
Alan Karns, supt. Fax 273-1030
www.generalmclane.org
Edinboro ES 400/K-4
5390 Route 6N 16412 814-273-1033
Sally Wagner, prin. Fax 273-1040
Parker MS 700/5-8
11781 Edinboro Rd 16412 814-273-1033
Annette Rilling, prin. Fax 273-1038
Other Schools – See Mc Kean

Eighty Four, Washington
Canon-McMillan SD
Supt. — See Canonsburg
Wylandville ES 200/K-4
1254 Route 519 15330 724-222-2507
Grace Lani, prin. Fax 225-5971

Elderton, Armstrong, Pop. 343
Armstrong SD
Supt. — See Ford City
Elderton ES 300/K-6
239 S Lytle St 15736 724-354-2131
Eric Ritzert, prin. Fax 354-4619

Eldred, McKean, Pop. 824
Otto-Eldred SD
Supt. — See Duke Center
Otto-Eldred ES 400/K-6
PO Box 309 16731 814-225-4779
Terry Stanley, prin. Fax 225-4917

Elizabeth, Allegheny, Pop. 1,505
Elizabeth Forward SD 2,500/K-12
401 Rock Run Rd 15037 412-896-2310
Dr. Bart Rocco, supt. Fax 751-9483
www.efsd.net
Central ES 300/K-5
401 Rock Run Rd 15037 412-896-2318
Susan Heatherington, prin. Fax 751-0692
Elizabeth Forward MS 700/6-8
401 Rock Run Rd 15037 412-896-2335
Michael Routh, prin. Fax 751-6669
Other Schools – See Mc Keesport, Monongahela

Elizabethtown, Lancaster, Pop. 11,892
Elizabethtown Area SD 4,000/K-12
600 E High St 17022 717-367-1521
Dr. Amy Slamp, supt. Fax 367-1920
www.etownschools.org
East High Street ES 600/K-5
800 E High St 17022 717-361-0099
Annette Spagnolo, prin. Fax 367-3826
Elizabethtown Area MS 1,000/6-8
600 E High St 17022 717-361-7525
Randall Fox, prin. Fax 361-2597
Fairview ES 100/K-5
8853 Elizabethtown Rd 17022 717-367-7099
Dr. Carol Myers, prin. Fax 361-2503
Mill Road ES 300/K-5
35 Elm Ave 17022 717-361-7424
Dr. Carol Myers, prin. Fax 361-0184
Other Schools – See Bainbridge, Rheems

Lower Dauphin SD
Supt. — See Hummelstown
Conewago ES 200/K-5
2809 Hershey Rd 17022 717-367-7233
Edward Gnall, prin. Fax 367-6893

Mt. Calvary Christian S 400/PK-12
PO Box 508 17022 717-367-1649
Kenneth Howard, supt. Fax 367-5672
St. Peters Catholic S 100/PK-5
61 E Washington St 17022 717-367-1678
Suzanne Wood, prin. Fax 367-3081

Elkins Park, Montgomery, Pop. 4,700
Abington SD
Supt. — See Abington
McKinley ES 600/K-6
370 Cedar Rd 19027 215-663-0430
Charles Lentz, prin. Fax 663-0593

Cheltenham Township SD 4,500/K-12
2000 Ashbourne Rd 19027 215-886-9500
Dr. William Kiefer, supt. Fax 884-3029
www.cheltenham.org
Elkins Park S 700/5-6
8149 New Second St 19027 215-881-4941
Carol Nejman, prin. Fax 635-7492
Myers ES 400/K-4
7609 Montgomery Ave 19027 215-517-4540
Andrew Kuhn, prin. Fax 635-7437
Other Schools – See Cheltenham, Glenside, Wyncote

St. James S 200/PK-8
8306 Brookside Rd 19027 215-635-4673
Nancy Peluso, prin. Fax 635-3521

Elkland, Tioga, Pop. 1,722
Northern Tioga SD 2,400/K-12
117 Coates Ave 16920 814-258-5642
Timothy Bowers, supt. Fax 258-7083
www.ntiogasd.org
Wood ES 300/K-6
112 Ellison Rd 16920 814-258-5131
Jess Millard, prin. Fax 258-7484
Other Schools – See Tioga, Westfield

Elliottsburg, Perry
West Perry SD 2,900/K-12
2606 Shermans Valley Rd 17024 717-789-3934
Rhonda Brunner, supt. Fax 789-4997
www.westperry.org/
West Perry MS 700/6-8
2620 Shermans Valley Rd 17024 717-789-3012
Bernard Danko, prin. Fax 789-3393
Other Schools – See Blain, New Bloomfield, Shermans Dale

Ellsworth, Washington, Pop. 1,039
Bentworth SD
Supt. — See Bentleyville
Bentworth MS 200/7-8
89 Pine St 15331 724-239-4431
David Schreiber, prin. Fax 239-5889

Ellwood City, Lawrence, Pop. 8,262
Ellwood City Area SD 2,100/K-12
501 Crescent Ave 16117 724-752-1591
Frank Aloi, supt. Fax 752-0743
www.ellwood.k12.pa.us
Hartman ES 300/K-6
Crescent Ave and 4th 16117 724-758-3241
George Garda, prin. Fax 758-0534
North Side ES 400/K-6
Orchard and North Sts 16117 724-752-1381
Christine Gibson, prin. Fax 758-0329
Perry Township ES 300/K-6
Portersville Rd 16117 724-758-9458
George Garda, prin.
Walnut Ridge ES 100/K-6
Aetna Dr and Sunset 16117 724-758-5609
Christine Gibson, prin.

Riverside Beaver County SD 1,800/K-12
318 Country Club Dr 16117 724-758-7512
David Anney, supt. Fax 758-2070
www.riverside.k12.pa.us
Riverside IS 400/4-6
302 Country Club Dr 16117 724-758-7512
Stephen Girting, prin. Fax 758-0919
Riverside MS 300/7-8
302 Country Club Dr 16117 724-758-7512
Stephen Girting, prin. Fax 758-0919
Riverside PS 400/K-3
300 Country Club Dr 16117 724-758-7512
Raymond Santillo, prin. Fax 758-7519

Holy Redeemer S 100/PK-8
311 Lawrence Ave 16117 724-758-5591
Sr. Ellamae McDonald, prin. Fax 758-0705

Elverson, Chester, Pop. 1,164
Twin Valley SD 3,200/K-12
4851 N Twin Valley Rd 19520 610-286-8611
Dr. Robert Pleis, supt. Fax 286-8608
www.tvsd.org
Twin Valley ES 400/K-4
50 Mast Dr 19520 610-286-8670
Gail Porrazzo, prin. Fax 286-8672
Twin Valley MS 800/5-8
770 Clymer Hill Rd 19520 610-286-8660
Dr. Gerald Catagnus, prin. Fax 286-8662
Other Schools – See Birdsboro, Honey Brook

Emmaus, Lehigh, Pop. 11,351
East Penn SD 7,700/K-12
800 Pine St 18049 610-966-8300
Dr. Thomas Seidenberger, supt. Fax 966-8339
www.eastpenn.k12.pa.us/
Jefferson ES 300/K-5
520 Elm St 18049 610-965-1644
Cheryl Wetzel, prin. Fax 966-8349
Lincoln ES 400/K-5
233 Seem St 18049 610-965-1636
Other Schools – See Alburtis, Macungie, Wescosville

St. Ann S 300/PK-8
435 S 6th St 18049 610-965-9220
Diana Kile, prin. Fax 967-1099

Emporium, Cameron, Pop. 2,362
Cameron County SD 900/K-12
601 Woodland Ave 15834 814-486-4000
Clyde Moate, supt. Fax 486-1721
www.cameroncountyschools.org/
Woodland ES 400/K-6
601 Woodland Ave 15834 814-486-4000
Lynn Newcomer, prin. Fax 486-3150

Enola, Cumberland, Pop. 5,961
Cumberland Valley SD
Supt. — See Mechanicsburg
Shaull ES 400/K-5
1 Shaull Dr 17025 717-732-2460
Christopher Baldrige, prin. Fax 732-8664

East Pennsboro Area SD 2,900/K-12
890 Valley St 17025 717-732-3601
Dr. Linda Bigos, supt. Fax 732-8927
www.epasd.k12.pa.us
East Pennsboro Area MS 800/5-8
529 N Enola Dr 17025 717-732-0771
Stephen Andrejack, prin.
East Pennsboro ES 600/K-4
840 Panther Pkwy 17025 717-732-0441
Christine Frenchek, prin.
Other Schools – See Camp Hill

Ephrata, Lancaster, Pop. 13,092
Ephrata Area SD 4,000/K-12
803 Oak Blvd 17522 717-721-1400
Dr. Gerald Rosati, supt. Fax 733-1841
easdpa.org
Clay ES 500/K-5
250 Clay School Rd 17522 717-721-1100
Joy Darkes, prin. Fax 721-7082
Ephrata MS 900/6-8
957 Hammon Ave 17522 717-721-1468
Kevin Fillgrove, prin. Fax 738-1930
Fulton ES 400/K-5
51 E Fulton St 17522 717-721-1130
Gary Oberly, prin. Fax 721-1133
Highland ES 500/K-5
99 Highland Ave 17522 717-721-1160
Gangi Cucciuffo, prin. Fax 721-1167
Other Schools – See Akron

Ephrata Mennonite S 200/K-10
598 Stevens Rd 17522 717-738-4266
Fax 738-4266
Hinkletown Mennonite S 200/K-8
272 Wanner Rd 17522 717-354-7100
Kathy Stoltzfus, prin. Fax 354-8438
Our Mother of Perpetual Help S 300/PK-8
330 Church Ave 17522 717-738-2414
Margaret Gardner, prin. Fax 738-3280
Pleasant Valley Mennonite S 100/1-12
144 Pleasant Valley Rd 17522 717-738-1833
Larry Weaver, prin. Fax 738-3941

Erdenheim, Montgomery

Philadelphia-Montgomery Christian Acad. 400/PK-12
35 Hillcrest Rd 19038 215-233-0782
Donald Beebe, hdmstr. Fax 233-0829

Erie, Erie, Pop. 102,612
Erie CSD 12,300/K-12
148 W 21st St 16502 814-874-6000
Dr. James Barker, supt. Fax 874-6010
eriesd.org
Burton ES 300/K-5
1661 Buffalo Rd 16510 814-874-6850
Carla Johnson, prin. Fax 874-6856
Cleveland S 600/K-8
1540 W 38th St 16508 814-874-6670
Teresa Szumigala, prin. Fax 874-6675
Connell S 700/K-8
1820 E 38th St 16510 814-874-6785
Joseph Orlando, prin. Fax 874-6789
Diehl S 400/K-8
2327 Fairmont Pkwy 16510 814-874-6585
Jeannette Barczynski, prin. Fax 874-6589
Edison ES 300/K-5
1921 E Lake Rd 16511 814-874-6470
Brenda McWilliams, prin. Fax 874-6475
Emerson-Gridley ES 500/K-6
816 Park Ave S 16502 814-874-6450
Malinda Bostick, prin. Fax 874-6456
Glenwood ES 400/K-6
3503 Peach St 16508 814-874-6570
Dianne Bernard, prin. Fax 874-6575
Harding S 600/K-8
820 Lincoln Ave 16505 814-874-6550
Leslee Hutchinson, prin. Fax 874-6556
Irving ES 400/K-6
2310 Plum St 16502 814-874-6770
Michelle Fiorelli, prin. Fax 874-6775
Jefferson S 600/K-8
230 E 38th St 16504 814-874-6650
Diane Madara, prin. Fax 874-6656
Lincoln ES 500/K-5
831 E 31st St 16504 814-874-6685
Linda Cappabianca, prin. Fax 874-6689
McKinley ES 500/K-5
933 E 22nd St 16503 814-874-6870
Kristen Boyd, prin. Fax 874-6875
Perry S 500/K-8
955 W 29th St 16508 814-874-6485
Timothy Sabol, prin. Fax 874-6489
Pfeiffer-Burleigh S 700/K-8
235 E 11th St 16503 814-874-6750
Rose Sheridan, prin. Fax 874-6756
Roosevelt MS 400/7-8
2501 Plum St 16502 814-874-6800
Fabienne Mir, prin. Fax 874-6807
Wayne S 600/K-8
650 East Ave 16503 814-874-6700
James Smith, prin. Fax 874-6707
Wilson MS 500/6-8
718 E 28th St 16504 814-874-6600
Scherry Prater, prin. Fax 874-6607

Fort LeBoeuf SD
Supt. — See Waterford
Robison ES 400/K-5
1651 Robison Rd W 16509 814-868-5565
Cindy Hargest, prin. Fax 864-2017

Harbor Creek SD
Supt. — See Harborcreek
Clark ES 300/K-6
3650 Depot Rd 16510 814-897-2100
Donna Rose, prin. Fax 897-8723
Klein ES 300/K-6
5325 E Lake Rd 16511 814-897-2100
Fax 898-0225
Rolling Ridge ES 500/K-6
3700 Ridge Pkwy 16510 814-897-2100
Cynthia Zajac, prin. Fax 898-1916

Iroquois SD, 800 Tyndall Ave 16511 900/K-12
Dr. Sam Signorino, supt. 814-899-7643
isd.iu5.org/
Iroquois ES, 4231 Morse St 16511 300/K-6
Brenda Evans, prin. 814-899-7643

Millcreek Township SD 7,500/K-12
3740 W 26th St 16506 814-835-5300
Frank Bova, supt. Fax 835-5371
www.mtsd.org
Belle Valley ES 600/K-5
5300 Henderson Rd 16509 814-835-5600
Jon Colinear, prin. Fax 835-5623
Chestnut Hill ES 400/K-5
1001 W 54th St 16509 814-835-5577
Elizabeth Detisch, prin. Fax 835-5590
Grandview ES 600/K-5
4301 Lancaster Rd 16506 814-835-5496
Geoffrey Groves, prin. Fax 835-5466
Ridgefield ES 300/K-5
3227 Highland Rd 16506 814-835-5395
Jeremiah Bull, prin. Fax 835-5376
Tracy ES 600/K-5
2624 W 6th St 16505 814-835-5800
Donald Stark, prin. Fax 835-5810
Vernondale ES 200/K-5
1432 Wilkins Rd 16505 814-835-5493
Dr. Marilyn Kendall, prin. Fax 835-5467
Westlake MS 600/6-8
4330 W Lake Rd 16505 814-835-5756
Marty Kaverman, prin. Fax 835-5770
Wilson MS 500/6-8
900 W 54th St 16509 814-835-5510
John Cavanagh, prin. Fax 835-5542
Other Schools – See Fairview

Wattsburg Area SD 1,600/K-12
10782 Wattsburg Rd 16509 814-824-3400
Jay Badams, supt. Fax 824-5200
www.wattsburg.org/
Wattsburg Area ES 600/K-4
10780 Wattsburg Rd 16509 814-824-3400
Chad Porter, prin. Fax 825-0302
Wattsburg Area MS 500/5-8
10774 Wattsburg Rd 16509 814-824-3400
Douglas McGarvey, prin. Fax 825-6337

Bethel Christian S of Erie 100/K-12
1781 W 38th St 16508 814-868-2365
Dennis Gillenwater, admin. Fax 864-7674
Blessed Sacrament S 500/PK-8
2510 Greengarden Rd 16502 814-455-1387
Sheri Kurczewski, prin. Fax 461-0247
Erie Day S 200/PK-8
1372 W 6th St 16505 814-452-4273
Michael Mullin, hdmstr. Fax 455-5184
Erie First Christian Academy 200/PK-12
8150 Oliver Rd 16509 814-866-6979
John Richardson, admin. Fax 866-5829
Holy Family S 100/PK-8
1153 E 9th St 16503 814-452-4720
Sr. M. Kevin Berdis, prin. Fax 453-2275
Lake Erie Adventist S 50/1-8
190 Hunter Willis Rd 16509 814-824-6169
Luther Memorial Learning Center 200/K-8
220 W 11th St 16501 814-454-0106
Susan Belott, prin.
Our Lady of Mt. Carmel S 200/PK-8
1531 E Grandview Blvd 16510 814-825-2822
Veronica Antoske, prin. Fax 825-7437
Our Lady of Peace S 500/PK-8
2401 W 38th St Unit B 16506 814-838-3548
Jeffrey Lipiec, prin. Fax 838-9133
Our Lady's Christian S 400/PK-8
606 Lowell Ave 16505 814-838-7676
Fay Nelson, prin. Fax 838-6860
St. Boniface S 100/PK-8
9363 Wattsburg Rd 16509 814-825-4238
Barbara Portenier, prin. Fax 825-4274
St. George S 700/PK-8
1612 Bryant St 16509 814-864-4821
Lawrence Neubauer, prin. Fax 866-8297
St. James S 300/PK-8
2602 Buffalo Rd 16510 814-899-3429
Sr. Colette Hilow, prin. Fax 898-8285
St. John/Holy Rosary East Side Cath S 200/PK-8
504 E 27th St 16504 814-452-6874
Joseph Wachter, prin. Fax 455-0358
St. Luke S 400/PK-8
425 E 38th St 16504 814-825-7105
Marietta Stalsky, prin. Fax 825-7169
St. Peter Cathedral S 300/PK-8
160 W 11th St 16501 814-452-4276
Kathleen Lane, prin. Fax 452-0479
Villa Maria S 400/PK-8
2551 W 8th St Ste A 16505 814-838-5451
Damon Finazzo, prin. Fax 833-6132

Essington, Delaware
Interboro SD
Supt. — See Prospect Park
Tinicum S 300/K-8
91 Seneca St 19029 610-521-4450
David Criscuolo, prin. Fax 521-5775

Etters, York, Pop. 797
West Shore SD
Supt. — See Lewisberry
Newberry ES 400/K-5
2055 Old Trail Rd 17319 717-938-2111
Robert Detz, prin.
Red Mill ES, 700 Red Mill Rd 17319 600/K-5
Michael Zang, prin. 717-938-3778

Evans City, Butler, Pop. 1,957
Seneca Valley SD
Supt. — See Harmony
Evans City ES 600/K-4
345 W Main St 16033 724-538-8800
Fax 538-3660
Evans City MS 500/5-6
345 W Main St 16033 724-538-8800
Thomas Hallman, prin. Fax 538-3660

Everett, Bedford, Pop. 1,888
Everett Area SD 1,500/K-12
427 E South St 15537 814-652-9114
Royce Ann Boyd, supt. Fax 652-6191
www.everett.k12.pa.us
Everett Area ES 500/K-6
165 E 1st Ave 15537 814-652-9114
Shawn Kovac, prin. Fax 652-9640
Everett Area MS 200/7-8
1 Renaissance Cir 15537 814-652-9114
James Hollis, prin. Fax 652-0107
Other Schools – See Breezewood, Clearville

Snake Spring Valley Christian Academy 50/PK-12
377 Upper Snake Spring Rd 15537 814-623-2840
Sean LaMarche, admin. Fax 623-4864

Exeter, Luzerne, Pop. 6,007
Wyoming Area SD 2,600/K-12
20 Memorial St 18643 570-655-3733
Raymond Bernardi, supt. Fax 883-1280
www.wyomingarea.org
Kennedy ES 200/K-4
58 Penn Ave 18643 570-655-2146
Margaret Grimes, prin. Fax 602-0943
Other Schools – See Pittston, West Pittston, Wyoming

Wyoming Area Catholic S 200/PK-8
1690 Wyoming Ave 18643 570-654-7982
Lucille Procopio, prin. Fax 654-0605

Export, Westmoreland, Pop. 856
Kiski Area SD
Supt. — See Leechburg
Mamont ES 300/K-6
230 Mamont Dr 15632 724-327-4057
Christine Ross, prin. Fax 733-0689

Exton, Chester, Pop. 2,550
Downingtown Area SD
Supt. — See Downingtown
Lionville MS 1,500/6-8
550 W Uwchlan Ave 19341 610-524-6300
Judy Groh, prin. Fax 524-0152

West Chester Area SD
Supt. — See West Chester
Exton ES 500/K-5
301 Hendricks Ave 19341 484-266-1400
Roberta Gettis, prin. Fax 266-1499

SS. Philip & James S 600/PK-8
721 E Lincoln Hwy 19341 610-363-6536
Sr. Marita Barber, prin. Fax 363-6495

Factoryville, Wyoming, Pop. 1,197
Lackawanna Trail SD 1,300/K-12
PO Box 85 18419 570-945-5184
Matthew Rakauskas, supt. Fax 945-3154
www.ltsd.org
Lackawanna Trail ES 600/K-6
PO Box 85 18419 570-945-5153
Jeffrey Gregory, prin. Fax 945-3154

Fairchance, Fayette, Pop. 2,097
Albert Gallatin Area SD
Supt. — See Uniontown
Wilson ES 200/K-5
100 AL Wilson Dr 15436 724-564-7434
Veronica Murray, prin. Fax 564-7423

Fairfield, Adams, Pop. 511
Fairfield Area SD 1,300/K-12
4840 Fairfield Rd 17320 717-642-8228
William Chain, supt. Fax 642-2036
www.fairfieldpaschools.org/
Fairfield Area ES 500/K-4
4842 Fairfield Rd 17320 717-642-8228
Babara Richwine, prin. Fax 642-2016
Fairfield Area MS 400/5-8
4840 Fairfield Rd 17320 717-642-8228
Beth Bender, prin. Fax 642-2005

Fairless Hills, Bucks, Pop. 9,026
Bristol Township SD
Supt. — See Levittown
Armstrong MS 400/7-8
475 Wistar Rd 19030 215-945-4940
Larry Funk, prin. Fax 945-1664

Pennsbury SD
Supt. — See Fallsington
Oxford Valley ES 500/K-5
430 Trenton Rd 19030 215-949-6808
Fran Nitkin, prin. Fax 949-6810
Village Park ES 300/K-5
75 Unity Dr 19030 215-949-6740
Helen Stopper, prin. Fax 269-1911

Calvary Christian S 100/PK-8
676 Lincoln Hwy 19030 215-736-2391
Robin Laskey, dir. Fax 295-6691
Childrens House of Bucks County 100/PK-6
840 Trenton Rd 19030 215-943-3656
Susan Weir, prin. Fax 946-3088
Pen Ryn S 200/PK-8
235 S Olds Blvd 19030 215-547-1800
Liz Morton, hdmstr. Fax 946-2877
St. Frances Cabrini S 300/K-8
10 Goble Ct 19030 215-946-6334
Mary Katz, prin. Fax 946-0316

Fairview, Erie, Pop. 212
Fairview SD 1,700/K-12
7460 McCray Rd 16415 814-474-2600
Larry Kessler, supt. Fax 474-5497
www.fairviewschools.org/
Fairview ES 500/K-4
5145 Avonia Rd 16415 814-474-2600
Dr. Ben Horn, prin. Fax 474-2719

Fairview MS 600/5-8
4967 Avonia Rd 16415 814-474-2600
Steve Ferringer, prin. Fax 474-1640

Millcreek Township SD
Supt. — See Erie
Asbury ES 600/K-5
5875 Sterrettania Rd 16415 814-835-5512
Terry Costello, prin. Fax 835-6100
Walnut Creek MS 600/6-8
5901 Sterrettania Rd 16415 814-835-5700
Darcie Moseley, prin. Fax 835-5710

Leadership Christian Academy 100/PK-7
5900 Sterrettania Rd 16415 814-833-0286
Diane Price, prin. Fax 833-4155

Fairview Village, Montgomery

Fairview Village Adventist S 50/K-8
PO Box 360 19409 610-489-5960
Fax 489-5960

Fallsington, Bucks
Pennsbury SD 9,500/K-12
134 Yardley Ave 19054 215-428-4100
Dr. Paul Long, admin. Fax 295-8912
www.pennsbury.k12.pa.us
Fallsington ES 200/K-5
134 Yardley Ave 19054 215-428-4170
David Hughes, prin. Fax 428-5210
Other Schools – See Fairless Hills, Levittown, Morrisville, Yardley

---

St. Joseph the Worker S 200/PK-8
9160 New Falls Rd 19054 215-945-4312
John Mundy, prin. Fax 945-8733

Farmington, Fayette
Uniontown Area SD
Supt. — See Uniontown
Wharton ES, 136 Elliotsville Rd 15437 200/K-5
Edward Fearer, prin. 724-329-5510

Farrell, Mercer, Pop. 5,999
Farrell Area SD 1,100/PK-12
1600 Roemer Blvd 16121 724-346-6585
Dr. Lawrence Connelly, supt. Fax 346-0223
www.farrellareaschools.com
Farrell Area ES 600/PK-6
1600 Roemer Blvd 16121 724-346-6585
Carole Borkowski, prin. Fax 509-1109

Monsignor Geno Monti S 100/K-8
1225 Union St 16121 724-347-1440
Alice Connelly, prin. Fax 347-1440

Fawn Grove, York, Pop. 465
South Eastern SD 3,300/K-12
377 Main St 17321 717-382-4843
Dr. Tracy Shank, supt. Fax 382-4769
www.sesdweb.net/
Fawn Area ES 300/K-4
504 Main St 17321 717-382-4220
Jennifer Herman, prin. Fax 382-1326
South Eastern MS - East 600/7-8
375 Main St 17321 717-382-4851
Jill Kling, prin. Fax 382-9033
South Eastern MS West 600/5-6
417 Main St 17321 717-382-4851
Kimberly Rauscher, prin. Fax 382-4786
Other Schools – See Delta, Stewartstown

Fayette City, Fayette, Pop. 684
Frazier SD
Supt. — See Perryopolis
Central ES 200/K-5
Central School Rd 15438 724-326-4576
Kenneth Meadows, prin. Fax 736-0688

Fayetteville, Franklin, Pop. 3,033
Chambersburg Area SD
Supt. — See Chambersburg
Fayetteville ES, 8 E Main St 17222 300/K-5
Barbara Wolf, prin. 717-352-2774

Feasterville, Bucks, Pop. 6,696
Neshaminy SD
Supt. — See Langhorne
Ferderbar ES, 300 Heights Ln 19053 600/K-5
Judy Brown, prin. 215-809-6370
Lower Southampton ES 400/K-5
7 School Ln 19053 215-809-6350
Matt Walsh, prin.

Assumption BVM S 300/K-8
55 E Bristol Rd 19053 215-357-5499
Sr. Patricia McKee, prin. Fax 357-2283

Fenelton, Butler
Butler Area SD
Supt. — See Butler
Clearfield Township ES 200/K-6
719 Clearfield Rd 16034 724-287-8721
Jack Ratica, prin. Fax 287-2106

Finleyville, Washington, Pop. 452
Ringgold SD
Supt. — See New Eagle
Gastonville ES 400/K-5
3685 Finleyville Elrama Rd 15332 724-348-7205
Wendy Burke, prin. Fax 348-8839
Ringgold MS 500/6-8
6023 State Route 88 15332 724-348-7154
Jeffrey Matty, prin. Fax 348-8839

Fishertown, Bedford
Chestnut Ridge SD 1,700/K-12
3281 Valley Rd 15539 814-839-4195
Joseph Kimmel, supt. Fax 839-2088
www.crsd.k12.pa.us/
Chestnut Ridge MS 500/5-8
3281 Valley Rd 15539 814-839-4195
Max Shoemaker, prin. Fax 839-2088
Other Schools – See New Paris

Fleetwood, Berks, Pop. 4,006
Brandywine Heights Area SD
Supt. — See Topton
Rockland Center ES 100/K-2
73 Lyons Rd 19522 610-682-5161
Andrew Potteiger, prin. Fax 682-5164

Fleetwood Area SD 2,700/K-12
801 N Richmond St 19522 610-944-9598
Dr. Paul Eaken, supt. Fax 944-9408
www.fleetwoodasd.k12.pa.us
Fleetwood Area MS 800/5-8
407 N Richmond St 19522 610-944-7634
Christopher Redding, prin. Fax 944-5307
Fleetwood ES 200/K-4
109 W Vine St 19522 610-944-8404
Lori Koehler, prin. Fax 944-5341
Richmond ES 200/K-4
14432 Kutztown Rd 19522 610-944-8279
Michelle Jackson, prin. Fax 944-8342
Other Schools – See Blandon

Flinton, Cambria
Glendale SD 900/K-12
1466 Beaver Valley Rd 16640 814-687-3402
Dr. Patrick Lukasavich, supt. Fax 687-3341
www.gsd1.org
Glendale ES 400/K-6
1500 Beaver Valley Rd 16640 814-687-4263
Ed DiSabato, prin. Fax 687-4083

Flourtown, Montgomery, Pop. 4,754
Springfield Township SD
Supt. — See Oreland
Springfield Twp ES - Erdenheim Campus 400/K-4
500 Haws Ln 19031 215-233-6000
Christine Bradley, prin. Fax 233-6094

St. Genevieve S 200/K-8
1237 Bethlehem Pike 19031 215-836-5644
Sr. Theresa Maugle, prin. Fax 836-0159

Folcroft, Delaware, Pop. 6,906
Southeast Delco SD 3,800/K-12
1560 Delmar Dr 19032 610-522-4300
Stephen Butz, supt. Fax 461-4874
www.sedelco.org
Delcroft S 600/1-8
799 School Ln 19032 610-522-4360
Ed Small, prin. Fax 534-3717
Other Schools – See Collingdale, Glenolden, Sharon Hill

Folsom, Delaware, Pop. 8,173
Ridley SD 5,900/K-12
901 Morton Ave 19033 610-534-1900
Dr. Nicholas Ignatuk, supt. Fax 534-2335
www.ridleysd.k12.pa.us
Edgewood ES 300/K-5
525 8th Ave 19033 610-534-1900
Dr. Wayne Goldey, prin. Fax 328-1840
Other Schools – See Eddystone, Morton, Ridley Park, Swarthmore, Woodlyn

Ford City, Armstrong, Pop. 3,258
Armstrong SD 5,100/K-12
410 Main St 16226 724-763-7151
Dr. William Kerr, supt. Fax 763-7295
www.asd.k12.pa.us
Lenape ES 800/K-6
2300 Center Ave 16226 724-763-5299
Thomas Dinga, prin. Fax 763-2552
Other Schools – See Dayton, Elderton, Kittanning, Rural Valley

---

Divine Redeemer S 200/PK-6
726 4th Ave 16226 724-763-3761
Dr. John Shaner, prin. Fax 763-4112

Forest City, Susquehanna, Pop. 1,795
Forest City Regional SD 900/PK-12
100 Susquehanna St 18421 570-785-2400
Dr. Robert Vadella, supt. Fax 785-9557
www.forestcityschool.org/
Forest City Regional ES 500/PK-6
100 Susquehanna St 18421 570-785-2483
Kenneth Swartz, prin. Fax 785-2354

Forest Hills, Allegheny, Pop. 6,424

Christ Lutheran S 100/PK-8
400 Barclay Ave 15221 412-271-7173
Lois Frerking, prin. Fax 271-4921

Fort Washington, Montgomery, Pop. 3,699
Upper Dublin SD
Supt. — See Maple Glen
Fort Washington ES 500/K-5
1264 Fort Washington Ave 19034 215-643-8961
William Del Collo, prin. Fax 643-8967

Germantown Academy 1,100/PK-12
340 Morris Rd 19034 215-646-3300
James Connor, hdmstr. Fax 646-1216
Open Door Christian Academy 200/PK-8
1260 Fort Washington Ave 19034 215-542-9795
Dr. Donald Dawes, hdmstr. Fax 646-6822

Forty Fort, Luzerne, Pop. 4,331
Wyoming Valley West SD
Supt. — See Kingston
Dana Street ES 600/K-5
50 Dana St 18704 570-283-0591
Irvin DeRemer, prin. Fax 283-1802

Wyoming Seminary-Lower S 400/PK-8
1560 Wyoming Ave 18704 570-718-6600
Kip Nygren, pres. Fax 718-6649

Foxburg, Clarion, Pop. 269
Allegheny-Clarion Valley SD 900/K-12
PO Box 100 16036 724-659-5820
Brenda Brinker, supt. Fax 659-2963
www.acvsd.org/
Allegheny-Clarion Valley ES 400/K-6
PO Box 347 16036 724-659-3555
Jon Fair, prin. Fax 659-2963

Franklin, Venango, Pop. 6,879
Franklin Area SD 2,300/K-12
417 13th St 16323 814-432-8917
Ronald Paranick, supt. Fax 437-5754
www.fasd.k12.pa.us/
Central ES 300/K-6
1276 Otter St 16323 814-432-8419
Dr. Pamela Dye, prin. Fax 437-7819
Franklin Area MS 400/7-8
246 Pone Ln 16323 814-432-2224
Dale Ishman, prin. Fax 437-1491
Sandycreek ES 200/K-6
297 Pone Ln 16323 814-432-3819
Brenda Fry, prin. Fax 437-7924
Seventh Street ES 100/K-6
310 7th St 16323 814-432-5562
Dr. James Ruby, prin. Fax 432-5237
Other Schools – See Harrisville, Polk, Utica

Valley Grove SD 600/K-12
429 Wiley Ave 16323 814-432-4919
Jeffrey Clark, supt. Fax 437-1243
www.vgsd.org/
Valley Grove ES 100/K-6
389 Sugarcreek Dr 16323 814-432-3861
Sherry Griswold, prin. Fax 432-5223

St. Patrick S 100/PK-8
952 Buffalo St 16323 814-432-8689
Carol Long, prin. Fax 437-6538

Frederick, Montgomery
Boyertown Area SD
Supt. — See Boyertown
New Hanover-Upper Frederick ES 700/K-6
2547 Big Rd 19435 610-754-9580
M. Stephanie Wilson, prin.

Fredericksburg, Lebanon, Pop. 3,607
Northern Lebanon SD 2,500/K-12
PO Box 100 17026 717-865-2117
Dr. Don Bell, supt. Fax 865-0606
www.norleb.k12.pa.us
Fredericksburg ES 300/K-6
PO Box 27 17026 717-865-4107
Dr. Christopher Garchinsky, prin. Fax 865-0807
Northern Lebanon MS 400/7-8
PO Box 100 17026 717-865-2117
David Yavoich, prin. Fax 865-5835
Other Schools – See Annville, Jonestown

Fredericktown, Washington, Pop. 1,237
Bethlehem-Center SD 1,400/K-12
194 Crawford Rd 15333 724-267-4910
Dr. Karen Downie, supt. Fax 267-4904
www.bc.k12.pa.us
Bethlehem-Center ES 600/K-5
194 Crawford Rd 15333 724-267-4922
Madeleine Rieger, prin. Fax 267-4905
Bethlehem-Center MS 300/6-8
136 Crawford Rd 15333 724-267-4935
William Henderson, prin. Fax 267-4937

Freedom, Beaver, Pop. 1,665
Ambridge Area SD
Supt. — See Ambridge
Ambridge Area JHS 500/7-8
401 1st St 15042 724-266-2833
Megan Mealie, prin. Fax 869-5321
Economy ES 700/K-6
1000 1st St 15042 724-266-2833
Sandra Rudar, prin. Fax 869-3490

Freedom Area SD 1,400/K-12
1701 8th Ave 15042 724-775-5464
Dr. Ronald Sofo, supt. Fax 775-7434
www.freedom.k12.pa.us
Big Knob ES 400/K-4
205 Fezell Rd 15042 724-775-7881
Richard Edder, prin. Fax 775-3672
Freedom Area MS 300/5-8
1701 8th Ave 15042 724-775-7641
Robert Gallagher, prin. Fax 775-7748
Other Schools – See Conway

Freeland, Luzerne, Pop. 3,455
Hazleton Area SD
Supt. — See Hazleton
Freeland S 900/K-8
400 Alvin St 18224 570-636-2300
Joseph Barletta, prin. Fax 636-0868

Freemansburg, Northampton, Pop. 1,973
Bethlehem Area SD
Supt. — See Bethlehem
Freemansburg ES 400/K-5
501 Monroe St 18017 610-866-6681
Leigh Rusnak, prin. Fax 807-5988

Freeport, Armstrong, Pop. 1,854
Freeport Area SD
Supt. — See Sarver
Freeport Area JHS 300/7-8
325 4th St 16229 724-295-9020
Robert Isenberg, prin. Fax 295-4630
Freeport K Center 100/K-K
408 High St 16229 724-295-9250
Thomas Saulle, prin. Fax 295-9210

South Buffalo ES 300/1-6
562 Freeport Rd 16229 724-295-9510
Thomas Saulle, prin. Fax 295-4860

Frenchville, Clearfield
Clearfield Area SD
Supt. — See Clearfield
Girard-Goshen ES 100/K-4
8962 Gillingham Rd 16836 814-263-4898
Mary Sayers, prin. Fax 263-4311

Friedens, Somerset, Pop. 1,576
Somerset Area SD
Supt. — See Somerset
Friedens ES 200/K-3
1936 Stoystown Rd 15541 814-445-6436
Karen Maust, prin. Fax 445-1950

Friedensburg, Schuylkill
Blue Mountain SD
Supt. — See Orwigsburg
Blue Mountain ES West 300/K-5
PO Box 220 17933 570-739-4461
Heath Renninger, prin. Fax 739-4822

Friendsville, Susquehanna, Pop. 89
Montrose Area SD
Supt. — See Montrose
Choconut Valley ES 400/K-6
4458 Stanley Lake Rd 18818 570-553-2102
Christopher McComb, prin. Fax 553-2738

Furlong, Bucks
Central Bucks SD
Supt. — See Doylestown
Bridge Valley ES 900/K-6
2280 Sugar Bottom Rd 18925 267-893-3700
Nadine Garvin, prin. Fax 893-5825

Galeton, Potter, Pop. 1,301
Galeton Area SD 400/PK-12
25 Bridge St 16922 814-435-6571
David Wishard, supt. Fax 435-1187
www.edline.net/pages/Galeton_Area_School
Galeton Area S 400/PK-12
25 Bridge St 16922 814-435-6571
Larry Smith, prin. Fax 435-6981

Gallitzin, Cambria, Pop. 1,666
Penn Cambria SD
Supt. — See Cresson
Penn Cambria MS 400/5-8
401 Division St 16641 814-886-4181
Jeff Baird, prin. Fax 886-9308

Gap, Lancaster, Pop. 1,226
Pequea Valley SD
Supt. — See Kinzers
Salisbury ES 400/K-5
422 School Lane Rd 17527 717-442-8268
Linda Dwight, prin. Fax 442-9781

Garnet Valley, Delaware
Garnet Valley SD
Supt. — See Glen Mills
Bethel Springs ES 600/K-5
3280 Foulk Rd, 610-579-3000
Steven Piasecki, prin.

Geigertown, Berks

High Point Baptist Academy 300/PK-12
PO Box 188 19523 610-286-5942
Brian Williams, prin. Fax 286-7525

Gettysburg, Adams, Pop. 8,014
Gettysburg Area SD 3,300/K-12
900 Biglerville Rd 17325 717-334-6254
Dr. William Hall, supt. Fax 334-5220
www.gettysburg.k12.pa.us
Eisenhower ES 200/K-3
120 E Broadway 17325 717-334-6254
Joan Peck, prin. Fax 337-4430
Gettysburg Area MS 700/6-8
37 Lefever St 17325 717-334-6254
Steven Litten, prin. Fax 334-6999
Gettys ES 400/K-3
898 Biglerville Rd 17325 717-334-6254
Roger Morrill, prin. Fax 337-4434
Lincoln ES 400/4-5
98 Lefever St 17325 717-334-6254
Cathy Harner, prin. Fax 337-4437
Other Schools – See Cashtown

Adams County Christian Academy 100/PK-12
1865 Biglerville Rd 17325 717-334-9177
Charles Garcia, admin. Fax 334-7691
Freedom Christian S 100/PK-12
3185 York Rd 17325 717-624-3884
Karen Trout, admin. Fax 624-1562
Gettysburg SDA S 50/PK-8
1493 Biglerville Rd 17325 717-338-0131
Marian Baker, prin. Fax 338-0131
St. Francis Xavier S 200/K-8
45 W High St 17325 717-334-4221
Sr. Phyllis Simmons, prin. Fax 334-8883

Gibsonia, Allegheny, Pop. 3,500
Hampton Township SD
Supt. — See Allison Park
Poff ES 300/K-5
2990 Haberlein Rd 15044 412-492-6335
Dr. Michael Mooney, prin. Fax 443-4429

Pine-Richland SD 3,300/K-12
702 Warrendale Rd 15044 724-625-7773
Dr. James Manley, supt. Fax 625-1490
www.pinerichland.org
Eden Hall Upper ES 4-6
3900 Bakerstown Rd 15044 724-443-1450
Robert Cooper, prin. Fax 443-1451
Hance ES 400/K-3
5518 Molnar Dr 15044 724-443-1541
Dr. Richard Psych, prin. Fax 443-1290
Pine-Richland MS 700/7-8
100 Logan Rd 15044 724-625-3111
Dr. Kathleen Harrington, prin. Fax 625-3144
Richland ES 400/K-3
3811 Bakerstown Rd 15044 724-443-1558
Dr. Guy Rossi, prin. Fax 443-2180
Other Schools – See Wexford

Aquinas Academy 300/K-12
2308 W Hardies Rd 15044 724-444-0722
Leslie Mitros, hdmstr. Fax 444-0750

Gilbertsville, Montgomery, Pop. 3,994
Boyertown Area SD
Supt. — See Boyertown
Gilbertsville ES, 36 Congo Rd 19525 700/K-6
Ronald Christman, prin. 610-369-7485

Gillett, Bradford
Athens Area SD
Supt. — See Athens
Burnham ES 100/K-5
5252 Monkey Run Rd 16925 570-596-2102
Andrew Latcford, prin. Fax 596-2602

Girard, Erie, Pop. 3,017
Girard SD 2,000/K-12
1203 Lake St 16417 814-774-5666
Dr. James Tracy, supt. Fax 774-4220
girardsd.org
Rice Avenue MS 700/5-8
1100 Rice Ave 16417 814-774-5604
David Koma, prin. Fax 774-5259
Other Schools – See Lake City

Girard Alliance Christian Academy 100/PK-12
229 Rice Ave 16417 814-774-9537
Karen Brumagin, admin. Fax 774-2552

Gladwyne, Montgomery, Pop. 4,000
Lower Merion SD
Supt. — See Ardmore
Gladwyne ES 600/K-5
230 Righters Mill Rd 19035 610-645-1440
Dr. James Johnson, prin.

Gladwyne Montessori S 300/PK-6
920 Youngs Ford Rd 19035 610-649-1761
Abigail Miller, hdmstr. Fax 649-7978

Glen Mills, Delaware
Garnet Valley SD, 80 Station Rd 19342 4,600/K-12
Dr. Anthony Costello, supt. 610-579-7300
www.garnetvalleyschools.com/
Concord ES, 114 Station Rd 19342 700/K-2
Patricia Dunn, prin. 610-579-6100
Garnet Valley ES 800/3-5
599 Smithbridge Rd 19342 610-579-4150
Christine Menzel, prin. Fax 579-4139
Garnet Valley MS 1,100/6-8
601 Smithbridge Rd 19342 610-579-5100
Christopher Marchese, prin.
Other Schools – See Garnet Valley

St. Thomas the Apostle S 400/K-8
430 Valleybrook Rd 19342 610-459-8134
Barbara Virga, prin. Fax 459-8120

Glenmoore, Chester
Downingtown Area SD
Supt. — See Downingtown
Springton Manor ES K-5
400 Fairview Rd 19343 610-384-9030
Leigh Abbott, prin. Fax 466-0914

Glenolden, Delaware, Pop. 7,309
Interboro SD
Supt. — See Prospect Park
Glenolden S 700/K-8
198 S MacDade Blvd 19036 610-237-6430
Joseph Flynn, prin. Fax 586-1738

Southeast Delco SD
Supt. — See Folcroft
Darby Township S 700/1-8
801 W Ashland Ave 19036 610-522-4375
Dr. Darla Glantz, prin. Fax 522-9065
Kindergarten Center K-K
1 School Ln 19036 610-522-4365
Susan Vaites, prin. Fax 522-1686

Upper Darby SD
Supt. — See Drexel Hill
Senkow ES, 15 Lamont Ave 19036 200/1-5
Sean Burns, prin. 610-957-5114

Glen Rock, York, Pop. 1,853
Southern York County SD 3,200/K-12
PO Box 128 17327 717-235-4811
Thomas Hensley, supt. Fax 235-0863
www.syc.k12.pa.us
Friendship ES 400/K-6
PO Box 128 17327 717-235-4811
Beth Koontz, prin. Fax 235-0302
Shrewsbury ES 600/K-6
PO Box 128 17327 717-235-4811
Sandra Lemmon, prin. Fax 227-2294
Southern ES 600/K-6
PO Box 128 17327 717-235-4811
Michael Shirey, prin. Fax 235-8790
Southern MS 500/7-8
PO Box 128 17327 717-235-4811
Kevin Helmeczi, prin. Fax 227-9681

Glenshaw, Allegheny
Shaler Area SD 4,100/K-12
1800 Mount Royal Blvd 15116 412-492-1200
Donald Lee, supt. Fax 492-1293
www.sasd.k12.pa.us
Jeffery PS 200/K-3
201 Wetzel Rd 15116 412-492-1200
Kara Eckert, prin. Fax 492-1287
Rogers PS 200/K-3
705 Scott Ave 15116 412-492-1200
Leah McCord, prin. Fax 487-0293
Shaler Area ES 800/4-6
700 Scott Ave 15116 412-492-1200
Cynthia Foht, prin. Fax 492-1317
Shaler Area MS 400/7-8
1810 Mount Royal Blvd 15116 412-492-1200
Eloise Groegler, prin. Fax 492-1237
Other Schools – See Allison Park, Pittsburgh

Montessori Centre Academy 100/PK-6
1014 William Flynn Hwy 15116 412-486-6239
Yolanda Sweenie, prin. Fax 486-2930
St. Bonaventure S 500/PK-8
2001 Mount Royal Blvd Ste 2 15116 412-486-2608
Jacqueline Easley, prin. Fax 486-4583
St. Mary S 400/PK-8
2510 Middle Rd 15116 412-486-7611
Antoinette Pilarski, prin. Fax 487-9509

Glenside, Montgomery, Pop. 8,704
Abington SD
Supt. — See Abington
Copper Beech ES 900/K-6
825 N Easton Rd 19038 215-881-2000
Janice Kline, prin. Fax 881-2002

Cheltenham Township SD
Supt. — See Elkins Park
Glenside ES 300/K-4
400 Harrison Ave 19038 215-881-6440
Bruce Williams, prin. Fax 886-6797

St. Luke the Evangelist S 300/K-8
2336 Fairhill Ave 19038 215-884-0843
Sr. William Adele, prin. Fax 884-4607

Glenville, York
South Western SD
Supt. — See Hanover
Manheim ES 200/K-5
5778 Blooming Grove Rd 17329 717-229-2930
Brian Cromer, prin. Fax 227-9059

Grampian, Clearfield, Pop. 422
Curwensville Area SD
Supt. — See Curwensville
Penn-Grampian ES 100/K-4
178 Walltown Rd 16838 814-236-1411
Susan Wingard, prin. Fax 236-2240

Grantville, Dauphin
Lower Dauphin SD
Supt. — See Hummelstown
East Hanover ES 400/K-5
2673 Sand Beach Rd 17028 717-469-2686
Gary Messinger, prin. Fax 469-0539

Graysville, Greene
West Greene SD
Supt. — See Waynesburg
Graysville ES 300/K-5
1029 W Roy Furman Hwy 15337 724-428-3592
Donald Painter, prin. Fax 428-3933

Greencastle, Franklin, Pop. 3,838
Greencastle-Antrim SD 2,900/K-12
500 Leitersburg St 17225 717-597-3226
C. Gregory Hoover, supt. Fax 597-2180
www.greencastle.k12.pa.us
Greencastle-Antrim ES 600/3-5
500 Leitersburg St 17225 717-597-3226
Chad Stover, prin. Fax 597-3652
Greencastle-Antrim MS 700/6-8
370 S Ridge Ave 17225 717-597-3226
Mark Herman, prin. Fax 597-6468
Greencastle-Antrim PS 600/K-2
504 Leitersburg St 17225 717-597-3226
Angela Singer, prin. Fax 597-1306

Shady Grove Mennonite S 200/1-10
1442 Buchanan Trl E 17225 717-597-0843
Wilmer Eby, prin.

Green Lane, Montgomery, Pop. 585
Upper Perkiomen SD
Supt. — See Pennsburg
Marlborough ES 600/K-5
1450 Gravel Pike 18054 215-234-4387
Lesley Motruk, prin. Fax 234-8842

Greensboro, Greene, Pop. 279
Southeastern Greene SD 700/K-12
1000 Mapletown Rd 15338 724-943-3630
Michael Caruso, supt. Fax 943-3052
www.segsd.org
Other Schools – See Bobtown

Greensburg, Westmoreland, Pop. 15,569
Greater Latrobe SD
Supt. — See Latrobe
Mountain View ES 600/K-6
1010 Mountain View Dr 15601 724-834-7399
Robin Pynos, prin. Fax 834-5338

Greensburg Salem SD 3,200/K-12
1 Academy Hill Pl 15601 724-832-2901
Thomas Yarabinetz, supt. Fax 832-2968
www.greensburgsalem.org
Greensburg Salem MS 700/6-8
301 N Main St 15601 724-832-2930
Todd McMillen, prin. Fax 832-2937

Hutchinson ES 600/K-5
810 Welty St 15601 724-832-2885
Lisa Hauswirth, prin. Fax 832-2874
Nicely ES 300/K-5
55 McLaughlin Dr 15601 724-832-2865
Kathryn Hricenak, prin. Fax 832-2860
Other Schools – See New Alexandria

Hempfield Area SD 6,300/K-12
4347 State Route 136 15601 724-834-2590
Terry Foriska, supt. Fax 850-2298
www.hempfieldarea.k12.pa.us
Bovard ES 200/K-5
840 Bovard Luxor Rd 15601 724-850-5230
Don McIlvaine, prin. Fax 850-5231
Ft. Allen ES 600/K-5
560 Baltzer Meyer Pike 15601 724-850-2501
Marty Rovedatti-Jackson, prin. Fax 850-2502
Harrold MS 500/6-8
1368 Middletown Rd 15601 724-850-2301
Jason Lochner, prin. Fax 850-2302
Maxwell ES 400/K-5
1101 Old Salem Rd 15601 724-850-3500
Debra Schoming, prin. Fax 850-3501
Wendover MS 500/6-8
425 Arthur Pl 15601 724-838-4070
Deanna Mikesic, prin. Fax 838-4071
West Point ES 200/K-5
533 Saint Andrews Dr 15601 724-850-2270
Roseanna Duda, prin. Fax 850-2271
Other Schools – See Irwin, New Stanton

Aquinas Academy 400/PK-8
340 N Main St 15601 724-834-7940
Cherie Rullo, prin. Fax 836-0497
Seton Montessori S 50/PK-K
294 Frye Farm Rd 15601 724-837-8500
Sr. Anita Schulte, prin. Fax 836-0772
Westmoreland Christian Academy 50/PK-12
538 Rugh St 15601 724-853-8308
Melody Stoltenberg, prin. Fax 836-7472

Greenville, Mercer, Pop. 6,355
Greenville Area SD 1,600/K-12
9 Donation Rd 16125 724-588-2502
Dr. Patricia Homer, supt. Fax 588-5024
www.greenville.k12.pa.us
East ES 400/4-6
71 Columbia Ave 16125 724-588-1173
Nancy Castor, prin. Fax 588-1319
Hempfield ES 400/K-3
60 Fredonia Rd 16125 724-588-1018
Nancy Castor, prin. Fax 588-5036

Reynolds SD 1,400/K-12
531 Reynolds Rd 16125 724-646-5501
Maddox Stokes Ph.D., supt. Fax 646-5505
www.reynolds.k12.pa.us
Reynolds ES 700/K-6
1609 Brentwood Dr 16125 724-646-5601
Ronald Bradley, prin. Fax 646-5605

Living Word Christian S 100/PK-12
21 S Maysville Rd 16125 724-588-2140
Jan Chapin, admin. Fax 588-8742
St. Michael S 200/PK-8
80 N High St 16125 724-588-7050
Mary Jo Lipani, prin. Fax 588-7056

Grove City, Mercer, Pop. 7,764
Grove City Area SD 2,700/K-12
511 Highland Ave 16127 724-458-6733
Dr. Robert Post, supt. Fax 458-5868
www.grovecity.k12.pa.us
Grove City Area MS 400/7-8
130 E Main St 16127 724-458-8040
James Anderson, prin. Fax 450-0780
Highland ES 300/1-2
611 Highland Ave 16127 724-458-8101
Jennifer Connelly, prin. Fax 458-4399
Hillview ES 700/3-6
482 E Main Street Ext 16127 724-458-7570
Dr. David Foley, prin. Fax 458-0444
Washington K 200/K-K
301 N Madison Ave 16127 724-458-9620
Jennifer Connelly, prin. Fax 458-4399

Grove City Christian Academy 100/PK-10
1333 W Main St 16127 724-458-5253
Kennedy Henriquez, prin. Fax 458-5259

Guys Mills, Crawford

Faith Builders Christian S 100/1-12
PO Box 127 16327 814-789-2303
Gerald Miller, prin. Fax 789-3396

Gwynedd, Montgomery

Gwynedd Friends K 100/PK-K
PO Box 142 19436 215-699-5392
Pam Callantine, dir.

Hadley, Mercer
Commodore Perry SD 600/K-12
3002 Perry Hwy 16130 724-253-3255
Michael Stahlman, supt. Fax 253-3467
www.cppanthers.org/
Perry ES 300/K-6
3002 Perry Hwy 16130 724-253-2025
Pamela J. Slatcoff, prin. Fax 253-3467

Halifax, Dauphin, Pop. 844
Halifax Area SD 1,200/K-12
3940 Peters Mountain Rd 17032 717-896-3416
Robert Hassinger, supt. Fax 896-3976
www.hasd.us
Enders-Fisherville ES 200/K-1
791 Enders Rd 17032 717-362-9259
Fax 362-6358
Halifax Area ES 300/2-5
3940 Peters Mountain Rd 17032 717-896-3416
Fax 896-8337
Halifax Area MS 300/6-8
3940 Peters Mountain Rd 17032 717-896-3416
Gregory Milbrand, prin. Fax 896-3976

Hamburg, Berks, Pop. 4,183
Hamburg Area SD 2,200/K-12
Windsor St 19526 610-562-2241
Steven Keifer, supt. Fax 562-2634
www.hasdhawks.org
Hamburg Area MS 700/6-8
Windsor St 19526 610-562-3990
Kenneth Buck, prin. Fax 562-1425
Tilden ES, 524 W State St 19526 300/K-5
Shaun Fitzpatrick, prin. 610-562-0291
Other Schools – See Shoemakersville

Blue Mountain SDA S 50/PK-8
45 Woodland Ter 19526 610-562-5052
Frank Stahl, prin. Fax 562-1321

Hamlin, Wayne
Western Wayne SD
Supt. — See South Canaan
Hamlin ES 400/PK-2
PO Box 55 18427 570-689-2632
Ellen Faliskie, prin. Fax 689-5139

Hanover, York, Pop. 14,990
Conewago Valley SD
Supt. — See New Oxford
Conewago Township ES 600/K-3
1189 W Elm Ave 17331 717-624-2157
Lawrence Sanders, prin. Fax 632-6553

Hanover Public SD 1,600/K-12
403 Moul Ave 17331 717-637-9000
Dr. Alan Moyer, supt. Fax 630-4617
www.hpsd.k12.pa.us
Clearview ES 200/K-4
801 Randolph St 17331 717-637-9000
Jay Czap, prin. Fax 630-4637
Hanover MS 500/5-8
300 Keagy Ave 17331 717-637-9000
Pamela Smith, prin. Fax 630-4632
Hanover Street ES 300/K-4
101 E Hanover St 17331 717-637-9000
Mark Hershner, prin. Fax 630-4636
Washington ES 100/K-4
301 Moul Ave 17331 717-637-9000
Dr. Thomas Krout, prin. Fax 630-4635

South Western SD 4,100/K-12
225 Bowman Rd Ste 2 17331 717-632-2500
Barbara Rupp, supt. Fax 632-7993
www.swsd.k12.pa.us/
Baresville ES 500/K-5
135 Sanford Ave 17331 717-632-2500
Kathleen Lambe, prin. Fax 637-4241
Markle IS 1,000/6-8
225 Bowman Rd Ste 1 17331 717-632-2500
Kevin Duckworth, prin. Fax 633-7073
Park Hills ES 500/K-5
137 W Granger St 17331 717-632-2500
Mary Kay Kelly, prin. Fax 633-1262
West Manheim ES 600/K-5
2000 Baltimore Pike 17331 717-632-2500
Kristine Strausbaugh, prin. Fax 637-2011
Other Schools – See Glenville

Sacred Heart S 200/K-8
55 Basilica Dr 17331 717-632-8715
Sr. Eileen Kean, prin. Fax 632-6596
St. Joseph MS 100/6-8
5125 Grandview Rd 17331 717-632-0118
Susan Mummert, prin. Fax 632-0030
St. Joseph S 200/K-5
236 Baltimore St 17331 717-632-1335
Susan Mummert, prin. Fax 632-5147
St. Vincent DePaul S 100/K-8
224 3rd St 17331 717-637-5190
Linda Billig, prin. Fax 637-0666

Hanover Twp, Lehigh
Hanover Area SD 2,000/K-12
1600 Sans Souci Pkwy 18706 570-831-2313
Anthony Podczasy, supt. Fax 822-6776
www.hanoverarea.org
Hanover Area Memorial ES 300/5-6
80 W Saint Marys Rd 18706 570-822-5102
Terry Schnee, prin. Fax 823-3096
Hanover Green S 200/K-K
555 Main Rd 18706 570-824-3941
Cecilia Pecaitis, prin. Fax 824-3941
Lee Park ES 300/1-2
99 Lee Park Ave 18706 570-824-4741
Ann Marie Mantione, prin. Fax 824-5714
Lynwood ES 300/3-4
2 Colley St 18706 570-824-3732
Bill Jones, prin. Fax 821-6171

Harborcreek, Erie
Harbor Creek SD 1,400/K-12
6375 Buffalo Rd 16421 814-897-2100
Dr. Richard Lansberry, supt. Fax 897-2142
www.hcsd.iu5.org
Harbor Creek JHS 400/7-8
6375 Buffalo Rd 16421 814-897-2100
Linda Allen, prin. Fax 897-2121
Other Schools – See Erie

Harleysville, Montgomery, Pop. 7,405
North Penn SD
Supt. — See Lansdale
Nash ES 500/K-6
1560 Liberty Bell Dr 19438 215-368-2407
Ronald Martiello, prin. Fax 368-7804

Souderton Area SD
Supt. — See Souderton
Indian Valley MS 1,100/6-8
130 Maple Ave 19438 215-256-8896
Dr. Dale Burkhard, prin. Fax 256-1288
Lower Salford ES 400/K-5
250 Maple Ave 19438 215-256-9121
Donna Huff, prin. Fax 256-4603
Oak Ridge ES 600/K-5
465 Moyer Rd 19438 215-256-6633
Thomas Ferlick, prin. Fax 256-9258
Salford Hills ES 400/K-5
2720 Barndt Rd 19438 610-287-9197
Maryellen Myers, prin. Fax 287-4030

Harmony, Butler, Pop. 902
Seneca Valley SD 7,500/K-12
124 Seneca School Rd 16037 724-452-6040
Dr. Donald Tylinski, supt. Fax 452-6105
www.svsd.net/
Seneca Valley MS 1,200/7-8
122 Seneca School Rd 16037 724-452-6040
Sean McCarty, prin. Fax 452-0331
Other Schools – See Cranberry Township, Evans City, Zelienople

Harrisburg, Dauphin, Pop. 47,472
Central Dauphin SD 10,500/K-12
600 Rutherford Rd 17109 717-545-4703
Dr. Luis Gonzalez, supt. Fax 545-5624
www.cdschools.org
Central Dauphin East MS 500/6-8
628 Rutherford Rd 17109 717-545-4703
Robert Holbrook, prin. Fax 657-4987
Central Dauphin MS 800/6-8
4600 Locust Ln 17109 717-540-4606
James Miller, prin. Fax 545-6931
Chambers Hill ES 100/K-5
6450 Chambers Hill Rd 17111 717-561-1655
Steven Epstein, prin. Fax 561-4977
Lawnton ES 300/K-5
4400 Franklin St 17111 717-558-9430
Erika Willis, prin. Fax 558-7780
Linglestown ES 400/K-5
1044 N Mountain Rd 17112 717-657-3211
Mary Dougherty, prin. Fax 657-9698
Linglestown MS 500/6-8
1200 N Mountain Rd 17112 717-657-3060
Kenneth Miller, prin. Fax 657-0537
Mountain View ES 400/K-5
400 Gibbel Rd 17112 717-657-8585
Fax 657-9733
North Side ES 500/K-5
4520 Devonshire Rd 17109 717-657-3201
Mary Nardo, prin. Fax 654-9770
Paxtang ES 200/K-5
3530 Rutherford St 17111 717-561-1781
Robert Stewart, prin. Fax 561-4992
Paxtonia ES 600/K-5
6135 Jonestown Rd 17112 717-657-3202
Thomas Toone, prin. Fax 657-9780
Phillips ES 300/K-5
100 Oakmont Rd 17109 717-657-3203
Deborah Stover, prin. Fax 657-9790
Rutherford ES 300/K-5
6500 Clearfield St 17111 717-561-1990
Robert Miller, prin. Fax 561-5004
South Side ES 500/K-5
4525 Union Deposit Rd 17111 717-657-3204
Kelly Fowlkes, prin. Fax 657-9757
West Hanover ES 400/K-5
7740 Manor Dr 17112 717-657-3210
Lewis Correale, prin. Fax 657-9767
Other Schools – See Dauphin, Steelton

Harrisburg City SD 7,700/PK-12
2101 N Front St Bldg 2 17110 717-703-4000
Dr. Gerald Kohn, supt. Fax 703-4115
www.hbgsd.k12.pa.us
Camp Curtin S 700/K-8
2900 N 6th St 17110 717-703-4200
Christopher Cherny, prin. Fax 703-4225
Downey S 500/K-8
1313 Monroe St 17103 717-703-1240
Susan Nock, prin. Fax 703-1245
Foose S 700/K-8
1301 Sycamore St 17104 717-703-1280
Lisa Crum, prin. Fax 703-1245
Franklin S K-8
1205 N 6th St 17102 717-703-1200
Rose Sampson, prin. Fax 703-1215
Hamilton S 400/K-8
1701 N 6th St 17102 717-703-1320
Karen Wright, prin. Fax 703-1330
Lincoln S 300/K-8
1601 State St 17103 717-703-1360
Stacey Jones, prin. Fax 703-1375
Marshall S 500/K-8
301 Hale Ave 17104 717-703-1400
Nancy Snyder, prin. Fax 703-1420
Melrose S 300/K-8
2041 Berryhill St 17104 717-703-1440
Tiffany Sparkman, prin. Fax 703-1455
Rowland S 700/K-8
1842 Derry St 17104 717-703-4500
Barbara Hasan, prin. Fax 703-4520
Scott S 500/PK-3
1900 Derry St 17104 717-703-4560
Marisol Craig, prin. Fax 703-4580
Steele S 300/K-8
2537 N 5th St 17110 717-703-1560
Barbara Batts, prin. Fax 703-1570

Susquehanna Township SD 3,200/K-12
3550 Elmerton Ave 17109 717-657-5100
David Volkman, supt. Fax 657-2919
www.hannasd.org
Carter K Center 200/K-K
150 S Progress Ave 17109 717-657-5113
Sabina Grant-Spencer, prin. Fax 657-2919

Holtzman ES 700/3-5
1910 Linglestown Rd 17110 717-657-5158
Michael Selvenis, prin. Fax 657-2919
Lindemuth PS 500/1-2
1201 N Progress Ave 17109 717-657-5122
Sabina Grant-Spencer, prin. Fax 657-2919
Susquehanna Township MS 800/6-8
801 Wood St 17109 717-657-5125
Travis Waters, prin. Fax 657-2919

Cathedral S 200/PK-8
212 State St 17101 717-234-3797
Sr. Mary Shurer, prin. Fax 213-2000
Covenant Christian Academy 200/K-12
6098 Locust Ln 17109 717-540-9885
Joseph Sanelli, hdmstr. Fax 540-7176
Harrisburg Adventist S 50/1-8
424 N Progress Ave 17109 717-545-7300
Timothy Brown, prin. Fax 545-7300
Harrisburg Christian S 300/K-12
PO Box 6464 17112 717-545-3728
Tom Wieland, hdmstr. Fax 545-9370
Hillside Adventist S 50/1-8
1301 Cumberland St 17103 717-234-7388
Holy Family S 200/K-8
555 S 25th St 17104 717-232-2551
Sr. M. Margaret Ann Quinn, prin. Fax 232-9661
Holy Name of Jesus S 600/K-8
6190 Allentown Blvd 17112 717-657-1704
Dr. Ann Licata, prin. Fax 657-9135
Londonderry S 200/PK-8
1800 Bamberger Rd 17110 717-540-0543
Rhoda Barasch, prin. Fax 540-5335
Rabbi David L Silver Yeshiva Academy 100/PK-8
3301 N Front St 17110 717-238-8775
Danielle Houser, admin. Fax 238-8773
St. Catherine LaBoure S 400/PK-8
4020 Derry St 17111 717-564-1760
Jennifer Wicht, prin. Fax 564-3010
St. Margaret Mary S 400/PK-8
2826 Herr St 17103 717-232-3771
Joyce Haug, prin. Fax 232-0776
St. Stephen's Episcopal S 200/PK-8
215 N Front St 17101 717-238-8590
Ruth Graffius, hdmstr. Fax 238-0565

Harrison City, Westmoreland
Penn-Trafford SD 4,600/K-12
PO Box 530 15636 724-744-4496
Dr. Deborah Kolonay, supt. Fax 744-4016
www.penntrafford.org
Other Schools – See Irwin, Jeannette, Trafford

Harrisville, Butler, Pop. 908
Franklin Area SD
Supt. — See Franklin
Victory ES 200/K-6
1819 Georgetown Rd 16038 814-786-7311
Dr. James Ruby, prin. Fax 786-7889

Slippery Rock Area SD
Supt. — See Slippery Rock
Har-Mer ES 100/K-5
220 W Prairie St 16038 724-735-2548
Cory Hake, prin. Fax 735-0053

Harveys Lake, Luzerne, Pop. 2,868
Lake-Lehman SD
Supt. — See Lehman
Lake-Noxen ES 300/K-6
RR 3 Box 270 18618 570-639-1129
Debra Deming, prin. Fax 639-3288

Hatboro, Montgomery, Pop. 7,288
Hatboro-Horsham SD
Supt. — See Horsham
Blair Mill ES 400/K-5
109 Bender Rd 19040 215-420-5200
Nancy Doherty, prin. Fax 420-5252
Crooked Billet ES 300/K-5
70 Meadowbrook Ave 19040 215-420-5300
Monica Taylor, prin. Fax 420-5350
Pennypack ES 200/K-5
130 Spring Ave 19040 215-420-5400
Amy Roslevege, prin. Fax 420-5436

Upper Moreland Township SD
Supt. — See Willow Grove
Upper Moreland IS 700/3-5
3990 Orangemans Rd 19040 215-325-1700
Dr. Joseph Waters, prin. Fax 325-1701
Upper Moreland MS 800/6-8
4000 Orangemans Rd 19040 215-674-4185
Charles Hafele, prin. Fax 956-1906
Upper Moreland PS 600/K-2
3980 Orangemans Rd 19040 215-325-1400
Sean Arney, prin. Fax 325-1401

St. John Bosco S 200/PK-8
215 E County Line Rd 19040 215-675-1484
Sr. Rita Marrota, prin. Fax 675-7084

Hatfield, Montgomery, Pop. 2,872
North Penn SD
Supt. — See Lansdale
Hatfield ES 500/K-6
1701 Fairgrounds Rd 19440 215-368-1585
Fax 368-6762
Kulp ES 500/K-6
801 Cowpath Rd 19440 215-368-3061
Erik Huebner, prin. Fax 368-7835

St. Maria Goretti S 200/K-8
2980 Cowpath Rd 19440 215-721-9098
Theresa Madden, prin. Fax 721-3394
Stepping Stones K, PO Box 57 19440 100/PK-K
Lori Bezanis, dir. 215-368-2052

Haverford, Montgomery, Pop. 6,000

Friends S Haverford 200/PK-6
851 Buck Ln 19041 610-642-2334
Martha Bryans, hdmstr. Fax 642-0870
Haverford S 1,000/PK-12
450 Lancaster Ave 19041 610-642-3020
Joseph Cox, hdmstr. Fax 649-4898

Havertown, Delaware, Pop. 30,000
Haverford Township SD 5,200/K-12
50 E Eagle Rd 19083 610-853-5900
William Keilbaugh Ed.D., supt. Fax 853-5942
www.haverford.k12.pa.us
Chatham Park ES 600/K-5
400 Allston Rd 19083 610-853-5900
Daniel Marsella, prin. Fax 853-5974
Haverford MS 1,300/6-8
1701 Darby Rd 19083 610-853-5900
Carol Restifo, prin. Fax 853-5937
Lynnewood ES 500/K-5
1400 Lawrence Rd 19083 610-853-5900
Susan Mingey, prin. Fax 853-5977
Manoa ES 500/K-5
101 S Manoa Rd 19083 610-853-5900
Norbert Paga, prin. Fax 853-5978
Other Schools – See Ardmore, Bryn Mawr

Annunciation BVM S 300/PK-8
421 Brookline Blvd 19083 610-446-8430
Eileen Kearney, prin. Fax 446-0627
Sacred Heart S 200/PK-8
105 Wilson Ave 19083 610-446-9198
Sr. Irene Cassady, prin. Fax 446-4861
St. Denis S 400/PK-8
300 E Eagle Rd 19083 610-446-4608
Jacqueline Coccia, prin. Fax 446-5705
Stratford Friends S 100/K-6
5 Llandillo Rd 19083 610-446-3144
Dr. Timothy Madigan, dir. Fax 446-6381

Hawley, Pike, Pop. 1,292
Wallenpaupack Area SD 3,800/K-12
2552 Route 6 18428 570-226-4557
Michael Silsby, supt. Fax 226-0638
www.wallenpaupack.org/
Hawley K Center 100/K-K
500 Academy St 18428 570-226-4557
Gwyn Devendorf, prin.
Wallenpaupack Area MS 900/6-8
139 Atlantic Ave 18428 570-226-4557
Diane Szader, prin. Fax 251-3165
Wallenpaupack North IS 500/4-5
187 Atlantic Ave 18428 570-226-4557
William Walker, prin. Fax 226-1976
Wallenpaupack PS 400/1-3
158 Atlantic Ave 18428 570-226-4557
Anthony Cavallaro, prin. Fax 251-3151
Other Schools – See Newfoundland

Hawthorn, Clarion, Pop. 558
Redbank Valley SD
Supt. — See New Bethlehem
Redbank-Hawthorn ES 200/K-6
1306 Truittsburg Rd 16230 814-365-5141
Jason Huffman, prin. Fax 365-2427

Hazleton, Luzerne, Pop. 22,125
Hazleton Area SD 10,000/K-12
1515 W 23rd St 18202 570-459-3111
Samuel Marolo, supt. Fax 459-3118
www.hasd.k12.pa.us
Arthur Street ES 400/K-6
424 E 9th St 18201 570-459-0166
Maureen DeRose, prin. Fax 459-3128
Hazleton S 800/K-8
700 N Wyoming St 18201 570-459-3186
Maureen DeRose, prin. Fax 450-6547
Heights Terrace S 1,100/K-8
275 Mill St 18201 570-459-3166
Dr. Frank Antonelli, prin. Fax 459-1394
Other Schools – See Drums, Freeland, Mc Adoo, Sugarloaf, West Hazleton

---

Hazleton Trinity K 50/K-K
100 N Church St 18201 570-454-8123
Linda Sims, dir. Fax 454-1014
Holy Family Academy 400/PK-8
1700 W 22nd St 18202 570-459-9431
Stan Pavlick, prin. Fax 455-2847
Immanuel Christian S 100/K-12
725 N Locust St 18201 570-459-1111
Kelly Knowlden, hdmstr. Fax 459-6920

Hellam, York, Pop. 1,408
Eastern York SD
Supt. — See Wrightsville
Kreutz Creek ES 400/K-5
50 N Lee St 17406 717-757-9682
Andrea Moyers-Bloss, prin. Fax 757-2087

Hellertown, Northampton, Pop. 5,615
Saucon Valley SD 2,400/K-12
2097 Polk Valley Rd 18055 610-838-7026
Sandra Fellin, supt. Fax 838-6419
www.svpanthers.org
Saucon Valley ES 1,000/K-5
2085 Polk Valley Rd 18055 610-838-9331
Roseria Frey, prin. Fax 838-7473
Saucon Valley MS 600/6-8
2095 Polk Valley Rd 18055 610-838-7071
Pamela Bernardo, prin. Fax 838-7473

St. Theresa S 200/K-8
300 Leonard St 18055 610-838-8161
Louise Glass, prin. Fax 838-1915

Hereford, Berks
Upper Perkiomen SD
Supt. — See Pennsburg
Hereford ES 500/K-5
1043 Gravel Pike 18056 215-679-4151
Theodore Mucellin, prin. Fax 679-6355

Herminie, Westmoreland
Yough SD 2,500/K-12
915 Lowber Rd 15637 724-446-7272
Lawrence Nemec, supt. Fax 446-5017
www.yough.net
Good ES 300/K-4
1464 Herminie W Newton Rd 15637 724-446-5503
Sharon Luzier, prin. Fax 446-5509
Other Schools – See Ruffs Dale, West Newton

Hermitage, Mercer, Pop. 16,571
Hermitage SD 1,500/K-12
411 N Hermitage Rd 16148 724-981-8750
Dr. Daniel Bell, supt. Fax 981-5080
www.hermitage.k12.pa.us
Artman ES 400/K-3
343 N Hermitage Rd 16148 724-981-8750
Brian Schaller, prin. Fax 981-5080
Delahunty MS 200/6-7
419 N Hermitage Rd 16148 724-981-8750
Eric Trosch, prin. Fax 981-5080
Ionta ES 100/4-5
375 N Hermitage Rd 16148 724-981-8750
Eric Trosch, prin. Fax 981-5080

Notre Dame S 300/PK-8
2335 Highland Rd 16148 724-342-2205
Victoria Wagner, prin. Fax 704-7397

Herndon, Northumberland, Pop. 362
Line Mountain SD 1,200/K-12
185 Line Mountain Rd 17830 570-758-2640
David Campbell, supt. Fax 758-2842
www.linemountain.com
Other Schools – See Dalmatia, Leck Kill, Trevorton

Hershey, Dauphin, Pop. 11,860
Derry Township SD 3,500/K-12
PO Box 898 17033 717-534-2501
Dr. Linda Brewer, supt. Fax 533-4357
www.hershey.k12.pa.us
Hershey ECC 500/K-1
PO Box 898 17033 717-531-2211
Jacqueline Castleman, prin. Fax 531-2351
Hershey IS 500/4-5
PO Box 898 17033 717-531-2277
Lori Dixon, prin. Fax 508-2271
Hershey MS 900/6-8
PO Box 898 17033 717-531-2222
Sue King, prin. Fax 531-2245
Hershey PS 500/2-3
PO Box 898 17033 717-531-2277
Joy Mackenzie, prin. Fax 508-2266

Lower Dauphin SD
Supt. — See Hummelstown
South Hanover ES 400/K-5
15 W 3rd St 17033 717-566-2564
Patricia Rhine, prin. Fax 566-1157

Hershey S 1,700/PK-12
PO Box 830 17033 717-520-2000
John O'Brien, pres. Fax 520-2002
St. Joan of Arc S 300/PK-8
329 W Areba Ave 17033 717-533-2854
Sr. Eileen McGowan, prin. Fax 534-0755

Hilltown, Bucks

St. Agnes-Sacred Heart MS 100/5-8
Route 152 and Broad St 18927 215-822-9174
Margaret Graham, prin. Fax 822-7942

Holland, Bucks, Pop. 5,300
Council Rock SD
Supt. — See Newtown
Hillcrest ES 600/K-6
420 E Holland Rd 18966 215-944-1600
Nakia Jones-Tate, prin. Fax 944-1692
Holland ES 500/K-6
597 Beverly Rd 18966 215-944-1500
Andrew Sanko, prin. Fax 944-1597
Holland MS 700/7-8
400 E Holland Rd 18966 215-944-2700
Michael Lecker, prin. Fax 944-2789
Rolling Hills ES 500/K-6
340 Middle Holland Rd 18966 215-944-2000
Joseph MacClay, prin. Fax 944-2097

St. Bede the Venerable S 400/K-8
1053 Holland Rd 18966 215-357-4720
Florence Viola, prin. Fax 355-9526

Hollidaysburg, Blair, Pop. 5,519
Hollidaysburg Area SD 3,700/K-12
201 Jackson St 16648 814-695-8702
Dr. Paul Gallagher, supt. Fax 695-2315
www.tigerwires.com
Frankstown ES 700/K-6
RR 3 Box 592 16648 814-695-4961
Frank Filkosky, prin. Fax 695-4833
Longer ES 400/K-6
1320 Union St 16648 814-695-4431
Timothy Gildea, prin. Fax 695-5091
Other Schools – See Duncansville

Hollidaysburg Catholic S 200/PK-8
PO Box 599 16648 814-695-6112
Elaine Spencer, prin. Fax 696-8960
Penn-Mont Academy 100/K-6
131 Holliday Hills Dr 16648 814-696-8801
Michelle Hartye, prin. Fax 696-5893

Hollsopple, Somerset

Johnstown Christian S 200/PK-12
125 Christian School Rd 15935 814-288-2588
Dr. Kathy Keafer, admin. Fax 288-1447

Holtwood, Lancaster
Penn Manor SD
Supt. — See Lancaster
Martic ES 400/K-6
266 Martic Heights Dr 17532 717-284-4128
Corly McPherson, prin. Fax 284-5954

Home, Indiana
Marion Center Area SD
Supt. — See Marion Center
Rayne ES 100/K-4
2535 Route 119 Hwy N 15747 724-463-8615
Donna Bruder-Smith, prin.

Homer City, Indiana, Pop. 1,755
Homer-Center SD 1,000/K-12
65 Wildcat Ln 15748 724-479-8080
Dr. Vincent Delconte, supt. Fax 479-3967
homercenter.org/
Homer-Center ES 500/K-6
45 Wildcat Ln 15748 724-479-9077
Michael Stofa, prin. Fax 479-3967

Homestead, Allegheny, Pop. 3,535
Steel Valley SD
Supt. — See Munhall
Barrett ES 300/1-5
221 E 12th Ave 15120 412-464-3600
Sharon Fisher, prin. Fax 464-3632

Honesdale, Wayne, Pop. 4,849
Wayne Highlands SD 3,200/K-12
474 Grove St 18431 570-253-4661
Thomas Jenkins, supt. Fax 253-9409
www.waynehighlands.org
Lakeside ES 500/3-5
129 Lakeside Dr 18431 570-253-6820
Sandra Rickard, prin. Fax 253-6826
Stourbridge Primary Center 500/K-2
123 ABC Dr 18431 570-253-3010
Paula Brennan, prin. Fax 253-3236
Wayne Highlands MS 600/6-8
482 Grove St 18431 570-253-5900
Timothy Morgan, prin. Fax 253-5259
Other Schools – See Damascus, Lakewood

Honey Brook, Lancaster, Pop. 1,388
Twin Valley SD
Supt. — See Elverson
Honey Brook ES 500/K-4
1530 Walnut Rd 19344 610-273-3615
Jamie Whye, prin. Fax 273-7053

Honey Grove, Juniata
Juniata County SD
Supt. — See Mifflintown
Lack-Tuscarora ES 100/K-5
3044 Middle Rd 17035 717-734-3172
Valerie Ricedorf, prin. Fax 734-3147

Hookstown, Beaver, Pop. 144
South Side Area SD 1,300/K-12
4949 Route 151 15050 724-573-9581
Dr. Michael Bjalobok, supt. Fax 573-0414
www.sssd.k12.pa.us/
South Side ES 500/K-5
4949 Route 151 15050 724-573-9581
Michael Lewis, prin. Fax 573-2273
South Side MS 300/6-8
4949 Route 151 15050 724-573-9581
Timothy Strader, prin. Fax 573-0449

Horsham, Montgomery, Pop. 15,051
Hatboro-Horsham SD 5,400/K-12
229 Meetinghouse Rd 19044 215-420-5000
Dr. William Lessa, supt. Fax 420-5262
www.hatboro-horsham.org
Hallowell ES 400/K-5
200 Maple Ave 19044 215-420-5900
Steven Glaize, prin. Fax 420-5951
Keith Valley MS 1,300/6-8
227 Meetinghouse Rd 19044 215-420-5050
Jonathan Kircher, prin. Fax 420-5291
Simmons ES 800/1-5
411 Babylon Rd 19044 215-420-5700
Karen Kanter, prin. Fax 420-5885
Other Schools – See Ambler, Hatboro

Quaker S at Horsham 100/PK-8
250 Meetinghouse Rd 19044 215-674-2875
Ruth Joray, hdmstr. Fax 674-9913
St. Catherine of Siena S 300/K-8
317 Witmer Rd 19044 215-674-1904
Sr. Alicia Perna, prin. Fax 674-1466

Houston, Washington, Pop. 1,276
Chartiers-Houston SD 1,200/K-12
2020 W Pike St 15342 724-746-1400
John George, supt. Fax 746-3971
www.chbucs.k12.pa.us/
Allison Park ES 600/K-6
803 McGovern Rd 15342 724-745-4700
Annette Caruso, prin. Fax 745-1710

Central Christian Academy 200/PK-8
145 McGovern Rd 15342 724-746-4902
Kate Giacalone, admin. Fax 746-5053

Houtzdale, Clearfield, Pop. 902
Moshannon Valley SD 1,000/K-12
4934 Green Acre Rd 16651 814-378-7609
Cheryl Pataky, supt. Fax 378-7100
www.movalley.org
Moshannon Valley ES 500/K-6
5026 Green Acre Rd 16651 814-378-7683
Connie Chihon-Godin, prin. Fax 378-5988

Howard, Centre, Pop. 665
Bald Eagle Area SD
Supt. — See Wingate
Howard ES 100/K-6
PO Box 406 16841 814-625-2423
Michael Hall, prin. Fax 625-2785

Hughesville, Lycoming, Pop. 2,114
East Lycoming SD 1,700/K-12
349 Cemetery St 17737 570-584-2131
Dr. Susan Bigger, supt. Fax 584-5701
www.eastlycoming.net
Ashkar ES 500/K-6
350 S Broad St 17737 570-584-5121
Suzanne Foresman, prin. Fax 584-6391
Other Schools – See Lairdsville, Picture Rocks

Hummelstown, Dauphin, Pop. 4,402
Lower Dauphin SD 3,900/K-12
291 E Main St 17036 717-566-5300
Sherri Smith, supt. Fax 566-3670
www.ldsd.org
Lower Dauphin MS 1,000/6-8
251 Quarry Rd 17036 717-566-5310
Daniel Berra, prin. Fax 566-5383
Nye ES 400/K-5
200 S John St 17036 717-566-0300
Douglas Winner, prin. Fax 566-4814
Other Schools – See Elizabethtown, Grantville, Hershey, Middletown

---

Hershey Christian S 300/K-12
1525 Sand Hill Rd 17036 717-533-4900
Timothy Rockafellow, admin. Fax 533-0908

Huntingdon, Huntingdon, Pop. 6,876
Huntingdon Area SD 2,300/K-12
2400 Cassady Ave Ste 2 16652 814-643-4140
Jill Adams, supt. Fax 643-6244
www.hasd.tiu.k12.pa.us/
Huntingdon Area MS 500/6-8
2500 Cassady Ave 16652 814-643-2900
Patricia Wargo, prin. Fax 643-6513
Jackson-Miller ES 100/K-5
13006 Greenwood Rd 16652 814-667-3767
Jeffrey Coppes, prin. Fax 667-3190
Southside ES 300/K-5
10906 Station Rd 16652 814-627-1100
Jeffrey Coppes, prin. Fax 627-0301
Standing Stone ES 400/K-5
10 W 29th St 16652 814-643-0771
Jeffrey Coppes, prin. Fax 643-5947
Other Schools – See Mill Creek

Calvary Christian Academy 100/K-12
300 Standing Stone Ave 16652 814-643-4075
Tim Jones, prin. Fax 643-4094

Huntingdon Valley, Montgomery, Pop. 10,000
Abington SD
Supt. — See Abington
Rydal East ES 300/2-6
1160 Huntingdon Pike 19006 215-884-1308
Laura Ann Pladus, prin. Fax 884-8955

Lower Moreland Township SD 2,000/K-12
2551 Murray Ave 19006 215-938-0270
Dr. Mary Feeley, supt. Fax 947-6933
www.lmtsd.org
Murray Avenue MS 800/4-8
2551 Murray Ave 19006 215-938-0230
Jennifer Dilks, prin. Fax 947-3697
Pine Road ES 600/K-3
3737 Pine Rd 19006 215-938-0290
Donna Blakeman, prin. Fax 502-4248

Huntingdon Valley Christian Academy 100/PK-10
1845 Byberry Rd 19006 215-947-6595
Gary Davis, prin. Fax 947-4277
St. Albert the Great S 500/K-8
214 Welsh Rd 19006 215-947-2332
Cynthia Koons, prin. Fax 938-9360
Valley Christian S 100/PK-6
2364 Huntingdon Pike 19006 215-947-4581
Susan Caler, admin. Fax 947-4583

Huntington Mills, Luzerne
Northwest Area SD
Supt. — See Shickshinny
Huntington Mills S 300/K-6
PO Box 28 18622 570-542-0128
Joseph Gorham, prin. Fax 864-0836

Hyndman, Bedford, Pop. 978
Bedford Area SD
Supt. — See Bedford
Hyndman/Londonderry ES 200/K-5
233 School Dr 15545 814-842-3216
Fax 842-9471

Immaculata, Chester

Villa Maria Academy 400/K-8
1140 King Rd 19345 610-644-4864
Sr. Mary Tennity, prin. Fax 647-6403

Imperial, Allegheny, Pop. 3,449
West Allegheny SD
Supt. — See Oakdale
West Allegheny MS 800/6-8
207 W Allegheny Rd 15126 724-695-8979
Rick Smith, prin. Fax 695-8211
Wilson ES 500/K-5
100 Bruno Ln 15126 724-695-3300
Kathleen Sites, prin. Fax 695-0610

Indiana, Indiana, Pop. 15,016
Indiana Area SD 3,000/K-12
501 E Pike Rd 15701 724-463-8713
Dr. Deborah Clawson, supt. Fax 463-0868
www.iasd.cc
East Pike ES 400/K-6
501 E Pike Rd 15701 724-463-8567
Donald Springer, prin. Fax 463-0868
Eisenhower ES 300/K-6
1460 School St 15701 724-463-8566
Scott Poloff, prin. Fax 465-8612
Franklin ES 400/K-6
95 Ben Franklin Rd S 15701 724-465-5637
Michael Minnick, prin. Fax 465-1070
Mann ES 300/K-6
205 S 5th St 15701 724-463-8560
Denise Dragich, prin. Fax 463-9140

St. Bernard S 200/PK-6
300 Clairvaux Dr 15701 724-465-7139
John Lipchik, prin. Fax 465-0803
Seeds of Faith Christian Academy 100/PK-8
640 Church St 15701 724-463-7719
Paula Detar, prin. Fax 463-8097

Industry, Beaver, Pop. 1,845
Western Beaver County SD
Supt. — See Midland
Snyder ES 100/5-6
215 Engle Rd 15052 724-643-4910
Gabriel Engel, prin. Fax 643-5568

Irwin, Westmoreland, Pop. 4,187
Hempfield Area SD
Supt. — See Greensburg
West Hempfield ES 600/K-5
469 Wendel Rd 15642 724-850-2780
Randall Sarnelli, prin. Fax 850-2781
West Hempfield MS 600/6-8
156 Northumberland Dr 15642 724-850-2140
David Waryanka, prin. Fax 850-2141

Penn-Trafford SD
Supt. — See Harrison City
Sunrise ES 500/K-5
171 Sunrise Dr 15642 724-864-6700
Joseph Marasti, prin. Fax 864-0226

Jamestown, Mercer, Pop. 604
Jamestown Area SD 600/K-12
PO Box 217 16134 724-932-5557
Shane Murray, supt. Fax 932-5632
www.jamestown.k12.pa.us
Jamestown Area ES 300/K-6
PO Box 217 16134 724-932-3181
Tracy Reiser, prin.

Jamison, Bucks
Central Bucks SD
Supt. — See Doylestown
Jamison ES 800/K-6
2090 Land Rd 18929 267-893-3500
Lois Benton, prin. Fax 343-9585
Warwick ES 400/K-6
1340 Almshouse Rd 18929 267-893-4050
Chad Watters, prin. Fax 343-9425

Jeannette, Westmoreland, Pop. 10,196
Jeannette CSD 1,300/K-12
198 Park St 15644 724-523-5497
Sharon Marks, supt. Fax 523-3289
www.jeannette.k12.pa.us/
Jeannette McKee E'S 500/K-5
1000 Lowry Ave 15644 724-523-6522
Dr. Richard King, prin. Fax 523-9418
Jeannette McKee MS 300/6-8
1000 Lowry Ave 15644 724-527-1591
Matthew Jones, prin. Fax 523-6792

Penn-Trafford SD
Supt. — See Harrison City
Harrison Park ES 500/K-5
10 Dell Ave 15644 724-744-2161
Jeff Swartz, prin. Fax 744-1865
McCullough ES 400/K-5
213 Watt Rd 15644 724-744-7441
Joseph Marasti, prin. Fax 744-1076
Penn MS 700/6-8
11 Penn Middle Way 15644 724-744-4431
James Simpson, prin. Fax 744-1215

Christian Fellowship Academy 200/PK-12
2005 Ridge Rd 15644 724-523-2358
Shelli Prindle, prin. Fax 523-5439

Jefferson, Greene, Pop. 979
Jefferson-Morgan SD 800/K-12
PO Box 158 15344 724-883-2310
Donna Furnier, supt. Fax 883-4942
www.jmsd.org/
Jefferson-Morgan ES 500/K-6
PO Box 263 15344 724-883-2310
Sam Silbaugh, prin. Fax 883-2390
Jefferson-Morgan MS 7-8
PO Box 158 15344 724-883-2310
Carol Korber, prin. Fax 883-3786

Jefferson Hills, Allegheny, Pop. 9,642
West Jefferson Hills SD 2,900/K-12
835 Old Clairton Rd 15025 412-655-8450
Terry Kinavey, supt. Fax 655-9544
www.wjhsd.net
Gill Hall ES 300/K-5
829 Gill Hall Rd 15025 412-655-4732
Tina Mayer, prin. Fax 655-3888
Jefferson ES 600/K-5
875 Old Clairton Rd 15025 412-655-4163
Dennis Peterson, prin. Fax 655-4973
Other Schools – See Pittsburgh

Jenkintown, Montgomery, Pop. 4,404
Jenkintown SD 500/K-12
325 Highland Ave 19046 215-885-3722
Dr. Timothy Wade, supt. Fax 885-2090
www.jenkintown.org/

Jenkintown ES 300/K-6
325 Highland Ave 19046 215-884-2933
Thomas Roller, prin.

Abington Friends S 700/PK-12
575 Washington Ln 19046 215-886-4350
Richard Nourie, hdmstr. Fax 886-9143
Immaculate Conception S 200/K-8
606 West Ave 19046 215-887-1312
Diane Greco, prin. Fax 887-5517

Jermyn, Lackawanna, Pop. 2,244
Lakeland SD 1,600/K-12
1355 Lakeland Dr 18433 570-254-9485
Dr. Margaret Billings-Jones, supt. Fax 254-9224
www.lakelandsd.org
Lakeland ES 500/K-6
1333 Lakeland Dr 18433 570-254-9484
Alan King, prin. Fax 254-9224
Other Schools – See Mayfield

Jerome, Somerset, Pop. 1,074
Conemaugh Township Area SD
Supt. — See Davidsville
Conemaugh Township Area PS 200/K-2
PO Box 396 15937 814-479-4084
James Carr, prin. Fax 479-2540

Jersey Shore, Lycoming, Pop. 4,426
Jersey Shore Area SD 2,800/K-12
175 A and P Dr 17740 570-398-1561
Richard Emery, supt. Fax 398-5089
www.jsasd.k12.pa.us
Avis ES 200/K-5
1088 Third St 17740 570-753-5220
Kenneth Dady, prin. Fax 753-3460
Jersey Shore Area ES 500/K-5
601 Locust St 17740 570-398-7120
Laura Milarch, prin. Fax 398-5624
Jersey Shore Area MS 700/6-8
601 Thompson St 17740 570-398-7400
Reed Mellinger, prin. Fax 398-5618
Salladasburg ES 200/K-5
3490 State Route 287 17740 570-398-2931
John Herman, prin. Fax 398-5066
Other Schools – See Williamsport

Jessup, Lackawanna, Pop. 4,579

LaSalle Academy 400/PK-8
309 1st Ave 18434 570-489-2010
Sr. Donna Cerminaro, prin. Fax 489-3887

Jim Thorpe, Carbon, Pop. 4,892
Jim Thorpe Area SD 2,100/K-12
410 Center Ave 18229 570-325-3691
Babara Conway, supt. Fax 325-3699
www.jtasd.org/
Morris S 800/K-8
150 W 10th St 18229 570-325-2703
Holly Mordaunt, prin. Fax 325-8098
Other Schools – See Albrightsville

St. Joseph Regional Academy 100/K-8
25 W 6th St 18229 570-325-3186
Jo Ann Novatnack, prin. Fax 325-9451

Johnsonburg, Elk, Pop. 2,817
Johnsonburg Area SD 700/K-12
315 High School Rd 15845 814-965-2536
Walter Fitch, supt. Fax 965-5809
www.johnsonburgareaschooldistrict.com/
Johnsonburg Area ES 300/K-6
1356 Wilcox Rd 15845 814-965-2577
Dennis Crotzer, prin. Fax 965-4101

Johnstown, Cambria, Pop. 22,539
Central Cambria SD
Supt. — See Ebensburg
Jackson ES 300/K-5
3704 William Penn Ave 15909 814-749-8421
Beverly Ricketts, prin. Fax 749-8856

Conemaugh Township Area SD
Supt. — See Davidsville
Conemaugh Township Area IS 300/3-6
1516 Tire Hill Rd 15905 814-479-4080
Nicole Dull, prin. Fax 479-7497

Conemaugh Valley SD 1,000/K-12
1451 Frankstown Rd 15902 814-535-3957
William Rushin, supt. Fax 536-8902
Conemaugh Valley ES 400/K-6
1451 Frankstown Rd 15902 814-535-6970
William Kanich, prin. Fax 536-8370
East Taylor ES 100/K-4
1340 William Penn Ave 15906 814-539-6524
William Kanich, prin. Fax 536-4826

Ferndale Area SD 800/K-12
100 Dartmouth Ave 15905 814-535-1507
Carole Kakabar, supt. Fax 535-8527
www.fasdk12.org
Ferndale ES 500/K-6
100 Dartmouth Ave 15905 814-535-6724
Justin Zahorchak, prin. Fax 536-6506

Greater Johnstown SD 3,200/PK-12
1091 Broad St 15906 814-533-5651
Barbara Parkins, supt. Fax 533-5655
www.gjsd.net
East Side ES 700/PK-5
220 Messenger St 15902 814-533-5551
Douglas Henry, prin. Fax 533-5548
Greater Johnstown MS 700/6-8
280 Decker Ave 15906 814-533-5570
Darren Buchko, prin. Fax 533-5564
West Side ES 800/PK-5
196 Westgate Dr 15905 814-533-5542
Robert Beatty, prin. Fax 533-5592

Richland SD 1,400/K-12
340 Theatre Dr 15904 814-266-6063
Thomas Fleming, supt. Fax 266-7349
www.richlandsd.com/
Richland ES 700/K-6
321 Schoolhouse Rd 15904 814-266-5757
Edward Moran, prin. Fax 269-3499

Westmont Hilltop SD 1,800/K-12
827 Diamond Blvd 15905 814-255-6751
Dr. Susan Anderson, supt. Fax 255-7735
www.whsd.org
Westmont Hilltop ES 600/K-4
675 Goucher St 15905 814-255-8707
Samuel Brunatti, prin. Fax 255-8793
Westmont Hilltop MS 600/5-8
827 Diamond Blvd 15905 814-255-8704
Nicole Kuzmiak, prin. Fax 255-8783

Cambria County Christian S 100/K-12
561 Pike Rd 15909 814-749-7406
Charlie Fenchak, admin. Fax 749-7028
Cathedral Catholic Academy 200/PK-8
110 Lindberg Ave 15905 814-255-1964
Rosemary Batzel, prin. Fax 255-2623
Davidsville Christian S 50/PK-12
197 Pender Rd 15905 814-479-2525
Melissa Allison, admin. Fax 479-7908
Our Mother of Sorrows S 300/PK-8
430 Tioga St 15905 814-539-5315
Pamela Seidel, prin. Fax 539-5315
St. Andrew S 100/PK-8
1621 Ferndale Ave 15905 814-288-2811
Grace Guaetta, prin. Fax 288-6750
St. Benedict S 300/PK-8
2306 Bedford St 15904 814-266-3837
Sr. Carol Ann Ziecina, prin. Fax 266-7718

Jones Mills, Westmoreland
Mt. Pleasant Area SD
Supt. — See Mount Pleasant
Donegal ES 200/K-6
138 School House Ln 15646 724-547-4100
Scott Bryer, prin. Fax 547-7713

Jonestown, Lebanon, Pop. 1,008
Northern Lebanon SD
Supt. — See Fredericksburg
Jonestown ES 400/K-6
PO Box 839 17038 717-865-3193
Marian Robidas, prin. Fax 865-0805
Lickdale ES 300/K-6
40 Fisher Ave 17038 717-865-4012
Melissa McInerney, prin. Fax 865-5396

Blue Mountain Christian S 100/PK-12
14 Silvertown Rd 17038 717-865-9650
Janet Catani, coord. Fax 865-4732

Kane, McKean, Pop. 3,893
Kane Area SD 1,200/K-12
400 W Hemlock Ave 16735 814-837-9570
Sandra Chlopecki, supt. Fax 837-7450
www.kasd.net
Chestnut Street ES 500/K-5
226 Chestnut St 16735 814-837-7555
Linda Lorenzo, prin. Fax 837-9207
Kane Area MS 300/6-8
400 W Hemlock Ave 16735 814-837-6030
James Fryzlewicz, prin. Fax 837-9133

Karns City, Butler, Pop. 234
Karns City Area SD 1,800/K-12
1446 Kittanning Pike 16041 724-756-2030
Larry Henry, supt. Fax 756-2121
www.karnscity.k12.pa.us
Other Schools – See Bruin, Chicora, Cowansville

Kempton, Berks
Kutztown Area SD
Supt. — See Kutztown
Albany ES 100/K-5
3656 Route 737 19529 610-756-6926
Peter Miller, prin. Fax 756-3049

Kennerdell, Venango
Cranberry Area SD
Supt. — See Seneca
Rockland ES 100/K-5
164 Rockland Cranberry Rd 16374 814-498-2221
George Svolos, prin. Fax 498-2216

Kennett Square, Chester, Pop. 5,292
Kennett Consolidated SD 4,100/K-12
300 E South St 19348 610-444-6600
Dr. Rudolph Karkosak, supt. Fax 444-6614
kcsd.org
Greenwood ES 700/K-5
420 Greenwood Rd 19348 610-388-5990
Tracey Marino, prin.
Lang ES, 409 Center St 19348 400/K-5
Susan McArdle, prin. 610-444-6260
Other Schools – See Landenberg, Toughkenamon

Unionville-Chadds Ford SD 4,100/K-12
740 Unionville Rd 19348 610-347-0970
Sharon Parker, supt. Fax 347-0976
www.ucfsd.org
Patton MS 1,000/6-8
760 Unionville Rd 19348 610-347-2000
Bruce Vosburgh, prin. Fax 347-0421
Unionville ES 500/K-5
1775 W Doe Run Rd 19348 610-347-1700
Clifton Beaver, prin. Fax 347-1443
Other Schools – See Chadds Ford, West Chester

London Grove Friends K 50/K-K
500 W Street Rd 19348 610-268-8466
Cynthia Leahan, lead tchr.

St. Patrick S 200/K-8
210 Meredith St 19348 610-444-3104
Theresa Waters, prin. Fax 444-3166
Upland Country Day S 200/PK-9
420 W Street Rd 19348 610-444-3035
David Suter, hdmstr. Fax 444-2961

Kersey, Elk
Saint Marys Area SD
Supt. — See Saint Marys
Fox Township ES 200/K-5
376 Main St 15846 814-885-8076
Christine Kuhar, prin. Fax 885-6331

St. Boniface S 100/PK-5
359 Main St 15846 814-885-8093
Marie Giazzoni, prin. Fax 885-8611

Kimberton, Chester

Kimberton Waldorf S 300/PK-12
PO Box 350 19442 610-933-3635
Lisa Faranda, chrpsn. Fax 935-6985
St. Basil the Great S 200/PK-8
PO Box 858 19442 610-933-2453
Angela Ruffo, prin. Fax 933-7590

King of Prussia, Montgomery, Pop. 18,406
Upper Merion Area SD 3,600/K-12
435 Crossfield Rd 19406 610-205-6401
Dr. Melissa Jamula, supt. Fax 205-6433
www.umasd.org
Caley Road ES 400/K-4
725 Caley Rd 19406 610-205-3651
Jennifer Dilks, prin. Fax 205-3699
Candlebrook ES 400/K-4
310 Prince Frederick St 19406 610-205-3701
Anthony Sparano, prin. Fax 205-3749
Upper Merion MS 1,100/5-8
450 Keebler Rd 19406 610-205-8801
John Adiletto, prin. Fax 205-8999
Other Schools – See Bridgeport, Wayne

Mother of Divine Providence S 300/PK-8
405 Allendale Rd 19406 610-265-2323
Theresa Garvin, prin. Fax 265-1816

Kingsley, Susquehanna
Mountain View SD 1,300/K-12
11748 State Route 106 18826 570-434-2180
Dr. Andrew Chichura, supt. Fax 434-2404
www.mvsd.net
Mountain View ES 700/K-6
11748 State Route 106 18826 570-434-2181
Susan Pipitone, prin. Fax 434-2755

Kingston, Luzerne, Pop. 13,176
Wyoming Valley West SD 5,100/K-12
450 N Maple Ave 18704 570-288-6551
Dr. Michael Garzella, supt. Fax 288-1564
www.wvwspartans.org
Chester Street ES 300/1-5
110 Chester St 18704 570-287-2438
Raymond Whalen, prin. Fax 714-4140
Pringle Street ES 100/K-5
230 Pringle St 18704 570-287-5338
Erin Keating, prin. Fax 714-5086
Schuyler Avenue ES 200/K-5
715 Schuyler Ave 18704 570-287-6041
Irvin DeRemer, prin. Fax 714-7329
State Street ES 500/K-5
355 E State St 18704 570-779-5381
Erin Keating, prin. Fax 779-2023
Third Avenue ES 200/K-5
111 3rd Ave 18704 570-288-2282
Raymond Whalen, prin. Fax 714-3511
Wyoming Valley West MS 1,300/6-8
201 Chester St 18704 570-287-2131
Deborah Troy, prin. Fax 287-6343
Other Schools – See Forty Fort, Plymouth

Good Shepherd Academy 500/PK-8
316 N Maple Ave 18704 570-288-1404
James Jones, prin. Fax 288-6634
United Hebrew Institute/Israel Ben Zion 100/PK-8
1 Institute Ln 18704 570-287-9600
Rabbi Raphael Nemetsky, prin. Fax 718-0699
Wyoming Valley Montessori S 100/PK-8
851 W Market St 18704 570-288-3708
Mark DiPippa, prin. Fax 331-0279

Kintnersville, Bucks
Palisades SD 2,000/K-12
39 Thomas Free Dr 18930 610-847-5131
Francis Barnes Ph.D., supt. Fax 847-8116
www.palisadessd.org
Durham-Nockamixon ES 300/K-5
41 Thomas Free Dr 18930 610-847-5131
Janet Link, prin. Fax 847-6960
Palisades MS 500/6-8
4710 Durham Rd 18930 610-847-5131
Edward Baumgartner, prin. Fax 847-2691
Other Schools – See Pipersville, Quakertown

Kinzers, Lancaster
Pequea Valley SD 1,700/K-12
PO Box 130 17535 717-768-5530
Patrick Hallock, supt. Fax 768-7176
www.pvsd.k12.pa.us
Pequea Valley IS 400/6-8
PO Box 257 17535 717-768-5535
Erik Orndorff, prin. Fax 768-5656
Other Schools – See Gap, Paradise

Kittanning, Armstrong, Pop. 4,454
Armstrong SD
Supt. — See Ford City
Kittanning Area JHS 400/6-8
210 N Mckean St 16201 724-543-1295
Timothy Sedgwick, prin. Fax 543-1155

Kittanning Township ES 300/K-6
598 Silvis Hollow Rd 16201 724-548-7696
Eric Ritzert, prin. Fax 548-4112
West Hills IS 4-6
175 Heritage Park Dr 16201 724-543-1121
Sue Kreidler, prin. Fax 548-8765
West Hills PS 300/K-3
181 Heritage Park Dr 16201 724-548-7651
Ann Miranda, prin.

Grace Christian S 100/PK-6
215 Arthur St 16201 724-543-4019
Sandy Hankinson, admin. Fax 545-6738

Klingerstown, Schuylkill
Tri-Valley SD
Supt. — See Valley View
Mahantongo ES 100/K-6
1200 Ridge Rd 17941 570-648-6062
Gerald Anderson, prin. Fax 648-8739

Knox, Clarion, Pop. 1,122
Keystone SD 1,200/K-12
451 Huston Ave 16232 814-797-5921
Dr. Jean Gool, supt. Fax 797-2382
www.keyknox.com
Keystone ES 600/K-6
451 Huston Ave 16232 814-797-1251
Shawn Corcetti, prin. Fax 797-0205

Kresgeville, Monroe
Pleasant Valley SD
Supt. — See Brodheadsville
Polk ES 400/K-4
Route 209 18333 610-681-4044
Amy Braxmeier, prin. Fax 681-3121

Kunkletown, Monroe
Pleasant Valley SD
Supt. — See Brodheadsville
Eldred ES 200/K-4
RR 2 Box 11 18058 610-381-3634
Joseph Kondisko, prin. Fax 381-5073
Pleasant Valley ES 1,400/K-4
RR 3 Box 505 18058 610-681-3091
Penny Derr, prin. Fax 681-3018
Pleasant Valley IS 1,600/5-7
RR 3 Box 498 18058 610-681-8591
James Storm, prin. Fax 681-8666

Kutztown, Berks, Pop. 4,926
Kutztown Area SD 1,700/K-12
50 Trexler Ave 19530 610-683-7361
Robert Gross, supt. Fax 683-7230
www.kasd.org
Kutztown Area MS 400/6-8
10 Deisher Ln 19530 610-683-3575
James Brown, prin. Fax 683-5460
Kutztown ES 300/K-5
40 Normal Ave 19530 610-683-3557
James Orwig, prin. Fax 683-0254
Maxatawny ES 100/K-5
251 Long Lane Rd 19530 610-683-6771
James Orwig, prin. Fax 683-0388
Other Schools – See Kempton, Lenhartsville

Northwestern Lehigh SD
Supt. — See New Tripoli
Weisenberg ES 400/K-4
2665 Golden Key Rd 19530 610-298-8661
Renee Cartier, prin. Fax 285-2677

Laceyville, Wyoming, Pop. 378
Wyalusing Area SD
Supt. — See Wyalusing
Laceyville ES 100/K-6
RR 2 Box 2255 18623 570-869-1229
Joseph Darrow, prin. Fax 869-1006

Lafayette Hill, Montgomery, Pop. 6,700
Colonial SD
Supt. — See Plymouth Meeting
Whitemarsh ES 400/K-3
4120 Joshua Rd 19444 610-828-9092
Donna Drizin, prin. Fax 828-1516

St. Philip Neri S 400/PK-8
3015 Chestnut St 19444 610-828-3082
Berenice Annechini, prin. Fax 828-2943

Lahaska, Bucks, Pop. 200

Buckingham Friends S 200/K-8
PO Box 159 18931 215-794-7491
Scott Baytosh, hdmstr. Fax 794-7955

Lairdsville, Lycoming
East Lycoming SD
Supt. — See Hughesville
Renn ES 200/K-6
183 School Ln 17742 570-584-3070
William Knapsack, prin. Fax 584-5393

Lake Ariel, Wayne
North Pocono SD
Supt. — See Moscow
Jefferson ES 300/K-3
825 Lions Rd 18436 570-689-2656
Laura Davis, prin. Fax 689-3825

Western Wayne SD
Supt. — See South Canaan
Lake Ariel ES 300/3-5
111 Gravity Rd 18436 570-698-5119
Ellen Faliskie, prin. Fax 698-7316
Western Wayne MS 500/6-8
1970B Easton Tpke 18436 570-937-3010
Peter Chapla, prin. Fax 937-3440

Canaan Christian Academy 200/PK-12
30 Hemlock Rd 18436 570-937-4848
David Marquette, prin. Fax 937-4800

Lake City, Erie, Pop. 2,981
Girard SD
Supt. — See Girard
Elk Valley ES 700/K-4
2556 Maple Ave 16423 814-774-5602
Donna Miller, prin. Fax 774-8885

Lakewood, Wayne
Wayne Highlands SD
Supt. — See Honesdale
Preston S 200/K-8
1493 Crosstown Hwy 18439 570-798-2516
Chris Pietraszewski, prin. Fax 798-2677

Lampeter, Lancaster
Lampeter-Strasburg SD 2,400/K-12
PO Box 428 17537 717-464-3311
Robert Frick Ed.D., supt. Fax 464-4699
www.l-spioneers.org
Herr ES 3-5
PO Box 428 17537 717-464-3311
Andrew Godfrey, prin. Fax 509-0300
Lampeter ES 300/K-2
PO Box 428 17537 717-464-3311
Kathy Focht, prin. Fax 358-1880
Meylin MS 800/6-8
PO Box 428 17537 717-464-3311
Michael Burcin, prin. Fax 509-0289
Other Schools – See Strasburg

Lancaster, Lancaster, Pop. 54,757
Conestoga Valley SD 3,900/K-12
2110 Horseshoe Rd 17601 717-397-2421
Dr. Gerald Huesken, supt. Fax 397-0442
www.cvsd.k12.pa.us
Conestoga Valley MS 600/7-8
500 Mount Sidney Rd 17602 717-397-1294
Robert Houghton, prin. Fax 397-4404
Fritz ES 600/K-6
845 Hornig Rd 17601 717-397-5246
Colleen Hovanec, prin. Fax 397-6481
Smoketown ES 600/K-6
2426 Old Philadelphia Pike 17602 717-394-0555
Randall McCarty, prin. Fax 394-2792
Other Schools – See Brownstown, Leola

Hempfield SD
Supt. — See Landisville
Centerville ES 500/K-6
901 Centerville Rd 17601 717-898-5575
Janet Baer, prin. Fax 898-5557
Centerville MS 700/7-8
865 Centerville Rd 17601 717-898-5580
James Dague, prin. Fax 898-5647
Rohrerstown ES 500/K-6
2200 Noll Dr 17603 717-299-7126
Kathleen Swantner, prin. Fax 618-0997

Lancaster SD 11,200/K-12
1020 Lehigh Ave 17602 717-291-6121
Pedro Rivera, supt. Fax 291-6002
www.lancaster.k12.pa.us
Buchanan ES 400/K-5
340 S West End Ave 17603 717-291-6151
Fax 391-8608
Burrowes ES 400/K-5
1001 E Orange St 17602 717-291-6159
Gary Hess, prin. Fax 391-8607
Carter & MacRae ES 400/K-5
251 S Prince St 17603 717-396-6842
Ollie Jones, prin. Fax 295-7842
Fulton ES 500/K-5
225 W Orange St 17603 717-291-6110
Matt Stem, prin. Fax 396-6800
Hamilton ES 400/K-5
1300 Wabank Rd 17603 717-291-6166
Paula Wilson, prin. Fax 390-2575
Hand MS 500/6-8
431 S Ann St 17602 717-291-6161
Larry Mays, prin. Fax 391-8600
King ES 600/K-5
466 Rockland St 17602 717-291-6178
Lynette Waller, prin. Fax 391-8616
Lafayette ES 500/K-5
1000 Saint Joseph St 17603 717-291-6183
Fax 295-7847
Lincoln MS 700/6-8
1001 Lehigh Ave 17602 717-291-6187
Josh Keene, prin. Fax 399-6408
Martin ES 300/K-5
1900 Wabank Rd 17603 717-291-6193
Barbara Andrews, prin. Fax 390-2562
Price ES 500/K-5
615 Fairview Ave 17603 717-291-6252
Fax 291-6118
Reynolds MS 600/6-8
605 W Walnut St 17603 717-291-6257
Mark Simms, prin. Fax 396-6823
Ross ES 400/K-5
840 N Queen St 17603 717-291-6268
Camille Hopkins, prin. Fax 390-2576
Washington ES 600/K-5
545 S Ann St 17602 717-291-6275
Dr. Janette Hewitt, prin. Fax 390-2563
Wharton ES 200/K-5
705 N Mary St 17603 717-291-6281
Jackie Hair, prin. Fax 390-2561
Wheatland MS 700/6-8
919 Hamilton Park Dr 17603 717-291-6285
Marty Slaugh, prin. Fax 399-6411
Wickersham ES 500/K-5
401 N Reservoir St 17602 717-291-6291
Dr. Bernard James, prin. Fax 390-2577

Manheim Township SD
Supt. — See Lititz
Brecht ES 300/K-5
1250 Lititz Pike 17601 717-291-1733
Travis Bash, prin. Fax 735-0939
Bucher ES 300/K-5
450 Candlewyck Rd 17601 717-569-4291
Jennifer Mack, prin. Fax 569-3060
Manheim Township MS 900/6-8
PO Box 5134 17606 717-560-3111
Heather Nuneviller, prin. Fax 569-1670
Neff - 6th Grade S 400/6-6
PO Box 5134 17606 717-581-9124
Jason Reifsnyder, prin. Fax 569-8226
Neff ES 400/K-5
PO Box 5134 17606 717-569-8502
Drew Scheffey, prin. Fax 569-8226
Nitrauer ES 600/K-5
811 Ashbourne Ave 17601 717-569-4239
Patricia Zanghi, prin. Fax 569-7973
Schaeffer ES 400/K-5
875 Pleasure Rd 17601 717-392-6797
Anthony Aldinger, prin. Fax 392-0267

Penn Manor SD 5,300/K-12
2950 Charlestown Rd 17603 717-872-9500
Michael Leichliter, supt. Fax 872-9505
www.pennmanor.net
Hambright ES 400/K-6
2121 Temple Ave 17603 717-393-3818
Gerard Egan, prin. Fax 399-1583
Manor MS 500/7-8
2950 Charlestown Rd 17603 717-872-9510
Dana Edwards, prin. Fax 872-9505
Other Schools – See Conestoga, Holtwood, Millersville, Pequea, Washington Boro, Willow Street

---

Dayspring Christian Academy 300/PK-12
1008 New Holland Ave 17601 717-295-6400
Michael Myers, hdmstr. Fax 295-6410
Lancaster Adventist S 50/K-8
1721 Conard Rd 17602 717-464-2591
Lancaster Christian S 300/K-12
651 Lampeter Rd 17602 717-392-8092
Dr. Sandy Outlar, hdmstr. Fax 509-3094
Lancaster Country Day S 500/PK-12
725 Hamilton Rd 17603 717-392-2916
Stephen Lisk, prin. Fax 392-0425
Lancaster Mennonite S - Locust Grove 200/PK-8
2257 Old Philadelphia Pike 17602 717-394-7107
Richard Thomas, supt. Fax 394-4944
Lancaster Mennonite S - New Danville 100/PK-6
393 Long Ln 17603 717-872-2506
Judi Mollenkof, admin. Fax 872-5201
Living Word Academy 300/PK-12
2384 New Holland Pike 17601 717-556-0711
Mark Cote, hdmstr. Fax 656-4868
Montessori Academy of Lancaster 200/PK-3
2750 Weaver Rd 17601 717-560-0815
Karen Rubenstein, prin. Fax 560-0817
New S of Lancaster 300/PK-8
935 Columbia Ave 17603 717-397-7655
Mary Cae Williams, hdmstr. Fax 397-2538
Resurrection MS 100/4-8
521 E Orange St 17602 717-392-3083
Brenda Weaver, prin. Fax 735-7793
Resurrection S 100/K-3
32 W Vine St 17603 717-397-3136
Brenda Weaver, prin. Fax 295-8475
Sacred Heart of Jesus S 200/PK-8
235 Nevin St 17603 717-393-8433
Sr. Mary Deering, prin. Fax 393-1028
St. Anne S 200/PK-8
108 E Liberty St 17602 717-394-6711
Dr. Christopher Kennedy, admin. Fax 394-8628
St. Leo the Great S 300/PK-8
2427 Marietta Ave 17601 717-392-2441
Georgia Steinbacher, prin. Fax 392-4080
St. Philip the Apostle Preschool PK-PK
2111 Millersville Pike 17603 717-872-2166
Linda Simpson, prin.
San Juan Baptista Learning Center PK-PK
425 S Duke St 17602 717-283-0270
Wonder Club S 100/PK-K
PO Box 7267 17604 717-394-9723
Jere Shertzer, pres. Fax 393-4966

Landenberg, Chester
Kennett Consolidated SD
Supt. — See Kennett Square
Kennett MS, 195 Sunny Dell Rd 19350 1,000/6-8
John Carr, prin. 610-268-5800

Landenberg Christian Academy 50/PK-6
109 Gypsy Hill Rd 19350 610-255-5805
Julie Malone, admin.

Landisville, Lancaster, Pop. 4,239
Hempfield SD 7,200/K-12
200 Church St 17538 717-898-5564
Brenda Becker, supt. Fax 898-5628
www.hempfieldsd.org
Landisville IS 400/4-6
300 Church St 17538 717-898-5590
Richard Bentley, prin. Fax 618-0996
Landisville MS 500/7-8
340 Mumma Dr 17538 717-898-5607
Dr. Nancy Herr, prin. Fax 898-1603
Landisville Primary Center 600/K-3
320 Mumma Dr 17538 717-898-5519
Ronald Swantner, prin. Fax 618-1009
Other Schools – See East Petersburg, Lancaster, Mount Joy, Mountville

Langhorne, Bucks, Pop. 1,974
Neshaminy SD 9,200/K-12
2001 Old Lincoln Hwy 19047 215-809-6500
Paul Kadri, supt. Fax 809-6502
www.neshaminy.k12.pa.us
Heckman ES, 201 Cherry St 19047 500/K-5
Brian Kern, prin. 215-809-6330
Hoover ES, 501 Trenton Rd 19047 600/K-5
Mike Stanford, prin. 215-809-6340
Other Schools – See Feasterville, Levittown

Lansdale, Montgomery, Pop. 15,913
Methacton SD
Supt. — See Eagleville
Worcester ES 500/K-5
3017 Skippack Pike 19446 610-489-5000
Bruce MacGregor, prin. Fax 831-5326

North Penn SD 13,000/K-12
401 E Hancock St 19446 215-368-0400
Dr. Robert Hassler, supt. Fax 368-3161
www.npenn.org
Bridle Path ES 600/K-6
200 Bridle Path Rd 19446 215-362-2200
Scott Mitchell, prin. Fax 362-7517
Gwynedd Square ES 500/K-6
1641 Supplee Rd 19446 215-855-4331
Lou Ann Justice, prin. Fax 412-7982
Inglewood ES 400/K-6
1313 Allentown Rd 19446 215-368-2992
Maureen Coffey, prin. Fax 368-7808
Knapp ES 600/K-6
698 Knapp Rd 19446 215-368-2054
Joseph Mazza, prin. Fax 368-6932
Oak Park ES 500/K-6
500 Squirrel Ln 19446 215-368-4017
Bonnie Rosen, prin. Fax 368-7862
Walton Farm ES 500/K-6
1610 Allentown Rd 19446 215-855-8800
Sylvannya Dantzler, prin. Fax 412-8695
York Avenue ES 300/K-6
700 York Ave 19446 215-368-6002
Dr. Charles D'Alfonso, prin. Fax 368-7875
Other Schools – See Harleysville, Hatfield, North Wales

Calvary Baptist Christian S 300/PK-12
1380 S Valley Forge Rd 19446 215-368-1100
Fax 368-1003
Corpus Christi S 500/K-8
920 Sumneytown Pike 19446 215-368-0582
Wanda Costello, prin. Fax 361-5927
St. Stanislaus S 400/K-8
493 E Main St 19446 215-368-0995
Diane McCaughan, prin. Fax 393-4869

Lansdowne, Delaware, Pop. 10,789
William Penn SD 5,000/K-12
100 Green Ave 19050 610-284-8000
Joseph Bruni, supt. Fax 284-8053
www.wpsd.k12.pa.us
Ardmore Avenue ES 500/K-6
161 Ardmore Ave 19050 610-623-7900
Jason Harris, prin. Fax 284-2226
Other Schools – See Aldan, Colwyn, Darby, East Lansdowne, Yeadon

---

Lansdowne Friends S 100/PK-6
110 N Lansdowne Ave 19050 610-623-2548
Susan Stone, hdmstr. Fax 623-3637
St. Philomena S 200/K-8
13 N Highland Ave 19050 610-259-6817
Patricia Walsh, prin. Fax 259-5656

Lansford, Carbon, Pop. 4,210
Panther Valley SD 1,700/K-12
1 Panther Way 18232 570-645-4248
Rosemary Porembo, supt. Fax 645-6232
www.panthervalley.org/
Panther Valley MS 400/6-8
678 Panther Pride Way 18232 570-645-2175
Lisa Mace, prin. Fax 645-9723
Other Schools – See Nesquehoning

Our Lady of the Angels Academy 100/K-8
123 E Water St 18232 570-645-7101
Sr. Regina Elinich, prin. Fax 645-5278

Laporte, Sullivan, Pop. 276
Sullivan County SD
Supt. — See Dushore
Sullivan County ES 200/K-6
PO Box 115 18626 570-946-7471
Mary McClintock, prin. Fax 946-4272

Latrobe, Westmoreland, Pop. 8,654
Derry Area SD
Supt. — See Derry
Loyalhanna ES 100/K-1
314 Loyalhanna School Rd 15650 724-537-6751
Marty Rovedatti-Jackson, prin. Fax 537-3263

Greater Latrobe SD 4,200/K-12
410 Main St 15650 724-539-4200
Judith Swigart, supt. Fax 539-4202
www.glsd.k12.pa.us
Baggaley ES 700/K-6
4080 State Route 982 15650 724-539-4531
Michael Porembka, prin. Fax 539-0448
Latrobe ES 800/K-6
1501 Ligonier St 15650 724-539-9777
Sherri Holler, prin. Fax 539-4224
Other Schools – See Greensburg

Christ the Devine Teacher S 300/PK-8
323 Chestnut St 15650 724-539-1561
Timothy Larouere, prin. Fax 532-3873

Laureldale, Berks, Pop. 3,752
Muhlenberg SD 3,100/K-12
801 E Bellevue Ave 19605 610-921-8000
Dr. Theresa Haught, supt. Fax 921-8076
www.muhlsdk12.org
Cole IS 300/5-6
3630 Kutztown Rd 19605 610-921-8212
Ryan Giffing, prin. Fax 741-1198
Muhlenberg ES 1,100/K-4
Sharp Ave and Kutztown Rd 19605 610-921-8028
Barbara Moyer, prin. Fax 921-7905
Muhlenberg MS 600/7-8
801 E Bellevue Ave 19605 610-921-8034
Donna Albright, prin. Fax 921-8038

Lebanon, Lebanon, Pop. 23,986
Cornwall-Lebanon SD 4,800/K-12
105 E Evergreen Rd 17042 717-272-2031
Joseph Kristobak, supt. Fax 274-2786
www.clsd.k12.pa.us
Cedar Crest MS 1,100/6-8
101 E Evergreen Rd 17042 717-272-2032
Mariah Rackley, prin. Fax 228-1437
Cornwall ES 500/K-5
45 Burd Coleman Rd 17042 717-273-4571
Charles Kindt, prin. Fax 273-5287
Ebenezer ES 600/K-5
1600 Colonial Cir 17046 717-272-1969
Cynthia Geesey, prin. Fax 272-6701
South Lebanon ES 500/K-5
1825 S 5th Ave 17042 717-273-4546
Barry Ferguson, prin. Fax 273-3634
Union Canal ES 400/K-5
400 Narrows Dr 17046 717-270-7227
Tracie Clemens, prin. Fax 270-7229

Lebanon SD 4,400/PK-12
1000 S 8th St 17042 717-273-9391
Dr. Marianne Bartley, supt. Fax 270-6778
www.lebanon.k12.pa.us
Harding ES, 622 Chestnut St 17042 600/PK-5
Cheryl Champion, prin. 717-273-9391
Houck ES, 315 E Lehman St 17046 300/PK-5
Robert Okonak, prin. 717-273-9391
Lebanon MS 1,000/6-8
350 N 8th St 17046 717-273-9391
Mary Garrett, prin. Fax 270-6859
Northwest ES, 900 Maple St 17046 800/PK-5
Neil Young, prin. 717-273-9391
Southeast ES 300/PK-5
499 E Pershing Ave 17042 717-273-9391
Michael Habecker, prin.
Southwest ES 300/PK-5
1500 Woodland St 17042 717-273-9391
Kenneth Travis, prin.

Lebanon Catholic S 400/K-12
1400 Chestnut St 17042 717-273-3731
Michele Ambrosia, admin. Fax 274-5167
Lebanon Christian Academy 100/K-12
875 Academy Dr 17046 717-273-8114
Fax 272-1886
New Covenant Christian S 200/PK-12
452 Ebenezer Rd 17046 717-274-2423
Bill Litman, admin. Fax 274-9830

Leck Kill, Northumberland
Line Mountain SD
Supt. — See Herndon
Leck Kill ES 100/K-6
3664 Old State Rd 17836 570-425-3671
Thea Tafner, prin. Fax 425-2888

Leechburg, Armstrong, Pop. 2,269
Kiski Area SD 4,300/K-12
250 Hyde Park Rd 15656 724-845-2022
Dr. John Meighan, supt. Fax 842-0444
www.kiskiarea.com
Allegheny-Hyde Park ES 600/K-6
1048 School Rd 15656 724-845-2032
Brian Kutchak, prin. Fax 845-0984
Kiski Area IS 700/7-8
260 Hyde Park Rd 15656 724-845-2219
Scott Koter, prin. Fax 845-3208
Other Schools – See Apollo, Export, Salina, Vandergrift

Leechburg Area SD 800/K-12
210 Penn Ave 15656 724-842-9681
James Budzilek, supt. Fax 845-2241
www.leechburg.k12.pa.us
Leechburg Area JHS 200/7-8
215 1st St 15656 724-842-0571
Cynthia Portman, prin. Fax 845-4761
Leech ES 400/K-6
200 Siberian Ave 15656 724-845-6071
Cynthia Portman, prin. Fax 845-9723

Leesport, Berks, Pop. 1,916
Schuylkill Valley SD 1,900/K-12
929 Lakeshore Dr 19533 610-916-0957
Dr. Solomon Lausch, supt. Fax 926-3960
www.schuylkillvalley.org/
Schuylkill Valley ES 700/K-4
62 Ashley Way 19533 610-926-4165
Bernadette Meck, prin. Fax 916-5048
Schuylkill Valley MS 500/5-8
114 Ontelaunee Dr 19533 610-926-7111
Michael Mitchell, prin. Fax 926-3321

Lehighton, Carbon, Pop. 5,523
Lehighton Area SD 2,400/K-12
1000 Union St 18235 610-377-4490
James Kraky, supt. Fax 577-0035
www.lehighton.org/
East Penn ES 100/K-4
496 W Lizard Creek Rd 18235 610-377-6094
Gretchen Laviolette, prin.
Franklin ES 300/K-4
1122 Fairyland Rd 18235 610-377-6163
Gretchen Laviolette, prin. Fax 577-0067
Lehighton Area MS 700/5-8
301 Beaver Run Rd 18235 610-377-6535
Timothy Kach, prin. Fax 377-6503
Mahoning ES 200/K-4
2466 Mahoning Dr E 18235 570-386-4678
Aaron Sebelin, prin. Fax 577-1009
Shull-David ES 300/K-4
200 Beaver Run Rd 18235 610-377-7880
Aaron Sebelin, prin. Fax 377-0908

Palmerton Area SD
Supt. — See Palmerton
Towamensing ES 400/K-6
7920 Interchange Rd 18235 610-681-4024
Gary Bruch, prin. Fax 681-6410

SS. Peter & Paul S 100/PK-8
307 Coal St 18235 610-377-4466
Sherry Ambrose, prin. Fax 377-8881

Lehman, Luzerne
Lake-Lehman SD 2,200/K-12
PO Box 38 18627 570-675-2165
James McGovern, supt. Fax 675-7657
www.lake-lehman.k12.pa.us/
Lehman-Jackson ES 500/K-6
PO Box 38 18627 570-675-2165
Marilyn Glogowski, prin. Fax 674-5907
Other Schools – See Harveys Lake, Sweet Valley

Lemoyne, Cumberland, Pop. 3,952
West Shore SD
Supt. — See Lewisberry
Lemoyne MS, 701 Market St 17043 400/6-8
Thomas Haupt, prin. 717-761-6345
Washington Heights ES 400/K-5
531 Walnut St 17043 717-761-8040
Deborah Schwager, prin.

Lenhartsville, Berks, Pop. 171
Kutztown Area SD
Supt. — See Kutztown
Greenwich-Lenhartsville ES 200/K-5
1457 Krumsville Rd 19534 610-756-6948
Peter Miller, prin. Fax 756-6858

Leola, Lancaster, Pop. 5,685
Conestoga Valley SD
Supt. — See Lancaster
Leola ES 400/K-6
11 School Dr 17540 717-656-2068
Colleen Pavlovec, prin. Fax 656-3247

Veritas Academy 200/K-12
26 Hillcrest Ave 17540 717-556-0690
G. Tyler Fischer, hdmstr. Fax 556-0736

Levittown, Bucks, Pop. 53,700
Bristol Township SD 5,700/K-12
6401 Mill Creek Rd 19057 215-943-3200
Ellen Budman, supt. Fax 949-2210
www.btsd.us/
Barton ES 500/K-6
5 Blue Lake Rd 19057 215-945-4177
George Ciarrocchi, prin. Fax 945-2463
Buchanan ES 400/K-6
2200 Haines Rd 19055 215-946-5922
Evy Clark, prin. Fax 946-8592
Emerson ES 400/K-6
6501 Mill Creek Rd 19057 215-945-0222
Jacqueline Cubberly, prin. Fax 547-8814
Fitch ES 300/K-6
101 Greenbrook Dr 19055 215-946-0232
Karen Snedeker, prin. Fax 946-2888
Lincoln ES 300/K-6
10 Plumtree Pl 19056 215-945-7487
Theresa Giardine, prin. Fax 945-2229
Washington ES 400/K-6
275 Crabtree Dr 19055 215-945-9482
Christopher Schoettle, prin. Fax 946-1390
Other Schools – See Bristol, Croydon, Fairless Hills

Neshaminy SD
Supt. — See Langhorne
Buck ES, 143 Top Rd 19056 400/K-5
Paul Mahoney, prin. 215-809-6300
Everitt ES, Forsythia Dr S 19056 400/K-5
Andre Modica, prin. 215-809-6320
Miller ES, 10 Cobalt Ridge Dr S 19057 400/K-5
Joan Chak, prin. 215-809-6360
Schweitzer ES, 10 Harmony Rd 19056 400/K-5
Stephanie Miguelez, prin. 215-809-6380

Pennsbury SD
Supt. — See Fallsington
Disney ES 400/K-5
200 Lakeside Dr 19054 215-949-6868
Fay Manicke, prin. Fax 949-6815
Manor ES 400/K-5
401 Penn Valley Rd 19054 215-949-6770
Richard Houseknecht, prin. Fax 949-6772
Penn Valley ES 300/K-5
180 NorthTurn Ln 19054 215-949-6800
Dr. Peggy Schiavone, prin. Fax 269-4827

Hope Lutheran S 100/PK-8
2600 Haines Rd 19055 215-946-3467
Doug Puls, prin. Fax 946-5926
Immaculate Conception S 200/K-8
3810 Bristol Oxford Valley 19057 215-949-2848
Sr. Mary Anne Winterberg, prin. Fax 946-2149
Queen of the Universe S 200/PK-8
2443 Trenton Rd 19056 215-945-1866
Joan Stulz, prin. Fax 945-0413
St. Michael the Archangel S 400/PK-8
130 Levittown Pkwy 19054 215-943-0222
Susan Gallagher, prin. Fax 943-9068

Lewisberry, York, Pop. 389
West Shore SD 8,200/K-12
507 Fishing Creek Rd 17339 717-938-9577
Jemry Small, supt. Fax 938-2779
www.wssd.k12.pa.us
Crossroads MS 600/6-8
535 Fishing Creek Rd 17339 717-932-1295
David Zuilkoski, prin.
Fishing Creek ES 400/K-5
510 Fishing Creek Rd 17339 717-938-6565
Kathleen Wagner, prin.
Mt. Zion ES, 850 Lewisberry Rd 17339 200/K-2
Julie Farrell, prin. 717-938-2621
Other Schools – See Camp Hill, Etters, Lemoyne, Mechanicsburg, New Cumberland

Lewisburg, Union, Pop. 5,562
Lewisburg Area SD 1,900/K-12
PO Box 351 17837 570-523-3220
Dr. Mark DiRocco, supt. Fax 522-3278
www.dragon.k12.pa.us
Eichhorn MS 400/6-8
2057 Washington Ave 17837 570-523-3220
Tracy Krum, prin. Fax 522-3331
Kelly ES 600/K-3
325 Hospital Dr 17837 570-523-3220
Dustin Dalton, prin. Fax 522-3296
Linntown ES 300/4-5
1951 Washington Ave 17837 570-523-3220
Paula Reber, prin. Fax 522-3330

Mifflinburg Area SD
Supt. — See Mifflinburg
Buffalo Cross Roads ES 100/K-3
954 Johnson Mill Rd 17837 570-996-8370
Leo Weidner, prin. Fax 996-8372

Lewistown, Mifflin, Pop. 8,649
Mifflin County SD 5,900/K-12
201 8th St 17044 717-248-0148
David Runk, supt. Fax 248-5345
www.mcsdk12.org
Buchanan ES 200/K-5
100 Franklin Ave 17044 717-248-0179
Dr. Linda Mohler, prin. Fax 248-8001
East Derry ES 300/K-5
2316 Back Maitland Rd 17044 717-543-5615
Dr. Linda Mohler, prin. Fax 543-6301
Highland Park Area ES 500/K-5
490 6th St 17044 717-248-0145
Dr. Joseph Maginnis, prin. Fax 248-0147
Lewiston ES 600/K-5
1 Manor Dr 17044 717-242-5823
Mark Hidlay, prin. Fax 242-5810
Lewistown MS 400/6-8
212 Green Ave 17044 717-242-5801
D. Robert Reeder, prin. Fax 242-5804
Other Schools – See Belleville, Mc Veytown, Milroy, Reedsville

Sacred Heart of Jesus S 100/K-5
110 N Dorcas St 17044 717-248-5351
Sr. Marie Luu, prin. Fax 248-1516

Liberty, Tioga, Pop. 2,810
Southern Tioga SD
Supt. — See Blossburg
Liberty ES 300/K-6
8622 Route 414 16930 570-324-2521
Albert Lindner, prin. Fax 324-2440

Ligonier, Westmoreland, Pop. 1,622
Ligonier Valley SD 2,100/K-12
339 W Main St 15658 724-238-5696
Christine Oldham Ed.D., supt. Fax 238-7877
lvsd.schoolwires.com/lvsd/site/
Ligonier Valley MS 400/5-8
536 Bell Street Ext 15658 724-238-6412
David Steimer, prin. Fax 238-2358
Mellon ES 400/K-4
559 Bell Street Ext 15658 724-238-5663
Diane Ravis, prin. Fax 238-6335
Other Schools – See New Florence

Holy Trinity S 100/K-8
327 W Vincent St 15658 724-238-6430
Barbara Sabo, prin. Fax 238-6688

Lilly, Cambria, Pop. 895
Penn Cambria SD
Supt. — See Cresson
Penn Cambria IS 100/3-4
376 Wood St 15938 814-886-8532
Cindy Pacifico, prin. Fax 886-5389
Penn Cambria PS 100/1-2
400 Main St 15938 814-886-2151
Cindy Pacifico, prin. Fax 886-5419

Limerick, Montgomery
Spring-Ford Area SD
Supt. — See Collegeville
Evans ES K-4
125 Sunset Rd 19468 610-705-6012
Jacqueline Havrilla, prin. Fax 705-6231

Linesville, Crawford, Pop. 1,122
Conneaut SD 2,700/K-12
219 W School Dr 16424 814-683-5900
Richard Rossi, supt. Fax 683-4127
conneautsd.org
Schafer ES 500/K-6
220 W School Dr 16424 814-683-5755
Susan Uzelac, prin. Fax 683-4972
Other Schools – See Conneaut Lake, Conneautville

Linwood, Delaware, Pop. 3,425
Chichester SD
Supt. — See Aston
Linwood ES 300/K-4
1403 Huddell Ave 19061 610-485-7351
Judith A. Edwards, prin. Fax 485-7366

Holy Saviour-St. John Fisher S 200/K-8
122 E Ridge Rd 19061 610-485-0363
Mary Rose Worrilow, prin. Fax 485-7809

Lititz, Lancaster, Pop. 9,008
Manheim Township SD 5,600/K-12
2933 Lititz Pike 17543 717-569-8231
Gene Freeman, supt. Fax 569-3729
www.mtwp.k12.pa.us
Reidenbaugh ES 500/K-5
1001 Buckwalter Rd 17543 717-626-1000
Mike Brominski, prin. Fax 627-3887
Other Schools – See Lancaster

Warwick SD 4,700/K-12
301 W Orange St 17543 717-626-3734
Dr. April Hershey, supt. Fax 626-3850
www.warwicksd.org/
Beck ES 600/K-6
418 E Lexington Rd 17543 717-626-3704
Lisa Himes, prin. Fax 627-6093
Bonfield ES 600/K-6
101 N Oak St 17543 717-626-3705
Dr. Peggy Montgomery, prin. Fax 626-3890
Kissel Hill ES 600/K-6
215 Landis Valley Rd 17543 717-626-3703
Melanie Calender, prin. Fax 627-6130
Lititz ES 600/K-6
20 S Cedar St 17543 717-626-3702
Dr. Joseph Elder, prin. Fax 627-6608
Warwick MS 700/7-8
401 Maple St 17543 717-626-3701
Larry Zeamer, prin. Fax 627-6089

Lititz Area Mennonite S 300/K-8
1050 E Newport Rd 17543 717-626-9551
Ken Fry, prin. Fax 626-0430
Lititz Christian S 300/PK-12
501 W Lincoln Ave 17543 717-626-9518
Rick Bernhardt, admin. Fax 626-5683
New Haven Mennonite S 100/1-12
225 Crest Rd 17543 717-626-1603

Littlestown, Adams, Pop. 4,131
Littlestown Area SD 2,300/K-12
162 Newark St 17340 717-359-4146
Dr. Donald Wills, supt. Fax 359-9617
www.lasd.k12.pa.us
Alloway Creek IS 300/4-5
162 Newark St 17340 717-359-4146
Timothy Mitzel, prin. Fax 359-9617
Maple Avenue MS 500/6-8
75 Maple Ave 17340 717-359-4146
Eric Naylor, prin. Fax 359-9617
Rolling Acres ES 600/K-3
150 E Myrtle St 17340 717-359-4146
Lawrence Ott, prin. Fax 359-8149

Littlestown Christian Academy 100/PK-12
2075 Fish and Game Rd 17340 717-359-8633
Ivan Cornwell, admin. Fax 359-0903

Liverpool, Juniata, Pop. 884
Juniata County SD
Supt. — See Mifflintown
Susquehanna Township ES 100/K-5
RR 1 Box 134 17045 717-444-3457
Debra Wagner, prin. Fax 694-3788

Llewellyn, Schuylkill
Minersville Area SD
Supt. — See Minersville
Llewellyn ECC 200/PK-K
Llewellyn Rd 17944 570-544-4453
Judith McGrory, prin. Fax 544-5998

Lock Haven, Clinton, Pop. 8,784
Keystone Central SD 4,500/K-12
110 E Bald Eagle St 17745 570-893-4900
Dr. John DiNunzio, supt. Fax 893-4923
www.kcsd.k12.pa.us
Dickey ES 300/K-5
102 S Fairview St 17745 570-748-2101
Nick Verrelli, prin. Fax 893-4949
Robb ES 400/K-5
400 E Church St 17745 570-748-3501
Robin Taranto, prin. Fax 893-4951
Woodward ES 300/K-5
35 King St 17745 570-748-4025
Robin Taranto, prin. Fax 893-4952
Other Schools – See Blanchard, Loganton, Mill Hall, Renovo

Lock Haven Catholic S 100/K-6
311 W Water St 17745 570-748-7252
Michele Alexander, prin. Fax 748-1939

Loganton, Clinton, Pop. 431
Keystone Central SD
Supt. — See Lock Haven
Sugar Valley Area S 100/K-5
98 E South St 17747 570-725-3521
Ralonda Pote, prin. Fax 748-7711

Loretto, Cambria, Pop. 1,166

St. Michael S 200/K-8
PO Box 67 15940 814-472-9117
Judith Noel, prin. Fax 472-9117

Lower Burrell, Westmoreland, Pop. 12,444
Burrell SD 2,100/K-12
1021 Puckety Church Rd 15068 724-334-1406
George Staudenmaier, supt. Fax 334-1429
www.burrell.k12.pa.us
Bon Air ES 500/K-5
3260 Leechburg Rd 15068 724-337-1463
Gregory Egnor, prin. Fax 334-1479
Huston MS 500/6-8
1020 Puckety Church Rd 15068 724-334-1443
Matt Conner, prin. Fax 334-1434
Stewart ES 400/K-5
2880 Leechburg Rd 15068 724-334-1483
Amy Lenart, prin. Fax 334-1490

Loysburg, Bedford
Northern Bedford County SD 1,200/PK-12
152 NBC Dr 16659 814-766-2221
Scott King, supt. Fax 766-3772
www.nbcsd.org/
Northern Bedford County ES 600/PK-5
217 NBC Dr 16659 814-766-2221
Carol Louden, prin. Fax 766-2232

Loysville, Perry

Heritage Christian S 50/K-8
2401 Fort Robinson Rd 17047 717-789-0008
Alicia Miller, admin. Fax 789-0008

Lucinda, Clarion

St. Joseph S 100/PK-6
PO Box 9 16235 814-226-8018
Sr. Monica Steiner, prin. Fax 223-9620

Lurgan, Franklin
Chambersburg Area SD
Supt. — See Chambersburg
Lurgan ES 200/K-5
8888 Roxbury Rd 17232 717-532-6125
E. Sue Kiley, prin. Fax 532-7533

Luthersburg, Clearfield
Du Bois Area SD
Supt. — See Du Bois
Luthersburg ES 200/K-5
2672 Helvetia Rd 15848 814-583-5544
Donald Mowrey, prin. Fax 583-7757

Lykens, Dauphin, Pop. 1,862
Upper Dauphin Area SD 1,300/K-12
5668 State Route 209 17048 717-362-8134
Elaine Eib Ed.D., supt. Fax 362-3050
www.udasd.org/
Upper Dauphin Area ES 500/K-4
5668 State Route 209 17048 717-362-4511
Evan Williams, prin. Fax 362-0988
Upper Dauphin Area MS 400/5-8
5668 State Route 209 17048 717-362-8177
Abbeu Walshaw-Wertz, prin. Fax 362-6567

Mc Adoo, Schuylkill, Pop. 2,320
Hazleton Area SD
Supt. — See Hazleton
McAdoo-Kelayres ES 500/K-6
15 Kelayres Rd, 570-929-2568
James Chapman, prin. Fax 929-1581

McAdoo Catholic S 100/K-8
35 N Cleveland St, 570-929-1442
Sr. Amy Summers, prin. Fax 929-3016

Mc Alisterville, Juniata
Juniata County SD
Supt. — See Mifflintown
Fayette Township ES 200/K-6
145 School St 17049 717-463-2236
Andy Kinzer, prin. Fax 463-2275

Juniata Mennonite S 200/K-12
PO Box 278 17049 717-463-2898
Andrew Meiser, prin. Fax 463-0134

Mc Clellandtown, Fayette
Albert Gallatin Area SD
Supt. — See Uniontown
Gallatin North MS 500/6-8
113 College Ave 15458 724-737-5423
James Patitucci, prin. Fax 737-5312
Plava ES 400/K-5
120 Puritan Rd 15458 724-737-5424
Jessica Marchezak, prin. Fax 737-5120

Mc Clure, Fayette
Midd-West SD
Supt. — See Middleburg
West Beaver ES 300/K-4
21 S Zeller St 17841 570-658-7341
David Harrison, prin. Fax 658-8022

Mifflin County Christian Academy 100/PK-12
5113 Back Maitland Rd 17841 717-543-2200
Craig Todd, admin. Fax 543-2207

Mc Connellsburg, Fulton, Pop. 1,079
Central Fulton SD 1,100/PK-12
151 E Cherry St 17233 717-485-3183
Dr. Julia Cigola, supt. Fax 485-5984
www.cfsd.info
Mc Connellsburg ES 500/PK-5
151 E Cherry St 17233 717-485-4438
Alicia Mellott, prin. Fax 485-9002
Mc Connellsburg MS 200/6-8
151 E Cherry St 17233 717-485-3195
Todd Beatty, prin. Fax 485-0175

Mc Donald, Washington, Pop. 2,246
Canon-McMillan SD
Supt. — See Canonsburg
Cecil IS 400/5-6
3676 Millers Run Rd 15057 724-745-2623
Scott Chambers, prin. Fax 873-5227

Fort Cherry SD 1,200/K-12
110 Fort Cherry Rd 15057 724-796-1551
Robert Dinnen Ph.D., supt. Fax 796-0065
www.fortcherry.org
Fort Cherry ES 600/K-6
110 Fort Cherry Rd 15057 724-796-1551
Jill Jacoby, prin. Fax 356-2770

South Fayette Township SD 2,100/K-12
3680 Old Oakdale Rd 15057 412-221-4542
Dr. Linda Hippert, supt. Fax 693-0490
www.southfayette.org
South Fayette Township ES 800/K-4
3620 Old Oakdale Rd 15057 412-221-4542
Denise Beverina-Moore, prin. Fax 693-2762
South Fayette Township MS 700/5-8
3700 Old Oakdale Rd 15057 412-221-4542
Karen Labutta, prin. Fax 693-0860

Mc Kean, Erie, Pop. 380
General McLane SD
Supt. — See Edinboro
Mc Kean ES 400/K-4
5120 West Rd 16426 814-273-1033
Michael Getz, prin. Fax 273-1048

Mc Keesport, Allegheny, Pop. 23,343
Elizabeth Forward SD
Supt. — See Elizabeth
Greenock ES 100/K-2
1101 Greenock Buena Vista 15135 412-896-2324
Jennifer Meliton, prin. Fax 751-3818
Mt. Vernon ES 100/3-5
2400 Greenock Buena Vista 15135 412-896-2327
Jennifer Meliton, prin. Fax 751-1345

McKeesport Area SD 4,300/K-12
3590 Oneil Blvd 15132 412-664-3610
Dr. Shirley Golofski, supt. Fax 664-3638
www.mckasd.com
Centennial ES 400/K-3
1601 Beaver St 15132 412-664-3750
Pam Gordon, prin. Fax 664-3756
Cornell IS 600/4-6
1600 Cornell St 15132 412-664-3720
Tamara Sanders, prin. Fax 664-3736
Founders Hall MS 700/7-8
3600 Oneil Blvd 15132 412-664-3690
Harry Bauman, prin. Fax 664-3768
Washington ES 500/K-3
1818 Sumac St 15132 412-664-3770
Stacey Fitzpatrick, prin. Fax 664-3777
Other Schools – See White Oak

South Allegheny SD 1,400/K-12
2743 Washington Blvd 15133 412-675-3070
Elaine Brown, supt. Fax 672-2836
www.southallegheny.org
South Allegheny ECC 200/K-1
1 Glendale St 15133 412-675-3070
Alisa King, prin. Fax 673-3991
South Allegheny ES 600/2-6
1707 Washington Blvd 15133 412-675-3070
Alisa King, prin. Fax 672-8541
South Allegheny MS 7-8
2743 Washington Blvd 15133 412-675-3070
Jeff Solomon, prin. Fax 673-4905

St. Joseph Regional S 200/PK-8
1125 Romine Ave 15133 412-678-0659
Frank Napoli, prin. Fax 678-1301

Mc Kees Rocks, Allegheny, Pop. 7,235
Montour SD 2,700/K-12
223 Clever Rd 15136 412-490-6500
Patrick Dworakowski, supt. Fax 490-0828
www.montourschools.com
Burkett ES 300/K-4
5501 Steubenville Pike 15136 412-787-0408
Dr. Joseph Findley, prin. Fax 787-2558
Other Schools – See Coraopolis, Pittsburgh

Sto-Rox SD 1,500/K-12
600 Russellwood Ave 15136 412-778-8871
Fran Serenka, supt. Fax 771-5205
www.srsd.k12.pa.us
Sto-Rox ES 600/K-4
300 Ewing Rd 15136 412-771-8091
Dr. Maureen Ungarean, prin. Fax 771-8641
Sto-Rox MS 300/5-8
298 Ewing Rd 15136 412-771-3213
Dr. Janell Logue-Belden, prin. Fax 771-3848

Holy Trinity S 300/PK-8
5720 Steubenville Pike 15136 412-787-2656
Kimberly Stevenson, prin. Fax 787-9487
Robinson Township Christian S 100/PK-12
77 Phillips Ln 15136 412-787-5919
Brett Wirebaugh, hdmstr. Fax 787-1558
St. John of God S 200/PK-8
3 Desiderio Way 15136 412-331-8501
Sr. Annamarie Gaglia, prin. Fax 331-8500

Mc Murray, Washington, Pop. 4,082
Peters Township SD 4,300/K-12
631 E McMurray Rd 15317 724-941-6251
Dr. Nina Zetty, supt. Fax 941-6565
www.ptsd.k12.pa.us
Mc Murray ES 1,000/4-6
626 E McMurray Rd 15317 724-941-5020
Dr. Robert Freado, prin. Fax 941-2769
Peters Township MS 600/7-8
625 E McMurray Rd 15317 724-941-2688
Dr. Anthony Merante, prin. Fax 941-1426
Pleasant Valley ES 500/K-3
250 E McMurray Rd 15317 724-941-6260
Mary Yavelak, prin. Fax 941-0708
Other Schools – See Venetia

Mc Sherrystown, Adams, Pop. 3,702

Annunciation BVM S 300/K-8
316 North St 17344 717-637-3135
Sr. Ann Wierman, prin. Fax 637-1715
St. Joseph Academy 50/PK-PK
90 Main St 17344 717-630-9990
Sr. Anne Leonard, prin. Fax 637-2441

Macungie, Lehigh, Pop. 3,111
East Penn SD
Supt. — See Emmaus
Eyer MS, 5616 Buckeye Rd 18062 800/6-8
Dr. Douglas Wells, prin. 610-965-1600
Lower Macungie ES K-K
6043 Lower Macungie Rd 18062 610-395-2341
Tara Desiderio, prin. Fax 391-0574
Lower Macungie MS 1,100/6-8
6299 Lower Macungie Rd 18062 610-395-8593
Suzanne Vincent, prin. Fax 398-4385
Macungie ES 500/1-5
4062 Brookside Rd 18062 610-965-1617
James Best, prin. Fax 966-7583
Shoemaker ES 700/1-5
4068 N Fairview St 18062 610-965-1626
Lynn Brinckman, prin. Fax 965-2977

Hillside S 100/K-6
2697 Brookside Rd 18062 610-967-3701
Dr. Sue Straeter, hdmstr. Fax 965-7683
Salem Christian S 200/PK-12
8031 Salem Bible Church Rd 18062 610-966-5823
Warren Skuret, admin. Fax 965-8368

Mc Veytown, Mifflin, Pop. 389
Mifflin County SD
Supt. — See Lewistown
Strodes Mills ES 400/K-5
185 Chestnut Ridge Rd 17051 717-248-5072
E. Terry Styers, prin. Fax 244-5839
Strodes Mills MS 200/6-8
205 Chestnut Ridge Rd 17051 717-248-5488
E. Terry Styers, prin. Fax 242-5839

Mahaffey, Clearfield, Pop. 384
Purchase Line SD
Supt. — See Commodore
Purchase Line North ES 200/K-6
5995 Fire Tower Rd 15757 814-277-6602
Carol Ayers, prin. Fax 277-8833

Mahanoy City, Schuylkill, Pop. 4,462
Mahanoy Area SD 1,100/K-12
1 Golden Bear Dr 17948 570-773-3443
Anthony Crimaldi, supt. Fax 773-2913
www.mabears.net
Mahanoy Area ES 400/K-4
1 Golden Bear Dr 17948 570-773-3443
Judy Filanowski, prin. Fax 773-1821
Mahanoy Area MS 300/5-8
1 Golden Bear Dr 17948 570-773-3443
Joie Green, prin. Fax 773-4034

Academy of the BVM 100/K-8
29 S Catawissa St 17948 570-773-2668
Karen Rogers, prin. Fax 773-2015

Malvern, Chester, Pop. 3,100
Great Valley SD 3,600/K-12
47 Church Rd 19355 610-889-2100
Melody Wilt, supt. Fax 889-2120
www.gvsd.org
Charlestown ES 300/K-5
2060 Charlestown Rd 19355 610-935-1555
Christopher Pickell, prin. Fax 935-4963
Great Valley MS 900/6-8
255 Phoenixville Pike 19355 610-644-6440
Edward Souders, prin. Fax 889-1166
Markley ES 500/K-5
354 Swedesford Rd 19355 610-644-1790
Juliette Pennyman, prin. Fax 407-0720
Sugartown ES K-5
611 Sugartown Rd 19355 610-699-1500
Karen Schneck, prin. Fax 699-1512
Wayne ES 500/K-5
20 Devon Rd 19355 610-647-6651
Bonnie Citron, prin. Fax 889-2118

Christ Memorial Lutheran S 100/PK-K
89 Line Rd 19355 610-296-0650
Jodie Merow, dir. Fax 644-4677
St. Patrick S 400/K-8
115 Channing Ave 19355 610-644-5797
Dr. JoAnne McAdams, prin. Fax 647-0535

Manchester, York, Pop. 2,436
Northeastern York SD 3,300/K-12
41 Harding St 17345 717-266-3667
Robert Tabachini, supt. Fax 266-5792
www.nesd.k12.pa.us
Orendorf ES 400/K-3
101 S Hartman St 17345 717-266-5621
Todd Monos, prin. Fax 266-2058
Shallow Brook IS 4-6
213 S Hartman St 17345 717-266-7030
Thomas Shaffer, prin. Fax 266-7042
Spring Forge IS 500/4-6
100 S Hartman St 17345 717-266-9833
Devin Moyer, prin. Fax 266-1693
Other Schools – See Mount Wolf, York, York Haven

Manheim, Lancaster, Pop. 4,659
Manheim Central SD 2,700/K-12
71 N Hazel St 17545 717-665-3422
Carol Saylor, supt. Fax 665-7631
www.manheimcentral.org
Burgard ES 500/K-6
111 S Penn St 17545 717-665-2209
James Hale, prin. Fax 665-4600
Doe Run ES 400/K-6
281 Doe Run Rd 17545 717-665-9766
George Way, prin. Fax 665-6105
Manheim Central MS 500/7-8
261 White Oak Rd 17545 717-665-2246
Dr. Clifton VanArtsdalen, prin. Fax 665-9108
Stiegel ES 300/K-6
3 S Hazel St 17545 717-665-6836
Dr. Jacy Hess, prin. Fax 665-7736

Manheim Christian S 200/PK-8
686 Lebanon Rd 17545 717-665-4300
Ray Kratz, prin. Fax 664-4253

Mansfield, Tioga, Pop. 3,354
Southern Tioga SD
Supt. — See Blossburg
Miller ES 500/K-6
1 Dorsett Dr 16933 570-662-2192
Doris Sargent, prin. Fax 662-3180

New Covenant Academy 100/PK-12
310 Extension St 16933 570-662-2996
Terry Mickey, hdmstr. Fax 662-0272

Maple Glen, Montgomery, Pop. 5,881
Upper Dublin SD 4,400/K-12
1580 Fort Washington Ave 19002 215-643-8800
Michael Pladus Ed.D., supt. Fax 643-8803
www.udsd.org
Maple Glen ES 400/K-5
1581 Fort Washington Ave 19002 215-643-3421
Thomas Sigafoos, prin. Fax 540-0988
Other Schools – See Dresher, Fort Washington, Willow Grove

St. Alphonsus S 400/K-8
29 Conwell Dr 19002 215-646-0150
Sr. Ruth Hennessy, prin. Fax 646-7150

Mapleton Depot, Huntingdon, Pop. 498
Mt. Union Area SD
Supt. — See Mount Union
Mapleton-Union ES 100/K-6
13606 Smith Valley Rd 17052 814-542-4401
David Hummel, prin. Fax 542-8633

Marcus Hook, Delaware, Pop. 2,266
Chichester SD
Supt. — See Aston
Marcus Hook ES 300/K-4
8th & Market Sts 19061 610-485-9780
Michael A. Rocco, prin. Fax 485-7210

Marienville, Forest
Forest Area SD
Supt. — See Tionesta
East Forest ES 100/K-6
120 W Birch St 16239 814-927-6688
William Jordan, prin. Fax 927-8452

Marietta, Lancaster, Pop. 2,603
Donegal SD
Supt. — See Mount Joy
Donegal Kindergarten Center K-K
420 Coffee Goss Rd 17547 717-426-1680
Sharon Hagenberger, prin. Fax 426-4893
Donegal MS 700/6-8
1175 River Rd 17547 717-426-4915
Judy Haugh, prin. Fax 426-2417
Riverview ES 200/1-5
1179 River Rd 17547 717-426-1561
Dana Blair, prin. Fax 426-3105

Susquehanna Waldorf S 200/PK-8
15 W Walnut St 17547 717-426-4506
Maria Wherley, contact Fax 426-3326

Marion, Franklin
Chambersburg Area SD
Supt. — See Chambersburg
Marion ES, PO Box 248 17235 100/K-5
Frederick Nickey, prin. 717-375-2360

Marion Center, Indiana, Pop. 428
Marion Center Area SD 1,900/PK-12
PO Box 156 15759 724-397-5551
Chris DeVivo, supt. Fax 397-9144
www.mcasd.net/
Marion Center Area ES 600/PK-4
2535 Route 119 Hwy N 15759 724-463-1989
Donna Bruder-Smith, prin. Fax 463-8002
Marion Center Area MS 500/5-8
PO Box 199 15759 724-397-5551
Matt Jioio, prin. Fax 397-9093
Other Schools – See Creekside, Home, Rochester Mills

Markleton, Somerset
Rockwood Area SD
Supt. — See Rockwood
Kingwood ES 100/K-6
5957 Kingwood Rd 15551 814-926-2597
Samuel Romesberg, prin. Fax 926-2631

Markleysburg, Fayette, Pop. 273
Uniontown Area SD
Supt. — See Uniontown
Marclay ES, 111 Bruceton Rd 15459 100/K-5
Edward Fearer, prin. 724-329-4248
McMullen MS 200/6-8
4773 National Pike 15459 724-329-8811
Edward Fearer, prin.

Mars, Butler, Pop. 1,707
Mars Area SD 2,300/K-12
545 Route 228 16046 724-625-1518
Dr. William Pettigrew, supt. Fax 625-1060
www.marsk12.org
Mars Area Centennial S 5-6
100 Winfield Manor Dr 16046 724-625-2601
Todd Lape, prin. Fax 625-2660
Mars Area ES 400/2-4
549 Route 228 16046 724-625-3161
Robert Zaccari, prin. Fax 625-3499
Mars Area MS 500/7-8
1775 Three Degree Rd 16046 724-625-3145
Richard Cornell, prin. Fax 625-4470
Mars Area Primary Center 500/K-1
547 Route 228 16046 724-625-1588
Dr. Elizabeth McMahon, prin. Fax 625-2280

Martinsburg, Blair, Pop. 2,157
Spring Cove SD
Supt. — See Roaring Spring
Martinsburg ES 300/K-5
415 E Spring St 16662 814-793-2014
Jeanne Hileman, prin. Fax 793-9447

Masontown, Fayette, Pop. 3,469
Albert Gallatin Area SD
Supt. — See Uniontown

Masontown ES 200/K-5
201 W Spring Ave 15461 724-583-1091
Tim Krupa, prin. Fax 583-1893

All Saints S 100/PK-6
100 S Washington St 15461 724-583-2141
Bernard Kubitza, prin. Fax 583-0232

Mayfield, Lackawanna, Pop. 1,713
Lakeland SD
Supt. — See Jermyn
Mayfield ES 300/K-6
501 Linden St 18433 570-876-2950
Kevin Sullivan, prin. Fax 876-3410

Maytown, Lancaster, Pop. 1,720
Donegal SD
Supt. — See Mount Joy
Maytown ES 200/1-5
PO Box 37 17550 717-426-3416
Sharon Hagenberger, prin. Fax 426-1639

Meadowbrook, Montgomery

Meadowbrook S 200/PK-6
1641 Hampton Rd 19046 215-884-3238
David Stephens, prin. Fax 884-9143

Meadville, Crawford, Pop. 13,368
Crawford Central SD 4,100/K-12
11280 Mercer Pike 16335 814-724-3960
Michael Dolecki, supt. Fax 333-8731
www.craw.org
East End ES 300/K-6
640 Walnut St 16335 814-724-6585
Kurt Meader, prin. Fax 337-7090
First District ES 300/K-6
725 N Main St 16335 814-724-1124
Delta Zahniser, prin. Fax 337-5990
Meadville Area MS 500/7-8
974 North St 16335 814-333-1188
Rebecca James, prin. Fax 333-2799
Neason Hill ES 300/K-6
11293 Williamson Rd 16335 814-724-7886
Stephanie Beauchat, prin. Fax 337-2329
Second District ES 200/K-6
1216 S Main St 16335 814-724-7073
Tamara Clark, prin. Fax 337-5835
West End ES 500/K-6
12068 Brooks Rd 16335 814-724-1450
John Karns, prin. Fax 337-5886
Other Schools – See Cochranton

Calvary Baptist Christian Academy 200/PK-12
543 Randolph St 16335 814-724-6606
Durwood Abbey, prin. Fax 337-4357
Seton S 200/PK-8
385 Pine St 16335 814-336-2320
Regina Merritt, prin. Fax 336-2328

Mechanicsburg, Cumberland, Pop. 8,818
Cumberland Valley SD 7,700/K-12
6746 Carlisle Pike 17050 717-697-8261
William Harner, supt. Fax 506-3302
www.cvschools.org
Eagle View MS 1,000/6-8
6746 Carlisle Pike 17050 717-766-0217
John Gallagher, prin. Fax 506-3806
Good Hope MS 800/6-8
451 Skyport Rd 17050 717-761-1865
Gary Quigley, prin. Fax 761-5910
Green Ridge ES 500/K-5
1 Green Ridge Rd 17050 717-766-4911
Chad Runkle, prin. Fax 796-2482
Hampden ES 600/K-5
441 Skyport Rd 17050 717-737-4513
Patricia Hillery, prin. Fax 761-6780
Silver Spring ES 500/K-5
6746 Carlisle Pike 17050 717-766-3332
Michelle Virtue, prin. Fax 506-3711
Sporting Hill ES 500/K-5
210 S Sporting Hill Rd 17050 717-761-5052
Stephanie Bowen, prin. Fax 761-6311
Other Schools – See Boiling Springs, Carlisle, Enola

Mechanicsburg Area SD 3,500/K-12
100 E Elmwood Ave 17055 717-691-4500
Joseph Hood, supt. Fax 691-3438
www.mbgsd.org
Broad Street ES 200/1-5
200 S Broad St 17055 717-691-4574
Krista Archibald, prin. Fax 697-7392
Elmwood ES 400/1-5
100 E Elmwood Ave 17055 717-691-4578
John McIntosh, prin. Fax 691-3655
Kindergarten Academy K-K
505 S Filbert St 17055 717-506-0852
Kathleen Healey, prin. Fax 506-0853
Mechanicsburg Area MS 900/6-8
1750 S Market St 17055 717-691-4560
Leonard Ference, prin. Fax 791-7977
Northside ES 200/1-5
411 N Walnut St 17055 717-691-4581
Laurie Benner, prin. Fax 697-8674
Shepherdstown ES 200/1-2
1849 S York St 17055 717-691-4589
Carole Capriotti, prin. Fax 691-2474
Upper Allen ES 300/3-5
1790 S Market St 17055 717-691-4594
Judith Ingram, prin. Fax 697-9107

West Shore SD
Supt. — See Lewisberry
Rossmoyne ES 200/3-5
1225 Rossmoyne Rd 17055 717-697-8578
Deborah Rundall, prin.

Emmanuel Baptist Christian Academy 100/PK-12
4681 E Trindle Rd 17050 717-761-7000
F. Ross Ritchey, prin. Fax 761-3207
Faith Tabernacle S 200/1-12
1410 Good Hope Rd 17050 717-975-0641
St. Joseph S 400/K-8
420 E Simpson St 17055 717-766-2564
Sr. Michael Ann Orlik, prin. Fax 766-1226

Media, Delaware, Pop. 5,451
Rose Tree Media SD 3,900/K-12
308 N Olive St 19063 610-627-6000
Dr. Denise Kerr, supt. Fax 891-0959
www.rtmsd.org
Glenwood ES 400/K-5
122 S Pennell Rd 19063 610-627-6900
William Dougherty, prin. Fax 892-7193
Indian Lane ES 400/K-5
309 S Old Middletown Rd 19063 610-627-7100
William Bennett, prin. Fax 566-6582
Media ES 400/K-5
120 E Front St 19063 610-627-6800
Maria Kotch, prin. Fax 566-3745
Rose Tree ES 300/K-5
1101 First Ave 19063 610-627-7200
Karen Daugherty, prin. Fax 566-5087
Springton Lake MS 900/6-8
1900 N Providence Rd 19063 610-627-6500
Joyce Jeuell, prin. Fax 566-8665

Benchmark S 200/1-8
2107 N Providence Rd 19063 610-565-3741
Robert Gaskins, hdmstr. Fax 565-3872
Media-Providence Friends S 200/PK-8
125 W Third St 19063 610-565-1960
Lynn Oberfield, prin. Fax 565-9866
Nativity BVM S 200/PK-8
30 E Franklin St 19063 610-566-6881
Mary Anne Johnston, prin. Fax 566-3910
St. Mary Magdalene S 400/K-8
2430 N Providence Rd 19063 610-565-1822
Patricia Miniszak, prin. Fax 627-9670
Walden S 200/PK-8
901 N Providence Rd 19063 610-892-8000
Cynthia Wein, prin. Fax 892-8060

Mehoopany, Wyoming
Tunkhannock Area SD
Supt. — See Tunkhannock
Mehoopany ES 200/K-4
400 Scottsville Rd 18629 570-833-5181
Patrick Mulhern, prin. Fax 833-2850

Melcroft, Fayette
Connellsville Area SD
Supt. — See Connellsville
Pritts ES 300/K-6
1542 Indian Creek Valley Rd 15462 724-455-3500
Robin Martin, prin. Fax 455-3560

Melrose Park, Montgomery, Pop. 6,500

Perelman Jewish Day S 200/K-5
7601 Old York Rd 19027 215-635-3130
Chagit Nusbaum, prin. Fax 635-3136
Saligman MS 200/6-8
7613 Old York Rd 19027 215-635-3303
Susan Friedman, prin. Fax 635-3325

Mercer, Mercer, Pop. 2,297
Mercer Area SD 1,400/K-12
545 W Butler St 16137 724-662-5100
Dr. William Gathers, supt. Fax 662-5109
www.mercer.k12.pa.us
Mercer Area ES 700/K-6
301 Lamor Rd 16137 724-662-5102
Claudia Sigmund, prin. Fax 662-5103
Mercer Area MS 200/7-8
545 W Butler St 16137 724-662-5105
Timothy Dadich, prin. Fax 662-2993

Mercersburg, Franklin, Pop. 1,549
Tuscarora SD 2,700/K-12
118 E Seminary St 17236 717-328-3127
Dr. Rebecca Erb, supt. Fax 328-9316
www.tus.k12.pa.us/
Buchanan MS 600/6-8
5191 Fort Loudon Rd 17236 717-328-5221
Charles Rahauser, prin. Fax 328-9081
Mercersburg ES 300/K-5
30 S Park Ave 17236 717-328-5278
Michelle Bennett, prin. Fax 328-5628
Montgomery ES 300/K-5
9138 Fort Loudon Rd 17236 717-328-2023
Brett Kagarise, prin. Fax 328-9723
Mountain View ES 300/K-5
2311 Lemar Rd 17236 717-328-2191
Brett Kegarise, prin. Fax 328-9591
Other Schools – See Saint Thomas

Merion Station, Montgomery, Pop. 700
Lower Merion SD
Supt. — See Ardmore
Merion ES, 549 S Bowman Ave 19066 500/K-5
Anne Heffron, prin. 610-645-1470

Waldron Mercy Academy 400/PK-8
513 Montgomery Ave 19066 610-664-9847
Sr. Patricia Smith, prin. Fax 664-6364

Mertztown, Berks
Brandywine Heights Area SD
Supt. — See Topton
Longswamp ES 100/K-2
1160 State St 19539 610-682-5151
Andrew Potteiger, prin. Fax 682-5153

Gateway Christian S 100/PK-12
245 Fredericksville Rd 19539 610-682-2748
Arthur Dexter, prin. Fax 682-9670

Meyersdale, Somerset, Pop. 2,340
Meyersdale Area SD 1,000/K-12
309 Industrial Park Rd 15552 814-634-5123
Tracey Karlie, supt. Fax 634-0832
www.masd.net
Meyersdale Area ES 400/K-5
1345 Shaw Mines Rd 15552 814-634-8313
Jackie Baer, prin.
Meyersdale Area MS 200/6-8
1353 Shaw Mines Rd 15552 814-634-1437
Julie Stahl, lead tchr.

Middleburg, Snyder, Pop. 1,356
Midd-West SD 2,400/K-12
568 E Main St 17842 570-837-0046
Wesley Knapp, supt. Fax 837-3018
www.mwsd.cc
Middleburg ES 600/K-5
600 Wagenseller St 17842 570-837-5524
Gregg Wetzel, prin. Fax 837-0579
Middleburg MS 400/6-8
10 Dock Hill Rd 17842 570-837-0551
Donna Samuelson, prin. Fax 837-5061
Other Schools – See Beaver Springs, Mc Clure, Mount Pleasant Mills

Middletown, Dauphin, Pop. 8,944
Lower Dauphin SD
Supt. — See Hummelstown
Londonderry ES 400/K-5
260 Schoolhouse Rd 17057 717-944-9462
J. Michael Lausch, prin. Fax 944-9529

Middletown Area SD 2,400/K-12
55 W Water St Ste 2 17057 717-948-3300
Richard Weinstein Ed.D., supt. Fax 948-3329
www.raiderweb.org
Fink ES 200/K-5
150 N Race St 17057 717-948-3370
Chelton Hunter, prin. Fax 948-3409
Kunkel ES 400/K-5
2401 Fulling Mill Rd 17057 717-939-6862
Thomas Shaffer, prin. Fax 939-3487
Middletown Area MS 600/6-8
215 Oberlin Rd 17057 717-948-3390
Kevin Cook, prin. Fax 948-3392
Reid ES 500/K-5
201 Oberlin Rd 17057 717-948-3360
Earl Bright, prin. Fax 702-1219

Middletown Christian S 50/PK-K
1325 Vine St 17057 717-944-0173
Ron Murphy, pres.
Seven Sorrows of BVM S 300/PK-8
280 N Race St 17057 717-944-5371
Loretta Miller, prin. Fax 944-5419

Midland, Beaver, Pop. 2,969
Midland Borough SD 300/PK-8
173 7th St 15059 724-643-8650
Sean Tanner, supt. Fax 643-4887
www.midlandpa.org
Midland S 300/PK-8
173 7th St 15059 724-643-5094
Nick Trombetta, prin. Fax 643-4887

Western Beaver County SD 900/K-12
343 Ridgemont Dr 15059 724-643-9310
Robert Postupac, supt. Fax 643-8048
www.westernbeaver.org/
Fairview ES 300/K-4
343 Ridgemont Dr 15059 724-643-9680
Gabriel Engel, prin. Fax 643-8048
Other Schools – See Industry

Mifflin, Juniata, Pop. 620
Juniata County SD
Supt. — See Mifflintown
Mountain View ES 200/K-5
23215 Route 35 S 17058 717-436-6816
Valerie Ricedorf, prin. Fax 436-0011

Mifflinburg, Union, Pop. 3,578
Mifflinburg Area SD 2,000/K-12
PO Box 285 17844 570-966-8200
Barry Tomasetti, supt. Fax 966-8210
www.mifflinburg.org
Mifflinburg Area IS 600/4-5
250 Mabel St 17844 570-966-8270
Scott Zimmerman, prin. Fax 966-8273
Mifflinburg Area MS 6-8
100 Mabel St 17844 570-966-8290
Marion Lynn, prin. Fax 966-8304
Mifflinburg ES 400/K-3
115 Shipton St 17844 570-966-8320
Leo Weidner, prin. Fax 966-8339
Other Schools – See Lewisburg, Millmont, New Berlin

Mifflintown, Juniata, Pop. 846
Juniata County SD 3,100/K-12
75 S 7th St 17059 717-436-2111
Dr. Kenneth Albaugh, supt. Fax 436-2777
Fermanagh-Mifflintown ES 200/K-5
75 S 7th St 17059 717-436-2111
Mark Sanders, prin. Fax 436-2777
Tuscarora MS 500/6-8
3873 William Penn Hwy 17059 717-436-2165
Ralph Baker, prin. Fax 436-5999
Walker Township ES 100/K-5
7864 William Penn Hwy 17059 717-436-6469
Mark Sanders, prin. Fax 436-2275
Other Schools – See Honey Grove, Liverpool, Mc Alisterville, Mifflin, Port Royal, Richfield, Thompsontown

Mildred, Sullivan
Sullivan County SD
Supt. — See Dushore
Turnpike Area ES 100/K-6
PO Box 265 18632 570-928-8341
Mary McClintock, prin. Fax 928-7337

Milford, Pike, Pop. 1,214
Delaware Valley SD 4,700/K-12
236 Route 6 and 209 18337 570-296-1800
Dr. Candis Finan, supt. Fax 296-3172
www.dvsd.org
Delaware Valley ES 600/K-6
244 Route 6 and 209 18337 570-296-1820
Kim Buitaitis, prin. Fax 296-3163
Delaware Valley MS 400/7-8
258 Route 6 and 209 18337 570-296-1830
Peter Ioppolo, prin. Fax 296-3162
Other Schools – See Dingmans Ferry, Shohola

St. Vincent de Paul Preschool 50/PK-PK
101 Saint Vincent Dr 18337 570-686-1867
Denise Spinnetta, dir. Fax 565-1762

Mill Creek, Huntingdon, Pop. 335
Huntingdon Area SD
Supt. — See Huntingdon
Brady-Henderson Mill Creek ES 100/K-5
11893 Technology Dr 17060 814-643-3038
Jeffrey Coppes, prin. Fax 643-6920

Millersburg, Dauphin, Pop. 2,491
Millersburg Area SD 900/K-12
799 Center St 17061 717-692-2108
Sheree-Lee Knorr, supt. Fax 692-2895
www.mlbgsd.k12.pa.us/
Lenkerville ES, 520 S Market St 17061 400/K-5
John Welker, prin. 717-692-3072
Millersburg Area MS 200/6-8
799 Center St 17061 717-692-2108
Jeffrey Prouse, prin.

Northern Dauphin Christian S 50/K-8
1072 State Route 25 17061 717-692-1940
Fax 692-1940

Millerstown, Perry, Pop. 682
Greenwood SD 900/K-12
405 E Sunbury St 17062 717-589-3117
Ed Burns, supt. Fax 589-3013
www.greenwoodsd.org
Greenwood ES 400/K-6
405 E Sunbury St 17062 717-589-3115
Inez McClure, prin. Fax 589-3013
Greenwood MS 100/7-8
405 E Sunbury St 17062 717-589-3116
Nicholas Guarente, prin. Fax 589-7096

Millersville, Lancaster, Pop. 7,583
Penn Manor SD
Supt. — See Lancaster
Eshleman ES 300/K-6
545 Leaman Ave 17551 717-872-9540
Anne Carroll, prin. Fax 872-9508

Millerton, Tioga
Troy Area SD
Supt. — See Troy
Wells Township ES 100/K-4
RR 2 Box 74 16936 570-537-2959
Susan Shipman, prin. Fax 537-6333

Mill Hall, Clinton, Pop. 1,490
Keystone Central SD
Supt. — See Lock Haven
Central Mountain MS 1,000/6-8
200 Ben Ave 17751 570-726-3141
Norman Palovcsik, prin. Fax 726-7227
Lamar Township ES 100/K-5
34 E End Mountain Rd 17751 570-726-3478
Steve Kreger, prin. Fax 726-7843
Mill Hall ES 300/K-5
210 Kyler Ave 17751 570-726-3105
Ralonda Pote, prin. Fax 726-7014

Millmont, Union
Mifflinburg Area SD
Supt. — See Mifflinburg
Laurelton ES 100/K-3
105 Weikert Rd 17845 570-966-8360
Leo Weidner, prin. Fax 966-8362

Mill Village, Erie, Pop. 393
Fort LeBoeuf SD
Supt. — See Waterford
Mill Village ES 100/K-5
PO Box 56L 16427 814-796-2060
Sean Wolfrom, prin. Fax 796-4850

Millville, Columbia, Pop. 957
Millville Area SD 700/K-12
PO Box 260 17846 570-458-5538
Kathleen Stark Ed.D., supt. Fax 458-5584
www.millville.k12.pa.us
Millville Area ES 400/K-6
PO Box 300 17846 570-458-5538
John Fetterman, prin. Fax 458-4715

Greenwood Friends S 100/PK-8
PO Box 438 17846 570-458-5532
Brenda Boggess, hdmstr. Fax 458-5533

Milmont Park, Delaware

Our Lady of Peace S 100/PK-8
200 Milmont Ave 19033 610-534-0689
Sr. Denise Clifford, prin. Fax 534-4856

Milroy, Mifflin, Pop. 1,456
Mifflin County SD
Supt. — See Lewistown
Armagh Township ES 200/K-5
PO Box 308 17063 717-667-2153
Michael LaMarca, prin. Fax 667-2126

Milton, Northumberland, Pop. 6,484
Milton Area SD 2,400/K-12
700 Mahoning St 17847 570-742-7614
Dr. William Clark, supt. Fax 742-4523
www.milton.k12.pa.us
Baugher ES 500/K-5
60 Brenda Rovenolt Dr 17847 570-742-7631
Dave Slater, prin. Fax 742-6025
Milton Area MS 500/6-8
700 Mahoning St 17847 570-742-7685
V. David Brown, prin. Fax 742-4857
Other Schools – See Montandon, New Columbia

Meadowbrook Christian S 300/PK-12
363 Stamm Rd 17847 570-742-2638
Rodney Baughman, admin. Fax 742-4710

Minersville, Schuylkill, Pop. 4,337
Minersville Area SD 1,200/PK-12
PO Box 787 17954 570-544-4764
M. Joseph Brady, supt. Fax 544-6162
www.battlinminers.com
Minersville Area ES 500/1-6
PO Box 787 17954 570-544-2077
Judith McGrory, prin. Fax 544-1404
Other Schools – See Llewellyn

Good Shepherd Regional S 100/K-8
301 Heffner St 17954 570-544-3766
Kimberly Fetter, prin. Fax 544-4870
St. Nicholas S 100/K-8
515 N Front St 17954 570-544-2800
Thomas Dando, prin. Fax 544-6471

Mohnton, Berks, Pop. 3,071
Governor Mifflin SD
Supt. — See Shillington
Brecknock ES 500/K-3
1332 Alleghenyville Rd 19540 610-775-5079
Dr. Maryellen Kueny, prin. Fax 685-3798

Mohrsville, Berks

King's Academy 200/K-12
1562 Main St 19541 610-926-9639
Daniel Tubbs, admin. Fax 926-8089

Monaca, Beaver, Pop. 5,973
Central Valley SD 2,300/K-12
160 Baker Rd Ext 15061 724-775-5600
Dr. Daniel Matsook, supt. Fax 775-4302
www.centralvalleysd.org/District
Center MS 500/6-8
160 Baker Rd Ext 15061 724-775-8200
Michael McCullough, prin. Fax 775-4302
Todd Lane ES 400/3-5
113 Todd Ln 15061 724-775-1050
Debbie DeDominicis, prin. Fax 775-2799
Other Schools – See Aliquippa

St. John the Baptist S 200/PK-8
1501 Virginia Ave 15061 724-775-5774
Stefanie Coley, prin. Fax 775-2997

Monessen, Westmoreland, Pop. 8,307
Monessen CSD 1,000/K-12
1275 Rostraver St 15062 724-684-3600
Dr. Cynthia Chelen, supt. Fax 684-6782
www.monessen.k12.pa.us/index.html
Monessen Elementary Center 400/K-5
1275 Rostraver St 15062 724-684-4456
Bethanne Natali, prin. Fax 684-6782
Monessen MS 200/6-8
1245 State Rd 15062 724-684-6282
Sherry Castaneda, prin. Fax 684-7931

Monongahela, Washington, Pop. 4,562
Elizabeth Forward SD
Supt. — See Elizabeth
Penn ES 300/K-5
392 William Penn Rd 15063 412-896-2330
Brad Simala, prin. Fax 384-4311

Ringgold SD
Supt. — See New Eagle
Monongahela ES 600/K-5
1200 Chess St 15063 724-258-2911
Dr. Michael Tominello, prin. Fax 258-2295

Monroeville, Allegheny, Pop. 28,591
Gateway SD 4,300/K-12
9000 Gateway Campus Blvd 15146 412-372-5300
Dr. Cleveland Steward, supt. Fax 373-5731
www.gatewayk12.org
Evergreen ES 300/K-4
3831 Evergreen Dr 15146 412-373-5842
Dr. Karen Shiner, prin. Fax 373-5845
Gateway MS 700/7-8
4450 Old William Penn Hwy 15146 412-373-5780
Aaron Johnson, prin. Fax 373-5794
Moss Side ES 300/K-4
5000 Gateway Campus Blvd 15146 412-373-5874
Fax 858-0457
Moss Side MS 600/5-6
9000 Gateway Campus Blvd 15146 412-373-5830
Linda Echard, prin. Fax 373-5885
Ramsey ES 300/K-4
2200 Ramsey Rd 15146 412-373-5856
Michael Fisher, prin. Fax 373-1058
University Park ES 300/K-4
320 Noel Dr 15146 724-327-4113
Carolyn Hankinson, prin. Fax 733-9436
Other Schools – See Pitcairn

Greater Works Christian S 100/PK-12
301 College Park Dr 15146 724-327-6500
Fax 325-4602
North American Martyrs S 100/PK-8
2526 Haymaker Rd 15146 412-373-0889
James Churilla, prin. Fax 380-1306

St. Bernadette S 300/PK-8
245 Azalea Dr 15146 412-372-7255
Sr. Carol Arch, prin. Fax 372-7649

Montandon, Northumberland
Milton Area SD
Supt. — See Milton
Montandon ES 200/K-5
PO Box 130 17850 570-523-3218
Brian Parise, prin. Fax 524-9665

Montgomery, Lycoming, Pop. 1,619
Montgomery Area SD 1,000/K-12
120 Penn St 17752 570-547-1608
Daphne Ross, supt. Fax 547-6271
www.montasd.org
Montgomery ES 300/K-5
120 Penn St 17752 570-547-1608
Karen Snyder, prin. Fax 547-6055
Montgomery MS 200/6-8
120 Penn St 17752 570-547-1608
Michael Prowant, prin. Fax 547-6755
Other Schools – See Allenwood

Montoursville, Lycoming, Pop. 4,628
Loyalsock Township SD 1,400/K-12
1720 Sycamore Rd 17754 570-326-6508
Dr. Richard Mextorf, supt. Fax 326-0770
www.ltsd.k12.pa.us
Schick ES 600/K-5
2800 Four Mile Dr 17754 570-326-3554
Scott Mato, prin. Fax 326-1498
Other Schools – See Williamsport

Montoursville Area SD 2,100/K-12
50 N Arch St 17754 570-368-2491
Dominic Cavallaro, supt. Fax 368-3501
www.montoursville.k12.pa.us/
Loyalsock Valley ES 300/K-4
3790 State Route 87 17754 570-435-0446
Mare Haas, prin. Fax 435-3214
Lyter ES 400/K-4
900 Spruce St 17754 570-368-2614
Craig Kurtz, prin. Fax 368-3535
McCall MS 600/5-8
600 Willow St 17754 570-368-2441
Jeffrey Moore, prin. Fax 368-3521

Montrose, Susquehanna, Pop. 1,596
Montrose Area SD 1,900/K-12
80 High School Rd 18801 570-278-6221
Michael Ognosky, supt. Fax 278-2426
www.masd.info/
Lathrop Street ES 500/K-6
14 Lathrop St 18801 570-278-0310
Gregory Adams, prin. Fax 278-4799
Other Schools – See Friendsville

Moon Township, Allegheny, Pop. 10,187
Moon Area SD 3,800/K-12
8353 University Blvd 15108 412-264-9440
Donna Milanovich, supt. Fax 264-3268
www.moonarea.net
Allard ES 200/K-5
170 Shafer Rd 15108 412-262-2500
James McElroy, prin. Fax 262-2581
Bon Meade ES 600/K-5
1595 Brodhead Rd 15108 724-457-7471
Joseph Garrity, prin. Fax 457-0919
Brooks ES 600/K-5
1720 Hassam Rd 15108 412-264-6540
Lynnette Conti Dinello, prin. Fax 264-4743
Hyde ES 200/K-5
110 Wallridge Dr 15108 412-262-2700
Joseph Johnson, prin. Fax 262-4617
McCormick ES K-5
2801 Beaver Grade Rd 15108 412-893-0421
Julie Moore, prin. Fax 893-0428
Moon Area MS 900/6-8
8353 University Blvd 15108 412-262-4140
Melissa Heasley, prin. Fax 264-3013

Rhema Christian S 200/PK-8
1301 Coraopolis Heights Rd 15108 412-269-9555
Dante Malamisuro, prin. Fax 269-1914

Moosic, Lackawanna, Pop. 5,738
Riverside SD
Supt. — See Taylor
Riverside ES East 400/K-6
900 School St 18507 570-562-2121
Joseph Fialko, prin. Fax 341-8298

Morgantown, Lancaster

Conestoga Christian S 300/K-12
2760 Main St 19543 610-286-0353
Susan Yoder, admin. Fax 286-0350

Morrisdale, Clearfield
West Branch Area SD 1,300/K-12
516 Allport Cutoff 16858 814-345-5615
Fax 345-5220
www.westbranch.org
West Branch Area ES 700/K-6
356 Allport Cutoff 16858 814-345-5627
William Hayward, prin. Fax 345-5220

Morrisville, Bucks, Pop. 9,810
Morrisville Borough SD 900/PK-12
550 W Palmer St 19067 215-736-2681
Elizabeth Hammond Yonson Ed.D., supt. Fax 736-2413
mv.org
Grandview ES 200/3-5
80 Grandview Ave 19067 215-736-5280
Kate Taylor, prin. Fax 736-5281
Reiter ES 200/PK-2
Harper and Hillcrest 19067 215-736-5270
Fax 736-5274

Pennsbury SD
Supt. — See Fallsington
Roosevelt ES 500/K-5
185 Walton Dr 19067 215-428-4256
Robert Wurst, prin. Fax 428-4263

Holy Trinity S 200/K-8
210 Stockham Ave 19067 215-295-6900
Barbara Nuzzolo, prin. Fax 337-9079
St. John the Evangelist S 200/K-8
728 Big Oak Rd 19067 215-295-0629
Sr. Joan Irene, prin. Fax 295-6258

Morton, Delaware, Pop. 2,665
Ridley SD
Supt. — See Folsom
Amosland ES 500/K-5
549 Amosland Rd 19070 610-534-1900
Dr. Bernadette Zeleznick, prin. Fax 237-8000

Our Lady of Perpetual Help S 300/K-8
2130 Franklin Ave 19070 610-543-8350
Sr. Deborah Krist, prin. Fax 544-3203

Moscow, Lackawanna, Pop. 1,916
North Pocono SD 2,600/K-12
701 Church St 18444 570-842-7659
Kurt Eisele, supt. Fax 842-0886
www.npsd.org/
Moscow ES 300/K-3
851 Church St 18444 570-842-8464
Robert Barrett, prin. Fax 842-8905
North Pocono IS 100/4-5
701 Church St 18444 570-842-7676
Daniel Powell, prin. Fax 842-4027
North Pocono MS 800/6-8
701 Church St 18444 570-842-4588
Edward Bugno, prin. Fax 842-1783
Other Schools – See Lake Ariel

St. Catherine Preschool 100/PK-PK
PO Box 250 18444 570-848-1258
Kathy Pierre, dir.

Mountain Top, Luzerne
Crestwood SD 3,100/K-12
281 S Mountain Blvd 18707 570-474-6782
Dave McLaughlin-Smith, supt. Fax 474-2254
www.csdcomets.org/
Crestwood MS 500/7-8
281 S Mountain Blvd 18707 570-474-6782
Brian Baddick, prin. Fax 474-2254
Fairview ES 700/K-6
117 Spruce St 18707 570-474-5942
Ronald Grevera, prin. Fax 403-0496
Rice ES 800/K-6
3700 Church Rd 18707 570-868-3161
Kevin Seyer, prin. Fax 868-3147

St. Jude S 300/K-8
422 S Mountain Blvd 18707 570-474-5803
Mary Ann Olszewski, prin. Fax 403-6159
Wyoming Valley Adventist S 50/1-8
476 3rd St 18707 570-868-5958

Mount Carmel, Northumberland, Pop. 6,053
Mt. Carmel Area SD 1,700/PK-12
600 W 5th St 17851 570-339-1500
Cheryl Latorre, supt. Fax 339-0487
www.mca.k12.pa.us
Mt. Carmel Area ES 900/PK-6
630 W 5th St 17851 570-339-1500
Mary Ann Krakowski, prin. Fax 339-0487

Mount Holly Springs, Cumberland, Pop. 1,911
Carlisle Area SD
Supt. — See Carlisle
Mt. Holly Springs ES 200/K-5
110 Mooreland Ave 17065 717-240-6800
Ruth-Ann Snyder, prin. Fax 486-3089

South Middleton SD
Supt. — See Boiling Springs
Rice ES 600/K-3
805 Holly Pike 17065 717-258-6484
David Boley, prin. Fax 486-3654

Mount Joy, Lancaster, Pop. 6,944
Donegal SD 2,600/K-12
1051 Koser Rd 17552 717-653-1447
Shelly Riedel Ed.D., supt. Fax 492-1350
www.donegal.k12.pa.us
Donegal Springs ES 600/1-5
1055 Koser Rd 17552 717-653-8812
Deborah Ault, prin. Fax 492-1341
Other Schools – See Marietta, Maytown

Hempfield SD
Supt. — See Landisville
Farmdale ES 500/K-6
695 Prospect Rd 17552 717-684-2206
Rachel Martin, prin. Fax 618-1007

Janus S 100/K-12
205 Lefever Rd 17552 717-653-0025
Deborah Kost, hdmstr. Fax 653-0696
Lancaster Mennonite S - Kraybill Campus 400/PK-8
598 Kraybill Church Rd 17552 717-653-5236
John Weber, prin. Fax 653-7334

Mount Lebanon, Allegheny, Pop. 32,900

Mount Lebanon Montessori S 200/PK-6
550 Sleepy Hollow Rd 15228 412-563-2858
Adrienne Benestelli, prin. Fax 563-5053

Mount Morris, Greene
Central Greene SD
Supt. — See Waynesburg

Perry ES 100/K-5
PO Box 100 15349 724-324-2687
Scott Headlee, prin. Fax 324-9285

Mount Penn, Berks, Pop. 2,994
Antietam SD
Supt. — See Reading
Mount Penn ES 400/2-6
2310 Cumberland Ave 19606 610-779-3547
Kerry Hoffman, prin. Fax 779-6937

Mount Pleasant, Westmoreland, Pop. 4,531
Mt. Pleasant Area SD 1,900/K-12
271 State St 15666 724-547-4100
Terry Struble, supt. Fax 547-0629
www.mpasd.net
Norvelt ES 400/K-6
163 Lilac Ln 15666 724-547-4100
Scott Bryer, prin. Fax 423-2733
Ramsay ES 300/2-6
300 Eagle St 15666 724-547-4100
Lance Benteler, prin. Fax 547-0564
Rumbaugh ES 200/K-1
2414 School St 15666 724-547-4100
Lance Benteler, prin. Fax 547-1860
Other Schools – See Jones Mills

Verna Montessori S 100/PK-8
268 Prittstown Rd 15666 724-887-8810
Fax 887-2977

Mount Pleasant Mills, Snyder
Midd-West SD
Supt. — See Middleburg
Perry-West Perry ES 100/K-5
10594 Route 35 17853 570-539-2620
Gregg Wetzel, prin. Fax 539-2099

Mount Union, Huntingdon, Pop. 2,392
Mt. Union Area SD 1,500/K-12
28 W Market St 17066 814-542-8631
James Estep, supt. Fax 542-8633
www.muasd.org/
Mount Union-Kistler ES 300/K-6
154 School St 17066 814-542-2595
Tonya DeVecchis-Kerr, prin. Fax 542-8633
Shirley Township ES 300/K-6
14188 2nd St 17066 814-542-9381
Frank Miller, prin. Fax 542-8633
Other Schools – See Mapleton Depot

Mountville, Lancaster, Pop. 2,746
Hempfield SD
Supt. — See Landisville
Mountville ES 500/K-6
200 College Ave 17554 717-285-5501
Christopher Jahnke, prin. Fax 618-1006

Mount Wolf, York, Pop. 1,345
Northeastern York SD
Supt. — See Manchester
Mt. Wolf ES 300/K-3
PO Box 1013 17347 717-266-6570
Randi Payne, prin. Fax 266-6516
Northeastern MS 600/7-8
4855 Board Rd 17347 717-266-3676
Michael Alessandroni, prin. Fax 266-9735

Muncy, Lycoming, Pop. 2,533
Muncy SD 1,100/K-12
46 S Main St Ste 1 17756 570-546-3125
Dr. Portia Brandt, supt. Fax 546-6676
www.muncysd.org
Myers ES 600/K-6
125 New St 17756 570-546-3129
William Ramsey, prin. Fax 546-7744

Munhall, Allegheny, Pop. 11,513
Steel Valley SD 1,900/K-12
220 E Oliver Rd 15120 412-464-3600
Dr. William Kinavey, supt. Fax 464-3626
www.svsd.k12.pa.us
Franklin Primary Center 100/K-K
220 E Oliver Rd 15120 412-464-3600
Sharon Fisher, prin. Fax 464-3626
Park ES 400/1-5
4100 Main St 15120 412-464-3600
Dr. Beth Tully, prin. Fax 464-3661
Steel Valley MS 500/6-8
3114 Main St 15120 412-464-3600
Kevin Walsh, prin. Fax 464-3642
Other Schools – See Homestead

St. Therese S 300/PK-8
3 Saint Therese Ct 15120 412-462-8163
Sr. Eileen Johnston, prin. Fax 462-5865

Murrysville, Westmoreland, Pop. 19,098
Franklin Regional SD 3,800/K-12
3210 School Rd 15668 724-327-5456
Dr. P. Emery D'Arcangelo, supt. Fax 327-6149
www.franklinregional.k12.pa.us
Franklin Regional MS 900/6-8
4660 Old William Penn Hwy 15668 724-327-5456
Christopher Kelly, prin. Fax 733-0949
Heritage ES 600/K-5
3240 School Rd 15668 724-327-5456
Samuel King, prin. Fax 327-8298
Newlonsburg ES 200/K-5
3170 School Rd 15668 724-327-5456
Tina Gillen, prin. Fax 327-4903
Sloan ES 700/K-5
4121 Sardis Rd 15668 724-327-5456
Judith Morrison, prin. Fax 733-5487

Mother of Sorrows S 300/PK-8
3264 Evergreen Dr 15668 724-733-8840
Joseph Rice, prin. Fax 325-1144

Muse, Washington
Canon-McMillan SD
Supt. — See Canonsburg
Muse ES 200/K-4
PO Box 430 15350 724-745-9014
Robert Kleinhans, prin. Fax 873-5233

Myerstown, Lebanon, Pop. 3,106
Eastern Lebanon County SD 2,500/K-12
180 Elco Dr 17067 717-866-7117
Dr. Richard Nilsen, supt. Fax 866-7084
www.elcosd.org/
Eastern Lebanon County MS 600/6-8
60 Evergreen Dr 17067 717-866-6591
Keith DuBois, prin. Fax 866-5837
Jackson ES 300/K-5
558 W Main Ave 17067 717-866-2624
Laurie Bowersox, prin. Fax 866-9690
Myerstown ES 300/K-5
101 S Railroad St 17067 717-866-4521
Laurie Bowersox, prin. Fax 866-6791
Other Schools – See Richland, Schaefferstown

Lebanon Valley Christian S 100/1-12
7821 Lancaster Ave 17067 717-933-5171
Myerstown Mennonite S 200/1-12
739 E Lincoln Ave 17067 717-866-5667

Nanticoke, Luzerne, Pop. 10,382
Greater Nanticoke Area SD 2,200/K-12
427 Kosciuszko St 18634 570-735-1270
Anthony Perrone, supt. Fax 735-1350
www.gnasd.com
GNA Elementary Center 500/3-5
601 Kosciuszko St 18634 570-735-1320
Dr. Mariellen Scott, prin. Fax 733-1006
Greater Nanticoke Area Ed Center 400/6-7
600 E Union St 18634 570-735-2770
Joseph Long, prin. Fax 740-2792
Kennedy S 200/2-2
513 Kosciuszko St 18634 570-735-6450
Dr. Mariellen Scott, prin. Fax 740-2757
Smith ES 300/K-1
25 Robert St 18634 570-735-3740
Joseph Long, prin. Fax 740-2704

Nanty Glo, Cambria, Pop. 3,024
Blacklick Valley SD 700/K-12
555 Birch St 15943 814-749-9211
Donald Thomas, supt. Fax 749-8627
www.bvsd.k12.pa.us
Blacklick Valley ES 300/K-6
1000 W Railroad St 15943 814-749-9211
Luke Lansberry, prin. Fax 749-8710

Narberth, Montgomery, Pop. 4,154
Lower Merion SD
Supt. — See Ardmore
Penn Valley ES 400/K-5
301 Righters Mill Rd 19072 610-645-1460
Alice Reyes, prin.
Welsh Valley MS, 325 Tower Ln 19072 800/6-8
Dr. Deitra Spence, prin. 610-658-3920

St. Margaret S 200/PK-8
227 N Narberth Ave 19072 610-664-2640
Sr. Corinne Ritchie, prin. Fax 664-4677

Natrona Heights, Allegheny, Pop. 11,400
Highlands SD 2,800/PK-12
PO Box 288 15065 724-226-2400
Dr. Louis Baldassare, supt. Fax 226-8437
www.goldenrams.com
Fawn ES 300/K-5
5591 Ridge Rd 15065 724-224-4844
Kathleen Shirey, prin. Fax 224-9243
Highlands MS 700/6-8
1350 Broadview Blvd 15065 724-226-0600
Catherine Russo, prin. Fax 226-3287
Natrona Heights ES 300/K-5
1415 Freeport Rd 15065 724-224-0774
Gene Nicastro, prin. Fax 224-1217
Other Schools – See Brackenridge, Tarentum

Our Lady of the Most Blessed Sacrament S 200/PK-8
800 Montana Ave 15065 724-226-2345
William Heasley, prin. Fax 226-4934

Nazareth, Northampton, Pop. 6,023
Nazareth Area SD 3,700/K-12
1 Education Plz 18064 610-759-1170
Dr. Victor Lesky, supt. Fax 759-9637
www.nazarethasd.k12.pa.us
Bushkill ES 400/K-3
960 Bushkill Center Rd 18064 610-759-1118
Gregory Shoemaker, prin. Fax 759-0454
Lower Nazareth ES 500/K-3
4422 Newburg Rd 18064 610-759-7311
Michael Santos, prin. Fax 759-7922
Nazareth Area IS 4-6
355 Tatamy Rd 18064 484-292-1111
Joseph Yanek, prin.
Nazareth Area MS 800/7-8
94 Freidensthal Ave 18064 610-759-3350
Robert Kern, prin. Fax 759-3725
Shafer ES 400/K-3
49 S Liberty St 18064 610-759-5228
William Mudlock, prin. Fax 759-2253

Pen Argyl Area SD
Supt. — See Pen Argyl
Plainfield ES 500/K-3
539 School Rd 18064 610-746-4436
Philip Giaquinto, prin. Fax 759-4227

Holy Family S 300/K-8
17 N Convent Ave 18064 610-759-5642
Colette Fisher, prin. Fax 759-0386

Needmore, Fulton

Fulton County Community Christian S 100/PK-12
PO Box 235 17238 717-573-4400
Russell Cheek, prin. Fax 573-2731

Nescopeck, Luzerne, Pop. 1,452
Berwick Area SD
Supt. — See Berwick
Nescopeck ES 300/K-5
315 Dewey St 18635 570-759-6400
Robert Croop, prin. Fax 759-4380

Nesquehoning, Carbon, Pop. 3,356
Panther Valley SD
Supt. — See Lansford
Panther Valley ES 800/K-5
1 N Mermon Ave 18240 570-669-9411
William Lombardo, prin. Fax 669-6043

New Albany, Bradford, Pop. 295
Wyalusing Area SD
Supt. — See Wyalusing
New Albany ES 100/K-6
RR 1 Box 2A 18833 570-363-2165
Joseph Darrow, prin. Fax 363-2102

New Alexandria, Westmoreland, Pop. 581
Greensburg Salem SD
Supt. — See Greensburg
Metzgar ES 400/K-5
140 Cc Hall Dr 15670 724-668-2237
Justine Federico, prin. Fax 668-8297

New Berlin, Union, Pop. 830
Mifflinburg Area SD
Supt. — See Mifflinburg
New Berlin ES 100/K-3
535 Liberty St 17855 570-966-8380
Leo Weidner, prin. Fax 966-8382

New Bethlehem, Clarion, Pop. 1,007
Redbank Valley SD 1,300/K-12
920 Broad St 16242 814-275-2426
John Cornish Ed.D., supt. Fax 275-2428
www.redbankvalley.net/
Mahoning Township ES 200/K-6
330 Pheasant Farm Rd 16242 814-275-1550
Jason Huffman, prin. Fax 275-1665
New Bethlehem-South Bethlehem ES 300/K-6
600 Vine St 16242 814-275-2680
Jason Huffman, prin. Fax 275-4110
Other Schools – See Hawthorn

New Bloomfield, Perry, Pop. 1,084
West Perry SD
Supt. — See Elliottsburg
New Bloomfield ES 400/K-5
300 W High St 17068 717-582-4318
Dianne Conaway, prin. Fax 582-7579

New Brighton, Beaver, Pop. 6,275
New Brighton Area SD 1,800/K-12
3225 43rd St 15066 724-843-1795
David Pietro Ed.D., supt. Fax 843-6144
www.nbsd.k12.pa.us
New Brighton Area ES 800/K-5
3200 43rd St Ste 1 15066 724-843-1194
Jason Hall, prin. Fax 843-8769
New Brighton Area MS 400/6-8
901 Penn Ave 15066 724-846-8100
Joe Guarino, prin. Fax 846-2337

New Britain, Bucks, Pop. 2,313
Central Bucks SD
Supt. — See Doylestown
Pine Run ES 600/K-6
383 W Butler Ave 18901 267-893-4450
Amanda Mumford Ed.D., prin. Fax 345-8827

New Castle, Lawrence, Pop. 25,030
Laurel SD 1,400/K-12
2497 Harlansburg Rd 16101 724-658-8940
Dr. Sandra L. Hennon, supt. Fax 658-2992
www.laurel.k12.pa.us
Laurel ES 700/K-6
223 McCaslin Rd 16101 724-658-2673
Dennis Devorick, prin. Fax 658-1167

Neshannock Township SD 1,400/K-12
3834 Mitchell Rd 16105 724-658-4793
Dr. Mary Todora, supt. Fax 658-1828
www.neshannock.k12.pa.us
Neshannock Memorial ES 700/K-6
3832 Mitchell Rd 16105 724-652-8709
Matthew Heasley, prin. Fax 657-9721

New Castle Area SD 3,600/PK-12
420 Fern St 16101 724-656-4756
George Gabriel, supt. Fax 656-4767
www.ncasd.com
Croton Pre K Center 100/PK-PK
420 Fern St 16101 724-656-4815
Terence Meehan, prin. Fax 656-4783
Kennedy PS 300/1-3
326 Laurel Blvd 16101 724-656-4738
Carmen Nocera, prin. Fax 658-8082
Lockley K 300/K-K
900 E Main St 16101 724-656-4735
Debra DeBlasio, prin. Fax 658-8037
Stevens PS 300/1-3
831 Harrison St 16101 724-656-4750
Debra DeBlasio, prin. Fax 658-8724
Washington IS 800/4-6
101 E Euclid Ave 16105 724-656-4729
Mark Elisco, prin. Fax 658-7219
West Side PS 200/1-3
708 W Washington St 16101 724-656-4753
Carmen Nocera, prin. Fax 658-9137

Shenango Area SD 1,400/K-12
2501 Old Pittsburgh Rd 16101 724-658-7287
Dr. Daniel Bell, supt. Fax 658-5370
Shenango ES 700/K-6
2501 Old Pittsburgh Rd 16101 724-658-5566
Marilyn Sanfilippo, prin. Fax 658-7871

Union Area SD 600/K-12
500 S Scotland Ln 16101 724-658-4775
Dr. Alfonso Angelucci, supt. Fax 658-5151
www.union.k12.pa.us/
Union Memorial ES 300/K-4
500 S Scotland Ln 16101 724-652-6683
Linda O'Neill, prin. Fax 658-5151

New Castle Christian Academy 100/PK-8
1701 Albert St 16105 724-658-5858
Marcia Votaw, admin. Fax 658-5861
St. Vitus S 100/PK-8
915 S Jefferson St 16101 724-654-9297
James Dailey, prin. Fax 654-9364

New Columbia, Union
Milton Area SD
Supt. — See Milton
White Deer ES 300/K-5
631 New Columbia Rd 17856 570-568-6201
Brian Parise, prin. Fax 568-0566

New Cumberland, Cumberland, Pop. 7,127
West Shore SD
Supt. — See Lewisberry
Fairview ES, 480 Lewisberry Rd 17070 200/3-5
Julie Farrell, prin. 717-774-2970
Hillside ES, 516 7th St 17070 400/K-5
Amy Rehmeyer, prin. 717-774-1321
New Cumberland MS 400/6-8
331 8th St 17070 717-774-0162
Karen Hertzler, prin.

St. Theresa S 500/PK-8
1200 Bridge St 17070 717-774-7464
Michael Tracy, prin. Fax 774-3154

New Derry, Westmoreland
Derry Area SD
Supt. — See Derry
New Derry ES 100/K-1
314 Pittsburgh St 15671 724-694-5771
Marty Rovedatti-Jackson, prin. Fax 694-0668

New Eagle, Washington, Pop. 2,276
Ringgold SD 3,000/K-12
400 Main St 15067 724-258-9329
Gary Hamilton, supt. Fax 258-5363
www.ringgold.org
Other Schools – See Donora, Finleyville, Monongahela

New Florence, Westmoreland, Pop. 749
Ligonier Valley SD
Supt. — See Ligonier
Laurel Valley ES 400/K-6
137 Education Ln 15944 724-238-5476
Victoria Hazlett, prin. Fax 235-9413

Newfoundland, Wayne
Wallenpaupack Area SD
Supt. — See Hawley
Wallenpaupack South ES 500/K-6
989 Main St 18445 570-676-3335
Dr. Nancy Simon, prin. Fax 676-3389

New Freedom, York, Pop. 3,889

St. John the Baptist Preschool 100/PK-PK
315 N Constitution Ave 17349 717-235-3525
Kathy Rohr, prin. Fax 235-8595
Shrewsbury Christian Academy 200/PK-8
701 Windy Hill Rd 17349 717-235-5763
Ronald Hill, hdmstr. Fax 235-5357

New Freeport, Greene
West Greene SD
Supt. — See Waynesburg
Springhill-Freeport ES 100/K-5
1055 Deep Valley Rd 15352 724-447-2331
Donald Painter, prin. Fax 447-2313

New Holland, Lancaster, Pop. 5,140
Eastern Lancaster County SD 3,300/K-12
PO Box 609 17557 717-354-1500
Dr. Robert Hollister, supt. Fax 354-1512
www.elanco.org/
Garden Spot MS 600/7-8
PO Box 609 17557 717-354-1560
Dr. Susan Sneath, prin. Fax 354-1129
New Holland ES 600/K-6
126 Eastern School Rd 17557 717-354-1520
Dr. Brenda Leiby, prin. Fax 354-1541
Other Schools – See Denver, East Earl

Friendship Baptist Academy 50/K-10
753 Meetinghouse Rd 17557 717-355-2615
Don Hagen, prin.

New Hope, Bucks, Pop. 2,276
New Hope-Solebury SD 1,100/K-12
180 W Bridge St 18938 215-862-2552
Raymond Boccuti, supt. Fax 744-6012
www.nhsd.org/
New Hope-Solebury MS 400/6-8
184 W Bridge St 18938 215-862-0608
Joyce Mundy, prin. Fax 862-2862
New Hope-Solebury Upper ES 300/3-5
186 W Bridge St 18938 215-862-8026
Amy Mangano, prin. Fax 862-8027
Other Schools – See Solebury

St. Martin of Tours S 200/PK-7
1 Riverstone Cir 18938 215-862-2075
Anne Florian, prin. Fax 862-6471

New Kensington, Westmoreland, Pop. 14,085
New Kensington-Arnold SD 2,300/PK-12
701 Stevenson Blvd 15068 724-335-8581
George Batterson Ed.D., supt. Fax 337-6519
nkasd.com
Ft. Crawford ES 200/K-3
255 3rd St 15068 724-337-8851
Patricia Johnson, prin. Fax 337-5550
Greenwald Memorial ES 200/K-3
110 Elmtree Rd 15068 724-335-6271
Lynn Buczynski, prin. Fax 335-1450
Martin ES 300/PK-3
1800 7th St 15068 724-335-3167
Donna Holtzman, prin. Fax 334-7850
Other Schools – See Arnold

Mary Queen of Apostles S 100/PK-8
1129 Leishman Ave 15068 724-339-4411
Catherine Collett, prin. Fax 337-6457

New Milford, Susquehanna, Pop. 845
Blue Ridge SD 1,200/PK-12
5058 School Rd 18834 570-465-3141
Chris Dyer, supt. Fax 465-3148
www.brsd.org
Blue Ridge ES 500/PK-5
5058 School Rd 18834 570-465-3141
Matthew Button, prin. Fax 465-3148
Blue Ridge MS 300/6-8
5058 School Rd 18834 570-465-3177
Matthew Nebzydoski, prin. Fax 465-3148

Faith Mountain Christian Academy 50/K-7
PO Box 567 18834 570-465-2220
Lois Frantz, prin. Fax 465-2220

New Oxford, Adams, Pop. 1,773
Conewago Valley SD 3,900/K-12
130 Berlin Rd 17350 717-624-2157
Dr. Daniel Trimmer, supt. Fax 624-5020
www.conewago.k12.pa.us
Conewago Valley IS 900/4-6
175 700 Rd 17350 717-624-2157
Kenneth Armacost, prin. Fax 624-6667
New Oxford ES 600/K-3
116 N Berlin Ave 17350 717-624-2157
Misti Wildasin, prin. Fax 624-6570
New Oxford MS 600/7-8
130 Berlin Rd 17350 717-624-2157
Gretchen Gates, prin. Fax 624-6560
Other Schools – See Hanover

Immaculate Conception BVM S 200/PK-8
101 N Peter St 17350 717-624-2061
Dianne Giampietro, prin. Fax 624-9711

New Paris, Bedford, Pop. 205
Chestnut Ridge SD
Supt. — See Fishertown
Chestnut Ridge Central ES 400/K-4
2534 Quaker Valley Rd 15554 814-839-4195
Kenneth Grace, prin. Fax 839-4418
New Paris Center ES 300/K-4
4401 Cortland Rd 15554 814-839-4195
Kenneth Grace, prin. Fax 839-4441

Newport, Perry, Pop. 1,467
Newport SD 900/K-12
PO Box 9 17074 717-567-3806
Dr. Kerry Helm, supt. Fax 567-6468
www.newportsd.org
Newport ES 500/K-5
PO Box 9 17074 717-567-3806
Michael Smith, prin. Fax 567-9485
Newport MS 6-8
PO Box 9 17074 717-567-3806
Joseph Stroup, prin. Fax 567-7402

Greater Perry Comm Christian Academy 50/K-12
55 W Shortcut Rd 17074 717-567-9990
Linda Daniel, admin. Fax 597-0441

New Providence, Lancaster
Solanco SD
Supt. — See Quarryville
Providence ES 400/K-5
137 Truce Rd 17560 717-786-3582
Shirley Hunter, prin. Fax 786-1532

New Ringgold, Schuylkill, Pop. 283
Tamaqua Area SD
Supt. — See Tamaqua
West Penn Township ES 300/K-5
185 School Dr 17960 570-386-5051
Steven Behr, prin. Fax 386-3226

Newry, Blair, Pop. 237

St. Patrick's Parish S 100/PK-8
PO Box 400 16665 814-695-3819
Joan Keller, prin. Fax 695-5274

New Salem, Fayette, Pop. 640
Brownsville Area SD
Supt. — See Brownsville
Cardale ES 300/1-6
192 Filbert Orient Rd 15468 724-246-8828
Frank Berdar, prin. Fax 246-1975

New Stanton, Westmoreland, Pop. 2,055
Hempfield Area SD
Supt. — See Greensburg
Stanwood ES 600/K-5
255 Arona Rd 15672 724-838-4000
Raymond Burk, prin. Fax 838-4001

Newtown, Bucks, Pop. 2,256
Council Rock SD 12,600/K-12
30 N Chancellor St 18940 215-944-1000
Mark Klein, supt. Fax 944-1031
www.crsd.org

Feinstone ES 800/K-6
1090 Eagle Rd 18940 215-944-2400
John Harlan, prin. Fax 944-2497
Goodnoe ES 700/K-6
298 Frost Ln 18940 215-944-2100
Nicole Crawford, prin. Fax 944-2197
Newtown ES 800/K-6
1 Wrights Rd 18940 215-944-2200
Kevin King, prin. Fax 944-2297
Newtown MS 900/7-8
116 Richboro Newtown Rd 18940 215-944-2600
Richard Hollahan, prin. Fax 944-2698
Other Schools – See Churchville, Holland, Richboro, Wrightstown

Newtown Friends S 300/PK-8
1450 Newtown Langhorne Rd 18940 215-968-2225
Steven Nierenberg, hdmstr. Fax 968-9346
St. Andrew S 900/PK-8
51 Wrights Rd 18940 215-968-2685
Nancy Matteo, prin. Fax 968-4795

Newtown Square, Delaware, Pop. 11,300
Marple Newtown SD 3,500/K-12
40 Media Line Rd Ste 209 19073 610-359-4200
Merle Horowitz, supt. Fax 723-3340
www.mnsd.net
Culbertson ES 400/K-5
3530 Goshen Rd 19073 610-359-4340
James Orwig, prin. Fax 353-4183
Other Schools – See Broomall

Delaware County Christian ES 300/PK-5
2 Bishop Hollow Rd 19073 610-353-6931
Stephen Dill, supt. Fax 353-5577
Episcopal Academy 1,100/PK-12
1785 Bishop White Dr 19073 484-424-1400
Hamilton Clark, hdmstr. Fax 424-1600
St. Anastasia S 600/PK-8
3309 W Chester Pike 19073 610-356-6225
Brad Kohlhepp, prin. Fax 356-5748

New Tripoli, Lehigh
Northwestern Lehigh SD 2,400/K-12
6493 Route 309 18066 610-298-8661
Suzanne Meixsell Ph.D., supt. Fax 298-8002
www.nwlehighsd.org
Northwestern Lehigh ES 400/K-4
6493 Route 309 18066 610-298-8661
Jill Berlet, prin. Fax 298-8002
Northwestern Lehigh MS 700/5-8
6636 Northwest Rd 18066 610-298-8661
Laurie Hoppes, prin. Fax 298-8178
Other Schools – See Kutztown

Newville, Cumberland, Pop. 1,323
Big Spring SD 2,900/K-12
45 Mount Rock Rd 17241 717-776-2000
Richard Fry, supt. Fax 776-4428
www.bigspring.k12.pa.us
Big Spring MS 800/6-8
47 Mount Rock Rd 17241 717-776-2000
Linda Wilson, prin. Fax 776-2468
Mt. Rock ES K-5
47 Mount Rock Rd 17241 717-776-2000
Linda Slusser, prin.
Newville ES 400/K-5
100 Steelstown Rd 17241 717-776-2035
William August, prin. Fax 776-2038
Oak Flat ES 500/K-5
334 Centerville Rd 17241 717-776-2045
Steven Smith, prin. Fax 776-2495
Other Schools – See Carlisle

New Wilmington, Lawrence, Pop. 2,480
Wilmington Area SD 1,500/K-12
300 Wood St 16142 724-656-8866
C. Joyce Nicksick, supt. Fax 946-8982
www.wilmington.k12.pa.us/
New Wilmington ES 300/K-4
450 Wood St 16142 724-656-8866
George Endrizzi, prin.
Wilmington Area MS 500/5-8
400 Wood St 16142 724-656-8866
Benjamin Fennick, prin.
Other Schools – See Pulaski, Volant

Nicktown, Cambria

Northern Cambria Catholic S 100/PK-8
PO Box 252 15762 814-948-8900
Sr. Mary Lee Przybylski, prin. Fax 948-8720

Normalville, Fayette
Connellsville Area SD
Supt. — See Connellsville
Springfield Township ES 300/K-6
PO Box 317 15469 724-455-3191
Robin Martin, prin. Fax 455-3114

Norristown, Montgomery, Pop. 30,689
Norristown Area SD 6,300/K-12
401 N Whitehall Rd 19403 610-630-5000
Dr. Janet Samuels, supt. Fax 630-5013
www.nasd.k12.pa.us
Cole Manor ES 400/K-4
2350 Springview Rd 19401 610-275-5525
Nicole Poncheri, prin. Fax 272-0529
East Norriton MS 800/5-8
330 Roland Dr 19401 610-275-6520
Stephen Brandt, prin. Fax 272-0531
Eisenhower MS 500/5-8
1601 Markley St 19401 610-277-8720
Christina Taylor, prin. Fax 270-2901
Fly ES 500/K-4
2920 Potshop Rd 19403 610-630-0380
Victoria Velazquez, prin. Fax 630-1519
Gotwals ES 300/K-4
1 E Oak St 19401 610-275-1077
Maryanne Hoskins, prin. Fax 277-4622
Hancock ES 400/K-4
1520 Arch St 19401 610-275-5522
Joanne Gillespie, prin. Fax 272-0547
Marshall Street ES 500/K-4
1525 W Marshall St 19403 610-630-8550
John Sweeney, prin. Fax 630-1378
Stewart MS 500/5-8
1315 W Marshall St 19401 610-275-6870
Rachel Holler, prin. Fax 272-0560
Whitehall ES 400/K-4
399 N Whitehall Rd 19403 610-630-6000
Deborah Donnelly, prin. Fax 630-1540

Penn Christian Academy 200/PK-8
50 W Germantown Pike 19401 610-279-6628
Vivian Dippold, admin. Fax 279-1956
St. Francis of Assisi S 200/PK-8
601 Buttonwood St 19401 610-272-0501
Constance DiBonaventure, prin. Fax 272-8011
St. Teresa of Avila S 200/PK-8
2550 S Parkview Dr 19403 610-666-6069
Janet Lazorcheck, prin. Fax 666-0195
St. Titus S 200/PK-8
3000 Keenwood Rd 19403 610-279-6043
Joanne Zinn, prin. Fax 279-8090
Visitation BVM S 700/PK-8
190 N Trooper Rd 19403 610-539-6080
Sr. Diane Marie, prin. Fax 630-7946

Northampton, Northampton, Pop. 9,699
Northampton Area SD 5,800/K-12
2014 Laubach Ave 18067 610-262-7811
Dr. Linda Firestone, supt. Fax 262-1150
www.northampton.k12.pa.us
Northampton Area MS 900/7-8
1617 Laubach Ave 18067 610-262-7817
Patrice Turner, prin. Fax 262-6583
Northampton Borough ES 900/K-6
1677 Lincoln Ave 18067 610-262-6430
Lori Gibbs, prin. Fax 262-6461
Other Schools – See Bath, Walnutport

Our Lady of Hungary S 200/PK-8
1300 Newport Ave 18067 610-262-9171
Sr. Deborah Reho, prin. Fax 262-2202

North East, Erie, Pop. 4,331
North East SD 1,900/K-12
50 E Division St 16428 814-725-8671
Dr. Judith Miller, supt. Fax 725-9380
www.nesd1.k12.pa.us/
Davis PS 400/K-2
50 E Division St 16428 814-725-8671
Timothy Welsh, prin. Fax 725-0821
North East IS 400/3-5
50 E Division St 16428 814-725-8671
Glen Zewe Ph.D., prin. Fax 725-8643
North East MS 500/6-8
1903 Freeport Rd 16428 814-725-8671
Gregory Beardsley, prin. Fax 725-1086

Creekside Christian S 50/PK-8
43 S Lake St 16428 814-725-2407
Leslie Brown, prin. Fax 725-0069
St. Gregory S 100/PK-8
140 W Main St 16428 814-725-4571
Nancy Pierce, prin. Fax 725-4572

Northern Cambria, Cambria, Pop. 4,022
Northern Cambria SD 1,100/K-12
601 Joseph St 15714 814-948-5481
Dr. Thomas Estep, supt. Fax 948-6058
www.ncsd.k12.pa.us/
Northern Cambria ES 500/K-5
601 Joseph St 15714 814-948-5880
Robert Williams, prin. Fax 948-6058
Northern Cambria MS 300/6-8
601 Joseph St 15714 814-948-5880
Thomas Rocco, prin.

North Huntingdon, Westmoreland, Pop. 28,158
Norwin SD 4,800/K-12
281 McMahon Dr 15642 724-861-3000
Dr. John Boylan, supt. Fax 863-9467
www.norwinsd.org
Hahntown ES K-4
791 Entry Rd 15642 724-861-3020
Daryl Clair, prin. Fax 861-3020
Hillcrest IS 800/5-6
11091 Mockingbird Dr 15642 724-861-3015
Rosemarie Dvorchak, prin. Fax 864-7203
Norwin MS 900/7-8
10870 Mockingbird Dr 15642 724-863-5707
Robert Suman, prin. Fax 863-5408
Sheridan Terrace ES 500/K-4
1219 Morris St 15642 724-861-3025
Dr. M. Joanne Elder, prin. Fax 863-4380
Stewartsville ES 500/K-4
101 Carpenter Ln 15642 724-861-3030
Doreen Harris, prin. Fax 863-9010
Sunset Valley ES 500/K-4
11605 Dickens Dr 15642 724-861-3035
Natalie McCracken, prin. Fax 863-4096

Queen of Angels S 900/PK-8
1 Main St 15642 724-978-0144
Linda Holsopple, prin. Fax 978-0171

Northumberland, Northumberland, Pop. 3,586
Shikellamy SD
Supt. — See Sunbury
Priestley ES, 423 Cannery Rd 17857 400/K-5
Dixie Barth, prin. 570-473-3261
Rice MS 300/6-8
400 Hanover St 17857 570-473-3547
Frank Boyer, prin. Fax 473-4483

Northumberland Christian S 200/K-12
351 5th St 17857 570-473-9786
John Rees, prin. Fax 473-8405
Sunbury Christian Academy 100/PK-12
135 Spruce Hollow Rd 17857 570-473-7592
Nancy Gross, admin. Fax 473-7531

North Versailles, Allegheny, Pop. 12,302
East Allegheny SD 1,400/PK-12
1150 Jacks Run Rd 15137 412-824-8012
Roger D'Emidio, supt. Fax 824-1062
www.eawildcats.net
Early Learning Center 100/PK-K
1150 Jacks Run Rd 15137 412-824-9700
Sean Gildea, prin. Fax 646-3026
Green Valley PS 200/1-3
3290 Crestview Dr 15137 412-673-9737
Sean Gildea, prin. Fax 673-0196
Logan MS 400/4-8
1154 Jacks Run Rd 15137 412-824-6053
Harriet Hopper, prin. Fax 824-6095

Praise Christian Academy 100/K-8
245 Foster Rd 15137 412-829-0400
Mary Ann Jacobs, prin. Fax 829-2325

North Wales, Montgomery, Pop. 3,299
North Penn SD
Supt. — See Lansdale
Gwyn-Nor ES 600/K-6
139 Hancock Rd 19454 215-368-7105
Elizabeth Santoro, prin. Fax 368-7884
Montgomery ES 700/K-6
1221 Stump Rd 19454 215-368-6614
Orlando Taylor, prin. Fax 368-7882
North Wales ES 400/K-6
201 Summit St 19454 215-699-4471
Ineke McCrea, prin. Fax 616-0521

Mary Mother of the Redeemer S 700/K-7
1321 Upper State Rd 19454 215-412-7101
Denise Judge, prin. Fax 412-7197
St. Rose of Lima S 200/K-8
425 S Pennsylvania Ave 19454 215-699-8831
Elizabeth Venziale, prin. Fax 661-1691

North Warren, Warren
Warren County SD 5,500/K-12
185 Hospital Dr Ste F 16365 814-723-6900
Dr. Robert Terrill, supt. Fax 723-4244
www.wcsdpa.org
Other Schools – See Clarendon, Russell, Sheffield, Sugar Grove, Warren, Youngsville

Norwood, Delaware, Pop. 5,852
Interboro SD
Supt. — See Prospect Park
Norwood S 600/K-8
558 Seneca Ave 19074 610-237-6425
Dr. Paulette Bradley, prin. Fax 237-1481

St. Gabriel S 200/K-8
233 Mohawk Ave 19074 610-532-3234
Patricia Grady, prin. Fax 532-5523

Oakdale, Allegheny, Pop. 1,466
West Allegheny SD 3,300/K-12
600 Donaldson Rd 15071 724-695-3422
John DiSanti Ph.D., supt. Fax 695-3788
www.westallegheny.k12.pa.us/
Donaldson ES 400/K-5
600 Donaldson Rd 15071 724-213-1010
Patricia Nolan, prin. Fax 213-1002
McKee ES 600/K-5
1501 Oakdale Rd 15071 724-693-8451
Thomas Orr, prin. Fax 693-0924
Other Schools – See Imperial

Oakmont, Allegheny, Pop. 6,587
Riverview SD 1,200/K-12
701 10th St 15139 412-828-1800
C. Erdeljac, supt. Fax 828-9346
www.rsd.k12.pa.us
Tenth Street ES 400/K-6
701 10th St 15139 412-828-1800
Gary Winkler, prin. Fax 828-7373
Other Schools – See Verona

Redeemer Lutheran S 100/PK-8
1261 Pennsylvania Ave 15139 412-828-9323
Gail Holzer, prin. Fax 828-1860
St. Irenaeus S 100/PK-8
637 4th St 15139 412-828-8444
Sr. Carol Papp, prin. Fax 828-8749

Oaks, Montgomery
Spring-Ford Area SD
Supt. — See Collegeville
Oaks ES 600/K-4
PO Box 396 19456 610-705-6008
Mark Moyer, prin. Fax 705-6247

Oil City, Venango, Pop. 10,942
Oil City Area SD 2,400/K-12
PO Box 929 16301 814-676-1867
Joseph Carrico, supt. Fax 676-2211
www.ocasd.org
Hasson Heights ES 600/K-5
833 Grandview Rd 16301 814-677-8021
Todd Lape, prin. Fax 677-2225
Oil City Area MS 500/6-8
8 Lynch Blvd 16301 814-676-5702
Bill Hall, prin. Fax 676-2306
Seventh Street ES 200/3-5
102 W 7th St 16301 814-677-3029
Lynda Weller, prin. Fax 677-3390
Smedley Street ES 200/K-2
310 Smedley St 16301 814-676-2294
Lynda Weller, prin. Fax 676-9314
Other Schools – See Cooperstown

St. Stephen S 200/K-8
214 Reed St 16301 814-677-3035
Marge Hajduk, prin. Fax 677-2053

Old Forge, Lackawanna, Pop. 8,558
Old Forge SD 900/K-12
300 Marion St 18518 570-457-6721
Roseann Brutico, supt. Fax 457-8389
www.ofsd.cc/
Old Forge ES 400/K-6
401 Melmore St 18518 570-457-8391
Nicole Van Luvender, prin. Fax 414-0516

Triboro Christian Academy 100/PK-12
100 S Main St 18518 570-457-5392
Erika Weber, admin. Fax 451-0807

Oley, Berks
Oley Valley SD 2,100/K-12
17 Jefferson St 19547 610-987-4100
Jeffrey Zackon Ed.D., supt. Fax 987-4138
www.oleyvalleysd.org
Oley Valley ES 900/K-5
3257 Friedensburg Rd 19547 610-987-4100
Sheila Simyak, prin. Fax 987-4173
Oley Valley MS 500/6-8
3247 Friedensburg Rd 19547 610-987-4100
Dan Marks, prin. Fax 987-4240

Orefield, Lehigh
Parkland SD
Supt. — See Allentown
Kernsville ES 600/K-5
5051 Kernsville Rd 18069 610-351-5840
Michael Gehringer, prin. Fax 351-5849
Orefield MS 1,200/6-8
2675 PA Route 309 18069 610-351-5750
Dr. Rodney Troutman, prin. Fax 351-5799

St. Joseph the Worker S 500/PK-8
1858 Applewood Dr 18069 610-395-7221
Jody Myers, prin. Fax 395-7904

Oreland, Montgomery, Pop. 5,695
Springfield Township SD 2,100/K-12
1901 Paper Mill Rd 19075 215-233-6000
Roseann Nyiri Ed.D., supt. Fax 233-5815
www.sdst.org
Springfield Township ES - Enfield Campus 400/K-4
1118 Church Rd 19075 215-233-6000
Karen Alston, prin. Fax 233-4688
Springfield Township MS 500/5-7
1901 Paper Mill Rd 19075 215-233-6000
Alice Snare, prin. Fax 233-6091
Other Schools – See Flourtown

Holy Martyrs S 200/PK-8
121 Allison Rd 19075 215-887-2044
David Hayden, prin. Fax 887-0024

Orwigsburg, Schuylkill, Pop. 2,995
Blue Mountain SD 3,000/K-12
PO Box 188 17961 570-366-0515
Dr. Joyce Romberger, supt. Fax 366-0838
www.bmsd.org
Blue Mountain ES East 700/K-5
675 Reddale Rd 17961 570-366-1066
Jeffrey Zwiebel, prin. Fax 366-1797
Blue Mountain MS 700/6-8
PO Box 279 17961 570-366-0546
James McGonigle, prin. Fax 366-2513
Other Schools – See Cressona, Friedensburg

Osceola Mills, Clearfield, Pop. 1,188
Philipsburg-Osceola Area SD
Supt. — See Philipsburg
Osceola Mills ES 300/K-6
400 Coal St 16666 814-339-6812
Linda Smutz, prin. Fax 339-7814

Ottsville, Bucks

St. John the Baptist S 200/PK-8
4040 Durham Rd 18942 610-847-5523
Vivian Zimmerman, prin. Fax 847-8357

Oxford, Chester, Pop. 4,682
Oxford Area SD 3,200/K-12
125 Bell Tower Ln 19363 610-932-6600
Dr. Raymond Fischer, supt. Fax 932-6603
www.oxford.k12.pa.us
Elk Ridge S 500/1-2
200 Wickersham Rd 19363 610-932-6670
Herbert Hayes, prin. Fax 932-7836
Hopewell ES, 602 Garfield St 19363 5-6
Nicole Addis, prin. 484-365-6150
Jordan Bank ES 200/K-K
536 Hodgson St 19363 610-932-6625
Herbert Hayes, prin. Fax 932-6662
Nottingham S 800/2-4
736 Garfield St 19363 610-932-6632
Paula Voshell, prin. Fax 932-4630
Penn's Grove S 600/7-8
301 S 5th St 19363 610-932-6615
David Hamburg, prin. Fax 932-6619

Bethany Christian S 400/PK-8
1137 Shadyside Rd 19363 610-998-0877
L. Linda Lewis, prin. Fax 998-0253
Sacred Heart S 300/K-8
203 Church Rd 19363 610-932-3633
Kathleen McCabe, prin. Fax 932-6051

Palmerton, Carbon, Pop. 5,279
Palmerton Area SD 1,800/K-12
680 4th St 18071 610-826-7101
Carol Boyce, supt. Fax 826-4958
www.palmerton.org/
Palmer ES 500/2-6
298 Lafayette Ave 18071 610-826-7101
Paul Rearden, prin. Fax 826-7528
Palmerton Area JHS 400/7-8
3529 Fireline Rd 18071 610-826-2492
Thaddeus Kosciolek, prin. Fax 826-2366
Parkside Education Center K-1
680 4th St 18071 610-826-4914
Paul Rearden, prin. Fax 826-4915
Other Schools – See Lehighton

St. John Neuman S 100/K-8
259 Lafayette Ave 18071 610-826-2354
Sr. Virginia Bator, prin. Fax 826-6444

Palmyra, Lebanon, Pop. 6,957
Palmyra Area SD 3,100/K-12
1125 Park Dr 17078 717-838-3144
Dr. Larry Schmidt, supt. Fax 838-5105
www.pasd.us
Forge Road ES 400/K-5
400 S Forge Rd 17078 717-838-1843
Anne Hoover, prin. Fax 838-9481
Northside ES 500/K-5
301 E Spruce St 17078 717-838-2447
Gary Zellner, prin. Fax 838-0253
Palmyra Area MS 700/6-8
50 W Cherry St 17078 717-838-2119
Janet Kaltreider, prin. Fax 838-4402
Pine Street ES 500/K-5
50 W Pine St 17078 717-838-2616
Donna Kuntz, prin. Fax 838-6792

Paoli, Chester, Pop. 5,603

St. Norbert S 200/K-8
6 Greenlawn Rd 19301 610-644-1670
Theresa Garvin, prin. Fax 644-0201

Paradise, Lancaster, Pop. 1,043
Pequea Valley SD
Supt. — See Kinzers
Paradise ES 200/K-5
20 N Belmont Rd 17562 717-768-5560
Beth Reinhart, prin. Fax 768-5654

Linville Hill Mennonite S 200/K-8
295 S Kinzer Rd 17562 717-442-4447
Vicky Zeng, admin. Fax 442-9283

Parkesburg, Chester, Pop. 3,445

Our Lady's Little Lambs S 50/PK-PK
603 W 2nd Ave 19365 610-857-1163
Janice Dagney, prin. Fax 857-2353

Parkside, Delaware, Pop. 2,212
Penn-Delco SD
Supt. — See Aston
Parkside ES 300/K-5
2 E Forestview Rd, 610-497-6300
Teresa Ford, prin. Fax 876-0943

Patton, Cambria, Pop. 1,923
Cambria Heights SD 1,500/K-12
PO Box 66 16668 814-674-6072
Dr. Joseph Macharola, supt. Fax 674-5411
chsd.k12.pa.us
Cambria Heights MS 400/6-8
PO Box 216 16668 814-674-6290
David Caldwell, prin. Fax 674-5054
Other Schools – See Carrolltown

Peckville, See Blakely
Valley View SD
Supt. — See Archbald
Valley View ES 500/K-2
901 Main St 18452 570-489-7579
James McKane, prin. Fax 489-7243

Pen Argyl, Northampton, Pop. 3,670
Pen Argyl Area SD 1,900/K-12
1620 Teels Rd 18072 610-863-3191
William Haberl Ed.D., supt. Fax 863-7040
www.penargyl.k12.pa.us
Wind Gap MS 800/4-8
1620 Teels Rd 18072 610-863-9093
Terry Barry, prin. Fax 863-3817
Other Schools – See Nazareth

Immaculate Conception S 100/K-6
PO Box 6 18072 610-863-4816
Sr. Maria Luz, prin. Fax 863-8158

Penfield, Clearfield
Du Bois Area SD
Supt. — See Du Bois
Penfield ES 100/K-5
201 Hoovertown Rd 15849 814-637-5652
Shawna Grim, prin. Fax 637-5641

Penndel, Bucks, Pop. 2,397

Our Lady of Grace S 500/K-8
300 Hulmeville Ave 19047 215-757-5287
Denise Lewis, prin. Fax 757-6199

Pennsburg, Montgomery, Pop. 3,371
Upper Perkiomen SD 3,000/K-12
2229 E Buck Rd 18073 215-679-7961
Dr. Timothy Kirby, supt. Fax 679-6214
www.upsd.org/
Other Schools – See East Greenville, Green Lane, Hereford

Penns Creek, Snyder

Penn View Christian Academy 100/PK-12
125 Penn View Dr 17862 570-837-1855
David Destefano, prin. Fax 837-1865

Pequea, Lancaster
Penn Manor SD
Supt. — See Lancaster
Marticville MS 400/7-8
356 Frogtown Rd 17565 717-291-9854
Richard Eby, prin. Fax 284-5954

Perkasie, Bucks, Pop. 8,736
Pennridge SD 6,700/K-12
1200 N 5th St 18944 215-257-5011
Dr. Robert Kish, supt. Fax 453-8699
www.pennridge.org
Bedminster ES 500/K-5
2914 Fretz Valley Rd 18944 215-795-2929
Christine Koegler, prin. Fax 795-2156
Deibler ES 400/K-5
1122 W Schwenkmill Rd 18944 215-257-1146
Deb Brady, prin. Fax 257-1173
Guth ES 400/K-5
601 N 7th St 18944 215-257-8057
Dr. Susan Mowrer-Benda, prin. Fax 257-1389
Pennridge Central MS 600/6-8
144 N Walnut St 18944 215-258-0939
Dr. Thomas Rutter, prin. Fax 258-0938
Pennridge North MS 6-8
1500 N 5th St 18944 215-453-6932
Dr. Margaret Kantes, prin. Fax 453-7867
Pennridge South MS 500/6-8
610 S 5th St 18944 215-257-0467
Felicia McAllister, prin. Fax 257-3094
Seylar ES 500/K-5
820 Callowhill Rd 18944 215-257-6272
David Wagner, prin. Fax 257-2418
Other Schools – See Sellersville

Perryopolis, Fayette, Pop. 1,748
Frazier SD 1,100/K-12
142 Constitution St 15473 724-736-4432
Dennis Spinella Ph.D., supt. Fax 736-0688
www.frazierschooldistrict.org
Frazier MS 300/6-8
142 Constitution St 15473 724-736-4428
Michael Turek, prin. Fax 736-0688
Perry ES 300/K-5
142 Constitution St 15473 724-736-4391
Kenneth Meadows, prin. Fax 736-0688
Other Schools – See Fayette City

Philadelphia, Philadelphia, Pop. 1,463,281
Philadelphia CSD 159,000/PK-12
440 N Broad St 19130 215-400-4000
Arlene Ackerman Ed.D., supt.
www.phila.k12.pa.us
Adaire S 500/K-8
1300 E Palmer St 19125 215-291-4712
Robert McGrogan, prin. Fax 291-6350
Alcorn S 600/K-8
3200 Dickinson St 19146 215-952-6219
Yvette Jackson, prin. Fax 952-0853
Allen S 400/K-8
3200 W Lehigh Ave 19132 215-227-4404
Romesa Scott, prin. Fax 227-2971
Allen S 900/K-8
6329 Battersby St 19149 215-537-2530
Jim Sierpello, prin. Fax 537-2599
Anderson S 500/K-8
1034 S 60th St 19143 215-471-2903
Donald Bandel, prin. Fax 471-2745
Arthur S 200/K-8
2000 Catharine St 19146 215-875-5774
Renee Musgrove, prin. Fax 875-8057
Bache-Martin S 500/K-8
2201 Brown St 19130 215-684-5074
Yvette Duperon, prin. Fax 684-5446
Baldi MS 1,200/6-8
8801 Verree Rd 19115 215-961-2003
Eugene McLaughlin, prin. Fax 961-2116
Barratt MS 400/6-8
1599 Wharton St 19146 215-952-6217
Roy McKinney, prin. Fax 952-8583
Barry S 300/K-8
5900 Race St 19139 215-471-2744
Darlene Beasley, prin. Fax 471-6320
Barton ES 700/K-2
4600 Rosehill St 19120 215-456-3007
Daniel Lazar, prin. Fax 456-5578
Beeber MS 700/6-8
5925 Malvern Ave 19131 215-581-5513
Joseph Starinieri, prin. Fax 581-5694
Bethune S 600/K-8
3301 Old York Rd 19140 215-227-4433
Arvel Wells, prin. Fax 227-8658
Birney S 600/K-8
900 Lindley Ave 19141 215-456-3000
Andrea Ingram-Mayo, prin. Fax 457-6695
Blaine S 400/K-8
3001 W Berks St 19121 215-684-5085
Gianeen Powell, prin. Fax 684-8858
Blankenburg S 400/K-8
4600 W Girard Ave 19131 215-581-5505
Dr. Christina Spink, prin. Fax 581-5922
Bluford ES 700/K-6
5801 Media St 19131 215-581-5502
Authurea Smith, prin. Fax 581-5725
Bregy S 400/K-8
1700 Bigler St 19145 215-952-6218
Marion Daniel, prin. Fax 952-0858
Bridesburg ES 400/K-5
2824 Jenks St 19137 215-537-2515
Elmer Boehringer, prin. Fax 537-3145
Brown ES 400/K-5
1946 E Sergeant St 19125 215-291-4717
Dawn Moore, prin. Fax 291-5836
Brown ES 600/K-6
3600 Stanwood St 19136 215-335-5650
Ellen Denofa, prin. Fax 335-5381
Bryant S 700/PK-8
6001 Cedar Ave 19143 215-471-2910
Jala Pearson, prin. Fax 471-8379

Carnell S 1,300/K-8
1100 Devereaux Ave 19111 215-537-2527
Woolworth Davis, prin. Fax 537-6305
Cassidy ES 600/K-6
6523 Lansdowne Ave 19151 215-581-5506
Beverly Crawl, prin. Fax 581-5581
Catharine ES 700/K-5
6600 Chester Ave 19142 215-727-2155
Carol Weick-Kofsky, prin. Fax 727-2264
Cayuga ES 400/K-5
4344 N 5th St 19140 215-456-3167
Evelyn Cortez, prin. Fax 456-5622
Childs S 400/K-8
1541 S 17th St 19146 215-952-6213
Alphonso Evans, prin. Fax 952-6254
Clemente MS 1,100/5-8
122 W Erie Ave 19140 215-291-5400
Carmen Garcia-Collins, prin. Fax 291-5036
Cleveland S 500/K-8
3701 N 19th St 19140 215-227-4415
Erica Green, prin. Fax 227-7197
Clymer S 500/K-8
1201 W Rush St 19133 215-227-8610
Kia Green, prin. Fax 227-4770
Comegys ES 600/PK-6
5100 Greenway Ave 19143 215-727-2162
Geraldine Fitzpatrick-Do, prin. Fax 727-2329
Comly ES 400/K-5
1001 Byberry Rd 19116 215-961-2008
Margaret Carnvale, prin. Fax 961-2555
Conwell MS 900/5-8
1849 E Clearfield St 19134 215-291-4722
Ed Hoffman, prin. Fax 291-5019
Cooke S 600/K-8
1300 W Louden St 19141 215-456-3002
Judy Burns, prin. Fax 456-3185
Cook-Wissahickon S 400/K-8
201 E Salaignac St 19128 215-487-4463
Anna Jenkins, prin. Fax 487-4808
Cramp ES 700/K-6
3449 N Mascher St 19140 215-291-4704
Milagros De Jesus, prin. Fax 291-5694
Creighton S 900/K-8
5401 Tabor Ave 19120 215-537-2531
Katherine Carter, prin. Fax 537-8398
Crossan ES 300/K-5
7350 Bingham St 19111 215-728-5014
William Griffin, prin. Fax 728-5955
Daroff S 900/K-8
5630 Vine St 19139 215-471-2905
Bonnie Berman, prin. Fax 471-3159
Day S 500/K-8
6342 Crittenden St 19138 215-276-5250
Karen Dean, prin. Fax 276-5817
DeBurgos Bilingual Magnet S 900/K-8
401 W Lehigh Ave 19133 215-291-4065
Maria Burgos, prin. Fax 291-4084
Decatur S 800/K-8
3500 Academy Rd 19154 215-281-2606
Charles Connor, prin. Fax 281-5803
Dick S 300/K-8
2498 W Diamond St 19121 215-684-5081
Amy Agree-Williams, prin. Fax 684-8995
Disston S 900/K-8
6801 Cottage St 19135 215-335-5661
Susan Smith, prin. Fax 335-5030
Dobson S 300/K-8
4667 Umbria St 19127 215-487-4460
Patricia Cruice, prin. Fax 487-4804
Douglass S 600/PK-8
2118 W Norris St 19121 215-684-5063
Edward Roulhac, prin. Fax 684-8916
Drew S 300/K-8
3724 Warren St 19104 215-823-8204
Huie Douglas, prin. Fax 823-5702
Duckrey S 400/K-8
1501 W Diamond St 19121 215-684-5066
David Baugh, prin. Fax 684-8927
Dunbar S 300/K-8
1750 N 12th St 19122 215-684-5065
Lisa Bellamy, prin. Fax 684-8945
Edmonds ES 600/K-6
8025 Thouron Ave 19150 215-276-5261
Sharen Finzimer, prin. Fax 276-5811
Edmunds S 1,200/K-8
1197 Haworth St 19124 215-537-2520
Leroy Baker, prin. Fax 537-2861
Elkin ES 1,100/K-4
3199 D St 19134 215-291-4701
Cheryl-Kennedy Gregory, prin. Fax 291-4876
Ellwood ES 400/K-6
6701 N 13th St 19126 215-276-5286
Bette Kleckley, prin. Fax 276-5289
Emlen ES 500/K-5
6501 Chew Ave 19119 215-951-4010
Richard Raisman, prin. Fax 951-4131
Fairhill S 600/K-8
601 W Somerset St 19133 215-227-4406
Luisa Garcia-Soler, prin. Fax 227-2986
Farrell S 900/K-8
8300 Castor Ave 19152 215-728-5009
Marie McCarthy, prin. Fax 728-5225
Fell S 500/K-8
900 W Oregon Ave 19148 215-952-6237
Dr. Eleanor Walls, prin. Fax 952-6239
Feltonville Arts & Sciences MS 800/6-8
210 E Courtland St 19120 215-456-5603
Nelson Reyes, prin. Fax 456-5614
Feltonville IS 800/3-5
238 E Wyoming Ave 19120 215-456-3012
Lisa Matthews, prin. Fax 456-0122
Ferguson S 500/K-8
2000 N 7th St 19122 215-684-5092
Sheila Drapiewski, prin. Fax 684-8880
Finletter S 1,000/K-8
6100 N Front St 19120 215-276-5265
Joanne Beaver, prin. Fax 276-5285

Fitler S 400/1-8
140 W Seymour St 19144 215-951-4009
Willete Jones, prin. Fax 951-4502
Fitzpatrick S 800/K-8
11061 Knights Rd 19154 215-281-2602
Cheryl Glaser, prin. Fax 281-3330
Forrest ES 900/K-6
7300 Cottage St 19136 215-335-5652
Patricia Epps, prin. Fax 335-5983
Fox Chase ES 300/K-5
500 Rhawn St 19111 215-728-5016
Karen Duckett, prin. Fax 728-5006
Frank ES 900/K-5
2000 Bowler St 19115 215-961-2005
Ellen Cooper, prin. Fax 961-2551
Franklin S 1,100/K-8
5735 Rising Sun Ave 19120 215-728-5017
Roslynn Sample-Green, prin. Fax 728-5992
Fulton S 400/K-8
60 E Haines St 19144 215-951-4005
Deborah Lee, prin. Fax 951-4056
Gideon S 300/K-8
2817 W Glenwood Ave 19121 215-684-5072
Jeannie Hendricks, prin. Fax 684-8917
Gillespie MS 400/7-8
1801 W Pike St 19140 215-227-4409
Jane Adams, prin. Fax 227-4676
Girard ES 500/K-4
1800 Snyder Ave 19145 215-952-8554
Thomas Koger, prin. Fax 952-6397
Gompers ES 400/K-6
5701 Wynnefield Ave 19131 215-581-5503
Phillip Deluca, prin. Fax 581-5686
Greenberg S 700/K-8
600 Sharon Ln 19115 215-961-2002
Gina Hubbard, prin. Fax 961-2560
Greenfield S 600/K-8
2200 Chestnut St 19103 215-299-3566
Dr. Ernie Angiolillo, prin. Fax 299-3567
Hackett ES 400/K-6
2161 E York St 19125 215-291-4706
Jill Coffey, prin. Fax 291-4169
Hamilton S 700/K-8
5640 Spruce St 19139 215-471-2911
Annette Gittleman, prin. Fax 471-2724
Hancock ES 500/K-5
3700 Morrell Ave 19114 215-281-2604
Rosemary Cataldi, prin. Fax 281-5900
Harding MS 1,100/6-8
2000 Wakeling St 19124 215-537-2528
Michael Calderone, prin. Fax 537-2850
Harrington ES 500/K-6
5300 Baltimore Ave 19143 215-471-2914
Mary Digiacomo, prin. Fax 471-5087
Harrison S 200/K-8
1012 W Thompson St 19122 215-684-5067
Marion McCloskey-Mueller, prin. Fax 684-8984
Harrity S 800/PK-8
5601 Christian St 19143 215-471-2908
Patricia Bainbridge, prin. Fax 471-3807
Hartranft S 500/K-8
720 W Cumberland St 19133 215-684-5088
Dr. Judith McMonagle, prin. Fax 765-6515
Henry S 500/K-8
601 Carpenter Ln 19119 215-951-4006
Caren Trantas, prin. Fax 951-4505
Heston S 500/PK-8
1621 N 54th St 19131 215-581-5514
Icilyn Wilson-Greene, prin. Fax 581-5724
Hill S 400/PK-8
3133 Ridge Ave Ste 1 19121 215-684-5077
Tamara Smith, prin. Fax 684-5125
Holme ES 500/K-6
9120 Academy Rd 19114 215-335-5656
Dontae Wilson, prin. Fax 335-5033
Hopkinson S 1,100/K-8
4001 L St 19124 215-537-2526
Candace Straff, prin. Fax 537-2900
Houston S 600/K-8
7300 Rural Ln 19119 215-248-6603
Kimberly Newman, prin. Fax 248-6683
Howe ES 300/K-5
5800 N 13th St 19141 215-276-5270
Doaquin Jessup, prin. Fax 276-5380
Huey S 800/K-8
5200 Pine St 19143 215-471-2901
Aaron Starke, prin. Fax 471-2720
Hunter S 600/K-8
2400 N Front St 19133 215-291-4710
James Douglass, prin. Fax 291-5177
Jackson S 300/K-8
1213 S 12th St 19147 215-952-6223
Sherry Ann Lewis, prin. Fax 952-6488
Jenks ES 400/K-4
2501 S 13th St 19148 215-952-6224
Siouda Chestnut, prin. Fax 952-6407
Jenks S 500/K-8
8301 Germantown Ave 19118 215-248-6604
Mary Lynskey, prin. Fax 248-6681
Jones MS 900/5-8
2950 Memphis St 19134 215-291-4709
Ernest Lowe, prin. Fax 291-4754
Juniata Park Academy K-8
801 E Hunting Park Ave 19124 215-289-7930
Patricia Mazzucca, prin. Fax 289-7949
Kearny S 400/K-8
601 Fairmount Ave 19123 215-351-7343
Eileen Spagnola, prin. Fax 351-7129
Kelley S 400/K-8
1601 N 28th St 19121 215-684-5071
Michael Garafola, prin. Fax 684-5179
Kelly ES 800/K-6
5116 Pulaski Ave 19144 215-951-4011
Dr. John Hackman, prin. Fax 951-4182
Kenderton S 500/PK-8
1500 W Ontario St 19140 215-227-4412
Robin Wilkins, prin. Fax 227-8778

Key ES 300/K-6
2230 S 8th St 19148 215-952-6216
Norris Eldridge, prin. Fax 952-8505
Kinsey S 500/K-8
6501 Limekiln Pike 19138 215-276-5266
Ennis Manns, prin. Fax 276-5394
Kirkbride S 400/K-8
1501 S 7th St 19147 215-952-6214
Victoria Magness, prin. Fax 952-6253
LaBrum MS 300/6-8
10800 Hawley Rd 19154 215-281-2607
Barbara Deni, prin. Fax 281-5800
Lamberton S 700/K-8
7501 Woodbine Ave 19151 215-581-5650
Marla Jones, prin. Fax 581-5707
Lawton ES 700/K-5
6101 Jackson St 19135 215-335-5659
Anita Urofsky, prin. Fax 335-5325
Lea S 400/K-8
4700 Locust St 19139 215-471-2915
Lisa Bells-Chiles, prin. Fax 471-4355
Leeds MS 400/6-8
1100 E Mount Pleasant Ave 19150 215-248-6602
Stephanie Mitchell, prin. Fax 248-6623
Leidy S 300/K-8
1301 Belmont Ave 19104 215-581-5500
Lorna Horsey, prin. Fax 581-5926
Levering S 300/K-8
6000 Ridge Ave 19128 215-487-4462
Dr. Glenn Douglas, prin. Fax 487-6477
Lingelbach S 400/K-8
6340 Wayne Ave 19144 215-951-4001
Tamera Conaway, prin. Fax 951-4514
Locke S 400/K-8
4550 Haverford Ave 19139 215-823-8202
Dr. Vernadine Cartwright, prin. Fax 823-5721
Loesche ES 700/K-5
595 Tomlinson Rd 19116 215-961-2000
Kari King-Hill, prin. Fax 961-2559
Logan ES 400/K-5
1700 Lindley Ave 19141 215-456-3006
Mark Wilicki, prin. Fax 456-3114
Longstreth S 600/PK-8
5700 Willows Ave 19143 215-727-2158
Robin Cooper, prin. Fax 727-2260
Lowell ES 1,000/K-4
450 W Nedro Ave 19120 215-276-5272
Rochelle Bock, prin. Fax 276-5278
Ludlow S 300/PK-8
550 W Master St 19122 215-684-5060
Charlotte Buonassisi, prin. Fax 684-4387
Mann ES 400/K-5
5376 W Berks St 19131 215-581-5516
Michael Smith, prin. Fax 581-5610
Marshall ES 500/K-5
4500 Griscom St 19124 215-537-2521
Renee Morley, prin. Fax 537-2847
Marshall S 600/K-8
5120 N 6th St 19120 215-456-0170
Edward Penn, prin. Fax 456-0187
Mayfair S 800/K-8
3001 Princeton Ave 19149 215-335-5651
Roberta Besden, prin. Fax 335-5035
McCall S 500/K-8
325 S 7th St 19106 215-351-7350
Carol Domb, prin. Fax 351-7349
McCloskey ES 300/K-5
8500 Pickering St 19150 215-248-6600
John Underwood, prin. Fax 248-6235
McClure ES 600/K-4
600 W Hunting Park Ave 19140 215-456-3001
Lillian Tearte, prin. Fax 456-5587
McDaniel ES 400/K-5
1801 S 22nd St 19145 215-952-8600
Darlynn Gray, prin. Fax 952-6379
McKinley S 400/K-8
2101 N Orkney St 19122 215-291-4702
Marilyn Mejia, prin. Fax 291-5613
McMichael S 500/K-8
3543 Fairmount Ave 19104 215-823-8205
Angela Gaddie-Edwards, prin. Fax 386-3549
Meade S 500/K-8
1600 N 18th St 19121 215-684-5062
Frank Murphy, prin. Fax 684-7006
Meehan MS 700/7-8
3001 Ryan Ave 19152 215-335-5654
Mary Jackson, prin. Fax 335-5992
Meredith S 400/K-8
725 S 5th St 19147 215-351-7360
Cindy Farlino, prin. Fax 351-7190
Mifflin S, 3624 Conrad St 19129 200/K-8
Charles Ray, prin. 215-951-4007
Mitchell ES 600/K-5
5600 Kingsessing Ave 19143 215-727-2160
Jackie Haltie, prin. Fax 727-2218
Moffet ES 500/K-5
127 W Oxford St 19122 215-291-4721
Olivia Dreibelbis, prin. Fax 291-5190
Moore ES 1,100/K-5
6900 Summerdale Ave 19111 215-728-5011
Colleen Wisler, prin. Fax 728-5692
Morrison S 900/K-8
5100 N 3rd St 19120 215-456-3004
Christopher Byrd, prin. Fax 456-5564
Morris S 400/K-8
2600 W Thompson St 19121 215-684-5087
Ruth King, prin. Fax 684-8881
Morton ES 800/K-5
2501 S 63rd St 19142 215-727-2164
Zena Sacks, prin. Fax 727-2341
Munoz-Marin S 900/K-8
3300 N 3rd St 19140 215-291-8825
Abigail Jimenez-Padron, prin. Fax 291-8845
Nebinger S 300/K-8
601 Carpenter St 19147 215-952-6202
Stephanie Phillips, prin. Fax 952-6392
Olney S 800/K-8
5301 N Water St 19120 215-456-3003
Dr. Henry Barsky, prin. Fax 456-5566

Overbrook ES 400/PK-5
2032 N 62nd St 19151 215-581-5691
Michelle Hayes-Flores, prin. Fax 581-5710
Pastorius S 600/K-8
5650 Sprague St 19138 215-951-4008
Kimberly Weston-Williams, prin. Fax 951-7307
Patterson ES 800/K-4
7000 Buist Ave 19142 215-492-6453
Anibal Soler, prin. Fax 492-6827
Peirce ES 400/K-6
2300 W Cambria St 19132 215-227-4411
Terrell Parris, prin. Fax 227-4699
Penn Alexander S 500/K-8
4209 Spruce St 19104 215-823-5465
Sheila Sydnor, prin. Fax 382-2031
Pennell ES 400/K-5
1800 Nedro Ave 19141 215-276-5267
Gina Kaplan, prin. Fax 276-5820
Penn Treaty MS 700/5-8
600 E Thompson St 19125 215-291-4715
Sam Howell, prin. Fax 291-5172
Pennypacker ES 500/K-6
1858 E Washington Ln 19138 215-276-5271
Sharon Glodek, prin. Fax 276-5843
Penrose ES 600/K-6
2515 S 78th St 19153 215-492-6455
Katherine Pendino, prin. Fax 492-6985
Pepper MS 800/5-8
2901 S 84th St 19153 215-492-6457
Yolanda Armstrong, prin. Fax 492-1844
Pollock ES 600/K-6
2850 Welsh Rd 19152 215-961-2004
Marilyn Carr, prin. Fax 961-2597
Potter-Thomas S 600/K-8
3001 N 6th St 19133 215-227-4423
Tania Kukulski, prin. Fax 227-7196
Powell ES 300/K-4
301 N 36th St 19104 215-823-8201
Margarite Holiday, prin. Fax 823-8215
Pratt ES 400/PK-6
2200 N 22nd St 19132 215-684-5083
Denise Young, prin. Fax 684-5058
Prince Hall ES 500/K-5
6101 N Gratz St 19141 215-276-5255
Sharon Patton Thaxton, prin. Fax 276-5803
Reynolds S 400/K-8
1429 N 24th St 19121 215-684-5061
Cheryl Hackett, prin. Fax 684-8888
Rhawnhurst ES 500/K-5
7809 Castor Ave 19152 215-728-5013
Karen Howell-Toomer, prin. Fax 728-5931
Rhoads S 500/K-8
4901 Parrish St 19139 215-581-5504
Ernestiine Caldwell, prin. Fax 581-3405
Richmond ES 700/K-5
2944 Belgrade St 19134 215-291-4718
Dr. Anthony Ciampoli, prin. Fax 291-4141
Roosevelt MS 400/6-8
430 E Washington Ln 19144 215-951-4170
Stefanie Ressler, prin. Fax 951-7762
Rowen ES 500/K-5
6841 N 19th St 19126 215-276-5251
Joyce Guy-Patton, prin. Fax 276-5806
Sharswood S 400/K-8
2300 S 2nd St 19148 215-952-6212
Maureen Skalski, prin. Fax 952-6405
Shaw MS 400/7-8
5400 Warrington Ave 19143 215-727-2161
Kwand Lang, prin. Fax 727-2248
Shawmont S 600/K-8
535 Shawmont Ave 19128 215-487-4466
Michael Graff, prin. Fax 487-4815
Sheppard ES 300/K-4
120 W Cambria St 19133 215-291-4711
James Otto, prin. Fax 291-4156
Sheridan ES 900/K-4
800 E Ontario St 19134 215-291-4724
Carmen Navarro-Maldonado, prin. Fax 291-4834
Sheridan West ES 200/5-8
3701 Frankford Ave 19124 215-537-2920
Bestainda Ortiz, prin. Fax 537-2962
Smedley ES 600/K-5
1790 Bridge St 19124 215-537-2523
Dr. James Cantwell, prin. Fax 537-2860
Smith ES 400/K-6
1900 Wharton St 19146 215-952-6222
Robert Frazier, prin. Fax 952-8669
Solis-Cohen ES 1,000/K-6
7001 Horrocks St 19149 215-728-5012
Joseph Bahm, prin. Fax 728-5982
Southwark S 500/K-8
1835 S 9th St 19148 215-952-8606
Jill Silverstein, prin. Fax 952-8670
Spring Garden S 300/K-8
1146 Melon St 19123 215-684-5070
Elois Dupree, prin. Fax 684-5059
Spruance S 1,300/K-8
6401 Horrocks St 19149 215-537-2514
Betty Klear, prin. Fax 537-2933
Stanton S 200/K-8
1700 Christian St 19146 215-875-3185
Diane Highsmith, prin. Fax 875-3711
Stanton S 400/K-8
2539 N 16th St 19132 215-227-4434
Malika Brooks, prin. Fax 227-4983
Stearne ES 600/PK-6
1655 Unity St 19124 215-537-2522
Darlene Vaughn, prin. Fax 537-2918
Steel ES 500/K-6
4301 Wayne Ave 19140 215-456-3008
Mary Bonner, prin. Fax 457-1466
Stetson MS 800/5-8
3200 B St 19134 215-291-4720
Renato Lajara, prin. Fax 291-4168
Sullivan ES 700/K-5
5300 Ditman St 19124 215-537-2524
Rumelle Scott, prin. Fax 537-2984

Sulzberger MS 300/8-8
4725 Fairmount Ave 19139 215-581-5633
Kathleen Fitzpatrick, prin.
Taggart S 500/K-8
400 W Porter St 19148 215-952-6228
Dr. Dianne Scott, prin. Fax 952-8502
Taylor ES 600/K-5
3698 N Randolph St 19140 215-227-4435
Debra Drossner, prin. Fax 227-4900
Tilden MS 600/6-8
6601 Elmwood Ave 19142 215-492-6454
Michelle Burns, prin. Fax 492-6128
Turner MS 200/8-8
5900 Baltimore Ave 19143 215-471-2906
Veronica Alston, prin. Fax 471-8745
Vare MS 500/5-8
2100 S 24th St 19145 215-952-8611
Dr. Patricia Cox, prin. Fax 952-8520
Vare S 400/K-8
1621 E Moyamensing Ave 19148 215-952-8620
Joanne Caprioti, prin. Fax 952-8508
Wagner MS 700/6-8
1701 W Chelten Ave 19126 215-276-5252
Penny Nixon, prin. Fax 276-5849
Waring ES 200/K-6
1801 Green St 19130 215-684-5073
Brianna Dunn, prin. Fax 684-5479
Washington Jr. MS 1,100/5-8
201 E Olney Ave 19120 215-456-0422
Gerald Branch, prin. Fax 456-2181
Washington S 300/K-8
1198 S 5th St 19147 215-952-6209
Margaret Bavwidinsi, prin. Fax 952-6431
Washington S 300/K-8
766 N 44th St 19104 215-823-8203
Carolynn Jackson, prin. Fax 823-8292
Webster ES 900/K-5
3400 Frankford Ave 19134 215-537-2525
Christine Connor, prin. Fax 537-2517
Welsh S 600/K-8
2331 N 4th St 19133 215-291-4708
Jeanette Fernandez, prin. Fax 291-4153
Whittier ES 500/K-6
3001 N 27th St 19132 215-227-4410
Betty Sago, prin. Fax 227-4777
Willard ES 800/K-4
2900 Emerald St 19134 215-291-4714
Ron Reilly, prin. Fax 291-4161
Wilson ES 300/K-6
1300 S 46th St 19143 215-823-8206
Sonya Harrison, prin. Fax 823-8233
Wilson MS 1,200/6-8
1800 Cottman Ave 19111 215-728-5015
Joel Boyd, prin. Fax 728-5051
Wister ES 400/K-6
67 E Bringhurst St 19144 215-951-4003
Donna Smith, prin. Fax 951-4534
Wright ES 400/K-6
2700 W Dauphin St 19132 215-684-5076
Anita Duke, prin. Fax 684-7018
Ziegler S 400/K-8
5935 Saul St 19149 215-537-2510
Linda Saxon, prin. Fax 537-2987

Al-Aqsa Islamic S 300/PK-12
1501 Germantown Ave 19122 215-765-6660
Abdur Rahman, prin. Fax 765-6640
All Saints' Episcopal S 100/PK-K
9601 Frankford Ave 19114 215-637-8788
Annunciation BVM S 200/PK-8
1150 Wharton St 19147 215-465-1416
Regina Tanghe, prin. Fax 465-0308
Ascension of Our Lord S 200/PK-8
735 E Westmoreland St 19134 215-739-6226
Teresa Richardson, prin. Fax 739-7317
Beulah Baptist Christian Day S 100/K-8
5001 Spruce St 19139 215-747-3347
Judith Barksdale, prin. Fax 747-7871
Blair Christian Academy 200/PK-12
220 W Upsal St 19119 215-438-6557
Dr. Karen Jenkins, admin. Fax 438-0661
Calvary Christian Academy 1,000/PK-12
13500 Philmont Ave 19116 215-969-1579
Dr. Samuel Pennington, hdmstr. Fax 969-9732
Calvary Temple Christian Academy 100/PK-8
3301 S 20th St 19145 215-462-2822
Dr. Virginia Voight, admin. Fax 551-7951
Cedar Grove Christian Academy 300/PK-8
6445 Bingham St 19111 215-725-3383
Arthur Hummel, hdmstr. Fax 725-7476
Chalutzim Academy 50/PK-6
7501 Haverford Ave 19151 215-477-4443
Linda Brown, admin. Fax 477-8710
Chestnut Hill Academy 600/PK-12
500 W Willow Grove Ave 19118 215-247-4700
Francis Steel, hdmstr. Fax 247-8516
Christian Stronghold Learning Academy 100/K-6
4701 Lancaster Ave 19131 215-878-6331
Reginald Dunstan, dir. Fax 878-7470
Christ the King S 500/K-8
3205 Chesterfield Rd 19114 215-632-1375
Sr. Trudy Helder, prin. Fax 632-0734
Cornerstone Christian Academy 200/K-8
PO Box 5520 19143 215-724-6858
Deborah Lee, prin. Fax 724-2827
Crooked Places Made Straight Chr Academy 300/K-12
711 S 50th St 19143 215-726-4151
Epiphany of Our Lord S 200/PK-8
1248 Jackson St 19148 215-467-5385
Patricia Cody, prin. Fax 336-5103
Faith Tabernacle S 200/1-12
3611 N Randolph St Ste 15 19140 215-221-0909
First Century Gospel S 100/1-10
6807 Rising Sun Ave 19111 215-742-6615
Frankford Friends S 100/PK-8
1500 Orthodox St 19124 215-533-5368
Penny Colgan-Davis, hdmstr. Fax 533-5523

Friends Select S 500/PK-12
1651 Benjamin Franklin Pkwy 19103 215-561-5900
Rose Hagan, hdmstr. Fax 864-2979
Germantown Friends S 900/K-12
31 W Coulter St 19144 215-951-2300
Richard Wade, hdmstr. Fax 951-2312
Gesu S 500/PK-8
1700 W Thompson St 19121 215-763-3660
Sr. Ellen Convey, prin. Fax 763-9844
Girard College S 700/1-12
2101 S College Ave 19121 215-787-2600
Dominic Cermele, pres. Fax 787-4435
Good Shepherd Lutheran S 100/PK-K
7234 Erdrick St 19135 215-331-0133
Graves Christian Academy 100/K-12
5447 Chester Ave 19143 215-727-7795
Sharon Flythe, admin. Fax 727-7804
Greene Street Friends S 200/PK-8
5511 Greene St 19144 215-438-7545
Edward Marshall, hdmstr. Fax 438-1121
High Street Christian Academy 50/PK-5
222 E High St 19144 215-848-8170
Linda Poole, admin. Fax 848-8170
Holmesburg Baptist Christian Academy 200/PK-8
7927 Frankford Ave 19136 215-335-4323
Linda Lewis, admin. Fax 335-2013
Holy Child S 400/PK-8
242 Hermitage St 19127 215-487-2796
Roselee Maddaloni, prin. Fax 242-0214
Holy Cross S 200/PK-8
144 E Mount Airy Ave 19119 215-242-0414
Sr. Rosanne Orchon, prin. Fax 242-0414
Holy Innocents Area S 300/K-8
1312 E Bristol St 19124 215-743-5909
Sr. Regina Mullen, prin. Fax 743-0199
Holy Redeemer S 300/K-8
915 Vine St 19107 215-922-0999
Lisa Cancelliere, prin. Fax 922-6674
Holy Spirit S 200/PK-8
1845 Hartranft St 19145 215-389-0715
Patricia Grady, prin. Fax 389-7527
Hope Church S 200/PK-12
6707 Old York Rd 19126 215-927-7770
Hunting Park Christian Academy 200/PK-8
4400 N 6th St 19140 215-324-1050
Tanya Figueiredo, dir. Fax 329-1310
Immaculate Heart of Mary S 500/PK-8
815 E Cathedral Rd 19128 215-482-2029
Kimberly Szypula, prin. Fax 482-1075
Immanuel Lutheran S 200/PK-8
1015 Cottman Ave 19111 215-725-7265
Alan Slawter, prin. Fax 725-2145
Incarnation of Our Lord S 400/K-8
425 Lindley Ave 19120 215-457-2779
Sr. Agnes Logan, prin. Fax 457-1328
La Salle Academy 100/3-8
1434 N 2nd St 19122 215-739-5804
Teresa Diamond, prin. Fax 739-1664
Logan Hope S 50/K-8
4934 N 13th St 19141 215-455-7442
Kenneth MacBain, dir. Fax 455-7176
Mary Mother of Peace Area Catholic S 400/K-8
6328 Buist Ave 19142 215-729-3603
Sr. Janet Mary Walters, prin. Fax 724-8728
Maternity BVM S 600/PK-8
9322 Old Bustleton Ave 19115 215-673-0235
Kathleen Veasy, prin. Fax 671-1347
Mother of Divine Grace S 200/K-8
2612 E Monmouth St 19134 215-426-7325
Jane Ellen White, prin. Fax 426-0753
Mt. Airy Christian Day S 100/PK-K
6401 Ogontz Ave 19126 215-276-2990
Rose Joseph, dir. Fax 270-1406
Mt. Sinai Christian Academy 50/PK-2
7282 Woodland Ave 19142 215-937-0417
Craig Davis, prin. Fax 937-0950
Nazareth Academy 200/1-8
4701 Grant Ave 19114 215-637-7777
Sr. Mary Allton, prin. Fax 637-5695
New Life Alternatives Christian Academy 100/PK-2
1993 N 63rd St 19151 215-877-3440
Bonita Patterson, admin. Fax 877-3743
Norwood Fontbonne Academy 500/PK-8
8891 Germantown Ave 19118 215-247-3811
Sr. Jean Laurich, prin. Fax 247-8405
Our Lady of Calvary S 900/PK-8
11023 Kipling Ln 19154 215-637-1648
Sr. Mildred Chesnavage, prin. Fax 637-3810
Our Lady of Consolation S 300/K-8
4816 Princeton Ave 19135 215-624-0505
Stephen DiCicco, prin. Fax 624-0536
Our Lady of Hope S 200/K-8
5218 N Broad St 19141 215-324-4211
Katherine Butler, prin. Fax 324-4142
Our Lady of Lourdes S 200/PK-8
1940 N 63rd St 19151 215-877-2727
Sr. M. Rosemary, prin. Fax 877-6042
Our Lady of Mt. Carmel S 300/1-8
2329 S 3rd St 19148 215-334-0584
Sr. Rosemarie O'Neill, prin. Fax 336-4519
Our Lady of Port Richmond S PK-8
3233 E Thompson St 19134 215-739-1920
Sr. Mary Ripp, prin.
Our Lady of Ransom S 200/K-8
6740 Roosevelt Blvd 19149 215-332-4352
Grace McGuirl, prin. Fax 332-6811
Our Lady of the Blessed Sacrament S 300/PK-8
344 N Felton St 19139 215-474-4011
Marguerittte Henry, prin. Fax 474-7807
Our Mother of Consolation S 200/PK-8
17 E Chestnut Hill Ave 19118 215-247-1060
Norman Hagy, prin. Fax 247-0590
Our Mother of Sorrows S 200/PK-8
1020 N 48th St 19131 215-473-5828
Sr. Patricia Bonner, prin. Fax 477-3096
Philadelphia Christian Academy 100/PK-8
6007 Larchwood Ave 19143 215-474-4530

Philadelphia S 400/PK-8
2501 Lombard St 19146 215-545-5323
Amy Vorenberg, hdmstr. Fax 546-1798
Politz Hebrew Academy 300/PK-8
9225 Old Bustleton Ave 19115 215-969-5960
Bessie Katz, dir. Fax 969-1037
Pope John Paul II Regional S 300/K-8
4435 Almond St 19137 215-535-3446
Linda Osik, prin. Fax 535-3858
Resurrection of Our Lord S 600/PK-8
2020 Shelmire Ave 19152 215-742-1127
Lucille Hillerman, prin. Fax 742-0947
Sacred Heart of Jesus S 200/PK-8
1329 E Moyamensing Ave 19147 215-462-4129
Sr. Patricia Mount, prin. Fax 462-9429
St. Anne S 200/PK-8
2343 E Tucker St 19125 215-634-4231
Sr. Margaret Duffy, prin. Fax 427-0608
St. Anselm S 500/K-8
12650 Dunks Ferry Rd 19154 215-632-1133
Geraldine Murphy, prin. Fax 632-3264
St. Athanasius-Immaculate Conception S 300/K-8
7105 Limekiln Pike 19138 215-424-5045
Sr. Joan Alminde, prin. Fax 927-6615
St. Benedict S 200/K-8
1935 Medary Ave 19141 215-424-8073
Lisa McLish, prin. Fax 424-5073
St. Bernard S 200/K-8
7360 Jackson St 19136 215-624-5204
Elaine McDowell, prin. Fax 624-8806
St. Bridget S 200/PK-8
3636 Stanton St 19129 215-844-4126
Susan Canio, prin. Fax 843-1413
St. Cecilia S 700/K-8
525 Rhawn St 19111 215-725-8588
Sr. Lisa Ann Golden, prin. Fax 725-0247
St. Christopher S 700/PK-8
13305 Proctor Rd 19116 215-673-5787
Patricia Kilbride, prin. Fax 673-8511
St. Cyprian S 200/K-8
6225 Cedar Ave 19143 215-748-4450
Paula Hawkins, prin. Fax 747-7794
St. Dominic S 400/PK-8
8510 Frankford Ave 19136 215-333-6703
Sr. Shaun Thomas, prin. Fax 333-9930
St. Donato S 200/PK-8
405 N 65th St 19151 215-748-2994
Amelia Luci, prin. Fax 748-0288
St. Francis DeSales S 500/K-8
917 S 47th St 19143 215-387-1749
Sr. Constance Touey, prin. Fax 387-6605
St. Francis Xavier S 200/PK-8
641 N 24th St 19130 215-763-6564
Dolores Butler, prin. Fax 236-2818
St. Gabriel S 200/PK-8
2917 Dickinson St 19146 215-468-7230
Sr. Noreen Friel, prin. Fax 468-2554
St. George S 200/PK-8
2700 E Venango St 19134 215-634-8803
Daniel Markowski, prin. Fax 634-3694
St. Helena S 300/PK-8
6101 N 5th St 19120 215-549-2947
Carol Volpe, prin. Fax 549-5947
St. Hugh of Cluny S 200/PK-8
3501 N Mascher St 19140 215-634-3060
Marilyn Benson, prin. Fax 634-2690
St. Ignatius of Loyola S 100/K-8
636 N 43rd St 19104 215-222-3626
Sr. Patricia Bonner, prin. Fax 222-8444
St. Jerome S 600/PK-8
3031 Stamford St 19136 215-624-0637
Sharon Nendza, prin. Fax 624-5711
St. Josaphat S 200/PK-8
4521 Longshore Ave 19135 215-332-8008
Fax 332-1876
St. Katherine of Siena S 600/K-8
9738 Frankford Ave 19114 215-637-2181
Sr. M. John, prin. Fax 637-4867
St. Laurentius S 200/K-8
1612 E Berks St 19125 215-423-8834
Sr. Rita Aponik, prin. Fax 426-4675
St. Malachy S 200/K-8
1419 N 11th St 19122 215-232-0696
Ruth Thornton Payne, prin. Fax 236-1434
St. Martha S 500/K-8
11321 Academy Rd 19154 215-632-0320
Karen Donofry, prin. Fax 632-5546
St. Martin De Porres S 400/K-8
2300 W Lehigh Ave 19132 215-223-6872
Sr. Nancy Fitzgerald, prin. Fax 233-4126
St. Martin De Porres S 200/K-8
44 W Logan St 19144 215-842-1266
Sr. Cheryl Hillig, prin. Fax 842-1400
St. Martin of Tours S 700/PK-8
999 E Sanger St 19124 215-533-3050
Sr. M. Stephen Meyer, prin. Fax 533-1579
St. Mary Interparochial S 200/K-8
247 S 5th St 19106 215-923-7522
Jeanne Meredith, prin. Fax 923-8502
St. Matthew S 1,100/K-8
3040 Cottman Ave 19149 215-333-3142
Sr. Kathleen Touey, prin. Fax 332-7242
St. Monica MS 200/5-8
16th and Porter Sts 19145 215-467-5338
Sr. Rita Murphy, prin. Fax 467-4599
St. Monica S 300/K-4
1720 W Ritner St 19145 215-334-3777
Sr. Rita Murphy, prin. Fax 389-0355
St. Nicholas of Tolentine S 400/PK-8
913 Pierce St 19148 215-468-0353
Sr. Mary Esther Carsele, prin. Fax 334-4255
St. Peter's S 200/PK-8
319 Lombard St 19147 215-925-3963
David Costello, hdmstr. Fax 925-3351
St. Peter the Apostle S 300/PK-8
1009 N 5th St 19123 215-922-5958
Sr. Rosalia Federici, prin. Fax 922-1015

St. Raymond of Penafort S 300/PK-8
7940 Williams Ave 19150 215-548-1919
Patricia Wright, prin. Fax 548-1925
St. Richard S 300/PK-8
1826 Pollock St 19145 215-467-5430
Stephen Hewitt, prin. Fax 468-3161
St. Rose of Lima S 200/K-8
1522 N Wanamaker St 19131 215-473-6030
Sr. Eileen Gillespie, prin. Fax 473-2338
St. Thomas Aquinas S 500/PK-8
1719 Morris St 19145 215-334-0878
Mary DiArenzo, prin. Fax 334-2357
St. Timothy S 900/PK-8
3033 Levick St 19149 215-338-9797
Dr. Joan Ciccone, prin. Fax 331-6457
St. Veronica S 200/K-8
3521 N 6th St 19140 215-225-1575
Sr. Koreen Cote, prin. Fax 225-2595
St. William S 400/PK-8
6238 Rising Sun Ave 19111 215-342-4488
Sr. Catherine Clark, prin. Fax 342-3115
Sharon Christian Academy 50/K-3
3955 Conshohocken Ave 19131 215-473-3446
Colona Roberts, prin. Fax 473-6711
Spring Garden Academy 100/PK-1
PO Box 15191 19130 215-563-9192
Pat Wegner, dir. Fax 563-8116
Springside S 700/PK-12
8000 Cherokee St 19118 215-247-7200
Priscilla Sands Ed.D., hdmstr. Fax 248-6377
Spruce Hill Christian S 200/K-8
4115 Baltimore Ave 19104 215-382-7839
Seth Cohen, hdmstr. Fax 382-7848
Stella Maris S 300/PK-8
814 Bigler St 19148 215-467-6262
Sr. L. Elizabeth Sandoli, prin. Fax 389-6040
Timothy Academy 200/PK-8
2637 N 4th St 19133 215-423-0416
Gwen Freeman, prin. Fax 423-4964
Trinity Christian S 100/PK-8
2300 S 18th St 19145 215-334-6657
Kelliann Link, prin.
Visitation BVM S 500/PK-8
300 E Lehigh Ave 19125 215-634-7280
Sr. Dolores Egner, prin. Fax 634-4062
Waldorf S of Philadelphia 200/PK-8
7500 Germantown Ave 19119 215-248-1662
Fax 248-6167
West Oak Lane Christian Academy 100/PK-5
7401 Limekiln Pike 19138 215-548-3450
Wynnefield Academy 200/PK-4
5200 Wynnefield Ave 19131 215-477-2422
Zion Christian Day S 50/PK-K
5307 N Front St 19120 215-329-4051

Philipsburg, Centre, Pop. 2,942
Philipsburg-Osceola Area SD 2,000/K-12
200 Short St 16866 814-342-1050
Dr. Stephen Benson, supt. Fax 342-7208
www.pomounties.org/
North Lincoln Hill ES 300/K-6
200 Short St 16866 814-342-4906
Robin Stewart, prin. Fax 342-7532
Philipsburg ES 400/K-6
1810 Black Moshannon Rd 16866 814-342-2870
Jeffrey Baker, prin. Fax 342-7526
Philipsburg-Osceola JHS 400/7-8
100 N 6th St 16866 814-342-4860
Robert Rocco, prin. Fax 342-7529
Other Schools – See Osceola Mills

Phoenixville, Chester, Pop. 15,420
Phoenixville Area SD 3,300/K-12
PO Box 809 19460 484-927-5000
Dr. Barbara Burke-Stevenson, supt. Fax 983-3729
www.pasd.com
Barkley ES 400/1-5
320 2nd Ave 19460 484-927-5300
Stephanie Zdrazil, prin. Fax 933-6471
East Pikeland ES 300/1-5
1191 Hares Hill Rd 19460 484-927-5350
Maryann Cox, prin. Fax 917-8437
Phoenixville Area K 200/K-K
100 School Ln 19460 484-927-5450
Karen Coldwell, prin. Fax 917-2125
Phoenixville Area MS 700/6-8
1330 Main St 19460 484-927-5200
Dr. Troy Czukoski, prin. Fax 933-6121
Schuylkill ES 600/1-5
290 S Whitehorse Rd 19460 484-927-5400
Dr. Frank Garritano, prin. Fax 933-6237

Holy Family S 400/PK-8
221 3rd Ave 19460 610-933-7562
Patricia Dura, prin. Fax 933-8823
Valley Forge Kinder House Montessori S 50/PK-5
865 Main St 19460 610-489-5757
Susan Kelly, hdmstr. Fax 489-6050

Picture Rocks, Lycoming, Pop. 682
East Lycoming SD
Supt. — See Hughesville
Ferrell ES 100/K-6
Center St 17762 570-584-3341
William Knapsack, prin. Fax 584-5467

Pine Forge, Berks

Wagner S 50/1-8
PO Box 345 19548 610-323-0340

Pine Grove, Schuylkill, Pop. 2,079
Pine Grove Area SD 1,700/K-12
103 School St 17963 570-345-2731
Dr. Terence Maher, supt. Fax 345-6473
www.pgasd.com
Pine Grove Area MS 500/5-8
105 School St 17963 570-345-2731
Steve Brill, prin. Fax 345-6075

Pine Grove ES 600/K-4
107 School St 17963 570-345-2731
Jennifer Bowen, prin. Fax 345-4356

Pine Grove Mills, Centre, Pop. 1,129
State College Area SD
Supt. — See State College
Ferguson Township ES 300/K-5
PO Box 237 16868 814-231-4119
Charlotte Zmyslo, prin. Fax 231-4163

Pipersville, Bucks
Palisades SD
Supt. — See Kintnersville
Tinicum ES 300/K-5
162 E Dark Hollow Rd 18947 610-294-9311
Scott Davis, prin. Fax 294-9182

Pitcairn, Allegheny, Pop. 3,449
Gateway SD
Supt. — See Monroeville
Pitcairn ES 200/K-4
435 Agatha St 15140 412-373-5850
Mary Catherine Reljac, prin. Fax 373-5853

Pittsburgh, Allegheny, Pop. 316,718
Avonworth SD 1,400/K-12
258 Josephs Ln 15237 412-369-8738
Dr. Valerie McDonald, supt. Fax 369-8746
www.avonworth.k12.pa.us
Avonworth ES 600/K-5
1320 Roosevelt Rd 15237 412-366-7170
Regis Mullen, prin. Fax 366-4146
Avonworth MS 300/6-8
256 Josephs Ln 15237 412-366-9650
Thomas Ralston, prin. Fax 358-9621

Baldwin-Whitehall SD 4,000/K-12
4900 Curry Rd 15236 412-885-7810
Dr. Lawrence Korchnak, supt. Fax 885-7802
www.bwschools.net/
Harrison MS 1,000/6-8
129 Windvale Dr 15236 412-885-7530
Rachel Gray, prin. Fax 885-6766
McAnnulty ES 300/K-1
5151 McAnulty Rd 15236 412-714-2020
Daniel Emanuelson, prin. Fax 714-2024
Paynter ES 700/K-5
3454 Pleasantvue Dr 15227 412-885-7535
Darlene DeFilippo, prin. Fax 885-6641
Whitehall ES, 4900 Curry Rd 15236 500/2-5
Andrea Dorfzaun, prin. 412-885-7525

Bethel Park SD
Supt. — See Bethel Park
Lincoln ES 300/K-4
1524 Hamilton Rd 15234 412-854-8618
Dorothy Stark, prin. Fax 833-5010

Brentwood Borough SD 1,300/K-12
3601 Brownsville Rd 15227 412-881-2227
Dr. Ronald Dufalla, supt. Fax 881-1640
www.brentwoodpgh.k12.pa.us
Brentwood MS 300/6-8
3601 Brownsville Rd 15227 412-881-4940
Lawrence Kushner Ph.D., prin. Fax 881-4170
Moore ES 200/K-5
3809 Dalewood St 15227 412-881-7776
Robert Monaghan, prin. Fax 881-8994
Other Schools – See Brentwood

Chartiers Valley SD 3,500/K-12
2030 Swallow Hill Rd 15220 412-429-2201
Anthony Skender, supt. Fax 429-2237
www.cvsd.net
Chartiers Valley IS 700/3-5
2030 Swallow Hill Rd 15220 412-429-2233
Ronald Yasher, prin. Fax 429-2380
Other Schools – See Bridgeville

Fox Chapel Area SD 4,600/K-12
611 Field Club Rd 15238 412-963-9600
Dr. Anne Stephens, supt. Fax 967-0697
www.fcasd.edu
Dorseyville MS 1,100/6-8
3732 Saxonburg Blvd 15238 412-967-2520
Rox Serrao, prin. Fax 967-2531
Fairview ES 300/K-5
710 Dorseyville Rd 15238 412-967-2401
Sari McNamara, prin. Fax 967-2408
Hartwood ES 400/K-5
3730 Saxonburg Blvd 15238 412-967-2480
Dr. Jacqueline Rauzan, prin. Fax 967-2531
Kerr ES 500/K-5
341 Kittanning Pike 15215 412-967-2490
Paul Noro, prin. Fax 967-2497
O'Hara ES 700/K-5
115 Cabin Ln 15238 412-967-2501
Dr. Vincent Delconte, prin. Fax 967-2510

Keystone Oaks SD 2,400/K-12
1000 Kelton Ave 15216 412-571-6000
Dr. William Urbanek, supt. Fax 571-6006
www.kosd.org
Aiken ES 200/K-5
881 Greentree Rd 15220 412-921-9166
Bobbi-Ann Barnes, prin. Fax 571-6164
Dormont ES 400/K-5
3200 Annapolis Ave 15216 412-571-6152
George Shevchik, prin. Fax 571-6151
Keystone Oaks MS 500/6-8
1002 Kelton Ave 15216 412-571-6146
Annette Todd, prin. Fax 571-6092
Myrtle Ave ES 300/K-5
3724 Myrtle Ave 15234 412-571-6137
Joseph Arcuri, prin. Fax 571-6051

Montour SD
Supt. — See Mc Kees Rocks
Ingram ES 200/K-4
40 Vancouver St 15205 412-921-2727
Jennifer Kosanovic, prin. Fax 920-7599

Mt. Lebanon SD 5,400/K-12
7 Horsman Dr 15228 412-344-2077
Dr. Timothy Steinhauer, supt. Fax 344-2047
www.mtlsd.org
Foster ES 300/K-5
700 Vermont Ave 15234 412-344-2162
Patrick Comeaux, prin. Fax 344-1121
Hoover ES 300/K-5
37 Robb Hollow Rd 15243 412-276-7411
Mary Ann Schnirel, prin. Fax 276-5524
Howe ES 300/K-5
400 Broadmoor Ave 15228 412-344-2157
David Zolkowski, prin. Fax 344-2236
Jefferson ES 200/K-5
11 Moffett St 15243 412-344-2167
Michael Schnirel, prin. Fax 344-0870
Jefferson MS 600/6-8
21 Moffett St 15243 412-344-2123
Joan Zacharias, prin. Fax 344-1252
Lincoln ES 400/K-5
2 Ralston Pl 15216 412-344-2147
James Salerno, prin. Fax 344-0813
Markham ES 300/K-5
165 Crescent Dr 15228 412-344-2152
Robert Mallery, prin. Fax 344-7088
Mellon MS 700/6-8
11 Castle Shannon Blvd 15228 412-344-2122
Brian McFeeley, prin. Fax 344-0590
Washington ES 400/K-5
735 Washington Rd 15228 412-344-2142
Emily Kirkham, prin. Fax 344-3314

North Allegheny SD 8,000/K-12
200 Hillvue Ln 15237 412-366-2100
Dr. Patricia Green, supt. Fax 369-5513
www.northallegheny.org
Carson MS, 200 Hillvue Ln 15237 700/6-8
Katherine Jenkins, prin. 412-369-5520
Ingomar ES 400/K-5
602 W Ingomar Rd 15237 412-366-9665
Dr. Paul Chmara, prin. Fax 366-5679
Ingomar MS 500/6-8
1521 Ingomar Heights Rd 15237 412-348-1470
Tammy Andreyko, prin. Fax 366-4487
McKnight ES 700/K-5
500 Cumberland Rd 15237 412-635-4105
Steve Parks, prin. Fax 635-4115
Peebles ES 400/K-5
8625 Peebles Rd 15237 412-366-9667
Susie Bjalobok, prin. Fax 635-2464
Other Schools – See Allison Park, Bradfordwoods, Sewickley, Wexford

North Hills SD 4,400/K-12
135 6th Ave 15229 412-318-6000
Dr. Joseph Goodnack, supt. Fax 318-1084
www.nhsd.net
Highcliff ES 200/K-6
156 Peony Ave 15229 412-318-1582
Beth Williams, prin. Fax 318-1584
McIntyre ES 300/K-6
200 McIntyre Rd 15237 412-318-1622
Amy Mathieu, prin. Fax 318-1624
Perrysville ES 200/K-6
950 Perry Hwy 15237 412-318-1602
Elaine Obidowski, prin. Fax 318-1604
Ross ES 600/K-6
90 Houston Rd 15237 412-318-1542
David Lieberman, prin. Fax 318-1544
Seville ES 200/K-6
100 Enger Ave 15214 412-318-1662
Lindsay Hauck, prin. Fax 318-1664
West View ES 500/K-6
47 Chalfonte Ave 15229 412-318-1502
Frank Brettschnneider, prin. Fax 318-1504

Northgate SD 1,400/K-12
591 Union Ave 15202 412-732-3300
Dr. Reggie Bonfield, supt. Fax 734-8008
www.northgate.k12.pa.us
Avalon ES 200/K-6
721 California Ave 15202 412-732-3300
Francesca Lattari, prin. Fax 734-8054
Other Schools – See Bellevue

Penn Hills SD 4,900/K-12
309 Collins Dr 15235 412-793-7000
Dr. Joseph Carroll, supt. Fax 793-6402
www.phsd.k12.pa.us
Dible ES 500/K-5
1079 Jefferson Rd 15235 412-372-1841
Kathleen Little, prin. Fax 373-1726
Penn Hebron ES 500/K-5
102 Duff Rd 15235 412-242-7770
Sandra Barker, prin. Fax 242-7905
Washington ES 400/K-5
2501 Main St 15235 412-793-2800
Thomas Iaquinta, prin. Fax 793-1414
Other Schools – See Verona

Pittsburgh SD 26,800/PK-12
341 S Bellefield Ave 15213 412-622-3600
Mark Roosevelt, supt. Fax 622-3604
www.pps.k12.pa.us
Allegheny Traditional Academy 400/K-5
810 Arch St 15212 412-323-4100
Viola Burgess, prin. Fax 323-4109
Allegheny Traditional Academy 300/6-8
810 Arch St 15212 412-323-4115
Toni Kendrick, prin. Fax 323-4114
Arlington IS 300/3-8
2500 Jonquil St 15210 412-488-3641
Dr. Cindi Muehlbauer, prin. Fax 488-3760
Arlington PS K-2
2429 Charcot St 15210 412-488-3700
Dr. Cindi Muehlbauer, prin. Fax 488-4709
Arsenal ES PK-5
215 39th St 15201 412-622-7307
Kerry Francis, prin. Fax 622-7310
Arsenal MS 500/6-8
220 40th St 15201 412-622-5740
Debra Rucki, prin. Fax 622-5743
Banksville ES 200/PK-5
1001 Carnahan Rd 15216 412-571-7400
Dr. Patricia Washington, prin. Fax 571-7398
Beechwood ES 400/PK-5
810 Rockland Ave 15216 412-571-7390
Sally Rifugiato, prin. Fax 571-7393
Brookline S 500/K-8
500 Woodbourne Ave 15226 412-571-7380
Valerie Lucas, prin. Fax 571-7386
Carmalt Science & Technology Academy 600/PK-8
1550 Breining St 15226 412-885-7760
Dr. Sandra Och, prin. Fax 885-7764
Chartiers ECC PK-PK
3799 Chartiers Ave 15204 412-928-6560
Fax 928-6564
Colfax S 600/K-8
2332 Beechwood Blvd 15217 412-422-3525
David May-Stein, prin. Fax 422-4896
Concord ES 300/K-5
2350 Brownsville Rd 15210 412-885-7755
Susan Barie, prin. Fax 885-7758
Dilworth Traditional Academy 400/PK-5
6200 Stanton Ave 15206 412-665-5000
Monica Lamar, prin. Fax 665-5012
Faison Arts IS 50/5-8
8080 Bennett St 15221 412-247-7840
Kevin McGuire, prin. Fax 247-7850
Faison Arts PS K-4
7430 Tioga St 15208 412-247-0305
Yvona Smith, prin. Fax 247-0105
Fort Pitt ES 500/PK-5
5101 Hillcrest St 15224 412-665-2020
Verna Arnold, prin. Fax 665-2247
Fulton Academy 300/PK-5
5799 Hampton St 15206 412-665-4590
Kevin Bivins, prin. Fax 665-4969
Grandview ES 300/K-5
845 McLain St 15210 412-488-6605
Dr. Ethel Flam, prin. Fax 488-6846
Greenfield S 500/K-8
1 Alger St 15207 412-422-3535
Eric Rosenthall, prin. Fax 422-4879
Homewood ECC PK-PK
7100 Hamilton Ave 15208 412-665-3996
Fax 665-2035
King S 700/PK-8
50 Montgomery Pl 15212 412-323-4160
Joan Murphy, prin. Fax 323-4165
Liberty ES 400/K-5
601 Filbert St 15232 412-622-8450
Barbara Soroczak, prin. Fax 622-8499
Lincoln IS 100/5-8
7109 Hermitage St 15208 412-247-7880
Dr. Regina Holley, prin. Fax 247-7888
Lincoln PS 200/K-4
328 Lincoln Ave 15206 412-665-3980
Dr. Regina Holley, prin. Fax 665-4959
Linden ES 400/K-5
725 S Linden Ave 15208 412-665-3996
Carla Berdnik, prin. Fax 665-2035
Manchester S 300/PK-8
1612 Manhattan St 15233 412-323-3100
Henry Stephens, prin. Fax 323-3015
McCleary ECC PK-PK
5251 Holmes St 15201 412-622-5740
Fax 622-5743
Mifflin S 500/PK-8
1290 Mifflin Rd 15207 412-464-4350
Edward Littlehale, prin. Fax 464-4355
Miller African Centered Academy 300/PK-8
2055 Bedford Ave 15219 412-338-3830
Alvin Gipson, prin. Fax 338-3834
Minadeo ES 600/PK-5
6502 Lilac St 15217 412-422-3520
Glory Getty, prin. Fax 422-4889
Morrow ES 500/PK-5
1611 Davis Ave 15212 412-734-6600
Dr. Annette Piper, prin. Fax 734-6606
Murray S 500/PK-8
800 Rectenwald St 15210 412-488-6815
James Nath, prin. Fax 488-2569
Northview Elementary Academy 300/PK-5
310 Mount Pleasant Rd 15214 412-323-3130
David May, prin. Fax 323-3197
Phillips ES 300/K-5
1901 Sarah St 15203 412-488-5190
Rodney Necciai, prin. Fax 488-4200
Pittsburgh Classical Academy 300/6-8
1463 Chartiers Ave 15220 412-928-3110
Valerie Merlo, prin. Fax 928-3106
Pittsburgh Montessori S 300/PK-8
201 S Graham St 15206 412-665-2010
Cynthia Wallace, prin. Fax 665-2038
Rogers CAPA Academy 300/6-8
5525 Columbo St 15206 412-665-2000
Ronald Jones, prin. Fax 665-2006
Rooney MS 300/6-8
3530 Fleming Ave 15212 412-732-6700
Jennifer Mikula, prin. Fax 732-6706
Roosevelt IS 2-5
17 W Cherryhill St 15210 412-885-7780
Vincent Lewandowski, prin. Fax 885-7784
Roosevelt PS 200/PK-1
200 The Blvd 15210 412-885-7788
Vincent Lewandowski, prin. Fax 885-7789
Schaeffer IS 100/4-8
3128 Allendale St 15204 412-778-2170
Dr. Cynthia Zurchin, prin. Fax 778-2174
Schaeffer PS 200/K-3
1235 Clairhaven St 15205 412-928-6560
LaVerne Anthony, prin. Fax 928-6564
Schiller Classical Academy 300/6-8
1018 Peralta St 15212 412-323-4190
Paula Heinzman, prin. Fax 323-4192
South Brook MS 400/6-8
779 Dunster St 15226 412-572-8170
Gina Reichert, prin. Fax 572-8177
South Hills MS 500/6-8
595 Crane Ave 15216 412-572-8130
Dr. Deborah Ann Cox, prin. Fax 572-8148
Spring Garden ECC PK-PK
1502 Spring Garden Ave 15212 412-323-3000
Fax 323-3008
Spring Hill ES 200/K-5
1351 Damas St 15212 412-323-3000
Todd Van Horn, prin. Fax 323-3008
Sterrett Classical Academy 400/6-8
7100 Reynolds St 15208 412-247-7870
Sarah Sumpter, prin. Fax 247-7877
Stevens S 300/K-8
822 Crucible St 15220 412-928-6550
Virginia Hill, prin. Fax 928-6554
Sunnyside S 400/K-8
4801 Stanton Ave 15201 412-665-2040
Laura Dadey, prin. Fax 665-2042
Vann S 200/K-8
631 Watt St 15219 412-622-8455
Derrick Hardy, prin. Fax 622-5739
Weil Technology Institute 200/PK-8
2250 Centre Ave 15219 412-338-3840
Mark McClinchie, prin. Fax 338-3848
West Liberty ES 300/K-5
785 Dunster St 15226 412-571-7420
Kathy Moran, prin. Fax 571-7424
Westwood S 400/K-8
508 Shadyhill Rd 15205 412-928-6570
Denyse Littles-Cullens, prin. Fax 928-6577
Whittier ES 300/K-5
150 Meridan St 15211 412-488-8211
Elaine Wallace, prin. Fax 488-4255
Woolslair ES 300/K-5
501 40th St 15224 412-623-8800
Victoria Burgess, prin. Fax 623-8810

Plum Borough SD 4,300/K-12
900 Elicker Rd 15239 412-795-0100
Lillian Naccarati Ed.D., supt. Fax 795-9115
www.pbsd.k12.pa.us
Center ES 500/K-6
201 Center New Texas Rd 15239 412-795-4420
Judith Mahoney, prin. Fax 795-1650
Holiday Park ES 500/K-6
4795 Havana Dr 15239 412-795-4430
Fran Sciullo, prin. Fax 795-1723
O'Block JHS 700/7-8
440 Presque Isle Dr 15239 724-733-2400
Joseph Fishell, prin. Fax 327-6880
Pivik ES 500/K-6
100 School Rd 15239 412-795-4580
Gail Yamnitzky, prin. Fax 795-2824
Regency Park ES 300/K-6
606 Millers Ln 15239 412-795-0660
Marla Wagner, prin. Fax 795-2923
Stevenson ES 400/K-6
313 Holiday Park Dr 15239 724-733-1500
D. Jason Knisely, prin. Fax 325-4876

Shaler Area SD
Supt. — See Glenshaw
Marzolf PS 400/K-3
101 Marzolf Rd Ext 15209 412-492-1200
Martin Martynuska, prin. Fax 486-8702
Reserve PS 200/K-3
2107 Lonsdale St 15212 412-492-1200
Frederick Pelkofer, prin. Fax 321-4507

Upper St. Clair SD
Supt. — See Upper Saint Clair
Baker ES 400/K-4
2300 Morton Rd 15241 412-833-1600
Dr. Ruth Ann Matyuf, prin. Fax 221-5283
Boyce MS 600/5-6
1500 Boyce Rd 15241 412-833-1600
Karen Brown, prin. Fax 854-2161
Eisenhower ES 500/K-4
100 Warwick Dr 15241 412-833-1600
Mark Miller, prin. Fax 854-1295
Ft. Couch MS 700/7-8
515 Fort Couch Rd 15241 412-833-1600
Joseph DeMar, prin. Fax 854-3095
Streams ES 400/K-4
1560 Ashlawn Dr 15241 412-833-1600
Dr. Claire Miller, prin. Fax 854-4374

West Jefferson Hills SD
Supt. — See Jefferson Hills
McClellan ES 300/K-5
360 School Ln 15236 412-655-2700
Margaret Sollon, prin. Fax 655-3526
Pleasant Hills MS 600/6-8
404 Old Clairton Rd 15236 412-655-8680
Daniel Como, prin. Fax 655-5691

Woodland Hills SD 4,900/K-12
2430 Greensburg Pike 15221 412-731-1300
Walter Calinger Ph.D., supt. Fax 731-1562
www.whsd.k12.pa.us
Dickson IS 400/4-6
7301 Schoyer Ave 15218 412-731-5816
Allison Kline, prin. Fax 731-5818
Edgewood PS 600/K-3
241 Maple Ave 15218 412-731-2238
Jean McAteer-Livingston, prin. Fax 731-2256
Shaffer PS 300/K-3
37 Garden Ter 15221 412-371-4535
Mary Duncan, prin. Fax 371-4571
Wilkins PS 500/K-3
362 Churchill Rd 15235 412-824-3231
Karen Bloch, prin. Fax 824-3244
Woodland Hills JHS - West 600/7-8
7600 Evans St 15218 412-351-0698
Janet Wilson-Carter, prin. Fax 351-5841
Other Schools – See Braddock, Rankin

Assumption S 200/K-8
35 N Jackson Ave 15202 412-761-7887
Joanne Britt, prin. Fax 761-7620
Bishop John McDowell Regional S 100/PK-8
3198 Schieck St 15227 412-884-5676
Mark Grgurich, prin. Fax 884-8610
Bishop Leonard-St. Mary of the Mount S 200/PK-8
115 Bigham St 15211 412-431-4645
Cynthia Baldrige, prin. Fax 381-0770
Brookline Regional S 200/PK-8
2690 Waddington Ave 15226 412-563-0858
Janet Salley-Rakoczy, prin. Fax 341-5610
Campus S 300/PK-8
3333 5th Ave 15213 412-578-6158
Dr. Anne-Marie Balzano, prin. Fax 578-6676
Cardinal Wright S 200/K-8
711 W Commons 15212 412-231-8248
Kenneth Macek, prin. Fax 231-0835
Community Day S 300/K-8
6424 Forward Ave 15217 412-521-1100
Ms. Avi Baron Munro, hdmstr. Fax 521-4511
Eden Christian Academy - Berkeley Hills 400/PK-6
206 Siebert Rd 15237 412-364-8055
Maureen Maier, prin. Fax 364-8330
Elizabeth Seton S 200/PK-8
3021 Landis St 15204 412-331-4529
Sarah Tonski, prin. Fax 331-8734
Ellis S 500/PK-12
6425 5th Ave 15206 412-661-5992
Mary Grant Ph.D., hdmstr. Fax 661-3979
Falk S 300/K-8
4060 Allequippa St 15261 412-624-8020
Dr. Wendell McConnaha, dir. Fax 624-1303
Fox Chapel Country Day S 100/PK-5
620 Squaw Run Rd E 15238 412-963-8644
Camille Wright, hdmstr. Fax 963-7123
Hillel Academy of Pittsburgh 200/K-12
5685 Beacon St 15217 412-521-8131
Daniel Kraut, dir. Fax 521-5150
Holy Rosary S 200/K-8
7120 Kelly St 15208 412-731-2567
Ednarita Canton, prin. Fax 731-3476
Holy Spirit S 100/K-8
100 Howard St 15209 412-821-4805
Linda Bechtol, prin. Fax 821-4714
Imani Christian Academy 200/K-12
235 Eastgate Dr 15235 412-731-7982
Milton Raiford, hdmstr. Fax 731-7343
Immaculate Conception S 200/PK-8
321 Edmond St 15224 412-621-5199
Sr. Mary Cook, prin. Fax 621-5601
Jubilee Christian S 100/K-6
255 Washington Rd 15216 412-561-5917
Mary Wolling, prin. Fax 561-2857
Mt. Nazareth Learning Center 100/PK-K
285 Bellevue Rd 15229 412-931-9761
Sr. Audrey Merski, prin. Fax 931-4533
Our Lady of Grace S 300/PK-8
1734 Bower Hill Rd 15243 412-279-6611
Lindsay Pfister, prin. Fax 279-6755
Pittsburgh Urban Christian S 100/K-8
809 Center St 15221 412-244-1779
Bob Phelps, prin. Fax 244-9027
Sacred Heart S 400/PK-8
325 Emerson St 15206 412-441-1582
Sr. Lynn Rettinger, prin. Fax 441-2798
St. Agnes S 200/K-8
120 Robinson St 15213 412-682-1129
Patricia Coffield, prin. Fax 687-8091
St. Anne S 200/PK-8
4040 Willow Ave 15234 412-561-7720
Cathy Jakubowski, prin. Fax 561-7927
St. Athanasius S 100/PK-8
2 Wentworth Ave 15229 412-931-6633
Gabrielle Yingling, prin. Fax 459-0104
St. Bartholomew S 100/PK-8
111 Erhardt Dr 15235 412-242-2511
Linda Pricer, prin. Fax 242-8317
St. Bede S 400/PK-8
6920 Edgerton Ave 15208 412-661-9425
Mary Drummond, prin. Fax 661-0447
St. Benedict the Moor S 200/K-8
2900 Bedford Ave 15219 412-682-3755
Sr. Margery Kundar, prin. Fax 682-4058
St. Bernard S 400/PK-8
401 Washington Rd 15216 412-341-5444
Dan Wagner, prin. Fax 341-2044
St. Cyril of Alexandria S 200/PK-8
3854 Brighton Rd 15212 412-761-5043
Margaret Bookser, prin. Fax 761-0840
St. Edmund's Academy 300/PK-8
5705 Darlington Rd 15217 412-521-1907
Dr. William Kindler, hdmstr. Fax 521-1260
St. Elizabeth S 500/PK-8
1 Grove Pl Ste 5 15236 412-881-2958
Maureen Richardson, prin. Fax 882-0111
St. Gabriel S 400/K-8
5200 Greenridge Dr 15236 412-882-3353
Barbara Sawyer, prin. Fax 882-2125
St. James S 200/K-8
721 Rebecca Ave 15221 412-242-3515
Sr. Marie Wolf, prin. Fax 241-3199
St. John Neumann S 100/K-8
250 44th St 15201 412-682-5096
Sr. Coletta Adelsberg, prin. Fax 682-0811
St. John the Baptist S 300/K-8
418 Unity Center Rd 15239 412-793-0555
Sandra Stonebraker, prin. Fax 793-4001
St. Louise de Marillac S 400/K-8
310 McMurray Rd 15241 412-835-0600
Dianne Tima, prin. Fax 835-2898
St. Margaret S 300/PK-8
915 Alice St 15220 412-922-4765
Catherine Millitzer, prin. Fax 922-4647
St. Maurice S 300/K-8
2001 Ardmore Blvd 15221 412-351-5403
Sr. Judith Stojhovic, prin. Fax 273-9114
St. Phillip S 400/PK-8
52 W Crafton Ave 15205 412-928-2742
Sr. Geraldine Marr, prin. Fax 920-7310
St. Raphael S 200/PK-8
1154 Chislett St 15206 412-661-0288
Sr. Judith Kenaan, prin. Fax 661-0428
St. Rosalia Academy 200/PK-8
411 Greenfield Ave 15207 412-521-3005
Sr. Delia McNeirney, prin. Fax 521-2763
St. Sebastian S 400/K-8
307 Siebert Rd 15237 412-364-8999
Diane Dickson, prin. Fax 364-5891
St. Sylvester S 200/PK-8
30 W Willock Rd 15227 412-882-9900
Kathleen Fox, prin. Fax 882-0153
St. Teresa of Avila S 300/PK-8
800 Avila Ct 15237 412-367-9001
Sr. Karen Brink, prin. Fax 364-1172
St. Thomas More S 200/PK-8
134 Fort Couch Rd 15241 412-833-1412
Sheila Riley, prin. Fax 833-5597
Shady Side Academy Junior S 200/PK-5
400 S Braddock Ave 15221 412-473-4400
Cheryl Little, hdmstr. Fax 473-4420
Shady Side Academy MS 200/6-8
500 Squaw Run Rd E 15238 412-968-3100
Thomas Southard, hdmstr. Fax 968-3008
SS. Simon & Jude S 100/PK-8
1625 Greentree Rd 15220 412-563-1353
Sr. Norma Zanieski, prin. Fax 563-8617
Trinity Christian S 300/K-12
299 Ridge Ave 15221 412-242-8886
Dale McLane, supt. Fax 242-8859
Waldorf S of Pittsburgh 100/PK-5
201 S Winebiddle St 15224 412-441-5792
K. Christopherson-Clark, admin. Fax 441-5179
Winchester Thurston S 600/PK-12
555 Morewood Ave 15213 412-578-7500
Gary Niels, hdmstr. Fax 578-7504
Word of God S 300/PK-8
7436 McClure Ave 15218 412-371-8587
Sr. Mary Powers, prin. Fax 371-0268
Yeshiva S 100/PK-12
PO Box 81868 15217 412-422-7300
Rabbi Yisroel Rosenfeld, dean Fax 422-5930

Pittston, Luzerne, Pop. 7,689
Pittston Area SD 3,200/K-12
5 Stout St 18640 570-654-2271
Dr. Ross Scarantino, supt. Fax 654-5548
www.pittstonarea.com
Pittston Area MS 700/6-8
120 New St 18640 570-655-2927
Patrick Bilbow, prin. Fax 654-0862
Pittston Area PS 400/1-2
210 Rock St 18640 570-655-3786
Teresa McAndrew, prin. Fax 883-1381
Pittston City IS 700/3-5
110 New St 18640 570-654-7176
Stanley Waleski, prin. Fax 883-1385
Other Schools – See Dupont

Wyoming Area SD
Supt. — See Exeter
Dymond ES 200/K-6
Sutton Creek Rd 18643 570-388-6527
Robert Kaluzavich, prin. Fax 388-2720

St. Mary Assumption S 200/K-8
41 Carroll St 18640 570-654-8313
Mary Jane Kozick, prin. Fax 654-7052
St. Mary ECC 200/PK-PK
535 N Main St 18640 570-654-8188
Mary Jane Kozick, prin. Fax 654-0195

Plains, Luzerne, Pop. 4,694
Wilkes-Barre Area SD
Supt. — See Wilkes Barre
Solomon/Plains ES 800/K-6
41 Abbott St 18705 570-826-7222
Sean Flynn, prin. Fax 820-3736
Solomon/Plains JHS 500/7-8
43 Abbott St 18705 570-826-7224
John Wuloski, prin. Fax 820-3715

Pleasant Gap, Centre, Pop. 1,699
Bellefonte Area SD
Supt. — See Bellefonte
Pleasant Gap ES 300/K-5
230 S Main St 16823 814-359-2739
Tammie Burnaford, prin. Fax 359-4552

Pleasantville, Venango, Pop. 1,039
Titusville Area SD
Supt. — See Titusville
Pleasantville ES, 374 N Main St 16341 200/1-5
Ted Wells, prin. 814-827-2715

Plymouth, Luzerne, Pop. 6,161
Wyoming Valley West SD
Supt. — See Kingston
Main Street ES 400/K-5
165 W Main St 18651 570-779-9529
Raymond Whalen, prin. Fax 779-2161

Plymouth Meeting, Montgomery, Pop. 6,241
Colonial SD 4,600/K-12
230 Flourtown Rd 19462 610-834-1670
Dr. Vincent Cotter, supt. Fax 834-7535
www.colonialsd.org
Colonial ES 700/4-5
230 Flourtown Rd 19462 610-941-0426
Therese Boegly, prin. Fax 834-8701
Colonial MS 1,100/6-8
716 Belvoir Rd 19462 610-275-5100
Robert Fahler, prin. Fax 278-2447
Plymouth ES 400/K-3
542 Plymouth Rd 19462 610-825-8190
Judith Lipson, prin. Fax 825-7853
Other Schools – See Conshohocken, Lafayette Hill

Epiphany of Our Lord S 200/PK-8
3040 Walton Rd 19462 610-825-0160
Miriam Havey, prin. Fax 825-0460
Plymouth Meeting Friends S 200/PK-6
2150 Butler Pike 19462 610-828-2288
Anne Javsicas, hdmstr. Fax 828-2390

Pocono Pines, Monroe, Pop. 824
Pocono Mountain SD
Supt. — See Swiftwater
Tobyhanna Elementary Center 700/K-5
HC 89 Box 36 18350 570-839-7121
Dr. Anastasia D'Angelo, prin. Fax 646-6147

Character Builders Christian Academy 50/PK-3
PO Box 179 18350 570-643-7002
Herman Simpson, admin. Fax 643-4108

Point Marion, Fayette, Pop. 1,276
Albert Gallatin Area SD
Supt. — See Uniontown
Friendship Hill ES 200/K-5
218 New Geneva Rd 15474 724-725-9515
Lara Bezjak, prin. Fax 725-9515
Gallatin South MS 400/6-8
224 New Geneva Rd 15474 724-725-5241
Ralph Garcia, prin. Fax 725-5424

Polk, Venango, Pop. 1,009
Franklin Area SD
Supt. — See Franklin
Polk ES 100/K-6
PO Box 976 16342 814-437-3411
Brenda Fry, prin. Fax 432-7405

Portage, Cambria, Pop. 2,686
Portage Area SD 700/PK-12
84 Mountain Ave 15946 814-736-9636
Richard Bernazzoli, supt. Fax 736-9634
portage.schoolwires.com
Portage Area ES 300/PK-7
84 Mountain Ave 15946 814-736-9636
Melodie Brunett, prin. Fax 736-4165

Port Allegany, McKean, Pop. 2,260
Port Allegany SD 1,100/K-12
20 Oak St 16743 814-642-2596
Martin Flint, supt. Fax 642-9574
www.pahs.net
Port Allegany ES 500/K-6
85 Clyde Lynch Dr 16743 814-642-9557
Terry Kriner, prin. Fax 642-7778

Port Carbon, Schuylkill, Pop. 1,919

St. Stephen Regional S 100/K-8
214 Valley St 17965 570-622-3063
Mildred Scarbinsky, prin. Fax 622-3689

Portersville, Butler, Pop. 261

Portersville Christian S 300/PK-12
343 E Portersville Rd 16051 724-368-8787
Jeffrey DeSantes, admin. Fax 368-3100

Port Matilda, Centre, Pop. 630
Bald Eagle Area SD
Supt. — See Wingate
Port Matilda ES 200/K-6
PO Box 558 16870 814-692-7429
Betsy Dickey, prin. Fax 692-8703

State College Area SD
Supt. — See State College
Gray's Woods ES 400/K-5
160 Brackenbourne Dr 16870 814-235-6100
Linda Colangelo, prin. Fax 272-8152

Port Royal, Juniata, Pop. 973
Juniata County SD
Supt. — See Mifflintown
Tuscarora Valley ES 100/K-5
401 8th St 17082 717-527-4635
Andy Kinzer, prin. Fax 436-2777

Pottstown, Montgomery, Pop. 21,551
Owen J. Roberts SD 4,300/K-12
901 Ridge Rd 19465 610-469-5100
Dr. Myra Forrest, supt. Fax 469-0748
www.ojrsd.com
East Coventry ES 600/K-6
932 Sanatoga Rd 19465 610-469-5103
Ryan Monaghan, prin. Fax 495-0346
French Creek ES 400/K-6
3590 Coventryville Rd 19465 610-469-5104
Malinda McKillip, prin. Fax 469-5738
North Coventry ES 600/K-6
475 Kemp Rd 19465 610-469-5105
Dr. James Melchor, prin. Fax 469-5864
Roberts MS 700/7-8
881 Ridge Rd 19465 610-469-5102
Dr. Robert Salladino, prin. Fax 469-5832
Other Schools – See Chester Springs, Spring City

Pottsgrove SD 3,200/K-12
1301 Kauffman Rd 19464 610-327-2277
Dr. Bradley Landis, supt. Fax 327-2530
www.pgsd.org
Lower Pottsgrove ES 700/K-5
1329 Buchert Rd 19464 610-323-7510
Ellen Siegel, prin. Fax 323-1911
Pottsgrove MS 800/6-8
1351 N Hanover St 19464 610-326-8243
Dr. William Ziegler, prin. Fax 718-0581
Ringing Rocks ES 400/K-5
1401 Kauffman Rd 19464 610-323-0903
Irene Klucar, prin. Fax 327-8893
Other Schools – See Stowe

Pottstown SD 3,200/PK-12
230 Beech St 19464 610-323-8200
David Krem, supt. Fax 326-6540
www.pottstownschools.com
Barth ES 300/PK-5
467 W Walnut St 19464 610-970-6675
Robert Giering, prin. Fax 970-4715
Edgewood ES 300/PK-5
920 Morris St 19464 610-970-6635
Dr. Angela Tuck, prin. Fax 327-1800
Franklin ES 300/PK-5
970 N Franklin St 19464 610-970-6640
Mia DiPaolo, prin. Fax 970-6742
Lincoln ES 400/PK-5
461 N York St 19464 610-970-6646
Loretta Hoch, prin. Fax 970-6743
Pottstown MS 700/6-8
600 N Franklin St 19464 610-970-6665
Gail Cooper, prin. Fax 970-8738
Rupert ES 300/PK-5
1230 South St 19464 610-970-6660
Matthew Moyer, prin. Fax 970-4188

Coventry Christian S 300/PK-4
962 E Schuylkill Rd 19465 610-326-3366
Mark Niehls, supt. Fax 326-9370
St. Aloysius S 400/K-8
220 N Hanover St 19464 610-326-6167
Sr. Wanda Marie Schlager, prin. Fax 970-9960
West-Mont Christian Academy 300/PK-12
873 S Hanover St 19465 610-326-7690
Dr. James Smock, admin. Fax 326-7126
Wyndcroft S 200/PK-8
1395 Wilson St 19464 610-326-0544
Dr. Kathleen Wunner, hdmstr. Fax 326-9931

Pottsville, Schuylkill, Pop. 14,764
Pottsville Area SD 3,100/K-12
1501 Laurel Blvd 17901 570-621-2900
Dr. James Gallagher, supt. Fax 621-2025
www.pottsville.k12.pa.us/
Clarke ES 1,100/K-4
601 N 16th St 17901 570-621-2945
Richard Boris, prin. Fax 622-7136
Lengel MS 800/5-8
1541 Laurel Blvd 17901 570-621-2923
Edward Hauck, prin. Fax 621-2999

All Saints Catholic S 100/PK-8
112 S 7th St 17901 570-622-0106
Kimberly Fetter, prin. Fax 622-4737
Trinity Center for Children 100/PK-6
200 S 2nd St 17901 570-621-3222
Susan Reier, dir. Fax 621-3222

Primos, Delaware

St. Eugene S 200/K-8
110 S Oak Ave 19018 610-622-2909
Jane Magnatta, prin. Fax 622-6358

Primos Secane, See Darby
Upper Darby SD
Supt. — See Drexel Hill
Primos ES, 861 Bunting Ln 19018 400/K-5
Gregory Manfre, prin. 610-622-6755

Prospect, Butler, Pop. 1,273
Slippery Rock Area SD
Supt. — See Slippery Rock
Moraine ES 400/K-5
350 Main St 16052 724-865-2010
Matt Lafko, prin. Fax 865-0023

Prospect Park, Delaware, Pop. 6,449
Interboro SD 3,900/K-12
900 Washington Ave 19076 610-461-6700
Dr. Lois Snyder, supt. Fax 583-1678
www.interborosd.org
Kindergarten Academy 300/K-K
900 Washington Ave 19076 610-957-5401
Bernadette Reiley, prin. Fax 957-5403
Prospect Park S 600/K-8
901 Pennsylvania Ave 19076 610-237-6420
Paul Korinth, prin. Fax 586-7704
Other Schools – See Essington, Glenolden, Norwood

Pulaski, Lawrence
Wilmington Area SD
Supt. — See New Wilmington
Pulaski ES, 320 Shenango St 16143 100/K-3
George Endrizzi, prin. 724-656-8866

Punxsutawney, Jefferson, Pop. 6,036
Punxsutawney Area SD 2,400/K-12
475 Beyer Ave 15767 814-938-5151
Dr. J. Frantz, supt. Fax 938-6677
www.punxsy.k12.pa.us/
Bell Township ES 100/K-6
662 Airport Rd 15767 814-938-5116
Sharon Weber, prin.
Jenks Hill ES, 200 Jenks Ave 15767 100/K-6
Travis Monroe, prin. 814-938-5117
Longview ES 100/K-6
19466 Route 119 Hwy N 15767 814-938-5118
Travis Monroe, prin.
Mapleview ES, 9329 Route 536 15767 200/K-6
Sharon Weber, prin. 814-938-5119
Punxsutawney Area MS 500/7-8
465 Beyer Ave 15767 814-938-5151
Richard Britten, prin.
West End ES, 300 Center St 15767 100/K-6
Travis Monroe, prin. 814-938-5122
Wilson ES, 407 E Mahoning St 15767 300/K-6
Sharon Weber, prin. 814-938-5161
Other Schools – See Anita

Punxsutawney Christian S 200/PK-12
105 W Mahoning St 15767 814-939-7010
Patricia Woods, prin. Fax 939-7011

SS. Cosmas & Damian S 200/PK-8
205 N Chestnut St 15767 814-938-4224
Dawn Bressler, prin. Fax 939-3759

Quakertown, Bucks, Pop. 8,823
Palisades SD
Supt. — See Kintnersville
Springfield ES 300/K-5
1950 Route 212 18951 610-346-7582
Andrea Farina, prin. Fax 346-8124

Quakertown Community SD 5,500/K-12
100 Commerce Dr 18951 215-529-2000
Lisa Andrejko Ed.D., supt. Fax 529-2042
www.qcsd.org/
Haycock ES 100/1-5
1014 Old Bethlehem Rd 18951 215-529-2662
Dr. Kathleen Winters, prin. Fax 529-2661
Milford MS 500/6-8
2255 Allentown Rd 18951 215-529-2210
Derek Peiffer, prin. Fax 529-2211
Neidig ES 300/K-5
201 N Penrose St 18951 215-529-2360
Tom Murray, prin. Fax 529-2361
Pfaff ES 500/K-5
1600 Sleepy Hollow Rd 18951 215-529-2850
Dr. Deborah Lock, prin. Fax 529-2851
Quakertown ES 300/K-5
123 S 7th St 18951 215-529-2410
Dr. Kathleen Winters, prin. Fax 529-2411
Richland ES 400/K-5
500 Fairview Ave 18951 215-529-2450
Leslie Staffeld Ed.D., prin. Fax 529-2451
Strayer MS 800/6-8
1200 Ronald Reagan Dr 18951 215-529-2290
Cynthia Lapinski, prin. Fax 529-2291
Tohickon Valley ES 400/K-5
2360 N Old Bethlehem Pike 18951 215-529-2500
Scott Godshalk, prin. Fax 529-2501
Trumbauersville ES 500/K-5
101 Woodview Dr 18951 215-529-2550
James Moczydlowski, prin. Fax 529-2551

Quakertown Christian S 300/PK-12
50 E Paletown Rd 18951 215-536-6970
Phillip Swartley, admin. Fax 536-2115
St. Isidore S 300/PK-8
603 W Broad St 18951 215-536-6052
Janet Radcliffe, prin. Fax 536-8647
United Friends S 100/PK-8
1018 W Broad St 18951 215-538-1733
Nancy Donnelly, hdmstr. Fax 538-3140

Quarryville, Lancaster, Pop. 2,101
Solanco SD 4,000/K-12
121 S Hess St 17566 717-786-8401
Martin Hudacs Ed.D., supt. Fax 786-8245
www.solanco.k12.pa.us
Clermont ES 500/K-5
1868 Robert Fulton Hwy 17566 717-548-2742
Beverly Kreeger, prin. Fax 548-6472
Quarryville ES 500/K-5
211 S Hess St 17566 717-786-2546
James O'Brien, prin. Fax 786-4997
Smith MS 500/6-8
645 Kirkwood Pike 17566 717-786-2244
James Close, prin. Fax 786-8796
Swift MS 400/6-8
1866 Robert Fulton Hwy 17566 717-548-2187
Suzanne Herr, prin. Fax 548-3350
Other Schools – See Christiana, New Providence

Radnor, Delaware, Pop. 31,300
Radnor Township SD
Supt. — See Wayne
Radnor ES 500/K-5
20 Matsonford Rd 19087 610-788-9300
Therese Borden, prin. Fax 788-2378

Armenian Sisters Academy 200/PK-8
440 Upper Gulph Rd 19087 610-687-4100
Sr. V. Louisa Kassarjian, prin. Fax 687-2430

Rankin, Allegheny, Pop. 2,168
Woodland Hills SD
Supt. — See Pittsburgh
Rankin IS 300/4-6
235 4th Ave 15104 412-271-2957
Reginald Hickman, prin. Fax 271-0298

Reading, Berks, Pop. 80,855
Antietam SD 1,100/K-12
100 Antietam Rd 19606 610-779-0554
Dr. Lawrence Mayes, supt. Fax 779-4424
www.antietamsd.org
Mount Penn PS 200/K-1
201 N 25th St 19606 610-370-2898
Shirley Feyers, prin. Fax 370-2981
Other Schools – See Mount Penn

Exeter Township SD 4,400/K-12
3650 Perkiomen Ave 19606 610-779-0700
Dr. Beverly Martin, supt. Fax 779-7104
www.exeter.k12.pa.us/
Exeter Township JHS 700/7-8
151 E 39th St 19606 610-779-3320
Eric Flamm, prin. Fax 370-0678
Jacksonwald ES 700/K-4
100 Church Lane Rd 19606 610-779-1820
Susan Cook, prin. Fax 779-8844
Lausch ES 400/K-4
200 Elm St 19606 610-779-3050
Joseph Schlaffer, prin. Fax 779-1085
Lorane ES 500/K-4
699 Rittenhouse Dr 19606 610-582-8608
Pamela Kiskaddon, prin. Fax 582-4225
Reiffton IS 700/5-6
4355 Dunham Dr 19606 610-779-7640
Gregory Fries, prin. Fax 779-6995

Reading SD 17,300/PK-12
800 Washington St 19601 610-371-5611
Dr. Thomas Chapman, supt. Fax 371-5971
www.readingsd.org
Ford ES 500/PK-5
901 Margaret St 19611 610-371-5928
Stanley Kuczawa, prin. Fax 320-6998
Glenside ES 400/PK-5
500 Lackawanna St 19601 610-371-5913
Melissa Fisher, prin. Fax 371-5916
Lauers Park ES 800/PK-5
251 N 2nd St 19601 610-371-5960
Gordon Hoodak, prin. Fax 371-5932
Millmont ES 200/PK-5
400 Summit Ave 19611 610-371-5853
Stanley Kuczawa, prin. Fax 371-5902
Northeast MS 1,100/6-8
1216 N 13th St 19604 610-371-5774
Alexander Brown, prin. Fax 371-5784
Northwest ES 800/PK-5
820 Clinton St 19601 610-371-5904
Michelle Wiley, prin. Fax 371-5614
Northwest MS 1,000/6-8
1000 N Front St 19601 610-371-5882
Dennis Campbell, prin. Fax 371-5881
Riverside ES 900/PK-5
1400 Centre Ave 19601 610-371-5896
Barbara Hoffman, prin. Fax 371-5899
Sixteenth and Haak ES 600/PK-5
1601 Haak St 19602 610-371-5760
Janet Heilman, prin. Fax 371-5840
Southern MS 800/6-8
931 Chestnut St 19602 610-371-5802
Joel Brigel, prin. Fax 371-5814
Southwest MS 600/6-8
300 Chestnut St 19602 610-371-5934
Dr. Lloyd Norman, prin. Fax 371-5950
Stout ES 700/PK-5
321 S 10th St 19602 610-371-5815
Susan Higginson, prin. Fax 371-5822
Tenth and Green ES 800/PK-5
400 N 10th St 19604 610-371-5756
Margaret Brown, prin. Fax 371-5630
Tenth and Penn ES 500/PK-5
955 Penn St 19601 610-320-6994
K. Castello-Stuchbury, prin. Fax 736-0491
Thirteenth and Green ES 600/1-5
501 N 13th St 19604 610-371-5766
Deborah Kopetsky, prin. Fax 371-5878
Thirteenth and Union ES 1,000/PK-5
1600 N 13th St 19604 610-371-5795
Dorothea Miller, prin. Fax 371-5801
Twelfth and Marion ES 500/1-5
1200 N 12th St 19604 610-371-5788
M. Renee Billops, prin. Fax 371-8776
Tyson-Schoener ES 700/PK-5
315 S 5th St 19602 610-371-5951
JuliAnneKline, prin. Fax 371-5877

Cabrini Academy 100/PK-8
240 Franklin St 19602 610-374-8483
Sr. Marita Olango, prin. Fax 374-0369
Fairview Christian S 200/K-12
410 S 14th St 19602 610-372-8826
Holy Guardian Angels S 400/PK-8
3125 Kutztown Rd 19605 610-929-4124
Maureen Wallin, prin. Fax 929-1623
Jacksonwald Learning Center 100/PK-K
250 Church Lane Rd 19606 610-779-1108
Reading Adventist Junior Academy 100/PK-10
309 N Kenhorst Blvd 19607 610-777-8424
Fax 603-0129
St. Catherine of Siena S 300/PK-8
2330 Perkiomen Ave 19606 610-779-5810
Sr. Kathleen Gorman, prin. Fax 779-6888
St. Margaret S 200/K-8
233 Spring St 19601 610-375-1882
Sr. Marian Michele Smith, prin. Fax 376-2291
St. Peter S 200/K-8
225 S 5th St 19602 610-374-2447
Sr. Jane McFadden, prin. Fax 374-3415

Reamstown, Lancaster, Pop. 2,649
Cocalico SD
Supt. — See Denver
Reamstown ES 500/PK-5
PO Box 248 17567 717-336-1531
Beth Haldeman, prin. Fax 336-1533

Rebersburg, Centre
Penns Valley Area SD
Supt. — See Spring Mills
Miles Township ES 100/K-4
80 Town Lane Rd 16872 814-349-8868
Carolyn Payne, prin. Fax 349-8870

Rector, Westmoreland

Valley S of Ligonier 200/K-9
153 Lupine Ln 15677 724-238-6652
Michael Kennedy, hdmstr. Fax 238-6838

Red Hill, Montgomery, Pop. 2,357

Red Hill Christian S 100/PK-4
501 Graber Aly 18076 215-679-6613
Karin Klein, admin. Fax 679-6613

Red Lion, York, Pop. 6,084
Red Lion Area SD 5,200/K-12
696 Delta Rd 17356 717-244-4518
Dr. Frank Herron, supt. Fax 244-2196
www.rlasd.k12.pa.us
Gable ES 500/K-6
100 E Prospect St 17356 717-244-5523
Susan Dunham, prin. Fax 417-1204
Macaluso ES, 1195 Windsor Rd 17356 K-6
Kitty Reinholt, prin. 717-244-4518

North Hopewell-Winterstown ES 300/K-6
12165 Winterstown Rd 17356 717-244-3164
Norina Bentzel, prin. Fax 417-1205
Pleasant View ES 500/K-6
700 Delta Rd 17356 717-244-5425
Cynthia Williams, prin. Fax 417-1202
Red Lion Area JHS 1,000/7-8
200 Country Club Rd 17356 717-244-1448
Kurt Fassnacht, prin. Fax 244-6160
Other Schools – See Brogue, Windsor, York

Red Lion Christian S 200/K-12
105 Springvale Rd 17356 717-244-3905
Fax 246-3738

Reedsville, Mifflin, Pop. 1,030
Mifflin County SD
Supt. — See Lewistown
Brown Township ES 200/K-5
96 Kish Rd 17084 717-667-3124
Michael LaMarca, prin. Fax 667-3755
Indian Valley MS 700/6-8
125 Kish Rd 17084 717-667-2123
Mark Crosson, prin. Fax 667-6608

Renfrew, Butler, Pop. 350
Butler Area SD
Supt. — See Butler
Connoquenessing ES 300/K-6
102 Connoquenessing Schl Rd 16053 724-287-8721
Jeff Mathieson, prin. Fax 789-7478

Renovo, Clinton, Pop. 1,243
Keystone Central SD
Supt. — See Lock Haven
Renovo ES 200/K-6
1301 Bucktail Ave 17764 570-923-2100
Justin Evey, prin. Fax 923-2857

Reynoldsville, Jefferson, Pop. 2,609
Du Bois Area SD
Supt. — See Du Bois
Johnson ES 300/K-5
923 Jackson St 15851 814-653-8254
Donald Mowery, prin. Fax 653-2378
Sykesville ES 100/K-5
1100 Sykesville School Rd 15851 814-894-2484
Elizabeth Shindledecker, prin. Fax 894-2769

Rheems, Lancaster, Pop. 1,044
Elizabethtown Area SD
Supt. — See Elizabethtown
Rheems ES 400/K-5
130 Alida St 17570 717-367-9121
Brad Sterner, prin. Fax 361-2537

Richboro, Bucks, Pop. 5,332
Council Rock SD
Supt. — See Newtown
Richboro ES 500/K-6
125 Upper Holland Rd 18954 215-944-1900
Rebecca Grimm, prin. Fax 944-1996
Richboro MS 500/7-8
98 Upper Holland Rd 18954 215-944-2500
William Bell, prin. Fax 944-2598

Richfield, Juniata
Juniata County SD
Supt. — See Mifflintown
Monroe Township ES 200/K-6
54 Main St 17086 717-694-3961
Debra Wagner, prin. Fax 694-3788

Richland, Lebanon, Pop. 1,479
Eastern Lebanon County SD
Supt. — See Myerstown
Ft. Zeller ES 200/K-5
243 N Sheridan Rd 17087 610-589-2575
Terrie Stauffer, prin. Fax 589-5815

Ridgway, Elk, Pop. 4,302
Ridgway Area SD 1,000/K-12
PO Box 447 15853 814-773-3146
Dr. Thomas Butler, supt. Fax 776-4299
www.ridgwayareaschooldistrict.com/
Ridgway Area MS 300/6-8
PO Box 447 15853 814-773-3156
William Connelly, prin. Fax 776-4239
Ridgway ES 400/K-5
PO Box 447 15853 814-776-2176
Anne Herzing, prin. Fax 776-4297

St. Leo S 200/PK-8
125 Depot St 15853 814-772-9775
Mary Detwiler, prin. Fax 772-9295

Ridley Park, Delaware, Pop. 7,062
Ridley SD
Supt. — See Folsom
Lakeview ES 400/K-5
333 Constitution Ave 19078 610-534-1900
Dr. Barbara White, prin. Fax 237-8013
Leedom ES 300/K-5
620 E Chester Pike 19078 610-534-1900
Dr. Richard Picard, prin. Fax 237-8019
Ridley MS 1,400/6-8
400 Free St 19078 610-237-8034
Gail Heinemeyer, prin. Fax 237-8032

SS. Madeline & Rose S 200/PK-8
500 Tome St 19078 610-583-3662
Mary Ann DiTomosso, prin. Fax 583-3683

Rimersburg, Clarion, Pop. 1,018
Union SD 700/K-12
354 Baker St Ste 2 16248 814-473-6311
Lawrence Bornak, supt. Fax 473-8201
www.unionsd.net/
Rimersburg ES, 88 School St 16248 200/4-6
Jean McCleary, prin. 814-473-3989
Other Schools – See Sligo

Ringtown, Schuylkill, Pop. 783
North Schuylkill SD
Supt. — See Ashland
Ringtown ES 200/K-6
PO Box 216 17967 570-889-3161
Neall Jones, prin. Fax 889-3595

Riverside, Northumberland, Pop. 1,820
Danville Area SD
Supt. — See Danville
Riverside ES 200/K-5
Avenue A and 5th St 17868 570-271-3268
John Bickhart, prin. Fax 271-4147

Roaring Spring, Blair, Pop. 2,309
Spring Cove SD 1,400/K-12
1100 E Main St 16673 814-224-5124
Rodney Green, supt. Fax 224-5516
springcove.schoolnet.com
Spring Cove ES K-5
137 Spring Cove Dr 16673 814-224-2311
Betsy Baker, prin. Fax 224-5595
Spring Cove MS 500/6-8
185 Spring Cove Dr 16673 814-224-2106
Frank Pannebaker, prin. Fax 224-2842
Other Schools – See Martinsburg

Robertsdale, Huntingdon
Tussey Mountain SD
Supt. — See Saxton
Robertsdale ES, PO Box 37 16674 100/K-6
Kathy Lazor, prin. 814-635-2708

Robesonia, Berks, Pop. 2,059
Conrad Weiser Area SD 3,000/K-12
44 Big Spring Rd 19551 610-693-8545
Dr. Robert Urzillo, supt. Fax 693-8586
www.conradweiser.org
Weiser MS 900/5-8
347 E Penn Ave 19551 610-693-8514
Joseph Torchia, prin. Fax 693-8543
Other Schools – See Wernersville, Womelsdorf

Rochester, Beaver, Pop. 3,804
Rochester Area SD 800/K-12
540 Reno St 15074 724-775-7500
Dr. C. Dean Galitsis, supt. Fax 775-6942
www.rasd.net/
Rochester Area ES 400/K-6
540 Reno St 15074 724-775-7500
Carolyn Wilkovich, prin. Fax 775-9266

Rochester Mills, Indiana
Marion Center Area SD
Supt. — See Marion Center
Canoe-Grant ES 100/K-4
4500 Richmond Rd 15771 724-286-9615
Donna Bruder-Smith, prin.

Rockhill Furnace, Huntingdon, Pop. 406
Southern Huntingdon County SD
Supt. — See Three Springs
Rockhill ES 200/K-5
PO Box 184 17249 814-447-3631
Cathie Brouse, prin. Fax 447-3892

Rockwood, Somerset, Pop. 933
Rockwood Area SD 900/K-12
439 Somerset Ave 15557 814-926-4913
Mark Bower, supt. Fax 926-2880
www.rockwoodschools.org
Rockwood Area ES 300/K-6
435 Somerset Ave 15557 814-926-4677
Samuel Romesberg, prin. Fax 926-2631
Other Schools – See Markleton

Rome, Bradford, Pop. 373
Northeast Bradford SD 900/K-12
RR 1 Box 211B 18837 570-744-2521
Heather McPherson, supt. Fax 744-2933
www.neb.k12.pa.us
Northeast Bradford ES 500/K-6
RR 1 Box 211B 18837 570-744-2521
Janice Otis, prin. Fax 744-2933

Rosemont, Montgomery

Irwin S 700/PK-12
275 S Ithan Ave 19010 610-525-8400
Dr. Mary Seppala, hdmstr. Fax 525-8908
Rosemount S of the Holy Child 300/PK-8
1344 Montgomery Ave 19010 610-922-1000
Sr. Mary Broderick, prin. Fax 525-7128

Roseto, Northampton, Pop. 1,662

Faith Christian S 200/K-12
122 Dante St 18013 610-588-3414
Robert Tomlinson, admin. Fax 588-8103
Our Lady of Mt. Carmel S 100/K-6
80 Ridge St 18013 610-588-2629
Joseph Yannuzzi, prin. Fax 588-3423

Rose Valley, Delaware, Pop. 928

School in Rose Valley 100/PK-6
20 School Ln 19063 610-566-1088
Donna Sanderson, prin. Fax 566-4640

Roslyn, Montgomery, Pop. 10,000
Abington SD
Supt. — See Abington
Roslyn ES 500/K-6
2565 Susquehanna Rd 19001 215-884-3368
Kevin Osborne, prin. Fax 884-2386

St. John of the Cross S 200/PK-8
2801 Woodland Rd 19001 215-659-1365
Marianne Garnham, prin. Fax 659-7996

Royersford, Montgomery, Pop. 4,330
Spring-Ford Area SD
Supt. — See Collegeville
Brooke ES 600/K-4
339 N Lewis Rd 19468 610-705-6006
Dr. Edward Mackel, prin. Fax 705-6248
Limerick ES 500/K-4
81 Limerick Center Rd 19468 610-705-6007
Mitchell Edmunds, prin. Fax 705-6246
Royersford ES 400/K-4
450 Spring St 19468 610-705-6005
David Willauer, prin. Fax 705-6250
Spring-Ford IS 1,200/5-6
833 S Lewis Rd Bldg 2 19468 610-705-6003
Edward Smith, prin. Fax 705-6254
Spring-Ford MS 7th Grade Center 600/7-7
833 S Lewis Rd Bldg 2 19468 610-705-6010
Dr. Theresa Weidenbaugh, prin. Fax 705-6238
Spring-Ford MS 8th Grade Center 500/8-8
700 Washington St 19468 610-705-6002
Michael Siggins, prin. Fax 705-6255
Upper Providence ES 700/K-4
833 S Lewis Rd Bldg 3 19468 610-705-6009
Dr. Melissa Patschke, prin. Fax 705-6236

Sacred Heart S 200/K-8
100 S Lewis Rd 19468 610-948-7206
Dorothy Gudz, prin. Fax 948-6508

Ruffs Dale, Westmoreland
Yough SD
Supt. — See Herminie
Mendon ES 300/K-4
164 State Route 31 15679 724-872-6484
John Janos, prin. Fax 872-6972
Yough MS 800/5-8
171 State Route 31 15679 724-872-5164
Thomas Paterline, prin. Fax 872-5319

Rural Valley, Armstrong, Pop. 874
Armstrong SD
Supt. — See Ford City
Shannock Valley ES 400/K-6
PO Box 325 16249 724-783-6991
Russell Carson, prin. Fax 783-7291

Russell, Warren
Warren County SD
Supt. — See North Warren
Russell ES 300/K-6
6820 Market St 16345 814-757-4507
Deborah Deppas, prin. Fax 757-8776

Calvary Chapel Christian S 50/PK-12
PO Box 579 16345 814-757-8744
James Stowe, admin. Fax 757-8745

Russellton, Allegheny, Pop. 1,691
Deer Lakes SD 2,000/K-12
PO Box 10 15076 724-265-5300
Mark King, supt. Fax 265-5025
www.deerlakes.net
Deer Lakes MS 500/6-8
PO Box 20 15076 724-265-5310
Dr. Thomas Lesniewski, prin. Fax 265-3711
East Union Intermediate Center 400/3-5
PO Box 30 15076 724-265-5330
James Schweinberg, prin. Fax 265-1699
Other Schools – See Tarentum

Rydal, Montgomery
Abington SD
Supt. — See Abington
Rydal West ES K-1
1231 Meetinghouse Rd 19046 215-884-0192
Laura Ann Pladus, prin. Fax 572-7963

St. Hilary of Poitiers S 200/1-8
920 Susquehanna Rd 19046 215-887-4520
Jane Rowles, prin. Fax 887-6337

Saegertown, Crawford, Pop. 1,057
Penncrest SD 3,800/K-12
PO Box 808 16433 814-763-2323
Richard Borchilo, supt. Fax 763-5129
www.penncrest.iu5.org
Saegertown ES 600/K-6
18741 Highway 198 16433 814-763-2314
Julie McKay, prin. Fax 763-5125
Other Schools – See Cambridge Springs, Townville

French Creek Valley Christian S 100/PK-12
420 North St 16433 814-763-3282
Wendy Horning, prin. Fax 763-3283

Saint Clair, Schuylkill, Pop. 3,123
Saint Clair Area SD 600/K-8
227 S Mill St 17970 570-429-2716
Kendy Hinkel, supt. Fax 429-2862
www.saintclairsd.org/
Saint Clair Area S 600/K-8
227 S Mill St 17970 570-429-2716
Michael Maley, prin. Fax 429-2859

Saint Marys, Elk, Pop. 14,182
Saint Marys Area SD 2,400/K-12
977 S Saint Marys St 15857 814-834-7831
Anna Kearney, supt. Fax 781-2190
smasd.org
Saint Marys Area MS 600/6-8
979 S Saint Marys St 15857 814-834-7831
James Wortman, prin. Fax 781-2191
South St. Marys Street ES 600/K-5
370 S Saint Marys St 15857 814-834-3021
Robert Grumley, prin. Fax 834-7814
Other Schools – See Kersey, Weedville

St. Marys Catholic MS 200/6-8
325 Church St 15857 814-834-2665
Mary Agnes Marshall, prin. Fax 834-5339

St. Mary's Catholic S 400/PK-5
114 Queens Rd 15857 814-834-4169
Mary Beth Schaut, prin. Fax 834-7830

Saint Thomas, Franklin
Tuscarora SD
Supt. — See Mercersburg
Saint Thomas ES 400/K-5
70 School House Rd 17252 717-369-3123
Dr. Nadine Sanders, prin. Fax 369-3183

Salina, Westmoreland
Kiski Area SD
Supt. — See Leechburg
Bell Avon ES 300/K-6
238 Stewart St 15680 724-697-4571
Christine Ross, prin. Fax 697-5461

Salisbury, Somerset, Pop. 829
Salisbury-Elk Lick SD 300/PK-12
PO Box 68 15558 814-662-2733
Lawrence Cogley, supt. Fax 662-2544
www.selsd.com
Salisbury-Elk Lick ES 100/K-6
PO Box 68 15558 814-662-2733
Joseph Renzi, prin. Fax 662-2544
Salisbury-Elk Lick Preschool PK-PK
PO Box 68 15558 814-662-2733
Joseph Renzi, prin. Fax 662-2544

Saltsburg, Indiana, Pop. 907
Blairsville-Saltsburg SD
Supt. — See Blairsville
Saltsburg ES 400/K-6
250 3rd St 15681 724-639-3556
Tracy Richards, prin. Fax 639-9322

Sarver, Butler
Freeport Area SD 2,000/K-12
621 S Pike Rd 16055 724-295-5141
Stan Chapp Ed.D., supt. Fax 295-3001
www.freeport.k12.pa.us
Buffalo ES 600/1-6
500 Sarver Rd 16055 724-353-9577
Steven Poleski, prin. Fax 353-1595
Other Schools – See Freeport

Evangel Heights Christian Academy 300/PK-12
120 Beale Rd 16055 724-295-9199
Gary Bracewell, dir. Fax 295-9009

Saxonburg, Butler, Pop. 1,636
South Butler County SD 2,900/K-12
328 Knoch Rd 16056 724-352-1700
Dr. Frank Prazenica, supt. Fax 352-3622
www.southbutler.k12.pa.us
Knoch MS 700/6-8
754 Dinnerbell Rd 16056 724-352-1700
James George, prin. Fax 352-0170
South Butler IS 400/4-5
340 Knoch Rd 16056 724-352-1700
Thomas Tibbott, prin. Fax 352-0380
South Butler PS 700/K-3
328 Knoch Rd 16056 724-352-1700
Greg Hajek, prin. Fax 352-8848

Saxton, Bedford, Pop. 772
Tussey Mountain SD 1,200/K-12
199 Front St 16678 814-635-3670
Dr. Ronald McCahan, supt. Fax 635-3928
www.tmsd.net/
Saxton-Liberty ES 300/K-6
1110 Mifflin St 16678 814-635-2934
Kathy Lazor, prin.
Other Schools – See Defiance, Robertsdale

Sayre, Bradford, Pop. 5,606
Sayre Area SD 1,200/PK-12
333 W Lockhart St 18840 570-888-7615
Dean Hosterman, supt. Fax 888-8248
www.sayresd.org
Litchfield Township ES 100/K-4
RR 1 Box 106a 18840 570-888-7198
Michelle Murrelle, prin. Fax 888-0921
Snyder ES 600/PK-6
130 Warren St 18840 570-888-7742
Michelle Murrelle, prin. Fax 888-6037

Epiphany S 100/K-8
627 Stevenson St 18840 570-888-5802
Sr. Kathleen Kelly, prin. Fax 888-2362

Schaefferstown, Lebanon
Eastern Lebanon County SD
Supt. — See Myerstown
Schaefferstown ES 300/K-5
PO Box 346 17088 717-949-6818
Terrie Stauffer, prin. Fax 949-8488

Schnecksville, Lehigh, Pop. 1,780
Parkland SD
Supt. — See Allentown
Schnecksville ES 500/K-5
4260 Sand Spring Rd 18078 610-351-5830
William Bowen, prin. Fax 351-5839

Schuylkill Haven, Schuylkill, Pop. 5,283
Schuylkill Haven Area SD 1,500/K-12
120 Haven St 17972 570-385-6705
Lorraine Felker, supt. Fax 385-6736
www.haven.k12.pa.us/
Schuylkill Haven ES 500/K-4
701 E Main St 17972 570-385-6731
Sarah Yoder, prin. Fax 385-6742
Schuylkill Haven MS 300/5-7
120 Haven St 17972 570-385-6708
Linda Berdanier, prin. Fax 385-6743

St. Ambrose S 100/PK-8
302 Randel St 17972 570-385-2377
Anne Curry, prin. Fax 385-2387

Schwenksville, Montgomery, Pop. 1,360
Perkiomen Valley SD
Supt. — See Collegeville
Schwenksville ES 500/K-5
55 2nd St 19473 610-879-8770
Pauline Galiardi, prin. Fax 879-8772

Blessed Teresa of Calcutta S 200/PK-8
256 Swamp Pike 19473 610-287-2500
Joan Rook, prin. Fax 287-2543
St. Mary S 300/PK-8
40 Spring Mount Rd 19473 610-287-7757
Kevin Conwell, prin. Fax 287-2562

Sciota, Monroe
Stroudsburg Area SD
Supt. — See Stroudsburg
Hamilton Township ES 300/K-2
HC 1 Box 218 18354 570-992-4960
Barbara Bradley, prin. Fax 992-9034

Scotland, Franklin
Chambersburg Area SD
Supt. — See Chambersburg
Scotland ES, 3832 Main St 17254 400/K-5
Barb DeSerio, prin. 717-709-4085

Scottdale, Westmoreland, Pop. 4,567
Southmoreland SD 1,600/K-12
609 Parker Ave 15683 724-887-2000
Dr. John Halfhill, supt. Fax 887-2055
www.southmoreland.net
Southmoreland ES 400/2-5
100 Scottie Way 15683 724-887-2022
John Lee, prin. Fax 887-2024
Southmoreland MS 400/6-8
200 Scottie Way 15683 724-887-2034
Dan Clara, prin. Fax 887-2032
Other Schools – See Alverton

St. John the Baptist S 100/PK-8
504 S Broadway St 15683 724-887-9550
Dr. Joseph Dreliszak, prin. Fax 887-9553

Scranton, Lackawanna, Pop. 73,120
Scranton SD 9,400/PK-12
425 N Washington Ave 18503 570-348-3400
Bill King, admin. Fax 348-3563
www.scrsd.org/
Adams ES 200/K-5
927 Capouse Ave 18509 570-348-3655
Sally Henry, prin. Fax 348-3163
Armstrong ES 500/PK-5
1500 N Lincoln Ave 18508 570-348-3661
Paul Stefani, prin. Fax 348-3599
Audubon ES 200/K-5
1801 Mulberry St 18510 570-348-3665
MaryAnn Cartegna, prin. Fax 348-3168
Bancroft ES 200/K-5
1002 Albright Ave 18508 570-348-3667
Gwendolyn Damiano, prin. Fax 348-3376
Kennedy ES 300/K-5
2300 Prospect Ave 18505 570-348-3673
John Kopicki, prin.
Lincoln-Jackson ES 200/K-5
Academy St & Hyde Park Ave 18505
Ann McDonough, prin. 570-348-3675
Marshall ES, 1415 Oram St 18504 400/PK-5
Linda Demuth, prin. 570-348-3677
McNichols Plaza ES 400/K-5
1111 S Irving Ave 18505 570-348-3685
Jeffrey McCreary, prin.
Morris ES, 1824 Boulevard Ave 18509 400/PK-5
Dave Bieri, prin. 570-348-3681
Northeast IS, 721 Adams Ave 18510 900/6-8
Eric Schaeffer, prin. 570-348-3651
Prescott ES, 838 Prescott Ave 18510 300/K-5
Albert O'Donnell, prin. 570-348-3683
South Scranton IS 500/6-8
355 Maple St 18505 570-348-3631
Barbara Dixon, prin.
Sumner ES, 372 N Sumner Ave 18504 300/PK-5
Daniel Williams, prin. 570-348-3688
West Scranton IS 800/6-8
1401 Fellows St 18504 570-348-3475
Dr. Charlotte Slocum, prin.
Whittier ES, 700 Orchard St 18505 300/K-5
Lawrence Miner, prin. 570-348-3690
Willard ES, 1100 Eynon St 18504 500/K-5
Jessica Leitzel, prin. 570-348-3692

All Saints Interparochial Academy 200/PK-8
1425 Jackson St 18504 570-343-8114
Michele Long, prin. Fax 343-0378
Immaculate Care Preschool 50/PK-PK
800 Taylor Ave 18510 570-344-4380
Ann Marie McDonald, prin.
Marian Interparochial S 300/PK-8
638 Hemlock St 18505 570-346-9922
Jeanne Rossi, prin. Fax 207-2652
St. Clare/St. Paul S-Main Campus 200/4-8
1527 Penn Ave 18509 570-343-7880
Elizabeth Murray, prin. Fax 343-0069
St. Clare/St. Paul S-Primary Campus 300/PK-3
2215 N Washington Ave 18509 570-343-2790
Elizabeth Murray, prin. Fax 343-4905
Scranton Hebrew Day S 100/K-8
540 Monroe Ave 18510 570-346-1576
Rabbi M. Nissel, prin. Fax 346-9310

Secane, Delaware

Our Lady of Fatima S 400/K-8
10 Fatima Dr 19018 610-586-7539
Sr. Ellen Giardino, prin. Fax 586-0117

Selinsgrove, Snyder, Pop. 5,417
Selinsgrove Area SD 2,500/K-12
401 18th St 17870 570-374-1144
Dr. Frederick Johnson, supt. Fax 372-2222
www.seal-pa.org/
Jackson-Penn K K-K
297 Route 204 17870 570-372-2295
Lorinda Krause, prin. Fax 372-2297
Selinsgrove Area MS 700/6-8
401 18th St 17870 570-372-2250
John Bohle, prin. Fax 372-2251
Selinsgrove ES 300/1-2
600 N Broad St 17870 570-372-2285
Lorinda Krause, prin. Fax 372-2287
Selinsgrove IS 500/3-5
301 18th St 17870 570-372-2270
Terry Heintzelman, prin. Fax 372-2272

Sellersville, Bucks, Pop. 4,496
Pennridge SD
Supt. — See Perkasie
Grasse ES 400/K-5
600 Rickert Rd 18960 215-723-7501
Anthony Rybarczyk, prin. Fax 723-0541
Sellersville ES 500/K-5
122 W Ridge Ave 18960 215-257-6591
Pricilla Ponist, prin. Fax 257-2169
West Rockhill ES 400/K-5
1000 Washington Ave 18960 215-257-9200
Dr. Donald Muenker, prin. Fax 257-2802

Faith Christian Academy 300/K-12
700 N Main St 18960 215-257-5031
Robert Clymer, prin. Fax 257-3327
St. Agnes-Sacred Heart PS 200/PK-4
393 N Main St 18960 215-257-3571
Margaret Graham, prin. Fax 257-8036
Upper Bucks Christian S 200/K-12
754 E Rockhill Rd 18960 215-536-9200
Russ Baun, prin. Fax 536-2229

Seneca, Venango, Pop. 1,029
Cranberry Area SD 1,300/K-12
3 Education Dr 16346 814-676-5628
Dr. Nicholas Bodnar, supt. Fax 677-5728
www.cranberrysd.org/
Cranberry ES 500/K-6
3 Education Dr 16346 814-676-1871
George Svolos, prin. Fax 677-9957
Other Schools – See Kennerdell, Venus

Christian Life Academy 100/PK-12
PO Box 207 16346 814-676-9360
Michael Lloyd, admin. Fax 676-2908

Sewickley, Allegheny, Pop. 3,674
North Allegheny SD
Supt. — See Pittsburgh
Franklin ES 400/K-5
2401 Rochester Rd 15143 412-366-9663
Jeff Anderchak, prin. Fax 366-5852

Quaker Valley SD 1,600/K-12
203 Graham St 15143 412-749-3600
Dr. Joseph Clapper, supt. Fax 749-3601
www.qvsd.org/qvsd/site/default.asp
Edgeworth ES, 200 Meadow Ln 15143 500/K-6
Amy Kern, prin. 412-749-3605
Osborne ES, 1414 Beaver St 15143 300/K-6
Dr. Jeanne Johnson, prin. 412-749-4003

Montessori Children's Community 100/PK-6
474 Chadwick St 15143 412-741-8982
Terri Modic, hdmstr. Fax 741-7614
St. James S 200/PK-8
201 Broad St 15143 412-741-5540
Jean Riley, prin. Fax 741-9038
Sewickley Academy 800/PK-12
315 Academy Ave 15143 412-741-2230
Kolia O'Connor, hdmstr. Fax 741-1411

Shade Gap, Huntingdon, Pop. 93
Southern Huntingdon County SD
Supt. — See Three Springs
Shade Gap ES 100/K-5
22251 Shade Valley Rd 17255 814-259-3137
Cathie Brouse, prin. Fax 259-3635

Shamokin, Northumberland, Pop. 7,581

Transfiguration S 50/K-8
129 N Shamokin St 17872 570-648-6435
Doreen Kushner, prin. Fax 648-6435

Shanksville, Somerset, Pop. 230
Shanksville-Stonycreek SD 300/PK-12
PO Box 128 15560 814-267-6499
Mr. Thomas McInroy, supt. Fax 267-4372
www.sssd.com
Shanksville-Stonycreek ES 200/PK-5
PO Box 128 15560 814-267-7140
Eloise Groegler, prin. Fax 267-7229

Sharon, Mercer, Pop. 15,504
Brookfield Local SD
Supt. — See Brookfield
Brookfield ES 400/K-3
115 Anson Way 16146 724-347-1851
Debra Gratz, prin. Fax 347-5241

Sharon CSD 2,200/K-12
215 Forker Blvd 16146 724-981-6390
John Sarandrea, supt. Fax 981-0844
sharoncitysd.schoolwires.com
Case Avenue ES 500/K-6
36 Case Ave 16146 724-983-4015
Traci Valentino, prin. Fax 983-4021
Musser ES 300/K-6
500 Cedar Ave 16146 724-981-4381
Michael Gay, prin. Fax 981-4600

West Hill ES 300/K-6
301 Ellsworth St 16146 724-981-4880
Sheila Schneider, prin. Fax 981-0482

St. Joseph S 200/PK-8
760 E State St 16146 724-983-8382
Marian Smith, prin. Fax 983-8383
SS. Peter & Paul Lutheran S 50/PK-PK
699 Stambaugh Ave 16146 724-347-5655
Fax 347-6336

Sharon Hill, Delaware, Pop. 5,357
Southeast Delco SD
Supt. — See Folcroft
Sharon Hill S 500/1-8
701 Coates St 19079 610-522-4355
Asia Ali-Hawkins, prin. Fax 522-4364

Sharpsville, Mercer, Pop. 4,281
Sharpsville Area SD 1,400/K-12
701 S 7th St 16150 724-962-7874
Mark Ferrara, supt. Fax 962-7873
www.sharpsville.k12.pa.us/
Sharpsville Area ES 600/K-5
100 Hittle Ave 16150 724-962-7455
Matt Dieter, prin. Fax 962-1003
Sharpsville Area MS 300/6-8
303 Blue Devil Way 16150 724-962-7863
John Vannoy, prin. Fax 962-7891

Sheffield, Warren, Pop. 1,294
Warren County SD
Supt. — See North Warren
Sheffield ES 100/K-5
PO Box 546 16347 814-968-3778
Deborah Dwyer, prin. Fax 968-3027

Shenandoah, Schuylkill, Pop. 5,296
Shenandoah Valley SD 1,100/PK-12
805 W Centre St 17976 570-462-1936
Dr. Stanley Rakowsky, supt. Fax 462-4611
www.shenandoah.k12.pa.us
Shenandoah Valley ES 600/PK-6
805 W Centre St 17976 570-462-2796
Barbara Wilkinson, prin. Fax 462-1943

Trinity Academy 100/PK-6
233 W Cherry St 17976 570-462-3927
Sr. Mary Ann Spaetti, prin. Fax 462-4603

Shermans Dale, Perry
West Perry SD
Supt. — See Elliottsburg
Carroll ES 500/K-5
6670 Spring Rd 17090 717-582-4256
Ronald Hummel, prin. Fax 582-3547

Shickshinny, Luzerne, Pop. 907
Northwest Area SD 1,400/K-12
243 Thorne Hill Rd 18655 570-542-4126
Nancy Tkatch, supt. Fax 542-0187
www.northwest.k12.pa.us/
Garrison Memorial ES 200/K-6
43 W Vine St 18655 570-542-0128
Joseph Gorham, prin. Fax 542-5884
Hunlock Creek S 300/K-6
21 Sunset Lake Rd 18655 570-542-0128
Joseph Gorham, prin. Fax 256-3216
Other Schools – See Huntington Mills

Shillington, Berks, Pop. 5,031
Governor Mifflin SD 4,300/K-12
10 S Waverly St 19607 610-775-1461
Dr. Mary Weiss, supt. Fax 775-6586
www.governormifflinsd.org
Cumru ES 600/K-3
601 Philadelphia Ave 19607 610-775-5081
James Watts, prin. Fax 685-0404
Mifflin IS 900/4-6
600 Governor Dr 19607 610-775-5083
Lee Umberger, prin. Fax 685-3761
Mifflin MS 700/7-8
10 S Waverly St 19607 610-775-1465
Kevin Hohl, prin. Fax 685-3760
Other Schools – See Mohnton

La Salle Academy 200/PK-8
440 Holland St 19607 610-777-7392
Patti Fisher, prin. Fax 777-1280

Shinglehouse, Potter, Pop. 1,190
Oswayo Valley SD 400/PK-12
PO Box 610 16748 814-697-7175
Charles Wicker, supt. Fax 697-7439
www.oswayo.com/
Oswayo Valley ES 200/PK-5
PO Box 610 16748 814-697-7161
Carolyn Fugate, prin. Fax 697-7799

Shippensburg, Cumberland, Pop. 5,605
Shippensburg Area SD 2,700/K-12
317 N Morris St 17257 717-530-2700
Kristin Carroll, supt. Fax 530-2724
www.edline.net/pages/Shippensburg_ASD
Burd ES 400/K-3
600 Brad St 17257 717-530-2780
Dr. Kenneth Jenkins, prin. Fax 530-2856
Grayson ES K-3
301 Lurgan Ave 17257 717-530-2770
Susan Martin, prin. Fax 530-2542
Luhrs University ES 100/K-5
1871 Old Main Dr 17257 717-477-1612
Fax 477-4072
Shippensburg Area IS 200/4-5
601 Hollar Ave 17257 717-530-3189
David Rice, prin. Fax 530-3627
Shippensburg Area MS 800/6-8
101 Park Pl W 17257 717-530-2750
Teri Mowery, prin. Fax 530-2757

Shiremanstown, Cumberland, Pop. 1,480

Bible Baptist S 500/PK-12
201 W Main St 17011 717-737-3550
George Wiedman, admin. Fax 761-3977
Children's Garden 100/PK-K
44 W Main St 17011 717-731-1095
LeighAnn Courtney, dir.

Shoemakersville, Berks, Pop. 2,118
Hamburg Area SD
Supt. — See Hamburg
Perry ES 400/K-5
201 4th St 19555 610-562-3024
Shawn Gravish, prin. Fax 562-0469

Shohola, Pike
Delaware Valley SD
Supt. — See Milford
Shohola ES 700/K-6
940 Twin Lakes Rd 18458 570-296-3600
Margaret Schaffer, prin. Fax 296-3161

Sidman, Cambria, Pop. 1,189
Forest Hills SD 2,300/K-12
PO Box 158 15955 814-487-7613
Donald Bailey, supt. Fax 487-7775
www.fhsd.k12.pa.us/
Forest Hills ES 1,100/K-6
PO Box 290 15955 814-487-7613
Antoinette Murphy, prin. Fax 487-2372

Sinking Spring, Berks, Pop. 3,443
Wilson SD
Supt. — See West Lawn
Cornwall Terrace ES 600/K-6
3100 Iroquois Ave 19608 610-670-0180
Jennifer Dianna, prin. Fax 334-6447
Green Valley ES K-6
270 Green Valley Rd 19608 610-670-0180
Dr. Dina Wert, prin. Fax 334-6442
Shiloh Hills ES 400/K-6
301 Sage Dr 19608 610-670-0180
Nancy Sinkus, prin. Fax 334-6443

Sipesville, Somerset
Somerset Area SD
Supt. — See Somerset
Sipesville ES 100/K-3
1036 Schoolhouse Rd 15561 814-445-7789
Karen Maust, prin. Fax 444-8613

Slatington, Lehigh, Pop. 4,413
Northern Lehigh SD 2,000/K-12
1201 Shadow Oaks Ln 18080 610-767-9800
Michael Michaels, supt. Fax 767-9809
www.nlsd.org
Northern Lehigh MS 300/7-8
600 Diamond St 18080 610-767-9812
Jill Chamberlain, prin. Fax 767-9850
Peters ES 400/K-2
4055 Friedens Rd 18080 610-767-9827
Karen Nicholas, prin. Fax 767-9857
Slatington ES 600/3-6
1201 Shadow Oaks Ln 18080 610-767-9821
Dr. Linda Marcincin, prin. Fax 767-9808

Sligo, Clarion, Pop. 701
Union SD
Supt. — See Rimersburg
Sligo ES 200/K-3
2013 Madison Street Ext 16255 814-745-2152
Jean McCleary, prin. Fax 745-3017

Slippery Rock, Butler, Pop. 3,210
Slippery Rock Area SD 2,400/K-12
201 Kiester Rd 16057 724-794-2960
Dr. Kathleen Nogay, supt. Fax 794-2001
www.slipperyrock.k12.pa.us
Slippery Rock Area ES 400/K-5
470 N Main St 16057 724-794-2960
W. Herbert Basham, prin. Fax 794-5461
Slippery Rock Area MS 600/6-8
201 Kiester Rd 16057 724-794-2960
Joseph Raykle, prin. Fax 794-6265
Other Schools – See Harrisville, Prospect

Smethport, McKean, Pop. 1,617
Smethport Area SD 1,000/PK-12
414 S Mechanic St 16749 814-887-5543
George Romanowski, supt. Fax 887-5544
www.smethportschools.com/
Smethport Area ES 500/PK-6
414 S Mechanic St 16749 814-887-5012
Larry Rondinelli, prin. Fax 887-5540

Smithfield, Fayette, Pop. 822
Albert Gallatin Area SD
Supt. — See Uniontown
Smithfield ES 300/K-5
23 Liberty St 15478 724-569-9570
Candice Jordon, prin. Fax 569-1608

Mount Moriah Christian S 100/PK-5
PO Box 903 15478 724-569-4890
Renee DuBois, prin. Fax 569-0798

Snow Shoe, Centre, Pop. 778
Bald Eagle Area SD
Supt. — See Wingate
Mountaintop Area ES 200/K-6
100 School Dr 16874 814-387-6861
Michael Hall, prin. Fax 387-4323

Solebury, Bucks
New Hope-Solebury SD
Supt. — See New Hope
New Hope-Solebury Lower ES K-2
3020 N Sugan Rd 18963 215-297-5438
Kenneth Silver, prin. Fax 297-0988

Trinity Church Day S 100/PK-K
PO Box 377 18963 215-297-5510
Cindy Bove, dir. Fax 297-0987

Somerset, Somerset, Pop. 6,500
Somerset Area SD 2,600/K-12
645 S Columbia Ave Ste 110 15501 814-443-2831
Dr. David Pastrick, supt. Fax 443-1964
sasdpa.us
Eagle View ES 500/4-6
191 Discovery Ln 15501 814-444-8455
Erick Fish, prin. Fax 445-3278
Maple Ridge ES 500/K-3
105 New Centerville Rd 15501 814-445-6677
Karen Maust, prin. Fax 445-1821
Other Schools – See Friedens, Sipesville

St. Peter S 100/1-6
433 W Church St 15501 814-445-6662
Jill Harris, prin. Fax 445-7766

Souderton, Montgomery, Pop. 6,691
Souderton Area SD 6,300/K-12
760 Lower Rd 18964 215-723-6061
Charles Amuso Ed.D., supt. Fax 723-8897
www.soudertonsd.org
Crouthamel ES 300/K-5
143 S School Ln 18964 215-723-5949
Deborah Alder, prin. Fax 723-1652
Franconia ES 500/K-5
366 Harleysville Pike 18964 215-723-2596
Gail Ryan, prin. Fax 723-4470
Indian Crest MS 500/6-8
139 Harleysville Pike 18964 215-723-9193
Jeff Pammer, prin. Fax 723-8897
West Broad Street ES 500/K-5
342 W Broad St 18964 215-723-1711
Marianne Boyd, prin. Fax 723-6909
Other Schools – See Harleysville, Telford

Penn View Christian S 600/PK-8
420 Godshall Rd 18964 215-723-1196
Robert Rutt, dir. Fax 723-0148

Southampton, Bucks, Pop. 11,500
Centennial SD
Supt. — See Warminster
Davis ES 300/K-5
475 Maple Ave 18966 215-364-5970
Kelley O'Leary, prin. Fax 364-6344
Klinger MS 700/6-8
1415 2nd Street Pike 18966 215-364-5950
Khalid Mumin, prin. Fax 364-5955
Stackpole ES 400/K-5
1350 Strathmann Dr 18966 215-364-5980
Michael Stanford, prin. Fax 364-6345

Our Lady of Good Counsel S 500/PK-8
611 Knowles Ave 18966 215-357-1300
Frank Mokriski, prin. Fax 357-4452

South Canaan, Wayne
Western Wayne SD 2,500/PK-12
PO Box 220 18459 570-937-4270
Andrew Falonk, supt. Fax 937-4105
www.westernwayne.org
Other Schools – See Hamlin, Lake Ariel, Waymart

South Park, Allegheny
South Park SD 2,200/K-12
2005 Eagle Ridge Dr 15129 412-655-3111
Richard Bucchianeri, supt. Fax 655-2952
www.sparksd.org
South Park ES 800/K-4
2001 Eagle Pride Ln 15129 412-655-8510
Dr. L. Robert Furman, prin. Fax 655-6540
South Park MS 700/5-8
2500 Stewart Rd 15129 412-831-7200
Kevin Monaghan, prin. Fax 831-7204

St. Joan of Arc S 200/PK-8
6470 Library Rd 15129 412-833-2433
Jonathan Cuniak, prin. Fax 835-1764

South Williamsport, Lycoming, Pop. 6,189
South Williamsport Area SD 1,400/K-12
515 W Central Ave 17702 570-327-1581
Thomas Farr, supt. Fax 326-0641
www.mounties.k12.pa.us
Central ES 500/K-4
555 W Mountain Ave 17702 570-323-3694
Kathy Furman, prin. Fax 320-4492
Rommelt MS 200/5-6
515 W Central Ave 17702 570-320-4470
Dwight Woodley, prin. Fax 327-0641

Mountain View Adventist S 50/1-8
305 Fleming St 17702 570-327-9238

Spartansburg, Crawford, Pop. 323
Corry Area SD
Supt. — See Corry
Spartansburg ES 100/K-6
PO Box 158 16434 814-654-7812
Daniel Daum, prin. Fax 654-7151

Spring Church, Armstrong
Apollo-Ridge SD
Supt. — See Apollo
Apollo-Ridge ES 700/K-5
1831 State Route 56 15686 724-478-6000
Travis Barta, prin. Fax 478-2967
Apollo-Ridge MS 400/6-8
1829 State Route 56 15686 724-478-6000
Ian Magness, prin. Fax 478-3730

Spring City, Chester, Pop. 3,284
Owen J. Roberts SD
Supt. — See Pottstown

East Vincent ES 600/K-6
340 Ridge Rd 19475 610-469-5106
Kathryn Brown, prin. Fax 469-5884

Spring-Ford Area SD
Supt. — See Collegeville
Spring City ES 100/K-4
190 S Wall St 19475 610-705-6004
Kathleen Gallagher-Kotch, prin. Fax 705-6253

Springdale, Allegheny, Pop. 3,597
Allegheny Valley SD
Supt. — See Cheswick
Colfax Upper ES 300/4-6
430 Colfax St 15144 724-274-7200
Roberta Rowan Ed.D., prin. Fax 274-2187

Springfield, Delaware, Pop. 24,160
Springfield SD 3,400/K-12
111 W Leamy Ave 19064 610-938-6000
Dr. James Capolupo, supt. Fax 938-6005
Richardson MS 1,000/5-8
20 W Woodland Ave 19064 610-938-6300
Frank McKnight, prin. Fax 938-6305
Sabold ES 600/K-4
468 E Thomson Ave 19064 610-938-6500
Cindy Morse, prin. Fax 938-6505
Scenic Hills ES 600/K-4
235 Hillview Dr 19064 610-938-6600
David Soslau, prin. Fax 938-6605

Holy Cross S 400/PK-8
240 N Bishop Ave 19064 610-626-1709
Barbara Rosini, prin. Fax 626-1859
St. Francis of Assisi S 300/K-8
112 Saxer Ave 19064 610-543-0546
Jill Carroll, prin. Fax 544-9431
St. Kevin S 200/PK-8
200 W Sproul Rd 19064 610-544-4455
Bernadette Dougherty, prin. Fax 544-7092

Spring Grove, York, Pop. 2,212
Spring Grove Area SD 3,800/K-12
100 E College Ave 17362 717-225-4731
Dr. Robert Lombardo, supt. Fax 225-6028
www.sgasd.org
Spring Grove Area IS 600/5-6
1480 Roth Church Rd 17362 717-225-4731
Craig Seelye, prin. Fax 225-7395
Spring Grove Area MS 600/7-8
1472 Roth Church Rd 17362 717-225-4731
Steve Guadagnino, prin. Fax 225-0146
Spring Grove ES 600/K-4
1450 Roth Church Rd 17362 717-225-4731
Jon Weaver, prin. Fax 225-9238
Other Schools – See Thomasville, York

Spring House, Montgomery, Pop. 2,782

Gwynedd Mercy Academy 500/K-8
PO Box 241 19477 215-646-4916
Sr. Anne Crampsie, prin. Fax 646-7250

Spring Mills, Centre
Penns Valley Area SD 1,600/K-12
4528 Penns Valley Rd 16875 814-422-8814
Brian Griffith, supt. Fax 422-8020
www.pennsvalley.org
Penns Valley Area ES 500/K-6
4528 Penns Valley Rd 16875 814-422-8824
Kurt Nyquist, prin. Fax 422-0374
Other Schools – See Centre Hall, Rebersburg

State College, Centre, Pop. 38,720
State College Area SD 7,200/K-12
131 W Nittany Ave 16801 814-231-1011
Dr. Patricia Best, supt. Fax 231-4130
www.scasd.org
Boalsburg/Panorama Village ES 300/K-5
240 Villa Crest Dr 16801 814-466-5040
Dr. Jean Vadella, prin. Fax 466-5058
Corl Street ES 300/K-5
235 Corl St 16801 814-231-1186
Charlotte Zmyslo, prin. Fax 235-4587
Easterly Parkway ES 400/K-5
234 Easterly Pkwy 16801 814-231-1170
Brian Peters, prin. Fax 272-8861
Houserville/Lemont ES 400/K-5
675 Elmwood St 16801 814-231-5026
Scott DeShong, prin. Fax 231-5004
Mount Nittany MS 800/6-8
656 Brandywine Dr 16801 814-466-5133
Jason Perrin, prin. Fax 466-5140
Park Forest ES 500/K-5
2181 School Dr 16803 814-231-5010
Donnan Stoicovy, prin. Fax 235-4558
Park Forest MS 800/6-8
2180 School Dr 16803 814-237-5301
Karen Wiser, prin. Fax 272-0196
Radio Park ES 400/K-5
800 W Cherry Ln 16803 814-231-4115
Deirdre Bauer, prin. Fax 235-4592
Other Schools – See Pine Grove Mills, Port Matilda

Grace Lutheran Dayschool 100/PK-K
205 S Garner St 16801 814-238-8110
Becky Krantweiss, dir. Fax 238-4104
Nittany Christian S 100/K-8
1221 W Whitehall Rd 16801 814-234-5652
Judy Firebaugh, prin. Fax 234-5632
Our Lady of Victory S 400/PK-8
800 Westerly Pkwy 16801 814-238-1592
Kathy Bechdel, prin. Fax 238-4553
State College Friends S 100/K-8
1900 University Dr 16801 814-237-8386
Dan Hendey, hdmstr. Fax 235-1446

Steelton, Dauphin, Pop. 5,667
Central Dauphin SD
Supt. — See Harrisburg

Swatara MS 400/6-8
1101 Highland St 17113 717-939-9363
Michael Jordan, prin. Fax 939-2156
Tri Community ES 400/K-5
255 Cypress St 17113 717-939-9591
Barbara Lamond, prin. Fax 939-5591

Steelton-Highspire SD 1,200/K-12
250 Reynders St 17113 717-704-3800
Deborah Wortham Ed.D., supt. Fax 704-3808
www.shsd.k12.pa.us
Steelton-Highspire ES 700/K-6
150 S 4th St 17113 717-704-3126
Tamara Willis, prin. Fax 704-3808

Prince of Peace S 100/K-8
245 Reynders St 17113 717-939-6357
Kimberly DePaulis, admin. Fax 939-3660

Stevens, Lancaster
Cocalico SD
Supt. — See Denver
Schoeneck ES 100/K-5
80 W Queen St 17578 717-336-1551
Timothy Butz, prin. Fax 336-1557

Stewartstown, York, Pop. 2,009
South Eastern SD
Supt. — See Fawn Grove
Stewartstown ES 500/K-4
17945 Barrens Rd N 17363 717-993-2725
Susan Seiple, prin. Fax 993-5256

Stoneboro, Mercer, Pop. 1,061
Lakeview SD 1,300/K-12
2482 Mercer St 16153 724-376-7911
Frank McClard, supt. Fax 376-7910
www.lakeview.k12.pa.us
Lakeview MS 400/5-8
2482 Mercer St 16153 724-376-7911
David Blakley, prin. Fax 376-7910
Oakview ES 500/K-4
1387 School Rd 16153 724-376-7911
Michele Rhule, prin. Fax 376-7910

Stowe, Montgomery, Pop. 3,598
Pottsgrove SD
Supt. — See Pottstown
West Pottsgrove ES 400/K-5
25 Grosstown Rd 19464 610-323-6510
Ruth Fisher, prin. Fax 718-0559

Stoystown, Somerset, Pop. 402
North Star SD
Supt. — See Boswell
North Star MS 100/5-8
3598 Whistler Rd 15563 814-893-5616
Thaddeus Kiesnowski, prin. Fax 893-5922

Strafford, Chester, Pop. 4,500

Woodlynde S 300/1-12
445 Upper Gulph Rd 19087 610-687-9660
John Murray, hdmstr. Fax 687-4752

Strasburg, Lancaster, Pop. 2,745
Lampeter-Strasburg SD
Supt. — See Lampeter
Strasburg ES 200/K-2
114 W Franklin St 17579 717-687-0444
William Bray Ed.D., prin. Fax 687-8993

Strattanville, Clarion, Pop. 515
Clarion-Limestone Area SD 1,100/K-12
4091 C L School Rd 16258 814-764-5111
Theodore Pappas, supt. Fax 764-5729
www.clasd.net/
Clarion-Limestone ES 600/K-6
4091 C L School Rd 16258 814-764-6006
Mary Wolf, prin. Fax 764-5806

Stroudsburg, Monroe, Pop. 6,264
Stroudsburg Area SD 5,900/K-12
123 Linden St 18360 570-421-1990
Dr. John Toleno, supt. Fax 424-5986
www.sburg.org
Arlington Heights ES 300/K-2
1100 N 9th St 18360 570-421-6952
Debra Eppley, prin. Fax 421-6065
Clearview ES 200/K-2
2000 N 5th St 18360 570-421-7277
Michael Romano, prin. Fax 421-5368
Morey ES 300/K-2
1044 W Main St 18360 570-421-6371
Cynthia Muffley, prin. Fax 421-4985
Ramsey ES 100/K-2
528 Thomas St 18360 570-421-3160
Michael Romano, prin. Fax 421-5359
Stroudsburg IS 900/3-4
2000 Chipperfield Dr 18360 570-421-4834
Jeffrey Walters, prin. Fax 421-5370
Stroudsburg MS 1,400/5-7
200 Pocono Commons 18360 570-213-0203
Karen Thomson, prin.
Other Schools – See Sciota

Rainbow Trail Child Care Center 100/PK-K
9 N 9th St 18360 570-424-1443
Stroudsburg Adventist S 50/PK-8
RR 2 Box 2085 18360 570-421-5577
Fax 421-5577

Sugar Grove, Warren, Pop. 576
Warren County SD
Supt. — See North Warren
Sugargrove ES 300/K-6
101 School St 16350 814-489-7851
Marcia Madigan, prin. Fax 489-0205

Sugarloaf, Luzerne
Hazleton Area SD
Supt. — See Hazleton

Valley S 1,200/K-8
79 Rock Glen Rd 18249 570-788-6044
Vincent Fayock, prin. Fax 788-4718

Sunbury, Northumberland, Pop. 10,086
Shikellamy SD 3,100/K-12
200 Island Blvd 17801 570-286-3720
Dr. Alan Lonoconus, supt. Fax 286-3776
www.shikbraves.org
Beck ES, 600 Arch St 17801 200/K-5
Susan Giberson, prin. 570-286-3725
Chief Shikellamy ES 300/K-5
RR 1 Box 246 17801 570-286-3728
Brett Misavage, prin. Fax 286-3730
Oaklyn ES 300/K-5
115 Oak St 17801 570-286-3731
Paul Renn, prin. Fax 286-3762
Sunbury MS 400/6-8
115 Fairmount Ave 17801 570-286-3736
Michael Hubicki, prin. Fax 286-3780
Other Schools – See Northumberland

St. Monica S 100/PK-8
109 Market St 17801 570-286-5983
Susan Bickhart, prin. Fax 286-7351

Susquehanna, Susquehanna, Pop. 1,702
Susquehanna Community SD 1,000/K-12
3192 Turnpike St 18847 570-853-4921
Bronson Stone, supt. Fax 853-3768
www.scschools.org/
Susquehanna Community ES 500/K-6
3192 Turnpike St 18847 570-853-4921
Robert Keyes, prin. Fax 853-3768

Swarthmore, Delaware, Pop. 6,146
Ridley SD
Supt. — See Folsom
Grace Park ES 300/K-5
1097 7th Ave 19081 610-534-1900
Bruce Horne, prin. Fax 328-0110

Wallingford-Swarthmore SD
Supt. — See Wallingford
Kid's Place 200/K-K
100 College Ave 19081 610-892-3470
Tronya Boylan, prin. Fax 938-9682
Swarthmore-Rutledge ES 500/1-5
100 College Ave 19081 610-892-3470
Dr. Gary Davis, prin. Fax 338-0609

Notre Dame DeLourdes S 400/PK-8
990 Fairview Rd 19081 610-328-9330
Barbara Burke, prin. Fax 328-3955

Sweet Valley, Luzerne
Lake-Lehman SD
Supt. — See Lehman
Ross ES 300/K-6
5148 Main Rd 18656 570-477-5050
Donald James, prin. Fax 477-2461

Swiftwater, Monroe
Pocono Mountain SD 11,500/K-12
PO Box 200 18370 570-839-7121
Dr. Dwight Pfennig, supt. Fax 895-4768
www.pmsd.org
Swiftwater Elementary Center 900/K-5
PO Box 200 18370 570-839-7121
Tamula Toleno, prin. Fax 839-5935
Swiftwater IS 400/6-7
PO Box 200 18370 570-839-7121
Krislin Ofalt, prin. Fax 839-5935
Other Schools – See Cresco, Pocono Pines, Tannersville, Tobyhanna

Tamaqua, Schuylkill, Pop. 6,754
Tamaqua Area SD 2,200/K-12
PO Box 112 18252 570-668-2570
Carol Makuta, supt. Fax 668-6850
www.tamaqua.k12.pa.us/
Rush ES 100/K-5
50 Meadow Ave 18252 570-668-6932
Steven Behr, prin. Fax 668-6858
Tamaqua Area MS 500/6-8
PO Box 90 18252 570-668-1210
Christopher Czapla, prin. Fax 668-5027
Tamaqua ES 500/K-5
Boyle Ave 18252 570-668-3306
Steven Behr, prin. Fax 668-3235
Other Schools – See New Ringgold

St. Jerome S 200/K-8
250 W Broad St 18252 570-668-2757
Mary Ann Mansell, prin. Fax 668-6101

Tannersville, Monroe
Pocono Mountain SD
Supt. — See Swiftwater
Pocono Elementary Center 700/K-5
Warner Rd 18372 570-839-7121
Dr. Cathy Sweeney, prin. Fax 629-8531

Tarentum, Allegheny, Pop. 4,677
Deer Lakes SD
Supt. — See Russellton
Curtisville Primary Center 500/K-2
1715 Saxonburg Blvd 15084 724-265-5340
Christopher Brough, prin. Fax 265-1488

Highlands SD
Supt. — See Natrona Heights
Grandview ES 500/PK-5
101 E 9th Ave 15084 724-224-0300
Patrick Graczyk, prin. Fax 224-3178

Taylor, Lackawanna, Pop. 6,227
Riverside SD 1,500/K-12
300 Davis St 18517 570-562-2121
David Woods, supt. Fax 562-3205
www.riversidesd.com/

Riverside ES West 300/K-4
300 Davis St 18517 570-562-2121
Paul Brennan, prin. Fax 562-1790
Other Schools – See Moosic

Telford, Montgomery, Pop. 4,633
Souderton Area SD
Supt. — See Souderton
Vernfield ES 400/K-5
960 Long Mill Rd 18969 215-721-0606
Sharon Fuhrman, prin. Fax 721-6909

Grace Christian S 100/K-6
320 N 3rd St 18969 215-723-5896
Lynn Hewett, admin. Fax 723-7136

Thomasville, York
Spring Grove Area SD
Supt. — See Spring Grove
Paradise ES 400/K-4
6923 Lincoln Hwy 17364 717-225-4731
Annette Julius, prin. Fax 225-4861

St. Rose of Lima S 200/PK-6
115 N Biesecker Rd 17364 717-792-0889
Peggy Rizzuto, prin. Fax 792-3959

Thompsontown, Juniata, Pop. 710
Juniata County SD
Supt. — See Mifflintown
Thompsontown-Delaware ES 100/K-6
6 School St 17094 717-535-5520
Debra Wagner, prin. Fax 535-5061

Thorndale, Chester, Pop. 3,518
Coatesville Area SD
Supt. — See Coatesville
Caln ES 500/K-5
3609 Lincoln Hwy 19372 610-383-3760
Mary Jean Wilson-Stenz, prin. Fax 383-3764

Three Springs, Huntingdon, Pop. 428
Southern Huntingdon County SD 1,400/K-12
10339 Pogue Rd 17264 814-447-5529
Grant Stiffler, supt. Fax 447-3967
www.shcsd.k12.pa.us
Spring Farms ES 200/K-5
12075 Old Plank Rd 17264 814-448-3411
Cathie Brouse, prin. Fax 448-9170
Other Schools – See Cassville, Rockhill Furnace, Shade Gap

Throop, Lackawanna, Pop. 3,949
Mid Valley SD 1,500/K-12
52 Underwood Rd 18512 570-307-1119
Randy Parry, supt. Fax 307-1107
www.mvsd.us
Mid Valley ES 800/K-5
50 Underwood Rd 18512 570-307-3241
Frank Mazur, prin. Fax 307-3239
Mid Valley MS 6-8
54 Underwood Rd 18512 570-307-2130
Debra Demming, prin. Fax 307-2193

Tioga, Tioga, Pop. 605
Northern Tioga SD
Supt. — See Elkland
Walter ES 500/K-6
65 Jct Cross Rd 16946 570-827-2171
Dennis Smith, prin. Fax 827-3451

Tionesta, Forest, Pop. 592
Forest Area SD 600/K-12
22318 Route 62 Unit 16 16353 814-755-4491
William Nichols, supt. Fax 755-2426
www.forestareaschools.org/
West Forest ES 200/K-6
22318 Route 62 Unit 15 16353 814-755-3302
Kevin Sprong, prin. Fax 755-2427
Other Schools – See Marienville

North Clarion County SD 600/K-12
10439 Route 36 16353 814-744-8536
David Stake, supt. Fax 744-9378
www.northclarion.org/
North Clarion County ES 300/K-6
10439 Route 36 16353 814-744-8541
David Stake, prin. Fax 744-9229

Titusville, Crawford, Pop. 5,862
Titusville Area SD 2,200/PK-12
221 N Washington St 16354 814-827-2715
Karen Jez, supt. Fax 827-7761
www.gorockets.org/
Early Childhood Learning Center 300/PK-K
330 E Spruce St 16354 814-827-2715
Diane Robbins, prin.
Hydetown ES 200/1-5
12294 Gresham Rd 16354 814-827-2715
Walter Funk, prin.
Main Street ES, 117 W Main St 16354 300/1-5
Robert Buchan, prin. 814-827-2715
Titusville MS, 415 Water St 16354 500/6-8
Michael McGaughey, prin. 814-827-2715
Other Schools – See Pleasantville

Tobyhanna, Monroe
Pocono Mountain SD
Supt. — See Swiftwater
Clear Run Elementary Center 900/K-5
3700 Memorial Blvd 18466 570-839-7121
Regina Schank, prin. Fax 894-1286
Clear Run Intermediate Center 1,000/6-7
3600 Memorial Blvd 18466 570-839-7121
Jessica Wenton, prin. Fax 894-9329
Coolbaugh Elementary Center 700/2-5
5800 Memorial Blvd 18466 570-839-7121
Karen Doughton, prin. Fax 894-2081
Coolbaugh Learning Center 200/K-1
194 Main St 18466 570-839-7121
Karen Doughton, prin. Fax 894-2079

Topton, Berks, Pop. 1,975
Brandywine Heights Area SD 1,900/K-12
200 W Weis St 19562 610-682-5100
Dr. Martin Handler, supt. Fax 682-5136
www.bhasd.org/
Brandywine Heights Area MS 600/5-8
200 W Weis St 19562 610-682-5131
Dr. Kathy Johnson, prin. Fax 682-5105
District-Topton ES 400/K-4
445 W Barkley St 19562 610-682-5171
Lawrence Rossi, prin. Fax 682-5176
Other Schools – See Fleetwood, Mertztown

Toughkenamon, Chester, Pop. 1,273
Kennett Consolidated SD
Supt. — See Kennett Square
New Garden ES 800/K-5
265 New Garden Rd 19374 610-268-6900
Barbara Decarlo, prin.

Towanda, Bradford, Pop. 2,915
Towanda Area SD 1,300/K-12
PO Box 231 18848 570-265-9894
Diane Place, supt. Fax 265-4881
www.tsd.k12.pa.us/
Morrow ES 400/K-2
101 N 4th St 18848 570-265-4991
Pamela Hosterman, prin. Fax 265-4881
Towanda Area ES 3-6
State and Western Ave 18848 570-265-6131
Pamela Hosterman, prin.

St. Agnes S 100/PK-8
102 3rd St 18848 570-265-6803
Kathleen DeWan, prin. Fax 265-3065

Tower City, Schuylkill, Pop. 1,343
Williams Valley SD 1,100/K-12
10330 Route 209 Rd 17980 717-647-2167
Olga Ehrhart, supt. Fax 647-2055
www.wvsd.k12.pa.us
Williams Valley ES 600/K-6
10400 Route 209 Rd 17980 717-647-2181
Paula Hromyak, prin. Fax 647-7543

Townville, Crawford, Pop. 293
Penncrest SD
Supt. — See Saegertown
Maplewood ES 700/K-6
32695 Highway 408 16360 814-967-2675
Ronald Cokain, prin. Fax 967-2136

Trafford, Westmoreland, Pop. 3,106
Penn-Trafford SD
Supt. — See Harrison City
Level Green ES 300/K-5
650 Cypress Ct 15085 412-372-6603
Jeff Swartz, prin. Fax 372-0114
Trafford ES 200/K-5
100 Brinton Ave 15085 412-372-6600
Karen Garner, prin. Fax 372-1554
Trafford MS 400/6-8
100 Brinton Ave 15085 412-372-6600
Karen Garner, prin. Fax 372-1554

Trevorton, Northumberland, Pop. 2,058
Line Mountain SD
Supt. — See Herndon
Trevorton ES 200/K-6
542 W Shamokin St 17881 570-797-3825
Thea Tafner, prin. Fax 797-4001

Troy, Bradford, Pop. 1,485
Troy Area SD 1,700/K-12
310 Elmira St 16947 570-297-2750
Robert W. Grantier, supt. Fax 297-1600
www.troyareasd.org/
Croman ES 300/K-4
250 Canton St 16947 570-297-3145
Susan Shipman, prin. Fax 297-3260
Troy Area MS 600/5-8
350 High St 16947 570-297-4565
Rebecca Stanfield, prin. Fax 297-5186
Troy ES East 200/K-4
RR 2 Box 300 16947 570-297-2138
Susan Shipman, prin. Fax 297-2200
Other Schools – See Millerton

Tunkhannock, Wyoming, Pop. 1,825
Tunkhannock Area SD 3,100/K-12
41 Philadelphia Ave 18657 570-836-3111
Michael Healey, supt. Fax 836-2942
www.tasd.net/
Evans Falls ES 300/K-4
2055 SR 29 S 18657 570-298-2195
Ann Way, prin. Fax 298-2514
Roslund ES 400/K-4
99 Digger Dr 18657 570-836-8243
Patrick Mulhern, prin. Fax 836-5622
Tunkhannock MS 1,000/5-8
200 Franklin Ave 18657 570-836-8235
Joseph Guglielmo, prin. Fax 836-5796
Other Schools – See Dalton, Mehoopany

Turbotville, Northumberland, Pop. 662
Warrior Run SD 1,800/K-12
4800 Susquehanna Trl 17772 570-649-5138
Daniel Scheaffer, supt. Fax 649-5475
www.wrsd.org
Turbotville ES 300/K-4
4800 Susquehanna Trl 17772 570-649-5164
Jay Gordon, prin.
Warrior Run MS 600/5-8
4800 Susquehanna Trl 17772 570-649-5135
Larry Boyer, prin.
Watsontown ES 400/K-4
4800 Susquehanna Trl 17772 570-538-5562
Susan Welteroth, prin.

Tyrone, Blair, Pop. 5,324
Tyrone Area SD 1,900/PK-12
701 Clay Ave 16686 814-684-0710
Dr. William Miller, supt. Fax 684-2678
www.tyrone.k12.pa.us/
Tyrone Area ES 700/PK-4
601 Clay Ave 16686 814-684-1342
Melissa Russell, prin. Fax 684-2149
Tyrone Area MS 600/5-8
1001 Clay Ave 16686 814-684-4240
Dr. John Vendetti, prin. Fax 682-1013

St. Matthew S 100/PK-6
1105 Cameron Ave 16686 814-684-3510
Melissa McMullen, prin. Fax 684-7833

Ulster, Bradford
Athens Area SD
Supt. — See Athens
Sheshequin-Ulster ES 200/K-5
PO Box 260 18850 570-358-3131
Andrew Latchford, prin. Fax 358-3547

North Rome Christian S 200/K-12
RR 1 Box 190A 18850 570-247-2800
Lee Ann Carmichael, admin. Fax 247-7288

Ulysses, Potter, Pop. 669
Northern Potter SD 600/K-12
745 Northern Potter Rd 16948 814-848-7506
Scott Graham, supt. Fax 848-7431
www.northernpottersd.org
Northern Potter Children's S 300/K-6
745 Northern Potter Rd 16948 814-848-7563
Michael Morgan, prin. Fax 848-7431

Union City, Erie, Pop. 3,364
Union City Area SD 1,300/K-12
107 Concord St 16438 814-438-3804
Sandra Myers, supt. Fax 438-2030
www.ucasd.org/
Union City ES 600/K-5
91 Miles St 16438 814-438-7611
Joyce Lansberry, prin. Fax 438-1085
Union City MS 300/6-8
105 Concord St 16438 814-438-7673
Joseph Neuch, prin. Fax 438-8079

Uniontown, Fayette, Pop. 11,935
Albert Gallatin Area SD 3,800/K-12
2625 Morgantown Rd 15401 724-564-7190
Walter Vicinelly, supt. Fax 564-7195
www.albertgallatin.k12.pa.us/
Swaney ES 400/K-5
1152 Township Dr 15401 724-564-9761
Jason Hutchinson, prin. Fax 564-4232
Other Schools – See Fairchance, Mc Clellandtown, Masontown, Point Marion, Smithfield

Laurel Highlands SD 3,600/K-12
304 Bailey Ave 15401 724-437-2821
Dr. Gary Brain, supt. Fax 437-8929
www.lhsd.org
Clark ES 400/K-5
200 Water St 15401 724-437-9600
Jeanne Moore, prin. Fax 437-9688
Hatfield ES 400/K-5
370 Derrick Ave 15401 724-437-7371
Edward Zelich, prin. Fax 437-9229
Hutchinson ES 300/K-5
213 Mountain View Rd 15401 724-437-6208
Richard Hauger, prin. Fax 437-9774
Laurel Highlands MS 900/6-8
18 Hookton Ave 15401 724-437-2865
Mary Macar, prin. Fax 437-8518
Marshall ES 400/K-5
335 Park St 15401 724-438-5851
Jesse Wallace, prin. Fax 438-7858

Uniontown Area SD 3,400/K-12
23 E Church St 15401 724-438-4501
Charles Machesky, supt. Fax 437-7007
www.uniontown.k12.pa.us
Franklin S 500/K-8
351 Morgantown St 15401 724-439-5020
Yolanda Defino, prin. Fax 439-5018
Lafayette ES 400/K-5
303 Connellsville St 15401 724-438-3581
Paula Work, prin.
Lafayette MS 200/6-8
303 Connellsville St 15401 724-438-3581
Joseph Galie, prin.
Menallen ES 400/K-6
7527 National Pike 15401 724-438-4160
Charles Yasechko, prin.
Other Schools – See Farmington, Markleysburg, Vanderbilt

Chestnut Ridge Christian Academy 100/PK-12
115 Downer Ave 15401 724-439-1090
Patricia D. Cowsert, prin. Fax 439-4540
Montessori S 50/PK-5
199 Edison St 15401 724-439-6116
Marjorie Murphy, dir. Fax 439-6116
St. John the Evangelist S 200/PK-8
52 Jefferson St 15401 724-438-8598
Christine Roskovensky, prin. Fax 438-8585
St. Mary S 200/PK-8
17 Gilmore St 15401 724-438-8471
Melvyn Sepic, prin. Fax 438-3321

Upland, Delaware, Pop. 2,910
Chester-Upland SD
Supt. — See Chester
Main Street S 300/PK-8
704 Main St 19015 610-447-3685
Karen Jones-Rodgers, prin. Fax 447-3684

Upper Black Eddy, Bucks

River Valley Waldorf S 100/PK-8
1395 Bridgeton Hill Rd, 610-982-5606
Klonda Speer, admin. Fax 982-5799

Upper Darby, See Darby
Upper Darby SD
Supt. — See Drexel Hill
Beverly Hills MS 1,500/6-8
1400 Garrett Rd 19082 610-626-9317
Dr. William Bailey, prin.
Bywood ES, 330 Avon Rd 19082 800/1-5
Daniel McGarry, prin. 610-352-6842
Highland Park ES 700/1-5
8301 W Chester Pike 19082 610-853-4530
John Council, prin.
Stonehurst Hills ES 700/1-5
7051 Ruskin Ln 19082 610-626-9111
Linda Sember, prin.

St. Laurence S 400/PK-8
8245 W Chester Pike 19082 610-789-2670
Sr. Helen Thomas McCann, prin. Fax 789-1128

Upper Saint Clair, Allegheny, Pop. 19,692
Upper St. Clair SD 4,100/K-12
1820 McLaughlin Run Rd 15241 412-833-1600
Dr. Patrick O'Toole, supt. Fax 833-5535
www.uscsd.k12.pa.us
Other Schools – See Pittsburgh

Utica, Venango, Pop. 200
Franklin Area SD
Supt. — See Franklin
Utica ES 100/K-6
3823 Academy St 16362 814-425-3279
Mary Peterson, prin. Fax 425-1338

Uwchland, Chester

St. Elizabeth S K-8
PO Box 780 19480 610-646-6540
Eileen Wilson, prin. Fax 321-0257
Windsor Christian Academy 100/K-5
PO Box 596 19480 610-458-7177
Jane McGrath, admin. Fax 458-2569

Valley View, Schuylkill, Pop. 4,660
Tri-Valley SD 900/K-12
110 W Main St 17983 570-682-9013
Mark Snyder, supt. Fax 682-9544
www.tri-valley.k12.pa.us
Hegins-Hubley ES 300/K-6
1801 W Main St 17983 570-682-9011
Gerald Anderson, prin. Fax 682-3124
Other Schools – See Klingerstown

Vanderbilt, Fayette, Pop. 530
Uniontown Area SD
Supt. — See Uniontown
Franklin ES 200/K-6
242 Buena Vista Rd 15486 724-628-6030
Charles Yasechko, prin.

Vandergrift, Westmoreland, Pop. 5,190
Kiski Area SD
Supt. — See Leechburg
Laurel Point ES 100/1-6
200 Poplar St 15690 724-568-2552
Jeff Jackson, prin. Fax 568-1972
Vandergrift ES 500/K-6
200 Poplar St 15690 724-567-6706
Jeff Jackson, prin. Fax 567-6261

Cardinal Maida Academy 100/K-8
315 Franklin Ave 15690 724-568-3304
Tom Stabile, prin. Fax 567-1900

Venetia, Washington
Peters Township SD
Supt. — See Mc Murray
Bower Hill ES 800/K-3
424 Bower Hill Rd 15367 724-941-0913
Kelly Gustafson, prin. Fax 941-0918

Venus, Venango
Cranberry Area SD
Supt. — See Seneca
Pinegrove ES 100/K-5
278 Pinegrove School Rd 16364 814-354-2264
Nicoletta McAninch, prin. Fax 354-2261

Verona, Allegheny, Pop. 2,931
Penn Hills SD
Supt. — See Pittsburgh
Forbes ES 400/K-5
5785 Saltsburg Rd 15147 412-793-2155
Kristin Brown, prin. Fax 793-4433

Riverview SD
Supt. — See Oakmont
Verner ES 200/K-6
700 1st St 15147 412-828-1800
Patty Friday, prin. Fax 828-8086

St. Joseph S 100/K-8
825 2nd St 15147 412-828-7213
Darlene Scopel, prin. Fax 828-4008

Villanova, Delaware

Villanova Academy 100/PK-6
1860 Montgomery Ave 19085 610-520-9624
Dr. Mustafa Ahmed, dir. Fax 520-1213

Volant, Lawrence, Pop. 109
Wilmington Area SD
Supt. — See New Wilmington

East Lawrence ES 100/K-3
1352 Golf Course Rd 16156 724-656-8866
George Endrizzi, prin.

Wallingford, Delaware
Wallingford-Swarthmore SD 3,600/K-12
200 S Providence Rd 19086 610-892-3470
Rudolph Rubeis, supt. Fax 892-3493
www.wssd.org
Nether Providence ES 300/1-5
410 Moore Rd 19086 610-892-3470
Jennifer Gaudioso, prin. Fax 874-3561
Strath Haven MS 900/6-8
200 S Providence Rd 19086 610-892-3470
George King, prin. Fax 892-3492
Wallingford ES 400/1-5
20 S Providence Rd 19086 610-892-3470
Dr. Ellen Milgrim, prin. Fax 891-0486
Other Schools – See Swarthmore

St. John Chrysostom S 200/PK-8
607 S Providence Rd 19086 610-876-7110
Kay Kelly, prin. Fax 876-5923

Walnutport, Northampton, Pop. 2,136
Northampton Area SD
Supt. — See Northampton
Lehigh Township ES 700/K-6
800 Blue Mountain Dr 18088 610-767-1191
Karen Fleming, prin. Fax 767-4731

Warfordsburg, Fulton
Southern Fulton SD 900/K-12
3072 Great Cove Rd Ste 100 17267 717-294-2203
Ralph Scott, supt. Fax 294-2207
sfsd.k12.pa.us
Southern Fulton ES 500/K-6
3072 Great Cove Rd 17267 717-294-3400
Kendra Trail, prin. Fax 294-6428

Warminster, Bucks, Pop. 32,400
Centennial SD 6,100/K-12
433 Centennial Rd 18974 215-441-6000
Dr. Thomas Turnbaugh, supt. Fax 441-8055
www.centennialsd.org/
Leary ES 400/K-5
157 Henry Ave 18974 215-441-6066
Dr. Donna Dunar, prin. Fax 441-6014
Log College MS 700/6-8
730 Norristown Rd 18974 215-441-6075
Dr. Harry Clark, prin. Fax 441-6073
Longstreth ES 400/K-5
999 Roberts Rd 18974 215-441-6087
W. Sewell-Wallace, prin. Fax 441-6015
McDonald ES 600/K-5
666 Reeves Ln 18974 215-441-6157
Keely Mahan, prin. Fax 441-6006
Willow Dale ES 500/K-5
720 Norristown Rd 18974 215-441-6093
Denise Wettstein, prin. Fax 441-6016
Other Schools – See Southampton

Nativity of Our Lord S 500/PK-8
585 W Street Rd 18974 215-675-2820
Susan Klunder, prin. Fax 675-9413

Warren, Warren, Pop. 9,648
Warren County SD
Supt. — See North Warren
Beaty-Warren MS 600/6-8
2 E 3rd Ave 16365 814-723-5200
Rhonda Decker, prin. Fax 723-9503
South Street Early Learning Center 400/K-1
713 Pennsylvania Ave E 16365 814-723-9340
Ann Buerkle, prin. Fax 723-9275
Warren Area ES 700/2-5
349 E 5th Ave 16365 814-723-4230
Ruth Nelson, prin. Fax 723-2361

St. Joseph S 100/K-4
608 Pennsylvania Ave W 16365 814-723-2030
Dr. Howard Ferguson, prin. Fax 723-6042

Warrington, Bucks, Pop. 7,000
Central Bucks SD
Supt. — See Doylestown
Barclay ES 700/K-6
2015 Palomino Dr 18976 267-893-4100
Daniel Estep, prin. Fax 343-0634
Mill Creek ES 1,200/K-6
638 Bellflower Blvd 18976 267-893-3600
Leonard Schwartz, prin. Fax 482-8214
Titus ES 600/K-6
2333 Lower Barness Rd 18976 267-893-4500
Carol Robinson, prin. Fax 343-0413

SS. Joseph & Robert S 100/K-4
40 Valley Rd 18976 215-672-0724
D. Jaster, prin. Fax 442-7972
SS. Joseph & Robert S 100/5-8
850 Euclid Ave 18976 215-343-5100
Donna Maria Meyers, prin. Fax 343-7434

Washington, Washington, Pop. 15,136
McGuffey SD
Supt. — See Claysville
Walker ES 300/K-4
2510 Park Ave 15301 724-222-3061
Sheryl Fleck, prin. Fax 222-2630

Trinity Area SD 3,600/K-12
231 Park Ave 15301 724-223-2000
Dr. R. Tim Marks, supt. Fax 228-2640
www.trinitypride.org
Trinity East ES 400/K-5
252 Cameron Rd 15301 724-225-8140
Jack Minnick, prin. Fax 225-4951
Trinity MS 800/6-8
50 Scenic Dr 15301 724-228-2112
Peter Keruskin, prin. Fax 228-1196

Trinity North ES 400/K-5
225 Midland Dr 15301 724-222-5064
Beth Tully, prin. Fax 229-1031
Trinity South ES 300/K-5
2500 S Main Street Ext 15301 724-225-7490
Michelle Ostrosky, prin. Fax 228-7658
Trinity West ES 400/K-5
1041 Gabby Ave 15301 724-222-4730
Gloria Nalepka, prin. Fax 222-0180

Washington SD 1,400/K-12
201 Allison Ave 15301 724-223-5112
Roberta DiLorenzo Ed.D., supt. Fax 223-5024
www.washington.k12.pa.us
Washington Park ES 500/K-3
801 E Wheeling St 15301 724-223-5150
Kelley Zebrasky, prin. Fax 223-5056
Washington Park ES 4-6
801 E Wheeling St 15301 724-223-5156
Kenneth Patterson, prin. Fax 223-5152
Washington Park MS 300/7-8
801 E Wheeling St 15301 724-223-5060
Cyril Walther, prin. Fax 223-5123

Faith Christian S 100/PK-12
524 E Beau St 15301 724-222-5440
Lucy Hall, prin. Fax 222-5442
Kennedy S 400/PK-8
111 W Spruce St 15301 724-225-1680
Michele Richter, prin. Fax 225-4651

Washington Boro, Lancaster
Penn Manor SD
Supt. — See Lancaster
Central Manor ES 500/K-6
3717 Blue Rock Rd 17582 717-872-1401
Deborah Holt, prin. Fax 872-9515
Letort ES 300/K-6
561 Letort Rd 17582 717-872-9530
Fax 872-9552

Waterfall, Fulton
Forbes Road SD 500/K-12
159 Red Bird Dr 16689 814-685-3866
Dr. Merrill Arnold, supt. Fax 685-3159
Forbes Road ES 200/K-6
143 Red Bird Dr 16689 814-685-3865
Byron Helsel, prin. Fax 685-3217

Waterford, Erie, Pop. 1,420
Fort LeBoeuf SD 2,300/K-12
PO Box 810 16441 814-796-2638
Dr. Michele Campbell, supt. Fax 796-6459
flb.fortleboeuf.net
Fort LeBoeuf MS 600/6-8
PO Box 516 16441 814-796-2681
Matthew Bennett, prin. Fax 796-4712
Waterford ES 500/K-5
PO Box 811 16441 814-796-4833
Jarrin Sperry, prin. Fax 796-3306
Other Schools – See Erie, Mill Village

Watsontown, Northumberland, Pop. 2,148

Watsontown Christian Academy 50/PK-12
1225 8th Street Dr 17777 570-538-9276
H. William Wilhelm, admin. Fax 538-9148

Waverly, Lackawanna
Abington Heights SD
Supt. — See Clarks Summit
Waverly ES 300/K-4
PO Box J 18471 570-585-6300
Mariellen Sluko, prin. Fax 586-4592

Waymart, Wayne, Pop. 1,447
Western Wayne SD
Supt. — See South Canaan
Wilson ES 500/PK-5
74 Belmont St 18472 570-488-6454
Maria Miller, prin. Fax 488-5151

Wayne, Delaware
Radnor Township SD 3,700/K-12
135 S Wayne Ave 19087 610-688-8100
Linda Grobman, supt. Fax 687-3318
www.rtsd.org/
Radnor MS 900/6-8
150 Louella Ave 19087 610-386-6300
Anthony Stevenson, prin. Fax 688-2491
Wayne ES 500/K-5
651 W Wayne Ave 19087 610-687-8480
Sharon McGrath-Johns, prin. Fax 293-0490
Other Schools – See Bryn Mawr, Radnor

Tredyffrin-Easttown SD 6,000/K-12
940 W Valley Rd Ste 1700 19087 610-240-1900
Dr. Daniel Waters, supt. Fax 240-1965
www.tesd.net/
New Eagle ES 400/K-4
507 Pugh Rd 19087 610-240-1550
Karen Whyte, prin. Fax 240-1561
Valley Forge ES 500/K-4
99 Walker Rd 19087 610-240-1600
Rebecca Wills, prin. Fax 240-1615
Valley Forge MS 900/5-8
105 W Walker Rd 19087 610-240-1300
Matthew Gibson, prin. Fax 240-1325
Other Schools – See Berwyn, Devon

Upper Merion Area SD
Supt. — See King of Prussia
Roberts ES 300/K-4
889 Croton Rd 19087 610-205-3751
Sharon Kuznick, prin. Fax 205-3799

Heritage S 200/PK-K
675 N Wayne Ave 19087 610-688-6342
Janet Chambers, dir. Fax 989-0591

St. Isaac Jogues Preschool 100/PK-PK
50 W Walker Rd 19087 610-687-2481
Anna Pawlewicz, dir. Fax 293-9529
St. Katherine of Siena S 400/K-8
229 Windermere Ave 19087 610-688-5451
Frank Tosti, prin. Fax 688-6796

Waynesboro, Franklin, Pop. 9,700
Waynesboro Area SD 4,200/K-12
210 Clayton Ave 17268 717-762-1191
James Robertson, supt. Fax 762-0028
www.wasd.k12.pa.us
Fairview Avenue ES 700/K-6
220 Fairview Ave 17268 717-762-1191
Dianne Eberhardt, prin. Fax 762-3939
Hooverville ES 300/K-6
10829 Buchanan Trl E 17268 717-762-1191
Rita Sterner-Hine, prin. Fax 762-4222
Mowrey ES 600/K-6
7891 Tomstown Rd 17268 717-762-1191
Sherian Diller, prin. Fax 749-5856
Summitview ES 600/K-6
840 E 2nd St 17268 717-762-1191
Aaron Taylor, prin. Fax 762-3764
Waynesboro Area MS 600/7-8
702 E 2nd St 17268 717-762-1191
Brian Richter, prin. Fax 762-6566

St. Andrew S 100/K-6
213 E Main St 17268 717-762-3221
Marilynn Noel, admin. Fax 762-8474

Waynesburg, Greene, Pop. 4,142
Central Greene SD 2,100/K-12
PO Box 472 15370 724-627-8151
Dr. Jerome Bartley, supt. Fax 627-9591
www.cgsd.org
Miller MS 500/6-8
126 E Lincoln St 15370 724-852-2722
John Lipscomb, prin. Fax 627-0637
Waynesburg Central ES 800/K-5
90 Zimmerman Dr 15370 724-627-3081
Debra Iams, prin. Fax 852-1160
Other Schools – See Mount Morris

West Greene SD 600/K-12
1367 Hargus Creek Rd 15370 724-499-5183
Thelma Szarell, supt. Fax 499-5623
www.wgsd.org/
Other Schools – See Graysville, New Freeport

Weatherly, Carbon, Pop. 2,621
Weatherly Area SD 800/K-12
602 6th St 18255 570-427-8681
Frank Victor, supt. Fax 427-8918
www.weatherlysd.org
Weatherly Area ES 300/K-5
602 6th St 18255 570-427-8687
Sandra Slavick, prin. Fax 427-8918
Weatherly Area MS 200/6-8
602 6th St 18255 570-427-8689
Sandra Slavick, prin. Fax 427-8918

Weedville, Elk
Saint Marys Area SD
Supt. — See Saint Marys
Bennetts Valley ES 100/K-5
Route 255 15868 814-787-5481
Christine Kuhar, prin. Fax 787-8766

Wellsboro, Tioga, Pop. 3,342
Wellsboro Area SD 1,600/K-12
227 Nichols St 16901 570-724-4424
Philip Waber, supt. Fax 724-5103
www.wellsborosd.k12.pa.us
Butler MS 500/5-8
9 Nichols St 16901 570-724-2306
David Krick, prin. Fax 724-4143
Gill ES 300/2-4
10 Sherman St 16901 570-724-1811
Wesley Kuratomi, prin. Fax 724-1057
Lappla ES 200/K-1
32 Meade St 16901 570-724-1941
Wesley Kuratomi, prin. Fax 723-1916

Comstock Adventist S 50/1-8
1292 Charleston Rd 16901 570-724-2321
Trinity Lutheran S 100/PK-6
53 West Ave 16901 570-724-7723
Janice Hughes, lead tchr. Fax 723-1053

Wellsville, York, Pop. 275
Northern York County SD
Supt. — See Dillsburg
Wellsville ES 200/K-5
1060 Zeigler Rd 17365 717-432-8691
Steve Lehman, prin. Fax 502-0861

Wernersville, Berks, Pop. 2,393
Conrad Weiser Area SD
Supt. — See Robesonia
Weiser East ES 600/K-4
200 Lincoln Dr 19565 610-678-9901
Lynne Hassler, prin. Fax 678-9279

Wescosville, Lehigh
East Penn SD
Supt. — See Emmaus
Wescosville ES 600/1-5
1064 Liberty Ln 18106 610-395-5851
Anthony Moyer, prin.

West Brandywine, Chester

Pope John Paul II Regional S 400/K-8
2875 Manor Rd, 610-384-5961
Sr. Helen Loretta, prin. Fax 384-5730

West Chester, Chester, Pop. 18,047
Unionville-Chadds Ford SD
Supt. — See Kennett Square
Pocopson ES 600/K-5
1105 Pocopson Rd 19382 610-793-9241
Dr. Andrew McLaughlin, prin. Fax 793-7792

West Chester Area SD 10,800/K-12
829 Paoli Pike 19380 484-266-1000
Dr. James Scanlon, supt. Fax 266-1175
www.wcasd.net
East Bradford ES 500/K-5
820 Frank Rd 19380 484-266-2100
Ann Helion, prin. Fax 266-2199
East Goshen ES 600/K-5
800 N Chester Rd 19380 484-266-1500
Dennis Brown, prin. Fax 266-1599
Fern Hill ES 500/K-5
915 Lincoln Ave 19380 484-266-1600
Dr. Sara Missett, prin. Fax 266-1699
Fugett MS 1,000/6-8
500 Ellis Ln 19380 484-266-2900
Joseph Morris, prin. Fax 266-2999
Glen Acres ES 500/K-5
1150 Delancey Pl 19382 484-266-1700
Dr. Susan Huber, prin. Fax 266-1799
Hillsdale ES 600/K-5
725 W Market St 19382 484-266-2000
Julianne Pecorella, prin. Fax 266-2099
Howse ES 500/K-5
641 W Boot Rd 19380 484-266-1300
Mary Powell, prin. Fax 266-1399
Peirce MS 900/6-8
1314 Burke Rd 19380 484-266-2500
Dr. Anthony Barber, prin. Fax 266-2599
Penn Wood ES 500/K-5
1470 Johnnys Way 19382 484-266-1900
Dr. Ellen Gacomis, prin. Fax 266-1999
Starkweather ES 600/K-5
1050 Wilmington Pike 19382 484-266-2200
Nancy Aronson, prin. Fax 266-2299
Stetson MS 900/6-8
1060 Wilmington Pike 19382 484-266-2700
LeRoy Whitehead, prin. Fax 266-2799
Westtown-Thornbury ES 400/K-5
750 Westbourne Rd 19382 484-266-1800
Timothy Krushinski, prin. Fax 266-1899
Other Schools – See Exton

Goshen Friends S 200/PK-5
814 N Chester Rd 19380 610-696-8869
Tom Richards, hdmstr. Fax 696-2578
St. Agnes S 400/PK-8
211 W Gay St 19380 610-696-1260
Sr. Joan Felicia, prin. Fax 436-9631
St. Maximillian Kolbe S 400/PK-8
300 Daly Dr 19382 610-399-8400
Anita Dixon, prin. Fax 399-4684
SS. Peter & Paul S 300/PK-5
1327 E Boot Rd 19380 610-696-1000
Margaret Egan, prin. Fax 631-0181
SS. Simon & Jude S 400/K-8
6 Cavanaugh Ct 19382 610-696-5249
Sr. Margaret Rose Adams, prin. Fax 696-4682
West Chester Christian S 200/K-12
1237 Paoli Pike 19380 610-692-3700
Dennis Quattlebaum, admin. Fax 631-0132
West Chester Friends S 100/PK-5
415 N High St 19380 610-696-2962
Matthew Bradley, hdmstr. Fax 431-1457
Westtown S 800/PK-12
975 Westtown Rd 19395 610-399-0123
John Baird, hdmstr. Fax 399-3760

Westfield, Tioga, Pop. 1,158
Northern Tioga SD
Supt. — See Elkland
Westfield Area ES 400/K-6
1355 Route 49 16950 814-367-2712
Cheryl Sottolano, prin. Fax 367-2776

West Grove, Chester, Pop. 2,640
Avon Grove SD 5,400/K-12
375 S Jennersville Rd 19390 610-869-2441
Dr. Augustus Massaro, supt. Fax 869-4335
www.avongrove.org/
Avon Grove IS 1,600/3-6
395 S Jennersville Rd 19390 610-869-2010
Todd Harvey, prin. Fax 667-4429
Engle MS 900/7-8
107 Schoolhouse Rd 19390 610-869-3022
Robert Fraser, prin. Fax 869-0827
Penn London ES 1,100/K-2
383 S Jennersville Rd 19390 610-869-9803
Marie DiGiulio, prin. Fax 869-4512

Assumption BVM S 200/K-8
290 State Rd 19390 610-869-9576
Danielle White, prin. Fax 869-4049

West Hazleton, Luzerne, Pop. 3,375
Hazleton Area SD
Supt. — See Hazleton
West Hazleton S 1,000/K-8
325 North St 18202 570-459-3160
Linda Mummey, prin. Fax 459-3122

West Lawn, Berks, Pop. 1,578
Wilson SD 5,200/K-12
2601 Grandview Blvd 19609 610-670-0180
Dr. Thomas Ruth, supt. Fax 334-6430
www.wilsonsd.org/
Lincoln Park ES 100/K-6
400 Dorchester Ave 19609 610-670-0180
Matthew Flannery, prin. Fax 334-6451
West Wyomissing ES 200/K-6
2173 Garfield Ave 19609 610-670-0180
Matthew Flannery, prin. Fax 334-6448
Whitfield ES 600/K-6
2700 Van Reed Rd 19609 610-670-0180
Brad Hart, prin. Fax 334-6446
Other Schools – See Sinking Spring, Wyomissing

St. Ignatius Loyola S 500/PK-8
2700 Saint Albans Dr 19609 610-678-0111
Robert Birmingham, prin. Fax 670-5795

West Middlesex, Mercer, Pop. 884
West Middlesex Area SD 1,200/K-12
3591 Sharon Rd 16159 724-634-3030
Alan Baldarelli, supt. Fax 528-0380
www.wmasd.k12.pa.us
Low ES 300/K-3
3591 Sharon Rd 16159 724-634-3030
J. Vincent Comiskey, prin. Fax 528-0380
Oakview ES 300/4-6
3591 Sharon Rd 16159 724-634-3030
J. Vincent Comiskey, prin. Fax 528-0380

West Mifflin, Allegheny, Pop. 21,236
West Mifflin Area SD 3,200/K-12
3000 Lebanon Church Rd 15122 412-466-9131
Patrick Risha, supt. Fax 466-9260
www.wmasd.org
Barton ES 200/K-5
764 Beverly Dr 15122 412-466-1820
Noelle Haney, prin. Fax 469-3357
Homeville ES 500/K-5
4315 Eliza St 15122 412-461-5946
Melissa Bracco, prin. Fax 461-5465
New Emerson ES 300/K-5
1922 Pennsylvania Ave 15122 412-466-3333
Cathryn Brundage, prin. Fax 469-3373
New England ES 300/K-5
2000 Clairton Rd 15122 412-466-1012
Michael Sable, prin. Fax 469-3367
West Mifflin Area MS 800/6-8
371 Camp Hollow Rd 15122 412-466-3200
David Deramo, prin. Fax 466-0836

St. Agnes S 100/PK-8
653 Saint Agnes Ln 15122 412-466-6238
Sr. Cynthia Wessel, prin. Fax 466-2013
Wilson Christian Academy 300/PK-12
1900 Clairton Rd 15122 412-466-1919
Fax 466-0303

West Newton, Westmoreland, Pop. 2,948
Yough SD
Supt. — See Herminie
West Newton ES 200/K-4
1208 Vine St 15089 724-872-5877
Fax 872-5609

Westover, Clearfield, Pop. 437
Harmony Area SD 400/PK-12
5239 Ridge Rd 16692 814-845-7918
David Goodin, supt. Fax 845-2305
www.harmonyowls.com/
Harmony Area ES 200/PK-6
5239 Ridge Rd 16692 814-845-2300
Ted Focht, prin. Fax 845-7396

West Pittston, Luzerne, Pop. 4,870
Wyoming Area SD
Supt. — See Exeter
Montgomery Avenue ES 500/K-6
100 Montgomery Ave 18643 570-654-1404
Robert Kaluzavich, prin. Fax 602-0555

West Reading, Berks, Pop. 4,005
Wyomissing Area SD
Supt. — See Wyomissing
West Reading ES 300/5-6
421 Chestnut St 19611 610-374-0739
Jamie Whye, prin. Fax 378-5739

Sacred Heart S 200/PK-8
701 Franklin St 19611 610-373-3316
Katherine Napolitano, prin. Fax 373-7299

West Sunbury, Butler, Pop. 100
Moniteau SD 1,700/K-12
1810 W Sunbury Rd 16061 724-637-2117
Dr. Trudy Peterman, supt. Fax 637-3862
www.moniteau.k12.pa.us
McKinney ES 800/K-6
391 Hooker Rd 16061 724-637-2321
Delores Bliss, prin. Fax 637-3877

Wexford, Allegheny
North Allegheny SD
Supt. — See Pittsburgh
Marshall ES 700/K-5
5135 Wexford Run Rd 15090 724-935-4044
Dr. James Bradley, prin. Fax 935-1064
Marshall MS 700/6-8
5145 Wexford Run Rd 15090 724-934-6060
Cynthia Kainaroi, prin. Fax 935-2474

Pine-Richland SD
Supt. — See Gibsonia
Wexford ES 400/K-3
250 Brown Rd 15090 724-935-4631
Rick Walsh, prin. Fax 935-3733

Eden Christian Academy - Wexford Campus 200/PK-6
12121 Perry Hwy 15090 724-935-9301
Carrie Powers, prin. Fax 935-9354
St. Alexis S 400/PK-8
10090 Old Perry Hwy 15090 724-935-3940
Sr. Patricia Montini, prin. Fax 935-0607
St. Alphonsus S 500/PK-8
201 Church Rd 15090 724-935-1152
Sr. Mariella Bradley, prin. Fax 935-1110

Whitehall, Lehigh, Pop. 13,744
Whitehall-Coplay SD 4,300/K-12
2940 MacArthur Rd 18052 610-439-1431
John Corby, supt. Fax 435-0124
www.whitehallcoplay.org
Gockley ES 500/K-1
2932 Zephyr Blvd 18052 610-433-7551
Dr. Mary Fekula, prin. Fax 433-2241

Steckel ES 900/2-4
2928 Zephyr Blvd 18052 610-435-1521
Glenn Noack, prin. Fax 435-4022
Whitehall-Coplay MS 1,400/5-8
2930 Zephyr Blvd 18052 610-439-1439
Peter Bugbee, prin. Fax 740-9308

Christ the King S 200/PK-8
3008 N Ruch St 18052 610-262-4177
Irene Quigley, prin. Fax 262-5632
Lehigh Valley Adventist S 100/PK-8
3950 Mechanicsville Rd 18052 610-799-2341
C. Rutt, prin. Fax 799-2342
Lehigh Valley Lutheran S 100/K-8
3355 MacArthur Rd 18052 610-351-8331
Jody Keim, dir. Fax 351-9811
St. Elizabeth S 200/K-8
433 Pershing Blvd 18052 610-264-0143
Sr. Bonita Smith, prin. Fax 264-1563
St. Stephen's Nursery S 200/PK-K
3900 Mechanicsville Rd 18052 610-435-4260
Fax 435-4156

White Oak, Allegheny, Pop. 8,185
McKeesport Area SD
Supt. — See Mc Keesport
McClure IS 300/4-6
500 Longvue Dr 15131 412-664-3740
Dr. Rula Skezas, prin. Fax 664-3747
White Oak ES 300/K-3
1415 California Ave 15131 412-664-3790
Anthony DeMaro, prin. Fax 664-3794

St. Angela Merici S 200/PK-8
1640 Fawcett Ave 15131 412-672-2360
Lynda McFarland, prin. Fax 672-0880

Wildwood, Allegheny

St. Catherine S 50/PK-PK
PO Box 246 15091 724-486-6001
Kate Morris, prin. Fax 486-6004

Wilkes Barre, Luzerne, Pop. 42,021
Wilkes-Barre Area SD 6,800/K-12
730 S Main St 18702 570-826-7131
Jeffrey Namey Ed.D., supt. Fax 829-5031
www.wbasd.k12.pa.us
Dodson ES 500/K-6
80 Jones St 18702 570-826-7185
Michael Croughn, prin. Fax 820-3717
Flood ES 500/K-6
565 N Washington St 18705 570-826-7245
Marlena Noeckley, prin. Fax 820-3732
Heights/Murray ES 700/K-6
1 S Sherman St 18702 570-826-7255
Brian Benedetti, prin. Fax 820-3733
Kistler ES 900/K-6
301 Old River Rd 18702 570-826-7230
Robert Anthony, prin. Fax 820-3734
Other Schools – See Plains

SS. Nicholas & Mary S 400/K-8
242 S Washington St 18701 570-823-8089
Sr. Mary Slattery, prin. Fax 823-1402
Wilkes-Barre Academy 200/PK-8
20 Stevens Rd 18702 570-823-7574
Janice Huntzinger, prin. Fax 823-9358

Wilkinsburg, Allegheny, Pop. 18,008
Wilkinsburg Borough SD 1,400/PK-12
718 Wallace Ave 15221 412-371-9667
Archie Perrin, supt. Fax 371-4058
www.wilkinsburgschools.org/
Johnston ES 200/PK-6
1256 Franklin Ave 15221 412-731-4680
Tanya Smith, prin. Fax 871-2227
Kelly ES 300/PK-6
400 Kelly Ave 15221 412-371-9504
Rosalind Fisher, prin. Fax 871-2217
Turner ES 300/PK-6
1833 Laketon Rd 15221 412-731-5883
Christine French, prin. Fax 871-2157
Wilkinsburg MS 200/7-8
747 Wallace Ave 15221 412-244-9303
Ella Rawlings, prin. Fax 871-2277

Williamsburg, Blair, Pop. 1,276
Williamsburg Community SD 600/K-12
515 W 3rd St 16693 814-832-2125
Linda Smith, supt. Fax 832-3657
www.williamsburg.k12.pa.us/
Williamsburg Community ES 300/K-6
607 Sage Hill Dr 16693 814-832-2125
Lisa Murgas, lead tchr. Fax 832-3042

Williamsport, Lycoming, Pop. 30,112
Jersey Shore Area SD
Supt. — See Jersey Shore
Nippenose Valley ES 300/K-5
7190 S State Route 44 17702 570-745-7111
Kenneth Dady, prin. Fax 745-3788

Loyalsock Township SD
Supt. — See Montoursville
Loyalsock Twp. MS 300/6-8
2101 Loyalsock Dr 17701 570-323-9439
Timothy Fausnaught, prin. Fax 323-5303

Williamsport Area SD 5,800/K-12
201 W 3rd St 17701 570-327-5500
Dr. Kathleen Kelley, supt. Fax 327-8122
www.wasd.org
Cochran ES 500/K-5
1500 Cherry St 17701 570-322-9731
David Michaels, prin. Fax 322-9733
Curtin MS 400/6-8
85 Eldred St 17701 570-323-4785
Brandon Pardoe, prin. Fax 323-4974
Jackson ES 600/K-5
2500 Newberry St 17701 570-323-1992
Kathryn Eshelman, prin. Fax 323-9006
Lycoming Valley MS 500/6-8
1825 Hayes Ave 17701 570-494-1700
James Dougherty, prin. Fax 494-1706
Roosevelt MS 500/6-8
2800 W 4th St 17701 570-323-6177
Reginald Fatherly, prin. Fax 326-6851
Round Hills ES 300/K-5
136 Grimesville Rd 17701 570-323-3786
Robert Williams, prin. Fax 323-2878
Sheridan ES 300/K-5
915 Sheridan St 17701 570-322-7851
Paul Daniels, prin. Fax 322-3465
Stevens ES 400/K-5
1150 Louisa St 17701 570-322-7853
Kirk Felix, prin. Fax 322-9949
Other Schools – See Cogan Station

Keystone Christian S 50/PK-5
1157 Market St 17701 570-323-7071
Jane Seaman, prin. Fax 323-7071
St. John Neumann Regional Academy 100/K-6
710 Franklin St 17701 570-326-3738
Susan Kaiser, prin. Fax 326-7385

Willow Grove, Montgomery, Pop. 16,325
Abington SD
Supt. — See Abington
Willow Hill ES 300/K-6
1700 Coolidge Ave 19090 215-657-3800
Damon Jordan, prin. Fax 657-4727

Upper Dublin SD
Supt. — See Maple Glen
Fitzwater ES 400/K-5
30 School Ln 19090 215-784-0381
Joanna Roger Ed.D., prin. Fax 784-0797

Upper Moreland Township SD 3,100/K-12
2900 Terwood Rd 19090 215-659-6800
Robert Milrod Ph.D., supt. Fax 659-3421
www.umtsd.org/
Other Schools – See Hatboro

St. David S 300/PK-8
401 Easton Rd 19090 215-659-6393
Sr. Angela Joseph, prin. Fax 659-6377

Willow Hill, Franklin
Fannett-Metal SD 400/K-12
PO Box 91 17271 717-349-7172
Dixie Paruch, supt. Fax 349-2748
www.edline.net/pages/fannett-metal
Fannett-Metal ES 200/K-5
PO Box 91 17271 717-349-2513
Michelle Hall, prin. Fax 349-2748

Willow Street, Lancaster, Pop. 5,817
Penn Manor SD
Supt. — See Lancaster
Pequea ES 400/K-6
802 Millwood Rd 17584 717-464-3831
Jennifer Sugar, prin. Fax 464-3809

Windber, Somerset, Pop. 4,119
Windber Area SD 1,400/PK-12
2301 Graham Ave 15963 814-467-5551
Rick Huffman, supt. Fax 467-4208
www.windberschools.org/wasdweb
Windber Area MS 300/6-8
2301 Graham Ave 15963 814-467-4620
Douglas Ledney, prin.
Windber ES 600/PK-5
421 Sugar Maple Dr 15963 814-467-5596
Fax 467-8594

Windsor, York, Pop. 1,311
Red Lion Area SD
Supt. — See Red Lion
Windsor Manor ES 300/K-6
2110 Windsor Rd 17366 717-246-9312
Timothy Gulley, prin. Fax 417-1201

Wingate, Centre
Bald Eagle Area SD 2,000/K-12
751 S Eagle Valley Rd 16823 814-355-4860
Daniel Fisher, supt. Fax 355-1028
www.beasd.org/
Wingate ES 500/K-6
751 S Eagle Valley Rd 16823 814-355-4872
James Orichosky, prin. Fax 355-5157
Other Schools – See Howard, Port Matilda, Snow Shoe

Womelsdorf, Berks, Pop. 2,766
Conrad Weiser Area SD
Supt. — See Robesonia
Weiser West ES 500/K-4
102 S 3rd St 19567 610-589-2501
Charles Rabuck, prin. Fax 589-9409

Woodlyn, Delaware, Pop. 10,151
Ridley SD
Supt. — See Folsom
Woodlyn ES 300/K-5
Colson Rd 19094 610-534-1900
Adam Staples, prin. Fax 833-2487

Wormleysburg, Cumberland, Pop. 2,651

Harrisburg Academy 500/PK-12
10 Erford Rd 17043 717-763-7811
Dr. James Newman, hdmstr. Fax 975-0894

Wrightstown, Bucks
Council Rock SD
Supt. — See Newtown
Wrightstown ES 400/K-6
729 Penns Park Rd 18940 215-944-2300
Susan Gormley, prin. Fax 944-2397

Wrightsville, York, Pop. 2,255
Eastern York SD 2,600/K-12
PO Box 150 17368 717-252-1555
Dr. Darla Pianowski, supt. Fax 478-6000
www.easternyork.com/
Eastern York MS 600/6-8
PO Box 2003 17368 717-252-3400
Wrightsville ES 400/K-5
320 Chestnut St 17368 717-252-3676
Donald Gillett, prin. Fax 252-9844
Other Schools – See East Prospect, Hellam

Wyalusing, Bradford, Pop. 549
Wyalusing Area SD 1,400/K-12
PO Box 157 18853 570-746-1605
Ray Fleming, supt. Fax 746-9156
www.wyalusingrams.com/
Camptown ES 100/K-6
RR 1 Box 41 18853 570-746-3018
Joseph Darrow, prin. Fax 746-6081
Wyalusing ES 400/K-6
RR 4 Box 4008 18853 570-746-1206
Joseph Darrow, prin. Fax 746-1928
Other Schools – See Laceyville, New Albany

Wyncote, Montgomery, Pop. 2,960
Cheltenham Township SD
Supt. — See Elkins Park
Cedarbrook MS 700/7-8
300 Longfellow Rd 19095 215-881-6423
Iris Parker, prin. Fax 576-5610
Wyncote ES 400/K-4
333 Rices Mill Rd 19095 215-881-6410
Crystal Clark, prin. Fax 881-6462

Ancillae-Assumpta Academy 500/PK-8
2025 Church Rd 19095 215-885-1636
Sr. Maureen Gillespie, prin. Fax 885-2740

Wynnewood, Montgomery, Pop. 7,800
Lower Merion SD
Supt. — See Ardmore
Penn Wynne ES 500/K-5
250 Haverford Rd 19096 610-645-1450
Shawn Bernatowicz, prin.

Friends' Central S - Lower PK-4
228 Old Gulph Rd 19096 610-642-7575
David Felsen, hdmstr.
Perleman Jewish Day S 300/K-5
49 Haverford Rd 19096 610-658-2518
Wendy Smith, prin. Fax 658-2922
Torah Academy of Greater Philadelphia 300/K-12
742 Argyle Rd 19096 610-642-7870
Rabbi Shmuel Jablon, prin. Fax 642-2265

Wyoming, Luzerne, Pop. 3,053
Wyoming Area SD
Supt. — See Exeter
Tenth Street ES 400/K-6
55 10th St 18644 570-693-1914
Margaret Grimes, prin. Fax 613-0298

Wyomissing, Berks, Pop. 10,434
Wilson SD
Supt. — See West Lawn
Spring Ridge ES 400/K-6
1211 Broadcasting Rd 19610 610-670-0180
Caroline DiCenso, prin. Fax 334-6449

Wyomissing Area SD 1,900/K-12
630 Evans Ave 19610 610-374-0739
Dr. Helen Larson, supt. Fax 374-0948
www.wyoarea.org/
Wyomissing Hills ES 600/K-4
110 Woodland Rd 19610 610-374-0739
Aaron Roberts, prin. Fax 374-8487
Other Schools – See West Reading

Yardley, Bucks, Pop. 2,542
Pennsbury SD
Supt. — See Fallsington
Afton ES 600/K-5
1673 Quarry Rd 19067 215-321-8540
Joseph Masgai, prin. Fax 321-3620
Boehm MS 800/6-8
866 Big Oak Rd 19067 215-428-4220
Theresa Ricci, prin. Fax 428-9605
Edgewood ES 800/K-5
899 Oxford Valley Rd 19067 215-321-2410
Michele Spack, prin. Fax 321-2412
Makefield ES 500/K-5
1939 Makefield Rd 19067 215-321-2420
Donna McCormick-Miller, prin. Fax 321-2422
Penn MS 1,000/6-8
1524 Derbyshire Rd 19067 215-428-4280
Larry Ricci, prin. Fax 428-1549
Pennwood MS 1,000/6-8
1523 Makefield Rd 19067 215-428-4237
Patricia Steckroat, prin. Fax 428-4265
Quarry Hill ES 600/K-5
1625 Quarry Rd 19067 215-321-2400
Karen Laarkamp, prin. Fax 369-0804

Abrams Hebrew Academy 200/K-8
31 W College Ave 19067 215-493-1800
Rabbi Ira Budow, dir. Fax 493-1165
Grey Nun Academy 200/PK-8
1750 Quarry Rd 19067 215-968-4151
Marianne Finnegan, prin. Fax 860-7418
St. Ignatius of Antioch S 200/PK-8
995 Reading Ave 19067 215-493-3867
Susan Tarrant, prin. Fax 573-3550

Yeadon, Delaware, Pop. 11,506
William Penn SD
Supt. — See Lansdowne
Bell Avenue ES 300/K-6
1000 Bell Ave 19050 610-284-6100
Phyllis Cubit, prin. Fax 284-2257

Evans ES 400/K-6
900 Baily Rd 19050 610-623-5975
Angela Ladson, prin. Fax 284-2310

York, York, Pop. 40,418
Central York SD 5,000/K-12
775 Marion Rd 17406 717-846-6789
Dr. Michael Snell, supt. Fax 840-0451
www.cysd.k12.pa.us
Central York MS 900/6-8
1950 N Hills Rd 17406 717-846-6789
Edmund McManama, prin.
Hayshire ES, 2801 Hayshire Dr 17406 600/K-3
Barbara Snare, prin. 717-846-6789
North Hills ES, 1330 N Hills Rd 17406 400/4-5
Kevin Youcheff, prin. 717-846-6789
Roundtown ES, 570 Church Rd 17404 500/K-3
Patricia Craig, prin. 717-846-6789
Sinking Springs ES 500/4-5
2850 N Susquehanna Trl 17406 717-846-6789
Charlet Miller, prin.
Stony Brook ES 500/K-3
250 Silver Spur Dr 17402 717-846-6789
Suzanne Drazba, prin.

Dallastown Area SD
Supt. — See Dallastown
Leaders Heights ES 300/K-5
49 Indian Rock Dam Rd 17403 717-741-1826
Charles Patterson, prin. Fax 741-6800
Loganville-Springfield ES 600/K-5
169 N Main St 17403 717-428-2240
Scott Carl, prin. Fax 428-2944
Ore Valley ES 800/K-5
2620 Springwood Rd 17402 717-505-5051
Greg Anderson, prin. Fax 741-2523
York Township ES 700/K-5
2500 S Queen St 17402 717-741-2281
Paula March, prin. Fax 741-2109

Northeastern York SD
Supt. — See Manchester
Conewago ES 200/K-3
570 Copenhaffer Rd 17404 717-266-1644
Joseph Snoke, prin. Fax 266-6365

Red Lion Area SD
Supt. — See Red Lion
Locust Grove ES 500/K-6
3620 E Prospect Rd 17402 717-757-2559
Tammy Grove, prin. Fax 755-9667

Spring Grove Area SD
Supt. — See Spring Grove
New Salem ES 400/K-4
3745 Salem Rd, 717-225-4731
Robert Shick, prin. Fax 792-0329

West York Area SD 3,200/K-12
2605 W Market St 17404 717-792-2796
Dr. Emilie Lonardi, supt. Fax 792-5114
www.wyasd.k12.pa.us
Lincolnway ES 500/2-5
2625 W Philadelphia St 17404 717-792-3902
Cynthia Renehan, prin. Fax 792-3902
Loucks ES 200/K-1
1381 W Poplar St 17404 717-843-6631
Cynthia Renehan, prin. Fax 845-6631
Trimmer ES 500/2-5
1900 Brenda Rd, 717-764-6586
Paula Rudy, prin. Fax 764-6586
Wallace ES 200/K-1
2065 High St, 717-764-6869
Paula Rudy, prin. Fax 764-6869
West York Area MS 800/6-8
1700 Bannister St 17404 717-845-1671
Chad Bumsted, prin. Fax 845-1671

York CSD 6,200/K-12
31 N Pershing Ave 17401 717-845-3571
Sharon Miller, supt. Fax 849-1394
www.ycs.k12.pa.us
Davis ES 400/K-5
300 S Ogontz St 17403 717-849-1246
Deloris Penn, prin. Fax 849-1416
Devers ES 600/K-5
801 Chanceford Ave 17404 717-849-1210
Carol Moore, prin. Fax 849-1416
Ferguson ES 400/K-5
525 N Newberry St 17404 717-849-1344
Sara Baker, prin. Fax 846-3825
Goode ES 700/K-5
251 N Broad St 17403 717-849-1314
Lu Lu Thomas, prin. Fax 846-4612
Jackson ES 500/K-5
177 E Jackson St 17401 717-849-1223
Deb Hummel, prin. Fax 846-4912
McKinley ES 400/K-5
600 Manor St 17401 717-849-1312
Erik Bentzel, prin. Fax 849-1240
Penn MS 900/6-8
415 E Boundary Ave 17403 717-849-1256
Kimberly Bell, prin. Fax 849-1362
Smith MS 800/6-8
701 Texas Ave 17404 717-849-1240
R. Jane Hines, prin. Fax 849-1418

York Suburban SD 2,800/K-12
1800 Hollywood Dr 17403 717-848-2814
Dr. Kathryn Orban, supt. Fax 843-6899
www.yssd.org/
East York ES 500/2-5
701 Erlen Dr 17402 717-755-1021
Dr. Mary Beth Grove, prin. Fax 840-4185
Indian Rock ES 300/2-5
1500 Indian Rock Dam Rd 17403 717-845-6651
Gregory Gulley, prin. Fax 843-3695
Valley View Center 400/K-1
850 Southern Rd 17403 717-843-0305
Dr. Tawn Ketterman, prin. Fax 843-3298
York Suburban MS 700/6-8
455 Sundale Dr 17402 717-755-2841
Victoria Gross, prin. Fax 751-0496

Bible Baptist Christian Academy 100/K-12
4190 N Susquehanna Trl 17404 717-266-0892
Christian S of York 400/PK-12
907 Greenbriar Rd 17404 717-767-6842
Dr. David Thompson, hdmstr. Fax 767-4904
Logos Academy 100/K-8
PO Box 1272 17405 717-846-4448
Traci Foster, hdmstr. Fax 846-9368
St. John Lutheran S 100/PK-6
2580 Mount Rose Ave 17402 717-755-4779
Timothy Gabbert, prin. Fax 840-1845
St. Joseph S 400/PK-6
2945 Kingston Rd 17402 717-755-1797
Patricia Byrnes, prin. Fax 751-0136
St. Patrick S 200/PK-6
235 S Beaver St 17401 717-854-8263
Sr. Mary Muir, prin. Fax 846-6049
York Country Day S 200/PK-12
1071 Regents Glen Blvd 17403 717-843-9805
Nathaniel Coffman, hdmstr. Fax 815-6769
York SDA S 50/PK-9
2220 Roosevelt Ave, 717-764-5603
Fax 764-5603

York Haven, York, Pop. 797
Northeastern York SD
Supt. — See Manchester
York Haven ES 200/K-3
PO Box 5 17370 717-266-5007
Raymond March, prin. Fax 266-7089

York Springs, Adams, Pop. 653
Bermudian Springs SD 2,200/K-12
7335 Carlisle Pike 17372 717-528-4113
Dr. Paul Healey, supt. Fax 528-7981
www.bermudian.org
Bermudian Springs ES 800/K-4
7335 Carlisle Pike 17372 717-528-4113
Roger Stroup, prin. Fax 528-4007
Bermudian Springs MS 700/5-8
7335 Carlisle Pike 17372 717-528-4113
Wade Hunt, prin. Fax 528-0034

Youngsville, Warren, Pop. 1,723
Warren County SD
Supt. — See North Warren
Youngsville S 700/K-8
232 2nd St 16371 814-563-7584
Eric Mineweaser, prin. Fax 563-9032

Warren County Christian S 100/K-12
165 Mead Run Rd 16371 814-563-4457
Richard Kolcharno, prin. Fax 563-7647

Zelienople, Butler, Pop. 4,010
Seneca Valley SD
Supt. — See Harmony
Connoquenessing Valley ES 800/K-4
300 S Pittsburgh St 16063 724-452-8280
DeeAnn Graham, prin. Fax 452-5640

St. Gregory S 200/K-8
115 Pine St 16063 724-452-9731
Mary Nock, prin. Fax 452-4748

Zieglerville, Montgomery
Perkiomen Valley SD
Supt. — See Collegeville
Perkiomen Valley West MS 600/6-8
220 Big Rd 19492 484-977-7210
Ryan Stanson-Marsh, prin. Fax 977-7212

RHODE ISLAND

RHODE ISLAND DEPARTMENT OF EDUCATION
255 Westminster St, Providence 02903-3400
Telephone 401-222-4600
Fax 401-277-6178
Website http://www.ride.ri.gov

Commissioner of Education Deborah Gist

RHODE ISLAND BOARD OF REGENTS
255 Westminster St, Providence 02903-3414

Chairperson Robert Flanders

PUBLIC, PRIVATE AND CATHOLIC ELEMENTARY SCHOOLS

Ashaway, Washington, Pop. 1,584
Chariho Regional SD
Supt. — See Wood River Junction
Ashaway ES 200/K-4
12A Hillside Ave 02804 401-377-2211
Dr. Linda Perra, prin. Fax 377-7735

Barrington, Bristol, Pop. 15,849
Barrington SD 3,500/PK-12
PO Box 95 02806 401-245-5000
Dr. Robert McIntyre, supt. Fax 245-5003
barringtonschools.org
Barrington MS 900/6-8
261 Middle Hwy 02806 401-247-3160
Richard Wheeler, prin. Fax 247-3164
Hampden Meadows ES 500/4-5
297 New Meadow Rd 02806 401-247-3166
Arlene Miguel, prin. Fax 245-5003
Nayatt ES 400/PK-3
400 Nayatt Rd 02806 401-247-3175
Christopher Kennedy, prin. Fax 245-5003
Primrose Hill ES 400/PK-3
60 Middle Hwy 02806 401-247-3170
Fax 245-5003
Sowams ES 200/K-3
364 Sowams Rd 02806 401-247-3180
James Callahan, prin. Fax 245-5003

Barrington Christian Academy 200/K-12
9 Old County Rd 02806 401-246-0113
Elsie Wright, hdmstr. Fax 246-2540
St. Andrew's S 50/3-12
63 Federal Rd 02806 401-246-1230
John Martin, hdmstr. Fax 246-0510
St. Luke S 200/PK-8
10 Waldron Ave 02806 401-246-0990
Maureen Jannetta, prin. Fax 246-2120

Block Island, Washington
New Shoreham SD 100/K-12
PO Box 1890 02807 401-466-7732
Leslie Ryan, supt. Fax 466-3249
www.bi.k12.ri.us
Block Island S 100/K-12
PO Box 1890 02807 401-466-5600
Davida Irving, prin. Fax 466-5610

Bradford, Washington, Pop. 1,604
Westerly SD
Supt. — See Westerly
Bradford ES 200/PK-4
15 Church St 02808 401-348-2283
Debra Pendola, prin. Fax 348-2288

Bristol, Bristol, Pop. 21,625
Bristol Warren Regional SD 3,000/PK-12
151 State St 02809 401-253-4000
Edward Mara Ed.D., supt. Fax 253-1740
www2.bw.k12.ri.us/
Colt Andrews ES 200/K-5
570 Hope St 02809 401-254-5991
Tracey McGee, prin. Fax 254-5941
Guiteras ES 300/K-5
35 Washington St 02809 401-254-5932
Sonya Whipp, prin. Fax 254-5942
Rockwell ES 300/PK-5
1225 Hope St 02809 401-254-5930
Dr. Karen Annotti, prin. Fax 247-3746
Other Schools – See Warren

Our Lady of Mt. Carmel S 200/PK-8
127 State St 02809 401-253-8455
Sr. Carmela Santarsiero, prin. Fax 254-8234

Central Falls, Providence, Pop. 19,159
Central Falls SD 3,400/PK-12
21 Hedley Ave 02863 401-727-7700
Frances Gallo, supt. Fax 727-7722
www.cfschools.net/
Calcutt MS 800/6-8
112 Washington St 02863 401-727-7726
Elizabeth Legault, prin. Fax 724-0870
Feinstein ES 200/1-5
405 Broad St 02863 401-727-7723
Sharon Cabeal, prin. Fax 724-1638
Hunt K 200/PK-K
14 Kendall St 02863 401-727-7720
Edda Carmadello, prin. Fax 724-0577
Risk ES 400/K-5
949 Dexter St 02863 401-727-7731
Maureen Azar, prin. Fax 725-5142
Robertson ES 200/K-5
135 Hunt St 02863 401-727-7733
Sharon Cabral, prin. Fax 724-0889
Veterans Memorial ES 500/K-5
150 Fuller Ave 02863 401-727-7740
Ann Lynch, prin. Fax 725-0941

St. Elizabeth Ann Seton Academy 200/PK-8
909 Lonsdale Ave 02863 401-728-6230
Paul Zona, prin. Fax 723-9532

Charlestown, Washington
Chariho Regional SD
Supt. — See Wood River Junction
Charlestown ES 400/PK-4
363 Carolina Back Rd 02813 401-364-7716
Donna L. Fitts, prin. Fax 364-1169

Chepachet, Providence
Foster-Glocester Regional SD 1,600/6-12
PO Box D 02814 401-568-4175
Michael Barnes Ed.D., supt. Fax 568-4178
www.fg.k12.ri.us/
Other Schools – See North Scituate

Glocester SD 700/PK-5
1145 Putnam Pike 02814 401-568-4175
Robert Wallace, supt. Fax 568-4178
www.fg.k12.ri.us
West Glocester ES 400/PK-5
111 Reynolds Rd 02814 401-567-0350
Dr. Lorraine Bowen, prin. Fax 568-4104
Other Schools – See North Scituate

Clayville, Providence
Scituate SD
Supt. — See North Scituate
Clayville ES 200/K-5
3 George Washington Hwy 02815 401-647-4115
Karen Cappelli, prin. Fax 647-4114

Coventry, Kent, Pop. 31,083
Coventry SD 5,600/PK-12
1675 Flat River Rd 02816 401-822-9400
Kenneth DiPietro, supt. Fax 822-9464
www.coventryschools.net
Blackrock ES 400/PK-5
12 La Casa Dr 02816 401-822-9450
Alicia Renieri-Castle, prin. Fax 822-9452
Feinstein MS of Coventry 1,400/6-8
15 Foster Dr 02816 401-822-9426
Dr. Michael Almeida, prin. Fax 822-9469
Hopkins Hill ES 400/K-5
95 Johnson Blvd 02816 401-822-9477
E. Murphy, prin. Fax 822-9478
Little Oaker Preschool 100/PK-PK
40 Reservoir Rd 02816 401-822-9477
E. Frances Murphy, prin. Fax 822-9492
Oak Haven ES 300/K-5
46 Pettine St 02816 401-822-9470
Kathleen Miner, prin. Fax 822-9472
Tiogue ES 400/K-5
170 E Shore Dr 02816 401-822-9460
Denise Richtarik, prin. Fax 822-9453
Washington Oak ES 500/PK-5
801 Read School House Rd 02816 401-397-1976
Dr. Donna Raptakis, prin. Fax 397-1094
Western Coventry ES 400/K-5
4588 Flat River Rd, Greene RI 02827 401-397-3355
Janice Sullivan, prin. Fax 397-4592

Father John Doyle S 500/PK-8
341 S Main St 02816 401-821-3756
Robert McDermott, prin. Fax 828-8513

Cranston, Providence, Pop. 81,614
Cranston SD 9,800/PK-12
845 Park Ave 02910 401-270-8000
M. Richard Scherza, supt. Fax 270-8703
www.cpsed.net
Arlington ES 200/K-6
155 Princess Ave 02920 401-270-8179
Michelle David, prin. Fax 270-8139
Bain MS 500/7-8
135 Gansett Ave 02910 401-270-8010
Thomas Barbieri, prin. Fax 270-8567
Barrows ES 200/K-6
9 Beachmont Ave 02905 401-270-8160
Joseph Rotz, prin. Fax 270-8506
Dutemple ES 200/K-6
32 Garden St 02910 401-270-8104
Mary Sue Mulligan, prin. Fax 270-8528
Eden Park ES 300/K-6
180 Oakland Ave 02910 401-270-8029
Cheryl Anderson, prin. Fax 270-8530
Edgewood Highland ES 200/PK-6
160 Pawtuxet Ave 02905 401-270-8065
Marlene Gamba, prin. Fax 270-8534
Garden City ES 300/PK-6
70 Plantation Dr 02920 401-270-8073
Mary Ann Casale, prin. Fax 270-8536
Gladstone Street ES 500/K-6
50 Gladstone St 02920 401-270-8080
Mark Garceau, prin. Fax 270-8540
Glen Hills ES 300/K-6
50 Glen Hills Dr 02920 401-270-8005
David Alba, prin. Fax 270-8544
Hope Highlands ES 300/K-6
300 Hope Rd 02921 401-270-8148
Don Cowart, prin. Fax 270-8706
Oak Lawn ES 300/PK-6
36 Stoneham St 02920 401-270-8004
Linda Stanelun, prin. Fax 270-8571
Orchard Farms ES 300/K-6
1555 Scituate Ave 02921 401-270-8801
Dennis Charpentier, prin. Fax 271-8805
Park View MS 500/7-8
25 Park View Blvd 02910 401-270-8090
John DeCristofaro, prin. Fax 270-8527
Peters ES 300/K-6
15 Mayberry St 02920 401-270-8199
Patricia Caporelli, prin. Fax 270-8577
Stadium ES 300/K-6
100 Crescent Ave 02910 401-270-8188
Susan Bryan, prin. Fax 270-8597
Stone Hill ES 200/K-6
21 Village Ave 02920 401-270-8022
Laura Albanese, prin. Fax 270-8636
Waterman ES 200/K-6
722 Pontiac Ave 02910 401-270-8013
Joanne Valk, prin. Fax 270-8614
Western Hills MS 700/7-8
400 Phenix Ave 02920 401-270-8030
Norma Cole, prin. Fax 270-8635
Woodridge ES 300/PK-6
401 Budlong Rd 02920 401-270-8007
Charlotte Josephs, prin. Fax 270-8708
Other Schools – See Providence

Cranston-Johnston Regional S 400/K-8
43 Poplar Dr 02920 401-942-7245
Sandra Jennings, prin. Fax 943-5738
St. Mary S 200/PK-8
85 Chester Ave 02920 401-944-4107
Lisa Lepore, prin. Fax 944-2395
St. Matthew S 100/K-8
1301 Elmwood Ave 02910 401-941-8954
Barbara Dwyer, prin. Fax 781-7722
St. Paul S 200/PK-8
1789 Broad St 02905 401-941-2030
John Corry, prin. Fax 941-0644

Cumberland, Providence
Cumberland SD 5,100/PK-12
2602 Mendon Rd 02864 401-658-1600
Donna Morelle Ed.D., supt. Fax 658-4620
www.cumberlandschools.org/

Ashton ES 400/K-5
130 Scott Rd 02864 401-333-0554
Nidia Karbonik, prin. Fax 334-1811
Community ES 700/K-5
15 Arnold Mills Rd 02864 401-333-5724
Robert Draper, prin. Fax 333-1412
Cumberland Preschool Center 100/PK-PK
364 Broad St 02864 401-723-3250
Kathleen Gibney, prin.
Garvin Memorial ES 400/K-5
1364 Diamond Hill Rd 02864 401-333-2557
Thomas Stepka, prin. Fax 333-2581
McCourt MS 600/6-8
45 Highland Ave 02864 401-725-2092
Armand Pires, prin. Fax 723-1188
McLaughlin Cumberland Hill ES 500/1-5
205 Manville Hill Rd 02864 401-658-1660
Donna Reinalda, prin. Fax 658-0046
North Cumberland MS 700/6-8
400 Nate Whipple Hwy 02864 401-333-6306
Richard Drolet, prin. Fax 333-1926
Norton ES 300/K-5
364 Broad St 02864 401-722-7610
Paula Maloney, prin. Fax 723-1084

Mercymount Country Day S 400/PK-8
75 Wrentham Rd 02864 401-333-5919
Sr. Martha Mulligan, prin. Fax 333-5150

East Greenwich, Kent, Pop. 11,865
East Greenwich SD 2,400/K-12
111 Peirce St 02818 401-398-1201
Charles Meyers, supt. Fax 886-3203
www.egsd.net/
Cole MS 400/7-8
100 Cedar Ave 02818 401-398-1213
Michael Zajac, prin. Fax 886-3283
Eldredge ES 300/4-6
101 1st Ave 02818 401-398-1204
Domenic Giusti, prin. Fax 886-3262
Frenchtown ES 300/K-3
1100 Frenchtown Rd 02818 401-398-1402
Cheryl Vaughn, prin. Fax 886-3204
Hanaford ES 300/4-6
200 Middle Rd 02818 401-886-3270
Christine Uhrin, prin. Fax 886-3267
Meadowbrook Farms ES 300/K-3
2 Chestnut Dr 02818 401-886-3245
Tara McAuliffe, prin. Fax 886-9657

Our Lady of Mercy Regional S 400/PK-8
55 4th Ave 02818 401-884-1618
Sr. Jeanne Barry, prin. Fax 885-3138
Rocky Hill S 300/PK-12
530 Ives Rd 02818 401-884-9070
James Young, hdmstr. Fax 885-4985

East Providence, Providence, Pop. 49,515
East Providence SD 5,800/PK-12
80 Burnside Ave 02915 401-433-6222
Mario Cirillo Ed.D., supt. Fax 433-6256
www.epschoolsri.com/
Hennessey ES 300/K-5
75 Fort St 02914 401-435-7831
Dave Britto, prin. Fax 435-7835
Kent Heights ES 300/K-5
2680 Pawtucket Ave 02914 401-435-7824
Fatima Avila, prin. Fax 435-7839
Martin MS 900/6-8
111 Brown St 02914 401-435-7819
Glenn Piros, prin. Fax 435-7851
Orlo Avenue ES 300/K-5
25 Orlo Ave 02914 401-435-7834
Cheryl Gibbs, prin. Fax 435-7825
Whiteknact ES 200/K-5
261 Grosvenor Ave 02914 401-435-7828
Linda Succi, prin. Fax 435-7862
Other Schools – See Riverside, Rumford

Gordon S 400/PK-8
45 Maxfield Ave 02914 401-434-3833
Ralph Wales, hdmstr. Fax 431-0320
Sacred Heart S 100/K-8
56 Purchase St 02914 401-434-1080
Sr. Nancy McClennon, prin. Fax 434-4638
St. Margaret S 200/PK-8
42 Bishop Ave 02916 401-434-2338
John Rezendes, prin. Fax 431-0266
St. Mary Academy-Bay View 500/PK-8
3070 Pawtucket Ave 02915 401-434-0113
Cynthia Lorincz, prin. Fax 434-4756

Esmond, Providence, Pop. 4,400
Smithfield SD 2,600/PK-12
49 Farnum Pike 02917 401-231-6606
Robert O'Brien, supt. Fax 232-0870
www.ri.net/schools/Smithfield/District/
Other Schools – See Greenville, Smithfield

Exeter, Washington
Exeter-West Greenwich Regional SD
Supt. — See West Greenwich
Metcalf ES 600/3-6
30 Nooseneck Hill Rd 02822 401-397-3375
Louise Boyce, prin. Fax 397-0011
Wawaloam ES 300/1-2
100 Victory Hwy 02822 401-295-8808
Melissa Marino, prin. Fax 295-5340

Foster, Providence
Foster SD 300/PK-5
160 Foster Center Rd 02825 401-647-5100
Robert Wallace, supt. Fax 647-3750
www.ri.net/schools/Foster/paine/HomePagex.html
Paine ES 300/PK-5
160 Foster Center Rd 02825 401-647-5100
Gary Moore, prin. Fax 647-3750

Greenville, Providence, Pop. 8,303
Smithfield SD
Supt. — See Esmond
Winsor ES 300/K-5
562 Putnam Pike 02828 401-949-2059
Bridget Morisseau, prin. Fax 949-7385

Harrisville, Providence, Pop. 1,654
Burrillville SD 2,500/PK-12
2300 Broncos Hwy 02830 401-568-1301
Steven Welford, supt. Fax 568-4111
www.bsd-ri.net/
Burrillville MS 600/6-8
2220 Broncos Hwy 02830 401-568-1320
Lois Short, prin. Fax 568-1317
Callahan ES 300/2-5
75 Callahan School St 02830 401-568-1330
David Brissette, prin. Fax 568-1328
Levy ES 400/PK-1
135 Harrisville Main St 02830 401-568-1340
Laurie Sullivan, prin. Fax 568-1318
Other Schools – See Pascoag

Hope, Providence
Scituate SD
Supt. — See North Scituate
Hope ES 300/K-5
391 North Rd 02831 401-821-3651
Janice Mowry, prin. Fax 823-4976

Hope Valley, Washington, Pop. 1,446
Chariho Regional SD
Supt. — See Wood River Junction
Hope Valley ES 300/PK-4
15 Thelma Dr 02832 401-539-2321
Richard Finlaw, prin. Fax 539-1354

Jamestown, Newport, Pop. 4,999
Jamestown SD 500/PK-8
76 Melrose Ave 02835 401-423-7020
Dr. Marcia Lukon, supt. Fax 423-7022
www.jamestownri.com/school
Jamestown ES 300/PK-4
76 Melrose Ave 02835 401-423-7020
Carole Melucci, prin. Fax 423-7022
Jamestown MS 200/5-8
55 Lawn Ave 02835 401-423-7010
Kathleen Almanzor, prin. Fax 423-7012

Johnston, Providence, Pop. 26,542
Johnston SD 2,900/PK-12
10 Memorial Ave 02919 401-233-1900
Margaret Iacovelli, supt. Fax 233-1907
www.ri.net/schools/johnston
Barnes ES 200/1-5
24 Barnes Ave 02919 401-231-8710
Bernard DiLullo, prin. Fax 231-7470
Brown Avenue ES 200/1-5
14 Brown Ave 02919 401-934-0270
Helina Dlugon, prin. Fax 934-2115
ECC 200/PK-K
10 Memorial Ave 02919 401-233-0054
Elizabeth Box, prin. Fax 233-0081
Ferri MS 800/6-8
10 Memorial Ave 02919 401-233-1930
Fax 233-1943
Thornton ES 200/1-5
4 School St 02919 401-943-7369
Louise Denham, prin. Fax 943-6940
Winsor Hill ES 300/1-5
100 Theresa St 02919 401-831-4619
Michele Zarcaro-Tampella, prin. Fax 421-5660

St. Rocco S 400/PK-8
931 Atwood Ave 02919 401-944-2993
Magdalen Chianese, prin. Fax 944-3019
Trinity Christian Academy 100/PK-12
2119 Hartford Ave 02919 401-934-0202
Jeremy McLellan, prin. Fax 934-1758

Lincoln, Providence, Pop. 18,045
Lincoln SD 4,200/PK-12
1624 Lonsdale Ave 02865 401-721-3300
Georgia Fortunato, supt. Fax 726-1813
www.lincolnps.org/
Fairlawn ES 200/PK-1
3 Fairlawn Way 02865 401-726-2930
Joyce Ruppell, prin. Fax 722-2650
Lincoln Central ES 300/2-5
1081 Great Rd 02865 401-334-2800
William Skitt, prin. Fax 334-4294
Lincoln MS 800/6-8
152 Jenckes Hill Rd 02865 401-721-3400
Bruce Macksoud, prin. Fax 333-9977
Lonsdale ES 200/2-5
270 River Rd 02865 401-725-4200
Jeannine Magliocco, prin. Fax 722-0920
Northern Early Learning Center 200/PK-1
315 New River Rd 02865 401-765-8698
Monique Latessa, prin. Fax 765-0530
Saylesville ES 300/2-5
50 Woodland St 02865 401-723-5240
Margaret Knowlton, prin. Fax 722-1090
Other Schools – See Manville

Lincoln SDA S 50/K-8
PO Box 153 02865 401-723-7999
Venetta Jarvis, prin. Fax 724-4364

Little Compton, Newport
Little Compton SD 300/K-8
PO Box 178 02837 401-635-2351
Dr. Harold Devine, supt. Fax 635-2191
www.littlecomptonschools.org
Wilbur & McMahon S 300/K-8
PO Box 178 02837 401-635-2351
James Gibney, prin. Fax 635-2191

Manville, Providence, Pop. 3,000
Lincoln SD
Supt. — See Lincoln
Northern Lincoln ES 300/2-5
315 New River Rd 02838 401-769-0261
Linda Cliff, prin. Fax 765-0560

Matunuck, Washington
South Kingstown SD
Supt. — See Wakefield
Matunuck ES 300/K-5
310 Matunuck Beach Rd 02879 401-360-1234
Debra Zepp, prin. Fax 360-1235

Middletown, Newport, Pop. 3,400
Middletown SD 1,900/PK-12
26 Oliphant Ln 02842 401-849-2122
Rosemarie Kraeger, supt. Fax 849-0202
www.ri.net/middletown/
Aquidneck ES 300/PK-3
70 Reservoir Rd 02842 401-847-4921
Michelle Fonseca, prin. Fax 846-7010
Forest Ave ES 200/PK-3
315 Forest Ave 02842 401-849-9434
Stephen Ponte, prin. Fax 846-4709
Gaudet MS 800/4-8
1113 Aquidneck Ave 02842 401-846-6395
Vincent Giuliano, prin. Fax 847-7580

All Saints Academy 200/K-8
915 W Main Rd 02842 401-848-4300
Dr. John Finnegan, prin. Fax 848-5587

Narragansett, Washington, Pop. 3,721
Narragansett SD 1,500/PK-12
25 5th Ave 02882 401-792-9450
Katherine Sipala, supt. Fax 792-9439
www.narragansett.k12.ri.us/
Narragansett ES 500/PK-4
55 Mumford Rd 02882 401-792-9420
Gail Dandurand, prin. Fax 792-9424
Narragansett Pier MS 500/5-8
235 S Pier Rd 02882 401-792-9430
Marie Ahern, prin. Fax 792-9436

Newport, Newport, Pop. 25,340
Newport SD 2,200/PK-12
437 Broadway 02840 401-847-2100
John Ambrogi Ed.D., supt. Fax 849-0170
www.newportrischools.org/
Carey ES 200/K-5
32 Narragansett Ave 02840 401-847-1690
Kimberly Behan, prin. Fax 842-0210
Coggeshall ES 200/K-5
134 Van Zandt Ave 02840 401-847-0363
Michael Franco, prin. Fax 842-0421
Cranston-Calvert ES 300/K-5
15 Cranston Ave 02840 401-847-1660
Jennifer Booth, prin. Fax 847-1665
Sullivan ES 200/PK-5
35 Dexter St 02840 401-847-2023
Maria Mare Schulz, prin. Fax 842-0601
Thompson MS 500/6-8
55 Broadway 02840 401-847-1493
Eric Thomas Ed.D., prin. Fax 849-3426
Underwood ES 200/K-5
90 Harrison Ave 02840 401-847-2785
Patricia Gablinske, prin. Fax 845-8558

St. Joseph of Cluny Sisters S 200/PK-8
75 Brenton Rd 02840 401-847-6043
Meredith Caswell, prin. Fax 848-5678
St. Michael's Country Day S 200/PK-8
180 Rhode Island Ave 02840 401-849-5970
Whitney Slade, hdmstr. Fax 849-7890

North Kingstown, Washington, Pop. 2,800
North Kingstown SD 4,500/K-12
100 Fairway Dr 02852 401-268-6200
Philip Thornton, supt. Fax 268-6405
www.nksd.net
Davisville ES 200/K-3
50 East Ct 02852 401-541-6340
Louise DiCarlo, prin. Fax 541-6350
Davisville MS 600/6-8
200 School St 02852 401-541-6300
Ruthanne Logan, prin. Fax 541-6310
Fishing Cove ES 300/K-3
110 Wickford Point Rd 02852 401-268-6580
Edie Dunn, prin. Fax 268-6590
Forest Park ES 200/K-3
50 Woodlawn Dr 02852 401-541-6380
Robert Vincze, prin. Fax 541-6390
Hamilton ES 400/4-5
25 Salisbury Ave 02852 401-268-6520
Morag Cronkite, prin. Fax 268-6530
Quidnessett ES 300/4-5
166 Mark Dr 02852 401-541-6360
Louise Denette, prin. Fax 541-6370
Stony Lane ES 500/K-3
825 Stony Ln 02852 401-268-6540
Joan Crothers, prin. Fax 268-6550
Wickford MS 500/6-8
250 Tower Hill Rd 02852 401-268-6470
Terry Merkel, prin. Fax 268-6480

South County Montessori S 100/PK-2
1239 Tower Hill Rd 02852 401-294-3575
Marika Moosbrugger, dir. Fax 295-8444
West Bay Christian Academy 200/K-8
475 School St 02852 401-884-3600
Dr. Richard Clarkson, dir. Fax 886-1650

North Providence, Providence, Pop. 32,500
North Providence SD 3,300/PK-12
2240 Mineral Spring Ave 02911 401-233-1100
Donna Ottaviano Ed.D., supt. Fax 233-1106

Birchwood MS 400/6-8
10 Birchwood Dr 02904 401-233-1120
Kenneth Ferrara, prin. Fax 353-6903
Centredale ES 200/PK-5
41 Angell Ave 02911 401-233-1145
Joan Piccardi, prin. Fax 232-5279
Greystone ES 200/K-5
100 Morgan Ave 02911 401-233-1130
Thomas Meagher, prin. Fax 232-5403
Marieville ES 300/K-5
1135 Mineral Spring Ave 02904 401-725-0099
Bruce Butler, prin. Fax 727-3249
McGuire ES 200/K-5
55 Central Ave 02911 401-233-1135
Lorraine Moschella, prin. Fax 232-5408
Olney ES 200/K-5
1378 Douglas Ave 02904 401-233-1160
Arthur Corsini, prin. Fax 353-4356
Ricci MS 400/6-8
51 Intervale Ave 02911 401-233-1170
Lucille Delasanta, prin. Fax 232-5421
Whelan ES 200/K-5
1440 Mineral Spring Ave 02904 401-233-1180
Paul Morry, prin. Fax 353-1465

North Scituate, Providence
Foster-Glocester Regional SD
Supt. — See Chepachet
Ponaganset MS 700/6-8
7 Rustic Hill Rd 02857 401-647-3361
Patricia Marcotte, prin. Fax 647-1792

Glocester SD
Supt. — See Chepachet
Fogarty Memorial ES 300/K-5
736 Snake Hill Rd 02857 401-568-6211
Richard Maresca, prin. Fax 568-3776

Scituate SD 1,800/PK-12
PO Box 188 02857 401-647-4100
Dr. Paul Lescault, supt. Fax 647-4102
www.scituateri.net
North Scituate ES 300/PK-5
46 Institute Ln 02857 401-647-4110
Marilyn DiMicco, prin. Fax 647-4112
Scituate MS 500/6-8
94 Trimtown Rd 02857 401-647-4123
Michael Zajac, prin. Fax 647-4104
Other Schools – See Clayville, Hope

North Smithfield, Providence, Pop. 10,497
North Smithfield SD
Supt. — See Slatersville
North Smithfield ES 600/PK-2
2214 Providence Pike 02896 401-765-2260
Carolyn Frayne, prin. Fax 765-8665
North Smithfield MS 300/6-8
1850 Providence Pike 02896 401-597-6100
John Lahar, prin. Fax 597-6121

Pascoag, Providence, Pop. 5,011
Burrillville SD
Supt. — See Harrisville
Steere Farm ES 400/PK-5
915 Steere Farm Rd 02859 401-568-1350
Cynthia Dunham, prin. Fax 568-1353

Fr. Holland Catholic Regional S 100/PK-7
180 Sayles Ave 02859 401-568-4589
Shawn Capron, prin. Fax 567-9069

Pawtucket, Providence, Pop. 73,742
Pawtucket SD 8,800/PK-12
PO Box 388 02862 401-729-6315
Dr. Hans Dellith, supt. Fax 727-1641
www.psdri.net
Baldwin ES 700/K-6
50 Whitman St 02860 401-729-6264
Raymond Dalton, prin. Fax 729-6269
Cunningham ES 500/K-6
40 Baldwin St 02860 401-729-6262
Darryl Luffborough, prin. Fax 729-9201
Curtis Memorial ES 300/K-6
582 Benefit St 02861 401-729-6252
Fax 721-2100
Curvin-McCabe ES 400/K-6
466 Cottage St 02861 401-729-6258
Fax 729-6538
Fallon Memorial ES 600/K-6
62 Lincoln Ave 02861 401-729-6254
Joan DiOrio, prin. Fax 729-6306
Goff JHS 500/7-8
974 Newport Ave 02861 401-729-6500
Lisa Benedetti Ramzi, prin. Fax 721-2105
Greene ES 500/PK-6
285 Smithfield Ave 02860 401-729-6260
Jackie Ash, prin. Fax 729-9200
Jenks JHS 500/7-8
350 Division St 02860 401-729-6520
Susan Pfeil, prin. Fax 729-6524
Little ES 400/K-6
60 S Bend St 02860 401-729-6256
Jean Friend, prin. Fax 729-6323
Potter-Burns ES 500/K-6
973 Newport Ave 02861 401-729-6250
Cheryl McWilliams, prin. Fax 729-6337
Slater JHS 600/7-8
281 Mineral Spring Ave 02860 401-729-6480
Fax 729-6490
Varieur ES 300/K-6
486 Pleasant St 02860 401-729-6266
Kathleen Suriani, prin. Fax 729-6544
Winters ES 500/K-6
481 Broadway 02860 401-729-6272
Keith Hemenway, prin. Fax 729-6414

St. Cecilia S 400/PK-8
755 Central Ave 02861 401-723-9463
Simone Kennedy, prin. Fax 722-1444

St. Teresa S 200/PK-8
140 Woodhaven Rd 02861 401-726-1414
Mary Carney, prin. Fax 722-6998
Woodlawn Catholic Regional S 200/K-8
61 Hope St 02860 401-723-3759
Veronica Procopio, prin. Fax 722-4090

Peace Dale, See Wakefield
South Kingstown SD
Supt. — See Wakefield
Curtis Corner MS 500/6-8
301 Curtis Corner Rd 02879 401-360-1333
Michele Humbyrd, prin. Fax 360-1334
Peace Dale ES 500/K-5
109 Kersey Rd 02879 401-360-1600
Pauline Lisi, prin. Fax 360-1601

Portsmouth, Newport, Pop. 3,600
Portsmouth SD 2,800/PK-12
29 Middle Rd 02871 401-683-1039
Susan Lusi Ph.D., supt. Fax 683-5204
portsmouthschoolsri.net
Elmhurst ES 300/K-5
1 Frank Coelho Dr 02871 401-683-3899
Robert Ettinger, prin. Fax 683-9087
Hathaway ES 400/K-5
53 Tallman Ave 02871 401-683-0500
Dr. Christina Martin, prin. Fax 683-0525
Melville ES 300/PK-5
1351 W Main Rd 02871 401-683-1650
Dr. Joanne Olson, prin. Fax 683-3412
Portsmouth MS 700/6-8
125 Jepson Ln 02871 401-849-3700
Joseph Amaral, prin. Fax 841-8420

Aquidneck Island Christian Academy 50/K-12
321 E Main Rd 02871 401-849-5550
Stephen Bailey, admin. Fax 849-6811
Pennfield S 200/PK-8
110 Sandy Point Ave 02871 401-849-4646
Robert Kelley, hdmstr. Fax 847-6720
St. Philomena S 400/K-8
324 Corys Ln 02871 401-683-0268
Donna Bettencourt-Glavin, prin. Fax 683-6554

Providence, Providence, Pop. 176,862
Cranston SD
Supt. — See Cranston
Rhodes ES 200/K-6
160 Shaw Ave 02905 401-270-8110
Kenneth Blackman, prin. Fax 270-8579

Providence SD 23,400/PK-12
797 Westminster St 02903 401-456-9100
Donnie Evans Ed.D., supt. Fax 456-9252
www.providenceschools.org
Bailey ES 400/PK-5
65 Gordon Ave 02905 401-456-1735
Joseph Picchione, prin. Fax 456-1786
Bridgham MS 600/6-8
1655 Westminster St 02909 401-456-9360
Thomas Montaquila, prin. Fax 453-8632
Carnevale ES 600/PK-6
50 Springfield St 02909 401-278-0554
Deborah Bessette, prin. Fax 278-0556
D'Abate ES 400/K-5
60 Kossuth St 02909 401-456-9416
Lucille Furia, prin. Fax 453-8647
Feinstein ES 400/K-5
1450 Broad St 02905 401-456-9367
Christine Riley, prin. Fax 456-9489
Feinstein ES 500/K-5
159 Sackett St 02907 401-456-9407
Mercedes Torres, prin. Fax 453-8658
Flynn ES 500/K-5
220 Blackstone St 02905 401-456-9373
Joyce Fitzpatrick, prin. Fax 453-8648
Fogarty ES 400/K-5
199 Oxford St 02905 401-456-9381
Steven Olsen, prin. Fax 453-8649
Fortes Academy 400/K-6
234 Daboll St 02907 401-278-0501
Lori Hughes, prin. Fax 278-0503
Fortes/Lima Annex ES 200/PK-1
65 Greenwich St 02907 401-278-2872
Andrea Riquetti, prin. Fax 278-2862
Greene MS 900/6-8
721 Chalkstone Ave 02908 401-456-9347
Dr. Nicole Mathis-Thomas, prin. Fax 453-8630
Gregorian ES 300/PK-6
455 Wickenden St 02903 401-456-9377
Anthony DeAngelis, prin. Fax 453-8650
Hopkins MS 600/6-8
480 Charles St 02904 401-456-9203
Albert Paranzino, prin. Fax 456-9226
Kennedy ES 500/K-6
195 Nelson St 02908 401-456-9403
Gina Picard, prin. Fax 453-8652
King ES 500/PK-6
35 Camp St 02906 401-456-9398
Michael Lazzareschi, prin. Fax 456-9497
Kizirian ES 600/K-6
60 Camden Ave 02908 401-456-9369
Deborah Ruggieri, prin. Fax 456-9496
Laurel Hill Avenue Annex ES 200/K-1
240 Laban St 02909 401-456-1783
Dorothy Smith, prin. Fax 456-1785
Laurel Hill Avenue ES 400/2-5
85 Laurel Hill Ave 02909 401-456-9389
Dorothy Smith, prin. Fax 453-8653
Lauro ES 800/PK-6
99 Kenyon St 02903 401-456-9391
Robin Mathis, prin. Fax 456-9246
Lima ES 300/2-6
222 Daboll St 02907 401-278-0504
Jose Valerio, prin. Fax 278-0506

Messer Annex ES 200/K-1
245 Althea St 02909 401-456-9441
Denise Missry-Milburn, prin. Fax 453-8654
Messer ES 300/2-5
158 Messer St 02909 401-456-9401
Denise Missry-Milburn, prin. Fax 456-9486
Perry MS 800/6-8
370 Hartford Ave 02909 401-456-9352
Frances Rotella, prin. Fax 453-8634
Pleasant View ES 500/PK-5
50 Obediah Brown Rd 02909 401-456-9325
Thomas Bacon, prin. Fax 453-8656
Reservoir Avenue ES 200/K-5
156 Reservoir Ave 02907 401-456-9406
Socorro Gomez-Potter, prin. Fax 453-8657
Springfield MS 500/6-8
152 Springfield St 02909 401-278-0557
Dinah Larbi, prin. Fax 278-0564
Stuart MS 800/6-8
188 Princeton Ave 02907 401-456-9341
Marc Catone, prin. Fax 453-8659
Veazie Street ES 600/K-6
211 Veazie St 02904 401-453-8601
Susan Chin, prin. Fax 453-8660
Webster Avenue ES 300/K-6
191 Webster Ave 02909 401-456-9414
Alicia Jones, prin. Fax 453-8661
West Broadway ES 500/PK-5
152 Springfield St 02909 401-456-9102
Frank Piccirilli, prin. Fax 456-9485
West ES 600/K-6
145 Beaufort St 02908 401-456-9337
Rachel Mellion, prin. Fax 456-9487
Williams MS 800/6-8
278 Thurbers Ave 02905 401-456-9355
Rudolph Mosely, prin. Fax 453-8631
Windmill Street ES 400/K-5
110 Paul St 02904 401-456-9419
Eusebio Lopes, prin. Fax 453-8662
Woods ES 400/K-5
674 Prairie Ave 02905 401-278-0515
Dr. Guy Alba, prin. Fax 278-0541
Young ES 300/K-6
674 Prairie Ave 02905 401-278-0517
Dr. Guy Alba, prin. Fax 278-0541

Barnard S 300/PK-6
600 Mount Pleasant Ave 02908 401-456-8127
Dr. Ronald Tibbetts, prin. Fax 456-8128
Bishop McVinney Regional S 200/PK-8
155 Gordon Ave 02905 401-781-2370
Louis Hebert, prin. Fax 785-2618
Blessed Sacrament S 300/PK-8
240 Regent Ave 02908 401-831-3993
June Spencer, prin. Fax 223-0536
Brown S 800/PK-12
250 Lloyd Ave 02906 401-831-7350
Joanne Hoffman, hdmstr. Fax 455-0084
Community Preparatory S 200/3-8
126 Somerset St 02907 401-521-9696
Dan Corley, hdmstr. Fax 521-9715
French-American S of Rhode Island 200/PK-8
75 John St 02906 401-274-3325
Dominique Thompson, hdmstr. Fax 455-3437
Holy Ghost S 200/PK-8
35 Swiss St 02909 401-421-4455
Carol Wood-Soltys, prin. Fax 421-5444
Jewish Community Day S of Rhode Island 200/PK-8
85 Taft Ave 02906 401-751-2470
Robert Sarkisian, hdmstr. Fax 351-7674
Lincoln S 400/PK-12
301 Butler Ave 02906 401-331-9696
Julia Eells, hdmstr. Fax 751-6670
Montessori Childrens House 100/PK-3
518 Lloyd Ave 02906 401-331-6120
Troy Locke, dir. Fax 331-0437
Providence Hebrew S 100/PK-12
450 Elmgrove Ave 02906 401-331-5327
Rabbi Peretz Scheinerman, dean Fax 331-0030
St. Augustine S 300/PK-8
635 Mount Pleasant Ave 02908 401-831-1213
Kathleen Morry, prin. Fax 831-4256
St. Patrick S 100/6-8
244 Smith St 02908 401-421-9300
Stephen Raymond, prin. Fax 421-0810
St. Pius V S 200/PK-8
49 Elmhurst Ave 02908 401-421-9750
Sr. Mary Agnes Greiffendorf, prin. Fax 455-3928
St. Thomas Regional S 200/K-8
15 Edendale Ave 02911 401-351-0403
Mary DiMuccio, prin. Fax 351-0403
Wheeler S 800/PK-12
216 Hope St 02906 401-421-8100
Dan Miller, hdmstr. Fax 751-7674

Riverside, See East Providence
East Providence SD
Supt. — See East Providence
Meadowcrest ECC 100/PK-K
60 Bart Dr 02915 401-433-6209
Jane Sylvia, prin. Fax 433-6247
Oldham ES 200/K-5
640 Bullocks Point Ave 02915 401-433-6250
Nadine Lima Ed.D., prin. Fax 433-6234
Riverside MS 500/6-8
179 Forbes St 02915 401-433-6230
Sandra Forand, prin. Fax 433-6261
Silver Spring ES 200/K-5
120 Silver Spring Ave 02915 401-435-7836
Nancy Cullion, prin. Fax 435-7826
Waddington ES 500/K-5
101 Legion Way 02915 401-433-6235
Patricia Barlow, prin. Fax 433-6207

Rumford, See East Providence
East Providence SD
Supt. — See East Providence

Francis ES — 400/K-5
64 Bourne Ave 02916 — 401-435-7829
Lloydanne Leddy, prin. — Fax 435-7853

Slatersville, Providence
North Smithfield SD — 1,600/PK-12
PO Box 72 02876 — 401-769-5492
Stephen Lindberg, supt. — Fax 769-5493
www.northsmithfieldschools.com/
Halliwell Memorial ES — 200/3-5
358 Victory Highway 02876 — 401-762-2793
Diane Jolin, prin. — Fax 765-8747
Other Schools – See North Smithfield

Smithfield, Providence, Pop. 19,163
Smithfield SD
Supt. — See Esmond
Gallagher MS — 600/6-8
10 Indian Run Trl 02917 — 401-949-2056
Laurie Beauvais, prin. — Fax 949-5697
LaPerche ES — 200/K-5
11 Limerock Rd 02917 — 401-231-6652
Donna Olson, prin. — Fax 231-1141
McCabe ES — 400/PK-5
100 Pleasant View Ave 02917 — 401-949-2058
Gloria Laramee, prin. — Fax 949-5773
Old County Road ES — 200/K-5
200 Old County Rd 02917 — 401-231-6613
Jill Barnhardt, prin. — Fax 231-2292

St. Philip S — 300/PK-8
618 Putnam Pike 02828 — 401-949-1130
Darlene Walsh, prin. — Fax 949-1141

Tiverton, Newport, Pop. 7,259
Tiverton SD — 2,100/K-12
100 N Brayton Rd 02878 — 401-624-8475
William Rearick, supt. — Fax 624-4086
www.tivertonschools.org/
Ft. Barton S — 200/K-4
99 Lawton Ave 02878 — 401-624-6114
Suzette Wordell, prin. — Fax 624-6115
Pocasset ES — 300/K-4
242 Main Rd 02878 — 401-624-6654
Fran Blaess, prin. — Fax 624-6655
Ranger ES — 200/K-4
278 N Brayton Rd 02878 — 401-624-8467
Thomas Gastall, prin. — Fax 624-8468
Tiverton MS — 600/5-8
10 Quintal Dr 02878 — 401-624-6668
Patricia Aull, prin. — Fax 624-6669

Wakefield, Washington, Pop. 7,134
South Kingstown SD — 3,800/PK-12
307 Curtis Corner Rd 02879 — 401-360-1307
Robert Hicks Ed.D., supt. — Fax 360-1330
www.skschools.net/
Broad Rock MS — 400/6-8
351 Broad Rock Rd 02879 — 401-782-6223
Sheila Sullivan, prin. — Fax 782-6282
Hazard S — 100/PK-PK
153 School St 02879 — 401-360-1200
Ruth Gallucci, coord. — Fax 360-1210
Wakefield ES — 300/K-5
101 High St 02879 — 401-360-1400
Michelle Little, prin. — Fax 360-1401
Other Schools – See Matunuck, Peace Dale, West Kingston

Monsignor Matthew F. Clarke Regional S — 300/PK-6
5074 Tower Hill Rd 02879 — 401-789-0860
Paula Bailey, prin. — Fax 789-3164

Warren, Bristol, Pop. 11,385
Bristol Warren Regional SD
Supt. — See Bristol
Cole ES — 300/PK-5
50 Asylum Rd 02885 — 401-245-1460
Charles Mello, prin. — Fax 245-8895
Kickemuit MS — 800/6-8
525 Child St 02885 — 401-245-2010
Michael Carbone, prin. — Fax 254-5960

Warwick, Kent, Pop. 87,233
Warwick SD — 10,400/PK-12
34 Warwick Lake Ave 02889 — 401-734-3100
Peter Horoschak Ed.D., supt. — Fax 734-3105
www.warwickschools.org
Aldrich JHS — 600/7-8
789 Post Rd 02888 — 401-734-3500
William Sangster, prin. — Fax 734-3508
Cedar Hill ES — 400/K-6
35 Red Chimney Dr 02886 — 401-734-3535
Joseph Peltier, prin. — Fax 734-3538
Drum Rock ECC — 300/K-6
575 Centerville Rd Ste 3 02886 — 401-734-3490
Kathryn Keenan, prin. — Fax 734-3493
Francis ES — 300/PK-6
325 Miantonomo Dr 02888 — 401-734-3340
Frank Ricci, prin. — Fax 734-3343
Gorton JHS — 500/7-8
69 Draper Ave 02889 — 401-734-3350
Mary Caporelli, prin. — Fax 734-3359
Greenwood ES — 300/K-6
93 Sharon St 02886 — 401-734-3290
Rosemary Hunter, prin. — Fax 734-3293
Holden ES — 300/K-6
61 Hoxsie Ave 02889 — 401-734-3455
Kenneth Rassler, prin. — Fax 734-3458
Holliman ES — 300/PK-6
70 Deborah Rd 02888 — 401-734-3170
John Vuono, prin. — Fax 734-3173
Hoxsie ES — 300/K-6
55 Glenwood Dr 02889 — 401-734-3555
Dr. Colleen Limoges, prin. — Fax 734-3558
Lippitt ES — 300/PK-6
30 Almy St 02886 — 401-734-3240
Roy Roberts, prin. — Fax 734-3243
Norwood ES — 200/PK-6
266 Norwood Ave 02888 — 401-734-3525
Nancy Plumb, prin. — Fax 734-3528
Oakland Beach ES — 400/PK-6
383 Oakland Beach Ave 02889 — 401-734-3420
Kathleen Adams, prin. — Fax 734-3423
Park ES — 300/PK-6
40 Asylum Rd 02886 — 401-734-3690
Marilyn Feeney, prin. — Fax 734-3693
Robertson ES — 200/PK-6
70 Nausauket Rd 02886 — 401-734-3470
Lynn Dambruch, prin. — Fax 734-3473
Scott ES — 300/PK-6
833 Centerville Rd 02886 — 401-734-3585
Virginia Bolano, prin. — Fax 734-3588
Sherman ES — 400/PK-6
120 Killey Ave 02889 — 401-734-3565
Michelle Paton, prin. — Fax 734-3568
Warwick Neck ES — 300/K-6
155 Rocky Point Ave 02889 — 401-734-3480
Ann Stratton, prin. — Fax 734-3483
Wickes ES — 300/K-6
50 Child Ln 02886 — 401-734-3575
Roy Costa, prin. — Fax 734-3578
Winman JHS — 600/7-8
575 Centerville Rd Ste 2 02886 — 401-734-3375
Joanne McInerney, prin. — Fax 734-3385
Wyman ES — 300/K-6
1 Columbia Ave 02888 — 401-734-3180
Judith Daniel, prin. — Fax 734-3183

St. Kevin S — 200/PK-8
39 Cathedral Rd 02889 — 401-737-7172
Roger Parent, prin. — Fax 738-1288
St. Peter S — 200/PK-8
120 Mayfair Rd 02888 — 401-781-9242
Joan Sickinger, prin. — Fax 467-5673
St. Rose of Lima S — 200/PK-8
200 Brentwood Ave 02886 — 401-739-6937
Jeannine Fuller, prin. — Fax 737-4632

Westerly, Washington, Pop. 16,477
Westerly SD — 2,900/PK-12
15 Highland Ave 02891 — 401-348-2700
Steven Welford, supt. — Fax 348-2707
www.westerly.k12.ri.us
Dunns Corners ES — 200/K-4
8 Plateau Rd 02891 — 401-348-2320
Christopher Haskins, prin. — Fax 348-2325
Springbrook ES — 300/K-4
39 Springbrook Rd 02891 — 401-348-2296
Victoria Ventura, prin. — Fax 348-2305
State Street ES — 200/K-4
25 State St 02891 — 401-348-2340
Audrey Faubert, prin. — Fax 348-2345
Westerly MS — 800/5-8
10 Sandy Hill Rd 02891 — 401-348-2750
Dennis Curran, prin. — Fax 348-2752
Other Schools – See Bradford

St. Pius X S — 200/K-8
32 Elm St 02891 — 401-596-5735
Henry Fiore, prin. — Fax 596-5791

West Greenwich, Kent, Pop. 3,492
Exeter-West Greenwich Regional SD — 2,000/PK-12
940 Nooseneck Hill Rd 02817 — 401-397-5125
Thomas Geismar, supt. — Fax 397-2407
www.ewg.k12.ri.us
Exeter-West Greenwich Regional JHS — 400/7-8
930 Nooseneck Hill Rd 02817 — 401-397-6897
Mark Thompson, prin. — Fax 392-0109
Lineham K — 100/PK-K
859 Nooseneck Hill Rd 02817 — 401-397-3771
Melissa Marino, prin. — Fax 392-0101
Other Schools – See Exeter

West Kingston, Washington
South Kingstown SD
Supt. — See Wakefield
West Kingston ES — 400/K-5
3119 Ministerial Rd 02892 — 401-360-1130
Nancy Nettik, prin. — Fax 360-1131

Meadowbrook Waldorf S — 200/PK-8
300 Kingstown Rd 02892 — 401-491-9570
Charlotte O'Brien, admin. — Fax 539-6003

West Warwick, Kent, Pop. 29,600
West Warwick SD — 3,700/PK-12
10 Harris Ave 02893 — 401-821-1180
Kenneth Sheehan, supt. — Fax 822-8463
www.westwarwickpublicschools.com/
Deering MS — 900/6-8
2 Webster Knight Dr 02893 — 401-822-8445
Brian Dillon, prin. — Fax 822-8474
Greenbush ES — 500/K-5
127 Greenbush Rd 02893 — 401-822-8454
Susan Buonanno, prin. — Fax 822-8478
Horgan ES — 400/K-5
124 Providence St 02893 — 401-822-8449
Donna Peluso, prin. — Fax 822-8475
Quinn ES — 400/PK-5
1 Brown St 02893 — 401-822-8456
Keith Remillard, prin. — Fax 822-8477
Wakefield Hills ES — 500/PK-5
505 Wakefield St 02893 — 401-822-8452
MaryLou Almonte, prin. — Fax 822-8476

St. Joseph S — 300/PK-8
850 Wakefield St 02893 — 401-821-3450
Richard Keenan, prin. — Fax 821-3516

Wood River Junction, Washington
Chariho Regional SD — 3,800/PK-12
455A Switch Rd 02894 — 401-364-7575
Barry Ricci, supt. — Fax 364-1176
www.chariho.k12.ri.us/
Chariho Regional MS — 1,100/5-8
455b Switch Rd 02894 — 401-364-0651
Gregory Zenion, prin. — Fax 364-1189
Other Schools – See Ashaway, Charlestown, Hope Valley, Wyoming

Woonsocket, Providence, Pop. 44,328
Woonsocket SD — 6,200/K-12
108 High St 02895 — 401-767-4600
Dr. Robert Gerardi, supt. — Fax 767-4607
www.woonsocketschools.com/
Bernon Heights ES — 400/K-5
657 Logee St 02895 — 401-767-4864
Margaret Tincknell, prin. — Fax 767-4865
Citizens Memorial ES — 300/3-5
250 Winthrop St 02895 — 401-767-4850
Nancy Zambarano, prin. — Fax 767-4851
Coleman ES — 300/3-5
96 2nd Ave 02895 — 401-767-4859
Thomas Hazard, prin. — Fax 767-4860
Fifth Avenue ES — 100/1-2
65 5th Ave 02895 — 401-767-4826
Robert DeRosier, prin. — Fax 767-4827
Globe Park ES — 500/K-5
192 Avenue A 02895 — 401-767-4830
Michael Capasso, prin. — Fax 767-4831
Harris ES — 300/K-5
60 High School St 02895 — 401-767-4855
Richard Pickett, prin. — Fax 767-4857
Pothier ES — 300/K-2
420 Robinson St 02895 — 401-767-4765
Donna Coderre, prin. — Fax 767-4652
Savoie ES — 300/K-5
980 Mendon Rd 02895 — 401-767-4820
Karen McBeth, prin. — Fax 767-4821
Social Street ES — 200/K-5
706 Social St 02895 — 401-767-4878
R. Ferguson, prin. — Fax 767-4879
Woonsocket MS — 1,500/6-8
357 Park Pl 02895 — 401-767-4600
Patrick McGee, prin. — Fax 767-4771

Good Shepherd Regional MS — 300/4-8
1210 Mendon Rd 02895 — 401-767-5906
Lawrence Poitras, prin. — Fax 767-5905
Monsignor Gadoury Regional PS — 100/PK-3
1371 Park Ave 02895 — 401-767-5902
Mary Chabot, prin. — Fax 767-5902

Wyoming, Washington
Chariho Regional SD
Supt. — See Wood River Junction
Richmond ES — 500/PK-4
190 Kingstown Rd 02898 — 401-539-2441
Laurie Weber, prin. — Fax 539-1357

SOUTH CAROLINA

SOUTH CAROLINA DEPARTMENT OF EDUCATION
1429 Senate St Ste 100, Columbia 29201-3799
Telephone 803-734-8500
Fax 803-734-3389
Website ed.sc.gov/

Superintendent of Education Jim Rex

SOUTH CAROLINA BOARD OF EDUCATION
1429 Senate St Ste 100, Columbia 29201-3730

Chairperson Kristin Maguire

PUBLIC, PRIVATE AND CATHOLIC ELEMENTARY SCHOOLS

Abbeville, Abbeville, Pop. 5,732
Abbeville County SD 2,800/K-12
400 Greenville St 29620 864-366-5427
Ivan Randolph, supt. Fax 366-8531
www.acsd.k12.sc.us/
Diamond Hill ES 300/K-7
104 Lake Secession Rd 29620 864-446-2600
Todd Ramey, prin. Fax 446-2602
Long Cane PS 200/K-2
815 E Greenwood St 29620 864-366-5924
Charles Costner, prin. Fax 366-4011
Westwood ES 200/3-5
124 Highway 28 Byp 29620 864-366-9604
Lori Brownlee-Brewton, prin. Fax 366-5297
Wright MS 400/6-8
111 Highway 71 29620 864-366-5998
Barry Jacks, prin. Fax 366-4282
Other Schools – See Calhoun Falls, Donalds

Aiken, Aiken, Pop. 27,490
Aiken County SD 24,100/K-12
1000 Brookhaven Dr 29803 803-641-2428
Elizabeth Everitt, supt. Fax 642-8903
www.aiken.k12.sc.us
Aiken ES 900/K-5
2050 Pine Log Rd 29803 803-641-2740
Sharon Cagle, prin. Fax 641-2526
Aiken MS 700/6-8
101 Gator Ln 29801 803-641-2570
Brooks Smith, prin. Fax 641-2578
Chukker Creek ES 700/K-5
1830 Chukker Creek Rd 29803 803-641-2474
Amy Gregory, prin. Fax 641-2537
East Aiken ES 500/K-5
223 Old Wagener Rd 29801 803-641-2450
Mary Robinson, prin. Fax 641-2527
Kennedy MS 900/6-8
274 E Pine Log Rd 29803 803-641-2470
Ben Osborne, prin. Fax 641-2405
Lever ES 600/K-5
2404 Columbia Hwy N 29805 803-641-2760
Renee Mack, prin. Fax 641-2402
Millbrook ES 600/K-5
255 E Pine Log Rd 29803 803-641-2580
Denise Huff, prin. Fax 641-2449
North Aiken ES 500/K-5
100 Bears Rock Rd 29801 803-641-2690
Rhonda Ray, prin. Fax 641-2674
Oakwood-Windsor ES 400/K-5
3773 Charleston Hwy 29801 803-641-2560
Janice Kitchings, prin. Fax 641-2561
Redcliffe ES 700/K-5
6741 Atomic Rd 29803 803-827-3350
Julie Revelle, prin. Fax 827-3354
Schofield MS 700/6-8
224 Kershaw St NE 29801 803-641-2770
Carl White, prin. Fax 641-2529
Other Schools – See Belvedere, Clearwater, Gloverville, Graniteville, Jackson, New Ellenton, North Augusta, Ridge Spring, Wagener, Warrenville

---

Aiken Preparatory S 100/PK-12
619 Barnwell Ave NW 29801 803-648-3223
Deborah Boehner, hdmstr. Fax 648-6482
St. Mary Help of Christians S 300/K-8
118 York St SE 29801 803-649-2071
Peggy Wertz, prin. Fax 643-0092
South Aiken Baptist Christian S 300/PK-12
980 Dougherty Rd 29803 803-648-7871
Randy Martin, prin. Fax 643-9533

Allendale, Allendale, Pop. 3,897
Allendale County SD
Supt. — See Fairfax
Allendale ES 600/PK-5
4561 Allendale Fairfax Hwy 29810 803-584-3476
Shelia Leath, prin. Fax 584-5346

Anderson, Anderson, Pop. 25,899
Anderson SD 5 12,100/PK-12
PO Box 439 29622 864-260-5000
Betty Bagley, supt. Fax 260-5074
www.anderson5.net
Calhoun Academy of the Arts 700/K-5
1520 E Calhoun St 29621 864-260-5090
Ann Self, prin. Fax 231-2802
Centerville ES 600/K-5
1529 Whitehall Rd 29625 864-260-5100
Kory Roberts, prin. Fax 260-5051
Concord ES 700/K-5
2701 Calrossie Rd 29621 864-260-5105
Beryl Barclay, prin. Fax 964-0424
Homeland Park ES 400/K-5
3519 Wilmont St 29624 864-260-5125
Greg Sweet, prin. Fax 375-2042
Lakeside MS 900/6-8
315 Pearman Dairy Rd 29625 864-260-5135
Martha Hanwell, prin. Fax 260-5885
McCants MS 1,300/6-8
2123 Marchbanks Ave 29621 864-260-5145
Jacky Stamps, prin. Fax 260-5846
McLees ES 700/K-5
4900 Dobbins Bridge Rd 29626 864-716-3600
Janet Mills, prin. Fax 716-3611
Midway ES 900/K-5
1221 Harriett Cir 29621 864-716-3800
Gary Bruhjell, prin. Fax 716-3811
Nevitt Forest ES 500/K-5
1401 Bolt Dr 29621 864-260-5190
Kelly Elrod, prin. Fax 375-2043
New Prospect ES 500/K-5
126 New Prospect Church Rd 29625 864-260-5195
Sylvia Thomas, prin. Fax 964-2854
South Fant ECC 200/PK-K
1700 S Fant St 29624 864-260-5225
Suzie Bannister, prin. Fax 964-2692
Southwood MS 500/6-8
1110 Southwood St 29624 864-260-5205
Evelyn Murphy, prin. Fax 964-2607
Varennes ES 400/K-5
1820 Highway 29 S 29626 864-260-5215
Dr. Mary Paul, prin. Fax 964-2677
West Market ECC PK-K
1901 Dobbins Bridge Rd 29626 864-260-5200
Suzie Bannister, prin. Fax 716-3820
Whitehall ES 500/K-5
702 Whitehall Rd 29625 864-260-5255
Kevin Snow, prin. Fax 375-2047

Montessori S of Anderson 300/PK-12
280 Sam McGee Rd 29621 864-226-5344
Paul Epstein Ph.D., prin. Fax 231-6562
St. Joseph S 100/PK-5
1200 Cornelia Rd 29621 864-225-2143
Mary Ann Wheeler, prin. Fax 225-6432

Andrews, Georgetown, Pop. 3,110
Georgetown County SD
Supt. — See Georgetown
Andrews ES 800/PK-5
13072 County Line Rd 29510 843-264-3419
Brian Clark, prin. Fax 264-5511
Rosemary MS 600/6-8
12804 County Line Rd 29510 843-264-9780
Michael Caviris, prin. Fax 264-9787

Aynor, Horry, Pop. 587
Horry County SD
Supt. — See Conway
Aynor ES 700/PK-5
516 Jordanville Rd 29511 843-488-7070
Reggie Gasque, prin. Fax 488-7071

Bamberg, Bamberg, Pop. 3,552
Bamberg SD 1 1,300/K-12
PO Box 526 29003 803-245-3053
Phyllis Schwarting, supt. Fax 245-3056
www.bamberg1.com
Bamberg-Ehrhardt MS 400/6-8
PO Box 548 29003 803-245-3058
Troy Phillips, prin. Fax 245-6501
Carroll ES 4-5
PO Box 949 29003 803-245-3047
Johnnie Smith, prin. Fax 245-3051
Carroll PS 400/K-3
PO Box 546 29003 803-245-3043
Ronald Bunch, prin. Fax 245-3078

Barnwell, Barnwell, Pop. 4,874
Barnwell SD 45 2,600/K-12
770 Hagood Ave 29812 803-541-1300
Roy Sapough, supt. Fax 541-1348
www.barnwell45.k12.sc.us
Barnwell ES 600/4-6
10524 Marlboro Ave 29812 803-541-1285
Jackie Sease, prin. Fax 541-1290
Barnwell PS 800/K-3
734 Hagood Ave 29812 803-541-1321
Robert Eubanks, prin. Fax 541-1313
Guinyard-Butler MS 400/7-8
779 Allen St 29812 803-541-1370
Senaca Baines, prin. Fax 541-1306

Batesburg, Lexington, Pop. 6,189
Lexington County SD 3 2,100/K-12
338 W Columbia Ave 29006 803-532-4423
Dr. Chester Floyd, supt. Fax 532-8000
www.lex3.k12.sc.us
Batesburg-Leesville MS 500/6-8
425 Shealy Rd 29006 803-532-3831
Angela Rye, prin. Fax 532-8021
Batesburg-Leesville PS 500/K-2
800 Summerland Ave 29006 803-532-4452
Tonya Watson, prin. Fax 532-4453
Other Schools – See Leesville

King Academy 200/K-12
1046 Sardis Rd 29006 803-532-6682
Dennis Gibson, hdmstr. Fax 604-0409

Beaufort, Beaufort, Pop. 12,058
Beaufort County SD 19,000/PK-12
PO Box 309 29901 843-322-2300
Dr. Valerie Page Truesdale, supt. Fax 322-2371
www.beaufort.k12.sc.us/
Beaufort ES 400/PK-5
1800 Prince St 29902 843-322-2600
Dr. Terry Hitch, prin. Fax 322-2685
Beaufort MS 600/6-8
2501 Mossy Oaks Rd 29902 843-322-5700
Carole Ingram, prin. Fax 322-5723
Broad River ES 400/PK-5
474 Broad River Blvd 29906 843-322-8400
Gail Wages, prin. Fax 322-8380
Coosa ES 600/PK-5
45 Middle Rd, 843-322-6100
Carmen Dillard, prin. Fax 322-6170
Mossy Oaks ES 400/K-5
2510 Mossy Oaks Rd 29902 843-322-2900
Donald Gruel, prin. Fax 322-2956
Shanklin ES 500/PK-5
121 Morrall Dr 29906 843-466-3400
Robert Grant, prin. Fax 466-3472
Shell Point ES 500/PK-5
81 Savannah Hwy 29906 843-322-2800
Mary Ellen Parks, prin. Fax 322-2827
Smalls MS 700/6-8
43 W K Alston Dr 29906 843-322-2500
Denise Smith, prin. Fax 322-2564
Other Schools – See Bluffton, Daufuskie Island, Hilton Head Island, Ladys Island, Okatie, Port Royal, Saint Helena Island, Seabrook

---

Beaufort Academy 400/PK-12
240 Sams Point Rd, 843-524-3393
Timothy Johnston, prin. Fax 524-1171
Beaufort SDA S 50/1-8
906 Church St 29902 843-846-1395
E.C. Montessori S 100/PK-4
15 Celadon Dr, 843-525-1141
Terri Powell, prin. Fax 525-9242
St. Peter S 200/PK-8
70 Ladys Island Dr, 843-522-2163
Chris Trott, prin. Fax 522-6513

Belton, Anderson, Pop. 4,568
Anderson SD 2
Supt. — See Honea Path
Belton ES 500/3-5
202 Watkins St 29627 864-338-7738
Adrienne Davenport, prin. Fax 338-3319
Belton MS 500/6-8
102 Cherokee Rd 29627 864-338-6595
Margaret Spivey, prin. Fax 338-3301

Marshall PS 500/K-2
218 Bannister St 29627 864-338-7611
Kimberley Clardy, prin. Fax 338-3309
Wright ES 200/K-6
1136 Wright School Rd 29627 864-296-1776
Tara Brice, prin. Fax 296-9951

Belvedere, Aiken, Pop. 6,133
Aiken County SD
Supt. — See Aiken
Belvedere ES 600/K-5
201 Rhomboid Pl 29841 803-442-6330
Alison Churm, prin. Fax 442-6131

Bennettsville, Marlboro, Pop. 9,351
Marlboro County SD 4,800/PK-12
PO Box 947 29512 843-479-4016
Frank Roberson, supt. Fax 479-5944
www.marlboro.k12.sc.us
Bennettsville ES 500/3-5
801 Country Club Dr 29512 843-479-5938
Parnell Miles, prin. Fax 479-1532
Bennettsville MS 500/6-8
701 Cheraw St 29512 843-479-5941
Diane Grant, prin. Fax 479-5943
Bennettsville PS 600/PK-2
301 Jefferson St 29512 843-479-5937
Stacey Jaillette, prin. Fax 454-2006
Other Schools – See Blenheim, Clio, Mc Coll, Wallace

Bethune, Kershaw, Pop. 362
Kershaw County SD
Supt. — See Camden
Bethune ES 100/K-5
PO Box 477 29009 843-334-6278
Theodore Jackson, prin. Fax 334-6275

Bishopville, Lee, Pop. 3,831
Lee County SD 2,200/K-12
PO Box 507 29010 803-484-5327
Dr. Cleo Richardson, supt. Fax 484-9107
www.leeschoolsk12.org/home.asp
Bishopville PS 500/K-3
603 N Dennis Ave 29010 803-484-9475
Lei Knight, prin. Fax 484-5156
Dennis IS 200/4-5
321 Roland St 29010 803-484-5386
Kwamine Simpson, prin. Fax 484-5825
Lee Central MS 100/6-8
41 Charlenes Ln 29010 803-428-2100
Deitra Johnson, prin. Fax 428-2174
Other Schools – See Mayesville, Rembert

Lee Academy 600/K-12
630 Cousar St 29010 803-484-5532
Phil Rizzo, prin. Fax 484-9491

Blacksburg, Cherokee, Pop. 1,898
Cherokee SD
Supt. — See Gaffney
Blacksburg ES 400/3-5
402 Hardin St 29702 864-839-2363
Janice Keller, prin. Fax 839-5922
Blacksburg MS 400/6-8
101 London St 29702 864-839-6476
Virgil Hampton, prin. Fax 839-2390
Blacksburg PS 500/PK-2
1010 E Cherokee St 29702 864-839-1106
Malinda Patterson, prin. Fax 839-1109

Blackville, Barnwell, Pop. 2,919
Barnwell SD 19 900/PK-12
297 Pascallas St 29817 803-284-5605
Teresa Pope Ph.D., supt. Fax 284-4417
www.barnwell19.k12.sc.us/
Blackville-Hilda JHS 100/7-8
PO Box 186 29817 803-284-5900
Marvin Foster, prin. Fax 284-0961
Macedonia ES 500/PK-6
PO Box 246 29817 803-284-5800
Teresa Reid, prin. Fax 284-0959

Barnwell Christian S 100/1-12
5675 SC Highway 70 29817 803-259-2100
Andrew Korver, prin. Fax 259-2100
Davis Academy 300/K-12
5061 Hilda Rd 29817 803-284-2476
Bryan England, hdmstr. Fax 284-5544

Blair, Fairfield
Fairfield County SD
Supt. — See Winnsboro
McCrorey-Liston ES 200/K-6
1978 State Highway 215 S 29015 803-635-9490
Chandra Bell, prin. Fax 635-1557

Blenheim, Marlboro, Pop. 133
Marlboro County SD
Supt. — See Bennettsville
Blenheim S 400/PK-8
PO Box 250 29516 843-528-3262
Gwen Dixon-Coe, prin. Fax 528-3202

Bluffton, Beaufort, Pop. 2,341
Beaufort County SD
Supt. — See Beaufort
Bluffton ES 1,000/PK-5
160 H E McCracken Cir 29910 843-706-8500
Christine Wright, prin. Fax 706-8542
McCracken MS 1,000/6-8
250 H E McCracken Cir 29910 843-706-8700
Phillip Shaw, prin. Fax 706-8778
Riley ES 700/PK-5
200 Burnt Church Rd 29910 843-706-8300
Jay Parks, prin. Fax 706-8378

Cross Schools 300/PK-10
495 Buckwalter Pkwy 29910 843-706-2000
Shawn Young, hdmstr. Fax 706-2010
May River Montessori S 100/PK-3
PO Box 2557 29910 843-757-2312
Sharon Haag, hdmstr. Fax 757-4374

St. Gregory the Great S PK-5
333 Fording Island Rd, 843-815-9988
Sr. Canice Adams, prin. Fax 815-3150

Blythewood, Richland, Pop. 655
Richland SD 2
Supt. — See Columbia
Bethel/Hanberry ES 700/PK-5
125 Boney Rd 29016 803-691-6880
Jeff Williams, prin. Fax 691-6883
Blythewood MS 1,000/6-8
2351 Longtown Rd E 29016 803-691-6850
Brenda Hafner, prin. Fax 691-6860
Center for Achievement K-5
1141A Kelly Mill Rd 29016 803-691-7216
Stephanie Courtney, prin. Fax 691-7218
Kelly Mill MS 1,000/6-8
1141 Kelly Mill Rd 29016 803-691-7210
Dr. Michaele Lemrow, prin. Fax 691-7211
Lake Carolina ES 900/PK-5
1151 Kelly Mill Rd 29016 803-714-1300
Dr. James Ann Lynch, prin. Fax 714-1301
Round Top ES 600/PK-5
449 Rimer Pond Rd 29016 803-691-8676
Jeaneen Tucker, prin. Fax 691-8677

Boiling Springs, Spartanburg, Pop. 3,522
Spartanburg SD 2 9,200/K-12
4606 Parris Bridge Rd 29316 864-578-0128
Scott Mercer, supt. Fax 578-8924
www.spartanburg2.k12.sc.us
Boiling Springs ES 900/K-4
700 Double Bridge Rd 29316 864-578-1231
Kim Ashby, prin. Fax 599-9163
Boiling Springs IS 1,200/5-6
2055 Hanging Rock Rd 29316 864-578-2884
Tammy Greer, prin. Fax 578-2426
Other Schools – See Chesnee, Inman, Mayo, Spartanburg

Bowman, Orangeburg, Pop. 1,179

Bowman Academy 100/K-12
PO Box 98 29018 803-829-2770
Ada Smith, prin. Fax 829-1340

Branchville, Orangeburg, Pop. 1,052
Orangeburg County Consolidated SD 4
Supt. — See Cope
Lockett ES 300/K-6
PO Box 218 29432 803-274-8588
Hercules Busby, prin. Fax 274-8650

Brunson, Hampton, Pop. 576
Hampton SD 1
Supt. — See Varnville
Brunson ES 200/PK-6
PO Box 130 29911 803-632-2531
Mary Hutto, prin. Fax 632-6695

Buffalo, Union, Pop. 1,569
Union County SD
Supt. — See Union
Buffalo ES 500/K-4
733 Main St 29321 864-429-1730
Melissa Inman, prin. Fax 429-2100

Cades, Williamsburg
Williamsburg County SD
Supt. — See Kingstree
Cades Hebron ES 300/K-6
3783 Green Rd 29518 843-389-3386
Fax 389-3308

Calhoun Falls, Abbeville, Pop. 2,264
Abbeville County SD
Supt. — See Abbeville
Calhoun ES 200/K-5
750 N Calhoun St 29628 864-447-8016
David Nixon, prin. Fax 447-8079

Camden, Kershaw, Pop. 7,000
Kershaw County SD 10,400/PK-12
1301 Dubose Ct 29020 803-432-8416
Dr. Frank Morgan, supt. Fax 425-8918
www.kershaw.k12.sc.us
Baron-DeKalb ES 200/PK-5
2684 Baron Dekalb Rd 29020 803-432-2483
Bettye Turner, prin. Fax 425-8979
Camden ES of the Creative Arts 500/K-5
1304 Lyttleton St 29020 803-425-8960
Ed Yount, prin. Fax 425-7708
Camden MS 800/6-8
902 McRae Rd 29020 803-425-8975
Jeff Jordan, prin. Fax 425-8954
Jackson S 400/K-5
1109 Campbell St 29020 803-425-8965
Gerald Gary, prin. Fax 425-7709
Pine Tree Hill ES 600/PK-5
938 Bishopville Hwy 29020 803-425-8970
Lisa Shannon, prin. Fax 425-7718
Other Schools – See Bethune, Cassatt, Elgin, Kershaw, Lugoff

Camden Adventist S 50/1-8
612 Boykin Rd 29020 803-432-0541
Emmanuel Christian S 100/K-9
PO Box 798 29021 803-432-8751
Grace Episcopal K 100/K-K
1315 Lyttleton St 29020 803-432-7621
Fax 432-7622

Campobello, Spartanburg, Pop. 464
Spartanburg SD 1 4,800/K-12
PO Box 218 29322 864-468-4542
James Littlefield, supt. Fax 472-2846
www.spart1.org/do/
Campobello-Gramling S 600/K-8
250 Fagan Ave 29322 864-468-4551
John Hodge, prin. Fax 468-4210

Holly Springs-Motlow ES 400/K-6
325 Motlow School Rd 29322 864-895-2453
David Craft, prin. Fax 895-0620
Other Schools – See Inman, Landrum

Cassatt, Kershaw
Kershaw County SD
Supt. — See Camden
Midway ES 400/PK-5
1892 Highway 1 N 29032 803-432-6122
Jewell Stanley, prin. Fax 425-8929

Cayce, Lexington, Pop. 12,432
Lexington County SD 2
Supt. — See West Columbia
Busbee Creative Arts Academy 400/6-8
501 Bulldog Blvd 29033 803-739-4070
C.R. Hall, prin. Fax 739-4133
Davis ES of Technology 400/K-5
2305 Frink St 29033 803-739-4080
Dr. Jesse Washington, prin. Fax 739-8396
Taylor ES 300/K-5
103 Ann Ln 29033 803-739-4180
Dr. Tracy Johnson, prin. Fax 739-3184

Central, Pickens, Pop. 4,039
Pickens County SD
Supt. — See Easley
Central ES 400/K-5
608 Johnson Rd 29630 864-639-2311
Elliott Southard, prin. Fax 639-5140
Edwards MS 800/6-8
1157 Madden Bridge Rd 29630 864-624-4423
Gary Culler, prin. Fax 624-4426

Chapin, Lexington, Pop. 676
Lexington/Richland Counties SD 5
Supt. — See Irmo
Chapin ES 700/PK-5
940 Old Bush River Rd 29036 803-345-2214
Harriet Wilson, prin. Fax 345-7129
Chapin MS 900/6-8
1130 Old Lexington Hwy 29036 803-345-1466
Jane Crawford, prin. Fax 345-7117
Lake Murray ES 800/K-5
1531 Three Dog Rd 29036 803-732-8151
Claire Thompson, prin. Fax 732-8157

Charleston, Charleston, Pop. 106,712
Berkeley County SD
Supt. — See Moncks Corner
Daniel Island S K-8
2365 Daniel Island Dr 29492 843-471-2301
Lori Dibble, prin. Fax 471-2304

Charleston County SD 37,500/PK-12
75 Calhoun St Fl 2 29401 843-937-6300
Dr. Nancy McGinley, supt. Fax 937-6307
www.ccsdschools.com/
Ashley River ES 500/K-5
1871 Wallace School Rd 29407 843-763-1555
Jayne Ellicott, prin. Fax 763-1567
Birney MS 700/6-8
7750 Pinehurst St 29420 843-764-2212
Carol Bartlett, prin. Fax 569-5466
Buist Academy for Advanced Studies 400/K-8
103 Calhoun St 29401 843-724-7750
Sallie Ballard, prin. Fax 724-1493
Burke MS 6-8
244 President St 29403 843-579-4815
Maurice Cannon-Dean, prin. Fax 579-4855
Burns ES 400/K-5
3750 Dorchester Rd 29405 843-745-7113
Elizabeth McCraw, prin. Fax 529-3906
Charleston Progressive Academy 300/K-7
382 Meeting St 29403 843-720-2967
Wanda Wright-Sheats, prin. Fax 577-1680
Chicora ES 300/K-5
1912 Success St 29405 843-745-7099
Camille Lee, prin. Fax 566-7792
Corcoran ES 500/K-5
8585 Vistavia Rd 29406 843-764-2218
Kenneth Plaster, prin. Fax 764-2234
Drayton Hall ES 500/K-4
3183 Ashley River Rd 29414 843-852-0678
John Cobb, prin. Fax 852-2069
Ford ES 400/K-5
3180 Thomasina McPherson 29405 843-745-7131
Cindy Smalls, prin. Fax 529-3927
Ft. Johnson MS 600/6-8
1825 Camp Rd 29412 843-762-2740
David Parler, prin. Fax 762-6212
Fraser ES 200/PK-6
63 Columbus St 29403 843-724-7767
Perren Peterson, prin. Fax 720-3137
Goodwin ES 500/K-5
5501 Dorchester Rd 29418 843-767-5911
Diane Ross, prin. Fax 767-5929
Harbor View ES 500/K-5
1576 Harbor View Rd 29412 843-762-2749
Tim Ellenburger, prin. Fax 762-6207
Hunley Park ES 500/K-5
1000 Michigan Ave 29404 843-767-5914
Michael Ard, prin. Fax 767-5932
James Island ES 500/K-5
1872 S Grimball Rd 29412 843-762-8240
Cathy Coleman, prin. Fax 762-8250
James Island MS 500/6-8
1484 Camp Rd 29412 843-762-2784
Gary McDonald, prin. Fax 762-6209
Lambs ES 400/K-5
6800 Dorchester Rd 29418 843-767-5900
Janice Timko, prin. Fax 767-5928
Memminger ES 300/PK-6
20 Beaufain St 29401 843-724-7778
Anthony Dixon, prin. Fax 720-3142
Midland Park ES 500/K-5
2415 Midland Park Rd 29406 843-574-2183
Robert Candillo, prin. Fax 569-5476
Mitchell ES 300/PK-6
2 Perry St 29403 843-724-7262
Dirk Bedford, prin. Fax 720-3128

Montessori Community S K-6
2120 Wood Ave 29414 843-769-0346
Kim Hay, admin. Fax 852-4879
Murray-Lasaine ES 200/K-5
691 Riverland Dr 29412 843-762-2765
Lara Latto, prin. Fax 762-6203
Oakland ES 400/K-4
2728 Arlington Dr 29414 843-763-1510
Jennifer Swearingen, prin. Fax 769-2598
St. Andrew's Magnet S of Math-Science 700/K-5
30 Chadwick Dr 29407 843-763-1503
Mark Shea, prin. Fax 769-2594
St. Andrews MS 400/6-8
721 Wappoo Rd 29407 843-763-1533
Benjamin Bragg, prin. Fax 763-1599
Sanders-Clyde ES 200/PK-6
805 Morrison Dr 29403 843-724-7783
Melvin Middleton, prin. Fax 720-3138
Simons ES 400/PK-6
741 King St 29403 843-805-6715
Laura Owings, prin. Fax 720-3128
Springfield ES 300/K-4
2741 Clover St 29414 843-763-1538
Dr. Jacqueline Dinge, prin. Fax 769-2236
Stiles Point ES 600/K-5
883 Mikell Dr 29412 843-762-2767
Stephen Burger, prin. Fax 762-2773
Stono Park ES 300/K-4
1699 Garden St 29407 843-763-1507
Ruth Taylor, prin. Fax 769-2248
West Ashley MS 400/7-8
1776 William Kennerty Dr 29407 843-763-1546
Jennifer Coker, prin. Fax 852-6557
Williams MS 700/5-8
640 Butte St 29414 843-763-1529
Robert Grimm, prin. Fax 763-5955
Other Schools – See Edisto Island, Hollywood, Johns Island, Ladson, Mc Clellanville, Mount Pleasant, North Charleston, Ravenel, Sullivans Island, Wadmalaw Island, Yonges Island

---

Addlestone Hebrew Academy 200/PK-8
1639 Raoul Wallenberg Blvd 29407 843-571-1105
Rabbi Achiya Delouya, prin. Fax 571-6116
Ashley Hall 600/PK-12
172 Rutledge Ave 29403 843-722-4088
Jill Muti, hdmstr. Fax 720-2868
Blessed Sacrament S 400/PK-8
7 Saint Teresa Dr 29407 843-766-2128
Roseann Tracy, prin. Fax 766-2154
Cathedral Academy 300/K-12
PO Box 41129 29423 843-760-1192
Keith Brown, hdmstr. Fax 760-1197
Charleston Catholic S 200/K-8
888 King St 29403 843-577-4495
Fred McKay, prin. Fax 577-6662
Charleston Day S 200/1-8
15 Archdale St 29401 843-722-7791
Brendan O'Shea, hdmstr. Fax 720-2143
Charleston SDA S 50/K-8
2518 Savannah Hwy 29414 843-571-7519
Chester Caswell, prin. Fax 571-7519
Charles Towne Montessori S 200/PK-6
56 Leinbach Dr 29407 843-571-1140
Edward Jackson, hdmstr. Fax 556-0493
First Baptist Church S 500/PK-12
48 Meeting St 29401 843-722-6646
Thomas Mullins, hdmstr. Fax 720-2521
James Island Christian S 200/PK-12
15 Crosscreek Dr 29412 843-795-1762
Dr. Rick Johnson, hdmstr. Fax 762-1619
Mason Prep S 300/1-8
56 Halsey Blvd 29401 843-723-0664
Dawn Howell, hdmstr. Fax 723-1104
Nativity S 100/PK-8
1125 Pittsford Cir 29412 843-795-3975
Patti Dukes, prin. Fax 795-7575
Porter-Gaud S 900/K-12
300 Albemarle Rd 29407 843-556-3620
Christian Proctor Ph.D., hdmstr. Fax 769-9926
St. John S 100/K-8
3921 Saint Johns Ave Stop 2 29405 843-744-3901
Carole Anne White, prin. Fax 744-3689
Trinity Montessori S 100/PK-8
1293 Orange Grove Rd 29407 843-556-6686
Melissa Aller, hdmstr. Fax 556-6664

Cheraw, Chesterfield, Pop. 5,474
Chesterfield County SD
Supt. — See Chesterfield
Cheraw IS 600/3-5
421 Chesterfield Hwy 29520 843-921-1030
Scott Eddins, prin. Fax 921-1036
Cheraw PS 600/K-2
321 High St 29520 843-921-1020
Gracyn Jackson, prin. Fax 921-1015
Long MS 600/6-8
1010 W Greene St 29520 843-921-1010
Dannie Blair, prin. Fax 921-1017

Chesnee, Spartanburg, Pop. 1,022
Spartanburg SD 2
Supt. — See Boiling Springs
Carlisle-Fosters Grove ES 500/K-4
625 Fosters Grove Rd 29323 864-578-2215
Nicha Jordan, prin. Fax 599-7376
Chesnee ES 500/K-5
985 Fairfield Rd 29323 864-461-7322
Dr. Robert Ledford, prin. Fax 431-7338
Chesnee MS 500/6-8
805 S Alabama Ave 29323 864-461-3900
Dale Campbell, prin. Fax 461-3950
Cooley Springs-Fingerville ES 300/K-5
140 Cooley Springs School 29323 864-592-1211
Denny Landrum, prin. Fax 592-3406

Chester, Chester, Pop. 6,199
Chester County SD 5,500/K-12
109 Hinton St 29706 803-385-6122
Larry Heath, supt. Fax 581-0863
www.chester.k12.sc.us/
Chester MS 800/6-8
1014 McCandless Rd 29706 803-377-8192
Gail Hamilton, prin. Fax 581-1875
Chester Park Ctr Literacy Through Tech 400/K-5
835 Lancaster Hwy 29706 803-581-7275
Kristin Langdale, prin. Fax 581-7277
Chester Park S of Inquiry 500/K-5
835 Lancaster Hwy 29706 803-581-5184
Dena Dunlap, prin. Fax 385-5435
Chester Park S of the Arts 500/K-5
835 Lancaster Hwy 29706 803-581-7279
Anne Stone, prin. Fax 581-7281
Other Schools – See Great Falls, Richburg

Chesterfield, Chesterfield, Pop. 1,338
Chesterfield County SD 7,800/K-12
401 West Blvd 29709 843-623-2175
Dr. John Williams, supt. Fax 623-3434
www.chesterfield.k12.sc.us
Chesterfield-Ruby MS 500/6-8
14445 Highway 9 29709 843-623-9401
Dr. Andrea Hampton, prin. Fax 623-9429
Edwards ES 500/K-5
2411 West Blvd 29709 843-623-2351
Vickie Buckner, prin. Fax 623-9412
Other Schools – See Cheraw, Jefferson, Mc Bee, Pageland, Patrick, Ruby

Clearwater, Aiken, Pop. 4,731
Aiken County SD
Supt. — See Aiken
Clearwater ES 400/K-5
PO Box 397 29822 803-593-7240
Susan Malcolm, prin. Fax 593-7120

Midland Valley Christian Academy 100/K-5
PO Box 645 29822 803-594-9945
David Winchester, admin. Fax 593-6615

Clemson, Pickens, Pop. 12,364
Pickens County SD
Supt. — See Easley
Clemson ES 700/K-5
581 Berkeley Dr 29631 864-654-2341
Dr. Ken Weichel, prin. Fax 624-4425

Holy Trinity Episcopal Day S 100/PK-K
193 Old Greenville Hwy 29631 864-654-0298
Rev. John Nieman, hdmstr. Fax 654-5066

Clinton, Laurens, Pop. 9,071
Laurens SD 56 2,700/PK-12
211 N Broad St Ste B 29325 864-833-0800
Dr. Wayne Brazell, supt. Fax 938-2301
www.laurens56.k12.sc.us
Bailey Child Development Ctr 50/PK-PK
625 Elizabeth St 29325 864-938-2553
Nancy Roland, dir. Fax 938-2320
Bell Street MS 500/6-8
600 Peachtree St 29325 864-833-0807
Maureen Tiller, prin. Fax 833-0810
Clinton ES 500/K-5
800 Chestnut St 29325 864-833-0812
Brenda Romines, prin. Fax 833-0814
District 56 Academy 6-8
625 Elizabeth St 29325 864-938-2569
Martha Brothers, dir. Fax 833-0838
Eastside ES 400/K-5
103 Old Colony Rd 29325 864-833-0827
Henry Simmons, prin. Fax 833-0829
Other Schools – See Joanna

Clio, Marlboro, Pop. 752
Marlboro County SD
Supt. — See Bennettsville
Clio S 300/PK-8
2635 Highway 9 E 29525 843-586-9391
Chris Brown, prin. Fax 586-9391

Clover, York, Pop. 4,251
Clover SD 2 5,500/PK-12
604 Bethel St 29710 803-810-8005
Marc Sosne, supt. Fax 222-8010
www.clover2.k12.sc.us
Bethany ES 300/PK-4
337 Maynard Grayson Rd 29710 803-810-8800
Cathy McCarter, prin. Fax 222-8055
Bethel ES 500/PK-4
6000 Highway 55 E 29710 803-831-7816
Tom Guinane, prin. Fax 631-2996
Clover JHS 900/7-8
1555 Highway 55 E 29710 803-810-8300
Mark Hopkins, prin. Fax 222-8034
Clover MS 500/5-6
300 Clinton Ave 29710 803-222-9503
Kathy Weathers, prin. Fax 222-8043
Crowders Creek ES 700/PK-4
5515 Charlotte Hwy 29710 803-831-2434
Millicent Dickey, prin. Fax 831-9471
Crowders Creek MS 5-6
5521 Charlotte Hwy 29710 803-831-1339
Will Largen, prin. Fax 831-2624
Griggs Road ES 500/PK-4
100 Griggs Rd 29710 803-222-5777
Pam Cato, prin. Fax 222-8066
Kinard ES 400/PK-4
201 Pressly St 29710 803-222-3071
Georgia Westmoreland, prin. Fax 222-8048

Columbia, Richland, Pop. 117,088
Lexington/Richland Counties SD 5
Supt. — See Irmo
Cross Roads MS 1,000/6-6
6949 Saint Andrews Rd 29212 803-732-8300
Barbara Turner, prin. Fax 732-8307
Harbison West ES 500/PK-5
257 Crossbow Dr 29212 803-476-3800
Franklin Foster, prin. Fax 476-3820
Irmo MS 1,000/7-8
6051 Wescott Rd 29212 803-476-3600
Marie Waldrop, prin. Fax 476-3620
Leaphart ES 500/K-5
120 Piney Grove Rd 29210 803-798-0030
Dr. Rebecca McKenzie-Appling, prin. Fax 750-3315
Nursery Road ES 600/K-5
6706 Nursery Rd 29212 803-732-8475
Christina Melton, prin. Fax 732-8474
Seven Oaks ES 600/K-5
2800 Ashland Rd 29210 803-476-8500
Ann Copelan, prin. Fax 476-8520

Richland SD 1 23,500/PK-12
1616 Richland St 29201 803-231-7000
Dr. Allen Coles, supt. Fax 231-7505
www.richlandone.org/
Alcorn MS 500/6-8
5125 Fairfield Rd 29203 803-735-3439
Fax 735-3487
Arden ES 300/K-5
1300 Ashley St 29203 803-735-3400
Dr. Diane James, prin. Fax 691-4321
Bradley ES 300/K-5
3032 Pine Belt Rd 29204 803-738-7200
Dr. Erica Fields, prin. Fax 736-7346
Brennen ES 700/K-5
4438 Devereaux Rd 29205 803-738-7204
Dr. Marian Crum-Mack, prin. Fax 738-7904
Brockman ES 300/PK-5
2245 Montclair Dr 29206 803-790-6743
Lynn Robertson, prin. Fax 790-6745
Burnside ES 300/K-5
7300 Patterson Rd 29209 803-783-5530
Dr. Felicia Butler, prin. Fax 783-5594
Burton-Pack ES 400/K-5
111 Garden Dr 29204 803-691-5550
Denise Collier, prin. Fax 691-5555
Carver-Lyon ES 300/K-5
2100 Waverly St 29204 803-343-2900
Dr. Dorothy Gallman, prin. Fax 253-5721
Caughman Road ES 600/K-5
7725 Caughman Rd 29209 803-783-5534
Jane Wyatt, prin. Fax 783-5537
Crayton MS 1,100/6-8
5000 Clemson Ave 29206 803-738-7224
Susan Childs, prin. Fax 738-7901
Forest Heights ES 400/K-5
2500 Blue Ridge Ter 29203 803-691-3780
Dr. Frank Robinson, prin. Fax 691-3782
Gibbes MS 400/6-8
500 Summerlea Dr 29203 803-343-2942
Rick Coleman, prin. Fax 733-3040
Hand MS 900/6-8
2600 Wheat St 29205 803-343-2947
Marisa Vickers, prin. Fax 733-6173
Hyatt Park ES 500/K-5
4200 Main St 29203 803-735-3421
Elizabeth Eason, prin. Fax 735-3391
Lewis Greenview ES 400/K-5
726 Easter St 29203 803-735-3417
Delores Gilliard, prin. Fax 735-3495
Logan ES 200/K-5
815 Elmwood Ave 29201 803-343-2915
Dr. Richard Moore, prin. Fax 929-3896
Meadowfield ES 600/K-5
525 Galway Ln 29209 803-783-5549
Paula Stephens, prin. Fax 695-3079
Mill Creek ES 300/K-5
925 Universal Dr 29209 803-783-5553
Steve Cannon, prin. Fax 783-5572
Moore ES 300/K-5
333 Etiwan Ave 29205 803-343-2910
Dr. Chantalle Baker-Parnell, prin. Fax 929-3882
Perry MS 400/6-8
2600 Barhamville Rd 29204 803-256-6347
Demetria Clemons, prin. Fax 255-2262
Pine Grove ES 400/K-5
111 Huffstetler Dr 29210 803-214-2380
Betty Prudence, prin. Fax 214-2385
Rhame ES 400/K-5
1300 Arrowwood Rd 29210 803-731-8900
Mikell Owens, prin. Fax 750-4040
Rosewood ES 400/K-5
3300 Rosewood Dr 29205 803-343-2930
Dr. Ted Wachter, prin. Fax 929-3849
St. Andrews MS 700/6-8
1231 Blue Field Dr 29210 803-731-8910
Ken Richardson, prin. Fax 731-8913
Sandel ES 500/K-5
2700 Seminole Rd 29210 803-731-8906
Fae Hutchins-Young, prin. Fax 731-8977
Sanders MS 500/6-8
136 Alida St 29203 803-735-3445
Andrenna Smith, prin. Fax 735-3679
Satchel Ford ES 700/K-5
5901 Satchelford Rd 29206 803-738-7209
Connie Alley, prin. Fax 738-7218
South Kilbourne ES 200/K-5
1400 S Kilbourne Rd 29205 803-738-7215
Sarah Smith, prin. Fax 790-6734
Taylor ES 200/K-5
200 McRae St 29203 803-343-2924
Debbie Hunter, prin. Fax 929-3851
Thomas ES 400/K-5
6001 Weston Ave 29203 803-735-3430
Evelyn Moore, prin. Fax 735-3369
Watkins-Nance ES 400/K-5
2525 Barhamville Rd 29204 803-733-4321
Dr. Evelyn Cohens, prin. Fax 733-4332
Other Schools – See Eastover, Gadsden, Hopkins

Richland SD 2 21,000/PK-12
6831 Brookfield Rd 29206 803-787-1910
Stephen Hefner Ed.D., supt. Fax 738-7393
www.richland2.org
Boyd S 200/PK-PK
7900 Brookmont Ln 29203 803-935-0124
Kelli Alridge, prin. Fax 935-1212
Center for Inquiry ES K-5
200 1/2 Summit Pkwy 29229 803-699-2969
Dr. Lyn Mueller, lead tchr. Fax 699-2963

Center for Knowledge ES K-5
3006 Appleby Ln 29223 803-699-2966
Dr. Jo Lane Hall, lead tchr. Fax 699-2967
Clemson Road CDC PK-PK
2621 Clemson Rd 29229 803-699-2536
Debbie Brady, prin. Fax 699-2695
Conder ES 600/PK-5
8040 Hunt Club Rd 29223 803-736-8720
Dr. Shirley Watson, prin. Fax 699-3688
Dent MS 1,200/6-8
2721 Decker Blvd 29206 803-699-2750
Randall Gary, prin. Fax 699-2754
Forest Lake ES 600/PK-5
6801 Brookfield Rd 29206 803-782-0470
Dr. Kappy Cannon, prin. Fax 738-7365
Keels ES 600/PK-5
7500 Springcrest Dr 29223 803-736-8754
Lynne Ladue, prin. Fax 736-8773
Killian ES 600/PK-5
2621 Clemson Rd 29229 803-699-2981
Eric Brown, prin. Fax 699-2971
Longleaf MS 6-8
1160 Longreen Pkwy 29229 803-691-4870
Katinia Davis, prin. Fax 691-4043
Nelson ES 500/PK-5
225 N Brickyard Rd 29223 803-736-8730
Dr. Maree Price, prin. Fax 699-3672
North Springs ES 800/PK-5
1300 Clemson Rd 29229 803-736-3183
Denise Barth, prin. Fax 699-2732
Polo Road ES K-5
1250 Polo Rd 29223 803-419-2226
Jane Fancher, prin. Fax 462-2173
Rice Creek ES 800/PK-5
4751 Hard Scrabble Rd 29229 803-699-2900
Jan Fickling, prin. Fax 699-2907
Sandlapper ES K-5
1001 Longtown Rd 29229 803-691-4045
Linda Hall, prin. Fax 691-1545
Summit Parkway MS 1,000/6-8
200 Summit Pkwy 29229 803-699-3580
Sig Tanner, prin. Fax 699-3682
Windsor ES 600/PK-5
9800 Dunbarton Dr 29223 803-736-8723
Eric Jeffcoat, prin. Fax 600-3648
Wright MS 1,200/6-8
2740 Alpine Rd 29223 803-736-8740
Lori Marrero, prin. Fax 736-8798
Other Schools – See Blythewood, Elgin

Covenant Christian S 100/PK-12
2801 Stepp Dr 29204 803-787-0225
Dr. T. Chris Crain, hdmstr. Fax 782-7309
Hammond S 1,000/PK-12
854 Galway Ln 29209 803-776-0295
Christopher Angel, prin. Fax 776-0122
Heathwood Hall Episcopal S 900/PK-12
3000 S Beltline Blvd 29201 803-765-2309
Charles Jones, hdmstr. Fax 748-4755
Lippen ES - Monticello Road 300/PK-5
7401 Monticello Rd 29203 803-807-4300
Eric Alfrey, prin. Fax 807-4333
Lippen ES - St. Andrews 100/PK-5
500 Saint Andrews Rd 29210 803-807-4400
Beverly Bandy, prin. Fax 807-4399
Montessori S of Columbia 100/PK-6
2807 Oceola St 29205 803-783-8838
Marla Schoolmeester, dir.
New Heights S 100/PK-6
5501 Broad River Rd 29212 803-798-5138
Linda Walsh, admin. Fax 772-6786
Reid S 400/PK-5
6005 David St 29203 803-735-9570
Carol Cooper, dir. Fax 754-0245
St. John Neumann S 400/PK-6
721 Polo Rd 29223 803-788-1367
Barbara Cole, prin. Fax 788-7330
St. Joseph S 300/PK-6
3700 Devine St 29205 803-254-6736
Rose Tindall, prin. Fax 540-1913
St. Martin de Porres S 100/PK-5
1500 Oak St 29204 803-254-5477
Sr. Roberta Fulton, prin. Fax 254-7335
St. Peter S 200/PK-6
1035 Hampton St 29201 803-252-8285
Kathy Preston, prin. Fax 799-2438
Sandhills S 50/1-9
1500 Hallbrook Dr 29209 803-695-1400
Anne Vickers, hdmstr. Fax 695-1214
Sloans S 100/K-12
171 Starlight Dr 29210 803-772-1677

Conway, Horry, Pop. 13,442
Horry County SD 33,800/PK-12
PO Box 260005 29528 843-488-6700
Cindy Elsberry, supt. Fax 488-6722
www.horrycountyschools.net
Black Water MS 6-8
900 E Cox Ferry Rd 29526 843-903-8440
Cindy Thibodeau, prin. Fax 903-8441
Conway Education Center PK-PK
1620 Sherwood Dr 29526 843-488-6239
Amy Edwards, prin. Fax 488-6233
Conway ES 800/K-5
1101 Snowhill Dr 29526 843-488-0696
Maquitta Davis, prin. Fax 488-0656
Conway MS 600/6-8
1104 Elm St 29526 843-488-6040
Mary Clark, prin. Fax 488-0611
Homewood ES 700/PK-5
108 N Clemson Cir 29526 843-365-2512
Penny Foye, prin. Fax 365-7211
Kingston ES 600/PK-5
4580 Highway 472 29526 843-365-3777
Mary Anderson, prin. Fax 365-2764
Pee Dee ES 600/PK-5
6555 Highway 134 29527 843-397-2579
Cheryl Banks, prin. Fax 397-1426
South Conway ES 600/PK-5
3001 4th Ave 29527 843-488-0272
Leon Hayes, prin. Fax 488-0605
Waccamaw ES 600/PK-5
251 Claridy Rd 29526 843-347-4684
Barbara Ammons, prin. Fax 347-0398
Whittemore Park MS 700/6-8
1808 Rhue St 29527 843-488-0669
Robbie Watkins, prin. Fax 488-0669
Other Schools – See Aynor, Galivants Ferry, Garden City, Green Sea, Little River, Loris, Myrtle Beach, North Myrtle Beach

---

Conway Christian S 200/K-12
PO Box 1245 29528 843-365-2005
Connie Smith, prin. Fax 365-2021

Cope, Orangeburg, Pop. 103
Orangeburg County Consolidated SD 4 4,100/PK-12
PO Box 68 29038 803-534-8081
Floride Calvert, supt. Fax 531-5614
www.orangeburg4.com
Other Schools – See Branchville, Cordova, Neeses, Orangeburg

Cordova, Orangeburg, Pop. 147
Orangeburg County Consolidated SD 4
Supt. — See Cope
Carver-Edisto MS 600/6-8
PO Box 65 29039 803-534-3554
Jeannie Monson, prin. Fax 535-0937
Edisto PS 600/K-2
PO Box 110 29039 803-536-4782
Susan Zeigler, prin. Fax 516-0789

Cottageville, Colleton, Pop. 708
Colleton County SD
Supt. — See Walterboro
Cottageville ES 300/K-5
648 Peirce Rd 29435 843-835-5716
Karl Naugle, prin. Fax 835-2095

Coward, Florence, Pop. 671
Florence County SD 3
Supt. — See Lake City
Lynch ES 300/K-5
PO Box 140 29530 843-389-3323
Franklin Foster, prin. Fax 389-3322

Cowpens, Spartanburg, Pop. 2,330
Spartanburg SD 3
Supt. — See Glendale
Cowpens ES 400/K-5
341 Foster St 29330 864-279-6300
Cindy Snead, prin. Fax 279-6303
Cowpens MS 500/6-8
150 Foster St 29330 864-279-6400
Rodney Goode, prin. Fax 279-6403

Cross, Berkeley
Berkeley County SD
Supt. — See Moncks Corner
Cross ES 400/K-6
1325 Ranger Dr 29436 843-899-8916
Dr. Carolyn Myers-Gillens, prin. Fax 899-8918

Dalzell, Sumter
Sumter SD 2
Supt. — See Sumter
Hillcrest MS 400/6-8
PO Box 151 29040 803-499-3341
Robert Barth, prin. Fax 499-3353

Darlington, Darlington, Pop. 6,525
Darlington County SD 11,000/K-12
PO Box 1117 29540 843-398-5100
Dr. Rainey Knight, supt. Fax 398-5198
www.darlington.k12.sc.us
Brockington Magnet ES 400/3-5
413 Brockington Rd 29532 843-398-5095
Allison Baker, prin. Fax 398-2495
Brunson-Dargan ES 300/3-5
400 Wells St 29532 843-398-5080
Ada Harper, prin. Fax 398-2534
Cain ES 400/K-2
607 1st St 29532 843-398-5020
Wanda Odom, prin. Fax 398-2452
Darlington MS 1,200/6-8
150 Pinedale Dr 29532 843-398-5088
Carlita Davis, prin. Fax 398-3390
Pate ES 400/K-2
1010 Indian Branch Rd 29532 843-398-5070
Terry Martin, prin. Fax 398-2397
St. John's ES 700/K-5
140 Park St 29532 843-398-5130
Jean Taylor, prin. Fax 398-5164
Other Schools – See Hartsville, Lamar, Society Hill

Daufuskie Island, Beaufort
Beaufort County SD
Supt. — See Beaufort
Daufuskie Island S 50/K-8
PO Box 54 29915 843-842-1251
Gretchen Keefner, prin. Fax 842-9831

Denmark, Bamberg, Pop. 3,130
Bamberg SD 2 900/PK-12
62 Holly Ave 29042 803-793-3346
Sacaida Howell Ph.D., supt. Fax 793-2006
Denmark-Olar ES 400/PK-5
1459 Sol Blatt Blvd 29042 803-793-3112
Isaiah Echols, prin. Fax 793-2020
Denmark-Olar MS 200/6-8
PO Box 383 29042 803-793-3383
Randy Mack, prin. Fax 793-2038

Dillon, Dillon, Pop. 6,366
Dillon SD 2 3,600/PK-12
405 W Washington St 29536 843-774-1200
D. Ray Rogers, supt. Fax 774-1203
www.dillon2.k12.sc.us
East ES 600/K-3
901 E Harrison St 29536 843-774-1222
Bobbie Walters, prin. Fax 841-3881
Gordon ES 800/4-6
926 Perry Ave 29536 843-774-1227
Ja-Novoice Richardson, prin. Fax 841-3607
Martin JHS 600/7-8
301 Martin Luther King Jr 29536 843-774-1212
Rodney Cook, prin. Fax 841-3616
South Dillon ES 300/PK-3
900 Patriot St 29536 843-774-1210
Carla Angus, prin. Fax 841-3685
Stewart Heights PS 400/PK-3
1001 W Calhoun St 29536 843-774-1219
Jayne Lee, prin. Fax 841-3689

Dillon Christian S 400/K-12
PO Box 151 29536 843-841-1000
John Davis, hdmstr. Fax 841-0810

Donalds, Abbeville, Pop. 346
Abbeville County SD
Supt. — See Abbeville
Cherokee Trail ES 400/K-7
6219 Highway 184 E 29638 864-379-8500
Chester King, prin. Fax 379-8509

Dorchester, Dorchester
Dorchester SD 4
Supt. — See Saint George
Harleyville-Ridgeville ES 400/PK-5
1650 E Main St 29437 843-462-7671
Dr. Morris Ravenell, prin. Fax 462-7647

Duncan, Spartanburg, Pop. 2,977
Spartanburg SD 5 6,300/K-12
PO Box 307 29334 864-949-2350
Dr. Scott Turner, supt. Fax 439-0051
www.spart5.net
Abner Creek ES K-4
2050 Abner Creek Rd 29334 864-949-2334
Pat Paul, prin. Fax 949-2307
Beech Springs IS 500/5-6
PO Box 411 29334 864-949-7600
Ginger Thompson, prin. Fax 949-7604
Berry Shoals IS 600/5-6
300 Shoals Rd 29334 864-949-2300
Mike Powell, prin. Fax 949-2304
Duncan ES 500/K-4
100 S Danzler Rd 29334 864-949-2373
Susan Hill, prin. Fax 949-2374
Florence Chapel MS 600/7-8
290 Shoals Rd 29334 864-949-2310
Steve Gambrell, prin. Fax 949-2315
Other Schools – See Lyman, Moore, Reidville, Wellford

Easley, Pickens, Pop. 18,852
Anderson SD 1
Supt. — See Williamston
Concrete PS 400/PK-2
535 Powdersville Main 29642 864-269-4571
Sherry Padgett, prin. Fax 269-6701
Hunt Meadows ES 700/PK-5
420 Hunt Rd 29642 864-850-3987
Torie Tourtellot, prin. Fax 850-3810

Pickens County SD 16,100/K-12
1348 Griffin Mill Rd 29640 864-855-8150
Dr. Lee D'Andrea, supt. Fax 855-8159
www.pickens.k12.sc.us
Crosswell ES 500/K-5
161 School Rd 29640 864-855-8160
Diane Brown, prin. Fax 855-8161
Dacusville ES 600/K-5
2671 Earls Bridge Rd 29640 864-859-7429
Dr. Michael Fleming, prin. Fax 850-2090
Dacusville MS 400/6-8
899 Thomas Mill Rd 29640 864-859-6049
Ellen Smith, prin. Fax 850-2094
East End ES 600/K-5
505 E 2nd Ave 29640 864-855-7860
Tammy Day, prin. Fax 855-7862
Forest Acres ES 600/K-5
401 Mcalister Rd 29642 864-855-7865
Stephanie Price, prin. Fax 855-7867
Gettys MS 1,300/6-8
105 Stewart Dr 29640 864-855-8170
Michael Corey, prin. Fax 855-6413
McKissick ES 400/K-5
156 Mckissick Rd 29640 864-855-7870
Dr. Thomas Polidor, prin. Fax 855-7872
West End ES 600/K-5
314 Pelzer Hwy 29642 864-855-8165
Angie Rodgers, prin. Fax 850-2083
Other Schools – See Central, Clemson, Liberty, Pickens, Six Mile

Eastover, Richland, Pop. 779
Richland SD 1
Supt. — See Columbia
Webber ES 300/K-5
140 Webber School Rd 29044 803-353-8771
Dorothy Ham, prin. Fax 353-4032

Edgefield, Edgefield, Pop. 4,520
Edgefield County SD
Supt. — See Johnston
Parker ES 500/K-5
41 Crest Rd 29824 803-637-4020
Gaye Holmes, prin. Fax 637-4058

Edisto Island, Charleston
Charleston County SD
Supt. — See Charleston
Edwards S 100/K-8
1960 Jane Edwards Rd 29438 843-559-4171
Susan Miles, prin. Fax 869-0627

Colleton County SD
Supt. — See Walterboro
Edisto Beach ES 50/K-5
42 Station Ct 29438 843-869-3542
Olivia Padgett, prin. Fax 869-3543

Effingham, Florence
Florence County SD 1
Supt. — See Florence
Carter ES 700/K-6
4937 S Irby St 29541 843-664-8479
Amy Poston, prin. Fax 673-5771
Savannah Grove ES 700/K-6
2348 Savannah Grove Rd 29541 843-664-8463
Chandra Anderson, prin. Fax 664-8185

Elgin, Kershaw, Pop. 954
Kershaw County SD
Supt. — See Camden
Blaney ES 600/PK-5
1621 Smyrna Rd 29045 803-438-3241
Lisa Carter, prin. Fax 408-0117
Stover MS 600/6-8
1649 Smyrna Rd 29045 803-438-7414
Dennis Reeder, prin. Fax 438-7014

Richland SD 2
Supt. — See Columbia
Bookman Road ES 700/PK-5
1245 Bookman Rd 29045 803-699-1724
Michael Guliano, prin. Fax 699-0892
Bridge Creek ES K-5
121 Bombing Range Rd 29045 803-462-3900
Felix Figueroa, prin. Fax 462-3901
Pontiac ES 700/PK-5
500 Spears Creek Church Rd 29045 803-699-2700
Beth Elliott, prin. Fax 699-2704
Spears Creek Road Child Development Ctr PK-PK
502 Spears Creek Church Rd 29045 803-865-5355
Sabino Mosso-Taylor, prin. Fax 865-5356

Elloree, Orangeburg, Pop. 709
Orangeburg County Consolidated SD 3
Supt. — See Holly Hill
Elloree S 400/K-8
PO Box 810 29047 803-897-2233
Mamie Dupree, prin. Fax 897-2034

Estill, Hampton, Pop. 2,394
Hampton SD 2 1,300/K-12
PO Box 1028 29918 803-625-5000
Kenneth Gardner, supt. Fax 625-2573
www.hampton2.k12.sc.us
Estill ES 500/K-5
PO Box 1027 29918 803-625-5030
Ron Youmans, prin. Fax 625-2373
Estill MS 300/6-8
PO Box 817 29918 803-625-5200
Julia Lee, prin. Fax 625-3588

Henry Academy 300/PK-12
8766 Savannah Hwy 29918 803-625-2440
Dr. Terry King, hdmstr. Fax 625-3110

Eutawville, Orangeburg, Pop. 334
Orangeburg County Consolidated SD 3
Supt. — See Holly Hill
St. James/Gaillard ES 300/K-5
PO Box 250 29048 803-492-7927
Michelle Wilson, prin. Fax 496-3728

Fairfax, Allendale, Pop. 3,178
Allendale County SD 1,700/PK-12
3249 Allendale Fairfax Hwy 29827 803-584-4603
Ora Watson Ph.D., supt. Fax 584-5303
www.acs.k12.sc.us
Allendale-Fairfax MS 400/6-8
3305 Allendale Fairfax Hwy 29827 803-584-3489
Brian Newsome, prin. Fax 584-5331
Fairfax ES 300/PK-6
PO Box 910 29827 803-632-2536
Dewey Carey, prin. Fax 632-2822
Other Schools – See Allendale

Florence, Florence, Pop. 31,269
Florence County SD 1 14,900/K-12
319 S Dargan St 29506 843-669-4141
Larry Jackson, supt. Fax 673-1108
www.fsd1.org
Briggs ES 600/K-6
1012 Congaree Dr 29501 843-664-8169
Martin Schmid, prin. Fax 664-8189
Carver ES 800/K-4
515 N Cashua Dr 29501 843-664-8156
Cynthia Young, prin. Fax 664-8177
Delmae Heights ES 800/K-4
1211 S Cashua Dr 29501 843-664-8448
Roy Ann Jolley, prin. Fax 673-5777
Greenwood ES 700/K-6
2300 E Howe Springs Rd 29505 843-664-8451
Susan Hartwig, prin. Fax 664-8182
Lester ES 400/K-6
3501 E Palmetto St 29506 843-664-8459
Greg Mingo, prin. Fax 679-6753
McLaurin ES 500/K-4
1400 Mcmillian Ln 29506 843-664-8457
Deborah Cribb, prin. Fax 664-8462
Moore IS 600/5-6
1101 Cheraw Dr 29501 843-664-8171
Barbara Hood, prin. Fax 664-8188
North Vista ES 600/K-6
1100 N Irby St 29501 843-664-8159
Sharon Dixon, prin. Fax 679-6752
Royall ES 700/K-6
1400 Woods Rd 29501 843-664-8167
Julie Smith-Koon, prin. Fax 292-1573
Sneed MS 900/7-8
1102 S Ebenezer Rd 29501 843-673-1199
Tony Lunsford, prin. Fax 679-6890
Southside MS 800/7-8
200 E Howe Springs Rd 29505 843-664-8467
Craig Washington, prin. Fax 673-5766
Timrod ES 400/K-6
1901 E Old Marion Hwy 29506 843-664-8454
Thurmond Williams, prin. Fax 664-8180
Wallace-Gregg ES 400/K-6
515 Francis Marion Rd 29506 843-664-8481
Gloria Mudrow, prin. Fax 664-8181
Williams MS 700/7-8
1119 N Irby St 29501 843-664-8162
Leon McCray, prin. Fax 664-8178
Other Schools – See Effingham

All Saints Episcopal S 300/PK-6
1425 Cherokee Rd 29501 843-662-8134
Joan Pennstrom, prin. Fax 662-9641
Byrnes Schools 300/PK-12
1201 E Ashby Rd 29506 843-662-0131
John Colby, hdmstr. Fax 669-2466
Christian Assembly S 200/PK-12
401 Pamplico Hwy 29505 843-667-1975
Audrey Streit, prin. Fax 664-0389
Florence Christian S 700/PK-12
PO Box 12809 29504 843-662-0454
Jim Berry, prin. Fax 661-4301
Hannah Academy & Day Care 50/K-8
803 Oakland Ave 29506 843-669-3777
King's Academy 300/K-12
1015 S Ebenezer Rd 29501 843-661-7464
Don Wilson, hdmstr. Fax 661-7647
Maranatha Christian S 200/PK-12
2624 W Palmetto St 29501 843-665-6395
Chad Reel, prin. Fax 629-0510
Montessori S of Florence 100/PK-6
510 W Palmetto St 29501 843-629-2920
Phyllis Thomas, dir. Fax 629-0870
St. Anthony S 300/PK-8
2536 Hoffmeyer Rd 29501 843-662-1910
Phyllis Brandis, prin. Fax 662-5335

Fort Mill, York, Pop. 8,257
Lancaster County SD
Supt. — See Lancaster
Indian Land ES 800/K-5
4137 Dobys Bridge Rd, 803-548-2916
Elizabeth Blum, prin. Fax 548-3011

York SD 4 7,200/K-12
120 E Elliott St 29715 803-548-2527
Dr. V. Keith Callicutt, supt. Fax 547-4696
www.fort-mill.k12.sc.us
Fort Mill ES 800/K-5
192 Springfield Pkwy 29715 803-547-7546
Karen Helms, prin. Fax 547-7559
Fort Mill MS 600/6-8
200 Springfield Pkwy 29715 803-547-5553
Fax 548-2911
Orchard Park ES 800/K-5
474 Third Baxter St 29708 803-548-8170
Linda Locklier, prin. Fax 548-8174
Riverview ES 600/K-5
1434 Harris Rd 29715 803-548-4677
Annette Chinchilla, prin. Fax 548-4747
Springfield ES 700/K-5
1691 Springfield Pkwy 29715 803-548-8150
Scott Frattaroli, prin. Fax 548-8154
Springfield MS 6-8
1711 Springfield Pkwy 29715 803-548-8199
Keith Griffin, prin. Fax 547-1013
Other Schools – See Tega Cay

Fountain Inn, Greenville, Pop. 6,729
Greenville County SD
Supt. — See Greenville
Fountain Inn ES 800/K-5
608 Fairview St 29644 864-355-5100
Glenn Wile, prin. Fax 355-5164

Gadsden, Richland
Richland SD 1
Supt. — See Columbia
Gadsden ES 200/K-5
1660 S Goodwin Cir 29052 803-353-2231
Dr. Charles DeLaughter, prin. Fax 691-3782

Gaffney, Cherokee, Pop. 12,934
Cherokee SD 9,000/PK-12
PO Box 460 29342 864-902-3500
Dr. William James, supt. Fax 902-3541
www.cherokee1.k12.sc.us
Alma ES 200/K-5
213 Alma St 29340 864-489-4742
Kim Camp, prin. Fax 902-3595
Bramlett ES 300/K-5
301 Spruce St 29340 864-489-2831
Dr. Tom Abbott, prin. Fax 487-1236
Corinth ES 400/K-5
128 Corinth Rd 29340 864-489-2163
Brenda Sharts, prin. Fax 487-7444
Draytonville ES 300/K-5
2373 Wilkinsville Hwy 29340 864-487-1240
Janice Ford, prin. Fax 487-1218
Ewing MS 500/6-8
171 E Junior High Rd 29340 864-489-3176
Dr. Denise Wooten, prin. Fax 489-8534
Gaffney MS 700/6-8
805 E Frederick St 29340 864-902-3630
Jean Brewington, prin. Fax 902-3637
Goucher ES 200/K-5
604 Goucher School Rd 29340 864-487-1246
Ashley Clary, prin. Fax 487-1248
Granard MS 500/6-8
815 W Rutledge Ave 29341 864-489-6833
Shirley Sealy, prin. Fax 488-1553
Grassy Pond ES 400/K-5
1146 Boiling Springs Hwy 29341 864-487-1256
Nan Ruppe, prin. Fax 487-1255
Lee ES 400/K-5
401 Overbrook Dr 29341 864-489-5748
Sharon Jefferies, prin. Fax 902-3642
Limestone-Central ES 400/K-5
727 Pacolet Hwy 29340 864-487-1249
Clay Fowler, prin. Fax 487-1251
Northwest ES 500/K-5
840 Green River Rd 29341 864-487-1243
Cathy Bloise, prin. Fax 487-1245
Vaughan ES 300/K-5
192 Vaughn Rd 29341 864-489-2424
Dr. Ron Cope, prin. Fax 487-1253
Other Schools – See Blacksburg

Galivants Ferry, Horry
Horry County SD
Supt. — See Conway
Midland ES 500/K-5
3011 Nichols Hwy 29544 843-358-3036
Jennifer Parker, prin. Fax 358-0643

Garden City, Horry, Pop. 6,305
Horry County SD
Supt. — See Conway
Seaside ES 700/K-5
1605 Woodland Drive Ext 29576 843-650-3490
Beth Selander, prin. Fax 650-3479

Gaston, Lexington, Pop. 1,389
Lexington County SD 4
Supt. — See Swansea
Mack PS 700/PK-2
161 Gaston St 29053 803-794-8369
Donna Goodwin, prin. Fax 794-5946
Sandhills MS 500/7-8
582 Meadowfield Rd 29053 803-926-1890
Justin Nutter, prin. Fax 926-1910

Georgetown, Georgetown, Pop. 8,941
Georgetown County SD 10,400/PK-12
2018 Church St 29440 843-436-7000
Dr. Randy Dozier, supt. Fax 436-7171
www.gcsd.k12.sc.us
Browns Ferry ES 200/PK-5
7292 Browns Ferry Rd 29440 843-527-1325
Bethany Giles-Burgess, prin. Fax 546-2138
Georgetown MS 900/6-8
2400 Anthuan Maybank St 29440 843-527-4495
Rosemary Gray, prin. Fax 527-2290
Kensington ES 700/PK-5
86 Kensington Blvd 29440 843-546-8511
Fedrick Cohens, prin. Fax 546-0605
Maryville ES 600/PK-5
2125 Poplar St 29440 843-546-8423
Stephanie Bell, prin. Fax 546-5038
McDonald ES 600/PK-5
532 McDonald Rd 29440 843-527-3485
Miriam Daniels, prin. Fax 546-8674
Plantersville ES 100/PK-5
1668 Exodus Dr 29440 843-546-8453
Shawn Johnson, prin. Fax 527-2869
Sampit ES 400/PK-5
69 Woodland Ave 29440 843-527-4411
Maudest Rhue-Scott, prin. Fax 546-1226
Other Schools – See Andrews, Hemingway, Pawleys Island

Gilbert, Lexington, Pop. 552
Lexington County SD 1
Supt. — See Lexington
Gilbert ES 600/3-5
314 Main St 29054 803-821-1600
Tim Oswald, prin. Fax 821-1603
Gilbert MS 700/6-8
120 Rikard Cir 29054 803-821-1700
Benji Ricard, prin. Fax 821-1703
Gilbert PS 600/K-2
520 Main St 29054 803-821-1400
Loretta Arnette, prin. Fax 821-1403

Glendale, Spartanburg
Spartanburg SD 3 3,000/K-12
PO Box 267 29346 864-279-6000
Dr. Jim Ray, supt. Fax 279-6003
www.spa3.k12.sc.us
Other Schools – See Cowpens, Pacolet, Spartanburg

Gloverville, Aiken, Pop. 2,753
Aiken County SD
Supt. — See Aiken
Gloverville ES 400/K-5
114 Gloria Rush Cir 29828 803-593-7280
Michelle Padgett, prin. Fax 593-7281

Goose Creek, Berkeley, Pop. 32,516
Berkeley County SD
Supt. — See Moncks Corner
Boulder Bluff ES 600/K-5
400 Judy Dr 29445 843-553-1223
Diane White, prin. Fax 820-4086
Devon Forest ES 1,100/K-5
1127 Dorothy St 29445 843-820-3880
Christen Mitchum Ed.D., prin. Fax 820-3883
Goose Creek PS 600/K-2
200 Foster Creek Rd 29445 843-820-8008
Kathy Sullivan, prin. Fax 820-8016
Howe Hall AIMS ES 400/K-5
115 Howe Hall Rd 29445 843-820-3899
Marty French, prin. Fax 820-5428
Marrington ES 50/K-5
109 Gearing St 29445 843-572-0313
Arnold Coull, prin. Fax 820-4063
Marrington MS, 109 Gearing St 29445 6-8
Jim Spencer, prin. 843-572-3373
Sedgefield IS 600/3-5
225 Garwood Dr 29445 843-820-4090
Susan Best, prin. Fax 820-5433
Sedgefield MS 800/6-8
131 Charles B Gibson Blvd 29445 843-797-2620
Mike Lucas, prin. Fax 820-5401
Westview ES 400/4-5
100 Westview Dr 29445 843-797-2992
Rusty Boston, prin. Fax 820-4012
Westview MS 1,200/6-8
101 Westview Dr 29445 843-572-1700
Jerome Davis, prin. Fax 820-3728
Westview PS 900/PK-3
98 Westview Dr 29445 843-820-3898
Dr. Luci Carter, prin. Fax 820-4078

St. Timothys Childrens Center 100/PK-PK
PO Box 807 29445 843-553-7175
Mary Ann Smith, dir.

Graniteville, Aiken
Aiken County SD
Supt. — See Aiken
Byrd ES 500/K-5
1225 Weldon Way 29829 803-663-4320
Russell Gunter, prin. Fax 663-4321
Leavelle-McCampbell MS 400/6-8
82 Canal St 29829 803-663-4300
Jacquelyn Barnwell, prin. Fax 663-4302

Gray Court, Laurens, Pop. 1,005
Laurens SD 55
Supt. — See Laurens
Gray Court - Owings ES K-5
PO Box 128 29645 864-876-2131
Mark Adams, prin. Fax 876-9597
Gray Court-Owings MS 200/6-8
PO Box 187 29645 864-876-2171
Marilyn Ramsey, prin. Fax 876-2965
Hickory Tavern ES 400/K-5
163 Neely Ferry Rd 29645 864-575-2126
Mary Ann Crouch, prin. Fax 575-3428
Hickory Tavern MS 300/6-8
163 Neely Ferry Rd 29645 864-575-4301
Russell Scott, prin. Fax 575-4305

Great Falls, Chester, Pop. 2,095
Chester County SD
Supt. — See Chester
Great Falls ES 400/K-4
301 Dearborn St 29055 803-482-2214
Jerry Digh, prin. Fax 482-6800
Great Falls MS 300/5-8
409 Sunset Ave 29055 803-482-2220
Wendell Sumter, prin. Fax 482-6025

Greeleyville, Williamsburg, Pop. 419
Williamsburg County SD
Supt. — See Kingstree
Greeleyville ES 300/K-6
PO Box 128 29056 843-426-2116
Sam Giles, prin. Fax 426-2141

Green Sea, Horry
Horry County SD
Supt. — See Conway
Green Sea-Floyds ES 700/PK-6
5000 Tulip Grove Rd 29545 843-392-1078
Shirley Huggins, prin. Fax 392-1090

Greenville, Greenville, Pop. 56,676
Anderson SD 1
Supt. — See Williamston
Powdersville ES 400/3-5
139 Hood Rd 29611 864-269-4431
Debra Gill, prin. Fax 269-4426
Powdersville MS 500/6-8
135 Hood Rd 29611 864-269-1821
Monty Oxendine, prin. Fax 269-0795

Greenville County SD 66,400/PK-12
PO Box 2848 29602 864-355-3100
Dr. Phinnize Fisher, supt. Fax 241-4195
www.greenville.k12.sc.us/
Alexander ES 300/K-5
1601 W Bramlett Rd 29611 864-355-1000
Leda Young, prin. Fax 355-1044
Armstrong ES 500/K-5
8601 White Horse Rd 29617 864-355-1100
Jackie Goggins, prin. Fax 355-1158
Augusta Circle ES 500/K-5
100 Winyah St 29605 864-355-1200
Kerry Bannister, prin. Fax 355-1212
Beck Academy 900/6-8
901 Woodruff Rd 29607 864-355-1400
Dr. J. Brodie Bricker, prin. Fax 355-1490
Berea ES 500/K-5
100 Berea Dr 29617 864-355-1500
Patricia Booker-Christy, prin. Fax 355-1558
Berea MS 900/6-8
151 Berea Middle School Rd 29617 864-355-1700
Robin Mill, prin. Fax 355-1777
Blythe Academy of Languages 800/K-5
100 Blythe Dr 29605 864-355-4400
Sandra Griffin, prin. Fax 355-4412
Cashion ES 600/K-5
1500 Fork Shoals Rd 29605 864-355-8000
Shirley Chapman, prin. Fax 355-8021
Cherrydale ES 400/K-5
302 Perry Rd 29609 864-355-3300
Scarlet Black, prin. Fax 355-3361
Collins ES 800/K-5
1200 Parkins Mill Rd 29607 864-355-3200
Alice Arrington, prin. Fax 355-3290
Duncan Chapel ES 700/K-5
210 Duncan Chapel Rd 29617 864-355-2700
Regina McClain, prin. Fax 355-2769
East North Street Academy 600/K-5
1720 E North St 29607 864-355-2900
W. Lavelle McCray, prin. Fax 355-2980
Greenbrier ES 600/K-5
853 Log Shoals Rd 29607 864-355-5300
Nicky Andrews, prin. Fax 355-5327
Greenville Middle Academy 700/6-8
339 Lowndes Ave 29607 864-355-5600
Dr. Robert Palmer, prin. Fax 355-5682
Hollis Academy 500/K-5
200 Goodrich St 29611 864-355-4800
Miki Golden, prin. Fax 355-4826
Hughes Academy 900/6-8
122 Deoyley Ave 29605 864-355-6200
Dr. Patrick Mark, prin. Fax 355-6275
Kerns ES K-5
6650 Frontage Rd 29605 864-355-1300
Judy Mulkey, prin. Fax 355-1351
Lake Forest ES 600/K-5
16 Berkshire Ave 29615 864-355-4000
Cindy Coggins, prin. Fax 355-4072
Lakeview MS 500/6-8
3801 Old Buncombe Rd 29617 864-355-6400
Dr. Tracy Hall, prin. Fax 355-6416
League Academy 800/6-8
125 Twin Lake Rd 29609 864-355-8100
Merry Cox, prin. Fax 355-8160
Mitchell Road ES 500/K-5
4124 E North St 29615 864-355-6700
Nerissa Lewis, prin. Fax 355-6719
Monaview ES 400/K-5
10 Monaview St 29617 864-355-4300
Sharon Dowell, prin. Fax 355-4314
Northwest Cresent Child Development Ctr PK-K
925 N Franklin Rd 29617 864-355-4080
Doris Santanello, prin. Fax 355-4097
Overbrook Child Development Center 700/K-K
111 Laurens Rd 29607 864-355-7350
Doris Santanello, prin. Fax 355-7373
Pelham Road ES 600/K-5
100 All Star Way 29615 864-355-7600
Nancy Brantley, prin. Fax 355-7658
Sevier MS 700/6-8
1004 Piedmont Park Rd 29609 864-355-8200
Karen Kapp, prin. Fax 355-8255
Sterling S K-8
99 John McCarroll Way 29607 864-355-4480
David Johnstone, prin. Fax 355-4490
Stone Academy 500/K-5
115 Randall St 29609 864-355-8400
Edward Holliday, prin. Fax 355-8455
Summit Drive ES 300/K-5
424 Summit Dr 29609 864-355-8800
Megan Mitchell, prin. Fax 355-8817
Tanglewood MS 700/6-8
44 Merriwoods Dr 29611 864-355-4500
William Price, prin. Fax 355-4512
Welcome ES 600/K-5
36 E Welcome Rd 29611 864-355-3900
Christine Phillips, prin. Fax 355-3961
Westcliffe ES 300/K-5
105 Eastbourne Rd 29611 864-355-0300
Carolyn Morgan, prin. Fax 355-0360
Other Schools – See Fountain Inn, Greer, Marietta, Pelzer, Piedmont, Simpsonville, Taylors, Travelers Rest

---

Christ Church Episcopal Preschool 200/PK-K
10 N Church St 29601 864-233-7612
Heather Meadors, dir. Fax 235-9412
Christ Church Episcopal S 1,000/K-12
245 Cavalier Dr 29607 864-299-1522
Dr. Leland Cox, hdmstr. Fax 299-4285
First Presbyterian Academy 200/PK-2
200 W Washington St 29601 864-235-0122
Michael Everhart, hdmstr. Fax 235-0698
Greenville SDA S 50/K-8
1704 E North St 29607 864-232-8885
Sonja Eberhart, prin. Fax 232-8885
Hampton Park Christian S 700/K-12
875 State Park Rd 29609 864-233-0556
Bruce Mizell, admin. Fax 235-5621
Jones ES 800/PK-6
1700 Wade Hampton Blvd 29614 864-770-1392
Fax 770-1318
Jones JHS 200/7-8
1700 Wade Hampton Blvd 29614 864-770-1393
Fax 271-7278
Mitchell Road Christian Academy 400/PK-8
207 Mitchell Rd 29615 864-268-2210
Bob Schmidt, hdmstr. Fax 268-3184
Montessori S of Greenville 50/K-3
305 Pelham Rd 29615 864-232-3447
Robin Bylenga, prin. Fax 232-1919
Mt. Zion Christian S 300/PK-8
724 Garlington Rd 29615 864-297-6646
Lisa Muse, prin. Fax 627-1101
Our Lady of the Rosary S 200/K-8
2 James Dr 29605 864-277-5350
John Harrington, prin. Fax 277-7745
Our Saviour Lutheran S 50/PK-PK
2600 Wade Hampton Blvd 29615 864-268-4714
Mary Glover, dir. Fax 268-5169
St. Anthony of Padua S 100/PK-5
309 Gower St 29611 864-271-0167
Sr. Catherine Noecker, prin. Fax 271-2936
St. Mary S 300/K-8
101 Hampton Ave 29601 864-271-3870
Sr. Mary John, prin. Fax 271-0159
Shannon Forest Christian S 600/PK-12
829 Garlington Rd 29615 864-678-5107
Brenda Hillman, hdmstr. Fax 281-9372

Greenwood, Greenwood, Pop. 22,378
Greenwood SD 50 8,800/PK-12
PO Box 248 29648 864-941-5400
Darrell Johnson, supt. Fax 941-5427
www.gwd50.org
Brewer MS, 1000 Emerald Rd 29646 700/6-8
Chad Evans, prin. 864-941-5500
Greenwood 50 ECC PK-PK
1125 Cambridge Ave E 29646 864-941-5520
Rex Coates, prin. Fax 941-3497
Lakeview ES 600/K-5
660 Center St 29649 864-941-5760
Virginia Metts, prin. Fax 941-3498
Mathews ES, 725 Marshall Rd 29646 400/K-5
Doris Watson, prin. 864-941-5680
Merrywood ES 500/K-5
329 Deadfall Rd W 29649 864-941-5700
Debra Green, prin.
Northside MS 800/6-8
431 Deadfall Rd W 29649 864-941-5780
Beth Pinson, prin. Fax 941-3434
Oakland ES 500/K-5
1802 Durst Ave E 29649 864-941-5660
Mark Blackwell, prin. Fax 388-2401
Pinecrest ES 500/K-5
220 Northside Dr E 29649 864-941-5580
Susan Buchanan, prin. Fax 229-5284
Springfield ES 600/K-5
1608 Florida Ave 29646 864-941-5535
Bonnie Corbitt, prin. Fax 388-2402
Westview MS 700/6-8
1410 W Alexander Ave 29646 864-229-4301
Cynthia Storer, prin. Fax 229-4827
Woodfields ES 500/K-5
1032 Emerald Rd 29646 864-941-5540
Jean Craig, prin.
Other Schools – See Hodges

Calvary Christian S 100/K-12
2775 Montague Avenue Ext 29649 864-229-6553
Cindy Stanley, prin.
Cambridge Academy 100/PK-8
103 Eastman St 29649 864-229-2875
Don Frazier, hdmstr. Fax 229-6712
Greenwood Christian S 400/PK-12
2026 Woodlawn Rd 29649 864-229-2427
Michael Edds, hdmstr. Fax 852-5278
Palmetto Christian Academy of Greenwood 50/PK-12
330 Deadfall Rd W 29649 864-223-0391
Joan Gore, prin. Fax 223-1692

Greer, Greenville, Pop. 21,421
Greenville County SD
Supt. — See Greenville
Blue Ridge MS 900/6-8
2423 E Tyger Bridge Rd 29651 864-355-1900
Rebecca Greene, prin. Fax 355-1966
Buena Vista ES 800/K-5
310 S Batesville Rd 29650 864-355-2200
Ann K. Mohr, prin. Fax 355-2214
Chandler Creek ES 800/K-5
301 Chandler Rd 29651 864-355-2400
Kathryn Bayne, prin. Fax 355-2420
Crestview ES 700/K-5
509 American Legion Rd 29651 864-355-2600
Margaret Thomason, prin. Fax 355-2613
Dunbar Child Development Center PK-PK
200 Morgan St 29651 864-355-2270
Doris Santanello, prin. Fax 355-2295
Greer MS 1,000/6-8
3032 E Gap Creek Rd 29651 864-355-5800
Scott Rhymer, prin. Fax 355-5880
Riverside MS 1,000/6-8
615 Hammett Bridge Rd 29650 864-355-7900
Ron Harrison, prin. Fax 355-7918
Skyland ES 600/K-7
4221 N Highway 14 29651 864-355-7200
Carolyn Styles, prin. Fax 355-7215
Woodland ES 1,000/K-5
1730 Gibbs Shoals Rd 29650 864-355-0400
Wanda Mote, prin. Fax 355-0477

Gresham, Marion
Marion SD 7
Supt. — See Mullins
Brittons Neck ES 100/1-5
223 Gresham Rd 29546 843-362-3510
Tammy Martin, prin. Fax 362-3519

Hampton, Hampton, Pop. 2,799
Hampton SD 1
Supt. — See Varnville
Hampton ES 400/4-6
PO Box 687 29924 803-943-3251
Eric Robinson, prin. Fax 943-4128
Hazel PS 400/PK-3
628 Railroad Ave W 29924 803-943-3659
Bonnie Wilson, prin. Fax 943-0532

Hanahan, Berkeley, Pop. 13,818
Berkeley County SD
Supt. — See Moncks Corner
Hanahan ES 900/K-5
4000 Mabeline Rd 29410 843-553-3290
Tom Sparkman, prin. Fax 820-5421
Hanahan MS 700/5-8
5815 Murray Dr 29410 843-820-3800
Robin Rogers, prin. Fax 820-3804

Divine Redeemer S 200/PK-8
1104 Fort Dr 29410 843-553-1521
Jean Steinhoff, prin. Fax 553-7109

Hardeeville, Jasper, Pop. 1,843
Jasper County SD
Supt. — See Ridgeland
Hardeeville ES 600/PK-5
150 Hurricane Alley 29927 843-784-8400
Dr. Barbara Baxter, prin. Fax 784-8409

Hartsville, Darlington, Pop. 7,414
Darlington County SD
Supt. — See Darlington
Carolina ES 200/1-5
719 W Carolina Ave 29550 843-383-3112
Donna Barrett, prin. Fax 857-3232
Hartsville MS 1,200/6-8
1427 14th St 29550 843-383-3121
Meredith Taylor, prin. Fax 857-4510
North Hartsville ES 800/1-5
110 School Dr 29550 843-383-3115
Kristi Austin, prin. Fax 857-3190
Southside ECC 400/K-K
1615 Blanding Dr 29550 843-383-3105
Patricia Toney, prin. Fax 857-3315
Thornwell ES for the Arts 300/1-5
437 W Carolina Ave 29550 843-383-3127
P.J. Casey, prin. Fax 383-6043
Washington Street ES 400/1-3
325 W Washington St 29550 843-383-3141
Valerie Sawyer, prin. Fax 857-3351
West Hartsville ES 200/4-5
214 Clyde Rd 29550 843-383-3144
Dr. Kay Howell, prin. Fax 857-3272

Emmanuel Christian S 400/PK-12
1001 N Marquis Hwy 29550 843-332-0164
Fax 878-0501
Hart Academy 200/PK-8
852 Flinns Rd 29550 843-332-4991
John Horlbeck, hdmstr. Fax 383-9523

Heath Springs, Lancaster, Pop. 860
Lancaster County SD
Supt. — See Lancaster
Heath Springs ES 400/K-5
158 Solar Rd 29058 803-273-3176
Sherri Watson, prin. Fax 273-3717

Hemingway, Williamsburg, Pop. 524
Georgetown County SD
Supt. — See Georgetown
Carvers Bay MS 400/6-8
13000 Choppee Rd 29554 843-545-0918
Darryl Stanley, prin. Fax 558-6937
Pleasant Hill ES 400/PK-5
127 Schoolhouse Dr 29554 843-558-9417
Teddy Graham, prin. Fax 558-7017

Williamsburg County SD
Supt. — See Kingstree
Hemingway ES K-6
160 Baxley Rd 29554 843-558-4444
Cynthia Brown, prin. Fax 558-4440

Hickory Grove, York, Pop. 374
York SD 1
Supt. — See York
Hickory Grove-Sharon ES 400/PK-6
4901 Hickory Grove Rd 29717 803-925-2116
Dietrich Long, prin. Fax 925-2218

Hilton Head Island, Beaufort, Pop. 34,497
Beaufort County SD
Supt. — See Beaufort
Hilton Head Island ECC 400/PK-K
165 Pembroke Dr 29926 843-689-0400
Adrienne Sutton, prin. Fax 689-7455
Hilton Head Island Intl Baccalaureate ES 900/1-5
30 School Rd 29926 843-342-4100
Jill McAden, prin. Fax 342-4299
Hilton Head Island MS 900/6-8
55 Wilborn Rd 29926 843-689-4500
Sherry DeSimone, prin. Fax 689-4600
Hilton Head Island S for Creative Arts 600/1-5
10 Wilborn Rd 29926 843-342-4380
Gretchen Keefner, prin. Fax 689-7455

Hilton Head Christian Academy 500/K-12
55 Gardner Dr 29926 843-681-2878
Mike Lindsay, hdmstr. Fax 681-9758
Hilton Head Prep S 500/K-12
8 Foxgrape Rd 29928 843-671-2286
Dr. Anthony Kandel, hdmstr. Fax 671-7624
St. Francis By the Sea S 200/PK-8
45 Beach City Rd 29926 843-681-6501
Michael Rockers, prin. Fax 689-3725

Hodges, Greenwood, Pop. 166
Greenwood SD 50
Supt. — See Greenwood
Hodges ES, 4717 Main St 29653 300/K-5
Roger Richburg, prin. 864-374-5000

Holly Hill, Orangeburg, Pop. 1,364
Orangeburg County Consolidated SD 3 3,200/K-12
PO Box 98 29059 803-496-3288
Dr. Cynthia Cash-Greene, supt. Fax 496-5850
www.obg3.k12.sc.us
Holly Hill ES 500/K-5
PO Box 278 29059 803-496-5219
Carol Szorosy, prin. Fax 496-3526
Holly Hill-Roberts MS 600/6-8
PO Box 879 29059 803-496-3818
JoAnne Lawton, prin. Fax 496-7584
Other Schools – See Elloree, Eutawville, Vance

Holly Hill Academy 300/K-12
PO Box 757 29059 803-496-3243
John Gasque, hdmstr. Fax 496-9778

Hollywood, Charleston, Pop. 4,307
Charleston County SD
Supt. — See Charleston
Hughes ES 100/K-5
8548 Willtown Rd 29449 843-889-2976
Marguerite Middleton, prin. Fax 889-6758
Schroder MS 300/6-8
7224 Highway 162 29449 843-889-2391
Sheryl Biss, prin. Fax 889-6539

Honea Path, Anderson, Pop. 3,597
Anderson SD 2 3,700/K-12
10990 Belton Honea Path Hwy 29654 864-369-7364
Thomas Chapman, supt. Fax 369-4006
www.anderson2.k12.sc.us
Honea Path ES 500/K-4
806 E Greer St 29654 864-369-7612
Mark Robertson, prin. Fax 369-4030
Honea Path MS 400/5-8
107 Brock Ave 29654 864-369-7641
John Snead, prin. Fax 369-4034
Other Schools – See Belton

Hopkins, Richland
Richland SD 1
Supt. — See Columbia
Hopkins ES 300/K-5
6120 Cabin Creek Rd 29061 803-783-5541
Angela Brown, prin. Fax 783-5569
Hopkins MS 500/6-8
1601 Clarkson Rd 29061 803-695-3331
Goler Collins, prin. Fax 695-3320
Horrell Hill ES 600/K-5
517 Horrell Hill Rd 29061 803-783-5545
Parthenia Satterwhite, prin. Fax 783-5593

Southeast MS 700/6-8
731 Horrell Hill Rd 29061 803-695-5700
Jeannetta Scott, prin. Fax 695-5703

Huger, Berkeley
Berkeley County SD
Supt. — See Moncks Corner
Cainhoy S 300/K-8
2434 Cainhoy Rd 29450 843-899-8975
John Spagnolia, prin. Fax 899-8970

Indian Land, York
Lancaster County SD
Supt. — See Lancaster
Indian Land MS 6-8
8361 Charlotte Hwy, 803-578-2500
David McDonald, prin. Fax 578-2549

Inman, Spartanburg, Pop. 1,918
Spartanburg SD 1
Supt. — See Campobello
Inman ES 400/K-3
25 Oakland Ave 29349 864-472-8403
Beth Young, prin. Fax 472-7839
Inman IS 300/4-6
10 W Miller St 29349 864-472-1510
Debbie Wright, prin. Fax 472-1511
Mabry JHS 400/7-8
35 Oakland Ave 29349 864-472-8402
Brian Batson, prin. Fax 472-7438
New Prospect ES 300/K-6
9251 Highway 9 29349 864-592-1970
Chris Price, prin. Fax 592-2010

Spartanburg SD 2
Supt. — See Boiling Springs
Boiling Springs JHS 1,100/7-8
4801 Highway 9 29349 864-578-5954
Donald Barnette, prin. Fax 599-5489
Oakland ES 600/K-4
151 Mud Creek Rd 29349 864-814-3870
James Moore, prin. Fax 814-3806

Irmo, Richland, Pop. 11,223
Lexington/Richland Counties SD 5 16,100/PK-12
1020 Dutch Fork Rd 29063 803-476-8000
Dr. Herbert Berg, supt. Fax 476-8017
www.lex5.k12.sc.us
Ballentine ES 700/K-5
1040 Bickley Rd 29063 803-476-4500
Dr. Barbara Brockhard, prin. Fax 475-4520
Corley ES 700/PK-5
1500 Chadford Rd 29063 803-476-4001
Dr. Judy Franchini, prin. Fax 476-4020
Dutch Fork ES 500/K-5
7900 Broad River Rd 29063 803-476-3900
June M. Lominack, prin. Fax 476-3920
Dutch Fork MS 1,000/7-8
1528 Old Tamah Rd 29063 803-732-8167
Roderic Taylor, prin. Fax 732-8171
Irmo ES 500/K-5
7401 Gibbes St 29063 803-732-8275
Shannon McAlister, prin. Fax 732-8035
Oak Pointe ES K-5
1 River Bottom Rd 29063 803-476-4100
James Stephens, prin. Fax 476-4120
River Springs ES 600/K-5
115 Connie Wright Rd 29063 803-732-8147
Sandra Williamson, prin. Fax 732-8158
Other Schools – See Chapin, Columbia

Islandton, Colleton

New Hope Christian S of Islandton 50/PK-12
PO Box 55 29929 843-866-2608
Mark Givens, prin.

Iva, Anderson, Pop. 1,180
Anderson SD 3 2,500/K-12
PO Box 118 29655 864-348-6196
L. Hugh Smith, supt. Fax 348-6198
www.anderson3.k12.sc.us
Iva ES 500/K-5
803 Antreville Hwy 29655 864-348-6400
Eric Hughes, prin. Fax 348-7071
Other Schools – See Starr

Jackson, Aiken, Pop. 1,644
Aiken County SD
Supt. — See Aiken
Jackson MS 400/6-8
8217 Atomic Rd 29831 803-279-3525
Marc Funderburk, prin. Fax 471-2202

Jefferson, Chesterfield, Pop. 703
Chesterfield County SD
Supt. — See Chesterfield
Jefferson ES 300/K-5
809 W Elizabeth 29718 843-658-3295
Wendy Folsom, prin. Fax 658-3309
New Heights MS 600/6-8
5738 Highway 151 29718 843-658-6830
Larry Stinson, prin. Fax 658-6812

Joanna, Laurens, Pop. 1,735
Laurens SD 56
Supt. — See Clinton
Joanna-Woodson ES 300/K-5
510 S Ellis St 29351 864-697-6480
Melodie Edwards, prin. Fax 697-4302

Johns Island, Charleston
Charleston County SD
Supt. — See Charleston
Angel Oak ES 400/K-5
6134 Chisolm Rd 29455 843-559-6412
Rodney Moore, prin. Fax 559-6415
Haut Gap MS 300/6-8
1861 Bohicket Rd 29455 843-559-6418
Paul Padron, prin. Fax 559-6439
Mt. Zion ES 200/K-5
3464 River Rd 29455 843-559-3841
Deborah Fordham, prin. Fax 559-6440

Charleston Collegiate S 300/PK-12
2024 Academy Rd 29455 843-559-5506
J. Robert Shirley Ph.D., prin. Fax 559-6172

Johnsonville, Florence, Pop. 1,460
Florence County SD 5 1,600/PK-12
PO Box 98 29555 843-386-2358
A. Dale Strickland, supt. Fax 386-3139
www.flo5.k12.sc.us
Johnsonville ES 700/PK-4
160 E Marion St 29555 843-386-2955
Dayne Coker, prin. Fax 386-3574
Johnsonville MS 400/5-8
PO Box 67 29555 843-386-2066
Stevie Phillips, prin. Fax 386-3786

Johnston, Edgefield, Pop. 2,352
Edgefield County SD 3,800/K-12
3 Par Dr 29832 803-275-4601
Mary Rice-Crenshaw, supt. Fax 275-4426
www.edgefield.k12.sc.us
JET MS 600/6-8
1095 Columbia Rd 29832 803-275-1997
Louis Scott, prin. Fax 275-1783
Johnston ES 400/K-5
514 Lee St 29832 803-275-1755
Bridget Clark, prin. Fax 275-1785
Other Schools – See Edgefield, North Augusta, Trenton

Wardlaw Academy 200/PK-12
1296 Columbia Rd 29832 803-275-4794
Ben Couch, hdmstr. Fax 275-4873

Jonesville, Union, Pop. 927
Union County SD
Supt. — See Union
Jonesville ES 300/K-6
514 Alman St 29353 864-674-5518
Floyd Lyles, prin. Fax 674-1890
Jonesville MS 100/7-8
131 N Main St 29353 864-674-5272
Michelle James, prin. Fax 674-5280

Kershaw, Lancaster, Pop. 1,631
Kershaw County SD
Supt. — See Camden
Mt. Pisgah ES 100/K-5
5160 Mount Pisgah Rd 29067 803-475-6791
Duane Pate, prin. Fax 475-0602
North Central MS 400/6-8
805 Keys Ln 29067 803-424-2740
Burchell Richardson Ed.D., prin. Fax 424-2742

Lancaster County SD
Supt. — See Lancaster
Jackson MS 500/6-8
6865 Kershaw Camden Hwy 29067 803-475-6021
Theodore Dutton, prin. Fax 475-8256
Kershaw ES 500/K-5
108 N Rollins Dr 29067 803-475-6655
Jennifer Etheridge, prin. Fax 475-5784

Kingstree, Williamsburg, Pop. 3,363
Williamsburg County SD 4,300/K-12
PO Box 1067 29556 843-355-5571
Ralph Fennell, supt. Fax 355-3213
wcsd.k12.sc.us/
Anderson PS 700/K-3
500 Lexington Ave 29556 843-355-5493
Dr. Teresa Wright, prin. Fax 355-7111
Kingstree ES 500/4-6
1503 Woodland Dr 29556 843-355-7233
Fax 355-9371
Kingstree JHS 500/7-8
710 3rd Ave 29556 843-355-6823
Margie Myers, prin. Fax 355-9207
St. Mark ES 200/K-6
6628 Thurgood Marshall Hwy 29556 843-382-3935
Rumell Taylor, prin. Fax 382-3940
Other Schools – See Cades, Greeleyville, Hemingway, Salters

Williamsburg Academy 300/K-12
PO Box 770 29556 843-355-9400
Joan Thompson, prin. Fax 355-7734

Ladson, Berkeley, Pop. 13,540
Berkeley County SD
Supt. — See Moncks Corner
College Park ES 800/K-5
100 Davidson Dr 29456 843-797-2711
Amanda Prince, prin. Fax 820-4022
College Park MS 700/6-8
713 College Park Rd 29456 843-553-8300
Ingrid Dukes, prin. Fax 820-4026
Sangaree MS 800/6-8
1050 Discovery Dr 29456 843-821-4028
Jude Gehlmann, prin. Fax 871-8974

Charleston County SD
Supt. — See Charleston
Ladson ES 400/K-5
3321 Ladson Rd 29456 843-764-2225
Reginald Bright, prin. Fax 569-5468

Dorchester SD 2
Supt. — See Summerville
Oakbrook ES 1,100/K-5
306 Old Fort Dr 29456 843-821-1165
Monica O'Dea, prin. Fax 821-3984
Oakbrook MS 1,200/6-8
286 Old Fort Dr 29456 843-873-9750
Garland Crump, prin. Fax 821-3931

Grace Christian Academy 100/PK-12
PO Box 749 29456 843-553-1373
Rev. Randy Wade, prin. Fax 553-1378

Ladys Island, Beaufort
Beaufort County SD
Supt. — See Beaufort

Ladys Island ES 400/PK-5
73 Chowan Creek Blf, 843-322-2240
Terry Dingle, prin. Fax 322-2281
Ladys Island MS 700/6-8
30 Cougar Dr, 843-322-3100
Terry Bennett, prin. Fax 322-3179

Lake City, Florence, Pop. 6,690
Florence County SD 3 3,600/K-12
PO Box 1389 29560 843-374-8652
Beth Wright, supt. Fax 374-2946
www.florence3.k12.sc.us/
Lake City ES 400/K-5
PO Box 1717 29560 843-374-2353
Renee Kirby, prin. Fax 374-5480
Main Street ES 400/K-5
PO Box 1509 29560 843-374-2221
Angelia Scott, prin. Fax 374-8697
McNair MS 500/6-8
PO Box 1209 29560 843-374-8651
Margie Myers, prin. Fax 374-8504
Truluck MS 400/6-8
PO Box 1239 29560 843-374-8685
Katherene Tisdale, prin. Fax 374-7341
Other Schools – See Coward, Olanta, Scranton

Carolina Academy 200/K-12
351 N Country Club Rd 29560 843-374-5485
Anna Floyd, hdmstr. Fax 374-0164

Lake View, Dillon, Pop. 792
Dillon SD 1 800/K-12
PO Box 644 29563 843-759-3001
Stephen Laird, supt. Fax 759-3000
www.lakeviewschools.com
Lake View ES 300/K-4
1311 Scott St 29563 843-759-3003
Kimberly Scott, prin. Fax 759-3005
Lake View MS 200/5-7
1501 Scott St 29563 843-759-3005
Vandy Gaffney, prin. Fax 759-3008

Lamar, Darlington, Pop. 1,003
Darlington County SD
Supt. — See Darlington
Lamar ES 300/K-2
214 N Darlington Ave 29069 843-326-7575
Garry Flowers, prin. Fax 326-7050
Spaulding ES 200/3-5
204 E Pearl St 29069 843-326-5347
Vernisa Bodison, prin. Fax 326-1086
Spaulding MS 200/6-8
400 Cartersville Hwy 29069 843-326-5335
Derrick Glover, prin. Fax 326-7656

Lancaster, Lancaster, Pop. 8,371
Lancaster County SD 10,800/PK-12
300 S Catawba St 29720 803-286-6972
R. Gene Moore, supt. Fax 416-8860
www.lancasterscschools.org/
Brooklyn Springs ES 600/K-5
1637 Billings Dr 29720 803-283-8471
Gwen Hinson, prin. Fax 285-8942
Buford ES 900/K-5
1906 N Rocky River Rd 29720 803-286-0026
Sandra Jones, prin. Fax 286-9986
Buford MS 500/6-8
1890 N Rocky River Rd 29720 803-285-8473
Sheri Wells, prin. Fax 283-2023
Clinton ES 400/K-5
110 Clinton School Rd 29720 803-285-5395
Rachel Ray, prin. Fax 283-3998
Erwin ES 400/K-5
1477 Locustwood Ave 29720 803-285-8484
Jane Gaston, prin. Fax 289-6332
McDonald Green ES 500/K-5
2763 Lynwood Dr 29720 803-285-7416
Michelle Crosby, prin. Fax 285-7417
North ES 600/K-5
1100 Roddey Dr 29720 803-283-9918
Linda Blackwell, prin. Fax 286-7769
Rucker MS 500/6-8
422 Old Dixie Rd 29720 803-416-8555
Phillip Mickles, prin. Fax 285-1534
South MS 700/6-8
1551 Billings Dr 29720 803-283-8416
Joyce Crimminger, prin. Fax 283-8417
Southside ECC 100/PK-PK
500 Hampton Rd 29720 803-283-3915
LaVilla Brevard, admin. Fax 313-9587
Other Schools – See Fort Mill, Heath Springs, Indian Land, Kershaw

Landrum, Spartanburg, Pop. 2,518
Spartanburg SD 1
Supt. — See Campobello
Earle ES 500/K-5
100 Redland Rd 29356 864-457-3416
Nita High, prin. Fax 457-3913
Landrum MS 300/6-8
104 Redland Rd 29356 864-457-2629
Crystral McSwain, prin. Fax 457-5372

Blue Ridge Christian Academy 100/PK-12
424 Highway 101 29356 864-895-9008
Jill Bird, hdmstr. Fax 895-8797

Latta, Dillon, Pop. 1,462
Latta SD 1,500/K-12
205 King St 29565 843-752-7101
Dr. John Kirby, supt. Fax 752-2081
www.dillon3.k12.sc.us
Latta ECC 200/K-1
134 Latimer St 29565 843-752-2711
Dollie Morrell, prin. Fax 752-2713
Latta ES 500/2-5
122 Latimer St 29565 843-752-5295
Debra Morris, prin. Fax 752-2713
Latta MS 400/6-8
612 N Richardson St 29565 843-752-7117
Martha Heyward, prin. Fax 752-2722

Laurens, Laurens, Pop. 9,824
Laurens SD 55 5,100/K-12
1029 W Main St 29360 864-984-3568
Billy Strickland, supt. Fax 984-8100
www.laurens55.k12.sc.us/
Ford ES 400/K-5
601 Lucas Ave 29360 864-984-3986
Dianne Simmons, prin. Fax 984-4724
Laurens ES 500/K-5
301 Henry St 29360 864-984-3067
Phillip Dean, prin. Fax 984-5749
Laurens MS 400/6-8
1035 W Main St 29360 864-984-2400
Rhett Harris, prin. Fax 984-6013
Morse ES 600/K-5
200 Parkview Dr 29360 864-984-7777
Ameca Carter, prin. Fax 984-2926
Sanders MS 300/6-8
609 Green St 29360 864-984-0354
George Ward, prin. Fax 984-2452
Other Schools – See Gray Court, Waterloo

Leesville, Lexington, Pop. 2,235
Lexington County SD 3
Supt. — See Batesburg
Batesburg-Leesville ES 400/3-5
403 S Lee St 29070 803-532-1155
Dr. Darlene Stephens, prin. Fax 532-8027

Lexington, Lexington, Pop. 13,586
Lexington County SD 1 18,300/K-12
PO Box 1869 29071 803-821-1000
Karen Woodward Ed.D., supt. Fax 821-1010
www.lexington1.net
Carolina Springs ES K-5
6340 Platt Springs Rd 29073 803-821-5100
W. Darrell Barringer Ph.D., prin. Fax 821-5103
Carolina Springs MS 6-8
6180 Platt Springs Rd 29073 803-821-4900
Alan Zwart, prin. Fax 821-4903
Lake Murray ES 1,100/K-5
205 Wise Ferry Rd 29072 803-821-3100
Lynn Boyleston, prin. Fax 821-3103
Lexington ES 900/K-5
116 Azalea Dr 29072 803-821-4000
Ruth Rish, prin. Fax 821-4003
Lexington IS 300/5-6
420 Hendrix St 29072 803-821-3900
Sherry Cariens, prin. Fax 821-3903
Lexington MS 1,000/6-8
702 N Lake Dr 29072 803-821-3700
Laura McMahan, prin. Fax 821-3703
Midway ES 1,000/K-4
180 Midway Rd 29072 803-821-0300
Cheryl Fralick, prin. Fax 821-0303
New Providence ES K-5
1118 Old Cherokee Rd 29072 803-821-3300
C. Van Bowers, prin. Fax 821-3303
Oak Grove ES 500/K-5
479 Oak Dr 29073 803-821-0100
Devona Price, prin. Fax 821-0103
Pleasant Hill ES K-5
664 Rawl Rd 29072 803-821-2800
Margaret Mitchum, prin. Fax 821-2803
Pleasant Hill MS 6-8
660 Rawl Rd 29072 803-821-2700
Dr. William Coon, prin. Fax 821-2703
Red Bank ES 1,000/K-5
246 Community Dr 29073 803-821-4600
Marie Watson, prin. Fax 821-4603
Saxe Gotha ES 800/K-5
100 Bill Williamson Ct 29073 803-821-4800
Beth Houck, prin. Fax 821-4803
Other Schools – See Gilbert, Pelion, West Columbia

Columbia Adventist Academy 50/PK-10
241 Riverchase Way 29072 803-796-0277
Nancy Chang, prin. Fax 796-2123

Liberty, Pickens, Pop. 3,004
Pickens County SD
Supt. — See Easley
Liberty ES 900/K-4
251 N Hillcrest St 29657 864-843-5820
Shaileen Riginos, prin. Fax 843-5822
Liberty MS 700/5-8
310 W Main St 29657 864-843-5855
Donivan Edwards, prin. Fax 843-5857

Little Mountain, Newberry, Pop. 259
Newberry County SD
Supt. — See Newberry
Little Mountain ES 300/K-5
692 Mill St 29075 803-945-7721
Rudolph Tarver, prin. Fax 945-1058

Little River, Horry, Pop. 3,470
Horry County SD
Supt. — See Conway
North Myrtle Beach ES 700/2-3
1283 Highway 57 S 29566 843-399-8800
Vicki Underwood, prin. Fax 399-8700
North Myrtle Beach IS 600/4-5
700 Sandridge Rd 29566 843-399-2204
Michelle Greene-Graham, prin. Fax 399-2250
North Myrtle Beach MS 1,000/6-8
11240 Highway 90 29566 843-399-6136
Virginia Horton, prin. Fax 399-2233

Lobeco, Beaufort

Agape Christian Academy 100/K-12
PO Box 719 29931 843-846-4835
Charles Lightsey, prin.

Lockhart, Union, Pop. 507
Union County SD
Supt. — See Union
Lockhart ES K-6
212 Lockhart Dr 29364 864-545-6501
James Sloan, prin. Fax 545-2175
Lockhart MS 100/7-8
PO Box 220 29364 864-545-6501
James Sloan, prin. Fax 545-2175

Longs, Horry

Holy Trinity S PK-8
1760 Living Stones Ln 29568 843-390-4108
Colette Ott, prin. Fax 390-4097

Loris, Horry, Pop. 2,305
Horry County SD
Supt. — See Conway
Daisy ES 600/PK-5
2801 Red Bluff Rd 29569 843-756-5136
Dr. Dawn Brooks, prin. Fax 756-3965
Loris ES 800/PK-5
901 Highway 9 Business E 29569 843-390-6860
Mark Porter, prin. Fax 390-6861
Loris MS 700/6-8
5209 Highway 66 29569 843-756-2181
Judy Beard, prin. Fax 756-0522

Lugoff, Kershaw, Pop. 3,211
Kershaw County SD
Supt. — See Camden
Doby's Mill ES 700/PK-5
1964 Fort Jackson Rd 29078 803-438-4055
Ginger Catoe, prin. Fax 438-7925
Lugoff ES 600/K-5
994 Ridgeway Rd 29078 803-438-8000
Melissa Lloyd, prin. Fax 438-8024
Lugoff-Elgin MS 600/6-8
1244 Highway 1 S 29078 803-438-3591
Dave Matthews, prin. Fax 438-8027
Wateree ES 600/K-5
424 Wildwood Ln 29078 803-438-8018
Janice Wood, prin. Fax 438-8020

Lyman, Spartanburg, Pop. 2,765
Spartanburg SD 5
Supt. — See Duncan
Hill MS 500/7-8
PO Box 1329 29365 864-949-2370
Terry Glasgow, prin. Fax 949-2369
Lyman ES K-4
PO Box 1119 29365 864-949-2330
Tim Henson, prin. Fax 949-2339

Mc Bee, Chesterfield, Pop. 674
Chesterfield County SD
Supt. — See Chesterfield
Mc Bee ES 400/K-6
PO Box 368 29101 843-335-8347
Dr. David Nutt, prin. Fax 335-5671

Mc Clellanville, Charleston, Pop. 334
Charleston County SD
Supt. — See Charleston
Mc Clellanville MS 100/6-8
711 Pinckney St 29458 843-577-0325
Chris Swetckie, prin. Fax 887-3002
St. James-Santee ES 200/K-5
8900 N Highway 17 29458 843-723-0863
Lerah Smith-Lee, prin. Fax 887-3357

Mc Coll, Marlboro, Pop. 2,722
Marlboro County SD
Supt. — See Bennettsville
Mc Coll S 700/PK-8
700 N Main St 29570 843-523-5371
Macky Norton, prin. Fax 523-9147

Mc Cormick, McCormick, Pop. 1,736
McCormick SD 900/K-12
821 N Mine St 29835 864-852-2435
Sandra Calliham Ed.D., supt. Fax 852-2883
www.mccormick.k12.sc.us/
Mc Cormick ES 400/K-5
6977 SC Highway 28 S 29835 864-443-2292
Eleanor Rice, prin. Fax 443-2755
Mc Cormick MS 200/6-8
6979 SC Highway 28 S 29835 864-443-2243
Cecily Morris, prin. Fax 443-3299

Manning, Clarendon, Pop. 4,025
Clarendon SD 2 3,200/PK-12
PO Box 1252 29102 803-435-4435
John Tindal, supt. Fax 435-8172
www.clarendon2.k12.sc.us
Manning ECC 600/PK-1
2759 Raccoon Rd 29102 803-473-4744
Betty Harrington, prin. Fax 473-4777
Manning ES 700/4-6
311 W Boyce St 29102 803-435-5066
Jerry Coker, prin. Fax 435-0340
Manning JHS 500/7-8
1101 W L Hamilton Rd 29102 803-435-8195
Preston Threatt, prin. Fax 435-6848
Manning PS 500/2-3
125 N Boundary St 29102 803-435-2268
Judy Holmes, prin. Fax 435-8737

Marietta, Greenville, Pop. 2,245
Greenville County SD
Supt. — See Greenville
Slater-Marietta ES 500/K-5
100 Baker Cir 29661 864-355-2000
Lindsey Cole, prin. Fax 355-2016

Marion, Marion, Pop. 6,997
Marion SD 1 2,900/K-12
719 N Main St 29571 843-423-1811
Michael Lupo, supt. Fax 423-8328
www.marion1.k12.sc.us
Easterling PS 700/K-2
600 E Northside Ave 29571 843-423-8335
Angie Grice, prin. Fax 423-8314
Johnakin MS 700/6-8
601 Gurley St 29571 843-423-8360
Jason Bryant, prin. Fax 423-8383

Marion IS 700/3-5
2320 N Highway 41A 29571 843-423-8345
Tim Felder, prin. Fax 423-8378

Mayesville, Sumter, Pop. 1,042
Lee County SD
Supt. — See Bishopville
Lower Lee ES 300/K-5
5142 St Charles Rd 29104 803-428-3637
David Montgomery, prin. Fax 428-3658

Mayo, Spartanburg, Pop. 1,569
Spartanburg SD 2
Supt. — See Boiling Springs
Mayo ES 300/K-5
PO Box 130 29368 864-461-2622
William Browning, prin. Fax 461-5102

Moncks Corner, Berkeley, Pop. 6,525
Berkeley County SD 26,200/PK-12
PO Box 608 29461 843-899-8600
Dr. Anthony Parker, supt. Fax 899-8791
www.berkeley.k12.sc.us
Berkeley ES 800/K-2
715 Highway 6 29461 843-899-8860
Tracy Gaskins, prin. Fax 899-8865
Berkeley IS 700/3-5
777 Stoney Landing Rd 29461 843-899-8870
Mike Shaw, prin. Fax 899-8873
Berkeley MS 1,200/6-8
320 N Live Oak Dr 29461 843-899-8840
Dr. Lee Westbury, prin. Fax 899-8846
Bonner ES 700/K-4
171 Macedonia Foxes Cir 29461 843-899-8950
Natalie Lockliear, prin. Fax 899-8928
Macedonia MS 600/5-8
200 Macedonia Foxes Cir 29461 843-899-8940
Janie Langley, prin. Fax 899-8929
Whitesville ES 600/K-5
324 Gaillard Rd 29461 843-899-8880
Julia Taylor, prin. Fax 899-8883
Other Schools – See Charleston, Cross, Goose Creek, Hanahan, Huger, Ladson, Pineville, Saint Stephen, Summerville

St. John Christian Academy 400/PK-12
204 W Main St 29461 843-761-8539
Eric Denton, hdmstr. Fax 899-5514

Moore, Spartanburg
Spartanburg SD 5
Supt. — See Duncan
River Ridge ES 600/K-4
5960 Reidville Rd 29369 864-949-7620
Dr. Glenda Bigby, prin. Fax 949-7627

Spartanburg SD 6
Supt. — See Roebuck
Anderson Mill ES 500/K-5
1845 Old Anderson Mill Rd 29369 864-576-6539
Beth Haun, prin. Fax 595-2452
Dawkins MS 800/6-8
1300 E Blackstock Rd 29369 864-576-8088
Kenneth Kiser, prin. Fax 595-2418

Mount Pleasant, Charleston, Pop. 57,932
Charleston County SD
Supt. — See Charleston
Belle Hall ES 700/K-5
385 Egypt Rd 29464 843-849-2841
Kevin Conklin, prin. Fax 849-2893
Cario MS 1,200/6-8
3500 Thomas Cario Blvd 29466 843-856-4595
Shari Bouis, prin. Fax 856-4599
Edwards ES 700/K-5
855 Von Kolnitz Rd 29464 843-849-2805
Thomas Lee, prin. Fax 849-2892
Laing MS 500/6-8
2213 N Highway 17 29466 843-849-2809
Deborah Price, prin. Fax 849-2895
Laurel Hill PS 800/K-2
3100 Thomas Cario Blvd 29466 843-849-2200
Michael Antonelli, prin. Fax 849-3377
Moore ES 600/K-5
1256 Hamlin Rd 29466 843-849-2815
Karen Felder, prin. Fax 849-2891
Moultrie MS 800/6-8
1560 Mathis Ferry Rd 29464 843-849-2819
Jean Siewicki, prin. Fax 849-2899
Mount Pleasant Academy 400/K-5
942 Whipple Rd 29464 843-849-2826
Jane McGee-Davis, prin. Fax 849-2897
Pinckney ES 800/K-5
3300 Thomas Cario Blvd 29466 843-856-4585
Leanne Sheppard, prin. Fax 856-4594
Whitesides ES 600/K-5
1120 Rifle Range Rd 29464 843-849-2838
Lona Pounder, prin. Fax 849-2884

Christ Our King / Stella Maris S 700/PK-8
1183 Russell Dr 29464 843-884-4721
Jean Moschella, prin. Fax 971-7850
Coastal Christian Preparatory S 200/K-12
681 McCants Dr 29464 843-884-3663
Chad Moore, hdmstr. Fax 884-9608
Palmetto Christian Academy 400/K-12
361 Egypt Rd 29464 843-881-9967
Mike Hiltibidal, hdmstr. Fax 881-4662
Trident Academy 100/K-12
1455 Wakendaw Rd 29464 843-884-7046
Joe Ferber, hdmstr. Fax 881-8320

Mullins, Marion, Pop. 4,855
Marion SD 2 1,800/PK-12
PO Box 689 29574 843-464-3700
Dr. Nathaniel Miller, supt. Fax 464-3705
www.marion2.k12.sc.us
McCormick ES 400/3-5
1123 Sandy Bluff Rd 29574 843-464-3760
Becky Ford, prin. Fax 464-3763
Mullins ECC PK-PK
111 Academy St 29574 843-464-3725
Paula Grant, prin. Fax 464-3728
North Mullins PS 300/K-2
105 Charles St 29574 843-464-3750
Dr. Mike Sutton, prin. Fax 464-3755
Palmetto MS 500/6-8
305 ONeal St 29574 843-464-3730
Coleman Barbour, prin. Fax 464-3736

Marion SD 7 600/PK-12
3559 S Highway 501 29574 843-423-2891
Everette Dean Ed.D., supt. Fax 423-7987
www.marion7.k12.sc.us
Rains Centenary ECC 100/PK-K
3549 S Highway 501 29574 843-362-1974
Angela Huggins, prin. Fax 423-9692
Other Schools – See Gresham

Pee Dee Academy 400/K-12
PO Box 449 29574 843-423-1771
Hal Townsend, prin. Fax 423-0301

Murrells Inlet, Horry, Pop. 3,334

St. Michael S 200/K-8
542 Cypress Ave 29576 843-651-6795
Miriam Jones, prin. Fax 651-6803

Myrtle Beach, Horry, Pop. 26,593
Horry County SD
Supt. — See Conway
Burgess ES K-5
9645 Scipio Ln 29588 843-650-4600
Donna Hooks, prin. Fax 650-4602
Carolina Forest ES 900/K-5
285 Carolina Forest Blvd 29579 843-236-0001
Melissa Spearman, prin. Fax 236-0152
Forestbrook ES 800/K-5
4000 Panthers Pkwy 29588 843-236-8100
John Calder, prin. Fax 236-8103
Forestbrook MS 1,000/6-8
4430 Gator Ln 29588 843-236-7300
Margaret Sordian, prin. Fax 236-8065
Lakewood ES 700/K-5
1675 Highway 396 29575 843-650-6768
Tom Rex, prin. Fax 650-6748
Myrtle Beach ES 500/2-3
3101 N Oak St 29577 843-448-1774
Janice Christy, prin. Fax 448-1115
Myrtle Beach IS 500/4-5
3301 N Oak St 29577 843-626-5831
Cathy Slater, prin. Fax 626-8528
Myrtle Beach MS 800/6-8
950 Seahawk Way 29577 843-448-3932
Roger Gray, prin. Fax 448-1182
Myrtle Beach PS 800/PK-1
612 29th Ave N 29577 843-448-1658
Dr. June Moorehead, prin. Fax 448-0139
Ocean Bay ES K-5
950 International Dr 29579 843-903-8400
Nancy Ward, prin. Fax 903-8401
Ocean Bay MS 6-8
905 International Dr 29579 843-903-8420
Connie Huddle, prin. Fax 903-8421
Palmetto Bays ES 700/PK-5
8900 Highway 544 29588 843-236-6200
David James, prin. Fax 236-7900
St. James ES 1,100/K-5
9711 Saint James Rd 29588 843-650-8220
Mary Beth Heath, prin. Fax 650-7909
St. James MS 1,000/6-8
9775 Saint James Rd 29588 843-650-5543
Dr. Dwight Boykin, prin. Fax 650-5610
Socastee ES 600/PK-5
4950 Socastee Blvd 29588 843-650-2606
Deb Colliver, prin. Fax 650-2629

Calvary Christian S 300/PK-12
4511 Dick Pond Rd 29588 843-650-2829
Mark Roland, prin. Fax 215-4125
Chabad Academy 100/PK-8
2803 N Oak St 29577 843-448-0035
Christian Academy 200/K-12
PO Box 2250 29578 843-839-5855
Nancy Henry, admin. Fax 839-5856
Risen Christ Lutheran S 50/PK-12
10595 Highway 17 N 29572 843-272-8163
Kim Lavado, prin. Fax 272-4039
St. Andrew S 200/K-8
3601 N Kings Hwy 29577 843-448-6062
Molly Halasz, prin. Fax 626-8644
St. Phillip's Lutheran K 100/PK-K
6200 N Kings Hwy 29572 843-449-5345
Janice Myers, dir. Fax 449-5345

Neeses, Orangeburg, Pop. 402
Orangeburg County Consolidated SD 4
Supt. — See Cope
Hunter-Kinard-Tyler ES 400/PK-6
7066 Norway Rd 29107 803-263-4441
Debra Norman, prin. Fax 263-4404

Newberry, Newberry, Pop. 10,659
Newberry County SD 5,500/K-12
PO Box 718 29108 803-321-2600
Bennie Bennett, supt. Fax 321-2604
www.newberry.k12.sc.us/
Boundary Street ES 400/K-5
1406 Boundary St 29108 803-321-2616
Timothy Hunter, prin. Fax 321-2605
Gallman ES 400/K-5
255 Hawkins Rd 29108 803-321-2655
Cathryn Hartzog, prin. Fax 321-2657
Newberry ES 400/K-5
1829 Nance St 29108 803-321-2670
Lelia Caldwell, prin. Fax 321-2671
Newberry MS 600/6-8
125 ONeal St 29108 803-321-2640
Katrina Singletary, prin. Fax 321-2647
Reuben ES 200/K-5
3605 Spearman Rd 29108 803-321-2664
Gloria Owens, prin. Fax 321-2665
Other Schools – See Little Mountain, Pomaria, Prosperity, Whitmire

Newberry Academy 200/K-12
2055 Smith Rd 29108 803-276-2760
Bob Dawkins, hdmstr. Fax 276-2401

New Ellenton, Aiken, Pop. 2,259
Aiken County SD
Supt. — See Aiken
Greendale ES 400/K-5
505 S Boundary Ave 29809 803-652-8170
Rebecca Koelker, prin. Fax 652-8173
New Ellenton MS 200/6-8
814 Main St S 29809 803-652-8200
Elisa Sanders-Pee, prin. Fax 652-8203

Faith Christian S 50/PK-6
210 Pine St NW 29809 803-652-3037
Linda Anderson, admin.

New Zion, Clarendon
Clarendon SD 3
Supt. — See Turbeville
Walker-Gamble ES 600/K-5
2358 Walker Gamble Rd 29111 843-659-2102
Sheila Floyd, prin. Fax 659-2129

Ninety Six, Greenwood, Pop. 1,922
Greenwood SD 52 1,700/PK-12
605 Johnston Rd 29666 864-543-3100
Dan Powell Ph.D., supt. Fax 543-3704
www.greenwood52.org
Edgewood MS 400/6-8
200 Edgewood Cir 29666 864-543-3511
Wallace Hall, prin. Fax 543-4994
Ninety Six ES 400/3-5
810 Johnston Rd 29666 864-543-4995
Jane Calhoun, prin. Fax 543-4962
Ninety Six PS 400/PK-2
121 S Cambridge St 29666 864-543-3112
Cathy Anderson, prin. Fax 543-4427

North, Orangeburg, Pop. 788
Orangeburg County Consolidated SD 5
Supt. — See Orangeburg
Dover ES 300/K-6
PO Box 218 29112 803-247-2184
Cynthia Strozier, prin. Fax 247-5010

North Augusta, Aiken, Pop. 19,467
Aiken County SD
Supt. — See Aiken
Hammond Hill ES 600/K-5
901 W Woodlawn Ave 29841 803-442-6170
Janet Vaughan, prin. Fax 442-6112
Knox MS 600/6-8
1804 Wells Rd 29841 803-442-6300
John Murphy, prin. Fax 442-6302
Mossy Creek ES 700/K-5
421 W Five Notch Rd 29841 803-442-6090
Stephanie Hammond, prin. Fax 442-6092
North Augusta ES 600/K-5
400 E Spring Grove Ave 29841 803-442-6280
Laurie Reese, prin. Fax 442-6282
North Augusta MS 700/6-8
725 Old Edgefield Rd 29841 803-442-6200
Barry Head, prin. Fax 442-6202

Edgefield County SD
Supt. — See Johnston
Merriwether ES 800/K-5
PO Box 7190 29861 803-279-9993
Gene Huiet, prin. Fax 279-8898
Merriwether MS 400/6-8
430 Murrah Rd 29860 803-279-2511
Bobby Turner, prin. Fax 279-1710

Our Lady of Peace S 100/K-8
856 Old Edgefield Rd 29841 803-279-8396
Karen Wilcox, prin. Fax 279-5247
Victory Christian S 100/K-12
620 W Martintown Rd 29841 803-278-0125
Dr. Ed Martin, prin. Fax 278-7310

North Charleston, Charleston, Pop. 86,313
Charleston County SD
Supt. — See Charleston
Brentwood MS 400/6-8
2685 Leeds Ave 29405 843-745-7094
LaWanda Glears, prin. Fax 566-1838
Charlestowne Academy 500/K-12
5841 Rivers Ave 29406 843-746-1349
Kathy Penick, prin. Fax 746-1354
Child & Family Development Center PK-PK
2415 Avenue F 29405 843-529-3911
Latetia Staggers, dir. Fax 566-1952
Dunston ES 200/K-5
1825 Remount Rd 29406 843-745-7109
Janice Malone, prin. Fax 529-3905
Hursey ES 300/K-5
4542 Simms Ave 29405 843-745-7105
LaDene Conroy, prin. Fax 529-3903
Morningside MS 500/6-8
1999 Singley St 29405 843-745-2000
Kala Goodwine, prin. Fax 745-7191
North Charleston ES 500/K-5
4921 Durant Ave 29405 843-745-7107
Latisha Vaughn-Brandon, prin. Fax 554-5716
Pepperhill ES 500/K-5
3300 Creola Rd 29420 843-767-5905
Tanya Underwood, prin. Fax 767-5940

Dorchester SD 2
Supt. — See Summerville
Eagle Nest ES K-5
8640 River Oaks Dr 29420 843-695-2460
Karen Spillane, prin. Fax 695-2465

River Oaks MS — 6-8
8642 River Oaks Dr 29420 — 843-695-2470
Kathy Sobolewski, prin. — Fax 695-2475
Windsor Hill ES — 800/K-5
8600 William Moultrie Dr 29420 — 843-760-9820
Mary Davies, prin. — Fax 760-4469

Northside Christian S — 400/K-12
7800 Northside Dr 29420 — 843-797-2690
Dr. Cecil Beach, admin. — Fax 797-7402
Northwood Academy — 400/PK-5
2263 Otranto Rd 29406 — 843-572-0940
Larry Evanoff, dir. — Fax 764-2274

North Myrtle Beach, Horry, Pop. 14,096
Horry County SD
Supt. — See Conway
North Myrtle Beach PS — 800/PK-1
901 11th Ave N 29582 — 843-663-0195
Renea Fowler, prin. — Fax 249-8638

Lord's Children K — 100/PK-K
818 Jordan Rd 29582 — 843-280-5434

Okatie, Beaufort
Beaufort County SD
Supt. — See Beaufort
Okatie ES — 800/PK-5
53 Cherry Point Rd, — 843-322-7700
Jamie Pinckney, prin. — Fax 322-7710

Olanta, Florence, Pop. 628
Florence County SD 3
Supt. — See Lake City
Olanta ES — 200/K-5
PO Box 628 29114 — 843-396-4457
Rebecca Hobbs, prin. — Fax 396-9512

Orangeburg, Orangeburg, Pop. 14,460
Orangeburg County Consolidated SD 4
Supt. — See Cope
Edisto ES — 600/3-5
136 Woodolive St 29115 — 803-531-7646
Belinda Johnson, prin. — Fax 531-7614

Orangeburg County Consolidated SD 5 — 6,300/K-12
578 Ellis Ave 29115 — 803-534-5454
Melvin Smoak, supt. — Fax 533-7953
www.ocsd5schools.org/home.aspx
Clark MS — 800/5-8
919 Bennett St 29115 — 803-531-2200
Dr. Lana Williams, prin. — Fax 533-6503
Howard MS — 500/5-8
1255 Belleville Rd 29115 — 803-534-5470
Dr. Jacqueline Vogt, prin. — Fax 535-1606
Marshall ES — 600/K-4
1441 Marshall St 29118 — 803-534-7865
Jacqueline Jamieson, prin. — Fax 535-1645
Mellichamp ES — 200/K-4
350 Murray Rd 29115 — 803-534-8044
Beverly Stronan-Spires, prin. — Fax 533-6492
Rivelon ES — 200/K-4
350 Thomas Eklund Cir 29115 — 803-534-2949
Paulette Faust, prin. — Fax 533-6540
Sheridan ES — 500/K-4
1139 Hillsboro Rd 29115 — 803-534-7504
Xennie Weeks, prin. — Fax 535-1650
Whittaker ES — 500/K-4
790 Whittaker Pkwy 29115 — 803-534-6559
Dr. Bettie Hicks, prin. — Fax 533-6466
Other Schools – See North, Rowesville

Felton Laboratory S — 300/K-8
PO Box 7037 29117 — 803-536-7034
Dr. Vanessa Lancaster, dir. — Fax 533-3635
Orangeburg Prep S — 800/K-12
2651 North Rd 29118 — 803-534-7970
Kelley Mims, hdmstr. — Fax 535-2190

Pacolet, Spartanburg, Pop. 2,727
Spartanburg SD 3
Supt. — See Glendale
Pacolet ES — 400/K-5
150 McDowell St 29372 — 864-279-6500
Kenny Blackwood, prin. — Fax 279-6503
Pacolet MS — 200/6-8
850 Sunny Acres Rd 29372 — 864-279-6600
Cynthia James, prin. — Fax 279-6603

Pageland, Chesterfield, Pop. 2,544
Chesterfield County SD
Supt. — See Chesterfield
Pageland ES — 400/3-5
715 W McGregor St 29728 — 843-672-2400
Jim Heffner, prin. — Fax 672-5585
Petersburg PS — 400/K-2
326 N Arnold St 29728 — 843-672-6241
Marcus Sutton, prin. — Fax 672-5866

South Pointe Christian S — 200/PK-12
PO Box 188 29728 — 843-672-2760
Dan Wooten, prin. — Fax 672-3913

Pamplico, Florence, Pop. 1,158
Florence County SD 2 — 1,200/K-12
2121 S Pamplico Hwy 29583 — 843-493-2502
Robert Sullivan, supt. — Fax 493-1912
www.flo2.k12.sc.us/
Hannah-Pamplico S — 800/K-8
2131 S Pamplico Hwy 29583 — 843-493-5588
Debbie Carter, prin. — Fax 493-5461

New Prospect Christian S — 100/K-12
4221 Sheminally Rd 29583 — 843-493-2189

Patrick, Chesterfield, Pop. 353
Chesterfield County SD
Supt. — See Chesterfield
Plainview ES — 200/K-6
16002 Highway 102 29584 — 843-498-6633
Dennis McDaniel, prin. — Fax 498-6024

Pauline, Spartanburg
Spartanburg SD 6
Supt. — See Roebuck
Pauline-Glenn Springs ES — 400/K-5
PO Box 95 29374 — 864-583-1868
Jennifer Atkinson, prin. — Fax 573-8534

Pawleys Island, Georgetown, Pop. 144
Georgetown County SD
Supt. — See Georgetown
Waccamaw ES — 1,000/PK-5
1364 Waverly Rd 29585 — 843-237-4233
Vervatine Reid, prin. — Fax 237-2015
Waccamaw IS — 4-6
320 Wildcat Way 29585 — 843-237-7071
Dr. Timothy Carnahan, prin. — Fax 237-7031
Waccamaw MS — 600/6-8
247 Wildcat Way 29585 — 843-237-0106
William Dwyer, prin. — Fax 237-0237

Pawleys Island Christian Academy — 100/PK-8
10304 Ocean Hwy 29585 — 843-237-9293
Richard Kauffman, admin. — Fax 237-8960
St. Peters Lutheran S — 50/PK-K
65 Crooked Oak Dr 29585 — 843-237-2795

Pelion, Lexington, Pop. 587
Lexington County SD 1
Supt. — See Lexington
Forts Pond ES — K-5
7350 Fish Hatchery Rd 29123 — 803-821-2500
John Young, prin. — Fax 821-2503
Pelion ES — 900/K-5
1202 Pine St 29123 — 803-821-2000
Catherine Hodge, prin. — Fax 821-2003
Pelion MS — 600/6-8
758 Magnolia St 29123 — 803-821-2300
Dr. Sandra Jowers, prin. — Fax 821-2303

Pelzer, Anderson, Pop. 100
Greenville County SD
Supt. — See Greenville
Fork Shoals ES — 700/K-5
916 McKelvey Rd 29669 — 864-355-5000
Christopher Ross, prin. — Fax 355-5012
Riley Child Development Center — PK-K
9122 Augusta Rd 29669 — 864-355-3400
Doris Santanello, prin. — Fax 355-3440
Woodside ES — 600/K-5
9122 Augusta Rd 29669 — 864-355-4900
Stephanie Reese, prin. — Fax 355-4965

Pendleton, Anderson, Pop. 3,050
Anderson SD 4 — 2,800/K-12
PO Box 545 29670 — 864-646-8000
Dr. Maurice Lopez, supt. — Fax 646-8555
www.anderson4.k12.sc.us
La France ES — 500/K-5
550 Williams St 29670 — 864-646-8010
Hope Atyeo, prin. — Fax 646-8011
Mt. Lebanon ES — K-6
2850 Lebanon Rd 29670 — 864-403-2400
Mona Fleming, prin. — Fax 716-3654
Pendleton ES — 500/K-5
902 E Queen St 29670 — 864-646-8015
Gwen Massey, prin. — Fax 646-8016
Riverside MS — 700/6-8
458 Riverside St 29670 — 864-646-8020
Kevin Black, prin. — Fax 646-8025
Other Schools – See Townville

Pickens, Pickens, Pop. 2,974
Pickens County SD
Supt. — See Easley
Ambler ES — 300/K-5
838 Ambler School Rd 29671 — 864-898-5588
Carlton Lewis, prin. — Fax 898-5589
Hagood ES — 300/K-5
435 Sparks Ln 29671 — 864-878-8710
Karen Jackson, prin. — Fax 878-8719
Holly Springs ES — 200/K-5
120 Holly Springs School Rd 29671 — 864-898-5590
Donna Harden, prin. — Fax 898-5591
Lewis ES — 300/K-5
1755 Shady Grove Rd 29671 — 864-868-9047
Kathy Brazinski, prin. — Fax 868-4016
Pickens ES — 500/K-5
567 Hampton Ave 29671 — 864-878-8725
Dr. Del Freitag, prin. — Fax 898-5627
Pickens MS — 900/6-8
467 Sparks Ln 29671 — 864-878-8735
Dr. Libba Floyd, prin. — Fax 878-8734

Piedmont, Greenville, Pop. 4,143
Anderson SD 1
Supt. — See Williamston
Spearman ES — 500/PK-5
2001 Easley Hwy 29673 — 864-947-9787
Jason Lesley, prin. — Fax 947-1162
Wren ES — 700/PK-5
226 Roper Rd 29673 — 864-850-5950
Rhonda Tunstall, prin. — Fax 850-5951
Wren MS — 800/6-8
1010 Wren School Rd 29673 — 864-850-5930
Robin Fulbright, prin. — Fax 850-5941

Greenville County SD
Supt. — See Greenville
Cleveland ES — 600/K-5
375 Woodmont School Rd Ext 29673 — 864-355-4200
Karen Chambers, prin. — Fax 355-4215
Grove ES — 600/K-5
1220 Old Grove Rd 29673 — 864-355-5900
Amy Mims, prin. — Fax 355-5965
Woodmont MS — 900/6-8
325 N Flat Rock Rd 29673 — 864-355-8500
Greg Scott, prin. — Fax 355-8587

Pineville, Berkeley
Berkeley County SD
Supt. — See Moncks Corner

Gourdin ES — 200/K-5
1649 Highway 45 29468 — 843-567-3637
Lorene Bradley, prin. — Fax 567-3069

Pinewood, Sumter, Pop. 501
Sumter SD 2
Supt. — See Sumter
Manchester ES — 500/K-5
200 W Clark St 29125 — 803-452-5454
Dr. Laura Brown, prin. — Fax 452-5423

Pomaria, Newberry, Pop. 180
Newberry County SD
Supt. — See Newberry
Pomaria/Garmany ES — 400/K-5
7288 US Highway 176 29126 — 803-321-2651
Beth Brooks, prin. — Fax 321-2652

Port Royal, Beaufort, Pop. 9,347
Beaufort County SD
Supt. — See Beaufort
Port Royal ES — 300/PK-5
1214 Paris Ave 29935 — 843-322-0820
Kay Keeler, prin. — Fax 322-0841

Prosperity, Newberry, Pop. 1,098
Newberry County SD
Supt. — See Newberry
Mid-Carolina MS — 600/6-8
6834 US Highway 76 29127 — 803-364-3634
Deedee Westwood, prin. — Fax 364-4877
Prosperity/Rikard ES — 500/K-5
381 S Wheeler Ave 29127 — 803-364-2321
Tim Lyden, prin. — Fax 364-4484

Ravenel, Charleston, Pop. 2,306
Charleston County SD
Supt. — See Charleston
Ellington ES — 200/K-6
5600 Ellington School Rd 29470 — 843-889-9411
Karen Hollinshead-Brown, prin. — Fax 889-2205

Reidville, Spartanburg, Pop. 502
Spartanburg SD 5
Supt. — See Duncan
Reidville ES — 400/K-4
PO Box 189 29375 — 864-949-2388
Elizabeth Sima, prin. — Fax 949-2390

Rembert, Sumter
Lee County SD
Supt. — See Bishopville
West Lee ES — 200/K-5
55 W Lee School Rd 29128 — 803-428-3147
Robert Ervin, prin. — Fax 428-3184

Sumter SD 2
Supt. — See Sumter
Rafting Creek ES — 200/K-5
4100 Highway 261 N 29128 — 803-432-2994
Ida Barboza, prin. — Fax 425-7386

Sumter Academy — 500/PK-12
5265 Camden Hwy 29128 — 803-499-3378
Debbie Nix, hdmstr. — Fax 499-3391

Richburg, Chester, Pop. 321
Chester County SD
Supt. — See Chester
Lewisville ES — 600/K-5
4006 Lewisville High School 29729 — 803-789-5164
Carl Carpenter, prin. — Fax 789-3954
Lewisville MS — 300/6-8
PO Box 280 29729 — 803-789-5858
H.L. Erwin, prin. — Fax 789-6159

Ridgeland, Jasper, Pop. 2,618
Jasper County SD — 2,800/PK-12
PO Box 848 29936 — 843-717-1100
Dr. Delacy Sanford, supt. — Fax 717-1199
www.jcsd.net
Ridgeland ES — 900/PK-5
250 Jaguar Trl 29936 — 843-717-1300
Sharyn Taylor-Cox, prin. — Fax 717-1309
Ridgeland MS — 500/6-8
PO Box 250 29936 — 843-717-1400
Ranell Williams, prin. — Fax 717-1409
Other Schools – See Hardeeville

Heyward Academy — 500/PK-12
1727 Malphrus Rd 29936 — 843-726-3673
John Rogers, hdmstr. — Fax 726-5773

Ridge Spring, Saluda, Pop. 797
Aiken County SD
Supt. — See Aiken
Ridge Spring-Monetta S — 700/K-8
422 Hazzard Cir 29129 — 803-685-2000
Jim Hooper, prin. — Fax 685-2008

Ridgeville, Dorchester, Pop. 1,960
Dorchester SD 4
Supt. — See Saint George
Clay Hill MS — 100/6-8
387 S Railroad Ave 29472 — 843-851-7386
Kenneth Pinkney, prin. — Fax 873-0571

Ridgeway, Fairfield, Pop. 331
Fairfield County SD
Supt. — See Winnsboro
Geiger ES — 300/K-6
300 S Coleman St 29130 — 803-337-8288
Joe Seibles, prin. — Fax 337-8185

Rock Hill, York, Pop. 59,554
Rock Hill SD 3 — 17,100/PK-12
PO Box 10072 29731 — 803-981-1000
Lynn Moody Ed.D., supt. — Fax 981-1094
www.rock-hill.k12.sc.us/
Belleview ES — 600/K-5
501 Belleview Rd 29730 — 803-981-1181
John Kirell, prin. — Fax 981-1193

Castle Heights MS 900/6-8
2382 Fire Tower Rd 29730 803-981-1400
Kelly Kane, prin. Fax 981-1430
Central Child Development Center 300/PK-PK
414 E Black St 29730 803-980-2060
Sylvia Echols, coord. Fax 980-2070
Children's ES at Sylvia Circle 300/K-5
929 Sylvia Cir 29730 803-981-1380
Sandra Lindsay-Brown, prin. Fax 981-1494
Dutchman Creek MS 6-8
4757 Mount Gallant Rd 29732 803-981-1360
Norris Williams, prin.
Ebenezer Avenue ES 400/K-5
242 Ebenezer Ave 29730 803-981-1435
Tanya Campbell, prin. Fax 981-1925
Ebinport ES 500/K-5
2142 India Hook Rd 29732 803-981-1550
Shane Goodwin, prin. Fax 981-1492
Finley Road ES 500/K-5
1089 Finley Rd 29730 803-981-1280
Deborah Maynard, prin. Fax 981-1294
Independence ES 500/K-5
132 W Springdale Rd 29730 803-981-1135
Mary Chandler-McVann, prin. Fax 981-2010
India Hook ES K-5
2068 Yukon Dr 29732 803-985-1600
Crystal Guyton, prin. Fax 985-1620
Leslie ES 500/K-5
250 Neely Store Rd 29730 803-981-1910
Seberina Myles, prin. Fax 981-1916
Mt. Gallant ES 600/K-5
4664 Mount Gallant Rd 29732 803-981-1360
Latoya Dixon, prin. Fax 981-1366
Mount Holly ES, 1800 Porter Rd 29730 K-5
Chris Beard, prin. 803-985-1650
Northside ES 500/K-5
840 Annafrel St 29730 803-981-1570
Linda Crute, prin. Fax 981-1926
Oakdale ES 600/K-5
1129 Oakdale Rd 29730 803-981-1585
Neil McVann, prin. Fax 981-1593
Old Pointe ES 700/K-5
380 Old Pointe School Rd 29732 803-980-2040
Al Bogan, prin. Fax 980-2045
Rawlinson Road MS 1,100/6-8
2631 W Main St 29732 803-981-1500
Jean Dickson, prin. Fax 981-1532
Richmond Drive ES 600/K-5
1162 Richmond Dr 29732 803-981-1930
Pat Maness, prin. Fax 981-1929
Rosewood ES 700/K-5
2240 Rosewood Dr 29732 803-981-1540
Stephen Ward, prin. Fax 981-1568
Saluda Trail MS 900/6-8
2300 Saluda Rd 29730 803-981-1800
Brenda Campbell, prin. Fax 981-1819
Sullivan MS 1,100/6-8
1825 Eden Ter 29730 803-981-1450
Michael Waiksnis, prin. Fax 981-1456
Sunset Park ES 300/K-5
1036 Ogden Rd 29730 803-981-1260
Tammy White, prin. Fax 981-1268
York Road ES 500/K-5
2254 W Main St 29732 803-981-1950
Patrick Robinson, prin. Fax 981-1961

St. Anne S 300/PK-8
1698 Bird St 29730 803-324-4814
Anthony Perrini, prin. Fax 324-0189
Trinity Christian S 200/PK-12
505 University Dr 29730 803-366-3121
Stephen Ehrhart, admin. Fax 366-8339
Westminster Catawba Christian S 600/PK-12
2650 India Hook Rd 29732 803-366-4119
John Gabrenas, admin. Fax 328-5465

Roebuck, Spartanburg, Pop. 1,966
Spartanburg SD 6 9,600/K-12
1390 Cavalier Way 29376 864-576-4212
Dr. Darryl Owings, supt. Fax 574-6265
www.spartanburg6.k12.sc.us
Gable MS 700/6-8
198 Otts Shoals Rd 29376 864-576-3500
Karen Bush, prin. Fax 595-2428
Roebuck ES 800/K-5
2401 E Blackstock Rd 29376 864-576-6151
Annie Means, prin. Fax 595-2429
Other Schools – See Moore, Pauline, Spartanburg

Rowesville, Orangeburg, Pop. 366
Orangeburg County Consolidated SD 5
Supt. — See Orangeburg
Bethune-Bowman ES 300/K-5
4857 Charleston Hwy 29133 803-533-6371
Charlene Stokes, prin. Fax 533-6373

Ruby, Chesterfield, Pop. 347
Chesterfield County SD
Supt. — See Chesterfield
Ruby ES 300/K-5
249 Thurman Ave 29741 843-634-6310
Nelson Hendrick, prin. Fax 634-5013

Ruffin, Colleton
Colleton County SD
Supt. — See Walterboro
Bells ES 300/K-5
12088 Bells Hwy 29475 843-866-2417
Cordelia Jenkins, prin. Fax 866-7361
Ruffin MS 400/6-8
155 Patriot Ln 29475 843-562-2291
Harry Jenkins, prin. Fax 562-8028

Saint George, Dorchester, Pop. 2,097
Dorchester SD 4 2,300/PK-12
500 Ridge St 29477 843-563-4535
Jerry Montjoy, supt. Fax 563-9269
www.dorchester4.k12.sc.us
Saint George MS 400/6-8
600 Minus St 29477 843-563-3171
Dr. Gwendolyn Boyd Wright, prin. Fax 563-5936

Williams Memorial ES 700/PK-5
290 S Metts St 29477 843-563-3231
Jeffrey Beckwith, prin. Fax 563-5929
Other Schools – See Dorchester, Ridgeville

Dorchester Academy 400/K-12
PO Box 901 29477 843-563-9511
Kimberly Brock, hdmstr. Fax 563-4764

Saint Helena Island, Beaufort
Beaufort County SD
Supt. — See Beaufort
St. Helena Early Learning Center PK-1
1031 Sea Island Pkwy 29920 843-838-6900
Chris Porter, prin. Fax 838-0372
St. Helena ES 300/2-5
1025 Sea Island Pkwy 29920 843-838-0300
Priscilla Drake, prin. Fax 838-0372

Saint Matthews, Calhoun, Pop. 2,093
Calhoun County SD 1,800/PK-12
PO Box 215 29135 803-655-7310
James Westbury, supt. Fax 655-7393
Ford MS 400/6-8
304 Agnes St 29135 803-655-7222
Hughie Peterson, prin. Fax 655-7506
Guinyard ES 700/PK-5
125 Herlong Ave 29135 803-874-3314
Jacqueline Mayo, prin. Fax 874-4107
Other Schools – See Swansea

Calhoun Academy 500/PK-12
PO Box 526 29135 803-874-2734
Milly McLauchlin, hdmstr. Fax 655-5096
Upward Way Christian Academy 50/K-12
3941 Old State Rd 29135 803-655-9026
Shelby Neil, admin.

Saint Stephen, Berkeley, Pop. 1,749
Berkeley County SD
Supt. — See Moncks Corner
Saint Stephen ES 300/K-5
1053 Russellville Rd 29479 843-567-2813
Elaine Norton, prin. Fax 567-3064
Saint Stephen MS 300/6-8
225 Carolina Dr 29479 843-567-3128
Brenda Jamison, prin. Fax 567-8162

Salters, Williamsburg
Williamsburg County SD
Supt. — See Kingstree
Cooper ES 200/K-6
4568 Seaboard Rd 29590 843-387-5426
Dr. Kerry Singleton, prin. Fax 387-5444

Saluda, Saluda, Pop. 2,969
Saluda SD 2,200/PK-12
404 N Wise Rd 29138 864-445-8441
David Mathis, supt. Fax 445-9585
www.saludak-12.org
Hollywood ES 400/K-5
1261 Hollywood Rd 29138 864-445-8333
Tammie Shore, prin. Fax 445-3518
Saluda ES 300/3-5
400 W Butler Ave 29138 864-445-2564
Marcie Enlow, prin. Fax 445-8833
Saluda MS 500/6-8
140 Ivory Key Rd 29138 864-445-3767
Shawn Love, prin. Fax 445-3980
Saluda PS 400/PK-2
200 Matthews Dr 29138 864-445-2469
Carey Burns, prin. Fax 445-4374

Scranton, Florence, Pop. 999
Florence County SD 3
Supt. — See Lake City
Scranton ES 300/K-5
PO Box 129 29591 843-389-2531
Darlene Matthews, prin. Fax 389-2548

Seabrook, Beaufort
Beaufort County SD
Supt. — See Beaufort
Davis ES 400/PK-5
364 Kean Neck Rd 29940 843-466-3600
Don Doggett, prin. Fax 466-3581
Whale Branch ES 300/PK-5
15 Stuart Point Rd 29940 843-466-1000
Mark Mansell, prin. Fax 466-1075
Whale Branch MS 400/6-8
2009 Trask Pkwy 29940 843-466-3000
MonaLise Dickson, prin. Fax 466-3087

Seneca, Oconee, Pop. 7,962
Oconee County SD
Supt. — See Walhalla
Blue Ridge ES PK-5
995 S Oak St 29678 864-886-4550
Kathy Eichler, prin. Fax 886-4551
Keowee ES 300/K-5
7051 Keowee School Rd 29672 864-886-4475
Michelle DeLoache, prin. Fax 886-4474
Northside ES 300/PK-5
710 N Townville St 29678 864-886-4445
Geoff Smith, prin. Fax 886-4446
Ravenel ES 500/K-5
150 Ravenel School Rd 29678 864-885-5026
Tommy Bolger, prin. Fax 885-5063
Seneca MS 800/6-8
810 W South 4th St 29678 864-886-4455
Al LeRoy, prin. Fax 886-4452

Oconee Christian Academy 200/PK-12
150 His Way Cir 29672 864-882-6925
Thad Cloer, admin. Fax 882-7217

Shaw AFB, Sumter
Sumter SD 2
Supt. — See Sumter
High Hills IS 400/4-5
4971 Frierson Rd 29152 803-499-3327
Elizabeth Compton, prin. Fax 499-9553

Shaw Heights ES 500/2-3
5121 Frierson Rd 29152 803-666-2335
Stella Hall, prin. Fax 666-3719

Simpsonville, Greenville, Pop. 15,135
Greenville County SD
Supt. — See Greenville
Bells Crossing ES 1,200/K-5
804 Scuffletown Rd 29681 864-355-3800
Barbara A. Barlow, prin. Fax 355-3885
Bethel ES 1,100/K-5
111 Bethel School Rd 29681 864-355-4100
Brenda Byrd, prin. Fax 355-4180
Bryson ES 1,000/K-5
703 Bryson Dr 29681 864-355-3600
Tom Chambers, prin. Fax 355-3696
Bryson MS 1,300/6-8
3657 S Industrial Dr 29681 864-355-2100
Phillip Davie, prin. Fax 355-2194
Chandler MS 6-8
4231 Fork Shoals Rd 29680 864-452-0300
Rita Mantooth, prin. Fax 452-0365
Golden Strip Family & Child Dev Ctr PK-K
1102 Howard Dr 29681 864-688-2247
Doris Santanello, prin. Fax 964-7043
Gordon ES K-5
1507 Scuffletown Rd 29681 864-452-0200
Jackie Parker, prin. Fax 450-0242
Hillcrest MS 1,200/6-8
510 Garrison Rd 29681 864-355-6100
Keith Russell, prin. Fax 355-6120
Mauldin ES 1,100/K-5
1194 Holland Rd 29681 864-355-3700
Michael Parker, prin. Fax 355-3783
Mauldin MS 1,200/6-8
1190 Holland Rd 29681 864-355-6770
Rosia Gardner, prin. Fax 355-6988
Oakview ES 1,200/K-5
515 Godfrey Rd 29681 864-355-7100
Phillip Reavis, prin. Fax 355-7115
Plain ES 900/K-5
506 Neely Ferry Rd 29680 864-355-7700
Deborah Mihalic, prin. Fax 355-7774
Simpsonville ES 700/K-5
200 Morton Ave 29681 864-355-8300
Jan James, prin. Fax 355-8360

Five Oaks Academy 100/PK-8
1101 Jonesville Rd 29681 864-228-1881
Kathleen Grant, dir. Fax 228-9888
Greenville Classical Academy 100/K-12
2519 Woodruff Rd 29681 864-329-9884
Tim Cockrell, dean
Southside Christian S 900/PK-12
2211 Woodruff Rd 29681 864-234-7595
Stephen Reel Ph.D., supt. Fax 234-7048

Six Mile, Pickens, Pop. 553
Pickens County SD
Supt. — See Easley
Six Mile ES 500/K-5
777 N Main St 29682 864-868-2352
Clif Alexander, prin. Fax 868-4011

Society Hill, Darlington, Pop. 697
Darlington County SD
Supt. — See Darlington
Rosenwald S 200/K-8
508 Church St 29593 843-378-4011
Kimberly Mason, prin. Fax 398-2694

Spartanburg, Spartanburg, Pop. 38,379
Spartanburg SD 2
Supt. — See Boiling Springs
Hendrix ES 700/K-4
1084 Springfield Rd 29316 864-578-1288
Dawn Neely, prin. Fax 578-6162

Spartanburg SD 3
Supt. — See Glendale
Cannons ES 300/K-5
1315 Old Converse Rd 29307 864-279-6100
Karen Grimm, prin. Fax 279-6103
Clifdale ES 400/K-5
451 Heritage Hills Dr 29307 864-279-6200
Jan Scott, prin. Fax 279-6203

Spartanburg SD 6
Supt. — See Roebuck
Arcadia ES 300/K-5
375 Spring St 29301 864-576-1371
Dr. Charles Bagwell, prin. Fax 595-2408
Bobo ES 300/K-5
495 Powell Mill Rd 29301 864-576-2085
Patrick Suber, prin. Fax 576-3180
Fairforest ES 600/K-5
1005 Mount Zion Rd 29303 864-576-4886
Stephen Krawczyk, prin. Fax 576-0402
Fairforest MS 800/6-8
4120 N Blackstock Rd 29301 864-576-1270
Ty Dawkins, prin. Fax 576-2600
Lone Oak ES 300/K-5
7314 Lone Oak Rd 29303 864-503-9088
Verotta Kennedy, prin. Fax 503-9090
West View ES 700/K-5
400 Oak Grove Rd 29301 864-576-1833
Shawn Wootton, prin. Fax 595-2436
Woodland Heights ES 400/K-5
1216 John B White SR Blvd 29306 864-576-0506
Dr. Cindy Pridgen, prin. Fax 595-2439

Spartanburg SD 7 7,300/K-12
PO Box 970 29304 864-594-4400
Thomas White, supt. Fax 594-4398
www.spart7.org
Boyd ES 500/K-6
1505 Fernwood Glendale Rd 29307 864-594-4430
Bob Grant, prin. Fax 594-6143
Chapman ES 500/K-6
210 Bryant Rd 29303 864-594-4440
Eric Mathison, prin. Fax 594-6145

Cleveland ES 500/K-6
151 Franklin St 29303 864-594-4444
Fred Logan, prin. Fax 594-6146
Houston ES 300/K-6
1475 Skylyn Dr 29307 864-594-4448
Tommy Stokes, prin. Fax 594-6147
Park Hills ES 500/K-6
301 Crescent Ave 29306 864-594-4465
Donald Mims, prin. Fax 594-6149
Pine Street ES 700/K-6
500 S Pine St 29302 864-594-4470
Anne Chapman-Jeter, prin. Fax 594-6150
Todd ES 600/K-6
150 Old Canaan Rd 29306 864-594-4475
Marc Zachary, prin. Fax 594-6152
Wright ES 300/K-6
457 S Church St 29306 864-594-4477
Wanda Owens-Jackson, prin. Fax 594-6144

Eddlemon Adventist S 50/K-8
1217 John B White Sr Blvd 29306 864-576-2234
Sheri Blake, prin. Fax 587-9623
Montessori Academy of Spartanburg PK-8
384 S Spring St 29306 864-585-3046
Karen Royals, admin.
St. Paul the Apostle S 100/PK-8
152 Alabama St 29302 864-582-6645
Patricia Lanthier, prin. Fax 582-1225
Spartanburg Christian Academy 500/PK-12
8740 Asheville Hwy 29316 864-578-4238
Robert McDonald, hdmstr. Fax 542-1846
Spartanburg Day S 500/PK-12
1701 Skylyn Dr 29307 864-582-7539
Christopher Dorrance, hdmstr. Fax 948-0026
Westgate Christian S 200/K-12
1990 Old Reidville Rd 29301 864-576-4953
Fred Seiber, prin. Fax 576-7581

Starr, Anderson, Pop. 188
Anderson SD 3
Supt. — See Iva
Starr ES 700/K-5
400 Professor Brown Ln 29684 864-352-6154
Valerie Neal, prin. Fax 352-6158
Starr-Iva MS 600/6-8
1034 Rainey Rd 29684 864-352-6146
Michael Ruthsatz, prin. Fax 352-2095

Sullivans Island, Charleston, Pop. 1,574
Charleston County SD
Supt. — See Charleston
Sullivans Island ES 300/K-6
2015 Ion Ave 29482 843-883-3118
Susan King, prin. Fax 883-3134

Summerton, Clarendon, Pop. 1,053
Clarendon SD 1 600/PK-12
PO Box 38 29148 803-485-2325
Dr. Rose Wilder, supt. Fax 485-3308
www.clarendon1.k12.sc.us
St. Paul ES 100/3-5
3074 Liberty Hill Rd 29148 803-478-2286
Patricia Middleton, prin. Fax 478-2579
Scott's Branch MS 200/6-8
1154 4th St 29148 803-485-2043
Dr. Gwendolyn Harris, prin. Fax 485-7012
Summerton ECC PK-2
12 S Church St 29148 803-485-2102
Tamika Riley, prin.

Clarendon Hall S 200/K-12
PO Box 609 29148 803-485-3550
Kimberly Fleming, prin. Fax 485-3205

Summerville, Dorchester, Pop. 37,714
Berkeley County SD
Supt. — See Moncks Corner
Sangaree ES 700/K-2
1460 Royle Rd 29483 843-820-3868
Alan Wilson, prin. Fax 820-3874
Sangaree IS 600/3-5
201 School House Ln 29483 843-820-3850
Angel Siegling, prin. Fax 820-3854

Dorchester SD 2 19,800/K-12
102 Green Wave Blvd 29483 843-873-2901
Joseph Pye, supt. Fax 821-3959
www.dorchester2.k12.sc.us
Alston MS 900/6-8
500 Bryan St 29483 843-873-3890
Sam Clark, prin. Fax 821-3978
Beech Hill ES 900/K-5
1001 Beech Hill Rd 29485 843-821-3970
Rene Harris, prin. Fax 821-3979
DuBose MS 1,000/6-8
1005 DuBose School Rd 29483 843-875-7012
Kenneth Farrell, prin. Fax 821-3995
Flowertown ES 1,000/K-5
20 King Charles Cir 29485 843-871-7400
Donna Goodwin, prin. Fax 821-3980
Fort Dorchester ES 1,500/K-5
5201 Old Glory Ln 29485 843-832-5550
Carol Farris, prin. Fax 832-5553
Gregg MS 1,200/6-8
500 Greenwave Blvd 29483 843-871-3150
Lori Phillips, prin. Fax 821-3992
Knightsville ES 1,200/K-5
847 Orangeburg Rd 29483 843-873-4851
Anita Putillion, prin. Fax 821-3983
Newington ES 900/K-5
10 King Charles Cir 29485 843-871-3230
Camilla Groome, prin. Fax 821-3981
Reeves ES K-5
1003 DuBose School Rd 29483 843-695-2450
Laura Blanchard, prin. Fax 695-2455
Rollings MS of the Arts 600/6-8
815 S Main St 29483 843-873-3610
Elena Furnari, prin. Fax 821-3985
Spann ES 800/K-5
901 John Mckissick Way 29483 843-873-3050
Wanda Carroll, prin. Fax 821-3987
Summerville ES 800/K-5
835 S Main St 29483 843-873-2372
Fax 821-3988
Other Schools – See Ladson, North Charleston

Faith Christian S 300/PK-12
337 Farmington Rd 29483 843-873-8464
Rev. Doug Wolfrath, hdmstr. Fax 873-4288
Oaks Christian S 200/PK-8
505 Gahagan Rd 29485 843-875-7667
Phil Wrenn, hdmstr. Fax 871-2629
Pinewood Prep S 800/PK-12
1114 Orangeburg Rd 29483 843-873-1643
Glyn Cowlishaw, hdmstr. Fax 821-4257
Summerville Catholic S 300/K-8
226 Black Oak Blvd 29485 843-873-9310
Lisa Tanner, prin. Fax 873-5709

Sumter, Sumter, Pop. 39,679
Sumter SD 17 8,700/PK-12
1109 N Pike W 29153 803-469-8536
Zona Jefferson Ph.D., supt. Fax 469-6006
district.sumter17.k12.sc.us/
Alice Drive ES 700/PK-5
251 Alice Dr 29150 803-775-0857
Debra Thomas, prin. Fax 775-7580
Alice Drive MS 800/6-8
40 Miller Rd 29150 803-775-0821
Rick Avins, prin. Fax 778-2929
Bates MS 800/6-8
715 Estate St 29150 803-775-0711
Dr. Vanessa Lancaster, prin. Fax 775-0715
Chestnut Oaks MS 400/7-8
1200 Oswego Hwy 29153 803-775-7272
Dr. Cornelius Leach, prin. Fax 775-7601
Crosswell Drive ES 700/PK-5
301 Crosswell Dr 29150 803-775-0679
Dr. Ayesha Hunter, prin. Fax 778-2857
Kingsbury ES 600/PK-5
825 Kingsbury Dr 29154 803-775-6244
Phillip Jackson, prin. Fax 775-7021
Lemira ES 500/PK-5
952 Fulton St 29153 803-775-0658
Delcia Harper-Baxter, prin. Fax 778-2730
Millwood ES 700/PK-5
24 Pinewood Rd 29150 803-775-0648
Dr. John Hilton, prin. Fax 436-2987
Sixth Grade Oaks Academy 6-6
1200 Oswego Hwy 29153 803-775-7272
Dr. Cornelius Leach, prin. Fax 775-7601
Wilder ES 500/PK-5
975 S Main St 29150 803-773-5723
Maria Newton-Ta'Bon, prin. Fax 778-2918
Willow Drive ES 600/PK-5
26 Willow Dr 29150 803-773-5796
Dr. Melissa O'Connor, prin. Fax 778-2847

Sumter SD 2 8,700/K-12
1345 Wilson Hall Rd 29150 803-469-6900
Frank Baker, supt. Fax 469-3769
www.sumter2.org
Cherryvale ES 500/K-5
1420 Furman Dr 29154 803-494-8200
Jeannie Pressley, prin. Fax 494-8233
Davis ES 400/K-5
345 Eastern School Rd 29153 803-495-3247
Ann McFadden, prin. Fax 495-3211
Ebenezer MS 500/6-8
3440 Ebenezer Rd 29153 803-469-8571
Marlene DeWit, prin. Fax 469-8575
Furman MS 900/6-8
3400 Bethel Church Rd 29154 803-481-8510
John Feeney, prin. Fax 481-8923
Mayewood MS 200/6-8
4300 E Brewington Rd 29153 803-495-8014
Dr. Mary Hallums, prin. Fax 495-8016
Oakland ES 500/K-1
5415 Oakland Dr 29154 803-499-3366
Shirley Tomlin, prin. Fax 499-3361
Pocalla Springs ES 900/K-5
2060 Bethel Church Rd 29154 803-481-5800
Lucille McQuilla, prin. Fax 481-5813
Other Schools – See Dalzell, Pinewood, Rembert, Shaw AFB, Wedgefield

---

Berea Junior Academy 50/K-8
675 S Lafayette Dr 29150 803-773-6875
St. Anne S 100/K-5
11 S Magnolia St 29150 803-775-3632
Kristi Doyle, prin. Fax 938-9074
Sumter Christian S 400/PK-12
420 S Pike W 29150 803-773-1902
Ron Davis, prin. Fax 775-1676
Wilson Hall S 800/PK-12
520 Wilson Hall Rd 29150 803-469-3475
Fred Moulton, hdmstr. Fax 469-3477

Swansea, Lexington, Pop. 686
Calhoun County SD
Supt. — See Saint Matthews
Sandy Run ES 200/PK-5
450 Old Swamp Rd 29160 803-791-8866
George Kiernan, prin. Fax 791-8975

Lexington County SD 4 3,700/PK-12
607 E 5th St 29160 803-568-1000
Dr. Linda Hawkins, supt. Fax 568-1020
www.lexington4.net
Sandhills ES 500/3-4
130 Lewis Rast Rd 29160 803-568-1200
Lisa Evans, prin. Fax 568-1210
Sandhills IS 500/5-6
140 Lewis Rast Rd 29160 803-568-1250
Sara Ankrapp, prin. Fax 568-1260
Swansea PS 400/PK-2
1195 I W Hutto Rd 29160 803-568-1050
Lillian Atkins, prin. Fax 568-1052
Other Schools – See Gaston

Tamassee, Oconee
Oconee County SD
Supt. — See Walhalla
Tamassee-Salem ES 300/PK-5
9950 N Highway 11 29686 864-886-4540
Shanon Lusk, prin. Fax 886-4539

Taylors, Greenville, Pop. 19,619
Greenville County SD
Supt. — See Greenville
Brook Glenn ES 500/K-5
2003 E Lee Rd 29687 864-355-4700
Bernice Jackson, prin. Fax 355-4755
Brushy Creek ES 800/K-5
1344 Brushy Creek Rd 29687 864-355-5400
DeeDee Washington, prin. Fax 355-5413
Mountain View ES 700/K-5
6350 Mountain View Rd 29687 864-355-6800
Tom Hughes, prin. Fax 355-6856
Northwood MS 800/6-8
710 Ikes Rd 29687 864-355-7000
Richard Griffin, prin. Fax 355-7077
Paris ES 600/K-5
32 E Belvue Rd 29687 864-355-4260
David Wise, prin. Fax 355-4391
Taylors ES 600/K-5
809 Reid School Rd 29687 864-355-7450
Vaughn Overman, prin. Fax 355-7477
Tigerville ES 300/K-5
25 Tigerville Elem School 29687 864-355-4600
Regina Urueta, prin. Fax 355-4646

Prince of Peace S 200/PK-5
1209 Brushy Creek Rd 29687 864-322-2233
Michael Pennell, prin. Fax 331-2153

Tega Cay, York, Pop. 4,372
York SD 4
Supt. — See Fort Mill
Gold Hill ES 800/K-5
1000 Dave Gibson Blvd 29708 803-548-8250
Terry Brewer, prin. Fax 548-8373
Gold Hill MS 600/6-8
1025 Dave Gibson Blvd 29708 803-548-8300
Tommy Johnston, prin. Fax 548-8322

Timmonsville, Florence, Pop. 2,385
Florence County SD 4 1,000/PK-12
220 N Pinckney St 29161 843-346-5391
Dr. Bertha McCants, supt. Fax 346-3145
www.florence4.k12.sc.us
Brockington ES 500/PK-5
304 Kemper St 29161 843-346-4953
Angela Jacobs, prin. Fax 346-5197
Johnson MS 200/6-8
304 Kemper St 29161 843-346-4685
Robert McDonald, prin. Fax 346-5199

Townville, Anderson
Anderson SD 4
Supt. — See Pendleton
Townville ES 200/K-5
PO Box 10 29689 864-287-3994
Denise Fredericks, prin. Fax 287-5716

Travelers Rest, Greenville, Pop. 4,237
Greenville County SD
Supt. — See Greenville
Gateway ES 600/K-5
200 Hawkins Rd 29690 864-355-5200
Glenn Wright, prin. Fax 355-5259
Heritage ES 600/K-5
1592 Geer Hwy 29690 864-355-6000
Martha Kinard, prin. Fax 355-6046
Northwest MS 900/6-8
1606 Geer Hwy 29690 864-355-6900
Lee Givins, prin. Fax 355-6920

Trenton, Edgefield, Pop. 301
Edgefield County SD
Supt. — See Johnston
Douglas ES 300/K-5
215 Samuel E Diggs Rd 29847 803-275-1752
Bruce Lee, prin. Fax 275-1751

Turbeville, Clarendon, Pop. 724
Clarendon SD 3 900/K-12
PO Box 270 29162 843-659-2188
Connie Dennis, supt. Fax 659-3204
www.clarendon3.org/
East Clarendon MS 6-8
PO Box 153 29162 843-659-2187
Carol Lenderman, prin. Fax 659-2192
Other Schools – See New Zion

Union, Union, Pop. 8,321
Union County SD 4,200/K-12
PO Box 907 29379 864-429-1740
Dr. David Eubanks, supt. Fax 429-1745
www.union.k12.sc.us
Excelsior MS 500/5-6
212 Culp St 29379 864-429-1725
Kathy Taylor, prin. Fax 429-2811
Foster Park ES 500/K-4
901 Arthur Blvd 29379 864-429-1737
Barbara Palmer, prin. Fax 429-1799
Monarch ES 400/K-4
218 Monarch School Dr 29379 864-429-1733
Anita Maness, prin. Fax 429-1789
Sims JHS 600/7-8
200 Sims Dr 29379 864-429-1755
Mickey Connolly, prin. Fax 429-1798
Other Schools – See Buffalo, Jonesville, Lockhart

Vance, Orangeburg, Pop. 202
Orangeburg County Consolidated SD 3
Supt. — See Holly Hill
Vance/Providence ES 300/K-5
633 Camden Rd 29163 803-492-7766
James Myers, prin. Fax 492-3961

Varnville, Hampton, Pop. 2,048
Hampton SD 1 2,900/PK-12
372 E Pine St 29944 803-943-4576
Doug McTeer, supt. Fax 943-5943
www.hampton1.org
North District MS 400/7-8
PO Box 368 29944 803-943-3507
Mark Dean, prin. Fax 943-4074
Varnville ES 400/PK-6
PO Box 367 29944 803-943-2376
Donna Kinard, prin. Fax 943-5715
Other Schools – See Brunson, Hampton, Yemassee

Wadmalaw Island, Charleston
Charleston County SD
Supt. — See Charleston
Frierson ES 100/K-6
6133 Maybank Hwy 29487 843-559-1182
Blondell Adams, prin. Fax 559-6438

Wagener, Aiken, Pop. 872
Aiken County SD
Supt. — See Aiken
Busbee ES 600/K-5
20 Corbett Cir 29164 803-564-1000
Rose Marshall, prin. Fax 564-1010
Corbett MS 300/6-8
10 Corbett Cir 29164 803-564-1050
Dr. Deborah Bass, prin. Fax 564-1058

Walhalla, Oconee, Pop. 3,727
Oconee County SD 10,300/PK-12
414 S Pine St 29691 864-886-4400
Dr. Mike Lucas, supt. Fax 886-4408
www.oconee.k12.sc.us
Brown ES 700/PK-5
225 Coffee Rd 29691 864-886-4470
Michelle Grant, prin. Fax 886-4471
Walhalla ES 500/K-5
PO Box 370 29691 864-886-4480
Steven Hanvey, prin. Fax 886-4481
Walhalla MS 700/6-8
177 Razorback Ln 29691 864-886-4485
Charles Middleton, prin. Fax 886-4483
Other Schools – See Seneca, Tamassee, Westminster

Wallace, Marlboro
Marlboro County SD
Supt. — See Bennettsville
Wallace S 400/PK-8
3643 Highway 9 W 29596 843-537-7493
Janice Henson, prin. Fax 537-2572

Walterboro, Colleton, Pop. 5,548
Colleton County SD 6,200/PK-12
213 N Jefferies Blvd 29488 843-782-4510
Charles Gale, supt. Fax 549-2606
www.colleton.k12.sc.us
Black Street ES 500/K-5
256 Smith St 29488 843-549-7702
Tracy McDonald, prin. Fax 549-1343
Colleton MS 500/6-8
603 Colleton Loop 29488 843-549-2690
Dr. Kenneth Jenkins, prin. Fax 549-1222
ECC PK-PK
214 Bailey St 29488 843-549-1727
Martha Strickland, prin. Fax 549-6220
Forest Circle MS 600/6-8
500 Forest Cir 29488 843-549-2361
Scott Matthews, prin. Fax 549-5061
Forest Hills ES 700/K-5
633 Hiers Corner Rd 29488 843-549-2119
Cindy Riley, prin. Fax 549-1557
Hendersonville ES 400/K-5
6089 Hendersonville Hwy 29488 843-844-2025
Jessica Williams, prin. Fax 844-7361
Northside ES 700/K-5
1929 Industrial Rd 29488 843-538-4350
Barbara Steele, prin. Fax 538-3478
Other Schools – See Cottageville, Edisto Island, Ruffin

Colleton Prep Academy 400/K-12
PO Box 1426 29488 843-538-8959
Arthur Ellis, hdmstr. Fax 538-8260
Family Christian Academy 100/PK-8
2107 Hampton St 29488 843-893-3536
Pam Taylor, coord. Fax 893-2174

Ware Shoals, Greenwood, Pop. 2,377
Greenwood SD 51 1,100/PK-12
25 E Main St 29692 864-456-7496
Fay Sprouse, supt. Fax 456-3578
www.gwd51.k12.sc.us
Ware Shoals ES 200/4-6
45 W Main St 29692 864-456-2711
Nancy Brown, prin. Fax 456-4470
Ware Shoals PS 400/PK-3
15269 Indian Mound Rd 29692 864-861-2261
Dr. Frank Cason, prin. Fax 861-4338

Warrenville, Aiken
Aiken County SD
Supt. — See Aiken
Jefferson ES 500/K-5
170 Flint Dr 29851 803-593-7180
Pam Hart, prin. Fax 593-7112
Langley-Bath-Clearwater MS 500/6-8
29 Lions Trl 29851 803-593-7260
Brenda DeLoache, prin. Fax 593-7119
Warrenville ES 400/K-5
569 Howlandville Rd 29851 803-663-4270
Brenda Smith, prin. Fax 663-4271

Waterloo, Laurens, Pop. 204
Laurens SD 55
Supt. — See Laurens
Waterloo ES 300/K-6
10457 Highway 221 S 29384 864-677-4670
Taria Stokes, prin. Fax 677-4674

Wedgefield, Sumter
Sumter SD 2
Supt. — See Sumter
Delaine ES 200/K-5
5355 Cane Savannah Rd 29168 803-494-2661
Roosevelt Miott, prin. Fax 494-2675

Wellford, Spartanburg, Pop. 2,282
Spartanburg SD 5
Supt. — See Duncan
Wellford ES 600/K-4
684 Syphrit Rd 29385 864-949-2385
Angie Showalter, prin. Fax 949-2386

West Columbia, Lexington, Pop. 13,413
Lexington County SD 1
Supt. — See Lexington
White Knoll ES 900/K-5
132 White Knoll Way 29170 803-821-4500
Janet H. Malone, prin. Fax 821-4503
White Knoll MS 1,400/6-8
116 White Knoll Way 29170 803-821-4300
Nancy Turner Ph.D., prin. Fax 821-4303

Lexington County SD 2 8,800/PK-12
715 9th St 29169 803-796-4708
Dr. Venus Holland, supt. Fax 739-4063
www.lex2.k12.sc.us
Brookland-Cayce ES #1 300/K-5
114 Hook Ave 29169 803-739-4075
Walter Clark, prin. Fax 739-8384
Congaree ES 400/2-5
1221 Ramblin Rd 29172 803-755-7430
Jeff Becker, prin. Fax 755-7405
Congaree-Wood ECC 600/PK-1
739 Pine Ridge Dr 29172 803-755-7474
Victoria Thompkins, prin. Fax 755-7482
Fulmer MS 600/6-8
1614 Walterboro St 29170 803-822-5660
Dixon Brooks, prin. Fax 822-5664
Northside MS 600/6-8
157 Cougar Dr 29169 803-739-4190
David Sims, prin. Fax 739-3188
Pair ES 300/K-5
2325 Platt Springs Rd 29169 803-739-4085
Wanda Whatley, prin. Fax 739-3195
Pine Ridge MS 500/6-8
735 Pine Ridge Dr 29172 803-755-7400
Cindy Hall, prin. Fax 755-7449
Pineview ES 500/K-5
3035 Leaphart Rd 29169 803-739-4090
Cynthia Stiltner, prin. Fax 739-3190
Saluda River Academy for the Arts 400/K-5
1520 Duke St 29169 803-739-4095
Tonya Fryer, prin. Fax 739-3198
Springdale ES 400/K-5
361 Wattling Rd 29170 803-739-4175
Shane Thackston, prin. Fax 739-3198
Wood ES 500/2-5
737 Pine Ridge Dr 29172 803-755-7420
Dr. Vicki Traufler, prin. Fax 755-7447
Other Schools – See Cayce

Glenforest S 100/K-12
1041 Harbor Dr 29169 803-796-7622
Fax 796-1603

Westminster, Oconee, Pop. 2,669
Oconee County SD
Supt. — See Walhalla
Fair-Oak ES 500/PK-3
1964 Oakway Rd 29693 864-886-4505
Carolyn Harris, prin. Fax 886-4506
Oakway IS 300/4-5
150 School House Rd Ste B 29693 864-886-4510
Ann Miller, prin. Fax 886-4511
Orchard Park ES 500/PK-5
600 Toccoa Hwy 29693 864-886-4515
Kathy Whitmire, prin. Fax 886-4516
Westminster ES 500/PK-5
206 Hamilton Dr 29693 864-886-4520
Mike McLeod, prin. Fax 886-4521
West Oak MS 400/6-8
501 Westminster Hwy 29693 864-886-4525
Jami Verderosa, prin. Fax 886-4524

Poplar Springs SDA S 50/1-8
4279A S Highway 11 29693 864-638-5963
Judy Harward, prin. Fax 638-5911

West Pelzer, Anderson, Pop. 899
Anderson SD 1
Supt. — See Williamston
West Pelzer ES 400/PK-5
10 W Stewart St, 864-947-6424
Dr. Stacy Hashe, prin. Fax 947-2014

Whitmire, Newberry, Pop. 1,526
Newberry County SD
Supt. — See Newberry
Whitmire Community S 300/K-12
2597 Hwy 66 29178 803-694-2320
Joey Haney, prin. Fax 694-3835

Williamston, Anderson, Pop. 3,878
Anderson SD 1 8,800/PK-12
PO Box 99 29697 864-847-7344
Dr. Wayne Fowler, supt. Fax 847-3543
www.anderson1.k12.sc.us
Cedar Grove ES 600/PK-5
107 Melvin Ln 29697 864-847-3500
Dr. Eunice Williams, prin. Fax 847-3502
Palmetto ES 700/PK-5
1 Roberts Blvd 29697 864-847-5442
Jerome Hudson, prin. Fax 847-3504
Palmetto MS 700/6-8
803 N Hamilton St 29697 864-847-4333
Barry Knight, prin. Fax 847-3529
Other Schools – See Easley, Greenville, Piedmont, West Pelzer

Williston, Barnwell, Pop. 3,260
Williston SD 29 1,000/PK-12
12255 Main St 29853 803-266-7878
Alexia Clamp, supt. Fax 266-3879
www.williston.k12.sc.us
Edwards ES 500/PK-5
1071 Elko St 29853 803-266-3737
Donna Selvey, prin. Fax 266-7061
Williston-Elko MS 300/6-8
12333 Main St 29853 803-266-3430
Dr. Eavon Hickson, prin. Fax 266-7623

Winnsboro, Fairfield, Pop. 3,612
Fairfield County SD 3,400/PK-12
PO Box 622 29180 803-635-4607
Dr. Samantha Ingram, supt. Fax 635-6578
www.fairfield.k12.sc.us/
Fairfield IS 400/4-6
1647 US Highway 321 Byp N 29180 803-635-4810
Moni Cheagle, prin. Fax 635-1803
Fairfield MS 500/7-8
728 US Highway 321 Byp S 29180 803-635-4270
Leevette Malloy, prin. Fax 635-9108
Fairfield PS 600/K-3
175 Medley Rd 29180 803-635-5594
Brenda Gilchrist, prin. Fax 635-1721
Gordon ECC 200/PK-PK
560 Fairfield St 29180 803-635-4859
Lillian Potter-Arnold, prin. Fax 635-1379
Miller ES 300/K-6
255 Kelly Miller Rd 29180 803-635-2961
Lillian Arnold, prin. Fax 635-4564
Other Schools – See Blair, Ridgeway

Winn Academy 300/K-12
PO Box 390 29180 803-635-5494
Ken Atkerson, hdmstr. Fax 635-4310

Woodruff, Spartanburg, Pop. 4,105
Spartanburg SD 4 3,000/PK-12
118 McEdco Rd 29388 864-476-3186
Dr. W. Rallie Liston, supt. Fax 476-8616
www.spartanburg4.org
Woodruff ES 700/3-5
915 Cross Anchor Rd 29388 864-476-3123
Aaron Fulmer, prin. Fax 476-6193
Woodruff MS 700/6-8
205 SJ Workman Hwy 29388 864-476-3150
Denise Brown, prin. Fax 476-6036
Woodruff PS 800/PK-2
200 Lucy P Edwards Rd 29388 864-476-3174
Kim McAbee, prin. Fax 476-7067

Yemassee, Hampton, Pop. 839
Hampton SD 1
Supt. — See Varnville
Fennell ES 300/PK-6
PO Box 427 29945 843-589-2032
Willie Coker, prin. Fax 589-8043

Yonges Island, Charleston
Charleston County SD
Supt. — See Charleston
Blaney ES 200/K-6
7184 Highway 162 29449 843-889-3992
Michelle Simmons, prin. Fax 889-6518

York, York, Pop. 7,233
York SD 1 5,200/PK-12
PO Box 770 29745 803-684-9916
Vernon Prosser, supt. Fax 684-1903
www.york.k12.sc.us
Cotton Belt ES 700/PK-5
1176 Black Hwy 29745 803-684-1947
Mark Hendry, prin. Fax 684-1949
Hunter Street ES 800/PK-5
1100 Hunter St 29745 803-684-1926
Kevin Hood, prin. Fax 684-1931
Jefferson ES 600/PK-5
1543 Chester Hwy 29745 803-684-1942
Jane Wallace, prin. Fax 684-1944
Johnson MS 700/6-7
400 E Jefferson St 29745 803-684-2311
Keith McSwain, prin. Fax 684-1918
Other Schools – See Hickory Grove

Blessed Hope Baptist S 200/K-12
410 Blessed Hope Rd 29745 803-684-9819

SOUTH DAKOTA

SOUTH DAKOTA DEPARTMENT OF EDUCATION
700 Governors Dr, Pierre 57501
Telephone 605-773-5669
Fax 605-773-6139
Website http://www.state.sd.us/deca

Secretary of Education Thomas Oster

SOUTH DAKOTA BOARD OF EDUCATION
700 Governors Dr, Pierre 57501

President Kelly Duncan

PUBLIC, PRIVATE AND CATHOLIC ELEMENTARY SCHOOLS

Aberdeen, Brown, Pop. 24,098
Aberdeen SD 6-1 3,700/K-12
1224 S 3rd St 57401 605-725-7100
Dr. Gary Harms, supt. Fax 725-7199
www.aberdeen.k12.sd.us
Holgate MS 400/6-8
2200 N Dakota St 57401 605-725-7700
Dr. Greg Aas, prin. Fax 725-7799
Lee ES 400/K-5
1900 N State St 57401 605-725-7500
Eric Kline, prin. Fax 725-7599
Lincoln ES 300/K-5
414 S 10th St 57401 605-725-7200
Robbie Gellhaus, prin. Fax 725-7299
Overby ES 300/K-5
612 14th Ave SE 57401 605-725-7300
Mike Neubert, prin. Fax 725-7399
Simmons ES 300/K-5
1500 S 3rd St 57401 605-725-7600
Knute Reierson, prin. Fax 725-7699
Simmons MS 400/6-8
1300 S 3rd St 57401 605-725-7900
Kelly Northrup, prin. Fax 725-7999
Tiffany ES 300/K-5
819 8th Ave NE 57401 605-725-7400
Earl Martell, prin. Fax 725-7499

Aberdeen Christian S 100/PK-6
1500 E Melgaard Rd 57401 605-225-2053
Jarvis Wipf, admin. Fax 226-2106
Roncalli MS 200/3-6
501 3rd Ave SE 57401 605-229-4100
Mary Schwab, prin. Fax 229-4101
Roncalli PS 200/PK-2
419 1st Ave NE 57401 605-225-3460
Mary Schwab, prin. Fax 229-4101
Trinity Lutheran S 50/K-8
923 S Dakota St 57401 605-229-4697
Phillip Rehberger, prin.

Alcester, Union, Pop. 889
Alcester-Hudson SD 61-1 300/PK-12
PO Box 198 57001 605-934-1890
Jerry Joachim, supt. Fax 934-1936
www.alcester-hudson.k12.sd.us
Alcester-Hudson ES 200/PK-6
PO Box 198 57001 605-934-2171
Jerry Joachim, prin. Fax 934-1765
Alcester-Hudson JHS 100/7-8
PO Box 198 57001 605-934-1890
LeeAnn Haisch, prin. Fax 934-1936

Alexandria, Hanson, Pop. 676
Hanson SD 30-1 300/PK-12
PO Box 490 57311 605-239-4387
James Bridge, supt. Fax 239-4293
www.hanson.k12.sd.us/
Hanson ES 100/PK-5
PO Box 490 57311 605-239-4387
Susan Blankenship, prin. Fax 239-4293
Hanson JHS 50/6-8
PO Box 490 57311 605-239-4387
Kevin Lein, prin. Fax 239-4293
Oaklane Colony S 50/K-8
PO Box 490 57311 605-239-4387
Susan Blankenship, prin. Fax 239-4293
Other Schools – See Mitchell

Mitchell SD 17-2
Supt. — See Mitchell
Rockport Colony S 50/K-8
25209 Rockport Rd 57311 605-239-4214
Joe Childs, prin. Fax 239-4372

Arlington, Kingsbury, Pop. 952
Arlington SD 38-1 300/K-12
PO Box 359 57212 605-983-5597
Chris Lund, supt. Fax 983-4652
www.arlington.k12.sd.us
Arlington ES 200/K-6
PO Box 359 57212 605-983-5741
Rhonda Gross, prin. Fax 983-4652
Arlington JHS 100/7-8
PO Box 359 57212 605-983-5598
Rhonda Gross, prin. Fax 983-4652

Oldham-Ramona SD 39-5
Supt. — See Ramona
Spring Lake S 50/K-8
21727 452nd Ave 57212 605-482-8014
John Bjorkman, prin.

Armour, Douglas, Pop. 736
Armour SD 21-1 200/K-12
PO Box 640 57313 605-724-2153
Burnell Glanzer, supt. Fax 724-2977
www.armour.k12.sd.us/
Armour ES 100/K-4
PO Box 640 57313 605-724-2698
Burnell Glanzer, prin. Fax 724-2977
Armour MS 50/5-8
PO Box 640 57313 605-724-2698
Burnell Glanzer, prin. Fax 724-2799

Astoria, Deuel, Pop. 136
Deubrook Area SD 5-6
Supt. — See White
Astoria ES 50/K-1
PO Box 38 57213 605-794-1152
Cristy Olsen, prin. Fax 794-2492

Avon, Bon Homme, Pop. 543
Avon SD 4-1 300/PK-12
PO Box 407 57315 605-286-3291
Tom Culver, supt. Fax 286-3712
www.avon.k12.sd.us/
Avon ES 100/PK-6
PO Box 407 57315 605-286-3291
Tom Culver, prin. Fax 286-3712
Avon JHS 50/7-8
PO Box 407 57315 605-286-3291
Joe Kramer, prin. Fax 286-3510

Baltic, Minnehaha, Pop. 932
Baltic SD 49-1 400/PK-12
PO Box 309 57003 605-529-5464
Robert Sittig, supt. Fax 529-5443
www.baltic.k12.sd.us/
Baltic ES 200/PK-5
PO Box 309 57003 605-529-5464
Robert Sittig, prin. Fax 529-5443
Baltic MS 100/6-8
PO Box 309 57003 605-529-5461
James Aisenbery, prin. Fax 529-5467

Bancroft, Kingsbury, Pop. 35
Willow Lake SD 12-3
Supt. — See Willow Lake
Collin Colony S 57353 K-8
Kevin Quimby, prin. 605-625-5945
Fax 625-3103

Batesland, Shannon, Pop. 97
Shannon County SD 65-1 900/PK-8
PO Box 109 57716 605-288-1921
Dan Elwood, supt. Fax 288-1814
www.shannon.ws
Batesland S 100/PK-8
PO Box 49 57716 605-288-1948
Connie Kaltenbach, prin. Fax 288-1986
Other Schools – See Hermosa, Pine Ridge, Porcupine

Belle Fourche, Butte, Pop. 4,675
Belle Fourche SD 9-1 1,300/PK-12
2305 13th Ave 57717 605-723-3355
Steve Willard, supt. Fax 723-3366
www.bellefourche.k12.sd.us/
Belle Fourche MS 400/5-8
2305 13th Ave 57717 605-723-3367
Kevin Smidt, prin. Fax 723-3374
North Park K 100/K-K
2305 13th Ave 57717 605-723-3379
Patrick Deering, prin. Fax 723-3381
South Park ES 400/PK-PK, 1-
2305 13th Ave 57717 605-723-3382
Patrick Deering, prin. Fax 723-3384

Beresford, Union, Pop. 2,027
Beresford SD 61-2 700/PK-12
301 W Maple St 57004 605-763-4293
Brian Field, supt. Fax 763-5305
www.beresford.k12.sd.us/
Beresford ES 300/PK-5
209 S 4th St 57004 605-763-5012
Kevin Nelson, prin. Fax 763-2205
Beresford MS 200/6-8
205 W Maple St 57004 605-763-2139
Mike Radke, prin. Fax 763-5305

Big Stone City, Grant, Pop. 570
Big Stone CSD 25-1 100/PK-8
655 Walnut St 57216 605-862-8108
Daniel Swartos, supt. Fax 862-8640
www.bigstonecity.k12.sd.us
Big Stone City ES 100/PK-5
655 Walnut St 57216 605-862-8108
Daniel Swartos, prin. Fax 862-8640
Big Stone City JHS 50/6-8
655 Walnut St 57216 605-862-8108
Daniel Swartos, prin. Fax 862-8640

Bison, Perkins, Pop. 342
Bison SD 52-1 100/K-12
PO Box 9 57620 605-244-5271
Shawn Winthers, admin. Fax 244-5276
www.bison.k12.sd.us/
Bison ES 100/K-6
PO Box 9 57620 605-244-5273
Shawn Winthers, prin. Fax 244-5276
Bison JHS 50/7-8
PO Box 9 57620 605-244-5961
Shawn Winthers, prin. Fax 244-5276

Blackhawk, Meade, Pop. 1,995
Rapid City Area SD 51-4
Supt. — See Rapid City
Black Hawk ES 300/K-5
7108 Seeaire St, 605-787-6701
Jacqueline Higlin, prin. Fax 787-6654

Blunt, Hughes, Pop. 360
Agar-Blunt-Onida SD 58-3
Supt. — See Onida
Blunt ES 100/K-6
PO Box 207 57522 605-962-6297
Kathryn Hirchert, prin. Fax 962-6390

Bonesteel, Gregory, Pop. 270
South Central SD 26-5 100/PK-12
PO Box 410 57317 605-654-2314
Erik Person, supt.
www.southcentral.k12.sd.us/
South Central ES, PO Box 410 57317 100/PK-6
J.D. Evans, prin. 605-654-2314
South Central JHS, PO Box 410 57317 50/7-8
J.D. Evans, prin. 605-654-2314

Bowdle, Edmunds, Pop. 523
Bowdle SD 22-1 100/K-12
PO Box 563 57428 605-285-6272
Larry Gauer, supt. Fax 285-6830
www.bowdle.k12.sd.us
Bowdle ES 100/K-6
PO Box 563 57428 605-285-6590
Larry Gauer, prin. Fax 285-6830
Bowdle JHS 50/7-8
PO Box 563 57428 605-285-6590
Larry Gauer, prin. Fax 285-6830

Box Elder, Pennington, Pop. 2,992
Douglas SD 51-1 2,300/PK-12
400 Patriot Dr 57719 605-923-0000
Dr. Loren Scheer, supt. Fax 923-0018
www.dsdk12.net
Badger Clark/Carrousel ES 400/K-1
401 Don Williams Dr 57719 605-923-0080
Michelle Henrich, prin. Fax 923-0081
Case ES 400/2-3
441 Don Williams Dr 57719 605-923-0070
Jeannie Clark, prin. Fax 923-0071
Douglas MS 500/6-8
401 Tower Rd 57719 605-923-0050
Dan Baldwin, prin. Fax 923-0051
Douglas Preschool PK-PK
400 Patriot Dr 57719 605-923-0013
Joan Dunmire, prin. Fax 923-0018
Vandenburg ES 400/4-5
600 N Ellsworth Rd 57719 605-923-0060
Mona Terwilliger, prin. Fax 923-0061

Brandon, Minnehaha, Pop. 7,176
Brandon Valley SD 49-2 2,900/PK-12
300 S Splitrock Blvd 57005 605-582-2049
David Pappone, supt. Fax 582-7456
www.brandonvalleyschools.com
Bennis ES 600/PK-5
2001 S Sioux Blvd 57005 605-582-8010
Karen Heyden, prin. Fax 582-8012
Brandon ES 700/PK-5
501 E Holly Blvd 57005 605-582-6315
Merle Horst, prin. Fax 582-2709
Brandon Valley MS 700/6-8
700 E Holly Blvd 57005 605-582-3214
Dan Pansch, prin. Fax 582-7206
Other Schools – See Sioux Falls, Valley Springs

Bridgewater, McCook, Pop. 592
Bridgewater SD 43-6 200/PK-12
PO Box 350 57319 605-729-2541
Jason Bailey, admin. Fax 729-2580
www.bridgewater.k12.sd.us/
Bridgewater ES 100/PK-5
PO Box 350 57319 605-729-2541
Kim Aman, prin. Fax 729-2580
Bridgewater MS 50/6-8
PO Box 350 57319 605-729-2541
Christena Schultz, prin. Fax 729-2580

Britton, Marshall, Pop. 1,282
Britton-Hecla SD 45-4 500/PK-12
PO Box 190 57430 605-448-2234
Donald Kirkegaard, supt. Fax 448-5994
www.britton.k12.sd.us/
Britton-Hecla ES 200/PK-6
PO Box 190 57430 605-448-2234
Shad Storley, prin. Fax 448-5994
Britton-Hecla JHS 100/7-8
PO Box 190 57430 605-448-2234
Marcia Forrester, prin. Fax 448-5994
Sunset Colony S 50/K-8
PO Box 190 57430 605-448-2234
Shad Storley, prin. Fax 448-5994
Westwood Rural S PK-8
499 Westwood Rd 57430 605-448-2234
Shad Storley, prin. Fax 448-5994

Brookings, Brookings, Pop. 18,715
Brookings SD 5-1 2,100/K-12
2130 8th St S 57006 605-696-4700
Dr. Roger DeGroot, supt. Fax 696-4704
www.brookings.k12.sd.us/
Camelot IS, 1401 15th St S 57006 4-5
David Fiedler, prin. 605-696-4400
Hillcrest ES 300/K-3
304 15th Ave 57006 605-696-4600
Gary Thomas, prin. Fax 696-4642
Medary ES 400/K-3
718 5th St S 57006 605-696-4300
Richard Brubakken, prin. Fax 696-4362
Mickelson MS 600/6-8
1801 12th St S 57006 605-696-4500
Dan Neiles, prin. Fax 696-4506

Peace Lutheran S 50/PK-K
1910 12th St S 57006 605-692-5272

Buffalo, Harding, Pop. 341
Harding County SD 31-1 200/K-12
PO Box 367 57720 605-375-3241
Ruth Krogh, supt. Fax 375-3246
www.hardingcounty.k12.sd.us/
Buffalo ES 100/K-6
PO Box 367 57720 605-375-3241
Josh Page, prin. Fax 375-3246
Harding County JHS 50/7-8
PO Box 367 57720 605-375-3241
Josh Page, prin. Fax 375-3246
Other Schools – See Camp Crook, Ludlow

Burke, Gregory, Pop. 606
Burke SD 26-2 200/K-12
PO Box 382 57523 605-775-2644
Jack Broome, supt. Fax 775-2468
Burke ES 100/K-5
PO Box 382 57523 605-775-2246
Brian Daughters, prin. Fax 775-2468
Burke JHS 100/6-8
PO Box 382 57523 605-775-2645
Brian Daughters, prin. Fax 775-2468

Camp Crook, Harding, Pop. 50
Harding County SD 31-1
Supt. — See Buffalo
Camp Crook S 50/K-8
Box 58 / 3rd N 57724 605-375-3241
Josh Page, prin. Fax 375-3246

Canistota, McCook, Pop. 700
Canistota SD 43-1 200/K-12
PO Box 8 57012 605-296-3458
Chad Janzen, supt. Fax 296-3158
www.canistota.k12.sd.us
Canistota ES 100/K-6
PO Box 8 57012 605-296-3458
Ryan Nielsen, prin. Fax 296-3158
Canistota JHS 50/7-8
PO Box 8 57012 605-296-3458
Ryan Nielsen, prin. Fax 296-3158

Canton, Lincoln, Pop. 3,165
Canton SD 41-1 800/PK-12
800 N Main St 57013 605-764-2706
Terry Majeres, supt. Fax 764-2700
www.canton.k12.sd.us
Canton MS 200/6-8
800 N Main St 57013 605-764-2706
Terry Gerber, prin. Fax 764-2700
Lawrence ES 300/PK-5
724 N Sanborn St 57013 605-764-2579
James Jibben, prin. Fax 764-5003

Carpenter, Beadle
Clark SD 12-2
Supt. — See Clark
Fordham Colony S 50/K-8
533 Fordham Dr 57322 605-532-3606
Jerry Hartley, prin. Fax 532-3608

Willow Lake SD 12-3
Supt. — See Willow Lake
Shamrock Colony S 50/K-8
19087 413th Ave 57322 605-625-5945
Kevin Quimby, prin. Fax 625-3103

Carthage, Miner, Pop. 167
Carthage SD 48-2 50/K-6
141 Town Rd W 57323 605-772-4435
Lori Wehlander, supt. Fax 772-4435
Carthage ES 50/K-6
141 Town Rd W 57323 605-772-4435
Lori Wehlander, prin. Fax 772-4435

Castlewood, Hamlin, Pop. 681
Castlewood SD 28-1 300/K-12
310 E Harry St 57223 605-793-2351
Keith Fodness, supt. Fax 793-2679
www.castlewood.k12.sd.us/
Castlewood ES 100/K-6
310 E Harry St 57223 605-793-2351
Terri Tillma, prin. Fax 793-2679
Castlewood JHS 50/7-8
310 E Harry St 57223 605-793-2351
Keith Fodness, prin. Fax 793-2679
Claremont Colony S 50/K-8
46271 184th St 57223 605-793-2351
Terri Tillma, prin. Fax 793-2679

Centerville, Turner, Pop. 864
Centerville SD 60-1 300/PK-12
PO Box 100 57014 605-563-2291
Doug Voss, supt. Fax 563-2615
www.centerville.k12.sd.us
Centerville ES 100/PK-6
PO Box 100 57014 605-563-2291
Doug Voss, prin. Fax 563-2615
Centerville JHS 50/7-8
PO Box 100 57014 605-563-2291
Jim Nelson, prin. Fax 563-2615

Chamberlain, Brule, Pop. 2,259
Chamberlain SD 7-1 900/PK-12
PO Box 119 57325 605-234-4477
Tim Mitchell, supt. Fax 234-4479
www.chamberlain.k12.sd.us
Chamberlain ES 500/PK-6
PO Box 119 57325 605-234-4460
Andy Wilkins, prin. Fax 234-4479
Chamberlain MS 100/7-8
PO Box 119 57325 605-234-4467
Deb Johnson, prin. Fax 234-4479

St. Joseph Indian S 200/1-8
PO Box 89 57325 605-734-6021
Fr. Steve Huffstetter, prin. Fax 734-3483

Chancellor, Turner, Pop. 315
Lennox SD 41-4
Supt. — See Lennox
Chancellor ES 100/K-5
401 1st St 57015 605-647-2754
Kym Johnston, prin. Fax 647-6044

Chester, Lake
Chester Area SD 39-1 400/PK-12
PO Box 159 57016 605-489-2411
Mark Greguson, supt. Fax 489-2413
www.chester.k12.sd.us
Chester ES 200/PK-6
PO Box 159 57016 605-489-2412
Faith Stratton, prin. Fax 489-2413
Chester JHS 100/7-8
PO Box 159 57016 605-489-2411
Michael Reinhiller, prin. Fax 489-2413

Other Schools – See Madison

Claremont, Brown, Pop. 125
Langford SD 45-2
Supt. — See Langford
Newport Colony S 50/K-8
11796 414th Ave 57432 605-493-6454
Monte Nipp, prin. Fax 493-6447

Clark, Clark, Pop. 1,186
Clark SD 12-2 400/PK-12
220 N Clinton St 57225 605-532-3603
Brian Heupel, supt. Fax 532-3600
clark.k12.sd.us/
Clark ES 100/PK-6
200 2nd Ave NW 57225 605-532-3606
Jerry Hartley, prin. Fax 532-3608
Clark JHS 100/7-8
220 N Clinton St 57225 605-532-3605
Brian Heupel, prin. Fax 532-3600
Other Schools – See Carpenter, Garden City

Clear Lake, Deuel, Pop. 1,243
Deuel SD 19-4 500/PK-12
PO Box 770 57226 605-874-2163
Dean Christensen, supt. Fax 874-8585
www.deuel.k12.sd.us/
Deuel ES 200/PK-5
PO Box 770 57226 605-874-2163
Tim Steffensen, prin. Fax 874-8585
Deuel MS 100/6-8
PO Box 770 57226 605-874-2163
Tim Steffensen, prin. Fax 874-8585

Colman, Moody, Pop. 559
Colman-Egan SD 50-5 300/K-12
PO Box I 57017 605-534-3534
Darold Rounds, supt. Fax 534-3670
www.colman-egan.k12.sd.us
Colman-Egan JHS 50/7-8
PO Box I 57017 605-534-3534
Terrance Stulken, prin. Fax 534-3670
Colman ES 100/K-6
PO Box I 57017 605-534-3534
Terrance Stulken, prin. Fax 534-3670

Colome, Tripp, Pop. 312
Colome SD 59-1 200/K-12
PO Box 367 57528 605-842-1624
Alan Armstrong, supt. Fax 842-0783
www.colome.k12.sd.us/
Colome ES 100/K-6
PO Box 367 57528 605-842-0583
Alan Armstrong, prin. Fax 842-0783
Colome JHS 50/7-8
PO Box 367 57528 605-842-1624
Alan Armstrong, prin. Fax 842-0783

Colton, Minnehaha, Pop. 658
Tri-Valley SD 49-6 900/PK-12
46450 252nd St 57018 605-446-3538
Terry Eckstaine, supt. Fax 446-3520
www.tri-valley.k12.sd.us/
Tri-Valley ES 500/PK-6
46450 252nd St 57018 605-446-3538
Marice Highstreet, prin. Fax 446-3520
Tri-Valley MS 100/7-8
46450 252nd St 57018 605-446-3538
Tim Pflanz, prin. Fax 446-3520

Conde, Spink, Pop. 171
Conde SD 56-1 100/PK-12
PO Box 10 57434 605-382-5231
Jerry McPartland, supt. Fax 382-5650
www.conde.k12.sd.us/
Conde ES 50/PK-6
PO Box 10 57434 605-382-5231
Matt Pollock, prin. Fax 382-5650
Conde JHS 50/7-8
PO Box 10 57434 605-382-5231
Matt Pollock, prin. Fax 382-5650

Corsica, Douglas, Pop. 625
Corsica SD 21-2 200/PK-12
120 S Napoleon Ave 57328 605-946-5475
Vern DeGeest, supt. Fax 946-5607
www.corsica.k12.sd.us
Corsica ES 100/PK-5
120 S Napoleon Ave 57328 605-946-5684
June Holbeck, prin. Fax 946-5607
Corsica MS 50/6-8
120 S Napoleon Ave 57328 605-946-5475
Brittney Eide, prin. Fax 946-5607

Dakota Christian S 100/PK-12
37614 SD Highway 44 57328 605-243-2211
Barry Miedema, prin. Fax 243-2379

Custer, Custer, Pop. 1,991
Custer SD 16-1 1,000/PK-12
147 N 5th St 57730 605-673-3154
Dr. Tim Creal, supt. Fax 673-5607
www.csd.k12.sd.us
Custer ES 300/PK-5
371 Crook St 57730 605-673-4483
Carol Veit, prin. Fax 673-4515
Custer MS 200/6-8
527 Montgomery St 57730 605-673-4540
Eric Pingrey, prin. Fax 673-3079
Other Schools – See Fairburn, Hermosa

Deadwood, Lawrence, Pop. 1,296
Lead-Deadwood SD 40-1
Supt. — See Lead
Lead-Deadwood ES 300/PK-5
716 Main St 57732 605-717-3884
Tim Kosters, prin. Fax 717-2823

Dell Rapids, Minnehaha, Pop. 3,188
Dell Rapids SD 49-3 900/PK-12
1216 N Garfield Ave 57022 605-428-5473
Thomas Ludens, supt. Fax 428-5609
www.dellrapids.k12.sd.us/district
Dell Rapids ES 300/PK-4
1216 N Garfield Ave 57022 605-428-3192
Dr. John Jewett, prin. Fax 428-5631
Dell Rapids MS 300/5-8
1216 N Garfield Ave 57022 605-428-5473
Fran Ruesink, prin. Fax 428-5609

St. Mary S 100/PK-6
812 N State Ave 57022 605-428-3459
Kelly Neill, prin. Fax 428-5377

De Smet, Kingsbury, Pop. 1,089
De Smet SD 38-2 300/K-12
PO Box 157 57231 605-854-3423
Jim Altenburg, admin. Fax 854-9138
www.desmet.k12.sd.us
De Smet MS 100/6-8
PO Box 157 57231 605-854-3423
Jim Altenburg, prin. Fax 854-9138
Wilder ES 100/K-5
PO Box 157 57231 605-854-3963
Jay Nelson, prin. Fax 854-9138

Doland, Spink, Pop. 270
Doland SD 56-2 200/K-12
PO Box 385 57436 605-635-6302
Jerry McPartland, supt. Fax 635-6504
www.doland.k12.sd.us/
Doland ES 50/K-6
PO Box 385 57436 605-635-6241
Jim Hulscher, prin. Fax 635-6504
Doland JHS 50/7-8
PO Box 385 57436 605-635-6241
Jim Hulscher, prin. Fax 635-6504
Hillside Colony S 50/K-8
18248 Hillside Ln 57436 605-635-5302
Jerry McPartland, prin. Fax 635-6504
Other Schools – See Raymond

Dupree, Ziebach, Pop. 450
Dupree SD 64-2 300/PK-12
PO Box 10 57623 605-365-5140
Bruce Johnson, supt. Fax 365-5514
www.dupree.k12.sd.us/
Dupree ES 200/PK-6
PO Box 10 57623 605-365-5140
Wayne Blankenbiller, prin. Fax 365-5514
Dupree JHS 100/7-8
PO Box 10 57623 605-365-5140
Quinn Lenk, prin. Fax 365-5514

Eagle Butte, Dewey, Pop. 1,817
Eagle Butte SD 20-1 400/K-12
PO Box 260 57625 605-964-4911
Dr. Edward Slocum, supt. Fax 964-4912
Eagle Butte JHS 100/7-8
PO Box 672 57625 605-964-7841
Jesse Mendoza, prin. Fax 964-1224
Eagle Butte Lower ES 3-4
PO Box 260 57625 605-964-2702
Cindy Lindskov, prin. Fax 964-6779
Eagle Butte PS 100/K-2
PO Box 672 57625 605-964-7920
Kevin White Bull, prin. Fax 964-7923
Eagle Butte Upper ES 100/5-6
PO Box 260 57625 605-964-2702
Cora Petersen, prin. Fax 964-4912

Edgemont, Fall River, Pop. 823
Edgemont SD 23-1 200/K-12
PO Box 29 57735 605-662-7294
David Cortney, supt. Fax 662-7721
edgemont.k12.sd.us
Edgemont ES 100/K-6
PO Box 29 57735 605-662-7254
David Cortney, dean Fax 662-7721
Edgemont JHS 50/7-8
PO Box 29 57735 605-662-7254
Linda Tidball, dean Fax 662-7721

Elk Mountain SD 16-2 50/K-6
10222 Valley Rd 57735 605-749-2258
Gloria Schaffer, supt. Fax 749-2258
Elk Mountain ES 50/K-6
10222 Valley Rd 57735 605-749-2258
Gloria Schaffer, prin. Fax 749-2258

Elk Point, Union, Pop. 1,836
Elk Point-Jefferson SD 61-7 700/PK-12
PO Box 578 57025 605-356-5950
Brian Shanks, supt. Fax 356-5953
www.epj.k12.sd.us/
Elk Point-Jefferson ES 400/PK-6
PO Box 578 57025 605-356-5800
Douglas Brusseau, prin. Fax 356-5802
Elk Point-Jefferson MS 100/7-8
PO Box 578 57025 605-356-5900
Janet Ries, prin. Fax 356-5999

Elkton, Brookings, Pop. 619
Elkton SD 5-3 300/K-12
PO Box 190 57026 605-542-5361
Tony Simons, supt. Fax 542-4441
elkton.k12.sd.us
Elkton ES 100/K-6
PO Box 190 57026 605-542-2541
Brian Jandahl, prin. Fax 542-4441
Elkton JHS 50/7-8
PO Box 190 57026 605-542-2541
Brian Jandahl, prin. Fax 542-4441
Newdale Colony S 50/K-8
21336 484th Ave 57026 605-542-2541
Brian Jandahl, prin. Fax 542-4441
Other Schools – See White

Emery, Hanson, Pop. 526
Emery SD 30-2 200/PK-12
PO Box 265 57332 605-449-4271
Jason Bailey, supt. Fax 449-4270
www.emery.k12.sd.us/
Emery ES 100/PK-5
PO Box 265 57332 605-449-4271
Kim Aman, prin. Fax 449-4270
Emery JHS 50/6-8
PO Box 265 57332 605-449-4271
Christena Schultz, prin. Fax 449-4270

Enning, Meade
Meade SD 46-1
Supt. — See Sturgis
Enning S 50/K-8
Highway 34 Box 22 57737 605-269-2264
Bev Rosenboom, prin. Fax 269-2099

Estelline, Hamlin, Pop. 687
Estelline SD 28-2 200/K-12
PO Box 306 57234 605-873-2201
Chip Sundberg, supt. Fax 873-2102
www.estelline.k12.sd.us
Estelline S 100/K-8
PO Box 306 57234 605-873-2203
Sharon Delzer, prin. Fax 873-2102

Ethan, Davison, Pop. 318
Ethan SD 17-1 200/PK-12
PO Box 169 57334 605-227-4211
Terry Mathis, supt. Fax 227-4236
www.ethan.k12.sd.us/
Ethan ES 100/PK-5
PO Box 169 57334 605-227-4211
Joel Bergeson, prin. Fax 227-4236
Ethan MS 50/6-8
PO Box 169 57334 605-227-4211
Joel Bergeson, prin. Fax 227-4236

Parkston SD 33-3
Supt. — See Parkston
New Elm Spring Colony S 50/K-8
41844 269th St 57334 605-928-3040
Robert Monson, prin. Fax 928-7284

Eureka, McPherson, Pop. 988
Eureka SD 44-1 200/K-12
PO Box 10 57437 605-284-2875
Bo Beck, supt. Fax 284-2810
www.eureka.k12.sd.us/
Eureka ES 100/K-6
PO Box 10 57437 605-284-2875
Bo Beck, prin. Fax 284-2810
Eureka JHS 50/7-8
PO Box 10 57437 605-284-2521
Bo Beck, prin. Fax 284-2810

Fairburn, Custer, Pop. 80
Custer SD 16-1
Supt. — See Custer
Fairburn S 50/K-8
PO Box 135 57738 605-255-4349
Chip Franke, prin. Fax 255-4590

Faith, Meade, Pop. 474
Faith SD 46-2 200/K-12
PO Box 619 57626 605-967-2152
Mel Dutton, supt. Fax 967-2153
www.faith.k12.sd.us/
Faith ES 100/K-6
PO Box 619 57626 605-967-2152
Michelle Becker, prin. Fax 967-2153
Faith JHS 50/7-8
PO Box 619 57626 605-967-2152
Michelle Becker, prin. Fax 967-2153
Maurine S 50/K-8
PO Box 619 57626 605-967-2152
Michelle Becker, prin. Fax 967-2153

Faulkton, Faulk, Pop. 703
Faulkton Area SD 24-3 300/K-12
PO Box 308 57438 605-598-6266
Joel Price, supt. Fax 598-6666
www.faulkton.k12.sd.us
Brentwood S 50/K-8
15442 343rd Ave 57438 605-598-4333
Jennifer Knecht, prin. Fax 598-6576
Evergreen Colony S 50/K-8
35691 156th St 57438 605-324-3303
Jennifer Knecht, prin.
Faulkton ES 100/K-6
PO Box 308 57438 605-598-6266
Joel Price, prin. Fax 598-6666
Faulkton JHS 50/7-8
PO Box 308 57438 605-598-6266
Craig Cassens, prin. Fax 598-6666

Other Schools – See Wecota

Flandreau, Moody, Pop. 2,327
Flandreau SD 50-3 600/K-12
600 W Community Dr 57028 605-997-3263
Rick Weber, supt. Fax 997-2457
www.flandreau.k12.sd.us
Flandreau ES 300/K-5
500 W Community Dr 57028 605-997-2780
Brad Olinger, prin. Fax 997-2457
Flandreau MS 100/6-8
700 W Community Dr 57028 605-997-2705
Brian Relf, prin. Fax 997-2457
Pleasant Valley S 50/K-8
22941 487th Ave 57028 605-997-2780
Brad Olinger, prin. Fax 997-2559

Florence, Codington, Pop. 297
Florence SD 14-1 200/PK-12
PO Box 66 57235 605-758-2412
Gary Leighton, supt. Fax 758-2433
www.florence.k12.sd.us/
Florence ES 100/PK-6
PO Box 66 57235 605-758-2412
Jean Case, lead tchr. Fax 758-2433
Florence JHS 50/7-8
PO Box 66 57235 605-758-2412
Gary Leighton, prin. Fax 758-2433

Forestburg, Sanborn
Sanborn Central SD 55-5 200/K-12
40405 SD Highway 34 57314 605-495-4183
Linda Whitney, supt. Fax 495-4185
www.sanborncentral.com/
Sanborn Central ES 100/K-5
40405 SD Highway 34 57314 605-495-4183
Connie Vermeulen, prin. Fax 495-4185
Sanborn Central MS 50/6-8
40405 SD Highway 34 57314 605-495-4183
Connie Vermeulen, prin. Fax 495-4185
Upland Colony S 50/K-8
40405 SD Highway 34 57314 605-495-4183
Connie Vermeulen, prin. Fax 495-4185

Fort Pierre, Stanley, Pop. 2,069
Stanley County SD 57-1 400/K-12
PO Box 370 57532 605-223-7741
Don Hotalling, supt. Fax 223-7750
www.stanleycounty.k12.sd.us
Orton S 50/K-8
PO Box 370 57532 605-223-7745
Merry Bleeker, prin. Fax 223-7760
Parkview ES 3-5
PO Box 370 57532 605-223-7745
Merry Bleeker, prin. Fax 223-7760
Stanley County ES 100/K-2
PO Box 370 57532 605-223-7745
Merry Bleeker, prin. Fax 223-7760
Stanley County MS 100/6-8
PO Box 370 57532 605-223-7743
Brian Doherty, prin. Fax 223-7751
Other Schools – See Hayes

Frankfort, Spink, Pop. 152
Hitchcock-Tulare SD 56-6
Supt. — See Tulare
Hitchcock-Tulare Glendale Colony S 50/K-8
17866 Glendale Dr 57440 605-596-4171
Scott Pudwill, prin. Fax 596-4175
Hitchcock-Tulare Spink Colony S 100/K-8
18206 Spink Ln 57440 605-596-4171
Scott Pudwill, prin. Fax 596-4175

Frederick, Brown, Pop. 243
Frederick Area SD 6-2 200/PK-12
PO Box 486 57441 605-329-2145
Randall Barondeau, supt. Fax 329-2722
www.frederickarea.k12.sd.us/
Frederick ES 100/PK-6
PO Box 486 57441 605-329-2145
Ann Hegge, prin. Fax 329-2722
Frederick JHS 50/7-8
PO Box 486 57441 605-329-2145
Randy Barondeau, prin. Fax 329-2722

Freeman, Hutchinson, Pop. 1,223
Freeman SD 33-1 400/K-12
PO Box 220 57029 605-925-4214
Don Hotchkiss, supt. Fax 925-4814
www.freeman.k12.sd.us/
Freeman ES 200/K-6
PO Box 220 57029 605-925-4216
Ryan Mors, prin. Fax 925-4814
Freeman JHS 50/7-8
PO Box 220 57029 605-925-4214
Kim Krull, prin. Fax 925-4814
Other Schools – See Olivet

Garden City, Clark, Pop. 65
Clark SD 12-2
Supt. — See Clark
Hillcrest Colony S 50/K-8
1024 Hillcrest Dr 57236 605-532-3606
Jerry Hartley, prin. Fax 532-3608

Garretson, Minnehaha, Pop. 1,152
Garretson SD 49-4 500/PK-12
PO Box C 57030 605-594-3451
Robert Arend, supt. Fax 594-3443
www.garretson.k12.sd.us/
Garretson ES 300/PK-5
PO Box C 57030 605-594-3453
Teresa Johnson, prin. Fax 594-3443

Garretson MS 100/6-8
PO Box C 57030 605-594-3452
Chris Long, prin. Fax 594-3443

Gayville, Yankton, Pop. 393
Gayville-Volin SD 63-1 300/K-12
PO Box 158 57031 605-267-4476
Jason Selchert, supt. Fax 267-4294
www.gayvillevolin.k12.sd.us/
Gayville-Volin ES 100/K-5
PO Box 158 57031 605-267-4476
Jesse Sealey, prin. Fax 267-4294
Gayville-Volin MS 100/6-8
PO Box 158 57031 605-267-4476
Tom Rice, prin. Fax 267-4294

Gettysburg, Potter, Pop. 1,169
Gettysburg SD 53-1 300/K-12
100 E King Ave 57442 605-765-2436
Jeff Marlette, supt. Fax 765-2249
www.gettysburg.k12.sd.us/
Gettysburg ES 100/K-5
100 E King Ave 57442 605-765-2436
Jeff Marlette, prin. Fax 765-2249
Gettysburg JHS 50/6-8
100 E King Ave 57442 605-765-2436
Scott Kortan, prin. Fax 765-2249

Gregory, Gregory, Pop. 1,186
Gregory SD 26-4 400/K-12
PO Box 438 57533 605-835-8771
David Nicholas, supt. Fax 835-8744
www.gregory.k12.sd.us/
Gregory ES 200/K-5
PO Box 438 57533 605-835-8771
David Nicholas, prin. Fax 835-8744
Gregory MS 100/6-8
PO Box 438 57533 605-835-9672
Michael Dacy, prin. Fax 835-8146

Groton, Brown, Pop. 1,365
Groton Area SD 6-6 600/PK-12
PO Box 410 57445 605-397-2351
Laura Schuster, supt. Fax 397-8453
www.groton.k12.sd.us/
Groton ES 300/PK-6
PO Box 410 57445 605-397-2317
Susan Foster, prin. Fax 397-2344
Groton JHS 100/7-8
PO Box 410 57445 605-397-8381
Todd Sweeter, prin. Fax 397-8453

Hamill, Tripp
Winner SD 59-2
Supt. — See Winner
Hamill S 50/K-8
31905 Dejong Rd 57534 605-842-8125
Bill Kaiser, prin. Fax 842-8121

Harrisburg, Lincoln, Pop. 1,875
Harrisburg SD 41-2 1,500/PK-12
PO Box 187 57032 605-743-2567
James Holbeck, supt. Fax 743-2569
www.harrisburg.k12.sd.us
Harrisburg Liberty ES 400/PK-5
PO Box 306 57032 605-743-2567
Tanja Pederson, prin. Fax 743-2569
Harrisburg MS 300/6-8
PO Box 309 57032 605-743-2567
Rich Schneider, prin. Fax 743-2569
Other Schools – See Sioux Falls

Harrold, Hughes, Pop. 206
Highmore-Harrold SD 34-2
Supt. — See Highmore
Harrold ES 50/K-6
206 S Nixon St 57536 605-852-2276

Hartford, Minnehaha, Pop. 2,065
West Central SD 49-7 1,100/PK-12
PO Box 730 57033 605-528-3217
Jeff Danielsen, supt. Fax 528-3219
www.westcentral.k12.sd.us/
Hartford ES 200/PK-2
PO Box 730 57033 605-528-3215
Dianna Tyler, prin. Fax 528-3399
West Central MS 300/6-8
PO Box 730 57033 605-528-3799
Guy Johnson, prin. Fax 528-3702
Other Schools – See Humboldt

Hayes, Stanley
Stanley County SD 57-1
Supt. — See Fort Pierre
Cheyenne S 50/K-8
24882 196th St 57537 605-223-7745
Merry Bleeker, prin. Fax 223-7760
Hayes S 50/K-8
25431 US Highway 14/34 57537 605-223-7745
Merry Bleeker, prin. Fax 223-7760

Hayti, Hamlin, Pop. 362
Hamlin SD 28-3 600/PK-12
44577 188th St 57241 605-783-3631
Joel Jorgenson, supt. Fax 783-3632
www.hamlin.k12.sd.us/
Hamlin ES 300/PK-6
44577 188th St 57241 605-783-3631
Mary Pietila, prin. Fax 783-3632
Hamlin MS 100/7-8
44577 188th St 57241 605-783-3631
Richard Schneider, prin. Fax 783-3632

Henry, Codington, Pop. 258
Henry SD 14-2 200/K-12
PO Box 8 57243 605-532-5364
Brian Sieh, supt. Fax 532-3795
www.henry.k12.sd.us/
Henry ES 100/K-5
PO Box 8 57243 605-532-5364
Brian Sieh, prin. Fax 532-3795
Henry JHS 50/6-8
PO Box 8 57243 605-532-5364
Joel Hedtke, prin. Fax 532-5364

Hereford, Meade
Meade SD 46-1
Supt. — See Sturgis
Hereford S 50/K-8
15998 Cross S Rd 57785 605-269-2264
Bev Rosenboom, prin. Fax 269-2099

Hermosa, Custer, Pop. 335
Custer SD 16-1
Supt. — See Custer
Hermosa S 100/K-8
PO Box 27 57744 605-255-4345
Chip Franke, prin. Fax 255-4190
Spring Creek S 50/K-8
15942 Lower Spring Creek Rd 57744 605-255-4171
Chip Franke, prin. Fax 255-4560

Shannon County SD 65-1
Supt. — See Batesland
Red Shirt S 50/K-8
HC 83 Box 313 57744 605-255-4224
Barbara Ice, prin. Fax 255-5396

Herreid, Campbell, Pop. 415
Herreid SD 10-1 100/K-12
PO Box 276 57632 605-437-2263
Jack Adkins, supt. Fax 437-2264
Herreid ES 100/K-5
PO Box 276 57632 605-437-2263
Jack Adkins, prin. Fax 437-2264
Herreid JHS 50/6-8
PO Box 276 57632 605-437-2263
Steve Volk, prin. Fax 437-2264

Highmore, Hyde, Pop. 808
Highmore-Harrold SD 34-2 300/PK-12
PO Box 416 57345 605-852-2275
Elsie Baye, supt. Fax 852-2295
www.highmore.k12.sd.us/
Highmore ES 100/PK-6
PO Box 416 57345 605-852-2276
Elsie Baye, prin. Fax 852-2295
Highmore JHS 50/7-8
PO Box 416 57345 605-852-2275
James Jones, prin. Fax 852-2295
Other Schools – See Harrold

Hill City, Pennington, Pop. 846
Hill City SD 51-2 500/PK-12
PO Box 659 57745 605-574-3030
Mark Naugle, supt. Fax 574-3031
www.hillcity.k12.sd.us
Hill City ES 200/PK-5
PO Box 659 57745 605-574-3015
Dave Larson, prin. Fax 574-3028
Hill City MS 100/6-8
PO Box 659 57745 605-574-3005
Todd Satter, prin. Fax 574-3040

Hitchcock, Beadle, Pop. 100
Hitchcock-Tulare SD 56-6
Supt. — See Tulare
Hitchcock-Tulare ES 50/K-6
235 Palm St 57348 605-266-2151
Scott Pudwill, prin. Fax 266-2160

Hot Springs, Fall River, Pop. 4,102
Hot Springs SD 23-2 900/PK-12
1609 University Ave 57747 605-745-4145
Dr. Donald Marchant, supt. Fax 745-4178
www.hssd.k12.sd.us
Hot Springs ES 400/PK-5
1609 University Ave 57747 605-745-4149
Lynette Powell, prin. Fax 745-4165
Hot Springs MS 200/6-8
1609 University Ave 57747 605-745-4146
John Fitzgerald, prin. Fax 745-6387

Bethesda Lutheran S 50/PK-5
1537 Baltimore Ave 57747 605-745-6676
Carol Hagedorn, dean Fax 745-6676

Hoven, Potter, Pop. 436
Hoven SD 53-2 100/K-12
PO Box 128 57450 605-948-2252
Peggy Petersen, supt. Fax 948-2477
www.hoven.k12.sd.us/
Hoven ES 100/K-6
PO Box 188 57450 605-948-2252
Peggy Petersen, prin. Fax 948-2477
Hoven JHS 50/7-8
PO Box 128 57450 605-948-2252
Peggy Petersen, prin. Fax 948-2477

Howard, Miner, Pop. 945
Howard SD 48-3 400/PK-12
500 N Section Line St 57349 605-772-5515
Mike Cullen, supt. Fax 772-5516
www.howard.k12.sd.us/
Howard ES 200/PK-6
201 N Minnie St 57349 605-772-4443
Christopher Noid, prin. Fax 772-4445
Howard JHS 100/7-8
500 N Section Line St 57349 605-772-5515
Mike Cullen, prin. Fax 772-5516
Shannon Colony S 50/K-8
43955 SD Highway 34, 605-772-4443
Christopher Noid, prin. Fax 772-4445

Humboldt, Minnehaha, Pop. 549
West Central SD 49-7
Supt. — See Hartford
Humboldt ES 300/K-5
PO Box 136 57035 605-363-3131
Jill Olson, prin. Fax 363-3818

Hurley, Turner, Pop. 399
Hurley SD 60-2 200/K-12
PO Box 278 57036 605-238-5221
Shane Voss, supt. Fax 238-5223
www.hurleybulldogs.com/
Hurley ES 100/K-6
PO Box 278 57036 605-238-5221
Shane Voss, prin. Fax 238-5223
Hurley JHS 50/7-8
PO Box 278 57036 605-238-5221
Barb Hansen, prin. Fax 238-5223

Huron, Beadle, Pop. 11,086
Huron SD 2-2 2,000/K-12
PO Box 949 57350 605-353-6990
Ross Opsal, supt. Fax 353-6993
www.huron.k12.sd.us
Buchanan ES 100/K-5
5 Mellette Ave SW 57350 605-353-7875
Heather Rozell, prin. Fax 353-7877
Huron Colony S 50/K-8
RR 1 57350 605-353-6978
Heather Rozell, prin. Fax 353-6993
Huron MS 500/6-8
1045 18th St SW 57350 605-353-6900
Michael Taplett, prin. Fax 353-6913
Jefferson ES 100/K-5
855 Utah Ave SE 57350 605-353-7880
Beth Foss, prin. Fax 353-7883
Madison ES 200/K-5
1634 Idaho Ave SE 57350 605-353-7885
Heather Rozell, prin. Fax 353-7888
Riverside Colony S 50/K-8
RR 1 57350 605-353-6980
Heather Rozell, prin. Fax 353-6993
Washington ES 300/K-5
1451 McClellan Dr 57350 605-353-7895
Beth Foss, prin. Fax 353-7898

Holy Trinity S 100/PK-5
425 21st St SW 57350 605-352-9344
Michelle Schoenfelder, prin. Fax 352-0889
James Valley Christian S 100/PK-12
1550 Dakota Ave N 57350 605-352-7737
Jim Friesen, supt. Fax 352-9893

Interior, Jackson, Pop. 77
Kadoka Area SD 35-2
Supt. — See Kadoka
Interior S 50/PK-8
PO Box 1 57750 605-837-2173
Roger Jensen, prin. Fax 837-2176

Ipswich, Edmunds, Pop. 887
Ipswich SD 22-6 400/PK-12
PO Box 306 57451 605-426-6561
Mark DeGroot, supt. Fax 426-6029
www.ipswich.k12.sd.us/
Deerfield Colony S 50/PK-8
PO Box 306 57451 605-426-6832
Camille Geditz, prin. Fax 426-6029
Ipswich ES 100/PK-6
PO Box 306 57451 605-426-6832
Camille Geditz, prin. Fax 426-6029
Ipswich JHS 50/7-8
PO Box 306 57451 605-426-6571
Trent Osborne, prin. Fax 426-6029
Pembrook Colony S 50/PK-8
PO Box 306 57451 605-426-6832
Camille Geditz, prin. Fax 426-6029
Other Schools – See Leola

Holy Cross S 50/PK-6
PO Box 324 57451 605-426-6222
Diane Geditz, prin. Fax 426-6588

Irene, Yankton, Pop. 410
Irene-Wakonda SD 13-3 100/PK-12
PO Box 5 57037 605-263-3311
Larry Johnke, supt. Fax 263-3316
www.irene-wakonda.k12.sd.us/
Other Schools – See Wakonda

Iroquois, Kingsbury, Pop. 258
Iroquois SD 2-3 200/K-12
PO Box 98 57353 605-546-2210
Mark Sampson, supt. Fax 546-8540
www.iroquois.k12.sd.us/
Iroquois ES 100/K-5
PO Box 98 57353 605-546-2262
Mark Sampson, prin. Fax 546-8540
Iroquois MS 50/6-8
PO Box 98 57353 605-546-2426
Rick Soma, prin. Fax 546-8540

Pearl Creek Colony S 50/K-8
PO Box 98 57353 605-546-2210
Mark Sampson, prin. Fax 546-8540

Jefferson, Union, Pop. 590

St. Peter S 50/PK-PK
PO Box 98 57038 605-966-5529
Erin Hammitt, prin. Fax 966-5746

Kadoka, Jackson, Pop. 668
Kadoka Area SD 35-2 400/PK-12
PO Box 99 57543 605-837-2175
Mary Austad, supt. Fax 837-2176
kadoka.k12.sd.us/
Kadoka S 200/PK-8
PO Box 99 57543 605-837-2173
Roger Jensen, prin. Fax 837-2176
Other Schools – See Interior, Longvalley, Midland

Kennebec, Lyman, Pop. 284
Lyman SD 42-1
Supt. — See Presho
Kennebec ES 100/K-5
PO Box 188 57544 605-869-2213
Doug Eppard, prin. Fax 869-2283
Lyman MS 100/6-8
PO Box 188 57544 605-869-2213
Doug Eppard, prin. Fax 869-2283

Kimball, Brule, Pop. 693
Kimball SD 7-2 200/K-12
PO Box 479 57355 605-778-6232
Bill Thompson, supt. Fax 778-6393
www.kimball.k12.sd.us
Grass Ranch S 50/K-8
PO Box 479 57355 605-778-6231
Sheri Hardman, prin. Fax 778-6393
Kimball ES 100/K-6
PO Box 479 57355 605-778-6231
Sheri Hardman, prin. Fax 778-6393
Kimball JHS 50/7-8
PO Box 479 57355 605-778-6231
Sheri Hardman, prin. Fax 778-6393

Kranzburg, Codington, Pop. 179

Holy Rosary S 50/PK-6
PO Box 137 57245 605-886-8114
Carolyn Westby, prin. Fax 886-2715

Lake Andes, Charles Mix, Pop. 783
Andes Central SD 11-1 400/PK-12
PO Box 40 57356 605-487-7671
Darrell Mueller, supt. Fax 487-7051
www.andescentral.k12.sd.us/
Andes Central ES 200/PK-6
PO Box 67 57356 605-487-5243
William Kitchenmaster, prin. Fax 487-7656
Andes Central JHS 100/7-8
PO Box 40 57356 605-487-5207
Rocky Brinkman, prin. Fax 487-7051
Lakeview Colony S 50/PK-9
PO Box 67 57356 605-487-7655
William Kitchenmaster, prin. Fax 487-7671

Lake Preston, Kingsbury, Pop. 677
Lake Preston SD 38-3 200/K-12
300 1st St NE 57249 605-847-4455
Tim Casper, supt. Fax 847-4311
www.lakepreston.k12.sd.us
Lake Preston ES 100/K-6
300 1st St NE 57249 605-847-4464
Joan Olson, prin. Fax 847-4311
Lake Preston JHS 50/7-8
300 1st St NE 57249 605-847-4455
Tim Casper, prin. Fax 847-4311

Langford, Marshall, Pop. 283
Langford SD 45-2 200/K-12
PO Box 127 57454 605-493-6454
Monte Nipp, supt. Fax 493-6447
www.langford.k12.sd.us/
Langford ES 100/K-6
PO Box 127 57454 605-493-6454
Monte Nipp, prin. Fax 493-6447
Langford JHS 50/7-8
PO Box 127 57454 605-493-6454
Toni Brown, prin. Fax 493-6447
Other Schools – See Claremont

Lead, Lawrence, Pop. 2,891
Lead-Deadwood SD 40-1 800/PK-12
320 S Main St 57754 605-717-3890
Dr. Dan Leikvold, supt. Fax 717-2813
www.lead-deadwood.k12.sd.us/
Lead-Deadwood MS 200/6-8
234 S Main St 57754 605-717-3898
Nick Gottlob, prin. Fax 717-2821
Other Schools – See Deadwood

Lemmon, Perkins, Pop. 1,229
Lemmon SD 52-2 300/PK-12
209 3rd St W 57638 605-374-3762
Rick Herbel, supt. Fax 374-3562
www.lemmon.k12.sd.us
Lemmon ES 100/PK-6
905 5th Ave W 57638 605-374-3784
Linda O'Donnell, prin. Fax 374-3562
Lemmon JHS 100/7-8
209 3rd St W 57638 605-374-3762
Rick Herbel, prin. Fax 374-3562
Other Schools – See Meadow

Lennox, Lincoln, Pop. 2,092
Lennox SD 41-4 900/PK-12
PO Box 38 57039 605-647-2202
Pat Jones, supt. Fax 647-2201
www.lennox.k12.sd.us
Lennox ES 200/PK-5
PO Box 38 57039 605-647-2204
Kym Johnston, prin. Fax 647-6043
Lennox MS 200/6-8
PO Box 38 57039 605-647-2204
Darren Ellwein, prin. Fax 647-6043
Other Schools – See Chancellor, Worthing

Leola, McPherson, Pop. 411
Ipswich SD 22-6
Supt. — See Ipswich
Rosette Colony S 50/PK-8
12465 359th Ave 57456 605-426-6832
Camille Geditz, prin. Fax 426-6029

Leola SD 44-2 300/PK-12
PO Box 350 57456 605-439-3143
Jamie Hermann, supt. Fax 439-3206
www.leola.k12.sd.us/
Leola ES 100/PK-6
PO Box 350 57456 605-439-3143
Jamie Hermann, prin. Fax 439-3206
Leola JHS 50/7-8
PO Box 350 57456 605-439-3143
Brett Schwann, prin. Fax 439-3206
Other Schools – See Westport, Wetonka

Longvalley, Jackson
Kadoka Area SD 35-2
Supt. — See Kadoka
Longvalley S 50/K-8
PO Box 25, 605-837-2173
Roger Jensen, prin. Fax 837-2176

Ludlow, Harding
Harding County SD 31-1
Supt. — See Buffalo
Ludlow S 50/K-8
HC 63 57755 605-375-3241
Josh Page, prin. Fax 375-3246

Mc Intosh, Corson, Pop. 302
Mc Intosh SD 15-1 200/PK-12
PO Box 80 57641 605-273-4227
Dick Schaffan, supt. Fax 273-4531
www.mcintosh.k12.sd.us/
Mc Intosh ES 100/PK-6
PO Box 80 57641 605-273-4227
Brad Zachow, prin. Fax 273-4531
Mc Intosh JHS 50/7-8
PO Box 80 57641 605-273-4227
Dick Schaffan, prin. Fax 273-4531

Mc Laughlin, Corson, Pop. 799
Mc Laughlin SD 15-2 500/PK-12
PO Box 880 57642 605-823-4484
Lorie Hach, supt. Fax 823-4886
www.mclaughlin.k12.sd.us/
Mc Laughlin ES 200/PK-5
PO Box 880 57642 605-823-4483
Michael Donner, prin. Fax 823-4886
Mc Laughlin MS 100/6-8
PO Box 880 57642 605-823-4484
Robin Cook, prin. Fax 823-4886

Madison, Lake, Pop. 6,223
Chester Area SD 39-1
Supt. — See Chester
Rustic Acres S 50/K-8
24243 40056th Ave 57042 605-489-2412
Faith Stratton, prin. Fax 489-2413

Madison Central SD 39-2 700/K-12
800 NE 9th St 57042 605-256-7700
Vincent Schaefer, supt. Fax 256-7711
www.madison.k12.sd.us
Madison ES K-5
700 NW 9th St 57042 605-256-7721
Daniel Walsh, prin. Fax 256-7729
Madison MS 300/6-8
830 NE 9th St 57042 605-256-7717
Cotton Koch, prin. Fax 256-7728
Other Schools – See Winfred

St. Thomas S 100/PK-5
401 N Van Eps Ave 57042 605-256-4419
Colleen Davis, prin. Fax 256-3953

Marion, Turner, Pop. 833
Marion SD 60-3 200/PK-12
PO Box 207 57043 605-648-3615
Denise Fox, supt. Fax 648-3652
www.marion.k12.sd.us
Marion ES 100/PK-6
PO Box 207 57043 605-648-3615
Denise Fox, prin. Fax 648-3652
Marion JHS 50/7-8
PO Box 207 57043 605-648-3615
Adam Shaw, prin. Fax 648-3617

Martin, Bennett, Pop. 1,048
Bennett County SD 3-1 500/K-12
PO Box 580 57551 605-685-6697
Wayne Semmler, supt. Fax 685-6694
www.bennettco.k12.sd.us/
Bennett County JHS 100/7-8
PO Box 580 57551 605-685-6330
James Rotert, prin. Fax 685-6935

Martin ES 300/K-6
PO Box 580 57551 605-685-6717
Belinda Ready, prin. Fax 685-6147

Meadow, Perkins
Lemmon SD 52-2
Supt. — See Lemmon
Progress S 50/K-8
19327 SD Highway 20 57644 605-374-3784
Linda O'Donnell, prin. Fax 374-3562

Mellette, Spink, Pop. 227
Northwestern Area SD 56-7 300/PK-12
PO Box 45 57461 605-887-3467
Ray Sauerwein, supt. Fax 887-3101
www.northwestern.k12.sd.us
Northwestern ES 100/PK-5
PO Box 45 57461 605-887-3467
Richard Osborn, prin. Fax 887-3101
Northwestern MS 100/6-8
PO Box 45 57461 605-887-3467
Richard Osborn, prin. Fax 887-3101

Menno, Hutchinson, Pop. 697
Menno SD 33-2 300/PK-12
PO Box 346 57045 605-387-5161
Dr. Chris Christensen, supt. Fax 387-5171
www.menno.k12.sd.us/
Menno ES 100/PK-5
PO Box 346 57045 605-387-5161
Terry Quam, prin. Fax 387-5171
Menno MS 100/6-8
PO Box 346 57045 605-387-5161
Terry Quam, prin. Fax 387-5171
Other Schools – See Scotland, Utica

Midland, Haakon, Pop. 158
Kadoka Area SD 35-2
Supt. — See Kadoka
Midland ES 50/K-6
PO Box 226 57552 605-843-2561
Roger Jensen, prin. Fax 843-2562

Milbank, Grant, Pop. 3,357
Milbank SD 25-4 800/PK-12
1001 E Park Ave 57252 605-432-5579
Marlin Smart, supt. Fax 432-4137
www.milbank.k12.sd.us
Koch ES 400/PK-6
400 E 10th Ave 57252 605-432-6730
Merlin Smart, prin. Fax 432-6286
Milbank MS 100/7-8
1001 E Park Ave 57252 605-432-5510
Dan Snaza, prin. Fax 432-6610

St. Lawrence S 100/PK-6
113 S 6th St 57252 605-432-5673
Sheryl Monson, prin. Fax 432-5846

Milesville, Haakon
Haakon SD 27-1
Supt. — See Philip
Cheyenne S 50/K-8
21380 SD Hwy 34 57553 605-859-2001
Keven Morehart, prin. Fax 859-3005
Milesville S 50/K-8
22061 200th St 57553 605-859-2001
Keven Morehart, prin. Fax 859-3005

Millboro, Tripp
Winner SD 59-2
Supt. — See Winner
Millboro S 50/K-8
29877 310th Ave 57580 605-842-8101
Judy Audiss, prin. Fax 842-8120

Miller, Hand, Pop. 1,364
Miller SD 29-4 500/PK-12
PO Box 257 57362 605-853-2614
Michael Ruth, supt. Fax 853-3041
www.miller.k12.sd.us/
Millerdale Colony S 50/K-8
PO Box 257 57362 605-853-2711
Shawn Oligmueller, prin. Fax 853-3041
Miller ES 200/PK-6
PO Box 257 57362 605-853-2711
Shawn Oligmueller, prin. Fax 853-3041
Miller JHS 100/7-8
PO Box 257 57362 605-853-2455
Gerry Hunter, prin. Fax 853-3041

Sunshine Bible Academy 100/K-12
400 Sunshine Dr 57362 605-853-3071
Larry Mehlhaff, supt. Fax 853-3072

Mission, Todd, Pop. 949
Todd County SD 66-1 1,900/PK-12
PO Box 87 57555 605-856-4457
Margo Heinert, supt. Fax 856-2449
www.tcsdk12.org/
North ES 300/K-3
PO Box 308 57555 605-856-4561
Karen Fox, prin. Fax 856-2432
South ES 200/4-5
PO Box 48 57555 605-856-4812
Patrice Wright, prin. Fax 856-2136
Todd County MS 400/6-8
PO Box 248 57555 605-856-2341
Peggy Diekhoff, prin. Fax 856-2032
Other Schools – See O Kreek, Parmelee, Rosebud, Saint Francis

White Eagle Christian Academy 50/PK-8
PO Box 1326 57555 605-856-2476
Jack Moore, pres. Fax 856-2194

Mitchell, Davison, Pop. 14,696
Hanson SD 30-1
Supt. — See Alexandria
Millbrook Colony S 50/K-8
41659 256th St 57301 605-239-4387
Susan Blankenship, prin. Fax 239-4293

Mitchell SD 17-2 2,500/K-12
800 W 10th Ave 57301 605-995-3010
Joseph Graves, supt. Fax 995-3089
www.mitchell.k12.sd.us
Longfellow ES 200/K-5
929 E 2nd Ave 57301 605-995-3092
Joe Childs, prin. Fax 995-3084
Mitchell MS 600/6-8
800 W 10th Ave 57301 605-995-3051
Brad Berens, prin. Fax 995-3037
Rogers ES 400/K-5
1301 N Kimball St 57301 605-995-3091
Vicki Harmdierks, prin. Fax 996-6610
Rosedale Colony S 50/K-8
25986 Rosedale Rd 57301 605-239-4215
Joe Childs, prin. Fax 239-4346
Williams ES 500/K-5
1420 W University Ave 57301 605-995-3090
Becky Roth, prin. Fax 996-5286
Other Schools – See Alexandria

John Paul II S 200/PK-6
1510 W Elm Ave 57301 605-996-2365
Michelle Omens, prin. Fax 995-0378
Mitchell Christian S 200/PK-12
805 W 18th Ave 57301 605-996-8861
Brian Held, admin. Fax 996-3642

Mobridge, Walworth, Pop. 3,279
Mobridge-Pollock SD 62-6 600/PK-12
114 10th St E 57601 605-845-7227
Terry Kraft, supt. Fax 845-3455
www.mobridge-pollock.k12.sd.us/
Beadle ES 100/3-5
114 10th St E 57601 605-845-3797
Brian Liedtke, prin. Fax 845-3455
Davis ES 100/PK-2
114 10th St E 57601 605-845-3360
Brian Liedtke, prin. Fax 845-3455
Mobridge MS 100/6-8
114 10th St E 57601 605-845-2768
Tim Frederick, prin. Fax 845-3455
Other Schools – See Pollock

Zion Lutheran S 50/K-8
620 9th St W 57601 605-845-2702
Barbara Naumann, prin. Fax 845-5024

Montrose, McCook, Pop. 476
Montrose SD 43-2 200/K-12
309 S Church Ave 57048 605-363-5025
Dean Kueter, supt. Fax 363-3513
www.montroseschool.k12.sd.us/
Montrose ES 100/K-6
309 S Church Ave 57048 605-363-5026
Dean Kueter, prin. Fax 363-3513
Montrose JHS 50/7-8
309 S Church Ave 57048 605-363-5025
Kenneth Greeno, prin. Fax 363-3513
Orland Colony S 50/K-8
309 S Church Ave 57048 605-363-3902
Dean Kueter, prin. Fax 363-3513

Mount Vernon, Davison, Pop. 461
Mount Vernon SD 17-3 200/K-12
PO Box 46 57363 605-236-5237
Patrick Mikkonen, supt. Fax 236-5604
www.mtvernon.k12.sd.us/
Mount Vernon ES 100/K-5
PO Box 46 57363 605-236-5237
Margaret Freidel, prin. Fax 236-5604
Mount Vernon MS 100/6-8
PO Box 46 57363 605-236-5237
Margaret Freidal, prin. Fax 236-5604

Murdo, Jones, Pop. 535
Jones County SD 37-3 100/PK-12
PO Box 109 57559 605-669-2297
Gary Knispel, supt. Fax 669-3248
www.jonesco.k12.sd.us/
Jones County ES 100/PK-6
PO Box 109 57559 605-669-2297
Gary Knispel, prin. Fax 669-3248
Jones County MS 50/7-8
PO Box 109 57559 605-669-2258
Larry Ball, prin. Fax 669-2904

New Effington, Roberts, Pop. 226
Sisseton SD 54-2
Supt. — See Sisseton
New Effington ES 100/K-6
10587 464th Ave 57255 605-637-5231
Dan Yost, prin. Fax 637-5234

Newell, Butte, Pop. 641
Newell SD 9-2 400/K-12
PO Box 99 57760 605-456-2393
Tim McCann, supt. Fax 456-2395
www.newell.k12.sd.us
Newell ES 100/K-5
PO Box 99 57760 605-456-0102
Donavan DeBoer, prin. Fax 456-2395
Newell MS 100/6-8
PO Box 99 57760 605-456-0102
Donavan DeBoer, prin. Fax 456-2395

New Underwood, Pennington, Pop. 653
New Underwood SD 51-3 300/K-12
PO Box 128 57761 605-754-6485
Dr. Julie Ertz, supt. Fax 754-6492
www.newunderwood.k12.sd.us
New Underwood ES 100/K-6
PO Box 128 57761 605-754-6485
Dr. Julie Ertz, prin. Fax 754-6492
New Underwood JHS 50/7-8
PO Box 128 57761 605-754-6485
Steve Elwood, prin. Fax 754-6492

North Sioux City, Union, Pop. 2,494
Dakota Valley SD 61-8 800/K-12
1150 Northshore Dr 57049 605-422-3800
Al Leber, supt. Fax 422-3807
www.dakotavalley.k12.sd.us/
Dakota Valley ES 400/K-4
1150 Northshore Dr 57049 605-422-3840
Tami Hummel, prin. Fax 422-3847
Dakota Valley MS 100/5-8
1150 Northshore Dr 57049 605-422-3830
Harlan Halverson, prin. Fax 422-3837

Oelrichs, Fall River, Pop. 145
Oelrichs SD 23-3 100/K-12
PO Box 65 57763 605-535-2631
Dr. Alberta Moore, supt. Fax 535-2046
www.oelrichs.k12.sd.us/
Oelrichs ES 100/K-6
PO Box 65 57763 605-535-2251
Connie Carson, prin. Fax 535-2046
Oelrichs JHS 50/7-8
PO Box 65 57763 605-535-2251
Connie Carson, prin. Fax 535-2046

O Kreek, Todd, Pop. 170
Todd County SD 66-1
Supt. — See Mission
O'Kreek ES 50/K-6
PO Box 180, 605-856-4930
Liane Christensen, lead tchr. Fax 856-2081

Olivet, Hutchinson, Pop. 67
Freeman SD 33-1
Supt. — See Freeman
Tschetter Colony S 50/K-8
27709 Tschetter Ave 57052 605-925-4216
Ryan Mors, prin. Fax 925-4814
Wolf Creek Colony S 50/K-8
42906 Colony Rd 57052 605-925-4216
Ryan Mors, prin. Fax 925-4814

Onida, Sully, Pop. 665
Agar-Blunt-Onida SD 58-3 300/K-12
PO Box 205 57564 605-258-2619
Kevin Pickner, supt. Fax 258-2361
www.abo.k12.sd.us
Onida ES 100/K-6
PO Box 205 57564 605-258-2617
Kathryn Hirchert, prin. Fax 258-2361
Sully Buttes JHS 50/7-8
PO Box 205 57564 605-258-2618
Mike Lodmel, prin. Fax 258-2361
Other Schools – See Blunt

Opal, Meade
Meade SD 46-1
Supt. — See Sturgis
Opal S 50/K-8
18010 Opal Rd 57758 605-269-2264
Bev Rosenboom, prin. Fax 269-2099

Parker, Turner, Pop. 1,001
Parker SD 60-4 400/K-12
PO Box 517 57053 605-297-3456
Tracey Olson, supt. Fax 297-4381
parker.k12.sd.us
Parker ES 200/K-6
PO Box 517 57053 605-297-3237
Tracey Olson, prin. Fax 297-4381
Parker JHS 100/7-8
PO Box 517 57053 605-297-3456
Joe Meyer, prin. Fax 297-4381

Parkston, Hutchinson, Pop. 1,560
Parkston SD 33-3 600/K-12
102C S Chapman Dr 57366 605-928-3368
Shayne McIntosh, supt. Fax 928-7284
www.parkston.k12.sd.us
Old Elm Spring Colony S 50/K-8
42023 268th St 57366 605-928-3368
Robert Monson, prin. Fax 928-7284
Parkston ES 300/K-6
102C S Chapman Dr 57366 605-928-3368
Robert Monson, prin. Fax 928-7284
Parkston JHS 100/7-8
102A S Chapman Dr 57366 605-928-3368
Joseph Kollmann, prin. Fax 928-4032
Other Schools – See Ethan

Parmelee, Todd, Pop. 618
Todd County SD 66-1
Supt. — See Mission

He Dog ES 100/PK-6
PO Box 260 57566 605-747-2438
Deb Boyd, prin. Fax 747-5168

Philip, Haakon, Pop. 756
Haakon SD 27-1 300/PK-12
PO Box 730 57567 605-859-2679
Keven Morehart, supt. Fax 859-3005
www.philip.k12.sd.us
Philip ES 100/PK-6
PO Box 730 57567 605-859-2001
Keven Morehart, prin. Fax 859-3005
Philip MS 50/7-8
PO Box 730 57567 605-859-2680
Jeff Rieckman, prin. Fax 859-3550
Other Schools – See Milesville

Piedmont, Meade
Meade SD 46-1
Supt. — See Sturgis
Piedmont/Stagebarn ES 400/K-6
12380 Sturgis Rd 57769 605-787-5295
Ethan Dschaak, prin. Fax 787-5954

Pierre, Hughes, Pop. 14,052
Pierre SD 32-2 2,500/PK-12
211 S Poplar Ave 57501 605-773-7300
Dr. Kelly Glodt, supt. Fax 773-7304
www.pierre.k12.sd.us
Buchanan ES 300/PK-5
100 N Buchanan Ave 57501 605-773-7310
Heath Larson, prin. Fax 773-7314
Jefferson ES 400/PK-5
321 W 5th St 57501 605-773-7320
Kevin MutchelKnaus, prin. Fax 773-7318
McKinley ES 100/PK-5
716 E Dakota Ave 57501 605-773-7380
Rob Coverdale, prin. Fax 773-7379
Morse MS 600/6-8
309 E Capitol Ave 57501 605-773-7330
Troy Wiebe, prin. Fax 773-7338
Washington ES 300/K-5
106 S Monroe Ave 57501 605-773-7370
Rob Coverdale, prin. Fax 773-7374

Pierre SDA S 50/PK-8
1206 E Robinson Ave 57501 605-224-9891
St. Joseph S 200/PK-5
210 E Broadway Ave 57501 605-224-7185
Darlene Braun, prin. Fax 224-1014

Pine Ridge, Shannon, Pop. 2,596
Shannon County SD 65-1
Supt. — See Batesland
Wolf Creek S 400/PK-8
PO Box 469 57770 605-867-5174
Russell Budmayr, prin. Fax 867-5067

Red Cloud Indian S 400/PK-12
100 Mission Dr 57770 605-867-5888
Bob Brave Heart, supt. Fax 867-2528

Plankinton, Aurora, Pop. 567
Plankinton SD 1-1 100/PK-12
PO Box 190 57368 605-942-7743
Donald Quimby, supt. Fax 942-7453
www.plankinton.k12.sd.us
Plankinton S 100/PK-12
PO Box 190 57368 605-942-7743
Lee Ann Nussbaum, prin. Fax 942-7453

Platte, Charles Mix, Pop. 1,318
Platte-Geddes SD 11-5 400/K-12
PO Box 140 57369 605-337-3391
Anton Glass, supt. Fax 337-2549
www.platte-geddes.k12.sd.us/
Cedar Grove Colony S 50/K-8
PO Box 140 57369 605-337-2468
Jared Ahlberg, prin. Fax 337-2549
Platte Colony S 50/K-8
PO Box 140 57369 605-337-2468
Jared Ahlberg, prin. Fax 337-2549
Platte ES 200/K-6
PO Box 140 57369 605-337-2468
Jared Ahlberg, prin. Fax 337-2549
Platte JHS 100/7-8
PO Box 140 57369 605-337-3391
Steve Randall, prin. Fax 337-2549

Pollock, Campbell, Pop. 289
Mobridge-Pollock SD 62-6
Supt. — See Mobridge
Pollock ES 50/K-6
PO Box 207 57648 605-889-2831
Brian Liedtke, prin. Fax 889-2543

Porcupine, Shannon, Pop. 783
Shannon County SD 65-1
Supt. — See Batesland
Rockyford S 300/PK-8
HC 49 Box 175 57772 605-455-6300
Monica Horse, prin. Fax 455-2091

Our Lady of Lourdes S 100/K-8
PO Box 9 57772 605-455-6406
Fax 867-5874

Presho, Lyman, Pop. 628
Lyman SD 42-1 400/K-12
PO Box 1000 57568 605-895-2579
Bruce Carrier, supt. Fax 895-2216
www.lyman.k12.sd.us/

Presho ES 100/K-5
PO Box 1000 57568 605-895-2579
Doug Eppard, prin. Fax 895-2216
Other Schools – See Kennebec

Ramona, Lake, Pop. 185
Oldham-Ramona SD 39-5 100/PK-12
PO Box 8 57054 605-482-8244
John Bjorkman, supt. Fax 482-8282
www.oldhamramona.k12.sd.us
Oldham-Ramona ES 100/PK-6
PO Box 8 57054 605-482-8244
Jane Lee, lead tchr. Fax 482-8282
Oldham-Ramona JHS 50/7-8
PO Box 8 57054 605-482-8244
John Bjorkman, prin. Fax 482-8282
Other Schools – See Arlington

Rapid City, Pennington, Pop. 62,167
Rapid City Area SD 51-4 12,700/K-12
300 6th St Ste 2 57701 605-394-4031
Dr. Peter Wharton, supt. Fax 394-2514
www.rcas.org
Beadle ES 300/K-5
10 Van Buren St 57701 605-394-1841
Robin Gillespie, prin. Fax 394-1739
Canyon Lake ES 300/K-5
1500 Evergreen Dr 57702 605-394-1817
Jackie Talley, prin. Fax 355-3013
Corral Drive ES 400/K-5
4503 Park Dr 57702 605-394-6789
Gregg McNabb, prin. Fax 394-3341
Dakota MS 800/6-8
615 Columbus St 57701 605-394-4092
Brad Tucker, prin. Fax 394-6935
Grandview ES 600/K-5
3301 Grandview Dr 57701 605-394-1829
Shannon Schaefers, prin. Fax 394-5831
Knollwood Heights ES 500/K-5
1701 Downing St 57701 605-394-1851
Deborah Warr, prin. Fax 394-5391
Mann ES 200/K-5
902 Anamosa St 57701 605-394-1847
Deborah Warr, prin. Fax 394-4194
Meadowbrook ES 500/K-5
3125 W Flormann St 57702 605-394-1821
Michael Donohoe, prin. Fax 394-1780
North MS 500/6-8
1501 N Maple Ave 57701 605-394-4042
Jeanne Burckhard, prin. Fax 394-6120
Pinedale ES 400/K-5
4901 W Chicago St 57702 605-394-1805
Rick Owen, prin. Fax 394-5830
Rapid Valley ES 500/K-5
2601 Covington St 57703 605-393-2221
Valerie Nefzger, prin. Fax 393-1973
Robbinsdale ES 400/K-5
424 E Indiana St 57701 605-394-1825
Patty Hamm, prin. Fax 394-1827
South Canyon ES 300/K-5
218 Nordby Ln 57702 605-394-1801
Cary Minnick, prin. Fax 355-3019
South MS 600/6-8
2 Indiana St 57701 605-394-4024
Larry Stevens, prin. Fax 394-5834
South Park ES 300/K-5
207 Flormann St 57701 605-394-1833
Rod Haugen, prin. Fax 394-1853
Southwest MS 400/6-8
4501 Park Dr 57702 605-394-6792
Gordon Kendall, prin. Fax 355-3095
Valley View ES 500/K-5
4840 Homestead St 57703 605-393-2812
Wayne Rosby, prin. Fax 393-2861
West MS 600/6-8
1003 Soo San Dr 57702 605-394-4033
Doug Foley, prin. Fax 394-1889
Wilson ES 300/K-5
827 Franklin St 57701 605-394-1837
Kathy Conlon, prin. Fax 394-1832
Other Schools – See Blackhawk

Calvary Christian S 100/PK-7
PO Box 2434 57709 605-348-5175
Mary Causey, prin. Fax 342-0773
Memorial Christian S 200/PK-6
4905 S Highway 16 57701 605-342-8265
Joyce Beebe, prin. Fax 342-6848
Rapid City SDA S 50/K-8
305 N 39th St 57702 605-343-2785
Nora Kertzman, prin. Fax 343-0673
St. Elizabeth Seton S 600/K-8
431 Oakland St 57701 605-348-1477
Colleen Lecy, prin. Fax 342-4367
St. Paul's Lutheran S 100/K-8
835 E Fairmont Blvd 57701 605-341-5385
Jared Rathje, prin. Fax 342-8717
Zion Lutheran S 200/PK-5
4550 S Highway 16 57701 605-342-5749
Priscilla Sayles, prin. Fax 342-4469

Raymond, Spink, Pop. 78
Doland SD 56-2
Supt. — See Doland
Clark Colony S 50/K-8
41181 179th St 57258 605-635-6302
Jerry McPartland, prin. Fax 635-6504

Redfield, Spink, Pop. 2,318
Redfield SD 56-4 600/PK-12
PO Box 560 57469 605-472-4520
Randy Joyce, supt. Fax 472-4525
www.redfield.k12.sd.us
Redfield ES 300/PK-6
PO Box 560 57469 605-472-4520
Jerold Bender, prin. Fax 472-4525
Redfield JHS 100/7-8
PO Box 560 57469 605-472-4520
Rob Lewis, prin. Fax 472-4525

Renner, Minnehaha
Sioux Falls SD 49-5
Supt. — See Sioux Falls
Renberg ES 100/K-5
47260 258th St 57055 605-543-5273
Larry Larsen, prin. Fax 543-5076

Revillo, Grant, Pop. 141
Grant-Deuel SD 25-3 200/PK-12
16370 482nd Ave 57259 605-623-4241
Grant VanderVorst, supt. Fax 623-4215
www.grant-deuel.k12.sd.us/
Grant-Deuel ES 100/PK-6
16370 482nd Ave 57259 605-623-4241
Grant VanderVorst, prin. Fax 623-4215
Grant-Deuel JHS 50/7-8
16370 482nd Ave 57259 605-623-4241
Grant VanderVorst, prin. Fax 623-4215

Roscoe, Edmunds, Pop. 297
Edmunds Central SD 22-5 100/K-12
PO Box 317 57471 605-287-4251
Lew Paulson, supt. Fax 287-4813
www.echs.k12.sd.us/
Edmunds Central ES 50/K-5
PO Box 317 57471 605-287-4251
Lew Paulson, prin. Fax 287-4813
Edmunds Central JHS 50/6-8
PO Box 317 57471 605-287-4251
Lew Paulson, prin. Fax 287-4813

Rosebud, Todd, Pop. 1,538
Todd County SD 66-1
Supt. — See Mission
Rosebud ES 300/K-5
PO Box 310 57570 605-747-2411
Linda Bordeaux, prin. Fax 747-4334

Rosholt, Roberts, Pop. 439
Rosholt SD 54-4 200/PK-12
PO Box 106 57260 605-537-4283
Carolyn Eide, supt. Fax 537-4285
www.rosholt.k12.sd.us/
Rosholt ES 100/PK-6
PO Box 106 57260 605-537-4283
Dan Dalchow, prin. Fax 537-4285
Rosholt JHS 50/7-8
PO Box 106 57260 605-537-4278
Dan Dalchow, prin. Fax 537-4285
White Rock Colony S 50/K-8
PO Box 106 57260 605-537-4790
Molly Howson, prin. Fax 537-4285

Roslyn, Day, Pop. 204
Roslyn SD 18-2 100/K-12
PO Box 196 57261 605-486-4311
Marc Frankenstein, supt. Fax 486-4635
www.roslyn-eden.k12.sd.us/default.htm
Roslyn ES 50/K-6
PO Box 196 57261 605-486-4561
Marc Frankenstein, prin. Fax 486-4635
Roslyn JHS 50/7-8
PO Box 196 57261 605-486-4311
Marc Frankenstein, prin. Fax 486-4635

Rutland, Lake
Rutland SD 39-4 100/K-12
102 School St 57057 605-586-4352
Carl Fahrenwald, supt. Fax 586-4343
www.rutland.k12.sd.us
Rutland ES 100/K-6
102 School St 57057 605-586-4352
Ron Swier, prin. Fax 586-4343
Rutland JHS 50/7-8
102 School St 57057 605-586-4352
Ron Swier, prin. Fax 586-4343

Saint Francis, Todd, Pop. 705
Todd County SD 66-1
Supt. — See Mission
Spring Creek S 100/K-8
233 Yellow Cloud Dr 57572 605-747-2541
Erin McCloskey, prin. Fax 747-4369

Salem, McCook, Pop. 1,393
McCook Central SD 43-7 400/PK-12
PO Box 310 57058 605-425-2264
Dr. Carol Pistulka, supt. Fax 425-2079
www.mccookcentral.k12.sd.us/
McCook Central ES 100/PK-4
PO Box 310 57058 605-425-2264
Dr. Deb Eichacker, prin. Fax 425-2079
McCook Central MS 100/5-8
PO Box 310 57058 605-425-2264
Brad Seamer, prin. Fax 425-2079

St. Mary S 100/K-8
PO Box 40 57058 605-425-2607
Steve McCormick, prin. Fax 425-3310

Scotland, Bon Homme, Pop. 830
Menno SD 33-2
Supt. — See Menno
Maxwell Colony S 50/K-8
42805 Maxwell Rd 57059 605-387-5161
Terry Quam, prin. Fax 387-5171
Scotland SD 4-3 300/PK-12
711 4th St 57059 605-583-2237
Damon Alvey, supt. Fax 583-2239
www.scotland.k12.sd.us
Scotland ES 100/PK-5
711 4th St 57059 605-583-2717
Damon Alvey, prin. Fax 583-2718
Scotland MS 100/6-8
711 4th St 57059 605-583-2237
Ryan Bruns, prin. Fax 583-2239

Selby, Walworth, Pop. 690
Selby Area SD 62-5 200/PK-12
PO Box 324 57472 605-649-7818
Darrel McFarland, supt. Fax 649-7282
www.selby.k12.sd.us/
Selby Area ES 100/PK-6
PO Box 324 57472 605-649-7818
Tony Siebrecht, prin. Fax 649-7282
Selby Area JHS 50/7-8
PO Box 324 57472 605-649-7818
Tony Siebrecht, prin. Fax 649-7282

Sioux Falls, Minnehaha, Pop. 139,517
Brandon Valley SD 49-2
Supt. — See Brandon
Assam ES K-5
7700 E Willow Wood 57110 605-582-1500
Susan Foster, prin. Fax 332-0947

Harrisburg SD 41-2
Supt. — See Harrisburg
Harrisburg Explorer ES 400/PK-5
4010 W 82nd St 57108 605-743-2567
Mike Munzke, prin. Fax 367-4695
Harrisburg Journey ES PK-5
6801 S Grange Ave 57108 605-743-2567
John Snobeck, prin. Fax 367-0017

Sioux Falls SD 49-5 20,000/PK-12
201 E 38th St 57105 605-367-7900
Dr. Pam Homan, supt. Fax 367-4637
www.sf.k12.sd.us
Anderson ES 200/K-5
1600 N Wayland Ave 57103 605-367-6130
Kirk Zeeck, prin. Fax 367-6064
Axtell Park MS 600/6-8
201 N West Ave 57104 605-367-7647
Steve Cain, prin. Fax 367-8326
Cleveland ES 700/K-5
1000 S Edward Dr 57103 605-367-6150
Dr. Jackie McNamara, prin. Fax 367-6066
Discovery ES 700/K-5
1506 S Discovery Ave 57106 605-362-3530
Anne Williams, prin. Fax 362-3535
Dunn ES 500/K-5
2400 S Bahnson Ave 57103 605-371-4120
Teresa Boysen, prin. Fax 371-4122
Edison MS 700/6-8
2101 S West Ave 57105 605-367-7643
Steve Griffith, prin. Fax 367-8457
Field ES 200/K-5
501 S Highland Ave 57103 605-367-6160
Dr. Kathy Coulter, prin. Fax 367-6069
Frost ES 400/PK-5
3101 S 4th Ave 57105 605-367-6170
Colleen Werner, prin. Fax 367-6071
Garfield ES 300/K-5
2421 W 15th St 57104 605-367-6180
Nancy Duncan, prin. Fax 367-6072
Harris ES 600/K-5
3501 E 49th St 57103 605-371-4111
Nancy Hagen, prin. Fax 371-4110
Hawthorne ES 400/PK-5
601 N Spring Ave 57104 605-367-4580
Cheryl Larson, prin. Fax 367-6074
Hayward ES 500/PK-5
400 N Valley View Rd 57107 605-367-4590
Kiersta Machacek, prin. Fax 367-6075
Henry MS 1,100/6-8
2200 S 5th Ave 57105 605-367-7639
Steve Albrecht, prin. Fax 367-7693
Howe ES 500/K-5
2801 S Valley View Rd 57106 605-362-2752
Dr. Celeste Uthe-Burow, prin. Fax 362-2724
Jefferson ES 300/K-5
1610 S Lake Ave 57105 605-367-4530
Teresa Luecke, prin. Fax 367-7101
Kennedy ES 700/K-5
4501 S Holbrook Ave 57106 605-362-2784
Larry Bandy, prin. Fax 362-2776
Longfellow ES 300/K-5
1116 S 4th Ave 57105 605-367-4550
Jeffery Sheets, prin. Fax 367-6078
Lowell ES 300/K-5
710 W 18th St 57104 605-367-8378
Twaine Fink, prin. Fax 367-6079
Mann ES 200/K-5
1401 E 26th St 57105 605-367-6190
Tara Eckstaine, prin. Fax 367-6080
Memorial MS 1,000/6-8
1401 S Sertoma Ave 57106 605-362-2785
Carrie Aaron, prin. Fax 362-2790

Parks ES K-5
5701 E Red Oak Dr 57110 605-371-4170
June Gaston, prin. Fax 371-4174
Pettigrew ES 300/K-5
7900 W 53rd St 57106 605-362-3560
Fax 362-3564
Redlin ES 400/PK-5
1721 E Austin St 57103 605-367-6140
Mitch Sheaffer, prin. Fax 367-6065
Sullivan ES 700/PK-5
3701 E 3rd St 57103 605-367-6084
Lois Running, prin. Fax 367-6088
Twain ES 200/K-5
315 W 27th St 57105 605-367-4560
Mary Peterson, prin. Fax 367-6082
Whittier MS 1,000/6-8
930 E 6th St 57103 605-367-7620
Dr. Diana Messick, prin. Fax 367-8357
Wilder ES 400/K-5
2300 S Lyndale Ave 57105 605-367-4570
Dr. Linda Haugan, prin. Fax 367-8487
Other Schools – See Renner

Bethel Lutheran S 50/K-8
1801 S Valley View Rd 57106 605-362-8231
Benjamin Priebe, prin.
Christian Center S 200/K-5
6300 W 41st St 57106 605-361-8002
Dr. Victor Fordyce, prin. Fax 361-3670
Christ the King S 200/PK-6
1801 S Lake Ave 57105 605-338-5103
Stephanie Wilson, prin. Fax 335-1231
Good Shepherd Lutheran S 100/PK-8
4800 S Southeastern Ave 57103 605-371-0072
Peter Markgraf, prin. Fax 371-0072
Holy Spirit S 400/PK-6
4309 S Bahnson Ave 57103 605-371-1481
Carol Loeffelholz, prin. Fax 371-1483
O'Gorman JHS 400/7-8
3100 W 41st St 57105 605-988-0546
Colly Broveleit, prin. Fax 336-9839
St. Lambert's S 200/K-6
1000 S Bahnson Ave 57103 605-338-7042
Barbara Lockwood, prin. Fax 336-8727
St. Mary S 300/K-6
2001 S 5th Ave 57105 605-334-9881
Courtney Tielke, prin. Fax 334-9224
St. Michael's S 400/K-6
1600 S Marion Rd 57106 605-361-0021
Lisa Huemoeller, prin. Fax 361-0094
Sioux Falls Christian S 300/PK-3
6120 S Charger Cir 57108 605-334-7397
Matt Covey, prin. Fax 334-5717
Sioux Falls Lutheran S 300/PK-8
308 W 37th St 57105 605-335-1923
Rodney Lenz, prin. Fax 335-1930
Sioux Falls SDA S 50/1-8
1604 S Sierra Cir 57110 605-333-0197

Sisseton, Roberts, Pop. 2,540
Sisseton SD 54-2 900/K-12
516 8th Ave W 57262 605-698-7613
Dr. Stephen Schulte, supt. Fax 698-3032
www.sisseton.k12.sd.us/
Thollehauge MS 300/5-8
516 8th Ave W 57262 605-698-7613
Karen Whitney, prin. Fax 698-7487
Westside ES 300/K-4
516 8th Ave W 57262 605-698-7613
Dan Yost, prin. Fax 698-7404
Other Schools – See New Effington

South Shore, Codington, Pop. 260
Waverly SD 14-5
Supt. — See Waverly
South Shore ES 50/PK-6
203 S School St 57263 605-756-4120
Laura Morrow, prin. Fax 756-4201

Spearfish, Lawrence, Pop. 9,355
Spearfish SD 40-2 1,900/PK-PK, 1-
525 E Illinois St 57783 605-717-1229
Dave Peters, supt. Fax 717-1200
www.spearfish.k12.sd.us
East ES 400/3-5
400 E Hudson St 57783 605-717-1210
Dan Olson, prin. Fax 717-1231
Spearfish MS 500/6-8
1600 N Canyon St 57783 605-717-1215
Tom Riedel, prin. Fax 717-6926
West ES 300/PK-PK, 1-
920 W King St 57783 605-717-1205
Paul Soriano, prin. Fax 717-1232

Black Hills Christian Academy 50/PK-8
PO Box 1089 57783 605-722-1276
Jullie Totino, admin. Fax 722-1217
Black Hills Classical Christian S 100/PK-12
PO Box 723 57783 605-717-4019
Michele Thomson, admin.

Springfield, Bon Homme, Pop. 1,522
Bon Homme SD 4-2
Supt. — See Tyndall
Springfield ES 50/K-5
1008 Walnut St 57062 605-369-2282
Michael Duffek, prin. Fax 369-2438

Stickney, Aurora, Pop. 308
Stickney SD 1-2 100/K-12
PO Box 67 57375 605-732-4221
Robert Krietlow, supt. Fax 732-4281
www.stickney.k12.sd.us/
Stickney JHS 50/8-8
PO Box 67 57375 605-732-4221
Robert Krietlow, prin. Fax 732-4281
Stickney S 100/K-7
PO Box 67 57375 605-732-4221
Ferra Kemp, prin. Fax 732-4281

Sturgis, Meade, Pop. 6,260
Meade SD 46-1 2,500/K-12
1230 Douglas St 57785 605-347-2523
James Heinert, supt. Fax 347-0005
meade.k12.sd.us
Alkali S 50/K-8
14758 Alkali Rd 57785 605-269-2264
Bev Rosenboom, prin. Fax 269-2099
Sturgis ES 500/K-5
1121 Ballpark Rd 57785 605-347-2386
Norman Graham, prin. Fax 347-0005
Sturgis Williams MS 500/6-8
1425 Cedar St 57785 605-347-5232
Lonny Harter, prin. Fax 720-0190
Other Schools – See Enning, Hereford, Opal, Piedmont, Union Center, Wasta, Whitewood

Summit, Roberts, Pop. 273
Summit SD 54-6 100/PK-12
PO Box 791 57266 605-398-6211
Ellen Helgeson, supt. Fax 398-6311
www.summit.k12.sd.us
Summit ES 100/PK-6
PO Box 791 57266 605-398-6211
Ellen Helgeson, prin. Fax 398-6311
Summit JHS 50/7-8
PO Box 791 57266 605-398-6211
Ellen Helgeson, prin. Fax 398-6311

Tabor, Bon Homme, Pop. 384
Bon Homme SD 4-2
Supt. — See Tyndall
Hutterische Colony S 50/K-8
31232 Colony Rd 57063 605-589-3388
Dr. Bryce Knudson, prin. Fax 589-3468
Tabor ES 50/K-5
227 N Lidice Ave 57063 605-463-2271
Michael Duffek, prin. Fax 463-9511

Tea, Lincoln, Pop. 2,455
Tea Area SD 41-5 900/K-12
PO Box 488 57064 605-498-2700
Jerry Schutz, supt. Fax 498-2702
www.teaschools.k12.sd.us/
Tea ES 400/K-3
PO Box 488 57064 605-498-2700
Betsy Drew, prin. Fax 498-4134
Tea MS 200/4-8
PO Box 488 57064 605-498-2700
Chris Fechner, prin. Fax 498-1161

Timber Lake, Dewey, Pop. 441
Timber Lake SD 20-3 300/K-12
PO Box 1000 57656 605-865-3654
Frank Seiler, supt. Fax 865-3294
www.tls.k12.sd.us/
Timber Lake ES 100/K-5
PO Box 1000 57656 605-865-3654
Sarah Schweitzer, prin. Fax 865-3294
Timber Lake MS 100/6-8
PO Box 1000 57656 605-865-3654
Chris Bohlander, prin. Fax 865-3294

Toronto, Deuel, Pop. 179
Deubrook Area SD 5-6
Supt. — See White
Toronto ES 100/2-6
PO Box 399 57268 605-794-1151
Cristy Olsen, prin. Fax 629-3701

Tripp, Hutchinson, Pop. 666
Tripp-Delmont SD 33-5 100/PK-12
PO Box 430 57376 605-935-6766
Lynn Vlasman, supt. Fax 935-6507
www.tridel.k12.sd.us/
Tripp-Delmont S 50/PK-8
PO Box 430 57376 605-935-6766
Kelly Hansen, prin. Fax 935-6507

Tulare, Spink, Pop. 202
Hitchcock-Tulare SD 56-6 300/K-12
PO Box 108 57476 605-596-4171
Scott Pudwill, supt. Fax 596-4175
www.hitchcock-tulare.k12.sd.us/
Hitchcock-Tulare JHS 50/7-8
PO Box 108 57476 605-596-4171
Jeff Clark, prin. Fax 596-4150
Other Schools – See Frankfort, Hitchcock

Tyndall, Bon Homme, Pop. 1,155
Bon Homme SD 4-2 600/PK-12
PO Box 28 57066 605-589-3388
Dr. Bryce Knudson, supt. Fax 589-3468
www.bonhomme.k12.sd.us/
Bon Homme MS 100/6-8
PO Box 28 57066 605-589-3387
Ed Mitzel, prin. Fax 589-3468
Tyndall ES 200/PK-5
PO Box 28 57066 605-589-3389
Michael Duffek, prin. Fax 589-3468
Other Schools – See Springfield, Tabor

Union Center, Meade
Meade SD 46-1
Supt. — See Sturgis
Atall S 50/K-8
16375 Atall Rd 57787 605-269-2264
Bev Rosenboom, prin. Fax 269-2099
Union Center S 50/K-8
1700 SD Highway 34 57787 605-269-2264
Bev Rosenboom, prin. Fax 269-2099

Utica, Yankton, Pop. 85
Menno SD 33-2
Supt. — See Menno
Jamesville Colony S 50/K-8
43582 NE Jim River Rd 57067 605-387-5161
Terry Quam, prin. Fax 387-5171

Valley Springs, Minnehaha, Pop. 809
Brandon Valley SD 49-2
Supt. — See Brandon
Valley Springs ES 100/K-5
PO Box 130 57068 605-757-6285
Bill Freking, prin. Fax 582-6795

Vermillion, Clay, Pop. 9,964
Vermillion SD 13-1 1,200/PK-12
17 Prospect St 57069 605-677-7000
Dr. Mark Froke, supt. Fax 677-7002
www.vermillion.k12.sd.us
Austin ES 200/PK-1
300 High St 57069 605-677-7010
Dr. Liz Oaks-Pifer, prin. Fax 677-7014
Jolley ES 300/2-5
224 S University St 57069 605-677-7015
Mark Upward, prin. Fax 677-7022
Vermillion MS 300/6-8
422 Princeton St 57069 605-677-7025
Pat Anderson, prin. Fax 677-7028

St. Agnes S 100/PK-5
909 Lewis St 57069 605-624-4144
Darla Hamm, prin. Fax 624-4478

Viborg, Turner, Pop. 799
Viborg SD 60-5 300/PK-12
PO Box 397 57070 605-766-5418
Patrick Kraning, supt. Fax 766-5635
www.viborg.k12.sd.us/
Viborg ES 100/PK-6
PO Box 397 57070 605-766-5418
Dawn Wirth, prin. Fax 766-5635
Viborg JHS 50/7-8
PO Box 397 57070 605-766-5418
Patrick Kraning, prin. Fax 766-5635

Volga, Brookings, Pop. 1,442
Sioux Valley SD 5-5 600/PK-12
PO Box 278 57071 605-627-5657
Dean Johnson, supt. Fax 627-5291
www.svs.k12.sd.us/
Sioux Valley ES 300/PK-5
PO Box 278 57071 605-627-5657
Sandra McGeough, prin. Fax 627-5291
Sioux Valley MS 100/6-8
PO Box 278 57071 605-627-5657
David Colberg, prin. Fax 627-5291

Volga Christian S 100/PK-8
223 E 6th St 57071 605-627-9286
Bruce Lucas, prin. Fax 627-9286

Wagner, Charles Mix, Pop. 1,601
Wagner Community SD 11-4 500/PK-12
101 Walnut Ave SW 57380 605-384-3677
Susan Smit, supt. Fax 384-3678
www.wagner.k12.sd.us/
Wagner ES 1-4
101 Walnut Ave SW 57380 605-384-3393
Carol Ersland, prin. Fax 384-3200
Wagner JHS 100/5-8
101 Walnut Ave SW 57380 605-384-3913
Steve Petry, prin. Fax 384-3678
Wagner K 200/PK-K
101 Walnut Ave SW 57380 605-384-4354
Lori Bouza, prin. Fax 384-3888

Wakonda, Clay, Pop. 345
Irene-Wakonda SD 13-3
Supt. — See Irene
Wakonda ES 100/PK-6
PO Box 268 57073 605-267-2644
Debra Lyle, prin. Fax 267-2645

Wakpala, Corson
Smee SD 15-3 200/PK-12
PO Box B 57658 605-845-3040
Keith McVay, supt. Fax 845-7244
www.smee.k12.sd.us
Wakpala S 100/PK-8
PO Box B 57658 605-845-3040
Shirley Boyd, prin. Fax 845-7244

Wall, Pennington, Pop. 808
Wall SD 51-5 100/K-12
PO Box 414 57790 605-279-2156
Dennis Rieckman, supt. Fax 279-2613
www.wall.k12.sd.us
Big White ES 50/K-6
PO Box 414 57790 605-279-2156
Charles Sykora, prin. Fax 279-2613

Warner, Brown, Pop. 430
Warner SD 6-5 300/PK-12
PO Box 20 57479 605-225-6397
Kirk Easton, supt. Fax 225-0007
www.warner.k12.sd.us/
Warner ES 200/PK-5
PO Box 20 57479 605-225-6194
Donneley Kay, prin. Fax 225-0007
Warner MS 100/6-8
PO Box 20 57479 605-225-6194
Charles Welke, prin. Fax 225-0007

Wasta, Pennington, Pop. 75
Meade SD 46-1
Supt. — See Sturgis
Elm Springs S 50/K-8
21309 Elm Springs Rd 57791 605-269-2264
Bev Rosenboom, prin. Fax 269-2099

Watertown, Codington, Pop. 20,265
Watertown SD 14-4 3,700/PK-12
PO Box 730 57201 605-882-6312
Dr. Lesli Hanson, supt. Fax 882-6327
www.watertown.k12.sd.us/
Jefferson ES 500/PK-6
1701 N Maple 57201 605-882-6390
Laura Morrow, prin. Fax 882-6391
Lincoln ES 500/K-6
1100 13th St NE 57201 605-882-6340
Dr. Susan Patrick, prin. Fax 882-6343
McKinley ES 300/K-6
5 12th St SW 57201 605-882-6350
Darrell Stacey, prin. Fax 882-6351
Mellette ES 300/K-6
619 2nd St NW 57201 605-882-6385
John Decker, prin. Fax 882-6382
Roosevelt ES 300/K-6
412 2nd St SE 57201 605-882-6360
Gregg DeSpeigler, prin. Fax 882-6361
Watertown MS 600/7-8
601 11th St NE 57201 605-882-6370
Daniel Albertsen, prin. Fax 886-6372

Immaculate Conception S 100/K-6
109 3rd St SE 57201 605-886-3883
Carol Dagel, prin. Fax 886-0199
St. Martin Lutheran S 100/K-8
1200 2nd St NE 57201 605-886-4976
Mark Renner, prin. Fax 886-6362
Watertown Christian S 100/PK-12
15 12th Ave NE 57201 605-882-0949
Dave Florey, admin. Fax 882-5935

Waubay, Day, Pop. 607
Waubay SD 18-3 200/PK-12
202 W School Rd 57273 605-947-4529
Al Stewart, supt. Fax 947-4243
www.waubay.k12.sd.us/
Waubay ES 100/PK-6
202 W School Rd 57273 605-947-4529
Loren Lutz, prin. Fax 947-4243
Waubay JHS 50/7-8
202 W School Rd 57273 605-947-4529
Al Stewart, prin. Fax 947-4243

Waverly, Codington
Waverly SD 14-5 200/PK-12
319 Mary Pl 57201 605-886-9174
Laura Morrow, supt. Fax 886-6630
www.waverly.k12.sd.us
Waverly ES 100/PK-6
319 Mary Pl, 605-886-9174
Laura Morrow, prin. Fax 886-6630
Waverly JHS 50/7-8
319 Mary Pl, 605-886-9174
Laura Morrow, prin. Fax 886-6630
Other Schools – See South Shore

Webster, Day, Pop. 1,751
Webster SD 18-4 500/PK-12
102 E 9th Ave 57274 605-345-3548
James Block, supt. Fax 345-4421
www.webster.k12.sd.us/
Webster ES 200/PK-5
102 E 9th Ave 57274 605-345-4651
Craig Case, prin. Fax 345-4421
Webster MS 100/6-8
102 E 9th Ave 57274 605-345-4653
Craig Case, prin. Fax 345-4421

Wecota, Faulk
Faulkton Area SD 24-3
Supt. — See Faulkton
Blumengard Colony S 50/K-8
35075 148th St 57438 605-324-3243
Jennifer Knecht, prin.
Thunderbird Colony S 50/K-8
15185 346th Ave 57438 605-324-3241
Jennifer Knecht, prin.

Wessington Springs, Jerauld, Pop. 926
Wessington Springs SD 36-2 300/PK-12
PO Box 449 57382 605-539-9391
Lance Witte, supt. Fax 539-1029
www.wessingtonsprings.k12.sd.us
Spring Valley Colony S 50/K-8
PO Box 449 57382 605-539-1754
Jason Kolousek, prin. Fax 539-1583
Wessington Springs ES 100/PK-5
PO Box 449 57382 605-539-1754
Jason Kolousek, prin. Fax 539-1583
Wessington Springs MS 100/6-8
PO Box 449 57382 605-539-1754
Jason Kolousek, prin. Fax 539-1583

Westport, Brown, Pop. 121
Leola SD 44-2
Supt. — See Leola
Grassland Colony S 50/K-8
11865 370th Ave 57481 605-439-3143
Jamie Hermann, prin. Fax 439-3206

Wetonka, McPherson, Pop. 11
Leola SD 44-2
Supt. — See Leola
Longlake Colony S 50/K-8
36848 123rd St 57481 605-439-3143
Jamie Hermann, prin. Fax 439-3206

White, Brookings, Pop. 499
Deubrook Area SD 5-6 400/K-12
PO Box 346 57276 605-629-1100
Kevin Keenaghan, supt. Fax 629-3701
www.deubrook.com
Deubrook MS 100/7-8
PO Box 346 57276 605-629-1114
Don Ray, prin. Fax 629-3701
Norfeld Colony S K-8
PO Box 346 57276 605-794-1152
Cristy Olsen, prin. Fax 629-3701
Other Schools – See Astoria, Toronto

Elkton SD 5-3
Supt. — See Elkton
Rolland Colony S 50/K-6
48088 210th St 57276 605-542-2541
Brian Jandahl, prin. Fax 542-4441

White Lake, Aurora, Pop. 389
White Lake SD 1-3 200/K-12
PO Box 246 57383 605-249-2251
Berle Johnson, supt. Fax 249-2725
www.whitelake.k12.sd.us/
White Lake ES 100/K-6
PO Box 246 57383 605-249-2251
Berle Johnson, prin. Fax 249-2725
White Lake JHS 50/7-8
PO Box 246 57383 605-249-2251
Berle Johnson, prin. Fax 249-2725

White River, Mellette, Pop. 586
White River SD 47-1 400/PK-12
PO Box 273 57579 605-259-3311
Thomas Cameron, supt. Fax 259-3133
www.whiteriver.k12.sd.us/
Norris ES 50/K-6
PO Box 273 57579 605-259-3137
Abi Van Regenmorter, prin. Fax 259-3133
Prairie View S 50/K-8
PO Box 273 57579 605-259-3137
Abi Van Regenmorter, prin. Fax 259-3133
White River ES 100/PK-5
PO Box 273 57579 605-259-3137
Abi Van Regenmorter, prin. Fax 259-3133
White River MS 100/6-8
PO Box 273 57579 605-259-3135
Kendra Becker, prin. Fax 259-3133

Whitewood, Lawrence, Pop. 826
Meade SD 46-1
Supt. — See Sturgis
Whitewood ES 100/K-6
603 Garfield St 57793 605-269-2264
Bev Rosenboom, prin. Fax 269-2099

Willow Lake, Clark, Pop. 266
Willow Lake SD 12-3 200/PK-12
PO Box 170 57278 605-625-5945
Kevin Quimby, supt. Fax 625-3103
www.willowlake.k12.sd.us/
Mayfield Colony S 50/K-8
PO Box 170 57278 605-625-5945
Kevin Quimby, prin. Fax 625-3103
Willow Lake ES 100/PK-6
PO Box 170 57278 605-625-5945
Kevin Quimby, prin. Fax 625-3103
Willow Lake JHS 50/7-8
PO Box 170 57278 605-625-5924
Kerry Stobbs, prin. Fax 625-3103
Other Schools – See Bancroft, Carpenter

Wilmot, Roberts, Pop. 531
Wilmot SD 54-7 300/PK-12
PO Box 100 57279 605-938-4647
Tim Graf, supt. Fax 938-4185
www.wilmot.k12.sd.us
Wilmot ES 100/PK-6
PO Box 100 57279 605-938-4647
Mike Schmidt, prin. Fax 938-4185
Wilmot JHS 50/7-8
PO Box 100 57279 605-938-4647
Larry Hulscher, prin. Fax 938-4185

Winfred, Lake, Pop. 53
Madison Central SD 39-2
Supt. — See Madison
Gracevale Colony S 50/K-8
23843 446th Ave 57076 605-256-7721
Dan Walsh, prin. Fax 256-7729

Winner, Tripp, Pop. 2,917
Winner SD 59-2 800/K-12
PO Box 231 57580 605-842-8101
Mike Hanson, supt. Fax 842-8120
www.winner.k12.sd.us
Winner ES 200/K-4
PO Box 231 57580 605-842-8170
Stacy Halverson, prin. Fax 842-8123
Winner MS 200/5-8
PO Box 231 57580 605-842-8150
Brian Naasz, prin. Fax 842-8122
Other Schools – See Hamill, Millboro

Wolsey, Beadle, Pop. 388
Wolsey Wessington SD 2-6 200/K-12
375 Ash St SE 57384 605-883-4221
James Cutshaw, supt. Fax 883-4720
Wolsey Wessington ES 100/K-4
375 Ash St SE 57384 605-883-4221
Carol Rowen, prin. Fax 883-4720
Wolsey Wessington MS 100/5-8
375 Ash St SE 57384 605-883-4221
Carol Rowen, prin. Fax 883-4720

Wood, Mellette, Pop. 67
Wood SD 47-2 50/K-8
PO Box 458 57585 605-452-3251
Chris Anderson, supt. Fax 452-3252
Witten S 50/K-8
114 S Dakota St 57585 605-879-2336
Mary Elder, prin. Fax 452-3252
Wood S 50/K-8
PO Box 458 57585 605-452-3251
Mary Elder, prin. Fax 452-3252

Woonsocket, Sanborn, Pop. 676
Woonsocket SD 55-4 200/K-12
PO Box 428 57385 605-796-4431
Rodrick Weber, supt. Fax 796-4352
www.woonsocket.k12.sd.us/
Woonsocket S 100/K-8
PO Box 428 57385 605-796-4431
Paula Lynch, prin. Fax 796-4432

Worthing, Lincoln, Pop. 745
Lennox SD 41-4
Supt. — See Lennox
Worthing ES 100/K-5
230 Cedar St 57077 605-372-4114
Darin Eich, prin. Fax 372-6046

Yankton, Yankton, Pop. 13,716
Yankton SD 63-3 3,000/PK-12
PO Box 738 57078 605-665-3998
Joseph Gertsema, supt. Fax 665-1422
www.ysd.k12.sd.us
Beadle ES 400/K-5
PO Box 738 57078 605-665-2282
Carey Mitzel, prin. Fax 655-5961
Lincoln ES 400/K-5
PO Box 738 57078 605-665-7392
Paul Struck, prin. Fax 665-0301
Stewart ES 300/PK-5
PO Box 738 57078 605-665-5765
Jerome Klimisch, prin. Fax 668-0762
Webster ES 200/K-5
PO Box 738 57078 605-665-2484
Melanie Ryken, prin. Fax 655-0006
Yankton MS 700/6-8
PO Box 738 57078 605-665-2419
Kathleen Wagner, prin. Fax 665-6239

Sacred Heart MS 100/5-8
504 Capitol St 57078 605-665-1808
Regan Manning, prin. Fax 260-9787
Sacred Heart S 200/PK-4
1500 Saint Benedict Dr 57078 605-665-5841
Regan Manning, prin. Fax 260-3400

TENNESSEE

TENNESSEE DEPARTMENT OF EDUCATION
710 James Robertson Pkwy, Nashville 37243-1219
Telephone 615-741-2731
Fax 615-532-4791
Website http://www.state.tn.us/education

Commissioner of Education Tim Webb

TENNESSEE BOARD OF EDUCATION
400 Deaderick St Ste 200, Nashville 37243-1403

Executive Director Dr. Gary Nixon

PUBLIC, PRIVATE AND CATHOLIC ELEMENTARY SCHOOLS

Adamsville, McNairy, Pop. 2,062
Hardin County SD
Supt. — See Savannah
West Hardin ES 200/K-5
25105 Highway 69 38310 731-632-0413
Kenny Harris, prin. Fax 632-0253

McNairy County SD
Supt. — See Selmer
Adamsville ES 600/K-6
220 S Elm St 38310 731-632-0934
Danny Combs, prin. Fax 632-5007

Afton, Greene
Greene County SD
Supt. — See Greeneville
Chuckey Doak MS 500/6-8
120 Chuckey Doak Rd 37616 423-787-2038
Amy Brooks, prin. Fax 787-2096

Alamo, Crockett, Pop. 2,380
Alamo CSD 600/PK-6
264 E Park St 38001 731-696-5515
Reecha Black, supt. Fax 696-2541
www.alamoschool.org
Alamo ES 600/PK-6
264 E Park St 38001 731-696-5515
Joyce Nanney, prin. Fax 696-2541

Crockett County SD 1,900/PK-12
102 N Cavalier Dr 38001 731-696-2604
Stan Black, supt. Fax 696-4734
www.ccschools.net
Crockett County MS 500/6-8
497 N Cavalier Dr 38001 731-696-5583
Bobby Mullins, prin. Fax 696-2034
Other Schools – See Friendship, Gadsden, Maury City

Alcoa, Blount, Pop. 8,388
Alcoa CSD 1,600/K-12
524 Faraday St 37701 865-984-0531
Tom Shamblin, supt. Fax 984-5832
www.alcoaschools.net/
Alcoa ES 600/K-4
1200 Springbrook Rd 37701 865-982-3120
Merna Schott, prin. Fax 984-4458
Alcoa MS 500/5-8
1325 Springbrook Rd 37701 865-982-5211
James Kirk, prin. Fax 380-2533

Algood, Putnam, Pop. 3,188
Putnam County SD
Supt. — See Cookeville
Algood S 1,100/K-8
540 Dry Valley Rd, Cookeville TN 38506
931-537-6141
Leann Taylor, prin. Fax 537-3700

Allardt, Fentress, Pop. 657
Fentress County SD
Supt. — See Jamestown
Allardt S 400/PK-8
PO Box 129 38504 931-879-9515
Mike Allen, prin. Fax 879-2702

Allons, Overton
Clay County SD
Supt. — See Celina
Maple Grove S 50/K-8
368 Cleo Johnson Rd 38541 931-823-4838
Jerry Collins, prin. Fax 823-8734

Overton County SD
Supt. — See Livingston
Allons S 300/K-8
321 Old Celina Rd 38541 931-823-5921
Wayne Sells, prin. Fax 823-7496

Altamont, Grundy, Pop. 1,166
Grundy County SD 2,300/PK-12
PO Box 97 37301 931-692-3467
Joel Hargis, dir. Fax 692-2188
volweb.utk.edu/Schools/grundyco/grundy.index.html
North S 300/PK-8
PO Box 7 37301 931-692-3710
Dr. David Dickerson, prin. Fax 692-2664
Other Schools – See Coalmont, Gruetli Laager, Palmer, Pelham, Tracy City

Andersonville, Anderson
Anderson County SD
Supt. — See Clinton
Andersonville ES 400/PK-5
1951 Mountain Rd 37705 865-494-7695
Beth Roeder, prin. Fax 494-5484

Antioch, Davidson
Metropolitan Nashville SD
Supt. — See Nashville
Antioch MS 900/5-8
5050 Blue Hole Rd 37013 615-333-5642
Dr. Stephanie Kraft, prin. Fax 333-5053
Apollo MS 500/5-8
631 Richards Rd 37013 615-333-5025
Ron Woodard, prin. Fax 333-5029
Cole ES 700/K-4
5060 Colemont Dr 37013 615-333-5043
Chad High, prin. Fax 298-8052
Edison ES 600/PK-5
6130 Mount View Rd 37013 615-501-8800
Ronald Powe, prin. Fax 262-6656
Kelley ES, 5834 Pettus Rd 37013 500/K-4
Marsha Dunn, prin. 615-941-7535
Kennedy MS 1,100/6-8
2087 Hobson Pike 37013 615-501-7900
Ron Anderson, prin.
Marshall MS, 5832 Pettus Rd 37013 1,000/5-8
Dr. Barbara Ide, prin. 615-941-7515
Maxwell ES 500/K-4
5535 Blue Hole Rd 37013 615-333-7180
Lucia Ashworth, prin. Fax 333-7183
Moss ES 800/K-4
4701 Bowfield Dr 37013 615-333-5200
Alison Effinger, prin. Fax 333-5208
Mt. View ES 800/K-5
3820 Murfreesboro Pike 37013 615-641-9393
Dr. Kimberly Fowler, prin. Fax 641-9395

Ezell-Harding Christian S 800/PK-12
574 Bell Rd 37013 615-367-0532
Jim Morris, pres. Fax 399-8747
Lighthouse Christian S 500/K-12
5100 Blue Hole Rd 37013 615-331-6286
Brian Sweatt, admin. Fax 331-2491

Apison, Hamilton
Hamilton County SD
Supt. — See Chattanooga
Apison ES 500/K-5
10433 E Brainerd Rd 37302 423-236-4322
Ronald Hughes, prin. Fax 236-4000

Apison S 50/1-8
11429 Bates Rd 37302 423-236-4926
Mark Seargent, prin. Fax 236-4926

Arlington, Shelby, Pop. 3,534
Shelby County SD
Supt. — See Memphis
Arlington ES 900/K-5
11825 Douglass St 38002 901-867-6000
Gina Gore, prin. Fax 867-6006
Arlington MS 1,200/6-8
5470 Lamb Rd 38002 901-867-6015
Patricia Prescott, prin. Fax 867-6080
Barrets Chapel ES 300/K-5
10280 Godwin Rd 38002 901-873-8160
Barbara Hodge, prin. Fax 829-2343
Shadowlawn MS 900/6-8
4734 Shadowlawn Rd 38002 901-373-2654
John McDonald, prin. Fax 373-1363

Macon Road Baptist S - East 200/K-12
11017 Highway 64 38002 901-867-8161
Jeremy Errett, prin. Fax 766-1610

Ashland City, Cheatham, Pop. 4,550
Cheatham County SD 7,000/PK-12
102 Elizabeth St 37015 615-792-5664
Lynn Seifert, dir. Fax 792-2551
cheatham.k12tn.net
Ashland City ES 500/PK-4
108 Elizabeth St 37015 615-792-4296
Dr. Betty Steen, prin. Fax 792-2030
Cheatham MS 700/5-8
700 Scoutview Rd 37015 615-792-2334
Robin Norris, prin. Fax 792-2337
East Cheatham ES 400/PK-4
3201 Bearwallow Rd 37015 615-746-5251
Dawn Young, prin. Fax 746-4594
Other Schools – See Chapmansboro, Kingston Springs, Pegram, Pleasant View

Athens, McMinn, Pop. 13,878
Athens CSD 1,800/PK-9
943 Crestway Dr 37303 423-745-2863
Dr. Craig Rigell, supt. Fax 745-9041
www.athenscityschools.net
City Park ES 400/K-3
203 Keith Ln 37303 423-745-3862
Holly Rhome-Owens, prin. Fax 745-9577
Four Star Academy 100/PK-PK
625 S Matlock Ave 37303 423-745-0912
Janey Morris, prin. Fax 507-1244
Ingelside ES 400/K-3
200 Guille St 37303 423-745-3671
Teresa Riggin, prin. Fax 745-9665
North City ES 200/4-6
1601 Palos St 37303 423-745-4210
Debbie Harrison, prin. Fax 745-9306
Westside ES 300/4-6
700 Westside St 37303 423-745-4721
Ann Dodson, prin. Fax 745-0621

McMinn County SD 6,000/PK-12
216 N Jackson St 37303 423-745-1612
David Pierce, supt. Fax 744-1641
www.mcminn.k12.tn.us/
Baker S 300/PK-8
1044 County Road 172 37303 423-745-2760
Lee Parkison, prin. Fax 745-5986
Rogers Creek S 400/PK-8
137 County Road 82 37303 423-745-2123
Jeff Derrick, prin. Fax 745-4286
Other Schools – See Calhoun, Englewood, Etowah, Niota, Riceville

---

Fairview Christian Academy 100/K-12
261 County Road 439 37303 423-745-6781
Greg Ranck, prin.

Atoka, Tipton, Pop. 5,676
Tipton County SD
Supt. — See Covington
Atoka ES 900/K-5
870 Rosemark Rd 38004 901-837-5650
Charlotte Fisher, prin. Fax 837-5662

Atwood, Carroll, Pop. 982
West Carroll Special SD 1,000/K-12
1415 Highway 77 38220 731-669-5005
Eric Williams, supt. Fax 669-3860
www.wcssd.org
Other Schools – See Mc Lemoresville, Trezevant

Auburntown, Cannon, Pop. 257
Cannon County SD
Supt. — See Woodbury
Auburn S 100/K-8
150 Vantrease Ave 37016 615-464-4342
Roger Turney, prin. Fax 464-4344

Bartlett, Shelby, Pop. 43,263
Shelby County SD
Supt. — See Memphis
Altruria ES 800/K-5
6641 Deermont Dr 38134 901-373-2600
Marva Johnson, prin. Fax 373-1418
Appling MS 800/6-8
3700 Appling Rd 38133 901-373-1410
Odell Foster, prin. Fax 373-1360

Bartlett ES 1,000/K-5
3932 Billy Maher Rd 38135 901-373-2610
Page Watson, prin. Fax 373-1394
Bon Lin ES 700/K-5
3940 N Germantown Rd 38133 901-937-2344
Kay Williams, prin. Fax 937-3387
Bon Lin MS 6-8
3862 N Germantown Rd 38133 901-347-1520
Dr. Russell Dyer, prin. Fax 347-1491
Ellendale ES 600/K-5
6950 Dawnhill Rd 38135 901-373-2636
Dr. Bess Anne Mcknight, prin. Fax 373-1395
Elmore Park MS 700/6-8
6330 Althorne Rd 38134 901-373-2642
Marjorie Lowe, prin. Fax 373-1361
Oak ES 700/K-5
3573 Oak Rd 38135 901-373-2646
Patricia Rowland, prin. Fax 373-1415
Rivercrest ES 900/K-5
4825 Rivercrest Ln 38135 901-373-1373
Portia Tate, prin. Fax 373-1380

Bartlett Baptist Preschool 100/PK-K
3465 Kirby Whitten Pkwy 38135 901-373-8919
Pam Crawford, dir.

Baxter, Putnam, Pop. 1,333
Putnam County SD
Supt. — See Cookeville
Baxter ES 500/K-4
125 Elmore Town Rd 38544 931-858-3110
Tammy Hoover, prin. Fax 858-4644
Cornerstone MS 500/5-8
371 1st Ave S 38544 931-858-6601
Garry Lee, prin. Fax 858-6637

Bean Station, Grainger, Pop. 2,773
Grainger County SD
Supt. — See Rutledge
Bean Station S 600/PK-6
200 Bean Station School Rd 37708 865-767-2131
Dwayne Brabson, prin. Fax 767-2248

Beech Bluff, Madison
Jackson-Madison County SD
Supt. — See Jackson
Beech Bluff ES 300/PK-4
4488 Beech Bluff Rd 38313 731-422-1572
Pam Betler, prin. Fax 423-8045

Bells, Crockett, Pop. 2,307
Bells CSD 400/PK-5
4532 Highway 88 S 38006 731-663-2739
Charles Williams, supt. Fax 663-2161
www.bellscityschool.org
Bells ES 400/PK-5
4532 Highway 88 S 38006 731-663-2739
Elaine Clement, prin. Fax 663-2161

Benton, Polk, Pop. 1,103
Polk County SD 2,800/PK-12
PO Box 665 37307 423-338-4506
James Jones, supt. Fax 338-2691
www.polk-schools.com
Benton ES 600/PK-5
PO Box 190 37307 423-338-4510
Pam Thomas, prin. Fax 338-7977
Chilhowee MS 500/6-8
PO Box 977 37307 423-338-3102
Ronnie German, prin. Fax 338-3158
Other Schools – See Copperhill, Oldfort

Bethel Springs, McNairy, Pop. 771
McNairy County SD
Supt. — See Selmer
Bethel Springs S 500/K-8
4733 Main St 38315 731-934-7288
Terry Moore, prin. Fax 934-0046

Bethpage, Sumner
Sumner County SD
Supt. — See Gallatin
Bethpage ES 200/K-5
420 Old Highway 31 E 37022 615-841-3212
Bill Johnson, prin. Fax 841-3998
North Sumner ES 200/K-5
1485 N Sumner Rd 37022 615-888-2281
Terry Herndon, prin. Fax 888-3560

Big Rock, Stewart
Stewart County SD
Supt. — See Dover
North Stewart ES 400/PK-5
2201 Highway 79 37023 931-232-5505
Debbie Grasty, prin. Fax 232-8139

Big Sandy, Benton, Pop. 518
Benton County SD
Supt. — See Camden
Big Sandy S 400/K-12
13305 Highway 69A 38221 731-593-3221
Mike Bell, prin. Fax 593-3245

Birchwood, Hamilton
Hamilton County SD
Supt. — See Chattanooga
Birchwood ES 200/PK-5
5623 Highway 60 37308 423-961-2444
Julie Legg, prin. Fax 961-2069

Blountville, Sullivan, Pop. 2,605
Sullivan County SD 12,200/PK-12
PO Box 306 37617 423-354-1000
Jack Barnes, supt. Fax 354-1004
www.sullivank12.net
Blountville ES 300/K-5
155 School Ave 37617 423-354-1650
Evangeline Montgomery, prin. Fax 354-1656
Blountville MS 500/6-8
1651 Blountville Blvd 37617 423-354-1600
Michael Wilson, prin. Fax 354-1606
Central Heights ES 300/K-5
158 Central Heights Rd 37617 423-354-1575
Jeff Hickam, prin. Fax 354-1581
Holston ES 300/K-5
2348 Highway 75 37617 423-354-1550
John Weaver, prin. Fax 354-1555
Holston MS 500/6-8
2348 Highway 75 37617 423-354-1500
Bill Miller, prin. Fax 354-1505
Other Schools – See Bluff City, Bristol, Kingsport, Piney Flats

Bluff City, Sullivan, Pop. 1,602
Sullivan County SD
Supt. — See Blountville
Bluff City ES 500/K-5
282 Maple Dr 37618 423-354-1825
Kerwin Nelson, prin. Fax 354-1831
Bluff City MS 500/6-8
337 Carter St 37618 423-354-1801
Jack Walling, prin. Fax 354-1818

Bolivar, Hardeman, Pop. 5,652
Hardeman County SD 4,300/PK-12
PO Box 112 38008 731-658-2510
Donald Hopper Ph.D., dir. Fax 658-2061
www.hardemancountyschools.org
Bolivar ES 900/PK-5
445 Nuckolls Rd 38008 731-658-3981
Bobby Doyle, prin. Fax 658-2641
Bolivar MS 400/6-8
915 Pruitt St 38008 731-658-3656
Warner Ross, prin. Fax 658-6625
Other Schools – See Grand Junction, Hornsby, Middleton, Toone, Whiteville

Bradford, Gibson, Pop. 1,073
Bradford Special SD 600/K-12
PO Box 220 38316 731-742-3180
Dan Black, supt. Fax 742-3994
www.bradfordssd.com/
Bradford ES 300/K-6
PO Box 99 38316 731-742-2118
Andy Leach, prin. Fax 742-3062

Bradyville, Cannon
Cannon County SD
Supt. — See Woodbury
Woodland S 400/K-8
8383 Jim Cummings Hwy 37026 615-765-5498
Charles Heath, prin. Fax 765-7496

Brentwood, Williamson, Pop. 32,426
Metropolitan Nashville SD
Supt. — See Nashville
Granbery ES 600/K-4
5501 Hill Rd 37027 615-333-5112
Lori Donahue, prin. Fax 262-6901

Williamson County SD
Supt. — See Franklin
Brentwood MS 1,000/6-8
5324 Murray Ln 37027 615-472-4250
Bill Harlin, prin. Fax 472-4263
Crockett ES 600/K-5
9019 Crockett Rd 37027 615-472-4340
Robert Bohrer, prin. Fax 472-4351
Edmondson ES 600/K-5
851 Edmondson Pike 37027 615-472-4360
Julie Sparrow, prin. Fax 472-4371
Grassland ES 700/K-5
6803 Manley Ln 37027 615-472-4480
Dr. Ann Gordon, prin. Fax 472-4492
Kenrose ES 700/K-5
1702 Raintree Pkwy 37027 615-472-4630
Dr. Marilyn Webb, prin. Fax 472-4646
Lipscomb ES 600/PK-5
8011 Concord Rd 37027 615-472-4650
Michelle Contich, prin. Fax 472-4661
Scales ES 600/K-5
6430 Murray Ln 37027 615-472-4830
Rick West, prin. Fax 472-4841
Sunset ES 900/K-5
100 Sunset Trl 37027 615-472-5020
Dr. Tim Brown, prin. Fax 472-5030
Sunset MS 400/6-8
200 Sunset Trl 37027 615-472-5040
Dr. Jason Pearson, prin. Fax 472-5050
Woodland MS 800/6-8
1500 Volunteer Pkwy 37027 615-472-4930
Priscilla Fizer, prin. Fax 472-4941

Currey Ingram Academy 400/K-12
6544 Murray Ln 37027 615-507-3242
Kathleen Rayburn, hdmstr. Fax 507-3170
Montessori Academy 200/PK-8
6021 Cloverland Dr 37027 615-833-3610
Linda Bernstorf, hdmstr. Fax 833-3680

Briceville, Anderson
Anderson County SD
Supt. — See Clinton
Briceville ES 100/K-5
103 Slatestone Rd 37710 865-426-2289
Karen Cupples, prin. Fax 426-6451

Brighton, Tipton, Pop. 2,441
Tipton County SD
Supt. — See Covington
Brighton ES 1,100/K-5
1201 Old Highway 51 S 38011 901-837-5860
Michael Hughes, prin. Fax 837-5879
Brighton MS 1,000/6-8
7785 Highway 51 S 38011 901-837-5600
John Combs, prin. Fax 837-5625

Bristol, Sullivan, Pop. 24,994
Bristol CSD 3,800/PK-12
615 Martin Luther King Blvd 37620 423-652-9451
Gary Lilly, supt. Fax 652-9238
www.btcs.org
Anderson ES 300/PK-6
901 9th St 37620 423-652-9444
Andrew Brown, prin. Fax 652-9497
Avoca ES 500/K-6
2440 Volunteer Pkwy 37620 423-652-9445
Myra Newman, prin. Fax 652-4616
Fairmount/Central ES 200/K-6
735 Martin Luther King Blvd 37620 423-652-9311
Rachel Walk, prin. Fax 652-9436
Haynesfield ES 400/K-6
201 Bluff City Hwy 37620 423-652-9292
Amy Scott, prin. Fax 652-9241
Holston View ES 400/K-6
1840 King College Rd 37620 423-652-9470
Tom Parker, prin. Fax 652-9472
Vance MS 700/7-8
815 Edgemont Ave 37620 423-652-9449
Rigby Kind, prin. Fax 652-9297

Sullivan County SD
Supt. — See Blountville
Akard Memorial ES 200/K-5
224 Mount Area Dr 37620 423-354-1675
Garry Booker, prin. Fax 354-1681
Emmett ES 200/K-5
753 Emmett Rd 37620 423-354-1865
Robin McClellan, prin. Fax 354-1871
Holston Valley MS 200/6-8
1717 Bristol Caverns Hwy 37620 423-354-1880
Jess Lockhart, prin. Fax 354-1891
Valley Pike ES 100/K-5
2125 Carolina Ave 37620 423-354-1855
Dr. Mary Rouse, prin. Fax 354-1861
Weaver ES 300/K-5
3341 Weaver Pike 37620 423-354-1853
Randy Gentry, prin. Fax 354-1849

Mountain Empire Baptist S 100/K-12
1317 Weaver Pike 37620 423-968-7116
Zach Wagner, prin. Fax 968-7206
Tri-Cities Christian S - Bristol 200/PK-6
2031 Broad St 37620 423-968-3574
Alicia Holder, prin.

Brownsville, Haywood, Pop. 10,720
Haywood County SD 3,500/PK-12
900 E Main St 38012 731-772-9613
Marlon King, supt. Fax 772-3275
www.haywood.k12.tn.us
Anderson ECC 500/PK-K
620 W Main St 38012 731-772-9053
Mary Colling, prin. Fax 772-7621
East Side ES 500/3-4
1315 E Jefferson St 38012 731-772-1233
Tammie Canada, prin. Fax 772-0991
Haywood ES 500/1-2
312 N Grand Ave 38012 731-772-0732
Jean Wills, prin. Fax 779-1995
Haywood JHS 600/7-8
1201 Haralson St 38012 731-772-3265
Dontye Bradford, prin. Fax 772-3352
Sunny Hill ES 500/5-6
2401 Anderson Ave 38012 731-772-3401
Dorothy Bond, prin. Fax 772-3401

Bruceton, Carroll, Pop. 1,486
Hollow Rock-Bruceton Special SD 700/K-12
PO Box 135 38317 731-586-7657
Rod Sturdivant, supt. Fax 586-7419
www.hrbk12.org
Central ES 300/K-5
PO Box 135 38317 731-586-2171
Jennie Nunamaker, prin. Fax 586-7419
Central MS 200/6-8
PO Box 135 38317 731-586-2161
Tim Gilmer, prin. Fax 586-7419

Buchanan, Henry
Henry County SD
Supt. — See Paris
Lakewood ES 500/PK-5
6745 Highway 79 N Ste A 38222 731-644-1600
Barbra Thoeming, prin. Fax 644-0680
Lakewood MS 300/6-8
6745 Highway 79 N Ste B 38222 731-644-1600
Barbra Thoeming, prin. Fax 644-0680

Bulls Gap, Hawkins, Pop. 716
Hawkins County SD
Supt. — See Rogersville
Bulls Gap S 400/K-8
315 Allen Dr 37711 423-235-5201
Sharon Southern, prin. Fax 235-7687
St. Clair ES 200/K-5
1350 Melinda Ferry Rd 37711 423-235-2721
Thomas Floyd, prin. Fax 235-2721

Burns, Dickson, Pop. 1,402
Dickson County SD
Supt. — See Dickson
Stuart-Burns ES 700/K-5
3201 Highway 96 37029 615-446-2791
Lisa Cooper, prin. Fax 441-4140

Butler, Carter
Carter County SD
Supt. — See Elizabethton
Little Milligan S 100/K-8
4226 Highway 321 37640 423-768-4400
J.R. Campbell, prin. Fax 768-4403

Byrdstown, Pickett, Pop. 875
Pickett County SD 700/K-12
141 Skyline Dr 38549 931-864-3123
Diane Elder, supt. Fax 864-7185

Pickett County S 500/K-8
1016 Woodlawn Dr 38549 931-864-3496
Kenny Tompkins, prin. Fax 864-3258

Calhoun, McMinn, Pop. 513
McMinn County SD
Supt. — See Athens
Calhoun S 400/PK-8
PO Box 129 37309 423-336-2974
Larson Frerichs, prin. Fax 336-3878

Camden, Benton, Pop. 3,736
Benton County SD 2,600/K-12
197 Briarwood St 38320 731-584-6111
Randall Robertson, supt. Fax 584-8142
www.bcos.org/index/
Briarwood IS 400/3-5
169 Briarwood St 38320 731-584-4257
Sharon Latendresse, prin. Fax 593-3245
Camden ES 400/K-2
208 Washington Ave 38320 731-584-4918
Lori Cantrell, prin. Fax 584-0554
Camden JHS 400/6-8
75 Schools Dr 38320 731-584-4518
Michelle Leonard, prin. Fax 584-4493
Other Schools – See Big Sandy, Holladay

Carthage, Smith, Pop. 2,268
Smith County SD 3,500/PK-12
126 Smith Co Middle Sch Ln 37030 615-735-9625
Roger Lewis, supt. Fax 735-8271
boe.smithcounty.com/
Carthage ES 500/PK-6
149 Skyline Dr 37030 615-735-0433
Tim Nesbitt, prin. Fax 735-8256
Defeated S 200/K-8
451 Defeated Creek Hwy 37030 615-774-3150
Meranda Cook, prin.
Smith County MS 400/5-8
134 Smith Co Mid School Ln 37030 615-735-8277
Ronnie Scudder, prin. Fax 735-8255
Union Heights S 300/K-8
663 Lebanon Hwy 37030 615-735-1975
Richard Anderson, prin. Fax 736-0667
Other Schools – See Elmwood, Gordonsville

Caryville, Campbell, Pop. 2,380
Campbell County SD
Supt. — See Jacksboro
Caryville ES 300/PK-5
140 Lake Rd 37714 423-562-2687
Sandra Chaniott, prin. Fax 566-8918

Cedar Grove, Bedford

Leach Christian S 50/1-8
9575 Highway 70 38321 731-987-3778
Ken McHenry, prin.

Cedar Hill, Robertson, Pop. 310
Robertson County SD
Supt. — See Springfield
Byrns ES 500/PK-5
6399 Highway 41 N 37032 615-696-0533
Sherry Hall, prin. Fax 696-0795

Celina, Clay, Pop. 1,369
Clay County SD 1,100/K-12
PO Box 469 38551 931-243-3310
Donnie Cherry, supt. Fax 243-3706
www.clay-lea.k12.tn.us/
Celina S 500/K-8
PO Box 409 38551 931-243-2391
Joann McLerran, prin. Fax 243-4428
Other Schools – See Allons, Red Boiling Springs

Centerville, Hickman, Pop. 4,002
Hickman County SD 4,000/PK-12
115 Murphree Ave 37033 931-729-3391
Dr. Jerry Nash, dir. Fax 729-3834
www.hickman.k12tn.net/
Centerville ES 500/PK-2
104 Maryfield Ave 37033 931-729-2212
Misty Shelton, prin. Fax 729-6094
Centerville IS 400/3-5
110 Maryfield Ave 37033 931-729-2748
Alicia Baker, prin. Fax 729-5497
Hickman County MS 400/6-8
1639 Bulldog Blvd 37033 931-729-4234
Vicky Smith, prin. Fax 729-5688
Other Schools – See Lyles

Martin Memorial S 50/1-8
900 Highway 50 37033 931-729-9856
Marcia Kesselring, prin. Fax 729-9856

Chapel Hill, Marshall, Pop. 1,019
Marshall County SD
Supt. — See Lewisburg
Chapel Hill ES 800/K-6
415 S Horton Pkwy 37034 931-364-3435
Dean Delk, prin. Fax 364-3540

Chapmansboro, Cheatham
Cheatham County SD
Supt. — See Ashland City
West Cheatham ES 400/K-4
3120 Highway 12 N 37035 615-792-5167
Amber Raymer, prin. Fax 792-1230

Charleston, Bradley, Pop. 644
Bradley County SD
Supt. — See Cleveland
Charleston ES 300/K-5
PO Box 435 37310 423-336-2232
Jodie Grannan, prin. Fax 336-3692

Charlotte, Dickson, Pop. 1,155
Dickson County SD
Supt. — See Dickson
Charlotte ES 500/PK-5
PO Box 70 37036 615-740-5803
Malissa Johnson, prin. Fax 789-6388
Charlotte MS 400/6-8
PO Box 40 37036 615-740-6060
Ray Lecomte, prin. Fax 789-7033

Chattanooga, Hamilton, Pop. 154,762
Hamilton County SD 40,500/PK-12
3074 Hickory Valley Rd 37421 423-209-8460
Dr. Jim Scales, supt. Fax 209-8601
www.hcde.org
Alpine Crest ES 300/K-5
4700 Stagg Rd 37415 423-874-1921
Karen Day, prin. Fax 874-1939
Barger Academy of Fine Arts 400/K-5
4808 Brainerd Rd 37411 423-493-0348
Gregory Bagby, prin. Fax 493-0354
Battle Academy 400/K-5
1601 S Market St 37408 423-209-5747
Ruth White, prin. Fax 209-5748
Brown Academy 400/PK-5
718 E 8th St 37403 423-209-5760
Lea Ann Burk, prin. Fax 209-5761
Chattanooga Arts & Sciences ES 400/K-5
865 E 3rd St 37403 423-209-5816
William Fain, prin. Fax 209-5817
Chattanooga S for Liberal Arts 400/K-8
6579 E Brainerd Rd 37421 423-855-2614
Ismahen Kangles, prin. Fax 855-9429
Clifton Hills ES 400/PK-5
1815 E 32nd St 37407 423-493-0357
Krystal Scarborough, prin. Fax 493-0362
Dalewood MS 300/6-8
1300 Shallowford Rd 37411 423-493-0323
Linda Darden, prin. Fax 493-0327
Donaldson ES 300/PK-5
927 W 37th St 37410 423-825-7337
Valerie Brown, prin. Fax 825-7335
DuPont ES 300/K-5
4134 Hixson Pike 37415 423-870-0615
Anita Coleman, prin. Fax 870-0631
East Brainerd ES 500/K-5
7453 E Brainerd Rd 37421 423-855-2600
Bryan Stewart, prin. Fax 855-2610
East Lake Academy of Fine Arts 400/6-8
2700 E 34th St 37407 423-493-0334
Charles Joynes, prin. Fax 493-0343
East Lake ES 300/PK-5
3600 13th Ave 37407 423-493-0366
Neelie Parker, prin. Fax 493-0370
East Ridge ES 300/K-5
1014 John Ross Rd 37412 423-493-9296
Sharon Watts, prin. Fax 493-9298
East Ridge MS 700/6-8
4400 Bennett Rd 37412 423-867-6214
Steven Robinson, prin. Fax 867-6226
East Side ES 600/K-5
1603 S Lyerly St 37404 423-493-7780
Emily Baker, prin. Fax 493-7784
Hardy ES 600/PK-5
2100 Glass St 37406 423-493-0301
Natalie Elder, prin. Fax 493-0302
Hillcrest ES 300/K-5
4302 Bonny Oaks Dr 37416 423-855-2602
Katrina Lawrence, prin. Fax 855-2604
Lakeside Academy 500/PK-5
4850 Jersey Pike 37416 423-855-2605
Marsha Drake, prin. Fax 855-2607
Lookout Valley ES 300/PK-5
701 Browns Ferry Rd 37419 423-825-7370
Judy Solovey, prin. Fax 825-7371
McBrien ES 500/PK-5
1501 Tombras Ave 37412 423-867-6209
Madeline Bell, prin. Fax 867-6225
Normal Park Museum Magnet Lower S 300/PK-5
1009 Mississippi Ave 37405 423-209-5900
Jill Levine, prin. Fax 209-5901
Normal Park Museum Magnet Upper S 300/6-8
1219 W Mississippi Ave 37405 423-209-5914
Jill Levine, admin. Fax 209-5920
Orchard Knob ES 300/PK-5
400 N Orchard Knob Ave 37404 423-493-0385
Marthel Young, prin. Fax 493-0388
Orchard Knob MS 400/6-8
500 N Highland Park Ave 37404 423-493-7793
Maryo Beck, prin. Fax 493-7795
Red Bank ES 700/K-5
1100 Mountain Creek Rd 37405 423-874-1917
Stephanie Hinton, prin. Fax 874-1918
Red Bank MS 600/6-8
3715 Dayton Blvd 37415 423-874-1908
Kathryn Obrien, prin. Fax 874-1938
Rivermont ES 300/PK-5
3330 Hixson Pike 37415 423-870-0610
Leesa Kerns, prin. Fax 870-0611
Shepherd ES 500/K-5
7126 Tyner Rd 37421 423-855-2611
Ray Evans, prin. Fax 855-2668
Spring Creek ES 500/PK-5
1100 Spring Creek Rd 37412 423-855-6138
Paula Burgner, prin. Fax 855-6150
Tyner Middle Academy 400/6-8
6837 Tyner Rd 37421 423-855-2648
Delia Price, prin. Fax 855-2699
Westview ES 700/K-5
9629 E Brainerd Rd 37421 423-855-6141
Margo Williams, prin. Fax 892-2199
Woodmore ES 400/PK-5
800 Woodmore Ln 37411 423-493-0394
Visa Harper, prin. Fax 493-0396
Other Schools – See Apison, Birchwood, Harrison, Hixson, Lookout Mountain, Ooltewah, Sale Creek, Signal Mountain, Soddy Daisy

---

Avondale SDA S 50/PK-8
1201 N Orchard Knob Ave 37406 423-698-5028
Mari Edi Gardner, prin. Fax 697-7803
Belvoir Christian Academy 200/PK-8
800 Belvoir Ave 37412 423-622-3755
Frank Streufert, prin. Fax 622-0177
Boyd-Buchanan S 900/PK-12
4626 Bonnieway Dr 37411 423-622-6177
Lanny Witt, pres. Fax 508-2219
Brainerd Baptist S 300/PK-5
PO Box 8099 37414 423-622-3873
Sean Corcoran, prin. Fax 624-5164
Bright S 400/PK-5
1950 Hixson Pike 37405 423-267-8546
O.J. Morgan, hdmstr. Fax 265-0025
Calvary Christian S 100/PK-12
4601 North Ter 37411 423-622-2181
Tim Rowe, prin.
Chattanooga Christian S 1,100/K-12
3354 Charger Dr 37409 423-265-6411
Don Holwerda, pres. Fax 756-4044
Grace Baptist Academy 400/PK-12
7815 Shallowford Rd 37421 423-892-8224
David Patrick, hdmstr. Fax 892-1194
Hickory Valley Christian S 200/K-8
6605 Shallowford Rd 37421 423-894-3200
Ginny Young, prin. Fax 894-8665
Montessori S 200/PK-8
300 Montessori Way 37404 423-622-6366
Roberta Spink, prin. Fax 622-6027
Our Lady of Perpetual Help S 300/K-8
505 S Moore Rd 37412 423-622-1481
Jeri McInturff, prin. Fax 622-2016
St. Jude S 400/PK-8
930 Ashland Ter Ste 1 37415 423-877-6022
Jamie Goodhard, prin. Fax 875-8920
St. Nicholas S 200/PK-5
7525 Min Tom Dr 37421 423-899-1999
Mark Fallo, hdmstr. Fax 899-0109
St. Peter's Episcopal S 200/PK-5
848 Ashland Ter 37415 423-870-1794
Kathleen Lanza, hdmstr. Fax 877-2604
Silverdale Baptist Academy 700/K-12
7236 Bonny Oaks Dr 37421 423-892-2319
Rebecca Hansard, hdmstr. Fax 648-7600
Standifer Gap SDA S 100/PK-8
8255 Standifer Gap Rd 37421 423-892-6013
Sheryl Stull, prin. Fax 664-4891
Tennessee Temple Academy 300/PK-12
1907 Bailey Ave 37404 423-493-4337
William Basham, prin. Fax 643-8360

Christiana, Rutherford
Rutherford County SD
Supt. — See Murfreesboro
Christiana ES 600/K-5
4701 Shelbyville Pike 37037 615-896-0614
Julie Benson, prin. Fax 896-3715
Christiana MS 900/6-8
4675 Shelbyville Pike 37037 615-904-3885
Dr. John Ash, prin. Fax 904-3886

Chuckey, Greene
Greene County SD
Supt. — See Greeneville
Chuckey ES 400/PK-5
1605 Chuckey Hwy 37641 423-257-2108
Teresa Taylor, prin. Fax 257-3938

Washington County SD
Supt. — See Jonesborough
South Central S 300/K-8
2955 Highway 107 37641 423-753-1135
Mike Edmonds, prin. Fax 753-1135

Church Hill, Hawkins, Pop. 6,370
Hawkins County SD
Supt. — See Rogersville
Carters Valley ES 500/K-5
1006 N Central Ave 37642 423-357-7450
Lisa Webb, prin. Fax 357-5169
Church Hill ES 400/K-5
400 Old Stage Rd 37642 423-357-5621
Richard Hutson, prin. Fax 357-4422
Church Hill MS 700/6-8
PO Box 38 37642 423-357-3051
William Christian, prin. Fax 357-9873
McPheeters Bend ES 100/K-5
1115 Goshen Valley Rd 37642 423-357-6822
Renee Bernard, prin. Fax 357-5437

Clairfield, Claiborne
Claiborne County SD
Supt. — See Tazewell
Clairfield S 100/K-8
6360 Highway 90 37715 423-784-6052
Linda Keck, prin. Fax 784-6052

Clarksburg, Carroll, Pop. 375
South Carroll County Special SD 400/PK-12
PO Box 219 38324 731-986-4534
Diana Collins, supt. Fax 986-4562
www.rocketsonline.org/
Clarksburg S 400/PK-12
PO Box 219 38324 731-986-3165
Trey Crews, prin. Fax 986-4562

Clarksville, Montgomery, Pop. 112,878
Clarksville-Montgomery County SD 27,100/PK-12
621 Gracey Ave 37040 931-920-7808
Michael Harris, supt. Fax 648-5612
www.cmcss.net
Barkers Mill ES 900/K-5
1230 Little Bobcat Ln 37042 931-906-7235
Rhonda Kennedy, prin. Fax 503-2643
Barksdale ES 600/K-5
1920 Madison St 37043 931-648-5685
Peggy Vaden, prin. Fax 533-2087

Burt ES 200/4-5
110 Bailey St 37040 931-648-5630
Irene Gudgeon, prin. Fax 553-2088
Cumberland Heights ES 700/K-5
2093 Ussery Rd S 37040 931-648-5695
Tonya Cunningham, prin. Fax 503-3400
Darden ES 600/K-5
609 E St 37042 931-648-5615
Michelle Rayle, prin. Fax 553-2089
East Montgomery ES 800/K-5
230 McAdoo Creek Rd 37043 931-358-2868
Yvonne Hackney, prin. Fax 358-4092
Glenellen ES 1,100/K-5
825 Needmore Rd 37040 931-920-6158
Cindy Adams, prin. Fax 920-6163
Hazelwood ES 700/PK-5
2623 Tiny Town Rd 37042 931-553-2075
Rosanne Sanford, prin. Fax 503-3403
Kenwood ES 800/K-5
1101 Peachers Mill Rd 37042 931-553-2059
Sallie Oden, prin. Fax 503-3401
Kenwood MS 1,000/6-8
241 E Pine Mountain Rd 37042 931-553-2080
Frank Wilson, prin. Fax 552-3080
Liberty ES 600/K-5
849 S Liberty Church Rd 37042 931-905-5729
Kim Masters, prin. Fax 905-5734
Minglewood ES 800/K-5
215 Cunningham Ln 37042 931-648-5646
Jane Winter, prin. Fax 503-3402
Moore ES 400/K-5
1350 Madison St 37040 931-648-5635
Laura Black, prin. Fax 503-3404
New Providence MS 1,000/6-8
146 Cunningham Ln 37042 931-648-5655
Laura Barnett, prin. Fax 503-3409
Northeast ES 900/K-5
3705 Trenton Rd 37040 931-648-5662
Jane Lezon, prin. Fax 553-6986
Northeast MS 1,400/6-8
3703 Trenton Rd 37040 931-648-5665
Tracy Hollinger, prin. Fax 503-3410
Richview MS 900/6-8
2350 Memorial Drive Ext 37043 931-648-5620
Mary Gist, prin. Fax 551-8111
Ringgold ES 800/K-5
240 Ringgold Rd 37042 931-648-5625
Melinda Harris, prin. Fax 503-3406
Rossview ES K-5
2235 Cardinal Ln 37043 931-645-1403
Paula Ford, prin. Fax 920-9949
Rossview MS 1,000/6-8
2265 Cardinal Ln 37043 931-920-6150
Anna Neubauer, prin. Fax 920-6147
St. Bethlehem ES 600/K-3
2450 Old Russellville Pike 37040 931-648-5670
Gina Biter, prin. Fax 503-3408
Sango ES 1,000/K-5
3585 Sango Rd 37043 931-358-4093
Priscilla Story, prin. Fax 358-4098
Smith ES 500/K-5
740 Greenwood Ave 37040 931-648-5660
Maribeth Sisk, prin. Fax 503-3405
West Creek ES K-5
1201 W Creek Coyote Trl 37042 931-802-8637
Beth Unfried, prin. Fax 920-9977
West Creek MS 6-8
1202 W Creek Coyote Trl 37042 931-503-3288
Matthew Blake, prin. Fax 503-3296
Other Schools – See Cunningham, Woodlawn

Clarksville Academy 500/PK-12
710 N 2nd St 37040 931-647-6311
Kay Drew, hdmstr. Fax 906-0610
Clarksville Christian S 100/PK-8
501 Highway 76 37043 931-647-8180
Lisa Tucker, prin.
St. Mary S 100/PK-8
1901 Madison St 37043 931-645-1865
Denise Tucker, prin. Fax 645-1160
Tabernacle Christian S 50/PK-5
303 Market St 37042 931-552-9431
Katobwa Stallworth, prin. Fax 552-9148
Unity Christian Academy 50/1-12
1800 Memorial Dr 37043 931-645-6003
Jacqueline Hale, prin. Fax 645-6226

Cleveland, Bradley, Pop. 38,186
Bradley County SD 10,500/K-12
800 S Lee Hwy 37311 423-476-0620
Johnny McDaniel, supt. Fax 476-0485
www.bradleyschools.org
Black Fox ES 400/K-5
3119 Varnell Rd SW 37311 423-478-8800
Kim Fisher, prin. Fax 478-8850
Blue Springs ES 200/K-5
4832 Blue Springs Rd 37311 423-478-8801
Debra Bailey, prin. Fax 478-8851
Hopewell ES 500/K-5
5350 Freewill Rd NW 37312 423-478-8802
Tim Riggs, prin. Fax 478-8804
Lake Forest MS 1,200/6-8
610 Kile Lake Rd SE 37323 423-478-8821
Ritchie Stevenson, prin. Fax 478-8832
Michigan Avenue ES 600/K-5
188 Michigan Avenue School 37323 423-478-8807
Sheena Newman, prin. Fax 478-8856
North Lee ES 500/K-5
205 Sequoia Rd NW 37312 423-478-8809
Nat Akiona, prin. Fax 478-8811
Oak Grove ES 500/K-5
400 Durkee Rd SE 37323 423-478-8812
Melvin Bryson, prin. Fax 478-8866
Ocoee MS 1,300/6-8
2250 N Ocoee St 37311 423-476-0630
Ron Spangler, prin. Fax 476-0588
Prospect ES 400/K-5
2450 Prospect School Rd NW 37312 423-478-8814
Steve Montgomery, prin. Fax 478-8815
Taylor ES 400/K-5
5265 Bates Pike SE 37323 423-478-8817
Sherry Shroyer, prin. Fax 478-8853
Valley View ES 300/K-5
5607 Spring Place Rd SE 37323 423-478-8825
Sherrie Ledford, prin. Fax 478-8526
Waterville ES 600/K-5
4081 Dalton Pike SE 37323 423-478-8827
Charlene Cofer, prin. Fax 478-8873
Other Schools – See Charleston

Cleveland CSD 4,500/K-12
4300 Mouse Creek Rd NW 37312 423-472-9571
Dr. Frederick Denning, dir. Fax 472-3390
www.clevelandschools.org
Arnold ES 300/K-5
473 8th St NW 37311 423-472-2241
Kellye Bender, prin. Fax 472-9877
Blythe-Bower ES 500/K-5
604 20th St SE 37311 423-479-5121
Kelly Kiser, prin. Fax 472-2459
Cleveland MS 1,000/6-8
3635 Georgetown Rd NW 37312 423-479-9641
Jeffrey Elliott, prin. Fax 479-9553
Mayfield ES 300/K-5
501 20th St NE 37311 423-472-4541
Dee Dee Finison, prin. Fax 472-2539
Ross ES 400/3-5
4340 Mouse Creek Rd NW 37312 423-479-7274
Doug Moore, prin. Fax 472-9763
Stuart ES 400/K-5
802 20th St NW 37311 423-476-8246
Randall Stephens, prin. Fax 479-5016
Yates PS 400/K-2
750 Mouse Creek Rd NW 37312 423-479-1723
Carolyn Ingram, prin. Fax 472-2388

Bowman Hills SDA S 100/K-8
300 Westview Dr NE 37312 423-476-6014
Larry Robbins, prin. Fax 476-6063
Cleveland Christian S 100/K-12
PO Box 3596 37320 423-476-2642
Linda King, prin.
Shenandoah Baptist Academy 100/K-12
PO Box 5207 37320 423-339-0992
Robert Nelms, prin. Fax 339-0117
Tennessee Christian Academy 200/PK-12
4995 N Lee Hwy 37312 423-559-8939
Kathi Douglas, hdmstr. Fax 476-4974

Clifton, Wayne, Pop. 2,679
Wayne County SD
Supt. — See Waynesboro
Hughes S 300/PK-12
PO Box A 38425 931-676-3325
Marlon Davis, prin. Fax 676-3903

Clinton, Anderson, Pop. 9,381
Anderson County SD 7,100/PK-12
101 S Main St 37716 865-463-2800
Larry Foster, supt. Fax 457-9157
www.acs.ac
Clinton MS 700/6-8
110 N Hicks St 37716 865-457-3451
Bob Stokes, prin. Fax 457-9486
Dutch Valley ES 200/PK-5
1044 Old Dutch Valley Rd 37716 865-457-2599
Mike Harmening, prin. Fax 457-0152
Grand Oaks ES 300/PK-5
1033 Oliver Springs Hwy 37716 865-435-7506
Katrina Oakley, prin. Fax 435-5346
Other Schools – See Andersonville, Briceville, Heiskell, Lake City, Norris, Oliver Springs, Powell

Clinton CSD 900/PK-6
212 N Hicks St 37716 865-457-0225
Vicki Violette, dir. Fax 463-0668
www.clintonschools.org
Clinton ES 400/PK-6
210 N Hicks St 37716 865-457-0616
Jamie Jordan, prin. Fax 457-1024
North Clinton ES 200/K-6
305 Beets St 37716 865-457-2784
Matt Murphy, prin. Fax 457-1193
South Clinton ES 300/PK-6
242 Hiway Dr 37716 865-457-2684
Lori Collins, prin. Fax 457-1089

Coalfield, Morgan
Morgan County SD
Supt. — See Wartburg
Coalfield S 500/K-12
PO Box 98 37719 865-435-7332
Robert Bennett, prin. Fax 435-2646

Coalmont, Grundy, Pop. 971
Grundy County SD
Supt. — See Altamont
Coalmont S 200/PK-8
PO Box 148 37313 931-592-9453
Dr. Russell Ladd, prin. Fax 592-9455

Cumberland Heights SDA S 50/K-8
67 Old Highway 56 37313 931-692-3982
Pamela Cross, prin.

Collegedale, Hamilton, Pop. 7,215

Spalding SDA S 400/K-8
PO Box 568 37315 423-396-2122
Murray Cooper, prin. Fax 396-2218

College Grove, Williamson
Williamson County SD
Supt. — See Franklin
College Grove ES 200/PK-5
6668 Arno College Grove Rd 37046 615-472-4320
Dr. Melonye Lowe, prin. Fax 472-4331

Collierville, Shelby, Pop. 37,564
Shelby County SD
Supt. — See Memphis
Bailey Station ES 800/K-5
3435 Bailey Station Rd 38017 901-853-6380
Sherry Roper, prin.
Collierville ES 800/K-5
590 Peterson Lake Rd 38017 901-853-3300
Louise Claney, prin. Fax 853-3326
Collierville MS 900/6-8
146 College St 38017 901-853-3320
Ingrid Warren, prin. Fax 853-3327
Crosswind ES 700/K-5
831 Shelton Rd 38017 901-853-3330
Kim Lampkins, prin. Fax 854-2343
Schilling Farms MS 1,000/6-8
935 Colbert St S 38017 901-854-2345
Sherry Phillips, prin. Fax 854-8200
Sycamore ES 700/K-5
1155 Sycamore Rd 38017 901-854-8202
Dr. Patricia Butler, prin. Fax 854-8207
Tara Oaks ES 900/K-5
600 E Harpers Ferry Dr 38017 901-853-3337
Patricia Russell, prin. Fax 854-2349

Central Day S 400/K-8
2005 E Winchester Blvd 38017 901-255-8134
John Spice, prin. Fax 255-8203
Incarnation S 200/PK-8
360 Bray Station Rd 38017 901-853-7804
Connie Berman, prin. Fax 854-0536

Collinwood, Wayne, Pop. 1,045
Wayne County SD
Supt. — See Waynesboro
Collinwood ES 400/PK-4
450 N Trojan Blvd 38450 931-724-9118
Judy England, prin. Fax 724-5447
Collinwood MS 300/5-8
300 4th Ave N 38450 931-724-9510
Robert Vandiver, prin. Fax 924-2519

Columbia, Maury, Pop. 33,777
Maury County SD 12,100/PK-12
501 W 8th St 38401 931-388-8403
Eddie Hickman, supt. Fax 840-4410
www.mauryk12.org/
Baker ES 400/K-5
1301 Hampshire Pike 38401 931-388-3319
Della Matlock, prin. Fax 840-4414
Brown ES 300/K-5
301 Cord Dr 38401 931-388-3601
Tina Weatherford, prin. Fax 380-4670
Cox MS 700/6-8
633 Bear Creek Pike 38401 931-840-3902
Dr. Debbie Steen, prin. Fax 840-3903
Highland Park ES 400/K-5
1606 Highland Ave 38401 931-388-7325
Wanda Dunn, prin. Fax 380-4862
Howell ES 800/K-5
653 Bear Creek Pike 38401 931-540-1032
Connie Brown, prin. Fax 540-2977
McDowell ES 300/K-5
714 W 7th St 38401 931-840-4418
Kevin Eady, prin. Fax 381-2320
Riverside ES 500/K-5
203 Carter St 38401 931-840-4422
Ken Wiles, prin. Fax 380-4696
Whitthorne MS 1,100/6-8
1325 Hampshire Pike 38401 931-388-2558
Linda Lester, prin. Fax 380-4684
Woodard ES 600/PK-5
207 Rutherford Ln 38401 931-380-2872
Bonnie Rodgers, prin. Fax 380-4667
Other Schools – See Culleoka, Hampshire, Mount Pleasant, Santa Fe, Spring Hill

---

Columbia Academy 600/K-12
1101 W 7th St 38401 931-388-5363
Jon Bennett, prin. Fax 380-8506
Zion Christian Academy 400/PK-12
6901 Old Zion Rd 38401 931-388-5731
Don Wahlman, hdmstr. Fax 388-5842

Cookeville, Putnam, Pop. 27,743
Jackson County SD
Supt. — See Gainesboro
Dodson Branch S 200/K-8
16221 Dodson Branch Hwy 38501 931-268-0761
Tammy Woolbright, prin.

Putnam County SD 10,500/PK-12
1400 E Spring St 38506 931-526-9777
Dr. Kathleen Airhart, dir. Fax 528-6942
www.putnamcountyschools.com
Cane Creek ES 400/PK-4
1500 W Jackson St 38501 931-520-1173
Donna Shanks, prin. Fax 520-1426
Capshaw ES 600/K-4
1 Cougar Ln 38501 931-526-2414
Kim Wright, prin. Fax 372-0383
Northeast ES 500/PK-4
575 N Old Kentucky Rd 38501 931-526-2978
Fay Borden, prin. Fax 372-0385
Park View ES 500/PK-4
545 Scott Ave 38501 931-526-2516
Bobby Winningham, prin. Fax 520-0209
Prescott Central MS 900/5-6
242 E 10th St 38501 931-528-3647
Sandra Joslin, prin. Fax 520-2018
Sycamore ES 400/PK-4
452 Ellis Ave 38501 931-526-9322
Ed Wheaton, prin. Fax 372-0387

Trace MS 800/7-8
230 Raider Dr 38501 931-520-2200
Linda Nash, prin. Fax 520-2204
Whitson ES 400/PK-4
288 E Main St 38506 931-526-6575
Teri Anderson, prin. Fax 372-0384
Other Schools – See Algood, Baxter, Monterey

Cookeville Christian S 50/K-8
2660 Highway 111 N 38506 931-537-3561
Eleanor Langford, prin. Fax 526-8195
Daniel 1 Academy 100/1-12
1654 Burgess Falls Rd 38506 931-432-1496
Cynthia Holman, prin. Fax 432-1498
Heavenly Host Lutheran S 200/PK-8
777 S Willow Ave 38501 931-520-3766
Elizabeth Wickersham, prin. Fax 372-2016
Highland Rim Academy 100/K-7
PO Box 3022 38502 931-526-4472
Daniel Bailey, prin. Fax 526-4472

Copperhill, Polk, Pop. 482
Polk County SD
Supt. — See Benton
Copper Basin ES 500/PK-6
206 Cougar Dr 37317 423-496-3271
Doris Housley, prin. Fax 496-3272

Cordova, Shelby
Memphis CSD
Supt. — See Memphis
Cordova ES 700/K-4
750 N Sanga Rd 38018 901-416-1700
Tamera Avanzi, prin. Fax 416-1701
Cordova MS 1,100/5-8
900 N Sanga Rd 38018 901-416-2189
Joy Whitehead, prin. Fax 416-2191

Shelby County SD
Supt. — See Memphis
Chimneyrock ES 1,100/K-4
8601 Chimneyrock Blvd 38016 901-756-2316
Daphanie Swife, prin. Fax 759-3019
Dexter ES 1,000/K-4
7105 Dexter Rd 38016 901-373-3526
Cherry Davidson, prin. Fax 373-8561
Dexter MS 600/5-8
6998 Raleigh LaGrange Rd 38018 901-373-3134
Phyllis Jones, prin. Fax 373-3378
Macon-Hall ES 1,000/K-5
9800 Macon Rd 38016 901-759-4530
Mary Anne Spencer, prin. Fax 759-4536
Mt. Pisgah MS 1,200/5-8
1444 Pisgah Rd 38016 901-756-2386
John Gilmer, prin. Fax 756-2306

Briarcrest Christian S - Leawood Campus 200/PK-5
1620 N Houston Levee Rd 38016 901-737-1356
Carol Hughey, prin. Fax 737-0463
First Assembly Christian S 800/PK-12
8650 Walnut Grove Rd 38018 901-458-5543
Wendell Meadows, supt. Fax 324-3558
Harding Academy of Memphis - Cordova 300/1-6
8360 Macon Rd 38018 901-624-0522
Pamela Womack, pres. Fax 322-3037
Harding Acad of Memphis - Cordova Kndgtn 100/K-K
8350 Macon Rd 38018 901-757-1008
Beth Kelley, dir.
Lamplighter Montessori S 200/PK-8
8563 Fay Rd 38018 901-751-2000
Terrie Sampson, prin. Fax 758-3200
St. Francis of Assisi S 1,000/PK-8
2100 N Germantown Pkwy 38016 901-388-7321
Beth York, prin. Fax 388-8201

Cornersville, Marshall, Pop. 937
Marshall County SD
Supt. — See Lewisburg
Cornersville ES 500/K-6
485 N Main St 37047 931-293-2327
Bonnie Reese, prin. Fax 293-6829

Corryton, Knox, Pop. 100
Knox County SD
Supt. — See Knoxville
Corryton ES 200/K-5
7200 Corryton Rd 37721 865-687-4573
Brandon Pratt, prin. Fax 689-0867
Gibbs ES 700/K-5
7715 Tazewell Pike 37721 865-689-1497
Adam Parker, prin. Fax 688-0712

New Hope Christian S 100/PK-8
7602 Bud Hawkins Rd 37721 865-688-5330
Emily Pursiful, prin. Fax 688-3052

Cosby, Cocke
Cocke County SD
Supt. — See Newport
Cosby S 600/K-8
3320 Cosby Hwy 37722 423-487-3850
Nora Wilson, prin. Fax 487-2845
Smoky Mountain S 200/K-8
135 S Highway 32 37722 423-487-2255
Joe Burchette, prin. Fax 487-5382

Sevier County SD
Supt. — See Sevierville
Jones Cove S 200/PK-8
4554 Jones Cove Rd 37722 865-453-9325
Dr. Shannon Sullivan, prin. Fax 453-2779

Cottontown, Sumner
Sumner County SD
Supt. — See Gallatin
Oakmont ES 100/K-5
3323 Highway 76 37048 615-325-5313
Lynne Porter, prin. Fax 325-5316

Counce, Hardin
Hardin County SD
Supt. — See Savannah
South Side S 200/K-8
1970 Highway 57 38326 731-689-5185
Jennifer Copeland, prin. Fax 689-5214

Covington, Tipton, Pop. 9,018
Tipton County SD 12,500/PK-12
1580 Highway 51 S 38019 901-476-7148
Dr. Tim Fite, supt. Fax 476-4870
www.tipton-county.com
Covington Integrated Arts Academy 700/K-8
760 Bert Johnston Ave 38019 901-476-1444
Jan Sanford, prin. Fax 475-2786
Crestview ES 900/PK-4
151 Mark Walker Dr 38019 901-475-5925
Betty Glass, prin. Fax 475-2632
Crestview MS 900/5-8
201 Mark Walker Dr 38019 901-475-5900
James Fields, prin. Fax 475-2607
Peay ES 800/K-5
474 Academic Dr 38019 901-475-5121
Leisa Bennett, prin. Fax 475-2793
Other Schools – See Atoka, Brighton, Drummonds, Munford

Cowan, Franklin, Pop. 1,756
Franklin County SD
Supt. — See Winchester
Cowan ES 300/PK-5
501 Cumberland St E 37318 931-967-7353
Cynthia Young, prin. Fax 967-7915
South MS 500/6-8
601 Cumberland St W 37318 931-967-7355
Sandra Stewart, prin. Fax 967-1413

Crab Orchard, Cumberland, Pop. 900
Cumberland County SD
Supt. — See Crossville
Crab Orchard S 400/PK-8
240 School Rd 37723 931-484-7400
Rebecca Richards, prin. Fax 456-5655

Crawford, Overton
Overton County SD
Supt. — See Livingston
Wilson S 200/K-8
2210 Hanging Limb Hwy 38554 931-445-3335
Christy Lee, prin. Fax 445-3005

Cross Plains, Robertson, Pop. 1,517
Robertson County SD
Supt. — See Springfield
East Robertson ES 600/K-5
5177 E Robertson Rd 37049 615-654-3874
Mark Stubblefield, prin. Fax 654-4029

Crossville, Cumberland, Pop. 10,424
Cumberland County SD 7,400/PK-12
368 4th St 38555 931-484-6135
Aarona Vanwinkle, supt. Fax 484-6491
ccschools.k12tn.net/
Brown S 500/K-8
3766 Dunbar Rd 38572 931-788-2248
Christie Thompson, prin. Fax 788-2489
Homestead S 700/PK-8
3889 Highway 127 S 38572 931-456-8344
Robin Perry, prin. Fax 456-8342
Martin S 600/K-8
1362 Miller Ave 38555 931-484-7547
Christie Lewis, prin. Fax 484-8785
North Cumberland S 700/PK-8
7657 Highway 127 N 38571 931-484-5174
Kathy Allen, prin. Fax 707-5556
South Cumberland S 700/PK-8
3536 Lantana Rd 38572 931-788-6713
Darrell Threet, prin. Fax 788-1116
Stone S 600/PK-8
1219 Cook Rd 38555 931-456-5636
Susanne Wilson, prin. Fax 456-5369
Other Schools – See Crab Orchard, Pleasant Hill, Rockwood

Christian Academy of the Cumberlands 200/PK-12
325 Braun St 38555 931-707-9540
Alicia Jones, prin. Fax 707-9545
Crossville Christian S 50/PK-5
28 Rock Quarry Rd 38555 931-484-0026
Julia Palumbo, hdmstr. Fax 484-0041

Culleoka, Maury
Maury County SD
Supt. — See Columbia
Culleoka S 1,000/K-12
1921 Warrior Way 38451 931-987-2511
Jeff Quirk, prin. Fax 987-2594

Hopewell Church Covenant Family S 50/1-12
3886 Hopewell Rd 38451 931-381-2605
Charles Mangum, admin. Fax 381-8952

Cunningham, Montgomery
Clarksville-Montgomery County SD
Supt. — See Clarksville
Montgomery Central ES 400/K-5
4011 Highway 48 37052 931-387-3208
Nancy Grant, prin. Fax 387-2565
Montgomery Central MS 700/6-8
3941 Highway 48 37052 931-387-2575
Dee-Etta Whitlock, prin. Fax 387-3391

Dandridge, Jefferson, Pop. 2,347
Jefferson County SD 7,500/PK-12
PO Box 190 37725 865-397-3194
Connie Campbell, dir. Fax 397-3301
jc-schools.net/
Dandridge ES 800/K-5
780 Highway 92 S 37725 865-397-3127
Sandra Austin, prin. Fax 397-1465

Maury MS 600/6-8
965 Maury Cir 37725 865-397-3424
Dr. Amie Lambert, prin. Fax 397-4253
Piedmont ES 400/K-5
1100 W Dumplin Valley Rd 37725 865-397-2939
Michael Horner, prin. Fax 397-1865
Other Schools – See Jefferson City, New Market, Strawberry Plains, Talbott, White Pine

Dayton, Rhea, Pop. 6,443
Dayton CSD 700/PK-8
520 Cherry St 37321 423-775-8414
Richard Fisher, supt. Fax 775-4135
www.daytoncity.net
Dayton City S 700/PK-8
520 Cherry St 37321 423-775-8412
Michael Latham, prin. Fax 775-4135

Rhea County SD 4,300/PK-12
305 California Ave 37321 423-775-7812
Dallas Smith, supt. Fax 775-7831
www.rheacounty.org
Frazier ES 300/K-5
3900 Double S Rd 37321 423-775-7854
Gayle Kelly, prin. Fax 775-6754
Graysville ES 300/PK-5
606 Long St 37321 423-775-7850
Elizabeth Brown, prin. Fax 775-7862
Rhea Central S 1,200/K-8
1005 Delaware Ave 37321 423-775-7842
Doug Keylon, prin. Fax 775-7843
Other Schools – See Spring City

Laurelbrook SDA S 50/1-8
114 Campus Dr 37321 423-775-0563
Chuck Hess, prin. Fax 775-6052
Rhea County Academy 50/K-8
PO Box 925 37321 423-775-2826
Tim Wehse, admin.

Decatur, Meigs, Pop. 1,450
Meigs County SD 1,800/K-12
PO Box 1039 37322 423-334-5793
Donald Roberts, supt. Fax 334-1462
www.meigscounty.net
Meigs MS 400/6-8
564 N Main St 37322 423-334-9187
Allen Roberts, prin. Fax 334-1353
Meigs North ES 400/K-5
22015 State Highway 58 N 37322 423-334-5454
Margaret Templeton, prin. Fax 334-1366
Meigs South ES 400/K-5
9638 State Highway 58 S 37322 423-334-5444
Jane Rogers, prin. Fax 334-1801

Decaturville, Decatur, Pop. 846
Decatur County SD 1,600/PK-12
PO Box 369 38329 731-852-2391
Dr. Michael Price, supt. Fax 852-2960
www.decaturcountytn.org
Decaturville ES 200/PK-5
820 S West St 38329 731-852-4616
Danny Adkisson, prin. Fax 852-2009
Other Schools – See Parsons

Decherd, Franklin, Pop. 2,190
Franklin County SD
Supt. — See Winchester
Decherd ES 500/PK-5
401 N Bratton St 37324 931-967-5483
Alison Spears, prin. Fax 967-2525

Good Shepherd S 100/PK-8
2037 Decherd Blvd 37324 931-967-5673
Kelly Doyle, prin. Fax 967-3569

Deer Lodge, Morgan, Pop. 300

Meister Memorial SDA S 50/1-8
1145 Meister Hills Rd 37726 931-863-4944
Michelle White, prin.

Del Rio, Cocke
Cocke County SD
Supt. — See Newport
Del Rio S 100/K-8
500 Highway 107 S 37727 423-487-5570
Jan Dellinger, prin. Fax 487-5411

Denmark, Madison
Jackson-Madison County SD
Supt. — See Jackson
Denmark ES 300/PK-4
535 Denmark Jackson Rd 38391 731-427-5986
Tiffany Taylor, prin. Fax 427-3083
West MS 400/7-8
317 Denmark Rd 38391 731-988-3810
Ricky Catlett, prin. Fax 988-3810

Dickson, Dickson, Pop. 12,873
Dickson County SD 7,900/PK-12
817 N Charlotte St 37055 615-446-7571
Johnny Chandler, dir. Fax 441-1375
www.dicksoncountyschools.org/
Centennial ES 600/K-5
198 Upper Lake Dr 37055 615-446-0355
Crysti Sheley, prin. Fax 446-8186
Dickson ES 300/K-5
120 W Broad St 37055 615-740-5837
Eva Larkins, prin. Fax 441-4136
Dickson MS 800/7-8
401 E College St 37055 615-446-2273
David Bradford, prin. Fax 441-4139
Discovery S 200/K-5
101 Henslee Dr 37055 615-441-4163
Debbie Bogdan, prin. Fax 740-6679
Oakmont ES 700/PK-5
630 Highway 46 S 37055 615-446-2435
Janey Thomas, prin. Fax 441-4138

Other Schools – See Burns, Charlotte, Vanleer, White Bluff

Dickson Adventist S 50/1-8
PO Box 706 37056 615-446-7030
Diane Capps, prin. Fax 446-7030
United Christian Academy 200/K-12
784 Highway 46 S 37055 615-446-0322
Faith Bybee, prin. Fax 446-0249

Dover, Stewart, Pop. 1,495
Stewart County SD 2,300/PK-12
PO Box 433 37058 931-232-5176
Dr. Phillip Wallace, supt. Fax 232-5390
www.stewartcountyschools.net
Dover ES 600/K-5
PO Box 130 37058 931-232-5442
Brian Saunders, prin. Fax 232-3106
Stewart County MS 500/6-8
PO Box 1001 37058 931-232-9112
Jane Lancaster, prin.
Other Schools – See Big Rock

Doalnara Academy 50/K-12
802 Upper Standing Rock Rd 37058 931-232-8903
Ted Lee, hdmstr. Fax 232-6362

Doyle, White, Pop. 552
White County SD
Supt. — See Sparta
Doyle ES 200/PK-5
174 W Gooseneck Rd 38559 931-657-2287
Brenda Knox, prin. Fax 657-5041

Dresden, Weakley, Pop. 2,703
Weakley County SD 4,900/K-12
8319 Highway 22 Ste A 38225 731-364-2247
Richard Barber, supt. Fax 364-2662
www.weakleycountyschools.com
Dresden ES 500/K-4
759 Linden St Ste B 38225 731-364-3401
Mike Laughrey, prin. Fax 364-5537
Dresden MS 400/5-8
759 Linden St Ste A 38225 731-364-2407
Pam Harris, prin. Fax 364-5840
Other Schools – See Gleason, Greenfield, Martin, Sharon

Drummonds, Tipton
Tipton County SD
Supt. — See Covington
Drummonds ES 800/K-5
5068 Drummonds Rd 38023 901-837-3571
Patricia Mills, prin. Fax 837-5799

Duff, Campbell
Campbell County SD
Supt. — See Jacksboro
White Oak S 100/PK-8
5634 White Oak Rd 37729 423-784-6051
Harry Chitwood, prin. Fax 784-9386
Wynn-Habersham S 200/K-8
174 Habersham Rd 37729 423-784-9482
Roger Walden, prin. Fax 784-9380

Dunlap, Sequatchie, Pop. 4,681
Sequatchie County SD 2,200/PK-12
PO Box 488 37327 423-949-3617
Johnny Cordell, supt. Fax 949-5257
www.sequatchie.k12.tn.us/
Griffith ES 900/PK-4
PO Box 819 37327 423-949-2105
Sarai Carbaugh, prin. Fax 949-6872
Sequatchie County MS 700/5-8
PO Box 789 37327 423-949-4149
Donald Johnson, prin. Fax 949-4140

Dunlap Adventist S 50/K-8
105 Appache Ln 37327 423-949-2920
David Bartlett, prin.
Sequatchie Valley Preparatory Academy 50/K-12
1050 Ray Hixson Rd 37327 423-554-4677
Robert Young, admin. Fax 554-4398

Dyer, Gibson, Pop. 2,418
Gibson County SD 3,000/PK-12
PO Box 60 38330 731-692-3803
Robert Galloway, dir. Fax 692-4375
www.gcssd.org
Dyer S 500/PK-8
PO Box 220 38330 731-692-2444
Brad Garner, prin. Fax 692-2751
Other Schools – See Kenton, Medina, Rutherford, Trenton, Yorkville

Dyersburg, Dyer, Pop. 17,466
Dyer County SD 3,400/PK-12
159 Everett Ave 38024 731-285-6712
Dr. Dwight Hedge, supt. Fax 286-6721
www.dyercs.net
Fifth Consolidated ES 300/K-5
PO Box 1270 38025 731-285-2840
Greg Cherry, prin. Fax 285-2915
Powell ES 200/K-5
988 Highway 210 38024 731-285-1994
Alice Seratt, prin. Fax 285-9108
Three Oaks MS 300/6-8
3200 Upper Finley Rd 38024 731-285-3100
Betty Jackson, prin. Fax 285-3360
Other Schools – See Finley, Newbern, Trimble

Dyersburg CSD 3,500/PK-12
PO Box 1507 38025 731-286-3600
Lloyd Ramer, supt. Fax 286-2754
www.dcs.k12tn.net/dcs/index.html
Dyersburg IS 800/3-5
725 Tibbs St 38024 731-286-3620
Lou Newbill, prin. Fax 286-3622
Dyersburg MS 900/6-8
400 Frank Maynard Dr 38024 731-286-3625
Tyles Davenport, prin. Fax 286-3624
Dyersburg PS 900/PK-2
1425 Frank Maynard Dr 38024 731-286-3615
Linda DeBerry, prin. Fax 286-3617

Christ Classical Academy 100/PK-8
1005 US Highway 51 Byp W 38024 731-285-3727
Janice Young, prin. Fax 285-3726

Eads, Shelby

Evangelical Christian S 600/PK-5
11893 Macon 38028 901-850-9652
Joanne Lamberth, prin. Fax 850-9653

Eagleville, Rutherford, Pop. 458
Rutherford County SD
Supt. — See Murfreesboro
Eagleville S 700/K-12
500 Highway 99 37060 615-904-6710
Ronda Holton, prin. Fax 904-6711

Eidson, Hawkins
Hawkins County SD
Supt. — See Rogersville
Clinch S 100/K-12
1010 Clinch Valley Rd 37731 423-272-3110
Linda Long, prin. Fax 272-3110

Elizabethton, Carter, Pop. 13,944
Carter County SD 6,000/PK-12
305 Academy St 37643 423-547-4000
Dallas Williams, supt. Fax 547-8338
carter.k12.tn.us
Happy Valley MS 500/5-8
163 Warpath Ln 37643 423-547-4070
Alex Payne, prin. Fax 547-8352
Hunter S 500/PK-8
145 Hope St 37643 423-547-4074
Heather Smith, prin. Fax 547-4075
Keenburg S 300/PK-8
139 Keenburg Rd 37643 423-547-4047
Jason Hartley, prin. Fax 547-4048
Unaka S 300/K-8
120 Unaka Dr 37643 423-474-4110
Fax 474-4111
Valley Forge ES 300/PK-5
1485 Riverview Dr 37643 423-547-4085
Bud Hazelwood, prin. Fax 547-4081
Other Schools – See Butler, Hampton, Johnson City, Roan Mountain, Watauga

Elizabethton CSD 2,100/PK-12
804 S Watauga Ave 37643 423-547-8000
Edwin Alexander, supt. Fax 547-8101
www.ecschools.net
Dugger JHS 500/6-8
306 W E St 37643 423-547-8025
James Jacobs, prin. Fax 547-8021
Early Learning Center 100/PK-PK
104 Hudson Dr 37643 423-547-8035
Randy Lacy, dir. Fax 542-5955
East Side ES 200/K-5
800 Siam Rd 37643 423-547-8010
Joshua Wandell, prin. Fax 547-8038
McCormick ES 300/K-5
226 S Cedar Ave 37643 423-547-8020
Brian Culbert, prin. Fax 547-8120
West Side ES 200/K-5
1310 Burgie St 37643 423-547-8030
Douglas Mitchell, prin. Fax 547-8031

Elkton, Giles, Pop. 506
Giles County SD
Supt. — See Pulaski
Elkton S 400/PK-8
176 College St 38455 931-468-2285
Bob Polly, prin. Fax 468-2350

Elmwood, Smith
Smith County SD
Supt. — See Carthage
Forks River S 200/PK-8
611 Cookeville Hwy 38560 615-897-2676
Melinda Spivey, prin. Fax 897-2222

Englewood, McMinn, Pop. 1,666
McMinn County SD
Supt. — See Athens
Englewood S 700/PK-8
PO Box 47 37329 423-887-5260
David Decker, prin. Fax 887-7327

Erin, Houston, Pop. 1,442
Houston County SD 1,600/PK-12
PO Box 209 37061 931-289-4148
Cathy Harvey, supt. Fax 289-5543
houston.k12.tn.us/
Erin ES, 6500 Highway 13 37061 500/K-5
Elaine Hewitt, prin. 931-289-3127
Houston County MS 400/6-8
3460 W Main St 37061 931-289-5591
Ray Busey, prin.
Other Schools – See Tennessee Ridge

Erwin, Unicoi, Pop. 5,786
Unicoi County SD 2,600/PK-12
600 N Elm Ave 37650 423-743-1600
Denise Brown, dir. Fax 743-1615
www.unicoischools.com/
Love Chapel ES 300/K-4
1426 Love Station Rd 37650 423-743-1657
Janet Sutphin, prin. Fax 743-1662
Rock Creek ES 200/K-4
1121 E Erwin Rd 37650 423-743-1648
Stephen White, prin. Fax 743-1664
Temple Hill ES 100/K-4
797 Old Highway Rd 37650 423-743-1661
Larry Howell, prin. Fax 743-1663
Unicoi County MS 500/5-7
600 S Mohawk Dr 37650 423-743-1653
John English, prin. Fax 743-1638
Other Schools – See Unicoi

Estill Springs, Franklin, Pop. 2,179
Franklin County SD
Supt. — See Winchester
Rock Creek ES 500/PK-5
901 Rock Creek Rd 37330 931-649-5435
Danny Brown, prin. Fax 649-2040

Ethridge, Lawrence, Pop. 555
Lawrence County SD
Supt. — See Lawrenceburg
Ethridge S 500/K-8
33 Main St 38456 931-829-2167
Robin Thompson, prin. Fax 829-2186

Etowah, McMinn, Pop. 3,712
Etowah CSD 400/PK-8
858 8th St 37331 423-263-5483
David Green, supt. Fax 263-3401
www.etowahcityschool.com
Etowah S 400/PK-8
858 8th St 37331 423-263-5483
Linda Cheek, prin. Fax 263-3401

McMinn County SD
Supt. — See Athens
Mountain View S 700/K-8
145 County Road 627 37331 423-263-2498
Ed Rich, prin. Fax 263-5671

Fairview, Williamson, Pop. 7,190
Williamson County SD
Supt. — See Franklin
Fairview ES 500/PK-5
2640 Fairview Blvd 37062 615-472-4380
Joan Tidwell, prin. Fax 472-4391
Fairview MS 500/6-8
7200 Cumberland Dr 37062 615-472-4430
Brian Bass, prin. Fax 472-4441
Westwood ES 400/PK-5
7200 Tiger Trl 37062 615-472-4890
Nancy Simpkins, prin. Fax 472-4901

Fall Branch, Washington, Pop. 1,203
Washington County SD
Supt. — See Jonesborough
Fall Branch S 400/K-8
1061 Highway 93 37656 423-348-1200
Walter Huffine, prin. Fax 348-1207

Fayetteville, Lincoln, Pop. 7,034
Fayetteville CSD 1,000/PK-9
110 Elk Ave S Ste A 37334 931-433-5542
Bill Evans, supt. Fax 433-7499
www.fcsboe.org
Askins ES 400/PK-3
901 Shady Ln 37334 931-433-4319
Joel Hastings, prin. Fax 433-0513
Fayetteville IS 300/4-6
1800 Wilson Pkwy Ste A 37334 931-438-2533
Steve Giffin, prin. Fax 438-2539

Lincoln County SD 4,000/PK-12
206 Davidson St E 37334 931-433-3565
Dr. Wanda Shelton, dir. Fax 433-7397
www.lcdoe.org
Highland Rim S 700/K-8
111 Highland Rim Rd 37334 931-433-4197
Leonard McGrath, prin. Fax 438-1472
South Lincoln S 500/K-8
362 Smith Mill Rd 37334 931-937-7385
Greg Holder, prin. Fax 937-7886
Stone Bridge Academy 300/PK-8
1107 Hedgemont Ave 37334 931-433-3939
Tammy Shelton, prin. Fax 438-1707
Other Schools – See Flintville, Petersburg, Taft

Riverside Christian Academy 300/K-12
PO Box 617 37334 931-438-4722
Daniel Eldridge, prin.

Finger, McNairy, Pop. 358

Pioneer Christian S 50/K-10
802 Sweet Lips Rd 38334 731-934-7327
Salome Kinniburgh, admin. Fax 934-7327

Finley, Dyer
Dyer County SD
Supt. — See Dyersburg
Finley ES 300/PK-5
PO Box K 38030 731-285-7050
Dr. Mary Ellen Watkins, prin. Fax 288-0615

Flintville, Lincoln
Lincoln County SD
Supt. — See Fayetteville
Flintville S 400/K-8
37 Flintville School Rd 37335 931-937-8271
Terrell Bain, prin. Fax 937-6739

Franklin, Williamson, Pop. 53,311
Franklin Special SD 3,800/PK-8
507 New Highway 96 W 37064 615-794-6624
David Snowden Ph.D., supt. Fax 790-4716
www.fssd.org
Franklin ES 400/PK-4
1501 Figuers Dr 37064 615-794-1187
David Esslinger Ed.D., prin. Fax 591-2800
Freedom IS 600/5-6
840 Glass Ln 37064 615-790-4718
Dr. Hank Staggs, prin. Fax 790-4717

Freedom MS 700/7-8
750 New Highway 96 W 37064 615-794-0987
Kristi Jefferson, prin. Fax 790-4742
Johnson ES 400/PK-4
815 Glass Ln 37064 615-794-4837
Jan Cochran, prin. Fax 790-4749
Liberty ES 400/K-4
600 Liberty Pike 37064 615-790-0892
Jerre Ann Mathis, prin. Fax 790-4714
Moore ES 400/K-4
1061 Lewisburg Pike 37064 615-790-4700
Patricia Green, prin. Fax 790-4748
Poplar Grove ES 500/K-4
2959 Del Rio Pike 37069 615-790-4720
Lee Kirkpatrick, prin. Fax 790-4729
Poplar Grove MS 400/5-8
2959 Del Rio Pike 37069 615-790-4721
Vanessa Garcia, prin. Fax 790-4730

Williamson County SD 27,300/PK-12
1320 W Main St Ste 202 37064 615-472-4000
Dr. David Heath, supt. Fax 472-4003
www.wcs.edu
Grassland MS 1,000/6-8
2390 Hillsboro Rd 37069 615-472-4500
Dr. Susan Curtis, prin. Fax 472-4511
Hillsboro S 500/PK-8
5412 Pinewood Rd 37064 615-472-4560
Dr. Tracy Lampley, prin. Fax 472-4572
Hunters Bend ES 700/K-5
2121 Fieldstone Pkwy 37069 615-472-4580
Mike Parman, prin. Fax 472-4591
Oak View ES 500/K-5
2390 Henpeck Ln 37064 615-472-4710
Denise Goodwin, prin. Fax 472-4725
Page MS 800/6-8
6262 Arno Rd 37064 615-472-4760
Josie Jacobs, prin. Fax 472-4771
Trinity ES 700/PK-5
4410 Murfreesboro Rd 37067 615-472-4850
Chris Schwartz, prin. Fax 472-4861
Walnut Grove ES 700/K-5
326 Stable Rd 37069 615-472-4870
Jay Jordan, prin. Fax 472-4881
Winstead ES 700/PK-5
4080 Columbia Pike 37064 615-472-4910
Connie Kinder, prin. Fax 472-4921
Other Schools – See Brentwood, College Grove, Fairview, Nolensville, Primm Springs, Spring Hill, Thompsons Station

---

Battle Ground Academy 1,000/K-12
336 Ernest Rice Ln 37069 615-794-3501
Dr. John Griffith, hdmstr. Fax 567-8360
Eagles Nest Academy 200/PK-6
810 Del Rio Pike 37064 615-790-8556
Eric VanGorden, hdmstr. Fax 790-8617
Montessori S of Franklin 100/PK-6
1325 W Main St Ste G 37064 615-794-0567
Francie Beard, prin. Fax 794-2411
New Hope Academy 200/PK-6
1820 Downs Blvd 37064 615-595-0324
Stuart Tutler, hdmstr. Fax 261-4494
St. Matthew S 300/K-8
533 Sneed Rd W 37069 615-662-4044
Barby Magness, prin. Fax 662-6822
Willow Hall Academy 50/K-12
4092 Carters Creek Pike 37064 615-790-1975
Cavalyn Muller, prin. Fax 599-9692

Friendship, Crockett, Pop. 612
Crockett County SD
Supt. — See Alamo
Friendship ES 200/PK-5
6117 State Highway 189 38034 731-677-2718
Mary Marvin, prin. Fax 677-2331

Friendsville, Blount, Pop. 921
Blount County SD
Supt. — See Maryville
Friendsville ES 500/K-5
210 E 4th Ave 37737 865-980-1252
Ellen Jenkins, prin. Fax 980-1253
Union Grove ES K-5
330 S Old Grey Ridge Rd 37737 865-980-1515
Kristy Brewer, prin. Fax 980-1520
Union Grove MS 6-8
334 S Old Grey Ridge Rd 37737 865-980-1320
Alicia Lail, prin. Fax 980-1323

Gadsden, Crockett, Pop. 560
Crockett County SD
Supt. — See Alamo
Gadsden ES 100/PK-5
18989 Highway 79 38337 731-663-2453
Marsha Morphis, prin. Fax 663-3938

Gainesboro, Jackson, Pop. 859
Jackson County SD 1,700/K-12
711 School Dr 38562 931-268-0268
Joe Barlow, supt. Fax 268-3647
volweb.utk.edu/school/jackson/
Gainesboro ES 400/K-3
611 S Main St 38562 931-268-9775
Charles Breidert, prin. Fax 268-3674
Jackson County MS 600/4-8
170 Blue Devil Ln 38562 931-268-9779
Gail Myers, prin. Fax 268-9413
Other Schools – See Cookeville

Gallatin, Sumner, Pop. 26,720
Sumner County SD 25,400/PK-12
695 E Main St 37066 615-451-5200
Benny Bills, dir. Fax 451-5216
www.sumnerschools.org/
Bills ES 600/K-5
1030 Union School Rd 37066 615-451-6577
Ken Henderson, prin. Fax 451-6575
Doss MS 800/6-8
281 Big Station Camp Blvd 37066 615-206-0116
Mike Brown, prin. Fax 206-0165
Guild ES 500/PK-5
1018 S Water Ave 37066 615-452-5583
Lance Taylor, prin. Fax 451-6582
Howard ES 400/K-5
805 Long Hollow Pike 37066 615-452-3025
Cindy Swafford, prin. Fax 451-6567
Rucker-Stewart MS 600/6-8
350 Hancock St 37066 615-452-1734
Andrew Turner, prin. Fax 451-5297
Shafer MS 600/6-8
240 Albert Gallatin Ave 37066 615-452-9100
David Hallman, prin. Fax 451-6545
Station Camp ES K-5
1020 Bison Trl 37066 615-230-0387
Dr. Linda Cash, prin. Fax 230-8518
Stuart ES 600/K-5
780 Hart St 37066 615-452-1486
Dr. Brenda Valentine, prin. Fax 451-5281
Union ES 400/K-5
516 Carson St 37066 615-452-0737
Danny Sullivan, prin. Fax 451-6543
Other Schools – See Bethpage, Cottontown, Goodlettsville, Hendersonville, Portland, Westmoreland, White House

---

St. John Vianney S 200/PK-8
501 N Water Ave 37066 615-230-7048
Sr. Peter Marie, prin. Fax 206-9839
Sumner Academy 200/PK-8
464 Nichols Ln 37066 615-452-1914
William Hovenden, prin. Fax 452-1923

Gatlinburg, Sevier, Pop. 4,426
Sevier County SD
Supt. — See Sevierville
Pi Beta Phi S 500/K-8
125 Cherokee Orchard Rd 37738 865-436-5076
Glenn Bogart, prin. Fax 436-9494
Pittman Center S 200/K-8
2455 E Parkway 37738 865-436-4515
Susan Carr, prin. Fax 430-3068

Germantown, Shelby, Pop. 37,480
Shelby County SD
Supt. — See Memphis
Dogwood ES 700/K-5
8945 Dogwood Rd 38139 901-756-2310
Andrea Simpson, prin. Fax 751-7852
Farmington ES 700/K-5
2085 Cordes Rd 38139 901-756-2320
Lee Ann Kight, prin. Fax 756-2308
Germantown ES 700/K-5
2730 Cross Country Dr 38138 901-756-2330
Jennifer Payne, prin. Fax 756-2302
Germantown MS 800/6-8
7925 CD Smith Rd 38138 901-756-2338
Russell Joy, prin. Fax 759-4521
Houston MS 800/6-8
9400 Wolf River Blvd 38139 901-756-2366
Tamara Mason, prin. Fax 756-2346
Riverdale S 1,000/K-8
7391 Neshoba Rd 38138 901-756-2300
David Carlisle, prin. Fax 759-4520

Bodine S 100/1-8
2432 Yester Oaks Dr 38139 901-754-1800
Rene Lee, prin. Fax 751-8595
Evangelical Christian S 300/PK-5
1920 Forest Hill Irene Rd 38139 901-754-4420
Chuck Smith, prin. Fax 751-6782
Our Lady of Perpetual Help S 300/PK-8
8151 Poplar Ave 38138 901-753-1181
Pat Wyckoff, prin. Fax 754-1475
St. George's Independent S Germantown 600/PK-5
8250 Poplar Ave 38138 901-261-2300
Judy Shelton, admin. Fax 261-2311

Gladeville, Wilson
Wilson County SD
Supt. — See Lebanon
Gladeville ES 400/K-5
8840 Stewarts Ferry Pike 37071 615-444-5694
Monica Hopkins, prin. Fax 449-3435

Gleason, Weakley, Pop. 1,426
Weakley County SD
Supt. — See Dresden
Gleason S 600/K-12
92-99 State Championship Dr 38229 731-648-5351
Randy Frazier, prin. Fax 648-9199

Goodlettsville, Davidson, Pop. 15,320
Metropolitan Nashville SD
Supt. — See Nashville
Goodlettsville ES 400/K-4
514 Donald St 37072 615-859-8950
Michael Westveer, prin. Fax 783-2820
Goodlettsville MS 600/5-8
300 S Main St 37072 615-859-8956
Sarah Moore, prin. Fax 859-8965
Old Center ES 300/PK-4
1245 S Dickerson Rd 37072 615-859-8968
Barbara Edwards, prin. Fax 859-8970

Sumner County SD
Supt. — See Gallatin
Madison Creek ES 700/K-5
1040 Madison Creek Rd 37072 615-859-4991
Jim Daniels, prin. Fax 859-3963
Millersville ES 300/K-5
1248 Louisville Hwy 37072 615-859-1439
Olivia Isenberg, prin. Fax 859-5224

Gordonsville, Smith, Pop. 1,130
Smith County SD
Supt. — See Carthage
Gordonsville ES, 104 Main St E 38563 400/PK-6
Mark Medley, prin. 615-683-8245
New Middleton S 200/PK-8
402 New Middleton Hwy 38563 615-683-8411
Susie Woodard, prin. Fax 683-8422

Grand Junction, Hardeman, Pop. 316
Hardeman County SD
Supt. — See Bolivar
Grand Junction ES 200/PK-6
750 Pledge St 38039 731-764-2841
Linda Buggs, prin. Fax 764-6913

Gray, Washington, Pop. 1,071
Washington County SD
Supt. — See Jonesborough
Boones Creek ES 500/K-4
348 Christian Church Rd 37615 423-283-3500
Teresa Leonard, prin. Fax 283-3510
Gray S 1,000/K-8
755 Gray Station Rd 37615 423-477-1640
Paula Maupin, prin. Fax 477-1642
Rideview S K-8
252 Sam Jenkins Rd 37615 423-788-7340
Peggy Greene, prin.

Tri-City SDA S 50/K-8
314 Delmer Salts Rd 37615 423-477-8421
Joy Leffers, dir. Fax 477-8420

Greenback, Loudon, Pop. 997
Loudon County SD
Supt. — See Loudon
Greenback S 700/PK-12
400 Chilhowee Ave 37742 865-856-3028
Joey Breedlove, prin. Fax 856-5427

Greenbrier, Robertson, Pop. 6,054
Robertson County SD
Supt. — See Springfield
Greenbrier ES 700/K-5
2658 Highway 41 S 37073 615-643-4529
Mitzi Grogan, prin. Fax 643-0238
Greenbrier MS 600/6-8
2450 Highway 41 S 37073 615-643-7835
Kathy Hassler, prin.

Greeneville, Greene, Pop. 15,383
Greene County SD 7,400/PK-12
910 W Summer St 37743 423-639-4194
Dr. Joe Parkins, dir. Fax 639-1017
www.greenek12.org/
Baileyton S 400/K-8
6335 Horton Hwy 37745 423-234-6411
Kevin Ridley, prin. Fax 234-6411
Camp Creek S 300/PK-8
2941 Camp Creek Rd 37743 423-798-2644
Jane Bell, prin. Fax 798-0446
DeBusk S 300/K-8
740 Debusk Rd 37743 423-638-7233
Chris Malone, prin. Fax 638-8364
Doak ES 600/PK-5
70 West St 37745 423-638-3197
Jennifer Teague, prin. Fax 638-5276
Glenwood S 300/K-8
3860 Warrensburg Rd 37743 423-638-7120
Lynda Edwards, prin. Fax 638-8688
Nolachuckey S 400/PK-8
565 Nolichuckey Rd 37743 423-639-7731
Gerald Miller, prin. Fax 639-9480
Ottway S 300/PK-8
2705 Ottway Rd 37745 423-234-8511
Tim Shelton, prin. Fax 234-3281
West Pines S 300/PK-8
3500 W Pines Rd 37745 423-234-8022
Tim Harrison Ed.D., prin. Fax 234-3109
Other Schools – See Afton, Chuckey, Mohawk, Mosheim

Greeneville CSD 2,800/K-12
PO Box 1420 37744 423-787-8000
Lyle Ailshie, dir. Fax 638-2540
www.gcschools.net
Eastview ES 300/K-5
454 E Bernard Ave 37745 423-638-6351
Dale Landers, prin. Fax 638-2651
Greeneville MS 700/6-8
433 E Vann Rd 37743 423-639-7841
Shelly Smith, prin. Fax 639-4112
Henard ES 300/K-5
425 E Vann Rd 37743 423-638-3511
Ken Fay, prin. Fax 638-2900
Highland ES 100/K-5
208 N Highland Ave 37745 423-638-3341
Brenda Ottinger, prin. Fax 638-1780
Tusculum View ES 400/K-5
1725 Lafayette St 37745 423-639-2751
Pat Donaldson, prin. Fax 639-2198

Greeneville Adventist Academy 100/K-12
305 Takoma Ave 37743 423-639-2011
Keith Nelson, prin. Fax 639-5002
Towering Oaks Christian S 200/PK-8
1985 Buckingham Rd 37745 423-639-0791
Bob Cardinal, dir. Fax 638-6026

Greenfield, Weakley, Pop. 2,084
Weakley County SD
Supt. — See Dresden
Greenfield S 700/K-12
101 N Faxon St 38230 731-235-3424
Mike Riggs, prin. Fax 235-3480

Grimsley, Fentress
Fentress County SD
Supt. — See Jamestown
South Fentress S 600/PK-8
5018 Wilder Rd 38565 931-863-3131
Vicki McDonald, prin. Fax 863-3980

Gruetli Laager, Grundy, Pop. 1,910
Grundy County SD
Supt. — See Altamont
Swiss Memorial S 300/PK-8
PO Box 129 37339 931-779-3129
Jamie Ruehling, prin. Fax 779-3179

Faith Missionary Academy 100/K-12
495 Red Barn Rd 37339 931-779-3338
S.D. Smith, prin. Fax 779-4338

Halls, Lauderdale, Pop. 2,236
Lauderdale County SD
Supt. — See Ripley
Halls ES 800/PK-6
601 Carmen St 38040 731-836-9651
Pat Carmack, prin. Fax 836-5573
Halls JHS 200/7-8
800 W Tigrett St 38040 731-836-5579
Ned Lewis, prin. Fax 836-5579

Hampshire, Maury
Maury County SD
Supt. — See Columbia
Hampshire S 400/K-12
4235 Old State Rd 38461 931-285-2300
Leigh Ann Willey, prin. Fax 285-2612

Hampton, Carter
Carter County SD
Supt. — See Elizabethton
Hampton S 700/K-8
408 Highway 321 37658 423-725-5220
Jan Hickman, prin. Fax 725-5221

Harriman, Roane, Pop. 6,725
Roane County SD
Supt. — See Kingston
Bowers ES 300/PK-5
120 Breazeale St 37748 865-882-1185
Candace Lett, prin. Fax 882-3203
Dyllis ES 200/K-5
510 Dyllis Rd 37748 865-435-2298
Joan Turbyville, prin. Fax 435-3344
Harriman MS 300/6-8
1025 Cumberland St 37748 865-882-1727
David Stevens, prin. Fax 882-6285
Midtown ES 400/K-5
2830 Roane State Hwy 37748 865-882-1228
Robin Smith, prin. Fax 882-8165
Walnut Hill ES 300/K-5
215 Maple St 37748 865-882-2571
Glenna Treece, prin. Fax 882-2164

Harrison, Hamilton, Pop. 7,191
Hamilton County SD
Supt. — See Chattanooga
Brown MS 500/6-8
5716 Highway 58 37341 423-344-1439
John Stewart, prin. Fax 344-1471
Harrison ES 400/K-5
5637 Highway 58 37341 423-344-1428
Norma Faerber, prin. Fax 344-1430

Harrogate, Claiborne, Pop. 3,985
Claiborne County SD
Supt. — See Tazewell
Forge Ridge S 200/K-8
160 Hill Rd 37752 423-869-2768
Marty Cosby, prin. Fax 869-4977
Livesay MS 300/5-8
PO Box 460 37752 423-869-4663
Sandra Keck, prin. Fax 869-8389
Myers ES 300/K-4
275 Nettleton Rd 37752 423-869-2172
Karen Fultz, prin. Fax 869-0353

Hartford, Cocke
Cocke County SD
Supt. — See Newport
Grassy Fork S 100/K-8
4120 Big Creek Rd 37753 423-487-5835
Dr. Shannon Grooms, prin. Fax 487-5387

Hartsville, Trousdale, Pop. 2,373
Trousdale County SD 1,300/K-12
103 Lock Six Rd 37074 615-374-2193
Clint Satterfield, dir. Fax 374-1108
www.tcschools.org/
Satterfield MS 300/6-8
210 Damascus St 37074 615-374-2748
John Kerr, prin. Fax 374-2602
Trousdale County ES 600/K-5
115 Lock Six Rd 37074 615-374-3752
Patrice Swaffer, prin. Fax 374-1121

Heiskell, Anderson
Anderson County SD
Supt. — See Clinton
Fairview ES 300/PK-5
6715 Hickory Valley Rd 37754 865-494-7959
Sandra Patton, prin. Fax 494-6880

Henderson, Chester, Pop. 6,061
Chester County SD 2,800/PK-12
PO Box 327 38340 731-989-5134
John Pipkin, supt. Fax 989-4755
www.chestercountyschools.org
Chester County JHS 500/7-8
930 E Main St 38340 731-989-8135
Britt Eads, prin. Fax 989-8137
Chester County MS 600/4-6
634 E Main St 38340 731-989-8110
Randle Fenimore, prin. Fax 989-8117
East Chester County ES 400/PK-3
708 E Main St 38340 731-989-8145
Melinda Parker, prin. Fax 989-8147
West Chester County ES 300/K-3
1243 W Main St 38340 731-989-8150
Jimmy Dyer, prin. Fax 989-8151
Other Schools – See Jacks Creek

Hendersonville, Sumner, Pop. 44,876
Sumner County SD
Supt. — See Gallatin
Anderson ES 900/K-5
250 Shute Ln 37075 615-264-5830
Dr. Nancy Glover, prin. Fax 824-0470
Beech ES 500/PK-5
3120 Long Hollow Pike 37075 615-824-2700
Bobby Elrod, prin. Fax 264-6089
Berry ES 400/K-5
138 Indian Lake Rd 37075 615-822-3123
Dr. Kathy Kimble, prin. Fax 264-6009
Brown ES 500/K-5
115 Gail Dr 37075 615-824-8633
Doug Binkley, prin. Fax 264-5819
Ellis MS 600/6-8
100 Indian Lake Rd 37075 615-264-6093
Opal Poe, prin. Fax 264-5800
Hawkins MS 500/6-8
487A Walton Ferry Rd 37075 615-824-3456
Mike Shelton, prin. Fax 264-6003
Hunter MS 800/6-8
2101 New Hope Rd 37075 615-822-4720
Shelly Petty, prin. Fax 264-6036
Hyde Magnet S 600/K-12
128 Township Dr 37075 615-264-6543
Brad Schreiner, prin. Fax 264-6546
Indian Lake ES 600/K-5
505 Indian Lake Rd 37075 615-824-6810
Jewell McGhee, prin. Fax 264-6064
Lakeside Park ES 400/K-5
204 Dolphus Dr 37075 615-824-5151
Vicki Shelton, prin. Fax 264-6550
Walton Ferry ES 500/K-5
732 Walton Ferry Rd 37075 615-824-3217
Jeff Witt, prin. Fax 264-5809
Whitten ES 500/K-5
140 Scotch St 37075 615-824-3258
Adam Cripps, prin. Fax 264-6556

Aaron Academy, 645 E Main St 37075 1,300/K-12
David Longoria, prin. 615-826-2595
Hendersonville Christian Academy 200/K-12
355 Old Shackle Island Rd 37075 615-824-1550
William Slater, prin.

Henry, Henry, Pop. 529
Henry County SD
Supt. — See Paris
Henry S 400/PK-8
937 Pioneer Rd 38231 731-243-7114
Samuel Tharpe, prin. Fax 243-2951

Hermitage, See Nashville
Metropolitan Nashville SD
Supt. — See Nashville
Dodson ES 500/PK-4
4401 Chandler Rd 37076 615-885-8806
Tiffany Curtis, prin. Fax 262-6962
DuPont-Tyler MS 700/5-8
431 Tyler Dr 37076 615-885-8827
Cherish Piche, prin. Fax 847-7322
Hermitage ES 200/K-4
3800 Plantation Dr 37076 615-885-8838
Barbara Frazier, prin. Fax 321-8389
Tulip Grove ES 600/K-4
441 Tyler Dr 37076 615-885-8944
Denise Colon, prin. Fax 292-5154

Hilham, Overton
Overton County SD
Supt. — See Livingston
Hilham S 300/K-8
2305 Hilham Highway 38568 931-823-6816
Vickie Eldridge, prin. Fax 823-5203

Hillsboro, Coffee
Coffee County SD
Supt. — See Manchester
Hillsboro ES 500/PK-5
284 Winchester Hwy 37342 931-596-2775
Suzi Boyd, prin. Fax 596-2107

Hixson, See Chattanooga
Hamilton County SD
Supt. — See Chattanooga
Big Ridge ES 500/K-5
5210 Cassandra Smith Rd 37343 423-843-4793
Susan Hixson, prin. Fax 843-4794
Falling Water ES 200/K-5
715 Roberts Mill Rd 37343 423-843-4711
William Shadwick, prin. Fax 843-4732
Ganns-Middle Valley ES 500/K-5
1609 Thrasher Pike 37343 423-843-4700
Karen Hollis, prin. Fax 843-4731
Hixson ES 500/K-5
5950 Winding Ln 37343 423-870-0621
Sandra Jerardi, prin. Fax 870-0628
Hixson MS 500/6-8
5681 Old Hixson Pike 37343 423-847-4810
Sandra Barnwell, prin. Fax 847-4811
Loftis MS 800/6-8
8611 Columbus Rd 37343 423-843-4749
Harry Walter, prin. Fax 843-4758
McConnell ES 600/K-5
8629 Columbus Rd 37343 423-843-4704
Joy Black, prin. Fax 843-4706

Berean Academy 300/K-12
441 Berean Ln 37343 423-877-1288
Carol Calvert, prin. Fax 875-5965

Hohenwald, Lewis, Pop. 3,791
Lewis County SD 2,000/PK-12
206 S Court St 38462 931-796-3264
Benny Pace, supt. Fax 796-5127
www.lewis.k12.tn.us
Lewis County ES 500/PK-2
305 S Oak St 38462 931-796-5621
Dr. Mike Taylor, prin. Fax 796-5762
Lewis County IS 400/3-5
310 S Park St 38462 931-796-1029
Trent Hill, prin. Fax 796-7651
Lewis County MS 500/6-8
207 S Court St 38462 931-796-4586
Tim Watkins, prin. Fax 796-7601

Holladay, Benton
Benton County SD
Supt. — See Camden
Holladay S 200/K-8
148 Stokes Rd 38341 731-584-6874
Marty Arnold, prin. Fax 584-2985

Hornbeak, Obion, Pop. 424
Obion County SD
Supt. — See Union City
Black Oak S 400/K-8
365 N Shawtown Rd 38232 731-538-2271
Sheila Stone, prin. Fax 538-2271

Hornsby, Hardeman, Pop. 300
Hardeman County SD
Supt. — See Bolivar
Hornsby S 200/PK-8
PO Box 70 38044 731-658-5707
Ted Kessler, prin. Fax 658-9999

Humboldt, Gibson, Pop. 9,269
Humboldt CSD 1,500/PK-12
1421 Osborne St Ste 6 38343 731-784-2652
Garnett Twyman, supt. Fax 784-2480
www.humboldtschools.com
East End ES 500/PK-5
1560 N 30th Ave 38343 731-784-4171
Larry McCartney, prin. Fax 784-1343
Humboldt JHS 200/6-8
1811 Ferrell St 38343 731-784-9514
Lillian Shelton, prin. Fax 784-3274
Stigall ES 300/PK-PK, 5-
301 Westside Dr 38343 731-784-2825
Jennifer Stanfield, prin. Fax 784-9410

Huntingdon, Carroll, Pop. 4,186
Huntingdon Special SD 1,200/K-12
585 High St 38344 731-986-2222
Lynn Twyman, supt. Fax 986-4365
www.huntingdonschools.org/
Huntingdon MS 500/4-8
199 Browning Ave 38344 731-986-4544
Pat Dillahunty, prin. Fax 986-8689
Huntingdon PS 400/K-3
191 Cox St E 38344 731-986-3091
Alan Eubanks, prin. Fax 986-0525

Huntland, Franklin, Pop. 886
Franklin County SD
Supt. — See Winchester
Huntland S 600/PK-12
400 Gore St 37345 931-469-7506
Ken Bishop, prin. Fax 469-0590

Huntsville, Scott, Pop. 1,194
Scott County SD 2,700/PK-12
PO Box 37 37756 423-663-2159
Sharon Wilson, supt. Fax 663-9682
www.scottcounty.net
Fairview S 400/PK-8
8702 Baker Hwy 37756 423-663-3700
Denise Watson, prin. Fax 663-4447
Huntsville ES 400/PK-4
3221 Baker Hwy 37756 423-663-2520
Kevin Byrd, prin. Fax 663-2971
Huntsville MS 200/5-8
3101 Baker Hwy 37756 423-663-2192
Lamance Bryant, prin. Fax 663-2967
Other Schools – See Oneida, Robbins, Winfield

Huron, Henderson
Henderson County SD
Supt. — See Lexington
Westover S 500/PK-8
300 Crucifer Rd 38345 731-968-9846
Stacye Valle, prin. Fax 968-9699

Jacksboro, Campbell, Pop. 1,992
Campbell County SD 5,200/PK-12
PO Box 445 37757 423-562-8377
Dr. Michael Martin, supt. Fax 566-7562
www.campbell.k12.tn.us
Jacksboro ES 700/PK-5
PO Box 437 37757 423-562-7433
Lynn Ray, prin. Fax 566-8957
Jacksboro MS 500/6-8
150 Eagle Cir 37757 423-562-3773
Jamie Wheeler, prin. Fax 562-8994
Other Schools – See Caryville, Duff, Jellico, La Follette, Pioneer

Jacks Creek, Chester
Chester County SD
Supt. — See Henderson
Jacks Creek ES 200/K-3
PO Box 168 38347 731-989-8155
LaTasha Phillips, prin. Fax 989-8156

Jackson, Madison, Pop. 62,099
Jackson-Madison County SD 14,300/PK-12
310 N Parkway 38305 731-664-2592
Dr. Nancy Zambito, supt. Fax 664-2502
www.jmcss.net/
Alexander Magnet ES 300/PK-4
900 N Highland Ave 38301 731-422-1841
Fax 424-4801
Arlington International Leadership S 600/PK-4
701 Arlington Ave 38301 731-265-9784
Jimmy Bailey, prin. Fax 265-9803

Barker ES 800/K-4
1470 Ashport Rd 38305 731-668-8831
Linda Johnston, prin. Fax 668-8126
Bemis IS 400/5-6
230 D St 38301 731-427-3320
Tracey Vowell, prin. Fax 427-3290
East IS 500/5-6
2480 Ashport Rd 38305 731-988-3860
Bryan Chandler, prin. Fax 988-3866
Jackson Careers and Technology IS 600/5-6
668 Lexington Ave 38301 731-427-4581
Janis Perry, prin. Fax 427-2334
Jackson IS 500/5-6
211 Old Hickory Blvd 38305 731-668-8023
Jerome Maclin, prin. Fax 668-5933
Lane Technology Magnet ES 300/PK-4
746 Lexington Ave 38301 731-423-4720
Tisa Day, prin. Fax 423-4797
Lincoln Magnet ES 400/PK-4
425 Berry St 38301 731-988-3800
Lynne Shuttleworth, prin. Fax 988-3801
Malesus ES 400/K-4
610 Bolivar Hwy 38301 731-423-0634
Stan Parker, prin. Fax 427-6979
Northeast MS 600/7-8
2665 Christmasville Rd 38305 731-422-6687
Fax 423-1805
North Parkway ES 700/PK-4
1341 N Parkway 38305 731-427-3384
Versie Hamlett, prin. Fax 427-2591
Nova ES 400/K-5
248 Bedford White Rd 38305 731-424-1591
Kippi Jordan, prin. Fax 427-6177
Parkview Montessori Magnet S 300/PK-8
905 E Chester St 38301 731-422-3116
Melinda Harris, prin. Fax 422-6684
Pope ES 500/K-4
1071 Old Humboldt Rd 38305 731-668-0350
Sharon Murphy, prin. Fax 668-5348
Rose Hill MS 600/7-8
2233 Beech Bluff Rd 38301 731-423-6170
James Shaw, prin. Fax 423-6171
Tigrett MS 500/7-8
716 Westwood Ave 38301 731-988-3840
Janice Epperson, prin. Fax 988-3838
Whitehall ES 200/PK-4
532 Whitehall St 38301 731-427-6396
Deborah Montague, prin. Fax 423-6168
Other Schools – See Beech Bluff, Denmark, Pinson

Augustine S 100/PK-8
1171 Old Humboldt Rd 38305 731-660-6822
Donna Nelson, admin. Fax 660-6833
Hines Memorial SDA S 50/K-8
1902 Campbell St 38305 731-427-0012
Heather Barker, prin. Fax 427-1255
Jackson Christian S 900/PK-12
832 Country Club Ln 38305 731-668-8055
Dr. Rick Brooks, pres. Fax 664-5763
Montessori Center of Jackson 50/PK-4
2732 Highway 45 S 38301 731-668-9197
Teri Canady, prin. Fax 664-9207
St. Mary's S 400/K-8
1665 Highway 45 Byp 38305 731-668-2525
Sr. Mary Evelyn Potts, prin. Fax 668-1164
Trinity Christian Academy 800/PK-12
10 Windy City Rd 38305 731-668-8500
Dr. Sam Botta, hdmstr. Fax 668-3232
University S of Jackson 1,300/PK-12
232 Mcclellan Rd 38305 731-664-0812
Clay Liliensteren, hdmstr. Fax 664-5046

Jamestown, Fentress, Pop. 1,865
Fentress County SD 2,500/PK-12
1011 Old Highway 127 S 38556 931-879-9218
Mike Jones, supt. Fax 879-4050
www.fentress.k12tn.net
Pine Haven S 700/PK-8
800 N York Hwy 38556 931-879-9525
Daryl Rains, prin. Fax 879-2773
York S 500/PK-8
218 School Ave 38556 931-879-5832
John Cargile, prin. Fax 879-2739
Other Schools – See Allardt, Grimsley

Jasper, Marion, Pop. 3,082
Marion County SD 4,200/PK-12
204 Betsy Pack Dr 37347 423-942-3434
Mark Griffith, supt. Fax 942-4210
www.marionschools.org/
Jasper ES 600/K-4
495 Warrior Dr 37347 423-942-2110
Tim Bible, prin. Fax 942-8817
Jasper MS 500/5-8
601 Elm Ave 37347 423-942-6251
Ramona McEntyre, prin. Fax 942-0141
Other Schools – See Monteagle, South Pittsburg, Whitwell

Jasper Adventist Christian S 50/K-8
PO Box 787 37347 423-942-1819
Holly Abrams, prin. Fax 942-1819

Jefferson City, Jefferson, Pop. 7,931
Jefferson County SD
Supt. — See Dandridge
Jefferson ES 800/K-5
321 W Broadway Blvd 37760 865-475-4712
Lynn Husen, prin. Fax 475-8719
Jefferson MS 700/6-8
361 W Broadway Blvd 37760 865-475-6133
Joel Sanford, prin. Fax 471-6878

Jellico, Campbell, Pop. 2,514
Campbell County SD
Supt. — See Jacksboro
Jellico S 500/PK-8
551 Sunset Trl 37762 423-784-6565
Curtis Chitwood, prin. Fax 784-2997

Jellico SDA S 50/1-8
170 Adventist Ln 37762 423-784-9355
Joan Fos, prin. Fax 784-9355

Joelton, See Nashville
Metropolitan Nashville SD
Supt. — See Nashville
Joelton ES 300/K-4
7141 Whites Creek Pike 37080 615-876-5110
Dr. Alan Powell, prin. Fax 847-7336
Joelton MS 400/5-8
3500 Old Clarksville Pike 37080 615-876-5100
Patti Spann, prin. Fax 876-1469

Johnson City, Washington, Pop. 58,718
Carter County SD
Supt. — See Elizabethton
Central S 300/K-8
252 Taylortown Rd 37601 423-547-4045
Elaine Ellis, prin. Fax 547-4056
Happy Valley ES 600/K-4
1840 Milligan Hwy 37601 423-547-4028
Dale Potter, prin. Fax 547-8342

Johnson City CSD 7,000/PK-12
PO Box 1517 37605 423-434-5200
Dr. Richard Bales, supt. Fax 434-5237
www.jcschools.org
Cherokee ES 500/K-5
2100 Cherokee Rd 37604 423-434-5281
Mary Nell McIntyre, prin. Fax 434-5591
Fairmont ES 400/PK-5
1405 Lester Harris Rd 37601 423-434-5275
Carol McGill, prin. Fax 434-5278
Indian Trail MS 1,100/6-7
307 Car Mol Dr 37601 423-610-6000
Tammy Pearce, prin. Fax 610-6010
Lake Ridge ES 500/K-5
1001 Lake Ridge Sq 37601 423-610-6030
John Phillips, prin. Fax 610-6033
Mountain View ES 500/PK-5
907 King Springs Rd 37601 423-434-5260
Dr. Roger Walk, prin. Fax 434-5596
North Side ES 300/PK-5
1000 N Roan St 37601 423-434-5249
Richard Church, prin. Fax 434-5295
South Side ES 300/PK-5
1011 Southwest Ave 37604 423-434-5289
Amy Stover, prin. Fax 434-5291
Towne Acres ES 400/K-5
2310 Larkspur Dr 37604 423-854-4800
Steven Barnett, prin. Fax 854-4810
Woodland ES 400/PK-5
2303 Indian Ridge Rd 37604 423-434-5267
Dr. Tracey Crowe, prin. Fax 434-5298

Washington County SD
Supt. — See Jonesborough
Boones Creek MS 400/5-8
4352 N Roan St 37615 423-283-3520
Pam Page, prin. Fax 283-3524
University S, PO Box 70632 37614 500/K-12
Virginia Foley, dir. 423-929-4271

Ashley Academy 100/PK-8
1502 Knob Creek Rd 37604 423-929-7888
Jackie Maggard, prin. Fax 929-7666
Providence Academy 500/K-12
2788 Carroll Creek Rd 37615 423-854-9819
Jerry Williams, admin. Fax 854-8958
St. Mary S 200/K-8
2211 E Lakeview Dr 37601 423-282-3397
Randi McKee, prin. Fax 282-0224
Tri-Cities Christian S - Johnson City 100/PK-6
2423 Susannah St 37601 423-282-0422
Melody Archer, prin.

Jonesborough, Washington, Pop. 4,550
Washington County SD 9,000/PK-12
405 W College St 37659 423-753-1100
Ronald Dykes, supt. Fax 753-1114
www.wcde.org
Jonesborough ES 700/PK-4
306 Forrest Dr 37659 423-753-1180
Lisa Lady, prin. Fax 753-1181
Jonesborough MS 500/5-8
308 Forrest Dr 37659 423-753-1190
Terry Crowe, prin. Fax 753-1570
Lamar S 700/K-8
3261 Highway 81 S 37659 423-753-1130
Bill Smith, prin. Fax 753-1134
Sulphur Springs S 800/K-8
1518 Gray Station Sulphur 37659 423-753-1140
Deborah Mason, prin. Fax 753-1146
Other Schools – See Chuckey, Fall Branch, Gray, Johnson City, Limestone, Telford

Kenton, Gibson, Pop. 1,301
Gibson County SD
Supt. — See Dyer
Kenton ES 50/PK-4
101 Tommy Wade Dr 38233 731-749-0007
Renee Childs, prin. Fax 749-8023

Kingsport, Sullivan, Pop. 44,130
Kingsport CSD 6,500/PK-12
1701 E Center St 37664 423-378-2100
Dr. Richard Kitzmiller, supt. Fax 378-2120
www.k12k.com/
Jackson ES 400/PK-5
600 Jackson St 37660 423-378-2250
Carolyn Kennedy, prin. Fax 378-2242
Jefferson ES 500/K-5
2216 Westmoreland Ave 37664 423-378-2270
Brian Partin, prin. Fax 378-2277
Johnson ES 600/PK-5
1001 Ormond Dr 37664 423-378-2300
Lenore Kilgore, prin. Fax 378-2310
Kennedy ES 300/PK-5
1500 Woodland Ave 37665 423-857-2700
Dr. Janet Faulk, prin. Fax 378-2340
Lincoln ES 400/PK-5
1000 Summer St 37664 423-378-2360
Tammie Davis, prin. Fax 378-2375
Robinson MS 700/6-8
1517 Jessee St 37664 423-378-2200
Jim Nash, prin. Fax 378-2220
Roosevelt ES 200/K-5
1051 Lake St 37660 423-856-2600
Michael Hubbard, prin. Fax 378-2395
Sevier MS 700/6-8
1200 Wateree St 37660 423-378-2450
Jocelyn Lyons, prin. Fax 378-2430
Washington ES 500/K-5
1100 Bellingham Dr 37660 423-378-2480
Martha Greer, prin. Fax 378-2470

Sullivan County SD
Supt. — See Blountville
Brookside ES 200/PK-4
149 Brookside School Ln 37660 423-354-1730
Dr. Deborah Morelock, prin. Fax 354-1736
Cedar Grove ES 200/PK-4
100 Coley St 37660 423-354-1720
Clarence Marshall, prin. Fax 354-1726
Colonial Heights MS 600/6-8
415 Lebanon Rd 37663 423-354-1360
Cathy Horton, prin. Fax 354-1365
Indian Springs ES 500/K-5
333 Hill Rd 37664 423-354-1685
Karen Nave, prin. Fax 354-1691
Ketron IS 400/5-7
3301 Bloomingdale Rd 37660 423-354-1750
Mike Surgenor, prin. Fax 354-1759
Kingsley ES 300/PK-4
100 Emory Ln 37660 423-354-1740
Dr. Sandra Ramsey, prin. Fax 354-1746
Miller Perry ES 600/K-5
904 Fordtown Rd 37663 423-354-1760
Karen Broyles, prin. Fax 354-1766
Rock Springs ES 400/K-5
1238 Moreland Dr 37664 423-354-1380
Kim Harvey, prin. Fax 354-1389
Sullivan ES 300/K-5
209 Rosemont St 37660 423-354-1770
Tom Bowers, prin. Fax 354-1775
Sullivan MS 200/6-8
4154 Sullivan Gardens Dr 37660 423-354-1780
Zada Church, prin. Fax 354-1786

Appalachian Christian S 50/1-12
1044 New Beason Well Rd 37660 423-288-3352
Newl Dotson, dir. Fax 288-3354
Cedar View Christian School 300/K-12
PO Box 143 37662 423-245-6341
Dr. Jim Fields, prin.
St. Dominic S 100/PK-5
1474 E Center St 37664 423-245-8491
Debbie DePollo, prin. Fax 245-2907

Kingston, Roane, Pop. 5,472
Roane County SD 7,500/PK-12
105 Bluff Rd 37763 865-376-5592
Dr. Toni McGriff, supt. Fax 376-1284
www.roaneschools.com/
Cherokee MS 600/6-8
200 Paint Rock Ferry Rd 37763 865-376-9281
Elizabeth Rose, prin. Fax 376-8525
Kingston ES 800/K-5
2000 Kingston Hwy 37763 865-376-5252
Shelia Sitzlar, prin. Fax 376-8535
Midway ES 400/K-5
130 Laurel Bluff Rd 37763 865-376-2341
Keevin Woody, prin. Fax 376-8512
Other Schools – See Harriman, Oliver Springs, Rockwood, Ten Mile

Kingston Springs, Cheatham, Pop. 2,870
Cheatham County SD
Supt. — See Ashland City
Harpeth MS 600/5-8
170 Harpeth View Trl 37082 615-952-2293
Shannon Schwila, prin. Fax 952-4527
Kingston Springs ES 400/K-4
166 W Kingston Springs Rd 37082 615-952-9060
Jill Bramble, prin. Fax 952-3650

Knoxville, Knox, Pop. 180,130
Knox County SD 58,200/PK-12
PO Box 2188 37901 865-594-1800
Dr. James McIntyre, supt. Fax 594-1627
knoxschools.org/
Amherst ES 700/K-5
7205 Ball Camp Pike 37931 865-560-7001
Carolyn Lee, prin. Fax 560-7005
Ball Camp ES 500/K-5
9801 Middlebrook Pike 37931 865-539-7888
Susan Turner, prin. Fax 539-3042
Bearden ES 300/K-5
5717 Kingston Pike 37919 865-909-9000
Susan Dunlap, prin. Fax 909-9007
Bearden MS 1,100/6-8
1000 Francis Rd 37909 865-539-7839
Heather Karnes, prin. Fax 539-7851
Beaumont Magnet ES 500/K-5
1211 Beaumont Ave 37921 865-594-1272
Gwynn Carey, prin. Fax 594-1375
Belle Morris ES 500/K-5
2308 Washington Pike 37917 865-594-1277
Terry Hursey, prin. Fax 594-1125
Blue Grass ES 800/K-5
8901 Bluegrass Rd 37922 865-539-7864
Reggie Mosley, prin. Fax 531-2164

Bonny Kate ES 400/K-5
7608 Martin Mill Pike 37920 865-579-2108
Linda Norris, prin. Fax 579-8256
Brickey - McCloud ES 1,000/K-5
1810 Dry Gap Pike 37918 865-689-1499
Robbie Norman, prin. Fax 689-0814
Burnett ES 700/K-5
4521 Brown Gap Rd 37918 865-689-1474
Kathy Duggan, prin. Fax 689-1476
Cedar Bluff IS 600/3-5
709 N Cedar Bluff Rd 37923 865-539-7852
Susan Davis, prin. Fax 539-7854
Cedar Bluff MS 500/6-8
707 N Cedar Bluff Rd 37923 865-539-7891
Sonya Winstead, prin. Fax 539-7792
Cedar Bluff PS 600/K-2
705 N Cedar Bluff Rd 37923 865-539-7721
Richard Ward, prin. Fax 539-8667
Chilhowee IS 300/3-5
5005 Asheville Hwy 37914 865-594-1285
Linda Delaney, prin. Fax 594-1286
Christenberry ES 600/K-5
927 Oglewood Ave 37917 865-594-8500
Martha Jean Bratton, prin. Fax 594-8508
Dogwood ES 800/K-5
705 Tipton Ave 37920 865-579-5677
Lana Shelton-Lowe, prin. Fax 579-6051
Farragut IS 1,100/3-5
208 W End Ave, 865-966-6703
Kay Wellons, prin. Fax 671-7074
Farragut MS 1,200/6-8
200 W End Ave, 865-966-9756
Dick Dalhaus, prin. Fax 671-7048
Farragut PS 1,000/PK-2
509 N Campbell Station Rd, 865-966-5848
Julia Craze, prin. Fax 671-1787
Fountain City ES 500/K-5
2910 Montbelle Dr 37918 865-689-1445
Wendy Newton, prin. Fax 689-1491
Gap Creek ES 100/K-5
1920 Kimberlin Heights Rd 37920 865-577-4860
Patricia Moore, prin. Fax 579-2112
Greene Magnet Technology Academy 600/K-5
3001 Brooks Ave 37914 865-594-1328
George Anna Yarbro, prin. Fax 594-1169
Green Math Science Academy 400/K-5
801 Townview Dr 37915 865-594-1324
Sherry Hensley, prin. Fax 594-1938
Gresham MS 800/6-8
500 Gresham Rd 37918 865-689-1430
Donna Parker, prin. Fax 689-7437
Halls ES 800/K-5
7502 Andersonville Pike 37938 865-922-7445
Nancy Maland, prin. Fax 925-7409
Halls MS 1,000/6-8
4317 E Emory Rd 37938 865-922-7494
Doug Oliver, prin. Fax 925-7439
Hardin Valley ES 700/K-4
11445 Hardin Valley Rd 37932 865-470-2088
Tod Evans, prin. Fax 560-1480
Hill Family Community Center 100/K-K
1725 Delaware Ave 37921 865-594-3632
Mamosa Foster, prin. Fax 594-3847
Holston MS 700/6-8
600 N Chilhowee Dr 37924 865-594-1300
Tom Brown, prin. Fax 594-4429
Inskip ES 500/K-5
4701 High School Rd 37912 865-689-1450
Elisa Luna, prin. Fax 689-0806
Karns ES 600/K-2
8108 Beaver Ridge Rd 37931 865-539-7767
Darlene Miller, prin. Fax 539-7774
Karns MS 1,200/6-8
2925 Gray Hendrix Rd 37931 865-539-7732
Danny Trent, prin. Fax 539-7745
Lonsdale ES 200/K-5
1317 Louisiana Ave 37921 865-594-1330
Lisa Light, prin. Fax 594-1208
Lotts ES 1,200/K-5
9320 Westland Dr 37922 865-539-8611
Emily Lenn, prin. Fax 539-8632
Maynard ES 200/K-5
737 College St 37921 865-594-1333
Brenda Reliford, prin. Fax 594-1120
Mooreland Heights ES 300/K-5
5315 Magazine Rd 37920 865-579-2105
Roy Miller, prin. Fax 579-2189
Mt. Olive ES 300/K-5
2507 Maryville Pike 37920 865-579-2170
Angela Harrod, prin. Fax 579-2175
New Hopewell ES 300/K-5
757 Kimberlin Heights Rd 37920 865-579-2194
Melanie Harb, prin. Fax 579-2113
Northwest MS 900/6-8
5301 Pleasant Ridge Rd 37912 865-594-1345
Dr. Karen Loy, prin. Fax 594-1339
Norwood ES 600/K-5
1909 Merchant Dr 37912 865-689-1460
Janie Knight, prin. Fax 689-9140
Pleasant Ridge ES 400/K-5
3013 Walnoaks Rd 37921 865-594-1354
Bibi Burnett, prin. Fax 594-1355
Pond Gap ES 400/K-5
1400 Hollywood Rd 37909 865-909-9040
Susan Espiritu, prin. Fax 909-9012
Ritta ES 500/K-5
6228 Washington Pike 37918 865-689-1496
Christy Dowell, prin. Fax 689-0501
Rocky Hill ES 800/K-5
1200 Morrell Rd 37919 865-539-7844
Cory Smith, prin. Fax 539-7845
Sequoyah ES 500/K-5
942 Southgate Rd 37919 865-594-1360
Martha Hill, prin. Fax 594-1137
Shannondale ES 400/K-5
5316 Shannondale Rd 37918 865-689-1465
Reba Lane, prin. Fax 689-9158
South-Doyle MS 1,000/6-8
3900 Decatur Dr 37920 865-579-2133
Karen Harrel, prin. Fax 579-2128
South Knoxville ES 100/K-5
801 Sevier Ave 37920 865-579-2100
Muncie Cooper-Harbin, prin. Fax 579-2199
Spring Hill ES 600/K-5
4711 Mildred Dr 37914 865-594-1365
Lynn Draper, prin. Fax 594-1370
Sterchi ES 400/PK-5
900 Oaklett Dr 37912 865-689-1470
Cindy Bosse, prin. Fax 689-1471
Vine MS 500/6-8
1807 Martin Luther King Jr 37915 865-594-4461
Becky Ervin, prin. Fax 594-1702
West Haven ES 300/K-5
3620 Sisk Rd 37921 865-594-4467
Ina Langston, prin. Fax 594-3743
West Hills ES 800/K-5
409 Vanosdale Rd 37909 865-539-7850
Suzanne Oliver, prin. Fax 539-7876
West Valley MS 1,100/6-8
9118 George Williams Rd 37922 865-539-5145
Sheila Fugua, prin. Fax 539-5155
West View ES 200/K-5
1714 Mingle Ave 37921 865-594-4471
Sherry Hensley, prin. Fax 594-1669
Whittle Springs MS 600/6-8
2700 White Oak Ln 37917 865-594-4474
Vicki Neubert, prin. Fax 594-1132
Other Schools – See Corryton, Mascot, Powell, Strawberry Plains

---

Berean Christian S 400/K-12
2329 Prosser Rd 37914 865-521-6054
George Waller, hdmstr. Fax 522-5063
Cedar Springs Weekday S 300/PK-K
9132 Kingston Pike 37923 865-291-5252
Dr. Wanda Mooney, dir. Fax 693-6611
Christian Academy of Knoxville 1,200/PK-12
529 Academy Way 37923 865-690-4721
Scott Sandie, supt. Fax 690-4752
Christian Family Cooperative S 100/PK-8
PO Box 31733 37930 865-693-6779
Maynard Nordmoe, admin. Fax 693-2434
Concord Christian S 400/K-8
11704 Kingston Pike, 865-966-8858
Dr. Bill Wilson, dir. Fax 288-1617
Episcopal S of Knoxville 300/K-8
950 Episcopal School Way 37932 865-777-9032
Jay Secor, hdmstr. Fax 777-9034
First Lutheran S 200/PK-8
1207 N Broadway St 37917 865-524-0308
Roger Tessendorf, prin. Fax 524-5636
Freedom Christian Academy 200/PK-8
PO Box 6010 37914 865-525-7807
Melanie Stipes, admin. Fax 522-7729
Grace Christian Academy 800/K-12
5914 Beaver Ridge Rd 37931 865-691-3427
Donald Criss, hdmstr. Fax 342-3827
Knoxville Adventist S 100/K-10
3615 Kingston Pike 37919 865-522-9929
Shirley Watson, prin. Fax 522-8263
Knoxville Baptist Christian S 100/PK-12
2434 E 5th Ave 37917 865-524-3211
Robert Evans, admin. Fax 523-4814
Knoxville Christian S 100/PK-12
11549 Snyder Rd 37932 865-966-7060
William Childers, prin. Fax 671-2148
Nature's Way Montessori S 100/K-8
4710 Murphy Rd 37918 865-689-8976
Mary Smith, prin. Fax 687-5077
Paideia Academy 100/K-6
10825 Yarnell Rd 37932 865-670-0440
James Cowart, admin. Fax 670-0440
Rule Christian Academy 50/K-K
1210 Heiskell Ave 37921 865-546-1500
Terry Minor, hdmstr. Fax 546-0180
Sacred Heart S 600/PK-8
711 S Northshore Dr 37919 865-588-0415
Sedonna Prater, prin. Fax 558-4139
St. John Neumann S 400/K-8
625 Saint John Ct, 865-777-0077
Bill Derbyshire, prin. Fax 777-0087
St. Joseph S 200/K-8
1810 Howard Dr 37918 865-689-3424
Dr. Aurelia Montgomery, prin. Fax 687-7885
Tate's School of Discovery 200/PK-5
9215 Bob Gray Rd 37923 865-693-3021
Brenda Seagraves, prin.
Thackston S, 2023 Lake Ave 37916 100/PK-6
Kristi Wofford, prin. 865-522-0729
University SDA S 50/K-8
1837 Brandau St 37921 865-524-1424
Gloria Adi, prin. Fax 524-5066
Webb S of Knoxville 1,000/K-12
9800 Webb School Ln 37923 865-693-0011
Scott Hutchinson, pres. Fax 691-8057

Kodak, Sevier
Sevier County SD
Supt. — See Sevierville
Northview ES 700/K-4
3293 Douglas Dam Rd 37764 865-933-2415
Missy Wade, prin. Fax 932-4322
Northview MS 500/5-8
3295 Douglas Dam Rd 37764 865-933-7985
Julie Oliver, prin. Fax 933-7387

Lafayette, Macon, Pop. 4,177
Macon County SD 3,600/K-12
501 College St 37083 615-666-2125
Darrel Law, supt. Fax 666-7878
www.maconcountyschools.com/
Central ES 400/2-3
905 Sycamore St 37083 615-666-3265
Dawn Thompson, prin. Fax 666-4028
Fairlane ES 400/K-1
305 Fairlane Dr 37083 615-666-2970
Linda Smith, prin. Fax 666-7477
Lafayette MS 400/4-5
401 Meador Dr 37083 615-666-8868
Terry Marsh, prin. Fax 666-9489
Macon County JHS 700/6-8
1003 Highway 52 Byp E 37083 615-666-7545
Bobby Bransford, prin. Fax 666-9264
Other Schools – See Red Boiling Springs, Westmoreland

Lighthouse Academy 300/K-12
5576 Highway 52 W 37083 615-666-7151
Leon Keith, prin. Fax 666-7151

La Follette, Campbell, Pop. 8,166
Campbell County SD
Supt. — See Jacksboro
La Follette ES PK-5
195 Myers Ln 37766 423-562-3439
Jeanne Higdon, prin. Fax 562-3439
La Follette MS 600/6-8
1309 E Central Ave 37766 423-562-8448
John Turnblazer, prin. Fax 562-2107
Valley View ES 400/PK-5
1187 Old Middlesboro Hwy 37766 423-562-5278
Steve Rutherford, prin. Fax 562-8098

Christian Academy of Campbell County 100/PK-8
2709 Gnrl Carl W Stiner Hwy 37766 423-566-5294
Donnie Poston, prin. Fax 566-4115

La Grange, Fayette, Pop. 146

La Grange Montessori S 100/PK-8
PO Box 365 38046 901-878-1499
Kim Skinner, prin. Fax 878-1135

Lake City, Anderson, Pop. 1,844
Anderson County SD
Supt. — See Clinton
Lake City ES 600/PK-5
402 Lindsay Ave 37769 865-426-2108
John Faulconer, prin. Fax 426-2110
Lake City MS 300/6-8
1132 S Main St 37769 865-426-2609
Paula Sellers, prin. Fax 426-9319

Lakeland, Shelby, Pop. 7,388
Shelby County SD
Supt. — See Memphis
Lakeland ES 1,000/K-5
10050 Oakseed Ln 38002 901-867-7071
Nancy Rouse, prin. Fax 867-2801

Lascassas, Rutherford
Rutherford County SD
Supt. — See Murfreesboro
Lascassas S 800/K-8
6300 Lascassas Pike 37085 615-893-0758
Lyndal Duke, prin. Fax 893-1275

Laurel Bloomery, Johnson
Johnson County SD
Supt. — See Mountain City
Laurel ES 100/K-6
300 Gentry Creek Rd 37680 423-727-2685
Teresa Cunningham, prin. Fax 727-2631

La Vergne, Rutherford, Pop. 25,885
Rutherford County SD
Supt. — See Murfreesboro
LaVergne Lake ES K-5
201 Davids Way 37086 615-904-6730
Jeff McCann, prin. Fax 904-6731
La Vergne MS 900/6-8
382 Stones River Rd 37086 615-904-3877
Dirk Ash, prin. Fax 904-3878
La Vergne PS 1,100/PK-2
220 Stones River Rd 37086 615-904-6735
Angela Thomas-Maupin, prin. Fax 904-6736
Rock Springs ES 800/PK-5
1000 Waldron Rd 37086 615-904-3820
Stephen Lewis, prin. Fax 904-3821
Waldron S 800/3-5
125 Floyd Mayfield Dr 37086 615-904-3785
Dr. Polly Pewitt, prin. Fax 904-3786

Lawrenceburg, Lawrence, Pop. 10,911
Lawrence County SD 6,900/PK-12
700 Mahr Ave 38464 931-762-3581
Dr. Bill Heath, supt. Fax 762-7299
www.lcss.us/
Coffman MS 400/7-8
111 Lafayette Ave 38464 931-762-6395
Bernard Fuller, prin. Fax 762-7176
Crockett ES 500/PK-6
2301 Waynesboro Hwy 38464 931-762-2288
Anne Ray, prin. Fax 766-0683
Lawrenceburg ES 400/PK-6
600 Prosser Rd 38464 931-762-3282
Gari Lynn, prin. Fax 766-5605
New Prospect S 600/PK-8
4520 Pulaski Hwy 38464 931-762-2934
Jerry Dryden, prin. Fax 762-3820
Sowell ES 400/K-6
510 7th St 38464 931-762-4438
Dr. Gina Haddix, prin. Fax 762-4487
Other Schools – See Ethridge, Leoma, Loretto, Summertown

Egly SDA S, 11 Valley Rd 38464 50/K-8
Jim Morgan, prin. 931-762-6297
Sacred Heart S 100/PK-8
220 Berger St 38464 931-762-6125
Rosemary Harris, prin. Fax 762-6125

Lebanon, Wilson, Pop. 23,043
Lebanon Special SD 3,000/K-8
701 Coles Ferry Pike 37087 615-449-6060
Dr. Sharon Roberts, dir. Fax 449-5673
www.lssd.org
Baird MS 600/7-8
131 WJB Pride Ln 37087 615-444-2190
Scott Benson, prin. Fax 453-2690
Byars Dowdy ES 600/K-4
900 Hickory Ridge Rd 37087 615-444-6651
Lorie Blackburn, prin. Fax 443-0212
Castle Heights Upper ES 600/5-6
1007 N Castle Heights Ave 37087 615-444-2483
Terry Trice, prin. Fax 443-6314
Coles Ferry ES 700/K-4
511 Coles Ferry Pike 37087 615-443-1946
Chip Bevis, prin. Fax 443-0215
Houston ES 600/K-4
207 Oakdale Dr 37087 615-444-7494
Julie Beasley, prin. Fax 443-0243

Wilson County SD 14,800/PK-12
351 Stumpy Ln 37090 615-444-3282
Mike Davis, dir. Fax 449-3858
www.wcschools.com
Carroll-Oakland S 600/K-8
4664 Hunters Point Pike 37087 615-444-5208
Carol Ferrell, prin. Fax 449-3914
Southside S 800/K-8
1224 Murfreesboro Rd 37090 615-444-6330
Danny Hill, prin. Fax 443-2668
Tuckers Crossroads S 500/K-8
5905 Trousdale Ferry Pike 37087 615-444-3956
Susie Breedwell, prin. Fax 444-3958
Other Schools – See Gladeville, Mount Juliet, Watertown

Covenant Life S 50/PK-4
113 S Hartmann Dr 37087 615-443-4845
Genese Sink, dir.
Friendship Christian S 700/PK-12
5400 Coles Ferry Pike 37087 615-449-1573
Jim Wilson, prin. Fax 449-2769

Lenoir City, Loudon, Pop. 7,675
Lenoir CSD 2,200/PK-12
2145 Harrison Ave 37771 865-986-8058
Wayne Miller, supt. Fax 988-6732
www.lenoircityschools.com/
Lenoir City ES 700/PK-5
203 Kelly Ln 37771 865-986-2009
Skip Overstreet, prin. Fax 988-7250
Lenoir City MS 400/6-8
2141 Harrison Ave 37771 865-986-2038
Chip Orr, prin. Fax 988-1964

Loudon County SD
Supt. — See Loudon
Eaton ES 700/PK-4
423 Hickory Creek Rd 37771 865-986-2420
Jennifer Malone, prin. Fax 988-5550
Highland Park ES 400/PK-4
4404 Highway 11 E 37772 865-986-2241
David Clinton, prin. Fax 988-7495
North MS 900/5-8
421 Hickory Creek Rd 37771 865-986-9944
Tim Berry, prin. Fax 988-9089

Crossroads Christian Academy 100/PK-12
1963 Martel Rd 37772 865-986-9823
Shannon Klenkel, admin.

Leoma, Lawrence
Lawrence County SD
Supt. — See Lawrenceburg
Leoma S 500/PK-8
2612 Highway 43 S 38468 931-852-2542
Kathy Burns, prin. Fax 852-2536

Lewisburg, Marshall, Pop. 10,790
Marshall County SD 5,200/K-12
700 Jones Cir 37091 931-359-1581
Stan Curtis, supt. Fax 270-8816
www.mcs.marshall.k12tn.net
Lewisburg MS 400/7-8
500 Tiger Blvd 37091 931-359-1265
Randy Hubbell, prin. Fax 359-4030
Marshall ES 500/K-2
401 Tiger Blvd 37091 931-359-7149
Dr. Patsey Thomas, prin. Fax 359-8669
Oak Grove ES 500/K-6
1645 Franklin Pike 37091 931-270-1855
Patsey Thomas, prin. Fax 270-8053
Westhills IS 600/3-6
1351 W Ellington Pkwy 37091 931-359-3909
Sherry Park, prin. Fax 359-3999
Other Schools – See Chapel Hill, Cornersville

Lexington, Henderson, Pop. 7,667
Henderson County SD 3,700/PK-12
35 E Wilson St 38351 731-968-3661
Steve Wilkinson, supt. Fax 968-9457
www.henderson-lea.henderson.k12.tn.us/
Bargerton S 300/K-8
6141 Poplar Spgs Bargerton 38351 731-968-7484
Danny Leasure, prin. Fax 968-9498
Pin Oak S 400/K-8
19925 Highway 412 E 38351 731-968-7341
Lori Leasure, prin. Fax 968-9490
South Haven S 300/PK-8
5455 Highway 22A 38351 731-968-6890
Janet Hays, prin. Fax 968-9705
Other Schools – See Huron, Reagan, Scotts Hill, Wildersville

Lexington CSD 1,100/PK-8
70 Dixon St 38351 731-967-5591
Joe Wood, supt. Fax 967-0794
www.caywood.org
Caywood ES 800/PK-5
162 Monroe Ave 38351 731-968-8457
Angela Blankenship, prin. Fax 968-2938
Lexington MS 300/6-8
112 Airways Dr 38351 731-968-8457
Shannon Taylor, prin. Fax 967-7130

Liberty, DeKalb, Pop. 382
DeKalb County SD
Supt. — See Smithville
Dekalb West S 400/PK-8
101 Bull Dog Ln 37095 615-536-5332
Danny Parkerson, prin. Fax 536-5350

Limestone, Washington
Washington County SD
Supt. — See Jonesborough
West View S 600/K-8
2847 Old State Route 34 37681 423-753-1175
Patton Gamble, prin. Fax 753-1583

Linden, Perry, Pop. 981
Perry County SD 1,100/PK-12
333 S Mill St 37096 931-589-2102
Gil Webb, dir. Fax 589-5110
www.perryboe.com/
Linden ES 300/PK-4
331 Brooklyn Ave 37096 931-589-2531
Janie Burkett, prin. Fax 589-2158
Linden MS 200/5-8
130 College Ave 37096 931-589-5000
Donna Tucker, prin. Fax 589-3685
Other Schools – See Lobelville

Livingston, Overton, Pop. 3,489
Overton County SD 3,400/K-12
302 Zachary St 38570 931-823-1287
Matt Eldridge, supt. Fax 823-4673
www.overtoncountyschools.net
Livingston MS 400/5-8
216 Bilbrey St 38570 931-823-5917
Doug Smith, prin. Fax 823-7549
Roberts ES 600/K-4
301 Zachary St 38570 931-823-5551
Bridgett Carwile, prin. Fax 823-5965
Other Schools – See Allons, Crawford, Hilham, Rickman

Lobelville, Perry, Pop. 909
Perry County SD
Supt. — See Linden
Lobelville S 300/PK-8
196 E Fourth Ave 37097 931-593-2354
Eric Lomax, prin. Fax 593-2613

Lookout Mountain, Hamilton, Pop. 1,898
Hamilton County SD
Supt. — See Chattanooga
Lookout Mountain ES 200/K-5
321 N Bragg Ave 37350 423-821-6116
Paula Gossett, prin. Fax 825-7384

Loretto, Lawrence, Pop. 1,710
Lawrence County SD
Supt. — See Lawrenceburg
South Lawrence S 700/PK-8
PO Box 310 38469 931-853-4965
Kylie Weathers, prin. Fax 853-4945

Sacred Heart S 100/PK-8
PO Box 277 38469 931-853-4388
Catherine Bradley, prin. Fax 853-4388

Loudon, Loudon, Pop. 4,745
Loudon County SD 5,200/PK-12
100 River Rd 37774 865-458-5411
M. Wayne Honeycutt, dir. Fax 458-6138
www.loudoncounty.org/
Ft. Loudoun MS 400/6-8
1703 Roberts Rd 37774 865-458-2026
Tiffany Ratledge, prin. Fax 458-6611
Loudon ES 500/PK-5
2175 Roberts Rd 37774 865-458-2001
Kim Greenway, prin. Fax 458-1405
Steekee ES 300/PK-5
4500 Steekee School Rd 37774 865-458-3322
Scott MacIntosh, prin. Fax 458-9921
Other Schools – See Greenback, Lenoir City, Philadelphia

Louisville, Blount, Pop. 2,157
Blount County SD
Supt. — See Maryville
Middlesettlements ES 400/K-5
3105 Miser Station Rd 37777 865-983-6644
Cynthia Schneitman, prin. Fax 982-6137

Luttrell, Union, Pop. 955
Union County SD
Supt. — See Maynardville
Luttrell ES 300/PK-5
241 Tazewell Pike 37779 865-992-3441
Sonja Saylor, prin. Fax 992-9154

Lyles, Hickman
Hickman County SD
Supt. — See Centerville
East Hickman ES 500/PK-2
5191 Highway 100 37098 931-670-3044
Joni Prince, prin. Fax 670-5433
East Hickman IS 500/3-5
5198 E Eagle Dr 37098 931-670-0227
Kathy Dick, prin. Fax 670-4360
East Hickman MS 500/6-8
9414 E Eagle Dr 37098 931-670-4237
Julia Thomasson, prin. Fax 670-4239

Lynchburg, Moore, Pop. 5,241
Moore County SD 1,000/K-12
PO Box 219 37352 931-759-7303
Chad Moorehead, supt. Fax 759-6386
Lynchburg ES 500/K-6
276 Mechanic St N 37352 931-759-7388
Brantley Smith, prin.

Lynnville, Giles, Pop. 339
Giles County SD
Supt. — See Pulaski
Richland ES 500/PK-4
10333 Columbia Hwy 38472 931-527-0663
Valena Newton, prin. Fax 527-3279

Mc Ewen, Humphreys, Pop. 1,480
Humphreys County SD
Supt. — See Waverly
McEwen ES 400/K-5
220 Swift St E 37101 931-582-6913
Vicki Spann, prin. Fax 582-3267
McEwen JHS 200/6-8
360 Melrose St 37101 931-582-8417
T. Coleman, prin. Fax 582-8418

St. Patrick S 100/PK-8
175 Saint Patrick St 37101 931-582-3493
Sr. Mary Raymond, prin. Fax 582-6386

Mc Kenzie, Carroll, Pop. 5,363
Mc Kenzie Special SD 1,400/PK-12
114 Bell Ave 38201 731-352-2246
James Ward, supt. Fax 352-7550
www.mckenzieschools.org
Mc Kenzie ES 600/PK-4
165 Brooks Ave 38201 731-352-5272
Richard Davy, prin. Fax 352-6076
Mc Kenzie MS 400/5-8
80 Woodrow Ave 38201 731-352-2792
Lynn Watkins, prin. Fax 352-4709

Mc Lemoresville, Carroll, Pop. 288
West Carroll Special SD
Supt. — See Atwood
West Carroll PS 200/K-2
PO Box 219 38235 731-986-8359
Claudia Argo, prin. Fax 986-4509

Mc Minnville, Warren, Pop. 12,060
Warren County SD 6,200/K-12
2548 Morrison St 37110 931-668-4022
Dr. Jerry Hale, dir. Fax 815-2685
www.warrenschools.com
Centertown S 400/K-8
376 Warrior Blvd 37110 931-939-2261
Janie Moore, prin. Fax 939-2050
Dibrell S 400/K-8
1759 Mike Muncey Rd 37110 931-934-2301
Robbie Hitchcock, prin. Fax 934-2092
Hickory Creek ES 600/K-5
270 Pioneer Ln 37110 931-668-5100
Donald Prater, prin. Fax 668-7260
Irving College S 200/K-8
115 Dry Creek Rd 37110 931-668-8693
Mike Mansfield, prin. Fax 668-9351
Ray Memorial ES 500/K-5
504 N Chancery St 37110 931-473-9006
Beverly Ramsey, prin. Fax 506-5245
Warren County MS 800/6-8
200 Caldwell St 37110 931-473-6557
Betty Wood, prin. Fax 473-2432
West ES 600/K-5
400 Clark Blvd 37110 931-473-3801
Marsha Newman, prin. Fax 473-0863
Other Schools – See Morrison, Rock Island

Boyd Christian S 200/PK-12
806 Morrison St 37110 931-473-9631
Robert Harper, prin. Fax 473-9632
Faulkner Springs Christian S 50/1-8
201 Bluff Springs Rd 37110 931-668-4092
Alicia Reeve, prin. Fax 668-3694

Madison, See Nashville
Metropolitan Nashville SD
Supt. — See Nashville
Amqui ES 600/PK-4
319 Anderson Ln 37115 615-612-3678
Sharon Elrod, prin. Fax 612-3684
Chadwell ES 300/PK-4
321 Port Dr 37115 615-860-1459
Clementine Chamberlain, prin. Fax 860-1462
Gateway ES 200/K-4
1524 Monticello Ave 37115 615-860-1465
Constance Hayes, prin. Fax 291-6326
Neelys Bend ES 400/K-4
1300 Neelys Bend Rd 37115 615-860-1471
Rick Binkley, prin.
Neelys Bend MS 700/5-8
1251 Neelys Bend Rd 37115 615-860-1477
Dr. Antoinette Williams, prin. Fax 612-3669
Stratton ES 500/PK-4
310 W Old Hickory Blvd 37115 615-860-1486
Steve Perkins, prin. Fax 262-6957

Goodpasture Christian S 900/PK-12
619 W Due West Ave 37115 615-868-2600
Lindsey Judd, prin. Fax 865-1766
Madison Campus S 200/K-8
1515 Sutherland Dr 37115 615-865-4575
Arthur Cheney, prin. Fax 612-4409
Metro Christian Academy 300/K-12
730 Neelys Bend Rd 37115 615-868-6674
Gae Wofford, prin. Fax 868-2116
St. Joseph S 400/PK-8
1225 Gallatin Pike S 37115 615-865-1491
Sr. Martha Ann, prin. Fax 612-0228

Madisonville, Monroe, Pop. 4,352
Monroe County SD 5,400/K-12
205 Oak Grove Rd 37354 423-442-2373
Michael Lowry, dir. Fax 442-1389
www.monroe.k12.tn.us/
Madisonville IS 500/3-5
1000 Green Rd 37354 423-442-2454
Terry Moser, prin. Fax 442-1534
Madisonville MS 500/6-8
175 Oak Grove Rd 37354 423-442-4137
Augusta Davis, prin. Fax 442-9338
Madisonville PS 500/K-2
268 Warren St 37354 423-442-2236
David Hester, prin. Fax 442-2215
Other Schools – See Tellico Plains, Vonore

Achievement Academy of Monroe County 50/1-10
380 Oak Grove Rd 37354 423-420-1821
Julia Atchley-Pace, prin. Fax 420-1821

Manchester, Coffee, Pop. 9,497
Coffee County SD 4,900/PK-12
1343 McArthur St 37355 931-723-5150
Kenny Casteel, supt. Fax 723-5153
www.coffeecountyschools.com/
Coffee County MS 1,000/6-8
865 McMinnville Hwy 37355 931-723-5177
Jimmy Davis, prin. Fax 723-5180
East Coffee ES 400/K-5
6264 McMinnville Hwy 37355 931-723-5185
Kelvin Shores, prin. Fax 723-3231
New Union ES 400/PK-5
3320 Woodbury Hwy 37355 931-723-5187
Bill Bryan, prin. Fax 723-5197
North Coffee ES 500/PK-5
6790 Murfreesboro Hwy 37355 931-723-5183
Kim Aaron, prin. Fax 723-3230
Other Schools – See Hillsboro, Tullahoma

Manchester CSD 1,300/PK-9
215 E Fort St 37355 931-728-2316
Dr. Prater Powell, supt. Fax 728-7075
www.manchestercitysch.org/
College Street ES 500/PK-6
405 College St 37355 931-728-2805
Lisa Yates, prin. Fax 728-5100
Westwood ES 600/PK-6
912 Oakdale St 37355 931-728-3412
Sandra Morris, prin. Fax 723-0221

Martin, Weakley, Pop. 10,151
Weakley County SD
Supt. — See Dresden
Martin ES 500/3-5
300 S College St 38237 731-587-2290
Teresa Jackson, prin. Fax 587-2877
Martin MS 500/6-8
700 Fowler Rd 38237 731-587-2346
Nate Holmes, prin. Fax 588-0529
Martin PS 500/K-2
215 S College St 38237 731-587-9033
Athalia Donaldson, prin. Fax 587-6699

Maryville, Blount, Pop. 25,851
Blount County SD 10,600/K-12
831 Grandview Dr 37803 865-984-1212
Rob Britt, dir. Fax 980-1002
www.blountk12.org
Blount ES 600/K-5
131 S Old Glory Rd 37801 865-980-1430
Sandy Bell, prin. Fax 980-1428
Carpenters ES 600/K-5
915 Huffstetler Rd 37803 865-980-1490
Fred Goins, prin. Fax 980-1495
Carpenters MS 700/6-8
920 Huffstetler Rd 37803 865-980-1414
Mike Crabtree, prin. Fax 980-1404
Eagleton ES 500/K-5
708 Sam Houston School Rd 37804 865-980-1455
Jerry Bailey, prin. Fax 980-1451
Eagleton MS 400/6-8
2610 Cinema Dr 37804 865-982-3211
Becky Stone, prin. Fax 982-4203
Fairview ES 400/K-5
2130 Old Niles Ferry Rd 37803 865-982-0630
Greg England, prin. Fax 977-0712
Heritage MS 700/6-8
3737 E Lamar Alexander Pkwy 37804 865-980-1300
Dr. Jesse Robinette, prin. Fax 980-1281
Lanier ES 400/K-5
6006 Lanier Rd 37801 865-980-1075
Teresa Robinson, prin. Fax 980-1053
Montvale ES 400/K-5
3128 Montvale Rd 37803 865-983-2666
Gary Leatherwood, prin. Fax 977-0240
Porter ES 700/K-5
4520 Wildwood Springs Rd 37804 865-983-4071
Deborah Craig, prin. Fax 981-4928
Other Schools – See Friendsville, Louisville, Rockford, Townsend, Walland

Maryville CSD 4,800/PK-12
833 Lawrence Ave 37803 865-982-7121
Stephanie Thompson, supt. Fax 977-5055
www.maryvillecityschools.k12.tn.us/
Foothills ES 500/K-4
520 Sandy Springs Rd 37803 865-681-0364
Amy Vagnier, prin. Fax 681-0366
Fort Craig ES 300/PK-4
520 S Washington St 37804 865-983-4371
Ramona Best, prin. Fax 977-0724
Houston ES 500/PK-4
330 Melrose St 37803 865-983-3241
Scott Blevins, prin. Fax 977-0756
Maryville IS 700/5-6
835 Montgomery Ln 37803 865-980-0590
Jan Click, prin. Fax 980-0589
Maryville MS 800/7-8
805 Montvale Station Rd 37803 865-983-2070
Lisa McGinley, prin. Fax 977-9413
Sevier ES 600/PK-4
2001 Sequoyah Ave 37804 865-983-8551
Rick Wilson, prin. Fax 977-0725

Maryville Christian S 400/PK-12
2525 Morganton Rd 37801 865-681-3205
Glenn Slater, admin. Fax 681-4086
Maryville SDA S, PO Box 4128 37802 50/1-8
Gail Jorgensen, prin. 865-982-7584

Mascot, Knox, Pop. 2,138
Knox County SD
Supt. — See Knoxville
East Knox County ES 500/K-5
9315 Rutledge Pike 37806 865-933-3493
Kay Dawson, prin. Fax 933-8178

Mason, Fayette, Pop. 1,145
Fayette County SD
Supt. — See Somerville
Northwest ES 100/PK-5
5245 Highway 70 38049 901-594-5113
Santita Wright, prin. Fax 594-5029

Maury City, Crockett, Pop. 717
Crockett County SD
Supt. — See Alamo
Maury City ES 200/PK-5
PO Box 68 38050 731-656-2244
Melissa Glenn, prin. Fax 656-2936

Maynardville, Union, Pop. 1,915
Union County SD 3,000/PK-12
PO Box 10 37807 865-992-5466
Wayne Goforth, dir. Fax 992-0126
www.ucps.org/
Big Ridge ES 200/K-5
3420 Hickory Valley Rd 37807 865-992-8687
Roger Flatford, prin. Fax 992-8647
Maynard MS 700/6-8
PO Box 669 37807 865-992-1030
Josh Williams, prin. Fax 992-1060
Maynardville ES 800/PK-5
PO Box 339 37807 865-992-8391
Joel McBrayer, prin. Fax 992-8392
Other Schools – See Luttrell, Sharps Chapel

Medina, Gibson, Pop. 1,290
Gibson County SD
Supt. — See Dyer
Medina ES 500/PK-3
PO Box 99 38355 731-783-3660
Calvin Bailey, prin. Fax 783-3778
Medina MS 500/4-8
PO Box 369 38355 731-783-1962
Steve Maloan, prin. Fax 783-1964

Memphis, Shelby, Pop. 672,277
Memphis CSD 108,900/PK-12
2597 Avery Ave 38112 901-416-5300
Dr. Kriner Cash, supt. Fax 416-5578
www.mcsk12.net
Airways MS 500/6-8
2601 Ketchum Rd 38114 901-416-5006
Sharon Griffin, prin. Fax 416-5009
Alcy ES 400/K-5
1750 E Alcy Rd 38114 901-416-7800
Dr. Murphysteen Counts, prin. Fax 416-7862
Alton ES 400/K-4
2020 Alton Ave 38106 901-416-7430
Barbara Beaver, prin. Fax 416-7414
American Way MS 1,000/6-8
3805 American Way 38118 901-416-1250
Russell Heaston, prin. Fax 416-1251
Balmoral/Ridgeway ES 300/K-5
5905 Grosvenor Ave 38119 901-416-2128
Robyn Liebenhaut, prin. Fax 416-2130
Bellevue MS 400/6-8
575 S Bellevue Blvd 38104 901-416-4488
Kevin Malone, prin. Fax 416-4490
Berclair ES 400/K-6
810 N Perkins Rd 38122 901-416-8800
Dr. Sam Shaw, prin. Fax 416-8802
Bethel Grove ES 400/K-5
2459 Arlington Ave 38114 901-416-5012
Shirley Jenkins, prin. Fax 416-5005
Bond ES 1,000/K-5
2727 Kate Bond Rd 38133 901-416-0020
Lyle Conley, prin. Fax 416-0021
Brewster ES 400/K-5
2605 Sam Cooper Blvd 38112 901-416-7150
Shondra Huery, prin. Fax 416-7151
Brookmeade ES 300/K-6
3777 Edenburg Dr 38127 901-416-3920
Harold Beaver, prin. Fax 416-8546
Brownsville Road ES 700/K-5
5292 Banbury Ave 38135 901-416-4300
Charles Newborn, prin. Fax 416-4302
Bruce ES 500/K-6
581 S Bellevue Blvd 38104 901-416-4495
Martha Tipton, prin. Fax 416-4494
Caldwell ES 300/PK-5
230 Henry Ave 38107 901-416-3200
LaWanda Hill, prin. Fax 416-3211
Campbell ES 700/K-6
3232 Birchfield Dr 38127 901-416-1000
Margaret McLaurin, prin.
Campus ES 300/1-6
535 Zach Curlin Rd 38152 901-678-2285
Susan Copeland, prin. Fax 678-4235
Carnes ES 300/K-5
943 J W Williams Ln 38105 901-416-3206
Terry Boone, prin. Fax 416-3208
Charjean ES 300/K-5
2140 Charjean Rd 38114 901-416-5016
Angela Mickey, prin. Fax 416-5018
Cherokee ES 500/K-5
3061 Kimball Ave 38114 901-416-5028
Barbara Campbell, prin. Fax 416-5010
Chickasaw MS 500/7-8
4060 Westmont Rd 38109 901-416-8134
Corey Williams, prin. Fax 416-8139
Church ES 600/K-5
4100 Millbranch Rd 38116 901-416-0198
Elizabeth Stewart, prin. Fax 416-2248
Coleman ES 600/K-5
3210 Raleigh Millington Rd 38128 901-416-4306
Victoria Matthews, prin. Fax 416-4432
Colonial MS 1,000/6-8
4778 Sea Isle Rd 38117 901-416-8980
Marty Pettigrew, prin. Fax 416-8996
Corning ES 400/K-6
1662 Dabbs Ave 38127 901-416-3926
Arcinko Chandler, prin. Fax 416-3928
Coro Lake ES 200/PK-6
1560 Drew Rd 38109 901-416-8140
Lequite Manning, prin. Fax 416-8142
Corry MS 400/6-8
2230 Corry Rd 38106 901-416-7804
Dr. Canidra Henderson, prin. Fax 416-7863
Craigmont MS 1,000/6-8
3455 Covington Pike 38128 901-416-7780
Reggie Jackson, prin. Fax 416-1454
Cromwell ES 400/K-5
4989 Cromwell Ave 38118 901-416-2500
Evette Smith, prin. Fax 416-2517
Crump ES 1,000/K-5
4405 Crump Rd 38141 901-416-1970
Alonzo Brown, prin. Fax 416-1973
Cummings ES 500/K-5
1037 Cummings St 38106 901-416-7810
Lisa Frieson, prin. Fax 416-7812
Cypress MS 400/6-8
2109 Howell Ave 38108 901-416-4524
Jeanna Brandon, prin. Fax 416-4528
Delano ES 300/K-6
1716 Delano Ave 38127 901-416-3932
Patrice Shipp, prin. Fax 416-3934
Denver ES 300/K-6
1940 Frayser Blvd 38127 901-416-3936
Beverly Becton, prin. Fax 416-3938
Double Tree ES 500/K-6
4560 Double Tree Rd 38109 901-416-8144
Peggy Herring, prin. Fax 416-8149
Douglass ES 300/K-6
1650 Ash St 38108 901-416-5946
Angela Brown, prin. Fax 416-8085
Downtown ES 600/K-6
10 N 4th St 38103 901-416-8400
Marcia Wunderlich, prin. Fax 416-8406
Dunbar ES 300/K-5
2606 Select Ave 38114 901-416-5000
Lori Phillips, prin. Fax 416-5002
Egypt ES 900/K-5
4160 Karen Cv 38128 901-416-4150
Rita White, prin. Fax 416-4163
Evans ES 600/K-5
4949 Cottonwood Rd 38118 901-416-2504
Cynthia Alexander, prin. Fax 416-8475
Fairley ES 400/K-5
4950 Fairley Rd 38109 901-416-8080
Dr. Trina Holly, prin. Fax 416-8081
Fairview MS 200/6-8
750 E Parkway S 38104 901-416-4536
Cassandra Smith, prin. Fax 416-4539
Florida-Kansas ES 400/PK-5
90 W Olive Ave 38106 901-416-7874
Tracie Greer, prin. Fax 416-7887
Ford Road ES 700/PK-6
3336 Ford Rd 38109 901-416-8150
Anthony Harris, prin. Fax 416-8156
Fox Meadows ES 600/K-5
2960 Emerald St 38115 901-416-2530
Rhonda Bowles Howard, prin. Fax 416-2550
Frayser ES 500/K-6
1602 Dellwood Ave 38127 901-416-3840
Elaine Stewart-Price, prin. Fax 416-4836
Freeman S 600/1-8
5250 Tulane Rd 38109 901-416-3156
Elaine Parks, prin. Fax 416-3127
Gardenview ES 500/K-5
4075 Hartz Dr 38116 901-416-3068
Faye Anderson, prin. Fax 416-6773
Geeter MS 600/6-8
4649 Horn Lake Rd 38109 901-416-8157
Dr. Chloe Sims, prin. Fax 416-8160
Georgia Avenue ES 600/PK-5
690 Mississippi Blvd 38126 901-416-7200
Raychellet Williamson, prin. Fax 416-7252
Georgian Hills ES 400/K-6
3930 Leweir St 38127 901-416-3750
Cowinta Key, prin. Fax 416-3903
Germanshire ES 800/K-5
3965 S Germantown Rd 38125 901-416-3733
Jacqueline Coleman, prin. Fax 416-3723
Getwell ES 600/K-5
2795 Getwell Rd 38118 901-416-0267
Bobby Walker, prin. Fax 416-6774
Goodlett ES 400/K-5
3001 S Goodlett St 38118 901-416-2510
Dr. Linda Campbell, prin. Fax 416-2512
Gordon ES 300/K-5
815 Breedlove St 38107 901-416-3212
Thelma Roberson, prin. Fax 416-3214
Graceland ES 500/K-5
3866 Patte Ann Dr 38116 901-416-3074
Clinton Coleman, prin. Fax 416-4965
Grahamwood ES 1,000/K-6
3950 Summer Ave 38122 901-416-5952
Pete Johnson, prin. Fax 416-5954
Grandview Heights ES 600/K-6
2342 Clifton Ave 38127 901-416-3940
Jeffrie Akins, prin. Fax 416-3923

Graves ES 500/K-6
3398 Graves Rd 38116 901-416-3086
Sandra Woodard, prin. Fax 416-3088

Guthrie ES 300/PK-5
951 Chelsea Ave 38107 901-416-3220
Barbara Buford, prin. Fax 416-3222

Hamilton ES 500/K-5
1378 Ethlyn Ave 38106 901-416-7826
Debra Stanford, prin. Fax 416-7827

Hamilton MS 700/6-8
1478 Wilson St 38106 901-416-7832
Robert Gordon, prin. Fax 416-3314

Hanley ES 700/PK-5
680 Hanley St 38114 901-416-5958
Ruby Payne, prin. Fax 416-5961

Havenview MS 700/6-8
1481 Hester Rd 38116 901-416-3092
Corey Kelly, prin. Fax 416-3093

Hawkins Mill ES 400/PK-6
4295 Mountain Terrace St 38127 901-416-3944
Carla Franklin, prin. Fax 416-3948

Hickory Ridge ES 800/K-5
3890 Hickory Hill Rd 38115 901-416-1195
Pamela McReynolds, prin. Fax 416-1474

Hickory Ridge MS 900/6-8
3920 Ridgeway Rd 38115 901-416-9337
Cedric Smith, prin. Fax 416-9210

Hill ES 500/K-5
345 E Olive Ave 38106 901-416-7844
Tyrone Hobson, prin. Fax 416-7890

Holmes Road ES 700/K-5
1083 E Holmes Rd 38116 901-416-6469
Eugene Lockhart, prin. Fax 416-2469

Humes MS 600/6-8
659 N Manassas St 38107 901-416-3226
Deartis Barber, prin. Fax 416-2815

Idlewild ES 500/K-6
1950 Linden Ave 38104 901-416-4566
Natalie Catchings, prin. Fax 416-4492

Jackson ES 400/K-6
3925 Wales Ave 38108 901-416-4222
Yolanda Heidelberg, prin. Fax 416-4277

Keystone ES 500/K-6
4301 Old Allen Rd 38128 901-416-3924
Dee Weedon, prin. Fax 416-3947

Kingsbury ES 400/K-5
4055 Bayliss Ave 38108 901-416-6020
Anne Allen, prin. Fax 416-6041

Kirby MS 900/6-8
6670 E Raines Rd 38115 901-416-1980
Jason Bolden, prin. Fax 416-0974

Klondike ES 400/PK-5
1250 Vollintine Ave 38107 901-416-4572
Joyce Anderson, prin. Fax 416-4575

Knight Road ES 500/K-5
3237 Knight Rd 38118 901-416-2514
Dr. Yvette Williams-Renfro, prin. Fax 416-2516

Lakeview ES 200/PK-5
5132 Jonetta St 38109 901-416-8163
Dr. Susie Hodge, prin. Fax 416-8168

Lanier MS 700/6-8
817 Brownlee Rd 38116 901-416-3128
Michelle Brock-Demps, prin. Fax 416-9875

LaRose ES 200/PK-5
864 S Wellington St 38126 901-416-7848
Tonya Cooper, prin. Fax 416-7850

Lester ES 500/PK-6
320 Carpenter St 38112 901-416-5969
Cedrick Gray, prin. Fax 416-5971

Levi ES 400/K-6
135 W Levi Rd 38109 901-416-8166
Janice Tankson, prin. Fax 416-8167

Lincoln ES 300/PK-5
1566 S Orleans St 38106 901-416-7860
Barbara Milligan, prin. Fax 416-7858

Magnolia ES 500/PK-6
2061 Livewell Cir 38114 901-416-4578
Thomas Johnson, prin. Fax 416-4580

Manor Lake ES 400/K-5
4900 Horn Lake Rd 38109 901-416-8170
Velma Pritchard, prin. Fax 416-8172

Newberry ES 600/K-5
5540 Newberry Ave 38115 901-416-2518
Yolanda Williamson, prin. Fax 416-8184

Norris ES 200/K-5
1490 Norris Rd 38106 901-416-7876
Yolanda Jordan, prin. Fax 416-7878

Oak Forest ES 800/K-5
7447 Nonconnah View Cv 38119 901-416-2257
Dr. Kathleen Joyner, prin. Fax 416-2264

Oakhaven ES 700/K-6
3795 Bishops Bridge Rd 38118 901-416-2320
Pauletta Ogilvie, prin. Fax 416-2335

Oakshire ES 400/K-5
1765 E Holmes Rd 38116 901-416-3140
Thomas Rogers, prin. Fax 416-3142

Orleans ES 200/K-5
1400 McMillan St 38106 901-416-7880
Dorothy Murrell, prin. Fax 416-7881

Peabody ES 400/K-6
2086 Young Ave 38104 901-416-4606
Kongsouly Jones, prin. Fax 416-4611

Rainshaven ES 400/K-5
430 Ivan Rd 38109 901-416-3146
Lois Johnson, prin. Fax 416-3148

Raleigh-Bartlett Meadows ES 500/K-5
5195 Twin Woods Ave 38134 901-416-4336
Dr. Daphyne Smith, prin. Fax 416-4339

Raleigh-Egypt MS 1,000/6-8
4215 Alice Ann Dr 38128 901-416-4141
Rogenia Conley-Finnie, prin. Fax 416-4110

Richland ES 700/K-6
5440 Rich Rd 38120 901-416-2148
Sharon McNary, prin. Fax 416-2150

Ridgeway MS 1,100/6-8
6333 Quince Rd 38119 901-416-1588
Lisa Henry, prin. Fax 416-1477

Riverview ES 400/PK-5
260 Joubert Ave 38109 901-416-7360
Samuel Polk, prin. Fax 416-7372

Riverview MS 500/6-8
241 Majuba Ave 38109 901-416-7340
Betty Parks, prin. Fax 416-7343

Ross ES 1,100/K-5
4890 Ross Rd 38141 901-416-1990
Roy Stone, prin. Fax 416-1964

Rozelle ES 400/K-6
993 Roland St 38114 901-416-4612
Carl Johnson, prin. Fax 416-4619

Scenic Hills ES 400/K-5
3450 Scenic Hwy 38128 901-416-4342
William Jones, prin. Fax 416-4343

Sea Isle ES 500/K-5
5250 Sea Isle Rd 38117 901-416-2104
Dr. Teri Evans, prin. Fax 416-2109

Shady Grove ES 400/K-6
5360 Shady Grove Rd 38120 901-416-2166
Janet Robbins, prin. Fax 416-2168

Shannon ES 300/PK-5
2248 Shannon Ave 38108 901-416-4616
Tisha Stewart, prin. Fax 416-4516

Sharpe ES 400/K-5
3431 Sharpe Ave 38111 901-416-5020
Gary Zimmerman, prin. Fax 416-5022

Sheffield ES 400/K-5
4290 Chuck Ave 38118 901-416-2360
Vanessa Wesley, prin. Fax 416-2371

Shelby Oaks ES 1,000/K-6
6053 Summer Ave 38134 901-416-4305
Catherine Diezi, prin. Fax 416-4311

Sherwood ES 800/PK-5
1156 Robin Hood Ln 38111 901-416-4864
Tonya Miller, prin. Fax 416-4869

Sherwood MS 900/6-8
3480 Rhodes Ave 38111 901-416-4870
Eric Cooper, prin. Fax 416-4881

Snowden S 1,600/K-8
1870 N Parkway 38112 901-416-4621
Randy Thompson, prin. Fax 416-4620

South Park ES 400/K-5
1736 Getwell Rd 38111 901-416-5024
Rebecca Dapper, prin. Fax 416-5025

South Side MS 300/6-8
1880 Prospect St 38106 901-416-7420
Kobie Sweeton, prin. Fax 416-7381

Springdale ES 300/K-5
880 N Hollywood St 38108 901-416-4883
JeVon Marshall, prin. Fax 416-9280

Spring Hill ES 500/K-5
3796 Frayser Raleigh Rd 38128 901-416-4346
Raymond Vassar, prin. Fax 416-4348

Treadwell ES 900/K-6
3538 Given Ave 38122 901-416-6130
Renita Perry, prin. Fax 320-6132

Vance MS 400/6-8
673 Vance Ave 38126 901-416-3256
Leviticus Pointer, prin. Fax 416-3257

Vollentine ES 400/K-5
1682 Vollintine Ave 38107 901-416-4632
Katrina Finley, prin. Fax 416-3603

Walker MS 900/6-8
1900 E Raines Rd 38116 901-416-1030
Tonya McBride, prin. Fax 416-1075

Wells Academy 100/7-8
995 S Lauderdale St 38126 901-416-3210
Tamika Carwell, prin. Fax 416-3205

Wells Station ES 500/K-6
1610 Wells Station Rd 38108 901-416-2172
Bobbie Williams, prin. Fax 416-2175

Westhaven ES 400/PK-5
4585 Hodge Rd 38109 901-416-8202
Dr. Angela Whitelaw, prin. Fax 416-8154

Westside ES 500/K-6
3347 Dawn Dr 38127 901-416-3725
Michael Rowland, prin. Fax 416-3729

Westside MS 200/7-8
3389 Dawn Dr 38127 901-416-3700
Willie Williams, prin. Fax 416-3701

Westwood ES 400/K-6
778 Parkrose Rd 38109 901-416-8020
Gloria Golden, prin. Fax 416-8036

Whitehaven ES 500/K-5
4783 Elvis Presley Blvd 38116 901-416-7431
Monica Smith, prin. Fax 416-9358

White's Chapel ES 200/K-6
3966 Sewanee Rd 38109 901-416-8206
Carolyn Crawford, prin. Fax 416-8209

White Station ES 700/K-6
4840 Chickasaw Rd 38117 901-416-8900
Vickie Sneed, prin. Fax 416-8911

White Station MS 800/7-8
5465 Mason Rd 38120 901-416-2184
Eric Sullivan, prin. Fax 416-2187

Whitney ES 600/K-6
1219 Whitney Ave 38127 901-416-3949
Regina Nichols, prin. Fax 416-3953

Willow Oaks ES 700/K-5
4417 Willow Rd 38117 901-416-2196
Shawn Page, prin. Fax 416-2198

Winchester ES 600/PK-5
3587 Boeingshire Dr 38116 901-416-3152
Flora Childres, prin. Fax 416-3154

Winridge ES 900/K-5
3500 Ridgeway Rd 38115 901-416-6618
Janice Cross, prin. Fax 416-4467

Wooddale MS 1,100/6-8
3467 Castleman St 38118 901-416-2420
Tamala Boyd, prin. Fax 416-2426

Other Schools – See Cordova

Shelby County SD 46,100/K-12
160 S Hollywood St 38112 901-321-2500
Bobby Webb Ed.D., supt. Fax 321-2559
www.scsk12.org/

Highland Oaks ES 800/2-5
5252 Annandale Dr 38125 901-756-2343
Carol Macon, prin. Fax 756-2304

Highland Oaks PS 400/K-1
5270 Riverdale Rd 38141 901-756-5290
Jacqueline Webster, prin. Fax 756-5390

Northhaven ES 500/K-5
5157 N Circle Rd 38127 901-353-8580
Louis Padgett, prin. Fax 353-8586

Southwind ES 1,100/K-5
8155 Meadow Vale Dr 38125 901-756-2325
Sue L. Jones, prin. Fax 759-4559

Southwind MS 1,100/6-8
7740 Lowrance Rd 38125 901-759-3000
Marcia Crouch, prin. Fax 759-3011

Other Schools – See Arlington, Bartlett, Collierville, Cordova, Germantown, Lakeland, Millington

---

Alcy SDA Junior Academy 100/K-8
1325 E Alcy Rd 38106 901-775-3960
JoAnn Wade, prin. Fax 775-0142

Bornblum Solomon Schechter S 200/1-8
6641 Humphreys Blvd 38120 901-747-2665
Brenda Bluestein, hdmstr. Fax 747-4641

Briarcrest Christian S 1,100/PK-8
6000 Briarcrest Ave 38120 901-765-4600
Carol Roebuck, prin. Fax 765-4667

Central Baptist S 300/K-12
5470 Raleigh Lagrange Rd 38134 901-386-8161
Jeremy Cordova, prin. Fax 386-9165

Christ Methodist S 400/PK-6
411 S Grove Park Rd 38117 901-683-6873
Steven Jackson, prin. Fax 761-5759

Christ the King Lutheran S 300/PK-8
5296 Park Ave 38119 901-682-8405
Tom Wilt, prin. Fax 682-7687

Christ the Rock Christian Academy 100/K-6
8800 Winchester Rd 38125 901-751-7122
Karen Swihart, prin. Fax 869-4056

Creative Life Preparatory S 50/K-9
1222 Riverside Blvd 38106 901-775-0304
Dr. Carolyn Bibbs, admin. Fax 946-5433

De La Salle S at Blessed Sacrament 100/K-8
2540 Hale Ave 38112 901-866-9084
Br. Mark Snodgrass, prin. Fax 866-9086

Elliston Baptist Academy 100/PK-12
4179 Elliston Rd 38111 901-743-4250
Fax 743-4257

Evangelical Christian S 600/PK-5
735 Ridge Lake Blvd 38120 901-683-9013
Dr. Barbara Harris, prin. Fax 683-6702

Gateway Christian S 1,300/1-12
4070 Macon Rd 38122 901-458-4276
Donna Bumgardner, dir. Fax 323-0914

Grace-St. Luke's Episcopal S 500/PK-8
246 S Belvedere Blvd 38104 901-278-0200
Tom Beazley, hdmstr. Fax 272-7119

Harding Academy of Memphis - Southwind 100/K-6
8220 E Shelby Dr 38125 901-755-5662
Carol Knight, prin. Fax 755-5122

Harding Acad of Memphis - White Station 200/K-6
1106 Colonial Rd 38117 901-767-2093
Bonnie Jamerson, prin. Fax 767-6387

Holy Names S 100/3-8
709 Keel Ave 38107 901-507-1503
Sr. Donna Banfield, prin. Fax 507-1507

Holy Rosary S 500/PK-8
4841 Park Ave 38117 901-685-1231
Darren Mullis, prin. Fax 818-0335

Hutchison S 900/PK-12
1740 Ridgeway Rd 38119 901-761-2220
Annette Smith Ed.D., hdmstr. Fax 683-3510

Immaculate Conception Cathedral S 200/PK-12
1695 Central Ave 38104 901-725-2705
Sally Hermsdorfer, prin. Fax 725-2709

Immanuel Lutheran S 200/PK-8
6319 Raleigh Lagrange Rd 38134 901-388-0205
Scott Browning, prin. Fax 377-7371

Lausanne Collegiate S 800/PK-12
1381 W Massey Rd 38120 901-474-1000
Stuart McCathie, hdmstr. Fax 682-1696

Little Flower S 100/PK-2
1666 Jackson Ave 38107 901-725-9900
Barbara Pettit, prin. Fax 725-5779

Macon Road Baptist S - Berclair 300/PK-12
1082 Berclair Rd 38122 901-683-6363
Trent Thorell, prin.

Margolin Hebrew Academy 200/PK-12
390 S White Station Rd 38117 901-682-2400
Gil Perl, dean Fax 767-1871

Maria Montessori S 100/PK-8
740 Harbor Bend Rd 38103 901-527-3444
Maria Cole, admin. Fax 527-6273

Memphis Junior Academy 100/K-10
50 N Mendenhall Rd 38117 901-683-1061
Suzette York, prin. Fax 683-1012

Neighborhood S 100/PK-8
175 Tillman St 38111 901-323-4092
Charles Beady Ph.D., pres. Fax 888-7952

New Hope Christian Academy 400/PK-6
3000 University St 38127 901-358-3183
Trent Williamson, hdmstr. Fax 358-3184

Our Lady of Sorrows S 100/PK-8
3690 Thomas St 38127 901-358-7431
Julia Willhite, prin. Fax 353-1153

Pleasant View S 100/PK-8
1888 Bartlett Rd 38134 901-380-0122
Wesam Salem, prin.

Presbyterian Day S 700/PK-6
4025 Poplar Ave 38111 901-842-4600
A. Lee Burns, hdmstr. Fax 327-7564

Resurrection S PK-3
3572 Emerald St 38115 901-546-9926
Debbie Bell, prin. Fax 546-9928
St. Agnes Academy-St. Dominic S 500/PK-8
30 Avon Rd 38117 901-767-1356
Barbara Daush, pres. Fax 681-0047
St. Anne S 200/PK-8
670 S Highland St 38111 901-323-1344
Cristy Perry, prin. Fax 458-5215
St. Ann S 600/K-8
6529 Stage Rd 38134 901-386-3328
Kathy Brooks, prin. Fax 386-1030
St. Augustine S 100/PK-6
1169 Kerr Ave 38106 901-942-8002
LaTonya Rayford, prin. Fax 942-4564
St. Dominic S for Boys 200/PK-8
30 Avon Rd 38117 901-767-1356
Barbara Daush, prin. Fax 681-0047
St. George's Independent S Memphis 100/PK-5
3749 Kimball Ave 38111 901-261-2200
Judy Shelton, admin. Fax 261-2211
St. John S 100/PK-6
2718 Lamar Ave 38114 901-743-6700
Teddi Niedzwiedz, prin. Fax 743-6720
St. Joseph S 100/PK-6
3825 Neely Rd 38109 901-344-0021
Phil Amido, prin. Fax 348-0787
St. Louis S 500/K-8
5192 Shady Grove Rd 38117 901-682-9692
Richard Orians, prin. Fax 680-0571
St. Mary's Episcopal S 900/PK-12
60 Perkins Ext 38117 901-537-1472
Marlene Shaw, hdmstr. Fax 682-0119
St. Michael S 100/PK-8
3880 Forrest Ave 38122 901-323-2162
Christina Ostrowski, prin. Fax 323-0481
St. Patrick S 100/PK-6
287 S 4th St 38126 901-521-3252
Kenneth Bernardini, prin. Fax 521-8265
St. Paul S 300/PK-6
1425 E Shelby Dr 38116 901-346-0862
Sr. Helen Marie Glaser, prin. Fax 396-2677
Westminster Academy 300/K-12
2500 Ridgeway Rd 38119 901-380-9192
Dr. Michael Johnson, hdmstr. Fax 405-2019
Woodland Presbyterian S 400/PK-8
5217 Park Ave 38119 901-685-0976
Adam Moore, hdmstr. Fax 761-2406
Word of Faith Christian Academy 100/PK-12
3528 Sharpe Ave 38111 901-744-4061
Debra Smith, prin.
World Overcomers Christian Academy 50/K-3
6655 Winchester Rd 38115 901-473-3030
Jacqueline Bridges, admin. Fax 473-3088

Michie, McNairy, Pop. 663
McNairy County SD
Supt. — See Selmer
Michie S 400/K-8
6418 Highway 57 E 38357 731-632-3602
Lynda Walters, prin. Fax 632-4945

Middleton, Hardeman, Pop. 622
Hardeman County SD
Supt. — See Bolivar
Middleton ES 500/PK-6
PO Box 537 38052 731-376-0160
Richard Bishop, prin. Fax 376-9111

Milan, Gibson, Pop. 7,823
Milan Special SD 2,200/PK-12
1165 S Main St 38358 731-686-0844
Mary Reel, dir. Fax 686-8781
www.milanssd.org
Milan ES 1,000/PK-4
1100 Middle Rd 38358 731-686-0840
Jill Gallemore, prin. Fax 686-3282
Milan MS 600/5-8
4040 Middle Rd 38358 731-686-7232
Lacee Mallard, prin. Fax 723-8872

Millington, Shelby, Pop. 10,306
Shelby County SD
Supt. — See Memphis
Harrold ES 400/K-5
4943 W Union Rd 38053 901-873-8165
Tanya Mabry, prin. Fax 873-8121
Jeter ES 200/K-5
7662 Benjestown Rd 38053 901-873-8170
Paulette Bond, prin. Fax 876-3600
Lucy ES 600/K-5
6269 Amherst Rd 38053 901-873-8175
Detris Anderson, prin. Fax 873-8116
Millington ES 700/K-5
6445 William L Osteen Dr 38053 901-873-8433
Rickey Lunsford, prin.
Millington MS 600/6-8
4964 Cuba Millington Rd 38053 901-873-8130
Dr. Michael Lowe, prin. Fax 873-8136
Woodstock MS 600/6-8
5885 Woodstock Cuba Rd 38053 901-353-8590
Eric Linsy, prin. Fax 353-8599

Faith Heritage Christian Academy 200/K-12
PO Box 157 38083 901-872-0828
M.O. Eckel, hdmstr. Fax 872-0803
Lighthouse Christian Academy 100/K-12
3660 Shelby Rd 38053 901-873-3353
Shari Keough, prin.
Tipton Rosemark Academy 700/PK-12
8696 Rosemark Rd 38053 901-829-4221
John Scott, hdmstr. Fax 829-4292

Minor Hill, Giles, Pop. 428
Giles County SD
Supt. — See Pulaski
Minor Hill S 500/PK-8
PO Box 139 38473 931-565-3117
Lisa Stogner, prin. Fax 565-4504

Mohawk, Greene
Greene County SD
Supt. — See Greeneville
McDonald S 400/PK-8
8120 McDonald Rd 37810 423-235-5406
Donna Smith, prin. Fax 235-7778

Monteagle, Marion, Pop. 1,220
Marion County SD
Supt. — See Jasper
Monteagle S 300/PK-8
120 E Main St 37356 931-924-2136
Janet Layne, prin. Fax 924-2104

Monterey, Putnam, Pop. 2,791
Putnam County SD
Supt. — See Cookeville
Burks MS 300/5-8
300 Crossville St 38574 931-839-7641
Denette Kolbe, prin. Fax 839-6683
Uffelman ES 400/K-4
112 N Elm St 38574 931-839-2791
Eddie Nipper, prin. Fax 839-6071

Mooresburg, Hawkins
Hawkins County SD
Supt. — See Rogersville
Mooresburg ES 200/K-5
305 Highway 31 37811 423-272-9597
Melville Bailey, prin. Fax 272-9597

Morrison, Warren, Pop. 700
Warren County SD
Supt. — See Mc Minnville
Morrison S 400/K-8
601 School St 37357 931-635-2512
Kim Cantrell, prin. Fax 635-3233

Morristown, Hamblen, Pop. 26,187
Hamblen County SD 10,000/K-12
210 E Morris Blvd 37813 423-586-7700
Dr. Dale Lynch, supt. Fax 586-7747
www.hcboe.net
Alpha ES 700/K-5
5620 Old Highway 11E 37814 423-586-3332
Dr. Julia Price, prin. Fax 585-3737
Fairview-Marguerite ES 500/K-5
2125 Fairview Rd 37814 423-586-4098
Suzanne Wampler, prin. Fax 585-3746
Hay ES 300/K-5
501 Britton Ct 37814 423-586-1080
Kim Dyke, prin. Fax 586-1080
Hillcrest ES 600/K-5
407 S Liberty Hill Rd 37813 423-586-7472
John Clawson, prin. Fax 585-3750
Lincoln Heights ES 400/K-5
215 Lincoln Ave 37813 423-586-2062
Janet Dalton, prin. Fax 585-3757
Lincoln Heights MS 500/6-8
219 Lincoln Ave 37813 423-581-3200
James Templin, prin. Fax 585-3763
Manley ES 600/K-5
551 W Economy Rd 37814 423-586-7400
Rebekah Barnard, prin. Fax 585-3766
Meadowview MS 600/6-8
1623 Meadowview Ln 37814 423-581-6360
Ron Wright, prin. Fax 585-3771
Union Heights ES 300/K-5
3366 Old Enka Hwy 37813 423-586-1502
Lynn Sullivan, prin. Fax 585-3822
West ES 400/K-5
235 W Converse St 37814 423-586-1263
Paula Combs, prin. Fax 585-3810
West View MS 600/6-8
1 Indian Path 37813 423-581-2407
Scott Walker, prin. Fax 585-3807
Witt ES 200/K-5
4650 S Davy Crockett Pkwy 37813 423-586-2862
Stan Harville, prin. Fax 585-3754
Other Schools – See Russellville, Whitesburg

All Saints' Episcopal S 200/PK-8
3275 Maple Valley Rd 37813 423-586-3280
Dr. Henry Selby, hdmstr. Fax 586-9355
Cornerstone Academy 100/K-8
PO Box 3040 37815 423-307-1189
Dan Peterson, hdmstr. Fax 586-1637
Morristown SDA S 50/K-8
360 W Economy Rd 37814 423-586-4198
Evelyn Heath, prin.

Moscow, Fayette, Pop. 541
Fayette County SD
Supt. — See Somerville
LaGrange-Moscow ES 300/PK-5
15655 Highway 57 38057 901-877-6854
Latonya Mercer, prin. Fax 877-3165

Mosheim, Greene, Pop. 1,775
Greene County SD
Supt. — See Greeneville
Mosheim S 1,000/PK-8
297 W School St 37818 423-422-4123
Yhona Jones, prin. Fax 422-7547

Mountain City, Johnson, Pop. 2,419
Johnson County SD 2,400/PK-12
211 N Church St 37683 423-727-2640
Morris Woodring, dir. Fax 727-2663
www.jocoed.k12tn.net
Doe ES 200/PK-6
7164 Highway 67 W 37683 423-727-2682
Bridgette Hackett, prin. Fax 727-2698
Johnson County MS 400/7-8
500 Fairground Ln 37683 423-727-2600
Emogene South, prin. Fax 727-2608
Mountain City ES 400/PK-6
301 Donnelly St 37683 423-727-2621
Gay Triplett, prin. Fax 727-2631
Roan Creek ES 500/PK-6
2410 Roan Creek Rd 37683 423-727-4964
Dana Stafford, prin. Fax 727-2164
Other Schools – See Laurel Bloomery, Shady Valley

Mount Carmel, Hawkins, Pop. 5,270
Hawkins County SD
Supt. — See Rogersville
Mt. Carmel ES 400/K-5
127 Cherry St 37645 423-357-7221
Bobby Wines, prin. Fax 357-9863

Mount Juliet, Wilson, Pop. 18,099
Wilson County SD
Supt. — See Lebanon
Lakeview ES 700/K-5
6211 Saundersville Rd 37122 615-758-5619
Stan Moss, prin. Fax 758-5600
Mount Juliet ES 900/K-5
2521 W Division St 37122 615-758-5654
Steve Brown, prin. Fax 758-5602
Mount Juliet MS 1,100/6-8
3565 N Mount Juliet Rd 37122 615-754-6688
Tim Bell, prin. Fax 754-7566
Patton ES, 1003 Woodridge Pl 37122 K-5
Lori Hassell, prin. 615-444-3282
Rutland ES 500/K-5
1995 S Rutland Rd 37122 615-754-1800
Yvonne Kittrell, prin. Fax 754-1801
Stoner Creek ES 500/K-5
1035 N Mount Juliet Rd 37122 615-754-6300
Kathy Stivender, prin. Fax 754-5784
West ES 400/K-5
9315 Lebanon Rd 37122 615-758-5846
Adam Bannach, prin. Fax 754-5798
West Wilson MS 1,000/6-8
935 N Mount Juliet Rd 37122 615-758-5152
Wendell Marlowe, prin. Fax 758-5283
Wright ES 700/K-5
5017 Market Pl 37122 615-754-6200
Jill Giles, prin. Fax 754-5282

Heritage Christian Academy - Mt. Juliet 200/K-12
PO Box 1135 37121 615-754-7946
Katrina Hagerty, prin.
Mt. Juliet Christian Academy 600/PK-12
735 N Mount Juliet Rd 37122 615-758-2427
Greg Scheck, hdmstr. Fax 758-3662

Mount Pleasant, Maury, Pop. 4,452
Maury County SD
Supt. — See Columbia
Mount Pleasant ES 500/K-4
600 Locust St 38474 931-379-5040
Larry Brown, prin. Fax 379-2095
Mt. Pleasant MS of Visual/Performing Art 400/6-8
410 Gray Ln 38474 931-379-1100
Elliotte Kinzer, prin. Fax 379-1108

Munford, Tipton, Pop. 5,652
Tipton County SD
Supt. — See Covington
Munford ES 1,000/K-5
1200 McLaughlin Dr 38058 901-837-0152
Mary Haywood, prin. Fax 837-5778
Munford MS 900/6-8
100 Education Ave 38058 901-837-1700
Glenn Turner, prin. Fax 837-5749

Murfreesboro, Rutherford, Pop. 86,793
Murfreesboro CSD 6,700/PK-6
2552 S Church St 37127 615-893-2313
Marilyn Mathis, supt. Fax 893-2352
www.cityschools.net
Bellwood-Bowdoin PreSchool 400/PK-PK
1165 Middle Tennessee Blvd 37130 615-895-2123
Dena Oneal, prin. Fax 898-7155
Black Fox ES 700/K-6
1753 S Rutherford Blvd 37130 615-893-6395
Joe Thompson, prin. Fax 893-0121
Bradley Academy 400/K-6
511 Mercury Blvd 37130 615-895-2672
Regina Payne, prin. Fax 898-7131
Cason Lane Academy ES 900/K-6
1330 Cason Ln 37128 615-898-7145
Chad Fletcher, prin. Fax 898-7156
Discovery S at Reeves-Rogers 700/K-6
1807 Greenland Dr 37130 615-895-4973
Dr. Linda Clark, prin. Fax 898-7110
Hobgood ES 300/K-6
307 S Baird Ln 37130 615-895-2744
Barbara Sales, prin. Fax 896-3627
Mitchell-Neilson ES 400/3-6
711 W Clark Blvd 37129 615-890-7841
Greg Lyles, prin. Fax 904-2416
Mitchell-Neilson PS 400/PK-2
1303 Jones Blvd 37129 615-895-2904
Robin Newell, prin. Fax 848-5300
Northfield ES 700/PK-6
550 W Northfield Blvd 37129 615-895-7324
Dr. Gene Loyd, prin. Fax 898-7158
Pittard ES K-6
745 DeJarnette Ln 37130 615-396-0240
Roseann Barton, prin. Fax 396-0248
Scales ES 900/K-6
2340 Saint Andrews Dr 37128 615-895-5279
Catherine Stephens, prin. Fax 217-2482
Siegel ES 1,000/K-6
135 W Thompson Ln 37129 615-904-1002
Barbara Tuckson, prin. Fax 904-1007

Rutherford County SD 34,600/PK-12
2240 Southpark Dr 37128 615-893-5812
Harry Gill, supt. Fax 898-7940
www.rcs.k12.tn.us
Barfield ES 1,000/PK-5
350 Barfield Crescent Rd 37128 615-904-3810
Judy Goodwin, prin. Fax 904-3811

Blackman ES 1,000/K-5
586 Fortress Blvd 37128 615-904-3795
Cynthia Ford, prin. Fax 904-3796
Blackman MS 900/6-8
3945 Blaze Dr 37128 615-904-3860
Will Shelton, prin. Fax 904-3861
Buchanan S 600/K-8
6050 Manchester Pike 37127 615-893-3651
Mike Swanson, prin. Fax 893-6222
Central MS 1,000/7-8
701 E Main St 37130 615-893-8262
Cary Holman, prin. Fax 898-7964
Hill ES 400/K-5
6309 Lebanon Rd 37129 615-893-8046
Butch Campbell, prin. Fax 848-5272
McFadden S of Excellence 400/K-8
221 Bridge Ave 37129 615-893-7251
Clark Blair, prin. Fax 898-7724
Pittard Campus S 300/K-6
923 E Lytle St 37130 615-895-1030
Dr. Stan Baskin, prin. Fax 904-7502
Siegel MS 1,100/6-8
355 W Thompson Ln 37129 615-904-3830
Tom Delbridge, prin. Fax 904-3831
Wilson ES 700/K-5
1545 Cutoff Rd 37129 615-904-3840
Jon Dinkins, prin. Fax 904-3841
Other Schools – See Christiana, Eagleville, Lascassas, La Vergne, Readyville, Rockvale, Smyrna

---

Franklin Road Christian S 300/K-12
3124 Franklin Rd 37128 615-890-0894
David Justice, prin. Fax 893-7837
Middle Tennessee Christian S 800/PK-12
100 E MTCS Rd 37129 615-893-0602
Fax 895-8815
Providence Christian Academy 300/K-12
410 Dejarnette Ln 37130 615-904-0902
Butch Vaughn, hdmstr. Fax 904-0859
St. Rose of Lima S 300/K-8
1601 N Tennessee Blvd 37130 615-898-0555
Sr. Mary Cecilia, prin. Fax 890-0977
Victory Christian S 50/K-12
PO Box 2220 37133 615-893-5683
Adam Swanson, admin. Fax 896-1111

Nashville, Davidson, Pop. 545,915
Metropolitan Nashville SD 72,400/PK-12
2601 Bransford Ave 37204 615-259-4636
Chris Hensen, supt. Fax 259-8492
www.mnps.org
Allen MS 500/5-8
500 Spence Ln 37210 615-291-6385
Ganet Johnson, prin. Fax 291-6066
Bailey MS 300/5-8
2000 Greenwood Ave 37206 615-262-6670
Jim Murrell, prin. Fax 262-6979
Bass MS 400/5-8
5200 Delaware Ave 37209 615-298-8065
Janet Murphy, prin. Fax 292-5548
Baxter MS 600/5-8
350 Hart Ln 37207 615-262-6710
David Martin, prin. Fax 262-6743
Bellevue MS 500/5-8
655 Colice Jeanne Rd 37221 615-662-3000
Kimber Halliburton, prin. Fax 662-5728
Bellshire Design Center ES 400/PK-4
1128 Bell Grimes Ln 37207 615-860-1452
Donna Wilburn, prin. Fax 860-9810
Binkley ES 400/PK-4
4700 W Longdale Dr 37211 615-333-5037
Dr. Carol Hammond, prin. Fax 333-5041
Bordeaux Enhanced Option ES 400/PK-4
1910 S Hamilton Rd 37218 615-291-6355
Jackie Kinzer, prin. Fax 291-6313
Brick Church MS 600/5-8
2835 Brick Church Pike 37207 615-262-6665
Chirelle Jefferson, prin. Fax 262-6966
Brookmeade ES 300/K-4
1015 Davidson Rd 37205 615-353-2000
Rob Hancock, prin. Fax 353-4628
Buena Vista Enhanced Option ES 300/PK-4
1531 9th Ave N 37208 615-291-6762
Julie Hopkins, prin. Fax 291-6768
Caldwell Enhanced Option ES 200/PK-4
401 Meridian St 37207 615-291-6361
Carlos Comer, prin. Fax 291-6363
Cameron MS 600/5-8
1034 1st Ave S 37210 615-291-6365
Beverly Walker Bell, prin. Fax 291-6072
Carter-Lawrence Magnet ES 400/PK-4
1118 12th Ave S 37203 615-291-7333
Kesha Moore, prin. Fax 291-7323
Charlotte Park ES 600/PK-4
480 Annex Ave 37209 615-353-2006
Angela Vaughn, prin. Fax 353-2008
Cockrill ES 600/PK-4
4701 Indiana Ave 37209 615-298-8075
Catherine Prentis, prin. Fax 783-2806
Cotton ES 500/PK-4
1033 W Greenwood Ave 37206 615-262-6981
Dr. Karen Hamilton, prin. Fax 333-5659
Creswell Magnet MS 500/5-8
3500 John Mallette Dr 37218 615-291-6515
Dr. Dorothy Gunn, prin. Fax 291-5326
Crieve Hall ES 300/K-4
498 Hogan Rd 37220 615-333-5059
Linda Mickle, prin. Fax 329-8183
Croft Design Center MS 800/5-8
482 Elysian Fields Rd 37211 615-332-0217
Juana Grandberry, prin. Fax 333-5650
Cumberland ES 400/PK-4
4247 Cato Rd 37218 615-291-6370
Renita Perkins, prin. Fax 332-0645
Donelson MS 700/5-8
110 Stewarts Ferry Pike 37214 615-884-4080
Dr. Cecilia Arbuckle, prin. Fax 885-8970

Eakin ES 400/K-4
2500 Fairfax Ave 37212 615-298-8076
Roxanne Ross, prin. Fax 298-8497
Early - Paideia S 200/5-8
1000 Cass St 37208 615-291-6369
Karen Bryant, prin. Fax 298-8497
Ewing Park MS 400/5-8
3410 Knight Dr 37207 615-876-5115
Jeanna Collins, prin. Fax 299-1018
Fall-Hamilton Enhanced Option ES 300/PK-4
510 Wedgewood Ave 37203 615-291-6380
Marsha McGill, prin. Fax 291-6317
Glencliff ES 400/K-4
120 Antioch Pike 37211 615-333-5105
Jeanette Smith, prin. Fax 333-5003
Glendale ES 300/PK-4
800 Thompson Ave 37204 615-279-7970
Mary Sue Clark, prin. Fax 279-7978
Glengarry ES 400/PK-4
200 Finley Dr 37217 615-360-2900
Laurie Smith Ed.D., prin. Fax 279-7978
Glenn Enhanced Option ES 200/PK-4
322 Cleveland St 37207 615-262-6682
Dr. Laura Snyder, prin. Fax 360-2932
Glenview ES 500/PK-4
1020 Patricia Dr 37217 615-360-2906
Claudia Russell, prin. Fax 262-6667
Gower ES 500/PK-4
650 Old Hickory Blvd 37209 615-353-2012
Miatta Alexander, prin. Fax 859-8961
Gra-Mar MS 600/5-8
575 Joyce Ln 37216 615-262-6685
Dr. Barry Potts, prin. Fax 262-6901
Green ES 400/K-4
3500 Hobbs Rd 37215 615-298-8082
Dr. Eileen Wills, prin. Fax 783-2814
Harpeth Valley ES 700/K-4
7840 Learning Ln 37221 615-662-3015
Peggy Brodein, prin. Fax 662-3011
Haynes Health/Medical Science Design Ctr 400/5-8
510 W Trinity Ln 37207 615-262-6688
Robert Blankenship, prin. Fax 298-8084
Haywood ES 600/PK-4
3790 Turley Dr 37211 615-333-5118
Melanie Potts, prin. Fax 333-5646
Head Magnet S 500/5-8
1830 Jo Johnston Ave 37203 615-329-8160
Dr. Angela Carr, prin. Fax 321-8389
Hickman ES 500/K-4
112 Stewarts Ferry Pike 37214 615-884-4020
Dorothy Critchlow, prin. Fax 884-4028
Hill MS 600/5-8
150 Davidson Rd 37205 615-353-2020
Connie Gwinn, prin. Fax 884-4028
Howe ES 300/PK-4
1928 Greenwood Ave 37206 615-262-6675
Thelma Smith, prin. Fax 262-6763
Inglewood ES 400/PK-4
1700 Riverside Dr 37216 615-262-6697
Bertha Brown, prin. Fax 860-7541
Jones Paideia Magnet ES 300/K-4
1800 9th Ave N 37208 615-291-6382
Pam Greer, prin.
Joy ES 500/PK-4
2201 Jones Ave 37207 615-262-6724
LaTonya White, prin. Fax 258-1079
Kirkpatrick ES 400/PK-4
1000 Sevier St Ste 2 37206 615-262-6708
Pippa Meriwether, prin. Fax 262-6615
Lakeview Design Center ES 800/K-5
455 Rural Hill Rd 37217 615-360-2912
Robin Shumate, prin. Fax 360-2915
Lillard ES 300/K-4
3200 Kings Ln 37218 615-876-5126
Debra Thompson, prin. Fax 876-5104
Litton MS 300/5-8
4601 Hedgewood Dr 37216 615-262-6700
Dr. Tonya Hutchinson, prin. Fax 262-6995
Lockeland Design Center ES 300/PK-4
105 S 17th St 37206 615-258-1330
Emily Spencer, prin. Fax 258-1336
Major ES 500/K-4
5141 John Hager Rd, 615-232-2203
Teresa Dennis, prin. Fax 232-7108
McGavock ES 300/K-4
275 Mcgavock Pike 37214 615-885-8912
Dr. Sharon Williams, prin. Fax 316-7752
McKissack S 300/PK-8
915 38th Ave N 37209 615-329-8170
Sharon Braden, prin. Fax 329-8183
McMurray MS 700/5-8
520 McMurray Dr 37211 615-333-5126
Deloris Burke, prin. Fax 333-5125
Meigs Magnet MS 700/5-8
713 Ramsey St 37206 615-271-3222
Jon Hubble, prin. Fax 271-3223
Mills ES 400/PK-4
4106 Kennedy Ave 37216 615-262-6677
Patti Yon, prin. Fax 226-4796
Moore MS 500/5-8
4425 Granny White Pike 37204 615-298-8095
Jill Pittman, prin. Fax 298-8452
Napier Enhanced Option ES 400/PK-4
60 Fairfield Ave 37210 615-291-6400
Michael Ross, prin. Fax 291-6003
Oliver MS 500/5-8
6211 Nolensville Pike 37211 615-332-3011
Dr. LeAnn Kelly, prin. Fax 332-3019
Paragon Mills ES 700/PK-4
260 Paragon Mills Rd 37211 615-333-5170
Jane Johnson, prin. Fax 333-5615
Park Avenue Enhanced Option ES 200/PK-4
3703 Park Ave 37209 615-298-8412
Deltina Braden, prin. Fax 298-6751
Pennington ES 300/K-4
2817 Donna Hill Dr 37214 615-885-8918
Carolyn Wood, prin. Fax 885-8920

Priest ES 400/K-4
1700 Otter Creek Rd 37215 615-298-8416
Melinda Williams, prin. Fax 665-8283
Robertson Academy PK-6
835 Robertson Academy Rd 37220 615-333-5175
Beth O'Shea, prin. Fax 333-5178
Rosebank ES 300/PK-4
1012 Preston Dr 37206 615-262-6720
Diane Brooks, prin. Fax 333-5178
Rose Park Math/Science MS 300/5-8
1025 9th Ave S 37203 615-291-6405
Rise Pope, prin. Fax 262-6717
Ross ES 200/PK-4
601 McFerrin Ave 37206 615-262-6721
Amelia Brown, prin. Fax 262-6638
Shayne ES 600/PK-4
6217 Nolensville Pike 37211 615-332-3020
Debbie Brown, prin. Fax 262-6638
Shwab ES 300/PK-4
1500 Dickerson Pike 37207 615-262-6725
Diane Gilbert, prin. Fax 332-3028
Stanford Montesori Design Center ES 400/PK-4
2417 Maplecrest Dr 37214 615-885-8822
Melva Stricklin, prin. Fax 885-8928
Sylvan Park Paideia Design Center 400/K-4
4801 Utah Ave 37209 615-298-8423
Evalina Cheadle, prin. Fax 292-5154
Tusculum ES 600/PK-4
4917 Nolensville Pike 37211 615-333-5179
Diane Beckman, prin. Fax 885-8965
Two Rivers MS 600/5-8
2991 Mcgavock Pike 37214 615-885-8931
William Moody, prin. Fax 333-5641
Una ES 800/K-4
2018 Murfreesboro Pike 37217 615-360-2921
Dr. Kay Shepard, prin. Fax 885-8954
Vaught MS 400/5-8
160 Rural Ave 37209 615-353-2081
Elaine Fahrner, prin. Fax 353-2090
Warner Enhanced Option ES 200/PK-4
626 Russell St 37206 615-291-6395
Lori Flemming, prin. Fax 353-2090
West End MS, 3529 W End Ave 37205 400/5-8
Greg Hutchings, prin. 615-298-8425
Westmeade ES 400/PK-4
6641 Clearbrook Dr 37205 615-353-2066
Stephen Breese, prin. Fax 298-8450
Whitsitt ES 500/PK-4
110 Whitsett Rd 37210 615-333-5600
Stephen Caraway, prin. Fax 876-5134
Wright MS 900/5-8
180 McCall St 37211 615-333-5189
Jud Haynie, prin. Fax 333-5635
Other Schools – See Antioch, Brentwood, Goodlettsville, Hermitage, Joelton, Madison, Old Hickory, Whites Creek

---

Abintra Montessori S 100/PK-9
914 Davidson Dr 37205 615-352-4317
Sherry Knott, prin. Fax 352-1529
Akiva Community Day S 100/K-6
809 Percy Warner Blvd 37205 615-356-1880
Robert Berk Ph.D., hdmstr. Fax 356-1850
Artios Academy 50/K-6
PO Box 150834 37215 615-834-7878
Tim McCoy, hdmstr. Fax 837-9132
Born Again Christian Academy 100/PK-2
PO Box 78307 37207 615-228-1430
Wilbert Peoples, admin. Fax 228-9598
Cedarcreek Schoolhouse Academy 800/K-12
621 Berry Rd 37204 615-383-7002
Beth Buchanan, dir. Fax 383-7002
Christ Presbyterian Academy 900/K-12
2323A Old Hickory Blvd 37215 615-373-9550
Richard Anderson, hdmstr. Fax 370-0884
Christ the King S 200/PK-8
3105 Belmont Blvd 37212 615-292-9465
Dr. Christine Gebhardt, prin. Fax 292-2477
Covenant S 100/PK-6
33 Burton Hills Blvd 37215 615-467-2313
Bobby Huff, hdmstr. Fax 467-2315
Davidson Academy 900/PK-12
1414 Old Hickory Blvd 37207 615-860-5300
Bill Chaney Ed.D., hdmstr. Fax 868-7918
Donelson Christian Academy 900/PK-12
300 Danyacrest Dr 37214 615-883-2926
Dr. Daniel Kellum, hdmstr. Fax 883-2998
Ensworth S 1,000/K-12
211 Ensworth Pl 37205 615-383-0661
William Moseley, hdmstr. Fax 269-4840
Franklin Road Academy 900/PK-12
4700 Franklin Pike 37220 615-832-8845
Dr. Margaret Wade, hdmstr. Fax 834-4137
Harding Academy 500/K-8
170 Windsor Dr 37205 615-356-5510
Ian Craig, hdmstr. Fax 356-0441
Holy Rosary Academy 500/K-8
190 Graylynn Dr 37214 615-883-1108
Mary Hart, prin. Fax 885-5100
Jenkins S 100/K-8
814 Youngs Ln 37207 615-227-8992
Queen Robinson, prin. Fax 227-8644
Linden Waldorf S 100/PK-8
3201 Hillsboro Pike 37215 615-354-0270
Fax 354-0247
Lipscomb Campus S 1,400/PK-12
3901 Granny White Pike 37204 615-966-6355
Dr. Michael Hammond, dir. Fax 966-7633
Nashville Christian S 500/K-12
7555 Sawyer Brown Rd 37221 615-356-5600
Paula Caruthers, prin. Fax 352-1324
Oak Hill S 500/PK-6
4815 Franklin Pike 37220 615-297-6544
Bill Campbell, hdmstr. Fax 298-9555
Our Savior Lutheran Academy 100/PK-8
5110 Franklin Pike 37220 615-833-1500
Wendy Morris, prin. Fax 833-3761

Overbrook S 300/PK-8
4210 Harding Pike Ste 1 37205 615-292-5134
Sr. Marie Blanchette, prin. Fax 783-0560
St. Ann S 200/PK-8
5105 Charlotte Pike 37209 615-269-0568
John Foreman, prin. Fax 297-1383
St. Bernard Academy 300/PK-8
2020 24th Ave S 37212 615-385-0440
Carl Sabo, prin. Fax 783-0241
St. Edward S 500/PK-8
190 Thompson Ln 37211 615-833-5770
Dr. Sue Baumgartner, prin. Fax 833-9739
St. Henry S 600/PK-8
6401 Harding Pike 37205 615-352-1328
Sr. Ann Hyacinth, prin. Fax 356-9293
St. Paul Christian Academy 300/PK-6
5035 Hillsboro Pike 37215 615-269-4751
Kenneth Cheeseman, hdmstr. Fax 269-6838
St. Pius X Classical Academy 200/PK-8
2750 Tucker Rd 37218 615-255-2049
Katherine Kendall, prin. Fax 255-2049
University S of Nashville 1,000/K-12
2000 Edgehill Ave 37212 615-321-8000
Vincent Durnan, dir. Fax 321-0889

Newbern, Dyer, Pop. 3,089
Dyer County SD
Supt. — See Dyersburg
Newbern ES 500/PK-5
320 Washington St 38059 731-627-2139
Betty Jackson, prin. Fax 627-9610
Northview MS 500/6-8
820 Williams St 38059 731-627-3713
Anthony Jones, prin. Fax 627-4823

New Johnsonville, Humphreys, Pop. 1,964
Humphreys County SD
Supt. — See Waverly
Lakeview S 400/K-8
802 Long St 37134 931-535-2513
Danon Hooper, prin. Fax 535-3593

New Market, Jefferson, Pop. 1,318
Jefferson County SD
Supt. — See Dandridge
New Market ES 300/K-5
1559 W Old A J Hwy 37820 865-475-3551
Vickie Forgety, prin. Fax 475-7122

Newport, Cocke, Pop. 7,299
Cocke County SD 4,800/K-12
305 Hedrick Dr 37821 423-623-7821
Manney Moore, supt. Fax 625-3947
www.cocke-lea.cocke.k12.tn.us
Bridgeport S 300/K-8
1935 Edwina Bridgeport Rd 37821 423-623-2215
April Cody, prin. Fax 623-3440
Centerview S 300/K-8
2400 Highway 160 37821 423-623-4947
Pam Messer, prin. Fax 623-2038
Edgemont S 600/K-8
375 Carson Springs Rd 37821 423-623-2288
Connie Ball, prin. Fax 623-0345
Northwest S 300/K-8
344 Woodson Rd 37821 423-623-4697
Regina Gregg, prin. Fax 623-3432
Other Schools – See Cosby, Del Rio, Hartford, Parrottsville

Newport CSD 700/K-8
301 College St 37821 423-625-0686
David Bible, dir. Fax 613-8029
www.newportgrammar.com
Newport Grammar S 700/K-8
301 College St 37821 423-623-3811
Sandra Burchette, prin. Fax 623-4599

New Tazewell, Claiborne, Pop. 2,882
Claiborne County SD
Supt. — See Tazewell
Alpha Preschool 100/PK-PK
901 Alpha Dr 37825 423-626-3323
Dr. Elizabeth Fugate, prin. Fax 626-3634
Midway S 500/K-8
4411 Clouds Rd 37825 423-626-3067
Sharon Tolliver, prin. Fax 626-1864
Tazewell New Tazewell ES 600/K-4
501 Davis Dr 37825 423-626-9502
Portia Smith, prin. Fax 626-0484

Niota, McMinn, Pop. 796
McMinn County SD
Supt. — See Athens
Niota S 600/PK-8
418 S Burn Rd 37826 423-568-2247
Lois Preece, prin. Fax 568-2687

Nolensville, Williamson, Pop. 2,571
Williamson County SD
Supt. — See Franklin
Nolensville ES 400/K-5
2338 Rocky Fork Rd 37135 615-472-4690
Beth Ferguson, prin. Fax 472-4701

Norris, Anderson, Pop. 1,439
Anderson County SD
Supt. — See Clinton
Norris ES 300/K-5
PO Box 949 37828 865-494-7422
Jess Ann Cole, prin. Fax 494-9764
Norris MS 500/6-8
PO Box 980 37828 865-494-7171
Jeff Harshbarger, prin. Fax 494-6693

Oakdale, Morgan, Pop. 239
Morgan County SD
Supt. — See Wartburg
Oakdale S 600/K-12
225 Clifty Creek Rd 37829 423-369-3885
Diana Smith, prin. Fax 369-2821

Oakland, Fayette, Pop. 2,469
Fayette County SD
Supt. — See Somerville
Oakland ES 600/PK-3
PO Box 388 38060 901-465-3804
Stephanie Kelly, prin. Fax 465-1284
West JHS 300/6-8
13100 Highway 194 38060 901-465-9213
Dr. Walter Owens, prin. Fax 465-1599

Oak Ridge, Anderson, Pop. 27,297
Oak Ridge CSD 4,500/PK-12
PO Box 6588 37831 865-425-9001
Dr. Thomas Bailey, supt. Fax 425-9070
www.ortn.edu
Glenwood ES 300/K-4
125 Audubon Rd 37830 865-425-9401
Pearl Goins, prin. Fax 425-9360
Jefferson MS 600/5-8
200 Fairbanks Rd 37830 865-425-9301
Bruce Lay, prin. Fax 425-9339
Linden ES 400/K-4
700 Robertsville Rd 37830 865-425-5701
Roger Ward, prin. Fax 425-5713
Oak Ridge Preschool 200/PK-PK
PO Box 6588 37831 865-425-9101
Dr. Marian Phillips, prin. Fax 425-9120
Robertsville MS 600/5-8
245 Robertsville Rd 37830 865-425-9201
Mike Baker, prin. Fax 425-9236
Willow Brook ES 400/K-4
298 Robertsville Rd 37830 865-425-3201
Mardee Miller, prin. Fax 425-3268
Woodland ES 400/K-4
168 Manhattan Ave 37830 865-425-9501
Nancy West, prin. Fax 425-9432

St. Mary S 200/PK-8
323 Vermont Ave 37830 865-483-9700
Andrea Graham, prin. Fax 483-8305

Oldfort, Polk
Polk County SD
Supt. — See Benton
South Polk ES 400/PK-5
PO Box 100 37362 423-338-4512
Richard Warren, prin. Fax 338-5683

Old Hickory, See Nashville
Metropolitan Nashville SD
Supt. — See Nashville
Dupont ES 400/PK-4
1311 9th St 37138 615-847-7305
Stephanie Hoskins, prin. Fax 847-7311
DuPont-Hadley MS 600/5-8
1901 Old Hickory Blvd 37138 615-847-7300
Amy Downey, prin. Fax 847-7311
Jackson ES 500/K-4
110 Shute Ln 37138 615-847-7317
Ann Marie Gleason, prin. Fax 847-7336

Oliver Springs, Morgan, Pop. 3,275
Anderson County SD
Supt. — See Clinton
Norwood ES 300/PK-5
809 E Tri County Blvd 37840 865-435-2519
Wayne Patton, prin. Fax 435-2758
Norwood MS 200/6-8
803 E Tri County Blvd 37840 865-435-7749
Danny Richards, prin. Fax 435-5426

Morgan County SD
Supt. — See Wartburg
Petros-Joyner S 300/K-8
125 Petros Joyner School Rd 37840 423-324-8600
David Treece, prin. Fax 324-2558

Roane County SD
Supt. — See Kingston
Oliver Springs S 600/K-8
317 Roane St 37840 865-435-0011
Gwen Johnson, prin. Fax 435-1621

Oneida, Scott, Pop. 3,677
Oneida Special SD 1,300/PK-12
PO Box 4819 37841 423-569-8912
S. Henry Baggett, supt. Fax 569-2201
www.oneidaschools.org/
Oneida ES 600/PK-5
330 Claude Terry Dr 37841 423-569-8340
Melinda Miller, prin. Fax 569-2406
Oneida MS 300/6-8
376 N Main St 37841 423-569-2475
Cheryl Butler, prin. Fax 569-5977

Scott County SD
Supt. — See Huntsville
Burchfield S 400/PK-8
112 W 3rd Ave 37841 423-569-4935
Randy Shelton, prin. Fax 569-1756

Ooltewah, Hamilton, Pop. 4,903
Hamilton County SD
Supt. — See Chattanooga
Hunter MS 800/6-8
6810 Teal Ln 37363 423-344-1474
Robert Alford, prin. Fax 344-1485
Ooltewah ES 400/K-5
9232 Lee Hwy 37363 423-238-4204
Thomas Arnold, prin. Fax 238-4250
Ooltewah MS 1,100/6-8
5100 Ooltewah Ringgold Rd 37363 423-238-5732
Margaret Abernathy, prin. Fax 238-5735
Smith ES 700/K-5
6930 Teal Ln 37363 423-344-1425
Billie Jenno, prin. Fax 344-1462
Snow Hill ES 500/K-5
9042 Career Ln 37363 423-344-1456
Shane Harwood, prin. Fax 344-1472

Wolftever Creek ES 400/PK-5
5080 Ooltewah Ringgold Rd 37363 423-238-7300
Ralph Fernandez, prin. Fax 238-6502

Ooltewah Adventist S 100/K-8
9209 Amos Rd 37363 423-238-4449
Kim Thompson, prin. Fax 238-4577

Palmer, Grundy, Pop. 738
Grundy County SD
Supt. — See Altamont
Palmer S 200/PK-8
PO Box 9 37365 931-779-3383
Sadie Smartt, prin. Fax 779-3445

Paris, Henry, Pop. 9,874
Henry County SD 3,100/PK-12
217 Grove Blvd 38242 731-642-9733
John Hinson, supt. Fax 642-8073
www.henryk12.net/
Other Schools – See Buchanan, Henry, Puryear

Paris Special SD 1,500/K-8
1219 Highway 641 S 38242 731-642-9322
Mike Brown, supt. Fax 642-9327
www.parisssd.org/
Inman MS 500/6-8
400 Harrison St 38242 731-642-8131
Clay Lindsey, prin. Fax 642-8209
Paris ES 500/3-5
650 Volunteer Dr Ste B 38242 731-642-3675
Leah Watkins, prin. Fax 644-0734
Rhea ES 600/K-2
115 S Wilson St 38242 731-642-0961
Scott Owens, prin. Fax 642-5171

Holy Cross Preschool PK-PK
1210 E Wood St 38242 731-642-4681
Angie Taylor, dir. Fax 644-9668

Parrottsville, Cocke, Pop. 217
Cocke County SD
Supt. — See Newport
Parrottsville S 500/K-8
1901 Highway 321 37843 423-623-1612
Lanny Trentham, prin. Fax 623-3332

Parsons, Decatur, Pop. 2,445
Decatur County SD
Supt. — See Decaturville
Decatur County MS 500/5-8
2740 Highway 641 S 38363 731-847-6510
Chris Villaflor, prin. Fax 847-6572
Parsons ES 400/K-4
182 W 4th St 38363 731-847-7317
Renae Lomax, prin. Fax 847-6669

Pegram, Cheatham, Pop. 2,166
Cheatham County SD
Supt. — See Ashland City
Pegram ES 300/K-4
4552 Dogwood Ln 37143 615-646-6637
Glenna Barrow, prin. Fax 662-4736

Pelham, Grundy
Grundy County SD
Supt. — See Altamont
Pelham S 100/PK-8
PO Box 37 37366 931-467-3276
Lloyd Carden, prin. Fax 467-2262

Petersburg, Lincoln, Pop. 596
Lincoln County SD
Supt. — See Fayetteville
Unity S 300/K-8
259 Boonshill Petersburg Rd 37144 931-732-4136
Dennis Eakin, prin. Fax 732-4374

Philadelphia, Loudon, Pop. 572
Loudon County SD
Supt. — See Loudon
Philadelphia S 600/PK-8
300 Spring St 37846 865-458-6801
Mary Hill, prin. Fax 458-6805

Pigeon Forge, Sevier, Pop. 5,784
Sevier County SD
Supt. — See Sevierville
Pigeon Forge MS 500/5-8
300 Wears Valley Rd 37863 865-453-2401
Troy Kelley, prin. Fax 453-0799

Pikeville, Bledsoe, Pop. 1,863
Bledsoe County SD 2,000/PK-12
PO Box 369 37367 423-447-2914
Philip Kiper, dir. Fax 447-7135
www.bledsoe.k12.tn.us/
Bledsoe County MS 400/6-8
PO Box 147 37367 423-447-3212
Bridgett Loyd, prin. Fax 447-3085
Pikeville ES 500/PK-5
41068 SR 30 37367 423-447-2457
James Ellis, prin. Fax 447-6230
Rigsby ES 200/K-5
8231 New Harmony Rd 37367 423-447-2891
Carl Brown, prin. Fax 447-7369
Wheeler ES 300/PK-5
33073 SR 30 37367 423-881-3394
Cristy Pendergrass, prin. Fax 881-3867

Pikeville SDA S 50/1-8
52 Cumberland Ave 37367 423-447-3026
Tim Grove, prin.

Piney Flats, Sullivan
Sullivan County SD
Supt. — See Blountville
Hughes S 500/K-8
240 Austin Springs Rd 37686 423-354-1835
Bryan Mason, prin. Fax 354-1841

Pinson, Madison
Jackson-Madison County SD
Supt. — See Jackson
South ES 200/PK-4
570 Stone Rd 38366 731-988-5413
Lois Mays, prin. Fax 988-5463

Pioneer, Campbell
Campbell County SD
Supt. — See Jacksboro
Elk Valley S 100/K-8
6691 Highway 297 37847 423-784-6866
Gilbert Lay, prin. Fax 784-5826

Pleasant Hill, Cumberland, Pop. 600
Cumberland County SD
Supt. — See Crossville
Pleasant Hill S 600/PK-8
PO Box 10 38578 931-277-3677
Mary Ann Kotus-Huff, prin. Fax 277-3387

Pleasant View, Cheatham, Pop. 3,453
Cheatham County SD
Supt. — See Ashland City
Pleasant View ES 600/K-4
2625 Church St 37146 615-746-5031
Mickey Dyce, prin. Fax 746-8215
Sycamore MS 900/5-8
1025 Old Clarksville Pike 37146 615-746-8852
Judy Bell, prin. Fax 746-5770

Pleasant View Christian S 400/K-12
160 Hicks Edgen Rd 37146 615-746-8555
Ken Riggs, admin. Fax 746-2646

Portland, Sumner, Pop. 10,342
Sumner County SD
Supt. — See Gallatin
Portland MS 900/6-8
604 S Broadway 37148 615-325-4146
Jim Butler, prin. Fax 325-5320
Riggs ES 500/K-5
211 Fountain Head Rd 37148 615-325-2391
Steve Hilgadiack, prin. Fax 325-5315
Watt-Hardison ES 600/K-5
300 Gibson St 37148 615-325-3233
Theresa Levatino, prin. Fax 325-5305
Wiseman ES 600/K-5
922 S Broadway 37148 615-325-8580
Dale Wix, prin. Fax 325-8581

Highland S 100/PK-8
234 Highland Circle Dr 37148 615-325-3184
Catherine Langsdale, prin. Fax 325-0349
Portland Montessori Academy 50/PK-12
613 College St 37148 615-323-1065
Renee Wood, prin. Fax 323-0575

Powell, Knox, Pop. 7,534
Anderson County SD
Supt. — See Clinton
Claxton ES 600/PK-5
2218 Clinton Hwy 37849 865-945-2222
Myles Hebrard, prin. Fax 945-3797

Knox County SD
Supt. — See Knoxville
Copper Ridge ES 600/K-5
2502 E Brushy Valley Rd 37849 865-938-7002
Terry Frost, prin. Fax 947-4336
Powell ES 900/K-5
1711 Spring St 37849 865-938-2048
Kelly Johnson, prin. Fax 947-1805
Powell MS 900/6-8
3329 W Emory Rd 37849 865-938-9008
Gary Critselous, prin. Fax 947-4357

First Baptist Academy 100/K-7
7706 Ewing Rd 37849 865-947-8503
Jennifer Green, prin. Fax 761-6474
Temple Baptist Academy 300/K-12
PO Box 159 37849 865-938-8180
Dwayne Hickman, prin. Fax 938-8147

Primm Springs, Williamson
Williamson County SD
Supt. — See Franklin
Pinewood ES 100/K-5
7510 Pinewood Rd 38476 615-472-4780
Dr. David Davis, prin. Fax 472-4791

Pulaski, Giles, Pop. 7,917
Giles County SD 4,800/PK-12
270 Richland Dr 38478 931-363-4558
Tee Jackson, dir. Fax 363-8975
www.giles-lea.giles.k12.tn.us
Bridgeforth MS 500/6-8
1051 Bridgeforth Cir 38478 931-363-7526
J.B. Smith, prin. Fax 424-7021
Pulaski ES 500/PK-2
606 S Cedar Ln 38478 931-363-5233
William Holt, prin. Fax 424-7027
Southside ES 500/3-5
707 S Cedar Ln 38478 931-424-7005
Carole Swimford, prin. Fax 424-1644
Other Schools – See Elkton, Lynnville, Minor Hill

Bright Beginnings Christian Preschool 100/PK-K
1827 Mill St 38478 931-363-4144
Tina Jet, admin. Fax 424-6568

Puryear, Henry, Pop. 670
Henry County SD
Supt. — See Paris
Harrelson S 500/PK-8
143 Puryear Country Club Rd 38251 731-247-3152
Beverly Fridy, prin. Fax 247-3154

Ramer, McNairy, Pop. 361
McNairy County SD
Supt. — See Selmer
Ramer S 300/K-8
PO Box 8 38367 731-645-3996
Jim Petty, prin. Fax 645-3990

Readyville, Cannon
Cannon County SD
Supt. — See Woodbury
West Side S 300/K-8
3714 Murfreesboro Rd 37149 615-563-4482
Robert Sain, prin. Fax 563-1911

Rutherford County SD
Supt. — See Murfreesboro
Kittrell S 500/PK-8
7801 Old Woodbury Pike 37149 615-893-7604
Sherry Chaffin, prin. Fax 849-2187

Reagan, Henderson
Henderson County SD
Supt. — See Lexington
South Side S 300/K-8
29855 Highway 104 S 38368 731-549-3718
Neal Wright, prin. Fax 549-2431

Red Boiling Springs, Macon, Pop. 1,059
Clay County SD
Supt. — See Celina
Hermitage Springs S 300/K-8
17580 Clay County Hwy 37150 615-699-2414
Cherry Ann Denton, prin. Fax 699-2410

Macon County SD
Supt. — See Lafayette
Red Boiling Springs ES K-6
415 Hillcrest Dr 37150 615-699-2222
Michael Owens, prin. Fax 699-3445

Riceville, McMinn
McMinn County SD
Supt. — See Athens
Riceville S 700/PK-8
3592 Highway 11 S 37370 423-462-2294
Diane Vinson, prin. Fax 462-2534

Rickman, Overton, Pop. 750
Overton County SD
Supt. — See Livingston
Rickman S 700/K-8
631 Rickman Monterey Hwy 38580 931-498-2825
Amy Brown, prin. Fax 498-2095

Ridgely, Lake, Pop. 1,593
Lake County SD
Supt. — See Tiptonville
Kendall S 500/PK-8
200 N College St 38080 731-264-5586
Suzanne Keefe, prin. Fax 264-5587

Ridgetop, Robertson, Pop. 1,680
Robertson County SD
Supt. — See Springfield
Watauga ES 500/K-5
PO Box 190 37152 615-859-5252
Kelley Armstrong, prin. Fax 859-5933

Ridgetop Adventist S 50/K-8
PO Box 829 37152 615-859-0259
Kathy Trumper, prin. Fax 859-3631

Ripley, Lauderdale, Pop. 7,772
Lauderdale County SD 4,500/PK-12
PO Box 350 38063 731-635-2941
Joey Hassell, supt. Fax 635-7985
www.lced.net
Lauderdale MS 700/6-8
309 Charles Griggs St 38063 731-635-1391
Gregory Billings, prin. Fax 635-0028
Ripley ES 700/3-5
100 Highway 19 E 38063 731-221-3066
Pennye Thurmond, prin. Fax 221-3055
Ripley PS 900/PK-2
225 Volz Ave 38063 731-635-0691
Drayton Hawkins, prin. Fax 635-0312
Other Schools – See Halls

Abundant Life Christian S 100/PK-6
446 S Washington St 38063 731-635-7005
Karen Taylor, dir. Fax 635-7005

Roan Mountain, Carter, Pop. 1,220
Carter County SD
Supt. — See Elizabethton
Cloudland ES 400/K-6
8540 Highway 19 E 37687 423-772-5310
Dawn Winters, prin. Fax 772-5311

Robbins, Scott
Scott County SD
Supt. — See Huntsville
Robbins S 300/PK-8
355 School House Rd 37852 423-627-4354
Marva Robbins, prin. Fax 627-2200

Rockford, Blount, Pop. 813
Blount County SD
Supt. — See Maryville
Rockford ES 400/K-5
3728 Williams Mill Rd 37853 865-982-1415
Carol Chastain, prin. Fax 681-1788

Rock Island, Warren
Warren County SD
Supt. — See Mc Minnville
Eastside S 400/K-8
2121 Old Rock Island Rd 38581 931-686-2392
Doug Reed, prin. Fax 686-2118

Rockvale, Rutherford
Rutherford County SD
Supt. — See Murfreesboro
Rockvale ES 600/PK-5
6550 Highway 99 37153 615-904-3881
Donald Johnson, prin. Fax 904-3882
Rockvale MS 300/6-8
6551 Highway 99 37153 615-904-6745
Fred Barlow, prin. Fax 904-6746

Rockwood, Roane, Pop. 5,426
Cumberland County SD
Supt. — See Crossville
Pine View S 200/PK-8
349 Daysville Rd 37854 865-354-1986
Pat Allen, prin. Fax 354-1922

Roane County SD
Supt. — See Kingston
Ridge View ES 800/K-5
625 Pumphouse Rd 37854 865-354-2111
Kevin Ayers, prin. Fax 354-5150
Rockwood MS 300/6-8
434 W Rockwood St 37854 865-354-0931
William Thompson, prin. Fax 354-5160

Rogersville, Hawkins, Pop. 4,283
Hawkins County SD 7,600/K-12
200 N Depot St 37857 423-272-7629
Charlotte Britton, dir. Fax 272-2207
www.hawkinsschools.net
Hawkins ES 400/3-5
1121 E Main St 37857 423-272-2632
Barry Bellamy, prin. Fax 272-9066
Keplar ES 100/K-5
1914 Burem Rd 37857 423-272-9390
Sandra Williams, prin. Fax 272-9390
Rogers PS 500/K-2
2001 E Main St 37857 423-272-9110
Charlotte Webb, prin. Fax 272-7211
Rogersville MS 500/6-8
958 E Mckinney Ave 37857 423-272-7603
Dr. John Carroll, prin. Fax 272-7603
Other Schools – See Bulls Gap, Church Hill, Eidson, Mooresburg, Mount Carmel, Surgoinsville

Rogersville CSD 600/PK-8
116 W Broadway St 37857 423-272-7651
Sherry Terry, supt. Fax 272-7790
www.rcschool.net
Rogersville S 600/PK-8
116 W Broadway St 37857 423-272-7651
William Walker, prin. Fax 272-7790

Rossville, Fayette, Pop. 479

Rossville Christian Academy 300/K-12
PO Box 369 38066 901-853-0200
Mike Coggins, hdmstr.

Russellville, Hamblen
Hamblen County SD
Supt. — See Morristown
Russellville ES 700/K-5
5655 Old Russellville Pike 37860 423-586-6560
Samuel Taylor, prin. Fax 585-3796

Rutherford, Gibson, Pop. 1,245
Gibson County SD
Supt. — See Dyer
Rutherford S 400/K-8
PO Box 70 38369 731-665-6180
Ken White, prin. Fax 665-6638

Rutledge, Grainger, Pop. 1,261
Grainger County SD 3,200/PK-12
PO Box 38 37861 865-828-3611
Terry Acuff, supt. Fax 828-4357
www.grainger.k12.tn.us/
Joppa S 500/PK-6
4745 Rutledge Pike 37861 865-828-5721
Pam Roach, prin. Fax 828-5603
Rutledge ES 300/2-6
7480 Rutledge Pike 37861 865-828-5530
Tim Collins, prin. Fax 828-5797
Rutledge MS 100/7-8
140 Pioneer Dr 37861 865-828-3366
Roger Blanken, prin. Fax 828-3364
Rutledge PS 100/PK-1
470 Water St 37861 865-828-5614
April Sell, prin. Fax 828-5849
Other Schools – See Bean Station, Washburn

New System S 400/K-12
250 Tampico Church Rd 37861 865-828-4488
Brenda Young, prin.

Sale Creek, Hamilton
Hamilton County SD
Supt. — See Chattanooga
North Hamilton County ES 400/K-5
601 Industrial Blvd 37373 423-332-8848
Penny Leffew, prin. Fax 332-8850

Santa Fe, Maury
Maury County SD
Supt. — See Columbia
Santa Fe S 700/K-12
2629 Santa Fe Pike 38482 931-682-2172
Cathy Cook, prin. Fax 682-2606

Savannah, Hardin, Pop. 7,200
Hardin County SD 3,800/K-12
155 Guinn St 38372 731-925-3943
John Thomas, supt. Fax 925-7313
www.hardin.k12.tn.us
Hardin County MS 800/6-8
299 Lacefield Dr 38372 731-925-9037
Steve Haffly, prin. Fax 925-0253

Nixon ES 100/K-5
4455 Highway 128 38372 731-925-3752
Todd Buczynski, prin. Fax 926-2831
North Savannah ES 400/K-5
200 Tennessee St 38372 731-925-3986
Billy Garrard, prin. Fax 925-7451
Parris South ES 400/K-5
169 Lacefield Dr 38372 731-925-2480
Jeremy Davis, prin. Fax 925-4022
Walker ES 200/K-5
9380 Highway 128 38372 731-925-5650
Patricia White, prin. Fax 926-2331
Walnut Grove ES 100/K-5
4355 Highway 69 38372 731-925-3814
Linda Gean, prin. Fax 925-3814
Whites ES 100/K-5
110 School Dr 38372 731-925-5267
Martha Holt, prin. Fax 925-6243
Other Schools – See Adamsville, Counce

Savannah Christian Academy 100/K-8
PO Box 730 38372 731-926-1504
Kristine Smith, prin. Fax 926-3009

Scotts Hill, Decatur, Pop. 914
Henderson County SD
Supt. — See Lexington
Scotts Hill S 300/K-8
1 Highway 114 S 38374 731-549-3145
Wanda Small, prin. Fax 549-2430

Selmer, McNairy, Pop. 4,618
McNairy County SD 4,300/K-12
170 W Court Ave 38375 731-645-3267
Charles Miskelly, supt. Fax 645-8085
www.mcnairy.org
Selmer ES 500/K-4
533 E Poplar Ave 38375 731-645-3131
Carolyn Giesler, prin. Fax 645-9756
Selmer MS 400/5-8
635 E Poplar Ave 38375 731-645-7977
Joel Boyd, prin. Fax 645-6377
Other Schools – See Adamsville, Bethel Springs, Michie, Ramer

Sevierville, Sevier, Pop. 14,788
Sevier County SD 14,200/PK-12
226 Cedar St 37862 865-453-4671
Dr. Jack Parton, supt. Fax 522-1497
www.sevier.org
Boyds Creek S 600/K-8
1729 Indian Warpath Rd 37876 865-774-8285
John Wade, prin. Fax 429-2083
Catlettsburg S K-8
1409 Catlettsburg Rd 37862 865-453-4671
Jerry Wear, prin.
Catons Chapel S 400/K-8
3135 Catons Chapel Rd 37876 865-453-2132
Bill Hatcher, prin. Fax 453-2693
Lawson ECC 50/PK-PK
550 Eastgate Rd 37862 865-453-1036
Dr. Fran Harmon, prin. Fax 453-3112
New Center S 900/K-8
2701 Old Newport Hwy 37876 865-453-2123
Dr. Nancy Sims, prin. Fax 453-7321
Pigeon Forge PS 600/K-4
1766 Waldens Creek Rd 37862 865-428-3016
Nancye Williams, prin. Fax 428-3053
Sevierville IS 700/3-5
416 High St 37862 865-428-8925
Terri Dodge, prin. Fax 428-7846
Sevierville MS 700/6-8
520 High St 37862 865-453-0311
Jayson Nave, prin. Fax 428-2316
Sevierville PS 700/K-2
1146 Blanton Dr 37862 865-453-2824
Harriet Berrier, prin. Fax 428-5443
Wearwood S 200/K-8
3150 Wearwood Dr 37862 865-453-2252
Bruce Wilson, prin. Fax 453-8943
Other Schools – See Cosby, Gatlinburg, Kodak, Pigeon Forge, Seymour

---

Covenant Christian Academy 300/PK-12
PO Box 5080 37864 865-429-4324
Dr. Douglas Mills, hdmstr. Fax 509-3885

Sewanee, Franklin, Pop. 2,128
Franklin County SD
Supt. — See Winchester
Sewanee ES 200/PK-5
PO Box 696 37375 931-598-5951
Mike Maxon, prin. Fax 598-0943

Seymour, Sevier, Pop. 7,026
Sevier County SD
Supt. — See Sevierville
Seymour IS 700/3-5
212 N Pitner Rd 37865 865-609-0030
Peggy Oakes, prin. Fax 609-2258
Seymour MS 800/6-8
737 Boyds Creek Hwy 37865 865-579-0730
Faye Nelson, prin. Fax 579-0905
Seymour PS 700/K-2
717 Boyds Creek Hwy 37865 865-577-5970
Jannese Moore, prin. Fax 573-9236

Kings Academy 400/PK-12
202 Smothers Rd 37865 865-573-8321
Walter Grubb, hdmstr. Fax 573-8323

Shady Valley, Johnson
Johnson County SD
Supt. — See Mountain City
Shady Valley ES 100/K-6
423 Highway 133 37688 423-739-2422
E. Richard Price, prin. Fax 739-9278

Sharon, Weakley, Pop. 935
Weakley County SD
Supt. — See Dresden
Sharon S 200/K-8
254 N Woodlawn Ave 38255 731-456-2672
Don High, prin. Fax 456-2750

Sharps Chapel, Union
Union County SD
Supt. — See Maynardville
Sharps Chapel ES 100/PK-5
1550 Sharps Chapel Rd 37866 865-278-3294
Bryan Shoffner, prin. Fax 278-3993

Shelbyville, Bedford, Pop. 18,648
Bedford County SD 7,600/K-12
500 Madison St 37160 931-684-3284
Ed Gray, supt. Fax 684-1133
www.bedfordk12tn.com/
Eakin PS 600/K-3
1100 Glenoaks Rd 37160 931-684-7852
Fax 684-0553
East Side PS 400/K-3
421 Elliott St 37160 931-684-7112
Fax 684-7108
Harris MS 800/6-8
570 Eagle Blvd 37160 931-684-5195
Bill Pietkiewicz, prin. Fax 685-9455
Liberty S 700/K-8
500 Snell Rd 37160 931-684-7809
Tim Harwell, prin. Fax 685-0627
Southside PS 400/K-3
903 S Cannon Blvd 37160 931-684-7545
Reita Vaughn, prin. Fax 685-0912
Thomas IS 500/4-5
515 Tate Ave 37160 931-684-6818
Dee McCullough, prin. Fax 684-7174
Other Schools – See Unionville, Wartrace

Victory Baptist Academy 100/K-12
PO Box 1030 37162 931-684-8115
Lyn Warren, prin.

Signal Mountain, Hamilton, Pop. 7,146
Hamilton County SD
Supt. — See Chattanooga
Nolan ES 500/K-5
4435 Shackleford Ridge Rd 37377 423-886-0898
Ken Barker, prin. Fax 886-0897
Thrasher ES 500/K-5
1301 James Blvd 37377 423-886-0882
Aimee Randolph, prin. Fax 886-0888

Signal Mountain Christian S 50/K-5
2502 Fairmount Pike 37377 423-886-1115
Danette Kelley, dir. Fax 886-1115

Smithville, DeKalb, Pop. 4,160
DeKalb County SD 2,900/PK-12
110 S Public Sq 37166 615-597-4084
Mark Willoughby, supt. Fax 597-6326
web.dekalb.k12tn.net/
DeKalb MS 500/6-8
1132 W Broad St 37166 615-597-7987
Randy Jennings, prin. Fax 597-2640
Northside ES 500/3-5
400 N Congress Blvd 37166 615-597-1575
Dr. Gayle Redmon, prin. Fax 597-1585
Smithville ES 600/PK-2
221 E Bryant St 37166 615-597-4415
Dr. Bill Tanner, prin. Fax 597-7547
Other Schools – See Liberty

Smyrna, Rutherford, Pop. 33,497
Rutherford County SD
Supt. — See Murfreesboro
Cedar Grove ES 900/K-5
354 Chaney Rd 37167 615-904-3777
Kellye Goostree, prin. Fax 904-3760
Colemon ES 400/PK-5
100 Wise Dr 37167 615-904-6740
Dr. Joe Phillips, prin. Fax 459-0936
Francis S 800/K-8
221 Todd Ln 37167 615-459-4128
Dr. Andria Helton, prin. Fax 459-7710
Rock Springs MS 900/6-8
3301 Rock Springs Rd 37167 615-904-3825
Dr. Pat Essary, prin. Fax 904-3826
Smyrna ES 600/K-5
1001 Sam Davis Rd 37167 615-904-6725
Regina Joiner, prin. Fax 904-6726
Smyrna MS 800/6-8
712 Hazelwood Dr 37167 615-904-3845
Dr. Linda Kennedy, prin. Fax 904-3846
Smyrna PS 500/PK-5
200 Walnut St 37167 615-904-6720
Dr. Gale Vogel, prin. Fax 355-5609
Stewartsboro ES 1,000/K-5
10479 Old Nashville Hwy 37167 615-904-6705
Gary Seymore, prin. Fax 459-6249
Stewarts Creek ES 800/K-5
200 Red Hawk Blvd 37167 615-904-6750
Richard Zago, prin. Fax 904-6751
Stewarts Creek MS 700/6-8
400 Red Hawk Blvd 37167 615-904-6700
Larry Creasy, prin. Fax 904-6701
Youree ES 700/K-5
250 Todd Ln 37167 615-904-6775
Steve Luker, prin. Fax 904-6776

Lancaster Christian Academy 300/PK-12
150 Soccer Way 37167 615-223-0451
Sherry Lancaster, prin. Fax 223-6946

Sneedville, Hancock, Pop. 1,317
Hancock County SD 1,000/K-12
PO Box 629 37869 423-733-2591
Mike Antrican, dir. Fax 733-8757
www.hancockcountyschools.com/
Hancock County ES 500/K-5
373 Newmans Ridge Rd 37869 423-733-2534
Marta Stapleton, prin. Fax 733-9820

Soddy Daisy, Hamilton, Pop. 8,884
Hamilton County SD
Supt. — See Chattanooga
Allen ES 500/K-5
9811 Dallas Hollow Rd 37379 423-843-4713
Barbara Weeks, prin. Fax 843-4714
Daisy ES 500/K-5
620 Sequoyah Rd 37379 423-332-8815
Kirk Shrum, prin. Fax 332-8816
Soddy Daisy MS 600/6-8
200 Turner Rd 37379 423-332-8800
Dr. Robert Jenkins, prin. Fax 332-8810
Soddy ES 300/PK-5
260 School St 37379 423-332-8823
LeeAnn Mills, prin. Fax 332-8843

Somerville, Fayette, Pop. 2,907
Fayette County SD 3,100/PK-12
PO Box 9 38068 901-465-5260
Myles Wilson, supt. Fax 466-3725
www.fayette.k12.tn.us
Central ES 300/PK-5
10425 Highway 76 S 38068 901-465-3208
Trudi Royston, prin. Fax 465-5377
East JHS 300/6-8
400 Leach Dr 38068 901-465-3151
Earl LeFlore, prin. Fax 465-5084
Jefferson ES 200/PK-5
13955 Highway 59 38068 901-465-2086
Sandra Bryant, prin. Fax 466-9749
Somerville ES 200/PK-5
12690 S Main St 38068 901-465-2761
Debra Lewis, prin. Fax 465-0179
Other Schools – See Mason, Moscow, Oakland, Williston

Fayette Academy 700/K-12
PO Box 130 38068 901-465-3241
Nita Armour, prin. Fax 465-2141

South Fulton, Obion, Pop. 2,452
Obion County SD
Supt. — See Union City
South Fulton ES 400/K-5
209 John C Jones Pkwy 38257 731-479-2304
Elise Braswell, prin. Fax 479-1447

South Pittsburg, Marion, Pop. 3,123
Marion County SD
Supt. — See Jasper
South Pittsburg ES 500/PK-6
310 Elm Ave 37380 423-837-6117
Donna Blansett, prin. Fax 837-6168

Richard CSD 400/K-12
1620 Hamilton Ave 37380 423-837-7282
Grant Barham, supt. Fax 837-0641
www.richardhardy.org
Hardy Memorial S 400/K-12
1620 Hamilton Ave 37380 423-837-7282
Stan Mannon, prin. Fax 837-0641

Sparta, White, Pop. 4,766
White County SD 4,100/PK-12
136 Baker St 38583 931-836-2229
Donny Haley, supt. Fax 836-8128
www.whitecountyschools.org
Bon De Croft ES 200/PK-5
8095 Crossville Hwy 38583 931-935-2359
Gary Alspaugh, prin. Fax 935-2399
Cassville ES 200/PK-5
261 Will Thompson Rd 38583 931-761-2277
Geeta McMillan, prin. Fax 761-5102
Findlay ES 400/PK-5
576 Hale St 38583 931-738-2412
Gary Alspaugh, prin. Fax 738-3007
Northfield ES 300/K-5
570 S Bunker Hill Rd 38583 931-761-7979
Kurt Dronebarger, prin. Fax 761-7969
White County MS 900/6-8
300 Turn Table Rd 38583 931-738-9238
Paul Steele, prin. Fax 738-9271
Woodland Park ES 500/PK-5
88 Panther Dr 38583 931-738-3505
Craig Lynn, prin. Fax 738-5071
Other Schools – See Doyle, Walling

Speedwell, Claiborne
Claiborne County SD
Supt. — See Tazewell
Powell Valley S 400/K-8
255 Powell Valley School Ln 37870 423-869-4659
Early Perkins, prin. Fax 869-8343

Spencer, Van Buren, Pop. 1,694
Van Buren County SD 800/PK-12
PO Box 98 38585 931-946-2242
Michael Martin, dir. Fax 946-2858
www.vanburenschools.org
Spencer ES 300/PK-5
PO Box 218 38585 931-946-2171
Denise Whittenberg, prin. Fax 946-7113

Spring City, Rhea, Pop. 2,009
Rhea County SD
Supt. — See Dayton
Spring City ES 600/PK-5
270 E Jackson Ave 37381 423-365-6451
Shane Johnston, prin. Fax 365-7075
Spring City MS 300/6-8
751 Wassom Memorial Hwy 37381 423-365-9105
Buddy Jackson, prin. Fax 365-9102

Springfield, Robertson, Pop. 15,916
Robertson County SD 10,600/PK-12
PO Box 130 37172 615-384-5588
Daniel Whitlow, supt. Fax 384-9749
www.robcoschools.org
Bransford ES 300/PK-K
700 Bransford Dr 37172 615-384-4313
Harold Barbee, prin. Fax 384-3213
Cheatham Park ES 400/1-5
301 Locust St 37172 615-384-0232
Raymond Woodard, prin. Fax 382-2305
Coopertown ES 400/K-3
3746 Highway 49 W 37172 615-384-7642
Lori Smith, prin. Fax 384-1176
Coopertown MS 300/4-8
3820 Highway 49 W 37172 615-382-4166
Shirley Whitley, prin. Fax 382-4171
Krisle ES 400/PK-5
6712 Highway 49 E 37172 615-384-2596
Suzann Brown, prin. Fax 384-9022
Springfield MS 600/6-8
715 5th Ave W 37172 615-384-4821
Dr. Mike Morris, prin. Fax 384-7890
Westside ES 400/1-5
309 Alsup Dr 37172 615-384-8495
Lisa Cobb, prin. Fax 384-0230
Other Schools – See Cedar Hill, Cross Plains, Greenbrier, Ridgetop, White House

---

South Haven Christian S 200/K-12
112 Academy Dr 37172 615-384-5073
Dr. Steve Blaser, prin. Fax 425-2403

Spring Hill, Maury, Pop. 17,148
Maury County SD
Supt. — See Columbia
Spring Hill ES 500/K-5
5359 Main St 37174 931-486-2291
Sharron Cantrell, prin. Fax 486-2294
Wright ES 400/K-5
4714 Derryberry Ln 37174 931-388-8403
Jerry Harrison, prin. Fax 486-3588

Williamson County SD
Supt. — See Franklin
Chapman's Retreat ES 1,000/PK-5
1000 Secluded Ln 37174 615-472-4300
Dr. Renee Garriss, prin. Fax 472-4312
Longview ES K-5
2929 Commonwealth Dr 37174 615-472-5060
Dr. Jonathan Ullrich, prin. Fax 472-5071

Strawberry Plains, Jefferson
Jefferson County SD
Supt. — See Dandridge
Rush Strong S 700/PK-8
3081 W Old Andrew Johnson 37871 865-933-5313
Ruth Pohlman, prin. Fax 933-3331

Knox County SD
Supt. — See Knoxville
Carter ES 500/K-5
9304 College St 37871 865-933-4172
Julie Thompson, prin. Fax 932-8190
Carter MS 700/6-8
204 N Carter School Rd 37871 865-933-3426
Jewel Brock, prin. Fax 932-8170

Blue Springs Christian Academy 50/K-12
3265 Blue Springs Rd 37871 865-932-7603
June Ingram, prin.

Summertown, Lawrence
Lawrence County SD
Supt. — See Lawrenceburg
Summertown ES 600/PK-6
319 Corbin St 38483 931-964-3614
Debbie Hughes, prin. Fax 964-4164

Sunbright, Morgan, Pop. 590
Morgan County SD
Supt. — See Wartburg
Sunbright S 600/K-12
PO Box 129 37872 423-628-2244
Carolyn Shannon, prin. Fax 628-2120

Surgoinsville, Hawkins, Pop. 1,744
Hawkins County SD
Supt. — See Rogersville
Surgoinsville ES 400/K-4
1010 Main St 37873 423-345-2153
Susan Trent, prin. Fax 345-2154
Surgoinsville MS 300/5-8
1044 Main St 37873 423-345-2252
Zada Church, prin. Fax 345-3598

Sweetwater, Monroe, Pop. 6,117
Sweetwater CSD 1,500/PK-8
PO Box 231 37874 423-337-7051
Dr. Keith Hickey, supt. Fax 337-6773
www.compurdy.com/scs2/
Brown IS 300/5-6
135 Starrett St 37874 423-337-5905
Melanie Miller, prin. Fax 337-0791
Sweetwater ES 300/3-4
301 Broad St 37874 423-337-7062
Diana Howard, prin. Fax 337-7609
Sweetwater JHS 300/7-8
1013 Cannon Ave 37874 423-337-7336
Rodney Boruff, prin. Fax 337-7360
Sweetwater PS 600/PK-2
500 Highway 322 E 37874 423-351-7004
Darrin Nichols, prin. Fax 351-7089

Covenant Baptist Academy 50/PK-12
PO Box 89 37874 423-337-7000
Sandy Murdock, prin. Fax 337-2328

Cross Creek Christian S 100/PK-12
501 N East St 37874 423-337-9330
Randy Nelson, pres. Fax 337-9335

Taft, Lincoln
Lincoln County SD
Supt. — See Fayetteville
Blanche S 300/K-8
1649 Ardmore Hwy 38488 931-425-6141
Rickey Stafford, prin. Fax 425-9160

Talbott, Jefferson
Jefferson County SD
Supt. — See Dandridge
Talbott ES 200/K-5
848 Talbott Kansas Rd 37877 865-475-2988
Dr. Judy Walters, prin. Fax 475-8808

Tazewell, Claiborne, Pop. 2,150
Claiborne County SD 5,200/PK-12
PO Box 179 37879 423-626-3543
Eddie Shoffner, supt. Fax 626-5945
www.clairbornecountyschools.com
Soldiers Memorial MS 600/5-8
1510 Legion St 37879 423-626-3531
Lynn Barnard, prin. Fax 626-2151
Springdale ES 400/K-6
1915 Highway 25E S 37879 423-626-9142
Joy Collingsworth, prin. Fax 626-3936
Other Schools – See Clairfield, Harrogate, New Tazewell, Speedwell

Telford, Washington
Washington County SD
Supt. — See Jonesborough
Grandview S K-8
2891 Highway 11 E 37690 423-257-7400
J.W. McKinney, prin.

Tellico Plains, Monroe, Pop. 930
Monroe County SD
Supt. — See Madisonville
Coker Creek S 100/K-8
130 Ruritan Rd 37385 423-261-2241
Jill Franklin, prin. Fax 261-2394
Rural Vale S 200/K-8
395 Daugherty Spring Rd 37385 423-253-3551
Stanley Shadden, prin. Fax 253-2009
Tellico Plains ES 400/K-4
121 Old High School Rd 37385 423-253-2626
Robert Hooper, prin. Fax 253-7962
Tellico Plains JHS 300/5-8
120 Old High School Rd 37385 423-253-2250
Missy Carter, prin. Fax 253-7824

Ten Mile, Roane
Roane County SD
Supt. — See Kingston
Midway MS 200/6-8
104 Dogtown Rd 37880 865-717-5464
Nadine Jackson, prin. Fax 376-0948

Tennessee Ridge, Houston, Pop. 1,311
Houston County SD
Supt. — See Erin
Tennessee Ridge ES 300/PK-5
135 School St 37178 931-721-3780
Judy Stephen, prin.

Thompsons Station, Williamson, Pop. 914
Williamson County SD
Supt. — See Franklin
Bethesda ES 600/PK-5
4907 Bethesda Rd 37179 615-472-4200
Steve Fisher, prin. Fax 472-4211
Heritage ES 900/PK-5
4801 Columbia Pike 37179 615-472-4520
Dr. Laura LaChance, prin. Fax 472-4531
Heritage MS 900/6-8
4803 Columbia Pike 37179 615-472-4540
Paula Pulliam, prin. Fax 472-4553

Tiptonville, Lake, Pop. 4,099
Lake County SD 1,000/PK-12
PO Box 397 38079 731-253-6601
Amy Floyd, supt. Fax 253-7111
www.lake.k12.tn.us/
Newton ES 300/PK-5
819 Church St 38079 731-253-7253
Sherry Darnell, prin. Fax 253-7178
Other Schools – See Ridgely

Toone, Hardeman, Pop. 358
Hardeman County SD
Supt. — See Bolivar
Toone S 300/PK-8
PO Box 68 38381 731-658-5606
Rebecca Watson, prin. Fax 658-9880

Townsend, Blount, Pop. 258
Blount County SD
Supt. — See Maryville
Townsend ES 100/K-5
PO Box 399 37882 865-980-1202
John Dalton, prin. Fax 980-1205

Tracy City, Grundy, Pop. 1,698
Grundy County SD
Supt. — See Altamont
Tracy S 400/PK-8
276 3rd St 37387 931-592-5741
Russell Fugate, prin. Fax 592-5750

Trenton, Gibson, Pop. 4,577
Gibson County SD
Supt. — See Dyer
Spring Hill S 100/K-8
84 State Route 188 38382 731-559-4223
Joey Harrison, prin. Fax 559-4337

Trenton Special SD 1,500/PK-12
201 W 10th St 38382 731-855-1191
Sandra Harper, supt. Fax 855-1414
voyager.rtd.utk.edu/~trenton/
Trenton ES 600/PK-4
811 S College St 38382 731-855-0971
Jonathan Criswell, prin. Fax 855-2732
Trenton MS 400/5-8
2065 US Highway 45 Byp S 38382 731-855-2422
Juanita Johnson, prin. Fax 855-1826

Trezevant, Carroll, Pop. 893
West Carroll Special SD
Supt. — See Atwood
West Carroll ES 300/3-6
PO Box 278 38258 731-669-3851
Travis Carter, prin. Fax 669-3173

Trimble, Dyer, Pop. 726
Dyer County SD
Supt. — See Dyersburg
Trimble ES 200/K-5
256 College St 38259 731-297-5512
Vicki Williams, prin. Fax 297-5514

Troy, Obion, Pop. 1,249
Obion County SD
Supt. — See Union City
Hillcrest S 600/K-8
605 S Main St 38260 731-536-4222
Melinda McCullough, prin. Fax 536-4609

Tullahoma, Coffee, Pop. 18,909
Coffee County SD
Supt. — See Manchester
Hickerson ES 200/PK-5
5017 Old Manchester Hwy 37388 931-455-9576
Angela Harris, prin. Fax 455-3758

Franklin County SD
Supt. — See Winchester
North Lake ES 300/PK-5
10626 Old Tullahoma Rd 37388 931-455-6239
George Butler, prin. Fax 455-6273

Tullahoma CSD 3,500/PK-12
510 S Jackson St 37388 931-454-2600
Dr. Dan Lawson, dir. Fax 454-2642
www.tullahomacityschools.net/
Bel Aire ES 300/K-5
500 Stone Blvd 37388 931-454-2610
Donna Rhoton, prin. Fax 454-2656
East Lincoln ES 300/PK-5
700 E Lincoln St 37388 931-454-2612
Jane Fisher, prin. Fax 454-2609
East MS 400/6-8
908 Country Club Dr 37388 931-454-2632
Debbie Edens, prin. Fax 454-2660
Farrar ES 400/PK-5
215 Westside Dr 37388 931-454-2608
Mickey Shuran, prin. Fax 454-2658
Lee ES 400/K-5
313 Layne St 37388 931-454-2637
Dr. Gail Holland, prin. Fax 454-2649
West MS 400/6-8
90 Hermitage Dr 37388 931-454-2605
Dr. Greg Carter, prin. Fax 454-2661

St. Paul the Apostle S 100/K-8
306 W Grizzard St 37388 931-455-4221
Susan Molvik, prin. Fax 455-8298
Tullahoma SDA Christian S 50/K-8
231 Turkey Creek Dr 37388 931-455-1924
Sharon Brooks, prin. Fax 455-1924

Unicoi, Unicoi, Pop. 3,481
Unicoi County SD
Supt. — See Erwin
Unicoi ES 500/PK-4
404 Massachusetts Ave 37692 423-743-1665
Mike Lamie, prin. Fax 743-1667

Union City, Obion, Pop. 10,788
Obion County SD 4,300/K-12
316 S 3rd St 38261 731-885-9743
David Huss, supt. Fax 885-4902
www.obioncountyschools.com
Lake Road S 700/K-8
1130 E Highway 22 38261 731-885-5304
Dennis Buckelew, prin. Fax 885-5304
Ridgemont S 600/K-8
1285 N Highway 45 W 38261 731-536-5171
Randy Pitts, prin. Fax 536-0664
Other Schools – See Hornbeak, South Fulton, Troy

Union CSD 1,400/K-12
PO Box 749 38281 731-885-3922
Gary Houston, supt. Fax 885-6033
www.union-city-hs.obion.k12.tn.us/
Union City ES 700/K-5
1100 S Miles Ave 38261 731-885-1632
Michael Miller, prin. Fax 885-9699
Union City MS 300/6-8
1111 High School Dr 38261 731-885-2901
Dan Boykin, prin. Fax 885-3677

Unionville, Bedford
Bedford County SD
Supt. — See Shelbyville
Community ES 800/K-6
3480 Highway 41A N 37180 931-685-1417
Jeff Yoes, prin. Fax 294-2444

Vanleer, Dickson, Pop. 314
Dickson County SD
Supt. — See Dickson
Vanleer ES 300/K-5
PO Box 7 37181 615-740-5760
Rachel Weaver, prin. Fax 763-3100

Vonore, Monroe, Pop. 1,383
Monroe County SD
Supt. — See Madisonville
Vonore ES 400/K-4
PO Box 159 37885 423-884-6392
Priscilla Gregory, prin. Fax 884-6981
Vonore MS 200/5-8
414 Hall St 37885 423-884-2730
Debra Tipton, prin. Fax 884-2731

Walland, Blount
Blount County SD
Supt. — See Maryville
Walland ES 300/K-5
247 E Millers Cove Rd 37886 865-983-2801
Phyllis Garner, prin. Fax 681-6219

Walling, White
White County SD
Supt. — See Sparta
Central View ES 100/K-5
14484 Old Kentucky Rd 38587 931-761-2907
Deborah Roberts, prin. Fax 761-2906

Wartburg, Morgan, Pop. 913
Morgan County SD 3,600/K-12
136 Flat Fork Rd 37887 423-346-6214
Mike Davis, dir. Fax 346-6043
mcs.k12tn.net
Central ES 600/K-5
1315 Knoxville Hwy 37887 423-346-6683
David Hodgen, prin. Fax 346-5556
Central MS 300/6-8
146 Liberty Rd 37887 423-346-2800
Larry Davis, prin. Fax 346-2805
Other Schools – See Coalfield, Oakdale, Oliver Springs, Sunbright

Wartrace, Bedford, Pop. 564
Bedford County SD
Supt. — See Shelbyville
Cascade ES 700/K-5
2998 Fairfield Pike 37183 931-389-0031
Martha Fisher, prin. Fax 389-0032

Washburn, Grainger
Grainger County SD
Supt. — See Rutledge
Washburn S 700/PK-12
7925 Highway 131 37888 865-497-2557
Ginny McElhaney, prin. Fax 497-2934

Watauga, Carter, Pop. 431
Carter County SD
Supt. — See Elizabethton
Range S 100/K-8
655 Watauga Rd 37694 423-547-4037
Elizabeth Banks, prin. Fax 547-4038

Watertown, Wilson, Pop. 1,392
Wilson County SD
Supt. — See Lebanon
Watertown ES 600/PK-6
PO Box 127 37184 615-237-3821
Anita Christian, prin. Fax 237-9544

Waverly, Humphreys, Pop. 4,134
Humphreys County SD 3,100/PK-12
2443 Highway 70 E 37185 931-296-2568
James Long, supt. Fax 296-6501
www.hcss.org
Waverly ES 500/PK-3
612 E Main St 37185 931-296-2371
Shirley Link, prin. Fax 296-6515
Waverly JHS 500/4-8
520 E Main St 37185 931-296-4514
Andy Daniels, prin. Fax 296-6507
Other Schools – See Mc Ewen, New Johnsonville

Waynesboro, Wayne, Pop. 2,175
Wayne County SD 2,500/PK-12
PO Box 658 38485 931-722-3548
Wanda Johnston, supt. Fax 722-7579
Waynesboro ES 400/PK-4
PO Box 219 38485 931-722-5580
Julia Bevis, prin. Fax 722-3006
Waynesboro MS 300/5-8
407 S Main St 38485 931-722-5545
Ryan Keaton, prin. Fax 722-3953
Other Schools – See Clifton, Collinwood

Westmoreland, Sumner, Pop. 2,165
Macon County SD
Supt. — See Lafayette
Westside ES 300/K-5
8025 Old Highway 52 37186 615-666-3128
David Flynn, prin. Fax 666-6873

Sumner County SD
Supt. — See Gallatin
Westmoreland ES 400/K-5
3012 Thompson Ln 37186 615-644-2340
Dr. David Stafford, prin. Fax 644-3924
Westmoreland MS 400/6-8
4128 Hawkins Dr 37186 615-644-3003
Danny Robinson, prin. Fax 644-5584

White Bluff, Dickson, Pop. 2,372
Dickson County SD
Supt. — See Dickson
James MS 300/6-8
PO Box 169 37187 615-740-5770
Louise Buchanan, prin. Fax 797-6401
White Bluff ES 500/K-5
377 School Rd 37187 615-740-5775
Gail Mosley, prin. Fax 797-6400

White House, Sumner, Pop. 8,723
Robertson County SD
Supt. — See Springfield
Woodall ES 700/K-5
300 Edenway Dr 37188 615-672-7772
Kathy Maynard, prin. Fax 672-7276

Sumner County SD
Supt. — See Gallatin
White House MS 600/6-8
2020 Highway 31 W 37188 615-672-4379
Jerry Apple, prin. Fax 672-6409
Williams ES 700/K-5
115 S Palmers Chapel Rd 37188 615-672-6432
Ellen Brown, prin. Fax 672-0996

Heritage and Hope Academy 200/PK-12
506 Hester Dr 37188 615-672-6949
Tom Thornton, hdmstr. Fax 672-8222
White House Christian Academy 200/PK-12
PO Box 927 37188 615-672-9422
Dr. Richard Jones, prin. Fax 672-9116

White Pine, Jefferson, Pop. 2,055
Jefferson County SD
Supt. — See Dandridge
White Pine S 800/K-8
3060 Roy Messer Hwy 37890 865-674-2596
Bill Walker, prin. Fax 674-8383

Whitesburg, Hamblen
Hamblen County SD
Supt. — See Morristown
East Ridge MS 600/6-8
6595 Saint Clair Rd 37891 423-581-3041
Marcia Carlyle, prin. Fax 585-3763
Whitesburg ES 200/K-5
7859 E Andrew Johnson Hwy 37891 423-235-2547
William Southern, prin. Fax 585-6315

Whites Creek, See Nashville
Metropolitan Nashville SD
Supt. — See Nashville
Green ES 300/PK-4
3921 Lloyd Rd 37189 615-876-5105
Brenda Steele, prin. Fax 333-5667

Whiteville, Hardeman, Pop. 4,489
Hardeman County SD
Supt. — See Bolivar
Whiteville S 400/PK-8
2510 US Highway 64 38075 731-254-8013
Mamie Griggs-Polk, prin. Fax 254-9528

Whitwell, Marion, Pop. 1,604
Marion County SD
Supt. — See Jasper
Whitwell ES 600/PK-4
150 Tiger Trl 37397 423-658-5313
David Smith, prin. Fax 658-0306
Whitwell MS 400/5-8
1 Butterfly Ln 37397 423-658-5635
Linda Hooper, prin. Fax 658-6949

Wildersville, Henderson
Henderson County SD
Supt. — See Lexington
Beaver S 200/K-8
19830 Highway 22 N 38388 731-968-2109
Mike Bevis, prin. Fax 968-9706

Williston, Fayette, Pop. 359
Fayette County SD
Supt. — See Somerville
Southwest ES 50/4-5
8095 Highway 194 38076 901-465-8317
Rodney Parks, prin. Fax 466-1981

Winchester, Franklin, Pop. 7,752
Franklin County SD 6,000/PK-12
215 S College St 37398 931-967-0626
Dr. Rebecca Sharber, supt. Fax 967-7832
franklincountyschools.k12tn.net
Broadview ES 300/PK-5
4980 Lynchburg Rd 37398 931-967-0132
Sandy Schultz, prin. Fax 967-0292
Clark Memorial ES 500/PK-5
500 N Jefferson St 37398 931-967-2407
David Carson, prin. Fax 967-9655
North MS 800/6-8
2990 Decherd Blvd 37398 931-967-5323
Linda Jones, prin. Fax 967-1413
Other Schools – See Cowan, Decherd, Estill Springs, Huntland, Sewanee, Tullahoma

Winfield, Scott, Pop. 979
Scott County SD
Supt. — See Huntsville
Winfield S 200/PK-8
23370 Scott Hwy 37892 423-569-8288
Sharon Stanley, prin. Fax 569-9835

Woodbury, Cannon, Pop. 2,524
Cannon County SD 2,300/K-12
301 W Main St Ste 100 37190 615-563-5752
Edward Diden, supt. Fax 563-2716
www.cannoncounty.net
East Side S 100/K-8
5658 McMinnville Hwy 37190 615-563-4196
Karen King, prin. Fax 563-6252
Short Mountain S 200/K-8
5988 Short Mountain Rd 37190 615-563-4418
Robert Pitts, prin. Fax 563-4596
Woodbury S 400/K-8
530 W Adams St 37190 615-563-2220
Gerald Tidwell, prin. Fax 563-6153
Other Schools – See Auburntown, Bradyville, Readyville

Woodbury SDA S 50/1-8
PO Box 290 37190 615-765-5330
Joan Zollinger, prin. Fax 765-5330

Woodlawn, Montgomery
Clarksville-Montgomery County SD
Supt. — See Clarksville
Woodlawn ES 700/K-5
2250 Woodlawn Rd 37191 931-648-5680
Janet Staggs, prin. Fax 503-3407

Yorkville, Gibson, Pop. 289
Gibson County SD
Supt. — See Dyer
Yorkville S 200/PK-8
PO Box 37 38389 731-643-6598
David Brewer, prin. Fax 643-6635

TEXAS

TEXAS EDUCATION AGENCY
1701 Congress Ave, Austin 78701-1494
Telephone 512-463-9734
Fax 512-463-9838
Website http://www.tea.state.tx.us

Commissioner of Education Robert Scott

TEXAS BOARD OF EDUCATION
1701 Congress Ave, Austin 78701-1402

Chairperson Gail Lowe

REGIONAL EDUCATION SERVICE CENTERS (RESC)

Region 1 ESC
Jack Damron, dir. 956-984-6000
1900 W Schunior St, Edinburg Fax 984-6299
www.esc1.net/

Region 2 ESC
Dr. Linda Villarreal, dir. 361-561-8400
209 N Water St Fax 883-3442
Corpus Christi 78401
www.esc2.net

Region 3 ESC
Dr. Julius Cano, dir. 361-573-0731
1905 Leary Ln, Victoria 77901 Fax 576-4804
www.esc3.net/

Region 4 ESC
Dr. William McKinney, dir. 713-462-7708
7145 W Tidwell Rd, Houston 77092 Fax 744-6514
www.esc4.net/

Region 5 ESC
Dr. R. Steve Hyden, dir. 409-838-5555
2295 Delaware St Fax 833-9755
Beaumont 77703
www.esc5.net

Region 6 ESC
Thomas Poe, dir. 936-435-8400
3332 Montgomery Rd Fax 435-8484
Huntsville 77340
www.esc6.net/

Region 7 ESC
Elizabeth Abernethy, dir. 903-988-6700
1909 N Longview St, Kilgore 75662 Fax 988-6735
www.esc7.net/

Region 8 ESC
Harvey Hohenberger, dir. 903-572-8551
PO Box 1894 Fax 575-2611
Mount Pleasant 75456
www.reg8.net/

Region 9 ESC
Anne Poplin, dir. 940-322-6928
301 Loop 11, Wichita Falls 76306 Fax 767-3836
www.esc9.net

Region 10 ESC
Wilburn Echols, dir. 972-348-1700
400 E Spring Valley Rd Fax 231-3642
Richardson 75081
www.ednet10.net/

Region 11 ESC
Richard Ownby, dir. 817-740-3600
3001 North Fwy, Fort Worth 76106 Fax 740-7600
www.esc11.net

Region 12 ESC
Dr. Tom Norris, dir. 254-297-1212
PO Box 23409, Waco 76702 Fax 666-0823
www.esc12.net

Region 13 ESC
Dr. Pat Pringle, dir. 512-919-5313
5701 Springdale Rd, Austin 78723 Fax 919-5374
www5.esc13.net/

Region 14 ESC
Ronnie Kincaid, dir. 325-675-8600
1850 State Highway 351 Fax 675-8659
Abilene 79601
www.esc14.net/

Region 15 ESC
Scot Goen, dir. 325-658-6571
PO Box 5199, San Angelo 76902 Fax 658-6571
www.netxv.net/

Region 16 ESC
John Bass, dir. 806-677-5000
5800 Bell St, Amarillo 79109 Fax 677-5001
www.esc16.net/

Region 17 ESC
Dr. Kyle Wargo, dir. 806-792-4000
1111 W Loop 289, Lubbock 79416 Fax 792-1523
www.esc17.net/

Region 18 ESC
Charles Greenawalt, dir. 432-563-2380
PO Box 60580, Midland 79711 Fax 567-3290
www.esc18.net

Region 19 ESC
Dr. James Vasquez, dir. 915-780-1919
PO Box 971127, El Paso 79997 Fax 780-6537
www.esc19.net/

Region 20 ESC
Dr. Terry Smith, dir. 210-370-5200
1314 Hines, San Antonio 78208 Fax 370-5750
www.esc20.net

PUBLIC, PRIVATE AND CATHOLIC ELEMENTARY SCHOOLS

Abbott, Hill, Pop. 328

Abbott ISD 300/PK-12
PO Box 226 76621 254-582-9442
Bill Tarleton, supt. Fax 582-5430
www.abbottisd.org

Abbott S 300/PK-12
PO Box 226 76621 254-582-3011
Travis Walker, prin. Fax 582-5430

Abernathy, Hale, Pop. 2,762

Abernathy ISD 800/PK-12
505 7th St 79311 806-298-2007
Herb Youngblood, supt. Fax 298-2400
www.abernathyisd.com

Abernathy ES 400/PK-5
505 7th St 79311 806-298-2001
Shawn Bearden, prin. Fax 298-2400

Abernathy JHS 200/6-8
505 7th St 79311 806-298-2002
Harold Bufe, prin. Fax 298-4775

Abilene, Taylor, Pop. 114,757

Abilene ISD 16,200/PK-12
PO Box 981 79604 325-677-1444
Dr. David Polnick, supt. Fax 794-1325
www.abileneisd.org/

Austin ES 600/K-5
2341 Greenbriar Dr 79605 325-690-3920
Candy Scarborough, prin. Fax 690-3932

Bassetti ES 600/K-5
5749 US Highway 277 S 79606 325-690-3720
Stacy Evans, prin. Fax 690-3731

Bonham ES 600/K-5
4250 Potomac Ave 79605 325-690-3745
Diane Rose, prin. Fax 690-3758

Bowie ES 500/K-5
1733 S 20th St 79602 325-671-4770
Tina Jones, prin. Fax 671-4784

Clack MS 700/6-8
1610 Corsicana Ave 79605 325-692-1961
Rodney Brown, prin. Fax 690-3547

College Heights ES 300/K-5
1450 N 17th St 79601 325-671-4795
Kathryn Walker, prin. Fax 671-4806

Craig MS 900/6-8
702 S Judge Ely Blvd 79602 325-794-4100
Gustavo Villanueva, prin. Fax 794-1385

Dyess ES 400/K-5
402 Delaware Rd 79607 325-690-3795
Mike Newton, prin. Fax 690-3991

Fannin ES 400/K-5
2726 N 18th St 79603 325-671-4820
Kim Farmer, prin. Fax 671-4832

Jackson ES 500/PK-5
2650 S 32nd St 79605 325-690-3602
Linda Case, prin. Fax 690-3614

Johnston ES 500/K-5
3602 N 12th St 79603 325-671-4845
Roger Thomas, prin. Fax 671-4860

Lee ES 400/K-5
1026 N Pioneer Dr 79603 325-671-4895
Andy Blessing, prin. Fax 671-4906

Locust ECC 300/PK-PK
625 S 8th St 79602 325-671-4569
Cheryl Cunningham, dir. Fax 671-4580

Long ES 300/K-5
3600 Sherry Ln 79603 325-671-4920
Kari Leong, prin. Fax 671-4933

Madison MS 1,000/6-8
3145 Barrow St 79605 325-692-5661
Jennifer Raney, prin. Fax 690-3584

Mann MS 500/6-8
2545 Mimosa Dr 79603 325-672-8493
Joe Alcorta, prin. Fax 671-4405

Ortiz ES 500/PK-5
2550 Vogel St 79603 325-671-4945
Karen Munoz, prin. Fax 671-4954

Reagan ES 400/K-5
5340 Hartford St 79605 325-690-3627
Michael Kozelsky, prin. Fax 690-3641

Taylor ES 600/K-5
916 E North 13th St 79601 325-671-4970
David Adams, prin. Fax 671-4983

Thomas ES 500/K-5
1240 Lakeside Dr 79602 325-671-4995
Cam Hurst, prin. Fax 671-5007

Ward ES 600/K-5
3750 Paint Brush Dr 79606 325-690-3666
Steve Hodges, prin. Fax 690-3664

Woodson ECC 400/PK-PK
520 N 9th St 79601 325-671-4594
Cheryl Cunningham, prin. Fax 671-4602

Wylie ISD 2,600/PK-12
6249 Buffalo Gap Rd 79606 325-692-4353
Joey Light, supt. Fax 695-3438
www.wylie.esc14.net

Wylie ECC 100/PK-PK
6249 Buffalo Gap Rd 79606 325-437-2350
Nadine Davis, prin. Fax 437-2351

Wylie ES 400/K-2
7650 Hardwick Rd 79606 325-692-6554
Debbie Lambert, prin. Fax 695-4645

Wylie IS 400/3-5
3158 Beltway S 79606 325-692-7961
Terry Hagler, prin. Fax 695-4647

Wylie JHS 700/6-8
4010 Beltway S 79606 325-695-1910
Tommy Vaughn, prin. Fax 692-5786

Abilene Christian S 300/PK-12
2550 N Judge Ely Blvd 79601 325-672-9200
Craig Fisher, pres. Fax 672-1262

Abilene Jr. Academy 50/1-8
PO Box 239 79604 325-676-2785

Cornerstone Christian S 100/PK-5
PO Box 55 79604 325-676-8232
Kathi Russell, admin. Fax 437-2432

St. John's Episcopal S 100/PK-5
1600 Sherman Dr 79605 325-695-8870
Simone Simpson, hdmstr. Fax 698-1532

Ackerly, Dawson, Pop. 231

Sands Consolidated ISD 200/PK-12
PO Box 218 79713 432-353-4888
Wayne Blount, supt. Fax 353-4650
sands.esc17.net

Sands S 200/PK-12
PO Box 218 79713 432-353-4888
Zelda Bilbo, prin. Fax 353-4650

Addison, Dallas, Pop. 13,667

Greenhill S 1,200/PK-12
4141 Spring Valley Rd 75001 972-628-5400
Scott Griggs, hdmstr. Fax 404-8217

Trinity Christian Academy 1,500/K-12
17001 Addison Rd 75001 972-931-8325
David Delph, hdmstr. Fax 931-8923

Adkins, Bexar

Salem Sayers Baptist Academy 100/PK-12
PO Box 397 78101 210-649-1178
Teresa Sandoval, admin. Fax 649-3385

Adrian, Oldham, Pop. 154
Adrian ISD 100/K-12
PO Box 189 79001 806-538-6203
David Johnson, supt. Fax 538-6291
www.adrianisd.net
Adrian S 100/K-12
PO Box 189 79001 806-538-6203
Scott Vincent, prin. Fax 538-6291

Afton, Dickens
Patton Springs ISD 100/PK-12
PO Box 32 79220 806-689-2220
Larry McClenny, supt. Fax 689-2253
www.pattonsprings.net
Patton Springs S 100/PK-12
PO Box 32 79220 806-689-2220
Mike Norrell, prin. Fax 689-2470

Agua Dulce, Nueces, Pop. 729
Agua Dulce ISD 400/PK-12
PO Box 250 78330 361-998-2542
Donna Hilliard, supt. Fax 998-2816
www.adisd.esc2.net
Agua Dulce ES 200/PK-5
PO Box 250 78330 361-998-2335
Penny Pillack, prin. Fax 998-2333

Alamo, Hidalgo, Pop. 15,976
Donna ISD
Supt. — See Donna
Salinas II ES 800/PK-5
333 E Business Highway 83 78516 956-783-1332
Ida M. Garcia, prin. Fax 782-9175

Pharr-San Juan-Alamo ISD
Supt. — See Pharr
Alamo MS 1,100/6-8
1819 W US Highway 83 78516 956-702-5887
Iris Guajardo, prin. Fax 702-5893
Bowie ES 600/PK-5
811 E Bowie Ave 78516 956-702-5839
Rosario Coplea, prin. Fax 702-5842
Farias ES 600/PK-5
205 N Alamo Rd 78516 956-702-5734
Joe Jilpas, prin. Fax 702-5742
Franklin ES 400/PK-5
900 E Birch Ave 78516 956-702-5811
Irma Cano, prin. Fax 781-5029
Guerra ES 700/PK-5
807 State Highway 495 78516 956-783-2833
Sylvia Casiano, prin. Fax 783-2840
North Alamo ES 600/PK-5
733 N Alamo Rd 78516 956-702-6090
Sylvia Hernandez, prin. Fax 781-6687

Valley Christian Heritage S 100/PK-12
932 N Alamo Rd 78516 956-787-9743
Mary Rydl, admin. Fax 787-1977

Alba, Wood, Pop. 479
Alba-Golden ISD 800/PK-12
1373 County Road 2377 75410 903-768-2472
Dwayne Ellis, supt. Fax 768-2130
www.agisd.com
Alba-Golden ES 400/PK-5
1373 County Road 2377 75410 903-768-2472
Gary Simms, prin. Fax 768-2130

Albany, Shackelford, Pop. 1,833
Albany ISD 600/PK-12
PO Box 188 76430 325-762-2823
Shane Fields, supt. Fax 762-3876
www.albany.esc14.net
Smith ES 300/PK-6
PO Box 2499 76430 325-762-3384
Doyleen Terrell, prin. Fax 762-3070

Aledo, Parker, Pop. 2,524
Aledo ISD 4,200/PK-12
1008 Bailey Ranch Rd 76008 817-441-8327
Don Daniel, supt. Fax 441-5144
www.aledo.k12.tx.us
Aledo MS 700/7-8
416 S FM 1187 76008 817-441-5198
Dan Peterson, prin. Fax 441-5133
Coder ES 600/PK-5
12 Vernon Rd 76008 817-441-6095
Amy Sadler, prin. Fax 441-5135
McAnally IS 300/6-6
151 S FM 5 76008 817-441-8347
Bob Harmon, prin. Fax 441-5177
Stuard ES 700/K-5
200 Thunderhead Ln 76008 817-441-5103
Robin Seay, prin. Fax 441-5116
Vandagriff ES 500/K-5
408 S FM 1187 76008 817-441-8771
Bill Warden, prin. Fax 441-5150
Other Schools – See Willow Park

Aledo Christian S 100/PK-12
PO Box 117 76008 817-441-7357
Kay Ross, prin. Fax 441-7476

Alice, Jim Wells, Pop. 19,519
Alice ISD 5,300/K-12
2 Coyote Trl 78332 361-664-0981
Dr. Salvador Cavazos, supt. Fax 660-2113
www.aliceisd.net/
Adams MS 700/7-8
901 E 3rd St 78332 361-660-2055
Lucinda Munoz, prin. Fax 660-2094
Dubose IS 400/5-6
1000 Lantana St 78332 361-664-7512
Sandra Knezek, prin. Fax 660-2157
Garcia ES 200/K-4
3051 Old Kingsville Rd 78332 361-660-2050
Deborah Aucompaugh, prin. Fax 660-2161
Hillcrest ES 200/K-4
1400 Morningside Dr 78332 361-660-2098
Paula Garcia, prin. Fax 660-2163
Memorial IS 400/5-6
900 W 3rd St 78332 361-660-2080
Gloria Garcia, prin. Fax 660-2160
Noonan ES 400/K-4
701 W 3rd St 78332 361-664-7591
Evey Guerra, prin. Fax 660-2166
Saenz ES 500/K-4
400 Palo Blanco St 78332 361-664-4981
Nora Lopez, prin. Fax 660-2167
Salazar ES 300/K-4
1028 Pierce St 78332 361-664-6263
Monica Oliveira, prin. Fax 660-2168
Schallert ES 500/K-4
1001 Jim Wells Dr 78332 361-664-6361
Patricia Garcia, prin. Fax 660-2169

Alice Christian S 50/PK-12
1200 N Stadium Rd 78332 361-668-6618
St. Elizabeth S 200/PK-6
615 E 5th St 78332 361-664-6271
Selina Garcia, prin. Fax 668-4250
St. Joseph S 100/PK-6
311 Dewey Ave 78332 361-664-4642
Mary Sandoval, prin. Fax 664-4642

Allen, Collin, Pop. 69,222
Allen ISD 15,400/PK-12
PO Box 13 75013 972-727-0511
Dr. Ken Helvey, supt. Fax 727-0518
www.allenisd.org
Anderson ES 900/K-6
305 N Alder Dr 75002 972-396-6924
Leslie Norris, prin. Fax 396-6929
Boon ES 800/K-6
1050 Comanche Dr 75013 972-747-3331
Tammie James, prin. Fax 727-3335
Boyd ES 600/K-6
800 S Jupiter Rd 75002 972-727-0560
Shannon Fuller, prin. Fax 727-0566
Chandler ES 500/K-6
1000 Water Oak Dr 75002 469-467-1400
Cindy Blair, prin. Fax 467-1410
Curtis MS 700/7-8
1530 Rivercrest Blvd 75002 972-727-0340
Becky Kennedy, prin. Fax 727-0345
Ereckson MS 7-8
450 Tatum Dr 75013 972-747-3308
Phyllis Spain, prin. Fax 747-3311
Evans ES K-6
1225 Walnut Springs Dr 75013 972-747-3373
Pam Hale, prin. Fax 747-3374
Ford MS 800/7-8
630 Park Place Dr 75002 972-727-0590
Susan Horowitz, prin. Fax 727-0596
Green ES 800/K-6
1315 Comanche Dr 75013 972-727-0370
Kelly Campman, prin. Fax 727-0373
Kerr ES 800/K-6
1325 Glendover Dr 75013 214-495-6765
Ardath Streitmatter, prin. Fax 495-6771
Marion ES 900/K-6
PO Box 13 75013 214-495-6784
Johnna Walker, prin. Fax 495-6787
Norton ES 500/PK-6
1120 Newport Dr 75013 972-396-6918
Gayle Smith, prin. Fax 396-6923
Olson ES PK-6
1751 E Exchange Pkwy 75002 972-562-1800
Kim McLaughlin, prin. Fax 562-1835
Reed ES 700/K-6
1200 Rivercrest Blvd 75002 972-727-0580
Rachel Kaiser, prin. Fax 727-0588
Rountree ES 600/PK-6
800 E Main St 75002 972-727-0550
Cristie McClain, prin. Fax 727-0555
Story ES 800/PK-6
1550 Edelweiss Dr 75002 972-727-0570
George Junco, prin. Fax 727-0573
Vaughan ES 700/K-6
820 Cottonwood Dr 75002 972-727-0470
Honey Gray, prin. Fax 727-0579
Other Schools – See Parker

Lovejoy ISD 1,400/K-12
259 Country Club Rd 75002 972-562-5077
Ted Moore, supt. Fax 562-9924
www.lovejoyisd.net/
Lovejoy ES 700/K-5
259 Country Club Rd 75002 469-742-8100
Patty Jackson, prin. Fax 742-8101
Other Schools – See Fairview, Lucas

Plano ISD
Supt. — See Plano
Beverly ES 600/K-5
715 Duchess Dr 75013 469-752-0400
Liz Kirby, prin. Fax 752-0401

Heritage Montessori Academy of Allen 100/PK-4
1222 N Alma Dr 75013 972-908-2463
Aline Lage, prin. Fax 908-2907

Alpine, Brewster, Pop. 6,065
Alpine ISD 1,000/PK-12
704 W Sul Ross Ave 79830 432-837-7700
Jose Cervantes, supt. Fax 837-7740
www.alpine.esc18.net
Alpine ES 400/PK-4
200 W Avenue A 79830 432-837-7730
Kendall Burling, prin. Fax 837-7744
Alpine MS 300/5-8
801 Middle School Dr 79830 432-837-7720
Panchi Scown, prin. Fax 837-7795

Altair, Colorado
Rice Consolidated ISD 1,300/PK-12
PO Box 338 77412 979-234-3531
Michael Lanier Ph.D., supt. Fax 234-3409
www.ricecisd.org/
Other Schools – See Eagle Lake, Garwood, Sheridan

Alto, Cherokee, Pop. 1,156
Alto ISD 700/PK-12
244 County Road 2429 75925 936-858-7101
Dr. Ray Despain, supt. Fax 858-2101
www.alto.esc7.net/
Alto ES 400/PK-4
244 County Road 2429 75925 936-858-7170
Melody Witt, prin. Fax 858-4382
Alto MS 200/5-8
244 County Road 2429 75925 936-858-7149
Kelly West, prin. Fax 858-4579

Alton, Hidalgo, Pop. 7,057
Mission Consolidated ISD
Supt. — See Mission
Alton ES 600/PK-5
6631 N Chicago St, 956-323-7600
David Bourbois, prin. Fax 323-7617
Alton Memorial JHS 600/6-8
521 S Los Ebanos Blvd, 956-323-5000
Sylvia Garcia, prin. Fax 323-5045
Cantu ES 600/PK-5
920 W Main Ave, 956-323-7400
Joe Lopez, prin. Fax 323-7415
Cavazos ES 700/PK-5
803 S Los Ebanos Blvd, 956-323-7200
Joyce Geary, prin. Fax 323-7225
Salinas ES 600/PK-5
6 3/4 Mile N Conway, 956-323-6200
Diana Elizondo, prin. Fax 323-6219
Waitz ES 500/PK-5
842 W Saint Francis Ave, 956-323-6600
Ester Espericueta, prin. Fax 323-6618

Alvarado, Johnson, Pop. 3,977
Alvarado ISD 3,100/PK-12
PO Box 387 76009 817-783-6800
Dr. Chester Juroska, supt. Fax 783-3844
www.alvaradoisd.net/
Alvarado ES North 400/PK-3
PO Box 387 76009 817-783-6863
Lori Nunez, prin. Fax 783-6871
Alvarado ES South 400/PK-3
PO Box 387 76009 817-783-6880
Dandy Early, prin. Fax 783-6889
Alvarado IS 500/4-6
PO Box 387 76009 817-783-6825
Chris Everett, prin. Fax 783-6837
Alvarado JHS 500/7-8
PO Box 387 76009 817-783-6840
Melodye Broods, prin. Fax 783-6844
Lillian ES 400/PK-3
PO Box 387 76009 817-783-6815
Gary Davault, prin. Fax 783-6823

Alvin, Brazoria, Pop. 22,171
Alvin ISD 13,200/PK-12
301 E House St 77511 281-388-1130
Dr. Robby McGowen, supt. Fax 388-0566
www.alvinisd.net/
Alvin ES 300/3-5
1910 Rosharon Rd 77511 281-245-2511
Carol Nelson, prin. Fax 331-2217
Alvin JHS 700/6-8
2300 W South St 77511 281-245-2772
Trent Thrasher, prin. Fax 331-5926
Alvin PS 700/PK-2
2200 W Park Dr 77511 281-585-2531
Diane Peltier, prin. Fax 331-9888
Disney ES 300/3-5
5000 Mustang Rd 77511 281-245-2378
Lee Courville, prin. Fax 585-6503
Fairview JHS 6-8
2600 County Road 190 77511 281-245-3100
Kelly Jackson, prin.
Harby JHS 800/6-8
1500 Heights Rd 77511 281-585-6626
Nancy Flores, prin. Fax 388-2247
Hood-Case ES 800/PK-5
1450 Heights Rd 77511 281-585-5786
Donna McMillan, prin. Fax 388-0447
Longfellow ES 300/3-5
1300 E House St 77511 281-585-3397
Dee Dee Baker, prin. Fax 331-1190
Passmore ES 700/PK-5
600 Kost Rd 77511 281-585-6696
Kim Wells, prin. Fax 331-6697
Stevenson PS 800/PK-3
4715 Mustang Rd 77511 281-245-2353
Cathy Baccigalopi, prin. Fax 331-2234
Twain PS 900/PK-3
610 E Clements St 77511 281-585-5318
Brenda Vincent, prin. Fax 331-2584
Other Schools – See Manvel, Pearland

Living Stones Christian S 200/K-12
1407 Victory Ln 77511 281-331-0086
Judy Jandl, admin. Fax 331-6747
Next Generation Learning Center 50/PK-6
415 W Adoue St 77511 281-388-3723
Andrea Jackson, admin.

Alvord, Wise, Pop. 1,309
Alvord ISD 700/PK-12
PO Box 70 76225 940-427-5975
William Branum, supt. Fax 427-2313
www.alvordisd.net/
Alvord ES 300/PK-5
PO Box 70 76225 940-427-2881
Keith Crutsinger, prin. Fax 427-2213
Alvord MS 200/6-8
PO Box 70 76225 940-427-5511
Larry Hicks, prin. Fax 427-2461

Amarillo, Potter, Pop. 183,021
Amarillo ISD 30,600/PK-12
7200 W Interstate 40 79106 806-326-1000
Rod Schroder, supt. Fax 354-4378
www.amaisd.org
Allen 6th Grade Campus 200/6-6
700 N Lincoln St 79107 806-326-3770
Sandy Whitlow, prin. Fax 371-5829
Austin MS 700/6-8
1808 Wimberly Rd 79109 806-326-3000
David Vincent, prin. Fax 356-4802
Avondale ES 400/PK-5
1500 S Avondale St 79106 806-326-4000
Doug Burke, prin. Fax 354-4498
Belmar ES 200/K-5
6342 Adirondack Trl 79106 806-326-4050
Genie Baca, prin. Fax 354-5081
Bivins ES 500/PK-5
1500 S Fannin St 79102 806-326-4100
Tom Panger, prin. Fax 371-6133
Bonham MS 800/6-8
5600 SW 49th Ave 79109 806-326-3100
Dr. Curtis Crump, prin. Fax 356-4865
Bowie MS 1,100/6-8
3001 SE 12th Ave 79104 806-326-3200
Saul Guillen, prin. Fax 371-6016
Carver Academy ES 400/PK-5
1905 NW 12th Ave 79107 806-326-4150
Steffanie Chew, prin. Fax 371-6081
Carver Early Childhood Academy 400/PK-1
1800 N Travis St 79107 806-326-4200
Denise Wiltcher, prin. Fax 371-6178
Coronado ES 400/PK-5
3210 Wimberly Rd 79109 806-326-4250
Mike Manchee, prin. Fax 356-4821
Crockett MS 700/6-8
4720 Floyd Ave 79106 806-326-3300
Lisa Loan, prin. Fax 356-4873
de Zavala MS 300/5-8
2801 N Coulter St 79124 806-326-3400
Angie Noel, prin. Fax 354-4286
Eastridge ES 700/PK-5
1314 Evergreen St 79107 806-326-4300
Linda Vaughn, prin. Fax 381-7333
Emerson ES 600/PK-5
600 N Cleveland St 79107 806-326-4350
Melissa Schooler, prin. Fax 371-6055
Fannin MS 600/6-8
4627 S Rusk St 79110 806-326-3500
Tammie Villarreal, prin. Fax 354-4588
Forest Hill ES 600/PK-5
3515 E Amarillo Blvd 79107 806-326-4400
Kevin Word, prin. Fax 381-7221
Glenwood ES 400/PK-5
2407 S Houston St 79103 806-326-4450
Brandy Self, prin. Fax 371-5848
Hamlet ES 400/PK-5
705 Sycamore St 79107 806-326-4500
Kym Daniel, prin. Fax 381-7366
Houston MS 800/6-8
815 S Independence St 79106 806-326-3600
David Bishop, prin. Fax 371-5577
Humphrey's-Highland ES 600/PK-5
1301 S Dallas St 79104 806-326-4550
Debby Rutherford, prin. Fax 371-5822
Lamar ES 400/PK-5
3800 S Lipscomb St 79110 806-326-4600
Melody Fox, prin. Fax 356-4871
Landergin ES 500/PK-5
3209 S Taylor St 79110 806-326-4650
Kim Lackey, prin. Fax 371-6034
Lawndale ES 400/PK-5
2215 S Bivins St 79103 806-326-4700
Shirley Thomas, prin. Fax 371-5687
Lee ES 300/PK-5
119 NE 15th Ave 79107 806-326-4750
Roscoe Guest, prin. Fax 371-6046
Mann MS 400/6-8
610 N Buchanan St 79107 806-326-3700
Renee Mott, prin. Fax 371-5617
Mesa Verde ES 400/PK-5
4011 Beaver Dr 79107 806-326-4800
Shelley Baloglou, prin. Fax 381-7323
Oak Dale ES 500/PK-5
2711 S Hill St 79103 806-326-4850
Ann McClarty, prin. Fax 371-6106
Olsen Park ES 400/PK-5
2409 Anna St 79106 806-326-4900
Alan Nickson, prin. Fax 356-4944
Paramount Terrace ES 300/PK-5
3906 Cougar Dr 79109 806-326-4950
Kris Schellhamer, prin. Fax 354-4623
Pleasant Valley ES 300/PK-5
4413 River Rd 79108 806-326-5000
Lisa Neese, prin. Fax 381-7372
Puckett ES 400/K-5
6700 Oakhurst Dr 79109 806-326-5050
Jeanine Powell, prin. Fax 356-4833
Ridgecrest ES 500/PK-5
5306 SW 37th Ave 79109 806-326-5100
Chris Altman, prin. Fax 356-4835
Rogers ES 500/PK-5
920 N Mirror St 79107 806-326-5150
Terri Huseman, prin. Fax 371-5718
Sanborn ES 500/PK-5
700 S Roberts St 79102 806-326-5250
Margaret Mehringer, prin. Fax 371-6171
San Jacinto ES 600/PK-5
3400 SW 4th Ave 79106 806-326-5200
Doug Curry, prin. Fax 371-5843
Sleepy Hollow ES 400/K-5
3435 Reeder Dr 79121 806-326-5300
Doneice Ray, prin. Fax 354-5079
South Georgia ES 400/PK-5
5018 Susan Dr 79110 806-326-5350
Stephanie Friemel, prin. Fax 356-4959
South Lawn ES 400/PK-5
4719 Bowie St 79110 806-326-5400
Chris Tatum, prin. Fax 356-4879
Sunrise ES 300/PK-5
5123 SE 14th Ave 79104 806-326-5450
Bea Enevoldsen, prin. Fax 371-5841
Tradewind ES 400/K-5
4300 S Williams St 79118 806-326-5500
Kim Bentley, prin. Fax 371-6535
Travis MS 800/6-8
2815 Martin Rd 79107 806-326-3800
Dr. Dana West, prin. Fax 381-7207
Western Plateau ES 400/K-5
4927 Shawnee Trl 79109 806-326-5550
Leslie Frith, prin. Fax 356-4872
Whittier ES 500/PK-5
2004 N Marrs St 79107 806-326-5600
Tim White, prin. Fax 381-7322
Wills ES 400/PK-5
3500 SW 11th Ave 79106 806-326-5650
Karen Atkinson, prin. Fax 371-5842
Windsor ES 500/K-5
6700 Hyde Pkwy 79109 806-326-5700
Charla Cobb, prin. Fax 356-4999
Wolflin ES 400/PK-5
2026 S Hughes St 79109 806-326-5750
Kelly Simpson, prin. Fax 371-6101
Woodlands ES 400/K-4
2501 N Coulter St 79124 806-326-5800
Dalea Tatum, prin. Fax 356-4926

Canyon ISD
Supt. — See Canyon
Arden Road ES 600/K-4
6801 Learning Tree Ln 79119 806-677-2360
Marc Hamil, prin. Fax 677-2379
City View ES K-4
3400 Knoll St 79119 806-677-2500
Andrew Burgoon, prin. Fax 677-2519
Greenways IS 700/5-6
8100 Pineridge Dr 79119 806-677-2460
Steve West, prin. Fax 677-2499
Hillside ES K-4
9600 Perry Ave 79119 806-677-2520
Janet Laughter, prin. Fax 677-2539
Howe ES 500/K-4
5108 Pico Blvd 79110 806-677-2380
Yolanda Thurman, prin. Fax 677-2399
Lakeview ES 400/PK-4
6407 Lair Rd 79118 806-677-2830
Heather Wright, prin. Fax 677-2849
Sundown Lane ES 400/PK-4
4715 W Sundown Ln 79118 806-677-2400
David Faver, prin. Fax 677-2419
Westover Park JHS 800/7-8
7200 Pinnacle Dr 79119 806-677-2420
Doug Voran, prin. Fax 677-2439

Highland Park ISD 900/PK-12
PO Box 30430 79120 806-335-2823
Bill Mayfield, supt. Fax 335-3547
www.hpisd.net
Highland Park ES 500/PK-5
PO Box 30430 79120 806-335-1334
Pam Hicks, prin. Fax 335-3184
Highland Park MS 200/6-8
PO Box 30430 79120 806-335-2821
Shelley Collins, prin. Fax 335-3215

River Road ISD 1,400/PK-12
9500 N US Highway 287 79108 806-381-7800
Randy Owen, supt. Fax 381-1357
www.rrisd.net
River Road MS 300/6-8
7600 Pavillard Dr 79108 806-383-8721
Richard Kelley, prin. Fax 381-7815
Rolling Hills ES 700/PK-5
2800 W Cherry Ave 79108 806-383-8621
Doug Rawlins, prin. Fax 381-7814

Arbor Christian Academy 400/K-12
5000 Hollywood Rd 79118 806-355-7207
Kiley Murray, admin. Fax 353-8969
Heritage Classical Academy 200/PK-12
4100 Republic Ave 79109 806-463-2427
Dennis Rawls, admin. Fax 463-2433
Our Lady of Guadalupe S 100/PK-5
1108 S Houston St 79102 806-372-2629
Sr. Minerva Salvador, prin. Fax 372-2225
St. Andrews Episcopal S 300/PK-8
1515 S Georgia St 79102 806-376-9501
Ron Ferguson, hdmstr. Fax 376-8421
St. Joseph S 100/PK-5
4118 S Bonham St 79110 806-359-1604
Angie Seidenberger, prin. Fax 355-5622
St. Mary S 200/PK-5
1200 S Washington St 79102 806-376-9112
Kathi Lewis, prin. Fax 376-4314
San Jacinto Christian Academy 600/PK-12
PO Box 3428 79116 806-372-2285
Mark McKnight, supt. Fax 376-6712
Trinity Lutheran S 100/PK-6
5005 W Interstate 40 79106 806-352-5620
Rick Ryan, prin. Fax 353-7785

Amherst, Lamb, Pop. 765
Amherst ISD 200/K-12
PO Box 248 79312 806-246-3501
Joel Rodgers, supt. Fax 246-7729
www.amherstisd.com/
Amherst S 200/K-12
PO Box 248 79312 806-246-3221
Joel Henry, prin. Fax 246-3649

Anahuac, Chambers, Pop. 2,083
Anahuac ISD 1,400/PK-12
PO Box 369 77514 409-267-3600
Dr. Linda Kay Barnhart, supt. Fax 267-3855
www.anahuac.isd.esc4.net
Anahuac ES 700/PK-5
PO Box 399 77514 409-267-3600
Rose Womack, prin. Fax 267-6119
Anahuac MS 400/6-8
PO Box 849 77514 409-267-3600
LynnDell Turner, prin. Fax 267-3643

Anderson, Grimes, Pop. 274
Anderson - Shiro Consolidated ISD 600/PK-12
1139 Highway 90 N 77830 936-873-2802
Fred Brent, supt. Fax 873-2673
www.ascisd.net
Anderson - Shiro ES 200/PK-4
1139 Highway 90 N 77830 936-873-2801
Debra Lynn, prin. Fax 873-2581

Andrews, Andrews, Pop. 9,391
Andrews ISD 2,500/PK-12
405 NW 3rd St 79714 432-523-3640
Bobby Azam, supt. Fax 523-3343
andrews.esc18.net
Andrews MS 600/6-8
405 NW 3rd St 79714 432-523-3640
Penny Bane, prin. Fax 524-1904
Clearfork ES 400/PK-1
405 NW 3rd St 79714 432-523-3640
Estella Vasquez, prin. Fax 523-1903
Devonian ES 300/2-3
405 NW 3rd St 79714 432-523-3640
Belma Avena, prin. Fax 524-1905
Underwood ES 200/4-5
405 NW 3rd St 79714 432-523-3640
Linda Marquez, prin. Fax 524-1906

Angleton, Brazoria, Pop. 18,761
Angleton ISD 6,300/PK-12
1900 N Downing Rd 77515 979-864-8024
Dr. Heath Burns, supt. Fax 864-8070
www.angletonisd.net/
Angleton IS 1,000/7-8
1800 N Downing Rd 77515 979-849-4318
Roy Gardner, prin. Fax 849-8652
Angleton MS 900/5-6
1001 W Mulberry St 77515 979-848-8990
Robin Braun, prin. Fax 864-8686
Early Childhood Campus 700/PK-K
429 E Locust St 77515 979-849-1226
Annette Jones, prin. Fax 864-8704
Frontier ES 300/1-4
5200 Airline Rd 77515 979-849-8241
Vicki Harmon, prin. Fax 864-8715
Northside ES 500/1-4
1000 Ridgecrest St 77515 979-849-6189
Liz Comeaux, prin. Fax 864-8696
Rancho Isabella ES 400/1-4
100 Corral Loop 77515 979-849-2418
Johnny Briseno, prin. Fax 864-8725
Southside ES 400/1-4
1200 Park Ln 77515 979-849-5245
Jerry Crowell, prin. Fax 864-8730
Westside ES 300/1-4
300 S Walker St 77515 979-849-6288
Sidney Hamilton, prin. Fax 864-8736

Angleton Christian S 50/PK-7
237 E Locust St 77515 979-849-4311
Dr. Rochelle Brunson, admin. Fax 849-4323

Anna, Collin, Pop. 1,750
Anna ISD 1,900/PK-12
501 S Sherley Ave 75409 972-924-3955
Dr. Joe Wardell, supt. Fax 924-3321
www.annaisd.net
Anna MS 400/6-8
501 S Sherley Ave 75409 972-924-2380
Todd Southard, prin. Fax 924-2856
Bryant ES 1,000/PK-5
501 S Sherley Ave 75409 972-924-3353
Courtney Green, prin. Fax 924-2857
Rattan ES PK-5
501 S Sherley Ave 75409 972-924-8237
Sue Akins, prin. Fax 924-8271

Anson, Jones, Pop. 2,332
Anson ISD 800/PK-12
1431 Commercial Ave 79501 325-823-3671
Jay Baccus, supt. Fax 823-4444
www.ansontigers.com
Anson ES 400/PK-5
922 Avenue M 79501 325-823-3361
Will Brewer, prin. Fax 823-3127
Anson MS 200/6-8
1120 Avenue M 79501 325-823-2771
David Hagler, prin. Fax 823-3667

Anthony, El Paso, Pop. 4,072
Anthony ISD 800/PK-12
840 6th St 79821 915-886-6500
Ronald Haugen, supt. Fax 886-3835
www.anthonyisd.net
Anthony ES 400/PK-5
610 6th St 79821 915-886-6510
Crescencio Cardona, prin. Fax 886-3205
Anthony MS 200/6-8
813 6th St 79821 915-886-6530
David Gregory, prin. Fax 886-3875

Anton, Hockley, Pop. 1,172
Anton ISD 300/PK-12
PO Box 309 79313 806-997-2301
Dwayne Chenault, supt. Fax 997-2062
www.antonisd.org
Anton ES 200/PK-6
PO Box 309 79313 806-997-5221
Kelly Priest, prin. Fax 997-2062

Apple Springs, Trinity
Apple Springs ISD 200/PK-12
PO Box 125 75926 936-831-3344
Gregg Spivey, supt. Fax 831-2824
www.asisd.com/
Apple Springs ES 100/PK-5
PO Box 125 75926 936-831-2241
Cody Moree, prin. Fax 831-2824

Aquilla, Hill, Pop. 149
Aquilla ISD 200/PK-12
404 N Richards 76622 254-694-3770
James Gwaltney, supt. Fax 694-6237
www.aquillaisd.net
Aquilla S 200/PK-12
404 N Richards 76622 254-694-3770
David Edison, prin. Fax 694-6237

Aransas Pass, San Patricio, Pop. 8,877
Aransas Pass ISD 2,100/PK-12
244 W Harrison Blvd 78336 361-758-3466
Dr. Sue Thomas, supt. Fax 758-2962
www.apisd.org
Blunt MS 300/7-8
2103 Demory Ln 78336 361-758-2711
Bryan O'Bryant, prin. Fax 758-4690
Faulk ECC 500/PK-1
430 S 8th St 78336 361-758-3141
Martha Rose, prin. Fax 758-5493
Kieberger ES 300/2-3
748 W Goodnight Ave 78336 361-758-3113
Naomi Hansen, prin. Fax 758-3605
Marshall ES 500/4-6
2300 McMullen Ln 78336 361-758-3455
Clint Houston, prin. Fax 758-3046

Highland Avenue Christian S 100/K-12
1630 W Highland Ave 78336 361-758-8196
Steve Hale, prin. Fax 758-5214

Archer City, Archer, Pop. 1,859
Archer City ISD 500/PK-12
PO Box 926 76351 940-574-4536
Randel Beaver, supt. Fax 574-4051
www.esc9.net/acisd
Archer City ES 200/PK-6
PO Box 926 76351 940-574-4506
Vance Morris, prin. Fax 574-4051

Argyle, Denton, Pop. 2,969
Argyle ISD 1,500/PK-12
800 Eagle Dr 76226 940-464-7241
Dr. Telena Wright, supt. Fax 464-7297
www.argyleisd.com
Argyle IS 100/5-6
800 Eagle Dr 76226 940-464-5100
Conrad Streeter, prin. Fax 464-5101
Argyle MS 300/7-8
800 Eagle Dr 76226 940-246-2126
Chris Daniel, prin. Fax 246-2128
Hilltop ES 600/PK-4
800 Eagle Dr 76226 940-464-0564
Robin McWhorter, prin. Fax 464-4017

Denton ISD
Supt. — See Denton
Blanton ES K-5
9501 Stacee Ln 76226 940-369-0700
Karen Satterwhite, prin. Fax 241-1423
Harpool MS 6-8
9601 Stacee Ln 76226 940-369-1700
Mike Vance, prin. Fax 241-1342
Rayzor ES 700/K-5
377 Rayzor Rd 76226 940-369-4100
Happy Carrico, prin. Fax 455-2658

Liberty Christian S 1,100/PK-12
1301 S US Highway 377 76226 940-294-2000
Rodney Haire, pres. Fax 294-2045

Arlington, Tarrant, Pop. 362,805
Arlington ISD 62,900/PK-12
1203 W Pioneer Pkwy 76013 682-867-4611
Jerry McCullough, supt. Fax 459-7299
www.aisd.net
Amos ES 600/PK-6
3100 Daniel Dr 76014 682-867-4700
Rodney Rinn, prin. Fax 419-4705
Anderson ES 700/PK-6
1101 Timberlake Dr 76010 682-867-7750
Kyle Bunker, prin. Fax 652-7975
Ashworth ES 600/PK-6
6700 Silo Rd 76002 682-867-4800
Lynn Allen, prin. Fax 419-4805
Atherton ES 1,100/PK-6
2101 Overbrook Dr 76014 682-867-4900
Stephanie Hawthorne, prin. Fax 419-4905
Bailey JHS 800/7-8
2411 Winewood Ln 76013 682-867-0700
Jimmy Walker, prin. Fax 801-0705
Barnett JHS 1,000/7-8
2101 E Sublett Rd 76018 682-867-5000
Cindy Elwood, prin. Fax 419-5005
Bebensee ES 900/PK-6
5900 Inks Lake Dr 76018 682-867-5100
John Walkinshaw, prin. Fax 419-5105
Beckham ES 700/PK-6
1700 Southeast Pkwy 76018 682-867-6600
Lisa Strickland, prin. Fax 375-6605
Berry ES 700/PK-6
1800 Joyce St 76010 682-867-0850
Dr. Kathy Link, prin. Fax 801-0905
Blanton ES 600/PK-6
1900 S Collins St 76010 682-867-1000
Stephen Paulsen, prin. Fax 801-0955
Boles JHS 700/7-8
3900 SW Green Oaks Blvd 76017 682-867-8000
Fernando Benavides, prin. Fax 561-8005
Bryant ES 700/PK-6
2201 Havenwood Dr 76018 682-867-5200
Nancy Simko, prin. Fax 419-5205
Burgin ES 900/PK-6
401 E Mayfield Rd 76014 682-867-1300
Sheila Madden, prin. Fax 419-1416
Butler ES 700/K-6
2121 Margaret Dr 76012 682-867-1010
Sara Coulter, prin. Fax 801-1015
Carter JHS 800/7-8
701 Tharp St 76010 682-867-1700
Rashel Stevens, prin. Fax 801-1705
Corey ES 800/PK-6
5200 Kelly Elliott Rd 76017 682-867-3900
Steve Howell, prin. Fax 561-3905
Crow ES 600/PK-6
1201 Coke Dr 76010 682-867-1850
Sally Amendola, prin. Fax 801-1855
Ditto ES 700/PK-6
3001 Quail Ln 76016 682-867-3100
Julie Harcrow, prin. Fax 492-3105
Duff ES 600/K-6
3100 Lynnwood Dr 76013 682-867-2000
Cynthia Harbison, prin. Fax 801-2005
Dunn ES 600/K-6
2201 Woodside Dr 76013 682-867-3200
Debbie Williams, prin. Fax 492-3205
Ellis ES 900/PK-6
2601 Shadow Ridge Dr 76006 682-867-7900
Beverly Behgam, prin. Fax 652-7905
Ferguson JHS 500/7-8
600 SE Green Oaks Blvd 76018 682-867-1600
David Tapia, prin. Fax 472-1605
Fitzgerald ES 700/PK-6
5201 Creek Valley Dr 76018 682-867-5300
Robert Cox, prin. Fax 419-5305
Foster ES 600/PK-6
1025 High Point Rd 76015 682-867-5350
Joshua Garcia, prin. Fax 419-5355
Goodman ES 600/PK-6
1400 Rebecca Ln 76014 682-867-2200
Tera Albert, prin. Fax 801-2205
Gunn JHS 500/7-8
3000 S Fielder Rd 76015 682-867-5400
Lesia Rodawalt, prin. Fax 419-5405
Hale ES 600/K-6
2400 E Mayfield Rd 76014 682-867-1530
Elizabeth Ricles, prin. Fax 419-1535
Hill ES 600/K-6
2020 W Tucker Blvd 76013 682-867-2300
Bryan Shippey, prin. Fax 801-2305
Hutcheson JHS 700/7-8
2101 Browning Dr 76010 682-867-2400
Rose Bolden, prin. Fax 801-2415
Johns ES 1,000/PK-6
1900 Sherry St 76010 682-867-2500
Tammy Rogers, prin. Fax 801-2505
Key ES 500/K-6
3621 Roosevelt Dr 76016 682-867-5500
Debbi Chumchal, prin. Fax 419-5505
Knox ES 600/PK-6
2315 Stonegate St 76010 682-867-2051
Yvonne Harris-Dupont, prin. Fax 801-2056
Kooken Education Center 400/PK-PK
423 N Center St 76011 682-867-7152
Dr. Connie Spence, prin.
Little ES 700/K-6
3721 Little Rd 76016 682-867-3300
Barbara Lindley, prin. Fax 492-3305
Miller ES 900/PK-6
6401 W Pleasant Ridge Rd 76016 682-867-8400
Chris Chamberlain, prin. Fax 561-8405
Moore ES 600/K-6
5500 Park Springs Blvd 76017 682-867-8900
Vivian Johnson, prin. Fax 561-8905
Morton ES 1,000/PK-6
2900 Barrington Pl 76014 682-867-5600
John Peterson, prin. Fax 419-5605
Nichols JHS 900/7-8
2201 Ascension Blvd 76006 682-867-2600
Sandra Knox, prin. Fax 801-2605
Ousley JHS 700/7-8
950 Southeast Pkwy 76018 682-867-5700
Lora Thurston, prin. Fax 419-5705
Pearcy ES 600/PK-6
601 E Harris Rd 76002 682-867-5555
Melissa Haubrich, prin. Fax 419-5554
Pope ES 600/PK-6
901 Chestnut Dr 76012 682-867-2750
Celina Kilgore, prin. Fax 801-2755
Rankin ES 800/PK-6
1900 Oleander St 76010 682-867-2800
Deanna McClellan, prin. Fax 801-2805
Roark ES 600/PK-6
2401 Roberts Cir 76010 682-867-2900
Marsha Tucker, prin. Fax 801-2905
Roquemore ES 700/PK-6
2001 Van Buren Dr 76011 682-867-3500
Suzie Swan, prin. Fax 801-3505
Shackelford JHS 700/7-8
2000 N Fielder Rd 76012 682-867-3600
Carolyn Galvan, prin. Fax 801-3605
Sherrod ES 800/PK-6
2626 Lincoln Dr 76006 682-867-3700
Jeanine Johnson, prin. Fax 801-3705
Short ES 600/PK-6
2000 California Ln 76015 682-867-5850
Katherine McCollum, prin. Fax 419-5855
South Davis ES 600/PK-6
2001 S Davis Dr 76013 682-867-3800
Erma Nichols, prin. Fax 801-3805
Speer ES 900/PK-6
811 Fuller St 76012 682-867-4000
Linda DeLeon, prin. Fax 801-4005
Swift ES 600/PK-6
1101 S Fielder Rd 76013 682-867-4100
Patti Casey, prin. Fax 801-4105
Thornton ES 700/PK-6
2301 E Park Row Dr 76010 682-867-4200
David Gutierrez, prin. Fax 801-4205
Webb ES 800/PK-6
1200 N Cooper St 76011 682-867-4300
Michael Martin, prin. Fax 801-4305
Williams ES 900/PK-6
4915 Red Birch Dr 76018 682-867-5900
Dana Goode, prin. Fax 419-5905
Wimbish ES 600/PK-6
1601 Wright St 76012 682-867-6000
Russell Berrong, prin. Fax 801-6005
Wood ES 900/PK-6
3300 Pimlico Dr 76017 682-867-1100
Sandra White, prin. Fax 419-1105
Workman JHS 600/7-8
701 E Arbrook Blvd 76014 682-867-1200
David Bellile, prin. Fax 419-1205
Young JHS 900/7-8
3200 Woodside Dr 76016 682-867-3400
Roger Jones, prin. Fax 492-3405
Other Schools – See Grand Prairie

Kennedale ISD
Supt. — See Kennedale
Patterson ES 500/K-4
6621 Kelly Elliott Rd 76001 817-563-8600
Tara Sublette, prin. Fax 483-3638

Mansfield ISD
Supt. — See Mansfield
Anderson ES 800/PK-4
5615 Fox Hunt Dr 76017 817-472-3200
Miller Beaird, prin. Fax 472-3216
Brockett ES 600/PK-4
810 Dove Meadows Dr 76002 817-299-6620
Chuck Roe, prin. Fax 453-6835
Coble MS 1,100/7-8
1200 Ballweg Rd 76002 817-299-6400
Derrell Douglas, prin. Fax 453-7331
Cross Timber IS 1,000/5-6
2934 Russell Rd 76001 817-561-3800
Gerald Kokenes, prin. Fax 561-3814
Davis ES 900/PK-4
900 Eden Rd 76001 817-472-3260
Holly Smith, prin. Fax 472-3267
Gideon ES 500/PK-4
1201 Mansfield Webb Rd 76002 817-472-3299
Imelda Little, prin. Fax 472-3292
Harmon ES 800/PK-4
5700 Petra Dr 76017 817-472-3225
Sharon Ferguson, prin. Fax 472-3228
Holt ES 600/PK-4
7321 Ledbetter Rd 76001 817-299-6460
Kelly Campbell, prin. Fax 561-3888
Howard MS 1,000/7-8
7501 Calender Rd 76001 817-299-3500
Jimmy Neal, prin. Fax 561-3840
Icenhower IS 1,000/5-6
8100 Webb Ferrell Rd 76002 817-299-2700
Duane Thurston, prin. Fax 453-6890
Jones ES 700/PK-4
7650 S Watson Rd 76002 817-299-6940
Dameon Gray, prin. Fax 472-3247
Morris ES 700/K-4
7900 Tin Cup Dr 76001 817-473-5353
Debbie Clanton, prin. Fax 473-5362
Reid ES 700/PK-4
500 Country Club Dr 76002 817-299-6960
Elizabeth Hostin, prin. Fax 453-7360

Arlington Faith Academy 50/K-6
PO Box 170718 76003 817-483-0119
Gerald Waite, admin. Fax 483-4292
Burton Adventist Academy 300/PK-12
4611 Kelly Elliott Rd 76017 817-572-0081
Gerald Coy, prin. Fax 561-4237
Fellowship Academy 200/K-12
7000 US 287 Hwy 76001 817-563-5913
Monica Collier, prin. Fax 563-5427
Grace Lutheran S 100/PK-8
308 W Park Row Dr 76010 817-274-1654
Steve Stigler, prin. Fax 277-9353
High Point Preparatory Academy 200/K-12
2500 E Arbrook Blvd 76014 817-394-3100
Beth Featherston, prin. Fax 394-3101
Holy Rosary Catholic S 500/PK-8
2015 SW Green Oaks Blvd 76017 817-419-6800
Lynn Day, prin. Fax 419-7080
Montessori Academy 300/PK-6
3428 W Arkansas Ln 76016 817-274-1548
Pam Dunbar, prin. Fax 274-6951
Oakridge S 900/PK-12
5900 W Pioneer Pkwy 76013 817-451-4994
Jonathan Kellam, hdmstr. Fax 457-6681
Pantego Christian Academy 800/PK-12
2201 W Park Row Dr 76013 817-460-3315
Steve Newby, hdmstr. Fax 277-6749
St. Maria Goretti S 400/PK-8
1200 S Davis Dr 76013 817-275-5081
Mary Ellen Doskocil, prin. Fax 277-4193
St. Pauls Preparatory Academy 300/PK-12
PO Box 121234 76012 817-561-3500
Janice Wood, prin. Fax 561-3408
Tate Springs Christian S 200/PK-6
4201 Little Rd 76016 817-478-7091
Fax 483-8283

Arp, Smith, Pop. 932
Arp ISD 900/PK-12
PO Box 70 75750 903-859-8482
Toney Lowery, supt. Fax 859-2621
www.arp.sprnet.org
Arp ES 400/PK-5
PO Box 70 75750 903-859-4650
Wendy Popescu, prin. Fax 859-3683
Arp JHS 200/6-8
PO Box 70 75750 903-859-4936
Dwight Thomas, prin. Fax 859-3980

Asherton, Dimmit, Pop. 1,331
Carrizo Springs Consolidated ISD
Supt. — See Carrizo Springs
Asherton ES 100/PK-6
1295 May Ave 78827 830-468-3592
Silvestre Cavasos, prin. Fax 468-3721

Aspermont, Stonewall, Pop. 831
Aspermont ISD 200/PK-12
PO Box 549 79502 940-989-3355
Cliff Gilmore, supt. Fax 989-3353
www.aspermont.esc14.net
Aspermont ES 100/PK-6
PO Box 549 79502 940-989-3323
Ron Taylor, prin. Fax 989-2954

Atascosa, Bexar
Southwest ISD
Supt. — See San Antonio
Elm Creek ES 600/PK-5
11535 Pearsall Rd 78002 210-622-4430
J. Luis Rojas, prin. Fax 622-4431

Athens, Henderson, Pop. 12,559
Athens ISD 3,200/PK-12
104 Hawn St 75751 903-677-6900
Dr. Fred Hayes, supt. Fax 677-6908
www.athensisd.net
Athens Annex S 200/PK-PK
601 E College St 75751 903-677-6940
Renee Campbell, prin. Fax 677-6956
Athens IS 500/4-5
307 Madole St 75751 903-677-6960
Janie Sims, prin. Fax 677-6987
Athens MS 400/6-8
6800 State Highway 19 S 75751 903-677-3030
Louis DeRosa, prin. Fax 677-2111
Bel Air ES 500/2-3
215 Willowbrook Dr 75751 903-677-6980
Renee Campbell, prin. Fax 677-6986
South Athens ES 500/K-1
718 Robbins Rd 75751 903-677-6970
Tina Eaton, prin. Fax 677-3470

Athens Christian Academy 100/K-8
105 S Carroll St 75751 903-675-5135
Carter Gates, admin. Fax 675-4708

Atlanta, Cass, Pop. 5,677
Atlanta ISD 2,000/PK-12
106 W Main St 75551 903-796-4194
Roger Hailey, supt. Fax 799-1004
www.atlisd.net/
Atlanta ES 400/3-5
902 Abc Ln 75551 903-796-7164
Dianne Whatley, prin. Fax 799-1018
Atlanta MS 400/6-8
600 High School Ln 75551 903-796-7928
Rex Stone, prin. Fax 799-1021
Atlanta PS 500/PK-2
505 Rabbit Blvd 75551 903-796-8115
Melba Foster, prin. Fax 799-1014

Aubrey, Denton, Pop. 2,210
Aubrey ISD 1,400/PK-12
415 Tisdell Ln 76227 940-668-0060
Dr. James Monaco, supt. Fax 365-2627
www.aubreyisd.net/
Aubrey MS 400/6-8
815 W Sherman Dr 76227 940-668-0200
Delore Jones, prin. Fax 365-3135
Brockett ES 300/K-5
900 Chestnut St 76227 940-668-0036
Mark Furlow, prin. Fax 365-0118
Monaco ES 400/PK-5
9350 Cape Cod Blvd 76227 940-668-0000
Shannon Saylor, prin. Fax 668-0001

Denton ISD
Supt. — See Denton
Navo MS 600/6-8
1701 Navo Rd 76227 972-347-7500
Shaun Perry, prin. Fax 346-2562
Paloma Creek ES 400/K-5
1600 Navo Rd 76227 972-347-7300
Romeo Mungia, prin. Fax 346-9501
Providence ES 600/K-5
1000 FM 2931 76227 940-369-1900
Susan Bolte, prin. Fax 369-4202
Savannah ES 500/K-5
1101 Cotton Exchange Dr 76227 972-347-7400
Michael McWilliams, prin. Fax 346-3352

Austin, Travis, Pop. 690,252
Austin ISD 88,400/PK-12
1111 W 6th St 78703 512-414-1700
Dr. Pascal Forgione, supt. Fax 414-1707
www.austinisd.org
Allan ES 400/PK-5
4900 Gonzales St 78702 512-414-2304
Leticia Botello, prin. Fax 385-2512
Allison ES 500/PK-6
515 Vargas Rd 78741 512-414-2004
Guadalupe Velasquez, prin. Fax 385-0905
Andrews ES 600/PK-5
6801 Northeast Dr 78723 512-414-1770
Laurie Barber, prin. Fax 926-6635
Bailey MS 1,200/6-8
4020 Lost Oasis Holw 78739 512-414-4990
Julia Fletcher, prin. Fax 292-0898
Baranoff ES 800/K-5
12009 Buckingham Gate Rd 78748 512-841-7100
Linda Purvis, prin. Fax 841-7104
Barrington ES 700/PK-6
400 Cooper Dr 78753 512-414-2008
Susan Stamy, prin. Fax 836-4077
Barton Hills ES 400/K-6
2108 Barton Hills Dr 78704 512-414-2013
Katie Achtermann, prin. Fax 841-3849
Becker ES 200/PK-5
906 W Milton St 78704 512-414-2019
Carolyn Wirth, prin. Fax 442-1759
Bedichek MS 1,000/6-8
6800 Bill Hughes Rd 78745 512-414-3265
Dan Diehl, prin. Fax 444-4382
Blackshear ES 300/PK-5
1712 E 11th St 78702 512-414-2021
Thelma Longoria, prin. Fax 477-7640
Blanton ES 600/PK-5
5408 Westminster Dr 78723 512-414-2026
Leslie Dusing, prin. Fax 926-8553
Blazier ES 400/PK-5
8601 Vertex Blvd 78747 512-841-8800
Dora Fabelo, prin. Fax 841-8801
Boone ES 600/PK-5
8101 Croftwood Dr 78749 512-414-2537
Kathleen Noack, prin. Fax 280-3307
Brentwood ES 400/PK-5
6700 Arroyo Seco 78757 512-414-2039
K. Williams-Carter, prin. Fax 453-8928
Brooke ES 400/PK-5
3100 E 4th St 78702 512-414-2043
Olivia del Valle, prin. Fax 385-3862
Brown ES 500/PK-6
505 W Anderson Ln 78752 512-414-2047
Veronica Sharp, prin. Fax 452-6097
Bryker Woods ES 400/K-6
3309 Kerbey Ln 78703 512-414-2054
Nancy Hobbs, prin. Fax 459-9047
Burnet MS 1,000/6-8
8401 Hathaway Dr 78757 512-414-3225
Antonio Medina, prin. Fax 452-0695
Campbell ES 400/PK-5
2613 Rogers Ave 78722 512-414-2056
Dovie Wherry-Boykins, prin. Fax 841-1246
Casey ES 900/PK-5
9400 Texas Oaks Dr 78748 512-841-6900
Patricia Fuller, prin. Fax 841-6925
Casis ES 700/PK-5
2710 Exposition Blvd 78703 512-414-2062
Patricia Martin, prin. Fax 477-1776
Clayton ES 600/K-5
7525 La Crosse Ave 78739 512-841-9200
Dru McGovern-Robinett, prin. Fax 841-9201
Cook ES 800/K-5
1511 Cripple Creek Dr 78758 512-414-2510
Orlando Salazar, prin. Fax 837-5983
Covington MS 900/6-8
3700 Convict Hill Rd 78749 512-414-3276
Candace Hughs, prin. Fax 892-4547
Cowan ES 600/PK-5
2817 Kentish Dr 78748 512-841-2700
April Clinch-Glenn, prin. Fax 841-2755
Cunningham ES 500/PK-5
2200 Berkeley Ave 78745 512-414-2067
Denise Kelly, prin. Fax 441-6006
Davis ES 700/PK-5
5214 Duval Rd 78727 512-414-2580
Douglas Hall, prin. Fax 346-7384
Dawson ES 400/PK-5
3001 S 1st St 78704 512-414-2070
Shannon Sellstrom, prin. Fax 442-5765
Dobie MS 900/6-8
1200 E Rundberg Ln 78753 512-414-3270
Carol Chapman, prin. Fax 836-8411
Doss ES 700/PK-5
7005 Northledge Dr 78731 512-414-2365
Sharon Raven, prin. Fax 345-0013
Fulmore Magnet S 1,000/6-8
201 E Mary St 78704 512-841-4916
Dr. Mary Anne Wilkenson, dir. Fax 841-4915
Fulmore MS 1,000/6-8
201 E Mary St 78704 512-414-3207
Lisa Bush, prin. Fax 441-3129
Galindo ES 700/PK-5
3800 S 2nd St 78704 512-414-1756
Donna Marie Linn, prin. Fax 414-0448
Garcia MS Gustavo L. 600/6-8
7414 Johnny Morris Rd 78724 512-841-9400
Dr. Helen Johnson, prin. Fax 841-9401
Govalle ES 400/PK-5
3601 Govalle Ave 78702 512-414-2078
Nancy Maniscalco, prin. Fax 926-4820
Graham ES 700/PK-5
11211 Tom Adams Dr 78753 512-414-2395
Blaine Helwig, prin. Fax 835-4562
Gullett ES 400/K-5
6310 Treadwell Blvd 78757 512-414-2082
Janie Ruiz, prin. Fax 451-2036
Harris ES 700/PK-5
1711 Wheless Ln 78723 512-414-2085
Gloria Arredondo, prin. Fax 929-7347
Hart ES 900/PK-5
8301 Furness Dr 78753 512-841-2100
Elia Diaz-Ortiz, prin. Fax 841-2190
Highland Park ES 500/K-5
4900 Fairview Dr 78731 512-414-2090
Tammy Workman, prin. Fax 414-2626
Hill ES 700/PK-5
8601 Tallwood Dr 78759 512-414-2369
Connie Giles, prin. Fax 841-8105
Houston ES 900/PK-5
5409 Ponciana Dr 78744 512-414-2517
Elia Diaz-Camarillo, prin. Fax 448-4869
Jordan ES 700/PK-5
6711 Johnny Morris Rd 78724 512-414-2578
Diana Vallejo, prin. Fax 926-8299
Joslin ES 400/PK-5
4500 Manchaca Rd 78745 512-414-2094
Sandra Creswell, prin. Fax 443-3011
Kealing Magnet Program 1,200/6-8
1607 Pennsylvania Ave 78702 512-414-3180
Mary Ramberg, dir. Fax 414-6704
Kealing MS 1,200/6-8
1607 Pennsylvania Ave 78702 512-414-3214
Lynda Redler, prin. Fax 478-9133
Kiker ES 700/K-5
5913 La Crosse Ave 78739 512-414-2584
Lori Schneider, prin. Fax 288-5779
Kocurek ES 700/PK-5
9800 Curlew Dr 78748 512-414-2547
Christopher Summers, prin. Fax 282-7824
Lamar MS 700/6-8
6201 Wynona Ave 78757 512-414-3217
Eleanor Duncan, prin. Fax 467-6862
Langford ES 800/PK-5
2206 Blue Meadow Dr 78744 512-414-1765
Armando Cisneros, prin. Fax 447-4808
Lee ES 400/K-6
3308 Hampton Rd 78705 512-414-2098
Elyse Smith, prin. Fax 478-4463
Linder ES 900/PK-5
2800 Metcalfe Rd 78741 512-414-2398
Beverly Odom, prin. Fax 447-3222
Maplewood ES 300/PK-6
3808 Maplewood Ave 78722 512-414-4402
Luiz Lazaro, prin. Fax 472-8559
Martin MS 700/6-8
1601 Haskell St 78702 512-414-3243
Susan Galvan, prin. Fax 320-0125
Mathews ES 400/PK-6
906 Westlynn St 78703 512-414-4406
Amy Kinkade, prin. Fax 476-2108
McBee ES 600/K-5
1001 W Braker Ln 78758 512-841-2500
Lucy Duncan, prin. Fax 841-2333
Mendez MS 1,100/6-8
5106 Village Square Dr 78744 512-414-3284
Connie Barr, prin. Fax 442-5738
Metz ES 700/PK-5
84 Robert T Martinez Jr St 78702 512-414-4408
Valerie Galbraith, prin. Fax 472-3412
Mills ES 900/PK-5
6201 Davis Ln 78749 512-841-2400
Patricia Butler, prin. Fax 841-2490
Murchison MS 1,200/6-8
3700 N Hills Dr 78731 512-414-3254
Kimiko Cartwright, prin. Fax 343-1710
Norman ES 600/PK-5
4001 Tannehill Ln 78721 512-414-2347
Floretta Andrews, prin. Fax 926-6321
Oak Hill ES 900/PK-5
6101 Patton Ranch Rd 78735 512-414-2336
Teresa Whistler, prin. Fax 892-2279
Oak Springs ES 300/PK-5
3601 Webberville Rd 78702 512-414-4413
Monica Woods, prin. Fax 472-5005
Odom ES 800/PK-5
1010 Turtle Creek Blvd 78745 512-414-2388
Sharon Richards, prin. Fax 443-6170
O'Henry MS 800/6-8
2610 W 10th St 78703 512-414-3229
Peter Price, prin. Fax 477-7428
Ortega ES 300/PK-5
1135 Garland Ave 78721 512-414-4417
Anna Pedroza, prin. Fax 929-7906
Overton ES 500/PK-5
7201 Colony Loop Dr 78724 512-841-9300
Gilbert Hicks, prin. Fax 841-9301
Palm ES 700/PK-5
7601 Dixie Dr 78744 512-414-2545
Norma Silva-Quinn, prin. Fax 280-2769
Paredes MS 1,100/6-8
10100 S Mary Moore Searight 78748 512-841-6800
Raul Moreno, prin. Fax 841-7036
Patton ES 800/PK-5
6001 Westcreek Dr 78749 512-414-1780
Allan Neal Stevens, prin. Fax 892-6541
Pearce MS 800/6-8
6401 N Hampton Dr 78723 512-414-3234
James Troutman, prin. Fax 926-6146
Pease ES 200/K-6
1106 Rio Grande St 78701 512-414-4428
Beth Ellis, prin. Fax 477-3009
Pecan Springs ES 500/PK-5
3100 Rogge Ln 78723 512-414-4445
Elaine McKinney, prin. Fax 926-0001
Perez ES 600/PK-5
7500 S Pleasant Valley Rd 78744 512-841-9100
David Kauffman, prin. Fax 841-9101
Pickle ES 700/PK-5
1101 Wheatley Ave 78752 512-841-8400
Joel De La Garza, prin. Fax 841-8444
Pillow ES 500/PK-5
3025 Crosscreek Dr 78757 512-414-2350
Tonya King, prin. Fax 467-2513
Pleasant Hill ES 700/PK-5
6405 Circle S Rd 78745 512-414-4453
Sharon Stoner, prin. Fax 442-4741
Read Preschool PK-PK
2608 Richcreek Rd 78757 512-414-9400
Janice Darrington-Weston, prin.
Reilly ES 300/PK-5
405 Denson Dr 78752 512-414-4464
Anna Garza, prin. Fax 453-1193
Richards S for Young Women Leaders 200/6-7
2206 Prather Ln 78704 512-414-3236
Jeanne Goka, prin. Fax 441-5208
Ridgetop ES 200/PK-5
5005 Caswell Ave 78751 512-414-4469
Joaquin Gloria, prin. Fax 459-9187
Rodriguez ES 900/PK-5
4400 Franklin Park Dr 78744 512-841-7200
Suzie Cunningham, prin. Fax 841-7205
St. Elmo ES 500/PK-5
600 W Saint Elmo Rd 78745 512-414-4477
Adriana Gonzales, prin. Fax 442-6871
Sanchez ES 700/PK-5
73 San Marcos St 78702 512-414-4423
Azucena Garcia, prin. Fax 472-9493
Sims ES 400/PK-5
1203 Springdale Rd 78721 512-414-4488
Freda Mills, prin. Fax 841-1282
Small MS 1,100/6-8
4801 Monterey Oaks Blvd 78749 512-841-6700
Amy Taylor, prin. Fax 841-6703
Summitt ES 600/PK-5
12207 Brigadoon Ln 78727 512-414-4484
Ann Lilie, prin. Fax 832-1458
Sunset Valley ES 400/PK-5
3000 Jones Rd 78745 512-414-2392
Kim Placker, prin. Fax 892-7206

Travis Heights ES 600/PK-5
2010 Alameda Dr 78704 512-414-4495
Lisa Robertson, prin. Fax 442-9537
Walnut Creek ES 900/PK-5
401 W Braker Ln 78753 512-414-4499
Valerie Taylor-Schkade, prin. Fax 837-6789
Webb MS 700/6-8
601 E Saint Johns Ave 78752 512-414-3258
Reynaldo Garcia, prin. Fax 452-9683
Widen ES 800/PK-5
5605 Nuckols Crossing Rd 78744 512-414-2556
Julie Pryor, prin. Fax 441-8971
Williams ES 600/PK-5
500 Mairo St 78748 512-414-2525
Lisa Mock, prin. Fax 292-3041
Winn ES 700/PK-5
3500 Susquehanna Ln 78723 512-414-2390
Ruth Harvin, prin. Fax 926-9211
Wooldridge ES 1,000/PK-5
1412 Norseman Ter 78758 512-414-2353
Celia Glick, prin. Fax 339-6583
Wooten ES 600/PK-5
1406 Dale Dr 78757 512-414-2315
Ron Bolek, prin. Fax 459-9227
Zavala ES 500/PK-6
310 Robert T Martinez Jr St 78702 512-414-2318
Rosa Pena, prin. Fax 477-2361
Zilker ES 400/PK-6
1900 Bluebonnet Ln 78704 512-414-2327
Randall Thomson, prin. Fax 442-3992
Other Schools – See Manchaca

Del Valle ISD
Supt. — See Del Valle
Baty ES 700/PK-5
2101 Faro Dr 78741 512-386-3450
Dawn Cochran, prin. Fax 386-3455
Hillcrest ES 600/PK-5
6910 E William Cannon Dr 78744 512-386-3550
Sara Guerra, prin. Fax 386-3555
Hornsby-Dunlap ES 800/PK-5
13901 FM 969 78724 512-386-3650
Laurie Jurado, prin. Fax 386-3655
Ojeda MS 600/6-8
4900 McKinney Falls Pkwy 78744 512-386-3500
Timica Patton, prin. Fax 386-3505
Smith ES 500/PK-5
4209 Smith School Rd 78744 512-386-3850
Ray Thomason, prin. Fax 386-3855

Eanes ISD 7,200/PK-12
601 Camp Craft Rd 78746 512-732-9001
Dr. Nola Wellman, supt. Fax 732-9005
www.eanesisd.net/
Barton Creek ES 400/PK-5
1370 Patterson Rd 78733 512-732-9180
John Andrews, prin. Fax 732-9189
Bridge Point ES 900/PK-5
6401 Cedar St 78746 512-732-9200
Brad Wirht, prin. Fax 732-9209
Cedar Creek ES 400/PK-5
3301 Pinnacle Rd 78746 512-732-9120
Lisa Streun, prin. Fax 732-9129
Eanes ES 500/PK-5
4101 Bee Caves Rd 78746 512-732-9100
Cynthia Acosta, prin. Fax 732-9109
Hill Country MS 800/6-8
1300 Walsh Tarlton Ln 78746 512-732-9220
Kathleen Sullivan, prin. Fax 732-9229
West Ridge MS 900/6-8
9201 Scenic Bluff Dr 78733 512-732-9240
Karl Waggoner, prin. Fax 732-9249
Other Schools – See West Lake Hills

Lake Travis ISD 5,600/PK-12
3322 Ranch Rd 620 S 78738 512-533-6000
Dr. Rockwell Kirk, supt. Fax 533-6001
www.laketravis.txed.net
Hudson Bend MS 500/6-8
15600 Lariat Trl 78734 512-533-6400
Debbie Aceves, prin. Fax 533-6401
Lake Pointe ES 600/K-5
11801 Sonoma Dr 78738 512-533-6500
Heidi Gudelman, prin. Fax 533-6501
Lake Travis ES 700/PK-5
15303 Kollmeyer Dr 78734 512-533-6300
Karen Miller-Kopp, prin. Fax 533-6301
Lake Travis MS 800/6-8
3328 Ranch Road 620 S 78738 512-533-6200
Russell Maedgen, prin. Fax 533-6201
Lakeway ES 700/K-5
1701 Lohmans Crossing Rd 78734 512-533-6350
Samuel Hicks, prin. Fax 533-6351
Serene Hills ES K-5
3301 Serene Hills Dr 78738 512-533-7400
Allison Cobb, prin. Fax 533-7401
Other Schools – See Bee Cave

Leander ISD
Supt. — See Leander
Bush ES 1,100/PK-5
12600 Country Trails Ln 78732 512-435-4750
Terri Breaux, prin. Fax 435-4763
Canyon Ridge MS 800/6-8
12601 Country Trl 78732 512-434-7550
Susan Sullivan, prin. Fax 434-7555
Grandview Hills ES 300/K-5
12024 Vista Parke Dr 78726 512-434-7266
Brenda Cruz, prin. Fax 434-7280
River Place ES 600/K-5
6500 Sitio Del Rio Blvd 78730 512-434-7026
Paul Smith, prin. Fax 434-7040
River Ridge ES K-5
12900 Tierra Grande Trl 78732 512-570-7310
Jim Rose, prin. Fax 570-4635
Rutledge ES 600/PK-5
11501 Staked Plains Dr 78717 512-435-4626
Jana Rueter, prin. Fax 435-4635
Steiner Ranch ES 900/K-5
4001 N Quinlan Park Rd 78732 512-434-7100
Shirley Bennett, prin. Fax 434-7105

Manor ISD
Supt. — See Manor
Bluebonnet Trail ES 800/PK-5
11316 Farmhaven Rd 78754 512-278-4125
Debby Ewald, prin. Fax 278-4140
Decker ES 900/PK-5
8500 Decker Ln 78724 512-278-4141
Leslie Whitworth, prin. Fax 278-4142
Decker MS 6-8
8104 Decker Ln 78724 512-278-4630
J. Manuel Garcia, prin. Fax 278-4017
Oak Meadows ES PK-5
5600 Decker Ln 78724 512-278-4328
Deborah Manhart, prin. Fax 278-4017

Pflugerville ISD
Supt. — See Pflugerville
Copperfield ES 800/PK-5
12135 Thompkins Dr 78753 512-594-5800
Dr. Sandra Bell, prin. Fax 594-5805
Delco PS 600/PK-2
12900 Dessau Rd Ste A 78754 512-594-6200
Tammy Rebecek, prin. Fax 594-6205
Dessau ES 500/3-5
1501 Dessau Ridge Ln 78754 512-594-4600
Araceli Soliz, prin. Fax 594-4605
Dessau MS 1,000/6-8
12900 Dessau Rd 78754 512-594-2600
Diana Sustaita, prin. Fax 594-2605
Northwest ES 500/PK-5
14014 Thermal Dr 78728 512-594-4400
Criss Wakefield, prin. Fax 594-4405
Parmer Lane ES 700/PK-5
1806 W Parmer Ln 78727 512-594-4000
Mario Acosta, prin. Fax 594-4005
River Oaks ES 500/PK-5
12401 Scofield Farms Dr 78758 512-594-5000
Jasmin Khan, prin. Fax 594-5005
Westview MS 800/6-8
1805 Scofield Ln 78727 512-594-2200
Ronald Gonzales, prin. Fax 594-2205

Round Rock ISD
Supt. — See Round Rock
Anderson Mill ES 400/PK-5
10610 Salt Mill Holw 78750 512-428-3700
Rebecca Lavender, prin. Fax 428-3790
Canyon Creek ES 600/K-5
10210 Ember Glen Dr 78726 512-428-2800
Eleece Moffatt, prin. Fax 428-2890
Canyon Vista MS 1,000/6-8
8455 Spicewood Springs Rd 78759 512-464-8100
Barbara Paris, prin. Fax 464-8210
Caraway ES 500/PK-5
11104 Oak View Dr 78759 512-464-5500
Shelly Hohmann, prin. Fax 464-5590
Cedar Valley MS 1,400/6-8
8139 Racine Trl 78717 512-428-2300
Jane Miller, prin. Fax 428-2420
Deerpark MS 1,100/6-8
8849 Anderson Mill Rd 78729 512-464-6600
Sonya Hayes, prin. Fax 464-6740
Forest North ES 700/PK-5
13414 Broadmeade Ave 78729 512-464-6750
Mary Patterson, prin. Fax 464-6794
Grisham MS 700/6-8
10805 School House Ln 78750 512-428-2650
Mary Brinkman, prin. Fax 428-2790
Jollyville ES 500/PK-5
6720 Corpus Christi Dr 78729 512-428-2200
Sonja Howard, prin. Fax 428-2299
Laurel Mountain ES 800/K-5
10111 D K Ranch Rd 78759 512-464-4300
Jan Richards, prin. Fax 464-4390
Live Oak ES 500/PK-5
8607 Anderson Mill Rd 78729 512-428-3800
Mary Morris, prin. Fax 428-3890
Pond Springs ES 700/PK-5
7825 Elkhorn Mountain Trl 78729 512-464-4200
Edie Binns, prin. Fax 464-4290
Purple Sage ES 400/PK-5
11801 Tanglebriar Trl 78750 512-428-3500
Cindy Walker, prin. Fax 428-3590
Sommer ES K-5
16200 Avery Ranch Blvd 78717 512-704-0600
Mark Pratz, prin. Fax 704-0690
Spicewood ES 700/PK-5
11601 Olson Dr 78750 512-428-3600
Beth June, prin. Fax 428-3690
Wells Branch ES 800/PK-5
14650 Merriltown Rd 78728 512-428-3400
Belinda Cini, prin. Fax 428-3490

All Saints' Episcopal S 100/PK-K
209 W 27th St 78705 512-472-8866
Cindy LaPorte, dir. Fax 477-5215
Austin Adventist Junior Academy 50/K-10
PO Box 340370 78734 512-459-8976
Rhonda Hight, prin. Fax 419-7868
Austin City Academy 50/K-12
PO Box 92737 78709 512-288-4883
Stan Whitmore, prin. Fax 857-0765
Austin Montessori S 300/PK-9
5006 Sunset Trl 78745 512-892-0253
Donna Goertz, admin. Fax 891-9875
Austin Waldorf S 400/K-12
8700 S View Rd 78737 512-288-5942
Susan Darcy, admin. Fax 301-8997
Bannockburn Baptist S 100/PK-8
7100 Brodie Ln 78745 512-892-0000
Brenda Russell, prin. Fax 892-7669
Brentwood Christian S 800/PK-12
11908 N Lamar Blvd 78753 512-835-5983
Marquita Moss, pres. Fax 835-2184
Cathedral of St. Mary S 200/PK-8
910 San Jacinto Blvd 78701 512-476-1480
David O'Connell, prin. Fax 476-9922
Children's S 200/PK-2
2825 Hancock Dr 78731 512-453-1126
Sheryl Wallin, prin. Fax 302-0320
City S 100/PK-8
1700 Woodland Ave 78741 512-416-7744
Chris Fisher, dir. Fax 444-7553
Girls' School of Austin 100/K-8
2007 McCall Rd 78703 512-478-7827
Lisa Schmitt, hdmstr. Fax 478-5456
Good Shepherd Episcopal S 200/PK-K
2206 Exposition Blvd 78703 512-476-4393
Jeanie Stark, hdmstr. Fax 476-1167
Hill Country Christian S of Austin 500/PK-12
12124 Ranch Road 620 N 78750 512-331-7036
Bill McGee, hdmstr. Fax 257-4190
Holy Family Catholic S 500/PK-8
9400 Neenah Ave 78717 512-246-4455
Falba Turner, prin. Fax 246-4454
Holy Word Lutheran S 100/K-8
10601 Bluff Bend Dr 78753 512-836-0660
Kyle Raymond, prin. Fax 836-2135
Hyde Park Baptist S 800/K-12
3901 Speedway 78751 512-465-8333
Brian Littlefield, supt. Fax 371-1433
Legacy Oaks Christian S 100/PK-12
7915 Manchaca Rd 78745 512-326-2286
Gail Padovani, dir. Fax 326-9014
Menachem Hebrew Academy 50/PK-8
7010 Village Center Dr 78731 512-343-2500
Our Savior Lutheran S 100/PK-5
1513 E Yager Ln 78753 512-836-9600
Donn Trautner, prin. Fax 836-4660
Rawson-Saunders School 100/1-8
2600 Exposition Blvd 78703 512-476-8382
Laura Steinbach, hdmstr. Fax 476-1132
Reedemer Lutheran S 500/PK-8
1500 W Anderson Ln 78757 512-451-6478
Glen Kieschnick, prin. Fax 610-8809
Regents S of Austin 800/K-12
3230 Travis Country Cir 78735 512-899-8095
Roderick Gilbert, hdmstr. Fax 899-8623
St. Andrew's Episcopal S 500/1-8
1112 W 31st St 78705 512-299-9800
Lucy Nazro, hdmstr. Fax 299-9822
St. Austin S 200/K-8
1911 San Antonio St 78705 512-477-3751
Donna Woodard, prin. Fax 477-3079
St. Gabriel's Catholic S 400/PK-8
2500 Wimberly Ln 78735 512-327-7755
Misty Poe, prin. Fax 327-4334
St. Ignatius Martyr S 300/PK-8
120 W Oltorf St 78704 512-442-8547
Todd Blahnik, prin. Fax 442-8685
St. Louis S 400/PK-8
2114 Saint Joseph Blvd 78757 512-454-0384
Carol Bruns, prin. Fax 454-7252
St. Martin's Lutheran S 200/PK-K
606 W 15th St 78701 512-476-4037
Linda Easterwood, dir. Fax 473-2946
St. Matthew's Episcopal S 200/PK-K
8134 Mesa Dr 78759 512-345-3040
Pam Littlefield, dir. Fax 345-5866
St. Paul Lutheran S 200/PK-8
3407 Red River St 78705 512-472-3313
Mary Eifert, prin. Fax 469-0785
St. Theresa's S 400/PK-8
4311 Small Dr 78731 512-451-7105
Gracie Burback, prin. Fax 451-8808
Shoreline Christian S 200/PK-6
15201 Burnet Rd 78728 512-310-7358
Richard Tankersley, hdmstr. Fax 255-5955
Strickland Christian S 200/K-8
PO Box 150413 78715 512-447-1447
Fax 447-6225
Trinity Episcopal S of Austin 300/K-8
3901 Bee Caves Rd 78746 512-472-9525
Liza Lee, hdmstr. Fax 472-2337

Avalon, Ellis

Avalon ISD 200/PK-12
PO Box 455 76623 972-627-3251
David Del Bosque, supt. Fax 627-3220
avalon.tx.schoolwebpages.com/education/
Avalon S 200/PK-12
PO Box 455 76623 972-627-3251
Margret Day, prin. Fax 627-3220

Avery, Red River, Pop. 440

Avery ISD 300/PK-12
150 San Antonio St 75554 903-684-3460
Barry Bassett, supt. Fax 684-3294
www.averyisd.net/
Avery ES 200/PK-5
150 San Antonio St 75554 903-684-3116
Sue Jackson, prin. Fax 684-3294

Avinger, Cass, Pop. 455

Avinger ISD 100/K-12
245 Conner 75630 903-562-1271
Douglas Carter, supt. Fax 562-1271
www.avingerisd.net/
Avinger ES 100/K-6
245 Conner 75630 903-562-1355
Kenny Abernathy, prin. Fax 562-1271

Axtell, McLennan

Axtell ISD 600/PK-12
308 Ottawa 76624 254-863-5301
Stanley Harris, supt. Fax 863-5651
www.axtellisd.net/
Axtell ES 300/PK-5
1178 Longhorn Pkwy 76624 254-863-5419
Betty Somers, prin. Fax 863-5944
Axtell MS 200/6-8
308 Ottawa 76624 254-863-5301
Dale Monsey, prin. Fax 863-5651

Azle, Tarrant, Pop. 10,350

Azle ISD 5,800/PK-12
300 Roe St 76020 817-444-3235
Waldon Hafley, supt. Fax 444-6866
www.azleisd.net

Azle ES 500/5-6
301 Church St 76020 817-444-1312
Darcy Simmons, prin. Fax 444-6934
Azle JHS 500/7-8
201 School St 76020 817-444-2564
Stacey Summerhill, prin. Fax 270-0880
Cross Timbers ES 500/K-4
831 Jackson Trl 76020 817-444-3802
Dee Gilley, prin. Fax 444-0730
Forte JHS 400/7-8
479 Sandy Beach Rd 76020 817-270-1133
David McClellan, prin. Fax 270-1157
Hoover ES 400/5-6
484 Sandy Beach Rd 76020 817-444-7766
Lynne Trevino, prin. Fax 270-1425
Liberty ES 400/PK-4
11450 Liberty School Rd 76020 817-444-1317
Debra Vaughan, prin. Fax 444-1937
Silver Creek ES 400/K-4
10300 S FM 730 76020 817-444-0257
Jackie Spitzer, prin. Fax 270-2383
Walnut Creek ES 500/PK-4
1010 Boyd Rd 76020 817-444-4045
Todd Smith, prin. Fax 270-1576
Other Schools – See Fort Worth

Springtown ISD
Supt. — See Springtown
Reno ES 500/PK-4
172 W Reno Rd 76020 817-221-5001
Traunsa Reeves, prin. Fax 677-1214

Azle Christian S 100/K-12
1801 S Stewart St 76020 817-444-9964
Randy Rosamond, admin. Fax 444-9914
Royal Christian Academy 50/K-8
PO Box 96 76098 817-925-3774
Delma Sue Nielsen, dir.

Bacliff, Galveston, Pop. 5,549
Dickinson ISD
Supt. — See Dickinson
Little ES 900/PK-4
622 Oklahoma Ave 77518 281-229-7000
Melissa Williams, prin. Fax 229-7001

Baird, Callahan, Pop. 1,680
Baird ISD 300/PK-12
PO Box 1147 79504 325-854-1400
Edgar Camacho, supt. Fax 854-2058
www.baird.esc14.net
Baird S 200/PK-8
PO Box 1147 79504 325-854-1400
Jarod Bellar, prin. Fax 854-2327

Balch Springs, Dallas, Pop. 19,475
Mesquite ISD
Supt. — See Mesquite
Gray ES 600/PK-6
3500 Pioneer Rd 75180 972-882-7280
Karen Lloyd, prin. Fax 882-7288
Hodges ES 600/PK-6
14401 Spring Oaks Dr 75180 972-290-4040
Elaine Whitlock, prin. Fax 290-4046

Ballinger, Runnels, Pop. 4,019
Ballinger ISD 1,000/PK-12
PO Box 231 76821 325-365-3588
Laura Strube, supt. Fax 365-5920
ballinger.netxv.net/
Ballinger ES 500/PK-5
PO Box 231 76821 325-365-3527
Brian Arrott, prin. Fax 365-2943
Ballinger JHS 200/6-8
PO Box 231 76821 325-365-3537
Mike Carter, prin. Fax 365-5420

Balmorhea, Reeves, Pop. 472
Balmorhea ISD 200/PK-12
PO Box 368 79718 432-375-2223
Mary Lou Carrasco, supt. Fax 375-2511
www.bisdbears.esc18.net
Balmorhea S 200/PK-12
PO Box 368 79718 432-375-2223
Teri Barragan, prin. Fax 375-2511

Bandera, Bandera, Pop. 1,123
Bandera ISD 2,500/PK-12
PO Box 727 78003 830-796-3313
Kevin Dyes Ed.D., supt. Fax 796-6238
www.banderaisd.net
Alkek ES 600/PK-5
PO Box 727 78003 830-796-6223
Jon Orozco, prin. Fax 796-6232
Bandera MS 600/6-8
PO Box 727 78003 830-796-6270
Gary Bitzkie, prin. Fax 796-6277
Other Schools – See Pipe Creek

Bangs, Brown, Pop. 1,623
Bangs ISD 1,000/PK-12
PO Box 969 76823 325-752-6612
Bill Foster, supt. Fax 752-6253
www.bangsisd.net
Bangs MS 300/5-8
PO Box 969 76823 325-752-6088
John Schaefer, prin. Fax 752-6367
Stephens ES 500/PK-4
PO Box 969 76823 325-752-7236
Mike Cofresi, prin. Fax 752-6974

Banquete, Nueces
Banquete ISD 900/PK-12
PO Box 369 78339 361-387-2551
Jim Rumage, supt. Fax 387-7188
www.banqueteisd.esc2.net/
Banquete ES 400/PK-5
PO Box 369 78339 361-387-4329
Debra Litton, prin. Fax 767-8105
Banquete JHS 200/6-8
PO Box 369 78339 361-387-6504
Eusebio Torres, prin. Fax 387-7051

Barksdale, Edwards
Nueces Canyon Consolidated ISD 300/K-12
PO Box 118 78828 830-234-3514
Russ Perry, supt. Fax 234-3435
www.nccisd.net/
Other Schools – See Camp Wood

Bartlett, Bell, Pop. 1,701
Bartlett ISD 400/PK-12
PO Box 170 76511 254-527-4247
Michael Mayfield, supt. Fax 527-3340
www.bartlett.txed.net/
Bartlett ES 200/PK-6
PO Box 170 76511 254-527-3352
Allen Reese, prin. Fax 527-3441

Bastrop, Bastrop, Pop. 7,297
Bastrop ISD 8,200/PK-12
906 Farm St 78602 512-321-2292
Roderick Emanuel, supt. Fax 321-7469
www.bastrop.isd.tenet.edu
Bastrop IS 600/5-6
509 Old Austin Hwy 78602 512-321-6023
Merv Doherty, prin. Fax 321-4348
Bastrop MS 600/7-8
709 Old Austin Hwy 78602 512-321-3911
James Richardson, prin. Fax 321-1557
Bluebonnet ES 600/PK-4
416 FM 1209 78602 512-308-1325
Richard Batlle, prin. Fax 308-1306
Emile ES 500/K-4
601 Martin Luther King Dr 78602 512-321-4451
Terrell King, prin. Fax 321-3564
Lost Pines ES 700/PK-4
151 Tiger Woods Dr 78602 512-321-2086
Denise Rogers, prin. Fax 321-2385
Mina ES 600/PK-4
1203 Hill St 78602 512-321-2565
Kelly McBride, prin. Fax 321-4354
Other Schools – See Cedar Creek, Red Rock

Batesville, Zavala, Pop. 1,313
Uvalde Consolidated ISD
Supt. — See Uvalde
Batesville S 100/PK-8
Highway 117 78829 830-376-4221
Mary Diaz, prin. Fax 376-4223

Bay City, Matagorda, Pop. 18,323
Bay City ISD 3,700/PK-12
520 7th St 77414 979-245-5766
Keith Brown, supt. Fax 245-3175
www.bcblackcats.net
Bay City IS 300/4-5
2417 16th St 77414 979-245-4864
Heath Koenig, prin. Fax 245-5920
Bay City JHS 600/6-8
1507 Sycamore Ave 77414 979-245-6345
Brandon Hood, prin. Fax 245-1419
Cherry ES 400/PK-3
2509 8th St 77414 979-245-6341
Barbara Gordon, prin. Fax 245-1702
Holmes ES 600/PK-3
3200 5th St 77414 979-245-4818
Jessica Estlinbaum, prin. Fax 245-1645
McAllister IS 300/4-5
4100 Hiram Brandon Dr 77414 979-245-5591
Lisa Moya, prin. Fax 245-1451
Roberts ES 400/PK-3
1212 Whitson St 77414 979-245-8331
Melissa Carroll, prin. Fax 245-1573

Holy Cross S 100/K-6
2001 Katy Ave 77414 979-245-5632
Sr. Geraldine Pavlik, prin. Fax 245-6120

Baytown, Harris, Pop. 68,371
Goose Creek Consolidated ISD 20,400/PK-12
PO Box 30 77522 281-420-4800
Dr. Toby York, supt. Fax 420-4815
www.gccisd.net/
Alamo ES 600/K-5
302 W Wye Dr 77521 281-420-4595
Ruth Perrin, prin. Fax 420-4905
Austin ES 1,000/K-5
3022 Massey Tompkins Rd 77521 281-420-4620
Laura Smith, prin. Fax 420-4899
Baytown JHS 800/6-8
7707 Bayway Dr 77520 281-420-4560
Steve Koester, prin. Fax 420-4908
Bowie ES 600/PK-5
2200 Clayton Dr 77520 281-420-4605
Ginger McKay, prin. Fax 420-4609
Carver ES 700/PK-5
600 S Pruett St 77520 281-420-4600
Rachel DeLeon, prin. Fax 420-4983
Cedar Bayou JHS 1,000/6-8
2610 Elvinta St 77520 281-420-4570
Barbara Ardoin, prin. Fax 420-4909
Crockett ES 800/PK-5
4500 Barkaloo Rd 77521 281-420-4645
Jaime Lannou, prin. Fax 420-4649
De Zavala ES 800/PK-5
305 Tri City Beach Rd 77520 281-420-4920
Robin Stoerner, prin. Fax 420-4342
Gentry JHS 1,000/6-8
1919 E Archer Rd 77521 281-420-4590
Tammy Edwards, prin. Fax 420-4909
Harlem ES 700/PK-5
3333 East Fwy 77521 281-420-4910
Michael Wahl, prin. Fax 426-5358
Lamar ES 900/PK-5
816 N Pruett St 77520 281-420-4625
Greg Lynd, prin. Fax 420-4626
Mann JHS 1,000/6-8
310 S Highway 146 77520 281-420-4585
Michael Coopersmith, prin. Fax 420-4664
San Jacinto ES 500/PK-5
2615 Virginia St 77520 281-420-4670
Becky Robins, prin. Fax 420-4599

Smith ES 700/PK-5
403 E James St 77520 281-420-4615
Suzanna Raymundo, prin. Fax 420-4940
Travis ES 800/PK-5
100 Robin Rd 77520 281-420-4660
Brenda Hastings-Gongora, prin. Fax 420-4986
Walker ES 700/PK-5
4711 Seabird St 77521 281-420-1800
Suzanne Keith, prin. Fax 421-3204
Other Schools – See Highlands

Baytown Christian Academy 200/PK-4
302 W Cedar Bayou Lynchburg 77521
281-421-2597
Dr. Carolyn Brock, hdmstr. Fax 421-9845
St. Joseph S 100/PK-6
1811 Carolina St 77520 281-422-9749
Ann Mullins, prin. Fax 422-3044
San Jacinto Christian Academy 100/PK-12
301 Ilfrey St 77520 281-424-9525
Fax 424-1600

Beasley, Fort Bend, Pop. 673
Lamar Consolidated ISD
Supt. — See Rosenberg
Beasley ES 300/PK-5
PO Box 121 77417 832-223-1100
Doris Goates, prin. Fax 223-1101

Beaumont, Jefferson, Pop. 111,799
Beaumont ISD 18,600/PK-12
3395 Harrison Ave 77706 409-899-9972
Dr. Carrol Thomas, supt. Fax 923-1025
www.beaumont.k12.tx.us
Amelia ES 400/PK-5
565 S Major Dr 77707 409-617-6000
Holley Hancock, prin. Fax 617-6024
Austin MS 500/6-8
3410 Austin St 77706 409-617-5800
Dr. Aaron Covington, prin. Fax 617-5823
Bingman ES 200/K-5
5265 Kenneth Ave 77705 409-838-5259
Lisa Bolton, prin. Fax 785-3453
Blanchette ES 200/K-5
5265 Kenneth Ave 77705 409-617-6275
Barbara Hardeman, prin. Fax 617-6298
Caldwood ES 600/PK-5
102 Berkshire Ln 77707 409-835-3818
Jim Melanson, prin. Fax 785-3501
Curtis ES 600/K-5
6225 N Circuit Dr 77706 409-617-6050
Susan Brown, prin. Fax 617-6073
Dishman ES 700/PK-5
3475 Champions Dr 77707 409-617-6250
Paul Shipman, prin. Fax 617-6274
Dunbar ES 400/PK-5
825 Jackson St 77701 409-832-7617
Iris Williams, prin. Fax 617-6098
Fehl ES 300/K-5
3350 Blanchette St 77701 409-835-3871
Cynthia Washington, prin. Fax 617-3871
Field ES 300/PK-5
4315 Concord Rd 77703 409-892-1661
Philip Brooks, prin. Fax 617-6348
Fletcher ES 600/K-5
1055 Avenue F 77701 409-833-3831
Mike Gonzales, prin. Fax 617-6123
French ES 300/K-5
3525 Cleveland St 77703 409-832-6631
Jackie Lavergne, prin. Fax 617-6346
Guess ES 700/PK-5
8055 Voth Rd 77708 409-892-9702
Hoyt Simmons, prin. Fax 923-5280
Homer Drive ES 400/PK-5
8950 Homer Dr 77708 409-892-9420
Ava Colbert, prin. Fax 617-6248
King MS 400/6-8
1400 Avenue A 77701 409-617-5850
Michael Shelton, prin. Fax 617-5873
Lucas ES 400/K-5
1750 E Lucas Dr 77703 409-892-9683
Martha Fowler, prin. Fax 617-6446
Marshall MS 800/6-8
6455 Gladys Ave 77706 409-617-5900
Shannon Pier, prin. Fax 617-5924
Martin ES 500/PK-5
3500 Pine St 77703 409-617-6425
Ted Stuberfield, prin. Fax 617-6448
Odom Academy 800/6-8
2550 W Virginia St 77705 409-617-5925
Tillie Hickman, prin. Fax 617-5949
Ogden ES 300/K-5
2300 Victoria St 77701 409-833-2313
Wayne Wells, prin. Fax 617-6173
Pietzsch/MacArthur ES 900/PK-5
4301 Highland Ave 77705 409-835-2505
Linda Thomas, prin. Fax 617-6498
Price ES 200/PK-5
3350 Waverly St 77705 409-617-6375
Rachel Jones, prin. Fax 617-3757
Regina-Howell ES 700/PK-5
5850 Regina Ln 77706 409-892-5045
Rose Hardy, prin. Fax 923-5203
Smith MS 400/6-8
4415 Concord Rd 77703 409-617-5825
Carol Batiste, prin. Fax 617-5848
South Park MS 400/6-8
4500 Highland Ave 77705 409-617-5875
Odis Norris, prin. Fax 617-5899
Vincent MS 900/6-8
350 Eldridge Dr 77707 409-617-5950
Randall Maxwell, prin. Fax 617-5974

Hamshire-Fannett ISD
Supt. — See Hamshire
Hamshire-Fannett ES 500/PK-3
23395 Burrell Wingate Rd 77705 409-794-1412
Karen Reneau, prin. Fax 794-1049

Hamshire-Fannett IS 400/4-6
11407 Dugat Rd 77705 409-794-1558
Stephen Edwards, prin. Fax 794-1787
Hamshire-Fannett MS 300/7-8
11375 Dugat Rd 77705 409-794-2361
Mark Martin, prin. Fax 794-3042

All Saints Episcopal S 400/PK-8
4108 Delaware St 77706 409-892-1755
Scootie Clark, hdmstr. Fax 892-0166
Cathedral Christian S 200/PK-6
2350 Eastex Fwy 77703 409-892-1503
Jeb Airey, dir. Fax 898-1506
Montessori S on 11th Street 50/PK-4
2510 N 11th St Ste C 77703 409-899-5002
LaVonne Dobson, prin.
Our Mother of Mercy S 100/PK-5
3360 Sarah St 77705 409-842-5534
Dolores Fulton, prin. Fax 842-4001
St. Anne S 600/PK-8
375 N 11th St 77702 409-832-5939
Kathy Attaway Ph.D., prin. Fax 832-4655
St. Anthony Cathedral S 200/PK-8
850 Forsythe St 77701 409-832-3486
Phyllis Walters, prin. Fax 838-9051

Beckville, Panola, Pop. 760
Beckville ISD 600/PK-12
PO Box 37 75631 903-678-3311
Devin Tate, supt. Fax 678-2157
www.beckvilleisd.net/
Beckville Sunset ES 300/PK-5
PO Box 37 75631 903-678-3601
Bruce Hawkins, prin. Fax 678-2257

Bedford, Tarrant, Pop. 48,390
Hurst-Euless-Bedford ISD 20,200/PK-12
1849 Central Dr Ste A 76022 817-283-4461
Gene Buinger Ed.D., supt. Fax 354-3311
www.hebisd.edu
Bedford Heights ES 700/K-6
1000 Cummings Dr 76021 817-788-3150
Brad Mengwasser, prin. Fax 788-3112
Bell Manor ES 700/PK-6
1300 Winchester Way 76022 817-354-3370
Stephanie Smith, prin. Fax 354-3374
Meadow Creek ES 600/PK-6
3001 Harwood Rd 76021 817-354-3500
Mike Wagner, prin. Fax 354-3329
Shady Brook ES 600/K-6
2601 Shady Brook Dr 76021 817-354-3513
Monica Stennis, prin. Fax 354-3336
Spring Garden ES 600/PK-6
2400 Cummings Dr 76021 817-354-3395
Paul McCollum, prin. Fax 354-3337
Stonegate ES 600/K-6
900 Bedford Rd 76022 817-285-3250
Sharon Wynn, prin. Fax 285-3210
Other Schools – See Euless, Fort Worth, Hurst

St. Vincent's Cathedral S 200/PK-8
1300 Forest Ridge Dr 76022 817-354-7979
Dr. Mary Dickerson, hdmstr. Fax 354-5073

Bee Cave, Travis, Pop. 1,538
Lake Travis ISD
Supt. — See Austin
Bee Cave ES 600/K-5
14300 Hamilton Pool Rd 78738 512-533-6250
Janie Braxdale, prin. Fax 533-6251

Beeville, Bee, Pop. 13,560
Beeville ISD 3,100/PK-12
2400 N Saint Marys St 78102 361-358-7111
Dr. John Hardwick, supt. Fax 358-7837
www.beevilleisd.net/
FMC ES 400/1-5
100 Pfeil Ln 78102 361-362-6050
Joni Barber, prin. Fax 362-6054
Hall ES 400/1-5
1100 W Huntington St 78102 361-362-6060
Martina Villarreal, prin. Fax 362-6059
Hampton-Moreno-Dugat ECC 400/PK-K
2000 S Mussett 78102 361-362-6040
Belinda Aguirre, prin. Fax 362-6049
Jefferson ES 200/1-5
701 E Hayes St 78102 361-362-6070
Sarah Jaure, prin. Fax 362-6069
Moreno MS 600/6-8
301 N Minnesota St 78102 361-358-6262
Jean Blankenship, prin. Fax 362-6092

First Baptist Church S 100/PK-6
PO Box 519 78104 361-358-4161
Yolanda Silva, dir. Fax 358-4163
St. Philip's Episcopal S 100/PK-6
105 N Adams St 78102 361-358-6242
Sandra Keller, hdmstr. Fax 358-8232

Bellaire, Harris, Pop. 17,206
Houston ISD
Supt. — See Houston
Condit ES 600/PK-5
7000 S 3rd St 77401 713-295-5255
Frederick Bowyer, prin. Fax 668-5738
Gordon ES 400/PK-5
6300 Avenue B 77401 713-295-5276
Trealla Epps, prin. Fax 662-3527
Horn ES 500/K-5
4535 Pine St 77401 713-295-5264
Sarah Cordray-Harrington, prin. Fax 295-5286
Pin Oak MS 1,200/6-8
4601 Glenmont St 77401 713-295-6500
Michael McDonough, prin. Fax 295-6511

Post Oak S 300/PK-8
4600 Bissonnet St 77401 713-661-6688
John Long, hdmstr. Fax 661-4959

Veritas Christian Academy of Houston 200/PK-8
7000 Ferris St 77401 713-773-9605
Lamia Raad, hdmstr. Fax 773-9753

Bellevue, Clay, Pop. 397
Bellevue ISD 200/K-12
PO Box 38 76228 940-928-2104
Dean Gilstrap, supt. Fax 928-2583
www.bellevueisd.org/
Bellevue S 200/K-12
PO Box 38 76228 940-928-2104
Terry Davis, prin. Fax 928-2583

Bells, Grayson, Pop. 1,270
Bells ISD 800/PK-12
PO Box 7 75414 903-965-7721
Joe D. Moore, supt. Fax 965-7036
bells.ednet10.net/
Bells ES 400/PK-6
PO Box 7 75414 903-965-7725
Rebeckah Pritchard, prin. Fax 965-0140
Prichard JHS 100/7-8
PO Box 7 75414 903-965-4835
Sara Baker, prin. Fax 965-7428

Bellville, Austin, Pop. 4,303
Bellville ISD 2,200/PK-12
518 S Mathews St 77418 979-865-3133
John Conley, supt. Fax 865-8591
www.bellville.k12.tx.us
Bellville JHS 500/6-8
518 S Mathews St 77418 979-865-5966
Laura Bailey, prin. Fax 865-7060
O'Bryant IS 200/4-5
518 S Mathews St 77418 979-865-3671
Natalie Neumann, prin. Fax 865-7049
O'Bryant PS 500/PK-3
518 S Mathews St 77418 979-865-5907
Paul Aschenbeck, prin. Fax 865-7039
Other Schools – See Industry

Faith Academy 200/PK-12
12177 Highway 36 77418 979-865-1811
Merlene Byler, admin. Fax 865-2454

Belton, Bell, Pop. 15,530
Belton ISD 8,400/PK-12
PO Box 269 76513 254-215-2000
Dr. Vivian Baker, supt. Fax 215-2001
www.bisd.net
Belton MS 900/6-8
1704 Sparta Rd 76513 254-215-2800
Joe Brown, prin. Fax 215-2801
Lakewood ES 700/K-5
11200 FM 2305 76513 254-215-3100
Judy Schiller, prin. Fax 215-3101
Leon Heights ES 300/PK-5
1501 N Main St 76513 254-215-3200
Barrett Pollard, prin. Fax 215-3201
Miller Heights ES 400/PK-5
1110 Fairway Dr 76513 254-215-3300
Tammy Becker, prin. Fax 215-3301
Southwest ES 500/K-5
611 Saunders St 76513 254-215-3500
Roxanne Sanders, prin. Fax 215-3501
Sparta ES 700/PK-5
1800 Sparta Rd 76513 254-215-3600
Amy Armstrong, prin. Fax 215-3601
Tyler ES 600/PK-5
501 E 4th Ave 76513 254-215-3700
Sybil Collins, prin. Fax 215-3701
Other Schools – See Temple

Benavides, Duval, Pop. 1,591
Benavides ISD 500/PK-12
PO Box P 78341 361-256-3000
Dr. Ignacio Salinas, supt. Fax 256-3002
www.benavidesisd.net/
Benavides ES 300/PK-6
PO Box P 78341 361-256-3030
Rick Kee, prin. Fax 256-3032

Ben Bolt, Jim Wells
Ben Bolt-Palito Blanco ISD 600/PK-12
PO Box 547 78342 361-664-9904
Dr. Grace Everett, supt. Fax 668-0446
www.bbpbisd.org/
Ben Bolt MS 200/4-8
PO Box 547 78342 361-664-9568
Gloria Venecia, prin. Fax 664-5235
Palito Blanco ES 200/PK-3
PO Box 547 78342 361-664-3201
Robert Lopez, prin. Fax 668-0549

Benbrook, Tarrant, Pop. 21,922
Fort Worth ISD
Supt. — See Fort Worth
Benbrook ES 500/K-5
800 Mercedes St 76126 817-249-7100
Shelly Anderson, prin. Fax 249-7104
Leonard MS 900/7-8
8900 Chapin Rd 76116 817-560-5630
Richard Pritchett, prin. Fax 560-5639
Leonard Sixth Grade S 400/6-6
4921 Benbrook Hwy 76116 817-570-4060
Nicole Houston Johnson, prin. Fax 570-4065
Waverly Park ES 800/PK-5
3604 Cimmaron Trl 76116 817-560-5660
Mary Marshall, prin. Fax 560-5685
Westpark ES 400/PK-5
10117 Westpark Dr 76126 817-249-7150
Richard Penland, prin. Fax 249-7164

Benjamin, Knox, Pop. 239
Benjamin ISD 100/K-12
PO Box 166 79505 940-459-2231
Olivia Gloria, supt. Fax 459-2007
www.benjaminisd.net/
Benjamin S 100/K-12
PO Box 166 79505 940-459-2231
Danny Copeland, prin. Fax 459-2007

Ben Wheeler, Van Zandt
Martins Mill ISD 500/PK-12
301 FM 1861 75754 903-479-3872
Todd Schneider, supt. Fax 479-3711
www.martinsmillisd.net
Martins Mill ES 300/PK-6
301 FM 1861 75754 903-479-3706
Suzzette Stringer, prin. Fax 479-3754

Bertram, Burnet, Pop. 1,304
Burnet Consolidated ISD
Supt. — See Burnet
Bertram ES 400/K-5
315 Main St 78605 512-355-2111
Carla Denison, prin. Fax 355-2261

Big Bend National Park, Brewster, Pop. 250
San Vicente ISD 50/K-8
PO Box 195 79834 432-477-2220
Shirley Coleman, supt. Fax 477-2221
www.svisd.com
San Vicente S 50/K-8
PO Box 195 79834 432-477-2220
Shirley Coleman, prin. Fax 477-2221

Big Lake, Reagan, Pop. 2,591
Reagan County ISD 700/PK-12
1111 E 12th St 76932 325-884-3705
Marshall Harrison, supt. Fax 884-3021
rcisd.esc18.net
Reagan County ES 400/PK-5
501 N Texas Ave 76932 325-884-3741
Ty Stevens, prin. Fax 884-2194
Reagan County MS 100/6-8
500 N Pennsylvania Ave 76932 325-884-3728
Glenn Byrd, prin. Fax 884-2327

Big Sandy, Upshur, Pop. 1,349
Big Sandy ISD 700/PK-12
PO Box 598 75755 903-636-5287
Scott Beene, supt. Fax 636-5111
www.bigsandyisd.org
Big Sandy ES 400/PK-5
PO Box 598 75755 903-636-5287
Donna Varnado, prin. Fax 636-5111
Big Sandy JHS 200/6-8
PO Box 598 75755 903-636-5287
Byron Jordan, prin. Fax 636-5111

Harmony ISD 1,000/PK-12
9788 State Highway 154 W 75755 903-725-5492
Jed Whitaker, supt. Fax 725-6737
www.harmonyeagles.com
Harmony JHS 200/6-8
9788 State Highway 154 W 75755 903-725-5485
Perry Cowan, prin. Fax 725-7270
Irons-Smith IS 200/4-5
9788 State Highway 154 W 75755 903-725-7077
Ginger Cargal, prin. Fax 725-7370
Poole ES 300/PK-3
9788 State Highway 154 W 75755 903-725-5496
Cara Rendon, prin. Fax 725-7078

Big Spring, Howard, Pop. 24,253
Big Spring ISD 3,800/K-12
708 E 11th Pl 79720 432-264-3600
Michael Stevens, supt. Fax 264-3646
bsisd.esc18.net/
Bauer Magnet ES 300/K-4
708 E 11th Pl 79720 432-264-4121
Wenda Christopher, prin. Fax 264-3646
Big Spring JHS 600/7-8
708 E 11th Pl 79720 432-264-4135
Coby Norman, prin. Fax 264-3646
Goliad IS 600/5-6
708 E 11th Pl 79720 432-264-4111
Tim Tannehill, prin. Fax 264-3646
Kentwood ES 200/K-4
708 E 11th Pl 79720 432-264-4130
Dana Byrd, prin. Fax 264-3646
Marcy ES 500/K-4
708 E 11th Pl 79720 432-264-4144
Brenda Dunlap, prin. Fax 264-3646
Moss ES 300/K-4
708 E 11th Pl 79720 432-264-4148
George Martin, prin. Fax 264-3646
Washington ES 300/K-4
708 E 11th Pl 79720 432-264-4126
Ruben Cervantes, prin. Fax 264-3646

Forsan ISD
Supt. — See Forsan
Elbow ES 300/K-5
5001 Nichols Rd 79720 432-398-5444
Steve Osborn, prin. Fax 398-5465

Big Wells, Dimmit, Pop. 750
Carrizo Springs Consolidated ISD
Supt. — See Carrizo Springs
Big Wells ES 100/PK-6
1312 Missouri 78830 830-457-2201
Ana Sulaica, prin. Fax 457-0024

Bishop, Nueces, Pop. 3,204
Bishop Consolidated ISD 1,200/PK-12
719 E 6th St 78343 361-584-3591
Christina Gutierrez, supt. Fax 584-3593
www.bishopcisd.esc2.net/
Bishop ES 200/4-6
200 S Fir Ave 78343 361-584-3571
Carmen Gonzalez, prin. Fax 584-3571
Bishop PS 300/PK-3
705 W Main St 78343 361-584-2434
Debbie Gonzalez, prin. Fax 584-7600
Luehrs JHS 200/7-8
701 E 6th St 78343 361-584-3576
Dan True, prin. Fax 584-3576
Other Schools – See Robstown

St. Paul Lutheran S 50/PK-3
801 E Main St 78343 361-584-2778
Susan Moerbe, prin. Fax 584-2691

Blackwell, Nolan, Pop. 348
Blackwell Consolidated ISD 100/PK-12
PO Box 505 79506 325-282-2311
James Bible, supt. Fax 282-2027
www.blackwell.esc14.net/
Blackwell S 100/PK-12
PO Box 505 79506 325-282-2311
Gary Smith, prin. Fax 282-2027

Blanco, Blanco, Pop. 1,609
Blanco ISD 1,000/PK-12
814 11th St 78606 830-833-4414
Dr. Jon Ford, supt. Fax 833-2019
www.blancoisd.com/
Blanco ES 400/PK-5
814 11th St 78606 830-833-4338
Scott Kvapil, prin. Fax 833-4389
Blanco MS 200/6-8
814 11th St 78606 830-833-5570
Jesse Salazar, prin. Fax 833-2507

Blanket, Brown, Pop. 404
Blanket ISD 200/K-12
901 Avenue H 76432 325-748-5311
Kevy Allred, supt. Fax 748-3391
blanket.netxv.net/
Blanket S 100/K-6
901 Avenue H 76432 325-748-3341
Brenda Tunnell, prin. Fax 748-2110

Blessing, Matagorda
Tidehaven ISD
Supt. — See Elmaton
Blessing ES 200/PK-5
PO Box 170 77419 361-588-6622
Kim Marceaux, prin. Fax 588-1150

Bloomburg, Cass, Pop. 371
Bloomburg ISD 200/PK-12
PO Box 156 75556 903-728-5151
Michael White, supt. Fax 728-5190
www.bloomburgisd.net
Bloomburg ES 100/PK-6
PO Box 156 75556 903-728-5216
Brian Stroman, prin. Fax 728-5399

Blooming Grove, Navarro, Pop. 918
Blooming Grove ISD 900/PK-12
PO Box 258 76626 903-695-2541
Michael Baldree, supt. Fax 695-2594
www.bgisd.org
Blooming Grove ES 400/PK-5
PO Box 258 76626 903-695-4401
David Brewer, prin. Fax 695-2009
Blooming Grove JHS 200/6-8
PO Box 258 76626 903-695-4201
Doyle Bell, prin. Fax 695-4601

Bloomington, Victoria, Pop. 1,888
Bloomington ISD 1,000/PK-12
PO Box 158 77951 361-897-1652
Brad Williams, supt. Fax 897-1214
www.bisd-tx.org/
Bloomington ES 300/PK-3
PO Box 668 77951 361-897-1121
Israel Salinas, prin. Fax 897-0212
Bloomington MS 100/7-8
PO Box 158 77951 361-897-2260
James Pieper, prin. Fax 897-3822
Other Schools – See Placedo

Blossom, Lamar, Pop. 1,486
Prairiland ISD
Supt. — See Pattonville
Blossom S 300/PK-8
310 High St 75416 903-982-5230
Glen Martin, prin. Fax 982-5260

Blue Ridge, Collin, Pop. 939
Blue Ridge ISD 600/PK-12
10688 County Road 504 75424 972-752-5554
Todd Lintzen, supt. Fax 752-9084
brisd.com
Blue Ridge ES 300/PK-5
425 N Church St 75424 972-752-5857
Andrew Seigrist, prin. Fax 752-9950
Blue Ridge S 100/6-8
318 School St 75424 972-752-4243
Danny Henderson, prin. Fax 752-5363

Bluff Dale, Erath
Bluff Dale ISD 100/K-8
PO Box 101 76433 254-728-3277
Ben Chaplin, supt. Fax 728-3298
www.bdisd.net/
Bluff Dale S 100/K-8
PO Box 101 76433 254-728-3277
Ben Chaplin, prin. Fax 728-3298

Blum, Hill, Pop. 443
Blum ISD 300/PK-12
PO Box 520 76627 254-874-5231
Nicholas Brown, supt. Fax 874-5233
www.blumisd.net
Blum ES 200/PK-5
PO Box 520 76627 254-874-5231
Mark Brandenberger, prin. Fax 874-5233

Boerne, Kendall, Pop. 8,054
Boerne ISD 6,200/PK-12
123 Johns Rd 78006 830-357-2000
Dr. John Kelly, supt. Fax 357-2009
www.boerne-isd.net
Cibolo Creek ES 500/K-6
300 Herff Ranch Blvd 78006 830-357-4400
Laurel Babb, prin. Fax 357-4499
Curington ES 700/PK-6
601 Adler St 78006 830-357-4000
Jean Perry, prin. Fax 357-4099
Fabra ES 700/PK-6
238 Lohmann St 78006 830-357-4200
Susan Light, prin. Fax 357-4299
Kendall ES 600/K-6
141 Old San Antonio Rd 78006 830-357-4600
Debbie Williams, prin. Fax 357-4699
Other Schools – See Fair Oaks Ranch

Geneva S 300/K-10
113 Cascade Caverns Rd 78015 830-775-6101
Brad Ryden, hdmstr. Fax 755-6102
Hill Country Montessori S 100/PK-6
50 Stone Wall Dr 78006 830-229-5377
Madellaine Costello, hdmstr. Fax 229-5378
Vanguard Christian Institute 100/PK-12
43360 Interstate 10 W 78006 830-537-5244
Walter Tracy, supt. Fax 537-5785

Bogata, Red River, Pop. 1,314
Rivercrest ISD 800/PK-12
4100 US Highway 271 S 75417 903-632-5203
Rickey Logan, supt. Fax 632-4691
www.rivercrestisd.net
Rivercrest ES 400/PK-5
4220 US Highway 271 S 75417 903-632-5214
Karla Coker, prin. Fax 632-2424
Rivercrest JHS 200/6-8
4100 US Highway 271 S 75417 903-632-0878
Stanley Jessee, prin. Fax 632-4691

Boling, Wharton, Pop. 1,119
Boling ISD 1,000/PK-12
PO Box 160 77420 979-657-2770
Charles Butcher, supt. Fax 657-3265
www.bolingisd.net
Iago JHS 200/6-8
PO Box 89 77420 979-657-2826
Bryan Blanar, prin. Fax 657-2828
Newgulf ES 500/PK-5
PO Box 9 77420 979-657-2837
Gerald Floyd, prin. Fax 657-3604

Bonham, Fannin, Pop. 10,556
Bonham ISD 1,900/K-12
PO Box 490 75418 903-583-5526
Sonny Cruse, supt. Fax 583-8463
www.bonhamisd.org/
Evans MS 400/4-6
1301 N Main St 75418 903-583-2914
Linda Staton, prin. Fax 583-7133
Finley-Oates ES 600/K-3
1901 Albert Broadfoot St 75418 903-640-4090
Mary Lou Fox, prin. Fax 640-8140
Rather JHS 300/7-8
1200 N Main St 75418 903-583-7474
Karol Alexander, prin. Fax 583-3713

Booker, Lipscomb, Pop. 1,330
Booker ISD 400/PK-12
PO Box 288 79005 806-658-4501
Mike Lee, supt. Fax 658-4503
www.bookerisd.net/
Booker ES, PO Box 288 79005 200/PK-4
Lisa Yauck, prin. 806-658-4559

Borger, Hutchinson, Pop. 13,305
Borger ISD 3,200/PK-12
200 E 9th St 79007 806-273-6481
Clifton Stephens, supt. Fax 273-1066
www.borgerisd.net
Belton ECC 400/PK-K
800 N McGee St 79007 806-273-1059
De'Lila Holder, prin. Fax 273-1070
Borger IS 600/5-5
1321 S Florida St 79007 806-273-4342
Randal Hatfield, prin. Fax 273-4343
Borger MS 600/6-8
1321 S Florida St 79007 806-273-1037
Matt Ammerman, prin. Fax 273-1069
Crockett ES 400/3-4
400 Kaye St 79007 806-273-1054
Jayson Hataway, prin. Fax 203-1067
Gateway ES 400/1-2
401 Tristram St 79007 806-273-1044
Kenneth Rosser, prin. Fax 273-1071

Bovina, Parmer, Pop. 1,804
Bovina ISD 500/PK-12
PO Box 70 79009 806-251-1336
Bill Bizzell, supt. Fax 251-1578
www.esc16.net/bovinaisd/
Bovina ES 200/PK-5
PO Box 70 79009 806-251-1316
Darla Sealey, prin. Fax 251-1578
Bovina JHS 100/6-8
PO Box 70 79009 806-251-1377
David Newhouse, prin. Fax 251-1578

Bowie, Montague, Pop. 5,543
Bowie ISD 1,500/PK-12
PO Box 1168 76230 940-872-1151
Greg Evans, supt. Fax 872-5979
www.bowieisd.net/
Bowie ES 600/PK-3
405 Lovers Ln 76230 940-872-3696
Anthony Taksin, prin. Fax 872-3041
Bowie IS 200/4-5
801 E Tarrant St 76230 940-872-1153
Steven Monkres, prin. Fax 872-8978
Bowie JHS 300/6-8
501 E Tarrant St 76230 940-872-1152
Tom McEwen, prin. Fax 872-8921

Gold-Burg ISD 200/K-12
468 Prater Rd 76230 940-872-3562
Kenny Miller, supt. Fax 872-5933
www.esc9.net/gold-burg/
Other Schools – See Ringgold

Boyd, Wise, Pop. 1,300
Boyd ISD 1,000/PK-12
PO Box 92308 76023 940-433-2327
Gregory Stone, supt. Fax 433-9569
www.boydisd.net
Boyd ES 300/PK-3
PO Box 92308 76023 940-433-2327
Furman Clark, prin. Fax 433-9536
Boyd IS 200/4-6
PO Box 92308 76023 940-433-2327
Anke Bracey, prin. Fax 433-9548
Boyd MS 200/7-8
PO Box 92308 76023 940-433-2327
Shawn Bryans, prin. Fax 433-9565

Boys Ranch, Oldham
Boys Ranch ISD 300/K-12
PO Box 219 79010 806-534-2221
Vita Sotelo, supt. Fax 534-2384
www.boysranchisd.org/
Blakemore MS 100/6-8
PO Box 219 79010 806-534-2361
Derek Davis, prin. Fax 534-0041
Farley ES 100/K-5
PO Box 219 79010 806-534-2248
Chester Dunavin, prin. Fax 534-0111

Brackettville, Kinney, Pop. 1,830
Brackett ISD 700/PK-12
PO Box 586 78832 830-563-2491
Paula Renken, supt. Fax 563-9264
www.brackett.k12.tx.us
Brackett IS 100/5-6
PO Box 586 78832 830-563-2492
Alma Gutierrez, prin. Fax 563-9355
Brackett JHS 100/7-8
PO Box 586 78832 830-563-2480
Frank Taylor, prin. Fax 563-9559
Jones ES 300/PK-4
PO Box 586 78832 830-563-2492
Alma Gutierrez, prin. Fax 563-9355

Brady, McCulloch, Pop. 5,345
Brady ISD 1,300/PK-12
100 W Main St 76825 325-597-2301
Jeffrey Brasher, supt. Fax 597-3984
www.bradyisd.org
Brady ES 500/1-5
100 W Main St 76825 325-597-2590
Kelley Hirt, prin. Fax 597-0490
Brady MS 300/6-8
100 W Main St 76825 325-597-8110
Bryan Shipman, prin. Fax 597-4166
North Ward S 200/PK-K
100 W Main St 76825 325-597-8392
Jenny Roberts, prin. Fax 597-0034

Brazoria, Brazoria, Pop. 2,897
Columbia-Brazoria ISD
Supt. — See West Columbia
Barrow ES 700/PK-6
112 Gaines St 77422 979-799-1700
Patricia Heidel, prin. Fax 798-6784
West Brazos JHS 500/7-8
20022 N Highway 36 77422 979-799-1730
Alice Batchelor, prin. Fax 798-8000
Wild Peach ES 300/PK-5
County Road 353 77422 979-799-1750
Gwendolyn Sandles, prin. Fax 798-9198

Breckenridge, Stephens, Pop. 5,649
Breckenridge ISD 1,700/PK-12
PO Box 1738 76424 254-559-2278
Jennings Teel, supt. Fax 559-2353
Breckenridge JHS 300/7-8
502 W Lindsey St 76424 254-559-6581
Lee Garner, prin. Fax 559-1082
East ES 400/PK-1
1310 E Elm St 76424 254-559-6531
Molly Peterson, prin. Fax 559-3001
North ES 200/2-3
300 W 7th St 76424 254-559-6511
Susan Fambrough, prin. Fax 559-3670
South ES 400/4-6
1001 W Elliott St 76424 254-559-6554
Jerry Overman, prin. Fax 559-2307

Bremond, Robertson, Pop. 896
Bremond ISD 400/PK-12
PO Box 190 76629 254-746-7145
Walter Fenn, supt. Fax 746-7726
www.bremondisd.net
Bremond ES 200/PK-5
PO Box 190 76629 254-746-7145
Ronnie Groholski, prin. Fax 746-7726
Bremond MS 100/6-8
PO Box 190 76629 254-746-7145
Donna Thompson, prin. Fax 746-7726

Brenham, Washington, Pop. 14,161
Brenham ISD 4,900/PK-12
PO Box 1147 77834 979-277-3700
Sam Bell, supt. Fax 277-3701
www.brenhamisd.net
Alton ES 500/PK-4
304 Kerr St 77833 979-277-3870
Calvin Kossie, prin. Fax 277-3871
Brenham ES 800/PK-4
1000 S Blue Bell Rd 77833 979-277-3880
Kim Rocka, prin. Fax 277-3881
Brenham JHS 700/7-8
1200 Carlee Dr 77833 979-277-3830
Artis Edwards, prin. Fax 277-3831
Brenham MS 600/5-6
1600 S Blue Bell Rd 77833 979-277-3845
Bonnie Brinkmeyer, prin. Fax 277-3846
Krause ES 700/PK-4
2201 E Stone St 77833 979-277-6545
Joy Nelson, prin. Fax 277-6549

Brenham Christian Academy 100/3-12
2111 S Blue Bell Rd 77833 979-830-8480
Noel Scoggins, hdmstr. Fax 830-1687
First Baptist Church S 200/PK-6
302 Pahl St 77833 979-836-6411
Nancy Fritz, admin. Fax 836-3269

Grace Lutheran S 100/PK-8
1212 W Jefferson St 77833 979-836-2030
Jacob Hollatz, prin. Fax 836-0510
St. Paul's Christian S 200/PK-4
305 W Third St 77833 979-836-1145
Sherrie Winkelmann, dir. Fax 836-5795

Bridge City, Orange, Pop. 8,800
Bridge City ISD 2,500/PK-12
1031 W Round Bunch Rd 77611 409-735-1602
Dr. Jamey Harrison, supt. Fax 735-1694
www.bridgecityisd.net/
Bridge City IS 600/3-5
1029 W Round Bunch Rd 77611 409-792-8800
Tara Fountain, prin. Fax 792-8827
Bridge City MS 600/6-8
300 Bower Dr 77611 409-735-1513
Kelly McBride, prin. Fax 735-1517
Hatton S 300/PK-K
1035 W Round Bunch Rd 77611 409-735-1600
Norman Gaspard, prin. Fax 735-1656
Sims ES 400/1-2
350 Bower Dr 77611 409-735-1700
Kent Broussard, prin. Fax 735-1726

Bridgeport, Wise, Pop. 5,659
Bridgeport ISD 2,200/PK-12
2107 15th St 76426 940-683-5124
Eddie Bland, supt. Fax 683-4268
www.bridgeportisd.net
Bridgeport ES 600/PK-2
1408 Elementary Dr 76426 940-683-5955
Ron Gordon, prin. Fax 683-5079
Bridgeport IS 500/3-5
1400 US Highway 380 76426 940-683-5784
Gina Florence, prin. Fax 683-4086
Bridgeport MS 500/6-8
702 17th St 76426 940-683-2273
Robert Haynes, prin. Fax 683-5812

Briscoe, Wheeler
Fort Elliott Consolidated ISD 200/PK-12
PO Box 138 79011 806-375-2454
Carl Baker, supt. Fax 375-2327
www.fortelliott.com/
Ft. Elliott S 200/PK-12
PO Box 138 79011 806-375-2454
Roy Baker, prin. Fax 375-2327

Broaddus, San Augustine, Pop. 187
Broaddus ISD 400/PK-12
PO Box 58 75929 936-872-3041
Dr. Jerry Meador, supt. Fax 872-3699
www.broaddus.esc7.net
Broaddus ES 200/PK-6
PO Box 58 75929 936-872-3315
Kim Boatman, prin. Fax 872-3439

Brock, Parker
Brock ISD 800/K-12
100 Grindstone Rd 76087 817-594-7642
Richard Tedder, supt. Fax 599-3246
www.brockisd.net
Brock ES 400/K-5
100 Grindstone Rd 76087 817-594-8017
Dee Mills, prin. Fax 599-5117
Brock MS 200/6-8
100 Grindstone Rd 76087 817-594-3195
Chad Massey, prin. Fax 594-3191

Bronte, Coke, Pop. 981
Bronte ISD 300/PK-12
PO Box 670 76933 325-473-2511
Alan Richey, supt. Fax 473-2313
www.bronteisd.net/
Bronte ES 200/PK-6
PO Box 670 76933 325-473-2251
Donna Poehls, prin. Fax 473-2313

Brookeland, Sabine
Brookeland ISD 300/PK-12
RR 2 Box 18 75931 409-698-2677
Lana Comeaux, supt. Fax 698-2533
www.brookelandisd.net
Brookeland ES 200/PK-5
RR 2 Box 18 75931 409-698-2152
Judy Soucie, prin. Fax 698-9874

Brookesmith, Brown
Brookesmith ISD 200/PK-12
PO Box 706 76827 325-643-3023
Bryan Swartz, supt. Fax 643-3378
www.brookesmithisd.net/
Brookesmith S 100/PK-8
PO Box 706 76827 325-646-3791
James Oliver, prin. Fax 646-3378

Brownfield, Terry, Pop. 9,173
Brownfield ISD 1,800/PK-12
601 E Tahoka Rd 79316 806-637-2591
Jerry Jones, supt. Fax 637-9208
www.brownfieldisd.net/
Brownfield MS 300/6-8
1001 E Broadway St 79316 806-637-7521
Brandon Hays, prin. Fax 637-2919
Colonial Heights ES 400/PK-1
1100 E Reppto St 79316 806-637-4282
Tom Gaither, prin. Fax 637-1815
Oak Grove ES 500/2-5
1000 E Cactus Ln 79316 806-637-6455
Anthony Sorola, prin. Fax 637-3636

Brownsboro, Henderson, Pop. 856
Brownsboro ISD 2,800/PK-12
PO Box 465 75756 903-852-3701
Elton Caldwell, supt. Fax 852-3957
www.brownsboro.k12.tx.us
Brownsboro ES 400/PK-3
PO Box 465 75756 903-852-6461
Brian Ralson, prin. Fax 852-2718
Brownsboro IS 300/4-6
PO Box 465 75756 903-852-7325
Jennifer Settle, prin. Fax 852-2054
Brownsboro JHS 400/7-8
PO Box 465 75756 903-852-6931
Yolanda Larkin, prin. Fax 852-5238
Chandler IS 300/4-6
PO Box 465 75756 903-849-6436
Marianne Jones, prin. Fax 849-3019
Other Schools – See Chandler

Brownsville, Cameron, Pop. 167,493
Brownsville ISD 48,400/PK-12
1900 Price Rd 78521 956-548-8000
Hector Gonzales, supt. Fax 548-8019
www.bisd.us/
Aiken ES 800/PK-5
6290 Southmost Rd 78521 956-986-5200
E.J. Martinez, prin. Fax 554-5208
Benavides ES 800/PK-5
3101 McAllen Rd 78520 956-350-3250
Sherry Stout, prin. Fax 350-3273
Besteiro MS 900/6-8
6280 Southmost Rd 78521 956-544-3900
Alma Cardenas-Rubio, prin. Fax 544-3927
Brite ES 700/PK-5
450 S Browne Ave 78521 956-698-3000
Frank Ortiz, prin. Fax 831-5146
Burns ES 1,200/PK-5
1974 E Alton Gloor Blvd 78526 956-548-8490
Mario Fajardo, prin. Fax 548-8489
Canales ES 700/PK-5
1811 International Blvd 78521 956-548-8900
Loyda Poy, prin. Fax 548-8919
Castaneda ES 600/PK-5
3201 Lima St 78521 956-548-8800
Nora Camargo, prin. Fax 548-8807
Champion ES 1,000/PK-5
4750 Bowie Rd 78521 956-832-6200
Berta Presas, prin. Fax 832-6225
Cromack ES 800/PK-5
3200 E 30th St 78521 956-548-8820
Carmelita Rodriguez, prin. Fax 548-8824
Cummings MS 1,000/6-8
1800 Cummings Pl 78520 956-548-8630
Jennifer Gonzales, prin. Fax 548-8218
Del Castillo ES 600/PK-5
105 Morningside Rd 78521 956-982-2600
Jose Luis Poy, prin. Fax 982-2622
Egly ES 1,100/PK-5
445 Land O Lakes Dr 78521 956-548-8850
Christina Bridgwater, prin. Fax 982-3074
El Jardin ES 600/PK-5
6911 Boca Chica Blvd 78521 956-831-6000
Esmeralda Tamez, prin. Fax 831-6024
Faulk MS 900/6-8
2000 Roosevelt St 78521 956-548-8500
Mario Rodriguez, prin. Fax 982-2894
Gallegos ES 800/PK-5
2700 Rancho Viejo Ave 78526 956-547-4230
Lucy Green, prin. Fax 547-4232
Garcia MS 1,000/6-8
5701 FM 802 78526 956-832-6300
Dr. Oscar Cantu, prin. Fax 832-6304
Garden Park ES 800/PK-5
855 Military Rd 78520 956-982-2630
Victor Caballero, prin. Fax 982-2644
Garza ES 800/PK-5
200 Esperanza Rd 78521 956-982-2660
Carlos Garza, prin. Fax 982-2682
Gonzalez ES 1,100/PK-5
4350 Coffeeport Rd 78521 956-831-6030
Yolanda Kruger, prin. Fax 831-6040
Hudson ES 1,200/PK-5
2980 FM 802 78526 956-574-6400
Dr. Rita Hernandez, prin. Fax 574-6403
Longoria ES 400/PK-5
2400 E Van Buren St 78520 956-982-2700
Marina Flores, prin. Fax 982-2703
Lucio MS 1,100/6-8
300 N Vermillion Ave 78521 956-831-4550
Rose Longoria, prin. Fax 838-2298
Martin ES 700/PK-5
1701 Stanford Ave 78520 956-982-2730
Gilda Jo Pena, prin. Fax 982-3032
Morningside ES 800/PK-5
1025 Morningside Rd 78521 956-982-2760
Dolores Emerson, prin. Fax 982-2787
Oliveira MS 1,200/6-8
444 Land O Lakes Dr 78521 956-548-8530
Alonzo Barbosa, prin. Fax 544-3968
Ortiz ES 700/PK-5
2500 W Alton Gloor Blvd 78520 956-698-1100
Sandra Lopez, prin. Fax 546-6611
Palm Grove ES 700/PK-5
7942 Southmost Rd 78521 956-982-3850
Lily Cazares, prin. Fax 986-5070
Paredes ES 1,200/PK-5
3700 Heritage Trl 78526 956-574-5582
Julie Trevino, prin. Fax 574-5584
Perez ES 700/PK-5
2514 Shidler Dr 78521 956-982-2800
Ruben Martinez, prin. Fax 982-2806
Perkins MS 900/6-8
4750 Austin Rd 78521 956-831-8770
Blanca Lambarri, prin. Fax 831-8789
Putegnat ES 500/PK-5
730 E 8th St 78520 956-548-8930
Ernestina Trevino, prin. Fax 548-8947
Resaca ES 300/PK-5
901 E Filmore St 78520 956-982-2900
Carlos Paredes, prin. Fax 982-2916
Russell ES 1,000/PK-5
800 Lakeside Blvd 78520 956-548-8960
Bill Gutierrez, prin. Fax 548-8889
Sharp ES 600/PK-5
1439 Palm Blvd 78520 956-982-2930
Fax 982-2948
Skinner ES 800/PK-5
411 W Saint Charles St 78520 956-982-2830
Kim Moore, prin. Fax 982-2849
Southmost ES 600/PK-5
5245 Southmost Rd 78521 956-548-8870
Jimmy Haynes, prin. Fax 554-4245
Stell MS 1,000/6-8
1105 E Los Ebanos Blvd 78520 956-548-8560
Acacia Ameel, prin. Fax 548-8666
Stillman MS 1,200/6-8
2977 W Tandy Rd 78520 956-698-1000
Maricela Zarate, prin. Fax 350-3231
Vela MS 1,000/6-8
4905 Paredes Line Rd 78526 956-548-7770
Robert Gonzales, prin. Fax 548-7780
Vermillion ES 1,200/PK-5
6895 FM 802 78526 956-831-6060
Jay Harris, prin. Fax 831-1093
Victoria Heights ES 500/PK-5
2801 E 13th St 78521 956-982-2960
Michael Moreno, prin. Fax 982-2988
Villa Nueva ES 400/PK-5
7455 Old Military Rd 78520 956-542-3957
Jose Martinez, prin. Fax 544-0720
Yturria ES 1,100/PK-5
2955 W Tandy Rd 78520 956-698-0870
Norma Torres, prin. Fax 350-3207

Los Fresnos Consolidated ISD
Supt. — See Los Fresnos
Olmito ES 900/PK-5
2500 Arroyo Blvd 78526 956-233-3950
Valarie Londrie, prin. Fax 350-8835

Brownsville SDA S 50/K-8
243 Old Port Isabel Rd 78521 956-542-5536
Episcopal Day S 400/PK-6
34 N Coria St 78520 956-542-5231
Teresa Hoskins, prin. Fax 504-9486
First Baptist S 300/PK-12
1600 Boca Chica Blvd 78520 956-542-4854
Deborah Batsell, prin. Fax 542-6188
Guadalupe Regional MS 100/6-8
1214 Lincoln St 78521 956-504-5568
Michael Motyl, prin. Fax 504-9393
Incarnate Word Academy 300/PK-8
244 Resaca Blvd 78520 956-546-4486
Christina Moreno, pres. Fax 504-3960
Livingway Christian S 200/PK-12
PO Box 3731 78523 956-548-2223
Dr. Anne Moore, dir. Fax 548-1970
St. Luke S 200/PK-6
2850 Price Rd 78521 956-544-7982
Ana Gomez, prin. Fax 544-4874
St. Mary's S 500/PK-6
1300 E Los Ebanos Blvd 78520 956-546-1805
Juan M. Barreda, prin. Fax 546-0787

Brownwood, Brown, Pop. 19,566
Brownwood ISD 3,500/PK-12
PO Box 730 76804 325-643-5644
Reece Blincoe, supt. Fax 643-5640
www.brownwoodisd.org
Brownwood IS 500/5-6
800 Rogan St 76801 325-646-0462
Connie Easterwood, prin. Fax 646-9317
Brownwood MS 500/7-8
PO Box 1286 76804 325-646-9545
Bryan Allen, prin. Fax 646-3785
Coggin ES 200/4-4
1005 Avenue B 76801 325-646-8919
Todd Lewis, prin. Fax 646-1250
East ES 300/PK-3
2700 Vincent St 76801 325-646-2937
Nanda Wilbourn, prin. Fax 646-5900
Northwest ES 600/PK-3
311 Bluffview Dr 76801 325-646-0707
Stacy Smith, prin. Fax 646-2449
Woodland Heights ES 500/PK-3
3900 4th St 76801 325-646-8633
Bob Turner, prin. Fax 641-0109

Victory Life Academy 100/PK-12
PO Box 940 76804 325-641-2223
Cathy Roberts, admin. Fax 643-9772

Bruni, Webb
Webb Consolidated ISD 400/PK-12
PO Box 206 78344 361-747-5415
Dr. David Jones, supt. Fax 747-5202
www.webb.esc1.net/
Bruni MS 100/6-8
PO Box 206 78344 361-747-5415
Steve Myers, prin. Fax 747-5298
Other Schools – See Oilton

Bryan, Brazos, Pop. 66,306
Bryan ISD 14,500/PK-12
101 N Texas Ave 77803 979-209-1000
Michael Cargill, supt. Fax 209-1004
www.bryanisd.org
Austin MS 900/6-8
801 S Ennis St 77803 979-209-6700
Patti Moore, prin. Fax 209-6741
Bonham ES 600/PK-5
3100 Wilkes St 77803 979-209-1200
Ken Newbold, prin. Fax 209-1218
Bowen ES 400/PK-5
3870 Copperfield Dr 77802 979-209-1300
Amy Anding, prin. Fax 209-1306
Branch ES 600/PK-5
2040 W Villa Maria Rd 77807 979-209-2900
David Ogden, prin. Fax 209-2910
Carver ECC 400/PK-PK
1401 W Martin L King Jr St 77803 979-209-3700
Mary Blackburn, prin. Fax 209-3701
Crockett ES 500/PK-5
401 Elm Ave 77801 979-209-2960
Judy Joiner, prin. Fax 209-2965
Davila MS 6-8
2751 N Earl Rudder Fwy 77803 979-209-7150
Joshua Garcia, prin. Fax 209-7151

Fannin ES 500/PK-5
1200 Baker Ave 77803 979-209-3800
Ronny Werner, prin. Fax 209-3826
Henderson ES 400/PK-5
801 Matous Dr 77802 979-209-1560
Edward Fellows, prin. Fax 209-1566
Houston ES 500/PK-5
4501 Canterbury Dr 77802 979-209-1360
Holly Scott, prin. Fax 209-1462
Johnson ES 400/PK-5
3800 Oak Hill Dr 77802 979-209-1460
Carol Happ, prin. Fax 209-1462
Jones ES 600/PK-5
1400 Pecan St 77803 979-209-3900
Stephanie Mosqueda, prin. Fax 209-3912
Kemp ES 400/PK-5
1601 W Mrtn Lthr King Jr St 77803 979-209-3760
Kelli Deegear, prin. Fax 209-3764
Long MS 1,000/6-8
1106 N Harvey Mitchell Pkwy 77803 979-209-6500
Lindsay Harris, prin. Fax 209-6566
Milam ES 600/PK-5
1201 Ridgedale St 77803 979-209-3960
Tracy Spies, prin. Fax 209-3969
Mitchell ES 500/PK-5
2500 Austins Colony Pkwy 77808 979-209-1400
Karen Kaspar, prin. Fax 209-1420
Navarro ES 600/PK-5
4619 Northwood Dr 77803 979-209-1260
Marilyn Rosas, prin. Fax 209-1270
Neal ES 400/PK-5
801 W Martin Luther King Jr 77803 979-209-3860
Linda Asberry, prin. Fax 209-3863
Rayburn MS 1,200/6-8
1048 N Earl Rudder Fwy 77802 979-209-6600
Paul Hord, prin. Fax 209-6611
Sul Ross ES 300/PK-5
3300 Parkway Ter 77802 979-209-1500
Holly Havemann, prin. Fax 209-1513

Allen Academy 300/PK-12
3201 Boonville Rd 77802 979-776-0731
Mark Bloom, hdmstr. Fax 774-7769
Brazos Christian S 300/PK-12
3000 W Villa Maria Rd 77807 979-823-1000
Robert Armstrong, hdmstr. Fax 823-1774
St. Joseph ES 200/K-5
901 E Wm J Bryan Pkwy 77803 979-822-6643
Dr. Esther Miranda, prin. Fax 779-2810
St. Michael's Academy 200/PK-12
2500 S College Ave 77801 979-822-2715
Betty Creamer, prin. Fax 823-4971

Bryson, Jack, Pop. 537
Bryson ISD 300/PK-12
PO Box 309 76427 940-392-3281
Jack Coody, supt. Fax 392-2086
www.brysonisd.net
Bryson S 300/PK-12
PO Box 309 76427 940-392-2601
Debbie Hearne, prin. Fax 392-2086

Buckholts, Milam, Pop. 406
Buckholts ISD 200/PK-12
PO Box 248 76518 254-593-3011
Kent Dutton, supt. Fax 593-2270
www.buckholtsisd.net
Buckholts S 200/PK-12
PO Box 248 76518 254-593-2744
John Clark, prin. Fax 593-2270

Buda, Hays, Pop. 3,948
Hays Consolidated ISD
Supt. — See Kyle
Barton MS 700/6-8
4950 Jack C Hays Trl 78610 512-268-1472
Chris Ulcak, prin. Fax 268-1610
Buda ES 300/3-5
PO Box 1290 78610 512-268-8439
Lauri Schroeder, prin. Fax 295-4014
Buda PS 300/PK-2
PO Box 1410 78610 512-295-8449
Lauri Schroeder, prin. Fax 295-2946
Dahlstrom MS 700/6-8
3600 FM 967 78610 512-268-8441
Hilda Gartzke, prin. Fax 295-5346
Elm Grove ES 600/K-5
801 S FM 1626 78610 512-268-8440
Irma Flores-Brothers, prin. Fax 295-6809
Green ES 700/PK-5
1301 Old Goforth Rd 78610 512-268-8438
Robin Kelley-Broadway, prin. Fax 295-4107

Santa Cruz Catholic S PK-2
PO Box 160 78610 512-312-2137
Martha Owan, prin. Fax 312-2143

Buffalo, Leon, Pop. 1,910
Buffalo ISD 800/PK-12
708 Cedar Creek Rd 75831 903-322-3765
Jack Thomason, supt. Fax 322-3091
www.buffaloisd.com
Buffalo ES 400/PK-5
1700 E Commerce St 75831 903-322-3562
Johnny Veretto, prin. Fax 322-4077
Buffalo JHS 200/6-8
355 Bison Trl 75831 903-322-4340
Lacy Freeman, prin. Fax 322-4803

Buffalo Gap, Taylor, Pop. 446
Jim Ned Consolidated ISD
Supt. — See Tuscola
Buffalo Gap ES 200/PK-5
PO Box 608 79508 325-572-3533
John Mayes, prin. Fax 572-3850

Bullard, Smith, Pop. 1,562
Bullard ISD 1,200/PK-12
PO Box 250 75757 903-894-6639
Keith Bryant, supt. Fax 894-9291
www.bullardisd.net
Bullard ES, PO Box 250 75757 300/2-4
Lisa Williams, prin. 903-894-2930
Bullard IS 100/5-6
PO Box 250 75757 903-894-6793
Tommy Wade, prin. Fax 894-3982
Bullard MS 300/7-8
PO Box 250 75757 903-894-6533
Lisa Williams, prin. Fax 894-7592
Bullard PS PK-1
PO Box 250 75757 903-894-6389
Michelle Hurst, prin. Fax 894-5937

Brook Hill S 500/PK-12
PO Box 668 75757 903-894-5000
Rod Fletcher, hdmstr. Fax 894-6332

Bulverde, Comal, Pop. 4,446
Comal ISD
Supt. — See New Braunfels
Rahe Bulverde ES 500/PK-5
1781 E Ammann Rd 78163 830-885-1600
Merrie Fox, prin. Fax 885-1601

Bracken Christian S 300/PK-12
670 Old Boerne Rd 78163 830-438-3211
Craig Walker, admin. Fax 980-2327
Lighthouse Christian Learning Center 100/PK-1
2420 Bulverde Rd 78163 830-980-9016
Denise Harris, dir. Fax 980-9018

Buna, Jasper, Pop. 2,127
Buna ISD 1,500/PK-12
PO Box 1087 77612 409-994-5101
Byron Terrier, supt. Fax 994-4808
www.bunaisd.net
Buna ES 700/PK-5
PO Box 1087 77612 409-994-4840
Michelle Hughes, prin. Fax 994-4808
Buna JHS 400/6-8
PO Box 1087 77612 409-994-4860
Thomas Saunders, prin. Fax 994-4808

Burkburnett, Wichita, Pop. 10,378
Burkburnett ISD 3,700/PK-12
416 Glendale St 76354 940-569-3326
Danny Taylor, supt. Fax 569-4776
www.burkburnettisd.org
Burkburnett MS 700/6-8
108 S Avenue D 76354 940-569-3381
Brad Owen, prin. Fax 569-7116
Evans ES 500/PK-5
1015 S Berry St 76354 940-569-3311
Scott Slater, prin. Fax 569-2719
Hardin ES 700/PK-5
100 N Avenue D 76354 940-569-5253
Don Fritsche, prin. Fax 569-1509
Other Schools – See Wichita Falls

Burkeville, Newton
Burkeville ISD 300/PK-12
PO Box 218 75932 409-565-2201
Keith Langfitt, supt. Fax 565-2012
www.burkeville.org/
Burkeville ES 200/PK-6
PO Box 218 75932 409-565-4284
David Erickson, prin. Fax 565-2012

Burleson, Johnson, Pop. 29,613
Burleson ISD 8,500/PK-12
1160 SW Wilshire Blvd 76028 817-245-1000
Dr. Mark Jackson, supt. Fax 447-5737
www.burlesonisd.net
Academy at Nola Dunn 500/K-5
900 SW Hillside Dr 76028 817-447-5895
Tani Simons, prin. Fax 447-5898
Bransom ES 600/PK-5
820 S Hurst Rd 76028 817-447-5875
April Chiarelli, prin. Fax 447-5888
Brock ES K-5
12000 Oak Grove Rd S 76028 817-245-3800
Philo Waters, prin.
Frazier ES 400/PK-5
1125 NW Summercrest Blvd 76028 817-245-3000
Christy Strayhorn, prin.
Hajek ES, 555 NE McAlister Rd 76028 K-5
Cretia Basham, prin. 817-245-3700
Hughes MS 900/6-8
316 SW Thomas St 76028 817-447-5750
Sean Scott, prin. Fax 447-5748
Kerr MS 1,000/6-8
517 SW Johnson Ave 76028 817-447-5810
Kim Cantu, prin. Fax 447-5742
Mound ES 700/PK-5
205 SW Thomas St 76028 817-447-5765
Oteka Gibson, prin. Fax 447-5845
Norwood ES 700/PK-5
619 Evelyn Ln 76028 817-447-5770
Aaron McWilliams, prin. Fax 447-5831
Stribling ES 600/PK-5
1881 E Renfro St 76028 817-447-5755
Melissa Button, prin. Fax 447-5835
Taylor ES 700/PK-5
400 NE Alsbury Blvd 76028 817-447-5775
Elida Silva, prin. Fax 447-5841

Joshua ISD
Supt. — See Joshua
North Joshua ES 600/PK-6
100 Ranchway Dr 76028 817-202-2500
Susan Haertner, prin. Fax 295-9836

Mansfield ISD
Supt. — See Mansfield
Tarver-Rendon ES 500/PK-4
12350 Rendon Rd 76028 817-561-3850
Janet McDade, prin. Fax 561-3864

Burleson Adventist S 100/PK-8
1635 Fox Ln 76028 817-295-6812
Larry Howerton, prin. Fax 295-8001

Holy Cross Christian Academy 200/PK-6
PO Box 3113 76097 817-295-7232
Kristy Werner, admin. Fax 295-6307

Burnet, Burnet, Pop. 5,562
Burnet Consolidated ISD 3,300/PK-12
208 E Brier Ln 78611 512-756-2124
Jeffrey Hanks, supt. Fax 756-7498
www.burnet.txed.net
Burnet ES 400/PK-1
608 N Vanderveer St 78611 512-756-2126
Jo McDonald, prin. Fax 756-6993
Burnet MS 700/6-8
1401 N Main St 78611 512-756-6182
Mindy Evans, prin. Fax 756-7955
Richey ES 400/4-5
500 E Graves St 78611 512-756-2609
Jill Wittekiend, prin. Fax 756-2624
Shady Grove ES 400/2-3
1001 Shady Grove Pkwy 78611 512-756-8090
Terra Singletary, prin. Fax 756-6856
Other Schools – See Bertram

Burton, Washington, Pop. 367
Burton ISD 300/PK-12
PO Box 37 77835 979-289-3131
James Palmer, supt. Fax 289-3076
www.burtonisd.net
Burton ES 200/PK-6
PO Box 129 77835 979-289-2175
Cheryl Dabera, prin. Fax 289-0170

Bushland, Potter
Bushland ISD 1,000/PK-12
PO Box 60 79012 806-359-6683
John Lemons, supt. Fax 359-6769
bushlandisd.org/
Bushland ES 400/PK-4
PO Box 60 79012 806-359-5410
Bobbye Morgan, prin. Fax 355-4658
Bushland MS 400/5-8
PO Box 60 79012 806-359-5418
Mark Reasor, prin. Fax 355-2841

Byers, Clay, Pop. 530
Byers ISD 100/K-12
PO Box 286 76357 940-529-6102
Steve Wolf, supt. Fax 529-6104
www.esc9.net/byersisd/
Byers S 100/K-12
PO Box 286 76357 940-529-6101
Burt Montgomery, prin. Fax 529-6104

Bynum, Hill, Pop. 246
Bynum ISD 200/PK-12
PO Box 68 76631 254-623-4251
Brenda Speer, supt. Fax 623-4290
www.bynumisd.net/
Bynum S 200/PK-12
PO Box 68 76631 254-623-4251
Amy Feller, prin. Fax 623-4290

Cactus, Moore, Pop. 2,629
Dumas ISD
Supt. — See Dumas
Cactus ES 400/PK-6
PO Box 368 79013 806-966-5102
Carla Tafoya, prin. Fax 966-5561

Caddo Mills, Hunt, Pop. 1,211
Caddo Mills ISD 1,400/PK-12
PO Box 160 75135 903-527-6056
Vicki Payne, supt. Fax 527-4883
www.caddomillsisd.org/caddomillsisd/site/default.asp
Caddo Mills ES 600/PK-5
PO Box 160 75135 903-527-3162
Sandi Stroope, prin. Fax 527-0166
Caddo Mills MS 300/6-8
PO Box 160 75135 903-527-3161
Michael Powell, prin. Fax 527-2379
Griffis ES, PO Box 160 75135 PK-5
Courtney Painter, prin. 903-527-3525

Caldwell, Burleson, Pop. 3,862
Caldwell ISD 1,900/PK-12
203 N Gray St 77836 979-567-9000
Randall Berryhill, supt. Fax 567-9876
www.caldwell.k12.tx.us/
Caldwell ES 500/PK-2
203 N Gray St 77836 979-567-4126
Dana Degarmo, prin. Fax 567-9422
Caldwell IS 400/3-5
203 N Gray St 77836 979-567-4266
Tracy Meyer, prin. Fax 567-7131
Caldwell MS 400/6-8
203 N Gray St 77836 979-567-6270
Kim McManus, prin. Fax 567-6272

First Baptist S 100/PK-8
PO Box 687 77836 979-567-3771
Rhonda Hadley, admin. Fax 567-3771

Calvert, Robertson, Pop. 1,403
Calvert ISD 100/PK-12
PO Box 7 77837 979-364-2824
K.L. Groholski, supt. Fax 364-2468
www.calvertisd.com/
Calvert S 100/PK-12
PO Box 7 77837 979-364-2882
George Sheldon, prin. Fax 364-2468

Cameron, Milam, Pop. 5,900
Cameron ISD 1,600/PK-12
PO Box 712 76520 254-697-3512
Rodney Fausett, supt. Fax 697-2448
www.cameronisd.net
Cameron ES 300/3-5
PO Box 712 76520 254-697-2381
Tammy Witten, prin. Fax 605-0356
Cameron JHS 300/6-8
PO Box 712 76520 254-697-2131
Missi Giesenschlag, prin. Fax 605-0379

Milam ES 500/PK-2
PO Box 712 76520 254-697-3641
Ronny Welborn, prin. Fax 605-0354

Campbell, Hunt, Pop. 779
Campbell ISD 400/PK-12
409 W North St 75422 903-862-3259
Strike Franklin, supt. Fax 862-2222
www.ednet10.net/campbell
Campbell ES 200/PK-6
409 W North St 75422 903-862-3253
Dr. Gerald Rosebure, prin. Fax 862-3546

Camp Wood, Real, Pop. 864
Nueces Canyon Consolidated ISD
Supt. — See Barksdale
Nueces Canyon ES 200/K-6
Highway 337 78833 830-597-3218
David Velky, prin. Fax 597-6197

Canadian, Hemphill, Pop. 2,258
Canadian ISD 600/PK-12
800 Hillside Ave 79014 806-323-5393
Frank Belcher, supt. Fax 323-8143
www.canadianisd.net
Baker ES 100/3-5
800 Hillside Ave 79014 806-323-5386
Jim Knight, prin. Fax 323-9916
Canadian ES 200/PK-2
800 Hillside Ave 79014 806-323-9331
Kirk Saul, prin. Fax 323-6852
Canadian MS 100/6-8
800 Hillside Ave 79014 806-323-5351
Sam Hancock, prin. Fax 323-8791

Canton, Van Zandt, Pop. 3,591
Canton ISD 1,900/PK-12
225 W Elm St 75103 903-567-4179
Dr. Jerome Stewart, supt. Fax 567-2370
cantonisd.net
Canton ES 500/PK-2
1163 S Buffalo St 75103 903-567-6521
Kelly Lamar, prin. Fax 567-5373
Canton IS 400/3-5
1190 W Highway 243 75103 903-567-6418
Sandra Dunlap, prin. Fax 567-2956
Canton JHS 400/6-8
1115 S Buffalo St 75103 903-567-4329
Amy Autry, prin. Fax 567-1298

Lighthouse Christian Academy 50/K-12
597 Cherry Creek Ln 75103 903-567-9907
Julie Wright, hdmstr. Fax 567-9907
Victory Christian S 100/PK-8
PO Box 1078 75103 903-567-2072
Tammy Griffin, prin. Fax 567-6446

Canutillo, El Paso, Pop. 4,442
Canutillo ISD
Supt. — See El Paso
Alderete MS 600/6-8
PO Box 100 79835 915-877-6600
Annette Brigham, prin. Fax 877-6607
Canutillo ES 700/PK-5
PO Box 100 79835 915-877-7600
Monica Garcia, prin. Fax 877-7607
Canutillo MS 600/6-8
PO Box 100 79835 915-877-7900
Dr. Monica Reyes-Garcia, prin. Fax 877-7907
Childress ES 600/K-5
PO Box 100 79835 915-877-7700
Christine Althoff, prin. Fax 877-7707
Damian ES 800/PK-5
PO Box 100 79835 915-877-7655
Margarita Porras-Grant, prin. Fax 877-7670
Davenport ES 500/PK-5
PO Box 100 79835 915-886-6400
Marta Strobach, prin. Fax 886-6407

Canyon, Randall, Pop. 13,353
Canyon ISD 8,200/PK-12
PO Box 899 79015 806-677-2600
Mike Wartes, supt. Fax 677-2659
www.canyonisd.net
Canyon IS 700/5-6
506 8th St 79015 806-677-2800
Paul Kimbrough, prin. Fax 677-2829
Canyon JHS 500/7-8
910 9th Ave 79015 806-677-2700
Kirk Kear, prin. Fax 677-2739
Crestview ES 400/K-4
80 Hunsley Rd 79015 806-677-2780
Bridget Johnson, prin. Fax 677-2799
Reeves-Hinger ES 700/PK-4
1005 21st St 79015 806-677-2870
Brandi Parker, prin. Fax 677-2889
Other Schools – See Amarillo

Canyon Lake, Comal, Pop. 9,975
Comal ISD
Supt. — See New Braunfels
Startzville ES 700/PK-5
42111 FM 3159 78133 830-885-8000
Dr. Denise Kern, prin. Fax 885-8001

Carmine, Fayette, Pop. 230
Round Top - Carmine ISD 200/PK-12
PO Box 385 78932 979-278-4250
Ronald Goehring, supt. Fax 278-4251
www.rtcisd.net/
Other Schools – See Round Top

Carrizo Springs, Dimmit, Pop. 5,681
Carrizo Springs Consolidated ISD 2,500/PK-12
300 N 7th St 78834 830-876-2473
Dr. Cecilia Moreno, supt. Fax 876-9700
www.cscisd.net
Carrizo Springs ES 1,000/PK-4
300 N 7th St 78834 830-876-3513
Juan Ortiz, prin. Fax 876-2547
Carrizo Springs IS 300/5-6
300 N 7th St 78834 830-876-3561
Michelle Howard, prin. Fax 876-5132
Carrizo Springs JHS 300/7-8
300 N 7th St 78834 830-876-2496
Dirk Dykstra, prin. Fax 876-3655
Other Schools – See Asherton, Big Wells

Carrollton, Denton, Pop. 118,870
Carrollton-Farmers Branch ISD 26,100/PK-12
PO Box 115186 75011 972-968-6100
Annette Griffin Ed.D., supt. Fax 968-6210
www.cfbisd.edu
Blalack MS 1,200/6-8
1706 E Peters Colony Rd 75007 972-968-3500
Les Black, prin. Fax 968-3510
Blanton ES 400/PK-5
2525 Scott Mill Rd 75006 972-968-1100
Patti Fair, prin. Fax 968-1110
Carrollton ES 700/PK-5
1805 Pearl St 75006 972-968-1200
Phil Jackson, prin. Fax 968-1210
Central ES 700/K-5
1600 S Perry Rd 75006 972-968-1300
Rosa Olivera, prin. Fax 968-1310
Country Place ES 400/K-5
2115 Raintree Dr 75006 972-968-1400
Kathi Ferris-Robb, prin. Fax 968-1410
Davis ES 600/K-5
3205 Dorchester Dr 75007 972-968-1500
Lisa Williams, prin. Fax 968-1510
Furneaux ES 400/K-5
3210 Furneaux Ln 75007 972-968-1800
Jim Cunningham, prin. Fax 968-1810
Good ES 500/K-5
1012 Study Ln 75006 972-968-1900
Leslie Coney, prin. Fax 968-1910
Kelly Prekindergarten Center 400/PK-PK
2325 Heads Ln 75006 972-968-6000
Randi Wells, prin. Fax 968-6010
Kent ES 600/PK-5
1800 W Rosemeade Pkwy 75007 972-968-2000
Debbie Williams, prin. Fax 968-2010
McCoy ES 400/K-5
2425 Mccoy Rd 75006 972-968-2300
Dawn Rink, prin. Fax 968-2310
McLaughlin PS 300/K-2
1500 Webb Chapel Rd 75006 972-968-2500
Tracy Freeman, prin. Fax 968-2510
Perry MS 1,000/6-8
1709 E Belt Line Rd 75006 972-968-4400
Joe LaPuma, prin. Fax 968-4410
Polk MS 1,000/6-8
2001 Kelly Blvd 75006 972-968-4600
Michelle Bailey, prin. Fax 968-4610
Pre-Kindergarten Center 300/PK-PK
1820 Pearl St 75006 972-968-6600
Eva Medina-Walker, prin. Fax 968-6610
Rainwater ES 400/K-5
1408 E Frankford Rd 75007 972-968-2800
Robert Bostic, prin. Fax 968-2810
Rosemeade ES 300/K-5
3550 Kimberly Dr 75007 972-968-3000
M. Amy Miller, prin. Fax 968-3010
Thompson ES 500/K-5
2915 Scott Mill Rd 75007 972-968-3400
Angie Doak, prin. Fax 968-3410
Other Schools – See Coppell, Dallas, Farmers Branch, Irving

Dallas ISD
Supt. — See Dallas
Junkins ES 700/PK-5
2808 Running Duke Dr 75006 972-502-2400
Susan Walker, prin. Fax 502-2401

Lewisville ISD
Supt. — See Flower Mound
Arbor Creek MS 900/6-8
2109 Arbor Creek Dr 75010 469-713-5971
Chantell Upshaw, prin. Fax 350-9163
Coyote Ridge ES 600/K-5
4520 Maumee Dr 75010 469-713-5994
Cathy Grygar, prin. Fax 350-9026
Creek Valley MS 1,000/6-8
4109 Creek Valley Blvd 75010 469-713-5184
Dr. Glenda Edwards, prin. Fax 350-9172
Hebron Valley ES 700/PK-5
4108 Creek Valley Blvd 75010 469-713-5182
Felicia Sprayberry, prin. Fax 350-9068
Homestead ES 600/PK-5
1830 E Branch Hollow Dr 75007 469-713-5181
Sean Perry, prin. Fax 350-9083
Indian Creek ES 600/PK-5
2050 Arbor Creek Dr 75010 469-713-5180
Dr. Lucy Lambert-Guesnard, prin. Fax 350-9085
Polser ES 500/K-5
1520 Polser Rd 75010 469-713-5978
Mike Gibbs, prin. Fax 350-9134

American Heritage Academy 400/K-12
2660 E Trinity Mills Rd 75006 972-416-5437
Robert Anderson M.Ed., hdmstr. Fax 418-5768
Carrollton Christian Academy 500/PK-12
2205 E Hebron Pkwy 75010 972-242-6688
Dr. Alex Ward, hdmstr. Fax 245-0321
Prince of Peace Christian S 900/PK-12
4000 Midway Rd 75007 972-447-9887
Chris Hahn, prin. Fax 447-0877

Carthage, Panola, Pop. 6,611
Carthage ISD 2,800/PK-12
1 Bulldog Dr 75633 903-693-3806
J. Glenn Hambrick, supt. Fax 693-3650
www.carthageisd.org/
Baker-Koonce ES 600/4-6
1 Bulldog Dr 75633 903-693-8611
Fatha Burchette, prin. Fax 693-5948
Carthage JHS 400/7-8
1 Bulldog Dr 75633 903-693-2751
Mike Baysinger, prin. Fax 693-9582
Carthage PS 600/PK-1
1 Bulldog Dr 75633 903-693-2254
Kiley Schumacher, prin. Fax 693-3287
Libby ES 400/2-3
1 Bulldog Dr 75633 903-693-8862
Yolanda Brown, prin. Fax 693-4696

Castroville, Medina, Pop. 2,936
Medina Valley ISD 3,100/PK-12
8449 FM 471 S 78009 830-931-2243
James Stansberry, supt. Fax 931-4050
www.mvisd.com
Castroville ES 500/PK-5
1000 Madrid St 78009 830-931-2117
Brenda Mann, prin. Fax 931-3973
Medina Valley MS 800/6-8
8395 FM 471 S 78009 830-931-2243
John Slaton, prin. Fax 931-3258
Other Schools – See La Coste, San Antonio

St. Louis S 300/PK-5
610 Madrid St 78009 830-931-3544
Dr. Jose Ramos, prin. Fax 931-0155

Cayuga, Anderson
Cayuga ISD 600/PK-12
PO Box 427 75832 903-928-2102
Dr. Rick Webb, supt. Fax 928-2646
www.cayuga.esc7.net
Cayuga ES 300/PK-5
PO Box 427 75832 903-928-2295
Tracie Campbell, prin. Fax 928-2387
Cayuga MS 100/6-8
PO Box 427 75832 903-928-2699
Sherri McInnis, prin. Fax 928-2646

Cedar Creek, Bastrop
Bastrop ISD
Supt. — See Bastrop
Cedar Creek ES 600/PK-4
5582 FM 535 78612 512-332-0699
Jinger Myers, prin. Fax 321-6905
Cedar Creek IS 600/5-6
151 Voss Pkwy 78612 512-321-2292
Shawn Adams, prin. Fax 321-3484
Cedar Creek MS 600/7-8
125 Voss Pkwy 78612 512-332-2626
Jim Hallamek, prin. Fax 332-2631

Cedar Hill, Dallas, Pop. 41,582
Cedar Hill ISD 7,700/PK-12
PO Box 248 75106 972-291-1581
Horace Williams, supt. Fax 291-5231
www.chisd.net
Belt Line IS 300/5-6
PO Box 248 75106 972-291-2583
Dawn Brown, prin. Fax 291-7160
Bray ES 300/PK-4
PO Box 248 75106 972-291-4231
Robert Johansen, prin. Fax 291-6098
Coleman MS 500/7-8
PO Box 248 75106 972-293-4505
Michael Timms, prin. Fax 272-9445
Highlands ES 600/PK-4
PO Box 248 75106 972-291-0496
Sylvia Lewis, prin. Fax 291-5764
High Pointe ES 600/K-4
PO Box 248 75106 972-291-7874
Karen Crow, prin. Fax 291-5695
Lake Ridge ES 300/K-4
PO Box 248 75106 972-293-4501
Andrew Barbee, prin. Fax 291-5210
Permenter MS 800/7-8
PO Box 248 75106 972-291-5270
Dr. Denise Roache-Davis, prin. Fax 291-5296
Plummer ES 500/PK-4
PO Box 248 75106 972-291-4058
Linda Cronenberg, prin. Fax 291-4980
Waterford Oaks ES 600/PK-4
PO Box 248 75106 972-291-5290
Violet Maxwell, prin. Fax 293-2381
West IS 400/5-6
PO Box 248 75106 972-291-6060
Deborah Owens-Pinckney, prin. Fax 291-0646
Wilson IS 400/5-6
PO Box 248 75106 972-291-4502
Shauntee Mayfield, prin. Fax 291-5213

Ashleys Private S 100/PK-4
310 W Beltline Rd 75104 972-291-1313
Sharon Ashley, hdmstr. Fax 293-8056
Trinity Christian S 600/PK-12
1231 E Pleasant Run Rd 75104 972-291-2505
Dr. Kathleen Watts, supt. Fax 291-4739

Cedar Park, Williamson, Pop. 48,139
Leander ISD
Supt. — See Leander
Cedar Park MS 1,200/6-8
2100 Sun Chase Blvd 78613 512-434-5025
Sandra Stewart, prin. Fax 434-7539
Cox ES 800/PK-5
1001 Brushy Creek Rd 78613 512-435-4650
Sheri Hawthorn, prin. Fax 435-4655
Cypress ES 700/PK-5
2900 El Salido Pkwy 78613 512-434-7200
Coleen Meyer, prin. Fax 434-7205
Deer Creek ES 1,000/PK-5
2420 Zeppelin Dr 78613 512-434-7176
Vicki Price, prin. Fax 434-7180
Faubion ES 600/PK-5
1209 Cypress Creek Rd 78613 512-435-4950
Sarah Grissom, prin. Fax 435-4955
Giddens ES 700/PK-5
1500 Timberwood Dr 78613 512-434-7050
Susan Cole, prin. Fax 434-7055

Henry MS 1,000/6-8
100 N Vista Ridge Pkwy 78613 512-435-4800
Dr. David Ellis, prin. Fax 435-4805
Knowles ES 700/PK-5
2101 Cougar Country 78613 512-434-7650
Lisa Gibbs, prin. Fax 434-7655
Mason ES 700/PK-5
1501 N Lakeline Blvd 78613 512-434-7000
Jamie Klassen, prin. Fax 434-7005
Naumann ES 900/PK-5
1201 Brighton Bend Ln 78613 512-434-7250
Sande Powledge, prin. Fax 434-7255
Reagan ES PK-5
1700 E Park St 78613 512-570-7200
Kim Adcock, prin. Fax 570-7205
Running Brushy MS 1,100/6-8
2303 N Lakeline Blvd 78613 512-435-4700
Karin Johnson, prin. Fax 435-4705
Westside ES PK-5
300 Ryan Jordan Ln 78613 512-570-7000
Susie Villalpando, prin. Fax 570-7005

Cedar Park Montessori S 100/PK-6
400 E Whitestone Blvd 78613 512-259-8495
Kalika Sarathkumara, dir. Fax 259-3989
Good Shepherd Lutheran S 200/PK-K
700 W Whitestone Blvd 78613 512-258-7602
Ann Block, dir. Fax 258-2335
Harbor Christian Academy 50/PK-12
901 Royal Ln 78613 512-219-5673
Deborah Baker, supt. Fax 219-5679
Summit Christian Academy of Cedar Park 400/PK-12
2121 Cypress Creek Rd 78613 512-250-1369
Derek Cortez, supt. Fax 257-1851

Celeste, Hunt, Pop. 848
Celeste ISD 500/PK-12
PO Box 67 75423 903-568-4825
Collin Clark, supt. Fax 568-4495
www.celesteisd.org/
Celeste ES 300/PK-5
PO Box 67 75423 903-568-4530
Paula Lyon, prin. Fax 568-4651
Celeste JHS 100/6-8
PO Box 67 75423 903-568-4612
Paula Lyon, prin. Fax 568-4277

Celina, Collin, Pop. 3,716
Celina ISD 1,400/PK-12
205 S Colorado St 75009 469-742-9100
Rob O'Connor, supt. Fax 382-3607
www.celinaisd.com/
Celina ES 400/PK-2
550 S Utah St 75009 469-742-9103
Majorie Vasquez, prin. Fax 382-3789
Celina IS 200/3-5
507 E Malone St 75009 469-742-9104
Starlynn Wells, prin. Fax 382-4792
Celina MS 300/6-8
710 E Pecan St 75009 469-742-9101
Janet Calvert, prin. Fax 382-4258

Celina Christian Academy 50/K-6
PO Box 389 75009 972-382-2930
Kim Herron, prin. Fax 382-4055

Center, Shelby, Pop. 5,781
Center ISD 2,600/PK-12
404 Mosby St 75935 936-598-5642
James Hockenberry, supt. Fax 598-1515
www.centerisd.org/
Center ES 400/2-3
314 Nacogdoches St 75935 936-598-3625
Kurt Radnitzer, prin. Fax 598-1507
Center IS 300/4-5
624 Malone Dr 75935 936-598-6148
Linda Snell, prin. Fax 598-1555
Center MS 500/6-8
302 Kennedy St 75935 936-598-5619
Gayla Miller, prin. Fax 598-1534
Moffett PS 700/PK-1
294 Stadium Dr 75935 936-598-6266
Margie Blount, prin. Fax 598-1545

Excelsior ISD 100/PK-8
11270 State Highway 7 W 75935 936-598-5866
Johnny Lewis, supt. Fax 598-2076
www.excelsior.esc7.net
Excelsior S 100/PK-8
11270 State Highway 7 W 75935 936-598-5866
Johnny Lewis, prin. Fax 598-2076

Center Point, Kerr
Center Point ISD 600/PK-12
PO Box 377 78010 830-634-2171
Dr. Donna Smith, supt. Fax 634-2254
www.cpisd.net
Center Point ES 300/PK-5
PO Box 377 78010 830-634-2257
Virginia Weidenfeld, prin. Fax 634-2119
Center Point MS 100/6-8
PO Box 377 78010 830-634-2533
Janda Castillo, prin. Fax 634-7825

Centerville, Leon, Pop. 944
Centerville ISD 700/K-12
813 S Commerce St 75833 903-536-7812
Cathy Nichols, supt. Fax 536-3133
www.centerville.k12.tx.us
Centerville ES 400/K-6
813 S Commerce St 75833 903-536-2235
Jason Jeitz, prin. Fax 536-3525

Chandler, Henderson, Pop. 2,470
Brownsboro ISD
Supt. — See Brownsboro
Chandler ES 500/PK-3
615 N Broad St 75758 903-849-3400
Sonya McCoy, prin. Fax 849-3628

Channelview, Harris, Pop. 30,600
Channelview ISD 7,100/PK-12
1403 Sheldon Rd 77530 281-452-8002
Greg Ollis, supt. Fax 457-9073
www.channelview.isd.esc4.net
Channelview Pre K PK-PK
828 Sheldon Rd 77530 281-860-3827
Judy Lee, prin. Fax 860-3801
Cobb IS 200/6-6
915 Dell Dale St 77530 281-452-7788
Blake Smith, prin. Fax 452-7413
Crenshaw ES 600/K-5
16204 Wood Dr 77530 281-457-3080
Audry Lane, prin. Fax 457-5434
De Zavala ES 300/K-5
16150 2nd St 77530 281-452-6008
Manuel Escalante, prin. Fax 452-3562
Hamblen ES 600/K-5
1019 Dell Dale St 77530 281-457-8720
Janice Powell, prin. Fax 457-8724
Johnson JHS 1,200/7-8
15500 Proctor St 77530 281-452-8030
Peter Griffiths, prin. Fax 452-1022
McMullan ES 500/K-5
1290 Dell Dale St 77530 281-452-1154
Mike Niemeyer, prin. Fax 452-1367
Schochler ES 600/K-5
910 Deerpass Dr 77530 281-452-2880
Ann Garza, prin. Fax 452-3709
Other Schools – See Houston

Pecan Street Christian Academy 100/PK-8
1215 Pecan St 77530 281-452-1333
Alice Roebuck, admin. Fax 452-1941

Channing, Hartley, Pop. 356
Channing ISD 100/K-12
PO Box A 79018 806-235-3719
Robert McLain, supt. Fax 235-2609
Channing S 100/K-12
PO Box A 79018 806-235-3719
Forrest Herbert, prin. Fax 235-2609

Charlotte, Atascosa, Pop. 1,796
Charlotte ISD 500/PK-12
PO Box 489 78011 830-277-1431
Alfonso Obregon, supt. Fax 277-1551
charlotte.echalk.com
Charlotte ES 300/PK-5
PO Box 489 78011 830-277-1710
Denise Cruz, prin. Fax 277-1675
Charlotte JHS 100/6-8
PO Box 489 78011 830-277-1646
Charles Ervin, prin. Fax 277-1654

Cherokee, San Saba
Cherokee ISD 100/K-12
PO Box 100 76832 325-622-4298
Chris Perry, supt. Fax 622-4430
www.centex-edu.net/cherokee
Cherokee S 100/K-12
PO Box 100 76832 325-622-4298
Chris Perry, prin. Fax 622-4430

Chester, Tyler, Pop. 261
Chester ISD 200/K-12
PO Box 28 75936 936-969-2211
Mike Terry, supt. Fax 969-2080
www.esc5.net/chester/
Chester ES, PO Box 28 75936 100/K-5
Mike Terry, prin. 936-969-2211

Chico, Wise, Pop. 1,069
Chico ISD 700/PK-12
PO Box 95 76431 940-644-2228
Mike Jones, supt. Fax 644-5642
www.chicodragons.org
Chico ES 300/PK-5
PO Box 95 76431 940-644-2220
Lisa Slaughter, prin. Fax 644-5642
Chico MS 200/6-8
PO Box 95 76431 940-644-5550
Maury Martin, prin. Fax 644-5642

Childress, Childress, Pop. 6,606
Childress ISD 1,200/PK-12
PO Box 179 79201 940-937-2501
John Wilson, supt. Fax 937-2938
www.childressisd.net/
Childress ES 600/PK-5
300 3rd St SE 79201 940-937-6314
Janet Word, prin. Fax 937-2165
Childress JHS 200/6-8
700 Commerce St 79201 940-937-3641
Marsha Meacham, prin. Fax 937-8427

Chillicothe, Hardeman, Pop. 736
Chillicothe ISD 200/K-12
PO Box 418 79225 940-852-5391
James Rice, supt. Fax 852-5269
cisd-tx.net
Chillicothe ES 100/K-6
PO Box 538 79225 940-852-5521
Howard Tooley, prin. Fax 852-5012

Chilton, Falls
Chilton ISD 400/PK-12
PO Box 488 76632 254-546-1200
Benny Bobo, supt. Fax 546-1201
www.chiltonisd.org
Chilton ES 200/PK-5
PO Box 488 76632 254-546-1200
Gladys Graves, prin. Fax 546-1203

China, Jefferson, Pop. 1,079
Hardin-Jefferson ISD
Supt. — See Sour Lake
China ES 200/PK-4
PO Box 398 77613 409-981-6410
Sandra Sherman, prin. Fax 752-5995

China Spring, McLennan
China Spring ISD
Supt. — See Waco
China Spring ES 800/PK-4
200 Bob Johnson Rd 76633 254-836-4635
Judy Weeden, prin. Fax 836-4637
China Spring IS 300/5-6
412 E Cougar Ln 76633 254-836-0676
Brent Merritt, prin. Fax 836-0675
China Spring MS 300/7-8
7201 N River Xing 76633 254-836-4611
Bill Bratcher, prin. Fax 836-4777

Chireno, Nacogdoches, Pop. 408
Chireno ISD 300/K-12
PO Box 85 75937 936-362-2132
Roger Dees, supt. Fax 362-2490
www.chirenoisd.org/
Chireno S 200/K-8
PO Box 85 75937 936-362-2132
Heather Hagle, prin. Fax 362-2490

Christoval, Tom Green
Christoval ISD 400/K-12
PO Box 162 76935 325-896-2520
David Walker, supt. Fax 896-7405
www.christovalisd.org
Christoval ES 200/K-5
PO Box 162 76935 325-896-2446
Carolyn Reichenau, prin. Fax 896-1145

Cibolo, Guadalupe, Pop. 7,804
Schertz-Cibolo-Universal City ISD
Supt. — See Schertz
Dobie JHS 900/7-8
395 W Borgfeld Rd 78108 210-619-4100
Linda Cannon, prin. Fax 619-4142
Jordan IS 800/5-6
515 Thistle Creek Dr 78108 210-619-4250
Shannon Allen, prin. Fax 619-4277
Schlather IS 5-6
230 Schlather St 78108 210-619-4300
Marie Riley, prin. Fax 619-4340
Watts ES 700/K-4
100 Deer Mdw 78108 210-619-4400
Becky Stark, prin. Fax 619-4419
Wiederstein ES 400/PK-4
171 W Borgfeld Rd 78108 210-619-4550
Stacy Serna, prin. Fax 619-4590

Cisco, Eastland, Pop. 3,833
Cisco ISD 900/PK-12
PO Box 1645 76437 254-442-3056
Hal Porter, supt. Fax 442-1412
www.ciscoisd.net/
Cisco ES 400/PK-5
PO Box 1645 76437 254-442-1219
Darleen Hearne, prin. Fax 442-4836
Cisco JHS 200/6-8
PO Box 1645 76437 254-442-3004
Kelly West, prin. Fax 442-1832

Clarendon, Donley, Pop. 2,021
Clarendon ISD 500/PK-12
PO Box 610 79226 806-874-2062
Monty Hysinger, supt. Fax 874-2579
www.clarendon.k12.tx.us/
Clarendon ES 200/PK-5
PO Box 610 79226 806-874-3855
Mike Word, prin. Fax 874-2579
Clarendon JHS 100/6-8
PO Box 610 79226 806-874-3232
Marvin Elam, prin. Fax 874-9748

Clarksville, Red River, Pop. 3,611
Clarksville ISD 900/PK-12
1500 W Main St 75426 903-427-3891
Pam Bryant, supt. Fax 427-5071
www.clarksvilleisd.net/home.aspx
Cheatham MS 200/6-8
1500 W Main St 75426 903-427-3891
Tammie Bates, prin. Fax 427-4118
Clarksville ES 500/PK-5
1500 W Main St 75426 903-427-3891
Carrie Gray, prin. Fax 427-1601

Claude, Armstrong, Pop. 1,328
Claude ISD 400/PK-12
PO Box 209 79019 806-226-7331
Laura Zanchettin, supt. Fax 226-2244
www.claudeisd.net/
Claude ES 200/PK-5
PO Box 209 79019 806-226-3522
Reagan Oles, prin. Fax 226-2244

Cleburne, Johnson, Pop. 29,184
Cleburne ISD 6,500/PK-12
505 N Ridgeway Dr Ste 100 76033 817-202-1100
Dr. Ronny Beard, supt. Fax 202-1460
www.cleburne.k12.tx.us/
Adams ES 300/K-5
1492 Island Grove Rd 76031 817-202-2000
Richard Mitchell, prin. Fax 202-1482
Coleman ES 500/PK-5
920 W Westhill Dr 76033 817-202-2030
Kyle Boles, prin. Fax 202-1484
Cooke ES 600/K-5
902 Phillips St 76033 817-202-2060
Gary Buckingham, prin. Fax 202-1483
Gerard ES 400/K-5
1212 Hyde Park Blvd 76033 817-202-2130
Jay Lewis, prin. Fax 202-1485
Irving ES 300/PK-5
345 Hix Rd 76031 817-202-2100
Juanita Reyes, prin. Fax 202-1486
Marti ES 600/K-5
2020 W Kilpatrick St 76033 817-202-1650
Sharon Urban, prin. Fax 202-1487
Santa Fe ES 600/PK-5
221 Fergason Rd 76031 817-202-2300
Susie Sarchet, prin. Fax 202-1497

Smith MS 900/6-8
1710 Country Club Rd 76033 817-202-1500
Dr. Lylia King, prin. Fax 202-1475
Wheat MS 700/6-8
810 N Colonial Dr 76033 817-202-1300
David Diaz, prin. Fax 202-1479

Cleburne Adventist Christian S 50/K-8
111 Meadowview Dr 76033 817-645-4300
Cindy Read, prin.
Cleburne Community Christian S 100/PK-8
PO Box 2017 76033 817-641-2857
Joyce Ganong, prin. Fax 641-2863

Cleveland, Liberty, Pop. 8,032
Cleveland ISD 3,300/PK-12
316 E Dallas St 77327 281-592-8717
Kerry Cowart, supt. Fax 592-8283
www.clevelandisd.org
Cleveland JHS 700/6-8
2000 E Houston St 77327 281-593-1148
Patricia Curry, prin. Fax 593-3400
Eastside ES 500/4-5
1602 Shell Ave 77327 281-592-0125
Jacqueline Reist, prin. Fax 592-0277
Northside ES 600/2-3
1522 N Blair Ave 77327 281-592-4628
Gay Lynn Pruett, prin. Fax 592-9679
Southside ES 600/PK-1
303 E Fort Worth St 77327 281-592-0594
Katy Scott, prin. Fax 592-2185

Tarkington ISD 2,000/PK-12
2770 FM 163 Rd 77327 281-592-8781
John Kirchner, supt. Fax 592-3969
www.tarkingtonisd.net/
Tarkington IS 300/4-5
2770 FM 163 Rd 77327 281-592-6134
Jim Hair, prin. Fax 592-2453
Tarkington MS 500/6-8
2770 FM 163 Rd 77327 281-592-7737
John Johnson, prin. Fax 592-5241
Tarkington PS 600/PK-3
2770 FM 163 Rd 77327 281-592-7736
Maureen Cullen, prin. Fax 592-2361

Clifton, Bosque, Pop. 3,642
Clifton ISD 900/PK-12
1102 Key St 76634 254-675-2827
Rhoda White, supt. Fax 675-4351
www.clifton.k12.tx.us
Clifton ES 300/PK-5
706 W 11th St 76634 254-675-2827
Tonya Dansby, prin. Fax 675-8725
Clifton MS 300/6-8
1102 Key St 76634 254-675-2827
Billy Murrell, prin. Fax 675-2005

Clint, El Paso, Pop. 985
Clint ISD
Supt. — See El Paso
Clint JHS 400/6-8
13100 Alameda Ave 79836 915-926-8100
David Morales, prin. Fax 851-3459
Surratt ES 900/PK-5
12675 Alameda Ave 79836 915-926-8200
Robert Flores, prin. Fax 851-3489

Clute, Brazoria, Pop. 10,731
Brazosport ISD 12,800/PK-12
301 W Brazoswood Dr 77531 979-730-7000
Joe Ripple, supt. Fax 266-2486
www.brazosportisd.net
Clute IS 600/5-8
421 E Main St 77531 979-730-7230
Jay Whitehead, prin. Fax 730-7363
Griffith ES 500/PK-4
101 Lexington Ave 77531 979-730-7180
Dolores Trevino, prin. Fax 266-2469
Ogg ES 500/PK-4
208 N Lazy Ln 77531 979-730-7195
Eddie Damian, prin. Fax 266-2488
Other Schools – See Freeport, Jones Creek, Lake Jackson, Richwood

Clyde, Callahan, Pop. 3,673
Clyde Consolidated ISD 1,300/PK-12
PO Box 479 79510 325-893-4222
Dr. Gail Haterius, supt. Fax 893-4024
www.clyde.esc14.net
Clyde ES 400/PK-2
1811 Nottingham Ln 79510 325-893-4788
Kim Jones, prin. Fax 893-5642
Clyde IS 200/3-5
505 N Hays Rd 79510 325-893-2815
Traci Yandell, prin. Fax 893-3067
Clyde JHS 200/6-8
211 S 3rd St W 79510 325-893-5788
Greg Edwards, prin. Fax 893-5319

Eula ISD 300/PK-12
6040 FM 603 79510 325-529-3186
Tim Kelley, supt. Fax 529-4461
www.eulaisd.us
Eula ES 200/PK-6
6040 FM 603 79510 325-529-3212
Ann Clark, prin. Fax 529-4461

Coahoma, Howard, Pop. 915
Coahoma ISD 800/PK-12
PO Box 110 79511 432-394-4290
Randy Brown, supt. Fax 394-4302
www.coahomaisd.com/
Coahoma ES 400/PK-6
PO Box 110 79511 432-394-4323
Patricia Bennett, prin. Fax 394-4419
Coahoma JHS 100/7-8
PO Box 110 79511 432-394-4615
Dean Richters, prin. Fax 394-4052

Coldspring, San Jacinto, Pop. 763
Coldspring-Oakhurst Consolidated ISD 1,700/PK-12
PO Box 39 77331 936-653-1115
LaTonya Goffney, supt. Fax 653-2197
www.cocisd.org
Coldspring-Oakhurst IS 400/3-5
PO Box 39 77331 936-653-1152
D'Wayne Bryant, prin. Fax 653-3689
Lincoln JHS 400/6-8
PO Box 39 77331 936-653-1166
Andrea Seale, prin. Fax 653-3688
Street ES 400/PK-2
PO Box 39 77331 936-653-1187
Elizabeth Jarvis, prin. Fax 653-3690

Coleman, Coleman, Pop. 4,829
Coleman ISD 1,000/PK-12
PO Box 900 76834 325-625-3575
Royce Young, supt. Fax 625-4751
www.colemanisd.net/
Coleman ES 500/PK-5
303 15th St 76834 325-625-3546
Becky Jackson, prin. Fax 625-4064
Coleman JHS 200/6-8
301 15th St 76834 325-625-3593
Paula Ringo, prin. Fax 625-3358

College Station, Brazos, Pop. 72,388
College Station ISD 8,900/PK-12
1812 Welsh Ave 77840 979-764-5400
Dr. Eddie Coulson, supt. Fax 764-5535
www.csisd.org
A & M Consolidated MS 600/7-8
105 Holik St 77840 979-764-5575
Nkrumah Dixon, prin. Fax 764-4294
College Hills ES 600/PK-4
1101 Williams St 77840 979-764-5565
Jane Rankin, prin. Fax 764-2889
College Station MS 700/7-8
900 Rock Prairie Rd 77845 979-764-5545
Oliver Hadnot, prin. Fax 764-4015
Creek View ES PK-4
1001 Eagle Ave 77845 979-694-5890
Tami Laza, prin. Fax 764-5492
Cypress Grove IS 600/5-6
900 Graham Rd 77845 979-694-5600
Rick Hill, prin. Fax 694-3680
Forest Ridge ES 700/PK-4
1950 Greens Prairie Rd W 77845 979-694-5801
Terresa Katt, prin. Fax 694-2610
Oakwood IS 600/5-6
106 Holik St 77840 979-764-5530
Kate Schoen, prin. Fax 764-3891
Pebble Creek ES 600/PK-4
200 Parkview Dr 77845 979-764-5595
Donna Bairrington, prin. Fax 764-2489
Rock Prairie ES 600/PK-4
3400 Welsh Ave 77845 979-764-5570
Mike Martindale, prin. Fax 764-2276
South Knoll ES 700/PK-4
1220 Boswell St 77840 979-764-5580
Laura Richter, prin. Fax 764-3090
Southwood Valley ES 700/PK-4
2700 Brothers Blvd 77845 979-764-5590
Kristiana Hamilton, prin. Fax 764-2009

Brazos Valley Adventist S 50/PK-8
1350 Earl Rudder Fwy S 77840 979-595-1115
Agida Henderson, prin.
St. Thomas Early Learning Center 100/PK-PK, 1-
906 George Bush Dr 77840 979-696-1728
Laura Calvin, dir. Fax 696-1727

Colleyville, Tarrant, Pop. 22,394
Grapevine-Colleyville ISD
Supt. — See Grapevine
Bransford ES 500/K-5
601 Glade Rd 76034 817-788-4420
Sarah Hodges, prin. Fax 428-1203
Colleyville ES 600/K-5
5800 Colleyville Blvd 76034 817-788-4440
Fax 498-2062
Colleyville MS 800/6-8
1100 Bogart Dr 76034 817-788-4400
Toni Thalken, prin. Fax 498-9764
Glenhope ES 500/K-5
6600 Glenhope Cir N 76034 817-251-5720
Wynette Griffin, prin. Fax 329-5618
Heritage MS 900/6-8
5300 Heritage Ave 76034 817-358-4790
Pete Valamides, prin. Fax 267-9929
Taylor ES 500/K-5
5300 Pool Rd 76034 817-358-4870
David Kinney, prin. Fax 540-3940

Keller ISD
Supt. — See Keller
Liberty ES 400/K-4
1101 W McDonwell School Rd 76034 817-744-6000
Janet Travis, prin. Fax 743-0314

Covenant Christian Academy 500/PK-12
901 Cheek Sparger Rd 76034 817-281-4333
Keith Castello, hdmstr. Fax 281-4674
Crown of Life Lutheran S 100/PK-8
6605 Pleasant Run Rd 76034 817-251-1881
Tim Walz, prin. Fax 421-9263
Gordon Montessori S 200/PK-6
1513 Hall Johnson Rd 76034 817-354-6670
Laura Roark, hdmstr. Fax 354-6665

Collinsville, Grayson, Pop. 1,471
Collinsville ISD 600/PK-12
PO Box 49 76233 903-429-6272
Tim Wright, supt. Fax 429-6665
www.collinsvilleisd.org
Collinsville IS 100/5-6
PO Box 49 76233 903-429-6272
Ken Kemp, prin. Fax 429-6665
Collinsville PS 300/PK-4
PO Box 49 76233 903-429-3077
Sheila Riddle, prin. Fax 429-1004

Colmesneil, Tyler, Pop. 631
Colmesneil ISD 600/K-12
PO Box 37 75938 409-837-5757
Elton Hightower, supt. Fax 837-5759
www.esc5.net/colmesneil
Colmesneil ES 200/K-5
PO Box 37 75938 409-837-2229
Yvette Carlton, prin. Fax 837-9119
Colmesneil MS 100/6-8
PO Box 37 75938 409-837-5272
Rodney Haught, prin. Fax 837-2307

Colorado City, Mitchell, Pop. 4,018
Colorado ISD 1,000/PK-12
PO Box 1268 79512 325-728-3721
Jim White, supt. Fax 728-8471
www.ccity.esc14.net
Colorado MS 200/6-8
312 E 12th St 79512 325-728-2673
Mark Merrell, prin. Fax 728-1051
Hutchinson ES 200/3-5
440 Cedar St 79512 325-728-5215
Kathlyn Arthur, prin. Fax 728-1037
Kelley ES 300/PK-2
1435 Elm St 79512 325-728-3471
Denise Farmer, prin. Fax 728-1036

Columbus, Colorado, Pop. 3,934
Columbus ISD 1,600/PK-12
105 Cardinal Ln 78934 979-732-5704
Randall Hoyer, supt. Fax 732-5960
www.columbusisd.org/
Columbus ES 700/PK-5
1324 Bowie St 78934 979-732-2078
Michael Koehl, prin. Fax 732-8627
Columbus JHS 300/6-8
702 Rampart St 78934 979-732-2891
Wayne Zimmerhanzel, prin. Fax 732-9081

St. Anthony S 200/PK-8
635 Bonham St 78934 979-732-5505
John O'Leary, prin. Fax 732-9758

Comanche, Comanche, Pop. 4,302
Comanche ISD 1,200/PK-12
1414 N Austin St 76442 325-356-2727
Rick Howard, supt. Fax 356-2312
www.comancheisd.net
Comanche ES 400/PK-3
200 E Highland Ave 76442 325-356-2440
Curtis Stankhe, prin. Fax 356-1838
Comanche MS 200/4-6
308 FM 3381 76442 325-356-3900
Susan Carruth, prin. Fax 356-3990
Jeffries JHS 200/7-8
1 Valley Forge Dr 76442 325-356-5220
Mary Jane McPherren, prin. Fax 356-1949

Combes, Cameron, Pop. 2,840
Harlingen Consolidated ISD
Supt. — See Harlingen
Dishman ES 500/PK-5
PO Box 249 78535 956-427-3100
Eloisa Ackerman, prin. Fax 427-3103

Comfort, Kendall, Pop. 1,477
Comfort ISD 1,300/PK-12
PO Box 398 78013 830-995-6400
John Chapman, supt. Fax 995-2236
www.comfort.txed.net
Comfort ES 600/PK-5
PO Box 157 78013 830-995-6410
Angeli Willson, prin. Fax 995-4153
Comfort MS 300/6-8
PO Box 187 78013 830-995-6420
Christopher Yeschke, prin. Fax 995-2248

Commerce, Hunt, Pop. 8,971
Commerce ISD 1,700/PK-12
PO Box 1251 75429 903-886-3755
Larry Johnson, supt. Fax 886-6025
www.commerceisd.org/home.htm
Commerce ES 500/PK-2
PO Box 1251 75429 903-886-3757
Bobbie Thurman, prin. Fax 886-6112
Commerce MS 400/6-8
PO Box 1251 75429 903-886-3795
Wes Underwood, prin. Fax 886-6102
Williams ES 300/3-5
PO Box 1251 75429 903-886-3758
Julia Robinson, prin. Fax 886-6228

Como, Hopkins, Pop. 645
Como-Pickton Consolidated ISD 900/PK-12
PO Box 18 75431 903-488-3671
Sandra Billodeau, supt. Fax 488-3133
como.tx.schoolwebpages.com/
Como-Pickton ES 500/PK-5
PO Box 18 75431 903-488-3671
Randy Stuard, prin. Fax 488-3133
Como-Pickton JHS 200/6-8
PO Box 18 75431 903-488-3671
Penny Armstrong, prin. Fax 488-3133

Comstock, Val Verde
Comstock ISD 200/K-12
PO Box 905 78837 432-292-4444
Orlie Wolfenbarger, supt. Fax 292-4436
www.comstockisd.net/
Comstock S 200/K-12
PO Box 905 78837 432-292-4444
Toby Ward, prin. Fax 292-4436

Conroe, Montgomery, Pop. 47,042
Conroe ISD 43,200/PK-12
3205 W Davis St 77304 936-709-7751
Dr. Don Stockton, supt. Fax 760-7704
www.conroeisd.net/

Anderson ES 800/PK-4
1414 E Dallas St 77301 936-709-5300
Gilberto Lozano, prin. Fax 790-5312
Armstrong ES 700/PK-4
110 Gladstell St 77301 936-709-3400
Victor Uher, prin. Fax 709-3415
Austin ES 600/PK-4
14796 Highway 105 E 77306 936-709-8400
Cindy Lentz, prin. Fax 709-8403
Creighton ES 900/PK-4
12089 FM 1485 Rd 77306 936-709-2900
Jennifer Watson, prin. Fax 231-1135
Cryar IS 1,000/5-6
2375 Montgomery Park Blvd 77304 936-709-7300
Dr. Lloyd Swanson, prin. Fax 709-7313
Giesinger ES 700/PK-4
2323 White Oak Blvd 77304 936-709-2600
Jeri Alloway, prin. Fax 539-6109
Grangerland IS 900/5-6
13351 FM 1485 Rd 77306 936-709-3500
Tammy Hamilton, prin. Fax 709-3565
Houser ES 800/PK-4
27370 Oak Ridge School Rd 77385 281-863-4000
Paula Green, prin. Fax 863-4076
Houston ES 600/PK-4
1000 N Thompson St 77301 936-709-5100
Ivan Velasco, prin. Fax 709-5103
Milam ES 800/PK-4
16415 FM 3083 Rd 77302 936-709-5200
Judy Davis, prin. Fax 709-5203
Moorehead JHS 900/7-8
13475 FM 1485 Rd 77306 936-709-2400
Sarah Sanders, prin. Fax 709-2499
Oak Ridge ES 700/PK-4
19675 Interstate 45 S 77385 832-592-5900
Tara Vandermark, prin. Fax 592-5968
Peet JHS 1,000/7-8
400 Sgt Ed Holcomb Blvd N 77304 936-709-3700
Curtis Null, prin. Fax 709-3828
Reaves ES 500/K-4
1717 N Loop 336 W 77304 936-709-5400
Rebecca Page, prin. Fax 709-5407
Rice ES 600/PK-4
904 Gladstell Rd 77304 936-709-2700
Carrie Fitzpatrick, prin. Fax 788-6322
Runyan ES 600/PK-4
1101 Foster Dr 77301 936-709-2800
Tracy Voelker, prin. Fax 788-6319
San Jacinto ES 700/PK-4
17601 FM 1314 Rd 77302 281-465-7700
Renee O'Neal, prin. Fax 572-4853
Travis IS 600/5-6
1100 N Thompson St 77301 936-709-7000
Jean Anne Gloriod, prin. Fax 709-7019
Washington JHS 600/7-8
507 Dr Martin Luther King 77301 936-709-7400
Hartwell Brown, prin. Fax 709-7492
Other Schools – See Spring, The Woodlands

Adventist Christian Academy of Texas 100/PK-12
3601 S Loop 336 E 77301 936-756-5078
Carolyn Early, prin. Fax 760-4029
Calvary Baptist S 200/PK-12
3401 N Frazier St 77303 936-756-0743
Becky Burchett, prin. Fax 756-0764
Christ Community S 100/PK-6
1488 Wellman Rd 77384 936-321-6300
Kelle Castleberry, prin. Fax 273-5858
Conroe Christian S 50/K-12
1612 Odd Fellow St 77301 936-539-2989
Trent Smith, prin. Fax 539-2986
Covenant Christian S 300/PK-12
4503 Interstate 45 N 77304 936-890-8080
Dr. Charles Lloyd, admin. Fax 890-5343
First Baptist Academy 100/K-4
600 N Main St 77301 936-756-6622
Janice Archer, admin. Fax 756-2436
Lifestyle Christian S 200/K-12
3993 Interstate 45 N 77304 936-756-9383
Joshua Davenport, prin. Fax 760-3003
Oak Ridge Christian Academy 100/PK-9
27420 Robinson Rd 77385 281-298-5800
Matthew Duston, hdmstr. Fax 292-2818
Sacred Heart S 300/PK-8
615 McDade St 77301 936-756-3848
Gerard Kubelka, prin. Fax 756-4097
St. Mark Lutheran S 50/PK-5
2100 Tickner St 77301 936-756-3151
David Quail, hdmstr. Fax 756-3796

Converse, Bexar, Pop. 12,650

Judson ISD
Supt. — See Live Oak
Converse ES 600/PK-5
6720 FM 1516 N 78109 210-945-1210
Ted Haynes, prin. Fax 658-8162
Elolf ES 900/PK-5
6335 Beech Trail Dr 78109 210-661-1130
Cathy Hottle, prin. Fax 666-0536
Masters ES K-5
2650 Woodlake Pkwy 78109 210-945-1150
Melissa Arnell, prin. Fax 310-0650
Miller's Point ES 700/K-6
7027 Misty Ridge Dr 78109 210-945-5114
Michael McFalls, prin. Fax 590-4254

St. Monica S 300/1-8
PO Box 429 78109 210-658-6701
JoAnn Wood, prin. Fax 658-6945

Coolidge, Limestone, Pop. 882

Coolidge ISD 300/PK-12
PO Box 70 76635 254-786-2206
Dr. Chris Hulen, supt. Fax 786-4835
www.coolidge.k12.tx.us/
Coolidge ES 200/PK-5
PO Box 70 76635 254-786-4833
Terry Farnsworth, prin. Fax 786-4835

Cooper, Delta, Pop. 2,185

Cooper ISD 900/PK-12
PO Box 478 75432 903-395-2111
Jason Marshall, supt. Fax 395-2117
www.cooperisd.net/
Cooper ES 400/PK-5
PO Box 478 75432 903-395-2111
Doug Wicks, prin. Fax 395-2019
Cooper JHS 200/6-8
PO Box 478 75432 903-395-0509
Chris Kiser, prin. Fax 395-2382

Coppell, Dallas, Pop. 38,704

Carrollton-Farmers Branch ISD
Supt. — See Carrollton
Riverchase ES 400/PK-5
272 S MacArthur Blvd 75019 972-968-2900
Jody Williams, prin. Fax 968-2910

Coppell ISD 9,400/PK-12
200 S Denton Tap Rd 75019 214-496-6000
Dr. Jeff Turner, supt. Fax 496-6036
www.coppellisd.com
Austin ES 500/PK-5
161 S Moore Rd 75019 214-496-7300
Laurie O'Neill, prin. Fax 496-7306
Coppell MS East 700/6-8
400 Mockingbird Ln 75019 214-496-6600
Laura Springer, prin. Fax 496-6603
Coppell MS North 800/6-8
120 Natches Trce 75019 214-496-7100
Lynn Ojeda, prin. Fax 496-7103
Coppell MS West 900/6-8
1301 Wrangler Cir 75019 214-496-8600
Vernon Edin, prin. Fax 496-8606
Cottonwood Creek ES 500/PK-5
615 Minyard Dr 75019 214-496-8300
Dr. Andra Penny, prin. Fax 496-8306
Denton Creek ES 500/K-5
250 Natches Trce 75019 214-496-8100
Bryan McLain, prin. Fax 496-8106
Lakeside ES 500/K-5
1100 Village Pkwy 75019 214-496-7600
Gema Hall, prin. Fax 496-7606
Mockingbird ES 500/K-5
300 Mockingbird Ln 75019 214-496-8200
Pam Mitchell, prin. Fax 496-8206
Pinkerton ES 300/K-5
260 Southwestern Blvd 75019 214-496-6800
Kristi Mikkelsen, prin. Fax 496-6806
Town Center ES 500/K-5
185 N Heartz Rd 75019 214-496-7800
Penny Tramel, prin. Fax 496-7806
Wilson ES 400/K-5
200 S Coppell Rd 75019 214-496-7500
Deana Harrell, prin. Fax 496-7506
Other Schools – See Irving

Coppell Montessori Academy 100/PK-4
136 Fitness Ct 75019 972-462-8311
Carmen Sexton, prin. Fax 462-8312

Copperas Cove, Coryell, Pop. 30,643

Copperas Cove ISD 6,100/PK-12
703 W Avenue D 76522 254-547-1227
Dr. Rose Cameron, supt. Fax 547-1542
www.ccisd.com
Clements\Hollie Parsons ES 200/PK-5
1115 Northern Dancer Dr 76522 254-547-2235
Patti Monroe, prin. Fax 547-0845
Copperas Cove JHS 500/6-8
702 Sunny Ave 76522 254-547-6959
Randy Troub, prin. Fax 518-2620
Fairview\Miss Jewell ES 1,000/PK-5
1002 Veterans Ave 76522 254-547-4212
Sylvia Miller, prin. Fax 547-6980
Halstead ES 500/PK-5
910 N Main St 76522 254-547-3440
Mary Derrick, prin. Fax 547-6896
Lee JHS 600/6-8
1205 Courtney Ln 76522 254-542-7877
Kayleen Love, prin. Fax 542-8103
Stevens ES 400/PK-5
302 Manning Dr 76522 254-547-8289
Christy Slagle, prin. Fax 547-8325
Walker ES 500/PK-5
100 FM 3046 76522 254-547-2283
Jack Brown, prin. Fax 547-5984
Williams\Lovett Ledger ES 300/PK-5
909 Courtney Ln 76522 254-542-1001
Kevin Cameron, prin. Fax 542-2794

Corinth, Denton, Pop. 17,980

Denton ISD
Supt. — See Denton
Crownover MS 900/6-8
1901 Creekside Dr 76210 940-369-4700
Gwen Perkins, prin. Fax 321-0502

Lake Dallas ISD
Supt. — See Lake Dallas
Corinth ES 700/K-4
3501 Cliff Oaks Dr 76210 940-497-4010
Ellen Smith, prin. Fax 497-8479

Corpus Christi, Nueces, Pop. 283,474

Calallen ISD 3,900/PK-12
4205 Wildcat Dr 78410 361-242-5600
Arturo Almendarez, supt. Fax 242-5620
www.calallen.k12.tx.us
Calallen East PS 500/PK-3
3709 Lott Ave 78410 361-242-5938
Greer Parker, prin. Fax 242-5944
Calallen MS 900/6-8
4602 Cornett Dr 78410 361-242-5672
Lynnette Felder, prin. Fax 242-5680
Calallen/Wood River PS 600/PK-3
15118 Dry Creek Dr 78410 361-387-5566
Candy Morris, prin. Fax 387-3114

Magee IS 700/PK-PK, 4-
4201 Calallen Dr 78410 361-242-5900
Michael Gurleski, prin. Fax 242-5913

Corpus Christi ISD 38,600/PK-12
PO Box 110 78403 361-886-9200
Doyne Scott Elliff, supt. Fax 886-9109
www.corpuschristiisd.org
Allen ES 400/PK-5
1414 18th St 78404 361-878-2140
Joe Hernandez, prin. Fax 886-9874
Baker MS 900/6-8
3445 Pecan St 78411 361-878-4600
Darla Reid, prin. Fax 878-1834
Barnes ES 600/PK-5
2829 Oso Pkwy 78414 361-994-5051
Lisa Bowers, prin. Fax 994-0860
Browne MS 700/6-8
4301 Schanen Blvd 78413 361-878-1426
Donna Adams, prin. Fax 878-1836
Calk ES 400/PK-5
4621 Marie St 78411 361-878-1700
Susan Bateman, prin. Fax 878-1814
Carroll Lane ES 400/PK-5
4120 Carroll Ln 78411 361-878-2160
Dianne Moore, prin. Fax 878-2303
Casa Linda ES 400/PK-5
1540 Casa Grande Dr 78411 361-878-2180
Denise Woodson, prin. Fax 878-1816
Central Park ES 400/PK-5
3602 McArdle Rd 78415 361-878-2200
Norma Reyna, prin. Fax 878-1817
Chula Vista Fine Arts ES 400/1-5
1761 Hudson St 78416 361-878-1718
Robin Conde, prin. Fax 878-1818
Club Estates ES 500/K-5
5222 Merganser Dr 78413 361-994-3642
Dr. Lynda DeLeon, prin. Fax 994-3615
Crockett ES 600/PK-5
2625 Belton St 78416 361-878-2220
Rosa Sanchez, prin. Fax 878-2366
Cullen Place MS 500/6-8
5225 Greely Dr 78412 361-994-3630
Dr. Jennitta Rupp, prin. Fax 994-3624
Cunningham MS 500/6-8
4321 Prescott St 78416 361-878-4630
Dr. Patricia Castillo, prin. Fax 878-1838
Dawson ES 600/K-5
6821 Sanders Dr 78413 361-878-4800
Teresa Ybarguan-Garcia, prin. Fax 878-4805
Driscoll MS 700/6-8
3501 Kenwood Dr 78408 361-878-4660
Stella Olson-Torres, prin. Fax 886-9890
Early Childhood Development Center 50/PK-PK
6300 Ocean Dr 78412 361-825-3366
Susan Luis, prin. Fax 825-3301
Evans Special Emphasis ES 400/PK-5
1315 Comanche St 78401 361-878-2240
Arnoldo Barrera, prin. Fax 886-9877
Fannin ES 500/PK-5
2730 Gollihar Rd 78415 361-878-2260
Elodia Gutierrez, prin. Fax 878-1820
Galvan ES 600/PK-5
3126 Masterson Dr 78415 361-878-1786
Patti Heiland, prin. Fax 878-1821
Garcia ES 300/K-5
4401 Greenwood Dr 78416 361-878-2280
Norma DeLeon, prin. Fax 878-2367
Gibson ES 500/PK-5
5723 Hampshire Rd 78408 361-878-2500
Anna Fuentes, prin. Fax 289-7406
Grant MS 1,000/6-8
4350 Aaron Dr 78413 361-878-1860
Carla Rosa-Villarreal, prin. Fax 878-1871
Haas MS 500/6-8
6630 McArdle Rd 78412 361-994-3636
Deborah Scates, prin. Fax 994-3626
Hamlin MS 800/6-8
3900 Hamlin Dr 78411 361-878-1438
Debbie McAden, prin. Fax 878-1839
Houston ES 500/PK-5
363 Norton St 78415 361-878-2520
Olivia Ballesteros, prin. Fax 878-1823
Jones ES 600/PK-5
7533 Lipes Blvd 78413 361-994-3674
Galen Hoffstadt, prin. Fax 994-3616
Kaffie MS 1,000/6-8
5922 Brockhampton St 78414 361-994-3600
Rhonda Roberts, prin. Fax 994-3604
Kostoryz ES 800/PK-5
3602 Panama Dr 78415 361-878-2540
Angie Ramiraz, prin. Fax 878-2329
Lamar ES 500/PK-5
2212 Morris St 78405 361-878-2560
Christine Marroquin, prin. Fax 886-9219
Lexington Place ES 300/PK-5
2901 Mcardle Rd 78415 361-878-2580
Fax 878-2300
Los Encinos Special Emphasis ES 400/PK-5
1826 Frio St 78417 361-878-2600
Sylvia Prezas, prin. Fax 878-1826
Martin MS 600/6-8
3502 Greenwood Dr 78416 361-878-4690
Delma Yzaguirre, prin. Fax 878-2455
Meadowbrook ES 600/PK-5
901 Meadowbrook Dr 78412 361-878-2620
LaTricia Johnson, prin. Fax 994-3650
Menger ES, 2401 S Alameda St 78404 500/PK-5
Cynthia Wilson-Ferris, prin. 361-878-2640
Mireles ES 500/PK-5
7658 Cimarron Blvd 78414 361-994-6960
Josie Alvarez, prin. Fax 994-6970
Montclair ES 500/PK-5
5241 Kentner St 78412 361-994-3651
Kimberly Bissell, prin. Fax 994-6940
Moore ES 600/PK-5
6121 Durant Dr 78414 361-878-2660
Janie Vela, prin. Fax 994-3619

Oak Park Special Emphasis ES | 700/PK-5
3801 Leopard St 78408 | 361-878-2120
Maria Elena Zavala, prin. | Fax 878-2139
Prescott ES | 300/PK-5
1945 Gollihar Rd 78416 | 361-878-2680
Jaime Gonzales, prin. | Fax 878-1828
Sanders ES | 400/PK-5
4102 Republic Dr 78413 | 361-878-1761
Debra Miget, prin. | Fax 878-1829
Schanen Estates ES | 500/PK-5
5717 Killarmet Dr 78413 | 361-878-1766
Pamela Wright, prin. | Fax 878-1830
Seale Academy of Fine Arts | 700/6-8
1707 Ayers St 78404 | 361-878-4750
Angela Portis-Woodson, prin. | Fax 886-9892
Shaw Special Emphasis ES | 600/PK-5
2920 Soledad St 78405 | 361-878-2100
Rafael Silva, prin. | Fax 878-2109
Smith ES | 500/PK-5
6902 Williams Dr 78412 | 361-994-3660
Steve Barrera, prin. | Fax 994-3681
South Park MS | 600/6-8
3001 McArdle Rd 78415 | 361-878-4720
Sandra Clement, prin. | Fax 878-1844
Travis ES | 400/PK-5
3210 Churchill Dr 78415 | 361-878-2700
John Trevino, prin. | Fax 844-0341
Webb ES | 500/K-5
6953 Boardwalk Ave 78414 | 361-878-2740
Norma Cullum, prin. | Fax 878-2759
Wilson ES | 700/PK-5
3925 Fort Worth St 78411 | 361-878-1771
Sheila Thomas, prin. | Fax 878-1831
Windsor Park Gifted/Talent ES | 600/1-5
4525 S Alameda St 78412 | 361-994-3664
Dr. Victoria Smith, prin. | Fax 994-3621
Woodlawn ES | 400/PK-5
1110 Woodlawn Dr 78412 | 361-994-3669
Linda Bushell, prin. | Fax 994-3622
Yeager ES | 400/PK-5
5414 Tripoli Dr 78411 | 361-878-1778
Melissa Naranjo, prin. | Fax 878-1832
Zavala Special Emphasis ES | 600/PK-5
3102 Highland Ave 78405 | 361-878-2720
Rosemary Pompa, prin. | Fax 886-9884

Flour Bluff ISD | 5,300/PK-12
2505 Waldron Rd 78418 | 361-694-9200
Dr. Julie Carbajal, supt. | Fax 694-9809
www.flourbluffschools.net
Flour Bluff ECC | 500/PK-K
2505 Waldron Rd 78418 | 361-694-9036
Fax 694-9810
Flour Bluff ES | 700/3-4
2505 Waldron Rd 78418 | 361-694-9500
Linda Barganski, prin. | Fax 694-9805
Flour Bluff IS | 800/5-6
2505 Waldron Rd 78418 | 361-694-9400
Salvador Alvarado, prin. | Fax 694-9804
Flour Bluff JHS | 800/7-8
2505 Waldron Rd 78418 | 361-694-9300
Danny Glover, prin. | Fax 694-9803
Flour Bluff PS | 800/1-2
2505 Waldron Rd 78418 | 361-694-9600
Cindy Holder, prin. | Fax 694-9806

London ISD | 300/K-8
1306 FM 43 78415 | 361-855-0092
Charley McMath, supt. | Fax 855-0198
www.londonisd.net
London S | 300/K-8
1306 FM 43 78415 | 361-855-0092
Clay Campbell, prin. | Fax 855-0198

Tuloso-Midway ISD | 3,400/PK-12
PO Box 10900 78460 | 361-903-6400
Dr. Cornelio Gonzalez, supt. | Fax 241-5836
www.tmisd.esc2.net
Tuloso-Midway IS | 800/3-5
PO Box 10900 78460 | 361-903-6550
Ayme Morales, prin. | Fax 903-6572
Tuloso-Midway MS | 800/6-8
PO Box 10900 78460 | 361-903-6600
Thomas Walker, prin. | Fax 241-9829
Tuloso-Midway PS | 800/PK-2
PO Box 10900 78460 | 361-903-6500
Gloria Dornak, prin. | Fax 241-5617

West Oso ISD | 2,000/PK-12
5050 Rockford Dr 78416 | 361-806-5900
Dr. Crawford Helms, supt. | Fax 225-8308
www.westosoisd.esc2.net
Kennedy ES | 400/PK-1
5040 Rockford Dr 78416 | 361-806-5920
Gracie Stillman, prin. | Fax 225-8332
West Oso ES | 600/2-5
1526 Cliff Maus Dr 78416 | 361-806-5930
Terry Avery, prin. | Fax 225-8956
West Oso JHS | 400/6-8
5202 Bear Ln 78405 | 361-806-5950
Raela Johnson-Olivarez, prin. | Fax 299-3111

Annapolis Christian Academy | 200/PK-12
5633 S Staples St 78411 | 361-991-6004
Peter Hansen, hdmstr. | Fax 232-5629
Bishop Garriga MS | 100/6-8
3114 Saratoga Blvd 78415 | 361-851-0853
Rosario Davila, prin. | Fax 853-5145
Central Catholic S | 100/PK-5
1218 Comanche St 78401 | 361-883-3873
Sr. Anne Brigid Schlegel, prin. | Fax 883-5879
Christ the King S | 100/PK-6
1625 Arlington Dr 78415 | 361-883-5391
Perry LeGrange, prin. | Fax 888-9207
Coastal Bend Adventist Jr. Academy | 50/PK-8
6645 Downing St 78414 | 361-991-6968
Marcy Tanner, prin. | Fax 991-3617
First Baptist S | 200/PK-8
3115 Ocean Dr 78404 | 361-884-8931
Chris Verburgt, prin. | Fax 888-5905
Holy Family S | 300/PK-5
2526 Soledad St 78416 | 361-884-9142
Sr. Patricia Rodriguez, prin. | Fax 884-1750
Incarnate Word Academy | 300/PK-5
450 Chamberlain St 78404 | 361-883-0857
Sr. Camelia Herlihy, prin. | Fax 883-2185
Incarnate Word Academy | 300/6-8
2917 Austin St 78404 | 361-883-0857
Adolfo Garza, prin. | Fax 882-9193
Most Precious Blood S | 200/PK-5
3502 Saratoga Blvd 78415 | 361-852-4800
Nelda Bazan, prin. | Fax 855-8707
Our Lady of Perpetual Help Academy | 200/PK-7
5814 Williams Dr 78412 | 361-991-3305
Linda Cantu, prin. | Fax 994-1806
St. James Episcopal S | 300/PK-8
602 S Carancahua St 78401 | 361-883-0835
Patrick Roberts, hdmstr. | Fax 883-0837
St. Patrick S | 300/PK-6
3340 S Alameda St 78411 | 361-852-1211
Dr. Patricia Stegall, prin. | Fax 852-4855
St. Pius X S | 200/PK-6
737 Saint Pius Dr 78412 | 361-992-1343
Kathy Clark, prin. | Fax 992-0329
SS. Cyril & Methodius S | 100/PK-5
5002 Kostoryz Rd 78415 | 361-853-9392
Anna Peterson, prin. | Fax 853-0282
Yorktown Christian Academy | 200/PK-8
5025A Yorktown Blvd 78413 | 361-985-9960
John Cadena, admin. | Fax 985-9821

Corrigan, Polk, Pop. 1,931
Corrigan-Camden ISD | 1,100/PK-12
504 S Home St 75939 | 936-398-4040
Tom Bowman, supt. | Fax 398-4616
www.corrigan-camdenisd.net
Corrigan-Camden ES | 200/4-6
504 S Home St 75939 | 936-398-2501
Barbara Roden, prin. | Fax 398-5042
Corrigan-Camden JHS | 200/7-8
504 S Home St 75939 | 936-398-2962
Ray Bostick, prin. | Fax 398-4608
Corrigan-Camden PS | 400/PK-3
504 S Home St 75939 | 936-398-2503
Sue McMeans, prin. | Fax 398-9027

Corsicana, Navarro, Pop. 26,052
Corsicana ISD | 5,800/PK-12
601 N 13th St 75110 | 903-874-7441
Don Denbow, supt. | Fax 872-2100
www.cisd.org
Bowie ES | 700/K-5
1800 Bowie Dr 75110 | 903-872-6541
Billy Snow, prin. | Fax 872-6298
Carroll ES | 800/PK-5
1101 E 13th Ave 75110 | 903-872-3074
Darla Nolen, prin. | Fax 641-4153
Collins MS | 800/7-8
1500 Dobbins Rd 75110 | 903-872-3979
Lamont Smith, prin. | Fax 874-1423
Drane IS | 400/6-6
100 S 18th St 75110 | 903-874-8281
Herbrt O'Neil, prin. | Fax 641-4130
Fannin ES | 700/K-5
3201 N Beaton St 75110 | 903-874-3728
Steve Brownlee, prin. | Fax 874-0758
Houston ES | 200/PK-3
1213 W 4th Ave 75110 | 903-874-6971
Laurie Sharpley, prin. | Fax 641-4114
Navarro ES | 800/K-5
601 S 45th St 75110 | 903-874-1011
Debbie Cottar, prin. | Fax 874-3874

Mildred ISD | 700/K-12
5475 S US Highway 287 75109 | 903-872-6505
Douglas Lane, supt. | Fax 872-1341
www.mildredisd.org/
Mildred ES | 400/K-6
5475 S US Highway 287 75109 | 903-872-0381
Paula McNeel, prin. | Fax 641-0347

Collins Catholic S | 200/PK-8
3000 W State Highway 22 75110 | 903-872-1751
Jessica Starek, prin. | Fax 872-1186

Cotton Center, Hale
Cotton Center ISD | 200/PK-12
PO Box 350 79021 | 806-879-2160
Rocky Stone, supt. | Fax 879-2175
cottoncenter.esc17.net
Cotton Center S | 200/PK-12
PO Box 350 79021 | 806-879-2176
Andrew Hannon, prin. | Fax 879-2175

Cotulla, LaSalle, Pop. 3,655
Cotulla ISD | 1,200/PK-12
310 N Main St 78014 | 830-879-3073
Elizabeth Saenz, supt. | Fax 879-3609
www.cotullaisd.org
Newman MS | 200/6-8
310 N Main St 78014 | 830-879-2224
Ernesto Mendizabal, prin. | Fax 879-4357
Ramirez-Burks ES | 600/PK-5
310 N Main St 78014 | 830-879-2511
Kim Hoff, prin. | Fax 879-4361
Other Schools – See Encinal

Coupland, Williamson
Coupland ISD | 100/K-8
PO Box 217 78615 | 512-856-2422
Gary Chandler, supt. | Fax 856-2222
www.couplandtx.org/coupland_isd.htm
Coupland S | 100/K-8
PO Box 217 78615 | 512-856-2422
Gary Chandler, prin. | Fax 856-2222

Covington, Hill, Pop. 305
Covington ISD | 300/PK-12
PO Box 67 76636 | 254-854-2215
Diane Innis, supt. | Fax 854-2272
www.covingtonisd.org/
Covington S | 300/PK-12
PO Box 67 76636 | 254-854-2215
Hugh Ellison, prin. | Fax 854-2272

Crandall, Kaufman, Pop. 3,475
Crandall ISD | 2,100/PK-12
PO Box 128 75114 | 972-427-8000
Dr. Larry Watson, supt. | Fax 427-8001
www.crandall-isd.net
Crandall ES | 400/PK-1
PO Box 460 75114 | 972-427-8130
Jeannia Dykman, prin. | Fax 427-8131
Crandall IS | 500/3-5
PO Box 430 75114 | 972-427-8110
Ginger Sikes, prin. | Fax 427-8111
Crandall MS | 500/6-8
PO Box 490 75114 | 972-427-8080
Gail Barnes, prin. | Fax 427-8031
Raynes ES, PO Box 888 75114 | 100/2-2
Dennis Eastep, prin. | 972-427-8000

Crane, Crane, Pop. 3,044
Crane ISD | 1,000/PK-12
511 W 8th St 79731 | 432-558-1022
Larry Lee, supt. | Fax 558-1025
www.craneisd.com
Crane ES | 400/PK-5
511 W 8th St 79731 | 432-558-1050
Joy Armstrong, prin. | Fax 558-1077
Crane MS | 200/6-8
511 W 8th St 79731 | 432-558-1040
Paul Payne, prin. | Fax 558-1046

Cranfills Gap, Bosque, Pop. 353
Cranfills Gap ISD | 100/PK-12
PO Box 67 76637 | 254-597-2505
Jack Davis, supt. | Fax 597-0001
www.cranfillsgapisd.com/
Cranfills Gap S | 100/PK-12
PO Box 67 76637 | 254-597-2505
Jack Davis, prin. | Fax 597-0001

Crawford, McLennan, Pop. 789
Crawford ISD | 600/K-12
200 Pirate Dr 76638 | 254-486-2381
Kevin Noack, supt. | Fax 486-2198
www.crawfordisd.net/
Crawford ES | 200/K-4
200 Pirate Dr 76638 | 254-486-9083
Linda Stout, prin. | Fax 486-9085
Crawford MS | 200/5-8
200 Pirate Dr 76638 | 254-486-2381
Chuck Viladevall, prin. | Fax 486-2198

Creedmoor, Travis, Pop. 188
Del Valle ISD
Supt. — See Del Valle
Creedmoor ES | 700/PK-6
5604 FM 1327, | 512-386-3950
Patricia Rocha, prin. | Fax 386-3955

Crockett, Houston, Pop. 7,039
Crockett ISD | 1,300/PK-12
704 E Burnett Ave 75835 | 936-544-2125
Dr. Bill Like, supt. | Fax 544-5727
www.crockettisd.net
Crockett ECC | 200/PK-K
704 E Burnett Ave 75835 | 936-544-8276
Ianthia Fisher, prin. | Fax 544-9678
Crockett ES | 400/1-5
704 E Burnett Ave 75835 | 936-544-3758
Ann Fiolek, prin. | Fax 544-4404
Crockett JHS | 200/6-8
704 E Burnett Ave 75835 | 936-544-2149
Stephen Tuggle, prin. | Fax 544-4164

Jordan S | 100/PK-6
1303 E Houston Ave 75835 | 936-544-4049
Deborah Kelly, hdmstr. | Fax 546-0034

Crosby, Harris, Pop. 1,811
Crosby ISD | 4,700/PK-12
PO Box 2009 77532 | 281-328-9200
Michael Joseph, supt. | Fax 328-9208
www.crosbyisd.org
Barrett PS | 700/1-2
PO Box 2009 77532 | 281-328-9320
Bob York, prin. | Fax 328-9374
Crosby K | 500/PK-K
PO Box 2009 77532 | 281-328-9370
Ronald Davenport, prin. | Fax 328-9379
Crosby MS | 800/7-8
PO Box 2009 77532 | 281-328-9264
Karen Grey, prin. | Fax 328-9356
Drew IS | 700/5-6
PO Box 2009 77532 | 281-328-9306
Mary Jenkins, prin. | Fax 328-9376
Newport ES | 700/3-4
PO Box 2009 77532 | 281-328-9330
Christy Covan, prin. | Fax 328-9378

Sacred Heart S | 100/PK-8
907 Runneburg Rd 77532 | 281-328-6561
Ken Waguespack, prin. | Fax 462-0072

Crosbyton, Crosby, Pop. 1,749
Crosbyton Consolidated ISD | 500/PK-12
204 S Harrison St 79322 | 806-675-7331
Marvin Stewart, supt. | Fax 675-2409
www.crosbyton.k12.tx.us
Crosbyton ES | 200/PK-5
204 S Harrison St 79322 | 806-675-7331
Shelly Tate, prin. | Fax 675-2409
Crosbyton MS | 100/6-8
204 S Harrison St 79322 | 806-675-7331
Dennis Verkamp, prin. | Fax 675-2409

Cross Plains, Callahan, Pop. 1,118
Cross Plains ISD | 400/PK-12
700 N Main St 76443 | 254-725-6121
Jackie Tennison, supt. | Fax 725-6559
www.crossplains.esc14.net/

Cross Plains ES 200/PK-6
700 N Main St 76443 254-725-6123
Margie Sowell, prin. Fax 725-6559

Crowell, Foard, Pop. 1,062
Crowell ISD 300/PK-12
PO Box 239 79227 940-684-1403
Charles Hundley, supt. Fax 684-1616
www.crowellisd.net/
Crowell ES 100/PK-6
PO Box 239 79227 940-684-1878
Amie Bell, prin. Fax 684-1616

Crowley, Tarrant, Pop. 9,691
Crowley ISD 13,600/PK-12
PO Box 688 76036 817-297-5800
Greg Gibson, supt. Fax 297-5805
www.crowley.k12.tx.us
Crowley IS 5-6
10525 McCart Ave 76036 817-297-5960
Des Stewart, prin. Fax 297-5964
Deer Creek ES 600/PK-6
805 S Crowley Rd 76036 817-297-5880
Karla Ellis, prin. Fax 297-5884
Race ES 800/PK-6
537 S Heights Dr 76036 817-297-5080
Melissa Block, prin. Fax 297-5084
Stevens MS 900/7-8
940 N Crowley Rd 76036 817-297-5840
Lyndsae Benton, prin. Fax 297-5850
Summer Creek MS 7-8
10236 Summercreek Dr 76036 817-297-5090
Kathy Allen, prin. Fax 297-5094
Other Schools – See Fort Worth

Nazarene Christian Academy 300/K-12
2001 E Main St 76036 817-297-7003
Kathie Starks, prin. Fax 297-1509

Crystal City, Zavala, Pop. 7,224
Crystal City ISD 2,000/PK-12
805 E Crockett St 78839 830-374-2367
Raymundo Villarreal, supt. Fax 374-8004
www.crystalcityisd.org/
Fly JHS 300/7-8
805 E Crockett St 78839 830-374-2371
Theresa Ramirez, prin. Fax 374-8060
Juarez MS 300/5-6
805 E Crockett St 78839 830-374-8105
Irma Martinez, prin. Fax 374-0043
Rivera ES 500/PK-1
805 E Crockett St 78839 830-374-8078
Adelicia Leeper, prin. Fax 374-8024
Zavala ES 400/2-4
805 E Crockett St 78839 830-374-3418
Isabel Villarreal, prin. Fax 374-8092

First Baptist S 100/PK-6
PO Box 266 78839 830-374-2422

Cuero, DeWitt, Pop. 6,770
Cuero ISD 2,000/PK-12
405 Park Heights Dr 77954 361-275-3832
Henry Lind, supt. Fax 275-2981
www.cueroisd.org
Cuero IS 400/4-6
502 Park Heights Dr 77954 361-275-6638
Bill Hamilton, prin. Fax 275-9627
Cuero JHS 300/7-8
608 Jr High Dr 77954 361-275-2222
Jan Reeve, prin. Fax 275-6912
French K 200/PK-K
505 Henry St 77954 361-275-2121
Mark Iacoponelli, prin. Fax 275-5313
Hunt ES 400/1-3
805 N Hunt St 77954 361-275-6312
Paula Hamilton, prin. Fax 275-3474

St. Michael S 100/PK-6
208 N McLeod St 77954 361-277-3854
Judy Roeder, prin. Fax 275-3618

Cumby, Hopkins, Pop. 637
Cumby ISD 400/PK-12
303 Sayle St 75433 903-994-2260
Shaun Barnett, supt. Fax 994-2399
www.cumbyisd.net/
Cumby ES 200/PK-6
303 Sayle St 75433 903-994-2260
Shelly Slaughter, prin. Fax 994-2847

Miller Grove ISD 200/PK-12
7819 Farm Road 275 S 75433 903-459-3288
Steve Johnson, supt. Fax 459-3744
millergrove.esc8.net/
Miller Grove ES 100/PK-5
7819 Farm Road 275 S 75433 903-459-3724
Linda Bailey, prin. Fax 382-2121

Cushing, Nacogdoches, Pop. 653
Cushing ISD 500/PK-12
PO Box 337 75760 936-326-4890
Michael Davis, supt. Fax 326-4115
www.cushingisd.org
Cushing ES 200/PK-5
PO Box 337 75760 936-326-4234
Melanie Pettit, prin. Fax 326-4265

Cypress, Harris
Cypress-Fairbanks ISD
Supt. — See Houston
Andre ES 1,300/K-5
8111 Fry Rd 77433 281-463-5500
Marilyn Fredell, prin. Fax 463-5507
Arnold MS 1,300/6-8
11111 Telge Rd 77429 281-897-4700
Susan Higgins, prin. Fax 807-8610
Ault ES 1,000/PK-5
21010 Maple Village Dr 77433 281-373-2800
Donna Guthrie, prin. Fax 373-2823
Black ES 1,000/K-5
14155 Grant Rd 77429 281-320-7145
Lillian Chastain, prin. Fax 320-7144
Farney ES 800/K-5
14425 Barker Cypress Rd 77429 281-373-2850
Beth Coleman, prin. Fax 373-2855
Goodson MS 1,500/6-8
17333 Huffmeister Rd 77429 281-373-2350
Phyllis Hamilton, prin. Fax 373-2355
Hamilton ES 1,000/PK-5
12330 Kluge Rd 77429 281-370-0990
Catherine Bauer, prin. Fax 320-7067
Hamilton MS 1,300/6-8
12330 Kluge Rd 77429 281-320-7000
Ify Ogwumike, prin. Fax 320-7021
Hopper MS 1,300/6-8
7811 Fry Rd 77433 281-463-5353
Robert Borneman, prin. Fax 463-5354
Keith ES, 20550 Fairfield Grn 77433 1,100/PK-5
Patty Mooney, prin. 281-213-1744
Lamkin ES 1,000/PK-5
11521 Telge Rd 77429 281-897-4775
Gale Parker, prin. Fax 807-8163
Millsap ES 800/K-5
12424 Huffmeister Rd 77429 281-897-4470
Jodi Matteson, prin. Fax 807-8635
Postma ES 1,100/K-5
18425 West Rd 77433 281-345-3660
Kim Freed, prin. Fax 345-3545
Robison ES 1,500/PK-5
13600 Skinner Rd 77429 281-213-1700
Dan McIlduff, prin. Fax 213-1705
Sampson ES 1,200/K-5
16002 Coles Crossing Dr N 77429 281-213-1600
Cindy O'Brien, prin. Fax 213-1605
Spillane MS, 17500 Jarvis Rd 77429 1,600/6-8
Gary Kinninger, prin. 281-213-1645
Warner ES 1,300/K-5
19545 Cypress North Houston 77433 281-213-1660
Michael Maness, prin. Fax 213-1651

Covenant Academy 100/K-8
11711 Telge Rd 77429 281-373-2233
Timm Petersen, dir. Fax 588-8227
Longwood Montessori S 100/PK-3
12839 Louetta Rd 77429 281-655-5900
Victoria Turner, prin. Fax 655-0022
St. John Lutheran S 200/PK-PK
15238 Huffmeister Rd 77429 281-304-5546
Karen Schulze, dir. Fax 256-2708

Daingerfield, Morris, Pop. 2,470
Daingerfield-Lone Star ISD 1,400/PK-12
200 Tiger Dr 75638 903-645-2239
Pat Adams, supt. Fax 645-2137
www.dlsisd.org
Daingerfield JHS 300/6-8
200 Texas St 75638 903-645-2261
Justin Johnston, prin. Fax 645-4010
South ES 200/3-5
701 Linda Dr 75638 903-645-3501
Sandra Quarles, prin. Fax 645-2295
West ES 300/PK-2
1305 W W M Watson Blvd 75638 903-645-2901
Galen Smith, prin. Fax 645-7178
Other Schools – See Lone Star

Daisetta, Liberty, Pop. 1,090
Hull-Daisetta ISD 600/PK-12
PO Box 477 77533 936-536-6321
Mary Huckabay, supt. Fax 536-6251
www.hdisd.net/
Other Schools – See Hull, Raywood

Dalhart, Dallam, Pop. 7,146
Dalhart ISD 1,600/PK-12
701 E 10th St 79022 806-244-7810
David Foote, supt. Fax 244-7822
www.dalhart.k12.tx.us
Dalhart ES 600/PK-3
701 E 10th St 79022 806-244-7350
Karen Taft, prin. Fax 244-7352
Dalhart IS 200/4-5
701 E 10th St 79022 806-244-7380
Mark McCormick, prin. Fax 244-7387
Dalhart JHS 400/6-8
701 E 10th St 79022 806-244-7825
John Machel, prin. Fax 244-7835

Dalhart Christian Academy 100/PK-6
PO Box 987 79022 806-244-6482
Deborah Dunham, prin. Fax 244-3542
St. Anthony's S 100/PK-6
1302 Oak Ave 79022 806-244-4511
Nicole Barber, prin. Fax 244-4811

Dallardsville, Polk
Big Sandy ISD 500/PK-12
PO Box 188 77332 936-563-1000
Kenneth Graham, supt. Fax 563-1010
www.bigsandyisd.net/
Other Schools – See Livingston

Dallas, Dallas, Pop. 1,213,825
Carrollton-Farmers Branch ISD
Supt. — See Carrollton
Long MS 900/6-8
2525 Frankford Rd 75287 972-968-4100
Nicoloas Lasker, prin. Fax 968-4110
McKamy ES 500/PK-5
3443 Briargrove Ln 75287 972-968-2400
Bridget O'Connor, prin. Fax 968-2410
McWhorter ES 500/PK-5
3678 Timberglen Rd 75287 972-968-2800
Benita Gordon, prin. Fax 968-2810
Sheffield IS 400/3-5
18110 Kelly Blvd 75287 972-968-3200
Amy Miller, prin. Fax 968-3210
Sheffield PS 400/PK-2
18111 Kelly Blvd 75287 972-968-3100
Kathy Grieb, prin. Fax 968-3110

Dallas ISD 154,900/PK-12
3700 Ross Ave 75204 972-925-3700
Michael Hinojosa Ed.D., supt. Fax 925-3201
www.dallasisd.org
Adams ES 700/PK-5
8239 Lake June Rd 75217 972-794-1200
Jaime Sandoval, prin. Fax 794-1201
Adams ES 500/PK-5
12600 Welch Rd 75244 972-794-2600
Jean McGill, prin. Fax 794-2601
Alexander ES 500/PK-5
1830 Goldwood Dr 75232 972-749-3100
Roshanda Clayton-Brown, prin. Fax 749-3101
Anderson ES 800/PK-6
620 N Saint Augustine Dr 75217 972-749-6200
Silvia Garcia, prin. Fax 749-6201
Anderson Learning Center 600/6-8
3400 Garden Ln 75215 972-925-7900
Benita Noiel-Ashford, prin. Fax 925-7901
Arcadia Park ES 700/PK-6
1300 N Justin Ave 75211 972-502-5300
Diana Vega, prin. Fax 502-5301
Arlington Park Community Learning Center 200/PK-5
5606 Wayside Dr 75235 972-749-5500
Nikia Barnett-Smith, prin. Fax 749-5501
Atwell Law Academy 1,100/6-8
1303 Reynoldston Ln 75232 972-794-6400
Harnell Williams, prin. Fax 794-6401
Bayles ES 600/PK-5
2444 Telegraph Ave 75228 972-749-8900
Maria Tafur, prin. Fax 749-8901
Bethune ES 900/PK-6
1665 Duncanville Rd 75211 972-502-1300
Rocio Bernal, prin. Fax 502-1301
Blair ES 700/PK-6
7720 Gayglen Dr 75217 972-794-1600
Nicholas Johnson, prin. Fax 794-1601
Blanton ES 700/PK-5
8915 Greenmound Ave 75227 972-794-1700
Kathryn Carter, prin. Fax 794-1701
Bonham ES 400/PK-3
2617 N Henderson Ave 75206 972-749-5700
Sandra Fernandez, prin. Fax 749-5701
Botello ES 400/PK-5
225 S Marsalis Ave 75203 214-502-4600
Clarissa Plair, prin. Fax 932-5094
Bowie ES 700/PK-5
330 N Marsalis Ave 75203 972-925-6600
Abril Rivera, prin. Fax 925-6601
Brashear ES 800/PK-6
2959 S Hampton Rd 75224 972-502-2600
Deardra Hayes-Whigham, prin. Fax 502-2601
Browne MS 900/7-8
3333 Sprague Dr 75233 972-502-2500
Cedric Barrett, prin. Fax 502-2501
Bryan ES 600/PK-5
2001 Deer Path Dr 75216 972-502-8500
Orethann Price, prin. Fax 502-8501
Budd ES 600/PK-5
2121 S Marsalis Ave 75216 972-502-8400
Maya Lagbara, prin. Fax 502-8401
Burleson ES 700/PK-6
6300 Elam Rd 75217 972-749-4500
Yolanda Knight, prin. Fax 749-4501
Burnet ES 1,100/PK-5
3200 Kinkaid Dr 75220 972-794-3000
Shelly Vaughan, prin. Fax 794-3001
Bushman ES 800/PK-5
4200 Bonnie View Rd 75216 972-749-1800
Kellie Bell, prin. Fax 749-1801
Cabell ES 600/PK-5
12701 Templeton Trl 75234 972-794-2400
Barbara Banks, prin. Fax 794-2401
Caillet ES 700/PK-5
3033 Merrell Rd 75229 972-794-3200
Judith Meyer, prin. Fax 794-3201
Carpenter ES 500/PK-6
2121 Tosca Ln 75224 972-794-6000
Tanya Glover-Johnson, prin. Fax 794-6001
Carr ES 300/PK-5
1952 Bayside St 75212 972-794-4300
Christian Ruiz, prin. Fax 794-4301
Carver Learning Center 400/PK-5
3719 Greenleaf St 75212 972-794-3600
Harold Morgan, prin. Fax 794-3601
Cary MS 1,100/6-8
3978 Killion Dr 75229 972-502-7600
Santiago Camacho, prin. Fax 502-7601
Casa View ES 1,000/PK-5
2100 N Farola Dr 75228 972-749-7700
Mike Paschall, prin. Fax 749-7701
Chavez Learning Center 700/PK-5
1710 N Carroll Ave 75204 972-925-1000
Jose Munoz, prin. Fax 925-1001
Cigarroa ES 700/PK-5
9990 Webb Chapel Rd 75220 972-502-2900
Donna Trevino-Jones, prin. Fax 502-2901
City Park ES 200/PK-5
1738 Gano St 75215 972-794-7600
Graciela Pontus, prin. Fax 794-7601
Cochran ES 700/PK-6
6000 Keeneland Pkwy 75211 972-794-4600
Alejandra Lara, prin. Fax 794-4601
Comstock MS 900/7-8
7044 Hodde St 75217 972-794-1300
Marlon Brooks, prin. Fax 794-1301
Conner ES 500/PK-5
3037 Green Meadow Dr 75228 972-749-8200
Josette McMillian, prin. Fax 749-8201
Cowart ES 900/PK-6
1515 S Ravinia Dr 75211 972-794-5500
Marta Jourdan, prin. Fax 794-5501
Cuellar ES 900/PK-6
337 Pleasant Vista Dr 75217 972-749-6400
N. Lora Watson, prin. Fax 749-6401

Dade Learning Center 50/6-8
2801 Park Row Ave 75215 972-749-3800
David Welch, prin. Fax 749-3801
Dallas Environmental Science Academy 200/6-8
3635 Greenleaf St 75212 972-794-3950
Peter Cobelle, prin. Fax 794-3951
Darrell ES 300/PK-5
4730 S Lancaster Rd 75216 972-749-2100
Linda Smith-Ellis, prin. Fax 749-2101
Dealey Montessori Academy 400/PK-8
6501 Royal Ln 75230 972-794-8400
Johanna Bortnem, prin. Fax 794-8401
DeGolyer ES 400/K-5
3453 Flair Dr 75229 972-794-2800
Alecia Cobb, prin. Fax 794-2801
De Zavala ES 300/PK-5
3214 N Winnetka Ave 75212 972-892-6400
Ann Margaret Vincent, prin. Fax 892-6401
Donald ES 600/PK-6
1218 Phinney Ave 75211 972-794-5300
Rina Davis, prin. Fax 794-5301
Dorsey ES 500/PK-6
133 N Saint Augustine Dr 75217 972-749-6300
Zulema Marillo, prin. Fax 749-6301
Douglass ES 800/PK-6
226 N Jim Miller Rd 75217 972-794-1400
Sheryl Northcutt, prin. Fax 794-1401
Dunbar Learning Center 500/PK-5
4200 Metropolitan Ave 75210 972-794-6600
Grant Atai, prin. Fax 794-6601
Earhart Learning Center 400/PK-5
3531 N Westmoreland Rd 75212 972-794-3700
Andrea Nelson, prin. Fax 794-3701
Edison MS 1,000/6-8
2940 Singleton Blvd 75212 972-794-4100
Jimmy King, prin. Fax 794-4101
Ervin ES 700/PK-5
3722 Black Oak Dr 75241 972-749-3700
Marcus Paris, prin. Fax 749-3701
Fannin ES 400/PK-3
4800 Ross Ave 75204 972-794-7800
Linda Trujillo, prin. Fax 794-7801
Field ES 500/PK-5
2151 Royal Ln 75229 972-794-2700
Roslyn Carter, prin. Fax 794-2701
Florence MS 900/6-8
1625 N Masters Dr 75217 972-749-6000
Theodore Timms, prin. Fax 749-6001
Foster ES 900/PK-5
3700 Clover Ln 75220 972-794-8100
Anthony Chavez, prin. Fax 794-8101
Frank ES 1,200/PK-5
5201 Celestial Rd 75254 972-502-5900
Jonnice Legum-Berns, prin. Fax 502-5901
Franklin MS 700/6-8
6920 Meadow Rd 75230 972-502-7100
Ronald Jones, prin. Fax 502-7101
Frazier ES 100/K-3
4600 Spring Ave 75210 972-925-1900
Leslie Sharp, prin. Fax 925-1901
Garcia MS, 700 E 8th St 75203 800/6-8
Gary Auld, prin. 972-502-5500
Gaston MS 900/6-8
9565 Mercer Dr 75228 972-502-5400
Susie Stauss, prin. Fax 502-5401
Gill ES 1,000/PK-5
10910 Ferguson Rd 75228 972-749-8400
Brenda Campbell, prin. Fax 749-8401
Gonzalez ES 800/PK-6
6610 Lake June Rd 75217 972-502-3300
Baudel Fonseca, prin. Fax 502-3301
Gooch ES 500/PK-5
4030 Calculus Dr 75244 972-794-2500
Kenneth Fincher, prin. Fax 794-2501
Greiner Exploratory Arts Academy 1,500/6-8
501 S Edgefield Ave 75208 972-925-7100
David Blain, prin. Fax 925-7101
Guzick ES 800/PK-5
5000 Berridge Ln 75227 972-502-3900
Kimberly Robinson, prin. Fax 502-3901
Hall ES 600/PK-6
2120 Keats Dr 75211 972-794-5400
Jose Angel Cano, prin. Fax 794-5401
Harllee ES 200/PK-5
1216 E 8th St 75203 972-925-6500
Jonica Crowder-Lockwood, prin. Fax 925-6501
Hawthorne ES 500/PK-5
7800 Umphress Rd 75217 972-749-4700
James Wallace, prin. Fax 749-4701
Henderson ES 600/PK-6
2200 S Edgefield Ave 75224 972-749-2900
Ida Escobedo, prin. Fax 749-2901
Hernandez ES 500/PK-5
5555 Maple Ave 75235 972-925-2700
Eva Casas, prin. Fax 925-2701
Hexter ES 500/PK-5
9720 Waterview Rd 75218 972-502-5800
Joel Healey, prin. Fax 502-5801
Highland Meadows ES 700/PK-5
8939 Whitewing Ln 75238 972-502-5200
Janet Jones, prin. Fax 502-5201
Hill MS 700/6-8
505 Easton Rd 75218 972-502-5700
Salvador Sosa, prin. Fax 502-5701
Hogg ES 400/PK-5
1144 N Madison Ave 75208 972-502-8600
Sylvia Segura, prin. Fax 502-8601
Holmes Humanities/Comm Academy 1,300/6-8
2001 E Kiest Blvd 75216 972-925-8500
Keith Baker, prin. Fax 925-8501
Hood MS 1,400/6-8
7625 Hume Dr 75227 972-749-4100
Fred Davis, prin. Fax 749-4101
Hooe ES 500/PK-5
2419 Gladstone Dr 75211 972-794-6700
Yvonne Rojas, prin. Fax 794-6701
Hotchkiss ES 800/PK-5
6929 Town North Dr 75231 972-749-7000
Lea Beach, prin. Fax 749-7001

Houston ES 200/PK-5
2827 Throckmorton St 75219 972-749-5800
Oscar Nandayapa, prin. Fax 749-5801
Hulcy MS 900/6-8
9339 S Polk St 75232 214-932-7400
Roberto Ayala, prin. Fax 932-7401
Ireland ES 700/PK-5
1515 N Jim Miller Rd 75217 972-749-4900
Jennifer Clark, prin. Fax 749-4901
Jackson Center for Learning 100/6-8
2929 Stag Rd 75241 214-932-7900
Regina Rice, prin. Fax 932-7901
Jackson ES 500/K-5
5828 E Mockingbird Ln 75206 972-749-7200
Olivia Henderson, prin. Fax 749-7201
Johnston ES 600/PK-5
2020 Mouser Ln 75203 972-925-7400
Deborah Kilgore, prin. Fax 925-7401
Jones ES 1,000/PK-6
3901 Meredith Ave 75211 972-794-4700
Luis Valdez, prin. Fax 794-4701
Jordan ES 600/PK-5
1111 W Kiest Blvd 75224 972-925-8100
Lucy Hopkins, prin. Fax 925-8101
Kahn ES 800/PK-6
610 N Franklin St 75211 972-502-1400
Armando Rendon, prin. Fax 502-1401
Kennedy Learning Center 700/PK-5
1802 Moser Ave 75206 972-794-7100
Carolina Leon, prin. Fax 794-7101
Kiest ES 900/PK-5
2611 Healey Dr 75228 972-502-5600
Carolyn Lewis, prin. Fax 502-5601
King Learning Center 400/PK-5
1817 Warren Ave 75215 972-502-8100
Maria Freeman, prin. Fax 502-8101
Kleberg ES 900/PK-5
1450 Edd Rd 75253 972-749-6500
Marsha Burkley, prin. Fax 749-6501
Knight ES 700/PK-5
2615 Anson Rd 75235 972-749-5300
Enrique Escobedo, prin. Fax 749-5301
Kramer ES 500/PK-5
7131 Midbury Dr 75230 972-794-8300
Menay Harris, prin. Fax 794-8301
Lagow ES 700/PK-6
637 Edgeworth Dr 75217 972-749-6600
Gabriella Williams-Hill, prin. Fax 749-6601
Lakewood ES 500/PK-5
3000 Hillbrook St 75214 972-749-7300
Michelle Thompson, prin. Fax 749-7301
Lang MS, 1678 Chenault St 75228 1,100/6-8
Robert Peters, prin. 972-925-2400
Lanier Center for Arts 500/PK-5
1400 Walmsley Ave 75208 972-794-4400
Alyssa Peraza, prin. Fax 794-4401
Lee ES 300/PK-5
2911 Delmar Ave 75206 972-749-7400
Alicia Zapata, prin. Fax 749-7401
Lee ES 500/PK-5
7808 Racine Dr 75232 972-749-3900
Tondolyn Mosley, prin. Fax 749-3901
Lipscomb ES 400/PK-3
5801 Worth St 75214 972-794-7300
Yolanda Gonzalez, prin. Fax 794-7301
Lisbon ES 400/PK-5
4203 S Lancaster Rd 75216 972-749-1900
Curtis Holland, prin. Fax 749-1901
Longfellow Career Academy 400/6-8
5314 Boaz St 75209 972-749-5400
Shannon Tovar, prin. Fax 749-5401
Long MS 1,100/6-8
6116 Reiger Ave 75214 972-502-4700
Danielle Petters, prin. Fax 502-4701
Lowe ES 900/PK-5
7000 Holly Hill Dr 75231 972-502-1700
Connie Wallace, prin. Fax 502-1701
Macon ES 600/PK-6
650 Holcomb Rd 75217 972-794-1500
Kathleen Snyder, prin. Fax 794-1501
Maple Lawn ES 500/PK-5
3120 Inwood Rd 75235 972-925-2500
Roberto Basurto, prin. Fax 925-2501
Marcus ES 900/PK-5
2911 Northaven Rd 75229 972-794-2900
C. Rodriguez-Torres, prin. Fax 794-2901
Marsalis ES 500/PK-5
5640 S Marsalis Ave 75241 972-749-3500
Kimberly Richardson, prin. Fax 749-3501
Marsh MS 1,200/6-8
3838 Crown Shore Dr 75244 972-502-6600
Kyle Richardson, prin. Fax 502-6601
Martinez Learning Center 500/PK-5
4500 Bernal Dr 75212 972-794-6900
Rosa Linda Pena, prin. Fax 794-6901
Mata IS 400/4-5
7420 La Vista Dr 75214 972-749-7500
James Ramirez, prin. Fax 749-7501
McNair ES 800/PK-5
3150 Bainbridge Ave 75237 972-794-6200
Virginia Lockwood-Terry, prin. Fax 794-6201
McShan ES 500/PK-5
8307 Meadow Rd 75231 972-502-3800
Dirona Jackson-Robinson, prin. Fax 502-3801
Medrano ES 700/PK-5
2221 Lucas Dr 75219 972-794-3300
Ricardo Weir, prin. Fax 794-3301
Medrano MS 6-8
9815 Brockbank Dr 75220 972-925-1300
Constance Ramirez, prin. Fax 925-1301
Milam ES 200/PK-5
4200 Mckinney Ave 75205 972-749-5600
Anna Galvan, prin. Fax 749-5601
Miller ES 500/PK-5
3111 Bonnie View Rd 75216 972-502-8700
Sheila Aldredge, prin. Fax 502-8701
Mills ES 400/PK-5
1515 Lynn Haven Ave 75216 972-925-7500
Norma Martinez, prin. Fax 925-7501

Moreno ES 700/PK-6
2115 S Hampton Rd 75224 972-502-3100
Alba Marrero, prin. Fax 502-3101
Moseley ES 900/PK-6
10400 Rylie Rd 75217 972-749-6700
Alejandro Fernandez, prin. Fax 749-6701
Mt. Auburn ES 800/PK-3
6012 E Grand Ave 75223 972-749-8500
Mary Lou Martinez, prin. Fax 749-8501
Oliver ES 400/PK-5
4010 Idaho Ave 75216 972-749-3400
Karen Gosby, prin. Fax 749-3401
Peabody ES 600/PK-6
3101 Raydell Pl 75211 972-794-5200
Dee Anne Egan, prin. Fax 794-5201
Pease ES 400/PK-3
2914 Cummings St 75216 214-932-3800
Cheryl Freeman, prin. Fax 932-3801
Peeler ES 400/PK-5
810 S Llewellyn Ave 75208 972-502-8300
Helen Lopez, prin. Fax 502-8301
Pershing ES 400/PK-5
5715 Meaders Ln 75229 972-794-8600
Margarita Hernandez, prin. Fax 794-8601
Pleasant Grove ES 700/PK-5
1614 N Saint Augustine Dr 75217 972-892-5000
Ellen Perry, prin. Fax 892-5001
Polk Center for Talented & Gifted 500/PK-5
6911 Victoria Ave 75209 972-794-8900
Shirley Williams-Lewis, prin. Fax 794-8901
Preston Hollow ES 500/PK-5
6423 Walnut Hill Ln 75230 972-794-8500
David Chapasko, prin. Fax 794-8501
Quintanilla MS 1,000/7-8
2700 Remond Dr 75211 972-502-3200
Rodney Cooksy, prin. Fax 502-3201
Ray Learning Center 300/PK-5
2211 Caddo St 75204 972-794-7700
Bernette Austin, prin. Fax 794-7701
Reagan ES 400/PK-5
201 N Adams Ave 75208 972-502-8200
Sebastian Bozas, prin. Fax 502-8201
Reilly ES 500/PK-5
11230 Lippitt Ave 75218 972-749-7800
Ada McPhaul, prin. Fax 749-7801
Reinhardt ES 700/PK-5
10122 Losa Dr 75218 972-749-7900
Phoebe Montgomery, prin. Fax 749-7901
Rhoads Learning Center 500/PK-5
4401 S 2nd Ave 75210 972-749-1000
Renatte Palmer, prin. Fax 749-1001
Rice Learning Center 500/PK-5
2425 Pine St 75215 972-749-1100
Alpher Garrett-Jones, prin. Fax 749-1101
Roberts ES 500/PK-5
4919 E Grand Ave 75223 972-749-8700
Zuelma Ortiz, prin. Fax 749-8701
Rogers ES 700/PK-5
5314 Abrams Rd 75214 972-794-8800
Yolanda Rodriguez, prin. Fax 794-8801
Rosemont ES 400/3-5
719 N Montclair Ave 75208 972-749-5000
Anna Brining, prin. Fax 749-5001
Rosemont PS - Semos Campus 600/PK-2
1919 Stevens Forest Dr 75208 972-502-3850
Fax 502-3861
Rowe ES 500/PK-5
4918 Hovenkamp Dr 75227 972-749-8800
Jonathan Smith, prin. Fax 749-8801
Runyon ES 700/PK-5
10750 Cradlerock Dr 75217 972-749-6100
Sherry Williams, prin. Fax 749-6101
Rusk MS 600/6-8
2929 Inwood Rd 75235 972-925-2000
Evangelina Kircher, prin. Fax 925-2001
Russell ES 200/4-5
3031 S Beckley Ave 75224 972-925-8300
Mary Newsome-Haywood, prin. Fax 925-8301
Salazar ES 800/PK-6
1120 S Ravinia Dr 75211 972-502-1800
Jennifer Parvin, prin. Fax 502-1801
Saldivar ES 900/PK-5
9510 Brockbank Dr 75220 972-794-2000
Chaundra Macklin, prin. Fax 794-2001
Sanger ES 400/PK-5
8410 San Leandro Dr 75218 972-749-7600
Larry Allen, prin. Fax 749-7601
San Jacinto ES 800/PK-5
7900 Hume Dr 75227 972-749-4200
Clarita Rivera, prin. Fax 749-4201
Seagoville MS 1,000/6-8
950 N Woody Rd 75253 972-892-7100
Kathryn Kreger, prin. Fax 892-7101
Seguin Community Learning Center 600/PK-3
111 W Corning Ave 75224 972-925-8400
Yolanda Thompson, prin. Fax 925-8401
Sequoyah Learning Center 400/PK-5
3635 Greenleaf St 75212 972-794-3900
Stephanie Love, prin. Fax 794-3901
Silberstein ES 700/PK-5
5940 Hollis Ave 75227 972-794-1900
Rudy Mendoza, prin. Fax 794-1901
Soto ES 700/PK-6
4510 W Jefferson Blvd 75211 972-502-5100
Irene Aguilar, prin. Fax 502-5101
Spence Talented/Gifted Academy 1,200/6-8
4001 Capitol Ave 75204 972-925-2300
Clarkie Clark, prin. Fax 925-2301
Starks ES 500/PK-5
3033 Tips Blvd 75216 972-502-8800
Lynette Howard, prin. Fax 502-8801
Stemmons ES 900/PK-6
2727 Knoxville St 75211 972-794-4900
Luis Cowley, prin. Fax 794-4901
Stevens Park ES 900/PK-6
2615 W Colorado Blvd 75211 972-794-4200
Silvia Wright, prin. Fax 794-4201

Stockard MS 800/7-8
2300 S Ravinia Dr 75211 972-794-5700
Faustino Rivas, prin. Fax 794-5701
Stone ES at Vickery Meadows 300/PK-5
6606 Ridgecrest Rd 75231 972-502-7900
Rosalinda Pratt, prin. Fax 502-7901
Stone Montessori S 100/PK-8
4747 Veterans Dr 75216 972-794-3400
Lisa Curry, prin. Fax 794-3401
Storey MS 1,100/6-8
3000 Maryland Ave 75216 972-925-8700
Cassandra Asberry, prin. Fax 925-8701
Tasby MS 800/6-8
7001 Fair Oaks Ave 75231 972-502-1900
Jose Cardenas, prin. Fax 502-1901
Tatum ES 800/PK-5
3002 N Saint Augustine Dr 75227 972-502-2000
A. Tracie Brown, prin. Fax 502-2001
Terry ES 400/PK-5
6661 Greenspan Ave 75232 972-749-3200
Deborah Traylor, prin. Fax 749-3201
Thompson Learning Center 500/PK-5
5700 Bexar St 75215 972-502-8900
Kamalia Cotton, prin. Fax 502-8901
Thornton ES 500/PK-5
6011 Old Ox Rd 75241 972-794-8000
Clara Daniels, prin. Fax 794-8001
Titche ES 800/PK-5
9560 Highfield Dr 75227 972-794-2100
Leavetta Sasser-Phillips, prin. Fax 794-2101
Tolbert ES 500/PK-6
4000 Blue Ridge Blvd 75233 972-794-5900
Chanel Howard-Veazy, prin. Fax 794-5901
Travis Academy 100/4-8
3001 Mckinney Ave 75204 972-794-7500
Mari Smith, prin. Fax 794-7501
Truett ES 1,200/PK-5
1811 Gross Rd 75228 972-749-8000
Tiffany Barnett-Nemec, prin. Fax 749-8001
Turner ES 500/K-5
5505 S Polk St 75232 972-794-6300
Wendy Hawthorne, prin. Fax 794-6301
Twain Leadership Vanguard ES 400/PK-5
724 Green Cove Ln 75232 972-749-3000
Clifford Greer, prin. Fax 749-3001
Urban Park ES 800/PK-5
6901 Military Pkwy 75227 972-794-1100
Enid Rosenfeldt, prin. Fax 794-1101
Walker MS 200/6-8
12532 Nuestra Dr 75230 972-502-6100
Brian Lusk, prin. Fax 502-6101
Walnut Hill ES 400/PK-5
10115 Midway Rd 75229 972-502-7800
Tammie Brooks, prin. Fax 502-7801
Webster ES 600/PK-6
3815 S Franklin St 75233 972-794-6100
Constance Burton, prin. Fax 794-6101
Weiss ES 700/PK-5
8601 Willoughby Blvd 75232 972-749-4000
Tangela Carter, prin. Fax 749-4001
Wheatley ES 100/PK-3
2908 Metropolitan Ave 75215 972-749-1300
Nanette Watts-Weeks, prin. Fax 749-1301
Williams ES 300/PK-5
4518 Pomona Rd 75209 972-794-8700
Lorena Garay Hernandez, prin. Fax 794-8701
Winnetka ES 800/PK-5
1151 S Edgefield Ave 75208 972-749-5100
Manuel Rojas, prin. Fax 749-5101
Withers ES 400/PK-5
3959 Northaven Rd 75229 972-794-5000
Anita Hardwick, prin. Fax 794-5001
Young ES 400/PK-5
4601 Veterans Dr 75216 972-749-2000
Sandra Foster, prin. Fax 749-2001
Zaragosa ES 600/PK-5
4550 Worth St 75246 972-749-8600
Alejandra Lara, prin. Fax 749-8601
Zumwalt MS 600/6-8
2445 E Ledbetter Dr 75216 972-749-3600
Carlos Lee, prin. Fax 749-3601
Other Schools – See Carrollton, Mesquite, Seagoville

Duncanville ISD
Supt. — See Duncanville
Acton ES 500/PK-4
9240 County View Rd 75249 972-708-2400
Robbie Blacknall, prin. Fax 708-2424
Bilhartz ES 600/PK-4
6700 Wandt Dr 75236 972-708-6600
Barbara Jones, prin. Fax 708-6666
Hyman ES 600/PK-4
8441 Fox Creek Trl 75249 972-708-6700
Steve Hudson, prin. Fax 708-6767
Kennemer MS 700/7-8
7101 W Wheatland Rd 75249 972-708-3600
Elijah Granger, prin. Fax 708-3636

Highland Park ISD 6,300/PK-12
7015 Westchester Dr 75205 214-780-3000
Dr. Dawson Orr, supt. Fax 780-3099
www.hpisd.org
Armstrong ES 500/PK-4
3600 Cornell Ave 75205 214-780-3100
Dr. Mary Richey, prin. Fax 780-3199
Bradfield ES 600/K-4
4300 Southern Ave 75205 214-780-3200
Dr. Gloria McNutt, prin. Fax 780-3299
Highland Park MS 1,000/7-8
3555 Granada Ave 75205 214-780-3600
Laurie Norton, prin. Fax 780-3699
Hyer ES 600/K-4
3920 Caruth Blvd 75225 214-780-3300
Jeremy Gilbert, prin. Fax 780-3399
McCulloch IS 1,000/5-6
3555 Granada Ave 75205 214-780-3500
Laurie Norton, prin. Fax 780-3599
University Park ES 600/K-4
3505 Amherst Ave 75225 214-780-3400
Dr. Lynda Carter, prin. Fax 780-3499

Plano ISD
Supt. — See Plano
Frankford MS 1,200/6-8
7706 Osage Plaza Pkwy 75252 469-752-5200
Renee Godi, prin. Fax 752-5201
Haggar ES 600/K-5
17820 Campbell Rd 75252 469-752-1400
Robin Williams, prin. Fax 752-1401
Mitchell ES 600/PK-5
4223 Briargrove Ln 75287 469-752-2800
Linda Patrick, prin. Fax 752-2801

Richardson ISD
Supt. — See Richardson
Aikin ES 600/PK-6
12300 Pleasant Valley Dr 75243 469-593-1820
Sandra Pointer, prin. Fax 593-1763
Audelia Creek ES 600/PK-6
12600 Audelia Rd 75243 469-593-2900
Mike Savage, prin. Fax 593-2901
Bowie ES 500/K-6
7643 La Manga Dr 75248 469-593-6000
Staci Low, prin. Fax 593-6066
Brentfield ES 600/K-6
6767 Brentfield Dr 75248 469-593-5740
Steve Lemons, prin. Fax 593-5723
Bukhair ES 700/1-6
13900 Maham Rd 75240 469-593-4900
Suzanne Mann, prin. Fax 593-4901
RISD Academy 600/1-6
13630 Coit Rd 75240 469-593-3300
Keith Forte, prin. Fax 593-3307
Dobie PS 600/PK-1
14040 Rolling Hills Ln 75240 469-593-4100
Kay Reynolds, prin. Fax 593-4011
Forest Lane Academy 500/PK-6
9663 Forest Ln 75243 469-593-1850
Pam Aitken, prin. Fax 593-1919
Forest Meadow JHS 600/7-8
9373 Whitehurst Dr 75243 469-593-1500
Charles Bruner, prin. Fax 593-1461
Forestridge ES 700/PK-6
10330 Bunchberry Dr 75243 469-593-8500
Kathy Higgins, prin. Fax 593-8502
Hamilton Park Pacesetter Magnet ES 700/PK-6
8301 Towns St 75243 469-593-3900
Megan Timme Ed.D., prin. Fax 593-3950
Lake Highlands ES 600/PK-6
9501 Ferndale Rd 75238 469-593-2100
Kim Sullivan, prin. Fax 593-2088
Lake Highlands JHS 700/7-8
10301 Walnut Hill Ln 75238 469-593-1600
Veronica Escalante, prin. Fax 593-1606
Marshall ES 500/PK-6
9666 W Ferris Branch Blvd 75243 469-593-6800
Tonia Alexander Ph.D., prin. Fax 593-6801
Merriman Park ES 400/K-6
7101 Winedale Dr 75231 469-593-2800
Laurie Taylor, prin. Fax 593-2741
Moss Haven ES 400/K-6
9202 Moss Farm Ln 75243 469-593-2200
Philip Henderson, prin. Fax 593-2158
Northlake ES 500/PK-6
10059 Ravensway Dr 75238 469-593-2300
Glenda Howell, prin. Fax 593-2309
Northwood Hills ES 400/K-6
14532 Meandering Way 75254 469-593-4300
Mackie Kazdoy, prin. Fax 593-4301
Prestonwood ES 300/K-6
6525 La Cosa Dr 75248 469-593-6700
Nancy Stenberg, prin. Fax 593-6712
Skyview ES 500/K-6
9229 Meadowknoll Dr 75243 469-593-2400
Philip Bates, prin. Fax 593-2423
Spring Creek ES 300/PK-6
7667 Roundrock Rd 75248 469-593-4500
Candace Judd, prin. Fax 593-4501
Spring Valley ES 400/PK-6
13535 Spring Grove Ave 75240 469-593-4600
Kelly Colburn, prin. Fax 593-4609
Stults Road ES 500/PK-6
8700 Stults Rd 75243 469-593-2500
Darwin Spiller, prin. Fax 593-2521
Wallace ES 400/K-6
9921 Kirkhaven Dr 75238 469-593-2600
Debbie Evans, prin. Fax 593-2610
White Rock ES 600/K-6
9229 Chiswell Rd 75238 469-593-2700
Nancy Kinzie, prin. Fax 593-2706

Akiba Academy 300/PK-8
12324 Merit Dr 75251 214-295-3400
Mark Stolovitsky, hdmstr. Fax 295-3405
All Saints S 300/K-8
7777 Osage Plaza Pkwy 75252 214-217-3300
Marie Pishko, prin. Fax 217-3339
Arbor Acre Prep S 50/PK-8
8000 S Hampton Rd 75232 972-224-0511
Mary Cunningham, prin. Fax 224-0511
Bethel SDA S 50/K-8
2215 Lanark Ave 75203 903-832-6036
Fax 832-6216
Calvary Lutheran S 100/K-8
9807 Church Rd 75238 214-343-7457
James Henrickson, prin. Fax 348-1424
Christ the King S 500/K-8
4100 Colgate Ave 75225 214-365-1234
Rosemary Seltzer, prin. Fax 365-1236
Clay Academy 200/PK-8
3303 Potters House Way 75236 214-467-4143
Mildred Tolliver, admin. Fax 296-3029
Covenant S 300/K-12
7300 Valley View Ln 75240 214-358-5818
Kyle Queal, hdmstr. Fax 358-5809
Dallas Academy 200/K-12
950 Tiffany Way 75218 214-324-1481
James Richardson, hdmstr. Fax 327-8537

Dallas Adventist Junior Academy 100/PK-10
4025 N Central Expy 75204 214-528-6327
Darlene White, prin. Fax 528-6450
Dallas Montessori Academy 100/PK-8
5757 Samuell Blvd Ste 200 75228 214-388-0091
Dina Paulik, prin. Fax 388-3415
Douglass Academy 100/PK-4
2020 W Wheatland Rd 75232 972-228-5210
Cheryl Rischer, dir.
Episcopal S of Dallas-Colgate Campus 400/PK-4
4344 Colgate Ave 75225 214-353-5818
Rev. Stephen Swann, hdmstr. Fax 353-5861
Fairhill S 200/1-12
16150 Preston Rd 75248 972-233-1026
Jane Sego, dir. Fax 233-8205
Fellowship Christian Academy 600/PK-8
1821 W Camp Wisdom Rd 75232 214-672-9200
Shaliendra Thomas, admin. Fax 672-9201
First Baptist Academy 600/K-12
PO Box 868 75221 214-969-7861
William Walters, hdmstr. Fax 969-7797
Good Shepherd Episcopal S 600/PK-8
11110 Midway Rd 75229 214-357-1610
J. Robert Kohler, hdmstr. Fax 357-4105
Grace Academy 200/PK-6
11306A Inwood Rd 75229 214-696-5648
Jim Clarke, hdmstr. Fax 696-8713
Highland Park Presbyterian Day S 300/PK-4
3821 University Blvd 75205 214-525-6500
Carrie Parsons, dir. Fax 525-6501
Hockaday S 1,000/PK-12
11600 Welch Rd 75229 214-363-6311
Jeanne Whitman, hdmstr. Fax 363-0942
Holy Cross Lutheran S 200/PK-6
11425 Marsh Ln 75229 214-358-4396
Dennis Boldt, prin. Fax 350-9133
Holy Trinity S 200/PK-8
3815 Oak Lawn Ave 75219 214-526-5113
Ed Doherty, prin. Fax 526-4524
IBOC Christian Academy 300/PK-5
7710 S Westmoreland Rd 75237 972-572-4262
Julia Fuller, admin. Fax 709-3888
Kiest Park Christian Academy 100/PK-1
2719 S Hampton Rd 75224 214-331-1536
Armida Ortega, admin. Fax 330-0469
Lakehill Prep S 400/K-12
2720 Hillside Dr 75214 214-826-2931
Roger Perry, hdmstr. Fax 826-4623
Lakewood Montessori S 100/PK-5
6210 E Mockingbird Ln 75214 214-821-9466
Nancy Garoutte, prin. Fax 821-9426
Lamplighter S 300/PK-4
11611 Inwood Rd 75229 214-369-9201
Dr. Arnold Cohen, hdmstr. Fax 369-5540
Levine Academy 400/PK-8
18011 Hillcrest Rd 75252 972-248-3032
Dr. Fred Nathan, hdmstr. Fax 248-0695
Lighthouse Christian Academy 200/PK-6
PO Box 210217 75211 214-339-2207
Mary Sariego, admin. Fax 337-9636
Lobias Murray Christian Academy 200/K-12
330 E Ann Arbor Ave 75216 214-372-6466
Sharon Smith, prin. Fax 376-6763
Mary Immaculate S 500/K-8
14032 Dennis Ln 75234 972-243-7105
Nancy Russell, prin. Fax 241-7678
Montessori S of North Dallas 100/PK-3
18303 Davenport Rd 75252 972-985-8844
Monica Cook, dir. Fax 673-0118
Mount St. Michael S 100/PK-8
PO Box 225159 75222 214-337-0244
Gretchen Montgomery, prin. Fax 339-1702
Our Lady of Perpetual Help S 200/K-8
7625 Cortland Ave 75235 214-351-3396
Dan Quill, prin. Fax 351-9889
Our Redeemer Lutheran S 100/PK-6
7611 Park Ln 75225 214-368-1371
Lois Frischmann, prin. Fax 368-1473
Parish Episcopal S 1,200/PK-12
4101 Sigma Rd 75244 972-239-8011
Gloria Snyder, hdmstr. Fax 991-1237
St. Alcuin Montessori S 300/PK-8
6144 Churchill Way 75230 972-239-1745
Shaun Underhill, admin. Fax 934-8727
St. Augustine S 200/PK-8
1064 N Saint Augustine Dr 75217 214-391-1381
Michael Moretta, prin. Fax 391-8781
St. Bernard of Clairvaux S 200/PK-8
1420 Old Gate Ln 75218 214-321-2897
Faustino Leos, prin. Fax 321-4060
St. Cecilia S 200/PK-8
635 Mary Cliff Rd 75208 214-948-8628
Candice Barbosa, prin. Fax 948-4956
St. Elizabeth S 300/PK-8
4019 S Hampton Rd 75224 214-331-5139
Christina Clem, prin. Fax 467-4346
St. James Episcopal Montessori S 100/PK-4
9845 McCree Rd 75238 214-348-1349
Loree Birkenback, hdmstr. Fax 348-1368
St. John's Episcopal S 500/PK-8
848 Harter Rd 75218 214-328-9131
Walter Sorensen, prin. Fax 320-0205
St. Marks S of Texas 800/1-12
10600 Preston Rd 75230 214-346-8000
Arnold Holtberg, hdmstr. Fax 346-8002
St. Mary of Carmel S 100/PK-8
1716 Singleton Blvd 75212 214-748-2934
Thomas Suhy, prin. Fax 760-9052
St. Monica S 900/PK-8
4140 Walnut Hill Ln 75229 214-351-5688
Patricia Dulac, prin. Fax 352-2608
St. Patrick S 500/PK-8
9635 Ferndale Rd 75238 214-348-8070
Frances Thompson, prin. Fax 503-7230
St. Philip's S 200/PK-6
1600 Pennsylvania Ave 75215 214-421-5221
Dr. Terry Flowers, hdmstr. Fax 428-5371

St. Philip the Apostle S 200/K-8
8151 Military Pkwy 75227 214-381-4973
Fred Meyers, prin. Fax 381-0466
St. Pius X S 400/K-8
3030 Gus Thomasson Rd 75228 972-279-2339
Dr. Carol Newman, prin. Fax 613-2059
St. Rita S 700/K-8
12525 Inwood Rd 75244 972-239-3203
Dr. Elena Hines, prin. Fax 934-0657
St. Thomas Aquinas S 700/PK-8
3741 Abrams Rd 75214 214-826-0566
Patrick Magee, prin. Fax 826-0251
Santa Clara of Assisi S 200/PK-8
321 Calumet Ave 75211 214-333-9423
Stephanie Malous, prin. Fax 333-2556
Scofield Christian S 200/PK-6
7730 Abrams Rd 75231 214-349-6843
Stephanie Johnson-Martin, hdmstr. Fax 342-2061
Shelton S 800/PK-12
15720 Hillcrest Rd 75248 972-774-1772
Dr. Joyce Pickering, dir. Fax 991-3977
Southwest Adventist Jr. Academy 50/PK-8
1600 Bonnie View Rd 75203 214-948-1666
Fax 948-1125
Torah Day S 200/PK-8
6921 Frankford Rd 75252 972-964-0090
Rabbi Yerachmiel Udman, hdmstr. Fax 964-0091
Tyler Street Christian Academy 200/PK-12
915 W 9th St 75208 214-941-9717
Dr. Karen Egger, supt. Fax 941-0324
West Dallas Community S 100/PK-8
2320 Canada Dr 75212 214-634-1927
Tom Neuhoff, hdmstr. Fax 688-1928
White Rock Montessori 200/PK-8
1601 Oates Dr 75228 214-324-5580
Sue Henry, prin. Fax 324-5671
White Rock North S 200/PK-6
9727 White Rock Trl 75238 214-348-7410
Amy Adams, prin. Fax 348-3109
Winston S 200/1-12
5707 Royal Ln 75229 214-691-6950
Dr. Polly Peterson, hdmstr. Fax 691-1509
Zion Lutheran S 200/PK-8
6121 E Lovers Ln 75214 214-363-1630
Jeff Thorman, prin. Fax 361-2049

Damon, Brazoria
Damon ISD 200/PK-8
PO Box 429 77430 979-742-3457
Donald Rhodes, supt. Fax 742-3275
www.damonisd.net/
Damon S 200/PK-8
PO Box 429 77430 979-742-3457
Donald Rhodes, prin. Fax 742-3275

Danbury, Brazoria, Pop. 1,667
Danbury ISD 800/PK-12
PO Box 378 77534 979-922-1218
Eric Grimmett, supt. Fax 922-8246
www.danburyisd.org/
Danbury ES 400/PK-6
PO Box 716 77534 979-922-8787
Carol Shefcik, prin. Fax 922-1589
Danbury MS 100/7-8
PO Box 586 77534 979-922-1226
Kevin Rueb, prin. Fax 922-1051

Darrouzett, Lipscomb, Pop. 302
Darrouzett ISD 100/PK-12
PO Box 98 79024 806-624-2221
Danny Cochran, supt. Fax 624-4361
www.darrouzettisd.net
Darrouzett S 100/PK-12
PO Box 98 79024 806-624-3001
David Taylor, prin. Fax 624-4361

Dawson, Navarro, Pop. 906
Dawson ISD 500/PK-12
199 N School Ave 76639 254-578-1031
Arvel Rotan, supt. Fax 578-1721
www.dawsonisd.net/
Dawson ES 300/PK-6
199 N School Ave 76639 254-578-1416
Cynthia Pollard, prin. Fax 578-1721

Dayton, Liberty, Pop. 6,622
Dayton ISD 4,900/PK-12
PO Box 248 77535 936-258-2667
Greg Hayman, supt. Fax 258-5616
www.daytonisd.net/
Austin ES 700/K-1
PO Box 248 77535 936-258-2535
Mary Burke, prin. Fax 257-4138
Brown ES 700/4-5
PO Box 248 77535 936-257-2796
Liz Harris, prin. Fax 257-4154
Colbert ES 100/PK-PK
PO Box 248 77535 936-258-2727
Rita Gilmore, prin. Fax 257-4151
Nottingham S 400/6-6
PO Box 248 77535 936-257-4100
Rita Gilmore, prin. Fax 257-4110
Richter ES 800/2-3
PO Box 248 77535 936-258-7126
Lynn Sturrock, prin. Fax 257-4179
Wilson JHS 800/7-8
PO Box 248 77535 936-258-2309
Oran Hamilton, prin. Fax 257-4109

Decatur, Wise, Pop. 6,031
Decatur ISD 2,800/PK-12
501 E Collins St 76234 940-393-7100
Gerard Gindt Ed.D., supt. Fax 627-3141
www.decaturisd.us/
Carson ES 500/PK-4
2100 S Business 287 76234 940-393-7500
Kim Barker, prin. Fax 627-4792
Decatur IS 400/5-6
1200 W Eagle Dr 76234 940-393-7400
Dan Martin, prin. Fax 627-0082
Decatur MS 400/7-8
1201 W Thompson St 76234 940-393-7300
Dewayne Tamplen, prin. Fax 627-2497
Rann ES 600/PK-4
1300 Deer Park Rd 76234 940-393-7600
Melonie Christian, prin. Fax 627-6198

Deer Park, Harris, Pop. 28,993
Deer Park ISD 15,200/PK-12
203 Ivy Ave 77536 832-668-7000
Arnold Adair, supt. Fax 930-1945
www.dpisd.org
Bonnette JHS 700/6-8
5010 W Pasadena Blvd 77536 832-668-7700
Stephen Harrell, prin. Fax 930-4756
Carpenter ES 900/PK-5
5002 W Pasadena Blvd 77536 832-668-8400
Belinda Box, prin. Fax 930-4970
Dabbs ES 800/K-5
302 E Lambuth Ln 77536 832-668-8100
Marty Emmons, prin. Fax 930-4910
Deer Park ES 600/PK-5
2920 Luella Ave 77536 832-668-8000
Lisa McLaughlin, prin. Fax 930-4930
Deer Park JHS 800/6-8
410 E 9th St 77536 832-668-7500
Tiffany Regan, prin. Fax 930-4726
San Jacinto ES 800/K-5
601 E 8th St 77536 832-668-7900
Helen Boudreaux, prin. Fax 930-4950
Other Schools – See Pasadena

La Porte ISD
Supt. — See La Porte
College Park ES 800/PK-5
4315 Luella Ave 77536 281-604-4400
Deborah Shearer, prin. Fax 604-4460
Heritage ES 500/K-5
4301 East Blvd 77536 281-604-2600
Danette Tilley, prin. Fax 604-2605

De Kalb, Bowie, Pop. 1,790
De Kalb ISD 800/PK-12
101 Maple St 75559 903-667-2566
David Manley, supt. Fax 667-3791
www.dekalbisd.net
De Kalb ES 300/PK-4
101 W Fannin St 75559 903-667-2328
Kim Birdsong, prin. Fax 667-5151
De Kalb MS 200/5-8
929 W Grizzley St 75559 903-667-2834
Darnisha Carreathers, prin. Fax 667-5509

Hubbard ISD 100/PK-8
3347 US Highway 259 S 75559 903-667-2645
Traci Drake, supt. Fax 667-5835
hubbard.esc8.net/
Hubbard S 100/PK-8
3347 US Highway 259 S 75559 903-667-2645
Traci Drake, prin. Fax 667-5835

De Leon, Comanche, Pop. 2,386
De Leon ISD 600/PK-12
425 S Texas St 76444 254-893-5095
Dr. Randy Mohundro, supt. Fax 893-3101
www.deleon.esc14.net
De Leon ES 300/PK-4
425 S Texas St 76444 254-893-6889
Judd Gibson, prin. Fax 893-6004
Perkins MS 200/5-8
425 S Texas St 76444 254-893-6111
Mark Lewis, prin. Fax 893-7918

Dell City, Hudspeth, Pop. 408
Dell City ISD 100/K-12
PO Box 37 79837 915-964-2663
Tanya Lewis, supt. Fax 964-2473
Dell City S 100/K-12
PO Box 37 79837 915-964-2663
David Turrentine, prin. Fax 964-2473

Del Rio, Val Verde, Pop. 36,020
San Felipe-Del Rio Consolidated ISD 10,100/PK-12
PO Box 428002 78842 830-778-4000
Tommy Hall, supt. Fax 774-9892
www.sfdr-cisd.org
Buena Vista ES 700/K-5
PO Box 428002 78842 830-778-4600
Paula Bostick, prin. Fax 774-9875
Calderon ES 700/K-5
PO Box 428002 78842 830-778-4628
Jose Perez, prin. Fax 774-9975
Cardwell Preschool 400/PK-PK
PO Box 428002 78842 830-778-4650
Linda Guajanuato, prin. Fax 774-9855
Chavira ES 500/K-5
PO Box 428002 78842 830-778-4660
Aida Gomez, prin. Fax 778-4974
Del Rio MS 1,500/7-8
PO Box 428002 78842 830-778-4530
Carlos Rios, prin. Fax 778-4550
East Side ES 500/K-5
PO Box 428002 78842 830-778-4680
Tonya Senne, prin. Fax 774-9560
Garfield ES 700/K-5
PO Box 428002 78842 830-778-4700
Janell Runyan, prin. Fax 774-9928
Green ES 800/K-5
PO Box 428002 78842 830-778-4750
Dorothy Birkhead, prin. Fax 774-9532
Lamar ES 400/K-5
PO Box 428002 78842 830-778-4730
Maria Owens, prin. Fax 774-9493
North Heights ES 500/K-5
PO Box 428002 78842 830-778-4770
Denise Reyes, prin. Fax 778-4988
San Felipe Memorial MS 700/6-6
PO Box 428002 78842 830-778-4560
Sandra Hernandez, prin. Fax 774-9871

Sacred Heart S 300/PK-8
209 E Greenwood St 78840 830-775-3274
Aurora Guerra, prin. Fax 774-2800

Del Valle, Travis
Del Valle ISD 8,100/PK-12
5301 Ross Rd 78617 512-386-3000
Bernard Blanchard, supt. Fax 386-3015
www.del-valle.k12.tx.us
Del Valle ES 700/PK-6
5400 Ross Rd 78617 512-386-3350
Bertha Hernandez, prin. Fax 386-3355
Del Valle MS 700/6-8
5500 Ross Rd 78617 512-386-3400
Kenneth Storm, prin. Fax 386-3405
Popham ES 700/PK-5
7014 Elroy Rd 78617 512-386-3750
Dr. Joyce Bannerot, prin. Fax 386-3755
Other Schools – See Austin, Creedmoor

Denison, Grayson, Pop. 23,648
Denison ISD 4,500/PK-12
1201 S Rusk Ave 75020 903-462-7000
Henry Scott, supt. Fax 462-7002
denisonisd.net
Golden Rule ES 300/PK-5
811 W Florence St 75020 903-462-7250
Karen Sawyer, prin. Fax 462-7376
Houston ES 300/PK-5
1100 W Morgan St 75020 903-462-7300
Karen Musgrave, prin. Fax 462-7419
Hyde Park ES 300/K-5
1701 S Hyde Park Ave 75020 903-462-7350
Regina Prigge, prin. Fax 462-7455
Lamar ES 400/PK-5
1000 S 5th Ave 75021 903-462-7400
Janet Mobley, prin. Fax 462-7495
Layne ES 300/K-5
1000 Layne Dr 75020 903-462-7450
Ginger Brawley, prin. Fax 462-7532
Mayes ES 300/PK-5
201 Jennie Ln 75020 903-462-7500
Brent Hoy, prin. Fax 462-7563
McDaniel MS 1,000/6-8
400 S Lillis Ln 75020 903-462-7200
Alvis Dunlap, prin. Fax 462-7328
Terrell ES 500/PK-5
230 Martin Luther King St 75020 903-462-7550
Dr. David Kirkbride, prin. Fax 462-7609

St. Luke's Parish Day S 100/PK-5
427 W Woodard St 75020 903-465-2653
Rev. David Petrash, hdmstr. Fax 463-1128

Denton, Denton, Pop. 104,153
Denton ISD 20,500/PK-12
1307 N Locust St 76201 940-369-0000
Dr. Ray Braswell, supt. Fax 369-4982
www.dentonisd.org
Borman ES 600/PK-5
1201 Parvin St 76205 940-369-2500
Ruben Molinar, prin. Fax 369-4903
Calhoun MS 800/6-8
709 W Congress St 76201 940-369-2400
Anthony Sims, prin. Fax 369-4939
Evers Park ES 500/K-5
3300 Evers Pkwy 76207 940-369-2600
Jane Flores, prin. Fax 369-4906
Ginnings ES 600/K-5
2525 Yellowstone Pl 76209 940-369-2700
Missey Chavez, prin. Fax 369-4909
Hawk ES 800/K-5
2300 Oakmont Dr 76210 940-369-1800
Susannah O'Bara, prin. Fax 369-4911
Hodge ES 600/PK-5
3900 Grant Pkwy 76208 940-369-2800
Sam Kelley, prin. Fax 369-4912
Houston ES 700/PK-5
3100 Teasley Ln 76205 940-369-2900
Teresa Andress, prin. Fax 369-4915
Lee ES 600/K-5
800 Mack Dr 76209 940-369-3500
Laura Rodriguez, prin. Fax 369-4918
McMath MS 1,000/6-8
1900 Jason Dr 76205 940-369-3300
Dr. Debra Nobles, prin. Fax 369-4946
McNair ES 700/PK-5
1212 Hickory Creek Rd 76210 940-369-3600
Sean Flynn, prin. Fax 369-4921
Nelson ES 500/K-5
3909 Teasley Ln 76210 940-369-1400
Kaylene Tierce, prin. Fax 383-3534
Pecan Creek ES 700/K-5
4400 Lakeview Blvd 76208 940-369-4400
Aleta Atkinson, prin. Fax 369-4904
Rayzor ES 600/PK-5
1400 Malone St 76201 940-369-3700
Carlos Ramirez, prin. Fax 369-4924
Rivera ES 600/PK-5
701 Newton St 76205 940-369-3800
Robert Gonzalez, prin. Fax 369-4927
Ryan ES 600/K-5
201 W Ryan Rd 76210 940-369-4600
Gary Miller, prin. Fax 369-4936
Strickland MS 900/6-8
324 E Windsor Dr 76209 940-369-4200
Kathleen Carmona, prin. Fax 369-4950
Wilson ES 600/K-5
1306 E Windsor Dr 76209 940-369-4500
Audrey Staniszewski, prin. Fax 369-4933
Windle S for Young Children 300/PK-PK
901 Audra Ln 76209 940-369-3900
Dr. Ron Arrington, prin. Fax 369-4930
Other Schools – See Argyle, Aubrey, Corinth, Shady Shores

Denton Calvary Academy 300/1-12
PO Box 2414 76202 940-320-1944
Fax 591-9311

Hilltop Montessori 50/PK-8
1014 N Elm St 76201 940-387-0578
Julie Winnette, dir. Fax 387-0578
Immaculate Conception S 300/PK-8
2301 N Bonnie Brae St 76207 940-381-1155
Elaine Schad, prin. Fax 381-1837
Selwyn S 200/PK-12
3333 W University Dr 76207 940-382-6771
Sandy Doerge, hdmstr. Fax 383-0704

Denver City, Yoakum, Pop. 3,994
Denver City ISD 1,400/PK-12
501 Mustang Dr 79323 806-592-5900
Dagobert Azam, supt. Fax 592-5909
www.dcisd.org
Gravitt JHS 300/6-8
419 Mustang Dr 79323 806-592-5940
Howard Wright, prin. Fax 592-5949
Kelley / Dodson ES 700/PK-5
500 N Soland Ave 79323 806-592-5920
Kristy Kostelich, prin. Fax 592-5929

Deport, Lamar, Pop. 698
Prairiland ISD
Supt. — See Pattonville
Deport ES 200/PK-5
PO Box 218 75435 903-652-3325
Lanny Mathews, prin. Fax 652-2212

De Soto, Dallas, Pop. 39,440
De Soto ISD 8,800/PK-12
200 E Belt Line Rd, 972-223-6666
Lloyd Treadwell, supt. Fax 274-8209
www.desotoisd.org
Amber Terrace ES 400/PK-5
224 Amber Ln, 972-223-8757
Nikeesia Ranson, prin. Fax 274-8247
Cockrell Hill ES 700/PK-5
425 S Cockrell Hill Rd, 972-230-1692
Wanda Randall, prin. Fax 274-8081
De Soto East MS 600/6-8
601 E Belt Line Rd, 972-223-0690
Donna Blackburn, prin. Fax 274-8156
De Soto West MS 800/6-8
800 N Westmoreland Rd, 972-230-1820
Kevin Dixon, prin. Fax 274-8183
Meadows ES 300/PK-5
1016 The Meadows Pkwy, 972-224-0960
Teresa Angeles, prin. Fax 228-7908
Northside ES 500/PK-5
525 Ray Ave, 972-224-6709
Lisa Mott, prin. Fax 228-7925
Woodridge ES 700/PK-5
1001 Woodridge Dr, 972-223-3800
Robert Torres, prin. Fax 274-8204
Young ES 500/PK-5
707 N Young Blvd, 972-223-6505
Becky Sheppard, prin. Fax 274-8221
Other Schools – See Glenn Heights, Red Oak

Canterbury Episcopal S 300/K-12
1708 N Westmoreland Rd, 972-572-7200
Rev. Dick Cadigan, hdmstr. Fax 572-7400
Cross of Christ Lutheran S 100/PK-PK
512 N Cockrell Hill Rd, 972-223-9586
Linda Hinckley, lead tchr. Fax 223-0660

Detroit, Red River, Pop. 743
Detroit ISD 500/PK-12
110 E Garner St 75436 903-674-6131
Morris Lyon, supt. Fax 674-2478
www.detroiteagles.net
Detroit ES 200/PK-5
110 E Garner St 75436 903-674-3137
Chris Bradshaw, prin. Fax 674-2407
Detroit JHS 100/6-8
110 E Garner St 75436 903-674-2646
Misty Looney, prin. Fax 674-2206

Devers, Liberty, Pop. 437
Devers ISD 100/PK-8
PO Box 488 77538 936-549-7135
Larry Wadzeck, supt. Fax 549-7595
www.deversisd.net/
Devers ES 100/PK-5
PO Box 488 77538 936-549-7591
Larry Wadzeck, prin. Fax 549-7085
Devers JHS 100/6-8
PO Box 488 77538 936-549-7135
Danny Grimes, prin. Fax 549-7085

Devine, Medina, Pop. 4,409
Devine ISD 1,800/PK-12
205 W College Ave 78016 830-851-0795
Linda McAnelly, supt. Fax 663-6706
www.devineisd.org
Ciavarra ES 500/PK-2
112 Bentson Dr 78016 830-851-0395
Brenda Gardner, prin. Fax 663-6730
Devine IS 300/3-5
900 Atkins Ave 78016 830-851-0495
Scott Sostarich, prin. Fax 663-6746
Devine MS 400/6-8
400 Cardinal Dr 78016 830-851-0695
Lori Marek, prin. Fax 663-6769

Faith Christian Academy 50/PK-12
PO Box 172 78016 830-663-4718
Karen Bishop, dir. Fax 663-4718

Deweyville, Newton, Pop. 1,218
Deweyville ISD 700/PK-12
PO Box 408 77614 409-746-7702
Rick Summers, supt. Fax 746-3360
www.esc05.k12.tx.us/dewisd/
Deweyville ES 300/PK-5
PO Box 409 77614 409-746-2716
Phyllis Kingsbury, prin. Fax 746-7700
Deweyville MS 200/6-8
PO Box 109 77614 409-746-2924
Betty Foster, prin. Fax 746-2753

D Hanis, Medina
D'Hanis ISD 200/K-12
PO Box 307 78850 830-363-7216
Pam Seipp, supt. Fax 363-7390
dhanis.tx.schoolwebpages.com
Koch ES K-5
PO Box 307 78850 830-363-8102
Dorothy Saunders, prin. Fax 363-7390

Diana, Upshur
New Diana ISD 700/PK-12
1373 US Highway 259 S 75640 903-663-8000
Joyce Sloan, supt. Fax 663-9565
www.newdianaisd.net/
Hunt ES 200/PK-3
11150 State Highway 154 E 75640 903-663-8004
Jim Kilpatrick, prin. Fax 663-7575
New Diana IS 4-6
1379 US Highway 259 S 75640 903-663-8003
Donna McGuire, prin. Fax 663-9588
New Diana MS 100/7-8
11854 State Highway 154 E 75640 903-663-8002
Greg Pope, prin. Fax 663-1812

Diboll, Angelina, Pop. 5,441
Diboll ISD 1,900/PK-12
PO Box 550 75941 936-829-4718
Gary Martel, supt. Fax 829-5558
www.dibollisd.com
Diboll JHS 400/6-8
403 Dennis St 75941 936-829-5225
Mark Kettering, prin. Fax 829-5848
Diboll PS 400/PK-1
110 Ballenger St 75941 936-829-4671
Lara Kelley, prin. Fax 829-4977
Temple ES 600/2-5
400 Ash St 75941 936-829-5419
Laurie Burton, prin. Fax 829-5159

Dickinson, Galveston, Pop. 17,898
Dickinson ISD 8,300/PK-12
PO Box Z 77539 281-229-6000
Dr. Leland Williams, supt. Fax 229-6011
www.dickinsonisd.org
Barber MS 500/5-6
5651 FM 517 Rd E 77539 281-229-6900
Bonnie Fried, prin. Fax 229-6901
Bay Colony ES 1,100/PK-4
101 Bay Colony Elementary Dr 77539 281-534-8100
Kathy Velghe, prin. Fax 534-8125
Dunbar MS 500/5-6
2901 23rd St 77539 281-229-6600
Kevin Lankford, prin. Fax 229-6601
Hughes Road ES 800/PK-4
11901 Hughes Rd 77539 281-534-6877
Trish Lankford, prin. Fax 534-6879
McAdams JHS 1,100/7-8
11415 Hughes Rd 77539 281-229-7100
Traci Goodwin, prin. Fax 229-7101
Silbernagel ES 800/PK-4
4201 25th St 77539 281-534-6950
Michael Scruggs, prin. Fax 534-6952
Other Schools – See Bacliff, San Leon

Pine Drive Christian S 300/PK-12
705 FM 517 Rd E 77539 281-534-4881
Larry Bowles, admin. Fax 534-4318
True Cross S 200/PK-8
400 FM 517 Rd E 77539 281-337-5212
Marc Martinez, prin. Fax 337-5779

Dilley, Frio, Pop. 4,167
Dilley ISD 800/PK-12
245 W FM 117 78017 830-965-1912
Jack Seals, supt. Fax 965-4069
dilleyisd.net
Dilley ES 400/PK-5
245 W FM 117 78017 830-965-1313
Deborah Thompson, prin. Fax 965-1178
Harper MS 200/6-8
245 W FM 117 78017 830-965-2195
Trini Medina, prin. Fax 965-2171

Dime Box, Lee
Dime Box ISD 200/PK-12
PO Box 157 77853 979-884-2324
Donnie Reagan, supt. Fax 884-0106
dimebox.groupfusion.net
Dime Box S 200/PK-12
PO Box 157 77853 979-884-3366
Joshua Pinkerton, prin. Fax 884-0314

Dimmitt, Castro, Pop. 3,981
Dimmitt ISD 1,100/PK-12
608 W Halsell St 79027 806-647-3101
Charles Miller, supt. Fax 647-5433
www.dimmittisd.net
Dimmitt MS 300/5-8
805 W Jones St 79027 806-647-3108
Max Newman, prin. Fax 647-2996
Richardson ES 500/PK-4
708 W Stinson St 79027 806-647-4131
Doricell Davis, prin. Fax 647-4438

Dodd City, Fannin, Pop. 443
Dodd City ISD 300/PK-12
602 N Main St 75438 903-583-7585
Craig Reed, supt. Fax 583-9545
www.doddcityisd.org
Dodd City S 300/PK-12
602 N Main St 75438 903-583-7585
Lesia Bridges, prin. Fax 583-7586

Donna, Hidalgo, Pop. 15,846
Donna ISD 13,800/PK-12
116 N 10th St 78537 956-464-1600
Roberto Loredo, supt. Fax 464-1752
www.donnaisd.net
Adame ES 600/PK-5
116 N 10th St 78537 956-461-4010
Maria Partida, prin. Fax 461-4017
Caceres ES 500/PK-5
116 N 10th St 78537 956-464-1995
Rebecca Castaneda, prin. Fax 464-1743
Garza ES 800/PK-5
116 N 10th St 78537 956-464-1886
Emmy DeLaGarza, prin. Fax 464-1891
Guzman ES 400/PK-5
116 N 10th St 78537 956-464-1920
Tomas Tamez, prin. Fax 464-1926
Lenoir ES 600/PK-5
116 N 10th St 78537 956-464-1685
Elizabeth Gongora, prin. Fax 464-1877
Munoz ES 900/PK-5
116 N 10th St 78537 956-464-1310
Gloria Sutti, prin. Fax 464-1316
Ochoa ES 500/PK-5
116 N 10th St 78537 956-464-1900
Celia Martinez, prin. Fax 464-1918
Price ES 700/PK-5
116 N 10th St 78537 956-464-1303
Elisa Gonzalez, prin. Fax 464-1676
Rivas ES 400/PK-5
116 N 10th St 78537 956-464-1990
Maria Quintero, prin. Fax 464-1869
Runn ES 300/PK-5
116 N 10th St 78537 956-464-1864
Jose Vela, prin. Fax 464-1934
Salazar ES 700/PK-5
116 N 10th St 78537 956-464-1977
Maricela Valdez, prin. Fax 464-1983
Sauceda MS 900/6-8
116 N 10th St 78537 956-464-1360
Nancy Castillo, prin. Fax 464-1349
Singleterry ES 700/PK-5
116 N 10th St 78537 956-454-1845
Maria Alvarez, prin. Fax 454-1849
Solis MS 800/6-8
116 N 10th St 78537 956-464-1650
Chrsielda Saenz, prin. Fax 464-1786
Stainke ES 500/PK-5
116 N 10th St 78537 956-464-1940
Griselda Alvarez, prin. Fax 464-1941
Veterans MS 1,000/6-8
116 N 10th St 78537 956-464-1350
Kent Edwards, prin. Fax 464-1356
Other Schools – See Alamo

Doss, Gillespie
Doss Consolidated Common SD 50/K-8
11431 Ranch Road 648 78618 830-997-7502
Mark Stroeher, supt. Fax 997-9958
Doss S 50/K-8
11431 Ranch Road 648 78618 830-669-2411
Carrie Bierschwale, prin. Fax 669-2303

Douglass, Nacogdoches
Douglass ISD 300/PK-12
PO Box 38 75943 936-569-9804
Jay Hampton-Tullos, supt. Fax 569-9446
www.douglass.esc7.net
Douglass S 300/PK-12
PO Box 38 75943 936-569-9804
Eric Samford, prin. Fax 569-9446

Dripping Springs, Hays, Pop. 1,666
Dripping Springs ISD 4,500/PK-12
PO Box 479 78620 512-858-3002
Mard Herrick Ph.D., supt. Fax 858-3098
www.dripping-springs.k12.tx.us/
Dripping Springs ES 900/PK-5
PO Box 479 78620 512-858-3700
Deborah Albers, prin. Fax 858-3799
Dripping Springs MS 900/6-8
PO Box 479 78620 512-858-3400
Kim Gravell, prin. Fax 858-3499
Rooster Springs ES 700/PK-5
PO Box 479 78620 512-465-6200
Rhonda Whitman, prin. Fax 465-6299
Walnut Springs ES 800/PK-5
PO Box 479 78620 512-858-3800
Holly Cargill, prin. Fax 858-3899

Driscoll, Nueces, Pop. 822
Driscoll ISD 300/PK-8
PO Box 238 78351 361-387-7349
Cynthia Garcia, supt. Fax 387-6088
www.driscollisd.esc2.net
Driscoll ES 200/PK-5
PO Box 238 78351 361-387-7349
Lynn Landenberger, prin. Fax 387-6088
Driscoll MS 100/6-8
PO Box 238 78351 361-387-7349
Lynn Landenberger, prin. Fax 387-6088

Dublin, Erath, Pop. 3,662
Dublin ISD 1,200/PK-12
PO Box 169 76446 254-445-3341
Roy Neff, supt. Fax 445-3345
www.dublin.k12.tx.us
Dublin ES 400/PK-2
PO Box 169 76446 254-445-2577
Charlotte Pounds, prin. Fax 445-2570
Dublin IS 200/3-5
PO Box 169 76446 254-445-2618
Rebecca Owen, prin. Fax 445-3383
Dublin MS 300/6-8
PO Box 169 76446 254-445-2618
John Grimland, prin. Fax 445-2607

Dumas, Moore, Pop. 13,887
Dumas ISD 3,900/PK-12
PO Box 615 79029 806-935-6461
Larry Appel, supt. Fax 935-6275
www.dumas-k12.net/
Dumas JHS 600/7-8
PO Box 697 79029 806-935-4155
Danny Potter, prin. Fax 934-1434
Green Acres ES 600/PK-6
PO Box 736 79029 806-935-4157
Sharla Wilson, prin. Fax 934-1444

Hillcrest ES 400/PK-6
PO Box 715 79029 806-935-5629
Stephanie Schilling, prin. Fax 934-1439
Morningside ES 500/PK-6
PO Box 698 79029 806-935-4153
Stan Stroebel, prin. Fax 934-1438
Sunset ES 500/PK-6
PO Box 716 79029 806-935-2127
Philip Rhodes, prin. Fax 934-1441
Other Schools – See Cactus

Duncanville, Dallas, Pop. 35,150
Duncanville ISD 12,400/PK-12
802 S Main St 75137 972-708-2000
Dr. Alfred Ray, supt. Fax 708-2020
www.duncanvilleisd.org
Alexander ES 500/K-4
510 Softwood Dr 75137 972-708-2500
Linda Sorensen, prin. Fax 708-2525
Brandenburg IS 600/5-6
1903 Blueridge Dr 75137 972-708-3100
Dawn Smith, prin. Fax 708-3131
Byrd MS 700/7-8
1040 W Wheatland Rd 75116 972-708-3400
Gabe Trujillo, prin. Fax 708-3434
Central ES 500/PK-4
302 E Freeman St 75116 972-708-2600
Kathleen Brown, prin. Fax 708-2626
Daniel IS 600/5-6
1007 Springwood Ln 75137 972-708-3200
Mark Smythe, prin. Fax 708-3232
Fairmeadows ES 600/PK-4
101 E Fairmeadows Dr 75116 972-708-2700
Teresa Villarreal, prin. Fax 708-2727
Hardin IS 600/5-6
426 E Freeman St 75116 972-708-3300
Joyce Price, prin. Fax 708-3333
Hastings ES 400/PK-4
602 W Center St 75116 972-708-2800
Julie Hargrove, prin. Fax 708-2828
Merrifield ES 600/PK-4
102 E Vinyard Rd 75137 972-708-2900
Linda Snook, prin. Fax 708-2929
Reed MS 500/7-8
530 E Freeman St 75116 972-708-3500
John Matthews, prin. Fax 708-3535
Smith ES 500/K-4
1010 Big Stone Gap Rd 75137 972-708-3000
Bill Bryant, prin. Fax 708-3030
Other Schools – See Dallas

ChristWay Academy 200/PK-12
419 N Cedar Ridge Dr 75116 972-296-6525
Becky King, admin. Fax 239-2670

Eagle Lake, Colorado, Pop. 3,693
Rice Consolidated ISD
Supt. — See Altair
Eagle Lake ES 400/PK-5
701 Tate Ave 77434 979-234-3531
Sue Weller, prin. Fax 234-3409
Eagle Lake JHS 200/6-8
600 Johnnie D Hutchins 77434 979-234-3531
Mike Keenon, prin. Fax 234-3409

Eagle Pass, Maverick, Pop. 25,571
Eagle Pass ISD 11,900/PK-12
1420 Eidson Rd 78852 830-773-5181
Jesus Sanchez, supt. Fax 773-7252
www.eaglepassisd.net
Austin ES 200/1-6
587 Madison St 78852 830-758-7004
Alma Martinez, prin. Fax 773-2731
Benavides Heights ES 400/1-6
1750 Mesa Dr 78852 830-758-7006
Salvador Gonzalez, prin. Fax 758-0216
Darr ES 500/1-6
841 Memo Robinson Rd 78852 830-758-7060
Adelita Olivares, prin. Fax 758-0090
Eagle Pass JHS 1,000/7-8
1750 N Bibb Ave 78852 830-758-7037
Oscar Castillon, prin. Fax 757-1278
ECC 600/PK-K
636 Kelso Dr 78852 830-758-7027
Letty Sandoval, prin. Fax 757-1153
Gallego ES 400/1-6
300 Azucena St 78852 830-758-7132
Sylvia Saucedo, prin. Fax 757-5795
Glass ES 500/K-6
1501 Boehmer Ave 78852 830-758-7041
Rosa Castillon, prin. Fax 773-5989
Gonzalez ES 500/1-6
400 Balcones Blvd 78852 830-758-7099
Julian Lerma, prin. Fax 757-3274
Graves ES 600/1-6
1420 Eidson Rd 78852 830-758-7043
Alicia Charles, prin. Fax 758-0342
Houston ES 500/2-6
2789 FM 1021 78852 830-758-7069
Jesus Costilla, prin. Fax 757-6639
Kennedy Hall S 400/PK-K
1610 Del Rio Blvd Ste B 78852 830-758-7189
Lisa Ruiz, prin. Fax 758-7192
Language Development Center 500/PK-K
724 FM 3443 78852 830-758-7047
Rosella Even, prin. Fax 758-1528
Lee ES 500/1-6
300 S Monroe St 78852 830-758-7062
Annie Santleban, prin. Fax 773-3471
Liberty ES 600/1-6
1850 Flowers 78852 830-758-7156
Rosa Barcena, prin. Fax 757-3237
Memorial JHS 1,100/7-8
1800 Lewis St 78852 830-758-7053
Maria Sumpter, prin. Fax 773-8900
Rosita Valley ES 300/2-6
735 Rosita Valley Rd 78852 830-758-7065
Johnnie Lee Gonzalez, prin. Fax 757-2098
Rosita Valley Literacy Academy 400/PK-1
811 Rosita Valley Rd 78852 830-758-7067
Aida Pang-Villa, prin. Fax 773-8859
San Luis ES 500/1-6
2090 Williams St 78852 830-758-7071
Selina Jimenez, prin. Fax 773-1632
Seco Mines ES 400/1-6
2900 Diaz St 78852 830-758-7073
Maribel Martinez, prin. Fax 773-8725
Other Schools – See Quemado

Our Lady of Refuge S 200/PK-8
577 Washington St 78852 830-773-3531
Adolfo Olivarez, prin. Fax 773-7310

Early, Brown, Pop. 2,774
Early ISD 1,400/PK-12
PO Box 3315, Brownwood TX 76803 325-646-7934
Brett Koch, supt. Fax 646-9238
www.earlyisd.net/
Early ES 300/3-5
PO Box 3315, Brownwood TX 76803 325-646-5511
Aletha Patterson, prin. Fax 646-5469
Early MS 300/6-8
PO Box 3315, Brownwood TX 76803 325-643-5665
Randy Lancaster, prin. Fax 646-9972
Early PS 300/PK-2
PO Box 3315, Brownwood TX 76803 325-643-9622
Sherry Clark, prin. Fax 646-5336

Earth, Lamb, Pop. 1,077
Springlake-Earth ISD 400/PK-12
PO Box 130 79031 806-257-3310
Denver Crum, supt. Fax 257-3927
www.springlake-earth.org
Springlake S 300/PK-8
PO Box 130 79031 806-257-3863
Robert Conkin, prin. Fax 257-3927

East Bernard, Wharton, Pop. 2,275
East Bernard ISD 900/PK-12
723 College St 77435 979-335-7519
Garland Calhoun, supt. Fax 335-6561
www.ebisd.org/
East Bernard ES 400/PK-4
723 College St 77435 979-335-7519
Tim Pope, prin. Fax 335-6085
East Bernard JHS 300/5-8
723 College St 77435 979-335-7519
Emmett Tugwell, prin. Fax 335-6085

Eastland, Eastland, Pop. 3,813
Eastland ISD 1,200/PK-12
PO Box 31 76448 254-631-5120
Donald Hughes, supt. Fax 631-5126
www.eastland.esc14.net/
Eastland MS, PO Box 31 76448 300/6-8
Brett Ramsey, prin. 254-631-5040
Siebert ES, PO Box 31 76448 600/PK-5
Mary Jones, prin. 254-631-5080

Ector, Fannin, Pop. 632
Ector ISD 300/K-12
PO Box 128 75439 903-961-5405
Gary Bohannon, supt. Fax 961-2110
ector.ednet10.net
Ector ES 100/K-6
PO Box 128 75439 903-961-2355
Jim Shaw, prin. Fax 961-2110

Edcouch, Hidalgo, Pop. 4,426
Edcouch-Elsa ISD 5,200/PK-12
PO Box 127 78538 956-262-6000
Michael Sandroussi, supt. Fax 262-6032
www.eeisd.org
Garcia ES 400/1-4
PO Box 127 78538 956-262-6002
Adam Sabedra, prin. Fax 262-6004
Gutierrez ECC 800/PK-K
PO Box 127 78538 956-262-0040
Mari Segura, prin. Fax 262-0043
Rodriguez ES 400/1-4
PO Box 127 78538 956-262-6062
Mary Garza, prin. Fax 262-6061
Ybarra MS 400/5-6
PO Box 127 78538 956-262-8273
Tony Garza, prin. Fax 262-8313
Other Schools – See Elsa

Eddy, McLennan, Pop. 1,113
Bruceville-Eddy ISD 900/PK-12
1 Eagle Dr 76524 254-859-5832
Richard Kilgore, supt. Fax 859-4023
www.brucevilleeddyisd.net
Bruceville-Eddy ES, 1 Eagle Dr 76524 300/PK-3
April Weeden, prin. 254-859-5465
Bruceville-Eddy IS, 1 Eagle Dr 76524 200/4-6
Gary Herbert, prin. 254-859-5525

Eden, Concho, Pop. 2,447
Eden Consolidated ISD 300/K-12
PO Box 988 76837 325-869-4121
John Massey, supt. Fax 869-5210
www.edencisd.net
Eden ES 100/K-6
PO Box 988 76837 325-869-5261
Kathy Gonzales, prin. Fax 869-5672

Edgewood, Van Zandt, Pop. 1,451
Edgewood ISD 900/PK-12
PO Box 6 75117 903-896-4332
Jack Shellnutt, supt. Fax 896-7056
www.edgewood.esc7.net
Edgewood ES 200/PK-2
PO Box 6 75117 903-896-4773
Carolyn James, prin. Fax 896-7056
Edgewood IS 200/3-5
PO Box 6 75117 903-896-2134
Cavin Travis, prin. Fax 896-7056
Edgewood MS 200/6-8
PO Box 6 75117 903-896-1530
Terry Phillips, prin. Fax 896-7056

Edinburg, Hidalgo, Pop. 62,735
Edinburg Consolidated ISD 29,700/PK-12
PO Box 990 78540 956-289-2300
Gilberto Garza, supt. Fax 383-3576
www.ecisd.us/
Austin ES 300/PK-5
PO Box 990 78540 956-289-2331
Homero Cano, prin. Fax 316-7560
Avila ES 700/PK-5
PO Box 990 78540 956-289-2307
Marla Cavazos, prin. Fax 385-3330
Barrientes MS 1,000/6-8
PO Box 990 78540 956-289-2430
Eva Torres, prin. Fax 316-7749
Betts ES 600/PK-5
PO Box 990 78540 956-384-5300
Jesus Cantu, prin. Fax 384-5312
Brewster S 300/PK-8
PO Box 990 78540 956-289-2334
Cipriano Pena, prin. Fax 316-7510
Cano-Gonzales ES 600/PK-5
PO Box 990 78540 956-289-2380
Thelma Rodriguez, prin. Fax 316-7457
Canterbury ES 600/PK-5
PO Box 990 78540 956-289-2374
Dahlia Guzman, prin. Fax 316-7606
De Escandon ES 700/PK-5
PO Box 990 78540 956-316-7398
Gloria Rivera, prin. Fax 316-7647
De La Vina ES 600/PK-5
PO Box 990 78540 956-289-2366
Erika Playle, prin. Fax 316-7782
De Zavala ES 500/PK-5
PO Box 990 78540 956-289-2350
Dr. Graciela Perez, prin. Fax 316-7605
Edinburg South MS 1,600/6-8
PO Box 990 78540 956-316-7750
Anthony Garza, prin. Fax 316-8817
Eisenhower ES 800/PK-5
PO Box 990 78540 956-316-7272
Sonya Rodriguez, prin. Fax 316-7554
Esparza ES 500/PK-5
PO Box 990 78540 956-289-2308
Ernestina Cano, prin. Fax 385-3310
Garza MS 1,700/6-8
PO Box 990 78540 956-316-3100
Anibal Gorena, prin. Fax 316-3109
Gonzalez ES 700/PK-5
PO Box 990 78540 956-316-7408
Arnoldo Benavidez, prin. Fax 316-7420
Guerra ES 600/PK-5
PO Box 990 78540 956-384-5340
Sandra Avila, prin. Fax 384-5352
Harwell MS 1,400/6-8
PO Box 990 78540 956-289-2440
Gilda Sanchez, prin. Fax 386-7303
Jefferson ES 400/PK-5
PO Box 990 78540 956-289-2385
Ana Villalobos Salinas, prin. Fax 316-7427
Johnson ES 500/PK-5
PO Box 990 78540 956-289-2358
Trina Rendon, prin. Fax 316-7630
Kennedy ES 600/PK-5
PO Box 990 78540 956-384-5125
Belinda Figarelli, prin. Fax 384-5131
Lee ES 500/PK-5
PO Box 990 78540 956-289-2342
Nelda Gaytan, prin. Fax 316-7596
Lincoln ES 400/PK-5
PO Box 990 78540 956-384-5200
Eva Sandoval, prin. Fax 384-5208
Magee ES 600/PK-5
PO Box 990 78540 956-289-2306
Carla Zuazua, prin. Fax 385-3320
Memorial MS 1,600/6-8
PO Box 990 78540 956-316-7575
Carlos Guzman, prin. Fax 316-7581
Monte Cristo ES 600/PK-5
PO Box 990 78540 956-289-2362
Sandra Rodriguez, prin. Fax 316-7471
San Carlos ES 600/PK-5
PO Box 990 78540 956-289-2370
Vicky Martinez, prin. Fax 316-7364
Travis ES 500/PK-5
PO Box 990 78540 956-289-2354
Edna Olivarez, prin. Fax 316-7637
Trevino ES 700/PK-5
PO Box 990 78540 956-384-5360
Cynthia Saenz, prin. Fax 384-5372
Truman ES 700/PK-5
PO Box 990 78540 956-316-7520
Celia Avila, prin. Fax 316-7527
Villarreal ES 700/PK-5
PO Box 990 78540 956-289-2377
Carolina Desiga-Lozano, prin. Fax 381-4782
Other Schools – See Hargill, Mc Allen

South Texas ISD
Supt. — See Mercedes
South Texas Preparatory Academy 7-8
724 S Sugar Rd 78539 956-381-5522
Ana Castro, prin. Fax 381-1177

Discovery S 200/PK-6
1711 W Alberta Rd 78539 956-381-1117
Patricia Bader, prin. Fax 381-1007
St. Joseph S 300/PK-8
119 W Fay St 78539 956-383-3957
Sr. Kathleen Murray, prin. Fax 318-0681

Edna, Jackson, Pop. 5,870
Edna ISD 800/PK-12
PO Box 919 77957 361-782-3573
Robert Wells, supt. Fax 781-1002
www.ednaisd.org
Edna ES PK-5
PO Box 919 77957 361-782-2953
Kim Randolph, prin. Fax 781-1028

Pumphrey JHS 300/6-8
PO Box 919 77957 361-782-2351
Demetric Wells, prin. Fax 781-1025

El Campo, Wharton, Pop. 10,884
El Campo ISD 3,400/PK-12
700 W Norris St 77437 979-543-6771
Robert Pool, supt. Fax 543-1670
www.ecisd.org/
El Campo MS 700/6-8
1401 MLK Blvd 77437 979-543-6362
Rodney Montello, prin. Fax 541-5210
Hutchins ES 500/2-3
1006 Roberts St 77437 979-543-5481
Mauri Treybig, prin. Fax 543-2418
Myatt ES 600/PK-1
501 W Webb St 77437 979-543-7514
Liz Graves, prin. Fax 543-5188
Northside ES 500/4-5
2610 Meadow Ln 77437 979-543-5812
Diann Srubar, prin. Fax 578-0682

St. Philip S 300/PK-8
302 W Church St 77437 979-543-2901
Gwen Edwards, prin. Fax 578-8835

Eldorado, Schleicher, Pop. 1,809
Schleicher ISD 600/PK-12
PO Box W 76936 325-853-2514
Billy Collins, supt. Fax 853-2695
www.scisd.net
Eldorado ES 300/PK-4
PO Box W 76936 325-853-2770
Houston Hendryx, prin. Fax 853-2177
Eldorado MS 200/5-8
PO Box W 76936 325-853-3028
Kara Sue Garlitz, prin. Fax 853-2895

Electra, Wichita, Pop. 2,938
Electra ISD 500/PK-12
PO Box 231 76360 940-495-3683
Gary Nightingale, supt. Fax 495-3945
www.electraisd.net
Dinsmore ES 200/PK-4
700 S Main St 76360 940-495-3682
Fran Davis, prin. Fax 495-2625
Electra JHS 200/5-8
621 S Bailey St 76360 940-495-2533
Gene Jarvis, prin. Fax 495-4636

Elgin, Bastrop, Pop. 8,689
Elgin ISD 3,600/PK-12
PO Box 351 78621 512-281-9731
Bill Graves, supt. Fax 285-9935
www.elginisd.net
Elgin MS 800/6-8
1351 N Avenue C 78621 512-281-3382
David Bell, prin. Fax 281-9781
Elgin North ES 300/PK-2
1005 W 2nd St 78621 512-281-3457
Ricardo Reyes, prin. Fax 281-9772
Elgin South ES 300/3-5
902 W 2nd St 78621 512-281-3457
Ricardo Reyes, prin. Fax 281-9772
Neidig ES 600/PK-5
13700 County Line Rd 78621 512-281-9702
Glenell Bankhead, prin. Fax 281-9703
Washington ES 600/PK-5
510 M L K Dr 78621 512-281-3411
Virginia Caudle, prin. Fax 281-9749

Elkhart, Anderson, Pop. 1,260
Elkhart ISD 1,300/PK-12
301 E Parker St 75839 903-764-2952
Mike Moon, supt. Fax 764-2466
www.elkhartisd.org/
Elkhart ES, 301 E Parker St 75839 700/PK-5
Denise Ray, prin. 903-764-2979
Elkhart MS, 301 E Parker St 75839 300/6-8
Ron Mays, prin. 903-764-2459

Slocum ISD 400/PK-12
5765 E State Highway 294 75839 903-478-3624
Fred Fulton, supt. Fax 478-3030
www.slocum.esc7.net
Slocum ES 200/PK-6
5765 E State Highway 294 75839 903-478-3624
Cliff Lasiter, prin. Fax 478-3030

El Lago, Harris, Pop. 2,963
Clear Creek ISD
Supt. — See League City
White ES 500/K-5
1708 Les Talley Dr 77586 281-284-4300
Matthew Paulson, prin. Fax 284-4305

Elmaton, Matagorda
Tidehaven ISD 900/PK-12
PO Box 129 77440 361-588-6321
Dr. Suzanne Wesson, supt. Fax 588-7109
www.tidehavenisd.com
Tidehaven IS 200/6-8
PO Box 130 77440 361-588-6600
Debra Taska, prin. Fax 588-6600
Other Schools – See Blessing, Markham

Elm Mott, McLennan
Connally ISD
Supt. — See Waco
Connally JHS 400/7-8
100 Hancock Dr 76640 254-296-7700
Terry Dawson, prin. Fax 829-2354
Connally PS 600/K-2
100 Little Cadet Ln 76640 254-296-7600
Marlo Moore, prin. Fax 829-1273
Elm Mott Center 200/PK-PK
101 Mesquite 76640 254-750-7140
Helen Smith, prin. Fax 829-4005

El Paso, El Paso, Pop. 598,590
Canutillo ISD 5,900/PK-12
7965 Artcraft Rd 79932 915-877-7400
Dr. Pam Padilla, supt. Fax 877-7414
www.canutillo-isd.org
Garcia ES 500/PK-5
6550 Westside Dr 79932 915-877-7657
Sylvia Gonzalez, prin. Fax 877-7678
Other Schools – See Canutillo

Clint ISD 10,100/PK-12
14521 Horizon Blvd 79928 915-926-4000
Ricardo Estrada, supt. Fax 926-4009
www.clintweb.net
East Montana MS 800/6-8
14521 Horizon Blvd 79928 915-926-5200
Mario Acosta, prin. Fax 855-0821
Montana Vista ES 800/PK-5
14521 Horizon Blvd 79928 915-926-5300
Irene Ortega, prin. Fax 857-0631
Red Sands ES 900/PK-5
14521 Horizon Blvd 79928 915-926-5400
Michael Mackeben, prin. Fax 855-8294
Other Schools – See Clint, Horizon City

El Paso ISD 63,900/PK-12
PO Box 20100 79998 915-881-2700
Dr. Lorenzo Garcia, supt. Fax 887-5485
www.episd.org
Alta Vista ES 400/PK-5
1000 N Grama St 79903 915-231-2620
Manuel Mendoza, prin. Fax 566-0971
Aoy ES 700/PK-5
901 S Campbell St 79901 915-351-3220
Jimmy Snyder, prin. Fax 533-7038
Armendariz MS 800/6-8
2231 Arizona Ave 79930 915-546-9012
Patsy Smith, prin. Fax 577-0848
Barron ES 700/PK-5
11155 Whitey Ford St 79934 915-849-4220
Lugarda Dominic, prin. Fax 822-1460
Bassett MS 900/6-8
4400 Elm St 79930 915-231-2260
Mark Brooker, prin. Fax 565-1562
Beall ES 500/PK-5
320 S Piedras St 79905 915-496-8120
Alberto Reyes, prin. Fax 533-7044
Bliss ES 700/PK-5
4401 Sheridan Rd 79906 915-587-2540
Thomas O'Hara, prin. Fax 566-2806
Bond ES 900/PK-5
250 Lindbergh Ave 79932 915-832-6930
Haidi Appel, prin. Fax 581-1220
Bonham ES 300/K-5
7024 Cielo Vista Dr 79925 915-881-6950
Sylvia Haynes, prin. Fax 778-0525
Bradley ES 400/PK-5
5330 Sweetwater Dr 79924 915-849-2840
Richard Anderson, prin. Fax 821-0628
Brown MS 1,300/6-8
7820 Helen Of Troy Dr 79912 915-774-4080
Victoria York, prin. Fax 581-6424
Burleson ES 400/PK-5
4400 Blanco Ave 79905 915-351-3260
Irma Phillips, prin. Fax 533-0967
Burnet ES 400/PK-5
3700 Thomason Ave 79904 915-231-2580
Barbara Graham, prin. Fax 566-3951
Canyon Hills MS 1,000/6-8
8930 Eclipse St 79904 915-231-2240
Angie Silvaggio, prin. Fax 757-8067
Charles MS 600/6-8
4909 Trojan Dr 79924 915-849-3940
Michael Mendoza, prin. Fax 821-0505
Cielo Vista ES 400/PK-5
9000 Basil Ct 79925 915-626-2000
Taryn Bailey, prin. Fax 599-2965
Clardy ES 700/PK-5
5508 Delta Dr 79905 915-887-4040
Raquel Fraga, prin. Fax 778-1580
Clendenin ES 500/PK-5
2701 Harrison Ave 79930 915-231-2640
Ruben Acosta, prin. Fax 566-4459
Coldwell ES 400/PK-5
4101 Altura Ave 79903 915-231-2220
Jason Yturralde, prin. Fax 566-4634
Collins ES 600/PK-5
4860 Tropicana Ave 79924 915-231-2600
James Horan, prin. Fax 759-7315
Cooley ES 500/PK-5
107 N Collingsworth St 79905 915-780-1020
Ana Maria Acosta, prin. Fax 775-1272
Crockett ES 700/PK-5
3200 Wheeling Ave 79930 915-587-2640
Jesse Armendariz, prin. Fax 566-4950
Crosby ES 600/PK-5
5411 Wren Ave 79924 915-780-1040
Christine Mosier, prin. Fax 759-7409
Douglass ES 500/PK-6
101 S Eucalyptus St 79905 915-496-8070
James VanNosdale, prin. Fax 533-3716
Dowell ES 400/PK-5
5249 Bastille Ave 79924 915-231-2560
Pattie Calk, prin. Fax 759-7713
Fannin ES 700/PK-5
5425 Salem Dr 79924 915-849-3910
Barbara Gibson, prin. Fax 821-0680
Green ES 500/PK-5
5430 Buckley Dr 79912 915-231-2700
Cecilia Stephens, prin. Fax 833-8794
Guerrero ES 900/PK-5
7530 Lakehurst Rd 79912 915-231-2680
Joe Sheldon, prin. Fax 581-4418
Guillen MS 1,000/6-8
900 S Cotton St 79901 915-496-4620
Thomas Fraire, prin. Fax 532-1143
Hart ES 600/PK-5
1110 Park St 79901 915-496-8030
Armando Llanos, prin. Fax 533-3726

Hawkins ES 300/PK-5
5816 Stephenson Ave 79905 915-587-2660
Blanca Garcia, prin. Fax 775-2699
Henderson MS 900/6-8
5505 Robert Alva Ave 79905 915-887-3080
Lydia Muniz, prin. Fax 772-3425
Hillside ES 700/PK-5
4500 Clifton Ave 79903 915-587-2560
Adrian Botello, prin. Fax 566-5210
Hornedo MS 1,900/6-8
825 E Redd Rd 79912 915-231-2200
Victoria York, prin. Fax 587-5059
Houston ES 400/PK-5
2851 Grant Ave 79930 915-587-2620
Elco Ramos, prin. Fax 566-5964
Hughey ES 700/PK-5
6201 Hughey Cir 79925 915-832-6670
Edmund Brezinski, prin. Fax 779-6911
Johnson ES 700/PK-5
499 Cabaret Dr 79912 915-832-3940
Suzanne Splawn, prin. Fax 581-0917
Kohlberg ES 900/PK-5
1445 Nardo Goodman Dr 79912 915-832-4880
Marc Escareno, prin. Fax 833-4628
Lamar ES 600/PK-5
1440 E Cliff Dr 79902 915-351-3200
Bertha Martinez, prin. Fax 534-0083
Lee ES 700/PK-5
7710 Pandora St 79904 915-587-3560
Bonnie O'Leary, prin. Fax 759-8115
Lincoln MS 1,100/6-8
500 Mulberry Ave 79932 915-231-2180
Sandy Whitney, prin. Fax 581-1371
Logan ES 500/PK-5
3200 Ellerthorpe Ave 79904 915-231-2720
Joseph Garren, prin. Fax 566-8550
MacArthur S 700/K-8
8101 Whitus Dr 79925 915-587-2680
Leticia Guerra-Ramirez, prin. Fax 779-2281
Magoffin MS 900/6-8
4931 Hercules Ave 79904 915-774-4040
Raul Ruiz, prin. Fax 757-7675
Mesita ES 700/PK-5
3307 N Stanton St 79902 915-496-8180
Laila Ferris, prin. Fax 534-7010
Milam ES 300/PK-5
5000 Luke St 79908 915-587-2520
Irma Ludwig, prin. Fax 562-6448
Morehead MS 1,100/6-8
5625 Confetti Dr 79912 915-231-2140
James Lamonica, prin. Fax 587-5355
Moreno ES 400/PK-5
2300 San Diego Ave 79930 915-832-6650
Irma Thomas, prin. Fax 566-5163
Moye ES 600/PK-5
4825 Alps Dr 79904 915-774-4000
Alicia Ayala, prin. Fax 751-7810
Newman ES 600/PK-5
10275 Alcan St 79924 915-587-3580
Lucy Fischer, prin. Fax 759-8306
Nixon ES 800/PK-5
11141 Loma Roja Dr 79934 915-849-5700
Oscar Ontiveros, prin. Fax 821-6582
Park ES 500/PK-5
3601 Edgar Park Ave 79904 915-587-3540
Dolores Del Toro, prin. Fax 759-8315
Polk ES 700/K-5
940 Belvidere St 79912 915-832-6970
Ina Lachmann, prin. Fax 584-6124
Putnam ES 500/PK-5
6508 Fiesta Dr 79912 915-832-6700
Patricia Medlin, prin. Fax 585-2304
Richardson MS 800/6-8
11350 Loma Franklin Dr 79934 915-822-8829
Dianne Jones, prin. Fax 822-8812
Rivera ES 500/PK-5
6445 Escondido Dr 79912 915-231-2780
Carlene Cephus, prin. Fax 585-2337
Roberts ES 800/PK-5
341 Thorn Ave 79932 915-231-2660
Richard Chavez, prin. Fax 585-2729
Ross MS 800/6-8
6101 Hughey Cir 79925 915-887-3060
John Tanner, prin. Fax 771-6792
Rusk ES 500/PK-5
3601 N Copia St 79930 915-587-2580
Angie Cooper, prin. Fax 565-1666
Schuster ES 200/PK-5
5515 Will Ruth Ave 79924 915-231-2760
Jesus Medina, prin. Fax 759-9315
Stanton ES 600/PK-5
5414 Hondo Pass Dr 79924 915-587-3520
Vanessa Foreman, prin. Fax 759-9415
Terrace Hills MS 700/6-8
4835 Blossom Ave 79924 915-231-2120
Milton Jones, prin. Fax 759-0615
Tippin ES 800/PK-5
6541 Bear Ridge Dr 79912 915-585-4750
Donna Jerman, prin. Fax 833-2140
Travis ES 400/PK-5
5000 N Stevens St 79930 915-231-2740
Don Smelser, prin. Fax 565-2013
Vilas ES 300/PK-5
220 Lawton Dr 79902 915-351-3240
Sandra Uranga, prin. Fax 542-0971
Western Hills ES 500/K-5
530 Thunderbird Dr 79912 915-774-4060
Nancy Tovar, prin. Fax 875-0183
Whitaker ES 600/PK-5
4700 Rutherford Dr 79924 915-231-2820
Mary Elvia Rodriguez, prin. Fax 751-9436
White ES 600/PK-5
4256 Roxbury Dr 79922 915-832-4830
Raul Mendoza, prin. Fax 585-3619
Wiggs MS 800/6-8
1300 Circle Dr 79902 915-231-2100
Jesus Teran, prin. Fax 533-2902

Zavala ES 400/PK-5
51 N Hammett St 79905 915-496-8160
Olga Arreola, prin. Fax 542-1760

Socorro ISD 38,300/PK-12
PO Box 292800 79929 915-937-0000
Dr. Xavier DeLaTorre, supt. Fax 851-7572
www.sisd.net
Antwine S 800/K-8
3830 Rich Beem 79938 915-937-6400
Stacy Sonnier, prin. Fax 851-7830
Ball ES 1,000/PK-5
1950 Firehouse Dr 79936 915-937-8200
Lucia Borrego, prin. Fax 856-1478
Campestre ES 700/PK-5
11399 Socorro Rd 79927 915-937-7300
Isabel Andresen, prin. Fax 851-1715
Chavez ES 1,100/K-5
11720 Pebble Hills Blvd 79936 915-937-8300
Leslie Thomas, prin. Fax 856-9993
Clarke MS 900/6-8
1515 Bob Hope Dr 79936 915-937-5600
Chelaine Marion, prin. Fax 857-3765
Cooper ES 600/PK-5
1515 Rebecca Ann Dr 79936 915-937-7700
Carmen Moran, prin. Fax 855-7645
Desert Wind S 1,000/PK-8
1100 Colina de Paz 79928 915-937-7800
David Solis, prin. Fax 851-7840
Drugan S 700/PK-8
12451 Pellicano Dr 79928 915-937-6800
Susan Cook, prin. Fax 937-6815
Escontrias ES 600/2-5
205 Buford Rd 79927 915-937-4100
Dr. Magdalena Aguilar, prin. Fax 937-9212
Hambric S 1,400/K-8
3535 Nolan Richardson Dr 79936 915-937-4600
Danny Gurany, prin. Fax 851-7560
Hilley ES 800/PK-5
693 N Rio Vista Rd 79927 915-937-8400
Esther Gonzales, prin. Fax 860-3778
Hueco ES 600/PK-5
300 Old Hueco Tanks Rd 79927 915-937-7600
Lori Diaz, prin. Fax 860-1125
Ituarte ES 800/K-5
12860 Tierra Sonora 79938 915-937-7000
Carlos Amato, prin. Fax 937-7095
Jordan ES 500/K-5
13995 Jason Crandall Dr 79938 915-937-8801
Michelle Barton, prin. Fax 937-8889
Loma Verde ES 900/PK-5
12150 Ted Houghton 79936 915-937-8600
Rose Carreon, prin. Fax 851-7780
Lujan-Chavez ES 1,100/PK-5
2200 Sun Country Dr 79938 915-937-8700
Yvonne Walker, prin. Fax 851-7720
Martinez ES 800/PK-5
2640 Robert Wynn St 79936 915-937-8000
Marta Provenghi, prin. Fax 921-1509
Montwood MS 900/6-8
11710 Pebble Hills Blvd 79936 915-937-5800
Libby Tidwell, prin. Fax 856-9909
O'Shea-Keleher ES 900/PK-5
1800 Leroy Bonse Dr 79936 915-937-7200
Rosa Chavez-Avedician, prin. Fax 921-1506
Paso del Norte S 1,300/K-8
12300 Tierra Este Dr 79938 915-937-6200
Jeanette Williams, prin. Fax 851-7800
Rojas ES 600/PK-5
500 Bauman Rd 79927 915-937-8500
Arturo Gonzalez, prin. Fax 937-8513
Sanchez MS 800/6-8
321 N Rio Vista Rd 79927 915-937-5200
Clarice Jones, prin. Fax 859-6636
Serna S 700/PK-8
11471 Alameda Ave 79927 915-937-4800
Ricardo Damian, prin. Fax 851-7580
Shook ES 500/PK-5
13777 Paseo Del Este Dr 79928 915-937-7100
Adalberto Garcia, prin. Fax 937-7197
Sierra Vista ES 800/PK-5
1501 Bob Hope Dr 79936 915-937-8100
Rubina Rodriguez, prin. Fax 849-1263
Slider MS 1,000/6-8
11700 School Ln 79936 915-937-5400
Mitchell Ferguson, prin. Fax 857-5804
Socorro MS 700/6-8
321 Bovee Rd 79927 915-937-5000
Fax 859-6955
Sun Ridge MS 800/6-8
2210 Sun Country Dr 79938 915-937-6600
Dr. Kim Baxter, prin. Fax 851-7730
Sybert S 1,200/K-8
11530 Edgemere Blvd 79936 915-937-4400
Carol Bauer, prin. Fax 851-7777
Vista Del Sol ES 500/PK-5
11851 Vista Del Sol Dr 79936 915-937-7500
Irma Rodriguez, prin. Fax 855-7523
Other Schools – See Horizon City

Ysleta ISD 45,100/PK-12
9600 Sims Dr 79925 915-434-0000
Roger Parks, supt. Fax 591-4144
www.yisd.net
Ascarate ES 500/K-6
7090 Alameda Ave 79915 915-434-7400
Mauricio Cano, prin. Fax 772-8051
Cadwallader ES 300/PK-6
7988 Alameda Ave 79915 915-434-7500
Maria Rodriguez, prin. Fax 858-0873
Camino Real MS 700/6-8
9393 Alameda Ave 79907 915-434-8300
Dolores Chaparro, prin. Fax 858-3743
Capistrano ES 700/K-6
240 Mecca Dr 79907 915-434-8600
Espie Flores, prin. Fax 860-2750
Cedar Grove ES 700/PK-6
218 Barker Rd 79915 915-434-7600
Dora Magana, prin. Fax 772-8092
Chacon International S 700/K-8
221 S Prado Rd 79907 915-434-9200
Gloria Polanco-McNealy, prin. Fax 859-2131
Del Norte Heights ES 600/K-6
1800 Winslow Rd 79915 915-434-2400
Wendy Banegas, prin. Fax 591-8862
Desertaire ES 600/PK-6
6301 Tiger Eye Dr 79924 915-434-6400
Lisa Lopez, prin. Fax 821-0634
Desert View MS 600/7-8
1641 Billie Marie Dr 79936 915-434-5300
Michelle Kehrwald, prin. Fax 591-9327
Dolphin Terrace ES 700/K-6
9790 Pickerel Dr 79924 915-434-6500
Deborah Vasquez, prin. Fax 757-8073
East Point ES 800/K-6
2400 Zanzibar Rd 79925 915-434-4500
Catherine Kennedy, prin. Fax 591-8958
Eastwood Heights ES 700/PK-6
10530 Janway Dr 79925 915-434-4600
Lynn Musel, prin. Fax 591-8960
Eastwood Knolls S 700/K-8
10000 Buckwood Ave 79925 915-434-4400
Lorenzo Mata, prin. Fax 592-0339
Eastwood MS 600/7-8
2612 Chaswood St 79935 915-434-4300
Malinda Carri-Villalobos, prin. Fax 591-9426
Edgemere ES 700/K-6
10300 Edgemere Blvd 79925 915-434-4700
Maria Maldonado, prin. Fax 590-8335
Glen Cove ES 1,100/PK-6
10955 Sam Snead Dr 79936 915-434-5500
Elizabeth Ortiz, prin. Fax 591-9024
Hacienda Heights ES 600/K-6
7530 Acapulco Ave 79915 915-434-2500
Victor Perez, prin. Fax 591-9044
Hillcrest MS 600/7-8
8040 Yermoland Dr 79907 915-434-2200
Paul Covey, prin. Fax 591-9439
Hulbert ES 400/K-6
7755 Franklin Dr 79915 915-434-6900
Nellie Morales, prin. Fax 772-8166
Indian Ridge MS 600/7-8
11201 Pebble Hills Blvd 79936 915-434-5400
Grace Martinez, prin. Fax 591-9447
Kennedy Pre K 600/PK-PK
9009 Alameda Ave 79907 915-434-9100
Angel Nieto, prin. Fax 860-7530
Lancaster ES 700/K-6
9230 Elgin Dr 79907 915-434-3400
Dolores Acosta, prin. Fax 860-2315
Le Barron Park ES 1,100/K-6
920 Burgundy Dr 79907 915-434-3500
Steve Sanchez, prin. Fax 860-2817
Loma Terrace ES 800/K-6
8200 Ryland Ct 79907 915-434-2600
Susana Gonzalez, prin. Fax 591-9111
Marian Manor ES 500/K-6
8300 Forrest Haven Ct 79907 915-434-3600
Virginia Padilla, prin. Fax 591-9131
Mesa Vista ES 500/PK-6
8032 Alamo Ave 79907 915-434-2700
Connie Fattorini-Vasquez, prin. Fax 591-9171
Mission Valley ES 600/PK-6
8674 N Loop Dr 79907 915-434-3700
Ruben Cadena, prin. Fax 860-0049
North Loop ES 400/K-6
412 Emerson St 79915 915-434-2800
Anthony Fraga, prin. Fax 591-9202
North Star ES 600/K-6
5950 Sean Haggerty Dr 79924 915-434-6700
Terry Lopez, prin. Fax 822-9386
Parkland ES 600/PK-6
6330 Deer Ave 79924 915-434-6600
Margaret Bustamante, prin. Fax 757-9458
Parkland MS 700/7-8
6045 Nova Way 79924 915-434-6300
Ruben Flores, prin. Fax 757-6608
Pasodale ES 800/PK-5
8253 McElroy Ave 79907 915-434-8500
Antonio Acuna, prin. Fax 858-1269
Pebble Hills ES 900/PK-6
11145 Edgemere Blvd 79936 915-434-5600
Robert Martinez, prin. Fax 591-9222
Presa ES 500/K-5
128 Presa Pl 79907 915-434-8700
Rosa Lujan, prin. Fax 860-2810
Ramona ES 400/PK-6
351 Nichols Rd 79915 915-434-7700
Ana Silva, prin. Fax 772-8153
Ranchland Hills MS 500/7-8
7615 Yuma Dr 79915 915-434-2300
Felipe de Jesus Barraza, prin. Fax 592-0036
Rio Bravo MS 400/6-8
525 Greggerson Dr 79907 915-434-8400
Javier Suffle, prin. Fax 872-0269
Riverside MS 700/7-8
7615 Mimosa Ave 79915 915-434-7300
James Mesta, prin. Fax 772-7549
Sageland ES 500/K-6
7901 Santa Monica Ct 79915 915-434-2900
Elisa Aguilar, prin. Fax 591-9228
Scotsdale ES 800/PK-6
2901 Mcrae Blvd 79925 915-434-4800
Gloria Olivas, prin. Fax 591-9270
South Loop ES 500/K-5
520 Southside Rd 79907 915-434-8800
Kathleen Warren, prin. Fax 860-9075
Thomas Manor ES 500/K-6
7900 Jersey St 79915 915-434-7800
Marcelino Franco, prin. Fax 772-8301
Tierra Del Sol ES 700/K-6
1832 Tommy Aaron Dr 79936 915-434-5800
Nancy Evans, prin. Fax 591-9271
Valley View MS 700/7-8
8660 N Loop Dr 79907 915-434-3300
Carmen Crosse, prin. Fax 858-3615
Vista Hills ES 800/PK-6
10801 La Subida Dr 79935 915-434-5700
Mo Batres, prin. Fax 591-9305
Washington ES 600/K-6
3505 N Lee Trevino Dr 79936 915-434-5900
Pauline Muela, prin. Fax 590-6535
Ysleta ES 600/K-6
8624 Dorbandt Cir 79907 915-434-8900
Homero Silva, prin. Fax 859-9311
Ysleta MS 400/6-8
8691 Independence Dr 79907 915-434-8200
Irene Medina, prin. Fax 858-0261
Ysleta Preschool 700/PK-PK
7909 Ranchland Dr 79915 915-434-9500
Celia Salazar, prin. Fax 591-9325

Ascension Lutheran Day S 100/PK-PK
6520 Loma De Cristo Dr 79912 915-833-4849
Veronica Matthews, prin. Fax 581-3216
Bethel Christian S 200/PK-12
6301 Alabama St 79904 915-565-2222
Marsha Hodge-Cardenas, admin. Fax 565-2223
Christian Joy Center Academy 100/PK-6
1208 Sumac Dr 79925 915-595-1328
Debra Brown, admin. Fax 595-1493
Community of Faith Christian S 100/PK-8
4539 Emory Rd 79922 915-584-2561
Blanca Mixer, prin. Fax 584-3529
El Paso Country Day S 100/PK-12
220 E Cliff Dr 79902 915-533-4492
Dr. Laura Alpern, dir. Fax 533-9626
El Paso Jewish Academy 50/1-8
805 Cherry Hill Ln 79912 915-833-0808
Ilisa Cappell, dir. Fax 833-0808
Faith Christian Academy 500/PK-12
8960 Escobar Dr 79907 915-594-3305
Cesar Ramirez, prin. Fax 593-5474
Father Yermo S 200/2-8
237 Tobin Pl 79905 915-533-4693
Sr. Angelica Omana, prin. Fax 532-6807
Fr. Yermo Early Learning Center 100/PK-1
616 S Virginia St 79901 915-542-1253
Sr. Angelica Omana, prin. Fax 532-1121
Holy Trinity S 100/PK-8
10000 Pheasant Rd 79924 915-751-2566
Rosa Gandara, prin. Fax 751-2596
Immanuel Christian S 700/PK-12
1201 Hawkins Blvd 79925 915-778-6160
Donene O'Dell, admin. Fax 772-8207
Jesus Chapel S 200/PK-12
10200 Album Ave 79925 915-593-1153
Alba Wilcox, prin. Fax 593-1113
Loretto S 200/PK-5
4625 Clifton Ave 79903 915-566-8400
Jane German, prin. Fax 564-0563
Mt. Franklin Christian Academy 200/PK-8
201 E Sunset Rd 79922 915-581-4487
Deborah Crutcher, dir. Fax 581-0331
North Loop Christian Academy 100/K-8
8617 N Loop Dr 79907 915-859-8090
Bob Patterson, admin.
Our Lady of Assumption S 100/PK-8
4805 Byron St 79930 915-565-3411
Karen Biddle, prin. Fax 564-5724
Our Lady of the Valley S 200/PK-8
8600 Winchester Rd 79907 915-859-6448
Sr. Caroline Vasquez, prin. Fax 859-3908
Radford S 200/PK-12
2001 Radford St 79903 915-565-2737
John Doran, dir. Fax 565-2730
St. Clement's Episcopal S 400/PK-8
600 Montana Ave 79902 915-533-4248
Nick Cobos, hdmstr. Fax 544-1778
St. Joseph S 600/PK-8
1300 Lamar St 79903 915-566-1661
Br. Edwin Gallagher, prin. Fax 566-1664
St. Matthews S 300/PK-3
400 W Sunset Rd 79922 915-581-8801
Carol Montoya, prin. Fax 581-8816
St. Patrick S 500/PK-8
1111 N Stanton St 79902 915-532-4142
Liliana Esparza, prin. Fax 532-8297
St. Pius X S 500/PK-8
1007 Geronimo Dr 79905 915-772-6598
Carlos Gomez, prin. Fax 225-0010
St. Raphael S 500/PK-8
2310 Woodside Dr 79925 915-598-2241
Elizabeth Wiehe, prin. Fax 598-3002
Trinity Lutheran S 50/K-8
3800 Hondo Pass Dr 79904 915-755-7259
Harmon Butler, prin. Fax 755-6572
Zion Lutheran S 50/PK-K
2800 Pershing Dr 79903 915-565-7999
Nancy Cagann, prin. Fax 566-6677

Elsa, Hidalgo, Pop. 6,458
Edcouch-Elsa ISD
Supt. — See Edcouch
Johnson ES 500/1-4
S Fannin St 78543 956-262-6010
Mary Gonzales, prin. Fax 262-6012
Kennedy ES 400/1-4
Austin & 9th St 78543 956-262-6027
Noemi Hernandez, prin. Fax 262-6029
Truan JHS 700/7-8
E 9th St 78543 956-262-6082
Fred Aguilar, prin. Fax 262-6079

Elysian Fields, Harrison
Elysian Fields ISD 1,000/PK-12
PO Box 120 75642 903-633-2420
Dr. Bob Browning, supt. Fax 633-2498
www.elysian-fields.k12.tx.us/
Elysian Fields ES 500/PK-5
PO Box 119 75642 903-633-2465
Linda Marr, prin. Fax 633-2187
Elysian Fields JHS 200/6-8
PO Box 120 75642 903-633-2306
Maynard Chapman, prin. Fax 633-2326

Emory, Rains, Pop. 1,332
Rains ISD 1,600/PK-12
PO Box 247 75440 903-473-2222
David Seago, supt. Fax 473-3053
www.rains.k12.tx.us/
Rains ES 500/PK-3
PO Box 247 75440 903-473-2222
Angie Trull, prin. Fax 473-7259
Rains IS 200/4-5
PO Box 247 75440 903-473-2222
Maybeth McMahan, prin. Fax 473-5162
Rains JHS 400/6-8
PO Box 247 75440 903-473-2222
Denise Flagg, prin. Fax 473-5162

Encinal, LaSalle, Pop. 653
Cotulla ISD
Supt. — See Cotulla
Encinal ES 100/PK-4
503 Encinal Blvd 78019 956-948-5324
Ricardo Arias, prin. Fax 948-5534

Ennis, Ellis, Pop. 18,735
Ennis ISD 4,700/PK-12
PO Box 1420 75120 972-875-9027
Dr. Eddie Dunn, supt. Fax 875-8667
www.ennis.k12.tx.us
Austin ES 300/1-4
1500 Austin Dr 75119 972-875-5571
Jan White, prin. Fax 875-7216
Bowie ES 500/1-4
501 Jeter Dr 75119 972-875-1818
Kay Skuza, prin. Fax 875-3407
Early Childhood Development Center 600/PK-K
1701 W Lampasas St 75119 972-875-6982
Lisa Lowe, prin. Fax 872-9829
Ennis JHS 800/7-8
3101 Ensign Rd 75119 972-872-3850
Orlando Vargas, prin. Fax 875-1433
Houston ES 300/1-4
1701 S Hall St 75119 972-875-5531
Linda Southard, prin. Fax 875-4816
Sixth Grade Center 400/5-6
2200 W Lampasas St 75119 972-872-9253
Bobby White, prin. Fax 872-9370
Travis ES 300/1-4
200 N Shawnee St 75119 972-875-7325
Ryan McCabe, prin. Fax 875-4205

Era, Cooke
Era ISD 400/K-12
PO Box 98 76238 940-665-5961
Jeremy Thompson, supt. Fax 665-5311
www.eraisd.net
Era ES 200/K-5
PO Box 98 76238 940-665-5961
Autry Hardy, prin. Fax 665-3327

Etoile, Nacogdoches
Etoile ISD 100/K-8
PO Box 98 75944 936-854-2238
Andy Trekell, supt. Fax 854-2241
www.etoile.esc7.net
Etoile S 100/K-8
PO Box 98 75944 936-854-2238
Andy Trekell, prin. Fax 854-2241

Euless, Tarrant, Pop. 51,226
Grapevine-Colleyville ISD
Supt. — See Grapevine
Bear Creek ES 700/K-5
401 Bear Creek Dr 76039 817-358-4860
Brooke Moose, prin. Fax 267-3863

Hurst-Euless-Bedford ISD
Supt. — See Bedford
Lakewood ES 700/K-6
1600 Donley Dr 76039 817-354-3375
Julie McAvoy, prin. Fax 354-3525
Midway Park ES 700/PK-6
409 N Ector Dr 76039 817-354-3380
Doreen Mengwasser, prin. Fax 354-3332
North Euless ES 600/PK-6
1101 Denton Dr 76039 817-354-3505
Melissa Meadows, prin. Fax 354-3334
Oakwood Terrace ES 700/PK-6
700 Ranger St 76040 817-354-3386
Denise Rhodes, prin. Fax 354-3335
South Euless ES 700/PK-6
605 S Main St 76040 817-354-3521
Carma Schellhorn, prin. Fax 354-3523
Wilshire ES 600/PK-6
420 Wilshire Dr 76040 817-354-3529
Jonathan James, prin. Fax 354-3338

Metroplex Chapel Academy 50/PK-4
601 E Airport Fwy 76039 817-267-1000
Terry Lamkin, hdmstr. Fax 267-5000

Eustace, Henderson, Pop. 874
Eustace ISD 1,600/PK-12
PO Box 188 75124 903-425-5151
Dr. Coy Holcombe, supt. Fax 425-5147
www.eustaceisd.net/
Eustace IS 300/3-5
PO Box 188 75124 903-425-5181
Robert Reeve, prin. Fax 425-5294
Eustace MS 400/6-8
PO Box 188 75124 903-425-5171
Karyn Mullen, prin. Fax 425-5146
Eustace PS 500/PK-2
PO Box 188 75124 903-425-5191
Dianne Shaffer, prin. Fax 425-5148

Evadale, Jasper, Pop. 1,422
Evadale ISD 500/PK-12
PO Box 497 77615 409-276-1337
Rodney Cavness, supt. Fax 276-1908
www.esc5.net/evadale/
Evadale S 300/PK-8
PO Box 497 77615 409-276-1337
Robert Wilson, prin. Fax 276-1588

Evant, Coryell, Pop. 390
Evant ISD 300/PK-12
PO Box 339 76525 254-471-5536
Dr. Sid Pruitt, supt. Fax 471-5629
www.evantisd.org/
Evant ES 100/PK-6
PO Box 339 76525 254-471-5536
James Slone, prin. Fax 471-5629

Everman, Tarrant, Pop. 5,733
Everman ISD 4,500/PK-12
608 Townley Dr 76140 817-568-3500
Jeri Pfeifer, supt. Fax 568-3508
www.eisd.org
Bishop ES 600/PK-4
501 Vaughn Ave 76140 817-568-3575
Nikita Russell, prin. Fax 568-3572
Everman JHS 700/7-8
8901 Oak Grove Rd 76140 817-568-3530
Debra Carter, prin. Fax 568-3594
Hommel ES 300/PK-4
308 W Enon Ave 76140 817-568-3540
Colette Kotula, prin. Fax 568-3543
Souder ES 600/PK-4
201 N Forest Hill Dr 76140 817-568-3580
Pat Brady, prin. Fax 568-3589
Townley ES PK-4
2200 McPherson Rd 76140 817-568-3560
Nancy Kay, prin. Fax 568-5177
Other Schools – See Fort Worth

Fabens, El Paso, Pop. 5,599
Fabens ISD 2,100/PK-12
PO Box 697 79838 915-765-2600
Poncho Garcia, supt. Fax 764-3115
www.fabensisd.net/
Fabens MS 600/6-8
PO Box 697 79838 915-765-2630
Luis Liano, prin. Fax 764-7263
Fabens PS 500/PK-3
PO Box 697 79838 915-765-2650
Sandra Carbajal, prin. Fax 765-2655
O'Donnell ES 400/4-5
PO Box 697 79838 915-765-2640
Michele Gonzalez, prin. Fax 764-4358

Fairfield, Freestone, Pop. 3,508
Fairfield ISD 1,800/PK-12
615 Post Oak Rd 75840 903-389-2532
Tony Price, supt. Fax 389-7050
www.fairfield.k12.tx.us
Fairfield ES 700/PK-4
330 W Main St 75840 903-389-2148
Elisabeth Harris, prin. Fax 389-5314
Fairfield JHS 600/5-8
701 Post Oak Rd 75840 903-389-4210
Bryan Gawryszewski, prin. Fax 389-5454

Fair Oaks Ranch, Bexar, Pop. 5,715
Boerne ISD
Supt. — See Boerne
Fair Oaks Ranch ES 700/K-6
29085 Ralph Fair Rd 78015 830-357-4800
Sandi Killo, prin. Fax 357-4899

Fairview, Collin, Pop. 5,201
Lovejoy ISD
Supt. — See Allen
Puster ES K-5
856 Stoddard Rd 75069 469-742-8300
Janet Anders, prin. Fax 742-8301
Sloan Creek MS 6-8
440 Country Club Rd 75069 469-742-8400
Gavan Goodrich, prin. Fax 742-8401

Falfurrias, Brooks, Pop. 5,050
Brooks County ISD 1,600/PK-12
PO Box 589 78355 361-325-8000
Joe Trevino, supt. Fax 325-1913
www.bcisdistrict.net
Falfurrias ES 400/2-5
PO Box 589 78355 361-325-8041
Marie Vidaurri, prin. Fax 325-3067
Falfurrias JHS 300/6-8
PO Box 589 78355 361-325-8072
Israel Escobar, prin. Fax 325-2220
Lasater ES 300/PK-1
PO Box 589 78355 361-325-8060
Fax 325-9566

La Gloria ISD 100/PK-6
182 E County Road 401 78355 361-325-2330
David Braswell, supt. Fax 325-2533
www.lagloriaisd.esc2.net/
La Gloria ES 100/PK-6
182 E County Road 401 78355 361-325-2330
David Braswell, prin. Fax 325-2533

Falls City, Karnes, Pop. 606
Falls City ISD 300/K-12
PO Box 399 78113 830-254-3551
Linda Bettin, supt. Fax 254-3354
www.fcisd.net/
Falls City ES 200/K-6
PO Box 399 78113 830-254-3551
Christy Blocker, prin. Fax 254-3354

Farmers Branch, Dallas, Pop. 26,487
Carrollton-Farmers Branch ISD
Supt. — See Carrollton
Blair IS 500/3-5
14055 Heartside Pl 75234 972-968-1000
Lori Parker, prin. Fax 968-1010
Farmers Branch ES 500/K-5
13521 Tom Field Rd 75234 972-968-6100
Susan Lightsey, prin. Fax 968-6110
Field MS 1,100/6-8
13551 Dennis Ln 75234 972-968-3900
Dan Ford, prin. Fax 968-3910
Montgomery ES 600/K-5
2807 Amber Ln 75234 972-968-2700
Teri Walden, prin. Fax 968-2710
Stark ES 600/PK-5
12400 Josey Ln 75234 972-968-3200
Abby McCone, prin. Fax 968-3210
Strickland IS, 3030 Fyke Rd 75234 3-5
Tracy Smith, prin. 972-968-5700

Farmersville, Collin, Pop. 3,357
Farmersville ISD 1,400/PK-12
501A State Highway 78 N 75442 972-782-6601
Jeff Adams, supt. Fax 784-7293
www.farmersvilleisd.net/
Farmersville IS 400/2-5
807 N Main St 75442 972-782-8108
Hazel Johnson, prin. Fax 782-7527
Farmersville JHS 300/6-8
501 State Highway 78 N 75442 972-782-6202
Scott Farler, prin. Fax 782-7029
Tatum ES 300/PK-1
405 N Washington St 75442 972-782-7251
Scott Knight, prin. Fax 782-8109

Farwell, Parmer, Pop. 1,318
Farwell ISD 500/PK-12
PO Box F 79325 806-481-3371
Larry Gregory, supt. Fax 481-9275
www.farwellschools.org
Farwell ES 300/PK-5
PO Box F 79325 806-481-9131
Gary Cates, prin. Fax 481-3255
Farwell JHS 100/6-8
PO Box F 79325 806-481-9260
Jimmy Mace, prin. Fax 481-9258

Fate, Rockwall, Pop. 2,533
Royse City ISD
Supt. — See Royse City
Herndon IS 5-6
300 N Blackland Rd 75132 469-721-8101
Shanna Brown, prin. Fax 874-2186

Fayetteville, Fayette, Pop. 272
Fayetteville ISD 200/K-12
PO Box 129 78940 979-378-4242
Ron Eilers, supt. Fax 378-4246
www.fayettevilleisd.com
Fayetteville ES 100/K-5
PO Box 129 78940 979-378-4242
Ron Eilers, prin. Fax 378-4246

Ferris, Ellis, Pop. 2,298
Ferris ISD 2,100/PK-12
PO Box 459 75125 972-544-3858
Michael Bodine, supt. Fax 544-2784
www.ferrisisd.org
Ferris IS 500/4-6
PO Box 447 75125 972-544-8662
Anthony Spears, prin. Fax 544-3085
Ferris JHS 300/7-8
PO Box 459 75125 972-544-2279
Thomas Knight, prin. Fax 544-2281
Ingram ES 400/PK-K
PO Box 446 75125 972-544-3212
Steve Freeman, prin. Fax 544-3405
McDonald ES 300/1-3
PO Box 403 75125 972-544-2574
Jack Mitchell, prin. Fax 544-2116

Flatonia, Fayette, Pop. 1,421
Flatonia ISD 600/PK-12
PO Box 189 78941 361-865-2941
Dr. Alice Smith, supt. Fax 865-2940
www.esc13.net/flatonia/
Flatonia ES 300/PK-6
PO Box 189 78941 361-865-2947
Candace Wubbena, prin. Fax 865-2945

Flint, Smith

Carpenter's Cross Christian S 50/PK-4
18110 FM 344 W 75762 903-825-1011
Julie Lee, prin. Fax 825-3561

Florence, Williamson, Pop. 1,109
Florence ISD 1,000/PK-12
PO Box 489 76527 254-793-2850
John Van Dever, supt. Fax 793-3055
www.florence.k12.tx.us
Florence ES 500/PK-5
PO Box 489 76527 254-793-2497
Reagan Willman, prin. Fax 793-3158
Florence MS 200/6-8
PO Box 489 76527 254-793-2504
Steve Ham, prin. Fax 793-3054

Floresville, Wilson, Pop. 7,024
Floresville ISD 3,700/PK-12
908 10th St 78114 830-393-5300
David Vinson, supt. Fax 393-5399
www.fisd.us
Floresville ECC 400/PK-K
1200 5th St 78114 830-393-5700
Hazel Ramirez, prin. Fax 393-5714
Floresville ES 800/3-5
2000 Tiger Ln 78114 830-393-5325
Jean Hughes, prin. Fax 393-5320
Floresville MS 900/6-8
2601 B St 78114 830-393-5350
Jacque Baker, prin. Fax 393-5339
Floresville PS 500/1-2
1111 A St 78114 830-393-5310
Benny Villanueva, prin. Fax 393-5315

Sacred Heart S 100/PK-5
1007 Trail St 78114 830-393-2117
Kimberly Patek, prin. Fax 393-6968

Flower Mound, Denton, Pop. 63,526
Lewisville ISD 49,300/PK-12
1800 Timber Creek Rd 75028 972-713-5200
Dr. Jerry Roy, supt. Fax 350-9500
www.lisd.net

Bluebonnet ES 500/K-5
2000 Spinks Rd 75028 469-713-5195
Sharon Burris, prin. Fax 350-9005
Bridlewood ES 800/K-5
4901 Remington Park Dr 75028 469-713-5193
Mike Rogers, prin. Fax 350-9007
Donald ES 600/K-5
2400 Forest Vista Dr 75028 469-713-5198
Michelle Wooten, prin. Fax 350-9033
Downing MS 600/6-8
5555 Bridlewood Blvd 75028 469-713-5962
Lisa Lingren, prin. Fax 350-9176
Flower Mound ES 600/K-5
4101 Churchill Dr 75028 469-713-5955
Gayle Nurre, prin. Fax 350-9046
Forest Vista ES 600/PK-5
900 Forest Vista Dr 75028 469-713-5194
Dr. Patrick Schott, prin. Fax 350-9047
Forestwood MS 700/6-8
2810 Morriss Rd 75028 469-713-5972
Dave Tickner, prin. Fax 350-9184
Garden Ridge ES 500/PK-5
2220 S Garden Ridge Blvd 75028 469-713-5956
Dan Van Horne, prin. Fax 350-9052
Lamar MS 800/6-8
4000 Timber Creek Rd 75028 469-713-5966
Mike Fields, prin. Fax 350-9024
Liberty ES 800/PK-5
4600 Quail Run 75022 469-713-5958
Linda Holman, prin. Fax 350-9098
McKamy MS 1,000/6-8
2401 Old Settlers Rd 75022 469-713-5991
Peter Taggart, prin. Fax 350-9209
Old Settlers ES 800/PK-5
2525 Old Settlers Rd 75022 469-713-5993
Mary Lewis, prin. Fax 350-9126
Prairie Trail ES 700/K-5
5555 Timber Creek Rd 75028 469-713-5980
Chellie Adams, prin. Fax 350-9135
Shadow Ridge MS 700/6-8
2050 Aberdeen Dr 75028 469-713-5984
Gary Gibson, prin. Fax 350-9215
Timbercreek ES 600/K-5
1900 Timber Creek Rd 75028 469-713-5961
Victoria Abshier, prin. Fax 350-9146
Vickery ES 600/K-5
3301 Wager Dr 75028 469-713-5969
Kristen Streeter, prin. Fax 350-9157
Wellington ES 1,000/K-5
3900 Kenwood Dr 75022 469-713-5989
Dr. Robin Macke, prin. Fax 350-9160
Other Schools – See Carrollton, Frisco, Highland Village, Lewisville, The Colony

Lamb of God Lutheran S 400/PK-K
1401 Cross Timbers Rd 75028 972-539-0055
Linda Braun, dir. Fax 539-8194

Floydada, Floyd, Pop. 3,294
Floydada ISD 700/PK-12
226 W California St 79235 806-983-3498
Jerry Vaughn, supt. Fax 983-5739
www.floydadaisd.esc17.net
Floydada ES 200/PK-5
215 N White St 79235 806-983-4974
Gilbert Trevino, prin. Fax 983-4976
Floydada JHS 200/6-8
910 S 5th St 79235 806-983-2161
Mac Sherman, prin. Fax 983-5739

Follett, Lipscomb, Pop. 414
Follett ISD 200/K-12
PO Box 28 79034 806-653-2301
Jeff Northern, supt. Fax 653-2036
www.follettisd.net
Follett S 200/K-12
PO Box 28 79034 806-653-2301
Jamie Copley, prin. Fax 653-2036

Forestburg, Montague
Forestburg ISD 200/K-12
PO Box 415 76239 940-964-2323
Dr. Fonda Huneycutt, supt. Fax 964-2531
www.esc9.net/forestburgisd/
Forestburg S 200/K-12
PO Box 415 76239 940-964-2323
John Robertson, prin. Fax 964-2531

Forest Hill, Tarrant, Pop. 13,227
Fort Worth ISD
Supt. — See Fort Worth
Beal ES 500/PK-5
5615 Forest Hill Dr 76119 817-531-6460
Patricia Scott, prin. Fax 531-7738
Sellars ES 600/PK-5
4200 Dorsey St 76119 817-531-6430
Sonja Whitaker, prin. Fax 531-6156

Forney, Kaufman, Pop. 10,579
Forney ISD 6,200/PK-12
600 S Bois d Arc St 75126 972-564-4055
Dr. Darrell Brown, supt. Fax 564-7007
www.forneyisd.net
Blackburn ES 600/PK-6
2401 Concord St 75126 972-564-7008
Trudy Watson, prin. Fax 762-7190
Brown MS 800/7-8
1050 Windmill Farms Blvd 75126 972-564-3967
Jody Fadely, prin. Fax 564-7022
Claybon ES 600/K-6
1011 FM 741 75126 972-564-7023
Scott Fisher, prin. Fax 564-3499
Criswell ES 600/K-6
401 FM 740 N 75126 972-564-1609
Jeff Hutcheson, prin. Fax 564-3307
Crosby ES 500/K-6
495 Diamond Creek Dr 75126 972-564-7002
Justin Vercher, prin. Fax 762-3150
Henderson ES 700/K-6
12755 FM 1641 75126 972-564-7100
Stephen Chapman, prin. Fax 564-5612

Johnson ES 500/K-6
701 S Bois d Arc St 75126 972-564-3397
Bobby Milliorn, prin. Fax 564-7012
Lewis ES 400/K-6
1309 Luckenbach Dr 75126 972-564-7102
Shellie Baird, prin. Fax 355-2128
Nell Hill Rhea ES PK-6
240 Monitor Dr 75126 469-762-4157
Cecilia Cosper, prin. Fax 355-0191
Smith ES PK-6
1750 Iron Gate Blvd 75126 469-762-4158
Amy Childress, prin. Fax 355-0154
Warren MS 7-8
811 S Bois D Arc St 75126 469-762-4156
Kenneth Pearce, prin. Fax 552-1693

Forsan, Howard, Pop. 221
Forsan ISD 700/K-12
PO Box A 79733 432-457-2223
Randy Johnson, supt. Fax 457-2225
forsan.esc18.net
Other Schools – See Big Spring

Fort Davis, Jeff Davis
Fort Davis ISD 300/PK-12
PO Box 1339 79734 432-426-4440
Robert Sanford, supt. Fax 426-3841
www.fdisd.com
Dirks-Anderson ES 100/PK-6
PO Box 1339 79734 432-426-4454
Trava Baker, prin. Fax 426-4456

Fort Hancock, Hudspeth
Fort Hancock ISD 500/K-12
PO Box 98 79839 915-769-3811
Jose Franco, supt. Fax 769-3940
www.forthancockisd.net/
Fort Hancock MS 200/5-8
PO Box 98 79839 915-769-3811
Jasminka Speer, prin. Fax 769-0045
Martinez ES 200/K-4
PO Box 98 79839 915-769-3811
Yvonne Samaniego, prin. Fax 769-0043

Fort Hood, Bell, Pop. 33,700
Killeen ISD
Supt. — See Killeen
Clarke ES 600/PK-3
51612 Comanche Ave 76544 254-336-1510
Bill Diab, prin. Fax 539-3542
Clear Creek ES 800/PK-5
4800 Washington St 76544 254-336-1550
Maryann Ramos, prin. Fax 519-5640
Duncan ES 800/PK-5
52400 Muskogee Dr 76544 254-336-1620
Marie Davis, prin. Fax 539-6069
Meadows ES 700/PK-5
423 27th St 76544 254-336-1870
Karol Carlisle, prin. Fax 501-1893
Montague Village ES 500/K-5
84001 Clements Dr 76544 254-336-2230
Karen Hutchison, prin. Fax 539-3453
Murphy MS 600/6-8
53393 Sun Dance Dr 76544 254-200-6530
Mike Quinn, prin. Fax 616-5245
Oveta Culp Hobby ES 600/PK-5
51000 Tank Destroyer Blvd 76544 254-200-6500
Keith Moore, prin. Fax 616-6524
Smith MS 500/6-8
51000 Tank Destroyer Blvd 76544 254-336-1050
Sandra Forsythe, prin. Fax 532-1247
Venable Village ES 600/PK-5
60160 Venable Dr 76544 254-336-1980
Cynthia Potvin, prin. Fax 519-5632

Fort Stockton, Pecos, Pop. 7,268
Fort Stockton ISD 2,100/PK-12
101 W Division St 79735 432-336-4000
Ralph Traynham, supt. Fax 336-4008
www.fsisd.net/
Alamo ES 400/K-3
101 W Division St 79735 432-336-4016
Joe Baker, prin. Fax 336-4028
Apache ES 200/PK-3
101 W Division St 79735 432-336-4161
Estela Casas, prin. Fax 336-4167
Fort Stockton IS 300/4-5
101 W Division St 79735 432-336-4141
Zana Hanson, prin. Fax 336-4147
Fort Stockton MS 500/6-8
101 W Division St 79735 432-336-4131
Judy Espino, prin. Fax 336-4136

Fort Worth, Tarrant, Pop. 624,067
Azle ISD
Supt. — See Azle
Eagle Heights ES 500/PK-4
6505 Lucerne Dr 76135 817-237-4161
Paula Eagleton, prin. Fax 237-0656

Birdville ISD
Supt. — See Haltom City
Thomas Academy 600/PK-5
8200 O Brian Way 76180 817-547-3000
Sabrina Lindsey, prin. Fax 581-5490

Castleberry ISD 3,800/PK-12
315 Churchill Rd 76114 817-252-2000
Gary Jones, supt. Fax 738-1062
www.castleberryisd.net
Castleberry ES 2-3 400/2-3
5228 Ohio Garden Rd 76114 817-252-2300
Hollie Lancarte, prin. Fax 625-1884
Castleberry ES PK-1 1,000/PK-1
5228 Ohio Garden Rd 76114 817-252-2300
Deonna Courtney, prin. Fax 625-1884
Cato ES 400/4-5
1101 Merritt St 76114 817-252-2400
Leigh Turner, prin. Fax 625-9724
James ES 400/PK-5
5300 Buchanan St 76114 817-252-2500
Terry Johnson, prin. Fax 626-6921

Marsh MS 700/6-8
415 Hagg Dr 76114 817-252-2200
Stephanie Romeo, prin. Fax 738-3454

Crowley ISD
Supt. — See Crowley
Carden ES 600/PK-4
3701 Garden Springs Dr 76123 817-370-5600
Vivian Lincoln, prin. Fax 370-5604
Crouch IS 800/5-6
8036 Cedar Lake Ln 76123 817-370-5670
Stefani Allen, prin. Fax 370-5676
Crowley MS 1,300/7-8
3800 W Risinger Rd 76123 817-370-5650
Daryle Moffett, prin. Fax 370-5656
Dallas Park ES 900/PK-4
8700 Viridian Ln 76123 817-370-5620
Juan Castaneda, prin. Fax 370-5624
Hargrave ES 500/PK-4
9200 Poynter St 76123 817-370-5630
Teri Conley, prin. Fax 370-5635
Meadow Creek ES 600/PK-4
2801 Country Creek Ln 76123 817-370-5690
Ferrekk Yeokum, prin. Fax 370-5694
Oakmont ES 600/PK-4
6651 Oakmont Trl 76132 817-370-5610
Kim Scoggins, prin. Fax 370-5615
Parkway ES 600/PK-4
1320 W Everman Pkwy 76134 817-568-5710
Sharon Norwood, prin. Fax 568-5714
Poynter ES 600/PK-6
521 Ashdale Dr 76140 817-568-5730
La Creasha Stille, prin. Fax 568-5734
Sycamore ES 700/PK-6
1601 Country Manor Rd 76134 817-568-5700
Sherry Gore, prin. Fax 568-5704

Eagle Mtn.-Saginaw ISD 13,500/PK-12
1200 Old Decatur Rd 76179 817-232-0880
Dr. Cole Pugh, supt. Fax 847-6124
www.emsisd.com
Bryson ES 800/K-5
8601 Old Decatur Rd 76179 817-237-8306
Sheryl Sutherland, prin. Fax 238-8991
Chisholm Ridge ES 800/K-5
8301 Running River Ln 76131 817-232-0715
Sherry Grant, prin. Fax 306-4391
Comanche Springs ES 700/K-5
8100 Comanche Springs Dr 76131 817-847-8700
Melanie Caldwell, prin. Fax 847-0941
Creekview MS 1,000/6-8
6716 Bob Hanger St 76179 817-237-4261
Anthe Anagnostis, prin. Fax 237-2387
Eagle Mountain ES 600/K-5
9700 Boat Club Rd 76179 817-236-7191
Paul Jennings, prin. Fax 236-1461
Elkins ES 600/K-5
5787 WJ Boaz Rd 76179 817-237-0805
Dawn Battle, prin. Fax 237-0948
Gililland ES 700/K-5
701 Waggoman Rd 76131 817-232-0331
Belia Thompson, prin. Fax 232-8822
Greenfield ES K-5
6020 Ten Mile Bridge Rd 76135 817-237-0357
Cathe Bragg, prin. Fax 237-5809
Highland MS 1,000/6-8
1001 E Bailey Boswell Rd 76131 817-847-5143
Karen Pressley, prin. Fax 847-1922
Lake Pointe ES, 5501 Park Dr 76179 K-5
Sheri Larson, prin. 817-232-0880
Northbrook ES K-5
2500 Cantrell Sansom Rd 76131 817-232-0880
Angie Kraus, prin.
Parkview ES K-5
6225 Crystal Lake Dr 76179 817-232-0880
Shelly Butler, prin.
Prairie Vista MS 800/6-8
8000 Comanche Springs Dr 76131 817-847-9210
Stephen Griffin, prin. Fax 847-4255
Remington Point ES 800/K-5
6000 Old Decatur Rd 76179 817-232-1342
Betsy Brooks, prin. Fax 232-2594
Wayside MS 800/6-8
1300 Old Decatur Rd 76179 817-232-0541
Wendee Long, prin. Fax 232-2391
Other Schools – See Saginaw

Everman ISD
Supt. — See Everman
Powell IS 700/5-6
8875 Oak Grove Rd 76140 817-568-3523
Felicia Donaldson, prin. Fax 568-3533
Ray ES 400/PK-4
7309 Sheridan Rd 76134 817-568-3545
Mya Asberry, prin. Fax 568-3544

Fort Worth ISD 78,600/PK-12
100 N University Dr 76107 817-871-2000
Dr. Melody Johnson, supt. Fax 871-2112
www.fortworthisd.org
Bonnie Brea ES 300/K-5
3504 Kimbo Rd 76111 817-222-7500
Stephanie Hughes, prin. Fax 222-7595
Briscoe ES 400/PK-5
2751 Yuma Ave 76104 817-814-0300
Shawn Buchanan, prin. Fax 814-0350
Burton Hill ES 400/PK-5
519 Burton Hill Rd 76114 817-377-7390
Tamara Dugan, prin. Fax 377-7079
Carter Park ES 600/PK-5
1204 E Broadus Ave 76115 817-815-8600
Michael Buchenau, prin. Fax 815-8650
Chavez PS 600/PK-2
3710 Deen Rd 76106 817-378-5000
Elizabeth Vasquez, prin. Fax 378-5012
Clarke ES 600/PK-5
3300 S Henderson St 76110 817-814-6100
Antonio Martinez, prin. Fax 814-6150
Clayton ES 500/PK-5
2000 Park Place Ave 76110 817-922-6660
Beth McKenzie-Hollinger, prin. Fax 922-6932

Como ES 500/PK-5
4000 Horne St 76107 817-815-6500
Brenda Haynes, prin. Fax 815-6550
Como Montessori 400/PK-8
4001 Littlepage St 76107 817-377-7370
Janna Bennett, prin. Fax 377-7043
Contreras ES 900/PK-5
4100 Lubbock Ave 76115 817-814-7800
Diana Puente-Vargas, prin. Fax 814-7850
Daggett ES 600/PK-5
958 Page Ave 76110 817-814-5500
Melissa Green, prin. Fax 814-5550
Daggett MS 300/6-8
1108 Carlock St 76110 817-922-6550
Linda Villarreal, prin. Fax 922-6996
Daggett Montessori S 500/K-8
2309 Lipscomb St 76110 817-920-1200
Susan Wade, prin. Fax 920-1211
Davis ES 400/PK-5
4400 Campus Dr 76119 817-531-4650
Sheila Turner, prin. Fax 531-4670
De Zavala ES 400/PK-5
1419 College Ave 76104 817-814-5600
Roberto Santana, prin. Fax 814-5650
Diamond Hill ES 700/PK-5
2000 Dewey St 76106 817-815-0400
Keith Burgett, prin. Fax 815-0450
Dillow ES 500/PK-5
4000 Avenue N 76105 817-531-6415
Rochelle Colvin, prin. Fax 531-7741
Dunbar 6th Grade S 300/6-6
5100 Willie St 76105 817-815-3400
Keith Christmas, prin. Fax 815-3450
Dunbar MS 500/7-8
2501 Stalcup Rd 76119 817-496-7430
Crystal Goodman, prin. Fax 496-7697
Eastern Hills ES 600/PK-5
5917 Shelton St 76112 817-815-4500
Vernal Elliot, prin. Fax 815-4550
East Handley ES 400/PK-5
2617 Mims St 76112 817-815-4400
Susan Hill, prin. Fax 815-4450
Elder MS 1,100/6-8
709 NW 21st St 76164 817-814-4100
Carla Spaniel, prin. Fax 814-4150
Elliott ES 500/PK-5
2501 Cooks Ln 76120 817-815-4600
Pamela Henderson, prin. Fax 815-4650
Ellis PS 500/PK-K
215 NE 14th St 76164 817-378-5050
Shirley Monge, prin. Fax 378-5070
Forest Oak MS 700/6-8
3221 Pecos St 76119 817-531-6330
Gerald Batty, prin. Fax 531-4342
Glencrest 6th Grade S 400/6-6
4801 Eastline Dr 76119 817-815-8400
Paula Woods, prin. Fax 815-8450
Glen Park ES 800/PK-5
3601 Pecos St 76119 817-815-8800
Dr. Cassandra Morris-Surles, prin. Fax 815-8850
Greenbriar ES 500/PK-5
1605 Grady Lee St 76134 817-814-7400
Amelia Harden, prin. Fax 814-7450
Green ES 700/PK-5
4612 David Strickland Rd 76119 817-815-8900
Edra Bailey, prin. Fax 815-8950
Handley MS 700/6-8
2801 Patino Rd 76112 817-496-7450
Lewis Washington, prin. Fax 496-7653
Helbing ES 600/PK-5
3524 N Crump St 76106 817-815-0500
Betty Sandley, prin. Fax 815-0550
Hubbard Heights ES 800/PK-5
1333 W Spurgeon St 76115 817-814-7500
Dorene Benavidez, prin. Fax 814-7550
Huerta ES 600/PK-5
3309 W Long Ave 76106 817-740-5550
Yadira Martinez, prin. Fax 740-4892
James MS 1,100/6-8
1101 Nashville Ave 76105 817-531-6230
Rian Townsend, prin. Fax 531-6114
Jara ES 700/PK-5
2100 Lincoln Ave 76164 817-814-4500
Marta Plata, prin. Fax 814-4550
Kirkpatrick ES 400/PK-5
3229 Lincoln Ave 76106 817-814-4600
Cynthia Hernandez, prin. Fax 814-4650
Kirkpatrick MS 500/6-8
3201 Refugio Ave 76106 817-814-4200
Jason Oliver, prin. Fax 814-4250
Logan ES 500/PK-5
2300 Dillard St 76105 817-815-3700
Sonya Williams, prin. Fax 815-3750
Lowery Road ES 800/PK-5
7600 Lowery Rd 76120 817-492-7900
Debra Williamson, prin. Fax 492-7905
McDonald ES 600/PK-5
1850 Barron Ln 76112 817-496-7445
Anitra Perry, prin. Fax 492-7815
McLean MS 700/6-8
3816 Stadium Dr 76109 817-922-6830
John Engel, prin. Fax 922-4498
McLean Sixth Grade S 400/6-6
3201 S Hills Ave 76109 817-207-6700
Sarah Weeks, prin. Fax 207-6705
McRae ES 900/PK-5
3316 Avenue N 76105 817-814-0500
Kendall Miller, prin. Fax 814-0550
Meacham MS 700/6-8
3600 Weber St 76106 817-815-0200
Elodia Escamilla, prin. Fax 815-0250
Meadowbrook ES 800/PK-5
4330 Meadowbrook Dr 76103 817-815-4900
Franchesca Cain, prin. Fax 815-4950
Meadowbrook MS 1,000/6-8
2001 Ederville Rd S 76103 817-531-6250
Cherie Washington, prin. Fax 531-7709

Mendoza ES 500/PK-5
1412 Denver Ave 76164 817-814-4700
Blanca Galindo, prin. Fax 814-4750
Merrett ES 600/PK-5
7325 Kermit Ave 76116 817-377-7245
Melissa Bryan, prin. Fax 377-7045
Mitchell Blvd ES 500/PK-5
3601 Mitchell Blvd 76105 817-815-9000
Karen Lewis, prin. Fax 815-9050
Monnig MS 600/6-8
3136 Bigham Blvd 76116 817-377-7250
Laura Stegall, prin. Fax 377-7024
Moore ES 300/PK-5
1809 NE 36th St 76106 817-815-0600
Jose Diaz, prin. Fax 815-0650
Morningside ES 500/PK-5
2601 Evans Ave 76104 817-814-0600
Ronnita Carridine, prin. Fax 814-0650
Morningside MS 400/6-8
2751 Mississippi Ave 76104 817-815-8300
Andrew Chambers, prin. Fax 815-8350
Moss ES 400/PK-5
4108 Eastland St 76119 817-815-3600
Seretha Walker, prin. Fax 815-3650
Nash ES 400/PK-5
401 Samuels Ave 76102 817-814-9400
Pamela Day, prin. Fax 814-9450
North Hi Mount ES 300/PK-5
3801 W 7th St 76107 817-815-1500
Hilda Caballero, prin. Fax 815-1550
Oakhurst ES 700/PK-5
2700 Yucca Ave 76111 817-814-9500
Karen Molinar, prin. Fax 814-9550
Oaklawn ES 300/PK-5
3220 Hardeman St 76119 817-815-9100
Margarita Garcia, prin. Fax 815-9150
Pate ES 600/PK-5
3800 Anglin Dr 76119 817-815-3800
Erika Moody, prin. Fax 815-3850
Peak ES 500/PK-5
1201 E Jefferson Ave 76104 817-814-0700
Lear Linton, prin. Fax 814-0750
Phillips ES 500/PK-5
3020 Bigham Blvd 76116 817-377-7270
Patty Steen, prin. Fax 377-7036
Ridglea Hills ES 600/PK-5
6817 Cumberland Rd 76116 817-377-7345
Clifford Mayer, prin. Fax 377-7077
Riverside MS 900/6-8
1600 Bolton St 76111 817-814-9200
Daniel Scroggins, prin. Fax 814-9250
Rosemont 6th Grade S 400/6-6
3908 Mccart Ave 76110 817-814-7300
Kenneth Goodwin, prin. Fax 814-7350
Rosemont MS 900/7-8
1501 W Seminary Dr 76115 817-814-7200
Yassmin Lee, prin. Fax 814-7250
Rosen ES 400/K-5
2613 Roosevelt Ave 76164 817-814-4800
Maria Lewis, prin. Fax 814-4850
Sagamore Hill ES 800/PK-5
701 S Hughes Ave 76103 817-815-5000
Veronica Delgado, prin. Fax 815-5050
Seminary Hills Park ES 500/PK-5
5037 Townsend Dr 76115 817-920-1270
Aileen Martina, prin. Fax 920-1284
Shulkey ES 500/PK-5
5533 Whitman Ave 76133 817-370-5870
Alice Galban, prin. Fax 370-5898
Sims ES 800/PK-5
3500 Crenshaw Ave 76105 817-814-0800
Rudy Valdez, prin. Fax 814-0850
South Hills ES 800/PK-5
3009 Bilglade Rd 76133 817-814-5800
Priscila Dilley, prin. Fax 814-5850
South Hi Mount ES 600/K-5
4101 Birchman Ave 76107 817-377-7380
Carla Coscia, prin. Fax 377-7083
Springdale ES 500/PK-5
3207 Hollis St 76111 817-814-9600
Victorius Eugenio, prin. Fax 814-9650
Stevens ES 700/PK-5
6161 Wrigley Way 76133 817-370-5880
Ronald Schultze, prin. Fax 370-5773
Stripling MS 600/6-8
2100 Clover Ln 76107 817-815-1300
Terry Mossige, prin. Fax 815-1350
Sunrise-McMillian ES 400/PK-5
3409 Stalcup Rd 76119 817-815-3900
Marion Mouton, prin. Fax 815-3950
Tanglewood ES 600/PK-5
3060 Overton Park Dr W 76109 817-922-6815
Constance Smith, prin. Fax 922-6917
Terrell ES 200/K-5
1411 I M Terrell Cir S 76102 817-815-1900
Jo Ann Dickerson, prin. Fax 815-1950
Turner ES 600/PK-5
3001 Azle Ave 76106 817-814-4900
Norma Ayala, prin. Fax 814-4950
Van Zandt-Guinn ES 300/PK-5
501 Missouri Ave 76104 817-815-2000
Keith Besses, prin. Fax 815-2050
Walton ES 500/PK-5
5816 Rickenbacker Pl 76112 817-815-3300
Leonard Brasfield, prin. Fax 815-3350
Washington Heights ES 400/PK-5
3215 N Houston St 76106 817-815-0700
Sandra Garza, prin. Fax 815-0750
Wedgwood 6th Grade S 500/6-6
4212 Belden Ave 76132 817-370-5860
Kelli Taulton, prin. Fax 370-5868
Wedgwood MS 1,000/7-8
3909 Wilkie Way 76133 817-370-5830
Theodore Jarchow, prin. Fax 370-5733
Westcliff ES 400/PK-5
4300 Clay Ave 76109 817-922-6850
Sara Gillaspie, prin. Fax 922-6961

Westcreek ES 700/PK-5
3401 Walton Ave 76133 817-370-5850
Wilma Lovings, prin. Fax 370-5855
Western Hills ES 400/3-5
2805 Laredo Dr 76116 817-815-6800
Tracy Allen, prin. Fax 815-6850
Western Hills PS 700/PK-2
8300 Mojave Trl 76116 817-815-6900
Jana Marbut-Ray, prin. Fax 815-6950
West Handley ES 400/K-5
2749 Putnam St 76112 817-815-5100
Hector Martinez, prin. Fax 815-5150
Williams ES 500/PK-5
901 Baurline St 76111 817-814-9700
Carlos Meekins, prin. Fax 814-9750
Wilson ES 700/PK-5
900 W Fogg St 76110 817-814-7700
Elda Gonzalez, prin. Fax 814-7750
Woodway ES 800/PK-5
6701 Woodway Dr 76133 817-370-5890
Jerry Moore, prin. Fax 370-5724
Worth Heights ES 900/PK-5
519 E Butler St 76110 817-814-6200
Hilaria Ruiz, prin. Fax 814-6250
Other Schools – See Benbrook, Forest Hill, Haltom City

Hurst-Euless-Bedford ISD
Supt. — See Bedford
River Trails ES 700/PK-6
8850 Elbe Trl 76118 817-285-3235
Mary Stokic, prin. Fax 285-3238

Keller ISD
Supt. — See Keller
Basswood ES K-4
3100 Clay Mountain Trl 76137 817-744-6500
Tony Johnson, prin. Fax 750-5168
Bluebonnet ES 800/K-4
7000 Teal Dr 76137 817-744-4500
Ken McGuire, prin. Fax 581-3441
Chisholm Trail IS 1,000/5-6
3901 Summerfields Blvd 76137 817-744-3800
Dr. Leona McDade, prin. Fax 306-8393
Fossil Hill MS 1,000/7-8
3821 Staghorn Cir S 76137 817-744-3050
Dustin Blank, prin.
Hillwood MS 1,000/7-8
8250 Parkwood Hill Blvd 76137 817-744-3350
Jim Joros, prin. Fax 581-1810
North Riverside ES 700/K-4
7900 N Riverside Dr 76137 817-744-5300
Robyn Gibson, prin. Fax 306-1474
Park Glen ES 600/PK-4
5100 Glen Canyon Rd 76137 817-744-5400
Carol Wicker, prin. Fax 485-2067
Parkview ES 800/PK-4
6900 Bayberry Dr 76137 817-744-5500
Doreen Krebs, prin. Fax 232-8693
Parkwood Hill IS 1,000/5-6
8201 Parkwood Hill Blvd 76137 817-744-4000
Kathy Knowles, prin. Fax 581-0085

Lake Worth ISD
Supt. — See Lake Worth
Marine Creek ES 300/PK-4
4801 Huffines Blvd 76135 817-306-4270
Donna Bagwell, prin. Fax 238-6726
Miller ES 500/PK-4
5250 Estrella St 76106 817-306-4280
Brent McClain, prin. Fax 624-9007

Northwest ISD
Supt. — See Justin
Nance ES 600/PK-5
701 Tierra Vista Way 76131 817-698-1950
Connie Finley, prin. Fax 698-1960
Peterson ES K-5
2000 Winter Hawk Dr 76177 817-698-5000
Todd Rogers, prin.

White Settlement ISD 4,900/PK-12
401 S Cherry Ln 76108 817-367-1350
Dr. Audrey Arnold, supt. Fax 367-1351
www.wsisd.com/
Blue Haze ES 500/K-4
601 Blue Haze Dr 76108 817-367-2583
Ronda Wright, prin. Fax 367-1344
Fine Arts Academy K-5
8301 Downe Dr 76108 817-367-5396
Fax 367-1396
North ES 800/PK-4
9850 Legacy Dr 76108 817-367-1323
Eddie Lynge, prin. Fax 367-1308
Tannahill IS 800/5-6
701 American Flyer Blvd 76108 817-367-1370
Chris Jenkins, prin. Fax 367-1371
Other Schools – See White Settlement

All Saints Catholic S 100/PK-8
2006 N Houston St 76164 817-624-2670
Christina Mendez, prin. Fax 624-1221
All Saints' Episcopal S 800/K-12
9700 Saints Cir 76108 817-560-5700
Thaddeus Bird, hdmstr. Fax 560-5722
Bethesda Christian S 500/K-12
4700 N Beach St 76137 817-281-6446
Vicki Vaughn, admin. Fax 281-1560
Calvary Christian Academy 300/PK-12
1401 Oakhurst Scenic Dr 76111 817-332-3351
Sue Tidwell, admin. Fax 332-4621
Christian Life Preparatory S 200/K-12
6250 South Fwy 76134 817-293-1500
Deborah Henry, admin. Fax 293-1500
Ekklesia Christian S 50/PK-6
1200 Bessie St 76104 817-332-1202
Michelle Chambers, admin. Fax 335-6606
Fellowship Christian Academy 100/K-12
1140 Morrison Dr 76120 817-457-2345
Angela Cuppett, supt. Fax 457-2347

Fort Worth Academy 200/K-8
7301 Dutch Branch Rd 76132 817-370-1191
William Broderick, hdmstr. Fax 294-1323
Ft. Worth Adventist Jr Academy 100/PK-8
3040 Sycamore School Rd 76133 817-370-7177
Fax 370-8455
Fort Worth Christian S 900/PK-12
7517 Bogart Dr 76180 817-281-6504
Fax 281-7063
Fort Worth Country Day S 1,100/K-12
4200 Country Day Ln 76109 817-732-7718
Evan Peterson, hdmstr. Fax 377-3425
Fort Worth Save Our Children S 100/PK-7
4215 Avenue M 76105 817-536-6563
Vernon James, prin. Fax 536-3033
Glenview Christian S 200/PK-12
4805 NE Loop 820 76137 817-281-5155
Jerome Chenausky, admin. Fax 514-0760
Harvest Christian Academy 200/K-12
7200 Denton Hwy 76148 817-485-1660
Terry Caywood, hdmstr. Fax 514-6279
Harvest Christian S 100/K-12
7501 Crowley Rd 76134 817-568-0021
John Winner, admin. Fax 568-1395
Hill S of Ft. Worth 200/2-12
4817 Odessa Ave 76133 817-923-9482
Greg Owens, admin. Fax 923-4894
Holy Family Catholic S 200/PK-8
6146 Pershing Ave 76107 817-737-4201
Dr. John Shreve, prin. Fax 738-1542
Key S 100/PK-12
3947 E Loop 820 S 76119 817-446-3738
Mary Ann Key, dir. Fax 496-3299
Lake Country Christian S 400/PK-12
8777 Boat Club Rd 76179 817-236-8703
Nancy Purtell, admin. Fax 236-1103
Lighthouse Christian Academy 50/K-7
7200 Robertson Rd 76135 817-237-7641
Nanci Danielsen, admin. Fax 509-0457
Miss Endy's Christian Day S 50/PK-6
5837 Humbert Ave 76107 817-737-9031
Wilbernita Crosby, prin. Fax 377-1719
Montessori at Sundance Square 100/PK-K
201 Jones St 76102 817-334-0036
Amanda Phy, prin. Fax 334-0132
Montessori Children's House - Fort Worth 100/PK-6
3420 Clayton Rd E 76116 817-732-0252
Amy Henderson, prin. Fax 732-6601
Our Lady of Victory S 200/PK-8
3320 Hemphill St 76110 817-924-5123
Trudy Miller, prin. Fax 923-9621
Our Mother of Mercy S 100/PK-8
1007 E Terrell Ave 76104 817-923-0058
Dr. Carolyn Yusuf, prin. Fax 923-0060
Redeemer Lutheran S 100/PK-5
4513 Williams Rd 76116 817-560-0032
Paige Nickell, prin.
St. Andrews S 700/PK-8
3304 Dryden Rd 76109 817-924-8917
Clarice Peninger, prin. Fax 927-8507
St. George S 200/PK-8
824 Hudgins Ave 76111 817-222-1221
Dr. Olga Ferris, prin. Fax 838-0424
St. Paul Lutheran S 200/PK-8
1800 West Fwy 76102 817-332-2281
Larry Hoffschneider, prin. Fax 332-2640
St. Peter the Apostle S 200/PK-8
1201 S Cherry Ln 76108 817-246-2032
Erin Vader, prin. Fax 246-3686
St. Rita S 200/PK-8
712 Weiler Blvd 76112 817-451-9383
Charlene Hymel, prin. Fax 446-4465
Southwest Christian ES 300/K-6
6801 Dan Danciger Rd 76133 817-294-0350
Dr. Penny Armstrong, pres. Fax 294-0752
Temple Christian S 200/PK-6
1250 Jim Wright Fwy N 76108 817-244-1136
Dorothy Stringer, supt. Fax 457-0777
Temple Christian S of Ft. Worth 900/PK-12
6824 Randol Mill Rd 76120 817-457-0770
Dorothy Stringer, supt. Fax 457-0777
Trinity Valley S 1,000/K-12
7500 Dutch Branch Rd 76132 817-321-0100
Gary Krahn, hdmstr. Fax 321-0105

Franklin, Robertson, Pop. 1,489
Franklin ISD 900/PK-12
PO Box 909 77856 979-828-1900
Timothy Lowry, supt. Fax 828-1910
www.franklinisd.net/
Franklin MS 200/6-8
PO Box 909 77856 979-828-5434
Gerald Hancock, prin. Fax 828-3134
Reynolds ES 400/PK-5
PO Box 909 77856 979-828-7300
Susan Nelson, prin. Fax 828-5048

Frankston, Anderson, Pop. 1,233
Frankston ISD 800/PK-12
PO Box 428 75763 903-876-2556
Austin Thacker, supt. Fax 876-4558
www.frankston.esc7.net
Frankston ES 400/PK-5
PO Box 428 75763 903-876-2214
Melissa McIntire, prin. Fax 876-4558
Frankston MS 200/6-8
PO Box 428 75763 903-876-2215
Richard Hamilton, prin. Fax 876-4558

Fred, Tyler
Warren ISD
Supt. — See Warren
Fred ES 200/PK-5
PO Box 10 77616 409-429-3240
Chris Carter, prin. Fax 429-3488

Fredericksburg, Gillespie, Pop. 10,432
Fredericksburg ISD 2,800/PK-12
234 Friendship Ln 78624 830-997-9551
Marc Williamson, supt. Fax 997-6164
www.fisd.org/
Fredericksburg ES 900/1-5
1608 N Adams St 78624 830-997-9595
Ann Moore, prin. Fax 997-7209
Fredericksburg MS 600/6-8
110 W Travis St 78624 830-997-7657
Kevan Webb, prin. Fax 997-1927
Fredericksburg PS 200/PK-K
1110 S Adams St 78624 830-997-7421
Missy Garcia-Stevens, prin. Fax 990-0002
Other Schools – See Stonewall

Fredericksburg Christian S 50/K-12
1208 N Milam St 78624 830-997-9193
Linda Williams, prin.
Heritage S 200/K-12
PO Box 1217 78624 830-997-6597
Nancy Hierholzer, hdmstr. Fax 997-4900
St. Mary S 300/PK-8
202 S Orange St 78624 830-997-3914
Billy Pahl, prin. Fax 997-2382

Freeport, Brazoria, Pop. 12,605
Brazosport ISD
Supt. — See Clute
Fleming ES 300/PK-4
PO Box Z 77542 979-730-7175
George Robinson, prin. Fax 237-6332
Freeport IS 600/7-8
PO Box Z 77542 979-730-7240
Kristine Traylor, prin. Fax 237-6329
Long ES 500/PK-4
PO Box Z 77542 979-730-7185
Lorrie Kloss, prin. Fax 237-6356
O'Hara Lanier MS 500/5-6
PO Box Z 77542 979-730-7220
Grace Walkes-Cahee, prin. Fax 237-6348
Velasco ES 600/PK-4
PO Box Z 77542 979-730-7210
Laura Morris, prin. Fax 237-6318

Freer, Duval, Pop. 3,081
Freer ISD 900/PK-12
PO Box 240 78357 361-394-6025
Alberto Gonzales, supt. Fax 394-5005
www.freerisd.org/
Freer JHS 200/6-8
PO Box 240 78357 361-394-7102
Linda Garza, prin. Fax 394-5016
Thomas ES 400/PK-5
PO Box 240 78357 361-394-6800
Frances Perez, prin. Fax 394-5014

Fresno, Fort Bend, Pop. 3,182
Fort Bend ISD
Supt. — See Sugar Land
Burton ES 900/K-5
1625 Hunter Green Ln 77545 281-634-5080
Ida Watkins, prin. Fax 634-5094
Goodman ES 1,000/K-5
1100 W Sycamore St 77545 281-634-5985
Lisa Langston, prin. Fax 634-6000
Parks ES 400/K-5
19101 Chimney Rock 77545 281-634-6390
Christina Hopkins, prin. Fax 327-6390

Friendswood, Galveston, Pop. 33,094
Clear Creek ISD
Supt. — See League City
Brookside IS 800/6-8
3535 E FM 528 Rd 77546 281-482-9710
Deanna Daws, prin. Fax 992-7858
Landolt ES 700/PK-5
2104 Pilgrims Point Dr 77546 281-284-5200
Yolanda Jones, prin. Fax 284-5205
Wedgewood ES 800/PK-5
4000 Friendswood Link Rd 77546 281-284-5700
Ann Arrington, prin. Fax 284-5705
West Brook IS 1,300/6-8
302 W El Dorado Blvd 77546 281-284-3800
Dr. Lori Broughton, prin. Fax 284-3805

Friendswood ISD 5,800/K-12
302 Laurel Dr 77546 281-482-1267
Trish Hanks, supt. Fax 996-2513
www.fisdk12.net
Bales IS 600/4-6
211 Stadium Ln 77546 281-482-8255
Joel Hannemann, prin. Fax 996-2551
Cline ES 800/K-3
505 Briarmeadow Ave 77546 281-482-1201
Debbie Smith, prin. Fax 996-2557
Friendswood JHS 1,000/7-8
402 Laurel Dr 77546 281-482-7818
Dana Drew, prin. Fax 996-2529
Westwood ES 800/K-3
506 W Edgewood Dr 77546 281-482-3341
Lynn Hobratschk, prin. Fax 996-2542
Windsong IS 700/4-6
2100 W Parkwood Ave 77546 281-482-0111
Nelda Guerra, prin. Fax 996-2594

Lord of Life Lutheran S 50/PK-8
4425 FM 2351 Rd 77546 281-482-0481
Andrew Van Weele, prin. Fax 648-4189

Friona, Parmer, Pop. 3,735
Friona ISD 1,300/PK-12
909 E 11th St 79035 806-250-2747
Kenny Austin, supt. Fax 250-3805
www.frionaisd.com
Friona ES 400/2-5
909 E 11th St 79035 806-250-3340
Becky Riethmayer, prin. Fax 250-5078
Friona JHS 300/6-8
909 E 11th St 79035 806-250-2788
Kevin Wiseman, prin. Fax 250-8155
Friona PS 300/PK-1
909 E 11th St 79035 806-250-2240
Tracy Ellis, prin. Fax 250-3937

Frisco, Collin, Pop. 70,793
Frisco ISD 27,400/K-12
6942 Maple St 75034 469-633-6000
Rick Reedy, supt. Fax 633-6050
www.friscoisd.org
Allen ES K-5
5800 Legacy Dr 75034 469-633-3800
Teresa Wilkinson, prin. Fax 633-3810
Ashley ES 800/K-5
15601 Christopher Ln 75035 469-633-3700
Kathy Kazanski, prin. Fax 633-3710
Bledsoe ES 600/K-5
1900 Timber Ridge Dr 75034 469-633-3600
Beverly Woodson, prin. Fax 633-3610
Boals ES 800/K-5
2035 Jaguar Dr 75034 469-633-3300
Anna Koenig, prin. Fax 633-3350
Bright ES 500/K-5
7600 Woodstream Dr 75034 469-633-2700
Susie Graham, prin. Fax 633-2750
Carroll ES 400/K-5
4380 Throne Hall Dr 75034 469-633-3725
Melissa Colbert, prin. Fax 633-3735
Christie ES 600/K-5
10300 Huntington Rd 75035 469-633-2400
Manuel Gonzales, prin. Fax 633-2450
Clark MS 900/6-8
4600 Colby Dr 75035 469-633-4600
Joel Partin, prin. Fax 633-4650
Corbell ES 700/K-5
11095 Monarch Dr 75034 469-633-3550
David Wehmeyer, prin. Fax 633-3560
Curtsinger ES 800/K-5
12450 Jereme Trl 75035 469-633-2100
Angela Borgarello, prin. Fax 633-2150
Fisher ES 600/K-5
2500 Old Orchard Rd 75034 469-633-2600
Nancy Lawson, prin. Fax 633-2650
Griffin MS 900/6-8
3703 Eldorado Pkwy 75034 469-633-4900
Elizabeth Holcomb, prin. Fax 633-4950
Gunstream ES 500/K-5
7600 Rockyridge Dr 75035 469-633-3100
David Smolka, prin. Fax 633-3150
Isbell ES 600/K-5
6000 Maltby Dr 75035 469-633-3400
Ginger Lemons, prin. Fax 633-3450
Pink ES 700/K-5
3650 Overhill Dr 75034 469-633-3500
Bethany Rowan, prin. Fax 633-3510
Pioneer Heritage MS 700/6-8
1649 High Shoals Dr 75034 469-633-4700
Todd Fouche, prin. Fax 633-4750
Roach MS 800/6-8
12499 Independence Pkwy 75035 469-633-5000
Terri Gladden, prin. Fax 633-5010
Rogers ES 700/K-5
10500 Rogers Rd 75034 469-633-2000
Susan Nesmith, prin. Fax 633-2050
Sem ES 700/K-5
12721 Honey Grove Dr 75035 469-633-3575
Dianna High, prin. Fax 633-3585
Shawnee Trail ES 800/K-5
10701 Preston Vineyard Dr 75035 469-633-2500
Sherri Wakeland, prin. Fax 633-2550
Smith ES 800/K-5
9800 Sean Dr 75035 469-633-2200
Matt Kimball, prin. Fax 633-2250
Sparks ES 500/K-5
8200 Otis Dr 75034 469-633-3000
Marilee McMichael, prin. Fax 633-3050
Spears ES 600/K-5
8500 Wade Blvd 75034 469-633-2900
Martha Moroch, prin. Fax 633-2950
Stafford MS 6-8
2288 Little River Rd 75034 469-633-5100
Robin Scott, prin. Fax 633-5110
Staley MS 700/6-8
6927 Stadium Ln 75034 469-633-4500
Dennis McDonald, prin. Fax 633-4550
Tadlock ES K-5
12515 Godfrey Dr 75035 469-633-3775
Kellie Rapp, prin. Fax 633-3785
Wester MS 800/6-8
12293 Shepherds Hill Ln 75035 469-633-4800
Angela Romney, prin. Fax 633-4850
Other Schools – See Little Elm, Mc Kinney, Plano

Lewisville ISD
Supt. — See Flower Mound
Hicks ES 400/K-5
3651 Compass Dr 75034 469-713-5981
Ann Beckel, prin. Fax 350-9075

Little Elm ISD
Supt. — See Little Elm
Hackberry ES 400/K-4
7200 Snug Harbor Cir 75034 972-547-3505
Kevin Moffitt, prin. Fax 547-3916

Frisco Montessori Academy 300/PK-5
8890 Meadow Hill Dr 75034 972-712-7400
Jody Rosen, prin. Fax 712-6441
Legacy Christian Academy 600/PK-12
5000 Academy Dr 75034 469-633-1330
Chris Harmon, hdmstr. Fax 633-1348
Starwood Montessori S 200/PK-6
6600 Lebanon Rd 75034 972-712-8080
Anita Hanks, prin. Fax 712-5458

Fritch, Hutchinson, Pop. 2,089
Sanford-Fritch ISD 900/PK-12
PO Box 1290 79036 806-857-3122
Daymun White, supt. Fax 857-3795
www.sfisd.net/
Sanford-Fritch ES 400/PK-5
PO Box 1290 79036 806-857-3126
Vicki McClellan, prin. Fax 857-9492

Sanford-Fritch JHS 200/6-8
PO Box 1290 79036 806-857-9268
Edith Allen, prin. Fax 857-9431

Frost, Navarro, Pop. 709
Frost ISD 400/PK-12
PO Box K 76641 903-682-2711
Jim Revill, supt. Fax 682-2107
www.frostisd.org
Frost ES 200/PK-6
PO Box K 76641 903-682-2541
Becky Melton, prin. Fax 682-2107

Fruitvale, Van Zandt, Pop. 453
Fruitvale ISD 400/PK-12
PO Box 77 75127 903-896-1191
Bill Boyd, supt. Fax 896-1011
www.fruitvaleisd.com
Fruitvale MS 100/6-8
PO Box 77 75127 903-896-4363
Bill Boyd, prin. Fax 896-1011
Randall ES 200/PK-5
PO Box 77 75127 903-896-4466
Peggy Brumit, prin. Fax 896-1011

Fulshear, Fort Bend, Pop. 936
Lamar Consolidated ISD
Supt. — See Rosenberg
Huggins ES 500/PK-5
1 Huggins Dr 77441 832-223-1600
Veronica Williams, prin. Fax 223-1601

Fulton, Aransas, Pop. 1,663
Aransas County ISD
Supt. — See Rockport
Fulton 4-5 Learning Center 500/4-5
502 N Mesquite St 78358 361-790-2240
Jeremy Saegert, prin. Fax 790-2274

Gail, Borden
Borden County ISD 100/K-12
PO Box 95 79738 806-756-4313
Jimmy Thomas, supt. Fax 756-4310
www.bcisd.net/
Borden S 100/K-12
PO Box 95 79738 806-756-4314
Bart McMeans, prin. Fax 756-4310

Gainesville, Cooke, Pop. 16,569
Callisburg ISD 1,100/PK-12
148 Dozier St 76240 940-665-0540
Dr. Charles Holloway, supt. Fax 668-2706
www.cisdtx.net
Callisburg ES 600/PK-6
148 Dozier St 76240 940-612-4196
Rusty Clark, prin. Fax 612-4804

Gainesville ISD 2,900/PK-12
800 S Morris St 76240 940-665-4362
Bill Gravitt, supt. Fax 665-4473
www.gainesvilleisd.org
Chalmers ES 700/2-4
600 Radio Hill Rd 76240 940-665-4147
Patti Mercer, prin. Fax 665-9290
Edison ES 600/PK-1
1 Edison Dr 76240 940-665-6091
Tammy Fuhrmann, prin. Fax 665-5728
Gainesville JHS 400/7-8
421 N Denton St 76240 940-665-4062
Rhett King, prin. Fax 665-1432
Lee IS 400/5-6
2100 N Grand Ave 76240 940-668-6662
Vance Wells, prin. Fax 668-0353

Sivells Bend ISD 100/PK-8
1053 County Road 403 76240 940-665-6411
Phil Newton, supt. Fax 665-2527
www.sivellsbendisd.net
Sivells Bend S 100/PK-8
1053 County Road 403 76240 940-665-6411
Phil Newton, prin. Fax 665-2527

Walnut Bend ISD 100/PK-8
47 County Road 198 76240 940-665-5990
Tommy Hunter, supt. Fax 665-9660
www.walnutbendisd.net
Walnut Bend S 100/PK-8
47 County Road 198 76240 940-665-5990
Tommy Hunter, prin. Fax 665-9660

St. Mary Catholic S 200/PK-8
931 N Weaver St 76240 940-665-5395
John Metzler, prin. Fax 665-9538

Galena Park, Harris, Pop. 10,221
Galena Park ISD
Supt. — See Houston
Galena Park ES 600/PK-5
401 N Main St 77547 832-386-1670
Lance Lyles, prin. Fax 386-1692
Galena Park MS 900/6-8
400 Keene St 77547 832-386-1700
Chris Blake, prin. Fax 386-1738
MacArthur ES 800/PK-5
1801 N Main St 77547 832-386-4630
Lina Esquivel, prin. Fax 386-4631

Our Lady of Fatima S 100/PK-6
1702 9th St 77547 713-674-5832
Frances Ramsey, prin. Fax 674-3877

Galveston, Galveston, Pop. 57,466
Galveston ISD 7,900/PK-12
PO Box 660 77553 409-766-5100
Lynne Cleveland, supt. Fax 766-5106
www.gisd.org/gisd/site/default.asp
Austin Magnet MS 400/6-8
1514 Avenue N 1/2 77550 409-765-9373
Cathy Vanness, prin. Fax 765-5946
Burnet ES 600/PK-5
5501 Avenue S 77551 409-740-0256
Lillian Wiley, prin. Fax 744-8264
Central MS 600/6-8
3014 Avenue I 77550 409-765-2101
Connie Hebert, prin. Fax 765-2141
Morgan ES 600/PK-5
1410 37th St 77550 409-763-1333
Annette Dailey, prin. Fax 763-0211
Oppe ES 600/K-5
2915 81st St 77554 409-744-8962
Helena Aucoin, prin. Fax 744-1905
Parker ES 600/K-5
6802 Jones Dr 77551 409-744-5257
Melvin Bouldin, prin. Fax 744-8312
Rosenberg ES 500/PK-5
721 10th St 77550 409-765-5731
Fax 765-8952
Scott ES 600/PK-5
4116 Avenue N 1/2 77550 409-765-7633
Felicia Garrett, prin. Fax 763-0704
Weis MS 700/6-8
7100 Stewart Rd 77551 409-740-5100
Canzetta Hollis, prin. Fax 744-8936
Other Schools – See Port Bolivar

Galveston Catholic S 200/PK-8
2601 Ursuline St 77550 409-765-6607
Madeleine Nix, prin. Fax 765-5154
Trinity Episcopal S 200/PK-8
720 Tremont St 77550 409-765-9391
Rev. David Dearman, hdmstr. Fax 765-9491

Ganado, Jackson, Pop. 1,871
Ganado ISD 700/PK-12
PO Box 1200 77962 361-771-4200
Jeff Black, supt. Fax 771-2280
www.ganadoisd.org/
Ganado ES 400/PK-6
PO Box 1200 77962 361-771-4250
Virgil Knowlton, prin. Fax 771-2280

Garden City, Glasscock
Glasscock County ISD 300/PK-12
PO Box 9 79739 432-354-2230
Steve Long, supt. Fax 354-2503
www.gckats.net/
Glasscock County ES 200/PK-6
PO Box 9 79739 432-354-2243
Randy Gartman, prin. Fax 354-2503

Garland, Dallas, Pop. 216,346
Garland ISD 57,700/PK-12
PO Box 469026 75046 972-494-8201
Dr. Curtis Culwell, supt. Fax 485-4928
www.garlandisd.net
Abbett ES 700/K-5
730 W Muirfield Rd 75044 972-675-3000
Winston Ferrell, prin. Fax 675-3005
Austin Academy for Excellence MS 900/6-8
1125 Beverly Dr 75040 972-926-2620
Dr. Ann Poore, prin. Fax 926-2633
Beaver Technology ES 500/K-5
3232 March Ln 75042 972-494-8301
Mida Milligan, prin. Fax 494-8702
Bradfield ES 400/PK-5
3817 Bucknell Dr 75042 972-494-8303
Mary Johnston, prin. Fax 494-8729
Bullock ES 500/PK-5
3909 Edgewood Dr 75042 972-494-8308
Linda Sires, prin. Fax 494-8704
Bussey MS 900/6-8
1204 Travis St 75040 972-494-8391
Harry Farley, prin. Fax 494-8971
Caldwell ES 500/PK-5
3400 Saturn Rd 75041 972-926-2500
Kathy Markham, prin. Fax 926-2505
Carver ES 400/PK-5
2200 Wynn Joyce Rd 75043 972-487-4415
Jennifer Porter, prin.
Centerville ES 300/PK-5
600 E Keen Dr 75041 972-926-2510
Ramona Aguilar, prin. Fax 926-2515
Cisneros Preschool 700/PK-PK
2826 S 5th St 75041 972-271-7160
Celia Nejera, prin. Fax 271-7165
Classical Center at Brandenburg MS 1,100/6-8
626 Nickens Rd 75043 972-926-2630
Carra King, prin. Fax 926-2633
Classical Center at Vial ES 600/PK-5
126 Creekview Dr 75043 972-240-3710
Wendy Eldredge, prin. Fax 240-3711
Club Hill ES 600/K-5
1330 Colonel Dr 75043 972-926-2520
James Love, prin. Fax 926-2526
Cooper ES 600/K-5
1200 Kingsbridge Dr 75040 972-675-3010
Darlene Cravens, prin. Fax 675-3015
Couch ES 800/PK-5
4349 Waterhouse Blvd 75043 972-240-1801
Susanne Hill, prin. Fax 240-9276
Daugherty ES 400/PK-5
500 W Miller Rd 75041 972-926-2530
Deborah Henson, prin. Fax 926-2535
Davis ES 600/PK-5
1621 McCallum Dr 75042 972-494-8205
Kenda Willingham, prin. Fax 494-8707
Ethridge ES 700/K-5
2301 Sam Houston Dr 75044 972-675-3020
Patricia Opon, prin. Fax 675-3025
Freeman ES 400/PK-5
1220 W Walnut St 75040 972-494-8371
Dr. Rebecca Orona, prin. Fax 494-8835
Golden Meadows ES 600/PK-5
1726 Travis St 75042 972-494-8373
Barbara McCain, prin. Fax 494-8709
Handley ES 600/K-5
3725 Broadway Blvd 75043 972-926-2540
Loyed Jones, prin. Fax 926-2545
Heather Glen ES 600/K-5
5119 Heather Glen Dr 75043 972-270-2881
John Drummond, prin. Fax 681-0078
Hickman ES 700/PK-5
3114 Pinewood Dr 75044 972-675-3150
Chris Grey, prin. Fax 675-3155
Hillside Academy for Excellence 400/K-5
2014 Dairy Rd 75041 972-926-2550
Wanda Marks, prin. Fax 926-2555
Houston MS 700/6-8
2232 Sussex Dr 75041 972-926-2640
Don Hernandez, prin. Fax 926-2647
Hudson MS 1,200/6-8
4405 Hudson Park 75048 972-675-3070
Don Hernandez, prin. Fax 675-3077
Jackson Tech Center for Math & Science 1,100/6-8
1310 Bobbie Ln 75042 972-494-8362
David Dunphy, prin. Fax 494-8802
Kimberlin Academy for Excellence 500/K-5
1520 Cumberland Dr 75040 972-926-2560
Fred Dillard, prin. Fax 926-2565
Lister ES 700/K-5
3131 Mars Dr 75040 972-675-3030
Deborah Wilkerson, prin. Fax 675-3036
Luna ES 500/K-5
1050 Lochness Ln 75044 972-675-3040
James Howard, prin. Fax 675-3045
Lyles MS 1,000/6-8
4655 S Country Club Rd 75043 972-240-3720
Nikki Hunter, prin. Fax 240-3723
Montclair ES 600/PK-5
5200 Marketplace Dr 75043 972-279-4041
Grayson Toperzer, prin. Fax 681-0565
Northlake ES 700/PK-5
1626 Bosque Dr 75040 972-494-8359
Dr. Kathy Metzinger, prin. Fax 494-8717
O'Banion MS 1,000/6-8
700 Birchwood Dr 75043 972-279-6103
John Tucci, prin. Fax 613-9532
Park Crest ES 500/K-5
2232 Parkcrest Dr 75041 972-926-2571
Don Drummond, prin. Fax 926-2575
Parsons Preschool 600/PK-PK
2202 Richoak Dr 75044 972-675-8065
Dr. Bonnie Barrett, prin. Fax 675-8061
Roach ES 400/PK-5
1811 Mayfield Ave 75041 972-926-2580
Jeanette O'Neal, prin. Fax 926-2585
Sellers MS 800/6-8
1009 Mars Dr 75040 972-494-8337
William Woods, prin. Fax 494-8607
Sewell ES 700/PK-5
4400 Hudson Park 75048 972-675-3050
Susan Craig, prin. Fax 675-3055
Shorehaven ES 400/PK-5
600 Shorehaven Dr 75040 972-494-8346
Dr. Patricia Tremmel, prin. Fax 494-8720
Shugart ES 700/K-5
4726 Rosehill Rd 75043 972-240-3700
Kelly Williams, prin. Fax 240-3701
Southgate ES 500/K-5
1115 Mayfield Ave 75041 972-926-2590
Clyde Schilling, prin. Fax 926-2595
Spring Creek ES 600/K-5
1510 Spring Creek Dr 75040 972-675-3060
Sue Sheridan, prin. Fax 675-3065
Toler ES 600/K-5
3520 Guthrie Rd 75043 972-226-3922
Patricia Tatum, prin. Fax 226-0262
Walnut Glen Academy For Excellence 500/K-5
3101 Edgewood Dr 75042 972-494-8330
Sylvia McCloskey, prin. Fax 494-8725
Watson Technology Ctr for Math & Science 600/K-5
2601 Dairy Rd 75041 972-926-2600
Jenny Roberson, prin. Fax 926-2606
Weaver ES 500/PK-5
805 Pleasant Valley Rd 75040 972-494-8311
Mary Garcia, prin. Fax 494-8721
Webb MS 1,200/6-8
1610 Spring Creek Dr 75040 972-675-3080
Jim Lewis, prin. Fax 675-3089
Williams ES 300/K-5
1821 Oldgate Ln 75042 972-926-2610
Ellen Mooney, prin. Fax 926-2615
Other Schools – See Rowlett, Sachse

Mesquite ISD
Supt. — See Mesquite
Price ES 500/K-6
630 Stroud Ln 75043 972-290-4100
Larry Sanford, prin. Fax 290-4110

Richardson ISD
Supt. — See Richardson
Big Springs ES 500/K-6
3301 W Campbell Rd 75044 469-593-8100
Denise May, prin. Fax 593-8114
Henry ES 400/PK-6
4100 Tynes Dr 75042 469-593-8200
Carol Mixon, prin. Fax 593-8221

Firewheel Christian Academy 200/PK-8
5500 Lavon Dr 75040 972-495-0851
Michelle Chapman, prin. Fax 495-3927
Garland Christian Academy 400/K-12
1516 Lavon Dr 75040 972-487-0043
Linda Glassel, admin. Fax 276-4079
Good Shepherd S 200/PK-8
214 S Garland Ave 75040 972-272-6533
Gail Richardson-Bassett, prin. Fax 272-0512
Mount Hebron Christian Academy 100/PK-4
901 Dairy Rd 75040 972-272-8095
Carolyn Primm, dir. Fax 494-2094
Quanah's Academy 50/PK-4
5840 N Garland Ave 75044 972-496-6777
Cheryl Robinson, admin. Fax 496-6777

Garrison, Nacogdoches, Pop. 846
Garrison ISD 700/PK-12
459 N US Highway 59 75946 936-347-7000
Arnie Kelley, supt. Fax 347-2529
www.garrisonisd.com

Garrison ES 300/PK-5
459 N US Highway 59 75946 936-347-7010
Lisa McKnight, prin. Fax 347-7004
Garrison MS 100/6-8
459 N US Highway 59 75946 936-347-7020
Allan Metcalf, prin. Fax 347-7004

Garwood, Colorado
Rice Consolidated ISD
Supt. — See Altair
Garwood S 200/K-8
Highway 71 S 77442 979-234-3531
John Post, prin. Fax 234-3409

Gary, Panola
Gary ISD 300/K-12
PO Box 189 75643 903-685-2291
Todd Greer, supt. Fax 685-2639
www.gary.esc7.net
Gary S 300/K-12
PO Box 189 75643 903-685-2291
Todd Greer, prin. Fax 685-2639

Gatesville, Coryell, Pop. 15,651
Gatesville ISD 2,800/PK-12
311 S Lovers Ln 76528 254-865-7251
Stewart Speer, supt. Fax 865-2279
www.gatesvilleisd.org/
Gatesville ES 400/2-3
311 S Lovers Ln 76528 254-865-7262
Pamela Bone, prin. Fax 248-0077
Gatesville IS 600/4-6
311 S Lovers Ln 76528 254-865-2526
Charles Ament, prin. Fax 865-2932
Gatesville JHS 400/7-8
311 S Lovers Ln 76528 254-865-8271
Bobby Cole, prin. Fax 865-2252
Gatesville PS 500/PK-1
311 S Lovers Ln 76528 254-865-7264
Scott Harper, prin. Fax 865-2160

Gause, Milam
Gause ISD 200/PK-8
PO Box 38 77857 979-279-5891
Perry Bell, supt. Fax 279-5142
www.gauseisd.net
Gause S 200/PK-8
PO Box 38 77857 979-279-5891
Perry Bell, prin. Fax 279-5142

Georgetown, Williamson, Pop. 39,015
Georgetown ISD 9,400/PK-12
603 Lakeway Dr 78628 512-943-5000
Dr. Abbe Boring, supt. Fax 943-5004
www.georgetownisd.org
Benold MS 700/6-8
3407 Northwest Blvd 78628 512-943-5090
Leslie Michalik, prin. Fax 943-5099
Carver ES 400/PK-2
1200 W 17th St 78626 512-943-5070
Patsy Reyna-Henry, prin. Fax 943-5079
Cooper ES 500/K-5
1921 NE Inner Loop 78626 512-943-5060
Beth Foss, prin. Fax 943-5069
Eagle Wings Child Development Center PK-PK
2200 N Austin Ave 78626 512-943-5123
Ashley Tenney, dir.
Forbes MS 600/6-8
1911 NE Inner Loop 78626 512-943-5150
Leonard Rhoads, prin. Fax 943-5159
Ford ES 500/PK-5
210 Woodlake Dr, 512-943-5180
Jennifer Mauldin, prin. Fax 943-5189
Frost ES 500/PK-2
711 Lakeway Dr 78628 512-943-5020
Annette Vierra, prin. Fax 943-5028
McCoy ES 500/3-5
1313 Williams Dr 78628 512-943-5030
Mary Norris, prin. Fax 943-5039
Pickett ES 400/3-5
1100 Thousand Oaks Blvd 78628 512-943-5050
Laurie McIntyre, prin. Fax 943-5059
Purl ES 700/PK-2
1700 Laurel St 78626 512-943-5080
Brian Dawson, prin. Fax 943-5089
Tippit MS 800/6-8
1601 Leander Rd 78628 512-943-5040
Carlos Cantu, prin. Fax 943-5049
Village ES 400/K-5
400 Village Commons Blvd, 512-943-5140
Alma Guzman, prin. Fax 943-5149
Williams ES 500/3-5
507 E University Ave 78626 512-943-5160
Cheryl Lang, prin. Fax 943-5169

Leander ISD
Supt. — See Leander
Parkside ES PK-5
301 Garner Park Dr 78628 512-570-7100
Sharon Hejl, prin. Fax 570-7105

Community Montessori S 100/PK-6
500 Pleasant Valley Dr 78626 512-863-7920
Rebecca Lowe, dir. Fax 819-9617
Covenant Christian Academy 100/PK-12
1351 FM 1460 78626 512-863-6946
Rev. William Wright M.Ed., admin. Fax 863-4756
Grace Academy of Georgetown 100/K-12
PO Box 5005 78627 512-864-9500
Dr. Tim Deibler, hdmstr. Fax 868-5429
St. Helen Catholic S 200/PK-8
2700 E University Ave 78626 512-868-0744
Sr. Mary Jean Olsovsky, prin. Fax 863-8558
Zion Lutheran S 200/PK-8
6101 FM 1105 78626 512-863-5345
Howard Voelker, prin. Fax 869-5659

George West, Live Oak, Pop. 2,342
George West ISD 1,200/PK-12
913 Houston St 78022 361-449-1914
Ty Sparks, supt. Fax 449-1426
www.gwisd.esc2.net/
George West ES 300/4-6
910 Houston St 78022 361-449-1914
Tommy Williams, prin. Fax 449-1426
George West JHS 200/7-8
900 Houston St 78022 361-449-1914
Heather Lee, prin. Fax 449-3909
George West PS 300/PK-3
405 Travis St 78022 361-449-1914
Pat James, prin. Fax 449-8921

Geronimo, Guadalupe
Navarro ISD
Supt. — See Seguin
Navarro JHS 300/7-8
PO Box 10 78115 830-401-5550
Luke Morales, prin. Fax 379-3135

Giddings, Lee, Pop. 5,442
Giddings ISD 1,900/PK-12
PO Box 389 78942 979-542-2854
Michael Kuhrt, supt. Fax 542-9264
www.giddings.txed.net
Giddings ES 600/PK-3
PO Box 389 78942 979-542-2886
Charlotte Penn, prin. Fax 542-1153
Giddings IS 400/4-6
PO Box 389 78942 979-542-4403
Chris Gersch, prin. Fax 542-4327
Giddings MS 300/7-8
PO Box 389 78942 979-542-2057
Shane Holman, prin. Fax 542-3941

Immanual Lutheran S 200/K-8
382 N Grimes St 78942 979-542-3319
Daniel Schaefer, prin. Fax 542-9084
St. Paul Lutheran S 100/PK-8
1578 County Road 211 78942 979-366-2218
David Birnbaum, prin. Fax 366-2200

Gilmer, Upshur, Pop. 5,141
Gilmer ISD 2,400/PK-12
500 S Trinity St 75644 903-841-7400
Rick Albritton, supt. Fax 843-5279
www.gilmerisd.org
Bruce JHS 300/7-8
111 Bruce St 75645 903-841-7500
Dawn Harris, prin. Fax 843-6108
Gilmer ES 1,000/PK-4
1625 US Highway 271 N 75644 903-841-7700
Connie Isabell, prin. Fax 843-4754
Gilmer IS 300/5-6
1623 US Highway 271 N 75644 903-841-7800
Hoby Holder, prin. Fax 797-6346

Union Hill ISD 300/PK-12
2197 FM 2088 75644 903-762-2140
Sharon Richardson, supt. Fax 762-6845
www.uhisd.com/
Richardson ES 100/PK-5
2197 FM 2088 75644 903-762-2139
Brad Watson, prin. Fax 762-6845

Gladewater, Gregg, Pop. 6,295
Gladewater ISD 2,200/PK-12
500 W Quitman Ave 75647 903-845-6991
Mike Morrison, supt. Fax 845-6994
www.gladewaterisd.com
Broadway ES 300/2-3
200 Broadway Ave 75647 903-845-6971
Darren Richardson, prin. Fax 845-2229
Gay Avenue PS 400/PK-1
100 W Gay Ave 75647 903-845-2254
Mickey Bryce, prin. Fax 845-2555
Gladewater MS 500/6-8
700 Melba Ave 75647 903-845-2243
James Griffin, prin. Fax 844-1738
Weldon IS 300/4-5
314 Saunders St 75647 903-845-6921
Quentin Woods, prin. Fax 845-6923

Sabine ISD 1,300/PK-12
5424 FM 1252 W 75647 903-984-8564
Stacey Bryce, supt. Fax 984-6108
www.sabine.esc7.net
Sabine ES 600/PK-5
5219 Old Highway 135 N 75647 903-984-5320
Teri Bass, prin. Fax 984-4101
Sabine MS 300/6-8
5424 FM 1252 W 75647 903-984-4767
Durwin Cooley, prin. Fax 984-8823

Union Grove ISD 600/PK-12
PO Box 1447 75647 903-845-5509
Brian Gray, supt. Fax 845-6178
www.uniongroveisd.org
Union Grove ES 400/PK-5
PO Box 1447 75647 903-845-3481
Craig Attaway, prin. Fax 845-6270

Glenn Heights, Dallas, Pop. 9,324
De Soto ISD
Supt. — See De Soto
McCowan MS 800/6-8
1500 Majestic Meadows Dr 75154 972-274-8090
Sissy Lowe, prin. Fax 274-8099

Red Oak ISD
Supt. — See Red Oak
Red Oak IS 800/5-6
401 E Ovilla Rd 75154 972-617-2685
Cristi Watts, prin. Fax 617-4388
Shields ES 500/K-4
223 W Ovilla Rd 75154 972-223-1499
Tina North, prin. Fax 230-0495

Community Christian Academy 50/K-12
1931 S Hampton Rd 75154 972-274-0015
Dr. Nancie Rowe, admin. Fax 274-0078

Glen Rose, Somervell, Pop. 2,567
Glen Rose ISD 1,700/PK-12
PO Box 2129 76043 254-898-3900
Wayne Rotan, supt. Fax 897-3651
www.grisd.net
Glen Rose ES 400/PK-2
PO Box 2129 76043 254-898-3500
Jill Power, prin. Fax 897-3086
Glen Rose IS 400/3-5
PO Box 2129 76043 254-898-3600
Susan McCarty, prin. Fax 897-9707
Glen Rose JHS 400/6-8
PO Box 2129 76043 254-898-3700
Shirley Craft, prin. Fax 897-4059

Godley, Johnson, Pop. 992
Godley ISD 1,500/PK-12
512 W Links Dr 76044 817-389-2536
Paul Smithson, supt. Fax 389-2543
www.godleyisd.net/
Godley ES 400/PK-2
604 N Pearson St 76044 817-389-3838
Toni O'Dowd, prin. Fax 389-4404
Godley IS 300/3-5
309 N Pearson St 76044 817-389-2383
Melinda Reynolds, prin. Fax 389-2394
Godley MS 400/6-8
409 N Pearson St 76044 817-389-2121
David Williams, prin. Fax 389-4357

Goldthwaite, Mills, Pop. 1,824
Goldthwaite ISD 600/PK-12
PO Box 608 76844 325-648-3531
Vincent Gilbert, supt. Fax 648-2456
www.centex-edu.net/goldthwaiteisd
Goldthwaite ES 300/PK-5
PO Box 608 76844 325-648-3055
Phyllis Morris, prin. Fax 648-3528
Goldthwaite MS 100/6-8
PO Box 608 76844 325-648-3630
Brad Jones, prin. Fax 648-3571

Goliad, Goliad, Pop. 2,006
Goliad ISD 1,600/PK-12
PO Box 830 77963 361-645-3259
Sam Atwood, supt. Fax 645-3614
www.goliadisd.org
Goliad ES 400/PK-3
PO Box 830 77963 361-645-3206
Virginia McDaniel, prin. Fax 645-2578
Goliad IS 500/4-6
PO Box 830 77963 361-645-3206
De Helmer, prin. Fax 645-2578
Goliad MS 200/7-8
PO Box 830 77963 361-645-3146
Mary Tippin, prin. Fax 645-8040

Gonzales, Gonzales, Pop. 7,514
Gonzales ISD 2,500/PK-12
PO Box 157 78629 830-672-9551
Victor Salazar, supt. Fax 672-7159
www.gonzales.txed.net
East Avenue PS 500/PK-1
1615 Saint Louis St 78629 830-672-2826
Christi Leonhardt, prin. Fax 672-6161
Gonzales ES 500/2-4
1600 Saint Andrew St 78629 830-672-1467
Gwen Hodges, prin. Fax 672-5758
Gonzales JHS 400/7-8
426 N College St 78629 830-672-8641
Willie Black, prin. Fax 672-6466
North Avenue IS 400/5-6
1023 N Saint Joseph St 78629 830-672-9557
Wanda Fryer, prin. Fax 672-4350

Goodrich, Polk, Pop. 276
Goodrich ISD 300/PK-12
PO Box 789 77335 936-365-1112
Guylene Robertson, supt. Fax 365-3518
www.goodrichisd.net
Goodrich ES 100/PK-5
PO Box 789 77335 936-365-1131
Dr. Kathryn Washington, prin. Fax 365-2375
Goodrich MS, PO Box 789 77335 100/6-8
Dr. Kathryn Washington, prin. 936-365-1112

Gordon, Palo Pinto, Pop. 465
Gordon ISD 200/K-12
PO Box 47 76453 254-693-5582
Jon Hartgraves, supt. Fax 693-5503
gordon.onlineisd.com
Gordon S 200/K-12
PO Box 47 76453 254-693-5342
David Low, prin. Fax 693-5503

Goree, Knox, Pop. 288
Munday Consolidated ISD
Supt. — See Munday
Munday JHS 100/7-8
PO Box 156 76363 940-422-5233
Kristi Bufkin, prin. Fax 422-4429

Gorman, Eastland, Pop. 1,258
Gorman ISD 400/PK-12
PO Box 8 76454 254-734-3171
David Perry, supt. Fax 734-3393
www.gorman.esc14.net/
Maxfield ES 200/PK-6
PO Box 8 76454 254-734-2617
Mary Reeves, prin. Fax 734-3445

Graford, Palo Pinto, Pop. 602
Graford ISD 300/PK-12
400 W Division Ave 76449 940-664-3101
Chance Welch, supt. Fax 664-2123
www.grafordisd.net

Graford ES | 200/PK-6
400 W Division Ave 76449 | 940-664-5821
Angela Myrick, prin. | Fax 664-2765

Graham, Young, Pop. 8,715
Graham ISD | 2,400/PK-12
400 3rd St 76450 | 940-549-0595
Beau Rees, supt. | Fax 549-8656
www.grahamisd.com
Crestview ES | 500/1-3
1317 Old Jacksboro Rd 76450 | 940-549-6023
Clay Wright, prin. | Fax 549-6025
Graham JHS | 600/6-8
1000 2nd St 76450 | 940-549-2002
Robert Loomis, prin. | Fax 549-6991
Pioneer K | 300/PK-K
1425 1st St 76450 | 940-549-2442
Greg Melton, prin. | Fax 549-2460
Woodland ES | 300/4-5
1219 Cliff Dr 76450 | 940-549-4090
Joe Gordy, prin. | Fax 549-4093

Open Door Christian S | 100/PK-8
735 Oak St 76450 | 940-549-2339
Linda Sims, prin. | Fax 549-6436

Granbury, Hood, Pop. 7,360
Granbury ISD | 6,700/PK-12
600 W Pearl St 76048 | 817-408-4000
Ron Mayfield, supt. | Fax 408-4014
www.granburyisd.org
Acton ES | 700/PK-5
3200 Acton School Rd 76049 | 817-408-4200
Ralph Purget, prin. | Fax 408-4299
Acton MS | 800/6-8
1300 James Rd 76049 | 817-408-4800
Jimmy Dawson, prin. | Fax 408-4849
Baccus ES | 500/PK-5
901 Loop 567 76048 | 817-408-4300
Beverly Huffman, prin. | Fax 408-4399
Brawner IS | 400/3-5
1520 S Meadows Dr 76048 | 817-408-4950
Stacie Brown, prin. | Fax 408-4999
Granbury MS | 800/6-8
2000 Crossland Rd 76048 | 817-408-4850
Diane Fullerton, prin. | Fax 408-4899
Mambrino ES | 600/PK-5
3835 Mambrino Hwy 76048 | 817-408-4900
Rebecca Johnson, prin. | Fax 408-4949
Oak Woods IS | 400/PK-5
311 Davis Rd 76049 | 817-408-4750
Donnie Cody, prin. | Fax 408-4799
Roberson ES | 500/PK-2
1500 Misty Meadow Dr 76048 | 817-408-4500
Kellie Lambert, prin. | Fax 408-4599

Cornerstone Christian Academy | 100/PK-12
603 Meander Rd 76049 | 817-573-6485
Ellie Kotton, admin. | Fax 573-7604
Happy Hill Farm Academy | 100/K-12
3846 N Highway 144 76048 | 254-897-4822
Dru Pruitt, prin. | Fax 897-7650

Grandfalls, Ward, Pop. 371
Grandfalls-Royalty ISD | 100/PK-12
PO Box 10 79742 | 432-547-2266
Robert Westbrook, supt. | Fax 547-2960
www.grisd.com/
Grandfalls-Royalty S | 100/PK-12
PO Box 10 79742 | 432-547-2266
Tammie White, prin. | Fax 547-2960

Grand Prairie, Dallas, Pop. 144,337
Arlington ISD
Supt. — See Arlington
Crouch ES | 900/PK-6
2810 Prairie Hill Dr 75051 | 682-867-0200
Aaron Perales, prin. | Fax 595-0205
Farrell ES | 800/PK-6
3410 Paladium Dr 75052 | 682-867-0300
Jeanne Pakele, prin. | Fax 595-0309
Larson ES | 700/PK-6
2620 E Avenue K 75050 | 682-867-0000
Richard Longgrear, prin. | Fax 595-0005
Remynse ES | 600/PK-6
2720 Fall Dr 75052 | 682-867-0500
Madonna Kennedy, prin. | Fax 595-0505
Starrett ES | 800/PK-6
2675 Fairmont Dr 75052 | 682-867-0400
John Wofford, prin. | Fax 595-0405
West ES | 800/K-6
2911 Kingswood Blvd 75052 | 682-867-0100
Yleen George, prin. | Fax 595-0105

Grand Prairie ISD | 24,700/PK-12
PO Box 531170 75053 | 972-264-6141
Dr. Susan Simpson, supt. | Fax 237-5440
www.gpisd.org
Adams MS | 800/6-8
833 W Tarrant Rd 75050 | 972-262-1934
MeShelley White, prin. | Fax 522-3099
Arnold MS | 800/6-8
1204 E Marshall Dr 75051 | 972-642-5137
Raymond Edwards, prin. | Fax 343-7499
Austin ES | 400/PK-5
815 NW 7th St 75050 | 972-262-4615
Tanya Gilliam, prin. | Fax 343-4699
Bonham ES | 600/PK-5
1301 E Coral Way 75051 | 972-262-4255
Mark Edens, prin. | Fax 522-3199
Bowie ES | 500/PK-5
425 Alice Dr 75051 | 972-262-7348
Michelle Ailara, prin. | Fax 264-6219
Bush ES | 500/PK-5
511 E Springdale Ln 75052 | 972-237-1628
Pat Blanchard, prin. | Fax 237-1059
Crockett ES | 600/PK-5
1340 Skyline Rd 75051 | 972-262-5353
Suzy Meyer, prin. | Fax 343-6299

Daniels Elementary Academy | 500/K-5
801 SW 19th St 75051 | 972-264-7803
Sterlin McGruder, prin. | Fax 343-4574
Dickinson ES | 700/K-5
1902 Palmer Trl 75052 | 972-641-1664
Tim Harkrider, prin. | Fax 641-8601
Eisenhower ES | 400/K-5
2102 N Carrier Pkwy 75050 | 972-262-3717
Emily Brinkley, prin. | Fax 264-9473
Fannin ES | 400/K-5
301 NE 28th St 75050 | 972-262-8668
Donnie Bartlett, prin. | Fax 343-4799
Garcia ES | 500/K-5
2444 Graham St 75050 | 972-237-0001
Olga Silva, prin. | Fax 237-9660
Garner ES | 500/K-5
145 W Polo Rd 75052 | 972-262-5000
Vikki Wiggins, prin. | Fax 264-9476
Hill ES | 600/PK-5
4213 S Robinson Rd 75052 | 972-264-0802
Traci Davis, prin. | Fax 264-9475
Houston ES | 600/PK-5
1502 College St 75050 | 972-262-8629
Christy Hanson, prin. | Fax 642-9638
Jackson MS | 1,000/6-8
3504 Corn Valley Rd 75052 | 972-264-2704
Michael Brinkley, prin. | Fax 343-7599
Johnson ES | 500/PK-5
650 Stonewall Dr 75052 | 972-262-1066
Tonia Walker, prin. | Fax 642-8298
Kennedy MS | 900/6-8
2205 SE 4th St 75051 | 972-264-8651
John Walsh, prin. | Fax 522-3699
Lee MS | 800/6-8
401 E Grand Prairie Rd 75051 | 972-262-6785
Donna Grant, prin. | Fax 343-6099
Marshall ES | 400/K-5
1160 W Warrior Trl 75052 | 972-522-7200
Whitney Carlisle, prin. | Fax 522-7299
Milam ES | 400/K-5
2030 Proctor Dr 75051 | 972-262-7131
Lisa Molinar, prin. | Fax 264-9492
Moore ES | 600/PK-5
3150 Waterwood Dr 75052 | 972-660-2261
Angela Lesley, prin. | Fax 343-4899
Moseley ES | 500/PK-5
1851 W Camp Wisdom Rd 75052 | 972-522-2800
Vanessa Alba, prin. | Fax 522-2899
Powell ES | 600/PK-5
5009 S Carrier Pkwy 75052 | 972-642-3961
Thelma Jones, prin. | Fax 642-4049
Rayburn ES | 500/PK-5
2800 Reforma Dr 75052 | 972-264-8900
Debbie Austin, prin. | Fax 264-9493
Reagan MS | 700/6-8
4616 Bardin Rd 75052 | 972-522-7300
Justin Marchel, prin. | Fax 522-7399
Seguin ES | 600/K-5
1450 SE 4th St 75051 | 972-522-7100
Susanna Ramirez, prin. | Fax 522-7199
Travis ES | 500/PK-5
525 NE 15th St 75050 | 972-262-2990
Ann Potucek, prin. | Fax 343-6198
Truman MS | 700/6-8
1501 Coffeyville Trl 75052 | 972-641-7676
Charles Lester, prin. | Fax 641-8666
Whitt ES | 600/PK-5
3320 S Edelweiss Dr 75052 | 972-264-5024
Alisha Crumley, prin. | Fax 343-4999
Zavala ES | 500/K-5
3501 Mark Dr 75052 | 972-642-0448
Mary Smith, prin. | Fax 264-9495

Mansfield ISD
Supt. — See Mansfield
Cabaniss ES | PK-4
6080 Mirabella Blvd 75052 | 972-299-6480
Gema Padgett, prin. | Fax 472-3030
Daulton ES | 500/K-4
2607 N Grand Peninsula Dr 75054 | 817-299-6640
Erwann Wilson, prin. | Fax 453-6570
Spencer ES | 300/K-4
3140 S Camino Lagos 75054 | 817-299-6680
Tammy Rountree, prin. | Fax 453-6580

Immaculate Conception S | 100/PK-8
400 NE 17th St 75050 | 972-264-8777
Linda Santos, prin. | Fax 264-7742

Grand Saline, Van Zandt, Pop. 3,228
Grand Saline ISD | 1,100/PK-12
400 Stadium Dr 75140 | 903-962-7546
Mark Keahey, supt. | Fax 962-7464
www.gsisd.esc7.net
Grand Saline ES | 300/PK-2
900 N Oleander St 75140 | 903-962-7526
Brandi Dyer, prin. | Fax 962-7438
Grand Saline IS | 300/3-5
200 Stadium Dr 75140 | 903-962-5515
Brenda English, prin. | Fax 962-3783
Grand Saline MS | 200/6-8
400 Stadium Dr 75140 | 903-962-7537
Brad Swain, prin. | Fax 962-7474

Grandview, Johnson, Pop. 1,567
Grandview ISD | 1,100/PK-12
PO Box 310 76050 | 817-866-2450
Keith Scharnhorst, supt. | Fax 866-3351
www.gvisd.org
Grandview ES | 300/PK-2
PO Box 310 76050 | 817-866-2473
Kristi Griffith, prin. | Fax 866-4882
Grandview IS | 200/3-5
PO Box 310 76050 | 817-866-2701
Kristi Griffith, prin. | Fax 866-2452
Grandview JHS | 300/6-8
PO Box 310 76050 | 817-866-2492
Jeff Hudson, prin. | Fax 866-3912

Granger, Williamson, Pop. 1,331
Granger ISD | 500/PK-12
PO Box 578 76530 | 512-859-2613
Stephen White, supt. | Fax 859-2446
www.grangerisd.net
Granger S | 500/PK-12
PO Box 578 76530 | 512-859-2173
Chris Buerger, prin. | Fax 859-2446

SS. Cyril & Methodius S | 100/PK-6
PO Box 248 76530 | 512-859-2927
Dr. Norlene Kunkel, prin. | Fax 859-2649

Grapeland, Houston, Pop. 1,421
Grapeland ISD | 500/PK-12
PO Box 249 75844 | 936-687-4619
E. D. Sumrall, supt. | Fax 687-4624
www.grapelandisd.net/
Grapeland ES | 300/PK-6
PO Box 249 75844 | 936-687-2317
Jim Wise, prin. | Fax 687-2341
Grapeland JHS | 100/7-8
PO Box 249 75844 | 936-687-2351
Fax 687-9739

Grapevine, Tarrant, Pop. 47,460
Carroll ISD | 7,700/PK-12
3051 Dove Rd 76051 | 817-949-8282
Dr. David Faltys, supt. | Fax 949-8228
www.southlakecarroll.edu
Other Schools – See Southlake

Grapevine-Colleyville ISD | 13,900/PK-12
3051 Ira E Woods Ave 76051 | 817-251-5501
Dr. Kay Waggoner, supt. | Fax 481-2907
www.gcisd-k12.org
Cannon ES | 500/PK-5
1300 W College St 76051 | 817-251-5680
Tona Taylor, prin. | Fax 421-0982
Cross Timbers MS | 900/6-8
2301 Pool Rd 76051 | 817-251-5320
Linda Tidmore, prin. | Fax 424-4296
Dove ES | 500/K-5
1932 Dove Rd 76051 | 817-251-5700
Becky Lamb, prin. | Fax 481-6730
Grapevine ES | 500/K-5
1801 Hall Johnson Rd 76051 | 817-251-5735
Jim Calvin, prin. | Fax 481-6451
Grapevine MS | 700/6-8
301 Pony Pkwy 76051 | 817-251-5660
Tim Hughes, prin. | Fax 424-1626
Heritage ES | 500/K-5
4500 Heritage Ave 76051 | 817-358-4820
Stacey Voigt, prin. | Fax 540-2892
Silver Lake ES | 500/K-5
1301 N Dooley St 76051 | 817-251-5750
Lisa Dunn, prin. | Fax 329-4536
Timberline ES | 700/PK-5
3220 Timberline Dr 76051 | 817-251-5770
Cody Spielmann, prin. | Fax 329-5666
Other Schools – See Colleyville, Euless

Faith Christian S | 600/K-12
730 E Worth St 76051 | 817-442-9144
Dr. Ed Smith, pres. | Fax 442-9904
Holy Trinity Catholic S | 400/PK-8
3750 William D Tate Ave 76051 | 817-421-8000
Sr. Bernice Knapek, prin. | Fax 421-4468

Greenville, Hunt, Pop. 25,637
Bland ISD
Supt. — See Merit
Bland ES | 200/PK-4
4320 Highway 380 75401 | 903-527-3211
Janis Hodo, prin. | Fax 527-3214

Greenville ISD | 4,800/PK-12
PO Box 1022 75403 | 903-457-2500
Donald Jefferies, supt. | Fax 457-2504
www.greenvilleisd.com
Bowie ES | 400/K-5
6005 Stonewall St 75402 | 903-457-2676
Carol Petty, prin. | Fax 457-0725
Carver ES | 500/K-5
2110 College St 75401 | 903-457-0777
Isela Montes, prin. | Fax 457-0786
Crockett ES | 200/K-5
1316 Wolfe City Dr 75401 | 903-457-2684
Amy Pool, prin. | Fax 457-0722
Greenville 6th Grade Center | 400/6-6
3201 Stanford St 75401 | 903-457-2660
David Gish, prin. | Fax 457-2533
Greenville MS | 700/7-8
3611 Texas St 75401 | 903-457-2620
Mike Clyde, prin. | Fax 457-2628
Lamar ES | 600/K-5
6321 Jack Finney Blvd 75402 | 903-457-0765
James Evans, prin. | Fax 457-0774
Travis ES | 300/K-5
3005 Division St 75401 | 903-457-2696
Judy Evans, prin. | Fax 457-0741
Waters ECC | 300/PK-PK
2504 Carver St 75401 | 903-457-2680
Ralph Sanders, prin. | Fax 457-0745

Greenville Christian S | 200/PK-12
8420 Jack Finney Blvd 75402 | 903-454-1111
Julie Robinson, hdmstr. | Fax 455-8470

Gregory, San Patricio, Pop. 2,264
Gregory-Portland ISD
Supt. — See Portland
Austin ES | 300/PK-4
308 N Gregory Ave 78359 | 361-777-4252
Suzy Hartman, prin. | Fax 777-4261

Groesbeck, Limestone, Pop. 4,353
Groesbeck ISD 1,600/PK-12
PO Box 559 76642 254-729-4100
Dr. Harold Ramm, supt. Fax 729-5167
www.groesbeck.k12.tx.us
Groesbeck ES 700/PK-5
801 S Ellis St 76642 254-729-4104
Lea Hardison, prin. Fax 729-2798
Groesbeck MS 400/6-8
410 Elwood Enge Dr 76642 254-729-4102
Ladena King, prin. Fax 729-8763

Groom, Carson, Pop. 587
Grandview-Hopkins ISD 50/K-6
11676 FM 293 79039 806-669-3831
William Cook, supt. Fax 669-3044
Grandview-Hopkins ES 50/K-6
11676 FM 293 79039 806-669-3831
William Cook, prin. Fax 669-3044

Groom ISD 100/K-12
PO Box 598 79039 806-248-7557
Terry Stevens, supt. Fax 248-7949
www.groomisd.net
Groom S 100/K-12
PO Box 598 79039 806-248-7474
Terry Stevens, prin. Fax 248-7949

Groves, Jefferson, Pop. 15,006
Port Neches-Groves ISD
Supt. — See Port Neches
Groves ES 300/4-5
3901 Cleveland Ave 77619 409-962-1531
Scarlett Hammersmith, prin. Fax 963-2481
Groves MS 600/6-8
5201 Wilson St 77619 409-962-0225
Ken Cummings, prin. Fax 963-1898
Preschool Center 100/PK-PK
5840 W Jefferson St 77619 409-962-8446
Dr. Stacey Arnold, prin. Fax 960-6870
Van Buren ES 300/K-3
6400 Van Buren St 77619 409-962-6511
David Guidry, prin. Fax 962-2043

Triangle Adventist S 50/PK-8
PO Box H 77619 409-963-3806

Groveton, Trinity, Pop. 1,138
Centerville ISD 200/PK-12
10327 N State Highway 94 75845 936-642-1597
Craig Quincy Davis, supt. Fax 642-2810
www.centervilleisd.net/internet/
Centerville ES 100/PK-6
10327 N State Highway 94 75845 936-642-1597
Charles Brantner, prin. Fax 642-2810

Groveton ISD 600/K-12
PO Box 728 75845 936-642-1473
Joe Driskell, supt. Fax 642-1628
www.grovetonisd.net
Groveton ES 300/K-5
PO Box 580 75845 936-642-1182
Mickey Gilbert, prin. Fax 642-3254

Grulla, Starr, Pop. 1,613
Rio Grande City ISD
Supt. — See Rio Grande City
Grulla MS 700/6-8
PO Box 338 78548 956-487-5558
Pablo Martinez, prin. Fax 487-5633

Gruver, Hansford, Pop. 1,122
Gruver ISD 400/PK-12
PO Box 650 79040 806-733-2001
David Teal, supt. Fax 733-5416
www.gruverisd.net
Gruver ES 100/PK-4
PO Box 1139 79040 806-733-2031
Debby Mayhew, prin. Fax 733-5412
Gruver JHS 100/5-8
PO Box 709 79040 806-733-2081
Micah Davis, prin. Fax 733-5523

Gun Barrel City, Henderson, Pop. 5,962
Mabank ISD
Supt. — See Mabank
Lakeview ES 400/PK-4
306 Harbor Point Rd, 903-880-1360
Kevyn Pate, prin. Fax 880-1363

Gunter, Grayson, Pop. 1,561
Gunter ISD 900/PK-12
PO Box 109 75058 903-433-4750
Kevin Worthy, supt. Fax 433-1053
www.gunterisd.org
Gunter ES 300/PK-4
PO Box 109 75058 903-433-5315
Cheyrl Cohagan, prin. Fax 433-1184
Gunter MS 200/5-8
PO Box 109 75058 903-433-1545
Pat Autry, prin. Fax 433-9306

Gustine, Comanche, Pop. 447
Gustine ISD 200/PK-12
503 W Main St 76455 325-667-7981
Ken Baugh, supt. Fax 667-7281
www.gustine.esc14.net/
Gustine S 200/PK-12
503 W Main St 76455 325-667-7303
Robert Rauch, prin. Fax 667-0203

Guthrie, King
Guthrie Common SD 100/PK-12
PO Box 70 79236 806-596-4466
Gary Harrell, supt. Fax 596-4519
www.guthriejags.com/
Guthrie S 100/PK-12
PO Box 70 79236 806-596-4466
Roddy Shipman, prin. Fax 596-4519

Hale Center, Hale, Pop. 2,180
Hale Center ISD 600/PK-12
PO Box 1210 79041 806-839-2451
Rick Teran, supt. Fax 839-2195
www.halecenter.esc17.net
Akin ES 300/PK-4
PO Box 1210 79041 806-839-2121
Jackie King, prin. Fax 839-4404
Carr MS 200/5-8
PO Box 1210 79041 806-839-2141
Christian Rabone, prin. Fax 839-4417

Hallettsville, Lavaca, Pop. 2,497
Ezzell ISD 100/K-8
20500 FM 531 77964 361-798-4448
Carl Krug, supt. Fax 798-9331
www.ezzellisd.org
Ezzell S 100/K-8
20500 FM 531 77964 361-798-4448
Carl Krug, prin. Fax 798-9331

Hallettsville ISD 900/K-12
PO Box 368 77964 361-798-2242
Dr. JoAnn Bludau, supt. Fax 798-5902
www.hisdbrahmas.org
Hallettsville ES 300/K-4
200 N Ridge St 77964 361-798-2242
Trina Patek, prin. Fax 798-4349
Hallettsville JHS 200/5-8
410 S Russell St 77964 361-798-2242
Sophie Teltschik, prin. Fax 798-3573

Vysehrad ISD 100/K-8
595 County Road 182 77964 361-798-4118
Paul Darilek, supt. Fax 798-3131
www.vysehrad.k12.tx.us
Vysehrad S 100/K-8
595 County Road 182 77964 361-798-4118
Paul Darilek, prin. Fax 798-3131

Sacred Heart S 300/PK-12
313 S Texana St 77964 361-798-4251
David Smolik, prin. Fax 798-4970

Hallsville, Harrison, Pop. 2,897
Hallsville ISD 3,700/PK-12
PO Box 810 75650 903-668-5990
Greg Wright, supt. Fax 668-5990
www.hisd.com
Hallsville ES 300/2-2
PO Box 810 75650 903-668-5990
Kerri Brice, prin. Fax 668-5990
Hallsville IS 600/3-4
PO Box 810 75650 903-668-5990
Cristi Parsons, prin. Fax 668-5990
Hallsville JHS 600/7-8
PO Box 810 75650 903-668-5990
Dr. Amber Daub, prin. Fax 668-5990
Hallsville MS 600/5-6
PO Box 810 75650 903-668-5990
Brandon Jones, prin. Fax 668-5990
Hallsville PS 400/K-1
PO Box 810 75650 903-668-5990
Lawrence Coleman, prin. Fax 668-5990
Little Cats Learning Center 100/PK-PK
PO Box 810 75650 903-668-5990
Barbara Stevens, coord. Fax 668-5990

Haltom City, Tarrant, Pop. 39,875
Birdville ISD 22,500/PK-12
6125 E Belknap St 76117 817-847-5700
Stephen Waddell Ed.D., supt. Fax 838-7261
www.birdville.k12.tx.us
Academy at West Birdville 700/PK-5
3001 Layton St 76117 817-547-2500
Lindi Andrews, prin. Fax 831-5795
Birdville ES 400/PK-5
3126 Bewley St 76117 817-547-1500
Michael Sandoval, prin. Fax 831-5736
Francisco ES 400/PK-5
3701 Layton St 76117 817-547-1700
Janelle Rayfield, prin. Fax 831-5724
Haltom MS 800/6-8
5000 Hires Ln 76117 817-547-4000
Susan Taylor, prin. Fax 831-5778
North Oaks MS 500/6-8
4800 Jordan Park Dr 76117 817-547-4600
Bob Koerner, prin. Fax 581-5352
Smith ES 500/PK-5
3701 Haltom Rd 76117 817-547-1600
Scott Gregory, prin. Fax 831-5817
South Birdville ES 400/PK-5
2600 Solona St 76117 817-547-2300
Han Arthurs, prin. Fax 831-5798
Spicer ES 600/PK-5
4300 Estes Park Rd 76137 817-547-3300
Mike Dukes, prin. Fax 581-5497
Stowe ES 500/PK-5
4201 Rita Ln 76117 817-547-2400
Mike Moon, prin. Fax 581-5328
Other Schools – See Fort Worth, Hurst, North Richland Hills, Richland Hills, Watauga

Fort Worth ISD
Supt. — See Fort Worth
Howell ES 400/PK-5
1324 Kings Hwy 76117 817-814-9300
Carlos Mendoza, prin. Fax 814-9350

Hamilton, Hamilton, Pop. 2,920
Hamilton ISD 900/PK-12
PO Box 392 76531 254-386-3149
Sam Bell, supt. Fax 386-8885
www.hamilton.k12.tx.us
Hamilton MS 200/6-8
PO Box 392 76531 254-386-8168
Mona Gloff, prin. Fax 386-8885
Whitney ES 400/PK-5
PO Box 392 76531 254-386-8166
Jennifer Zschiesche, prin. Fax 386-8885

Hamlin, Jones, Pop. 2,018
Hamlin ISD 500/PK-12
PO Box 338 79520 325-576-2722
Tony Daniel, supt. Fax 576-2152
www.hamlin.esc14.net
Hamlin ES 200/PK-5
405 NW 5th St 79520 325-576-3191
Lonnie Powell, prin. Fax 576-2358
Hamlin MS 100/6-8
250 SW Avenue F 79520 325-576-2933
Laura O'Rear, prin. Fax 576-2317

Hamshire, Jefferson
Hamshire-Fannett ISD 1,800/PK-12
PO Box 223 77622 409-243-2517
Keith Elliott, supt. Fax 243-3437
www.hfisd.net/
Other Schools – See Beaumont

Happy, Swisher, Pop. 615
Happy ISD 200/K-12
PO Box 458 79042 806-558-5331
Dr. Billy Howell, supt. Fax 558-2070
www.happyisd.net
Happy ES, PO Box 458 79042 100/K-6
Doug McCause, prin. 806-558-2561

Hardin, Liberty, Pop. 797
Hardin ISD 1,300/PK-12
PO Box 330 77561 936-298-2112
Bob Parker, supt. Fax 298-9161
www.hardin.isd.esc4.net/
Hardin ES 500/PK-4
PO Box 330 77561 936-298-2114
Silas Hare, prin. Fax 298-9153
Hardin IS 200/5-6
PO Box 330 77561 936-298-2054
Dr. Michael Bearden, prin. Fax 298-3264
Hardin MS 200/7-8
PO Box 330 77561 936-298-2054
Alan Tidwell, prin. Fax 298-3264

Hargill, Hidalgo
Edinburg Consolidated ISD
Supt. — See Edinburg
Hargill ES 300/PK-5
4th and Wilson 78549 956-289-2338
Diane Willis, prin. Fax 845-6337

Harker Heights, Bell, Pop. 21,337
Killeen ISD
Supt. — See Killeen
Eastern Hills MS 800/6-8
300 Indian Trl 76548 254-336-1100
Jamie Blassingame, prin. Fax 680-6606
Harker Heights ES 700/PK-5
726 S Ann Blvd 76548 254-336-2050
Carolyn Dugger, prin. Fax 680-3592
Mountain View ES 800/PK-5
500 Mountain Lion Rd 76548 254-336-1900
Nancy Varljen, prin. Fax 680-2479
Skipcha ES 800/PK-5
515 Prospector Trl 76548 254-200-6690
Carrie Parker, prin. Fax 690-3581
Union Grove MS 50/6-8
101 E Iowa Dr 76548 254-200-6580
Robin Champagne, prin. Fax 690-5042

Harleton, Harrison
Harleton ISD 700/PK-12
PO Box 510 75651 903-777-2372
Dr. Craig Coleman, supt. Fax 777-2406
www.harletonisd.net/
Harleton ES 300/PK-5
PO Box 400 75651 903-777-4092
Wendy Newman, prin. Fax 777-3009
Harleton JHS 200/6-8
PO Box 610 75651 903-777-3010
Craig Evers, prin. Fax 777-3009

Harlingen, Cameron, Pop. 62,318
Harlingen Consolidated ISD 17,500/PK-12
407 N 77 Sunshine Strip 78550 956-430-9503
Dr. Steve Flores, supt. Fax 430-9514
www.harlingen.isd.tenet.edu
Austin ES 500/PK-5
700 E Austin Ave 78550 956-427-3060
Debra Valenzuela, prin. Fax 427-3063
Bonham ES 900/PK-5
2400 E Jefferson Ave 78550 956-427-3070
Cathy Silstorf, prin. Fax 427-3073
Bowie ES 300/PK-5
309 W Lincoln Ave 78550 956-427-3080
Susan Salinas, prin. Fax 427-3083
Coakley MS 900/6-8
1402 S 6th St 78550 956-427-3000
Kevin Brackmeyer, prin. Fax 427-3006
Crockett ES 400/PK-5
1406 W Jefferson Ave 78550 956-427-3090
Juan Garcia, prin. Fax 427-3093
Gutierrez MS 800/6-8
3205 Wilson Rd 78552 956-430-4400
Dr. Marsha Marchbanks, prin. Fax 430-4480
Houston ES 300/PK-5
301 E Taft Ave 78550 956-427-3110
Diana Rodriguez, prin. Fax 427-3114
Jefferson ES 400/PK-5
601 S J St 78550 956-427-3120
Manuel Olivo, prin. Fax 427-3127
Lamar ES 700/PK-5
1100 McLarry Rd 78550 956-427-3130
Daniel Garza, prin. Fax 427-3133
Long ES 1,000/PK-5
2601 N 7th St 78550 956-427-3140
Lori Romero, prin. Fax 427-3144
Means ES, 1201 E Loop 499 78550 PK-5
Elizabeth Maldonado, prin. 956-427-3100
Memorial MS 700/6-8
300 N 13th St 78550 956-427-3020
Alex Gonzalez, prin. Fax 427-3024

Milam ES 500/PK-5
1215 S Rangerville Rd 78552 956-427-3150
Rosa Linda Cobarrubias, prin. Fax 427-3153
Rodriguez ES 600/K-5
8402 Wilson Rd 78552 956-430-4060
Traci Gonzalez, prin. Fax 430-4065
Stuart Place ES 600/K-5
6701 W Business 83 78552 956-427-3160
Vivian Bauer, prin. Fax 427-3159
Travis ES 600/PK-5
600 E Polk St 78550 956-427-3170
Joe Rodriguez, prin. Fax 427-3173
Treasure Hills ES 700/K-5
2525 Haine Dr 78550 956-427-3180
Linda Krabill, prin. Fax 427-3187
Vela MS 800/6-8
801 S Palm Blvd 78552 956-427-3479
Dr. Alicia Noyola, prin. Fax 427-3549
Vernon MS 700/6-8
125 S 13th St 78550 956-427-3040
Gracie Gutierrez, prin. Fax 427-3046
Wilson ES 600/PK-5
16495 Dolores St 78552 956-427-3190
Doroteo Enriquez, prin. Fax 427-3197
Zavala ES 400/PK-5
1111 N B St 78550 956-427-3200
Yvonne Montemayor, prin. Fax 427-3203
Other Schools – See Combes

Calvary Christian S 400/PK-8
1815 N 7th St 78550 956-425-1882
Karen Zeissel, prin. Fax 412-0324
Destiny Christian Academy 50/K-8
2601 Bothwell Rd 78552 956-440-0659
Ronnie Rodriguez, prin. Fax 425-2012
Harlingen Adventist S 50/1-8
PO Box 532785 78553 956-428-2926
St. Alban's Episcopal S 300/PK-6
1417 E Austin Ave 78550 956-428-2326
Mary Katherine Duffy, prin. Fax 428-8457
St. Anthony S 300/PK-8
1015 E Harrison Ave 78550 956-423-2486
Esther Flores, prin. Fax 412-0084
St. Paul Lutheran S 100/PK-8
1920 E Washington Ave 78550 956-423-3926
Julie Walther, prin. Fax 423-0926

Harper, Gillespie
Harper ISD 600/PK-12
PO Box 68 78631 830-864-4044
Pari Whitten, supt. Fax 864-4060
www.harper.txed.net/
Harper ES 200/PK-5
PO Box 68 78631 830-864-4044
Jay Harper, prin. Fax 864-4748
Harper MS 100/6-8
PO Box 68 78631 830-864-4044
Chris Stevenson, prin. Fax 864-4748

Harrold, Wilbarger
Harrold ISD 100/K-12
PO Box 400 76364 940-886-2213
David Thweatt, supt. Fax 886-2215
www.harroldisd.net/
Harrold S 100/K-12
PO Box 400 76364 940-886-2213
Craig Templeton, prin. Fax 886-2215

Hart, Castro, Pop. 1,101
Hart ISD 300/PK-12
PO Box 490 79043 806-938-2143
David Rivera, supt. Fax 938-2610
www.hartisd.net/
Hart ES 200/PK-6
PO Box 490 79043 806-938-2142
Emilio Olivares, prin. Fax 938-2610

Hartley, Hartley
Hartley ISD 200/K-12
PO Box 408 79044 806-365-4458
Larry Hulsey, supt. Fax 365-4459
www.hartleytx.com/hartleyisd
Hartley S 200/K-12
PO Box 408 79044 806-365-4458
Larry Hulsey, prin. Fax 365-4459

Haskell, Haskell, Pop. 2,782
Haskell Consolidated ISD 600/PK-12
PO Box 937 79521 940-864-2602
Bill Alcorn, supt. Fax 864-8096
www.haskell.esc14.net/
Haskell ES 400/PK-6
PO Box 937 79521 940-864-2654
James Lisle, prin. Fax 864-2369
Rochester JHS 100/7-8
PO Box 937 79521 940-743-3260
Reida Penman, prin. Fax 864-8096

Paint Creek ISD 100/K-12
4485 FM 600 79521 940-864-2471
Don Ballard, supt. Fax 864-8038
www.paintcreek.esc14.net
Paint Creek S 100/K-12
4485 FM 600 79521 940-864-2471
Jim Raughton, prin. Fax 864-8038

Haslet, Tarrant, Pop. 1,449
Northwest ISD
Supt. — See Justin
Haslet ES 500/K-5
501 Schoolhouse Rd 76052 817-215-0850
Julie Nerby, prin. Fax 215-0870
Sendera Ranch ES K-5
1216 Diamond Back Ln 76052 817-698-3500
Suzie McNeese, prin.

Hawkins, Wood, Pop. 1,471
Hawkins ISD 800/PK-12
PO Box 1430 75765 903-769-2181
Dan Rose, supt. Fax 769-0505
www.hawkinsisd.org
Hawkins ES 400/PK-5
PO Box 1430 75765 903-769-0536
Letha Wuerch, prin. Fax 769-0513
Hawkins MS 200/6-8
PO Box 1430 75765 903-769-0552
David Ledkins, prin. Fax 769-0583

Hawley, Jones, Pop. 603
Hawley ISD 800/PK-12
PO Box 440 79525 325-537-2214
Glenn Coles, supt. Fax 537-2265
www.hawley.esc14.net
Hawley ES 300/PK-5
PO Box 440 79525 325-537-2721
Brian Hunt, prin. Fax 537-2265
Hawley MS 200/6-8
PO Box 440 79525 325-537-2070
Nikki Grisham, prin. Fax 537-2265

Hearne, Robertson, Pop. 4,710
Hearne ISD 1,100/PK-12
900 Wheelock St 77859 979-279-3200
David Deaver, supt. Fax 279-3631
www.hearne.k12.tx.us/
Hearne ES 600/PK-6
1210 Hackberry St 77859 979-279-3341
David Saul, prin. Fax 279-8011
Hearne JHS 100/7-8
1201B W Brown St 77859 979-279-2449
Robert Garcia, prin. Fax 279-8033

Heath, Rockwall, Pop. 6,418
Rockwall ISD
Supt. — See Rockwall
Parks-Heath ES 700/K-6
330 Laurence Dr 75032 972-772-4300
Dan Crawford, prin. Fax 772-2098

Hebbronville, Jim Hogg, Pop. 4,465
Jim Hogg County ISD 1,100/PK-12
PO Box 880 78361 361-527-3203
Pedro Lopez, supt. Fax 527-4823
www.jhcisd.net/
Hebbronville ES 600/K-5
PO Box 880 78361 361-527-3203
Sandra Perez, prin. Fax 527-2133
Hebbronville JHS 200/6-8
PO Box 880 78361 361-527-3203
Patricia Gonzalez, prin. Fax 527-5986

Hedley, Donley, Pop. 377
Hedley ISD 200/PK-12
PO Box 69 79237 806-856-5323
Bryan Hill, supt. Fax 856-5372
Hedley S 200/PK-12
PO Box 69 79237 806-856-5323
Bryan Hill, prin. Fax 856-5372

Helotes, Bexar, Pop. 6,187
Northside ISD
Supt. — See San Antonio
Beard ES 1,100/K-5
8725 Sonoma Pkwy 78023 210-397-6600
Mark Rustan, prin. Fax 695-3849
Helotes ES 600/K-5
13878 Riggs Rd 78023 210-397-3800
Rhonda Smith, prin. Fax 695-3827
Kuentz ES K-5
12303 Leslie Rd 78023 210-397-8500

Hemphill, Sabine, Pop. 1,069
Hemphill ISD 1,000/PK-12
PO Box 1950 75948 409-787-3371
Glenn Pearson, supt. Fax 787-4005
www.hemphill.esc7.net
Hemphill ES 400/PK-4
PO Box 1950 75948 409-787-3371
Susan Smith, prin. Fax 787-4005
Hemphill MS 300/5-8
PO Box 1950 75948 409-787-3371
Paula Pruitt, prin. Fax 787-4005

Hempstead, Waller, Pop. 6,546
Hempstead ISD 1,400/PK-12
PO Box 1007 77445 979-826-3304
Gene Glover, supt. Fax 826-5510
www.hempstead.isd.esc4.net
Hempstead ECC 400/PK-2
PO Box 1007 77445 979-826-2452
Joy Toney, prin. Fax 826-5564
Hempstead ES 300/3-5
PO Box 1007 77445 979-826-2452
Tonya Bronikowski, prin. Fax 826-5524
Hempstead MS 300/6-8
PO Box 1007 77445 979-826-2530
Amy Lacey, prin. Fax 826-5583

Henderson, Rusk, Pop. 11,496
Henderson ISD 2,300/PK-12
PO Box 728 75653 903-657-8511
Bobby Brown, supt. Fax 657-9271
www.hendersonisd.org/
Henderson MS 800/6-8
PO Box 728 75653 903-657-1491
Richard Cooper, prin. Fax 657-6499
Northside ES 500/4-5
PO Box 728 75653 903-657-1511
Kerrie Jennings, prin. Fax 657-5238
Wylie ES, PO Box 728 75653 1-3
Clay Freeman, prin. 903-657-8511
Wylie PS, PO Box 728 75653 PK-K
Kim Buckner, prin. 903-657-8511

Full Armor Christian Academy 200/PK-12
PO Box 2035 75653 903-655-8489
Stephen Scogin, admin. Fax 657-8267

Henrietta, Clay, Pop. 3,325
Henrietta ISD 1,000/PK-12
1801 E Crafton St 76365 940-720-7900
Jeff McClure, supt. Fax 538-7505
www.henrietta-isd.net
Henrietta ES 500/PK-5
1600 E Crafton St 76365 940-720-7910
Kendra Bennett, prin. Fax 538-7515
Henrietta JHS 200/6-8
308 E Gilbert St 76365 940-720-7920
Quana West, prin. Fax 538-7525

Midway ISD 100/PK-12
12142 State Highway 148 S 76365 940-476-2215
Hollis Adams, supt. Fax 476-2226
www.esc9.net/midway
Midway S 100/PK-12
12142 State Highway 148 S 76365 940-476-2222
Jimmie Lee, prin. Fax 476-2226

Hereford, Deaf Smith, Pop. 14,472
Hereford ISD 3,800/K-12
601 N 25 Mile Ave 79045 806-363-7600
Kelli Moulton, supt. Fax 363-7647
www.herefordisd.net
Aikman ES, 900 Avenue K 79045 400/K-3
Sandy Maldonado, prin. 806-363-7640
Bluebonnet IS, 221 16th St 79045 300/4-5
Linda Gonzalez, prin. 806-363-7650
Hereford JHS, 704 La Plata St 79045 900/6-8
Susan Perrin, prin. 806-363-7630
Northwest ES, 400 Moreman St 79045 400/K-3
David Fanning, prin. 806-363-7660
Tierra Blanca ES 300/K-3
615 Columbia Dr 79045 806-363-7680
Sharon Hodges, prin.
West Central IS 200/4-5
120 Campbell St 79045 806-363-7690
Cuca Salinas, prin.

Walcott ISD 200/PK-6
4275 Highway 214 79045 806-289-5222
Dr. Bill McLaughlin, supt. Fax 289-5371
www.walcottisd.net
Walcott ES 200/PK-6
4275 Highway 214 79045 806-289-5222
Dr. Bill McLaughlin, prin. Fax 289-5224

Nazarene Christian Academy 100/PK-6
1410 La Plata St 79045 806-364-1697
Dr. Ron Muller, dir. Fax 364-7973
St. Anthonys S 100/PK-6
120 W Park Ave 79045 806-364-1952
Ann Lueb, prin. Fax 364-0969

Hermleigh, Scurry
Hermleigh ISD 200/K-12
1026 School Ave 79526 325-863-2772
Gary Rotan, supt. Fax 863-2713
www.hermleigh.esc14.net/
Hermleigh S 200/K-12
1026 School Ave 79526 325-863-2451
Joe Bible, prin. Fax 863-2713

Hewitt, McLennan, Pop. 12,987
Midway ISD
Supt. — See Waco
Hewitt ES 600/PK-4
900 W Panther Way 76643 254-761-5750
Jason Bunting, prin. Fax 666-7540
Midway MS 1,000/7-8
800 N Hewitt Dr 76643 254-761-5680
Jennifer Allison, prin. Fax 761-5775
Spring Valley ES 600/K-4
610 W Spring Valley Rd 76643 254-761-5710
Maudie Monroe, prin. Fax 666-4654

Hico, Hamilton, Pop. 1,337
Hico ISD 700/PK-12
PO Box 218 76457 254-796-2181
Rod Townsend, supt. Fax 796-2446
www.hico-isd.net
Hico ES 300/PK-5
PO Box 218 76457 254-796-2183
Kathryn Heinrichs, prin. Fax 796-4214
Hico JHS 200/6-8
PO Box 218 76457 254-796-2182
Shelli Stegall, prin. Fax 796-9830

Hidalgo, Hidalgo, Pop. 10,889
Hidalgo ISD 3,300/PK-12
PO Box D 78557 956-843-3100
Eduardo Cancino Ph.D., supt. Fax 843-3343
www.hidalgo-isd.com/
Diaz JHS 700/6-8
PO Box D 78557 956-843-3140
Olivia Hernandez, prin. Fax 843-3198
Hidalgo ES 400/PK-5
PO Box D 78557 956-843-3150
Raquel Reyes, prin. Fax 843-7035
Hidalgo Park ES 400/PK-5
PO Box D 78557 956-781-4074
Maribel Sepulveda, prin. Fax 781-4631
Salinas ES 400/PK-5
PO Box D 78557 956-843-3351
Silverio Macias, prin. Fax 843-3357
Other Schools – See Pharr

Valley View ISD
Supt. — See Pharr
Lucas ES 500/PK-5
1300 N McColl St 78557 956-843-3036
Sylvia Ibarra, prin. Fax 843-3039
Valley View South ES 400/PK-5
900 S McColl St 78557 956-843-7742
Nancy Montemayor, prin. Fax 843-3021

Higgins, Lipscomb, Pop. 437
Higgins ISD 100/K-12
PO Box 218 79046 806-852-2171
Hope Appel, supt. Fax 852-3502
www.region16.net/higginsisd/
Higgins S 100/K-12
PO Box 218 79046 806-852-2631
Hope Appel, prin. Fax 852-3502

High Island, Galveston
High Island ISD 200/K-12
PO Box 246 77623 409-286-5317
Paula Quick, supt. Fax 286-5351
www.esc5.net/hiisd/
High Island ES 100/K-5
PO Box 246 77623 409-286-5314
Audie Tackett, prin. Fax 286-2120
High Island MS 50/6-8
PO Box 246 77623 409-286-5314
Audie Tackett, prin. Fax 286-2120

Highlands, Harris, Pop. 6,632
Goose Creek Consolidated ISD
Supt. — See Baytown
Highlands ES 900/2-5
200 E Wallisville Rd 77562 281-420-4900
Judy Duncan, prin. Fax 426-5099
Highlands JHS 700/6-8
1212 E Wallisville Rd 77562 281-420-4695
Kevin Foxworth, prin. Fax 426-4301
Hopper PS 600/PK-1
405 E Houston St 77562 281-420-4685
Karen Thomas, prin. Fax 426-5179

Highland Village, Denton, Pop. 15,105
Lewisville ISD
Supt. — See Flower Mound
Briarhill MS 1,000/6-8
2100 Briarhill Blvd 75077 469-713-5975
Chris Mattingly, prin. Fax 350-9167
Heritage ES 800/PK-5
100 Barnett Dr 75077 469-713-5985
Belinda Nikkel, prin. Fax 350-9072
Highland Village ES 400/K-5
301 Brazos Blvd 75077 469-713-5957
Sherry Wagner, prin. Fax 350-9079
McAuliffe ES 600/PK-5
2300 Briarhill Blvd 75077 469-713-5959
Jennifer Mattingly, prin. Fax 350-9116

Hillsboro, Hill, Pop. 9,000
Hillsboro ISD 1,600/PK-12
121 E Franklin St 76645 254-582-8585
Buck Gilcrease, supt. Fax 582-4165
www.hillsboroisd.org
Franklin Preschool 200/PK-PK
103 Country Club Rd 76645 254-582-4130
Lynda Duncan, prin. Fax 582-4133
Hillsboro ES 300/K-2
115 Jane Ln 76645 254-582-4140
Lynda Duncan, prin. Fax 582-4145
Hillsboro IS 300/3-6
1000 Old Bynum Rd 76645 254-582-4170
Tommy McEwen, prin. Fax 582-4175
Hillsboro JHS 200/7-8
210 E Walnut St 76645 254-582-4120
Cathryn Patterson, prin. Fax 582-4122

Hitchcock, Galveston, Pop. 7,193
Hitchcock ISD 1,100/PK-12
8117 Highway 6 77563 409-986-5514
Michael Bergman Ed.D., supt. Fax 986-5141
www.hitchcockisd.org
Crosby MS 300/5-8
7801 Neville Ave 77563 409-986-5528
Pat Fox, prin. Fax 986-9254
Stewart ES 500/PK-4
7013 Stewart St 77563 409-986-5561
Barbara Trahan, prin. Fax 986-5563

Our Lady of Lourdes S 100/PK-6
10114 Highway 6 77563 409-925-3224
Earl Routh, prin. Fax 925-5094

Hockley, Harris
Waller ISD
Supt. — See Waller
Roberts Road ES 600/PK-4
24920 Zube Rd 77447 281-256-2343
Scott Lowell, prin. Fax 373-3164

Holland, Bell, Pop. 1,090
Holland ISD 600/PK-12
PO Box 217 76534 254-657-0175
Cindy Gunn, supt. Fax 657-0172
www.holland.k12.tx.us
Bowman MS 100/6-8
PO Box 217 76534 254-657-2224
Mike Mazoch, prin. Fax 657-2250
Holland ES 300/PK-5
PO Box 217 76534 254-657-2525
Shane Downing, prin. Fax 657-2845

Holliday, Archer, Pop. 1,681
Holliday ISD 800/PK-12
PO Box 689 76366 940-586-1281
Clarke Boyd, supt. Fax 586-1492
www.hollidayisd.net
Holliday ES 400/PK-5
PO Box 978 76366 940-586-1986
Shannon Owen, prin. Fax 586-0538
Holliday MS 200/6-8
PO Box 977 76366 940-586-1314
Kelly Carver, prin. Fax 583-4480

Hondo, Medina, Pop. 8,779
Hondo ISD 2,200/PK-12
PO Box 308 78861 830-426-3027
Clay Rosenbaum, supt. Fax 426-7683
www.hondo.k12.tx.us
McDowell JHS 500/6-8
1602 27th St S 78861 830-426-2261
Larry Carroll, prin. Fax 426-7624
Meyer ES 600/PK-2
2502 Avenue Q 78861 830-426-3161
Ellen Schueling, prin. Fax 426-7679
Woolls IS 500/3-5
2802 Avenue Q 78861 830-426-7666
Jimmy Gouard, prin. Fax 426-7669

Honey Grove, Fannin, Pop. 1,836
Honey Grove ISD 700/PK-12
540 6th St 75446 903-378-2264
Jan Cummins, supt. Fax 378-2991
www.honeygroveisd.net/
Honey Grove ES 300/PK-5
540 6th St 75446 903-378-2264
Michael Brinkley, prin. Fax 378-3288
Honey Grove MS 200/6-8
540 6th St 75446 903-378-2264
Robert Milton, prin. Fax 378-2095

Hooks, Bowie, Pop. 2,924
Hooks ISD 1,100/PK-12
100 E 5th St 75561 903-547-6077
Kathy Allen, supt. Fax 547-2943
www.hooksisd.net/
Hooks ES 400/PK-4
401 Precinct Rd 75561 903-547-2291
Jean Trout, prin. Fax 547-3172
Hooks JHS 300/5-8
PO Box 249 75561 903-547-2568
Shane Krueger, prin. Fax 547-2595

Leary ISD 100/PK-8
PO Box 519 75561 903-838-8960
Jim Tankersley, supt. Fax 838-6036
www.learyisd.net/
Leary S 100/PK-8
PO Box 519 75561 903-838-8960
Jennifer Brown, prin. Fax 838-6036

Horizon City, El Paso, Pop. 8,695
Clint ISD
Supt. — See El Paso
Desert Hills ES 800/PK-3
300 N Kenazo Ave 79928 915-926-4500
Bob Bowermaster, prin. Fax 852-3570
Horizon MS 1,100/6-8
400 N Kenazo Ave 79928 915-926-4700
Josie Perez, prin. Fax 852-9274
Macias ES 1,000/PK-3
14400 Golden Eagle Dr 79928 915-926-4600
Emi Gonzalez, prin. Fax 852-7547
Welch IS 700/4-5
14510 McMahon Ave 79928 915-926-4400
Charles Vass, prin. Fax 852-7230

Socorro ISD
Supt. — See El Paso
Ensor MS 600/6-8
13600 Ryderwood Dr 79928 915-937-6000
Jason Long, prin. Fax 851-7590
Horizon Heights ES 1,200/PK-5
13601 Ryderwood Dr 79928 915-937-7400
Leticia Salas, prin. Fax 937-7497

Houston, Harris, Pop. 2,016,582
Aldine ISD 58,600/PK-12
14910 Aldine Westfield Rd 77032 281-449-1011
Dr. Wanda Bamberg, supt. Fax 449-4291
www.aldine.k12.tx.us
Aldine MS 900/7-8
14908 Aldine Westfield Rd 77032 281-985-6580
Marcus Pruitt, prin. Fax 985-6480
Anderson Academy 700/1-3
7401 Wheatley St 77088 281-878-0370
Stephanie Rhodes, prin. Fax 591-8549
Bethune Academy 600/3-4
2500 S Victory Dr 77088 281-878-0380
Theresa Craft, prin. Fax 878-0383
Black ES 700/K-4
160 Mill Stream Ln 77060 281-878-0350
Lori Garcia, prin. Fax 878-0389
Bussey ES 700/K-4
11555 Airline Dr 77037 281-878-1501
Lidia Maza, prin. Fax 878-1506
Calvert ES 900/K-4
1925 Marvell Dr 77032 281-985-6360
Cheryl LaFleur, prin. Fax 985-6364
Caraway IS 800/5-6
3031 Ellington St 77088 281-878-0320
Cheryl Matthews, prin. Fax 878-0326
Carmichael ES 700/K-4
6902 Silver Star Dr 77086 281-878-0345
Monica Stogsdill, prin. Fax 878-0379
Carroll Academy 1,000/K-4
423 W Gulf Bank Rd 77037 281-878-0340
Resie Wilson, prin. Fax 591-8527
Carter Academy 900/K-4
3111 Fallbrook Dr 77038 281-878-7760
Robert Graham, prin. Fax 878-7767
Conley ES 800/K-4
3345 W Greens Rd 77066 281-537-5418
Katie Roede, prin. Fax 895-5005
deSantiago Pre K Center 700/PK-PK
1420 Aldine Meadows Rd 77032 281-985-7500
Rosa Mattern, prin. Fax 985-7509
Drew Academy 600/6-8
1910 W Little York Rd 77091 281-878-0360
Earnest Washington, prin. Fax 447-4694
Dunn ES 1,200/K-4
2003 WW Thorne Blvd 77073 281-233-4320
Terrie Sanchez, prin. Fax 233-4328
Eckert IS 900/5-6
1430 Aldine Meadows Rd 77032 281-985-6380
Todd Armelin, prin. Fax 985-6681
Ermel ES 700/K-4
7103 Woodsman Trl 77040 713-466-5220
Everette Taylor, prin. Fax 856-4256
Escamilla IS 900/5-6
5241 Mount Houston Rd 77093 281-985-6390
Milo Ortiz, prin. Fax 985-6137
Francis ES 800/K-4
14815 Lee Rd 77032 281-985-6500
Gina Rodgers, prin. Fax 985-6504
Goodman ES 800/K-4
9325 Deer Trail Dr 77088 281-878-0355
Camelia Chester, prin. Fax 878-0330

Grantham Academy 900/7-8
13300 Chrisman Rd 77039 281-985-6590
Benjamin Ibarra, prin. Fax 985-6595
Gray ES 600/K-4
700 West Rd 77038 281-878-0660
Kimberly Martin, prin. Fax 878-0664
Hambrick MS 1,000/7-8
4600 Aldine Mail Rd 77039 281-985-6570
Cindy Rogers, prin. Fax 442-9036
Harris Academy 800/K-4
3130 Holder Forest Dr 77088 281-878-7900
Kathy Bacy, prin. Fax 878-7913
Hill IS 1,000/5-6
2625 W Mount Houston Rd 77038 281-878-7775
Donnie King, prin. Fax 878-7779
Hinojosa Pre K Center 700/PK-PK
1620 Lauder Rd 77039 281-985-4750
Sandra Arredondo, prin. Fax 985-4754
Hoffman MS 900/7-8
6101 W Little York Rd 77091 713-613-7670
Rhonda Johnson, prin. Fax 613-7675
Houston Academy 700/5-6
8103 Carver Rd 77088 281-878-7745
Ruby Allen, prin. Fax 878-7755
Johnson ES 800/K-4
5801 Hamill Rd 77039 281-985-6510
Rebecca Hoyt, prin. Fax 985-6494
Keeble Pre K Center 800/PK-PK
203 W Gulf Bank Rd 77037 281-878-6860
Maria Galindo, prin. Fax 878-6869
Kujawa ECC PK-PK
7111 Fallbrook Dr 77086 281-878-1514
Deborah Hagood, prin. Fax 878-1545
Kujawa ES 700/K-4
7007 Fallbrook Dr 77086 281-878-1530
Debera Thomas, prin. Fax 878-1536
Marcella IS 900/5-6
16250 Cotillion Dr 77060 281-878-0860
Kathleen Sandoval, prin. Fax 878-0805
Mendel ES 300/K-4
3735 Topping St 77093 713-694-8002
Ann Stockwell, prin. Fax 696-4157
Odom ES 800/K-4
14701 Henry Rd 77060 281-878-0390
Lori Wooley, prin. Fax 878-0397
Oleson ES 900/K-4
12345 Vickery St 77039 281-985-6530
Cassandra Cosby, prin. Fax 985-6143
Orange Grove ES 800/K-4
4514 Mount Houston Rd 77093 281-985-6540
Betty Morrow, prin. Fax 985-6544
Parker IS 1,100/5-6
19850 E Hardy Rd 77073 281-233-8930
Candace Hardin, prin. Fax 233-8935
Plummer MS 900/7-8
11429 Spears Rd 77067 281-539-4000
Isaac Carrier, prin. Fax 539-4017
Raymond Academy 800/K-4
1605 Connorvale Rd 77039 281-985-6550
Linda Miller, prin. Fax 985-6555
Reece Academy 600/PK-K
2223 Esther Dr 77088 281-878-0800
Sherrie Batro, prin. Fax 878-0808
Reed Academy 900/5-6
1616 Lauder Rd 77039 281-985-6670
Gina Rigsby, prin. Fax 985-6679
Sammons ES 700/K-4
2301 Frick Rd 77038 281-878-0955
Maria Valdez, prin. Fax 591-8546
Shotwell MS 1,000/7-8
6515 Trail Valley Way 77086 281-878-0960
Wanda Walker, prin. Fax 591-8564
Smith Academy 800/K-4
5815 W Little York Rd 77091 713-613-7650
Dana Stelly, prin. Fax 613-7653
Spence ES 900/K-4
1300 Gears Rd 77067 281-539-4050
Debra Carrington, prin. Fax 539-4054
Stehlik IS 900/5-6
400 West Rd 77038 281-878-0300
Janet Ray, prin. Fax 878-0305
Stephens ES 1,000/K-4
2402 Aldine Mail Rd 77039 281-985-6560
Raymond Stubblefield, prin. Fax 985-6564
Stovall Academy 700/K-4
3025 Ellington St 77088 281-591-8500
Acquenette LeBlanc, prin. Fax 591-8507
Stovall MS 1,000/7-8
11201 Airline Dr 77037 281-878-0670
Raul Fonseca, prin. Fax 448-0636
Thompson ES 600/K-4
220 Casa Grande Dr 77060 281-878-0333
Sara McClain, prin. Fax 878-0339
Vines Pre K Center 700/PK-PK
7220 Inwood Park Dr 77088 281-878-7950
Dorothea Pickens, prin. Fax 878-7959
Wilson IS 1,000/5-6
3131 Fallbrook Dr 77038 281-878-0990
Mable Holt, prin. Fax 878-0995
Worsham ES 900/K-4
3007 Hartwick Rd 77093 281-985-6520
Denise Meister, prin. Fax 985-6524
Other Schools – See Humble

Alief ISD 43,700/PK-12
4250 Cook Rd 77072 281-498-8110
Louis Stoerner Ed.D., supt. Fax 498-8730
www.aliefisd.net/
Albright MS 1,300/7-8
6315 Winkleman Rd 77083 281-983-8411
Patrick Cherry, prin. Fax 983-8443
Alexander ES 900/PK-4
8500 Brookwulf Dr 77072 281-983-8300
Melissa Scott, prin. Fax 983-8454
Alief MS 1,000/6-8
4415 Cook Rd 77072 281-983-8422
Vinson Lewis, prin. Fax 983-8053
Best ES 800/PK-4
10000 Centre Pkwy 77036 713-988-6445
Lorena Augustus, prin. Fax 272-3211

Boone ES 800/PK-4
11400 Bissonnet St 77099 281-983-8308
Angela Chapman, prin. Fax 983-8035
Budewig IS 1,200/5-6
12570 Richmond Ave 77082 281-988-3200
Rosalind Burroughs, prin. Fax 497-7293
Bush ES 800/PK-4
9730 Stroud Dr 77036 713-272-3220
Gloria Price, prin. Fax 272-3230
Chambers ES 700/PK-4
10700 Carvel Ln 77072 281-983-8313
Jannae Jernberg, prin. Fax 983-8493
Chancellor ES 900/PK-5
4350 Boone Rd 77072 281-983-8318
Lisa Saarie, prin. Fax 983-8033
Collins ES 900/PK-5
9829 Town Park Dr 77036 713-272-3250
Paul Baez, prin. Fax 272-3260
Cummings ES 600/PK-4
10455 S Kirkwood Rd 77099 281-983-8328
Kathy Navel, prin. Fax 983-8096
Hearne ES 1,100/PK-4
13939 Rio Bonito Rd 77083 281-983-8333
Bertran Bilton, prin. Fax 983-8060
Heflin ES 800/PK-5
3303 Synott Rd 77082 281-531-1144
Robin Human, prin. Fax 531-3418
Hicks ES 1,300/PK-4
8520 Hemlock Hill Dr 77083 281-983-8040
Mary Kesler, prin. Fax 983-8064
Holmquist ES 1,000/PK-4
15040 Westpark Dr 77082 281-988-3024
Nancy Lewin, prin. Fax 556-1050
Holub MS 1,100/7-8
9515 S Dairy Ashford St 77099 281-983-8433
Pat Brown, prin. Fax 983-8398
Horn ES 900/PK-4
10734 Bissonnet St 77099 281-988-3223
Kathy Jahn, prin. Fax 530-5262
Kennedy ES 900/PK-4
10200 Huntington Place Dr 77099 281-983-8338
Cindy Rouse, prin. Fax 983-8390
Killough MS 1,000/7-8
7600 Synott Rd 77083 281-983-8444
Luis Olivas, prin. Fax 983-8067
Klentzman IS 1,100/5-6
11100 Stancliff Rd 77099 281-983-8477
Sonya Vaden, prin. Fax 983-8373
Landis ES 700/PK-4
10255 Spice Ln 77072 281-983-8343
Chris Pichon, prin. Fax 983-8072
Liestman ES 1,200/PK-4
7610 Synott Rd 77083 281-983-8348
Ava Montgomery, prin. Fax 983-8086
Mahanay ES 800/PK-5
13215 High Star Dr 77083 281-983-8355
Jo Nell Keller, prin. Fax 983-8083
Martin ES 1,000/PK-4
11718 Hendon Ln 77072 281-983-8363
Sandy Taylor, prin. Fax 983-7705
Mata IS 1,000/5-6
9225 S Dairy Ashford St 77099 281-983-7800
Janet Spurlock, prin. Fax 983-7810
Miller IS 1,000/5-6
15025 Westpark Dr 77082 281-531-3430
Janine Hoke, prin. Fax 531-3446
O'Donnell MS 1,200/6-8
14041 Alief Clodine Rd 77082 281-495-6000
Janie Saxton, prin. Fax 568-5029
Olle MS 1,000/7-8
9200 Boone Rd 77099 281-983-8455
Cassandra Dyson, prin. Fax 983-8077
Outley ES 1,000/PK-6
12355 Richmond Ave 77082 281-584-0655
Pam Pecheux, prin. Fax 531-3421
Owens IS 1,000/5-6
6900 Turtlewood Dr 77072 281-983-8466
Amador Velasquez, prin. Fax 983-8098
Petrosky ES 800/PK-4
6703 Winkleman Rd 77083 281-983-8366
Bernadette Bentley, prin. Fax 983-7708
Rees ES 900/PK-4
16305 Kensley Dr 77082 281-531-1444
Kim Winans, prin. Fax 531-3429
Smith ES 800/PK-4
11300 Stancliff Rd 77099 281-983-8380
MaryAnne Bronson, prin. Fax 983-7710
Sneed ES 1,100/PK-5
9855 Pagewood Ln 77042 713-789-6979
Jan Garrett, prin. Fax 260-7307
Youens ES 900/PK-5
12141 High Star Dr 77072 281-983-8383
Nancy Trent, prin. Fax 983-8055
Youngblood IS 1,100/5-6
8410 Dairy View Ln 77072 281-983-8020
Pam Bruner, prin. Fax 983-8051

Channelview ISD
Supt. — See Channelview
Brown ES 900/K-5
16550 Wallisville Rd 77049 281-860-1400
David Walker, prin. Fax 860-9716

Clear Creek ISD
Supt. — See League City
Bayou ES 600/PK-5
16000 Hickory Knoll Dr 77059 281-284-5100
Jane Kelling, prin. Fax 284-5105
Brookwood ES 800/PK-5
16850 Middlebrook Dr 77059 281-284-5600
Cathy Homer, prin. Fax 284-5605
Clear Lake City ES 500/PK-5
1707 Fairwind Rd 77062 281-284-4200
Leslie Dragg, prin. Fax 284-4205
Clear Lake IS 1,000/6-8
15545 El Camino Real 77062 281-488-1296
Brett Lemley, prin. Fax 488-8795
Falcon Pass ES 600/K-5
2465 Falcon Pass 77062 281-284-6200
Monica Grubbs, prin. Fax 284-6205
North Pointe ES 800/PK-5
3200 Almond Creek Dr 77059 281-284-5900
Laurie O'Neill, prin. Fax 284-5905
Space Center IS 1,200/6-8
17400 Saturn Ln 77058 281-284-3300
Susan Stuart, prin. Fax 284-3305
Ward ES 700/PK-5
1440 Bouldercrest Dr 77062 281-284-5400
Katherine Gouger, prin. Fax 284-5405
Weber ES 800/K-5
11955 Blackhawk Blvd 77089 281-284-6300
Teresa Snider, prin. Fax 284-6305
Whitcomb ES 800/PK-5
900 Reseda Dr 77062 281-284-4900
Dana Biddy, prin. Fax 284-4905

Cypress-Fairbanks ISD 96,300/PK-12
PO Box 692003 77269 281-897-4000
David Anthony Ed.D., supt. Fax 897-4125
www.cfisd.net
Adam ES 900/PK-5
11303 Honey Grove Ln 77065 281-897-4485
Beth May, prin. Fax 517-2089
Aragon MS 1,600/6-8
16823 West Rd 77095 281-856-5100
Jill Smith, prin. Fax 856-5105
Bane ES 900/PK-5
5805 Kaiser St 77040 713-460-6140
Virginia Marez, prin. Fax 460-7847
Bang ES 900/PK-5
8900 Rio Grande Dr 77064 281-897-4760
Cindy Barclift, prin. Fax 517-2095
Birkes ES 900/K-5
8500 Queenston Blvd 77095 281-345-3300
Carla Brosnahan, prin. Fax 345-3305
Bleyl MS 1,500/6-8
10800 Mills Rd 77070 281-897-4340
Barbara Crook, prin. Fax 897-4353
Campbell MS 1,400/6-8
11415 Bobcat Rd 77064 281-897-4300
Dr. Robert Hatcher, prin. Fax 807-8634
Cook MS 1,400/6-8
9111 Wheatland Dr 77064 281-897-4400
Sherma Duck, prin. Fax 897-3850
Copeland ES 1,000/PK-5
18018 Forest Heights Dr 77095 281-856-1400
Linda Jefferson, prin. Fax 463-5510
Danish ES, 11850 Fallbrook Dr 77065 900/K-5
Sandra Oliver, prin. 281-955-4981
Dean MS 1,300/6-8
14104 Reo St 77040 713-460-6153
Chris Hecker, prin. Fax 460-6197
Emmott ES 800/PK-5
11750 Steeple Way Blvd 77065 281-897-4500
Mary Ann Smith, prin. Fax 897-3888
Fiest ES 1,000/PK-5
8425 Pine Falls Dr 77095 281-463-5838
Ronda Rickett, prin. Fax 856-1174
Francone ES 900/PK-5
11250 Perry Rd 77064 281-897-4512
Sue Romanowsky, prin. Fax 897-4518
Frazier ES 1,000/PK-5
8300 Little River Rd 77064 713-896-3475
Jeff LaCoke, prin. Fax 896-5013
Gleason ES 900/PK-5
9203 Willowbridge Park Blvd 77064 281-517-6800
Sandra McNeely, prin. Fax 517-6805
Hairgrove ES 900/PK-5
7120 N Eldridge Pkwy 77041 713-896-5015
Lesa Cain, prin. Fax 896-5020
Hancock ES 900/PK-5
13801 Schroeder Rd 77070 281-897-4523
Louanne Shaffer, prin. Fax 807-8166
Holbrook ES 800/PK-5
6402 Langfield Rd 77092 713-460-6165
Howard Diacon, prin. Fax 460-7866
Holmsley ES 1,100/PK-5
7315 Hudson Oaks Dr 77095 281-463-5885
Christina Cole, prin. Fax 463-5529
Horne ES 1,000/PK-5
14950 W Little York Rd 77084 281-463-5954
Janna Barnhart, prin. Fax 856-1451
Kahla MS 1,500/6-8
16212 W Little York Rd 77084 281-345-3260
Marvin Webster, prin.
Kirk ES 900/PK-5
12421 Tanner Rd 77041 713-849-8250
Doug Ogilvie, prin. Fax 849-8255
Labay MS 1,400/6-8
15435 Willow River Dr 77095 281-463-5800
Dr. Cheryl Johns, prin. Fax 463-5804
Lee ES, 12900 W Little York Rd 77041 1,000/K-5
Barbara Fine, prin. 713-849-8281
Lieder ES 1,000/PK-5
17003 Kieth Harrow Blvd 77084 281-463-5928
Missy Edgerton, prin. Fax 463-5531
Lowery ES 900/PK-5
15950 Ridge Park Dr 77095 281-463-5900
Brenda Trial, prin. Fax 463-5516
Matzke ES 900/PK-5
13102 Jones Rd 77070 281-897-4450
Anne Odum, prin. Fax 897-4454
Metcalf ES 1,300/PK-5
6100 Queenston Blvd 77084 281-856-1152
John Steward, prin. Fax 856-1154
Moore ES 1,000/K-5
13734 Lakewood Forest Dr 77070 281-370-4040
Laura Harman, prin. Fax 320-7978
Owens ES 1,000/PK-5
7939 Jackrabbit Rd 77095 281-463-5915
Laura Barrett, prin. Fax 463-5526
Post ES 1,000/PK-5
7600 Equador St 77040 713-896-3488
Missy Kilday, prin. Fax 896-3497
Reed ES 1,000/PK-5
8700 Tami Renee Ln 77040 713-896-5035
Leslie Thomas, prin. Fax 896-5051
Tipps ES 1,000/K-5
5611 Queenston Blvd 77084 281-345-3350
Pam Redd, prin. Fax 345-3355
Truitt MS 1,400/6-8
6600 Addicks Satsuma Rd 77084 281-856-1100
Robert Hull, prin. Fax 856-1104
Watkins MS 1,400/6-8
4800 Cairnvillage St 77084 281-463-5850
Jose Martinez, prin. Fax 463-5508
Willbern ES 1,000/PK-5
10811 Goodspring Dr 77064 281-897-3820
Dr. Carrie Marz, prin. Fax 517-2162
Wilson ES 900/K-5
18015 Kieth Harrow Blvd 77084 281-463-5941
Pamela Link, prin. Fax 463-5944
Yeager ES 900/PK-5
13615 Champion Forest Dr 77069 281-440-4914
Susan Brenz, prin. Fax 587-7516
Other Schools – See Cypress, Katy

Fort Bend ISD
Supt. — See Sugar Land
Blue Ridge ES 500/PK-5
6241 McHard Rd 77053 281-634-4520
Deirdre Holloway, prin. Fax 634-4533
Fleming ES 900/PK-5
14850 Bissonnet St 77083 281-634-4600
Katina Brown, prin. Fax 634-4615
Hodges Bend MS 1,900/6-8
16510 Bissonnet St 77083 281-634-3000
Lillie Vega, prin. Fax 634-3028
Holley ES 700/K-5
16655 Bissonnet St 77083 281-634-3850
Michele Riggs, prin. Fax 634-3856
McAuliffe MS 1,000/6-8
16650 S Post Oak Rd 77053 281-634-3360
Sharon Delesbore, prin. Fax 634-3393
Mission Bend ES 800/K-5
16200 Beechnut St 77083 281-634-4240
Carole Hale, prin. Fax 634-4250
Mission Glen ES 800/PK-5
16053 Mission Glen Dr 77083 281-634-4280
Carol Allin, prin. Fax 634-4296
Mission West ES 900/PK-5
7325 Clodine Reddick Rd 77083 281-634-4320
Dr. Deana Cady, prin. Fax 634-4334
Ridgegate ES 800/PK-5
6015 W Ridgecreek Dr 77053 281-634-4840
Nita White, prin. Fax 634-4855
Ridgemont ES 800/PK-5
4910 Raven Ridge Dr 77053 281-634-4880
Lita Skinner, prin. Fax 634-4896

Galena Park ISD 23,600/PK-12
14705 Woodforest Blvd 77015 832-386-1000
Dr. Mark Henry, supt. Fax 386-1298
www.galenaparkisd.com
Cimarron ES 1,000/PK-5
816 Cimarron St 77015 832-386-3240
Amy Cole, prin. Fax 386-3241
Cloverleaf ES 900/PK-5
1035 Frankie St 77015 832-386-3200
Lee Brown, prin. Fax 386-3201
Cobb Sixth Grade Campus 1,200/6-6
6722 Uvalde Rd 77049 832-386-2100
Aneka Van Court, prin. Fax 386-2101
Cunningham MS 900/6-8
14110 Wallisville Rd 77049 832-386-4470
Billy Foster, prin. Fax 386-4471
Green Valley ES 900/PK-5
13350 Woodforest Blvd 77015 832-386-4390
Cheri Dixon, prin. Fax 386-4391
Havard ES 800/PK-5
15150 Wallisville Rd 77049 832-386-3710
Fran Keal, prin. Fax 386-3711
Houston ES PK-5
4101 E Sam Houston Pkwy N 77015 832-386-4430
Ofelia Garza, prin. Fax 386-4431
Jacinto City ES 800/PK-5
10910 Wiggins St 77029 832-386-4600
James Keal, prin. Fax 386-4601
Normandy Crossing ES 600/PK-5
12500 Normandy Crossing Dr 77015 832-386-1600
Dianne Edwards, prin. Fax 386-1642
North Shore ES 1,100/PK-5
14310 Duncannon Dr 77015 832-386-4660
Esmeralda Perez, prin. Fax 386-4661
North Shore MS 1,400/6-8
120 Castlegory Rd 77015 832-386-2600
Paul Drexler, prin. Fax 386-2643
Purple Sage ES 700/PK-5
6500 Purple Sage Rd 77049 832-386-3100
Robin Blount, prin. Fax 386-3106
Pyburn ES 700/PK-5
12302 Coulson St 77015 832-386-3150
Grace Devost, prin. Fax 386-3168
Tice ES 600/PK-5
14120 Wallisville Rd 77049 832-386-4050
Judy Holbrook, prin. Fax 386-4053
Williamson ES 500/PK-5
6720 New Forest Pkwy 77049 832-386-4000
Terri Moore, prin. Fax 386-4025
Woodland Acres ES 400/PK-5
12936 Sarahs Ln 77015 832-386-2220
Gloria Vasquez, prin. Fax 386-2221
Woodland Acres MS 500/6-8
12947 Myrtle Ln 77015 832-386-4700
Julissa Alcantar, prin. Fax 386-4701
Other Schools – See Galena Park

Houston ISD 189,100/PK-12
4400 W 18th St 77092 713-556-6300
Dr. Abelardo Saavedra, supt. Fax 556-6323
www.houstonisd.org/
Alcott ES 500/PK-5
5859 Bellfort St 77033 713-732-3540
Marshall Scott, prin. Fax 732-3542
Allen ES 400/PK-5
400 Victoria Dr 77022 713-696-2755
Nicola Esch, prin. Fax 696-2757
Almeda ES 700/PK-6
14249 Bridgeport Rd 77047 713-434-5620
Beverly Cage, prin. Fax 434-5622

Anderson ES 700/PK-5
5727 Ludington Dr 77035 713-726-3600
Roslyn Vaughn, prin. Fax 726-3603

Ashford ES 500/PK-4
1815 Shannon Valley Dr 77077 281-368-2120
Mary Polhemus, prin. Fax 368-2123

Askew ES 900/PK-4
11200 Wood Lodge Dr 77077 281-368-2100
Alvin Abraham, prin. Fax 368-2103

Atherton ES 400/PK-6
2011 Solo St 77020 713-671-4100
Albert Lemons, prin. Fax 671-4104

Attucks MS 900/6-8
4330 Bellfort St 77051 713-732-3670
Renaldo Wallace, prin. Fax 732-3677

Barrick ES 700/PK-5
12001 Winfrey Ln 77076 281-405-2500
Yolanda Garrido, prin. Fax 405-2502

Bastian ES 500/PK-5
5051 Bellfort St 77033 713-732-5830
Bruce Goffney, prin. Fax 732-5837

Bell ES 700/PK-5
12323 Shaftsbury Dr 77031 281-983-2800
Paula Viebrock, prin. Fax 983-2802

Bellfort Academy 300/4-5
7647 Bellfort St 77061 713-640-0950
Rosa Martinez, prin. Fax 640-0957

Benavidez ES 1,000/PK-5
6262 Gulfton St 77081 713-778-3350
Kimberly Valera, prin. Fax 778-3358

Benbrook ES 500/PK-5
4026 Bolin Rd 77092 713-613-2502
Dana Darden, prin. Fax 613-2281

Berry ES 600/PK-5
2310 Berry Rd 77093 713-696-2700
Deborah Silber, prin. Fax 696-2701

Black MS 700/6-8
1575 Chantilly Ln 77018 713-613-2505
Meilin Jao, prin. Fax 613-2533

Blackshear ES 400/PK-6
2900 Holman St 77004 713-942-1481
Linda Bellard, prin. Fax 942-1486

Bonham ES 1,100/PK-5
8302 Braes River Dr 77074 713-778-3480
Daphane Carter, prin. Fax 778-3482

Bonner ES 900/PK-5
8100 Elrod St 77017 713-943-5740
Linda M. Rodriguez, prin. Fax 943-5741

Braeburn ES 900/PK-5
7707 Rampart St 77081 713-295-5210
Santos Reyes, prin. Fax 295-5289

Briargrove ES 1,000/PK-5
6145 San Felipe St 77057 713-917-3600
Martin Garza, prin. Fax 917-3601

Briscoe ES 500/PK-6
321 Forest Hill Blvd 77011 713-924-1740
Juan M. Gonzalez, prin. Fax 924-1742

Brookline ES 1,000/PK-5
6301 South Loop E 77087 713-845-7400
Sandra Gonzales, prin. Fax 847-4717

Browning ES 500/PK-5
607 Northwood St 77009 713-867-5140
John Baker, prin. Fax 867-5148

Bruce ES 400/PK-6
510 Jensen Dr 77020 713-226-4560
Joseph Gonzales, prin. Fax 226-4562

Burbank ES 800/PK-5
216 Tidwell Rd 77022 713-696-2690
Elizabeth Rios, prin. Fax 696-2691

Burbank MS 1,200/6-8
315 Berry Rd 77022 713-696-2720
Jose Espinosa, prin. Fax 696-2723

Burnet ES 700/PK-6
5403 Canal St 77011 713-924-1780
Cynthia Galaviz, prin. Fax 924-1783

Burrus ES 400/PK-6
701 E 33rd St 77022 713-867-5180
Jessie Woods, prin. Fax 867-5182

Bush ES 1,000/PK-5
13800 Westerloch Dr 77077 281-368-2150
Theresa Rose, prin. Fax 368-2153

Carrillo ES 700/PK-5
960 S Wayside Dr 77023 713-924-1870
Mary Hallinan, prin. Fax 924-1873

Clifton MS 1,100/6-8
6001 Golden Forest Dr 77092 713-613-2516
Beverly Teal, prin. Fax 613-2523

Codwell ES 700/PK-6
5225 Tavenor Ln 77048 713-732-3580
Valerie Orum, prin. Fax 732-3582

Concord ECC 50/PK-PK
4901 Lockwood Dr 77026 713-671-4185
Exerta Mackie, prin. Fax 671-4187

Cook ES 300/PK-5
7115 Lockwood Dr 77016 713-636-6040
Laquetta Kennedy, prin. Fax 636-6088

Coop ES 700/PK-5
10130 Aldine Westfield Rd 77093 713-696-2630
Scott Goetz, prin. Fax 696-2633

Cornelius ES 900/PK-5
7475 Westover St 77087 713-845-7405
Karen Jackson, prin. Fax 845-7448

Crawford ES 300/PK-6
1510 Jensen Dr 77020 713-226-2634
Gloria Gorham, prin. Fax 226-2636

Crespo ES 900/PK-5
7500 Office City Dr 77012 713-845-7492
Celestina Martinez, prin. Fax 847-4716

Crockett ECC PK-K
1417 Houston Ave 77007 713-226-2620
Elida Troutman, prin.

Cullen MS 800/6-8
6900 Scott St 77021 713-746-8180
Lynett Hookfin, prin. Fax 746-8181

Cunningham ES 700/PK-5
5100 Gulfton St 77081 713-295-5223
Nancy Mercado, prin. Fax 668-6217

Daily ES 700/K-5
12909 Briar Forest Dr 77077 281-368-2111
Merrie Bonnette, prin. Fax 368-7463

Davila ES 700/PK-5
7610 Dahlia St 77012 713-924-1851
Diana Martinez, prin. Fax 924-1853

Deady MS 1,200/6-8
2500 Broadway St 77012 713-845-7411
Sherry Blasco, prin. Fax 845-5645

De Chaumes ES 700/PK-5
155 Cooper Rd 77076 713-696-2676
Sandy Gaw, prin. Fax 696-2680

De Zavala ES 600/PK-6
7521 Avenue H 77012 713-924-1888
Javier Villarreal, prin. Fax 924-1891

Dodson ES 500/PK-6
1808 Sampson St 77003 713-226-2685
Gwendolyn Hunter, prin. Fax 226-2687

Dogan ES 400/PK-6
4202 Liberty Rd 77026 713-671-4140
Joseph Williams, prin. Fax 671-4142

Dowling MS 1,800/6-8
14000 Stancliff St 77045 713-434-5603
Barrett Brooks, prin. Fax 434-5608

Durham ES 500/PK-5
4803 Brinkman St 77018 713-613-2527
Daniel Breiman, prin. Fax 613-2515

Durkee ES 700/PK-5
7301 Nordling Rd 77076 713-696-2835
Diane Tanguma, prin. Fax 696-2837

Edison MS 1,000/6-8
6901 Avenue I 77011 713-924-1800
George Martin, prin. Fax 924-1316

Eliot ES 600/PK-5
6411 Laredo St 77020 713-671-3670
Rozino Gene Smith, prin. Fax 671-3676

Elrod ES 500/PK-5
6230 Dumfries Dr 77096 713-778-3330
Vickie Rumrill, prin. Fax 778-3333

Emerson ES 700/PK-5
9533 Skyline Dr 77063 713-917-3630
Dr. Frances Godwin, prin. Fax 917-3634

Farias ECC 400/PK-PK
515 E Rittenhouse St 77076 713-691-8730
Altha Oliver, prin.

Field ES 400/PK-5
703 E 17th St 77008 713-867-5190
John Hendrickson, prin. Fax 867-5194

Fleming MS 500/6-8
4910 Collingsworth St 77026 713-671-4170
Marla McNeal-Sheppard, prin. Fax 671-4176

Foerster ES 700/PK-5
14200 Fonmeadow Dr 77035 713-726-3604
Pamela Farinas, prin. Fax 726-3629

Fondren ES 400/PK-6
12405 Carlsbad St 77085 713-726-3611
Michael Walker, prin. Fax 726-3646

Fondren MS 800/6-8
6333 S Braeswood Blvd 77096 713-778-3360
Brenda Rangel-Ganter, prin. Fax 778-3362

Fonville MS 1,200/6-8
725 E Little York Rd 77076 713-696-2825
Efrain Olivo, prin. Fax 696-2829

Foster ES 500/PK-5
3919 Ward St 77021 713-746-8260
Marthea Raney, prin. Fax 746-8263

Franklin ES 600/PK-6
7101 Canal St 77011 713-924-1820
Salvador Vega, prin. Fax 924-1823

Frost ES 500/PK-5
5650 Selinsky Rd 77048 713-732-3491
Elbert White, prin. Fax 732-3498

Gallegos ES 600/PK-5
7415 Harrisburg Blvd 77011 713-924-1830
Xochitl Rodriguez-Davila, prin. Fax 924-1833

Garcia ES 800/PK-5
9550 Aldine Westfield Rd 77093 713-696-2900
Rebecca Mir, prin. Fax 696-2904

Garden Oaks ES 600/PK-6
901 Sue Barnett Dr 77018 713-696-2930
Lindsey Pollock, prin. Fax 696-2932

Garden Villas ES 1,000/PK-5
7185 Santa Fe Dr 77061 713-845-7484
Vesta Terry-Autry, prin. Fax 847-4714

Golfcrest ES 800/PK-5
7414 Fairway Dr 77087 713-845-7425
Freddy R. Delgado, prin. Fax 847-4705

Grady MS 500/6-8
5215 San Felipe St 77056 713-625-1411
Gretchen Kasper-Hoffman, prin. Fax 625-1415

Gregg ES 700/PK-5
6701 Roxbury Rd 77087 713-845-7432
David Jackson, prin. Fax 847-4708

Gregory-Lincoln Education Center 200/PK-8
1101 Taft St 77019 713-942-1400
Johnnie Jackson, prin. Fax 942-1406

Grimes ES 400/PK-5
9220 Jutland Rd 77033 713-732-3460
Lashawn Porter, prin. Fax 732-3463

Grissom ES 700/PK-5
4900 Simsbrook Dr 77045 713-434-5660
Cynthia Smith, prin. Fax 434-5664

Gross ES 800/PK-5
12583 S Gessner Dr 77071 713-778-8450
Barbara Gravesbrown, prin. Fax 778-8454

Halpin ECC 400/PK-K
10901 Sandpiper Dr 77096 713-778-6720
Patricia Thomas, prin. Fax 778-6724

Hamilton MS 1,300/6-8
139 E 20th St 77008 713-802-4725
Roger A. Bunnell, prin. Fax 802-4731

Harris ES 800/PK-5
801 Broadway St 77012 713-924-1860
Steven Harding, prin. Fax 924-1863

Harris ES 600/PK-5
1262 Mae Dr 77015 713-450-7100
Nicole Moore, prin. Fax 450-7103

Hartman MS 1,500/6-8
7111 Westover St 77087 713-845-7435
Joseph Addison, prin. Fax 847-4706

Hartsfield ES 400/PK-5
5001 Perry St 77021 713-746-8280
Joyce Williams, prin. Fax 746-8283

Harvard ES 600/PK-5
810 Harvard St 77007 713-867-5210
Kevin Beringer, prin. Fax 867-5215

Helms Community Learning Center 500/PK-5
503 W 21st St 77008 713-867-5130
Theresa Campos, prin. Fax 867-5133

Henderson ES 800/PK-5
1800 Dismuke St 77023 713-924-1730
Herlinda Garcia, prin. Fax 924-1735

Henderson North ES 400/PK-6
701 Solo St 77020 713-671-4195
Diane Blakely, prin. Fax 671-4197

Henry MS 1,100/6-8
10702 E Hardy Rd 77093 713-696-2650
Christian Sanders, prin. Fax 696-2657

Herod ES 700/PK-5
5627 Jason St 77096 713-778-3315
Jerri Nixon, prin. Fax 778-3317

Herrera ES 900/PK-5
525 Bennington St 77022 713-696-2800
Maria Rodriguez, prin. Fax 696-2804

Hines-Caldwell ES 900/PK-5
5515 W Orem Dr 77085 713-726-3700
Bonita Morgan, prin.

Hobby ES 700/PK-5
4021 Woodmont Dr 77045 713-434-5650
Ivalyn Patterson, prin. Fax 434-5652

Hogg MS 800/6-8
1100 Merrill St 77009 713-802-4700
Imelda Medrano, prin. Fax 802-4708

Hohl ES 500/PK-6
5320 Yale St 77091 713-696-2810
Lenita Kelly, prin. Fax 696-2812

Holland MS 800/6-8
1600 Gellhorn Dr 77029 713-671-3860
Brian McDonald, prin. Fax 671-3874

Houston Gardens ES 400/PK-6
6820 Homestead Rd 77028 713-636-6979
Tarawa Groves, prin. Fax 636-6983

Isaacs ES 600/PK-6
3830 Pickfair St 77026 713-671-4120
Gloria Gaines, prin. Fax 671-4122

Jackson MS 1,100/6-8
5100 Polk St 77023 713-924-1760
Ana Zamarripa, prin. Fax 924-1768

Janowski ES 600/PK-5
7500 Bauman Rd 77022 713-696-2844
Myrna Bazan, prin. Fax 696-2847

Jefferson ES 600/PK-5
5000 Sharman St 77009 713-696-2778
Kerry Hamilton, prin. Fax 696-2784

Johnston MS 1,400/6-8
10410 Manhattan Dr 77096 713-726-3616
Dave Wheat, prin. Fax 726-3622

Jones ES 300/PK-5
1810 Stuart St 77004 713-942-1430
Brian Flores, prin. Fax 942-1433

Kashmere Gardens ES 500/PK-6
4901 Lockwood Dr 77026 713-671-4160
Exerta Mackie, prin. Fax 671-4163

Kelso ES 600/PK-5
5800 Southmund St 77033 713-845-7451
Debra Hayes, prin. Fax 847-4710

Kennedy ES 500/PK-6
306 Crosstimbers St 77022 713-696-2686
Daryl Sherman, prin. Fax 696-2689

Ketelsen ES 500/K-5
600 Quitman St 77009 713-220-5050
Cynthia Banda, prin. Fax 220-5074

Key MS 700/6-8
4000 Kelley St 77026 713-636-6000
Mable Caleb, prin. Fax 636-6008

King ECC 400/PK-PK
3930 W Fuqua St 77045 713-797-7900
Gabrielle Coleman, prin. Fax 797-7904

Kolter ES 500/PK-5
9710 Runnymeade Dr 77096 713-726-3630
Marguerite Stewart, prin. Fax 726-3663

Lantrip ES 700/PK-6
100 Telephone Rd 77023 713-924-1670
Matilda Orozco, prin. Fax 924-1672

Las Americas MS 100/6-8
6501 Bellaire Blvd 77074 713-773-5300
Marie Moreno, prin. Fax 773-5303

Laurenzo ECC 300/PK-PK
205 N Delmar St 77011 713-924-0350
Carmen Rogina, prin. Fax 924-0390

Law ES 500/PK-5
12401 S Coast Dr 77047 713-732-3630
Hannah Harvey, prin. Fax 732-3633

Lewis ES 800/PK-3
7649 Rockhill St 77061 713-845-7453
Cheryl Lewis, prin. Fax 847-4711

Lockhart ES 500/PK-5
3501 Southmore Blvd 77004 713-942-1950
Felicia Adams, prin. Fax 942-1953

Longfellow ES 600/K-5
3617 Norris Dr 77025 713-295-5268
Thomas O'Neill, prin. Fax 295-5257

Long MS 1,300/6-8
6501 Bellaire Blvd 77074 713-778-3380
Diana De La Rosa, prin. Fax 778-3387

Looscan ES 500/PK-5
3800 Robertson St 77009 713-696-2760
Robert J. Pollock, prin. Fax 696-2765

Love ES 500/PK-5
1120 W 13th St 77008 713-867-0840
Robert Chavarria, prin. Fax 867-0841

Lovett ES 600/K-5
8814 S Rice Ave 77096 713-295-5258
Susan Monaghan, prin. Fax 295-5291

Lyons ES 900/PK-5
800 Roxella St 77076 713-696-2870
Cecilia Gonzales, prin. Fax 696-2877
MacArthur ES 400/PK-5
5909 England St 77021 713-746-8290
Alma Perez, prin. Fax 746-8292
MacGregor ES 400/K-5
4801 La Branch St 77004 713-942-1990
Patricia Allen, prin. Fax 942-1993
Mading ES 600/PK-5
8511 Crestmont St 77033 713-732-3560
Benté Gage, prin. Fax 732-3563
Marshall MS 1,000/6-8
1115 Noble St 77009 713-226-2600
Jorge Medina, prin. Fax 226-2605
Martinez ES 700/PK-5
901 Hays St 77009 713-224-1424
Patricia Gonzales, prin. Fax 224-1304
Martinez ES 600/PK-5
7211 Market St 77020 713-671-3680
Elba Carrion, prin. Fax 671-3684
McDade ES 400/PK-6
5815 Hirsch Rd 77026 713-636-6950
Beverly Cashaw, prin. Fax 636-6954
McNamara ES 800/PK-5
8714 McAvoy Dr 77074 713-778-3460
Tiffany Chenier, prin. Fax 778-3431
McReynolds MS 600/6-8
5910 Market St 77020 713-671-3650
Jorge Arredondo, prin. Fax 671-3657
Memorial ES 400/PK-5
6401 Arnot St 77007 713-867-5150
Art Castillo, prin. Fax 867-5151
Milne ES 700/PK-5
7800 Portal Dr 77071 713-778-3420
Clayton Crook, prin. Fax 778-3424
Mistral ECC 400/PK-PK
6203 Jessamine St 77081 713-773-6253
Mechiel Rozas, prin.
Mitchell ES 1,100/PK-5
10900 Gulfdale Dr 77075 713-991-8190
Sylvia Perez, prin. Fax 991-8193
Montgomery ES 700/PK-5
4000 Simsbrook Dr 77045 713-434-5640
Tammie Daily, prin. Fax 434-5643
Moreno ES 700/PK-5
620 E Canino Rd 77037 281-405-2150
Adriana Abarca-Castro, prin. Fax 405-2176
Neff ES 1,100/PK-5
8200 Carvel Ln 77036 713-778-3470
Anita Lundvall, prin. Fax 778-3473
Northline ES 700/PK-5
821 E Witcher Ln 77076 713-696-2890
Brian Doyle, prin. Fax 696-2894
Oak Forest ES 700/K-5
1401 W 43rd St 77018 713-613-2536
Kimberly Hobbs, prin. Fax 613-2244
Oates ES 400/PK-6
10044 Wallisville Rd 77013 713-671-3800
Isabel Palacios, prin. Fax 671-3803
Ortiz MS 1,100/6-8
6767 Telephone Rd 77061 713-845-5650
Yolanda Alleman, prin. Fax 845-5646
Paige ES 400/PK-5
7501 Curry Rd 77093 713-696-2855
Betty Pouncey, prin. Fax 696-2858
Parker ES 800/PK-5
10626 Atwell Dr 77096 713-726-3634
Carol Selig, prin. Fax 726-3660
Park Place ES 1,000/PK-5
8235 Park Place Blvd 77017 713-845-7458
Kim Heckman, prin. Fax 845-7460
Patterson ES 800/K-5
5302 Allendale Rd 77017 713-943-5750
Jennie Castano, prin. Fax 943-5755
Peck ES 400/PK-5
5130 Arvilla Ln 77021 713-845-7463
Carlotta Brown, prin. Fax 845-4701
Pershing MS 1,700/6-8
3838 Blue Bonnet Blvd 77025 713-295-5240
Robin Lowe, prin. Fax 295-5252
Petersen ES 800/PK-6
14404 Waterloo Dr 77045 713-434-5630
Linda Kalantar, prin. Fax 434-5634
Pilgrim Academy 700/PK-7
6302 Skyline Dr 77057 713-458-4672
Diana Castillo, prin. Fax 458-4693
Piney Point ES 900/PK-5
8921 Pagewood Ln 77063 713-917-3610
Bobbie Swaby, prin. Fax 917-3613
Pleasantville ES 500/PK-5
1431 Gellhorn Dr 77029 713-671-3840
Tarrynce Robinson, prin. Fax 671-3844
Poe ES 700/PK-5
5100 Hazard St 77098 713-535-3780
Claudia Gonzales, prin. Fax 535-3784
Port Houston ES 300/PK-6
1800 Mccarty St 77029 713-671-3890
Jarrett Whitaker, prin. Fax 671-3893
Pugh ES 500/PK-5
1147 Kress St 77020 713-671-3820
Lydia Guerrero, prin. Fax 671-3825
Red ES 500/PK-5
4520 Tonawanda Dr 77035 713-726-3638
Dawn Randle, prin. Fax 726-3698
Revere MS 1,100/6-8
10502 Briar Forest Dr 77042 713-917-3500
Anastasia Lindo, prin. Fax 917-3505
Reynolds ES 400/PK-6
9601 Rosehaven Dr 77051 713-731-5590
Sandra Pipkin, prin. Fax 731-5598
Rhoads ES 300/PK-6
4103 Brisbane St 77047 713-732-3650
Debra Balthazar, prin. Fax 732-3653
Rice S 700/K-8
7550 Seuss Dr 77025 713-349-1800
Linda Lazenby, prin. Fax 349-1828
River Oaks ES 700/K-5
2008 Kirby Dr 77019 713-942-1460
Kelly McBride, prin. Fax 942-1463
Roberts ES 600/K-5
6000 Greenbriar St 77030 713-295-5272
Linda Smith, prin. Fax 295-5282
Robinson ES 600/K-6
12425 Wood Forest Dr 77013 713-450-7108
Tracy Cooper, prin. Fax 450-7129
Rodriguez ES 900/PK-5
5858 Chimney Rock Rd 77081 713-295-3870
Elena Martinez Buley, prin. Fax 295-3875
Rogers S 300/K-8
5840 San Felipe St 77057 713-917-3565
Cathryn White, prin. Fax 917-3555
Roosevelt ES 500/PK-5
6700 Fulton St 77022 713-696-2820
Maria Rodriguez, prin. Fax 696-2821
Ross ES 400/PK-5
2819 Bay St 77026 713-226-4550
David Terrell, prin. Fax 226-4554
Rucker ES 700/PK-5
5201 Vinett St 77017 713-845-7467
Linda Boas, prin. Fax 845-5083
Rusk ES 300/PK-7
2805 Garrow St 77003 713-226-4543
Steven Gutierrez, prin. Fax 226-4546
Ryan MS 600/6-8
2610 Elgin St 77004 713-942-1932
Ruby Andrews, prin. Fax 942-1943
Sanchez ES 600/PK-5
2700 Berkley St 77012 713-845-7472
Jesse Herrera, prin. Fax 847-4755
Sands Point ES 400/PK-5
10550 Westoffice Dr 77042 713-334-1273
Lilly McIntyre, prin. Fax 334-1281
Scarborough ES 800/PK-5
3021 Little York Rd 77093 713-696-2710
Susan Bargaleski, prin. Fax 696-2712
School at St. George Place 500/K-5
5430 Hidalgo St 77056 713-625-1499
Drue McClure, prin. Fax 985-7455
Scott ES 400/PK-6
3300 Russell St 77026 713-671-4110
Dr. Artice Hedgemon, prin. Fax 671-4114
Scroggins ES 600/PK-5
400 Boyles St 77020 713-671-4130
San Juana Elizondo, prin. Fax 671-4133
Seguin ES 600/PK-5
5905 Waltrip St 77087 713-845-5600
Angie Miranda, prin. Fax 845-5615
Shadowbriar ES 500/3-5
2650 Shadowbriar Dr 77077 281-368-2160
Patricia May, prin. Fax 368-2170
Sharpstown MS 1,100/6-8
8330 Triola Ln 77036 713-778-3440
Jeffrey Amerson, prin. Fax 778-3444
Shearn ES 400/PK-5
9802 Stella Link Rd 77025 713-295-5236
Clifford Buck, prin. Fax 295-5253
Sherman ES 500/PK-5
1909 Mckee St 77009 713-226-2627
Amelia Cardenas Aguilar, prin. Fax 236-8417
Sinclair ES 500/K-5
6410 Grovewood Ln 77008 713-867-5161
Bonnie Clark, prin. Fax 867-5162
Smith Education Center 200/1-8
1701 Bringhurst St 77020 713-226-2668
Ray Gatlin, prin. Fax 226-2680
Smith ES 800/PK-5
4802 Chrystell Ln 77092 713-613-2542
Gloria Salazar, prin. Fax 613-2578
Southmayd ES 600/PK-5
1800 Coral St 77012 713-924-1720
Siomara Saenz-Phillips, prin. Fax 924-1722
Stevens ES 600/PK-5
1910 Lamonte Ln 77018 713-613-2546
Lucy Anderson, prin. Fax 613-2541
Stevenson ES 400/PK-5
5410 Cornish St 77007 713-802-4772
Norma Perez-Gwynn, prin. Fax 802-4774
Stevenson MS 1,200/6-8
9595 Winkler Dr 77017 713-943-5700
Alisa Zapata, prin. Fax 943-5711
Sugar Grove ES 400/PK-5
8405 Bonhomme Rd 77074 713-271-0214
Robert Taylor, prin. Fax 771-9342
Sutton ES 1,000/PK-5
7402 Albacore Dr 77074 713-778-3400
Sarah Cripps-Rains, prin. Fax 778-3407
Thomas MS 700/6-8
5655 Selinsky Rd 77048 713-732-3500
Bill Sorrells, prin. Fax 732-3511
Thompson ES 600/PK-5
6121 Tierwester St 77021 713-746-8250
Billie Joe Johnson, prin. Fax 746-8253
Tijerina ES 700/PK-6
6501 Sherman St 77011 713-924-1790
Paola Daniels, prin. Fax 924-1792
Tinsley ES 700/1-5
11035 Bob White Dr 77096 713-778-8400
Brenda Artega, prin. Fax 778-8405
Travis ES 700/PK-5
3311 Beauchamp St 77009 713-802-4790
Susan T. Walker, prin. Fax 802-4795
Turner ES 300/PK-5
3200 Rosedale St 77004 713-942-1490
Verlinda Higgins, prin. Fax 942-1494
Twain ES 800/PK-5
7500 Braes Blvd 77025 713-295-5230
Joyce Dauber, prin. Fax 295-5283
Valley West ES 600/PK-5
10707 S Gessner Dr 77071 713-773-6151
Sandra Little, prin. Fax 773-6156
Wainwright ES 600/PK-5
5330 Milwee St 77092 713-613-2550
John Barrerra, prin. Fax 613-2549
Walnut Bend ES 700/PK-5
10620 Briar Forest Dr 77042 713-917-3540
Julie Fernandez, prin. Fax 917-3656
Welch MS 1,400/6-8
11544 S Gessner Dr 77071 713-778-3300
Cynthia Iyamu, prin. Fax 995-6067
West Briar MS 1,300/6-8
13733 Brimhurst Dr 77077 281-368-2140
Geoffrey Ohl, prin. Fax 368-2194
West University ES 1,000/PK-5
3756 University Blvd 77005 713-295-5215
John Threet, prin. Fax 667-8514
Wharton ES 400/PK-6
900 W Gray St 77019 713-535-3771
Imelda Alamia, prin. Fax 535-3772
Whidby ES 600/PK-5
7625 Springhill St 77021 713-746-8170
Cheryl York, prin. Fax 746-8173
White ES 800/PK-5
9001 Triola Ln 77036 713-778-3490
T.M. Le-Thai, prin. Fax 778-3493
Whittier ES 500/PK-5
10511 La Crosse St 77029 713-671-3810
Lori Lueptow, prin. Fax 671-3812
Wilson ES 400/PK-5
2100 Yupon St 77006 713-942-1470
Gayle Curtis, prin. Fax 942-1472
Windsor Village ES 800/PK-5
14440 Polo St 77085 713-726-3642
Lana Edwards, prin. Fax 726-3647
Woodson S 800/PK-8
10720 Southview St 77047 713-732-3600
Linda Whitley, prin. Fax 732-3606
Young ES 300/PK-5
3555 Bellfort St 77051 713-732-3590
Denese V. Wolff, prin. Fax 732-3592
Other Schools – See Bellaire

Humble ISD
Supt. — See Humble
Summerwood ES 700/K-5
14000 Summerwood Lakes Dr 77044 281-641-3000
Terre McKinney, prin. Fax 641-3017

Katy ISD
Supt. — See Katy
Bear Creek ES 600/K-5
4815 Hickory Downs Dr 77084 281-237-5600
Lisa Leetham, prin. Fax 644-1500
Mayde Creek ES 1,000/PK-5
2698 Greenhouse Rd 77084 281-237-3950
Kerri Finnesand, prin. Fax 644-1555
Mayde Creek JHS 1,400/6-8
2700 Greenhouse Rd 77084 281-237-3900
Dr. Cazilda Steele, prin. Fax 644-1650
Schmalz ES 1,100/K-5
18605 Green Land Way 77084 281-237-4500
Karen Ladner, prin. Fax 644-1615
Wolfe ES 400/K-5
502 Addicks Howell Rd 77079 281-237-2250
Dr. Jacob LeBlanc, prin. Fax 644-1620

Klein ISD
Supt. — See Klein
Eiland ES 700/PK-5
6700 N Klein Circle Dr 77088 832-484-6900
Greg Jones, prin. Fax 484-7854
Epps Island ES 800/PK-5
7403 Smiling Wood Ln 77086 832-484-5800
Fax 484-7856
Greenwood Forest ES 700/PK-5
12100 Misty Valley Dr 77066 832-484-5700
Maryanne Straub, prin. Fax 484-7858
Kaiser ES 900/PK-5
13430 Bammel N Houston Rd 77066 832-484-6100
Dr. Rebecca Lancaster, prin. Fax 484-7864
Klein IS 1,100/6-8
4710 W Mount Houston Rd 77088 832-249-4900
Bob Anderson, prin. Fax 249-4046
Klenk ES 900/PK-5
6111 Bourgeois Rd 77066 832-484-6800
Sandra Simi, prin. Fax 484-7866
McDougle ES 800/PK-5
10410 Kansack Ln 77086 832-484-7550
Lynn Brown, prin. Fax 484-7699
Nitsch ES 900/PK-5
4702 W Mount Houston Rd 77088 832-484-6400
Carol James, prin. Fax 484-7878
Wunderlich IS 1,300/6-8
11800 Misty Valley Dr 77066 832-249-5200
Patricia Crittendon, prin. Fax 249-4050

North Forest ISD 6,600/PK-12
PO Box 23278 77228 713-633-1600
William Jones Ph.D., supt. Fax 636-7946
www.nfisd.org
Elmore MS 600/6-8
8200 Tate St 77028 713-672-7466
Gwenette Ferguson, prin. Fax 671-3565
Fonwood ES 700/K-5
10719 Seneca St 77016 713-633-0781
Edith Mahone, prin. Fax 636-7940
Kirby MS 700/6-8
9706 Mesa Dr 77078 713-633-0670
Rubye Gilbert, prin. Fax 636-7895
Lakewood ES 700/PK-5
8800 Grandriver Dr 77078 713-631-7730
Jerrell Purvis, prin. Fax 636-7858
Marshall S 1,000/PK-K
6200 Winfield Rd 77050 281-442-8467
Sharon Ratliff, prin. Fax 986-6475
Oak Village MS 700/6-8
6602 Winfield Rd 77050 281-449-6561
Jacquelyn Hopkins, prin. Fax 671-7650
Rogers ES 500/K-5
10550 J L Reaux St 77016 713-633-1860
Tatyanna Williams, prin. Fax 636-7959
Shadydale ES 700/K-5
5905 Tidwell Rd 77016 713-633-5150
Angelanette Allen, prin. Fax 636-7925

Pasadena ISD
Supt. — See Pasadena
Atkinson ES 600/K-5
9602 Kingspoint Rd 77075 713-740-0520
Lena Rohne-Ortiz, prin. Fax 740-4128
Beverly Hills IS 1,400/6-8
11111 Beamer Rd 77089 713-740-0420
Alyta Harrell, prin. Fax 740-4051
Burnett ES 700/K-5
11828 Teaneck Dr 77089 713-740-0536
Cindy Amador-Henderson, prin. Fax 740-4130
Bush ES 500/K-4
9100 Blackhawk Blvd 77075 713-740-0928
Debbie Barrett, prin. Fax 740-4126
Frazier ES 600/K-5
10503 Hughes Rd 77089 713-740-0560
Rhonda Parmer, prin. Fax 740-4132
Freeman ES 600/K-5
2323 Theta St 77034 713-740-0568
Kaye Post, prin. Fax 740-4107
Garfield ES 1,000/PK-5
10301 Hartsook St 77034 713-740-0584
Scott Harrell, prin. Fax 740-4134
Genoa ES 900/K-5
12900 Almeda Genoa Rd 77034 713-740-0592
Tiffany Bennett, prin. Fax 740-4135
Jessup ES 800/PK-5
9301 Almeda Genoa Rd 77075 713-740-0616
Emily Simancas, prin. Fax 740-4112
Meador ES 600/PK-5
10701 Seaford Dr 77089 713-740-0648
Darlene Davis, prin. Fax 740-4105
Milstead MS 800/5-6
338 Gilpin St 77034 713-740-5238
Shannon Trejo, prin. Fax 740-4176
Moore ES 600/K-5
8880 Southbluff Blvd 77089 713-740-0656
Jill Lacamu, prin. Fax 740-4140
Morris MS 700/5-6
10415 Fuqua St 77089 713-740-0672
Susan Blalock, prin. Fax 740-4047
Schneider MS 800/5-6
8420 Easthaven Blvd 77075 713-740-0920
Marsha Jones, prin. Fax 740-4125
Stuchbery ES 600/PK-5
11210 Hughes Rd 77089 713-740-0752
Jackie Salisbury, prin. Fax 740-4147
Thompson IS 1,100/6-8
11309 Sagedowne Ln 77089 713-740-0510
Dr. Angela Stallings, prin. Fax 740-4083

Sheldon ISD 5,200/PK-12
11411 C E King Pkwy 77044 281-727-2000
Dr. Vickey Giles, supt. Fax 727-2085
www.sheldonisd.com/
Carroll ES 1-5
10210 C E King Pkwy 77044 281-436-8300
James Webster, prin.
Cravens ECC 700/PK-K
13210 Tidwell Rd 77044 281-727-2100
Shereen James, prin. Fax 727-2160
King MS 800/6-8
8530 C E King Pkwy 77044 281-727-4300
Shawne Smith, prin. Fax 459-7452
Monahan ES 700/1-5
8901 Deep Valley Dr 77044 281-459-7480
Brenda Emanuel, prin. Fax 454-2975
Royalwood ES 900/1-5
7715 Royalwood Dr 77049 281-459-7400
Kristi Amarantos, prin. Fax 454-2775
Sheldon ES 600/1-5
17203 Hall Shepperd Rd 77049 281-456-6700
Christie Gates, prin. Fax 456-6775

Spring Branch ISD 30,900/PK-12
955 Campbell Rd 77024 713-464-1511
Duncan Klussmann Ed.D., supt. Fax 365-4071
www.springbranchisd.com/
Bear Blvd S 300/PK-PK
8860 Westview Dr 77055 713-365-4101
Jim Felle, dir. Fax 365-4106
Buffalo Creek ES 600/PK-5
2801 Blalock Rd 77080 713-329-6600
David Rodriquez, prin. Fax 329-6605
Bunker Hill ES 600/PK-5
11950 Taylorcrest Rd 77024 713-365-5050
Valerie Martinez, prin. Fax 365-5059
Cedar Brook ES 600/PK-5
2121 Ojeman Rd 77080 713-365-5020
Veleta Madsen, prin. Fax 365-5027
Edgewood ES 800/PK-5
8655 Emnora Ln 77080 713-365-4010
Suzanne Mercado, prin. Fax 365-4007
Frostwood ES 600/PK-5
12214 Memorial Dr 77024 713-365-5080
Jan Griffin, prin. Fax 365-5086
Hollibrook ES 700/PK-5
3602 Hollister St 77080 713-329-6430
Elsa Delgado, prin. Fax 329-6440
Housman ES 600/PK-5
6705 Housman St 77055 713-613-1700
Mary Lou Davalos, prin. Fax 613-1706
Hunters Creek ES 700/PK-5
10650 Beinhorn Rd 77024 713-365-4930
Stefanie Roach, prin. Fax 365-4937
Landrum MS 700/6-8
2200 Ridgecrest Dr 77055 713-365-4020
Luis Pratts, prin. Fax 365-4040
Lion Lane S 300/PK-PK
2210 Ridgecrest Dr 77055 713-365-4360
Sharee Cantrell, dir. Fax 365-4364
Meadow Wood ES 400/PK-5
14230 Memorial Dr 77079 281-560-7400
Robye Snyder, prin. Fax 560-7409
Memorial Drive ES 500/PK-5
11202 Smithdale Rd 77024 713-365-4960
Anick Watson, prin. Fax 365-4967
Memorial MS 1,100/6-8
12550 Vindon Dr 77024 713-365-5400
Lisa Weir, prin. Fax 365-5411

Northbrook MS 600/6-8
3030 Rosefield Dr 77080 713-329-6510
Valerie Johnson, prin. Fax 329-6523
Nottingham ES 500/K-5
570 Nottingham Oaks Trl 77079 281-560-7460
Frederick Larry, prin. Fax 560-7469
Panda Path S 100/PK-PK
8575 Pitner Rd 77080 713-329-6690
Sara Hannes, dir. Fax 329-6696
Pine Shadows ES 600/PK-5
9900 Neuens Rd 77080 713-365-4260
Alexia Greiner, prin. Fax 365-4274
Ridgecrest ES 800/PK-5
2015 Ridgecrest Dr 77055 713-365-4060
Patricia Thomas, prin. Fax 365-4067
Rummel Creek ES 700/PK-5
625 Brittmoore Rd 77079 713-365-5450
Nancy Harn, prin. Fax 365-5462
Shadow Oaks ES 700/PK-5
1335 Shadowdale Dr 77043 713-365-4580
Julie Baggerly, prin. Fax 365-4585
Sherwood ES 400/PK-5
1700 Sherwood Forest St 77043 713-365-4800
Anita Jacobs, prin. Fax 365-4806
Spring Branch ES 600/PK-5
1700 Campbell Rd 77080 713-365-4150
Sue Bryant, prin. Fax 365-4159
Spring Branch MS 1,000/6-8
1000 Piney Point Rd 77024 713-365-5500
Robert Salek, prin. Fax 365-5515
Spring Forest MS 800/6-8
14240 Memorial Dr 77079 281-560-7500
Shawn Bird, prin. Fax 560-7509
Spring Oaks MS 800/6-8
2150 Shadowdale Dr 77043 713-365-4515
David Sablatura, prin. Fax 365-4522
Spring Shadows ES 700/PK-5
9725 Kempwood Dr 77080 713-329-6470
Cathie Erickson, prin. Fax 329-6480
Spring Woods MS 800/6-8
9810 Neuens Rd 77080 713-365-4110
Cynthia Chai, prin. Fax 365-4115
Terrace ES 600/PK-5
10400 Rothbury St 77043 713-329-6400
Karen Sanders, prin. Fax 329-6406
Thornwood ES 500/PK-5
14400 Fern Dr 77079 281-560-7430
Karen Liska, prin. Fax 560-7439
Tiger Trail S 300/PK-PK
10406 Tiger Trl 77043 713-365-4575
Vidal Garza, dir. Fax 365-4578
Treasure Forest ES 700/PK-5
7635 Amelia Rd 77055 713-613-1720
Imelda De La Guardia, prin. Fax 613-1724
Valley Oaks ES 600/PK-6
8390 Westview Dr 77055 713-365-4080
Gary Henry, prin. Fax 365-4086
Westwood ES 600/PK-5
2100 Shadowdale Dr 77043 713-365-4550
Kay Kennard, prin. Fax 365-4555
Wilchester ES 600/PK-5
13618 Saint Marys Ln 77079 713-365-4900
Carol Emerson, prin. Fax 365-4912
Wildcat Way S 300/PK-PK
12754 Kimberley Ln 77024 713-365-4740
Tim Ashford, dir. Fax 365-4745
Woodview ES 700/PK-5
9749 Cedardale Dr 77055 713-365-4285
Neda Scanlan, prin. Fax 365-4294

Spring ISD 32,000/PK-12
16717 Ella Blvd 77090 281-891-6000
Ralph Draper Ed.D., supt. Fax 891-6026
www.springisd.org
Bammel ES 600/PK-5
17309 Red Oak Dr 77090 281-891-8152
Terri Williams, prin. Fax 891-6652
Bammel MS 1,700/6-8
16711 Ella Blvd 77090 281-891-7900
Cleotis Wadley, prin. Fax 891-7901
Beneke ES 900/PK-5
3840 Briarchase Dr 77014 281-891-8450
Helen Livers, prin. Fax 891-8451
Booker ES PK-5
22352 Imperial Valley Dr 77073 281-891-8753
Keisha Womack, prin. Fax 891-6063
Clark IS 700/3-5
1825 Rushworth Dr 77014 281-891-8540
Beth Lopez, prin. Fax 891-8541
Clark PS 900/PK-2
12625 River Laurel Dr 77014 281-891-8600
Monica Lewis, prin. Fax 891-8601
Claughton MS 1,400/6-8
3000 Spears Rd 77067 281-891-7950
Becky Hernandez, prin. Fax 891-7951
Cooper ES 1,200/PK-5
18655 Imperial Valley Dr 77073 281-891-8660
Leticia Gonzalez, prin. Fax 209-0035
Heritage ES 700/PK-5
12255 T C Jester Blvd 77067 281-891-8510
Barbra Jones, prin. Fax 891-8511
Lewis ES 800/PK-5
3230 Spears Rd 77067 281-891-8720
Barbara Jones, prin. Fax 440-8676
Link ES 800/PK-5
2815 Ridge Hollow Dr 77067 281-891-8390
Berky Hernandez, prin. Fax 891-8391
Meyer ES 1,200/PK-5
16330 Forest Way Dr 77090 281-891-8270
Serena Pierson, prin. Fax 895-0807
Ponderosa ES 800/PK-5
17202 Butte Creek Rd 77090 281-891-8180
Debbie Graham, prin. Fax 891-8181
Reynolds ES 800/PK-5
3975 Gladeridge Dr 77068 281-891-8240
Carolyn Mays, prin. Fax 891-8241
Thompson ES 800/PK-5
12470 Walters Rd 77014 281-891-8480
Cynthia Gomez, prin. Fax 891-8481

Wells MS 1,300/6-8
4033 Gladeridge Dr 77068 281-891-7750
Stephen Clark, prin. Fax 891-7751
Other Schools – See Spring

Abiding Word Lutheran S 100/K-8
17123 Red Oak Dr 77090 281-895-7048
Shawn Herkstroeter, prin. Fax 895-7048
Annunciation Orthodox S 700/PK-8
3600 Yoakum Blvd 77006 713-470-5600
Mark Kelly, hdmstr. Fax 470-5605
Ascension Episcopal S 100/PK-5
2525 Seagler Rd 77042 713-783-0260
Linda Pitkin, hdmstr. Fax 787-9162
Awty International S 1,200/PK-12
7455 Awty School Ln 77055 713-686-4850
Dr. David Watson, hdmstr. Fax 686-4956
Banff S 100/PK-12
13726 Cutten Rd 77069 281-444-9326
Deborah Wasser, prin. Fax 444-3632
Bay Area Montessori S 100/PK-6
PO Box 891083 77289 281-480-7022
Tommie Hebert, admin. Fax 461-3597
Bayou Montessori S 100/PK-4
16204 Hickory Knoll Dr 77059 281-480-1648
Kathleen Burchfield, prin. Fax 480-8880
Beren Academy 300/PK-12
11333 Cliffwood Dr 77035 713-723-7170
Rabbi Ari Segal, hdmstr. Fax 723-8343
Beth Yeshurun S 200/PK-5
4525 Beechnut St 77096 713-666-1884
Mindy Rosenthal, prin. Fax 666-2924
Branch S 100/PK-5
1424 Sherwood Forest St 77043 713-465-0288
Emily Smith, hdmstr. Fax 465-0337
Briarwood S 300/K-12
12207 Whittington Dr 77077 281-493-1070
Carole Wills, hdmstr. Fax 493-1343
Carethers Adventist S 50/PK-10
5874 Bellfort St 77033 713-733-1351
Central Christian Academy 100/K-12
2217 Bingle Rd 77055 713-468-3248
Scott Jacobs, admin. Fax 468-7322
Champions Christian Academy 100/K-5
2113 Cypress Landing Dr 77090 281-440-1155
Theresa Colletti-Barajas, admin. Fax 440-5055
Christ Lutheran S 50/PK-K
6603 Uvalde Rd 77049 281-458-3231
Fax 458-4625
Christ Memorial Lutheran S 100/PK-K
14200 Memorial Dr 77079 281-497-2055
Barb Tanz, prin. Fax 293-7734
Christ the Lord Lutheran S 100/PK-8
4410 S Kirkwood Rd 77072 281-498-2634
Steven Vasold, prin. Fax 498-7963
Clay Road Baptist S 200/PK-8
9151 Clay Rd 77080 713-939-1023
Kevin Thames, prin. Fax 939-8121
Clear Lake Christian S 300/K-12
14325 Crescent Landing Dr 77062 281-488-4883
Bruce Guillot, supt. Fax 480-3287
Corpus Christi S 200/PK-8
4005 Cheena Dr 77025 713-664-3351
Claire Mueller, prin. Fax 664-6095
Cypress Christian S 500/K-12
11123 Cypress N Houston Rd 77065 281-469-8829
Dr. Glenn Holzman, admin. Fax 469-6040
Duchesne Academy Lower S 200/PK-4
10202 Memorial Dr 77024 713-468-8211
Debra Johnson, prin. Fax 465-9809
Duchesne Academy MS 200/5-8
10202 Memorial Dr 77024 713-468-8211
Julie Meyer, prin. Fax 465-9809
Epiphany Lutheran S 200/PK-7
8101 Senate Ave 77040 713-896-1843
Linda Wimberley, prin. Fax 896-7568
Eternity Christian S 50/K-3
1122 West Rd 77038 281-999-5107
Beth Bashinski, admin. Fax 999-0107
Family Christian Academy 300/PK-12
14718 Woodford Dr 77015 713-455-4483
Robert Anderson, admin. Fax 450-3730
First Baptist Academy 500/PK-8
7450 Memorial Woods Dr 77024 713-290-2500
Olivia Elmore, hdmstr. Fax 290-2508
Gloria Dei Lutheran S 100/PK-K
18220 Upper Bay Rd 77058 281-333-3323
Kathie Walker, prin. Fax 335-0574
Grace S 400/PK-8
10219 Ella Lee Ln 77042 713-782-4421
Dr. Liz Walgamuth, prin. Fax 267-5056
Gulfhaven Christian S 100/PK-9
10716 Sabo Rd 77089 713-944-1619
Holy Ghost S 100/PK-8
6920 Chimney Rock Rd 77081 713-668-5327
Sr. Judy Scheffler, prin. Fax 667-4410
Holy Name S 100/PK-8
1912 Marion St 77009 713-227-9529
Tina Lewis, prin. Fax 227-0224
Holy Spirit Episcopal S 300/PK-8
12535 Perthshire Rd 77024 713-468-5138
Nancy Clausey, hdmstr. Fax 465-6972
Holy Trinity Episcopal S 100/PK-8
11810 Lockwood Rd 77044 281-459-4323
Dr. Shirley Ellisor, hdmstr. Fax 459-4302
Imani S 400/PK-8
12401 S Post Oak Rd 77045 713-723-0616
Patricia Hogan Williams, hdmstr. Fax 723-6143
Immanuel Lutheran S 100/PK-8
306 E 15th St 77008 713-861-8787
Cheryl Burmeister, prin. Fax 861-8787
John Paul II S 700/PK-8
1400 Parkway Plaza Dr 77077 281-496-1500
Jamie Hengst, prin. Fax 496-2943
Joy S 100/K-8
1 Chelsea Blvd 77006 713-523-0660
Shara Bumgarner, hdmstr. Fax 523-5660

Kinkaid S 1,400/PK-12
201 Kinkaid School Dr 77024 713-782-1640
Donald North, hdmstr. Fax 782-3543
Living Word Christian Academy 100/K-8
6601 Antoine Dr 77091 713-686-5538
Everette Cannings, supt. Fax 686-6840
Lutheran South Academy 700/PK-12
12555 Ryewater Dr 77089 281-464-8299
Dr. Micah Parker, hdmstr. Fax 464-6119
Memorial Christian Academy 100/PK-6
1315 S Dairy Ashford St 77077 281-493-3700
Linda Keathley, prin. Fax 493-6233
Memorial Lutheran S 100/PK-8
5800 Westheimer Rd 77057 713-782-4022
Rev. J. Bart Day, hdmstr. Fax 782-1749
Mission Bend Christian Academy 200/PK-6
3710 Highway 6 S 77082 281-497-4057
Marita Foreman, hdmstr. Fax 497-3395
Montessori Country Day S 100/PK-6
30 Oakdale St 77006 713-520-0738
Marge Ellison, prin. Fax 524-0569
Montessori Learning Institute 100/PK-6
5701 Beechnut St 77074 713-774-6952
My Le Vo, prin. Fax 774-4484
Mt. Olive Lutheran S 50/PK-PK
10310 Scarsdale Blvd 77089 281-922-4453
Bobbie Ledbetter, prin. Fax 922-5914
New Heights Christian Academy 200/PK-12
1700 W 43rd St 77018 713-861-9101
Dr. Richard Walters, prin. Fax 426-4525
Northland Christian S 800/PK-12
4363 Sylvanfield Dr 77014 281-440-1060
Cliff Kraner, prin. Fax 440-7572
Oaks Adventist Christian S 100/PK-12
11903C Tanner Rd 77041 713-896-0071
Michelle Battistone, prin. Fax 896-0721
Our Lady of Guadalupe S 200/PK-8
2405 Navigation Blvd 77003 713-224-6904
Katherine Costello, prin. Fax 225-2122
Our Lady of Mt. Carmel S 100/PK-8
6703 Whitefriars Dr 77087 713-643-0676
Stephanie Couty, prin. Fax 649-1835
Our Mother of Mercy S 100/PK-8
2010 Benson St 77020 713-673-1862
Mary Ashley, prin. Fax 673-1041
Our Redeemer Lutheran North S 50/PK-8
215 Rittenhouse St 77076 713-694-0332
Ladeina Brush, dir. Fax 699-1032
Our Savior Lutheran S 200/PK-8
5000 W Tidwell Rd 77091 713-290-8277
Lance Gerard, prin. Fax 290-0850
Pilgrim Lutheran S 100/PK-8
8601 Chimney Rock Rd 77096 713-432-7082
David Glienke, prin. Fax 666-6585
Presbyterian S 500/PK-8
5300 Main St 77004 713-520-0284
Raymond Johnson, hdmstr. Fax 620-6510
Queen of Peace S 200/PK-8
2320 Oakcliff St 77023 713-921-1558
Rebecca Bogard, prin. Fax 921-0855
Redd S 300/PK-8
4820 Strack Rd 77069 281-440-1106
Denna Baskin, prin. Fax 440-3225
Regis S 200/PK-8
7330 Westview Dr 77055 713-682-8383
Dr. Nancy Taylor, hdmstr. Fax 682-8388
Resurrection S 100/PK-8
916 Majestic St 77020 713-674-5545
Danny Brogee, prin. Fax 678-4036
River Oaks Baptist S 800/PK-8
2300 Willowick Rd 77027 713-623-6938
Nancy Hightower, hdmstr. Fax 621-8216
St. Ambrose S 500/PK-8
4213 Mangum Rd 77092 713-686-6990
Judy Fritsch, prin. Fax 686-6902
St. Andrew Lutheran S 100/PK-PK
1353 Witte Rd 77055 713-468-0026
Shatha Razzook, dir. Fax 468-1064
St. Anne S 500/PK-8
2120 Westheimer Rd 77098 713-526-3279
Kathy Barnosky, prin. Fax 526-8025
St. Augustine S 200/PK-8
5500 Laurel Creek Way 77017 713-946-9050
Rose Garcia-Filteau, prin. Fax 943-3444
St. Catherine's Montessori S 200/PK-9
9821 Timberside Dr 77025 713-665-2195
Judy McCullough, prin. Fax 665-1478
St. Cecilia S 500/PK-8
11740 Joan of Arc Dr 77024 713-468-9515
Dr. Carol Everling, prin. Fax 468-4698
St. Charles Borromeo S 200/PK-5
501 Tidwell Rd 77022 713-692-4898
Joshua Raab, prin. Fax 692-1376
St. Christopher S 300/PK-8
8134 Park Place Blvd 77017 713-649-0009
JoAnn Prater, prin. Fax 649-1104
St. Christopher's Day S PK-K
1656 Blalock Rd 77080 713-465-6035
Fax 465-2086
St. Clare of Assisi S 200/PK-8
3131 El Dorado Blvd 77059 281-286-3395
Alfred Varisco, prin. Fax 286-1256
St. Elizabeth Ann Seton S 500/K-8
6646 Addicks Satsuma Rd 77084 281-463-1444
Jan Krametbauer, prin. Fax 463-8707
St. Francis De Sales S 400/PK-8
8100 Roos Rd 77036 713-774-4447
Diane Wooten, prin. Fax 271-6744
St. Francis Episcopal Day S 800/PK-8
335 Piney Point Rd 77024 713-458-6100
Dr. Susan Lair, hdmstr. Fax 782-4720
St. Francis of Assisi S 200/PK-8
5100 Dabney St 77026 713-674-1966
Dr. Clarice Campbell, prin. Fax 674-9901
St. James S 100/PK-8
3129 Southmore Blvd 77004 713-521-9884
Vanita Reed, prin. Fax 526-0887

St. Jerome S 300/K-8
8825 Kempwood Dr 77080 713-468-7946
Sharon Makulski, prin. Fax 464-0325
St. John's S 1,200/K-12
2401 Claremont Ln 77019 713-850-0222
John Allman, hdmstr. Fax 850-4089
St. Mark Lutheran S 300/PK-8
1515 Hillendahl Blvd 77055 713-468-2623
Herb Mock, prin. Fax 468-6735
St. Mark's Episcopal S 400/PK-8
3816 Bellaire Blvd 77025 713-667-7030
Dr. David Pitre, hdmstr. Fax 349-0419
St. Mary of the Purification S 200/PK-5
3006 Rosedale St 77004 713-522-9276
Mazie McCoy, prin. Fax 522-1879
St. Michael S 500/PK-8
1833 Sage Rd 77056 713-621-6847
Stephen Parsons, prin. Fax 877-8812
St. Nicholas S 100/PK-5
10420 Mullins Dr 77096 713-726-0221
Monica Jolivet, prin. Fax 726-0225
St. Peter the Apostle MS 50/6-8
6220 La Salette St 77021 713-747-9484
Sr. Felicia Omole, prin. Fax 842-7055
St. Phillip Neri S 100/PK-5
PO Box 330190 77233 713-733-2343
Melina Harris, prin. Fax 733-4759
St. Rose of Lima S 100/PK-5
3600 Brinkman St 77018 713-691-0104
Maria Luisa Rodriguez, prin. Fax 692-8073
St. Stephen's Episcopal School Houston 200/PK-12
1800 Sul Ross St 77098 713-821-9100
Betty Sierra, hdmstr. Fax 821-9156
St. Theresa S 200/PK-8
6622 Haskell St 77007 713-864-4536
Audrey Nelson, prin. Fax 869-5184
St. Thomas' Episcopal S 600/K-12
4900 Jackwood St 77096 713-666-3111
Michael Cusack, hdmstr. Fax 668-3887
St. Thomas More S 600/PK-8
5927 Wigton Dr 77096 713-729-3434
Nadine Mouser, prin. Fax 721-5644
St. Thomas the Apostle Episcopal S 100/PK-5
18300 Upper Bay Rd 77058 281-333-1340
Fax 333-9113
St. Vincent De Paul S 500/PK-8
6802 Buffalo Speedway 77025 713-666-2345
Carolyn Sears, prin. Fax 663-3562
School of the Woods 400/PK-12
1321 Wirt Rd 77055 713-686-8811
Sherry Herron, hdmstr. Fax 686-1936
Second Baptist S 1,100/PK-12
6410 Woodway Dr 77057 713-365-2310
Brett Jacobsen Ed.D., hdmstr. Fax 365-2355
Sephardic Gan of Houston PK-3
9730 Hillcroft St 77096 713-721-3900
Seton Catholic JHS 100/6-8
801 Roselane St 77037 281-447-2132
Patrick Clark, prin. Fax 447-1825
Shady Acres Christian S 50/1-12
7330 Vogel Rd 77088 281-999-2040
Marsha Farley, prin. Fax 999-2040
Sherwood Forest Montessori S 50/PK-6
1331 Sherwood Forest St 77043 713-464-5791
Sara Norton, prin. Fax 464-5810
Shlenker S 300/PK-5
5600 N Braeswood Blvd 77096 713-270-6127
Ricki Komiss, hdmstr. Fax 270-6114
Smaller Scholars Montessori S 400/PK-6
1685 S Dairy Ashford St 77077 281-558-3515
Noreen Martin, hdmstr. Fax 558-0917
Southhampton Montessori S 300/PK-6
5012 Morningside Dr 77005 713-526-7458
Gloria Blake, prin. Fax 526-7173
Southwest Christian Academy 200/PK-12
7400 Eldridge Pkwy 77083 281-561-7400
Paula Thurmond, prin. Fax 240-9606
Sunshine Children's World Academy 50/K-3
11410 Hall Rd 77089 281-481-3630
Linda Goudeau, prin. Fax 481-3665
Texas Christian S 200/PK-12
17810 Kieth Harrow Blvd 77084 281-550-6060
Herc Palmquist, admin. Fax 550-2400
Torah Day S 100/PK-8
10900 Fondren Rd 77096 713-777-2000
Rabbi Shimon Lazeroff, dean Fax 776-0036
Trinity Lutheran S 200/PK-8
800 Houston Ave 77007 713-224-7265
Amy Boatman, prin. Fax 224-1163
Village S 700/PK-12
13077 Westella Dr 77077 281-496-7900
Betty Moore, prin. Fax 496-7799
Westbury Christian S 500/PK-12
10420 Hillcroft St 77096 713-723-8377
Greg Glenn, prin. Fax 551-8117
Westside Montessori S 100/PK-4
13555 Briar Forest Dr 77077 281-556-5970
Diane Musgrove, prin. Fax 556-5961
Windwood Christian Academy 700/PK-5
10555 Spring Cypress Rd 77070 281-257-7862
Michelle Asous, dir. Fax 257-7887
Yellowstone Academy 200/PK-8
3000 Trulley St 77004 713-741-8000
Kim Hensen, dir. Fax 741-8006
Yorkshire Academy 200/PK-5
14120 Memorial Dr 77079 281-531-6088
Janet Howard, prin. Fax 531-6097

Howe, Grayson, Pop. 2,709
Howe ISD 1,000/PK-12
105 W Tutt St 75459 903-532-5518
Kevin Wilson, supt. Fax 532-9378
www.howeisd.net
Howe ES 400/PK-4
315 Roberts St 75459 903-532-6014
Ritchie Bowling, prin. Fax 532-9909
Howe MS 300/5-8
300 Beatrice St 75459 903-532-6013
Greg Masters, prin. Fax 537-0113

Hubbard, Hill, Pop. 1,680
Hubbard ISD 500/PK-12
PO Box 218 76648 254-576-2564
Walter Padgett, supt. Fax 576-5019
www.hubbardisd.com/
Hubbard ES 200/PK-5
PO Box 218 76648 254-576-2359
Steven Slaughter, prin. Fax 576-5018
Hubbard MS 100/6-8
PO Box 218 76648 254-576-2758
Lance Johnson, prin. Fax 576-5017

Huffman, Harris
Huffman ISD 2,900/PK-12
PO Box 2390 77336 281-324-1871
Douglas Killian Ph.D., supt. Fax 324-3293
www.huffmanisd.net
Bowen ECC 500/PK-1
PO Box 2390 77336 281-324-1399
Jack Fillbrandt, prin. Fax 324-1646
Copeland ES 200/2-3
PO Box 2390 77336 281-324-7100
Jay Pratt, prin. Fax 324-2076
Huffman IS 500/4-5
PO Box 2390 77336 281-324-9380
Jay Pratt, prin. Fax 324-9369
Huffman MS 700/6-8
PO Box 2390 77336 281-324-2598
Janet Bryant, prin. Fax 324-2710

Hughes Springs, Cass, Pop. 1,876
Hughes Springs ISD 1,000/PK-12
871 Taylor St 75656 903-639-3800
Rick Ogden, supt. Fax 639-2624
www.hsisd.net
Hughes Springs ES 500/PK-5
PO Box 879 75656 903-639-3881
Theresa Jennings, prin. Fax 639-3930
Hughes Springs JHS 200/6-8
PO Box 1389 75656 903-639-3812
Brian Nation, prin. Fax 639-3929

Hull, Liberty, Pop. 850
Hull-Daisetta ISD
Supt. — See Daisetta
Hull-Daisetta ES 300/PK-5
7243 FM 834E 77564 936-536-6667
Kelley Berry, prin. Fax 536-3800

Humble, Harris, Pop. 14,803
Aldine ISD
Supt. — See Houston
Jones ECC PK-PK
8003 Forest Point Dr 77338 281-446-1576
Gladys Moton, prin. Fax 985-6010
Jones ES K-4
7903 Forest Point Dr 77338 281-446-6168
Cheryl Fontenot, prin. Fax 985-6022
Magrill ES 1,200/K-4
21701 Rayford Rd 77338 281-233-4300
Robin Williams, prin. Fax 233-4303
Teague MS 1,100/7-8
21700 Rayford Rd 77338 281-233-4310
Michael Gallien, prin. Fax 233-4318

Humble ISD 34,100/PK-12
PO Box 2000 77347 281-641-1000
Dr. Guy Sconzo, supt. Fax 641-1050
www.humble.k12.tx.us./
Atascocita MS 1,700/6-8
18810 W Lake Houston Pkwy 77346 281-641-4600
Thyrun Hurst, prin. Fax 641-4617
Eagle Springs ES 700/PK-5
12500 Will Clayton Pkwy 77346 281-641-3100
Karen Geffert, prin. Fax 641-3117
Fall Creek ES PK-5
14435 Mesa Dr 77396 281-641-3400
Cathy Airola, prin. Fax 641-3417
Fields ES 700/PK-5
2505 S Houston Ave 77396 281-641-2700
Karen Weeks, prin. Fax 641-2717
Humble ES 700/PK-5
20252 Fieldtree Dr 77338 281-641-1100
Kathy Shealy, prin. Fax 641-1117
Humble MS 1,200/6-8
11207 Will Clayton Pkwy 77346 281-641-4000
Marie Flynn, prin. Fax 641-4017
Lakeland ES 700/PK-5
1500 Montgomery Ln 77338 281-641-1200
Sharon Lee, prin. Fax 641-1217
Maplebrook ES 800/PK-5
7935 Farmingham Rd 77346 281-641-2900
Marsha Reineking, prin. Fax 641-2917
North Belt ES 500/PK-5
8105 E North Belt 77396 281-641-1300
Colleen Killingsworth, prin. Fax 641-1317
Oak Forest ES 700/PK-5
6400 Kingwood Glen Dr 77346 281-641-2800
Marty Bragg, prin. Fax 641-2817
Oaks ES 700/PK-5
5858 Upper Lake Dr 77346 281-641-1890
Cindy Blankenship, prin. Fax 641-1817
Park Lakes ES 800/PK-5
4400 Wilson Rd 77396 281-641-3200
Sarah Ballard, prin. Fax 641-3217
Pine Forest ES 700/PK-5
19702 W Lake Houston Pkwy 77346 281-641-2100
Nancy Morrison, prin. Fax 641-2117
River Pines ES 700/PK-5
2400 Cold River Dr 77396 281-641-3300
Betsy Cross, prin. Fax 641-3317
Sterling MS 900/6-8
1131 Wilson Rd 77338 281-641-6000
Penne Leifer, prin. Fax 641-6017
Timbers ES 800/PK-5
6910 Lonesome Woods Trl 77346 281-641-2000
Pat Winkler, prin. Fax 641-2017
Timberwood MS 1,300/6-8
18450 Timber Forest Dr 77346 281-641-3800
Carol Atwood, prin. Fax 641-3817

Whispering Pines ES 800/PK-5
17321 Woodland Hills Dr 77346 281-641-2500
Glenda Holder, prin. Fax 641-2517
Other Schools – See Houston, Kingwood

Christian Life Center Academy 200/PK-12
600 Charles St 77338 281-319-0077
Richard Rodriguez, admin. Fax 446-5501
Humble Christian S 300/PK-12
16202 Old Humble Rd 77396 281-441-1313
Ted Howell, admin. Fax 441-1329
Lamb of God Lutheran S 100/PK-1
1400 FM 1960 Bypass Rd E 77338 281-446-5262
Fax 446-0289
Pines Montessori S 200/PK-6
3535 Cedar Knolls Dr 77339 281-358-8933
Patricia Sobelman, hdmstr. Fax 358-3162
St. Mary Magdalene S 300/PK-8
530 Ferguson St 77338 281-446-8535
Jean Johnson, prin. Fax 446-8527

Hunt, Kerr
Hunt ISD 200/PK-12
PO Box 259 78024 830-238-4893
David Kelm, supt. Fax 238-4691
www.huntisd.com
Hunt S 200/PK-12
PO Box 259 78024 830-238-4893
David Kelm, prin. Fax 238-4691

Huntington, Angelina, Pop. 2,073
Huntington ISD 1,700/PK-12
PO Box 328 75949 936-876-4287
Dr. Eric Wright, supt. Fax 876-3212
www.huntingtonisd.com/
Huntington ES 600/PK-3
PO Box 328 75949 936-876-5194
Melanie Stubblefield, prin. Fax 422-4450
Huntington IS 300/4-5
PO Box 328 75949 936-876-3432
Ben Wilroy, prin. Fax 422-4419
Huntington MS 400/6-8
PO Box 328 75949 936-876-4722
Glenn Frank, prin. Fax 876-4009

Huntsville, Walker, Pop. 36,699
Huntsville ISD 5,700/PK-12
441 FM 2821 Rd E 77320 936-295-3421
Dr. Richard Montgomery, supt. Fax 291-3444
www.huntsville-isd.org
Gibbs Prekindergarten Center 50/PK-PK
441 FM 2821 Rd E 77320 936-293-2837
Rosa Valles, prin. Fax 293-2822
Houston ES 400/K-4
441 FM 2821 Rd E 77320 936-439-1200
Stacey Bennett, prin. Fax 439-1223
Huntsville ES 500/K-4
441 FM 2821 Rd E 77320 936-293-2888
Connie Lott, prin. Fax 293-2896
Huntsville IS 900/5-6
441 FM 2821 Rd E 77320 936-293-2717
Angee Andrus, prin. Fax 293-2712
Johnson ES 500/K-4
441 FM 2821 Rd E 77320 936-293-2866
Delanise Taylor, prin. Fax 293-2876
Mance Park JHS 1,000/7-8
441 FM 2821 Rd E 77320 936-293-2755
Beth Burt, prin. Fax 293-2759
Stewart ES 600/K-4
441 FM 2821 Rd E 77320 936-293-2811
Amber Rodriguez, prin. Fax 293-2809

Alpha Omega Academy 300/K-12
PO Box 8419 77340 936-438-8833
Paul Davidhizar, hdmstr. Fax 438-8844
Faith Lutheran S 100/PK-2
111 Sumac Rd 77340 936-291-1706
Kristie Pacher, prin. Fax 295-8266
Summit Christian Academy 100/PK-6
PO Box 1590 77342 936-295-9601
Joyce Parrish, admin. Fax 295-9236

Hurst, Tarrant, Pop. 37,967
Birdville ISD
Supt. — See Haltom City
Porter ES 400/PK-5
2750 Prestondale Dr 76054 817-547-2900
Jaimie Smith, prin. Fax 581-5381

Hurst-Euless-Bedford ISD
Supt. — See Bedford
Bellaire ES 600/PK-6
501 Bellaire Dr 76053 817-285-3230
Livia Mansour, prin. Fax 285-3203
Donna Park ES 500/PK-6
1125 Scott Dr 76053 817-285-3285
Aungelique Brading, prin. Fax 285-3289
Harrison Lane ES 600/PK-6
1000 Harrison Ln 76053 817-285-3270
Donna Stevens, prin. Fax 285-3207
Hurst Hills ES 500/PK-6
525 Billie Ruth Ln 76053 817-285-3295
Georgeann Gallian, prin. Fax 285-3208
Shady Oaks ES 500/PK-6
1400 Cavender Dr 76053 817-285-3240
Gina Mayfield, prin. Fax 285-3209
West Hurst ES 500/PK-6
501 Precinct Line Rd 76053 817-285-3290
Debra Day, prin. Fax 285-3212

Red Apple Lutheran S 200/PK-K
941 W Bedford Euless Rd 76053 817-284-7833
Marian Hamre, dir. Fax 284-3950

Hutto, Williamson, Pop. 7,401
Hutto ISD 4,400/PK-12
PO Box 430 78634 512-759-3771
Dr. David Borrer, supt. Fax 759-4796
www.hutto.txed.net
Cottonwood Creek ES 600/PK-5
3160 Limmer Loop 78634 512-759-5430
Jacqueline Tealer, prin. Fax 759-5431
Farley MS 6-8
303 County Road 137 78634 512-759-2050
Dorothy Struble, prin. Fax 759-2033
Hutto ES 600/PK-5
100 Mager Ln 78634 512-759-2094
Fax 759-4778
Hutto MS 800/6-8
1005 Exchange Blvd 78634 512-759-4541
Dale Mitchell, prin. Fax 759-4753
Johnson ES 700/PK-5
955 Carl Stern Blvd 78634 512-759-5400
Tammy Jordan, prin. Fax 759-5401
Ray ES 700/PK-5
225 Swindoll Ln 78634 512-759-5450
Janet Reichardt, prin. Fax 759-5451
Other Schools – See Round Rock

Idalou, Lubbock, Pop. 2,046
Idalou ISD 900/PK-12
PO Box 1338 79329 806-892-2501
Jim Waller, supt. Fax 892-3204
www.idalouisd.net/
Idalou ES 300/PK-4
PO Box 1399 79329 806-892-2524
Southern Bush, prin. Fax 892-2666
Idalou MS 300/5-8
PO Box 1353 79329 806-892-2133
Steve Gunter, prin. Fax 892-2388

Imperial, Pecos
Buena Vista ISD 100/PK-12
PO Box 310 79743 432-536-2225
David Dillard, supt. Fax 536-2469
www.bvisd.esc18.net/
Buena Vista S 100/PK-12
PO Box 310 79743 432-536-2225
Guy Birdwell, prin. Fax 536-2469

Industry, Austin, Pop. 333
Bellville ISD
Supt. — See Bellville
West End ES 200/K-5
7453 Ernst Pkwy 78944 979-357-2595
Charles Abel, prin. Fax 357-4799

Inez, Victoria, Pop. 1,371
Industrial ISD
Supt. — See Vanderbilt
Industrial ES West 200/PK-5
599 FM 444 S 77968 361-284-3226
Dianne Juroske, prin. Fax 782-0010

Ingleside, San Patricio, Pop. 9,531
Ingleside ISD 2,300/PK-12
PO Box 1320 78362 361-776-7631
Troy Mircovich, supt. Fax 776-0267
www.inglesideisd.org
Blaschke/Sheldon ES 300/5-6
2624 Mustang Dr 78362 361-776-3050
Stephanie McNew, prin. Fax 776-7912
Ingleside PS 500/PK-1
2100 Achievement Blvd 78362 361-776-3060
Chip Johnston, prin. Fax 775-2070
Mircovich ES 500/2-4
2720 Big Oak Ln 78362 361-776-1683
James Bonorden, prin. Fax 776-0509
Taylor JHS 300/7-8
2739 Mustang Dr 78362 361-776-2232
Reymundo Gonzalez, prin. Fax 776-2192

Ingram, Kerr, Pop. 1,838
Ingram ISD 1,400/PK-12
510 College St 78025 830-367-5517
James Stroder, supt. Fax 367-5631
www.ingramisd.net
Ingram ES 600/PK-5
510 College St 78025 830-367-5751
Sharon Kubenka, prin. Fax 367-7333
Ingram MS 300/6-8
510 College St 78025 830-367-4012
Jill Dworsky, prin. Fax 367-7335

Iola, Grimes
Iola ISD 500/PK-12
PO Box 159 77861 936-394-2361
Douglas Devine, supt. Fax 394-2132
www.iolaisd.net
Iola ES 300/PK-6
PO Box 159 77861 936-394-2361
Danny Mallett, prin. Fax 394-2132

Iowa Park, Wichita, Pop. 6,175
Iowa Park Consolidated ISD 1,900/PK-12
PO Box 898 76367 940-592-4193
Jerry Baird, supt. Fax 592-2136
www.ipcisd.net/
Bradford ES 400/3-5
800 Texowa Rd 76367 940-592-5841
Vickie Jordan, prin. Fax 592-2059
George MS 400/6-8
412 E Cash St 76367 940-592-2196
Darla Biddy, prin. Fax 592-2801
Kidwell ES 400/PK-2
1200 N 3rd St 76367 940-592-4322
Debra Brandt, prin. Fax 592-2487

Ira, Scurry
Ira ISD 300/K-12
6143 W FM 1606 79527 325-573-2629
Dr. Skip Casey, supt. Fax 573-5825
Ira S 300/K-12
6143 W FM 1606 79527 325-573-2628
Jay Waller, prin. Fax 573-9887

Iraan, Pecos, Pop. 1,172
Iraan-Sheffield ISD 500/PK-12
PO Box 486 79744 432-639-2512
Kevin Allen, supt. Fax 639-2501
isisd.esc18.net
Iraan ES 200/PK-5
PO Box 486 79744 432-639-2524
Blake Andrews, prin. Fax 639-2501
Iraan JHS 100/6-8
PO Box 486 79744 432-639-2867
Randy Doege, prin. Fax 639-2501

Iredell, Bosque, Pop. 380
Iredell ISD 100/PK-12
PO Box 39 76649 254-364-2411
Bryan Lee, supt. Fax 364-2206
www.iredell-isd.com
Iredell S 100/PK-12
PO Box 39 76649 254-364-2411
Bryan Lee, prin. Fax 364-2206

Irving, Dallas, Pop. 193,649
Carrollton-Farmers Branch ISD
Supt. — See Carrollton
Bush MS 600/6-8
515 Cowboys Pkwy 75063 972-968-3700
Lynda Opitz, prin. Fax 968-3710
Freeman ES 500/K-5
8757 Valley Ranch Pkwy W 75063 972-968-1700
Walter Peterson, prin. Fax 968-1710
Landry ES 500/PK-5
265 Red River Trl 75063 972-968-2100
Lance Hamlin, prin. Fax 968-2110
Las Colinas ES 500/PK-5
2200 Kinwest Pkwy 75063 972-968-2200
Kelly Calvery, prin. Fax 968-2210
La Villita ES PK-5
1601 Camino Lago 75039 972-968-6900
Deama Mayfield, prin.

Coppell ISD
Supt. — See Coppell
Valley Ranch ES 400/K-5
9800 Rodeo Dr 75063 214-496-8500
Cynthia Arterbery, prin. Fax 496-8506

Irving ISD 32,900/PK-12
PO Box 152637 75015 972-215-5000
Dr. Neil Dugger, supt. Fax 215-5201
www.irvingisd.net
Austin MS 900/6-8
825 E Union Bower Rd 75061 972-721-3100
David Saenz, prin. Fax 721-3105
Barton ES 800/K-5
2931 Conflans Rd 75061 972-313-4100
Jane Lampton, prin. Fax 313-4110
Bowie MS 1,000/6-8
600 E 6th St 75060 972-721-3000
Joe Moreno, prin. Fax 721-3044
Brandenburg ES 900/K-5
2800 Hillcrest Dr 75062 972-258-7100
Pam Meredith, prin. Fax 258-7199
Britain ES 800/K-5
631 Edmondson Dr 75060 972-554-3800
Brenda Bingham, prin. Fax 554-3899
Brown ES 800/K-5
2501 10th St 75060 972-513-4000
Dr. Adam Grinage, prin. Fax 513-4099
Clifton ECC 600/PK-PK
3950 Pleasant Run Rd 75038 972-261-2800
Mary Rudisell, prin. Fax 261-2849
Crockett MS 1,000/6-8
2431 Hancock St 75061 972-313-4700
Angie Gaylord, prin. Fax 313-4770
Davis ES 800/K-5
310 Davis Dr 75061 972-313-4900
John Ringhauser, prin. Fax 313-4949
de Zavala MS 1,000/6-8
707 W Pioneer Dr 75061 972-273-8900
John Rose, prin. Fax 273-8924
Elliott ES 800/K-5
1900 S Story Rd 75060 972-313-4300
Jill Tokumoto, prin. Fax 313-4316
Farine ES 800/K-5
615 Metker St 75062 972-261-2700
Julie Miller, prin. Fax 261-2799
Gilbert ES 800/K-5
1501 E Pioneer Dr 75061 972-721-8400
Michael Crotty, prin. Fax 721-8480
Good ES 800/K-5
1200 E Union Bower Rd 75061 972-721-3300
Yanira Oliveras, prin. Fax 721-3379
Haley ES 800/K-5
1100 Schulze Dr 75060 972-273-6600
Robyn Bowling, prin. Fax 273-6608
Haley ES 700/K-5
3601 Cheyenne St 75062 972-261-2500
Lisa Molinar, prin. Fax 261-2599
Hanes ES 600/K-5
2730 Cheyenne St 75062 972-261-2900
Stacey Blevins, prin. Fax 261-2950
Houston MS 1,000/6-8
3033 Country Club Dr W 75038 972-261-2300
Robert Abel, prin. Fax 261-2399
Johnston ES 700/K-5
2801 Rutgers Dr 75062 972-659-7700
Tina Richard, prin. Fax 659-7799
Keyes ES 800/K-5
1501 N Britain Rd 75061 972-721-3400
Irma Vega-Zadeh, prin. Fax 721-3405
Kinkeade ECC 600/PK-PK
2333 Cameron Pl 75060 972-273-6500
Myrna Baker, prin. Fax 273-6549
Lamar MS 1,100/6-8
219 Crandall Rd 75060 972-313-4400
Rocci Malone, prin. Fax 313-4499
Lee ES 700/K-5
1600 Carlisle St 75062 972-261-2600
Maria Elena Coronado, prin. Fax 261-2629
Lively ES 900/K-5
1800 Plymouth Dr W 75061 972-273-6700
Patty Notgrass, prin. Fax 273-6710
Pierce ECC 700/PK-PK
901 N Britain Rd 75061 972-554-3700
Linda Tucker, prin. Fax 554-3749

Schulze ES 600/K-5
1200 S Irving Heights Dr 75060 972-785-3500
Erin Yacho, prin. Fax 785-3599
Stipes ES 400/K-5
3100 Cross Timbers Dr 75060 972-986-4500
Jackie Gorena, prin. Fax 986-4598
Townley ES 800/K-5
1030 W Vilbig St 75060 972-273-6800
Doug Sevier, prin. Fax 273-6877
Townsell ES 800/K-5
3700 Pleasant Run Rd 75038 972-215-5500
Linda Willett, prin. Fax 215-5599
Travis MS 1,100/6-8
1600 Finley Rd 75062 972-261-2400
Terry Cooper, prin. Fax 261-2450

Berean Christian Academy 50/PK-6
1000 E 6th St 75060 972-438-1440
Leon Adkins, pres. Fax 554-6807
Highlands S 400/PK-12
1451 E Northgate Dr 75062 972-554-1980
Dr. Paul Sullivan, hdmstr. Fax 721-1691
Holy Family of Nazareth S 200/PK-8
2323 Cheyenne St 75062 972-255-0205
Dennis Poyant, prin. Fax 252-0448
Redeemer Montessori S 100/PK-3
2700 Warren Cir 75062 972-257-3517
Jennifer Davey, prin. Fax 258-9882
St. Luke S 200/PK-8
1023 Schulze Dr 75060 972-253-8285
Cathy Quattrochi, prin. Fax 253-5535
Sloan S 100/K-5
3131 N O Connor Rd 75062 972-659-1199
Darin Sloan, admin. Fax 255-6070
StoneGate Christian Academy 100/PK-12
2833 W Shady Grove Rd 75060 972-790-0070
Rhonda Tuttle, hdmstr. Fax 790-6560

Italy, Ellis, Pop. 2,091
Italy ISD 600/PK-12
300 College 76651 972-483-1815
Jimmie Malone, supt. Fax 483-6152
www.italyisd.org/
Stafford ES 300/PK-6
300 College 76651 972-483-6342
Carolyn Maevers, prin. Fax 483-6892

Itasca, Hill, Pop. 1,618
Itasca ISD 600/PK-12
123 N College St 76055 254-687-2922
Glenn Pittman, supt. Fax 687-2637
www.itasca.k12.tx.us
Itasca ES 300/PK-4
300 N Files St 76055 254-687-2922
Karon Farquhar, prin. Fax 687-2637
Itasca MS 100/5-8
208 N Files St 76055 254-687-2922
Larry Mynarcik, prin. Fax 687-2637

Ivanhoe, Fannin
Sam Rayburn ISD 400/PK-12
9363 E FM 273 75447 903-664-2255
Jeff Irvin, supt. Fax 664-2406
www.samrayburnisd.org/
Rayburn ES 200/PK-6
9363 E FM 273 75447 903-664-2005
Jim Shaw, prin. Fax 664-2406

Jacksboro, Jack, Pop. 4,610
Jacksboro ISD 1,000/PK-12
812 W Belknap St 76458 940-567-7203
Dennis Bennett, supt. Fax 567-2214
www.jacksboroisd.net/
Jacksboro ES 500/PK-5
1677 N Main St 76458 940-567-7206
Patricia Zeitler, prin. Fax 567-2603
Lowrance MS 200/6-8
117 N 4th St 76458 940-567-7205
Don O'Steen, prin. Fax 567-2681

Jacksonville, Cherokee, Pop. 14,395
Jacksonville ISD 5,000/PK-12
PO Box 631 75766 903-586-6511
Stuart Bird, supt. Fax 586-3133
www.jacksonvilleisd.org
Douglass ES 700/PK-4
PO Box 631 75766 903-586-6519
Amber Penn, prin. Fax 589-4341
East Side ES 700/PK-4
PO Box 631 75766 903-586-5146
Laurie Greathouse, prin. Fax 589-4977
Jacksonville MS 700/7-8
PO Box 631 75766 903-586-3686
Lisa Herron, prin. Fax 586-8071
Nichols IS 700/5-6
PO Box 631 75766 903-541-0213
Tammy Jones, prin. Fax 541-0199
West Side ES 500/PK-4
PO Box 631 75766 903-586-5165
Sandi Jones, prin. Fax 586-6196
Wright ES 500/PK-4
PO Box 631 75766 903-586-5286
Brad Stewart, prin. Fax 589-8108

Jacksonville Christian S 100/PK-6
PO Box 869 75766 903-586-8801
Sharon Beall, admin. Fax 586-0438

Jarrell, Williamson, Pop. 1,406
Jarrell ISD 700/PK-12
PO Box 9 76537 512-746-2124
Dr. Jamie Mattison, supt. Fax 746-2518
www.esc13.net/jarrell
Jarrell ES 300/PK-5
PO Box 9 76537 512-746-2170
Becky Snow, prin. Fax 746-2575
Jarrell MS 200/6-8
PO Box 9 76537 512-746-4180
Abbe Lester, prin. Fax 746-4280

Jasper, Jasper, Pop. 7,531
Jasper ISD 2,900/PK-12
128 Park Ln 75951 409-384-2401
Dr. Jimmy Creet, supt. Fax 382-1084
www.jasperisd.net
Few PS 900/PK-2
225 Bulldog Ave 75951 409-489-9808
Vanessa Phillips, prin. Fax 382-1399
Jasper JHS 400/7-8
211 2nd St 75951 409-384-3585
Mervin Cleveland, prin. Fax 382-1160
Parnell ES 400/3-4
151 Park Ln 75951 409-384-2212
Betty Powers, prin. Fax 382-1114
Rowe IS 400/5-6
750 E Gibson St 75951 409-384-4461
Victor Williams, prin. Fax 382-1192

Jayton, Kent, Pop. 472
Jayton-Girard ISD 100/PK-12
PO Box 168 79528 806-237-2991
Tim Seymore, supt. Fax 237-2670
www.jaytonjaybirds.com
Jayton S 100/PK-12
PO Box 168 79528 806-237-2991
Jodie Reel, prin. Fax 237-2670

Jefferson, Marion, Pop. 1,992
Jefferson ISD 1,300/PK-12
1600 Martin Luther King Dr 75657 903-665-2461
Sharon Ross, supt. Fax 665-7367
jeffersonisd.org/
Jefferson ES 400/1-4
301 W Harrison St 75657 903-665-2461
Melissa McIntosh, prin. Fax 665-6401
Jefferson JHS 400/5-8
804 N Alley St 75657 903-665-2461
John McCoy, prin. Fax 665-8914
Jefferson PS 100/PK-K
304 W Broadway St 75657 903-665-2461
Lonnie Taylor, prin. Fax 665-7092

Cypress Bend Adventist S 50/PK-8
2997 FM 728 75657 903-665-7402
Peggy Dyke, prin. Fax 665-9759

Jewett, Leon, Pop. 922
Leon ISD 700/PK-12
PO Box 157 75846 903-626-1400
Jay Winn, supt. Fax 626-1420
www.leonisd.net/
Leon ES 300/PK-5
PO Box 157 75846 903-626-1426
Dana Anderson, prin. Fax 626-1440
Leon JHS 200/6-8
PO Box 157 75846 903-626-1451
Darin Hale, prin. Fax 626-1455

Joaquin, Shelby, Pop. 946
Joaquin ISD 700/PK-12
11109 US Highway 84 E 75954 936-269-3128
Phil Worsham, supt. Fax 269-3615
www.joaquinisd.net/
Joaquin ES 400/PK-6
11109 US Highway 84 E 75954 936-269-3128
Sherry Scruggs, prin. Fax 269-3324
Joaquin JHS 100/7-8
11109 US Highway 84 E 75954 936-269-3128
Mid Johnson, prin. Fax 269-9123

Johnson City, Blanco, Pop. 1,469
Johnson City ISD 700/PK-12
PO Box 498 78636 830-868-7410
David Shanley, supt. Fax 868-7375
Johnson ES 300/PK-4
PO Box 498 78636 830-868-4028
Shannon Helmke, prin. Fax 868-7375
Johnson MS 200/5-8
PO Box 498 78636 830-868-9025
Cammie Ockman, prin. Fax 868-7375

Jonesboro, Coryell
Jonesboro ISD 200/K-12
PO Box 125 76538 254-463-2111
Larry Robinson, supt. Fax 463-2275
jonesboroisd.net
Jonesboro S 200/K-12
PO Box 125 76538 254-463-2111
Mike Kelly, prin. Fax 463-2275

Jones Creek, Brazoria, Pop. 2,130
Brazosport ISD
Supt. — See Clute
Austin ES 300/PK-6
7351 Stephen F Austin Rd 77541 979-730-7160
Melania Gutierrez, prin. Fax 237-6341

Joshua, Johnson, Pop. 5,500
Joshua ISD 4,500/PK-12
PO Box 40 76058 817-202-2500
Ray Dane, supt. Fax 641-2738
www.joshuaisd.org
Caddo Grove ES 500/PK-6
7301 FM 1902 76058 817-202-2500
Kathryn Cockerham, prin. Fax 645-6420
Elder ES 500/PK-6
513 Henderson St 76058 817-202-2500
Lance Cathey, prin. Fax 641-2951
Loflin MS 700/7-8
520 Stadium Dr 76058 817-202-2500
Dr. Clark Cavin, prin. Fax 202-9140
Plum Creek ES 500/PK-6
500 Plum St 76058 817-202-2500
Jim Moon, prin. Fax 202-9133
Staples ES 400/PK-6
505 S Main St 76058 817-202-2500
Pam McCoy, prin. Fax 556-0450
Other Schools – See Burleson

Joshua Adventist Multi Grade S 100/PK-8
PO Box 329 76058 817-556-2109
David Stair, prin.
Joshua Christian S 200/PK-12
PO Box 1379 76058 817-295-7377
Dr. Gene Wolfenbarger, supt. Fax 484-2415

Jourdanton, Atascosa, Pop. 4,235
Jourdanton ISD 1,200/PK-12
200 Zanderson Ave 78026 830-769-3548
Dr. Lana Collavo, supt. Fax 769-3272
www.jourdantonisd.net/
Jourdanton ES 600/PK-5
200 Zanderson Ave 78026 830-769-2121
Michele Hartung, prin. Fax 769-3272
Jourdanton JHS 200/6-8
200 Zanderson Ave 78026 830-769-2234
Robert Rutkowski, prin. Fax 769-3272

Junction, Kimble, Pop. 2,654
Junction ISD 700/PK-12
1700 College St 76849 325-446-3580
Renee Schulze, supt. Fax 446-4413
www.junctionisd.net
Junction ES 300/PK-5
1700 College St 76849 325-446-2055
Kara Fluty, prin. Fax 446-4569
Junction MS 200/6-8
1700 College St 76849 325-446-2464
Melissa Hoggett, prin. Fax 446-2255

Justin, Denton, Pop. 2,938
Northwest ISD 10,800/PK-12
2001 Texan Dr 76247 817-215-0000
Dr. Karen Rue, supt. Fax 215-0170
www.nisdtx.org
Hatfield ES 600/K-5
2051 Texan Dr 76247 817-215-0350
Cathy Sager, prin. Fax 215-0369
Justin ES 600/PK-5
425 Boss Range Rd 76247 817-215-0800
Anita Chaney, prin. Fax 215-0840
Pike MS 800/6-8
2200 Texan Dr 76247 817-215-0400
Mike Blankenship, prin. Fax 215-0425
Other Schools – See Fort Worth, Haslet, Keller, Newark, Rhome, Roanoke, Trophy Club

Karnack, Harrison
Karnack ISD 200/PK-12
PO Box 259 75661 903-679-3117
Cozzetta Robinson, supt. Fax 679-4252
www.karnackisd.org/
Carver ES 100/PK-6
PO Box 259 75661 903-679-3111
Joyce Stuart, prin. Fax 679-3163

Karnes City, Karnes, Pop. 3,430
Karnes City ISD 1,000/PK-12
314 N Highway 123 78118 830-780-2321
Frances Penland, supt. Fax 780-3823
www.kcisd.net
Karnes City JHS 200/6-8
410 N Highway 123 78118 830-780-2321
Jeanette Winn, prin. Fax 780-4382
Sides ES 500/PK-5
221 N Esplanade St 78118 830-780-2321
Julie Braun, prin. Fax 780-4427

Katy, Harris, Pop. 13,255
Cypress-Fairbanks ISD
Supt. — See Houston
Duryea ES 1,100/PK-5
20150 Arbor Creek Dr 77449 281-856-5174
Deborah Harbin, prin.
Hemmenway ES K-5
20400 W Little York Rd 77449 281-856-9870
Rhonda Frewin, prin.
Jowell ES 1,300/PK-5
6355 Greenhouse Rd 77449 281-463-5966
Julie Manuel, prin. Fax 345-3628
McFee ES 1,100/K-5
19315 Plantation Cove Ln 77449 281-463-5380
Donna Teel Harden, prin. Fax 463-5680
Robinson ES K-5
4321 Westfield Village Dr 77449 281-855-1240
Kathleen Dickson, prin.
Sheridan ES 1,300/PK-5
19790 Kieth Harrow Blvd 77449 281-856-1420
Anne Wilcox, prin. Fax 856-1461
Thornton MS 1,700/6-8
19802 Kieth Harrow Blvd 77449 281-856-1500
Mark McCord, prin. Fax 856-1548
Walker ES 1,300/PK-5
6424 Settlers Village Dr 77449 281-345-3200
Melissa Ehrhardt, prin. Fax 345-3205

Katy ISD 50,300/PK-12
PO Box 159 77492 281-396-6000
Alton Frailey, supt. Fax 644-1800
www.katyisd.org/
Alexander ES 1,100/K-5
6161 S Fry Rd 77494 281-237-7100
Kristin Harper, prin. Fax 644-1585
Beckendorff JHS 1,300/6-8
8200 S Fry Rd 77494 281-237-8800
Ted Viering, prin. Fax 644-1635
Beck JHS 1,100/6-8
5200 S Fry Rd 77450 281-237-3300
James Cross, prin. Fax 644-1630
Cardiff JHS 6-8
3900 Dayflower Dr 77449 281-234-0600
Richard Hull, prin. Fax 644-1855
Cimarron ES 800/K-5
1100 S Peek Rd 77450 281-237-6900
Mindy Dickerson, prin. Fax 644-1505
Cinco Ranch JHS 1,100/6-8
23420 Cinco Ranch Blvd 77494 281-237-7300
Dr. Steven Robertson, prin. Fax 644-1640

Creech ES 900/K-5
5905 S Mason Rd 77450 281-237-8850
Dr. Patricia Paetow, prin. Fax 644-1605
Exley ES 1,000/PK-5
21800 Westheimer Pkwy 77450 281-237-8400
Elizabeth Kuylen, prin. Fax 644-1535
Fielder ES 900/K-5
2100 Greenway Village Dr 77494 281-237-6450
Mark Vigario, prin. Fax 644-1515
Franz ES 1,200/PK-5
2751 N Westgreen Blvd 77449 281-237-8600
Georgia Bartlett, prin. Fax 644-1520
Golbow ES 900/PK-5
3535 Lakes of Bridgewater 77449 281-237-5350
Terri Majors, prin. Fax 644-1525
Griffin ES 900/K-5
7800 S Fry Rd 77494 281-237-8700
Jackie Keithan, prin. Fax 644-1850
Hayes ES 800/K-5
21203 Park Timbers Ln 77450 281-237-3200
Rhonda Henderson, prin. Fax 644-1541
Holland ES K-5
23720 Seven Meadows Pkwy 77494 281-234-0500
Carra Fleming, prin. Fax 644-1695
Hutsell ES 800/PK-5
5360 Franz Rd 77493 281-237-6500
Keiko Davidson, prin. Fax 644-1530
Katy ES 600/PK-5
5726 George Bush Dr 77493 281-237-6550
Leslie Smuts, prin. Fax 644-1550
Katy JHS 1,200/6-8
5350 Franz Rd 77493 281-237-6800
Dr. Scott Sheppard, prin. Fax 644-1645
Kilpatrick ES 1,100/K-5
26100 Cinco Ranch Blvd 77494 281-237-7600
Malynn Rodriguez, prin. Fax 644-1570
King ES 800/K-5
1901 Charlton House Ln 77493 281-237-6850
Melvin Nash, prin. Fax 644-1595
McDonald JHS 1,300/6-8
3635 Lakes of Bridgewater 77449 281-237-5300
Ed Keeney, prin. Fax 644-1655
McMeans JHS 1,200/6-8
21000 Westheimer Pkwy 77450 281-237-8000
Dr. Susan Rice, prin. Fax 644-1660
McRoberts ES 1,200/PK-5
3535 N Fry Rd 77449 281-237-2000
Chris Salenga, prin. Fax 644-1580
Memorial Parkway ES 700/PK-5
21603 Park Tree Ln 77450 281-237-5850
Olga Leonard, prin. Fax 644-1560
Memorial Parkway JHS 1,000/6-8
21203 Highland Knolls Dr 77450 281-237-5800
Dr. Joe Graham, prin. Fax 644-1665
Morton Ranch ES K-5
2502 S Mason Rd 77450 281-234-0300
Elisa Farris, prin. Fax 644-1685
Morton Ranch JHS 1,200/6-8
2498 N Mason Rd 77449 281-237-7400
Becky Bracewell, prin. Fax 644-1670
Nottingham Country ES 700/K-5
20500 Kingsland Blvd 77450 281-237-5500
Marlene Bourgeois, prin. Fax 644-1566
Pattison ES 800/PK-5
19910 Stonelodge St 77450 281-237-5450
Debra Barker, prin. Fax 644-1575
Rhodes ES 900/PK-5
19711 Clay Rd 77449 281-237-8500
Cheryl Rankin, prin. Fax 644-1590
Rylander ES 1,000/K-5
24831 Westheimer Pkwy 77494 281-237-8300
Lisa Simmons, prin. Fax 644-1600
Stephens ES K-5
2715 N Fry Rd 77449 281-234-0200
Stephanie Jaterka, prin. Fax 644-1680
Sundown ES 800/PK-5
20100 Saums Rd 77449 281-237-5400
Steven Pustejovsky, prin. Fax 644-1610
West Memorial ES 600/PK-5
22605 Provincial Blvd 77450 281-237-6600
Kathleen Leonard, prin. Fax 644-1625
West Memorial JHS 800/6-8
22311 Provincial Blvd 77450 281-237-6400
Marcus Forney, prin. Fax 644-1675
Williams ES 1,000/K-5
3900 S Peek Rd 77450 281-237-7200
Ronnie Lee, prin. Fax 644-1545
Winborn ES 900/PK-5
22555 Prince George Ln 77449 281-237-6650
Kelly Ricks, prin. Fax 644-1510
Woodcreek ES K-5
1155 Woodcreek Bend Ln 77494 281-234-0100
Ronnie Mosher, prin. Fax 644-1690
Woodcreek JHS 6-8
1801 Woodcreek Bend Ln 77494 281-234-0800
Patti Shafer, prin. Fax 644-1860
Other Schools – See Houston

CrossPoint Christian S 300/PK-K
700 Westgreen Blvd 77450 281-398-6464
Connie Robinson, prin. Fax 599-9446
Faith West Academy 600/PK-12
2225 Porter Rd 77493 281-391-5683
Kirk Rightmire, hdmstr. Fax 391-2606
Katy Adventist Christian S 50/K-8
1913 East Ave 77493 281-392-5603
Edgar Browning, prin.
Memorial Lutheran S 50/PK-K
5810 3rd St 77493 281-391-0172
Linda Stahmer, dir. Fax 391-7579

Kaufman, Kaufman, Pop. 7,872
Kaufman ISD 3,600/PK-12
1000 S Houston St 75142 972-932-2622
Todd Williams, supt. Fax 932-0812
kaufman.ednet10.net
Edwards ECC 500/PK-K
1605 Rand Rd 75142 972-932-0800
Mica Cooper, prin. Fax 932-6850
Monday PS 500/1-2
905 S Madison St 75142 972-932-3513
Jenny Sunderlin, prin. Fax 932-2758
Nash IS 600/5-6
1002 S Houston St 75142 972-932-6415
Linda Mott, prin. Fax 932-4028
Norman JHS 500/7-8
3701 S Houston St 75142 972-932-2410
Jeri Ann Campbell, prin. Fax 932-7771
Phillips ES 500/3-4
1501 Royal Dr 75142 972-932-4500
Carla Crouch, prin. Fax 932-7633

Kaufman Christian S 100/PK-6
401 N Shannon St 75142 972-932-6111
Christy Butler, admin. Fax 932-6111

Keene, Johnson, Pop. 5,952
Keene ISD 700/PK-12
PO Box 656 76059 817-774-5200
Kevin Sellers, supt. Fax 774-5400
www.keeneisd.org/
Keene ES 300/PK-5
PO Box 656 76059 817-774-5320
Eric Ribble, prin. Fax 774-5303
Keene JHS 200/6-8
PO Box 656 76059 817-774-5270
Billie Hopps, prin. Fax 774-5402

Keene Adventist S 300/PK-8
302 Pecan St 76059 817-645-9125
Donna Berkner, prin. Fax 645-9271

Keller, Tarrant, Pop. 35,706
Keller ISD 28,800/PK-12
350 Keller Pkwy 76248 817-744-1000
Dr. James Veitenheimer, supt. Fax 337-3261
www.kellerisd.net
Bear Creek IS 900/5-6
801 Bear Creek Pkwy 76248 817-744-3650
Tedna Taylor, prin. Fax 337-5200
Caprock ES PK-4
12301 Grey Twig Dr 76244 817-744-6400
Angie Nayfa, prin. Fax 741-5203
Eagle Ridge ES 600/K-4
4600 Alta Vista Rd 76244 817-744-6300
Lorene Ownby, prin.
Freedom ES 600/PK-4
5401 Wall Price Rd 76248 817-744-4800
Vickie Miles, prin. Fax 741-9913
Friendship ES 600/K-4
5400 Shiver Rd 76244 817-744-6200
Bronwyn Sullenberger, prin. Fax 741-5853
Heritage ES 700/PK-4
4001 Thompson Rd 76244 817-744-4900
Christy Johnson, prin.
Hidden Lakes ES 800/K-4
900 Preston Ln 76248 817-744-5000
Melanie Graham, prin. Fax 741-1260
Independence ES 700/K-4
11773 Bray Birch Ln 76244 817-744-6100
Kathleen Vaghy, prin. Fax 741-6338
Indian Springs MS 1,000/7-8
305 Bursey Rd 76248 817-744-3200
Carrie Jackson, prin. Fax 431-4432
Keller-Harvel ES 500/PK-4
635 Norma Ln 76248 817-744-5100
Patsy Wheaton, prin. Fax 337-3551
Keller MS 800/7-8
300 College Ave 76248 817-744-2900
Sandra Chapa, prin. Fax 337-3500
Lone Star ES 700/PK-4
4647 Shiver Rd 76244 817-744-5200
Steve Hurst, prin. Fax 379-6231
Perot ES 800/K-4
9345 General Worth Dr 76244 817-744-4600
Cory Wilson, prin. Fax 741-3659
Shady Grove ES 500/PK-4
1400 Sarah Brooks Dr 76248 817-744-5600
Gary Mantz, prin. Fax 428-2895
South Keller IS 900/5-6
201 Bursey Rd 76248 817-744-4150
Deborah Cano, prin. Fax 431-6616
Trinity Meadows IS 800/5-6
3500 Keller Hicks Rd 76244 817-744-4300
Ron Myers, prin. Fax 741-6923
Trinity Springs MS 700/7-8
3550 Keller Hicks Rd 76244 817-744-3500
Lindsay Anderson, prin. Fax 741-6353
Willis Lane ES 700/PK-4
1620 Willis Ln 76248 817-744-5700
Cheryl Hudson, prin. Fax 337-3830
Woodland Springs ES 700/PK-4
12120 Woodland Springs Dr 76244 817-744-5900
Linda Lammers, prin. Fax 741-0354
Other Schools – See Colleyville, Fort Worth, Southlake, Watauga

Northwest ISD
Supt. — See Justin
Granger ES 400/K-5
12771 Saratoga Spring Cir 76248 817-698-1100
Kimmie Etheredge, prin. Fax 698-1170

Messiah Lutheran S 100/K-12
1308 Whitley Rd 76248 817-431-5486
Ray Main, hdmstr. Fax 898-0365
St. Elizabeth Ann Seton S 700/PK-8
2016 Willis Ln 76248 817-431-4845
Kay Burrell, prin. Fax 431-4165

Kemah, Galveston, Pop. 2,386
Clear Creek ISD
Supt. — See League City
Stewart ES 600/PK-5
330 Marina Bay Dr 77565 281-284-4700
Britani Moses, prin. Fax 284-4705

Kemp, Kaufman, Pop. 1,258
Kemp ISD 1,700/PK-12
905 S Main St 75143 903-498-1314
Dr. Peter Running, supt. Fax 498-1315
kemp.ednet10.net
Kemp IS 300/4-6
101 Old State Highway 40 Rd 75143 903-498-1362
Kim McDowell, prin. Fax 498-1379
Kemp JHS 300/7-8
204 W 17th St 75143 903-498-1343
Phil Edwards, prin. Fax 498-1359
Kemp PS 500/PK-3
601 E 8th St 75143 903-498-2125
Lisa Lowe, prin. Fax 498-2136

Kendleton, Fort Bend, Pop. 522
Kendleton ISD 100/PK-6
PO Box 705 77451 979-532-2855
Mildred West Ph.D., supt. Fax 532-0295
www.kendletonisd.net/
Powell Point ES 100/PK-6
PO Box 705 77451 979-532-2855
Mildred West, prin. Fax 532-0295

Kenedy, Karnes, Pop. 3,408
Kenedy ISD 700/PK-12
401 FM 719 78119 830-583-4100
Jan LaCour Ed.D., supt. Fax 583-9950
www.kenedy.isd.tenet.edu
Kenedy ES 400/PK-5
401 FM 719 78119 830-583-4100
Melanie Witte, prin. Fax 583-2597
Kenedy MS 200/6-8
401 FM 719 78119 830-583-4100
Randy Tiemann, prin. Fax 583-9519

Kennard, Houston, Pop. 319
Kennard ISD 300/PK-12
PO Box 38 75847 936-655-2008
Gary Jacobs, supt. Fax 655-2327
www.kennardisd.net/
Kennard ES 200/PK-6
PO Box 38 75847 936-655-2724
Ginger Arbuckle, prin. Fax 655-2327

Kennedale, Tarrant, Pop. 6,547
Kennedale ISD 3,000/K-12
PO Box 467 76060 817-563-8000
Gary Dugger, supt. Fax 483-3610
www.kennedale.net
Arthur IS 500/5-6
PO Box 448 76060 817-563-8300
Danny Greenfield, prin. Fax 483-3628
Delaney ES 600/K-4
PO Box 1287 76060 817-563-8400
Wanda Hibbetts, prin. Fax 483-3653
Kennedale JHS 500/7-8
PO Box 489 76060 817-563-8200
Larry Westmoreland, prin. Fax 483-3655
Other Schools – See Arlington

Kerens, Navarro, Pop. 1,803
Kerens ISD 700/PK-12
PO Box 310 75144 903-396-2924
Kevin Stanford, supt. Fax 396-2334
www.kerens.k12.tx.us/
Kerens S 700/PK-12
PO Box 310 75144 903-396-2931
David Tyson, prin. Fax 396-2334

Kermit, Winkler, Pop. 5,281
Kermit ISD 1,300/PK-12
601 S Poplar St 79745 432-586-1000
Santos Lujan, supt. Fax 586-1016
www.kisd.esc18.net/
East PS 400/PK-2
601 S Poplar St 79745 432-586-1020
Lupe Singh, prin. Fax 586-1023
Kermit JHS 300/6-8
601 S Poplar St 79745 432-586-1040
Roxane Greer, prin. Fax 586-1045
Purple Sage ES 300/PK-PK, 3-
601 S Poplar St 79745 432-586-1030
Lupe Singh, prin. Fax 586-1033

Kerrville, Kerr, Pop. 22,010
Kerrville ISD 4,600/PK-12
1009 Barnett St 78028 830-257-2200
Dan Troxell Ph.D., supt. Fax 257-2249
www.kerrvilleisd.net
Daniels ES 600/K-5
2002 Singing Wind Dr 78028 830-257-2208
Amy Billeiter, prin. Fax 257-1310
Nimitz ES 500/PK-5
100 Valley View Dr 78028 830-257-2209
Wade Ivy, prin. Fax 895-7905
Peterson MS 700/7-8
1607 Sidney Baker St 78028 830-257-2204
Sharon Mock, prin. Fax 257-1300
Starkey ES 600/PK-5
1030 W Main St 78028 830-257-2210
Diane Stern, prin. Fax 792-3727
Tally ES 500/K-5
1840 Goat Creek Rd 78028 830-257-2222
Buck Thompson, prin. Fax 257-2288
Wilson Sixth Grade S 300/6-6
1010 Barnett St 78028 830-257-2207
Donna Jenschke, prin. Fax 257-1316

Hill Country SDA S 50/K-8
611 Harper Rd 78028 830-257-3903
Brendia Bennett, prin. Fax 257-3903
Holy Cross Lutheran S 50/K-6
210 Spence St 78028 830-257-6750
Fax 257-4436
Notre Dame S 200/PK-8
907 Main St 78028 830-257-6707
Sandra Garcia, prin. Fax 792-4370

Kilgore, Gregg, Pop. 11,858
Kilgore ISD 3,800/PK-12
301 N Kilgore St 75662 903-984-2073
Jody Clements, supt. Fax 983-3212
www.kisd.org/
Chandler ES 800/1-3
301 N Kilgore St 75662 903-984-2534
Tamara Dean, prin. Fax 986-8026
Kilgore Heights K 500/PK-K
301 N Kilgore St 75662 903-984-3022
Duane Deen, prin. Fax 984-2176
Kilgore IS 500/4-5
301 N Kilgore St 75662 903-984-1280
Andy Adams, prin. Fax 984-7879
Laird MS 800/6-8
301 N Kilgore St 75662 903-984-5072
Jody Sanders, prin. Fax 984-6225

Killeen, Bell, Pop. 100,233
Killeen ISD 35,000/PK-12
PO Box 967 76540 254-336-0006
Dr. Robert Muller, supt. Fax 526-3103
www.killeenisd.org
Bellaire ES 500/PK-5
108 W Jasper Dr 76542 254-336-1410
David House, prin. Fax 519-5596
Brookhaven ES 700/PK-5
3221 Hilliard Ave 76543 254-336-1440
Rose Englebrecht, prin. Fax 680-6604
Cedar Valley ES 700/PK-5
4801 Chantz Dr 76542 254-336-1480
Janet Wyrick, prin. Fax 680-6600
Clifton Park ES 500/PK-5
2200 Trimmier Rd 76541 254-336-1580
Catherine Snyder, prin. Fax 680-6605
Cross ES 700/PK-5
1910 Herndon Dr 76543 254-336-2550
Cassandra Spearman, prin. Fax 680-1795
East Ward ES 500/PK-5
1608 E Rancier Ave 76541 254-336-1650
Hilda Arnold, prin. Fax 519-5648
Fowler ES 400/PK-5
1020 Trimmier Rd 76541 254-336-1760
Debra Drever, prin. Fax 680-6635
Hay Branch ES 700/PK-5
6101 Westcliff Rd 76543 254-336-2080
Sue Kozora, prin. Fax 680-6602
Iduma ES 1,000/PK-5
PO Box 967 76540 254-333-2590
Judy Tyson, prin. Fax 526-9046
Liberty Hill MS 800/6-8
4500 Kit Carson Trl 76542 254-336-1370
Brandon Bringhurst, prin. Fax 953-4367
Live Oak Ridge MS 800/6-8
2600 Robinett Rd 76549 254-336-2490
Brenda Alexander, prin. Fax 554-2170
Manor MS 700/6-8
1700 S W S Young Dr 76543 254-336-1310
Jan Rainwater, prin. Fax 680-7029
Maxdale ES 600/K-5
2600 Westwood Dr 76549 254-336-2460
Paula Finnessey, prin. Fax 634-6135
Nolan MS 700/6-8
505 E Jasper Dr 76541 254-336-1150
Lolly Garcia, prin. Fax 519-5598
Palo Alto MS 700/6-8
2301 W Elms Rd 76549 254-336-1200
Matt Widacki, prin. Fax 519-5577
Patterson MS 6-8
8383 W Trimmier Rd 76542 254-336-7100
Jill Balzer, prin.
Peebles ES 700/PK-5
1800 N W S Young Dr 76543 254-336-2120
Gayle Dudley, prin. Fax 519-5631
Pershing Park ES 700/PK-5
1500 W Central Texas Expy 76549 254-336-1790
Linda Butler, prin. Fax 519-5610
Rancier MS 700/6-8
3301 Hilliard Ave 76543 254-336-1250
David Manley, prin. Fax 680-6601
Reeces Creek ES 700/PK-5
400 W Stan Schlueter Loop 76542 254-336-2150
Michelle Taylor, prin. Fax 519-5630
Saegert Ranch ES 800/PK-5
5600 Schorn Dr 76542 254-200-6660
Gail Charles-Walters, prin. Fax 554-3824
Sugar Loaf ES 500/PK-5
1517 Barbara Ln 76549 254-336-1940
Karl Bradley, prin. Fax 519-5595
Timber Ridge ES 600/PK-5
5402 White Rock Dr 76542 254-200-6630
Dana Coleman, prin. Fax 690-2337
Trimmier ES 700/PK-5
4400 Success Dr 76542 254-336-2270
Penny Batts, prin. Fax 519-1539
West Ward ES 500/PK-5
709 W Dean Ave 76541 254-336-1830
Maureen Adams, prin. Fax 520-1024
Willow Springs ES 700/PK-5
2501 W Stan Schlueter Loop 76549 254-336-2020
Linda Olson, prin. Fax 519-5606
Other Schools – See Fort Hood, Harker Heights, Nolanville

Grace Lutheran S 100/PK-K
1007 Bacon Ranch Rd 76542 254-634-4424
Naomi Matthys, admin. Fax 634-5475
Killeen Adventist Junior Academy 100/PK-8
3412 Lake Rd 76543 254-699-9466
Fran Wilson, prin. Fax 699-0519
Memorial Christian Academy 200/PK-9
PO Box 11269 76547 254-526-5403
Jackie Shiller, admin. Fax 634-2030
New Beginnings Christian Academy 100/PK-6
3621 E Vtrans Memorial Blvd 76543 254-680-8277
Ernestine Williams, prin. Fax 680-4031
St. Joseph S 100/PK-5
2901 E Rancier Ave 76543 254-634-7272
Becky Kirkland, prin. Fax 634-1224

Kingsland, Llano, Pop. 2,725
Llano ISD
Supt. — See Llano
Packsaddle ES 500/PK-5
150 Pioneer Ln 78639 325-388-8129
Annette Moresco, prin. Fax 388-7000

Kingsville, Kleberg, Pop. 24,740
Kingsville ISD 4,100/PK-12
PO Box 871 78364 361-592-3387
Emilio Castro, supt. Fax 595-7805
www.kvisd.esc2.net
Gillett IS 600/5-6
PO Box 871 78364 361-592-3309
Dolores Hernandez, prin. Fax 595-9008
Harrel ES 300/PK-1
PO Box 871 78364 361-592-9305
Leo Ramos, prin. Fax 516-1313
Harvey ES 300/PK-1
PO Box 871 78364 361-592-4327
Fax 595-9130
Kleberg ES 400/2-4
PO Box 871 78364 361-592-2615
Diana Guerrero-Pena, prin. Fax 595-9145
Lamar ES 400/PK-1
PO Box 871 78364 361-592-5246
Dawn Mireles, prin. Fax 592-2368
Memorial MS 500/7-8
PO Box 871 78364 361-595-5771
Jose Mireles, prin. Fax 592-4198
Perez ES 500/2-4
PO Box 871 78364 361-592-8511
Melba Franco, prin. Fax 516-1468

Ricardo ISD 500/PK-8
138 W County Road 2160 78363 361-592-6465
Dr. Vita Canales, supt. Fax 592-3101
Ricardo ES 300/PK-4
138 W County Road 2160 78363 361-592-6465
Denise Rosenauer, prin. Fax 593-0704
Ricardo MS 200/5-8
138 W County Road 2160 78363 361-592-6465
Karen Unterbrink, prin. Fax 593-0707

Santa Gertrudis ISD 400/PK-12
PO Box 592 78364 361-592-3937
Mary Springs, supt. Fax 592-2836
www.sgisd.net
Santa Gertrudis S 200/PK-8
PO Box 592 78364 361-592-7582
Mary Springs, prin. Fax 592-2836

St. Gertrude S 100/PK-6
400 E Caesar Ave 78363 361-592-6522
Beverly Lanmon, prin. Fax 592-0100

Kingwood, Harris, Pop. 37,397
Humble ISD
Supt. — See Humble
Bear Branch ES 600/PK-5
3500 Garden Lake Dr 77339 281-641-1600
Kay Pruitt, prin. Fax 641-1617
Creekwood MS 1,100/6-8
3603 W Lake Houston Pkwy 77339 281-641-4400
Walt Winicki, prin. Fax 641-4417
Deerwood ES 600/PK-5
2920 Forest Garden Dr 77345 281-641-2200
Carol Suell, prin. Fax 641-2217
Elm Grove ES 600/PK-5
2815 Clear Ridge Dr 77339 281-641-1700
Donna Fife, prin. Fax 641-1717
Foster ES 600/PK-5
1800 Trailwood Village Dr 77339 281-641-1400
Terry VeDepo, prin. Fax 641-1417
Greentree ES 800/PK-5
3502 Brook Shadow Dr 77345 281-641-1900
Nancy Pinkerton, prin. Fax 641-1917
Hidden Hollow ES 500/PK-5
4104 Appalachian Trl 77345 281-641-2400
Janice Wiederhold, prin. Fax 641-2417
Kingwood MS 900/6-8
2407 Pine Terrace Dr 77339 281-641-4200
Robert Atteberry, prin. Fax 641-4217
Riverwood MS 1,100/6-8
2910 High Valley Dr 77345 281-641-4800
Greg Joseph, prin. Fax 641-4817
Shadow Forest ES 700/PK-5
2300 Mills Branch Dr 77345 281-641-2600
Nancy Arnold, prin. Fax 641-2617
Willow Creek ES 600/PK-5
2002 Willow Terrace Dr 77345 281-641-2300
Deborah Thomas, prin. Fax 641-2317
Woodland Hills ES 600/PK-5
2222 Tree Ln 77339 281-641-1500
Pat Buttermore, prin. Fax 641-1517

New Caney ISD
Supt. — See New Caney
Kings Manor ES 700/PK-5
21111 Royal Crossing Dr 77339 281-577-2940
Penny Peacock, prin. Fax 359-6391

Christian S of Kingwood 200/PK-8
2901 Woodland Hills Dr 77339 281-359-4929
Linda Copeland, prin. Fax 359-2514
Good Shepherd Episcopal S 200/PK-K
2929 Woodland Hills Dr 77339 281-359-1895
Jan Lopez, dir. Fax 358-3155
Kingwood Montessori S 50/PK-6
2510 Mills Branch Dr Ste 10 77345 281-548-1452
Janet Ebach, prin. Fax 548-1456
Northeast Christian Academy 200/PK-12
1711 Hamblen Rd 77339 281-359-1090
Brad Baggett, hdmstr. Fax 359-5560
St. Martha S 400/PK-8
2411 Oak Shores Dr 77339 281-358-5523
Leslie Flickinger, prin. Fax 358-5526

Kirbyville, Jasper, Pop. 2,029
Kirbyville Consolidated ISD 1,500/PK-12
206 E Main St 75956 409-423-7520
Richard Hazlewood, supt. Fax 423-2367
www.kirbyvillecisd.org/
Kirbyville ES 800/PK-6
2100 S Margaret Ave 75956 409-423-8526
Beverly Hall, prin. Fax 423-3753
Kirbyville JHS 200/7-8
2200 S Margaret Ave 75956 409-420-0692
Micah Dyer, prin. Fax 423-6654

Klein, Harris, Pop. 12,000
Klein ISD 43,500/PK-12
7200 Spring Cypress Rd 77379 832-249-4000
Dr. Jim Cain, supt. Fax 249-4055
www.kleinisd.net
Benfer ES 700/PK-5
18027 Kuykendahl Rd Ste B 77379 832-484-6000
Loraine Lambert, prin. Fax 484-7850
Benignus ES 1,000/PK-5
7225 Alvin A Klein Dr 77379 832-484-7750
Misty Kainer, prin. Fax 484-7796
Brill ES 700/PK-5
9102 Herts Rd 77379 832-484-6150
Karen Smith, prin. Fax 484-7851
Doerre IS 1,400/6-8
18218 Theiss Mail Route Rd 77379 832-249-5700
Cecilia Saccomanno, prin. Fax 249-4054
Ehrhardt ES 700/PK-5
6603 Rosebrook Ln 77379 832-484-6200
Dean Borg, prin. Fax 484-7853
Frank ES 800/PK-5
9225 Crescent Clover Dr 77379 832-375-7000
Eve Messina, prin. Fax 375-7100
Hassler ES 1,100/PK-5
9325 Lochlea Ridge Dr 77379 832-484-7100
Carol Randall, prin. Fax 484-7860
Kleb IS 1,100/6-8
7425 Louetta Rd 77379 832-249-5500
Pam Bourgeois, prin. Fax 249-4053
Krahn ES 1,000/PK-5
9502 Eday Dr 77379 832-484-6500
Charmaine Villere, prin. Fax 484-7868
Krimmel IS 1,200/6-8
7070 FM 2920 Rd 77379 832-375-7200
Scott Crowe, prin. Fax 375-7150
Kuehnle ES 600/PK-5
5510 Winding Ridge Dr 77379 832-484-6650
Mignon Johnson, prin. Fax 484-7870
Mittelstadt ES 700/PK-5
7525 Kleingreen Ln 77379 832-484-6700
Cynthia Levy, prin. Fax 484-7876
Mueller ES, 7074 FM 2920 Rd 77379 PK-5
Sharon Firestone, prin. 832-375-7300
Strack IS 1,200/6-8
18027 Kuykendahl Rd Ste S 77379 832-249-5400
Steve Owen, prin. Fax 249-4051
Theiss ES 700/PK-5
17510 Theiss Mail Route Rd 77379 832-484-5900
JoAnn Keenan, prin. Fax 484-7886
Other Schools – See Houston, Spring, Tomball

Trinity Lutheran S 600/PK-8
18926 Klein Church Rd 77379 281-376-5810
Keith Goedecke, prin. Fax 251-1987

Knippa, Uvalde
Knippa ISD 300/PK-12
PO Box 99 78870 830-934-2176
Michael Thompson, supt. Fax 934-2490
www.knippa.net/
Knippa S 300/PK-12
PO Box 99 78870 830-934-2177
Michael Thompson, prin. Fax 934-2490

Knox City, Knox, Pop. 1,083
Knox City-O'Brien Consolidated ISD 300/PK-12
606 E Main St 79529 940-657-3521
Louis Baty, supt. Fax 657-3379
www.esc9.net/knoxcity/
Knox City ES 100/PK-4
606 E Main St 79529 940-658-3147
Marsha McGaughey, prin. Fax 658-3379
Other Schools – See O Brien

Kopperl, Bosque
Kopperl ISD 300/PK-12
PO Box 67 76652 254-889-3502
Kenneth Bateman, supt. Fax 889-3443
www.kopperlisd.org
Kopperl S 300/PK-12
PO Box 67 76652 254-889-3502
Katrina Adcock, prin. Fax 889-3443

Kountze, Hardin, Pop. 2,153
Kountze ISD 1,300/PK-12
PO Box 460 77625 409-246-3352
Diane Daniels, supt. Fax 246-3217
kountzeisd.org
Kountze ES 400/PK-3
PO Box 460 77625 409-246-3877
Brad McEachern, prin. Fax 246-4138
Kountze IS 200/4-6
PO Box 460 77625 409-246-8168
Dustin Rutherford, prin. Fax 246-3857
Kountze MS 200/7-8
PO Box 460 77625 409-246-3551
John Ferguson, prin. Fax 246-8907

Kress, Swisher, Pop. 779
Kress ISD 200/K-12
200 E 5th St 79052 806-684-2652
Doug Setliff, supt. Fax 684-2687
www.kressonline.net
Kress ES 100/K-6
401 Ripley Ave 79052 806-684-2326
Doug Setliff, prin. Fax 684-2778

Krum, Denton, Pop. 3,368
Krum ISD 1,000/PK-12
809 E McCart St 76249 940-482-6000
Mike Davis, supt. Fax 482-3929
www.krumisd.net
Dodd IS 200/4-5
809 E McCart St 76249 940-482-6000
Lila Wright, prin. Fax 482-3368
Dyer ES 100/2-3
809 E McCart St 76249 940-482-6000
Debbie Hudson, prin. Fax 482-8203
Krum Early Education Center PK-1
809 E McCart St 76249 940-482-6000
Tammy Morris, prin. Fax 482-6232
Krum MS 300/6-8
809 E McCart St 76249 940-482-6000
Michelle Pieniazek, prin. Fax 482-6299

Kyle, Hays, Pop. 17,770
Hays Consolidated ISD 11,900/PK-12
21003 Interstate 35 78640 512-268-2141
Dr. Jeremy Lyon, supt. Fax 268-2147
www.hayscisd.net
Chapa MS 700/6-8
3311 Dacy Ln 78640 512-268-8500
Lisa Islas, prin. Fax 295-7824
Fuentes ES 600/PK-5
901 Goforth Rd 78640 512-268-7827
Jodie Wymore, prin. Fax 268-5968
Hemphill ES 1,000/PK-5
3995 E FM 150 78640 512-268-4688
Mike Hanson, prin. Fax 268-6208
Kyle ES 600/PK-5
500 W Blanco St 78640 512-268-3311
Elaine Meyer, prin. Fax 268-1417
Negley ES 600/PK-5
5940 McNaughton 78640 512-268-8501
Will Webber, prin. Fax 268-8582
Science Hall ES 700/PK-5
1510 Bebee Rd 78640 512-268-8502
Angela Nelson, prin. Fax 268-8784
Simon MS, 3839 E FM 150 78640 6-8
Michelle Chae, prin. 512-268-8507
Tobias ES 800/PK-5
1005 E FM 150 78640 512-268-8437
Kristi Jackson, prin. Fax 268-8447
Wallace MS 600/6-8
1500 W Center St 78640 512-268-2891
Brenda Agnew, prin. Fax 268-1853
Other Schools – See Buda, Niederwald, San Marcos

La Coste, Medina, Pop. 1,204
Medina Valley ISD
Supt. — See Castroville
LaCoste ES 300/PK-5
PO Box 280 78039 830-985-3421
Marinda Santos, prin. Fax 985-3732

Ladonia, Fannin, Pop. 699
Fannindel ISD 200/PK-12
601 W Main St 75449 903-367-7251
H.L. Milton, supt. Fax 367-7252
fannindel.esc8.net/
Other Schools – See Pecan Gap

La Feria, Cameron, Pop. 6,815
La Feria ISD 2,500/PK-12
PO Box 1159 78559 956-797-2612
Nabor Cortez, supt. Fax 797-3737
www.laferiaisd.net/
Dominguez ES 500/5-6
600 Pancho Maples Dr 78559 956-797-1712
Jane Castillo, prin. Fax 797-2600
Green JHS 500/7-8
501 N Canal St 78559 956-797-1512
Michael Torres, prin. Fax 797-2157
Houston K 400/PK-K
505 N Villarreal St 78559 956-797-1814
Nora Delos Santos, prin. Fax 797-2032
Sanchez ES 1-2
1601 S Main St 78559 956-797-8550
Dennis Amstutz, prin. Fax 797-3737
Vail ES 300/3-4
209 W Jessamine Ave 78559 956-797-5523
Isaac Rodriguez, prin. Fax 797-3429

Lago Vista, Travis, Pop. 5,573
Lago Vista ISD 1,200/PK-12
PO Box 4929 78645 512-267-8300
Dr. Barbara Qualls, supt. Fax 267-8304
www.lagovista.txed.net/
Lago Vista MS 300/6-8
PO Box 4929 78645 512-267-8305
Paul Bixler, prin. Fax 267-8329
Other Schools – See Leander

La Grange, Fayette, Pop. 4,620
La Grange ISD 2,000/PK-12
PO Box 100 78945 979-968-7000
Dr. Randy Albers, supt. Fax 968-8155
www.lgisd.net/
Hermes ES 600/PK-3
PO Box 100 78945 979-968-4100
Cheryl Schmidt, prin. Fax 968-8155
La Grange IS 400/4-6
PO Box 100 78945 979-968-4700
David Ehler, prin. Fax 968-8155
La Grange MS 300/7-8
PO Box 100 78945 979-968-4747
Neal Miller, prin. Fax 968-8155

Sacred Heart S 200/PK-6
545 E Pearl St 78945 979-968-3223
Elmer Faykus, prin. Fax 968-5740

Laguna Vista, Cameron, Pop. 2,600

Laguna Madre Christian Academy 50/PK-6
1441 Santa Isabel Blvd 78578 956-943-4446
Carole Smith, dir. Fax 943-4462

Laird Hill, Rusk
Leveretts Chapel ISD 200/PK-12
PO Box 669 75666 903-834-6675
Donna Johnson, supt. Fax 834-6602
www.lcisd.esc7.net/
Other Schools – See Overton

La Joya, Hidalgo, Pop. 4,486
La Joya ISD 25,800/PK-12
201 E Expressway 83 78560 956-580-5000
Dr. Alda Benavides, supt. Fax 580-5444
www.lajoyaisd.com
De Zavala MS 900/6-8
603 Tabasco Rd 78560 956-580-5472
Le-Ann Alaniz-Herrera, prin. Fax 580-5494
Tabasco ES 800/PK-5
223 S Leo Ave 78560 956-580-8810
Velma Ochoa, prin. Fax 580-8825
Other Schools – See Mission, Palmview, Penitas, Sullivan City

Lake Dallas, Denton, Pop. 7,000
Lake Dallas ISD 4,000/PK-12
PO Box 548 75065 940-497-4039
Gayle Stinson, supt. Fax 497-3737
www.ldisd.net
Lake Dallas IS 300/5-5
PO Box 548 75065 940-497-4056
Deon Quisenberry, prin. Fax 497-8475
Lake Dallas MS 900/6-8
PO Box 548 75065 940-497-4037
Jim Parker, prin. Fax 497-4028
Lake Dallas PS 200/PK-K
PO Box 548 75065 940-497-2222
Deon Quisenberry, prin. Fax 497-2807
Other Schools – See Corinth, Shady Shores

Lake Jackson, Brazoria, Pop. 27,386
Brazosport ISD
Supt. — See Clute
Beutel ES 500/PK-4
300 Ligustrum St 77566 979-730-7165
Kathy Vickers, prin. Fax 292-2821
Brannen ES 500/PK-4
802 That Way St 77566 979-730-7170
Julie Evans, prin. Fax 292-2834
Lake Jackson IS 900/7-8
100 Oyster Creek Dr 77566 979-730-7250
Danny Massey, prin. Fax 292-2804
Ney ES 600/PK-4
308 Winding Way St 77566 979-730-7190
Mary Randazzo, prin. Fax 292-2829
Rasco MS 900/5-6
92 Lake Rd 77566 979-730-7225
Robin Pelton, prin. Fax 292-2817
Roberts ES 500/PK-4
110 Cedar St 77566 979-730-7205
Judy Thacker, prin. Fax 292-2825

Brazosport Christian S 300/PK-12
200B Willow Dr 77566 979-297-0563
David Diamond, hdmstr. Fax 297-8455

Lake Worth, Tarrant, Pop. 4,681
Lake Worth ISD 2,300/PK-12
6805 Telephone Rd 76135 817-306-4200
Dr. Janice Cooper, supt. Fax 237-5131
www.lwisd.org/
Collins MS 300/7-8
3651 Santos Dr, 817-306-4200
Kathy Harmon, prin. Fax 624-7058
Howry IS 100/5-6
4000 Dakota Trl 76135 817-306-4240
Karen Miller, prin. Fax 237-3687
Morris ES 400/PK-4
3801 Merrett Dr 76135 817-306-4260
Eric Moore, prin. Fax 237-3625
Tadpole Learning Center PK-PK
6817 Telephone Rd 76135 817-306-4225
Paula Thornton, prin. Fax 238-0639
Other Schools – See Fort Worth

La Marque, Galveston, Pop. 13,860
La Marque ISD 3,700/PK-12
PO Box 7 77568 409-938-4251
Ecomet Burley, supt. Fax 908-5012
www.lmisd.net
Early Childhood Learning Center 500/PK-K
PO Box 7 77568 409-935-3020
Joanne Stringfellow, prin. Fax 908-5022
Highlands ES 400/1-5
PO Box 7 77568 409-935-6321
Tyra Stemley, prin. Fax 908-5044
Inter-City ES 400/1-5
PO Box 7 77568 409-935-8043
Brenda Mullins, prin. Fax 908-5048
La Marque MS 800/6-8
PO Box 7 77568 409-938-4286
Sonya Sonia, prin. Fax 908-5071
Westlawn ES 300/1-5
PO Box 7 77568 409-908-5100
Krystal Harris, prin. Fax 908-5094
Other Schools – See Texas City

Lamesa, Dawson, Pop. 9,321
Klondike ISD 200/PK-12
2911 County Road H 79331 806-462-7334
Steve McLaren, supt. Fax 462-7333
klondike.esc17.net
Klondike S 200/PK-12
2911 County Road H 79331 806-462-7332
Steve McLaren, prin. Fax 462-7323

Lamesa ISD 2,000/PK-12
PO Box 261 79331 806-872-5461
Scott Davis, supt. Fax 872-6220
www.lamesa.esc17.net
Lamesa MS 400/6-8
PO Box 261 79331 806-872-8301
Chris Riggins, prin. Fax 872-2949
North ES 500/3-5
PO Box 261 79331 806-872-5428
Diane Page, prin. Fax 872-8324
South ES 700/PK-2
PO Box 261 79331 806-872-5401
Stacy Leonard, prin. Fax 872-9161

Lampasas, Lampasas, Pop. 7,465
Lampasas ISD 3,500/PK-12
207 W 8th St 76550 512-556-6224
Brant Myers Ed.D., supt. Fax 556-8711
www.lampasas.k12.tx.us
Hanna Springs IS 1,000/3-6
604 E Avenue F 76550 512-556-2152
Nancy Yeary, prin. Fax 556-0225
Kline Whitis ES 800/PK-2
500 S Willis St 76550 512-556-8291
Mitzi Stripling, prin. Fax 556-8285
Lampasas MS 500/7-8
207 E Avenue A 76550 512-556-3101
Dwain Brock, prin. Fax 556-0245

Lancaster, Dallas, Pop. 32,233
Lancaster ISD 6,300/PK-12
PO Box 400 75146 972-218-1400
Dr. Larry Lewis, supt. Fax 218-1401
www.lancasterisd.org
Beltline ES 500/PK-5
1355 W Belt Line Rd 75146 972-218-1608
Patty Cunningham, prin. Fax 218-1620
Houston ES 700/PK-5
2929 Marquis Ln 75134 972-218-1512
Diane Burns, prin. Fax 218-1524
Lancaster ES 400/PK-5
1109 W Main St 75146 972-218-1590
Vanessa Alba, prin. Fax 218-1607
Lancaster MS 1,400/6-8
822 W Pleasant Run Rd 75146 972-218-1660
Demetrus Liggins, prin. Fax 218-3080
Parks/Millbrook ES 400/PK-5
630 Millbrook Dr 75146 972-218-1564
Helena Mosley, prin. Fax 218-3420
Pleasant Run ES 300/PK-5
427 W Pleasant Run Rd 75146 972-218-1538
Cindy Lynch, prin. Fax 218-1550
Rolling Hills ES 500/PK-5
450 Rolling Hills Pl 75146 972-218-1525
Gene Morrow, prin. Fax 218-1537
West Main ES 200/PK-5
531 W Main St 75146 972-218-1551
Priscilla Maxfield, prin. Fax 218-1563

Laneville, Rusk
Laneville ISD 200/PK-12
7415 FM 1798 W 75667 903-863-5353
Ron Tidwell, supt. Fax 863-2736
Laneville S 200/PK-12
7415 FM 1798 W 75667 903-863-5353
Carolyn Reeves, prin. Fax 863-2376

La Porte, Harris, Pop. 33,136
La Porte ISD 8,300/PK-12
1002 San Jacinto St 77571 281-604-7000
Lloyd Graham, supt. Fax 604-7020
www.lpisd.org
Baker Sixth Grade Campus 600/6-6
1002 San Jacinto St 77571 281-604-6872
Cynthia Chism, prin. Fax 604-6885
Bayshore ES 400/PK-5
1002 San Jacinto St 77571 281-604-4600
P. Herrerra-Johnson, prin. Fax 604-4680
La Porte ES 600/K-5
1002 San Jacinto St 77571 281-604-4700
Jewel Whitfield, prin. Fax 604-4787
La Porte JHS 600/7-8
1002 San Jacinto St 77571 281-604-6600
Vicki Defee, prin. Fax 604-6605
Lomax ES 600/K-5
1002 San Jacinto St 77571 281-604-4300
Vicki Gentile, prin. Fax 604-4355
Lomax JHS 500/7-8
1002 San Jacinto St 77571 281-604-6701
Stephanie Cox, prin. Fax 604-6730
Reid ES 600/K-5
1002 San Jacinto St 77571 281-604-4500
Dan Eubank, prin. Fax 604-4555
Rizzuto ES 800/PK-5
1002 San Jacinto St 77571 281-604-6500
Angie Garza-Viator, prin. Fax 604-6555
Other Schools – See Deer Park

La Pryor, Zavala, Pop. 1,343
La Pryor ISD 500/PK-12
PO Box 519 78872 830-365-4000
Eddie Ramirez, supt. Fax 365-4006
www.lapryor.net
La Pryor ES 300/PK-6
PO Box 519 78872 830-365-4009
Lisa Taylor, admin. Fax 365-4021

Laredo, Webb, Pop. 208,754
Laredo ISD 24,800/PK-12
1702 Houston St 78040 956-795-3200
Ronald McLeod Ed.D., supt. Fax 795-3205
www.laredoisd.org/
Bruni ES 700/PK-5
1508 San Eduardo Ave 78040 956-795-3910
Lucy Flores, prin. Fax 795-3913
Christen MS 1,400/6-8
2001 Santa Maria Ave 78040 956-795-3725
Carlos Cruz, prin. Fax 795-3732
Cigarroa MS 1,400/6-8
2600 Palo Blanco St 78046 956-795-3700
Laura Flores, prin. Fax 795-3711
Daiches ES 600/PK-5
1401 Green St 78040 956-795-3930
Rebecca Pulido, prin. Fax 795-3933
Dovalina ES 600/PK-5
1700 Anna Ave 78040 956-795-3940
Sylvia Moreno, prin. Fax 795-3943

Farias ES 900/PK-5
1510 Chicago St 78041 956-795-3950
Sam Sanchez, prin. Fax 795-3954
Gallego ES 600/PK-5
520 Clark Blvd 78040 956-795-3920
San Juana Garza, prin. Fax 795-3923
Hachar ES 500/PK-5
3000 Guadalupe St 78043 956-795-3960
Sarah Appling, prin. Fax 795-3963
Heights ES 300/PK-5
1208 Market St 78040 956-795-3970
Adriana Padilla, prin. Fax 795-3973
Kawas ES 700/PK-5
2100 S Milmo Ave 78046 956-795-3980
Yolanda Montemayor, prin. Fax 795-3982
Lamar MS 1,300/6-8
1818 N Arkansas Ave 78043 956-795-3750
Virginia Salinas, prin. Fax 795-3766
Leyendecker ES 500/PK-5
1311 Garden St 78040 956-795-3990
Maria Felicitas Oviedo, prin. Fax 795-3992
Ligarde ES 600/PK-PK, 1-
2800 S Canada Ave 78046 956-795-4000
Jacobita Laurel, prin. Fax 795-4002
MacDonell ES 700/PK-5
1606 Benavides St 78040 956-795-4010
Cynthia Conchas, prin. Fax 795-4012
Martin ES 700/PK-5
310 W Locust St 78040 956-795-4020
Lorenia Torres, prin. Fax 795-4025
Memorial MS 900/6-8
2002 Marcella Ave 78040 956-795-3775
Connie Vela, prin. Fax 795-3780
Milton ES 900/PK-5
2500 E Ash St 78043 956-795-4030
Elsa Flores, prin. Fax 795-4033
Pierce ES 900/PK-5
800 E Eistetter St 78041 956-795-4050
Josefina Torres, prin. Fax 795-4053
Ryan ES 900/PK-5
2401 Clark Blvd 78043 956-795-4060
Sandra Munoz, prin. Fax 795-4061
Sanchez/Ochoa ES 900/PK-5
211 E Ash St 78040 956-795-4040
Dr. Adriana Guzman, prin. Fax 795-4042
Santa Maria ES 700/PK-5
3817 Santa Maria Ave 78041 956-795-4080
Nora Santos, prin. Fax 795-4082
Santo Nino ES 800/PK-5
2701 Bismark St 78043 956-795-4090
Myrtala Ramirez, prin. Fax 795-4093
Tarver ES 700/PK-5
3200 Tilden Ave 78040 956-795-4100
Ana Maria Campos, prin. Fax 795-4103
Zachry ES 700/PK-5
3200 Chacota St 78046 956-795-4120
Diana Martinez, prin. Fax 795-4122

United ISD 37,700/PK-12
201 Lindenwood Dr 78045 956-473-6201
Roberto Santos, supt. Fax 473-6476
www.uisd.net
Arndt ES 1,000/PK-5
610 Santa Martha Blvd 78046 956-473-2800
Juanita Zepeda, prin. Fax 473-2899
Benavides ES 900/PK-5
10702 Kirby Dr 78045 956-473-4900
Dr. Myrtha Villarreal, prin. Fax 473-4999
Borchers ES 600/PK-5
9551 Backwoods Trl 78045 956-473-7200
Dinorah Wickstrom, prin. Fax 473-7299
Centeno ES 700/PK-5
2710 La Pita Mangana Rd 78046 956-473-8800
Maria Arambula Ruiz, prin. Fax 473-8899
Clark ES 600/PK-5
500 W Hillside Rd 78041 956-473-4600
Clemen Bell, prin. Fax 473-4699
Clark MS 800/6-8
500 W Hillside Rd 78041 956-473-7500
Rene Rodriguez, prin. Fax 473-7599
Cuellar ES 1,000/PK-5
6431 Casa Del Sol Blvd 78043 956-473-2700
Sylvia Ruiz, prin. Fax 473-2799
De Llano ES 700/PK-5
1415 Shiloh Dr 78045 956-473-4000
Maria Campos, prin. Fax 473-4099
Fasken ES 900/PK-5
11111 Atlanta Dr 78045 956-473-4700
Elouisa Diaz, prin. Fax 473-4799
Finley ES 500/PK-5
2001 Lowry Rd 78045 956-473-4500
Claudia Benavides, prin. Fax 473-4599
Garcia ES 1,100/PK-5
1453 Concord Hills Blvd 78046 956-764-8900
Clarissa Flores, prin. Fax 764-8999
Garcia MS 600/6-8
499 Pena Dr 78046 956-473-5000
Gerardo Gonzalez, prin. Fax 473-5099
Gonzalez MS 800/6-8
5208 Santa Claudia 78043 956-473-7000
Adriana Ramirez, prin. Fax 473-7099
Gutierrez ES 800/PK-5
505 Calle Del Norte 78041 956-473-4400
Claudia Guzman, prin. Fax 473-4499
Juarez-Lincoln ES 400/PK-5
1600 Espejo Molina Rd 78046 956-473-4300
Melissa Cruz, prin. Fax 473-4399
Kazen ES 700/PK-5
9620 Albany Dr 78045 956-473-4200
Cordelia Gutierrez, prin. Fax 473-4299
Kennedy-Zapata ES 600/PK-5
3809 Espejo Molina Rd 78046 956-473-4100
Thelma Martinez, prin. Fax 473-4199
Killiam ES, 5511 Fairfield Dr 78043 PK-5
Linda Vera, prin. 956-473-6201
Lamar Bruni-Vergar MS 700/6-8
5910 Saint Luke 78046 956-473-6600
Annabel Rubio, prin. Fax 473-6699

Los Obispos MS 800/6-8
4801 S Ejido Ave 78046 956-473-7800
Armando Salazar, prin. Fax 473-1899
Malakoff ES 800/PK-5
2810 Havana 78045 956-473-4800
Anna Torres, prin. Fax 473-4899
Muller ES 700/PK-5
4430 Muller Blvd 78045 956-473-3900
Mayra Solorio, prin. Fax 473-3999
Newman ES 600/PK-5
1300 Alta Vista Dr 78041 956-473-3800
Zulema Gutierrez, prin. Fax 473-3899
Nye ES 800/PK-5
101 E Del Mar Blvd 78041 956-473-3700
Patricia Lanas, prin. Fax 473-3799
Perez ES 900/PK-5
500 Sierra Vista Blvd 78046 956-473-3600
Maria de Lourdes Viloria, prin. Fax 473-3699
Prada ES 800/PK-5
510 Soria Dr 78046 956-473-3500
Maria Aguilar, prin. Fax 473-3599
Roosevelt ES 800/PK-5
3301 Sierra Vista Blvd 78046 956-473-3400
Sylvia Reash, prin. Fax 473-3499
Ruiz ES 900/PK-5
1717 Los Presidentes Ave 78046 956-473-3300
David Garza, prin. Fax 473-3399
Salinas ES 900/PK-5
1000 Century Dr W 78046 956-473-3200
Abraham Rodriguez, prin. Fax 473-3299
Trautmann ES 900/PK-5
810 Lindenwood Dr 78045 956-473-3100
Cynthia Rodriguez, prin. Fax 473-3199
Trautmann MS 1,400/6-8
8501 Curly Ln 78045 956-473-7400
Raymundo Gonzalez, prin. Fax 473-7499
United D.D. Hachar ES 500/PK-5
1003 Espejo Molina Rd 78046 956-473-3000
Fernando Garcia, prin. Fax 473-3099
United MS 900/6-8
700 E Del Mar Blvd 78041 956-473-7300
David Canales, prin. Fax 473-7399
United South MS 1,100/6-8
3707 Los Presidentes Ave 78046 956-473-7700
Selma Santos, prin. Fax 473-7799
Washington MS 1,100/6-8
10306 Riverbank Dr 78045 956-473-7600
David Gonzalez, prin. Fax 473-7699
Zaffirini ES 1,000/PK-5
5210 Santa Claudia 78043 956-473-2900
Anna Wirsching, prin. Fax 473-2999

Blessed Sacrament S 100/K-7
1501 N Bartlett Ave 78043 956-722-1222
Esther Gutierrez, prin. Fax 722-5635
Champions Christian Academy 50/PK-2
4020 Santa Maria Ave 78041 956-791-1322
Haydee Diaz, dir. Fax 723-4969
Mary Help of Christians S 600/PK-8
10 E Del Mar Blvd 78041 956-722-3966
Sr. Suzanne Miller, prin. Fax 722-1413
Our Lady of Guadalupe S 100/PK-5
400 Callaghan St 78040 956-722-3915
Herlinda Martinez, prin. Fax 727-2840
St. Augustine S 400/PK-8
1300 Galveston St 78040 956-724-1176
Sylvia Cortez, prin. Fax 724-9891
St. Peters Memorial S 100/PK-6
PO Box 520 78042 956-723-6302
Dr. Linda Mitchell, prin. Fax 725-2671
United Day S 500/PK-8
1701 San Isidro Pkwy 78045 956-723-7261
Rita Peters, prin. Fax 718-4048

La Rue, Henderson
La Poynor ISD 500/K-12
13155 US Highway 175 E, 903-876-4057
Dr. B.L. Davis, supt. Fax 876-4541
www.lapoynorisd.net/
La Poynor ES 200/K-5
13155 US Highway 175 E, 903-876-5293
Marsha Mills, prin. Fax 876-4541
La Poynor JHS 100/6-8
13155 US Highway 175 E, 903-876-1085
Ken Barrow, prin. Fax 876-4541

Lasara, Willacy
Lasara ISD 300/PK-12
PO Box 57 78561 956-642-3598
Rolando Pena, supt. Fax 642-3546
www.lasaraisd.net/
Lasara S 300/PK-8
PO Box 57 78561 956-642-3271
Sulema Osuna, prin. Fax 642-3546

Latexo, Houston, Pop. 275
Latexo ISD 500/K-12
PO Box 975 75849 936-544-5664
Dr. Roy Tucker, supt. Fax 544-5332
www.latexoisd.net
Latexo ES 200/K-6
PO Box 975 75849 936-546-5630
Dr. Stacy Easterly, prin. Fax 546-2220

La Vernia, Wilson, Pop. 1,087
La Vernia ISD 2,800/PK-12
13600 US Highway 87 W 78121 830-779-2181
Dr. Tom Harvey, supt. Fax 779-2304
www.lvisd.org
La Vernia ES 600/4-6
369 S FM 1346 78121 830-779-2181
Becky Johanson, prin. Fax 779-2304
La Vernia JHS 400/7-8
110 D L Vest 78121 830-779-2181
Maria Wildenstein, prin. Fax 779-2728
La Vernia PS 900/PK-3
249 S FM 1346 78121 830-779-2181
Sheri Boos, prin. Fax 779-7031

La Villa, Hidalgo, Pop. 1,455
La Villa ISD 600/PK-12
PO Box 9 78562 956-262-4755
Dr. Norma Salaiz, supt. Fax 262-7323
www.lavillaisd.org
La Villa MS 100/6-8
PO Box 9 78562 956-262-4760
Vilma Gomez, prin. Fax 262-5243
Munoz ES 300/PK-5
PO Box 9 78562 956-262-9357
Debbie Winslow, prin. Fax 262-9452

Lavon, Collin, Pop. 421
Community ISD
Supt. — See Nevada
NeSmith ES K-5
801 Presidents Blvd 75166 972-843-8620
Julie Meek, prin. Fax 843-8621

Lawn, Taylor, Pop. 349
Jim Ned Consolidated ISD
Supt. — See Tuscola
Lawn ES 200/PK-5
PO Box 118 79530 325-583-2256
Glenda Bowden, prin. Fax 583-2511

Lazbuddie, Parmer
Lazbuddie ISD 100/PK-12
PO Box 9 79053 806-965-2156
Karl Vaughn, supt. Fax 965-2892
www.lazbuddieisd.org
Lazbuddie S 100/PK-12
PO Box 9 79053 806-965-2152
John Jones, prin. Fax 965-2892

League City, Galveston, Pop. 61,490
Clear Creek ISD 36,700/PK-12
PO Box 799 77574 281-284-0000
Dr. Greg Smith, supt. Fax 284-0005
www.ccisd.net
Bauerschlag ES 800/K-5
2051 W League City Pkwy 77573 281-284-6100
Trudy Knight, prin. Fax 284-6105
Creekside IS 800/6-8
4320 W Main St 77573 281-284-3500
Pete Caterina, prin. Fax 284-3505
Ferguson ES 900/PK-5
1910 S Compass Rose Blvd 77573 281-284-5500
Elaine Sanders, prin. Fax 284-5505
Gilmore ES 800/PK-5
3552 W League City Pkwy 77573 281-284-6400
Suzanne Jones, prin. Fax 284-6405
Goforth ES 800/K-5
2610 Webster St 77573 281-284-6000
Kimberly Noell, prin. Fax 284-6005
Hall ES 500/K-5
5931 Meadowside St 77573 281-284-5300
Stephanie King, prin. Fax 284-5305
Hyde ES 700/PK-5
3700 FM 518 Rd E 77573 281-284-5800
Kelly Chapman, prin. Fax 284-5805
League City ES 600/PK-5
709 E Wilkins St 77573 281-284-4400
Carla Massa, prin. Fax 284-4405
League City IS 1,200/6-8
2588 Webster St 77573 281-284-3400
Kimberly Brouillard, prin. Fax 284-3405
Ross ES 600/PK-5
2401 W Main St 77573 281-284-4500
Mark Smith, prin. Fax 284-4505
Victory Lakes IS 1,000/6-8
2880 W Walker St 77573 281-284-3700
Barry Beck, prin. Fax 284-3705
Other Schools – See El Lago, Friendswood, Houston, Kemah, Seabrook, Webster

---

Bay Area Christian S 700/K-12
4800 W Main St 77573 281-332-4814
Freddie Cullins, admin. Fax 554-5495
St. Mary S 300/PK-8
1612 E Walker St 77573 281-332-4014
Ruth Winsor, prin. Fax 332-5148

Leakey, Real, Pop. 372
Leakey ISD 200/PK-12
PO Box 1129 78873 830-232-5595
Fred McNiel, supt. Fax 232-5535
www.leakey.k12.tx.us/
Leakey S 200/PK-12
PO Box 1129 78873 830-232-5595
Lorri Gonzalez, prin. Fax 232-5535

Leander, Williamson, Pop. 17,851
Lago Vista ISD
Supt. — See Lago Vista
Lago Vista ES 600/PK-5
20311 Dawn Dr 78645 512-267-8340
Beth Mohler, prin. Fax 267-8362

Leander ISD 24,800/PK-12
PO Box 218 78646 512-434-5000
Bret Champion Ed.D., supt. Fax 434-5387
www.leanderisd.org
Bagdad ES 700/PK-5
800 Deercreek Ln 78641 512-435-4600
Cathy White, prin. Fax 435-4605
Block House Creek ES 800/PK-5
401 Creek Run Dr 78641 512-434-7150
Dr. Deana Cady, prin. Fax 434-7155
Leander MS 600/6-8
410 S West Dr 78641 512-434-7800
Sandy Trujillo, prin. Fax 434-7805
Plain ES 500/PK-5
501 S Brook Dr 78641 512-435-4926
Jenna Sanders, prin. Fax 435-4935
Pleasant Hill ES 1,000/PK-5
1800 Horizon Park Blvd 78641 512-434-7076
Lana Collier, prin. Fax 434-7080
Whitestone ES 600/PK-5
2000 Crystal Falls Pkwy 78641 512-434-5300
Beckie Webster, prin. Fax 434-5305

Wiley MS 700/6-8
1701 County Road 271 78641 512-435-4850
Sylvia Flannery, prin. Fax 435-4851
Winkley ES PK-5
2100 Pow Wow 78641 512-435-4976
Donna Brady, prin. Fax 435-4977
Other Schools – See Austin, Cedar Park, Georgetown

Summit Christian Academy of Leander 200/PK-6
1303 Leander Dr 78641 512-259-4416
Derek Cortez, supt. Fax 259-0814

Lefors, Gray, Pop. 540
Lefors ISD 100/PK-12
PO Box 390 79054 806-835-2533
Clay Montgomery, supt. Fax 835-2238
www.region16.net/leforsisd/
Lefors S 100/PK-12
PO Box 390 79054 806-835-2533
Jeff Nicklas, prin. Fax 835-2238

Leggett, Polk
Leggett ISD 200/PK-12
PO Box 68 77350 936-398-2804
Vicki Jones, supt. Fax 398-2078
www.leggettisd.net/
Leggett ES 100/PK-6
PO Box 68 77350 936-398-2412
Richard Perry, prin. Fax 398-0889

Leming, Atascosa
Pleasanton ISD
Supt. — See Pleasanton
Leming ES 100/PK-K
25 E Fifth St 78050 830-281-3267
Jackie Russell, prin. Fax 569-6598

Lenorah, Martin
Grady ISD 200/PK-12
3500 FM 829 79749 432-459-2444
John Tubb, supt. Fax 459-2729
grady.tx.schoolwebpages.com
Grady S 200/PK-12
3500 FM 829 79749 432-459-2445
Leandro Gonzales, prin. Fax 459-2729

Leonard, Fannin, Pop. 2,071
Leonard ISD 900/PK-12
1 Tiger Aly 75452 903-587-2318
Larry LaFavers, supt. Fax 587-2845
www.leonardisd.net
Leonard ES 300/PK-3
1 Tiger Aly 75452 903-587-2316
Brad Maxwell, prin. Fax 587-2392
Leonard IS 100/4-5
1 Tiger Aly 75452 903-587-8303
Brandi Savage, prin. Fax 587-4414
Leonard JHS 200/6-8
1 Tiger Aly 75452 903-587-2315
Brad Connelly, prin. Fax 587-2228

Levelland, Hockley, Pop. 12,777
Levelland ISD 2,600/PK-12
704 11th St 79336 806-894-9628
Mark Holcomb, supt. Fax 894-2583
www.levelland.isd.tenet.edu
Cactus ES 300/1-3
704 11th St 79336 806-894-3323
Karl Race, prin. Fax 894-2234
Levelland Academic Beginnings Center 500/PK-K
1412 E Ellis St 79336 806-894-6959
Donna Pugh, prin. Fax 894-5512
Levelland IS 200/4-5
704 11th St 79336 806-894-3060
Gary Bridges, prin. Fax 894-8957
Levelland MS 400/6-8
1402 E Ellis St 79336 806-894-6355
Kenny Berry, prin. Fax 894-8935
South ES 300/1-3
704 11th St 79336 806-894-6255
Rodney Caddell, prin. Fax 894-1283

Levelland Christian S 100/PK-8
1905 Cactus Dr 79336 806-894-6019
Amber Beadles, admin. Fax 897-0522

Lewisville, Denton, Pop. 90,348
Lewisville ISD
Supt. — See Flower Mound
Castle Hills ES 500/PK-5
1025 Holy Grail Dr 75056 469-713-5952
Venita Blake, prin. Fax 350-9018
Central ES 1,100/PK-5
400 High School Dr 75057 469-713-5976
Raul Pena, prin. Fax 350-9019
College Street ES 200/K-5
350 W College St 75057 469-713-5965
Patty Ruth, prin. Fax 350-9024
Creekside ES 500/K-5
901 Valley View Dr 75067 469-713-5953
Rod McGinnis, prin. Fax 350-9027
Degan ES 700/PK-5
1680 College Pkwy 75077 469-713-5967
Brenda Rogers, prin. Fax 350-9028
Delay MS 700/6-8
136 W Purnell Rd 75057 469-713-5191
Pam Flores, prin. Fax 350-9174
Durham MS 800/6-8
2075 S Edmonds Ln 75067 469-713-5963
Scot Finch, prin. Fax 350-9182
Hedrick ES 500/K-5
1532 Bellaire Blvd 75067 469-713-5189
Esteva Bargo, prin. Fax 350-9071
Hedrick MS 600/6-8
1526 Bellaire Blvd 75067 469-713-5188
Barbara Hamric, prin. Fax 350-9196
Huffines MS 1,000/6-8
1440 N Valley Pkwy 75077 469-713-5990
James Hill, prin. Fax 350-9199
Independence ES PK-5
2511 Windhaven Pkwy 75056 469-713-5212
Teddie Winslow, prin. Fax 350-9479
Jackson ECC 500/PK-PK
1651 S Valley Pkwy 75067 469-713-5986
Dulia Longoria, prin. Fax 350-9103
Killian MS 500/6-8
2561 FM 544 75056 469-713-5977
Alan Cassel, prin. Fax 350-9200
Lakeland ES 800/PK-5
800 Fox Ave 75067 469-713-5992
James Crockett, prin. Fax 350-9092
Parkway ES 500/PK-5
2100 S Valley Pkwy 75067 469-713-5979
Judy Miers, prin. Fax 350-9132
Rockbrook ES 700/K-5
2751 Rockbrook Dr 75067 469-713-5968
Elisa Wittrock, prin. Fax 350-9139
Southridge ES 700/PK-5
495 W Corporate Dr 75067 469-713-5187
Julie Sheriff, prin. Fax 350-9140
Valley Ridge ES 800/K-5
1604 N Garden Ridge Blvd 75077 469-713-5982
Charlotte Cauthen, prin. Fax 350-9155

Lakeland Christian Academy 200/PK-8
397 S Stemmons Fwy 75067 972-219-3939
Tena Mitchell, dir. Fax 219-9601
Miller Adventist S 50/PK-8
1471 W Corporate Dr 75067 972-353-3981
Fax 353-3981
Temple Christian Academy 300/PK-12
1010 Bellaire Blvd 75067 972-436-3480
Dr. Richard Wallace, admin. Fax 219-5639

Lexington, Lee, Pop. 1,245
Lexington ISD 1,000/PK-12
8731 N Highway 77 78947 979-773-2254
Chuck Holt, supt. Fax 773-4455
www.lexington.isd.tenet.edu
Lexington ES 500/PK-5
8731 N Highway 77 78947 979-773-2525
Lynette Brown, prin. Fax 773-4455
Lexington MS 200/6-8
8731 N Highway 77 78947 979-773-2255
Sarah Garrison, prin. Fax 773-4455

Liberty, Liberty, Pop. 8,433
Liberty ISD 2,300/PK-12
1600 Grand Ave 77575 936-336-7213
Mona Chadwick, supt. Fax 336-2283
www.libertyisd.net
Liberty ES 700/2-5
1002 Bowie St 77575 936-336-3603
Tom Connelly, prin. Fax 336-6077
Liberty MS 500/6-8
2515 Jefferson Dr 77575 936-336-3582
David Taylor, prin. Fax 336-1021
San Jacinto ES 500/PK-1
2525 Grand Ave 77575 936-336-3161
Donna Eckols, prin. Fax 336-5751

Liberty Hill, Williamson, Pop. 1,491
Liberty Hill ISD 2,300/PK-12
14001 W State Highway 29 78642 512-260-5580
Dr. Rob Hart, supt. Fax 260-5581
www.libertyhill.txed.net
Liberty Hill Bill Burden ES 600/2-4
315 Stonewall Pkwy 78642 512-260-4400
Terrie Chambers, prin. Fax 260-4410
Liberty Hill ES 400/PK-1
1400 Loop 332 78642 512-515-6514
Jan Tredemeyer, prin. Fax 778-5942
Liberty Hill IS 300/5-6
301 Forrest St 78642 512-515-6516
Kathy Major, prin. Fax 778-6419
Liberty Hill MS 400/7-8
101 Loop 332 78642 512-515-5636
Chad Pirtle, prin. Fax 778-5937

Lindale, Smith, Pop. 4,030
Lindale ISD 3,400/PK-12
PO Box 370 75771 903-881-4001
Stan Surratt, supt. Fax 881-4004
www.lindaleeagles.org
Lindale ECC 300/PK-K
PO Box 370 75771 903-881-4400
Belinda Neal, prin. Fax 881-4401
Lindale IS 500/5-6
PO Box 370 75771 903-881-4200
Mike Griffin, prin. Fax 882-0994
Lindale JHS 500/7-8
PO Box 370 75771 903-881-4150
Vicki Thrasher, prin. Fax 882-2842
Lindale PS 500/1-2
PO Box 370 75771 903-881-4350
Robbie Lyons, prin. Fax 881-4351
Penny ES 500/3-4
PO Box 370 75771 903-881-4250
Monica Moore, prin. Fax 881-4251

Linden, Cass, Pop. 2,201
Linden-Kildare Consolidated ISD 800/PK-12
205 Kildare Rd 75563 903-756-5027
Clint Coyne, supt. Fax 756-7242
www.lkcisd.net
Linden ES 400/PK-5
205 Kildare Rd 75563 903-756-5471
Marcella Young, prin. Fax 756-5022
Linden-Kildare JHS 200/6-8
205 Kildare Rd 75563 903-756-5381
Jerry Hankins, prin. Fax 756-8832

Lindsay, Cooke, Pop. 956
Lindsay ISD 500/K-12
PO Box 145 76250 940-668-8923
Dennis Holt, supt. Fax 668-2662
www.lindsayisd.org/
Lindsay ES 300/K-6
PO Box 145 76250 940-668-8923
Kim Otto, prin. Fax 668-2662

Lingleville, Erath
Lingleville ISD 200/PK-12
PO Box 134 76461 254-968-2596
Dennis Hughes, supt. Fax 965-5821
www.lingleville.k12.tx.us/
Lingleville S 200/PK-12
PO Box 134 76461 254-968-2596
Mike Thompson, prin. Fax 965-5821

Lipan, Hood, Pop. 488
Lipan ISD 200/PK-8
211 N Kickapoo St 76462 254-646-2266
Mike Vinyard, supt. Fax 646-3499
www.lipanindians.net/
Lipan ES 100/PK-6
211 N Kickapoo St 76462 254-646-2266
Sharon Mills, prin. Fax 646-3498
Lipan JHS 50/7-8
211 N Kickapoo St 76462 254-646-2266
Mike Permenter, prin. Fax 646-3499

Little Elm, Denton, Pop. 18,012
Frisco ISD
Supt. — See Frisco
Robertson ES 600/K-5
2501 Woodlake Pkwy 75068 469-633-3675
James Iorio, prin. Fax 633-3685

Little Elm ISD 5,200/PK-12
500 Lobo Ln 75068 972-292-1847
Steve Murray, supt. Fax 294-1107
www.leisd.ws/
Brent IS 400/5-6
500 Witt Rd 75068 972-668-2991
Jason Huffman, prin. Fax 668-2995
Chavez ES 700/K-4
2600 Hart Rd 75068 972-294-1670
Teresa Starrett, prin. Fax 294-0172
King Pre K 300/PK-PK
101 Main St 75068 972-292-1908
Laura Griffin, prin. Fax 292-3368
Lakeside JHS 700/7-8
400 Lobo Ln 75068 972-292-3200
Larry Winget, prin. Fax 292-3009
Lakeview ES 600/K-4
1800 Waterside Dr 75068 972-547-3575
Cyndy Mika, prin. Fax 362-0709
Powell IS 400/5-6
520 Lobo Ln 75068 972-547-3515
Dee Owen, prin. Fax 292-3272
Zellars ES 500/K-4
300 Lobo Ln 75068 972-292-0720
Debbie Clark, prin. Fax 294-1858
Other Schools – See Frisco, Oak Point

Littlefield, Lamb, Pop. 6,329
Littlefield ISD 1,600/PK-12
1207 E 14th St 79339 806-385-3844
Jerry Blakely, supt. Fax 385-6297
www.littlefield.k12.tx.us
Littlefield ES 300/3-5
1207 E 14th St 79339 806-385-6217
Tom Whistler, prin. Fax 385-9174
Littlefield JHS 300/6-8
1207 E 14th St 79339 806-385-3922
Pam Moore, prin. Fax 385-5603
Littlefield PS 500/PK-2
1207 E 14th St 79339 806-385-4551
Jan Richards, prin. Fax 385-9173

Trinity Christian S 50/PK-3
PO Box 966 79339 806-385-5749
Andrew Melton, admin. Fax 385-5749

Little River, Bell, Pop. 1,512
Academy ISD 1,000/PK-12
704 E Main St 76554 254-982-4304
Kevin Sprinkles, supt. Fax 982-0023
www.academy.k12.tx.us/
Academy ES 400/PK-4
311 N Bumblebee Dr 76554 254-982-4621
Vicki Slye, prin. Fax 982-4584
Academy JHS 300/5-8
501 E Main St 76554 254-982-4620
Stephen Ash, prin. Fax 982-4776

Live Oak, Bexar, Pop. 10,942
Judson ISD 20,700/PK-12
8012 Shin Oak Dr 78233 210-945-5100
Dr. Willis Mackey, supt. Fax 945-6900
www.judsonisd.org
Crestview ES 600/K-5
7710 Narrow Pass St 78233 210-945-5111
Dr. Nancy Gerhard, prin. Fax 590-4300
Other Schools – See Converse, San Antonio, Universal City

Livingston, Polk, Pop. 6,401
Big Sandy ISD
Supt. — See Dallardsville
Big Sandy S 500/PK-12
FM 1276 77351 936-563-1000
Kevin Foster, prin. Fax 563-1010

Livingston ISD 4,100/PK-12
PO Box 1297 77351 936-328-2100
Dr. Darrell Myers, supt. Fax 328-2109
www.livingstonisd.com
Livingston IS 600/4-5
819 W Church St 77351 936-328-2150
Lana Smith, prin. Fax 328-2159
Livingston JHS 1,000/6-8
1801 Highway 59 Loop N 77351 936-328-2120
Michael Woodard, prin. Fax 328-2139
Pine Ridge ES 700/PK-3
1200 Mill Rdg 77351 936-328-2160
Janel Sewell, prin. Fax 328-2179
Timber Creek ES 600/K-3
701 N Willis Ave 77351 936-328-2180
Kyle Rice, prin. Fax 328-2199

Llano, Llano, Pop. 3,348
Llano ISD 2,000/PK-12
200 E Lampasas St 78643 325-247-4747
Dennis Hill, supt. Fax 247-5623
www.llano.k12.tx.us
Llano ES 500/PK-5
1600 Oatman St 78643 325-247-5718
Keeva Frazier, prin. Fax 247-5731
Llano JHS 400/6-8
400 E State Highway 71 E 78643 325-247-4659
Harper Stewart, prin. Fax 247-5916
Other Schools – See Kingsland

Lockhart, Caldwell, Pop. 13,567
Lockhart ISD 4,500/PK-12
PO Box 120 78644 512-398-0000
Joe Parra, supt. Fax 398-0025
www.lockhartisd.org
Bluebonnet ES 500/PK-5
211 Mockingbird Ln 78644 512-398-0900
Becky Kibby, prin. Fax 398-0901
Carver K 400/PK-K
371 Carver St 78644 512-398-0060
Barbara Bernal, prin. Fax 398-0110
Clear Fork ES 400/1-5
1102 Clearfork St 78644 512-398-0450
Deanna Juarez, prin. Fax 398-0536
Lockhart JHS 1,000/6-8
500 City Line Rd 78644 512-398-0770
Lora Hardway, prin. Fax 398-0772
Navarro ES 400/1-5
715 N Medina St 78644 512-398-0690
Susan Masur, prin. Fax 398-0692
Plum Creek ES 500/1-5
710 Flores St 78644 512-398-0570
Evangelina Orta, prin. Fax 398-0572

Lockney, Floyd, Pop. 1,878
Lockney ISD 600/PK-12
PO Box 428 79241 806-652-2115
Phil Cotham, supt. Fax 652-2729
www.lockney.isd.tenet.edu/
Lockney ES 300/PK-5
PO Box 127 79241 806-652-3321
Jean Anne Williams, prin. Fax 652-2956
Lockney JHS 100/6-8
PO Box 550 79241 806-652-2236
Craig Setliff, prin. Fax 652-4920

Lohn, McCulloch
Lohn ISD 100/PK-12
PO Box 277 76852 325-344-5749
Leon Freeman, supt. Fax 344-5789
www.centex-edu.net/lohn
Lohn S 100/PK-12
PO Box 277 76852 325-344-5749
Heidi Gardner, prin. Fax 344-5789

Lometa, Lampasas, Pop. 853
Lometa ISD 300/PK-12
PO Box 250 76853 512-752-3384
David Rice, supt. Fax 752-3424
www.centex-edu.net/lometa/
Lometa S 300/PK-12
PO Box 250 76853 512-752-3384
Kip Bullock, prin. Fax 752-3424

Lone Oak, Hunt, Pop. 554
Lone Oak ISD 900/PK-12
PO Box 38 75453 903-662-5427
Eddie White, supt. Fax 662-5290
loisd.echalk.com/
Lone Oak ES 400/PK-4
8163 US Highway 69 S 75453 903-662-5022
Judy Steadham, prin. Fax 662-0973
Lone Oak MS 300/5-8
8161 US Highway 69 S 75453 903-662-5121
Kim White, prin. Fax 662-5017

Lone Star, Morris, Pop. 1,589
Daingerfield-Lone Star ISD
Supt. — See Daingerfield
Lone Star ES 200/PK-5
100 Milam St 75668 903-656-2351
Lesia Lewis, prin. Fax 656-2621

Longview, Gregg, Pop. 75,609
Longview ISD 7,800/PK-12
PO Box 3268 75606 903-381-2200
Dr. James Wilcox, supt. Fax 753-5389
www.lisd.org
Bramlette ES 500/PK-5
PO Box 3268 75606 903-758-8353
Vernessa Gentry, prin. Fax 758-8378
Everhart ES 300/1-3
PO Box 3268 75606 903-758-5622
Linda Lister, prin. Fax 758-7870
Forest Park MS 600/6-8
PO Box 3268 75606 903-758-9971
Darrin Bickham, prin. Fax 758-6964
Foster MS 700/6-8
PO Box 3268 75606 903-753-1692
Sedric Clark, prin. Fax 758-1571
Foster PS 400/PK-K
PO Box 3268 75606 903-758-2254
Jacqueline Burnett, prin. Fax 758-7872
Hudson ES 400/1-5
PO Box 3268 75606 903-753-7472
Sue Wilson, prin. Fax 753-8256
Johnston ES 300/3-5
PO Box 3268 75606 903-663-1118
Sarah Sheppard, prin. Fax 663-1320
Judson MS 500/6-8
PO Box 3268 75606 903-663-0206
Brian Kasper, prin. Fax 663-0275
McClure ES 300/4-5
PO Box 3268 75606 903-758-8373
Cynthia Wise, prin. Fax 757-8419
McQueen PS 400/PK-2
PO Box 3268 75606 903-663-2125
John York, prin. Fax 663-2135
South Ward ES 500/PK-5
PO Box 3268 75606 903-753-2961
Dr. Carl Briley, prin. Fax 757-9458
Valley View ES 500/PK-5
PO Box 3268 75606 903-753-1821
Melinda Anderson, prin. Fax 753-8884
Ware ES 400/PK-5
PO Box 3268 75606 903-758-8612
Karen Bonds, prin. Fax 758-0721

Pine Tree ISD 4,200/PK-12
PO Box 5878 75608 903-295-5000
Lynn Whitaker, supt. Fax 295-5004
www.ptisd.org
Pine Tree 5th/6th Grade S 700/5-6
PO Box 5878 75608 903-295-5160
Debbie Terry, prin. Fax 295-5162
Pine Tree ES 700/1-2
PO Box 5878 75608 903-295-5120
Suzanne Mitchell, prin. Fax 295-5126
Pine Tree IS 700/3-4
PO Box 5878 75608 903-295-5151
Cliff Lightfoot, prin. Fax 295-5155
Pine Tree JHS 300/7-8
PO Box 5878 75608 903-295-5081
Clay Gillentine, prin. Fax 295-5082
Pine Tree PS 400/PK-K
PO Box 5878 75608 903-295-5095
Jeanette Doddy, prin. Fax 295-5098

Spring Hill ISD 1,800/PK-12
3101 Spring Hill Rd 75605 903-759-4404
Wes Jones, supt. Fax 297-0141
www.springhill.esc7.net
Spring Hill IS 300/3-4
3101 Spring Hill Rd 75605 903-323-7701
Dana Robertson, prin. Fax 323-7762
Spring Hill JHS 300/7-8
3101 Spring Hill Rd 75605 903-323-7718
David Reed, prin. Fax 323-7765
Spring Hill MS 200/5-6
3101 Spring Hill Rd 75605 903-323-7708
Kelly Stansell, prin. Fax 323-7753
Spring Hill PS 500/PK-2
3101 Spring Hill Rd 75605 903-323-7848
Peggy Mayfield, prin. Fax 323-7847

Bibleway Christian Learning Center 50/PK-6
PO Box 8292 75607 903-643-8085
Vincentia Williams, admin. Fax 643-8277
Christian Heritage S 200/K-12
2715 FM 1844 75605 903-663-4151
Debbie McGinness, dean Fax 663-4587
East Texas Christian S 200/PK-12
PO Box 8053 75607 903-757-7891
Philip Brown, admin. Fax 619-0349
Longview Christian S 200/PK-12
2101 W Marshall Ave 75604 903-297-3501
Karen Williams, prin. Fax 759-4415
St. Mary's S 200/PK-8
405 Hollybrook Dr 75605 903-753-1657
Amy Allen, prin. Fax 758-7347
Trinity S of Texas 300/PK-12
215 N Teague St 75601 903-753-0612
Rev. Charlene Miller, hdmstr. Fax 753-4812

Loop, Gaines
Loop ISD 100/PK-12
PO Box 917 79342 806-487-6411
Phil Mitchell, supt. Fax 487-6416
www.loopisd.net/
Loop S 100/PK-12
PO Box 917 79342 806-487-6411
Vick Orlando, prin. Fax 487-6416

Loraine, Mitchell, Pop. 617
Loraine ISD 100/PK-12
PO Box 457 79532 325-737-2235
Eric Stoddard, supt. Fax 737-2019
www.loraine.esc14.net/
Loraine S 100/PK-12
PO Box 457 79532 325-737-2225
Eric Stoddard, prin. Fax 737-2603

Lorena, McLennan, Pop. 1,595
Lorena ISD 1,600/PK-12
PO Box 97 76655 254-857-3239
Sandra Talbert, supt. Fax 857-4533
www.lorenaisd.net
Lorena ES 300/2-4
PO Box 97 76655 254-857-4613
Lowell Anderson, prin. Fax 857-9019
Lorena MS 500/5-8
PO Box 97 76655 254-857-4621
Rusty Grimm, prin. Fax 857-3419
Lorena PS 300/PK-1
PO Box 97 76655 254-857-8909
Kathy Lina, prin. Fax 857-8815

Lorenzo, Crosby, Pop. 1,288
Lorenzo ISD 300/PK-12
PO Box 520 79343 806-634-5591
Dick Van Hoose, supt. Fax 634-5928
lorenzo.esc17.net/
Lorenzo ES 200/PK-6
PO Box 520 79343 806-634-5593
Suzanne McGuire, prin. Fax 634-8419

Los Fresnos, Cameron, Pop. 5,192
Los Fresnos Consolidated ISD 8,900/PK-12
PO Box 309 78566 956-254-5010
Gonzalo Salazar, supt. Fax 233-4031
www.lfcisd.net
Las Yescas ES 500/PK-5
PO Box 309 78566 956-233-6955
Oscar De La Rosa, prin. Fax 748-2540
Liberty Memorial MS 500/6-8
PO Box 309 78566 956-233-3900
Glafira Braga, prin. Fax 233-1074
Lopez-Riggins ES 600/PK-5
PO Box 309 78566 956-233-6916
Norma Castillo, prin. Fax 233-3706
Los Cuates MS 600/6-8
PO Box 309 78566 956-254-5182
Pablo Leal, prin. Fax 233-6265
Los Fresnos ES 700/PK-5
PO Box 309 78566 956-233-6900
Martha Barreda, prin. Fax 233-6296
Palmer-Laakso ES 700/PK-5
PO Box 309 78566 956-254-5121
Alma Atkinson, prin. Fax 233-3659
Rancho Verde ES, PO Box 309 78566 PK-5
Ada Amaro-Sibaja, prin. 956-254-5232
Reseca MS 700/6-8
PO Box 309 78566 956-254-5159
Jimmy McDonough, prin. Fax 233-6209
Other Schools – See Brownsville, Rancho Viejo, San Benito

Lott, Falls, Pop. 672
Rosebud-Lott ISD 600/PK-12
1789 Highway 77 76656 254-583-4510
Howell Wright, supt. Fax 583-2602
www.rlisd.org/
Lott ES 100/3-5
513 S 5th St 76656 254-584-4251
Natalie Parcus, prin. Fax 584-4050
Rosebud-Lott MS 100/6-8
1789 Highway 77 76656 254-583-4962
Jaime Velasco, prin. Fax 583-7036
Other Schools – See Rosebud

Westphalia ISD 100/K-8
124 County Road 3000 76656 254-584-4988
Ryan Steele, supt. Fax 584-2963
www.westphaliaisd.org/
Westphalia S 100/K-8
124 County Road 3000 76656 254-584-4988
Ryan Steele, prin. Fax 584-2963

Louise, Wharton
Louise ISD 400/PK-12
PO Box 97 77455 979-648-2982
Andrew Peters, supt. Fax 648-2520
louiseisd.org
Louise S 200/PK-8
PO Box 97 77455 979-648-2262
Donna Kutac, prin. Fax 648-2520

Lovelady, Houston, Pop. 611
Lovelady ISD 600/PK-12
PO Box 99 75851 936-636-7616
John Reynolds, supt. Fax 636-2212
www.loveladyisd.net
Lovelady S 400/PK-8
PO Box 250 75851 936-636-7832
Debbie Harrelson, prin. Fax 636-2529

Lubbock, Lubbock, Pop. 209,737
Frenship ISD
Supt. — See Wolfforth
Crestview ES 700/K-5
6020 81st St 79424 806-794-3661
Stacy Davis, prin. Fax 798-2373
North Ridge ES 700/PK-5
6302 11th Pl 79416 806-793-6686
Cheryl Booher, prin. Fax 792-3798
Oak Ridge ES, 6514 68th St 79424 PK-5
Doug Smith, prin. 806-794-5200
Terra Vista MS 600/6-8
1111 Upland Ave 79416 806-796-0076
Brent Lowrey, prin. Fax 796-1540
Westwind ES 600/PK-5
6401 43rd St 79407 806-799-3731
Beth Epps, prin. Fax 799-1087
Willow Bend ES 500/PK-5
8816 13th St 79416 806-796-0090
Kathy Dawson, prin. Fax 796-1517

Lubbock ISD 24,900/PK-12
1628 19th St 79401 806-766-1000
Wayne Havens, supt. Fax 766-1210
www.lubbockisd.org
Alderson MS 400/6-8
219 Walnut Ave 79403 806-766-1500
George Love, prin. Fax 766-1490
Arnett ES 200/K-5
701 E Queens St 79403 806-766-1644
Myrna Porras, prin. Fax 766-1956
Atkins MS 300/6-8
5401 Avenue U 79412 806-766-1522
Chris Huber, prin. Fax 766-2226
Ballenger ECC 300/PK-PK
1110 40th St 79412 806-766-1600
Bill Fuller, prin. Fax 766-1604
Bayless ES 600/K-5
2115 58th St 79412 806-766-1655
Elsa Montes, prin. Fax 766-1651
Bean ES 500/K-5
3001 Avenue N 79411 806-766-1666
Debbie Alderson, prin. Fax 766-1663
Bowie ES 300/K-5
2902 Chicago Ave 79407 806-766-0822
Anita Rangel, prin. Fax 766-0816
Bozeman ES 400/K-5
3101 E 2nd St 79403 806-766-1677
Amy Stephens, prin. Fax 766-1676
Brown ES 400/K-5
2315 36th St 79412 806-766-0833
Lori Alexander, prin. Fax 766-0832
Cavazos MS 500/6-8
210 N University Ave 79415 806-766-6600
Mike Worth, prin. Fax 766-6627
Centennial ES 400/K-5
1301 N Utica Ave 79416 806-766-1980
Glenn Teal, prin.
Dunbar MS 500/6-8
2010 E 26th St 79404 806-766-1300
Jimmy Moore, prin. Fax 766-1320

Dupre ES 300/K-5
2008 Avenue T 79411 806-766-1688
Robin Conkwright, prin. Fax 766-1691
Evans MS 500/6-8
4211 58th St 79413 806-766-0722
Jack Purkeypile, prin. Fax 766-0570
Guadulupe ES 200/K-5
101 N Avenue P 79401 806-766-1699
Edwina Medrano, prin. Fax 766-1702
Hardwick ES 600/K-5
1420 Chicago Ave 79416 806-766-0844
Melissa Portwood, prin. Fax 766-0842
Harwell ES 400/K-5
4101 Avenue D 79404 806-766-1711
Severo Alvarado, prin. Fax 766-1713
Haynes ES 300/K-5
3802 60th St 79413 806-766-0855
Nancy Merrill, prin. Fax 766-0852
Hodges ES 500/K-5
5001 Avenue P 79412 806-766-1722
Robert Guerrero, prin. Fax 766-1730
Honey ES 500/K-5
3615 86th St 79423 806-766-0866
Phillip Neeb, prin. Fax 766-0864
Hutchinson MS 500/6-8
3102 Canton Ave 79410 806-766-0755
Heidi Dye, prin. Fax 766-0538
Iles ES 300/K-5
2401 Date Ave 79404 806-766-1755
Dr. Brian Yearwood, prin. Fax 766-1757
Irons MS 400/6-8
5214 79th St 79424 806-766-2044
Doug Young, prin. Fax 766-2070
Jackson ES 200/K-5
201 Vernon Ave 79415 806-766-1766
Edwina Medrano, prin. Fax 766-1760
MacKenzie MS 400/6-8
5402 12th St 79416 806-766-0777
Larry Hines, prin. Fax 766-0510
Maedgen ES 300/K-5
4401 Nashville Ave 79413 806-766-0877
Kelly Smiley, prin. Fax 766-0990
Mahon ECC 200/PK-PK
2010 Cornell St 79415 806-766-1913
Janice Dudley, prin. Fax 766-1773
Martin ECC 300/PK-PK
3315 E Broadway 79403 806-766-1788
Beth Burkhalter, prin. Fax 766-1967
McWhorter ES 400/K-5
2711 1st St 79415 806-766-1799
Luis Cardenas, prin. Fax 766-1790
Murfee ES 300/K-5
6901 Nashville Dr 79413 806-766-0888
Kathy Rollo, prin. Fax 766-0886
Overton ES 300/K-5
2902 Louisville Ave 79410 806-766-0899
Shana Underwood, prin. Fax 766-0895
Parkway ES 300/K-5
406 N Zenith Ave 79403 806-766-1811
Eddie Fitzgerald, prin. Fax 766-1803
Parsons ES 500/K-5
2811 58th St 79413 806-766-0911
Bob Wood, prin. Fax 766-0902
Roberts ES 400/K-5
7901 Ave P 79423 806-766-6220
Joe Williams, prin. Fax 766-6222
Rush ES 500/K-5
4702 15th St 79416 806-766-0933
Jady English, prin. Fax 766-0929
Slaton MS 500/6-8
1602 32nd St 79411 806-766-1555
Shelly Bratcher, prin. Fax 766-1571
Smith ES 600/K-5
8707 Dover Ave 79424 806-766-2022
Jim Andrus, prin. Fax 766-2042
Stewart ES 400/K-5
4815 46th St 79414 806-766-0944
Johnna Weatherbee, prin. Fax 766-0943
Stubbs ECC 300/PK-PK
3516 Toledo Ave 79414 806-766-0569
Kathy Davis, prin. Fax 766-0574
Tubbs ES 300/K-5
3311 Bates St 79415 806-766-1855
David Pierce, prin. Fax 766-1848
Waters ES 600/K-5
3006 78th St 79423 806-766-6207
Karen Thornton, prin. Fax 766-6209
Wester ES 400/K-5
4602 Chicago Ave 79414 806-766-0966
Julee Becker, prin. Fax 766-0962
Wheatley ES 200/K-5
1802 E 28th St 79404 806-766-1877
Margaret Randle, prin. Fax 766-1875
Wheelock ES 300/K-5
3008 42nd St 79413 806-766-0977
Delmira Lopez, prin. Fax 766-0972
Whiteside ES 600/K-5
7508 Albany Ave 79424 806-766-2088
Chris Brown, prin. Fax 766-2081
Williams ES 400/K-5
4812 58th St 79414 806-766-0988
Suzanne Christopher, prin. Fax 766-0979
Wilson ES 400/K-5
2807 25th St 79410 806-766-0922
Paula Finney, prin. Fax 766-0525
Wilson MS 300/6-8
4402 31st St 79410 806-766-0799
Cindy Wallace, prin. Fax 766-0814
Wolffarth ES 400/K-5
3202 Erskine St 79415 806-766-1899
John Ysasaga, prin. Fax 766-1890
Wright ES 100/K-5
1302 Adrian St 79403 806-766-1911
Myrna Porras, prin. Fax 766-1906

Lubbock-Cooper ISD 2,900/PK-12
16302 Loop 493 79423 806-863-2282
Pat Henderson, supt. Fax 863-3130
www.lcisd.net
Lubbock-Cooper MS 600/6-8
16302 Loop 493 79423 806-863-2282
Edna Parr, prin. Fax 863-2654
Lubbock-Cooper North ES 900/PK-5
3202 108th St 79423 806-687-2700
Rita McDaniel, prin. Fax 687-2714
Lubbock-Cooper South ES 700/PK-5
16302 Loop 493 79423 806-863-2282
Jim Rose, prin. Fax 863-3830
Lubbock-Cooper West ES PK-5
10101 Fulton Ave 79424 806-776-0700
Cherie Nettles, prin. Fax 771-9970

Roosevelt ISD 1,100/PK-12
1406 County Road 3300 79403 806-842-3282
Berhl Robertson, supt. Fax 842-3266
www.roosevelt.k12.tx.us/
Roosevelt ES 500/PK-5
1406 County Road 3300 79403 806-842-3284
Karen Bayer, prin. Fax 842-3930
Roosevelt JHS 300/6-8
1406 County Road 3300 79403 806-842-3218
Kayla Morrison, prin. Fax 842-3337

All Saints Episcopal S 300/PK-9
3222 103rd St 79423 806-745-7701
Dr. Mike Bennett, prin. Fax 748-0454
Christ the King S 400/PK-12
4011 54th St 79413 806-795-8283
Christine Wanjura, prin. Fax 795-9715
Hope Lutheran S 200/PK-K
PO Box 65113 79464 806-798-2747
Jenni Marsh, dir. Fax 798-3019
Lubbock Christian S 400/PK-12
2604 Dover Ave 79407 806-796-8700
Peter Dahlstrom, supt. Fax 791-3569
Southcrest Christian S 200/PK-8
3801 S Loop 289 79423 806-797-7400
Linda Merriott, prin. Fax 776-0546
Trinity Christian S 400/PK-6
7002 Canton Ave 79413 806-791-6581
Jill Roberts, prin. Fax 791-6596

Lucas, Collin, Pop. 3,971
Lovejoy ISD
Supt. — See Allen
Hart ES 500/K-5
450 Country Club Rd, 469-742-8200
Kathy Foster, prin. Fax 742-8201

Lucas Christian Academy 300/K-12
415 W Lucas Rd, 972-429-4362
Julie Montgomery, admin. Fax 429-5141

Lueders, Jones, Pop. 277
Lueders-Avoca ISD 100/PK-12
334 S McHarg St 79533 325-228-4211
Roger Huber, supt. Fax 228-4513
laisd.com
Lueders-Avoca S 100/PK-8
334 S McHarg St 79533 325-228-4211
Rebecca Russell, prin. Fax 228-4513

Lufkin, Angelina, Pop. 33,522
Hudson ISD 2,400/PK-12
6735 Ted Trout Dr 75904 936-875-3351
Mary Ann Whiteker, supt. Fax 875-9209
www.hudsonisd.org
Bonner ES 500/2-4
536 FM 3258 75904 936-875-9212
Suzanne Jones, prin. Fax 875-9314
Hudson MS 700/5-8
6735 Ted Trout Dr 75904 936-875-9292
Stanley Tupman, prin. Fax 875-9317
Peavy PS 500/PK-1
6920 State Highway 94 75904 936-875-9344
Tom Miller, prin. Fax 875-9378

Lufkin ISD 8,600/PK-12
PO Box 1407 75902 936-634-6696
Roy Knight, supt. Fax 634-8864
www.lufkinisd.org
Anderson ES 300/3-5
381 Champions Dr 75901 936-632-5527
Barbara Lazarine, prin. Fax 632-5487
Brandon ES 400/3-5
1612 Sayers St 75904 936-632-5513
Kathy Jost, prin. Fax 632-5617
Brookhollow ES 300/3-5
1009 Live Oak Ln 75904 936-634-8415
Don Jackson, prin. Fax 634-8543
Burley PS, 502 Joyce Ln 75901 400/K-2
Jason Davis, prin. 936-634-6696
Coston ES 400/3-5
707 Trenton St 75901 936-639-3118
Pablo Torres, prin. Fax 639-3289
Dunbar PS 300/1-2
1806 Mrtn Lthr King Jr Blvd 75904 936-630-4500
Dorinda Wade, prin. Fax 630-4511
Garrett K 400/PK-K
507 Kurth Dr 75904 936-634-8418
Kelly Ford-Proutt, prin. Fax 634-8406
Hackney S 300/PK-PK
708 Lubbock St 75901 936-634-3324
Shirley Jolley, prin. Fax 634-0463
Herty PS 400/PK-2
2804 Paul Ave 75901 936-639-2241
Cindy Tierney, prin. Fax 639-2480
Kurth PS 400/PK-2
521 York Dr 75901 936-639-3279
Karen Vinson, prin. Fax 639-3415
Lufkin MS 1,700/6-8
900 E Denman Ave 75901 936-630-4444
Vickie Evans, prin. Fax 632-4444

Slack ES 300/3-5
1305 Fuller Springs Dr 75901 936-639-2279
Robin Stowe, prin. Fax 639-3693
Trout PS 400/PK-2
1014 Allendale Dr 75904 936-639-3274
Janis Compton, prin. Fax 639-3873

Harmony Christian S 100/PK-8
1601 Rice Dr 75901 936-632-1905
Flo Davis, admin. Fax 632-1909
St. Cyprians Episcopal S 200/PK-5
1115 S John Redditt Dr 75904 936-632-1720
Brinn Williford, hdmstr. Fax 632-3852
St. Patrick S 100/PK-8
2116 Lowry St 75901 936-634-6719
Steve Coryell, prin. Fax 639-2776

Luling, Caldwell, Pop. 5,386
Luling ISD 1,500/PK-12
212 E Bowie St 78648 830-875-3191
Mark Weisner, supt. Fax 875-3193
www.luling.txed.net
Luling JHS 300/6-8
214 E Bowie St 78648 830-875-2121
Brian Thompson, prin. Fax 875-5482
Luling PS 200/1-2
118 W Bowie St 78648 830-875-2223
Leslie Hernandez, prin. Fax 875-6712
Rosenwald K 200/PK-K
102 W Newton St 78648 830-875-5319
Leslie Hernandez, prin. Fax 875-9744
Shanklin ES 300/3-5
122 E Houston St 78648 830-875-2515
Duane Limbaugh, prin. Fax 875-6708

Lumberton, Hardin, Pop. 9,637
Lumberton ISD 3,600/PK-12
121 S Main St 77657 409-923-7580
Ron Sims, supt. Fax 755-7848
www.lumberton.k12.tx.us
Lumberton Early Childhood S 600/K-1
1170 S Main St 77657 409-923-7695
Kevin Wing, prin. Fax 755-6607
Lumberton IS 800/4-6
107 S LHS Dr 77657 409-923-7790
John McMillian, prin. Fax 755-6716
Lumberton MS 500/7-8
123 S Main St 77657 409-923-7581
Lynn Bilberry, prin. Fax 751-0641
Lumberton PS 700/PK-PK, 2-
128 E Candlestick Dr 77657 409-923-7490
Sheila Barry, prin. Fax 923-7444

Lyford, Willacy, Pop. 1,986
Lyford Consolidated ISD 1,500/PK-12
PO Box 220 78569 956-347-3900
Eduardo Infante, supt. Fax 347-5588
www.lyfordcisd.net
Lyford ES 700/PK-5
PO Box 220 78569 956-347-3911
Dina Escamilla, prin. Fax 347-3577
Lyford MS 300/6-8
PO Box 220 78569 956-347-3910
Dana Yates, prin. Fax 347-2351

Lytle, Atascosa, Pop. 2,646
Lytle ISD 1,600/PK-12
PO Box 745 78052 830-709-5100
Michelle Carroll Smith, supt. Fax 709-5104
www.lytle-isd.net/
Lytle ES 500/2-5
PO Box 1060 78052 830-709-5130
Kenneth Dykes, prin. Fax 709-5136
Lytle JHS 300/6-8
PO Box 825 78052 830-709-5115
Izamare Marcrum, prin. Fax 709-5119
Lytle PS 300/PK-1
PO Box 460 78052 830-709-5140
JoAnn Buchanan, prin. Fax 709-5142

Mabank, Kaufman, Pop. 2,622
Mabank ISD 2,900/PK-12
310 E Market St 75147 903-880-1300
Dr. Russell Marshall, supt. Fax 880-1303
www.mabankisd.net
Central ES 500/PK-4
310 E Market St 75147 903-880-1380
Terri Watson, prin. Fax 880-1383
Mabank IS 5-6
310 E Market St 75147 903-880-1640
James Pate, prin. Fax 880-1643
Mabank JHS 500/7-8
310 E Market St 75147 903-880-1670
Dr. Darin Jolly, prin. Fax 880-1673
Southside ES 400/PK-4
310 E Market St 75147 903-880-1340
Julie Wiebersch, prin. Fax 880-1343
Other Schools – See Gun Barrel City

Lake Pointe Christian Academy 50/K-12
2611 W Main St, 903-887-5428
Tanyau Boatright, admin. Fax 432-1898

Mc Allen, Hidalgo, Pop. 113,877
Edinburg Consolidated ISD
Supt. — See Edinburg
Cavazos ES 500/PK-5
1501 Freddy Gonzales Rd 78504 956-384-5140
Sandra Guerra, prin. Fax 384-5147

Mc Allen ISD 25,200/PK-12
2000 N 23rd St 78501 956-618-6000
Yolanda Chapa, supt. Fax 631-7206
www.mcallenisd.org/
Alvarez ES 600/PK-5
2606 Gumwood Ave 78501 956-971-4471
Cynthia Rodriguez, prin. Fax 972-5668
Bonham ES 400/PK-5
2400 Jordan Ave 78503 956-971-4440
Lorena Saenz, prin. Fax 971-4284

Brown MS 800/6-8
2700 S Ware Rd 78503 956-632-8700
Carlos Hernandez, prin. Fax 632-8709
Castaneda ES 1,000/PK-5
4100 N 34th St 78504 956-632-8882
Eulalia Tijerina, prin. Fax 632-3627
Cathey MS 900/6-8
1800 N Cynthia St 78501 956-971-4300
Joe Gonzalez, prin. Fax 632-2811
Crockett ES 500/PK-5
2112 N Main St 78501 956-971-4414
Mariselda Morales, prin. Fax 971-4462
De Leon MS 1,100/6-8
4201 N 29th Ln 78504 956-632-8800
Philip Grossweiler, prin. Fax 632-8805
Escandon ES 500/PK-5
2901 Colbath Ave 78503 956-971-4511
Gloria Corpus, prin. Fax 971-4508
Fields ES 500/PK-5
500 Dallas Ave 78501 956-971-4344
Cynthia Hatzold, prin. Fax 971-4351
Fossum MS, 2000 N 23rd St 78501 6-8
Joanetta Ellis, prin. 956-971-1105
Garza ES 1,000/PK-5
6300 N 29th St 78504 956-971-4554
Katie Shults, prin. Fax 971-4235
Gonzalez ES 900/PK-5
201 E Martin Ave 78504 956-971-4577
Christina Hernandez, prin. Fax 971-4575
Hendricks ES PK-5
3900 Goldcrest Ave 78504 956-971-1145
Sandra Salinas, prin.
Houston ES 600/PK-5
3221 Olga Ave 78503 956-971-4484
Sonia Casas, prin. Fax 971-4295
Jackson ES 700/PK-5
501 W Harvey St 78501 956-971-4277
Joe Garza, prin. Fax 632-5179
Lincoln MS 800/6-8
1601 N 27th St 78501 956-971-4200
Rosalinda Martinez, prin. Fax 971-4273
McAuliffe ES 900/PK-5
3000 Daffodil Ave 78501 956-971-4400
Sandra Pitchford, prin. Fax 971-4482
Milam ES 900/PK-5
3800 N Main St 78501 956-971-4333
Linda McGurk, prin. Fax 972-5649
Morris MS 900/6-8
1400 Trenton Rd 78504 956-618-7300
Matt Weber, prin. Fax 632-3666
Navarro ES 400/PK-5
2100 W Hackberry Ave 78501 956-971-4455
Leticia Infante, prin. Fax 972-5692
Perez ES 500/PK-5
7801 N Main St 78504 956-971-1125
LouAnn Sarachene, prin. Fax 632-2880
Rayburn ES 1,100/PK-5
7000 N Main St 78504 956-971-4363
Nancy Dillard, prin. Fax 632-8453
Roosevelt ES 700/PK-5
4801 S 26th St 78503 956-971-4424
Yolanda Ramirez, prin. Fax 618-7362
Sanchez ES 500/PK-5
2901 Incarnate Word Ave 78504 956-971-1100
Hector Guerra, prin. Fax 618-9705
Seguin ES 700/PK-5
2200 N 29th St 78501 956-971-4565
Diana Cortez, prin. Fax 971-4589
Thigpen/Zavala ES 400/PK-5
2500 Galveston Ave 78501 956-971-4377
Maria DeLeon, prin. Fax 972-5660
Travis MS 800/6-8
600 Houston Ave 78501 956-971-4242
Trecia Munal, prin. Fax 632-8454
Wilson ES 500/PK-5
1200 E Hackberry Ave 78501 956-971-4525
Mariella Gorena, prin. Fax 971-4597

Sharyland ISD
Supt. — See Mission
Bentsen ES 600/PK-6
2101 S Taylor Rd 78503 956-668-1415
Dora Gonzalez, prin. Fax 668-0430
Sharyland North JHS 700/7-8
5100 W Dove Ave 78504 956-686-1415
Leticia Leal, prin. Fax 668-0425
Wernecke ES 500/PK-6
4500 W Dove Ave 78504 956-928-1063
Karen Meadors, prin. Fax 928-0221

Central Christian S 200/PK-6
1320 W Nolana Ave 78504 956-687-2340
Mary Shimotsu, dir. Fax 682-6049
Covenant Christian Academy 300/PK-8
4201 N Ware Rd 78504 956-686-7886
Milton Gonzalez, prin. Fax 686-9470
Our Lady of Sorrows S 600/PK-8
1100 Gumwood Ave 78501 956-686-3651
Fred Valle, prin. Fax 686-1996
St. Paul Lutheran S 200/PK-8
300 Pecan Blvd 78501 956-682-2345
Dr. Kathryn Lang, prin. Fax 682-7148
South Texas Christian Academy 300/PK-12
7001 N Ware Rd 78504 956-682-1117
Jim Donlon, prin. Fax 682-7398
Taylor Christian S 50/PK-8
2021 W Jackson Ave 78501 956-686-7574
Carolina Bocanegra, dir. Fax 686-7574

Mc Camey, Upton, Pop. 2,028
Mc Camey ISD 500/PK-12
PO Box 1069 79752 432-652-3666
Donny Wiley, supt. Fax 652-4219
www.mcisd.esc18.net/
Mc Camey MS 100/5-8
PO Box 1069 79752 432-652-3666
Scott Allen, prin. Fax 652-4246
Mc Camey PS 200/PK-4
PO Box 1069 79752 432-652-3666
Shane Thedford, prin. Fax 652-4247

Mc Dade, Bastrop
Mc Dade ISD 200/PK-8
PO Box 400 78650 512-273-0292
Bill Kelly, supt. Fax 273-2101
www.mcdadeisd.net
Mc Dade S 200/PK-8
PO Box 400 78650 512-273-2522
Waylon Cooksey, prin. Fax 273-2101

Mc Gregor, McLennan, Pop. 4,940
Mc Gregor ISD 1,200/PK-12
PO Box 356 76657 254-840-2828
Kevin Houchin, supt. Fax 840-4077
www.mcgregor-isd.org
Isbill JHS 300/5-8
PO Box 356 76657 254-840-3251
Paul Miller, prin. Fax 840-4077
Mc Gregor ES 500/PK-4
PO Box 356 76657 254-840-3204
Cheri Zacharias, prin. Fax 840-4077

Mc Kinney, Collin, Pop. 73,081
Frisco ISD
Supt. — See Frisco
Elliott ES K-5
3721 Hudson Xing 75070 469-633-3750
Susan Murphy, prin. Fax 633-3760
Mooneyham ES 500/K-5
2301 Eden Dr 75070 469-633-3650
Michele Lott, prin. Fax 633-3660
Ogle ES 800/K-5
4200 Big Fork Trl 75070 469-633-3525
Laurie Tinsley, prin. Fax 633-3535
Scoggins MS 6-8
7070 Stacy Rd 75070 469-633-5150
Barbara Warner, prin. Fax 633-5160

Mc Kinney ISD 22,700/PK-12
1 Duvall St 75069 469-742-4000
Tom Crowe, supt. Fax 742-4071
www.mckinneyisd.net
Bennett ES 900/K-5
7760 Coronado Dr 75070 469-742-5400
Amy Holderman, prin. Fax 742-5401
Burks ES 400/PK-5
1801 Hill St 75069 469-742-6200
Pam Bendorf, prin. Fax 742-6201
Caldwell ES 400/K-5
601 W Louisiana St 75069 469-742-5500
Chris Clark, prin. Fax 742-5501
Cockrill MS 900/6-8
1351 Hardin Rd 75071 469-742-7900
Dr. Melinda DeFelice, prin. Fax 742-7901
Dowell MS 1,200/6-8
301 Ridge Rd 75070 469-742-6700
Dr. Logan Faris, prin. Fax 742-6701
Eddins ES 600/K-5
311 Peregrine Dr 75070 469-742-6600
Melanie Raleeh, prin. Fax 742-6601
Evans MS 1,400/6-8
6998 W Eldorado Pkwy 75070 469-742-7100
Todd Young, prin. Fax 742-7101
Faubion MS 1,000/6-8
2000 Rollins St 75069 469-742-6900
Stella Uribe, prin. Fax 742-6901
Finch ES 600/K-5
1205 S Tennessee St 75069 469-742-5600
Harry Long, prin. Fax 742-5601
Glen Oaks ES 600/K-5
6100 Glen Oaks Dr 75070 469-742-6400
Rhonda Gilliam, prin. Fax 742-6401
Johnson ES 800/K-5
3400 Ash Ln 75070 469-742-6500
Suzy Woodard, prin. Fax 742-6501
Johnson MS 1,100/6-8
3400 Community Blvd 75071 469-742-4900
Mitch Curry, prin. Fax 742-4901
Lawson Early Childhood Center PK-PK
500 Dowell St 75070 469-742-2400
Paige Hanks, prin. Fax 742-2401
Malvern ES 700/K-5
1100 W Eldorado Pkwy 75069 469-742-5300
Sandra Barber, prin. Fax 742-5301
McGowen ES 600/K-5
4300 Columbus Dr 75070 469-742-7500
Michael Forsyth, prin. Fax 742-7501
McNeil ES 700/K-5
3650 Hardin Blvd 75070 469-742-5200
Deborah Kanar, prin. Fax 742-5201
Minshew ES 800/PK-5
300 Joplin Dr 75071 469-742-7300
Susie Towber, prin. Fax 742-7301
Naomi Press ES 400/K-5
4101 Shawnee Rd 75071 469-742-7600
Judy Fessenden, prin. Fax 742-7601
Slaughter ES 600/K-5
2706 Wolford St 75071 469-742-6100
Nick DeFelice, prin. Fax 742-6101
Valley Creek ES 600/K-5
2800 Valley Creek Trl 75070 469-742-4800
Linda Garvey, prin. Fax 742-4801
Vega ES 800/K-5
2511 Cattleman Dr 75071 469-742-5100
Wendy Tiemann, prin. Fax 742-5101
Walker ES 700/K-5
4000 Cockrill Dr 75070 469-742-4600
Deborah Sanchez, prin. Fax 742-4601
Webb ES 400/K-5
810 E Louisiana St 75069 469-742-6000
Amber Epperson, prin. Fax 742-6001
Wilmeth ES 600/K-5
901 Lacima Dr 75071 469-742-7400
Judy Bragg, prin. Fax 742-7401
Wolford ES 700/K-5
6951 Berkshire Rd 75070 469-742-4700
Francine Gratt, prin. Fax 742-4701

Prosper ISD
Supt. — See Prosper
Baker ES 600/PK-5
3125 Blue Wood Dr 75071 972-529-1208
Stacy Morris, prin. Fax 529-1142

Centennial Montessori Academy 100/PK-4
7508 W Eldorado Pkwy 75070 972-548-9000
Monisha Chatterjee, dir.
Concordia Christian Academy 100/K-3
2708 Virginia Pkwy 75071 972-562-9944
Steve Winkelman, prin. Fax 548-7425
Cornerstone Christian Academy 200/PK-12
4100 W Eldorado Pkwy # 100 75070 972-529-1818
Jeff Guleserian, hdmstr.
Faith Christian Academy 100/PK-12
115 Industrial Blvd Ste A 75069 972-562-5323
Tony Gore, dir. Fax 562-0581
Good Shepherd Montessori S 100/PK-8
7701 Virginia Pkwy 75071 972-547-4767
Laurann Sutton, prin. Fax 547-6917
Mc Kinney Christian Academy 400/PK-12
3601 Bois D Arc Rd 75071 214-544-2658
Kevin Fields, hdmstr. Fax 542-5056

Mc Lean, Gray, Pop. 764
Mc Lean ISD 200/PK-12
PO Box 90, 806-779-2301
Walter Cox, supt. Fax 779-2248
Mc Lean ES 100/PK-6
PO Box 90, 806-779-2671
Jay Lamb, prin. Fax 779-2248

Mc Leod, Cass
Mc Leod ISD 400/K-12
PO Box 350 75565 903-796-7181
Cathy May, supt. Fax 796-8443
www.mcleodisd.net
Mc Leod ES 200/K-5
PO Box 350 75565 903-796-7181
Kirby McCord, prin. Fax 796-8443
Mc Leod MS 100/6-8
PO Box 350 75565 903-796-7181
Karan Tidwell, prin. Fax 796-8443

Mc Queeney, Guadalupe, Pop. 2,063
Seguin ISD
Supt. — See Seguin
Mc Queeney ES 500/K-5
8860 FM 725 78123 830-557-5856
Paige Meloni, prin. Fax 557-5160

Madisonville, Madison, Pop. 4,250
Madisonville Consolidated ISD 2,300/PK-12
PO Box 879 77864 936-348-2797
Keith Smith, supt. Fax 348-2751
www.madisonvillecisd.org
Madisonville ES 700/PK-2
PO Box 849 77864 936-348-2261
Rhodena Brooks, prin. Fax 349-8028
Madisonville IS 500/3-5
PO Box 635 77864 936-348-2921
Marc Hodges, prin. Fax 348-2249
Madisonville JHS 500/6-8
PO Box 819 77864 936-348-3587
C. Keith Smith, prin. Fax 348-5603

Magnolia, Montgomery, Pop. 1,187
Magnolia ISD 10,900/PK-12
PO Box 88 77353 281-356-3571
Todd Stephens Ph.D., supt. Fax 356-1328
www.magnoliaisd.org
Bear Branch 6th Grade Campus 400/6-6
PO Box 1559 77353 281-252-2031
Tommy Burns, prin. Fax 252-2032
Bear Branch ES 800/K-5
PO Box 999 77353 281-356-4771
Susan Ward, prin. Fax 252-2074
Bear Branch JHS 800/7-8
PO Box 606 77353 281-356-6088
Gerald Evans, prin. Fax 252-2060
Ellisor ES 700/K-5
PO Box 909 77353 281-252-7400
Foy Campbell, prin. Fax 252-2301
Lyon ES 800/PK-5
PO Box 907 77353 281-356-8115
Tammy Haley, prin. Fax 356-2170
Magnolia 6th Grade Campus 400/6-6
PO Box 1540 77353 281-252-2033
Tim Owen, prin. Fax 252-2024
Magnolia ES 600/K-5
PO Box 638 77353 281-356-6434
Jennifer Ward, prin. Fax 252-2150
Magnolia JHS 900/7-8
PO Box 476 77353 281-356-1327
Mark Weatherly, prin. Fax 252-2125
Magnolia Parkway ES PK-5
11745 FM 1488 Rd 77354 281-252-7440
Mona Johnston, prin. Fax 252-7446
Nichols Sawmill ES 600/PK-5
PO Box 450 77353 281-252-2133
Linda Kenjura, prin. Fax 252-2138
Smith ES 700/PK-5
PO Box 1166 77353 281-252-2300
Kristin Craft, prin. Fax 252-2304
Williams ES 800/PK-5
PO Box 320 77353 281-356-6866
Amy Locker, prin. Fax 356-2204

Tomball ISD
Supt. — See Tomball
Decker Prairie ES 700/PK-4
27427 Decker Prairie Rosehl 77355 281-357-3134
Teresa Sullivan, prin. Fax 357-3293

Malakoff, Henderson, Pop. 2,370
Cross Roads ISD 600/PK-12
14434 FM 59 75148 903-489-2001
Clay Tompkins, supt. Fax 489-2527
www.crossroadsisd.org/

Cross Roads ES 300/PK-5
14434 FM 59 75148 903-489-1774
Charles Taylor, prin. Fax 489-1843
Cross Roads JHS 100/6-8
14434 FM 59 75148 903-489-2667
Glenda Wisenbaker, prin. Fax 489-3840

Malakoff ISD 1,300/PK-12
1308 FM 3062 75148 903-489-1152
John Spies Ed.D., supt. Fax 489-2566
www.malakoff.esc7.net
Malakoff ES 500/PK-5
310 N Terry St 75148 903-489-0313
Ronny Snow, prin. Fax 489-1536
Malakoff MS 200/6-8
106 N Cedar St 75148 903-489-0264
Quinton Watkins, prin. Fax 489-1812
Other Schools – See Tool

Malone, Hill, Pop. 301
Malone ISD 100/PK-8
PO Box 38 76660 254-533-2321
Linda Buffe, supt. Fax 533-5660
www.maloneisd.org
Malone S 100/PK-8
PO Box 38 76660 254-533-2321
Linda Buffe, prin. Fax 533-5660

Manchaca, Travis
Austin ISD
Supt. — See Austin
Menchaca ES 900/PK-5
PO Box 759 78652 512-414-2333
John Rocha, prin. Fax 282-4043

Manor, Travis, Pop. 1,877
Manor ISD 5,800/PK-12
PO Box 359 78653 512-278-4000
Andrew Kim, supt. Fax 278-4017
www.manorisd.net
Blake Manor ES 700/PK-5
18010 Blake Manor Rd 78653 512-278-4200
Courtney Thomas, prin. Fax 278-4198
Manor ES 800/PK-5
PO Box 348 78653 512-278-4100
Dan Santema, prin. Fax 278-4104
Manor MS 1,000/6-8
PO Box 388 78653 512-278-4000
Don Wise, prin. Fax 278-4295
Presidential Meadows ES 400/PK-5
13252 George Bush St 78653 512-278-4820
Tara Bowens, prin. Fax 278-4231
Other Schools – See Austin

Mansfield, Tarrant, Pop. 37,976
Mansfield ISD 30,900/PK-12
605 E Broad St 76063 817-299-6300
Bob Morrison, supt. Fax 473-5465
www.mansfieldisd.org
Boren ES 700/PK-4
1400 Country Club Dr 76063 817-473-5665
John Williams, prin. Fax 473-5727
Brooks Wester MS 900/7-8
1520 N Walnut Creek Dr 76063 817-299-7000
Scott Shafer, prin. Fax 453-7213
Brown ES 600/K-4
1860 Cannon Dr 76063 817-473-5399
Marilyn Varner, prin. Fax 473-5392
Jobe MS 7-8
2491 Gertie Barrett Rd 76063 817-299-7040
Demetrus Liggins, prin. Fax 453-6521
Jones MS 500/7-8
4500 E Broad St 76063 817-276-6200
Travis Moore, prin. Fax 453-7380
Lillard IS 700/5-6
1301 N Day Miar Rd 76063 817-276-6260
Donna O'Brian, prin. Fax 453-7100
Low IS 5-6
1526 N Walnut Creek Dr 76063 817-299-3640
Jason Short, prin. Fax 453-6577
Nash ES 700/PK-4
1050 Magnolia St 76063 817-299-6900
Rennda Branson, prin. Fax 453-7300
Orr IS 900/5-6
2900 E Broad St 76063 817-299-5820
Alma Martinez, prin. Fax 473-5747
Perry ES PK-4
1261 S Main St 76063 817-299-3600
Sondra Thomas, prin. Fax 453-6760
Ponder ES 500/PK-4
102 Pleasant Ridge Dr 76063 817-473-5661
Jennifer Stoecker, prin. Fax 473-5658
Shepard IS 900/5-6
1280 Highway 1187 76063 817-299-5940
Chuck Roberts, prin. Fax 453-6812
Sheppard ES 500/PK-4
1701 Highway 1187 76063 817-299-6600
Gary Manns, prin. Fax 453-6870
Smith ES 500/PK-4
701 S Holland Rd 76063 817-299-6980
Rita Ashley, prin. Fax 453-7340
Tipps ES 700/PK-4
3001 N Walnut Creek Dr 76063 817-299-6920
Elna Davis, prin. Fax 453-7320
Worley MS 900/7-8
500 Pleasant Ridge Dr 76063 817-473-5668
Christie Alfred, prin. Fax 473-5623
Other Schools – See Arlington, Burleson, Grand Prairie

Pantego Christian Academy - Mansfield 100/PK-2
PO Box 360 76063 817-460-3315
Cindy Sherrill, prin. Fax 453-6342
St. John Lutheran S 50/PK-PK
1218 E Debbie Ln 76063 817-473-0303
Bobette Stegall M.Ed., dir. Fax 473-3661

Manvel, Brazoria, Pop. 3,287
Alvin ISD
Supt. — See Alvin
Jeter ES 900/PK-5
2455 County Road 58 77578 281-489-3920
Kim Smith, prin. Fax 489-3982
Manvel JHS 600/6-8
7380 Lewis Ln 77578 281-245-2078
Kathy Windsor, prin. Fax 489-8169
Mason ES 600/PK-5
7400 Lewis Ln 77578 281-245-2844
Fulvia Shaw, prin. Fax 489-9181

Marathon, Brewster
Marathon ISD 100/PK-12
PO Box 416 79842 432-386-4431
Conrad Arriola, supt. Fax 386-4395
www.marathonisd.com/
Marathon S 100/PK-12
PO Box 416 79842 432-386-4431
Deborah Dannelley, prin. Fax 386-4395

Marble Falls, Burnet, Pop. 6,745
Marble Falls ISD 4,000/PK-12
2001 Broadway St 78654 830-693-4357
Dr. Ryder Warren, supt. Fax 693-5685
www.mfisd.txed.net
Colt ES 700/PK-5
2200 Manzano Mile 78654 830-693-3474
Linda Romano, prin. Fax 693-7092
Highland Lakes ES 600/PK-5
8200 W FM 1431 78654 830-798-3650
Keith Powell, prin. Fax 598-9349
Marble Falls ES 500/PK-5
901 Avenue U 78654 830-693-2385
Andy Reddock, prin. Fax 693-5421
Marble Falls MS 900/6-8
1511 Pony Dr 78654 830-693-4439
John Schumacher, prin. Fax 693-7788
Other Schools – See Spicewood

Faith Academy of Marble Falls 200/1-12
PO Box 1240 78654 830-798-1333
Mark Earwood, admin. Fax 798-1332
St. Peters S 50/PK-K
1803 FM 1431 78654 830-798-2253
Jan Starkey B.A., dir. Fax 693-6772

Marfa, Presidio, Pop. 1,978
Marfa ISD 400/PK-12
PO Box T 79843 432-729-4252
Teloa Swinnea, supt. Fax 729-4310
www.marfaisd.com
Marfa ES 200/PK-6
PO Box T 79843 432-729-4252
Liana Sawyer, prin. Fax 729-3417

Marion, Guadalupe, Pop. 1,118
Marion ISD 1,400/PK-12
PO Box 189 78124 830-914-2803
James Hartman, supt. Fax 420-2300
www.marion.txed.net
Krueger ES Karrer Campus 300/3-5
PO Box 189 78124 830-914-2803
Roxana Rutledge, prin. Fax 420-3258
Krueger PS 300/PK-2
PO Box 189 78124 830-914-2803
Kathy Dittrich, prin. Fax 420-3776
Marion MS 300/6-8
PO Box 189 78124 830-914-2803
Daryl Wendel, prin. Fax 420-2300

Markham, Matagorda, Pop. 1,206
Tidehaven ISD
Supt. — See Elmaton
Markham ES 200/PK-5
PO Box 317 77456 979-843-5015
Robert Franco, prin. Fax 843-5018

Marlin, Falls, Pop. 6,206
Marlin ISD 1,200/PK-12
130 Coleman St 76661 254-883-3585
Ray Matthews, supt. Fax 883-6612
www.marlinisd.org
Marlin ES 600/PK-5
602 Donohoo St 76661 254-883-3232
Curtis Hurst, prin. Fax 883-5237
Marlin MS 300/6-8
678 Success Dr 76661 254-883-9241
Gene Hicks, prin. Fax 883-2839

Marshall, Harrison, Pop. 24,006
Marshall ISD 5,700/PK-12
1305 E Pinecrest Dr 75670 903-927-8701
Kenn Franklin, supt. Fax 935-0203
www.marshallisd.com
Carver ES 200/K-4
2302 Holland St 75670 903-927-8870
James Moye, prin. Fax 927-8871
Crockett ES 600/K-4
700 Jasper Dr 75672 903-927-8880
Lara Cavin, prin. Fax 927-8885
Houston MS 400/5-6
2905 E Travis St 75672 903-927-8860
Richele Langley, prin. Fax 927-8863
Lee ES 300/K-4
1315 Calloway St 75670 903-927-8890
Greg Morris, prin. Fax 927-8891
Marshall JHS 900/7-8
700 W Houston St 75670 903-927-8830
Stephanie Richard, prin. Fax 927-8837
Moore ES 400/K-4
2303 Norwood St 75670 903-927-8760
Shelley Price, prin. Fax 927-8761
South Marshall ES 300/K-4
1600 Meadow St 75670 903-927-8770
Wilma Jamerson, prin. Fax 927-8771
Travis ES 300/K-4
300 W Carolanne Blvd 75672 903-927-8780
Amy Dickson, prin. Fax 927-8782
Washington ECC 300/PK-PK
1202 Evans St 75670 903-927-8790
Tara Murray, prin. Fax 927-8794
Young MS 400/5-6
1501 Sanford St 75670 903-927-8850
Kenny Barron, prin. Fax 927-8853

St. Joseph S K-1
2307 S Garrett St 75672 903-935-5502
Philip Verhalen, prin. Fax 935-5502
Trinity Episcopal S 300/PK-6
2905 Rosborough Springs Rd 75672 903-938-3513
Sherry Henderson, prin. Fax 938-8725

Mart, McLennan, Pop. 2,531
Mart ISD 600/PK-12
PO Box 120 76664 254-876-2523
Todd Gooden, supt. Fax 876-3028
www.martisd.org/
Mart ES 200/PK-4
PO Box 120 76664 254-876-2112
Jennifer Kyle, prin. Fax 876-3301
Mart MS 200/5-8
PO Box 120 76664 254-876-2762
Linda Delaney, prin. Fax 876-2792

Martinsville, Nacogdoches
Martinsville ISD 300/PK-12
PO Box 100 75958 936-564-3455
Kevin Burton, supt. Fax 569-0498
www.martinsville.esc7.net
Martinsville ES 200/PK-6
PO Box 100 75958 936-564-3455
Brady Taylor, prin. Fax 569-0498

Mason, Mason, Pop. 2,211
Mason ISD 600/PK-12
PO Box 410 76856 325-347-1144
Matt Underwood, supt. Fax 347-5877
www.masonisd.net/
Mason ES 300/PK-4
PO Box 410 76856 325-347-1122
Pam Kruse, prin. Fax 347-5461
Mason JHS 200/5-8
PO Box 410 76856 325-347-1122
Pam Kruse, prin. Fax 347-5461

Matador, Motley, Pop. 673
Motley County ISD 200/PK-12
PO Box 310 79244 806-347-2676
Dr. Tom Alvis, supt. Fax 347-2871
www.motleyco.org
Motley S 200/PK-12
PO Box 310 79244 806-347-2676
William Cochran, prin. Fax 347-2871

Matagorda, Matagorda
Matagorda ISD 100/PK-6
PO Box 657 77457 979-863-7693
Laura Shay, supt. Fax 863-2230
www.matagordaisd.org/
Matagorda ES 100/PK-6
PO Box 657 77457 979-863-7693
Fax 863-2230

Mathis, San Patricio, Pop. 5,462
Mathis ISD 1,900/PK-12
PO Box 1179 78368 361-547-3378
Dr. Maria Rodriguez-Casas, supt. Fax 547-4198
www.mathisisd.org
Mathis IS 400/4-6
PO Box 1179 78368 361-547-2472
Moises Alfaro, prin. Fax 547-4119
McCraw JHS 300/7-8
PO Box 1179 78368 361-547-2381
Daniel Ceballos, prin. Fax 547-4156
Weber-Hardin ES 700/PK-3
PO Box 1179 78368 361-547-4106
Adell Cueva, prin. Fax 547-4162

Maud, Bowie, Pop. 1,015
Maud ISD 500/PK-12
PO Box 1028 75567 903-585-2219
Robert Stinnett, supt. Fax 585-5451
www.maud.esc8.net
Maud S 500/PK-12
PO Box 1028 75567 903-585-2219
Jackie Smith, prin. Fax 585-5451

May, Brown
May ISD 300/K-12
3400 E County Road 411 76857 254-259-2091
Donald Rhodes, supt. Fax 259-3514
www.mayisd.com
May ES 100/K-6
3400 E County Road 411 76857 254-259-3711
Matt Behal, prin. Fax 259-2135

Maypearl, Ellis, Pop. 876
Maypearl ISD 1,000/PK-12
PO Box 40 76064 972-435-1000
Arvell Lynn Dehart, supt. Fax 435-1001
www.maypearlisd.org/
Kirkpatrick ES 400/PK-4
PO Box 40 76064 972-435-1010
Barbara Truby, prin. Fax 435-1011
Maypearl IS 200/5-6
PO Box 40 76064 972-435-1015
Janet Stinson, prin. Fax 435-1016
Maypearl JHS 200/7-8
PO Box 40 76064 972-435-1020
Kay Day, prin. Fax 435-1021

Meadow, Terry, Pop. 631
Meadow ISD 100/PK-12
604 4th St 79345 806-539-2246
Cody Carroll, supt. Fax 539-2529
meadow.esc17.net
Burleson ES PK-5
604 4th St 79345 806-539-2527
Ann Callaway, prin. Fax 539-2529

Meadows, Fort Bend, Pop. 6,141
Fort Bend ISD
Supt. — See Sugar Land

Meadows ES 400/K-5
12037 Pender Ln, 281-634-4720
Irma Cobos, prin. Fax 634-4734

Medina, Bandera
Medina ISD 300/K-12
PO Box 1470 78055 830-589-2855
Ross Hord, supt. Fax 589-7150
www.medinaisd.org
Medina ES 200/K-6
PO Box 1470 78055 830-589-2731
Dale Naumann, prin. Fax 589-7150

Melissa, Collin, Pop. 2,435
Melissa ISD 800/PK-12
1904 Cooper St 75454 972-837-2411
Loyd Jason Smith, supt. Fax 837-4233
www.melissaisd.org
McKillop ES 400/PK-4
3509 Liberty Way 75454 972-837-2632
Cheryle Gonzales, prin. Fax 837-2836
Melissa Ridge IS 200/5-6
2950 Cardinal Dr 75454 972-837-4530
Christy Fiori, prin. Fax 837-4497

Memphis, Hall, Pop. 2,403
Memphis ISD 500/PK-12
PO Box 460 79245 806-259-2443
Tanya Monroe, supt. Fax 259-2515
memphisisd.net/
Austin ES 100/3-5
PO Box 460 79245 806-259-2581
Ed Bailey, prin. Fax 259-2786
Memphis MS 100/6-8
PO Box 460 79245 806-259-3400
Patrick Shaffer, prin. Fax 259-2051
Travis ES 100/PK-2
PO Box 460 79245 806-259-2141
Nori Banda, prin. Fax 259-3119

Menard, Menard, Pop. 1,538
Menard ISD 400/PK-12
PO Box 729 76859 325-396-2404
Martha Ellis, supt. Fax 396-2143
www.menardisd.net
Menard ES 200/PK-5
PO Box 729 76859 325-396-2348
Kyle Chambers, prin. Fax 396-2761
Menard JHS 100/6-8
PO Box 729 76859 325-396-2348
Kyle Chambers, prin. Fax 396-2761

Mercedes, Hidalgo, Pop. 14,185
Mercedes ISD 5,200/PK-12
PO Box 419 78570 956-514-2000
Beto Gonzalez, supt. Fax 514-2033
www.misdtx.net
Hinojosa ES 600/1-4
500 S Rio Rico Rd 78570 956-514-2277
Michelle Guajardo, prin. Fax 514-2292
Kennedy ES 800/5-6
837 S Ohio Ave 78570 956-514-2300
Mary Alice Gonzalez, prin. Fax 514-2311
Mercedes ECC 700/PK-K
950 W 6th St 78570 956-514-2344
Evangelina Gracia, prin. Fax 514-2341
Mercedes JHS 700/7-8
PO Box 419 78570 956-514-2200
Jeanne Venecia, prin. Fax 514-2233
North ES, PO Box 419 78570 1-4
Rene Guajardo, prin.
Taylor ES 500/1-4
900 N Missouri Ave 78570 956-514-2388
Edward Churchill, prin. Fax 514-2377
Travis ES 600/1-4
1551 S Georgia Ave 78570 956-514-2322
Perla Guerrero, prin. Fax 514-2326

South Texas ISD 2,100/7-12
100 Med High Dr 78570 956-565-2454
Marla Guerra Ed.D., supt. Fax 565-9129
www.stisd.net
Other Schools – See Edinburg

Immanuel Lutheran S 50/PK-3
703 W 3rd St 78570 956-565-1518
Virginia Guzman, prin. Fax 565-3208

Meridian, Bosque, Pop. 1,527
Meridian ISD 500/PK-12
PO Box 349 76665 254-435-2081
Eli Casey, supt. Fax 435-2025
www.meridianisd.org
Meridian ES 300/PK-6
PO Box 349 76665 254-435-2731
Kim Edwards, prin. Fax 435-6099

Merit, Hunt
Bland ISD 600/PK-12
PO Box 216 75458 903-776-2239
Bryan Clark, supt. Fax 776-2240
www.blandisd.net
Bland MS 200/5-8
PO Box 216 75458 903-776-2373
John Orozco, prin. Fax 776-2853
Other Schools – See Greenville

Merkel, Taylor, Pop. 2,592
Merkel ISD 1,200/PK-12
PO Box 430 79536 325-928-5813
William Hood, supt. Fax 928-3910
www.merkel.esc14.net
Merkel ES 200/PK-3
PO Box 430 79536 325-928-4795
Dee Dee Wright, prin. Fax 928-3174
Merkel IS 100/4-5
PO Box 430 79536 325-928-5464
Dee Dee Wright, prin. Fax 928-3266
Merkel MS 300/6-8
PO Box 430 79536 325-928-5511
David Acevedo, prin. Fax 928-3138

Tye ES 200/PK-5
PO Box 430 79536 325-692-3809
Gayle Maxey, prin. Fax 793-2690

Mertzon, Irion, Pop. 833
Irion County ISD 400/PK-12
PO Box 469 76941 325-835-6111
Brenda Mendiola, supt. Fax 835-2017
Irion County ES 200/PK-6
PO Box 469 76941 325-835-3991
Maela Edmonson, prin. Fax 835-2281

Mesquite, Dallas, Pop. 129,902
Dallas ISD
Supt. — See Dallas
Smith ES 700/PK-5
5299 Gus Thomasson Rd 75150 972-502-4800
Lora Morris, prin. Fax 502-4801

Mesquite ISD 35,100/PK-12
405 E Davis St 75149 972-288-6411
Dr. Linda Henrie, supt. Fax 882-7787
www.mesquiteisd.org
Achziger ES PK-5
3300 Ridgeranch Rd 75181 972-290-4180
Kim Johnson, prin. Fax 290-4190
Agnew MS 800/7-8
729 Wilkinson Dr 75149 972-882-5750
Donna Gallegos, prin. Fax 882-5760
Austin ES 500/K-6
3020 Poteet Dr 75150 972-882-7220
Jenifer Piepenbrink, prin. Fax 882-7225
Beasley ES 400/K-6
919 Green Canyon Dr 75150 972-882-5160
Leigh Kovalcik, prin. Fax 882-5161
Berry MS 900/6-8
2675 Bear Dr 75181 972-882-5850
Sandra Bibb, prin. Fax 882-5888
Black ES 600/K-6
328 Newsome Rd 75149 972-882-7240
Darla Franklin, prin. Fax 882-7250
Cannaday ES 600/K-6
2701 Chisolm Trl 75150 972-882-5060
Jonathan Royle, prin. Fax 882-5070
Florence ES 600/PK-6
4621 Gleneagle St 75150 972-290-4080
Vickie Compton, prin. Fax 290-4088
Floyd ES 700/PK-5
3025 Hickory Tree Rd 75180 972-882-7100
Kim Broadway, prin. Fax 882-7110
Galloway ES 700/PK-6
200 Clary Dr 75149 972-882-5101
Wanda Mingle, prin. Fax 882-5110
Gentry ES 800/PK-6
1901 Twin Oaks Dr 75181 972-290-4140
Lynne Noe, prin. Fax 290-4150
Hanby ES 900/PK-5
912 Cascade St 75149 972-882-5040
Debra Bassinger, prin. Fax 882-5050
Kimball ES 300/K-6
4010 Coryell Way 75150 972-290-4120
Dr. Bill Sefzik, prin. Fax 290-4130
Kimbrough MS 700/7-8
3900 N Galloway Ave 75150 972-882-5900
Dr. Alane Malone, prin. Fax 882-5942
Lawrence ES 400/PK-6
3811 Richman Dr 75150 972-882-7000
Paige Dewitt, prin. Fax 882-7010
Mackey ES 800/K-5
14900 N Spring Ridge Cir 75180 972-290-4160
Lisa Millsaps, prin. Fax 290-4179
McDonald MS 900/7-8
2930 N Town East Blvd 75150 972-882-5700
Cathy Swann, prin. Fax 882-5710
McKenzie ES 500/K-6
3535 Stephens Green Dr 75150 972-882-5140
Aimee Lewis, prin. Fax 882-5151
McWhorter ES 700/PK-6
1700 Hickory Tree Rd 75149 972-882-7020
Dr. Poppy Airhart, prin. Fax 882-7030
Moss ES 600/K-6
1208 New Market Rd 75149 972-882-7130
Stephanie Davis, prin. Fax 882-7146
Motley ES 300/K-6
3719 Moon Dr 75150 972-882-5080
Sherri La Barbera, prin. Fax 882-5090
New MS 1,200/6-8
3700 S Belt Line Rd 75181 972-882-5600
Marvin Daniel, prin. Fax 882-5620
Pirrung ES 500/PK-5
1500 Creek Valley Rd 75181 972-882-7170
Cara Jackson, prin. Fax 882-7189
Porter ES 500/PK-6
517 Via Avenida 75150 972-290-4000
Becky Rasco, prin. Fax 290-4004
Range ES 600/K-6
2600 Bamboo St 75150 972-882-5180
Sherrie Beard, prin. Fax 882-5190
Rugel ES 300/K-6
2701 Sybil Dr 75149 972-882-7260
Renee Duckworth, prin. Fax 882-7270
Rutherford ES 500/K-5
1607 Sierra Dr 75149 972-290-4060
Deborah Shewmake, prin. Fax 290-4068
Seabourn ES 600/PK-6
2300 Sandy Ln 75149 972-882-7040
Debi Tanton, prin. Fax 882-7050
Shands ES 700/K-6
4836 Shands Dr 75150 972-290-4020
Daron Aston, prin. Fax 290-4030
Shaw ES 700/K-6
707 Purple Sage Trl 75149 972-882-7060
Chassordee Willie, prin. Fax 882-7070
Smith ES 600/K-5
2300 Mesquite Valley Rd 75149 972-882-7080
Cindy Heiman, prin. Fax 882-7090
Terry MS 6-8
2351 Edwards Church Rd 75181 972-882-5650
Karyn Cummings, prin. Fax 882-5660

Thompson ES 800/K-5
2525 Helen Ln 75181 972-882-7190
Dr. Anjanette Murry, prin. Fax 882-7197
Tisinger ES 700/PK-5
1701 Hillcrest St 75149 972-882-5120
Vicki Carpenter, prin. Fax 882-5130
Tosch ES 700/K-6
2424 Larchmont Dr 75150 972-882-5000
Betsy Adams, prin. Fax 882-5010
Vanston MS 600/7-8
3230 Karla Dr 75150 972-882-5801
Carmen Ayo, prin. Fax 882-5848
Wilkinson MS 800/6-8
2100 Crest Park Dr 75149 972-882-5950
Valerie Nelson, prin. Fax 882-5988
Other Schools – See Balch Springs, Garland

Dallas Christian S 600/K-12
1515 Republic Pkwy 75150 972-270-5495
Fax 270-7581

Mexia, Limestone, Pop. 6,742
Mexia ISD 2,200/PK-12
PO Box 2000 76667 254-562-4000
Dr. Jason Ceyanes, supt. Fax 562-4007
www.mexia.k12.tx.us/
McBay ES 800/PK-3
PO Box 2000 76667 254-562-4030
Donna Savage, prin. Fax 562-0074
Mexia JHS 500/6-8
PO Box 2000 76667 254-562-4020
Russ Meggs, prin. Fax 562-5053
Sims IS 300/4-5
PO Box 2000 76667 254-562-4025
William Matthews, prin. Fax 562-4028

Meyersville, DeWitt
Meyersville ISD 100/K-8
PO Box 1 77974 361-277-5817
Laura Whitson, supt. Fax 275-5034
www.meyersvilleisd.org
Meyersville S 100/K-8
PO Box 1 77974 361-275-3639
Laura Whitson, prin. Fax 275-5034

Miami, Roberts, Pop. 543
Miami ISD 200/K-12
PO Box 368 79059 806-868-3971
Donna Gill, supt. Fax 868-3171
www.miamiisd.net
Miami S 200/K-12
PO Box 368 79059 806-868-3971
Kelly Carrell, prin. Fax 868-3171

Midland, Midland, Pop. 99,227
Greenwood ISD 1,600/PK-12
2700 FM 1379 79706 432-685-7800
Doug Young, supt. Fax 685-7804
www.greenwood.esc18.net/
Brooks MS 300/7-8
2700 FM 1379 79706 432-685-7837
Byron Moreland, prin. Fax 685-7838
Greenwood IS 300/4-6
2700 FM 1379 79706 432-685-7819
Terri Rimer, prin. Fax 685-7826
Greenwood PS 500/PK-3
2700 FM 1379 79706 432-685-7821
John-Paul Huber, prin. Fax 685-7822

Midland ISD 18,900/PK-12
615 W Missouri Ave 79701 432-689-1000
Dr. Sylvester Perez, supt. Fax 689-1976
www.midlandisd.net/
Abell JHS 800/7-8
3201 Heritage Blvd 79707 432-689-6200
Debbie Jordan, prin. Fax 689-6217
Alamo JHS 800/7-8
3800 Storey Ave 79703 432-689-1700
Leann Hopkins, prin. Fax 689-1712
Bonham ES 600/K-6
909 Bonham St 79703 432-689-1770
Jennifer Galloway, prin. Fax 689-1776
Bowie ES 400/K-6
805 Elk Ave 79701 432-689-1400
Trudie Thomason, prin. Fax 689-5121
Bunche ECC 400/PK-PK
700 S Jackson St 79701 432-689-1410
Jodie Baugh, prin. Fax 689-1417
Burnet ES 500/K-6
900 Raymond Rd 79703 432-689-1780
Hector Herrera, prin. Fax 689-1783
Bush ES 600/K-6
5001 Preston Dr 79707 432-689-1870
Jill Arthur, prin. Fax 689-1879
Carver Center 4-6
1300 E Wall St 79701 432-689-1420
Judy Bridges, prin. Fax 689-1426
Crockett ES 500/K-6
401 E Parker Ave 79701 432-689-1430
Jennifer Ruiz, prin. Fax 689-1429
De Zavala ES 300/K-6
705 N Lee St 79701 432-689-1440
Terri Matthews, prin. Fax 689-5048
Emerson ES 500/K-6
2800 Moss Ave 79705 432-689-1790
Adelina Baiza, prin. Fax 689-6271
Fannin ES 500/K-6
2400 Fannin Ave 79705 432-689-1450
Kathy Robinson, prin. Fax 689-1346
Goddard JHS 800/7-8
2500 Haynes Dr 79705 432-689-1300
Rick Wood, prin. Fax 689-1321
Greathouse ES 600/PK-6
5107 Greathouse Ave 79707 432-689-6250
Amanda Magallan, prin. Fax 689-6261
Henderson ES 500/K-6
4800 Graceland Dr 79703 432-689-1801
Geta Mitchell, prin. Fax 689-1807
Houston ES 600/K-6
2000 W Louisiana Ave 79701 432-689-1460
Sha Burdsal, prin. Fax 689-5026

Jones ES 500/K-6
4919 Shadylane Dr 79703 432-689-1810
Angela Henry, prin. Fax 689-1816
Lamar ES 500/K-6
3200 Kessler Ave 79701 432-689-1820
Rene Flores, prin. Fax 689-1893
Long ES 500/K-6
4200 Cedar Spring Dr 79703 432-689-1830
Linda Hall, prin. Fax 689-1836
Milam ES 300/K-6
301 E Dormard Ave 79705 432-689-1470
Thomas Miller, prin. Fax 689-1473
Parker ES 500/K-6
3800 Norwood St 79707 432-689-1840
Lisa Neighbors, prin. Fax 689-1843
Pease Technology & Communication S 400/K-6
1700 Magnolia Ave 79705 432-689-1480
Lillian Porter, prin. Fax 689-1489
Rusk ES 400/K-6
2601 Wedgwood St 79707 432-689-1850
Vicki Shenk, prin. Fax 689-1856
San Jacinto JHS 700/7-8
1400 N N St 79701 432-689-1350
Joanna Rowley, prin. Fax 689-1385
Santa Rita ES 400/K-6
5306 Whitman Dr 79705 432-689-1490
Kellie Ebenstein, prin. Fax 689-5094
Scharbauer ES 600/K-6
2115 Hereford Blvd 79707 432-689-1860
Kim Lee, prin. Fax 689-6286
South ES 400/K-6
201 W Dakota Ave 79701 432-689-1550
J.R. Silva, prin. Fax 689-1539
Travis ES 500/K-6
900 E Gist Ave 79701 432-689-1560
K'Lynn Easley, prin. Fax 689-5054
Washington Math & Science Institute 500/K-6
1800 E Wall St 79701 432-689-1570
Nicole Gabriel, prin. Fax 689-1593
West ECC 300/PK-PK
2101 W Missouri Ave 79701 432-689-1580
Lorena Gonzales, prin. Fax 689-1294

Midland Christian S 1,000/PK-12
2001 Culver Dr 79705 432-694-1661
Eddie Lee, supt. Fax 694-5281
St. Anns Catholic S 300/PK-8
2000 W Texas Ave 79701 432-684-4563
Joan Wilmes, prin. Fax 687-2468
Trinity S of Midland 500/PK-12
3500 W Wadley Ave 79707 432-697-3281
Geoffrey Butler, hdmstr. Fax 697-7403

Midlothian, Ellis, Pop. 13,188
Midlothian ISD 6,500/PK-12
100 Walter Stephenson Rd 76065 972-775-8296
Dr. J.D. Kennedy, supt. Fax 775-1757
www.midlothian-isd.net
Baxter ES 600/PK-5
1050 Park Place Blvd 76065 972-775-8281
Nena Challenner, prin. Fax 775-3154
Irvin ES 400/K-5
700 W Avenue H 76065 972-775-8239
Jean Embry, prin. Fax 775-3179
Longbranch ES 700/K-5
6631 FM 1387 76065 972-775-2830
Kelly Madden, prin. Fax 775-2054
Miller ES PK-5
2800 Sudith Ln 76065 972-775-4497
Beth Van Amburgh, prin. Fax 775-4316
Mountain Peak ES 700/PK-5
5201 FM 663 76065 972-775-2881
Karen Childers, prin. Fax 775-2054
Seale MS 700/6-8
700 George Hopper Rd 76065 972-775-6145
Dee Arterburn, prin. Fax 775-1502
Vitovsky ES 500/K-5
333 Church St 76065 972-775-5536
Cherie Wagoner, prin. Fax 775-5532
Walnut Grove MS 800/6-8
990 N Walnut Grove Rd 76065 972-775-5355
Brian Blackwell, prin. Fax 775-8127

Milano, Milam, Pop. 421
Milano ISD 400/PK-12
PO Box 145 76556 512-455-2533
Lindy Robinson, supt. Fax 455-9311
www.milanoisd.net
Milano ES 200/PK-5
PO Box 124 76556 512-455-2062
Stephanie Longoria, prin. Fax 455-2267
Milano JHS 100/6-8
PO Box 145 76556 512-455-6701
Lee Hafley, prin. Fax 455-9311

Miles, Runnels, Pop. 815
Miles ISD 400/PK-12
PO Box 308 76861 325-468-2861
Robert Gibson, supt. Fax 468-2179
miles.netxv.net/index.htm
Miles ES 200/PK-6
PO Box 308 76861 325-468-2861
Sharla Arp, prin. Fax 468-2179

Milford, Ellis, Pop. 726
Milford ISD 200/K-12
PO Box 545 76670 972-493-2911
Don Clingenpeel, supt. Fax 493-2429
www.milfordisd.org
Milford S 200/K-12
PO Box 545 76670 972-493-2921
Marilee Byrne, prin. Fax 493-4600

Millsap, Parker, Pop. 390
Millsap ISD 800/PK-12
305 Pine St 76066 940-682-3101
Jerry Hunkapiller, supt. Fax 682-4476
www.millsapisd.net
Millsap ES 300/PK-5
305 Pine St 76066 940-682-4489
Wayne Hubik, prin. Fax 682-4476
Millsap MS 200/6-8
305 Pine St 76066 940-682-4994
Shanna Coker, prin. Fax 682-4476

Mineola, Wood, Pop. 4,994
Mineola ISD 1,600/PK-12
1000 W Loop 564 75773 903-569-2448
Mary Lookadoo, supt. Fax 569-5155
www.mineolaisd.net
Mineola ES 300/3-5
1000 W Loop 564 75773 903-569-2466
David Sauer, prin. Fax 569-3061
Mineola MS 300/6-8
1000 W Loop 564 75773 903-569-5338
Bob Simmons, prin. Fax 569-5339
Mineola PS 400/PK-2
1000 W Loop 564 75773 903-569-5488
Rod Allen, prin. Fax 569-5489

Mineral Wells, Palo Pinto, Pop. 16,919
Mineral Wells ISD 3,700/PK-12
906 SW 5th Ave 76067 940-325-6404
Dr. James Collins, supt. Fax 325-6378
www.mwisd.net/
Houston ES 600/2-3
300 SW 13th St 76067 940-325-3427
Kelly Wilkerson, prin. Fax 325-7683
Lamar ES 700/PK-1
2012 SE 12th St 76067 940-325-5303
Parisa Lerma, prin. Fax 328-0152
Mineral Wells JHS 600/7-8
1301 SE 14th Ave 76067 940-325-0711
Jay Walsworth, prin. Fax 328-0450
Travis ES 800/4-6
1001 SE Martin Luther King 76067 940-325-7801
Natalie Griffin, prin. Fax 328-0972

Community Christian S 50/PK-12
2501 Garrett Morris Pkwy 76067 940-328-1333
Karen Horton, admin. Fax 328-1277

Mission, Hidalgo, Pop. 60,146
La Joya ISD
Supt. — See La Joya
Bentsen ES 400/PK-5
2916 W Mile 3 Rd, 956-519-5746
Silvia Palacios, prin. Fax 519-5752
Camarena ES 800/PK-5
2612 N Moorefield Rd, 956-584-0827
Jose Garcia, prin. Fax 584-0830
Cavazos ES 900/PK-5
4563 N Minnesota Rd, 956-580-8850
Marisa Garza, prin. Fax 580-8865
Chapa ES 800/PK-5
5670 N Doffing Rd, 956-580-6150
Raul Valdez, prin. Fax 580-6157
Chavez MS 900/6-8
78 Showers Rd 78572 956-580-6182
Daniel Villareal, prin. Fax 580-6169
De Escandon ES 800/PK-5
700 S Schuerbach Rd 78572 956-580-6132
Dianabel Gomez-Villareal, prin. Fax 580-6146
De La Garza ES 700/PK-5
5441 N La Homa Rd, 956-580-6000
Irene Fernandez, prin. Fax 580-6017
Diaz-Villarreal ES 900/PK-5
5543 N La Homa Rd, 956-580-6170
Magda Villarreal, prin. Fax 580-6016
Flores ES 800/PK-5
1913 Roque Salinas Rd 78572 956-580-6100
Maria Flores, prin. Fax 580-6113
Garcia MS 900/6-8
933 Paula Dr, 956-584-0800
Paz Etizondo, prin. Fax 584-0817
Gonzalez ES 800/PK-5
3912 N Goodwin Rd, 956-580-8870
Yolanda Meave, prin. Fax 580-8885
Leo ES 700/PK-5
1625 Roque Salinas Rd 78572 956-580-6030
Maria Flores-Guerra, prin. Fax 580-6047
Memorial MS 1,000/6-8
2610 N Moorefield Rd, 956-580-6087
Dalee Garcia, prin. Fax 580-6084
Paredes ES 700/PK-5
5301 N Bentsen Palm Dr, 956-584-0871
Irma Vela, prin. Fax 584-0877
Perez ES 600/PK-5
4431 N Minnesota Rd, 956-580-8830
Belinda de la Rosa, prin. Fax 580-8845
Seguin ES 700/PK-5
8500 Western Ave, 956-580-8511
Marta Castillo, prin. Fax 580-8515
Zapata ES 800/PK-5
9100 N La Homa Rd, 956-519-5760
Bertha Perez, prin. Fax 519-5767

Mission Consolidated ISD 14,400/PK-12
1201 Bryce Dr 78572 956-323-5505
Oscar Rodriguez, supt. Fax 323-5891
www.mcisd.net/
Bryan ES 700/PK-5
1201 Bryce Dr 78572 956-323-4800
Ana Reyna, prin. Fax 323-4819
Castro ES 600/PK-5
1201 Bryce Dr 78572 956-323-6800
Fax 323-6818
Escobar/Rios ES 3-5
1201 Bryce Dr 78572 956-323-8400
Sara Paz, prin. Fax 323-8480
Leal ES 600/PK-5
1201 Bryce Dr 78572 956-323-4600
Ramon Benevides, prin. Fax 323-4615
Marcell ES 600/PK-5
1201 Bryce Dr 78572 956-323-5635
Michelle Rodriguez, prin. Fax 323-5641
Mims ES 700/PK-5
1201 Bryce Dr 78572 956-323-4400
Yvonne Zamora, prin. Fax 323-4418
Mission JHS 700/6-8
1201 Bryce Dr 78572 956-323-3300
Raul Sanchez, prin. Fax 323-3338
O'Grady ES 800/PK-5
1201 Bryce Dr 78572 956-323-4200
Monico Rodriguez, prin. Fax 323-4220
Pearson ES 600/PK-6
1201 Bryce Dr 78572 956-323-4000
Melissa Davis, prin. Fax 323-4015
White JHS 900/6-8
1201 Bryce Dr 78572 956-323-3600
Pete Garcia, prin. Fax 323-3632
Other Schools – See Alton, Palmhurst

Sharyland ISD 9,200/PK-12
1106 N Shary Rd 78572 956-580-5200
Scott Owings, supt. Fax 585-2972
www.sharylandisd.org/
Garza ES 900/PK-6
1106 N Shary Rd 78572 956-580-5353
Rainer Clover, prin. Fax 580-5363
Gray JHS 600/7-8
1106 N Shary Rd 78572 956-580-5333
Cynthia Sandoval, prin. Fax 580-5346
Hinojosa ES 800/PK-6
1106 N Shary Rd 78572 956-584-4990
Dr. Debra Arce, prin. Fax 584-4998
Jensen ES 700/PK-6
1106 N Shary Rd 78572 956-580-5252
Margarita Gonzalez, prin. Fax 580-5266
Martinez ES 600/PK-6
1106 N Shary Rd 78572 956-584-4900
Rosa O'Donnell, prin. Fax 584-4908
Shary ES 800/PK-6
1106 N Shary Rd 78572 956-580-5282
Pam Montalvo, prin. Fax 580-5294
Shimotsu ES 500/PK-6
1106 N Shary Rd 78572 956-583-5643
Anthony Limon, prin. Fax 519-1079
Other Schools – See Mc Allen

Agape Christian S 100/PK-6
1401 E 24th St, 956-585-9773
Jane Eason, dir. Fax 585-9775
Our Lady of Guadalupe K 50/PK-K
PO Box 1047 78573 956-585-6445
Sr. Cynthia Mello, prin. Fax 584-5856
World Center Leadership Academy 100/PK-7
2214 W Griffin Pkwy, 956-585-7000
David Hill, prin. Fax 585-7000

Missouri City, Fort Bend, Pop. 69,941
Fort Bend ISD
Supt. — See Sugar Land
Armstrong ES K-6
3440 Independence Blvd 77459 281-634-9410
Joanna Dodson, prin. Fax 327-9409
Baines MS 1,100/6-8
9000 Sienna Ranch Rd 77459 281-634-6870
David Yaffie, prin. Fax 634-6880
Briargate ES 600/PK-5
15817 Blueridge Rd 77489 281-634-4560
Faye McNeil, prin. Fax 634-4576
Glover ES 700/PK-5
1510 Columbia Blue Dr 77489 281-634-4920
Vonda Washington, prin. Fax 634-4934
Hunters Glen ES 700/PK-5
695 Independence Blvd 77489 281-634-4640
Angela Dow, prin. Fax 634-4656
Jones ES 700/PK-5
302 Martin Ln 77489 281-634-4960
Robert Arena, prin. Fax 634-4974
Lake Olympia MS 1,200/6-8
3100 Lake Olympia Pkwy 77459 281-634-3520
Kevin Shipley, prin. Fax 634-3549
Lantern Lane ES 600/K-5
3323 Mission Valley Dr 77459 281-634-4680
Sheila Emery, prin. Fax 634-4694
Lexington Creek ES 800/K-5
2335 Dulles Ave 77459 281-634-5000
Lucretia DeFlora, prin. Fax 634-5014
Missouri City MS 1,100/6-8
202 Martin Ln 77489 281-634-3440
Trevor Lemon, prin. Fax 634-3473
Palmer ES 900/PK-5
4208 Crow Valley Dr 77459 281-634-4760
Pat Shoffit, prin. Fax 634-4773
Quail Valley ES 800/PK-5
3500 Quail Village Dr 77459 281-634-5040
Amelia Perez, prin. Fax 634-5054
Quail Valley MS 1,200/6-8
3019 FM 1092 Rd 77459 281-634-3600
Lee Crews, prin. Fax 634-3632
Scanlan Oaks ES 1,300/PK-5
9000 Camp Sienna Trl 77459 281-634-3950
Pamela Browning, prin. Fax 634-3915
Schiff ES K-5
7400 Discovery Ln 77459 281-634-9450
Mary Brewster, prin. Fax 327-9449
Sienna Crossing ES 900/K-5
10011 Steep Bank Trce 77459 281-634-3680
Linda Ruckman, prin. Fax 634-3799

Excel Adventist Academy 100/K-8
7950 W Fuqua Dr 77489 281-835-0770
Ramsarran Shakuntala, prin. Fax 835-1275
Southminster S 300/PK-5
4200 Cartwright Rd 77459 281-261-8872
Kristin Correll, hdmstr. Fax 499-4430

Monahans, Ward, Pop. 6,325
Monahans-Wickett-Pyote ISD 1,800/PK-12
606 S Betty Ave 79756 432-943-6711
Keith Richardson, supt. Fax 943-2307
mwpisd.esc18.net
Cullender K 200/PK-K
1100 S Leon Ave 79756 432-943-5252
Chad Smith, prin. Fax 943-4768

Sudderth ES 300/4-6
Carol and E 79756 432-943-2414
Bonnie Richardson, prin. Fax 943-2685
Tatom ES 400/1-3
1600 S Calvin Ave 79756 432-943-2769
Doug Doege, prin. Fax 943-2179
Walker JHS 300/7-8
800 S Faye Ave 79756 432-943-4622
Jeff Jones, prin. Fax 943-3723

Montague, Montague
Montague ISD 100/PK-8
PO Box 78 76251 940-894-2811
David Freeman, supt. Fax 894-6605
www.montagueisd.org/
Montague S 100/PK-8
PO Box 78 76251 940-894-2811
Kenda Cox, prin. Fax 894-6605

Mont Belvieu, Chambers, Pop. 2,525
Barbers Hill ISD 3,600/PK-12
PO Box 1108 77580 281-576-2221
Greg Poole, supt. Fax 576-3410
www.bhisd.net/
Barbers Hill ES 600/3-4
PO Box 1108 77580 281-576-3421
Sue Chatham, prin. Fax 576-3420
Barbers Hill IS 500/5-6
PO Box 1108 77580 281-576-3403
Rick Kana, prin. Fax 576-3350
Barbers Hill K 300/PK-K
PO Box 1108 77580 281-576-3407
Lisa Watkins, prin. Fax 576-3412
Barbers Hill MS 500/7-8
PO Box 1108 77580 281-576-3351
Lance Murphy, prin. Fax 576-3353
Barbers Hill PS 600/1-2
PO Box 1108 77580 281-576-3405
Kirven Tillis, prin. Fax 576-3415

Monte Alto, Hidalgo
Monte Alto ISD 600/PK-8
25149 1st St 78538 956-262-1381
Gabriel Farias, supt. Fax 262-5535
www.montealtoisd.org
Monte Alto ES 400/PK-5
25149 1st St 78538 956-262-6101
Olivia Almanza, prin. Fax 262-5535
Monte Alto MS 200/6-8
25149 1st St 78538 956-262-1374
Ramiro Gomez, prin. Fax 262-1377

Montgomery, Montgomery, Pop. 538
Montgomery ISD 5,600/PK-12
PO Box 1475 77356 936-582-1333
Dr. Jim Gibson, supt. Fax 582-6447
www.misd.org
Lone Star ES 800/PK-4
16600 FM 2854 Rd 77316 936-588-6100
Carolyn Fiaschetti, prin. Fax 588-5941
Madeley Ranch ES 100/PK-4
3500 Madeley Ranch Rd 77356 936-582-7500
Sonja Lopez, prin.
Montgomery ES 600/PK-4
20774 Eva St 77356 936-597-6333
Wendy Graves, prin. Fax 597-6339
Montgomery IS 400/5-5
700 Dr M L King Jr Dr 77356 936-597-6494
Jada Mullins, prin. Fax 597-6497
Montgomery JHS 900/7-8
19000 Stewart Creek Rd 77356 936-582-6400
Duane McFadden, prin. Fax 582-6329
Montgomery MS 400/6-6
13755 Liberty St 77316 936-597-7070
Sheryl Moore, prin. Fax 597-7074
Stewart Creek ES 700/PK-4
18990 Stewart Creek Rd 77356 936-582-5355
Linda Hylander, prin. Fax 582-5360

Moody, McLennan, Pop. 1,393
Moody ISD 800/PK-12
107 Cora Lee Ln 76557 254-853-2172
Allen Law, supt. Fax 853-2886
www.moodyisd.org
Moody ES 300/K-4
107 Cora Lee Ln 76557 254-853-2155
Kent Coker, prin. Fax 853-3009
Moody MS 200/5-8
107 Cora Lee Ln 76557 254-853-2182
Josh Carty, prin. Fax 853-2886
Moody Preschool 50/PK-PK
107 Cora Lee Ln 76557 254-853-2181
Stephanie Bailey, lead tchr.

Moran, Shackelford, Pop. 223
Moran ISD 100/PK-12
PO Box 98 76464 325-945-3101
Reggy Spencer, supt. Fax 945-2741
www.moran.esc14.net/
Moran S 100/PK-12
PO Box 98 76464 325-945-3101
Reggy Spencer, prin. Fax 945-2741

Morgan, Bosque, Pop. 518
Morgan ISD 100/PK-12
PO Box 300 76671 254-635-2311
Charles McGehee, supt. Fax 635-2224
www.morganisd.org
Morgan S 100/PK-12
PO Box 300 76671 254-635-2311
Pamela Miller, prin. Fax 635-2224

Morgan Mill, Erath
Morgan Mill ISD 100/K-8
PO Box 8 76465 254-968-4814
Dean Edwards, supt. Fax 968-4921
www.morganmill.esc11.net
Morgan Mill S 100/K-8
PO Box 8 76465 254-968-4814
Shirley Couch, prin. Fax 968-4921

Morse, Hansford
Pringle-Morse Consolidated ISD 100/PK-8
PO Box 109 79062 806-733-2507
Kent Hargis, supt. Fax 733-5417
www.pringlemorsecisd.net
Pringle-Morse S 100/PK-8
PO Box 109 79062 806-733-2507
Kent Hargis, prin. Fax 733-5417

Morton, Cochran, Pop. 1,962
Morton ISD 500/PK-12
500 Champion Dr 79346 806-266-5505
Fredda Schooler, supt. Fax 266-5449
www.mortonisd.net/
Morton ES 300/PK-5
500 Champion Dr 79346 806-266-5505
Kellye Kuehler, prin. Fax 266-5123
Morton JHS 100/6-8
500 Champion Dr 79346 806-266-5505
Hurlon Kirkland, prin. Fax 266-5739

Moulton, Lavaca, Pop. 930
Moulton ISD 300/K-12
PO Box C 77975 361-596-4609
Michael Novotny, supt. Fax 596-7578
www.moultonisd.net
Moulton ES 200/K-6
PO Box C 77975 361-596-4605
Nathan Brown, prin. Fax 596-7578

Mountain Home, Kerr
Divide ISD 50/PK-6
120 Divide School Rd 78058 830-640-3322
Bill Bacon, supt. Fax 640-3323
Divide ES 50/PK-6
120 Divide School Rd 78058 830-640-3322
Bill Bacon, prin. Fax 640-3323

Mount Calm, Hill, Pop. 341
Mount Calm ISD 100/PK-8
PO Box 105 76673 254-993-2611
Phil Gerik, supt. Fax 993-1022
mountcalmisd.org
Mount Calm S 100/PK-8
PO Box 105 76673 254-993-2611
Barbara Lane, prin. Fax 993-1022

Mount Enterprise, Rusk, Pop. 528
Mount Enterprise ISD 400/PK-12
301 NW 3rd St 75681 903-822-3721
Dean Evans, supt. Fax 822-3633
www.meisd.esc7.net
Mount Enterprise ES 200/PK-5
301 NW 3rd St 75681 903-822-3545
Tammy Van Schoubroek, prin. Fax 822-3633

Mount Pleasant, Titus, Pop. 14,760
Chapel Hill ISD 800/PK-12
PO Box 1257 75456 903-572-8096
Marc Levesque, supt. Fax 572-1086
chisd.echalk.com/
Chapel Hill ES 300/PK-5
PO Box 1257 75456 903-572-4586
Missy Walley, prin. Fax 577-9176
Chapel Hill JHS 100/6-8
PO Box 1257 75456 903-572-3925
Mike Clifton, prin. Fax 572-9747

Harts Bluff ISD 400/PK-8
3506 Farm Road 1402 75455 903-572-5427
Eddie Johnson, supt. Fax 572-4699
hbisd.schoolwebpages.com
Harts Bluff S 400/PK-8
3506 Farm Road 1402 75455 903-577-1146
Carole Dickerson, prin. Fax 577-8710

Mount Pleasant ISD 5,400/PK-12
PO Box 1117 75456 903-575-2000
Terry Myers, supt. Fax 575-2014
www.mpisd.net
Brice ES 500/K-4
PO Box 1117 75456 903-575-2057
Regina Conroy, prin. Fax 575-2061
Child Development Center 600/PK-PK
PO Box 1117 75456 903-575-2092
Deborah Cody, prin. Fax 575-2077
Corprew ES 400/K-4
PO Box 1117 75456 903-575-2050
LaWanda McCowan, prin. Fax 575-2052
Fowler ES 500/K-4
PO Box 1117 75456 903-575-2070
Pam McCollum, prin. Fax 575-2075
Mount Pleasant JHS 700/7-8
PO Box 1117 75456 903-575-2110
Brian McAdams, prin. Fax 575-2117
Sims ES 500/K-4
PO Box 1117 75456 903-575-2062
Michael Lide, prin. Fax 575-2064
Wallace MS 800/5-6
PO Box 1117 75456 903-575-2040
Rodney Huffman, prin. Fax 575-2047

Mount Vernon, Franklin, Pop. 2,583
Mount Vernon ISD 1,600/PK-12
PO Box 98 75457 903-537-2546
Richard Flanagan, supt. Fax 537-4784
www.mtvernonisd.com/
Mount Vernon ES 500/PK-3
PO Box 1139 75457 903-537-2266
David Rains, prin. Fax 537-2057
Mount Vernon IS 300/4-6
PO Box 1139 75457 903-537-3402
Kathie Thompson, prin. Fax 537-7093
Mount Vernon JHS 300/7-8
PO Box 1139 75457 903-537-2267
Kelly Baird, prin. Fax 537-3601

Muenster, Cooke, Pop. 1,665
Muenster ISD 500/PK-12
PO Box 608 76252 940-759-2281
John Kaufman, supt. Fax 759-5200
www.muensterisd.net
Muenster ES 300/PK-6
PO Box 608 76252 940-759-2282
Lou Heers, prin. Fax 759-5201

Sacred Heart S 300/PK-12
PO Box 588 76252 940-759-2511
Chad Riley, prin. Fax 759-4422

Muleshoe, Bailey, Pop. 4,579
Muleshoe ISD 1,500/PK-12
514 W Avenue G 79347 806-272-7400
Gene Sheets, supt. Fax 272-4120
www.muleshoeisd.net
DeShazo ES 300/3-5
514 W Avenue G 79347 806-272-7364
Debbie Gallman, prin. Fax 272-7370
Dillman ES 500/PK-2
514 W Avenue G 79347 806-272-7383
Todd Newberry, prin. Fax 272-7388
Watson JHS 300/6-8
514 W Avenue G 79347 806-272-7349
Alex Salazar, prin. Fax 272-4983

Mullin, Mills, Pop. 178
Mullin ISD 100/PK-12
PO Box 128 76864 325-985-3374
C.L. Hammond, supt. Fax 985-3915
www.centex-edu.net/mullin/
Mullin ES 100/PK-6
PO Box 128 76864 325-985-3374
Sumer Alexander, prin. Fax 985-3372

Mumford, Robertson
Mumford ISD 500/PK-12
PO Box 268 77867 979-279-3678
Pete Bienski, supt. Fax 279-5044
www.mumford.k12.tx.us
Mumford ES 300/PK-6
PO Box 268 77867 979-279-3678
Pete Bienski, prin. Fax 279-5044

Munday, Knox, Pop. 1,349
Munday Consolidated ISD 400/PK-12
PO Box 300 76371 940-422-4241
Robert Dillard, supt. Fax 422-5331
www.esc9.net/munday
Munday ES 200/PK-6
PO Box 300 76371 940-422-4322
Todd Wilson, prin. Fax 422-5331
Other Schools – See Goree

Murchison, Henderson, Pop. 636
Murchison ISD 100/K-8
PO Box 538 75778 903-469-3636
Shirley Rowe, supt. Fax 469-3887
www.murchison.esc7.net
Murchison S 100/K-8
PO Box 538 75778 903-469-3636
Shirley Rowe, prin. Fax 469-3887

Murphy, Collin, Pop. 11,026
Plano ISD
Supt. — See Plano
Boggess ES 800/K-5
225 Glen Ridge Dr 75094 469-752-4000
Mark Speck, prin. Fax 752-4001
Hunt ES 500/K-5
415 Oriole Dr 75094 469-752-4400
Linda Engelking, prin. Fax 752-4401
Murphy MS 1,100/6-8
620 N Murphy Rd 75094 469-752-7000
Ann Aston, prin. Fax 752-7001

Wylie ISD
Supt. — See Wylie
Tibbals ES 600/PK-4
621 Waters Edge Way 75094 972-429-2520
Melinda Sarles, prin. Fax 429-2260

Heritage Montessori Academy 200/PK-3
120 Heritage Pkwy 75094 972-424-3137
Aline Lage, dir. Fax 424-9605

Nacogdoches, Nacogdoches, Pop. 30,806
Central Heights ISD 800/PK-12
10317 US Highway 259 75965 936-564-2681
Dr. Jeremy Glenn, supt. Fax 569-6889
www.centralhts.org
Central Heights ES 400/PK-6
10317 US Highway 259 75965 936-552-3424
Jana Muckleroy, prin. Fax 569-6889

Nacogdoches ISD 6,400/PK-12
PO Box 631521 75963 936-569-5000
Dr. Rodney Hutto, supt. Fax 569-5797
www.nacogdoches.k12.tx.us
Brooks-Quinn-Jones ES 800/PK-5
PO Box 631521 75963 936-569-5040
Rachel Johnson, prin. Fax 569-5796
Carpenter ES 400/K-5
PO Box 631521 75963 936-569-5070
Terrance Archie, prin. Fax 569-3165
Fredonia ES 500/K-5
PO Box 631521 75963 936-569-5080
Traci Barnes, prin. Fax 569-3168
Marshall ES 200/K-5
PO Box 631521 75963 936-569-5062
Shelton Jones, prin. Fax 569-5038
McMichael MS 700/6-8
PO Box 631521 75963 936-552-0519
Joe Zuniga, prin. Fax 552-0523
Moses MS 700/6-8
PO Box 631521 75963 936-569-5001
Steve Green, prin. Fax 569-5031
Raguet ES 400/K-5
PO Box 631521 75963 936-569-5052
Kristi Shofner, prin. Fax 569-5060
Rusk ES 700/K-5
PO Box 631521 75963 936-569-3100
Valerie Sheppard, prin. Fax 569-5759

Christ Episcopal S 100/PK-6
502 E Starr Ave 75961 936-564-0621
Linda Bass, prin. Fax 552-7120
Nacodoches Christian Academy 100/PK-8
211 SE Stallings Dr 75964 936-462-1021
Donna Baker, dir. Fax 462-1021

Nash, Bowie, Pop. 2,352
Texarkana ISD
Supt. — See Texarkana
Nash ES 400/PK-5
100 E Burton St 75569 903-838-4321
Bertie Norton, prin. Fax 831-7158

Natalia, Medina, Pop. 1,794
Natalia ISD 1,100/PK-12
PO Box 548 78059 830-663-4416
Joey Moczygemba, supt. Fax 663-4186
www.nataliaisd.net/
Natalia ECC 200/PK-1
PO Box 548 78059 830-663-9739
Carmen Ramirez, dean Fax 663-4186
Natalia ES 300/2-5
PO Box 548 78059 830-663-2837
Elvia de la Garza, prin. Fax 663-9693
Natalia JHS 200/6-8
PO Box 548 78059 830-663-4027
Henry Booth, prin. Fax 663-2347

Navasota, Grimes, Pop. 7,253
Navasota ISD 2,400/PK-12
PO Box 511 77868 936-825-4200
Rory Gesch, supt. Fax 825-4297
www.navasotaisd.org
High Point ES 300/PK-5
PO Box 511 77868 936-825-1130
Leah Russell, prin. Fax 894-3195
Navasota IS 300/4-5
PO Box 511 77868 936-825-4275
Cindy DeMott, prin. Fax 825-8523
Navasota JHS 600/6-8
PO Box 511 77868 936-825-4225
William Russell, prin. Fax 825-4260
Webb ES 400/PK-3
PO Box 511 77868 936-825-1120
Bill Murray, prin. Fax 825-2802

Nazareth, Castro, Pop. 337
Nazareth ISD 200/K-12
PO Box 189 79063 806-945-2231
Deborah Clinton, supt. Fax 945-2431
Nazareth S 200/K-12
PO Box 189 79063 806-945-2231
Deborah Clinton, prin. Fax 945-2431

Neches, Anderson
Neches ISD 400/K-12
PO Box 310 75779 903-584-3311
Randy Snider, supt. Fax 584-3686
www.nechesisd.com
Neches ES 200/K-6
PO Box 310 75779 903-584-3401
Kim Snider, prin. Fax 584-3278

Nederland, Jefferson, Pop. 16,751
Nederland ISD 5,000/PK-12
220 N 17th St 77627 409-724-2391
Beverly Gail Krohn, supt. Fax 724-4280
www.nederland.k12.tx.us
Central MS 700/5-8
220 N 17th St 77627 409-727-5765
Charles Jehlen, prin. Fax 724-4275
Helena Park ES 500/K-4
220 N 17th St 77627 409-722-0462
Darrell Evans, prin. Fax 726-2698
Highland Park ES 500/K-4
220 N 17th St 77627 409-722-0236
George Rienstra, prin. Fax 726-2694
Hillcrest ES 500/PK-4
220 N 17th St 77627 409-722-3484
Karen Noble, prin. Fax 726-2690
Langham ES 500/PK-4
220 N 17th St 77627 409-722-4324
Rosetta Morgan, prin. Fax 724-4286
Wilson MS 800/5-8
220 N 17th St 77627 409-727-6224
Scott Clemmons, prin. Fax 726-2699

Needville, Fort Bend, Pop. 3,288
Needville ISD 2,600/PK-12
PO Box 412 77461 979-793-4308
Curtis Rhodes, supt. Fax 793-3823
www.needvilleisd.com
Needville ES 1,000/PK-4
PO Box 412 77461 979-793-4241
Jeanna Sniffin, prin. Fax 793-2299
Needville JHS 400/7-8
PO Box 412 77461 979-793-4250
Karen Smart, prin. Fax 793-4575
Needville MS 400/5-6
PO Box 412 77461 979-793-3027
Marla Sebesta, prin. Fax 793-7665

Nevada, Collin, Pop. 621
Community ISD 1,300/PK-12
PO Box 400 75173 972-843-8400
Bud Nauyokas, supt. Fax 843-8401
www.communityisd.org
Community MS 300/6-8
PO Box 400 75173 972-843-8411
Rodney Rainey, prin. Fax 843-8412
McClendon ES 500/PK-5
PO Box 400 75173 972-843-8409
Timothy Novak, prin. Fax 843-8410
Other Schools – See Lavon

Newark, Tarrant, Pop. 1,054
Northwest ISD
Supt. — See Justin
Seven Hills ES 400/K-5
654 FM 3433 76071 817-215-0700
Mary Dunlevy, prin. Fax 215-0740

New Boston, Bowie, Pop. 4,624
Malta ISD 100/PK-8
6178 W US Highway 82 75570 903-667-2950
Linda Estill, supt. Fax 667-2984
www.maltaisd.net/
Malta S 100/PK-8
6178 W US Highway 82 75570 903-667-2950
Kelly Kinney, prin. Fax 667-2984

New Boston ISD 1,500/PK-12
600 N McCoy Blvd 75570 903-628-2521
Gary Van Deaver Ed.D., supt. Fax 628-2235
www.nbschools.net
Crestview ES 600/PK-4
604 N McCoy Blvd 75570 903-628-6521
Mary Lovelace, prin. Fax 628-4205
New Boston MS 400/5-8
1215 N State Highway 8 75570 903-628-6588
Glenn Barfield, prin. Fax 628-5132

New Braunfels, Comal, Pop. 47,168
Comal ISD 16,200/PK-12
1404 N Interstate 35 78130 830-221-2000
Dr. Marc Walker, supt. Fax 221-2001
www.comalisd.org
Canyon MS 1,100/6-8
2014 FM 1101 78130 830-221-2300
Patti Vlieger, prin. Fax 221-2301
Church Hill MS 400/6-8
1275 N Business IH 35 78130 830-221-2800
Dani Baylor, prin. Fax 221-2801
Comal ES 800/PK-5
6720 FM 482 78132 830-837-7000
Joni Coker, prin. Fax 837-7001
Frazier ES 1,400/PK-5
1441 N Business IH 35 78130 830-221-2225
Lyndon Langford, prin. Fax 221-2226
Freiheit ES 800/PK-5
2002 FM 1101 78130 830-221-2700
Betsy Nash, prin. Fax 221-2701
Hoffmann Lane ES 700/PK-5
4600 FM 306 78132 830-221-2500
Janice Tubb, prin. Fax 221-2501
Morningside ES 500/PK-5
3855 Morningside Dr 78132 830-837-7100
Jodi Cox, prin. Fax 837-7101
Mountain Valley MS 100/6-8
1165 Sattler Rd 78132 830-885-1300
Scott Hammond, prin. Fax 885-1301
Other Schools – See Bulverde, Canyon Lake, San Antonio, Spring Branch

New Braunfels ISD 7,000/PK-12
PO Box 311688 78131 830-643-5700
Michael Smith, supt. Fax 643-5701
www.newbraunfels.txed.net/
County Line ES 600/PK-5
1200 W County Line Rd 78130 830-627-6610
Deborah Cary, prin. Fax 627-6611
Klein Road ES K-5
2620 Klein Way 78130 830-221-1700
Kara Bock, prin. Fax 221-1701
Lamar PS 400/PK-5
240 N Central Ave 78130 830-627-6890
Shana Behling, prin. Fax 627-6891
Lone Star ES 400/2-3
2343 W San Antonio St 78130 830-627-6820
Curtis Wubbena, prin. Fax 627-6821
Memorial ES 700/K-5
1911 S Walnut Ave 78130 830-627-6470
Duane Trujillo, prin. Fax 627-6471
New Braunfels MS 1,100/7-8
656 S Guenther Ave 78130 830-627-6270
Dr. Demetria Cummins, prin. Fax 627-6271
Oakrun S 500/6-6
415 Oak Run Pt 78132 830-627-6400
Dr. David Simmons, prin. Fax 627-6401
Schurz ES 400/PK-5
633 W Coll St 78130 830-627-6680
Merry White, prin. Fax 627-6681
Seele ES 400/4-5
540 Howard St 78130 830-627-6750
Cris Vasquez, prin. Fax 627-6751
Walnut Springs ES 600/K-5
1900 S Walnut Ave 78130 830-627-6540
Kathy Kenney, prin. Fax 627-6541

Cross Lutheran S 100/PK-8
2171 Common St 78130 830-625-3969
Kevin Dierks, prin. Fax 625-5019
New Braunfels Christian Academy 500/PK-12
220 FM 1863 78132 830-629-1821
Barbara Smith, hdmstr. Fax 629-1880
SS. Peter & Paul S 200/PK-8
198 W Bridge St 78130 830-625-4531
John Pelicano, prin. Fax 606-6916

New Caney, Montgomery, Pop. 3,000
New Caney ISD 9,000/PK-12
21580 Loop 494 77357 281-577-8600
Richard Cowan, supt. Fax 354-2639
www.newcaneyisd.org
Aikin ES 500/PK-5
600 Dogwood 77357 281-577-2900
Trish Musick, prin. Fax 399-9946
Keefer Crossing MS 600/7-8
20350 FM 1485 Rd 77357 281-577-8840
Steve Freeman, prin. Fax 399-9859
New Caney ES 800/PK-5
20501 FM 1485 Rd 77357 281-399-1400
Betty Wyatt, prin. Fax 399-2174
Other Schools – See Kingwood, Porter

Newcastle, Young, Pop. 571
Newcastle ISD 200/PK-12
PO Box 129 76372 940-846-3551
Gordon Grubbs, supt. Fax 846-3452
esc9.net/newcastle
Newcastle ES 100/PK-6
PO Box 129 76372 940-846-3531
Cathy Creel, prin. Fax 846-3452

New Deal, Lubbock, Pop. 696
New Deal ISD 700/PK-12
PO Box 280 79350 806-746-5833
Jimmy Noland, supt. Fax 746-5707
www.newdealisd.net
New Deal ES 300/PK-4
PO Box 240 79350 806-746-5849
Kristi Mayo, prin. Fax 746-5142
New Deal MS 200/5-8
PO Box 308 79350 806-746-6633
Jerry Adams, prin. Fax 746-5244

New Home, Lynn, Pop. 316
New Home ISD 200/K-12
PO Box 248 79383 806-924-7542
Leland Zant, supt. Fax 924-7520
www.newhomeisd.org/
New Home S 200/K-12
PO Box 248 79383 806-924-7543
Shane Fiedler, prin. Fax 924-7520

New London, Rusk, Pop. 991
West Rusk ISD 800/PK-12
PO Box 168 75682 903-895-4503
Mike King, supt. Fax 895-2267
www.westrusk.esc7.net
West Rusk ES 400/PK-5
PO Box 168 75682 903-895-4503
Gwen Gilliam, prin. Fax 895-2267
West Rusk JHS 200/6-8
PO Box 168 75682 903-895-4428
Leah Bobbitt, prin. Fax 895-2267

New Summerfield, Cherokee, Pop. 1,037
New Summerfield ISD 400/PK-12
PO Box 6 75780 903-726-3306
Gregg Weiss, supt. Fax 726-3405
www.nsisd.sprnet.org/
New Summerfield S 400/PK-12
PO Box 6 75780 903-726-3306
Luther Taliaferro, prin. Fax 726-3405

Newton, Newton, Pop. 2,351
Newton ISD 1,200/PK-12
414 Main St 75966 409-379-8137
Gene Isabell, supt. Fax 379-2189
www.newtonisd.net
Newton ES 600/PK-5
414 Main St 75966 409-379-2491
Michelle Barrow, prin. Fax 379-2801
Newton MS 300/6-8
414 Main St 75966 409-379-8324
Julia House, prin. Fax 379-5082

New Waverly, Walker, Pop. 925
New Waverly ISD 900/PK-12
355 Front St 77358 936-344-6751
Dr. Clay Webb, supt. Fax 344-2438
www.new-waverly.k12.tx.us
New Waverly ES 300/PK-3
355 Front St 77358 936-344-2900
Justin Gray, prin. Fax 344-2905
New Waverly IS 100/4-5
355 Front St 77358 936-344-6601
Dr. Darol Hail, prin. Fax 344-2331
New Waverly JHS 200/6-8
355 Front St 77358 936-344-2246
Truman Goodwin, prin. Fax 344-8313

Niederwald, Caldwell, Pop. 487
Hays Consolidated ISD
Supt. — See Kyle
Camino Real ES K-5
170 Las Brisas Blvd 78640 512-268-8505
Marivel Sedillo, prin. Fax 398-5599

Nixon, Gonzales, Pop. 2,246
Nixon-Smiley Consolidated ISD 1,000/PK-12
PO Box 400 78140 830-582-1536
Cathy Booth Ph.D., supt. Fax 582-1920
www.esc13.net/nixon
Nixon-Smiley ES 500/PK-4
PO Box 400 78140 830-582-1536
Lynda Goetz, prin. Fax 582-2258
Other Schools – See Smiley

Nocona, Montague, Pop. 3,250
Nocona ISD 900/PK-12
220 Clay St 76255 940-825-3267
Vickie Gearheart, supt. Fax 825-4945
www.noconaisd.net/
Nocona ES 500/PK-5
220 Clay St 76255 940-825-3151
Gilpatrick Peyton, prin. Fax 825-4253
Nocona MS 200/6-8
220 Clay St 76255 940-825-3121
Norman Waters, prin. Fax 825-6151

Prairie Valley ISD 100/PK-12
12920 FM 103 76255 940-825-4425
W. Tucker, supt. Fax 825-4650
www.prairievalleyisd.net/
Prairie Valley ES 100/PK-5
12920 FM 103 76255 940-825-4425
Tim West, prin. Fax 825-4650

Nolanville, Bell, Pop. 2,257
Killeen ISD
Supt. — See Killeen
Cavazos ES, 1200 N 10th St 76559 K-5
Joe Gullekson, prin. 254-336-7000
Nolanville ES 800/PK-5
901 Old Nolanville Rd 76559 254-336-2180
Gabriela Morgan, prin. Fax 698-5315

Nordheim, DeWitt, Pop. 333
Nordheim ISD 100/PK-12
500 Broadway 78141 361-938-5211
Sonya Little, supt. Fax 938-5266
www.nordheimisd.org
Nordheim S 100/PK-12
500 Broadway 78141 361-938-5211
Sonya Little, prin. Fax 938-5266

Normangee, Leon, Pop. 763
Normangee ISD 500/PK-12
PO Box 219 77871 936-396-3111
Jerry Burger, supt. Fax 396-3112
www.normangeeisd.org
Normangee ES 300/PK-6
PO Box 219 77871 936-396-9999
Kristi Lee, prin. Fax 396-2609

North Richland Hills, Tarrant, Pop. 61,115
Birdville ISD
Supt. — See Haltom City
Foster Village ES 600/PK-5
6800 Springdale Ln 76182 817-547-3100
Ann Croxdale, prin. Fax 581-5382
Green Valley ES 500/PK-5
7900 Smithfield Rd 76182 817-547-3400
Dawn Boriack, prin. Fax 581-5477
Holiday Heights ES 700/PK-5
5221 Susan Lee Ln 76180 817-547-2600
Fax 581-5396
Mullendore ES 400/PK-5
4100 Flory St 76180 817-547-1900
Billy Pope, prin. Fax 581-5326
North Richland MS 900/6-8
4800 Rufe Snow Dr 76180 817-547-4200
Ernie Valamides, prin. Fax 581-5372
North Ridge ES 600/PK-5
7331 Holiday Ln 76182 817-547-3200
April Chiarelli, prin. Fax 581-5440
North Ridge MS 800/6-8
7332 Douglas Ln 76182 817-547-5200
Steve Ellis, prin. Fax 581-5460
Smithfield ES 500/PK-5
6724 Smithfield Rd 76182 817-547-2100
Greg Bicknell, prin. Fax 581-5377
Smithfield MS 700/6-8
8400 Main St 76182 817-547-5000
Jeff Russell, prin. Fax 581-5480
Snow Heights ES 300/PK-5
4801 Vance Rd 76180 817-547-2200
Carla Beth Horton, prin. Fax 581-5323
Walker Creek ES 500/PK-5
8780 Bridge St 76180 817-547-3500
Marta White, prin. Fax 581-2932

North Park Christian Academy 50/PK-5
7025 Mid Cities Blvd 76182 817-498-8456
Jane Edwards, admin. Fax 428-2060

North Zulch, Madison
North Zulch ISD 300/PK-12
PO Box 158 77872 936-399-1000
Roy Gilbert, supt. Fax 399-2025
www.northzulchisd.net
North Zulch ES 200/PK-6
PO Box 158 77872 936-399-1010
Rinza Stewart, prin. Fax 399-2038

Novice, Coleman, Pop. 135
Novice ISD 100/PK-12
PO Box 205 79538 325-625-4069
Wes Hays, supt. Fax 625-3915
novice.netxv.net/index.html
Novice S 100/PK-12
PO Box 205 79538 325-625-4500
Diana Dobbins, prin. Fax 625-3915

Nursery, Victoria
Nursery ISD 100/PK-5
PO Box 69 77976 361-575-6882
Suzanne Bell, supt. Fax 576-9212
www.nurseryisd.org
Nursery ES 100/PK-5
PO Box 69 77976 361-575-6882
Suzanne Bell, prin. Fax 576-9212

Oak Point, Denton, Pop. 2,391
Little Elm ISD
Supt. — See Little Elm
Oak Point ES K-4
401 Shahan Prairie Rd 75068 972-547-3585
Martha Werner, prin. Fax 362-0018

Oakwood, Leon, Pop. 497
Oakwood ISD 200/PK-12
631 N Holly St 75855 903-545-2140
Richard Scoggin, supt. Fax 545-1820
www.oakwoodisd.net/
Oakwood ES 100/PK-5
631 N Holly St 75855 903-545-2140
Richard Scoggin, prin. Fax 545-1820

O Brien, Haskell, Pop. 148
Knox City-O'Brien Consolidated ISD
Supt. — See Knox City
O'Brien MS 100/5-8
711 9th St 79539 940-658-3731
Mark Tucker, prin. Fax 658-3379

Odem, San Patricio, Pop. 2,484
Odem-Edroy ISD 1,200/PK-12
1 Owl Sq 78370 361-368-2561
Charles Zepeda, supt. Fax 368-2879
www.oeisd.org/
Odem ES 600/PK-5
1 Owl Sq 78370 361-368-3881
James Brannigan, prin. Fax 368-2317
Odem JHS 200/6-8
1 Owl Sq 78370 361-368-8121
Rosie Wood, prin. Fax 368-2033

Odessa, Ector, Pop. 93,546
Ector County ISD 26,100/PK-12
PO Box 3912 79760 432-334-7100
Hector Mendez, supt. Fax 335-8984
www.ectorcountyisd.org
Austin Montessori Magnet S 500/PK-6
PO Box 3912 79760 432-332-3453
Sylvia Sanchez, prin. Fax 334-5282
Blackshear Magnet ES 600/K-6
PO Box 3912 79760 432-332-8263
Mauricio Marquez, prin. Fax 334-0826
Blanton ES 400/K-6
PO Box 3912 79760 432-367-2779
Evelyn Garcia, prin. Fax 368-2251
Burleson ES 500/K-6
PO Box 3912 79760 432-362-3101
Lisa Anaya, prin. Fax 368-3241
Burnet ES 600/K-6
PO Box 3912 79760 432-366-8121
Lisa Wills, prin. Fax 368-2262
Cameron Dual Language Magnet ES 600/K-6
PO Box 3912 79760 432-331-7861
Monica Sarabia, prin. Fax 334-6744
Carver Early Education Center 400/PK-PK
PO Box 3912 79760 432-337-6481
Sally Navarro, prin. Fax 334-0737
Cavazos ES 700/K-6
PO Box 3912 79760 432-381-6476
Wayne Squiers, prin. Fax 385-2012
Dowling ES 600/K-6
PO Box 3912 79760 432-331-7862
Sherry Palmer, prin. Fax 334-6757
Fly ES 700/K-6
PO Box 3912 79760 432-385-2025
Carlton Johnson, prin. Fax 385-2031
Goliad ES 500/K-6
PO Box 3912 79760 432-366-4571
Donna Brasher, prin. Fax 368-2271
Gonzales ES 500/K-6
PO Box 3912 79760 432-366-8981
Tracy Taylor, prin. Fax 368-3274
Hays Magnet ES 400/K-6
PO Box 3912 79760 432-337-6691
Carolyn Gonzales, prin. Fax 334-0753
Houston ES 500/K-6
PO Box 3912 79760 432-366-8809
Marcos Lopez, prin. Fax 368-3293
Ireland Magnet ES 500/K-6
PO Box 3912 79760 432-368-3280
Pamela Walker, prin. Fax 368-3283
Johnson ES 800/K-6
PO Box 3912 79760 432-366-3465
Marilee Holmes, prin. Fax 368-3260
Jordan ES 700/K-6
PO Box 3912 79760 432-366-5799
Jan Brown, prin. Fax 368-2284
Lamar Early Education Center 400/PK-PK
PO Box 3912 79760 432-332-2583
Brenda Bentley, prin. Fax 334-6792
Milam Magnet ES 400/PK-6
PO Box 3912 79760 432-337-1561
Staci Ashley, prin. Fax 334-0705
Noel ES 700/K-6
PO Box 3912 79760 432-334-0860
Alicia Syverson, prin. Fax 334-0861
Pease ES 800/K-6
PO Box 3912 79760 432-337-6883
Annette Macias, prin. Fax 334-0718
Pond-Alamo ES 400/K-6
PO Box 3912 79760 432-332-2522
Amanda Warber, prin. Fax 334-6781
Reagan Magnet ES 600/K-6
PO Box 3912 79760 432-366-3321
Andrea Martin, prin. Fax 368-3251
Ross ES 500/K-6
PO Box 3912 79760 432-366-4761
Yolanda Hernandez, prin. Fax 368-2294
San Jacinto ES 600/K-6
PO Box 3912 79760 432-331-7865
Cindy Harbour, prin. Fax 334-6767
Travis Magnet ES 500/K-6
PO Box 3912 79760 432-334-0840
Bill Garcia, prin. Fax 334-0847
Zavala Magnet ES 600/K-6
PO Box 3912 79760 432-334-6712
Yesenia Sandoval, prin. Fax 334-0807

St. Johns Episcopal S 200/PK-6
401 N County Rd W 79763 432-337-6431
Fax 335-0815
St. Marys S 200/PK-6
1703 Adams Ave 79761 432-337-6052
Mary Jaramillo, prin. Fax 337-6052

O Donnell, Lynn, Pop. 1,070
O'Donnell ISD 300/PK-12
PO Box 487, 806-428-3241
Rodney Schneider, supt. Fax 428-3395
odonnell.esc17.net
O'Donnell ES 200/PK-5
PO Box 487, 806-428-3244
Penny Forbes, prin. Fax 428-3277
O'Donnell JHS 100/6-8
PO Box 487, 806-428-3247
Clay Burns, prin. Fax 428-3759

Oglesby, Coryell, Pop. 458
Oglesby ISD 200/K-12
PO Box 158 76561 254-456-2271
Edna Davis, supt. Fax 456-2522
www.oglesbyisd.net
Oglesby S 200/K-12
PO Box 158 76561 254-456-2271
Kendall Smith, prin. Fax 456-2916

Oilton, Webb
Webb Consolidated ISD
Supt. — See Bruni
Oilton ES 200/PK-5
301 Despain St 78371 361-747-5415
Maria Ramirez, prin. Fax 747-4939

Olney, Young, Pop. 3,340
Olney ISD 800/PK-12
809 W Hamilton St 76374 940-564-3519
Tom Bailey, supt. Fax 564-5205
www.olney-isd.net/
Olney ES 400/PK-5
801 W Hamilton St 76374 940-564-5608
Troy Batts, prin. Fax 564-3518
Olney JHS 200/6-8
300 S Avenue H 76374 940-564-3517
Terry Dunlap, prin. Fax 564-5882

Olton, Lamb, Pop. 2,275
Olton ISD 700/PK-12
PO Box 388 79064 806-285-2641
Brad Lane, supt. Fax 285-2724
www.oltonisd-esc17.net/
Olton JHS 100/6-8
PO Box 509 79064 806-285-2681
Mike Wiley, prin. Fax 285-3348
Webb ES 400/PK-5
PO Box 1007 79064 806-285-2657
Joe Becker, prin. Fax 285-2438

Omaha, Morris, Pop. 970
Pewitt Consolidated ISD 1,000/PK-12
PO Box 1106 75571 903-884-2804
David Fitts, supt. Fax 884-2866
www.pewittcisd.net
Pewitt ES 500/PK-5
PO Box 1106 75571 903-884-2404
Laurence Johnson, prin. Fax 884-3076
Pewitt JHS 200/6-8
PO Box 1106 75571 903-884-2505
Ronnie Herron, prin. Fax 884-3111

Onalaska, Polk, Pop. 1,355
Onalaska ISD 900/PK-12
PO Box 2289 77360 936-646-1000
David Kennedy, supt. Fax 646-2605
www.onalaskaisd.net
Onalaska ES 500/PK-6
PO Box 2289 77360 936-646-1010
Lynn Redden, prin. Fax 646-1019

Orange, Orange, Pop. 18,052
Little Cypress-Mauriceville Cons ISD 3,700/PK-12
6586 FM 1130 77632 409-883-2232
Pauline Hargrove, supt. Fax 883-3509
www.lcmcisd.org/
Little Cypress ES 600/PK-3
5723 Meeks Dr 77632 409-886-2838
Candace Clary, prin. Fax 886-8172
Little Cypress IS 300/4-5
2300 Allie Payne Rd 77632 409-886-4245
Julia Dickerson, prin. Fax 886-1828
Little Cypress JHS 500/6-8
6765 FM 1130 77632 409-883-2317
Keith Lindsey, prin. Fax 883-5044
Mauriceville ES 700/PK-5
20040 FM 1130 77632 409-745-1615
Buffy Knight, prin. Fax 745-5187
Mauriceville MS 400/6-8
19952 FM 1130 77632 409-745-1958
Todd Loupe, prin. Fax 745-3383

West Orange-Cove Consolidated ISD 2,700/PK-12
PO Box 1107 77631 409-882-5500
Dr. O. Taylor Collins, supt. Fax 882-5467
www.woccisd.net
Anderson ES 700/K-3
PO Box 1107 77631 409-882-5424
Benny Smith, prin. Fax 882-5454
North Early Learning Center 300/PK-PK
PO Box 1107 77631 409-882-5434
Shelia Perry, prin. Fax 882-5449
Oates ES 400/4-5
PO Box 1107 77631 409-882-5540
Bill Conway, prin. Fax 882-5457
West Orange-Stark MS 600/6-8
PO Box 1107 77631 409-882-5520
Anitrea Goodwin, prin. Fax 882-5545

Community Christian S 400/PK-12
3400 Martin Luther King Jr 77632 409-883-4531
Daniel Rose, admin. Fax 883-8855
St. Mary S 200/PK-8
2600 Bob Hall Rd 77630 409-883-8913
Susan Freiberg, prin. Fax 883-0827

Orangefield, Orange
Orangefield ISD 1,700/PK-12
PO Box 228 77639 409-735-5337
Philip Welch, supt. Fax 735-2080
www.orangefieldisd.com/
Orangefield ES 600/PK-4
PO Box 228 77639 409-735-5346
Larry Haynes, prin. Fax 735-3940
Orangefield JHS 500/5-8
PO Box 228 77639 409-735-6737
Brian Ousley, prin. Fax 792-9605

Orange Grove, Jim Wells, Pop. 1,402
Orange Grove ISD 1,700/PK-12
PO Box 534 78372 361-384-2495
Earl Luce, supt. Fax 384-2148
www.ogisd.esc2.net/
Orange Grove IS 500/2-5
PO Box 534 78372 361-384-9358
Ernest Henderson, prin. Fax 384-2186
Orange Grove JHS 400/6-8
PO Box 534 78372 361-384-2323
Arnold Diaz, prin. Fax 384-9579
Orange Grove PS 300/PK-1
PO Box 534 78372 361-384-2316
Herlinda Perez, prin. Fax 384-9171

Orchard, Fort Bend, Pop. 473
Brazos ISD
Supt. — See Wallis
Brazos ES 400/PK-5
PO Box 30 77464 979-478-6610
Jeannie Young, prin. Fax 478-6031

Ore City, Upshur, Pop. 1,166
Ore City ISD 900/PK-12
PO Box 100 75683 903-968-3300
Lynn Heflin, supt. Fax 968-3797
www.ocisd.net
Ore City ES 400/PK-5
PO Box 100 75683 903-968-3300
Claire Koonce, prin. Fax 968-6903
Ore City JHS 200/6-8
PO Box 100 75683 903-968-3300
Neil Hinson, prin. Fax 968-4913

Overton, Rusk, Pop. 2,321
Leveretts Chapel ISD
Supt. — See Laird Hill
Leveretts Chapel S 100/PK-8
8956 State Highway 42/135 N 75684 903-834-3181
Jolynn Browning, prin. Fax 834-6602

Overton ISD 400/PK-12
PO Box 130 75684 903-834-6145
Alan Umholtz, supt. Fax 834-6755
www.overtonisd.net/
Overton ES 300/PK-5
PO Box 130 75684 903-834-6144
Jennifer Driver, prin. Fax 834-3913
Overton MS 6-8
PO Box 130 75684 903-834-6146
T.J. Rucker, prin. Fax 834-3256

Ovilla, Dallas, Pop. 3,780

Ovilla Christian S 400/PK-12
3251 Ovilla Rd 75154 972-617-1177
Julie Weyand, admin. Fax 218-0135

Ozona, Crockett, Pop. 3,181
Crockett County Consolidated SD 800/PK-12
PO Box 400 76943 325-392-5501
Abe Gott, supt. Fax 392-5177
www.ozonaschools.net
Ozona IS 200/3-5
PO Box 400 76943 325-392-5501
Dan Webb, prin. Fax 392-5177
Ozona MS 200/6-8
PO Box 400 76943 325-392-5501
Benny Granger, prin. Fax 392-5177
Ozona PS 200/PK-2
PO Box 400 76943 325-392-5501
Dan Webb, prin. Fax 392-5177

Paducah, Cottle, Pop. 1,363
Paducah ISD 100/PK-12
PO Box P 79248 806-492-3524
John Brinson, supt. Fax 492-2432
www.paducahisd.org/
Goodwin S PK-8
810 Goodwin Ave 79248 806-492-3807
Bill Hutchinson, prin. Fax 492-2600

Paint Rock, Concho, Pop. 293
Paint Rock ISD 100/PK-12
PO Box 277 76866 325-732-4314
Brett Starkweather, supt. Fax 732-4384
paintrock.netxv.net/
Paint Rock S 100/PK-12
PO Box 277 76866 325-732-4314
Zach Gibson, prin. Fax 732-4384

Palacios, Matagorda, Pop. 5,166
Palacios ISD 1,600/PK-12
1209 12th St 77465 361-972-5491
Vicki Adams, supt. Fax 972-3567
www.palaciosisd.org/
Central ES 500/PK-3
1001 5th St 77465 361-972-2911
Lynne Mumme, prin. Fax 972-5539
East Side IS 400/4-6
901 2nd St 77465 361-972-2544
Carolyn Kubecka, prin. Fax 972-2695
Palacios JHS 200/7-8
200 Shark Dr 77465 361-972-2417
Joe Adams, prin. Fax 972-6372

Palestine, Anderson, Pop. 17,912
Palestine ISD 3,400/PK-12
1600 S Loop 256 75801 903-731-8000
Dr. Thomas Wallis, supt. Fax 729-5588
www.palestineschools.org/
Northside ECC 500/PK-K
2509 N State Highway 155 75803 903-731-8020
Barbara Dutton, prin. Fax 731-4006
Palestine MS 700/6-8
233 Ben Milam Dr 75801 903-731-8008
Todd Williams, prin. Fax 731-8010
Southside PS 600/1-2
201 E Gillespie St 75801 903-731-8023
Brandon Jayroe, prin. Fax 731-4120
Story ES 700/3-5
5300 N Loop 256 75801 903-731-8015
Larissa Loveless, prin. Fax 731-4121

Westwood ISD 1,800/PK-12
PO Box 260 75802 903-729-1776
Dr. Ed Lyman, supt. Fax 729-3696
www.westwoodisd.net
Westwood ES 500/3-6
PO Box 260 75802 903-729-1771
Sonya Brown, prin. Fax 723-0169
Westwood JHS 300/7-8
PO Box 260 75802 903-723-0423
Jennifer Williams, prin. Fax 723-6765
Westwood PS 500/PK-2
PO Box 260 75802 903-729-1787
Becky Rutledge, prin. Fax 729-8839

Christian Heritage Academy 100/K-6
1500 Crockett Rd 75801 903-723-4685
Tammy Patton, prin. Fax 729-1175

Palmer, Ellis, Pop. 2,074
Palmer ISD 1,100/PK-12
PO Box 790 75152 972-449-3389
Alan Oakley, supt. Fax 845-2112
www.palmer-isd.org
Palmer ES 300/PK-2
PO Box 790 75152 972-449-3132
Lynne Vallejo, prin. Fax 449-3472
Palmer IS 200/3-5
PO Box 790 75152 972-449-3832
Vikki Connor, prin. Fax 845-2509
Palmer MS 300/6-8
PO Box 790 75152 972-449-3319
Brian Warner, prin. Fax 845-3380

Palmhurst, Hidalgo, Pop. 4,991
Mission Consolidated ISD
Supt. — See Mission
Cantu JHS 6-8
5101 N Stewart Rd 78572 956-323-7800
Jose Rios, prin. Fax 323-7880
Midkiff ES 600/PK-5
4201 N Mayberry St, 956-323-7000
Leticia Leal, prin. Fax 323-7025

Palmview, Hidalgo, Pop. 4,421
La Joya ISD
Supt. — See La Joya
Reyna ES 700/PK-5
900 E Veterans Blvd 78572 956-580-5975
Alma Ortega, prin. Fax 580-5989
Richards MS 900/6-8
7005 Ann Richards Rd 78572 956-519-5710
Melba Lozano, prin. Fax 519-5726

Palo Pinto, Palo Pinto
Palo Pinto ISD 100/PK-6
PO Box 280 76484 940-659-2745
Eric Cederstrom, supt. Fax 659-2936
www.palopintoisd.net/
Palo Pinto ES 100/PK-6
PO Box 280 76484 940-659-2745
Teresa Mahan, prin. Fax 659-2936

Pampa, Gray, Pop. 16,744
Pampa ISD 3,400/PK-12
321 W Albert St 79065 806-669-4700
Barry Haenisch, supt. Fax 665-0506
www.pampaisd.net
Austin ES 400/K-5
1900 Duncan St 79065 806-669-4760
Beverly Underwood, prin. Fax 669-4731
Lamar ES 500/PK-5
1234 S Nelson St 79065 806-669-4880
Jan Cleek, prin. Fax 669-4735
Pampa JHS 700/6-8
2401 Charles St 79065 806-669-4901
Paul Nies, prin. Fax 669-4742
Travis ES 400/K-5
2300 Primrose Ln 79065 806-669-4901
Jill Faubion, prin. Fax 669-4737
Wilson ES 400/K-5
801 E Browning Ave 79065 806-669-4970
Melissa True, prin. Fax 669-4736

Community Christian S 50/PK-8
PO Box 51 79066 806-665-3393
Marsha Richardson, admin. Fax 665-3393
St. Vincent De Paul S 100/PK-5
2300 N Hobart St 79065 806-665-5665
Amy Unruh, prin. Fax 669-2559

Panhandle, Carson, Pop. 2,609
Panhandle ISD 700/PK-12
PO Box 1030 79068 806-537-3568
Gary Laramore, supt. Fax 537-5553
www.panhandleisd.net
Panhandle ES 300/PK-5
PO Box 1030 79068 806-537-3579
Blair Brown, prin. Fax 537-4230
Panhandle JHS 100/6-8
PO Box 1030 79068 806-537-3541
John Strother, prin. Fax 537-5725

Paradise, Wise, Pop. 515
Paradise ISD 1,000/PK-12
338 School House Rd 76073 940-969-2501
Robert Criswell, supt. Fax 969-5008
www.pisd.net
Paradise ES 300/PK-3
338 School House Rd 76073 940-969-2501
Stacie Meadows, prin. Fax 969-5043
Paradise IS 200/4-6
338 School House Rd 76073 940-969-2501
Andrea Chapman, prin. Fax 969-5031
Paradise JHS 100/7-8
338 School House Rd 76073 940-969-2501
Patti Seckman, prin. Fax 969-5025

Paris, Lamar, Pop. 26,539
Chisum ISD 900/PK-12
3250 S Church St 75462 903-737-2830
Diane Stegall, supt. Fax 737-2831
chisumisd.org
Chisum ES 400/PK-5
3230 S Church St 75462 903-737-2820
Johnny North, prin. Fax 737-2825
Chisum MS 200/6-8
3250 S Church St 75462 903-737-2806
Cliff Chadwick, prin. Fax 737-2805

North Lamar ISD 3,100/PK-12
3201 Lewis Ln 75460 903-737-2000
James Dawson, supt. Fax 669-0129
www.northlamar.net
Bailey IS 400/4-5
3201 Lewis Ln 75460 903-737-7971
Melecia Merritt, prin. Fax 669-0179
Everett ES 400/2-3
3201 Lewis Ln 75460 903-737-2061
Carey Malone, prin. Fax 669-0189
Higgins ES 400/PK-1
3201 Lewis Ln 75460 903-737-2081
Billy Douglas, prin. Fax 669-0189
Stone MS 700/6-8
3201 Lewis Ln 75460 903-737-2041
Steve Sparks, prin. Fax 669-0149
Other Schools – See Powderly

Paris ISD 3,700/PK-12
1920 Clarksville St 75460 903-737-7473
Paul Trull, supt. Fax 737-7484
www.parisisd.net
Aikin ES 1,100/1-5
3100 Pine Mill Rd 75460 903-737-7443
Patricia Gilbert, prin. Fax 737-7517
Crockett MS 500/6-7
655 S Collegiate Dr 75460 903-737-7450
Angela Chadwick, prin. Fax 737-7526
Givens K 400/PK-K
655 Martin Luther King Jr 75460 903-737-7466
Suzanne Patty, prin. Fax 737-7531
Justiss ES 400/1-5
401 18th St NW 75460 903-737-7458
Renee Elmore, prin. Fax 737-7530
Travis JHS 300/8-8
3270 Graham St 75460 903-737-7434
Mike Henry, prin. Fax 737-7534

Trinity Christian Academy 50/K-12
2060 Farm Road 79 75460 903-789-9557
Dr. Gary Ballard, prin. Fax 785-7372

Parker, Collin, Pop. 2,513
Allen ISD
Supt. — See Allen
Bolin ES 600/K-6
5705 Cheyenne Dr, Allen TX 75002 214-495-6750
Beverly Joyce, prin. Fax 495-6756

Pasadena, Harris, Pop. 143,852
Deer Park ISD
Supt. — See Deer Park
Deepwater ES 1,100/PK-PK, 3-
309 Glenmore Dr 77503 832-668-8300
Kim Edwards, prin. Fax 475-6150
Deepwater JHS 700/6-8
501 Glenmore Dr 77503 832-668-7600
Scott Davis, prin. Fax 475-6138
Fairmont ES 800/K-5
4315 Heathfield Dr 77505 832-668-8500
Ron McCallon, prin. Fax 998-4411
Fairmont JHS 700/6-8
4911 Holly Bay Ct 77505 832-668-7800
Donna Collom, prin. Fax 998-4456
Parkwood ES 800/K-2
404 Parkwood Dr 77503 832-668-8200
Allan Myers, prin. Fax 475-6180

Pasadena ISD 51,000/PK-12
1515 Cherrybrook Ln 77502 713-740-0000
Kirk Lewis, supt. Fax 475-7912
www.pasadenaisd.org
Bailey ES 800/K-5
2707 Lafferty Rd 77502 713-740-0528
Karyn Johnson, prin. Fax 740-4129
Bondy IS 1,000/6-8
5101 Keith Ave 77505 713-740-0430
Dan Connolly, prin. Fax 740-4152
DeZavala MS 700/5-6
101 Jackson Ave 77506 713-740-0544
Lolene Clark, prin. Fax 740-4159
Fisher ES 800/PK-5
2920 Watters Rd 77502 713-740-0552
Libby Escalante, prin. Fax 740-4131
Gardens ES 700/PK-5
1105 Harris Ave 77506 713-740-0576
Celia Layton, prin. Fax 740-4133
Golden Acres ES 500/PK-5
5232 Sycamore Ave 77503 713-740-0600
Gloria Chomenko, prin. Fax 740-4136
Jackson IS 1,100/6-8
1020 Thomas Ave 77506 713-740-0440
Paula Sword, prin. Fax 740-4109
Jensen ES 700/PK-5
3514 Tulip St 77504 713-740-0608
Candy Bernsen, prin. Fax 740-4137
Kruse ES 700/PK-5
400 Main St 77506 713-740-0624
Rosie Layne Prusz, prin. Fax 740-4138
Lomax MS 800/5-6
1519 Genoa Red Bluff Rd 77504 713-740-5230
Norma Penny, prin. Fax 740-4175
McMasters ES 600/K-5
1011 Bennett Dr 77503 713-740-0640
Mable Pratt, prin. Fax 740-4079
Miller IS 1,200/6-8
1002 Fairmont Pkwy 77504 713-740-0450
Joe Saavedra, prin. Fax 740-4106
Morales ES 700/PK-5
305 W Harris Ave 77506 713-740-0664
Kathy Connolly, prin. Fax 740-4104
Parks ES 600/PK-5
3302 San Augustine Ave 77503 713-740-0680
Frances Burley, prin. Fax 740-4141
Park View IS 1,000/6-8
3003 Dabney Dr 77502 713-740-0460
Rob Hasson, prin. Fax 740-4115
Pomeroy ES 800/PK-5
920 Burke Rd 77506 713-740-0696
Ruth Rabago, prin. Fax 740-4103
Queens IS 1,000/6-8
1112 Queens Rd 77502 713-740-0470
Troy Jones, prin. Fax 740-4102
Red Bluff ES 700/PK-5
416 Bearle St 77506 713-740-0704
Kathleen McElman, prin. Fax 740-4143
Richey ES 800/PK-5
610 Richey St 77506 713-740-0712
Gabriel Gonzales, prin. Fax 740-4098

San Jacinto IS 900/6-8
3102 San Augustine Ave 77503 713-740-0480
Dianna Walker, prin. Fax 740-4153
Smythe ES 700/K-5
2202 Pasadena Blvd 77502 713-740-0728
Quita Brown, prin. Fax 740-4114
Southmore IS 900/6-8
2000 Patricia Ln 77502 713-740-0500
Lana Stahl, prin. Fax 740-4154
South Shaver ES 700/PK-5
2020 Shaver St 77502 713-740-0842
Sharon Ainsworth, prin. Fax 740-4145
Sparks ES 600/PK-5
2503 Southmore Ave 77502 713-740-0744
Sherri Means, prin. Fax 740-4146
Teague ES 600/K-5
4200 Crenshaw Rd 77504 713-740-0760
Valorie Morris, prin. Fax 740-4148
Turner ES 600/PK-5
4333 Lily St 77505 713-740-0768
Keith Palmer, prin. Fax 740-4149
Williams ES 800/PK-5
1522 Scarborough Ln 77502 713-740-0776
Mel Capelo, prin. Fax 740-4150
Young ES 800/K-5
4221 Fox Meadow Ln 77504 713-740-0784
Shirlyn Ross, prin. Fax 740-4151
Other Schools – See Houston, South Houston

First Baptist Christian Academy 600/PK-12
7500 Fairmont Pkwy 77505 281-991-9191
Joyce Harding, admin. Fax 991-7092
St. Pius V S 200/PK-8
812 Main St 77506 713-472-5172
Sr. Krysia Pillon, prin. Fax 473-2731

Pattison, Waller, Pop. 448
Royal ISD 1,900/PK-12
PO Box 489 77466 281-934-1826
Nathaniel Richardson, supt. Fax 934-8339
www.royal.isd.esc4.net
Royal ECC 300/PK-K
PO Box 390 77466 281-934-3147
Susan Hopkins, prin. Fax 934-2846
Royal ES 700/1-5
PO Box 489 77466 281-934-2248
Robin Beaty, prin. Fax 934-3358
Royal MS 400/6-8
PO Box 528 77466 281-934-2241
Dr. Gary Bates, prin. Fax 934-2329

Pattonville, Lamar
Prairiland ISD 1,100/PK-12
466 Farm Road 196 75468 903-652-6476
James Morton, supt. Fax 652-3738
www.prairiland.net
Prairiland JHS 300/6-8
466 Farm Road 196 75468 903-652-5681
Jason Hostetler, prin. Fax 652-3232
Other Schools – See Blossom, Deport

Pawnee, Bee
Pawnee ISD 100/PK-8
PO Box 569 78145 361-456-7256
Elaine Richardson, supt. Fax 456-7388
www.pawneeisd.esc2.net
Pawnee S 100/PK-8
PO Box 569 78145 361-456-7256
Demetrio Garcia, prin. Fax 456-7388

Pearland, Brazoria, Pop. 56,790
Alvin ISD
Supt. — See Alvin
Marek ES 1,000/PK-6
1947 Kirby St 77584 281-245-3232
Lisa Butler, prin. Fax 436-3796
Ryan JHS 6-8
11500 Shadow Creek Pkwy 77584 281-245-3210
Deborah Roberson, prin.
Savannah Lakes ES K-5
5151 Savannah Pkwy 77584 281-245-3214
Terri Constantine, prin. Fax 245-3161
Wilder ES, 2225 Kingsley Dr 77584 PK-5
Terri Bruce, prin. 281-245-3090

Pearland ISD, PO Box 7 77588 18,000/PK-12
Dr. Bonny Cain, supt. 281-485-3203
www.pearlandisd.org
Alexander MS 700/5-6
3001 Old Alvin Rd 77581 832-736-6700
Annette Chambliss, prin.
Carleston ES, 3010 Harkey Rd 77584 700/PK-4
Katherine Drago, prin. 281-412-1412
Challenger ES 800/PK-4
9434 Hughes Ranch Rd 77584 281-485-7912
Lisa Nelson, prin.
Cockrell ES, 3500 McHard Rd 77581 500/PK-4
Gerri Roberts, prin. 832-736-6600
Harris ES, 2314 Schleider Dr 77581 900/PK-4
Ruth Cornett, prin. 281-485-4024
Jamison MS, 2506 Woody Rd 77581 800/5-6
Sharon Bradley, prin. 281-412-1440
Lawhon ES, 5810 Brookside Rd 77581 600/PK-4
Marlo Keller, prin. 281-412-1445
Magnolia ES, 5350 Magnolia St 77584 600/PK-4
Sharon Gifford, prin. 281-727-1750
Massey Ranch ES 900/PK-4
3900 Manvel Rd 77584 281-727-1700
Heather Block, prin.
Miller JHS, 3301 Manvel Rd 77584 7-8
Lonnie Leal, prin. 281-997-3900
Pearland East JHS 800/7-8
2315 Old Alvin Rd 77581 281-485-2481
Cynthia Henry, prin.
Pearland South JHS 800/7-8
4719 Bailey Rd 77584 281-727-1500
Mollye Dahlstrom, prin.
Pearland West JHS 700/7-8
2337 Galveston Ave 77581 281-412-1222
Pam Wilson, prin.

Rogers MS, 3121 Manvel Rd 77584 900/5-6
Kim Brooks, prin. 832-736-6400
Rustic Oak ES, 1302 Rustic Ln 77581 800/PK-4
Beth West, prin. 281-482-5400
Sablatura MS 700/5-6
2201 Galveston Ave 77581 281-412-1500
Lisa Nixon, prin.
Shadycrest ES 800/PK-4
2405 Shady Bend Dr 77581 281-412-1404
Angela Blair, prin.
Silvercrest ES 700/PK-4
3003 Southwyck Pkwy 77584 832-736-6000
Cortenay Colling, prin.
Silverlake ES 800/PK-4
2550 County Road 90 77584 713-436-8000
Lakesha Vaughn, prin.

Eagle Heights Christian Academy 300/PK-12
3005 Pearland Pkwy 77581 281-485-6330
John Stahl, prin. Fax 485-8682
Montessori S of Downtown Silverlake 100/PK-5
2525 County Road 90 77584 281-412-5763
D.S. Alhanut, prin. Fax 412-5245
St. Helen S 200/K-8
2213 Old Alvin Rd 77581 281-485-2845
Elaina Satsky, prin. Fax 485-7607
Silverline Montessori S 300/PK-4
2505 CR 89 77584 713-997-3700
Anuja Mehta, dir. Fax 997-0737

Pearsall, Frio, Pop. 7,772
Pearsall ISD 2,400/PK-12
318 Berry Ranch Rd 78061 830-334-8001
Mario Sotelo, supt. Fax 334-8007
www.pearsall.k12.tx.us
Flores ES 700/PK-2
321 W Pena St 78061 830-334-4108
Nicole Gonzales, prin. Fax 334-5047
Pearsall IS 500/3-5
415 E Florida St 78061 830-334-3316
Consuelo Arellano, prin. Fax 334-5007
Pearsall JHS 500/6-8
607 E Alabama St 78061 830-334-8021
Julian Hernandez, prin. Fax 334-8025

Pecan Gap, Delta, Pop. 221
Fannindel ISD
Supt. — See Ladonia
Fannindel ES 100/PK-5
409 W Main St 75469 903-359-6314
Perry Evans, prin. Fax 359-6315

Pecos, Reeves, Pop. 8,251
Pecos-Barstow-Toyah ISD 2,000/PK-12
PO Box 869 79772 432-447-7201
Manuel Espino, supt. Fax 447-3076
pbtisd.esc18.net
Austin ES 500/1-3
PO Box 869 79772 432-447-7541
Jim Workman, prin. Fax 447-4248
Crockett MS 400/6-8
PO Box 869 79772 432-447-7461
Steve Lucas, prin. Fax 447-4853
Haynes ES 300/4-5
PO Box 869 79772 432-447-7497
Victor Tarin, prin. Fax 445-1612
Pecos K 200/PK-K
PO Box 869 79772 432-447-7596
Omar Salgado, prin. Fax 445-4203

Penelope, Hill, Pop. 231
Penelope ISD 200/PK-12
PO Box 68 76676 254-533-2215
Scot Kelley, supt. Fax 533-2262
www.penelopeisd.org/
Penelope S 200/PK-12
PO Box 68 76676 254-533-2215
Gordon Vogel, prin. Fax 533-2262

Penitas, Hidalgo, Pop. 1,182
La Joya ISD
Supt. — See La Joya
Clinton ES 800/K-5
39202 Mile 7 Rd 78576 956-580-8500
Adriana Villarreal, prin. Fax 580-8509
Corina-Sanchez Pena ES PK-5
4800 Liberty Blvd 78576 956-580-5401
Sofia Villarreal, prin.
Kennedy ES 800/PK-5
1801 Diamond Ave 78576 956-584-4800
Diane Hinojosa, prin. Fax 584-4813
Saenz MS 700/6-8
39200 Mile 7 Rd 78576 956-580-8500
Lionel Perez, prin. Fax 580-8509

Perrin, Jack
Perrin-Whitt Consolidated ISD 400/K-12
216 N Benson St 76486 940-798-3718
Darren Francis, supt. Fax 798-3071
www.pwcisd.net
Perrin ES 200/K-6
216 N Benson St 76486 940-798-2395
David Wolf, prin. Fax 798-3071

Perryton, Ochiltree, Pop. 8,096
Perryton ISD 2,100/PK-12
PO Box 1048 79070 806-435-5478
Mike Jackson, supt. Fax 435-4689
www.perrytonisd.com
Perryton JHS 500/6-8
PO Box 1048 79070 806-435-3601
Jeff Vanlandingham, prin. Fax 435-3624
Perryton K 300/PK-K
PO Box 1048 79070 806-435-2463
Noah Cano, prin. Fax 435-6093
Williams IS 300/4-5
PO Box 1048 79070 806-435-3436
Robert Hall, prin. Fax 435-9231
Wright ES 500/1-3
PO Box 1048 79070 806-435-2371
Tina Clyburn, prin. Fax 434-8844

Victory Christian Academy 100/PK-4
PO Box 1267 79070 806-435-3476
Kathy Sparks, supt. Fax 435-9256

Petersburg, Hale, Pop. 1,255
Petersburg ISD 300/PK-12
PO Box 160 79250 806-667-3585
Joey Nichols, supt. Fax 667-3463
www.petersburgisd.net
Petersburg ES 200/PK-6
PO Box 160 79250 806-667-3577
Royce Roark, prin. Fax 667-3463

Petrolia, Clay, Pop. 806
Petrolia ISD 500/PK-12
PO Box 176 76377 940-524-3555
Derrith Welch, supt. Fax 524-3370
www.esc9.net/petrolia
Petrolia ES 200/PK-5
PO Box 176 76377 940-524-3212
Micki Wesley, prin. Fax 524-3370
Petrolia JHS 100/6-8
PO Box 176 76377 940-524-3433
Micki Wesley, prin. Fax 524-3202

Pettus, Bee
Pettus ISD 400/PK-12
PO Box D 78146 361-375-2296
Tucker Rackley, supt. Fax 375-2295
www.pettusisd.esc2.net
Pettus ES 200/PK-5
PO Box D 78146 361-375-2296
Cheryl Burris, prin. Fax 375-2930

Pflugerville, Travis, Pop. 27,531
Pflugerville ISD 20,100/PK-12
1401 Pecan St W 78660 512-594-0000
Charles Dupre, supt. Fax 594-0005
www.pflugervilleisd.net
Brookhollow ES 600/K-5
1200 N Railroad Ave 78660 512-594-5200
Philip Riley, prin. Fax 594-5205
Highland Park ES 800/K-5
428 Kingston Lacy Blvd 78660 512-594-6800
Christie Olivarez, prin. Fax 594-6805
Kelly Lane MS 800/6-8
18900 Falcon Pointe Blvd 78660 512-594-2800
Devin Padavil, prin. Fax 594-2805
Murchison ES 600/K-5
2215 Kelly Ln 78660 512-594-6000
Brian Ernest, prin. Fax 594-6005
Park Crest MS 900/6-8
1500 N Railroad Ave 78660 512-594-2400
Denise Monzingo, prin. Fax 594-2405
Pflugerville ES 500/K-5
701 Immanuel Rd 78660 512-594-3800
Genia Antoine, prin. Fax 594-3805
Pflugerville MS 1,100/6-8
1600 Settlers Valley Dr 78660 512-594-2000
Mary Kimmins, prin. Fax 594-2005
Spring Hill ES 600/K-5
600 Heatherwilde Blvd 78660 512-594-5400
Tere Ralston, prin. Fax 594-5405
Timmerman ES 500/PK-5
700 Pecan St W 78660 512-594-4200
Christy Chandler, prin. Fax 594-4205
Wieland ES 600/K-5
900 Tudor House Rd 78660 512-594-3900
Kevin Williams, prin. Fax 594-3905
Windermere ES 500/3-5
1100 Picadilly Dr 78660 512-594-4800
Angela Murski, prin. Fax 594-4805
Windermere PS 600/PK-2
429 Grand Avenue Pkwy 78660 512-594-5600
Christi Siegel, prin. Fax 594-5605
Other Schools – See Austin, Round Rock

Pharr, Hidalgo, Pop. 58,986
Hidalgo ISD
Supt. — See Hidalgo
Kelly ES 500/PK-5
201 W Las Milpas Rd 78577 956-781-6525
Trine Barron, prin. Fax 781-5972

Pharr-San Juan-Alamo ISD 29,300/PK-12
PO Box 1150 78577 956-702-5600
Dr. Daniel King, supt. Fax 702-5648
psja.schoolfusion.us/
Buckner ES 400/PK-5
1001 N Fir St 78577 956-702-5771
Priscilla Salinas, prin. Fax 702-5774
Carnahan ES 500/PK-5
317 W Gore Ave 78577 956-702-5678
Rafaela Romero, prin. Fax 702-5681
Chavez ES 800/PK-5
401 E Thomas Dr 78577 956-783-3343
Noimi Martinez, prin. Fax 783-3365
Ford ES 600/PK-5
1200 E Polk Ave 78577 956-702-5641
Rene Montero, prin. Fax 702-5647
Garcia ES 700/PK-5
1002 W Juan Balli Rd 78577 956-783-2848
Yolanda Castillo, prin. Fax 783-2858
Johnson MS 1,200/6-8
500 E Sioux Rd 78577 956-702-5657
Juan Serna, prin. Fax 702-5661
Liberty MS 1,400/6-8
1212 Fir Rdg 78577 956-702-5826
Marisela Zepeda, prin. Fax 783-2820
Long ES 700/PK-5
3700 N Raider 78577 956-702-5799
Janie Gomez, prin. Fax 702-6080
Longoria ES 700/PK-5
400 E Rendon St 78577 956-702-5725
Rosa Enna Zuniga, prin. Fax 702-5727
Napper ES 600/PK-5
903 N Flag St 78577 956-702-5717
Rosie Reyes, prin. Fax 702-5719
Palmer ES 700/PK-5
703 E Sam Houston Blvd 78577 956-702-5688
Rosie Rakay, prin. Fax 702-5695

Pharr ES 800/PK-5
500 E Sam Houston Blvd 78577 956-702-5816
Carmen Gutierrez, prin. Fax 702-5825
Ramirez ES 700/PK-5
1920 N Hibiscus St 78577 956-702-5790
Connie Casas, prin. Fax 702-5793
South Pharr ES 600/PK-5
1000 W Dicker Dr 78577 956-784-5800
Elida Newell, prin. Fax 784-5808
Whitney ES 600/PK-5
1600 W Kelly Ave 78577 956-702-5781
Eleticia Nava, prin. Fax 702-5783
Other Schools – See Alamo, San Juan

Valley View ISD 4,200/PK-12
9701 S Jackson Rd 78577 956-843-3025
Leonel Galaviz, supt. Fax 843-8688
www.vview.net
Valley View 6th Grade Campus 300/6-6
9701 S Jackson Rd 78577 956-843-3752
Cynthia Oliver, prin. Fax 843-3756
Valley View ES 700/PK-5
9701 S Jackson Rd 78577 956-843-2732
Jesus Cerda, prin. Fax 843-8526
Valley View JHS 600/7-8
9701 S Jackson Rd 78577 956-843-2452
Monica Luna, prin. Fax 843-7992
Valley View North ES 600/PK-5
9701 S Jackson Rd 78577 956-783-1134
Librado De Hoyos, prin. Fax 783-1163
Other Schools – See Hidalgo

Oratory Academy 500/PK-12
1407 W Moore Rd 78577 956-781-3056
Fr. Mario Aviles, prin. Fax 702-3047

Pilot Point, Denton, Pop. 4,042
Pilot Point ISD 1,500/PK-12
829 S Harrison St 76258 940-686-8700
Glenn Barber, supt. Fax 686-8705
www.pilotpointisd.com
Pilot Point ES 400/PK-2
829 S Jefferson St 76258 940-686-8710
Rae Ann Strittmatter, prin. Fax 686-8715
Pilot Point IS 400/3-6
501 Carroll St 76258 940-686-8720
Jill Johnson, prin. Fax 686-8725
Pilot Point MS - J. Earl Selz Campus 200/7-8
828 S Harrison St 76258 940-686-8730
Larry Shuman, prin. Fax 686-8735

Pineland, Sabine, Pop. 916
West Sabine ISD 600/K-12
PO Box 869 75968 409-584-2655
Travis Edwards, supt. Fax 584-2139
www.westsabine.esc7.net
West Sabine ES 300/K-6
PO Box 869 75968 409-584-2205
Pam Edwards, prin. Fax 584-3096

Pipe Creek, Bandera
Bandera ISD
Supt. — See Bandera
Hill Country ES 500/PK-5
6346 FM 1283 78063 830-535-6151
Renee Cadena, prin. Fax 535-5111

Pipe Creek Christian S 100/PK-12
PO Box 63778 78063 830-510-6131
Richard Cobler, admin. Fax 510-6131

Pittsburg, Camp, Pop. 4,553
Pittsburg ISD 2,300/PK-12
PO Box 1189 75686 903-856-3628
Judy Pollan, supt. Fax 856-0269
pittsburgisd.net
Pittsburg ES 400/2-4
110 Fulton St 75686 903-856-6472
Stephanie McConnell, prin. Fax 855-3370
Pittsburg IS 400/5-6
209 Lafayette St 75686 903-855-3395
Sarah Richmond, prin. Fax 855-3398
Pittsburg MS 400/7-8
313 Broach St 75686 903-856-6432
Terri Brown, prin. Fax 855-3357
Pittsburg PS 400/PK-1
405 Broach St 75686 903-856-6482
Vicki Rockett, prin. Fax 855-3385

Placedo, Victoria
Bloomington ISD
Supt. — See Bloomington
Placedo ES 200/4-6
PO Box 156 77977 361-897-1717
James Pieper, prin. Fax 897-3894

Plains, Yoakum, Pop. 1,457
Plains ISD 500/PK-12
PO Box 479 79355 806-456-7401
Michael Michaelson, supt. Fax 456-4325
plainsisd.net/
Plains ES, PO Box 479 79355 200/PK-4
Vernon Hise, prin. 806-456-7438
Plains MS, PO Box 479 79355 200/5-8
John Starcher, prin. 806-456-7490

Plainview, Hale, Pop. 21,991
Plainview ISD 5,900/PK-12
PO Box 1540 79073 806-296-6392
Dr. Ron Miller, supt. Fax 296-4014
www.plainview.k12.tx.us
Ash Sixth Grade Learning Center 400/6-6
908 Ash St 79072 806-296-4130
Dr. Brent Richburg, prin. Fax 296-4101
College Hill ES 400/PK-4
707 Canyon St 79072 806-296-4158
Linda Watson, prin. Fax 296-4102
Coronado JHS 400/7-7
2501 Joliet St 79072 806-296-4175
Tillie Becerra, prin. Fax 296-4177
Edgemere ES 500/PK-4
2600 W 20th St 79072 806-296-4105
Vickie Young, prin. Fax 296-4103
Estacado JHS 400/8-8
2500 W 20th St 79072 806-296-4165
Ritchie Thornton, prin. Fax 296-4169
Highland ES 400/K-4
1707 W 11th St 79072 806-296-4137
Becky Buxton, prin. Fax 296-4139
Hillcrest ES 500/PK-4
315 SW Alpine Dr 79072 806-296-4151
Greg Brown, prin. Fax 296-4106
Lakeside Fifth Grade Learning Center 400/5-5
1800 Joliet St 79072 806-296-4144
Brandon Shelton, prin. Fax 296-4107
La Mesa ES 500/PK-4
600 S Ennis St 79072 806-296-4110
Sharon Wright, prin. Fax 296-9425
Thunderbird ES 400/PK-4
1200 W 32nd St 79072 806-296-4123
Jimye Sadler, prin. Fax 296-4125

Plainview Christian Academy 200/PK-12
310 S Ennis St 79072 806-296-6034
Karen Earhart, admin. Fax 296-0074

Plano, Collin, Pop. 250,096
Frisco ISD
Supt. — See Frisco
Anderson ES 600/K-5
2800 Oakland Hills Dr 75025 469-633-2300
Monica Jackson, prin. Fax 633-2350
Borchardt ES 600/K-5
4300 Waskom Dr 75024 469-633-2800
Betty King, prin. Fax 633-2850
Fowler MS 700/6-8
3801 McDermott Rd 75025 469-633-5050
Donnie Wiseman, prin. Fax 633-5060
Riddle ES 400/K-5
8201 Robinson Rd 75024 469-633-3200
Rachel Taylor, prin. Fax 633-3250
Taylor ES 500/K-5
9865 Gillespie Dr 75025 469-633-3625
Tanya Kelly, prin. Fax 633-3635

Plano ISD 53,400/PK-12
2700 W 15th St 75075 469-752-8100
Dr. Douglas Otto, supt. Fax 752-8096
www.pisd.edu
Andrews ES 700/K-5
2520 Scenic Dr 75025 469-752-3900
Toni Strickland, prin. Fax 752-3901
Armstrong MS 800/6-8
3805 Timberline Dr 75074 469-752-4600
Donella Green, prin. Fax 752-4601
Barksdale ES 700/PK-5
2424 Midway Rd 75093 469-752-0100
Pam Murray, prin. Fax 752-0101
Barron ECC 600/PK-PK
3300 P Ave 75074 469-752-0200
Dr. Elaine Schmidt, prin. Fax 752-0201
Beaty ECC 400/PK-PK
1717 Nevada Dr 75093 469-752-4200
Susie Vaughan, prin. Fax 752-4201
Bethany ES 500/PK-5
2418 Micarta Dr 75025 469-752-0300
Denise Bleggi, prin. Fax 752-0301
Bowman MS 1,000/6-8
2501 Jupiter Rd 75074 469-752-4800
George King, prin. Fax 752-4801
Brinker ES 700/PK-5
3800 Clark Pkwy 75093 469-752-0500
Barbara Richardson, prin. Fax 752-0501
Carlisle ES 500/K-5
6525 Old Orchard Dr 75023 469-752-0600
Dr. Saul Laredo, prin. Fax 752-0601
Carpenter MS 1,000/6-8
1501 Cross Bend Rd 75023 469-752-5000
Shauna Koehne, prin. Fax 752-5001
Centennial ES 600/K-5
2609 Ventura Dr 75093 469-752-0700
Jason Myatt, prin. Fax 752-0701
Christie ES 800/PK-5
3801 Rainier Rd 75023 469-752-0800
Emelia Ahmed, prin. Fax 752-0801
Daffron ES 600/K-5
3900 Preston Meadow Dr 75093 469-752-0900
Cindy Guinn, prin. Fax 752-0901
Davis ES 300/PK-5
2701 Parkhaven Dr 75075 469-752-1000
Jill Shepperd, prin. Fax 752-1001
Dooley ES 500/PK-5
2425 San Gabriel Dr 75074 469-752-1100
Sue Loomis, prin. Fax 752-1101
Forman ES 600/K-5
3600 Timberline Dr 75074 469-752-1200
Tramy Tran, prin. Fax 752-1201
Gulledge ES 600/PK-5
6801 Preston Meadow Dr 75024 469-752-1300
Renee Rucker, prin. Fax 752-1301
Haggard MS 900/6-8
2401 Westside Dr 75075 469-752-5400
Julie-Anne Dean, prin. Fax 752-5401
Harrington ES 500/PK-5
1540 Baffin Bay Dr 75075 469-752-1500
Ann Irvine, prin. Fax 752-1501
Haun ES 700/K-5
4500 Quincy Ln 75024 469-752-1600
Jayne Smith, prin. Fax 752-1601
Hedgcoxe ES 500/K-5
7701 Prescott Dr 75025 469-752-1700
Kristi Graham, prin. Fax 752-1701
Hendrick MS 900/6-8
7400 Red River Dr 75025 469-752-5600
Sheila Spencer, prin. Fax 752-5601
Hickey ES 500/K-5
4100 Coldwater Creek Ln 75074 469-752-4100
Jacque Meziere, prin. Fax 752-4101
Hightower ES 500/K-5
2601 Decator Dr 75093 469-752-1800
Mariea Sprott, prin. Fax 752-1801
Huffman ES 500/K-5
5510 Channel Isle Dr 75093 469-752-1900
Len Stevens, prin. Fax 752-1901
Hughston ES 400/K-5
2601 Cross Bend Rd 75023 469-752-2000
Luanne Collins, prin. Fax 752-2001
Jackson ES 600/K-5
1101 Jackson Dr 75075 469-752-2100
Kris Benson, prin. Fax 752-2101
Mathews ES 600/K-5
7500 Marchman Way 75025 469-752-2300
Jane Ball, prin. Fax 752-2301
McCall ES 600/K-5
6601 Cloverhaven Way 75074 469-752-4500
Cathy Taylor, prin. Fax 752-4501
Meadows ES 400/PK-5
2800 18th St 75074 469-752-2400
Bryan Bird, prin. Fax 752-2401
Memorial ES 600/K-5
2600 R Ave 75074 469-752-2500
Maricela Helm, prin. Fax 752-2501
Mendenhall ES 600/PK-5
1313 18th St 75074 469-752-2600
Karen Noble, prin. Fax 752-2601
Pearson ECC 300/PK-PK
4000 Eagle Pass 75023 469-752-4300
Dr. Cheri Izbicki, prin. Fax 752-4301
Rasor ES 500/PK-5
945 Hedgcoxe Rd 75025 469-752-2900
Zack Pruett, prin. Fax 752-2901
Renner MS 1,200/6-8
5701 W Parker Rd 75093 469-752-5800
Bill McLaughlin, prin. Fax 752-5801
Rice MS 1,100/6-8
8500 Gifford Dr 75025 469-752-6000
Gail Stelter, prin. Fax 752-6001
Robinson MS 1,000/6-8
6701 Preston Meadow Dr 75024 469-752-6200
Kary Cooper, prin. Fax 752-6201
Saigling ES 400/PK-5
3600 Matterhorn Dr 75075 469-752-3000
Kellie Latimer, prin. Fax 752-3001
Schimelpfenig MS 1,000/6-8
2400 Maumelle Dr 75023 469-752-6400
Olga Sanchez-Grosscup, prin. Fax 752-6401
Shepard ES 500/PK-5
1000 Wilson Dr 75075 469-752-3100
Mary Spickler, prin. Fax 752-3101
Sigler ES 500/K-5
1400 Janwood Dr 75075 469-752-3200
Sandra Muzquiz, prin. Fax 752-3201
Skaggs ES 700/K-5
3201 Russell Creek Dr 75025 469-752-3300
Mary Ann Bargmann, prin. Fax 752-3301
Thomas ES 800/K-5
6537 Blue Ridge Trl 75023 469-752-3500
Lynn Swanson, prin. Fax 752-3501
Weatherford ES 500/PK-5
2941 Mollimar Dr 75075 469-752-3600
Arron Moeller, prin. Fax 752-3601
Wells ES 500/K-5
3427 Mission Ridge Rd 75023 469-752-3700
Stefanie Ramos, prin. Fax 752-3701
Wilson MS 1,000/6-8
1001 Custer Rd 75075 469-752-6700
Selenda Anderson, prin. Fax 752-6701
Wyatt ES 700/K-5
8900 Coit Rd 75025 469-752-3800
Debby Moilanen, prin. Fax 752-3801
Other Schools – See Allen, Dallas, Murphy, Richardson

Faith Lutheran S 200/PK-8
1701 E Park Blvd 75074 972-423-7448
Timothy Merritt, prin. Fax 423-9618
Messiah Lutheran Lambs S 200/PK-K
1801 W Plano Pkwy 75075 972-398-7560
Gail Winningham, dir. Fax 398-7598
Montessori Children's House - Plano 200/PK-4
1900 Hedgcoxe Rd 75025 972-517-5437
Effie Saifi, dir. Fax 517-5407
Plano Christian Academy 100/K-12
1501 H Ave 75074 972-422-1722
Brittany Burnette, admin. Fax 422-5497
Prestonwood Christian Academy 1,400/PK-12
6801 W Park Blvd 75093 972-820-5300
Larry Taylor, hdmstr. Fax 820-5058
Prince of Peace Catholic S 800/PK-8
5100 W Plano Pkwy 75093 972-380-5505
Cindy Kirsch, prin. Fax 380-5270
St. Mark Catholic S 700/PK-8
1201 Alma Dr 75075 972-578-0610
Suzanne Bacot, prin. Fax 423-3299
St. Timothy Academy 100/K-8
4550 Legacy Dr 75024 214-291-4701
Kathy Bryan, hdmstr. Fax 291-4696
West Plano Montessori S 300/PK-4
3425 Ashington Ln 75023 972-618-8844
Reena Khandpur, prin. Fax 398-1798

Plantersville, Grimes

School of Environmental Education 100/5-5
7738 Camp Kappe Rd 77363 936-894-2141
Sr. Thomas Ann LaCour, prin. Fax 894-2198

Pleasanton, Atascosa, Pop. 9,375
Pleasanton ISD 3,400/PK-12
831 Stadium Dr 78064 830-569-1200
Bernard Zarosky, supt. Fax 569-2171
www.pisd.us
Pleasanton ES 600/3-6
831 Stadium Dr 78064 830-569-1340
Debbie Drew, prin. Fax 569-3096
Pleasanton IS 500/5-6
831 Stadium Dr 78064 830-569-1310
Deborah Miles, prin. Fax 569-3145

Pleasanton JHS 500/7-8
831 Stadium Dr 78064 830-569-1280
Deborah Miles, prin. Fax 569-2514
Pleasanton PS 700/PK-2
831 Stadium Dr 78064 830-569-2000
Jackie Russell, prin. Fax 569-5208
Other Schools – See Leming

Point Comfort, Calhoun, Pop. 736
Calhoun County ISD
Supt. — See Port Lavaca
Point Comfort ES 100/PK-6
PO Box 500 77978 361-987-2212
Scott Norris, prin. Fax 987-2018

Pollok, Angelina
Central ISD 1,600/PK-12
7622 N US Highway 69 75969 936-853-2216
Allen Garner, supt. Fax 853-2215
www.centralisd.com
Central ES 400/3-5
7622 N US Highway 69 75969 936-853-9390
Dianne Croom, prin. Fax 853-9329
Central JHS 400/6-8
7622 N US Highway 69 75969 936-853-2115
Chad Smith, prin. Fax 853-2348
Central PS 400/PK-2
7622 N US Highway 69 75969 936-853-2710
Karen Shumaker, prin. Fax 853-9329

Ponder, Denton, Pop. 846
Ponder ISD 1,100/PK-12
PO Box 278 76259 940-479-8200
Bruce Yeager, supt. Fax 479-8209
www.ponderisd.net
Ponder ES 500/PK-5
PO Box 278 76259 940-479-8230
Janell Wilbanks, prin. Fax 479-8239
Ponder JHS 300/6-8
PO Box 278 76259 940-479-8220
Ted Heers, prin. Fax 479-8229

Poolville, Parker
Poolville ISD 500/K-12
PO Box 96 76487 817-594-4452
Jimmie Dobbs, supt. Fax 594-2651
www.poolville.net
Poolville ES 200/K-5
PO Box 96 76487 817-599-3308
Kathy Pierce, prin. Fax 599-2651
Poolville JHS 100/6-8
PO Box 96 76487 817-594-4539
Bill Sanders, prin. Fax 594-0081

Port Aransas, Nueces, Pop. 3,667
Port Aransas ISD 600/PK-12
100 S Station St 78373 361-749-1205
Dr. Sharon Doughty, supt. Fax 749-1215
www.port-aransas.k12.tx.us
Brundrett MS 100/6-8
100 S Station St 78373 361-749-1209
Bob Byrd, prin. Fax 749-1218
Olsen ES 200/PK-5
100 S Station St 78373 361-749-1212
Sylvia Buttler, prin. Fax 749-1219

Port Arthur, Jefferson, Pop. 56,684
Port Arthur ISD 9,100/PK-12
PO Box 1388 77641 409-989-6244
Dr. Johnny Brown, supt. Fax 989-6268
www.paisd.org
Austin MS 600/6-8
2441 61st St 77640 409-736-1521
Dr. Lisa Chambers, prin. Fax 736-0267
DeQueen ES 500/PK-5
740 DeQueen Blvd 77640 409-984-8900
Gladdie Fowler, prin. Fax 982-1843
Dowling ES 300/PK-5
6301 Pat Ave 77640 409-736-2571
Dwight Wagner, prin. Fax 736-2406
Edison MS 800/6-8
3501 12th St 77642 409-985-4311
Barbara Polk, prin. Fax 985-6945
Houston ES 1,000/PK-5
3245 36th St 77642 409-985-5525
Cathy Sandoval, prin. Fax 985-8701
Lee ES 700/PK-5
3900 10th St 77642 409-984-8300
Kim Vine, prin. Fax 983-1649
Travis ES 900/PK-5
1115 Lakeview Ave 77642 409-982-2891
Bessie Johnson, prin. Fax 982-8966
Tyrrell ES 800/PK-5
4401 Ferndale Dr 77642 409-962-7373
Emily Moore, prin. Fax 963-2765
Washington ES 300/PK-5
1300 Texas Ave 77640 409-984-8600
Dr. Ella Williams, prin. Fax 982-3569
Wheatley S of Early Childhood Programs 400/PK-PK
1100 Jefferson Dr 77642 409-985-9101
Madeline Savoy, prin. Fax 985-5487
Wilson Technology Theme S 500/PK-8
1001 10th St 77640 409-985-9347
LaSonya Baptiste, prin. Fax 982-2847

Port Neches-Groves ISD
Supt. — See Port Neches
Taft ES 400/K-3
2500 Taft Ave 77642 409-962-2262
Nathan Addison, prin. Fax 963-1923

St. Catherine S 200/PK-8
3840 Woodrow Dr 77642 409-962-3011
Michael Collins, prin. Fax 962-5019

Port Bolivar, Galveston
Galveston ISD
Supt. — See Galveston
Crenshaw S 200/PK-8
416 Highway 87 77650 409-684-8526
Bill Heuman, prin. Fax 684-7916

Porter, Montgomery, Pop. 7,000
New Caney ISD
Supt. — See New Caney
Bens Branch ES 600/PK-5
24160 Briar Berry Ln 77365 281-577-8800
Dr. Delinda Neal, prin. Fax 354-4296
Crippen ES 700/PK-5
18690 Cumberland Blvd 77365 281-354-6601
Sarah Hottman, prin. Fax 354-6823
New Caney 6th Grade Campus 600/6-6
22784 Highway 59 77365 281-577-8860
Jackie Wimberly, prin. Fax 354-8725
Porter ES 600/PK-5
22256 Ford Rd 77365 281-354-3267
Debra Johnson, prin. Fax 354-7583
Sorters Mill ES 500/PK-5
23300 Sorters Rd 77365 281-577-8780
Tricia Musick, prin. Fax 354-0164
Valley Ranch ES 600/PK-5
21700 Valley Rnch Crssng Dr 77365 281-577-8760
Gloria Hammack, prin. Fax 577-9209
White Oak MS 600/7-8
24161 Briar Berry Ln 77365 281-577-8800
Paula Burk, prin. Fax 354-5186

Port Isabel, Cameron, Pop. 5,373
Point Isabel ISD 2,600/PK-12
101 Port Rd 78578 956-943-0000
Dr. Estella Pineda, supt. Fax 943-0014
www.pi-isd.net/
Derry ES 500/3-5
101 Port Rd 78578 956-943-0070
Ana Holland, prin. Fax 943-0074
Garriga ES 800/PK-2
101 Port Rd 78578 956-943-0080
Nancy Gonzalez, prin. Fax 943-0085
Port Isabel JHS 500/6-8
101 Port Rd 78578 956-943-0060
Joel Garcia, prin. Fax 943-0055

Portland, San Patricio, Pop. 16,219
Gregory-Portland ISD 4,300/PK-12
608 College St 78374 361-777-1091
Dr. Paul Clore, supt. Fax 777-1093
www.g-pisd.org
Andrews ES 300/K-4
1100 Lang Rd 78374 361-777-4048
Marisa Eddins, prin. Fax 643-0775
Clark ES 600/PK-4
2250 Memorial Pkwy 78374 361-643-2361
Bobby Rister, prin. Fax 777-4046
East Cliff ES 400/K-4
200 Fulton Pl 78374 361-777-4255
Alma Munoz, prin. Fax 777-3207
Gregory-Portland IS 700/5-6
4200 Wildcat Dr 78374 361-643-4404
Leticia Villa, prin. Fax 643-8193
Gregory-Portland JHS 700/7-8
4600 Wildcat Dr 78374 361-777-4042
Xavier Barrera, prin. Fax 643-3187
Other Schools – See Gregory

Port Lavaca, Calhoun, Pop. 11,696
Calhoun County ISD 4,300/PK-12
525 N Commerce St 77979 361-552-9728
Larry Nichols, supt. Fax 551-2648
www.calcoisd.org
Harrison/Jefferson/Madison ES 800/PK-5
605 N Commerce St 77979 361-552-5253
Pam Weathersby, prin. Fax 551-2628
Jackson/Roosevelt ES 900/PK-5
1512 Jackson St 77979 361-552-3317
Mitzi McAfee, prin. Fax 551-2691
Travis MS 800/6-8
705 N Nueces St 77979 361-552-3784
Lina Moore, prin. Fax 551-2692
Other Schools – See Point Comfort, Port O Connor, Seadrift

Our Lady of the Gulf S 100/K-8
PO Box 87 77979 361-552-6140
Theresa Dent, prin. Fax 552-4300

Port Neches, Jefferson, Pop. 13,131
Port Neches-Groves ISD 4,600/PK-12
620 Avenue C 77651 409-722-4244
Dr. Lani Randall, supt. Fax 724-7864
www.pngisd.org
Port Neches ES 300/4-5
2101 Llano St 77651 409-722-2262
Amy Gil, prin. Fax 729-7003
Port Neches MS 500/6-8
2031 Llano St 77651 409-722-8115
Kyle Hooper, prin. Fax 727-8342
Ridgewood ES 400/K-3
2820 Merriman St 77651 409-722-7641
Julie Gauthier, prin. Fax 721-9721
Woodcrest ES 300/K-3
1522 Heisler St 77651 409-724-2309
Fae Sandifer, prin. Fax 729-9480
Other Schools – See Groves, Port Arthur

Port O Connor, Calhoun
Calhoun County ISD
Supt. — See Port Lavaca
Port O Connor ES 100/PK-5
PO Box 687 77982 361-983-2341
Lydia Strakos, prin. Fax 551-2605

Post, Garza, Pop. 3,802
Post ISD 800/PK-12
501 S Avenue K 79356 806-495-3343
Marlin Marcum, supt. Fax 495-2945
www.post.k12.tx.us
Post ES 400/PK-5
211 W 8th St 79356 806-495-3436
Staci Marts, prin. Fax 495-2381
Post MS 200/6-8
405 W 8th St 79356 806-495-2874
Marvin Self, prin. Fax 495-2426

First Baptist Christian S 50/PK-K
402 W Main St 79356 806-495-3554

Poteet, Atascosa, Pop. 3,626
Poteet ISD 1,600/PK-12
PO Box 138 78065 830-742-3567
Dr. Sharon Doughty, supt. Fax 742-3332
www.poteet.k12.tx.us
Poteet ES 600/PK-3
PO Box 138 78065 830-742-3503
Tina Gillespie, prin. Fax 742-8487
Poteet IS 200/4-6
PO Box 138 78065 830-742-3697
Carolina Gonzales, prin. Fax 742-3194
Poteet JHS 200/7-8
PO Box 138 78065 830-742-3571
Judith Gamez, prin. Fax 742-8495

Poth, Wilson, Pop. 2,145
Poth ISD 800/PK-12
PO Box 250 78147 830-484-3330
David Wehmeyer, supt. Fax 484-2961
www.pothisd.us
Poth ES 400/PK-5
PO Box 250 78147 830-484-3321
Norman Porter, prin. Fax 484-1271
Poth JHS 200/6-8
PO Box 250 78147 830-484-3323
Scott Caloss, prin. Fax 484-3682

Pottsboro, Grayson, Pop. 1,992
Pottsboro ISD 1,300/PK-12
PO Box 555 75076 903-786-3051
Dr. Kyle Collier, supt. Fax 786-9085
www.pottsboroisd.org/
Pottsboro ES 400/PK-3
PO Box 555 75076 903-786-9612
Gary Canada, prin. Fax 786-4903
Pottsboro IS 200/4-5
PO Box 555 75076 903-786-9770
Lucy Hansen, prin. Fax 786-9790
Pottsboro MS 300/6-8
PO Box 555 75076 903-786-9702
Wendi Russell, prin. Fax 786-4902

Powderly, Lamar
North Lamar ISD
Supt. — See Paris
Parker ES 300/PK-5
98 County Road 44112 75473 903-732-3066
Jacquelyn Neugent, prin. Fax 669-0139

Prairie Lea, Caldwell
Prairie Lea ISD 200/PK-12
PO Box 9 78661 512-488-2328
Jesus Lopez, supt. Fax 488-9006
www.prairielea.txed.net/
Prairie Lea S 200/PK-12
PO Box 9 78661 512-488-2328
Darren Kesselus, prin. Fax 488-2425

Premont, Jim Wells, Pop. 2,836
Premont ISD 800/PK-12
PO Box 530 78375 361-348-3915
Dr. Leobardo Cano, supt. Fax 348-2882
www.premontisd.net
Premont Central ES 300/PK-5
PO Box 1165 78375 361-348-3915
Richard Waterhouse, prin. Fax 348-2313
Premont JHS 200/6-8
PO Box 769 78375 361-348-3915
Adolfo Chapa, prin. Fax 348-2751

Presidio, Presidio, Pop. 4,775
Presidio ISD 1,500/PK-12
PO Box 1401 79845 432-229-3275
Dennis McEntire, supt. Fax 229-4228
www.presidio-isd.net
Franco MS 300/6-8
PO Box 1401 79845 432-229-3113
Teresa Porras, prin. Fax 229-4087
Presidio ES 700/PK-5
PO Box 1401 79845 432-229-3200
Yvette Machuca, prin. Fax 229-4267

Price, Rusk
Carlisle ISD 600/PK-12
PO Box 187 75687 903-861-3801
Michael Payne, supt. Fax 861-3932
www.carl.sprnet.org/cisd2.htm
Carlisle ES 400/PK-6
PO Box 187 75687 903-861-3612
Stephanie Rowan, prin. Fax 861-0063

Priddy, Mills
Priddy ISD 100/K-12
PO Box 40 76870 325-966-3323
Robby Stuteville, supt. Fax 966-3380
www.centex-edu.net/priddy/
Priddy S 100/K-12
PO Box 40 76870 325-966-3323
Adrianne Klein, prin. Fax 966-3380

Princeton, Collin, Pop. 4,115
Princeton ISD 2,400/PK-12
321 Panther Pkwy 75407 469-952-5400
Philip Anthony, supt. Fax 736-3505
www.princetonisd.net
Clark JHS 300/7-8
301 Panther Pkwy 75407 469-952-5400
Greg Tabor, prin. Fax 736-5903
Godwin ES 400/K-5
1019 N 6th St 75407 469-952-5400
Jodie Weddle, prin. Fax 736-3533
Harper ES K-5
8080 County Road 398 75407 469-952-5400
Anita Barch, prin. Fax 736-2621
Huddleston IS 200/6-6
301 N 5th St 75407 469-952-5400
Grant Sweeney, prin. Fax 736-6162

Lacy ES 700/PK-5
224 E College St 75407 469-952-5400
Rene Mullins, prin. Fax 736-6795

Progreso, Hidalgo, Pop. 5,082
Progreso ISD 1,500/PK-12
PO Box 610 78579 956-565-3002
Dr. Fernando Castillo, supt. Fax 565-2128
www.progreso-isd.net/
Progreso East ES 100/PK-5
PO Box 610 78579 956-565-0281
Yulia Molina, prin. Fax 565-2128
Progreso West ES 600/PK-5
PO Box 610 78579 956-565-1103
Diana Dominguez, prin. Fax 565-2128
Thompson MS 300/6-8
PO Box 610 78579 956-565-6539
Oscar Dominquez, prin. Fax 565-2128

Prosper, Collin, Pop. 4,207
Prosper ISD 2,500/PK-12
PO Box 100 75078 972-346-3316
Drew Watkins, supt. Fax 346-9247
www.prosper-isd.net
Folsom ES 600/PK-5
800 Sommerville Dr 75078 972-346-9230
Brenda Keener, prin. Fax 346-9245
Rogers MS 6-8
1001 S Coit Rd 75078 972-346-9114
Andy Baker, prin. Fax 346-9248
Rucker ES 700/PK-5
402 S Craig Rd 75078 972-346-2456
Holly Ferguson, prin. Fax 346-9249
Other Schools – See Mc Kinney

Quanah, Hardeman, Pop. 2,715
Quanah ISD 600/PK-12
PO Box 150 79252 940-663-2281
Terry Allen, supt. Fax 663-2875
www.qisd.net
Reagan ES 300/PK-6
PO Box 150 79252 940-663-2171
Albert Motsenbocker, prin. Fax 663-2209
Travis MS 100/7-8
PO Box 150 79252 940-663-2226
Mike Hale, prin. Fax 663-6361

Queen City, Cass, Pop. 1,591
Queen City ISD 1,100/PK-12
PO Box 128 75572 903-796-8256
Rob Barnwell, supt. Fax 796-0248
www.qcisd.net
Hileman ES 400/PK-4
PO Box 128 75572 903-796-6304
Carla Dupree, prin. Fax 799-5275
Upchurch MS 300/5-8
PO Box 128 75572 903-796-6412
Steve Holmes, prin. Fax 796-0834

Quemado, Maverick
Eagle Pass ISD
Supt. — See Eagle Pass
Kirchner ES 100/K-6
1st and Crockett St 78877 830-758-7045
Rosa Valderrama, prin. Fax 758-0328

Quinlan, Hunt, Pop. 1,457
Boles ISD 500/PK-12
9777 FM 2101 75474 903-883-4464
Dr. Graham Sweeney, supt. Fax 883-4531
boles.ednet10.net
Boles ES 200/PK-4
9777 FM 2101 75474 903-883-2161
Shirley Duran, prin. Fax 883-9094
Boles MS 200/5-8
9777 FM 2101 75474 903-883-4464
Mikayle Moreland, prin. Fax 883-3097

Quinlan ISD 2,700/PK-12
301 E Main St 75474 903-356-3293
Michael French, supt. Fax 356-2339
www.quinlanisd.net
Butler IS 400/4-5
410 Clardy Dr 75474 903-356-2153
Jacqulyn Cooper, prin. Fax 356-0034
Cannon ES 600/1-3
315 Business Highway 34 75474 903-356-3825
John Milton, prin. Fax 356-3952
Martin ECC 300/PK-K
401 Panther Path 75474 903-356-4400
Casey Johnson, prin. Fax 356-4418
Thompson MS 600/6-8
423 Panther Path 75474 903-356-2154
Michael Tull, prin. Fax 356-2414

Quitman, Wood, Pop. 2,198
Quitman ISD 1,100/PK-12
1101 E Goode St 75783 903-763-5000
Dr. Nancy Vaughan, supt. Fax 763-2710
www.quitmanisd.net/
Quitman ES 600/PK-6
902 E Goode St 75783 903-763-5000
Mary Nichols, prin. Fax 763-4151
Quitman JHS 200/7-8
1101 E Goode St 75783 903-763-5000
Garland Willis, prin. Fax 763-2589

Ralls, Crosby, Pop. 2,122
Ralls ISD 500/PK-12
810 Avenue I 79357 806-253-2509
Deanna Logan, supt. Fax 253-2508
ralls.esc17.net/
Ralls ES 300/PK-5
810 Avenue I 79357 806-253-2546
L'Rae Watson, prin. Fax 253-3112
Ralls MS 100/6-8
810 Avenue I 79357 806-253-2549
Michael Allbright, prin. Fax 253-4031

Rancho Viejo, Cameron, Pop. 1,799
Los Fresnos Consolidated ISD
Supt. — See Los Fresnos

Villareal ES 500/PK-5
7700 E Lakeside Blvd 78575 956-233-3975
Jeaneva Scoville, prin. Fax 350-2087

Randolph AFB, Bexar
Randolph Field ISD 1,200/PK-12
Building 1225 78148 210-357-2300
Billy Walker, supt. Fax 357-2469
www.randolph-field.k12.tx.us
Randolph ES 600/PK-5
Building 146 78148 210-357-2345
Karen Bessette, prin. Fax 357-2346
Randolph MS 300/6-8
Building 1225 78148 210-357-2400
Bruce Cannon, prin. Fax 357-2475

Ranger, Eastland, Pop. 2,535
Ranger ISD 400/PK-12
1842 E Loop 254 76470 254-647-1187
Doyle Russell, supt. Fax 647-5215
www.ranger.esc14.net
Ranger ES, 1842 E Loop 254 76470 200/PK-6
Kelly Kunkel, prin. 254-647-1138

Rankin, Upton, Pop. 725
Rankin ISD 200/PK-12
PO Box 90 79778 432-693-2461
Tena Gray, supt. Fax 693-2353
www.rankin.k12.tx.us
Gossett ES 100/PK-7
PO Box 90 79778 432-693-2455
Tena Gray, prin. Fax 693-2552

Raymondville, Willacy, Pop. 9,483
Raymondville ISD 2,400/PK-12
1 Bearkat Blvd 78580 956-689-2471
Johnny Pineda, supt. Fax 689-5869
www.raymondvilleisd.org/
Green MS 500/6-8
1 Bearkat Blvd 78580 956-689-2471
Sabrina Franco, prin. Fax 689-5330
Pittman ES 600/PK-5
1 Bearkat Blvd 78580 956-689-2471
Sylvia Hembree, prin. Fax 689-5997
Smith ES 600/PK-5
1 Bearkat Blvd 78580 956-689-2471
Gilbert Galvan, prin. Fax 689-5871

Raywood, Liberty
Hull-Daisetta ISD
Supt. — See Daisetta
Hull-Daisetta JHS 100/6-8
160 At Woodson School Rd 77582 936-536-6321
Quinn Godwin, prin. Fax 536-3839

Realitos, Duval
Ramirez Common SD 50/PK-6
10492 School St 78376 361-539-4343
Jose Leal, supt. Fax 539-4482
www.ramirezcsd.com
Ramirez ES 50/PK-6
10492 School St 78376 361-539-4343
Jose Leal, prin. Fax 539-4482

Red Oak, Ellis, Pop. 7,171
De Soto ISD
Supt. — See De Soto
Moates ES 800/PK-5
1500 Heritage Blvd 75154 972-230-2881
Wesley Pittman, prin. Fax 274-8073

Red Oak ISD 5,100/PK-12
PO Box 9000 75154 972-617-2941
Scott Niven, supt. Fax 617-4333
www.redoakisd.org
Eastridge ES 400/K-4
PO Box 9000 75154 972-617-2266
Bob Magier, prin. Fax 617-4417
Red Oak ES 600/PK-4
PO Box 9000 75154 972-617-3523
Sharon Graves, prin. Fax 576-3423
Red Oak JHS 800/7-8
PO Box 9000 75154 972-617-0066
Kathy Teer, prin. Fax 617-4377
Wooden ES 400/PK-4
PO Box 9000 75154 972-617-2977
Shondra Jones, prin. Fax 617-4404
Other Schools – See Glenn Heights

Red Rock, Bastrop
Bastrop ISD
Supt. — See Bastrop
Red Rock ES 500/PK-4
2401 FM 20 78662 512-332-2670
Bruce Nelson, prin. Fax 321-2038

Redwater, Bowie, Pop. 883
Redwater ISD 1,100/PK-12
PO Box 347 75573 903-671-3481
Anne Farris, supt. Fax 671-2019
www.redwaterisd.org/
Redwater ES 300/PK-3
PO Box 347 75573 903-671-3425
Kelly Lusk, prin. Fax 671-3196
Redwater JHS 200/7-8
PO Box 347 75573 903-671-3227
Bebe Hayes, prin. Fax 671-2019
Redwater MS 200/4-6
PO Box 347 75573 903-672-3412
Lindsey Crain, prin. Fax 671-2444

Refugio, Refugio, Pop. 2,797
Refugio ISD 700/PK-12
212 W Vance St 78377 361-526-2325
J. Robert Azam, supt. Fax 526-2326
www.refugioisd.net/
Refugio ES 400/PK-6
212 W Vance St 78377 361-526-4844
Jennifer Perez-Lara, prin. Fax 526-1063

Rhome, Wise, Pop. 866
Northwest ISD
Supt. — See Justin

Chisholm Trail MS 700/6-8
583 FM 3433 76078 817-215-0600
Dr. Rob Thornell, prin. Fax 215-0648
Prairie View ES 600/PK-5
609 FM 3433 76078 817-215-0550
Sandy Conklin, prin. Fax 215-0598

Rice, Ellis, Pop. 924
Rice ISD 700/PK-12
1302 SW McKinney St 75155 903-326-4287
Judith Pritchett, supt. Fax 326-4164
www.rice-isd.org
Rice ES 400/PK-5
PO Box 450 75155 903-326-4151
Regina Casaday, prin. Fax 326-4900

Richards, Grimes
Richards ISD 100/K-12
PO Box 308 77873 936-851-2364
Martey Ainsworth, supt. Fax 851-2210
www.richardsisd.net
Richards ES 100/K-6
PO Box 308 77873 936-851-2364
Marty Ainsworth, prin. Fax 851-2210

Richardson, Dallas, Pop. 99,187
Plano ISD
Supt. — See Plano
Aldridge ES 600/PK-5
720 Pleasant Valley Ln 75080 469-752-0000
Marilyn Carruthers, prin. Fax 752-0001
Miller ES 700/PK-5
5651 Coventry Dr 75082 469-752-2700
Jennifer Bero, prin. Fax 752-2701
Schell ES 600/K-5
5301 E Renner Rd 75082 469-752-6600
Susan Dantzler, prin. Fax 752-6601
Stinson ES 800/K-5
4201 Greenfield Dr 75082 469-752-3400
Barbara Salamone, prin. Fax 752-3401

Richardson ISD 31,800/PK-12
400 S Greenville Ave 75081 469-593-0000
Dr. Carolyn Bukhair, supt. Fax 593-0402
www.risd.org
Arapaho Classical Magnet S 500/K-6
1300 Cypress Dr 75080 469-593-6400
Nelwyn Shows, prin. Fax 593-6448
Canyon Creek ES 200/K-6
2100 Copper Ridge Dr 75080 469-593-6500
Beth Carstens, prin. Fax 593-6511
Dartmouth ES 300/K-6
417 Dartmouth Ln 75081 469-593-8400
Kathy Clayton, prin. Fax 593-8408
Dover ES 500/PK-6
700 Dover Dr 75080 469-593-4200
Brona Hudson, prin. Fax 593-4201
Greenwood Hills ES 400/PK-6
1313 W Shore Dr 75080 469-593-6100
Michele Zupa, prin. Fax 593-6111
Harben ES 400/PK-6
600 S Glenville Dr 75081 469-593-8800
Nicole Farrar-Myers, prin. Fax 593-8801
Math/Science/Technology Magnet ES 600/K-6
450 Abrams Rd 75081 469-593-7300
Angela Vaughan, prin. Fax 593-7301
Mohawk ES 300/K-6
1500 Mimosa Dr 75080 469-593-6600
Billie Snow, prin. Fax 593-6610
Northrich ES 500/PK-6
1301 Custer Rd 75080 469-593-6200
La'shon Easter, prin. Fax 593-6201
Prairie Creek ES 200/K-6
2120 E Prairie Creek Dr 75080 469-593-6300
Kyle Stuard, prin. Fax 593-6308
Richardson Heights ES 400/PK-6
101 N Floyd Rd 75080 469-593-4400
Jenny Lanier, prin. Fax 593-4401
Richardson Terrace ES 500/PK-6
300 N Dorothy Dr 75081 469-593-8700
Sharon Newman, prin. Fax 593-8781
Richland ES 600/PK-6
550 Park Bend Dr 75081 469-593-4650
Gregory Gaston, prin. Fax 593-4654
Springridge ES 400/PK-6
1801 E Spring Valley Rd 75081 469-593-8600
Charis Hunt, prin. Fax 593-8603
Twain ES 400/PK-6
1200 Larkspur Dr 75081 469-593-4800
Carmen Casamayor-Ryan, prin. Fax 593-4799
Yale ES 500/K-6
1900 E Collins Blvd 75081 469-593-8300
Stan Crawford, prin. Fax 593-8362
Other Schools – See Dallas, Garland

Canyon Creek Christian Academy 500/PK-12
2800 Custer Pkwy 75080 972-231-4890
Andy Wright, hdmstr. Fax 234-8414
North Dallas Adventist Academy 100/PK-6
1201 W Belt Line Rd 75080 972-238-1183
Melonie Wolfe, prin. Fax 644-3488
St. Joseph S, 600 S Jupiter Rd 75081 300/K-8
Phil Riley, prin. 972-234-4679
St. Paul the Apostle S 400/PK-8
720 S Floyd Rd 75080 972-235-3263
Carol Regeci, prin. Fax 690-1542

Richland Hills, Tarrant, Pop. 8,047
Birdville ISD
Supt. — See Haltom City
Binion ES 600/PK-5
7400 Glenview Dr 76180 817-547-1800
Paul Andreason, prin. Fax 595-5111
Richland ES 400/PK-5
3250 Scruggs Park Dr 76118 817-547-2000
Dee Dee Peacock, prin. Fax 595-5110
Richland MS 500/6-8
7400 Hovenkamp Ave 76118 817-547-4400
Cheri Sizemore, prin. Fax 595-5139

St. John the Apostle S 300/PK-8
7421 Glenview Dr 76180 817-284-2228
Dr. Cynthia Cummins, prin. Fax 284-1800

Richland Springs, San Saba, Pop. 340
Richland Springs ISD 200/K-12
700 W Coyote Trl 76871 325-452-3524
Travis Winn, supt. Fax 452-3230
www.rscoyotes.net
Richland Springs S 200/K-12
700 W Coyote Trl 76871 325-452-3434
Don Fowler, prin. Fax 452-3580

Richmond, Fort Bend, Pop. 13,262
Fort Bend ISD
Supt. — See Sugar Land
Crockett MS 1,200/6-8
19001 Beechnut St, 281-634-6380
Catherine O'Brien, prin. Fax 327-6380
Jordan ES 900/K-5
17800 W Oaks Village Dr, 281-634-2800
Dr. Yvette Blake, prin. Fax 634-2801
Oakland ES 800/K-5
4455 Waterside Estates Dr 77406 281-634-3730
Barbara Herrington, prin. Fax 634-3738
Pecan Grove ES 600/K-5
3330 Old South Dr 77406 281-634-4800
Sandra Campos, prin. Fax 634-4814

Lamar Consolidated ISD
Supt. — See Rosenberg
Austin ES 600/K-5
1630 Pitts Rd 77406 832-223-1000
Bud Whileyman, prin. Fax 223-1001
Briscoe JHS 1,400/6-8
4300 FM 723 Rd 77406 832-223-4000
Mike Semmler, prin. Fax 223-4001
Frost ES 900/PK-5
3306 Skinner Ln 77406 832-223-1500
Shannon Hood, prin. Fax 223-1501
Hutchison ES 600/PK-5
3602 Ransom Rd 77469 832-223-1700
Eric Nicholie, prin. Fax 223-1701
Long ES 500/PK-5
907 Main St 77469 832-223-1900
Vicki Stevenson, prin. Fax 223-1901
McNeill ES PK-5
7300 S Mason Rd, 832-223-2800
Ken Davis, prin. Fax 223-2801
Meyer ES 600/PK-5
1930 J Meyer Rd 77469 832-223-2000
Lisa McKey, prin. Fax 223-2001
Pink ES 600/PK-5
1001 Collins Rd 77469 832-223-2100
Chandra Woods, prin. Fax 223-2101
Seguin ES 300/PK-5
605 Mabel St 77469 832-223-2200
Teresa Neinast, prin. Fax 223-2201
Smith ES 600/PK-5
2014 Lamar Dr 77469 832-223-2300
Mark Melendez, prin. Fax 223-2301
Velasquez ES 600/PK-5
402 Macek Rd 77469 832-223-2600
Beth Dow, prin. Fax 223-2601
Williams ES 400/PK-5
5111 FM 762 Rd 77469 832-223-2700
Holly Haynes, prin. Fax 223-2701

Calvary Episcopal S 300/PK-12
1201 Austin St 77469 281-342-3161
Malcolm Smith, dir. Fax 232-9449

Richwood, Brazoria, Pop. 3,267
Brazosport ISD
Supt. — See Clute
Polk ES 500/PK-4
600 Audubon Woods Dr, Clute TX 77531
979-730-7200
Cindy Deska, prin. Fax 266-2478

Our Lady Queen of Peace S 300/PK-8
1600 Highway 2004, Clute TX 77531 979-265-3909
Debra Kyle, prin. Fax 265-9780

Riesel, McLennan, Pop. 1,004
Riesel ISD 600/PK-12
600 E Frederick St 76682 254-896-6411
Steve Clugston, supt. Fax 896-2981
www.rieselisd.org
Foster ES 300/PK-6
200 Williams 76682 254-896-2297
Rick Ford, prin. Fax 896-2319

Ringgold, Montague
Gold-Burg ISD
Supt. — See Bowie
Ringgold ES 50/K-5
PO Box 130 76261 940-934-6249
Cassie Freeman, prin. Fax 934-6227

Rio Grande City, Starr, Pop. 13,651
Rio Grande City ISD 9,500/PK-12
1 S Fort Ringgold St 78582 956-716-6702
Roel Gonzalez, supt. Fax 487-8506
www.rgccisd.org/
Alto Bonito ES 700/PK-5
753 N FM 2360 78582 956-487-6295
Adeline Cantu, prin. Fax 487-5755
Grulla ES 600/PK-5
433 Old Military Rd 78582 956-487-3306
Leticia Lopez, prin. Fax 716-8615
Guerra ES 800/PK-5
1600 W Main St 78582 956-716-6982
Virginia Gonzalez, prin. Fax 487-1046
Hinojosa ES 500/PK-5
2448 Embassy St 78582 956-487-3710
Olga Smedley, prin. Fax 487-4942
La Union ES 500/PK-5
6300 NE Highway 83 78582 956-487-3404
Paul Doyno, prin. Fax 487-4076
North Grammar ES 400/K-5
1400 N Lopez St 78582 956-716-6917
Ricardo Saenz, prin. Fax 488-2081
Ringgold ES 400/PK-5
1 S Fort Ringgold St 78582 956-716-6929
Elena Olivarez, prin. Fax 716-6930
Ringgold MS 1,500/6-8
1 S Fort Ringgold St 78582 956-716-6851
Adolfo Pena, prin. Fax 716-6807
Sanchez ES 700/PK-5
2801 W Eisenhower St 78582 956-487-7095
Cynthia Bazan, prin. Fax 487-7133
Veterans MS 6-8
2700 W Eisenhower St 78582 956-488-0252
Joel Trigo, prin. Fax 488-0261
Other Schools – See Grulla

Immaculate Conception S 200/PK-8
305 N Britton Ave 78582 956-487-2558
Rubirita Urbina, prin. Fax 487-6478

Rio Hondo, Cameron, Pop. 2,082
Rio Hondo ISD 2,300/PK-12
215 W Colorado St 78583 956-748-1000
Anneliese McMinn, supt. Fax 748-1038
www.riohondoisd.net
Rio Hondo ES 700/PK-2
215 W Colorado St 78583 956-748-1050
Juan Montez, prin. Fax 748-1054
Rio Hondo IS 500/3-5
215 W Colorado St 78583 956-748-1100
Annette Jaramillo, prin. Fax 748-1104
Rio Hondo JHS 500/6-8
215 W Colorado St 78583 956-748-1150
Ida Stevens, prin. Fax 748-1168

Rio Vista, Johnson, Pop. 728
Rio Vista ISD 900/PK-12
PO Box 369 76093 817-373-2241
Dr. Rock McNulty, supt. Fax 373-2076
www.rvisd.net
Rio Vista ES 400/PK-4
PO Box 369 76093 817-373-2151
Chris Nichols, prin. Fax 373-3042
Rio Vista MS 300/5-8
PO Box 369 76093 817-373-2009
Gary Peacock, prin. Fax 373-3046

Rising Star, Eastland, Pop. 842
Rising Star ISD 300/PK-12
PO Box 37 76471 254-643-2717
Dr. Max Thompson, supt. Fax 643-1922
www.risingstarisd.com/
Rising Star ES 100/PK-6
PO Box 37 76471 254-643-2431
Barbara Long, prin. Fax 643-1002

Riviera, Kleberg
Riviera ISD 500/PK-12
203 Seahawk Dr 78379 361-296-3101
Ernest Havner, supt. Fax 296-3108
www.rivieraisd.esc2.net
De La Paz MS 100/6-8
203 Seahawk Dr 78379 361-296-3610
Josephine Smith, prin. Fax 296-3890
Nanny ES 200/PK-5
203 Seahawk Dr 78379 361-296-3603
Rosalinda Trevino, prin. Fax 296-3461

Roanoke, Denton, Pop. 3,518
Northwest ISD
Supt. — See Justin
Hughes ES 700/K-5
13824 Lost Spurs Rd 76262 817-698-1900
Kim Caley, prin. Fax 698-1918
Roanoke ES 500/PK-5
606 N Walnut St 76262 817-215-0650
Deborah Merki, prin. Fax 215-0670

Robert Lee, Coke, Pop. 1,070
Robert Lee ISD 300/PK-12
1323 W Hamilton St 76945 325-453-4555
Aaron Hood, supt. Fax 453-2326
www.rlisd.net
Robert Lee ES 100/PK-6
1323 W Hamilton St 76945 325-453-4557
Roger Henderson, prin. Fax 453-2326

Robinson, McLennan, Pop. 9,062
Robinson ISD 2,200/PK-12
500 W Lyndale Ave 76706 254-662-0194
Micheal Hope, supt. Fax 662-0215
www.robinson.k12.tx.us
Robinson ES 300/2-3
500 W Lyndale Ave 76706 254-662-5000
Tamara Roznos, prin. Fax 662-3140
Robinson IS 300/4-5
500 W Lyndale Ave 76706 254-642-6113
Barry Gann, prin. Fax 662-6183
Robinson JHS 500/6-8
500 W Lyndale Ave 76706 254-662-3843
Lynn Ford, prin. Fax 662-1845
Robinson PS 300/PK-1
500 W Lyndale Ave 76706 254-662-0251
Craig Cox, prin. Fax 662-3361

Robstown, Nueces, Pop. 12,484
Bishop Consolidated ISD
Supt. — See Bishop
Petronila ES 100/PK-5
2391 County Road 67 78380 361-387-2834
Rick Gutierrez, prin. Fax 767-0429

Robstown ISD 3,600/PK-12
801 N 1st St 78380 361-767-6600
Dr. Roberto Garcia, supt. Fax 387-6311
www.robstownisd.org/
Lotspeich ES 300/PK-4
1000 Ruben Chavez Rd 78380 361-767-6655
Norma Castaneda, prin. Fax 767-6655
Martin ES 400/3-4
701 N 1st St 78380 361-767-6670
Laura Cueva, prin. Fax 767-6670
Ortiz IS 400/5-6
208 E Avenue H 78380 361-767-6662
Esmeralda Limon, prin. Fax 767-6662
Salazar ES 700/PK-2
400 W Ligustrum Blvd 78380 361-767-6641
Robin Pesek, prin. Fax 767-6641
San Pedro ES 300/PK-4
800 W Avenue D 78380 361-767-6648
Terry Castaneda, prin. Fax 767-6648
Seale JHS 500/7-8
401 E Avenue G 78380 361-767-6631
Roel Lara, prin. Fax 387-0202

St. Anthony S 100/PK-8
203 Dunne Ave 78380 361-387-3814
Sr. Paz Aribon, prin. Fax 387-3814

Roby, Fisher, Pop. 638
Roby Consolidated ISD 300/PK-12
PO Box 519 79543 325-776-2222
David Hale, supt. Fax 776-2823
www.roby.esc14.net/
Roby S 200/PK-8
PO Box 519 79543 325-776-2224
Keith Kent, prin. Fax 776-3215

Rochelle, McCulloch
Rochelle ISD 200/K-12
PO Box 167 76872 325-243-5224
Steve Butler, supt. Fax 243-5283
www.rochelleisd.net
Rochelle S 200/K-12
PO Box 167 76872 325-243-5224
Norman Fryar, prin. Fax 243-5283

Rockdale, Milam, Pop. 6,048
Rockdale ISD 1,800/PK-12
PO Box 632 76567 512-430-6000
Walter Pond, supt. Fax 446-3460
www.rockdaleisd.net
Rockdale ES 800/PK-5
PO Box 632 76567 512-430-6030
Pam Kaufmann, prin. Fax 446-5229
Rockdale JHS 400/6-8
PO Box 632 76567 512-430-6100
Brent Kirkpatrick, prin. Fax 446-2597

Rockport, Aransas, Pop. 9,041
Aransas County ISD 3,200/PK-12
PO Box 907 78381 361-790-2212
Joseph Patek, supt. Fax 790-2077
www.acisd.org
Little Bay PS 300/PK-K
PO Box 907 78381 361-790-2000
Kathy Stephenson, prin. Fax 790-2245
Live Oak 1-3 Learning Center 700/1-3
PO Box 907 78381 361-790-2260
Patricia Nelson, prin. Fax 790-2207
Rockport-Fulton MS 800/6-8
PO Box 907 78381 361-790-2230
Betty Williams, prin. Fax 790-2030
Other Schools – See Fulton

Coastal Oaks Christian S 50/PK-6
2002 FM 3036 78382 361-790-9597
Brenda Whitaker, dir. Fax 729-4481
Sacred Heart S 200/PK-5
111 N Church St 78382 361-729-2672
Katherine Barnes, prin. Fax 729-9382

Rocksprings, Edwards, Pop. 1,181
Rocksprings ISD 300/PK-12
PO Box 157 78880 830-683-4137
Ms. Henri Gearing, supt. Fax 683-4141
www.rockspringsisd.net
Rocksprings S 200/PK-8
PO Box 157 78880 830-683-2140
John Cook, prin. Fax 683-4141

Rockwall, Rockwall, Pop. 29,354
Rockwall ISD 13,500/PK-12
1050 Williams St 75087 972-771-0605
Dr. Gene Burton, supt. Fax 771-2637
www.rockwallisd.com
Cain MS 1,000/7-8
6620 FM 3097 75032 972-772-1170
Jason Johnston, prin. Fax 772-2414
Dobbs ES 500/K-6
101 S Clark St 75087 972-771-5232
Teresa Twedell, prin. Fax 772-1145
Hartman ES 700/PK-6
1325 Petaluma Dr 75087 972-772-2080
Rebecca Reidling, prin. Fax 772-5794
Hays ES 600/PK-6
1880 Tannerson Dr 75087 469-698-2800
Amy Anderson, prin. Fax 698-2809
Jones ES 800/PK-6
2051 Trail Gln 75032 972-772-1070
Angela Marcellus, prin. Fax 772-5789
Pullen ES 700/K-6
6492 FM 3097 75032 972-772-1177
J. Renee Demianovich, prin. Fax 772-2424
Reinhardt ES 400/K-6
615 Highland Dr 75087 972-771-5247
Kaylene Lavene, prin. Fax 772-2097
Rochell ES 600/PK-6
899 Rochell Ct 75032 972-771-3317
Terry Peters, prin. Fax 771-0829
Shannon ES 400/PK-6
3130 Fontana Blvd 75032 469-698-2900
Dr. Katrina Hasley, prin. Fax 698-2909
Springer ES 1,300/PK-6
3025 Limestone Hill Ln 75032 972-772-7160
Mike Pitcher, prin. Fax 772-2464
Williams ES 700/K-6
350 Dalton Rd 75087 972-772-0502
Karen Aikman, prin. Fax 772-2046

Williams MS 1,000/7-8
625 E FM 552 75087 972-771-8313
Billy Pringle, prin. Fax 772-2033
Other Schools – See Heath, Rowlett

Royse City ISD
Supt. — See Royse City
Vernon ES PK-4
100 Miss May Ave 75087 972-635-5006
Paula Walker, prin. Fax 722-8577

Heritage Christian Academy 200/PK-12
1408 S Goliad St 75087 972-772-3003
Dr. Ron Taylor, hdmstr. Fax 772-3770

Rogers, Bell, Pop. 1,102
Rogers ISD 800/PK-12
1 Eagle Dr 76569 254-642-3802
Katie Ryan, supt. Fax 642-3851
www.rogers.k12.tx.us
Rogers ES 400/PK-5
1 Eagle Dr 76569 254-642-3250
Garrett Layne, prin. Fax 642-3145
Rogers MS 200/6-8
1 Eagle Dr 76569 254-642-3011
Genie Allison, prin. Fax 642-0033

Roma, Starr, Pop. 10,900
Roma ISD 5,500/PK-12
PO Box 187 78584 956-849-1377
Jesus Guerra, supt. Fax 849-3118
www.romaisd.com/
Barrera ES 600/K-5
PO Box 187 78584 956-486-2475
Olga Gonzalez, prin. Fax 486-2474
Barrera MS 6-8
PO Box 187 78584 956-849-2341
Carlos Gonzalez, prin. Fax 549-2190
Canavan S 400/PK-K
PO Box 187 78584 956-849-1717
Hortadelia Barrera, prin. Fax 849-3854
Escobar ES 700/K-5
PO Box 187 78584 956-849-4800
Ruben Gonzalez, prin. Fax 849-4566
Roma MS 1,000/6-8
PO Box 187 78584 956-849-1434
Teresa Ramirez, prin. Fax 849-1895
Saenz ES K-5
PO Box 187 78584 956-849-7230
Yadira Diaz, prin. Fax 849-7250
Scott ES 600/K-5
PO Box 187 78584 956-849-1175
Diana Salinas, prin. Fax 849-7274
Vera ES 600/K-5
PO Box 187 78584 956-849-4552
Yvonne Reyes, prin. Fax 849-1118

Ropesville, Hockley, Pop. 524
Ropes ISD 300/PK-12
304 Ranch Rd 79358 806-562-4031
Gary Lehnen, supt. Fax 562-4059
www.ropesisd.com/
Ropes S 300/PK-12
304 Ranch Rd 79358 806-562-4031
Joel Willmon, prin. Fax 562-4059

Roscoe, Nolan, Pop. 1,273
Highland ISD 200/PK-12
6625 FM 608 79545 325-766-3652
Guy Nelson, supt. Fax 766-2281
www.highland.esc14.net/
Highland S 200/PK-12
6625 FM 608 79545 325-766-3652
Duane Hyde, prin. Fax 766-3869

Roscoe ISD 300/PK-12
PO Box 579 79545 325-766-3629
Kim Alexander, supt. Fax 766-3138
www.roscoe.esc14.net
Roscoe ES 100/PK-6
PO Box 129 79545 325-766-3323
Andrew Wilson, prin. Fax 766-3658

Rosebud, Falls, Pop. 1,394
Rosebud-Lott ISD
Supt. — See Lott
Rosebud PS 100/PK-2
PO Box 478 76570 254-583-7965
Boyd Rice, prin. Fax 583-2642

Rosenberg, Fort Bend, Pop. 30,322
Lamar Consolidated ISD 20,700/PK-12
3911 Avenue I 77471 832-223-0110
Dr. Thomas Randle, supt. Fax 223-0111
www.lcisd.org
Bowie ES 600/PK-5
2304 Bamore Rd 77471 832-223-1200
Rick Amick, prin. Fax 223-1201
George JHS 800/7-8
4601 Airport Ave 77471 832-223-3600
Kelly Waters, prin. Fax 223-3601
Jackson ES 400/PK-5
301 3rd St 77471 832-223-1800
Helen Morgan, prin. Fax 223-1801
Lamar JHS 1,100/7-8
4814 Mustang Ave 77471 832-223-3200
Victoria Bedo, prin. Fax 223-3201
Navarro MS 400/6-6
4700 Avenue N 77471 832-223-3700
Frances Hester, prin. Fax 223-3701
Ray ES 700/PK-5
2611 Avenue N 77471 832-223-2400
Diane Parks, prin. Fax 223-2401
Travis ES 700/PK-5
2700 Avenue K 77471 832-223-2500
Kevin Winter, prin. Fax 223-2501
Wertheimer MS 6-6
4240 FM 723 Rd 77471 832-223-4100
Irma Nurre, prin. Fax 223-4101
Wessendorff MS 500/6-6
5201 Mustang Ave 77471 832-223-3300
Diana Freudensprung, prin. Fax 223-3301
Other Schools – See Beasley, Fulshear, Richmond, Sugar Land

Holy Rosary S 200/PK-8
1408 James St 77471 281-342-5813
Nancy Moore, prin. Fax 344-1107
Living Water Christian S 100/PK-8
4808 Airport Ave 77471 281-238-8946
Betty Jo Frank, admin. Fax 342-9951

Rotan, Fisher, Pop. 1,486
Rotan ISD 300/PK-12
102 N McKinley Ave 79546 325-735-2332
Kent Ruffin, supt. Fax 735-2686
www.rotan.org
Rotan ES 100/PK-4
102 N McKinley Ave 79546 325-735-3182
David Hargrove, prin. Fax 735-2686
Rotan JHS 100/5-8
102 N McKinley Ave 79546 325-735-3162
Mickey Early, prin. Fax 735-2686

Round Rock, Williamson, Pop. 86,316
Hutto ISD
Supt. — See Hutto
Veterans Hill ES PK-5
555 Limmer Loop, 512-759-3030
Michele Bischoffberger, prin. Fax 759-3980

Pflugerville ISD
Supt. — See Pflugerville
Caldwell ES 700/PK-5
1718 Picadilly Dr 78664 512-594-6400
Sonya Collins, prin. Fax 594-6405

Round Rock ISD 39,000/PK-12
1311 Round Rock Ave 78681 512-464-5000
Jesus Chavez Ph.D., supt. Fax 464-5090
www.roundrockisd.org
Berkman ES 600/PK-5
400 W Anderson Ave 78664 512-464-8250
Trana Allen, prin. Fax 464-8315
Blackland Prairie ES 1,100/PK-5
2005 Via Sonoma Dr, 512-424-8600
MarySue Hildebrand, prin. Fax 424-8690
Bluebonnet ES 600/PK-5
1010 Chisholm Valley Dr 78681 512-428-7700
Lucy McVey, prin. Fax 428-7790
Brushy Creek ES 800/PK-5
3800 Stonebridge Dr 78681 512-428-3000
Barry Ryan, prin. Fax 428-3080
Cactus Ranch ES 1,100/K-5
2901 Goldenoak Cir 78681 512-424-8000
Vicki Crain, prin. Fax 424-8090
Caldwell Heights ES 600/PK-5
4010 Eagles Nest St, 512-428-7300
Amanda Estes, prin. Fax 428-7390
Callison ES K-5
1750 Thompson Trl 78664 512-704-0700
Elizabeth Sims, prin. Fax 704-0790
Chisholm Trail MS 1,000/6-8
500 Oakridge Dr 78681 512-428-2500
Robert Sormani, prin. Fax 428-2629
Deep Wood ES 400/K-5
705 Saint Williams Ave 78681 512-464-4400
Meredith Perkins, prin. Fax 464-4494
Double File Trail ES 900/PK-5
2400 Chandler Creek Blvd, 512-428-7400
Abigail Duffy, prin. Fax 428-7490
Fern Bluff ES 900/PK-5
17815 Park Valley Dr 78681 512-428-2100
Dr. Elizabeth Wilson, prin. Fax 428-2160
Forest Creek ES 1,100/PK-5
3505 Forest Creek Dr 78664 512-464-5350
Sheri Lehnick, prin. Fax 464-5430
Fulkes MS 700/6-8
300 W Anderson Ave 78664 512-428-3100
Nancy Guererro, prin. Fax 428-3240
Gattis ES 800/PK-5
2920 Round Rock Ranch Blvd, 512-428-2000
Jennifer Lucas, prin. Fax 428-2065
Great Oaks ES 1,000/PK-5
16455 S Great Oaks Dr 78681 512-464-6850
Jana Stowe, prin. Fax 464-6930
Hopewell MS 1,500/6-8
1535 Gulf Way, 512-464-5200
Anthony Watson, prin. Fax 464-5349
Old Town ES 800/PK-5
2200 Chaparral Dr 78681 512-428-7600
Sharon Wilkes, prin. Fax 428-7690
Ridgeview MS 1,200/6-8
2000 Via Sonoma Dr, 512-424-8400
Dr. Holly Galloway, prin. Fax 424-8540
Robertson ES 600/PK-5
1415 Bayland St 78664 512-428-3300
Patricia Ephlin, prin. Fax 428-3370
Teravista ES K-5
4419 Tera Vista Club Dr, 512-704-0500
Kristina Snow, prin. Fax 704-0590
Union Hill ES 800/PK-5
1511 Gulf Way, 512-424-8700
Julie Nelson, prin. Fax 424-8790
Voigt ES 700/PK-5
1201 Cushing Dr 78664 512-428-7500
Christine Nemetsky, prin. Fax 428-7590
Walsh MS 6-8
3850 Walsh Ranch Blvd 78681 512-704-0800
Toni Hicks, prin.
Other Schools – See Austin

Applegate Adventist Academy 50/PK-8
PO Box 729 78680 512-388-5016
Ingrid Stanley, prin.
Round Rock Christian Academy 500/PK-12
301 N Lake Creek Dr 78681 512-255-4491
Susan Owen, prin. Fax 255-6043

Round Top, Fayette, Pop. 78
Round Top - Carmine ISD
Supt. — See Carmine
Round Top - Carmine ES 100/PK-6
PO Box 6 78954 979-249-3200
Patricia Nauman, prin. Fax 249-4084

Rowena, Runnels
Olfen ISD 100/PK-8
1122 Private Road 2562 76875 325-442-4301
John King, supt. Fax 442-2133
olfen.netxv.net/
Olfen S 100/PK-8
1122 Private Road 2562 76875 325-442-4301
Cherri Franklin, prin. Fax 442-2133

Rowlett, Dallas, Pop. 53,664
Garland ISD
Supt. — See Garland
Back ES 600/K-5
7300 Bluebonnet Dr 75089 972-475-1884
Karen Jordan, prin. Fax 412-5245
Coyle MS 1,200/6-8
4500 Skyline Dr 75088 972-475-3711
Ray Merrill, prin. Fax 412-7222
Dorsey ES 700/K-5
6200 Dexham Rd 75089 972-463-5595
Debra Chisholm, prin. Fax 463-1805
Giddens-Steadham ES 800/PK-5
6200 Danridge Rd 75089 972-463-5887
Cheryl Alexander, prin. Fax 463-7147
Herfurth ES 600/K-5
7500 Miller Rd 75088 972-475-7994
Sherri Perkins, prin. Fax 475-7391
Keeley ES 900/PK-5
8700 Liberty Grove Rd 75089 972-412-2140
Dr. Penny Campbell, prin. Fax 412-7061
Liberty Grove ES 500/PK-5
10201 Liberty Grove Rd 75089 972-487-4416
Leigh Anne Hill, prin.
Pearson ES 700/PK-5
5201 Nita Pearson Dr 75088 972-463-7568
Vicki DeVantier, prin. Fax 463-7623
Rowlett ES 700/K-5
3315 Carla Dr 75088 972-475-3380
Lisa Alexander, prin. Fax 412-4485
Schrade MS 1,300/6-8
6201 Danridge Rd 75089 972-463-8790
Jim Thomas, prin. Fax 463-8793
Stephens ES 700/PK-5
3700 Cheyenne Dr 75088 972-463-5790
Dr. Michael Richey, prin. Fax 463-5794

Rockwall ISD
Supt. — See Rockwall
Cullins Lake Point ES 900/K-6
5701 Scenic Dr 75088 972-412-3070
Cory White, prin. Fax 412-7920

Rockwall Christian Academy 200/PK-12
6005 Dalrock Rd 75088 972-412-8266
Jeanne Zakem, supt. Fax 463-3746

Roxton, Lamar, Pop. 699
Roxton ISD 300/PK-12
PO Box 307 75477 903-346-3213
Dr. Kenneth Hall, supt. Fax 346-3356
www.roxtonisd.org/
Roxton ES 200/PK-6
PO Box 307 75477 903-346-3213
Todd Morrison, prin. Fax 346-3356

Royse City, Rockwall, Pop. 5,589
Royse City ISD 3,100/PK-12
PO Box 479 75189 972-635-2413
Randy Hancock, supt. Fax 635-7037
www.rcisd.org
Cherry IS 5-6
PO Box 479 75189 972-636-3301
Lloyd Blaine, prin. Fax 635-5008
Davis ES 500/PK-4
PO Box 479 75189 972-635-9549
Fax 635-2535
Fort ES 500/PK-4
PO Box 479 75189 972-636-3304
Danette Dodson, prin. Fax 635-2535
Royse City MS 600/7-8
PO Box 479 75189 972-635-9544
Jere Craighead, prin. Fax 635-2531
Scott ES 500/K-4
PO Box 479 75189 972-636-3300
Jimmy Hughes, prin. Fax 635-6503
Other Schools – See Fate, Rockwall

Rule, Haskell, Pop. 639
Rule ISD 200/PK-12
1100 Union Ave 79547 940-997-2521
David Parr, supt. Fax 997-2446
Rule S 200/PK-12
1100 Union Ave 79547 940-997-2246
Jimmy New, prin. Fax 997-2446

Runge, Karnes, Pop. 1,084
Runge ISD 300/PK-12
PO Box 158 78151 830-239-4315
Dr. Randy Ewing, supt. Fax 239-4816
www.rungeisd.org
Runge ES 200/PK-6
PO Box 158 78151 830-239-4315
Debbie Witte, prin. Fax 239-4816

Rusk, Cherokee, Pop. 5,234
Rusk ISD 2,000/PK-12
203 E 7th St 75785 903-683-5592
Dr. James Largent, supt. Fax 683-2104
www.ruskisd.net
Rusk ES 300/2-3
203 E 7th St 75785 903-683-2595
Jan Evans, prin. Fax 683-6104
Rusk IS 300/4-5
203 E 7th St 75785 903-683-1726
Carlene Clayton, prin. Fax 683-5167
Rusk JHS 400/6-8
203 E 7th St 75785 903-683-2502
John Burkhalter, prin. Fax 683-4363

Rusk PS 400/PK-1
203 E 7th St 75785 903-683-6106
Sandra Lenard, prin. Fax 683-6299

Sabinal, Uvalde, Pop. 1,656
Sabinal ISD 500/PK-12
PO Box 338 78881 830-988-2472
Richard Grill, supt. Fax 988-7151
www.sabinal.k12.tx.us
Sabinal ES 300/PK-6
PO Box 667 78881 830-988-2436
Joe Marks, prin. Fax 988-7142
Sabinal JHS 100/7-8
PO Box 338 78881 830-988-2475
Sean Johnston, prin. Fax 988-7170

Sabine Pass, Jefferson
Sabine Pass ISD 200/PK-12
PO Box 1148 77655 409-971-2321
Malcolm Nash, supt. Fax 971-2120
www.sabinepass.net
Sabine Pass S 200/PK-12
PO Box 1148 77655 409-971-2321
Kristi Heid, prin. Fax 971-2120

Sachse, Dallas, Pop. 17,009
Garland ISD
Supt. — See Garland
Armstrong ES 700/K-5
4750 Ben Davis Rd 75048 972-414-7480
Becky Ayars, prin. Fax 414-7488

Wylie ISD
Supt. — See Wylie
Cox ES 600/PK-4
7009 Woodbridge Pkwy 75048 972-429-2500
Renee Truncole, prin. Fax 429-4435
Whitt ES PK-4
7520 Woodcreek Way 75048 972-429-2560
Dr. Jon Slaten, prin. Fax 941-8564

Sadler, Grayson, Pop. 439
S & S Consolidated ISD 900/PK-12
PO Box 837 76264 903-564-6051
Robert Steeber, supt. Fax 564-3492
www.sandscisd.net
S & S Consolidated ES 400/PK-5
PO Box 837 76264 903-893-0767
Terry Martin, prin. Fax 891-9338
S & S Consolidated MS 200/6-8
PO Box 837 76264 903-564-7626
Dr. Lee Yeager, prin. Fax 564-7857

Saginaw, Tarrant, Pop. 17,701
Eagle Mtn.-Saginaw ISD
Supt. — See Fort Worth
Hafley Development Center 300/PK-PK
616 W McLeroy Blvd 76179 817-232-2071
Carol Renfro, prin. Fax 232-5126
High Country ES 800/K-5
1301 High Country Trl 76131 817-306-8007
Karen Sutton, prin. Fax 306-5852
Saginaw ES 500/K-5
301 W McLeroy Blvd 76179 817-232-0631
Jack Hamilton, prin. Fax 232-3357

Trinity Baptist Temple Academy 200/PK-12
6045 WJ Boaz Rd 76179 817-237-4255
Dr. James Godbey, supt. Fax 237-5233

Saint Jo, Montague, Pop. 969
Saint Jo ISD 300/PK-12
PO Box L 76265 940-995-2668
Larry Smith, supt. Fax 995-2026
www.saintjoisd.net
Saint Jo ES 200/PK-6
PO Box L 76265 940-995-2541
Denise Thurman, prin. Fax 995-2026

Salado, Bell, Pop. 1,970
Salado ISD 1,100/PK-12
PO Box 98 76571 254-947-5479
Billy Wiggins, supt. Fax 947-5605
www.saladoisd.org
Arnold ES 300/PK-2
PO Box 98 76571 254-947-5191
Lisa Nix, prin. Fax 947-6924
Salado IS 200/3-6
PO Box 98 76571 254-947-1700
Andrea Gonzalez, prin. Fax 947-6954
Salado JHS 200/7-8
PO Box 98 76571 254-947-6935
Joelle Jenkins, prin. Fax 947-6934

Saltillo, Hopkins
Saltillo ISD 300/PK-12
PO Box 269 75478 903-537-2386
Paul Jones, supt. Fax 537-2191
www.saltilloisd.net/
Saltillo S 300/PK-12
PO Box 269 75478 903-537-2386
Ben Tyler, prin. Fax 537-2191

Samnorwood, Collingsworth
Samnorwood ISD 100/PK-12
PO Box 765 79077 806-256-2039
Shawn Read, supt. Fax 256-3974
www.samnorwoodisd.net/
Samnorwood S 100/PK-12
PO Box 765 79077 806-256-2039
Fax 256-3974

San Angelo, Tom Green, Pop. 88,014
Grape Creek ISD 1,100/PK-12
8207 US Highway 87 N 76901 325-658-7823
Frank Walter, supt. Fax 658-8719
www.grapecreek.org
Grape Creek ES 500/PK-5
8207 US Highway 87 N 76901 325-655-1735
MaryAnn Waldrop, prin. Fax 658-2623
Grape Creek MS 300/6-8
8207 US Highway 87 N 76901 325-655-1735
Greg Baucom, prin. Fax 657-2997

San Angelo ISD 14,100/PK-12
1621 University Ave 76904 325-947-3700
Dr. Carol Bonds, supt. Fax 947-3771
www.saisd.org
Alta Loma ES 300/PK-5
1700 N Garfield St 76901 325-947-3914
Debra Ledford, prin. Fax 947-3952
Austin ES 500/PK-5
700 N Van Buren St 76901 325-659-3636
Alisen Sanders, prin. Fax 657-4089
Belaire ES 300/PK-5
700 Stephen St 76905 325-659-3639
Tia Agan, prin. Fax 657-4093
Blackshear Preschool 100/PK-PK
2223 Brown St 76903 325-659-3642
Robin Harmon, prin. Fax 658-7442
Bonham ES 500/K-5
4630 Southland Blvd 76904 325-947-3917
Cindy Lee, prin. Fax 947-3945
Bowie ES 500/K-5
3700 Forest Trl 76904 325-947-3921
Myra Stewart, prin. Fax 947-3947
Bradford ES 400/K-5
1202 E 22nd St 76903 325-659-3645
Rachel Taunton, prin. Fax 659-3692
Crockett ES 400/K-5
2104 Johnson Ave 76904 325-947-3925
Heidi Wierzowiecki, prin. Fax 947-3951
Day Preschool 200/PK-PK
3026 N Oakes St 76903 325-481-3395
Robin Harmon, prin.
Fannin ES 400/K-5
1702 Wilson St 76901 325-947-3930
Debbie Conn, prin. Fax 947-3944
Fort Concho ES 300/K-5
310 E Washington Dr 76903 325-659-3654
Lori Barton, prin. Fax 657-4083
Glenmore ES 400/PK-5
323 Penrose St 76903 325-659-3657
Cheri Braden, prin. Fax 657-4086
Glenn MS 800/6-8
2201 University Ave 76904 325-947-3841
Mary Stinnett, prin. Fax 947-3847
Goliad ES 600/PK-5
3902 Goliad St 76903 325-659-3660
Ginger Luther, prin. Fax 657-4097
Holiman ES 300/PK-5
1900 Ricks Dr 76905 325-659-3663
Judy Bragg, prin. Fax 659-3696
Lamar ES 600/K-5
3444 School House Dr 76904 325-947-3900
Lynn Schniers, prin. Fax 947-3901
Lee MS 700/6-8
2500 Sherwood Way 76901 325-947-3871
Elaine Stribling, prin. Fax 947-3890
Lincoln MS 900/6-8
255 E 50th St 76903 325-659-3550
Sue Taylor, prin. Fax 659-3559
McGill ES 300/PK-5
201 Millspaugh St 76901 325-947-3934
Connie Williams, prin. Fax 947-3946
Reagan ES 400/PK-5
1600 Volney St 76903 325-659-3666
Karen Clark, prin. Fax 657-4096
Rio Vista Preschool 200/PK-PK
2800 Ben Ficklin Rd 76903 325-659-3669
Robin Harmon, prin. Fax 659-3693
San Jacinto ES 400/PK-5
800 Spaulding St 76903 325-659-3675
Mary McGann, prin. Fax 657-4092
Santa Rita ES 400/K-5
615 S Madison St 76901 325-659-3672
Kay Scott, prin. Fax 657-4094

Angelo Catholic S 100/PK-6
19 S Oakes St 76903 325-655-3325
Lucy Thomas, prin. Fax 655-1286
Cornerstone Christian S 200/PK-12
1502 N Jefferson St 76901 325-655-3439
Grady Roe, prin. Fax 658-8998
Trinity Lutheran S 200/PK-9
3516 YMCA Dr 76904 325-947-1275
Ron Fritsche, prin. Fax 947-1377

San Antonio, Bexar, Pop. 1,256,509
Alamo Heights ISD 4,500/PK-12
7101 Broadway St 78209 210-824-2483
Dr. Kevin Brown, supt. Fax 822-2221
www.ahisd.net
Alamo Heights JHS 1,100/6-8
7607 N New Braunfels Ave 78209 210-824-3231
Stephanie Kershner, prin. Fax 832-5825
Cambridge ES 800/1-5
1001 Townsend Ave 78209 210-822-3611
David MacRoberts, prin. Fax 832-5840
Howard K 400/PK-K
7800 Broadway St 78209 210-832-5900
Wilma Sosa, prin. Fax 832-5898
Woodridge ES 800/1-5
100 Woodridge Dr 78209 210-826-8021
Dr. Cordell Jones, prin. Fax 832-5871

Comal ISD
Supt. — See New Braunfels
Specht ES 900/PK-5
25815 Overlook Pkwy 78260 830-885-1500
Linda Harlan, prin. Fax 885-1501
Timberwood Park ES PK-5
26715 S Glenrose Rd 78260 830-885-8500
Dr. Sean Maika, prin. Fax 885-8501

East Central ISD 8,500/PK-12
6634 New Sulphur Springs Rd 78263 210-648-7861
Gary Patterson, supt. Fax 648-0931
www.ecisd.net/
East Central Development Center 300/PK-PK
12271 Donop Rd 78223 210-633-3020
Debbie Grams, prin. Fax 633-0323
East Central Heritage MS 1,000/6-8
8004 New Sulphur Springs Rd 78263 210-648-4546
Robert Kosub, prin. Fax 648-3501
Glenn ES 500/K-3
7284 FM 1628 78263 210-649-2021
Debbie Santos, prin. Fax 649-1226
Harmony ES 500/K-3
10625 Green Lake St 78223 210-633-0231
Debbie Grams, prin. Fax 633-2176
Highland Forest ES 600/K-3
3736 SE Military Dr 78223 210-333-7385
Sharon Schaefer, prin. Fax 333-4069
Legacy MS 1,000/6-8
5903 SE Loop 410 78222 210-648-3118
Manuel Ornelas, prin. Fax 648-1068
Oak Crest IS 600/4-5
7806 New Sulphur Springs Rd 78263 210-648-9484
Damon Trainer, prin. Fax 648-6967
Pecan Valley ES 400/PK-3
3966 E Southcross Blvd 78222 210-333-1230
Dr. Rona Halbreich, prin. Fax 359-1352
Salado IS 700/4-5
3602 S WW White Rd 78222 210-648-3310
Melodye Pieniazek, prin. Fax 359-1245
Sinclair ES 500/K-3
6126 Sinclair Rd 78222 210-648-4620
Janice Williams, prin. Fax 648-0422

Edgewood ISD 11,900/PK-12
5358 W Commerce St 78237 210-444-4500
Dr. Elizabeth Garza, supt. Fax 444-4602
www.eisd.net/
Brentwood MS 600/6-8
1626 Thompson Pl 78226 210-444-7675
Gustavo Cordova, prin. Fax 444-7698
Cenizo Park ES 500/PK-5
4415 Monterey St 78237 210-444-7850
Gloria Martinez, prin. Fax 444-7873
Coronado/Escobar ES 600/PK-5
5622 W Durango Blvd 78237 210-444-7875
Bertha Prieto, prin. Fax 444-7898
Garcia MS 600/6-8
3306 Ruiz St 78228 210-444-8075
Sharon Luce, prin. Fax 444-8098
Gardendale ES 600/PK-5
1731 Athel Ave 78237 210-444-8150
Eva Del Bosque, prin. Fax 444-8173
Gonzalez ES 500/PK-5
2803 Castroville Rd 78237 210-444-7800
Rosemary Barrera, prin. Fax 444-7823
Johnson ES 600/PK-5
6515 W Commerce St 78227 210-444-8175
Maria Inco, prin. Fax 444-8198
Las Palmas ES 600/K-5
115 Las Palmas Dr 78237 210-444-8050
Eliseo Rodriguez, prin. Fax 444-8073
Loma Park ES 900/PK-5
400 Aurora Dr 78228 210-444-8250
Alicia Garcia, prin. Fax 444-8273
Perales ES 500/PK-5
1507 Ceralvo St 78237 210-444-8350
Alicia Garcia, prin. Fax 444-8373
Roosevelt ES 600/PK-5
3823 Fortuna Ct 78237 210-444-8375
Pamela Reece, prin. Fax 444-8398
Stafford ES 600/PK-5
611 SW 36th St 78237 210-433-8400
Sheila Ballagh, prin. Fax 444-8423
Truman MS 400/6-8
1018 NW 34th St 78228 210-444-8425
Fax 444-8448
Winston ES 600/PK-5
2525 S General Mcmullen Dr 78226 210-444-8450
Fax 444-8473
Wrenn MS 700/6-8
627 S Acme Rd 78237 210-444-8475
Michael Rodriguez, prin. Fax 444-8498

Fort Sam Houston ISD 1,200/PK-12
1902 Winans Rd 78234 210-368-8701
Dr. Gail Siller, supt. Fax 368-8741
www.fshisd.net/
Ft. Sam Houston ES 700/PK-5
3370 Nursery Rd 78234 210-368-8800
Tonya Hyde, prin. Fax 368-8801

Harlandale ISD 12,000/PK-12
102 Genevieve Dr 78214 210-989-4300
Robert Jaklich, supt. Fax 921-4334
www.harlandale.net
Adams ES 700/PK-5
135 E Southcross Blvd 78214 210-989-2800
Rita Rodriguez-Uresti, prin. Fax 977-1407
Bellaire ES 600/PK-5
142 E Amber St 78221 210-989-2850
Elias Hernandez, prin. Fax 977-1421
Bell ES 500/PK-5
2717 Pleasanton Rd 78221 210-989-2900
Gaila Booth, prin. Fax 977-1438
Collier ES 500/PK-5
834 W Southcross Blvd 78211 210-989-2950
Velma Perez, prin. Fax 977-1452
Columbia Heights ES 400/PK-5
1610 Fitch St 78211 210-989-3000
Priscilla Lighthall, prin. Fax 977-1466
Gilbert ES 500/PK-5
931 E Southcross Blvd 78214 210-989-3050
Rosemary Cooremans, prin. Fax 977-1496
Gillette ES 500/PK-5
625 Gillette Blvd 78221 210-989-3100
Kathleen Morones, prin. Fax 977-1511
Harlandale MS 900/6-8
300 W Huff Ave 78214 210-921-4507
Katherine Pena, prin. Fax 977-8764
Kingsborough MS 700/6-8
422 E Ashley Rd 78221 210-989-2200
William Hall, prin. Fax 977-9463
Leal MS 800/6-8
743 W Southcross Blvd 78211 210-989-2400
Marianela Gonzalez, prin. Fax 977-1459

Morrill ES 500/PK-5
5200 S Flores St 78214 210-989-3150
Linda Aleman, prin. Fax 977-1527

Rayburn ES 400/PK-5
635 Rayburn Dr 78221 210-989-3200
Maria Tovar, prin. Fax 977-1541

Schulze ES 500/PK-5
9131 Yett Blvd 78221 210-989-3250
Buster Fisher, prin. Fax 977-1571

Stonewall/Flanders ES 700/PK-5
804 Stonewall St 78211 210-977-1610
Diane Tudyk, prin. Fax 977-1481

Vestal ES 500/PK-5
1111 W Vestal Pl 78221 210-989-3350
John Worch, prin. Fax 977-1587

Wells MS 700/6-8
422 W Hutchins Pl 78221 210-989-2600
Aracelie Bunsen, prin. Fax 923-5126

Wright ES 400/PK-5
115 E Huff Ave 78214 210-989-3400
Kathleen Stark, prin. Fax 977-1596

Judson ISD
Supt. — See Live Oak

Candlewood ES 700/PK-5
3635 Candleglenn 78244 210-662-1060
Regina Florence, prin. Fax 662-9327

Franz ES 500/PK-5
12301 Welcome Dr 78233 210-655-6241
Cindy Barnhart, prin. Fax 590-4649

Hartman ES 700/PK-5
7203 Woodlake Pkwy 78218 210-564-1520
Monica Borrego, prin. Fax 590-3096

Hopkins ES 900/PK-5
2440 Ackerman Rd 78219 210-661-1120
Martin Silverman, prin. Fax 662-9585

Kirby MS 1,000/6-8
5441 Seguin Rd 78219 210-661-1140
Kristina Vidaurri, prin. Fax 661-1195

Metzger MS 1,300/6-8
7475 Binz Engleman Rd 78244 210-662-2210
Ken Matthews, prin. Fax 662-8390

Park Village ES 600/PK-5
5855 Midcrown Dr 78218 210-653-1822
Marsha Bellinger, prin. Fax 590-4302

Paschall ES 800/PK-5
6351 Lakeview Dr 78244 210-666-4113
Jayanna Kelly, prin. Fax 666-4129

Spring Meadows ES 600/K-5
7135 Elm Trail Dr 78244 210-662-1050
Ken Harbord, prin. Fax 662-9082

Woodlake ES 800/K-5
5501 Lakebend East Dr 78244 210-661-4274
Chad Broussard, prin. Fax 662-9338

Woodlake Hills MS 1,200/6-8
6625 Woodlake Pkwy 78244 210-661-1110
Marcus Anthony, prin. Fax 666-0169

Lackland ISD 900/PK-12
2460 Kenly Ave Bldg 8265 78236 210-357-5000
Dr. David Splitek, supt. Fax 357-5050
www.lacklandisd.net/

Lackland ES 600/PK-6
2460 Kenly Ave Bldg 8265 78236 210-357-5053
Kay Norton, prin. Fax 357-5060

Medina Valley ISD
Supt. — See Castroville

Potranco ES 500/PK-5
190 County Road 381 S 78253 830-931-2243
Edward Balderas, prin. Fax 931-9575

North East ISD 61,700/PK-12
8961 Tesoro Dr 78217 210-804-7000
Dr. Richard Middleton, supt. Fax 804-7017
www.neisd.net

Bradley MS 1,300/6-8
14819 Heimer Rd 78232 210-491-8300
Justin Oxley, prin. Fax 491-8314

Bulverde Creek ES 700/K-5
3839 Canyon Pkwy 78259 210-491-8325
Sally McBee, prin. Fax 491-8333

Bush MS 1,700/6-8
1500 Evans Rd 78258 210-491-8450
Randy Hoyer, prin. Fax 491-8471

Camelot ES 600/K-5
7410 Ray Bon Dr 78218 210-564-1775
Gloria Canada, prin. Fax 564-1782

Canyon Ridge ES 1,000/K-5
20522 Stone Oak Pkwy 78258 210-482-2285
Peggy Peterson, prin. Fax 482-2293

Castle Hills ES 500/K-5
200 Lemonwood Dr 78213 210-442-0600
Lori Gerdin, prin. Fax 442-0607

Clear Spring ES 500/K-5
4311 Clear Spring Dr 78217 210-650-1575
Adam Schwab, prin. Fax 650-1582

Coker ES 800/K-5
302 Heimer Rd 78232 210-491-8400
Glennie Lecocke, prin. Fax 491-8408

Colonial Hills ES 700/K-5
2627 Kerrybrook Ct 78230 210-442-0725
Diana Montemayor, prin. Fax 442-0730

Dellview ES 500/PK-5
7235 Dewhurst Rd 78213 210-442-0775
Ivonna Gonzales, prin. Fax 442-0781

Driscoll MS 1,000/6-8
17150 Jones Maltsberger Rd 78247 210-491-6450
Michael Cardona, prin. Fax 491-6467

East Terrell Hills ES 600/PK-5
4415 Bloomdale 78218 210-564-1600
Colleen Hermes, prin. Fax 564-1604

Eisenhower MS 1,200/6-8
8231 Blanco Rd 78216 210-442-0500
Tim Miller, prin. Fax 442-0537

El Dorado ES 600/K-5
12634 El Sendero St 78233 210-650-1450
Susan Peery, prin. Fax 650-1458

Encino Park ES 1,000/PK-5
2550 Encino Rio 78259 210-497-6225
Colleen Bohrmann, prin. Fax 497-6238

Fox Run ES 800/K-5
6111 Fox Creek St 78247 210-564-1725
John Hinds, prin. Fax 564-1732

Garner MS 900/6-8
4302 Harry Wurzbach Rd 78209 210-805-5100
Donna Newman, prin. Fax 805-5138

Hardy Oak ES 900/K-5
22900 Hardy Oak Blvd 78258 210-481-4000
Sharon Newman, prin. Fax 481-4004

Harmony Hills ES 700/PK-5
10727 Memory Ln 78216 210-442-0625
Alan Rochkus, prin. Fax 442-0631

Harris MS 1,300/6-8
5300 Knollcreek 78247 210-657-8880
Peggy Clemmons, prin. Fax 657-8892

Hidden Forest ES 600/K-5
802 Silver Spruce St 78232 210-491-8425
Tamara Van Cleave, prin. Fax 491-8432

Huebner Road ES 800/PK-5
16311 Huebner Rd 78248 210-408-5525
Teresa Neuman, prin. Fax 408-5529

Jackson-Keller ES 700/K-5
1601 Jackson Keller Rd 78213 210-442-0700
Evelyn Kompier, prin. Fax 442-0706

Jackson MS 900/6-8
4538 Vance Jackson Rd 78230 210-442-0550
Brian Hurley, prin. Fax 442-0580

Krueger MS 1,100/6-8
438 Lanark Dr 78218 210-650-1350
John Smith, prin. Fax 650-1374

Larkspur ES 800/PK-5
11330 Belair Dr 78213 210-442-0675
Jerry Zapata, prin. Fax 442-0682

Long's Creek ES 900/K-5
15806 OConnor Rd 78247 210-657-8750
Richard Cantrell, prin. Fax 657-8754

Lopez MS 1,000/6-8
23103 Hardy Oak Blvd 78258 210-481-4060
Barry Lanford, prin. Fax 481-4072

Montgomery ES 500/K-5
7047 Montgomery 78239 210-564-1750
Walter Allen, prin. Fax 564-1758

Nimitz Academy 800/6-8
5426 Blanco Rd 78216 210-442-0450
Thalia Chaney, prin. Fax 442-0489

Northern Hills ES 700/K-5
13901 Higgins Rd 78217 210-650-1475
Brent Brummet, prin. Fax 650-1482

Northwood ES 400/K-5
519 Pike Rd 78209 210-805-5150
June Sharrer, prin. Fax 805-5157

Oak Grove ES 500/PK-5
3250 Nacogdoches Rd 78217 210-650-1550
Lola Folkes, prin. Fax 650-1558

Oak Meadow ES 500/PK-5
2800 Hunters Green St 78231 210-408-5500
Judy Wells, prin. Fax 408-5512

Olmos ES 700/K-5
1103 Allena Dr 78213 210-442-0650
Lesha Dalton, prin. Fax 442-0654

Redland Oaks ES 500/K-5
16650 Redland Rd 78247 210-491-8375
Mary Longloy, prin. Fax 491-8383

Regency Place ES 500/K-5
2635 E Bitters Rd 78217 210-650-1525
Susan Del Toro, prin. Fax 650-1532

Ridgeview ES 600/PK-5
8223 Mccullough Ave 78216 210-805-5200
Susan Wood, prin. Fax 805-5208

Roan Forest ES 1,000/K-5
22710 Roan Park 78259 210-481-4045
Ruth Wayne, prin. Fax 481-4053

Royal Ridge ES 700/K-5
5933 Royal Rdg 78239 210-564-1615
Comelia Black, prin. Fax 564-1620

Serna ES 600/PK-5
2569 NE Loop 410 78217 210-650-1500
Jeff Price, prin. Fax 650-1508

Stahl ES 900/K-5
5222 Stahl Rd 78247 210-564-1675
Pita Canales, prin. Fax 564-1682

Steubing Ranch ES 900/K-5
5100 Knollcreek 78247 210-650-1240
Laura Holson, prin. Fax 650-1248

Stone Oak ES 900/K-5
21045 Crescent Oaks 78258 210-497-6200
Terri Chidgey, prin. Fax 497-6204

Tejeda MS 1,300/6-8
2909 E Evans Rd 78259 210-482-2260
John Mehlbrech, prin. Fax 482-2277

Thousand Oaks ES 900/K-5
16080 Henderson Pass 78232 210-491-8350
Janet Dietel, prin. Fax 491-8358

Walzem ES 600/K-5
4618 Walzem Rd 78218 210-564-1625
Laura Huggins, prin. Fax 564-1630

West Avenue ES 400/K-5
3915 West Ave 78213 210-442-0750
Victor Herrera, prin. Fax 442-0756

Wetmore ES 1,000/K-5
3250 Thousand Oaks Dr 78247 210-481-4029
Wilbert Morgan, prin. Fax 481-4037

White MS 1,000/6-8
7800 Midcrown Dr 78218 210-650-1400
Jennifer Baadsgaard, prin. Fax 650-1443

Wilderness Oak ES 1,100/K-5
21019 Wilderness Oak 78258 210-491-8363
Jane Jensen, prin. Fax 491-8371

Wilshire ES 400/PK-5
6523 Cascade Pl 78218 210-805-5175
Carol Ketzle, prin. Fax 805-5181

Windcrest ES 500/K-5
465 Faircrest Dr 78239 210-564-1650
Jeanie Wiedenbach, prin. Fax 564-1657

Wood MS 1,000/6-8
14800 Judson Rd 78233 210-650-1300
Brenda Shelton, prin. Fax 650-1309

Woodstone ES 800/PK-5
5602 Fountainwood St 78233 210-564-1700
James Huston, prin. Fax 564-1708

Northside ISD 82,100/PK-12
5900 Evers Rd 78238 210-397-8500
Dr. John Folks, supt. Fax 706-8772
www.nisd.net

Adams Hill ES 400/PK-5
9627 Adams Hl 78245 210-397-1400
Carin Adermann, prin. Fax 678-2937

Aue ES 600/K-5
24750 Baywater Stage 78255 210-397-6750
Maricia Gregory, prin. Fax 698-4422

Boone ES 1,000/PK-5
6614 Spring Time St 78249 210-397-1450
Michella Wheat, prin. Fax 561-5143

Brauchle ES 700/PK-5
8555 Bowens Crossing St 78250 210-397-1500
Eleanor Maxwell, prin. Fax 706-7448

Braun Station ES 600/PK-5
8631 Tezel Rd 78254 210-397-1550
Jody Fries, prin. Fax 706-7463

Burke ES 800/PK-5
10111 Terra Oak 78250 210-397-1300
Annette Lopez, prin. Fax 257-1305

Cable ES 500/PK-5
1706 Pinn Rd 78227 210-397-2850
Brenda Farias, prin. Fax 678-2878

Carnahan ES K-5
6839 Babcock Rd 78249 210-397-5850
Lisa Jackson, prin. Fax 561-2050

Carson ES 600/PK-5
8151 Old Tezel Rd 78250 210-397-1100
Vickie Tschirhart, prin. Fax 257-1103

Cody ES 1,000/PK-5
10403 Dugas Dr 78245 210-397-1650
Kittiya Johnson, prin. Fax 678-2797

Colonies North ES 500/PK-5
9915 Northampton Dr 78230 210-397-1700
Sonya Kirkham, prin. Fax 561-5240

Connally MS 1,200/6-8
8661 Silent Sunrise 78250 210-397-1000
Cornelius Phelps, prin. Fax 257-1004

Coon ES 800/PK-5
3110 Timber View Dr 78251 210-397-7250
Mary Lou Mendoza, prin. Fax 706-7288

Driggers ES 600/PK-5
6901 Shadow Mist 78238 210-397-5900
Mary Cover, prin. Fax 257-4993

Elrod ES 800/PK-5
8885 Heath Circle Dr 78250 210-397-1800
Daisy Whisenant, prin. Fax 706-7493

Esparza ES 800/PK-5
5700 Hemphill Dr 78228 210-397-1850
Melva Matkin, prin. Fax 431-5843

Evers ES 700/PK-5
1715 Richland Hills Dr 78251 210-397-2550
Jessica Palomares, prin. Fax 706-7564

Fernandez ES 800/PK-5
6845 Ridgebrook St 78250 210-397-1900
Thomas Mackey, prin. Fax 706-7376

Fisher ES K-5
3430 Barrel Pass 78245 210-397-4450
Thomas Knapp, prin. Fax 366-0770

Forester ES K-5
10726 Rousseau St 78245 210-397-0200
Jeff Davenport, prin. Fax 257-1030

Galm ES 900/PK-5
1454 Saxonhill Dr 78253 210-397-1150
Ben Muir, prin. Fax 678-2863

Garcia MS 6-8
14900 Kyle Seale Pkwy 78255 210-397-8500

Glass ES 600/PK-5
519 Clearview Dr 78228 210-397-1950
Patricia Lambert, prin. Fax 431-5817

Glenn ES 700/PK-5
2385 Horal St 78227 210-397-2250
Dr. Benito Resendiz, prin. Fax 678-2891

Glenoaks ES 600/PK-5
5103 Newcome Dr 78229 210-397-2300
Janette Felder, prin. Fax 617-5452

Hatchett ES 1,000/PK-5
10700 Ingram Rd 78245 210-397-6850
Debra Pinon, prin. Fax 645-5222

Hobby MS 1,000/6-8
11843 Vance Jackson Rd 78230 210-397-6300
Tracy Tietze, prin. Fax 690-6332

Hoffman ES K-5
12118 Volunteer Pkwy 78253 210-397-8500

Howsman ES 600/PK-5
11431 Vance Jackson Rd 78230 210-397-2350
Thomas Buente, prin. Fax 561-5047

Hull ES 500/PK-5
7320 Remuda Dr 78227 210-397-0950
Ron Tatsch, prin. Fax 678-2917

Jefferson MS 6-8
10900 Shaenfield Rd 78254 210-397-3700
Kevin Kearns, prin. Fax 257-4988

Jones MS 1,100/6-8
1256 Pinn Rd 78227 210-397-2100
Wendy Reyes, prin. Fax 678-2113

Jordan MS 1,700/6-8
1725 Richland Hills Dr 78251 210-397-6150
Jennifer Alvarez, prin. Fax 523-4876

Knowlton ES 800/PK-5
9500 Timber Path 78250 210-397-2600
Gilbert Rios, prin. Fax 706-7534

Krueger ES 1,000/K-5
9900 Wildhorse Pkwy 78254 210-397-3850
LaNeil Belko, prin. Fax 257-1130

Lackland City ES 600/PK-5
101 Dumont Dr 78227 210-397-0800
Jerry Allen, prin. Fax 678-2946

Langley ES K-5
14185 Bella Vista Pl 78253 210-397-8500

Leon Springs ES 800/K-5
23881 W Interstate 10 78257 210-397-4400
Dr. Kathy Dodge-Clay, prin. Fax 698-4407

Leon Valley ES 700/PK-5
7111 Huebner Rd 78240 210-397-4650
Scott Mckenzie, prin. Fax 706-7391
Lewis ES 900/K-5
1000 Seascape 78251 210-397-2650
Sharon Browne, prin. Fax 257-3004
Linton ES 600/PK-5
2103 Oakhill Rd 78238 210-397-0750
Emilio Landeros, prin. Fax 706-7186
Locke Hill ES 800/K-5
5050 De Zavala Rd 78249 210-397-1600
Cathy Cowan, prin. Fax 561-5062
Luna MS 1,400/6-8
200 Grosenbacher Rd N 78253 210-397-5300
Lynn Pierson, prin.
May ES 800/PK-5
15707 Chase Hill Blvd 78256 210-397-2000
Kay Montgomery, prin. Fax 561-2024
McDermott ES 700/PK-5
5111 Usaa Blvd 78240 210-397-5100
Debra Tatum, prin. Fax 561-5118
Mead ES 700/K-5
3803 Midhorizon Dr 78229 210-397-1750
Rebecca Flores, prin. Fax 366-0770
Meadow Village ES 500/PK-5
1406 Meadow Way Dr 78227 210-397-0650
Evelyn Cobarruvias, prin. Fax 678-2846
Michael ES 400/PK-5
3155 Quiet Plain Dr 78245 210-397-3900
Lori Shaw, prin. Fax 645-3905
Murnin ES 700/K-5
9019 Dugas Rd 78251 210-397-4550
Debbie Patlovany, prin. Fax 366-0770
Myers ES 900/PK-5
3031 Village Pkwy 78251 210-397-6650
Ellen Sutton, prin. Fax 706-6674
Neff MS 1,000/6-8
5227 Evers Rd 78238 210-397-4100
Sylvia Wade, prin. Fax 523-4566
Nichols ES 700/K-5
9560 Braun Rd 78254 210-397-4050
Sylvia Swayne, prin. Fax 767-5951
Northwest Crossing ES 700/PK-5
10255 Dover Rdg 78250 210-397-0600
Shirley Thompson, prin. Fax 706-7546
Oak Hills Terrace ES 500/K-5
5710 Cary Grant Dr 78240 210-397-0550
Marcy Blattman, prin. Fax 706-7348
Ott ES 1,200/PK-5
100 Grosenbacher Rd N 78253 210-397-5550
Shana Hansen, prin.
Passmore ES 600/PK-5
570 Pinn Rd 78227 210-397-0500
Patricia Sanchez, prin. Fax 678-2808
Pease MS 1,200/6-8
201 Hunt Ln 78245 210-397-2950
Barry Perez, prin. Fax 678-2974
Powell ES 700/PK-5
6003 Thunder Dr 78238 210-397-0450
De'Ann Upright, prin. Fax 706-7361
Raba ES 900/PK-5
9740 Raba Dr 78251 210-397-1350
Andy Kline, prin. Fax 257-1335
Rawlinson MS 1,300/6-8
14100 Vance Jackson Rd 78249 210-397-4900
Nancy Pena, prin. Fax 767-4055
Rayburn MS 900/6-8
1400 Cedarhurst Dr 78227 210-397-2150
Eric Tobias, prin. Fax 678-2181
Rhodes ES 700/K-5
5714 N Knoll 78240 210-397-4000
Robert Lehr, prin. Fax 697-4020
Ross MS 1,000/6-8
3630 Callaghan Rd 78228 210-397-6350
Deonna Dean, prin. Fax 431-6383
Rudder MS 1,100/6-8
6558 Horn Blvd 78240 210-397-5000
Scott Zolinski, prin. Fax 561-5022
Scarborough ES PK-5
12280 Silver Pointe 78254 210-397-8000
Jeannine Keairnes, prin.
Scobee ES 700/PK-5
11223 Cedar Park 78249 210-397-0700
Kathleen Gorsche, prin. Fax 561-5076
Steubing ES 500/PK-5
11655 Braefield 78249 210-397-4350
Beverly Pantuso, prin. Fax 706-4374
Stevenson MS 1,800/6-8
8403 Tezel Rd 78254 210-397-7300
Glenda Munson, prin. Fax 706-7336
Stinson MS 1,700/6-8
13200 Skyhawk Dr 78249 210-397-3600
Willie Frantzen, prin. Fax 561-3609
Thornton ES 700/PK-5
6450 Pembroke Rd 78240 210-397-3950
Marji Gray, prin. Fax 561-5128
Timberwilde ES 700/PK-5
8838 Timberwilde St 78250 210-397-0400
Judy Rosanno, prin. Fax 706-7478
Vale MS 6-8
2120 N Ellison Dr 78251 210-397-5700
Erika Foerster, prin. Fax 257-1000
Valley Hi ES 400/PK-5
8503 Ray Ellison Blvd 78227 210-397-0350
Paula Harris, prin. Fax 678-2928
Villarreal ES 700/PK-5
2902 White Tail Dr 78228 210-397-5800
Lori Gallegos, prin. Fax 431-5809
Wanke ES 800/K-5
10419 Old Prue Rd 78249 210-397-6700
Don Van Winkle, prin. Fax 366-0770
Ward ES, 8400 Cavern Hl 78254 1,100/K-5
Sunday Nelson, prin. 210-397-6800
Westwood Terrace ES 700/PK-5
2315 Hackamore Ln 78227 210-397-0300
Levinia Lara, prin. Fax 678-2786
Zachry MS 1,500/6-8
9410 Timber Path 78250 210-397-7400
Javier Martinez, prin. Fax 706-7432

Other Schools – See Helotes, Shavano Park

San Antonio ISD 45,100/PK-12
141 Lavaca St 78210 210-299-5500
Dr. Robert Duron, supt. Fax 299-5580
www.saisd.net
Arnold ES 600/PK-5
467 Freiling 78213 210-732-4962
Kathleen St. Clair, prin. Fax 732-5192
Ball ES 500/PK-5
343 Koehler Ct 78223 210-533-1164
Cynthia Bernal, prin. Fax 533-1215
Baskin ES 600/PK-6
630 Crestview Dr 78201 210-735-5921
Betty Damiani, prin. Fax 735-5962
Beacon Hill ES 500/PK-5
1411 W Ashby Pl 78201 210-735-6511
Jose Moreno, prin. Fax 735-6683
Bowden ES 500/PK-5
515 Willow 78202 210-226-3601
Alva Ibarra, prin. Fax 226-8150
Brackenridge ES 500/PK-8
1214 Guadalupe St 78207 210-224-4916
Noemi Saldivar, prin. Fax 224-4933
Brewer ES 500/PK-6
906 Merida St 78207 210-433-2691
Lisa Barrera, prin. Fax 433-3027
Cameron Academy 400/PK-8
3635 Belgium Ln 78219 210-224-0310
Carolyn McClure, prin. Fax 224-2954
Carvajal ES 400/PK-5
225 Arizona Ave 78207 210-432-6921
Norma Cano Scarcliff, prin. Fax 432-7828
Collins Garden ES 700/PK-5
167 Harriman Pl 78204 210-226-7423
Mary Macias, prin. Fax 226-9958
Connell MS 700/6-8
400 Hot Wells Blvd 78223 210-534-6511
Theresa Salinas, prin. Fax 534-6589
Cotton ES 400/PK-5
1616 Blanco Rd 78212 210-733-8641
Lelia Bagwell, prin. Fax 733-0830
Crockett ES 800/PK-5
2215 Morales St 78207 210-434-6201
Bertha Rubio, prin. Fax 434-6476
Davis MS 500/6-8
4702 E Houston St 78220 210-662-8184
Charlotte Gregory, prin. Fax 662-8189
De Zavala ES 600/PK-5
2311 San Luis St 78207 210-226-8563
Joseph Cerna, prin. Fax 226-8627
Douglass ES 400/PK-6
318 Martin Luther King Dr 78203 210-532-0603
Melanie Herr-Zepeda, prin. Fax 532-1618
Fenwick ES 400/PK-5
1930 Waverly Ave 78228 210-732-4411
Dessynie Edwards, prin. Fax 732-4693
Forbes ES 400/PK-5
2630 Sally Gay Dr 78223 210-534-2651
Anselma Chase, prin. Fax 534-2695
Foster ES 600/PK-5
6718 Pecan Valley Dr 78223 210-333-1771
Stacey Lewis, prin. Fax 333-1873
Franklin ES 600/PK-5
1915 W Olmos Dr 78201 210-733-8431
Belinda Hernandez, prin. Fax 733-8479
Graebner ES 900/PK-5
530 Hoover Ave 78225 210-923-3161
M. Lourdes Correa, prin. Fax 923-0626
Green ES 300/PK-5
122 W Whittier St 78210 210-534-6851
Karen Rose, prin. Fax 534-6865
Herff ES 300/PK-2
996 S Hackberry 78210 210-533-7500
Thomasine Chambers, prin. Fax 533-9500
Highland Hills ES 800/PK-5
734 Glamis Ave 78223 210-534-6461
Tambrey Johnson, prin. Fax 534-6484
Highland Park ES 700/PK-5
635 Rigsby Ave 78210 210-533-8051
Manuel Caballero, prin. Fax 533-8132
Hillcrest ES 500/PK-5
211 W Malone Ave 78214 210-534-3903
Christa Carreno, prin. Fax 534-0691
Hirsch ES 400/PK-5
4826 Seabreeze Dr 78220 210-648-1821
Mateen Diop, prin. Fax 648-1925
Huppertz ES 500/PK-5
247 Bangor Dr 78228 210-433-3141
Diane Stock, prin. Fax 433-4984
Japhet ES 600/PK-5
314 Astor St 78210 210-534-5321
Beatrice Aleman, prin. Fax 534-1665
Kelly ES 300/PK-5
1026 Thompson Pl 78226 210-223-6962
Deborah Guardia, prin. Fax 223-9065
King ES 500/PK-5
1001 Ceralvo St 78207 210-433-2231
Francisca Whitaker, prin. Fax 433-6477
Knox ES 300/PK-5
302 Tipton Ave 78204 210-533-5521
Homer Rivera, prin. Fax 533-5539
Lamar ES 300/PK-5
201 Parland Pl 78209 210-822-7823
Janet Mansmann, prin. Fax 822-7874
Longfellow MS 800/6-8
1130 E Sunshine Dr 78228 210-433-0311
Liz Solis, prin. Fax 433-0375
Madison ES 600/PK-5
2900 W Woodlawn Ave 78228 210-736-3323
Barbara Black, prin. Fax 736-3356
Margil ES 400/PK-5
1000 Perez St 78207 210-223-5187
John Gomez, prin. Fax 223-4984
Maverick ES 600/PK-5
107 Raleigh Pl 78201 210-735-5461
Linda Nance, prin. Fax 735-2444
Mission Academy PK-8
9210 S Presa St 78223 210-633-2546
Maria Elena Garza, prin. Fax 633-2561

Neal ES 600/PK-5
3407 Capitol Ave 78201 210-735-0791
Rebecca Atchley, prin. Fax 735-0839
Nelson ES 300/PK-5
1014 Waverly Ave 78201 210-733-9631
Cynthia Ann Perez, prin. Fax 733-9933
Ogden ES 600/PK-5
2215 Leal St 78207 210-432-8641
Graciela De La Garza, prin. Fax 432-0755
Page MS 500/6-8
401 Berkshire Ave 78210 210-533-7331
Gary Pollock, prin. Fax 533-7369
Pershing ES 400/PK-5
600 Sandmeyer St 78208 210-226-4623
Judy Ratlief, prin. Fax 226-4656
Poe MS 800/6-8
814 Aransas Ave 78210 210-534-6331
Maria Saenz, prin. Fax 534-7299
Rhodes MS 700/6-8
3000 Tampico St 78207 210-433-5092
Edward Garcia, prin. Fax 433-7299
Rodriguez ES 400/PK-5
3626 W Durango Blvd 78207 210-433-4251
Yolanda Vega, prin. Fax 433-6846
Rogers ES 700/PK-5
620 McIlvaine 78212 210-734-5721
Gloria Villalobos, prin. Fax 734-4026
Rogers MS 700/6-8
314 Galway St 78223 210-333-7551
Lemelle Taylor, prin. Fax 333-7954
Schenck ES 700/PK-5
101 Kate Schenck Ave 78223 210-333-0611
Donna Finch, prin. Fax 333-0680
Smith ES 600/PK-5
823 S Gevers St 78203 210-533-1041
Lianna Cano, prin. Fax 533-1066
Steele ES 400/PK-5
722 Haggin St 78210 210-533-5331
Anita O'Neal, prin. Fax 533-5394
Stewart ES 600/PK-5
1950 Rigsby Ave 78210 210-333-2570
Christina Clark, prin. Fax 333-2597
Tafolla MS 700/6-8
1303 W Durango Blvd 78207 210-227-3383
Sylvia Lopez, prin. Fax 227-7044
Twain MS 600/6-8
2411 San Pedro Ave 78212 210-732-4641
Monica Garcia, prin. Fax 738-0518
Tynan ES 300/PK-5
925 Gulf 78202 210-226-5453
Horace Franklin, prin. Fax 226-5799
Washington ES 500/PK-5
1823 Nolan 78202 210-226-6923
Oscar Lerma, prin. Fax 226-6589
Wheatley MS 400/6-8
415 Gabriel 78202 210-227-3921
Mona Lopez, prin. Fax 227-9972
White ES 500/PK-5
545 S WW White Rd 78220 210-333-3220
Marlon Davis, prin. Fax 333-3223
Wilson ES 500/PK-5
1421 Clower 78201 210-733-8521
Cynthia De La Garza, prin. Fax 733-8756
Woodlawn ES 600/PK-5
1717 W Magnolia Ave 78201 210-732-4741
Carlos Galvan, prin. Fax 732-2037
Woodlawn Hills ES 400/PK-5
110 W Quill Dr 78228 210-432-6151
Dr. Joanelda DeLeon, prin. Fax 432-5341

South San Antonio ISD 9,200/PK-12
2515 Bobcat Ln 78224 210-977-7000
Ron Durbon, supt. Fax 977-7021
www.southsanisd.net
Armstrong ES 500/PK-5
7111 Apple Valley Dr 78242 210-623-8787
Sherry Moore, prin. Fax 623-8792
Athens ES 500/PK-5
2707 W Gerald Ave 78211 210-977-7475
Patricia Annunzio, prin. Fax 977-7484
Benavidez ES 600/PK-5
8340 Interstate 35 S 78224 210-977-7175
Tim Tucker, prin. Fax 977-7184
Carrillo ES 500/PK-5
500 Price Ave 78211 210-977-7550
Christina Trevino, prin. Fax 977-7558
Dwight MS 500/6-8
2454 W Southcross Blvd 78211 210-977-7300
Tommy Fonseca, prin. Fax 977-7316
Five Palms ES 400/PK-5
7138 Five Palms Dr 78242 210-645-3850
Liz Pineda, prin. Fax 645-3855
Hutchins ES 600/PK-5
1919 W Hutchins Pl 78224 210-977-7200
David Abundis, prin. Fax 977-7211
Kazen MS 500/6-8
1520 Gillette Blvd 78224 210-977-7150
Steve Veazey, prin. Fax 977-7155
Kindred ES 500/PK-5
7811 Kindred St 78224 210-977-7575
Lupe Montez, prin. Fax 977-7586
Madla ES 500/PK-5
6100 Royalgate Dr 78242 210-645-3800
Elvia Perez, prin. Fax 645-3807
Palo Alto ES 700/PK-5
1725 Palo Alto Rd 78211 210-977-7125
Rosanna Mercado, prin. Fax 977-7132
Price ES 400/PK-5
245 Price Ave 78211 210-977-7225
Dolores Solis, prin. Fax 977-7236
Shepard MS 500/6-8
5558 Ray Ellison Blvd 78242 210-623-1875
Eusebio Vega, prin. Fax 623-1880
Zamora MS 500/6-8
2515 Bobcat Ln 78224 210-977-7000
Marcos Perez, prin. Fax 977-7021

Southside ISD 3,900/PK-12
1460 Martinez Losoya Rd 78221 210-882-1600
Dr. Juan Jasso, supt. Fax 626-0101
www.southsideisd.org/home.aspx
Freedom ES 400/PK-4
1460 Martinez Losoya Rd 78221 210-882-1603
Monica Villarreal, prin. Fax 626-9866
Gallardo ES 400/PK-4
1460 Martinez Losoya Rd 78221 210-882-1609
Yolanda Lujan, prin. Fax 626-2161
Losoya ES 100/5-6
1460 Martinez Losoya Rd 78221 210-882-1602
Norma Martinez, prin. Fax 626-0116
Pearce ES 400/PK-4
1460 Martinez Losoya Rd 78221 210-882-1605
Mary Bandy, prin. Fax 626-0117
Southside Heritage ES 600/PK-4
1460 Martinez Losoya Rd 78221 210-882-1607
Carl Scarbrough, prin. Fax 626-9788
Southside MS 700/7-8
1460 Martinez Losoya Rd 78221 210-882-1601
R. Chris Christian, prin. Fax 626-0113

Southwest ISD 10,300/PK-12
11914 Dragon Ln 78252 210-622-4300
Dr. Velma Villegas, supt. Fax 622-4301
www.swisd.net/
Big Country ES 500/K-5
11914 Dragon Ln 78252 210-645-7560
Pam Dahlquist, prin. Fax 645-7561
Hidden Cove ES 600/PK-5
11914 Dragon Ln 78252 210-623-6220
Ana Maria Solis, prin. Fax 623-6219
Hope ES 500/K-5
11914 Dragon Ln 78252 210-927-8180
Angelica Romero, prin. Fax 927-8181
Indian Creek ES 700/K-5
11914 Dragon Ln 78252 210-623-6520
Malcolm Williams, prin. Fax 623-6521
Kriewald Road ES 500/PK-5
11914 Dragon Ln 78252 210-645-7550
Joseph Guidry, prin. Fax 645-7551
McAuliffe MS 700/7-8
11914 Dragon Ln 78252 210-623-6260
Orlando Vera, prin. Fax 623-6261
McNair MS 700/6-6
11914 Dragon Ln 78252 210-622-4480
Jason Migura, prin. Fax 622-4481
Scobee MS 900/7-8
11914 Dragon Ln 78252 210-645-7500
Mark Figueroa, prin. Fax 645-7501
Sky Harbour ES 600/K-5
11914 Dragon Ln 78252 210-623-6580
Marina Avila, prin. Fax 623-6584
Southwest ES 600/PK-5
11914 Dragon Ln 78252 210-622-4420
Michael Wagner, prin. Fax 622-4421
Sun Valley ES 600/K-5
11914 Dragon Ln 78252 210-645-7570
Vanessa Trevino, prin. Fax 645-7571
Other Schools – See Atascosa

Antioch Christian Academy 100/PK-6
227 Eross 78202 210-222-0159
Earl Bullock, prin. Fax 222-0553
Atonement Academy 500/PK-12
15415 Red Robin Rd 78255 210-695-2240
Richard Arndt, hdmstr. Fax 695-9679
Believers Academy 100/K-12
13714 Lookout Rd 78233 210-656-2999
Trudie Elmer, admin. Fax 656-1226
Blessed Sacrament S 300/K-8
600 Oblate Dr 78216 210-824-3381
Michael Fierro, prin. Fax 826-6146
Carver Academy 100/PK-6
217 Robinson Pl 78202 210-277-6754
Brenda Murphy, hdmstr.
Castle Hills First Baptist S 300/K-12
2220 NW Military Hwy 78213 210-377-8485
Dr. Herbert Hartzler, supt. Fax 377-8473
Child Montessori S 100/PK-4
2829 Hunters Green St 78231 210-493-6550
Jean Stein, prin. Fax 493-6550
Christian Academy of San Antonio 600/PK-12
325 Castroville Rd 78207 210-436-2277
Yolanda Molina, supt. Fax 436-2210
Christian Heritage S 200/PK-12
16316 San Pedro Ave 78232 210-496-1644
Jahnnette Brandt, prin. Fax 496-1993
Concordia Lutheran S 500/PK-8
16801 Huebner Rd 78258 210-479-1477
Matthew Meier, prin. Fax 479-9416
Cornerstone Christian S 500/PK-12
4802 Vance Jackson Rd 78230 210-979-9203
Jerry Eshleman, supt. Fax 979-0310
Crossroads Christian Academy 100/K-8
5834 Ray Ellison Blvd 78242 210-623-4500
Anna Grajeda, dir. Fax 623-3758
Ewing Educational Center 50/K-12
4143 Gardendale St 78229 210-732-7550
Billy Burchfield, admin. Fax 617-4658
Gloryland Christian Academy 50/K-12
307 E Pyron Ave 78214 210-923-6720
Mary Faulkner, admin.
Harvest Academy 400/PK-12
1270 N Loop 1604 E 78232 210-496-2277
Jim Fleetwood, prin.
Holy Name S 300/PK-8
3814 Nash Blvd 78223 210-333-7356
Chad Mills, prin. Fax 333-7642
Holy Spirit S 500/PK-8
770 W Ramsey Rd 78216 210-349-1169
Sandy Galvan, prin. Fax 349-1247
Hope Lutheran Learning Center 100/PK-6
5714 Callaghan Rd 78228 210-433-2011
Linda Gonzalez, dir. Fax 433-4338
Keystone S 400/K-12
119 E Craig Pl 78212 210-735-4022
Hugh McIntosh, hdmstr. Fax 732-4905

Kolitz Academy 100/K-8
12500 NW Military Hwy # 150 78231 210-302-6900
Robert Scott, hdmstr. Fax 302-6913
Kriterion Montessori S PK-8
611 W Ashby Pl 78212 210-735-9778
Hanna Laven, dir.
Little Flower S 300/PK-8
905 Kentucky Ave 78201 210-732-9207
Rita Graves, prin. Fax 732-3214
Mac Arthur Park Lutheran Preschool 100/PK-PK
2903 Nacogdoches Rd 78217 210-822-5374
Laura Brown, dir. Fax 826-5146
Maranatha Adventist S 50/K-8
2526 Goliad Rd 78223 210-333-8861
Rebecka Sauls, prin. Fax 532-9796
Montessori School of San Antonio 300/PK-8
17722 Rogers Ranch Pkwy 78258 210-492-3553
Chuck Raymer, hdmstr. Fax 492-3484
Mt. Sacred Heart S 400/PK-8
619 Mount Sacred Heart Rd 78216 210-342-6711
Maria Casto, prin. Fax 342-4032
New Life Christian Academy 200/K-12
6622 W US Highway 90 78227 210-679-6001
Anthony Jackson, prin. Fax 679-6080
Northwest Hills Christian S 400/PK-8
8511 Heath Circle Dr 78250 210-522-1102
Corine Coleman, dir. Fax 522-1103
Our Savior Lutheran S 50/K-8
11503 Vance Jackson Rd 78230 210-696-2716
Joshua Rimpel, prin. Fax 558-0572
Providence Preparatory MS 100/6-8
1215 N Saint Marys St 78215 210-224-6651
Charlene Ibrom, prin. Fax 224-6214
Rainbow Hills Baptist S 300/PK-12
2255 Horal St 78227 210-674-0490
Rev. Dennis Wall, chncllr. Fax 674-3615
River City Christian S 100/1-12
5810 Blanco Rd 78216 210-384-0297
Ezzard Castillo, hdmstr. Fax 384-0446
Rolling Hills Academy 200/PK-8
21240 Gathering Oak 78260 210-497-0323
Sergio Teran, prin. Fax 497-1440
St. Anthony S 400/PK-8
205 W Huisache Ave 78212 210-732-8801
Dr. John Kennedy, prin. Fax 732-5968
St. Benedict S 100/PK-8
4547 Lord Rd 78220 210-648-1611
Susan Gonzales, prin. Fax 648-1722
St. Cecilia S 200/PK-8
118 Lowell St 78210 210-534-2711
Mary Crow, prin. Fax 533-8284
St. David's Episcopal S 100/PK-K
1300 Wiltshire Ave 78209 210-824-2481
Ashley Miles, hdmstr. Fax 824-7870
St. George Episcopal S 500/PK-8
6900 West Ave 78213 210-342-4263
Robert Devlin, hdmstr. Fax 342-4681
St. Gregory the Great S 600/PK-8
700 Dewhurst Rd 78213 210-342-0281
Martha Gomez, prin. Fax 308-7177
St. James the Apostle S 300/PK-8
907 W Theo Ave 78225 210-924-1201
Sr. Mary Link, prin. Fax 924-0201
St. John Berchmans S 300/PK-8
1147 Cupples Rd 78226 210-433-0411
Beverly Abbott, prin. Fax 433-2335
St. John Bosco S 400/PK-8
5630 W Commerce St 78237 210-432-8011
Sr. Rosann Ruiz, prin. Fax 432-5168
St. John Lutheran S 50/PK-K
502 E Nueva 78205 210-225-2392
St. John the Evangelist S 100/PK-8
128 S Audubon Dr 78212 210-735-3526
Warren Carter, prin. Fax 735-3526
St. Joseph S 100/PK-8
535 New Laredo Hwy 78211 210-922-0193
David Zuber, prin. Fax 922-2002
St. Leo the Great S 200/PK-8
119 Octavia Pl 78214 210-532-3166
Carol Johnson, prin. Fax 532-5997
St. Luke S 500/PK-8
4603 Manitou 78228 210-434-2011
Marcella Salazar, prin. Fax 432-2419
St. Luke's Episcopal S 400/PK-8
15 Saint Lukes Ln 78209 210-826-0664
Dr. Mark Reford, hdmstr. Fax 826-8520
St. Margaret Mary S 200/PK-8
1202 Fair Ave 78223 210-534-6137
Ramon Guerra, prin. Fax 534-2225
St. Mary Magdalen S 200/PK-8
1700 Clower 78201 210-735-1381
Miguel Mejia, prin. Fax 735-2406
St. Mary's Hall 900/PK-12
9401 Starcrest Dr 78217 210-483-9100
Bob Windham, hdmstr. Fax 483-9299
St. Matthew Catholic S 700/PK-8
10703 Wurzbach Rd 78230 210-478-5099
Alvin Caro, prin. Fax 696-7624
St. Paul S 400/PK-8
307 John Adams Dr 78228 210-732-2741
Sandra Sanchez, prin. Fax 732-7702
St. Peter Prince of Apostles S 300/PK-8
112 Marcia Pl 78209 210-824-3171
Ann Lauder, prin. Fax 822-4504
St. Philip of Jesus S 200/PK-8
134 E Lambert St 78204 210-222-2872
Graciela Luna, prin. Fax 229-1829
St. Pius X S 300/PK-8
7734 Robin Rest Dr 78209 210-824-6431
Karen DuPree, prin. Fax 824-7454
St. Thomas Episcopal S 200/PK-5
1416 N Loop 1604 E 78232 210-494-3509
Gregory Hutchinson, dir. Fax 494-0678
St. Thomas More S 200/PK-8
4427 Moana Dr 78218 210-655-2882
William Smith, prin. Fax 655-9603
San Antonio Academy 300/PK-8
117 E French Pl 78212 210-733-7331
John Webster, hdmstr. Fax 734-0711

San Antonio Christian ES 500/PK-5
19202 Redland Rd 78259 210-248-1625
Phil Paden, prin. Fax 342-0146
San Antonio Christian MS 200/6-8
19202 Redland Rd 78259 210-340-1864
Dr. Thomas Erbaugh, prin. Fax 348-6030
Scenic Hills SDA S 50/PK-8
11223 Bandera Rd 78250 210-523-2312
Sherry Clapp, prin.
Shepherd of the Hills Lutheran S 500/PK-8
6914 Wurzbach Rd 78240 210-614-3741
Sue Gary, prin. Fax 692-1639
Trinity Christian Academy 200/K-12
5401 N Loop 1604 E 78247 210-653-2800
Susan Oldfield, prin. Fax 653-0303
Valley High Baptist Academy 100/PK-PK
6623 SW Loop 410 78227 210-674-5300
Village Parkway Christian S 100/PK-6
3002 Village Pkwy 78251 210-680-8187
Irene Taylor, prin. Fax 509-3502
Winston S San Antonio 200/K-12
8565 Ewing Halsell Dr 78229 210-615-6544
Dr. Charles Karulak, prin. Fax 615-6627
Z-Place Child Development Center 50/PK-PK
702 Cincinnati Ave 78201 210-732-8105

San Augustine, San Augustine, Pop. 2,465
San Augustine ISD 900/PK-12
702 High School Dr 75972 936-275-2306
Walter Key, supt. Fax 275-9776
www.saisd.us/
San Augustine ES 400/PK-4
101 S Milam St 75972 936-275-3424
Zachary Weems, prin. Fax 275-9719
San Augustine IS 200/5-8
1002 Barrett St 75972 936-275-2318
Steve Coston, prin. Fax 275-2962

San Benito, Cameron, Pop. 24,699
Los Fresnos Consolidated ISD
Supt. — See Los Fresnos
Laureles ES 700/PK-5
31393 FM 2893 78586 956-254-5141
Melanie McCormick, prin. Fax 233-3690

San Benito Consolidated ISD 11,300/PK-12
240 N Crockett St 78586 956-361-6110
Antonio Limon, supt. Fax 361-6115
www.sbcisd.net
Booth ES 700/PK-5
705 Zaragosa St 78586 956-361-6860
Manuel Cruz, prin. Fax 361-6868
Cabaza MS 1,100/6-8
2901 Shafer Rd 78586 956-361-6600
William Snavely, prin. Fax 361-6608
Cash ES 600/PK-5
400 Poinciana St 78586 956-361-6700
Lupita Monsevalles, prin. Fax 361-6708
De La Fuente ES PK-5
2700 S Sam Houston St 78586 956-361-6110
Tim Moon, prin. Fax 361-6820
Downs ES 600/PK-5
1302 N Dick Dowling St 78586 956-361-6720
Rogelio Cano, prin. Fax 361-6728
Garza ES 700/PK-5
845 8th St 78586 956-361-6900
Elsa Lambert, prin. Fax 361-6908
Jordan MS 1,200/6-8
700 N McCullough St 78586 956-361-6650
Sam Mendez, prin. Fax 361-6658
La Encantada ES 500/PK-5
35001 FM 1577 78586 956-361-6760
Libby Flores, prin. Fax 361-6768
Landrum ES 400/PK-5
450 S Dick Dowling St 78586 956-361-6800
Theresa Servellon, prin. Fax 361-6808
La Paloma ES 700/PK-5
35076 Padilla St 78586 956-361-6780
Cecilia Rangel, prin. Fax 361-6788
Rangerville ES 500/PK-5
17558 Landrum Park Rd 78586 956-361-6840
Mary Alice Leal, prin. Fax 361-6848
Roberts ES 400/PK-5
451 Biddle St 78586 956-361-6740
Aurora Mendoza, prin. Fax 361-6748
San Benito Riverside MS 700/6-8
35428 Padilla St 78586 956-361-6110
Joel Wood, prin. Fax 361-6940
Sullivan ES 500/PK-5
900 Elizabeth St 78586 956-361-6880
Bobbie Jo Hushen, prin. Fax 361-6888

Sanderson, Terrell, Pop. 1,128
Terrell County ISD 100/PK-12
PO Box 747 79848 432-345-2515
Gary Hamilton, supt. Fax 345-2670
www.terrell.esc18.net
Sanderson ES 100/PK-5
PO Box 747 79848 432-345-2881
Scott Allen, prin. Fax 345-2671
Sanderson JHS 50/6-8
PO Box 747 79848 432-345-2601
Michael Poppell, prin. Fax 345-2670

San Diego, Duval, Pop. 4,589
San Diego ISD 1,400/PK-12
609 W Labbe St 78384 361-279-3382
Luis Pizzini, supt. Fax 279-3388
www.sdisd.esc2.net
Collins PS 300/PK-2
609 W Labbe St 78384 361-279-3382
Raynaldo Perez, prin. Fax 279-3388
Jaime JHS 300/6-8
609 W Labbe St 78384 361-279-3382
Sam Bueno, prin. Fax 279-3139
Parr ES 300/3-5
609 W Labbe St 78384 361-279-3382
Raynaldo Perez, prin. Fax 279-3388

San Elizario, El Paso, Pop. 4,385
San Elizario ISD 3,300/PK-12
PO Box 920 79849 915-872-3900
Mike Quatrini, supt. Fax 872-3903
www.seisd.net
Alarcon ES 600/1-5
PO Box 920 79849 915-872-3930
Mayela Sanchez, prin. Fax 872-3931
Loya PS 600/PK-K
PO Box 920 79849 915-872-3940
George Augustain, prin. Fax 872-3941
Sambrano ES 400/1-5
PO Box 920 79849 915-872-3950
Marta Alvarez, prin. Fax 872-3951
San Elizario MS 800/6-8
PO Box 920 79849 915-872-3960
Linda Rodriguez, prin. Fax 872-3961

Sanger, Denton, Pop. 6,354
Sanger ISD 1,900/PK-12
PO Box 2399 76266 940-458-7438
Jack Biggerstaff, supt. Fax 458-5140
sisd.sangerisd.net/
Butterfield ES PK-2
291 Indian Ln 76266 940-458-4377
Debbie Romines, prin. Fax 458-5591
Chisholm Trail ES 400/K-2
812 Keaton Rd N 76266 940-458-5297
Sandra Hensley, prin. Fax 458-2537
Clear Creek IS 400/3-5
1901 S Stemmons St 76266 940-458-7476
Anne Williams, prin. Fax 458-2539
Sanger 6th Grade Campus 6-6
508 N 7th St 76266 940-458-3699
Steve Skelton, prin. Fax 458-3795
Sanger MS 400/7-8
105 Berry St 76266 940-458-7916
Deana Steeber, prin. Fax 458-5111

San Isidro, Starr
San Isidro ISD 300/PK-12
PO Box 10 78588 956-481-3100
Miguel Garcia, supt. Fax 481-3597
www.sanisidroisd.org/
San Isidro S, PO Box 10 78588 200/PK-8
Miguel Garcia, prin. 956-481-3107

San Juan, Hidalgo, Pop. 30,773
Pharr-San Juan-Alamo ISD
Supt. — See Pharr
Austin MS 1,000/6-8
804 S Stewart Rd 78589 956-702-5849
Dalila Garcia, prin. Fax 702-5858
Carman ES 800/PK-5
100 Ridge Rd 78589 956-702-5761
Maria Jilpas, prin. Fax 702-5767
Clover ES 700/PK-5
800 Carroll Ln 78589 956-702-5754
Rosalinda Diaz, prin. Fax 783-2810
Doedyns ES 700/PK-5
1401 N Raul Longoria Rd 78589 956-702-5744
Frances Palacios, prin. Fax 702-5724
Garza-Pena ES 700/PK-5
230 E Sgt Leonel Trevino Rd 78589 956-702-5873
Oralia Castaneda, prin. Fax 782-7741
North San Juan ES 800/PK-5
2900 N Raul Longoria Rd 78589 956-702-6036
Diana Ruiz, prin. Fax 702-5871
Reed & Mock ES 800/PK-5
400 E Eldora Rd 78589 956-783-2260
Sylvia Cano, prin. Fax 783-9169
San Juan MS 1,200/6-8
1229 S I Rd 78589 956-783-3800
Nora Rivas, prin. Fax 783-3811
Sorensen ES 400/PK-5
715 S Standard Ave 78589 956-702-5700
Maricela Cortez, prin. Fax 702-5703
Trevino ES 400/PK-5
104 E Sgt Leonel Trevino Rd 78589 956-702-5863
Lucila Gutierrez, prin. Fax 782-4239

San Leon, Galveston, Pop. 3,328
Dickinson ISD
Supt. — See Dickinson
San Leon ES 600/PK-4
2655 Broadway St 77539 281-229-7400
Stephanie Williams, prin. Fax 229-7401

San Marcos, Hays, Pop. 46,111
Hays Consolidated ISD
Supt. — See Kyle
Blanco Vista ES K-5
2951 Blanco Vista Blvd 78666 512-268-8506
Cynthia Davis, prin. Fax 393-2082

San Marcos Consolidated ISD 7,200/PK-12
PO Box 1087 78667 512-393-6700
Dr. Patty Shafer, supt. Fax 393-6709
www.smcisd.net/
Bonham Preschool 400/PK-PK
211 Lee St 78666 512-393-6722
Rosemary Garza, prin. Fax 393-6785
Bowie ES 700/K-4
4020 Monterrey Oaks 78666 512-393-6200
Karen McGowan, prin. Fax 393-6210
Crockett ES 700/K-4
1300 Girard St 78666 512-393-6400
Rick LaBuhn, prin. Fax 393-3557
DeZavala ES 700/K-4
600 Staples Rd 78666 512-393-6250
Dolores Cruz, prin. Fax 393-7115
Goodnight JHS 500/7-8
1301 N State Highway 123 78666 512-393-6550
Steve Dow, prin. Fax 393-6560
Hernandez IS 1,000/5-6
333 Stagecoach Trl 78666 512-393-6100
Sandra Reyes, prin. Fax 393-6109
Miller JHS 500/7-8
301 Foxtail Run 78666 512-393-6660
Susan Brown, prin. Fax 393-6602
Travis ES 600/K-4
1437 Post Rd 78666 512-393-6450
Niki Konecki, prin. Fax 393-6476

Master's S 100/K-6
1664 Center Point Rd 78666 512-392-4322
Beth Heatwole, prin. Fax 754-6017
San Marcos Adventist Academy 50/PK-10
PO Box 801 78667 512-392-9475
Susan Nichols, prin. Fax 392-2693

San Perlita, Willacy, Pop. 689
San Perlita ISD 300/PK-12
PO Box 37 78590 956-248-5563
Albert Pena, supt. Fax 248-5561
www.spisd.org
San Perlita ES 100/PK-6
PO Box 37 78590 956-248-5250
Ramiro Moreno, prin. Fax 248-5103
San Perlita MS 50/7-8
PO Box 37 78590 956-248-5250
Ramiro Moreno, prin. Fax 248-5103

San Saba, San Saba, Pop. 2,615
San Saba ISD 700/PK-12
808 W Wallace St 76877 325-372-3771
Leigh Ann Glaze, supt. Fax 372-5977
www.san-saba.net
San Saba ES 300/PK-4
808 W Wallace St 76877 325-372-3019
Bruce Tabor, prin. Fax 372-6187
San Saba MS 200/5-8
808 W Wallace St 76877 325-372-3200
Jeff Pannell, prin. Fax 372-5228

Santa Anna, Coleman, Pop. 1,026
Santa Anna ISD 300/K-12
701 Bowie St 76878 325-348-3136
Wes Hays, supt. Fax 348-3141
santaanna.netxv.net/
Santa Anna ES 100/K-6
701 Bowie St 76878 325-348-3138
Debbie Bacon, prin. Fax 348-3142

Santa Fe, Galveston, Pop. 10,498
Santa Fe ISD 4,600/PK-12
PO Box 370 77510 409-925-3526
Leigh Wall, supt. Fax 925-4002
www.sfisd.org/
Barnett IS 600/5-6
PO Box 370 77510 409-925-3526
Rachel Blundell, prin. Fax 925-4002
Cowan ES 300/4-4
PO Box 370 77510 409-925-3526
Susan Hall, prin. Fax 925-4002
Kubacek ES 600/2-3
PO Box 370 77510 409-925-3526
Dr. Lupe Hernandez, prin. Fax 925-4002
Santa Fe JHS 800/7-8
PO Box 370 77510 409-925-3526
Rachel Blundell, prin. Fax 925-4002
Wollam ES 800/PK-1
PO Box 370 77510 409-925-3526
Donna Carlson, prin. Fax 925-4002

Santa Maria, Cameron, Pop. 500
Santa Maria ISD 600/PK-12
PO Box 448 78592 956-565-6308
Homero Garcia, supt. Fax 565-4422
www.smisd.net
Gonzalez ES, PO Box 448 78592 400/PK-5
Jesse Munoz, prin. 956-565-5348
Santa Maria MS 100/6-8
PO Box 448 78592 956-565-6309
Jesse Munoz, prin. Fax 565-6720

Santa Rosa, Cameron, Pop. 2,946
Santa Rosa ISD 1,200/PK-12
PO Box 368 78593 956-636-9800
Heriberto Villarreal, supt. Fax 636-9890
www.santarosaisd.org
Barrera ES 600/PK-5
PO Box 368 78593 956-636-9870
Deanna Sanchez, prin. Fax 636-2746
Nelson MS 300/6-8
PO Box 368 78593 956-636-9850
Raul Trevino, prin. Fax 636-9869

Santo, Palo Pinto
Santo ISD 500/PK-12
PO Box 67 76472 940-769-2835
G. Gilbert, supt. Fax 769-3116
www.santoisd.net/
Santo ES 200/PK-5
PO Box 67 76472 940-769-3215
Cathy Longley, prin. Fax 769-3116

Saratoga, Hardin
West Hardin County Consolidated ISD 600/PK-12
39227 Highway 105 77585 936-274-5061
Sharon Tule, supt. Fax 274-4321
www.esc5.net/whccisd
West Hardin ES 300/PK-5
39227 Highway 105 77585 936-274-5061
Pam Rasberry, prin. Fax 274-4321
West Hardin JHS 100/6-8
39227 Highway 105 77585 936-274-5061
Fran Bledsoe, prin. Fax 274-5671

Sarita, Kenedy
Kenedy County Wide Common SD 100/PK-6
PO Box 100 78385 361-294-5381
Noemy Garcia, supt. Fax 294-5718
Sarita ES 100/PK-6
PO Box 100 78385 361-294-5381
Noemy Garcia, prin. Fax 294-5718

Savoy, Fannin, Pop. 886
Savoy ISD 300/PK-12
302 W Hayes St 75479 903-965-5262
Brian Neal, supt. Fax 965-7282
www.savoyisd.org
Savoy ES 200/PK-6
302 W Hayes St 75479 903-965-7738
Robert Biggers, prin. Fax 965-7282

Schertz, Guadalupe, Pop. 26,668
Schertz-Cibolo-Universal City ISD 7,900/PK-12
1060 Elbel Rd 78154 210-945-6200
Dr. Belinda Pustka, supt. Fax 945-6252
www.scuc.txed.net
Corbett JHS 600/7-8
12000 Ray Corbett Dr 78154 210-619-4150
Jay Muennink, prin. Fax 619-4190
Green Valley ES 800/K-4
1694 Green Valley Rd 78154 210-619-4450
Veronica Goldhorn, prin. Fax 619-4478
Paschal ES 700/K-4
590 Savannah Dr 78154 210-619-4500
Allison Miller, prin. Fax 619-4518
Schertz ES 500/K-4
701 Curtiss St 78154 210-619-4650
Tina Trcka, prin. Fax 619-4690
Sippel ES PK-4
420 Fair Lawn 78154 210-619-4600
Kelley Mosley, prin. Fax 619-4630
Wilder IS 600/5-6
806 Savannah Dr 78154 210-619-4200
Julie Knox, prin. Fax 619-4220
Other Schools – See Cibolo, Universal City

Schulenburg, Fayette, Pop. 2,742
Schulenburg ISD 800/PK-12
521 North St 78956 979-743-3448
Dr. Dale Pitts, supt. Fax 743-4721
www.schulenburg.txed.net
Schulenburg ES 400/PK-6
300 Bucek St 78956 979-743-4221
Michelle Michaelsen, prin. Fax 743-4721

St. Rose of Lima S 100/PK-8
405 Black St 78956 979-743-3080
Rosanne Gallia, prin. Fax 743-4228

Scurry, Kaufman, Pop. 631
Scurry-Rosser ISD 900/PK-12
10705 S State Highway 34 75158 972-452-8823
Chris Couch, supt. Fax 452-8586
www.scurry-rosser.com/
Scurry-Rosser ES 400/PK-4
9511 Silver Creek Dr 75158 972-452-8823
Martha Blessing, prin. Fax 452-3434
Scurry-Rosser MS 300/5-8
10729 S State Highway 34 75158 972-452-8823
Stuart Andrus, prin. Fax 452-8902

Seabrook, Harris, Pop. 10,907
Clear Creek ISD
Supt. — See League City
Bay ES 700/PK-5
1502 Bayport Blvd 77586 281-284-4600
Erin Tite, prin. Fax 284-4605
Robinson ES 500/PK-5
451 Kirby Rd 77586 281-284-6500
Jim Stephens, prin. Fax 284-6505
Seabrook IS 1,000/6-8
2401 Meyer Rd 77586 281-284-3100
David Williams, prin. Fax 284-3105

Seadrift, Calhoun, Pop. 1,390
Calhoun County ISD
Supt. — See Port Lavaca
Seadrift S 300/PK-8
PO Box 979 77983 361-785-3451
Dwana Finster, prin. Fax 785-4006

Seagoville, Dallas, Pop. 11,112
Dallas ISD
Supt. — See Dallas
Central ES 500/3-5
902 Shady Ln 75159 972-749-6800
Daniel Salinas, prin. Fax 749-6801
Seagoville ES 700/PK-2
304 N Kaufman St 75159 972-892-7900
Susan Hanke, prin. Fax 892-7901

Robinwood Christian Academy 100/K-6
111 W Stark Rd 75159 972-287-1487

Seagraves, Gaines, Pop. 2,321
Seagraves ISD 700/PK-12
PO Box 577 79359 806-387-2035
Dr. Kevin Spiller, supt. Fax 387-2944
www.seagraves.esc17.net/
Seagraves ES 300/K-5
PO Box 1415 79359 806-387-2015
Chad Wright, prin. Fax 387-3339
Seagraves JHS 100/6-8
PO Box 938 79359 806-387-2646
Ovidio Martinez, prin. Fax 387-2451
Seagraves Preschool 100/PK-PK
1300 Avenue J 79359 806-546-2629
Fax 546-0059

Sealy, Austin, Pop. 6,038
Sealy ISD 2,600/PK-12
939 Tiger Ln 77474 979-885-3516
Pamela Morris, supt. Fax 885-6457
www.sealyisd.com
Sealy JHS 600/6-8
939 Tiger Ln 77474 979-885-3292
Scott Kana, prin. Fax 877-0743
Selman ES 900/PK-3
1741 Highway 90 W 77474 979-885-3517
Larea Gamble, prin. Fax 885-1338
Selman IS 400/4-5
1741 Highway 90 W 77474 979-885-3852
Stephanie McElroy, prin. Fax 885-0162

Seguin, Guadalupe, Pop. 24,230
Navarro ISD 1,400/PK-12
6450 N State Highway 123 78155 830-372-1930
Dee Carter, supt. Fax 372-1853
www.navarroisd.us

Navarro ES 500/PK-3
380 Link Rd 78155 830-372-1933
Les Dragon, prin. Fax 379-3145
Navarro IS 200/4-6
300 Link Rd 78155 830-372-1943
Robert Wiegand, prin. Fax 379-3170
Other Schools – See Geronimo

Seguin ISD 7,400/PK-12
1221 E Kingsbury St 78155 830-372-5771
Dr. Irene Garza, supt. Fax 379-0392
www.seguin.k12.tx.us
Ball ECC 300/PK-PK
620 W Krezdorn St 78155 830-372-2725
Jennie Hines, prin. Fax 372-2727
Barnes MS 500/7-8
1539 Joe Carrillo Blvd 78155 830-379-4717
Jesus Uranga, prin. Fax 379-4239
Briesemeister MS 500/7-8
1616 W Court St 78155 830-379-0600
Elisa Carter, prin. Fax 379-0615
Jefferson Avenue ES 400/K-5
215 Short Ave 78155 830-379-3882
Kim Schlichting, prin. Fax 379-0950
Koennecke ES 600/K-5
1441 Joe Carrillo Blvd 78155 830-372-5430
Yomeida Guerra, prin. Fax 372-3317
Patlan ES 400/K-5
2501 Breustedt St 78155 830-372-4960
Merry White, prin. Fax 372-4565
Rodriguez ES K-5
West Kingsbury St 78155 830-372-5771
Saegert 6th Grade Center 600/6-6
118 N Bowie St 78155 830-372-3218
Don Hastings, prin. Fax 379-6281
Seguin Pre-K 400/PK-PK
450 Dolle Ave 78155 830-379-2675
Jennie Hines, prin. Fax 379-5590
Vogel ES 600/K-5
16121 FM 725 78155 830-379-4231
Michael Skinner, prin. Fax 372-2124
Weinert ES 500/K-5
1112 N Heideke St 78155 830-379-4226
Rebecca Marsh, prin. Fax 372-2720
Other Schools – See Mc Queeney

First Baptist Christian Academy 100/PK-6
1314 E Cedar St 78155 830-379-4208
Lynn Garrett, prin. Fax 379-4223
Lifegate Christian S 200/K-12
395 Lifegate Ln 78155 830-372-0850
Judy Childress, prin. Fax 372-0895
St. James S 200/PK-8
507 S Camp St 78155 830-379-2878
Deanna Sanchez, prin. Fax 379-2878

Selma, Bexar, Pop. 2,286

Our Lady of Perpetual Help S 600/PK-8
16075 N Evans Rd 78154 210-651-6811
Jackie Palermo, prin. Fax 651-5516

Seminole, Gaines, Pop. 5,954
Seminole ISD 2,200/PK-12
207 SW 6th St 79360 432-758-3662
Doug Harriman, supt. Fax 758-9833
www.seminole.k12.tx.us
Seminole ES 300/4-5
401 SW Avenue B 79360 432-758-3615
Randy Clay, prin. Fax 758-9064
Seminole JHS 500/6-8
601 SW Avenue B 79360 432-758-9431
Cary Moring, prin. Fax 758-5795
Seminole PS 300/2-3
508 SW Avenue D 79360 432-758-5841
Judy Sage, prin. Fax 758-5299
Young ES 500/PK-1
2100 SW Avenue B 79360 432-758-3637
Sherry Bowers, prin. Fax 758-2066

Seymour, Baylor, Pop. 2,704
Seymour ISD 600/PK-12
409 W Idaho St 76380 940-889-3525
Dr. John Baker, supt. Fax 889-5340
www.seymour-isd.net/
Seymour ES 200/PK-4
409 W Idaho St 76380 940-889-2533
Kristi Exum, prin. Fax 889-8890
Seymour MS 200/5-8
409 W Idaho St 76380 940-889-4548
Dr. Greg Roach, prin. Fax 889-4962

Shady Shores, Denton, Pop. 2,108
Denton ISD
Supt. — See Denton
Stephens ES K-5
133 N Garza Rd 76208 940-369-0000
Rod Southard, prin. Fax 369-4927

Lake Dallas ISD
Supt. — See Lake Dallas
Shady Shores ES 700/PK-4
300 Dobbs Rd 76208 940-497-4035
Jennie Taylor, prin. Fax 497-4036

Shallowater, Lubbock, Pop. 2,170
Shallowater ISD 1,200/PK-12
1100 Avenue K 79363 806-832-4531
Phil Warren, supt. Fax 832-4350
www.shallowaterisd.net
Shallowater ES 400/PK-2
1100 Avenue K 79363 806-832-4531
Mary Hughes, prin. Fax 832-4534
Shallowater IS 200/3-4
1100 Avenue K 79363 806-832-4531
Donna Bowles, prin. Fax 832-1884
Shallowater MS 300/5-8
1100 Avenue K 79363 806-832-4531
Kenny Border, prin. Fax 832-5543

Shamrock, Wheeler, Pop. 1,841
Shamrock ISD 200/K-12
100 S Illinois St 79079 806-256-3492
Wes Beck, supt. Fax 256-3628
Shamrock S 100/K-8
100 S Illinois St 79079 806-256-3227
Pam Morlan, prin. Fax 256-3628

Shavano Park, Bexar, Pop. 2,290
Northside ISD
Supt. — See San Antonio
Blattman ES 500/K-5
3300 N Loop 1604 W 78231 210-397-4600
Carin Adermann, prin. Fax 408-6219

Shelbyville, Shelby
Shelbyville ISD 700/PK-12
PO Box 325 75973 936-598-2641
Dr. Ray West, supt. Fax 598-6842
www.shelbyville.k12.tx.us
Shelbyville S 700/PK-12
PO Box 325 75973 936-598-7323
Mario Osby, prin. Fax 598-6842

Shepherd, San Jacinto, Pop. 2,282
Shepherd ISD 1,800/PK-12
1401 S Byrd Ave 77371 936-628-3396
Jody Cronin, supt. Fax 628-3841
www.shepherdisd.net/
Shepherd IS 400/3-5
1401 S Byrd Ave 77371 936-628-6764
Charlene Lowe, prin. Fax 628-6507
Shepherd MS 400/6-8
1401 S Byrd Ave 77371 936-628-3377
Jan Page, prin. Fax 628-6749
Shepherd PS 500/PK-2
1401 S Byrd Ave 77371 936-628-3302
Rebecca Smith, prin. Fax 628-6459

Sheridan, Colorado
Rice Consolidated ISD
Supt. — See Altair
Sheridan S 100/K-8
F M 2437 77475 979-234-3531
Larry Varley, prin. Fax 234-3409

Sherman, Grayson, Pop. 36,790
Sherman ISD 6,100/PK-12
PO Box 1176 75091 903-891-6400
Dr. Al Hambrick, supt. Fax 891-6407
www.shermanisd.net
Crutchfield ES 500/PK-4
521 S Dewey Ave 75090 903-891-6565
Jill Parker, prin. Fax 891-6570
Dillingham IS 900/5-6
1701 Gallagher Dr 75090 903-891-6495
Deborah Romines, prin. Fax 891-6499
Douglass ECC 200/PK-K
505 E College St 75090 903-891-6545
Linda Woytasczyk, prin. Fax 891-6549
Fairview ES 500/PK-4
501 W Taylor St 75092 903-891-6580
DeAn Jeffrey, prin. Fax 891-6585
Jefferson ES 400/PK-4
608 N Lee St 75090 903-891-6610
Amy Elliott, prin. Fax 891-6615
Neblett ES PK-4
1505 Gallagher Dr 75090 903-891-6670
Linda Salinas, prin. Fax 893-0263
Piner MS 900/7-8
402 W Pecan St 75090 903-891-6470
Karla Wright, prin. Fax 891-6475
Sory ES PK-4
120 Binkley Park Dr 75092 903-891-6650
Steven Traw, prin. Fax 892-6307
Wakefield ES 600/K-4
400 Sunset Blvd 75092 903-891-6595
Tammy Hutchins, prin. Fax 891-6600
Washington ES 400/PK-4
815 S Travis St 75090 903-891-6700
Joanne Miller, prin. Fax 891-6726

St. Mary S 200/PK-7
713 S Travis St 75090 903-893-2127
Nancy Kirkpatrick, prin. Fax 893-3233
Texoma Christian S 400/PK-12
3500 W Houston St 75092 903-893-7076
Jeffrey Burley, hdmstr. Fax 891-8486

Shiner, Lavaca, Pop. 2,019
Shiner ISD 500/PK-12
PO Box 804 77984 361-594-3121
Trey Lawrence, supt. Fax 594-3925
www.shinerisd.net
Shiner ES 300/PK-6
PO Box 804 77984 361-594-3251
Sue Gottwald, prin. Fax 594-8106

Shiner Catholic S 300/PK-12
PO Box 725 77984 361-594-2313
Robert Whitworth, prin. Fax 594-8599

Sidney, Comanche
Sidney ISD 100/PK-12
PO Box 190 76474 254-842-5500
Doug Bowden, supt. Fax 842-5731
www.sidney.esc14.net/
Sidney S 100/PK-12
PO Box 190 76474 254-842-5500
Ben Carroll, prin. Fax 842-5731

Sierra Blanca, Hudspeth
Sierra Blanca ISD 200/K-12
PO Box 308 79851 915-369-3741
Henry Dyer, supt. Fax 369-2605
www.sierrablancaisd.com/
Sierra Blanca S 200/K-12
PO Box 308 79851 915-369-2781
Denise Mendoza, prin. Fax 369-2605

Silsbee, Hardin, Pop. 6,722
Silsbee ISD 2,800/K-12
415 Highway 327 W 77656 409-385-5286
Richard Bain, supt. Fax 385-6530
www.silsbeeisd.org
Edwards-Johnson Memorial Silsbee MS 700/6-8
1140 Highway 327 E 77656 409-385-2291
Kevin Wharton, prin. Fax 386-5792
Kirby ES 400/K-1
1205 N 5th St 77656 409-385-5506
Robbie Reeves, prin. Fax 385-0638
Read-Turrentine ES 500/2-3
730 S 7th St 77656 409-385-5218
Tammy Roy, prin. Fax 386-5765
Reeves IS 400/4-5
695 Woodrow St 77656 409-385-6472
Terry Deaver, prin. Fax 386-5744

Silverton, Briscoe, Pop. 706
Silverton ISD 200/PK-12
PO Box 608 79257 806-823-2476
Bill Wood, supt. Fax 823-2276
www.silvertonisd.net
Silverton S 200/PK-12
PO Box 608 79257 806-823-2476
Sheryl Weaver, prin. Fax 823-2276

Simms, Bowie
Simms ISD 600/PK-12
PO Box 9 75574 903-543-2219
Rex Burks, supt. Fax 543-2512
www.simmsisd.net/
Bowie ES 300/PK-5
PO Box 9 75574 903-543-2245
Stephanie Dunson, prin. Fax 543-2512
Bowie JHS 100/6-8
PO Box 9 75574 903-543-2275
Lisa Hudgeons, prin. Fax 543-2512

Simonton, Fort Bend, Pop. 858

Simonton Christian Academy 50/PK-8
PO Box 490 77476 281-346-2303
Dave Davies, admin. Fax 346-2393

Sinton, San Patricio, Pop. 5,509
Sinton ISD 1,600/PK-12
PO Box 1337 78387 361-364-6800
Steve VanMatre, supt. Fax 364-6905
www.sintonisd.net/
Sinton ES 300/3-5
200 S Bowie St 78387 361-364-6900
Abigayle Barton, prin. Fax 364-6914
Smith MS 300/6-8
900 S San Patricio St 78387 361-364-6840
Brayde McClure, prin. Fax 364-6856
Welder ES 400/PK-2
600 N Bowie St 78387 361-364-6600
Lori Trevino, prin. Fax 364-6608

Skellytown, Carson, Pop. 610
Spring Creek ISD 100/PK-6
9849 FM 2171 79080 806-273-6791
Bret Madsen, supt. Fax 273-7479
Spring Creek ES 100/PK-6
9849 FM 2171 79080 806-273-6791
Bret Madsen, prin. Fax 273-7479

Skidmore, Bee
Skidmore-Tynan ISD 800/PK-12
PO Box 409 78389 361-287-3426
Dr. Brett Belmarez, supt. Fax 287-3442
www.stisd.esc2.net
Skidmore-Tynan ES 300/PK-5
PO Box 409 78389 361-287-3426
Letricia Vasquez, prin. Fax 287-0104
Skidmore-Tynan JHS 200/6-8
PO Box 409 78389 361-287-3426
Dan Garza, prin. Fax 287-0714

Slaton, Lubbock, Pop. 5,727
Slaton ISD 1,300/PK-12
140 E Panhandle St 79364 806-828-6591
James Taliaferro, supt. Fax 828-5506
www.slatonisd.net/
Austin ES 200/4-5
740 S 7th St 79364 806-828-5813
Twilla Rex, prin. Fax 828-2079
Slaton JHS 300/6-8
300 W Jean St 79364 806-828-6583
Louie Spinks, prin. Fax 828-2080
Thomas ES 500/PK-3
615 W Lubbock St 79364 806-828-5805
Charles Thompson, prin. Fax 828-2046

St. Joseph S 100/PK-8
1305 W Division St 79364 806-828-6761
James Starkey, prin. Fax 828-5396

Slidell, Wise
Slidell ISD 300/PK-12
PO Box 69 76267 940-466-3118
Greg Enis, supt. Fax 466-3062
www.slidellisd.net/
Slidell ES 100/PK-5
PO Box 69 76267 940-466-3118
Marsha Griggs, prin. Fax 466-3016

Smiley, Gonzales, Pop. 482
Nixon-Smiley Consolidated ISD
Supt. — See Nixon
Nixon-Smiley MS 300/5-8
500 Anglin Rd 78159 830-587-6401
Gary Tausch, prin. Fax 587-6558

Smithville, Bastrop, Pop. 4,370
Smithville ISD 1,700/PK-12
PO Box 479 78957 512-237-2487
Gary Sage, supt. Fax 237-2775
www.smithvilleisd.org

Brown PS 400/PK-2
PO Box 479 78957 512-237-2519
Nina Brinker, prin. Fax 237-5635
Smithville ES 400/3-5
PO Box 479 78957 512-237-2406
Ana Murray, prin. Fax 237-5614
Smithville JHS 400/6-8
PO Box 479 78957 512-237-2407
David Edwards, prin. Fax 237-5624

Smyer, Hockley, Pop. 490
Smyer ISD 400/PK-12
PO Box 206 79367 806-234-2935
Dane Kerns, supt. Fax 234-2411
www.smyer-isd.org
Smyer ES 200/PK-6
PO Box 206 79367 806-234-2341
Jeff Brazil, prin. Fax 234-2411

Snook, Burleson, Pop. 591
Snook ISD 500/PK-12
PO Box 87 77878 979-272-8307
Larry Williams, supt. Fax 272-5041
www.snookisd.com
Snook ES 300/PK-5
PO Box 87 77878 979-272-8307
Leonora Owre, prin. Fax 272-5041
Snook MS 100/6-8
PO Box 87 77878 979-272-8307
Brad Vestal, prin. Fax 272-5041

Snyder, Scurry, Pop. 10,580
Snyder ISD 2,600/PK-12
2901 37th St 79549 325-573-5401
Jim Kirkland, supt. Fax 573-9025
www.snyder.esc14.net
Snyder ES 1,200/K-5
2901 37th St 79549 325-574-8600
Karen Saunders, prin. Fax 573-0342
Snyder JHS 600/6-8
2901 37th St 79549 325-573-6356
Kellye Starnes, prin. Fax 574-6024
Stanfield Preschool 100/PK-PK
2901 37th St 79549 325-573-7512
Thomas Fogleman, prin. Fax 574-6087

Somerset, Bexar, Pop. 1,779
Somerset ISD 3,200/PK-12
PO Box 279 78069 866-852-9858
Saul Hinojosa, supt. Fax 852-9860
www.sisdk12.net
Somerset ECC 500/PK-1
PO Box 279 78069 866-852-9865
Sonia Barclay, prin. Fax 667-2599
Somerset ES 500/2-4
PO Box 279 78069 866-852-9864
Grace Trevino, prin. Fax 667-2602
Somerset JHS 500/7-8
PO Box 279 78069 866-852-9862
Connie Rodriguez, prin. Fax 448-2738
Other Schools – See Von Ormy

Somerville, Burleson, Pop. 1,753
Somerville ISD 500/PK-12
PO Box 997 77879 979-596-2153
Charles Camarillo, supt. Fax 596-1778
www.somervilleisd.org
Somerville ES 200/PK-5
PO Box 997 77879 979-596-1502
Ron Steedly, prin. Fax 596-1778
Somerville JHS 100/6-8
PO Box 997 77879 979-596-1461
Sandra Labby, prin. Fax 596-2004

Sonora, Sutton, Pop. 3,008
Sonora ISD 1,000/PK-12
807 S Concho Ave 76950 325-387-6940
Don Gibson, supt. Fax 387-5090
www.sonoraisd.net/
Sonora ES 400/PK-4
807 S Concho Ave 76950 325-387-6940
Louise Dermody, prin. Fax 387-9604
Sonora JHS 300/5-8
807 S Concho Ave 76950 325-387-6940
John Berry, prin. Fax 387-2007

Sour Lake, Hardin, Pop. 1,716
Hardin-Jefferson ISD 2,100/PK-12
PO Box 490 77659 409-981-6400
Shannon Holmes, supt. Fax 287-2283
www.hjisd.net/
Henderson MS, PO Box 649 77659 500/6-8
Melanie Nunez, prin. 409-981-6420
Sour Lake ES 700/PK-5
PO Box 340 77659 409-981-6440
Danny McFarland, prin. Fax 287-3987
Other Schools – See China

South Houston, Harris, Pop. 16,219
Pasadena ISD
Supt. — See Pasadena
Matthys ES 800/PK-5
1500 Main St 77587 713-740-0632
Becky Vargas, prin. Fax 740-4139
Pearl Hall ES 800/PK-5
1504 9th St 77587 713-740-0688
Marilyn Pavone, prin. Fax 740-4142
Smith ES 900/PK-5
1401 Avenue A 77587 713-740-0720
Cathy Danna, prin. Fax 740-4113
South Houston ES 600/PK-5
900 Main St 77587 713-740-0736
Dr. Karen Holt, prin. Fax 740-4144
South Houston IS 800/6-8
900 College Ave 77587 713-740-0490
Laura Gomez, prin. Fax 740-4097

Southlake, Tarrant, Pop. 24,902
Carroll ISD
Supt. — See Grapevine
Carroll ES 500/K-4
1705 W Continental Blvd 76092 817-949-4300
Stacey Wagnon, prin. Fax 949-4343
Carroll MS 600/7-8
1101 E Dove Rd 76092 817-949-5400
Matt Miller, prin. Fax 949-5454
Dawson MS 700/7-8
400 S Kimball Ave 76092 817-949-5500
Ryan Wilson, prin. Fax 949-5555
Durham ES 500/PK-4
801 Shady Oaks Dr 76092 817-949-4400
Dr. Betty McIlvain, prin. Fax 949-4444
Durham IS 500/5-6
801 Shady Oaks Dr 76092 817-949-5300
Gary Brake, prin. Fax 949-5353
Eubanks IS 600/5-6
500 S Kimball Ave 76092 817-949-5200
Mark Terry, prin. Fax 949-5252
Johnson ES 700/PK-4
1301 N Carroll Ave 76092 817-949-4500
Lori Allison, prin. Fax 949-4545
Old Union ES 500/K-4
1050 S Carroll Ave 76092 817-949-4600
Mary Johnston, prin. Fax 949-4646
Rockenbaugh ES 600/K-4
301 Byron Nelson Pkwy 76092 817-949-4700
Karen White, prin. Fax 949-4747

Keller ISD
Supt. — See Keller
Florence ES 600/PK-4
3095 Johnson Rd 76092 817-744-4700
Mark Martin, prin. Fax 337-3607

Clariden S 200/PK-12
100 Clariden Ranch Rd 76092 682-237-0400
David Deuel, hdmstr. Fax 831-0300
Highland Meadow Montessori Academy 100/PK-6
1060 E Highland St 76092 817-488-2138
Pat Howard, prin. Fax 416-8006

Southland, Garza
Southland ISD 100/K-12
190 Eighth St 79364 806-996-5599
Toby Miller, supt. Fax 996-5342
www.southlandisd.net
Southland S 100/K-12
190 Eighth St 79364 806-996-5339
Brad Ellison, prin. Fax 996-5595

Spearman, Hansford, Pop. 2,924
Spearman ISD 800/PK-12
403 E 11th Ave 79081 806-659-3233
Rodney Sumner, supt. Fax 659-2079
www.spearmanisd.com
Birdwell ES 400/PK-5
511 Townsend St 79081 806-659-2565
P.J. Hanna, prin. Fax 659-3206
Spearman JHS 200/6-8
313 W 5th Ave 79081 806-659-2563
Shane Whiteley, prin. Fax 659-3933

Spicewood, Burnet
Marble Falls ISD
Supt. — See Marble Falls
Spicewood ES 200/PK-5
1005 Spur 191 78669 830-798-3675
Michael Pittard, prin. Fax 798-3676

Splendora, Montgomery, Pop. 1,394
Splendora ISD 2,800/PK-12
23419 FM 2090 Rd 77372 281-689-3129
Thomas Price, supt. Fax 689-7509
www.splendoraisd.org/
Greenleaf ES 700/PK-6
26275 FM 2090 Rd 77372 281-689-8020
Judy Jones, prin. Fax 689-3213
Peach Creek ES 700/PK-6
14455 Cox St 77372 281-689-3114
Bob Frost, prin. Fax 689-7128
Piney Woods ES PK-6
23395 FM 2090 Rd 77372 281-689-3073
Trina Young, prin. Fax 689-7975
Splendora JHS 500/7-8
23411 FM 2090 Rd 77372 281-689-6343
Phelitria Barnes, prin. Fax 689-8702

Spring, Harris, Pop. 37,100
Conroe ISD
Supt. — See Conroe
Broadway ES 400/K-4
2855 Spring Trails Bnd 77386 281-465-2900
Andrea Smith, prin. Fax 465-2903
Cox IS 5-6
3333 Waterbend Cv 77386 281-465-3200
Ken Sharples, prin. Fax 465-3299
Ford ES 800/PK-4
25460 Richards Rd 77386 832-592-5700
Debby Johnson, prin. Fax 592-5709
Kaufman ES 1,100/K-4
2760 Northridge Forest Dr 77386 832-592-5600
Jennifer Daw, prin. Fax 592-5617
Vogel IS 1,200/5-6
27125 Geffert Wright Rd 77386 281-465-3611
Shellie Winkler, prin. Fax 465-3659
York JHS 1,200/7-8
3515 Waterbend Cv 77386 832-592-8600
Jeff Fuller, prin. Fax 592-8684

Klein ISD
Supt. — See Klein
Haude ES 700/PK-5
3111 Louetta Rd 77388 832-484-5600
Sue Schuelke, prin. Fax 484-7862
Hildebrandt IS 2,000/6-8
22800 Hildebrandt Rd 77389 832-249-5100
Joffrey Jones, prin. Fax 249-4068
Kreinhop ES 1,000/PK-5
20820 Ella Blvd 77388 832-484-7400
Dora Williams, prin. Fax 484-7404
Lemm ES 700/PK-5
19034 Joanleigh Dr 77388 832-484-6300
Kathy Brown, prin. Fax 484-7872
Metzler ES 700/K-5
8500 W Rayford Rd 77389 832-484-7900
Christine Rigia, prin. Fax 484-4145
Northampton ES 800/PK-5
6404 Root Rd 77389 832-484-5550
Jane McKetta, prin. Fax 484-7880
Roth ES 600/PK-5
21623 Castlemont Ln 77388 832-484-6600
Ann Dristas, prin. Fax 484-7882
Schindewolf IS 1,400/6-8
20903 Ella Blvd 77388 832-249-5900
Debbie Hamilton, prin. Fax 249-4072

Spring ISD
Supt. — See Houston
Anderson ES 800/PK-5
6218 Lynngate Dr 77373 281-891-8360
Kathy Morrison, prin. Fax 891-8361
Bailey MS 900/6-8
3377 James Leo Dr 77373 281-891-8000
Veronica Vijil, prin. Fax 891-8001
Burchett ES 700/PK-5
3366 James Leo Dr 77373 281-891-8630
Joan Harding, prin. Fax 528-6351
Dueitt MS 900/6-8
1 Eagle Xing 77373 281-891-7800
Paul LeBlanc, prin. Fax 891-7801
Hirsch ES 800/PK-5
2633 Trailing Vine Rd 77373 281-891-8330
Shane Manning, prin. Fax 891-8331
Jenkins ES 800/PK-5
4615 Reynaldo Dr 77373 281-891-8300
Michelle Star, prin. Fax 891-8301
McNabb ES 700/PK-5
743 E Cypresswood Dr 77373 281-891-8690
Pam Dettwiler, prin. Fax 528-5780
Northgate Crossing ES PK-5
23437 Northgate Crossing Bl 77373 281-891-8783
Debbie McIver, prin. Fax 891-8331
Salyers ES 700/PK-5
25705 W Hardy Rd 77373 281-891-8570
Leticia Grounds, prin. Fax 891-8571
Smith ES 900/PK-5
26000 Cypresswood Dr 77373 281-891-8420
Peggy Husky, prin. Fax 891-8421
Twin Creeks MS 1,000/6-8
27100 Cypresswood Dr 77373 281-891-7850
Charlie Rooke, prin. Fax 891-7851
Winship ES 800/PK-5
2175 Spring Creek Dr 77373 281-891-8210
Greg Harberts, prin. Fax 528-7158

Abercrombie Academy 100/K-5
17102 Theiss Mail Route Rd 77379 281-370-0663
Cathy Abercrombie, dir. Fax 257-2207
Northwoods Catholic S 200/PK-8
5500 FM 2920 Rd 77388 281-350-0300
Susan Horne, prin. Fax 350-0330
St. Edward S 300/PK-8
2601 Spring Stuebner Rd 77389 281-353-4570
Gregory Sawka, prin. Fax 353-8255
Woodlands Preparatory S 200/K-12
27440 Kuykendahl Rd 77389 936-516-0600
Ken West, dir. Fax 516-1155

Spring Branch, Comal
Comal ISD
Supt. — See New Braunfels
Brown ES 800/PK-5
20410 State Highway 46 W 78070 830-885-1400
Ross McGlothlin, prin. Fax 885-1401
Rebecca Creek ES 600/PK-5
125 Quest Ave 78070 830-885-1800
Sharon Richardson, prin. Fax 885-1801
Seay ES 400/K-5
20911 State Highway 46 W 78070 830-885-8700
Dr. Judy Murray, prin. Fax 885-8701
Smithson Valley MS 800/6-8
6101 FM 311 78070 830-885-1200
Link Fuller, prin. Fax 885-1201
Spring Branch MS 900/6-8
21053 State Highway 46 W 78070 830-885-8800
Tammy Lind, prin. Fax 885-8801

Springtown, Parker, Pop. 2,639
Springtown ISD 3,600/PK-12
101 E 2nd St 76082 817-220-7243
Andrea Hungerford, supt. Fax 523-5766
www.springtownisd.net
Springtown ES 700/1-4
416 E 3rd St 76082 817-220-2498
Lois Larsen, prin. Fax 523-4094
Springtown IS 500/5-6
300 Po Jo Dr 76082 817-220-1219
Joe Brown, prin. Fax 220-0889
Springtown MS 500/7-8
500 Po Jo Dr 76082 817-220-7455
Mark Wilson, prin. Fax 220-2395
Springtown Watson ES 300/PK-K
301 E 5th St 76082 817-220-2621
Ford Roberson, prin. Fax 220-2482
Other Schools – See Azle

Spur, Dickens, Pop. 1,027
Spur ISD 100/PK-12
PO Box 250 79370 806-271-3272
Earl Jarrett, supt. Fax 271-4575
www.spurbulldogs.com/
Spur ES 100/PK-5
PO Box 250 79370 806-271-4531
Nick Scott, prin. Fax 271-4575

Spurger, Tyler
Spurger ISD 400/PK-12
PO Box 38 77660 409-429-3464
Angela Matterson, supt. Fax 429-3770
www.spurgerisd.org/

Spurger ES 300/PK-6
PO Box 38 77660 409-429-3464
Joseph Fisher, prin. Fax 429-3770

Stafford, Fort Bend, Pop. 19,227
Stafford Municipal SD 3,000/PK-12
1625 Staffordshire Rd 77477 281-261-9200
H.D. Chambers, supt. Fax 261-9249
www.stafford.msd.esc4.net
Stafford ES 600/2-4
1625 Staffordshire Rd 77477 281-261-9229
Sharon Benka, prin. Fax 261-9262
Stafford IS 500/5-6
1625 Staffordshire Rd 77477 281-208-6100
Patricia Suarez, prin. Fax 208-6111
Stafford MS 500/7-8
1625 Staffordshire Rd 77477 281-261-9215
Dr. Phyllis Tyler, prin. Fax 261-9349
Stafford PS 500/PK-1
1625 Staffordshire Rd 77477 281-261-9203
Kim Vu, prin. Fax 261-9348

Stamford, Jones, Pop. 3,253
Stamford ISD 600/PK-12
507 S Orient St 79553 325-773-2705
Brad Lewis, supt. Fax 773-5684
www.stamford.esc14.net
Oliver ES 300/PK-5
507 S Orient St 79553 325-773-5713
Susan Mueller, prin. Fax 773-4077
Stamford MS 100/6-8
507 S Orient St 79553 325-773-2651
Kevin White, prin. Fax 773-4052

Stanton, Martin, Pop. 2,262
Stanton ISD 700/PK-12
PO Box 730 79782 432-756-2244
David Carr, supt. Fax 756-2052
www.stanton.esc18.net/
Stanton ES 400/PK-5
PO Box 730 79782 432-756-2285
Sandy Louder, prin. Fax 756-2052
Stanton MS 200/6-8
PO Box 730 79782 432-756-2544
Albert Chavez, prin. Fax 756-2702

Star, Mills
Star ISD 100/K-12
PO Box 838 76880 325-948-3661
Barbara Marchbanks, supt. Fax 948-3398
www.centex-edu.net/star
Star S 100/K-12
PO Box 838 76880 325-948-3661
Jim Burnett, prin. Fax 948-3398

Stephenville, Erath, Pop. 15,948
Huckabay ISD 200/K-12
200 County Road 421 76401 254-968-8476
Cheryl Floyd, supt. Fax 965-3740
Huckabay S 200/K-12
200 County Road 421 76401 254-968-5274
Tylor Chaplin, prin. Fax 965-3140

Stephenville ISD 3,500/PK-12
2655 W Overhill Dr 76401 254-968-7990
Dr. Darrell Floyd, supt. Fax 968-5942
www.sville.us
Central ES 400/PK-K
780 W Washington St 76401 254-965-3716
Judy Walker, prin. Fax 965-5319
Chamberlin ES 500/1-2
1601 W Frey St 76401 254-968-2311
Barry Cavitt, prin. Fax 968-5396
Gilbert IS 500/5-6
950 N Dale Ave 76401 254-968-4664
Kristen Carey, prin. Fax 968-8696
Henderson JHS 600/7-8
2798 W Frey St 76401 254-968-6967
Bob Cervetto, prin. Fax 965-7018
Hook ES 500/3-4
1067 W Jones St 76401 254-968-3213
Kathy Haynes, prin. Fax 968-6758

Three Way ISD 100/PK-8
247 County Road 207 76401 254-965-6496
Cindy Edwards, supt. Fax 965-3357
www.twisd.us/
Three Way S 100/PK-8
247 County Road 207 76401 254-965-6496
Cindy Edwards, prin. Fax 965-3357

Stephenville Christian S 50/PK-6
1120 County Road 351 76401 254-965-4821
Jane Dameron, dir. Fax 965-6853

Sterling City, Sterling, Pop. 1,013
Sterling City ISD 200/K-12
PO Box 786 76951 325-378-4781
Ronnie Krejci, supt. Fax 378-2283
sterlingcity.netxv.net
Sterling City ES 100/K-5
PO Box 786 76951 325-378-5821
Glenn Coles, prin. Fax 378-2283
Sterling City JHS 100/6-8
PO Box 786 76951 325-378-5821
Glenn Coles, prin. Fax 378-2283

Stinnett, Hutchinson, Pop. 1,860
Plemons-Stinnett-Phillips Cons ISD 600/PK-12
PO Box 3440 79083 806-878-2858
Bill Wiggins, supt. Fax 878-3585
www.pspcisd.net
West Texas ES 300/PK-5
PO Box 3440 79083 806-878-2103
Garey Dozier, prin. Fax 878-3585
West Texas MS 100/6-8
PO Box 3440 79083 806-878-2247
Kevin Freriks, prin. Fax 878-3434

Stockdale, Wilson, Pop. 1,579
Stockdale ISD 700/K-12
PO Box 7 78160 830-996-3551
Vicki Wehmeyer, supt. Fax 996-1071
www.stockdaleisd.net
Stockdale ES 300/K-5
PO Box 7 78160 830-996-1612
Michelle Hartmann, prin. Fax 996-1071
Stockdale JHS 200/6-8
PO Box 7 78160 830-996-3153
Doug Wozniak, prin. Fax 996-1071

Stonewall, Gillespie
Fredericksburg ISD
Supt. — See Fredericksburg
Stonewall ES 100/K-5
220 Peach St 78671 830-644-2216
Wendy Dietrich, prin. Fax 644-5566

Stratford, Sherman, Pop. 1,923
Stratford ISD 600/PK-12
PO Box 108 79084 806-366-3300
Jerry Birdsong, supt. Fax 366-3304
www.stratfordisd.net
Allen ES 200/PK-4
PO Box 108 79084 806-366-3340
Misti McBryde, prin. Fax 366-3304
Stratford JHS 200/5-8
PO Box 108 79084 806-366-3320
Clint Seward, prin. Fax 366-3304

Strawn, Palo Pinto, Pop. 758
Strawn ISD 200/K-12
PO Box 428 76475 254-672-5313
Andrew Lindsey, supt. Fax 672-5662
www.strawnschool.net/
Strawn S 200/K-12
PO Box 428 76475 254-672-5776
Melanie Cormack, prin. Fax 672-5662

Sudan, Lamb, Pop. 1,040
Sudan ISD 400/PK-12
PO Box 249 79371 806-227-2431
Lyndell Lance, supt. Fax 227-2146
www.sudanisd.net
Sudan ES 200/PK-7
PO Box 249 79371 806-227-2431
Scott Harrell, prin. Fax 227-2146

Sugar Land, Fort Bend, Pop. 75,754
Fort Bend ISD 69,200/PK-12
16431 Lexington Blvd 77479 281-634-1000
Dr. Timothy Jenney, supt. Fax 634-1700
www.fortbend.k12.tx.us
Austin Parkway ES 900/PK-5
4400 Austin Pkwy 77479 281-634-4001
Donna Whisonant, prin. Fax 634-4014
Barrington Place ES 800/PK-5
2100 Squire Dobbins Dr 77478 281-634-4040
Dawn Carlson, prin. Fax 634-4057
Brazos Bend ES 1,000/PK-5
621 Cunningham Creek Blvd 77479 281-634-5180
Beverly Croucher, prin. Fax 634-5200
Colony Bend ES 500/K-5
2720 Planters St 77479 281-634-4080
Sue Sierra, prin. Fax 634-4092
Colony Meadows ES 600/PK-5
4510 Sweetwater Blvd 77479 281-634-4120
Eugene Dupont, prin. Fax 634-4136
Commonwealth ES 800/K-5
4909 Commonwealth Blvd 77479 281-634-5120
Julie Diaz, prin. Fax 634-5140
Cornerstone ES 400/K-5
1800 Chatham Ave 77479 281-634-6400
Christopher Winans, prin. Fax 327-6400
Drabek ES 900/K-5
11325 Lake Woodbridge Dr, 281-634-6570
Susan Cornelius, prin. Fax 634-6572
Dulles ES 800/K-5
630 Dulles Ave 77478 281-634-5830
Ginger Carrabine, prin. Fax 634-5843
Dulles MS 1,500/6-8
500 Dulles Ave 77478 281-634-5750
Michael Heinzen, prin. Fax 634-5781
First Colony MS 1,200/6-8
3225 Austin Pkwy 77479 281-634-3240
Dr. Jennifer Reichek, prin. Fax 634-3267
Fort Settlement MS 1,100/6-8
5440 Elkins Rd 77479 281-634-6440
Karon Crockett, prin. Fax 634-6456
Garcia MS 1,900/6-8
18550 Old Richmond Rd, 281-634-3160
Viretta West, prin. Fax 634-3207
Highlands ES 700/PK-5
2022 Colonist Park Dr 77478 281-634-4160
Dr. Latecha Bogle, prin. Fax 634-4176
Lakeview ES 600/K-5
314 Lakeview Dr, 281-634-4200
Janet Moring, prin. Fax 634-4214
Oyster Creek ES 900/PK-5
16425 Mellow Oaks Ln, 281-634-5910
Thomas Heinly, prin. Fax 634-5925
Sartartia MS 1,100/6-8
8125 Homeward Way 77479 281-634-6310
Dr. Sara Thurman, prin. Fax 634-6373
Settlers Way ES 500/PK-5
3015 Settlers Way Blvd 77479 281-634-4360
Kristi Durham, prin. Fax 634-4376
Sugar Land MS 1,600/6-8
321 7th St, 281-634-3080
Lisa Padron, prin. Fax 634-3108
Sugar Mill ES 600/PK-5
13707 Jess Pirtle Blvd, 281-634-4440
Elizabeth Graham, prin. Fax 634-4459
Townewest ES 800/PK-5
13927 Old Richmond Rd, 281-634-4480
Stephanie Houston, prin. Fax 634-4494
Walker Station ES 900/K-5
6200 Homeward Way 77479 281-634-4400
Christopher Morgan, prin. Fax 634-4413

Other Schools – See Fresno, Houston, Meadows, Missouri City, Richmond

Lamar Consolidated ISD
Supt. — See Rosenberg
Campbell ES 1,000/K-5
1000 Shadow Bend Dr 77479 832-223-1300
Michelle Koerth, prin. Fax 223-1301
Dickinson ES 700/K-5
7110 Greatwood Pkwy 77479 832-223-1400
Karen Mumphord, prin. Fax 223-1401

Cambridge Montessori S 200/PK-2
6380 Highway 90A, 281-491-2223
Monica Sakhuja, prin. Fax 241-7056
Faith Lutheran S 200/K-8
800 Brooks St 77478 281-242-4453
Gordon Stoneburner, admin. Fax 242-8749
Fellowship Christian Academy 100/PK-6
16425 Old Richmond Rd Ste A, 281-495-1814
Karen Bowen, prin. Fax 495-1831
Ft. Bend Baptist Academy 400/PK-5
1250 7th St 77478 281-263-9100
Margie Meyer, prin. Fax 263-9102
Ft. Bend Baptist Academy 200/6-8
1250 7th St 77478 281-263-9191
Ronald Bell, prin. Fax 242-7195
God's Rainbow Christian Academy 50/PK-12
13131 Alston Rd 77478 281-313-1485
Milagros Quinones, dir. Fax 474-8877
Honor Roll S 600/PK-8
4111 Sweetwater Blvd 77479 281-265-7888
Michael Statham, hdmstr. Fax 265-7880
Riverbend Montessori S 100/PK-5
4225 Elkins Rd 77479 281-980-4123
Carolyn Edgar, dir. Fax 980-8817
St. Laurence S 700/PK-8
2630 Austin Pkwy 77479 281-980-0500
Debra Haney, prin. Fax 980-0026
St. Theresa Academy PK-8
115 7th St, 281-494-1156
Jonathan Beeson, prin. Fax 242-1393
Sugar Mill Montessori S 50/PK-K
1120 Burney Rd, 281-242-2100
Kay Challa, prin. Fax 242-2103

Sullivan City, Hidalgo, Pop. 4,346
La Joya ISD
Supt. — See La Joya
Benavides ES 400/PK-5
1882 El Pinto Rd 78595 956-580-6175
Mary Garza-Ibarra, prin. Fax 485-1091
Fordyce ES 500/PK-5
801 FM 886 78595 956-580-8894
Myra Ramos, prin. Fax 485-2713

Sulphur Bluff, Hopkins
Sulphur Bluff ISD 200/PK-12
PO Box 30 75481 903-945-2460
Robert Ross, supt. Fax 945-2459
www.sulphurbluffisd.net/
Sulphur Bluff ES 100/PK-6
PO Box 30 75481 903-945-2460
Amy Northcutt, prin. Fax 945-2459

Sulphur Springs, Hopkins, Pop. 15,228
North Hopkins ISD 500/PK-12
1994 Farm Road 71 W 75482 903-945-2192
Tom Long, supt. Fax 945-2531
www.northhopkins.net/
North Hopkins ES 300/PK-6
1994 Farm Road 71 W 75482 903-945-2192
Jim Westbrook, prin. Fax 945-2531

Sulphur Springs ISD 4,100/PK-12
631 Connally St 75482 903-885-2153
Patsy Bolton, supt. Fax 439-6162
www.ssisd.net/
Austin ES 200/1-4
808 Davis St S 75482 903-885-4045
Juan Harrison, prin. Fax 439-6139
Bowie ES 400/1-4
1400 Mockingbird Ln 75482 903-885-3772
Carol Worsham, prin. Fax 885-5754
Douglas IS 300/5-5
600 Calvert St 75482 903-885-4516
Tona Sue Hudson, prin. Fax 439-1181
Early Childhood Learning Center 600/PK-K
390 N Hillcrest Dr 75482 903-439-6170
Sherry Finney, prin. Fax 439-6177
Lamar ES 300/1-4
825 Church St 75482 903-885-4550
Rowena Johnson, prin. Fax 439-6144
Sulphur Springs MS 900/6-8
829 Bell St 75482 903-885-7741
Glenn Wilson, prin. Fax 439-6126
Travis ES 400/1-4
130 Garrison St 75482 903-885-5246
Kristin Monk, prin. Fax 438-2251

Sundown, Hockley, Pop. 1,540
Sundown ISD 600/PK-12
PO Box 1110 79372 806-229-3021
Mike Motheral, supt. Fax 229-2004
www.sundownisd.com
Sundown ES 300/PK-5
PO Box 1110 79372 806-229-5021
Scott Marshall, prin. Fax 229-2004
Sundown JHS 100/6-8
PO Box 1110 79372 806-229-4691
Eddie Carter, prin. Fax 229-2004

Sunnyvale, Dallas, Pop. 3,817
Sunnyvale ISD 600/K-12
417 E Tripp Rd 75182 972-226-7601
Doug Williams, supt. Fax 226-6882
www.sunnyvaleisd.com
Sunnyvale ES 300/K-5
417 E Tripp Rd 75182 972-226-7601
Amy Tutle, prin. Fax 226-6882

Grace Fellowship Christian S 100/K-12
3052 N Belt Line Rd 75182 972-226-4499
Edris Carr, prin. Fax 226-0242

Sunray, Moore, Pop. 1,942

Sunray ISD 500/PK-12
PO Box 240 79086 806-948-4411
Michael Brown, supt. Fax 948-5274
www.sunrayisd.net
Sunray ES 200/PK-4
PO Box 240 79086 806-948-4222
Terry Mulbery, prin. Fax 948-4180
Sunray MS 200/5-8
PO Box 240 79086 806-948-4444
Aaron Lewis, prin. Fax 948-4208

Sweeny, Brazoria, Pop. 3,622

Sweeny ISD 2,100/PK-12
1310 N Elm St 77480 979-491-8000
Randy Miksch, supt. Fax 491-8030
www.sweeny.isd.esc4.net/
Sweeny ES 900/PK-5
1310 N Elm St 77480 979-491-8300
Brian Brooks, prin. Fax 491-8373
Sweeny JHS 500/6-8
1310 N Elm St 77480 979-491-8200
Raymond Washington, prin. Fax 491-8274

Sweet Home, Lavaca

Sweet Home ISD 100/PK-8
PO Box 326 77987 361-293-3221
Randy Meyer, supt. Fax 741-2499
www.sweethomeisd.org
Sweet Home S 100/PK-8
PO Box 326 77987 361-293-3221
Randy Meyer, prin. Fax 741-2499

Sweetwater, Nolan, Pop. 10,694

Sweetwater ISD 2,300/PK-12
207 Musgrove St 79556 325-235-8601
Terry Pittman, supt. Fax 235-5561
www.sweetwaterisd.net/
Cowen ECC 200/PK-PK
700 W 4th St 79556 325-235-3482
Kelli Wigington, dir. Fax 235-2771
East Ridge ES 400/PK-3
1700 E 12th St 79556 325-235-5282
Mike Marlett, prin. Fax 235-3740
Southeast ES 300/PK-3
1201 Mustang Dr 79556 325-235-9222
Vicki Mayberry, prin. Fax 235-0260
Sweetwater IS 300/4-5
705 E 3rd St 79556 325-235-3491
Heather Moore, prin. Fax 235-8016
Sweetwater MS 500/6-8
305 Lamar St 79556 325-236-6303
Kerry Birdwell, prin. Fax 236-6941

Taft, San Patricio, Pop. 3,429

Taft ISD 1,300/PK-12
400 College St 78390 361-528-2636
Dr. Chad Kelly, supt. Fax 528-2223
www.taftisd.net
East ES 300/3-5
1150 Gregory St 78390 361-528-2636
Laura Dobbins, prin. Fax 528-2717
Petty ES 400/PK-2
401 Peach St 78390 361-528-2636
Brenda Meyer, prin. Fax 528-2669
Taft JHS 300/6-8
727 McIntyre Ave 78390 361-528-2636
Ricardo Trevino, prin. Fax 528-5477

Tahoka, Lynn, Pop. 2,730

Tahoka ISD 600/PK-12
PO Box 1230 79373 806-561-4105
Jimmy Parker, supt. Fax 561-4160
www.tahoka.esc17.net
Tahoka ES 300/PK-5
PO Box 1560 79373 806-561-4350
Alecia Hancock, prin. Fax 561-5334
Tahoka MS 100/6-8
PO Box 1500 79373 806-561-4538
Tom Thomas, prin. Fax 561-6082

Tatum, Rusk, Pop. 1,188

Tatum ISD 1,300/PK-12
PO Box 808 75691 903-947-6482
Dee Hartt Ed.D., supt. Fax 947-3295
www.tatumisd.org/
Tatum ES 300/4-6
PO Box 808 75691 903-947-6484
Clifford Harkless, prin. Fax 947-3299
Tatum MS 200/7-8
PO Box 808 75691 903-947-6487
Bob Garcia, prin. Fax 947-2322
Tatum PS 400/PK-3
PO Box 808 75691 903-947-6485
Donna Stagner, prin. Fax 947-6532

Taylor, Williamson, Pop. 15,014

Taylor ISD 3,000/PK-12
602 W 12th St 76574 512-365-1391
Bruce Scott Ed.D., supt. Fax 365-3800
www.taylorisd.org
Johnson ES 700/3-5
3100 Duck Ln 76574 512-365-1091
Reta Katz, prin. Fax 365-8533
Pasemann ES 800/PK-2
2809 North Dr 76574 512-365-2278
Jennifer Patschke, prin. Fax 365-2280
Taylor MS 700/6-8
304 Carlos Parker Blvd NW 76574 512-365-8591
Danny Ward, prin. Fax 365-8589

St. Marys S 100/PK-8
520 Washburn St 76574 512-352-2313
Dr. Barbara Gibson, prin. Fax 365-5313
St. Paul Lutheran S 100/PK-5
610 Fowzer St 76574 512-365-6161
Lyn Parmer, dir. Fax 365-6161

Teague, Freestone, Pop. 4,630

Dew ISD 200/PK-8
606 County Road 481 75860 903-389-2828
Thomas Weeaks, supt. Fax 389-5104
www.dewisd.org
Dew S 200/PK-8
606 County Road 481 75860 903-389-2828
Thomas Weeaks, prin. Fax 389-5104

Teague ISD 1,200/PK-12
420 N 10th Ave 75860 254-739-3071
Ned Burns, supt. Fax 739-5223
www.teagueisd.org/
Teague ES 400/PK-3
420 N 10th Ave 75860 254-739-2611
Carol Ann Dawley, prin. Fax 739-3605
Teague IS 200/4-6
420 N 10th Ave 75860 254-739-3303
Vickey Little, prin. Fax 739-3561
Teague JHS 200/7-8
420 N 10th Ave 75860 254-739-3011
Donnie Osborn, prin. Fax 739-5896

Temple, Bell, Pop. 55,447

Belton ISD
Supt. — See Belton
Lake Belton MS 900/6-8
8818 Tarver Dr 76502 254-215-2900
Suzy McKinney, prin. Fax 215-2901
Pirtle ES 800/K-5
714 S Pea Ridge Rd 76502 254-215-3400
Pam Neves, prin. Fax 215-3401
Tarver ES 400/PK-5
7949 Stone Hollow 76502 254-215-3800
Lois Knox, prin. Fax 774-9684

Temple ISD 8,300/PK-12
PO Box 788 76503 254-215-8473
Dr. Robin Battershell, supt. Fax 215-6783
www.tisd.org
Bethune ECC 400/PK-PK
510 E Avenue J 76504 254-215-6700
Tina Coppin, prin. Fax 215-6728
Bonham MS 500/6-8
4600 Midway Dr 76502 254-215-6600
Judy Hundley, prin. Fax 215-6634
Cater ES 400/K-5
4111 Lark Trl 76502 254-215-7444
David Dixon, prin. Fax 215-7479
Garcia ES 600/K-5
2525 Lavendusky Dr 76501 254-215-6100
Ron Smith, prin. Fax 215-6122
Jefferson ES 500/K-5
400 W Walker Ave 76501 254-215-5500
Beth Giniewicz, prin. Fax 215-5545
Kennedy-Powell ES 500/K-5
3707 W Nugent Ave 76504 254-215-6000
Melissa Harper, prin. Fax 215-6032
Lamar MS 600/6-8
2120 N 1st St 76501 254-215-6444
Jennifer Mathesen, prin. Fax 215-6483
Meridith-Dunbar ES 300/PK-3
1717 E Avenue J 76501 254-215-5900
Wanda Reynolds, prin. Fax 215-5944
Raye-Allen ES 400/K-5
5015 S 5th St 76502 254-215-5800
Gale Leidy, prin. Fax 215-5843
Scott ES 300/K-5
2301 W Avenue P 76504 254-215-6222
Donna Lammert, prin. Fax 215-6251
Thornton ES 500/K-5
2900 Pin Oak Dr 76502 254-215-5700
Mark Fleming, prin. Fax 215-5746
Travis MS 700/6-8
1500 S 19th St 76504 254-215-6300
Eddy McNamara, prin. Fax 215-6352
Western Hills ES 500/K-5
600 Arapaho Dr 76504 254-215-5600
Pat Groholski, prin. Fax 215-5624

Central Texas Christian S 500/PK-12
4141 W FM 93 76502 254-939-5700
Ed Thomas, supt. Fax 939-5733
St. Marys S 300/PK-8
1019 S 7th St 76504 254-778-8141
Dr. Ardelle Hamilton, prin. Fax 778-1396

Tenaha, Shelby, Pop. 1,100

Tenaha ISD 300/PK-12
PO Box 318 75974 936-248-5000
Don Fallin, supt. Fax 248-3902
www.tenahaisd.com/
Tenaha ES 200/PK-5
PO Box 318 75974 936-248-5000
Terry Bowlin, prin. Fax 248-4216

Terlingua, Brewster

Terlingua Common SD 200/PK-12
PO Box 256 79852 432-371-2281
Kathy Killingsworth, supt. Fax 371-2245
terlingua.cdtc.us/
Terlingua S 100/PK-8
PO Box 256 79852 432-371-2281
Bobbie Jones, prin. Fax 371-2245

Terrell, Kaufman, Pop. 17,665

Terrell ISD 4,500/PK-12
700 N Catherine St 75160 972-563-7504
Kelly Rodgers, supt. Fax 551-2842
www.terrellisd.com/
Burnett ES 600/PK-K
921 S Rockwall St 75160 972-563-1452
Zachery Wiley, prin. Fax 563-4782
Furlough MS 600/7-8
1351 Colquitt Rd 75160 972-563-7501
Danielle Whiffen, prin. Fax 563-5721
Kennedy ES 700/1-2
1400 S Rockwall St 75160 972-563-1443
Dwight Malone, prin. Fax 563-4783
Long ES 700/3-6
300 Creekside Dr 75160 972-563-1448
Maria Johnson, prin. Fax 563-4780
Wood ES 700/3-6
121 Poetry Rd 75160 972-563-3750
Judy Mackey, prin. Fax 563-4774

Poetry Community Christian S 200/K-12
18688 FM 986 75160 972-563-7227
Anne Puidk Horan, admin. Fax 563-0025

Texarkana, Bowie, Pop. 35,746

Liberty-Eylau ISD 2,800/PK-12
2901 Leopard Dr 75501 903-832-1535
Micah Lewis, supt. Fax 838-9444
www.leisd.net
Liberty-Eylau C.K. Bender ES 600/2-4
2300 Buchanan Rd 75501 903-831-5347
Patti O'Bannon, prin. Fax 831-5393
Liberty-Eylau MS 800/5-8
5555 Leopard Dr 75501 903-838-5555
Regina Houff, prin. Fax 832-6700
Liberty-Eylau Pre - K Center 200/PK-PK
3105 Norris Cooley Dr 75501 903-831-5352
Joann Floyd, prin. Fax 831-5354
Liberty-Eylau PS 400/K-1
5492 US Highway 59 S 75501 903-831-5390
Amy Barron, prin. Fax 832-6497

Pleasant Grove ISD 2,000/PK-12
8500 N Kings Hwy 75503 903-831-4086
Margaret Davis, supt. Fax 831-4435
www.pgisd.net
Pleasant Grove ES 700/PK-4
6500 Pleasant Grove Rd 75503 903-838-0528
Pam Bradford, prin. Fax 831-3799
Pleasant Grove MS 600/5-8
5605 Cooks Ln 75503 903-831-4295
Linda Erie, prin. Fax 831-5501

Red Lick ISD 400/K-8
3511 N FM 2148 75503 903-838-8230
Dr. Richard Hervey, supt. Fax 831-6134
www.redlickisd.com
Red Lick ES 200/K-4
3511 N FM 2148 75503 903-838-8230
Phyllis Deese, prin. Fax 831-6134
Red Lick MS 100/5-8
3511 N FM 2148 75503 903-838-6006
Doyle Clark, prin. Fax 831-6134

Texarkana ISD 6,500/PK-12
4241 Summerhill Rd 75503 903-794-3651
James Russell, supt. Fax 792-2632
www.txkisd.net
Dunbar IS 300/2-5
2315 W 10th St 75501 903-794-8112
Kathy Owen, prin. Fax 794-5841
Highland Park ES 300/PK-5
401 W 25th St 75503 903-794-8001
David Burden, prin. Fax 793-1702
Jones Early Literacy Center 300/PK-1
2600 W 15th St 75501 903-793-4871
Jennell Ingram, prin. Fax 793-7596
Morriss Math & Engineering ES 400/K-5
4826 University Park 75503 903-791-2262
Rick Sandlin, prin. Fax 798-6875
Spring Lake Park ES 400/PK-5
4324 Ghio Fish Blvd 75503 903-794-7525
Debbie Roberts, prin. Fax 794-0633
Texas MS 1,300/6-8
2100 College Dr 75503 903-793-5631
George Moore, prin. Fax 792-2935
Westlawn ES 400/K-5
410 Westlawn Dr 75501 903-223-4252
Trisha Allen, prin. Fax 223-4262
Other Schools – See Nash, Wake Village

Liberty-Eylau Christian S 50/K-4
4903 Eylau Loop Rd 75501 903-838-8080
Carolyn Teel, admin. Fax 838-3949
St. James Day S 200/PK-6
5501 N State Line Ave 75503 903-793-5554
Audrey Russell, hdmstr. Fax 793-1775
Texarkana SDA S 50/K-8
3100 Pleasant Grove Rd 75503 903-831-4442

Texas City, Galveston, Pop. 44,274

La Marque ISD
Supt. — See La Marque
Simms ES 300/1-5
529 N Westward St 77591 409-935-2891
David Scurry, prin. Fax 908-5081

Texas City ISD 5,800/PK-12
PO Box 1150 77592 409-942-2713
Fax 942-2655
www.tcisd.org/
Blocker MS 900/7-8
500 14th Ave N 77590 409-942-2756
R. Carter, prin. Fax 942-2755
Fry IS 800/5-6
1400 5th Ave N 77590 409-942-2780
Susan Tortorici, prin. Fax 942-2429
Heights ES 700/PK-4
300 N Logan St 77590 409-942-2850
Nathan Jackson, prin. Fax 942-2450
Kohfeldt ES 500/K-4
701 14th St N 77590 409-942-2840
Terri Burchfield, prin. Fax 942-2421
Northside ES 600/K-4
2300 21st St N 77590 409-942-2820
Susan Wilson, prin. Fax 942-2839
Roosevelt-Wilson ES 600/K-4
301 16th Ave N 77590 409-942-2860
Jeffrey High, prin. Fax 942-2871

Living Word Christian S 50/PK-12
2121 6th St N 77590 409-692-5844
Jeanette Huwe, prin. Fax 948-2977

Our Lady of Fatima S 200/PK-6
1600 9th Ave N 77590 409-945-3326
Susan Flanagan, prin. Fax 945-3389

Texhoma, Texas, Pop. 335
Texhoma ISD 100/PK-4
PO Box 709, Texhoma OK 73949 806-827-7400
Mel Yates, supt. Fax 827-7657
www.texhomaisd.net/
Texhoma ES 100/PK-4
PO Box 709, Texhoma OK 73949 806-827-7400
Mel Yates, prin. Fax 827-7657

Texline, Dallam, Pop. 514
Texline ISD 100/K-12
PO Box 60 79087 806-362-4667
Gary Laramore, supt. Fax 362-4538
www.texlineisd.net
Texline S 100/K-12
PO Box 60 79087 806-362-4284
Jim Allison, prin. Fax 362-4938

The Colony, Denton, Pop. 37,972
Lewisville ISD
Supt. — See Flower Mound
Camey ES 600/PK-5
4949 Arbor Glen Rd 75056 469-713-5951
Livia Callahan, prin. Fax 350-9015
Ethridge ES 400/PK-5
6001 Ethridge Dr 75056 469-713-5954
Martha Gooding, prin. Fax 350-9036
Griffin MS 700/6-8
5105 N Colony Blvd 75056 469-713-5973
Jeff Kajs, prin. Fax 350-9187
Lakeview MS 800/6-8
4300 Keys Dr 75056 469-713-5974
Dr. Steve Nauman, prin. Fax 350-9202
Morningside ES 700/K-5
6350 Paige Rd 75056 469-713-5970
Rita Bacque, prin. Fax 350-9117
Owen ES 400/K-5
5640 Squires Dr 75056 469-713-5950
Linda Fontes, prin. Fax 350-9000
Peters Colony ES 600/K-5
5101 Nash Dr 75056 469-713-5179
Toni Hall, prin. Fax 350-9133
Stewarts Creek ES 400/PK-5
4431 Augusta St 75056 469-713-5960
Lea Land, prin. Fax 350-9145

The Woodlands, Montgomery, Pop. 63,000
Conroe ISD
Supt. — See Conroe
Buckalew ES 900/K-4
4909 Alden Bridge Dr 77382 281-465-3400
Linda Crews, prin. Fax 298-6898
Bush ES 600/K-4
7420 Crownridge Dr 77382 936-709-1600
Judy Mills, prin. Fax 273-5297
Collins IS 500/5-6
6020 Shadow Bend Pl 77381 281-298-3800
Norma Nardone, prin. Fax 298-3803
David ES 600/K-4
5301 Shadow Bend Pl 77381 281-298-4700
Lee Allen, prin. Fax 298-4703
Deretchin ES 800/K-6
11000 Merit Oaks Dr 77382 832-592-8700
Debbie Jones, prin. Fax 592-8780
Galatas ES 600/K-4
9001 Cochrans Crossing Dr 77381 936-709-5000
Marlene Lindsay, prin. Fax 709-5003
Glen Loch ES 600/PK-4
27505 Glen Loch Dr 77381 281-298-4900
Cassie Hertzenberg, prin. Fax 298-4903
Hailey ES 600/K-4
12051 Sawmill Rd 77380 281-863-4100
Dr. Pat Nichol, prin. Fax 681-4004
Knox JHS 1,100/7-8
12104 Sawmill Rd 77380 832-592-8400
Joe Daw, prin. Fax 592-8410
Lamar ES 600/K-4
1300 Many Pines Rd 77380 832-592-5800
Mary Kirbo, prin. Fax 592-5810
McCullough JHS 1,900/7-8
3800 S Panther Creek Dr 77381 832-592-5100
Chris McCord, prin. Fax 592-5116
Mitchell IS 1,200/5-6
6800 Alden Bridge Dr 77382 832-592-8500
Paula Klapesky, prin. Fax 592-8518
Powell ES 800/K-4
7332 Cochrans Crossing Dr 77381 936-709-1700
Lisa Garrison, prin. Fax 273-3783
Ride ES 400/K-4
4920 W Panther Creek Dr 77381 281-465-2800
Cindy Johnston, prin. Fax 465-2803
Tough ES 1,100/K-6
11660 Crane Brook Dr 77382 281-465-5900
Julie English, prin. Fax 465-5959
Wilkerson IS 700/5-6
12312 Sawmill Rd 77380 832-592-8900
Marie Hartley, prin. Fax 592-8910

Cooper S 1,000/PK-12
1 John Cooper Dr 77381 281-367-0900
Michael Maher, hdmstr. Fax 292-9201
Esprit Montessori 100/PK-8
4890 W Panther Creek Dr 77381 281-298-9200
Rosemary Brumbelow, prin. Fax 298-2622
Harvest S 50/PK-7
5125 Shadow Bend Pl 77381 281-298-8632
Tiffany Cooper, admin. Fax 298-8632
Legacy Preparatory Christian Academy 100/PK-12
6565 Research Forest Dr 77381 936-273-4511
Audra May, dir.
St. Anthony of Padua S 400/PK-8
7901 Bay Branch Dr 77382 281-296-0300
Renee Nunez, prin. Fax 296-7238
Woodlands Christian Academy 400/PK-12
5800 Academy Way 77384 936-273-2555
Julie Ambler, hdmstr. Fax 271-3115

Thorndale, Milam, Pop. 1,330
Thorndale ISD 500/K-12
PO Box 870 76577 512-898-2538
Robert Lindemann, supt. Fax 898-5356
www.thorndale.txed.net/
Thorndale ES 200/K-5
PO Box 870 76577 512-898-2912
Suzanne Lenz, prin. Fax 898-5541
Thorndale MS 100/6-8
PO Box 870 76577 512-898-2670
Heather Klotz, prin. Fax 898-5505

St. Paul Lutheran S 100/PK-8
PO Box 369 76577 512-898-2711
Cindy Melcher, prin. Fax 898-5298

Thrall, Williamson, Pop. 847
Thrall ISD 400/K-12
201 S Bounds St 76578 512-898-0062
Bruce Davis, supt. Fax 898-5349
www.thrallisd.com
Thrall ES 300/K-5
201 S Bounds St 76578 512-898-5293
Suzanne Lenz, prin. Fax 898-2879

Three Rivers, Live Oak, Pop. 1,764
Three Rivers ISD 600/PK-12
108 N School Rd 78071 361-786-3626
Mac Johanson, supt. Fax 786-2555
www.trisd.esc2.net
Three Rivers ES 300/PK-5
108 N School Rd 78071 361-786-3592
Dianne Dye, prin. Fax 786-2555
Three Rivers MS 200/6-8
108 N School Rd 78071 361-786-3803
Hortensia Brooks, prin. Fax 786-2555

Throckmorton, Throckmorton, Pop. 789
Throckmorton ISD 200/PK-12
210 College St 76483 940-849-2411
Scott Hogue, supt. Fax 849-3345
www.throck.org/
Throckmorton S 100/PK-8
210 College St 76483 940-849-2421
Robert Underwood, prin. Fax 849-3345

Tilden, McMullen
McMullen County ISD 200/PK-12
PO Box 359 78072 361-274-3315
Frank Franklin, supt. Fax 274-3665
www.mcisd.us
McMullen County S 200/PK-12
PO Box 359 78072 361-274-3371
Scott Higgins, prin. Fax 274-3580

Timpson, Shelby, Pop. 1,144
Timpson ISD 600/PK-12
PO Box 370 75975 936-254-2463
Dr. Leland Moore, supt. Fax 254-3878
www.timpsonisd.com
Timpson ES 200/PK-5
PO Box 370 75975 936-254-2462
Betty Ivins, prin. Fax 254-3263
Timpson MS 100/6-8
PO Box 370 75975 936-254-2078
Calvin Smith, prin. Fax 254-2355

Tioga, Grayson, Pop. 878
Tioga ISD 200/PK-8
PO Box 159 76271 940-437-2366
Neal Harrison, supt. Fax 437-9986
tioga.ednet10.net/
Tioga S 200/PK-8
PO Box 159 76271 940-437-2366
Fax 437-9986

Tivoli, Refugio
Austwell-Tivoli ISD 200/K-12
207 Redfish St 77990 361-286-3212
Dr. Antonio Aguirre, supt. Fax 286-3637
www.atisd.net
Austwell-Tivoli ES 100/K-6
207 Redfish St 77990 361-286-3222
Stephen Maldonado, prin. Fax 286-3637

Tolar, Hood, Pop. 643
Tolar ISD 500/PK-12
PO Box 368 76476 254-835-4718
Bruce Gibbs, supt. Fax 835-4704
www.tolarisd.org
Tolar ES 200/PK-5
PO Box 368 76476 254-835-4028
Paul Ryan, prin. Fax 835-4319
Tolar JHS 6-8
PO Box 368 76476 254-835-5207
Woody Martin, prin. Fax 835-5208

Tomball, Harris, Pop. 9,938
Klein ISD
Supt. — See Klein
Kohrville ES 1,200/K-5
11600 Woodland Shore Dr 77375 832-484-7200
Darrel Luedeker, prin. Fax 484-7890
Schultz ES 800/PK-5
7920 Willow Forest Dr 77375 832-484-7000
Sherri Bradley, prin. Fax 484-7884

Tomball ISD 9,100/PK-12
221 W Main St 77375 281-357-3100
John Neubauer, supt. Fax 357-3128
www.tomballisd.net
Beckendorf IS 300/5-6
1110 Baker Dr 77375 281-357-3200
Delores Guidry, prin. Fax 357-3276
Canyon Pointe ES PK-4
13002 Northpointe Blvd 77377 281-357-3100
Valerie Petrzelka, prin.
Lakewood ES 800/K-4
15614 Gettysburg Dr 77377 281-357-3260
Holly Jones, prin. Fax 357-3271
Northpointe IS 700/5-6
11855 Northpointe Blvd 77377 281-357-3020
Pam Liles, prin. Fax 357-3026
Rosehill ES 700/PK-4
17950 Tomball Waller Rd 77377 281-357-3075
Jeanine Deyoe, prin. Fax 357-3099
Tomball ES 500/PK-4
1110 Inwood St 77375 281-357-3280
Meredith Walker, prin. Fax 357-3288
Tomball IS 300/5-6
723 W Main St 77375 281-357-3150
Cindy Sorrells, prin. Fax 357-3148
Tomball JHS 600/7-8
30403 Quinn Rd 77375 281-357-3000
Linda Harry, prin. Fax 357-3027
Willow Creek ES 900/PK-4
18302 N Eldridge Pkwy 77377 281-357-3080
JoAnn Colson, prin. Fax 357-3092
Willow Wood JHS 800/7-8
11770 Gregson Rd 77377 281-357-3030
Dr. Kate Caffery, prin. Fax 357-3044
Other Schools – See Magnolia

Rosehill Christian S 300/PK-12
19830 FM 2920 Rd 77377 281-351-8114
Dean Unsicker, admin. Fax 516-3418
St. Anne S 300/PK-8
1111 S Cherry St 77375 281-351-0093
Margaret Morgan, prin. Fax 357-1905
Salem Lutheran S 500/PK-8
22607 Lutheran Church Rd 77377 281-351-8122
Mary Beth Gaertner, prin.
Step by Step Christian S 100/K-7
1119 S Cherry St 77375 281-351-2888
Nancy Davis, admin. Fax 516-0253
Zion Lutheran S 50/PK-2
911 Hicks St 77375 281-255-6203
Pat Karish, dir. Fax 255-8696

Tom Bean, Grayson, Pop. 995
Tom Bean ISD 800/K-12
PO Box 128 75489 903-546-6076
Kathy Garrison, supt. Fax 546-6104
www.tombean-isd.org
Tom Bean ES 400/K-5
PO Box 128 75489 903-546-6333
Eric Hough, prin. Fax 546-6572
Tom Bean MS 200/6-8
PO Box 128 75489 903-546-6161
Dewitt Smith, prin. Fax 546-6798

Tool, Henderson, Pop. 2,452
Malakoff ISD
Supt. — See Malakoff
Tool ES 200/PK-5
1201 S Tool Dr, 903-432-3459
Bill Morgan, prin. Fax 432-3666

Tornillo, El Paso
Tornillo ISD 1,200/PK-12
PO Box 170 79853 915-765-3000
Paul Vranish, supt. Fax 764-2120
www.tisd.us/
Tornillo ES 500/PK-3
PO Box 170 79853 915-765-3100
Severo Alcoset, prin. Fax 764-5675
Tornillo IS 300/4-6
PO Box 170 79853 915-765-3300
Adriana Cantu, prin. Fax 764-4848
Tornillo JHS 200/7-8
PO Box 170 79853 915-765-3400
Ruth Lara, prin. Fax 764-2020

Trent, Taylor, Pop. 313
Trent ISD 200/PK-12
PO Box 105 79561 325-862-6400
Greg Priddy, supt. Fax 862-6448
www.esc14.net/data/trent.pdf
Trent S 200/PK-12
PO Box 105 79561 325-862-6125
Nelda Priddy, prin. Fax 862-6448

Trenton, Fannin, Pop. 703
Trenton ISD 500/PK-12
PO Box 5 75490 903-989-2245
Jerry Don Cook, supt. Fax 989-2767
www.trentonisd.com
Trenton ES 300/PK-5
PO Box 5 75490 903-989-2244
Zachary Zastoupil, prin. Fax 989-2415
Trenton MS 100/6-8
PO Box 5 75490 903-989-2243
Rick Largent, prin. Fax 989-5173

Trinidad, Henderson, Pop. 1,147
Trinidad ISD 300/PK-12
PO Box 329 75163 903-778-2673
David Atkeisson, supt. Fax 778-4120
www.trinidadisd.com
Trinidad S 300/PK-12
PO Box 329 75163 903-778-2415
Pam Glover, prin. Fax 778-4120

Trinity, Trinity, Pop. 2,780
Trinity ISD 1,100/PK-12
PO Box 752 75862 936-594-3569
Dr. Bobby Rice, supt. Fax 594-8425
www.trinityisd.net/
Lansberry ES 600/PK-4
PO Box 752 75862 936-594-3567
Stacy Collard, prin. Fax 594-2646
Trinity IS 100/5-6
PO Box 752 75862 936-594-4258
Vanessa Franklin, prin. Fax 594-8425
Trinity JHS 100/7-8
PO Box 752 75862 936-594-2321
Jim Underwood, prin. Fax 594-2162

Trophy Club, Denton, Pop. 7,334
Northwest ISD
Supt. — See Justin

Beck ES 400/K-5
401 Parkview Dr 76262 817-215-0450
Deborah McCune, prin. Fax 215-0498
Lakeview ES 300/K-5
100 Village Trl 76262 817-215-0750
Shane Conklin, prin. Fax 215-0770
Medlin MS 900/6-8
601 Parkview Dr 76262 817-215-0500
Robin Ellis, prin. Fax 215-0548

Troup, Smith, Pop. 2,052
Troup ISD 1,000/PK-12
PO Box 578 75789 903-842-3067
Marvin Beaty, supt. Fax 842-4563
www.troupisd.org
Troup ES 500/PK-5
PO Box 578 75789 903-842-3071
Debbie Moxley, prin. Fax 842-4563
Troup MS 200/6-8
PO Box 578 75789 903-842-3081
Ava Johnson, prin. Fax 842-4563

Troy, Bell, Pop. 1,365
Troy ISD 1,300/PK-12
PO Box 409 76579 254-938-2595
Kerry Hansen, supt. Fax 938-7323
www.troyisd.org
Mays ES 200/PK-1
PO Box 409 76579 254-938-0304
Peggy Smith, prin. Fax 938-0233
Troy ES 400/2-5
PO Box 409 76579 254-938-2503
Kathy Dutton, prin. Fax 938-2080
Troy MS 300/6-8
PO Box 409 76579 254-938-2543
Jimmy Cox, prin. Fax 938-2880

Tulia, Swisher, Pop. 4,714
Tulia ISD 1,100/PK-12
702 NW 8th St 79088 806-995-4591
Dr. Ken Miller, supt. Fax 995-3169
portal.tulia-isd.net/
Swinburn ES 200/3-5
300 N Dallas Ave 79088 806-995-4309
Scott Burrow, prin. Fax 995-4448
Tulia Highland ES 300/PK-2
800 NW 9th St 79088 806-995-4141
Casey McBroom, prin. Fax 995-2265
Tulia JHS 200/6-8
421 NE 3rd St 79088 806-995-4842
Johnny Lara, prin. Fax 995-4498

Turkey, Hall, Pop. 492
Turkey-Quitaque ISD 200/K-12
PO Box 397 79261 806-455-1411
Jerry Smith, supt. Fax 455-1718
Valley S 200/K-12
PO Box 397 79261 806-455-1411
Jon Davidson, prin. Fax 455-1718

Tuscola, Taylor, Pop. 714
Jim Ned Consolidated ISD 1,000/PK-12
PO Box 9 79562 325-554-7500
Kent LeFevre, supt. Fax 554-7740
www.jimned.esc14.net/
Jim Ned MS 300/6-8
PO Box 9 79562 325-554-7870
Bob Easterling, prin. Fax 554-7750
Other Schools – See Buffalo Gap, Lawn

Tyler, Smith, Pop. 91,936
Chapel Hill ISD 3,000/PK-12
11134 County Road 2249 75707 903-566-2441
Joe Stubblefield, supt. Fax 566-8469
www.chapelhillisd.org
Chapel Hill MS 700/6-8
13174 State Highway 64 E 75707 903-566-1491
Lisa McCreary, prin. Fax 566-6441
Jackson ES 300/PK-2
16406 FM 2767 75705 903-566-3530
Ruther Causey, prin. Fax 566-2572
Kissam IS 700/3-5
12800 State Highway 64 E 75707 903-566-8334
Andrew Griffith, prin. Fax 566-9362
Wise ES 500/PK-2
10659 State Highway 64 E 75707 903-566-2271
Becky Chenevert, prin. Fax 566-4782

Tyler ISD 18,100/PK-12
PO Box 2035 75710 903-262-1000
Dr. Randall Reid, supt. Fax 262-1178
www.tylerisd.org
Austin ES 500/PK-5
1105 W Franklin St 75702 903-262-1765
Carolyn Williams, prin. Fax 262-1767
Bell ES 500/PK-5
1409 E Hankerson St 75701 903-262-1820
Keri Hampton, prin. Fax 262-1821
Birdwell ES 500/PK-5
1919 S Kennedy Ave 75701 903-262-1870
Donna Bundy, prin. Fax 262-1871
Bonner ES 500/PK-5
235 S Saunders Ave 75702 903-262-1920
Deborah Thompson, prin. Fax 262-1921
Boulter Creative Arts Magnet S 600/6-8
2926 Garden Valley Rd 75702 903-262-1390
Adrian Vega, prin. Fax 262-1392
Caldwell Elementary Arts Academy 600/PK-5
331 S College Ave 75702 903-262-2250
Sherrill Echols, prin. Fax 262-2252
Clarkston ES 400/PK-5
2819 Shenandoah Dr 75701 903-262-1980
Kathryn Letsinger, prin. Fax 262-1981
Dixie ES 500/PK-5
213 Patton Ln 75704 903-262-2040
Connie Thomas, prin. Fax 262-2041
Dogan MS 500/6-8
2621 N Border Ave 75702 903-262-1450
Onella Brown, prin. Fax 262-1451
Douglas ES 700/PK-5
1525 N Carlyle Ave 75702 903-262-2100
Christy Roach, prin. Fax 262-2101

Griffin ES 600/PK-5
3000 N Border Ave 75702 903-262-2310
Cynthia Howland, prin. Fax 262-2311
Hogg MS 600/6-8
920 S Broadway Ave 75701 903-262-1500
Jo Ann Burns, prin. Fax 262-1501
Hubbard MS 900/6-8
1300 Hubbard Dr 75703 903-262-1560
Anissa Kiener, prin. Fax 262-1566
Jones ES 300/PK-5
2521 W Front St 75702 903-262-2360
Patricia Lewis, prin. Fax 262-2362
Moore MST Magnet MS 900/6-8
1200 S Tipton Ave 75701 903-262-1640
Claude Lane, prin. Fax 262-1641
Orr ES 700/PK-5
3001 Orr Dr 75702 903-262-2400
Walter Perez, prin. Fax 262-2401
Owens ES 900/K-5
11780 County Road 168 75703 903-262-2175
Linda Payne, prin. Fax 262-2176
Peete ES 400/PK-5
1511 Bellwood Rd 75701 903-262-2460
Freeman Sterling, prin. Fax 262-2461
Ramey ES 500/PK-5
2000 N Forest Ave 75702 903-262-2505
Cynthia Johnson, prin. Fax 262-2506
Rice ES 1,000/PK-5
409 Carriage Dr 75703 903-262-2555
Jennifer Sturm, prin. Fax 262-2556
Stewart MS 400/6-8
2800 W Shaw St 75701 903-262-1710
Debra Robertson, prin. Fax 262-1711
Woods ES 700/K-5
809 Clyde Dr 75701 903-262-1280
Kami Hale, prin. Fax 262-1281

All Saints Episcopal S 700/PK-12
2695 S Southwest Loop 323 75701 903-579-6000
Art Burke, hdmstr. Fax 579-6002
Christian Heritage S 100/K-12
961 County Road 1143 75704 903-593-2702
James Kilkenny, hdmstr. Fax 531-2226
East Texas Christian Academy 200/PK-12
1797 Shiloh Rd 75703 903-561-8642
Scott Fossey, pres. Fax 561-9620
Good Shepherd S 100/PK-12
2525 Old Jacksonville Rd 75701 903-592-4045
Fr. Walter Banek, hdmstr. Fax 596-7149
Grace Community S 500/PK-5
3215 Old Jacksonville Rd 75701 903-593-1977
Karla Foreman, prin. Fax 593-2897
King's Academy Christian S 100/K-12
714 Shelley Dr 75701 903-534-9992
Bruce Inpyn, admin. Fax 534-9555
St. Gregory S 300/PK-5
500 S College Ave 75702 903-595-4109
Kathy Shieldes Harry, prin. Fax 592-8626
Trinity Lutheran S 200/PK-PK
2001 Hunter St 75701 903-593-7465
Kelly Moore, dir. Fax 593-7664
Tyler SDA S 50/K-8
2931 S Southeast Loop 323 75701 903-595-6706
Dwayne Clark, prin. Fax 593-1210

Universal City, Bexar, Pop. 16,653
Judson ISD
Supt. — See Live Oak
Coronado Village ES 400/PK-5
213 Amistad Blvd 78148 210-945-5110
Melinda Salinas, prin. Fax 659-0579
Kitty Hawk MS 1,300/6-8
840 Old Cimarron Trl 78148 210-945-1220
Mike Miller, prin. Fax 659-0687
Olympia ES 700/PK-5
8439 Athenian Dr 78148 210-945-5113
Terri LeBleu, prin. Fax 659-6172
Salinas ES K-5
10560 Old Cimarron Trl 78148 210-659-5045
Yvette Ross, prin. Fax 659-2367

Schertz-Cibolo-Universal City ISD
Supt. — See Schertz
Rose Garden ES 400/PK-4
506 North Blvd 78148 210-619-4350
Ricki Muennink, prin. Fax 619-4369

First Baptist Academy 400/PK-12
1401 Pat Booker Rd 78148 210-658-5331
Cissy Stubblefield, admin. Fax 658-7024

Utopia, Uvalde
Utopia ISD 200/K-12
PO Box 880 78884 830-966-1928
John Walts, supt. Fax 966-6162
www.utopiaisd.net
Utopia S 200/K-12
PO Box 880 78884 830-966-3339
James Phillips, prin. Fax 966-6162

Uvalde, Uvalde, Pop. 16,441
Uvalde Consolidated ISD 5,100/PK-12
PO Box 1909 78802 830-278-6655
Dr. Wendell Brown, supt. Fax 591-4909
www.ucisd.net
Anthon ES 600/1-4
PO Box 1909 78802 830-591-2988
Elaine Kiesling, prin. Fax 591-2993
Benson ES 400/K-4
PO Box 1909 78802 830-591-4954
Mary Helen Saiz, prin. Fax 591-4959
Dalton K 700/PK-K
PO Box 1909 78802 830-591-4933
Janice Estrada, prin. Fax 591-4936
Flores MS 600/5-6
PO Box 1909 78802 830-591-2976
Cleo Eddy, prin. Fax 591-2987
Robb ES 500/1-4
PO Box 1909 78802 830-591-4947
Josefina Ramirez, prin. Fax 591-4937

Uvalde JHS 700/7-8
PO Box 1909 78802 830-591-2980
Kenneth Mueller, prin. Fax 591-2975
Other Schools – See Batesville

Sacred Heart S 100/PK-6
401 W Leona St 78801 830-278-2661
David Emrich, prin. Fax 279-0634
St. Philip's Episcopal Day S 100/PK-6
343 N Getty St 78801 830-278-1350
Elisa Santos, prin. Fax 278-2093

Valentine, Jeff Davis, Pop. 193
Valentine ISD 50/PK-12
PO Box 188 79854 432-467-2671
George Elliott, supt. Fax 467-2004
valentineisd.esc18.net
Valentine S 50/PK-12
PO Box 188 79854 432-467-2671
Dawn Houy, prin. Fax 467-2004

Valera, Coleman
Panther Creek Consolidated ISD 200/PK-12
129 Private Road 3421 76884 325-357-4506
Dwin Nanny, supt. Fax 357-4470
www.panthercountry.net/
Panther Creek ES 100/PK-5
129 Private Road 3421 76884 325-357-4449
Phillip Ratliff, prin. Fax 357-4470

Valley Mills, Bosque, Pop. 1,145
Valley Mills ISD 600/PK-12
PO Box 518 76689 254-932-5210
Micky Virdell, supt. Fax 932-6601
www.vmisd.net
Valley Mills ES 400/PK-6
PO Box 518 76689 254-932-5526
Marcia Anderson, prin. Fax 932-6601
Valley Mills JHS 100/7-8
PO Box 518 76689 254-932-5251
Randy Anderson, prin. Fax 932-6601

Valley View, Cooke, Pop. 808
Valley View ISD 700/K-12
200 Newton St 76272 940-726-3659
Monica Parkhill, supt. Fax 726-3614
www.vvisd.net
Valley View ES 200/K-4
200 Newton St 76272 940-726-3681
Susan Smith, prin. Fax 726-3647
Valley View MS 200/5-8
200 Newton St 76272 940-726-3244
Matthew Chalmers, prin. Fax 726-3786

Van, Van Zandt, Pop. 2,574
Van ISD 1,900/PK-12
PO Box 697 75790 903-963-8328
Joddie Witte, supt. Fax 963-3904
www.van.sprnet.org
Rhodes ES 400/PK-1
PO Box 697 75790 903-963-8386
Dana Oatley, prin. Fax 963-5586
Van IS 200/2-3
PO Box 697 75790 903-963-8331
Marty Moore, prin. Fax 963-5582
Van JHS 300/7-8
PO Box 697 75790 903-963-8321
Don Dunn, prin. Fax 963-3277
Van MS 300/4-6
PO Box 697 75790 903-963-1461
Trent Goodwin, prin. Fax 963-1472

Van Alstyne, Grayson, Pop. 2,760
Van Alstyne ISD 1,200/PK-12
PO Box 518 75495 903-482-8802
Dr. Allen Seay, supt. Fax 482-6086
www.vanalstyneisd.org
Van Alstyne ES 500/PK-4
201 Newport 75495 903-482-8805
Terry Billups, prin. Fax 482-8896
Van Alstyne MS 200/5-8
PO Box 889 75495 903-482-8804
Ryan Coleman, prin. Fax 482-8890

Vanderbilt, Jackson
Industrial ISD 1,000/PK-12
PO Box 369 77991 361-284-3226
Anthony Williams, supt. Fax 284-3349
www.iisd1.org
Industrial ES East 200/PK-5
PO Box 368 77991 361-284-3226
Gary Thedford, prin. Fax 284-3377
Industrial JHS 300/6-8
PO Box 367 77991 361-284-3226
Monte Althaus, prin. Fax 284-3049
Other Schools – See Inez

Van Horn, Culberson, Pop. 2,157
Culberson County-Allamore ISD 600/PK-12
PO Box 899 79855 432-283-2245
Guillermo Mancha Ed.D., supt. Fax 283-9062
www.ccaisd.net/
Eagle ES 300/PK-5
PO Box 899 79855 432-283-2245
Dolores Upchurch, prin. Fax 283-9062
Van Horn JHS 100/6-8
PO Box 899 79855 432-283-2245
John Fabela, prin. Fax 283-9062

Van Vleck, Matagorda, Pop. 1,534
Van Vleck ISD 900/PK-12
142 4th St S 77482 979-245-8518
Dr. Cynthia Clary, supt. Fax 245-1214
www.vvisd.org
Herman MS 200/6-8
719 1st St 77482 979-245-6401
John O'Brien, prin. Fax 245-8538
Rudd IS 100/4-5
128 5th St 77482 979-245-6561
John Keys, prin. Fax 245-1214

Van Vleck ES 300/PK-3
178 S 4th St 77482 979-245-8681
David Holubec, prin. Fax 323-0479

Vega, Oldham, Pop. 898
Vega ISD 300/K-12
PO Box 190 79092 806-267-2123
Margo Knox, supt. Fax 267-2146
www.region16.net/vegaisd
Vega ES 100/K-6
PO Box 190 79092 806-267-2126
Mikala Stephens, prin. Fax 267-2146

Venus, Johnson, Pop. 2,229
Venus ISD 1,700/PK-12
PO Box 364 76084 972-366-3448
Robert Matthews, supt. Fax 366-8742
www.venusisd.net
Venus ES 500/2-5
PO Box 364 76084 972-366-3748
Nancy Kay, prin. Fax 366-8808
Venus MS 400/6-8
PO Box 364 76084 972-366-3358
Jill Bottelberghe, prin. Fax 366-1740
Venus PS 300/PK-1
PO Box 364 76084 972-366-3268
Jane Nelson, prin. Fax 366-1826

Veribest, Tom Green
Veribest ISD 200/PK-12
PO Box 475 76886 325-655-4912
Michael Steck, supt. Fax 655-3355
veribest.netxv.net/
Veribest S 100/PK-5
PO Box 475 76886 325-655-2851
Clint Askins, prin. Fax 653-0551

Vernon, Wilbarger, Pop. 11,077
Northside ISD 200/K-12
18040 US Highway 283 76384 940-552-2551
Ed Donahue, supt. Fax 553-4919
www.northsideisd.us/
Northside S 200/K-12
18040 US Highway 283 76384 940-552-2551
Cindy Riggins, prin. Fax 553-4919

Vernon ISD 2,100/PK-12
1713 Wilbarger St 76384 940-553-1900
Tom Woody, supt. Fax 553-3802
vernonisd.org/
Central ES 300/2-3
1300 Paradise St 76384 940-553-1859
Fred Bush, prin. Fax 553-1138
McCord ES 500/PK-1
2915 Sand Rd 76384 940-553-4381
Alcie Estes, prin. Fax 552-0056
Shive ES 300/4-5
3130 Bacon St 76384 940-553-4309
Charles Chesser, prin. Fax 552-5597
Vernon MS 500/6-8
2200 Yamparika St 76384 940-552-6231
Kenneth Kenner, prin. Fax 552-0504

St. Paul Lutheran S 100/PK-K
4405 Hospital Dr 76384 940-552-6651
Mary Neuberger, dir. Fax 552-6616

Victoria, Victoria, Pop. 61,790
Victoria ISD 12,800/PK-12
PO Box 1759 77902 361-576-3131
Bob Moore, supt. Fax 788-9643
www.visd.com
Aloe ES 500/PK-5
PO Box 1759 77902 361-788-9509
Linda Allen, prin. Fax 788-9662
Chandler ES 600/PK-5
PO Box 1759 77902 361-788-9587
Debbie Michalski, prin. Fax 788-9590
Crain MS 1,000/6-8
PO Box 1759 77902 361-573-7453
Lisa Blundell, prin. Fax 788-9566
De Leon ES 600/K-5
PO Box 1759 77902 361-788-9553
Selina Reyna, prin. Fax 788-9634
Dudley Magnet ES 500/PK-5
PO Box 1759 77902 361-788-9517
Diane Billo, prin. Fax 788-9523
Gross Montessori Magnet ES 500/PK-5
PO Box 1759 77902 361-788-9500
Tammy Sestak, prin. Fax 788-9504
Guadalupe ES 100/K-5
PO Box 1759 77902 361-788-9906
Tammy Nobles, prin. Fax 788-9357
Hopkins Academy 600/PK-5
PO Box 1759 77902 361-788-9527
Sulema Salinas, prin. Fax 788-9635
Howell MS 1,000/6-8
PO Box 1759 77902 361-578-1561
Debbie Crick, prin. Fax 788-9547
Linn Math & Science Magnet ES 400/PK-5
PO Box 1759 77902 361-788-9600
Toni Misak, prin. Fax 788-9603
Mission Valley ES 200/K-5
PO Box 1759 77902 361-788-9514
Sylvia Davila, prin. Fax 788-9689
O'Connor Magnet ES 600/PK-5
PO Box 1759 77902 361-788-9572
Jill Lau, prin. Fax 788-9575
Rowland ES 600/PK-5
PO Box 1759 77902 361-788-9549
Cherie Singleton, prin. Fax 788-9902
Schorlemmer ES, PO Box 1759 77902 100/K-5
Ginger Henry, prin. 361-788-2860
Shields Accelerated Learning Magnet ES 600/PK-5
PO Box 1759 77902 361-788-9593
Armando Villarreal, prin. Fax 788-9691
Smith ES 600/PK-5
PO Box 1759 77902 361-788-9605
Carol Tippins, prin. Fax 788-9688
Torres ES, PO Box 1759 77902 100/K-5
Sherry Gorsuch, prin. 361-788-2850
Vickers ES 600/PK-5
PO Box 1759 77902 361-788-9579
Steve Carroll, prin. Fax 788-9663
Welder Magnet MS 1,000/6-8
PO Box 1759 77902 361-575-4553
Dr. Carlos Garza, prin. Fax 788-9629
Wood ES 100/K-5
PO Box 1759 77902 361-788-9533
Tammy Nobles, prin. Fax 788-9912

Faith Academy 300/PK-12
PO Box 4824 77903 361-573-2484
Dr. Chris Royael, admin. Fax 572-4602
Nazareth Academy 300/PK-8
206 W Convent St 77901 361-573-6651
Scott Kloesel, prin. Fax 573-1829
Our Lady of Victory S 500/PK-8
1311 E Mesquite Ln 77901 361-575-5391
Sr. Leonita Barron, prin. Fax 575-3473
Victoria Christian S 100/PK-2
801 E Airline Rd 77901 361-573-5345
Richard Smith, prin. Fax 578-3367

Vidor, Orange, Pop. 11,290
Vidor ISD 4,900/PK-12
120 E Bolivar St 77662 409-951-8714
Willie Hayes, supt. Fax 769-0093
www.vidorisd.org/
Oak Forest ES 700/PK-4
2400 Highway 12 77662 409-951-8860
Jami Poteet, prin. Fax 769-2678
Pine Forest ES 700/PK-4
4150 N Main St 77662 409-951-8800
Roxanne Manuel, prin. Fax 786-1728
Vidor ES 600/PK-4
400 E Railroad St 77662 409-951-8830
Linda Durmon, prin. Fax 769-0211
Vidor JHS 700/7-8
945 N Tram Rd 77662 409-951-8970
Debra Jordan, prin. Fax 769-6754
Vidor MS 800/5-6
2500 Highway 12 77662 409-951-8880
Nancy Smith, prin. Fax 783-0309

Von Ormy, Bexar
Somerset ISD
Supt. — See Somerset
Barbera Veterans ES 300/PK-1
4135 Smith Rd 78073 866-465-8808
Shannon Boyd, prin. Fax 465-8818
Savannah Heights IS 500/5-6
5040 Smith Rd 78073 866-852-9863
Steve Ayers, prin. Fax 488-4341

Waco, McLennan, Pop. 120,465
Bosqueville ISD 500/PK-12
7636 Rock Creek Rd 76708 254-757-3113
James Hopper, supt. Fax 752-4909
www.bosqueville.k12.tx.us
Bosqueville ES 300/PK-6
7636 Rock Creek Rd 76708 254-757-3113
Kelly Bray, prin. Fax 752-4909

China Spring ISD 2,100/PK-12
6301 Sylvia St 76708 254-836-1115
George Kazanas Ed.D., supt. Fax 836-0559
www.chinaspringisd.net
Other Schools – See China Spring

Connally ISD 2,700/PK-12
200 Cadet Way 76705 254-296-6460
Keith Boles, supt. Fax 412-5530
www.connally.org/
Connally ES 400/3-4
300 Cadet Way 76705 254-750-7170
Larry Cumby, prin. Fax 412-5525
Connally IS 400/5-6
100 BB Brown Dr 76705 254-750-7100
Deborah Brown, prin. Fax 412-5522
Other Schools – See Elm Mott

Gholson ISD 100/K-8
137 Hamilton Dr 76705 254-829-1528
Patricia McFerrin, supt. Fax 829-0054
www.gholsonisd.org/
Gholson S 100/K-8
137 Hamilton Dr 76705 254-829-1528
Patricia McFerrin, prin. Fax 829-0054

Hallsburg ISD 100/K-6
2313 Hallsburg Rd 76705 254-875-2331
Kent Reynolds, supt. Fax 875-2436
www.hallsburgisd.net
Hallsburg ES 100/K-6
2313 Hallsburg Rd 76705 254-875-2331
Kent Reynolds, prin. Fax 875-2436

La Vega ISD 2,500/PK-12
3100 Bellmead Dr 76705 254-799-4963
Dr. Sharon Shields, supt. Fax 799-8642
www.lavegaisd.org
La Vega ES 400/2-3
3100 Wheeler St 76705 254-799-1721
Peggy Johnson, prin. Fax 799-4453
La Vega IS H.P Miles Campus 600/4-6
508 E Loop 340 76705 254-799-5553
Kristi Rizo, prin. Fax 799-9738
La Vega JHS George Dixon Campus 400/7-8
4401 Orchard Ln 76705 254-799-2428
Elicia Krumnow, prin. Fax 799-8943
La Vega PS 400/PK-1
4400 Harrison St 76705 254-799-6229
Carla Swann, prin. Fax 799-1369

Midway ISD 6,200/PK-12
1205 Foundation Dr 76712 254-761-5610
Dr. Brad Lancaster, supt. Fax 666-7785
www.midwayisd.org/
Midway IS 900/5-6
9400 Chapel Rd 76712 254-761-5690
Sarah Holland, prin. Fax 666-0928
South Bosque ES 500/PK-4
1 Wickson Rd 76712 254-761-5720
Mary Lou Glaesmann, prin. Fax 776-2493
Speegleville ES 200/K-4
101 Maywood Dr 76712 254-761-5730
Christopher Eberlein, prin. Fax 848-9751
Woodway ES 600/PK-4
325 Estates Dr 76712 254-761-5740
Michael Cooper, prin. Fax 761-5765
Other Schools – See Hewitt

Waco ISD 14,200/PK-12
PO Box 27 76703 254-755-9463
Dr. Roland Hernandez, supt. Fax 755-9690
www.wacoisd.org
Alta Vista Montessori Magnet ES 500/PK-6
3637 Alta Vista Dr 76706 254-662-3050
Dr. Rochelle Peters, prin. Fax 662-7353
Bells Hill ES 500/PK-5
2125 Cleveland Ave 76706 254-754-4171
Bevil Cohn, prin. Fax 750-3559
Brazos MS 300/6-8
2415 Cumberland Ave 76707 254-754-5491
Henri Lewis, prin. Fax 750-3576
Brook Avenue ES 400/PK-5
720 Brook Ave 76708 254-750-3562
Jessica Hicks, prin. Fax 750-3545
Carver Academy 500/6-8
1601 J J Flewellen Rd 76704 254-757-0787
Pamela Correa, prin. Fax 750-3442
Cedar Ridge ES 500/PK-4
2115 Meridian Ave 76708 254-756-1241
Andrea Nolan, prin. Fax 750-3531
Chavez MS 400/6-8
700 S 15th St 76706 254-750-3736
Alfredo Loredo, prin. Fax 750-3739
Crestview ES 500/PK-4
1120 N New Rd 76710 254-776-1704
Sonya Joyner, prin. Fax 741-4910
Dean-Highland ES 400/PK-4
1800 N 33rd St 76707 254-752-3751
Yolanda Williams, prin. Fax 750-3458
Hillcrest ES 300/PK-5
4225 Pine Ave 76710 254-772-4286
Lorraine Randazzo, prin. Fax 741-4938
Hines ES 400/PK-5
301 Garrison St 76704 254-753-1362
Archie Hatton, prin. Fax 750-3799
Kendrick ES 400/PK-5
1801 Kendrick Ln 76711 254-752-3316
Julie Sapaugh, prin. Fax 750-3472
Lake Air IS 200/5-6
4601 Cobbs Dr 76710 254-772-1910
Robin Wilson, prin. Fax 741-4945
Lake Waco Montessori Magnet S 300/PK-8
3005 Edna Ave 76708 254-752-5951
Robin McDurham, prin. Fax 750-3586
Meadowbrook ES 300/PK-5
4315 Beverly Dr 76711 254-752-4511
John Campbell, prin. Fax 750-3596
Miller ES 300/PK-5
2401 J J Flewellen Rd 76704 254-412-7900
Belinda Rubio, prin. Fax 412-7902
Mountainview ES 400/PK-4
5901 Bishop Dr 76710 254-772-2520
Bill Sheppard, prin. Fax 741-4961
North Waco ES 500/PK-5
2015 Alexander Ave 76708 254-753-2423
Jim Patton, prin. Fax 750-3510
Parkdale ES 400/PK-4
6400 Edmond Ave 76710 254-772-2170
Marsha Henry, prin. Fax 741-4979
Provident Heights ES 400/PK-5
2415 Bosque Blvd 76707 254-750-3930
Aaron Pena, prin. Fax 750-3934
South Waco ES 600/PK-5
2104 Gurley Ln 76706 254-753-6802
Ricky Edison, prin. Fax 750-3527
Sul Ross ES 400/PK-5
901 S 7th St 76706 254-753-3541
Debbie Sims, prin. Fax 750-3785
Tennyson MS 300/7-8
6100 Tennyson Dr 76710 254-772-1440
Nina LeBlanc, prin. Fax 741-4970
University MS 500/6-8
1820 Irving Lee St 76711 254-753-1533
Rick Hartley, prin. Fax 750-3486
Viking Hills ES 300/PK-4
7200 Viking Dr 76710 254-772-2341
Deborah North, prin. Fax 741-4984
West Avenue ES 400/PK-5
1101 N 15th St 76707 254-750-3900
Andreia Foster, prin. Fax 750-3904

Live Oak Classical S 200/PK-8
PO Box 647 76703 254-714-1007
Alison Moffatt, prin.
New Creation Christian S 50/1-8
800 W State Highway 6 76712 254-772-8775
Patsy Starr, prin. Fax 399-0159
St. Louis S 300/K-8
2208 N 23rd St 76708 254-754-2041
Louis Gonzales, prin. Fax 754-2091
St. Paul's Episcopal S 100/PK-6
517 Columbus Ave 76701 254-753-0246
Richard Webb, hdmstr. Fax 755-7488
Texas Christian Academy 200/PK-12
4600 Sanger Ave 76710 254-772-5474
Jim Stuard, admin. Fax 772-4485
Waco Montessori S 200/PK-6
1920 Columbus Ave 76701 254-754-3966
Shirley Jansing, prin. Fax 752-2922

Waelder, Gonzales, Pop. 1,009
Waelder ISD 200/K-12
PO Box 247 78959 830-788-7161
Dave Plymale, supt. Fax 788-7429
www.esc13.net/waelder/

Waelder ES 100/K-5
PO Box 247 78959 830-788-7221
Dr. Carlos Garza, prin. Fax 788-7429

Wake Village, Bowie, Pop. 5,226
Texarkana ISD
Supt. — See Texarkana
Wake Village ES 800/PK-5
400 Wildcat Dr 75501 903-838-4261
Donna McDaniel, prin. Fax 832-6809

Wall, Tom Green
Wall ISD 900/K-12
PO Box 259 76957 325-651-7790
Walter Holik, supt. Fax 651-5081
www.wallisd.net
Wall ES 400/K-5
PO Box 259 76957 325-651-7522
Matt Fore, prin. Fax 651-9630
Wall MS 200/6-8
PO Box 259 76957 325-651-7648
Ryan Snowden, prin. Fax 651-9664

Waller, Waller, Pop. 1,998
Waller ISD 5,100/PK-12
2214 Waller St 77484 936-931-3685
Richard McReavy, supt. Fax 372-5576
www.wallerisd.net
Fields Store ES 600/PK-4
31670 Giboney Rd 77484 936-931-4050
Mary Davis, prin. Fax 372-4100
Holleman ES 700/PK-4
2200 Brazeal St 77484 936-372-9196
Merilyn Godwin, prin. Fax 372-2468
Jones ES 200/PK-4
2214 Waller St 77484 936-857-3336
Carol Bates, prin. Fax 857-5050
Schultz MS 700/5-6
19010 Stokes Rd 77484 936-931-9103
Brian Merrell, prin. Fax 372-9302
Waller JHS 700/7-8
2402 Waller St 77484 936-931-1353
Dr. Mina Schnitta, prin. Fax 931-4044
Other Schools – See Hockley

Wallis, Austin, Pop. 1,271
Brazos ISD 800/PK-12
PO Box 819 77485 979-478-6551
Jack Ellis, supt. Fax 478-6413
www.brazosisd.net/
Brazos MS 200/6-8
PO Box 879 77485 979-478-6411
Clay Hudgins, prin. Fax 478-6042
Other Schools – See Orchard

Walnut Springs, Bosque, Pop. 805
Walnut Springs ISD 200/PK-12
PO Box 63 76690 254-797-2133
Pat Garrett, supt. Fax 797-2191
www.walnutspringsisd.net
Walnut Springs S 200/PK-12
PO Box 63 76690 254-797-2133
Craig Taylor, prin. Fax 797-2191

Warren, Tyler
Warren ISD 1,200/PK-12
PO Box 69 77664 409-547-2241
Mike Pate, supt. Fax 547-3405
www.warrenisd.net
Warren ES 400/PK-5
PO Box 550 77664 409-547-2247
James Applewhite, prin. Fax 547-0146
Warren JHS 200/6-8
PO Box 205 77664 409-547-2246
Ernestine Mitchell, prin. Fax 547-2740
Other Schools – See Fred

Waskom, Harrison, Pop. 2,129
Waskom ISD 700/PK-12
PO Box 748 75692 903-687-3361
Jimmy Cox, supt. Fax 687-3253
www.waskomisd.net
Waskom ES 300/PK-4
PO Box 748 75692 903-687-3361
Wade Youngblood, prin. Fax 687-3377
Waskom MS 200/5-8
PO Box 748 75692 903-687-3361
Stuart Musick, prin. Fax 687-3224

Watauga, Tarrant, Pop. 23,548
Birdville ISD
Supt. — See Haltom City
Hardeman ES 800/PK-5
6100 Whispering Ln 76148 817-547-2800
Fax 581-5496

Watauga ES 800/PK-5
5937 Whitley Rd 76148 817-547-2700
Sharon Heier, prin. Fax 581-5425
Watauga MS 700/6-8
6300 Maurie Dr 76148 817-547-4800
Shannon Houston, prin. Fax 581-5369

Keller ISD
Supt. — See Keller
Whitley Road ES 600/PK-4
7600 Whitley Rd 76148 817-744-5800
Traci Bond, prin. Fax 281-4023

Water Valley, Tom Green
Water Valley ISD 300/PK-12
PO Box 250 76958 325-484-2478
Jimmy Hannon, supt. Fax 484-3359
www.wvisd.net/
Water Valley ES 200/PK-6
PO Box 250 76958 325-484-3351
Jason Powers, prin. Fax 484-2478

Waxahachie, Ellis, Pop. 25,454
Waxahachie ISD 5,900/PK-12
411 N Gibson St 75165 972-923-4631
Thomas Collins, supt. Fax 923-4759
www.wisd.org

Clift MS 6-6
650 Parks School House Rd 75165 972-923-4631
Ruth Sutton, prin.
Dunaway ES 500/1-5
600 S Highway 77 75165 972-923-4646
Eric Brewster, prin. Fax 923-4752
Felty ES, 231 Park Place Blvd 75165 K-5
Linda Edmiston, prin. 972-923-4761
Finley 7th Grade Center 500/7-7
2401 Brown St 75165 972-923-4680
Ryder Appleton, prin. Fax 923-4687
Howard Eighth Grade Center 500/8-8
265 Broadhead Rd 75165 972-923-4631
Robert Woodhouse, prin.
Marvin K 600/PK-K
110 Brown St 75165 972-923-4670
Ora Jackson, prin. Fax 923-4677
Northside ES 600/1-5
801 Brown St 75165 972-923-4610
Debbie Gish, prin. Fax 923-4750
Shackelford ES 600/K-5
1001 Butcher Rd 75165 972-923-4666
Nancy Edwards, prin. Fax 923-4753
Wedgeworth ES 700/1-5
405 Solon Rd 75165 972-923-4631
Elizabeth McDaniel, prin. Fax 923-4751

St. Joseph S 100/PK-8
506 E Marvin Ave 75165 972-937-0956
Mary Kay Volker, prin. Fax 937-1742
Waxahachie Preparatory Academy 200/K-12
PO Box P 75168 972-937-0440
John Cullen, admin. Fax 937-5033

Weatherford, Parker, Pop. 23,315
Garner ISD 200/PK-8
2222 Garner School Rd 76088 940-682-4140
Marion Ferguson, supt. Fax 682-4141
www.garnerisd.net
Garner S 200/PK-8
2222 Garner School Rd 76088 940-682-7410
Steve Wallace, prin. Fax 682-4141

Peaster ISD 1,100/PK-12
3602 Harwell Lake Rd 76088 817-341-5000
Philip Bledsoe, supt. Fax 341-5003
www.peaster.net
Peaster ES 500/PK-5
3400 Harwell Lake Rd 76088 817-594-1884
Jonathan Scott, prin. Fax 594-1890
Peaster MS 300/6-8
8512 FM Road 920 76088 817-341-5000
Jeff Perkins, prin. Fax 341-5052

Weatherford ISD 7,200/PK-12
1100 Longhorn Dr 76086 817-598-2800
Dr. Deborah Cron, supt. Fax 598-2835
www.weatherfordisd.com
Austin ES 500/K-6
1776 Texas Dr 76086 817-598-2848
Jenny Morris, prin. Fax 598-2978
Crockett ES 600/PK-6
1015 Jameson St 76086 817-598-2811
Debbie Braudaway, prin. Fax 598-2813
Curtis ES 700/K-6
501 W Russell St 76086 817-598-2838
Racheal Rife, prin. Fax 598-2840
Hall MS 600/7-8
902 Charles St 76086 817-598-2822
Michelle Howard-Schwind, prin. Fax 598-2854
Ikard ES 500/K-6
100 Ikard Ln 76086 817-598-2818
Linda Starnes, prin. Fax 598-2805
Martin ES 500/K-6
719 N Oakridge Dr 76087 817-598-2910
Joy Bailey, prin. Fax 598-2912
Seguin ES 600/PK-6
499 E 8th St 76086 817-598-2814
Kathy Dorris, prin. Fax 598-2826
Tison MS 600/7-8
102 Meadowview Rd 76087 817-598-2960
Debbie Bradley, prin. Fax 598-2963
Wright ES 600/PK-6
1309 Charles St 76086 817-598-2828
Andy Pool, prin. Fax 598-2830

Victory Baptist Academy 100/PK-12
1311 E Bankhead Dr 76086 817-596-2711
Matthew Ticzkus, admin. Fax 596-8093
Weatherford Christian S 200/PK-12
111 E Columbia St 76086 817-596-7807
Van Gravitt, hdmstr. Fax 596-0529

Webster, Harris, Pop. 8,852
Clear Creek ISD
Supt. — See League City
Greene ES 700/PK-5
2903 Friendswood Link Rd 77598 281-284-5000
Stefanie McBride, prin. Fax 284-5005
McWhirter ES 700/PK-5
300 Pennsylvania St 77598 281-332-0521
Dr. Michael Marquez, prin. Fax 332-8371

Westminster Christian Academy 100/K-6
670 E Medical Center Blvd 77598 281-280-9829
Tim Sansbury, hdmstr. Fax 990-9739

Weimar, Colorado, Pop. 2,016
Weimar ISD 600/PK-12
506 W Main St 78962 979-725-9504
Dr. Colleen Netterville, supt. Fax 725-8737
www.weimarisd.org/
Weimar ES 200/PK-5
515 W Main St 78962 979-725-6009
Lisa Meysembourg, prin. Fax 725-9527
Weimar JHS 100/6-8
101 N West St 78962 979-725-9515
Karen Bellue, prin. Fax 725-8383

St. Michael S 200/PK-8
103 E North St 78962 979-725-8461
Sr. Kathleen Goike, prin. Fax 725-8344

Welch, Dawson
Dawson ISD 200/PK-12
PO Box 180 79377 806-489-7568
Lindsey Wallace, supt. Fax 489-7463
Dawson S 200/PK-12
PO Box 180 79377 806-489-7461
Marva Hogue, prin. Fax 489-7463

Wellington, Collingsworth, Pop. 2,090
Wellington ISD 500/PK-12
609 15th St 79095 806-447-2512
Carl Taylor, supt. Fax 447-5124
www.wellingtonisd.net
Wellington ES 200/PK-5
606 16th St 79095 806-447-2353
Marcy Sessions, prin. Fax 447-5097
Wellington JHS 100/6-8
1504 Amarillo St 79095 806-447-5726
Tim Webb, prin. Fax 447-5089

Wellman, Terry, Pop. 201
Wellman-Union Consolidated ISD 200/K-12
PO Box 69 79378 806-637-4910
Leslie Vann, supt. Fax 637-2585
wellman.esc17.net
Wellman-Union ES 100/K-5
PO Box 129 79378 806-637-4619
Nancy Tidwell, prin. Fax 637-2585

Wells, Cherokee, Pop. 792
Wells ISD 300/PK-12
PO Box 469 75976 936-867-4466
Dale Morton, supt. Fax 867-4466
www.wells.esc7.net
Wells S 200/PK-8
PO Box 469 75976 936-867-4400
Leslie Brown, prin. Fax 867-4466

Weslaco, Hidalgo, Pop. 31,442
Weslaco ISD 15,900/PK-12
PO Box 266 78599 956-969-6500
Richard Rivera, supt. Fax 969-2664
www.wisd.us
Airport ES 800/PK-5
410 N Airport Dr 78596 956-969-6770
Ida Cuadra, prin. Fax 968-4062
Central MS 1,000/6-8
700 S Bridge Ave 78596 956-969-6710
Lauren Arce, prin. Fax 969-0779
Cleckler/Heald ES 900/PK-5
1601 W Sugar Cane Dr 78596 956-969-6888
Elizabet Garza, prin. Fax 968-6808
Cuellar MS 700/6-8
1201 S Bridge Ave 78596 956-969-6720
Mario Hernandez, prin. Fax 973-9797
Garza MS 1,000/6-8
1111 W Sugar Cane Dr 78596 956-969-6774
John Garlic, prin. Fax 447-0484
Gonzalez ES 800/PK-5
3801 N Mile 5 1/2 W 78596 956-969-6760
Daniel Budimir, prin. Fax 969-9828
Hoge MS 900/6-8
2302 N International Blvd 78596 956-969-6730
Patricia Munoz, prin. Fax 514-0903
Houston ES 600/PK-5
608 N Cantu St 78596 956-969-6740
Abel Aguilar, prin. Fax 973-9404
Margo ES 1,200/PK-5
1701 S Bridge Ave 78596 956-969-6800
Rhonda Sellman, prin. Fax 969-8868
Memorial ES 900/PK-5
1700 S Border Ave 78596 956-969-6780
Rubelina Martinez, prin. Fax 968-5506
North Bridge ES 800/PK-5
2001 N Bridge Ave 78596 956-969-6810
Maria Lopez, prin. Fax 968-1521
Rico ES 900/PK-5
2202 N International Blvd 78596 956-969-6815
Yolanda Hernandez, prin. Fax 565-4676
Roosevelt ES 400/PK-5
814 E Plaza St 78596 956-969-6750
Linda Wallace, prin. Fax 968-6154
Silva ES 800/PK-5
1001 W Mile 10 N 78596 956-969-6790
Cris Valdez, prin. Fax 968-6937

San Martin de Porres S 100/PK-3
905 N Texas Blvd 78596 956-973-8642
Sr. Helen Rottier, prin. Fax 973-0522
Valley Grande Adventist Academy 200/PK-12
1000 S Bridge Ave 78596 956-968-0573
Bernardo Samano, prin. Fax 968-9814

West, McLennan, Pop. 2,711
West ISD 1,500/PK-12
801 N Reagan St 76691 254-826-7500
Jan Hungate Ed.D., supt. Fax 826-7503
www.westisd.net
West ES 400/PK-3
801 N Reagan St 76691 254-826-7540
Rob Fleming, prin. Fax 826-7543
West IS 200/4-5
801 N Reagan St 76691 254-826-7530
Michele Scott, prin. Fax 826-7533
West MS 300/6-8
801 N Reagan St 76691 254-826-7520
Grady Fulbright, prin. Fax 826-7524

St. Marys S 200/PK-8
PO Box 277 76691 254-826-5991
Ericka Sammon, prin. Fax 826-7047

Westbrook, Mitchell, Pop. 196
Westbrook ISD 200/PK-12
PO Box 99 79565 325-644-2971
Todd Burleson, supt. Fax 644-2951
www.westbrookisd.com
Westbrook S 200/PK-12
PO Box 99 79565 325-644-2311
Doc Rowell, prin. Fax 644-5101

West Columbia, Brazoria, Pop. 4,240
Columbia-Brazoria ISD 3,100/PK-12
PO Box 158 77486 979-345-5147
Carol Bertholf, supt. Fax 345-4890
www.cbisd.com
West Columbia ES 800/PK-6
PO Box 158 77486 979-345-5191
Kathy Humbird, prin. Fax 345-3170
Other Schools – See Brazoria

Westhoff, DeWitt
Westhoff ISD 50/PK-8
PO Box 38 77994 830-236-5519
Donald Garrison, supt. Fax 236-5583
www.westhoffisd.org
Westhoff S 50/PK-8
PO Box 38 77994 830-236-5519
Donald Garrison, prin. Fax 236-5583

West Lake Hills, Travis, Pop. 3,021
Eanes ISD
Supt. — See Austin
Forest Trail ES 600/K-5
1203 S Capital Of Texas Hwy 78746 512-732-9160
Charles McCasland, prin. Fax 732-9169
Valley View ES 400/K-5
1201 S Capital Of Texas Hwy 78746 512-732-9140
Jennifer Dusek, prin. Fax 732-9149

Wharton, Wharton, Pop. 9,374
Wharton ISD 1,200/PK-12
2100 N Fulton St 77488 979-532-6201
Dr. James Bartosh, supt. Fax 532-6228
Sivells ES, 1605 N Alabama Rd 77488 200/PK-1
Ethel Garrett, prin. 979-532-6866
Wharton ES 2-5
2030 E Boling Hwy 77488 979-532-6201
Steve May, prin.
Wharton JHS 400/6-8
1120 N Rusk St 77488 979-532-6840
Marilyn Clark, prin. Fax 532-6849

Faith Christian Academy 100/PK-9
5227 FM 1301 Rd 77488 979-531-1000
Carmen Tanner, prin. Fax 531-1001

Wheeler, Wheeler, Pop. 1,217
Kelton ISD 100/PK-8
16703 FM 2697 79096 806-826-5795
Jay Watson, supt. Fax 826-3601
keltonisd.com
Kelton S 100/PK-8
16703 FM 2697 79096 806-826-5708
Heather Hardcastle, prin. Fax 826-3601

Wheeler ISD 400/PK-12
PO Box 1010 79096 806-826-5241
Paul Mahler, supt. Fax 826-3118
www.thestangs.com/
Wheeler S 400/PK-12
PO Box 1010 79096 806-826-5534
Jack Noles, prin. Fax 826-3118

White Deer, Carson, Pop. 1,071
White Deer ISD 400/K-12
PO Box 517 79097 806-883-2311
Danny Ferrell, supt. Fax 883-2321
www.whitedeerisd.net/
White Deer S 300/K-8
PO Box 37 79097 806-883-2311
Miriam Lynch, prin. Fax 883-5008

Whiteface, Cochran, Pop. 407
Whiteface Consolidated ISD 300/PK-12
PO Box 7 79379 806-287-1154
Elbert Wuthrich, supt. Fax 287-1131
www.whiteface.k12.tx.us
Whiteface ES 100/PK-6
PO Box 117 79379 806-287-1285
Tim Walker, prin. Fax 287-1131

Whitehouse, Smith, Pop. 7,122
Whitehouse ISD 4,000/PK-12
106 Wildcat Dr 75791 903-839-5500
Daniel DuPree, supt. Fax 839-5515
www.whitehouseisd.org
Brown ES 300/PK-5
104 State Highway 110 N 75791 903-839-5610
Valencia Ray, prin. Fax 839-5607
Cain ES 600/PK-5
801 State Highway 110 S 75791 903-839-5600
Sherri Randall, prin. Fax 839-5604
Higgins ES 800/PK-5
306 Bascom Rd 75791 903-839-5580
Tom Luce, prin. Fax 839-5584
Holloway 6th Grade S 300/6-6
701 E Main St 75791 903-839-5656
Travis Splinter, prin. Fax 839-1568
Stanton - Smith ES PK-5
500 Zavala Trl 75791 903-839-5730
Curtis Williams, prin. Fax 839-5744
Whitehouse JHS 600/7-8
108 Wildcat Dr 75791 903-839-5590
David Smith, prin. Fax 839-5518

White Oak, Gregg, Pop. 6,130
White Oak ISD 1,400/PK-12
200 S White Oak Rd 75693 903-291-2000
Michael Gilbert, supt. Fax 291-2222
www.woisd.net
White Oak IS 300/3-5
200 S White Oak Rd 75693 903-291-2100
Karen Dickson, prin. Fax 291-2196
White Oak MS 300/6-8
200 S White Oak Rd 75693 903-291-2050
Ronnie Hinkle, prin. Fax 291-2035
White Oak PS 300/PK-2
200 S White Oak Rd 75693 903-291-2150
Key Amundson, prin. Fax 291-2132

Whitesboro, Grayson, Pop. 4,001
Whitesboro ISD 1,600/PK-12
115 4th St 76273 903-564-4200
Dr. Ray Lea, supt. Fax 564-9303
www.whitesboroisd.org
Hayes PS 400/PK-2
117 4th St 76273 903-564-4259
Terry Stone, prin. Fax 564-4123
Whitesboro IS 300/3-5
211 N College St 76273 903-564-4180
Gina Henley, prin. Fax 564-4159
Whitesboro MS 400/6-8
600 4th St 76273 903-564-4240
Patty Mitchell, prin. Fax 564-5939

White Settlement, Tarrant, Pop. 15,736
White Settlement ISD
Supt. — See Fort Worth
Brewer MS 800/7-8
1000 S Cherry Ln 76108 817-367-1267
Christie Beaty, prin. Fax 367-1268
Liberty ES 500/PK-4
7976 Whitney Dr 76108 817-367-1312
Coby Kirkpatrick, prin. Fax 367-1313
West ES 500/PK-4
8901 White Settlement Rd 76108 817-367-1334
Ron Shelton, prin. Fax 367-1333

Whitewright, Grayson, Pop. 1,780
Whitewright ISD 800/PK-12
PO Box 888 75491 903-364-2155
Steve Arthur, supt. Fax 364-2839
www.whitewrightisd.com
Whitewright ES 300/PK-5
PO Box 888 75491 903-364-2424
Beryl Sears, prin. Fax 364-5799
Whitewright MS 200/6-8
PO Box 888 75491 903-364-2151
Bobby Worthy, prin. Fax 364-5263

Whitharral, Hockley
Whitharral ISD 200/K-12
PO Box 225 79380 806-299-1184
Ed Sharp, supt. Fax 299-1257
www.whitharral.k12.tx.us/
Whitharral S 200/K-12
PO Box 225 79380 806-299-1135
Carla Kristinek, prin. Fax 299-1257

Whitney, Hill, Pop. 2,049
Whitney ISD 1,600/PK-12
PO Box 518 76692 254-694-2254
Gene Solis, supt. Fax 694-2064
www.whitney.k12.tx.us
Whitney ES 400/PK-2
PO Box 518 76692 254-694-3456
Melaney Watson, prin. Fax 694-2059
Whitney IS 400/3-5
PO Box 518 76692 254-694-7303
Chris Hestilow, prin. Fax 694-7029
Whitney MS 300/6-8
PO Box 518 76692 254-694-3446
Wayne Redding, prin. Fax 694-2064

Wichita Falls, Wichita, Pop. 99,846
Burkburnett ISD
Supt. — See Burkburnett
Tower ES 800/PK-5
5200 Hooper Dr 76306 940-855-3221
Stacey Darnall, prin. Fax 851-9812

City View ISD 1,000/PK-12
1025 City View Dr 76306 940-855-4042
Steve Harris, supt. Fax 851-8889
www.cityview-isd.net/
City View ES 600/PK-6
1023 City View Dr 76306 940-855-2351
Kim Davis, prin. Fax 855-7943

Wichita Falls ISD 12,800/PK-12
PO Box 97533 76307 940-235-1000
Dr. George Kazanas, supt.
www.wfisd.net
Alamo ES 500/K-6
1912 11th St 76301 940-720-3128
Laura Scott, prin. Fax 767-4662
Barwise JHS, 3807 Kemp Blvd 76308 500/7-8
Linda Muehlberger, prin. 940-235-1108
Brook Village ECC 200/PK-K
2222 Brook Ave 76301 940-720-3333
Rose Partridge, prin. Fax 720-3335
Burgess ES, 3106 Maurine St 76306 400/PK-6
Dalton Clark, prin. 940-235-1136
Crockett ES 600/K-6
3015 Avenue I 76309 940-720-3150
Cathy Rule, prin. Fax 720-3276
Cunningham ES 400/PK-6
4107 Phillips Dr 76308 940-720-3042
Christina Henry, prin. Fax 720-3061
Fain ES 600/PK-6
1562 Norman St 76302 940-720-3157
Clarissa Richie, prin. Fax 720-3218
Fowler ES, 5100 Ridgecrest Dr 76310 600/K-6
Tania Rushing, prin. 940-235-1152
Franklin ES 500/K-6
2112 Speedway Ave 76308 940-720-3142
Kim Meyer, prin. Fax 720-3074
Haynes ES 200/K-6
1705 Katherine Dr 76306 940-716-2875
Ronda Hall, prin. Fax 716-2877
Houston ES, 2500 Grant St 76309 400/PK-6
Omar Montemayor, prin. 940-235-1164
Jefferson ES 500/K-6
4628 Mistletoe Dr 76310 940-720-3050
Pat Page, prin. Fax 692-5893
Kirby JHS, 1715 Loop 11 76306 400/7-8
Dee Palmore, prin. 940-235-1113
Lamar ES, 2206 Lucas Ave 76301 400/PK-3
Gail Anderson, prin. 940-235-1172
McNiel JHS, 4712 Barnett Rd 76310 600/7-8
Carol English, prin. 940-235-1118
Milam ES, 2901 Boren Ave 76308 400/K-6
Pat Baggs, prin. 940-235-1176
Scotland Park ES PK-6
1415 N 5th St 76306 940-235-1180
Dotsie Mergerson, prin.
Sheppard A F B ES 300/K-6
301 Anderson Dr 76311 940-716-2950
Marvin Peevey, prin. Fax 716-2960
Southern Hills ES PK-6
3920 Armory Rd 76302 940-235-1188
Joyce Shepard, prin.
Washington-Jackson Math/Science ES 400/PK-6
1300 Harding St 76301 940-720-3145
Tim Callaway, prin. Fax 720-3168
West Foundation ES 400/K-6
5220 Lake Wellington Pkwy 76310 940-720-3080
Lisa Wester, prin. Fax 720-3082
Zundy JHS 400/7-8
1706 Polk St 76309 940-720-3170
Linda Young, prin. Fax 720-3172

Agape Christian S 100/PK-12
5600 Burkburnett Rd 76306 940-851-6727
Dr. Paula Burt, prin. Fax 851-6592
Christ Academy 200/PK-8
3801 Louis J Rodriguez Dr 76308 940-692-2853
Keven Robertson, prin. Fax 692-2657
Notre Dame S 200/PK-12
2821 Lansing Blvd 76309 940-692-6041
Cindy Huckabee, prin. Fax 692-2811

Wildorado, Oldham
Wildorado ISD 100/PK-6
PO Box 120 79098 806-426-3317
Matthew Branstine, supt. Fax 426-3523
www.wildorado.net
Wildorado ES 100/PK-6
PO Box 120 79098 806-426-3317
Matt Branstine, prin. Fax 426-3523

Willis, Montgomery, Pop. 4,172
Willis ISD 5,700/PK-12
204 W Rogers St 77378 936-856-1200
Dr. Brian Zemlicka, supt. Fax 856-5182
www.willisisd.org/
Brabham MS 600/6-8
10000 FM 830 Rd 77318 936-890-2312
Sheryl Burlison, prin. Fax 856-2910
Cannan ES 700/PK-5
7639 County Line Rd 77378 936-890-8660
Ali Parker, prin. Fax 890-2616
Hardy ES 700/PK-5
701 Gerald St 77378 936-856-1241
Debbie Cooper, prin. Fax 856-1242
Lucas MS 600/6-8
1304 N Campbell St 77378 936-856-1274
Lisa Severns, prin. Fax 856-1065
Meador ES PK-5
10020 FM 830 Rd 77318 936-890-7550
Karon Priest, prin. Fax 890-7540
Parmley ES 800/PK-5
600 N Campbell St 77378 936-856-1231
Janie Wiggins, prin. Fax 856-1239
Turner ES 600/PK-5
10101 N Highway 75 77378 936-856-1289
Glynda Anderson, prin. Fax 856-1677

Willow Park, Parker, Pop. 3,463
Aledo ISD
Supt. — See Aledo
McCall ES K-5
400 Scenic Trl 76087 817-441-4500
Jason Beaty, prin. Fax 441-4535

Trinity Christian Academy 400/PK-12
4954 E I 20 Service Rd S 76087 817-441-7901
Dr. Marsha Barber, admin. Fax 441-7912

Wills Point, Van Zandt, Pop. 3,855
Wills Point ISD 2,700/PK-12
338 W North Commerce St 75169 903-873-3161
Joe Oliver, supt. Fax 873-2462
www.wpisd.com/
Wills Point JHS 400/7-8
200 Tiger Dr 75169 903-873-4924
Thomas Harp, prin. Fax 873-4873
Wills Point MS 400/5-6
101 School St 75169 903-873-3617
Alan Prachyl, prin. Fax 873-2465
Wills Point PS 500/PK-1
447 Terrace Dr 75169 903-873-2491
Deborah Deen, prin. Fax 873-3051
Woods IS 600/2-4
307 Wingo Way 75169 903-873-2841
Vicki Overturf, prin. Fax 873-3134

Wilson, Lynn, Pop. 501
Wilson ISD 200/PK-12
PO Box 9 79381 806-628-6271
Michael Norman, supt. Fax 628-6441
wilson.esc17.net/
Wilson S 200/PK-12
PO Box 9 79381 806-628-6261
Michael Norman, prin. Fax 628-6441

Wimberley, Hays, Pop. 2,712
Wimberley ISD 1,900/PK-12
14401 Ranch Rd 12 78676 512-847-2414
Dwain York, supt. Fax 847-2142
www.wimberley.txed.net/
Bowen IS 400/3-5
14501 Ranch Rd 12 78676 512-847-5558
Linda Land, prin. Fax 847-6176

Scudder PS 400/PK-2
400 Green Acres Dr 78676 512-847-3407
Andrea Gonzales, prin. Fax 847-2738
Wimberley JHS 500/6-8
200 Texan Blvd 78676 512-847-2181
Jason Valentine, prin. Fax 847-7897

St. Stephen's Episcopal S 200/PK-8
6000 FM 3237 78676 512-847-9857
Dr. Richard Stark, hdmstr. Fax 847-5275

Windthorst, Archer, Pop. 443
Windthorst ISD 500/PK-12
PO Box 190 76389 940-423-6688
Don Windham, supt. Fax 423-6505
www.windthorstisd.net
Windthorst ES 300/PK-6
PO Box 190 76389 940-423-6679
Jean Ashton, prin. Fax 423-6505

Winfield, Titus, Pop. 528
Winfield ISD 100/K-8
PO Box 298 75493 903-524-2221
Danny Denton, supt. Fax 524-2410
www.winfieldisd.net/
Winfield S 100/K-8
PO Box 298 75493 903-524-2221
Tony Martin, prin. Fax 524-2410

Wink, Winkler, Pop. 883
Wink-Loving ISD 300/PK-12
PO Box 637 79789 432-527-3880
John Benham, supt. Fax 527-3505
wlisd.esc18.net
Wink ES 200/PK-6
PO Box 637 79789 432-527-3880
Eddie Boggess, prin. Fax 527-3505

Winnie, Chambers, Pop. 2,238
East Chambers ISD 1,200/PK-12
1955 State Highway 124 77665 409-296-6100
Scott Campbell, supt. Fax 296-3528
www.eastchambers.net
East Chambers ES 500/PK-4
316 E Fear Rd 77665 409-296-6100
Vicki Bauer, prin. Fax 296-3259
East Chambers IS 200/5-6
213 School Rd 77665 409-296-6100
Lou Ann Rainey, prin. Fax 296-8108
East Chambers JHS 200/7-8
1931 State Highway 124 77665 409-296-6100
Lou Ann Rainey, prin. Fax 296-2724

Winnsboro, Wood, Pop. 3,794
Winnsboro ISD 1,500/PK-12
207 E Pine St 75494 903-342-3737
Dr. Mark Bosold, supt. Fax 342-3380
www.winnsboroisd.org
Memorial MS 400/5-8
505 S Chestnut St 75494 903-342-5711
Nan Saucier, prin. Fax 342-6689
Winnsboro ES 600/PK-4
310 W Coke Rd 75494 903-342-3548
Kristie Amason, prin. Fax 342-6858

Winona, Smith, Pop. 605
Winona ISD 800/PK-12
611 Wildcat Dr 75792 903-939-4001
Wiley Vonner, supt. Fax 877-9387
www.winonaisd.org
Winona ES 300/PK-5
605 Wildcat Dr 75792 903-939-4800
Joshua Snook, prin. Fax 877-2457
Winona MS 200/6-8
605 Wildcat Dr 75792 903-939-4040
Oscar Rendon, prin. Fax 877-9150

Winters, Runnels, Pop. 2,728
Winters ISD 700/PK-12
603 N Heights St 79567 325-754-5574
David Hutton, supt. Fax 754-5374
www.wintersisd.net/
Winters ES 400/PK-6
603 N Heights St 79567 325-754-5577
Brilla Reagan, prin. Fax 754-4686
Winters JHS 100/7-8
603 N Heights St 79567 325-754-5518
Cherri Barker, prin. Fax 754-5085

Woden, Nacogdoches
Woden ISD 800/PK-12
PO Box 100 75978 936-564-2073
Brent Hawkins, supt. Fax 564-1250
www.woden.esc7.net/
Woden ES 400/PK-5
PO Box 100 75978 936-564-2386
Debbie Blackmon, prin. Fax 564-3322
Woden JHS, PO Box 100 75978 200/6-8
Latricia Jacobs, prin. 936-564-2481

Wolfe City, Hunt, Pop. 1,647
Wolfe City ISD 600/PK-12
553 W Dallas St 75496 903-496-2283
Rick Loesch, supt. Fax 496-7905
www.wcisd.net
Wolfe City ES 300/PK-5
505 W Dallas St 75496 903-496-2032
Ola Owens, prin. Fax 496-7905
Wolfe City MS 100/6-8
553 W Dallas St 75496 903-496-7333
Laura Rodgers, prin. Fax 496-7905

Wolfforth, Lubbock, Pop. 2,942
Frenship ISD 5,800/PK-12
PO Box 100 79382 806-866-2442
Dr. David Vroonland, supt. Fax 866-4135
www.frenship.us
Bennett ES 200/PK-5
PO Box 100 79382 806-866-4443
Rhonda Dillard, prin. Fax 866-4715
Frenship MS 800/6-8
PO Box 100 79382 806-866-4464
Jerry Jerabek, prin. Fax 866-2181
Other Schools – See Lubbock

Woodsboro, Refugio, Pop. 1,626
Woodsboro ISD 500/PK-12
PO Box 770 78393 361-543-4518
Steven Self, supt. Fax 543-4856
www.wisd.net
Woodsboro ES 300/PK-6
PO Box 770 78393 361-543-4380
Sean Finnessey, prin. Fax 543-5478

Woodson, Throckmorton, Pop. 259
Woodson ISD 100/PK-12
PO Box 287 76491 940-345-6528
Dan Bellah, supt. Fax 345-6549
www.esc9.net/woodson/
Woodson S 100/PK-12
PO Box 287 76491 940-345-6521
Gordon Thomas, prin. Fax 345-6549

Woodville, Tyler, Pop. 2,313
Woodville ISD 1,400/PK-12
505 N Charlton St 75979 409-283-3752
Glen Conner, supt. Fax 283-7962
www.esc05.k12.tx.us/woodville
Woodville ES 400/PK-2
505 N Charlton St 75979 409-283-2452
John Cooley, prin. Fax 331-3409
Woodville IS 300/3-5
505 N Charlton St 75979 409-283-2549
Dr. Joannie Atkinson, prin. Fax 331-3412
Woodville MS 300/6-8
505 N Charlton St 75979 409-283-7109
Wayne Ivey, prin. Fax 331-3418

Wortham, Freestone, Pop. 1,089
Wortham ISD 500/PK-12
PO Box 247 76693 254-765-3095
Albert Armer, supt. Fax 765-3473
www.worthamisd.org
Wortham ES 200/PK-5
PO Box 247 76693 254-765-3080
Lesley Lambert, prin. Fax 765-3473
Wortham MS 100/6-8
PO Box 247 76693 254-765-3094
Lynn Jantzen, prin. Fax 765-3473

Wylie, Dallas, Pop. 29,061
Wylie ISD 11,600/PK-12
PO Box 490 75098 972-429-3000
Dr. H. John Fuller, supt. Fax 442-5368
www.wylieisd.net
Akin ES 500/K-4
PO Box 490 75098 972-429-3400
Valerie Plumlee, prin. Fax 442-5744
Birmingham ES 700/PK-4
PO Box 490 75098 972-429-3420
Sherry Betts, prin. Fax 442-1215
Burnett JHS 600/7-8
PO Box 490 75098 972-429-3200
Kyle Craighead, prin. Fax 429-1447
Cooper JHS 400/7-8
PO Box 490 75098 972-429-3250
Tami Nauyokus, prin. Fax 941-9175
Davis IS 600/5-6
PO Box 490 75098 972-429-3325
Barbara Rudolph, prin. Fax 429-9792
Dodd ES 700/PK-4
PO Box 490 75098 972-429-3440
Mike Evans, prin. Fax 442-9856
Draper IS 500/5-8
PO Box 490 75098 972-429-3350
Beth Edge, prin. Fax 442-9317
Groves ES 600/PK-4
PO Box 490 75098 972-429-3460
Jill Vasquez, prin. Fax 429-7906
Harrison IS 500/5-6
PO Box 490 75098 972-429-3300
Dr. Kimberly Gilmore, prin. Fax 442-3971
Hartman ES 600/PK-4
PO Box 490 75098 972-429-3480
Jennifer Speicher, prin. Fax 442-7072
McMillan JHS 700/7-8
PO Box 490 75098 972-429-3225
Jon Peters, prin. Fax 941-6372
Smith ES 600/PK-4
PO Box 490 75098 972-429-2540
Scott Winn, prin. Fax 442-5493
Other Schools – See Murphy, Sachse

First Baptist S 100/PK-PK
100 N 1st St 75098 972-442-0416
Holly Elgin, dir. Fax 442-6154
Wylie Preparatory Academy 200/1-12
PO Box 2273 75098 972-442-1388
Fax 429-3568

Yantis, Wood, Pop. 359
Yantis ISD 400/PK-12
105 W Oak St 75497 903-383-2463
Michael Barnett, supt. Fax 383-7620
www.yantisisd.net
Yantis ES 200/PK-5
105 W Oak St 75497 903-383-2463
Cheryl Hughes, prin. Fax 383-7620

Yoakum, Lavaca, Pop. 5,720
Yoakum ISD 1,300/PK-12
PO Box 737 77995 361-293-3162
Tom Kelley, supt. Fax 293-6678
www.yoakumisd.net/
Yoakum IS 300/3-5
PO Box 737 77995 361-293-2741
Chad Rothbauer, prin. Fax 293-6562
Yoakum JHS 300/6-8
PO Box 737 77995 361-293-3111
Gabe Adamek, prin. Fax 293-5787
Yoakum PS 200/1-2
PO Box 737 77995 361-293-2011
Pat Brewer, prin. Fax 293-2688
Yoakum PS Annex PK-K
PO Box 737 77995 361-293-3312
Pat Brewer, prin. Fax 293-6937

St. Joseph S 100/PK-8
310 Orth St 77995 361-741-5362
Susan Kelly, prin. Fax 293-3004

Yorktown, DeWitt, Pop. 2,265
Yorktown ISD 700/PK-12
PO Box 487 78164 361-564-2252
Deborah Kneese, supt. Fax 564-2254
www.yisd.org
Yorktown ES 300/PK-5
PO Box 487 78164 361-564-2252
Patty Strieber, prin. Fax 564-2270
Yorktown JHS 200/6-8
PO Box 487 78164 361-564-2252
Sylvia Hernandez, prin. Fax 564-2289

Zapata, Zapata, Pop. 7,119
Zapata County ISD 3,500/PK-12
PO Box 158 78076 956-765-6546
Romeo Rodriguez, supt. Fax 765-8350
www.zcisd.org
Benavides ES 100/PK-5
17th & Carla 78076 956-765-5611
Gerardo Montes, prin. Fax 765-3942
Villarreal ES 500/1-5
PO Box 3637 78076 956-765-4238
Carmen Zavala, prin. Fax 765-9580
Zapata MS 700/6-8
PO Box 3636 78076 956-765-6542
Gerardo Garcia, prin. Fax 765-9204
Zapata North ECC 600/PK-K
PO Box 3224 78076 956-765-6921
Erica Ramirez, prin. Fax 765-8512
Zapata South ES 600/1-5
PO Box 2030 78076 956-765-4332
Pedro Morales, prin. Fax 765-3320

Faith Academy 50/PK-7
PO Box 577 78076 956-765-6549
Rev. Gerardo Rodriguez, admin. Fax 765-5626

Zavalla, Angelina, Pop. 656
Zavalla ISD 500/PK-12
PO Box 45 75980 936-897-2271
David Flowers, supt. Fax 897-2674
www.zavallaisd.net/
Zavalla ES 200/PK-5
PO Box 45 75980 936-897-2611
Kevin Frauenberger, prin. Fax 897-2674

Zephyr, Brown
Zephyr ISD 200/K-12
11625 County Road 281 76890 325-739-5331
David Whisenhunt, supt. Fax 739-2126
zephyr.netxv.net/
Zephyr ES 100/K-6
11625 County Road 281 76890 325-739-5331
Gary Bufe, prin. Fax 739-2126

UTAH

UTAH OFFICE OF EDUCATION
PO Box 144200, Salt Lake City 84114-4200
Telephone 801-538-7500
Fax 801-538-7768
Website http://www.usoe.k12.ut.us

Superintendent of Public Instruction Patti Harrington

UTAH BOARD OF EDUCATION
250 E 500 S, Salt Lake City 84111-3284

Chairperson Richard Sadler

REGIONAL SERVICE CENTERS (RSC)

Central Utah Educational Services
Glen Taylor, dir. 435-896-4469
195 E 500 N, Richfield 84701 Fax 896-4767

Northeastern Utah Educational Services
Duke Mossman, dir. 435-654-1921
755 S Main St, Heber City 84032 Fax 654-2403

Southeast Educational Service Center
J.J. Grant, dir. 435-637-1173
685 E 200 S, Price 84501 Fax 637-1178

Southwest Educational Development Ctr
Randy Johnson, dir. 435-586-2865
520 W 800 S, Cedar City 84720 Fax 586-2868

PUBLIC, PRIVATE AND CATHOLIC ELEMENTARY SCHOOLS

Alpine, Utah, Pop. 9,063
Alpine SD
Supt. — See American Fork
Alpine ES 700/K-6
400 E 300 N 84004 801-756-8525
David Stephenson, prin. Fax 756-8527
Westfield ES 800/K-6
380 Long Dr 84004 801-763-7040
Vickie Haws, prin. Fax 763-7044

Altamont, Duchesne, Pop. 183
Duchesne SD
Supt. — See Duchesne
Altamont ES 300/K-6
PO Box 40 84001 435-738-1375
Janalee Goodrich, prin. Fax 738-1396

American Fork, Utah, Pop. 21,372
Alpine SD 53,100/K-12
575 N 100 E 84003 801-756-8400
Dr. Vernon Henshaw, supt. Fax 756-8516
www.alpine.k12.ut.us/
Barratt ES 600/K-6
168 N 900 E 84003 801-756-8528
Brent Palmer, prin. Fax 756-8530
Forbes ES 600/K-6
281 N 200 W 84003 801-756-8531
Sam Rencher, prin. Fax 756-8571
Greenwood ES 600/K-6
50 E 200 S 84003 801-756-8534
Cathy Matheson, prin. Fax 756-8536
Legacy ES 900/K-6
28 E 1340 N 84003 801-756-8565
Gary Gibb, prin. Fax 756-8568
Shelley ES 1,000/K-6
602 N 200 W 84003 801-756-8540
Peggy Crandell, prin. Fax 763-7020
Other Schools – See Alpine, Cedar Fort, Cedar Hills, Eagle Mountain, Highland, Lehi, Lindon, Orem, Pleasant Grove, Saratoga Sprngs, Vineyard

Antimony, Garfield, Pop. 112
Garfield SD
Supt. — See Panguitch
Antimony ES 50/K-6
PO Box 120026 84712 435-624-3221
Julie Allen, lead tchr. Fax 624-3286

Bear River City, Box Elder, Pop. 800
Box Elder SD
Supt. — See Brigham City
Century ES 500/K-5
5820 N 4800 W 84301 435-279-2651
Colleen Shaffer, prin. Fax 279-2654

Beaver, Beaver, Pop. 2,558
Beaver SD 1,500/K-12
PO Box 31 84713 435-438-2291
Ray Terry, supt. Fax 438-5898
www.beaver.k12.ut.us
Belknap ES 500/K-6
PO Box 686 84713 435-438-2281
Brody Fails, prin. Fax 438-5385
Other Schools – See Milford, Minersville

Beryl, Iron
Iron SD
Supt. — See Cedar City
Escalante Valley ES 100/K-6
202 N Beryl Hwy 84714 435-439-5550
Pam Robinson, prin. Fax 439-5552

Bicknell, Wayne, Pop. 335
Wayne SD 500/K-12
PO Box 127 84715 435-425-3813
Jessie Pace, supt. Fax 425-3806
www.wayne.k12.ut.us
Wayne MS 100/6-8
PO Box 128 84715 435-425-3421
Mary Bray, lead tchr. Fax 425-3130
Other Schools – See Hanksville, Loa

Big Water, Kane, Pop. 415
Kane SD
Supt. — See Kanab
Big Water ES 50/K-6
PO Box 410126 84741 435-675-5821
Gerry Rankin, prin. Fax 675-5821

Blanding, San Juan, Pop. 3,135
San Juan SD 2,900/K-12
200 N Main St 84511 435-678-1200
Dr. Douglas Wright, supt. Fax 678-1204
www.sanjuanschools.org/
Blanding ES 500/K-5
302 S 100 W 84511 435-678-1872
Bob Bowring, prin. Fax 678-1877
Lyman MS 300/6-8
535 N 100 E 84511 435-678-1398
Chas DeWitt, prin. Fax 678-1399
Other Schools – See Bluff, La Sal, Mexican Hat, Montezuma Creek, Monticello

Bluff, San Juan
San Juan SD
Supt. — See Blanding
Bluff ES 100/K-6
PO Box 130 84512 435-678-1296
Verona McDermott, prin. Fax 678-1299

Boulder, Garfield, Pop. 179
Garfield SD
Supt. — See Panguitch
Boulder ES 50/K-6
PO Box 1447 84716 435-335-7322
Roy Suggett, lead tchr. Fax 335-7354

Bountiful, Davis, Pop. 41,085
Davis SD
Supt. — See Farmington
Adelaide ES 600/K-6
731 W 3600 S 84010 801-402-1250
Jean Parkin, prin. Fax 402-1251
Boulton ES 500/PK-6
2611 Orchard Dr 84010 801-402-1300
Laura Bond, prin. Fax 402-1301
Bountiful ES 400/K-6
1620 S 50 W 84010 801-402-1350
Ross Quist, prin. Fax 402-1351
Holbrook ES 400/K-6
1018 E 250 N 84010 801-402-1450
Shauna Lund, prin. Fax 402-1451
Meadowbrook ES 400/PK-6
700 N 325 W 84010 801-402-1600
Sharla Fillmore, prin. Fax 402-1601
Muir ES 600/K-6
2275 S Davis Blvd 84010 801-402-1550
Kevin Prusse, prin. Fax 402-1551
Oak Hills ES 400/PK-6
1235 Lakeview Dr 84010 801-402-1650
Julie Larsen, prin. Fax 402-1651
Tolman ES 400/PK-6
300 E 1200 N 84010 801-402-1900
David Pendergast, prin. Fax 402-1901
Valley View ES 400/PK-6
1395 S 600 E 84010 801-402-2050
Mary Memmott, prin. Fax 402-2051
Washington ES 400/PK-6
340 W 650 S 84010 801-402-1950
Liz Beck, prin. Fax 402-1951

St. Olaf S 200/K-8
1793 Orchard Dr 84010 801-295-5341
JoAnn Emery, prin. Fax 295-5915

Brigham City, Box Elder, Pop. 18,355
Box Elder SD 10,000/K-12
960 S Main St 84302 435-734-4800
Martell Menlove, supt. Fax 734-4833
www.besd.net
Bunderson ES 400/K-5
641 E 200 N 84302 435-734-4900
Scott Hunsaker, prin. Fax 734-4902
Discovery ES 500/K-5
810 N 500 W 84302 435-734-4910
Kim Lynch, prin. Fax 734-4912
Foothill ES 300/K-5
820 N 100 E 84302 435-734-4916
Wade Hyde, prin. Fax 734-4918
Lake View ES 300/K-5
851 S 200 W 84302 435-734-4922
Susan LaVelle, prin. Fax 734-4924
Mountain View ES 300/K-5
650 E 700 S 84302 435-734-4926
David Lee, prin. Fax 734-4928
Young IS 900/6-7
830 S Law Dr 84302 435-734-4940
Chris Chournos, prin. Fax 734-4950
Other Schools – See Bear River City, Fielding, Garland, Grouse Creek, Howell, Park Valley, Perry, Snowville, Tremonton, Willard

---

Northridge Learning Center 100/K-12
44 S Main St 84302 435-734-2550
Dixie Evans, dir. Fax 723-3903

Castle Dale, Emery, Pop. 1,615
Emery County SD
Supt. — See Huntington
Castle Dale ES 200/K-6
PO Box 539 84513 435-381-5221
Ralph Worthen, prin. Fax 381-5220

Cedar City, Iron, Pop. 23,983
Iron SD 6,600/K-12
2077 W Royal Hunte Dr 84720 435-586-2804
James Johnson, supt. Fax 586-2815
www.iron.k12.ut.us
Canyon View MS 6-8
1865 N Main St 84721 435-586-2830
Conrad Aitken, prin. Fax 586-2837
Cedar East ES 500/K-5
255 E College Ave 84720 435-586-2840
Steve Burton, prin. Fax 586-2841
Cedar MS 900/6-8
2215 W Royal Hunte Dr 84720 435-586-2810
Kendall Benson, prin. Fax 586-2829
Cedar North ES 400/K-5
550 W 200 N 84720 435-586-2845
Brent Bonner, prin. Fax 586-2846
Cedar South ES 600/K-5
499 W 400 S 84720 435-586-2850
Jerry Oldroyd, prin. Fax 586-2852
Fiddlers Canyon ES 600/K-5
475 E 1935 N 84721 435-586-2860
Ray Whittier, prin. Fax 586-2861

Iron Springs ES K-5
235 N 4050 W 84720 435-586-9485
Jane Twitchell, prin. Fax 586-8647
Three Peaks ES K-5
1685 W Midvalley Rd 84721 435-586-8871
Tim Taylor, prin. Fax 586-8934
Other Schools – See Beryl, Enoch, Parowan

Cedar Fort, Utah, Pop. 338
Alpine SD
Supt. — See American Fork
Cedar Valley ES 100/K-5
40 E Center St 84013 801-768-3542
Fax 766-1370

Cedar Hills, Utah, Pop. 7,790
Alpine SD
Supt. — See American Fork
Cedar Ridge ES 900/K-6
4501 W Cedar Hills Dr 84062 801-785-8726
Susan Mattinson, prin. Fax 785-8769
Deerfield ES 900/K-6
4353 Harvey Blvd 84062 801-796-3141
Jane Friel, prin. Fax 796-3145

Centerville, Davis, Pop. 14,898
Davis SD
Supt. — See Farmington
Centerville ES 500/PK-6
350 N 100 E 84014 801-402-1400
Cameron Forbush, prin. Fax 402-1401
Reading ES 700/K-6
360 W 2025 N 84014 801-402-1750
Dena Lund, prin. Fax 402-1751
Stewart ES 700/K-6
1155 N Main St 84014 801-402-1850
Vonzaa Hewitt, prin. Fax 402-1851
Taylor ES 300/K-6
293 E Pages Ln 84014 801-402-1500
Vicki Corwin, prin. Fax 402-1501

Circleville, Piute, Pop. 476
Piute SD
Supt. — See Junction
Circleville ES 100/PK-6
300 S Center St 84723 435-577-2912
Janetta Dalton, prin. Fax 577-2927

Clearfield, Davis, Pop. 27,413
Davis SD
Supt. — See Farmington
Antelope ES 800/PK-6
1810 S Main St 84015 801-402-2100
Jody Schaap, prin. Fax 402-2101
Hill Field ES 500/K-6
389 S 1000 E 84015 801-402-2350
Paul Bryner, prin. Fax 402-2351
Holt ES 700/PK-6
448 N 1000 W 84015 801-402-2400
John Zurbuchen, prin. Fax 402-2401
Parkside ES K-6
2262 N 1500 W 84015 801-402-1150
Roy Warren, prin. Fax 402-1151
South Clearfield ES 500/PK-6
990 E 700 S 84015 801-402-2500
Daren Allred, prin. Fax 402-2501
Wasatch ES 300/K-6
270 Center St 84015 801-402-2650
Kathy Scott, prin. Fax 402-2651

Cleveland, Emery, Pop. 510
Emery County SD
Supt. — See Huntington
Cleveland ES 200/K-6
PO Box 220 84518 435-653-2235
Edward Clark, prin. Fax 653-2370

Clinton, Davis, Pop. 17,735
Davis SD
Supt. — See Farmington
Clinton ES 700/PK-6
1101 W 1800 N 84015 801-402-2150
Christopher Laypath, prin. Fax 402-2151
West Clinton ES 1,000/PK-6
2826 W 1800 N 84015 801-402-2700
Steve Hammer, prin. Fax 402-2701

Coalville, Summit, Pop. 1,451
North Summit SD 1,000/PK-12
PO Box 497 84017 435-336-5654
Steven Carlsen, supt. Fax 336-2401
www.nsummit.k12.ut.us
North Summit ES 400/PK-4
PO Box 497 84017 435-336-2101
Lori O'Connor, prin. Fax 336-2064
North Summit MS 300/5-8
PO Box 497 84017 435-336-5678
Wade Murdock, prin. Fax 336-4474

Cottonwood Heights, Salt Lake, Pop. 27,500
Jordan SD
Supt. — See Sandy
Bella Vista ES 400/K-6
2131 Fort Union Blvd, 801-944-2911
Denis Lyons, prin. Fax 302-4906
Ridgecrest ES 500/K-6
1800 E 7200 S, 801-944-2904
Catherine Stoneman, prin. Fax 302-4951

Delta, Millard, Pop. 3,106
Millard SD 2,600/PK-12
285 E 450 N 84624 435-864-1000
David Taylor, supt. Fax 864-5684
www.millard.k12.ut.us
Delta ECC 100/PK-K
450 S Center St 84624 435-864-5670
Greg Chappell, prin. Fax 864-5679
Delta ES 300/K-4
50 N 100 E 84624 435-864-5680
David Noah, prin. Fax 864-5689
Delta MS 500/5-8
251 E 300 N 84624 435-864-5660
David Styler, prin. Fax 864-5669
Other Schools – See Fillmore, Garrison

Draper, Salt Lake, Pop. 35,119
Jordan SD
Supt. — See Sandy
Draper ES 600/K-6
1080 E 12660 S 84020 801-572-7005
Tamra Baker, prin. Fax 302-4920
Oak Hollow ES 800/K-6
884 E 14400 S 84020 801-572-7389
Rebecca Dallimore, prin. Fax 302-4943
Willow Springs ES K-6
13288 Lone Rock Dr 84020 801-523-8142
Sharyle Karren, prin. Fax 302-4978

Oxford Academy 50/PK-12
1259 Draper Pkwy 84020 801-501-0228
Millicent Jacobson, dir. Fax 501-0296
St. John the Baptist ES 500/PK-5
300 E 11800 S 84020 801-984-7123
Nikki Ward, prin. Fax 984-7649
St. John the Baptist MS 400/6-8
300 E 11800 S 84020 801-984-7613
Jim Markosian, prin. Fax 984-7649

Duchesne, Duchesne, Pop. 1,481
Duchesne SD 4,000/K-12
PO Box 446 84021 435-738-1240
John Aland, supt. Fax 738-1254
www.dcsd.org
Duchesne ES 300/K-6
PO Box 370 84021 435-738-1290
Guy Coleman, prin. Fax 738-1313
Other Schools – See Altamont, Myton, Neola, Roosevelt, Tabiona

Dugway, Tooele, Pop. 1,761
Tooele County SD
Supt. — See Tooele
Dugway ES 100/K-6
5000 Valdez Cir 84022 435-831-4259
Robin Nielson, prin. Fax 831-4469

Dutch John, Daggett
Daggett SD
Supt. — See Manila
Flaming Gorge ES 50/K-4
PO Box 187 84023 435-885-3112
Scott Taylor, prin. Fax 885-3218

Eagle Mountain, Utah
Alpine SD
Supt. — See American Fork
Hidden Hollow ES K-6
2546 Express Pony, 801-789-7804
Tom Tillman, prin.

Eden, Weber
Weber SD
Supt. — See Ogden
Valley ES 600/K-6
5821 E 1900 N 84310 801-452-4180
Tommy Lee, prin. Fax 452-4199

Enoch, Iron, Pop. 4,167
Iron SD
Supt. — See Cedar City
Enoch ES 600/K-5
4701 N Wagon Wheel Dr, 435-586-2855
Lenora Roundy, prin.

Enterprise, Washington, Pop. 1,419
Washington County SD
Supt. — See Saint George
Enterprise ES 300/K-6
PO Box 459 84725 435-878-2236
William Evan Johnson, prin. Fax 878-2510

Ephraim, Sanpete, Pop. 4,977
South Sanpete SD
Supt. — See Manti
Ephraim ES 400/PK-5
151 S Main St 84627 435-283-4171
Lynn Willardson, prin. Fax 283-6892
Ephraim MS 400/6-8
555 S 100 E 84627 435-283-4037
Kirk Anderson, prin. Fax 283-4885

Escalante, Garfield, Pop. 744
Garfield SD
Supt. — See Panguitch
Escalante ES 100/K-6
PO Box 248 84726 435-826-4247
Sue Bassett, lead tchr. Fax 826-4789

Eureka, Juab, Pop. 793
Tintic SD 300/PK-12
PO Box 210 84628 435-433-6363
Ron Barlow, supt. Fax 433-6643
www.tintic.k12.ut.us
Eureka ES 100/PK-6
PO Box 170 84628 435-433-6927
Ron Barlow, prin. Fax 433-6622
Other Schools – See Wendover

Fairview, Sanpete, Pop. 1,163
North Sanpete SD
Supt. — See Mount Pleasant
Fairview ES 300/K-6
651 E 150 N 84629 435-427-9204
John Allan, prin. Fax 427-9201

Farmington, Davis, Pop. 14,357
Davis SD 60,000/PK-12
PO Box 588 84025 801-402-5261
Dr. W. Bryan Bowles, supt. Fax 402-5249
www.davis.k12.ut.us
Eagle Bay ES 700/K-6
1933 Clark Ln 84025 801-402-3800
Ofelia Wade, prin. Fax 402-3801
Farmington ES 500/K-6
50 W 200 S 84025 801-402-2950
Bryan Tesch, prin. Fax 402-2951
Knowlton ES 700/PK-6
801 Shepard Ln 84025 801-402-3000
Grace Larsen, prin. Fax 402-3001
Other Schools – See Bountiful, Centerville, Clearfield, Clinton, Kaysville, Layton, North Salt Lake, South Weber, Sunset, Syracuse, West Bountiful, West Point, Woods Cross

Ferron, Emery, Pop. 1,571
Emery County SD
Supt. — See Huntington
Ferron ES 200/K-6
PO Box 910 84523 435-384-2383
Brian Dawes, prin. Fax 384-2550

Fielding, Box Elder, Pop. 439
Box Elder SD
Supt. — See Brigham City
Fielding ES 300/K-5
PO Box 98 84311 435-458-2700
Gerald Jackman, prin. Fax 458-2702

Fillmore, Millard, Pop. 2,178
Millard SD
Supt. — See Delta
Fillmore ES 400/K-4
555 W 400 S 84631 435-743-5670
Rhonda Harrison, prin. Fax 743-5679
Fillmore MS 300/5-8
435 S 500 W 84631 435-743-5660
George Richardson, prin. Fax 743-5669

Fountain Green, Sanpete, Pop. 941
North Sanpete SD
Supt. — See Mount Pleasant
Fountain Green ES 200/K-6
PO Box 38 84632 435-445-3316
Darrell White, prin. Fax 445-3305

Garland, Box Elder, Pop. 1,982
Box Elder SD
Supt. — See Brigham City
Garland ES 400/K-5
250 N Main St 84312 435-257-2600
Kristi Capener, prin. Fax 257-2602

Garrison, Millard
Millard SD
Supt. — See Delta
Garrison S 50/K-8
PO Box 10 84728 435-855-2321
Cecelia Phillips, admin. Fax 855-2195

Goshen, Utah, Pop. 775
Nebo SD
Supt. — See Spanish Fork
Goshen S 300/K-6
60 N Center 84633 801-667-3361
James Welburn, prin. Fax 667-3374

Grantsville, Tooele, Pop. 7,494
Tooele County SD
Supt. — See Tooele
Grantsville ES 700/3-6
175 W Main St 84029 435-884-4520
Jeff Wyatt, prin. Fax 884-4521
Grantsville JHS 600/7-8
318 S Hale St 84029 435-884-4510
Keith Davis, prin. Fax 884-4513
Willow ES 500/K-2
439 Willow St 84029 435-884-4527
Mark Brunsdale, prin. Fax 884-4528

Green River, Emery, Pop. 952
Emery County SD
Supt. — See Huntington
Book Cliff ES 100/K-6
PO Box 448 84525 435-564-8102
Nolan Johnson, prin. Fax 564-8327

Grouse Creek, Box Elder
Box Elder SD
Supt. — See Brigham City
Grouse Creek S 50/K-10
PO Box 16 84313 435-747-7321
Duane Runyan, prin. Fax 747-7182

Gunnison, Sanpete, Pop. 2,700
South Sanpete SD
Supt. — See Manti
Gunnison Valley ES 500/PK-5
PO Box 369 84634 435-528-7880
Grant Hansen, prin. Fax 528-7474
Gunnison Valley MS 200/6-8
PO Box 1090 84634 435-528-5337
Alan Peterson, prin. Fax 528-5397

Hanksville, Wayne, Pop. 196
Wayne SD
Supt. — See Bicknell
Hanksville ES 50/K-5
PO Box 69 84734 435-542-3291
Rae Lene Ekher, prin. Fax 542-2025

Heber City, Wasatch, Pop. 5,299
Wasatch SD 3,700/K-12
101 E 200 N 84032 435-654-0280
Terry Shoemaker, supt. Fax 654-4714
www.wasatch.edu/
Heber Valley ES 500/K-5
730 S 600 W 84032 435-654-0112
Eric Campbell, prin. Fax 654-7540
Old Mill ES K-5
1600 E 980 S 84032 435-657-3130
Douglas Hardy, prin. Fax 654-9055

Rocky Mountain MS 700/6-7
800 School House Way 84032 435-654-9350
Sheldon Case, prin. Fax 654-9343
Smith ES 500/K-5
235 E 500 N 84032 435-654-2201
DeAnna Lloyd, prin. Fax 654-0167
Other Schools – See Midway

Helper, Carbon, Pop. 1,878
Carbon SD
Supt. — See Price
Mauro ES 300/K-6
20 S 2nd Ave 84526 435-472-5311
Seth Allred, prin. Fax 472-3687

Herriman, Salt Lake, Pop. 11,226
Jordan SD
Supt. — See Sandy
Butterfield Canyon ES K-6
6860 Mary Leizan Ln, 801-254-0737
Shelly Davis, prin. Fax 302-4977
Herriman ES 1,000/K-6
13170 S 6000 W, 801-446-3215
Joel Pullan, prin. Fax 302-4936

Highland, Utah, Pop. 13,350
Alpine SD
Supt. — See American Fork
Freedom ES 1,000/K-6
10326 N 6800 W 84003 801-766-5270
Jim Melville, prin. Fax 766-5272
Highland ES 800/K-6
10865 N 6000 W 84003 801-756-8537
Reed Hodson, prin. Fax 763-7001
Ridgeline ES, 6250 W 11800 N 84003 K-6
Ken Higgins, prin. 801-492-0401

Hooper, Weber, Pop. 4,306
Weber SD
Supt. — See Ogden
Freedom ES 900/K-6
4555 W 5500 S 84315 801-452-4100
Rick Proffer, prin. Fax 452-4119
Hooper ES 600/K-6
5500 S 5900 W 84315 801-452-4320
Dave Gerstheimer, prin. Fax 452-4339

Howell, Box Elder, Pop. 233
Box Elder SD
Supt. — See Brigham City
Howell ES 50/K-5
16020 N 17400 W 84316 435-471-2741
Wendy Merrill, prin. Fax 471-2741

Huntington, Emery, Pop. 2,062
Emery County SD 2,300/K-12
PO Box 120 84528 435-687-9846
Kirk Sitterud, supt. Fax 687-9849
www.emery.k12.ut.us
Huntington ES 400/K-6
PO Box 190 84528 435-687-9954
Thomas Baltzer, prin. Fax 687-2796
Other Schools – See Castle Dale, Cleveland, Ferron, Green River, Orangeville

Hurricane, Washington, Pop. 10,989
Washington County SD
Supt. — See Saint George
Hurricane ES 500/K-5
63 S 100 W 84737 435-635-4668
Travis Wilstead, prin. Fax 635-4670
Hurricane IS 6-7
1325 S 700 W 84737 435-635-8931
Brad Christensen, prin. Fax 635-8937
Hurricane MS 300/6-8
395 N 200 W 84737 435-635-4634
Roy Hoyt, prin. Fax 635-4663
Three Falls ES 600/K-5
789 S 700 W 84737 435-635-7229
Brad Jolley, prin. Fax 635-7273

Hyde Park, Cache, Pop. 2,858
Cache County SD
Supt. — See Logan
Cedar Ridge MS 600/6-7
65 N 200 W 84318 435-563-6229
Scott Jeppesen, prin. Fax 563-3915

Hyrum, Cache, Pop. 6,061
Cache County SD
Supt. — See Logan
Canyon ES 500/K-5
270 S 1300 E 84319 435-792-7684
Kelly Rindlisbacher, prin. Fax 792-7685
Lincoln ES 400/K-5
90 S Center St 84319 435-245-6442
Lynette Riggs, prin. Fax 245-4411

Ibapah, Tooele
Tooele County SD
Supt. — See Tooele
Ibapah ES 50/K-6
116 Eagles Nest 84034 435-234-1113
Kent Parsons, prin. Fax 234-1175

Ivins, Washington, Pop. 6,738
Washington County SD
Supt. — See Saint George
Red Mountain ES 600/K-5
263 E 200 S 84738 435-656-3802
Betty Barnum, prin. Fax 656-3812

Junction, Piute, Pop. 167
Piute SD 300/PK-12
PO Box 69 84740 435-577-2912
Don Yates, supt. Fax 577-2561
www.piute.k12.ut.us/
Other Schools – See Circleville, Marysvale

Kamas, Summit, Pop. 1,502
South Summit SD 1,400/PK-12
375 E 300 S 84036 435-783-4301
Barry Walker, supt. Fax 783-4501
www.ssummit.k12.ut.us/
South Summit ES 700/PK-5
535 E 300 S 84036 435-783-4318
Louise Willoughby, prin. Fax 783-2805
South Summit MS 300/6-8
355 E 300 S 84036 435-783-4341
Wade Woolstenhulme, prin. Fax 783-2787

Kanab, Kane, Pop. 3,516
Kane SD 1,200/K-12
746 S 175 E 84741 435-644-2555
Robert Johnson, supt. Fax 644-2509
www.kane.k12.ut.us
Kanab ES 400/K-6
41 W 100 N 84741 435-644-2329
Pam Aziz, prin. Fax 644-5041
Kanab MS 100/7-8
690 Cowboy Way 84741 435-644-5800
Doug Jacobs, prin. Fax 644-5121
Other Schools – See Big Water, Lake Powell, Orderville

Kaysville, Davis, Pop. 22,510
Davis SD
Supt. — See Farmington
Burton ES 700/K-6
827 E 200 S 84037 801-402-3150
Sharolyn Knudsen, prin. Fax 402-3151
Columbia ES 600/PK-6
378 S 50 W 84037 801-402-3350
Janet Sumner, prin. Fax 402-3351
Creekside ES 700/K-6
275 W Mutton Hollow Rd 84037 801-402-3650
Vickie Jessen, prin. Fax 402-3651
Kaysville ES 800/PK-6
50 N 100 E 84037 801-402-3400
Cleve Dibble, prin. Fax 402-3401
Morgan ES 700/K-6
1065 Thornfield Rd 84037 801-402-3450
Michael Volmar, prin. Fax 402-3451
Snow Horse ES K-6
1095 Smith Ln 84037 801-402-7350
Kathleen Bagley, prin. Fax 402-7351
Windridge ES 800/PK-6
1300 S 700 E 84037 801-402-3550
Maren Zimmerman, prin. Fax 402-3551

Kearns, Salt Lake, Pop. 34,900
Granite SD
Supt. — See Salt Lake City
Bacchus ES 600/K-6
5925 Copper City Dr 84118 801-646-4762
Chad Christman, prin. Fax 646-4763
Beehive ES 800/K-6
5655 S 5220 W 84118 801-646-4768
Georgia Block, prin. Fax 646-4769
Gourley ES 700/K-6
4905 S 4300 W 84118 801-646-4846
Janet Thorpe, prin. Fax 646-4847
Oquirrh Hills ES 400/PK-6
5241 S 4280 W 84118 801-646-4948
Vicki Ricketts, prin. Fax 646-4949
Silver Hills ES 800/PK-6
5770 W 5100 S 84118 801-646-5014
Debbie Koji, prin. Fax 646-5015
Smith ES 600/K-6
2150 W 6200 S 84118 801-646-5020
JoAnn Crawley, prin. Fax 646-5021
South Kearns ES 500/PK-6
4430 W 5570 S 84118 801-646-5026
Marie Rose, prin. Fax 646-5027
Western Hills ES 500/PK-6
5190 Heath Ave 84118 801-646-5091
Dr. Cecilia Jabakumur, prin. Fax 646-5092
West Kearns ES 500/PK-6
4900 S 4620 W 84118 801-646-5073
Jolene Randall, prin. Fax 646-5074

Koosharem, Sevier, Pop. 288
Sevier SD
Supt. — See Richfield
Koosharem ES 100/K-6
75 E Center 84744 435-638-7303
Lorna Stapley, prin. Fax 638-7516

Lake Powell, San Juan, Pop. 15
Kane SD
Supt. — See Kanab
Lake Powell ES 50/K-6
PO Box 4345 84533 435-684-2268
Gordon Miller, prin. Fax 684-3821

Laketown, Rich, Pop. 184
Rich SD
Supt. — See Randolph
North Rich ES 100/K-5
PO Box 129 84038 435-946-3359
Kip Motta, prin. Fax 946-3366
Rich MS 100/6-8
PO Box 129 84038 435-946-3359
Kip Motta, prin. Fax 946-3366

Lapoint, Uintah
Uintah SD
Supt. — See Vernal
Lapoint ES 300/K-5
HC 67 Box 151 84039 435-247-2637
Dennis Atkin, prin. Fax 247-2639

La Sal, San Juan
San Juan SD
Supt. — See Blanding
La Sal ES 50/K-4
PO Box 367 84530 435-678-1292
Shelly Thayn, lead tchr. Fax 678-1293

La Verkin, Washington, Pop. 4,105
Washington County SD
Supt. — See Saint George
La Verkin ES 600/K-5
51 W Center St 84745 435-635-4619
Steve Leavenworth, prin. Fax 635-7953

Layton, Davis, Pop. 61,782
Davis SD
Supt. — See Farmington
Adams ES 600/K-6
2200 E Sunset Dr 84040 801-402-3100
Charollet Chambers, prin. Fax 402-3101
Crestview ES 300/PK-6
185 W Golden Ave 84041 801-402-3200
Jan Rawlins, prin. Fax 402-3201
East Layton ES 600/PK-6
2470 E Cherry Ln 84040 801-402-3250
Beth Johnston, prin. Fax 402-3251
Ellison Park ES K-6
800 N Cold Creek Way 84041 801-402-7300
Chuck Johnson, prin. Fax 402-7301
Heritage ES 1,100/PK-6
1354 Weaver Ln 84041 801-402-1200
Cheryl Christensen, prin. Fax 402-1201
King ES 700/K-6
601 E Gordon Ave 84041 801-402-3300
Buck Ekstrom, prin. Fax 402-3301
Layton ES 700/PK-6
369 W Gentile St 84041 801-402-3500
Darryl Denhalter, prin. Fax 402-3501
Lincoln ES 800/PK-6
591 W Antelope Dr 84041 801-402-2450
Christine Whitaker, prin. Fax 402-2451
Mountain View ES 800/PK-6
2025 E 3100 N 84040 801-402-3700
Lucinda Wagner, prin. Fax 402-3701
Sand Springs ES 1,000/K-6
242 N 3200 W 84041 801-402-3850
Rebecca Hunt, prin. Fax 402-3851
Vae View ES 500/PK-6
1750 W 1600 N 84041 801-402-2800
Helene VanNatter, prin. Fax 402-2801
Whitesides ES 400/PK-6
233 Colonial Ave 84041 801-402-3600
Karen Schleifer, prin. Fax 402-3601

Layton Christian Academy 700/PK-12
2352 E Highway 193 84040 801-771-7141
Greg Miller, admin. Fax 771-0170
Northridge Learning Center 200/K-12
2405 N Hillfield Rd 84041 801-776-4532
Dixie Evans, dir. Fax 776-0638
Trinity Lutheran Preschool and K 50/PK-K
385 W Golden Ave 84041 801-544-5770
Donna Hering, lead tchr.

Lehi, Utah, Pop. 31,730
Alpine SD
Supt. — See American Fork
Eaglecrest ES 800/K-6
2760 N 300 W 84043 801-768-7035
Rex Becker, prin. Fax 768-7039
Eagle Valley ES 800/K-6
4475 Heritage Dr, 801-789-8300
Keith Conley, prin. Fax 789-8304
Fox Hollow ES K-6
1450 W 3200 N 84043 801-768-2499
Sandi Akagi, prin. Fax 768-2742
Lehi ES 600/K-6
765 N Center St 84043 801-768-7020
Starlene Holm, prin. Fax 768-7022
Meadow ES 700/K-6
176 S 500 W 84043 801-768-7025
Carolyn Johnson, prin. Fax 768-7018
Pony Express ES 1,100/K-6
3985 Smith Ranch Rd, 801-789-2600
Doug Van Alfen, prin. Fax 789-2604
Saratoga Shores ES 900/K-6
1415 Parkside Dr, 801-766-8349
Glenn Martin, prin.
Sego Lily ES 800/K-6
550 E 900 N 84043 801-768-7030
Rod Tucker, prin. Fax 768-7034
Snow Springs ES 900/K-6
850 S 1700 W 84043 801-768-7045
Phil Armstrong, prin. Fax 768-7049

Challenger S 300/PK-8
3920 Traverse Mountain Blvd 84043 801-451-6555

Lewiston, Cache, Pop. 1,663
Cache County SD
Supt. — See Logan
Lewiston ES 500/K-5
107 E 200 S 84320 435-258-2923
Adam Baker, prin. Fax 258-2707

Lindon, Utah, Pop. 9,679
Alpine SD
Supt. — See American Fork
Lindon ES 500/K-6
30 N Main St 84042 801-785-8717
Jason Theler, prin. Fax 785-8749
Rocky Mountain ES, 55 S 500 E 84042 700/K-6
David Turner, prin. 801-717-4846

Loa, Wayne, Pop. 498
Wayne SD
Supt. — See Bicknell
Loa ES 200/K-5
PO Box 130 84747 435-836-2851
Burke Torgerson, prin. Fax 836-2335

Logan, Cache, Pop. 47,357
Cache County SD 13,500/K-12
2063 N 1200 E 84341 435-752-3925
Dr. Steven Norton, supt. Fax 753-2168
www.ccsdut.org

Greenville ES 500/3-5
2450 N 400 E 84341 435-750-7888
Dee Ashcroft, prin. Fax 755-0112
Nibley ES 600/K-5
2545 S 660 W 84321 435-752-8303
Sharyle Shaffer, prin. Fax 752-8401
North Park ES 500/K-2
2800 N 800 E 84341 435-752-5121
Gary Thomas, prin. Fax 752-5019
River Heights ES 600/K-5
780 E 600 S 84321 435-753-4948
Glen Harris, prin. Fax 753-4973
Other Schools – See Hyde Park, Hyrum, Lewiston, Mendon, Millville, Providence, Richmond, Smithfield, Wellsville

Logan CSD 5,600/K-12
101 W Center St 84321 435-755-2300
Marshal Garrett, supt. Fax 755-2311
www.loganschools.org
Adams ES 400/K-5
415 E 500 N 84321 435-755-2320
Jed Grunig, prin. Fax 755-2322
Bridger ES 500/K-5
1261 N 400 W 84341 435-755-2345
David Long, prin. Fax 755-2348
Ellis ES 400/K-5
348 W 300 N 84321 435-755-2330
Sue Sorenson, prin. Fax 755-2332
Hillcrest ES 500/K-5
960 N 1400 E 84321 435-755-2360
Eric Markworth, prin. Fax 755-2362
Mt. Logan MS 1,200/6-8
875 N 200 E 84321 435-755-2370
Mike Monson, prin. Fax 755-2370
Wilson ES 500/K-5
89 S 500 E 84321 435-755-2340
Sundee Ware, prin. Fax 755-2342
Woodruff ES 500/K-5
950 W 600 S 84321 435-755-2350
Daryl Guymon, prin. Fax 755-2352

Magna, Salt Lake, Pop. 17,829
Granite SD
Supt. — See Salt Lake City
Copper Hills ES 800/K-6
7635 W 3715 S 84044 801-646-4792
Janice Flanagan, prin. Fax 646-4793
Lake Ridge ES 700/K-6
7400 W 3400 S 84044 801-646-4888
Dr. Ted Williams, prin. Fax 646-4889
Magna ES 900/PK-6
8500 W 3100 S 84044 801-646-4900
Victoria Thomas, prin. Fax 646-4901
Pleasant Green ES 800/K-6
8201 W 2700 S 84044 801-646-4972
Jane Lindsay, prin. Fax 646-4973

Manila, Daggett, Pop. 304
Daggett SD 200/K-12
PO Box 249 84046 435-784-3174
Bruce Northcott, supt. Fax 784-3549
www.dsdf.org
Manila ES 100/K-6
PO Box 249 84046 435-784-3174
Scott Taylor, prin. Fax 784-3209
Other Schools – See Dutch John

Manti, Sanpete, Pop. 3,185
South Sanpete SD 2,900/PK-12
39 S Main St 84642 435-835-2261
Don Hill, supt. Fax 835-2265
www.ssanpete.k12.ut.us
Manti ES 400/PK-5
150 W 100 S 84642 435-835-2271
Barbara Eliason, prin. Fax 835-2278
Other Schools – See Ephraim, Gunnison

Mapleton, Utah, Pop. 5,972
Nebo SD
Supt. — See Spanish Fork
Hobble Creek ES 700/K-6
1145 E 1200 N 84664 801-489-2863
Garth Bird, prin. Fax 489-2868
Mapleton ES 700/K-6
120 W Maple St 84664 801-489-2850
Celeste Gledhill, prin. Fax 489-2887

Marysvale, Piute, Pop. 346
Piute SD
Supt. — See Junction
Oscarson ES 50/PK-6
160 W Sevier Ave 84750 435-326-4341
Shelley Blackwell, prin. Fax 326-4247

Mendon, Cache, Pop. 936
Cache County SD
Supt. — See Logan
Mountainside ES K-5
235 E 125 N 84325 435-792-7688
Greg Larsen, prin. Fax 792-7690

Mexican Hat, San Juan, Pop. 259
San Juan SD
Supt. — See Blanding
Mexican Hat ES 200/K-6
PO Box 310457 84531 435-678-1285
Aaron Brewer, prin. Fax 678-1244

Midvale, Salt Lake, Pop. 27,170
Jordan SD
Supt. — See Sandy
Copperview ES 400/K-6
8449 Monroe St 84047 801-565-7440
Brent Shaw, prin. Fax 302-4912
East Midvale ES 600/K-6
6990 S 300 E 84047 801-565-7450
Sally Sansom, prin. Fax 302-4922
Midvale ES 600/K-6
362 W Center St 84047 801-565-7462
Karen Kezerian, prin. Fax 302-4940
Midvalley ES 600/K-6
217 E 7800 S 84047 801-565-7464
Carla Burningham, prin. Fax 302-4944

Midway, Wasatch, Pop. 2,737
Wasatch SD
Supt. — See Heber City
Midway ES 500/K-5
225 S 100 E 84049 435-654-0472
Shawn Kelly, prin. Fax 654-7426

Milford, Beaver, Pop. 1,437
Beaver SD
Supt. — See Beaver
Milford ES 200/K-6
PO Box 309 84751 435-387-2841
Ben Dalton, prin. Fax 387-5050

Millville, Cache, Pop. 1,395
Cache County SD
Supt. — See Logan
Millville ES 400/K-5
67 S Main 84326 435-752-7162
Maria Nielsen, prin. Fax 755-5758

Minersville, Beaver, Pop. 838
Beaver SD
Supt. — See Beaver
Minersville S 100/K-8
PO Box 189 84752 435-386-2382
Richard Albrecht, prin. Fax 386-2484

Moab, Grand, Pop. 4,807
Grand SD 1,500/PK-12
264 S 400 E 84532 435-259-5317
Margaret Hopkins, supt. Fax 259-6212
www.grandschools.org
Grand County MS 200/7-8
439 S 100 E 84532 435-259-7158
Melinda Snow, prin. Fax 259-6221
Knight IS 300/4-6
168 W 400 N 84532 435-259-7350
Robert Farnsworth, prin. Fax 259-8094
Red Rock ES 400/K-3
685 Millcreek Dr 84532 435-259-7326
Sherrie Buckingham, prin. Fax 259-8095
Sundwall Preschool PK-PK
190 E 100 N 84532 435-259-5628
Taryn Kay, prin. Fax 259-6747

Mona, Juab, Pop. 1,140
Juab SD
Supt. — See Nephi
Mona ES 300/K-6
PO Box 9 84645 435-623-2082
Norman Wall, prin. Fax 623-2661

Monroe, Sevier, Pop. 1,831
Sevier SD
Supt. — See Richfield
Monroe ES 600/K-5
40 W Center St 84754 435-527-4691
Ted Chappell, prin. Fax 527-4660
Monroe Preschool, 25 N 100 W 84754 PK-PK
Ellen Batty, lead tchr. 435-527-3014
South Sevier MS 300/6-8
300 E Center St 84754 435-527-4607
William Jolley, prin. Fax 527-4636

Montezuma Creek, San Juan, Pop. 345
San Juan SD
Supt. — See Blanding
Montezuma Creek ES 200/K-6
PO Box 630 84534 435-678-1261
Rebecca Benally, prin. Fax 678-1850

Monticello, San Juan, Pop. 1,913
San Juan SD
Supt. — See Blanding
Monticello ES 300/K-6
PO Box 189 84535 435-678-1180
Lance Hatch, prin. Fax 678-1179

Monument Valley, San Juan

Monument Valley SDA Mission S 50/K-8
PO Box 360013 84536 435-727-3270

Morgan, Morgan, Pop. 2,932
Morgan SD 2,100/K-12
PO Box 530 84050 801-829-3411
Ronald Wolff, supt. Fax 829-3531
www.morgan.k12.ut.us
Morgan ES 800/K-4
344 E Young St 84050 801-829-3438
Laraine Whitear, prin. Fax 829-3531
Morgan MS 700/5-8
PO Box 470 84050 801-829-3467
Mike Madeo, prin. Fax 829-0645
Other Schools – See Mountain Grn

Moroni, Sanpete, Pop. 1,276
North Sanpete SD
Supt. — See Mount Pleasant
Moroni ES 300/K-6
98 N 200 W 84646 435-436-8291
Richard Squire, prin. Fax 436-8401
North Sanpete MS 300/7-8
PO Box 307 84646 435-436-8206
Randy Shelley, prin. Fax 436-8208

Mountain Grn, Morgan
Morgan SD
Supt. — See Morgan
Mountain Green ES K-5
6064 Silver Leaf Dr, 801-876-3041
Tom McFarland, prin. Fax 876-3518

Mount Pleasant, Sanpete, Pop. 2,703
North Sanpete SD 2,300/PK-12
220 E 700 S 84647 435-462-2485
Courtney Syme, supt. Fax 462-2480
www.nsanpete.k12.ut.us
Mount Pleasant ES 400/PK-6
55 E 100 S 84647 435-462-2077
Rena Orton, prin. Fax 462-3608
Other Schools – See Fairview, Fountain Green, Moroni, Spring City

Murray, Salt Lake, Pop. 44,555
Murray CSD 6,300/K-12
147 E 5065 S 84107 801-264-7400
Richard Tranter, supt. Fax 264-7456
www.murrayschools.org/
Grant ES 400/K-6
662 Bulldog Cir 84123 801-264-7416
Russell Klein, prin. Fax 264-7437
Horizon ES 500/K-6
5180 Glendon St 84123 801-264-7420
Martha Kupferschmidt, prin. Fax 264-7444
Liberty ES 400/K-6
140 W 6100 S 84107 801-264-7424
Connie Amos, prin. Fax 264-7449
Longview ES 500/K-6
6240 Longview Dr 84107 801-264-7428
Andy Forsyth, prin. Fax 264-7452
McMillan ES 400/K-6
315 E 5900 S 84107 801-264-7430
Connie Buckner, prin. Fax 264-7451
Parkside ES 500/K-6
5175 Parkside Dr 84107 801-264-7434
Jennifer Kranz, prin. Fax 264-7453
Viewmont ES 500/K-6
745 Anderson Ave 84123 801-264-7438
Darren Dean, prin. Fax 264-7454

Christ Lutheran S 200/PK-8
240 E 5600 S 84107 801-266-8714
Corey Brandenburger, prin. Fax 266-8799
Mt. Vernon Academy 100/K-12
184 E Vine St 84107 801-266-5521
Nancy Woodward, prin. Fax 269-8080

Myton, Duchesne, Pop. 559
Duchesne SD
Supt. — See Duchesne
Myton ES 100/K-5
PO Box 186 84052 435-725-4735
Fred Arko, prin. Fax 725-4746

Neola, Duchesne, Pop. 511
Duchesne SD
Supt. — See Duchesne
Neola ES 100/K-5
PO Box 220 84053 435-725-4715
Fred Arko, prin. Fax 725-4730

Nephi, Juab, Pop. 5,045
Juab SD 2,100/K-12
346 E 600 N 84648 435-623-1940
Kirk Wright, supt. Fax 623-1941
www.juab.ut.proschoolweb.com/
Juab JHS 300/7-8
555 E 800 N 84648 435-623-1541
Ken Rowley, prin. Fax 623-4995
Nebo View ES 300/K-6
475 E 800 N 84648 435-623-1812
Steven Paulsen, prin. Fax 623-5039
Red Cliff ES 500/K-6
1199 S Main St 84648 435-623-0328
Janet Ware, prin. Fax 623-4212
Other Schools – See Mona

North Salt Lake, Davis, Pop. 10,538
Davis SD
Supt. — See Farmington
Orchard ES 600/K-6
205 E Center St 84054 801-402-1700
Gwen Hill, prin. Fax 402-1701

Ogden, Weber, Pop. 78,309
Ogden CSD 7,900/K-12
1950 Monroe Blvd 84401 801-737-7300
Noel Zabriskie, supt. Fax 627-7654
www.ogdensd.org
Bonneville ES 500/K-6
490 Gramercy Ave 84404 801-737-8900
Jay Seese, prin. Fax 627-7681
Dee ES 500/K-6
550 E 22nd St 84401 801-737-8100
Scott Robertson, prin. Fax 625-1165
Gramercy ES 500/K-6
1270 Gramercy Ave 84404 801-737-7500
Becky Hale, prin. Fax 625-8795
Heritage ES K-6
373 S 150 W 84404 801-737-8000
Sandy Coroles, prin. Fax 737-8047
Hillcrest ES 500/K-6
130 N Eccles Ave 84404 801-737-7550
Lynae Butler, prin. Fax 334-4411
Lincoln ES 500/K-6
1235 Canfield Dr 84404 801-737-7650
Cheryl Rankin, prin. Fax 625-8816
Madison ES K-6
2563 Monroe Blvd 84401 801-737-8200
Ross Lunceford, prin. Fax 627-7606
Mann ES 400/K-6
1300 9th St 84404 801-737-7600
Linda Brown, prin. Fax 627-7694
Odyssey ES K-6
375 Goddard St 84401 801-737-7400
Charlotte Parry, prin. Fax 737-8511
Polk ES 400/K-6
2615 Polk Ave 84401 801-737-8300
Jeanne Clifton, prin. Fax 625-8829

Shadow Valley ES K-6
4911 S 1500 E 84403 801-737-8151
Leanne Rich, prin. Fax 625-8800
Smith ES 500/K-6
3295 Gramercy Ave 84403 801-737-8350
Misti Young, prin. Fax 627-7660
Wasatch ES 300/K-6
3370 Polk Ave 84403 801-737-8450
Suzanne Bolar, prin. Fax 627-7685

Weber SD 28,900/K-12
5320 S 500 E 84405 801-476-7800
Michael Jacobsen, supt. Fax 476-7893
www.weber.k12.ut.us/
Bates ES 700/K-6
850 E 3100 N 84414 801-452-4580
Kevin Sederholm, prin. Fax 452-4599
Child ES 600/K-6
655 E 5500 S 84405 801-452-4140
Blake Hadley, prin. Fax 452-4159
Club Heights ES 300/K-6
4150 S 100 E 84405 801-452-4240
Karen Neiswender, prin. Fax 452-4259
Farr West ES 700/K-6
2190 W 2700 N 84404 801-452-4360
Dave Wallace, prin. Fax 452-4379
Green Acres ES 600/K-6
640 E 1900 N 84414 801-452-4420
Marilyn Runolfson, prin. Fax 452-4439
Lomond View ES 700/K-6
3644 N 900 W 84414 801-452-4780
Brad Larsen, prin. Fax 452-4799
Majestic ES 700/K-6
425 W 2550 N 84414 801-452-4260
David Hales, prin. Fax 452-4279
Mar Lon Hills ES 400/K-6
4400 Madison Ave 84403 801-452-4500
Darlene Sangiorgio, prin. Fax 452-4519
North Ogden ES 500/K-6
530 E 2650 N 84414 801-452-4300
Ralph Aardema, prin. Fax 452-4319
Pioneer ES 600/K-6
250 N 1600 W 84404 801-452-4560
Lori Rasmussen, prin. Fax 452-4579
Plain City ES 600/K-6
2335 N 3600 W 84404 801-452-4220
Dave Rhees, prin. Fax 452-4239
Riverdale ES 500/K-6
1160 W 4400 S 84405 801-452-4540
Maloy Hales, prin. Fax 452-4559
Roosevelt ES 500/K-6
190 W 5100 S 84405 801-452-4520
Melanie Stokes, prin. Fax 452-4539
Uintah ES 600/K-6
6115 S 2250 E 84403 801-452-4980
Quinn Karlinsey, prin. Fax 452-4999
Washington Terrace ES 500/K-6
20 E 4600 S 84405 801-452-4200
Gloria Rasmussen, prin. Fax 452-4219
West Weber ES 400/K-6
4178 W 900 S 84404 801-452-4280
Kevin Chase, prin. Fax 452-4299
Other Schools – See Eden, Hooper, Roy, West Haven

Children's Classic S 200/PK-2
5820 Wasatch Dr 84403 801-479-0400
Justina Longman, dir. Fax 479-0409
Deamude Adventist Christian S 50/K-8
1765 W 2100 S 84401 801-731-3140
Mindy Meadows, prin. Fax 731-4314
Evergreen Montessori Academy PK-10
5875 S 500 E 84405 801-479-7799
Amy Van Vliet, prin. Fax 479-7797
St. Joseph S 500/PK-8
2980 Quincy Ave 84403 801-393-6051
Armando Venegas, prin. Fax 393-6177
St. Paul Lutheran S 200/PK-8
3329 Harrison Blvd 84403 801-392-2912
Paulette Herman, prin. Fax 392-7562

Orangeville, Emery, Pop. 1,353
Emery County SD
Supt. — See Huntington
Cottonwood ES 200/K-6
PO Box 679 84537 435-748-2481
Dennis Jones, prin. Fax 748-2130

Orderville, Kane, Pop. 586
Kane SD
Supt. — See Kanab
Valley ES 200/K-6
PO Box 129 84758 435-648-2277
Brent Blodgett, prin. Fax 648-2131

Orem, Utah, Pop. 89,713
Alpine SD
Supt. — See American Fork
Aspen ES 500/K-6
945 W 2000 N 84057 801-227-8700
Sherrie Holbrook, prin. Fax 227-8786
Bonneville ES 800/K-6
1245 N 800 W 84057 801-227-8703
Kim Roper, prin. Fax 227-8705
Cascade ES 500/K-6
160 N 800 E 84097 801-227-8707
Doug Finch, prin. Fax 227-8709
Cherry Hill ES 700/K-6
250 E 1650 S 84058 801-227-8710
Allisa Hart, prin. Fax 227-8712
Foothill ES 500/K-6
921 N 1240 E 84097 801-227-2465
Dr. Vallen Thomas, prin. Fax 227-2466
Geneva ES, 665 W 400 N 84057 500/K-6
Michael Parkes, prin. 801-717-4837
Hillcrest ES 400/K-6
651 E 1400 S 84097 801-227-8717
Darrin Johnson, prin. Fax 227-8719
Northridge ES 800/K-6
1660 N 50 E 84057 801-227-8720
Kimberly Bird, prin. Fax 227-8726
Orchard ES 700/K-6
1035 N 800 E 84097 801-227-8723
Barry Bezzant, prin. Fax 227-2433
Orem ES 700/K-6
450 W 400 S 84058 801-227-8727
Brad Davies, prin. Fax 227-8729
Scera Park ES 500/K-6
450 S 400 E 84097 801-227-8730
Tom Carter, prin. Fax 227-8732
Sharon ES 400/K-6
525 N 400 E 84097 801-227-8733
Linda Anderson, prin. Fax 227-8735
Suncrest ES, 668 W 150 N 84057 400/K-6
Tom Freeman, prin. 801-717-4836
Westmore ES 400/K-6
1150 S Main St 84058 801-227-8742
Barry Beckstrand, prin. Fax 227-8744
Windsor ES 600/K-6
1315 N Main St 84057 801-227-8745
Craig Jensen, prin. Fax 227-8747

Meridian S 200/PK-12
280 S 400 E 84097 801-374-5480
David H. Hennessey Ph.D., hdmstr. Fax 374-5491

Panguitch, Garfield, Pop. 1,477
Garfield SD 900/K-12
PO Box 398 84759 435-676-8821
Dr. George Park, supt. Fax 676-8266
www.garfield.k12.ut.us
Panguitch ES 200/K-6
PO Box 386 84759 435-676-8847
Nick Reynolds, prin. Fax 676-1346
Panguitch MS 100/7-8
PO Box 393 84759 435-676-8225
Betty Rember, prin. Fax 676-2518
Other Schools – See Antimony, Boulder, Escalante, Tropic

Park City, Summit, Pop. 8,066
Park City SD 4,300/K-12
2700 Kearns Blvd 84060 435-645-5600
Ray Timothy, supt. Fax 645-5609
www.parkcity.k12.ut.us
Ecker Hill International MS 700/6-7
2465 Kilby Rd 84098 435-645-5610
Greg Proffit, prin. Fax 645-5615
Jeremy Ranch ES 600/K-5
5060 Rasmussen Rd 84098 435-645-5670
Shawn Kuennen, prin. Fax 645-5675
McPolin ES 400/K-5
2270 Kearns Blvd 84060 435-645-5630
Bob Edmiston, prin. Fax 645-5633
Parley's Park ES 500/K-5
1002 Silver Springs Dr 84098 435-645-5620
Michele Wallace, prin. Fax 645-5623
Trailside ES 500/K-5
5700 Trailside Dr 84098 435-645-5680
Pat Flynn, prin. Fax 645-5681

Colby S 200/PK-8
3770 Highway 224 84060 435-655-3966
Dr. Amy Fehlberg, dir. Fax 658-2120
Park City Academy 100/PK-9
3120 Pinebrook Rd 84098 435-649-2791
Charles Sachs, hdmstr. Fax 649-6759
Soaring Wings Montessori S 100/PK-3
PO Box 682384 84068 435-649-3626
Duna Strachan, dir. Fax 649-8621
Soaring Wings Montessori S - Jeremy Rch 100/PK-3
PO Box 682384 84068 435-640-1350
Duna Strachan, dir.

Park Valley, Box Elder
Box Elder SD
Supt. — See Brigham City
Park Valley S 50/K-10
788 Education Dr 84329 435-871-4411
Brian Anderson, prin. Fax 871-4444

Parowan, Iron, Pop. 2,532
Iron SD
Supt. — See Cedar City
Parowan ES 400/K-6
100 N 128 W 84761 435-477-3368
Kevin Porter, prin. Fax 477-1108

Payson, Utah, Pop. 16,442
Nebo SD
Supt. — See Spanish Fork
Barnett ES 600/K-6
456 N 300 E 84651 801-465-6000
Ryan Pitcher, prin. Fax 465-6001
Park View ES 500/PK-6
360 S 100 E 84651 801-465-6010
Kristie Nevins, prin. Fax 465-6011
Spring Lake ES 600/K-6
1750 S 500 W 84651 801-465-6070
Spencer Sainsbury, prin. Fax 465-6075
Taylor ES 300/K-6
92 S 500 W 84651 801-465-6050
Frank Daybell, prin. Fax 465-6039
Wilson ES 500/PK-6
590 W 500 S 84651 801-465-6060
Ron Penrod, prin. Fax 465-6068

Perry, Box Elder, Pop. 3,081
Box Elder SD
Supt. — See Brigham City
Three Mile Creek S 3-5
2625 S 1050 W 84302 435-734-4930
Janet Coombs, prin. Fax 734-4932

Pleasant Grove, Utah, Pop. 29,376
Alpine SD
Supt. — See American Fork
Central ES 500/K-6
95 N 400 E 84062 801-785-8711
Dr. Vicki Carter, prin. Fax 785-8713
Grovecrest ES 700/K-6
200 E 1100 N 84062 801-785-8714
Kestin Mattinson, prin. Fax 785-8715
Manila ES 800/K-6
1726 N 600 W 84062 801-785-8720
Nancy Sorensen, prin. Fax 785-8784
Mt. Mahogany ES 900/K-6
618 N 1300 W 84062 801-785-8795
Scot Westover, prin. Fax 785-8798
Valley View ES 500/K-6
941 Orchard Dr 84062 801-785-8723
Clark Hansen, prin. Fax 785-8725

Price, Carbon, Pop. 8,081
Carbon SD 3,300/K-12
251 W 400 N 84501 435-637-1732
Patsy Bueno, supt. Fax 637-9417
www.carbon.k12.ut.us
Castle Heights ES 500/K-6
750 Homestead Blvd 84501 435-637-7177
Jan Cox, prin. Fax 637-4645
Creekview ES 400/K-6
590 W 500 S 84501 435-637-0828
Joan Atwood, prin. Fax 637-4902
Other Schools – See Helper, Sunnyside, Wellington

Providence, Cache, Pop. 5,516
Cache County SD
Supt. — See Logan
Providence ES 600/K-5
91 E Center St 84332 435-752-6010
Curt Jenkins, prin. Fax 753-1937
Spring Creek MS 600/6-7
350 W 100 N 84332 435-753-6200
Blake Pickett, prin. Fax 753-1979

Provo, Utah, Pop. 113,459
Provo CSD 12,700/K-12
280 W 940 N 84604 801-374-4800
Dr. Randall Merrill, supt. Fax 374-4808
www.provo.edu
Canyon Crest ES 500/K-6
4664 N Canyon Rd 84604 801-221-9873
Patricia Anderson, prin. Fax 221-9989
Centennial MS 1,000/7-8
305 E 2320 N 84604 801-374-4621
Mitch Swenson, prin. Fax 374-4626
Dixon MS 900/7-8
750 W 200 N 84601 801-374-4980
Rosanna Ungerman, prin. Fax 374-4884
Earhart ES 600/K-6
2585 W 200 S 84601 801-370-4630
Jason Cox, prin. Fax 370-4633
Edgemont ES 500/K-6
566 E 3650 N 84604 801-221-9984
Dennis Pratt, prin. Fax 221-9987
Farrer ES 400/K-6
100 N 600 E 84606 801-374-4940
Alex Judd, prin. Fax 374-4982
Franklin ES 500/K-6
350 S 600 W 84601 801-374-4925
Marlin Palmer, prin. Fax 374-4886
Lakeview ES K-6
2899 W 1390 N 84601 801-374-4990
Drew Daniels, prin. Fax 374-4991
Provost ES 400/K-6
629 S 1000 E 84606 801-374-4960
Steve Oliverson, prin. Fax 374-4962
Rock Canyon ES 600/K-6
2405 Timpview Dr 84604 801-374-4935
Dean Nielson, prin. Fax 374-5081
Spring Creek ES 600/K-6
1740 Nevada Ave 84606 801-370-4650
Jarod Sites, prin. Fax 370-4653
Sunset View ES 600/K-6
525 S 1600 W 84601 801-374-4950
Anne Marie Harrison, prin. Fax 374-4950
Timpanogos ES 600/K-6
1165 Birch Ln 84604 801-374-4955
Diane Bridge, prin. Fax 374-4958
Wasatch ES 600/K-6
1080 N 900 E 84604 801-374-4910
Colleen Densley, prin. Fax 374-4912
Westridge ES 800/K-6
1720 W 1460 N 84604 801-374-4870
Gaye Gibbs, prin. Fax 374-4873

Ivy Hall Academy 200/PK-8
1598 W 820 N 84601 801-356-1000
Susan Kirby, dir. Fax 356-0484

Randolph, Rich, Pop. 472
Rich SD 400/K-12
PO Box 67 84064 435-793-2135
Dale Lamborn, supt. Fax 793-2136
www.rich.k12.ut.us
South Rich ES 100/K-5
PO Box 67 84064 435-793-3195
Dale Lamborn, prin. Fax 793-2136
Other Schools – See Laketown

Richfield, Sevier, Pop. 7,044
Sevier SD 4,600/PK-12
180 E 600 N 84701 435-896-8214
Brent Thorne, supt. Fax 896-8804
www.sevier.k12.ut.us
Ashman ES 500/K-2
70 N 200 W 84701 435-896-8415
Teresa Robinson, prin. Fax 896-8416
Pahvant ES 500/3-5
520 N 300 W 84701 435-896-4403
Selena Terry, prin. Fax 896-9479
Red Hills MS 500/6-8
400 S 600 W 84701 435-896-6421
Brent Gubler, prin. Fax 896-6423

Richfield Preschool 100/PK-PK
80 W Center St 84701 435-896-8776
Dawnanna Topham, dir.
Other Schools – See Koosharem, Monroe, Salina

Richmond, Cache, Pop. 1,849
Cache County SD
Supt. — See Logan
Park ES 300/K-5
90 S 100 W 84333 435-258-2344
Mark Daines, prin. Fax 258-5202
White Pine MS 400/6-7
184 W 100 N 84333 435-258-2111
Curt Hanks, prin. Fax 258-2532

Riverdale, Weber, Pop. 7,934

Christian Heritage S 600/PK-12
5101 S 1050 W 84405 801-393-4475
Daniel Drews, prin. Fax 621-8452

Riverton, Salt Lake, Pop. 32,089
Jordan SD
Supt. — See Sandy
Bluffdale ES 1,000/K-6
14323 S 2700 W 84065 801-254-8090
Ken Westwood, prin. Fax 302-4909
Foothills ES 1,300/K-6
13717 Shaggy Peak Dr, 801-302-8599
Kyle Hansen, prin. Fax 302-4976
Midas Creek ES K-5
11901 Park Haven Ln, 801-254-7407
Kevin Pullan, prin. Fax 302-4919
Riverton ES 800/K-6
13150 S 1830 W 84065 801-254-8050
Steve Giles, prin. Fax 302-4952
Rosamond ES 900/K-6
12195 S 1975 W 84065 801-254-8043
Shelley Nordick, prin. Fax 302-4957
Rose Creek ES 1,000/K-6
12812 S 3600 W 84065 801-254-8082
Michelle Peterson, prin. Fax 302-4963
Southland ES 800/K-6
12675 S 2700 W 84065 801-254-8047
Terri Summers, prin. Fax 302-4961

Roosevelt, Duchesne, Pop. 4,553
Duchesne SD
Supt. — See Duchesne
East ES 700/K-3
700 E 400 N Ste 107-10 84066 435-725-4665
Kevin Heaton, prin. Fax 725-4709
Roosevelt JHS 400/7-8
350 W 200 S 84066 435-725-4585
Loyal Summers, prin. Fax 725-4622
Roosevelt MS 500/4-6
437 N 300 W Ste 425-2 84066 435-725-4630
Mary Ellen Kettle, prin. Fax 725-4661

Uintah SD
Supt. — See Vernal
Eagle View S K-8
RR 2 Box 2468 84066 435-722-2247
Robert Stearmer, prin. Fax 722-2240

Roy, Weber, Pop. 35,229
Weber SD
Supt. — See Ogden
Lakeview ES 400/K-6
2025 W 5000 S 84067 801-452-4380
Cami Alexander, prin. Fax 452-4399
Midland ES 700/K-6
3100 W 4800 S 84067 801-476-5400
Shelly Roberts, prin. Fax 476-5459
Municipal ES 400/K-6
5775 S 2200 W 84067 801-452-4120
Joel Frederiksen, prin. Fax 452-4139
North Park ES 400/K-6
4230 S 2175 W 84067 801-452-4340
Vickie Thalman, prin. Fax 452-4359
Roy ES 600/K-6
2888 W 5600 S 84067 801-452-4160
Linda Anderson, prin. Fax 452-4179
Valley View ES 500/K-6
2465 W 4500 S 84067 801-476-5200
Kirt Swalberg, prin. Fax 476-5219

Saint George, Washington, Pop. 56,382
Washington County SD 21,900/K-12
121 W Tabernacle St 84770 435-673-3553
Max Rose Ph.D., supt. Fax 673-3216
www.washk12.org
Bloomington ES 500/K-5
425 Man O War Rd 84790 435-673-6266
Kim Heki, prin. Fax 674-6497
Bloomington Hills ES 600/K-5
919 E Brigham Rd 84790 435-674-6495
Michelle North, prin. Fax 652-4703
Coral Cliffs ES 600/K-5
2040 W 2000 N 84770 435-652-4712
Teria Mortensen, prin. Fax 652-4716
Desert Hills MS 900/6-8
936 Desert Hills Dr 84790 435-628-0001
Brian Stevenson, prin. Fax 674-6477
Diamond Valley ES 400/K-5
1411 W Diamond Valley Dr 84770 435-574-2009
Kelly Mitchell, prin. Fax 574-2013
Downs ES 600/K-5
1795 W 1230 N 84770 435-673-8978
Dale Porter, prin. Fax 673-6303
East ES 700/K-5
453 S 600 E 84770 435-673-6191
Joe Eckman, prin. Fax 673-6248
Fossil Ridge IS 1,000/6-7
383 S Mall Dr 84790 435-652-4706
Bob Sonju, prin. Fax 652-4758
Heritage ES 500/K-5
747 E Riverside Dr 84790 435-628-4427
Steven Gregoire, prin. Fax 628-5771
Little Valley ES 500/K-5
2330 E Horsemans Park Dr 84790 435-652-4771
Rob Stevenson, prin. Fax 652-4770
Panorama ES 500/K-5
301 N 2200 E 84790 435-628-6881
Judy Turner, prin. Fax 634-1476
Sandstone ES 600/K-5
850 N 2450 E 84790 435-674-6460
Neil Cottam, prin. Fax 674-6463
Sunrise Ridge IS 6-7
3167 S 2350 E 84790 435-652-4772
Sandy Ferrell, prin. Fax 652-4777
Sunset ES 600/K-5
495 Westridge Dr 84770 435-673-5669
Nate Esplin, prin. Fax 673-3544
Tonaquint IS 6-7
1210 W Curly Hollow Dr 84770 435-688-2238
Barbara Garrett, prin. Fax 688-2504
Other Schools – See Enterprise, Hurricane, Ivins, La Verkin, Santa Clara, Springdale, Washington

---

Calvary Chapel Christian S 50/K-12
3922 S Pioneer Rd 84790 435-634-8309
Mark Wever, supt. Fax 674-4908
Hatch Academy 50/K-12
PO Box 910400 84791 435-673-6474
Trinity Lutheran S 100/PK-8
2260 Red Cliffs Dr 84790 435-628-6115
Duane Nyen, prin. Fax 628-1850

Salem, Utah, Pop. 4,725
Nebo SD
Supt. — See Spanish Fork
Foothills ES K-6
412 S 810 E 84653 801-423-9172
Ed Schollenberger, prin. Fax 423-6538
Mt. Loafer ES 400/K-6
1025 S 250 W 84653 801-423-2705
Alicia Rudd, prin. Fax 423-3593
Salem ES 400/K-6
140 W 100 S 84653 801-423-1182
Ken VanAusdal, prin. Fax 423-2746

Salina, Sevier, Pop. 2,382
Sevier SD
Supt. — See Richfield
North Sevier MS 200/6-8
135 N 100 W 84654 435-529-3841
Cade Douglas, prin. Fax 529-7377
Salina ES 500/K-5
210 W 300 N 84654 435-529-7462
Jade Shepherd, prin. Fax 529-7463
Salina Preschool, 210 W 300 N 84654 PK-PK
Janet Curtis, lead tchr. 435-529-3872

Salt Lake City, Salt Lake, Pop. 178,097
Granite SD 64,100/PK-12
2500 S State St 84115 801-646-5000
Dr. Stephen Ronnenkamp, supt. Fax 646-4128
www.graniteschools.org
Arcadia ES 600/K-6
3461 W 4850 S 84118 801-646-4756
Terri Roylance, prin. Fax 646-4757
Bennion ES 700/K-6
5775 Sierra Grande Dr 84118 801-646-4774
Walt Layton, prin. Fax 646-4775
Cottonwood ES 500/K-6
5205 Holladay Blvd 84117 801-646-4798
Karen Marberger, prin. Fax 646-4799
Crestview ES 600/K-6
2100 Lincoln Ln 84124 801-646-4804
Verneita Hunt, prin. Fax 646-4805
Driggs ES 700/K-6
4340 S 2700 E 84124 801-646-4810
Calvin Poulson, prin. Fax 646-4811
Eastwood ES 500/K-6
3305 Wasatch Blvd 84109 801-646-4816
Jim McCasland, prin. Fax 646-4817
Fox Hills ES 600/K-6
3775 W 6020 S 84118 801-646-4828
Alleson Peck, prin. Fax 646-4829
Fremont ES 600/K-6
4249 S 1425 W 84123 801-646-4834
J. Lynn Cooper, prin. Fax 646-4835
Lincoln ES 500/PK-6
450 E 3700 S 84115 801-646-4894
Karen Gregory, prin. Fax 646-4895
Mill Creek ES 400/PK-6
3761 S 1100 E 84106 801-646-4912
Tina West, prin. Fax 646-4913
Morningside ES 500/K-6
4170 S 3000 E 84124 801-646-4924
Joan Bramble, prin. Fax 646-4925
Moss ES 500/K-6
4399 S 500 E 84107 801-646-4930
Milicent Larsen, prin. Fax 646-4931
Oakridge ES 600/K-6
4325 Jupiter Dr 84124 801-646-4936
Rosanne Newell, prin. Fax 646-4937
Oakwood ES 400/K-6
5815 Highland Dr 84121 801-646-4942
Court DeSpain, prin. Fax 646-4943
Penn ES 600/K-6
1670 Siggard Dr 84106 801-646-4960
Carol Syroid, prin. Fax 646-4961
Plymouth ES 600/K-6
5220 S 1470 W 84123 801-646-4978
Sally Sanders, prin. Fax 646-4979
Roosevelt ES 400/K-6
3225 S 800 E 84106 801-646-4996
Karen Robinson, prin. Fax 646-4997
Rosecrest ES 500/K-6
2420 Fisher Ln 84109 801-646-5002
Kent Fuller, prin. Fax 646-5003
Spring Lane ES K-6
5315 S 1700 E 84117 801-646-4906
Shari Fraser, prin. Fax 646-4907
Stansbury ES 700/PK-6
3050 Constitution Blvd 84119 801-646-5032
Ernie Broderick, prin. Fax 646-5033
Taylorsville ES 600/K-6
2010 Mantle Ave 84119 801-646-5038
Jonathan Adams, prin. Fax 646-5039
Twin Peaks ES 400/K-6
5325 S 1045 E 84117 801-646-5049
Tracy Rose, prin. Fax 646-5051
Upland Terrace ES 600/K-6
3700 Sunnydale Dr 84109 801-646-5055
Brent Nelson, prin. Fax 646-5056
Vista ES 600/PK-6
4925 S 2200 W 84118 801-646-5067
Dr. Julianne Clarke, prin. Fax 646-5068
Westbrook ES 700/K-6
3451 W 6200 S 84118 801-646-5085
Mardel Higginson, prin. Fax 646-5086
Wilson ES 600/PK-6
2567 S Main St 84115 801-646-5102
Linda Hart, prin. Fax 646-5106
Woodstock ES 500/K-6
6015 S 1300 E 84121 801-646-5108
Amy Martz, prin. Fax 646-5109
Wright ES K-6
6760 W 3100 S 84128 801-646-5480
Marilyn Laughlin, prin. Fax 646-5481
Other Schools – See Kearns, Magna, West Jordan, West Valley

Jordan SD
Supt. — See Sandy
Butler ES 500/K-6
7000 S 2700 E 84121 801-944-2942
Edy McGee, prin. Fax 302-4908
Canyon View ES 700/K-6
3050 Bengal Blvd 84121 801-944-2953
Sharon Okumura, prin. Fax 302-4910

Salt Lake City SD 23,100/K-12
440 E 100 S 84111 801-578-8599
Dr. McKell Withers, supt. Fax 578-8248
www.slc.k12.ut.us
Backman ES 500/K-6
601 N 1500 W 84116 801-578-8100
Fern Wilkerson, prin. Fax 578-8155
Beacon Heights ES 500/K-6
1850 S 2500 E 84108 801-481-4814
Sue Heath, prin. Fax 481-4900
Bennion ES 300/K-6
429 S 800 E 84102 801-578-8108
Christine Pittam, prin. Fax 578-8111
Bonneville ES 400/K-6
1145 S 1900 E 84108 801-584-2913
Donna Reid, prin. Fax 584-2919
Bryant MS 500/7-8
40 S 800 E 84102 801-578-8118
Francis Battle, prin. Fax 578-8125
Clayton MS 500/7-8
1471 S 1800 E 84108 801-481-4810
Linda Richins, prin. Fax 481-4884
Dilworth ES 500/K-6
1953 S 2100 E 84108 801-481-4806
Kenneth Limb, prin. Fax 481-4924
Edison ES 600/K-6
466 Cheyenne St 84104 801-974-8300
James Martin, prin. Fax 974-8352
Emerson ES 400/K-6
1017 Harrison Ave 84105 801-481-4819
Ken Jones, prin. Fax 481-4914
Ensign ES 400/K-6
775 12th Ave 84103 801-578-8150
Randall Miller, prin. Fax 578-8107
Escalante ES 600/K-6
1810 W 900 N 84116 801-578-8496
Richard Aslett, prin. Fax 578-8499
Franklin ES 500/K-6
1115 W 300 S 84104 801-578-8158
Dahlia Cordova, prin. Fax 578-8163
Glendale MS 600/7-8
1430 Andrew Ave 84104 801-974-8319
Betty Valenzuela, prin. Fax 974-8356
Hawthorne ES 500/K-6
1675 S 600 E 84105 801-481-4824
Marian Broadhead, prin. Fax 481-4927
Highland Park ES 500/K-6
1738 E 2700 S 84106 801-481-4833
Susan Parker, prin. Fax 481-4920
Hillside MS 600/7-8
2375 Garfield Ave 84108 801-481-4828
Heidi Larsen, prin. Fax 481-4831
Indian Hills ES 500/K-6
2496 Saint Marys Dr 84108 801-584-2908
Dr. Lewis Gardiner, prin. Fax 584-2932
Jackson ES 600/K-6
750 W 200 N 84116 801-578-8165
Sandra Buendia, prin. Fax 578-8172
Lincoln ES 500/K-6
1090 Roberta St 84111 801-578-8180
Tracy Vandeventer, prin. Fax 578-8188
Meadowlark ES 500/K-6
497 N Morton Dr 84116 801-578-8529
Mike Sadler, prin. Fax 578-8534
Mountain View ES 600/K-6
1380 Navajo St 84104 801-974-8315
John Erlacher, prin. Fax 974-8332
Newman ES 500/K-6
1269 Colorado St 84116 801-578-8537
Craig Ruesch, prin. Fax 578-8544
Nibley Park ES 400/K-6
2785 S 800 E 84106 801-481-4842
Doug McLennan, prin. Fax 481-4899
North Star ES 600/K-6
1545 N Morton Dr 84116 801-578-8448
Earl Arnoldson, prin. Fax 578-8445
Northwest MS 800/7-8
1730 W 1700 N 84116 801-578-8547
Rod Goode, prin. Fax 578-8558

Parkview ES 500/K-6
970 Emery St 84104 801-974-8304
Jane Larson, prin. Fax 974-8329
Riley ES 600/K-6
1410 S 800 W 84104 801-974-8310
Bobbie Kirby, prin. Fax 974-8354
Rose Park ES 500/K-6
1105 W 1000 N 84116 801-578-8554
Rae Louie, prin. Fax 578-8373
Uintah ES 600/K-6
1571 E 1300 S 84105 801-584-2940
Heidi Kunzler, prin. Fax 584-2944
Wasatch ES 500/K-6
30 R St 84103 801-578-8564
Julie Miller, prin. Fax 578-8117
Washington ES 300/K-6
420 N 200 W 84103 801-578-8140
JoAnn Price, prin. Fax 578-8147
Whittier ES 600/K-6
1600 S 300 E 84115 801-481-4846
Jane Fitts, prin. Fax 481-4849

Carden Memorial S 400/PK-8
1452 E 2700 S 84106 801-486-4895
James Taylor, hdmstr. Fax 487-5076
Challenger S 200/PK-K
4555 S 2300 E 84117 801-278-4797
Brenda Salt, dir. Fax 278-4798
Challenger S 500/PK-8
1325 S Main St 84115 801-487-9984
Hollie Holman, dir. Fax 487-9986
Cosgriff Memorial S 300/K-8
2335 Redondo Ave 84108 801-486-3197
Betsy Hunt, prin. Fax 484-8270
Intermountain Christian S 300/PK-12
6515 Lion Ln 84121 801-942-8811
Layne Billings, prin. Fax 942-8813
Kearns-St. Ann S 300/K-8
430 E 2100 S 84115 801-486-0741
Kay McMahon, prin. Fax 486-0742
Madeleine Choir S 200/K-8
205 1st Ave 84103 801-323-9850
Christina McGill, prin. Fax 323-0581
McGillis S 200/1-8
668 S 1300 E 84102 801-583-0094
Matt Culberson, hdmstr. Fax 583-0720
Our Lady of Lourdes Catholic S 200/K-8
1065 E 700 S 84102 801-364-5624
Louise Herman, prin. Fax 364-0925
Prince of Peace Lutheran S 100/PK-8
1441 Tamarack Rd 84123 801-261-3808
Jeffrey Loberger, prin. Fax 261-3806
Realms of Inquiry S 100/PK-12
1140 S 900 E 84105 801-467-5911
Laurie Bragg, hdmstr. Fax 467-5932
Redeemer Lutheran S 200/K-8
1955 E Stratford Ave 84106 801-487-6283
Linda Tatomer, prin. Fax 463-7904
Reid S 200/PK-9
2965 Evergreen Ave 84109 801-466-4214
Dr. Ethna Reid, prin. Fax 466-4214
Rowland Hall-St. Marks ES 500/PK-5
720 Guardsman Way 84108 801-355-7485
Deborah Mohrman, prin. Fax 363-5521
Rowland Hall-St. Marks MS 200/6-8
970 E 800 S 84102 801-355-0272
Stephen Bennhoff, prin. Fax 359-8318
St. Francis Xavier S 300/PK-8
4501 W 5215 S 84118 801-966-1571
Fax 966-1639
St. Sophia Hellenic Orthodox S 100/PK-6
5341 Highland Dr 84117 801-424-1297
Susan Brady, dir. Fax 277-1026
St. Vincent de Paul S 300/PK-8
1385 Spring Ln 84117 801-277-6702
Mark Longe, prin. Fax 424-0450
Salt Lake Junior Academy 50/PK-8
965 E 3370 S 84106 801-467-1374
Trevor Kendall, prin. Fax 467-0704

Sandy, Salt Lake, Pop. 89,664
Jordan SD 75,300/K-12
9361 S 300 E 84070 801-567-8100
Barry Newbold Ed.D., supt. Fax 567-8078
www.jordandistrict.org/
Altara ES 700/K-6
800 E 11000 S 84094 801-572-7000
Scott Jameson, prin. Fax 302-4903
Alta View ES 600/K-6
10333 Crocus St 84094 801-572-7031
Valerie Shaw, prin. Fax 302-4904
Bell View ES 500/K-6
9800 S 800 E 84094 801-572-7022
Christine Webb, prin. Fax 302-4905
Brookwood ES 600/K-6
8640 Snowbird Dr 84093 801-944-2962
Michelle Clark, prin. Fax 302-4907
Crescent ES 700/K-6
11100 S 230 E 84070 801-572-7060
Debbie Shumard, prin. Fax 302-4916
East Sandy ES 700/K-6
8295 S 870 E 84094 801-565-7452
William Geist, prin. Fax 302-4923
Edgemont ES 600/K-6
1085 Galena Dr 84094 801-572-7010
Ronnie Mulqueen, prin. Fax 302-4924
Granite ES 600/K-6
9760 S 3100 E 84092 801-944-2968
Denise Orme, prin. Fax 302-4930
Lone Peak ES 800/K-6
11515 High Mesa Dr 84092 801-572-7073
Kathy Anderson, prin. Fax 302-4935
Oakdale ES 500/K-6
1900 Creek Rd 84093 801-944-2907
Ruth Peters, prin. Fax 302-4949
Park Lane ES 600/K-6
9955 Eastdell Dr 84092 801-944-2973
Karen Medlin, prin. Fax 302-4955
Peruvian Park ES 600/K-6
1545 E 8425 S 84093 801-565-7478
Laura Finlinson, prin. Fax 302-4950
Quail Hollow ES 600/K-6
2625 Newcastle Dr 84093 801-944-2937
Marilyn Williams, prin. Fax 302-4954
Sandy ES 600/K-6
8725 S 280 E 84070 801-565-7490
Sandra Houlihan, prin. Fax 302-4956
Silver Mesa ES 500/K-6
8920 S 1700 E 84093 801-565-7492
Joy Sanford, prin. Fax 302-4958
Sprucewood ES 900/K-6
12025 S 1000 E 84094 801-572-7077
Garth Anderson, prin. Fax 302-4964
Sunrise ES 700/K-6
1520 E 11265 S 84092 801-572-7016
Jill Durrant, prin. Fax 302-4959
Willow Canyon ES 500/K-6
9650 S 1700 E 84092 801-572-7020
Todd Theobald, prin. Fax 302-4974
Other Schools – See Cottonwood Heights, Draper, Herriman, Midvale, Riverton, Salt Lake City, South Jordan, West Jordan

---

Blessed Sacrament S 300/PK-8
1745 E 9800 S 84092 801-572-5311
Judy Julian, prin. Fax 572-0251
Challenger S 500/PK-K
1260 E 8600 S 84094 801-561-9494
Trin Anglin, dir. Fax 561-9495
Challenger S 400/PK-8
10693 S 1000 E 84094 801-572-6686
Elizabeth Black, prin. Fax 572-6687
Grace Lutheran S 200/PK-8
1815 E 9800 S 84092 801-572-3793
William Busacker, prin. Fax 553-2403
Oxford Learning Source 50/PK-12
8615 Highland Dr 84093 801-942-4449
Millicent Jacobsen, dir. Fax 943-0775
Waterford S 1,000/PK-12
1480 E 9400 S 84093 801-572-1780
Nancy Heuston, hdmstr. Fax 572-1787

Santa Clara, Washington, Pop. 5,864
Washington County SD
Supt. — See Saint George
Arrowhead ES 600/K-5
545 Arrowhead Trl 84765 435-674-2027
Susan Harrah, prin. Fax 674-2038
Lava Ridge IS 900/6-7
2425 Rachel 84765 435-652-4742
Kalyn Gubler, prin. Fax 652-4747
Santa Clara ES 500/K-5
2950 Crestview Dr 84765 435-628-2624
Nadine Hancey, prin. Fax 628-3785

Santaquin, Utah, Pop. 6,901
Nebo SD
Supt. — See Spanish Fork
Orchard Hills ES K-6
168 E 610 S 84655 801-754-3237
Kim Barlow, prin. Fax 754-5106
Santaquin ES 500/K-6
25 S 400 W 84655 801-754-3611
Chad Argyle, prin. Fax 754-3612

Saratoga Sprngs, Utah
Alpine SD
Supt. — See American Fork
Harvest ES K-6
2105 Providence Dr, 801-768-2833
Karl Bowman, prin.

Smithfield, Cache, Pop. 7,589
Cache County SD
Supt. — See Logan
Summit ES 600/3-5
80 W Center St 84335 435-563-6269
Trudy Wilson, prin. Fax 563-6422
Sunrise ES 600/K-2
225 S 455 E 84335 435-563-3866
Kathy Toolson, prin. Fax 563-6422

Snowville, Box Elder, Pop. 170
Box Elder SD
Supt. — See Brigham City
Snowville ES 50/K-5
160 North Stone Rd 84336 435-872-2771
Brian Anderson, prin. Fax 872-2772

South Jordan, Salt Lake, Pop. 40,209
Jordan SD
Supt. — See Sandy
Daybreak ES K-5
4544 Harvest Moon Dr 84095 801-302-0553
Doree Strauss, prin. Fax 302-4915
Eastlake ES K-6
4389 Isla Daybreak Rd 84095 801-446-0778
Jan Tanner, prin. Fax 567-8623
Elk Meadows ES 900/K-6
3448 W 9800 S 84095 801-446-3200
Howard Griffith, prin. Fax 302-4926
Jordan Ridge ES 1,000/K-6
2636 W 9800 S 84095 801-254-8025
Catherine Anderson, prin. Fax 302-4933
Monte Vista ES 1,000/K-6
11121 S 2700 W 84095 801-254-8040
Tom Little, prin. Fax 302-4946
South Jordan ES 1,000/K-6
11205 Black Cherry Way 84095 801-254-8000
Paul Bergera, prin. Fax 302-4960
Welby ES 1,100/K-6
4130 W 9580 S 84095 801-280-1456
Luann Leavitt, prin. Fax 302-4967

South Weber, Davis, Pop. 5,593
Davis SD
Supt. — See Farmington
South Weber ES 700/K-6
1285 Lester Dr 84405 801-402-3750
Marilyn Hales, prin. Fax 402-3751

Spanish Fork, Utah, Pop. 26,606
Nebo SD 21,300/PK-12
350 S Main St 84660 801-354-7400
Chris Sorensen, supt. Fax 798-4010
www.nebo.edu
Brockbank ES 700/PK-6
340 W 500 N 84660 801-798-4025
Alison Hansen, prin. Fax 798-4026
Canyon ES 600/K-6
1492 E 1240 S 84660 801-798-4610
Dave Harlan, prin. Fax 798-3493
East Meadows ES K-6
1287 S 2130 E 84660 801-798-4015
Dwight Liddiard, prin. Fax 798-4022
Larsen ES 500/K-6
1175 E Flonette Ave 84660 801-798-4035
Michael Johnson, prin. Fax 798-4036
Park ES 400/K-6
90 N 600 E 84660 801-798-4045
Rob Keddington, prin. Fax 798-4046
Rees ES 700/PK-6
574 N Rees Ave 84660 801-798-4055
Mike Larsen, prin. Fax 798-4056
Riverview ES K-6
628 Westpark Dr 84660 801-798-4050
Sandra Jarvis, prin. Fax 798-4051
Spanish Oaks ES 600/K-6
2701 E Canyon Crest Dr 84660 801-798-7411
Susan Huff, prin. Fax 794-2845
Other Schools – See Goshen, Mapleton, Payson, Salem, Santaquin, Springville

Spring City, Sanpete, Pop. 1,003
North Sanpete SD
Supt. — See Mount Pleasant
Spring City ES 100/K-6
PO Box 159 84662 435-462-2169
John Thomas, prin. Fax 462-3445

Springdale, Washington, Pop. 538
Washington County SD
Supt. — See Saint George
Springdale ES 50/K-6
PO Box 509 84767 435-772-3279
Chris Snodgress, prin. Fax 772-3124

Springville, Utah, Pop. 25,309
Nebo SD
Supt. — See Spanish Fork
Art City ES 800/K-6
121 N 900 E 84663 801-489-2820
David Rowe, prin. Fax 489-6042
Brookside ES 400/K-6
750 E 400 S 84663 801-489-2830
DeAnn Nielsen, prin. Fax 489-2834
Cherry Creek ES K-6
484 S 200 E 84663 801-489-2810
Mark Balzotti, prin. Fax 489-2814
Sage Creek ES 700/K-6
1050 S 700 E 84663 801-489-2860
Natalie Call, prin. Fax 489-2865
Westside ES 800/K-6
740 W Center St 84663 801-489-2800
Sara Matis, prin. Fax 489-2825

Stansbury Park, Tooele, Pop. 1,049
Tooele County SD
Supt. — See Tooele
Rose Springs ES 700/K-6
5349 Innsbrook Pl 84074 435-833-9015
Leon Jones, prin. Fax 833-9207
Stansbury Park ES 600/K-6
485 Country Clb 84074 435-833-1968
Xenia Young, prin. Fax 833-1972

Sunnyside, Carbon, Pop. 376
Carbon SD
Supt. — See Price
Bruin Point ES 100/K-6
PO Box 399 84539 435-888-4474
Melissa Hamilton, prin. Fax 888-9938

Sunset, Davis, Pop. 4,947
Davis SD
Supt. — See Farmington
Doxey ES 400/PK-6
944 N 250 W 84015 801-402-2250
Bernardo Villar, prin. Fax 402-2263
Fremont ES 400/K-6
2525 N 160 W 84015 801-402-2300
Dave Dau, prin. Fax 402-2301
Sunset ES 500/PK-6
2014 N 250 W 84015 801-402-2550
Donald Beatty, prin. Fax 402-2551

Syracuse, Davis, Pop. 17,938
Davis SD
Supt. — See Farmington
Bluff Ridge ES 1,100/K-6
2680 S 775 W 84075 801-402-2850
Michael Venable, prin. Fax 402-2851
Buffalo Point ES K-6
1924 Doral Dr 84075 801-402-8400
Richard Baird, prin. Fax 402-8401
Cook ES 800/PK-6
1175 W 1350 S 84075 801-402-2200
Becky Parkin, prin. Fax 402-2201
Syracuse ES 800/K-6
1503 S 2000 W 84075 801-402-2600
Sue Caldwell, prin. Fax 402-2601

Tabiona, Duchesne, Pop. 154
Duchesne SD
Supt. — See Duchesne

Tabiona ES 100/K-6
PO Box 470 84072 435-738-1320
Robert Park, prin. Fax 738-1332

Tooele, Tooele, Pop. 28,369
Tooele County SD 11,900/K-12
92 Lodestone Way 84074 435-833-1900
Terry Linares, supt. Fax 833-1912
www.tooelesd.org
Copper Canyon ES 600/K-6
1600 N Broadway 84074 435-843-3820
Clint Spindler, prin. Fax 843-3824
East ES 700/K-6
135 S 7th St 84074 435-833-1951
Shanz Leonelli, prin. Fax 833-1952
Harris ES 500/K-6
251 N 1st St 84074 435-833-1961
Cleo Riggs, prin. Fax 833-1965
Johnsen JHS 7-8
2152 N 400 W 84074 435-833-1900
Hal Strain, prin. Fax 843-3816
Middle Canyon ES 700/K-6
751 E 1000 N 84074 435-833-1906
Cheryl Miller, prin. Fax 843-3802
Northlake ES 700/K-6
268 N Coleman St 84074 435-833-1940
JoAn Coon, prin. Fax 833-1943
Overlake ES 600/K-6
2052 N 170 W 84074 435-843-3805
Janice Johnson, prin. Fax 843-3809
Settlement Canyon ES K-6
935 Timpie Rd 84074 435-833-1900
Gailynn Warr, prin. Fax 882-4597
Tooele JHS 600/7-8
412 W Vine St 84074 435-833-1921
Larry Abraham, prin. Fax 833-1923
West ES 700/K-6
451 W 300 S 84074 435-833-1931
Suzanne Owen, prin. Fax 833-1933
Other Schools – See Dugway, Grantsville, Ibapah, Stansbury Park, Vernon, Wendover

St. Marguerite S 200/PK-8
15 S 7th St 84074 435-882-0081
Marcella Burden, prin. Fax 882-3866

Tremonton, Box Elder, Pop. 6,286
Box Elder SD
Supt. — See Brigham City
Harris IS 600/6-7
515 N 800 W 84337 435-257-2560
Keith Klein, prin. Fax 257-4133
McKinley ES 600/K-5
120 W 500 S 84337 435-257-2590
Julie Palmer Gnotta, prin. Fax 257-2593
North Park ES 600/K-5
50 E 700 N 84337 435-257-2580
Bambi Slater, prin. Fax 257-2583

Tropic, Garfield, Pop. 463
Garfield SD
Supt. — See Panguitch
Bryce Valley ES 100/K-6
PO Box 286 84776 435-679-8619
Layne LeFevre, prin. Fax 679-8936

Vernal, Uintah, Pop. 7,960
Uintah SD 5,300/PK-12
635 W 200 S 84078 435-781-3100
Charles Nelson Ed.D., supt. Fax 781-3107
www.uintah.net/
Ashley ES 400/K-5
350 N 1150 W 84078 435-781-3170
Diedra Massey, prin. Fax 781-3173
Davis ES 500/K-5
4101 S 2500 E 84078 435-781-3155
Jayme Leyba, prin. Fax 781-3193
Discovery ES 500/K-5
650 W 1200 S 84078 435-781-3146
Kathleen Hawkins, prin. Fax 781-3147
Maeser ES 600/K-5
2670 W 1000 N 84078 435-781-3160
Carol Parrish, prin. Fax 781-3162
Naples ES 400/K-5
1640 E 1900 S 84078 435-781-3150
John Anderson, prin. Fax 781-3152
Uintah Specialized Preschool PK-PK
250 S Vernal Ave 84078 435-781-3125
Shannon Deets, coord. Fax 781-3127
Vernal MS 800/6-7
721 W 100 S 84078 435-781-3140
Deborah Chatham, prin. Fax 781-3143
Other Schools – See Lapoint, Roosevelt

Uintah Basin Christian Academy 100/PK-9
PO Box 1548 84078 435-789-9332
Theresa Bruch, admin. Fax 789-9332

Vernon, Tooele, Pop. 282
Tooele County SD
Supt. — See Tooele
Vernon ES 50/K-6
70 N Main St 84080 435-839-3433
Lana Thomas, prin. Fax 839-3433

Vineyard, Utah, Pop. 127
Alpine SD
Supt. — See American Fork
Vineyard ES 600/K-6
620 E Holdaway Rd 84058 801-227-8739
Sylvia Allan, prin. Fax 227-2454

Washington, Washington, Pop. 13,669
Washington County SD
Supt. — See Saint George
Coral Canyon ES K-5
3435 E Canyon Crest Ave 84780 435-652-4787
Robyn Bishop, prin. Fax 652-4792
Horizon ES K-5
1970 S Arabian Way 84780 435-652-4781
Mona Haslem, prin. Fax 652-4784
Riverside ES 600/K-5
2500 S Harvest Ln 84780 435-652-4760
Nadine Walters, prin. Fax 652-4765
Washington ES 500/K-5
300 N 300 E 84780 435-673-3012
Burke Staheli, prin. Fax 634-5748

Wellington, Carbon, Pop. 1,558
Carbon SD
Supt. — See Price
Wellington ES 400/K-6
PO Box 407 84542 435-637-2570
Kelly Martinez, prin. Fax 637-5043

Wellsville, Cache, Pop. 2,575
Cache County SD
Supt. — See Logan
Wellsville ES 400/K-5
90 E 100 S 84339 435-245-3764
Cody Dobson, prin. Fax 245-4586
Willow Valley MS 500/6-7
525 N 200 W 84339 435-245-0505
Lynn Archibald, prin. Fax 245-5269

Wendover, Tooele, Pop. 1,620
Tintic SD
Supt. — See Eureka
Callao S 50/K-8
Callao Route 225 84083 435-693-3142
Annette Garland, lead tchr. Fax 693-3142
West Desert ES 50/PK-6
440 Trout Creek 84083 435-693-3193
Edgar Alder, prin. Fax 693-3193

Tooele County SD
Supt. — See Tooele
Smith ES 200/K-6
PO Box 879 84083 435-665-0470
Kent Parsons, prin. Fax 665-7562

West Bountiful, Davis, Pop. 4,896
Davis SD
Supt. — See Farmington
West Bountiful ES 600/PK-6
750 W 400 N 84087 801-402-2000
Barbara White, prin. Fax 402-2001

West Haven, Weber, Pop. 5,558
Weber SD
Supt. — See Ogden
Country View ES 500/K-6
4650 W 4800 S 84401 801-452-4400
Mike Geilmann, prin. Fax 452-4419
Kanesville ES 700/K-6
3112 S 3500 W 84401 801-452-4680
Mel Hawkes, prin. Fax 452-4699
West Haven ES 600/K-6
4385 S 3900 W 84401 801-452-4960
Maurine Newton, prin. Fax 452-4979

West Jordan, Salt Lake, Pop. 91,444
Granite SD
Supt. — See Salt Lake City
Bridger ES 700/K-6
5368 Cyclamen Way, 801-646-4780
Paulette McMillan, prin. Fax 646-4781

Jordan SD
Supt. — See Sandy
Columbia ES 800/K-6
3505 W 7800 S 84088 801-280-3279
Kathe Riding, prin. Fax 302-4911
Copper Canyon ES 800/K-6
8917 Copperwood Dr, 801-260-0222
Diena Riddle, prin. Fax 302-4975
Falcon Ridge ES K-6
6111 W 7000 S, 801-282-2437
Karen Thomson, prin. Fax 302-4928
Hayden Peak ES 1,300/K-6
5120 Hayden Peak Dr, 801-280-0722
Dana Easton, prin. Fax 302-4931
Heartland ES 700/K-6
1451 W 7000 S 84084 801-565-7533
Trenton Goble, prin. Fax 302-4932
Jordan Hills ES 1,100/K-6
8892 S 4800 W 84088 801-280-0238
Annette Huff, prin. Fax 302-4934
Majestic ES 300/K-6
7430 Redwood Rd 84084 801-565-7458
Noel Grabl, prin. Fax 302-4938
Mountain Shadows ES 1,000/K-6
5255 W 7000 S, 801-963-0291
Spencer Jacobs, prin. Fax 302-4945
Oakcrest ES 1,400/K-6
8462 Hilltop Oak Dr, 801-280-7243
Norman Emerson, prin. Fax 302-4914
Oquirrh ES 800/K-6
7165 Paddington Rd 84084 801-565-7474
Nancy Ward, prin. Fax 302-4947
Riverside ES 800/K-6
8737 S 1220 W 84088 801-565-7484
William Hanvey, prin. Fax 302-4953
Terra Linda ES 600/K-6
8400 S 3400 W 84088 801-282-8036
Mary Ann Erdmann, prin. Fax 302-4962
West Jordan ES 600/K-6
7220 S 2370 W 84084 801-565-7506
David Vicchrilli, prin. Fax 302-4968
Westland ES 600/K-6
2925 W 7180 S 84084 801-565-7508
Karen Egan, prin. Fax 302-4970
Westvale ES 800/K-6
2300 Gardner Ln 84088 801-565-7510
Becky Gerber, prin. Fax 302-4969

Challenger S 500/PK-1
2247 W 8660 S 84088 801-565-1058
Cindee Winter, dir. Fax 565-1059
Children's Christian S 100/PK-8
3138 W 7000 S 84084 801-971-5085
Arlene Farr, dir. Fax 965-8216

West Point, Davis, Pop. 7,650
Davis SD
Supt. — See Farmington
Lakeside ES 800/K-6
2941 W 800 N 84015 801-402-2900
Don Holt, prin. Fax 402-2901
West Point ES 900/K-6
3788 W 300 N 84015 801-402-2750
Nannette Robertson, prin. Fax 402-2751

West Valley, Salt Lake, Pop. 111,254
Granite SD
Supt. — See Salt Lake City
Academy Park ES 700/K-6
4580 Westpoint Dr 84120 801-646-4750
Jean Gowans, prin. Fax 646-4751
Farnsworth ES 600/K-6
3751 Sunnyvale Dr 84120 801-646-4822
Judith Simmons-Kissell, prin. Fax 646-4823
Frost ES 500/K-6
3444 W 4400 S 84119 801-646-4840
Dona Harris, prin. Fax 646-4841
Granger ES 600/K-6
3702 S 1950 W 84119 801-646-4852
Wayne Williamson, prin. Fax 646-4853
Hillsdale ES 800/PK-6
3275 W 3100 S 84119 801-646-4864
Yvonne Pearson, prin. Fax 646-4865
Hillside ES 600/PK-6
4283 S 6000 W 84128 801-646-4870
Jan Winger, prin. Fax 646-4871
Hunter ES 700/K-6
4351 S 5400 W 84120 801-646-4876
Natalie Hansen, prin. Fax 646-4877
Jackling ES 700/K-6
3760 Atlas Way 84120 801-646-4882
Jennifer Reed, prin. Fax 646-4883
Monroe ES 700/PK-6
4450 W 3100 S 84120 801-646-4918
Launa Harvey, prin. Fax 646-4919
Orchard ES 700/PK-6
6744 W 3800 S 84128 801-646-4954
Rebecca Tesch, prin. Fax 646-4955
Pioneer ES 700/K-6
3860 S 3380 W 84119 801-646-4966
Julie Lorentzon, prin. Fax 646-4967
Redwood ES 600/PK-6
2650 S Redwood Rd 84119 801-646-4984
Heather Nicholas, prin. Fax 646-4985
Rolling Meadows ES 500/PK-6
2950 Whitehall Dr 84119 801-646-4990
Kayla MacKay, prin. Fax 646-4995
Sandburg ES 600/PK-6
3900 Rancho Vista Ln 84120 801-646-5008
Linda Call, prin. Fax 646-5009
Truman ES 500/K-6
4639 S 3200 W 84119 801-646-5044
Dorothea Gray, prin. Fax 646-5045
Valley Crest ES 800/K-6
5240 W 3100 S 84120 801-646-5061
Jane McClure, prin. Fax 646-5062
West Valley ES 700/K-6
6049 Brud Dr 84128 801-646-5079
Naomi Hopf, prin. Fax 646-5080
Whittier ES 700/K-6
3585 S 6000 W 84128 801-646-5096
Judy Giles, prin. Fax 646-5097

Dancing Moose Montessori S 100/PK-2
4428 Links Dr 84120 801-968-0100
Jennifer Duffield, prin. Fax 966-1135

Willard, Box Elder, Pop. 1,663
Box Elder SD
Supt. — See Brigham City
Willard ES 300/K-2
40 W 50 S 84340 435-734-4934
Jerry Jones, prin. Fax 734-4936

Woods Cross, Davis, Pop. 8,019
Davis SD
Supt. — See Farmington
Woods Cross ES 900/PK-6
745 W 1100 S 84087 801-402-1800
Eric Holmes, prin. Fax 402-1801

VERMONT

VERMONT DEPARTMENT OF EDUCATION
120 State St, Montpelier 05620-0002
Telephone 802-828-3135
Fax 802-828-3140
Website http://www.state.vt.us/educ/

Commissioner of Education Armando Vilaseca

VERMONT BOARD OF EDUCATION
120 State St, Montpelier 05620-0002

Chairperson Tom James

PUBLIC, PRIVATE AND CATHOLIC ELEMENTARY SCHOOLS

Albany, Orleans, Pop. 167
Orleans Central Supervisory Union
Supt. — See Barton
Albany S 100/K-8
351 Main St 05820 802-755-6168
Jill Chafee, prin. Fax 755-6263

Alburg, Grand Isle, Pop. 521
Grand Isle Supervisory Union
Supt. — See North Hero
Alburg Community S 200/K-8
14 N Main St 05440 802-796-3573
Barbara Burrington, prin. Fax 796-3068

Arlington, Bennington, Pop. 1,311
Battenkill Valley Supervisory Union 400/K-12
530 E Arlington Rd Ste A 05250 802-375-9744
Charles Sweetman, supt. Fax 375-2368
Fisher ES 100/K-5
504 E Arlington Rd 05250 802-375-6409
Deanne LaCoste, prin. Fax 375-1544

Ascutney, Windsor
Windsor Southeast Supervisory Union
Supt. — See Windsor
Weathersfield S 100/K-8
PO Box 279 05030 802-674-5400
Mario Bevacqua, prin. Fax 674-9963

Bakersfield, Franklin
Franklin Northeast Supervisory Union
Supt. — See Richford
Bakersfield S 200/K-8
PO Box 17 05441 802-827-6611
Debora Price, prin. Fax 827-3170

Barnard, Windsor
Windsor Central Supervisory Union
Supt. — See Woodstock
Barnard Academy 100/K-6
PO Box 157 05031 802-234-9763
Anne Koop, prin. Fax 234-9641

Barnet, Caledonia
Caledonia Central Supervisory Union
Supt. — See Danville
Barnet S 200/PK-8
163 Kid Row 05821 802-633-4978
Kerry Keenan, prin. Fax 633-4497

Barre, Washington, Pop. 9,128
Barre Supervisory Union 2,800/PK-12
120 Ayers St 05641 802-476-5011
John Bacon Ed.D., supt. Fax 476-4944
71.18.184.4/
Barre City S 900/PK-8
50 Parkside Ter 05641 802-476-6541
James Taffel, prin. Fax 476-1492
Barre Town S 1,000/PK-8
70 Websterville Rd 05641 802-476-6617
Timothy Crowley, prin. Fax 479-5723

Washington Central Supervisory Union 1,700/PK-12
22 E View Ln 05641 802-229-0553
Robbe Brook, supt. Fax 229-2761
www.wcsuonline.org
Other Schools – See Berlin, East Montpelier, Middlesex, Plainfield, Worcester

---

Central Vermont Academy 100/K-12
317 Vine St 05641 802-479-0868
Sherrie Wall, prin. Fax 479-4311
Central Vermont Catholic S 200/PK-8
79 Summer St 05641 802-476-5015
Pattie O'Mahoney, prin. Fax 476-0861

Barton, Orleans, Pop. 756
Orleans Central Supervisory Union 1,100/K-12
130 Kinsey Rd 05822 802-525-1204
Stephen Urgenson Ed.D., supt. Fax 525-1276
www.ocsu.org/
Barton Academy & Graded S 200/K-8
PO Box 588 05822 802-525-6244
George Vana, prin. Fax 525-1170
Other Schools – See Albany, Brownington, Glover, Irasburg, Orleans

---

St. Paul S 100/PK-8
54 Eastern Ave 05822 802-525-6578
Peter Close, prin. Fax 525-3869

Bellows Falls, Windham, Pop. 3,019
Windham Northeast Supervisory Union 1,300/K-12
25 Cherry St 05101 802-463-9958
Johanna Harpster, supt. Fax 463-9705
www.wnesu.org
Bellows Falls MS 300/5-8
15 School St 05101 802-463-4366
Cheryl McDaniel-Thomas, prin. Fax 463-9738
Central ES 200/K-4
50 School Street Ext 05101 802-463-4346
Bruce Downer, prin. Fax 463-0131
Other Schools – See Grafton, Putney, Saxtons River, Westminster

Bennington, Bennington, Pop. 9,532
Southwest Vermont Supervisory Union 3,000/K-12
246 S Stream Rd 05201 802-447-7501
George Carpenter, supt. Fax 447-0475
www.svsu.org
Bennington ES 200/K-5
128 Park St 05201 802-442-5256
Jim Law, prin. Fax 442-1272
Monument ES 100/K-5
66 Main St 05201 802-447-7979
Jean Michaels, prin. Fax 442-2822
Mt. Anthony Union MS 600/7-8
747 East Rd 05201 802-447-7541
Warren Roaf, prin. Fax 442-1262
Stark ES 300/K-6
181 Orchard Rd 05201 802-442-2692
Donna MacKenzie-King, prin. Fax 442-1736
Woodford Hollow ES 50/K-6
995 VT Route 9 05201 802-442-4071
Sandy Foster, prin. Fax 442-2996
Other Schools – See North Bennington, Pownal, Shaftsbury

Grace Christian S 200/PK-12
104 Kocher Dr 05201 802-447-2233
Joyce Lloyd, admin. Fax 442-8403
Sacred Heart/St Francis de Sales S 200/PK-8
307 School St 05201 802-442-2446
David Estes, prin. Fax 442-2446
Ward S, 404 Houghton Ln 05201 50/K-8
Linda Everhart, prin. 802-442-4579

Benson, Rutland
Addison-Rutland Supervisory Union
Supt. — See Fair Haven
Benson Village S 200/PK-8
32 School St 05743 802-537-2491
Kim Doty, prin. Fax 537-2494

Berlin, See Montpelier
Washington Central Supervisory Union
Supt. — See Barre
Berlin ES 200/PK-6
372 Paine Tpke N 05602 802-223-2796
Charles Watson, prin. Fax 229-0222

Bethel, Windsor
Windsor Northwest Supervisory Union
Supt. — See Pittsfield
Bethel ES 200/K-6
273 Pleasant St 05032 802-234-6607
John Poljacik, prin. Fax 234-5779

Bondville, Bennington

Mountain S at Winhall 100/K-8
9 School St 05340 802-297-2662
Daren Houck, hdmstr. Fax 297-2590

Bradford, Orange, Pop. 824
Orange East Supervisory Union 1,300/K-12
PO Box 396 05033 802-222-5216
Wendy Baker, supt. Fax 222-4451
orangeeast.k12.vt.us/
Bradford ES 200/K-6
143 Fairground Rd 05033 802-222-4077
Charles Barrett, prin. Fax 222-5196
Other Schools – See East Corinth, Newbury, Thetford

Brandon, Rutland, Pop. 1,902
Rutland Northeast Supervisory Union 1,800/PK-12
49 Court Dr 05733 802-247-5757
John Castle, supt. Fax 247-5548
www.rnesu.org
Neshobe ES 400/PK-6
17 Neshobe Cir 05733 802-247-3721
Judi Pulsifer, prin. Fax 247-5699
Other Schools – See Chittenden, Leicester, Pittsford, Sudbury, Whiting

Brattleboro, Windham, Pop. 8,612
Windham Southeast Supervisory Union 2,800/K-12
53 Green St 05301 802-254-3731
Ron Stahley, supt. Fax 254-3733
www.wssu.k12.vt.us
Academy S 400/K-6
860 Western Ave 05301 802-254-3743
Andrew Paciull, prin. Fax 254-3756
Brattleboro Area MS 300/7-8
109 Sunny Acres St 05301 802-451-3500
Ingrid Chrisco, prin. Fax 451-3502
Green Street ES 300/K-6
164 Green St 05301 802-254-3737
Robert Neubauer, prin. Fax 254-3753
Oak Grove ES 200/K-6
15 Moreland Ave 05301 802-254-3740
Michael Friel, prin. Fax 254-3633
Other Schools – See East Dummerston, Guilford, Putney, Vernon

---

St. Michael S 100/PK-8
48 Walnut St 05301 802-254-5666
Elaine Beam, prin. Fax 254-5229

Bridgewater, Windsor
Windsor Central Supervisory Union
Supt. — See Woodstock
Bridgewater Village ES 100/K-6
PO Box 131 05034 802-672-3464
Kelley Cherrington, prin. Fax 672-5061

Bridport, Addison
Addison Central Supervisory Union
Supt. — See Middlebury
Bridport Central ES 100/PK-6
3442 VT Route 22A 05734 802-758-2331
Georgette Childs, prin. Fax 758-2866

Bristol, Addison, Pop. 1,841
Addison Northeast Supervisory Union 1,800/K-12
15 Orchard Ter Ste 10 05443 802-453-3657
Evelyn Howard, supt. Fax 453-2029
www.mtabe.k12.vt.us/ANESU/index.htm
Bristol ES 300/K-6
57 Mountain St 05443 802-453-3227
Catrina DiNapoli, prin. Fax 453-4666
Lincoln Community S 100/K-6
795 E River Rd 05443 802-453-2119
Tory Riley, prin. Fax 453-3370
Other Schools – See Monkton, New Haven, Starksboro

Brookfield, Orange
Orange Southwest Supervisory Union
Supt. — See Randolph
Brookfield ES 100/K-6
1728 Ridge Rd 05036 802-276-3153
Scott Kalter, prin. Fax 276-3189

Brookline, Windham
Windham Central Supervisory Union
Supt. — See Townshend
Brookline ES 50/K-6
624 Grassy Brook Rd 05345 802-365-7552
Betty Ann Runge, prin. Fax 365-7608

Brownington, Orleans
Orleans Central Supervisory Union
Supt. — See Barton

Browningtn Central S 100/K-7
103 Chase Rd 05860 802-754-8467
JoAnn Vana, prin. Fax 754-6177

Brownsville, Windsor
Windsor Southeast Supervisory Union
Supt. — See Windsor
Albert Bridge ES 100/K-6
PO Box 88 05037 802-484-3344
Cathy Knight, prin. Fax 484-5105

Burlington, Chittenden, Pop. 38,531
Burlington SD 3,600/PK-12
150 Colchester Ave 05401 802-865-5332
Jeanne Collins, supt. Fax 864-8501
www.bsdvt.org/
Academy for Intgrtd Arts at H.O. Wheeler 200/PK-5
6 Archibald St 05401 802-864-8475
Joyce Irvine, prin. Fax 864-2162
Champlain ES 300/K-5
800 Pine St 05401 802-864-8477
Leslie Colomb, prin. Fax 864-2157
Edmunds ES 300/K-5
299 Main St 05401 802-864-1791
Paul Schreiber, prin. Fax 864-2166
Edmunds MS 400/6-8
275 Main St 05401 802-864-8486
Bonnie Johnson-Aten, prin. Fax 864-2218
Flynn ES 300/K-5
1645 North Ave, 802-864-8478
Graham Clarke, prin. Fax 864-2145
Hunt MS 400/6-8
1364 North Ave, 802-864-8469
Linda Carroll, prin. Fax 864-8467
Smith ES 300/K-5
332 Ethan Allen Pkwy, 802-864-8479
Lorie Carruth, prin. Fax 864-4923
Sustainability Academy at Barnes S 200/PK-5
123 North St 05401 802-864-8480
Abi Sessions, prin. Fax 864-2161

Christ the King S 200/PK-8
136 Locust St 05401 802-862-6696
Paulette Thibault, prin. Fax 658-6553
Mater Christi S 300/PK-8
50 Mansfield Ave 05401 802-658-3992
Beverly Broomhall, prin. Fax 863-1196
North Avenue Christian S 100/PK-5
901 North Ave, 802-863-2579
Susan Comeau, prin. Fax 864-3681
St. Joseph S 100/PK-8
20 Allen St 05401 802-864-5623
Evelyn Rogerson, prin. Fax 860-2627

Cabot, Washington, Pop. 247
Washington NE Supervisory Union
Supt. — See Plainfield
Cabot S 200/PK-12
PO Box 98 05647 802-563-2289
Regina Quinn, prin. Fax 563-2022

Cambridge, Chittenden, Pop. 230
Franklin West Supervisory Union
Supt. — See Fairfax
Fletcher ES 100/PK-6
340 School Rd 05444 802-849-6251
Jeffrey Teitelbaum, prin. Fax 849-6509

Canaan, Essex
Essex North Supervisory Union 300/K-12
PO Box 100 05903 802-266-3330
Christopher Masson Ed.D., supt. Fax 266-7085
www.canaanschools.org/
Canaan S 300/K-12
99 School St 05903 802-266-8910
Deborah Lynch, prin. Fax 266-7068

Castleton, Rutland
Addison-Rutland Supervisory Union
Supt. — See Fair Haven
Castleton ES 300/PK-6
PO Box 68 05735 802-468-5624
Carole Pickett, prin. Fax 468-5625
Castleton Village S 100/7-8
PO Box 68 05735 802-468-2203
Linda Peltier, prin. Fax 468-5131

Charlotte, Chittenden
Chittendon South Supervisory Union
Supt. — See Shelburne
Charlotte Central S 500/PK-8
408 Hinesburg Rd 05445 802-425-2771
Sandra Jump, prin. Fax 425-2122

Chelsea, Orange
Orange-Windsor Supervisory Union
Supt. — See South Royalton
Chelsea S 200/K-12
6 School St 05038 802-685-4551
Karoline Johnson, prin. Fax 685-3310

Wellspring S 100/PK-6
PO Box 291 05038 802-685-3181
Mary Savidge, prin. Fax 685-9941

Chester, Windsor, Pop. 1,057
Windsor Southwest Supervisory Union 1,100/K-12
89 VT Route 103 S 05143 802-875-3365
Joan Paustian, supt. Fax 875-3313
www.wswsu.org/
Chester-Andover ES 300/K-6
72 Main St 05143 802-875-2108
Penny Kraft, prin. Fax 875-3998
Other Schools – See Londonderry, Proctorsville

Chittenden, Rutland
Rutland Northeast Supervisory Union
Supt. — See Brandon

Barstow Memorial S 300/PK-8
223 Chittenden Rd 05737 802-773-3763
Karen Prescott, prin. Fax 747-4814

Colchester, Chittenden
Colchester SD 2,300/K-12
PO Box 27 05446 802-264-5999
Larry Waters, supt. Fax 863-4774
www.csdvt.org
Colchester MS 500/6-8
PO Box 30 05446 802-264-5800
Carolyn Dickinson, prin. Fax 264-5858
Malletts Bay ES 500/3-5
PO Box 28 05446 802-264-5900
Barbara Nason, prin. Fax 264-5901
Porters Point ES 200/K-2
PO Box 32 05446 802-264-5920
James Marshall, prin. Fax 862-6835
Union Memorial ES 200/K-2
PO Box 48 05446 802-264-5959
Chris Antonicci, prin. Fax 879-5350

Concord, Essex
Essex-Caledonia Supervisory Union 600/PK-12
PO Box 255 05824 802-695-3373
Jill Peck, supt. Fax 695-1334
Concord S 200/PK-12
173 School St 05824 802-695-2550
Karl Stein, prin. Fax 695-3311
Other Schools – See Gilman, Guildhall, Saint Johnsbury

Cornwall, Addison
Addison Central Supervisory Union
Supt. — See Middlebury
Bingham Memorial ES 100/K-6
112 School Rd 05753 802-462-2463
Denise Goodnow, prin. Fax 462-2462

Coventry, Orleans
North Country Supervisory Union
Supt. — See Newport
Coventry Village S 100/K-8
PO Box 92 05825 802-754-6464
Martha Perron, prin. Fax 754-8508

Craftsbury Common, Orleans
Orleans Southwest Supervisory Union
Supt. — See Hardwick
Craftsbury ES 100/K-6
PO Box 73 05827 802-586-9671
Chris Young, prin. Fax 586-7524

Danby, Rutland
Bennington-Rutland Supervisory Union
Supt. — See Sunderland
Currier Memorial ES 100/K-6
234 N Main St 05739 802-293-5191
Helen Richards-Peelle, prin. Fax 293-5518

Danville, Caledonia
Caledonia Central Supervisory Union 500/PK-8
PO Box 216 05828 802-684-3801
Martha Tucker, supt. Fax 684-1190
Danville S 200/PK-8
148 Peacham Rd 05828 802-684-3651
Meg Powden, prin. Fax 684-1192
Other Schools – See Barnet, Peacham, West Danville

Derby, Orleans, Pop. 725
North Country Supervisory Union
Supt. — See Newport
North Country Union JHS 300/7-8
57 Jr High Dr 05829 802-766-2276
Nicole Larose, prin. Fax 766-2287

Derby Line, Orleans, Pop. 798
North Country Supervisory Union
Supt. — See Newport
Derby ES 400/K-6
907 Elm St 05830 802-873-3162
Douglas Westin, prin. Fax 873-9106
Holland ES 100/K-6
26 School Rd 05830 802-895-4455
Linda Phalen, prin. Fax 895-4161

Dorset, Bennington
Bennington-Rutland Supervisory Union
Supt. — See Sunderland
Dorset S 200/K-8
130 School Dr 05251 802-362-2606
James Merryman, prin. Fax 362-0894

Duxbury, See Waterbury
Washington West Supervisory Union
Supt. — See Waitsfield
Crossett Brook MS 300/5-8
5672 VT Route 100 05676 802-244-6100
Tom Drake, prin. Fax 244-6899

East Barre, Washington, Pop. 2,189
Orange North Supervisory Union
Supt. — See Williamstown
Orange Center S 100/PK-8
357 US Route 302 05649 802-476-3278
Richard Jacobs, prin. Fax 476-1389

East Corinth, Orange
Orange East Supervisory Union
Supt. — See Bradford
Waits River Valley S 200/K-8
6 Waits River Vly School Rd 05040 802-439-5534
Sandra Jump, prin. Fax 439-6444

East Dover, Windham
Windham Central Supervisory Union
Supt. — See Townshend
Dover ES 100/K-6
9 Schoolhouse Rd 05341 802-464-5386
William Anton, prin. Fax 464-0562

East Dummerston, Windham
Windham Southeast Supervisory Union
Supt. — See Brattleboro
Dummerston S 200/K-8
52 School House Rd, 802-254-2733
Jo Carol Ratti, prin. Fax 257-5751

East Haven, Essex
Caledonia North Supervisory Union
Supt. — See Lyndonville
East Haven River S 50/K-8
64A Community Bldg Rd 05837 802-467-3029
Rebecca Young, prin. Fax 467-3751

East Montpelier, Washington
Washington Central Supervisory Union
Supt. — See Barre
East Montpelier ES 200/PK-6
665 Vincent Flats Rd 05651 802-223-7936
Roderick Cooke, prin. Fax 223-3736

Orchard Valley Waldorf S 100/PK-8
2290 VT Route 14 N 05651 802-456-7400
Deborah Reed, prin. Fax 456-7449

Eden, Lamoille
Lamoille North Supervisory Union
Supt. — See Hyde Park
Eden Central ES 100/PK-6
PO Box 29 05652 802-635-6630
Jeffrey Lindgren, prin. Fax 635-3670

Enosburg Falls, Franklin, Pop. 1,473
Franklin Northeast Supervisory Union
Supt. — See Richford
Enosburg Falls ES 200/K-5
PO Box 510 05450 802-933-2171
Michelle Lussier, prin. Fax 933-5013
Enosburg Falls MS 100/6-8
PO Box 417 05450 802-933-7777
Erik Remmers, prin. Fax 933-5013

Essex Junction, Chittenden, Pop. 8,841
Chittenden Central Supervisory Union 2,800/PK-12
51 Park St 05452 802-879-5579
Michael Deweese, supt. Fax 878-1370
www.ccsuvt.org
ECC PK-PK
17 Summit St 05452 802-878-1386
Laurie Redel, contact Fax 878-1370
Fleming ES 200/4-5
9 Prospect St 05452 802-878-1381
Daniel Ryan, prin. Fax 879-5598
Hiawatha ES 200/PK-3
34 Hiawatha Ave 05452 802-878-1384
Thomas Bochanski, prin. Fax 879-8190
Lawton MS 300/6-8
104 Maple St 05452 802-878-1388
Laurie Singer, prin. Fax 879-8175
Summit Street ES 200/PK-3
17 Summit St 05452 802-878-1377
Mary Hughes, prin. Fax 878-1380
Other Schools – See Westford

Essex Town SD 1,300/PK-8
58 Founders Rd 05452 802-878-8168
Jim Fitzpatrick, supt. Fax 878-5190
www.etsdvt.org
Essex ES 400/PK-2
1 Bixby Hill Rd 05452 802-878-2584
Greg Marino, prin. Fax 879-0602
Essex MS 400/6-8
60 Founders Rd 05452 802-879-7173
Ned Kirsch, prin. Fax 879-1363
Founders Memorial ES 400/3-5
33 Founders Rd 05452 802-879-6326
Kathy Barwin, prin. Fax 879-6139

Fairfax, Franklin
Franklin West Supervisory Union 700/PK-12
PO Box 108 05454 802-849-2283
Bruce Chattman, supt. Fax 849-2865
www.franklinwestsu.org/
Bellows Free Academy PK-12
75 Hunt St 05454 802-849-6711
D. Scott Lang, prin. Fax 849-2611
Other Schools – See Cambridge, Saint Albans

Fairfield, Franklin
Franklin Central Supervisory Union
Supt. — See Saint Albans
Fairfield Center S 300/PK-8
57 Park St 05455 802-827-6639
Jason Therrien, prin. Fax 827-3604

Fair Haven, Rutland, Pop. 2,432
Addison-Rutland Supervisory Union 1,600/PK-12
49 Main St 05743 802-265-4905
Ronald Ryan, supt. Fax 265-2158
www.arsu.org
Fair Haven S 400/PK-8
103 N Main St 05743 802-265-3883
Wayne Cooke, prin. Fax 265-2343
Other Schools – See Benson, Castleton, Orwell

Fairlee, Orange
Rivendell Interstate SD
Supt. — See Orford, NH
Morey ES 100/K-5
PO Box 66 05045 802-333-9755
Eloise Ginty, prin. Fax 333-9601

Fayston, Washington
Washington West Supervisory Union
Supt. — See Waitsfield
Fayston ES 100/PK-6
782 German Flats Rd 05673 802-496-3636
Chris Dodge, prin. Fax 496-5297

Ferrisburg, Addison
Addison Northwest Supervisory Union
Supt. — See Vergennes
Ferrisburgh Central ES 200/K-6
56 Little Chicago Rd 05456 802-877-3463
JoAnn Taft-Blakely, prin. Fax 877-6377

Franklin, Franklin
Franklin Northwest Supervisory Union
Supt. — See Swanton
Franklin Central ES 100/K-6
PO Box 146 05457 802-285-2100
Joyce Hakey, prin. Fax 285-2111

Gilman, Essex
Essex-Caledonia Supervisory Union
Supt. — See Concord
Lunenburg & Gilman S 100/PK-8
PO Box 97 05904 802-892-5969
Elizabeth Benoit, prin. Fax 892-9045

Glover, Orleans
Orleans Central Supervisory Union
Supt. — See Barton
Glover Community S 100/K-8
100 School St 05839 802-525-6958
Dale Burnash, prin. Fax 525-4955

Grafton, Windham
Windham Northeast Supervisory Union
Supt. — See Bellows Falls
Athens/Grafton ES 100/K-6
PO Box 226 05146 802-843-2495
Lisa Wilson, prin. Fax 843-2496

Grand Isle, Grand Isle
Grand Isle Supervisory Union
Supt. — See North Hero
Grand Isle S 200/K-8
224 US Route 2 05458 802-372-6913
Troy Watkins, prin. Fax 372-5292

Greensboro, Orleans
Orleans Southwest Supervisory Union
Supt. — See Hardwick
Lakeview Union ES 100/K-6
189 Lauredon Ave 05841 802-533-7066
Linda Aiken, prin. Fax 533-2962

Guildhall, Essex
Essex-Caledonia Supervisory Union
Supt. — See Concord
Guildhall ES 50/K-6
PO Box 142 05905 802-676-3955
Cheryl McVetty, prin. Fax 695-1334

Guilford, Windham
Windham Southeast Supervisory Union
Supt. — See Brattleboro
Guilford Central S 200/K-8
374 School Rd 05301 802-254-2271
John Gagnon, prin. Fax 258-2848

Hardwick, Caledonia
Orleans Southwest Supervisory Union 1,100/K-12
PO Box 338 05843 802-472-6531
Mark Andrews, supt. Fax 472-6250
ossu35.tripod.com/index.htm
Hardwick ES 300/K-6
PO Box 515 05843 802-472-5411
Marilyn Zophar, prin. Fax 472-3325
Other Schools – See Craftsbury Common, Greensboro, Wolcott, Woodbury

Hartland, Windsor
Windsor Southeast Supervisory Union
Supt. — See Windsor
Hartland S 300/K-8
97 Martinsville Rd 05048 802-436-2255
Judith Callens, prin. Fax 436-2091

Highgate Center, Franklin
Franklin Northwest Supervisory Union
Supt. — See Swanton
Highgate ES 400/K-6
PO Box 163 05459 802-868-4170
Madeline Young, prin. Fax 868-4572

Hinesburg, Chittenden
Chittendon South Supervisory Union
Supt. — See Shelburne
Hinesburg Community S 500/PK-8
10888 Route 116 05461 802-482-2106
Robert Goudreau, prin. Fax 482-2003

Huntington, Chittenden
Chittenden East Supervisory Union
Supt. — See Richmond
Brewster-Pierce ES 100/K-4
120 School St 05462 802-434-2074
Mark Trifilio, prin. Fax 434-5575

Hyde Park, Lamoille, Pop. 426
Lamoille North Supervisory Union 1,900/PK-12
95 Cricket Hill Rd 05655 802-888-3142
Dr. Debra Taylor, supt. Fax 888-7908
www.lnsu.org/
Hyde Park ES 200/PK-6
50 E Main St 05655 802-888-2237
Michelle Mathias, prin. Fax 888-8591
Lamoille Union MS 300/7-8
736 VT 15 W 05655 802-851-1300
Chris Hindes, prin. Fax 851-1397
Other Schools – See Eden, Jeffersonville, Johnson, Waterville

Irasburg, Orleans
Orleans Central Supervisory Union
Supt. — See Barton
Irasburg S 200/K-8
292 Route 58 E 05845 802-754-8810
Paul Simmons, prin. Fax 754-2855

Island Pond, Essex, Pop. 1,222
North Country Supervisory Union
Supt. — See Newport
Brighton S 100/K-8
PO Box 419 05846 802-723-4373
Phyllis Perkins, prin. Fax 723-4114

Isle La Motte, Grand Isle
Grand Isle Supervisory Union
Supt. — See North Hero
Isle La Motte ES 50/K-6
534 School St 05463 802-928-3231
Diane Reilly, prin. Fax 928-3702

Jamaica, Windham
Windham Central Supervisory Union
Supt. — See Townshend
Jamaica Village ES 100/K-6
PO Box 488 05343 802-874-4822
Laura Hazard, prin. Fax 874-7170

Jay, Orleans
North Country Supervisory Union
Supt. — See Newport
Jay/Westfield ES 100/K-6
257 Revoir Flat Rd 05859 802-988-4042
Dean Vervoort, prin. Fax 988-2944

Jeffersonville, Lamoille, Pop. 569
Lamoille North Supervisory Union
Supt. — See Hyde Park
Cambridge ES 300/PK-6
PO Box 160 05464 802-644-8821
Mary Anderson, prin. Fax 644-6531

Jericho, Chittenden, Pop. 1,405
Chittenden East Supervisory Union
Supt. — See Richmond
Browns River MS 500/5-8
20 River Rd 05465 802-899-3711
Nancy Guyette, prin. Fax 899-4281
Jericho ES 300/K-4
90 VT Route 15 05465 802-899-2272
Victoria Graf, prin. Fax 899-1059
Underhill I.D. ES 100/K-4
10 River Rd 05465 802-899-4680
Cindy Mackin, prin. Fax 899-4001

Johnson, Lamoille, Pop. 1,410
Lamoille North Supervisory Union
Supt. — See Hyde Park
Johnson ES 200/PK-6
57 College Hl 05656 802-635-2211
Brigid Scheffert, prin. Fax 635-7663

Killington, Rutland
Windsor Central Supervisory Union
Supt. — See Woodstock
Sherburne ES 100/K-6
686 Schoolhouse Rd 05751 802-422-3366
Loren Pepe, prin. Fax 422-3367

Lake Elmore, Lamoille
Lamoille South Supervisory Union
Supt. — See Morrisville
Lake Elmore ES 50/1-3
PO Box 122 05657 802-888-2966
Tracy Wrend, prin. Fax 888-2966

Leicester, Addison
Rutland Northeast Supervisory Union
Supt. — See Brandon
Leicester Central ES 100/PK-6
68 Schoolhouse Rd 05733 802-247-8825
Carol Eckels, prin. Fax 247-5619

Londonderry, Windham
Windsor Southwest Supervisory Union
Supt. — See Chester
Flood Brook S 300/K-8
PO Box 547 05148 802-824-6811
Patrick Walters, prin. Fax 824-4105

Lowell, Orleans
North Country Supervisory Union
Supt. — See Newport
Lowell Village S 100/K-8
52 Gelo Park Rd 05847 802-744-6641
Scott Boskind, prin. Fax 744-9989

Ludlow, Windsor, Pop. 1,037
Rutland Windsor Supervisory Union 400/K-12
8 High St 05149 802-228-2541
Judith Pullinen, supt. Fax 228-8359
www.rwsu.org/
Ludlow ES 100/K-6
45 Main St 05149 802-228-5151
Karen Trimboli, prin. Fax 228-5026
Other Schools – See Mount Holly, Plymouth

Lyndonville, Caledonia, Pop. 1,222
Caledonia North Supervisory Union 1,000/PK-8
PO Box 107 05851 802-626-6100
Victoria Scheufler, supt. Fax 626-3423
www.cnsu-schools.org/
Lyndon Town S 500/K-8
2591 Lily Pond Rd 05851 802-626-3209
Amy Gale, prin. Fax 626-5872
Other Schools – See East Haven, Sheffield, Sutton, West Burke

Manchester Center, Bennington, Pop. 1,574
Bennington-Rutland Supervisory Union
Supt. — See Sunderland
Manchester S 400/K-8
PO Box 1526 05255 802-362-1597
Jacqueline Wilson, prin. Fax 362-3883

Maple Street S 100/K-8
322 Maple St 05255 802-362-7137
Dr. Fran Bisselle, hdmstr. Fax 362-3492

Marlboro, Windham
Windham Central Supervisory Union
Supt. — See Townshend
Marlboro S 100/K-8
PO Box D 05344 802-254-2668
Francie Marbury, prin. Fax 254-8768

Middlebury, Addison, Pop. 6,007
Addison Central Supervisory Union 1,900/PK-12
49 Charles Ave 05753 802-382-1274
William Lee Sease, supt. Fax 388-0024
www.acsu.k12.vt.us/
Hogan ES 400/K-6
201 Mary Hogan Dr 05753 802-382-1400
Barbara Bourne, prin. Fax 382-1405
Middlebury Union MS 300/7-8
48 Deerfield Ln 05753 802-382-1600
Inga Duktig, prin. Fax 382-1215
Other Schools – See Bridport, Cornwall, Ripton, Salisbury, Shoreham, Weybridge

---

St. Mary S 100/PK-6
86 Shannon St 05753 802-388-8392
Monique Almquist, prin. Fax 388-8392

Middlesex, See Montpelier
Washington Central Supervisory Union
Supt. — See Barre
Rumney Memorial ES 200/PK-6
433 Shady Rill Rd 05602 802-223-5429
Adam Rosen, prin. Fax 223-0750

Middletown Springs, Rutland
Rutland Southwest Supervisory Union
Supt. — See Poultney
Middletown Springs ES 100/PK-6
PO Box 1267 05757 802-235-2365
Aaron Boynton, prin. Fax 235-9226

Milton, Chittenden, Pop. 1,557
Milton Town SD 1,800/PK-12
42 Herrick Ave 05468 802-893-3210
Martin Waldron, supt. Fax 893-3213
www.mtsd-vt.org
Milton ES 1,000/PK-6
42 Herrick Ave 05468 802-893-3215
Jennifer Wood, prin. Fax 893-3224
Milton JHS 300/7-8
17 Rebecca Lander Dr 05468 802-893-3230
Laurie Hodgdon, prin. Fax 893-3247

Monkton, Addison
Addison Northeast Supervisory Union
Supt. — See Bristol
Monkton Central ES 200/K-6
PO Box 40 05469 802-453-2314
Richard Jesset, prin. Fax 453-6123

Montgomery Center, Franklin
Franklin Northeast Supervisory Union
Supt. — See Richford
Montgomery S 100/K-8
249 School Dr 05471 802-326-4632
Beth O'Brien, prin. Fax 326-4618

Montpelier, Washington, Pop. 8,003
Montpelier SD 1,000/K-12
5 High School Dr Unit 1 05602 802-223-9796
Stephen Metcalf, supt. Fax 223-9795
www.mpsvt.org/MPS_district/index.htm
Main Street MS 200/6-8
170 Main St 05602 802-223-3404
Pamela Arnold, prin. Fax 223-9225
Union ES 400/K-5
1 Park Ave 05602 802-223-6343
Timothy Francke, prin. Fax 223-9219

Moretown, Washington
Washington West Supervisory Union
Supt. — See Waitsfield
Moretown ES 200/PK-6
940 Route 100 B 05660 802-496-3742
Deborah Lesure, prin. Fax 496-3749

Morgan, Orleans
North Country Supervisory Union
Supt. — See Newport
Hatton ES 50/K-6
PO Box 159 05853 802-895-2916
Miriam Benson, prin. Fax 895-4804

Morrisville, Lamoille, Pop. 2,057
Lamoille South Supervisory Union 1,700/K-12
PO Box 340 05661 802-888-4541
Tracy Wrend, supt. Fax 888-6710
www.lamoillesouthsu.org/
Morristown ES 400/K-5
548 Park St 05661 802-888-3101
Ed Oravec, prin. Fax 888-7550
Peoples Academy MS 300/6-8
202 Copley Ave 05661 802-888-1402
Wendy Baker, prin. Fax 888-6488
Other Schools – See Lake Elmore, Stowe

Bishop Marshall S 100/PK-8
680 Laporte Rd 05661 802-888-4758
Carrie Wilson, prin. Fax 888-3137

Mount Holly, Rutland
Rutland Windsor Supervisory Union
Supt. — See Ludlow
Mt. Holly ES 100/K-6
PO Box 45 05758 802-259-2392
Craig Hutt-Vater, prin. Fax 259-2692

Newbury, Orange, Pop. 431
Orange East Supervisory Union
Supt. — See Bradford
Newbury ES 100/K-6
PO Box 68 05051 802-866-5621
Carl Chambers, prin. Fax 866-3345

Newfane, Windham, Pop. 113
Windham Central Supervisory Union
Supt. — See Townshend
Newfane ES 100/K-6
14 School St 05345 802-365-7536
Bruce Garrow, prin. Fax 365-7177

New Haven, Addison
Addison Northeast Supervisory Union
Supt. — See Bristol
Beeman ES 100/K-6
50 North St 05472 802-453-2331
Steven Flint, prin. Fax 453-4637

Newport, Orleans, Pop. 5,207
North Country Supervisory Union 3,000/K-12
338 Highland Ave Ste 4 05855 802-334-5847
Robert Kern, supt. Fax 334-6528
www.northcountryschools.org
Newport City ES 300/K-6
166 Sias Ave 05855 802-334-2455
Robert Midi, prin. Fax 334-0161
Other Schools – See Coventry, Derby, Derby Line, Island Pond, Jay, Lowell, Morgan, Newport Center, North Troy, West Charleston

---

United Christian Academy 100/K-12
65 School St 05855 802-334-3112
Dr. Richard O'Hara, hdmstr. Fax 334-2305

Newport Center, Orleans
North Country Supervisory Union
Supt. — See Newport
Newport Town S 100/K-8
4212 VT Route 105 05857 802-334-5201
Natalie Wilcox, prin. Fax 334-7541

North Bennington, Bennington, Pop. 1,368
Southwest Vermont Supervisory Union
Supt. — See Bennington
North Bennington ES 100/K-6
PO Box 279 05257 802-442-5955
Tom Martin, prin. Fax 447-2397

North Clarendon, Rutland
Rutland South Supervisory Union 1,100/K-12
PO Box 87 05759 802-775-3264
Walter Goetz, supt. Fax 775-8063
www.rssu.org/
Clarendon ES 200/K-6
84 Grange Hall Rd 05759 802-775-5379
Ruth Ann Barker, prin. Fax 747-7584
Other Schools – See Shrewsbury, Wallingford

Northfield, Washington, Pop. 3,157
Washington South Supervisory Union 800/PK-12
37 Cross St 05663 802-485-7755
Michele Fagan Ed.D., supt. Fax 485-3348
wssu.org
Northfield ES 300/PK-5
10 Cross St 05663 802-485-6161
Risa Mancillas, prin. Fax 485-3471
Other Schools – See Roxbury

North Hero, Grand Isle
Grand Isle Supervisory Union 700/K-8
5038 US Route 2 05474 802-372-6921
Richard Taylor, supt. Fax 372-4898
www.gisu.org
North Hero S 100/K-8
6441 US Route 2 05474 802-372-8866
Joanna Bennink, prin. Fax 372-4867
Other Schools – See Alburg, Grand Isle, Isle La Motte, South Hero

North Troy, Orleans, Pop. 621
North Country Supervisory Union
Supt. — See Newport
Troy S 200/K-8
PO Box 110 05859 802-988-2565
Arlynn Abramson, prin. Fax 988-2635

Norwich, Windsor
Hanover SD
Supt. — See Hanover, NH
Cross ES K-6
PO Box 900 05055 802-649-1703
Linda Kelley, prin. Fax 649-3640

Orleans, Orleans, Pop. 847
Orleans Central Supervisory Union
Supt. — See Barton
Orleans S 100/K-8
53 School St 05860 802-754-6650
Sandra Stanley, prin. Fax 754-2636

Orwell, Addison
Addison-Rutland Supervisory Union
Supt. — See Fair Haven
Orwell Village S 100/K-8
494 Main St 05760 802-948-2871
Sue DeCarolis, prin. Fax 948-2754

Peacham, Caledonia
Caledonia Central Supervisory Union
Supt. — See Danville
Peacham ES 50/PK-6
PO Box 271 05862 802-592-3513
Wendy Nelson, prin. Fax 592-3517

Pittsfield, Rutland
Windsor Northwest Supervisory Union 600/PK-12
PO Box 830 05762 802-746-7974
Timothy Mock, supt. Fax 746-8647
www.wnwsu.org/
Other Schools – See Bethel, Rochester, Stockbridge

Pittsford, Rutland
Rutland Northeast Supervisory Union
Supt. — See Brandon
Lothrop ES 300/PK-6
3447 US Route 7 05763 802-483-6361
Gregory West, prin. Fax 483-2146

Plainfield, Washington
Washington Central Supervisory Union
Supt. — See Barre
Calais ES 100/PK-6
321 Lightning Ridge Rd 05667 802-454-7777
Grace Hoffman, prin. Fax 454-1580

Washington NE Supervisory Union 700/PK-12
PO Box 470 05667 802-454-9924
George Burlison, supt. Fax 454-9934
Twinfield Union S 400/PK-12
106 Nasmith Brook Rd 05667 802-426-3213
Owen Bradley, prin. Fax 426-4085
Other Schools – See Cabot

Plymouth, Windsor
Rutland Windsor Supervisory Union
Supt. — See Ludlow
Plymouth ES 50/K-6
35 School Dr 05056 802-672-3666
Susan O'Brien, prin. Fax 672-3066

Poultney, Rutland, Pop. 1,556
Rutland Southwest Supervisory Union 700/PK-12
168 York St 05764 802-287-5286
Joan Paustian Ed.D., supt. Fax 287-2284
www.rswsu.org
Poultney ES 200/K-6
96 School Cir 05764 802-287-5212
Kristen Caliguiri, prin. Fax 287-2470
Other Schools – See Middletown Springs, Tinmouth, Wells

Pownal, Bennington
Southwest Vermont Supervisory Union
Supt. — See Bennington
Pownal ES 200/K-6
94 Schoolhouse Rd 05261 802-823-7333
Joy Kitchell, prin. Fax 823-4031

Proctor, Rutland
Rutland Central Supervisory Union
Supt. — See Rutland
Proctor ES 200/PK-6
14 School St 05765 802-459-2225
Nancy Erickson, prin. Fax 459-2103

Proctorsville, Windsor
Windsor Southwest Supervisory Union
Supt. — See Chester
Cavendish Town ES 100/K-6
PO Box 236 05153 802-226-7758
George Thomson, prin. Fax 226-7312

Putney, Windham
Windham Northeast Supervisory Union
Supt. — See Bellows Falls
Westminster West ES 1-4
3724 Westminster West Rd 05346 802-387-5756
Steven Tullar, prin. Fax 387-4309

Windham Southeast Supervisory Union
Supt. — See Brattleboro
Putney Central S 200/K-8
182 Westminster Rd 05346 802-387-5521
Amelia Stone, prin. Fax 387-2776

Grammar S 100/PK-8
69 Hickory Ridge Rd S 05346 802-387-5364
Steve Lorenz, prin. Fax 387-4744
Greenwood S 50/4-9
14 Greenwood Ln 05346 802-387-4545
Stewart Miller, hdmstr. Fax 387-5396

Quechee, Windsor
Hartford SD
Supt. — See White River Junction
Ottauquechee S 200/PK-5
PO Box 353 05059 802-295-8655
Amos Kornfeld, prin. Fax 295-8656

Upper Valley Waldorf S 200/PK-8
PO Box 709 05059 802-296-2496
Alexandra Keats, admin. Fax 296-5075

Randolph, Orange
Orange Southwest Supervisory Union 1,000/K-12
24 Central St 05060 802-728-5052
Brent Kay, supt. Fax 728-4844
www.orangesw.k12.vt.us/
Braintree ES 100/K-6
66 Bent Hill Rd 05060 802-728-9373
Nancy Frenette, prin. Fax 728-5044
Randolph ES 300/K-6
40 Ayers Brook Rd 05060 802-728-9555
Shirley Stewart, prin. Fax 728-6709
Other Schools – See Brookfield

Reading, Windsor
Windsor Central Supervisory Union
Supt. — See Woodstock
Reading ES 50/K-6
PO Box 176 05062 802-484-7230
Ray Pentkowski, prin. Fax 484-3818

Readsboro, Bennington
Windham Southwest Supervisory Union
Supt. — See Wilmington
Readsboro S 100/PK-8
301 Phelps Ln 05350 802-423-7786
Debra Vaughan, prin. Fax 423-9914

Richford, Franklin, Pop. 1,417
Franklin Northeast Supervisory Union 1,700/K-12
PO Box 130 05476 802-848-7661
Jay Nichols, supt. Fax 848-3531
fnesu.net/
Berkshire S 200/K-8
4850 Water Tower Rd 05476 802-933-2290
Lynn Cota-Caforia, prin. Fax 933-2812
Richford ES 200/K-6
1 Elementary School Rd 05476 802-848-7453
Roger Gagne, prin. Fax 848-7720
Other Schools – See Bakersfield, Enosburg Falls, Montgomery Center

Richmond, Chittenden
Chittenden East Supervisory Union 2,800/K-12
PO Box 282 05477 802-434-2128
James Massingham, supt. Fax 434-2196
www.cesu.k12.vt.us
Camels Hump MS 400/5-8
173 School St 05477 802-434-2188
Mark Carbone, prin. Fax 434-2192
Richmond ES 300/K-4
125 School St 05477 802-434-2461
Lauren Wooden, prin. Fax 434-7241
Other Schools – See Huntington, Jericho, Underhill Center, Waterbury

Ripton, Addison
Addison Central Supervisory Union
Supt. — See Middlebury
Ripton ES 100/PK-6
PO Box 155 05766 802-388-2208
Jane Phinney, prin. Fax 388-2208

Rochester, Windsor
Windsor Northwest Supervisory Union
Supt. — See Pittsfield
Rochester S 200/K-12
222 S Main St 05767 802-767-3161
John Poljacik, prin. Fax 767-1130

Roxbury, Washington
Washington South Supervisory Union
Supt. — See Northfield
Roxbury Village ES 100/PK-6
1559 Roxbury Rd 05669 802-485-7768
Abigail Sessions, prin. Fax 485-9304

Rutland, Rutland, Pop. 17,046
Rutland Central Supervisory Union 1,100/PK-12
257 S Main St 05701 802-775-4342
Wendy Savery, supt. Fax 775-7319
www.rcsu.org
Rutland Town S 300/K-8
1612 Post Rd 05701 802-775-0566
Patricia Beaumont, prin. Fax 775-8951
Other Schools – See Proctor, West Rutland

Rutland City SD 2,700/K-12
6 Church St 05701 802-773-1900
Mary Moran, supt. Fax 773-1927
rutlandcitypublicschools.org/
Rutland IS 700/3-6
65 Library Ave 05701 802-773-1932
Jay Slenker, prin. Fax 773-1913
Rutland MS 400/7-8
65 Library Ave 05701 802-773-1960
Wilfred Cunningham, prin. Fax 773-1914
Rutland Northeast ES 300/K-2
117 Temple St 05701 802-773-1940
Robert Johnson, prin. Fax 773-1911
Rutland Northwest ES 300/K-2
80 Pierpoint Ave 05701 802-773-1946
Kristin Hubert, prin. Fax 773-1912

Christ the King S 200/PK-8
60 S Main St 05701 802-773-0500
Carol Wincowski, prin. Fax 773-0554
Green Mountain Christian S 50/1-9
158 Stratton Rd 05701 802-775-3178
Greg Barlow, prin.
Rutland Area Christian S 100/PK-9
112 Lincoln Ave 05701 802-775-0709
Dawn Doherty, prin. Fax 786-0111

Saint Albans, Franklin, Pop. 7,565
Franklin Central Supervisory Union 1,700/PK-12
28 Catherine St 05478 802-524-2600
Robert Rosane, supt. Fax 524-1540
www.franklincsu.org/
St. Albans City S 800/PK-8
29 Bellows St 05478 802-527-0565
Joan Cavallo, prin. Fax 527-0153
St. Albans Town Educational Center 700/PK-8
169 S Main St 05478 802-527-7191
Angela Stebbins, prin. Fax 527-7043
Other Schools – See Fairfield

Franklin West Supervisory Union
Supt. — See Fairfax
Georgia S 600/K-8
4416 Ethan Allen Hwy 05478 802-524-6358
Flora Hurteau, prin. Fax 524-1781

Saint Johnsbury, Caledonia, Pop. 6,424
Essex-Caledonia Supervisory Union
Supt. — See Concord
Waterford S 200/PK-8
276 Duck Pond Rd 05819 802-748-9393
Donald Van Nostrand, prin. Fax 748-2806

Saint Johnsbury SD 700/PK-8
257 Western Ave 05819 802-748-4744
Nicole Saginor Ed.D., supt. Fax 748-2542
www.stjsd.org/
Saint Johnsbury S 700/PK-8
257 Western Ave 05819 802-748-8912
Marion Anastasia, prin. Fax 748-1095

Good Shepherd S 200/PK-8
PO Box 384 05819 802-751-8223
Karen Haskins, prin. Fax 751-8223

St. Johnsbury S 50/1-8
54 Southard St 05819 802-748-9528
David Knott, prin. Fax 748-9528

Salisbury, Addison
Addison Central Supervisory Union
Supt. — See Middlebury
Salisbury Community ES 100/K-6
286 Kelly Cross Rd 05769 802-352-4291
Fernanda Canales, prin. Fax 352-1067

Saxtons River, Windham, Pop. 496
Windham Northeast Supervisory Union
Supt. — See Bellows Falls
Saxtons River ES 100/K-5
PO Box 308 05154 802-869-2637
David Lesser, prin. Fax 869-2631

Shaftsbury, Bennington
Southwest Vermont Supervisory Union
Supt. — See Bennington
Shaftsbury ES 200/K-6
150 Buck Hill Rd 05262 802-442-4373
Jim Harwood, prin. Fax 442-3588

Sharon, Windsor
Orange-Windsor Supervisory Union
Supt. — See South Royalton
Sharon ES 100/K-6
75 Vermont Route 132 05065 802-763-7425
Barrett Williams, prin. Fax 763-2056

Sheffield, Caledonia
Caledonia North Supervisory Union
Supt. — See Lyndonville
Millers Run S 200/PK-8
3249 VT Route 122 05866 802-626-9755
Nancy Croteau, prin. Fax 626-4316

Shelburne, Chittenden
Chittendon South Supervisory Union 4,200/PK-12
5420 Shelburne Rd Ste 300 05482 802-383-1234
Elaine Pinckney, admin. Fax 383-1242
www.cssu.org/
Shelburne Community S 800/PK-8
345 Harbor Rd 05482 802-985-3336
John Bossange, prin. Fax 985-8951
Other Schools – See Charlotte, Hinesburg, Williston

Lake Champlain Waldorf S 300/PK-8
359 Turtle Ln 05482 802-985-2827
Andrea Bayer, dir. Fax 985-2834
Renaissance S, PO Box 339 05482 100/K-7
Louise Piche, prin. 802-985-8209

Sheldon, Franklin
Franklin Northwest Supervisory Union
Supt. — See Swanton
Sheldon S 300/K-8
78 Poor Farm Rd 05483 802-933-4909
Leonard Rosenberg, prin. Fax 933-6405

Shoreham, Addison
Addison Central Supervisory Union
Supt. — See Middlebury
Shoreham ES 100/K-6
130 School Rd 05770 802-897-7181
Heather Best, prin. Fax 897-2463

Shrewsbury, Rutland
Rutland South Supervisory Union
Supt. — See North Clarendon
Shrewsbury ES 100/K-6
300 Mountain School Rd 05738 802-492-3435
Deb Fishwick, prin. Fax 492-6107

South Burlington, Chittenden, Pop. 16,993
South Burlington SD 2,500/K-12
550 Dorset St 05403 802-652-7250
John Everitt, supt. Fax 652-7257
www.sbschools.net
Chamberlin ES 300/K-5
262 White St 05403 802-652-7400
Judith Maynard, prin. Fax 658-9048
Marcotte Central ES 400/K-5
10 Market St 05403 802-652-7200
Susan Luck, prin. Fax 658-9047
Orchard ES 300/K-5
2 Baldwin Ave 05403 802-652-7300
Rick Ebel, prin. Fax 658-9037
Tuttle MS 600/6-8
500 Dorset St 05403 802-652-7100
Joseph O'Brien, prin. Fax 652-7152

South Hero, Grand Isle
Grand Isle Supervisory Union
Supt. — See North Hero
Folsom S 100/K-8
75 South St 05486 802-372-6600
Michael Freed-Thall, prin. Fax 372-5188

South Pomfret, Windsor
Windsor Central Supervisory Union
Supt. — See Woodstock
Pomfret ES 100/PK-6
PO Box 130 05067 802-457-1234
Peggy Spencer, prin. Fax 457-3366

South Royalton, Windsor
Orange-Windsor Supervisory Union 900/PK-12
3590 VT Route 14 05068 802-763-8840
David Bickford Ed.D., supt. Fax 763-3235
www.owsu.org/
South Royalton S 400/PK-12
223 S Windsor St 05068 802-763-8844
Shaun Pickett, prin. Fax 763-3233
Other Schools – See Chelsea, Sharon, South Strafford, Tunbridge

South Strafford, Orange
Orange-Windsor Supervisory Union
Supt. — See South Royalton

Newton S 100/K-8
PO Box 239 05070 802-765-4351
Fax 765-4785

Springfield, Windsor, Pop. 4,207
Springfield SD 1,400/K-12
60 Park St 05156 802-885-5141
Dr. Frank Perotti, supt. Fax 885-8169
www.ssdvt.org
Elm Hill ES 100/K-5
10 Hoover St 05156 802-885-5154
Jonni Nichols, prin. Fax 885-5159
Park Street ES 300/K-5
60 Park St 05156 802-885-4774
Joan Nagle, prin. Fax 885-1173
Riverside MS 300/6-8
13 Fairground Rd 05156 802-885-8490
Becky Read, prin. Fax 885-8442
Union Street ES 200/K-5
43 Union St 05156 802-885-5155
Cheryl Hoffman, prin. Fax 885-8481

Stamford, Bennington
Windham Southwest Supervisory Union
Supt. — See Wilmington
Stamford S 100/K-8
986 Main Rd 05352 802-694-1379
Beth Keplinger, prin. Fax 694-1636

Starksboro, Addison
Addison Northeast Supervisory Union
Supt. — See Bristol
Robinson ES 100/K-6
PO Box 10 05487 802-453-2949
Dan Noel, prin. Fax 453-6062

Stockbridge, Windsor
Windsor Northwest Supervisory Union
Supt. — See Pittsfield
Stockbridge Central ES 100/PK-6
2933 VT Route 107 05772 802-234-9248
Michele Ricci, prin. Fax 767-9248

Stowe, Lamoille, Pop. 500
Lamoille South Supervisory Union
Supt. — See Morrisville
Stowe ES 300/K-5
PO Box 760 05672 802-253-4154
Richard Smiles, prin. Fax 253-6915
Stowe MS 200/6-8
413 Barrows Rd 05672 802-253-6913
Melanie Carpenter, prin. Fax 253-5314

Sudbury, Rutland
Rutland Northeast Supervisory Union
Supt. — See Brandon
Sudbury Country S 50/PK-6
31 Schoolhouse Ln 05733 802-623-7771
Susan Coombs, prin. Fax 623-7772

Sunderland, Bennington
Bennington-Rutland Supervisory Union 1,000/K-8
6378 VT Route 7A 05250 802-362-2452
Daniel French, supt. Fax 362-2455
www.brsu.org/
Sunderland ES 100/K-6
98 Bear Ridge Rd 05250 802-375-6100
Melody Troy, prin. Fax 375-6555
Other Schools – See Danby, Dorset, Manchester Center, West Pawlet

Sutton, Caledonia
Caledonia North Supervisory Union
Supt. — See Lyndonville
Sutton Village S 100/K-8
95 Underpass Rd 05867 802-467-3492
Roberta Stradling, prin. Fax 467-3023

Swanton, Franklin, Pop. 2,573
Franklin Northwest Supervisory Union 2,500/PK-12
100 Robin Hood Dr 05488 802-868-4967
Dr. John McCarthy, supt. Fax 868-4265
www.fnwsu.org
Babcock ES 300/PK-2
113 Grand Ave 05488 802-868-5346
Julie Benay, prin. Fax 868-3389
Swanton Central ES 400/2-6
24 4th St 05488 802-868-5346
Julie Benay, prin. Fax 868-4861
Other Schools – See Franklin, Highgate Center, Sheldon

Thetford, Orange
Orange East Supervisory Union
Supt. — See Bradford
Thetford ES 200/K-6
PO Box 182 05074 802-785-2426
Alice Worth, prin. Fax 785-2645

Tinmouth, Rutland
Rutland Southwest Supervisory Union
Supt. — See Poultney
Tinmouth ES 50/PK-6
573 Route 140 05773 802-446-2458
Susan McKelvie, prin. Fax 446-2466

Townshend, Windham
Windham Central Supervisory Union 1,000/K-12
1219 VT Route 30 05353 802-365-9510
Dr. Steven John, supt. Fax 365-7934
www.wcsu46.org
Townshend ES 100/K-6
PO Box 236 05353 802-365-7506
Deborah Leggott, prin. Fax 365-7955
Other Schools – See Brookline, East Dover, Jamaica, Marlboro, Newfane, Wardsboro, Windham

Tunbridge, Orange
Orange-Windsor Supervisory Union
Supt. — See South Royalton
Tunbridge Central S 100/K-8
PO Box 8 05077 802-889-3310
Kathleen Ball, prin. Fax 889-3214

Underhill Center, Chittenden
Chittenden East Supervisory Union
Supt. — See Richmond
Underhill Central ES 100/K-4
6 Irish Settlement Rd 05490 802-899-4676
Michael Berry, prin. Fax 899-5173

Vergennes, Addison, Pop. 2,763
Addison Northwest Supervisory Union 1,200/K-12
48 Green St Ste 1 05491 802-877-3332
Thomas O'Brien, supt. Fax 877-3628
www.anwsu.org
Addison Central ES 100/K-6
121 VT Route 17 W 05491 802-759-2131
Wayne Howe, prin. Fax 759-2631
Vergennes Union ES 300/K-6
43 East St 05491 802-877-3761
Sanford Bassett, prin. Fax 877-1115
Other Schools – See Ferrisburg

Champlain Valley Christian S 100/K-12
2 Church St 05491 802-877-3640
Elaine North, admin. Fax 877-1103

Vernon, Windham
Windham Southeast Supervisory Union
Supt. — See Brattleboro
Vernon ES 200/K-6
381 Governor Hunt Rd 05354 802-254-5373
John Reed, prin. Fax 257-0988

Waitsfield, Washington
Washington West Supervisory Union 2,000/PK-12
1673 Main St Ste A 05673 802-496-2272
Brigid Scheffert, supt. Fax 496-6515
www.wwsu.org/
Waitsfield ES, 3951 Main St 05673 200/PK-6
Kaiya Korb, prin. 802-496-3643
Other Schools – See Duxbury, Fayston, Moretown, Warren, Waterbury

Wallingford, Rutland, Pop. 1,148
Rutland South Supervisory Union
Supt. — See North Clarendon
Wallingford ES 200/K-6
PO Box 309 05773 802-446-2141
Jason Morse, prin. Fax 446-3354

Wardsboro, Windham
Windham Central Supervisory Union
Supt. — See Townshend
Wardsboro ES 100/K-6
PO Box 107 05355 802-896-6210
Rosemary FitzSimons, prin. Fax 896-6687

Warren, Washington
Washington West Supervisory Union
Supt. — See Waitsfield
Warren ES, 293 School Rd 05674 100/PK-6
Andreas Lehner, prin. 802-496-2487

Washington, Orange
Orange North Supervisory Union
Supt. — See Williamstown
Washington Village S 100/PK-8
72 School Ln 05675 802-883-2312
Charles Witters, prin. Fax 883-5411

Waterbury, Washington, Pop. 1,683
Chittenden East Supervisory Union
Supt. — See Richmond
Smilie Memorial ES 100/K-4
2712 Theodore Roosevelt Hwy 05676 802-434-2757
Sheila Rivers, prin. Fax 434-2098

Washington West Supervisory Union
Supt. — See Waitsfield
Thatcher Brook PS 400/PK-4
47 Stowe St 05676 802-244-7195
Don Schneider, prin. Fax 244-1158

Waterville, Lamoille
Lamoille North Supervisory Union
Supt. — See Hyde Park
Waterville ES 100/PK-6
3414 VT Route 109 05492 802-644-2224
Bonny Grant, prin. Fax 644-2726

Websterville, Washington

Websterville Baptist Christian S 100/K-12
PO Box 1 05678 802-479-0141
William Croteau, admin. Fax 476-7834

Wells, Rutland
Rutland Southwest Supervisory Union
Supt. — See Poultney
Wells Village S 100/K-6
135 VT Route 30 05774 802-645-0386
Linda O'Leary, prin. Fax 645-1906

Wells River, Orange, Pop. 342
Blue Mountain SD 400/PK-12
2420 Route 302 05081 802-757-2766
Richard Pike, supt. Fax 757-2790
www.bmuschool.org
Blue Mountain Union S 21 400/PK-12
2420 Route 302 05081 802-757-2711
Carol Curtis, prin. Fax 757-3894

West Burke, Caledonia, Pop. 367
Caledonia North Supervisory Union
Supt. — See Lyndonville
Burke Town S 200/K-8
3293 Burke Hollow Rd 05871 802-467-3385
Janet Cerro, prin. Fax 467-3323
Newark Street S 50/K-8
1448 Newark St 05871 802-467-3401
Mary Riggie, prin. Fax 467-1001

West Charleston, Orleans
North Country Supervisory Union
Supt. — See Newport
Charleston S 100/K-8
255 Center School Rd 05872 802-895-2915
Audrone Rastonis, prin. Fax 895-2611

West Danville, Caledonia
Caledonia Central Supervisory Union
Supt. — See Danville
Walden S 100/PK-8
135 Cahoon Farm Rd 05873 802-563-3000
Martha Dubuque, prin. Fax 563-3030

West Fairlee, Orange
Rivendell Interstate SD
Supt. — See Orford, NH
Westshire ES 100/K-5
744 VT Route 113 05083 802-333-4668
Shawn Gonyaw, prin. Fax 333-4744

Westford, Chittenden
Chittenden Central Supervisory Union
Supt. — See Essex Junction
Westford S 200/PK-8
146 Brookside Rd 05494 802-878-5932
David Wells, prin. Fax 879-0874

West Halifax, Windham
Windham Southwest Supervisory Union
Supt. — See Wilmington
Halifax S 100/K-8
246 Branch Rd 05358 802-368-2888
Stephanie Aldrich, prin. Fax 368-7847

Westminster, Windham, Pop. 269
Windham Northeast Supervisory Union
Supt. — See Bellows Falls
Westminster Center ES 200/K-6
PO Box 145 05158 802-722-3241
Steven Tullar, prin. Fax 722-9536

West Pawlet, Rutland
Bennington-Rutland Supervisory Union
Supt. — See Sunderland
Mettawee Community S 200/K-6
5788 VT Route 153 05775 802-645-9009
Nancy Mark, prin. Fax 645-0907

West Rutland, Rutland, Pop. 2,246
Rutland Central Supervisory Union
Supt. — See Rutland
West Rutland S 400/PK-12
713 Main St 05777 802-438-2288
Joseph Bowen, prin. Fax 438-5708

Weybridge, Addison
Addison Central Supervisory Union
Supt. — See Middlebury
Weybridge ES 100/K-6
210 Quaker Village Rd 05753 802-545-2113
Christina Johnson, prin. Fax 545-2439

White River Junction, Windsor, Pop. 2,521
Hartford SD 1,800/PK-12
73 Highland Ave 05001 802-295-8600
Donald LaPlante, supt. Fax 295-8602
www.hartfordschools.net/
Dothan Brook S 300/K-5
2300 Christian St 05001 802-295-8647
Sarah Carter, prin. Fax 295-8649
Hartford Memorial MS 400/6-8
245 Highland Ave 05001 802-295-8640
John Grant, prin. Fax 295-8602
White River S 200/PK-5
102 Pine St 05001 802-295-8650
Christopher Ashley, prin. Fax 295-8652
Other Schools – See Quechee

Mid-Vermont Christian S 100/PK-12
399 W Gilson Ave 05001 802-295-6800
Robert Bracy, hdmstr. Fax 295-3748

Whiting, Addison
Rutland Northeast Supervisory Union
Supt. — See Brandon
Whiting ES 50/PK-6
87 S Main St 05778 802-623-7991
Donn Marcus, prin. Fax 623-7992

Whitingham, Windham
Windham Southwest Supervisory Union
Supt. — See Wilmington
Whitingham - Twin Valley S 100/PK-8
4299 VT Route 100 05361 802-368-2880
Lucy Johnson, prin. Fax 368-7382

Williamstown, Orange
Orange North Supervisory Union 800/PK-12
111 Brush Hill Rd 05679 802-433-5818
Douglas Shiok, supt. Fax 433-5825
www.onsu.org/
Williamstown ES 300/PK-5
100 Brush Hill Rd 05679 802-433-6653
Elaine Watson Ed.D., prin. Fax 433-6266
Other Schools – See East Barre, Washington

Williston, Chittenden
Chittendon South Supervisory Union
Supt. — See Shelburne
Brook PS K-4
497 Talcott Rd 05495 802-878-2762
John Terko, prin. Fax 879-5829
Williston Central S 1,100/K-8
195 Central School Dr 05495 802-878-2762
Jackie Parks, prin. Fax 879-5830

Wilmington, Windham
Windham Southwest Supervisory Union 700/PK-12
211 Route 9 W 05363 802-464-1300
M. Wright, supt. Fax 464-1303
www.windhamsw.k12.vt.us/
Deerfield Valley ES 200/PK-5
360 VT Route 100 N 05363 802-464-5177
Mario Cruz-Davis, prin. Fax 464-1246
Other Schools – See Readsboro, Stamford, West Halifax, Whitingham

Windham, Windham
Windham Central Supervisory Union
Supt. — See Townshend
Windham ES 50/K-6
5940 Windham Hill Rd 05359 802-874-4159
Fax 874-4929

Windsor, Windsor, Pop. 3,714
Windsor Southeast Supervisory Union 1,100/K-12
105 Main St Ste 200 05089 802-674-2144
Fax 674-6357
www.windsor.k12.vt.us/
Windsor State Street ES 200/K-6
127 State St 05089 802-674-2310
JoAnne Ladd, prin. Fax 674-9803
Other Schools – See Ascutney, Brownsville, Hartland

Winooski, Chittenden, Pop. 6,353
Winooski SD 800/PK-12
60 Normand St 05404 802-655-0485
Steve Perkins, supt. Fax 655-7602
www.winooski.k12.vt.us
Kennedy ES 400/PK-5
70 Normand St 05404 802-655-0411
Mary O'Rourke, prin. Fax 654-1032
Winooski MS 200/6-8
80 Normand St 05404 802-655-3530
Mary Woodruff, prin. Fax 655-6538

St. Francis Xavier S 200/PK-8
5 Saint Peter St 05404 802-655-2600
Jesse Gaudette, prin. Fax 655-3096

Wolcott, Lamoille
Orleans Southwest Supervisory Union
Supt. — See Hardwick
Wolcott ES 100/K-6
PO Box 179 05680 802-472-6551
Merri Greenia, prin. Fax 472-6295

Woodbury, Washington
Orleans Southwest Supervisory Union
Supt. — See Hardwick
Woodbury ES 100/K-6
PO Box 28 05681 802-472-5715
Sharon Fortune, prin. Fax 472-6923

Woodstock, Windsor, Pop. 961
Windsor Central Supervisory Union 1,100/PK-12
496 Woodstock Rd Ste 2 05091 802-457-1213
Meg Gallagher, supt. Fax 457-2989
www.wcsu.net/
Woodstock ES 200/K-6
15 South St 05091 802-457-2522
Karen White, prin. Fax 457-3732
Woodstock Union MS 200/7-8
496 Woodstock Rd Ste 1 05091 802-457-1330
Dana Peterson, prin. Fax 457-5048
Other Schools – See Barnard, Bridgewater, Killington, Reading, South Pomfret

Worcester, Washington
Washington Central Supervisory Union
Supt. — See Barre
Doty Memorial ES 100/PK-6
PO Box 162 05682 802-223-5656
David Hartnett, prin. Fax 223-0216

VIRGINIA

VIRGINIA DEPARTMENT OF EDUCATION
PO Box 2120, Richmond 23218-2120
Telephone 804-225-2020
Fax 804-371-2099
Website http://www.pen.k12.va.us

Superintendent of Public Instruction Dr. Patricia Wright

VIRGINIA BOARD OF EDUCATION
PO Box 2120, Richmond 23218-2120

President Dr. Mark Emblidge

PUBLIC, PRIVATE AND CATHOLIC ELEMENTARY SCHOOLS

Abingdon, Washington, Pop. 7,925
Washington County SD 7,500/PK-12
812 Thompson Dr 24210 276-739-3003
Dr. Alan Lee, supt. Fax 623-4137
www.wcs.k12.va.us
Abingdon ES 500/PK-5
19431 Woodland Hills Rd 24210 276-739-3400
Andy Cox, prin. Fax 623-4121
Greendale ES 400/PK-5
13092 McGuffie Rd 24210 276-739-3500
Sherry King, prin. Fax 623-4102
Stanley MS 700/6-8
297 Stanley St 24210 276-739-3300
Kathy Laster, prin. Fax 676-1945
Watauga ES 500/PK-5
23181 Watauga Rd 24211 276-739-3600
Dr. Ann Abel, prin. Fax 628-1847
Other Schools – See Bristol, Damascus, Glade Spring, Meadowview

Accomac, Accomack, Pop. 545
Accomack County SD 5,300/PK-12
PO Box 330 23301 757-787-5754
W. Richard Bull, supt. Fax 787-2951
sbo.accomack.k12.va.us
Accawmacke ES 500/PK-5
26230 Drummondtown Rd 23301 757-787-8013
Clara Chandler, prin. Fax 787-8032
Other Schools – See Chincoteague, Mappsville, Melfa, Oak Hall, Onley, Parksley, Tangier

Afton, Nelson
Nelson County SD
Supt. — See Lovingston
Rockfish River ES 400/PK-5
200 Chapel Hollow Rd 22920 434-361-1791
Nita Hughes, prin. Fax 361-1795

Alberta, Brunswick, Pop. 303
Brunswick County SD
Supt. — See Lawrenceville
Red Oak-Sturgeon ES 300/PK-5
PO Box 398 23821 434-949-7820
Carolyn Meredith, prin. Fax 949-7519

Aldie, Loudoun
Loudoun County SD
Supt. — See Ashburn
Aldie ES 100/PK-5
PO Box 25 20105 703-444-7400
Jennifer Rueckert, prin. Fax 444-7401
Arcola ES PK-5
41740 Tall Cedar Pkwy 20105 703-957-4390
Dr. Clark Bowers, prin. Fax 327-7801
Mercer MS 1,100/6-8
42149 Greenstone Dr 20105 703-957-4340
Ric Gauriloff, prin. Fax 444-8068
Pinebrook ES K-5
25480 Mindful Ct 20105 703-957-4325
Dawn Haddock, prin. Fax 542-7178

Alexandria, Alexandria, Pop. 135,337
Alexandria CSD 9,600/PK-12
2000 N Beauregard St 22311 703-824-6600
Dr. Morton Sherman, supt. Fax 824-6699
www.acps.k12.va.us
Adams ES 600/PK-5
5651 Rayburn Ave 22311 703-824-6970
Mary Gibson, prin. Fax 379-4853
Barrett ES 200/K-5
1115 Martha Custis Dr 22302 703-824-6960
Annetta Lawson, prin. Fax 379-3782
Hammond MS 1,100/6-8
4646 Seminary Rd 22304 703-461-4100
Randolph Mitchell, prin. Fax 461-4111
Henry ES 400/K-5
4643 Taney Ave 22304 703-461-4170
Coleen Mann, prin. Fax 823-3350
Jefferson-Houston S for Arts & Academics 400/PK-5
1501 Cameron St 22314 703-706-4400
Kimberly Graves, prin. Fax 836-7923
Kelly S for Math Science & Technology 400/K-5
3600 Commonwealth Ave 22305 703-706-4420
Brandon Davis, prin. Fax 706-4425
Lyles-Crouch Traditional Academy 300/K-5
530 S Saint Asaph St 22314 703-706-4430
Patricia Zissios, prin. Fax 684-0252
MacArthur ES 500/K-5
1101 Janneys Ln 22302 703-461-4190
Deborah Thompson, prin. Fax 370-2719
Mason ES 400/K-5
2601 Cameron Mills Rd 22302 703-706-4470
Dawn Feltman, prin. Fax 683-9011
Maury ES 200/K-5
600 Russell Rd 22301 703-706-4440
Lucretia Jackson, prin. Fax 683-5146
Mt. Vernon Community S 500/PK-5
2601 Commonwealth Ave 22305 703-706-4460
Scott Coleman, prin. Fax 706-4466
Polk ES 400/K-5
5000 Polk Ave 22304 703-461-4180
Michael Brown, prin. Fax 751-8614
Ramsay ES 600/K-5
5700 Sanger Ave 22311 703-824-6950
Kathy Taylor, prin. Fax 379-7824
Tucker ES 600/K-5
435 Ferdinand Day Dr 22304 703-933-6300
Loretta Scott, prin. Fax 212-8465
Washington MS 1,000/6-8
1005 Mount Vernon Ave 22301 703-706-4500
Keisha Boggan, prin. Fax 706-4507

Fairfax County SD
Supt. — See Falls Church
Belle View ES 400/K-6
6701 Fort Hunt Rd 22307 703-660-8300
Tom Kuntz, prin. Fax 660-8397
Bren Mar Park ES 400/K-5
6344 Beryl Rd 22312 703-914-7200
Anita Lynch, prin. Fax 914-7297
Bucknell ES 300/PK-6
6925 University Dr 22307 703-660-2900
Joanne Jackson, prin. Fax 660-2997
Bush Hill ES 400/K-6
5927 Westchester St 22310 703-924-5600
Jack Pitzer, prin. Fax 924-5697
Cameron ES 500/K-6
3434 Campbell Dr 22303 703-329-2100
George Towery, prin. Fax 329-2197
Clermont ES 400/K-6
5720 Clermont Dr 22310 703-921-2400
Janet Molan, prin. Fax 921-2497
Fort Hunt ES 600/K-6
8832 Linton Ln 22308 703-619-2600
Carol Coose, prin. Fax 619-2697
Franconia ES 500/K-6
6043 Franconia Rd 22310 703-822-2200
Merrell Dade, prin. Fax 822-2297
Glasgow MS 1,100/6-8
4101 Fairfax Pkwy 22312 703-813-8700
Deirdre Lavery, prin. Fax 813-8797
Groveton ES 500/K-6
6900 Harrison Ln 22306 703-718-8000
Richard Pollio, prin. Fax 718-8097
Hayfield ES 600/K-6
7633 Telegraph Rd 22315 703-924-4500
Barbara Vaccarella, prin. Fax 924-4597
Hollin Meadows ES 600/K-6
2310 Nordok Pl 22306 703-718-8300
Jon Gates, prin. Fax 718-8397
Holmes MS 700/6-8
6525 Montrose St Ste 1 22312 703-658-5900
Roberto Pamas, prin. Fax 658-5997
Hybla Valley ES 700/K-6
3415 Lockheed Blvd 22306 703-718-7000
Lauren Sheehy, prin. Fax 718-7097
Island Creek ES 700/PK-6
7855 Morning View Ln 22315 571-642-6300
Susan Owner, prin. Fax 642-6397
Lane ES 700/K-6
7137 Beulah St 22315 703-924-7700
Suzanne Montgomery, prin. Fax 924-7797
Mt. Eagle ES 300/K-6
6116 N Kings Hwy 22303 703-721-2100
Brian Butler, prin. Fax 721-2197
Mt. Vernon Woods ES 500/PK-6
4015 Fielding St 22309 703-619-2800
Marie Lemmon, prin. Fax 619-2897
Parklawn ES 600/K-5
4116 Braddock Rd 22312 703-914-6900
Susan Akroyd, prin. Fax 914-6997
Riverside ES 500/K-6
8410 Old Mount Vernon Rd 22309 703-799-6000
Lori Morton, prin. Fax 799-6097
Rose Hill ES 800/PK-6
6301 Rose Hill Dr 22310 703-313-4200
Terri Czarniak, prin. Fax 313-4297
Sandburg MS 1,200/7-8
8428 Fort Hunt Rd 22308 703-799-6100
Wendy Eaton, prin. Fax 799-6197
Stratford Landing ES 700/PK-6
8484 Riverside Rd 22308 703-619-3600
Maura Caulfield, prin. Fax 619-3697
Twain MS 900/7-8
4700 Franconia Rd 22310 703-313-3700
Aimee Holleb, prin. Fax 313-3797
Washington Mill ES 500/K-6
9100 Cherrytree Dr 22309 703-619-2500
Tish Howard, prin. Fax 619-2597
Waynewood ES 600/K-6
1205 Waynewood Blvd 22308 703-704-7100
James Meier, prin. Fax 704-7197
Weyanoke ES 400/K-5
6520 Braddock Rd 22312 703-813-5400
Annette Almedina-Cabrera, prin. Fax 813-5497
Whitman MS 900/7-8
2500 Parkers Ln 22306 703-660-2400
Otha Davis, prin. Fax 660-2497
Woodlawn ES 500/K-6
8505 Highland Ln 22309 703-619-4800
Stephanie Bisson, prin. Fax 619-4897
Woodley Hills ES 500/K-6
8718 Old Mount Vernon Rd 22309 703-799-2000
Sharon Eldredge, prin. Fax 799-2097

Alexandria Country Day S 200/K-8
2400 Russell Rd 22301 703-548-4804
Alexander Harvey, hdmstr. Fax 549-9022
Aquinas Montessori S 200/PK-6
8334 Mount Vernon Hwy 22309 703-780-8484
Kathleen Futrell, dir. Fax 360-2875
Blessed Sacrament S 300/PK-8
1417 W Braddock Rd 22302 703-998-4170
Valerie Garcia, prin. Fax 998-5033
Browne Academy 300/PK-8
5917 Telegraph Rd 22310 703-960-3000
Margot Durkin, hdmstr. Fax 960-4588
Burgundy Farm Country Day S 300/PK-8
3700 Burgundy Rd 22303 703-960-3431
Jeff Sindler, hdmstr. Fax 960-5056
Calvary Road Christian S 300/PK-8
6811 Beulah St 22310 703-971-8004
L. Harold Jones, admin. Fax 971-0130
Christian Center S 200/PK-8
5411 Franconia Rd 22310 703-971-0558
Kathy Sems, prin. Fax 971-4264
Grace Episcopal S 100/PK-5
3601 Russell Rd 22305 703-549-5067
Chris Byrnes, hdmstr. Fax 549-9545
Immanuel Lutheran S 50/K-8
1801 Russell Rd 22301 703-549-7323
Margaret Zensinger, prin. Fax 549-7323
Islamic Saudi Academy 800/1-12
8333 Richmond Hwy 22309 703-780-0606
Abdulralman Alghofaili, dir. Fax 780-8639
Montessori S of Alexandria 100/PK-6
6300 Florence Ln 22310 703-960-3498
Cindy Lanham, dir. Fax 960-4667
Queen of Apostles S 200/K-8
4409 Sano St 22312 703-354-0714
Joanne Yates, prin. Fax 354-1820
St. Louis S 400/K-8
2901 Popkins Ln 22306 703-768-7732
Daniel Baillargeon, prin. Fax 768-3836
St. Mary S 700/PK-8
400 Green St 22314 703-549-1646
Janet Cantwell, prin. Fax 519-0840
St. Rita S 200/K-8
3801 Russell Rd 22305 703-548-1888
Mary Schlickenmaier, prin. Fax 519-9389
St. Stephen's & St. Agnes S 400/K-5
400 Fontaine St 22302 703-212-2736
Joan Holden, hdmstr. Fax 838-0032
St. Stephen's & St. Agnes S 300/6-8
4401 W Braddock Rd 22304 703-212-2741
Joan Holden, hdmstr. Fax 751-7142

Altavista, Campbell, Pop. 3,385
Campbell County SD
Supt. — See Rustburg
Altavista ES 600/K-5
2190 Lynch Mill Rd 24517 434-369-5665
Andy McCracken, prin. Fax 369-2859

Alton, Halifax
Halifax County SD
Supt. — See Halifax
Cluster Springs ES 200/K-5
7091 Huell Matthews Hwy 24520 434-517-2600
Lisa Long, prin. Fax 517-2610

Amelia Court House, Amelia
Amelia County SD 1,700/PK-12
8701 Otterburn Rd Ste 101 23002 804-561-2621
Dr. David Gangel, supt. Fax 561-3057
www.amelia.k12.va.us
Amelia County ES 700/PK-4
8533 N Five Forks Rd 23002 804-561-2433
Kathy Stuart, prin. Fax 561-6524
Amelia County MS 400/5-8
8740 Otterburn Rd 23002 804-561-4422
Kathleen Farmer, prin. Fax 561-6525

Amelia Academy 200/K-12
PO Box 106 23002 804-561-2270
James Grizzard, hdmstr. Fax 561-4934
Love Covenant Christian S 50/PK-12
17897 W Pridesville Rd 23002 804-561-3750
Greg LeMaster, hdmstr. Fax 561-1449

Amherst, Amherst, Pop. 2,225
Amherst County SD 4,800/PK-12
PO Box 1257 24521 434-946-9387
Brian Ratliff Ed.D., supt. Fax 946-9346
www.amherst.k12.va.us
Amherst ES 400/PK-5
156 Davis St 24521 434-946-9704
Dr. Mark Angle, prin. Fax 946-9706
Amherst MS 500/6-8
165 Gordons Fairgrounds Rd 24521 434-946-0691
Christie Cundiff, prin. Fax 946-0258
Central ES 300/PK-5
575 Union Hill Rd 24521 434-946-9700
Stephanie Prokity, prin. Fax 946-9702
Temperance ES 100/PK-5
1981 Lowesville Rd 24521 434-946-2811
Kelly Holmes, prin. Fax 277-5594
Other Schools – See Madison Heights, Monroe

Annandale, Fairfax, Pop. 55,800
Fairfax County SD
Supt. — See Falls Church
Annandale Terrace ES 600/K-5
7604 Herald St 22003 703-658-5600
Christina Dickens, prin. Fax 658-5697
Braddock ES 500/PK-5
7825 Heritage Dr 22003 703-914-7300
Cindy Botzin, prin. Fax 914-1185
Camelot ES 400/K-6
8100 Guinevere Dr 22003 703-645-7000
Craig Gfeller, prin. Fax 645-7097
Canterbury Woods ES 700/PK-6
4910 Willet Dr 22003 703-764-5600
Barbara Messinger, prin. Fax 764-5697
Columbia ES 300/K-5
6720 Alpine Dr 22003 703-916-2500
Michael Cunningham, prin. Fax 916-2597
Poe MS 1,100/6-8
7000 Cindy Ln 22003 703-813-3800
Sonya Swansbrough, prin. Fax 813-3897

Holy Spirit S 300/PK-8
8800 Braddock Rd 22003 703-978-7117
Sarah Schmitt, prin. Fax 978-7438
Montessori S of Northern Virginia 100/PK-4
6820 Pacific Ln 22003 703-256-9577
Betsy Mitchell, hdmstr. Fax 256-9851
St. Ambrose S 200/K-8
3827 Woodburn Rd 22003 703-698-7171
Barbara Dalmut, prin. Fax 698-7170
St. Michael S 300/K-8
7401 Saint Michaels Ln 22003 703-256-1222
Sr. Therese Bauer, prin. Fax 256-3490
Westminster S 300/K-8
3819 Gallows Rd 22003 703-256-3620
Ellis Glover, hdmstr.

Appalachia, Wise, Pop. 1,771
Wise County SD
Supt. — See Wise
Appalachia S 400/PK-7
PO Box 430 24216 276-565-1115
Dr. Alice Hughes, prin. Fax 565-2333

Appomattox, Appomattox, Pop. 1,729
Appomattox County SD 2,300/PK-12
PO Box 548 24522 434-352-8251
Dr. Aldridge Boone, supt. Fax 352-0883
www.appomattox.k12.va.us
Appomattox ES 500/3-5
176 Kids Pl 24522 434-352-7463
Tom Yarber, prin. Fax 352-8134
Appomattox MS 500/6-8
2020 Church St 24522 434-352-8257
Martha Eagle, prin. Fax 352-5621
Appomattox PS 600/PK-2
185 Learning Ln 24522 434-352-5766
Katherine Paine, prin. Fax 352-7476

Appomattox SDA S 50/K-8
PO Box 2259 24522 434-352-2660
Barbara Core, lead tchr.
Cornerstone Christian Academy 100/K-12
PO Box 897 24522 434-352-2345
Marcie Jones, hdmstr.

Ararat, Patrick
Patrick County SD
Supt. — See Stuart
Blue Ridge ES 300/K-7
PO Box 30 24053 276-251-5271
Carolyn Deekens, prin. Fax 251-1354

Arlington, Arlington, Pop. 189,927
Arlington County SD 18,500/PK-12
1426 N Quincy St 22207 703-228-6000
Dr. Robert G. Smith, supt. Fax 228-6188
www.apsva.us
Abingdon ES 400/PK-5
3035 S Abingdon St 22206 703-228-6650
Joanne Uyeda, prin. Fax 931-1804
Arlington Science Focus ES 400/PK-5
1501 N Lincoln St 22201 703-228-7670
Mary Begley, prin. Fax 525-2452
Arlington Traditional ES 400/PK-5
855 N Edison St 22205 703-228-6290
Holly Hawthorne, prin. Fax 522-1482
Ashlawn ES 400/PK-5
5950 8th Rd N 22205 703-228-5270
Edgar Miranda, prin. Fax 534-3685
Barcroft ES 300/PK-5
625 S Wakefield St 22204 703-228-5838
Miriam Hughey-Guy, prin. Fax 271-0948
Barrett ES 400/PK-5
4401 N Henderson Rd 22203 703-228-6288
Theresa Bratt, prin. Fax 351-0023
Campbell ES 300/PK-5
737 S Carlin Springs Rd 22204 703-228-6770
Sandra Lochhead-Price, prin. Fax 578-9432
Carlin Springs ES 500/PK-5
5995 5th Rd S 22204 703-228-6645
Corina Coronel, prin. Fax 998-5341
Claremont Immersion ES 400/K-5
4700 S Chesterfield Rd 22206 703-228-2500
Cintia Johnson, prin. Fax 820-4264
Drew Model ES 500/PK-5
3500 23rd St S 22206 703-228-5825
Cheryl Relford, prin. Fax 979-0892
Glebe ES 300/PK-5
1770 N Glebe Rd 22207 703-228-6280
Jamie Borg, prin. Fax 527-2040
Gunston MS 600/6-8
2700 S Lang St 22206 703-228-6900
Margaret Gill, prin. Fax 519-9183
Henry ES 300/K-5
701 S Highland St 22204 703-228-5820
Dr. Lisa Piehota, prin. Fax 486-8971
Hoffman-Boston ES 300/PK-5
1415 S Queen St 22204 703-228-5845
Yvonne Dangerfield, prin. Fax 892-4526
Jamestown ES 500/PK-5
3700 N Delaware St 22207 703-228-5275
Laura Annan Glascoe, prin. Fax 538-2612
Jefferson MS 600/6-8
125 S Old Glebe Rd 22204 703-228-5900
Sharon Monde, prin. Fax 979-3744
Kenmore MS 800/6-8
200 S Carlin Springs Rd 22204 703-228-6800
Dr. John Word, prin. Fax 998-3069
Key ES 600/PK-5
2300 Key Blvd 22201 703-228-4210
Marjorie Myers, prin. Fax 524-2236
Long Branch ES 400/PK-5
33 N Fillmore St 22201 703-228-4220
Felicia Russo, prin. Fax 875-2868
McKinley ES 400/PK-5
1030 N Mckinley Rd 22205 703-228-5280
Patricia Anderson, prin. Fax 538-4982
Nottingham ES 400/PK-5
5900 Little Falls Rd 22207 703-228-5290
Mary Beth Pelosky, prin. Fax 228-2300
Oakridge ES 400/PK-5
1414 24th St S 22202 703-228-5840
Dr. LaDarla Haws, prin. Fax 271-0529
Randolph ES 300/PK-5
1306 S Quincy St 22204 703-228-5830
Dr. Renee Bostick, prin. Fax 521-2516
Swanson MS 800/6-8
5800 Washington Blvd 22205 703-228-5500
Chrystal Forrester, prin. Fax 536-2775
Taylor ES 600/PK-5
2600 N Stuart St 22207 703-228-6275
Robert Hindman, prin. Fax 875-8039
Tuckahoe ES 600/PK-5
6550 26th St N 22213 703-228-5288
Cynthia Brown, prin. Fax 237-1548
Williamsburg MS 1,000/6-8
3600 N Harrison St 22207 703-228-5450
Kathleen Francis, prin. Fax 536-2870

Holy Martyrs of Vietnam S PK-PK
915 S Wakefield St 22204 703-920-1049
Tamila Mostamandy, prin. Fax 553-0371
Our Lady Queen of Peace ECC PK-PK
2700 19th St S 22204 703-271-0692
Floretta Ramsuer, prin. Fax 979-5590
Our Savior Lutheran S 100/K-8
825 S Taylor St 22204 703-892-4846
Barbara Huehn, prin.
Potomac Crescent Waldorf S 50/PK-4
923 23rd St S 22202 703-624-1309
Fax 486-1309
Rivendell S 200/K-8
5700 Lee Hwy 22207 703-532-1200
Byron List, hdmstr. Fax 532-3003
St. Agnes S 400/PK-8
2024 N Randolph St 22207 703-527-5423
Kristine Carr, prin. Fax 525-4689
St. Ann S 200/PK-8
980 N Frederick St 22205 703-525-7599
Mary Therrell, prin. Fax 525-2687
St. Charles S 200/PK-8
3299 Fairfax Dr 22201 703-527-0608
Linda Lacot, prin. Fax 526-0262

St. Thomas More S 300/PK-8
105 N Thomas St 22203 703-528-1547
Eleanor McCormack, prin. Fax 528-5048

Arrington, Nelson
Nelson County SD
Supt. — See Lovingston
Tye River ES 500/PK-5
5198 Thomas Nelson Hwy 22922 434-263-8960
Greg Hill, prin. Fax 263-8964

Ashburn, Loudoun, Pop. 3,393
Loudoun County SD 49,200/PK-12
21000 Education Ct 20148 571-252-1000
Dr. Edgar Hatrick, supt. Fax 252-1669
www.loudoun.k12.va.us
Ashburn ES 700/PK-5
44062 Fincastle Dr 20147 571-252-2350
Dr. Barbara Holley, prin. Fax 771-6792
Belmont Station ES 600/PK-5
20235 Nightwatch St 20147 571-252-2240
Patricia McGinley, prin. Fax 223-3805
Carter ES K-5
43330 Loudoun Reserve Dr 20148 703-957-4490
Michele Freeman, prin. Fax 661-8313
Cedar Lane ES 700/PK-5
43700 Tolamac Dr 20147 571-252-2120
James Dallas, prin. Fax 771-6521
Creighton's Corner ES K-5
23171 Minerva Dr 20148 703-957-4480
Kimberly Berkey, prin. Fax 327-4164
Dominion Trail ES 800/PK-5
44045 Bruceton Mills Cir 20147 571-252-2340
Susan Mabee, prin. Fax 858-0978
Eagle Ridge MS 1,100/6-8
42901 Waxpool Rd 20148 571-252-2140
Janice Koslowski, prin. Fax 779-8977
Farmwell Station MS 1,100/6-8
44281 Gloucester Pkwy 20147 571-252-2320
Sherryl Loya, prin. Fax 771-6495
Hillside ES 800/PK-5
43000 Ellzey Dr 20148 571-252-2170
Mary Green, prin. Fax 858-0504
Legacy ES 1,000/K-5
22995 Minerva Dr 20148 703-957-4425
Robert Duckworth, prin. Fax 542-7193
Mill Run ES 1,000/K-5
42940 Ridgeway Dr 20148 571-252-2160
Paul Vickers, prin. Fax 779-8932
Newton-Lee ES 800/K-5
43335 Gloucester Pkwy 20147 571-252-1535
Julie Boyd, prin. Fax 223-0793
Sanders Corner ES 600/PK-5
43100 Ashburn Farm Pkwy 20147 571-252-2250
Kathleen Hwang, prin. Fax 771-6614
Stone Hill MS 6-8
23415 Evergreen Ridge Dr 20148 703-957-4420
Rodney Moore, prin. Fax 223-0585
Weller ES K-5
20700 Marblehead Dr 20147 571-252-2360
Janet Radcliffe, prin. Fax 223-2282
Other Schools – See Aldie, Hamilton, Leesburg, Lovettsville, Middleburg, Purcellville, Round Hill, South Riding, Sterling, Waterford

---

Boyd S - Broadlands 200/PK-3
42945 Waxpool Rd 20148 703-723-3364
Mary Stage, dir. Fax 723-5761
Christian Faith & Fellowship S 500/PK-12
21673 Beaumeade Cir Ste 600 20147 703-729-5968
Kevin Jeter, hdmstr. Fax 729-6635
Montessori Academy at Belmont Greene 100/PK-6
20300 Bowfonds St 20147 703-729-7200
Bart Theriot, hdmstr. Fax 729-6957
St. Theresa S 500/K-8
21370 St Theresa Ln 20147 703-729-3577
Carol Krichbaum, prin. Fax 729-8068
Virginia Academy PK-8
19790 Ashburn Rd 20147 571-209-5500
Dr. Fred Snowden, admin. Fax 209-5845
Willow Montessori S 50/PK-K
20854 Stubble Rd 20147 703-579-5755
Paru Rellen, prin. Fax 729-5950

Ashland, Hanover, Pop. 6,996
Hanover County SD 18,200/K-12
200 Berkley St 23005 804-365-4500
Dr. Stewart Roberson, supt. Fax 365-4680
www.hcps.us
Clay ES 300/K-2
310 S James St 23005 804-365-8120
Teresa Keck, prin. Fax 365-8139
Elmont ES 400/K-5
12007 Cedar Ln 23005 804-365-8100
Larry Hardy, prin. Fax 365-8111
Gandy ES 300/3-5
201 Archie Cannon Dr 23005 804-365-4640
Leigh Finch, prin. Fax 365-4659
Liberty MS 1,200/6-8
13496 Liberty School Rd 23005 804-365-8060
Donald Latham, prin. Fax 365-8061
Other Schools – See Beaverdam, Mechanicsville, Montpelier

Hanover Academy 100/PK-8
115 Frances Rd 23005 804-798-8413
Rebecca Thomas, hdmstr.

Atkins, Smyth, Pop. 1,130
Smyth County SD
Supt. — See Marion
Atkins ES 200/PK-5
5903 Lee Hwy 24311 276-783-3366
Reva Rhea, prin. Fax 783-0901

Austinville, Wythe
Carroll County SD
Supt. — See Hillsville

Laurel ES 300/K-5
26 Pleasantview Rd 24312 276-728-9247
Alvin Davidson, prin. Fax 728-5742

Wythe County SD
Supt. — See Wytheville
Jackson Memorial ES 200/K-5
4424 Fort Chiswell Rd 24312 276-699-6150
Tammy Watson, prin. Fax 699-9650

Axton, Henry
Henry County SD
Supt. — See Collinsville
Axton ES 200/PK-5
1500 Axton School Rd 24054 276-650-1193
Charles Easley, prin. Fax 650-1462
Irisburg ES 200/PK-5
6871 Irisburg Rd 24054 276-650-2183
Jo Ellen Hylton, prin. Fax 650-1441

Carlisle S 500/PK-12
300 Carlisle Rd 24054 276-632-7288
Simon Owen-Williams, hdmstr. Fax 632-9545

Bassett, Henry, Pop. 1,579
Henry County SD
Supt. — See Collinsville
Campbell Court ES 400/PK-5
220 Campbell Ct 24055 276-629-5344
Dr. Patricia Grandinetti, prin. Fax 629-3849
Sanville ES 300/PK-5
19 Sanville School Rd 24055 276-629-5301
Dr. Sally Rodgers, prin. Fax 629-4648

Bastian, Bland
Bland County SD 900/K-12
361 Bears Trl 24314 276-688-3361
Don Hodock, supt. Fax 688-4659
www.bland.k12.va.us
Other Schools – See Bland, Rocky Gap

Bealeton, Fauquier
Fauquier County SD
Supt. — See Warrenton
Cedar-Lee MS 600/6-8
11138 Marsh Rd 22712 540-439-3207
Steven Parker, prin. Fax 439-2051
Miller ES 600/PK-5
6248 Catlett Rd 22712 540-439-1913
Judith Williams, prin. Fax 439-1925
Walter ES 500/PK-5
4529 Morrisville Rd 22712 540-439-3279
Alex O'Dell, prin. Fax 439-3318

Beaverdam, Hanover
Hanover County SD
Supt. — See Ashland
Beaverdam ES 400/K-5
15485 Beaverdam School Rd 23015 804-449-6373
Michael Mudd, prin. Fax 449-6510

Bedford, Bedford, Pop. 6,211
Bedford County SD 11,000/K-12
PO Box 748 24523 540-586-1045
Dr. Douglas Schuch, supt. Fax 586-7747
www.bedford.k12.va.us
Bedford ES 600/2-6
806 Tiger Trl 24523 540-586-0275
Liza Winter, prin. Fax 586-7619
Bedford MS 500/7-8
503 Longwood Ave 24523 540-586-7735
Rhetta Watkins, prin. Fax 586-4957
Bedford PS 200/K-1
807 College St 24523 540-586-8339
D. Wayne Lyle, prin. Fax 586-7654
Body Camp ES 200/K-5
1051 Elementary Way 24523 540-297-7391
Dr. Marvin McGinnis, prin. Fax 297-8843
Other Schools – See Big Island, Forest, Goode, Goodview, Huddleston, Lynchburg, Moneta, Montvale, Thaxton

Bent Mountain, Roanoke
Roanoke County SD
Supt. — See Roanoke
Bent Mountain ES 100/K-5
10148 Tinsley Ln 24059 540-929-4281
Virginia Sharp, prin. Fax 929-9012

Berryville, Clarke, Pop. 3,157
Clarke County SD 2,100/PK-12
309 W Main St 22611 540-955-6100
Dr. Michael Murphy, supt. Fax 955-6109
www.clarke.k12.va.us
Berryville PS 200/PK-1
317 W Main St 22611 540-955-6110
Dr. Steve Geyer, prin. Fax 955-6111
Cooley ES 300/2-5
34 Westwood Rd 22611 540-955-6120
Dr. Steve Geyer, prin. Fax 955-6124
Johnson-Williams MS 500/6-8
200 Swan Ave 22611 540-955-6160
Evan Robb, prin. Fax 955-6169
Other Schools – See Boyce

Big Island, Bedford
Bedford County SD
Supt. — See Bedford
Big Island ES 200/K-6
1114 Schooldays Rd 24526 434-299-5863
Dr. Deborah Shelton, prin. Fax 299-6037

Big Stone Gap, Wise, Pop. 5,854
Wise County SD
Supt. — See Wise
Powell Valley MS 500/5-8
3137 2nd Ave E 24219 276-523-0195
Stephen Bonney, prin. Fax 523-4762
Powell Valley PS 600/PK-4
2945 2nd Ave E 24219 276-523-4900
Jody Evans, prin. Fax 523-4901

King's Christian Academy 50/K-8
PO Box 339 24219 276-523-0004
Allison Giles, admin. Fax 523-4864

Birchleaf, Dickenson
Dickenson County SD
Supt. — See Clintwood
Sandlick S 500/PK-8
PO Box 188 24220 276-865-5361
John Whitner, prin. Fax 865-4448

Blacksburg, Montgomery, Pop. 39,130
Montgomery County SD
Supt. — See Christiansburg
Beeks ES 400/PK-5
709 Airport Rd 24060 540-951-5700
Micah Mefford, prin. Fax 951-5703
Blacksburg MS 800/6-8
3109 Prices Fork Rd 24060 540-951-5800
John Wheeler, prin. Fax 951-5808
Harding Avenue ES 200/K-5
429 Harding Ave 24060 540-951-5732
Meggan Marshall, prin. Fax 951-5729
Kipps ES 500/PK-5
2801 Prices Fork Rd 24060 540-951-5760
Christopher Widrig, prin. Fax 951-5764
Linkous ES 400/PK-5
813 Toms Creek Rd 24060 540-951-5726
Carol Kahler, prin. Fax 951-5725
Prices Fork ES 200/PK-5
4237 Prices Fork Rd 24060 540-951-5736
Dollie Cottrill, prin. Fax 951-5735

Dayspring Christian Academy 200/K-12
PO Box 909 24063 540-552-7777
William Hampton, admin. Fax 552-7778

Blackstone, Nottoway, Pop. 3,558
Nottoway County SD
Supt. — See Nottoway
Blackstone PS 400/K-4
615 East St 23824 434-292-5300
Ruth Horn, prin. Fax 292-4802

Kenston Forest S 400/PK-12
75 Ridge Rd 23824 434-292-7218
James Milroy, hdmstr. Fax 292-7455

Blairs, Pittsylvania
Pittsylvania County SD
Supt. — See Chatham
Southside ES 500/K-5
440 E Witt Rd 24527 434-836-0006
Todd Sease, prin. Fax 836-3615

Bland, Bland
Bland County SD
Supt. — See Bastian
Bland ES 300/K-7
31 Rocket Dr 24315 276-688-3621
Dianna Tibbs, prin. Fax 688-3403

Bluefield, Tazewell, Pop. 4,989
Tazewell County SD
Supt. — See Tazewell
Abbs Valley-Boissevain ES 200/PK-5
7030 Abbs Valley Rd 24605 276-945-5969
Sharon Smith, prin. Fax 945-2395
Dudley PS 300/PK-2
1840 Tazewell Ave 24605 276-326-1507
Susan Maupin, prin. Fax 322-1197
Graham IS 300/3-5
808 Greever Ave 24605 276-326-3737
Todd Baker, prin. Fax 326-1440
Graham MS 400/6-8
1 Academic Cir 24605 276-326-1101
Deidra Hill, prin. Fax 322-1409

Blue Ridge, Botetourt, Pop. 2,840
Botetourt County SD
Supt. — See Fincastle
Colonial ES 500/PK-5
2941 Webster Rd 24064 540-977-6773
Tammy Riggs, prin. Fax 977-4219

Bon Air, Chesterfield, Pop. 16,413
Chesterfield County SD
Supt. — See Chesterfield
Bon Air ES 500/PK-5
8701 Polk St 23235 804-560-2700
Bruce Tetlow, prin. Fax 560-0309

Boones Mill, Franklin, Pop. 290
Franklin County SD
Supt. — See Rocky Mount
Boones Mill ES 400/PK-5
265 Taylors Rd 24065 540-334-4000
Bernice Cobbs, prin. Fax 334-4001

Bowling Green, Caroline, Pop. 995
Caroline County SD 3,900/PK-12
16221 Richmond Tpke 22427 804-633-5088
Dr. Gregory Killough, supt. Fax 633-5563
www.caroline.k12.va.us
Bowling Green ES 400/3-5
16261 Richmond Tpke 22427 804-633-6101
Cathy McConnell, prin. Fax 633-4201
Other Schools – See Milford, Ruther Glen

Boyce, Clarke, Pop. 453
Clarke County SD
Supt. — See Berryville
Boyce ES 400/K-5
119 W Main St 22620 540-955-6115
Susan Catlett, prin. Fax 955-6119

Powhatan S 300/K-8
49 Powhatan Ln 22620 540-837-1009
John Lathrop, hdmstr. Fax 837-2558

Boydton, Mecklenburg, Pop. 466
Mecklenburg County SD 4,700/PK-12
PO Box 190 23917 434-738-6111
Helen Hill, supt. Fax 738-6679
www.mcpsweb.org
Other Schools – See Chase City, Clarksville, La Crosse, Skipwith, South Hill

Bridgewater, Rockingham, Pop. 5,413
Rockingham County SD
Supt. — See Harrisonburg
Wayland ES 600/PK-5
801 N Main St 22812 540-828-6081
Dr. David Burchfield, prin. Fax 828-4439

Blue Ridge Christian S 200/PK-8
PO Box 207 22812 540-828-2233
John Barlow, admin. Fax 828-4372

Bristol, Bristol, Pop. 17,335
Bristol CSD 2,400/PK-12
222 Oak St 24201 276-821-5600
Ina Danko, supt. Fax 821-5601
www.bvps.org/
Highland View ES 200/PK-5
1405 Eads Ave 24201 276-821-5710
Debbie Leonard, prin. Fax 821-5711
Jackson ES 300/PK-5
2045 Euclid Ave 24201 276-821-5740
Dr. Linda Brittle, prin. Fax 821-5741
Van Pelt ES 400/PK-5
200 Spring Hill Ter 24201 276-821-5770
Dennis Staton, prin. Fax 821-5771
Virginia MS 500/6-8
501 Piedmont Ave 24201 276-821-5660
Gary Ritchie, prin. Fax 821-5661
Washington Lee ES 300/PK-5
900 Washington Lee Dr 24201 276-821-5800
Mike Braswell, prin. Fax 821-5801

Washington County SD
Supt. — See Abingdon
High Point ES 500/PK-5
14091 Sinking Creek Rd 24202 276-642-5600
Ann Cunningham, prin. Fax 645-2360
Valley Institute ES 400/PK-5
4350 Gate City Hwy 24202 276-642-5500
Beverley Fifer, prin. Fax 645-2394
Wallace MS 400/6-8
13077 Wallace Pike 24202 276-642-5400
Dr. Fred Keller, prin. Fax 645-2365

St. Anne Catholic S 200/PK-7
300 Euclid Ave 24201 276-669-0048
Richard Fenchak, prin. Fax 669-3523
Sullins Academy 200/PK-8
22218 Sullins Academy Dr 24202 276-669-4101
Ramona Harr, hdmstr. Fax 669-4294

Bristow, Prince William
Prince William County SD
Supt. — See Manassas
Bristow Run ES 1,000/K-5
8990 Worthington Dr 20136 703-753-7741
Andrew Buchheit, prin. Fax 753-7604
Cedar Point ES 1,000/K-5
12601 Braemar Pkwy 20136 703-365-0963
Rebecca Miller Ed.D., prin. Fax 365-0954
Marsteller MS 1,700/6-8
14000 Sudley Manor Dr 20136 703-393-7608
Roberta Knetter, prin. Fax 530-6327
Victory ES K-5
12001 Tygart Lake Dr 20136 703-257-0356
Donna Cude, prin.

Linton Hall S 200/PK-8
9535 Linton Hall Rd 20136 703-368-3157
Elizabeth Poole, prin. Fax 368-3036

Broadway, Rockingham, Pop. 2,460
Rockingham County SD
Supt. — See Harrisonburg
Hillyard MS 800/6-8
226 Hawks Hill Dr 22815 540-896-8961
Douglas Alderfer, prin. Fax 896-6641
Myers ES 500/PK-5
290 Raider Rd 22815 540-896-2297
Sandra Cupp, prin. Fax 896-1576

Brookneal, Campbell, Pop. 1,252
Campbell County SD
Supt. — See Rustburg
Brookneal ES 300/PK-5
PO Box 36 24528 434-376-2042
David Rubinberg, prin. Fax 376-2371

Buchanan, Botetourt, Pop. 1,236
Botetourt County SD
Supt. — See Fincastle
Buchanan ES 300/PK-5
PO Box 639 24066 540-254-2084
Debbie Garrett, prin. Fax 254-1473

Buckingham, Buckingham, Pop. 370
Buckingham County SD 2,100/K-12
PO Box 24 23921 434-969-6100
Gary Blair, supt. Fax 969-1176
www.bchs.k12.va.us
Buckingham County MS 500/6-8
1184 High School Rd 23921 434-983-2102
Cindy O'Brien, prin. Fax 983-1002
Buckingham PS 200/K-3
77 Buckingham Primary Sch 23921 434-969-4490
Joan Staton, prin. Fax 969-1004
Other Schools – See Dillwyn, New Canton

Central Virginia Christian S 50/K-5
PO Box 8 23921 434-969-2827
Cherie Brickhill, admin. Fax 969-4725

Buena Vista, Buena Vista, Pop. 6,437
Buena Vista CSD 1,200/K-12
2329 Chestnut Ave Ste A 24416 540-261-2129
Dr. Rebecca Gates, supt. Fax 261-2967
www.bvcps.org
Enderly Heights ES 300/K-4
101 Woodland Ave 24416 540-261-6151
Christine Wood, prin. Fax 261-7009
Kling ES 200/K-4
3400 Lombardy Ave 24416 540-261-6717
Richard Roberts, prin. Fax 261-1389
McCluer MS 400/5-8
2329 Chestnut Ave 24416 540-261-7340
Troy Clark, prin. Fax 261-3292

Rockbridge County SD
Supt. — See Lexington
Mountain View ES 100/K-5
20 Burger Cir 24416 540-261-2418
Lori Teague, prin. Fax 261-8082

Burke, Fairfax, Pop. 57,700
Fairfax County SD
Supt. — See Falls Church
Cherry Run ES 500/PK-6
9732 Ironmaster Dr 22015 703-923-2800
Steve Gossin, prin. Fax 923-2897
Terra Centre ES 600/PK-6
6000 Burke Centre Pkwy 22015 703-249-1400
Michelle Sims, prin. Fax 249-1497
White Oaks ES 800/K-6
6130 Shiplett Blvd 22015 703-923-1400
Connie Goodman, prin. Fax 923-1497

Nativity S 300/PK-8
6398 Nativity Ln 22015 703-455-2300
Maria Kelly, prin. Fax 569-8109

Burkeville, Nottoway, Pop. 474
Nottoway County SD
Supt. — See Nottoway
Burkeville ES 200/K-4
507 Miller St 23922 434-767-5236
Tommy Coleman, prin. Fax 767-2896

Callaway, Franklin
Franklin County SD
Supt. — See Rocky Mount
Callaway ES 300/PK-5
8451 Callaway Rd 24067 540-483-0364
Brenda Hopkins, prin. Fax 483-0523

Cana, Carroll
Carroll County SD
Supt. — See Hillsville
St. Paul S 400/K-7
231 Flower Gap Rd 24317 276-755-3512
Nancy Wilmoth, prin. Fax 755-3211

Cape Charles, Northampton, Pop. 1,423
Northampton County SD
Supt. — See Machipongo
Kiptopeke ES 400/K-5
24023 Fairview Rd 23310 757-678-5151
Gwendolyn Coghill, prin. Fax 331-3219

Capron, Southampton, Pop. 169
Southhampton County SD
Supt. — See Courtland
Capron ES 200/PK-5
PO Box 164 23829 434-658-4348
Sandra Pettigrew, prin. Fax 658-4118

Carrollton, Isle of Wight, Pop. 80
Isle of Wight County SD
Supt. — See Smithfield
Carrollton ES 500/PK-3
14440 New Town Haven Ln 23314 757-238-2452
Dr. Calvin Bullock, prin. Fax 238-2536

Carrsville, Isle of Wight
Isle of Wight County SD
Supt. — See Smithfield
Carrsville ES 200/K-5
5355 Carrsville Hwy 23315 757-562-4054
Jackie Carr, prin. Fax 562-2607

Castlewood, Russell, Pop. 3,036
Russell County SD
Supt. — See Lebanon
Castlewood ES 500/1-7
242 Blue Devil Cir 24224 276-762-2315
Kim Hooker, prin. Fax 762-9261
Copper Creek S 100/PK-K
23894 US Highway 58 24224 276-794-9306
Anthony Carrier, prin. Fax 794-7934

Catlett, Fauquier
Fauquier County SD
Supt. — See Warrenton
Pearson ES 500/PK-5
9347 Bastable Mill Rd 20119 540-788-9071
Cindy Carter, prin. Fax 788-1737

Cedar Bluff, Tazewell, Pop. 1,073
Tazewell County SD
Supt. — See Tazewell
Cedar Bluff ES 500/K-5
PO Box 1400 24609 276-963-5765
Charity McDaniel, prin. Fax 963-4253

Centreville, Fairfax, Pop. 56,700
Fairfax County SD
Supt. — See Falls Church
Bull Run ES 900/K-6
15301 Lee Hwy 20121 703-227-1400
Deborah Miller, prin. Fax 227-1497
Centre Ridge ES 900/K-6
14400 New Braddock Rd 20121 703-227-2600
James Baldwin, prin. Fax 227-2697
Centreville ES 900/K-6
14330 Green Trails Blvd 20121 703-502-3500
Dwayne Young, prin. Fax 502-3597
Cub Run ES 500/PK-6
5301 Sully Station Dr 20120 703-633-7500
Jennifer Coakley, prin. Fax 633-7597
Deer Park ES 700/PK-6
15109 Carlbern Dr 20120 703-802-5000
Carol Larsen, prin. Fax 802-5097
London Towne ES 800/K-6
6100 Stone Rd 20120 703-227-5400
Andrew Camarda, prin. Fax 227-5497
Powell ES 900/K-6
13340 Leland Rd 20120 571-522-6000
Brian Hull, prin. Fax 522-6097
Stone MS 1,000/7-8
5500 Sully Park Dr 20120 703-631-5500
Scott Phillips, prin. Fax 631-5598
Virginia Run ES 800/K-6
15450 Martins Hundred Dr 20120 703-988-8900
Teresa Hicks, prin. Fax 988-8997

Chantilly, Fairfax, Pop. 44,300
Fairfax County SD
Supt. — See Falls Church
Brookfield ES 800/K-6
4200 Lees Corner Rd 20151 703-814-8700
Kim Brown, prin. Fax 803-7695
Franklin MS 900/7-8
3300 Lees Corner Rd 20151 703-904-5100
Sharon Eisenberg, prin. Fax 904-5197
Poplar Tree ES 800/K-6
13440 Melville Ln 20151 703-633-7400
Sharon Smith Williams, prin. Fax 633-7497
Rocky Run MS 800/7-8
4400 Stringfellow Rd 20151 703-802-7700
Dan Parris, prin. Fax 802-7797

Boyd S - Westfields 300/PK-8
4550 Walney Rd 20151 571-321-0364
Chris Ford, dir. Fax 321-0366
Chesterbrook Academy 200/PK-6
3753 Centerview Dr 20151 703-397-0555
Francis Robison, prin.
Cornerstone Montessori S 100/PK-3
4455 Brookfield Corporate 20151 703-961-9779
Kristin Brown, prin.
St. Timothy S 600/PK-8
13809 Poplar Tree Rd 20151 703-378-6932
Patricia Kobyra, prin. Fax 378-1273
St. Veronica S 300/K-8
3460 Centreville Rd 20151 703-773-2020
Mary Baldwin, prin. Fax 689-4410

Charles City, Charles City
Charles City County SD 900/K-12
10910 Courthouse Rd 23030 804-652-4612
Dr. Janet Crawley, supt. Fax 829-6723
208.31.123.10/
Charles City County ES 400/K-5
10049 Courthouse Rd 23030 804-829-9256
Dr. Danielle Belton, prin. Fax 829-2512
Charles City County MS 200/6-8
10035 Courthouse Rd 23030 804-829-9252
Scott Jefferies, prin. Fax 829-2363

Charlotte Court House, Charlotte, Pop. 446
Charlotte County SD 2,200/PK-12
PO Box 790 23923 434-542-5151
Melody Hackney, supt. Fax 542-4261
www.ccps.k12.va.us
Central MS 500/6-8
PO Box 748 23923 434-542-4536
Michael Haskins, prin. Fax 542-4630
Early Learning Center 100/PK-PK
PO Box 508 23923 434-542-4463
Carolyn Baker, prin. Fax 542-4650
Jeffress ES 100/3-5
5015 Patrick Henry Hwy 23923 434-542-5410
Deborah Barksdale, prin. Fax 542-5527
Other Schools – See Keysville, Phenix, Saxe

Charlottesville, Charlottesville, Pop. 40,437
Albemarle County SD 12,600/PK-12
401 McIntire Rd 22902 434-296-5893
Dr. Pamela Moran, supt. Fax 296-5869
www.k12albemarle.org/
Agnor-Hurt ES 500/PK-5
3201 Berkmar Dr 22901 434-973-5211
Michelle Del Gallo, prin. Fax 974-7046
Baker-Butler ES 500/PK-5
2740 Proffit Rd 22911 434-974-7777
David Cushman, prin. Fax 964-4684
Burley MS 500/6-8
901 Rose Hill Dr 22903 434-295-5101
Marcha Howard, prin. Fax 984-4975
Cale ES 500/PK-5
1757 Avon Street Ext 22902 434-293-7455
Lisa Jones, prin. Fax 293-2067
Greer ES 400/PK-5
190 Lambs Ln 22901 434-973-8371
Matthew Landahl, prin. Fax 973-0629
Hollymead ES 500/PK-5
2775 Powell Creek Dr 22911 434-973-8301
Dr. Clare Keiser, prin. Fax 978-3687
Jouett MS 500/6-8
210 Lambs Ln 22901 434-975-9320
Kathryn Baylor, prin. Fax 975-9325
Lewis ES 400/PK-5
1610 Owensville Rd 22901 434-293-9304
Kimberly Cousins, prin. Fax 979-3850
Murray ES 300/PK-5
3251 Morgantown Rd 22903 434-977-4599
Andrew T. Grider, prin. Fax 979-5416
Stone-Robinson ES 400/PK-5
958 N Milton Rd 22911 434-296-3754
E. Ashby Kindler, prin. Fax 296-7645
Sutherland MS 600/6-8
2801 Powell Creek Dr 22911 434-975-0599
David Rogers, prin. Fax 975-0852
Walton MS 500/6-8
4217 Red Hill Rd 22903 434-977-5615
Elizabeth Agee, prin. Fax 296-6648
Woodbrook ES 300/PK-5
100 Woodbrook Dr 22901 434-973-6600
Dr. William Sterrett, prin. Fax 973-0317
Other Schools – See Crozet, Earlysville, Esmont, Keswick, North Garden, Scottsville

Charlottesville CSD 4,200/PK-12
1562 Dairy Rd 22903 434-245-2400
Dr. Rosa Atkins, supt. Fax 245-2603
www.ccs.k12.va.us
Buford MS 600/7-8
617 9th St SW 22903 434-245-2411
Eric Johnson, prin. Fax 245-2611
Burnley-Moran ES 300/PK-4
1300 Long St 22901 434-245-2413
Daphne Keiser, prin. Fax 245-2613
Clark ES 300/PK-4
1000 Belmont Ave 22902 434-245-2414
Gena Keller, prin. Fax 245-2614
Greenbrier ES 300/PK-4
2228 Greenbrier Dr 22901 434-245-2415
James Kyner, prin. Fax 245-2615
Jackson-Via ES 300/PK-4
508 Harris Rd 22903 434-245-2416
Dr. Elizabeth McCay, prin. Fax 245-2616
Johnson ES 300/PK-4
1645 Cherry Ave 22903 434-245-2417
Vernon Bock, prin. Fax 245-2617
Venable ES 300/PK-4
406 14th St NW 22903 434-245-2418
Jamie Mathieson, prin. Fax 245-2618
Walker Upper ES 600/5-6
1564 Dairy Rd 22903 434-245-2412
Terri Perkins, prin. Fax 245-2612

Charlottesville Catholic S 400/PK-8
1205 Pen Park Rd 22901 434-964-0400
Alan Yost, prin. Fax 964-1373
Charlottesville Waldorf S 200/PK-8
120 Waldorf School Rd 22901 434-973-4946
Fax 973-4109
Covenant S 700/PK-12
175 Hickory St 22902 434-220-7329
Dr. Ronald Sykes, hdmstr. Fax 220-7320
Montessori Community S 200/PK-8
305 Rolkin Rd 22911 434-979-8886
Wendy Fisher, hdmstr. Fax 979-6258
Peabody S K-8
1232 Stoney Ridge Rd 22902 434-296-6901
Renee Henslee, hdmstr.
St. Anne's Belfield S 800/PK-12
2132 Ivy Rd 22903 434-296-5106
David Lourie, hdmstr. Fax 979-1486

Chase City, Mecklenburg, Pop. 2,382
Mecklenburg County SD
Supt. — See Boydton
Chase City ES 500/PK-5
5450 Highway Forty Seven 23924 434-372-4770
Hilda Puryear, prin. Fax 372-5294

Chatham, Pittsylvania, Pop. 1,298
Pittsylvania County SD 9,400/PK-12
PO Box 232 24531 434-432-2761
James McDaniel, supt. Fax 432-9560
www.pcs.k12.va.us
Chatham ES 300/K-5
245 Chatham Elementary Rd 24531 434-432-5441
Jenny Eaton, prin. Fax 432-2227
Chatham MS 500/6-8
11650 US Highway 29 24531 434-432-2169
Cedric Hairston, prin. Fax 432-2842
Union Hall ES 300/PK-5
100 Union Hall Elem Cir 24531 434-724-7010
Carolyn Harris, prin. Fax 724-1850
Other Schools – See Blairs, Danville, Dry Fork, Gretna, Hurt, Ringgold

---

Woodlawn Academy 200/PK-8
956 Woodlawn Academy Rd 24531 434-432-9244
Steve Welch, hdmstr.

Check, Floyd
Floyd County SD
Supt. — See Floyd
Check ES 400/K-7
6810 Floyd Hwy N 24072 540-745-9410
Mike Greco, prin. Fax 745-9491

Chesapeake, Chesapeake, Pop. 218,968
Chesapeake CSD 39,800/K-12
PO Box 16496 23328 757-547-0165
Dr. W. Randolph Nichols, supt. Fax 547-0196
eclipse.cps.k12.va.us
Butts Road IS 800/3-5
1571 Mount Pleasant Rd 23322 757-482-4566
Grace Hopkins, prin. Fax 482-4066
Butts Road PS 600/K-2
1000 Mount Pleasant Rd 23322 757-482-5820
Elizabeth Stublen, prin. Fax 482-5095
Camelot ES 500/K-5
2901 Guenevere Dr 23323 757-558-5347
Dr. Stephanie Johnson, prin. Fax 558-5351
Carver IS 500/3-5
2601 Broad St 23324 757-494-7505
Dr. Cassandra Barksdale, prin. Fax 494-7685
Cedar Road ES 800/K-5
1605 Cedar Rd 23322 757-547-0166
Michael Bailey, prin. Fax 547-0538
Chittum ES 800/K-5
2008 Dock Landing Rd 23321 757-465-6300
Sherry Wilson, prin. Fax 465-6304
Crestwood IS 800/3-5
1240 Great Bridge Blvd 23320 757-494-7565
Michael Ward, prin. Fax 494-7598
Crestwood MS 600/6-8
1420 Great Bridge Blvd 23320 757-494-7560
Jacqueline Tate, prin. Fax 494-7599

Deep Creek Central ES 500/K-5
2448 Shipyard Rd 23323 757-558-5356
Curtis Lane, prin. Fax 558-5358
Deep Creek ES 700/K-5
2809 Forehand Dr 23323 757-558-5333
Dr. D. Jean Jones, prin. Fax 558-5337
Deep Creek MS 500/6-8
1955 Deal Dr 23323 757-558-5321
J. Coppage-Miller, prin. Fax 558-5320
Georgetown PS 700/K-3
436 Providence Rd 23325 757-578-7060
Dalphine Joppy, prin. Fax 578-7064
Grassfield ES 800/K-5
2248 Averill Dr 23323 757-558-8923
Thomas Rubin, prin. Fax 558-4486
Great Bridge IS 700/3-5
253 Hanbury Rd W 23322 757-482-4405
Dr. Rebecca Adams, prin. Fax 482-4027
Great Bridge MS 1,300/6-8
441 Battlefield Blvd S 23322 757-482-5128
Michelle Porter, prin. Fax 482-0210
Great Bridge PS 600/K-2
408 Cedar Rd 23322 757-547-1135
Brenda Wilson, prin. Fax 547-1820
Greenbrier IS 600/3-5
1701 River Birch Run N 23320 757-578-7080
Keith Hyater, prin. Fax 578-7084
Greenbrier MS 900/6-8
1016 Greenbrier Pkwy 23320 757-548-5309
Jeffrey Johnson, prin. Fax 548-8921
Greenbrier PS 500/K-2
1551 Eden Way S 23320 757-436-3428
Charles Barnes, prin. Fax 436-0208
Hickory ES 400/K-5
109 Benefit Rd 23322 757-421-7080
Kimberly Pinello, prin. Fax 421-7096
Hickory MS 1,700/6-8
1997 Hawk Blvd 23322 757-421-0468
Dr. Jean Infantino, prin. Fax 421-0475
Indian River MS 800/6-8
2300 Old Greenbrier Rd 23325 757-578-7030
Naomi Epps, prin. Fax 578-7036
Jolliff MS 800/6-8
1021 Jolliff Rd 23321 757-465-5246
Dr. Lee Fowler, prin. Fax 465-1646
Marshall ES 500/K-5
2706 Border Rd 23324 757-494-7515
Dr. Linda Woolard, prin. Fax 494-7651
Norfolk Highlands PS 300/K-3
1115 Myrtle Ave 23325 757-578-7092
Dr. Deborah Hutchens, prin. Fax 578-7096
Owens MS 1,100/6-8
1997 Horseback Run 23323 757-558-5382
Michael Perez, prin. Fax 558-5386
Portlock PS 500/K-2
1857 Varsity Dr 23324 757-494-7555
Nancy Cruz, prin. Fax 494-7650
Smith MS 1,000/6-8
2500 Rodgers St 23324 757-494-7590
Dr. Linda Scott, prin. Fax 494-7680
Southeastern ES 800/K-5
1853 Battlefield Blvd S 23322 757-421-7676
Leslie Wiggins, prin. Fax 421-7053
Southwestern ES 500/K-5
4410 Airline Blvd 23321 757-465-6310
Gayle Bartlett, prin. Fax 465-6314
Sparrow Road IS 500/4-5
1605 Sparrow Rd 23325 757-578-7050
Barbara Fortner, prin. Fax 578-7054
Treakle ES 400/K-5
2500 Gilmerton Rd 23323 757-558-5361
Hope Terrell, prin. Fax 558-5365
Truitt IS 300/3-5
1100 Holly Ave 23324 757-494-8014
Shirley Bryant, prin. Fax 494-8083
Western Branch IS 800/3-5
4013 Terry Dr 23321 757-638-7941
Terry Reitz, prin. Fax 638-7945
Western Branch MS 900/6-8
4201 Hawksley Dr 23321 757-638-7920
Craig Jones, prin. Fax 638-7926
Western Branch PS 600/K-2
4122 Terry Dr 23321 757-638-7951
Carol Stanek, prin. Fax 638-7954
Williams PS 700/K-2
1100 Battlefield Blvd N 23320 757-547-0238
Craig Mills, prin. Fax 547-3475
Wright PS 300/K-2
600 Park Ave 23324 757-494-7585
Brenda Hobbs, prin. Fax 494-7681

Cathedral of Faith Christian S 50/PK-K
2020 Portlock Rd 23324 757-545-8050
A.B. Small, prin. Fax 545-0953
Cedar Road Christian Academy 200/PK-4
916 Cedar Rd 23322 757-547-9553
Julia Kennedy, dir. Fax 549-1333
Chesapeake Montessori S 50/PK-4
516 Albemarle Dr 23322 757-547-7673
Shanna Honan, dir. Fax 547-7673
Cornerstone Christian S 100/PK-6
1212 Willow Ave 23325 757-424-7230
Sally Roberts, admin. Fax 424-2722
Faith Diamond Christian Academy 100/PK-8
1023 Deep Creek Blvd 23323 757-487-1800
Megan Cromwell-Corprew, prin. Fax 487-6311
Greenbrier Christian Academy 600/PK-12
311 Kempsville Rd 23320 757-547-9595
Dr. Ron White, supt. Fax 547-9569
Greenbrier Montessori S 50/PK-6
1100 Greenbrier Pkwy 23320 757-549-8584
Nneka Okala, prin. Fax 549-8674
Mt. Lebanon Christian Academy 100/PK-5
884 Bells Mill Rd 23322 757-547-9550
Darlene Northam, prin. Fax 410-9527
Stonebridge S 200/PK-12
PO Box 9247 23321 757-488-2214
Kathleen Mallory, hdmstr. Fax 465-7637

Tidewater Adventist Academy 100/K-12
1136 Centerville Tpke N 23320 757-479-0002
Fax 479-0008

Chester, Chesterfield, Pop. 14,986
Chesterfield County SD
Supt. — See Chesterfield
Carver MS 1,300/6-8
3800 Cougar Trl 23831 804-524-3620
Donald Ashburn, prin. Fax 520-0189
Chester MS 1,000/6-8
3900 W Hundred Rd 23831 804-768-6145
Brent Thomas, prin. Fax 768-6152
Curtis ES 800/PK-5
3600 W Hundred Rd 23831 804-768-6175
Teressa Clary, prin. Fax 768-9008
Davis MS 200/6-8
601 Corvus Ct 23836 804-541-4700
Sarah Fraher, prin. Fax 541-4701
Ecoff ES 900/PK-5
5200 Ecoff Ave 23831 804-768-6185
JoAnn Crowell Redd, prin. Fax 778-7247
Enon ES 600/PK-5
2001 E Hundred Rd 23836 804-530-5720
Mike Crusco, prin. Fax 530-1331
Harrowgate ES 700/PK-5
15501 Harrowgate Rd 23831 804-520-6015
Linda Wood, prin. Fax 520-6021
Scott ES 200/K-5
813 Beginners Trail Loop 23836 804-541-4660
Joan Temple, prin. Fax 541-4679
Wells ES 900/PK-5
13101 S Chester Rd 23831 804-768-6265
Virginia Patterson, prin. Fax 768-0356

Evangel Christian S 200/PK-12
16801 Harrow Gate Rd 23831 804-526-5941
Ada Dowdy, prin. Fax 526-3582

Chesterfield, Chesterfield
Chesterfield County SD 57,400/PK-12
PO Box 10 23832 804-748-1405
Dr. Marcus Newsome, supt. Fax 796-7178
www.chesterfield.k12.va.us
Chalkley ES 800/PK-5
3301 Turner Rd 23832 804-674-1300
Christopher Hart, prin. Fax 675-1478
Gates ES 900/PK-5
10001 Courthouse Rd 23832 804-768-6195
Kasey Shane, prin. Fax 768-0697
Jacobs Road ES 700/PK-5
8800 Jacobs Rd 23832 804-674-1320
James Raines, prin. Fax 276-9045
Winterpock ES K-5
9000 Elementary Way Loop 23832 804-763-5051
Dianne Smith, prin. Fax 763-5056
Other Schools – See Bon Air, Chester, Colonial Heights, Ettrick, Matoaca, Midlothian, Moseley, Richmond

---

Guardian Christian Academy 300/PK-8
6851 Courthouse Rd 23832 804-271-1891
Glenda Paul, dir. Fax 271-4195
Richmond Christian S 500/PK-12
6511 Belmont Rd 23832 804-276-3193
Cathy Danko, prin. Fax 276-9106

Chilhowie, Smyth, Pop. 1,787
Smyth County SD
Supt. — See Marion
Chilhowie ES 600/PK-5
PO Box 348 24319 276-646-8220
Dennis Carter, prin. Fax 646-2848
Chilhowie MS 300/6-8
PO Box 5018 24319 276-646-3942
Mike Davidson, prin. Fax 646-0210

Chincoteague, Accomack, Pop. 4,416
Accomack County SD
Supt. — See Accomac
Chincoteague ES 300/PK-5
6078 Hallie W Smith Dr 23336 757-336-5545
Dianne Olsen, prin. Fax 336-5586

Christiansburg, Montgomery, Pop. 17,926
Montgomery County SD 9,700/PK-12
200 Junkin St 24073 540-382-5100
Wall Shannon, supt. Fax 381-6127
www.mcps.org
Christiansburg ES 400/3-5
160 Wades Ln 24073 540-382-5172
Jason Garretson, prin. Fax 381-6143
Christiansburg MS 800/6-8
1205 Buffalo Dr 24073 540-394-2180
Ryan Hitchman, prin. Fax 394-2197
Christiansburg PS 500/PK-2
240 Betty Dr 24073 540-382-5175
Oliver Lewis, prin. Fax 381-6162
Falling Branch ES 600/PK-5
735 Falling Branch Rd 24073 540-381-6145
Julie Vanidestine, prin. Fax 381-6148
Other Schools – See Blacksburg, Elliston, Radford, Riner, Shawsville

---

Pathway Christian Academy 100/PK-12
896 Life Dr 24073 540-394-7300
Sheena Asconi, admin.

Church Road, Dinwiddie
Dinwiddie County SD
Supt. — See Dinwiddie
Midway ES 400/K-5
5511 Midway Rd 23833 804-265-4205
Kathleen Burgess, prin. Fax 265-4209

Churchville, Augusta
Augusta County SD
Supt. — See Fishersville
Churchville ES 300/K-5
3710 Churchville Ave 24421 540-337-6036
Laura Hodges, prin. Fax 337-8803

Clarksville, Mecklenburg, Pop. 1,289
Mecklenburg County SD
Supt. — See Boydton
Clarksville ES 400/PK-5
1696 Noblin Farm Rd 23927 434-374-8668
Ann Dalton, prin. Fax 374-8157

Clear Brook, Frederick
Frederick County SD
Supt. — See Winchester
Stonewall ES 500/K-5
3165 Martinsburg Pike 22624 540-662-2289
Darren Thomas, prin. Fax 723-8903

Cleveland, Russell, Pop. 143
Russell County SD
Supt. — See Lebanon
Cleveland ES 100/K-7
5168 Cleveland Rd 24225 276-889-6534
Larry Rasnake, prin. Fax 889-4259

Clifton, Fairfax, Pop. 206
Fairfax County SD
Supt. — See Falls Church
Clifton ES 400/K-6
7010 Clifton Rd 20124 703-988-8000
Arthur Polton, prin. Fax 988-8097
Liberty MS 1,100/7-8
6801 Union Mill Rd 20124 703-988-8100
Peggy Kelly, prin. Fax 988-8197
Union Mill ES 800/K-6
13611 Springstone Dr 20124 703-322-8500
Susan Shadis, prin. Fax 322-8597

St. Andrew the Apostle S 200/PK-8
6720 Union Mill Rd 20124 703-817-1774
Glenda Sigg, prin. Fax 817-1721

Clifton Forge, Alleghany, Pop. 4,077
Alleghany County SD
Supt. — See Low Moor
Sharon ES 200/PK-5
100 Sharon School Cir 24422 540-863-1712
Sherman Callahan, prin. Fax 863-1717

Clinchco, Dickenson, Pop. 413
Dickenson County SD
Supt. — See Clintwood
Clinchco ES 200/PK-7
198 Cardinal St 24226 276-835-8671
Ginger Patton, prin. Fax 835-8424

Clintwood, Dickenson, Pop. 1,518
Dickenson County SD 2,500/PK-12
PO Box 1127 24228 276-926-4643
Judy Compton, supt. Fax 926-6374
www.dickenson.k12.va.us
Clintwood S 400/PK-8
PO Box 585 24228 276-926-6088
Janie Vanover, prin. Fax 926-6505
Longs Fork S 300/PK-8
1280 Browning Holw 24228 276-926-6339
Jettie Mullins, prin. Fax 926-6651
Other Schools – See Birchleaf, Clinchco, Nora

Cloverdale, Botetourt, Pop. 1,689
Botetourt County SD
Supt. — See Fincastle
Cloverdale ES 400/K-5
PO Box 6 24077 540-992-1086
David Marcum, prin. Fax 992-8378
Read Mountain MS 700/6-8
182 Orchard Hill Dr 24077 540-966-8655
Michael Tetreault, prin. Fax 966-8656

Coeburn, Wise, Pop. 1,982
Wise County SD
Supt. — See Wise
Coeburn MS 400/5-8
PO Box 670 24230 276-395-2135
Scott Keith, prin. Fax 395-5453
Coeburn PS 500/PK-4
PO Box 1337 24230 276-395-6100
Susan Mullins, prin. Fax 395-3242

Collinsville, Henry, Pop. 7,280
Henry County SD 7,800/PK-12
PO Box 8958 24078 276-634-4700
Anthony Jackson, supt. Fax 638-2925
www.henry.k12.va.us
Collinsville PS 300/PK-2
15 Primary School Rd 24078 276-647-8932
Sandy Gammons, prin. Fax 647-9585
Fieldale-Collinsville MS 900/6-8
645 Miles Rd 24078 276-647-3841
Moriah Dollarhite, prin. Fax 647-4090
Smith ES 300/3-5
40 School Dr 24078 276-647-7676
Jalyn Daniels-Boyd, prin. Fax 647-9434
Other Schools – See Axton, Bassett, Martinsville, Ridgeway, Stanleytown

Colonial Beach, Westmoreland, Pop. 3,515
Colonial Beach SD 600/K-12
16 Irving Ave N 22443 804-224-0906
Robert Luttrell, supt. Fax 224-8357
www.cbschools.net
Colonial Beach ES 300/K-7
315 Douglas Ave 22443 804-224-9897
Kevin Newman, prin. Fax 224-0304

Westmoreland County SD
Supt. — See Montross
Washington District ES 400/PK-5
454 Oak Grove Rd 22443 804-224-9100
James Cook, prin. Fax 224-1644

Colonial Heights, Colonial Heights, Pop. 17,567
Chesterfield County SD
Supt. — See Chesterfield
Christian ES 1,000/PK-5
14801 Woods Edge Rd 23834 804-530-5733
Carolyn Tisdale, prin. Fax 530-0217

Colonial Heights CSD 2,900/K-12
512 Boulevard 23834 804-524-3400
Dr. Joseph Cox, supt. Fax 526-4524
www.colonialhts.net
Colonial Heights MS 700/6-8
500 Conduit Rd 23834 804-524-3420
Dr. Kim Evans, prin. Fax 526-9288
Lakeview ES 400/K-5
401 Taswell Ave 23834 804-524-3435
Valerie Wiggins, prin. Fax 520-4158
North ES 300/K-5
3201 Dale Ave 23834 804-524-3430
Thomas Pond, prin. Fax 526-8800
Tussing ES 600/K-5
5501 Conduit Rd 23834 804-524-3440
David Staples, prin. Fax 526-7938

Restoration Military Academy 100/K-12
1617 Boulevard Ste C 23834 804-862-1600
Latricia Brown, dir. Fax 526-4613

Concord, Campbell
Campbell County SD
Supt. — See Rustburg
Concord ES 300/K-5
9339 Village Hwy 24538 434-993-2257
Daniel Frazier, prin. Fax 993-3509

Council, Buchanan
Buchanan County SD
Supt. — See Grundy
Council S 200/PK-7
7608 Helen Henderson Hwy 24260 276-859-9329
Ransome Breeding, prin. Fax 859-0631

Courtland, Southampton, Pop. 1,251
Southhampton County SD 2,900/PK-12
PO Box 96 23837 757-653-2692
Charles Turner, supt. Fax 653-9422
www.southampton.k12.va.us/
Riverdale ES 400/PK-5
31023 Camp Pkwy 23837 757-562-3007
Andrea Ellis, prin. Fax 562-6424
Southampton MS 700/6-8
23450 Southampton Pkwy 23837 757-653-9250
Michael Booth, prin. Fax 653-7251
Other Schools – See Capron, Newsoms, Sedley

Southampton Academy 400/PK-12
26495 Old Plank Rd 23837 757-653-2512
Mercer Neale, hdmstr. Fax 653-0011

Covington, Covington, Pop. 6,205
Alleghany County SD
Supt. — See Low Moor
Boiling Spring ES 200/K-5
5403 Boiling Spring Cir 24426 540-965-1817
Debbie Farmer, prin. Fax 965-1819
Callaghan ES 200/K-5
4018 Midland Trl 24426 540-965-1810
Nancy Moga, prin. Fax 965-1814
Clifton MS 700/6-8
1000 Riverview Farm Rd 24426 540-863-1726
Brenda Siple, prin. Fax 863-1731
Mountain View ES 600/PK-5
100 Gleason Dr 24426 540-863-1737
Teresa Johnson, prin. Fax 863-1740

Covington CSD 900/PK-12
340 E Walnut St 24426 540-965-1400
Edward Graham, supt. Fax 965-1404
www.covington.k12.va.us/
Edgemont PS 300/PK-3
574 W Indian Valley Rd 24426 540-965-1420
Marc W. Smith, prin.
Jeter-Watson IS 300/4-7
560 W Indian Valley Rd 24426 540-965-1430
Annette Shupe, prin.

Craigsville, Augusta, Pop. 1,016
Augusta County SD
Supt. — See Fishersville
Craigsville ES 100/K-5
100 E 1st St 24430 540-997-9184
Nick Nycum, prin. Fax 997-0432

Crewe, Nottoway, Pop. 2,291
Nottoway County SD
Supt. — See Nottoway
Crewe PS 200/K-4
1953 Sunnyside Rd 23930 434-645-8149
Carrie Gravely, prin. Fax 645-1604
Nottoway IS 300/5-6
5285 Old Nottoway Rd 23930 434-292-5353
Daisy Hicks, prin. Fax 298-0612
Nottoway MS 300/7-8
5279 Old Nottoway Rd 23930 434-292-5375
George Smith, prin. Fax 292-7479

Critz, Patrick
Patrick County SD
Supt. — See Stuart
Hardin-Reynolds Memorial MS 300/4-7
PO Box 130 24082 276-694-3631
Ann Fulcher, prin. Fax 694-5805

Crozet, Albemarle, Pop. 2,256
Albemarle County SD
Supt. — See Charlottesville
Brownsville ES 400/PK-5
5870 Rockfish Gap Tpke 22932 434-823-4658
Jo A. Vining, prin. Fax 823-5120
Crozet ES 400/PK-5
1407 Crozet Ave 22932 434-823-4800
Karen Marcus, prin. Fax 823-6470
Henley MS 800/6-8
5880 Rockfish Gap Tpke 22932 434-823-4393
Patrick McLaughlin, prin. Fax 823-2711

Crozier, Goochland
Goochland County SD
Supt. — See Goochland

Randolph ES 400/K-5
1552 Sheppard Town Rd 23039 804-556-5385
Stacey Austin, prin. Fax 784-2674

Salem Christian S 200/PK-12
1701 Cardwell Rd 23039 804-784-4174
Norman Brooking, admin. Fax 784-0432

Culpeper, Culpeper, Pop. 12,047
Culpeper County SD 7,300/K-12
450 Radio Ln 22701 540-825-3677
Dr. Bobbi Johnson, supt. Fax 829-2111
www.culpeperschools.org
Binns MS 800/6-8
205 E Grandview Ave 22701 540-825-6894
Sherri Harkness, prin. Fax 829-9926
Culpeper County MS 900/6-8
14300 Achievement Dr 22701 540-825-4140
William Zierden, prin. Fax 825-7543
Emerald Hill ES 900/K-5
11245 Rixeyville Rd 22701 540-937-7361
Stacey Timmons, prin. Fax 937-7365
Farmington ES 400/K-5
500 Sunset Ln 22701 540-825-0713
Gail Brewer, prin. Fax 829-0865
Richardson ES 700/K-5
18370 Simms Dr 22701 540-825-0616
Susan Bridges, prin. Fax 825-5807
Sample ES 700/K-5
18480 Simms Dr 22701 540-825-5448
Karie Lane, prin. Fax 829-2118
Sycamore Park ES 700/K-5
451 Radio Ln 22701 540-825-8847
Russell Houck, prin. Fax 825-6384
Yowell ES K-5
701 Yowell Dr 22701 540-825-9484
Cathy Timmons, prin. Fax 825-7509

Culpeper Christian S 200/PK-8
810 Old Rixeyville Rd 22701 540-825-4208
Michael Owings, admin. Fax 829-0910
Epiphany S 200/PK-6
114 E Edmondson St 22701 540-825-9017
Barbara Terry, prin. Fax 825-8987
St. Luke's Lutheran S 200/PK-9
1200 Old Rixeyville Rd 22701 540-825-8890
David Kukielski, hdmstr. Fax 825-4471

Cumberland, Cumberland
Cumberland County SD 1,600/PK-12
PO Box 170 23040 804-492-4212
James Thornton, supt. Fax 492-4818
www.cucps.k12.va.us
Cumberland ES 700/PK-5
PO Box 190 23040 804-492-4212
Chip Jones, prin. Fax 492-9107
Cumberland MS 300/6-8
PO Box 184 23040 804-492-4212
Mark Mabey, prin. Fax 492-9326

Dahlgren, King George
King George County SD
Supt. — See King George
Potomac ES 500/K-6
PO Box 314 22448 540-663-3322
Elizabeth Gordon, prin. Fax 663-2947

Dale City, Prince William, Pop. 58,000

Holy Family S 300/PK-8
14160 Ferndale Rd 22193 703-670-3138
Louis Frisenda, prin. Fax 670-8323

Damascus, Washington, Pop. 1,083
Washington County SD
Supt. — See Abingdon
Damascus MS 200/6-8
32101 Government Rd 24236 276-739-4100
David Lambert, prin. Fax 475-4032

Danville, Danville, Pop. 46,143
Danville CSD 6,800/PK-12
PO Box 9600 24543 434-799-6400
Sue Davis Ed.D., supt. Fax 799-5008
web.dps.k12.va.us
Bonner MS 600/6-8
300 Apollo Ave 24540 434-799-6446
Dr. J. David Cochran, prin. Fax 797-8867
Forest Hills ES 200/PK-5
155 Mountain View Ave 24541 434-799-6430
Catherine Lassiter, prin. Fax 799-8922
Gibson MS 400/6-8
1215 Industrial Ave 24541 434-799-6426
Robin Owens, prin. Fax 797-8857
Glenwood ES 200/PK-5
1540 Halifax Rd 24540 434-799-5129
Darlene Logan, prin. Fax 799-6545
Grove Park Preschool 200/PK-PK
1070 S Main St 24541 434-799-6437
Lou Ann Long, prin. Fax 797-8921
Johnson ES 600/PK-5
680 Arnett Blvd 24540 434-799-6433
George Macklin, prin. Fax 797-8926
Lea ES 300/PK-5
439 Cedarbrook Dr 24541 434-799-6423
Catiia Greene, prin. Fax 797-8924
Park Avenue ES 500/PK-5
661 Park Ave 24541 434-799-6452
Melissa Newton, prin. Fax 797-8891
Schoolfield Academy 600/PK-5
1400 W Main St 24541 434-799-6455
Amy Turner, prin. Fax 797-8923
Taylor ES 300/PK-5
825 Piney Forest Rd 24540 434-799-6440
Joyce Tucker, prin. Fax 799-5289
Westwood MS 500/6-8
500 Apollo Ave 24540 434-797-8860
Christie Dawson, prin. Fax 797-8874

Wilson ES 200/PK-5
1005 Main St 24541 434-773-8204
Jocelyn Fitzgerald, prin. Fax 773-8102
Woodberry Hills ES 200/PK-5
614 Audubon Dr 24540 434-799-6466
Kimberly Yates, prin. Fax 797-8927

Pittsylvania County SD
Supt. — See Chatham
Brosville ES 300/K-5
195 Bulldog Ln 24541 434-685-7787
Felita Atkins, prin. Fax 685-3362
Stony Mill ES 500/PK-5
100 Stony Mill Elem Cir 24541 434-685-7545
Joyce Ferguson, prin. Fax 685-4328
Twin Spring ES 800/K-5
100 Twin Springs Elementary 24540 434-724-2666
Emma Austin, prin. Fax 724-2851

B & P Young SDA S 50/1-8
212 Ingram Rd 24541 434-822-0356
Julia Allen, prin. Fax 822-0356
Epiphany Episcopal S PK-12
115 Jefferson Ave 24541 434-792-4334
Rev. Samuel Colley-Toothaker, hdmstr. Fax 792-0786
Sacred Heart S 300/PK-9
540 Central Blvd 24541 434-793-2656
Kimberly Meadows, prin. Fax 793-2658
Westover Christian Academy 500/PK-12
5665 Riverside Dr 24541 434-822-0800
Shawn Weeks, admin. Fax 822-0441

Dayton, Rockingham, Pop. 1,345
Rockingham County SD
Supt. — See Harrisonburg
Ottobine ES 200/PK-5
8646 Waggys Creek Rd 22821 540-879-2091
Laura Evy, prin. Fax 879-2556
Pence MS 800/6-8
375 Bowman Rd 22821 540-879-2535
Mary Shifflett, prin. Fax 879-2179

Dendron, Surry, Pop. 294
Surry County SD
Supt. — See Surry
Jackson MS 300/5-8
4255 New Design Rd 23839 757-267-2810
Dr. Serbrenia Sims, prin. Fax 267-0809
Surry ES 400/PK-4
1600 Hollybush Rd 23839 757-267-2558
Geraldine Bailey, prin. Fax 267-0107

Dillwyn, Buckingham, Pop. 445
Buckingham County SD
Supt. — See Buckingham
Dillwyn ES 200/4-5
40 Frank Harris Rd 23936 434-983-2511
Elaine Duke, prin. Fax 983-2222
Dillwyn PS 300/K-3
52 Dillwyn Primary Rd 23936 434-983-2861
Pennie Allen, prin. Fax 983-1542

Dinwiddie, Dinwiddie
Dinwiddie County SD 3,700/K-12
PO Box 7 23841 804-469-4190
Dr. Charles Maranzano, supt. Fax 469-4197
www.dinwiddie.k12.va.us
Dinwiddie County MS 700/6-7
PO Box 340 23841 804-469-4380
Trenia Harris, prin. Fax 469-3350
Dinwiddie ES 400/K-5
13811 Boydton Plank Rd 23841 804-469-4580
Patricia Moody, prin. Fax 469-4585
Southside ES 400/K-5
10305 Boydton Plank Rd 23841 804-469-4480
Roberta Brown, prin. Fax 469-4484
Other Schools – See Church Road, Mc Kenney, Sutherland

Disputanta, Prince George
Prince George County SD
Supt. — See Prince George
Harrison ES 700/PK-5
12900 E Quaker Rd 23842 804-991-2242
Sharon O'Neill, prin. Fax 991-2123
Moore MS 1,000/6-7
11455 Prince George Dr 23842 804-733-2740
Willie Elliott, prin. Fax 733-2697
South ES 500/PK-5
13400 Prince George Dr 23842 804-733-2755
Robin Pruett, prin. Fax 732-5844

Dryden, Lee
Lee County SD
Supt. — See Jonesville
Dryden ES 300/1-5
RR 1 Box 1825 24243 276-546-4443
Mona Baker, prin. Fax 546-5158

Powell Valley Christian S 50/K-8
RR 1 Box 1015 24243 276-523-0464
Nicky Herron, lead tchr.

Dry Fork, Pittsylvania
Pittsylvania County SD
Supt. — See Chatham
Tunstall MS 600/6-8
1160 Tunstall High Rd 24549 434-724-7086
Rebecca Stevens, prin. Fax 724-7907

Dublin, Pulaski, Pop. 2,208
Pulaski County SD
Supt. — See Pulaski
Dublin ES 600/PK-5
600 Dunlap Rd 24084 540-643-0337
Jennifer Wall, prin. Fax 674-1351
Dublin MS 600/6-8
650 Giles Ave 24084 540-643-0367
Robin Keener, prin. Fax 674-0813
Newbern ES 100/K-5
5470 Lyons Rd 24084 540-643-0639
Joseph Reed, prin. Fax 674-6905

Duffield, Scott, Pop. 60
Lee County SD
Supt. — See Jonesville
Stickleyville ES 100/PK-7
RR 1 Box 141S 24244 276-546-1337
Mary Laster, prin. Fax 546-2364

Scott County SD
Supt. — See Gate City
Duffield PS 300/K-4
663 Duff Patt Hwy 24244 276-431-2244
Cindy Dorton, prin. Fax 431-2131
Rye Cove IS 200/5-7
158 Memorial School Ln 24244 276-940-2322
Renee Dishner, prin. Fax 940-4161

Dumfries, Prince William, Pop. 4,816
Prince William County SD
Supt. — See Manassas
Dumfries ES 400/K-5
3990 Cameron St 22026 703-221-3101
Melvina Michie, prin. Fax 221-0047
Henderson ES 500/K-5
3799 Waterway Dr, 703-670-2885
Lisa Reinshuttle, prin. Fax 670-5521
Montclair ES 600/K-5
4920 Tallowwood Dr, 703-730-1072
Tawnya Soltis, prin. Fax 878-0356
Pattie ES 600/K-5
16125 Dumfries Rd, 703-670-3173
Margaret Otterblad, prin. Fax 583-7233
Potomac MS 6-8
3130 Panther Pride Dr 22026 703-221-4996
Dr. Benita Stephens, prin.
Swans Creek ES 600/K-5
17700 Wayside Dr 22026 703-445-0930
Dr. Barry Rosenberg, prin. Fax 445-0546
Williams ES 700/K-5
3100 Panther Pride Dr 22026 703-445-8376
Paula Jackson, prin. Fax 445-8378

Dungannon, Scott, Pop. 307
Scott County SD
Supt. — See Gate City
Dungannon IS 100/4-7
113 Fifth Ave 24245 276-467-2281
Jennifer Meade, prin. Fax 467-2654

Eagle Rock, Botetourt
Botetourt County SD
Supt. — See Fincastle
Eagle Rock ES 200/PK-5
145 Eagles Nest Dr 24085 540-884-2421
Wanda Martin, prin. Fax 473-8377

Earlysville, Albemarle
Albemarle County SD
Supt. — See Charlottesville
Broadus Wood ES 300/PK-5
185 Buck Mountain Rd 22936 434-973-3865
Barbara Edwards, prin. Fax 973-3833

Elkton, Rockingham, Pop. 2,606
Rockingham County SD
Supt. — See Harrisonburg
Elkton ES 600/PK-5
302 W B St 22827 540-298-1511
Edward Powell, prin. Fax 298-1471
Elkton MS 400/6-8
21063 Blue and Gold Dr 22827 540-298-1228
Ramona Pence, prin. Fax 298-0029

Elliston, Montgomery, Pop. 1,243
Montgomery County SD
Supt. — See Christiansburg
Elliston-Lafayette ES 200/PK-5
5201 Tango Ln 24087 540-268-2291
Denise Boyle, prin. Fax 268-2639
Shawsville ES 200/PK-5
4390 Riffe St 24087 540-268-2208
Amy Williams, prin. Fax 268-4335

Emporia, Emporia, Pop. 5,587
Greensville County SD 2,700/PK-12
105 Ruffin St 23847 434-634-3748
Dr. Philip Worrell, supt. Fax 634-3495
www.greensville.k12.va.us/
Belfield ES, 515 Belfield Rd 23847 400/5-6
Curtis Young, prin. 434-634-5566
Greensville ES, 1101 Sussex Dr 23847 1,100/PK-4
James Callahan, prin. 434-336-0907
Wyatt MS 400/7-8
206 Slagles Lake Rd 23847 434-634-5159
Rochelle Anderson, prin. Fax 634-0442

First Baptist Christian Academy 50/K-8
1155 Sussex Dr 23847 434-634-1230
Brenda Robinson, dir. Fax 634-0254

Esmont, Albemarle
Albemarle County SD
Supt. — See Charlottesville
Yancey ES 200/PK-5
7625 Porters Rd 22937 434-974-8060
Alison Dwier-Selden, prin. Fax 974-8061

Ettrick, Chesterfield, Pop. 5,290
Chesterfield County SD
Supt. — See Chesterfield
Ettrick ES 500/PK-5
20910 Chesterfield Ave 23803 804-520-6005
Michael Courtney, prin. Fax 520-0430

Ewing, Lee
Lee County SD
Supt. — See Jonesville
Elydale ES 100/K-7
RR 2 Box 557 24248 276-445-4439
Tara Williams, prin. Fax 445-5267
Ewing ES 200/K-7
PO Box 279 24248 276-445-5311
Jerry Hounshell, prin. Fax 445-3101

Exmore, Northampton, Pop. 1,393
Northampton County SD
Supt. — See Machipongo
Occohannock ES 500/K-5
4208 Seaside Rd 23350 757-678-5151
Amy Austen, prin. Fax 442-6349

Broadwater Academy 500/PK-12
PO Box 546 23350 757-442-9041
Jeremy McLean, hdmstr. Fax 442-9615
Shore Christian Academy 50/PK-4
11624 Occohannock Rd 23350 757-442-9791
Charley Dohme, prin. Fax 442-9791

Fairfax, Fairfax, Pop. 21,963
Fairfax County SD
Supt. — See Falls Church
Bonnie Brae ES 700/K-6
5420 Sideburn Rd 22032 703-321-3900
Kathy Bruce, prin. Fax 321-3997
Daniels Run ES 700/K-6
3705 Old Lee Hwy 22030 703-279-8400
Kathleen Mullenix, prin. Fax 279-8497
Eagle View ES PK-6
4500 Dixie Hill Rd 22030 703-322-3100
Deborah Tyler, prin. Fax 322-3197
Fairfax Villa ES 400/PK-6
10900 Santa Clara Dr 22030 703-267-2800
Dale Mann, prin. Fax 267-2897
Fairhill ES 500/K-6
3001 Chichester Ln 22031 703-208-8100
Patricia Phillips, prin. Fax 208-8197
Frost MS 1,100/7-8
4101 Pickett Rd 22032 703-426-5700
Marti Jo Jackson, prin. Fax 426-5797
Greenbriar East ES 600/PK-6
13006 Point Pleasant Dr 22033 703-633-6400
Linda Cohen, prin. Fax 378-7790
Greenbriar West ES 700/K-6
13300 Poplar Tree Rd 22033 703-633-6700
Lori Cleveland, prin. Fax 633-6797
Lanier MS 1,000/7-8
3801 Jermantown Rd 22030 703-934-2400
Scott Poole, prin. Fax 934-2497
Laurel Ridge ES 800/K-6
10110 Commonwealth Blvd 22032 703-426-3700
Larry Burke, prin. Fax 426-3797
Lees Corner ES 700/K-6
13500 Hollinger Ave 22033 703-227-3500
Clay Sande, prin. Fax 227-3597
Little Run ES 400/PK-6
4511 Olley Ln 22032 703-503-3500
Sharon Baumgarten, prin. Fax 503-3597
Mantua ES 900/PK-6
9107 Horner Ct 22031 703-645-6300
Jan-Marie Fernandez, prin. Fax 645-6397
Mosby Woods ES 600/K-6
9819 Five Oaks Rd 22031 703-937-1600
Mahri Aste, prin. Fax 937-1697
Navy ES 800/K-6
3500 W Ox Rd 22033 703-262-7100
Katie Hand, prin. Fax 262-7197
Oak View ES 700/K-6
5004 Sideburn Rd 22032 703-764-7100
Bonnie Glazewski, prin. Fax 764-7197
Olde Creek ES 400/K-6
9524 Old Creek Dr 22032 703-426-3100
Melissa Kupferschmid, prin. Fax 426-3197
Providence ES 800/K-6
3616 Jermantown Rd 22030 703-460-4400
Joy Hanbury, prin. Fax 460-4497
Wakefield Forest ES 500/K-6
4011 Iva Ln 22032 703-503-2300
Sheri D'Amato, prin. Fax 503-2397
Willow Springs ES 700/K-6
5400 Willow Springs School 22030 703-679-6000
Elizabeth Rhein, prin. Fax 687-6097

Gesher Jewish Day S of Northern Virginia 200/K-8
4700 Shirley Gate Rd 22030 703-978-9789
Dr. Zvi Schoenburg, hdmstr. Fax 978-2668
Little Flock Christian S 100/PK-8
11911 Braddock Rd 22030 703-591-1216
Andrea Schultz, prin.
Merritt Academy 200/PK-8
9211 Arlington Blvd 22031 703-273-8000
Carol Edelstein, dir. Fax 591-1431
Northern Virginia Christian Academy 200/K-12
11000 Berry St 22030 703-273-0803
Dr. Michael Reed, prin. Fax 273-0805
St. Leo S 500/PK-8
3704 Old Lee Hwy 22030 703-273-1211
Dave DiPippa, prin. Fax 273-6913
St. Mary of Sorrows Preschool PK-PK
5222 Sideburn Rd 22032 703-978-4141
Elena Quartuccio, prin. Fax 978-2568
Trinity Christian S 600/K-12
11204 Braddock Rd 22030 703-273-0966
David Vanderpoel Ph.D., hdmstr. Fax 352-8522
Way of Faith Christian Academy 200/K-12
8800 Arlington Blvd 22031 703-573-7221
Ellen Blackwell, dir. Fax 573-7248

Fairfax Station, Fairfax
Fairfax County SD
Supt. — See Falls Church
Fairview ES 600/K-6
5815 Ox Rd 22039 703-503-3700
Easter Lancaster, prin. Fax 978-5492
Halley ES 600/PK-6
8850 Cross Chase Cir 22039 703-551-5700
Janet Funk, prin. Fax 551-5797
Silverbrook ES 1,200/K-6
9350 Crosspointe Dr 22039 703-690-5100
Melaney Mackin, prin. Fax 690-5197

Living Savior Lutheran S 100/PK-K
5500 Ox Rd 22039 703-352-4208
Janet Fagre, dir.

Fairfield, Rockbridge
Rockbridge County SD
Supt. — See Lexington
Fairfield ES 300/K-5
PO Box 162 24435 540-348-5202
Sheree Gillespie, prin. Fax 377-2601
Rockbridge MS 200/6-8
1200 Sterrett Rd 24435 540-348-5445
John Morris, prin. Fax 348-1016

Falls Church, Falls Church, Pop. 10,781
Fairfax County SD 161,600/PK-12
8115 Gatehouse Rd 22042 703-423-1000
Dr. Jack Dale, supt. Fax 423-1007
www.fcps.edu
Baileys ES for the Arts & Sciences 800/K-5
6111 Knollwood Dr 22041 703-575-6800
Jay McClain, prin. Fax 575-6897
Beech Tree ES 400/K-5
3401 Beechtree Ln 22042 703-531-2600
Terry Phillips, prin. Fax 237-7785
Belvedere ES 500/PK-5
6540 Columbia Pike 22041 703-916-6800
Sandra Allison-Harris, prin. Fax 916-6897
Glen Forest ES 700/K-5
5829 Glen Forest Dr 22041 703-578-8000
Elizabeth Aldonas, prin. Fax 578-8097
Graham Road ES 300/K-6
3036 Graham Rd 22042 703-226-2700
Molly Bensinger-Lacy, prin. Fax 226-2797
Haycock ES 700/K-6
6616 Haycock Rd 22043 703-531-4000
Maureen Boland, prin. Fax 531-4097
Jackson MS 900/7-8
3020 Gallows Rd 22042 703-204-8100
Louise Porter, prin. Fax 204-8197
Lemon Road ES 300/K-6
7230 Idylwood Rd 22043 703-714-6400
Carolyn Carter Miller, prin. Fax 714-6497
Longfellow MS 1,000/7-8
2000 Westmoreland St 22043 703-533-2600
Carole Kihm, prin. Fax 533-2697
Pine Spring ES 500/PK-6
7607 Willow Ln 22042 571-226-4400
Nancy Bradley, prin. Fax 226-4497
Shrevewood ES 400/K-6
7525 Shreve Rd 22043 703-645-6600
Shirley McCoy, prin. Fax 645-6697
Sleepy Hollow ES 300/K-5
3333 Sleepy Hollow Rd 22044 703-237-7000
Craig Rowland, prin. Fax 237-7097
Timber Lane ES 500/PK-6
2737 West St 22046 703-206-5300
Diane Connolly, prin. Fax 206-5397
Westgate ES 300/K-6
7500 Magarity Rd 22043 703-610-5700
Juanita Harris, prin. Fax 610-5797
Westlawn ES 600/K-6
3200 Westley Rd 22042 703-241-5100
Cecilia Vanderhye, prin. Fax 241-5197
Woodburn ES 400/K-6
3401 Hemlock Dr 22042 703-641-8200
Bridget Chapin, prin. Fax 641-8297
Other Schools – See Alexandria, Annandale, Burke, Centreville, Chantilly, Clifton, Fairfax, Fairfax Station, Fort Belvoir, Great Falls, Herndon, Lorton, Mc Lean, Oakton, Reston, Springfield, Vienna

Falls Church CSD 1,900/K-12
803 W Broad St Ste 300 22046 703-248-5600
Lois Berlin, supt. Fax 248-5613
www.fccps.org/
Henderson MS 400/5-7
7130 Leesburg Pike 22043 703-720-5700
Ann McCarty, prin. Fax 720-5710
Jefferson ES 400/2-4
601 S Oak St 22046 703-248-5660
Vincent Baxter, prin. Fax 248-5666
Mount Daniel PS 300/K-1
2328 N Oak St 22046 703-248-5640
Kathleen Halayko, prin. Fax 248-5642

Congressional Schools of Virginia 300/PK-8
3229 Sleepy Hollow Rd 22042 703-533-9711
Seth Ahlborn, hdmstr. Fax 532-5467
Corpus Christi ECC 100/PK-PK
7506 Saint Philips Ct 22042 703-573-4570
Amy Fry, prin. Fax 573-6832
Corpus Christi S 400/K-8
3301 Glen Carlyn Rd 22041 703-820-7450
Laura Zybrick, prin. Fax 820-9635
Grace Lutheran S 100/K-8
3233 Annandale Rd 22042 703-534-5517
Robert Rebers, prin. Fax 534-1394
Montessori S of Holmes Run 100/PK-8
3527 Gallows Rd 22042 703-573-4652
Judith Clarke, hdmstr. Fax 573-2807
St. James S 600/K-8
830 W Broad St 22046 703-533-1182
Sr. Nancy Kindelan, prin. Fax 532-8316
St. Joseph Preschool PK-PK
203 N Spring St 22046 703-533-8441
Rodney Torp, prin. Fax 462-8621

Falmouth, Stafford, Pop. 3,541
Stafford County SD
Supt. — See Stafford
Drew MS 400/6-8
501 Cambridge St 22405 540-371-1415
Catherine Williams, prin. Fax 371-1447
Falmouth ES 400/K-5
1000 Forbes St 22405 540-373-7458
Gayle Thyrring, prin. Fax 371-1757

Fancy Gap, Carroll
Carroll County SD
Supt. — See Hillsville
Fancy Gap ES 200/K-5
63 Winding Ridge Rd 24328 276-728-7504
Dr. Jeanne Edwards, prin. Fax 728-4619

Farmville, Prince Edward, Pop. 6,876
Prince Edward County SD 2,600/K-12
35 Eagle Dr 23901 434-315-2100
Dr. Patricia Watkins, supt. Fax 392-1911
www.pecps.k12.va.us
Prince Edward ES 1,000/K-4
35 Eagle Dr 23901 434-315-2110
Barbara Brown, prin. Fax 392-1583
Prince Edward MS 800/5-8
35 Eagle Dr 23901 434-315-2120
Michael Earl, prin. Fax 392-4286

Fuqua S, PO Box 328 23901 500/PK-12
Ruth Murphy, pres. 434-392-4131
New Life Christian Academy 100/PK-12
9 Mahan Rd 23901 434-392-6236
Dr. Betty Weaver, admin. Fax 392-4462

Ferrum, Franklin, Pop. 1,514
Franklin County SD
Supt. — See Rocky Mount
Ferrum ES 300/PK-5
660 Ferrum School Rd 24088 540-365-7194
Marcie Altice, prin. Fax 365-7307

Fincastle, Botetourt, Pop. 358
Botetourt County SD 4,900/PK-12
143 Poor Farm Rd 24090 540-473-8263
Dr. Anthony Brads, supt. Fax 473-8298
www.bcps.k12.va.us
Breckinridge ES 200/PK-5
331 Springwood Rd 24090 540-473-8386
Laura Camp, prin. Fax 473-8361
Central Academy MS 400/6-8
367 Poor Farm Rd 24090 540-473-8333
Vaneta McAlexander, prin. Fax 473-8398
Other Schools – See Blue Ridge, Buchanan, Cloverdale, Eagle Rock, Troutville

Fishersville, Augusta, Pop. 3,230
Augusta County SD 10,400/K-12
6 John Lewis Rd 22939 540-245-5100
Gary McQuain, supt. Fax 245-5115
www.augusta.k12.va.us
Wilson ES 300/K-5
127 Woodrow Wilson Ave 22939 540-245-5040
David K. Shriver, prin. Fax 245-5042
Wilson MS 6-8
232 Hornet Rd 22939 540-245-5185
Donald Curtis, prin. Fax 245-5189
Other Schools – See Churchville, Craigsville, Fort Defiance, Mount Solon, Staunton, Stuarts Draft, Verona, Waynesboro

Flint Hill, Rappahannock

Wakefield Country Day S 200/PK-12
PO Box 739 22627 540-635-8555
Kathleen Grove, hdmstr. Fax 636-1501

Floyd, Floyd, Pop. 434
Floyd County SD 2,100/PK-12
140 Harris Hart Rd NE 24091 540-745-9400
Terry Arbogast Ed.D., supt. Fax 745-9496
www.floyd.k12.va.us
Floyd ES 500/PK-7
531 Oak Hill Dr SE 24091 540-745-9440
Jack McKinley, prin. Fax 745-9494
Other Schools – See Check, Radford, Willis

Forest, Bedford, Pop. 5,624
Bedford County SD
Supt. — See Bedford
Forest ES 400/K-5
1 Scholar Ln 24551 434-525-2681
Lorri Manley, prin. Fax 525-7186
Forest MS 1,000/6-8
100 Ashwood Dr 24551 434-525-6630
Michelle Morgan, prin. Fax 525-1284
Jefferson ES 700/K-5
1255 Patriot Pl 24551 434-534-6159
Dr. Mac Duis, prin. Fax 534-6240
New London Academy ES 300/K-5
12400 E Lynchburg Salem Tpk 24551 434-525-2177
J. Andy Greenough, prin. Fax 525-0935

Timberlake Christian Schools 300/PK-12
202 Horizon Dr 24551 434-237-5943
William Heppding, admin. Fax 239-3319

Fork Union, Fluvanna
Fluvanna County SD
Supt. — See Palmyra
Fluvanna MS 800/6-8
9172 James Madison Hwy 23055 434-842-2222
Kathi Driver, prin. Fax 842-5150

Fort Belvoir, Fairfax, Pop. 8,590
Fairfax County SD
Supt. — See Falls Church
Fort Belvoir ES 1,200/K-6
5970 Meeres Rd 22060 703-781-2700
Jane Wilson, prin. Fax 781-2797

Fort Blackmore, Scott
Scott County SD
Supt. — See Gate City
Fort Blackmore ES 100/K-3
214 Big Stoney Creek Rd 24250 276-995-2471
Valerie Babb, prin. Fax 995-2654

Fort Defiance, Augusta
Augusta County SD
Supt. — See Fishersville
Clymore ES 700/K-5
184 Fort Defiance Rd 24437 540-245-5043
John Chase, prin. Fax 245-5095
Stewart MS 700/6-8
118 Fort Defiance Rd 24437 540-245-5046
Bill Roberts, prin. Fax 245-5049

Fort Eustis, See Newport News
Newport News CSD
Supt. — See Newport News
Stanford ES 600/K-5
929 Madison Ave 23604 757-888-3200
Victor Martinez, prin. Fax 888-3354

Franklin, Southampton, Pop. 8,594
Franklin CSD 1,400/PK-12
207 W 2nd Ave 23851 757-569-8111
Fax 516-1015
www.franklincity.k12.va.us
King MS 300/6-8
501 Charles St 23851 757-562-4631
Horatio Douglas, prin. Fax 562-0231
Morton ES 600/PK-5
300 Morton St 23851 757-562-5458
Donald Spengeman, prin. Fax 562-6178

Fredericksburg, Fredericksburg, Pop. 20,732
Fredericksburg CSD 2,500/K-12
817 Princess Anne St 22401 540-372-1130
Dr. David Melton, supt. Fax 372-1111
www.cityschools.com
Lafayette Upper ES 500/3-5
3 Learning Ln 22401 540-310-0029
John Russ, prin. Fax 310-0671
Mercer ES 600/K-2
2100 Cowan Blvd 22401 540-372-1115
Marjorie Tankersley, prin. Fax 372-6753
Walker-Grant MS 500/6-8
1 Learning Ln 22401 540-372-1145
Harry Thomas, prin. Fax 891-5449

Spotsylvania County SD 23,900/PK-12
8020 River Stone Dr 22407 540-834-2500
Dr. Jerry Hill, supt. Fax 834-2556
www.spotsylvania.k12.va.us
Battlefield ES 700/PK-5
11108 Leavells Rd 22407 540-786-4532
Susan Fines, prin. Fax 786-3149
Battlefield MS 800/6-8
11120 Leavells Rd 22407 540-786-4400
Sheila Smith, prin. Fax 786-7109
Cedar Forest ES K-5
3412 Massaponax Church Rd 22408 540-834-4569
David Strawn, prin. Fax 834-4577
Chancellor ES 400/K-5
5995 Plank Rd 22407 540-786-6123
Shawn Hudson, prin. Fax 786-5487
Chancellor MS 900/6-8
6320 Harrison Rd 22407 540-786-8099
Melvin Brown, prin. Fax 785-9392
Freedom MS 900/6-8
7315 Smith Station Rd 22407 540-548-1030
Alan Jacobs, prin. Fax 786-0782
Harrison Road ES 800/K-5
6230 Harrison Rd 22407 540-548-4864
Deborah Frazier, prin. Fax 548-4863
Lee Hill ES 800/K-5
3600 Lee Hill School Dr 22408 540-898-1433
Darnella Cunningham, prin. Fax 898-9223
Parkside ES 800/K-5
5620 Smith Station Rd 22407 540-710-5190
Thomas Eichenberg, prin. Fax 710-7451
Salem ES 600/K-5
4501 Jackson Rd 22407 540-786-8218
Harold Morton, prin. Fax 786-5006
Smith Station ES 800/K-5
7320 Smith Station Rd 22407 540-786-5443
Michelle Wright, prin. Fax 785-2880
Spotswood ES 600/K-5
400 Lorraine Ave 22408 540-898-1514
Mary Jane Perrault, prin. Fax 898-8571
Other Schools – See Spotsylvania

Stafford County SD
Supt. — See Stafford
Conway ES 800/PK-5
105 Primmer House Rd 22405 540-361-1455
Roxie Cooper, prin. Fax 361-4493
Dixon-Smith MS 6-8
503 Deacon Rd 22405 540-899-0860
Steve Trant, prin. Fax 899-0881
Ferry Farm ES 600/K-5
20 Pendleton Rd 22405 540-373-7366
Robert Freeman, prin. Fax 371-3788
Gayle MS 900/6-8
100 Panther Dr 22406 540-373-0383
Donald Upperco, prin. Fax 373-8856
Grafton Village ES 600/PK-5
501 Deacon Rd 22405 540-373-5454
Michael Sidebotham, prin. Fax 373-1498
Rocky Run ES 800/K-5
95 Reservoir Rd 22406 540-286-1956
JoAnne Baker, prin. Fax 286-1955

Faith Baptist S 400/PK-12
4105 Plank Rd 22407 540-786-4953
Kenneth Biggs, admin. Fax 786-3380
Fredericksburg Academy 600/PK-12
10800 Academy Dr 22408 540-898-0020
Robert Graves, hdmstr. Fax 898-8951
Fredericksburg Christian MS 400/4-8
2231 Jefferson Davis Hwy 22401 540-373-5357
Warren Aldrich, prin. Fax 899-6211
Fredericksburg Christian S 400/PK-3
11925 Burgess Ln 22407 540-786-4196
Phyllis Dibella, prin. Fax 786-2956
Holy Cross Academy 600/PK-8
250 Stafford Lakes Pkwy 22406 540-286-1600
Sr. Susan Eder, prin. Fax 286-1625
Odyssey Montessori S 100/PK-12
125 Olde Greenwich Dr 22408 540-891-9080
Wendy LaRue, prin. Fax 891-9877
St. Mary Preschool PK-PK
1009 Stafford Ave 22401 540-373-7770
Nanci Scharf, prin. Fax 371-0251
St. Patrick S 300/PK-8
9151 Elys Ford Rd 22407 540-786-2277
George Elliott, prin. Fax 785-2213
Tree of Life Christian Prep 50/1-8
6050 Plank Rd 22407 540-786-2019
Janet Armstrong, lead tchr. Fax 548-0877

Fries, Grayson, Pop. 573
Grayson County SD
Supt. — See Independence
Fries MS 100/4-7
PO Box 446 24330 276-744-7201
Elizabeth Brown, prin. Fax 744-3384
Providence ES 100/PK-3
56 Bainbridge Rd 24330 276-744-7228
Susie Funk, prin. Fax 744-2155

Front Royal, Warren, Pop. 14,499
Warren County SD 4,400/K-12
210 N Commerce Ave 22630 540-635-2171
Pamela McInnis, supt. Fax 636-4195
www.wcps.k12.va.us
Barbour ES 500/K-5
290 Westminster Dr 22630 540-622-8090
Joanne Waters, prin. Fax 636-1053
Jeffries ES 600/K-5
320 E Criser Rd 22630 540-636-6824
Lisa Rudacille, prin. Fax 635-3803
Keyser ES 500/K-5
1015 E Stonewall Dr 22630 540-635-3125
Brenda Ring, prin. Fax 635-6978
Morrison ES 400/K-5
40 Crescent St 22630 540-635-4188
Margaret Holmes, prin. Fax 635-5640
Rhodes ES 200/K-5
224 W Strasburg Rd 22630 540-635-4556
Cynthia Whittle, prin. Fax 635-2821
Warren County MS 800/6-7
500 W 15th St 22630 540-635-2194
Alan Fox, prin. Fax 635-6981

Bethel Christian S 100/PK-12
80 N Lake Ave 22630 540-635-6799
Richard Hewitt, dir. Fax 635-6152
Riverfront Christian S 200/PK-12
55 E Strasburg Rd 22630 540-635-8202
Cindy Martin, admin. Fax 636-4418
Royal Christian Academy 100/PK-12
1111 N Shenandoah Ave 22630 540-636-7940
Darlene Pfister, admin. Fax 636-7213

Fulks Run, Rockingham
Rockingham County SD
Supt. — See Harrisonburg
Fulks Run ES 200/PK-5
11089 Brocks Gap Rd 22830 540-896-7635
Dr. David Wenger, prin. Fax 896-1606

Gainesville, Prince William
Prince William County SD
Supt. — See Manassas
Buckland Mills ES K-5
10511 Wharfdale Pl 20155 703-530-1560
Janet Greer, prin.
Bull Run MS 1,700/6-8
6308 Catharpin Rd 20155 703-753-9969
William Bixby, prin. Fax 753-9610
Gainesville MS 6-8
8001 Limestone Dr 20155 703-753-1702
Dr. Sally MacLean, prin.
Glenkirk ES PK-5
8584 Sedge Wren Dr 20155 703-753-1702
Lisa Gilkerson, prin.
Tyler ES 600/K-5
14500 John Marshall Hwy 20155 703-754-7181
Matthew Phythian, prin. Fax 754-4869

Galax, Galax, Pop. 6,676
Carroll County SD
Supt. — See Hillsville
Gladeville ES 300/K-5
3117 Glendale Rd 24333 276-236-5449
Mary Jane Carico, prin. Fax 238-1625
Oakland ES 200/K-5
4930 Pipers Gap Rd 24333 276-236-3049
Ira Gentry, prin. Fax 236-5367

Galax CSD 1,300/K-12
223 Long St 24333 276-236-2911
Rebecca Cardwell, supt. Fax 236-5776
www.gcps.k12.va.us/
Galax ES 500/K-4
225 Academy Dr 24333 276-236-6159
Brian Stuart, prin. Fax 236-5839
Galax MS 300/5-7
202 Maroon Tide Dr 24333 276-236-6124
Kristina Legg, prin. Fax 236-4162

Grayson County SD
Supt. — See Independence
Baywood ES 100/PK-5
247 Grammer Ln 24333 276-236-4868
John Alexander, prin. Fax 236-3791
Fairview ES 100/K-5
2323 Fairview Rd 24333 276-236-2365
Michael Reavis, prin. Fax 236-6807

Gate City, Scott, Pop. 2,072
Scott County SD 3,800/K-12
340 E Jackson St 24251 276-386-6118
James Scott, supt. Fax 386-2684
scott.k12.va.us/
Shoemaker ES 500/K-6
218 Shoemaker Dr 24251 276-386-7002
Kathryn Musick, prin. Fax 386-7932
Yuma ES 200/K-6
130 Grover Cleveland Ln 24251 276-386-3109
Sammy Parks, prin. Fax 386-6183
Other Schools – See Duffield, Dungannon, Fort Blackmore, Hiltons, Nickelsville, Weber City

Gladehill, Franklin
Franklin County SD
Supt. — See Rocky Mount
Glade Hill ES 300/PK-5
8081 Old Franklin Tpke, 540-576-3010
Leavina Lee, prin. Fax 576-3404

Glade Spring, Washington, Pop. 1,537
Washington County SD
Supt. — See Abingdon
Glade Spring MS 300/6-8
33474 Stagecoach Rd 24340 276-739-3800
Scott Allen, prin. Fax 429-4211

Gladys, Campbell
Campbell County SD
Supt. — See Rustburg
Gladys ES 200/PK-5
PO Box 37 24554 434-283-5311
Lacy Webb, prin. Fax 283-5312

Glen Allen, Henrico, Pop. 9,010
Henrico County SD
Supt. — See Richmond
Colonial Trail ES K-5
12101 Bacova Dr 23059 804-364-0055
Philip Cantone, prin.
Echo Lake ES 700/K-5
5200 Francistown Rd 23060 804-527-4672
Jodie Brinkmann, prin. Fax 527-4674
Glen Allen ES 500/K-5
11101 Mill Rd 23060 804-756-3040
Dr. Yvonne Fawcett, prin. Fax 756-0486
Greenwood ES 500/K-5
10960 Greenwood Rd 23059 804-261-2970
Debra Smith, prin.
Hungary Creek MS 900/6-8
4909 Francistown Rd 23060 804-527-2640
Elizabeth Armbruster, prin.
Longdale ES 400/K-5
9500 Norfolk St 23060 804-261-5095
Marcia Muse, prin. Fax 515-1198
Rivers Edge ES 700/K-5
11600 Holman Ridge Rd 23059 804-935-6760
Johnna Riley, prin.
Shady Grove ES 800/K-5
12200 Wyndham Lake Dr 23059 804-360-0825
Dr. Regina Schwab, prin. Fax 364-0844
Short Pump MS 1,000/6-8
4701 Pouncey Tract Rd 23059 804-360-0800
Dr. Mark Chamberlain, prin. Fax 360-0808
Springfield Park ES 700/K-5
4301 Fort McHenry Pkwy 23060 804-527-4630
Tamara Jones, prin. Fax 527-4631
Twin Hickory ES 800/K-5
4900 Twin Hickory Lake Dr 23059 804-360-4700
Dr. Yvonnie Perrello, prin.

Gloucester, Gloucester
Gloucester County SD 6,100/PK-12
6489 Main St 23061 804-693-5300
Dr. Howard Kiser, supt. Fax 693-1426
gets.gc.k12.va.us/
Bethel ES 500/PK-5
2991 Hickory Fork Rd 23061 804-693-2360
Paul McLean, prin. Fax 693-0403
Botetourt ES 500/PK-5
6361 Main St 23061 804-693-2151
Michelle Cagnon, prin. Fax 693-3954
Page MS 600/6-8
5628 George Washington Mem 23061 804-693-2540
David Daniel, prin. Fax 693-6595
Peasley MS 900/6-8
2885 Hickory Fork Rd 23061 804-693-1499
Bryan Hartley, prin. Fax 693-1497
Petsworth ES 400/PK-5
10658 George Washington Mem 23061
804-693-6161
Evelyn Perhac, prin. Fax 693-1238
Walker ES 500/PK-5
6099 T C Walker Rd 23061 804-693-5445
Dr. Bambi Thompson, prin. Fax 693-6295
Other Schools – See Hayes

Gloucester Montessori S 100/PK-5
PO Box 1506 23061 804-693-6455
Pat Landau, hdmstr. Fax 693-9554
Ware Academy 100/PK-8
7936 John Clayton Mem Hwy 23061 804-693-3825
Tom Thomas, hdmstr. Fax 694-0695

Goochland, Goochland
Goochland County SD 2,100/K-12
PO Box 169 23063 804-556-5316
Linda Underwood, supt. Fax 556-3847
www.glnd.k12.va.us
Byrd ES 300/K-5
2704 Hadensville Fife Rd 23063 804-556-5380
James Hopkins, prin. Fax 457-9303
Goochland ES 300/K-5
3150 River Rd W 23063 804-556-5321
Dianna Gordon, prin. Fax 556-6054
Goochland MS 300/6-8
3250 River Rd W Ste B 23063 804-556-5320
Johnette Burdette, prin. Fax 556-6223
Other Schools – See Crozier

Goode, Bedford
Bedford County SD
Supt. — See Bedford
Otter River ES 200/K-5
1044 Otter River Dr 24556 540-586-9210
Georgia Hairston, prin. Fax 586-7635

Goodview, Bedford
Bedford County SD
Supt. — See Bedford
Goodview ES 500/K-5
1374 Rivermont Academy Rd 24095 540-892-5674
Edwin Zimmerman, prin. Fax 892-5677

Stewartsville ES 400/K-5
1138 Wildcat Rd 24095 540-890-2174
Kelly Brown, prin. Fax 890-0955

Gordonsville, Orange, Pop. 1,617
Orange County SD
Supt. — See Orange
Gordon-Barbour ES 400/K-5
500 W Baker St 22942 540-661-4500
William Berry, prin. Fax 661-4499

Grafton, York
York County SD
Supt. — See Yorktown
Grafton Bethel ES 600/K-5
410 Lakeside Dr 23692 757-898-0350
Karen Grass Ed.D., prin. Fax 898-0359

Great Falls, Fairfax, Pop. 6,945
Fairfax County SD
Supt. — See Falls Church
Forrestville ES 800/K-6
1085 Utterback Store Rd 22066 703-404-6000
Matt Harris, prin. Fax 404-6097
Great Falls ES 600/K-6
701 Walker Rd 22066 703-757-2100
Ernest Leighty, prin. Fax 757-2197

Siena Academy PK-5
1020 Springvale Rd 22066 703-759-4129
Maggie Radzik, prin. Fax 759-3753

Gretna, Pittsylvania, Pop. 1,222
Pittsylvania County SD
Supt. — See Chatham
Gretna ES 600/PK-5
PO Box 595 24557 434-656-2231
Dianne Travis, prin. Fax 656-2661
Gretna MS 500/6-8
201 Coffey St 24557 434-656-2217
Vera Glass, prin. Fax 656-6122
Mt. Airy ES 200/PK-5
100 Mount Airy Elem Cir 24557 434-335-5291
Joyce Wright, prin. Fax 335-5585

Grottoes, Rockingham, Pop. 2,168
Rockingham County SD
Supt. — See Harrisonburg
South River ES 400/PK-5
2101 Elm Ave 24441 540-249-4001
Larry Shifflett, prin. Fax 249-3110

Grundy, Buchanan, Pop. 1,004
Buchanan County SD 3,400/PK-12
PO Box 833 24614 276-935-4551
Tommy Justus, supt. Fax 935-7150
www.buc.k12.va.us
Bevins ES 100/PK-5
8668 Slate Creek Rd 24614 276-259-7202
Deborah Estep, prin. Fax 259-6329
Riverview S 900/PK-8
27382 Riverside Dr 24614 276-935-1613
Melanie Hibbitts, prin. Fax 935-0782
Other Schools – See Council, Hurley, Oakwood, Vansant

Hague, Westmoreland
Westmoreland County SD
Supt. — See Montross
Cople ES 400/PK-5
7114 Cople Hwy 22469 804-472-2081
Cathy Rice, prin. Fax 472-2759

Halifax, Halifax, Pop. 1,293
Halifax County SD 4,000/K-12
PO Box 1849 24558 434-476-2171
Paul Stapleton, supt. Fax 476-1858
www.halifax.k12.va.us
Sinai ES 200/K-5
1011 Sinai Elementary Dr 24558 434-476-6193
Michael Wilborne, prin. Fax 476-5478
Other Schools – See Alton, Nathalie, Scottsburg, South Boston

Hamilton, Loudoun, Pop. 718
Loudoun County SD
Supt. — See Ashburn
Hamilton ES 300/PK-5
54 S Kerr St 20158 540-751-2570
Carol Winters, prin. Fax 338-6882

Hampton, Hampton, Pop. 145,579
Hampton CSD 22,200/PK-12
1 Franklin St 23669 757-727-2000
Dr. Linda Shifflette, supt. Fax 727-2002
www.sbo.hampton.k12.va.us
Aberdeen ES 400/K-5
1424 Aberdeen Rd 23666 757-825-4624
Dr. Stacia Barreau, prin. Fax 825-4538
Armstrong ES 400/K-5
3401 Matoaka Rd 23661 757-727-1067
Linda Byrd, prin. Fax 727-1436
Asbury ES 400/K-5
140 Beach Rd 23664 757-850-5075
Dr. Penny McIntyre, prin. Fax 848-2332
Barron ES 400/K-5
45 Fox Hill Rd 23669 757-850-5100
Mary Wallen, prin. Fax 850-5126
Bassette ES 300/K-5
671 Bell St 23661 757-727-1071
Dr. Daniello Belton, prin. Fax 727-1275
Booker ES 400/K-5
160 Apollo Dr 23669 757-850-5096
Troy Latuch, prin. Fax 850-5283
Bryan ES 400/K-5
1021 N Mallory St 23663 757-727-1056
Patrice Calloway, prin. Fax 727-1467
Burbank ES 400/K-5
40 Tide Mill Ln 23666 757-825-4642
Brenda McIntyre-Odoms, prin. Fax 896-7806
Cary ES 400/K-5
2009 Andrews Blvd 23663 757-850-5092
Ronald Holloman, prin. Fax 850-5068

Cooper ES 300/K-5
200 Marcella Rd 23666 757-825-4645
Chevese Thomas, prin. Fax 825-4631
Davis MS 1,100/6-8
1435 Todds Ln 23666 757-825-4520
David Leech, prin. Fax 825-4533
Eaton MS 900/6-8
2108 Cunningham Dr 23666 757-825-4540
Dr. Kenneth Crum, prin. Fax 825-4551
Forrest ES 500/K-5
1406 Todds Ln 23666 757-825-4627
Kim Garvin-Richardson, prin. Fax 896-6731
Jones Magnet MS 600/6-8
1819 Nickerson Blvd 23663 757-850-7900
Daniel Bowling, prin. Fax 850-5395
Kraft ES 500/K-5
600 Concord Dr 23666 757-825-4634
Ralph Saunders, prin. Fax 825-4507
Langley ES 500/K-5
16 Rockwell Rd 23669 757-850-5105
Katherine Hermann, prin. Fax 850-5409
Lee ES 400/K-5
1646 Briarfield Rd 23669 757-825-4637
Levia Stovall, prin. Fax 825-4618
Lindsay MS 900/6-8
1636 Briarfield Rd 23661 757-825-4560
Fax 825-4839
Machen ES 500/K-5
20 Sacramento Dr 23666 757-766-5250
Patricia Clark, prin. Fax 766-5297
Mallory ES 400/K-5
331 Big Bethel Rd 23666 757-825-4638
Ursula Hill, prin. Fax 825-4673
Merrimack ES 400/K-5
2113 Woodmansee Dr 23663 757-850-5084
Eric Stone, prin. Fax 850-5627
Moton ECC 100/PK-PK
339 Old Buckroe Rd 23663 757-727-1061
Joanne Drew, prin. Fax 727-8615
Phillips ES 400/K-5
703 Lemaster Ave 23669 757-850-5079
Anita Owens, prin. Fax 850-5622
Smith ES 400/K-5
379 Woodland Rd 23669 757-850-5088
Dr. Lawrence Myers, prin. Fax 850-5455
Spratley MS 800/6-8
339 Woodland Rd 23669 757-850-5032
Mark Hudson, prin. Fax 850-5186
Syms MS 1,200/6-8
170 Fox Hill Rd 23669 757-850-5050
Elondra Miles, prin. Fax 850-5413
Tarrant ES 300/K-5
1589 Wingfield Dr 23666 757-825-4639
Mike Stutt, prin. Fax 896-8105
Tucker-Capps ES 500/K-5
113 Wellington Dr 23666 757-825-4641
Susan Johnson, prin. Fax 825-4698
Tyler ES 500/K-5
57 Salina St 23669 757-727-1075
Jeffrey Blowe, prin. Fax 727-1439
Wythe ES 300/K-5
200 Claremont Ave 23661 757-926-2555
Donna Warthan, prin. Fax 926-2589

Calvary Christian Academy 200/PK-3
2311 Tower Pl 23666 757-825-1133
Nan Williams, admin. Fax 825-8771
Calvary Classical S 100/PK-8
403 Whealton Rd 23666 757-262-0062
Lori Rogers, prin. Fax 826-5389
Faith Outreach Education Center 100/PK-12
3105 W Mercury Blvd 23666 757-838-8949
Tina Gravely, prin. Fax 838-4434
Gloria Dei Lutheran S 500/PK-5
250 Fox Hill Rd 23669 757-851-6292
Linda Robinson, prin. Fax 850-3935
Hampton Christian ES 200/PK-5
2424 N Armistead Ave 23666 757-838-2355
Frank Carvell, supt. Fax 838-1998
St. Mary Star of the Sea S 200/PK-8
14 N Willard Ave 23663 757-723-6358
Mary Mueller, prin. Fax 723-6544

Harrisonburg, Harrisonburg, Pop. 40,438
Harrisonburg CSD 4,100/K-12
317 S Main St 22801 540-434-9916
Donald Ford, supt. Fax 434-5196
www.harrisonburg.k12.va.us
Harrison MS 900/5-8
1311 W Market St 22801 540-434-1949
Elisabeth Dunnenberger, prin. Fax 434-4052
Keister ES 400/K-4
100 Maryland Ave 22801 540-434-6585
Anne Lintner, prin. Fax 434-4452
Skyline MS 5-8
470 Linda Ln 22802 540-434-6862
Joe Glick, prin. Fax 434-6453
Smithland ES K-4
474 Linda Ln 22802 540-434-6075
Gary Painter, prin. Fax 434-6059
Spotswood ES 400/K-4
400 Mountain View Dr 22801 540-434-3429
Ann Conners, prin. Fax 434-4453
Stone Spring ES 500/K-4
1575 Peach Grove Ave 22801 540-574-1199
Lynn Sprouse, prin. Fax 432-0053
Waterman ES 500/K-4
451 Chicago Ave 22802 540-434-8352
Linda McCormick, prin. Fax 434-9996

Rockingham County SD 11,800/PK-12
100 Mount Clinton Pike 22802 540-564-3200
Dr. Carol Fenn, supt. Fax 564-3241
www.rockingham.k12.va.us/
Lacey Spring ES 400/PK-5
8621 N Valley Pike 22802 540-433-7819
Donna Robinson, prin. Fax 433-0838
Mountain View ES 500/PK-5
2800 Rawley Pike 22801 540-438-1965
Debi Rhodes, prin. Fax 438-0455

Pleasant Valley ES 400/PK-5
215 Pleasant Valley Rd 22801 540-434-4557
Paula Frazier, prin. Fax 433-3528
Other Schools – See Bridgewater, Broadway, Dayton, Elkton, Fulks Run, Grottoes, Linville, Mc Gaheysville, Penn Laird, Timberville

---

Cornerstone Christian S 200/PK-8
197 Cornerstone Dr 22802 540-432-9816
Rev. Rick Martin, prin. Fax 438-0116
Eastern Mennonite S 300/K-12
801 Parkwood Dr 22802 540-432-4500
Paul Leaman, prin. Fax 432-4528

Hartwood, Stafford
Stafford County SD
Supt. — See Stafford
Hartwood ES 600/K-5
14 Shackleford Well Rd, 540-752-4441
Catherine Walker, prin. Fax 752-4320

Hayes, Gloucester
Gloucester County SD
Supt. — See Gloucester
Abingdon ES 500/PK-5
7087 Powhatan Dr 23072 804-642-9885
Brenda Martin, prin. Fax 642-9692
Achilles ES 300/PK-5
9306 Guinea Rd 23072 804-642-9140
Molly Broderson, prin. Fax 642-9406

Haymarket, Prince William, Pop. 1,083
Prince William County SD
Supt. — See Manassas
Alvey ES 900/K-5
5300 Waverly Farm Rd 20169 571-261-2556
Candace Rotruck, prin. Fax 261-2557
Gravely ES PK-5
4670 Waverly Farm Rd 20169 571-248-4930
Michele Salzano, prin.
Mountain View ES 800/K-5
5600 Mcleod Way 20169 703-754-4161
Kirsten Fisher, prin. Fax 754-8416

Heathsville, Northumberland
Northumberland County SD
Supt. — See Lottsburg
Northumberland ES 700/PK-5
757 Academic Ln 22473 804-580-8032
Arnette Butler, prin.
Northumberland MS 300/6-8
9020 Northumberland Hwy 22473 804-580-5753
Robert Bailey, prin.

Henry, Franklin
Franklin County SD
Supt. — See Rocky Mount
Henry ES 200/PK-5
200 Henry School Rd 24102 540-483-5676
Lisa Bowman, prin. Fax 483-0399

Herndon, Fairfax, Pop. 21,965
Fairfax County SD
Supt. — See Falls Church
Carson MS 1,100/7-8
13618 McLearen Rd 20171 703-925-3600
August Frattali, prin. Fax 925-3697
Clearview ES 600/PK-6
12635 Builders Rd 20170 703-708-6000
Elaine Wellner, prin. Fax 708-6097
Crossfield ES 800/K-6
2791 Fox Mill Rd 20171 703-295-1100
Jerry Kovalcik, prin. Fax 295-1197
Dranesville ES 700/K-6
1515 Powells Tavern Pl 20170 703-326-5200
Susie McCallum, prin. Fax 326-5297
Floris ES 800/K-6
2708 Centreville Rd 20171 703-561-2900
Karen Siple, prin. Fax 561-2997
Fox Mill ES 700/K-6
2601 Viking Dr 20171 703-262-2700
Patricia Sheehy, prin. Fax 262-2797
Herndon ES 700/K-6
630 Dranesville Rd 20170 703-326-3100
Carolyn Gannaway, prin. Fax 326-3197
Herndon MS 1,100/7-8
901 Locust St 20170 703-904-4800
Justine Klena, prin. Fax 904-4897
Hutchison ES 600/K-6
13209 Parcher Ave 20170 703-925-8300
Judith Baldwin, prin. Fax 925-8397
McNair ES 900/PK-6
2499 Thomas Jefferson Dr 20171 703-793-4800
Theresa West, prin. Fax 793-4897
Oak Hill ES 900/K-6
3210 Kinross Cir 20171 703-467-3500
Amy Goodloe, prin. Fax 467-3597

Boyd S - Reston 100/PK-4
11579 Cedar Chase Rd 20170 703-404-9733
Mary Stage, prin. Fax 404-9734
Montessori S of Herndon 100/PK-6
840 Dranesville Rd 20170 703-437-8229
Nasim Mallick Khan, prin. Fax 956-6094
Mt. Pleasant Baptist Christian Academy 50/PK-5
2516 Squirrel Hill Rd 20171 703-793-1196
Margaret Aghayere, dir. Fax 793-1197
Nysmith S 700/PK-8
13625 Eds Dr 20171 703-713-3332
Carole Nysmith, dir. Fax 713-3336
St. Joseph S 600/K-8
750 Peachtree St 20170 703-437-3014
Joan Cargill, prin. Fax 437-0765
Temple Baptist S 200/PK-12
1545 Dranesville Rd 20170 703-437-7400
Samuel Dalton, admin. Fax 437-7430

Highland Springs, Henrico, Pop. 13,823
Henrico County SD
Supt. — See Richmond
Fair Oaks ES 300/K-5
201 Jennings Rd 23075 804-328-4085
Emily Steele, prin. Fax 328-4028
Highland Springs ES 600/K-5
600 Pleasant St 23075 804-328-4045
Jonathan Hochman, prin. Fax 328-4038

Hillsville, Carroll, Pop. 2,716
Carroll County SD 4,100/K-12
605 Pine St Ste 9 24343 276-728-3191
James Smith, supt. Fax 728-3195
www.ccpsd.k12.va.us
Gladesboro ES 200/K-5
7845 Snake Creek Rd 24343 276-398-2493
Linda King, prin. Fax 398-3384
Hillsville ES 500/K-5
90 Patriot Ln 24343 276-728-7312
Ross Scott, prin. Fax 728-3943
Other Schools – See Austinville, Cana, Fancy Gap, Galax, Woodlawn

Hiltons, Scott
Scott County SD
Supt. — See Gate City
Hilton ES 200/K-6
303 Academy Rd 24258 276-386-7430
Timothy Spicer, prin. Fax 386-3192

Hiwassee, Pulaski
Pulaski County SD
Supt. — See Pulaski
Snowville ES 300/PK-5
4858 Lead Mine Rd 24347 540-643-0766
Janis Carter, prin. Fax 639-0842

Honaker, Russell, Pop. 921
Russell County SD
Supt. — See Lebanon
Honaker ES 600/K-7
PO Box 744 24260 276-873-6301
Gary Hess, prin. Fax 873-7263

Hopewell, Hopewell, Pop. 22,690
Hopewell CSD 4,100/K-12
103 N 12th Ave 23860 804-541-6400
Dr. Winston Odom, supt. Fax 541-6401
www.hopewell.k12.va.us
Copeland ES 700/K-5
400 Westhill Rd 23860 804-541-6410
Susan Jones, prin. Fax 541-6411
Dupont ES 600/K-5
300 S 18th Ave 23860 804-541-6406
Tina Barringer, prin. Fax 541-6407
James ES 600/K-5
1807 Arlington Rd 23860 804-541-6408
Sandra Morton, prin. Fax 541-6409
Woodson MS 900/6-8
1000 Winston Churchill Dr 23860 804-541-6404
Cheryl Webb, prin. Fax 541-6405

Hot Springs, Bath
Alleghany County SD
Supt. — See Low Moor
Falling Spring ES 200/PK-5
100 Falling Spring Cir 24445 540-965-1815
Deborah Farmer, prin. Fax 965-1829

Bath County SD
Supt. — See Warm Springs
Valley ES 300/K-7
98 Panther Dr 24445 540-839-5395
Les Balgavy, prin. Fax 839-5392

Huddleston, Bedford
Bedford County SD
Supt. — See Bedford
Huddleston ES 200/K-5
1027 Huddleston Dr 24104 540-297-5144
Gus Exstrom, prin. Fax 297-8230

Hurley, Buchanan
Buchanan County SD
Supt. — See Grundy
Hurley S 400/PK-7
6911 Hurley Rd 24620 276-566-8523
Timothy Prater, prin. Fax 566-7751

Hurt, Pittsylvania, Pop. 1,245
Pittsylvania County SD
Supt. — See Chatham
Hurt ES 300/PK-5
315 Prospect Rd 24563 434-324-7231
Vickie Murphy, prin. Fax 324-7233

Faith Christian Academy 200/PK-12
PO Box 670 24563 434-324-8276
Lisa Moore, admin. Fax 324-8279

Independence, Grayson, Pop. 921
Grayson County SD 1,900/PK-12
PO Box 888 24348 276-773-2832
Elizabeth Thomas, supt. Fax 773-2939
www.edline.net/pages/Grayson_County_Schools
Bridle Creek ES 100/K-5
77 Bridle Creek Rd 24348 276-773-2611
Clark Nuckolls, prin. Fax 773-0389
Independence ES 200/K-5
PO Box 429 24348 276-773-2722
Susan Mitchell, prin. Fax 773-9566
Independence MS 400/6-8
PO Box 155 24348 276-773-3020
Judy Greear, prin. Fax 773-0479
Other Schools – See Fries, Galax, Whitetop

Irvington, Lancaster, Pop. 658

Chesapeake Academy 100/PK-8
PO Box 8 22480 804-438-5575
Deborah Cook, hdmstr. Fax 438-6146

Isle of Wight, Isle of Wight

Isle of Wight Academy 600/PK-12
PO Box 105 23397 757-357-3866
Benjamin Vaughan, hdmstr. Fax 357-6886

Jarratt, Sussex, Pop. 562
Sussex County SD
Supt. — See Sussex
Jefferson ES 200/K-5
PO Box 307 23867 434-535-8810
Shannon Smith, prin. Fax 535-0016

Jonesville, Lee, Pop. 980
Lee County SD 3,500/PK-12
5 Park St 24263 276-346-2107
Fred Marion, supt. Fax 346-0307
www.leectysch.com/
Flatwoods ES 400/PK-5
RR 1 Box 552 24263 276-346-2799
Lisa Poe, prin. Fax 346-4162
Jonesville MS 300/6-8
RR 1 Box 104H 24263 276-346-1011
Connie Daugherty, prin. Fax 346-1411
Other Schools – See Dryden, Duffield, Ewing, Keokee, Pennington Gap, Rose Hill, Saint Charles

Kenbridge, Lunenburg, Pop. 1,319
Lunenburg County SD 1,800/PK-12
1009 Main St 23944 434-676-2467
Wayne Staples, supt. Fax 676-1000
www.lun.k12.va.us
Kenbridge ES 400/PK-5
PO Box 907 23944 434-676-2491
Grayson Bagley, prin. Fax 676-8636
Other Schools – See Victoria

Keokee, Lee
Lee County SD
Supt. — See Jonesville
Keokee ES 100/PK-7
PO Box 93 24265 276-565-0637
Lisa Willis, prin. Fax 565-4109

Keswick, Albemarle
Albemarle County SD
Supt. — See Charlottesville
Stony Point ES 300/PK-5
3893 Stony Point Rd 22947 434-973-6405
Carrie Neeley, prin. Fax 973-9751

Keysville, Charlotte, Pop. 782
Charlotte County SD
Supt. — See Charlotte Court House
Eureka ES 400/K-5
315 Eureka School Rd 23947 434-736-8458
Andrew Heintzleman, prin. Fax 736-9830

Kilmarnock, Lancaster, Pop. 1,215
Lancaster County SD 1,500/PK-12
PO Box 2000 22482 804-435-3183
Susan Sciabbarrasi, supt. Fax 435-3309
www.lcs.k12.va.us
Lancaster MS 500/4-8
191 School St 22482 804-435-1681
Craig Kauffman, prin. Fax 435-0589
Other Schools – See Lancaster

King and Queen Court House, King and Queen
King & Queen County SD 800/K-12
PO Box 97 23085 804-785-5981
Richard Layman, supt. Fax 785-5686
www.kqps.net
Other Schools – See Mattaponi, Saint Stephens Church

King George, King George
King George County SD 3,800/K-12
PO Box 1239 22485 540-775-5833
Dr. Candace Brown, supt. Fax 775-2165
www.kgcs.k12.va.us
King George ES 800/K-6
10381 Ridge Rd 22485 540-775-5411
Ronald Monroe, prin. Fax 775-2715
King George MS 600/7-8
8246 Dahlgren Rd 22485 540-775-2331
Seidah Ashshaheed, prin. Fax 775-0263
Sealston ES 700/K-6
11048 Fletchers Chapel Rd 22485 540-775-3400
Christopher Bryant, prin. Fax 775-9953
Other Schools – See Dahlgren

King William, King William
King William County SD 2,100/PK-12
PO Box 185 23086 804-769-3434
Dr. Mark Jones, supt. Fax 769-3312
www.kwcps.k12.va.us
Acquinton ES 500/3-5
18550 King William Rd 23086 804-769-3739
Beverly Young, prin.
Cool Spring PS 500/PK-2
7301 Acquinton Church Rd 23086 804-769-7644
Dr. David Rorick, prin.
Hamilton-Holmes MS 500/6-8
18444 King William Rd 23086 804-769-3316
Dr. Stanley Waskiewicz, prin.

La Crosse, Mecklenburg, Pop. 604
Mecklenburg County SD
Supt. — See Boydton
La Crosse ES 300/PK-5
1000 School Cir 23950 434-757-7374
Nan Alga, prin. Fax 757-1378

Lancaster, Lancaster
Lancaster County SD
Supt. — See Kilmarnock
Lancaster PS 500/PK-3
36 Primary Cir 22503 804-435-3196
Lorena Watrous, prin. Fax 435-0989

Langley AFB, See Hampton
York County SD
Supt. — See Yorktown

Bethel Manor ES 500/K-5
1797 1st St 23665 757-867-7439
Betsy Poulsen Ed.D., prin. Fax 867-7435

Lawrenceville, Brunswick, Pop. 1,157
Brunswick County SD 2,300/PK-12
1718 Farmers Field Rd 23868 434-848-3138
Dr. Oliver Spencer, supt. Fax 848-4001
www.brun.k12.va.us
Meherrin-Powellton ES 300/PK-5
11555 Dry Bread Rd 23868 434-577-5000
Sandra King, prin. Fax 577-5001
Russell MS 500/6-8
19400 Christanna Hwy 23868 434-848-2132
Dr. Virginia Berry, prin. Fax 848-6201
Totaro ES 500/PK-5
19350 Christanna Hwy 23868 434-848-3209
Dr. Mark Harrison, prin.
Other Schools – See Alberta

Brunswick Academy 400/PK-12
2100 Planters Rd 23868 434-848-2220
Jean Grizzard, hdmstr. Fax 848-4729

Lebanon, Russell, Pop. 3,225
Russell County SD 3,800/PK-12
PO Box 8 24266 276-889-6500
Lorraine Turner, supt. Fax 889-6508
www.russell.k12.va.us
Lebanon ES 3-5
PO Box 668 24266 276-889-6531
Phillip Henley, prin. Fax 889-2008
Lebanon MS 300/6-8
PO Box 577 24266 276-889-6548
Joey Long, prin. Fax 889-4262
Lebanon PS 300/K-2
PO Box 187 24266 276-889-4507
Rita Street, prin. Fax 889-4509
Other Schools – See Castlewood, Cleveland, Honaker, Rosedale, Swords Creek

Leesburg, Loudoun, Pop. 36,269
Loudoun County SD
Supt. — See Ashburn
Ball's Bluff ES 600/PK-5
821 Battlefield Pkwy NE 20176 571-252-2880
Dr. Melinda Carper, prin. Fax 779-8804
Belmont Ridge MS 1,100/6-8
19045 Upper Belmont Pl 20176 571-252-2220
Timothy Flynn, prin. Fax 669-1455
Catoctin ES 600/PK-5
311 Catoctin Cir SW 20175 703-771-6770
Rebecca Moyer, prin. Fax 771-6773
Cool Spring ES 700/PK-5
501 Tavistock Dr SE 20175 703-771-6760
Jill Broaddus, prin. Fax 771-6764
Evergreen Mill ES 800/PK-5
491 Evergreen Mill Rd SE 20175 571-252-2900
Laurie McDonald, prin. Fax 779-8837
Harper Park MS 800/6-8
701 Potomac Station Dr NE 20176 571-252-2820
William Shipp, prin. Fax 779-8867
Leesburg ES 600/PK-5
323 Plaza St NE 20176 703-771-6720
C. Magruder, prin. Fax 771-6725
Lucketts ES 200/PK-5
14550 James Monroe Hwy 20176 703-771-6690
Michael Pellegrino, prin. Fax 771-6692
Reid ES 800/PK-5
800 N King St 20176 571-252-2050
Lisbeth Fye, prin. Fax 669-1469
Seldens Landing ES 900/K-5
43345 Coton Commons Dr 20176 571-252-2260
Jacquelyn Brownell, prin. Fax 779-8953
Simpson MS 800/6-8
490 Evergreen Mill Rd SE 20175 571-252-2840
Chad Runfola, prin. Fax 771-6643
Smart's Mill MS 900/6-8
850 N King St 20176 571-252-2030
Eric Steward, prin. Fax 252-2043
Sycolin Creek ES K-5
21100 Evergreen Mills Rd 20175 571-252-2910
Sharon Keegan-Coppels, prin. Fax 771-9616
Tolbert ES 800/K-5
691 Potomac Station Dr NE 20176 571-252-2870
Elaine Layman, prin. Fax 779-8989

Dominion Academy 300/PK-8
835 Lee Ave SW 20175 703-737-0157
Ann Ashcraft, admin. Fax 771-9512
Loudoun Country Day S 300/PK-8
20600 Red Cedar Dr 20175 703-777-3841
Dr. Randall Hollister, hdmstr. Fax 771-1346
Montessori S of Leesburg 100/PK-K
166 Fort Evans Rd NE 20176 703-779-7791
Rabia Mallick, prin. Fax 779-3711
St. John the Apostle Preschool PK-PK
101 Oakcrest Manor Dr NE 20176 703-777-7873
Jane Taylor, prin. Fax 771-9016

Lexington, Lexington, Pop. 6,776
Lexington CSD 500/K-8
300 Diamond St 24450 540-463-7146
Dr. Daniel Lyons, supt. Fax 464-5230
www.lexedu.org/
Harrington-Waddell ES 300/K-5
100 Pendelton Pl 24450 540-463-5353
Lisa Clark, prin. Fax 463-6309
Lylburn-Downing MS 200/6-8
302 Diamond St 24450 540-463-3532
Richard Dowd, prin.

Rockbridge County SD 2,900/K-12
1972 Big Spring Dr 24450 540-463-7386
John Reynolds, supt. Fax 463-7823
www.rockbridge.k12.va.us/
Central ES 400/K-5
85 Central Rd 24450 540-463-4500
Ryan Barber, prin. Fax 463-2225

Effinger ES 100/K-5
2893 Collierstown Rd 24450 540-463-4459
Melanie Falls, prin. Fax 463-4824
Maury River MS 400/6-8
600 Waddell St 24450 540-463-3129
Phillip Thompson, prin. Fax 464-4838
Other Schools – See Buena Vista, Fairfield, Natural Bridge Station

Rockbridge Christian Academy 100/PK-8
21 Snowy Egret Ln 24450 540-463-5456
Mary Phillips, admin. Fax 463-3485

Linville, Rockingham
Rockingham County SD
Supt. — See Harrisonburg
Linville-Edom ES 200/PK-5
3653 Linville Edom Rd 22834 540-833-6916
Karen Thomsen, prin. Fax 833-2267

Locust Grove, Orange
Orange County SD
Supt. — See Orange
Locust Grove ES 700/K-5
31230 Constitution Hwy 22508 540-661-4420
Jesse Magruder, prin. Fax 661-4419
Locust Grove MS 600/5-8
31208 Constitution Hwy 22508 540-661-4444
Martha Roby, prin. Fax 661-4447

Locust Hill, Middlesex
Middlesex County SD
Supt. — See Saluda
Middlesex ES 500/PK-5
PO Box 375 23092 804-758-2496
Joanie Banks, prin. Fax 758-2369
St. Clare Walker MS 300/6-8
PO Box 9 23092 804-758-2561
James Lane, prin. Fax 758-0834

Lorton, Fairfax, Pop. 15,385
Fairfax County SD
Supt. — See Falls Church
Gunston ES 600/K-6
10100 Gunston Rd 22079 703-541-3600
Tonya Cox, prin. Fax 541-3697
Lorton Station ES 1,000/K-6
9298 Lewis Chapel Rd 22079 571-642-6000
Susan Garrison, prin. Fax 642-6097

Lottsburg, Northumberland
Northumberland County SD 1,500/PK-12
2172 Northumberland Hwy 22511 804-529-6134
Clint Stables, supt. Fax 529-6449
www.nucps.net
Other Schools – See Heathsville

Louisa, Louisa, Pop. 1,510
Louisa County SD
Supt. — See Mineral
Jefferson ES 800/PK-5
1782 Jefferson Hwy 23093 540-967-0492
Teresa Byers, prin. Fax 967-0337
Trevilians ES 700/PK-5
2035 S Spotswood Trl 23093 540-967-1108
Tarnee Kendell-Hudson, prin. Fax 967-3695

Lovettsville, Loudoun, Pop. 1,160
Loudoun County SD
Supt. — See Ashburn
Lovettsville ES 500/PK-5
49 S Loudoun St 20180 540-771-6700
Kimberly Forcino, prin. Fax 771-6703

Lovingston, Nelson
Nelson County SD 2,000/PK-12
PO Box 276 22949 434-263-7100
Dr. Roger Dale Collins, supt. Fax 263-7115
www.nelson.k12.va.us
Nelson MS 500/6-8
6925 Thomas Nelson Hwy 22949 434-263-4801
Jody Ray, prin. Fax 263-4483
Other Schools – See Afton, Arrington

Low Moor, Alleghany
Alleghany County SD 2,900/PK-12
PO Box 140 24457 540-863-1800
Sarah Campbell, supt. Fax 863-1804
www.alleghany.k12.va.us/
Other Schools – See Clifton Forge, Covington, Hot Springs

Luray, Page, Pop. 4,865
Page County SD 3,700/PK-12
735 W Main St 22835 540-743-6533
Dr. Randall Thomas, supt. Fax 743-7784
www.pagecounty.k12.va.us
Luray ES 700/PK-7
555 1st St 22835 540-743-4078
Karin Blay, prin. Fax 743-1014
Other Schools – See Rileyville, Shenandoah, Stanley

Lynchburg, Lynchburg, Pop. 66,973
Bedford County SD
Supt. — See Bedford
Boonsboro ES 300/K-5
1234 Eagle Cir 24503 434-384-2881
Nancy Sale, prin. Fax 384-4661

Campbell County SD
Supt. — See Rustburg
Brookville MS 700/6-8
320 Bee Dr 24502 434-239-9267
Edwin Martin, prin. Fax 237-8974
Leesville Road ES 600/PK-5
25 Lewis Way 24502 434-239-0303
Katherine Bowles, prin. Fax 239-0355
Tomahawk ES 700/PK-5
155 Bee Dr 24502 434-237-4090
Debbie Elliott, prin. Fax 239-2162

Lynchburg CSD 8,800/PK-12
PO Box 2497 24505 434-522-3700
Dr. Paul McKendrick, supt. Fax 846-1500
www.lynchburg.org
Bass ES 200/K-5
1730 Seabury Ave 24501 434-522-3769
Leverne Marshall, prin. Fax 522-2374
Bedford Hills ES 500/K-5
4330 Morningside Dr 24503 434-384-2221
Robert Quel, prin. Fax 384-1703
Dearington ES for Innovation 200/K-5
210 Smyth St 24501 434-522-3757
Terrie Haley, prin. Fax 522-2351
Dunbar MS for Innovation 600/6-8
1200 Polk St 24504 434-522-3740
Brian Wray, prin. Fax 522-3727
Heritage ES 400/PK-5
501 Leesville Rd 24502 434-582-1130
Sharon Anderson, prin. Fax 582-1175
Hutcherson Early Learning Center PK-PK
2401 High St 24504 434-522-3756
Judy Trent, prin. Fax 522-2323
Linkhorne ES 500/PK-5
2501 Linkhorne Dr 24503 434-384-6611
Fax 384-9620
Linkhorne MS 700/6-8
2525 Linkhorne Dr 24503 434-384-5150
Robert Kerns, prin. Fax 384-2810
Miller ES for Innovation 200/K-5
600 Mansfield Ave 24501 434-522-3717
April Bruce, prin. Fax 522-2301
Munro ES 300/PK-5
4641 Locksview Rd 24503 434-384-1721
Donna Bear, prin. Fax 386-3067
Payne ES 500/PK-5
1201 Floyd St 24501 434-522-3762
John Blakely, prin. Fax 522-3791
Perrymont ES 400/PK-5
409 Perrymont Ave 24502 434-582-1100
Karen Nelson, prin. Fax 582-1108
Sandusky ES 400/K-5
5828 Apache Ln 24502 434-582-1111
Barbara Wickham, prin. Fax 582-1184
Sandusky MS 600/6-8
805 Chinook Pl 24502 434-582-1120
James E. Sales, prin. Fax 582-1183
Sheffield ES 400/PK-5
115 Kenwood Pl 24502 434-582-1115
Diane Swain, prin. Fax 582-1174

Branches Academy 50/PK-5
2812 Greenview Dr 24502 434-455-0294
Dr. Fay Andrist, admin. Fax 455-5952
Doss Junior Academy 100/K-10
19 George St 24502 434-237-1899
Stephen Doss, prin. Fax 237-0820
Holy Cross S 200/PK-12
2125 Langhorne Rd 24501 434-847-5436
William Coursey, prin. Fax 847-4156
James River Day S 200/K-8
5039 Boonsboro Rd 24503 434-384-7385
Mary Riser, hdmstr. Fax 384-5937
Liberty Christian Academy 1,800/PK-12
100 Mountain View Rd 24502 434-832-2000
Dr. Todd Campo, supt. Fax 832-2027

Mc Gaheysville, Rockingham
Rockingham County SD
Supt. — See Harrisonburg
Mc Gaheysville ES 400/PK-5
9508 Spotswood Trl 22840 540-289-3004
Rebecca Rhodes, prin. Fax 289-6832

Machipongo, Northampton
Northampton County SD 1,500/K-12
7207 Young St 23405 757-678-5151
Dr. Richard Bowmaster, supt. Fax 678-7267
www.ncps.k12.va.us
Other Schools – See Cape Charles, Exmore

Mc Kenney, Dinwiddie, Pop. 390
Dinwiddie County SD
Supt. — See Dinwiddie
Sunnyside ES 300/K-5
PO Box 250 23872 804-478-2313
Wanda Snodgrass, prin. Fax 478-2315

Mc Lean, Fairfax, Pop. 39,100
Fairfax County SD
Supt. — See Falls Church
Chesterbrook ES 500/K-6
1753 Kirby Rd 22101 703-714-8200
Robert Fuqua, prin. Fax 448-0971
Churchill Road ES 700/K-6
7100 Churchill Rd 22101 703-288-8400
Donald Hutzel, prin. Fax 288-8497
Cooper MS 900/7-8
977 Balls Hill Rd 22101 703-442-5800
Arlene Randall, prin. Fax 442-5897
Kent Gardens ES 900/K-6
1717 Melbourne Dr 22101 703-394-5600
Robyn Hooker, prin. Fax 394-5697
Sherman ES 400/PK-6
6630 Brawner St 22101 703-506-7900
Vicki Duling, prin. Fax 506-7997
Spring Hill ES 800/K-6
8201 Lewinsville Rd 22102 703-506-3400
Roger Vanderhye, prin. Fax 506-3497

Brooksfield S 100/PK-3
1830 Kirby Rd 22101 703-356-5437
Wendie Marsh, prin. Fax 356-6620
Langley S 500/PK-8
1411 Balls Hill Rd 22101 703-356-1920
Doris Cottam, prin. Fax 790-9712
Montessori S of McLean 200/PK-6
1711 Kirby Rd 22101 703-790-1049
Meredith Wood, prin. Fax 790-1962

Potomac S 900/K-12
PO Box 430 22101 703-356-4101
Geoffrey Jones, hdmstr. Fax 883-9031
St. John Academy 200/PK-8
6422 Linway Ter 22101 703-356-7554
Peter Schultz, prin. Fax 448-3811
St. Luke S 200/K-8
7005 Georgetown Pike 22101 703-356-1508
Renee White, prin. Fax 356-1141

Madison, Madison, Pop. 213
Madison County SD 1,900/K-12
PO Box 647 22727 540-948-3780
Dr. Brenda Tanner, supt. Fax 948-6988
www.madisonschools.k12.va.us
Madison PS 400/K-2
158 Primary School Dr 22727 540-948-3781
Mike Allers, prin. Fax 948-3365
Wetsel MS 400/6-8
186 Mountaineer Ln 22727 540-948-3783
David Covington, prin. Fax 948-4809
Yowell ES 400/3-5
1809 N Main St 22727 540-948-4511
Karen Allen, prin. Fax 948-3969

Madison Heights, Amherst, Pop. 11,700
Amherst County SD
Supt. — See Amherst
Amelon ES 500/PK-5
132 Amer Court 24572 434-528-6498
Nick Pontius, prin. Fax 929-1547
Elon ES 300/PK-5
147 Younger Dr 24572 434-528-6496
Ashley Wallace, prin. Fax 386-9300
Madison Heights ES 500/PK-5
287 Learning Ln 24572 434-846-2151
Darlene Mack, prin. Fax 845-5109
Monelison MS 700/6-8
257 Trojan Rd 24572 434-846-1307
Kathleen M. Pierce, prin. Fax 846-5318

Temple Christian S 400/PK-12
PO Box 970 24572 434-846-0024
Stephanie Sweat, prin. Fax 846-1807

Manassas, Manassas, Pop. 37,569
Manassas CSD 5,400/K-12
9000 Tudor Ln 20110 703-257-8808
Dr. Gail Pope, supt. Fax 257-8807
www.manassas.k12.va.us
Baldwin ES 500/K-4
9705 Main St 20110 703-257-8650
Dr. Ashley Cramp, prin. Fax 257-8654
Dean ES 500/K-4
9601 Prince William St 20110 703-257-8700
Robin Toogood, prin. Fax 257-8688
Haydon ES 500/K-4
9075 Park Ave 20110 703-257-8730
Rebecca Stone, prin. Fax 257-8708
Mayfield IS 5-6
8550 Signal Hill Rd 20110 703-257-8808
Jeffrey Abt, prin. Fax 257-8634
Metz JHS 1,000/7-8
9700 Fairview Ave 20110 703-257-8600
Melissa Saunders, prin. Fax 257-8615
Round ES 400/K-4
10100 Hastings Dr 20110 703-257-8750
John Durko, prin. Fax 257-8759
Weems ES 600/K-4
8750 Weems Rd 20110 703-257-8799
Angela Burnett, prin. Fax 257-8786

Prince William County SD 66,500/PK-12
PO Box 389 20108 703-791-7200
Steven Walts Ph.D., supt. Fax 791-7309
www.pwcs.edu
Ashland ES 800/K-5
15300 Bowmans Folly Dr 20112 703-583-8774
Amy Jordan, prin. Fax 583-9542
Bennett ES 800/K-5
8800 Old Dominion Dr 20110 703-361-8261
Sharon Fogarty, prin. Fax 361-1147
Benton MS 1,200/6-8
7411 Hoadly Rd 20112 703-791-0727
Linda Leibert, prin. Fax 791-0977
Coles ES 500/K-5
7405 Hoadly Rd 20112 703-791-3141
Alfie Turner, prin. Fax 791-4761
Ellis ES 600/K-5
10400 Kim Graham Ln 20109 703-365-0287
Jewell W. Moore, prin. Fax 365-0257
Loch Lomond ES 300/K-5
7900 Augusta Rd 20111 703-368-4128
William Horan, prin. Fax 257-8438
Marshall ES 700/K-5
12505 Kahns Rd 20112 703-791-2099
Kay Hermeling, prin. Fax 791-0032
Mullen ES 700/K-5
8000 Rodes Dr 20109 703-330-0427
Kathy Notyce, prin. Fax 330-7415
Parkside MS 1,100/6-8
8602 Mathis Ave 20110 703-361-3106
Rita Goss Ed.D., prin. Fax 361-8993
Pennington S 600/1-8
9305 Stonewall Rd 20110 703-369-6644
Joyce Boyd, prin. Fax 369-4206
Saunders MS 1,000/6-8
13557 Spriggs Rd 20112 703-670-9188
Myca Gray, prin. Fax 670-3078
Signal Hill ES 900/K-5
9553 Birmingham Dr 20111 703-530-7541
Cynthia Wrenn, prin. Fax 530-7542
Sinclair ES 500/K-5
7801 Garner Dr 20109 703-361-4811
Donna Fagerholm Ed.D., prin. Fax 361-7787
Stonewall MS 1,000/6-8
10100 Lomond Dr 20109 703-361-3185
John G. Miller, prin. Fax 368-1266
Sudley ES 500/K-5
9744 Copeland Dr 20109 703-361-3444
Pamela Moody, prin. Fax 361-8795
West Gate ES 500/K-5
8031 Urbanna Rd 20109 703-368-4404
Nikishia Lluvera-Holman, prin. Fax 361-0503
Woodbine Preschool Center 200/PK-PK
13225 Canova Dr 20112 703-791-3151
Mary Ann Adams, admin. Fax 791-2669
Yorkshire ES 500/K-5
7610 Old Centreville Rd 20111 703-361-3124
Damon Cerrone, prin. Fax 361-6184
Other Schools – See Bristow, Dumfries, Gainesville, Haymarket, Nokesville, Triangle, Woodbridge

---

All Saints S 500/PK-8
9294 Stonewall Rd 20110 703-368-4400
David Conroy, prin. Fax 393-2157
Emmanuel Christian S 200/PK-12
8302 Spruce St 20111 703-369-3950
Lawrence Landin, hdmstr. Fax 330-9285
Manassas Adventist Preparatory S 50/K-8
8225 Barrett Dr 20109 703-361-5593
Fax 361-5593

Manassas Park, Manassas Park, Pop. 11,622
Manassas Park CSD 2,500/PK-12
1 Park Center Ct Ste A 20111 703-335-8850
Dr. Thomas DeBolt, supt. Fax 361-4583
www.mpark.net
Cougar ES 900/PK-3
9330 Brandon St 20111 703-392-1317
Patricia Miller, prin. Fax 392-7204
Manassas Park ES 300/4-5
101 Tremont St 20111 703-368-2032
Stacey Mamon, prin. Fax 396-7172
Manassas Park MS 600/6-8
8202 Euclid Ave 20111 703-361-1510
Eric Neff, prin. Fax 331-3538

Mappsville, Accomack
Accomack County SD
Supt. — See Accomac
Kegotank ES 600/K-5
PO Box 28 23407 757-824-4756
Judith Byam, prin. Fax 824-4601

Marion, Smyth, Pop. 6,164
Smyth County SD 5,000/PK-12
121 Bagley Cir Ste 300 24354 276-783-3791
Dr. Michael Robinson, supt. Fax 783-3291
www.scsb.org
Marion IS 400/3-5
820 Stage St 24354 276-783-2609
Steven Miller, prin. Fax 783-9463
Marion MS 600/6-8
134 Wilden St 24354 276-783-4466
Brandon Ratliff, prin. Fax 783-4952
Marion PS 400/PK-2
1142 Highland Dr 24354 276-783-3021
Kimberly Williams, prin. Fax 781-2053
Other Schools – See Atkins, Chilhowie, Saltville, Sugar Grove

Marshall, Fauquier
Fauquier County SD
Supt. — See Warrenton
Thompson ES 200/PK-5
3284 Rectortown Rd 20115 540-364-2218
Marypat Warter, prin. Fax 364-1998

Fresta Valley Christian S 300/PK-12
6428 Wilson Rd 20115 540-364-1929
Kevin Worsham, admin. Fax 364-4603

Martinsville, Martinsville, Pop. 14,925
Henry County SD
Supt. — See Collinsville
Carver ES 500/PK-5
220 Trott Cir 24112 276-957-2226
Danny Cannaday, prin. Fax 957-4234
Laurel Park MS 800/6-8
280 Laurel Park Ave 24112 276-632-7216
Florence Simpson, prin. Fax 632-4865
Mt. Olivet ES 200/PK-5
255 Lancer Ln 24112 276-638-1022
Sherri Lewis, prin. Fax 638-2281
Rich Acres ES 300/PK-5
400 Rich Acres School Rd 24112 276-638-3366
William Bullins, prin. Fax 638-2462

Martinsville CSD 2,200/PK-12
PO Box 5548 24115 276-403-5820
Dr. Scott Kizner, supt. Fax 403-5825
www.martinsville.k12.va.us/
Clearview Preschool 200/PK-PK
800 Ainsley St 24112 276-634-5800
Pat Paige, dir. Fax 638-3031
Harris ES 500/K-5
710 Smith Rd 24112 276-403-5838
Natasha Rowell, prin. Fax 632-3069
Henry ES 100/K-5
1810 E Church Street Ext 24112 276-403-5812
Dr. Joan Montgomery, prin. Fax 656-1928
Martinsville MS 600/6-8
201 Brown St 24112 276-403-5886
Cynthia Tarpley, prin. Fax 638-4140

Mathews, Mathews
Mathews County SD 1,300/K-12
PO Box 369 23109 804-725-3909
David Holleran Ed.D., supt. Fax 725-3951
www.mathews.k12.va.us
Hunter MS 400/5-8
PO Box 339 23109 804-725-2434
Mike Comer, prin. Fax 725-2337
Lee-Jackson ES 400/K-4
PO Box 219 23109 804-725-2580
Andrew Greve, prin. Fax 725-3428

Matoaca, Chesterfield
Chesterfield County SD
Supt. — See Chesterfield
Matoaca ES 500/PK-5
6627 River Rd 23803 804-590-3100
Gloria Cooper, prin. Fax 590-1323
Matoaca MS 1,100/6-8
20300 Halloway Ave 23803 804-590-3130
Dr. Carla Mathews, prin. Fax 590-3136

Mattaponi, King and Queen
King & Queen County SD
Supt. — See King and Queen Court House
King & Queen ES 300/K-7
24667 The Trl 23110 804-785-5830
Harry Morgan, prin. Fax 785-3611

Max Meadows, Wythe
Wythe County SD
Supt. — See Wytheville
Ft. Chiswell MS 400/6-8
101 Pioneer Trl 24360 276-637-4400
Rebecca James, prin. Fax 637-4452
Max Meadows ES 200/K-5
PO Box 326 24360 276-637-3211
Beverly Quesenberry, prin. Fax 637-6568

Covenant Christian Academy 50/K-12
122 Apache Run 24360 276-637-4522
Dwight Haynes, admin. Fax 637-4523

Meadows of Dan, Patrick
Patrick County SD
Supt. — See Stuart
Meadows of Dan ES 100/K-7
3003 Jeb Stuart Hwy 24120 276-952-2424
Jeannie King, prin. Fax 952-1160

Meadowview, See Emory
Washington County SD
Supt. — See Abingdon
Meadowview ES 700/PK-5
14050 Glenbrook Ave 24361 276-739-3900
Dr. Beth Litz, prin. Fax 944-2113
Rhea Valley ES 500/PK-5
31305 Rhea Valley Rd 24361 276-739-4200
Debbie Anderson, prin. Fax 475-4055

Mechanicsville, Hanover, Pop. 22,027
Hanover County SD
Supt. — See Ashland
Battlefield Park ES 800/K-5
5501 Mechanicsville Tpke 23111 804-723-3600
Judy Bradley, prin. Fax 723-3605
Chickahominy MS 1,200/6-8
9450 Atlee Station Rd 23116 804-723-2160
Debbie Arco, prin. Fax 723-2191
Cold Harbor ES 600/K-5
6740 Cold Harbor Rd 23111 804-723-3620
Sarah Calveric, prin. Fax 723-3630
Cool Spring ES 800/K-5
9964 Honey Meadows Rd 23116 804-723-3560
Dr. Paula Brown, prin. Fax 723-3564
Jackson MS 1,200/6-8
8021 Lee Davis Rd 23111 804-723-2260
Dr. Anita Wallace, prin. Fax 723-2261
Kersey Creek ES K-5
10004 Learning Ln 23116 804-723-3440
Dr. Deborah Waters, prin. Fax 723-3450
Laurel Meadow ES K-5
8248 Lee Davis Rd 23111 804-723-2040
Karen Carpenter, prin. Fax 723-2058
Mechanicsville ES 700/K-5
7425 Mechanicsville Elem Dr 23111 804-723-3640
Dr. Amy Woodward, prin. Fax 723-3643
Oak Knoll MS 900/6-8
10295 Chamberlayne Rd 23116 804-365-4740
Caroline Harris, prin. Fax 365-4741
Pearsons Corner ES 500/K-5
8290 New Ashcake Rd 23116 804-723-3660
Stephen Smith, prin. Fax 723-3663
Pole Green ES 1,000/K-5
8993 Pole Green Park Ln 23116 804-365-4700
Rhonda Epling, prin. Fax 365-4717
Rural Point ES 700/K-5
7161 Studley Rd 23116 804-723-3580
Dr. Dana Gresham, prin. Fax 723-3594
Washington-Henry ES 500/K-5
9025 Washington Henry Dr 23116 804-723-2300
Jennifer Lenz, prin. Fax 723-2301

Liberty Christian S 200/PK-7
8094 Liberty Cir 23111 804-746-3062
Margaret Greer, admin. Fax 559-6533

Melfa, Accomack, Pop. 448
Accomack County SD
Supt. — See Accomac
Pungoteague ES 500/PK-5
28480 Bobtown Rd 23410 757-787-4032
Jennifer Annis, prin. Fax 787-1838

Middleburg, Loudoun, Pop. 880
Loudoun County SD
Supt. — See Ashburn
Banneker ES 200/PK-5
35231 Snake Hill Rd 20117 540-751-2480
Deborah Lee, prin. Fax 771-6782
Middleburg ES 100/PK-5
101 N Madison St 20117 540-751-2490
Gary Wilkers, prin. Fax 771-6682

Hill S 200/K-8
PO Box 65 20118 540-687-5897
Thomas Northrup, hdmstr. Fax 687-3132

Middletown, Frederick, Pop. 1,098
Frederick County SD
Supt. — See Winchester

Middletown ES 500/K-5
190 Mustang Ln 22645 540-869-4615
Grant Javersak, prin. Fax 869-5150

Midland, Fauquier, Pop. 1,905

Midland Christian Academy 100/PK-8
10456 Old Carolina Rd 22728 540-439-2606
Lynne Richman Cox, admin. Fax 439-2766

Midlothian, Chesterfield
Chesterfield County SD
Supt. — See Chesterfield
Bailey Bridge MS 1,600/6-8
12501 Bailey Bridge Rd 23112 804-739-6200
Donald Skeen, prin. Fax 739-6211
Clover Hill ES 900/PK-5
5700 Woodlake Village Pkwy 23112 804-739-6220
Amy Bosher, prin. Fax 739-6227
Crenshaw ES 800/PK-5
11901 Bailey Bridge Rd 23112 804-739-6250
David McCrum, prin. Fax 763-4479
Evergreen ES 900/PK-5
1701 E Evergreen Pkwy 23114 804-378-2400
Joyce Lanier, prin. Fax 378-2403
Midlothian MS 1,400/6-8
13501 Midlothian Tpke 23113 804-378-2460
Patrick Stanfield, prin. Fax 378-7556
Robious ES 700/PK-5
2801 Robious Crossing Dr 23113 804-378-2500
Anne O'Toole, prin. Fax 378-2507
Robious MS 1,300/6-8
2701 Robious Crossing Dr 23113 804-378-2510
Javaid Siddiqi, prin. Fax 378-2519
Smith ES 800/PK-5
13200 Bailey Bridge Rd 23112 804-739-6295
Virginia Lee Horgan, prin. Fax 739-0583
Spring Run ES 1,300/PK-5
13901 Spring Run Rd 23112 804-639-6352
Sandra Blankenship, prin. Fax 639-9015
Swift Creek ES 700/PK-5
13800 Genito Rd 23112 804-739-6305
Donald Bechtel, prin. Fax 739-6309
Swift Creek MS 1,500/6-8
3700 Old Hundred Rd S 23112 804-739-6315
Mary Robinson, prin. Fax 739-6322
Tomahawk Creek MS 6-8
1600 Learning Place Loop 23114 804-378-7120
Jeff Ellick, prin. Fax 794-2672
Watkins ES 800/PK-5
501 Coalfield Rd 23114 804-378-2530
Dr. Marlene Scott, prin. Fax 378-5182
Weaver ES 900/PK-5
3600 James River Rd 23113 804-378-2540
Holly Richard, prin. Fax 379-4555
Woolridge ES 800/PK-5
5401 Timber Bluff Pkwy 23112 804-739-6330
June Edwards, prin. Fax 639-5422

Millwood S 300/K-8
15100 Millwood School Ln 23112 804-639-3200
Dr. Louise Robinson, hdmstr.

Milford, Caroline
Caroline County SD
Supt. — See Bowling Green
Bowling Green PS 500/PK-2
17176 Richmond Tpke 22514 804-633-6401
Debra Holt, prin. Fax 633-2151
Caroline MS 900/6-8
13325 Devils Three Jump Rd 22514 804-633-6561
Derrick Scarborough, prin. Fax 633-9014

Millboro, Bath
Bath County SD
Supt. — See Warm Springs
Millboro ES 200/K-7
411 Church St 24460 540-997-5452
Wes Eary, prin. Fax 997-0123

Millers Tvrn, King and Queen

Aylett Country Day S 200/PK-8
PO Box 70, 804-443-3214
Nancy Haynes, hdmstr.

Mineral, Louisa, Pop. 459
Louisa County SD 4,600/PK-12
PO Box 7 23117 540-894-5115
Dr. Deborah Pettit, supt. Fax 894-0252
www.lcps.k12.va.us
Jouett ES 600/PK-5
315 Jouett School Rd 23117 540-872-3931
Paula Szalankiewicz, prin. Fax 872-4323
Louisa MS 1,100/6-8
PO Box 448 23117 540-894-5457
Thomas Schott, prin. Fax 894-5096
Other Schools – See Louisa

Moneta, Bedford
Bedford County SD
Supt. — See Bedford
Moneta ES 200/K-5
12718 N Old Moneta Rd 24121 540-297-4411
Barbara Rezzonico, prin. Fax 297-3280
Staunton River MS 800/6-8
1293 Golden Eagle Dr 24121 540-297-4152
Patty Johnson, prin. Fax 297-4076

Monroe, Amherst
Amherst County SD
Supt. — See Amherst
Pleasant View ES 100/PK-5
229 Dancing Creek Rd 24574 434-528-6492
Kelly Holmes, prin. Fax 922-7773

Monterey, Highland, Pop. 149
Highland County SD 300/PK-12
PO Box 250 24465 540-468-6300
Percy Nowlin, supt. Fax 468-6306
www.highland.k12.va.us
Highland ES 100/PK-5
PO Box 310 24465 540-468-6360
Teresa Kay Blum, prin. Fax 468-6333

Montpelier, Hanover
Hanover County SD
Supt. — See Ashland
South Anna ES 700/K-5
13122 Waltons Tavern Rd 23192 804-883-6089
Dr. Cyndee Blount, prin. Fax 730-2576

Montross, Westmoreland, Pop. 305
Westmoreland County SD 1,900/PK-12
141 Opal Ln 22520 804-493-8018
A. Elaine Fogliani, supt. Fax 493-9323
www.wmlcps.org/
Montross MS 400/6-8
8884 Menokin Rd 22520 804-493-9818
Jane Geyer, prin. Fax 493-0918
Other Schools – See Colonial Beach, Hague

Montvale, Bedford
Bedford County SD
Supt. — See Bedford
Montvale ES 300/K-6
1 Little Patriot Dr 24122 540-947-2241
Janet Brouhard, prin. Fax 947-5300

Moseley, Chesterfield
Chesterfield County SD
Supt. — See Chesterfield
Grange Hall ES 900/PK-5
19301 Hull Street Rd 23120 804-739-6265
Kathy Sefrin, prin. Fax 639-5403

Mount Solon, Augusta
Augusta County SD
Supt. — See Fishersville
North River ES 300/K-5
3395 Scenic Hwy 22843 540-350-2463
Katherine Ralston, prin. Fax 886-8550

Narrows, Giles, Pop. 2,150
Giles County SD
Supt. — See Pearisburg
Narrows S 600/K-7
401 Wolf St 24124 540-726-2391
Richard Franklin, prin. Fax 726-7345

Nathalie, Halifax
Halifax County SD
Supt. — See Halifax
Jennings ES 200/K-5
1011 Sydnor Jennings Rd 24577 434-349-1013
David Duffer, prin. Fax 349-1076
Meadville ES 200/K-5
1011 Meadville School Loop 24577 434-349-1012
Brenda Fuller, prin. Fax 349-5619

Natural Bridge Station, Rockbridge
Rockbridge County SD
Supt. — See Lexington
Natural Bridge ES 300/K-5
PO Box 280 24579 540-291-2292
Matthew Crossman, prin. Fax 291-2966

New Baltimore, Fauquier
Fauquier County SD
Supt. — See Warrenton
Ritchie ES 600/PK-5
4416 Broad Run Church Rd 20187 540-349-0460
A. Lee Bell, prin. Fax 349-0469

New Canton, Buckingham
Buckingham County SD
Supt. — See Buckingham
Gold Hill ES 200/K-5
59 Gold Hill Elementary Sch 23123 434-581-3342
Daisy Hicks, prin. Fax 581-1123

New Castle, Craig, Pop. 175
Craig County SD 700/K-12
PO Box 245 24127 540-864-5191
Ronnie Gordon, supt. Fax 864-6885
www.craig.k12.va.us/
McCleary ES 300/K-5
25345 Craigs Creek Rd 24127 540-864-5173
Scott Critzen, prin. Fax 864-8349

New Kent, New Kent
New Kent County SD 2,700/K-12
PO Box 110 23124 804-966-9650
J. Roy Geiger, supt. Fax 966-9879
www.nkcps.k12.va.us
New Kent County MS 600/6-8
PO Box 190 23124 804-966-9655
Howard Ormond, prin. Fax 966-2703
New Kent County PS 600/K-2
PO Box 170 23124 804-966-9663
Frederick Balmer, prin. Fax 966-2506
Other Schools – See Quinton

New Market, Shenandoah, Pop. 1,831

Shenandoah Valley Adventist S 100/K-8
115 Bindery Rd 22844 540-740-8237
Richard Maloon, prin. Fax 740-4562

Newport News, Newport News, Pop. 179,899
Newport News CSD 31,000/PK-12
12465 Warwick Blvd 23606 757-591-4500
Dr. Ashby Kilgore, supt. Fax 599-8270
www.sbo.nn.k12.va.us
Achievable Dream Academy 800/K-5
726 16th St 23607 757-928-6827
Catina Bullard-Clark, prin. Fax 247-1720
Carver ES 700/K-5
6160 Jefferson Ave 23605 757-591-4950
Alicia Spencer, prin. Fax 827-7936
Charles ES 500/K-5
701 Menchville Rd 23602 757-886-7750
John Tupponce, prin. Fax 988-1673
Crittenden MS 1,000/6-8
6158 Jefferson Ave 23605 757-591-4900
Felicia Barnett, prin. Fax 838-8261
Deer Park ES 500/K-5
11541 Jefferson Ave 23601 757-591-7470
Mark Kirk, prin. Fax 591-7448
Denbigh ECC 500/PK-PK
14302 Old Courthouse Way 23602 757-886-7789
Dr. Cynthia Pugh, prin. Fax 988-1676
Dozier MS 800/6-8
432 Industrial Park Dr 23608 757-888-3300
Angela Seiders, prin. Fax 887-3662
Dutrow ES 500/K-5
60 Curtis Tignor Rd 23608 757-886-7760
Marguerite Pittman, prin. Fax 989-0932
Epes ES 500/K-5
855 Lucas Creek Rd 23608 757-886-7755
Camisha Davis, prin. Fax 989-0015
Gildersleeve MS 1,200/6-8
1 Minton Dr 23606 757-591-4862
Benjamin Hogan, prin. Fax 596-2059
Greenwood ES 700/K-5
13460 Woodside Ln 23608 757-886-7744
Karen Lynch, prin. Fax 989-0231
Hall ECC 200/PK-PK
17346 Warwick Blvd 23603 757-888-3329
Lucyann Hancock, prin. Fax 888-3352
Hall ES 600/K-5
17346 Warwick Blvd 23603 757-888-3320
Amanda Corbin-Staton, prin. Fax 888-0212
Hidenwood ES 500/K-5
501 Blount Point Rd 23606 757-591-4766
Brian Nichols, prin. Fax 599-4451
Hilton ES 400/K-5
225 River Rd 23601 757-591-4772
Mary Jo Anastasio, prin. Fax 599-4382
Hines MS 1,200/6-8
561 McLawhorne Dr 23601 757-591-4878
Aaron Smith, prin. Fax 591-0119
Huntington MS 800/6-8
3401 Orcutt Ave 23607 757-928-6846
Cleo Holloway, prin. Fax 245-8451
Jenkins ES 400/K-5
80 Menchville Rd 23602 757-881-5400
Amelia Hunt, prin. Fax 881-9211
Kiln Creek ES 700/K-5
1501 Kiln Creek Pkwy 23602 757-886-7961
Deborah Pack, prin. Fax 989-0153
Magruder ECC 300/PK-PK
1712 Chestnut Ave 23607 757-928-6838
Johnnie Brown, prin. Fax 928-6718
Magruder PS 400/K-2
1712 Chestnut Ave 23607 757-928-6838
Tiffany Black, prin. Fax 247-0422
Marshall ES 300/K-2
743 24th St 23607 757-928-6832
Lorie Dildy, prin. Fax 247-0530
McIntosh ES 500/K-5
185 Richneck Rd 23608 757-886-7767
Barbara Jenkins, prin. Fax 989-0326
Nelson ES 600/K-5
826 Moyer Rd 23608 757-886-7783
Kimberly Brock, prin. Fax 989-0381
Newsome Park ES 700/K-5
4200 Marshall Ave 23607 757-928-6810
Diane Willis, prin. Fax 247-3218
Palmer ES 500/K-5
100 Palmer Ln 23602 757-881-5000
Izzie Brown, prin. Fax 249-4261
Passage MS 1,000/6-8
400 Atkinson Way 23608 757-886-7600
Dr. Kipp Rogers, prin. Fax 886-7661
PEEP 200/PK-PK
1241 Gatewood Rd 23601 757-591-4963
Heather Jankovich, admin. Fax 591-4695
Richneck ES 700/K-5
205 Tyner Dr 23608 757-886-7772
Cheryl Flemings, prin. Fax 874-6315
Riverside ES 500/PK-5
1100 Country Club Rd 23606 757-591-4740
Shannon Panko, prin. Fax 599-4518
Sanford ES 500/K-5
480 Colony Rd 23602 757-886-7778
Timothy Edwards, prin. Fax 989-0385
Saunders ES 500/K-5
853 Harpersville Rd 23601 757-591-4781
Sue Waxman, prin. Fax 599-4571
Sedgefield ES 500/K-5
804 Main St 23605 757-591-4788
Sherry Wolfson, prin. Fax 599-5064
South Morrison ES 600/K-5
746 Adams Dr 23601 757-591-4792
Barbara Nagel, prin. Fax 599-4981
Washington MS 6-8
3700 Chestnut Ave 23607 757-928-6860
Deborah Fields, prin. Fax 247-1119
Watkins ECC PK-PK
21 Burns Dr 23601 757-591-4815
Alan Romyak, admin. Fax 591-7690
Yates ES 500/K-5
73 Maxwell Ln 23606 757-881-5450
Raquel Cox, prin. Fax 930-1417
Other Schools – See Fort Eustis

Calvary Seventh-Day Adventist S 50/K-8
1200 17th St 23607 757-244-0913
Theresa Brinkley, prin. Fax 244-0716
Denbigh Baptist Christian S 600/K-12
13010 Mitchell Point Rd 23602 757-249-2654
Greg Hardy, admin. Fax 249-9480
Denbigh Christian Academy 200/K-8
1233 Shields Rd 23608 757-874-8661
Norman Rush, admin. Fax 234-4377
First Baptist Church Denbigh CDC 100/PK-5
3628 Campbell Rd 23602 757-833-7261
Hattie Harris, dir. Fax 877-7328
Hampton Roads Academy 500/PK-12
739 Academy Ln 23602 757-884-9100
Thomas Harvey, hdmstr. Fax 884-9137

Orcutt Baptist Christian S 100/PK-5
653 Baxter Ln 23602 757-249-2323
Claire Born, prin. Fax 249-9367
Our Lady of Mt. Carmel S 500/PK-8
52 Harpersville Rd 23601 757-596-2754
John Paul Myers, prin. Fax 596-1570
Resurrection Lutheran S 100/PK-5
765 J Clyde Morris Blvd 23601 757-596-5808
Ann Ezell, admin. Fax 596-5010
Rhema Christian Center Academy 100/PK-3
1700 27th St 23607 757-244-1258
Alice McDade, dir. Fax 244-4246
St. Andrew's Episcopal S 200/PK-5
45 Main St 23601 757-596-6261
Margaret Delk Moore, hdmstr. Fax 596-7218
Summit Christian Academy 100/PK-6
69 Saunders Rd 23601 757-599-9424
Sue Freeman, prin. Fax 599-1898
Trinity Lutheran S 300/PK-8
6812 River Rd 23607 757-245-2576
Lynn Fritzinger, hdmstr. Fax 245-4111
Warwick River Christian S 300/PK-8
252 Lucas Creek Rd 23602 757-877-2941
Greg Sommers, admin. Fax 877-6510

Newsoms, Southampton, Pop. 282
Southhampton County SD
Supt. — See Courtland
Meherrin ES 300/PK-5
28600 Grays Shop Rd 23874 757-654-6461
Syretha Wright, prin. Fax 654-6028

Nickelsville, Scott, Pop. 435
Scott County SD
Supt. — See Gate City
Nickelsville ES 300/K-7
PO Box 136 24271 276-479-2676
Kelsey Taylor, prin. Fax 479-2121

Nokesville, Prince William
Fauquier County SD
Supt. — See Warrenton
Greenville ES PK-5
7389 Academic Ave 20181 540-349-8925
Margie Riley, prin.

Prince William County SD
Supt. — See Manassas
Nokesville ES 400/K-5
12625 Fitzwater Dr 20181 703-594-2155
Bruce McDaniel Ed.D., prin. Fax 594-2478

Nora, Dickenson
Dickenson County SD
Supt. — See Clintwood
Ervinton ES 200/PK-7
PO Box 519 24272 276-835-9818
Anthony Robinson, prin. Fax 835-8796

Norfolk, Norfolk, Pop. 231,954
Norfolk CSD 35,200/PK-12
PO Box 1357 23501 757-628-3830
Dr. Stephen Jones, supt. Fax 628-3820
www.npsk12.com
Azalea Gardens MS 900/6-8
7721 Azalea Garden Rd 23518 757-531-3000
Dr. Reuthenia Clark, prin. Fax 531-3013
Bay View ES 700/PK-5
1434 E Bayview Blvd 23503 757-531-3030
Dr. Deborah Mansfield, prin. Fax 531-3025
Berkley/Compostella ECC 200/PK-PK
1530 Cypress St 23523 757-494-3870
Cheryl Bunch, prin. Fax 494-3290
Blair MS 1,100/6-8
730 Spotswood Ave 23517 757-628-2400
Jeanne Kruger, prin. Fax 628-2422
Bowling ES 500/PK-5
2861 E Princess Anne Rd 23504 757-628-2515
Brenda Shepherd, prin. Fax 628-2512
Calcott ES 500/PK-5
137 E Westmont Ave 23503 757-531-3039
Lillian Akers, prin. Fax 531-3041
Calvert Square ECC PK-PK
975 Bagnall Rd 23504 757-628-3412
Rosetta Woodhouse, prin. Fax 625-7084
Camp Allen ES 600/K-5
501 C St 23505 757-451-4170
Sherri Archer, prin. Fax 451-4172
Campostella ES 700/PK-5
1106 Campostella Rd 23523 757-494-3850
Dr. Laguna Foster, prin. Fax 494-3860
Chesterfield Academy 500/PK-5
2915 Westminster Ave 23504 757-628-2544
Sterling White, prin. Fax 628-2541
Coleman Place ES 700/PK-5
2445 Palmyra St 23513 757-852-4641
Callie Richardson, prin. Fax 852-4648
Crossroads ES 600/PK-5
7920 Tidewater Dr 23505 757-531-3050
Mary K. Beers, prin. Fax 531-3046
Dreamkeepers Academy 400/PK-5
2600 E Princess Anne Rd 23504 757-628-2555
Dr. Doreatha White, prin. Fax 628-2548
Easton Preschool 200/PK-PK
6045 Curlew Dr 23502 757-892-3290
Sharon Carson, prin. Fax 892-3285
Fairlawn ES 500/PK-5
1132 Wade St 23502 757-892-3260
Dennis Fifer, prin. Fax 892-3255
Ghent S 500/K-8
200 Shirley Ave 23517 757-628-2565
Christina Boone, prin. Fax 628-2564
Granby ES 600/PK-5
7101 Newport Ave 23505 757-451-4150
Vincent Darby, prin. Fax 451-4157
Ingleside ES 500/K-5
976 Ingleside Rd 23502 757-892-3270
Dwana White, prin. Fax 892-3265
Jacox ES 600/PK-5
1300 Marshall Ave 23504 757-628-2433
Kimberly Gray, prin. Fax 628-2435

Lafayette-Winona MS 900/6-8
1701 Alsace Ave 23509 757-628-2477
Cassandra Goodwyn, prin. Fax 628-2486
Lake Taylor MS 1,000/6-8
1380 Kempsville Rd 23502 757-892-3230
Michelle Williams-Moore, prin. Fax 892-3240
Larchmont ES 500/K-5
1145 Bolling Ave 23508 757-451-4180
Patricia Melise, prin. Fax 451-4188
Larrymore ES 500/K-5
7600 Halprin Dr 23518 757-531-3070
Dr. Thomas McAnulty, prin. Fax 531-3071
Lindenwood ES 400/PK-5
2700 Ludlow St 23504 757-628-2577
Pamela Hunter, prin. Fax 628-2576
Little Creek ES 700/PK-5
7900 Tarpon Pl 23518 757-531-3080
T. Michele Logan, prin. Fax 531-3083
Monroe ES 400/PK-5
520 W 29th St 23508 757-628-3500
Cassandra Washington, prin. Fax 628-3563
Northside MS 1,000/6-8
8720 Granby St 23503 757-531-3150
Richard Fraley, prin. Fax 531-3144
Norview ES 500/PK-5
6401 Chesapeake Blvd 23513 757-852-4660
Sandra Cox, prin. Fax 852-4658
Norview MS 1,100/6-8
6325 Sewells Point Rd 23513 757-852-4600
Reba Jacobs-Miller, prin. Fax 852-4590
Oakwood ES 300/PK-5
900 Asbury Ave 23513 757-852-4570
Shelia Holas, prin. Fax 852-4573
Oceanair ECC PK-PK
600 Dudley Ave 23503 757-531-3096
Lawrence Taylor, prin. Fax 531-3099
Oceanair ES 500/K-5
600 Dudley Ave 23503 757-531-3095
Lawrence Taylor, prin. Fax 531-3099
Ocean View ES 600/PK-5
9501 Mason Creek Rd 23503 757-531-3105
Lauren Campsen, prin. Fax 531-3111
Poplar Halls ES 400/PK-5
5523 Pebble Ln 23502 757-892-3280
Dr. Phyllis Clark-Freeman, prin. Fax 892-3275
Rosemont MS 600/6-8
1330 Branch Rd 23513 757-852-4610
Tracey Flemings, prin. Fax 852-4615
Ruffner Academy 900/6-8
610 May Ave 23504 757-628-2466
Kenyetta Goshen, prin. Fax 628-2465
St. Helena ES 300/PK-5
903 S Main St 23523 757-494-3884
Vandelyn Hodges, prin. Fax 494-3888
School of International Studies 300/6-8
7620 Shirland Ave 23505 757-451-4133
Dr. Lynnell Gibson, prin. Fax 451-4136
Sewells Point ES 600/K-5
7928 Hampton Blvd 23505 757-451-4160
Mary Wrushen, prin. Fax 451-4165
Sherwood Forest ES 700/PK-5
3035 Sherwood Forest Ln 23513 757-852-4550
Cheryl Jordan, prin. Fax 852-4532
Suburban Park ES 500/PK-5
310 Thole St 23505 757-531-3118
Bernette Brock, prin. Fax 531-3120
Tanners Creek ES 700/PK-5
1335 Longdale Dr 23513 757-852-4555
Kathleen Mein, prin. Fax 852-4553
Tarrallton ES 400/PK-5
2080 Tarrallton Dr 23518 757-531-1800
Diane Gibson, prin. Fax 531-1802
Taylor ES 400/PK-5
1122 W Princess Anne Rd 23507 757-628-2525
Mary Ann Bowen, prin. Fax 628-2531
Tidewater Park ES 400/PK-5
1045 E Brambleton Ave 23504 757-628-2500
Rosetta Woodhouse, prin. Fax 628-2501
Willard Model ES 500/K-5
1511 Willow Wood Dr 23509 757-628-2721
Maritsa Alger, prin. Fax 628-3997
Willoughby ES 300/PK-5
9500 4th View St 23503 757-531-3126
Sharon Phillips, prin. Fax 531-3125
Young ES 500/PK-5
543 E Olney Rd 23510 757-628-2588
Alana Balthazar, prin. Fax 628-2582

Calvary Christian S 400/PK-12
2331 E Little Creek Rd 23518 757-583-9730
Cheryl Finch Ph.D., hdmstr. Fax 480-5689
Christ the King S 300/PK-8
3401 Tidewater Dr 23509 757-625-4951
Rachel Chatham, prin. Fax 623-5212
Faith Academy S of Excellence 100/PK-8
1010 E 26th St 23504 757-624-1724
Sharon Riley, dir. Fax 961-7369
First Baptist READY Academy 100/PK-3
418 E Bute St 23510 757-622-5650
Robert Murray, admin. Fax 622-5653
Greenhill Farms Academy 50/K-5
969 Philpotts Rd 23513 757-853-0111
Doris Land, admin. Fax 853-1117
Holy Trinity S 200/PK-8
154 W Government Ave 23503 757-583-1873
Deneane Nofplot, prin. Fax 587-3677
McDonald Montessori 50/PK-3
4200 Granby St 23504 757-423-1800
Ellen McDonald, prin. Fax 423-1800
Norfolk Academy 1,200/1-12
1585 Wesleyan Dr 23502 757-461-6236
Dennis Manning, hdmstr. Fax 455-3181
Norfolk Christian Lower S 300/PK-5
255 Thole St 23505 757-423-5812
Dr. Karen Upton, prin. Fax 423-2009
Norfolk Christian MS 200/6-8
255 Thole St 23505 757-423-5770
Aimee Phillips, prin. Fax 440-5388

Norfolk Collegiate Lower S 300/K-5
5429 Tidewater Dr 23509 757-625-0471
Barbara Hall, admin. Fax 623-9246
Ocean View Christian Academy 50/PK-9
9504 Selby Pl 23503 757-583-4211
Amber Bornheimer, dir. Fax 583-5706
St. Pius X S 300/PK-8
7800 Halprin Dr 23518 757-588-6171
Sr. Linda Taber, prin. Fax 587-6580
Trinity Evangelical Lutheran S 100/PK-5
6001 Granby St 23505 757-489-2732
Judy Sykes, admin. Fax 489-8413
Williams S 200/K-8
419 Colonial Ave 23507 757-627-1383
John Mahoney, hdmstr. Fax 627-0869

North Garden, Albemarle
Albemarle County SD
Supt. — See Charlottesville
Red Hill ES 200/PK-5
3901 Red Hill School Rd 22959 434-293-5332
Arthur Stow, prin. Fax 293-7300

North Tazewell, See Tazewell
Tazewell County SD
Supt. — See Tazewell
North Tazewell ES 400/PK-5
300 W Riverside Dr 24630 276-988-4510
Sarah Reid, prin. Fax 988-8237
Springville ES 200/PK-5
144 Schoolhouse Rd 24630 276-322-5900
Rodney Gillespie, prin. Fax 322-1132

Norton, Norton, Pop. 3,677
Norton CSD 800/PK-12
PO Box 498 24273 276-679-2330
Dr. Lee Brannon, supt. Fax 679-4315
www.nortoncityschools.org/
Norton ES 500/PK-7
205 E Park Ave 24273 276-679-0971
Kaye Mink, prin. Fax 679-5914

Nottoway, Nottoway
Nottoway County SD 2,200/K-12
10321 E Colonial Trail Hwy 23955 434-645-9596
Dr. Daniel Grounard, supt. Fax 645-1266
www.nottowayschools.org/
Other Schools – See Blackstone, Burkeville, Crewe

Oak Hall, Accomack
Accomack County SD
Supt. — See Accomac
Arcadia MS 500/6-8
PO Box 220 23416 757-824-4862
Skip Oakley, prin. Fax 824-6618

Oakton, Fairfax, Pop. 24,610
Fairfax County SD
Supt. — See Falls Church
Oakton ES 600/K-6
3000 Chain Bridge Rd 22124 703-937-6100
Beverly Worek, prin. Fax 937-6197
Waples Mill ES 800/PK-6
11509 Waples Mill Rd 22124 703-390-7700
Linda Thetford, prin. Fax 390-7797

Dominion Christian S 100/K-8
PO Box 3068 22124 703-758-1055
Flint Hill S 1,100/PK-12
3320 Jermantown Rd 22124 703-584-2300
John Thomas, hdmstr. Fax 584-2369
Montessori S of Oakton 100/PK-6
12113 Vale Rd 22124 703-715-0611
Carolyn Linke, prin.

Oakwood, Buchanan
Buchanan County SD
Supt. — See Grundy
Twin Valley S 400/PK-7
9017 Riverside Dr 24631 276-498-4537
Sandra Cole, prin. Fax 498-7046

Onley, Accomack, Pop. 496
Accomack County SD
Supt. — See Accomac
Nandua MS 500/6-8
20330 Warrior Dr 23418 757-787-7037
John Killmon, prin. Fax 787-8807

Orange, Orange, Pop. 4,429
Orange County SD 4,800/PK-12
200 Dailey Dr 22960 540-661-4550
Larry Massie, supt. Fax 661-4599
www.ocss-va.org
Orange ES 600/PK-5
230 Montevista Ave 22960 540-661-4450
Daniel Phillips, prin. Fax 661-4449
Prospect Heights MS 500/6-8
202 Dailey Dr 22960 540-661-4400
Frank Leech, prin. Fax 661-4399
Other Schools – See Gordonsville, Locust Grove, Unionville

Grymes Memorial S 200/PK-8
PO Box 1160 22960 540-672-1010
Elizabeth Work, hdmstr.

Palmyra, Fluvanna
Fluvanna County SD 3,600/K-12
PO Box 419 22963 434-589-8208
Thomas Smith, supt. Fax 589-2248
www.fluco.org
Central ES 1,400/K-5
3340 Central Plains Rd 22963 434-589-8318
Sarah Pinckney, prin. Fax 589-4275
Columbia ES 100/K-2
563 Wilmington Rd 22963 434-589-8613
Sue Davies, prin. Fax 589-1959
Cunningham ES 200/K-2
479 Cunningham Rd 22963 434-842-3197
Sue Davies, prin. Fax 842-2502
Other Schools – See Fork Union

Parksley, Accomack, Pop. 833
Accomack County SD
Supt. — See Accomac
Metompkin ES 600/PK-5
24501 Parksley Rd 23421 757-665-1299
Faye Williams, prin. Fax 665-5283

Patrick Springs, Patrick
Patrick County SD
Supt. — See Stuart
Patrick Springs ES 300/K-3
75 Elementary Ln 24133 276-694-3396
Andrea Cassell, prin. Fax 694-5806

Pearisburg, Giles, Pop. 2,768
Giles County SD 2,600/K-12
151 School Rd 24134 540-921-1421
Dr. Terry Arbogast, supt. Fax 921-1424
sbo.gilesk12.org/
McClaugherty S 600/K-7
1001 Henson Ave 24134 540-921-1363
Jared Rader, prin. Fax 921-3130
Other Schools – See Narrows, Pembroke

Pembroke, Giles, Pop. 1,167
Giles County SD
Supt. — See Pearisburg
Eastern S 500/K-7
6899 Virginia Ave 24136 540-626-7281
Gregory Canaday, prin. Fax 626-7175

Penhook, Franklin
Franklin County SD
Supt. — See Rocky Mount
Snow Creek ES 200/PK-5
5393 Snow Creek Rd 24137 540-483-5599
Ken Grindstaff, prin. Fax 483-5604

Pennington Gap, Lee, Pop. 1,753
Lee County SD
Supt. — See Jonesville
Elk Knob ES 300/K-5
RR 2 Box 193 24277 276-546-1837
Lisa Stewart, prin. Fax 546-4161
Pennington MS 300/6-8
201 Middle School Dr 24277 276-546-1453
Otis Belcher, prin. Fax 546-3515

Penn Laird, Rockingham
Rockingham County SD
Supt. — See Harrisonburg
Montevideo MS 600/6-8
7648 McGaheysville Rd 22846 540-289-3401
Lisa Milliken, prin. Fax 289-3601
Peak View ES 600/PK-5
641 Lawyer Rd 22846 540-289-7510
Marcy Williams, prin. Fax 289-7439

Petersburg, Petersburg, Pop. 32,604
Petersburg CSD 3,900/PK-12
255 E South Blvd 23805 804-732-0510
Dr. James Victory, supt. Fax 732-0514
www.petersburg.k12.va.us/home.asp
Hill ES 400/K-5
1450 Talley Ave 23803 804-862-7002
Phyllis Byrd, prin. Fax 862-7182
Lee ES 300/K-5
51 Gibbons Ave 23803 804-862-7007
Barbara Patterson, prin. Fax 861-5041
Peabody MS 400/6-7
725 Wesley St 23803 804-862-7075
Cheryl Perkins, prin. Fax 733-6091
Stuart ES 300/PK-5
100 Pleasants Ln 23803 804-862-7013
Kori Reddick, prin. Fax 861-2197
Walnut Hill ES 600/K-5
300 W South Blvd 23805 804-862-7005
Zelda Lynch, prin. Fax 861-4032
Westview Early Childhood Ed Center PK-PK
1100 Patterson St 23803 804-862-7010
QuVarda Bailey, prin.

Lewis Christian S 50/K-8
300 Poplar Dr 23805 804-732-4733
Jacqueline Gonzalez, prin. Fax 732-7915
Rock Church Academy 100/PK-12
2301 County Dr 23803 804-733-3973
Kristen Davis, prin. Fax 733-3093
St. Joseph S 100/PK-6
123 Franklin St 23803 804-732-3931
Diane Young, prin. Fax 732-6479

Phenix, Charlotte, Pop. 191
Charlotte County SD
Supt. — See Charlotte Court House
Phenix ES 100/PK-2
400 Red House Rd 23959 434-542-5570
Deborah Barksdale, prin. Fax 542-5572

Poquoson, Poquoson, Pop. 11,811
Poquoson CSD 2,600/PK-12
500 City Hall Ave 23662 757-868-3055
Dr. Jennifer Parish, supt. Fax 868-3107
www.sbo.poquoson.k12.va.us
Poquoson ES 500/3-5
1033 Poquoson Ave 23662 757-868-6921
Dr. Jeff Carroll, prin. Fax 868-8058
Poquoson MS 600/6-8
985 Poquoson Ave 23662 757-868-6031
Todd Perelli, prin. Fax 868-4220
Poquoson PS 500/PK-2
19 Odd Rd 23662 757-868-4403
Susan Butler, prin. Fax 868-6846

Portsmouth, Portsmouth, Pop. 100,169
Portsmouth CSD 15,000/PK-12
PO Box 998 23705 757-393-8751
Dr. David Stuckwisch, supt. Fax 393-5236
www.pps.k12.va.us
Brighton ES 700/K-6
1100 Portsmouth Blvd 23704 757-393-8870
Barbara Shears-Walker, prin. Fax 393-5133
Churchland Academy 1,000/K-6
4061 River Shore Rd 23703 757-686-2527
Venessa Whichard Harris, prin. Fax 686-2529
Churchland ES 700/PK-6
5601 Michael Ln 23703 757-686-2523
Michele Ramey, prin. Fax 686-2526
Churchland MS 900/7-8
4051 River Shore Rd 23703 757-686-2512
Dr. Karen Giacometti, prin. Fax 686-2515
Churchland S 600/PK-6
5700 Hedgerow Ln 23703 757-686-2519
Cora Freeman, prin. Fax 686-2521
Cradock MS 700/7-8
21 Alden Ave 23702 757-393-8788
Dr. Rosalyn Sanderlin, prin. Fax 393-5020
Douglass Park ES 700/K-6
34 Grand St 23701 757-393-8646
Barbara Jones Smith, prin. Fax 393-8286
Hodges Manor ES 500/K-6
1201 Cherokee Rd 23701 757-465-2921
Dr. Faye Felton, prin. Fax 465-2922
Hurst ES 800/K-6
18 Dahlgren Ave 23702 757-558-2811
Evelyn Whitley, prin. Fax 558-2812
Lakeview ES 600/K-6
1300 Horne Ave 23701 757-465-2901
Queen Malone, prin. Fax 405-1895
Mt. Hermon Preschool PK-PK
3000 North St 23707 757-393-8825
Dr. Sandra Smith, prin. Fax 393-1349
Olive Branch ES 500/PK-6
415 Mimosa Rd 23701 757-465-2926
Darlene Bright, prin. Fax 465-2927
Park View ES 400/PK-6
260 Elm Ave 23704 757-393-8647
Gwendolyn Watkins, prin. Fax 393-8126
Simonsdale ES 300/K-6
132 Byers Ave 23701 757-465-2917
Karen Clark, prin. Fax 465-2918
Spong Preschool PK-PK
2200 Piedmont Ave 23704 757-393-5247
Francis Gill, prin. Fax 397-4514
Tyler ES 700/K-6
3649 Hartford St 23707 757-393-8879
J. Wayne Williams, prin. Fax 393-5876
Victory ES K-6
2828 Greenwood Dr 23701 757-393-8806
E. Ann Horne, prin. Fax 393-5139
Waters MS 600/7-8
600 Roosevelt Blvd 23701 757-558-2813
Dr. Eric Fischer, prin. Fax 485-2829
Westhaven ES 600/K-6
3701 Clifford St 23707 757-393-8855
Patricia Williams, prin. Fax 393-8410

Alliance Christian S 200/PK-12
5809 Portsmouth Blvd 23701 757-488-5552
Duane Ranard, admin. Fax 488-3192
Central Christian Academy 100/PK-8
1200 Hodges Ferry Rd 23701 757-488-4477
Krista Ryan, prin. Fax 488-4836
Christopher Academy 200/PK-5
3300 Cedar Ln 23703 757-484-6776
Phyllis Shannon, hdmstr. Fax 484-6774
Court Street Academy 100/K-8
447 Court St 23704 757-393-2312
Joyous Sound Education Center 100/PK-2
205 Gust Ln 23701 757-558-2880
Alvita Byrd, admin. Fax 558-2885
Portsmouth Catholic S 200/PK-8
2301 Oregon Ave 23701 757-488-6744
Mary Paul, prin. Fax 465-8833
Portsmouth Christian S 800/PK-12
3214 Elliott Ave 23702 757-393-0725
Bruce Devers, admin. Fax 397-7487
Toras Chaim S 100/PK-8
3110 Sterling Point Dr 23703 757-686-2480
Fax 686-4636

Potomac Falls, Loudoun

Our Lady of Hope S 200/K-7
46633 Algonkian Pkwy 20165 703-433-6760
Mary Pittman, prin. Fax 433-6761

Pound, Wise, Pop. 1,087
Wise County SD
Supt. — See Wise
Adams Combined S 600/PK-8
10824 Orby Cantrell Hwy 24279 276-796-5419
George Barton, prin. Fax 796-4698

Powhatan, Powhatan
Powhatan County SD 4,400/K-12
2320 Skaggs Rd 23139 804-598-5700
Margaret Meara, supt. Fax 598-5705
www.powhatan.k12.va.us
Flat Rock ES K-4
2210 Batterson Rd 23139 804-598-5443
Tanja Atkins-Nelson, prin. Fax 598-8235
Pocahontas ES 800/K-4
4294 Anderson Hwy 23139 804-598-5717
Linda Dail, prin. Fax 598-6320
Pocahontas MS 600/5-6
4290 Anderson Hwy 23139 804-598-5720
Lynne Prince, prin. Fax 598-1485
Powhatan ES 900/K-4
4111 Old Buckingham Rd 23139 804-598-5730
Constance Deal, prin. Fax 598-1484
Powhatan JHS 700/7-8
4135 Old Buckingham Rd 23139 804-598-5782
Richard Stewart, prin. Fax 403-3065

Blessed Sacrament S 500/PK-12
2501 Academy Rd 23139 804-598-4211
Joseph Oley, pres. Fax 598-1053

Prince George, Prince George
Prince George County SD 6,200/PK-12
PO Box 400 23875 804-733-2700
Dr. R. Francis Moore, supt. Fax 733-2737
pgs.k12.va.us
Beazley ES 600/PK-5
6700 Courthouse Rd 23875 804-733-2745
James Scruggs, prin. Fax 732-1627
North ES 300/PK-5
11100 Old Stage Rd 23875 804-458-8922
Vera Abbott-Young, prin. Fax 541-6251
Walton ES 600/PK-5
4101 Courthouse Rd 23875 804-733-2750
Jan Peyrot, prin. Fax 732-1592
Other Schools – See Disputanta

Woodlawn Christian S 100/PK-8
6764 Billy Williams Mem Dr 23875 804-732-3245
Sonya Adkins, hdmstr. Fax 732-7870

Pulaski, Pulaski, Pop. 9,088
Pulaski County SD 5,000/PK-12
202 N Washington Ave 24301 540-643-0200
Donald Stowers Ed.D., supt. Fax 643-0437
www.pcva.us
Critzer ES 400/PK-5
100 Critzer Dr 24301 540-643-0274
Harold Malcolm, prin. Fax 980-8627
Pulaski ES 600/PK-5
2004 Morehead Ln 24301 540-643-0737
Linda Edwards, prin. Fax 643-0990
Pulaski MS 500/6-8
500 Pico Ter 24301 540-643-0767
Michael Perry, prin. Fax 980-8571
Other Schools – See Dublin, Hiwassee, Radford

Purcellville, Loudoun, Pop. 4,680
Loudoun County SD
Supt. — See Ashburn
Blue Ridge MS 1,100/6-8
551 E A St 20132 540-751-2520
Roberta Griffith, prin. Fax 338-6823
Emerick ES 500/PK-5
440 S Nursery Ave 20132 540-338-6870
Deborah Cookus, prin. Fax 338-6876
Hillsboro ES 100/K-5
37110 Charles Town Pike 20132 540-751-2560
David Michener, prin. Fax 771-6732
Lincoln ES 200/PK-5
18048 Lincoln Rd 20132 703-751-2430
Albert Johnson, prin. Fax 338-6862
Mountain View ES 800/PK-5
36803 Allder School Rd 20132 540-751-2550
Douglas Martin, prin. Fax 338-0821

Quicksburg, Shenandoah
Shenandoah County SD
Supt. — See Woodstock
Ashby Lee ES 600/K-5
480 Stonewall Ln 22847 540-477-2927
Holly Rusher, prin. Fax 477-2844
North Fork MS 400/6-8
1018 Caverns Rd 22847 540-477-2953
Shelby Kline, prin. Fax 477-2562

Quinton, New Kent
New Kent County SD
Supt. — See New Kent
Watkins ES 600/3-5
PO Box 10 23141 804-966-9660
Russell Macomber, prin. Fax 932-8459

Radford, Radford, Pop. 14,575
Floyd County SD
Supt. — See Floyd
Indian Valley ES 200/K-7
4130 Indian Valley Rd NW 24141 540-745-9420
Carolyn Quinn, prin. Fax 745-9490

Montgomery County SD
Supt. — See Christiansburg
Belview ES 300/PK-5
3187 Peppers Ferry Rd 24141 540-633-3200
Rhonda Baker, prin. Fax 639-5235

Pulaski County SD
Supt. — See Pulaski
Riverlawn ES 300/PK-5
6671 Riverlawn Ct 24141 540-643-0748
John Bowler, prin. Fax 639-0882

Radford CSD 1,500/PK-12
1612 Wadsworth St 24141 540-731-3647
Dr. Chuck Bishop, supt. Fax 731-4419
www.rcps.org/
Belle Heth ES 300/4-6
810 2nd Ave 24141 540-731-3653
Kenneth Alderman, prin. Fax 731-3697
Dalton IS 200/7-8
60 Dalton Dr 24141 540-731-3651
Walter Smith, prin. Fax 731-5033
McHarg ES 500/PK-3
700 12th St 24141 540-731-3652
Rob Graham, prin. Fax 731-3696

Radiant, Madison

Cornerstone Christian S of the Piedmont 50/PK-4
2930 Beautiful Run Rd 22732 540-672-0512
John Higginbotham, hdmstr.

Raven, Tazewell, Pop. 2,640
Tazewell County SD
Supt. — See Tazewell
Raven ES 200/PK-5
22 School St 24639 276-964-9437
Sarah Cromer, prin. Fax 964-9437

Remington, Fauquier, Pop. 676
Fauquier County SD
Supt. — See Warrenton

Pierce ES 600/PK-5
12074 James Madison St 22734 540-439-3213
Christine Wolfe, prin. Fax 439-8519

Reston, Fairfax, Pop. 58,200
Fairfax County SD
Supt. — See Falls Church
Aldrin ES 500/PK-6
11375 Center Harbor Rd 20194 703-904-3800
Marty Marinoff, prin. Fax 904-3897
Armstrong ES 400/K-6
11900 Lake Newport Rd 20194 703-375-4800
Shane Wolfe, prin. Fax 375-4897
Dogwood ES 600/K-6
12300 Glade Dr 20191 703-262-3100
Robyn Cochran, prin. Fax 262-3197
Forest Edge ES 800/K-6
1501 Becontree Ln 20190 703-925-8000
Franklin Bensinger, prin. Fax 925-8097
Hughes MS 900/7-8
11401 Ridge Heights Rd 20191 703-715-3600
Aimee Monticchio, prin. Fax 715-3697
Hunters Woods ES for the Arts & Sciences 900/K-6
2401 Colts Neck Rd 20191 703-262-7400
Olivia Toatley, prin. Fax 262-7497
Lake Anne ES 500/K-6
11510 N Shore Dr 20190 703-326-3500
Linda Hajj, prin. Fax 326-3597
Sunrise Valley ES 500/K-6
10824 Cross School Rd 20191 703-715-3800
Elizabeth English, prin. Fax 715-3897
Terraset ES 400/K-6
11411 Ridge Heights Rd 20191 703-390-5600
Ellen Cury, prin. Fax 390-5697

Academy of Christian Education 200/PK-6
1808A Michael Faraday Ct 20190 703-471-2132
Donna Strater, admin. Fax 471-5790
Reston Montessori S 200/PK-3
1928 Isaac Newton Sq W 20190 703-481-2922
Kathleen Lanfear, prin. Fax 435-9308
Sunset Hills Montessori 200/PK-8
11180 Ridge Heights Rd 20191 703-476-7477
Eileen Minarik, prin. Fax 476-7233

Richlands, Tazewell, Pop. 4,116
Tazewell County SD
Supt. — See Tazewell
Richlands ES 500/PK-5
309 Front St 24641 276-964-4112
Wendy Barringer, prin. Fax 964-4278
Richlands MS 600/6-8
185 Learning Ln 24641 276-963-5370
Glayde Brown, prin. Fax 963-0210

Richmond, Richmond, Pop. 193,777
Chesterfield County SD
Supt. — See Chesterfield
Bellwood ES 400/PK-5
9536 Dawnshire Rd 23237 804-743-3600
Robin Morgan, prin. Fax 275-3227
Bensley ES 500/PK-5
6600 Strathmore Rd 23237 804-743-3610
Bessie Cooper, prin. Fax 271-2670
Beulah ES 600/PK-5
4216 Beulah Rd 23237 804-743-3620
Mary Jean Hunt, prin. Fax 271-3894
Crestwood ES 600/PK-5
7600 Whittington Dr 23225 804-560-2710
Lisa Rockwell, prin. Fax 320-8520
Davis ES 700/PK-5
415 S Providence Rd 23236 804-674-1310
Barbara Lowery, prin. Fax 675-0243
Falling Creek ES 600/PK-5
4800 Hopkins Rd 23234 804-743-3630
Pamela Johnson, prin. Fax 275-9269
Falling Creek MS 1,000/6-8
4724 Hopkins Rd 23234 804-743-3640
Stephanie Crutchfield, prin. Fax 743-3644
Gordon ES 600/PK-5
11701 Gordon School Rd 23236 804-378-2410
David Joyner, prin. Fax 379-2983
Greenfield ES 500/PK-5
10751 Savoy Rd 23235 804-560-2720
Tina Martin, prin. Fax 272-6739
Hening ES 1,000/PK-5
5230 Chicora Dr 23234 804-743-3655
Matthew Maher, prin. Fax 743-3658
Hopkins Road ES 600/PK-5
6000 Hopkins Rd 23234 804-743-3665
Donna Venable, prin. Fax 743-3671
Manchester MS 1,600/6-8
7401 Hull Street Rd 23235 804-674-1385
Jeff McGee, prin. Fax 674-1394
Providence ES 600/PK-5
11001 W Providence Rd 23236 804-674-1345
Steve DeGaetani, prin. Fax 745-2339
Providence MS 900/6-8
900 Starlight Ln 23235 804-674-1355
Tameshia Grimes, prin. Fax 674-1361
Reams Road ES 600/PK-5
10141 Reams Rd 23236 804-674-1370
Mary Dunn, prin. Fax 745-3391
Salem Church ES 600/K-5
9600 Salem Church Rd 23237 804-768-6215
Carol Lewellyn, prin. Fax 796-9499
Salem Church MS 900/6-8
9700 Salem Church Rd 23237 804-768-6225
Kenneth Butta, prin. Fax 768-6230

Henrico County SD 47,500/PK-12
PO Box 23120 23223 804-652-3600
Fred Morton, supt. Fax 652-3856
www.henrico.k12.va.us
Adams ES 600/K-5
600 S Laburnum Ave 23223 804-226-8745
Roy Holloway, prin. Fax 226-8768
Ashe ES 500/K-5
1001 Cedar Fork Rd 23223 804-343-6550
Dana Moore, prin. Fax 343-6514
Baker ES 500/K-5
6651 Willson Rd 23231 804-226-8755
Theodore Durniak, prin. Fax 226-8769
Brookland MS 1,200/6-8
9200 Lydell Dr 23228 804-261-5000
Martha Fouad, prin. Fax 261-5003
Byrd MS 1,200/6-8
9400 Quioccasin Rd 23238 804-750-2630
Sharon Pope, prin. Fax 750-2629
Carver ES, 1801 Lauderdale Dr 23238 500/K-5
Joanne Gutkin, prin. 804-750-2640
Chamberlayne ES 400/K-5
8200 St Charles Rd 23227 804-261-5030
Rebecca Grant, prin. Fax 261-1734
Crestview ES 200/K-5
1901 Charles St 23226 804-673-3775
Karen Rawlyk, prin. Fax 673-3742
Davis ES 500/K-5
8801 Nesslewood Dr 23229 804-527-4620
Bryan Almasian, prin. Fax 527-4658
Dumbarton ES 600/K-5
9000 Hungary Spring Rd 23228 804-756-3030
Eileen Traveline, prin. Fax 756-3014
Fairfield MS 1,400/6-8
5121 Nine Mile Rd 23223 804-328-4020
John Mayo, prin. Fax 328-4031
Gayton ES 500/K-5
12481 Church Rd 23233 804-360-0820
Peggy Wingfield, prin. Fax 360-0811
Glen Lea ES 400/K-5
3909 Austin Ave 23222 804-228-2725
Kimberly Lee, prin. Fax 228-2732
Harvie ES PK-5
3401 Harvie Rd 23223 804-343-7010
Dr. M. McQueen-Williams, prin. Fax 343-7013
Holladay ES 500/K-5
7300 Galaxie Rd 23228 804-261-5040
Charles Joseph, prin. Fax 261-5054
Johnson ES 500/K-5
5600 Bethlehem Rd 23230 804-673-3735
Constance Walters, prin. Fax 673-3753
Laburnum ES 600/K-5
500 Meriwether Ave 23222 804-228-2720
Peggy Taylor, prin. Fax 228-2733
Lakeside ES 400/K-5
6700 Cedar Croft St 23228 804-261-5050
Herbert Monroe, prin. Fax 261-5069
Longan ES 400/K-5
9200 Mapleview Ave 23294 804-527-4640
W. Richard Hall, prin. Fax 527-4639
Maybeury ES 600/K-5
901 Maybeury Dr 23229 804-750-2650
Eric Armbruster, prin. Fax 750-2649
Mehfoud ES 300/K-2
8320 Buffin Rd 23231 804-795-7020
Amy Hand, prin. Fax 795-7023
Montrose ES 400/K-5
2820 Williamsburg Rd 23231 804-226-8765
Linda Magliocca, prin. Fax 226-8771
Moody MS 1,000/6-8
7800 Woodman Rd 23228 804-261-5015
Arthur Raymond, prin. Fax 261-5024
Mount Vernon MS 100/6-8
7850 Carousel Ln 23294 804-527-4660
Victor Oliver, prin. Fax 527-4665
New Bridge S 100/3-8
5915 Nine Mile Rd 23223 804-328-6125
Dorothy Hutcheson, prin. Fax 328-5502
Nuckols Farm ES 600/K-5
12351 Graham Meadows Dr 23233 804-364-0840
Mary Cox, prin. Fax 364-0843
Pemberton ES 300/K-5
1400 Pemberton Rd 23238 804-750-2660
Kim Olsen, prin. Fax 750-2663
Pinchbeck ES 500/K-5
1225 Gaskins Rd 23238 804-750-2670
Kirk Eggleston, prin. Fax 750-2664
Pocahontas MS 800/6-8
12000 Three Chopt Rd 23233 804-364-0830
Tracie Weston, prin.
Ratcliffe ES 500/K-5
2901 Thalen St 23223 804-343-6535
Ingrid Grant, prin. Fax 343-6516
Ridge ES 500/K-5
8910 Three Chopt Rd 23229 804-673-3745
Robin Exton, prin. Fax 673-3754
Rolfe MS 1,500/6-8
6901 Messer Rd 23231 804-226-8730
Andrew Armstrong, prin. Fax 226-8739
Short Pump ES 600/K-5
3425 Pump Rd 23233 804-360-0812
Melissa Passehl, prin. Fax 364-0845
Skipwith ES 400/K-5
2401 Skipwith Rd 23294 804-527-4650
Dr. Kaye Thomas, prin. Fax 527-4664
Three Chopt ES 300/K-5
1600 Skipwith Rd 23229 804-673-3755
Robert Spotts, prin. Fax 673-3748
Trevvett ES 500/K-5
2300 Trevvett Dr 23228 804-261-5060
Sharon Vecchione, prin. Fax 515-1199
Tuckahoe ES 600/K-5
701 Forest Ave 23229 804-673-3765
Cindy Patterson, prin. Fax 673-3749
Tuckahoe MS 1,300/6-8
9000 Three Chopt Rd 23229 804-673-3720
Brian Fellows, prin. Fax 673-3731
Varina ES 400/3-5
2551 New Market Rd 23231 804-795-7010
Markam Tyler, prin. Fax 795-7028
Ward ES 500/K-5
3400 Darbytown Rd 23231 804-795-7030
David Burgess, prin. Fax 795-7017
Wilder MS 900/6-8
6900 Wilkinson Rd 23227 804-515-1100
Christie Forrest, prin. Fax 515-1110
Other Schools – See Glen Allen, Highland Springs, Sandston

Richmond CSD 23,100/PK-12
301 N 9th St 23219 804-780-7700
Dr. Yvonne Brandon, supt. Fax 780-4122
www.richmond.k12.va.us
Bellevue Model ES 300/PK-5
2301 E Grace St 23223 804-780-4417
Sherry Wharton-Carey, prin. Fax 780-8153
Binford MS 500/6-8
1701 Floyd Ave 23220 804-780-6231
Peter Glessman, prin. Fax 780-6057
Blackwell Annex ES PK-5
238 E 14th St 23224 804-780-5064
Conrad Davis, prin. Fax 319-3012
Blackwell ES 500/K-5
300 E 15th St 23224 804-780-5078
Conrad Davis, prin. Fax 319-3012
Boushall MS 600/6-8
3400 Hopkins Rd 23234 804-780-5016
Sheron Carter-Gunter, prin. Fax 780-5396
Broad Rock ES 300/PK-5
4615 Ferguson Ln 23234 804-780-5048
Carmen Rush, prin. Fax 780-5011
Brown MS 700/6-8
6300 Jahnke Rd 23225 804-319-3013
Denise Lewis, prin. Fax 319-3009
Carver ES 500/PK-5
1110 W Leigh St 23220 804-780-6247
Arcelius Brickhouse, prin. Fax 780-8046
Cary ES 300/PK-5
3021 Maplewood Ave 23221 804-780-6252
Brenda Phillips, prin. Fax 780-8407
Chimborazo ES 600/PK-5
3000 E Marshall St 23223 804-780-8392
Cheryl Burke, prin. Fax 780-8154
Clark Springs ES 200/PK-5
1101 Dance St 23220 804-780-6234
Cynthia Tedder, prin. Fax 780-8408
Elkhardt MS 500/6-8
6300 Hull Street Rd 23224 804-745-3600
Eric Jones, prin. Fax 674-5518
Fairfield Court ES 400/PK-5
2510 Phaup St 23223 804-780-4639
Irene Williams Ph.D., prin. Fax 780-4087
Fisher Model ES 400/PK-5
3701 Garden Rd 23235 804-327-5612
Charlene Brooks, prin. Fax 327-5611
Fox ES 400/PK-5
2300 Hanover Ave 23220 804-780-6259
Daniela Jacobs, prin. Fax 780-8409
Francis ES 500/PK-5
5146 Snead Rd 23224 804-745-3702
Daisy Greene, prin. Fax 319-3030
Ginter Park Annex S PK-5
4011 Moss Side Ave 23222 804-780-8463
Cathy Randolph, prin. Fax 780-4313
Ginter Park ES 500/PK-5
3817 Chamberlayne Ave 23227 804-780-8193
Cathy Randolph, prin. Fax 780-4313
Greene ES 500/PK-5
1745 Catalina Dr 23224 804-780-5082
Linda Sims, prin. Fax 319-3022
Henderson MS 500/6-8
4319 Old Brook Rd 23227 804-780-8288
Jeanine Turner, prin. Fax 228-5357
Hill MS 500/6-8
3400 Patterson Ave 23221 804-780-6107
Michael Kight, prin. Fax 780-8754
Holton ES 500/PK-5
1600 W Laburnum Ave 23227 804-228-5310
David Hudson, prin. Fax 262-1501
Jones ES 500/PK-5
200 Beaufont Hills Dr 23225 804-319-3185
Shelia Scott, prin. Fax 319-3187
King MS 700/6-8
1000 Mosby St 23223 804-780-8011
Aaron Dixon, prin. Fax 780-5590
Mason ES 400/PK-5
813 N 28th St 23223 804-780-4401
Sandra Bynum, prin. Fax 780-8155
Maymont ES 200/PK-5
1211 S Allen Ave 23220 804-780-6263
Wilma Battle, prin. Fax 780-8411
Munford ES 500/PK-5
211 Westmoreland St 23226 804-780-6267
Gregory Muzik, prin. Fax 780-6051
Oak Grove-Bellemeade ES K-5
2409 Webber Ave 23224 804-780-5073
Jannie Laursen, prin. Fax 780-5063
Oak Grove ES 400/K-5
2220 Ingram Ave 23224 804-780-5008
Jannie Laursen, prin. Fax 319-3024
Overby-Sheppard ES 400/PK-5
2300 1st Ave 23222 804-329-2515
Susan Stokes, prin. Fax 780-4321
Redd ES 500/PK-5
5601 Jahnke Rd 23225 804-780-5061
Regina Farr, prin. Fax 319-3025
Reid ES 600/PK-5
1301 Whitehead Rd 23225 804-745-3550
Reginald Williams, prin. Fax 319-3029
Southampton ES 400/PK-5
3333 Cheverly Rd 23225 804-320-2434
Linda Bennett, prin. Fax 560-2853
Stuart ES 300/PK-5
3101 Fendall Ave 23222 804-780-4879
Jennifer Moore, prin. Fax 780-4320
Summer Hill Annex ES K-5
2001 Ruffin Rd 23234 804-780-5024
Indira Williams, prin. Fax 319-3026
Summer Hill ES 500/PK-5
2717 Alexander Ave 23234 804-780-5041
Indira Williams, prin. Fax 319-3026
Swansboro ES 400/PK-5
3160 Midlothian Tpke 23224 804-780-5030
Mary Pierce, prin. Fax 319-3027
Thompson MS 600/6-8
7825 Forest Hill Ave 23225 804-272-7554
Rickie Hopkins, prin. Fax 560-5115

Westover Hills ES — 400/PK-5
1211 Jahnke Rd 23225 — 804-780-5002
Sarah Pitts, prin. — Fax 319-3028
Woodville ES — 600/PK-5
2000 N 28th St 23223 — 804-780-4821
Rosalind Taylor, prin. — Fax 780-8156

All Saints Catholic S — 200/PK-8
3418 Noble Ave 23222 — 804-329-7524
Kenneth Soistman, prin. — Fax 329-4201
All Saints Letsy Ann Memorial S — 50/K-5
2001 Royall Ave 23224 — 804-232-3159
Lona Rogers, dir. — Fax 232-2669
Banner Christian S — 200/PK-12
PO Box 74010 23236 — 804-276-5200
Patricia Burkett, hdmstr. — Fax 276-7620
Central Montessori S of Virginia — 50/PK-4
323 N 20th St 23223 — 804-447-7493
Anita Pishko, prin. — Fax 447-7494
Collegiate S — 1,600/K-12
103 N Mooreland Rd 23229 — 804-740-7077
Keith Evans, hdmstr. — Fax 741-9797
East End Christian Academy — 100/PK-12
3294 Britton Rd 23231 — 804-795-9266
Daniel Helland, admin. — Fax 795-2222
Elijah House Academy — 100/K-10
6255 Old Warwick Rd 23224 — 804-755-7051
Dr. William Kell, dir. — Fax 377-6800
Ephesus Adventist S — 100/K-8
3700 Midlothian Tpke 23224 — 804-233-4582
Keith Wallace, prin. — Fax 291-9180
Faith Life Academy — 50/K-6
420 Oronoco Ave 23222 — 804-321-1333
Dr. Barbara Reis, admin. — Fax 329-8980
Good Shepherd Episcopal S — 100/PK-8
4207 Forest Hill Ave 23225 — 804-231-1452
Charles Britton, hdmstr. — Fax 231-1651
Grove Avenue Christian S — 300/PK-12
8701 Ridge Rd 23229 — 804-741-2860
Heidi Ashley, admin. — Fax 754-8534
Luther Memorial S — 200/PK-8
1301 Robin Hood Rd 23227 — 804-321-6420
Dave Berlin, prin. — Fax 321-2884
Minnieland Private Day S — 200/PK-6
11211 W Huguenot Rd 23235 — 804-323-6804
Lori Marano, prin. — Fax 323-1452
Orchard House S — 100/5-8
500 N Allen Ave 23220 — 804-228-2436
Nancy Davies, dir. — Fax 228-1069
Our Lady of Lourdes S — 400/PK-8
8250 Woodman Rd 23228 — 804-262-1770
Lucy Reilley, prin. — Fax 262-1437
Richmond Academy of SDA — 100/K-12
3809 Patterson Ave 23221 — 804-353-0036
Angie Weems, prin. — Fax 358-8797
Richmond Montessori S — 300/PK-8
499 N Parham Rd 23229 — 804-741-0040
Susanne Gregory, hdmstr. — Fax 741-5341
Richmond Preparatory Christian Academy — 100/PK-8
217 W Grace St 23220 — 804-344-0051
Patricia Grant, prin. — Fax 344-0059
Richmond Waldorf S — 100/PK-6
1000 Westover Hills Blvd 23225 — 804-377-8024
Pete Svoboda, admin. — Fax 377-8027
Rudlin Torah Academy — 200/K-12
12285 Patterson Ave 23238 — 804-784-9050
Rabbi Hal Klestzick, prin. — Fax 784-9005
Sabot at Stony Point — 200/PK-8
3400 Stony Point Rd 23235 — 804-272-1341
Irene Carney, hdmstr.
St. Andrews S — 100/K-5
227 S Cherry St 23220 — 804-648-4545
Mary Wickham, hdmstr. — Fax 648-3428
St. Benedict S — 200/K-8
3100 Grove Ave 23221 — 804-254-8850
Sean Cruess, prin. — Fax 254-9163
St. Bridget S — 500/K-8
6011 York Rd 23226 — 804-288-1994
Charlene Bechely, prin. — Fax 288-5730
St. Catherine's S — 900/PK-12
6001 Grove Ave 23226 — 804-288-2804
Laura Erickson, hdmstr. — Fax 285-8169
St. Christopher's S — 1,000/PK-12
711 Saint Christophers Rd 23226 — 804-282-3185
Charles Stillwell, hdmstr. — Fax 285-3914
St. Edward-Epiphany S — 400/PK-8
10701 W Huguenot Rd 23235 — 804-272-2881
Georgette Richards, prin. — Fax 327-0788
St. Mary S — 400/PK-8
9501 Gayton Rd 23229 — 804-740-1048
Thomas Dertinger, prin. — Fax 740-1310
St. Michael's Episcopal S — 400/K-8
8706 Quaker Ln 23235 — 804-272-3514
Edgar Hubbard, hdmstr. — Fax 323-3280
Steward S — 600/K-12
11600 Gayton Rd 23238 — 804-740-3394
Kenneth Seward, hdmstr. — Fax 740-1464
Veritas Classical Christian S — 200/K-12
6627B Jahnke Rd 23225 — 804-272-9517
Steve Diehl, hdmstr. — Fax 272-9518
Victory Christian Academy — 100/K-12
8491 Chamberlayne Rd 23227 — 804-262-8256
Andrea Cassidy, prin. — Fax 553-1905
Webber Community Christian S — 200/PK-5
7800 Salem Church Rd 23237 — 804-271-4705
Debbie Davis, prin. — Fax 271-4358
West End Montessori S — 100/PK-4
9307 Quioccasin Rd 23229 — 804-523-7536
Janet Gallagher, prin. — Fax 523-4396

Ridgeway, Henry, Pop. 798
Henry County SD
Supt. — See Collinsville
Ridgeway ES — 400/PK-5
380 Church St 24148 — 276-956-3626
Wendy Durham, prin. — Fax 956-1851

Rileyville, Page
Page County SD
Supt. — See Luray
Springfield ES — 300/PK-7
158 Big Spring Ln 22650 — 540-743-3750
Teresa Day, prin. — Fax 743-4699

Riner, Montgomery
Montgomery County SD
Supt. — See Christiansburg
Auburn ES — 600/PK-5
4315 Riner Rd 24149 — 540-381-6521
Kenneth Moles, prin. — Fax 381-6530
Auburn MS — 300/6-8
4069 Riner Rd 24149 — 540-382-5165
Guylene Wood-Setzer, prin. — Fax 381-6562

Ringgold, Pittsylvania
Pittsylvania County SD
Supt. — See Chatham
Dan River MS — 500/6-8
5875 Kentuck Rd 24586 — 434-822-6027
Sherri Crumpton, prin. — Fax 822-6548
Kentuck ES — 600/PK-5
100 Kentuck Elementary Cir 24586 — 434-822-5944
Dr. Robert Gentry, prin. — Fax 822-5923

Roanoke, Roanoke, Pop. 92,631
Roanoke CSD — 13,200/PK-12
PO Box 13145 24031 — 540-853-2381
Dr. Rita Bishop, supt. — Fax 853-2951
www.rcps.info
Addison Aerospace Magnet MS — 500/6-8
1220 5th St NW 24016 — 540-853-2681
Robert Johnson, prin. — Fax 853-2842
Breckinridge MS — 400/6-8
3901 Williamson Rd NW 24012 — 540-853-2251
Asia Jones, prin. — Fax 853-6505
Crystal Spring ES — 300/K-5
2620 Carolina Ave SW 24014 — 540-853-2976
David Merritt, prin. — Fax 853-1930
Fairview Magnet ES — 400/PK-5
648 Westwood Blvd NW 24017 — 540-853-2978
Dr. Julie Bush, prin. — Fax 853-1038
Fallon Park ES — 600/PK-5
502 19th St SE 24013 — 540-853-2535
Cindy Delp, prin. — Fax 853-2094
Fishburn Park ES — 300/PK-5
3057 Colonial Ave SW 24015 — 540-853-2931
David Amos, prin. — Fax 853-1122
Forest Park Magnet ES — 300/PK-5
2730 Melrose Ave NW 24017 — 540-853-2923
Gloria Randolph-King, prin. — Fax 853-1773
Garden City ES — 300/PK-5
3718 Garden City Blvd SE 24014 — 540-853-2971
Rebecca Smith, prin. — Fax 853-1237
Grandin Court ES — 300/PK-5
2815 Spessard Ave SW 24015 — 540-853-2867
Theresa Pritchard, prin. — Fax 853-1399
Highland Park Magnet ES — 200/PK-5
1212 5th St SW 24016 — 540-853-2963
Debra Doss, prin. — Fax 853-1692
Huff Lane IS — 200/3-5
4412 Huff Ln NW 24012 — 540-853-2973
Dayl Graves, prin. — Fax 853-2402
Hurt Park ES — 200/PK-5
1525 Salem Ave SW 24016 — 540-853-2986
Carlton Bell, prin. — Fax 853-2397
Jackson MS — 500/6-8
1004 Montrose Ave SE 24013 — 540-853-6040
Stephanie Hogan, prin. — Fax 853-6027
Lincoln Terrace ES — 300/PK-5
1802 Liberty Rd NW 24012 — 540-853-2994
Freida Hines, prin. — Fax 853-1054
Madison MS — 500/6-8
1160 Overland Rd SW 24015 — 540-853-2351
Debra Dietrich, prin. — Fax 853-1050
Monterey ES — 400/PK-5
4501 Oliver Rd NE 24012 — 540-853-2933
Ann Kreft, prin. — Fax 853-1126
Morningside ES — 300/PK-5
1716 Wilson St SE 24013 — 540-853-2991
April Holmes, prin. — Fax 853-1552
Oakland IS — 200/3-5
3229 Williamson Rd NW 24012 — 540-853-6391
Gregory Johnston, prin. — Fax 853-2343
Preston Park PS — 300/PK-2
3142 Preston Ave NW 24012 — 540-853-2996
Karen McClung, prin. — Fax 853-1168
Raleigh Court ES — 400/PK-5
2202 Grandin Rd SW 24015 — 540-853-2655
Babette Cribbs, prin. — Fax 853-1106
Roanoke Academy/Math & Science — 400/PK-5
1616 19th St NW 24017 — 540-853-2751
Toni Belton, prin. — Fax 853-1192
Round Hill Montessori PS — 300/PK-2
2020 Oakland Blvd NW 24012 — 540-853-2756
Kathleen Tate, prin. — Fax 853-1118
Ruffner MS — 500/6-8
3601 Ferncliff Ave NW 24017 — 540-853-2605
Mark Hairston, prin. — Fax 853-1350
Virginia Heights ES — 300/PK-5
1210 Amherst St SW 24015 — 540-853-2937
Sybil Taylor, prin. — Fax 853-2496
Wasena ES — 300/PK-5
1125 Sherwood Ave SW 24015 — 540-853-2914
Eric Fisher, prin. — Fax 853-1189
Westside ES — 600/PK-5
1441 Westside Blvd NW 24017 — 540-853-2967
Dr. Melva Belcher, prin. — Fax 853-1429
Wilson MS — 500/6-8
1813 Carter Rd SW 24015 — 540-853-2358
Archie Freeman, prin. — Fax 853-2004

Roanoke County SD — 14,900/K-12
5937 Cove Rd 24019 — 540-562-3700
Dr. Lorraine Lange, supt. — Fax 562-3994
www.rcs.k12.va.us
Back Creek ES — 300/K-5
7130 Bent Mountain Rd 24018 — 540-772-7565
Karen Mabry, prin. — Fax 776-7144
Bonsack ES — 500/K-5
5437 Crumpacker Dr 24019 — 540-977-5870
Melissa Jones, prin. — Fax 977-5879
Burlington ES — 400/K-5
6533 Peters Creek Rd 24019 — 540-561-8165
Amy Shank, prin. — Fax 561-8162
Cave Spring ES — 500/K-5
5404 Springlawn Ave 24018 — 540-772-7558
Jodi Poff, prin. — Fax 776-7145
Cave Spring MS — 600/6-8
4880 Brambleton Ave 24018 — 540-772-7560
Steven Boyer, prin. — Fax 772-2195
Clearbrook ES — 200/K-5
5205 Franklin Rd SW 24014 — 540-772-7555
Karen Pendleton, prin. — Fax 776-7148
Glen Cove ES — 500/K-5
5901 Cove Rd 24019 — 540-561-8135
Jan Nichols, prin. — Fax 561-8164
Green Valley ES — 400/K-5
3838 Overdale Rd 24018 — 540-772-7556
Tammy Newcomb, prin. — Fax 776-7149
Hidden Valley MS — 800/6-8
4902 Hidden Valley School 24018 — 540-772-7570
Ken Nicely, prin. — Fax 772-7519
Mountain View ES — 500/K-5
5901 Plantation Cir 24019 — 540-561-8175
Leigh Smith, prin. — Fax 561-8167
Mt. Pleasant ES — 300/K-5
3216 Mount Pleasant Blvd 24014 — 540-427-1879
Ellen Walton, prin. — Fax 427-5779
Northside MS — 800/6-8
6810 Northside High School 24019 — 540-561-8145
Lori Wimbush, prin. — Fax 561-8152
Oak Grove ES — 500/K-5
5005 Grandin Rd Ext 24018 — 540-772-7580
Christina Flippen, prin. — Fax 776-7150
Penn Forest ES — 600/K-5
6328 Merriman Rd 24018 — 540-772-7590
Linda Wright, prin. — Fax 776-7151
Other Schools – See Bent Mountain, Salem, Vinton

Faith Christian S — 300/K-12
3585 Buck Mountain Rd 24018 — 540-769-5200
Samuel Cox, hdmstr. — Fax 769-6030
New Vista Montessori S — 50/PK-K
2005 Langdon Rd SW 24015 — 540-342-1173
Stewart Putney, dir. — Fax 342-1169
North Cross S — 500/PK-12
4254 Colonial Ave 24018 — 540-989-6641
Tim Seeley, hdmstr. — Fax 989-7299
Parkway Christian Academy — 200/PK-12
3230 King St NE 24012 — 540-982-2400
Troy Dixon, admin. — Fax 982-0128
Roanoke Adventist Prep S — 50/K-8
PO Box 4144 24015 — 540-342-1133
Dianne Watts, lead tchr. — Fax 342-8628
Roanoke Catholic S — 500/PK-12
621 N Jefferson St 24016 — 540-982-3532
Ray Correia, pres. — Fax 345-0785
Roanoke Valley Christian S — 400/K-12
6520 Williamson Rd 24019 — 540-366-2432
Rick Brown, admin. — Fax 366-9719

Rocky Gap, Bland
Bland County SD
Supt. — See Bastian
Rocky Gap ES — 300/K-7
PO Box 339 24366 — 276-928-1086
William Miller, prin. — Fax 928-0151

Rocky Mount, Franklin, Pop. 4,568
Franklin County SD — 7,600/PK-12
25 Bernard Rd 24151 — 540-483-5138
Dr. Charles Lackey, supt. — Fax 483-5806
www.frco.k12.va.us
Franklin MS East — 600/6-6
375 Middle School Rd 24151 — 540-483-5105
Terri Robertson, prin. — Fax 483-5501
Franklin MS West — 900/7-8
225 Middle School Rd 24151 — 540-483-5105
Terri Robertson, prin. — Fax 483-5501
Rocky Mount ES — 300/PK-5
555 School Board Rd 24151 — 540-483-5040
S. Jerome Johnson, prin. — Fax 483-5454
Sontag ES — 400/PK-5
3101 Sontag Rd 24151 — 540-483-5667
William Robey, prin. — Fax 483-5656
Waid ES — 400/PK-5
540 E Court St 24151 — 540-483-5736
John Bono, prin. — Fax 483-9674
Other Schools – See Boones Mill, Callaway, Ferrum, Gladehill, Henry, Penhook, Wirtz

---

Christian Heritage Academy — 100/PK-12
625 Glennwood Dr 24151 — 540-483-5855
Ed Roller, admin. — Fax 483-9355

Rosedale, Russell
Russell County SD
Supt. — See Lebanon
Belfast - Elk Garden ES — 200/K-6
PO Box G 24280 — 276-880-2283
Juanita Musick, prin. — Fax 880-1330

Rose Hill, Lee, Pop. 12,675
Lee County SD
Supt. — See Jonesville
Rose Hill ES — 200/PK-7
RR 1 Box 136 24281 — 276-445-4094
Lynn Metcalfe, prin. — Fax 445-5315

Round Hill, Loudoun, Pop. 639
Loudoun County SD
Supt. — See Ashburn
Round Hill ES — 500/PK-5
17115 Evening Star Dr 20141 — 540-751-2450
Nancy McManus, prin. — Fax 338-6834

Ruckersville, Greene
Greene County SD
Supt. — See Stanardsville
Ruckersville ES — 600/K-5
105 Progress Pl 22968 — 434-985-1472
Mike Coiner, prin. — Fax 990-9432

Rural Retreat, Wythe, Pop. 1,354
Wythe County SD
Supt. — See Wytheville
Rural Retreat ES 400/K-5
100 Martha Deborad Way 24368 276-686-4125
Mary Walters, prin. Fax 686-4467
Rural Retreat MS 300/6-8
321 E Buck Ave 24368 276-686-5200
Marion Haga, prin. Fax 686-4944

Rustburg, Campbell
Campbell County SD 8,800/PK-12
PO Box 99 24588 434-332-3458
Dr. Robert Johnson, supt. Fax 528-1655
www.campbell.k12.va.us
Rustburg ES 600/PK-5
25 Webbs Way 24588 434-332-5215
Lee Shearer, prin. Fax 332-1151
Rustburg MS 700/6-8
PO Box 130 24588 434-332-5141
Richard Burge, prin. Fax 332-2058
Yellow Branch ES 500/PK-5
377 Dennis Riddle Dr 24588 434-821-1021
Mary Arnold, prin. Fax 821-5871
Other Schools – See Altavista, Brookneal, Concord, Gladys, Lynchburg

Ruther Glen, Caroline
Caroline County SD
Supt. — See Bowling Green
Lewis & Clark ES 300/PK-5
18101 Clark And York Blvd 22546 804-448-0175
Harold Pellegreen, prin. Fax 448-0293
Madison ES 600/PK-5
9075 Chance Pl 22546 804-448-2171
Michelle Hinegardner, prin. Fax 448-4395

Carmel Christian Academy 100/PK-12
PO Box 605 22546 804-448-3288
John Carneal, admin. Fax 448-3146
Ladysmith Baptist Academy 100/PK-12
18290 Jefferson Davis Hwy 22546 804-448-3860
Milton Bush, prin. Fax 448-5806

Saint Charles, Lee, Pop. 154
Lee County SD
Supt. — See Jonesville
Saint Charles ES 200/PK-7
PO Box O 24282 276-383-4531
Brian Dean, prin. Fax 383-4422

Saint Paul, Wise, Pop. 969
Wise County SD
Supt. — See Wise
Saint Paul S 300/PK-7
PO Box 1067 24283 276-762-5941
Larry Greear, prin. Fax 762-0481

Saint Stephens Church, King and Queen
King & Queen County SD
Supt. — See King and Queen Court House
Lawson-Marriott ES 200/K-7
1599 Newtown Rd 23148 804-769-3116
Linda Via, prin. Fax 769-4091

Salem, Salem, Pop. 24,654
Roanoke County SD
Supt. — See Roanoke
Ft. Lewis ES 200/K-5
3115 W Main St 24153 540-387-6594
Kim Bradshaw, prin. Fax 387-6348
Glenvar ES 300/K-5
4507 Malus Dr 24153 540-387-6540
Dan Guard, prin. Fax 387-6351
Glenvar MS 500/6-8
4555 Malus Dr 24153 540-387-6322
Juliette Meyers, prin. Fax 387-6283
Masons Cove ES 200/K-5
3370 Bradshaw Rd 24153 540-387-6530
Ashley McCallum, prin. Fax 384-6087

Salem CSD 4,000/PK-12
510 S College Ave 24153 540-389-0130
Dr. H. Alan Seibert, supt. Fax 389-4135
www.salem.k12.va.us
Carver ES 500/K-5
6 E 4th St 24153 540-387-2492
Trula Byington, prin. Fax 375-4105
East Salem ES 400/PK-5
1765 Roanoke Blvd 24153 540-375-7001
Diane Rose, prin. Fax 343-6623
Lewis MS 900/6-8
616 S College Ave 24153 540-387-2513
Jerome Campbell, prin. Fax 389-8914
South Salem ES 400/K-5
1600 Carolyn Rd 24153 540-387-2478
Margaret Humphrey, prin. Fax 389-4810
West Salem ES 400/K-5
520 N Bruffey St 24153 540-387-2503
John Millard, prin. Fax 389-4923

Saltville, Smyth, Pop. 2,267
Smyth County SD
Supt. — See Marion
Northwood MS 200/6-8
156 Long Hollow Rd 24370 276-624-3341
Jeffrey Comer, prin. Fax 624-3535
Rich Valley ES 200/PK-5
196 Long Hollow Rd 24370 276-624-3314
Tamela Johnson, prin. Fax 624-3426
Saltville ES 200/PK-5
PO Box C 24370 276-496-4751
Brenda Boone, prin. Fax 496-3958

Saluda, Middlesex
Middlesex County SD 1,300/PK-12
PO Box 205 23149 804-758-2277
Donald Fairheart, supt. Fax 758-3727
www.mcps.k12.va.us/
Other Schools – See Locust Hill

Sandston, Henrico, Pop. 3,630
Henrico County SD
Supt. — See Richmond
Donahoe ES 400/K-5
1801 Graves Rd 23150 804-328-4035
Susan Thomas, prin. Fax 328-4022
Elko MS, 5901 Elko Rd 23150 6-8
Katrise Perera, prin. 804-328-4110
Sandston ES 200/K-5
7 Naglee Ave 23150 804-328-4055
Tracey Seamster, prin. Fax 328-4017
Seven Pines ES 500/K-5
301 Beulah Rd 23150 804-328-4065
Paul Llewellyn, prin. Fax 328-4043

New Bridge Academy 100/K-12
5701 Elko Rd 23150 804-737-7833
Stanford Stone, hdmstr. Fax 737-1181

Saxe, Charlotte
Charlotte County SD
Supt. — See Charlotte Court House
Bacon District ES 200/PK-5
840 Bacon School Rd 23967 434-735-8612
Sylvia Lockett, prin. Fax 735-8505

Scottsburg, Halifax, Pop. 148
Halifax County SD
Supt. — See Halifax
Clays Mill ES 200/K-5
1011 Clays Mill School Rd 24589 434-476-3022
Sherry Cowan, prin. Fax 476-1891
Scottsburg ES 200/K-5
1010 Scottsburg School Trl 24589 434-454-6454
Barbara Tune, prin. Fax 454-3175

Scottsville, Albemarle, Pop. 564
Albemarle County SD
Supt. — See Charlottesville
Scottsville ES 200/PK-5
7868 Scottsville School Rd 24590 434-974-8040
Nancy Teel, prin. Fax 286-2442

Seaford, York
York County SD
Supt. — See Yorktown
Seaford ES 500/K-5
1105 Seaford Rd 23696 757-898-0352
Lisa Pennycuff, prin. Fax 898-0413

Sedley, Southampton
Southhampton County SD
Supt. — See Courtland
Nottoway ES 400/PK-5
13093 Ivor Rd 23878 757-859-6539
Debra Hicks, prin. Fax 859-9392

Shawsville, Montgomery, Pop. 1,260
Montgomery County SD
Supt. — See Christiansburg
Shawsville MS 300/6-8
4179 Oldtown Rd 24162 540-268-2262
David Dickinson, prin. Fax 268-1868

Shenandoah, Page, Pop. 1,870
Page County SD
Supt. — See Luray
Grove Hill ES 200/PK-7
7979 US Highway 340 22849 540-652-8544
Daniel Smith, prin. Fax 652-1753
Shenandoah ES 400/PK-7
529 4th St 22849 540-652-8621
Chad Hensley, prin. Fax 652-1711

Skipwith, Mecklenburg
Mecklenburg County SD
Supt. — See Boydton
Bluestone MS 500/6-8
250 Middle School Rd 23968 434-372-3266
Mona Rainey, prin. Fax 372-3362

Smithfield, Isle of Wight, Pop. 6,840
Isle of Wight County SD 5,400/PK-12
820 W Main St 23430 757-357-0449
Michael McPherson Ed.D., supt. Fax 357-0849
www.iwcs.k12.va.us
Hardy ES 500/PK-3
9311 Hardy Cir 23430 757-357-3204
Joyce McDowell, prin. Fax 365-0236
Smithfield MS 600/7-8
14175 Turner Dr 23430 757-365-4100
Dr. Garett Smith, prin. Fax 365-4222
Westside ES 800/4-6
800 W Main St 23430 757-357-3021
Dr. John Caggiano, prin. Fax 357-2602
Other Schools – See Carrollton, Carrsville, Windsor

South Boston, Halifax, Pop. 8,115
Halifax County SD
Supt. — See Halifax
Halifax MS 1,000/6-8
1011 Middle School Cir 24592 434-572-4100
Beverly Crowder, prin. Fax 572-4106
South Boston ES K-5
2320 Parker Ave 24592 434-517-2620
Pamela Eakes, prin. Fax 517-2630

South Hill, Mecklenburg, Pop. 4,607
Mecklenburg County SD
Supt. — See Boydton
Buckhorn ES 300/PK-5
500 Gordon Lake Rd 23970 434-447-3075
Joan Covington, prin. Fax 955-2814
Park View MS 600/6-8
365 Dockery Rd 23970 434-447-3761
Michelle Mateka, prin. Fax 447-4920
South Hill ES 600/PK-5
1290 Plank Rd 23970 434-447-8134
Connie Puckett, prin. Fax 447-6511

South Riding, See Fairfax
Loudoun County SD
Supt. — See Ashburn
Hutchison Farm ES 900/PK-5
42819 Center St 20152 703-957-4350
Irene Ellis, prin. Fax 444-8020
Liberty ES K-5
25491 Riding Center Dr 20152 703-957-4370
Angela Gwynne-Atwater, prin. Fax 327-5118
Little River ES 1,000/PK-5
43464 Hyland Hills St 20152 703-957-4360
Joyce Hardcastle, prin. Fax 444-8005

Speedwell, Wythe
Wythe County SD
Supt. — See Wytheville
Speedwell ES 100/K-5
PO Box B 24374 276-621-4622
Allan Rouse, prin. Fax 621-4687

Spotsylvania, Spotsylvania
Spotsylvania County SD
Supt. — See Fredericksburg
Berkeley ES 300/K-5
5979 Partlow Rd, 540-582-5141
Mike Brown, prin. Fax 582-8110
Brock Road ES 800/PK-5
10207 Brock Rd 22553 540-972-3870
Barbara Dickinson, prin. Fax 972-3170
Courthouse Road ES 800/K-5
9911 Courthouse Rd 22553 540-891-0400
George McCrum, prin. Fax 891-0405
Courtland ES 700/K-5
6601 Smith Station Rd 22553 540-898-5422
Sherri Steele, prin. Fax 891-4658
Lee ES 500/K-5
7415 Brock Rd 22553 540-582-5445
Robin Nemeth, prin. Fax 582-3462
Livingston ES 500/K-5
6057 Courthouse Rd, 540-895-5101
Terrie Cagle, prin. Fax 895-9338
Ni River MS 800/6-8
11632 Catharpin Rd 22553 540-785-3990
Veronne Davis, prin. Fax 785-0658
Post Oak MS 800/6-8
6959 Courthouse Rd, 540-582-7517
Keith Wolfe, prin. Fax 582-7510
Riverview ES 700/K-5
7001 N Roxbury Mill Rd, 540-582-7617
Dianne Holmes, prin. Fax 582-7622
Spotsylvania MS 800/6-8
8801 Courthouse Rd 22553 540-582-6341
Mark Beckett, prin. Fax 582-3207
Thornburg MS 700/6-8
6929 N Roxbury Mill Rd, 540-582-7600
Kirk Tower, prin. Fax 582-7606
Wilderness ES 800/K-5
11600 Catharpin Rd 22553 540-786-9817
Carol Flenard, prin. Fax 785-2652

Springfield, Fairfax, Pop. 23,706
Fairfax County SD
Supt. — See Falls Church
Cardinal Forest ES 600/K-6
8600 Forrester Blvd 22152 703-923-5200
Karen Kenna, prin. Fax 923-5297
Crestwood ES 500/K-6
6010 Hanover Ave 22150 703-923-5400
Mary Person, prin. Fax 923-5497
Forestdale ES 400/PK-6
6530 Elder Ave 22150 703-313-4300
Cheryl Toth, prin. Fax 313-4397
Garfield ES 300/K-6
7101 Old Keene Mill Rd 22150 703-923-2900
Maureen Marshall, prin. Fax 923-2997
Hunt Valley ES 600/K-6
7107 Sydenstricker Rd 22152 703-913-8800
Pat Small, prin. Fax 913-8897
Irving MS 1,100/7-8
8100 Old Keene Mill Rd 22152 703-912-4500
Danny Little, prin. Fax 912-4597
Keene Mill ES 600/PK-6
6310 Bardu Ave 22152 703-644-4700
Nicholas Rousos, prin. Fax 644-4797
Key MS 800/7-8
6402 Franconia Rd 22150 703-313-3900
Penny Myers, prin. Fax 313-3997
Kings Glen ES 500/4-6
5401 Danbury Forest Dr 22151 703-239-4000
Samuel Elson, prin. Fax 239-4097
Kings Park ES 700/K-3
5400 Harrow Way 22151 703-426-7000
Sarah Skerker, prin. Fax 426-7097
Lynbrook ES 400/K-6
5801 Backlick Rd 22150 703-866-2940
Mary McNamee, prin. Fax 866-2997
Newington Forest ES 600/K-6
8001 Newington Forest Ave 22153 703-923-2600
John Kren, prin. Fax 923-2697
North Springfield ES 500/PK-5
7602 Heming Ct 22151 703-658-5500
Alice Alexander, prin. Fax 658-5597
Orange Hunt ES 900/K-6
6820 Sydenstricker Rd 22152 703-913-6800
Judy Ryan, prin. Fax 913-6897
Ravensworth ES 600/PK-6
5411 Nutting Dr 22151 703-426-3600
Pam O'Connor, prin. Fax 426-3697
Rolling Valley ES 500/K-6
6703 Barnack Dr 22152 703-923-2700
Debbie Lane, prin. Fax 923-2797
Sangster ES 700/K-6
7420 Reservation Dr 22153 703-644-8200
Gail Kinsey, prin. Fax 644-8297
Saratoga ES 700/K-6
8111 Northumberland Rd 22153 703-440-2600
Patricia Conklin, prin. Fax 440-2697
Springfield Estates ES 600/K-6
6200 Charles Goff Dr 22150 703-921-2300
Mary Randolph, prin. Fax 921-2397
West Springfield ES 400/K-6
6802 Deland Dr 22152 703-912-4400
Kathryn Woodley, prin. Fax 912-4457

Immanuel Christian S 400/PK-8
6915 Braddock Rd 22151 703-941-1220
Stephen Danish, admin. Fax 813-1945
Prince of Peace Lutheran S 300/PK-K
8306 Old Keene Mill Rd 22152 703-451-6177
Cindy Deatherage, prin. Fax 569-0978
St. Bernadette S 400/K-8
7602 Old Keene Mill Rd 22152 703-451-8696
Patricia Beeks, prin. Fax 451-8221
Word of Life Christian Academy 300/PK-12
5225 Backlick Rd 22151 703-354-4222
David Dawdy, prin. Fax 750-1306

Stafford, Stafford
Stafford County SD 24,700/PK-12
31 Stafford Ave 22554 540-658-6000
David Sawyer, supt. Fax 658-5963
stafford.schoolfusion.us/
Barrett ES 700/K-5
150 Duffey Dr, 540-658-6464
Kim Austin, prin. Fax 658-6465
Brent ES 700/K-5
2125 Mountain View Rd, 540-658-6790
Dorothy Truslow, prin. Fax 658-6799
Burns ES K-5
60 Gallery Rd 22554 540-658-6800
Nancy Coll, prin. Fax 658-6807
Garrisonville ES 700/PK-5
100 Wood Dr, 540-658-6260
Pamela Kahle, prin. Fax 658-6255
Hampton Oaks ES 500/K-5
107 Northampton Blvd 22554 540-658-6280
Daria Groover, prin. Fax 658-6276
Heim MS 6-8
320 Telegraph Rd 22554 540-658-5910
Mary McGraw, prin. Fax 658-0329
Moncure ES 700/K-5
75 Moncure Ln, 540-658-6300
Gregory Machi, prin. Fax 658-6292
Park Ridge ES 700/PK-5
2000 Parkway Blvd 22554 540-658-6320
Christine Primo, prin. Fax 658-6314
Poole MS 1,100/6-8
800 Eustace Rd 22554 540-658-6190
Greg Daniel, prin. Fax 658-6176
Rockhill ES 600/K-5
50 Wood Dr, 540-658-6360
Marilyn Butters, prin. Fax 658-6355
Stafford ES 600/K-5
1349 Courthouse Rd 22554 540-658-6340
Mary Foreman, prin. Fax 658-6332
Stafford MS 1,100/6-8
101 Spartan Dr 22554 540-658-6210
Steven Butters, prin. Fax 658-6204
Thompson MS 1,200/6-8
75 Walpole St 22554 540-658-6420
Gwendolyn Payne, prin. Fax 658-6430
Widewater ES 700/PK-5
101 Den Rich Rd 22554 540-658-6380
Kristen McKinney-Nash, prin. Fax 658-6378
Winding Creek ES 700/PK-5
475 Winding Creek Rd 22554 540-658-6400
Elliot Bolles, prin. Fax 658-6401
Wright MS 800/6-8
100 Wood Dr, 540-658-6240
William Boatwright, prin. Fax 658-6238
Other Schools – See Falmouth, Fredericksburg, Hartwood

Fredericksburg Christian S 200/K-8
101 Shepherds Way, 540-659-1279
Susan Underwood, admin. Fax 659-4914
Grace Preparatory S 100/K-12
2202 Jefferson Davis Hwy 22554 540-657-4500
Cheryl Hinzman, admin.
St. William of York S 200/K-8
3130 Jefferson Davis Hwy 22554 540-659-5207
Sr. Lisa Lorenz, prin. Fax 659-5637

Stanardsville, Greene, Pop. 501
Greene County SD 2,800/PK-12
PO Box 1140 22973 434-985-5254
David Jeck, supt. Fax 985-4686
www.greenecountyschools.com
Greene County PS 400/PK-2
64 Monroe Dr 22973 434-985-5279
Jason Davis, prin. Fax 985-1321
Greene ES 400/3-5
8094 Spotswood Trl 22973 434-985-5275
Mary Wheeler, prin. Fax 985-5287
Monroe MS 600/6-8
148 Monroe Dr 22973 434-985-5240
Kyle Pursel, prin. Fax 985-1359
Other Schools – See Ruckersville

Stanley, Page, Pop. 1,331
Page County SD
Supt. — See Luray
Stanley ES 600/PK-7
306 Aylor Grubbs Ave 22851 540-778-2612
Catherine Marston, prin. Fax 778-1913

Stanley SDA S 50/K-8
118 Church Ave 22851 540-778-3377
Joy Lipscomb, lead tchr. Fax 740-3377

Stanleytown, Henry, Pop. 1,563
Henry County SD
Supt. — See Collinsville
Stanleytown ES 400/PK-5
74 Edgewood Dr 24168 276-629-5084
Laryssa Penn, prin. Fax 629-2925

Staunton, Staunton, Pop. 23,337
Augusta County SD
Supt. — See Fishersville
Beverley Manor ES 400/K-5
116 Cedar Green Rd 24401 540-885-8024
Dawn Young, prin. Fax 885-8040
Beverley Manor MS 800/6-8
58 Cedar Green Rd 24401 540-886-5806
Nancy Miller, prin. Fax 886-4019
Riverheads ES 500/K-5
17 Howardsville Rd 24401 540-337-2535
Forrest Burgdorf, prin. Fax 337-1454

Staunton CSD 2,700/K-12
PO Box 900 24402 540-332-3920
Dr. Steve Nichols, supt. Fax 332-3924
www.staunton.k12.va.us
Dixon ES 300/K-5
1751 Shutterlee Mill Rd 24401 540-332-3934
Sharon Barker, prin. Fax 332-3973
McSwain ES 300/K-5
1101 N Coalter St 24401 540-332-3936
Kim Crocker, prin. Fax 332-3955
Shelburne MS 600/6-8
300 Grubert Ave 24401 540-332-3930
Richard Fletcher, prin. Fax 332-3933
Ware ES 300/K-5
330 Grubert Ave 24401 540-332-3938
Linda Mahler, prin. Fax 332-3957
Weller ES 200/K-5
600 Greenville Ave 24401 540-332-3940
Chris Bryant, prin. Fax 332-3959

Grace Christian S 200/PK-6
511 Thornrose Ave 24401 540-886-0937
Joanne Kinder, prin. Fax 886-2761
Richards Jr Academy 100/K-10
414 Sterling St 24401 540-886-4984
Beccy Ivins, prin. Fax 886-7087
Stuart Hall S 300/K-12
PO Box 210 24402 540-885-0356
Mark Eastham, hdmstr. Fax 886-2275

Stephens City, Frederick, Pop. 1,247
Frederick County SD
Supt. — See Winchester
Aylor MS 600/6-8
901 Aylor Rd 22655 540-869-3736
Donald Williams, prin. Fax 867-2756
Bass-Hoover ES 600/K-5
471 Aylor Rd 22655 540-869-4700
Gay Yowell, prin. Fax 869-0668

Shenandoah Valley Christian Academy 300/PK-12
PO Box 1360 22655 540-869-4600
Robert Quinn, supt. Fax 869-4662

Sterling, Loudoun, Pop. 20,512
Loudoun County SD
Supt. — See Ashburn
Algonkian ES 500/PK-5
20196 Carter Ct 20165 703-444-7410
Heidi Latham, prin. Fax 444-1917
Countryside ES 500/K-5
20624 Countryside Blvd 20165 571-434-3250
Arlene Glaser, prin. Fax 444-8055
Forest Grove ES 600/PK-5
46245 Forest Ridge Dr 20164 571-434-4560
Nancy Torregrossa, prin. Fax 444-7598
Guilford ES 400/PK-5
600 W Poplar Rd 20164 571-434-4550
David Stewart, prin. Fax 444-7424
Horizon ES 700/PK-5
46665 Broadmore Dr 20165 571-434-3260
William Raye, prin. Fax 444-7418
Lowes Island ES 600/PK-5
20755 Whitewater Dr 20165 571-434-4450
Bruce Shafferman, prin. Fax 430-6355
Meadowland ES 500/PK-5
729 Sugarland Run Dr 20164 571-434-4440
Laura Seck, prin. Fax 444-7435
Potowmack ES 500/PK-5
46465 Esterbrook Cir 20165 571-434-3270
Jennifer Abel, prin. Fax 444-7526
River Bend MS 1,100/6-8
46240 Algonkian Pkwy 20165 571-434-3220
Bennett Lacy, prin. Fax 444-7578
Rolling Ridge ES 400/PK-5
500 E Frederick Dr 20164 571-434-4540
Andrew Davis, prin. Fax 444-7442
Seneca Ridge MS 900/6-8
98 Seneca Ridge Dr 20164 571-434-4420
Mark McDermott, prin. Fax 444-7567
Sterling ES 500/PK-5
200 W Church Rd 20164 571-434-4580
Teri Finn, prin. Fax 450-1583
Sterling MS 900/6-8
201 W Holly Ave 20164 571-434-4520
Nereida Gonzalez-Sales, prin. Fax 444-7492
Sugarland ES 400/PK-5
65 Sugarland Run Dr 20164 571-434-4460
Angela Robinson, prin. Fax 444-7463
Sully ES 400/PK-5
300 Circle Dr 20164 703-444-7470
Timothy Martino, prin. Fax 444-7473

Chesterbrook Academy 200/PK-8
46100 Woodshire Dr 20166 703-404-0202
Lydia Soto, prin.

Strasburg, Shenandoah, Pop. 4,269
Shenandoah County SD
Supt. — See Woodstock
Sandy Hook ES 900/K-5
162 Stickley Loop 22657 540-465-8281
Stacey Leitzel, prin. Fax 465-5443
Signal Knob MS 500/6-8
687 Sandy Hook Rd 22657 540-465-3422
Melissa Hensley, prin. Fax 465-5412

Stuart, Patrick, Pop. 925
Patrick County SD 2,600/K-12
PO Box 346 24171 276-694-3163
Dr. Roger Morris, supt. Fax 694-3170
www.patrick.k12.va.us
Stuart ES 400/K-7
314 Staples Ave 24171 276-694-7139
Cynthia Williams, prin. Fax 694-5807
Other Schools – See Ararat, Critz, Meadows of Dan, Patrick Springs, Woolwine

Stuarts Draft, Augusta, Pop. 5,087
Augusta County SD
Supt. — See Fishersville
Stuarts Draft ES 600/K-5
63 School Blvd 24477 540-337-2951
Diane Bates, prin. Fax 946-7620
Stuarts Draft MS 600/6-8
1088 Augusta Farms Rd 24477 540-946-7611
Scott Musick, prin. Fax 946-7613
Stump ES 400/K-5
115 Draft Ave 24477 540-337-1549
Jane Wright, prin. Fax 337-1761

Suffolk, Suffolk, Pop. 78,994
Suffolk CSD 13,200/PK-12
PO Box 1549 23439 757-925-6750
Dr. Milton Liverman, supt. Fax 925-6751
www.sps.k12.va.us
Benn ES 700/PK-5
1253 Nansemond Pkwy 23434 757-925-5645
Melodie Griffin, prin. Fax 925-5644
Bowser ES 200/PK-1
4540 Nansemond Pkwy 23435 757-538-5410
Cheryl Riddick, prin. Fax 538-5408
Creekside ES PK-5
1000 Bennetts Creek Park Rd 23435 757-923-4251
Katrina Rountree-Bowers, prin. Fax 686-2640
Driver ES 400/2-5
4270 Driver Ln 23435 757-538-5405
Chanel Bryant, prin. Fax 538-5407
Elephants Fork ES 600/K-5
2316 William Reid Dr 23434 757-925-5555
Veleka Gatling, prin. Fax 925-5596
Forest Glen MS 500/6-8
200 Forest Glen Dr 23434 757-925-5550
Melvin Bradshaw, prin. Fax 925-5557
Hillpoint ES, 1101 Hillpoint Rd 23434 K-5
Ronald Leigh, prin. 757-925-6750
Kennedy MS 700/6-8
2325 E Washington St 23434 757-925-5560
Vivian Covington, prin. Fax 925-5594
Kilby Shores ES 700/PK-5
111 Kilby Shores Dr 23434 757-925-5575
Seazante Oliver, prin. Fax 925-5569
King's Fork MS 1,100/6-8
350 Kings Fork Rd 23434 757-925-5750
Talmadge Darden, prin. Fax 925-5754
Mt. Zion ES 400/PK-5
3264 Pruden Blvd 23434 757-925-5585
Frances Barnes, prin. Fax 925-5582
Nansemond Parkway ES 500/K-5
3012 Nansemond Pkwy 23434 757-538-5425
Keith Hubbard, prin. Fax 538-5415
Northern Shores ES 700/PK-5
6701 Respass Beach Rd 23435 757-925-5566
Elizabeth Bennett, prin. Fax 925-5602
Oakland ES 500/K-5
5505 Godwin Blvd 23434 757-925-5505
Christopher Phillips, prin. Fax 925-5622
Robertson ES 200/K-5
132 Robertson St 23438 757-925-5515
Rhonda Jones, prin. Fax 925-5591
Southwestern ES 400/K-5
9301 Southwestern Blvd 23437 757-925-5595
Nancy Harrell, prin. Fax 925-5592
Washington ES 500/PK-5
204 Walnut St 23434 757-925-5535
Patricia Montgomery, prin. Fax 925-5558
Yeates MS 1,000/6-8
4901 Bennetts Pasture Rd 23435 757-538-5400
Daniel O'Leary, prin. Fax 538-5416

First Baptist Christian S 300/K-12
237 N Main St 23434 757-925-0274
Kacee Griffin, hdmstr. Fax 539-2575
Nansemond-Suffolk Academy 900/PK-12
3373 Pruden Blvd 23434 757-539-8789
Colley Bell, hdmstr. Fax 934-8363

Sugar Grove, Smyth
Smyth County SD
Supt. — See Marion
Sugar Grove S 200/PK-8
242 Teas Rd 24375 276-677-3311
Gary Roberts, prin. Fax 677-3846

Surry, Surry, Pop. 254
Surry County SD 1,100/PK-12
PO Box 317 23883 757-294-5229
Lloyd Hamlin, supt. Fax 294-5263
www.surryschools.net/
Other Schools – See Dendron

Sussex, Sussex
Sussex County SD 1,400/K-12
PO Box 1368 23884 434-246-1099
Charles Harris, supt. Fax 246-8214
www.sussex.k12.va.us/
Sussex Central MS 300/6-8
PO Box 1387 23884 434-246-2251
Adriene Stephenson, prin. Fax 246-8912
Other Schools – See Jarratt, Wakefield, Waverly

Sutherland, Dinwiddie
Dinwiddie County SD
Supt. — See Dinwiddie
Sutherland ES K-5
6000 R B Pamplin Dr 23885 804-732-4168
Becky Baskerville, prin. Fax 732-4620

Swords Creek, Russell
Russell County SD
Supt. — See Lebanon

Givens ES 100/K-2
8153 Swords Creek Rd 24649 276-991-0001
Allison Steele, prin. Fax 991-1236
Swords Creek ES 100/3-7
3867 Swords Creek Rd 24649 276-991-0016
Allison Steele, prin. Fax 991-0102

Tangier, Accomack, Pop. 694
Accomack County SD
Supt. — See Accomac
Tangier S 100/K-12
PO Box 245 23440 757-891-2234
Nina Pruitt, prin. Fax 891-2572

Tappahannock, Essex, Pop. 2,155
Essex County SD 1,700/PK-12
PO Box 756 22560 804-443-4366
Thomas Saville, supt. Fax 443-4498
www.essex.k12.va.us
Essex MS 500/5-8
PO Box 609 22560 804-443-3040
Wendy Ellis, prin. Fax 445-1079
Tappahannock ES 600/PK-4
PO Box 399 22560 804-443-5301
Michael Daddario, prin. Fax 443-1176

Tappahannock Junior Academy 100/PK-10
PO Box 790 22560 804-443-5076
Kim Peterson, prin. Fax 443-5076

Tazewell, Tazewell, Pop. 4,404
Tazewell County SD 6,800/PK-12
PO Box 927 24651 276-988-5511
Dr. Brenda Lawson, supt. Fax 988-6765
tazewell.k12.va.us
Tazewell ES 600/PK-5
101 Parkview Dr 24651 276-988-4441
Suzanne Grindstaff, prin. Fax 988-0445
Tazewell MS 500/6-8
100 Bull Dog Ave 24651 276-988-6513
Kristina Welch, prin. Fax 988-6514
Other Schools – See Bluefield, Cedar Bluff, North Tazewell, Raven, Richlands

Thaxton, Bedford
Bedford County SD
Supt. — See Bedford
Thaxton ES 200/K-6
1081 Monorail Cir 24174 540-586-3821
Judy Reynolds, prin. Fax 586-0300

The Plains, Fauquier, Pop. 287
Fauquier County SD
Supt. — See Warrenton
Coleman ES 400/K-5
4096 Zulla Rd 20198 540-364-1515
Joy Seward, prin. Fax 364-4249
Marshall MS 500/6-8
4048 Zulla Rd 20198 540-364-1551
Christine Moschetti, prin. Fax 364-4699

Wakefield S 500/PK-12
PO Box 107 20198 540-253-7500
Peter Quinn, hdmstr. Fax 253-5422

Timberville, Rockingham, Pop. 1,703
Rockingham County SD
Supt. — See Harrisonburg
Plains ES 600/PK-5
225 American Legion Dr 22853 540-896-8956
J.W. Kile, prin. Fax 896-8908

Toano, James City
Williamsburg-James City County SD
Supt. — See Williamsburg
Toano MS 900/6-8
7817 Richmond Rd 23168 757-566-4251
Theresa Redd, prin. Fax 566-3006

Triangle, Prince William, Pop. 4,740
Prince William County SD
Supt. — See Manassas
Graham Park MS 800/6-8
3613 Graham Park Rd 22172 703-221-2118
Gary Anderson, prin. Fax 221-1079
Triangle ES 500/K-5
3615 Lions Field Rd 22172 703-221-4114
Mark Marinoble Ed.D., prin. Fax 221-3956

Calvary Christian S 200/PK-12
4345 Inn St 22172 703-221-2016
John Wallace, admin. Fax 221-7698
St. Francis of Assisi S 300/PK-8
18825 Fuller Heights Rd 22172 703-221-3868
Dr. Tricia Barber, prin. Fax 221-0700
Star of Bethlehem Christian Academy 100/PK-6
PO Box 409 22172 703-221-4111
Shirley Williams, dir. Fax 221-2823

Troutville, Botetourt, Pop. 432
Botetourt County SD
Supt. — See Fincastle
Greenfield ES 400/PK-5
288 Etzler Rd 24175 540-992-4416
Beth Umbarger, prin. Fax 992-3174
Troutville ES 300/K-5
12 Barron Dr 24175 540-992-1871
Karen Crush, prin. Fax 992-8382

Unionville, Orange
Orange County SD
Supt. — See Orange
Lightfoot ES 300/3-5
11360 Zachary Taylor Hwy 22567 540-661-4520
Judy Anderson, prin. Fax 661-4519
Unionville ES 300/PK-2
10285 Zachary Taylor Hwy 22567 540-661-4540
Jennifer Curtis, prin. Fax 661-4539

Vansant, Buchanan, Pop. 1,187
Buchanan County SD
Supt. — See Grundy
Prater ES 100/PK-5
8433 Lovers Gap Rd 24656 276-597-7552
David Bevins, prin. Fax 597-2473

Verona, Augusta, Pop. 3,479
Augusta County SD
Supt. — See Fishersville
Verona ES 400/K-5
1011 Lee Hwy 24482 540-248-0141
Marguerite McDonald, prin. Fax 248-0562

Victoria, Lunenburg, Pop. 1,789
Lunenburg County SD
Supt. — See Kenbridge
Lunenburg MS 400/6-8
583 Tomlinson Rd 23974 434-696-2161
Lisa Krause, prin. Fax 696-2162
Victoria ES 400/K-5
1521 8th St 23974 434-696-2163
James Abernathy, prin. Fax 696-2096

Vienna, Fairfax, Pop. 14,842
Fairfax County SD
Supt. — See Falls Church
Archer ES 700/K-6
324 Nutley St NW 22180 703-937-6200
Michelle Makrigiorgos, prin. Fax 937-6297
Colvin Run ES 800/K-6
1400 Trap Rd 22182 703-757-3000
Stephen Hockett, prin. Fax 757-3097
Cunningham Park ES 400/K-6
1001 Park St SE 22180 703-255-5600
Rebecca Baenig, prin. Fax 255-5697
Flint Hill ES 700/K-6
2444 Flint Hill Rd 22181 703-242-6100
Salvador Rivera, prin. Fax 242-6197
Freedom Hill ES 500/PK-6
1945 Lord Fairfax Rd 22182 703-506-7800
Timothy Stanley, prin. Fax 506-7897
Kilmer MS 1,100/7-8
8100 Wolftrap Rd 22182 703-846-8800
Deborah Hernandez, prin. Fax 846-8897
Marshall Road ES 600/K-6
730 Marshall Rd SW 22180 703-937-1500
Jennifer Heiges, prin. Fax 937-1597
Stenwood ES 400/K-6
2620 Gallows Rd 22180 703-208-7600
Laraine Edwards, prin. Fax 208-7697
Thoreau MS 800/7-8
2505 Cedar Ln 22180 703-846-8000
Mark Greenfelder, prin. Fax 846-8097
Vienna ES 400/PK-6
128 Center St S 22180 703-937-6000
Jeanette Black, prin. Fax 937-6000
Westbriar ES 400/K-6
1741 Pine Valley Dr 22182 703-937-1700
Jeannette Martino, prin. Fax 937-1700
Wolftrap ES 600/K-6
1903 Beulah Rd 22182 703-319-7300
Anita Blain, prin. Fax 319-7397

Fairfax Christian S 200/PK-12
1624 Hunter Mill Rd 22182 703-759-5100
Jo Thoburn, admin. Fax 759-2143
Green Hedges S 200/PK-8
415 Windover Ave NW 22180 703-938-8323
Fred Williams, hdmstr. Fax 938-1485
Our Lady of Good Counsel S 500/K-8
8601 Wolftrap Rd 22182 703-938-3600
Austin Poole, prin. Fax 255-1543
St. Mark S 400/PK-8
9972 Vale Rd 22181 703-281-9103
Roberta Etzel, prin. Fax 281-0675
Vienna Adventist Academy 100/PK-8
340 Courthouse Rd SW 22180 703-938-6200
C. Nicole Agbonkhese M.Ed., prin. Fax 938-3934

Vinton, Roanoke, Pop. 7,734
Roanoke County SD
Supt. — See Roanoke
Byrd MS 900/6-8
2910 E Washington Ave 24179 540-890-1035
Janet Womack, prin. Fax 890-0703
Cundiff ES 500/K-5
1200 Hardy Rd 24179 540-857-5009
Sherry Bryant, prin. Fax 857-5065
Horn ES 400/K-5
1002 Ruddell Rd 24179 540-857-5007
Susan Brown, prin. Fax 857-5062

Mineral Springs Christian S 100/PK-8
1030 Bible Ln 24179 540-890-4465
Rev. Bobby Harris, prin. Fax 890-3185

Virginia Beach, Virginia Beach, Pop. 438,415
Virginia Beach CSD 72,500/PK-12
PO Box 6038 23456 757-263-1000
Dr. James Merrill, supt. Fax 263-1397
www.vbschools.com/
Alanton ES 600/PK-5
1441 Stephens Rd 23454 757-648-2000
Jeanne Crocker, prin. Fax 496-6841
Arrowhead ES 600/K-5
5549 Susquehanna Dr 23462 757-648-2040
Constance James, prin. Fax 473-5101
Bayside ES 500/K-5
5649 Bayside Rd 23455 757-648-2080
Lori Hasher, prin. Fax 460-7513
Bayside MS 1,100/6-8
965 Newtown Rd 23462 757-648-4400
Dr. Barbara Cooper, prin. Fax 473-5185
Birdneck ES 1,100/PK-5
957 S Birdneck Rd 23451 757-648-2120
Irvin Beard, prin. Fax 473-4792
Brandon MS 1,300/6-8
1700 Pope St 23464 757-648-4450
Dr. Catherine Rogers, prin. Fax 366-4550
Brookwood ES 500/PK-5
601 S Lynnhaven Rd 23452 757-648-2160
Benjamin Gillikin, prin. Fax 431-4631
Centerville ES 700/PK-5
2201 Centerville Tpke 23464 757-648-2200
Dorianne Sharp, prin. Fax 502-0324
Christopher Farms ES 700/K-5
2828 Pleasant Acres Dr, 757-648-2240
Amy Cashwell, prin. Fax 427-3656
College Park ES 500/K-5
1110 Bennington Rd 23464 757-648-2280
Liz Warren, prin. Fax 366-4532
Cooke ES 500/PK-5
1501 Mediterranean Ave 23451 757-648-2320
Barbara Sessoms, prin. Fax 437-4711
Corporate Landing ES 600/PK-5
1590 Corporate Landing Pkwy 23454 757-648-2360
David French, prin. Fax 437-4760
Corporate Landing MS 1,500/6-8
1597 Corporate Landing Pkwy 23454 757-648-4500
Lauralee Grim, prin. Fax 437-6487
Creeds ES 300/K-5
920 Princess Anne Rd 23457 757-426-7792
Robin Davenport, prin. Fax 426-7837
Dey ES 700/K-5
1900 N Great Neck Rd 23454 757-648-2440
Lee Capwell, prin. Fax 496-6784
Diamond Springs ES K-1
5225 Learning Cir 23462 757-648-4240
Shirann Lewis, prin. Fax 493-5458
Fairfield ES 500/K-5
5428 Providence Rd 23464 757-648-2480
Dr. Sophia Stubblefield, prin. Fax 366-4530
Glenwood ES 1,000/PK-5
2213 Round Hill Dr 23464 757-648-2520
Susan Stuhlman, prin. Fax 471-5817
Great Neck MS 1,000/6-8
1848 N Great Neck Rd 23454 757-648-4550
Dr. John Smith, prin. Fax 496-6774
Green Run ES 500/PK-5
1200 Green Garden Cir, 757-648-2560
Ron Sykes, prin. Fax 427-6558
Hermitage ES 500/PK-5
1701 Pleasure House Rd 23455 757-648-2600
Holly Coggin, prin. Fax 460-7138
Holland ES 600/PK-5
3340 Holland Rd 23452 757-648-2640
Lionel Jackson, prin. Fax 427-0028
Independence MS 1,400/6-8
1370 Dunstan Ln 23455 757-648-4600
Cheryl Woodhouse, prin. Fax 460-0508
Indian Lakes ES 600/PK-5
1240 Homestead Dr 23464 757-648-2680
Kathleen Starr, prin. Fax 474-8454
Kemps Landing Magnet MS 600/6-8
4722 Jericho Rd 23462 757-648-4650
Charles Foster, prin. Fax 473-5106
Kempsville ES 500/PK-5
570 Kempsville Rd 23464 757-648-2720
Dr. Nancy Chandler, prin. Fax 474-8513
Kempsville Meadows ES 500/K-5
736 Edwin Dr 23462 757-474-8435
Douglas Daughtry, prin. Fax 474-8489
Kempsville MS 1,000/6-8
860 Churchill Dr 23464 757-648-4700
Dr. James Smith, prin. Fax 474-8449
Kings Grant ES 600/K-5
612 N Lynnhaven Rd 23452 757-648-2800
Sheila Wynn, prin. Fax 431-4092
Kingston ES 600/K-5
3532 Kings Grant Rd 23452 757-648-2840
Gregory Furlich, prin. Fax 431-4017
Landstown ES 800/PK-5
2212 Recreation Dr 23456 757-648-2880
Gregory Anderson, prin. Fax 430-2775
Landstown MS 1,600/6-8
2204 Recreation Dr 23456 757-648-4750
Peggy Peebles, prin. Fax 430-3247
Larkspur MS 1,700/6-8
4696 Princess Anne Rd 23462 757-648-4800
Dr. Dianne Cunningham, prin. Fax 474-8598
Linkhorn Park ES 700/K-5
977 First Colonial Rd 23454 757-648-2920
Linda Sidone, prin. Fax 496-6750
Luxford ES 500/PK-5
4808 Haygood Rd 23455 757-473-5014
Joanne D'Agostino, prin. Fax 473-5103
Lynnhaven ES 400/PK-5
210 Dillon Dr 23452 757-648-3000
Katherine Everett, prin. Fax 431-4634
Lynnhaven MS 1,200/6-8
1250 Bayne Dr 23454 757-648-4850
Dr. Randi Riesbeck, prin. Fax 496-6793
Malibu ES 300/PK-5
3632 Edinburgh Dr 23452 757-431-4098
Pam Bennis, prin. Fax 431-4099
New Castle ES 700/PK-5
4136 Dam Neck Rd 23456 757-648-3080
Lesley Hughes, prin. Fax 430-8977
Newtown ES 600/PK-5
5277 Learning Cir 23462 757-648-3120
Laverne Chatman, prin. Fax 493-5461
North Landing ES 600/PK-5
2929 N Landing Rd 23456 757-648-3160
Julie Risney, prin. Fax 427-6086
Ocean Lakes ES 600/PK-5
1616 Upton Dr 23454 757-648-3200
Charles Grindle, prin. Fax 721-4009
Parkway ES 500/K-5
4180 Ohare Dr, 757-648-3280
Nanocie Diggs, prin. Fax 471-5818
Pembroke ES 500/PK-5
4622 Jericho Rd 23462 757-473-5025
Dr. Linda Hayes, prin. Fax 473-5624
Pembroke Meadows ES 500/K-5
820 Cathedral Dr 23455 757-648-3360
Dr. Charles Spivey, prin. Fax 473-5261
Plaza ES 400/K-5
641 Carriage Hill Rd 23452 757-648-3400
Dr. Mary Daniels, prin. Fax 431-4639

Plaza MS 1,200/6-8
3080 S Lynnhaven Rd 23452 757-648-4900
Violet Hoyle, prin. Fax 431-5331

Point O'View ES 500/K-5
5400 Parliament Dr 23462 757-648-3440
Edward Timlin, prin. Fax 473-5262

Princess Anne ES 500/PK-5
2444 Seaboard Rd 23456 757-648-3480
Krista Barton-Arnold, prin. Fax 427-1447

Princess Anne MS 1,500/6-8
2509 Seaboard Rd 23456 757-648-4950
James Pohl, prin. Fax 430-0972

Providence ES 600/K-5
4968 Providence Rd 23464 757-648-3520
Jennifer Carstens, prin. Fax 474-8522

Red Mill ES 700/PK-5
1860 Sandbridge Rd 23456 757-648-3560
Dr. Steven Scarcelli, prin. Fax 426-9600

Rosemont ES 300/K-5
1257 Rosemont Rd, 757-648-3600
Dr. Miriam Freeman, prin. Fax 427-6411

Rosemont Forest ES 500/K-5
1716 Grey Friars Chase 23456 757-648-3640
David Portis, prin. Fax 471-5816

Salem ES 500/K-5
3961 Salem Lakes Blvd 23456 757-648-3680
Janet Zitt, prin. Fax 471-5813

Salem MS 1,200/6-8
2380 Lynnhaven Pkwy 23464 757-648-5000
Dr. Eugene Soltner, prin. Fax 474-8467

Seatack ES 300/K-5
912 S Birdneck Rd 23451 757-648-3720
Larry Ames, prin. Fax 437-7747

Shelton Park ES 400/PK-5
1700 Shelton Rd 23455 757-460-7577
Lou Anne Metzger, prin. Fax 460-7515

Strawbridge ES 800/PK-5
2553 Strawbridge Rd 23456 757-427-5562
Kelly Coon, prin. Fax 427-5031

Tallwood ES 600/PK-5
2025 Kempsville Rd 23464 757-648-3840
Thomas Chowns, prin. Fax 502-0308

Thalia ES 700/PK-5
421 Thalia Rd 23452 757-648-3880
Geoffrey Timlin, prin. Fax 431-4641

Thoroughgood ES 600/PK-5
1444 Dunstan Ln 23455 757-648-3920
Dr. Cheryl Zigrang, prin. Fax 460-7516

Three Oaks ES 600/PK-5
2201 Elson Green Ave 23456 757-648-3960
Lisa Hannah, prin. Fax 430-3758

Trantwood ES 600/K-5
2344 Inlynnview Rd 23454 757-648-4000
Dr. Patricia Slaughter, prin. Fax 496-6785

Virginia Beach MS 700/6-8
600 25th St 23451 757-648-5050
Rita Simpson, prin. Fax 437-4708

White Oaks ES 700/PK-5
960 Windsor Oaks Blvd 23462 757-648-4040
Gloria Costen, prin. Fax 474-8515

Williams ES 700/PK-5
892 Newtown Rd 23462 757-648-4080
George MacKay, prin. Fax 473-5263

Windsor Oaks ES 500/PK-5
3800 Van Buren Dr 23452 757-648-4120
Michael Maloney, prin. Fax 431-4637

Windsor Woods ES 400/K-5
233 Presidential Blvd 23452 757-648-4160
C. Drummond Ball, prin. Fax 431-4638

Woodstock ES 600/K-5
6016 Providence Rd 23464 757-366-4590
Tonilee Oliverio, prin. Fax 366-4578

Atlantic Shores Christian S 400/PK-6
1861 Kempsville Rd 23464 757-479-1125
Gaye Webb, prin. Fax 479-8742

Cape Henry Collegiate S 1,000/PK-12
1320 Mill Dam Rd 23454 757-481-2446
Dr. John Lewis, hdmstr. Fax 481-9194

Chesapeake Bay Academy 200/K-12
821 Baker Rd 23462 757-497-6200
Mary Ann Dukas, prin. Fax 497-6304

Coastal Christian Academy 50/1-12
640 Kempsville Rd 23464 757-217-2151
Dr. Anne Giminez, prin. Fax 467-5298

Hebrew Academy of Tidewater 100/PK-6
5000 Corporate Woods Dr 23462 757-424-4327
Dr. Zena Herod, prin. Fax 420-0915

Hope Lutheran S 50/PK-K
5350 Providence Rd 23464 757-424-4894
Fax 424-7626

Kempsville Presbyterian Church Day S 100/PK-K
805 Kempsville Rd 23464 757-495-4611
Phyllis Nix, dir. Fax 248-5704

Kings Grant Day S 100/PK-3
873 Little Neck Rd 23452 757-431-9744
Sharon Clark, admin. Fax 431-9472

New Light Baptist S of Excellence 100/PK-5
5549 Indian River Rd 23464 757-420-0945
Kathy Booker, dir. Fax 420-0413

Norfolk Christian S - Beach Campus 300/PK-5
1265 Laskin Rd 23451 757-428-1284
Wanda Scott, prin. Fax 428-4002

Old Donation Episcopal Day S 100/PK-K
4449 N Witchduck Rd 23455 757-499-2283
Janet Brown, dir. Fax 497-9291

Parish Day S 200/PK-2
2020 Laskin Rd 23454 757-491-6130
Jean Edwards, dir. Fax 437-8461

St. Gregory the Great S 700/PK-8
5343 Virginia Beach Blvd 23462 757-497-1811
Mary Chapman, prin. Fax 497-7005

St. John the Apostle S 200/PK-8
1968 Sandbridge Rd 23456 757-821-1100
Joseph Badali, prin. Fax 821-1047

St. Matthew S 600/PK-8
3316 Sandra Ln 23464 757-420-2455
Barbara White, prin. Fax 420-4880

Star of the Sea S 400/PK-8
309 15th St 23451 757-428-8400
Cathy Whisman, prin. Fax 428-2794

Virginia Beach Friends S 200/PK-12
1537 Laskin Rd 23451 757-428-7534
Jonathan Alden, hdmstr. Fax 428-7511

Wakefield, Sussex, Pop. 971

Sussex County SD
Supt. — See Sussex

Chambliss ES 200/K-3
PO Box 580 23888 757-899-5391
Diane Brown, prin. Fax 899-5002

Tidewater Academy 200/PK-12
PO Box 1000 23888 757-899-5401
Rodney Taylor, hdmstr. Fax 899-2521

Warm Springs, Bath

Bath County SD 800/K-12
PO Box 67 24484 540-839-2722
Dr. K. David Smith, supt. Fax 839-3040
www.bath.k12.va.us

Other Schools – See Hot Springs, Millboro

Warrenton, Fauquier, Pop. 8,635

Fauquier County SD 11,100/PK-12
320 Hospital Dr Ste 40 20186 540-351-1000
Jonathan Lewis, supt. Fax 347-1026
www.fcps1.org

Auburn MS 500/6-8
7270 Riley Rd 20187 540-428-3750
Jim Angelo, prin. Fax 428-3760

Bradley ES 500/PK-5
674 Hastings Ln 20186 540-347-6130
Debra Bell, prin. Fax 341-4253

Brumfield ES 600/PK-5
550 Alwington Blvd 20186 540-347-6180
Linda Clark, prin. Fax 341-7816

Smith ES 600/K-5
6176 Dumfries Rd 20187 540-347-6150
Patty Comstock, prin. Fax 347-7818

Taylor MS 400/6-8
350 E Shirley Ave 20186 540-347-6140
Ruth Nelson, prin. Fax 347-6145

Warrenton MS 400/6-8
244 Waterloo St 20186 540-347-6160
Barbara Bannister, prin. Fax 347-6169

Other Schools – See Bealeton, Catlett, Marshall, New Baltimore, Nokesville, Remington, The Plains

---

Cornerstone Christian Academy 100/PK-12
PO Box 861472 20187 540-349-4989
Karen Morris, prin. Fax 349-3177

Highland S 600/PK-12
597 Broadview Ave 20186 540-878-2700
Hank Berg, prin. Fax 878-2731

St. John the Evangelist S 200/PK-8
111 King St 20186 540-347-2458
Ed Hoffman, prin. Fax 349-8007

Warsaw, Richmond, Pop. 1,366

Richmond County SD 1,200/K-12
PO Box 1507 22572 804-333-3681
Dr. Marilyn Barr, supt. Fax 333-5586
www.richmond-county.k12.va.us

Richmond County ES 500/K-5
PO Box 213 22572 804-333-3510
Davis Roberts, prin. Fax 333-3930

Richmond County IS 300/6-8
PO Box 519 22572 804-333-3560
Dr. Daniel Bowling, prin. Fax 333-5387

Washington, Rappahannock, Pop. 182

Rappahannock County SD 1,000/K-12
6 School House Rd 22747 540-987-8773
Robert Chappell, supt. Fax 987-8896
www.rappahannock.k12.va.us

Rappahannock ES 600/K-7
34 School House Rd 22747 540-987-8259
Carol Johnson, prin. Fax 987-1130

Waterford, Loudoun

Loudoun County SD
Supt. — See Ashburn

Waterford ES 200/PK-5
15513 Loyalty Rd 20197 703-771-6660
Dr. Patricia Lynn, prin. Fax 771-6662

Waverly, Sussex, Pop. 2,176

Sussex County SD
Supt. — See Sussex

Jackson ES 100/4-5
PO Box 258 23890 804-834-2281
Diane Brown, prin. Fax 834-8297

Waynesboro, Waynesboro, Pop. 21,269

Augusta County SD
Supt. — See Fishersville

Cassell ES 500/K-5
1301 Rockfish Rd 22980 540-946-7635
Dr. Mindy Garber, prin. Fax 946-7637

Ladd ES 300/K-5
1930 Rosser Ave 22980 540-946-7630
Dr. Kathleen Overstreet, prin. Fax 946-7631

Waynesboro CSD 3,100/PK-12
301 Pine Ave 22980 540-946-4600
Dr. Robin Crowder, supt. Fax 946-4608
www.waynesboro.k12.va.us

Berkeley Glenn ES 300/PK-5
1020 Jefferson Ave 22980 540-946-4680
Sharon Tooley, prin. Fax 946-4684

Collins MS 700/6-8
1625 Ivy St 22980 540-946-4635
Carol Butler, prin. Fax 946-4642

Perry ES 500/PK-5
840 King Ave 22980 540-946-4650
Jeremy Weaver, prin. Fax 946-4656

Wenonah ES 200/PK-5
125 N Bayard Ave 22980 540-946-4660
Rebecca Jarvis, prin. Fax 946-4663

Westwood Hills ES 500/PK-5
548 Rosser Ave 22980 540-946-4670
Renee Deffenbaugh, prin. Fax 946-4673

Weber City, Scott, Pop. 1,283

Scott County SD
Supt. — See Gate City

Weber City ES 400/K-6
322 Jennings St 24290 276-386-7981
Kellie Johnson, prin. Fax 386-9289

West Point, King William, Pop. 3,013

West Point SD 800/K-12
PO Box T 23181 804-843-4368
Dr. Jeffrey Smith, supt. Fax 843-4421
www.wpps.k12.va.us

West Point ES 400/K-5
1060 Thompson Ave 23181 804-843-2030
Trena Hatcher, prin. Fax 843-3557

West Point MS 200/6-8
1040 Thompson Ave 23181 804-843-9810
Jeffrey Jackson, prin. Fax 843-9812

Whitetop, Grayson

Grayson County SD
Supt. — See Independence

Mt. Rogers S 100/PK-12
11337 Highlands Pkwy 24292 276-388-3489
Karen Blevins, prin. Fax 388-3103

Williamsburg, Williamsburg, Pop. 11,751

Williamsburg-James City County SD 10,100/K-12
101 Mounts Bay Rd Bldg D 23185 757-253-6777
Gary Mathews, supt. Fax 229-3027
www.wjcc.k12.va.us/

Baker ES 800/K-5
3131 Ironbound Rd 23185 757-221-0949
Bruce Brelsford, prin. Fax 229-1591

Berkeley MS 900/6-8
1118 Ironbound Rd 23188 757-229-8051
David Gaston, prin. Fax 229-6133

Blair MS 700/6-8
117 Ironbound Rd 23185 757-229-1341
Byron Bishop, prin. Fax 229-7057

Byrd ES 500/K-5
112 Laurel Ln 23185 757-229-7597
Wes Eary, prin. Fax 229-0237

James River ES 500/K-5
8901 Pocahontas Trl 23185 757-887-1768
Lynn Turner, prin. Fax 887-2162

Matoaka ES K-5
4001 Brick Bat Rd 23188 757-564-4001
Andy Jacobs, prin. Fax 564-4000

Montague ES 800/K-5
5380 Centerville Rd 23188 757-258-3022
Sammy Fudge, prin. Fax 258-5605

Norge ES 600/K-5
7311 Richmond Rd 23188 757-564-3372
Nancy Catano, prin. Fax 220-1763

Stonehouse ES 700/K-5
3651 Rochambeau Dr 23188 757-566-4300
Elizabeth Beckhouse, prin. Fax 566-2323

Whaley ES 600/K-5
301 Scotland St 23185 757-229-1931
Kathleen Noonan, prin. Fax 221-0286

Other Schools – See Toano

York County SD
Supt. — See Yorktown

Magruder ES 600/K-5
700 Penniman Rd 23185 757-220-4067
Mary Ahearn, prin. Fax 220-4081

Queens Lake MS 500/6-8
124 W Queens Dr 23185 757-220-4080
Kendra Crump Ed.D., prin. Fax 220-4074

Waller Mill Fine Arts Magnet S 300/K-5
314 Waller Mill Rd 23185 757-220-4060
Jennifer Goodwin, prin. Fax 220-4063

Greenwood Christian Academy 200/PK-4
5100 John Tyler Hwy 23185 757-345-0905
Elaine Milsark, prin. Fax 564-7739

Providence Classical S 100/K-8
116 Palace Ln 23185 757-565-2900
Susan Oweis, hdmstr. Fax 565-3720

Walsingham Academy Lower S 500/PK-7
PO Box 8702 23187 757-229-2642
Peter Bender, prin. Fax 259-1404

Williamsburg Christian Academy 300/PK-12
101 School House Ln 23188 757-220-1978
Gwendolyn Martin, hdmstr. Fax 741-4009

Williamsburg Montessori S 100/PK-6
4214 Longhill Rd 23188 757-565-0977
Sandy Andrews, prin. Fax 220-6655

Willis, Floyd

Floyd County SD
Supt. — See Floyd

Willis ES 200/K-7
PO Box 10 24380 540-745-9430
Sandra Montgomery, prin. Fax 745-9493

Winchester, Winchester, Pop. 25,119

Frederick County SD 11,900/K-12
1415 Amherst St 22601 540-662-3888
Patricia Taylor, supt. Fax 722-2788
www.frederick.k12.va.us

Apple Pie Ridge ES 500/K-5
349 Apple Pie Ridge Rd 22603 540-662-4781
Joseph Strong, prin. Fax 722-3918

Armel ES 500/K-5
2239 Front Royal Pike 22602 540-869-1657
Carolyn Maccubbin, prin. Fax 869-5342

Byrd MS 800/6-8
134 Rosa Ln 22602 540-662-0500
Mark Whittle, prin. Fax 662-7790

Evendale ES K-5
220 Rosa Ln 22602 540-662-0531
Sue Ellen Gossard, prin. Fax 662-6530
Frederick County MS 800/6-8
441 Linden Dr 22601 540-667-4233
Sharon Riggleman, prin. Fax 667-2392
Gainesboro ES 200/K-5
4651 N Frederick Pike 22603 540-888-4550
Christopher Cebrzynski, prin. Fax 888-4579
Indian Hollow ES 600/K-5
1548 N Hayfield Rd 22603 540-877-2283
Deanna Lock, prin. Fax 877-2353
Orchard View ES 500/K-5
4275 Middle Rd 22602 540-869-8642
Susan Bott, prin. Fax 868-2035
Redbud Run ES 600/K-5
250 First Woods Dr 22603 540-678-1868
Sherry Hall, prin. Fax 678-0703
Senseny Road ES 400/K-5
1481 Senseny Rd 22602 540-667-7863
Kristin Waldrop, prin. Fax 678-4852
Wood MS 800/6-8
1313 Amherst St 22601 540-667-7500
Teresa Miller, prin. Fax 667-7500
Other Schools – See Clear Brook, Middletown, Stephens City

Winchester CSD 3,800/K-12
PO Box 551 22604 540-667-4253
Ricky Leonard, supt. Fax 722-3583
www.wps.k12.va.us
Douglass ES 400/K-4
100 Cedarmeade Ave 22601 540-662-7656
Nancy Lee, prin. Fax 665-1081
Kerr ES 300/K-4
536 Jefferson St 22601 540-662-3945
Anita Jenkins, prin. Fax 662-4728
Morgan MS 1,100/5-8
48 S Purcell Ave 22601 540-667-7171
Sarah Kish, prin. Fax 723-8897
Quarles ES 400/K-4
1310 S Loudoun St 22601 540-662-3575
Jackie Ruff, prin. Fax 662-8449
Virginia Avenue / DeHart ES 400/K-4
559 Virginia Ave 22601 540-665-6330
Kathy Wetsel, prin. Fax 665-6334

Crossroads Christian Academy 100/K-12
PO Box 4339 22604 540-722-8660
Greg Roberts, prin. Fax 722-8667
Mountain View Christian Academy 200/K-12
153 Narrow Ln 22602 540-868-1231
Minta Hardman, admin. Fax 869-8976
Sacred Heart Academy 200/PK-8
110 Keating Dr 22601 540-662-7177
Rebecca McTavish, prin. Fax 722-2894
Sharon's Centre 50/PK-12
1855 Senseny Rd Ste 19 22602 540-667-7002
Sharon Jackson, prin.
Winchester Academy 50/PK-8
915 S Cameron St 22601 540-542-1100
Debra Hodgson, admin. Fax 542-1601
Winchester Montessori S 100/PK-8
1090 W Parkins Mill Rd 22602 540-667-1184
Jennifer Sheehy, prin. Fax 667-9880

Windsor, Isle of Wight, Pop. 2,429
Isle of Wight County SD
Supt. — See Smithfield
Windsor ES 600/PK-5
20008 Courthouse Hwy 23487 757-242-4193
Susan Goetz, prin. Fax 242-3842
Windsor MS 400/6-8
23320 N Court St 23487 757-242-3229
Stenette Byrd, prin. Fax 242-3405

Wirtz, Franklin
Franklin County SD
Supt. — See Rocky Mount
Burnt Chimney ES 500/PK-5
80 Burnt Chimney Rd 24184 540-721-2936
Antionette Wade, prin. Fax 721-2003
Dudley ES 400/PK-5
7250 Brooks Mill Rd 24184 540-721-2621
Keith Pennington, prin. Fax 721-3741

Smith Mountain Lake Christian Academy 50/K-8
2485 Lost Mountain Rd # B 24184 540-719-1192
Deke Andrews, admin. Fax 721-4627

Wise, Wise, Pop. 3,282
Wise County SD 6,700/PK-12
PO Box 1217 24293 276-328-8017
Dr. Jeff Perry, supt. Fax 328-3350
www.wise.k12.va.us
Addington MS 500/5-8
PO Box 977 24293 276-328-8821
James Bryant, prin. Fax 328-2044
Wise PS 600/PK-4
PO Box 947 24293 276-328-8019
Mark Giles, prin. Fax 328-6809
Other Schools – See Appalachia, Big Stone Gap, Coeburn, Pound, Saint Paul

---

Wise County Christian S 100/PK-12
PO Box 3297 24293 276-328-3297
Gary Hill, admin. Fax 328-3248

Woodbridge, Prince William, Pop. 33,300
Prince William County SD
Supt. — See Manassas
Antietam Road ES 500/K-5
12000 Antietam Rd 22192 703-497-7619
Linda Moniuszko, prin. Fax 491-7603
Bel Air ES 500/K-5
14151 Ferndale Rd 22193 703-670-4050
Clint Mitchell, prin. Fax 670-5593
Belmont ES 400/K-5
751 Norwood Ln 22191 703-494-4945
Bridget Outlaw, prin. Fax 491-2650
Beville MS 1,100/6-8
4901 Dale Blvd 22193 703-878-2593
Dr. Karen Giacometti, prin. Fax 730-1274
Dale City ES 500/K-5
14450 Brook Dr 22193 703-670-2208
Cindy Crow-Miller, prin. Fax 670-8425
Enterprise ES 500/K-5
13900 Lindendale Rd 22193 703-590-1558
Melanie McClure, prin. Fax 878-0404
Featherstone ES 400/K-5
14805 Blackburn Rd 22191 703-491-1156
Linda Dockery, prin. Fax 491-2052
Fitzgerald ES PK-5
15500 Benita Fitzgerald Dr 22193 703-583-4195
Deraine Simpson, prin.
Godwin MS 1,000/6-8
14800 Darbydale Ave 22193 703-670-6166
Veronica Abrams, prin. Fax 670-9888
Kerrydale ES 500/K-5
13199 Kerrydale Rd 22193 703-590-1262
Anthony Leonard, prin. Fax 670-6259
Kilby ES 300/K-5
1800 Horner Rd 22191 703-494-6677
Carolyn DeLaFleur, prin. Fax 497-7371
King ES 500/K-5
13224 Nickleson Dr 22193 703-590-1617
Laura Pumphrey, prin. Fax 590-0304
Lake Ridge ES 500/K-5
11970 Hedges Run Dr 22192 703-494-9153
Stefanie Sanders, prin. Fax 494-2272
Lake Ridge MS 1,200/6-8
12350 Mohican Rd 22192 703-494-5154
Jo Fitzgerald, prin. Fax 494-8246
Leesylvania ES 900/K-5
15800 Neabsco Rd 22191 703-670-8268
Mark Boyd, prin. Fax 670-9235
Lynn MS 900/6-8
1650 Prince William Pkwy 22191 703-494-5157
J. Harrison Coleman, prin. Fax 491-5141
Marumsco Hills ES 400/K-5
14100 Page St 22191 703-494-3252
Mary Joanne Alvey, prin. Fax 494-9789
McAuliffe ES 500/K-5
13540 Princedale Dr 22193 703-680-7270
Cynthia West, prin. Fax 897-1960
Minnieville ES 500/K-5
13639 Greenwood Dr 22193 703-670-6106
Glynis Taylor, prin. Fax 878-0695
Neabsco ES 800/K-5
3800 Cordell Ave 22193 703-670-2147
Linda Trexler, prin. Fax 670-0892
Occoquan ES 600/K-5
12915 Occoquan Rd 22192 703-494-2195
Sandra Carrillo, prin. Fax 494-2158
Old Bridge ES 600/K-5
3051 Old Bridge Rd 22192 703-491-5614
Anita G. Flemons, prin. Fax 491-0561
Parks ES K-5
13446 Princedale Dr 22193 703-580-9664
Jarcelynn Hart, prin. Fax 580-9667
Penn ES 600/K-5
12980 Queen Chapel Rd 22193 703-590-0344
Jane Wheeless, prin. Fax 590-1528
Porter S 600/1-8
15311 Forest Grove Dr 22191 703-580-6501
Darci Whitehead, prin. Fax 580-6646
Potomac View ES 600/K-5
14601 Lamar Rd 22191 703-491-1126
Susan Porter, prin. Fax 491-1292
Rippon MS 800/6-8
15101 Blackburn Rd 22191 703-491-2171
Shelia Coleman, prin. Fax 491-2487
River Oaks ES 600/K-5
16950 McGuffeys Trl 22191 703-441-0052
Aerica Williams, prin. Fax 441-1012
Rockledge ES 500/K-5
2300 Mariner Ln 22192 703-491-2108
Amy Schott, prin. Fax 491-0240
Springwoods ES 600/K-5
3815 Marquis Pl 22192 703-590-9874
Virginia Ripperger, prin. Fax 590-1457
Vaughan ES 600/K-5
2200 York Dr 22191 703-494-3220
Lillie Jessie, prin. Fax 497-4774
Westridge ES 600/K-5
12400 Knightsbridge Dr 22192 703-590-3711
Patricia Hayden, prin. Fax 590-0074
Woodbridge MS 1,000/6-8
2201 York Dr 22191 703-494-3181
Skyles Calhoun, prin. Fax 491-1441

Cardinal Montessori S 100/PK-4
1424 G St 22191 703-491-3810
Erick Gallegos, prin. Fax 499-9994
Christ Chapel Academy 500/PK-12
13909 Smoketown Rd 22192 703-670-3822
Rev. Paul Miklich, admin. Fax 590-6695
Riverview Baptist Day S 100/PK-2
1722 Florida Ave 22191 703-491-3023
Cindy Johnson, dir. Fax 491-3231
St. Thomas Aquinas Regional S 500/PK-8
13750 Marys Way 22191 703-491-4447
Sr. Marie Goretti, prin. Fax 492-8828
Victory Christian Academy 100/PK-6
14747 Arizona Ave 22191 703-491-7100
Michelle Sawyer, prin. Fax 490-8489

Woodlawn, Carroll
Carroll County SD
Supt. — See Hillsville
Woodlawn MS 500/6-7
745 Woodlawn Rd 24381 276-236-9931
Jerry King, prin. Fax 236-0345

Woodstock, Shenandoah, Pop. 4,229
Shenandoah County SD 6,100/K-12
600 N Main St Ste 200 22664 540-459-6222
Dr. B. Keith Rowland, supt. Fax 459-6707
www.shenandoah.k12.va.us
Muhlenberg MS 500/6-8
1251 Susan Ave 22664 540-459-2941
Gina Stetter, prin. Fax 459-5965
Robinson ES 1,100/K-5
1231 Susan Ave 22664 540-459-5155
James Grimley, prin. Fax 459-5992
Other Schools – See Quicksburg, Strasburg

Community Christian S Shenandoah Valley 100/PK-8
23749 Old Valley Pike 22664 540-459-5832
Nancy Ritenour, prin. Fax 459-5832

Woolwine, Patrick
Patrick County SD
Supt. — See Stuart
Woolwine ES 200/K-7
9993 Woolwine Hwy 24185 276-930-2811
William Sroufe, prin. Fax 694-1238

Wytheville, Wythe, Pop. 8,038
Wythe County SD 4,300/K-12
1570 W Reservoir St 24382 276-228-5411
Fax 228-9192
wcps.wythe.k12.va.us
Scott Memorial MS 400/6-8
950 S 7th St 24382 276-228-2851
Sidney Crockett, prin. Fax 228-8261
Sheffey ES 200/K-5
621 Piney Mountain Rd 24382 276-699-1771
Joe Phillips, prin. Fax 699-1031
Spiller ES 700/K-5
330 Tazewell St 24382 276-228-3561
Kim Ingo, prin. Fax 228-7277
Other Schools – See Austinville, Max Meadows, Rural Retreat, Speedwell

Yale, Sussex, Pop. 50

Yale SDA S 50/K-8
19183 Courthouse Rd 23897 434-246-6300
Todd Coulter, lead tchr. Fax 246-6300

Yorktown, York
York County SD 12,600/K-12
302 Dare Rd 23692 757-898-0300
Dr. Eric Williams, supt. Fax 890-0771
www.yorkcountyschools.org
Coventry ES 600/K-5
200 Owen Davis Blvd 23693 757-898-0402
Catherine Cheney, prin. Fax 867-7446
Dare ES 400/K-5
300 Dare Rd 23692 757-898-0362
Richard Carter, prin. Fax 898-0371
Grafton MS 900/6-8
405 Grafton Dr 23692 757-898-0525
Edward Holler Ed.D., prin. Fax 898-0534
Mt. Vernon ES 500/K-5
310 Mount Vernon Dr 23693 757-867-7440
Fax 867-7444
Tabb ES 500/K-5
3711 Big Bethel Rd 23693 757-898-0372
Cheryl Parr, prin. Fax 867-7433
Tabb MS 1,000/6-8
300 Yorktown Rd 23693 757-898-0320
Susan Rhew, prin. Fax 867-7425
Yorktown Math/Science/Tech Magnet S 500/K-5
131 Siege Ln 23692 757-898-0358
Michael Lombardo, prin. Fax 898-0415
Yorktown MS 700/6-8
11201 George Washington Mem 23690
757-898-0360
Candi Skinner, prin. Fax 898-0412
Other Schools – See Grafton, Langley AFB, Seaford, Williamsburg

---

Living Word Academy 100/PK-7
110 Industry Dr 23693 757-867-8024
Brenda Ashe, prin. Fax 867-9061

WASHINGTON

WASHINGTON DEPARTMENT OF EDUCATION
PO Box 47200, Olympia 98504-7200
Telephone 360-725-6000
Fax 360-753-6712
Website http://www.k12.wa.us

Superintendent of Public Instruction Randy Dorn

WASHINGTON BOARD OF EDUCATION
PO Box 47206, Olympia 98504-7206

Chairperson Mary Jean Ryan

EDUCATIONAL SERVICE DISTRICTS (ESD)

North Central ESD 171
Dr. Richard McBride, supt. 509-665-2610
PO Box 1847, Wenatchee 98807 Fax 662-9027
www.ncesd.org

Northwest ESD 189
Dr. Gerald Jenkins, supt. 360-299-4000
1601 R Ave, Anacortes 98221 Fax 299-4070
www.nwesd.org/

ESD 113
Dr. Bill Keim, supt. 360-464-6700
601 McPhee Rd SW Fax 464-6900
Olympia 98502
www.esd113.k12.wa.us

Olympic ESD 114
Dr. Walt Bigby, supt. 360-479-0993
105 National Ave N Fax 478-6869
Bremerton 98312
www.oesd.wednet.edu

ESD 123
Bruce Hawkins, supt. 509-547-8441
3918 W Court St, Pasco 99301 Fax 544-5795
www.esd123.org

Puget Sound ESD
Dr. Monte Bridges, supt. 800-664-4549
800 Oakesdale Ave SW Fax 917-7777
Renton 98057
www.psesd.org

ESD 101
Michael Dunn, supt. 509-789-3800
4202 S Regal St, Spokane 99223 Fax 456-2999
www.esd101.net

ESD 112
Dr. Twyla Barnes, supt. 360-750-7500
2500 NE 65th Ave Fax 750-9706
Vancouver 98661
www.esd112.org

ESD 105
Dr. Jane Gutting, supt. 509-575-2885
33 S 2nd Ave, Yakima 98902 Fax 575-2918
www.esd105.wednet.edu

PUBLIC, PRIVATE AND CATHOLIC ELEMENTARY SCHOOLS

Aberdeen, Grays Harbor, Pop. 16,358
Aberdeen SD 5 3,700/PK-12
216 N G St 98520 360-538-2000
Martin Kay, supt. Fax 538-2014
www.asd5.org
Central Park ES 200/K-6
601 School Rd 98520 360-538-2170
Tita Mallory, prin. Fax 538-2172
Gray ES 300/PK-6
1516 N B St 98520 360-538-2140
Noreen Sampson, prin. Fax 538-2142
Hopkins Preschool Center 50/PK-PK
1313 Pacific Ave 98520 360-538-2190
Nancy Liedtke, coord. Fax 538-2192
McDermoth ES 400/K-6
409 N K St 98520 360-538-2120
Jim Sawin, prin. Fax 538-2122
Miller JHS 500/7-8
100 E Lindstrom St 98520 360-538-2100
Jean Prochaska, prin. Fax 538-2106
Stevens ES 500/PK-6
301 S Farragut St 98520 360-538-2150
Kathleen Werner, prin. Fax 538-2156
West ES 400/PK-6
1801 Bay Ave 98520 360-538-2130
William O'Donnell, prin. Fax 538-2132

Wishkah Valley SD 117 200/K-12
4640 Wishkah Rd 98520 360-532-3128
Ray Yoder, supt. Fax 533-4638
www.wishkah.org
Wishkah Valley S 200/K-12
4640 Wishkah Rd 98520 360-532-3128
Joel Tyndell, prin. Fax 533-4638

St. Mary S 200/PK-8
518 N H St 98520 360-532-1230
Kathleen Beyer, prin. Fax 532-1209

Acme, Whatcom
Mt. Baker SD 507
Supt. — See Deming
Acme ES 200/K-6
PO Box 9 98220 360-383-2045
Kent Rogers, prin. Fax 383-2049

Addy, Stevens
Summit Valley SD 202 100/K-8
2360 Addy Gifford Rd 99101 509-935-6362
Bill Glidewell, supt. Fax 935-6364
www.svalley.k12.wa.us
Summit Valley S 100/K-8
2360 Addy Gifford Rd 99101 509-935-6362
Bill Glidewell, prin. Fax 935-6364

Adna, Lewis
Adna SD 226 600/PK-12
PO Box 118 98522 360-748-0362
Edward Rothlin, supt. Fax 748-9217
www.adna.k12.wa.us
Adna ES 300/PK-5
PO Box 28 98522 360-748-1752
Elizabeth Dallas, prin. Fax 740-9419

Airway Heights, Spokane, Pop. 4,647
Cheney SD 360
Supt. — See Cheney
Sunset ES 400/PK-5
12824 W 12th Ave 99001 509-559-4600
Sean Dotson, prin. Fax 244-0906

Almira, Lincoln, Pop. 301
Almira SD 17 100/K-8
PO Box 217 99103 509-639-2414
Shauna Schmerer, supt. Fax 639-2620
www.achsd.org
Almira S 100/K-8
PO Box 217 99103 509-639-2414
Shauna Schmerer, prin. Fax 639-2620

Amanda Park, Grays Harbor
Lake Quinault SD 97 200/K-12
PO Box 38 98526 360-288-2260
Rich DuBois, supt. Fax 288-2732
www.quinault.k12.wa.us/
Lake Quinault S 100/K-8
PO Box 38 98526 360-288-2414
Beth Daneker, prin. Fax 288-2209

Amboy, Clark
Battle Ground SD 119
Supt. — See Brush Prairie
Amboy MS 600/5-8
22115 NE Chelatchie Rd 98601 360-885-6050
Shayla Ebner, prin. Fax 885-6055

Anacortes, Skagit, Pop. 16,083
Anacortes SD 103 2,800/PK-12
2200 M Ave 98221 360-293-1200
Chris Borgen, supt. Fax 293-1222
www.asd103.org/
Anacortes MS 400/7-8
2200 M Ave 98221 360-293-1230
Patrick Harrington, prin. Fax 293-1231
Fidalgo ES 400/K-6
13590 Gibralter Rd 98221 360-293-9545
Tara Dowd, prin. Fax 299-1852
Island View ES 400/K-6
2501 J Ave 98221 360-293-3149
Bernard Selting, prin. Fax 299-1853
Mount Erie ES 400/K-6
1313 41st St 98221 360-293-9541
Bob Knorr, prin. Fax 299-1854
Whitney S 100/PK-K
1200 M Ave 98221 360-293-9536
Kevin Schwartz, prin. Fax 299-1845

Lopez Island SD 144
Supt. — See Lopez Island
Decatur Island S 50/K-8
0 Decatur Is 98221 360-375-6004
Kelli Fisher, lead tchr. Fax 375-6005

Anderson Island, Pierce
Steilacoom Historical SD 1
Supt. — See Steilacoom
Anderson Island ES 50/K-5
13005 Camus Rd 98303 253-884-4901
Nancy McClure, prin. Fax 884-7835

Ariel, Cowlitz
Woodland SD 404
Supt. — See Woodland
Yale ES 50/K-5
11842 Lewis River Rd 98603 360-231-4246
Mark Houk, prin. Fax 231-4446

Arlington, Snohomish, Pop. 15,277
Arlington SD 16 5,600/PK-12
315 N French Ave 98223 360-618-6200
Kristine McDuffy Ed.D., supt. Fax 618-6221
www.asd.wednet.edu
Eagle Creek ES 500/K-5
1216 E 5th St 98223 360-618-6270
Denise Putnam, prin. Fax 618-6275
Haller MS 600/6-8
600 E 1st St 98223 360-618-6400
Eric DeJong, prin. Fax 618-6411
Kent Prairie ES 500/K-5
8110 207th St NE 98223 360-618-6260
Kathy Engell, prin. Fax 618-6265
Pioneer ES 600/K-5
8213 Eaglefield Dr 98223 360-618-6230
Karl Olson, prin. Fax 618-6234
Post MS 600/6-8
1220 E 5th St 98223 360-618-6450
Brian Beckley, prin. Fax 618-6455
Presidents ES 600/PK-5
505 E 3rd St 98223 360-618-6240
Terri Bookey, prin. Fax 618-6245
Trafton ES 200/K-5
12616 Jim Creek Rd 98223 360-435-3250
Ed Aylesworth, prin. Fax 435-1312

Lakewood SD 306
Supt. — See Marysville
Cougar Creek ES 400/K-5
16216 11th Ave NE 98223 360-652-4517
Priscilla Brady, prin. Fax 652-4519

Academy Northwest / Family Academy 300/K-12
23420 Jordan Rd 98223 360-435-9423
Diana McAlister, admin.
Arlington Christian S 100/PK-12
PO Box 3337 98223 360-652-2988
Art Watson, prin. Fax 652-2921
Highland Christian S 100/K-12
135 S French Ave 98223 360-403-8351
Darlene Hartley, admin. Fax 403-4821

Ashford, Pierce
Eatonville SD 404
Supt. — See Eatonville
Columbia Crest ES 100/K-6
24503 State Route 706 E 98304 360-569-2567
Janna Rush, prin. Fax 569-2917

Asotin, Asotin, Pop. 1,124
Asotin-Anatone SD 420 600/K-12
PO Box 489 99402 509-243-1100
Greg Godwin, supt. Fax 243-4251
www.aasd.wednet.edu/index.htm
Asotin ES 300/K-6
PO Box 489 99402 509-243-4147
Wes Nicholas, prin. Fax 243-7720

Auburn, King, Pop. 47,086
Auburn SD 408 14,800/K-12
915 4th St NE 98002 253-931-4900
Dr. Kip Herren, supt. Fax 931-8006
www.auburn.wednet.edu
Cascade MS 800/6-8
1015 24th St NE 98002 253-931-4995
Isaiah Johnson, prin. Fax 833-7580
Chinook ES 400/K-5
3502 Auburn Way S 98092 253-931-4980
Lenny Holloman, prin. Fax 931-4728
Evergreen Heights ES 300/K-5
5602 S 316th St 98001 253-931-4974
Anne Gayman, prin. Fax 931-4860
Gildo Rey ES 400/K-5
1005 37th St SE 98002 253-931-4952
Robin Logan, prin. Fax 931-4731
Hazelwood ES 600/K-5
11815 SE 304th St 98092 253-931-4740
Sally Colburn, prin. Fax 804-4520
Ilalko ES 500/K-5
301 Oravetz Pl SE 98092 253-931-4748
Adam Couch, prin. Fax 804-4522
Jacobsen ES 400/K-5
29205 132nd Ave SE 98092 253-630-2441
Eric Daniel, prin. Fax 630-1323
Lakeland Hills ES 600/K-5
1020 Evergreen Way SE 98092 253-876-7711
Ryan Foster, prin. Fax 876-7714
Lake View ES 400/K-5
16401 SE 318th St 98092 253-931-4830
Mike Weibel, prin. Fax 931-4832
Lea Hill ES 600/K-5
30908 124th Ave SE 98092 253-931-4982
Ed Herda, prin. Fax 931-4733
Mt. Baker MS 800/6-8
620 37th St SE 98002 253-804-4555
Darin Adams, prin. Fax 931-0661
Olympic MS 700/6-8
1825 K St SE 98002 253-931-4966
Jason Hill, prin. Fax 939-2753
Pioneer ES 400/K-5
2301 M St SE 98002 253-931-4986
Debra Gary, prin. Fax 931-4734
Rainier MS 800/6-8
30620 116th Ave SE 98092 253-931-4843
Ben Talbert, prin. Fax 939-4318
Scobee ES 400/K-5
1031 14th St NE 98002 253-931-4984
Greg Brown, prin. Fax 804-4514
Terminal Park ES 400/K-5
1101 D St SE 98002 253-931-4978
Tim Carstens, prin. Fax 804-4532
Washington ES 400/K-5
20 E St NE 98002 253-931-4988
Pauline Thomas, prin. Fax 931-4736
Other Schools – See Pacific

Federal Way SD 210
Supt. — See Federal Way
Camelot ES 300/PK-5
4041 S 298th St 98001 253-945-2500
Paul Marquardt, prin. Fax 945-2525
Kilo MS 700/6-8
4400 S 308th St 98001 253-945-4700
Patricia Larson, prin. Fax 945-4747
Lake Dolloff ES 500/PK-5
4200 S 308th St 98001 253-945-2800
Sara Gill, prin. Fax 945-2828
Lakeland ES 400/K-5
35827 32nd Ave S 98001 253-945-3000
Jeff Soltez, prin. Fax 945-3030
Rainier View ES 400/PK-5
3015 S 368th St 98003 253-945-3700
John Trujillo, prin. Fax 945-3737
Sequoyah MS 700/6-8
3425 S 360th St 98001 253-945-3670
Vince Blauser, prin. Fax 945-3699
Valhalla ES 500/K-5
27847 42nd Ave S 98001 253-945-4300
Maria Verhaar, prin. Fax 945-4343

Buena Vista SDA S 200/K-8
3320 Academy Dr SE 98092 253-833-0718
Ron Trautwein, prin. Fax 833-0385
Holy Family S 200/K-8
505 17th St SE 98002 253-833-5130
Ann Leichleiter, prin. Fax 833-9311
RCS Kent View Christian S 200/PK-6
20 49th St NE 98002 253-852-5145
Tess Johnson, admin. Fax 850-8825
Valley Christian S 200/PK-8
1312 2nd St SE 98002 253-833-3541
Gloria Butz, admin. Fax 833-4239

Bainbridge Island, Kitsap, Pop. 21,951
Bainbridge Island SD 303 4,100/K-12
8489 Madison Ave NE 98110 206-842-4714
Faith Chapel, supt. Fax 842-2928
www.bainbridge.wednet.edu
Blakely ES 400/K-4
4704 Blakely Ave NE 98110 206-842-4752
Ric Jones, prin. Fax 780-2040
Odyssey Multi-Age Program 100/K-8
9530 NE High School Rd 98110 206-780-1646
Catherine Camp, prin. Fax 855-0511
Ordway ES 400/K-4
8555 Madison Ave NE 98110 206-842-7637
Dr. Robert Lewis, prin. Fax 780-1560
Sonoji Sakai IS 600/5-6
9343 Sportsman Club Rd NE 98110 206-780-6500
Jim Corsetti, prin. Fax 780-6565
Wilkes ES 400/K-4
12781 Madison Ave NE 98110 206-842-4411
Sheryl Belt, prin. Fax 780-3000
Woodward MS 600/7-8
9125 Sportsman Club Rd NE 98110 206-842-4787
Mary O'Neill, prin. Fax 780-4525

Madrona S 100/PK-6
PO Box 11371 98110 206-855-8041
Fax 855-0668
St. Cecilia S 100/PK-7
1310 Madison Ave N 98110 206-842-2017
Elizabeth Chamberlin, prin. Fax 842-6988
Voyager Montessori S 50/1-6
PO Box 11252 98110 206-780-5661
Renee Kok, hdmstr.

Battle Ground, Clark, Pop. 13,237
Battle Ground SD 119
Supt. — See Brush Prairie
Chief Umtuch MS 800/5-8
PO Box 200 98604 360-885-6350
Linda Allen, prin. Fax 885-6355
Daybreak MS, PO Box 200 98604 5-8
Shelly Whitten, prin. 360-885-6900
Daybreak PS, PO Box 200 98604 K-4
Jill Dutchess, prin. 360-885-6950
Maple Grove MS 700/5-8
PO Box 200 98604 360-885-6700
Bill Penrose, prin. Fax 885-6701
Maple Grove PS 900/K-4
PO Box 200 98604 360-885-6750
Barbara Baird, prin. Fax 885-6754
Strong ES 600/K-4
PO Box 200 98604 360-885-6400
Cindy Arnold, prin. Fax 885-6401
Tukes Valley MS 5-8
PO Box 200 98604 360-885-6250
Diana Harris, prin. Fax 885-6297
Tukes Valley PS K-4
PO Box 200 98604 360-885-6200
Laurie Sundby, prin. Fax 885-6247

Firm Foundation Christian S 400/PK-12
19919 NE 107th Ave 98604 360-687-8382
Scott Grove, admin. Fax 687-8799
Meadow Glade Adventist S 200/K-8
18717 NE 109th Ave 98604 360-687-5121
Brian Allison, prin. Fax 687-7166

Belfair, Mason
North Mason SD 403 2,000/K-12
71 E Campus Dr 98528 360-277-2300
David Peterson, supt. Fax 277-2320
www.nmsd.wednet.edu/
Belfair ES 500/K-5
22900 NE State Route 3 98528 360-277-2233
Robert Ditch, prin. Fax 275-8842
Hawkins MS 400/6-8
300 E Campus Dr 98528 360-277-2302
Thomas Worlund, prin. Fax 277-2324
Sand Hill ES 400/K-5
791 NE Sand Hill Rd 98528 360-277-2330
Ray Lucas, prin. Fax 277-2307

Bellevue, King, Pop. 117,137
Bellevue SD 405 16,300/PK-12
PO Box 90010 98009 425-456-4000
Karen Clark, supt. Fax 456-4176
www.bsd405.org
Ardmore ES 300/K-5
16616 NE 32nd St 98008 425-456-4700
Angela Dunavant, prin. Fax 456-4706
Bennett ES 400/K-5
17900 NE 16th St 98008 425-456-4800
Chris Thomas, prin. Fax 456-4824
Cherry Crest ES 400/K-5
12400 NE 32nd St 98005 425-456-4900
Michelle Carroll, prin. Fax 456-4911
Chinook MS 800/6-8
2001 98th Ave NE 98004 425-456-6300
Maria Frieboes, prin. Fax 456-6304
Clyde Hill ES 500/K-5
9601 NE 24th St 98004 425-456-5000
Jennifer Benson, prin. Fax 456-5036
Eastgate ES 400/K-5
4255 153rd Ave SE 98006 425-456-5100
Cathi Barnes, prin. Fax 456-5119
Enatai ES 400/K-5
10615 SE 23rd St 98004 425-456-5200
Heather Blust, prin. Fax 456-5213
Highland MS 600/6-8
15027 Bel Red Rd 98007 425-456-6400
Anissa Bereano, prin. Fax 456-6499
Lake Hills ES 500/K-5
14310 SE 12th St 98007 425-456-5300
Johnnie Gregory, prin. Fax 456-5302
Newport Heights ES 500/K-5
5225 119th Ave SE 98006 425-456-5500
Stephen Marafino, prin. Fax 456-5506
Odle MS 600/6-8
14401 NE 8th St 98007 425-456-6600
Jerry Schaefer, prin. Fax 456-6616
Phantom Lake ES 300/K-5
1050 160th Ave SE 98008 425-456-5600
Tracy Maury, prin. Fax 456-5606
Sherwood Forest ES 400/K-5
16411 NE 24th St 98008 425-456-5700
Gail McDonald, prin. Fax 456-5702
Somerset ES 600/K-5
14100 SE Somerset Blvd 98006 425-456-5800
Betty Hannaford, prin. Fax 456-5804
Spiritridge ES 300/K-5
16401 SE 24th St 98008 425-456-5900
Laura Bang-Knudsen, prin. Fax 456-5967
Stevenson ES 600/K-5
14220 NE 8th St 98007 425-456-6000
Christy Lindquist, prin. Fax 456-6015
Tillicum MS 600/6-8
16020 SE 16th St 98008 425-456-6700
Dion Yahoudy, prin. Fax 456-6770
Tyee MS 800/6-8
13630 SE Allen Rd 98006 425-456-6800
Judy Buckmaster, prin. Fax 456-6859
Woodridge ES 400/PK-5
12619 SE 20th Pl 98005 425-456-6200
Liz Ritz, prin. Fax 456-6204

Other Schools – See Medina

Issaquah SD 411
Supt. — See Issaquah
Cougar Ridge ES 600/K-5
4630 167th Ave SE 98006 425-837-7300
Jackie Tanner, prin. Fax 837-7230
Sunset ES 600/PK-5
4229 W Lake Sammamish Pkwy 98008
425-837-5600
Wayne Hamasaki, prin. Fax 837-5660

America's Child Montessori S 100/PK-4
14340 NE 21st St 98007 425-641-5437
Linda Kebely, dir. Fax 401-7135
Ark at Cross of Christ Lutheran S 50/PK-PK
411 156th Ave NE 98007 425-644-5414
Jan Galbraith, dir. Fax 746-9345
Bellevue Childrens Academy 200/PK-6
14600 NE 24th St 98007 425-649-0791
Yuka Shimizu, dir. Fax 643-8679
Bellevue Montessori - Park Campus K-6
10909 NE 24th St 98004 425-454-7439
Christine Hoffman, prin. Fax 454-1038
Bellevue Montessori S 200/PK-K
2411 112th Ave NE 98004 425-454-7439
Christine Hoffman, dir. Fax 454-1038
Cedar Park Christian International S 100/PK-6
625 140th Ave NE 98005 425-746-3258
Dr. Clint Behrends, supt. Fax 274-0469
Chestnut Hill Academy 100/K-1
2610 116th Ave NE 98004 425-576-1212
Jodel Kovich, admin. Fax 576-9411
Dartmoor S 100/1-12
13401 Bel-Red Rd 98005 425-603-1975
Jeffrey Woolley, hdmstr. Fax 603-0038
Eastside Christian S 300/PK-8
14615 SE 22nd St 98007 425-641-5570
Dr. Brian Fitch, prin. Fax 746-3155
Eton S 300/PK-8
2701 Bel Red Rd 98008 425-881-4230
Dr. Patricia Feltin, dir. Fax 861-8011
French Immersion S of Washington 200/PK-5
4211 W Lake Sammamish Pkwy 98008
425-653-3970
Veronique Dussud, dir. Fax 643-2938
Jewish Day S of Metro Seattle 300/PK-8
15749 NE 4th St 98008 425-460-0200
Maria Erlitz, hdmstr. Fax 460-0201
Little S 100/PK-6
2812 116th Ave NE 98004 425-827-8708
Laurel Seid, hdmstr. Fax 827-3814
Open Window S 200/K-8
6128 168th Pl SE 98006 425-747-2911
Wilder Dominick, hdmstr. Fax 562-4035
Sacred Heart S 400/K-8
9450 NE 14th St 98004 425-451-1773
David Burroughs, prin. Fax 450-3918
St. Louise S 500/K-8
133 156th Ave SE 98007 425-746-4220
Dan Fitzpatrick, prin. Fax 644-3294
St. Madeleine Sophie S 100/PK-8
4400 130th Pl SE 98006 425-747-6770
Dan Sherman, prin. Fax 747-1825
Three Cedars Waldorf S 100/PK-8
556 124th Ave NE 98005 425-401-9874
Briana Bennitt, dir. Fax 865-9093

Bellingham, Whatcom, Pop. 74,547
Bellingham SD 501 10,300/PK-12
1306 Dupont St 98225 360-676-6400
Ken Vedra, supt. Fax 676-2793
www.bham.wednet.edu
Alderwood ES 300/K-5
3400 Hollywood Ave 98225 360-676-6404
Stephanie Korn, prin. Fax 647-6896
Birchwood ES 300/K-5
3200 Pinewood Ave 98225 360-676-6466
David Adams, prin. Fax 647-6875
Columbia ES 200/K-5
2508 Utter St 98225 360-676-6413
Missy Ferguson, prin. Fax 647-6880
Cozier ES 400/K-5
1330 Lincoln St, 360-676-6410
Tom Venable, prin. Fax 676-6578
ECC PK-PK
3408 Redwood Ave 98225 360-676-6514
Fax 647-6809
Fairhaven MS 500/6-8
110 Parkridge Rd 98225 360-676-6450
Deirdre O'Neill, prin. Fax 647-6887
Geneva ES 600/K-5
1401 Geneva St, 360-676-6416
John Heritage, prin. Fax 647-6893
Happy Valley ES 500/K-5
1041 24th St 98225 360-676-6420
Karen Tolliver, prin. Fax 676-4989
King ES K-5
2155 Yew Street Rd, 360-647-6840
Rob McElroy, prin. Fax 647-6841
Kulshan MS 600/6-8
1250 Kenoyer Dr, 360-676-4886
Jeannie Hayden, prin. Fax 647-6892
Larrabee ES 200/K-5
1409 18th St 98225 360-676-6424
Eric Paige, prin. Fax 647-6885
Northern Heights ES 500/K-5
4000 Magrath Rd 98226 360-647-6820
Wendy Barrett, prin. Fax 647-6824
Parkview ES 300/K-5
3033 Coolidge Dr 98225 360-676-6433
Jane Tromburg, prin. Fax 647-6882
Roosevelt ES 400/K-5
2900 Yew St 98226 360-676-6440
Steve Morse, prin. Fax 647-6895
Shuksan MS 500/6-8
2713 Alderwood Ave 98225 360-676-6454
Andrew Mark, prin. Fax 647-6879

Silver Beach ES 400/K-5
4101 Academy St 98226 360-676-6443
Gregory Holmgren, prin. Fax 647-6884
Sunnyland ES 400/K-5
2800 James St 98225 360-676-6446
Mary Anne Stuckart, prin. Fax 647-6891
Whatcom MS 600/6-8
810 Halleck St 98225 360-676-6460
Jeffrey Coulter, prin. Fax 647-6899

Meridian SD 505 1,500/PK-12
214 W Laurel Rd 98226 360-398-7111
Timothy Yeomans, supt. Fax 398-8966
www.meridian.wednet.edu
Other Schools – See Everson, Lynden

Mt. Baker SD 507
Supt. — See Deming
Harmony ES 400/K-6
5060 Sand Rd 98226 360-383-2050
Bridget Rossman, prin. Fax 383-2054

Assumption S 400/PK-8
2116 Cornwall Ave 98225 360-733-6133
Roses Goeres, prin. Fax 647-4372
Baker View Christian S 50/PK-8
5353 Waschke Rd 98226 360-384-8155
Anthea Lindsey, dir. Fax 383-0151
Bellingham Christian S 200/PK-8
1600 E Sunset Dr 98226 360-733-7303
Bob Sampson, admin. Fax 647-0683
Catch the Son K 100/PK-PK
2600 Lakeway Dr, 360-715-8471
Sharon Reichstein, dir.
Evergreen Christian S 100/PK-6
4604 Cable St, 360-738-8248
Mary Enfield, admin. Fax 738-1020
St. Paul's Academy 400/PK-10
3000 Northwest Ave 98225 360-733-1750
Stephanie Sadler, hdmstr. Fax 738-8558
Whatcom Day Academy 100/PK-9
5217 Northwest Dr 98226 360-312-1103
Susan Donnelly, hdmstr. Fax 312-1804
Whatcom Hills Waldorf S 200/PK-8
941 Austin St, 360-733-3164
Carla Hasche, admin. Fax 733-0526

Benge, Adams
Benge SD 122 50/K-6
2978 E Benge Winona Rd 99105 509-887-2370
Mary Ault, admin. Fax 887-2360
Benge ES 50/K-6
2978 E Benge Winona Rd 99105 509-887-2370
Mary Ault, admin. Fax 887-2360

Benton City, Benton, Pop. 2,971
Kiona-Benton City SD 52 1,600/PK-12
1107 Grace 99320 509-588-2000
Rom Castilleja, supt. Fax 588-5580
www.owt.com/kibe/
Kiona-Benton City ES 700/PK-5
1107 Grace 99320 509-588-2090
Kevin Pearl, prin. Fax 588-2729
Kiona-Benton City MS 400/6-8
1107 Grace 99320 509-588-2040
Vance Wing, prin. Fax 588-2905

Bickleton, Klickitat
Bickleton SD 203 100/K-12
PO Box 10 99322 509-896-5473
Ric Palmer, supt. Fax 896-2071
www.bickletonschools.org
Bickleton S 100/K-12
PO Box 10 99322 509-896-5473
Ric Palmer, prin. Fax 896-2071

Black Diamond, King, Pop. 3,929
Enumclaw SD 216
Supt. — See Enumclaw
Black Diamond ES 300/K-5
PO Box 285 98010 360-802-7570
Gerrie Garton, prin. Fax 802-7610

Kent SD 415
Supt. — See Kent
Sawyer Woods ES 400/K-6
31135 228th Ave SE 98010 253-373-7750
Tim Helgeson, prin. Fax 373-7757

Blaine, Whatcom, Pop. 4,330
Blaine SD 503 2,200/PK-12
765 H St 98230 360-332-5881
Ron Spanjer, supt. Fax 332-7568
www.blaine.k12.wa.us
Blaine ES 500/3-5
836 Mitchell Ave 98230 360-332-5213
Kathy Newport, prin. Fax 332-7568
Blaine MS 500/6-8
975 H St 98230 360-332-8226
Darren Benson, prin. Fax 332-7568
Blaine PS 500/PK-2
820 Boblett St 98230 360-332-1300
Nancy Bakarich, prin. Fax 332-7568
Other Schools – See Point Roberts

Bonney Lake, Pierce, Pop. 14,611
Sumner SD 320
Supt. — See Sumner
Bonney Lake ES 500/K-5
18715 80th St E, 253-891-4450
Sandy Miller, prin. Fax 891-4472
Crestwood ES 300/K-5
3914 W Tapps Dr E, 253-891-4550
Kay Gallo, prin. Fax 891-4572
Emerald Hills ES 400/K-5
19515 S Tapps Dr E, 253-891-4750
Chuck Eychaner, prin. Fax 891-4772
Lakeridge MS 600/6-8
5909 Myers Rd E, 253-891-5100
Steve Fulkerson, prin. Fax 891-5145

Liberty Ridge ES 500/K-5
12202 209th Avenue Ct E, 253-891-4800
Margie Bellmer, prin. Fax 891-4822
Mountain View MS 600/6-8
10921 199th Avenue Ct E, 253-891-5200
Laurie Dent-Cleveland, prin. Fax 891-5245
Victor Falls ES 600/K-5
11401 188th Avenue Ct E, 253-891-4700
Beth Dykman, prin. Fax 891-4722

Bothell, King, Pop. 30,916
Everett SD 2
Supt. — See Everett
Cedar Wood ES 800/PK-5
3414 168th St SE 98012 425-385-7700
David Jones, prin. Fax 385-7702
Woodside ES 600/K-5
17000 23rd Ave SE 98012 425-385-7800
Betty Cobbs, prin. Fax 385-7802

Northshore SD 417 19,700/PK-12
3330 Monte Villa Pkwy 98021 425-408-7701
Larry Francois, supt. Fax 408-7702
www.nsd.org
Canyon Creek ES 600/K-6
21400 35th Ave SE 98021 425-408-5700
Bill Bagnall, prin. Fax 408-5702
Crystal Springs ES 600/K-6
21615 9th Ave SE 98021 425-408-4300
Diane Goodwin, prin. Fax 408-4302
Fernwood ES 600/K-6
3933 Jewell Rd 98012 425-408-4500
Lew Dickert, prin. Fax 408-4502
Lockwood ES 500/K-6
24118 Lockwood Rd 98021 425-408-5800
Ann Madsen, prin. Fax 408-5802
Love ES 400/K-6
303 224th St SW 98021 425-408-4600
Scott Beebe, prin. Fax 408-4602
Maywood Hills ES 500/K-6
19510 104th Ave NE 98011 425-408-5000
David Hoffman, prin. Fax 408-5002
Shelton View ES 300/K-6
23400 5th Ave W 98021 425-408-5200
Bob Jones, prin. Fax 408-5202
Sorenson ECC 100/PK-PK
19705 88th Ave NE 98011 425-408-5570
Annette McNabb, dir. Fax 408-5572
Westhill ES 500/PK-6
19515 88th Ave NE 98011 425-408-5500
Anne Cullum, prin. Fax 408-5502
Woodin ES 500/K-6
12950 NE 195th St 98011 425-408-5400
Jill Crivello, prin. Fax 408-5402
Woodmoor ES 800/K-6
12225 NE 160th St 98011 425-408-5600
Angela Kerr, prin. Fax 408-5602
Other Schools – See Kenmore, Redmond, Woodinville

Cedar Park Christian S 1,700/PK-12
16300 112th Ave NE 98011 425-488-9778
Clint Behrends, supt. Fax 483-5765
Evergreen Academy 100/PK-5
16017 118th Pl NE 98011 425-488-8000
Dana Mott, prin. Fax 488-0994
Heritage Christian Academy 300/PK-9
10310 NE 195th St 98011 425-485-2585
Jeff Michaelson, prin. Fax 486-2895
St. Brendan S 300/K-8
10049 NE 195th St 98011 425-483-8300
Chris Lunn, prin. Fax 483-2839
Whole Earth Montessori S 100/PK-6
2930 228th St SE 98021 425-486-3037
Dianna Galante, prin. Fax 482-1178
Woodinville Montessori S - North Creek 300/PK-9
19102 N Creek Pkwy Ste 100 98011 425-482-3184
Mary Schneider, prin. Fax 482-3186

Bow, Skagit
Burlington-Edison SD 100
Supt. — See Burlington
Allen S 500/K-8
17145 Cook Rd 98232 360-757-3352
Chris Pearson, prin. Fax 757-2503
Edison S 500/K-8
5801 Main St 98232 360-757-3375
Brenda Naish, prin. Fax 766-6272

Bremerton, Kitsap, Pop. 37,828
Bremerton SD 100-C 5,000/PK-12
134 Marion Ave N 98312 360-473-1000
Flip Herndon, supt. Fax 473-1040
www.bremertonschools.org
Crownhill ES 400/K-5
1500 Rocky Point Rd NW 98312 360-473-4200
Jill Carlson, prin. Fax 473-4240
Jahr ES 500/K-5
800 Dibb St 98310 360-473-4100
Mike Sellers, prin. Fax 473-4140
Kitsap Lake ES 400/K-5
1111 Carr Blvd 98312 360-473-4300
Flint Walpole, prin. Fax 473-4340
Mountain View MS 1,100/6-8
2400 Perry Ave 98310 360-473-0600
Michaeleen Gelhaus, prin. Fax 473-0640
Naval Avenue Early Learning Center 200/PK-3
900 Olympic Ave 98312 360-473-4400
John Welsh, prin. Fax 473-4440
View Ridge ES 500/PK-5
3250 Spruce Ave 98310 360-473-4500
Sandra Crabtree-Gessner, prin. Fax 473-4540
West Hills ES 300/PK-5
520 S National Ave 98312 360-473-4600
Lisa Heaman, prin. Fax 473-4640

Central Kitsap SD 401
Supt. — See Silverdale
Brownsville ES 500/K-6
8795 Illahee Rd NE 98311 360-662-8000
Sandra Horst, prin. Fax 662-8001

Cottonwood ES 300/K-6
330 NE Foster Rd 98311 360-662-8300
Paul Nash, prin. Fax 662-8301
Esquire Hills ES 500/K-6
2650 NE John Carlson Rd 98311 360-662-8600
Sue Corey, prin. Fax 662-8601
Green Mountain ES 400/K-6
3860 Boundary Trl NW 98312 360-662-8700
Melinda Reynvaan, prin. Fax 662-8701
Jackson Park ES 300/K-6
2900 Austin Dr 98312 360-662-9000
Tess Danubio, prin. Fax 662-9001
PineCrest ES 400/K-6
5530 Pine Rd NE 98311 360-662-9200
Connie Gates, prin. Fax 662-9201
Woodlands ES 400/K-6
7420 Central Valley Rd NE 98311 360-662-9700
Jeff McCormick, prin. Fax 662-9701

Christ the King Lutheran S 100/PK-8
8065 Chico Way NW 98312 360-692-8798
Bruce Babler, prin. Fax 307-9179
Kings West S 400/K-12
4012 Chico Way NW 98312 360-377-7700
Bryan Peterson, hdmstr. Fax 377-7795
Kitsap Adventist Christian S 50/K-9
5088 NW Taylor Rd 98312 360-377-4542
Heather Phelps, prin. Fax 377-3743
Our Lady Star of the Sea S 200/K-8
1516 5th St 98337 360-373-5162
Sally Merriwether, prin. Fax 377-1143
Peace Lutheran S 200/PK-8
1234 NE Riddell Rd 98310 360-373-2116
Douglas J. Eisele, prin. Fax 377-0686
Sylvan Way Christian S 300/PK-8
900 Sylvan Way 98310 360-373-5028
Judy Belcher, prin. Fax 373-3337

Brewster, Okanogan, Pop. 2,140
Brewster SD 111 800/PK-12
PO Box 97 98812 509-689-3418
Aaron Chavez, supt. Fax 689-2892
www.brewster.wednet.edu
Brewster ES 500/PK-6
PO Box 97 98812 509-689-2581
Eric Driessen, prin. Fax 689-3303

Brewster Adventist S 50/1-8
115 Valley Rd 98812 509-689-3213
Fax 689-9050

Bridgeport, Douglas, Pop. 2,043
Bridgeport SD 75 700/PK-12
PO Box 1060 98813 509-686-5656
Gene Schmidt, supt. Fax 686-2221
www.bridgeport.wednet.edu
Bridgeport ES 400/PK-5
PO Box 1060 98813 509-686-2201
Michael Porter, dean Fax 686-0773
Bridgeport MS 200/6-8
PO Box 1060 98813 509-686-9501
Scott Sattler, prin. Fax 686-4052

Brier, Snohomish, Pop. 6,344
Edmonds SD 15
Supt. — See Lynnwood
Brier ES 400/K-6
3625 232nd St SW 98036 425-431-7854
Tori Thomas, prin. Fax 431-7853
Brier Terrace MS 600/7-8
22200 Brier Rd 98036 425-431-7834
Kevin Allen, prin. Fax 431-7836

Brinnon, Jefferson
Brinnon SD 46 50/PK-8
46 Schoolhouse Rd 98320 360-796-4646
Nancy Thompson, admin. Fax 796-4113
Brinnon S 50/PK-8
46 Schoolhouse Rd 98320 360-796-4646
Nancy Thompson, prin. Fax 796-4113

Brush Prairie, Clark, Pop. 2,650
Battle Ground SD 119 10,500/K-12
11104 NE 149th St 98606 360-885-5300
Shonny Bria Ph.D., supt. Fax 885-5310
www.bgsd.k12.wa.us/
Other Schools – See Amboy, Battle Ground, Vancouver, Yacolt

Hockinson SD 98 2,100/K-12
17912 NE 159th St 98606 360-448-6400
Margaret Bates, supt. Fax 448-6409
www.hock.k12.wa.us/
Hockinson Heights IS 500/3-5
19912 NE 164th St 98606 360-448-6430
Lisa Swindell, prin. Fax 448-6439
Hockinson Heights PS 400/K-2
20000 NE 164th St 98606 360-448-6420
Colleen Anders, prin. Fax 448-6429
Hockinson MS 500/6-8
15916 NE 182nd Ave 98606 360-448-6440
Peter Rosenkranz, prin. Fax 448-6449

Buckley, Pierce, Pop. 4,473
White River SD 416 3,700/K-12
PO Box 2050 98321 360-829-0600
Tom Lockyer, supt. Fax 829-3843
www.whiteriver.wednet.edu
Elk Ridge ES 300/K-5
PO Box 1685 98321 360-829-3354
Christine Ellenwood, prin. Fax 829-3392
Foothills ES 500/K-5
PO Box 2210 98321 360-829-3355
Mark Cushman, prin. Fax 829-3381
Glacier MS 400/6-8
PO Box 1976 98321 360-829-3395
Andy McGrath, prin. Fax 829-3391
Mountain Meadow ES 500/K-5
PO Box 2390 98321 360-829-3356
Adam Uhler, prin. Fax 829-3388
Other Schools – See Wilkeson

Burbank, Walla Walla, Pop. 1,745
Columbia SD 400 900/PK-12
755 Maple St 99323 509-547-2136
Dr. Lou Gates, supt. Fax 546-0603
www.csd.wednet.edu
Columbia ES 400/PK-5
977 Maple St 99323 509-547-9393
Ian Yale, prin. Fax 545-6382
Columbia MS 200/6-8
835 Maple St 99323 509-545-8571
Mike Taylor, prin. Fax 547-4277

Burien, King, Pop. 30,737
Highline SD 401 17,600/K-12
PO Box 66100 98166 206-433-0111
John Welch, supt. Fax 433-2351
www.hsd401.org
Cedarhurst ES 500/K-6
611 S 132nd St 98168 206-631-3600
Roberta Giammona, prin. Fax 631-3604
Gregory Heights ES 500/K-6
16201 16th Ave SW 98166 206-433-2323
Phil Robinson, prin. Fax 439-4423
Hazel Valley ES 600/K-6
402 SW 132nd St 98146 206-433-2434
Johnathan Letcher, prin. Fax 433-2118
McMicken Heights ES 500/K-6
15631 Des Moines Memorial 98148 206-433-2276
Steve Grubb, prin. Fax 433-2473
Parkside ES 600/K-6
440 S 186th St 98148 206-433-2485
Robin Lamoureux, prin. Fax 433-2433
Seahurst ES 600/K-6
14603 14th Ave SW 98166 206-433-2531
Chris Larsen, prin. Fax 433-2599
Shorewood ES 400/K-6
2725 SW 116th St 98146 206-631-4900
Deborah Holcomb, prin. Fax 631-4999
Sylvester MS 700/7-8
16222 Sylvester Rd SW 98166 206-433-2401
Vicki Fisher, prin. Fax 433-2530
Other Schools – See Des Moines, Normandy Park, SeaTac, Seattle

---

Glendale Lutheran S 100/PK-6
13455 2nd Ave SW 98146 206-244-6085
Karin Manns, prin. Fax 244-0601
St. Francis of Assisi S 500/K-8
15216 21st Ave SW 98166 206-243-5690
Sheila Keaton, prin. Fax 433-8593
Three Tree Montessori S 100/PK-6
220 SW 160th St 98166 206-242-5100
Paula Walters, dir. Fax 242-5112

Burlington, Skagit, Pop. 8,247
Burlington-Edison SD 100 3,900/K-12
927 E Fairhaven Ave 98233 360-757-3311
Laurel Browning, supt. Fax 755-9198
www.be.wednet.edu/
Bay View S 600/K-8
15241 Josh Wilson Rd 98233 360-757-3322
Aaron Darragh, prin. Fax 757-1582
Umbarger S 700/K-8
820 S Skagit St 98233 360-757-3366
Scott Niemann, prin. Fax 755-0047
West View S 400/K-8
515 W Victoria Ave 98233 360-757-3391
Meagan Dawson, prin. Fax 757-3306
Other Schools – See Bow

Skagit Adventist S 200/PK-12
530 N Section St 98233 360-755-9261
Ken Knudsen, admin. Fax 755-9931

Camano Island, See Stanwood
Stanwood-Camano SD 401
Supt. — See Stanwood
Elger Bay ES 400/K-5
1810 Elger Bay Rd 98282 360-629-1290
Dr. Jon Evavold, prin. Fax 629-1291
Utsalady ES 500/K-5
608 Arrowhead Rd 98282 360-629-1260
Colleen Keller, prin. Fax 629-1261

Camas, Clark, Pop. 16,671
Camas SD 117 5,600/K-12
1919 NE Ione St 98607 360-833-5400
Dr. Mike Nerland, supt. Fax 833-5401
www.camas.wednet.edu/
Baller ES 500/K-5
1954 NE Garfield St 98607 360-833-5720
Jerry Moss, prin. Fax 833-5721
Fox ES 500/K-5
2623 NW Sierra St 98607 360-833-5700
Cathy Sork, prin. Fax 833-5701
Lacamas Heights ES 500/K-5
4600 NE Garfield St 98607 360-833-5740
Jan Strohmaier, prin. Fax 833-5741
Liberty MS 700/6-8
1612 NE Garfield St 98607 360-833-5850
Marilyn Boerke, prin. Fax 833-5851
Prune Hill ES 600/K-5
1601 NW Tidland St 98607 360-833-5730
Julie Swan, prin. Fax 833-5731
Skyridge MS 600/6-8
5220 NW Parker St 98607 360-833-5800
Ann Perrin, prin. Fax 833-5801
Zellerbach ES 400/K-5
841 NE 22nd Ave 98607 360-833-5710
Patricia Erdmann, prin. Fax 833-5711

Evergreen SD 114
Supt. — See Vancouver
Illahee ES 600/K-5
19401 SE 1st St 98607 360-604-3350
Joel Hauge, prin. Fax 604-3352

Pacific Crest Academy 200/PK-8
PO Box 1031 98607 360-834-9913
Dr. Leslie White, prin. Fax 834-9926

Carbonado, Pierce, Pop. 608
Carbonado Historical SD 19 200/K-8
PO Box 131 98323 360-829-0121
Scott Hubbard, supt. Fax 829-0471
www.carbonado.k12.wa.us/
Carbonado S 200/K-8
PO Box 131 98323 360-829-0121
Scott Hubbard, prin. Fax 829-0471

Carnation, King, Pop. 1,828
Riverview SD 407 3,000/K-12
32240 NE 50th St 98014 425-844-4500
Conrad Robertson, supt. Fax 844-4502
www.riverview.wednet.edu
Carnation ES 400/K-5
4950 Tolt Ave 98014 425-844-4550
Doug Poage, prin. Fax 844-4552
Stillwater ES 500/K-5
11530 320th Ave NE 98014 425-844-4680
Amy Wright, prin. Fax 844-4682
Tolt MS 700/6-8
3740 Tolt Ave 98014 425-844-4600
Janet Gavigan, prin. Fax 844-4602
Other Schools – See Duvall

Carrolls, Cowlitz
Kelso SD 458
Supt. — See Kelso
Carrolls ES 100/K-5
PO Box 3 98609 360-501-1380
Mark Connolly, lead tchr. Fax 501-1370

Carson, Skamania
Stevenson-Carson SD 303
Supt. — See Stevenson
Carson ES 200/3-6
351 Hot Springs Ave 98610 509-427-5939
Kim Meche, prin. Fax 427-5874
Wind River MS 200/7-8
441 Hot Springs Ave 98610 509-427-8952
Kathleen Browning, prin. Fax 427-8614

Cashmere, Chelan, Pop. 2,985
Cashmere SD 222 1,500/PK-12
210 S Division St 98815 509-782-3355
Glenn Johnson, supt. Fax 782-4747
www.cashmere.wednet.edu
Cashmere MS 500/5-8
300 Tigner Rd 98815 509-782-2001
Rolf Oxos, prin. Fax 782-2547
Vale ES 500/PK-4
101 Pioneer Ave 98815 509-782-2211
Jeanette Bowers, prin. Fax 782-1214

Castle Rock, Cowlitz, Pop. 2,104
Castle Rock SD 401 1,400/PK-12
600 Huntington Ave S 98611 360-501-2940
Susan Barker, supt. Fax 501-3140
www.castlerock.wednet.edu
Castle Rock ES 700/PK-6
700 Huntington Ave S 98611 360-501-2910
Henry Karnofski, prin. Fax 501-3121
Castle Rock MS 200/7-8
615 Front Ave SW 98611 360-501-2920
Tiffaney Golden, prin. Fax 501-3125

Cathlamet, Wahkiakum, Pop. 547
Wahkiakum SD 200 500/K-12
PO Box 398 98612 360-795-3971
Bob Garrett, supt. Fax 795-0545
Thomas MS 100/6-8
PO Box 398 98612 360-795-3261
Theresa Libby, prin. Fax 795-3205
Wendt ES 200/K-5
PO Box 398 98612 360-795-3261
Theresa Libby, prin. Fax 795-3205

Centerville, Klickitat
Centerville SD 215 100/K-8
2315 Centerville Hwy 98613 509-773-4893
Mike Lindhe, supt. Fax 773-4902
Centerville S 100/K-8
2315 Centerville Hwy 98613 509-773-4893
Mike Lindhe, prin. Fax 773-4902

Centralia, Lewis, Pop. 15,404
Centralia SD 401 3,500/K-12
PO Box 610 98531 360-330-7600
Steven Bodnar, supt. Fax 330-7604
www.centralia.wednet.edu
Centralia MS 500/7-8
901 Johnson Rd 98531 360-330-7619
Greg Domingos, prin. Fax 330-7622
Edison ES 300/K-3
607 H St 98531 360-330-7631
Neal Kirby, prin. Fax 807-6223
Fords Prairie ES 500/K-3
1620 Harrison Ave 98531 360-330-7633
David Roberts, prin. Fax 330-7698
Jefferson-Lincoln ES 400/K-3
400 W Summa St 98531 360-330-7636
Glenn Spinnie, prin. Fax 330-7803
Oakview ES 400/4-6
201 E Oakview Ave 98531 360-330-7638
David Carthum, prin. Fax 330-7812
Washington ES 300/4-6
800 Field Ave 98531 360-330-7641
Danielle Vekich, prin. Fax 330-7815

Centralia Christian S 200/PK-8
PO Box 1209 98531 360-736-7657
Denny Taylor, admin. Fax 807-9161

Chattaroy, Spokane
Riverside SD 416 1,800/PK-12
34515 N Newport Hwy 99003 509-464-8201
Roberta Kramer, supt. Fax 464-8206
www.riversidesd.org
Chattaroy ES 300/K-5
25717 N Yale Rd 99003 509-464-8250
Juanita Murray, prin. Fax 464-8294

Riverside ES 400/PK-5
3802 E Deer Park Milan Rd 99003 509-464-8350
Lynn Rowse, prin. Fax 464-8365
Riverside MS 400/6-8
3814 E Deer Park Milan Rd 99003 509-464-8450
Lynn Rowse, prin. Fax 464-8453

Chehalis, Lewis, Pop. 7,205
Chehalis SD 302 2,800/K-12
310 SW 16th St 98532 360-807-7200
Dr. Greg Kirsch, supt. Fax 748-8899
www.chehalis.k12.wa.us
Bennett ES 400/2-3
233 S Market Blvd 98532 360-807-7220
Kimberly Camren, prin. Fax 748-7256
Cascade ES 400/K-1
89 SW 3rd St 98532 360-807-7215
Christopher Simpson, prin. Fax 748-6167
Chehalis MS 700/6-8
1060 SW 20th St 98532 360-807-7230
James Budgett, prin. Fax 740-1849
Olympic ES 400/4-5
2057 SW Salsbury Ave 98532 360-807-7225
Brett Ellingson, prin. Fax 740-1952

Lewis County Adventist S 100/PK-10
2104 S Scheuber Rd 98532 360-748-3213
Dan Baker, prin. Fax 748-6399
St. Joseph S 200/PK-8
123 SW 6th St 98532 360-748-0961
Kendra Meek, prin. Fax 748-8502

Chelan, Chelan, Pop. 3,684
Lake Chelan SD 129 1,300/K-12
PO Box 369 98816 509-682-3515
Dr. Jim Busey, supt. Fax 682-5842
www.chelanschools.org/
Chelan MS 300/6-8
PO Box 369 98816 509-682-4073
Chris Anderson, prin. Fax 682-5001
Morgen Owings ES 500/K-5
PO Box 369 98816 509-682-4031
Jeff Peck, prin. Fax 682-3373

Cheney, Spokane, Pop. 10,356
Cheney SD 360 3,400/PK-12
520 4th St 99004 509-559-4599
Lawrence Keller, supt. Fax 559-4508
www.cheneysd.org
Betz ES 400/K-5
317 N 7th St 99004 509-559-4800
Kent Martin, prin. Fax 559-4837
Cheney MS 800/6-8
2716 N 6th St 99004 509-559-4400
Erika Burden, prin. Fax 559-4479
Salnave ES 300/K-5
1015 Salnave Rd 99004 509-559-4700
Debbie Maurus, prin. Fax 559-4740
Other Schools – See Airway Heights, Spokane

Chewelah, Stevens, Pop. 2,285
Chewelah SD 36 1,000/K-12
PO Box 47 99109 509-685-6800
Marcus Morgan, supt. Fax 935-8605
www.chewelah.k12.wa.us
Gess ES 400/K-5
PO Box 7 99109 509-685-6800
Jerry Pugh, prin. Fax 935-4860
Jenkins MS 200/6-8
PO Box 1099 99109 509-685-6800
C. Jean Homer, prin. Fax 935-4404

Chimacum, Jefferson
Chimacum SD 49 1,100/PK-12
PO Box 278 98325 360-732-4090
Mike Blair, supt. Fax 732-4336
www.csd49.org
Chimacum ES 200/3-5
PO Box 278 98325 360-732-4090
Mark Barga, prin. Fax 732-0274
Chimacum MS 200/6-8
PO Box 278 98325 360-732-4090
Whitney Meissner, prin. Fax 732-6859
Other Schools – See Port Hadlock

Clallam Bay, Clallam
Cape Flattery SD 401
Supt. — See Sekiu
Clallam Bay S 200/K-12
PO Box 337 98326 360-963-2324
Val Rieger, prin. Fax 963-2228

Clarkston, Asotin, Pop. 7,304
Clarkston SD J 250-185 2,700/K-12
PO Box 70 99403 509-758-2531
Pete Lewis, supt. Fax 758-3326
www.csdk12.org
Grantham ES 200/K-6
1253 Poplar St 99403 509-758-2503
Don Lee, prin. Fax 758-1639
Heights ES 400/K-6
1917 4th Ave 99403 509-758-8180
Samantha Ogden, prin. Fax 758-8212
Highland ES 300/K-6
1432 Highland Ave 99403 509-758-5531
Heather Lang, prin. Fax 758-5532
Lincoln MS 400/7-8
1945 4th Ave 99403 509-758-5506
Dan LejaMeyer, prin. Fax 758-7838
Parkway ES 300/K-6
1103 4th St 99403 509-758-2553
Eileen Loughney, prin. Fax 758-5020

Holy Family S 100/PK-6
1002 Chestnut St 99403 509-758-6621
Maribeth Richardson, prin. Fax 758-4997

Clearlake, Skagit
Sedro-Woolley SD 101
Supt. — See Sedro Woolley

Clearlake ES 200/K-6
PO Box 128 98235 360-855-3530
Henk Kruithof, prin. Fax 855-3531

Cle Elum, Kittitas, Pop. 1,796
Cle Elum-Roslyn SD 404 1,000/K-12
2690 State Route 903 98922 509-649-4850
Mark Flatau, supt. Fax 649-2404
www.cleelum.wednet.edu
Cle Elum-Roslyn ES 400/K-5
2696 State Route 903 98922 509-649-4700
Matt Chase, prin. Fax 649-3634
Strom MS 200/6-8
2694 State Route 903 98922 509-649-4800
Kim Headrick, prin. Fax 649-3634

Clinton, Island, Pop. 1,564

Whidbey Island Waldorf S 100/PK-8
PO Box 469 98236 360-341-5686
Maureen Marklin, admin. Fax 341-5689

Clyde Hill, King, Pop. 2,943

Bellevue Christian JHS 200/7-8
1601 98th Ave NE 98004 425-454-4028
Mike Olson, prin. Fax 454-4418

Colbert, Spokane
Mead SD 354
Supt. — See Mead
Colbert ES 600/K-6
4625 E Greenbluff Rd 99005 509-465-6300
Jared Hoadley, prin. Fax 465-6320
Midway ES 700/K-6
821 E Midway Rd 99005 509-465-6700
Ralph Thayer, prin. Fax 465-6720
Mountainside MS 600/7-8
4717 E Day Mount Spokane Rd 99005509-465-7400
Craig Busch, prin. Fax 465-7420

Colfax, Whitman, Pop. 2,780
Colfax SD 300 700/K-12
1110 N Morton St 99111 509-397-3042
Michael Morgan, supt. Fax 397-5835
www.colfax.k12.wa.us
Jennings S 400/K-8
1207 N Morton St 99111 509-397-2181
Tom Arlt, prin. Fax 397-6741

College Place, Walla Walla, Pop. 8,945
College Place SD 250 800/K-8
1755 S College Ave 99324 509-525-4827
Timothy Payne, supt. Fax 525-3741
www.cpps.org
Davis ES 300/K-3
31 SE Ash Ave 99324 509-525-5110
Chris Drabek, prin. Fax 525-0170
Meadow Brook IS 300/4-6
1775 S College Ave 99324 509-522-3265
Bill Varady, prin. Fax 522-3306
Sager MS 200/7-8
1755 S College Ave 99324 509-525-5300
Bill Varady, prin. Fax 525-3306

Rogers SDA S 300/K-8
200 SW Academy Way 99324 509-529-1850
Jim Weller, prin. Fax 529-3622

Colton, Whitman, Pop. 366
Colton SD 306 200/K-12
706 Union St 99113 509-229-3385
C. Dale Foley, supt. Fax 229-3374
www.colton.k12.wa.us
Colton S, 706 Union St 99113 200/K-12
Nate Smith, prin. 509-229-3386

Guardian Angel/St. Boniface S 50/1-8
PO Box 48 99113 509-229-3579
Lori Becker, prin.

Colville, Stevens, Pop. 5,029
Colville SD 115 1,900/K-12
217 S Hofstetter St 99114 509-684-7850
Ken Emmil, supt. Fax 684-7855
www.colsd.org
Colville JHS 400/7-8
990 S Cedar St 99114 509-684-7820
Paul Dumas, prin. Fax 684-7825
Fort Colville ES 400/3-6
1212 E Ivy Ave 99114 509-684-7830
Clayton Allen, prin. Fax 684-7831
Hofstetter ES 400/K-3
640 N Hofstetter St 99114 509-684-7690
Sherry Cowbrough, prin. Fax 684-7691

Onion Creek SD 30 50/K-8
2006 Lotze Creek Rd 99114 509-732-4240
Edwina Hargrave, supt. Fax 732-6114
www.ocsd30.org/
Onion Creek S 50/K-8
2006 Lotze Creek Rd 99114 509-732-4240
Edwina Hargrave, prin. Fax 732-6114

Colville Valley Junior Academy 50/K-10
139 E Cedar Loop 99114 509-684-6830
Richard Bergeson, prin. Fax 684-1084

Concrete, Skagit, Pop. 800
Concrete SD 11 600/K-12
45389 Airport Way 98237 360-853-8141
Barbara Hawkings, supt. Fax 853-7521
www.concrete.k12.wa.us
Concrete S 400/K-8
7838 S Superior Ave 98237 360-853-8145
Matt Whitten, prin. Fax 853-8149

Connell, Franklin, Pop. 2,980
North Franklin SD J 51-162 1,800/K-12
PO Box 829 99326 509-234-2021
Gregg Taylor, supt. Fax 234-9200
www.nfsd.k12.wa.us
Connell ES 500/K-6
PO Box 829 99326 509-234-4381
Pat Nunan, prin. Fax 234-4444
Olds JHS 300/7-8
PO Box 829 99326 509-234-3931
Jim Jacobs, prin. Fax 234-8171
Other Schools – See Mesa

Cook, Skamania
Mill A SD 31 100/K-8
1142 Jessup Rd, 509-538-2522
Dennis O'Hara, supt. Fax 538-2181
www.milla.k12.wa.us
Mill A S 100/K-8
1142 Jessup Rd, 509-538-2522
Dennis O'Hara, prin. Fax 538-2181

Cosmopolis, Grays Harbor, Pop. 1,646
Cosmopolis SD 99 200/PK-6
PO Box 479 98537 360-532-7181
Tami Hickle, supt. Fax 532-1535
www.cosmopolisschool.com/
Cosmopolis ES 200/PK-6
PO Box 479 98537 360-532-7181
Tami Hickle, prin. Fax 532-1535

North River SD 200 100/K-12
2867 N River Rd 98537 360-532-3079
David Pickering, supt. Fax 532-1738
North River S 100/K-12
2867 N River Rd 98537 360-532-3079
David Pickering, prin. Fax 532-1738

Coulee City, Grant, Pop. 637
Coulee-Hartline SD 151 100/K-12
410 Locust W 99115 509-632-8642
Dr. Edward Fisk, supt. Fax 632-5166
www.achsd.org
Coulee City S 100/K-5
410 Locust W 99115 509-632-5231
Kelley Schafer, prin. Fax 632-5166

Coulee Dam, Okanogan, Pop. 1,080
Grand Coulee Dam SD 301J 700/K-12
110 Stevens Ave 99116 509-633-2143
Jeff Loe, supt. Fax 633-2530
www.gcdsd.org
Other Schools – See Grand Coulee

Coupeville, Island, Pop. 1,813
Coupeville SD 204 1,100/K-12
2 S Main St 98239 360-678-4522
Patty Page, supt. Fax 678-4834
www.coupeville.k12.wa.us
Coupeville ES 500/K-5
6 S Main St 98239 360-678-4551
Fran McCarthy, prin. Fax 678-6810
Coupeville MS 300/6-8
501 S Main St 98239 360-678-4409
David Ebersole, prin. Fax 678-0540

Covington, King, Pop. 16,610
Kent SD 415
Supt. — See Kent
Cedar Heights MS 900/7-8
19640 SE 272nd St 98042 253-373-7620
Angela Grutko, prin. Fax 373-7628
Cedar Valley ES 400/K-6
26500 Timberlane Way SE 98042 253-373-7649
Chad Golden, prin. Fax 373-7651
Covington ES 500/K-6
17070 SE Wax Rd 98042 253-373-7652
Audrey Farris, prin. Fax 373-7654
Crestwood ES 500/K-6
25225 180th Ave SE 98042 253-373-7634
Linda Butts, prin. Fax 373-7636
Jenkins Creek ES 400/K-6
26915 186th Ave SE 98042 253-373-7331
Cathy Lendosky, prin. Fax 373-7333
Mattson MS 600/7-8
16400 SE 251st St 98042 253-373-7670
Steve Beck, prin. Fax 373-7673

Rainier Christian MS 100/7-8
26201 180th Ave SE 98042 253-639-7715
Ed Parr, admin. Fax 639-3184

Cowiche, Yakima
Highland SD 203 1,100/K-12
PO Box 38 98923 509-678-4173
Gary Masten, supt. Fax 678-4177
www.highland.wednet.edu/
Whitman-Cowiche ES 300/K-3
1181 Thompson Rd 98923 509-678-4435
Janice Sauve, prin. Fax 678-5494
Other Schools – See Tieton

Creston, Lincoln, Pop. 231
Creston SD 73 100/K-12
PO Box 17 99117 509-636-2721
William Wadlington, supt. Fax 636-2910
www.creston.wednet.edu
Creston ES 100/K-6
PO Box 17 99117 509-636-2721
William Wadlington, prin. Fax 636-2910

Curlew, Ferry
Curlew SD 50 200/K-12
PO Box 370 99118 509-779-4931
Steve McCullough, supt. Fax 779-4938
www.curlew.wednet.edu/default.htm
Curlew S 200/K-12
PO Box 370 99118 509-779-4931
Brett Simpson, prin. Fax 779-4938

Curtis, Lewis
Boistfort SD 234 100/PK-8
983 Boistfort Rd 98538 360-245-3343
Richard Apperson, supt. Fax 245-3451
Boistfort S 100/PK-8
983 Boistfort Rd 98538 360-245-3343
Richard Apperson, prin. Fax 245-3451

Cusick, Pend Oreille, Pop. 221
Cusick SD 59 300/PK-12
305 Monumental Rd 99119 509-445-1125
Dan Read, supt. Fax 445-1598
www.cusick.wednet.edu/
Herian ES 100/PK-6
305 Monumental Rd 99119 509-445-1125
Kathy Christiansen, prin. Fax 445-1598

Custer, Whatcom
Ferndale SD 502
Supt. — See Ferndale
Custer ES 400/K-6
7660 Custer School Rd 98240 360-383-9500
Kellie Larrabee, prin. Fax 383-9502

Dallesport, Klickitat
Lyle SD 406
Supt. — See Lyle
Dallesport ES 200/K-6
PO Box 529 98617 509-767-1132
Martin Huffman, prin. Fax 767-2000

Darrington, Snohomish, Pop. 1,333
Darrington SD 330 500/K-12
PO Box 27 98241 360-436-1323
Larry Johnson, supt. Fax 436-2045
www.dsd.k12.wa.us
Darrington ES 300/K-6
PO Box 27 98241 360-436-1313
Melissa Delgado, prin. Fax 436-0592

Davenport, Lincoln, Pop. 1,726
Davenport SD 207 600/PK-12
801 7th St 99122 509-725-1481
Jim Kowalkowski, supt. Fax 725-2260
www.davenport.wednet.edu/
Davenport ES 300/PK-6
1101 7th St 99122 509-725-1261
Jill Freeze, prin. Fax 725-2260

Dayton, Columbia, Pop. 2,703
Dayton SD 2 600/PK-12
609 S 2nd St 99328 509-382-2543
Richard Stewart, supt. Fax 382-2081
www.dayton.wednet.edu/
Dayton ES 300/PK-6
302 E Park St 99328 509-382-2507
Katie Leid, prin. Fax 382-2081
Dayton MS 100/7-8
609 S 2nd St 99328 509-382-2522
Katie Leid, prin. Fax 381-2081

Dayton Adventist Christian S 50/1-8
PO Box 227 99328 509-382-3139
Lana Ash, admin.

Deer Park, Spokane, Pop. 3,105
Deer Park SD 414 1,900/K-12
PO Box 490 99006 509-464-5500
Mick Miller, supt. Fax 464-5510
www.dpsd.org
Arcadia ES 400/3-5
PO Box 610 99006 509-464-5700
Bonnie Bantis, prin. Fax 464-5710
Deer Park ES 400/K-2
PO Box 609 99006 509-464-5600
Michele Miller, prin. Fax 464-5610
Deer Park MS 400/6-8
PO Box 882 99006 509-464-5800
Brent Seedall, prin. Fax 464-5810

Precious Moments Preschool 50/PK-PK
PO Box 1428 99006 509-276-5268
Kim Ferrell, dir. Fax 276-5268

Deming, Whatcom
Mt. Baker SD 507 2,300/K-12
PO Box 95 98244 360-383-2000
Dr. Richard Gantman, supt. Fax 383-2009
www.mtbaker.wednet.edu
Mt. Baker JHS 400/7-8
PO Box 95 98244 360-383-2030
Derek Forbes, prin. Fax 383-2039
Other Schools – See Acme, Bellingham, Maple Falls

Des Moines, King, Pop. 28,767
Federal Way SD 210
Supt. — See Federal Way
Woodmont S 400/K-8
26454 16th Ave S 98198 253-945-4500
Donna Bogle, prin. Fax 945-4545

Highline SD 401
Supt. — See Burien
Des Moines ES 400/K-6
22001 9th Ave S 98198 206-631-3700
Karin Jones, prin. Fax 631-3747
Midway ES 500/K-6
22447 24th Ave S 98198 206-631-4400
Ben Gauyan, prin. Fax 631-4499
North Hill ES 600/K-6
19835 8th Ave S 98148 206-433-2137
Nancy Melius, prin. Fax 433-2263
Pacific MS 700/7-8
22705 24th Ave S 98198 206-433-2581
Cecilia Beaman, prin. Fax 433-2451

Des Moines Creek Academy 50/PK-9
18635 8th Ave S 98148 206-824-4468
John Savage, hdmstr. Fax 824-7749
Grace Lutheran S 100/PK-PK
22975 24th Ave S 98198 206-878-5048

Holy Trinity Lutheran S — 100/PK-8
2021 S 260th St 98198 — 253-839-6516
Stephan Rodmyre, prin. — Fax 839-7921
St. Philomena S — 200/K-8
1815 S 220th St 98198 — 206-824-4051
Joe Budde, prin. — Fax 878-8646

Dixie, Walla Walla
Dixie SD 101 — 50/K-5
PO Box 40 99329 — 509-525-5339
Mark Wegner, supt. — Fax 525-1062
Dixie ES — 50/K-5
PO Box 40 99329 — 509-525-5339
Mark Wegner, prin. — Fax 525-1062

DuPont, Pierce, Pop. 5,374
Steilacoom Historical SD 1
Supt. — See Steilacoom
Clark ES — 400/K-3
1700 Palisade Blvd 98327 — 253-583-7100
Gary Yoho, prin. — Fax 964-0935
Pioneer MS — 500/6-8
1750 Bobs Hollow Ln 98327 — 253-983-2400
Kristi Webster, prin. — Fax 589-4892

Duvall, King, Pop. 5,710
Riverview SD 407
Supt. — See Carnation
Cherry Valley ES — 400/K-5
26701 NE Cherry Valley Rd 98019 — 425-844-4750
Darcy Becker, prin. — Fax 844-4752
Eagle Rock Multi-Age — 100/K-5
29300 NE 150th St 98019 — 425-844-4900
Judy Harris, prin. — Fax 844-4902

Duvall Christian S — 100/PK-5
PO Box 1209 98019 — 425-788-3636
Jacque Sims, prin. — Fax 788-1616

Easton, Kittitas
Easton SD 28 — 100/PK-12
PO Box 8 98925 — 509-656-2317
Patrick Dehuff, supt. — Fax 656-2585
Easton S — 100/PK-12
PO Box 8 98925 — 509-656-2317
Ron Woodruff, prin. — Fax 656-2585

Eastsound, San Juan
Orcas Island SD 137 — 500/K-12
557 School Rd 98245 — 360-376-2284
Barbara Kline, supt. — Fax 376-2283
www.orcasislandschools.org
Orcas Island ES — 200/K-6
611 School Rd 98245 — 360-376-2286
Tom Gobeske, prin. — Fax 376-5410
Orcas Island MS — 100/7-8
611 School Rd 98245 — 360-376-2287
Tom Gobeske, prin. — Fax 376-6078
Other Schools – See Waldron

Orcas Christian Day S — 100/K-12
PO Box 669 98245 — 360-376-6683
Tom Roosma, prin. — Fax 376-7642

East Wenatchee, Douglas, Pop. 8,819
Eastmont SD 206 — 5,500/K-12
460 9th St NE 98802 — 509-884-7169
Garn Christensen, supt. — Fax 884-4210
www.eastmont206.com/distoff/main/
Cascade ES — 500/K-4
2330 N Baker Ave 98802 — 509-884-0523
Robin Kirkpatrick, prin. — Fax 884-7067
Clovis Point IS — 600/5-7
1855 4th St SE 98802 — 509-888-1400
Dennis Gibson, prin. — Fax 888-1401
Grant ES — 400/K-4
1430 1st St SE 98802 — 509-884-0557
Spencer Taylor, prin. — Fax 886-7219
Kenroy ES — 400/K-4
601 N Jonathan Ave 98802 — 509-884-1443
Jon Abbott, prin. — Fax 884-0732
Lee ES — 500/K-4
1455 N Baker Ave 98802 — 509-884-1497
David Woods, prin. — Fax 886-1419
Sterling IS — 700/5-7
600 N James Ave 98802 — 509-884-7115
Chris Hall, prin. — Fax 886-7503
Other Schools – See Rock Island

Eatonville, Pierce, Pop. 2,328
Eatonville SD 404 — 2,200/K-12
PO Box 698 98328 — 360-879-1000
Raymond Arment, supt. — Fax 879-1086
cruiser.eatonville.wednet.edu/
Eatonville ES — 400/K-5
PO Box 669 98328 — 360-879-1600
Diane Heersink, prin. — Fax 879-1640
Eatonville MS — 500/6-8
PO Box 910 98328 — 360-879-1400
Ken Andersen, prin. — Fax 879-1480
Weyerhaeuser ES — 400/K-5
6105 365th St E 98328 — 360-879-1650
Pam Burke, prin. — Fax 879-1662
Other Schools – See Ashford

Edgewood, Pierce, Pop. 9,718
Fife SD 417
Supt. — See Fife
Hedden ES — 400/2-5
11313 8th St E 98372 — 253-517-1500
Julia Grubiak, prin. — Fax 517-1505

Puyallup SD 3
Supt. — See Puyallup
Mountain View ES — 300/PK-6
3411 119th Ave E 98372 — 253-841-8739
Nancy Strobel, prin. — Fax 840-8949
Northwood ES — 300/PK-6
9805 24th St E 98371 — 253-841-8740
Lisa Russell-Nolan, prin. — Fax 840-8973

Slavic Christian Academy - Edgewood — 100/K-12
10622 8th St E 98372 — 253-952-7163
Vadim Hetman, prin. — Fax 952-7164

Edmonds, Snohomish, Pop. 39,937
Edmonds SD 15
Supt. — See Lynnwood
Chase Lake Community S — 400/K-6
21603 84th Ave W 98026 — 425-431-7495
Karen Nilson, prin. — Fax 431-7493
Edmonds ES — 300/K-6
1215 Olympic Ave 98020 — 425-431-7374
Melissa Oliver, prin. — Fax 431-7372
Madrona S — 600/K-8
9300 236th St SW 98020 — 425-431-7979
Lynda Fischer, prin. — Fax 431-7985
Seaview ES — 400/K-6
8426 188th St SW 98026 — 425-431-7383
Jo Kish, prin. — Fax 431-7389
Sherwood ES — 400/K-6
22901 106th Ave W 98020 — 425-431-7460
Christine Kessler, prin. — Fax 431-7464
Westgate ES — 400/K-6
9601 220th St SW 98020 — 425-431-7470
Rob Baumgartner, prin. — Fax 431-7473

Mukilteo SD 6
Supt. — See Everett
Picnic Point ES — 400/K-5
5819 140th St SW 98026 — 425-356-1305
Lynn Olsen, prin. — Fax 356-1351
Serene Lake ES — 400/K-5
4709 Picnic Point Rd 98026 — 425-356-1307
Karen Reid, prin. — Fax 710-4334

Holy Rosary S — 200/PK-8
PO Box 206 98020 — 425-778-3197
Dr. Kathy Carr, prin. — Fax 771-8144
Westgate Chapel Preschool & K — 100/PK-K
22901 Edmonds Way 98020 — 425-775-2776
Bonnie Worthen, dir. — Fax 776-4673

Edwall, Lincoln

Christian Heritage S — 100/K-12
PO Box 118 99008 — 509-236-2224
Marty Klein, admin. — Fax 236-2224

Ellensburg, Kittitas, Pop. 16,914
Damman SD 7 — 50/K-5
41 Manastash Rd 98926 — 509-962-9079
Marsha Smith, supt. — Fax 925-2591
Damman ES — 50/K-5
41 Manastash Rd 98926 — 509-962-9076
Jacqueline Pratt, lead tchr. — Fax 962-9085

Ellensburg SD 401 — 3,000/K-12
1300 E 3rd Ave 98926 — 509-925-8000
Paul Farris, supt. — Fax 925-8025
wonders.eburg.wednet.edu/
Lincoln ES — 400/K-5
200 S Sampson St 98926 — 509-925-8050
Kevin Weberg, prin. — Fax 925-8056
Morgan MS — 700/6-8
400 E 1st Ave 98926 — 509-925-8200
Michelle Bibich, prin. — Fax 925-8202
Mount Stuart ES — 500/K-5
705 W 15th Ave 98926 — 509-925-8400
Paul Abbott, prin. — Fax 925-8407
Valley View ES — 400/K-5
1508 E 3rd Ave 98926 — 509-925-7316
Mike Nolan, prin. — Fax 925-8134

Ellensburg Christian S — 100/K-9
PO Box 426 98926 — 509-925-2411
Anna Ng, prin. — Fax 925-2435

Elma, Grays Harbor, Pop. 3,164
Elma SD 68 — 1,800/K-12
1235 Monte Elma Rd 98541 — 360-482-2822
Howard King, supt. — Fax 482-2092
www.elma.wednet.edu
Elma ES — 700/K-5
1235 Monte Elma Rd 98541 — 360-482-2632
Mark Keating, prin. — Fax 482-4565
Elma MS — 400/6-8
1235 Monte Elma Rd 98541 — 360-482-2237
Dave Demiglio, prin. — Fax 482-4872

Mary M. Knight SD 311 — 200/PK-12
2987 W Matlock Brady Rd 98541 — 360-426-6767
Tim Adsit, supt. — Fax 427-5516
mary.wa.schoolwebpages.com
Knight ES — 100/PK-6
2987 W Matlock Brady Rd 98541 — 360-426-6767
Yolanda Paez, prin. — Fax 427-5516

Endicott, Whitman, Pop. 322
Endicott SD 308 — 100/K-8
308 School Dr 99125 — 509-657-3523
Rick Winters, supt. — Fax 657-3521
www.sje.wednet.edu
Endicott ES — 50/K-6
308 School Dr 99125 — 509-657-3523
Suzanne Schmick, prin. — Fax 657-3521
Endicott-St. John MS — 50/7-8
308 School Dr 99125 — 509-657-3523
Suzanne Schmick, prin. — Fax 657-3521

Entiat, Chelan, Pop. 999
Entiat SD 127 — 400/K-12
2650 Entiat Way 98822 — 509-784-1800
Michael Wyant, supt. — Fax 784-2986
www.entiatschools.org
Rumburg ES — 200/K-6
2650 Entiat Way 98822 — 509-784-1314
Miles Caples, prin. — Fax 784-2986

Enumclaw, King, Pop. 10,896
Enumclaw SD 216 — 4,600/K-12
2929 McDougall Ave 98022 — 360-802-7100
Mike Nelson, supt. — Fax 802-7140
www.enumclaw.wednet.edu/
Enumclaw MS — 500/6-8
550 Semanski St 98022 — 360-802-7150
Steve Rabb, prin. — Fax 802-7224
Kibler ES — 500/K-5
2057 Kibler Ave 98022 — 360-802-7263
Julene Miller, prin. — Fax 802-7300
Southwood ES — 300/K-5
3240 McDougall Ave 98022 — 360-802-7370
Susan Arbury, prin. — Fax 802-7374
Sunrise ES — 400/K-5
899 Osceola St 98022 — 360-802-7425
Chris Beals, prin. — Fax 802-7427
Thunder Mountain MS — 600/6-8
42018 264th Ave SE 98022 — 360-802-7492
Virginia Callison, prin. — Fax 802-7500
Westwood ES — 400/K-5
21200 SE 416th St 98022 — 360-802-7620
Keri Marquand, prin. — Fax 802-7622
Other Schools – See Black Diamond

Gateway Christian S — 100/K-8
825 Dickson Ave 98022 — 360-802-2117
Dave Rohland, admin. — Fax 825-7671

Ephrata, Grant, Pop. 7,178
Ephrata SD 165 — 2,100/K-12
499 C St NW 98823 — 509-754-2474
Dr. Jerry Simon, supt. — Fax 754-4712
www.ephrataschools.org
Columbia Ridge ES — 400/K-4
60 H St SE 98823 — 509-754-2882
Andrea Sperline, prin. — Fax 754-4086
Ephrata MS — 400/7-8
384 A St SE 98823 — 509-754-4659
Jill Palmquist, prin. — Fax 754-5625
Grant ES — 400/K-4
451 3rd Ave NW 98823 — 509-754-4676
Shannon Criss, prin. — Fax 754-4512
Parkway ES — 300/5-6
1101 Parkway Blvd 98823 — 509-754-9729
Dawn Millard, prin. — Fax 754-5429

New Life Christian S — 100/PK-12
911 E Division Ave 98823 — 509-754-5558
Joseph Johnson, admin. — Fax 754-3540
St. Rose of Lima S — 100/PK-6
520 Nat Washington Way 98823 — 509-754-4901
Jon Lane, prin. — Fax 754-9274

Everett, Snohomish, Pop. 96,604
Everett SD 2 — 19,000/PK-12
PO Box 2098 98213 — 425-385-4000
Dr. Gary Cohn, supt. — Fax 385-4012
www.everett.k12.wa.us
Eisenhower MS — 700/6-8
10200 25th Ave SE 98208 — 425-385-7500
Sherri Kokx, prin. — Fax 385-7502
Emerson ES — 600/K-5
8702 7th Ave SE 98208 — 425-385-6200
Cynthia Jones, prin. — Fax 385-6202
Evergreen MS — 900/6-8
7621 Beverly Ln 98203 — 425-385-5700
Joyce Stewart, prin. — Fax 385-5702
Forest View ES — 400/K-5
5601 156th St SE 98208 — 425-385-7900
Brenda Fuglevand, prin. — Fax 385-7902
Garfield ES — 400/K-5
2215 Pine St 98201 — 425-385-4700
Shannon Arnim, prin. — Fax 385-4702
Gateway MS — 1,000/6-8
15404 Silver Firs Dr 98208 — 425-385-6600
Peter Scott, prin. — Fax 385-6602
Hawthorne ES — 500/PK-5
1110 Poplar St 98201 — 425-385-4600
Sara Hahn, prin. — Fax 385-4602
Jackson ES — 400/K-5
3700 Federal Ave 98201 — 425-385-5600
Janelle Phinney, prin. — Fax 385-5602
Jefferson ES — 500/K-5
2500 Cadet Way 98208 — 425-385-7400
Concie Pedroza, prin. — Fax 385-7402
Lowell ES — 500/PK-5
5010 View Dr 98203 — 425-385-5300
Colleen Welsh, prin. — Fax 385-5302
Madison ES — 500/PK-5
616 Pecks Dr 98203 — 425-385-5900
Mark Toland, prin. — Fax 385-5902
Monroe ES — 600/K-5
10901 27th Ave SE 98208 — 425-385-7300
Gerard Holzman, prin. — Fax 385-7302
North MS — 600/6-8
2514 Rainier Ave 98201 — 425-385-4800
Kelly Shepherd, prin. — Fax 385-4802
Penny Creek ES — 800/K-5
4117 132nd St SE 98208 — 425-385-7200
Shelley Petillo, prin. — Fax 385-7202
Silver Firs ES — 500/K-5
5909 146th Pl SE 98208 — 425-385-6500
Kimberly Gilmore, prin. — Fax 385-6502
Silver Lake ES — 600/PK-5
12815 Bothell Everett Hwy 98208 — 425-385-6900
Mary O'Brien, prin. — Fax 385-6902
View Ridge ES — 500/PK-5
202 Alder St 98203 — 425-385-5400
Kert Lenseigne, prin. — Fax 385-5402
Whittier ES — 400/PK-5
916 Oakes Ave 98201 — 425-385-4300
Carla Barton, prin. — Fax 385-4302
Other Schools – See Bothell, Mill Creek

Lake Stevens SD 4
Supt. — See Lake Stevens
Glenwood ES — 500/K-5
2221 103rd Ave SE 98205 — 425-335-1510
Laura Clift, prin. — Fax 335-1595

Hillcrest ES 600/PK-5
9315 4th St SE 98205 425-335-1545
Steve Burleigh, prin. Fax 335-1522
Lake Stevens MS 500/6-7
1031 91st Ave SE 98205 425-335-1544
Maureen McCoy, prin. Fax 335-1564
Skyline ES 600/K-5
1033 91st Ave SE 98205 425-335-1520
Dave Bartlow, prin. Fax 335-1587

Mukilteo SD 6 14,300/K-12
9401 Sharon Dr 98204 425-356-1274
Marci Larsen, supt. Fax 356-1310
www.mukilteo.wednet.edu
Challenger ES 600/K-5
9600 Holly Dr 98204 425-356-1250
Dirk Adkinson, prin. Fax 356-1270
Discovery ES 600/K-5
11700 Meridian Ave S 98208 425-356-1735
Rosalynn Schott, prin. Fax 710-4300
Explorer MS 900/6-8
9600 Sharon Dr 98204 425-356-1240
Ali Williams, prin. Fax 356-1288
Fairmount ES 700/K-5
11401 Beverly Park Rd 98204 425-356-1301
Tim Redmond, prin. Fax 710-4311
Horizon ES 700/K-5
222 W Casino Rd 98204 425-356-1333
Leslie Clauson, prin. Fax 356-1313
Odyssey ES 700/K-5
13025 17th Ave W 98204 425-356-1303
Cheryl Boze, prin. Fax 710-4317
Olivia Park ES 600/K-5
200 108th St SW 98204 425-356-1302
Edie Reclusado, prin. Fax 356-1317
Voyager MS 900/6-8
11711 4th Ave W 98204 425-356-1730
Wes Bailey, prin. Fax 290-3747
Other Schools – See Edmonds, Mukilteo

Snohomish SD 201
Supt. — See Snohomish
Seattle Hill ES 800/K-6
12711 51st Ave SE 98208 360-563-4675
Paula Nelson, prin. Fax 563-4680

Cedar Park Christian S 200/PK-8
13000 21st Dr SE 98208 425-337-6992
Curt Frunz, prin. Fax 357-9399
Everett Christian S 100/PK-8
2221 Cedar St 98201 425-259-3213
Matthew Kamps, prin. Fax 259-0721
Forest Park Adventist Christian S 50/K-8
4120 Federal Ave 98203 425-258-6911
Sheri Rodman, prin. Fax 339-8896
Immaculate Conception S 400/PK-8
2508 Hoyt Ave 98201 425-349-7777
Pat Green, prin. Fax 349-7048
Montessori S of Snohomish County 200/PK-12
1804 Puget Dr 98203 425-355-1311
Kathleen Gunnell, admin. Fax 347-1000
Northshore Christian Academy 700/PK-8
5700 23rd Dr W 98203 425-407-1119
Holly Leach, prin. Fax 407-1317
St. Mary Magdalen S 400/PK-8
8615 7th Ave SE 98208 425-353-7559
Sr. Joanne McCauley Ed.D., prin. Fax 356-2687
Valley View Christian S 50/PK-12
9717 31st Ave SE 98208 425-337-8868
Richard Wold, prin. Fax 337-9229
Zion Lutheran S 200/PK-8
3923 103rd Ave SE 98205 425-334-5064
Lynne Hereth, prin. Fax 334-4106

Everson, Whatcom, Pop. 2,067
Meridian SD 505
Supt. — See Bellingham
Reither PS 400/PK-3
954 E Hemmi Rd 98247 360-398-2111
Lynne Jermunson, prin. Fax 398-8340
Ten Mile Creek ES 200/4-5
960 E Hemmi Rd 98247 360-398-8018
David Forsythe, prin. Fax 398-1097

Nooksack Valley SD 506 1,700/PK-12
3326 E Badger Rd 98247 360-988-4754
Mark Johnson, supt. Fax 988-8983
www.nooksackschools.org
Everson ES 200/K-5
216 Everson Goshen Rd 98247 360-966-2030
Kevin DeVere, prin. Fax 966-0945
Nooksack ES 300/K-5
3333 Breckenridge Rd 98247 360-966-3321
Cindy Tjoelker, prin. Fax 966-7512
Other Schools – See Nooksack, Sumas

Fairchild AFB, Spokane, Pop. 4,854
Medical Lake SD 326
Supt. — See Medical Lake
Anderson ES 500/PK-6
400 W Fairchild Hwy 99011 509-565-3600
Mandi Poindexter, prin. Fax 565-3601

Fall City, King, Pop. 1,582
Snoqualmie Valley SD 410
Supt. — See Snoqualmie
Chief Kanim MS 700/6-8
PO Box 639 98024 425-831-8225
Kirk Dunckel, prin. Fax 831-8290
Fall City ES 600/K-5
PO Box 220 98024 425-831-4000
Dan Schlotfeldt, prin. Fax 831-4010

Farmington, Whitman, Pop. 142

Farmington SDA S, PO Box 187 99128 50/1-8
Jennifer Wintermeyer, lead tchr. 509-287-2601

Federal Way, King, Pop. 83,088
Federal Way SD 210 22,500/PK-12
31405 18th Ave S 98003 253-945-2000
Tom Murphy, supt. Fax 945-2001
www.fwps.org
Adelaide ES 400/K-5
1635 SW 304th St 98023 253-945-2300
Jason Smith, prin. Fax 945-2323
Brigadoon ES 400/K-5
3601 SW 336th St 98023 253-945-2400
Christine Odell, prin. Fax 945-2424
Enterprise ES 400/PK-5
35101 5th Ave SW 98023 253-945-2600
Margot Hightower, prin. Fax 945-2626
Green Gables ES 400/PK-5
32607 47th Ave SW 98023 253-945-2700
Diane Holt, prin. Fax 945-2727
Hill ES 400/PK-5
5830 S 300th St 98001 253-945-3200
Cindy Kelsey, prin. Fax 945-3232
Illahee MS 700/6-8
36001 1st Ave S 98003 253-945-4600
Stacy Lucas, prin. Fax 945-4646
Lake Grove ES 400/K-5
303 SW 308th St 98023 253-945-2900
Kristi White, prin. Fax 945-2929
Lakota MS 700/6-8
1415 SW 314th St 98023 253-945-4800
Pam Tuggle, prin. Fax 945-4848
Mirror Lake ES 400/K-5
625 S 314th St 98003 253-945-3300
Kent Cross, prin. Fax 945-3333
Nautilus S 400/K-8
1000 S 289th St 98003 253-945-3400
Cynthia Black, prin. Fax 945-3434
Olympic View ES 400/K-5
2626 SW 327th St 98023 253-945-3500
Cindy Dracobly, prin. Fax 945-3535
Panther Lake ES 400/K-5
34424 1st Ave S 98003 253-945-3600
Rudy Baca, prin. Fax 945-3636
Sacajawea MS 700/6-8
1101 S Dash Point Rd 98003 253-945-4900
Randy Kaczor, prin. Fax 945-4949
Saghalie MS 600/6-8
33914 19th Ave SW 98023 253-945-5000
Damon Hunter, prin. Fax 945-5050
Sherwood Forest ES 500/K-5
34600 12th Ave SW 98023 253-945-3800
Barbara Bergman, prin. Fax 945-3838
Silver Lake ES 500/K-5
1310 SW 325th Pl 98023 253-945-3900
Michael Swartz, prin. Fax 945-3939
Twain ES 500/PK-5
2450 S Star Lake Rd 98003 253-945-3100
Douglas Rutherford, prin. Fax 945-3131
Twin Lakes ES 400/PK-5
4400 SW 320th St 98023 253-945-4200
Guy Gamble, prin. Fax 945-4242
Wildwood ES 500/PK-5
2405 S 300th St 98003 253-945-4400
Jenna Brown, prin. Fax 945-4444
Other Schools – See Auburn, Des Moines, Kent

Brooklake Christian S 400/PK-8
629 S 356th St 98003 253-838-7522
Cathy Guy, admin. Fax 661-7366
Christian Faith S 300/PK-12
33645 20th Ave S 98003 253-943-2500
Dr. Natalie Ellington, prin. Fax 943-2493
Life Academy of Puget Sound 100/1-12
414 SW 312th St 98023 253-839-7378
Sue Austin, admin. Fax 839-1031
St. Luke Lutheran S 200/PK-K
515 S 312th St 98003 253-941-3000
Mitzie Ollila, dir. Fax 941-8994
St. Vincent De Paul S 300/K-8
30527 8th Ave S 98003 253-839-3532
Wanda Stewart, prin. Fax 946-1247
Spring Valley Montessori S 100/PK-8
36605 Pacific Hwy S 98003 253-927-2557
Gulsevin Kayihan, dir. Fax 838-5193

Ferndale, Whatcom, Pop. 9,977
Ferndale SD 502 4,700/PK-12
PO Box 698 98248 360-383-9200
Linda Quinn, supt. Fax 383-9201
www.ferndale.wednet.edu
Cascadia ES PK-6
PO Box 2009 98248 360-383-2300
Nick Payne, prin. Fax 383-2302
Central ES 300/K-6
PO Box 187 98248 360-383-9600
Mischa Burnett, prin. Fax 383-9602
Eagleridge ES 600/PK-6
PO Box 1127 98248 360-383-9700
K. John Fairbairn, prin. Fax 383-9702
Horizon MS 400/7-8
PO Box 1769 98248 360-383-9850
David Hutchinson, prin. Fax 383-9852
Mountain View ES 400/PK-6
PO Box 935 98248 360-383-9650
Georgia Dellinger, prin. Fax 383-9652
Skyline ES 500/PK-6
PO Box 905 98248 360-383-9450
Linda Melland, prin. Fax 383-9452
Vista MS 400/7-8
PO Box 1328 98248 360-383-9370
Mary Kanikeberg, prin. Fax 383-9372
Other Schools – See Custer, Lummi Island

Fife, Pierce, Pop. 5,567
Fife SD 417 3,300/K-12
5802 20th St E 98424 253-517-1000
Dr. Stephen McCammon, supt. Fax 517-1055
www.fifeschools.com
Other Schools – See Edgewood, Milton

Forks, Clallam, Pop. 3,192
Queets-Clearwater SD 20 50/K-8
146000 Highway 101 98331 360-962-2395
Michael Ferguson, supt. Fax 962-2038
Queets-Clearwater S 50/K-8
146000 Highway 101 98331 360-962-2395
Michael Ferguson, prin. Fax 962-2038

Quillayute Valley SD 402 1,200/PK-12
411 S Spartan Ave 98331 360-374-6262
Diana Reaume, supt. Fax 374-6990
www.forks.wednet.edu
Forks ES 500/PK-5
301 S Elderberry Ave 98331 360-374-6262
Lisa White, prin. Fax 374-2363
Forks MS 300/6-8
121 S Spartan Ave 98331 360-374-6262
Patti Fouts, prin. Fax 374-2362

Fort Lewis, Pierce, Pop. 22,224
Clover Park SD 400
Supt. — See Lakewood
Beachwood ES 500/K-5
8583 American Lake Ave 98433 253-583-5200
Josh Zarling, prin. Fax 583-5208
Clarkmoor ES 300/K-5
2090 S Division St 98433 253-583-5220
Molly Click, prin. Fax 583-5228
Evergreen ES 700/PK-5
9010 Blaine St 98433 253-583-5250
Holly Shaffer, prin. Fax 583-5258
Greenwood ES 300/PK-5
5190 N Division St 98433 253-583-5260
Angela Wolfe, prin. Fax 583-5268
Hillside ES 400/K-5
6399 Magnolia Blvd 98433 253-583-5280
Harjeet Sandhu-Fuller, prin. Fax 583-5288

Friday Harbor, San Juan, Pop. 2,096
San Juan Island SD 149 900/K-12
PO Box 458 98250 360-378-4133
Michael Soltman, supt. Fax 378-6276
www.sjisd.wednet.edu
Friday Harbor ES 400/K-5
PO Box 458 98250 360-378-5209
Gary Pflueger, prin. Fax 378-3405
Friday Harbor MS 200/6-8
PO Box 458 98250 360-378-5214
Ann Spratt, prin. Fax 378-9750
Other Schools – See Stuart Island

Garfield, Whitman, Pop. 632
Garfield SD 302 100/PK-8
PO Box 398 99130 509-635-1331
Zane Wells, supt. Fax 635-1332
www.garpal.wednet.edu
Garfield ES 50/PK-5
PO Box 398 99130 509-635-1331
Zane Wells, prin. Fax 635-1332
Garfield-Palouse MS 50/6-8
PO Box 398 99130 509-635-1331
Zane Wells, prin. Fax 635-1332

Gifford, Stevens
Evergreen SD 205 50/K-6
3341 Addy Gifford Rd 99131 509-722-6084
Lois Patterson, supt. Fax 722-6085
Evergreen ES 50/K-6
3341 Addy Gifford Rd 99131 509-722-6384
Windy Esvelt, lead tchr. Fax 722-6384

Gig Harbor, Pierce, Pop. 6,620
Peninsula SD 401 9,400/PK-12
14015 62nd Ave NW 98332 253-530-1000
Terry Bouck, supt. Fax 530-1010
www.peninsula.wednet.edu
Artondale ES 600/PK-5
6219 40th St NW 98335 253-530-1100
Kathy Weymiller, prin. Fax 530-1120
Discovery ES 500/K-5
4905 Rosedale St NW 98335 253-530-1200
David Brooks, prin. Fax 530-1220
Goodman MS 600/6-8
3701 38th Ave NW 98335 253-530-1600
Scott McDaniel, prin. Fax 858-5515
Harbor Heights ES 600/PK-5
4002 36th St NW 98335 253-530-1800
Mary Godwin-Austen, prin. Fax 530-1820
Harbor Ridge MS 500/6-8
9010 Prentice Ave 98332 253-530-1900
Connie West, prin. Fax 530-1920
Kopachuck MS 600/6-8
10414 56th St NW 98335 253-530-4100
Iva Scott, prin. Fax 265-8810
Minter Creek ES 400/K-5
12617 118th Ave NW 98329 253-530-4300
Steve Leitz, prin. Fax 530-4320
Purdy ES 600/PK-5
13815 62nd Ave NW 98332 253-530-4600
Jim Rudsit, prin. Fax 530-4620
Voyager ES 600/K-5
5615 Kopachuck Dr NW 98335 253-530-4800
Patty McClelland, prin. Fax 530-4820
Other Schools – See Lakebay, Vaughn

Gig Harbor Academy 100/PK-5
6820 32nd St NW 98335 253-265-2150
Vince Fragasso, hdmstr. Fax 265-8124
Harbor Montessori 100/PK-8
5414 Comte Dr NW 98335 253-851-5722
Sonya Cary, dir. Fax 851-5976
Hosanna Christian S 100/PK-8
3114 45th Street Ct NW 98335 253-851-8952
Laurie Zurinsky, prin. Fax 851-9971
Lighthouse Christian S 400/K-8
3008 36th St NW 98335 253-858-5962
Debbie Schindler, admin. Fax 858-8911
Peninsula Lutheran S 50/PK-PK
6509 38th Ave NW 98335 253-851-3511
Judy Summerer, dir.

Providence Christian S of Gig Harbor 50/K-7
PO Box 582 98335 253-858-5437
Carolyn Curles, admin.
St. Nicholas S 200/K-8
3555 Edwards Dr 98335 253-858-7632
Michael Sweeney, prin. Fax 858-1597

Glenwood, Klickitat
Glenwood SD 401 50/K-12
PO Box 12 98619 509-364-3438
Dr. Shane Couch, supt. Fax 364-3689
www.glenwood.k12.wa.us/
Glenwood S 50/K-12
PO Box 12 98619 509-364-3438
Dr. Shane Couch, prin. Fax 364-3689

Gold Bar, Snohomish, Pop. 2,286
Sultan SD 311
Supt. — See Sultan
Gold Bar ES 400/K-5
419 Lewis Ave 98251 360-793-9840
Deloris Babcock, prin. Fax 793-4158

Goldendale, Klickitat, Pop. 3,713
Goldendale SD 404 1,100/K-12
604 E Brooks St 98620 509-773-5177
Mark Heid, supt. Fax 773-6028
www.golden.wednet.edu
Goldendale MS 300/5-8
520 E Collins St 98620 509-773-4323
Dave Barta, prin. Fax 773-4579
Goldendale PS 400/K-4
820 S Schuster Ave 98620 509-773-4665
Thaynan Knowlton, prin. Fax 773-6602

Goldendale SDA S 50/1-8
PO Box 241 98620 509-773-3120
Lois Potterton, admin.

Graham, Pierce
Bethel SD 403
Supt. — See Spanaway
Centennial ES 700/K-6
24323 54th Ave E 98338 253-683-7700
Tamie Wright, prin. Fax 683-7798
Graham ES 800/K-6
10026 204th St E 98338 253-683-8500
Rob Haugen, prin. Fax 683-8598
Kapowsin ES 500/K-6
10412 264th St E 98338 253-683-8600
Machelle Beilke, prin. Fax 683-8698
Nelson ES PK-6
22109 108th Ave E 98338 253-683-6400
Kelley Boynton, prin. Fax 683-6498
North Star ES 600/K-6
7719 224th St E 98338 253-683-8800
Kris Hillius, prin. Fax 683-8898
Rocky Ridge ES 600/K-6
6514 260th St E 98338 253-683-5000
Leita Earl, prin. Fax 683-5098

South Sound Christian S 200/PK-6
25713 70th Ave E 98338 253-847-2643
Robert White, supt. Fax 847-4899

Grand Coulee, Grant, Pop. 925
Grand Coulee Dam SD 301J
Supt. — See Coulee Dam
Center ES 200/K-4
PO Box F 99133 509-633-0730
Susan Hinton, prin. Fax 633-2652
Grand Coulee Dam MS 200/5-8
PO Box J 99133 509-633-1520
Lisa Lakin, prin. Fax 633-2257

Grandview, Yakima, Pop. 8,908
Grandview SD 200 3,200/K-12
913 W 2nd St 98930 509-882-8500
Kevin Chase, supt. Fax 882-2029
www.grandview.wednet.edu
Grandview MS 700/6-8
1401 W 2nd St 98930 509-882-8600
Jack Dalton, prin. Fax 882-3538
McClure ES 600/K-5
811 W 2nd St 98930 509-882-7100
Jose Rivera, prin. Fax 882-5041
Smith ES 500/K-5
205 Fir St 98930 509-882-8700
Jared Lind, prin. Fax 882-5871
Thompson ES 500/K-5
1105 W 2nd St 98930 509-882-8550
Julie Wysong, prin. Fax 882-5947

Grandview Junior Academy 50/PK-8
106 N Elm St 98930 509-882-3817
Sandra Olson, prin.

Granger, Yakima, Pop. 2,836
Granger SD 204 1,400/PK-12
701 E Ave 98932 509-854-1515
Timothy Dunn, supt. Fax 854-1126
www.gsd.wednet.edu
Granger MS 500/5-8
501 Bailey Ave 98932 509-854-1003
Lisa Rosberg, prin. Fax 854-1083
Roosevelt ES 600/PK-4
405 Bailey Ave 98932 509-854-1420
Janet Wheaton, prin. Fax 854-1281

Granite Falls, Snohomish, Pop. 2,863
Granite Falls SD 332 2,400/K-12
307 N Alder St 98252 360-691-7717
Karen Koschak, supt. Fax 691-4459
www.gfalls.wednet.edu
Granite Falls MS 600/6-8
205 N Alder St 98252 360-691-7710
Dave Bianchini, prin. Fax 691-3726
Monte Cristo ES 500/K-5
1201 100th St NE 98252 360-691-7718
Kari Henderson-Burke, prin. Fax 691-2673
Mountain Way ES 600/K-5
702 N Granite Ave 98252 360-691-7719
Cathie West, prin. Fax 691-3724

Grapeview, Mason, Pop. 1,526
Grapeview SD 54 200/K-8
822 E Mason Benson Rd 98546 360-426-4921
Dale Almlie, supt. Fax 427-8975
gsd54.org/
Grapeview S 200/K-8
822 E Mason Benson Rd 98546 360-426-4921
Joan Jensen, prin. Fax 427-8975

Harrah, Yakima, Pop. 508
Mount Adams SD 209
Supt. — See White Swan
Harrah ES 600/PK-6
PO Box 159 98933 509-848-2935
Charles Cook, prin. Fax 848-2770

Harrah Community Christian S 50/PK-8
PO Box 68 98933 509-848-2418
Marie Wegmuller, admin. Fax 848-2662

Harrington, Lincoln, Pop. 420
Harrington SD 204 100/K-12
PO Box 204 99134 509-253-4331
Monte Swenson, supt. Fax 456-6306
www.harrsd.k12.wa.us
Harrington ES 100/K-6
PO Box 204 99134 509-253-4331
Cindy Leonard, prin. Fax 456-6306

Hoquiam, Grays Harbor, Pop. 9,030
Hoquiam SD 28 2,000/K-12
305 Simpson Ave 98550 360-538-8200
Mike Parker, supt. Fax 538-8202
Central ES 300/2-6
310 Simpson Ave 98550 360-538-8230
Mia Benjamin, prin. Fax 538-8232
Emerson ES 200/K-1
101 W Emerson Ave 98550 360-538-8240
Traci Sandstrom, prin. Fax 538-8242
Hoquiam MS 300/7-8
200 Spencer St 98550 360-538-8220
Diane Golob, prin. Fax 538-8222
Lincoln ES 200/2-6
700 Wood Ave 98550 360-538-8250
Sheryl O'Brien, prin. Fax 538-8252
Washington ES 200/2-6
3003 Cherry St 98550 360-538-8260
Wes Harris, prin. Fax 538-8262

Hunters, Stevens
Columbia SD 206 200/PK-12
PO Box 7 99137 509-722-3311
B. Paul Turner, supt. Fax 722-3310
www.columbia206.k12.wa.us/
Columbia S 200/PK-12
PO Box 7 99137 509-722-3311
Chuck Wyborney, prin. Fax 722-3310

Inchelium, Ferry, Pop. 393
Inchelium SD 70 100/K-12
PO Box 285 99138 509-722-6181
Ron Washington, supt. Fax 722-6192
www.inchelium.wednet.edu
Inchelium S 100/K-12
PO Box 285 99138 509-722-6181
Ricke Swaim, prin. Fax 722-6192

Index, Snohomish, Pop. 162
Index SD 63 50/PK-7
PO Box 237 98256 360-793-1330
Martin Boyle, supt. Fax 793-2835
www.index.k12.wa.us
Index ES 50/PK-7
PO Box 237 98256 360-793-1330
Martin Boyle, prin. Fax 793-2835

Issaquah, King, Pop. 17,059
Issaquah SD 411 16,100/PK-12
565 NW Holly St 98027 425-837-7000
Steve Rasmussen, supt. Fax 837-7005
www.issaquah.wednet.edu
Beaver Lake MS 1,000/6-8
25025 SE 32nd St 98029 425-837-4150
Josh Almy, prin. Fax 837-4195
Challenger ES 600/K-5
25200 SE Klahanie Blvd 98029 425-837-7550
Robin Earl, prin. Fax 837-5159
Clark ES 300/K-5
500 2nd Ave SE 98027 425-837-6300
Sue McPeak, prin. Fax 837-6251
Discovery ES 600/PK-5
2300 228th Ave SE 98075 425-837-4100
Tera Coyle, prin. Fax 837-4030
Endeavour ES 600/K-5
26205 SE Issqh Fall City Rd 98029 425-837-7350
Jodi Bongard, prin. Fax 837-7335
Grand Ridge ES 700/K-5
1739 NE Park Dr 98029 425-837-7925
Barb Walton, prin. Fax 837-7926
Issaquah MS 900/6-8
400 1st Ave SE 98027 425-837-6800
Corrine DeRosa, prin. Fax 837-6855
Issaquah Valley ES 400/K-5
555 NW Holly St 98027 425-837-7200
Jennell Hawthorne, prin. Fax 837-7175
Pine Lake MS 900/6-8
3200 228th Ave SE 98075 425-837-5700
Roy Adler, prin. Fax 837-5762
Sunny Hills ES 600/K-5
3200 Issqah Pine Lake Rd SE 98075 425-837-7400
Sarah White, prin. Fax 837-7402
Other Schools – See Bellevue, Newcastle, Renton, Sammamish

St. Joseph S 400/PK-8
220 Mt Park Blvd SW 98027 425-313-9129
Peg Johnston, prin. Fax 313-7296
Sammamish Christian S & Noah's Ark Pre S 300/PK-3
4221 228th Ave SE Ste B 98029 425-392-7470
Fax 392-3395

Joyce, Clallam
Crescent SD 313 200/K-12
PO Box 20 98343 360-928-3311
Tom Anderson, supt. Fax 928-3066
www.crescent.wednet.edu
Cresent ES 100/K-6
PO Box 20 98343 360-928-3311
Tom Anderson, prin. Fax 928-3066

Kahlotus, Franklin, Pop. 231
Kahlotus SD 56 100/K-12
PO Box 69 99335 509-282-3338
Randy Behrens, supt. Fax 282-3339
Kahlotus ES 50/K-6
PO Box 69 99335 509-282-3338
Ron Hopkins, prin. Fax 282-3339

Kalama, Cowlitz, Pop. 1,938
Kalama SD 402 1,000/K-12
548 China Garden Rd 98625 360-673-5282
James Sutton, supt. Fax 673-5228
www.kalama.k12.wa.us
Kalama ES 400/K-5
548 China Garden Rd 98625 360-673-5207
Jeanne Klahn, prin. Fax 673-5265

Keller, Ferry
Keller SD 3 50/K-6
PO Box 367 99140 509-634-4325
Dave Iverson, supt. Fax 634-4330
www.keller.k12.wa.us
Keller ES 50/K-6
PO Box 367 99140 509-634-4325
Dave Iverson, prin. Fax 634-4330

Kelso, Cowlitz, Pop. 11,854
Kelso SD 458 5,300/PK-12
601 Crawford St 98626 360-501-1900
Glenys Hill, supt. Fax 501-1902
www.kelso.wednet.edu
Barnes ES 400/PK-5
401 Barnes St 98626 360-501-1500
Brenda Ward, prin. Fax 501-1510
Butler Acres ES 400/K-5
1609 Burcham St 98626 360-501-1600
Cindy Cromwell, prin. Fax 501-1610
Catlin ES 300/K-5
404 Long Ave 98626 360-501-1550
Nancy Gill, prin. Fax 501-1560
Coweeman MS 600/6-8
2000 Allen St 98626 360-501-1750
Randy Heath, prin. Fax 501-1782
Huntington JHS 600/6-8
500 Redpath St 98626 360-501-1700
Elaine Cockrell, prin. Fax 501-1723
Rose Valley ES 200/K-5
1502 Rose Valley Rd 98626 360-501-1400
Tom Markley, prin. Fax 501-1420
Wallace ES 300/K-5
410 Elm St 98626 360-501-1650
Don Iverson, prin. Fax 501-1660
Other Schools – See Carrolls, Longview

Kelso-Longview SDA S 100/PK-8
96 Garden St 98626 360-423-9250
Tracy Lang, admin. Fax 578-5907

Kenmore, King, Pop. 19,564
Northshore SD 417
Supt. — See Bothell
Arrowhead ES 400/K-6
6725 NE Arrowhead Dr 98028 425-408-4000
Peter Misner, prin. Fax 408-4002
Kenmore ES 500/K-6
19121 71st Ave NE 98028 425-408-4800
Nancy Young, prin. Fax 408-4802
Moorlands ES 600/K-6
15115 84th Ave NE 98028 425-408-5100
Bethel Santos, prin. Fax 408-5102

Kennewick, Benton, Pop. 60,997
Finley SD 53 1,000/PK-12
224606 E Game Farm Rd 99337 509-586-3217
Suzanne Feeney, supt. Fax 586-4408
www.finleysd.org
Finley ES 400/PK-5
213504 E Cougar Rd 99337 509-586-7577
LaVonne DeFilippis, prin. Fax 586-8239
Finley MS 200/6-8
37208 S Finley Rd 99337 509-586-7561
Michael Harrington, prin. Fax 582-8452

Kennewick SD 17 14,600/K-12
524 S Auburn St 99336 509-222-5000
Dave Bond, supt. Fax 222-5050
www.ksd.org
Amistad ES 500/K-5
930 W 4th Ave 99336 509-222-5100
Lori McCord, prin. Fax 222-5101
Canyon View ES 500/K-5
1229 W 22nd Ave 99337 509-222-5200
Brenda Mehlenbacher, prin. Fax 222-5201
Cascade ES 500/K-5
505 S Highland Dr 99337 509-222-5300
Chad Foltz, prin. Fax 222-5301
Desert Hills MS 800/6-8
6011 W 10th Pl 99338 509-222-6600
Steve Jones, prin. Fax 222-6601
Eastgate ES 500/K-5
910 E 10th Ave 99336 509-222-5400
Mark Stephens, prin. Fax 222-5401
Edison ES 400/K-5
201 S Dawes St 99336 509-222-5500
Bruce Cannard, prin. Fax 222-5501
Hawthorne ES 500/K-5
3520 W John Day Ave 99336 509-222-5600
Craig Miller, prin. Fax 222-5601

Highlands MS 800/6-8
425 S Tweedt St 99336 509-222-6700
Scott Parker, prin. Fax 222-6701
Horse Heaven Hills MS 900/6-8
3500 S Vancouver St 99337 509-222-6800
Susan Denslow, prin. Fax 222-6801
Lincoln ES 500/K-5
4901 W 20th Ave 99338 509-222-5700
Doug Campbell, prin. Fax 222-5701
Park MS 800/6-8
1011 W 10th Ave 99336 509-222-6900
Kevin Pierce, prin. Fax 222-6901
Ridge View ES 500/K-5
7001 W 13th Ave 99338 509-222-5800
Lori Butler, prin. Fax 222-5801
Southgate ES 600/K-5
3121 W 19th Ave 99337 509-222-5900
Mary Ann Kautzky, prin. Fax 222-5901
Sunset View ES 600/K-5
711 N Center Pkwy 99336 509-222-6000
Debra Mensik, prin. Fax 222-6001
Vista ES 400/K-5
1701 N Young St 99336 509-222-6100
Matt Scott, prin. Fax 222-6101
Washington ES 500/K-5
105 W 21st Ave 99337 509-222-6200
Rob Phillips, prin. Fax 222-6201
Westgate ES 400/K-5
2514 W 4th Ave 99336 509-222-6300
Dale Kern, prin. Fax 222-6301

Bethlehem Lutheran S 200/PK-8
1409 S Garfield St 99337 509-582-5624
Linda Hardy, prin. Fax 586-6702
St. Joseph S 400/PK-8
901 W 4th Ave 99336 509-586-0481
Kathleen Cleary, prin. Fax 585-9781

Kent, King, Pop. 81,800
Federal Way SD 210
Supt. — See Federal Way
Star Lake ES 500/K-5
4014 S 270th St 98032 253-945-4000
Mindy Thompson, prin. Fax 945-4040
Sunnycrest ES 400/K-5
24629 42nd Ave S 98032 253-945-4100
Tom Capp, prin. Fax 945-4141
Totem MS 700/6-8
26630 40th Ave S 98032 253-945-5100
Christine Baker, prin. Fax 945-5151

Kent SD 415 26,900/K-12
12033 SE 256th St 98030 253-373-7000
Dr. Barbara Grohe, supt. Fax 373-7231
www.kent.k12.wa.us
Daniel ES 400/K-6
11310 SE 248th St, 253-373-7615
Janet Muldrow, prin. Fax 373-7617
East Hill ES 600/K-6
9825 S 240th St 98031 253-373-7455
Kyle Good, prin. Fax 373-7457
Emerald Park ES 500/K-6
11800 SE 216th St 98031 253-373-3850
Dean Ficken, prin. Fax 373-3852
Grass Lake ES 400/K-6
28700 191st Pl SE 98042 253-373-7661
Sandra Hart, prin. Fax 373-7663
Horizon ES 600/K-6
27641 144th Ave SE 98042 253-373-7313
Melanie Strey, prin. Fax 373-7324
Kent ES 500/K-6
24700 64th Ave S 98032 253-373-7497
Sherilyn Ulland, prin. Fax 373-7499
Lake Youngs ES 500/K-6
19660 142nd Ave SE 98042 253-373-7646
Chris Banks, prin. Fax 373-7648
Meadow Ridge ES 600/K-6
27710 108th Ave SE, 253-373-7870
Bonnie Wong, prin. Fax 373-7877
Meridian ES 700/K-6
25621 140th Ave SE 98042 253-373-7664
Stan Jaskot, prin. Fax 373-7666
Meridian MS 600/7-8
23480 120th Ave SE 98031 253-373-7383
Doug Boushey, prin. Fax 373-7395
Mill Creek MS 700/7-8
620 Central Ave N 98032 253-373-7446
Anthony Brown, prin. Fax 373-7478
Millennium ES 500/K-6
11919 SE 270th St, 253-373-3900
Carla Janes, prin. Fax 373-3905
Neely-O'Brien ES 600/K-6
6300 S 236th St 98032 253-373-7434
Jody Metzger, prin. Fax 373-7458
Panther Lake ES 500/K-6
20831 108th Ave SE 98031 253-373-7470
Beth Wallen, prin. Fax 373-7472
Park Orchard ES 500/K-6
11010 SE 232nd St 98031 253-373-7473
Christine Castillo, prin. Fax 373-7475
Pine Tree ES 500/K-6
27825 118th Ave SE, 253-373-7687
LaWonda Smith, prin. Fax 373-7688
Scenic Hill ES 500/K-6
26025 Woodland Way S, 253-373-7479
Wallace Clausen, prin. Fax 373-7481
Soos Creek ES 400/K-6
12651 SE 218th Pl 98031 253-373-7690
Patty Drobny, prin. Fax 373-7692
Sortun ES 500/K-6
12711 SE 248th St, 253-373-7314
Greg Kroll, prin. Fax 373-7316
Springbrook ES 400/K-6
20035 100th Ave SE 98031 253-373-7485
Gaynell Walker, prin. Fax 373-7487
Sunrise ES 500/K-6
22300 132nd Ave SE 98042 253-373-7630
Jennifer Reuland, prin. Fax 373-7632
Other Schools – See Black Diamond, Covington, Renton

Sunbeams Lutheran S 100/PK-2
23810 112th Ave SE 98031 253-854-3240
Denise Pacilli, dir. Fax 854-2721

Kettle Falls, Stevens, Pop. 1,588
Kettle Falls SD 212 800/K-12
PO Box 458 99141 509-738-6625
Greg Goodnight, supt. Fax 738-6375
www.kettlefalls.wednet.edu/
Kettle Falls ES 300/K-4
PO Box 458 99141 509-738-6725
Val McKern, prin. Fax 738-2234
Kettle Falls MS 300/5-8
PO Box 458 99141 509-738-6014
Tom Graham, prin. Fax 738-2401

Kingston, Kitsap, Pop. 1,270
North Kitsap SD 400
Supt. — See Poulsbo
Gordon ES 500/PK-5
26331 Barber Cut Off Rd NE 98346 360-394-6700
Claudia Alves, prin. Fax 394-6701
Kingston MS 500/6-8
9000 NE West Kingston Rd 98346 360-394-4900
Susan Wistrand, prin. Fax 394-4901
Wolfle ES 400/PK-5
27089 Highland Rd NE 98346 360-394-6800
Ben Degnin, prin. Fax 394-6801

Kirkland, King, Pop. 45,814
Lake Washington SD 414
Supt. — See Redmond
Bell ES 400/K-6
11212 NE 112th St 98033 425-822-7450
Curtis Anderson, prin. Fax 822-0794
Community ES 100/1-6
11133 NE 65th St 98033 425-827-0735
Cindy Duenas, prin. Fax 827-0760
Discovery Community S 100/1-6
12801 84th Ave NE 98034 425-820-3776
Mark Blomquist, prin.
Franklin ES 500/K-6
12434 NE 60th St 98033 425-822-7460
Kim Fricke, prin. Fax 739-0607
Frost ES 400/K-6
11801 NE 140th St 98034 425-821-8238
Sue Ann Sullivan, prin. Fax 821-4947
Juanita ES 300/K-6
9635 NE 132nd St 98034 425-823-8136
Paul Luczak, prin. Fax 820-2312
Keller ES 400/K-6
13820 108th Ave NE 98034 425-821-7060
Tim Stonich, prin. Fax 821-6814
Kirk ES 500/K-6
1312 6th St 98033 425-822-7449
Sandy Dennehy, prin. Fax 889-8359
Lakeview ES 400/K-6
10400 NE 68th St 98033 425-822-4517
Linda Hughes, prin. Fax 827-2045
Muir ES 400/K-6
14012 132nd Ave NE 98034 425-825-7680
Jeff DeGallier, prin. Fax 821-2546
Rose Hill ES 400/K-6
8110 128th Ave NE 98033 425-822-9578
Joyce Teshima, prin. Fax 822-7494
Sandburg ES 500/K-6
12801 84th Ave NE 98034 425-823-8670
Mark Blomquist, prin. Fax 823-3542
Thoreau ES 300/K-6
8224 NE 138th St 98034 425-823-4350
Mindy Mallon, prin. Fax 814-4986
Twain ES 600/K-6
9525 130th Ave NE 98033 425-828-3210
Rick Burden, prin. Fax 828-3213

Holy Family S 300/PK-8
7300 120th Ave NE 98033 425-827-0444
Jacqueline Degel, prin. Fax 827-0150
Kirkland SDA S 100/K-8
5320 108th Ave NE 98033 425-822-7554
Rick Serns, prin. Fax 828-0856

Kittitas, Kittitas, Pop. 1,133
Kittitas SD 403 600/K-12
PO Box 599 98934 509-968-3115
Monty Sabin, supt. Fax 968-4730
www.kittitas.wednet.edu
Kittitas ES 300/K-5
PO Box 1049 98934 509-968-3014
Derek Larsen, prin. Fax 968-3630

Klickitat, Klickitat
Klickitat SD 402 100/K-12
PO Box 37 98628 509-369-4145
Jerry Lynch, supt. Fax 369-3422
www.klickitat.wednet.edu/
Klickitat ES 100/K-6
PO Box 37 98628 509-369-4145
Kevin Davis, prin. Fax 369-3422

La Center, Clark, Pop. 1,873
La Center SD 101 1,500/K-12
PO Box 1840 98629 360-263-2131
Mark Mansell, supt. Fax 263-1140
www.lacenterschools.org
La Center ES 700/K-5
PO Box 1810 98629 360-263-2134
Carol Patton, prin. Fax 263-2133
La Center MS 300/6-8
PO Box 1750 98629 360-263-2136
David Cooke, prin. Fax 263-5936

Highland Lutheran Church Preschool & K 100/PK-K
38809 NE 41st Ave 98629 360-263-2303

Lacey, Thurston, Pop. 33,368
North Thurston SD 3 12,900/PK-12
305 College St NE 98516 360-412-4400
Dr. James Koval, supt. Fax 412-4410
www.nthurston.k12.wa.us
Chinook MS 700/7-8
4301 6th Ave NE 98516 360-412-4760
Monica Sweet, prin. Fax 412-4769
Evergreen Forest ES 500/PK-6
3025 Marvin Rd SE 98503 360-412-4670
Karen Johnson, prin. Fax 412-4679
Horizons IS 200/5-6
5900 54th Ave SE 98513 360-412-4730
Jennifer Keck, prin. Fax 412-4739
Horizons PS PK-4
4601 67th Ave SE 98513 360-412-4710
Tim Fries, prin. Fax 412-4719
Komachin MS 800/7-8
3650 College St SE 98503 360-412-4740
Julie Phipps, prin. Fax 412-4749
Lacey ES 600/K-6
1800 Homann Dr SE 98503 360-412-4650
Gary Culbertson, prin. Fax 412-4659
Lakes ES 700/PK-6
6211 Mullen Rd SE 98503 360-412-4600
Mike McDonald, prin. Fax 412-4609
Meadows ES 500/K-6
836 Deerbrush Dr SE 98513 360-412-4690
Carol O'Connell, prin. Fax 412-4699
Mountain View ES 600/K-6
1900 College St SE 98503 360-412-4630
Randy Weeks, prin. Fax 412-4639
Nisqually MS 600/7-8
8100 Steilacoom Rd SE 98503 360-412-4770
Karen Owen, prin. Fax 493-2756
Olympic View ES 500/K-6
1330 Horne St NE 98516 360-412-4660
Bob Richards, prin. Fax 412-4669
Pleasant Glade ES 500/PK-6
1920 Abernethy Rd NE 98516 360-412-4620
Bruce Walton, prin. Fax 412-4629
Seven Oaks ES 700/PK-6
1800 7 Oaks Rd SE 98503 360-412-4700
Ron Sisson, prin. Fax 412-4709
South Bay ES 600/K-6
3845 Sleater Kinney Rd NE 98506 360-412-4640
Kathi Weight, prin. Fax 412-4649
Other Schools – See Olympia

Community Christian Academy 200/PK-8
4706 Park Center Ave NE 98516 360-493-2223
Bob Willey, supt. Fax 412-0910
Faith Lutheran S 200/PK-6
7075 Pacific Ave SE 98503 360-491-1733
Carla Tranum, prin. Fax 491-3784
Holy Family S 200/PK-8
PO Box 3700 98509 360-491-7060
Barbara Dettlaff, prin. Fax 456-3725

La Conner, Skagit, Pop. 784
La Conner SD 311 700/K-12
PO Box 2103 98257 360-466-3171
Tim Bruce, supt. Fax 466-3523
lcsd.wednet.edu/index.htm
La Conner ES, PO Box 2103 98257 300/K-5
Lori Knudson, prin. 360-466-3172
La Conner MS, PO Box 2103 98257 100/6-8
K. C. Knudson, prin. 360-466-4113

La Crosse, Whitman, Pop. 355
LaCrosse SD 126 100/K-12
111 Hill Ave 99143 509-549-3591
Gary Wargo, supt. Fax 549-3529
www.lax.wednet.edu
LaCrosse ES 50/K-5
111 Hill Ave 99143 509-549-3592
Doug Curtis, prin. Fax 549-3529

Lakebay, Pierce
Peninsula SD 401
Supt. — See Gig Harbor
Evergreen ES 200/PK-5
1820 Key Peninsula Hwy S 98349 253-530-1300
Jacque Crisman, prin. Fax 530-1320
Key Peninsula MS 500/6-8
5510 Key Peninsula Hwy N 98349 253-530-4200
Jeri Goebel, prin. Fax 530-4220

Lake Forest Park, King, Pop. 12,476
Shoreline SD 412
Supt. — See Shoreline
Brookside ES 500/K-6
17447 37th Ave NE, 206-368-4140
Kathryn Noble, prin. Fax 368-4149
Lake Forest Park ES 400/K-6
18500 37th Ave NE, 206-368-4130
Linda Butler, prin. Fax 368-4139

Lake Stevens, Snohomish, Pop. 7,558
Lake Stevens SD 4 7,500/PK-12
12309 22nd St NE 98258 425-335-1500
David Burgess, supt. Fax 335-1549
www.lkstevens.wednet.edu
Highland ES 500/K-5
3220 113th Ave NE 98258 425-335-1585
Gina Anderson, prin. Fax 335-1600
Mt. Pilchuck ES 400/PK-5
12806 20th St NE 98258 425-335-1525
Chris Larson, prin. Fax 335-1568
North Lake MS 700/6-7
2202 123rd Ave NE 98258 425-335-1530
Gary Taber, prin. Fax 335-1576
Sunnycrest East ES 700/K-5
3411 99th Ave NE 98258 425-335-1535
Tim Haines, prin. Fax 335-1596
Other Schools – See Everett

Lakewood, Pierce, Pop. 57,671
Clover Park SD 400 11,500/PK-12
10903 Gravelly Lake Dr SW 98499 253-583-5000
Debbie LeBeau, supt. Fax 583-5198
www.cloverpark.k12.wa.us/
Carter Lake ES 400/K-5
3415 Lincoln Blvd SW 98439 253-583-5210
Paul Douglas, prin. Fax 583-5218

Custer ES 300/PK-5
7700 Steilacoom Blvd SW 98498 253-583-5230
Bev Eastman, prin. Fax 583-5238
Dower ES 200/PK-5
7817 John Dower Rd W 98499 253-583-5240
Kevin Brooks, prin. Fax 583-5248
Hudtloff MS 600/6-8
7702 Phillips Rd SW 98498 253-583-5400
Moureen David, prin. Fax 583-5408
Idlewild ES 300/PK-5
10806 Idlewild Rd SW 98498 253-583-5290
Penny Melton, prin. Fax 583-5298
Lake Louise ES 400/K-5
11014 Holden Rd SW 98498 253-583-5310
Patty Mitchell, prin. Fax 583-5318
Lakeview Hope Academy 400/K-5
3230 85th St S 98499 253-583-5300
Jo Dee Owens, prin. Fax 583-5308
Lochburn MS 600/6-8
5431 Steilacoom Blvd SW 98499 253-583-5420
Helen Wilson, prin. Fax 583-5428
Mann MS 500/6-8
11509 Holden Rd SW 98498 253-583-5440
Ron Banner, prin. Fax 583-5448
Oakbrook ES 300/K-5
7802 83rd Ave SW 98498 253-583-5330
Jeff Murrell, prin. Fax 583-5338
Oakwood ES 300/PK-5
3230 85th St S 98499 253-583-5340
John Mitchell, prin. Fax 583-5348
Park Lodge ES 400/K-5
6300 100th St SW 98499 253-583-5350
Eric Richards, prin. Fax 583-5358
Southgate ES 400/PK-5
10202 Earley Ave SW 98499 253-583-5360
Charlotte Clouse, prin. Fax 583-5368
Tillicum ES 300/PK-5
8514 Maple St SW 98498 253-583-5370
Taj Jensen, prin. Fax 583-5378
Tyee Park ES 400/K-5
11920 Seminole Rd SW 98499 253-583-5380
Tina Williams, prin. Fax 583-5388
Woodbrook MS 600/6-8
14920 Spring St SW 98439 253-583-5460
Nancy LaChapelle, prin. Fax 583-5468
Other Schools – See Fort Lewis

St. Frances Cabrini S 200/PK-8
5621 108th St SW 98499 253-584-3850
Stephanie Van Leuven, prin. Fax 584-3852
St. Mary's Christian S 100/PK-5
10630 Gravelly Lake Dr SW 98499 253-984-9475
Fax 588-6693

Lamont, Whitman, Pop. 99
Lamont SD 264 50/6-8
602 Main St 99017 509-257-2463
Mark Stedman, supt. Fax 257-2316
Lamont MS 50/6-8
602 Main St 99017 509-257-2463
Joseph Whipple, prin. Fax 257-2316

Langley, Island, Pop. 1,018
South Whidbey SD 206 1,600/K-12
PO Box 346 98260 360-221-6100
Fred McCarthy, supt. Fax 221-3835
www.sw.wednet.edu
Langley MS 400/6-8
PO Box 370 98260 360-221-5100
Rod Merrell, prin. Fax 221-8545
South Whidbey ES 400/K-5
PO Box 308 98260 360-221-4600
Jamie Boyd, prin. Fax 221-6929

Leavenworth, Chelan, Pop. 2,206
Cascade SD 228 1,300/PK-12
330 Evans St 98826 509-548-5885
Rob Clark, supt. Fax 548-6149
www.cascade.wednet.edu/
Beaver Valley ES 50/K-4
19265 Beaver Valley Rd 98826 509-763-3309
Carla Hudson, lead tchr. Fax 763-3309
Icicle River MS 300/6-8
10195 Titus Rd 98826 509-548-4042
Kenny Renner-Singer, prin. Fax 548-6646
Osborn ES 300/3-5
225 Central Ave 98826 509-548-5839
Kelli Doherty, prin. Fax 548-6856
Other Schools – See Peshastin

Upper Valley Christian S 100/K-12
111 Ski Hill Dr 98826 509-548-5292
John Bangsund, admin. Fax 548-5293

Liberty Lake, Spokane, Pop. 5,613
Central Valley SD 356
Supt. — See Spokane Valley
Liberty Lake ES 600/K-5
23606 E Boone Ave 99019 509-228-4300
Linda uphus, prin. Fax 228-4311

Lind, Adams, Pop. 576
Lind SD 158 200/PK-12
PO Box 340 99341 509-677-3481
John McGregor, supt. Fax 677-3463
www.lind.k12.wa.us
Lind ES 100/PK-6
PO Box 340 99341 509-677-3481
John McGregor, prin. Fax 677-3463

Littlerock, Thurston
Tumwater SD 33
Supt. — See Tumwater
Littlerock ES 400/K-6
PO Box C 98556 360-709-7250
Nate Pulley, prin. Fax 709-7252

Long Beach, Pacific, Pop. 1,386
Ocean Beach SD 101 900/K-12
PO Box 778 98631 360-642-3739
Rainer Houser, supt. Fax 642-1298
www.ocean.k12.wa.us
Long Beach ES 200/K-6
PO Box 758 98631 360-642-3242
Todd Carper, prin. Fax 642-1226
Other Schools – See Ocean Park

Longview, Cowlitz, Pop. 36,137
Kelso SD 458
Supt. — See Kelso
Beacon Hill ES 500/K-5
257 Alpha Dr 98632 360-501-1450
Ron Hutchison, prin. Fax 501-1455

Longview SD 122 7,300/K-12
2715 Lilac St 98632 360-575-7000
Dr. Suzanne Cusick, supt. Fax 575-7022
www.longview.k12.wa.us
Cascade MS, 2821 Parkview Dr 98632 500/6-8
Bruce Holway, prin. 360-577-2703
Columbia Heights ES 400/K-5
2820 Parkview Dr 98632 360-575-7461
Jay Opgrande, prin.
Columbia Valley Gardens ES 400/K-5
2644 30th Ave 98632 360-575-7502
Cheryl Kolano, prin.
Gray ES, 4622 Ohio St 98632 600/K-5
Scott Moultine, prin. 360-575-7302
Kessler ES 400/K-5
1902 E Kessler Blvd 98632 360-575-7580
Mike Mendenhall, prin.
Mint Valley ES, 2745 38th Ave 98632 500/K-5
Patrick Kelley, prin. 360-575-7581
Monticello MS, 1225 28th Ave 98632 600/6-8
Bill Marshall, prin. 360-575-7050
Mt. Solo MS, 5300 Mt Solo Rd 98632 500/6-8
Lori Cournyer, prin. 360-577-2800
Northlake ES 400/K-5
2210 Olympia Way 98632 360-575-7630
Ken Hermanson, prin.
Olympic ES, 1324 30th Ave 98632 300/K-5
Debbie Morgan, prin. 360-575-7084
St. Helens ES, 431 27th Ave 98632 300/K-5
Mary Ann Robbins, prin. 360-575-7362

St. Rose S 200/PK-8
720 26th Ave 98632 360-577-6760
Rosemary Griggs, prin. Fax 577-3689
Three Rivers Christian S 200/PK-6
2610 Ocean Beach Hwy 98632 360-423-4510
James Chenoweth, admin. Fax 423-1180

Loon Lake, Stevens
Loon Lake SD 183 100/PK-6
4001 Maple St 99148 509-233-2212
Steven Waunch, supt. Fax 233-2537
www.loonlakeschool.org
Loon Lake ES 100/PK-6
4001 Maple St 99148 509-233-2212
Steven Waunch, prin. Fax 233-2537

Lopez Island, San Juan
Lopez Island SD 144 300/K-12
86 School Rd 98261 360-468-2202
Bill Evans, supt. Fax 468-2212
www.lopez.k12.wa.us
Lopez Island ES 100/K-5
86 School Rd 98261 360-468-2201
Fax 468-2235
Other Schools – See Anacortes

Lummi Island, Whatcom
Ferndale SD 502
Supt. — See Ferndale
Beach ES 100/K-6
3786 Centerview Rd 98262 360-383-9440
Michael Berres, admin. Fax 383-9442

Lyle, Klickitat
Lyle SD 406 400/K-12
PO Box 368 98635 509-365-2191
Martin Huffman, supt. Fax 365-5000
www.lyleschools.org/
Lyle MS 50/7-8
PO Box 368 98635 509-365-2211
Phil Williams, prin. Fax 365-2665
Other Schools – See Dallesport

Lyman, Skagit, Pop. 420
Sedro-Woolley SD 101
Supt. — See Sedro Woolley
Lyman ES 200/K-6
PO Box 1308 98263 360-855-3535
Mark Nilson, prin. Fax 855-3536

Lynden, Whatcom, Pop. 10,697
Lynden SD 504 2,700/K-12
1203 Bradley Rd 98264 360-354-4443
Dennis Carlson Ed.D., supt. Fax 354-7662
www.lynden.wednet.edu
Fisher ES 400/K-5
501 14th St 98264 360-354-4291
Brad Jernberg, prin. Fax 354-0952
Isom ES 400/K-5
8461 Benson Rd 98264 360-354-1992
David VanderYacht, prin. Fax 354-5494
Lynden MS 600/6-8
516 Main St 98264 360-354-2952
Kris Petersen, prin. Fax 354-6631
Vossbeck ES 400/K-5
1301 Bridgeview Dr 98264 360-354-0488
Becky Midboe, prin. Fax 318-8318

Meridian SD 505
Supt. — See Bellingham
Meridian MS 400/6-8
861 Ten Mile Rd 98264 360-398-2291
Gerald Sanderson, prin. Fax 398-8131

Cornerstone Christian S 100/1-12
8872 Northwood Rd 98264 360-318-0663
Otto Bouwman, prin. Fax 318-8175
Ebenezer Christian S 100/K-8
9390 Guide Meridian Rd 98264 360-354-2632
Jim Buss, prin. Fax 354-7093
Lynden Christian MS 300/5-8
503 Lyncs Dr 98264 360-354-3358
Aaron Bishop, prin. Fax 354-6690
Lynden Christian S 500/PK-4
307 Drayton St 98264 360-354-5492
Jeff Boersma, prin. Fax 354-6690

Lynnwood, Snohomish, Pop. 33,504
Edmonds SD 15 19,600/PK-12
20420 68th Ave W 98036 425-431-7000
Nick Brossoit Ed.D., supt. Fax 431-7182
www.edmonds.wednet.edu
Alderwood ECC PK-PK
2000 200th Pl SW 98036 425-431-7595
Dennis Burkhardt, admin. Fax 431-7599
Alderwood MS 700/7-8
20000 28th Ave W 98036 425-431-7579
Mike VanOrden, prin. Fax 431-7580
Beverly ES 500/K-6
5221 168th St SW 98037 425-431-7732
Carol Frodge, prin. Fax 431-7738
Cedar Valley Community ES 400/K-6
19200 56th Ave W 98036 425-431-7390
Charlotte Beyer, prin. Fax 431-7395
College Place ES 500/K-6
20401 76th Ave W 98036 425-431-7620
Justin Irish, prin. Fax 431-7626
College Place MS 600/7-8
7501 208th St SW 98036 425-431-7451
Thea Gardner, prin. Fax 431-7449
Hazelwood ES 400/K-6
3300 204th St SW 98036 425-431-7884
Tim Parnell, prin. Fax 431-7883
Hilltop ES 500/K-6
20425 Damson Rd 98036 425-431-7604
Susan Ardissono, prin. Fax 431-7608
Lynndale ES 400/K-6
7200 191st Pl SW 98036 425-431-7365
David Zwaschka, prin. Fax 431-7363
Lynnwood ES 500/K-6
18638 44th Ave W 98037 425-431-7615
Chris Lindblom, prin. Fax 431-7617
Martha Lake ES 600/K-6
17500 Larch Way 98037 425-431-7766
Jeanne Moore, prin. Fax 431-7764
Meadowdale ES 500/K-6
6505 168th St SW 98037 425-431-7754
Daniel Davis, prin. Fax 431-7758
Meadowdale MS 700/7-8
6500 168th St SW 98037 425-431-7707
Christine Avery, prin. Fax 431-7714
Oak Heights ES 500/K-6
15500 18th Ave W, 425-431-7744
Greg Willis, prin. Fax 431-7747
Spruce ES 500/K-6
17405 Spruce Way 98037 425-431-7720
Margaret Mesaros, prin. Fax 431-7726
Other Schools – See Brier, Edmonds, Mountlake Terrace

Brighton S, 6717 212th St SW 98036 300/PK-8
David Locke, prin. 425-672-4430
Cedar Park Christian S - Lynwood Campus 200/PK-6
17931 64th Ave W 98037 425-742-9518
Philip Bir, prin. Fax 745-9306
Cypress Adventist S 100/K-8
21500 Cypress Way 98036 425-775-3578
Lowell Dunston, prin. Fax 775-3579
Providence Classical Christian S 200/PK-12
21500 Cypress Way Ste B 98036 425-774-6622
Ryan Evans, hdmstr. Fax 672-5796
St. Thomas More S 200/K-8
6511 176th St SW 98037 425-743-4242
Teresa Fewel, prin. Fax 745-8367
Soundview S 100/PK-8
6515 196th St SW 98036 425-778-8572
Inae Piercy, prin. Fax 640-9416
Trinity Lutheran Preschool & K 50/PK-K
6215 196th St SW 98036 425-771-8433

Mabton, Yakima, Pop. 2,038
Mabton SD 120 900/K-12
PO Box 37 98935 509-894-4852
Sandra Pasiero-Davis, supt. Fax 894-4769
www.mabton.wednet.edu
Artz-Fox ES 500/K-6
PO Box 40 98935 509-894-4941
Jonathan Braack, prin. Fax 894-5110
Mabton MS, PO Box 38 98935 200/7-8
Denny Brown, dir. 509-894-2160

Mc Cleary, Grays Harbor, Pop. 1,547
Mc Cleary SD 65 300/K-8
611 S Main St 98557 360-495-3204
Dan Bolender, supt. Fax 495-4589
www.mccleary.wednet.edu
Mc Cleary S 300/K-8
611 S Main St 98557 360-495-3204
Dan Bolender, prin. Fax 495-4589

Mansfield, Douglas, Pop. 331
Mansfield SD 207 100/PK-12
PO Box 188 98830 509-683-1012
Eugene Nelson, supt. Fax 683-1281
www.mansfield.wednet.edu/
Mansfield S 100/PK-12
PO Box 188 98830 509-683-1012
Eugene Nelson, prin. Fax 683-1281

Manson, Chelan
Manson SD 19 600/PK-12
PO Box A 98831 509-687-3140
Matt Charlton, supt. Fax 687-9877
www.manson.org

Manson ES 300/PK-6
PO Box A 98831 509-687-9502
Heather Ireland, prin. Fax 687-9537

Maple Falls, Whatcom
Mt. Baker SD 507
Supt. — See Deming
Kendall ES 500/K-6
7547 Kendall Rd 98266 360-383-2055
Charles Burleigh, prin. Fax 383-2059

Maple Valley, King, Pop. 15,153
Tahoma SD 409 7,000/K-12
25720 Maple Valley Black Di 98038 425-413-3400
Mike Maryanski, supt. Fax 413-3455
www.tahomasd.us
Cedar River MS 500/6-7
22615 Sweeney Rd SE 98038 425-413-5400
Mark Koch, prin. Fax 413-5455
Glacier Park ES 900/K-5
23700 SE 280th Pl 98038 425-432-7294
Emilie Hard, prin. Fax 432-6795
Lake Wilderness ES 900/K-5
24216 Witte Rd SE 98038 425-413-3500
Laurel Menard, prin. Fax 425-3555
Rock Creek ES 800/K-5
25700 Maple Valley Black Di 98038 425-413-3300
Fritz Gere, prin. Fax 413-3355
Shadow Lake ES 500/K-5
22620 Sweeney Rd SE 98038 425-413-6100
Chris Everett, prin. Fax 413-6113
Tahoma MS 600/6-7
24425 SE 216th St 98038 425-413-3600
Amy Doyle, prin. Fax 413-3655

Marysville, Snohomish, Pop. 29,889
Lakewood SD 306 2,600/PK-12
17110 16th Dr NE 98271 360-652-4500
Dr. Dennis Haddock, supt. Fax 652-4502
www.lwsd.wednet.edu
English Crossing ES 400/3-5
16728 28th Dr NE 98271 360-652-4515
Bill Landry, prin. Fax 654-2036
Lakewood ES 400/PK-2
17000 16th Dr NE 98271 360-652-4500
Dr. Sheila Woods, prin. Fax 654-2039
Lakewood MS 600/6-8
16800 16th Dr NE 98271 360-652-4510
Crystal Knight, prin. Fax 652-4512
Other Schools – See Arlington

Marysville SD 25 8,300/PK-12
4220 80th St NE 98270 360-653-7058
Dr. Larry Nyland, supt. Fax 629-1990
www.msvl.k12.wa.us
Allen Creek ES 600/K-5
6505 60th Dr NE 98270 360-653-0660
Kristin DeWitte, prin. Fax 629-1986
Cascade ES 600/K-5
5200 100th St NE 98270 360-653-0620
Christine Sampley, prin. Fax 653-6897
Cedarcrest MS 900/6-8
6400 88th St NE 98270 360-653-0850
Sheila Gerrish, prin. Fax 657-6470
Grove ES K-5
6510 Grove St 98270 360-653-0647
Jeanne Tennis, prin. Fax 629-1850
Liberty ES 500/PK-5
1919 10th St 98270 360-653-0625
Scott Irwin, prin. Fax 657-0229
Marshall ES 500/PK-5
4407 116th St NE 98271 360-653-0630
Michelle Gurnee, prin. Fax 658-9690
Marsh ES 600/K-5
6325 91st St NE 98270 360-653-0643
John Waldrop, prin. Fax 657-6779
Marysville MS 1,100/6-8
4923 67th St NE 98270 360-657-6396
Susan Hegeberg, prin. Fax 659-2576
Pinewood ES 600/K-5
5115 84th St NE 98270 360-653-0635
Breeze Williams, prin. Fax 658-9573
Quil Ceda ES 300/K-5
2415 74th St NE 98271 360-653-0890
Dave McKellar, prin. Fax 651-0769
Shoultes ES 400/PK-5
13525 51st Ave NE 98271 360-653-0640
Janelle McFalls, prin. Fax 658-9791
Sunnyside ES 600/K-5
3707 Sunnyside Blvd 98270 360-653-0645
Todd Christensen, prin. Fax 397-0320
Tenth Street MS 200/6-8
7204 27th Ave NE 98271 360-653-0665
Frank Redmon, prin. Fax 629-1950
Totem MS 500/6-8
1605 7th St 98270 360-653-0610
Judy Albertson, prin. Fax 657-6297
Tulalip ES 200/K-5
7730 36th Ave NW 98271 360-653-0650
Teresa Iyall, prin. Fax 658-9596

Bethlehem Christian S 200/PK-K
7215 51st Ave NE 98270 360-653-2882
Kelly Stadum, dir. Fax 651-2772
Grace Academy 300/PK-12
8521 67th Ave NE 98270 360-659-8517
Timothy Lugg, prin. Fax 653-5899
Legacy S of Arts and Classics 50/PK-1
11911 State Ave 98271 360-653-4520
Aaron Thompson, admin. Fax 651-1109

Mattawa, Grant, Pop. 3,287
Wahluke SD 73 1,900/PK-12
PO Box 907 99349 509-932-4565
Gary Greene, supt. Fax 932-4571
www.wsd73.wednet.edu
Mattawa ES 400/PK-1
PO Box 907 99349 509-932-4433
Mia Benjamin, prin. Fax 932-5265
Saddle Mountain IS 500/2-4
PO Box 907 99349 509-932-5693
Melissa Stevenson, prin. Fax 932-4586
Schott MS 300/5-6
PO Box 907 99349 509-932-3877
Dale Hedman, prin. Fax 932-3911
Wahluke JHS 300/7-8
PO Box 907 99349 509-932-4455
Fax 932-4282

Mead, Spokane
Mead SD 354 9,500/K-12
12828 N Newport Hwy 99021 509-465-6000
Thomas Rockefeller, supt. Fax 465-6020
www.mead354.org
Meadow Ridge ES 600/K-6
15601 N Freya St 99021 509-465-6600
Marilyn Brennan, prin. Fax 465-6620
Other Schools – See Colbert, Spokane

Medical Lake, Spokane, Pop. 4,190
Medical Lake SD 326 2,200/PK-12
PO Box 128 99022 509-565-3100
Dr. Pam Veltri, supt. Fax 565-3102
www.mlsd.org/
Hallett ES 300/4-6
PO Box 128 99022 509-565-3400
Dan Mueller, prin. Fax 565-3401
Medical Lake ES 300/PK-3
PO Box 128 99022 509-565-3500
Cindy McSmith, prin. Fax 565-3501
Medical Lake MS 300/7-8
PO Box 128 99022 509-565-3300
Sylvia Campbell, prin. Fax 565-3301
Other Schools – See Fairchild AFB

Medina, King, Pop. 3,032
Bellevue SD 405
Supt. — See Bellevue
Medina ES 500/K-5
8001 NE 8th St 98039 425-456-5400
Jennifer Rose, prin. Fax 456-5404

St. Thomas S 200/PK-6
8300 NE 12th St 98039 425-454-5880
Dr. Kirk Wheeler, prin. Fax 454-1921
Three Points Christian S 400/PK-6
7800 NE 28th St 98039 425-454-3977
Steve Kennedy, prin. Fax 454-5379

Mercer Island, King, Pop. 22,862
Mercer Island SD 400 4,000/K-12
4160 86th Ave SE 98040 206-236-3300
Dr. Gary Plano, supt. Fax 236-3333
www.misd.k12.wa.us
Islander MS 1,000/6-8
8225 SE 72nd St 98040 206-236-3400
MaryJo Budzius, prin. Fax 236-3408
Island Park ES 500/K-5
5437 Island Crest Way 98040 206-236-3410
Dr. Nancy Loorem, prin. Fax 230-6251
Lakeridge ES 500/K-5
8215 SE 78th St 98040 206-236-3415
Ralph Allen, prin. Fax 230-6232
West Mercer ES 600/K-5
4141 81st Ave SE 98040 206-236-3430
Rich Mellish, prin. Fax 230-6043

French-American S of Puget Sound 300/PK-8
3795 E Mercer Way 98040 206-275-3533
Andree McGiffin, hdmstr. Fax 812-0231
St. Monica S 200/K-8
4320 87th Ave SE 98040 206-232-5432
Pam Dellino, prin. Fax 275-2874

Mesa, Franklin, Pop. 425
North Franklin SD J 51-162
Supt. — See Connell
Basin City ES 400/K-6
303 Bailie Blvd 99343 509-269-4224
Lisa Flatau, prin. Fax 269-4215
Mesa ES 200/K-6
200 E Pepiot Rd 99343 509-265-4229
Marci Cox, prin. Fax 265-4238

Metaline Falls, Pend Oreille, Pop. 232
Selkirk SD 70 300/PK-12
PO Box 129 99153 509-446-2951
Nancy Lotze, supt. Fax 446-2929
www.selkirk.k12.wa.us
Selkirk ES 100/PK-6
PO Box 68 99153 509-446-4225
Don Hawpe, prin. Fax 446-4804

Mill Creek, Snohomish, Pop. 13,501
Everett SD 2
Supt. — See Everett
Heatherwood MS 800/6-8
1419 Trillium Blvd SE 98012 425-385-6300
Janet Gillingham, prin. Fax 385-6302
Mill Creek ES 600/K-5
3400 148th St SE 98012 425-385-6800
Mary Ann Opperud, prin. Fax 385-6802

Milton, Pierce, Pop. 6,468
Fife SD 417
Supt. — See Fife
Discovery PS 400/K-1
1205 19th Ave 98354 253-517-1200
Julie Bartlett, prin. Fax 517-1205
Endeavour IS 500/2-5
1304 17th Ave 98354 253-517-1400
Kevin Alfano, prin. Fax 517-1405
Surprise Lake MS 500/6-7
2001 Milton Way 98354 253-517-1300
John McCrossin, prin. Fax 517-1305

Monroe, Snohomish, Pop. 15,653
Monroe SD 103 6,400/K-12
200 E Fremont St 98272 360-804-2500
Dr. Ken Hoover, supt. Fax 804-2529
www.monroe.wednet.edu
Fryelands ES 500/K-5
15286 Fryelands Blvd SE 98272 360-804-3400
Jeff Presley, prin. Fax 804-3499
Monroe MS 500/6-8
351 Short Columbia St 98272 360-804-4200
Linda Boyle, prin. Fax 804-4299
Park Place MS 600/6-8
1408 W Main St 98272 360-804-4300
JoAnn Carbonetti, prin. Fax 804-4399
Salem Woods ES 500/K-5
12802 Wagner Rd 98272 360-804-3600
Janna Dmochowsky, prin. Fax 804-3699
Wagner ES 400/K-5
639 W Main St 98272 360-804-3200
Robin Fitch, prin. Fax 804-3299
Other Schools – See Snohomish

Cornerstone Academy 100/PK-6
14377 Fryelands Blvd SE 98272 425-273-5804
Michelle Jones, hdmstr. Fax 794-9847
Little Doves Preschool 100/PK-K
202 Dickinson Ave 98272 360-794-7230
Linda Herman, dir.
Monroe Christian S 200/PK-8
1009 W Main St 98272 360-794-8200
Elaine Obbink, prin. Fax 863-9270
Monroe Montessori S 100/PK-6
733 Village Way 98272 360-794-4622
Allan Washburn, prin.
Sky Valley SDA S 50/K-8
200 Academy Way 98272 360-794-7655
Angie Campanello, prin. Fax 794-7655

Montesano, Grays Harbor, Pop. 3,399
Montesano SD 66 1,300/PK-12
302 N Church St 98563 360-249-3942
Dr. Marti Harruff, supt. Fax 249-3391
www.monte.wednet.edu
Beacon Avenue ES 400/PK-3
1717 E Beacon Ave 98563 360-249-4528
Craig Loucks, prin. Fax 249-3884
Simpson Avenue S 300/4-6
519 W Simpson Ave 98563 360-249-4331
Judy Holliday, prin. Fax 249-4820

Grays Harbor Adventist Christian S 50/K-8
1216 US Highway 12 98563 360-249-1115
Adria Hay, prin. Fax 249-1129

Morton, Lewis, Pop. 1,083
Morton SD 214 400/K-12
PO Box 1219 98356 360-496-5300
Tom Manke, supt. Fax 586-3208
www.morton.wednet.edu
Morton ES 200/K-5
PO Box L 98356 360-496-5143
Kip Henderson, prin. Fax 496-0327

Moses Lake, Grant, Pop. 16,793
Moses Lake SD 161 7,200/K-12
920 W Ivy Ave 98837 509-766-2650
Steven Chestnut, supt. Fax 766-2678
www.moseslakeschools.org
Chief Moses MS 800/6-8
1111 E Nelson Rd 98837 509-766-2661
Mark Johnson, prin. Fax 766-2680
Frontier MS 700/6-8
517 W 3rd Ave 98837 509-766-2662
Chris Lupo, prin. Fax 766-2663
Garden Heights ES 600/K-5
707 E Nelson Rd 98837 509-766-2651
Kristi Hofheins, prin. Fax 766-3951
Knolls Vista ES 500/K-5
454 W Ridge Rd 98837 509-766-2652
Mike Riggs, prin. Fax 766-3955
Lakeview Terrace ES 400/K-5
780 S Clover Dr 98837 509-766-2653
Ryan Pike, prin. Fax 766-3956
Larson Heights ES 400/K-5
700 Lindberg Ln 98837 509-766-2655
Eric Johnson, prin. Fax 766-3960
Longview ES 600/K-5
9783 Apple Rd NE 98837 509-766-2656
Robbie Mason, prin. Fax 766-2665
Midway Learning Center 300/K-5
502 S C St 98837 509-766-2657
Chris Hendricks, prin. Fax 766-3952
North ES 400/K-5
1200 W Craig St 98837 509-766-2654
Shannon Dahl, prin. Fax 766-3958
Peninsula ES 600/K-5
2406 W Texas St 98837 509-766-2658
Doug Luiten, prin. Fax 766-3950

Crestview Christian S 50/1-9
1601 W Valley Rd 98837 509-765-4632
Richard Wilson, admin.
Moses Lake Christian Academy 300/PK-12
1475 Nelson Rd NE Ste A 98837 509-765-9704
David White, prin. Fax 765-3698

Mossyrock, Lewis, Pop. 504
Mossyrock SD 206 700/K-12
PO Box 478 98564 360-983-3181
Dr. Karen Ernest, supt. Fax 983-8111
www.mossyrock.k12.wa.us
Mossyrock ES 300/K-6
PO Box 455 98564 360-983-3184
Randy Torrey, prin. Fax 983-8190
Mossyrock JHS 100/7-8
PO Box 454 98564 360-983-3183
Karl Miler, prin. Fax 983-3188

Mountlake Terrace, Snohomish, Pop. 20,251
Edmonds SD 15
Supt. — See Lynnwood
Cedar Way ES 400/K-6
22222 39th Ave W 98043 425-431-7864
Hawkins Cramer, prin. Fax 431-7862

Mountlake Terrace ES 300/K-6
22001 52nd Ave W 98043 425-431-7894
Doug Johnson, prin. Fax 431-7899
Terrace Park S 400/K-8
5409 228th St SW 98043 425-431-7482
Mary Freitas, prin. Fax 431-7486

St. Pius X S 100/K-8
22105 58th Ave W 98043 425-778-9861
Ruth Foisy, prin. Fax 776-2663

Mount Vernon, Skagit, Pop. 29,271
Conway SD 317 400/K-8
19710 State Route 534 98274 360-445-5785
Dr. Wayne Robertson, supt. Fax 445-4511
www.conway.k12.wa.us
Conway S 400/K-8
19710 State Route 534 98274 360-445-5785
Claudine Berry, prin. Fax 445-4511

Mount Vernon SD 320 5,700/K-12
124 E Lawrence St 98273 360-428-6110
Carl Bruner, supt. Fax 428-6172
www.mv.k12.wa.us
Centennial ES 600/K-6
3100 E Martin Rd 98273 360-428-6138
Erwin Stroosma, prin. Fax 428-6158
Jefferson ES 500/K-6
1801 E Blackburn Rd 98274 360-428-6128
Peggy Zappone, prin. Fax 428-6159
LaVenture MS 400/7-8
1200 N Laventure Rd 98273 360-428-6116
Dan Berard, prin. Fax 428-6189
Lincoln ES 300/K-6
1005 S 11th St 98274 360-428-6135
Kristine Wollan, prin. Fax 428-6170
Little Mountain ES 600/K-6
1514 S LaVenture Rd 98274 360-428-6125
Brian Auckland, prin. Fax 428-6164
Madison ES 400/K-6
907 E Fir St 98273 360-428-6131
Evelyn Morse, prin. Fax 428-6171
Mount Baker MS 400/7-8
2310 E Section St 98274 360-428-6127
Beth Ashley, prin. Fax 428-6155
Washington ES 500/K-6
1020 Mclean Rd 98273 360-428-6122
W. Rosborough-Gillins, prin. Fax 428-6162

Sedro-Woolley SD 101
Supt. — See Sedro Woolley
Big Lake ES 200/K-6
16802 Lake View Blvd 98274 360-855-3525
Brian Isakson, prin. Fax 855-3526

Foothills Christian S 50/PK-8
PO Box 2537 98273 360-420-9749
William McKenzie, admin.
Immaculate Conception S 200/PK-8
1321 E Division St 98274 360-428-3912
Kathleen Cartee, prin. Fax 424-8838
Mt. Vernon Christian S 300/PK-12
820 W Blackburn Rd 98273 360-424-9157
Patrick DeJong, prin. Fax 424-9256

Moxee, Yakima, Pop. 1,411
East Valley SD 90
Supt. — See Yakima
East Valley Central MS 400/7-8
408 E Seattle Ave 98936 509-573-7500
Jeri Young, prin. Fax 573-7540
Moxee ES 500/K-3
PO Box 69 98936 509-573-7700
Monica Masias, prin. Fax 573-7740

Mukilteo, Snohomish, Pop. 19,857
Mukilteo SD 6
Supt. — See Everett
Columbia ES 500/K-5
10520 Harbour Pointe Blvd 98275 425-356-6685
Wendy Eidbo, prin. Fax 356-6689
Endeavour ES 400/K-5
12300 Harbour Pointe Blvd 98275 425-356-6696
Ann Jordan, prin. Fax 710-4306
Harbour Pointe MS 800/6-8
5000 Harbour Pointe Blvd 98275 425-356-6658
Nikki Cannon, prin. Fax 356-6660
Mukilteo ES 500/K-5
2600 Mukilteo Speedway 98275 425-356-1304
Pat Cushing, prin. Fax 710-4321
Olympic View MS 800/6-8
2602 Mukilteo Speedway 98275 425-356-1308
Nancy Coogan, prin. Fax 356-1332

Naches, Yakima, Pop. 681
Naches Valley SD JT3 1,500/K-12
PO Box 99 98937 509-653-2220
Duane Lyons, supt. Fax 653-1211
www.naches.wednet.edu
Naches Valley IS 200/3-4
PO Box 39 98937 509-653-2701
Todd Hilmes, prin. Fax 653-2729
Naches Valley MS 500/5-8
PO Box 39 98937 509-653-2725
Todd Hilmes, prin. Fax 653-2729
Other Schools – See Yakima

Nile Christian S / Hope Academy 50/K-12
370 Flying H Loop 98937 509-658-2990
Bruce Gillespie, dir. Fax 658-2009

Napavine, Lewis, Pop. 1,449
Napavine SD 14 700/PK-12
PO Box 840 98565 360-262-3303
Doug Skinner, supt. Fax 262-9737
www.napa.k12.wa.us
Napavine ES 400/PK-6
PO Box 837 98565 360-262-3345
Robert Hunt, prin. Fax 266-0452

Naselle, Pacific
Naselle-Grays River Valley SD 155 300/K-12
793 State Route 4 98638 360-484-7121
Alan Bennett, supt. Fax 484-3191
www.naselle.wednet.edu
Naselle-Grays River Valley S 200/K-12
793 State Route 4 98638 360-484-7121
Karen Wirkkala, prin. Fax 484-3191

Neah Bay, Clallam, Pop. 916
Cape Flattery SD 401
Supt. — See Sekiu
Neah Bay S 200/K-12
PO Box 86 98357 360-645-2221
Ann Renker, prin. Fax 645-2574

Nespelem, Okanogan, Pop. 207
Nespelem SD 14 200/PK-8
PO Box 291 99155 509-634-4541
Lloyd Olson, supt. Fax 634-4551
www.nespelemeagles.org/
Nespelem S 200/PK-8
PO Box 291 99155 509-634-4541
Lloyd Olson, prin. Fax 634-4551

Newcastle, King, Pop. 9,287
Issaquah SD 411
Supt. — See Issaquah
Newcastle ES 400/K-5
8400 136th Ave SE 98059 425-837-5800
Christy Otley, prin. Fax 837-5850

Renton SD 403
Supt. — See Renton
Hazelwood ES 500/K-5
6928 116th Ave SE 98056 425-204-4550
Cynthia Addis, prin. Fax 204-4552

Newman Lake, Spokane
East Valley SD 361
Supt. — See Spokane
East Farms ES 400/K-5
26203 E Rowan Ave 99025 509-226-3039
Charlene Wellington, prin. Fax 226-3668
Mountain View MS 400/6-8
6011 N Chase Rd 99025 509-226-1379
Jim McAdam, prin. Fax 226-3082

Newport, Pend Oreille, Pop. 2,157
Newport SD 56-415 1,200/PK-12
PO Box 70 99156 509-447-3167
Teresa von Marbod, supt. Fax 447-2553
www.newport.wednet.edu
Halstead MS 400/5-8
PO Box 70 99156 509-447-2426
Janet Burcham, prin. Fax 447-4914
Stratton ES 400/PK-4
PO Box 70 99156 509-447-0656
Teresa Holmes, prin. Fax 447-2612

Nine Mile Falls, Spokane
Nine Mile Falls SD 325 1,700/PK-12
10110 W Charles Rd 99026 509-340-4300
Brian Talbott, supt. Fax 340-4301
www.9mile.org
Lakeside MS 400/6-8
6169 Highway 291 99026 509-340-4100
Jeff Baerwald, prin. Fax 340-4101
Lake Spokane ES 500/PK-5
6015 Highway 291 99026 509-340-4040
Kevin Simpson, prin. Fax 340-4041
Nine Mile Falls ES 200/K-5
10102 W Charles Rd 99026 509-340-4010
Len Mortlock, prin. Fax 340-4011

Nooksack, Whatcom, Pop. 885
Nooksack Valley SD 506
Supt. — See Everson
Nooksack Valley MS 400/6-8
404 W Columbia St, 360-966-7561
Joel VanderYacht, prin. Fax 966-7805

Normandy Park, King, Pop. 6,178
Highline SD 401
Supt. — See Burien
Marvista ES 500/K-6
19800 Marine View Dr SW 98166 206-631-4200
Rebekah Kim, prin. Fax 433-2468

North Bend, King, Pop. 4,589
Snoqualmie Valley SD 410
Supt. — See Snoqualmie
North Bend ES 500/K-5
400 E 3rd St 98045 425-831-8400
Jim Frazier, prin. Fax 831-8410
Opstad ES 600/K-5
1345 Stilson Ave SE 98045 425-831-8300
John Jester, prin. Fax 831-8333
Twin Falls MS 6-8
46910 SE Middle Fork Rd 98045 425-831-4150
Ruth Moen, prin. Fax 831-4140

North Bend Montessori S 200/PK-K
PO Box 2300 98045 425-831-5766
Susan Weigel, dir. Fax 831-6330

Northport, Stevens, Pop. 338
Northport SD 211 200/K-12
PO Box 1280 99157 509-732-4441
Patsy Guglielmino, supt. Fax 732-6606
www.northportschools.org
Northport Grade S 100/K-8
PO Box 1280 99157 509-732-4441
Patsy Guglielmino, prin. Fax 732-6606

Oakesdale, Whitman, Pop. 395
Oakesdale SD 324 100/K-12
PO Box 228 99158 509-285-5296
Jake Dingman, supt. Fax 285-5121
www.oakesdale.wednet.edu
Oakesdale S 50/K-8
PO Box 228 99158 509-285-5296
Jake Dingman, prin. Fax 285-5121

Oak Harbor, Island, Pop. 22,327
Oak Harbor SD 201 5,200/PK-12
350 S Oak Harbor St 98277 360-279-5000
Dr. Rick Schulte, supt. Fax 279-5070
www.ohsd.net
Broadview ES 400/K-5
473 SW Fairhaven Dr 98277 360-279-5250
Joyce Swanson, prin. Fax 279-5299
Crescent Harbor ES 400/K-5
330 E Crescent Harbor Rd 98277 360-279-5650
Kathleen Schreck, prin. Fax 279-5699
Hillcrest ES 500/K-5
1500 NW 2nd Ave 98277 360-279-5200
Laura Schonberg, prin. Fax 279-5249
North Whidbey MS 700/6-8
67 NE Izett St 98277 360-279-5500
Laura Aesoph, prin. Fax 279-5516
Oak Harbor ES 500/PK-5
151 SE Midway Blvd 98277 360-279-5100
Dorothy Day, prin. Fax 279-5149
Oak Harbor MS 600/6-8
150 SW 6th Ave 98277 360-279-5300
Shane Evans, prin. Fax 279-5399
Olympic View ES 500/PK-5
380 NE Regatta Dr 98277 360-279-5150
Martha Adams, prin. Fax 279-5199

Oak Harbor Christian S 300/PK-8
675 E Whidbey Ave 98277 360-675-2831
Dave Zylstra, prin. Fax 675-4216
Whidbey Christian S 50/1-8
31830 State Route 20 98277 360-279-1812

Oakville, Grays Harbor, Pop. 688
Oakville SD 400 200/K-12
PO Box H 98568 360-273-0171
Kathy Lorton, supt. Fax 273-6724
Oakville ES 100/K-3
PO Box H 98568 360-273-5946
Kathy Lorton, prin. Fax 858-1359
Oakville MS 100/4-8
PO Box H 98568 360-273-5947
Tom Phimister, prin. Fax 273-8229

Ocean Park, Pacific, Pop. 1,409
Ocean Beach SD 101
Supt. — See Long Beach
Ocean Park ES 300/K-6
PO Box 1220 98640 360-665-4815
Bette Arne, prin. Fax 665-1275

Ocean Shores, Grays Harbor, Pop. 4,467
North Beach SD 64 700/K-12
PO Box 159 98569 360-289-2447
Stanley Pinnick, supt. Fax 289-2492
www.northbeach.k12.wa.us
North Beach MS 100/7-8
PO Box 969 98569 360-289-3888
Bill Duncanson, prin. Fax 289-0996
Ocean Shores ES 300/K-6
300 Mount Olympus Ave SE 98569 360-289-2147
Karen Ellingson, prin. Fax 289-0120
Other Schools – See Pacific Beach

Odessa, Lincoln, Pop. 942
Odessa SD 105-157-166 J 200/K-12
PO Box 248 99159 509-982-2668
Douglas Johnson, supt. Fax 982-0163
www.odessa.wednet.edu/
Jantz ES 100/K-5
PO Box 248 99159 509-982-2603
Ken Schutz, prin. Fax 982-0163

Okanogan, Okanogan, Pop. 2,398
Okanogan SD 105 1,000/K-12
PO Box 592 98840 509-422-3629
Dr. Richard Johnson, supt. Fax 422-1525
www.oksd.wednet.edu
Grainger ES 400/K-5
PO Box 592 98840 509-422-3580
Dean Radke, prin. Fax 422-1639
Okanogan MS 200/6-8
PO Box 592 98840 509-422-2680
Brett Baum, prin. Fax 422-0068

Olalla, Kitsap
South Kitsap SD 402
Supt. — See Port Orchard
Olalla ES 400/K-6
6100 SE Denny Bond Blvd 98359 360-443-3350
Karen Butler, prin. Fax 443-3399

Olympia, Thurston, Pop. 44,114
Griffin SD 324 700/K-8
6530 33rd Ave NW 98502 360-866-4918
Dr. Donald Brannam, supt. Fax 866-9684
www.griffin.k12.wa.us
Griffin S 700/K-8
6530 33rd Ave NW 98502 360-866-2515
Greg Woods, prin. Fax 866-9684

North Thurston SD 3
Supt. — See Lacey
Hawk ES 500/K-6
7600 5th Ave SE 98503 360-412-4610
Charles Harrington, prin. Fax 412-4619
Woodland ES 500/K-6
4630 Carpenter Rd SE 98503 360-412-4680
Stan Koep, prin. Fax 412-4689

Olympia SD 111 8,900/K-12
1113 Legion Way SE 98501 360-596-6100
Bill Lahmann, supt. Fax 596-6111
osd.wednet.edu
Boston Harbor ES 200/K-5
7300 Zangle Rd NE 98506 360-596-6200
Michael Havens, prin. Fax 596-6201
Brown ES 300/K-5
2000 26th Ave NW 98502 360-596-6800
Maureen Spacciante, prin. Fax 596-6801

Centennial ES 500/K-5
2637 45th Ave SE 98501 360-596-8300
Alice Drummer, prin. Fax 596-8301
Garfield ES 400/K-5
325 Plymouth St NW 98502 360-596-6900
Bob Hodges, prin. Fax 596-6901
Hansen ES 400/K-5
1919 Rd 65 NW 98502 360-596-7400
Ernie Rascon, prin. Fax 596-7401
Jefferson MS 400/6-8
2200 Conger Ave NW 98502 360-596-3200
Michael Cimino, prin. Fax 596-3201
Lincoln ES 300/K-5
213 21st Ave SE 98501 360-596-6400
Marcela Abadi, prin. Fax 596-6401
Madison ES 200/K-5
1225 Legion Way SE 98501 360-596-6300
Gayle Mar-Chun, prin. Fax 596-6301
Marshall MS 400/6-8
3939 20th Ave NW 98502 360-596-7600
John Hitchman, prin. Fax 596-7601
McKenny ES 400/K-5
3250 Morse Merryman Rd SE 98501 360-596-8400
Brendon Chertok, prin. Fax 596-8401
McLane ES 300/K-5
200 Delphi Rd SW 98502 360-596-6600
Joe Bremgartner, prin. Fax 596-6601
Pioneer ES 300/K-5
1655 Carlyon Ave SE 98501 360-596-6500
Chris Woods, prin. Fax 596-6501
Reeves MS 400/6-8
2200 Quince St NE 98506 360-596-3400
Aaron Davis, prin. Fax 596-3401
Roosevelt ES 400/K-5
1417 San Francisco Ave NE 98506 360-596-6700
Domenico Spatolo-Knoll, prin. Fax 596-6701
Washington MS 700/6-8
3100 Cain Rd SE 98501 360-596-3000
Pat Robinson, prin. Fax 596-3001

Tumwater SD 33
Supt. — See Tumwater
Black Lake ES 500/K-6
6345 Black Lake Blmre Rd SW 98512 360-709-7350
Misty Hutson, prin. Fax 709-7352
East Olympia ES 500/K-6
8700 Rich Rd SE 98501 360-709-7150
Patricia Kilmer, prin. Fax 709-7152

Cornerstone Christian S 100/K-8
5501 Wiggins Rd SE 98501 360-923-0071
Mary Kinsella, admin. Fax 923-9307
Evergreen Christian S 400/PK-8
1010 Black Lake Blvd SW 98502 360-357-5590
Lynette Vandekieft, admin. Fax 596-5864
Gospel Outreach Christian S 100/1-12
1925 S Bay Rd NE 98506 360-786-0070
Jon Swanzy, prin. Fax 357-1417
Olympia Christian S 100/PK-10
1416 26th Ave NE 98506 360-352-1831
Anita McKown, prin. Fax 352-1195
Olympia Waldorf S 200/PK-8
8126 Normandy St SE 98501 360-493-0906
Jesse Michener, admin. Fax 493-0835
St. Michael S 300/K-8
1204 11th Ave SE 98501 360-754-5131
Jack Nelson, prin. Fax 753-6090

Omak, Okanogan, Pop. 4,755
Omak SD 19 1,500/PK-12
PO Box 833 98841 509-826-0320
Arthur Himmler, supt. Fax 826-7689
www.omaksd.wednet.edu
East Omak ES 300/3-5
PO Box 833 98841 509-826-3003
Ted Pearson, prin. Fax 826-8231
ECC PK-PK
PO Box 833 98841 509-826-4908
Sheila Crowder, coord. Fax 826-8166
North Omak ES 400/K-2
PO Box 833 98841 509-826-2380
Susan Bell, prin. Fax 826-8166
Omak MS 200/6-8
PO Box 833 98841 509-826-2320
Kathy Miller, prin. Fax 826-7696

Omak Adventist Christian S 50/1-8
PO Box 3294 98841 509-826-5341
Jennifer Hoffpauir, lead tchr.

Onalaska, Lewis
Onalaska SD 300 1,000/PK-12
540 Carlisle Ave 98570 360-978-4111
Dale McDaniel, supt. Fax 978-4185
www.onysd.wednet.edu
Onalaska ES 400/PK-5
540 Carlisle Ave 98570 360-978-4111
Taj Jensen, prin. Fax 978-6142
Onalaska MS 400/6-8
540 Carlisle Ave 98570 360-978-4115
Glen Dickason, prin. Fax 978-6142

Orient, Ferry
Orient SD 65 100/K-8
PO Box 1419 99160 509-684-6873
Mark Selle, supt. Fax 684-3469
www.orient.k12.wa.us
Orient S 100/K-8
PO Box 1419 99160 509-684-6873
Tara Holmes, prin. Fax 684-3469

Orondo, Douglas
Orondo SD 13 200/PK-7
PO Box 71 98843 509-784-2443
Millie Watkins, supt. Fax 784-0633
www.orondo.wednet.edu/
Orondo ES 200/PK-7
PO Box 71 98843 509-784-1333
Millie Watkins, prin. Fax 784-1754

Oroville, Okanogan, Pop. 1,599
Oroville SD 410 700/PK-12
816 Juniper St 98844 509-476-2281
Dr. Ernie Bartelson, supt. Fax 476-2190
www.oroville.wednet.edu/
Oroville ES 300/PK-6
816 Juniper St 98844 509-476-3332
Joe Worsham, prin. Fax 476-3832

Orting, Pierce, Pop. 4,789
Orting SD 344 2,100/K-12
120 Washington Ave N 98360 360-893-6500
Jeff Davis, supt. Fax 893-2300
www.orting.wednet.edu
Orting MS 500/6-8
111 Whitehawk Blvd NE 98360 360-893-3565
Patrick Kelly, prin. Fax 893-2919
Orting PS 500/K-2
316 Washington Ave N 98360 360-893-2248
Jeanette Bergen, prin. Fax 893-4489
Partnership S of Science K-8
805 Old Pioneer Way NW 98360 360-893-7047
Jerry Black, prin. Fax 893-7185
Ptarmigan Ridge IS 500/3-5
805 Old Pioneer Way NW 98360 360-893-0595
L.B. Gilmer, prin. Fax 893-0603

Othello, Adams, Pop. 6,221
Othello SD 147-163-55 3,200/K-12
615 E Juniper St 99344 509-488-2659
George Juarez, supt. Fax 488-5876
www.othello.wednet.edu
Hiawatha ES 600/K-6
506 N 7th Ave 99344 509-488-3389
Scott Pass, prin. Fax 488-4793
Lutacaga ES 500/K-5
795 S 7th Ave 99344 509-488-9669
Aurora Garza, prin. Fax 488-4890
McFarland MS 500/6-8
790 S 10th Ave 99344 509-488-3326
Dennis Adams, prin. Fax 488-4844
Scootney Springs ES 600/K-6
695 S 14th Ave 99344 509-488-9625
Gary Street, prin. Fax 488-4592

Mid Columbia Christian S 50/PK-3
PO Box 713 99344 509-488-2554
Drew Roosma, admin.

Otis Orchards, Spokane, Pop. 5,811
East Valley SD 361
Supt. — See Spokane
Otis Orchards ES 300/K-5
22000 E Wellesley Ave 99027 509-924-9823
Suzanne Savall, prin. Fax 926-0786

Outlook, Yakima
Sunnyside SD 201
Supt. — See Sunnyside
Outlook ES 500/1-5
3800 Van Belle Rd 98938 509-837-3352
Robert Bowman, prin. Fax 837-7855

Pacific, King, Pop. 5,722
Auburn SD 408
Supt. — See Auburn
Alpac ES 500/K-5
310 Milwaukee Blvd N 98047 253-931-4976
Diane Collier, prin. Fax 931-4720

Pacific Beach, Grays Harbor
North Beach SD 64
Supt. — See Ocean Shores
Pacific Beach ES 100/K-6
PO Box U 98571 360-276-4512
Lynette Reime, prin. Fax 276-4510

Palisades, Douglas
Palisades SD 102 50/K-5
1114 Palisades Rd 98845 509-884-8071
Russ Elliott, supt. Fax 886-0615
www.palisades.wednet.edu
Palisades ES 50/K-5
1114 Palisades Rd 98845 509-884-8071
Russ Elliott, prin. Fax 886-0615

Palouse, Whitman, Pop. 945
Palouse SD 301 200/PK-12
600 E Alder St 99161 509-878-1921
Bev Fox, supt. Fax 878-1948
www.garpal.wednet.edu
Palouse ES 100/PK-5
600 E Alder St 99161 509-878-1921
Bev Fox, prin. Fax 878-1675

Pasco, Franklin, Pop. 46,494
Pasco SD 1 12,000/K-12
1215 W Lewis St 99301 509-543-6700
Saundra Hill, supt. Fax 546-2685
www.pasco.wednet.edu
Angelou ES 800/K-5
6001 N Road 84 99301 509-543-6748
LeAnn Nunamaker, prin. Fax 543-6749
Chess ES 600/K-5
715 N 24th Ave 99301 509-543-6789
Kristi Docken, prin. Fax 546-2897
Emerson ES 600/K-5
1616 W Octave St 99301 509-543-6792
Josette Mendoza, prin. Fax 546-2698
Frost ES 600/K-5
1915 N 22nd Ave 99301 509-543-6795
Carla Lobos, prin. Fax 546-2837
Livingston ES 700/K-5
2515 N Road 84 99301 509-546-2688
Susan Sparks, prin. Fax 546-2690
Longfellow ES 500/K-5
301 N 10th Ave 99301 509-547-2429
Diana Cissne, prin. Fax 543-6793
Markham ES 300/K-5
4031 Elm Rd 99301 509-543-6790
Wendy Lechelt-Polster, prin. Fax 543-6791

McGee ES 600/K-5
4601 Horizon Dr 99301 509-547-6583
Robin Hay, prin. Fax 546-2844
McLoughlin MS 1,200/6-8
2803 N Road 88 99301 509-547-4542
Michelle Whitney, prin. Fax 543-6797
Ochoa MS 800/6-8
1801 E Sheppard St 99301 509-543-6742
Jackie Ramirez, prin. Fax 543-6744
Stevens MS 800/6-8
1120 N 22nd Ave 99301 509-543-6798
Robert Elizondo, prin. Fax 546-2854
Twain ES 600/K-5
1801 N Road 40 99301 509-543-6794
Jody Hughes, prin. Fax 546-2847
Whittier ES 600/K-5
616 N Wehe Ave 99301 509-543-6750
Valerie Najera-Aragon, prin. Fax 543-6751

Star SD 54 50/K-6
24180 Pasco Kahlotus Rd 99301 509-547-2704
Don Anderson, supt. Fax 586-6537
www.starsd.wednet.edu
Star ES 50/K-6
24180 Pasco Kahlotus Rd 99301 509-547-2704
Don Anderson, prin. Fax 586-6537

Kingspoint Christian S 200/PK-12
7900 W Court St 99301 509-547-6498
Georgia Perkins, admin. Fax 547-6788
St. Patrick S 300/PK-8
1016 N 14th Ave 99301 509-547-7261
Tono Vegas, prin. Fax 547-2352
Tri-City Junior Academy 100/K-10
4115 W Henry St 99301 509-547-8092
Anthony Oucharek, prin. Fax 547-8516

Pateros, Okanogan, Pop. 624
Pateros SD 122 200/K-12
PO Box 98 98846 509-923-2751
Lois Davies, supt. Fax 923-2283
www.pateros.org
Pateros S 200/K-12
PO Box 98 98846 509-923-2343
Laura Christian, prin. Fax 923-2283

Paterson, Benton
Paterson SD 50 100/K-8
PO Box 189 99345 509-875-2601
Peggy Douglas, supt. Fax 875-2067
www.patersonschools.org
Paterson S 100/K-8
PO Box 189 99345 509-875-2601
Peggy Douglas, prin. Fax 875-2067

Pe Ell, Lewis, Pop. 680
Pe Ell SD 301 300/K-12
PO Box 368 98572 360-291-3244
Scott Fenter, supt. Fax 291-3823
www.peell.k12.wa.us/
Pe Ell S 300/K-12
PO Box 368 98572 360-291-3244
Kyle MacDonald, prin. Fax 291-3823

Peshastin, Chelan
Cascade SD 228
Supt. — See Leavenworth
Peshastin/Dryden ES 200/PK-2
PO Box 373 98847 509-548-5832
Brenda Anderson, prin. Fax 548-6752

Point Roberts, Whatcom
Blaine SD 503
Supt. — See Blaine
Point Roberts PS 50/K-3
PO Box 910 98281 360-945-2223
Fax 945-2230

Pomeroy, Garfield, Pop. 1,480
Pomeroy SD 110 300/K-12
PO Box 950 99347 509-843-3393
Kim Spacek, supt. Fax 843-3046
www.psd.wednet.edu
Pomeroy ES 200/K-6
PO Box 950 99347 509-843-1651
Kim Spacek, prin. Fax 843-8246

Port Angeles, Clallam, Pop. 18,927
Port Angeles SD 121 3,700/PK-12
216 E 4th St 98362 360-457-8575
Gary Cohn, supt. Fax 457-4649
www.portangelesschools.org/
Dry Creek ES 400/K-6
25 Rife Rd 98363 360-457-5050
Kate Wenzl, prin. Fax 417-8019
Franklin ES 500/K-6
2505 S Washington St 98362 360-457-9111
Nancy Pack, prin. Fax 417-2066
Hamilton ES 400/PK-6
1822 W 7th St 98363 360-452-6819
Loren Engel, prin. Fax 452-6359
Jefferson ES 300/PK-6
218 E 12th St 98362 360-457-4231
Michelle Olsen, prin. Fax 457-4296
Roosevelt ES 100/K-6
106 Monroe Rd 98362 360-452-8973
Doug Hayman, prin. Fax 452-4011
Stevens MS 300/7-8
1139 W 14th St 98363 360-452-5590
Charles Lisk, prin. Fax 457-5709

Olympic Christian S 200/PK-12
43 OBrien Rd 98362 360-457-4640
Brian Clark, prin. Fax 457-4612
Queen of Angels S 200/PK-8
1007 S Oak St 98362 360-457-6903
Debra Brines, prin. Fax 457-6866

Port Hadlock, Jefferson, Pop. 2,742
Chimacum SD 49
Supt. — See Chimacum

Chimacum Creek PS 200/PK-2
313 Ness Corner Rd 98339 360-344-3270
Mark Barga, prin. Fax 344-3271

Cedarbrook Adventist Christian S 50/K-8
PO Box 150 98339 360-385-4610
Greg Reseck, prin.
Sunfield Farm and S PK-5
PO Box 85 98339 360-385-3658
Jennifer Conway, admin.

Port Orchard, Kitsap, Pop. 7,986
South Kitsap SD 402 10,500/K-12
1962 Hoover Ave SE 98366 360-874-7000
Dave Larose, supt. Fax 874-7068
www.skitsap.wednet.edu
Burley-Glenwood ES 500/K-6
100 SW Lakeway Blvd 98367 360-443-3110
Derek Grant, prin. Fax 874-3169
East Port Orchard ES 500/K-6
1964 Hoover Ave SE 98366 360-443-3170
Kristi Smith, prin. Fax 443-3229
Glen ES 700/K-6
500 SW Birch Rd 98367 360-443-3400
Jason Shdo, prin. Fax 443-3469
Hidden Creek ES 500/K-6
5455 Converse Ave SE 98367 360-443-3050
Jean de la Pena, prin. Fax 443-3109
Manchester ES 500/K-6
1901 California Ave E 98366 360-443-3230
A.J. Callan, prin. Fax 443-3289
Mullenix Ridge ES 600/K-6
3900 SE Mullenix Rd 98367 360-443-3290
Anita Chandler, prin. Fax 443-3349
Orchard Heights ES 700/K-6
2288 Fircrest Dr SE 98366 360-443-3530
Nancy Pack, prin. Fax 443-3604
South Colby ES 500/K-6
3281 Banner Rd SE 98366 360-443-3000
Brian Pickard, prin. Fax 443-3049
Sunnyslope ES 500/K-6
4183 Sunnyslope Rd SW 98367 360-443-3470
Robert Leslie, prin. Fax 443-3529
Other Schools – See Olalla

Burley Christian S 100/PK-12
14687 Olympic Dr SE 98367 253-851-8619
Dennis Myers, admin. Fax 857-0093
Luther Center for Learning 50/K-8
3901 SE Mullenix Rd 98367 360-895-1782
Barb Haueisen, prin. Fax 895-9191
South Kitsap Christian S 200/PK-12
1780 Lincoln Ave SE 98366 360-876-5595
Sandy Jennings, admin. Fax 876-2206

Port Townsend, Jefferson, Pop. 9,001
Port Townsend SD 50 1,200/K-12
450 Fir St 98368 360-379-4502
Thomas Opstad, supt. Fax 385-3617
www.ptschools.org/
Blue Heron MS 300/4-8
3939 San Juan Ave 98368 360-379-4540
Mark Decker, prin. Fax 379-4548
Grant Street ES 200/K-3
1637 Grant St 98368 360-379-4535
Steve Finch, prin. Fax 379-4261

Poulsbo, Kitsap, Pop. 7,593
North Kitsap SD 400 6,400/PK-12
18360 Caldart Ave NE 98370 360-779-8704
Dr. Richard Jones, supt. Fax 697-3175
www.nkschools.org
Breidablik ES 300/PK-5
25142 Waghorn Rd NW 98370 360-779-8802
Lynn Jorgenson, prin. Fax 779-8807
Pearson ES 300/PK-5
15650 Central Valley Rd NW 98370 360-697-6266
Jeannette Wolfe, prin. Fax 779-8730
Poulsbo ES 500/K-5
18531 Noll Rd NE 98370 360-779-2911
Wally Lis, prin. Fax 598-1077
Poulsbo MS 500/6-8
2003 NE Hostmark St 98370 360-779-4453
Matt Vandeleur, prin. Fax 598-1041
Vinland ES 500/K-5
22104 Rhododendron Ln NW 98370 360-779-8990
Charles McCabe, prin. Fax 779-8946
Other Schools – See Kingston, Suquamish

Christ the King Academy 200/K-9
PO Box 2460 98370 360-779-9189
DeAnna Henning, admin. Fax 394-4148
Poulsbo Adventist S 50/1-8
1700 NE Lincoln Rd 98370 360-779-6290
Kerry Trethewey, prin.

Prescott, Walla Walla, Pop. 327
Prescott SD 402-37 200/K-12
PO Box 65 99348 509-849-2216
Dr. Carolyn Marsh, supt. Fax 849-2800
www.prescott.k12.wa.us/
Prescott ES, PO Box 65 99348 100/K-6
Dr. Carolyn Marsh, prin. 509-849-2217

Prosser, Benton, Pop. 5,140
Prosser SD 116 2,800/K-12
1126 Meade Ave Ste A 99350 509-786-3323
Dr. Ray Tolcacher, supt. Fax 786-2062
www.prosserschools.org/
Housel MS 700/6-8
2001 Highland Dr 99350 509-786-1732
Deanna Flores, prin. Fax 786-2814
Keene-Riverview ES 500/K-2
832 Park Ave 99350 509-786-2020
Shellie Hatch, prin. Fax 786-4271
Prosser Heights ES 500/3-5
2008 Miller Ave 99350 509-786-2633
Kris Moore, prin. Fax 786-3121

Whitstran ES 300/K-5
102101 W Foisy Rd 99350 509-973-2345
Sally Juzeler, prin. Fax 973-2500

Pullman, Whitman, Pop. 25,262
Pullman SD 267 2,200/K-12
240 SE Dexter St 99163 509-332-3581
Paul Sturm, supt. Fax 334-0375
www.psd267.wednet.edu
Franklin ES 300/K-5
850 SE Klemgard St 99163 509-334-5641
Brian Moore, prin. Fax 332-0864
Jefferson ES 400/K-5
1150 NW Bryant St 99163 509-332-2617
Craig Nelson, prin. Fax 332-0680
Lincoln MS 500/6-8
315 SE Crestview St 99163 509-334-3411
Cameron Grow, prin. Fax 334-9678
Sunnyside ES 300/K-5
425 SW Shirley St 99163 509-334-1800
Rick Bates, prin. Fax 332-0329

Pullman Christian S 100/PK-12
345 SW Kimball Dr 99163 509-332-3545
Sherri Goetze, prin. Fax 332-5433

Puyallup, Pierce, Pop. 35,861
Bethel SD 403
Supt. — See Spanaway
Frederickson ES 100/PK-6
17418 74th Ave E 98375 253-683-6300
Ellen Eddy, prin. Fax 683-6398

Puyallup SD 3 22,000/PK-12
PO Box 370 98371 253-841-1301
Dr. Tony Apostle, supt. Fax 840-8959
www.puyallup.k12.wa.us
Brouillet ES 800/K-6
17207 94th Ave E 98375 253-841-8670
Lisa Berry, prin. Fax 840-8871
Carson ES 800/K-6
8615 184th St E 98375 253-840-8808
Arturo Gonzalez, prin. Fax 840-8987
Edgerton ES 600/K-6
16528 127th Avenue Ct E 98374 253-840-8809
Guy Kovacs, prin. Fax 840-8993
Firgrove ES 1,000/K-6
13918 Meridian S 98373 253-841-8733
Char Krause, prin. Fax 840-8948
Fruitland ES 600/PK-6
1515 S Fruitland 98371 253-841-8734
Laurie Orheim, prin. Fax 840-8915
Hunt ES 800/K-6
12801 144th St E 98374 253-841-8690
Rebecca Williams, prin. Fax 840-8939
Karshner ES 400/PK-6
1328 8th Ave NW 98371 253-841-8736
Jeanie Schneider, prin. Fax 435-6278
Maplewood ES 300/K-6
1110 W Pioneer 98371 253-841-8737
Liz Knox, prin. Fax 840-8947
Meeker ES 400/K-6
409 5th St SW 98371 253-841-8738
Kevin Hampton, prin. Fax 435-2396
Pope ES 1,200/K-6
15102 122nd Ave E 98374 253-841-8755
Dave Sunich, prin. Fax 841-8684
Ridgecrest ES 500/PK-6
12616 Shaw Rd E 98374 253-841-8753
Dana Harris, prin. Fax 840-8944
Shaw Road ES 600/K-6
1106 Shaw Rd 98372 253-841-8675
Judy Piger, prin. Fax 840-8945
Spinning ES 400/K-6
1306 E Pioneer 98372 253-841-8742
Laura King, prin. Fax 840-8942
Stewart ES 300/K-6
426 4th Ave NE 98372 253-841-8743
Ann Hoban, prin. Fax 840-8955
Sunrise ES 500/PK-6
2323 39th Ave SE 98374 253-841-8744
Terrie Garrison, prin. Fax 840-8972
Wildwood Park ES 600/PK-6
1601 26th Ave SE 98374 253-841-8746
Glenn Malone, prin. Fax 840-8940
Woodland ES 700/PK-6
7707 112th St E 98373 253-841-8747
Eric Molver, prin. Fax 840-8885
Zeiger ES 800/K-6
13008 94th Ave E 98373 253-841-8663
Cory Crawford, prin. Fax 841-8704
Other Schools – See Edgewood, Tacoma

Sumner SD 320
Supt. — See Sumner
McAlder ES 500/K-5
15502 96th St E 98372 253-891-4500
Susie Black, prin. Fax 891-4522

All Saints S 300/PK-8
504 2nd St SW 98371 253-845-5025
Stephen Morissette, prin. Fax 435-9841
Cascade Christian/Puyallup ES 400/K-6
601 9th Ave SE Unit B 98372 253-841-2091
Joyce Blum, prin. Fax 841-2095
Northwest Christian S 100/PK-8
904 Shaw Rd 98372 253-845-5722
Marshall Merklin, prin.

Quilcene, Jefferson
Quilcene SD 48 200/K-12
PO Box 40 98376 360-765-3363
David Andersen, supt. Fax 765-4183
www.quilcene.wednet.edu
Quilcene S 200/K-12
PO Box 40 98376 360-765-3363
Jim Betteley, prin. Fax 765-4183

Quincy, Grant, Pop. 5,568
Quincy SD 144-101 2,400/K-12
119 J St SW 98848 509-787-4571
Dr. Burton Dickerson, supt. Fax 787-4336
www.qsd.wednet.edu
George ES 100/K-4
401 Washington Way 98848 509-785-2244
Nik Bergman, prin. Fax 787-8955
Monument ES 500/4-6
1400 13th Ave SW 98848 509-787-9826
Don Francis, prin. Fax 787-8974
Mountain View ES 300/K-1
119 D St NW 98848 509-787-4548
Kathie Brown, prin. Fax 787-9025
Pioneer ES 300/2-4
224 J St SE 98848 509-787-1595
Donna Kiehn, prin. Fax 787-2583
Quincy JHS 300/7-8
417 C St SE 98848 509-787-4435
Scott Ramsey, prin. Fax 787-8949

Rainier, Thurston, Pop. 1,649
Rainier SD 307 900/K-12
PO Box 98 98576 360-446-2207
Dennis Friedrich, supt. Fax 446-2918
www.rainier.wednet.edu
Rainier ES 400/K-5
PO Box 98 98576 360-446-4020
Paulette Johnson, prin. Fax 446-4022
Rainier MS 200/6-8
PO Box 98 98576 360-446-2206
Christopher Pollard, prin. Fax 446-7414

Randle, Lewis
White Pass SD 303 500/PK-12
PO Box 188 98377 360-497-3791
Richard Linehan, supt. Fax 497-2560
www.wpsd.wednet.edu
White Pass ES 200/PK-6
127 Kindle Rd 98377 360-497-7300
Kathy Tully, prin. Fax 497-2126

Raymond, Pacific, Pop. 2,995
Raymond SD 116 600/K-12
1016 Commercial St 98577 360-942-3415
Stephen Holland, supt. Fax 942-3416
www.raymond.k12.wa.us
Raymond ES 300/K-6
825 Commercial St 98577 360-942-2435
Jessica Bryant, prin. Fax 942-2503

Willapa Valley SD 160 400/K-12
22 Viking Way 98577 360-942-5855
Dr. Paula Akerlund, supt. Fax 942-3216
www.willapa.wednet.edu
Menlo MS, 22 Viking Way 98577 100/6-8
Rob Friese, prin. 360-942-2006
Willapa ES 200/K-5
845 Willapa Fourth St 98577 360-942-3311
Jay Pearson, prin.

Reardan, Lincoln, Pop. 610
Reardan-Edwall SD 9 500/K-12
PO Box 225 99029 509-796-2701
Doug Asbjornsen, supt. Fax 796-4954
www.reardan.net
Reardan ES 300/K-6
PO Box 109 99029 509-796-2511
Dwight Cooper, prin. Fax 796-2161

Redmond, King, Pop. 47,579
Lake Washington SD 414 23,400/K-12
PO Box 97039 98073 425-702-3200
Dr. Chip Kimball, supt. Fax 702-3213
www.lwsd.org
Alcott ES 600/K-6
4213 228th Ave NE 98053 425-868-1008
Karen Mason, prin. Fax 836-8903
Audubon ES 400/K-6
3045 180th Ave NE 98052 425-881-9575
Karen Dickens, prin. Fax 882-3422
Dickinson ES 500/K-6
7040 208th Ave NE 98053 425-836-6650
Ellen Challenger, prin. Fax 836-4658
Einstein ES 400/K-6
18025 NE 116th St 98052 425-558-7973
Jack Tobin, prin. Fax 867-0797
Explorer Community S 100/1-6
7040 208th Ave NE 98053 425-836-6650
Ellen Challenger, prin. Fax 836-4658
Mann ES 400/K-6
17001 NE 104th St 98052 425-881-9696
Megan Spaulding, prin. Fax 556-0874
McAuliffe ES 700/K-6
23823 NE 22nd St 98074 425-836-6680
Tracey Miller, prin. Fax 836-4238
Mead ES 600/K-6
1725 216th Ave NE 98074 425-868-0760
Shawna Rothaus, prin. Fax 868-4721
Parks ES 400/K-6
22845 NE Cedar Park Cres 98053 425-836-6660
Jeffrey Newport, prin. Fax 836-1350
Redmond ES 400/K-6
16800 NE 80th St 98052 425-702-3419
Janice Heid, prin. Fax 702-3420
Rockwell ES 500/K-6
11125 162nd Ave NE 98052 425-702-3450
Tina Livingston, prin. Fax 885-5528
Rush ES 400/K-6
6101 152nd Ave NE 98052 425-881-6047
Kimo Spray, prin. Fax 881-2752
Smith ES 800/K-6
23305 NE 14th St 98074 425-868-5116
Justin Blasko, prin. Fax 836-8258
Stella Schola S 100/6-8
13505 NE 75th St 98052 425-558-0842
Steve Mezich, prin. Fax 556-0629
Other Schools – See Kirkland, Sammamish, Woodinville

Northshore SD 417
Supt. — See Bothell
Sunrise ES 400/K-6
14075 172nd Ave NE 98052 425-408-5300
Paul Bodnar, prin. Fax 408-5302

Bear Creek S 200/K-6
19315 NE 95th St 98053 425-885-9401
Patrick Carruth, hdmstr. Fax 885-9663
Bear Creek S 600/K-12
8905 208th Ave NE 98053 425-898-1720
Patrick Carruth, hdmstr. Fax 898-1430
Faith Lutheran S 50/PK-3
9041 166th Ave NE 98052 425-885-1810
Barbara Deming, admin. Fax 885-2820
Medina Academy 100/PK-6
PO Box 2682 98073 425-497-8848
Saman Hassan, prin. Fax 497-8848
Montessori Children's House 50/PK-4
5003 218th Ave NE 98053 425-868-7805
Jennifer Wheelhouse, hdmstr. Fax 458-4330
Sammamish Montessori S 300/PK-4
7655 178th Pl NE 98052 425-883-3271
Joan Starling, prin. Fax 869-2639

Renton, King, Pop. 55,817
Issaquah SD 411
Supt. — See Issaquah
Apollo ES 400/K-5
15025 SE 117th St 98059 425-837-7500
Marla Erath, prin. Fax 837-7508
Briarwood ES 400/K-5
17020 SE 134th St 98059 425-837-5000
Drew Terry, prin. Fax 837-5037
Maple Hills ES 400/K-5
15644 204th Ave SE 98059 425-837-5100
Monique Beane, prin. Fax 837-5108
Maywood MS 900/6-8
14490 168th Ave SE 98059 425-837-6900
Patrick Murphy, prin. Fax 837-6910

Kent SD 415
Supt. — See Kent
Carriage Crest ES 500/K-6
18235 140th Ave SE 98058 253-373-7597
Susanne Wick, prin. Fax 373-7563
Fairwood ES 400/K-6
16600 148th Ave SE 98058 253-373-7491
Patricia Hoyle, prin. Fax 373-7492
Glenridge ES 500/K-6
19405 120th Ave SE 98058 253-373-7494
Scott Abernathy, prin. Fax 373-7495
Meeker MS 500/7-8
12600 SE 192nd St 98058 253-373-7284
Jeff Pelzel, prin. Fax 373-7560
Northwood MS 500/7-8
17007 SE 184th St 98058 253-373-7780
Colleen Nelson, prin. Fax 373-7788
Ridgewood ES 600/K-6
18030 162nd Pl SE 98058 253-373-7482
Andy Song, prin. Fax 373-7483

Renton SD 403 13,100/K-12
300 SW 7th St 98057 425-204-2300
Dr. Mary Alice Heuschel, supt. Fax 204-2456
www.rentonschools.us
Benson Hill ES 500/K-5
18665 116th Ave SE 98058 425-204-3300
Martha Flemming, prin. Fax 204-3313
Cascade ES 500/K-5
16022 116th Ave SE 98058 425-204-3350
Shannon Harvey, prin. Fax 204-3357
Highlands ES 600/K-5
2720 NE 7th St 98056 425-204-4600
Janet Fawcett, prin. Fax 204-4616
Kennydale ES 500/K-5
1700 NE 28th St 98056 425-204-4700
Bill Tarter, prin. Fax 204-4747
Maplewood Heights ES 500/K-5
13430 144th Ave SE 98059 425-204-4750
Judy Busch, prin. Fax 204-4798
McKnight MS 1,100/6-8
1200 Edmonds Ave NE 98056 425-204-3600
Mary Merritt, prin. Fax 204-3680
Nelson MS 1,100/6-8
2403 Jones Ave S 98055 425-204-3000
Colin Falk, prin. Fax 204-3079
Renton Park ES 400/K-5
16828 128th Ave SE 98058 425-204-2950
JoEllen Tapper, prin. Fax 204-2957
Sierra Heights ES 600/K-5
9901 132nd Ave SE 98059 425-204-4650
Nanci Davis, prin. Fax 204-4659
Talbot Hill ES 500/K-5
2300 Talbot Rd S 98055 425-204-4900
Sheryl Dunton, prin. Fax 204-4948
Tiffany Park ES 400/1-5
1601 Lake Youngs Way SE 98058 425-204-4850
Irene Olson, prin. Fax 204-4857
Other Schools – See Newcastle, Seattle

Cedar River Montessori S 100/PK-6
15828 SE Jones Rd 98058 425-271-9614
Charis Sharp Ph.D., hdmstr. Fax 271-6934
King of Kings Lutheran S 100/PK-PK
18207 108th Ave SE 98055 425-255-8520
Debra Timm, dir. Fax 226-4119
RCS Highlands Christian S 100/PK-6
PO Box 2578 98056 425-228-9897
Paula Satterberg, admin. Fax 228-7401
RCS Maple Valley Christian S 300/PK-6
PO Box 58129 98058 425-226-4640
Weldo Melvin, admin. Fax 228-1934
Renton Christian S 500/PK-8
15717 152nd Ave SE 98058 425-226-0820
Erik Konsmo, hdmstr. Fax 264-0291
St. Anthony S 500/K-8
336 Shattuck Ave S 98057 425-255-0059
Sr. Linda Riggers, prin. Fax 235-6555

Republic, Ferry, Pop. 988
Republic SD 309 400/K-12
30306 E Highway 20 99166 509-775-3173
Teena McDonald, supt. Fax 775-3712
www.republic.wednet.edu
Republic ES 200/K-5
30306 E Highway 20 99166 509-775-3327
Shawn Anderson, prin. Fax 775-2674
Republic JHS 100/6-8
30306 E Highway 20 99166 509-775-3171
Shawn Anderson, prin. Fax 775-1098

Richland, Benton, Pop. 44,317
Richland SD 400 10,000/K-12
615 Snow Ave 99352 509-967-6000
Jean Lane, supt. Fax 942-2401
www.rsd.edu
Badger Mountain ES 700/K-5
1515 Elementary St 99352 509-967-6225
Gail Ledbetter, prin. Fax 628-2702
Carmichael MS 900/6-8
620 Thayer Dr 99352 509-967-6425
Tim Praino, prin. Fax 942-2471
Chief Joseph MS 600/6-8
504 Wilson St, 509-967-6400
Jon Lobdell, prin. Fax 942-2492
Jefferson ES 400/K-5
1525 Hunt Ave, 509-967-6250
Roni Ramsey, prin. Fax 942-2569
Lee ES 700/K-5
1702 Van Giesen St, 509-967-6475
Kathy Page, prin. Fax 942-2556
Lewis & Clark ES 400/K-5
800 Downing St 99352 509-967-6275
Martin Brewer, prin. Fax 942-2377
Sacajawea ES 400/K-5
518 Catskill St, 509-967-6325
Jim Bruce, prin. Fax 371-2681
Whitman ES 400/K-5
1704 Gray St 99352 509-967-6300
Paul Dann, prin. Fax 942-2388
Other Schools – See West Richland

Christ the King S 400/K-8
1122 Long Ave, 509-946-6158
Joe Jisa, prin. Fax 943-8402
Liberty Christian S of the Tri-Cities 500/PK-12
2200 Williams Blvd, 509-946-0602
Dr. Mac Culver, supt. Fax 943-5623

Ridgefield, Clark, Pop. 2,869
Ridgefield SD 122 2,000/K-12
2724 S Hillhurst Rd 98642 360-619-1300
Art Edgerly, supt. Fax 619-1397
www.ridge.k12.wa.us
South Ridge ES 500/K-6
502 NW 199th St 98642 360-619-1500
Vern Yoshioka, prin. Fax 619-1559
Union Ridge ES 600/K-6
330 N 5th Ave 98642 360-750-7600
Connie Ford, prin. Fax 750-7659
View Ridge MS 300/7-8
510 Pioneer St 98642 360-619-1400
Chris Griffith, prin. Fax 619-1459

Cedar Tree Classical Christian S 100/K-10
20601 NE 29th Ave 98642 360-887-0190
Tom Bradshaw, hdmstr.
Mountain View Christian S 200/PK-6
2810 NE 259th St 98642 360-887-4019
Michelle Geer, prin. Fax 887-0717

Ritzville, Adams, Pop. 1,721
Ritzville SD 160-67 400/PK-12
209 E Wellsandt Rd 99169 509-659-1660
Dwight Remick, supt. Fax 659-0927
www.ritzville.wednet.edu
Ritzville S 200/PK-8
401 E 6th Ave 99169 509-659-0232
Deborah O'Brien, prin. Fax 659-4119

Rochester, Thurston, Pop. 1,250
Rochester SD 401 2,100/K-12
PO Box 457 98579 360-273-5536
James Anderson, supt. Fax 273-5547
www.rochester.wednet.edu/
Grand Mound ES 500/3-5
7710 James Rd SW 98579 360-273-5512
Clarence Surridge, prin. Fax 273-8917
Rochester MS 500/6-8
PO Box 398 98579 360-273-5958
Will Maus, prin. Fax 273-2045
Rochester PS 500/K-2
7440 James Rd SW 98579 360-273-5161
Karla Kyes, prin. Fax 273-2582

Rockford, Spokane, Pop. 494
Freeman SD 358 900/K-12
15001 S Jackson Rd 99030 509-291-3695
Sergio Hernandez, supt. Fax 291-3636
www.freemansd.org
Freeman ES 400/K-5
14917 S Jackson Rd 99030 509-291-4791
Lisa Phelan, prin. Fax 291-7339
Freeman MS 200/6-8
14917 S Jackson Rd 99030 509-291-7301
Jim Straw, prin. Fax 291-7339

Rock Island, Douglas, Pop. 858
Eastmont SD 206
Supt. — See East Wenatchee
Rock Island ES 200/K-4
5645 Rock Island Rd 98850 509-884-5023
Sue Kane, prin. Fax 884-1720

Roosevelt, Klickitat
Roosevelt SD 403 50/K-6
PO Box 248 99356 509-384-5462
Ken BeLieu, supt. Fax 384-5621
Roosevelt ES 50/K-6
PO Box 248 99356 509-384-5462
Fax 384-5621

Rosalia, Whitman, Pop. 600
Rosalia SD 320 300/K-12
916 S Josephine Ave 99170 509-523-3061
Dr. Thomas Crowley, supt. Fax 523-3861
www.rosaliaschools.com
Rosalia S 300/K-12
916 S Josephine Ave 99170 509-523-3061
Darrell Kuhn, prin. Fax 523-3861

Roy, Pierce, Pop. 683
Bethel SD 403
Supt. — See Spanaway
Roy ES 300/K-6
PO Box 238 98580 253-683-5100
Christoph Green, prin. Fax 683-5198

Royal City, Grant, Pop. 1,952
Royal SD 160 1,400/K-12
PO Box 486 99357 509-346-2222
Rosemarie Search, supt. Fax 346-8746
www.royal.wednet.edu/
Red Rock ES 700/K-5
PO Box 486 99357 509-346-2206
Theresa Eilers, prin. Fax 346-2207
Royal MS 300/6-8
PO Box 486 99357 509-346-2268
David Jaderlund, prin. Fax 346-2269

Saint John, Whitman, Pop. 552
St. John SD 322 200/PK-12
301 W Nob Hill Rd 99171 509-648-3336
Rick Winters, supt. Fax 648-3451
www.sje.wednet.edu/index.html
St. John ES, 301 W Nob Hill Rd 99171 100/PK-6
Rob Roettger, prin. 509-648-3336

Sammamish, King, Pop. 34,364
Issaquah SD 411
Supt. — See Issaquah
Cascade Ridge ES 600/K-5
2020 Trossachs Blvd SE 98075 425-837-5500
Colleen Shields, prin. Fax 837-5505

Lake Washington SD 414
Supt. — See Redmond
Blackwell ES 600/K-6
3225 205th Pl NE 98074 425-836-7300
Stephen Bryant, prin. Fax 836-7305
Carson ES, 1035 244th Ave NE 98074 K-6
Mary Cronin, prin. 425-936-2750

Arbor S 100/PK-8
1107 228th Ave SE 98075 425-392-3866
Mary O'Brien, pres. Fax 557-0175
TLC Academy 100/PK-K
21512 NE 16th St 98074 425-868-1943
Janet Bequette, dir. Fax 868-3774

Satsop, Grays Harbor
Satsop SD 104 100/K-6
PO Box 96 98583 360-482-5330
Marsha Hendrick, supt. Fax 482-5724
Satsop ES 100/K-6
PO Box 96 98583 360-482-5330
Marsha Hendrick, prin. Fax 482-5724

SeaTac, King, Pop. 25,081
Highline SD 401
Supt. — See Burien
Bow Lake ES 400/K-6
18237 42nd Ave S 98188 206-631-3500
Diana Garcia, prin. Fax 631-3573
Chinook MS 500/7-8
18650 42nd Ave S 98188 206-631-5700
Evie Livingston, prin. Fax 631-5770
Madrona ES 600/K-6
20301 32nd Ave S 98198 206-433-2478
Daniel Yarbrough, prin. Fax 433-2500

Seattle Christian S 700/K-12
18301 Military Rd S 98188 206-246-8241
Gloria Hunter, supt. Fax 246-9066

Seattle, King, Pop. 573,911
Highline SD 401
Supt. — See Burien
Beverly Park ES 500/K-6
1201 S 104th St 98168 206-631-3400
Katherine Anderson, prin. Fax 631-3452
Cascade MS 600/7-8
11212 10th Ave SW 98146 206-631-5500
Colin Ryan, prin. Fax 631-5568
Hilltop ES 600/K-6
12250 24th Ave S 98168 206-433-2371
Rick Wisen, prin. Fax 433-2346
Mount View ES 600/K-6
10811 12th Ave SW 98146 206-631-4500
Mark Demick, prin. Fax 631-4506
Southern Heights ES 300/K-6
11249 14th Ave S 98168 206-631-5000
Anne Coxon, prin. Fax 631-5042
White Center Heights ES 500/K-6
10015 6th Ave SW 98146 206-433-2437
Dave Darling, prin. Fax 433-2476

Renton SD 403
Supt. — See Renton
Bryn Mawr ES 400/1-5
8212 S 118th St 98178 425-204-4150
Tammy Watanabe, prin. Fax 204-4195
Campbell Hill ES 400/1-5
6418 S 124th St 98178 425-204-4000
Jon Stadler, prin. Fax 204-4013
Dimmitt MS 900/6-8
12320 80th Ave S 98178 425-204-2800
John Schmitz, prin. Fax 204-2812

Lakeridge ES 300/1-5
7400 S 115th St 98178 425-204-4100
Ginny Knox, prin. Fax 204-4145

Seattle SD 1 44,100/PK-12
PO Box 34165 98124 206-252-0000
Maria Goodloe-Johnson Ph.D., supt. Fax 252-0102
www.seattleschools.org

Adams ES 400/K-5
6110 28th Ave NW 98107 206-252-1300
Anne Johnson, prin. Fax 252-1301

African American Academy 300/K-8
8311 Beacon Ave S 98118 206-252-6650
Christopher Carter, prin. Fax 252-6651

Alki ES 300/PK-5
3010 59th Ave SW 98116 206-252-9050
Joanne Hill, prin. Fax 252-9051

Arbor Heights ES 300/K-5
3701 SW 104th St 98146 206-252-9250
Carol Coram, prin. Fax 252-9251

Bagley ES 300/K-5
7821 Stone Ave N 98103 206-252-5110
Kimberly Kinzer, prin. Fax 252-5111

Beacon Hill ES 400/K-5
2025 14th Ave S 98144 206-252-2700
Susie Murphy, prin. Fax 252-2701

Blaine S 500/K-8
2550 34th Ave W 98199 206-252-1920
Heather Swanson, prin. Fax 252-1921

Brighton ES 300/K-5
6725 45th Ave S 98118 206-252-6770
Beverly Raines, prin. Fax 252-6771

Broadview-Thompson S 500/K-8
13052 Greenwood Ave N 98133 206-252-4080
Jeanne Smart, prin. Fax 252-4081

Bryant ES 500/K-5
3311 NE 60th St 98115 206-252-5200
Kim Fox, prin. Fax 252-5201

Coe ES 400/K-5
2424 7th Ave W 98119 206-252-2000
David Elliott, prin. Fax 252-2001

Concord ES 300/K-5
723 S Concord St 98108 206-252-8100
Sandra Scott, prin. Fax 252-8101

Cooper ES 200/K-5
1901 SW Genesee St 98106 206-252-8170
Cathy Rutherford, prin. Fax 252-8171

Day ES 300/K-5
3921 Linden Ave N 98103 206-252-6010
Susan McCloskey, prin. Fax 252-6011

Dearborn Park ES 300/K-5
2820 S Orcas St 98108 206-252-6930
Ellen Punyon, prin. Fax 252-6931

Denny MS 600/6-8
8402 30th Ave SW 98126 206-252-9000
Jeff Clarke, prin. Fax 252-9001

Dunlap ES 400/PK-5
4525 S Cloverdale St 98118 206-252-7000
Greg Imel, prin. Fax 252-7001

Eckstein MS 1,200/6-8
3003 NE 75th St 98115 206-252-5010
Kim Whitworth, prin. Fax 252-5011

Emerson ES 200/K-5
9709 60th Ave S 98118 206-252-7100
Marion Vinson, prin. Fax 252-7101

Gatewood ES 300/K-5
4320 SW Myrtle St 98136 206-252-9400
Rhonda Claytor, prin. Fax 252-9401

Gatzert ES 300/K-5
1301 E Yesler Way 98122 206-252-2810
Norma Zavala, prin. Fax 252-2811

Graham Hill ES 300/PK-5
5149 S Graham St 98118 206-252-7140
Chris Morningstar, prin. Fax 252-7141

Green Lake ES 200/K-5
2400 N 65th St 98103 206-252-5320
Cheryl Gringer, prin. Fax 252-5321

Greenwood ES 200/K-5
144 NW 80th St 98117 206-252-1400
Walter Trotter, prin. Fax 252-1401

Hamilton International MS 700/6-8
4400 Interlake Ave N 98103 206-252-5810
Katie Leary, prin. Fax 252-5811

Hawthorne ES 300/PK-5
4100 39th Ave S 98118 206-252-7210
Sumiko Huff, prin. Fax 252-7211

Hay ES 500/K-5
201 Garfield St 98109 206-252-2100
Dan Warren, prin. Fax 252-2101

Highland Park ES 400/K-5
1012 SW Trenton St 98106 206-252-8240
Ann Gray, prin. Fax 252-8241

Kimball ES 500/K-5
3200 23rd Ave S 98144 206-252-7280
Anne Fitzpatrick, prin. Fax 252-7281

Kurose MS 600/6-8
3928 S Graham St 98118 206-252-7700
Mia Williams, prin. Fax 252-7701

Lafayette ES 500/K-5
2645 California Ave SW 98116 206-252-9500
Virginia Turner, prin. Fax 252-9501

Laurelhurst ES 500/K-5
4530 46th Ave NE 98105 206-252-5400
Kathy Jolly, prin. Fax 252-5401

Lawton ES 400/K-5
4000 27th Ave W 98199 206-252-2130
Ed Noh, prin. Fax 252-2131

Leschi ES 200/K-5
135 32nd Ave 98122 206-252-2950
Jo Lute-Ervin, prin. Fax 252-2951

Lowell ES 500/PK-5
1058 E Mercer St 98102 206-252-3020
Julie Breidenbach, prin. Fax 252-3021

Loyal Heights ES 400/K-5
2511 NW 80th St 98117 206-252-1500
Cashel Toner, prin. Fax 252-1501

Madison MS 900/6-8
3429 45th Ave SW 98116 206-252-9200
Jill Hudson, prin. Fax 252-9201

Madrona S 500/K-8
1121 33rd Ave 98122 206-252-3100
Kaaren Andrews, prin. Fax 252-3101

Maple ES 400/K-5
4925 Corson Ave S 98108 206-252-8310
Pat Hunter, prin. Fax 252-8311

Marshall ES 300/PK-5
2401 S Irving St 98144 206-252-2800
Winifred Todd, prin. Fax 252-2801

McClure MS 600/6-8
1915 1st Ave W 98119 206-252-1900
Sarah Pritchett, prin. Fax 252-1901

McGilvra ES 300/K-5
1617 38th Ave E 98112 206-252-3160
Jo Shapiro, prin. Fax 252-3161

Meany MS 500/6-8
301 21st Ave E 98112 206-252-2500
Stacey McGrath-Smith, prin. Fax 252-2501

Mercer MS 700/6-8
1600 S Columbian Way 98108 206-252-8000
Andhra Lutz, prin. Fax 252-8001

Minor ES 200/PK-5
1700 E Union St 98122 206-252-3230
Gregory King, prin. Fax 252-3231

Montlake ES 200/K-5
2409 22nd Ave E 98112 206-252-3300
Claudia Allan, prin. Fax 252-3301

Muir ES 300/K-5
3301 S Horton St 98144 206-252-7400
Awnie Thompson, prin. Fax 252-7401

New S at South Shore 200/K-8
3528 S Ferdinand St 98118 206-252-7600
Sherrie Encarnacion, prin. Fax 252-6561

North Beach ES 300/K-5
9018 24th Ave NW 98117 206-252-1510
Joanne Bowers, prin. Fax 252-1511

Northgate ES 200/K-5
11725 1st Ave NE 98125 206-252-4180
Ed Jefferson, prin. Fax 252-4181

Olympic Hills ES 200/K-5
13018 20th Ave NE 98125 206-252-4300
Zoe Jenkins, prin. Fax 252-4301

Olympic View ES 400/K-5
504 NE 95th St 98115 206-252-5500
Justin Baeder, prin. Fax 252-5501

Rogers ES 300/K-5
4030 NE 109th St 98125 206-252-4320
Marcia Boyd, prin. Fax 252-4321

Roxhill ES 300/PK-5
9430 30th Ave SW 98126 206-252-9570
Carmela Dellino, prin. Fax 252-9571

Sacajawea ES 300/K-5
9501 20th Ave NE 98115 206-252-5550
Barry Dorsey, prin. Fax 252-5551

Sanislo ES 300/K-5
1812 SW Myrtle St 98106 206-252-8380
Debbie Nelsen, prin. Fax 252-8381

Schmitz Park ES 300/K-5
5000 SW Spokane St 98116 206-252-9700
Gerrit Kischner, prin. Fax 252-9701

Stanford International ES 400/K-5
4057 5th Ave NE 98105 206-252-6080
Kelly Aramaki, prin. Fax 252-6081

Stevens ES 300/K-5
1242 18th Ave E 98112 206-252-3400
Jenniffer Reinig, prin. Fax 252-3401

Van Asselt ES 400/PK-5
7201 Beacon Ave S 98108 206-252-7500
Eldoris Turner, prin. Fax 252-7501

View Ridge ES 400/PK-5
7047 50th Ave NE 98115 206-252-5600
Terri Skjei, prin. Fax 252-5601

Washington MS 1,100/6-8
2101 S Jackson St 98144 206-252-2600
Jon Halfaker, prin. Fax 252-2601

Wedgewood ES 400/K-5
2720 NE 85th St 98115 206-252-5670
Denise Espania, prin. Fax 252-5671

West Seattle ES 200/PK-5
6760 34th Ave SW 98126 206-252-9450
Gayle Everly, prin. Fax 252-9451

West Woodland ES 400/K-5
5601 4th Ave NW 98107 206-252-1600
Marilyn Loveness, prin. Fax 252-1601

Whitman MS 1,000/6-8
9201 15th Ave NW 98117 206-252-1200
Michael Starosky, prin. Fax 252-1201

Whittier ES 400/PK-5
1320 NW 75th St 98117 206-252-1650
Cothron McMillian, prin. Fax 252-1651

Wing Luke ES 300/K-5
3701 S Kenyon St 98118 206-252-7630
Davy Muth, prin. Fax 252-7631

Tukwila SD 406
Supt. — See Tukwila

Cascade View ES 400/K-5
13601 32nd Ave S 98168 206-901-7700
Jeffrey Baker, prin. Fax 901-7707

Amazing Grace Christian S 200/PK-6
10056 Renton Ave S 98178 206-723-5526
Gloria Zimmerman, admin.

Assumption-St. Bridget S 500/K-8
6220 32nd Ave NE 98115 206-524-7452
Kathi Hand, prin. Fax 524-6757

Bertschi S 200/PK-5
2227 10th Ave E 98102 206-324-5476
Brigitte Bertschi, prin. Fax 329-4806

Billings MS 100/6-8
7217 Woodlawn Ave NE 98115 206-547-4614
Ted Kalmus, hdmstr. Fax 545-8505

Bright Water S 200/PK-8
1501 10th Ave E Ste 100 98102 206-624-6176
Laura Crandall, dir. Fax 322-7893

Bush S 600/K-12
3400 E Harrison St 98112 206-322-7978
Frank Magusin, hdmstr. Fax 860-3876

Christ the King S 200/PK-8
415 N 117th St 98133 206-364-6890
Terence Maguire, prin. Fax 364-8325

Concordia Lutheran S 100/PK-8
7040 36th Ave NE 98115 206-525-7407
Dave Meyer, admin. Fax 526-2082

Epiphany S 200/PK-5
3710 E Howell St 98122 206-323-9011
Matt Neely, hdmstr. Fax 324-2127

Explorer West MS 100/6-8
10015 28th Ave SW 98146 206-935-0495
Evan Hundley, hdmstr. Fax 932-7113

Fairview Christian S 100/PK-8
844 NE 78th St 98115 206-526-0762
Gary Madsen, admin. Fax 526-0763

Giddens S 200/PK-5
620 20th Ave S 98144 206-324-4847
Alvin Gilmore, hdmstr. Fax 322-0923

Holy Family S 200/PK-8
9615 20th Ave SW 98106 206-767-6640
Frank Cantwell, prin. Fax 767-9466

Holy Rosary S 500/K-8
4142 42nd Ave SW 98116 206-937-7255
Kris Brown, prin. Fax 937-2610

Hope Lutheran S 200/PK-8
4446 42nd Ave SW 98116 206-935-8500
Fax 937-9332

King's ES 700/PK-6
19303 Fremont Ave N 98133 206-546-7258
Evelyn Huling, prin. Fax 546-7586

King's JHS 200/7-8
19303 Fremont Ave N 98133 206-546-7243
Jordana Halkett, prin. Fax 546-7250

Lake Forest Park Montessori Academy 100/PK-K
19935 19th Ave NE 98155 206-367-4404
Eve Buckle, dir. Fax 367-0021

Lakeside MS 300/5-8
13510 1st Ave NE 98125 206-368-3630
Bernie Noe, hdmstr. Fax 440-2777

Menachem Mendel Seattle Cheder 100/PK-12
4541 19th Ave NE 98105 206-523-9766
Dr. Marcia Rodes, prin. Fax 524-6105

Meridian S 200/K-5
4649 Sunnyside Ave N 98103 206-632-7154
Ron Waldman, hdmstr. Fax 633-1864

Northgate Christian Academy 50/K-12
10510 Stone Ave N 98133 206-525-5699
Dale Cluck, prin. Fax 525-0614

Northwest Montessori S 100/PK-6
4910 Phinney Ave N 98103 206-634-1347
Barbara Madsen, admin. Fax 634-0667

Our Lady of Fatima S 300/K-8
3301 W Dravus St 98199 206-283-7031
Susan Burdett, prin. Fax 352-4588

Our Lady of Guadalupe S 50/K-8
3401 SW Myrtle St 98126 206-935-0651
Kristen Dixon, prin. Fax 938-3695

Our Lady of the Lake S 200/K-8
3520 NE 89th St 98115 206-525-9980
Vince McGovern, prin. Fax 523-2858

Pacific Crest S 100/PK-8
600 NW Bright St 98107 206-789-7889
Jacquie Maughan, dir. Fax 784-8944

St. Alphonsus S 200/PK-8
5816 15th Ave NW 98107 206-782-4363
Maureen Reid, prin. Fax 789-5709

St. Anne S 200/K-8
101 W Lee St 98119 206-282-3538
Patricia Durand, prin. Fax 284-4191

St. Benedict S 200/PK-8
4811 Wallingford Ave N 98103 206-633-3375
Maureen Blum, prin. Fax 632-3236

St. Bernadette S 200/K-8
1028 SW 128th St 98146 206-244-4934
Bob Rutledge, prin. Fax 244-4943

St. Catherine S 300/PK-8
8524 8th Ave NE 98115 206-525-0581
Dr. Nancy Wilson, prin. Fax 985-0253

St. Edward S 100/K-8
4212 S Mead St 98118 206-725-1774
Mary Lundeen, prin. Fax 725-4569

St. George S 200/PK-8
5117 13th Ave S 98108 206-762-0656
Bernadette O'Leary, prin. Fax 763-3220

St. John S 500/PK-8
120 N 79th St 98103 206-783-0337
Agnes Jacobson, prin. Fax 706-2704

St. Joseph S 600/K-8
700 18th Ave E 98112 206-329-3260
George Hofbauer, prin. Fax 324-7773

St. Matthew S 200/K-8
1230 NE 127th St 98125 206-362-2785
Lillian Zadra, prin. Fax 440-9476

St. Paul S 200/PK-8
10001 57th Ave S 98178 206-725-0780
Wayne Melonson, prin. Fax 722-5732

St. Therese S 200/K-8
900 35th Ave 98122 206-324-0460
Eileen Gray, prin. Fax 324-8464

Seattle Academy of Arts & Sciences 200/6-8
1432 15th Ave 98122 206-676-6880
Jean Orvis, dir. Fax 676-6880

Seattle Country Day S 300/K-8
2619 4th Ave N 98109 206-284-6220
Michael Murphy, hdmstr. Fax 283-4251

Seattle Girls' S 100/5-8
PO Box 22576 98122 206-709-2228
Marja Brandon, hdmstr. Fax 329-1580

Seattle Hebrew Academy 200/PK-8
1617 Interlaken Dr E 98112 206-323-5750
Rivy Kletenik, hdmstr. Fax 323-5751

Seattle Waldorf S 200/PK-8
2728 NE 100th St 98125 206-524-5320
Geraldine Kline, dir. Fax 523-3920

Shorewood Christian S 200/PK-9
10300 28th Ave SW 98146 206-933-1056
Tim Lorenz, prin. Fax 932-9002

Spruce Street S 100/K-5
914 Virginia St 98101 206-621-9211
Briel Schmitz, dir. Fax 624-2832

University Child Development S — 300/PK-5
5062 9th Ave NE 98105 — 206-547-8237
Paula Smith, hdmstr. — Fax 547-3615
Valley S — 100/PK-5
309 31st Ave E 98112 — 206-328-4475
Barry Wright, dir. — Fax 328-5877
Villa Academy — 400/PK-8
5001 NE 50th St 98105 — 206-524-8885
Polly Skinner, prin. — Fax 523-7131
Westside S — 200/PK-5
10015 28th Ave SW 98146 — 206-932-2511
Jo Ann Yockey, hdmstr. — Fax 935-2813
Zion Preparatory Academy — 100/K-6
4730 32nd Ave S 98118 — 206-723-0580
Ven Lucas, dir. — Fax 723-2990

Sedro Woolley, Skagit, Pop. 7,506
Sedro-Woolley SD 101 — 4,400/K-12
801 Trail Rd 98284 — 360-855-3500
Mark Venn, supt. — Fax 855-3574
www.swsd.k12.wa.us
Cascade MS — 600/7-8
201 N Township St 98284 — 360-855-3520
Michelle Kuss-Cybula, prin. — Fax 855-3521
Central ES — 400/K-6
601 Talcott St 98284 — 360-855-3560
Kevin Loomis, prin. — Fax 855-3561
Evergreen ES — 500/K-6
1007 McGarigle Rd 98284 — 360-855-3545
Matt Mihelich, prin. — Fax 855-3546
Purcell ES — 400/K-6
700 Bennett St 98284 — 360-855-3555
Rebecca Goertzel, prin. — Fax 855-3556
Samish ES — 200/K-6
23953 Prairie Rd 98284 — 360-855-3540
Rob Matthews, prin. — Fax 855-3541
Other Schools – See Clearlake, Lyman, Mount Vernon

Sekiu, Clallam
Cape Flattery SD 401 — 300/K-12
PO Box 109 98381 — 360-963-2329
Kandy Ritter, supt. — Fax 963-2373
www.capeflattery.wednet.edu
Other Schools – See Clallam Bay, Neah Bay

Selah, Yakima, Pop. 6,875
Selah SD 119 — 3,400/K-12
105 W Bartlett Ave 98942 — 509-697-0706
Dr. Steve Chestnut, supt. — Fax 697-0823
www.selah.k12.wa.us
Campbell ES — 600/K-4
408 N 1st St 98942 — 509-697-0725
Chad Quigley, prin. — Fax 697-0688
Lince ES — 700/K-4
316 W Naches Ave 98942 — 509-697-0675
Susan Petterson, prin. — Fax 697-0681
Selah IS — 800/5-7
1401 W Fremont Ave 98942 — 509-698-0400
Jim Merz, prin. — Fax 698-0403

Sequim, Clallam, Pop. 5,162
Sequim SD 323 — 3,000/K-12
503 N Sequim Ave 98382 — 360-582-3260
Bill Bentley, supt. — Fax 683-6303
www.sequim.k12.wa.us/
Greywolf ES — 500/K-5
171 Carlsborg Rd 98382 — 360-582-3300
Patricia Grenquist, prin. — Fax 582-9555
Haller ES — 600/K-5
350 W Fir St 98382 — 360-582-3200
Vince Riccobene, prin. — Fax 681-8543
Sequim MS — 600/6-8
301 W Hendrickson Rd 98382 — 360-582-3500
Brian Jones, prin. — Fax 582-9486

Five Acre S, 515 Lotzgesell Rd 98382 — 100/PK-6
William Jevne, prin. — 360-681-7255
Mountain View Christian S — 50/K-8
255 Medsker Rd 98382 — 360-683-6170
Larry Arnott, prin. — Fax 683-6193

Shaw Island, San Juan
Shaw Island SD 10 — 50/K-8
PO Box 426 98286 — 360-468-2570
Dr. Marie Phillips, supt. — Fax 468-2585
www.shaw.k12.wa.us
Shaw Island S — 50/K-8
PO Box 426 98286 — 360-468-2570
Dr. Marie Phillips, prin. — Fax 468-2585

Shelton, Mason, Pop. 9,065
Hood Canal SD 404 — 300/PK-8
111 N State Route 106 98584 — 360-877-9700
Tom Churchill, supt. — Fax 877-9123
www.hoodcanal.wednet.edu
Hood Canal S — 300/PK-8
111 N State Route 106 98584 — 360-877-5463
Tom Churchill, prin. — Fax 877-9123

Pioneer SD 402 — 700/PK-8
611 E Agate Rd 98584 — 360-426-9115
Daniel Winter, supt. — Fax 426-1036
www.psd402.org
Pioneer MS — 400/4-8
611 E Agate Rd 98584 — 360-426-8291
Heidi Bunker, prin. — Fax 426-1036
Pioneer PS — 300/PK-3
110 E Spencer Lake Rd 98584 — 360-427-2737
Peggy Sanderson, admin. — Fax 427-2933

Shelton SD 309 — 4,300/PK-12
700 S 1st St 98584 — 360-426-1687
Joan Zook, supt. — Fax 427-8610
www.sheltonschools.org
Bordeaux ES — 500/PK-5
350 E University Ave 98584 — 360-426-3253
Carey Murray, prin. — Fax 462-7392
Evergreen ES — 500/PK-5
900 W Franklin St 98584 — 360-426-8281
Steve Warner, prin. — Fax 426-8576
Mountain View ES — 600/PK-5
534 E K St 98584 — 360-426-8564
Chuck Brock, prin. — Fax 426-3446
Olympic MS — 500/6-7
800 E K St 98584 — 360-462-6671
Eric Barkman, prin. — Fax 462-6676

Southside SD 42 — 300/K-7
161 SE Collier Rd 98584 — 360-426-8437
Tim Garchow, supt. — Fax 426-9970
www.southside.k12.wa.us
Southside ES — 300/K-7
161 SE Collier Rd 98584 — 360-426-8437
Tim Garchow, prin. — Fax 426-9970

Mason County Christian S — 100/PK-8
470 E Eagle Ridge Dr 98584 — 360-426-7616
David Roller, supt. — Fax 426-6582
Shelton Valley Christian S — 50/K-8
PO Box 773 98584 — 360-426-4198
Judy McCain, admin. — Fax 426-1726

Shoreline, King, Pop. 52,024
Shoreline SD 412 — 8,600/PK-12
18560 1st Ave NE 98155 — 206-367-6111
Sue Walker, supt. — Fax 361-4204
www.shorelineschools.org
Briarcrest ES — 300/K-6
2715 NE 158th St 98155 — 206-368-4170
Jonathan Nessan, prin. — Fax 368-4174
Echo Lake ES — 400/K-6
19345 Wallingford Ave N 98133 — 206-361-4338
Mary Koontz, prin. — Fax 361-4335
Einstein MS — 800/7-8
19343 3rd Ave NW 98177 — 206-368-4730
Stephanie Clark-Lander, prin. — Fax 368-4735
Highland Terrace ES — 300/K-6
100 N 160th St 98133 — 206-361-4341
Miriam Tencate, prin. — Fax 361-4348
Kellogg MS — 700/7-8
16045 25th Ave NE 98155 — 206-368-4783
Lori Longo, prin. — Fax 368-4780
Meridian Park ES — 600/K-6
17077 Meridian Ave N 98133 — 206-361-4251
Amy Jessee, prin. — Fax 361-4259
Parkwood ES — 400/K-6
1815 N 155th St 98133 — 206-368-4150
Laura Ploudre, prin. — Fax 368-4158
Ridgecrest ES — 300/K-6
16516 10th Ave NE 98155 — 206-361-4272
Cinco Delgado, prin. — Fax 368-4193
Shoreline Children's Center — PK-PK
1900 N 170th St 98133 — 206-361-4256
Dr. Linda Averill, prin. — Fax 361-4258
Syre ES — 500/K-6
19545 12th Ave NW 98177 — 206-368-4165
David Tadlock, prin. — Fax 368-4164
Other Schools – See Lake Forest Park

Evergreen S — 400/PK-8
15201 Meridian Ave N 98133 — 206-364-2650
Margaret Wagner, hdmstr. — Fax 365-1827
St. Luke S — 400/K-8
17533 Saint Luke Pl N 98133 — 206-542-1133
Dr. Karen Matthews, prin. — Fax 546-8693
St. Mark S — 200/PK-8
18033 15th Pl NE 98155 — 206-364-1633
Kathryn Keck, prin. — Fax 367-3919
Shoreline Christian S — 300/PK-12
2400 NE 147th St 98155 — 206-364-7777
Timothy Visser, prin. — Fax 364-0349

Silverdale, Kitsap, Pop. 7,660
Central Kitsap SD 401 — 11,200/K-12
PO Box 8 98383 — 360-662-1610
Gregory Lynch, supt. — Fax 662-1611
www.cksd.wednet.edu
Clear Creek ES — 400/K-6
PO Box 8 98383 — 360-662-8100
Ninette Haynes, prin. — Fax 662-8101
Cougar Valley ES — 400/K-6
PO Box 8 98383 — 360-662-8400
Chris Visserman, prin. — Fax 662-8401
Emerald Heights ES — 500/K-6
PO Box 8 98383 — 360-662-8500
Greg Cleven, prin. — Fax 662-8501
Silverdale ES — 500/K-6
PO Box 8 98383 — 360-662-9400
Peggy Ellis, prin. — Fax 662-9401
Silver Ridge ES — 400/K-6
PO Box 8 98383 — 360-662-9500
Julie McKean, prin. — Fax 662-9501
Other Schools – See Bremerton

Skamania, Skamania
Skamania SD 2 — 100/K-8
122 Butler Loop Rd 98648 — 509-427-8239
JoAnn Fritz, supt. — Fax 427-8921
skamania.k12.wa.us/
Skamania S — 100/K-8
122 Butler Loop Rd 98648 — 509-427-8239
JoAnn Fritz, prin. — Fax 427-8921

Skykomish, King, Pop. 207
Skykomish SD 404 — 50/K-12
PO Box 325 98288 — 360-677-2623
Desiree L. Gould, supt. — Fax 677-2418
Skykomish ES — 50/K-6
PO Box 325 98288 — 360-677-2623
Desiree L. Gould, prin. — Fax 677-2418

Snohomish, Snohomish, Pop. 8,720
Monroe SD 103
Supt. — See Monroe
Chain Lake ES — 500/K-5
12125 Chain Lake Rd 98290 — 360-804-3100
Linda Martin, prin. — Fax 804-3199
Hidden River MS — 300/6-8
9224 Paradise Lake Rd 98296 — 360-804-4100
Steve Shurtleff, prin. — Fax 804-4199
Maltby ES — 400/K-5
9700 212th St SE 98296 — 360-804-3500
Sonja Hoeft, prin. — Fax 804-3599

Snohomish SD 201 — 9,600/PK-12
1601 Avenue D 98290 — 360-563-7300
William Mester Ph.D., supt. — Fax 563-7373
www.sno.wednet.edu
Cascade View ES — 600/K-6
2401 Park Ave 98290 — 360-563-7000
Lyla Meyer, prin. — Fax 563-7004
Cathcart ES — 600/K-6
8201 188th St SE 98296 — 360-563-7075
Casey Howard, prin. — Fax 563-7078
Centennial MS — 800/7-8
3000 S Machias Rd 98290 — 360-563-4525
Scott Peacock, prin. — Fax 563-4585
Central ES — 400/PK-2
221 Union Ave 98290 — 360-563-4600
Heidi Rothgeb, prin. — Fax 563-4604
Dutch Hill ES — 500/K-6
8231 131st Ave SE 98290 — 360-563-4450
Donna Kapustka, prin. — Fax 563-4455
Emerson ES — 400/3-6
1103 Pine Ave 98290 — 360-563-7150
Craig Church, prin. — Fax 563-7157
Little Cedars ES — K-6
7408 144th Pl SE 98296 — 360-563-2900
Becky Brockman, prin.
Machias ES — 500/K-6
231 147th Ave SE 98290 — 360-563-4825
Ginny Schilaty, prin. — Fax 563-4828
Riverview ES — 400/K-6
7322 64th St SE 98290 — 360-563-4375
Tamera Jones, prin. — Fax 563-4378
Totem Falls ES — 800/K-6
14211 Snohomish Cascade Dr 98296 — 360-563-4750
Mike Cosgrove, prin. — Fax 563-4756
Valley View MS — 800/7-8
14308 Broadway Ave 98296 — 360-563-4225
Nancy Rhoades, prin. — Fax 563-4236
Other Schools – See Everett

St. Michael S — PK-3
1512 Pine Ave 98290 — 360-568-0821
Suzanne Siekawitch, prin. — Fax 568-6426

Snoqualmie, King, Pop. 6,082
Snoqualmie Valley SD 410 — 5,700/PK-12
PO Box 400 98065 — 425-831-8000
Joel Aune, supt. — Fax 831-8040
www.svsd410.org/
Cascade View ES — 700/K-5
34816 SE Ridge St 98065 — 425-831-4100
Ray Wilson, prin. — Fax 831-4110
Snoqualmie ES — 500/K-5
39801 SE Park St 98065 — 425-831-8050
Cori Pflug-Tilton, prin. — Fax 831-8047
Snoqualmie MS — 600/6-8
9200 Railroad Ave SE 98065 — 425-831-8450
Vernie Newell, prin. — Fax 831-8440
Other Schools – See Fall City, North Bend

Soap Lake, Grant, Pop. 1,844
Soap Lake SD 156 — 500/PK-12
PO Box 158 98851 — 509-246-1822
John Adkins, supt. — Fax 246-0669
www.slschools.org
Soap Lake ES — 200/PK-5
PO Box 908 98851 — 509-246-1323
Judi Jensen, prin. — Fax 246-0669
Soap Lake MS — 100/6-8
PO Box 878 98851 — 509-246-1201
Dan Andrews, prin. — Fax 246-0669

South Bend, Pacific, Pop. 1,831
South Bend SD 118 — 600/PK-12
PO Box 437 98586 — 360-875-6041
Mike Morris, supt. — Fax 875-6062
www.southbend.wednet.edu/
Davis ES — 300/K-6
PO Box 437 98586 — 360-875-5615
Kresta Byington, prin. — Fax 875-6032
South Bend Early Learning Center — 100/PK-PK
PO Box 437 98586 — 360-875-5327
Laurie May, dir. — Fax 875-5379

Spanaway, Pierce, Pop. 15,001
Bethel SD 403 — 17,900/PK-12
516 176th St E 98387 — 253-683-6000
Tom Seigel, supt. — Fax 683-6059
www.bethelsd.org
Camas Prairie ES — 700/K-6
320 176th St E 98387 — 253-683-7400
Sean McKenzie, prin. — Fax 683-7498
Elk Plain S of Choice — 500/PK-6
22015 22nd Ave E 98387 — 253-683-7900
Mike Merrin, prin. — Fax 683-7998
Evergreen ES — 600/PK-6
1311 172nd St E 98387 — 253-683-8200
Brad Graham, prin. — Fax 683-8298
Pioneer Valley ES — 900/PK-6
7315 Eustis Hunt Rd 98387 — 253-683-8900
Stephen Rushing, prin. — Fax 683-8998
Shining Mountain ES — 700/PK-6
21615 38th Ave E 98387 — 253-683-5200
Mary Sewright, prin. — Fax 683-5298
Spanaway ES — 400/PK-6
7319 Eustis Hunt Rd 98387 — 253-683-5300
Kimberly Hanson, prin. — Fax 683-5398
Other Schools – See Graham, Puyallup, Roy, Tacoma

Spangle, Spokane, Pop. 234
Liberty SD 362 — 500/K-12
29818 S North Pine Creek Rd 99031 — 509-624-4415
Bill Motsenbocker, supt. — Fax 245-3288
www.liberty.wednet.edu/
Liberty S — 300/K-8
29818 S North Pine Creek Rd 99031 — 509-245-3211
Lori Johnson, prin. — Fax 245-3530

Upper Columbia Academy 50/1-8
3025 E Spangle Waverly Rd 99031 509-245-3629
Karen Sharpe, prin. Fax 245-3690

Spokane, Spokane, Pop. 196,818
Cheney SD 360
Supt. — See Cheney
Windsor ES 500/PK-5
5504 W Hallett Rd 99224 509-559-4200
Kaye Aucutt, prin. Fax 624-9107

East Valley SD 361 4,100/K-12
12325 E Grace Ave 99216 509-924-1830
John Glenewinkel, supt. Fax 927-9500
www.evsd.org
Continuous Curriculum S 200/K-8
16924 E Wellesley Ave 99216 509-927-9501
Chiere Martyn, prin. Fax 927-3211
East Valley MS 500/6-8
4920 N Progress Rd 99216 509-924-9383
Mark Purvine, prin. Fax 927-3214
Skyview ES 200/K-5
16924 E Wellesley Ave 99216 509-927-3210
Chiere Martyn, prin. Fax 921-7301
Trent ES 500/K-5
3303 N Pines Rd 99206 509-924-2622
Kyle Rydell, prin. Fax 927-3209
Trentwood ES 300/K-5
14701 E Wellesley Ave 99216 509-927-3215
Sigrid Brannan, prin. Fax 927-3216
Other Schools – See Newman Lake, Otis Orchards

Great Northern SD 312 50/K-6
3115 N Spotted Rd 99224 509-747-7714
Glenn Frizzell, supt. Fax 838-5670
www.gnsd.k12.wa.us/
Great Northern ES 50/K-6
3115 N Spotted Rd 99224 509-747-7714
Glenn Frizzell, prin. Fax 838-5670

Mead SD 354
Supt. — See Mead
Brentwood ES 600/K-6
406 W Regina Ave 99218 509-465-6200
Roger Pike, prin. Fax 465-6220
Evergreen ES 700/K-6
215 W Eddy Ave 99208 509-465-6400
Jon Iverson, prin. Fax 465-6420
Farwell ES 600/K-6
13005 N Crestline St 99208 509-465-6500
Barb Pybus, prin. Fax 465-6520
Northwood MS 800/7-8
13120 N Pittsburg St 99208 509-465-7500
Dave Stenersen, prin. Fax 465-7520
Prairie View ES 500/K-6
2606 W Johansen Rd 99208 509-465-7800
Becky Cooke, prin. Fax 465-7820
Shiloh Hills ES 500/K-6
505 E Stonewall Ave 99208 509-465-6800
Heather Havens, prin. Fax 465-6820

Orchard Prairie SD 123 100/K-7
7626 N Orchard Prairie Rd 99217 509-467-9517
Duane Reidenbach, supt. Fax 467-0590
www.orchardprairie.org/
Orchard Prairie ES 100/K-7
7626 N Orchard Prairie Rd 99217 509-467-9517
Fax 467-0590

Spokane SD 81 30,300/PK-12
200 N Bernard St 99201 509-354-5900
Nancy Stowell Ph.D., supt. Fax 354-5965
www.spokaneschools.org
Adams ES 400/PK-6
2909 E 37th Ave 99223 509-354-2000
Mary Weber, prin. Fax 354-2020
Arlington ES 600/K-6
6363 N Smith St 99217 509-354-2100
Sue Unruh, prin. Fax 354-2121
Audubon ES 500/PK-6
2020 W Carlisle Ave 99205 509-354-2140
Brent Perdue, prin. Fax 354-2141
Balboa ES 400/K-6
3010 W Holyoke Ave 99208 509-354-2220
Patricia Lynass, prin. Fax 354-2222
Bemiss ES 500/K-6
2323 E Bridgeport Ave 99207 509-354-2300
Jennifer Keck, prin. Fax 354-2310
Browne ES 500/PK-6
5102 N Driscoll Blvd 99205 509-354-2400
Lou Haymond, prin. Fax 354-2424
Chase MS 800/7-8
4747 E 37th Ave 99223 509-354-5000
John Andes, prin. Fax 354-5100
Cooper ES 600/PK-6
3200 N Ferrall St 99217 509-354-2500
Rona Williams, prin. Fax 354-2510
Finch ES 600/PK-6
3717 N Milton St 99205 509-354-2600
Kim Harmon, prin. Fax 354-2616
Franklin ES 300/K-6
2627 E 17th Ave 99223 509-354-2620
Mickey Hanson, prin. Fax 354-2666
Garfield ES 500/PK-6
222 W Knox Ave 99205 509-354-2700
Karen Cloninger, prin. Fax 354-2727
Garry MS 600/7-8
725 E Joseph Ave 99208 509-354-5200
Brenda Meenach, prin. Fax 354-5212
Glover MS 700/7-8
2404 W Longfellow Ave 99205 509-354-5400
Travis Schulhauser, prin. Fax 354-5399
Grant ES 500/K-6
1300 E 9th Ave 99202 509-354-2800
Dr. Julie Perron, prin. Fax 354-2828
Hamblen ES 500/K-6
2121 E Thurston Ave 99203 509-354-2900
Rita Forsythe, prin. Fax 354-2888
Holmes ES 400/K-6
2600 W Sharp Ave 99201 509-354-2990
Steve Barnes, prin. Fax 354-2991
Hutton ES 500/K-6
908 E 24th Ave 99203 509-354-3030
Chuck Demarest, prin. Fax 354-3040
Indian Trail ES 400/PK-6
4102 W Woodside Ave 99208 509-354-3100
Paul Gannon, prin. Fax 354-3110
Jefferson ES 500/K-6
3612 S Grand Blvd 99203 509-354-3200
Mary-Dean Wooley, prin. Fax 354-3210
Lidgerwood ES 300/K-6
5510 N Lidgerwood St 99208 509-354-3225
Valorie Buller, prin. Fax 354-3235
Lincoln Heights ES 400/PK-6
3322 E 22nd Ave 99223 509-354-3300
Mike McGinnis, prin. Fax 354-3333
Linwood ES 400/PK-6
906 W Weile Ave 99208 509-354-3400
Gina Naccarato-Keele, prin. Fax 354-3404
Logan ES 500/PK-6
1001 E Montgomery Ave 99207 509-354-3434
Lisa Pacheco, prin. Fax 354-3499
Longfellow ES 500/PK-6
800 E Providence Ave 99207 509-354-3500
Julia Lockwood, prin. Fax 354-3535
Madison ES 300/K-6
319 W Nebraska Ave 99205 509-354-3600
Greg Baerlocher, prin. Fax 354-3636
Moran Prairie ES 500/PK-6
4224 E 57th Ave 99223 509-354-3700
Matt Handelman, prin. Fax 354-3666
Mullan Road ES 500/K-6
2616 E 63rd Ave 99223 509-354-3800
Paul Stone, prin. Fax 354-3777
Regal ES 500/K-6
2707 E Rich Ave 99207 509-354-3900
Mallory Thomas, prin. Fax 354-3940
Ridgeview ES 400/K-6
5610 N Maple St 99205 509-354-4000
Kathy Williams, prin. Fax 354-3999
Roosevelt ES 400/PK-6
333 W 14th Ave 99204 509-354-4040
Shari Farris, prin. Fax 354-4080
Sacajawea MS 900/7-8
401 E 33rd Ave 99203 509-354-5500
Jeremy Ochse, prin. Fax 354-5505
Salk MS 700/7-8
6411 N Alberta St 99208 509-354-5600
Mark Gorman, prin. Fax 354-5542
Shaw MS 700/7-8
4106 N Cook St 99207 509-354-5800
Christine Lynch, prin. Fax 354-5899
Sheridan ES 500/K-6
3737 E 5th Ave 99202 509-354-4100
Pete Hall, prin. Fax 354-4101
Stevens ES 500/PK-6
1717 E Sinto Ave 99202 509-354-4200
Mike Crabtree, prin. Fax 354-4220
Westview ES 400/PK-6
6104 N Moore St 99205 509-354-4300
Cathy Comfort, prin. Fax 354-4303
Whitman ES 500/K-6
5400 N Helena St 99207 509-354-4320
Bev Lund, prin. Fax 354-4323
Willard ES 600/K-6
500 W Longfellow Ave 99205 509-354-4444
Steve Indgjerd, prin. Fax 354-4474
Wilson ES 300/K-6
911 W 25th Ave 99203 509-354-4500
Tony Ressa, prin. Fax 354-4520
Woodridge ES 400/K-6
5100 W Shawnee Ave 99208 509-354-4600
Brian Melody, prin. Fax 354-4604

West Valley SD 363 3,500/PK-12
PO Box 11739 99211 509-924-2150
Dr. Polly Crowley, supt. Fax 922-5295
www.wvsd.com
Centennial MS 600/6-8
915 N Ella Rd 99212 509-922-5482
Karen Bromps, prin. Fax 891-9520
Millwood ECC 50/PK-PK
8818 E Grace Ave 99212 509-922-5478
Connie Kliewer, prin. Fax 921-5259
Ness ES 300/K-5
9612 E Cataldo Ave 99206 509-922-5470
Mike Lollar, prin. Fax 927-9905
Orchard Center ES 300/K-5
7519 E Buckeye Ave 99212 509-922-5473
Travis Peterson, prin. Fax 927-1141
Pasadena Park ES 400/K-5
8508 E Upriver Dr 99212 509-922-5480
Robyn Davis, prin. Fax 891-9529
West Valley City MS 200/5-8
8920 E Valleyway Ave 99212 509-921-2836
Dusty Andres, prin. Fax 921-2849
Woodard ES 300/K-5
7401 E Mission Ave 99212 509-921-2160
Pam Francis, prin. Fax 927-1148

All Saints MS 200/5-8
1428 E 33rd Ave 99203 509-624-5712
Katherine Hicks, prin. Fax 624-7752
All Saints S 300/K-4
3510 E 18th Ave 99223 509-534-1098
Katherine Hicks, prin. Fax 534-1529
Assumption S 200/PK-8
3618 W Indian Trail Rd 99208 509-328-1115
Sonia Flores-Davis, prin. Fax 328-7872
Cataldo S 300/K-8
455 W 18th Ave 99203 509-624-8759
Stephanie Johnson, prin. Fax 624-8763
Concordia Lutheran S 50/K-K
7307 N Nevada St 99208 509-483-4218
Fax 483-4293
Countryside S 50/1-8
12107 W Seven Mile Rd 99224 509-466-8982
Phyllis Radu, admin. Fax 466-8982
Discovery S 100/PK-6
323 S Grant St 99202 509-838-0606
Gayle Peterson, hdmstr. Fax 838-5668
Northwest Christian S 400/PK-6
1412 W Central Ave 99205 509-328-4400
Terry Meyer, admin. Fax 328-4403
St. Aloysius S 300/PK-8
611 E Mission Ave 99202 509-489-7825
Kerrie Rowland, prin. Fax 487-0975
St. Charles S 300/PK-8
4515 N Alberta St 99205 509-327-9575
Skip Bonuccelli, prin. Fax 325-9353
St. George's S 400/K-12
2929 W Waikiki Rd 99208 509-466-1636
Mo Copeland, hdmstr. Fax 467-3258
St. John Vianney S 200/PK-8
501 N Walnut Rd 99206 509-926-7987
Rick Pelkie, prin. Fax 922-5282
St. Mary's Catholic S 200/K-8
14601 E 4th Ave 99216 509-924-4300
Laurene Nauditt, prin. Fax 922-8139
St. Matthew's Lutheran S 100/PK-8
6917 N Country Homes Blvd 99208 509-327-5601
David Sauer, prin. Fax 326-6751
St. Patrick S 100/PK-8
2706 E Queen Ave 99217 509-487-2830
Rick Pelkie, prin. Fax 484-3101
St. Thomas More S 300/K-8
515 W Saint Thomas Moore 99208 509-466-3811
Doug Banks, prin. Fax 466-0220
Slavic Christian Academy - Spokane 300/K-12
8913 N Nettleton Ln 99208 509-924-4618
Elena Solodyankin, supt. Fax 443-6278
Southside Christian S 200/PK-8
401 E 30th Ave 99203 509-838-8139
Heidi Bauer, admin. Fax 835-8050
Spokane Christian Academy 100/K-8
8909 E Bigelow Gulch Rd 99217 509-924-4888
Dave Harton, prin. Fax 924-0432
Spokane Junior Academy 100/K-10
1888 N Wright Dr 99224 509-325-1985
Brian Harris, prin. Fax 324-8904
Trinity S 200/PK-8
1306 W Montgomery Ave 99205 509-327-9369
Sandra Nokes, prin. Fax 328-4128
Westgate Christian S 100/PK-6
7111 N Nine Mile Rd 99208 509-325-2252
Mendi Juntunen, dir. Fax 327-4219

Spokane Valley, Spokane
Central Valley SD 356 11,600/PK-12
19307 E Cataldo Ave 99016 509-228-5400
Ben Small, supt. Fax 228-5409
www.cvsd.org
Adams ES 400/K-5
14707 E 8th Ave, 509-228-4000
Jeff Dufresne, prin. Fax 228-4009
Bowdish MS 600/6-8
2109 S Skipworth Rd, 509-228-4700
Dave Bouge, prin. Fax 228-4714
Broadway ES 400/PK-5
11016 E Broadway Ave, 509-228-4100
Eileen Utecht, prin. Fax 228-4109
Central Valley K K-K
1512 N Barker Rd, 509-228-5380
Joanne Comer, prin. Fax 228-4855
Chester ES 300/K-5
3525 S Pines Rd, 509-228-4150
Cindy Sothen, prin. Fax 228-4159
Evergreen MS 600/6-8
14221 E 16th Ave, 509-228-4780
John Parker, prin. Fax 228-4789
Greenacres ES 500/K-5
17915 E 4th Ave, 509-228-4200
Susan Rasmussen, prin. Fax 228-4209
Greenacres MS 700/6-8
17409 E Sprague Ave, 509-228-4860
Vern DiGiovanni, prin. Fax 228-4869
Horizon MS 400/6-8
3915 S Pines Rd, 509-228-4940
Jesse Hardt, prin. Fax 228-4983
McDonald ES 400/K-5
1512 S McDonald Rd, 509-228-4350
Kevin Longworth, prin. Fax 228-4359
North Pines MS 400/6-8
701 N Pines Rd, 509-228-5020
Gordon Grassi, prin. Fax 228-5029
Opportunity ES 400/K-5
1109 S Wilbur Rd, 509-228-4550
Molly Carolan, prin. Fax 228-4559
Ponderosa ES 400/K-5
10105 E Cimmaron Dr, 509-228-4450
Jerrol Olson, prin. Fax 228-4459
Progress ES 300/K-5
710 N Progress Rd, 509-228-4500
Matthew Chisholm, prin. Fax 228-4509
South Pines ES 400/PK-5
12021 E 24th Ave, 509-228-4400
Walt Clemons, prin. Fax 228-4409
Summit S 300/K-8
13313 E Broadway Ave, 509-228-4050
Lyle Krislock, prin. Fax 228-4059
Sunrise ES 600/K-5
14603 E 24th Ave, 509-228-4600
Sue McCollum, prin. Fax 228-4609
University ES 300/PK-5
1613 S University Rd, 509-228-4650
Sue Lennick, prin. Fax 228-4659
Other Schools – See Liberty Lake

Christ Lutheran Preschool 100/PK-K
13009 E Broadway Ave, 509-928-0231
Oaks-A Classical Christian Academy 300/K-12
PO Box 141146, 509-536-5955
Bruce Williams, hdmstr. Fax 536-7877
Spokane Valley Adventist S 100/PK-9
1603 S Sullivan Rd, 509-926-0955
Terry Lee, prin. Fax 922-0471
Valley Christian S 100/K-6
15618 E Broadway Ave, 509-924-0392
Debbie Heden, prin. Fax 924-3296

Sprague, Lincoln, Pop. 489
Sprague SD 8 100/K-12
PO Box 305 99032 509-257-2591
Mark Stedman, supt. Fax 257-2539
www.sprague.wednet.edu
Sprague ES 50/K-5
PO Box 305 99032 509-257-2591
Mark Stedman, prin. Fax 257-2539

Springdale, Stevens, Pop. 287
Mary Walker SD 207 400/PK-12
PO Box 159 99173 509-258-4534
Kevin Jacka, supt. Fax 258-4707
www.marywalker.org/
Springdale ES 200/PK-5
PO Box 159 99173 509-258-7357
Cheryl Henjum, prin. Fax 258-7756
Springdale MS 100/6-8
PO Box 159 99173 509-258-7357
Cheryl Henjum, prin. Fax 258-7756

Stanwood, Snohomish, Pop. 5,068
Stanwood-Camano SD 401 5,400/K-12
26920 Pioneer Hwy 98292 360-629-1200
Dr. Jean Shumate, supt. Fax 629-1242
www.stanwood.wednet.edu
Cedarhome ES 500/K-5
27911 68th Ave NW 98292 360-629-1280
Jeff Lofgren, prin. Fax 629-1289
Port Susan MS 600/6-8
7506 267th St NW 98292 360-629-1360
Michael Olson, prin. Fax 629-1365
Stanwood ES 400/K-5
10227 273rd Pl NW 98292 360-629-1250
Victor Hanzeli, prin. Fax 629-1252
Stanwood MS 600/6-8
9405 271st St NW 98292 360-629-1350
Barbara Marsh, prin. Fax 629-1354
Twin City ES 300/K-5
26211 72nd Ave NW 98292 360-629-1270
Pam Gentz, prin. Fax 629-1279
Other Schools – See Camano Island

Cedarhome Adventist Christian S 50/1-8
28505 68th Ave NW 98292 360-629-5340
Frank Meidell, prin.
Our Saviours Lutheran Preschool 50/PK-PK
27201 99th Ave NW 98292 360-629-3767

Starbuck, Columbia, Pop. 130
Starbuck SD 35 50/K-8
PO Box 188 99359 509-399-2381
Paul Boeckman, supt. Fax 399-2381
Starbuck S 50/K-8
PO Box 188 99359 509-399-2381
Fax 399-2381

Stehekin, Chelan
Stehekin SD 69, PO Box 37 98852 50/K-8
Stehekin S, PO Box 37 98852 50/K-8
Ron Scutt, prin.

Steilacoom, Pierce, Pop. 6,140
Steilacoom Historical SD 1 2,100/K-12
510 Chambers St 98388 253-983-2200
Dr. Arthur Himmler, supt. Fax 584-7198
www.steilacoom.k12.wa.us
Cherrydale PS 200/K-3
1201 Galloway St 98388 253-983-2500
Dr. Deva Ward, prin. Fax 583-8478
Salters Point ES 200/4-5
908 3rd St 98388 253-983-2600
Nilsa Sotomayor, prin. Fax 581-9083
Taylor ES 50/K-4
510 Chambers St 98388 253-588-5052
Nancy McClure, prin. Fax 984-1290
Other Schools – See Anderson Island, DuPont

Steptoe, Whitman
Steptoe SD 304 50/1-8
PO Box 138 99174 509-397-3119
Kay Frizzell, supt. Fax 397-6393
Steptoe S 50/1-8
PO Box 138 99174 509-397-3119
Eric Patton, prin. Fax 397-6393

Stevenson, Skamania, Pop. 1,256
Stevenson-Carson SD 303 800/K-12
PO Box 850 98648 509-427-5674
Dr. William Hundley, supt. Fax 427-4028
www.scsd.k12.wa.us
Stevenson ES 100/K-2
PO Box 850 98648 509-427-5672
Karen Douglass, prin. Fax 427-7413
Other Schools – See Carson

Stuart Island, See Friday Harbor
San Juan Island SD 149
Supt. — See Friday Harbor
Stuart Island S, HC, 50/K-8
Ann Spratt, prin. 360-378-5214

Sultan, Snohomish, Pop. 3,943
Sultan SD 311 2,200/K-12
514 4th St 98294 360-793-9800
Dan Chaplik, supt. Fax 793-9890
www.sultan.k12.wa.us
Sultan ES 600/K-5
501 Date Ave 98294 360-793-9830
Laurel Anderson, prin. Fax 793-9836
Sultan MS 600/6-8
301 High Ave 98294 360-793-9850
Robin Briganti, prin. Fax 793-9859
Other Schools – See Gold Bar

Sumas, Whatcom, Pop. 1,069
Nooksack Valley SD 506
Supt. — See Everson
Sumas ES 200/PK-5
1024 Lawson St 98295 360-988-9423
Kathy Winslow, prin. Fax 988-0505

Sumner, Pierce, Pop. 9,298
Dieringer SD 343 1,200/K-8
1320 178th Ave E, 253-862-2537
Dr. Judy Neumeier-Martinson, supt. Fax 862-8472
www.dieringer.wednet.edu
Dieringer Heights ES 400/K-K, 4-5
21727 34th St E, 253-826-4937
Kevin Anderson, prin. Fax 826-4908
Lake Tapps ES 400/1-3
1320 178th Ave E, 253-862-6600
Connie GeRoy, prin. Fax 862-3176
North Tapps MS 400/6-8
20029 12th St E, 253-862-2776
Pat Keaton, prin. Fax 862-2587

Sumner SD 320 8,300/K-12
1202 Wood Ave 98390 253-891-6000
Dr. Gil Mendoza, supt. Fax 891-6097
www.sumner.wednet.edu
Daffodil Valley ES 400/K-5
1509 Valley Ave E 98390 253-891-4600
Marcie Belfield, prin. Fax 891-4622
Maple Lawn ES 500/K-5
230 Wood Ave 98390 253-891-4400
Mike McCartin, prin. Fax 891-4422
Sumner MS 700/6-8
1508 Willow St 98390 253-891-5000
Steve Sjolund, prin. Fax 891-5045
Other Schools – See Bonney Lake, Puyallup

Sunnyside, Yakima, Pop. 14,426
Sunnyside SD 201 5,100/K-12
1110 S 6th St 98944 509-836-8701
Dr. Richard Cole, supt. Fax 837-0535
www.sunnyside.wednet.edu
Chief Kamiakin ES 600/1-5
1700 E Lincoln Ave 98944 509-837-6444
Julie Schmick, prin. Fax 837-0456
Harrison MS 600/6-8
810 S 16th St 98944 509-837-3601
Janie Hernandez, prin. Fax 837-0450
Pioneer ES 600/1-5
2101 E Lincoln Ave 98944 509-836-2200
Kris Diddens, prin. Fax 836-2220
Sierra Vista MS 700/6-8
916 N 16th St 98944 509-836-8500
Doug Rogers, prin. Fax 836-8515
Sun Valley ES K-K
1220 N 16th St 98944 509-836-6532
Heidi Hellner-Gomez, prin. Fax 837-5841
Washington ES 600/1-5
800 Jackson Ave 98944 509-837-3641
Gwyn Trull, prin. Fax 837-0454
Other Schools – See Outlook

Calvary Lutheran S 100/PK-K
PO Box 507 98944 509-837-6771
Fax 837-6771
Sunnyside Christian S 200/PK-8
811 North Ave 98944 509-837-3044
Delwin Dykstra, prin. Fax 837-4086
Trinity Reformed Christian S 50/1-8
1505 Grant Ave 98944 509-837-2880
Maaike Van Wingerden, dir. Fax 837-7188

Suquamish, Kitsap, Pop. 3,105
North Kitsap SD 400
Supt. — See Poulsbo
Suquamish ES 400/PK-5
18950 Park Blvd NE 98392 360-598-4219
Joe Davalos, prin. Fax 779-8977

Tacoma, Pierce, Pop. 195,898
Bethel SD 403
Supt. — See Spanaway
Clover Creek ES 600/K-6
16715 36th Ave E 98446 253-683-7800
Don Garrick, prin. Fax 683-7898
Naches Trail ES 800/K-6
15305 Waller Rd E 98446 253-683-8700
Nancy Sonnenburg, prin. Fax 683-8798
Thompson ES 500/PK-6
303 159th St E 98445 253-683-5800
Suzanne Gayda, prin. Fax 683-5898

Franklin Pierce SD 402 7,600/PK-12
315 129th St S 98444 253-298-3000
Frank Hewins, supt. Fax 298-3015
www.fp.k12.wa.us
Brookdale ES 400/PK-5
611 132nd St S 98444 253-298-3100
Barbara Rupert, prin. Fax 298-3115
Central Avenue ES 400/K-5
4505 104th St E 98446 253-298-3200
Debra Knesal, prin. Fax 298-3215
Christensen ES 400/K-5
10232 Barnes Ln S 98444 253-298-3300
Tim Enfield, prin. Fax 298-3315
Collins ES 400/K-5
4608 128th St E 98446 253-298-3400
Carrie Adrian, prin. Fax 298-3415
Elmhurst ES 400/K-5
420 133rd St E 98445 253-298-3500
Shaun Carey, prin. Fax 298-3515
Ford MS 900/6-8
1602 104th St E 98445 253-298-3600
Gary Benson, prin. Fax 298-3615
Harvard ES 500/K-5
1709 85th St E 98445 253-298-4100
Paul Elery, prin. Fax 298-4115
Keithley MS 900/6-8
12324 12th Ave S 98444 253-298-4300
Joyce Knowles, prin. Fax 298-4315
Midland ES 500/K-5
2300 105th St E 98445 253-298-4500
Nancy Brown, prin. Fax 298-4515
Sales ES 400/K-5
11213 Sheridan Ave S 98444 253-298-4200
Kristen Schroeder, prin. Fax 298-4215

Puyallup SD 3
Supt. — See Puyallup
Waller Road ES 300/K-6
6312 Waller Rd E 98443 253-841-8745
Conchita Oliver-Moore, prin. Fax 840-8941

Tacoma SD 10 28,900/PK-12
PO Box 1357 98401 253-571-1000
Dr. Arthur Jarvis, supt. Fax 571-1440
www.tacomaschools.org/
Arlington ES 200/PK-5
3002 S 72nd St 98409 253-571-3200
Lawrence West, prin. Fax 571-3201
Baker MS 700/6-8
8320 S I St 98408 253-571-5000
Steve Holmes, prin. Fax 571-5090
Birney ES 400/PK-5
1202 S 76th St 98408 253-571-4600
Christine Hinds, prin. Fax 571-4608
Blix ES 400/PK-5
1302 E 38th St 98404 253-571-7400
Paul Wieneke, prin. Fax 571-7525
Boze ES 500/PK-5
1140 E 65th St 98404 253-571-4688
Wendy Pye-Carter, prin. Fax 571-4690
Browns Point ES 400/K-5
1526 51st St NE 98422 253-571-7600
Patricia Moncure-Thomas, prin. Fax 571-7665
Bryant Montessori S 400/PK-8
717 S Grant Ave 98405 253-571-2800
Paula Bond, prin. Fax 571-2801
Crescent Heights ES 600/K-5
4110 Nassau Ave NE 98422 253-571-5500
John Blix, prin. Fax 571-5546
DeLong ES 400/K-5
4901 S 14th St 98405 253-571-5800
Ed Schau, prin. Fax 571-5799
Downing ES 300/PK-5
2502 N Orchard St 98406 253-571-7100
Susan Goerger, prin. Fax 571-7151
Edison ES 600/PK-5
5830 S Pine St 98409 253-571-1700
Renee Rossman, prin. Fax 571-1672
Fawcett ES 400/K-5
126 E 60th St 98404 253-571-4700
Zeek Edmond, prin. Fax 571-4754
Fern Hill ES 300/PK-5
8442 S Park Ave 98444 253-571-3888
Tammy Larsen, prin. Fax 571-3889
First Creek MS 500/6-8
1801 E 56th St 98404 253-571-2700
Delores Beason, prin. Fax 571-2717
Franklin ES 300/K-5
1402 S Lawrence St 98405 253-571-1400
Tracye Ferguson, prin. Fax 571-1790
Geiger ES 200/K-5
621 S Jackson Ave 98465 253-571-6800
Paula Bond, prin. Fax 571-6850
Giaudrone MS 600/6-8
4902 S Alaska St 98408 253-571-5811
Michael Robinson, prin. Fax 571-5812
Grant ES 400/PK-5
1018 N Prospect St 98406 253-571-5400
Fax 571-5425
Gray MS 600/6-8
6229 S Tyler St 98409 253-571-5200
Yvonne Bullock, prin. Fax 571-5201
Hunt MS 500/6-8
6501 S 10th St 98465 253-571-2400
Mary Chapman, prin. Fax 571-2481
Jefferson ES 200/PK-5
4302 N 13th St 98406 253-571-2261
Avance Byrd, prin. Fax 571-3982
Larchmont ES 400/K-5
8601 E B St 98445 253-571-6200
Cynthia Horner, prin. Fax 571-6262
Lee MS 500/6-8
602 N Sprague Ave 98403 253-571-1395
Jon Kellett, prin. Fax 571-1466
Lister ES 400/PK-5
2106 E 44th St 98404 253-571-2900
Rafael Maltos, prin. Fax 571-2969
Lowell ES 400/K-5
810 N 13th St 98403 253-571-7200
Robert Dahl, prin. Fax 571-7202
Lyon ES 300/PK-5
101 E 46th St 98404 253-571-2090
Kelly Wedum, prin. Fax 571-2174
Madison ECC PK-PK
3101 S 43rd St 98409 253-571-1900
Leslie Meisner, dir. Fax 571-1894
Manitou Park ES 600/PK-5
4330 S 66th St 98409 253-571-5300
Mary Wilson, prin. Fax 571-5369
Mann ES 500/PK-5
1002 S 52nd St 98408 253-571-6300
Patricia Kennedy, prin. Fax 571-6301
Mason MS 800/6-8
3901 N 28th St 98407 253-571-7000
Patrice Sulkosky, prin. Fax 571-7091
McCarver ES 400/PK-5
2111 S J St 98405 253-571-4900
Scott Rich, prin. Fax 571-4950
McKinley ES 300/PK-5
3702 McKinley Ave 98404 253-571-4340
Anita Roth, prin. Fax 571-4342
Meeker MS 800/6-8
4402 Nassau Ave NE 98422 253-571-6500
Kevin Ikeda, prin. Fax 571-6503
Northeast Tacoma ES 500/K-5
5412 29th St NE 98422 253-571-6933
Anne Tsuneishi, prin. Fax 571-6934
Point Defiance ES 400/PK-5
4330 N Visscher St 98407 253-571-6900
Olga Lay, prin. Fax 571-6922
Reed ES 500/PK-5
1802 S 36th St 98418 253-571-2072
Katherine Boyd, prin. Fax 571-2132

Roosevelt ES 200/PK-5
3550 E Roosevelt Ave 98404 253-571-4400
Darrell Johnston, prin. Fax 571-4468
Sheridan ES 600/K-5
5317 McKinley Ave 98404 253-571-2076
Kelly Evans, prin. Fax 571-2168
Sherman ES 300/K-5
4415 N 38th St 98407 253-571-5488
Connie Wick, prin. Fax 571-5484
Skyline ES 300/PK-5
2301 N Mildred St 98406 253-571-7800
Fax 571-7799
Stafford ES 300/K-5
1615 S 92nd St 98444 253-571-4300
Cynthia Evans, prin. Fax 571-4301
Stanley ES 300/PK-5
1712 S 17th St 98405 253-571-4500
Cynthia Johnson, prin. Fax 571-4553
Stewart MS 600/6-8
5010 Pacific Ave 98408 253-571-4200
Krestin Bahr, prin. Fax 571-4244
Truman MS 700/6-8
5801 N 35th St 98407 253-571-5600
Brenda McBrayer, prin. Fax 571-5680
Wainwright ES 300/PK-5
130 Alameda Ave 98466 253-571-3444
Dorothy William, prin. Fax 571-3446
Washington-Hoyt ES 400/K-5
3701 N 26th St 98407 253-571-5700
John Knight, prin. Fax 571-5738
Whitman ES 400/PK-5
1120 S 39th St 98418 253-571-7272
Connie Hedman, prin. Fax 571-7270
Whittier ES 400/K-5
777 Elm Tree Ln 98466 253-571-7500
Dan Tharp, prin. Fax 571-7586

Cascade Christian/Frederickson ES 200/PK-6
3425 176th St E 98446 253-537-9339
Mary Severeid, prin. Fax 531-4699
Cascade Christian/Tacoma ES 200/PK-6
1819 E 72nd St 98404 253-473-0590
Bonita Cheshier, prin. Fax 473-0591
Concordia Lutheran S 400/PK-8
202 E 56th St 98404 253-475-9513
Ellen Malzahn, prin. Fax 475-5445
Faith Lutheran S 100/PK-8
113 S 96th St 98444 253-537-2696
Philip Adickes, prin. Fax 537-2696
First Presbyterian Church S 200/PK-5
20 Tacoma Ave S 98402 253-272-7145
Dr. Jim Thoburn, hdmstr. Fax 404-0769
Holy Rosary S 100/K-8
504 S 30th St 98402 253-272-7012
Rudy Navarro, prin. Fax 404-1804
Life Christian S 900/PK-12
1717 S Union Ave 98405 253-756-5317
Ross Hjelseth, hdmstr. Fax 761-9798
Parkland Evangelical Lutheran S 100/PK-8
120 123rd St S 98444 253-537-1901
Larry Rude, prin. Fax 537-0172
Puget Sound Christian S 100/PK-6
1740 S 84th St 98444 253-537-6870
Shana Kinsella, admin. Fax 535-3822
St. Charles Borromeo S 500/K-8
7112 S 12th St 98465 253-564-6511
Patrick Feist, prin. Fax 566-5461
St. Patrick S 500/PK-8
1112 N G St 98403 253-272-2297
Francie Jordan, prin. Fax 383-2003
Tacoma Baptist S 400/PK-12
2052 S 64th St 98409 253-475-7226
Robert White, supt. Fax 471-9949
Tacoma SDA Christian S 1-8
230 S 94th St 98444 253-537-2555
Tacoma Waldorf S 100/PK-5
3315 S 19th St 98405 253-383-8711
Melissa Turner, admin.
Trinity Lutheran Childcare 50/PK-K
12115 Park Ave S 98444 253-535-2699
Lynn Cooper, dir.
Visitation S 200/PK-8
3306 S 58th St 98409 253-474-6424
Sheila Harrison, prin. Fax 474-6718
Wright S 500/PK-12
827 N Tacoma Ave 98403 253-272-2216
Rick Clarke, hdmstr. Fax 572-3616

Taholah, Grays Harbor, Pop. 788
Taholah SD 77 100/PK-12
PO Box 249 98587 360-276-4780
Rick Lindblad, supt. Fax 276-4370
www.taholah.k12.wa.us/
Taholah S 100/PK-12
PO Box 249 98587 360-276-4514
Rick Lindblad, prin. Fax 276-4370

Tekoa, Whitman, Pop. 772
Tekoa SD 265 200/PK-12
PO Box 869 99033 509-284-3281
Wayne Massie, supt. Fax 284-2045
www.tekoa.wednet.edu
Tekoa ES 100/PK-6
PO Box 869 99033 509-284-2781
Rebecca McHargue, prin. Fax 284-4027

Tenino, Thurston, Pop. 1,584
Tenino SD 402 1,400/PK-12
PO Box 4024 98589 360-264-3400
Russ Pickett, supt. Fax 264-3438
www.teninoschools.org/
Parkside ES 300/PK-2
PO Box 4024 98589 360-264-3800
Brock Williams, prin. Fax 264-3838
Tenino ES 300/3-5
PO Box 4024 98589 360-264-3700
David Ford, prin. Fax 264-3738
Tenino MS 300/6-8
PO Box 4024 98589 360-264-3600
Richard Staley, prin. Fax 264-3638

Thorp, Kittitas
Thorp SD 400 200/K-12
PO Box 150 98946 509-964-2107
James Hainer, supt. Fax 964-2313
www.thorp.wednet.edu
Thorp S 200/K-12
PO Box 150 98946 509-964-2107
James Hainer, prin. Fax 964-2313

Valley Christian S 50/K-8
270 Mission Rd 98946 509-964-2112
Fax 964-9161

Tieton, Yakima, Pop. 1,171
Highland SD 203
Supt. — See Cowiche
Tieton IS 300/4-6
PO Box 6 98947 509-673-3141
Andrew Woehler, prin. Fax 673-2771

Toledo, Lewis, Pop. 676
Toledo SD 237 1,000/PK-12
PO Box 469 98591 360-864-6325
Sharon Bower, supt. Fax 864-6326
www.toledo.k12.wa.us
Toledo ES 400/PK-5
PO Box 549 98591 360-864-4761
Ron Reynolds, prin. Fax 864-8146
Toledo MS 200/6-8
PO Box 668 98591 360-864-2395
Bill Waag, prin. Fax 864-8147

Tonasket, Okanogan, Pop. 970
Tonasket SD 404 1,200/PK-12
35 Highway 20 98855 509-486-2126
Randall Hauff, supt. Fax 486-1263
www.tonasket.wednet.edu
Tonasket ES 500/PK-5
35 Highway 20 98855 509-486-4933
Jeff Cravy, prin. Fax 486-2164
Tonasket MS 300/6-8
35 Highway 20 98855 509-486-2147
Ed Morgan, prin. Fax 486-1576

Peaceful Valley Christian S 50/K-8
PO Box 1062 98855 509-486-4345
Jackie Jager, lead tchr.

Toppenish, Yakima, Pop. 9,207
Toppenish SD 202 3,300/PK-12
306 Bolin Dr 98948 509-865-4455
Steve Myers, supt. Fax 865-2067
www.toppenish.wednet.edu/
Garfield ES 400/K-5
505 Madison Ave 98948 509-865-4575
Matt Piper, prin. Fax 865-8407
Kirkwood ES 400/K-5
403 S Juniper St 98948 509-865-4750
Anastasia Sanchez, prin. Fax 865-3223
Lincoln ES 400/K-5
309 N Alder St 98948 509-865-4555
Teri Martin, prin. Fax 865-7511
Preschool PK-PK
407 S Juniper St 98948 509-865-8179
Katherine Cove, dir. Fax 865-2476
Toppenish MS 700/6-8
104 Goldendale Ave 98948 509-865-2730
Dawn Weddle, prin. Fax 865-7503
Valley View ES 400/K-5
515 Zillah Ave 98948 509-865-8240
Robert Roybal, prin. Fax 865-8234

Touchet, Walla Walla
Touchet SD 300 300/K-12
PO Box 135 99360 509-394-2352
Dan McDonald, supt. Fax 394-2952
www.touchet.org/
Touchet ES, PO Box 135 99360 100/K-5
Danny McDonald, prin. 509-394-2923

Toutle, Cowlitz
Toutle Lake SD 130 600/K-12
5050 Spirit Lake Hwy 98649 360-274-6182
Scott Grabenhorst, supt. Fax 274-7608
www.toutlesd.k12.wa.us
Toutle Lake ES 300/K-6
5050 Spirit Lake Hwy 98649 360-274-6142
Vicky Frandsen, prin. Fax 274-7608

Trout Lake, Klickitat
Trout Lake SD R-400 200/K-12
PO Box 488 98650 509-395-2571
Doug Dearden, supt. Fax 395-2399
www.troutlake.k12.wa.us/
Trout Lake ES 100/K-4
PO Box 488 98650 509-395-2571
Doug Dearden, prin. Fax 395-2399

Tukwila, King, Pop. 16,969
Tukwila SD 406 2,700/K-12
4640 S 144th St 98168 206-901-8000
Ethelda Burke, supt. Fax 901-8016
www.tukwila.wednet.edu
Showalter MS 600/6-8
4628 S 144th St 98168 206-901-7800
Brett Christopher, prin. Fax 901-7807
Thorndyke ES 400/K-5
4415 S 150th St 98188 206-901-7600
Brian Hutchison, prin. Fax 901-7607
Tukwila ES 500/K-5
5939 S 149th St 98168 206-901-7500
Steve Salisbury, prin. Fax 901-7507
Other Schools – See Seattle

Tumwater, Thurston, Pop. 13,331
Tumwater SD 33 6,500/K-12
621 Linwood Ave SW 98512 360-709-7000
Terry Borden, supt. Fax 709-7002
www.tumwater.k12.wa.us
Bush MS 500/7-8
2120 83rd Ave SW 98512 360-709-7400
Linda O'Shaughnessy, prin. Fax 709-7402
Schmidt ES 600/K-6
225 Dennis St SE 98501 360-709-7200
Jack Arend, prin. Fax 709-7202
Simmons ES 600/K-6
1205 S 2nd Ave SW 98512 360-709-7100
Trisha Smith, prin. Fax 709-7102
Tumwater Hill ES 400/K-6
3120 Ridgeview Ct SW 98512 360-709-7300
Brian Duke, prin. Fax 709-7302
Tumwater MS 500/7-8
6335 Littlerock Rd SW 98512 360-709-7500
Jon Wilcox, prin. Fax 709-7502
Other Schools – See Littlerock, Olympia

Union Gap, Yakima, Pop. 5,707
Union Gap SD 2 600/K-8
3200 2nd St 98903 509-248-3966
Kurt Hilyard, supt. Fax 575-1876
uniongap.org
Union Gap S 600/K-8
3200 2nd St 98903 509-248-3966
Michele Southwick, prin. Fax 575-1876

University Place, Pierce, Pop. 30,425
University Place SD 83 5,500/K-12
3717 Grandview Dr W 98466 253-566-5600
Patricia Banks, supt. Fax 566-5607
www.upsd.wednet.edu
Chambers PS 400/K-4
9101 56th St W 98467 253-566-5650
Kathy Drouhard, prin. Fax 566-5698
Drum IS 600/5-7
4909 79th Ave W 98467 253-566-5660
Susie Jensen, prin. Fax 566-5663
Evergreen PS 500/K-4
7102 40th St W 98466 253-566-5680
Lance Goodpaster, prin. Fax 566-5684
Narrows View IS 700/5-7
7813 44th St W 98466 253-566-5630
Eric Brubaker, prin. Fax 566-5634
Sunset PS 400/K-4
4523 97th Ave W 98466 253-566-5640
Kurt Hatch, prin. Fax 566-5642
University Place PS 400/K-4
2708 Grandview Dr W 98466 253-566-5620
Allison Drago, prin. Fax 566-5704

Heritage Christian S 200/K-8
5412 67th Ave W 98467 253-564-6276
Glenn Fisher, prin. Fax 460-1695
Wright Academy 700/PK-12
7723 Chambers Creek Rd W 98467 253-620-8300
Robert Camner, prin. Fax 620-8431

Valley, Stevens
Valley SD 070 200/K-8
3034 Huffman Rd 99181 509-937-2791
Mark Selle, supt. Fax 937-2204
www.valleysd.org/
Valley S 200/K-8
3034 Huffman Rd 99181 509-937-2413
Todd Smith, prin. Fax 937-2204

Vancouver, Clark, Pop. 157,493
Battle Ground SD 119
Supt. — See Brush Prairie
Glenwood Heights PS 700/K-4
9716 NE 134th St 98662 360-885-5250
Eric Hoglund, prin. Fax 885-5260
Laurin MS 600/5-8
13601 NE 97th Ave 98662 360-885-5200
JoDee McMillen, prin. Fax 885-5201
Pleasant Valley MS 400/5-8
14320 NE 50th Ave 98686 360-885-5500
Ward Holcomb, prin. Fax 885-5510
Pleasant Valley PS 500/K-4
14320 NE 50th Ave 98686 360-885-5550
Melissa Mitchell, prin. Fax 885-5551

Evergreen SD 114 27,200/PK-12
PO Box 8910 98668 360-604-4000
John Deeder, supt. Fax 892-5307
www.evergreenps.org/
Burnt Bridge Creek ES 600/K-5
PO Box 8910 98668 360-604-6750
Jan Davey, prin. Fax 604-6751
Burton ES 600/K-5
PO Box 8910 98668 360-604-4975
Bonnie Webberley, prin. Fax 604-4977
Cascade MS 900/6-8
PO Box 8910 98668 360-604-3600
Gary Price, prin. Fax 604-3602
Columbia Valley ES 500/K-5
PO Box 8910 98668 360-604-3375
James Fernandez, prin. Fax 604-3377
Covington MS 1,000/6-8
PO Box 8910 98668 360-604-6300
Byron Molle, prin. Fax 604-6302
Crestline ES 500/K-5
PO Box 8910 98668 360-604-3325
Bobbie Jacobson-Butler, prin. Fax 604-3327
Ellsworth ES 500/K-5
PO Box 8910 98668 360-604-6950
Jerry Evans, prin. Fax 604-6952
Endeavour ES, PO Box 8910 98668 400/K-5
Lauren Hopson, prin. 360-604-4920
Evergreen ECC 100/PK-K
PO Box 8910 98668 360-604-3925
Gaelynn Mills, prin. Fax 604-3927
Fircrest ES 500/K-5
PO Box 8910 98668 360-604-6925
Margaret Varkados, prin. Fax 604-6927
Fisher's Landing ES 700/K-5
PO Box 8910 98668 360-604-6650
Joe Segram, prin. Fax 604-6652
Frontier MS 1,000/6-8
PO Box 8910 98668 360-604-3200
Lisa Wagner, prin. Fax 604-3202
Harmony ES 800/K-5
PO Box 8910 98668 360-604-6600
Mary Horn, prin. Fax 604-6602

Hearthwood ES 500/K-5
PO Box 8910 98668 360-604-6875
Scott Munro, prin. Fax 604-6877
Image ES 800/K-5
PO Box 8910 98668 360-604-6850
Kathleen Keller, prin. Fax 604-6852
Marrion ES 500/K-5
PO Box 8910 98668 360-604-6825
Traci Haddad, prin. Fax 604-6827
Mill Plain ES 500/K-5
PO Box 8910 98668 360-604-6800
Deb Alden, prin. Fax 604-6802
Orchards ES 600/K-5
PO Box 8910 98668 360-604-6975
Vinh Nguyen, prin. Fax 604-6977
Pacific MS 1,100/6-8
PO Box 8910 98668 360-604-6500
Kathy Stellfox, prin. Fax 604-6502
Pioneer ES 700/K-5
PO Box 8910 98668 360-604-3300
Jenny Roberts, prin. Fax 604-3302
Riverview ES 500/K-5
PO Box 8910 98668 360-604-6625
Judi DesRochers, prin. Fax 604-6627
Shahala MS 1,000/6-8
PO Box 8910 98668 360-604-3800
Renee Bernazzani, prin. Fax 604-3802
Sifton ES 600/K-5
PO Box 8910 98668 360-604-6675
Angela Mitchell, prin. Fax 604-6677
Silver Star ES 500/K-5
PO Box 8910 98668 360-604-6775
Janet Locascio, prin. Fax 604-6777
Sunset ES 600/K-5
PO Box 8910 98668 360-604-6900
Michael Martin, prin. Fax 604-6902
Wy' East MS 900/6-8
PO Box 8910 98668 360-604-6400
Gary Tichenor, prin. Fax 604-6402
York ES 600/K-5
PO Box 8910 98668 360-604-3975
Dawn Harris, prin. Fax 604-3977
Other Schools – See Camas

Vancouver SD 37 22,000/PK-12
PO Box 8937 98668 360-313-1000
Dr. Steven Webb, supt. Fax 313-1001
www.vansd.org
Alki MS 600/6-8
1800 NW Bliss Rd 98685 360-313-3200
Curtis Smith, prin. Fax 313-3201
Anderson ES 700/K-5
2215 NE 104th St 98686 360-313-1500
Lucy Estrada-Guzman, prin. Fax 313-1501
Chinook ES 700/K-5
1900 NW Bliss Rd 98685 360-313-1600
Joe Lapidus, prin. Fax 313-1601
Discovery MS 700/6-8
800 E 40th St 98663 360-313-3300
Chris Olsen, prin. Fax 313-3301
Eisenhower ES 500/K-5
9201 NW 9th Ave 98665 360-313-1700
Doug Hood, prin. Fax 313-1701
Felida ES 700/K-5
2700 NW 119th St 98685 360-313-1750
Edna Nash, prin. Fax 313-1751
Franklin ES 200/K-5
5206 NW Franklin St 98663 360-313-1850
William Nicolay, prin. Fax 313-1851
Fruit Valley ES 200/K-5
3410 Fruit Valley Rd 98660 360-313-1900
Debra Elliott, prin. Fax 313-1901
Gaiser MS 800/6-8
3000 NE 99th St 98665 360-313-3400
Mike Lane, prin. Fax 313-3401
Harney ES 400/K-5
3212 E Evergreen Blvd 98661 360-313-2000
Karrie Olsen, prin. Fax 313-2001
Hazel Dell ES 500/K-5
511 NE Anderson St 98665 360-313-2050
Woody Howard, prin. Fax 313-2051
Hough ES 300/K-5
1900 Daniels St 98660 360-313-2100
Sean McMillan, prin. Fax 313-2101
Jefferson MS 800/6-8
3000 NW 119th St 98685 360-313-3700
Marianne Thompson, prin. Fax 313-3701
King ES 500/K-5
4801 Idaho St 98661 360-313-2200
Debra Hale, prin. Fax 313-2201
Lake Shore ES 400/K-5
9300 NW 21st Ave 98665 360-313-2250
Scott Leary, prin. Fax 313-2251
Lee MS 800/6-8
8500 NW 9th Ave 98665 360-313-3500
Susan Cone, prin. Fax 313-3501
Lincoln ES 400/K-5
4200 NW Daniels St 98660 360-313-2300
Craig Homnick, prin. Fax 313-2301
Marshall ES 400/K-5
6400 MacArthur Blvd 98661 360-313-2400
Julie Kassner, prin. Fax 313-2401
McLoughlin MS 800/6-8
5802 MacArthur Blvd 98661 360-313-3600
Richard Reeves, prin. Fax 313-3601
Minnehaha ES 500/K-5
2800 NE 54th St 98663 360-313-2500
Jackie Merz-Beck, prin. Fax 313-2501
Ogden ES 400/K-5
8100 NE 28th St 98662 360-313-2550
Marcie Ramberg, prin. Fax 313-2551
Roosevelt ES 600/K-5
2921 Falk Rd 98661 360-313-2600
Karen Leary, prin. Fax 313-2601
Sacajawea ES 400/K-5
700 NE 112th St 98685 360-313-2750
Kris Janati, prin. Fax 313-2751
Salmon Creek ES 500/K-5
1601 NE 129th St 98685 360-313-2800
Mary Ellen Brunaugh, prin. Fax 313-2801

Truman ES 500/K-5
4505 NE 42nd Ave 98661 360-313-2900
Darci Fronk, prin. Fax 313-2901
Vancouver ECC 200/PK-PK
301 S Lieser Rd 98664 360-313-4850
Laura Dilley, dir. Fax 313-4851
Walnut Grove ES 700/K-5
6103 NE 72nd Ave 98661 360-313-3000
Bobbi Geenty, prin. Fax 313-3001
Washington ES 400/K-5
2908 S St 98663 360-313-3050
Theresa David-Turner, prin. Fax 313-3051

Cascadia S 100/1-8
10606 NE 14th St 98664 360-944-8096
David Drakos, admin. Fax 256-7553
Cornerstone Christian S 400/PK-8
7708 NE 78th St 98662 360-256-9715
Robert Shadle, prin. Fax 882-7614
Gardner S 100/PK-8
16413 NE 50th Ave 98686 360-574-5752
Mark McGough, hdmstr. Fax 574-5701
Hosanna Christian S 300/PK-8
4120 NE St Johns Rd 98661 360-906-0941
Dean Carter, admin. Fax 694-0224
Kings Way Christian S 600/PK-12
3300 NE 78th St 98665 360-574-1613
Steve Jensen, prin. Fax 573-5895
Our Lady of Lourdes S 300/PK-8
4701 NW Franklin St 98663 360-696-2301
Brian Anderson, prin. Fax 696-6700
St. Joseph S 400/K-8
6500 Highland Dr 98661 360-696-2586
Lesley Harrison, prin. Fax 696-0977
Skinner Montessori S 100/PK-8
5001 NE 66th Ave 98661 360-696-4862
Peggy Skinner, admin.

Vashon, King
Vashon Island SD 402 1,500/PK-12
PO Box 547 98070 206-463-2121
Dr. Terry Lindquist, supt. Fax 463-6262
www.vashonsd.org
Chautauqua ES 600/PK-5
9309 SW Cemetery Rd 98070 206-463-2882
Kate Baehr, prin. Fax 463-0937
McMurray MS 300/6-8
9329 SW Cemetery Rd 98070 206-463-9168
Greg Allison, prin. Fax 463-9707

Vaughn, Pierce
Peninsula SD 401
Supt. — See Gig Harbor
Vaughn ES 400/PK-5
17521 Hall Rd Kp N 98394 253-530-4700
Mike Benoit, prin. Fax 530-4720

Wahkiacus, Klickitat

Wahkiacus SDA Church S 50/1-8
457 Wahkiacus Heights Rd 98670 509-369-3735
Tom Hunt, prin.

Waitsburg, Walla Walla, Pop. 1,224
Waitsburg SD 401-100 400/K-12
PO Box 217 99361 509-337-6301
Dr. Carol Clarke, supt. Fax 337-6042
www.waitsburgsd.org
Preston Hall MS 100/6-8
PO Box 217 99361 509-337-9474
Dr. Ben Christensen, prin. Fax 337-6170
Waitsburg ES 100/K-5
PO Box 217 99361 509-337-6461
Dr. Carol Clarke, prin. Fax 337-6902

Waldron, San Juan
Orcas Island SD 137
Supt. — See Eastsound
Waldron Island S 98297 50/K-8
Barbara Kline, prin. 360-317-8578

Walla Walla, Walla Walla, Pop. 30,989
Walla Walla SD 140 5,700/K-12
364 S Park St 99362 509-527-3000
Dr. Richard Carter, supt. Fax 529-7713
www.wwps.org
Berney ES 500/K-5
1718 Pleasant St 99362 509-527-3060
Donna Painter, prin. Fax 527-3096
Blue Ridge ES 300/K-5
1150 W Chestnut St 99362 509-527-3066
Kim Doepker, prin. Fax 522-4480
Edison ES 300/K-5
1315 E Alder St 99362 509-527-3072
Nancy Withycombe, prin. Fax 527-3062
Garrison MS 600/6-8
906 Chase Ave 99362 509-527-3040
Gina Yonts, prin. Fax 527-3048
Green Park ES 500/K-5
1105 E Isaacs Ave 99362 509-527-3077
Michael Lambert, prin. Fax 522-4487
Pioneer MS 600/6-8
450 Bridge St 99362 509-527-3050
Dana Jones, prin. Fax 526-5212
Prospect Point ES 600/K-5
55 Reser Rd 99362 509-527-3088
Chris Gardea, prin. Fax 522-4489
Sharpstein ES 400/K-5
410 S Howard St 99362 509-527-3098
Laura Quaresma, prin. Fax 527-3065

Assumption S 200/PK-5
2066 E Alder St 99362 509-525-9283
John Lesko, prin. Fax 527-0848
Liberty Christian S 100/PK-8
3172 Peppers Bridge Rd 99362 509-525-5082
Fax 525-5073

Wapato, Yakima, Pop. 4,619
Wapato SD 207 3,300/K-12
PO Box 38 98951 509-877-4181
Becky Imler, supt. Fax 877-6077
www.wapato.k12.wa.us/
Adams ES 400/K-5
1309 S Camas Ave 98951 509-877-4180
Sydney John, prin. Fax 877-2761
Camas ES 600/K-5
1010 S Camas Ave 98951 509-877-3134
Susan Steele, prin. Fax 877-3022
Satus ES 600/K-5
910 S Camas Ave 98951 509-877-2177
Carrie Hendricks, prin. Fax 877-7092
Wapato MS 800/6-8
1309 Kateri Ln 98951 509-877-2173
Kelly Garza, prin. Fax 877-6232

Warden, Grant, Pop. 2,635
Warden SD 146-161 1,000/PK-12
101 W Beck Way 98857 509-349-2366
Sandra Sheldon, supt. Fax 349-2367
www.warden.wednet.edu
Warden ES 500/PK-5
101 W Beck Way 98857 509-349-2311
Jill Massa, prin. Fax 349-2312
Warden MS 200/6-8
101 W Beck Way 98857 509-349-2902
Doug Kaplicky, prin. Fax 349-2531

Washougal, Clark, Pop. 10,732
Mount Pleasant SD 29-93 100/K-6
152 Marble Rd 98671 360-835-3371
Michael Hyde, supt. Fax 835-7040
Mount Pleasant ES 100/K-6
152 Marble Rd 98671 360-835-3371
Michael Hyde, prin. Fax 835-7040

Washougal SD 112-6 3,000/K-12
4855 Evergreen Way 98671 360-954-3000
Teresa Baldwin, supt. Fax 835-7776
www.washougal.k12.wa.us
Canyon Creek MS 200/6-8
9731 Washougal River Rd 98671 360-954-3500
Sandi Christensen, prin. Fax 837-1500
Cape Horn-Skye ES 400/K-5
9731 Washougal River Rd 98671 360-954-3600
Mary Lou Woody, prin. Fax 837-3906
Gause ES 600/K-5
1100 34th St 98671 360-954-3700
Rex Larson, prin. Fax 954-3799
Hathaway ES 500/K-5
630 24th St 98671 360-954-3800
Laura Bolt, prin. Fax 335-0511
Jemtegaard MS 400/6-8
35300 SE Evergreen Hwy 98671 360-954-3400
Khrista McBride, prin. Fax 835-9145

Riverside SDA S 50/PK-8
PO Box 367 98671 360-835-5600
Dan Wister, prin. Fax 835-7276

Washtucna, Adams, Pop. 258
Washtucna SD 109-43 50/K-12
PO Box 688 99371 509-646-3237
Steve Smedley, supt. Fax 646-3249
www.tucna.wednet.edu
Washtucna S 50/K-12
100 School St 99371 509-646-3237
Glenn Martin, prin. Fax 646-3249

Waterville, Douglas, Pop. 1,155
Waterville SD 209 300/K-12
PO Box 490 98858 509-745-8584
Raymond Reid, supt. Fax 745-9073
www.waterville.wednet.edu/
Waterville ES 100/K-6
PO Box 490 98858 509-745-8585
Cathi Nelson, prin. Fax 745-9073

Wellpinit, Stevens
Wellpinit SD 49 500/K-12
PO Box 390 99040 509-258-4535
Tim Ames, supt. Fax 258-4065
www.wellpinit.wednet.edu
Wellpinit ES 200/K-5
PO Box 390 99040 509-258-4535
Terry Bartolino, prin. Fax 258-7378
Wellpinit MS 100/6-8
PO Box 390 99040 509-258-4535
Terry Bartolino, prin. Fax 258-4091

Wenatchee, Chelan, Pop. 29,374
Wenatchee SD 246 7,300/K-12
PO Box 1767 98807 509-663-8161
Brian Flones, supt. Fax 663-3082
home.wsd.wednet.edu
Columbia ES 400/K-5
600 Alaska Ave 98801 509-662-7256
Fay Crawford, prin. Fax 664-2910
Foothills MS 600/6-8
1410 Maple St 98801 509-664-8961
John Waldren, prin. Fax 663-6610
Lewis & Clark ES 500/K-5
1130 Princeton Ave N 98801 509-663-5351
Alfonso Lopez, prin. Fax 663-5601
Lincoln ES 500/K-5
1224 Methow St 98801 509-663-5710
Tim Sheppard, prin. Fax 662-6831
Mission View ES 500/K-5
60 Terminal Ave 98801 509-663-5851
Jeff Jaeger, prin. Fax 667-1117
Newbery ES 500/K-5
850 N Western Ave 98801 509-664-8930
Patti Eggleston, prin. Fax 664-8940
Orchard MS 500/6-8
1024 Orchard Ave 98801 509-662-7745
Mike Hopkins, prin. Fax 663-8042
Pioneer MS 600/6-8
1620 Russell St 98801 509-663-7171
Mark Helm, prin. Fax 663-0453

Sunnyslope ES 300/K-5
3109 School St 98801 509-662-8803
Mark Goveia, prin. Fax 664-5094
Washington ES 500/K-5
1401 Washington St 98801 509-662-5504
Keith Collins, prin. Fax 662-9227

Cascade Christian Academy 200/K-12
600 N Western Ave 98801 509-662-2723
Mark Witas, prin. Fax 662-5892
River Academy 200/PK-12
PO Box 4485 98807 509-665-2415
Eric DeVries, hdmstr. Fax 662-9235
St. Joseph S 200/PK-5
600 Saint Joseph Pl 98801 509-663-2644
Sr. Agueda Durazo, prin. Fax 663-8474
St. Paul's Lutheran S 100/PK-6
PO Box 2219 98807 509-662-3659
Dr. Joseph Tensmeyer, prin. Fax 662-5274

Westport, Grays Harbor, Pop. 2,402
Ocosta SD 172 700/PK-12
2580 S Montesano St 98595 360-268-9125
Gail Sackman, supt. Fax 268-2540
www.ocosta.k12.wa.us/
Ocosta ES 400/PK-6
2580 S Montesano St 98595 360-268-9125
Heather Sweet, prin. Fax 268-6327

West Richland, Benton, Pop. 9,907
Richland SD 400
Supt. — See Richland
Enterprise MS 800/6-8
5200 Paradise Dr 99353 509-967-6200
Tony Howard, prin. Fax 967-5685
Tapteal ES 500/K-5
705 N 62nd Ave 99353 509-967-6350
Rhonda Pratt, prin. Fax 967-4101
Wiley ES 600/K-5
2820 S Highlands Blvd 99353 509-967-6375
Heidi Weisert-Peatow, prin. Fax 967-4122

White Salmon, Klickitat, Pop. 2,280
White Salmon Valley SD 405-17 1,100/K-12
PO Box 157 98672 509-493-1500
Dale Palmer, supt. Fax 493-2275
schools.gorge.net/whitesalmon
Henkle MS 400/5-8
PO Box 1309 98672 509-493-1502
Rick George, prin. Fax 493-3385
Whitson ES 500/K-4
PO Box 1279 98672 509-493-1560
Vicki Prendergast, prin. Fax 493-8214

White Swan, Yakima, Pop. 2,669
Mount Adams SD 209 1,000/PK-12
PO Box 578 98952 509-874-2611
Richard Foss, supt. Fax 874-2960
www.mtadams.wednet.edu
Mount Adams MS 200/7-8
PO Box 578 98952 509-874-8626
Jason Nelson, prin. Fax 874-2646
Other Schools – See Harrah

Wilbur, Lincoln, Pop. 901
Wilbur SD 200 200/K-12
PO Box 1090 99185 509-647-2221
Steve Gaub, supt. Fax 647-2509
www.wilbur.wednet.edu/
Wilbur ES 100/K-6
PO Box 1090 99185 509-647-5892
Tom Johnson, prin. Fax 647-2509

Wilkeson, Pierce, Pop. 405
White River SD 416
Supt. — See Buckley
Wilkeson ES 200/K-5
PO Box A 98396 360-829-3357
John Hellwich, prin. Fax 829-3386

Wilson Creek, Grant, Pop. 242
Wilson Creek SD 167-202 100/K-12
PO Box 46 98860 509-345-2541
Linda McKay, supt. Fax 345-2288
www.wilsoncreek.org
Wilson Creek ES 100/K-6
PO Box 46 98860 509-345-2541
Kevin Kemp, prin. Fax 345-2288

Winlock, Lewis, Pop. 1,209
Evaline SD 36 100/K-6
111 Schoolhouse Rd 98596 360-785-3460
Linda Godat, supt. Fax 785-0951
Evaline ES 100/K-6
111 Schoolhouse Rd 98596 360-785-3460
Ann Stout, lead tchr. Fax 785-0951

Winlock SD 232 700/PK-12
311 NW Fir St 98596 360-785-3582
Richard Conley, supt. Fax 785-3583
www.winlock.wednet.edu
Winlock MS 200/6-8
241 N Military Rd 98596 360-785-3046
Marshall Mayer, prin. Fax 785-3047
Winlock-Miller ES 300/K-5
405 NW Benton Ave 98596 360-785-3516
James Swan, prin. Fax 785-4891
Winlock Preschool PK-PK
405 NW Benton Ave 98596 360-785-3372
James Swan, prin. Fax 785-4891

Winthrop, Okanogan, Pop. 359
Methow Valley SD 350 500/PK-12
18 Twin Lakes Rd 98862 509-996-9205
Dr. Mark Wenzel, supt. Fax 996-9208
www.methow.org
Methow Valley ES 200/PK-6
18 Twin Lakes Rd 98862 509-996-2186
Raymond Leaver, prin. Fax 996-9202

Wishram, Klickitat
Wishram SD 94 100/PK-12
PO Box 8 98673 509-748-2551
Duane Grams, supt. Fax 748-2127
Wishram S 100/PK-12
PO Box 8 98673 509-748-2551
Duane Grams, prin. Fax 748-2127

Woodinville, King, Pop. 9,889
Lake Washington SD 414
Supt. — See Redmond
Wilder ES 500/K-6
22130 NE 133rd St, 425-869-1909
Steve Roetcisoender, prin. Fax 702-0114

Northshore SD 417
Supt. — See Bothell
Bear Creek ES 400/K-6
18101 Avondale Rd NE, 425-408-4100
Gary Keeler, prin. Fax 408-4102
Cottage Lake ES 400/K-6
15940 Avondale Rd NE, 425-408-4200
Shelley Habinecht, prin. Fax 408-4202
East Ridge ES 500/K-6
22150 NE 156th Pl, 425-408-4400
Stacy Murphy, prin. Fax 408-4402
Hollywood Hill ES 400/K-6
17110 148th Ave NE 98072 425-408-4700
Doug Hale, prin. Fax 408-4702
Kokanee ES 400/K-6
23710 57th Ave SE 98072 425-408-4900
Kosal Chea, prin. Fax 408-4902
Wellington ES 600/K-6
16501 NE 195th St 98072 425-408-5900
Marsha Moore, prin. Fax 408-5902

Chrysalis S 300/K-12
14241 NE Woodinville Duvall 98072 425-481-2228
Karen Fogle, dir. Fax 486-8107
Mack Christian S 200/PK-6
18250 168th Pl NE 98072 425-485-1824
Debbie Symonds, prin. Fax 481-1167
Woodinville Montessori S 300/PK-9
13965 NE 166th St 98072 425-481-2300
Mary Schneider, hdmstr. Fax 482-3186

Woodland, Cowlitz, Pop. 4,336
Green Mountain SD 103 100/K-8
13105 NE Grinnell Rd 98674 360-225-7366
Michael Grubbs, supt. Fax 225-2217
www.greenmountainschool.us
Green Mountain S 100/K-8
13105 NE Grinnell Rd 98674 360-225-7366
Michael Grubbs, prin. Fax 225-2217

Woodland SD 404 2,200/PK-12
800 3rd St 98674 360-225-9451
Michael Green, supt. Fax 225-8956
www.woodlandschools.org/
Woodland IS 500/4-6
2250 Lewis River Rd 98674 360-225-0414
Chris Wiseman, prin. Fax 225-6944
Woodland MS 400/7-8
755 Park St 98674 360-225-9416
Cari Thomson Ph.D., prin. Fax 225-6725
Woodland PS 600/PK-3
600 Bozarth Ave 98674 360-225-9472
Mark Houk, prin. Fax 225-7970
Other Schools – See Ariel

Yacolt, Clark, Pop. 1,192
Battle Ground SD 119
Supt. — See Brush Prairie
Yacolt PS 800/K-4
406 W Yacolt Rd 98675 360-885-6000
Ken Evans, prin. Fax 885-6001

Yakima, Yakima, Pop. 81,214
East Valley SD 90 2,700/K-12
2002 Beaudry Rd 98901 509-573-7300
John Schieche, supt. Fax 573-7340
www.evsd90.org/
East Valley IS 600/4-6
1951 Beaudry Rd 98901 509-573-7600
Stephen Merz, prin. Fax 573-7640
Terrace Heights ES 400/K-3
4300 Maple Ct 98901 509-573-7800
Robert Adamson, prin. Fax 573-7840
Other Schools – See Moxee

Naches Valley SD JT3
Supt. — See Naches
Naches Valley PS 300/K-2
2700 Old Naches Hwy 98908 509-966-5050
Allison Schnebly, prin. Fax 966-6004

West Valley SD 208 4,700/K-12
8902 Zier Rd 98908 509-972-6000
Dr. Peter Ansingh, supt. Fax 972-6001
www.wvsd208.org
Ahtanum Valley ES 300/K-5
3006 S Wiley Rd 98903 509-965-2031
Richard Pryor, prin. Fax 966-7034
Apple Valley ES 300/K-5
7 N 88th Ave 98908 509-965-2060
Heidi Sutton, prin. Fax 966-8470
Cottonwood ES 400/K-5
1041 S 96th Ave 98908 509-965-2052
Sherry Adams, prin. Fax 966-8648
Mountainview ES 200/K-5
830 Stone Rd 98908 509-965-2070
Georgia Bonari, prin. Fax 965-7973
Summitview ES 300/K-5
6305 W Chestnut Ave 98908 509-965-2050
Crystal McDonald, prin. Fax 965-5280
West Valley MS 800/6-7
1500 S 75th Ave 98908 509-972-5700
Dave Jaeger, prin. Fax 972-5701
Wide Hollow ES 400/K-5
1000 S 72nd Ave 98908 509-965-2023
Terry Faletto, prin. Fax 965-2127

Yakima SD 7 14,600/PK-12
104 N 4th Ave 98902 509-573-7000
Dr. Elaine Beraza, supt. Fax 573-7181
www.yakimaschools.org/
Adams ES 700/PK-5
723 S 8th St 98901 509-573-5100
Dave Chaplin, prin. Fax 573-5151
Barge-Lincoln ES 500/PK-5
219 E I St 98901 509-573-5200
Netty Hull, prin. Fax 573-5252
Discovery Lab S 200/1-8
2810 Castlevale Rd 98902 509-573-5400
Deb Lavis, prin. Fax 573-5490
Franklin MS 800/6-8
410 S 19th Ave 98902 509-573-2100
Bill Hilton, prin. Fax 573-2121
Garfield ES 500/K-5
612 N 6th Ave 98902 509-573-5700
Alan Matsumoto, prin. Fax 573-5757
Gilbert ES 500/K-5
4400 Douglas Dr 98908 509-573-5800
Anne Berg, prin. Fax 573-5858
Hoover ES 600/PK-5
400 W Viola Ave 98902 509-573-5900
Luz Juarez-Stump, prin. Fax 573-5959
King ES 500/K-5
2000 S 18th St 98903 509-573-1100
Phil Vasquez, prin. Fax 573-1111
Lewis & Clark MS 700/6-8
1114 W Pierce St 98902 509-573-2200
Victor Nourani, prin. Fax 573-2222
McClure ES 600/PK-5
1222 S 22nd Ave 98902 509-573-1300
Del Carmichael, prin. Fax 573-1313
McKinley ES 400/K-5
621 S 13th Ave 98902 509-573-1400
Lee Maras, prin. Fax 573-1414
Nob Hill ES 400/K-5
801 S 34th Ave 98902 509-573-1500
Steve Brownlow, prin. Fax 573-1515
Ridgeview ES 500/K-5
609 W Washington Ave 98903 509-573-1803
K.C. Mitchell, prin. Fax 573-1818
Robertson ES 500/K-5
2807 W Lincoln Ave 98902 509-573-1600
Mark Hummel, prin. Fax 573-1616
Roosevelt ES 500/K-5
120 N 16th Ave 98902 509-573-1700
Dan Williams, prin. Fax 573-1717
Washington MS 700/6-8
510 S 9th St 98901 509-573-2300
Lorenzo Alvarado, prin. Fax 573-2323
Whitney ES 500/K-5
4411 W Nob Hill Blvd 98908 509-573-1900
Jean Hawkins, prin. Fax 573-1919
Wilson MS 800/6-8
902 S 44th Ave 98908 509-573-2400
Ernesto Araiza, prin. Fax 573-2424

Grace Lutheran S 100/PK-8
1207 S 7th Ave 98902 509-457-6611
Matt Fager, prin. Fax 457-6611
McAuliffe Academy 500/K-12
4702 Tieton Dr Ste A 98908 509-575-4989
Christopher Geis, admin. Fax 575-4976
Riverside Christian S 500/PK-12
721 Keys Rd 98901 509-965-2602
Rick Van Beek, supt. Fax 966-7031
St. Joseph - Marquette S 300/PK-8
202 N 4th St 98901 509-575-5557
Gregg Pleger, prin. Fax 457-5621
St. Paul Cathedral S 200/PK-8
1214 W Chestnut Ave 98902 509-575-5604
Buck Marsh, prin. Fax 577-8817
Westpark Christian Academy 100/PK-12
3902 Summitview Ave 98902 509-966-1632
Rev. Colleen Sheahan, admin. Fax 966-6282
Yakima Adventist Christian S 100/K-10
1200 City Reservoir Rd 98908 509-966-1933
Patrick Frey, prin. Fax 966-3907

Yelm, Thurston, Pop. 4,543
Yelm Community SD 2 5,200/PK-12
PO Box 476 98597 360-458-1900
Andy Wolf, supt. Fax 458-6178
www.ycs.wednet.edu
Fort Stevens ES 500/K-6
PO Box 476 98597 360-458-4800
Scot Embrey, prin. Fax 458-6315
Lackamas ES 300/K-6
PO Box 476 98597 360-894-6000
Kurt Fourre, prin. Fax 894-6002
Mc Kenna ES 500/K-6
PO Box 476 98597 360-458-2400
Amy Sturdivant, prin. Fax 458-6282
Mill Pond ES 500/K-6
PO Box 476 98597 360-458-3400
Jeri Person, prin. Fax 458-8040
Southworth ES 400/K-6
PO Box 476 98597 360-458-2500
Lisa Cadero-Smith, prin. Fax 458-6303
Yelm Prairie ES 500/PK-6
PO Box 476 98597 360-458-3700
Debbie McLaren, prin. Fax 458-6326

Zillah, Yakima, Pop. 2,599
Zillah SD 205 1,300/PK-12
1301 Cutler Way 98953 509-829-5911
Kevin McKay, supt. Fax 829-6290
www.zillahschools.org/
Hilton ES 400/PK-3
211 4th Ave 98953 509-829-5400
Doug Burge, prin. Fax 829-6470
Zillah IS 300/4-6
303 2nd Ave 98953 509-829-5555
Paula Dasso, prin. Fax 829-3575
Zillah MS 200/7-8
1301 Cutler Way 98953 509-829-5511
Andy Boe, prin. Fax 829-6290

WEST VIRGINIA

WEST VIRGINIA DEPARTMENT OF EDUCATION
1900 Kanawha Blvd E Rm 358, Charleston 25305-0330
Telephone 304-558-2681
Fax 304-558-0048
Website wvde.state.wv.us

State Superintendent of Schools Steven Paine

WEST VIRGINIA BOARD OF EDUCATION
1900 Kanawha Blvd E Rm 358, Charleston 25305-0330

President Priscilla Haden

REGIONAL EDUCATION SERVICE AGENCIES (RESA)

RESA I
Keith Butcher, dir. 304-256-4712
400 Neville St, Beckley 25801 Fax 256-4683
resa1.k12.wv.us/
RESA II
Dr. Dee Cockrille, dir. 304-529-6205
2001 McCoy Rd, Huntington 25701 Fax 529-6209
resa2.k12.wv.us/
RESA III
Charles Nichols, dir. 304-766-7655
501 22nd St, Dunbar 25064 Fax 766-7915
resa3.k12.wv.us
RESA IV
Elmer Pritt, dir., 404 Old Main Dr 304-872-6440
Summersville 26651 Fax 872-6442
resa4.k12.wv.us/
RESA V
Ron Nichols, dir. 304-485-6513
2507 9th Ave, Parkersburg 26101 Fax 485-6515
resa5.k12.wv.us/
RESA VII
Gabriel Devono, dir. 304-624-6554
1201 N 15th St, Clarksburg 26301 Fax 624-5223
resa7.k12.wv.us/
RESA VIII
Jane Lynch, dir., 109 S College St 304-267-3595
Martinsburg 25401 Fax 267-3599
www.resa8.org/resa8/site/default.asp
RESA VI
Nick Zervos, dir. 304-243-0440
30 G C and P Rd, Wheeling 26003 Fax 243-0443
resa6.k12.wv.us/

PUBLIC, PRIVATE AND CATHOLIC ELEMENTARY SCHOOLS

Accoville, Logan
Logan County SD
Supt. — See Logan
Buffalo ES 200/PK-3
PO Box 310 25606 304-583-9132
Ray Albright, prin. Fax 583-7512

Alderson, Greenbrier, Pop. 1,092
Greenbrier County SD
Supt. — See Lewisburg
Alderson ES 200/PK-5
RR 1 Box 162F 24910 304-445-7241
Barbara Bowling, prin. Fax 445-9718

Alum Bridge, Lewis
Lewis County SD
Supt. — See Weston
Alum Bridge ES 100/PK-4
PO Box 1086 26321 304-269-8312
Dan Hoover, prin. Fax 269-8352

Alum Creek, Lincoln, Pop. 1,602
Lincoln County SD
Supt. — See Hamlin
Midway ES 300/K-5
RR 1 Box 130 25003 304-756-3121
Randall Peters, prin. Fax 756-1459

Anawalt, McDowell, Pop. 247
McDowell County SD
Supt. — See Welch
Anawalt S 100/PK-5
PO Box 280 24808 304-383-4849
Brenda Owens, prin. Fax 383-4674

Ansted, Fayette, Pop. 1,604
Fayette County SD
Supt. — See Fayetteville
Ansted ES 200/PK-4
PO Box 609 25812 304-658-5961
Victor Whitt, prin. Fax 658-5961
Ansted MS 200/5-8
PO Box 766 25812 304-658-5170
Mark Scaggs, prin. Fax 658-3059

Arnoldsburg, Calhoun
Calhoun County SD
Supt. — See Mount Zion
Arnoldsburg S 200/PK-4
PO Box 159 25234 304-655-8616
Bryan Sterns, prin. Fax 655-8618

Arthurdale, Preston
Preston County SD
Supt. — See Kingwood
Valley ES 500/K-5
PO Box 700 26520 304-864-3835
Craig Schmidl, prin. Fax 864-3583

Ashford, Boone
Boone County SD
Supt. — See Madison
Ashford-Rumble ES 100/K-6
1649 Ashford Nellis Rd 25009 304-836-5381
Roger Toney, prin. Fax 836-5381

Ashton, Mason
Mason County SD
Supt. — See Point Pleasant
Ashton ES 400/PK-6
997 Ashton Upland Rd 25503 304-576-9931
Aleisha Green, prin. Fax 576-9935

Athens, Mercer, Pop. 1,182
Mercer County SD
Supt. — See Princeton
Athens S 500/K-8
PO Box 568 24712 304-384-9229
Terry Quesenberry, prin. Fax 384-7946

Augusta, Hampshire
Hampshire County SD
Supt. — See Romney
Augusta ES 300/K-5
61 Poncion Loop 26704 304-496-7001
Jeff Pancione, prin. Fax 496-7001

Aurora, Preston
Preston County SD
Supt. — See Kingwood
Aurora ES 100/K-6
125 Aurora School Dr 26705 304-735-3781
Jacqueline McCrum, prin. Fax 735-6805

Avondale, McDowell
McDowell County SD
Supt. — See Welch
Bradshaw ES 200/PK-5
Route 80 24811 304-938-2904
Joseph Sparks, prin. Fax 938-2849
Sandy River MS 200/7-8
PO Box 419 24811 304-938-2407
William Campbell, prin. Fax 938-2418

Baker, Hardy
Hardy County SD
Supt. — See Moorefield
East Hardy S 600/PK-8
PO Box 260 26801 304-897-5970
Rebecca Brill, prin. Fax 897-6653

Barboursville, Cabell, Pop. 3,185
Cabell County SD
Supt. — See Huntington
Barboursville ES 600/PK-5
718 Central Ave 25504 304-733-3000
Terry Porter, prin. Fax 733-3036
Barboursville MS 800/6-8
1400 Central Ave 25504 304-733-3003
Jerry Lake, prin. Fax 733-3009
Davis Creek ES 200/PK-5
6330 Davis Creek Rd 25504 304-733-3024
Viki Caldwell, prin. Fax 733-3049
Martha ES 300/PK-5
3067 Martha Rd 25504 304-733-3027
Boyd Mynes, prin. Fax 733-3016
Nichols ES 200/PK-5
3505 Erwin Rd 25504 304-733-3031
Barbara Carlton, prin. Fax 733-3054

Covenant S 200/K-12
5800 US Route 60 E 25504 304-736-0000
Stephen Wilkins, hdmstr. Fax 736-5213

Barrackville, Marion, Pop. 1,290
Marion County SD
Supt. — See Fairmont
Barrackville S 400/PK-8
PO Box 150 26559 304-367-2128
Kevin Haugh, prin. Fax 367-2173

Beaver, Raleigh, Pop. 1,244

Victory Baptist Academy 100/K-12
PO Box 549 25813 304-255-4535

Beckley, Raleigh, Pop. 16,936
Raleigh County SD 11,700/PK-12
105 Adair St 25801 304-256-4500
Charlotte Hutchens Ed.D., supt. Fax 256-4707
boe.rale.k12.wv.us
Beckley ES 300/K-5
399 Grey Flats Rd 25801 304-256-4575
Patricia Day, prin. Fax 265-4581
Beckley-Stratton MS 700/6-8
401 Grey Flats Rd 25801 304-256-4616
Rachel Pauley, prin. Fax 256-4616
Cranberry-Prosperity ES 300/PK-5
4575 Robert C Byrd Dr 25801 304-256-4574
Jan Lafferty, prin. Fax 256-4574
Crescent ES 300/K-5
205 Crescent Rd 25801 304-256-4585
Dan Pettry, prin. Fax 256-4585
Maxwell Hill ES 200/K-5
1001 Maxwell Hill Rd 25801 304-256-4599
Larry Farley, prin. Fax 256-4584
Park MS 400/6-8
212 Park Ave 25801 304-256-4586
Marsha Smith, prin. Fax 256-4709
Stanaford ES 300/K-5
950 Stanaford Rd 25801 304-256-4626
Dreama Bell, prin. Fax 256-4587
Stratton ES 200/1-5
1129 S Fayette St 25801 304-256-4604
Dorothy Smith, prin. Fax 256-4604
Other Schools – See Clear Creek, Coal City, Crab Orchard, Daniels, Fairdale, Ghent, Glen Daniel, Lester, Mabscott, MacArthur, Mount Hope, Shady Spring, Sophia, Sundial

---

St. Francis de Sales S 200/PK-8
622 S Oakwood Ave 25801 304-252-4087
Karen Wynne, prin. Fax 252-4087
Trinity Christian Academy 100/PK-12
224 Pinewood Dr 25801 304-254-9600
J.S. Peterson, admin. Fax 254-9655

Beech Bottom, Brooke, Pop. 576
Brooke County SD
Supt. — See Wellsburg
Beech Bottom PS 100/K-4
PO Box 36 26030 304-394-5341
Richard Whitehead, prin. Fax 394-5342

Belington, Barbour, Pop. 1,814
Barbour County SD
Supt. — See Philippi
Belington ES 400/PK-5
RR 2 Box 344 26250 304-823-1411
Teresa Childers, prin. Fax 823-2414
Belington MS 200/6-8
RR 2 Box 343 26250 304-823-1281
H. Moke Post, prin. Fax 823-2403

Belle, Kanawha, Pop. 1,187
Kanawha County SD
Supt. — See Charleston
Belle ES 300/PK-5
401 E 6th St 25015 304-949-2612
Ryan Kittle, prin. Fax 949-5854
DuPont MS 400/6-8
1 Panther Dr 25015 304-348-1978
David Miller, prin. Fax 949-1793
Midland Trail ES 200/PK-5
200 Ferry St 25015 304-949-1823
Grant Davis, prin. Fax 949-1016

Belmont, Pleasants, Pop. 1,009
Pleasants County SD
Supt. — See Saint Marys
Belmont ES 200/PK-4
512 Riverview Dr 26134 304-665-2456
Rebecca Griffith, prin. Fax 665-2408
Pleasants County MS 400/5-8
510 Riverview Dr 26134 304-665-2415
Mike Wells, prin. Fax 665-2451

Benwood, Marshall, Pop. 1,496

SS. James & John S 100/PK-8
52 7th St 26031 304-232-1587
Jennifer Marsh, prin. Fax 232-4707

Berkeley Springs, Morgan, Pop. 756
Morgan County SD 2,700/PK-12
247 Harrison Ave 25411 304-258-2430
David Banks, supt. Fax 258-9146
www.edline.net/pages/morgan_county_schools
Greenwood ES 100/K-5
8989 Winchester Grade Rd 25411 304-258-2372
Barbara Miller, prin. Fax 258-2047
Warm Springs IS 400/3-5
575 Warm Springs Way 25411 304-258-0031
Joyce Ott, prin. Fax 258-0033
Warm Springs MS 600/6-8
271 Warm Springs Way 25411 304-258-1500
Gene Brock, prin. Fax 258-4600
Widmyer ES 500/PK-2
10 Myers Rd 25411 304-258-2024
Dan Reynolds, prin. Fax 258-7693
Other Schools – See Hedgesville, Paw Paw

Berkeley Springs SDA S 50/K-10
3606 Valley Rd 25411 304-258-3581

Beverly, Randolph, Pop. 656
Randolph County SD
Supt. — See Elkins
Beverly ES 200/K-5
PO Box 209 26253 304-636-9162
Paul Zickefoose, prin. Fax 636-9163

Big Sandy, McDowell
McDowell County SD
Supt. — See Welch
Fall River ES 200/PK-5
PO Box 70 24816 304-656-7665
Dennis Jarvis, prin. Fax 656-7530

Birch River, Nicholas
Nicholas County SD
Supt. — See Summersville
Birch River ES 100/PK-5
379 Birch River Rd 26610 304-649-2651
Ramona Beverage, prin. Fax 649-2651

Blacksville, Monongalia, Pop. 172
Monongalia County SD
Supt. — See Morgantown
Mason-Dixon ES 400/K-6
7041 Mason Dixon Hwy 26521 304-662-6113
Karen Collins, prin. Fax 662-6167

Bluefield, Mercer, Pop. 11,119
Mercer County SD
Supt. — See Princeton
Bluefield IS 300/3-5
1301 Southview Dr 24701 304-327-8339
Cathy Daniels, prin. Fax 327-8348
Bluefield MS 600/6-8
2002 Stadium Dr 24701 304-325-2481
Todd Browning, prin. Fax 325-2156
Bluewell ES 200/PK-5
205 Bluewell School Rd 24701 304-589-5057
Sharon Reed, prin. Fax 589-3723
Brushfork ES 200/K-5
RR 4 Box 93 24701 304-325-7066
J. Bryan Staten, prin. Fax 325-2574
Ceres ES 200/K-5
RR 2 Box 189 24701 304-327-6786
Mary Terry, prin. Fax 327-5516
Memorial PS 200/K-2
319 Memorial Ave 24701 304-327-8016
Steve Hayes, prin. Fax 327-3933
Mercer County Early Learning Center 300/PK-PK
3318 E Cumberland Rd 24701 304-325-7316
Jane Walthall, prin. Fax 323-2591
Whitethorn PS 200/K-2
1919 Maryland Ave 24701 304-327-6217
Lori Comer, prin. Fax 324-3894

Valley View SDA S 50/K-12
PO Box 6312 24701 304-325-8679
Rosalie Stockil, prin. Fax 325-8679

Bomont, Clay
Clay County SD
Supt. — See Clay
White ES 100/K-5
501 Bomont Rd 25030 304-548-7101
Mike Mullins, prin. Fax 548-7101

Branchland, Lincoln
Lincoln County SD
Supt. — See Hamlin
Guyan Valley MS 200/6-8
700 State Route 10 25506 304-824-3235
Kevin Prichard, prin. Fax 824-3459

Brandywine, Pendleton
Pendleton County SD
Supt. — See Franklin
Brandywine ES 200/PK-6
PO Box 247 26802 304-249-5381
Lincoln Propst, prin. Fax 249-5226

Brenton, Wyoming
Wyoming County SD
Supt. — See Pineville
Baileysville S 400/K-8
PO Box 409 24818 304-732-6399
Connie Lynn Walls, prin. Fax 732-8365

Bridgeport, Harrison, Pop. 7,486
Harrison County SD
Supt. — See Clarksburg
Bridgeport MS 600/6-8
413 Johnson Ave 26330 304-326-7142
Carole Crawford, prin. Fax 842-6275
Johnson ES 600/PK-5
531 Johnson Ave 26330 304-326-7109
Dennis Stromberg, prin. Fax 842-6562
Simpson ES 400/PK-5
250 Worthington Dr 26330 304-326-7060
Loria Reid, prin. Fax 842-2568

Heritage Christian S 200/PK-8
225 Newton Ave 26330 304-842-1740
Linda Simms, admin. Fax 842-1750

Bruceton Mills, Preston, Pop. 74
Preston County SD
Supt. — See Kingwood
Bruceton S 500/K-8
PO Box 141 26525 304-379-2593
Stephen Wotring, prin. Fax 379-4079

Buckeye, Pocahontas
Pocahontas County SD
Supt. — See Marlinton
Marlinton MS 200/5-8
RR 2 Box 52S 24924 304-799-6773
Joseph Riley, prin. Fax 799-7278

Buckhannon, Upshur, Pop. 5,687
Upshur County SD 3,500/K-12
102 Smithfield St 26201 304-472-5480
Scott Lampinen, supt. Fax 472-0258
boe.upsh.k12.wv.us
Buckhannon Academy ES 300/K-5
2 College Ave 26201 304-472-3310
Randall Roy, prin. Fax 472-3790
Buckhannon-Upshur MS 900/6-8
RR 6 Box 303 26201 304-472-1520
Renee Warner, prin. Fax 472-6864
Hodgesville ES 100/K-5
RR 5 Box 383 26201 304-472-3212
Ann Mickle, prin. Fax 472-3932
Rock Cave ES 100/K-5
RR 2 Box 2F 26201 304-924-6969
Amanda Craig, prin. Fax 924-6969
Tennerton ES 300/K-5
RR 6 Box 513 26201 304-472-1278
Cheryl Adams, prin. Fax 472-8530
Union ES 300/K-5
20 Heavner Grove Rd 26201 304-472-1394
Dr. Sara Stankus, prin. Fax 472-2780
Washington District ES 100/K-5
HC 36 Box 234 26201 304-472-6599
Peggy Hall, prin. Fax 472-6599
Other Schools – See French Creek

Bud, Wyoming
Wyoming County SD
Supt. — See Pineville
Herndon Consolidated S 200/PK-8
PO Box 309 24716 304-294-7668
Della Ann Houck, prin. Fax 294-8474

Buffalo, Putnam, Pop. 1,204
Putnam County SD
Supt. — See Winfield
Buffalo ES 300/K-5
RR 1 Box 93 25033 304-937-2651
Mike Mullins, prin. Fax 937-2651

Bunker Hill, Berkeley
Berkeley County SD
Supt. — See Martinsburg
Bunker Hill ES 300/K-3
58 Happy School Ave 25413 304-229-1980
Scott Albright, prin. Fax 229-1983
Mill Creek IS 400/4-5
8785 Winchester Ave 25413 304-229-4570
Kimberly Agee, prin. Fax 229-4793
Musselman MS 1,100/6-8
105 Pride Ave 25413 304-229-1965
James Holland, prin. Fax 229-1967

Burlington, Mineral
Mineral County SD
Supt. — See Keyser
Burlington PS 100/PK-5
RR 1 Box 126 26710 304-289-3073
Garrett Carskadon, prin. Fax 289-5116

Burnsville, Braxton, Pop. 472
Braxton County SD
Supt. — See Sutton
Burnsville ES 100/PK-4
PO Box 35 26335 304-853-2523
Kim Dennison, prin. Fax 853-2431

Cameron, Marshall, Pop. 1,142
Marshall County SD
Supt. — See Moundsville
Cameron ES 300/K-6
12 Church St 26033 304-686-3305
Wendy Clutter, prin. Fax 686-3502

Capon Bridge, Hampshire, Pop. 214
Hampshire County SD
Supt. — See Romney
Capon Bridge ES 400/PK-5
PO Box 127 26711 304-856-3329
Dr. Robert Carter, prin. Fax 856-3329
Capon Bridge MS 300/6-8
PO Box 147 26711 304-856-2534
Ann Downs, prin. Fax 856-3192

Cedar Grove, Kanawha, Pop. 823
Kanawha County SD
Supt. — See Charleston
Cedar Grove Community S 300/K-8
PO Box J 25039 304-949-1642
Joe McQuerrey, prin. Fax 949-3418

Ceredo, Wayne, Pop. 1,631
Wayne County SD
Supt. — See Wayne
Ceredo ES 200/PK-5
PO Box 635 25507 304-453-1511
Dianna Buchman, prin. Fax 453-1502
Ceredo-Kenova MS 300/6-8
PO Box 705 25507 304-453-3588
Barry Scragg, prin. Fax 453-4420

Chapmanville, Logan, Pop. 1,145
Logan County SD
Supt. — See Logan
Chapmanville East ES 300/PK-4
PO Box 340 25508 304-855-3302
Darrell Bias, prin. Fax 855-7568
Chapmanville MS 600/5-8
300 Vance St 25508 304-855-8378
Garland Elmore, prin. Fax 855-1307
West Chapmanville ES 400/PK-4
PO Box 310 25508 304-855-3209
Mark Adkins, prin. Fax 855-3376

Charleston, Kanawha, Pop. 51,176
Kanawha County SD 27,600/PK-12
200 Elizabeth St 25311 304-348-7731
Ronald Duerring Ed.D., supt. Fax 348-7735
kcs.kana.k12.wv.us/
Adams MS 700/6-8
2002 Presidential Dr 25314 304-348-6652
Lois Greene, prin. Fax 348-6592
Bonham ES 200/PK-5
RR 1 Box 425 25312 304-348-1912
Michael Pack, prin. Fax 348-1367
Chamberlain ES 200/K-5
4901 Venable Ave 25304 304-348-1969
Nancy Pfister, prin. Fax 348-1970
Chandler ES 200/PK-5
1900 School St 25312 304-348-1902
Mellow Lee, prin. Fax 348-1903
Elk Elementary Center 600/PK-5
3320 Pennsylvania Ave 25302 304-348-7776
Cathi Bradley, prin. Fax 965-6921
Flinn ES 600/K-5
2006 McClure Pkwy 25312 304-348-1960
Beth Scott, prin. Fax 348-1959
Glenwood ES 200/K-5
810 Grant St 25302 304-348-6610
Thomas Fisher, prin. Fax 348-6681
Grandview ES 200/PK-5
959 Woodward Dr 25312 304-348-1928
Cynthia Cummings, prin. Fax 746-0771
Holz ES 300/PK-5
1505 Hampton Rd 25314 304-348-1906
Karen Simon, prin. Fax 345-0387
Jackson MS 600/6-8
812 Park Ave 25302 304-348-6123
George Aulenbacher, prin. Fax 348-1999
Kanawha City ES 300/K-5
3601 Staunton Ave SE 25304 304-348-1985
Katherine Porter, prin. Fax 348-6537
Kenna ES 200/K-5
198 Eureka Rd 25314 304-348-6104
Clara Jett, prin. Fax 348-6107
Malden ES 200/K-5
4001 Salines Dr 25306 304-348-1973
Bruce Kolsun, prin. Fax 348-1974
Mann MS 400/6-8
4300 MacCorkle Ave SE 25304 304-348-1971
Mickey Blackwell, prin. Fax 348-6591
Overbrook ES 400/K-5
218 Oakwood Rd 25314 304-348-6179
Barbara Floren, prin. Fax 347-7494
Piedmont ES 200/K-5
203 Bradford St 25301 304-348-1910
Stephen Knighton, prin. Fax 348-1911
Robins ES 200/K-5
915 Beech Ave 25302 304-348-6631
Henry Nearman, prin. Fax 348-6634
Ruffner ES 300/PK-5
809 Litz Dr 25311 304-348-1130
Steve Foster, prin. Fax 348-1131
Ruthlawn ES 200/K-5
66 Pin Oak Dr 25309 304-744-9481
Natalie Laliberty, prin. Fax 744-9482
Shoals ES 300/PK-5
100 Dutch Rd 25302 304-348-1900
Margaret Bays, prin. Fax 348-1901
Tyler MS 100/6-8
4277 Washington St W 25313 304-348-6133
Wayman Wilson, prin. Fax 348-6690
Watts ES 200/K-5
230 Costello St 25302 304-348-6635
Eric Lutz, prin. Fax 348-6644

Weberwood ES 200/K-5
732 Gordon Dr 25303 304-348-1924
Mary Lou Munoz, prin. Fax 347-7421
Other Schools – See Belle, Cedar Grove, Clendenin, Cross Lanes, Dunbar, East Bank, Elkview, Marmet, Miami, Nitro, Pratt, Saint Albans, Sissonville, South Charleston, Tad, Tornado

---

Bible Center S 200/PK-6
1111 Oakhurst Dr 25314 304-346-0431
Michael Reynolds, admin. Fax 346-0433
Cross Lanes Christian S 300/K-12
5330 Floradale Dr 25313 304-776-5020
Steve Adams, admin. Fax 776-5074
Sacred Heart S 300/PK-5
1035 Quarrier St 25301 304-346-5491
Terri Maier, prin. Fax 342-0870
St. Agnes S 100/PK-5
4801 Staunton Ave SE 25304 304-925-4341
Theresa O'Leary, prin. Fax 925-4423
St. Anthony S 100/PK-8
1027 6th St 25302 304-346-8441
Susan Maddox, prin. Fax 346-8445

Charles Town, Jefferson, Pop. 3,704
Jefferson County SD 8,700/PK-12
110 Mordington Ave 25414 304-725-9741
Susan Wall, supt. Fax 725-6487
boe.jeff.k12.wv.us
Charles Town MS 900/6-8
193 High St 25414 304-725-7821
Charles Hampton, prin. Fax 725-7526
Denny ES 400/3-5
209 W Congress St 25414 304-725-2513
Chris Walter, prin. Fax 725-1721
Page-Jackson ES 400/K-2
370 Page Jackson School Rd 25414 304-728-9212
Tara Aycock, prin. Fax 725-2968
South Jefferson ES 500/K-5
4599 Summit Point Rd 25414 304-728-9216
Richard Jenkins, prin. Fax 725-6428
Other Schools – See Harpers Ferry, Kearneysville, Ranson, Shenandoah Junction, Shepherdstown

Chester, Hancock, Pop. 2,436
Hancock County SD
Supt. — See New Cumberland
Allison ES 400/K-4
600 Railroad St 26034 304-387-1915
Linda Robinson, prin. Fax 387-2114

Circleville, Pendleton
Pendleton County SD
Supt. — See Franklin
North Fork ES 100/PK-6
PO Box 186 26804 304-567-3193
John Jenkins, prin. Fax 567-3196

Clarksburg, Harrison, Pop. 16,439
Harrison County SD 10,800/PK-12
PO Box 1370 26302 304-624-3325
Susan Collins, supt. Fax 624-3361
www.harcoboe.com
Adamston ES 300/PK-5
1636 W Pike St 26301 304-326-7070
Dora Stutler, prin. Fax 624-3270
Irving MS 700/6-8
443 Lee Ave 26301 304-326-7420
William Tucker, prin. Fax 624-3388
Mountaineer MS 6-8
2 Mountaineer Dr 26301 304-326-7620
Pamela Leggett, prin. Fax 326-7632
North View ES 300/PK-5
1400 N 19th St 26301 304-326-7650
Richard Skinner, prin. Fax 624-3287
Nutter Fort IS 500/3-5
1302 Buckhannon Pike 26301 304-326-7501
Ricky San Julian, prin. Fax 624-3259
Nutter Fort PS 700/PK-2
1302 Buckhannon Pike 26301 304-326-7520
Frank Marino, prin. Fax 624-3382
Wilsonburg ES 200/PK-5
RR 4 Box 1 26301 304-326-7640
Rosalee Dolan, prin. Fax 624-3279
Other Schools – See Bridgeport, Lost Creek, Lumberport, Salem, Shinnston, Stonewood, West Milford

---

Emmanuel Christian S 100/PK-12
1318 N 16th St 26301 304-624-6125
St. Mary Central S 200/PK-6
107 E Pike St 26301 304-622-9831
Nicole Folio, prin. Fax 622-9831

Clay, Clay, Pop. 580
Clay County SD 2,100/PK-12
PO Box 120 25043 304-587-4266
Larry Gillespie, supt. Fax 587-4181
www.claycountyschools.org
Clay County MS 500/6-8
PO Box 489 25043 304-587-2343
Joe Paxton, prin. Fax 587-2759
Clay ES 500/PK-5
PO Box 600 25043 304-587-4276
Danny Brown, prin. Fax 587-4279
Other Schools – See Bomont, Duck, Lizemores

Clear Creek, Raleigh
Raleigh County SD
Supt. — See Beckley
Clear Fork District ES 100/PK-5
4851 Clear Fork Rd 25044 304-854-1000
John Greenwald, prin. Fax 854-2829

Clendenin, Kanawha, Pop. 1,056
Kanawha County SD
Supt. — See Charleston
Clendenin ES 300/PK-5
PO Box 462 25045 304-965-5311
Chad Holt, prin. Fax 548-7372

Coal City, Raleigh, Pop. 1,876
Raleigh County SD
Supt. — See Beckley
Coal City ES 300/PK-5
PO Box 1240 25823 304-683-5001
Phyllis Newcomb, prin. Fax 683-3165

Coalton, Randolph, Pop. 287
Randolph County SD
Supt. — See Elkins
Coalton ES 200/PK-5
PO Box 129 26257 304-636-9164
Mary Tacy, prin. Fax 636-9165

Colliers, Brooke
Brooke County SD
Supt. — See Wellsburg
Colliers PS 200/K-4
270 Pennsylvania Ave 26035 304-748-8188
JoEllen Goodall, prin. Fax 797-7242

Comfort, Boone
Boone County SD
Supt. — See Madison
Sherman ES 500/PK-6
PO Box 369 25049 304-837-8310
Brenda Hudson-Viars, prin. Fax 837-8342

Cottageville, Jackson
Jackson County SD
Supt. — See Ripley
Cottageville ES 100/PK-5
100 School St 25239 304-372-7330
Glenn Varney, prin. Fax 372-7342

Cowen, Webster, Pop. 506
Webster County SD
Supt. — See Webster Springs
Glade ES 300/PK-4
25 Mill St 26206 304-226-5353
Sue Anderson, prin. Fax 226-3666
Glade MS 300/5-8
25 Mill St 26206 304-226-5353
Stephen White, prin. Fax 226-3666

Crab Orchard, Raleigh, Pop. 2,919
Raleigh County SD
Supt. — See Beckley
Crab Orchard ES 300/K-5
PO Box 727 25827 304-256-4577
Rose Kelly, prin. Fax 256-4573

Craigsville, Nicholas, Pop. 1,955
Nicholas County SD
Supt. — See Summersville
Beaver ES 100/K-5
16414 Webster Rd 26205 304-742-5611
Jo Ann Gainer, prin. Fax 742-5611
Craigsville ES 300/PK-5
100 School St 26205 304-742-5271
Charles Frazee, prin. Fax 742-5279

Crawley, Greenbrier
Greenbrier County SD
Supt. — See Lewisburg
Western Greenbrier MS 300/6-8
315 Timberwolf Dr 24931 304-392-6446
Mark Keaton, prin. Fax 392-6785

Cross Lanes, Kanawha, Pop. 10,878
Kanawha County SD
Supt. — See Charleston
Cross Lanes ES 500/PK-5
5525 Big Tyler Rd 25313 304-776-2022
Vanessa Brown, prin. Fax 776-2029
Jackson MS 700/6-8
5445 Big Tyler Rd 25313 304-776-3310
Lisa Woo, prin. Fax 776-3305
Point Harmony ES 600/K-5
5312 Big Tyler Rd 25313 304-776-3482
Darlena Reynolds, prin. Fax 776-6476

Crum, Wayne
Wayne County SD
Supt. — See Wayne
Crum ES 200/PK-5
PO Box 69 25669 304-393-3447
Patrick Fluty, prin. Fax 393-3033
Crum MS 200/6-8
PO Box 9 25669 304-393-3200
Jim Fletcher, prin. Fax 393-4429

Culloden, Cabell, Pop. 2,907
Cabell County SD
Supt. — See Huntington
Culloden ES 200/PK-5
2100 US Highway 60 25510 304-743-7301
Deborah Smith, prin. Fax 743-7306

Cyclone, Wyoming
Wyoming County SD
Supt. — See Pineville
Road Branch S 200/PK-8
1165 Huff Creek Rd 24827 304-682-5916
Rebecca Stewart Cooke, prin. Fax 682-5916

Dailey, Randolph
Randolph County SD
Supt. — See Elkins
Homestead ES 100/K-5
PO Box 158 26259 304-338-4903
Diana Hull, prin. Fax 338-4908

Dallas, Marshall
Marshall County SD
Supt. — See Moundsville
Sand Hill ES 100/K-6
RR 1 Box 87 26036 304-547-5041
Joyce Cole, prin. Fax 547-5041

Danese, Fayette
Fayette County SD
Supt. — See Fayetteville
Danese ES 100/K-5
PO Box 69 25831 304-438-6827
Cheryl Altizer, prin. Fax 438-6827

Danese Christian S 50/PK-7
PO Box 177 25831 304-438-8116
Allen Whitt, prin. Fax 438-8113

Daniels, Raleigh, Pop. 1,714
Raleigh County SD
Supt. — See Beckley
Daniels ES 500/K-5
351 4H Lake Rd 25832 304-256-4622
Alvin James, prin. Fax 256-4622

Danville, Boone, Pop. 540
Boone County SD
Supt. — See Madison
Ramage ES 300/PK-5
15908 Spruce River Rd 25053 304-369-0763
Roger Barker, prin. Fax 369-0765

Davisville, Wood
Wood County SD
Supt. — See Parkersburg
Kanawha ES 300/K-5
6465 Staunton Tpke 26142 304-420-9557
Anne Monterosso, prin. Fax 420-9608

Delbarton, Mingo, Pop. 442
Mingo County SD
Supt. — See Williamson
Burch ES 500/PK-6
RR 3 Box 4B 25670 304-475-2141
Rocky Hall, prin. Fax 475-2627

Regional Christian S 100/PK-12
PO Box 236 25670 304-475-3468
Regina Bias, admin. Fax 475-5287

Diana, Webster
Webster County SD
Supt. — See Webster Springs
Diana S 100/PK-8
90 Eagle Ln 26217 304-847-2112
Rondlynn Cool, prin. Fax 847-5364

Dingess, Mingo
Mingo County SD
Supt. — See Williamson
Dingess ES 100/PK-4
PO Box 34 25671 304-752-7036
Don Spence, prin. Fax 752-7036

Dixie, Nicholas
Nicholas County SD
Supt. — See Summersville
Dixie ES 100/PK-5
PO Box 288 25059 304-632-1323
Teresa Morris, prin. Fax 623-1323

Duck, Clay
Clay County SD
Supt. — See Clay
Big Otter ES 300/K-5
59 Ossia Rd 25063 304-286-3111
Pam Mullins, prin. Fax 286-3112

Dunbar, Kanawha, Pop. 7,740
Kanawha County SD
Supt. — See Charleston
Dunbar IS 300/3-5
1330 Myers Ave 25064 304-766-1570
Cheryl Plear, prin. Fax 766-1573
Dunbar MS 400/6-8
325 27th St 25064 304-766-0363
Lynda Gilkeson, prin. Fax 766-0365
Dunbar PS 300/PK-2
2401 Myers Ave 25064 304-766-0367
Kay Lee, prin. Fax 766-0366
Shawnee Community Education Center 50/PK-PK
142 Marshall Ave 25064 304-766-0378
Fax 766-0378

Dunlow, Wayne
Wayne County SD
Supt. — See Wayne
Dunlow ES 100/PK-5
RR 1 Box 308 25511 304-385-4376
Shane Runyon, prin. Fax 385-1026

East Bank, Kanawha, Pop. 896
Kanawha County SD
Supt. — See Charleston
East Bank MS 400/6-8
PO Box 499 25067 304-595-2311
Candy Strader, prin. Fax 595-4676

East Lynn, Wayne
Wayne County SD
Supt. — See Wayne
East Lynn ES 200/PK-5
HC 85 Box 3 25512 304-849-3171
Rhonda Holland, prin. Fax 849-5608

Eleanor, Putnam, Pop. 1,491
Putnam County SD
Supt. — See Winfield
Washington ES 200/K-5
PO Box 680 25070 304-586-2184
Cynthia Frazier, prin. Fax 586-4275
Washington MS 300/6-8
PO Box 660 25070 304-586-2875
Joann Stewart, prin. Fax 586-3037

Elizabeth, Wirt, Pop. 972
Wirt County SD 1,000/PK-12
PO Box 189 26143 304-275-4279
Dan Metz, supt. Fax 275-4581

Wirt County MS 300/5-8
PO Box 699 26143 304-275-3977
J. D. Hoover, prin. Fax 275-4257
Wirt County PS 400/PK-4
PO Box 220 26143 304-275-4263
Dwight Goff, prin. Fax 275-4263

Elk Garden, Mineral, Pop. 211
Mineral County SD
Supt. — See Keyser
Elk Garden PS 100/PK-5
RR 1 Box 320 26717 304-446-5141
Charles Keller, prin. Fax 446-5425

Elkins, Randolph, Pop. 7,109
Randolph County SD 4,400/PK-12
1425 S Davis Ave 26241 304-636-9156
Terry George, supt. Fax 636-9157
boe.rand.k12.wv.us
Elkins MS 700/6-8
308 Robert E Lee Ave 26241 304-636-9176
David Roth, prin. Fax 636-9178
Elkins Third Ward ES 300/K-5
111 Nathan St 26241 304-636-9183
Barry Band, prin. Fax 636-9184
Jennings Randolph ES 300/PK-5
101 Scott Ford Rd 26241 304-636-9181
Rebecca Whiteman, prin. Fax 636-9166
Midland ES 300/K-5
150 Kennedy Dr 26241 304-636-9186
Terry Nelson, prin. Fax 636-9187
North ES 300/PK-5
RR 2 Box 320 26241 304-636-9188
Darlene Lindsay, prin. Fax 636-9188
Other Schools – See Beverly, Coalton, Dailey, Harman, Mill Creek, Pickens, Valley Head

---

Highland Adventist S 50/K-12
1 Old Leadsville Rd 26241 304-636-4274
Fax 636-4274

Elkview, Kanawha, Pop. 1,047
Kanawha County SD
Supt. — See Charleston
Bridge ES 100/K-5
5120 Elk River Rd 25071 304-965-5501
Jodie Hypes, prin. Fax 348-1125
Elkview MS 700/6-8
5090 Elk River Rd 25071 304-348-1947
Rick Messinger, prin. Fax 348-6590
Pinch ES 400/K-5
300 S Pinch Rd 25071 304-348-1943
Betty Moore, prin. Fax 348-1944

Elk Valley Christian S 200/PK-12
5110 Elk River Rd 25071 304-965-7063
Barbara Hamm, prin. Fax 965-7064

Ellenboro, Ritchie, Pop. 372
Ritchie County SD
Supt. — See Harrisville
Ellenboro ES 100/PK-5
PO Box 219 26346 304-869-3305
Steve Lewis, prin. Fax 869-3306
Ritchie County MS 400/6-8
105 Ritchie Co School Rd 26346 304-869-3512
Michael Dotson, prin. Fax 869-3519

Evans, Jackson
Jackson County SD
Supt. — See Ripley
Evans ES 200/PK-5
205 Schoolhouse Dr 25241 304-372-7333
Barbara Upton, prin. Fax 372-7317

Fairdale, Raleigh
Raleigh County SD
Supt. — See Beckley
Fairdale ES 400/K-5
PO Box 10 25839 304-934-7217
Gail Mills, prin. Fax 934-7835

Fairmont, Marion, Pop. 19,049
Marion County SD 8,200/PK-12
200 Gaston Ave 26554 304-367-2100
Thomas Deadrick, supt. Fax 367-2111
www.marionboe.com/
East Dale ES 600/K-6
RR 3 26554 304-367-2132
Diane Burnside, prin. Fax 366-2522
East Fairmont JHS 400/7-8
1 Orion Ln 26554 304-367-2123
Christine Miller, prin. Fax 367-2179
East Park ES 400/K-6
1025 Fairfax St 26554 304-367-2134
Carrie Hendershot, prin. Fax 367-2187
Jayenne ES 200/PK-4
1500 Country Club Rd 26554 304-367-2136
Andy Neptune, prin. Fax 367-2178
Pleasant Valley ES 300/PK-6
1858 Valley School Rd 26554 304-367-2148
Kim Middlemas, prin. Fax 367-2148
Watson ES 400/PK-4
1579 Mary Lou Retton Dr 26554 304-367-2156
Jane DeVaul, prin. Fax 366-0107
West Fairmont MS 600/5-8
110 10th St 26554 304-366-5631
Rockie DeLorenzo, prin. Fax 366-5636
White Hall ES 200/PK-4
38 Emerald Ln 26554 304-367-2158
Mike Williams, prin. Fax 367-2181
Other Schools – See Barrackville, Fairview, Mannington, Monongah, Rivesville

---

Fairmont S 200/K-8
416A Madison St 26554 304-363-5313
Sr. Mary DiDomenico, prin. Fax 363-7701

Fairview, Marion, Pop. 436
Marion County SD
Supt. — See Fairmont
Fairview ES 200/K-4
PO Box 39 26570 304-449-1752
L. Dick Werry, prin. Fax 449-1866
Fairview MS 100/5-8
17 Jesses Run Rd 26570 304-449-1312
Steve Rodriguez, prin. Fax 449-1305

Monongalia County SD
Supt. — See Morgantown
Daybrook ES 100/K-4
2097 Daybrook Rd 26570 304-798-3230
DeAnn Hartshorn, prin. Fax 798-3266
Jakes Run S 50/PK-PK
1265 Jakes Run Rd 26570 304-879-5158
Brenda Yohn, prin. Fax 879-5155

Falling Waters, Berkeley
Berkeley County SD
Supt. — See Martinsburg
Marlowe ES 300/K-2
9580 Williamsport Pike 25419 304-274-2291
Sharon Rogers, prin. Fax 274-8939

Fayetteville, Fayette, Pop. 2,657
Fayette County SD 6,700/PK-12
111 Fayette Ave 25840 304-574-1176
Chris Perkins, supt. Fax 574-3643
boe.faye.k12.wv.us
Fayetteville ES 400/K-5
200 W Wiseman Ave 25840 304-574-1011
Jeannie Ayers, prin. Fax 574-1011
Gatewood ES 100/K-6
RR 1 Box 156A 25840 304-574-2025
Steven Rhodes, prin. Fax 574-2025
Other Schools – See Ansted, Danese, Gauley Bridge, Lookout, Meadow Bridge, Mount Hope, Oak Hill, Scarbro, Smithers

Flatwoods, Braxton, Pop. 354
Braxton County SD
Supt. — See Sutton
Flatwoods ES 200/PK-4
PO Box 130 26621 304-765-5821
Barbara Adams, prin. Fax 765-3586

Flemington, Taylor, Pop. 290
Barbour County SD
Supt. — See Philippi
Mt. Vernon ES 100/PK-5
RR 1 Box 374C 26347 304-739-4696
Tammy Tucker, prin. Fax 739-4614

Taylor County SD
Supt. — See Grafton
Flemington ES 100/PK-4
RR 1 Box 30 26347 304-739-4749
Sue Murphy, prin. Fax 739-4671
West Taylor ES 200/PK-4
RR 1 Box 186B1 26347 304-842-0490
Kathy Green, prin. Fax 842-0492

Follansbee, Brooke, Pop. 2,971
Brooke County SD
Supt. — See Wellsburg
Follansbee MS 600/5-8
1400 Main St 26037 304-527-1942
Kim Johnson, prin. Fax 527-1954
Hooverson Heights PS 200/K-4
200 Rockdale Rd 26037 304-527-0870
Rhonda Combs, prin. Fax 527-2440
Jefferson PS 200/K-4
1098 Jefferson St 26037 304-527-2250
Nadine Sweda, prin. Fax 527-2014

Fort Ashby, Mineral, Pop. 1,288
Mineral County SD
Supt. — See Keyser
Fort Ashby PS 300/PK-2
PO Box 1050 26719 304-298-3632
William Pratt, prin. Fax 298-3200
Frankfort IS 200/3-4
RR 2 Box 500 26719 304-298-3616
Dawn Burke, prin. Fax 298-3557

Fort Gay, Wayne, Pop. 818
Wayne County SD
Supt. — See Wayne
Fort Gay ES 400/PK-5
8600 Orchard St 25514 304-648-5488
David Sammons, prin. Fax 648-7070
Fort Gay MS 200/6-8
PO Box 460 25514 304-648-5404
Donita Webb, prin. Fax 648-7082

Foster, Boone
Boone County SD
Supt. — See Madison
Brookview ES 600/PK-5
1 Learning Way 25081 304-369-1012
Karen Vickers, prin. Fax 369-1054

Frametown, Braxton
Braxton County SD
Supt. — See Sutton
Frametown ES 200/PK-4
HC 61 Box 14 26623 304-364-5526
Linda Sears, prin. Fax 364-8620

Frankford, Greenbrier
Greenbrier County SD
Supt. — See Lewisburg
Frankford ES 200/PK-5
18070 Seneca Trail N 24938 304-497-2921
Bedford McClintic, prin. Fax 497-2963

Franklin, Pendleton, Pop. 824
Pendleton County SD 1,100/PK-12
PO Box 888 26807 304-358-2207
Doug Lambert, supt. Fax 358-2936
pendletoncountyschools.com/
Franklin ES 300/PK-6
PO Box 848 26807 304-358-2206
Rick Linaburg, prin. Fax 358-7628
Other Schools – See Brandywine, Circleville

French Creek, Upshur
Upshur County SD
Supt. — See Buckhannon
French Creek ES 200/K-5
RR 2 Box 305 26218 304-924-6381
Jody Johnson, prin. Fax 924-6386

Gallipolis Ferry, Mason
Mason County SD
Supt. — See Point Pleasant
Beale ES 300/PK-6
12897 Huntington Rd 25515 304-675-1260
Pat Brumfield, prin. Fax 675-1261

Gassaway, Braxton, Pop. 884
Braxton County SD
Supt. — See Sutton
Davis ES 200/PK-4
113 5th St 26624 304-364-5291
Tim Via, prin. Fax 364-8547

Gauley Bridge, Fayette, Pop. 706
Fayette County SD
Supt. — See Fayetteville
Gauley Bridge ES 100/K-5
PO Box 519 25085 304-632-2661
Gary Hough, prin. Fax 632-0297

Genoa, Wayne
Wayne County SD
Supt. — See Wayne
Genoa ES 100/K-5
RR 1 Box 10 25517 304-385-4421
William Preece, prin. Fax 385-4427

Gerrardstown, Berkeley
Berkeley County SD
Supt. — See Martinsburg
Gerrardstown ES 200/K-3
15 Dominion Rd 25420 304-229-1985
Kevin McBee, prin. Fax 229-1988
Mountain Ridge IS 400/3-5
2691 Gerrardstown Rd 25420 304-229-6791
Michelle Martin, prin. Fax 229-6914

Ghent, Raleigh
Raleigh County SD
Supt. — See Beckley
Ghent ES 300/K-5
PO Box 350 25843 304-787-3631
Coleen Redden, prin. Fax 787-3474

Gilbert, Mingo, Pop. 399
Mingo County SD
Supt. — See Williamson
Gilbert ES 500/PK-6
PO Box 1900 25621 304-664-5042
Delmar Blankenship, prin. Fax 664-9723

Glen Dale, Marshall, Pop. 1,475
Marshall County SD
Supt. — See Moundsville
Glen Dale ES 200/K-5
407 7th St 26038 304-843-4427
John Lee, prin. Fax 843-4464

Glen Daniel, Raleigh
Raleigh County SD
Supt. — See Beckley
Trap Hill MS 400/6-8
665 Coal River Rd 25844 304-934-5392
Jerry Bawgus, prin. Fax 934-5393

Glen Fork, Wyoming
Wyoming County SD
Supt. — See Pineville
Glen Fork S 200/K-8
PO Box 50 25845 304-682-6423
Terri Lea Smith, prin. Fax 682-3160

Glenville, Gilmer, Pop. 1,482
Gilmer County SD 1,000/PK-12
201 N Court St 26351 304-462-7386
John Bennett, supt. Fax 462-5103
gilmercountyschools.org/
Glenville ES 200/PK-6
44 Vanhorn Dr 26351 304-462-7338
Toni Bishop, prin. Fax 462-5108
Other Schools – See Normantown, Sand Fork, Troy

Grafton, Taylor, Pop. 5,407
Taylor County SD 2,500/PK-12
PO Box 160 26354 304-265-2497
J. Diane Watt, supt. Fax 265-2508
www.taylorcountyboe.net
Jarvis ES 600/PK-4
650 N Pike St 26354 304-265-4090
Anita Hornor, prin. Fax 265-2560
Taylor County MS 700/5-8
RR 2 Box 148A 26354 304-265-0722
Pam Gallaher, prin. Fax 265-4623
Other Schools – See Flemington

Grantsville, Calhoun, Pop. 546
Calhoun County SD
Supt. — See Mount Zion
Pleasant Hill ES 200/PK-4
3254 N Calhoun Hwy 26147 304-354-6022
Jacqueline Shimer, prin. Fax 354-6070

Green Bank, Pocahontas
Pocahontas County SD
Supt. — See Marlinton

Green Bank S 300/PK-8
RR 1 Box 5 24944 304-456-4865
Ruth Bland, prin. Fax 456-5162

Griffithsville, Lincoln
Lincoln County SD
Supt. — See Hamlin
Duval S 200/PK-8
10300 State Route 3 25521 304-524-2101
Kim Clayton, prin. Fax 524-2732

Hacker Valley, Webster
Webster County SD
Supt. — See Webster Springs
Hacker Valley S 100/PK-8
PO Box 69 26222 304-493-6488
K. Howes, prin. Fax 493-6489

Hambleton, Tucker, Pop. 250
Tucker County SD
Supt. — See Parsons
Tucker Valley S 600/PK-8
100 Crest Ave 26269 304-478-3606
Joyce Carnico, prin. Fax 478-4888

Hamlin, Lincoln, Pop. 1,100
Lincoln County SD 2,700/PK-12
10 Marland Ave 25523 304-824-3033
David Roach, supt. Fax 824-7947
boe.linc.k12.wv.us/
Hamlin S 400/PK-8
8130 Court Ave 25523 304-824-3036
Patricia Faulknier, prin. Fax 824-5575
Other Schools – See Alum Creek, Branchland, Griffithsville, Harts, Ranger, West Hamlin

Hanover, Wyoming
Wyoming County SD
Supt. — See Pineville
Huff Consolidated S 300/PK-8
PO Box E 24839 304-938-3672
Phyllis Repass, prin. Fax 938-3672

Harman, Randolph, Pop. 126
Randolph County SD
Supt. — See Elkins
Harman S 200/K-12
PO Box 130 26270 304-227-4114
Debbie Schmidlen, prin. Fax 227-3610

Harpers Ferry, Jefferson, Pop. 313
Jefferson County SD
Supt. — See Charles Town
Blue Ridge ES 500/K-5
18866 Charles Town Rd 25425 304-725-2995
Susan Zigler, prin. Fax 728-7041
Harpers Ferry MS 500/6-8
1710 W Washington St 25425 304-535-6357
Joseph Spurgas, prin. Fax 535-6986
Shipley ES 400/K-5
652 Shipley School Rd 25425 304-725-4395
Mark Osbourn, prin. Fax 728-7388

Bolivar Christian Academy 100/PK-6
87 Old Taylor Ln 25425 304-535-6355
Becki Fitzwater, admin. Fax 535-6355

Harrisville, Ritchie, Pop. 1,861
Ritchie County SD 1,600/PK-12
134 S Penn Ave 26362 304-643-2991
Robert Daquilante, supt. Fax 643-2994
Harrisville ES 300/PK-5
1201 E Main St 26362 304-643-2220
Wesley Ezell, prin. Fax 643-2170
Other Schools – See Ellenboro, Pennsboro, Smithville

Harts, Lincoln, Pop. 2,332
Lincoln County SD
Supt. — See Hamlin
Harts IS 100/4-8
RR 1 Box 130 25524 304-855-4881
Belinda Toney, prin. Fax 855-7945
Harts PS 100/PK-3
RR 2 Box 28 25524 304-855-3173
Debbie Dingess, prin. Fax 855-3713

Logan County SD
Supt. — See Logan
Dingess ES 100/PK-4
RR 1 Box 607 25524 304-855-3585
Sam Dalton, prin. Fax 855-6600

Hedgesville, Berkeley, Pop. 244
Berkeley County SD
Supt. — See Martinsburg
Back Creek Valley ES 200/K-3
1962 Back Creek Valley Rd 25427 304-229-1975
Cynthia Barber, prin. Fax 229-1978
Hedgesville ES 600/PK-2
88 School House Dr 25427 304-754-3341
Paul Tyson, prin. Fax 754-6660
Hedgesville MS 600/6-8
334 School House Dr 25427 304-754-3313
Elizabeth Adams, prin. Fax 754-6613
Tomahawk IS 500/3-5
6665 Hedgesville Rd 25427 304-754-3171
John Spataro, prin. Fax 754-3201

Morgan County SD
Supt. — See Berkeley Springs
Pleasant View ES 100/PK-5
10500 Martinsburg Rd 25427 304-258-2606
Nicole Fox, prin. Fax 258-7993

Hewett, Boone
Boone County SD
Supt. — See Madison
Jeffrey-Spencer ES 100/PK-5
PO Box 319 25108 304-369-1342
Josh Bacchus, prin. Fax 369-1345

Hillsboro, Pocahontas, Pop. 234
Pocahontas County SD
Supt. — See Marlinton
Hillsboro ES 100/PK-5
HC 64 Box 399 24946 304-653-4221
Leonard Paranac, prin. Fax 653-4212

Hilltop, Fayette, Pop. 250

Mountainview Christian S 200/PK-12
2 Mountain View Rd 25855 304-465-0502
Rev. Rudell Bloomfield, hdmstr. Fax 465-5484

Hinton, Summers, Pop. 2,696
Summers County SD 1,600/PK-12
116 Main St 25951 304-466-6000
Vicki Hinerman, supt. Fax 466-6008
boe.summ.k12.wv.us
Hinton Area ES 400/PK-5
121 Park Ave 25951 304-466-6024
Michael Tabor, prin. Fax 466-6008
Summers MS 400/6-8
400 Temple St 25951 304-466-6030
Kitrick Durnan, prin. Fax 466-2271
Other Schools – See Jumping Branch, Talcott

Holden, Logan, Pop. 1,246
Logan County SD
Supt. — See Logan
Holden Central ES 200/K-4
PO Box M 25625 304-239-2771
Michael White, prin. Fax 239-2514

Hometown, Putnam
Putnam County SD
Supt. — See Winfield
Hometown ES 100/K-5
PO Box 249 25109 304-586-2395
Carol Graham, prin. Fax 586-2395

Huntington, Cabell, Pop. 49,198
Cabell County SD 11,700/PK-12
2850 5th Ave 25702 304-528-5000
William Smith, supt. Fax 528-5080
boe.cabe.k12.wv.us
Altizer ES 300/PK-5
250 3rd St 25705 304-528-5100
Judith Short, prin. Fax 528-5148
Beverly Hills MS 500/6-8
2901 Saltwell Rd 25705 304-528-5102
Gary Cook, prin. Fax 528-5197
Central City ES 500/PK-5
2100 Washington Ave 25704 304-528-5231
Patrick O'Neal, prin. Fax 528-5245
Enslow MS 200/6-8
2613 Collis Ave 25702 304-528-5121
Georgia Porter, prin. Fax 528-5097
Geneva Kent ES 300/K-5
68 Holley Ave 25705 304-528-5126
Connie Mize, prin. Fax 528-5150
Guyandotte ES 200/PK-5
605 5th Ave 25702 304-528-5128
Martha Evans, prin. Fax 528-5151
Highlawn ES 300/PK-5
2549 1st Ave 25703 304-528-5130
Robin Harmon, prin. Fax 528-5152
Hite-Saunders ES 200/PK-5
3708 Green Valley Rd 25701 304-528-5132
Brenda Horne, prin. Fax 528-5038
Huntington MS 200/6-8
1001 Jefferson Ave 25704 304-528-5180
Joe Brison, prin. Fax 528-5215
Meadows ES 200/PK-5
1601 Washington Blvd 25701 304-528-5166
Elizabeth Green, prin. Fax 528-5153
Peyton ES 200/PK-5
199 Rotary Rd 25705 304-528-5173
Marion Ward, prin. Fax 528-5195
Southside ES 200/PK-5
620 12th Ave 25701 304-528-5168
John Hanna, prin. Fax 528-5154
Spring Hill ES 400/PK-5
1901 Hall Ave 25701 304-528-5175
Pamela Bailey, prin. Fax 528-5177
Other Schools – See Barboursville, Culloden, Lesage, Milton, Ona, Salt Rock

Wayne County SD
Supt. — See Wayne
Kellogg ES 500/PK-5
4415 Piedmont Rd 25704 304-429-4441
Eugenia Webb Damron, prin. Fax 429-7200
Vinson MS 300/6-8
3851 Piedmont Rd 25704 304-429-1641
Tammy Forbush, prin. Fax 429-6162

Academy of Huntington 100/PK-8
2400 Johnstown Rd 25701 304-781-6540
Larry Crawford, hdmstr. Fax 522-6382
Grace Christian S 300/PK-12
1111 Adams Ave 25704 304-522-8635
Dr. Dan Brokke, admin. Fax 522-3240
Our Lady of Fatima S 300/PK-8
535 Norway Ave 25705 304-523-2861
John Downey, prin. Fax 525-0390
St. Joseph S 300/PK-6
520 13th St 25701 304-522-2644
Carol Templeton, prin. Fax 522-2512

Hurricane, Putnam, Pop. 5,968
Putnam County SD
Supt. — See Winfield
Conner Street ES 300/K-5
445 Conner St 25526 304-562-9351
Karen Fragale, prin. Fax 562-3635
Hurricane MS 900/6-8
518 Midland Trl 25526 304-562-9271
Greg LeMaster, prin. Fax 562-7163
Hurricane Town ES 300/K-5
300 Harbour Ln 25526 304-562-3610
Deborah Spicer, prin. Fax 562-3610
Lakeside ES 200/K-5
2550 US Route 60 25526 304-562-3630
Tammy Dill, prin. Fax 562-3630
Mountain View ES K-5
3967 Teays Valley Rd 25526 304-586-0500
Doug Pitzer, prin. Fax 757-5667
West Teays ES 800/K-5
3676 Teays Valley Rd 25526 304-757-6711
Valerie Fowler, prin. Fax 757-8098

Calvary Baptist Academy 200/K-12
3655 Teays Valley Rd 25526 304-757-6768
Lighthouse Christian Academy 100/PK-5
2440 US Route 60 25526 304-562-3900
Melanie White, admin. Fax 562-3990

Iaeger, McDowell, Pop. 314
McDowell County SD
Supt. — See Welch
Iaeger ES 300/PK-5
PO Box 359 24844 304-938-2227
A. Ray Bailey, prin. Fax 938-5289

Inwood, Berkeley, Pop. 1,360
Berkeley County SD
Supt. — See Martinsburg
Inwood PS 200/K-3
7864 Winchester Ave 25428 304-229-1990
Brent Sherrard, prin. Fax 229-1992

Jane Lew, Lewis, Pop. 409
Lewis County SD
Supt. — See Weston
Jane Lew ES 400/PK-4
6536 Main St 26378 304-884-7836
George Reynolds, prin. Fax 884-7185

Jumping Branch, Summers
Summers County SD
Supt. — See Hinton
Jumping Branch ES 100/PK-5
PO Box 9 25969 304-466-6025
Patricia Harvey, prin. Fax 466-6025

Junior, Barbour, Pop. 448
Barbour County SD
Supt. — See Philippi
Junior ES 100/PK-5
River Rd 26275 304-823-4229
Sue Talbot, prin. Fax 823-2895

Kearneysville, Jefferson
Jefferson County SD
Supt. — See Charles Town
North Jefferson ES 300/PK-5
6996 Charles Town Rd 25430 304-725-9587
Mary Jenkins, prin. Fax 728-7331

Country Day S 200/PK-8
449 Rose Hill Dr 25430 304-725-1438
Karen Stroup, hdmstr. Fax 728-8394

Kenna, Jackson
Jackson County SD
Supt. — See Ripley
Kenna ES 300/PK-5
650 Route 21 25248 304-372-7343
Mike King, prin. Fax 372-7313

Kenova, Wayne, Pop. 3,391
Wayne County SD
Supt. — See Wayne
Buffalo ES 500/PK-5
331 Buffalo Creek Rd 25530 304-429-2911
Michele Blatt, prin. Fax 429-3269
Buffalo MS 300/6-8
298 Buffalo Creek Rd 25530 304-429-6062
John Waugaman, prin. Fax 429-7245
Kenova ES 300/K-5
1400 Poplar St 25530 304-453-1521
Deidre Farley, prin. Fax 453-4415

Kermit, Mingo, Pop. 227
Mingo County SD
Supt. — See Williamson
Kermit S 300/K-8
PO Box 720 25674 304-393-4130
Dora Chaffin, prin. Fax 393-4137

Keyser, Mineral, Pop. 5,410
Mineral County SD 4,400/PK-12
1 Baker Pl 26726 304-788-4200
Skip Hackworth, supt. Fax 788-4204
boe.mine.k12.wv.us/
Fountain PS 100/K-4
RR 5 Box 390 26726 304-788-4215
Roberta Unger, prin. Fax 788-4229
Keyser S 1,200/PK-8
700 S Water St 26726 304-788-4220
John Campbell, prin. Fax 788-4225
Other Schools – See Burlington, Elk Garden, Fort Ashby, New Creek, Ridgeley, Wiley Ford

Kimball, McDowell, Pop. 360
McDowell County SD
Supt. — See Welch
Kimball ES 300/PK-5
PO Box 308 24853 304-585-7570
A. Brady Eanes, prin. Fax 585-7165

Kingwood, Preston, Pop. 2,926
Preston County SD 4,500/K-12
PO Box 566 26537 304-329-0580
John Lofink, supt. Fax 329-0720
www.prestonboe.com
Central Preston MS 300/6-8
100 E High St 26537 304-329-0033
Karen Ovesney, prin. Fax 329-2389

Kingwood ES 500/K-5
207 S Price St 26537 304-329-1034
Dorothy Nichols, prin. Fax 329-1035
Other Schools – See Arthurdale, Aurora, Bruceton Mills, Masontown, Rowlesburg, Terra Alta, Tunnelton

Lavalette, Wayne
Wayne County SD
Supt. — See Wayne
Lavalette ES 300/PK-5
PO Box 380 25535 304-525-3221
Jim Christain, prin. Fax 525-3245

Left Hand, Roane
Roane County SD
Supt. — See Spencer
Geary S 300/PK-8
PO Box 89 25251 304-565-3721
Brenda Chadwell, prin. Fax 565-3741

Lenore, Mingo
Mingo County SD
Supt. — See Williamson
Lenore S 500/K-8
General Delivery 25676 304-475-5231
Sabrina Runyon, prin. Fax 475-2411

Leon, Mason, Pop. 127
Mason County SD
Supt. — See Point Pleasant
Leon ES 100/K-6
138 Aylor St 25123 304-458-1710
Don Bower, prin. Fax 458-2049

Lerona, Mercer
Mercer County SD
Supt. — See Princeton
Sun Valley ES 100/K-5
PO Box 10 25971 304-384-7441
Kristal Filipek, prin. Fax 384-3114

Lesage, Cabell
Cabell County SD
Supt. — See Huntington
Cox Landing ES 200/PK-5
6358 Cox Ln 25537 304-733-3019
Laura Cooper, prin. Fax 733-3021

Lester, Raleigh, Pop. 316
Raleigh County SD
Supt. — See Beckley
Lester ES 200/PK-5
PO Box 727 25865 304-934-5885
Drexel Sammons, prin. Fax 934-6242

Levels, Hampshire
Hampshire County SD
Supt. — See Romney
Cornwell ES 100/K-5
HC 60 Box 72 25431 304-492-5520
Amy Haines, prin. Fax 492-5123

Lewisburg, Greenbrier, Pop. 3,595
Greenbrier County SD 5,300/PK-12
202 Chestnut St 24901 304-647-6470
John Curry, supt. Fax 647-6490
Lewisburg ES 400/PK-5
206 N Lee St 24901 304-647-6477
Leann Piercy-McMillian, prin. Fax 647-4838
Other Schools – See Alderson, Crawley, Frankford, Quinwood, Rainelle, Ronceverte, Rupert, Smoot, White Sulphur Springs

---

Greenbrier Valley Academy 50/K-10
235 N Court St 24901 304-647-5925
Suzan Wilson, prin. Fax 647-5925

Little Birch, Braxton
Braxton County SD
Supt. — See Sutton
Little Birch ES 100/PK-4
PO Box 10 26629 304-765-2042
Judy Shafer, prin. Fax 765-2042

Lizemores, Clay
Clay County SD
Supt. — See Clay
Lizemores ES 100/PK-5
PO Box 70 25125 304-587-4823
Tina Burnette, prin. Fax 587-2772

Logan, Logan, Pop. 1,547
Logan County SD 6,100/PK-12
PO Box 477 25601 304-792-2060
Wilma Zigmond, supt. Fax 752-3711
lc2.boe.loga.k12.wv.us/
Justice ES 100/PK-4
407 Circle Dr 25601 304-752-3250
Debra Lucas, prin. Fax 752-5456
Logan ES 300/K-4
12 Middleburg Is 25601 304-752-4180
Michael Johnson, prin. Fax 752-5463
Logan MS 900/5-8
14 Wildcat Way 25601 304-752-1804
Ernestine Sutherland, prin. Fax 752-0207
Other Schools – See Accoville, Chapmanville, Harts, Holden, Mallory, Man, Omar, Verdunville

Lookout, Fayette
Fayette County SD
Supt. — See Fayetteville
Divide ES 200/PK-4
PO Box 180 25868 304-574-1443
Bruce Williams, prin. Fax 574-0693
Nuttall MS 200/5-8
PO Box 130 25868 304-574-0429
Jeremy Pyle, prin. Fax 574-0491

Lost Creek, Harrison, Pop. 497
Harrison County SD
Supt. — See Clarksburg
Lost Creek ES 200/PK-5
PO Box 128 26385 304-326-7040
Pattae Kinney, prin. Fax 745-4393
South Harrison MS 400/6-8
RR 1 Box 58B 26385 304-326-7460
Phil Brown, prin. Fax 745-5587

Lumberport, Harrison, Pop. 969
Harrison County SD
Supt. — See Clarksburg
Lumberport ES 300/PK-5
PO Box 417 26386 304-326-7020
Vickie Luchuck, prin. Fax 584-5943
Lumberport MS 500/6-8
PO Box 309 26386 304-326-7540
Anthony Fratto, prin. Fax 584-4602

Mabscott, Raleigh, Pop. 1,364
Raleigh County SD
Supt. — See Beckley
Mabscott ES 300/PK-5
PO Box 174 25871 304-256-4595
Theresa Lewis, prin. Fax 256-4595

MacArthur, Raleigh, Pop. 1,595
Raleigh County SD
Supt. — See Beckley
Hollywood ES 200/K-5
PO Box 7, 304-256-4590
Doug Bird, prin. Fax 256-4579

Mc Mechen, Marshall, Pop. 2,019
Marshall County SD
Supt. — See Moundsville
Center Mc Mechen ES 200/K-5
800 Marshall St 26040 304-232-6530
Weldon Yoder, prin. Fax 232-6520

Madison, Boone, Pop. 2,634
Boone County SD 4,500/PK-12
69 Avenue B 25130 304-369-3131
Steve Pauley, supt. Fax 369-0855
www.boonecountyboe.org
Madison ES 300/K-5
150 Josephine Ave 25130 304-369-2241
Patricia Conaway, prin. Fax 369-2869
Madison MS 600/6-8
404 Riverside Dr W 25130 304-369-4464
Gary Bell, prin. Fax 369-5800
Other Schools – See Ashford, Comfort, Danville, Foster, Hewett, Nellis, Seth, Uneeda, Van, Wharton, Whitesville

Mallory, Logan, Pop. 1,126
Logan County SD
Supt. — See Logan
Man Central S 400/K-8
PO Box 390 25634 304-583-8316
Leah Perry, prin. Fax 583-7342

Man, Logan, Pop. 716
Logan County SD
Supt. — See Logan
South Man ES 100/PK-3
301 E Mcdonald Ave 25635 304-583-7522
David Adkins, prin. Fax 583-8046

Mannington, Marion, Pop. 2,080
Marion County SD
Supt. — See Fairmont
Blackshere ES 400/PK-4
77 Blackshere Dr 26582 304-986-2707
Scott Morris, prin. Fax 986-2715
Mannington MS 400/5-8
113 Clarksburg St 26582 304-986-1050
Mike Call, prin. Fax 986-1747

Marlinton, Pocahontas, Pop. 1,247
Pocahontas County SD 1,300/PK-12
926 5th Ave 24954 304-799-4505
Dr. Patrick Law, supt. Fax 799-4499
boe.poca.k12.wv.us
Marlinton ES 300/PK-4
926 5th Ave Ste A 24954 304-799-6551
Ron Hall, prin. Fax 799-6552
Other Schools – See Buckeye, Green Bank, Hillsboro

Marmet, Kanawha, Pop. 1,626
Kanawha County SD
Supt. — See Charleston
Chesapeake ES 200/PK-5
13620 MacCorkle Ave 25315 304-949-1121
Marianne Annie, prin. Fax 949-2351
Marmet ES 200/K-5
408 94th St 25315 304-949-2382
Michelle Settle, prin. Fax 949-6116

Martinsburg, Berkeley, Pop. 15,996
Berkeley County SD 16,100/PK-12
401 S Queen St 25401 304-267-3500
Manny Arvon, supt. Fax 267-3524
boe.berk.k12.wv.us
Bedington ES 200/PK-2
149 Bedington Rd, 304-274-2535
Linda Ghion, prin. Fax 274-3957
Berkeley Heights ES 600/K-3
726 Hack Wilson Way 25401 304-267-3520
Amber Boeckmann, prin. Fax 263-3798
Burke Street ES 100/PK-3
422 W Burke St 25401 304-267-3525
Todd Cutlip, prin. Fax 267-3527
Eagle IS 500/4-5
730 Eagle School Rd, 304-263-0422
Margaret Kursey, prin. Fax 263-6506
Martinsburg North MS 500/6-8
250 East Rd, 304-267-3540
Elizabeth Ward, prin. Fax 264-5066
Martinsburg South MS 900/6-8
150 Bulldog Blvd 25401 304-267-3545
David Rogers, prin. Fax 264-5062
Opequon ES 500/K-3
395 East Rd, 304-267-3550
Tana Petrucci, prin. Fax 267-3552
Orchard View IS 500/4-5
1455 Delmar Orchard Rd, 304-263-4143
Joyce Chapman, prin. Fax 263-4148
Potomack IS 600/3-5
5308 Williamsport Pike, 304-274-6592
Stephen Crowell, prin. Fax 274-6876
Rosemont ES 400/K-3
301 S Alabama Ave 25401 304-267-3560
Sandra Duffy, prin. Fax 263-3838
Spring Mills MS 600/6-8
255 Campus Dr, 304-274-5030
Marc Arvon, prin. Fax 274-3598
Tuscarora ES 300/K-3
2000 Tavern Rd 25401 304-267-3565
Larry Hitt, prin. Fax 264-5059
Valley View ES 500/K-3
140 Nadenbousch Ln, 304-229-1970
Frederick Johnson, prin. Fax 229-1973
Winchester Avenue ES 400/PK-3
650 Winchester Ave 25401 304-267-3570
Dean Warrenfeltz, prin. Fax 267-3572
Other Schools – See Bunker Hill, Falling Waters, Gerrardstown, Hedgesville, Inwood

---

Faith Christian Academy 300/PK-12
138 Greensburg Rd, 304-263-0011
Eric Kerns, admin. Fax 267-0638
Rocky Knoll SDA S 50/K-8
52 Advent Dr, 304-263-9894
St. Joseph S 400/PK-8
110 E Stephen St 25401 304-267-6447
Frances Odum, prin. Fax 267-6573

Masontown, Preston, Pop. 649
Preston County SD
Supt. — See Kingwood
West Preston MS 200/6-8
PO Box 70 26542 304-864-5221
Steve Plum, prin. Fax 864-5298

Matewan, Mingo, Pop. 501
Mingo County SD
Supt. — See Williamson
Matewan ES 300/PK-4
100 Chambers St 25678 304-426-4719
Teresa Jones, prin. Fax 426-4732
Matewan MS 200/5-8
200 Tiger Ln 25678 304-426-8569
Marsha Maynard, prin. Fax 426-4480

Matoaka, Mercer, Pop. 306
Mercer County SD
Supt. — See Princeton
Lashmeet-Matoaka S 400/PK-8
PO Box 408 24736 304-467-7477
Linda Richards, prin. Fax 467-7477

Maysville, Grant
Grant County SD
Supt. — See Petersburg
Maysville ES 200/PK-6
7147 Highway 42 S 26833 304-749-7441
Mark Nicol, prin. Fax 749-7442

Meadow Bridge, Fayette, Pop. 310
Fayette County SD
Supt. — See Fayetteville
Meadow Bridge ES 200/K-6
2725 Main St 25976 304-484-7914
Andrew Tokarz, prin. Fax 484-7599

Metz, Wetzel
Wetzel County SD
Supt. — See New Martinsville
Long Drain S 300/PK-8
RR 1 Box 108A 26585 304-775-4221
Paul Huston, prin. Fax 775-4261

Miami, Kanawha
Kanawha County SD
Supt. — See Charleston
Dawes ES 200/PK-5
PO Box 149 25134 304-595-3323
Ed Fauber, prin. Fax 595-3362

Middlebourne, Tyler, Pop. 853
Tyler County SD 1,600/PK-12
PO Box 25 26149 304-758-2145
Jeff Hoover, supt. Fax 758-4566
Borman ES 400/PK-5
PO Box 299 26149 304-758-2152
James Brown, prin. Fax 758-2148
Other Schools – See Sistersville

Mill Creek, Randolph, Pop. 658
Randolph County SD
Supt. — See Elkins
Ward ES 300/K-5
PO Box 278 26280 304-335-4975
Diana Arbogast, prin. Fax 335-4976

Milton, Cabell, Pop. 2,262
Cabell County SD
Supt. — See Huntington
Milton ES 600/PK-5
1201 Pike St 25541 304-743-7303
Kim Cooper, prin. Fax 743-7307
Milton MS 700/6-8
1 Panther Way 25541 304-743-7308
Dan Gleason, prin. Fax 743-7324

Mineral Wells, Wood, Pop. 1,698
Wood County SD
Supt. — See Parkersburg
Mineral Wells ES 600/PK-5
PO Box 40 26150 304-489-1670
Bill Matthews, prin. Fax 489-2637

Moatsville, Barbour
Barbour County SD
Supt. — See Philippi
Kasson S 200/PK-8
RR 1 Box 233A 26405 304-457-1485
Michelle Barb, prin. Fax 457-6186

Monongah, Marion, Pop. 912
Marion County SD
Supt. — See Fairmont
Monongah ES 300/PK-4
628 Walnut St 26554 304-367-2159
Carolyn Kerr, prin. Fax 367-2188
Monongah MS 200/5-8
500 Camden Ave 26554 304-367-2164
Steve Malnick, prin. Fax 367-2190

Moorefield, Hardy, Pop. 2,408
Hardy County SD 2,000/PK-12
510 Ashby St 26836 304-530-2348
Barbara Whitecotton, supt. Fax 530-2340
www.hardycountyschools.com/
Moorefield ES 400/PK-2
400 N Main St 26836 304-538-6356
Beverly Coppe, prin. Fax 538-2536
Moorefield IS 3-5
345 Caledonia Heights Rd 26836 304-530-3450
Bonnie Rogers, prin. Fax 530-3451
Moorefield MS 300/6-8
303 Caledonia Dr 26836 304-434-3000
Patrick McGregor, prin. Fax 434-3003
Other Schools – See Baker

Morgantown, Monongalia, Pop. 28,292
Monongalia County SD 10,100/PK-12
13 S High St 26501 304-291-9210
Frank Devono, supt. Fax 291-3015
boe.mono.k12.wv.us
Brookhaven ES 400/K-5
1215 Baker St 26508 304-291-9236
Davene Burks, prin. Fax 284-9355
Cheat Lake ES 600/K-4
154 Crosby Rd 26508 304-594-2772
Dr. Mary Lynn Cocco, prin. Fax 594-2283
Cheat Lake MS 600/5-8
160 Crosby Rd 26508 304-594-1165
Joanne Hines, prin. Fax 594-1677
Dorsey Center 100/PK-PK
1433 Dorsey Ave 26501 304-291-9330
Brenda Yohn, prin. Fax 291-9324
Easton ES 100/K-4
2901 Point Marion Rd 26505 304-291-9228
DeAnn Hartshorn, prin. Fax 284-9350
Mountainview ES 600/K-5
2100 Greenbag Rd 26508 304-291-9255
Stephen King, prin. Fax 291-9254
Mylan Park ES 500/PK-5
901 Mylan Park Ln 26501 304-983-7700
Debbie Tampoya, prin. Fax 983-7704
North ES 600/K-5
825 Chestnut Ridge Rd 26505 304-291-9280
Rosann Hardin, prin. Fax 291-9213
Ridgedale ES 300/K-5
1550 Goshen Rd 26508 304-291-9231
Liz Zuchowski, prin. Fax 291-9215
Skyview ES 400/PK-5
668 River Rd 26501 304-284-2890
Sandra Wolfe, prin. Fax 284-2894
South MS 700/6-8
500 E Parkway Dr 26501 304-291-9340
Dennis Gallon, prin. Fax 291-9306
Suncrest MS 500/6-8
360 Baldwin St 26505 304-291-9335
James Napolillo, prin. Fax 284-9362
Suncrest PS 200/PK-3
523 Junior Ave 26505 304-291-9347
Kenneth Wolfe, prin. Fax 284-9388
Westwood MS 500/6-8
670 River Rd 26501 304-291-9300
Leonard Haney, prin. Fax 284-9368
Woodburn ES 200/K-5
Parson and Fortney St 26505 304-291-9295
Linda Nakaishi, prin. Fax 284-9351
Other Schools – See Blacksville, Fairview

Covenant Christian S 100/PK-8
PO Box 342 26507 304-292-6050
Rev. David Friend, admin. Fax 292-9614
Lighthouse Christian Academy 50/K-12
980 Stewartstown Rd 26508 304-276-0731
Terry Sloane, admin. Fax 599-6163
St. Francis de Sales Central S 500/PK-8
41 Guthrie Ln 26508 304-291-5070
Sr. Patricia Foley, prin. Fax 291-5104
Trinity Christian S 300/PK-12
200 Trinity Way 26505 304-291-4659
Michael Staud, supt. Fax 291-4660

Moundsville, Marshall, Pop. 9,567
Marshall County SD 3,800/PK-12
PO Box 578 26041 304-843-4400
Alfred Renzella, supt. Fax 843-4409
boe.mars.k12.wv.us
Central ES 50/3-5
750 Tomlinson Ave 26041 304-843-4425
Karen Klamut, prin. Fax 843-4426
McNinch PS 200/PK-2
2600 4th St 26041 304-843-4431
Rita DeMundo, prin. Fax 843-4461
Moundsville MS 400/6-8
223 Tomlinson Ave 26041 304-843-4440
M. Jan Madden, prin. Fax 843-4446
Washington Lands ES 300/K-5
RR 4 Box 255 26041 304-843-4420
Michael Hince, prin. Fax 843-4459
Other Schools – See Cameron, Dallas, Glen Dale, Mc Mechen, Wheeling

---

St. Francis Xavier S 200/PK-8
600 Jefferson Ave 26041 304-845-2562
Cathy Frame, prin. Fax 845-0016

Mount Hope, Fayette, Pop. 1,411
Fayette County SD
Supt. — See Fayetteville
Mount Hope ES 200/PK-4
408 Lincoln St 25880 304-877-2891
Randall Rhodes, prin. Fax 877-6105

Raleigh County SD
Supt. — See Beckley
Bradley ES 500/PK-5
210 Bradley School Rd 25880 304-256-4605
Sandra Sheatsley, prin. Fax 256-4624

Mount Lookout, Nicholas
Nicholas County SD
Supt. — See Summersville
Mount Lookout ES 100/K-5
1945 E Mount Lookout Rd 26678 304-872-2731
Pam Butcher, prin. Fax 872-2731

Mount Nebo, Nicholas
Nicholas County SD
Supt. — See Summersville
Mount Nebo ES 100/PK-5
PO Box 160 26679 304-872-2440
R. Young, prin. Fax 872-2440

Mount Zion, Calhoun
Calhoun County SD 1,200/PK-12
HC 89 Box 119 26151 304-354-7011
Roger Propst, supt. Fax 354-7420
boe.calh.k12.wv.us
Other Schools – See Arnoldsburg, Grantsville

Mullens, Wyoming, Pop. 1,653
Wyoming County SD
Supt. — See Pineville
Mullens ES 200/K-4
2107 Caloric Rd 25882 304-294-5252
Carolyn Wilcox, prin. Fax 294-5252
Mullens MS 200/5-8
801 Moran Ave 25882 304-294-5757
Sidney Bradford, prin. Fax 294-5757

Nellis, Boone
Boone County SD
Supt. — See Madison
Nellis ES 100/PK-6
179 Memorial Dr 25142 304-836-5281
Jeff Nelson, prin. Fax 836-5281

Nettie, Nicholas
Nicholas County SD
Supt. — See Summersville
Panther Creek ES 300/PK-5
PO Box 39 26681 304-846-6808
Angie Amick, prin. Fax 846-2144

New Creek, Mineral
Mineral County SD
Supt. — See Keyser
New Creek PS 200/PK-5
General Delivery 26743 304-788-4249
Robin McDowell, prin. Fax 788-4208

New Cumberland, Hancock, Pop. 1,043
Hancock County SD 4,300/PK-12
PO Box 1300 26047 304-564-3411
Suzan Smith, supt. Fax 564-3990
www.hancockschools.org
New Manchester ES 300/PK-4
128 Frankfort Rd 26047 304-564-3242
Chris Humberson, prin. Fax 564-5084
Oak Glen MS 700/5-8
39 Golden Bear Dr 26047 304-387-2363
Donna Popovich, prin. Fax 387-4624
Other Schools – See Chester, Weirton

New Haven, Mason, Pop. 1,528
Mason County SD
Supt. — See Point Pleasant
New Haven ES 500/PK-6
PO Box 989 25265 304-882-2025
Cameron Moffett, prin. Fax 882-2037

New Martinsville, Wetzel, Pop. 5,791
Wetzel County SD 2,900/PK-12
333 Foundry St 26155 304-455-2441
William Jones, supt. Fax 455-3446
www.wetzelcountyschools.com
New Martinsville S 900/K-8
20 E Benjamin Dr 26155 304-455-2291
M. Fay Shank, prin. Fax 455-6436
Other Schools – See Metz, Paden City, Reader

Nitro, Kanawha, Pop. 6,750
Kanawha County SD
Supt. — See Charleston
Nitro ES 400/K-5
1921 19th St 25143 304-755-2451
Karen Price, prin. Fax 755-9215

Putnam County SD
Supt. — See Winfield
Rock Branch ES 200/K-5
4616 1st Ave 25143 304-755-1443
Sonya Shue, prin. Fax 755-0019

Normantown, Gilmer
Gilmer County SD
Supt. — See Glenville
Normantown ES 100/PK-6
10233 US Highway 33 W 25267 304-462-8035
Patty Lowther, prin. Fax 462-5329

Oak Hill, Fayette, Pop. 7,312
Fayette County SD
Supt. — See Fayetteville
Collins MS 700/5-8
601 Jones Ave 25901 304-469-3711
Charles Smallwood, prin. Fax 465-1352
Oak Hill East End ES 200/K-4
103 Ingram St 25901 304-469-3591
James Wells, prin. Fax 469-3591
Oak Hill ES 400/PK-4
140 School St 25901 304-469-4541
David Cavalier, prin. Fax 469-4310
Rosedale ES 300/K-4
4001 Summerlee Rd 25901 304-469-6661
Ted Dixon, prin. Fax 469-3569

SS. Peter & Paul S 100/PK-8
123 Elmore St 25901 304-465-5045
Aaron Kemlock, prin. Fax 465-8726

Oakvale, Mercer, Pop. 138
Mercer County SD
Supt. — See Princeton
Oakvale S 200/PK-8
PO Box 188, 304-898-3731
Ernest Adkins, prin. Fax 898-2031

Oceana, Wyoming, Pop. 1,478
Wyoming County SD
Supt. — See Pineville
Berlin McKinney ES 400/PK-4
HC 65 Box 402 24870 304-682-6481
Steve Anderson, prin. Fax 682-5234
Oceana MS 300/5-8
HC 65 Box 403 24870 304-682-6296
Jim Hopkins, prin. Fax 682-6296

Omar, Logan
Logan County SD
Supt. — See Logan
Omar ES 300/PK-4
PO Box 590 25638 304-946-2660
Darlene Adkins, prin. Fax 946-4236

Beth Haven Christian S 100/PK-12
PO Box 620 25638 304-946-4447

Ona, Cabell
Cabell County SD
Supt. — See Huntington
Ona ES 300/PK-5
Ona Drive Rd 25545 304-743-7318
Tim Hardesty, prin. Fax 743-7321

Paden City, Wetzel, Pop. 2,737
Wetzel County SD
Supt. — See New Martinsville
Paden City ES 200/K-6
510 N 2nd Ave 26159 304-337-2221
Tammy Chambers, prin. Fax 337-9049

Parkersburg, Wood, Pop. 32,020
Wood County SD 11,600/PK-12
1210 13th St 26101 304-420-9663
William Niday, supt. Fax 420-9513
www.netassoc.net/wcboe/
Blennerhassett ES 400/K-5
444 Jewell Rd 26101 304-863-5128
Keith Palmer, prin. Fax 863-5335
Blennerhassett JHS 400/6-8
444 Jewell Rd 26101 304-863-3356
Jim Hostuttle, prin. Fax 863-3357
Criss ES 200/K-5
2800 22nd St 26101 304-420-9522
Mary Vincent, prin. Fax 420-9523
Edison JHS 500/6-8
1201 Hillcrest St 26101 304-420-9525
Jean Mewshaw, prin. Fax 420-9527
Emerson ES 400/K-5
1605 36th St 26104 304-420-9528
Lori Lowers, prin. Fax 420-9632
Fairplains ES 200/PK-5
615 Broadway Ave 26101 304-420-9531
Liz Conrad, prin. Fax 420-9533
Franklin ES 300/PK-5
1511 Division Street Ext 26101 304-420-9534
Walt Ingles, prin. Fax 420-9537
Gihon ES 300/PK-5
2000 Belmont Rd 26101 304-420-9539
Betsy Patterson, prin. Fax 420-9540
Hamilton JHS 400/6-8
3501 Cadillac Dr 26104 304-420-9547
Mike Windland, prin. Fax 420-9567
Jefferson ES 500/PK-5
1103 Plum St 26101 304-420-9554
Judy Johnson, prin. Fax 420-9507
Lubeck ES 400/K-5
207 Lubeck Rd 26101 304-863-3321
Mary Thomas, prin. Fax 863-3848
Madison ES 400/PK-5
1426 32nd St 26104 304-420-9563
Heather Mannix, prin. Fax 420-9564
Martin ES 300/PK-5
1301 Hillcrest St 26101 304-420-9625
Ronda Lemon, prin. Fax 420-9578
McKinley ES 300/K-5
1130 19th St 26101 304-420-9581
Fred Shreve, prin. Fax 420-9582
Van Devender JHS 300/6-8
918 31st St 26104 304-420-9645
Steve Taylor, prin. Fax 420-9647
Worthington ES 200/K-5
2500 36th St 26104 304-420-9660
Joe Oliverio, prin. Fax 420-2459
Other Schools – See Davisville, Mineral Wells, Vienna, Waverly, Williamstown

---

North Christian S 100/K-5
3109 Emerson Ave 26104 304-485-0241
Wes Erwin, prin. Fax 428-3231

Parkersburg Academy 50/K-8
1800 38th St 26104 304-485-6901
Breta White, prin. Fax 422-4582
Parkersburg Catholic S 200/PK-6
810 Juliana St 26101 304-422-6694
Kevin Simonton, prin. Fax 422-2469

Parsons, Tucker, Pop. 1,400
Tucker County SD 1,200/PK-12
501 Chestnut St 26287 304-478-2771
Rick Hicks, supt. Fax 478-3422
www.tuckercountyschools.com
Other Schools – See Hambleton, Thomas

Paw Paw, Morgan, Pop. 507
Morgan County SD
Supt. — See Berkeley Springs
Paw Paw ES 100/PK-6
60 Pirate Cir 25434 304-947-7425
Michelle Fleming, prin. Fax 947-5513

Pennsboro, Ritchie, Pop. 1,196
Ritchie County SD
Supt. — See Harrisville
Creed Collins ES 200/PK-5
512 Collins Ave 26415 304-659-2140
Allen Laugh, prin. Fax 659-3322

Petersburg, Grant, Pop. 2,634
Grant County SD 2,000/PK-12
204 Jefferson Ave 26847 304-257-1011
Dr. Marsha Carr-Lambert, supt. Fax 257-2453
www.grantcountyschools.com
Dorcas ES 100/PK-6
HC 33 Box 1060 26847 304-257-1220
Dwayne Hedrick, prin. Fax 257-2876
Petersburg ES 600/PK-6
333 Rig St 26847 304-257-1110
Mitch Webster, prin. Fax 257-9658
Other Schools – See Maysville

Peterstown, Monroe, Pop. 497
Monroe County SD
Supt. — See Union
Peterstown ES 400/PK-4
108 College Dr 24963 304-753-4328
Leigh Boggess, prin. Fax 753-4786
Peterstown MS 400/5-8
36 College Dr 24963 304-753-4322
Lisa Canterbury, prin. Fax 753-5376

Philippi, Barbour, Pop. 2,826
Barbour County SD 2,600/PK-12
105 S Railroad St 26416 304-457-3030
DeEdra Lundeen, supt. Fax 457-3559
www.wvschools.com/barbourcountyschools/
Philippi ES 400/PK-5
RR 3 Box 38 26416 304-457-4229
Connie Mundy, prin. Fax 457-2287
Philippi MS 300/6-8
RR 3 Box 40 26416 304-457-2999
David Neff, prin. Fax 457-2561
Other Schools – See Belington, Flemington, Junior, Moatsville, Volga

---

Feed My Sheep Christian S 50/PK-8
311 Depot St 26416 304-457-1135
Sharon Arnett, admin. Fax 457-1135

Pickens, Randolph
Randolph County SD
Supt. — See Elkins
Pickens S 50/K-12
PO Box 146 26230 304-924-5525
Diane Betler, prin. Fax 924-6460

Pineville, Wyoming, Pop. 676
Wyoming County SD 4,100/PK-12
PO Box 69 24874 304-732-6262
Frank Blackwell, supt. Fax 732-7226
boe.wyom.k12.wv.us/
Pineville ES 400/PK-4
PO Box 700 24874 304-732-7966
Donald Wayne Clay, prin. Fax 732-7966
Pineville MS 300/5-8
PO Box 470 24874 304-732-6442
Deirdre Cline, prin. Fax 732-6737
Other Schools – See Brenton, Bud, Cyclone, Glen Fork, Hanover, Mullens, Oceana

Poca, Putnam, Pop. 1,028
Putnam County SD
Supt. — See Winfield
Poca ES 300/PK-5
PO Box 430 25159 304-755-7561
Lexie Damous, prin. Fax 755-7561
Poca MS 300/6-8
PO Box 647 25159 304-755-7343
Dale Eggleton, prin. Fax 755-8930

Point Pleasant, Mason, Pop. 4,481
Mason County SD 4,000/PK-12
1200 Main St 25550 304-675-4540
Dr. William Capehart, supt. Fax 675-7226
boe.maso.k12.wv.us/
Point Pleasant IS 400/3-6
1 Walden Roush Way 25550 304-675-1430
Paul Ashby, prin. Fax 675-2110
Point Pleasant PS 400/PK-2
2200 Lincoln Ave 25550 304-675-1420
Tim Click, prin. Fax 675-1474
Roosevelt ES 200/K-6
7953 Ripley Rd 25550 304-675-3337
Pam Hay, prin. Fax 675-7331
Other Schools – See Ashton, Gallipolis Ferry, Leon, New Haven

---

Christ Academy, PO Box 224 25550 50/K-12
Bree Ramey, prin. 304-521-2977

Pratt, Kanawha, Pop. 535
Kanawha County SD
Supt. — See Charleston
Pratt ES 300/PK-5
PO Box 36 25162 304-949-4838
David Anderson, prin. Fax 442-4541

Prichard, Wayne
Wayne County SD
Supt. — See Wayne
Prichard ES 100/K-5
PO Box 89 25555 304-486-5096
Bambi Cyrus, prin. Fax 486-5096

Princeton, Mercer, Pop. 6,222
Mercer County SD 9,500/PK-12
1403 Honaker Ave 24740 304-487-1551
Deborah Akers Ed.D., supt. Fax 425-5844
boe.merc.k12.wv.us/
Glenwood S 700/PK-8
1734 Glenwood Park Rd 24740 304-487-2445
Steve Comer, prin. Fax 487-0047
Melrose ES 200/K-5
HC 71 Box 257 24740 304-425-3757
Ernestine Battlo, prin. Fax 425-3757
Mercer County Early Learning Center 100/PK-PK
821 Broadway St 24740 304-425-4251
Jane Walthall, prin. Fax 425-5117
Mercer ES 300/3-5
1200 Mercer St 24740 304-425-3160
Betty Atwood, prin. Fax 487-3617
Princeton MS 600/6-8
300 N Johnston St 24740 304-425-7517
Danny Buckner, prin. Fax 487-2250
Princeton PS 500/K-2
219B Old Bluefield Rd 24740 304-487-3904
Jon Corbett, prin. Fax 487-2649
Straley ES 200/3-5
810 Straley Ave 24740 304-425-3173
Gayle Mills, prin. Fax 487-2724
Other Schools – See Athens, Bluefield, Lerona, Matoaka, Oakvale, Rock, Spanishburg

---

Mercer Christian Academy 100/PK-12
314 Oakvale Rd Ste A 24740 304-487-1603
Bob Brooks, admin. Fax 431-2514

Prosperity, Raleigh, Pop. 1,322

Greater Beckley Christian S 200/PK-12
PO Box 670 25909 304-255-1571
Dr. James Fritz, admin. Fax 582-0341

Quinwood, Greenbrier, Pop. 423
Greenbrier County SD
Supt. — See Lewisburg
Crichton ES 100/PK-5
PO Box 205 25981 304-438-6958
Patti Burdette, prin. Fax 438-5227

Rainelle, Greenbrier, Pop. 1,511
Greenbrier County SD
Supt. — See Lewisburg
Rainelle ES 200/PK-5
701 Kanawha Ave 25962 304-438-8861
John Lewis, prin. Fax 438-8875

Ranger, Lincoln
Lincoln County SD
Supt. — See Hamlin
Ranger ES 100/K-5
104 Ranger Bottom Rd 25557 304-778-3454
Christina Napier, prin. Fax 778-3454

Ranson, Jefferson, Pop. 2,891
Jefferson County SD
Supt. — See Charles Town
Ranson ES 400/PK-5
600 N Preston St 25438 304-725-7310
Debra Corbett, prin. Fax 725-1912

Ravenswood, Jackson, Pop. 3,991
Jackson County SD
Supt. — See Ripley
Kaiser ES 400/PK-2
804 Kaiser Ave 26164 304-273-2692
Jim Frazier, prin. Fax 273-3029
Ravenswood ES 300/3-5
RR 2 Box 22A 26164 304-273-5391
Gary Cross, prin. Fax 273-5392
Ravenswood MS 400/6-8
409 Sycamore St 26164 304-273-5480
Gary Higginbotham, prin. Fax 273-5746

Reader, Wetzel
Wetzel County SD
Supt. — See New Martinsville
Short Line S 500/PK-8
HC 60 Box 170 26167 304-386-4115
T. Jane Beckett, prin. Fax 386-4969

Red House, Putnam
Putnam County SD
Supt. — See Winfield
Confidence ES 200/K-5
HC 63 Box 163 25168 304-586-2041
Colleen Huston, prin. Fax 586-0748

Reedy, Roane, Pop. 191
Roane County SD
Supt. — See Spencer
Reedy ES 100/PK-6
66 Roosevelt St 25270 304-927-6433
Lori Gibson, prin. Fax 927-6433

Richwood, Nicholas, Pop. 2,369
Nicholas County SD
Supt. — See Summersville
Cherry River ES 200/PK-5
190 Riverside Dr 26261 304-846-6646
Tim Bennett, prin. Fax 846-6897
Richwood MS 300/6-8
2 Valley Ave 26261 304-846-2638
Mark Skaggs, prin. Fax 846-2639

Ridgeley, Mineral, Pop. 709
Mineral County SD
Supt. — See Keyser
Frankfort MS 500/5-8
RR 3 Box 170 26753 304-726-4339
Susan Ray, prin. Fax 726-4339

Ripley, Jackson, Pop. 3,266
Jackson County SD 5,100/PK-12
PO Box 770 25271 304-372-7300
Blaine Hess, supt. Fax 372-7312
boe.jack.k12.wv.us
Fairplain ES 300/PK-5
HC 80 Box 147 25271 304-372-7340
Keri Starcher, prin. Fax 372-7347
Ripley ES 700/PK-5
404 2nd Ave 25271 304-372-7345
Janet Postlethwait, prin. Fax 372-7364
Ripley MS 800/6-8
RR 2 Box 75A 25271 304-372-7350
Gail Varney, prin. Fax 372-7332
Other Schools – See Cottageville, Evans, Kenna, Ravenswood, Sandyville

Rivesville, Marion, Pop. 913
Marion County SD
Supt. — See Fairmont
Rivesville S 300/K-8
229 Phillips Ave 26588 304-278-5331
Mark Stutler, prin. Fax 278-5351

Roanoke, Lewis
Lewis County SD
Supt. — See Weston
Roanoke ES 200/PK-4
1176 Oil Creek Rd 26447 304-452-8887
Denise Sprouse, prin. Fax 452-0438

Rock, Mercer
Mercer County SD
Supt. — See Princeton
Montcalm ES 300/K-5
RR 2 Box 35 24747 304-589-5202
Ron Ball, prin. Fax 589-7095

Romney, Hampshire, Pop. 1,975
Hampshire County SD 3,700/PK-12
111 School St 26757 304-822-3528
Robin Lewis, supt. Fax 822-5382
boe.hamp.k12.wv.us/
Romney ES 500/PK-5
45 School St 26757 304-822-3018
Terrie Saville, prin. Fax 822-3018
Romney MS 500/6-8
111 School St 26757 304-822-5014
John Watson, prin. Fax 822-5744
Other Schools – See Augusta, Capon Bridge, Levels, Slanesville, Springfield

Ronceverte, Greenbrier, Pop. 1,544
Greenbrier County SD
Supt. — See Lewisburg
Eastern Greenbrier MS 900/6-8
RR 1 Box 150 24970 304-647-6498
Doug Clemons, prin. Fax 647-3087
Ronceverte ES 400/PK-5
246 Ronceverte School Dr 24970 304-647-6480
Andrea Stewart, prin. Fax 647-3086

Rowlesburg, Preston, Pop. 620
Preston County SD
Supt. — See Kingwood
Rowlesburg S 100/K-8
46 Center St 26425 304-454-9311
Pete Pell, prin. Fax 454-9313

Rupert, Greenbrier, Pop. 944
Greenbrier County SD
Supt. — See Lewisburg
Rupert ES 200/PK-5
PO Box D 25984 304-392-5235
Leatha Williams, prin. Fax 392-5234

Saint Albans, Kanawha, Pop. 11,167
Kanawha County SD
Supt. — See Charleston
Alban ES 400/K-5
2030 Harrison Ave 25177 304-722-0234
Chris Ketterly, prin. Fax 722-0235
Bailey ES 400/PK-5
405 Winfield Rd 25177 304-722-0230
Ed Rider, prin. Fax 722-0231
Central ES 400/K-5
900 Helene St 25177 304-722-0226
Tamela Moore, prin. Fax 722-0227
Hayes MS 500/6-8
830 Strawberry Rd 25177 304-722-0222
Scott Monty, prin. Fax 722-0247
Lakewood ES 200/K-5
2089 Lakewood Dr 25177 304-722-0200
Kriss Godfrey, prin. Fax 722-0456
McKinley JHS 300/6-8
3000 Kanawha Ter 25177 304-722-0218
Amy Scott, prin. Fax 722-0246
Weimer ES 200/PK-5
3040 Kanawha Ter 25177 304-722-0205
Suzanne Armstrong, prin. Fax 722-0206

St. Francis of Assisi S 100/PK-5
525 Holley St 25177 304-727-5690
Erin Sikora, prin. Fax 727-5690

Saint Marys, Pleasants, Pop. 1,979
Pleasants County SD 1,400/PK-12
2272 N Pleasants Hwy 26170 304-684-2215
Dr. Joe Super, supt. Fax 684-3569
www.edline.net/pages/pleasantscountyschools

Saint Marys ES 300/PK-4
315 Washington St 26170 304-684-3510
Thomas Hardbarger, prin. Fax 684-3295
Other Schools – See Belmont

Salem, Harrison, Pop. 1,976
Harrison County SD
Supt. — See Clarksburg
Salem ES 300/PK-5
RR 1 Box 10A 26426 304-326-7180
Freda Perkins, prin. Fax 782-1293

Miracle Meadows S 50/K-12
RR 1 Box 289B 26426 304-782-3628
Carol Bearce, prin. Fax 782-3660

Salt Rock, Cabell
Cabell County SD
Supt. — See Huntington
Salt Rock ES 200/PK-5
5570 Madison Creek Rd 25559 304-733-3037
Lisa Alexander, prin. Fax 733-3060

Sand Fork, Gilmer, Pop. 171
Gilmer County SD
Supt. — See Glenville
Sand Fork ES 100/PK-6
PO Box 260 26430 304-462-7605
Fax 462-5368

Sandyville, Jackson
Jackson County SD
Supt. — See Ripley
Gilmore ES 200/PK-5
RR 3 Box 28A 25275 304-273-3511
Paulette Anderson, prin. Fax 273-9560

Scarbro, Fayette
Fayette County SD
Supt. — See Fayetteville
Scarbro ES 100/K-4
93 Hambrick Rd 25917 304-469-4511
Lee Jones, prin. Fax 469-4511

Scott Depot, Putnam
Putnam County SD
Supt. — See Winfield
Scott Teays ES 500/K-5
4308 Teays Valley Rd 25560 304-757-7279
Beth Pitzer, prin. Fax 757-4114

Teays Valley Christian S 300/K-12
4373 Teays Valley Rd 25560 304-757-9550
Jack Davis, prin. Fax 757-2560

Seth, Boone
Boone County SD
Supt. — See Madison
Sherman JHS 200/7-8
PO Box AA 25181 304-837-3694
Cheryl Workman, prin. Fax 837-7603

Shady Spring, Raleigh, Pop. 1,929
Raleigh County SD
Supt. — See Beckley
Shady Spring ES 500/PK-5
PO Box 2009 25918 304-256-4633
Donald Price, prin. Fax 256-4592
Shady Spring MS 600/6-8
500 Flat Top Rd 25918 304-256-4570
Gary Nichols, prin. Fax 256-4612

Shenandoah Junction, Jefferson
Jefferson County SD
Supt. — See Charles Town
Lowery ES 600/PK-5
103 Shenandoah Junction Rd 25442 304-728-7250
Kristen Martin, prin. Fax 728-7631
Wildwood MS 600/6-8
1209 Shenandoah Junction Rd 25442 304-728-1988
Paul Brown, prin. Fax 728-9521

Shepherdstown, Jefferson, Pop. 1,158
Jefferson County SD
Supt. — See Charles Town
Shepherdstown ES 300/K-5
662 S Church St 25443 304-876-6270
Suzanne Offutt, prin. Fax 876-6964
Shepherdstown MS 400/6-8
54 Minden St 25443 304-876-6120
Betsey Best, prin. Fax 876-6428

Shinnston, Harrison, Pop. 2,240
Harrison County SD
Supt. — See Clarksburg
Big Elm ES 700/PK-5
200 Tetrick St 26431 304-326-7280
Julie Mancini, prin. Fax 592-3255

Sissonville, Kanawha, Pop. 4,290
Kanawha County SD
Supt. — See Charleston
Sissonville ES 200/PK-5
8324 Sissonville Dr 25320 304-348-1961
David Agnew, prin. Fax 348-6147
Sissonville MS 500/6-8
8316 Old Mill Rd 25320 304-348-1993
Brian Eddy, prin. Fax 348-6594

Sistersville, Tyler, Pop. 1,512
Tyler County SD
Supt. — See Middlebourne
Sistersville ES 300/PK-5
651 Terrace Cir 26175 304-652-2601
Robin Daquilante, prin. Fax 652-2603
Tyler Consolidated MS 400/6-8
1993 Silver Knight Dr 26175 304-758-9000
Norris Stombock, prin. Fax 758-9006

Slanesville, Hampshire
Hampshire County SD
Supt. — See Romney
Slanesville ES 200/K-5
PO Box 230 25444 304-496-7069
Joyce Malcolm, prin. Fax 496-1139

Smithers, Fayette, Pop. 858
Fayette County SD
Supt. — See Fayetteville
Valley ES 300/K-4
PO Box 215 25186 304-442-2321
DeAnn Bennett, prin. Fax 442-2337

Smithville, Ritchie
Ritchie County SD
Supt. — See Harrisville
Smithville ES 100/PK-5
PO Box 30 26178 304-477-3273
Debbie White, prin. Fax 477-3118

Smoot, Greenbrier
Greenbrier County SD
Supt. — See Lewisburg
Smoot ES 200/PK-5
Smoot School Rd 24977 304-392-5295
James Varner, prin. Fax 392-2152

Sophia, Raleigh, Pop. 1,260
Raleigh County SD
Supt. — See Beckley
Independence MS 600/6-8
PO Box 1171 25921 304-683-4542
Terry Poe, prin. Fax 683-4552
Sophia/Soak Creek ES 300/K-5
PO Box 487 25921 304-683-5191
Lori Knight, prin. Fax 683-4541

South Charleston, Kanawha, Pop. 12,700
Kanawha County SD
Supt. — See Charleston
Alum Creek ES 200/PK-5
RR 7 Box 279A 25309 304-348-1935
Karen Scheer, prin. Fax 348-1936
Bridgeview ES 400/PK-5
5100 Ohio St 25309 304-766-0383
William Reynolds, prin. Fax 766-0388
Montrose ES 300/K-5
631 Montrose Dr 25303 304-348-1930
Julie Hedge, prin. Fax 347-7409
Richmond ES 300/PK-5
4620 Spring Hill Ave 25309 304-766-0357
Teresa Sauvageot, prin. Fax 766-0358
South Charleston MS 400/6-8
400 3rd Ave 25303 304-348-1918
Henry Graves, prin. Fax 744-4869

Spanishburg, Mercer
Mercer County SD
Supt. — See Princeton
Spanishburg S 300/PK-8
PO Box 7 25922 304-425-5854
Phoebe Meadows, prin. Fax 425-1229

Spencer, Roane, Pop. 2,258
Roane County SD 2,600/PK-12
PO Box 609 25276 304-927-6400
Stephen Goffreda, supt. Fax 927-6402
www.roanecountyschools.com/
Spencer ES 500/PK-4
85 Clay Rd 25276 304-927-6428
William Chapman, prin. Fax 927-6429
Spencer MS 400/5-8
102 Chapman Ave 25276 304-927-6415
Kevin Campbell, prin. Fax 927-6416
Other Schools – See Left Hand, Reedy, Walton

Springfield, Hampshire
Hampshire County SD
Supt. — See Romney
Springfield-Green Spring ES 100/K-5
PO Box 309 26763 304-822-4317
Amy Haines, prin. Fax 822-4317

Stonewood, Harrison, Pop. 1,859
Harrison County SD
Supt. — See Clarksburg
Norwood ES 300/PK-5
208 Kidd Ave 26301 304-326-7050
Benny Guido, prin. Fax 624-3286

Summersville, Nicholas, Pop. 3,369
Nicholas County SD 4,100/PK-12
400 Old Main Dr 26651 304-872-3611
Beverly Kingery, supt. Fax 872-4626
boe.nich.k12.wv.us
Glade Creek ES 100/K-5
7950 Webster Rd 26651 304-872-2882
Lydia Young, prin. Fax 872-2882
Summersville ES 300/PK-5
307 McKees Creek Rd 26651 304-872-1421
Cindy Vance, prin. Fax 872-1444
Summersville MS 600/6-8
40 Grizzley Ln 26651 304-872-5092
Freddy Amick, prin. Fax 872-6314
Zela ES 100/PK-5
165 Country Rd 26651 304-872-1481
John Miller, prin. Fax 872-1481
Other Schools – See Birch River, Craigsville, Dixie, Mount Lookout, Mount Nebo, Nettie, Richwood

---

New Life Christian Academy 200/PK-12
899 Broad St 26651 304-872-1148
Margaret Campbell, prin. Fax 872-7477
Summersville Adventist S 50/K-8
70 Friends R Fun Dr 26651 304-872-6958

Sundial, Raleigh
Raleigh County SD
Supt. — See Beckley
Marsh Fork ES 200/K-5
8801 Coal River Rd 25140 304-854-1951
Shannon Pioch, prin. Fax 854-1054

Sutton, Braxton, Pop. 993
Braxton County SD 2,400/PK-12
411 N Hill Rd 26601 304-765-7101
Carolyn Long, supt. Fax 765-7148
boe.brax.k12.wv.us/
Braxton County MS 700/5-8
100 Carter Braxton Dr 26601 304-765-2644
Denver Drake, prin. Fax 765-2696
Sutton ES 200/PK-4
288 N Hill Rd 26601 304-765-5202
Don Johnson, prin. Fax 765-5547
Other Schools – See Burnsville, Flatwoods, Frametown, Gassaway, Little Birch

Tad, Kanawha
Kanawha County SD
Supt. — See Charleston
Ingles ES 200/K-5
PO Box 367 25201 304-348-1975
Tracy George, prin. Fax 348-1976

Talcott, Summers
Summers County SD
Supt. — See Hinton
Talcott ES 200/PK-5
PO Box 140 24981 304-466-6029
Rhonda Shaver, prin. Fax 466-6004

Terra Alta, Preston, Pop. 1,496
Preston County SD
Supt. — See Kingwood
Terra Alta/East Preston S 400/K-8
1103 E State Ave 26764 304-789-2596
Jeannie Gren, prin. Fax 789-2596

Thomas, Tucker, Pop. 411
Tucker County SD
Supt. — See Parsons
Davis-Thomas S 200/PK-8
PO Box 250 26292 304-463-4422
Daryla Rapp, prin. Fax 463-4424

Tornado, Kanawha, Pop. 1,006
Kanawha County SD
Supt. — See Charleston
Andrews Heights ES 400/K-5
PO Box 340 25202 304-722-0232
Karen Wellman, prin. Fax 722-0233

Triadelphia, Ohio, Pop. 796
Ohio County SD
Supt. — See Wheeling
Middle Creek ES 300/K-5
579 Middle Creek Rd 26059 304-243-0369
James Tecca, prin. Fax 243-0371

Troy, Gilmer
Gilmer County SD
Supt. — See Glenville
Troy ES 100/PK-6
3093 WV Highway 47 W 26443 304-462-8655
David Bishop, prin. Fax 462-5132

Tunnelton, Preston, Pop. 346
Preston County SD
Supt. — See Kingwood
Fellowsville ES 100/K-5
RR 1 Box 265 26444 304-892-3866
Stanley Shaver, prin. Fax 892-3866
South Preston MS 200/6-8
PO Box 400 26444 304-568-2331
Darrell Martin, prin. Fax 568-2759
Tunnelton-Denver ES 200/K-5
RR 2 Box 118B 26444 304-568-2292
Randy Zinn, prin. Fax 568-2372

Uneeda, Boone
Boone County SD
Supt. — See Madison
Madison Elementary Pre K Center PK-PK
PO Box 730 25205 304-369-0558
Patricia Conaway, prin. Fax 369-0629

Union, Monroe, Pop. 550
Monroe County SD 2,000/PK-12
PO Box 330 24983 304-772-3094
Dr. Lyn Guy, supt. Fax 772-5020
www.monroecountyschoolswv.org
Mountain View S 600/K-8
PO Box 620 24983 304-772-4903
Ray Lee, prin. Fax 772-4907
Other Schools – See Peterstown

Valley Head, Randolph
Randolph County SD
Supt. — See Elkins
Valley Head ES 100/PK-5
Route 219 S 26294 304-339-4950
Diane Hull, prin. Fax 339-4474

Van, Boone
Boone County SD
Supt. — See Madison
Van ES 100/PK-5
PO Box 360 25206 304-245-8811
Kirk King, prin. Fax 245-8816

Verdunville, Logan
Logan County SD
Supt. — See Logan
Verdunville ES 200/PK-4
PO Box J 25649 304-752-1656
Barbara Porter, prin. Fax 752-2142

Vienna, Wood, Pop. 10,770
Wood County SD
Supt. — See Parkersburg
Greenmont ES 300/K-5
209 58th St 26105 304-420-9544
Brett Ubbons, prin. Fax 420-9543

Jackson JHS 400/6-8
1601 34th St 26105 304-420-9551
Richard Summers, prin. Fax 295-9954
Neale ES 400/K-5
2305 Grand Central Ave 26105 304-420-9587
Mike Fling, prin. Fax 420-9589
Vienna ES 300/PK-5
700 41st St 26105 304-420-9648
Julie Handley, prin. Fax 420-9693

Volga, Barbour
Barbour County SD
Supt. — See Philippi
Volga-Century ES 100/PK-5
RR 1 Box 12S 26238 304-457-3239
Laura Dick, prin. Fax 457-2604

Walton, Roane
Roane County SD
Supt. — See Spencer
Walton S 400/PK-8
90 School Dr 25286 304-577-6731
Jerry Garner, prin. Fax 577-6228

War, McDowell, Pop. 692
McDowell County SD
Supt. — See Welch
Southside S K-8
PO Box 730 24892 304-875-2283
Ann Handy, prin. Fax 875-2238

Waverly, Wood
Wood County SD
Supt. — See Parkersburg
Waverly ES 100/K-6
422 Virginia St 26184 304-464-4250
Kay Bowling, prin. Fax 464-4263

Wayne, Wayne, Pop. 1,154
Wayne County SD 7,700/PK-12
PO Box 70 25570 304-272-5116
Gary Adkins, supt. Fax 272-6500
boe.wayn.k12.wv.us/
Wayne ES 600/PK-5
PO Box 308 25570 304-272-3226
Deborah Russell, prin. Fax 272-9072
Wayne MS 500/6-8
200 Pioneer Rd 25570 304-272-3227
Loren Perry, prin. Fax 272-5811
Other Schools – See Ceredo, Crum, Dunlow, East Lynn, Fort Gay, Genoa, Huntington, Kenova, Lavalette, Prichard

Webster Springs, Webster, Pop. 836
Webster County SD 1,600/PK-12
315 S Main St 26288 304-847-5638
A.J. Rogers, supt. Fax 847-2538
boe.webs.k12.wv.us/
Webster Springs S 400/PK-8
318 River Dr 26288 304-847-5321
Geoffrey Ezell, prin. Fax 847-5364
Other Schools – See Cowen, Diana, Hacker Valley

Weirton, Hancock, Pop. 19,544
Brooke County SD
Supt. — See Wellsburg
Millsop PS 100/K-4
1401 Legion Rd 26062 304-748-7760
Joyce Vogler, prin. Fax 748-8470

Hancock County SD
Supt. — See New Cumberland
Broadview ES 200/K-4
189 Circle Dr 26062 304-723-2525
Dawn Petrovich, prin. Fax 723-1525
Liberty ES 200/K-4
200 Culler Rd 26062 304-723-2818
Stephanie Brown, prin. Fax 723-3810
Weir MS 700/5-8
125 Sinclair Ave 26062 304-748-6080
Dan Enich, prin. Fax 748-0847
Weirton Heights ES 400/PK-4
160 S 12th St 26062 304-748-1950
Frank Carey, prin. Fax 748-4102

St. Joseph the Worker S 200/PK-8
151 Michael Way 26062 304-723-1970
Alfred Boniti, prin. Fax 723-5122
St. Paul S 200/PK-8
140 Walnut St 26062 304-748-5225
James Lesho, prin. Fax 748-4163

Welch, McDowell, Pop. 2,371
McDowell County SD 3,200/PK-12
30 Central Ave 24801 304-436-8441
Suzette Cook, supt. Fax 436-4008
boe.mcdo.k12.wv.us
Mount View MS 300/7-8
960 Mount View Rd 24801 304-436-4657
Adam Grygiel, prin. Fax 436-3472
Welch ES 300/PK-5
1235 Stewart St 24801 304-436-4645
Sandra Murensky, prin. Fax 436-4049
Other Schools – See Anawalt, Avondale, Big Sandy, Iaeger, Kimball, War

Wellsburg, Brooke, Pop. 2,727
Brooke County SD 3,500/K-12
1201 Pleasant Ave 26070 304-737-3481
Mary Hervey DeGarmo, supt. Fax 737-3480
bhs.broo.k12.wv.us/BOE4/
Franklin PS 200/K-4
1305 Washington Pike 26070 304-737-1760
Scott Donohew, prin. Fax 737-1760
Wellsburg MS 500/5-8
1447 Main St 26070 304-737-2922
Diane Higgins, prin. Fax 737-2976
Wellsburg PS 200/K-4
1448 Main St 26070 304-737-0133
Mark Rihel, prin. Fax 737-0463
Other Schools – See Beech Bottom, Colliers, Follansbee, Weirton

---

St. John S 50/PK-4
1340 Charles St 26070 304-737-0511
Cindy McDaniel, prin. Fax 737-0988

West Hamlin, Lincoln, Pop. 687
Lincoln County SD
Supt. — See Hamlin
West Hamlin ES 500/PK-5
RR 2 Box 112 25571 304-824-3630
Kirk King, prin. Fax 824-3630

West Milford, Harrison, Pop. 646
Harrison County SD
Supt. — See Clarksburg
West Milford ES 500/PK-5
226 School St 26451 304-326-7030
Wendy Imperial, prin. Fax 745-4488

Weston, Lewis, Pop. 4,241
Lewis County SD 2,700/PK-12
239 Court Ave 26452 304-269-8300
Dr. Joseph Mace, supt. Fax 269-8305
www.edline.net/pages/Lewis_County_School_District
Bland MS 800/5-8
358 Court Ave 26452 304-269-8325
Grace Talhammer, prin. Fax 269-8310
Peterson Central ES 400/PK-4
509 Berlin Rd 26452 304-269-8330
Steven W. Hall, prin. Fax 269-8351
Other Schools – See Alum Bridge, Jane Lew, Roanoke

St. Patrick S 100/PK-6
224 Center Ave 26452 304-269-5547
Paul Derico, prin. Fax 269-5547

West Union, Doddridge, Pop. 808
Doddridge County SD 1,200/PK-12
103 Sistersville Pike 26456 304-873-2300
Janice Michels, supt. Fax 873-2210
Doddridge County ES 500/PK-4
RR 2 Box 35D 26456 304-873-3294
Gregory Kuhns, prin. Fax 873-3297
Doddridge County MS 400/5-8
RR 2 Box 35C 26456 304-873-2390
Deborah Kuhns, prin. Fax 873-2541

Wharton, Boone
Boone County SD
Supt. — See Madison
Wharton ES 100/PK-5
PO Box 60 25208 304-247-6672
David Startzel, prin. Fax 247-6676

Wheeling, Ohio, Pop. 29,639
Marshall County SD
Supt. — See Moundsville
Hilltop ES, 1 Ram Dr 26003 K-5
Jane Duffy, prin. 304-232-8640
Sherrard MS 300/6-8
1000 Fairmont Pike 26003 304-233-3331
Joyce Cole, prin. Fax 233-6418

Ohio County SD 5,300/K-12
2203 National Rd 26003 304-243-0300
George Krelis, supt. Fax 243-0328
wphs.ohio.k12.wv.us/ocbe/
Bethlehem ES 100/K-5
22 Chapel Rd 26003 304-243-0350
Michelle Snyder, prin. Fax 243-0351
Bridge Street MS 300/6-8
19 Junior Ave 26003 304-243-0381
Amy Minch, prin. Fax 243-0385
Elm Grove ES 300/K-5
RR 2 Box 444 26003 304-243-0363
Richard Dunlevy, prin. Fax 243-0364
Madison ES 200/K-5
91 Zane St 26003 304-243-0366
Nicolette Kacmarik, prin. Fax 243-0457
Ritchie ES 300/K-5
3700 Wood St 26003 304-243-0372
John Jorden, prin. Fax 243-0373
Steenrod ES 300/K-5
100 Clarks Ln 26003 304-243-0354
Daniel Coram, prin. Fax 243-0357
Triadelphia MS 400/6-8
1636 National Rd 26003 304-243-0387
Walter Saunders, prin. Fax 243-0392

Warwood S 500/K-8
150 Viking Dr 26003 304-243-0394
Andy Garber, prin. Fax 243-0395
West Liberty ES 100/K-5
745 Van Meter Way 26003 304-336-7221
Michelle Snyder, prin. Fax 336-7222
Wheeling MS 200/6-8
3500 Chapline St 26003 304-243-0425
Patrick Riddle, prin. Fax 243-0426
Woodsdale ES 300/K-5
1 Bethany Pike 26003 304-243-0378
Mary Kay Reisinger, prin. Fax 243-0379
Other Schools – See Triadelphia

Corpus Christi S 200/PK-8
1512 Warwood Ave 26003 304-277-1220
Dick Taylor, prin. Fax 277-2823
Our Lady of Peace S 200/PK-8
640 Old Fairmont Pike 26003 304-242-1383
C'Ann Reilly, prin. Fax 243-5410
St. Michael S 400/PK-8
1221 National Rd 26003 304-242-3966
Marilyn Richardson, prin. Fax 214-6578
St. Vincent de Paul S 200/PK-8
127 Key Ave 26003 304-242-5844
Arica Holt, prin. Fax 243-1624
Speiro Academy 50/K-12
135 Stewarts Hill Rd 26003 304-243-0001
Susan Olinda Cline, prin. Fax 845-4047
Wheeling Catholic S 100/PK-8
77 14th St 26003 304-233-1515
Dr. Judith Stechly, prin. Fax 233-1516
Wheeling Country Day S 100/PK-5
8 Park Rd 26003 304-232-2430
Patricia Pockl, hdmstr. Fax 232-2434

White Sulphur Springs, Greenbrier, Pop. 2,352
Greenbrier County SD
Supt. — See Lewisburg
White Sulphur Springs ES 400/PK-5
150 Reed St 24986 304-536-2244
Ann Smith, prin. Fax 536-1930

Greenbrier Episcopal S 100/PK-12
10 Dry Creek Rd 24986 304-536-3636
Andrew Smith, prin. Fax 536-2900

Whitesville, Boone, Pop. 516
Boone County SD
Supt. — See Madison
Whitesville ES 100/PK-6
37949 Coal River Rd 25209 304-854-1301
Christopher Duncan, prin. Fax 854-1301

Wiley Ford, Mineral
Mineral County SD
Supt. — See Keyser
Wiley Ford PS 200/PK-2
PO Box 20 26767 304-738-0400
Paula Athey, prin. Fax 738-3633

Williamson, Mingo, Pop. 3,181
Mingo County SD 4,400/PK-12
RR 2 Box 310 25661 304-235-3333
Dwight Dials, supt. Fax 235-3410
mingoboe.us/
Riverside ES 300/PK-4
5 Parkway Dr 25661 304-235-2521
Cindy Caffee, prin. Fax 235-2520
Williamson MS 200/5-8
801 Alderson St 25661 304-235-3430
Helen Curry, prin. Fax 235-5567
Other Schools – See Delbarton, Dingess, Gilbert, Kermit, Lenore, Matewan

---

Sacred Heart S 50/PK-6
126 W 4th Ave 25661 304-235-3027
Sr. Lillian Jordan, prin. Fax 235-3027
Williamson Christian S 50/PK-7
PO Box 901 25661 304-235-3700
Christopher Blevins, admin. Fax 235-3949

Williamstown, Wood, Pop. 2,955
Wood County SD
Supt. — See Parkersburg
Williamstown ES 500/K-6
418 Williams Ave 26187 304-375-7675
Keith Enoch, prin. Fax 375-4894

Winfield, Putnam, Pop. 2,011
Putnam County SD 9,100/PK-12
9 Courthouse Dr 25213 304-757-5667
Harold Hatfiled, supt. Fax 757-5664
www.putnamschools.com
Eastbrook ES 300/K-5
1600 Bills Creek Rd 25213 304-755-9835
Gary Hoffman, prin. Fax 755-0012
Winfield ES 500/PK-5
2 Wall St 25213 304-586-2565
Rebecca Meadows, prin. Fax 586-5351
Winfield MS 600/6-8
3280 Winfield Rd 25213 304-586-3072
Clarence Woodworth, prin. Fax 586-0920
Other Schools – See Buffalo, Eleanor, Hometown, Hurricane, Nitro, Poca, Red House, Scott Depot

WISCONSIN

WISCONSIN DEPARTMENT PUBLIC INSTRUCTION
PO Box 7841, Madison 53707-7841
Telephone 608-266-3390
Fax 608-267-1052
Website http://www.dpi.state.wi.us

Superintendent of Public Instruction Tony Evers

COOPERATIVE EDUCATIONAL SERVICE AGENCIES (CESA)

CESA 1
Timothy Gavigan, admin. 262-787-9500
19601 W Bluemound Rd Fax 787-9501
Brookfield 53045
www.cesa1.k12.wi.us

CESA 2
Gary Albrecht, admin. 608-758-6232
448 E High St, Milton 53563 Fax 868-4864
www.cesa2.k12.wi.us

CESA 3
Nancy Hendrickson, admin. 608-822-3276
1300 Industrial Dr Fax 822-3760
Fennimore 53809
www.cesa3.k12.wi.us

CESA 4
Guy Leavitt, admin. 608-786-4800
923 E Garland St Fax 786-4801
West Salem 54669
www.cesa4.k12.wi.us

CESA 5
Wayne Moll, admin. 608-742-8811
PO Box 564, Portage 53901 Fax 742-2384
www.cesa5.k12.wi.us

CESA 6
Joan Wade, admin. 920-233-2372
PO Box 2568, Oshkosh 54903 Fax 424-3478
www.cesa6.k12.wi.us

CESA 7
Jeffery Dickert, admin. 920-492-5960
595 Baeten Rd, Green Bay 54304 Fax 492-5965
www.cesa7.k12.wi.us

CESA 8
Bob Kellogg, admin. 920-855-2114
PO Box 320, Gillett 54124 Fax 855-2299
www.cesa8.k12.wi.us

CESA 9
Jerome Fiene, admin. 715-453-2141
PO Box 449, Tomahawk 54487 Fax 453-7519
www.cesa9.k12.wi.us

CESA 10
Larry D. Annett, admin. 715-723-0341
725 W Park Ave Fax 720-2070
Chippewa Falls 54729
www.cesa10.k12.wi.us

CESA 11
Jesse Harness, admin. 715-986-2020
225 Ostermann Dr Fax 986-2040
Turtle Lake 54889
www.cesa11.k12.wi.us

CESA 12
Kenneth Kasinski, admin. 715-682-2363
618 Beaser Ave, Ashland 54806 Fax 682-7244
www.cesa12.k12.wi.us

PUBLIC, PRIVATE AND CATHOLIC ELEMENTARY SCHOOLS

Abbotsford, Clark, Pop. 1,901
Abbotsford SD 600/PK-12
PO Box 70 54405 715-223-6715
Reed Welsh, supt. Fax 223-4239
www.abbotsford.k12.wi.us
Abbotsford ES 300/PK-5
PO Box A 54405 715-223-4281
Gary Gunderson, prin. Fax 223-0691

Abrams, Oconto
Oconto Falls SD
Supt. — See Oconto Falls
Abrams ES 300/PK-5
3000 Elm St 54101 920-826-5819
George Georgia, prin. Fax 826-7858

Adams, Adams, Pop. 1,781
Adams-Friendship Area SD
Supt. — See Friendship
Adams-Friendship ES 400/PK-5
500 N Pierce St 53910 608-339-3016
Charlotte Preiss, prin. Fax 339-0416
Adams-Friendship MS 400/6-8
420 N Main St 53910 608-339-4064
Garret Gould, prin. Fax 339-2434

Albany, Green, Pop. 1,133
Albany SD 400/PK-12
PO Box 349 53502 608-862-3225
Stephen Guenther, supt. Fax 862-3230
www.albany.k12.wi.us
Albany ES 200/PK-5
PO Box 349 53502 608-862-3225
Stephen Guenther, prin. Fax 862-3230
Albany MS 100/6-8
PO Box 349 53502 608-862-3135
Traci Davis, prin. Fax 862-3230

Algoma, Kewaunee, Pop. 3,197
Algoma SD 200/PK-12
1715 Division St 54201 920-487-7001
Ronald Welch, supt. Fax 487-7016
www.alghs.k12.wi.us
Algoma S 200/PK-12
514 Fremont St 54201 920-487-7010
William Bush, prin. Fax 487-7015

St. Mary S 100/PK-8
214 Church St 54201 920-487-5004
Laura Krzysiak, prin. Fax 487-5002
St. Paul Lutheran S 100/K-8
1115 Division St 54201 920-487-5712
Brian Miller, prin. Fax 487-9733

Allenton, Washington
Slinger SD
Supt. — See Slinger
Allenton ES 400/PK-5
228 Weis St 53002 262-629-5546
Christopher Holt, prin. Fax 629-1821

Alma, Buffalo, Pop. 899
Alma SD 300/PK-12
S1618 State Road 35 54610 608-685-4416
Steven Sedlmayr, supt. Fax 685-4446
www.alma.k12.wi.us
Alma S 200/PK-8
S1618 State Road 35 54610 608-685-4416
Jane Bremer, prin. Fax 685-4446

Alma Center, Jackson, Pop. 449
Alma Center-Humbird-Merrillan SD 600/PK-12
PO Box 308 54611 715-964-8271
William VanMeer, supt. Fax 964-1005
www.achm.k12.wi.us
Lincoln JHS 100/7-8
PO Box 308 54611 715-964-5311
Jeffrey Arzt, prin. Fax 964-1005
Other Schools – See Merrillan

Almond, Portage, Pop. 431
Almond-Bancroft SD 300/PK-12
1336 Elm St 54909 715-366-2941
Dann Boxx, admin. Fax 366-2940
www.abschools.k12.wi.us
Almond-Bancroft S 300/PK-12
1336 Elm St 54909 715-366-2941
Jeff Rykal, prin. Fax 366-2943

Altoona, Eau Claire, Pop. 6,448
Altoona SD 1,500/PK-12
1903 Bartlett Ave 54720 715-839-6032
Gregory Fahrman, supt. Fax 839-6066
www.altoona.k12.wi.us
Altoona MS 400/5-8
1903 Bartlett Ave 54720 715-839-6030
Jack Wagener, prin. Fax 839-6099
Pedersen ES 600/PK-4
1827 Bartlett Ave 54720 715-839-6050
Chelsea Engen, prin. Fax 839-6166

Otter Creek Christian Academy 50/1-10
919 10th St W 54720 715-834-1782
Richard Bauer, prin.
St. Mary S 100/PK-6
1828 Lynn Ave 54720 715-830-2278
Fax 830-9573

Amery, Polk, Pop. 2,868
Amery SD 1,800/PK-12
543 Minneapolis Ave S 54001 715-268-9771
Stephen Schiell, supt. Fax 268-7300
www.amerysd.k12.wi.us
Amery IS 400/3-5
543 Minneapolis Ave S 54001 715-268-9771
Oralee Schock, prin. Fax 268-5612
Amery MS 400/6-8
501 Minneapolis Ave S 54001 715-268-9771
Thomas Bensen, prin. Fax 268-4967
Lien ES 400/PK-2
469 Minneapolis Ave S 54001 715-268-9771
Cheryl Meyer, prin. Fax 268-5633

Amherst, Portage, Pop. 973
Tomorrow River SD 900/PK-12
357 N Main St 54406 715-824-5521
LeAnn Chase, supt. Fax 824-7177
www.amherst.k12.wi.us
Amherst ES 400/PK-5
357 N Main St 54406 715-824-5523
Michael Toelle, prin. Fax 824-5474
Amherst MS 200/6-8
357 N Main St 54406 715-824-5524
Michael Toelle, prin. Fax 824-5454

Antigo, Langlade, Pop. 8,282
Antigo SD 2,600/PK-12
120 S Dorr St 54409 715-627-4355
Roxann Bornemann, supt. Fax 623-3279
www.antigo.k12.wi.us/
Antigo MS 600/6-8
815 7th Ave 54409 715-623-4173
Douglas Knol, prin. Fax 627-4982
Crestwood ES 100/K-5
W8464 County Road AA 54409 715-623-6557
Sharon Kind, prin. Fax 627-0805
East ES 100/PK-5
220 7th Ave 54409 715-623-2506
Sharon Kind, prin. Fax 623-3948
North ES 200/K-5
506 Graham Ave 54409 715-623-3515
Ryan Hammerschmidt, prin. Fax 627-2612
Pleasant View ES 100/K-5
W11141 County Road HH 54409 715-627-7700
John Lund, prin. Fax 627-0457
Spring Valley ES 100/K-5
N4754 County Road BB 54409 715-623-6900
Ryan Hammerschmidt, prin. Fax 627-0460
West ES 200/K-5
1232 7th Ave 54409 715-623-2508
John Lund, prin. Fax 627-0906
Other Schools – See Mattoon

All Saints S 200/PK-8
419 6th Ave 54409 715-623-4835
John Reetz, prin. Fax 627-2969
Peace Lutheran S 100/PK-8
300 Lincoln St 54409 715-623-2209
David Selmeyer, prin. Fax 627-4117

Appleton, Outagamie, Pop. 70,217
Appleton Area SD 13,300/PK-12
PO Box 2019 54912 920-832-6161
Lee Allinger, supt. Fax 832-1725
www.aasd.k12.wi.us
Badger ES 300/K-6
501 S Bluemound Dr 54914 920-832-6264
William McClone, prin. Fax 832-6149
Berry ES 500/K-6
3601 S Telulah Ave 54915 920-832-5750
Rick Waters, prin. Fax 832-2986
Columbus ES 200/K-6
913 N Oneida St 54911 920-832-6232
Jennifer Dordel, prin. Fax 832-6355
Edison ES 300/PK-6
412 N Meade St 54911 920-832-6235
James Donnellan, prin. Fax 993-7033
Einstein MS 400/7-8
324 E Florida Ave 54911 920-832-6240
Dave Boden, prin. Fax 832-6164
Ferber ES 700/PK-6
515 E Capitol Dr 54911 920-832-5755
Paul Cooney, prin. Fax 993-7069
Franklin ES 400/K-6
2212 N Jarchow St 54911 920-832-6246
Carrie Willer, prin. Fax 832-4464
Highlands ES 500/PK-6
2037 N Elinor St 54914 920-832-6250
Val Dreier, prin. Fax 832-4389
Horizons ES 400/K-6
2101 Schaefer Cir 54915 920-832-4600
Karen Brice, prin. Fax 832-1592

Houdini ES 600/PK-6
2305 W Capitol Dr 54914 920-832-4608
Jan Haven, prin. Fax 993-7078
Huntley ES 600/K-6
2224 N Ullman St 54911 920-832-6255
Thomas Kubisch, prin. Fax 832-6118
Jefferson ES 400/PK-6
1000 S Mason St 54914 920-832-6260
Tiffany Frerks, prin. Fax 993-7060
Johnston ES 500/PK-6
2725 E Forest St 54915 920-832-6265
Dominick Ferrito, prin. Fax 832-6199
Lincoln ES 300/PK-6
1000 N Mason St 54914 920-832-6270
Sheree Garvey, prin. Fax 832-6348
Madison MS 700/7-8
2020 S Carpenter St 54915 920-832-6276
Dave Hash, prin. Fax 832-6337
McKinley ES 500/PK-6
1125 E Taft Ave 54915 920-832-6285
Gary Mulry, prin. Fax 832-6326
Richmond ES 300/K-6
1441 E John St 54915 920-832-5779
Roberta Schmidt, prin. Fax 993-7044
Roosevelt MS 400/7-8
318 E Brewster St 54911 920-832-6294
Al Brant, prin. Fax 832-4605
Wilson MS 500/7-8
225 N Badger Ave 54914 920-832-6226
John Magas, prin. Fax 832-4857

Kimberly Area SD
Supt. — See Kimberly
Sunrise ES 500/PK-4
N9363 Exploration Ave 54915 920-954-1822
John Schultz, prin. Fax 954-5945
Woodland ES PK-4
N9085 N Coop Rd 54915 920-730-0924
Sean Fitzgerald, prin. Fax 423-4177
Woodland IS 5-6
N9085 N Coop Rd 54915 920-730-0924
Craig Miller, prin. Fax 423-4177

Appleton Catholic Central S 200/PK-5
313 S State St 54911 920-733-3709
Jeffrey Staddler, prin. Fax 733-8142
Celebration Lutheran S 100/PK-8
3100 E Evergreen Dr 54913 920-734-8218
Joan Klaas, admin. Fax 734-7890
Holy Spirit S 300/PK-8
W2796 County Road KK 54915 920-733-2651
Sue Simonsen, prin. Fax 733-5440
Mt. Olive Evangelical Lutheran S 200/PK-8
930 E Florida Ave 54911 920-739-9194
Douglas Enter, prin. Fax 739-9423
Riverview Lutheran S 100/K-8
136 W Seymour St 54915 920-733-3728
Ethan Hutchinson, prin. Fax 733-3728
St. Bernadette S 200/PK-5
2331 E Lourdes Dr 54915 920-739-5391
Elizabeth Watson, prin. Fax 739-0061
St. Edward S 50/K-5
N2944 State Road 47 54913 920-733-6276
Becky Morrin, prin. Fax 733-1005
St. Joseph MS 400/6-8
2626 N Oneida St 54911 920-730-8849
Brad Norcross, prin. Fax 730-4147
St. Paul Lutheran S 200/PK-8
225 E Harris St 54911 920-733-9061
Charles Sonnenburg, prin. Fax 733-4200
St. Peter Lutheran S 100/PK-8
N2740 French Rd 54913 920-739-2009
Philip Punzel, prin. Fax 739-3615
St. Pius X S 300/PK-5
500 W Marquette St 54911 920-733-4918
Sr. Carol Jean Peterson, prin. Fax 733-7269
St. Thomas More S 200/PK-5
1810 N Mcdonald St 54911 920-739-7826
David Callan, prin. Fax 739-1787

Arcadia, Trempealeau, Pop. 2,348
Arcadia SD 1,000/PK-12
756 Raider Dr 54612 608-323-3315
Lawrence Ferguson, supt. Fax 323-2256
www.arcadia.k12.wi.us/
Arcadia S 700/PK-8
358 E River St 54612 608-323-7500
Richard Hanson, prin. Fax 323-7015

Holy Family Catholic S 100/PK-8
341 Washington St 54612 608-323-3676
Maureen Munn, prin. Fax 323-7386

Arena, Iowa, Pop. 788
River Valley SD
Supt. — See Spring Green
Arena ES 100/K-5
314 Willow St 53503 608-753-2361
James Radtke, prin. Fax 753-2519

Argyle, Lafayette, Pop. 784
Argyle SD 300/PK-12
PO Box 256 53504 608-543-3318
Robert Gilpatrick, supt. Fax 543-3868
www.argyle.k12.wi.us
Argyle ES 200/PK-5
PO Box 256 53504 608-543-3318
Janet West, prin. Fax 543-3868

Arkansaw, Pepin
Durand SD
Supt. — See Durand
Arkansaw ES 200/1-6
N6290 N H St 54721 715-285-5315
Jan Lund, prin. Fax 285-5684

Arkdale, Adams
Adams-Friendship Area SD
Supt. — See Friendship

Roche A Cri ES 100/PK-5
1501 18th Ave 54613 608-564-7919
Barbara Albrecht, prin. Fax 564-7714

Arlington, Columbia, Pop. 608
Poynette SD
Supt. — See Poynette
Arlington ES 100/K-3
PO Box 50 53911 608-635-4760
Brian Sutton, prin. Fax 635-9470

Arpin, Wood, Pop. 320

Bethel Jr. Academy 50/1-8
8054 Bethel Rd 54410 715-652-2763
Holly Roy, prin.

Ashland, Ashland, Pop. 8,306
Ashland SD 2,200/PK-12
2000 Beaser Ave 54806 715-682-7080
Peggy Smith, supt. Fax 682-7097
www.ashland.k12.wi.us
Ashland MS 500/6-8
203 11th St E 54806 715-682-7087
Brian Anderson, prin. Fax 682-7944
Lake Superior IS 400/3-5
1101 Binsfield Rd 54806 715-682-7083
John Esposito, prin. Fax 682-7506
Lake Superior PS 400/PK-2
1101 Binsfield Rd 54806 715-682-7085
Chris Graff, prin. Fax 682-7946
Marengo Valley ES 200/K-5
62408 State Highway 112 54806 715-278-3286
John Esposito, prin. Fax 278-3586

Our Lady of the Lake S 100/PK-8
215 Lake Shore Dr E 54806 715-682-7622
Dan Bell, prin. Fax 682-7626

Athens, Marathon, Pop. 1,045
Athens SD 500/PK-12
PO Box F 54411 715-257-7511
Frank Harrington, supt. Fax 257-7502
www.athens.k12.wi.us
Athens ES 200/PK-5
PO Box 190 54411 715-257-7571
Dan Shumway, prin. Fax 257-9026
Athens MS 100/6-8
PO Box F 54411 715-257-7511
Timothy Micke, prin. Fax 257-7651

St. Anthony S 100/K-8
PO Box 1 54411 715-257-7541
Lucy McCarthy, prin. Fax 257-7541
Trinity Lutheran S 100/PK-8
PO Box 100 54411 715-257-7559
Dean Frick, prin. Fax 257-7559

Auburndale, Wood, Pop. 728
Auburndale SD 800/PK-12
PO Box 139 54412 715-652-2117
Gerald Eichman, supt. Fax 652-2836
www.aubschools.com
Auburndale ES 400/PK-5
PO Box 138 54412 715-652-2812
Andrew Place, prin. Fax 652-2836

Augusta, Eau Claire, Pop. 1,370
Augusta SD 400/PK-12
E19320 Bartig Rd 54722 715-286-3300
Stephen LaFave, supt. Fax 286-3336
www.augusta.k12.wi.us
Augusta ES 300/PK-5
E19320 Bartig Rd 54722 715-286-3303
Jane Kangas, prin. Fax 286-3335

Baldwin, Saint Croix, Pop. 3,509
Baldwin-Woodville Area SD 1,500/PK-12
550 US Highway 12 54002 715-684-3411
Russell Helland, supt. Fax 684-3168
www.bwsd.k12.wi.us/
Greenfield ES 600/PK-4
1160 14th Ave 54002 715-684-3334
Gary Hoffman, prin. Fax 684-5109
Other Schools – See Woodville

Baldwin Christian S 100/PK-8
896 US Highway 63 54002 715-684-2656
Kurt Swanson, pres.

Balsam Lake, Polk, Pop. 1,026
Unity SD 1,000/PK-12
PO Box 307 54810 715-825-3515
Brandon Robinson, supt. Fax 825-3517
www.unity.k12.wi.us/
Unity ES 400/PK-4
PO Box 307 54810 715-825-2101
Wayne Whitwam, prin. Fax 825-4034
Unity MS 300/5-8
PO Box 307 54810 715-825-2101
Elizabeth Jorgensen, prin. Fax 825-4410

Bangor, LaCrosse, Pop. 1,375
Bangor SD 600/K-12
PO Box 99 54614 608-486-2331
Roger Foegen, supt. Fax 486-4587
www.bangor.k12.wi.us
Bangor ES 200/K-5
PO Box 99 54614 608-486-2331
Lois Meinking, prin. Fax 486-4045

St. Paul's Evangelical Lutheran S 100/K-8
PO Box 257 54614 608-486-2641
Timothy Payne, prin. Fax 486-2394

Baraboo, Sauk, Pop. 10,927
Baraboo SD 3,000/PK-12
101 2nd Ave 53913 608-355-3950
Crystal Ritzenthaler Ed.D., supt. Fax 355-3960
www.baraboo.k12.wi.us
East ES 400/PK-5
815 6th St 53913 608-355-3920
Glenn Bildsten, prin. Fax 355-4677
South ES 300/PK-5
400 Mulberry St 53913 608-355-3910
Julie Cushman, prin. Fax 355-3971
West K 100/PK-K
707 Center St 53913 608-355-3905
James Ruder, prin. Fax 355-4679
Young MS 700/6-8
1531 Draper St 53913 608-355-3930
Scott Miller, prin. Fax 355-3998
Other Schools – See North Freedom, West Baraboo

St. John Lutheran S 200/K-8
515 5th St 53913 608-355-3860
John Hartwig, prin. Fax 355-3861
St. Joseph S 100/PK-5
310 2nd St 53913 608-356-3083
Timothy Lowe, prin. Fax 356-4024

Barneveld, Iowa, Pop. 1,148
Barneveld SD 400/K-12
PO Box 98 53507 608-924-4711
Joe Bertone, supt. Fax 924-1646
www.barneveld.k12.wi.us
Barneveld ES 200/K-5
PO Box 98 53507 608-924-4711
Kevin Knudson, prin. Fax 924-1646

Barron, Barron, Pop. 3,151
Barron Area SD 1,200/PK-12
100 W River Ave 54812 715-537-5612
Monti Hallberg, supt. Fax 637-5161
www.barron.k12.wi.us/
Almena ES 100/PK-3
100 W River Ave 54812 715-357-3263
Susan Wohlk, prin. Fax 357-6513
Riverview MS 300/5-8
135 W River Ave 54812 715-537-5641
Lance Northey, prin. Fax 637-5373
Woodland ES 300/PK-4
808 E Woodland Ave 54812 715-537-5621
Stephen Sprinkel, prin. Fax 637-9353
Other Schools – See Ridgeland

Bayfield, Bayfield, Pop. 602
Bayfield SD 400/PK-12
PO Box 5001 54814 715-779-3201
Linda Kunelius, supt. Fax 779-5268
www.bayfield.k12.wi.us
Bayfield ES 200/PK-5
PO Box 5001 54814 715-779-3201
Sheila Everhart, prin. Fax 779-5226
Bayfield MS 100/6-8
PO Box 5001 54814 715-779-3201
Sheila Everhart, prin. Fax 779-5226
La Pointe ES 50/K-6
300 N 4th St 54814 715-747-3605
Sheila Everhart, prin. Fax 779-5226

Beaver Dam, Dodge, Pop. 15,153
Beaver Dam SD 3,200/K-12
705 McKinley St 53916 920-885-7300
Donald Childs, supt. Fax 885-7305
www.beaverdam.k12.wi.us
Beaver Dam MS 700/6-8
108 4th St 53916 920-885-7365
Ben Jones, prin. Fax 885-7415
Jefferson ES 300/K-5
301 Brook St 53916 920-885-7392
Barbara Link, prin. Fax 885-7395
Lincoln ES 300/K-5
210 Gould St 53916 920-885-7396
Tanya Gubin, prin. Fax 885-7399
Prairie View ES 200/K-5
510 N Crystal Lake Rd 53916 920-885-7380
Jeff Rehberg, prin. Fax 885-7381
South Beaver Dam ES 100/K-5
W9787 County Road D 53916 920-885-7383
Kathy Lehman, prin. Fax 885-7384
Trenton ES 100/1-5
N8954 County Rd W 53916 920-885-7385
Sharon Bliefernicht, prin. Fax 885-7386
Washington ES 300/K-5
600 Grove St 53916 920-885-7376
Martha Hyke, prin. Fax 885-7379
Wilson ES 100/K-5
405 W 3rd St 53916 920-885-7373
Laura Maron, prin. Fax 885-7375

St. Katharine Drexel S 300/PK-8
503 S Spring St 53916 920-885-5558
Barbara Haase, prin. Fax 885-7610
St. Stephen Lutheran S 200/K-8
412 W Maple Ave 53916 920-885-6484
Roger Fenner, prin. Fax 885-3106

Belgium, Ozaukee, Pop. 2,008

St. Mary S 50/PK-5
675 County Road D 53004 262-285-3532
Joanne Karpin, prin. Fax 285-3532

Belleville, Dane, Pop. 2,114
Belleville SD 900/PK-12
PO Box 230 53508 608-424-3315
Dr. Randy Freese, supt. Fax 424-3486
www.belleville.k12.wi.us/
Belleville ES 200/PK-1
PO Box 230 53508 608-424-3337
Sally Baxter, prin. Fax 424-1687
Belleville IS 300/2-6
PO Box 230 53508 608-424-3371
Sally Baxter, prin. Fax 424-1409
Belleville MS 100/7-8
PO Box 230 53508 608-424-1902
Rick Conroy, prin. Fax 424-3692

Belmont, Lafayette, Pop. 894
Belmont Community SD 300/K-12
PO Box 348 53510 608-762-5131
Jim Siedenburg, supt. Fax 762-5129
www.belmont.k12.wi.us
Belmont ES 100/K-6
PO Box 348 53510 608-762-5131
Christy Larson, prin. Fax 762-5129

Beloit, Rock, Pop. 35,621
Beloit SD 7,000/PK-12
1633 Keeler Ave 53511 608-361-4000
Milt Thompson, supt. Fax 361-4122
www.sdb.k12.wi.us
Aldrich MS 700/6-8
1859 Northgate Dr 53511 608-361-3605
Walter James, prin. Fax 361-3620
Burdge ES 200/PK-5
321 Olympian Blvd 53511 608-361-2005
Deb Prosser, prin. Fax 361-2020
Converse ES 300/K-5
1602 Townline Ave 53511 608-361-2105
Stephanie Jacobs, prin. Fax 361-2120
Cunningham ES 300/PK-5
910 Townline Ave 53511 608-361-2205
Robert Pickett, prin. Fax 361-2220
Gaston ES 300/K-5
610 McKinley Ave 53511 608-361-2305
Melody Wirgau, prin. Fax 361-2320
Hackett ES 400/PK-5
533 W Grand Ave 53511 608-361-2405
Tom Hohnson, prin. Fax 361-2420
McLenegan ES 200/K-5
2639 Sunshine Ln 53511 608-361-2505
Carole Campbell, prin. Fax 363-7298
McNeel MS 800/6-8
1524 Frederick St 53511 608-361-3800
Anthony Bosco, prin. Fax 361-3820
Merrill ES 300/PK-5
1333 Copeland Ave 53511 608-361-2605
Brenda Atlas, prin. Fax 361-2620
Morgan ES 300/K-5
1811 Lee Ln 53511 608-361-2705
Tina Sciacca-Hansen, prin. Fax 361-2720
Robinson ES 300/K-5
1801 Cranston Rd 53511 608-361-2805
Sam Carter, prin. Fax 361-2820
Royce ES 300/K-5
825 Liberty Ave 53511 608-361-2905
Grace Okoli, prin. Fax 361-2920
Todd ES 300/K-5
1621 Oakwood Ave 53511 608-361-4205
Sonja Christensen, prin. Fax 364-3933
Wright ES 200/PK-5
1033 Woodward Ave 53511 608-361-4305
Sue Anne Green, prin. Fax 361-4320

Beloit Turner SD 1,300/PK-12
1237 E Inman Pkwy 53511 608-364-6372
Dennis McCarthy, supt. Fax 364-6373
www.fjturner.k12.wi.us
Powers ES 300/PK-2
620 Hillside Ave 53511 608-364-6360
Sue Brandenburg, prin. Fax 364-6362
Townview ES 300/3-5
2442 W Beloit Newark Rd 53511 608-364-6365
Karen Neas, prin. Fax 365-7549
Turner MS 300/6-8
1237 E Inman Pkwy 53511 608-364-6367
Randall McClellan, prin. Fax 364-6369

Parkview SD
Supt. — See Orfordville
Newark ES 100/K-4
11247 S Merlet Rd 53511 608-365-6156
Mark Miller, prin. Fax 365-9330

Brother Dutton S 100/PK-8
717 Hackett St 53511 608-364-2825
Edward O'Brien, prin. Fax 364-2827
Our Lady of Assumption S 200/PK-8
2222 Shopiere Rd 53511 608-365-4014
Arlene McMorran, prin. Fax 368-2832
St. John Lutheran S 50/PK-8
1000 Bluff St 53511 608-365-7838
Cheryl Stapleton, prin. Fax 361-0989

Benton, Lafayette, Pop. 979
Benton SD 300/PK-12
PO Box 7 53803 608-759-4002
Bruce Bradley, admin. Fax 759-3805
www.benton.k12.wi.us
Benton ES 100/PK-6
PO Box 7 53803 608-759-4002
Gary Neis, prin. Fax 759-3805
Benton S 100/PK-12
PO Box 7 53803 608-759-4002
Duane Schober, prin. Fax 759-3805

Berlin, Green Lake, Pop. 5,213
Berlin Area SD 1,700/PK-12
295 E Marquette St 54923 920-361-2004
Jerry Runice, supt. Fax 361-2170
www.berlin.k12.wi.us
Berlin MS 400/6-8
289 E Huron St 54923 920-361-2441
Diane Toraason, prin. Fax 361-2945
Clay Lamberton ES 600/PK-5
259 E Marquette St 54923 920-361-2442
Scott Bartol, prin. Fax 361-4352
Other Schools – See Poy Sippi

All Saints Catholic S 200/PK-8
151 S Grove St 54923 920-361-1781
Steven Zangl, prin. Fax 361-7379
St. John Lutheran S 100/PK-8
146 Mound St 54923 920-361-0555
Curtis Snow, prin. Fax 361-0555

Big Bend, Waukesha, Pop. 1,267
Mukwonago SD
Supt. — See Mukwonago
Big Bend ES 400/K-6
W230S8695 Big Bend Dr 53103 262-662-4401
Theresa Genneman, prin. Fax 662-1309

Christ Lutheran S 100/K-8
W229S8930 Clark St 53103 262-662-3355
Steven Janke, prin. Fax 662-3370
St. Joseph S 100/PK-8
W227S8930 Saint Joseph Dr 53103 262-662-2737
Bob Abshire, prin. Fax 662-2684

Birchwood, Washburn, Pop. 537
Birchwood SD 200/PK-12
300 S Wilson St 54817 715-354-3471
Frank Helquist, supt. Fax 354-3469
www.birchwood.k12.wi.us/
Birchwood S 100/PK-8
300 S Wilson St 54817 715-354-3471
Jeff Stanley, prin. Fax 354-3469

Birnamwood, Shawano, Pop. 779
Wittenberg-Birnamwood SD
Supt. — See Wittenberg
Birnamwood S 400/K-8
337 Main St 54414 715-449-2576
Guy Steckbauer, prin. Fax 449-2826

Black Creek, Outagamie, Pop. 1,224
Seymour Community SD
Supt. — See Seymour
Black Creek S 400/K-8
PO Box 237 54106 920-984-3396
Susan Kaphingst, prin. Fax 984-9303

Black Earth, Dane, Pop. 1,283
Wisconsin Heights SD
Supt. — See Mazomanie
Black Earth ES 100/PK-2
1133 Center St 53515 608-767-2251
Dale Green, prin. Fax 767-2545

Black River Falls, Jackson, Pop. 3,485
Black River Falls SD 1,800/PK-12
301 N 4th St 54615 715-284-4357
Fax 284-7064
www.brf.org
Black River Falls MS 400/6-8
1202 Pierce St 54615 715-284-5315
David Roou, prin. Fax 284-0364
Forrest Street ES 300/PK-1
720 Forrest St 54615 715-284-9406
Sherri Torkelson, prin. Fax 284-7064
Gebhardt ES 200/4-5
411 Gebhardt Rd 54615 715-284-5125
Shelley Severson, prin. Fax 284-7472
Third Street ES 300/2-3
206 N 3rd St 54615 715-284-7155
Jon Warmke, prin. Fax 284-7064

Blair, Trempealeau, Pop. 1,261
Blair-Taylor SD 600/PK-12
PO Box 125 54616 608-989-2881
Dennis Dervetski, supt. Fax 989-2451
btsd.k12.wi.us
Blair-Taylor ES 300/PK-6
PO Box 125 54616 608-989-9835
Connie Biedron, prin. Fax 989-2451

Blanchardville, Lafayette, Pop. 774
Pecatonica Area SD 400/PK-12
PO Box 117 53516 608-523-4248
Gary Neis, supt. Fax 523-4286
www.pecatonica.k12.wi.us
Other Schools – See Hollandale

Bloomer, Chippewa, Pop. 3,280
Bloomer SD 1,000/PK-12
1310 17th Ave 54724 715-568-2800
Dr. Mary Randall, supt. Fax 568-5315
www.bloomer.k12.wi.us
Bloomer ES 400/PK-4
1715 Oak St 54724 715-568-1042
Connie Stockman, prin. Fax 568-1045
Bloomer MS 200/5-8
600 Jackson St 54724 715-568-1025
Barry Kamrath, prin. Fax 568-3687

St. Paul Lutheran S 50/PK-8
1319 Larson St 54724 715-568-5544
Seth Jaeger, prin.
St. Paul S 200/PK-8
1210 Main St 54724 715-568-3233
Roxanne Kuss, prin. Fax 568-3244

Bloomington, Grant, Pop. 688
River Ridge SD
Supt. — See Patch Grove
River Ridge MS 100/4-8
PO Box 97 53804 608-994-2711
Dr. Kevin Shetler, prin. Fax 994-2714

St. Mary S 50/1-8
PO Box 35 53804 608-994-2435
Julie Zenz, prin. Fax 994-2551

Bonduel, Shawano, Pop. 1,390
Bonduel SD 900/PK-12
PO Box 310 54107 715-758-4860
Peter Behnke, supt. Fax 758-4869
www.bonduel.k12.wi.us
Bonduel ES 300/PK-5
PO Box 310 54107 715-758-4810
Margaret Jones, prin. Fax 758-4819
Bonduel MS 200/6-8
PO Box 310 54107 715-758-4840
Connie Rutledge, prin. Fax 758-4849

Navarino ES 100/K-5
W5153 State Highway 156 54107 715-758-4830
Margaret Jones, prin. Fax 758-4839

St. Paul Lutheran S 200/PK-8
PO Box 577 54107 715-758-8532
Gerald Schmidt, prin. Fax 758-6352

Boscobel, Grant, Pop. 3,373
Boscobel Area SD 900/PK-12
1110 Park St 53805 608-375-4164
Dr. Stephen Smith, supt. Fax 375-2378
www.boscobel.k12.wi.us
Boscobel ES 500/PK-6
200 Buchanan St 53805 608-375-4165
Rick Walters, prin. Fax 375-4197
Boscobel MS 200/7-8
300 Brindley St 53805 608-375-4161
Greg Bell, prin. Fax 375-2640

Bowler, Shawano, Pop. 336
Bowler SD 400/PK-12
PO Box 8 54416 715-793-4307
Scott Peterson, supt. Fax 793-1302
www.bowler.k12.wi.us
Bowler ES 200/PK-6
PO Box 8 54416 715-793-4302
Kathy DeLorme, prin. Fax 793-1302

Boyceville, Dunn, Pop. 1,034
Boyceville Community SD 900/PK-12
1003 Tiffany St 54725 715-643-4311
Charles Buckel, supt. Fax 643-3127
www.boyceville.k12.wi.us
Tiffany Creek ES 400/PK-6
1003 Tiffany St 54725 715-643-4331
Nicholas Kaiser, prin. Fax 643-7805

Boyd, Chippewa, Pop. 641
Stanley-Boyd Area SD
Supt. — See Stanley
Boyd ES 50/K-5
303 E Park St 54726 715-667-3221
Judy Gulcynski, prin. Fax 667-3094

Brandon, Fond du Lac, Pop. 888
Rosendale-Brandon SD
Supt. — See Rosendale
Brandon S 200/PK-8
200 W Bowen St 53919 920-346-2915
Douglas Nowak, prin. Fax 346-5490

Briggsville, Marquette
Wisconsin Dells SD
Supt. — See Wisconsin Dells
Neenah Creek ES 100/K-5
PO Box 68 53920 608-981-2342
Fax 981-2341

Brillion, Calumet, Pop. 2,910
Brillion SD 900/PK-12
315 S Main St 54110 920-756-2368
Dominick Madison, supt. Fax 756-3705
www.brillion.k12.wi.us
Brillion ES 300/PK-5
315 S Main St 54110 920-756-3624
Tiffanie Nigbor, prin. Fax 756-3705
Brillion MS 200/6-8
315 S Main St 54110 920-756-2166
Ann Hatch, prin. Fax 756-3705

Holy Family S 100/PK-8
209 N Custer St 54110 920-756-2502
Scott Smith, prin. Fax 756-9702
Trinity Evangelical Lutheran S 100/K-8
601 E National Ave 54110 920-756-3738
Mark Murphy, prin. Fax 756-9189

Bristol, Kenosha
Bristol SD 1 600/K-8
20121 83rd St 53104 262-857-2334
Gale Ryczek, supt. Fax 857-6644
www.bristol.k12.wi.us
Bristol S 600/K-8
20121 83rd St 53104 262-857-2334
Jeff Terry, prin. Fax 857-6644

Brodhead, Green, Pop. 3,068
Brodhead SD 1,200/PK-12
2501 W 5th Ave 53520 608-897-2141
Charles Deery, supt. Fax 897-2770
www.brodhead.k12.wi.us
Albrecht ES 500/PK-5
1400 21st St 53520 608-897-2146
Dave Novy, prin. Fax 897-2212
Brodhead MS 300/6-8
2100 W 9th Ave 53520 608-897-2184
Charles Urness, prin. Fax 897-2789

Brookfield, Waukesha, Pop. 39,656
Elmbrook SD 7,600/PK-12
PO Box 1830 53008 262-781-3030
Matthew Gibson, supt. Fax 783-0983
www.elmbrookschools.org
Brookfield ES 500/K-5
2530 N Brookfield Rd 53045 262-785-3930
Laura Myrah, prin. Fax 785-3932
Burleigh ES 800/PK-5
16185 Burleigh Pl 53005 262-781-5280
William Zahn, prin. Fax 790-0302
Dixon ES 400/K-5
2400 Pilgrim Square Dr 53005 262-785-3970
Ann Goebel, prin. Fax 785-3904
Hillside ES 400/K-5
2250 N Lynette Ln 53045 262-785-3940
Julie Kremer, prin. Fax 785-3944
Swanson ES 600/K-5
305 N Calhoun Rd 53005 262-789-2540
Anne Kreul, prin. Fax 789-3288

Wisconsin Hills MS 900/6-8
18700 W Wisconsin Ave 53045 262-785-3960
Robyn Martino, prin. Fax 785-3967
Other Schools – See Elm Grove

Waukesha SD
Supt. — See Waukesha
Pleasant Hill MS 100/4-6
175 S Barker Rd 53045 262-970-2100
Michael Sukawaty, prin. Fax 970-2120

Brookfield Academy 700/PK-12
3460 N Brookfield Rd 53045 262-783-3200
Dr. Robert Solsrud, hdmstr. Fax 783-3209
Brookfield Christian S 200/PK-8
14155 W Burleigh Rd 53005 262-782-4722
Robert Wiers, prin. Fax 782-0551
Christ the Lord Lutheran Evangelical S 100/K-8
1650 N Brookfield Rd 53045 262-782-3040
John Melso, prin. Fax 782-3504
Immanuel Lutheran S 200/PK-8
13445 Hampton Rd 53005 262-781-4135
Donald Rohde, prin. Fax 781-5460
St. Dominic Catholic S 400/K-8
18105 W Capitol Dr 53045 262-783-7565
John Chovanec, prin. Fax 783-5947
St. John Vianney S 500/K-8
17500 Gebhardt Rd 53045 262-796-3942
Jayme Hartmann, prin. Fax 796-3953
St. Luke Catholic S 100/K-8
1305 Davidson Rd 53045 262-782-0032
Judi Kelley, prin. Fax 782-6057

Brooklyn, Green, Pop. 1,148
Oregon SD
Supt. — See Oregon
Brooklyn ES 400/K-4
204 Division St 53521 608-455-4500
Anita Koehler, prin. Fax 455-2404

Brown Deer, Milwaukee, Pop. 11,611
Brown Deer SD 1,600/PK-12
8200 N 60th St 53223 414-371-6750
Deb Kerr, admin. Fax 371-6751
www.bdsd.k12.wi.us
Brown Deer MS 600/5-8
5757 W Dean Rd 53223 414-371-6900
Blake Peuse, prin. Fax 371-6901
Dean ES 300/PK-4
8355 N 55th St 53223 414-371-6800
Marirose Lucey, prin. Fax 371-6801

Brownsville, Dodge, Pop. 553

St. Paul Lutheran S 100/PK-8
PO Box 370 53006 920-583-4242
Kurt Callaway, prin. Fax 583-4274

Bruce, Rusk, Pop. 731
Bruce SD 500/PK-12
104 W Washington Ave 54819 715-868-2533
Debra Brown, supt. Fax 868-2534
www.bruce.k12.wi.us
Bruce ES 300/PK-6
104 W Washington Ave 54819 715-868-2585
David Hulback, prin. Fax 868-2534
Bruce MS 100/7-8
104 W Washington Ave 54819 715-868-2585
Larry Villiard, prin. Fax 868-2534

Brussels, Door
Southern Door SD 1,300/PK-12
2073 County Road DK 54204 920-825-7311
Joseph Innis, supt. Fax 825-7311
www.southerndoor.k12.wi.us
Southern Door ES 600/PK-5
2073 County Road DK 54204 920-825-7321
Laurie Connell, prin. Fax 825-7692
Southern Door MS 300/6-8
2073 County Road DK 54204 920-825-7321
Gary Langenberg, prin. Fax 825-7692

Burlington, Racine, Pop. 11,148
Burlington Area SD 3,500/K-12
100 N Kane St 53105 262-763-0210
Ronald Jandura, supt. Fax 763-0215
www.basd.k12.wi.us
Cooper ES 300/K-4
249 Conkey St 53105 262-763-0180
Daniel Armstrong, prin. Fax 763-5384
Dyer IS 500/5-6
201 S Kendrick Ave 53105 262-763-0220
Joyce Uglow, prin. Fax 767-5583
Karcher MS 600/7-8
225 Robert St 53105 262-763-0190
Marty McGinley, prin. Fax 767-5580
Lyons Center ES 200/K-4
1622 Mill St 53105 262-763-5380
Christine Anderson, prin. Fax 763-5382
Waller ES 400/K-4
195 Gardner Ave 53105 262-763-0185
Victoria Libbey, prin. Fax 763-0187
Winkler ES 200/K-4
34150 Fulton St 53105 262-539-2726
Linda Luger, prin. Fax 539-2217
Other Schools – See Kansasville

Randall J1 SD 800/K-8
37101 87th St 53105 262-877-3314
Steven Bloom, supt. Fax 537-2280
www.randall.k12.wi.us
Randall S 800/K-8
37101 87th St 53105 262-537-2211
Travis Lawrence, prin. Fax 537-2280

Wheatland J1 SD 400/K-8
6606 368th Ave 53105 262-537-2216
C. Scott Huth, admin. Fax 537-4059
www.wheatland.k12.wi.us
Wheatland Center S 400/K-8
6606 368th Ave 53105 262-537-2216
Patti Clements, prin. Fax 537-4059

St. Charles Borromeo S 200/K-8
449 Conkey St 53105 262-763-2848
Sr. Margaret Pietsch, prin. Fax 763-3818
St. John's Lutheran S 200/PK-8
198 Westridge Ave 53105 262-763-2377
Robert Dusseau, prin. Fax 763-6015
St. Mary S 300/K-8
225 W State St 53105 262-763-1515
Loretta Jackson, prin. Fax 763-1508

Butler, Waukesha, Pop. 1,822

St. Agnes Catholic S 200/K-8
12801 W Fairmount Ave 53007 262-781-4996
Susan Booth, prin. Fax 781-3512

Butternut, Ashland, Pop. 387
Butternut SD 100/PK-12
PO Box 247 54514 715-769-3434
Joni Weinert, supt. Fax 769-3712
www.butternut.k12.wi.us
Butternut S 100/PK-12
PO Box 247 54514 715-769-3434
Joni Weinert, prin. Fax 769-3712

Cadott, Chippewa, Pop. 1,313
Cadott Community SD 900/PK-12
PO Box 310 54727 715-289-3795
Joe Zydowsky, supt. Fax 289-3748
www.cadott.k12.wi.us
Cadott ES 500/PK-6
PO Box 310 54727 715-289-4213
Jeff Walsh, prin. Fax 289-3017
Cadott JHS 100/7-8
PO Box 310 54727 715-289-4211
Matthew McDonough, prin. Fax 289-3085

St. Joseph S, PO Box 159 54727 100/PK-8
JoDeane Lokemoen, prin. 715-289-4985

Caledonia, Racine

Trinity Lutheran S 100/PK-8
7900 Nicholson Rd 53108 262-835-4326
Michael Hertig, prin. Fax 835-0707

Cambria, Columbia, Pop. 789
Cambria-Friesland SD 400/PK-12
410 E Edgewater St 53923 920-348-5548
Tony Hinden, supt. Fax 348-5119
www.cf.k12.wi.us
Cambria-Friesland ES 200/PK-5
410 E Edgewater St 53923 920-348-5656
Rick Hammes, prin. Fax 348-5119

Cambridge, Dane, Pop. 1,227
Cambridge SD 900/PK-12
403 Blue Jay Way 53523 608-423-4345
Ronald Dayton, supt. Fax 423-9869
www.cambridge.k12.wi.us
Cambridge ES 400/PK-5
802 W Water St 53523 608-423-9727
Diana Lalor-Freye, prin. Fax 423-7078
Nikolay MS 200/6-8
211 South St 53523 608-423-7335
George Smith, prin. Fax 423-4499

Cameron, Barron, Pop. 1,655
Cameron SD 800/PK-12
PO Box 378 54822 715-458-4560
Randal Braun, supt. Fax 458-4822
www.cameron.k12.wi.us
Cameron ES 300/PK-4
PO Box 378 54822 715-458-2210
Patricia Schroeder, prin. Fax 458-0041
Cameron MS 300/5-8
PO Box 378 54822 715-458-4563
Thomas Spanel, prin. Fax 458-3436

Campbellsport, Fond du Lac, Pop. 1,930
Campbellsport SD 1,400/K-12
114 W Sheboygan St 53010 920-533-8381
Daniel Olson, admin. Fax 533-5726
www.csd.k12.wi.us
Campbellsport ES 400/K-6
751 Grandview Ave 53010 920-533-8032
Connie Strand, prin. Fax 533-3433
Campbellsport JHS 200/7-8
114 W Sheboygan St 53010 920-533-3411
Kristen Langer, prin. Fax 533-5726
Other Schools – See Eden

Kewaskum SD
Supt. — See Kewaskum
Wayne ES 100/K-5
5760 Mohawk Rd 53010 262-626-8427
Janet Molebash, prin. Fax 626-4401

St. Matthew S 100/K-8
PO Box 634 53010 920-533-4103
Joan Schlaefer, prin. Fax 533-8078
Waucousta Lutheran S 50/K-8
W2011 County Road F 53010 920-533-4792
David Wege, prin. Fax 533-4792

Camp Douglas, Juneau, Pop. 586
Tomah Area SD
Supt. — See Tomah
Camp Douglas ES 50/3-5
101 Junction St 54618 608-374-7091
Patricia Ellsworth, prin. Fax 372-5087

Cascade, Sheboygan, Pop. 696
Plymouth SD
Supt. — See Plymouth
Cascade ES 100/K-5
510 Lake Ct 53011 920-528-8322
Amy Flood, prin. Fax 892-5074

Casco, Kewaunee, Pop. 564
Luxemburg-Casco SD
Supt. — See Luxemburg
Luxemburg-Casco MS 300/7-8
619 Church Ave 54205 920-837-2205
Mike Snowberry, prin. Fax 837-7517

Holy Trinity S 100/PK-8
510 Church Ave 54205 920-837-7531
Kaye Jacobs, prin. Fax 837-2361

Cashton, Monroe, Pop. 1,018
Cashton SD 500/PK-12
PO Box 129 54619 608-654-5131
Bradford Saron, supt. Fax 654-5136
www.cashton.k12.wi.us
Cashton ES 200/PK-6
PO Box 129 54619 608-654-7377
Ryan Alderson, prin. Fax 654-7390

Sacred Heart S 50/PK-8
710 Kenyon St 54619 608-654-7733
Linda Gutierrez, lead tchr. Fax 654-7413

Cassville, Grant, Pop. 1,045
Cassville SD 300/PK-12
715 E Amelia St 53806 608-725-5116
Leland Kulland, supt. Fax 725-2353
www.cassvillesd.k12.wi.us
Cassville ES 100/PK-6
715 E Amelia St 53806 608-725-5307
Leland Kulland, prin. Fax 725-2353

St. Charles Borromeo S 100/1-8
PO Box 167 53806 608-725-5173
Barb Mason, prin. Fax 725-5179

Cato, Manitowoc

St. Mary / St. Michael S 100/PK-8
19 S County Road J 54230 920-775-4366
Ron Nesper, prin. Fax 775-4365

Cazenovia, Sauk, Pop. 338
Weston SD 400/PK-12
E2511A County Rd S 53924 608-986-2151
Eric Franzen, supt. Fax 986-2205
www.weston.k12.wi.us
Weston ES 200/PK-5
E2511A County Rd S 53924 608-986-2151
Eric Franzen, prin. Fax 986-2205
Weston MS 100/6-8
E2511A County Rd S 53924 608-986-2151
Eric Franzen, prin. Fax 986-2205

Cedarburg, Ozaukee, Pop. 11,298
Cedarburg SD 3,100/K-12
W68N611 Evergreen Blvd 53012 262-376-6100
Dr. Daryl Herrick, supt. Fax 376-6110
www.cedarburg.k12.wi.us
Parkview ES 400/K-5
W72N853 Harrison Ave 53012 262-376-6800
Jayne Holck, prin. Fax 376-6810
Thorson ES 500/K-5
W51N932 Keup Rd 53012 262-376-6700
Kandy Gibson, prin. Fax 376-6710
Webster MS 700/6-8
W75N624 Wauwatosa Rd 53012 262-376-6500
Robert Klimpke, prin. Fax 376-6510
Westlawn ES 300/K-5
W64N319 Madison Ave 53012 262-376-6900
Paul Sanders, prin. Fax 376-6992

First Immanuel Lutheran S 300/PK-8
W67N622 Evergreen Blvd 53012 262-377-6610
Robert Eberhart, prin. Fax 377-9606
St. Francis Borgia S 400/PK-8
N43W6005 Hamilton Rd 53012 262-377-2050
Dr. Sue Brandley, prin. Fax 377-4099

Cedar Grove, Sheboygan, Pop. 2,012
Cedar Grove-Belgium Area SD 1,100/PK-12
321 N 2nd St 53013 920-668-8686
Steven Shaw, supt. Fax 668-8605
www.cedargrovebelgium.k12.wi.us/
Cedar Grove-Belgium ES 500/PK-4
321 N 2nd St 53013 920-668-8518
Mary Wolf, prin. Fax 668-6933
Cedar Grove-Belgium MS 300/5-8
321 N 2nd St 53013 920-668-8518
Jeanne Courneene, prin. Fax 668-8566

Chetek, Barron, Pop. 2,150
Chetek SD 900/K-12
1001 Knapp St 54728 715-924-2226
Al Brown, supt. Fax 924-2376
www.chetek.k12.wi.us/
Chetek MS 200/6-8
1001 Knapp St 54728 715-924-3136
Bryan Yenter, prin. Fax 924-2921
Roselawn ES 400/K-5
1201 6th St 54728 715-924-2244
Jill Koenitzer, prin. Fax 924-2279

Chilton, Calumet, Pop. 3,617
Chilton SD 1,200/PK-12
530 W Main St 53014 920-849-8109
Claire Martin, supt. Fax 849-4539
www.chilton.k12.wi.us
Chilton ES 500/PK-4
530 W Main St 53014 920-849-9388
Pamela Schuster, prin. Fax 849-9457

Chilton MS 300/5-8
530 W Main St 53014 920-849-9152
Richard Appel, prin. Fax 849-7210

Chilton Area Catholic S 100/PK-6
60 E Washington St 53014 920-849-4141
Elisabeth Rollmann, prin. Fax 849-9092

Chippewa Falls, Chippewa, Pop. 13,374
Chippewa Falls Area SD 5,000/PK-12
1130 Miles St 54729 715-726-2417
Thomas Hughes, supt. Fax 726-2781
cfsd.chipfalls.k12.wi.us
Chippewa Falls MS 1,000/6-8
750 Tropicana Blvd 54729 715-726-2400
Janet Etmund, prin. Fax 726-2789
Halmstad ES 400/K-5
565 E South Ave 54729 715-726-2415
Beth Schultz, prin. Fax 720-3756
Hillcrest ES 400/K-5
1200 Miles St 54729 715-726-2405
Robert Vanderloop, prin. Fax 720-3754
Parkview ES 500/K-5
501 Jefferson Ave 54729 715-720-3750
Scott Nelson, prin. Fax 720-3755
Southview ES 600/PK-5
615 A St 54729 715-726-2411
Heidi White, prin. Fax 726-2798
Stillson ES 400/K-5
17250 County Highway J 54729 715-726-2412
Carol Wilczak, prin. Fax 720-3745
Other Schools – See Jim Falls

Holy Ghost S 100/4-6
436 S Main St 54729 715-723-6478
Mary Selz, prin. Fax 723-8990
Notre Dame MS 100/7-8
1316 Bel Air Blvd 54729 715-723-4777
Robert Vanderloop, prin. Fax 723-3353
St. Charles Borromeo PS 200/PK-3
429 W Spruce St 54729 715-723-5827
Mary Selz, prin.
St. Peter S 100/1-8
11370 County Highway Q 54729 715-288-6250
Tammy Christopher, prin. Fax 288-6250

Clayton, Polk, Pop. 584
Clayton SD 400/PK-12
PO Box 130 54004 715-948-2163
Cathleen Shimon, supt. Fax 948-2362
www.claytonsd.k12.wi.us
Clayton ES 200/PK-5
PO Box 130 54004 715-948-2163
Cathleen Shimon, prin. Fax 948-2362
Clayton MS 100/6-8
PO Box 130 54004 715-948-2163
Cathleen Shimon, prin. Fax 948-2362

Clear Lake, Polk, Pop. 1,077
Clear Lake SD 700/PK-12
1101 3rd St SW 54005 715-263-2114
Brad Ayer, supt. Fax 263-2933
www.clearlake.k12.wi.us
Clear Lake JHS 100/7-8
1101 3rd St SW 54005 715-263-2113
Chris Petersen, prin. Fax 263-3550
Nelson ES 300/PK-6
135 8th Ave 54005 715-263-2117
Nancy Becker, prin. Fax 263-3519

Cleveland, Manitowoc, Pop. 1,401
Sheboygan Area SD
Supt. — See Sheboygan
Cleveland ES 100/K-5
411 E Washington Ave 53015 920-693-8241
Deb Streblow, prin. Fax 693-8357

Clinton, Rock, Pop. 3,124
Clinton Community SD 1,200/PK-12
PO Box 566 53525 608-676-5482
Dr. Pamela Kiefert, supt. Fax 676-4444
www.clinton.k12.wi.us
Clinton ES 400/PK-4
PO Box 70 53525 608-676-2211
Joseph Bellante, prin. Fax 676-5717
Clinton MS 400/5-8
PO Box 559 53525 608-676-2275
Carol Langley, prin. Fax 676-5176

Clintonville, Waupaca, Pop. 4,399
Clintonville SD 1,600/PK-12
45 W Green Tree Rd 54929 715-823-7215
Tom O'Toole, supt. Fax 823-1315
www.clintonville.k12.wi.us
Clintonville MS 400/5-8
255 N Main St 54929 715-823-7215
Tom Dechant, prin. Fax 823-1443
Dellwood Early Learning Center 100/PK-PK
238 Harriet St 54929 715-823-7215
Kayrene Schultz, prin. Fax 823-1401
Rexford/Longfellow ES 500/K-4
105 S Clinton Ave 54929 715-823-7215
Kristine Strauman, prin. Fax 823-7140

St. Martin Lutheran S 200/PK-8
100 S Clinton Ave 54929 715-823-6538
Jerry Jiter, prin. Fax 823-1464
St. Rose S 100/PK-5
140 Auto St 54929 715-823-4360
Mary Morse, prin. Fax 823-3402

Cochrane, Buffalo, Pop. 406

Buffalo Lutheran S 50/PK-8
401 S Main St 54622 608-248-2387
Frank Krause, prin.

Colby, Clark, Pop. 1,664
Colby SD 1,000/PK-12
PO Box 139 54421 715-223-2301
J. Terry Downen, supt. Fax 223-4539
www.colby.k12.wi.us
Colby ES 300/K-5
PO Box 80 54421 715-223-3939
Lea Fildes, prin. Fax 223-2123
Colby MS 300/5-8
PO Box 110 54421 715-223-8869
Nancy Marcott, prin. Fax 223-6754
Little Stars Preschool PK-K
PO Box 140 54421 715-223-2044
Terry Downen, prin. Fax 223-4388

St. Mary S 100/1-8
PO Box 408 54421 715-223-3033
Scott Hudak, prin. Fax 223-0223

Coleman, Marinette, Pop. 706
Coleman SD 600/PK-12
343 Business 141 N 54112 920-897-4011
Dr. Robert Werley, supt. Fax 897-2015
www.coleman.k12.wi.us
Coleman ES 300/PK-5
347 Business 141 N 54112 920-897-2525
Robert Werley, prin. Fax 897-2015

Colfax, Dunn, Pop. 1,070
Colfax SD 900/PK-12
601 University Ave 54730 715-962-3773
Dennis Geissler, supt. Fax 962-4024
www.colfax.k12.wi.us/
Colfax S 600/PK-8
601 University Ave 54730 715-962-3676
William Yingst, prin. Fax 962-4024

Colgate, Washington
Germantown SD
Supt. — See Germantown
Belle ES 400/PK-5
3294 Willow Creek Rd 53017 262-253-3470
Brendan McCarthy, prin. Fax 253-3490

Richfield J1 SD
Supt. — See Richfield
Plat ES 100/PK-2
4908 Monches Rd 53017 262-628-1778
Dr. Elliott Moeser, prin. Fax 628-9959

Coloma, Waushara, Pop. 469
Westfield SD
Supt. — See Westfield
Coloma ES 100/K-6
210 N Linden St 54930 715-228-2851
Jennifer Johnson, prin. Fax 228-2860

Columbus, Columbia, Pop. 5,101
Columbus SD 1,100/PK-12
200 W School St 53925 920-623-5950
Mark Jansen, supt. Fax 623-5958
www.columbus.k12.wi.us
Columbus ES 300/PK-3
200 Fuller St 53925 920-623-5952
Susan Sewell, prin. Fax 623-6026
Columbus MS 400/4-8
400 S Dickason Blvd 53925 920-623-5954
Doug Waitrovich, prin. Fax 623-5742

Petersen SDA S 50/1-8
W1004 Hall Rd 53925 920-623-4056
Rose Paden, prin.
St. Jerome S 200/PK-8
1550 Farnham St 53925 920-623-5780
Jamie Cotter, prin. Fax 623-1115
Zion Lutheran S 100/K-8
822 Western Ave 53925 920-623-5180
Paul Ihde, prin. Fax 623-2352

Combined Locks, Outagamie, Pop. 3,000
Kimberly Area SD
Supt. — See Kimberly
Janssen ES 500/PK-4
420 Wallace St 54113 920-788-7915
Hercules Nikolaou, prin. Fax 788-7923

Coon Valley, Vernon, Pop. 748
Westby Area SD
Supt. — See Westby
Coon Valley ES 200/PK-4
PO Box 309 54623 608-452-3143
Mark Anderson, prin. Fax 452-3155

Cornell, Chippewa, Pop. 1,392
Cornell SD 500/PK-12
PO Box 517 54732 715-239-6577
Paul Schley, supt. Fax 239-6467
www.cornell.k12.wi.us
Cornell ES 300/PK-6
PO Box 517 54732 715-239-6577
Paul Schley, prin. Fax 239-6587

Cottage Grove, Dane, Pop. 5,271
Monona Grove SD
Supt. — See Monona
Cottage Grove ES 300/2-4
470 N Main St 53527 608-839-4576
Barbara Berg, prin. Fax 839-4439
Glacial Drumlin MS 5-8
801 Damascus Trl 53527 608-839-8437
Renee Tennant, prin. Fax 839-8984
Taylor Prairie ES 300/PK-1
900 N Parkview St 53527 608-839-8515
Connie Haessly, prin. Fax 839-8323

Crandon, Forest, Pop. 1,867
Crandon SD 900/PK-12
9750 US Highway 8 W 54520 715-478-3339
Dr. Richard Peters, supt. Fax 478-5130
www.crandon.k12.wi.us
Crandon ES 400/PK-5
9750 US Highway 8 W 54520 715-478-3723
Jim Engebretson, prin. Fax 478-5570
Crandon MS 200/6-8
9750 US Highway 8 W 54520 715-478-3713
Glen Pfeifer, prin. Fax 478-5570

Crivitz, Marinette, Pop. 1,030
Crivitz SD 700/PK-12
400 South Ave 54114 715-854-2721
Ronald Saari, supt. Fax 854-3755
www.crivitz.k12.wi.us
Crivitz ES 400/PK-6
718 Hall Hay St 54114 715-854-2721
Patrick Mans, prin. Fax 854-2050
Crivitz MS 100/7-8
718 Hall Hay St 54114 715-854-2721
Patrick Mans, prin. Fax 854-2050

Cross Plains, Dane, Pop. 3,418
Middleton-Cross Plains Area SD
Supt. — See Middleton
Glacier Creek MS 600/6-8
2800 Military Rd 53528 608-829-9420
Tim Keeler, prin. Fax 798-5425
Park ES 300/PK-5
1209 Park St 53528 608-829-9250
Karen Jones, prin. Fax 798-4943

St. Francis Xavier S 200/PK-8
2939 Thinnes St 53528 608-798-2422
Tom Young, prin. Fax 798-0898

Cuba City, Grant, Pop. 2,104
Cuba City SD 700/PK-12
101 N School St 53807 608-744-2847
Sam McGrew, supt. Fax 744-2324
www.cubacity.k12.wi.us
Cuba City S 400/PK-8
518 W Roosevelt St 53807 608-744-2174
James Boebel, prin. Fax 744-7469

St. Rose of Lima S 100/PK-8
218 N Jackson St 53807 608-744-2120
Sr. Georgianna Dorsey, prin. Fax 744-3709

Cudahy, Milwaukee, Pop. 18,316
Cudahy SD 2,800/PK-12
2915 E Ramsey Ave 53110 414-294-7400
James Heiden, supt. Fax 769-2319
www.cudahy.k12.wi.us/
Cudahy MS 400/7-8
5530 S Barland Ave 53110 414-294-2830
Mike Carolan, prin. Fax 489-3010
Jones ES 200/PK-6
5845 S Swift Ave 53110 414-294-7150
Matthew Orlowski, prin. Fax 489-3007
Kosciuszko ES 300/PK-6
5252 S Kirkwood Ave 53110 414-294-7200
Joel Katte, prin. Fax 769-1584
Lincoln ES 400/PK-6
4416 S Packard Ave 53110 414-294-2930
Karen Ebbers, prin. Fax 489-3008
Mitchell ES 300/PK-6
5950 S Illinois Ave 53110 414-294-7100
Matthew Geiger, prin. Fax 489-3006
Park View ES 300/PK-6
5555 S Nicholson Ave 53110 414-294-7250
Jacqueline Santi, prin. Fax 489-3009

St. Paul's Lutheran S 100/PK-8
3766 E Cudahy Ave 53110 414-744-9771
Lance List, prin. Fax 744-2717

Cumberland, Barron, Pop. 2,242
Cumberland SD 1,100/PK-12
1010 8th Ave 54829 715-822-5124
Barry Rose, supt. Fax 822-5136
www.cumberland.k12.wi.us/
Cumberland ES 400/PK-4
1530 2nd Ave 54829 715-822-5123
Jim Richie, prin. Fax 822-5135
Cumberland MS 300/5-8
980 8th Ave 54829 715-822-5122
Jim Sciacca, prin. Fax 822-5132

Custer, Portage

Sacred Heart S 50/PK-6
7379 Church St 54423 715-592-4902
Patrick Burkhart, prin.

Dane, Dane, Pop. 896

St. Michael S 50/K-8
PO Box 170 53529 608-849-5619
Sr. Jacqueline Tierney, prin. Fax 850-5610

Darien, Walworth, Pop. 1,635
Delavan-Darien SD
Supt. — See Delavan
Darien ES 300/K-5
125 S Walworth St 53114 262-728-2642
Kathleen Maher, prin. Fax 724-4147

Darlington, Lafayette, Pop. 2,341
Darlington Community SD 800/PK-12
11630 Center Hill Rd 53530 608-776-2006
Dr. Denise Wellnitz, supt. Fax 776-3407
www.darlington.k12.wi.us
Darlington S 500/PK-8
11630 Center Hill Rd 53530 608-776-4021
Michelle Savatski, prin. Fax 776-3510

Holy Rosary S 100/PK-4
744 Wells St 53530 608-776-3710
Diane Smith-Hole, prin. Fax 776-4059

Deerfield, Dane, Pop. 2,202
Deerfield Community SD 700/PK-12
300 Simonson Blvd 53531 608-764-5431
Michelle Jensen, supt. Fax 764-5433
www.deerfield.k12.wi.us
Deerfield ES 400/PK-6
340 W Quarry St 53531 608-764-5442
Mark Becker, prin. Fax 764-8652
Deerfield MS 100/7-8
300 Simonson Blvd 53531 608-764-5431
Jeffrey Stenroos, prin. Fax 764-5433

De Forest, Dane, Pop. 6,262
De Forest Area SD 3,200/PK-12
520 E Holum St 53532 608-842-6500
Jon Bales, supt. Fax 842-6592
www.deforest.k12.wi.us
De Forest Area MS 1,000/5-8
404 Yorktown Rd 53532 608-842-6000
Paul Herrick, prin. Fax 842-6015
Eagle Point ES 300/K-4
201 N Cleveland Ave 53532 608-842-6200
Ann Schoenberger, prin. Fax 842-6215
Holum PreKindergarten Center 50/PK-PK
520 E Holum St 53532 608-842-6200
Ann Schoenberger, prin. Fax 842-6215
Yahara ES 400/K-4
234 N Lexington Pkwy 53532 608-842-6400
Roy Bernards, prin. Fax 842-6415
Other Schools – See Morrisonville, Windsor

Delafield, Waukesha, Pop. 6,767
Kettle Moraine SD
Supt. — See Wales
Cushing ES 500/PK-5
227 Genesee St 53018 262-646-6700
Amanda Thompson, prin. Fax 646-6730

Delavan, Walworth, Pop. 8,370
Delavan-Darien SD 2,600/K-12
324 Beloit St 53115 262-728-2642
Wendy Overturf, supt. Fax 728-5954
www.ddschools.org
Phoenix MS 500/6-8
414 Beloit St 53115 262-728-2642
Steven Ferger, prin. Fax 728-0359
Turtle Creek ES 600/K-5
1235 Creek Rd 53115 262-728-2642
Deborah Maki, prin. Fax 728-6951
Wileman ES 300/K-5
1001 E Geneva St 53115 262-728-2642
Donna Sorensen, prin. Fax 728-6956
Other Schools – See Darien

Delavan Christian S 100/PK-8
848 Oak St 53115 262-728-5667
Enno Haan, prin. Fax 728-0092
Our Redeemer Lutheran S 200/PK-8
416 W Geneva St 53115 262-728-6589
James Breytung, prin. Fax 728-5581
St. Andrews S 100/K-8
115 S 7th St 53115 262-728-6211
Julie Supernaw, prin. Fax 728-3683

Denmark, Brown, Pop. 1,990
Denmark SD 1,600/PK-12
450 N Wall St 54208 920-863-4000
Tony Klaubauf, supt. Fax 863-4015
www.denmark.k12.wi.us
Denmark ECC 200/PK-K
450 N Wall St 54208 920-863-4175
David Harper, contact Fax 863-1923
Denmark ES 500/1-5
450 N Wall St 54208 920-863-4050
Ann Birdsall, prin. Fax 863-8302
Denmark MS 400/6-8
450 N Wall St 54208 920-863-4100
Dyan Pasono, prin. Fax 863-3184

All Saints S 100/PK-8
PO Box 787 54208 920-863-2449
LeRoy Meles, prin. Fax 863-5425

De Pere, Brown, Pop. 23,375
De Pere SD 3,600/PK-12
1700 Chicago St 54115 920-337-1032
Benjamin Villarruel, supt. Fax 337-1033
www.depere.k12.wi.us
Altmayer ES K-4
3001 Ryan Rd 54115 920-338-1894
Emmy Mayer, prin. Fax 338-1360
De Pere MS 500/7-8
700 Swan Rd 54115 920-337-1024
Tammy Woulf, prin. Fax 337-1049
Dickinson ES 600/PK-4
435 S Washington St 54115 920-337-1027
Debra Gagnon, prin. Fax 337-1043
Foxview IS 600/5-6
650 S Michigan St 54115 920-337-1036
Andy Bradford, prin. Fax 403-7390
Heritage ES 700/K-4
1250 Swan Rd 54115 920-337-1035
Kathleen Van Pay, prin. Fax 403-7381

West De Pere SD 2,200/PK-12
930 Oak St 54115 920-337-1393
John Zegers, supt. Fax 337-1398
www.wdpsd.com
Hemlock Creek ES PK-5
1900 Williams Grant Dr 54115 920-425-1900
Kathleen Held, prin. Fax 425-1914
West De Pere MS 500/6-8
1177 S 9th St 54115 920-337-1099
James Finley, prin. Fax 337-1380
Westwood ES 900/PK-5
1155 Westwood Dr 54115 920-337-1087
Jane Paluch, prin. Fax 337-1091

Green Bay Montessori Childrens World S 50/K-7
670 Main Ave 54115 920-983-3164
James Wildenberg, admin. Fax 983-3166
Immanuel Lutheran S 50/K-8
3737 Shirley Rd 54115 920-864-7787
Grant Barthel, prin. Fax 864-2424
Notre Dame S 300/K-8
221 S Wisconsin St 54115 920-337-1115
Mary Vanden Busch, prin. Fax 337-1117
Our Lady of Lourdes S 300/PK-8
1305 Lourdes Ave 54115 920-336-3091
Sue Sands, prin. Fax 337-6806

De Soto, Vernon, Pop. 369
De Soto Area SD 600/PK-12
615 Main St 54624 608-648-0102
David Strudthoff, supt. Fax 648-3959
www.desoto.k12.wi.us
De Soto MS 100/6-8
615 Main St 54624 608-648-0104
Martin Kirchhof, prin. Fax 648-0117
Prairie View ES 100/PK-5
E3245 County Rd N 54624 608-648-2227
George Andrews, prin. Fax 648-2224
Other Schools – See Stoddard

Dickeyville, Grant, Pop. 1,056

Holy Ghost/Immaculate Conception S 200/PK-8
PO Box 40 53808 608-568-7790
Rita Hesseling, prin. Fax 568-3872

Dodgeville, Iowa, Pop. 4,840
Dodgeville SD 1,300/PK-12
307 N Iowa St 53533 608-935-3307
Diane Messer, supt. Fax 935-3021
www.dsd.k12.wi.us/
Dodgeville ES 400/PK-4
404 N Johnson St 53533 608-935-3307
Julie Piper, prin. Fax 935-2824
Dodgeville MS 300/6-8
951 W Chapel St 53533 608-935-3307
Mitch Wainwright, prin. Fax 935-9643
Other Schools – See Ridgeway

St. Joseph S 200/PK-8
305 E Walnut St 53533 608-935-3392
Sharon Wimer, prin. Fax 935-1722

Dousman, Waukesha, Pop. 1,885
Kettle Moraine SD
Supt. — See Wales
Dousman ES 600/PK-5
341 E Ottawa Ave 53118 262-965-6550
Brian Stuckey, prin. Fax 965-6559
Kettle Moraine MS 1,000/6-8
301 E Ottawa Ave 53118 262-965-6500
David Carr, prin. Fax 965-6506

St. Bruno S 100/K-8
246 W Ottawa Ave 53118 262-965-2291
Michael Brown, prin. Fax 965-2249

Downsville, Dunn
Menomonie Area SD
Supt. — See Menomonie
Downsville ES 100/K-5
PO Box 78 54735 715-664-8546
Dudley Markham, prin. Fax 664-8548

Dresser, Polk, Pop. 844
St. Croix Falls SD
Supt. — See Saint Croix Falls
Dresser ES 100/PK-K
131 2nd St 54009 715-755-3165
Jeff Benoy, prin. Fax 483-3695

Drummond, Bayfield
Drummond Area SD 500/PK-12
PO Box 40 54832 715-739-6669
John Knight, supt. Fax 739-6345
www.dasdk12.net
Drummond ES 300/PK-6
PO Box 40 54832 715-739-6231
John Knight, prin. Fax 739-6345
Drummond MS 100/7-8
PO Box 40 54832 715-739-6231
Ellen Nelson, prin. Fax 739-6345

Durand, Pepin, Pop. 1,898
Durand SD 900/PK-12
604 7th Ave E 54736 715-672-8919
Jerry Walters, supt. Fax 672-8900
www.durand.k12.wi.us
Woodlawn Early Learning Center 100/PK-K
650 Auth St 54736 715-672-8977
Jan Lund, prin. Fax 672-8993
Other Schools – See Arkansaw

Holy Rosary S 100/K-3
N6217 County Road V 54736 715-672-4276
Theresa Kane, lead tchr. Fax 672-3485
St. Mary S 100/4-8
901 W Prospect St 54736 715-672-5617
Jill Gruber, lead tchr. Fax 672-3931
Thompson Lake Christian S 50/1-8
W6733 Church School Ln 54736 715-672-5037

Eagle, Waukesha, Pop. 1,769
Palmyra-Eagle Area SD
Supt. — See Palmyra
Eagle ES 300/K-6
PO Box 550 53119 262-594-2148
Sara Norton, prin. Fax 594-2820

Eagle River, Vilas, Pop. 1,608
Northland Pines SD 1,400/PK-12
1800 Pleasure Island Rd 54521 715-479-6487
Mike Richie, supt. Fax 479-7633
www.npsd.k12.wi.us/
Northland Pines/Eagle River ES 300/PK-5
1700 Pleasure Island Rd 54521 715-479-6471
Duane Frey, prin. Fax 477-6263
Northland Pines MS 300/6-8
1700 Pleasure Island Rd 54521 715-479-6479
Jacqueline Coghlan, prin. Fax 479-7303
Other Schools – See Land O Lakes, Saint Germain

Christ Lutheran S 50/K-8
201 N 3rd St 54521 715-479-8284
Christopher Mueller, prin. Fax 479-8284

East Troy, Walworth, Pop. 4,224
East Troy Community SD 1,700/K-12
2043 Division St 53120 262-642-6710
Christopher Hibner, supt. Fax 642-6712
www.easttroy.k12.wi.us
Byrnes ES 100/K-K
2031 Division St 53120 262-642-6725
Fax 642-6788
Doubek ES 200/1-2
2040 Beulah Ave 53120 262-642-6720
Fax 642-6723
East Troy MS 400/6-8
3143 Graydon Ave 53120 262-642-6740
Michael Willeman, prin. Fax 642-6743
Prairie View ES 300/3-5
2131 Townline Rd 53120 262-642-6720
Twila Voss, prin. Fax 642-6788

Good Shepherd Lutheran S 100/PK-5
1936 Emery St 53120 262-642-3310
Karl Sattler, prin. Fax 642-3310
St. Paul Lutheran S 100/PK-8
2665 North St 53120 262-642-3202
Kenneth White, prin. Fax 642-4132
St. Peter S 100/PK-8
3001 Elm St 53120 262-642-5533
Sarah Halbesna, prin. Fax 642-5897

Eau Claire, Eau Claire, Pop. 62,570
Eau Claire Area SD 9,900/PK-12
500 Main St 54701 715-852-3000
Dr. Ron Heilmann, supt. Fax 852-3004
www.ecasd.k12.wi.us
Davey ES 300/K-5
3000 Starr Ave 54703 715-852-3200
Kevin Mahoney, prin. Fax 852-3204
Delong MS 900/6-8
2000 Vine St 54703 715-852-4900
Dr. Tim O'Reilly, prin. Fax 852-4904
Flynn ES 300/K-5
1430 Lee St 54701 715-852-3300
Kim Hill Phelps, prin. Fax 852-3304
Lakeshore ES 400/PK-5
711 Lake St 54703 715-852-3400
Robert Hehli, prin. Fax 852-3404
Locust Lane ES 300/PK-5
3245 Locust Ln 54703 715-852-3700
Kaying Xiong, prin. Fax 852-3704
Longfellow ES 300/K-5
512 Balcom St 54703 715-852-3800
Sarah Fisher, prin. Fax 852-3804
Manz ES 400/K-5
1000 E Fillmore Ave 54701 715-852-3900
Heather Grant, prin. Fax 852-3904
Meadowview ES 400/K-5
4714 Fairfax St 54701 715-852-4000
Dr. Del Boley, prin. Fax 852-4004
Northstar MS 600/6-8
2711 Abbe Hill Dr 54703 715-852-5100
Michelle Golden, prin. Fax 852-5104
Northwoods ES 400/K-5
3600 Northwoods Ln 54703 715-852-4100
Lynn McNish, prin. Fax 852-4104
Putnam Heights ES 400/PK-5
633 W MacArthur Ave 54701 715-852-4200
Kim Koller, prin. Fax 852-4204
Robbins ES 400/PK-5
3832 E Hamilton Ave 54701 715-852-4600
Andrew Thiel, prin. Fax 852-4604
Roosevelt ES 300/K-5
3010 8th St 54703 715-852-4700
Joe Sanfelippo, prin. Fax 852-4704
Sherman ES 400/K-5
3110 Vine St 54703 715-852-4800
Chad Erickson, prin. Fax 852-4804
South MS 800/6-8
2115 Mitscher Ave 54701 715-852-5200
Mike Erickson, prin. Fax 852-5204

Crestview Academy 200/K-8
1519 Peterson Ave 54703 715-835-2275
Arnold Prokott, admin. Fax 836-9878
Eau Claire Academy 100/3-12
PO Box 1168 54702 715-834-6681
Laurie Van Beek, prin. Fax 834-9954
Eau Claire Lutheran S 100/PK-8
3031 Epiphany Ln 54703 715-835-9314
Jane Jaenke, prin. Fax 835-9166
Genesis Child Development Center 100/PK-PK
418 N Dewey St 54703 715-830-2275
Gayle Flaig, prin.
Immaculate Conception S 200/K-6
1703 Sherwin Ave 54701 715-830-2276
Joseph Eisenhuth, prin. Fax 830-9846
Messiah Lutheran S 100/K-8
2015 N Hastings Way 54703 715-834-2865
Seth Schaller, prin. Fax 834-8144
Regis Child Development Center 100/PK-PK
2114 Fenwick Ave 54701 715-830-2274
Gayle Flaig, prin.
Regis MS 100/7-8
2100 Fenwick Ave 54701 715-830-2272
William Uelmen, prin. Fax 830-5461
St. James the Greater S 100/K-6
2502 11th St 54703 715-830-2277
Linda Schultz, lead tchr. Fax 830-9861

St. Mark Lutheran S 100/PK-8
3307 State St 54701 715-834-5782
Chad Marohn, prin. Fax 834-7668

Eden, Fond du Lac, Pop. 725
Campbellsport SD
Supt. — See Campbellsport
Eden ES 300/K-6
PO Box 38 53019 920-477-3291
Thomas Koyen, prin. Fax 477-7203

Shepherd of the Hills S - Eden Campus 100/K-8
W1562 County Road B 53019 920-477-3551
Fax 477-3030

Edgar, Marathon, Pop. 1,327
Edgar SD 700/PK-12
PO Box 196 54426 715-352-2351
Mark Lacke, supt. Fax 352-3198
www.edgar.k12.wi.us/edgar/
Edgar ES 300/PK-5
PO Box 198 54426 715-352-2727
Lisa Witt, prin. Fax 352-3022
Edgar MS 100/6-8
PO Box 198 54426 715-352-2727
Lisa Witt, prin. Fax 352-3022

St. John the Baptist S 100/PK-8
PO Box 66 54426 715-352-3000
Lynelle Ellis, lead tchr. Fax 352-7517

Edgerton, Rock, Pop. 5,102
Edgerton SD 1,900/PK-12
200 Elm High Dr 53534 608-884-9402
Dr. Norman Fjelstad, supt. Fax 884-9327
www.edgerton.k12.wi.us
Community ES 800/PK-5
100 Elm High Dr 53534 608-884-9402
Bill Fry, prin. Fax 884-8548
Edgerton MS 400/6-8
300 Elm High Dr 53534 608-884-9402
Jerry Roth, prin. Fax 884-2279
Yahara Valley ES 100/1-5
100 Elm High Dr 53534 608-884-9402
Aundrea Kerkenbush, prin. Fax 884-4975

Oaklawn Academy 200/6-8
432 Liguori Rd 53534 608-884-3425
Javier Valenzuela, prin. Fax 884-8175

Egg Harbor, Door, Pop. 263

Zion Lutheran S 50/K-8
3937 County Road V 54209 920-743-2325
Adam Glodowski, prin. Fax 743-6067

Elcho, Langlade
Elcho SD 400/PK-12
PO Box 800 54428 715-275-3205
William Fisher, supt. Fax 275-4388
www.elcho.k12.wi.us
Elcho S 200/PK-8
PO Box 800 54428 715-275-3707
Andrew Blodgett, prin. Fax 275-4388

Elderon, Marathon, Pop. 175
Wittenberg-Birnamwood SD
Supt. — See Wittenberg
Elderon ES 100/K-4
PO Box 91 54429 715-454-6223
Nancy Resch, prin. Fax 454-7110

Eleva, Trempealeau, Pop. 655
Eleva-Strum SD
Supt. — See Strum
Eleva IS 100/4-6
26237 W Mondovi St 54738 715-287-4217
Craig Semingson, prin. Fax 287-3531

Elkhart Lake, Sheboygan, Pop. 1,068
Elkhart Lake - Glenbeulah SD 500/PK-12
PO Box K 53020 920-876-3381
Ann Buechel-Haack, supt. Fax 876-3511
Elkhart Lake - Glenbeulah S 300/PK-8
PO Box 518 53020 920-876-3307
Debbie Hammann, prin. Fax 876-3105

Elkhorn, Walworth, Pop. 9,021
Elkhorn Area SD 2,900/K-12
3 N Jackson St 53121 262-723-3160
Gregory Wescott, supt. Fax 723-4652
www.elkhorn.k12.wi.us
Elkhorn Area MS 700/6-8
627 E Court St 53121 262-723-6800
John Gendron, prin. Fax 723-4967
Jackson ES 400/K-5
13 N Jackson St 53121 262-723-1200
Tammy Fisher, prin. Fax 723-3719
Tibbets ES 400/K-5
W5218 County Road A 53121 262-742-2585
Gregory Wells, prin. Fax 742-4582
West Side ES 400/K-5
222 Sunset Dr 53121 262-723-3297
Sara Stone, prin. Fax 723-6790

First Lutheran S 100/PK-8
415 Devendorf St 53121 262-723-1091
Matthew Grow, prin. Fax 723-8912
St. Patrick S 100/PK-8
534 Sunset Dr 53121 262-723-4258
Julie Muellenbach, prin. Fax 723-1577

Elk Mound, Dunn, Pop. 815
Elk Mound Area SD 1,000/PK-12
405 University St 54739 715-879-5066
Ronald Walsh, supt. Fax 879-5846
www.elkmound.k12.wi.us
Elk Mound MS 300/5-8
302 University St 54739 715-879-5595
Eric Wright, prin. Fax 879-5846
Mound View ES 400/PK-4
455 University St 54739 715-879-5744
Eric Hanson, prin. Fax 879-5846

Ellsworth, Pierce, Pop. 3,060
Ellsworth Community SD 1,500/PK-12
PO Box 1500 54011 715-273-3900
Barry Cain, supt. Fax 273-5775
www.ellsworth.k12.wi.us
Ellsworth MS 500/5-8
PO Box 1500 54011 715-273-3908
Steve Broton, prin. Fax 273-6834
Hillcrest ES 300/PK-4
PO Box 1500 54011 715-273-3912
Leona Johnson, prin. Fax 273-6838
Other Schools – See Hager City

St. Francis S 100/K-5
PO Box 250 54011 715-273-4391
Jeanne McCoy, prin. Fax 273-6374

Elm Grove, Waukesha, Pop. 6,182
Elmbrook SD
Supt. — See Brookfield
Pilgrim Park MS 900/6-8
1500 Pilgrim Pkwy 53122 262-785-3920
Michael Sereno, prin. Fax 785-3933
Tonawanda ES 400/K-5
13605 Underwood River Pkwy 53122 262-785-3950
Alexis Kasmarick, prin. Fax 785-3956

Elm Grove Lutheran S 100/PK-8
945 Terrace Dr 53122 262-797-2970
Mark Angell, prin. Fax 797-2977
St. Mary's Visitation S 400/K-8
13000 Juneau Blvd 53122 262-782-7057
Lynn Ann Reesman, prin. Fax 782-3035

Elmwood, Pierce, Pop. 796
Elmwood SD 400/PK-12
213 S Scott St 54740 715-639-2711
Adam Zenner, supt. Fax 639-3110
www.elmwood.k12.wi.us
Elmwood ES 200/PK-6
213 S Scott St 54740 715-639-2711
Jon Hinzman, prin. Fax 639-3110
Elmwood MS 50/7-8
213 S Scott St 54740 715-639-2721
Jon Hinzman, prin. Fax 639-3110

Elroy, Juneau, Pop. 1,527
Royall SD 600/PK-12
PO Box 125 53929 608-462-2600
Scott Sarnow, supt. Fax 462-2618
www.royall.k12.wi.us
Elroy ES 200/PK-3
PO Box 125 53929 608-462-2605
Darcy Uppena, prin. Fax 462-2626
Other Schools – See Kendall

Endeavor, Marquette, Pop. 471
Portage Community SD
Supt. — See Portage
Endeavor ES 100/PK-6
414 S Church St 53930 608-587-2625
Ann Ostrowski, prin. Fax 587-2881

Ettrick, Trempealeau, Pop. 518
Gale-Ettrick-Trempealeau SD
Supt. — See Galesville
Ettrick ES 100/PK-5
22750 Washington St 54627 608-525-4571
Shelley Shirel, prin. Fax 525-8600

Evansville, Rock, Pop. 4,658
Evansville Community SD 1,800/PK-12
340 Fair St 53536 608-882-5224
Heidi Carvin, supt. Fax 882-6564
www.evansville.k12.wi.us
Leonard ES 500/PK-2
401 S 3rd St 53536 608-882-4606
Louisa Havlik, prin. Fax 882-5838
McKenna MS 400/6-8
307 S 1st St 53536 608-882-4780
Robert Flaherty, prin. Fax 882-5744
Robinson IS 400/3-5
420 S 4th St 53536 608-882-3888
Vicki Lecy Luebke, prin. Fax 882-3889

Fairchild, Eau Claire, Pop. 516
Osseo-Fairchild SD
Supt. — See Osseo
Fairchild ES 100/K-5
PO Box 100 54741 715-334-3311
Mary Kempf, prin. Fax 334-5461

Fall Creek, Eau Claire, Pop. 1,213
Fall Creek SD 900/PK-12
336 E Hoover Ave 54742 715-877-2123
Gary Frankiewicz, supt. Fax 877-2911
www.fallcreek.k12.wi.us
Fall Creek ES 400/PK-5
336 E Hoover Ave 54742 715-877-3331
Gayle Holte, prin. Fax 877-2911
Fall Creek MS 200/6-8
336 E Hoover Ave 54742 715-877-2511
Brian Schulner, prin. Fax 877-2911

Fall River, Columbia, Pop. 1,280
Fall River SD 500/PK-12
PO Box 116 53932 920-484-3333
Heidi Schmidt, supt. Fax 484-3600
www.fallriver.k12.wi.us
Fall River ES 300/PK-5
PO Box 116 53932 920-484-3333
Bradley Johnsrud, prin. Fax 484-3600

Fennimore, Grant, Pop. 2,357
Fennimore Community SD 800/PK-12
1397 9th St 53809 608-822-3243
Jamie Nutter, supt. Fax 822-3250
www.fennimore.k12.wi.us
Fennimore ES 400/PK-6
830 Madison St 53809 608-822-3285
Michael Berg, prin. Fax 822-3257

Fish Creek, Door
Gibraltar Area SD 600/PK-12
3924 State Highway 42 54212 920-868-3284
Stephen Seyfer, supt. Fax 868-2714
www.gibraltar.k12.wi.us
Gibraltar ES 300/PK-5
3924 State Highway 42 54212 920-868-3284
Judy Munsey, prin. Fax 868-2714
Gibraltar MS 100/6-8
3924 State Highway 42 54212 920-868-3284
Kirk Knutson, prin. Fax 868-2714

Fitchburg, Dane, Pop. 22,040
Verona Area SD
Supt. — See Verona
Savanna Oaks MS 400/6-8
5890 Lacy Rd 53711 608-845-4000
Stephanie Edwards, prin. Fax 845-4020
Stoner Prairie ES 400/K-5
5830 Devoro Rd 53711 608-845-4200
Chris Olson, prin. Fax 845-4220

Florence, Florence
Florence SD 500/PK-12
PO Box 440 54121 715-528-3217
Storm Carroll, supt. Fax 528-5338
www.florence.k12.wi.us
Florence ES 200/PK-6
PO Box 350 54121 715-528-3262
Deb Divoky, admin. Fax 528-5910
Florence MS 100/7-8
PO Box 440 54121 715-528-3215
Brandon Jerue, admin. Fax 528-5338

Fond du Lac, Fond du Lac, Pop. 42,435
Fond du Lac SD 7,000/K-12
72 W 9th St 54935 920-929-2900
James Sebert Ed.D., supt. Fax 929-6804
www.fonddulac.k12.wi.us
Chegwin ES 300/K-5
109 E Merrill Ave 54935 920-929-2820
Theresa Loehr, prin. Fax 929-7014
Evans ES 300/K-5
140 S Peters Ave 54935 920-929-2828
James Botting, prin. Fax 929-7060
Lakeshore ES 500/K-5
706 Prairie Rd 54935 920-929-2901
Michael Mockert, prin. Fax 929-6991
Parkside ES 200/K-5
475 W Arndt St 54935 920-929-2840
Delmar Coburn, prin. Fax 929-6156
Pier ES 400/K-5
259 Old Pioneer Rd 54935 920-929-2868
John Colwin, prin. Fax 929-6910
Riverside ES 300/K-5
396 Linden St 54935 920-929-2880
Sharon Simon, prin. Fax 929-6912
Roberts ES 400/K-5
270 Candy Ln 54935 920-929-2835
Richard Gregory, prin. Fax 929-6158
Rosenow ES 400/K-5
290 Weis Ave 54935 920-929-2996
Sara Austin, prin. Fax 929-6957
Sabish MS 500/6-8
100 N Peters Ave 54935 920-929-2800
Kelly Noble, prin. Fax 929-2807
Theisen MS 500/6-8
525 E Pioneer Rd 54935 920-929-2850
Kim Pahlow, prin. Fax 929-2854
Waters ES 400/K-5
495 Wabash Ave 54935 920-929-2845
Catherine Daniels, prin. Fax 929-2944
Woodworth MS 500/6-8
101 Morningside Dr 54935 920-929-6900
Steven Hill, prin. Fax 929-6944

FACES MS 300/3-8
PO Box 2138 54936 920-921-9610
Cheryl Jaeger, prin. Fax 921-0457
FACES PS 200/PK-2
95 E 2nd St 54935 920-921-5300
Cheryl Jaeger, prin. Fax 921-5908
Faith Lutheran S 200/K-8
55 Prairie Rd 54935 920-923-6313
Jon Woldt, prin. Fax 922-3278
Fond du Lac Christian S 100/K-12
720 Rienzi Rd 54935 920-924-2177
Matthew Bro, admin. Fax 322-9459
Redeemer Lutheran S 100/K-8
606 Forest Ave 54935 920-921-4020
David Nell, prin. Fax 921-4020
St. Peter Lutheran S 100/K-8
1600 S Main St 54937 920-922-1160
Michael Mathwig, prin. Fax 922-4042

Fontana, Walworth, Pop. 1,662
Fontana J8 SD 300/PK-8
450 S Main St 53125 262-275-6881
Mark Wenzel, admin. Fax 275-5360
www.fontana.k12.wi.us
Fontana S 300/PK-8
450 S Main St 53125 262-275-6881
Mark Wenzel, prin. Fax 275-5360

Footville, Rock, Pop. 757
Parkview SD
Supt. — See Orfordville
Footville ES 100/K-2
PO Box 327 53537 608-876-6091
Mark Miller, prin. Fax 876-4172

Fort Atkinson, Jefferson, Pop. 11,949
Fort Atkinson SD 2,700/PK-12
201 Park St 53538 920-563-7807
James Fitzpatrick, supt. Fax 563-7809
www.fortschools.org
Barrie ES 300/K-5
1000 Harriette St 53538 920-563-7817
Anthony Bolz, prin. Fax 563-7821
Fort Atkinson MS 600/6-8
310 S 4th St E 53538 920-563-7833
Robert Abbott, prin. Fax 563-7838
Luther ES 300/K-5
205 Park St 53538 920-568-4465
Dave Geiger, prin. Fax 568-7051
Purdy ES 400/PK-5
719 S Main St 53538 920-563-7822
Rick Brietzke, prin. Fax 563-7837
Rockwell ES 300/K-5
821 Monroe St 53538 920-563-7818
Vicki Wright, prin. Fax 568-3202

Faith Community Christian S 50/PK-8
W5949 Hackbarth Rd 53538 920-563-9954
Richard Doellstedt, admin. Fax 563-4754
St. Joseph S 100/PK-8
1650 Endl Blvd 53538 920-563-3029
David Podmolik, prin. Fax 563-3150
St. Paul's Lutheran S 200/K-8
309 Bluff St 53538 920-563-5349
Harlan Pelischek, prin. Fax 563-5061

Fountain City, Buffalo, Pop. 1,026
Cochrane-Fountain City SD 700/PK-12
S2770 State Road 35 54629 608-687-7771
Thomas Hiebert, supt. Fax 687-3312
www.cfc.k12.wi.us
Cochrane-Fountain City ES 400/PK-6
S2770 State Road 35 54629 608-687-4171
Steve Stoppelmoor, prin. Fax 687-6412

Fox Lake, Dodge, Pop. 1,458

St. John Lutheran S 100/K-8
110 Edgelawn Dr 53933 920-928-3296
John Schlavensky, prin. Fax 928-3296

Fox Point, Milwaukee, Pop. 6,741
Maple Dale-Indian Hill SD 400/PK-8
8377 N Port Washington Rd 53217 414-351-7380
Mary Dean, supt. Fax 351-8104
www.mapledale.k12.wi.us
Other Schools – See Milwaukee

St. Eugene S 200/PK-8
7600 N Port Washington Rd 53217 414-918-1120
Michael Taylor, prin. Fax 918-1122

Franklin, Milwaukee, Pop. 33,263
Franklin SD 4,100/K-12
8255 W Forest Hill Ave 53132 414-529-8220
Steve Patz, supt. Fax 529-8230
www.franklin.k12.wi.us
Country Dale ES 400/K-6
7380 S North Cape Rd 53132 414-529-8240
Larry Madsen, prin. Fax 529-8242
Forest Park MS 600/7-8
8225 W Forest Hill Ave 53132 414-529-8250
Matthew Lesar, prin. Fax 529-8249
Franklin ES 400/K-6
7620 S 83rd St 53132 414-529-8270
Phillip Posard, prin. Fax 529-8274
Pleasant View ES 500/K-6
4601 W Marquette Ave 53132 414-423-4650
Charles Wedig, prin. Fax 423-4653
Robinwood ES 500/K-6
10705 W Robinwood Ln 53132 414-529-8255
Thomas Reinke, prin. Fax 529-8256
Southwood Glen ES 400/K-6
9090 S 35th St 53132 414-761-1181
Carol Dixon, prin. Fax 761-1755

Indian Community S 300/PK-8
10405 W Saint Martins Rd 53132 414-525-6100
Alan Caldwell, admin. Fax 345-6160
St. Martin of Tours S 100/K-8
7933 S 116th St 53132 414-425-9200
Jeanne Johnson, prin. Fax 425-2527
St. Paul Lutheran S 100/K-8
6881 S 51st St 53132 414-421-1930
Gary Wille, prin. Fax 421-4299

Franksville, Racine
North Cape SD 200/K-8
11926 County Road K 53126 262-835-4069
Petra Walker, admin. Fax 835-2311
www.northcape.k12.wi.us
North Cape S 200/K-8
11926 County Road K 53126 262-534-3894
Petra Walker, prin. Fax 835-2311

Norway J7 SD 100/PK-8
21016 W 7 Mile Rd 53126 414-425-6020
Jeff Gorn, supt. Fax 425-6038
www.droughtschool.net
Drought S 100/PK-8
21016 W 7 Mile Rd 53126 414-425-6020
Jeff Gorn, prin. Fax 425-6038

Raymond SD 14 400/K-8
2659 76th St 53126 262-835-2929
George Slupski, supt. Fax 835-2087
www.raymondschool.com/
Raymond S 400/K-8
2659 76th St 53126 262-835-2929
George Slupski, prin. Fax 835-2087

Frederic, Polk, Pop. 1,233
Frederic SD 500/PK-12
1437 Clam Falls Dr 54837 715-327-5630
Gerald Tischer, supt. Fax 327-5609
www.frederic.k12.wi.us/
Frederic ES 300/PK-6
305 Birch St E 54837 715-327-4221
Kelly Steen, prin. Fax 327-8327

Frederic Adventist S 50/1-8
PO Box 430 54837 715-327-4956
Ron Wood, admin.

Fredonia, Ozaukee, Pop. 2,192
Northern Ozaukee SD 800/PK-12
401 Highland Dr 53021 262-692-2489
William Harbron, supt. Fax 692-6257
www.nosd.edu
Ozaukee ES 300/PK-4
401 Highland Dr 53021 262-692-2401
Cynthia Dallman, prin. Fax 692-2441
Ozaukee MS 200/5-8
401 Highland Dr 53021 262-692-2463
Pam Warner, prin. Fax 692-2313

Rosemary S 100/K-6
PO Box 250 53021 262-692-2141
Gerald Malueg, prin. Fax 692-3085

Freedom, Outagamie
Freedom Area SD 1,600/PK-12
N4021 County Rd E, Kaukauna WI 54130
920-788-7944
Lois Cuff, supt. Fax 788-7949
www.freedomschools.k12.wi.us
Freedom ES 700/PK-5
N3569 County Rd E, 920-788-7950
Jeanne Czech, prin. Fax 788-7956
Freedom MS 300/6-8
N4021 County Rd E, Kaukauna WI 54130
920-788-7945
Ken Fisher, prin. Fax 788-7701

St. Nicholas S 100/PK-8
W2035 County Rd S, Kaukauna WI 54130
Rosemary Perrino, prin. 920-788-9371

Fremont, Waupaca, Pop. 687
Weyauwega-Fremont SD
Supt. — See Weyauwega
Fremont ES 200/PK-5
PO Box 308 54940 920-446-2231
Kirk Delwiche, prin. Fax 446-2347

St. John Lutheran S 50/K-8
N6199 37th Ave 54940 920-446-3836
David Schulz, prin. Fax 446-3836

Friendship, Adams, Pop. 766
Adams-Friendship Area SD 1,800/PK-12
201 W 6th St 53934 608-339-3213
Steven Lavallee, supt. Fax 339-6213
www.af.k12.wi.us/pages/index.cfm
Pine Land ES 50/K-3
201 W 6th St 53934 608-564-7424
Mary Wisse, prin. Fax 564-7496
Other Schools – See Adams, Arkdale, Grand Marsh

Galesville, Trempealeau, Pop. 1,462
Gale-Ettrick-Trempealeau SD 1,200/PK-12
PO Box 4000 54630 608-582-2291
Troy Gunderson, supt. Fax 582-4263
www.getschools.k12.wi.us
Gale-Ettrick-Tremp MS 200/6-8
19650 Prairie Ridge Ln 54630 608-582-3500
Paul Uhren, prin.
Galesville ES 200/PK-5
PO Box 4001 54630 608-582-2241
Ron Jones, prin. Fax 582-4447
Other Schools – See Ettrick, Trempealeau

Genesee Depot, Waukesha
Kettle Moraine SD
Supt. — See Wales
Magee ES 300/PK-5
PO Box 37 53127 262-968-6450
Maria Kucharski, prin. Fax 968-6471

St. Paul S 100/K-8
PO Box 95 53127 262-968-3175
Linda Cooney, prin. Fax 968-5546

Genoa, Vernon, Pop. 266

St. Charles S 50/PK-8
PO Box 130 54632 608-689-2642
Heidi Balk, lead tchr. Fax 689-2811

Genoa City, Walworth, Pop. 2,742
Genoa City J2 SD 600/K-8
PO Box 250 53128 262-279-1051
Bill Lehner, supt. Fax 279-1052
Brookwood ES 400/K-4
PO Box 250 53128 262-279-6496
Aaron Griffin, prin. Fax 279-2098
Brookwood MS 300/5-8
PO Box 250 53128 262-279-1053
Kellie Bohn, prin. Fax 279-1052

Germantown, Washington, Pop. 19,245
Germantown SD 3,900/PK-12
N104W13840 Donges Bay Rd 53022 262-253-3900
Kenneth Rogers, supt. Fax 251-6999
www.germantown.k12.wi.us
County Line ES 500/PK-5
W159N9939 Butternut Rd 53022 262-253-3465
Catherine Schultz, prin. Fax 253-3491
Kennedy MS 900/6-8
W160N11836 Crusader Ct 53022 262-253-3450
Steven Bold, prin. Fax 253-3499
MacArthur ES 400/PK-5
W154N11492 Fond Du Lac Ave 53022
262-253-3468
Adrienne Schneider, prin. Fax 253-3496
Rockfield ES 300/PK-5
N132W18473 Rockfield Rd 53022 262-253-3472
Paul Bingen, prin. Fax 253-3497
Other Schools – See Colgate

Bethlehem Lutheran S - North 100/K-4
N108W14290 Bel Aire Ln 53022 262-257-0409
Daryl Weber, prin. Fax 257-0407
St. Boniface S 300/K-8
W204N11968 Goldendale Rd 53022 262-628-1955
Susan Nygaard, prin. Fax 628-1689

Gillett, Oconto, Pop. 1,188
Gillett SD 700/PK-12
PO Box 227 54124 920-855-2137
Stuart Rivard, supt. Fax 855-1557
www.gillett.k12.wi.us
Gillett ES 300/PK-5
PO Box 231 54124 920-855-2119
Marjorie Muller, prin. Fax 855-1502
Gillett MS 200/6-8
PO Box 227 54124 920-855-2137
Sam Santacroce, prin. Fax 855-6600

Gilman, Taylor, Pop. 460
Gilman SD 400/PK-12
325 N 5th Ave 54433 715-447-8216
Mark Heyerdahl, supt. Fax 447-8731
www.gilman.k12.wi.us
Gilman ES 200/PK-6
325 N 5th Ave 54433 715-447-8776
Dawn Randall, prin. Fax 447-8731

Gilmanton, Buffalo
Gilmanton SD 200/PK-12
PO Box 28 54743 715-946-3158
William Perry, supt. Fax 946-3474
www.ghs.k12.wi.us
Gilmanton ES 50/PK-5
PO Box 28 54743 715-946-3158
William Perry, prin. Fax 946-3474

Glendale, Milwaukee, Pop. 12,880
Glendale-River Hills SD 900/PK-8
2600 W Mill Rd 53209 414-351-7170
Larry Smalley, supt. Fax 434-0109
www.glendale.k12.wi.us
Glen Hills MS 500/4-8
2600 W Mill Rd 53209 414-351-7160
Haydee Smith, prin. Fax 351-8100
Parkway ES 500/PK-3
5910 N Milwaukee River Pkwy 53209 414-351-7190
Shannon Kilton, prin. Fax 351-8103

St. John Lutheran S 200/PK-8
7877 N Port Washington Rd 53217 414-352-4150
Tammy Langfield, prin. Fax 352-4221

Glenwood City, Saint Croix, Pop. 1,225
Glenwood City SD 700/K-12
850 Maple St 54013 715-265-4757
Timothy Emholtz, supt. Fax 265-4214
www.gcsd.k12.wi.us/
Glenwood City ES 300/K-6
857 320th St 54013 715-265-4231
James Celt, prin.
Glenwood City JHS 100/7-8
850 Maple St 54013 715-265-4266
Timothy Johnson, prin.

Glidden, Ashland
Glidden SD 100/PK-12
370 Grant St 54527 715-264-2141
Tim Kief, supt. Fax 264-3413
www.glidden.k12.wi.us
Glidden ES 100/PK-5
370 Grant St 54527 715-264-2141
Tim Kief, prin. Fax 264-3413
Glidden MS 6-8
370 Grant St 54527 715-264-2141
Tim Kief, prin. Fax 264-3413

Goodman, Marinette
Goodman-Armstrong Creek SD 200/PK-12
PO Box 160 54125 715-336-2575
Jeff Reeder, supt. Fax 336-2576
goodman.wi.schoolwebpages.com/
Goodman-Armstrong ES 100/PK-6
PO Box 160 54125 715-336-2575
Jeff Reeder, prin. Fax 336-2576

Grafton, Ozaukee, Pop. 11,625
Grafton SD 2,100/PK-12
1900 Washington St 53024 262-376-5400
Jeffrey Pechura, supt. Fax 376-5599
www.grafton.k12.wi.us/
Grafton ES 300/PK-5
1800 Washington St 53024 262-376-5700
Jeffrey Martyka, prin. Fax 376-5727
Kennedy ES 300/K-5
1629 11th Ave 53024 262-376-5650
Karen Sieber, prin. Fax 376-5660
Long MS 500/6-8
700 Hickory St 53024 262-376-5800
Greg Kabara, prin. Fax 376-5810
Woodview ES 200/K-5
600 5th Ave 53024 262-376-5750
Tyson Novinska, prin. Fax 376-5760

Our Savior Lutheran S 100/PK-8
1332 Arrowhead Rd 53024 262-377-7780
Joel Grulke, prin. Fax 377-9045

St. Joseph S — 200/K-8
1619 Washington St 53024 — 262-375-6505
Mary Stallmann, prin. — Fax 375-6509
St. Paul Lutheran S — 300/PK-8
701 Washington St 53024 — 262-377-4659
Michael Yurk, prin. — Fax 377-7808

Grand Marsh, Adams
Adams-Friendship Area SD
Supt. — See Friendship
Grand Marsh ES — 100/PK-5
620 County Rd E 53936 — 608-339-6556
Karen Doherty, prin. — Fax 339-7306

Granton, Clark, Pop. 402
Granton Area SD — 300/K-12
217 N Main St 54436 — 715-238-7292
Rick Rehm, supt. — Fax 238-7288
www.granton.k12.wi.us/
Granton S — 200/K-8
217 N Main St 54436 — 715-238-7292
Craig Anderson, prin. — Fax 238-7288

Grantsburg, Burnett, Pop. 1,397
Grantsburg SD — 1,000/PK-12
480 E James Ave 54840 — 715-463-5499
Joni Burgin, supt. — Fax 463-2534
www.gk12.net/
Grantsburg ES — 200/1-3
480 E James Ave 54840 — 715-463-2320
Kathleen Coppenbarger, prin. — Fax 463-5158
Grantsburg MS — 400/4-8
480 E James Ave 54840 — 715-463-2455
Brad Jones, prin. — Fax 463-3209
Nelson ES — 100/PK-K
480 E James Ave 54840 — 715-689-2421
Kathleen Coppenbarger, prin. — Fax 689-2421

Gratiot, Lafayette, Pop. 247
Black Hawk SD
Supt. — See South Wayne
Black Hawk MS — 100/4-8
PO Box 457 53541 — 608-922-6457
Charles McNulty, prin. — Fax 922-3376

Green Bay, Brown, Pop. 101,203
Ashwaubenon SD — 3,000/PK-12
1055 Griffiths Ln 54304 — 920-492-2900
David Schmidt, supt. — Fax 492-2911
www.ashwaubenon.k12.wi.us
Cormier S & Early Learning Center — 200/PK-K
2280 S Broadway 54304 — 920-448-2870
Maria Arena, prin. — Fax 448-2873
Parkview MS — 700/6-8
955 Willard Dr 54304 — 920-492-2940
Kris Hucek, prin. — Fax 492-2944
Pioneer ES — 400/1-5
1360 Ponderosa Ave 54313 — 920-492-2920
Pete Marto, prin. — Fax 492-2987
Valley View ES — 600/1-5
2200 True Ln 54304 — 920-492-2930
Kurt Weyers, prin. — Fax 492-2340

Green Bay Area SD — 19,800/PK-12
PO Box 23387 54305 — 920-448-2000
Gregory Maass, supt. — Fax 448-3562
www.greenbay.k12.wi.us
Baird ES — 300/PK-5
539 Laverne Dr 54311 — 920-391-2410
Annette Zernicke, prin. — Fax 391-2532
Beaumont ES — 300/PK-5
1505 Gatewood St 54304 — 920-492-2690
Cynthia Schneider, prin. — Fax 492-5565
Chappell ES — 200/PK-5
205 N Fisk St 54303 — 920-492-2630
Kristen Worden, prin. — Fax 492-5566
Danz ES — 500/PK-5
2130 Basten St 54302 — 920-391-2440
Theresa Willems, prin. — Fax 391-2533
Doty ES — 400/PK-5
525 Longview Ave 54301 — 920-337-2360
David Bridenhagen, prin. — Fax 337-2373
Edison MS — 1,100/6-8
442 Alpine Dr 54302 — 920-391-2450
Mark Smith, prin. — Fax 391-2531
Eisenhower ES — 400/PK-5
1770 Amy St 54302 — 920-391-2420
Claudia Orr, prin. — Fax 391-2534
Elmore ES — 200/PK-5
615 Ethel Ave 54303 — 920-492-2615
Kathryn Tillo, prin. — Fax 492-5567
Fort Howard ES — 300/PK-5
520 Dousman St 54303 — 920-448-2105
Curt Julian, prin. — Fax 448-3553
Franklin MS — 800/6-8
1234 W Mason St 54303 — 920-492-2670
Matthew Weller, prin. — Fax 492-5563
Howe ES — 400/PK-5
525 S Madison St 54301 — 920-448-2141
De Ann Lehman, prin. — Fax 448-3554
Jackson ES — 300/PK-5
1306 S Ridge Rd 54304 — 920-492-2620
Kathleen Costello, prin. — Fax 492-5568
Jefferson ES — 200/PK-5
905 Harrison St 54303 — 920-448-2106
Mary Ann Anderson, prin. — Fax 448-3555
Keller ES — 200/PK-5
1806 Bond St 54303 — 920-492-2685
Sherilyn Moon, prin. — Fax 492-5569
Kennedy ES — 300/PK-5
1754 9th St 54304 — 920-492-2640
Ann Barszcz, prin. — Fax 492-5570
King ES — 400/PK-5
1601 Dancing Dunes Dr 54313 — 920-492-2771
Diane Stelmach, prin. — Fax 492-5571
Langlade ES — 300/PK-5
400 Broadview Dr 54301 — 920-337-2370
Pamela Haugh, prin. — Fax 337-2374
Leopold S — 400/PK-8
622 Eliza St 54301 — 920-448-2140
Trina Lambert, prin. — Fax 448-3552
Lincoln ES — 200/PK-5
105 S Buchanan St 54303 — 920-492-2675
Kim Spychalla, prin. — Fax 492-5572
Lombardi MS — 900/6-8
1520 S Point Rd 54313 — 920-492-2625
Nancy Croy, prin. — Fax 492-5564
Mac Arthur ES — 300/PK-5
1331 Hobart Dr 54304 — 920-492-2680
Rebecca Swanson, prin. — Fax 492-5573
Martin ES — 400/PK-5
626 Pinehurst Ave 54302 — 920-391-2405
Carrie Shepherd, prin. — Fax 391-2500
McAuliffe ES — 600/PK-5
2071 Emerald Dr 54311 — 920-391-2436
Kelly Rollin, prin. — Fax 391-2535
Nicolet ES — 400/PK-5
1309 Elm St 54302 — 920-448-2142
Tammy Van Dyke, prin. — Fax 448-3556
Smith S — 800/PK-8
2765 Sussex Rd 54311 — 920-391-2425
Andrea Landwehr, prin. — Fax 391-2564
Sullivan ES — 600/PK-5
1567 Deckner Ave 54302 — 920-391-2470
Michael Fraley, prin. — Fax 391-2536
Tank ES — 200/PK-5
814 S Oakland Ave 54304 — 920-448-2104
Kathleen Mueller, prin. — Fax 448-3557
Washington MS — 900/6-8
314 S Baird St 54301 — 920-448-2095
Amy Bindas, prin. — Fax 448-3551
Webster ES — 300/PK-5
2101 S Webster Ave 54301 — 920-448-2143
Nancy Schultz, prin. — Fax 448-3558
Wequiock ES — 200/PK-5
3994 Wequiock Rd 54311 — 920-448-2477
Shirley Paulson, prin. — Fax 448-2234
Wilder ES — 500/PK-5
2590 Robinson Ave 54311 — 920-391-2460
Mark Allen, prin. — Fax 391-2537

Howard-Suamico SD — 5,100/K-12
2700 Lineville Rd 54313 — 920-662-7878
Damian LaCroix, supt. — Fax 662-9777
www.hssd.k12.wi.us
Bay View MS — 800/7-8
1217 Cardinal Ln 54313 — 920-662-8196
Steve Meyers, prin. — Fax 662-7979
Forest Glen ES — 700/K-4
1935 Cardinal Ln 54313 — 920-662-7958
Angela Sorenson, prin. — Fax 662-7900
Howard ES — 200/K-4
631 W Idlewild Ct 54303 — 920-662-9700
Vickie Dassler, prin. — Fax 662-9750
Lineville IS — 800/5-6
2700 Lineville Rd 54313 — 920-662-7871
Charles Templer, prin. — Fax 662-7822
Meadowbrook ES — 400/K-4
720 Hillcrest Hts 54313 — 920-662-5000
Kathleen Hoppe, prin. — Fax 662-5050
Suamico ES — 600/K-4
2153 School Ln 54313 — 920-662-9800
Ryan Welnetz, prin. — Fax 662-9888
Other Schools – See Suamico

Pulaski Community SD
Supt. — See Pulaski
Lannoye ES — 200/K-5
2007 County Road U 54313 — 920-865-6400
Pamela Engel, prin. — Fax 865-6402

Enterprise Academy — 200/PK-5
680 Cormier Rd 54304 — 920-496-1233
Kelley Roznik, prin. — Fax 496-3143
Green Bay Adventist Jr. Academy — 50/1-8
1422 Shawano Ave 54303 — 920-494-2741
David Smith, admin. — Fax 494-6507
Green Bay Trinity Lutheran S — 100/K-7
120 S Henry St 54302 — 920-655-4673
Kenneth Baumann, prin. — Fax 468-5757
Holy Cross S — 200/PK-8
3002 Bay Settlement Rd 54311 — 920-468-0625
Robin Jensen, prin. — Fax 468-0625
Holy Family S — 400/PK-8
1204 S Fisk St 54304 — 920-494-1931
Pamela Otto, prin. — Fax 494-4942
Pilgrim Lutheran S — 300/PK-8
1731 Saint Agnes Dr 54304 — 920-965-2244
Kenny Longmire, prin. — Fax 965-2255
Prince of Peace S — 100/PK-5
3542 Finger Rd 54311 — 920-468-7262
Theresa Williams, prin. — Fax 468-5713
Redeemer Lutheran S — 100/PK-8
205 Hudson St 54303 — 920-499-1033
Kevin Kuske, prin. — Fax 496-0795
Resurrection S — 200/PK-8
333 Hilltop Dr 54301 — 920-336-3230
Jane Schueller, prin. — Fax 336-1949
St. Bernard S — 500/PK-8
2020 Hillside Ln 54302 — 920-468-5026
Kay Franz, prin. — Fax 468-3478
St. John the Baptist S — 400/PK-8
2561 Glendale Ave 54313 — 920-434-3822
Vicki Marotz, prin. — Fax 434-5016
St. Mark Evangelical Lutheran S — 200/PK-8
1167 Kenwood St 54304 — 920-494-9113
Jeremy Bock, prin. — Fax 494-3028
St. Matthew S — 300/PK-8
2575 S Webster Ave 54301 — 920-432-5223
Renee Dercks-Engels, prin. — Fax 435-0065
St. Paul Lutheran S — 100/PK-8
514 S Clay St 54301 — 920-435-9852
Kenneth Kasten, prin. — Fax 437-3517
St. Thomas More S — 100/PK-8
650 S Irwin Ave 54301 — 920-432-8242
Eric Weydt, prin. — Fax 432-1562

Greendale, Milwaukee, Pop. 13,860
Greendale SD — 2,400/PK-12
5900 S 51st St 53129 — 414-423-2700
William Hughes, supt. — Fax 423-2723
www.greendale.k12.wi.us
Canterbury ES — 400/PK-5
7000 Enfield Ave 53129 — 414-423-2770
Christian Pleister, prin. — Fax 423-2994
College Park ES — 300/K-5
5701 W College Ave 53129 — 414-423-2850
Kerry Owens-Bur, prin. — Fax 423-2852
Greendale MS — 600/6-8
6800 Schoolway 53129 — 414-423-2800
John Weiss, prin. — Fax 423-2806
Highland View ES — 300/PK-5
5900 S 51st St 53129 — 414-423-2750
Leni Dietrich, prin. — Fax 423-0592

St. Alphonsus S — 300/K-8
6000 W Loomis Rd 53129 — 414-421-1760
Pat Wadzinski, prin. — Fax 421-8744

Greenfield, Milwaukee, Pop. 35,753
Greenfield SD — 3,300/PK-12
8500 W Chapman Ave 53228 — 414-529-9090
Conrad Farner, supt. — Fax 529-9478
www.greenfield.k12.wi.us
Edgewood ES — 300/PK-5
4711 S 47th St 53220 — 414-281-5750
Charlie Smith, prin. — Fax 281-3909
Glenwood ES — 200/PK-5
3550 S 51st St 53220 — 414-545-2280
Jeff Krumbein, prin. — Fax 545-5626
Greenfield MS — 700/6-8
3200 W Barnard Ave 53221 — 414-282-4700
Brad Iding, prin. — Fax 282-1017
Maple Grove ES — 400/PK-5
6921 W Coldspring Rd 53220 — 414-541-0600
Lisa Elliott, prin. — Fax 541-8070
Other Schools – See Milwaukee

Whitnall SD — 2,400/PK-12
5000 S 116th St 53228 — 414-525-8400
Karen Petric, supt. — Fax 525-8401
www.whitnall.com
Whitnall MS — 600/6-8
5025 S 116th St 53228 — 414-525-8650
Lynn Stadler, prin. — Fax 525-8651
Other Schools – See Hales Corners

Our Father Lutheran S — 100/PK-8
6023 S 27th St 53221 — 414-282-7500
John Mierow, prin. — Fax 282-9737
St. Jacobi Lutheran S — 200/PK-8
8605 W Forest Home Ave 53228 — 414-425-2040
David Hackmann, prin. — Fax 425-0583
St. John the Evangelist S — 200/K-8
8500 W Coldspring Rd 53228 — 414-321-8540
Mary Otto, prin. — Fax 321-4450

Green Lake, Green Lake, Pop. 1,125
Green Lake SD — 400/PK-12
PO Box 369 54941 — 920-294-6411
Ken Bates, supt. — Fax 294-6589
www.greenlakeschools.com
Green Lake ES — 200/PK-6
PO Box 369 54941 — 920-294-6411
E. Jon Tracy, prin. — Fax 294-6589

Peace Lutheran S — 100/K-8
435 Walker Ave 54941 — 920-294-3509
Todd Stoltz, prin.

Greenleaf, Brown, Pop. 470

St. Mary S — 100/PK-6
2218 Day St 54126 — 920-864-2586
Gloria Kennedy, prin. — Fax 864-2979
Zion Lutheran S — 100/K-8
7373 County Rd W 54126 — 920-864-2349
Brian Humann, prin.
Zion Lutheran S — 100/PK-8
8374 County Rd W 54126 — 920-864-2468
Ron Schroeder, prin. — Fax 864-2684

Greenville, Outagamie
Hortonville SD
Supt. — See Hortonville
Greenville ES — 700/PK-4
W6822 Greenridge Dr 54942 — 920-757-6971
Laurie Wagner, prin. — Fax 757-6972
Greenville MS — 500/5-8
N1450 Fawn Ridge Dr 54942 — 920-757-7140
Bruce Carew, prin. — Fax 757-7141

Grace Christian S — 50/K-6
N1615 Meadowview Dr 54942 — 920-733-9101
Anita Golz, prin. — Fax 757-0461
Immanuel Evangelical Lutheran S — 200/PK-8
W7265 School Rd 54942 — 920-757-6606
Richard Huebner, prin. — Fax 757-1151
St. Mary S — 200/PK-8
N2387 Municipal Dr 54942 — 920-757-5516
Debra Fuller, prin. — Fax 757-6560

Greenwood, Clark, Pop. 1,082
Greenwood SD — 400/PK-12
PO Box 310 54437 — 715-267-6101
Thomas Nykl, supt. — Fax 267-6113
www.greenwood.k12.wi.us/
Greenwood ES — 200/PK-6
PO Box 310 54437 — 715-267-7211
Thomas Nykl, prin. — Fax 267-7209

St. Mary S — 50/1-6
PO Box 129 54437 — 715-267-6477
Jeannine Raycher, prin. — Fax 267-4421

Gresham, Shawano, Pop. 585
Gresham SD 300/PK-12
501 Schabow St 54128 715-787-3211
Keary Mattson, supt. Fax 787-3951
Gresham S 100/PK-8
501 Schabow St 54128 715-787-3211
Keary Mattson, prin. Fax 787-3951

Hager City, Pierce
Ellsworth Community SD
Supt. — See Ellsworth
Lindgren Early Learning Center 100/PK-PK
N3470 US Highway 63 54014 715-792-2424
Mary Zimmerman, prin. Fax 792-5420
Prairie View ES 100/K-4
W7375 170th Ave 54014 715-792-5285
Mary Zimmerman, prin. Fax 792-2068

Hales Corners, Milwaukee, Pop. 7,535
Whitnall SD
Supt. — See Greenfield
Edgerton ES 400/PK-5
5145 S 116th St 53130 414-525-8900
Chris D'Acquisto, prin. Fax 525-8901
Hales Corners ES 500/K-5
11319 W Godsell Ave 53130 414-525-8800
Lori Komas, prin. Fax 525-8801

Hales Corners Lutheran S 500/PK-8
12300 W Janesville Rd 53130 414-529-6702
Eva Fronk, prin. Fax 529-6710
St. Mary Parish S 400/K-8
9553 W Edgerton Ave 53130 414-425-3100
Jeanne Siegenthaler, prin. Fax 425-6270

Hamburg, Marathon
Merrill Area SD
Supt. — See Merrill
Maple Grove ES 100/K-5
290 County Road F 54411 715-536-7684
Jeffrey Damrau, prin. Fax 536-4221

Hammond, Saint Croix, Pop. 1,695
St. Croix Central SD 1,300/PK-12
PO Box 118 54015 715-796-2256
David Bradley, supt. Fax 796-2460
www.scc.k12.wi.us
St. Croix Central MS 400/5-8
PO Box 118 54015 715-796-2256
Scott Woodington, prin. Fax 796-2460
Other Schools – See Roberts

Hartford, Washington, Pop. 13,017
Erin SD 400/PK-8
6901 County Road O 53027 262-673-3720
Keith Kriewaldt, admin. Fax 673-2659
www.erinschool.org
Erin S 400/PK-8
6901 County Road O 53027 262-673-3720
John Platais, prin. Fax 673-2659

Hartford J1 SD 1,600/PK-8
675 E Rossman St 53027 262-673-3155
Dr. Mark Smits, admin. Fax 673-3548
www.hartfordjt1.k12.wi.us
Central MS 500/6-8
1100 Cedar St 53027 262-673-8040
Wayne Thuecks, prin. Fax 673-7596
Lincoln ES 600/PK-5
755 S Rural St 53027 262-673-2100
Jacob Jilling, prin. Fax 673-0148
Rossman ES 500/PK-5
600 Highland Ave 53027 262-673-3300
Pam Pyzyk, prin. Fax 673-3543

Slinger SD
Supt. — See Slinger
Addison ES 400/PK-5
5050 Indian Dr 53027 262-644-8037
John Larkin, prin. Fax 644-1936

Peace Lutheran S 200/K-8
1025 Peace Lutheran Dr 53027 262-673-3811
James Rademan, prin. Fax 673-3897
St. Kilian S 200/PK-8
245 High St 53027 262-673-3081
Angela Little, prin. Fax 673-0412

Hartland, Waukesha, Pop. 8,672
Hartland-Lakeside J3 SD 1,400/PK-8
800 N Shore Dr 53029 262-369-6700
Glenn Schilling, supt. Fax 369-6755
www.hartlake.org
North ES 400/PK-5
232 Church St 53029 262-369-6710
Patrick Thome, prin. Fax 369-6711
North Shore MS 500/6-8
800 N Shore Dr 53029 262-369-6767
Michele Schmidt, prin. Fax 369-6766
South ES 500/PK-5
651 E Imperial Dr 53029 262-369-6720
David Risch, prin. Fax 369-6722

Lake Country SD 500/K-8
1800 Vettelson Rd 53029 262-367-3606
Mark Lichte, supt. Fax 367-3205
www.lcs.k12.wi.us
Lake Country S 500/K-8
1800 Vettelson Rd 53029 262-367-3606
Mark Lichte, prin. Fax 367-3205

Swallow SD 500/K-8
W299N5614 County Rd E 53029 262-367-2000
Jeff Klaisner, supt. Fax 367-5014
www.swallowschool.org
Swallow S 500/K-8
W299N5614 County Rd E 53029 262-367-2000
Bob Hall, prin. Fax 367-5014

Divine Redeemer Lutheran S 300/PK-8
N48W31385 W Hill Rd 53029 262-367-3664
Michael Oldenburg, prin. Fax 367-0824
St. Charles S 200/K-8
526 Renson Rd 53029 262-367-2040
Douglas Dunlop, prin. Fax 367-6960
University Lake S 300/PK-12
PO Box 290 53029 262-367-6011
Bradley Ashley, hdmstr. Fax 367-3146
Zion Lutheran S 100/PK-8
1023 E Capitol Dr 53029 262-367-3617
David Neujahr, prin. Fax 367-3617

Hatley, Marathon, Pop. 490
D.C. Everest Area SD
Supt. — See Schofield
Hatley ES 100/3-5
417 Emmonsville Rd 54440 715-446-3336
Julie Fondell, prin. Fax 446-3171

Haugen, Barron, Pop. 277
Rice Lake Area SD
Supt. — See Rice Lake
Haugen ES 100/K-5
615 5th St W 54841 715-234-7341
Drew Goeldner, prin. Fax 236-7598

Hayward, Sawyer, Pop. 2,293
Hayward Community SD 1,900/PK-12
PO Box 860 54843 715-634-2619
Michael Cox, supt. Fax 634-3560
www.hayward.k12.wi.us
Hayward IS 400/3-5
PO Box 860 54843 715-634-2619
John Becker, prin. Fax 934-2244
Hayward MS 500/6-8
PO Box 860 54843 715-634-2619
Craig Olson, prin. Fax 634-9953
Hayward PS 400/PK-2
PO Box 860 54843 715-634-2619
John Becker, prin. Fax 934-2246
Other Schools – See Stone Lake

Hazel Green, Grant, Pop. 1,205
Southwestern Wisconsin SD 600/PK-12
PO Box 368 53811 608-854-2261
James Egan, supt. Fax 854-2305
www.swsd.k12.wi.us
Southwestern Wisconsin S 400/PK-8
PO Box 368 53811 608-854-2261
Douglas McArthur, prin. Fax 854-2305

St. Joseph S 100/PK-8
780 County Road Z 53811 608-748-4442
Carol Gebhart, prin. Fax 748-5201

Helenville, Jefferson

St. Peters Lutheran S 100/K-8
W3255 US Highway 18 53137 920-674-3245
Craig Winkler, prin. Fax 674-3245

Highland, Iowa, Pop. 817
Highland SD 300/PK-12
PO Box 2850 53543 608-929-4525
David Romstad, supt. Fax 929-4527
www.highland.k12.wi.us
Highland ES 100/PK-5
PO Box 2850 53543 608-929-4525
David Romstad, prin. Fax 929-4527

Hilbert, Calumet, Pop. 1,087
Hilbert SD 500/PK-12
PO Box 390 54129 920-853-3558
Anthony Sweere, supt. Fax 853-7030
www.hilbert.k12.wi.us
Hilbert ES 200/PK-6
PO Box 390 54129 920-853-3531
Martha Albers, prin. Fax 853-3095
Hilbert MS 100/7-8
PO Box 390 54129 920-853-3558
Martha Albers, prin. Fax 853-7030

St. Mary S 50/K-6
PO Box 249 54129 920-853-3216
Chandra Sromek, prin. Fax 853-3560
St. Peter Lutheran S 50/PK-6
PO Box 190 54129 920-853-3851
Bonnie Teinert, prin. Fax 853-3851
Trinity Lutheran S 100/PK-8
N6081 W River Rd 54129 920-853-3134
Debbie Kline, prin. Fax 853-3134

Hillsboro, Vernon, Pop. 1,303
Hillsboro SD 600/PK-12
PO Box 526 54634 608-489-2221
Ron Benish, supt. Fax 489-2811
www.hillsboro.k12.wi.us
Hillsboro ES 300/PK-6
PO Box 526 54634 608-489-2225
Curt Bisarek, prin. Fax 489-3358

Holcombe, Chippewa
Lake Holcombe SD 400/PK-12
27331 262nd Ave 54745 715-595-4241
Tom Goulet, supt. Fax 595-6383
lakeholcombe.k12.wi.us
Holcombe S 300/PK-8
27331 262nd Ave 54745 715-595-4241
Mark Porter, prin. Fax 595-6383

Hollandale, Iowa, Pop. 266
Pecatonica Area SD
Supt. — See Blanchardville
Pecatonica ES 200/PK-5
PO Box 128 53544 608-523-4283
David McSherry, prin. Fax 967-1172

Holmen, LaCrosse, Pop. 7,446
Holmen SD 3,400/PK-12
1019 McHugh Rd 54636 608-526-6610
Dale Carlson, supt. Fax 526-1333
www.holmen.k12.wi.us
Evergreen ES 500/K-5
510 Long Coulee Rd 54636 608-526-9080
Joanne Stephens, prin. Fax 526-9540
Holmen MS 800/6-8
502 N Main St 54636 608-526-3391
Fax 526-6716
Prairie View ES K-5
1201 Newport Ln 54636 608-526-1600
Patrice Tronstad, prin.
Sand Lake ES 500/K-5
3600 Sandlake Rd 54636 608-781-0974
Neal Janssen, prin. Fax 781-2809
Viking ES 600/K-5
500 E Wall St 54636 608-526-3316
Teri Staloch, prin. Fax 526-9482
Other Schools – See Onalaska

Horicon, Dodge, Pop. 3,604
Horicon SD 900/PK-12
611 Mill St 53032 920-485-2898
Gary Berger, supt. Fax 485-3601
www.horicon.k12.wi.us
Van Brunt ES 300/PK-5
611 Mill St 53032 920-485-4423
Scott Miller, prin. Fax 485-4318
Van Brunt MS 200/6-8
611 Mill St 53032 920-485-4423
Scott Miller, prin. Fax 485-4318

Mountain Top Christian Academy 100/PK-12
W3941 State Road 33 53032 920-485-6630
Stacey Nummerdor, prin. Fax 485-0308
St. Stephen Lutheran S 100/PK-8
505 N Palmatory St 53032 920-485-6687
Joel Glawe, prin. Fax 485-2545

Hortonville, Outagamie, Pop. 2,630
Hortonville SD 3,300/PK-12
PO Box 70 54944 920-779-7900
William Prijic, supt. Fax 779-7903
www.hasd.org
Hortonville ES 400/PK-4
PO Box 70 54944 920-779-7911
Larry Sikowski, prin. Fax 779-7915
Hortonville MS 500/5-8
PO Box 70 54944 920-779-7922
John Brattlund, prin. Fax 779-7923
Other Schools – See Greenville

Bethlehem Evangelical Lutheran S 200/PK-8
PO Box 250 54944 920-779-6761
Eric Troge, prin. Fax 779-4320

Houlton, Saint Croix
Hudson SD
Supt. — See Hudson
Houlton ES 200/K-5
70 County Rd E 54082 715-377-3850
Ann Mitchell, prin. Fax 549-5797

Howards Grove, Sheboygan, Pop. 3,034
Howards Grove SD 900/K-12
403 Audubon Rd 53083 920-565-4454
John Eickholt, supt. Fax 565-4461
www.hgsd.k12.wi.us
Howards Grove MS 300/5-8
506 Kennedy Ave 53083 920-565-4452
Andy Hansen, prin. Fax 565-4460
Northview ES 300/K-4
902 Tyler Rd 53083 920-565-4457
Diane Weiland, prin. Fax 565-4458

St. Paul's Lutheran S 100/PK-8
441 Millersville Ave 53083 920-565-3780
Mark Nolte, prin. Fax 565-3781

Hubertus, Washington
Friess Lake SD 300/K-8
1750 State Road 164 53033 262-628-2380
John Engstrom, supt. Fax 628-2546
www.friesslakeschool.org
Friess Lake S 300/K-8
1750 State Road 164 53033 262-628-2380
John Engstrom, prin. Fax 628-2546

Crown of Life Lutheran S 50/K-8
1292 Tally Ho Trl 53033 262-628-2550
Wade Cohoon, prin. Fax 628-0893
St. Gabriel S 100/K-8
3733 Hubertus Rd 53033 262-628-1711
Dr. Judith Mortell, prin. Fax 628-0280

Hudson, Saint Croix, Pop. 11,367
Hudson SD 5,200/PK-12
644 Brakke Dr 54016 715-377-3700
Mary Bowen-Eggebraaten, supt. Fax 377-3726
www.hudson.k12.wi.us
Hudson MS 1,100/6-8
1300 Carmichael Rd 54016 715-377-3820
Dan Koch, prin. Fax 377-3821
Hudson Prairie ES 600/K-5
1400 Carmichael Rd 54016 715-377-3860
Susan Prather, prin. Fax 377-3861
North Hudson ES 500/K-5
510 Lemon St N 54016 715-377-3870
Dolf Schmidt, prin. Fax 377-3871
River Crest ES PK-5
535 County Road F 54016 715-377-3890
Patricia Hodges, prin. Fax 377-3891
Rock ES 600/K-5
340 13th St S 54016 715-377-3840
Amy Hamborg, prin. Fax 377-3841

Willow River ES 400/K-5
1118 4th St 54016 715-377-3880
David Grambow, prin. Fax 377-3881
Other Schools – See Houlton

St. Patrick S 400/PK-8
403 Saint Croix St 54016 715-386-3941
Mary Piasecki, prin. Fax 381-5125
Trinity Academy 200/PK-5
1205 6th St 54016 715-386-9349
Alison Johnson, prin. Fax 386-0137

Hurley, Iron, Pop. 1,678
Hurley SD 300/PK-12
5503 W Range View Dr 54534 715-561-4900
Christopher Patritto, supt. Fax 561-4953
www.hurley.k12.wi.us
Hurley S 300/PK-12
5503 W Range View Dr 54534 715-561-4900
Jeffrey Gulan, prin. Fax 561-4157

Hustisford, Dodge, Pop. 1,106
Hustisford SD 400/PK-12
PO Box 326 53034 920-349-8109
Ed Van Ravenstein, supt. Fax 349-3716
www.hustisford.k12.wi.us
Hustis ES 200/PK-6
PO Box 386 53034 920-349-3228
Keith Schneider, prin. Fax 349-8675

Bethany Lutheran S 50/K-8
PO Box 387 53034 920-349-3244
Douglas Stellick, prin. Fax 349-3245

Independence, Trempealeau, Pop. 1,246
Independence SD 300/PK-12
23786 Indee Blvd 54747 715-985-3172
Dave Laehn, supt. Fax 985-2303
www.indps.k12.wi.us
Independence S 200/PK-8
23786 Indee Blvd 54747 715-985-3172
Anne Gierok, prin. Fax 985-2303

SS. Peter & Paul S 100/PK-8
36100 Osseo Rd 54747 715-985-3719
Marge Baecker, prin. Fax 985-5288

Iola, Waupaca, Pop. 1,232
Iola-Scandinavia SD 800/PK-12
450 Division St 54945 715-445-2411
Joseph Price, supt. Fax 445-4468
www.iola.k12.wi.us/
Iola Scandinavia ES 400/PK-6
450 Division St 54945 715-445-2411
Tess Lecy-Wojcik, prin. Fax 445-4468

Iron Ridge, Dodge, Pop. 987

St. Matthew Lutheran S 50/K-8
308 Herman St 53035 920-387-2210
Jason Hagenow, prin.

Iron River, Bayfield
Maple SD
Supt. — See Maple
Iron River ES 100/K-5
PO Box 128 54847 715-372-4334
Steve Gustafson, prin. Fax 372-4319

Ixonia, Jefferson
Oconomowoc Area SD
Supt. — See Oconomowoc
Ixonia ES 100/K-4
N8425 North St 53036 262-560-8400
Deanna Burton, prin. Fax 560-8418

St. Pauls Evangelical Lutheran S 100/K-8
W1956 Gopher Hill Rd 53036 920-261-5589
Jon Lindemann, prin. Fax 261-3551

Jackson, Washington, Pop. 6,036
West Bend SD
Supt. — See West Bend
Jackson ES 500/K-5
W204N16850 Jackson Dr 53037 262-335-5474
Brian Heimark, prin. Fax 677-1594

Davids Star Lutheran S 100/PK-8
2750 Davids Star Dr 53037 262-677-2412
Timothy Gustafson, prin. Fax 677-8960
Morning Star Lutheran S 100/K-8
N171W20131 Highland Rd 53037 262-677-9196
James Brohn, prin. Fax 677-9772

Janesville, Rock, Pop. 61,962
Janesville SD 10,400/PK-12
527 S Franklin St, 608-743-5000
Thomas Evert, supt. Fax 743-5110
www.janesville.k12.wi.us/sdj
Adams ES 400/PK-5
1138 E Memorial Dr 53545 608-743-6300
Catherine Grant, prin. Fax 743-6337
Edison MS 800/6-8
1649 S Chatham St 53546 608-743-5900
Steve Sperry, prin. Fax 743-5910
Franklin MS 600/6-8
450 N Crosby Ave, 608-743-6000
Kim Ehrhardt, prin. Fax 743-6010
Harrison ES 300/K-5
760 Princeton Rd 53546 608-743-6400
Marlene Novota, prin. Fax 743-6437
Jackson ES 300/PK-5
441 W Burbank Ave 53546 608-743-6500
John Walczak, prin. Fax 743-6510
Jefferson ES 300/PK-5
1831 Mount Zion Ave 53545 608-743-6600
Alice Wilkens Mann, prin. Fax 743-6610
Kennedy ES 400/K-5
3901 Randolph Rd 53546 608-743-7500
Niel Bender, prin. Fax 743-7560
Lincoln ES 400/PK-5
1821 Conde St 53546 608-743-6700
Rodonna Amiel, prin. Fax 743-6710
Madison ES 400/PK-5
331 N Grant Ave, 608-743-6800
Susan Masterson, prin. Fax 743-6810
Marshall MS 900/6-8
25 S Pontiac Dr 53545 608-743-6200
Synthia Taylor, prin. Fax 743-6210
Monroe ES 400/PK-5
55 S Pontiac Dr 53545 608-743-6900
Lori Burns, prin. Fax 743-6937
Roosevelt ES 400/PK-5
316 S Ringold St 53545 608-743-7000
Lynn Karges, prin. Fax 743-7010
Van Buren ES 400/PK-5
1515 Lapham St 53546 608-743-7100
Kori Settersten, prin. Fax 743-7110
Washington ES 500/PK-5
811 N Pine St, 608-743-7200
Scott Garner, prin. Fax 743-7210
Wilson ES 400/PK-5
465 Rockport Rd, 608-743-7300
Becky Bicha, prin. Fax 743-7310

Milton SD
Supt. — See Milton
Consolidated ES 100/K-3
4838 N County Road F 53545 608-868-9595
Theresa Rusch, prin. Fax 752-5136
Harmony ES 200/K-3
4243 E Rotamer Rd 53546 608-868-9360
Jeanne Smith, prin. Fax 868-5664

Oakhill Christian S 100/K-12
1650 S Oakhill Ave 53546 608-754-2759
Jim Eaker, prin. Fax 754-2159
Rock County Christian S 100/PK-5
5122 S Driftwood Dr 53546 608-757-1000
Linda Hutson, prin. Fax 757-1058
Rock Prairie Montessori S 100/PK-3
5246 E Rotamer Rd 53546 608-868-4844
Bonnie Winkofsky, prin. Fax 868-5965
St. John Vianney S 300/PK-8
1250 E Racine St 53545 608-752-6802
Judi Dillon, prin. Fax 752-3095
St. Mary S 200/PK-8
307 E Wall St 53545 608-754-5221
Julie Garvin, prin. Fax 754-1871
St. Matthew Lutheran S 100/K-8
709 Milton Ave 53545 608-752-1304
Kevin Proeber, prin. Fax 757-9076
St. Patrick S 100/PK-8
305 Lincoln St, 608-752-2031
Michael Martinsen, prin. Fax 754-0357
St. Paul Lutheran S 300/PK-8
210 S Ringold St 53545 608-754-4471
James Sohl, prin. Fax 754-4050
St. Williams S 200/PK-8
1822 Ravine St, 608-755-5184
Diane Rebout, prin. Fax 755-5190
Woodland Christian S 50/K-8
4324 E Bingham Rd 53546 608-868-7560

Jefferson, Jefferson, Pop. 7,592
Jefferson SD 1,800/PK-12
206 S Taft Ave 53549 920-675-1000
Michael Swartz, supt. Fax 675-1020
www.jefferson.k12.wi.us
East ES 300/PK-5
120 S Sanborn Ave 53549 920-675-1400
Connie Pellmann, prin. Fax 675-1420
Jefferson MS 400/6-8
501 S Taft Ave 53549 920-675-1300
Mark Rollefson, prin. Fax 675-1320
West ES 300/PK-5
900 W Milwaukee St 53549 920-675-1200
Mike Howard, prin. Fax 675-1220
Other Schools – See Sullivan

St. John's Evangelical Lutheran S 100/K-8
232 E Church St 53549 920-674-2922
Douglas Gurgel, prin. Fax 674-5477
St. John the Baptist S 200/PK-8
333 E Church St 53549 920-674-5821
Mary Kilar, prin. Fax 674-2521

Jim Falls, Chippewa
Chippewa Falls Area SD
Supt. — See Chippewa Falls
Jim Falls ES 100/K-5
13643 198th St 54748 715-720-3260
Heidi White, prin. Fax 720-3262

Johnson Creek, Jefferson, Pop. 2,024
Johnson Creek SD 600/PK-12
PO Box 39 53038 920-699-2811
Michael Garvey Ph.D., supt. Fax 699-2801
www.johnsoncreek.k12.wi.us/
Johnson Creek ES 300/PK-6
PO Box 39 53038 920-699-2511
Kris Blakeley, prin. Fax 699-2603

Juda, Green
Juda SD 300/PK-12
N2385 Spring St 53550 608-934-5251
Gary Scheuerell, supt. Fax 934-5254
www.juda.k12.wi.us
Juda S 200/PK-8
N2385 Spring St 53550 608-934-5251
Gary Scheuerell, prin. Fax 934-5254

Junction City, Portage, Pop. 413
Stevens Point Area SD
Supt. — See Stevens Point
Kennedy ES 200/PK-6
616 W 2nd St 54443 715-345-5699
Peter Werner, prin. Fax 457-3101

Juneau, Dodge, Pop. 2,587
Dodgeland SD 800/PK-12
401 S Western Ave 53039 920-386-4404
Annette Thompson, supt. Fax 386-4498
www.dodgeland.k12.wi.us
Dodgeland ES 400/PK-5
401 S Western Ave 53039 920-386-4404
Jessica Johnson, prin. Fax 386-2602

St. John Lutheran S 100/PK-8
402 S Main St 53039 920-386-4644
Richard Cody, prin. Fax 386-4644

Kansasville, Racine
Brighton SD 1 200/K-8
1200 248th Ave 53139 262-878-2191
Laurie Wright, supt. Fax 878-2869
www.brighton.k12.wi.us/
Brighton S 200/K-8
1200 248th Ave 53139 262-878-2191
Laurie Wright, prin. Fax 878-2869

Burlington Area SD
Supt. — See Burlington
Dover Center ES 100/K-4
23303 Church Rd 53139 262-878-5700
Sue Mosher, prin. Fax 878-5701

Dover SD 1 100/K-8
4101 S Beaumont Ave 53139 262-878-3773
Giles Williams, supt. Fax 878-1231
www.kansasville.org
Kansasville S 100/K-8
4101 S Beaumont Ave 53139 262-878-3773
Giles Williams, prin. Fax 878-1231

Providence Catholic S - West Campus 5-8
1714 240th Ave 53139 262-878-2713
Wilson Shierk, prin. Fax 878-3299

Kaukauna, Outagamie, Pop. 14,656
Kaukauna Area SD 3,400/PK-12
1701 County Road CE 54130 920-766-6100
Lloyd McCabe, supt. Fax 766-6104
www.kaukauna.k12.wi.us
Haen ES 200/1-4
1130 Haen Dr 54130 920-766-6134
Ken Kortens, prin. Fax 766-6138
Park ES 100/1-4
509 Lawe St 54130 920-766-6129
Mary Weber, prin. Fax 766-6544
Quinney ES 400/1-4
2601 Sullivan Ave 54130 920-766-6116
Kelli Antoine, prin. Fax 766-6122
River View IS 500/5-6
101 Oak St 54130 920-766-6124
Stacy Knapp, prin. Fax 766-6545
River View MS 500/7-8
101 Oak St 54130 920-766-6111
Dan Joseph, prin. Fax 766-6109
Tanner ES 300/PK-K
2500 Fieldcrest Dr 54130 920-766-6150
Sharon Rath, prin. Fax 766-6550

Holy Cross S 300/3-8
220 Doty St 54130 920-766-0186
Jeanine Leege, prin. Fax 759-2428
St. Aloysius S 100/PK-2
2401 Main Ave 54130 920-766-5199
Jeanine Leege, prin. Fax 766-5229
Trinity Lutheran S 100/PK-8
800 Augustine St 54130 920-766-2029
Steven Lemke, prin. Fax 759-6170

Kendall, Monroe, Pop. 472
Royall SD
Supt. — See Elroy
Kendall ES 100/4-5
PO Box 10 54638 608-463-7133
Darcy Uppena, prin. Fax 463-7137

Kenosha, Kenosha, Pop. 95,240
Kenosha SD 21,100/PK-12
PO Box 340 53141 262-359-6300
Joseph Mangi, supt. Fax 359-7672
www.kusd.edu/
Bain S of Language & Art 800/PK-5
2600 50th St 53140 262-359-2300
Scott Kennow, prin. Fax 359-2400
Bose ES 300/K-5
1900 15th St 53140 262-359-4044
Margaret Zei, prin. Fax 359-4005
Brass Community ES PK-5
6400 15th Ave 53143 262-359-8000
Daniel Weyrauch, prin. Fax 359-8050
Bullen MS 800/6-8
2804 39th Ave 53144 262-359-4460
Kim Fischer, prin. Fax 359-4487
Columbus ES 200/K-5
6410 25th Ave 53143 262-359-6242
Fax 359-7481
Forest Park ES 500/K-5
6810 45th Ave 53142 262-359-6319
Gary Gayan, prin. Fax 359-6170
Frank ES 400/K-5
1816 57th St 53140 262-359-6324
Heather Connolly, prin. Fax 359-6393
Grant ES 300/PK-5
1716 35th St 53140 262-359-6346
Lisa KC, prin. Fax 359-6672
Grewenow ES 400/K-5
7714 20th Ave 53143 262-359-6362
Gay Voelz, prin. Fax 359-7706
Harvey ES 400/PK-5
2012 19th Ave 53140 262-359-4040
Starlynn Daley, prin. Fax 359-4020

Jefferson ES 300/K-5
1832 43rd St 53140 262-359-6390
Kathy Walsh, prin. Fax 359-7578
Jeffery ES 400/K-5
4011 87th St 53142 262-359-2100
Kurt Johnson, prin. Fax 359-2033
Lance MS 1,000/6-8
4515 80th St 53142 262-359-2240
Chad Dahlk, prin. Fax 359-2184
Lincoln MS 800/6-8
6729 18th Ave 53143 262-359-6296
Ernest Llanas, prin. Fax 359-5966
Mahone MS 900/6-8
6900 60th St 53144 262-359-8100
Brian Edwards, prin. Fax 359-6851
McKinley ES 300/PK-5
5520 32nd Ave 53144 262-359-6002
Theresa Giampietro, prin. Fax 359-7641
McKinley MS 600/6-8
5710 32nd Ave 53144 262-359-6367
Sharon Miller, prin. Fax 359-6089
Nash ES K-5
6801 99th Ave 53142 262-359-3500
Martin Pitts, prin. Fax 359-3550
Roosevelt ES 400/K-5
3322 Roosevelt Rd 53142 262-359-6097
Karen Davis, prin. Fax 359-6107
Somers ES 600/PK-5
1245 72nd Ave 53144 262-359-3200
Debra Schaefer, prin. Fax 359-3212
Southport ES 500/PK-5
723 76th St 53143 262-359-6309
Vicky Gabriel, prin. Fax 359-5952
Stocker ES 700/PK-5
6315 67th St 53142 262-359-2143
April Nelson, prin. Fax 359-2012
Strange ES 500/K-5
5414 49th Ave 53144 262-359-6024
Jonathan Bar-Din, prin. Fax 359-6247
Vernon ES 500/PK-5
8518 22nd Ave 53143 262-359-2113
Alicia Hribal, prin. Fax 359-2169
Washington MS 600/6-8
811 Washington Rd 53140 262-359-6291
Nancy Weirick, prin. Fax 359-6056
Wilson ES 300/K-5
4520 33rd Ave 53144 262-359-6094
Yolanda Jackson-Lewis, prin. Fax 359-5993
Other Schools – See Pleasant Prairie

Paris J1 SD 200/K-8
1901 176th Ave 53144 262-859-2350
Roger Gahart, supt. Fax 859-2641
www.paris.k12.wi.us
Paris S 200/K-8
1901 176th Ave 53144 262-859-2350
Roger Gahart, prin. Fax 859-2641

Armitage Academy 100/K-8
6032 8th Ave 53143 262-654-4200
Thomas Creighton, prin. Fax 654-4737
Bethany Lutheran S 100/K-8
2100 75th St 53143 262-654-3234
Christopher Avery, prin. Fax 654-3501
Christian Life S 800/PK-12
10700 75th St 53142 262-694-3900
Susan Nelson, admin. Fax 694-3312
Friedens Lutheran S 200/PK-8
5043 20th Ave 53140 262-652-3451
Don Eickmeyer, prin. Fax 654-1565
Kenosha Montessori S 50/K-6
2401 69th St 53143 262-654-6950
Jo Ann Miller-Cole, prin.
Our Lady of Mt. Carmel S 100/K-6
5400 19th Ave 53140 262-652-5057
Ken Anton, prin. Fax 652-2542
Our Lady of the Holy Rosary S 200/K-8
4400 22nd Ave 53140 262-652-2771
Jessica Knierim, prin. Fax 652-6179
St. Mark S 100/K-6
7207 14th Ave 53143 262-656-7360
Frank Germinaro, prin. Fax 656-7375
St. Marys Catholic S 300/K-8
7400 39th Ave 53142 262-694-6018
Sandra Wiercinski, prin. Fax 694-6048
St. Peter S 100/PK-6
2224 30th Ave 53144 262-551-8383
Jacqueline Grajera, prin. Fax 551-9833
St. Therese S 100/PK-6
2020 91st St 53143 262-694-8080
Carol Degen, prin. Fax 694-1982

Keshena, Menominee, Pop. 685
Menominee Indian SD 900/K-12
PO Box 1330 54135 715-799-3824
Wendell Waukau, supt. Fax 799-4659
www.misd.k12.wi.us
Keshena PS 400/K-5
PO Box 1410 54135 715-799-3828
Kristin Wells, prin. Fax 799-1342
Other Schools – See Neopit

Kewaskum, Washington, Pop. 3,607
Kewaskum SD 1,900/PK-12
PO Box 37 53040 262-626-8427
Michael Krumm, supt. Fax 626-2961
www.kewaskumschools.org
Farmington ES 200/K-5
8736 Boltonville Rd 53040 262-626-8427
Janet Molebash, prin. Fax 692-6863
Kewaskum ES 400/PK-5
PO Box 127 53040 262-626-8427
Tom Fischer, prin. Fax 626-4151
Kewaskum MS 400/6-8
PO Box 432 53040 262-626-8427
Ken Soerens, prin. Fax 626-4214
Other Schools – See Campbellsport

Holy Trinity S 100/K-8
PO Box 464 53040 262-626-2603
Sr. Katy LaFond, prin. Fax 626-8863
St. Lucas S 100/K-8
PO Box 86 53040 262-626-2680
David Stoltz, prin. Fax 626-8451

Kewaunee, Kewaunee, Pop. 2,877
Kewaunee SD 900/PK-12
915 2nd St 54216 920-388-3230
Jean Broadwater, supt. Fax 388-5174
www.kewaunee.k12.wi.us
Kewaunee ES 300/PK-2
921 3rd St 54216 920-388-2458
Tracy Ledvina, prin. Fax 388-5696
Kewaunee MS 300/3-8
921 3rd St 54216 920-388-2458
Marge Weichelt, prin. Fax 388-5696

Holy Rosary S 100/K-8
519 Kilbourn St 54216 920-388-2431
Richard Aebly, prin. Fax 388-3822

Kiel, Manitowoc, Pop. 3,507
Kiel Area SD 1,400/PK-12
PO Box 201 53042 920-894-2266
Jack Lewis, supt. Fax 894-5100
www.kiel.k12.wi.us/
Kiel MS 400/5-8
PO Box 197 53042 920-894-2264
David Slosser, prin. Fax 894-5121
Zielanis ES 500/PK-4
PO Box 217 53042 920-894-2265
Chad Ramminger, prin. Fax 894-5104

Divine Savior S 100/PK-8
423 Fremont St 53042 920-894-3533
Lawrence Konetzke, prin. Fax 894-4959
Trinity Lutheran S 100/PK-8
387 Cemetary Rd 53042 920-894-3012
Benjamin Rank, prin. Fax 894-4742

Kimberly, Outagamie, Pop. 6,230
Kimberly Area SD 3,300/PK-12
217 E Kimberly Ave 54136 920-788-7900
Bob Mayfield Ed.D., supt. Fax 788-7919
www.kimberly.k12.wi.us
Gerritts MS 600/7-8
545 S John St 54136 920-788-7905
Cathy Clarksen, prin. Fax 788-7914
Mapleview IS 100/5-6
125 E Kimberly Ave 54136 920-788-7910
Craig Miller, prin. Fax 788-7760
Westside ES 400/PK-4
746 W 3rd St 54136 920-739-3578
Jami Grall, prin. Fax 739-6212
Other Schools – See Appleton, Combined Locks

Appleton Christian S 100/PK-8
614 E Kimberly Ave 54136 920-687-2700
Patricia Tofte, admin. Fax 687-2715
Holy Spirit S 100/PK-5
614 E Kimberly Ave 54136 920-788-7650
Sue Simonson, prin. Fax 788-7652

Knapp, Dunn, Pop. 419
Menomonie Area SD
Supt. — See Menomonie
Knapp ES 100/PK-5
110 South St 54749 715-665-2131
Dudley Markham, prin. Fax 665-2344

Kohler, Sheboygan, Pop. 1,991
Kohler SD 600/PK-12
333 Upper Rd 53044 920-459-2920
Dr. Robert Kobylski, supt. Fax 459-2930
www.kohler.k12.wi.us
Kohler S 400/PK-8
333 Upper Rd 53044 920-459-2920
Susan Jaberg, prin. Fax 459-2930

Krakow, Oconto
Pulaski Community SD
Supt. — See Pulaski
Fairview ES 100/PK-5
2840 State Highway 32 54137 920-899-6300
Colleen Miner, prin. Fax 899-6302

Lac du Flambeau, Vilas, Pop. 1,423
Lac du Flambeau SD 1 400/PK-8
2899 State Highway 47 S 54538 715-588-3838
Larry Ouimette, supt. Fax 588-3243
www.ldf.k12.wi.us/
Lac du Flambeau S 400/PK-8
2899 State Highway 47 S 54538 715-588-3838
Ronald Grams, prin. Fax 588-3243

La Crosse, LaCrosse, Pop. 50,287
La Crosse SD 6,800/PK-12
807 East Ave S 54601 608-789-7600
Gerald Kember, supt. Fax 789-7960
www.lacrosseschools.com/
Emerson ES 300/PK-5
2101 Campbell Rd 54601 608-789-7990
Regina Siegel, prin. Fax 789-7171
Franklin ES 200/PK-5
1611 Kane St 54603 608-789-7970
Gerald Berns, prin. Fax 789-7172
Hamilton Early Learning Center 100/PK-2
1111 7th St S 54601 608-789-7695
Nancy Matchett, prin. Fax 789-7030
Hintgen ES 400/PK-5
3505 28th St S 54601 608-789-7767
Mark White, prin. Fax 789-7173
La Crosse Offsite Preschool 100/PK-PK
807 East Ave S 54601 608-789-7006
Jane Morken, prin. Fax 789-7960
Lincoln MS 400/6-8
510 9th St S 54601 608-789-7780
Fax 789-7181
Logan MS 500/6-8
1450 Avon St 54603 608-789-7740
Troy Harcey, prin. Fax 789-7754
Longfellow MS 600/6-8
1900 Denton St 54601 608-789-7670
Penny Reedy, prin. Fax 789-7975
North Woods ES 300/PK-5
2541 Sablewood Rd 54601 608-789-7000
Jane Morken, prin. Fax 789-7010
Roosevelt ES 100/PK-5
1307 Hayes St 54603 608-789-7760
Harvey Witzenburg, prin. Fax 789-7080
Southern Bluffs ES 400/PK-5
4010 Sunnyside Dr 54601 608-789-7020
Mary Lin Wershofen, prin. Fax 789-7176
Spence ES 400/PK-5
2150 Bennett St 54601 608-789-7773
Nancy Sikorsky, prin. Fax 789-7174
State Road ES 300/K-5
N1821 Hagen Rd 54601 608-789-7690
David Gluch, prin. Fax 789-7084
Summit ES 300/PK-5
1800 Lakeshore Dr 54603 608-789-7980
Dirk Hunter, prin. Fax 789-7175

Aquinas MS South Campus 200/7-8
315 11th St S 54601 608-784-0156
Patricia Kosmatka, prin. Fax 784-0229
Blessed Sacrament S 200/3-6
2404 King St 54601 608-782-5564
Kay Berra, prin. Fax 782-7765
First Evangelical Lutheran S 100/PK-8
520 West Ave S 54601 608-784-1050
David Niemi, prin. Fax 785-2417
Immanuel Lutheran S 100/K-8
806 Saint Paul St 54603 608-784-5712
Jonathan Mumm, prin.
Mary Mother of the Church ECC 100/PK-PK
2000 Weston St 54601 608-788-5225
Kathy Weisbecker, admin.
Mt. Calvary-Grace Lutheran S 100/PK-8
1614 Park Ave 54601 608-784-8223
Jon Biedenbender, prin. Fax 784-7305
St. Joseph Cathedral S 100/PK-2
1319 Ferry St 54601 608-782-5998
John Stellflue, prin. Fax 784-9933
Three Rivers Waldorf S 100/PK-8
901 Caledonia St 54603 608-782-8774
Alma Noll, admin. Fax 787-6914

Ladysmith, Rusk, Pop. 3,789
Ladysmith-Hawkins SD 1,000/PK-12
1700 Edgewood Ave E 54848 715-532-5277
Mario Friedel, supt. Fax 532-7445
www.lhsd.k12.wi.us/
Ladysmith ES 400/PK-4
624 E 6th St S 54848 715-532-5464
Mario Friedel, prin. Fax 532-3475
Ladysmith MS 300/5-8
115 E 6th St S 54848 715-532-5252
Chris Poradish, prin. Fax 532-7455

Our Lady of Sorrows S 100/K-8
105 Washington Ave 54848 715-532-3232
Tami Stewart, prin. Fax 532-7368

La Farge, Vernon, Pop. 799
La Farge SD 200/PK-12
301 W Adams St 54639 608-625-2400
Shawn Donovan, supt. Fax 625-0118
www.lafarge.k12.wi.us/
La Farge ES 100/PK-5
301 W Adams St 54639 608-625-2400
Shawn Donovan, prin. Fax 625-0152
La Farge MS 100/6-8
301 W Adams St 54639 608-625-2400
Shawn Donovan, prin. Fax 625-0152

Lake Delton, Sauk, Pop. 3,053
Wisconsin Dells SD
Supt. — See Wisconsin Dells
Lake Delton ES 200/K-5
PO Box 280 53940 608-253-4391
Teresa Regel, lead tchr. Fax 254-6765

Lake Geneva, Walworth, Pop. 8,223
Geneva J4 SD 100/PK-8
N2575 Snake Rd 53147 262-248-3816
Craig Cook, supt. Fax 248-7021
www.woodsschool.com/
Woods S 100/PK-8
N2575 Snake Rd 53147 262-248-3816
Craig Cook, prin. Fax 248-7021

Lake Geneva J1 SD 1,900/K-8
208 E South St 53147 262-348-1000
James Gottinger, supt. Fax 248-9704
www.lakegenevaschools.com
Central-Denison ES 600/K-5
900 Wisconsin St 53147 262-348-4000
Samantha Polek, prin. Fax 248-7321
Eastview ES 300/K-5
507 Sage St 53147 262-348-6000
Colin Nugent, prin. Fax 248-0456
Lake Geneva MS 600/6-8
600 N Bloomfield Rd 53147 262-348-3000
Joseph Lynch, prin. Fax 348-3092
Star Center ES 300/K-5
W1380 Lake Geneva Hwy 53147 262-348-7000
Betsy Schroeder, prin. Fax 279-7938

Linn J4 SD 100/PK-8
W3490 Linton Rd 53147 262-248-4067
Mary DeYoung, supt. Fax 248-1050
Traver S 100/PK-8
W3490 Linton Rd 53147 262-248-4067
Craig Collins, prin. Fax 248-1050

Linn J6 SD 100/PK-8
W4094 S Lakeshore Dr 53147 262-248-4120
Lillian Henderson, supt. Fax 248-5133
www.linn6.k12.wi.us
Reek S 100/PK-8
W4094 S Lakeshore Dr 53147 262-248-4120
Lillian Henderson, prin. Fax 248-5133

First Evangelical Lutheran S 100/K-8
1101 Logan St 53147 262-248-3374
Peter Lemke, prin. Fax 248-3317
Mount Zion Christian S 100/K-8
2330 State Road 120 53147 262-248-5255
Daniel Clement, prin. Fax 248-7648
St. Francis DeSales S 200/K-8
130 W Main St 53147 262-248-2778
David Wieters, prin. Fax 248-7860

Lake Mills, Jefferson, Pop. 5,241
Lake Mills Area SD 1,300/PK-12
120 E Lake Park Pl 53551 920-648-2215
Dean Sanders, supt. Fax 648-5795
www.lakemills.k12.wi.us
Lake Mills MS 300/6-8
318 College St 53551 920-648-2358
Terry Bothun, prin. Fax 648-8928
Prospect Street ES 600/PK-5
135 E Prospect St 53551 920-648-2338
Jeannie Jerde, prin. Fax 648-5490

St. Paul Evangelical Lutheran S 200/K-8
1530 S Main St 53551 920-648-2918
Fred Luehring, prin. Fax 648-2250

Lancaster, Grant, Pop. 3,977
Lancaster Community SD 1,000/PK-12
925 W Maple St 53813 608-723-2175
Robin Wagner, supt. Fax 723-6397
www.lancastersd.k12.wi.us
Lancaster MS 200/6-8
802 E Elm St 53813 608-723-6425
Mark Uppena, prin. Fax 723-6731
Winskill ES 400/PK-5
861 W Maple St 53813 608-723-4066
Quinn Rasmussen, prin. Fax 723-2608

St. Clement S 100/K-6
330 W Maple St 53813 608-723-7474
Josh Jensen, prin. Fax 723-4424

Land O Lakes, Vilas
Northland Pines SD
Supt. — See Eagle River
Northland Pines/Land O Lakes ES 100/K-5
6485 Town Hall Rd 54540 715-547-3619
Duane Frey, prin. Fax 547-3903

Lannon, Waukesha, Pop. 1,006
Hamilton SD
Supt. — See Sussex
Lannon ES 300/K-5
7145 N Lannon Rd 53046 262-255-6106
Richard Ladd, prin. Fax 255-4185

St. John Lutheran S 200/K-8
20813 W Forest View Dr 53046 262-251-2940
Daniel Brands, prin. Fax 251-3612

Laona, Forest
Laona SD 300/PK-12
PO Box 100 54541 715-674-2143
David Aslyn, supt. Fax 674-5904
www.laona.k12.wi.us
Robinson ES 200/PK-6
PO Box 100 54541 715-674-3801
David Aslyn, prin. Fax 674-5904

Larsen, Winnebago
Winneconne Community SD
Supt. — See Winneconne
Winchester ES 100/K-4
5270 Ann St 54947 920-836-2864
Lisa Hughes, prin. Fax 582-5816

La Valle, Sauk, Pop. 326
Reedsburg SD
Supt. — See Reedsburg
Ironton-La Valle ES 100/K-5
PO Box 329 53941 608-985-7716
Fax 985-7719

Lena, Oconto, Pop. 501
Lena SD 400/PK-12
304 E Main St 54139 920-829-5703
David Honish, supt. Fax 829-5122
www.lena.k12.wi.us
Lena ES 200/PK-5
304 E Main St 54139 920-829-5959
Carla Spice, prin. Fax 829-5122
Lena MS 100/6-8
304 E Main St 54139 920-829-5244
David Honish, prin. Fax 829-5122

Maranatha SDA S 50/1-8
5100 McCarthy Rd 54139 920-834-5247

Little Chute, Outagamie, Pop. 10,870
Little Chute Area SD 1,500/PK-12
325 Meulemans St Ste A 54140 920-788-7605
David Botz, supt. Fax 788-7603
www.littlechute.k12.wi.us
Little Chute ES 600/PK-5
901 Grand Ave 54140 920-788-7610
James Neubert, prin. Fax 788-7847
Little Chute MS 300/6-8
325 Meulemans St Ste B 54140 920-788-7607
Lori Van Handel, prin. Fax 788-7615

St. John Nepomucene S 300/PK-8
328 Grand Ave 54140 920-788-9082
Holly Rottier, prin. Fax 788-7046

Livingston, Iowa, Pop. 581
Iowa-Grant SD 800/PK-12
498 County Road IG 53554 608-943-6311
Terrance Slack, supt. Fax 943-8438
www.igs.k12.wi.us
Iowa-Grant S 500/PK-8
498 County Road IG 53554 608-943-6313
Claudia Quam, prin. Fax 943-8438

Lodi, Columbia, Pop. 3,030
Lodi SD 1,700/PK-12
115 School St 53555 608-592-3851
Michael Shimshak, supt. Fax 592-3852
www.lodi.k12.wi.us
Lodi ES 400/3-5
101 School St 53555 608-592-3842
Trevor Hovde, prin. Fax 592-1025
Lodi MS 400/6-8
900 Sauk St 53555 608-592-3854
David Dyb, prin. Fax 592-1035
Lodi PS 400/PK-2
103 Pleasant St 53555 608-592-3855
Lyle Hendrickson, prin. Fax 592-1015

Loganville, Sauk, Pop. 281
Reedsburg SD
Supt. — See Reedsburg
Loganville ES 100/K-5
S5864 State Road 23 53943 608-727-3401
Jennifer Gehri, prin. Fax 727-2715

Lomira, Dodge, Pop. 2,410
Lomira SD 1,000/K-12
1030 4th St 53048 920-269-4396
John Mason, admin. Fax 269-4996
www.lomira.k12.wi.us/
Lomira ES 200/K-5
1030 4th St 53048 920-269-4396
Robert Lloyd, prin. Fax 269-4996
Lomira JHS 100/6-8
1030 4th St 53048 920-269-4396
Robert Lloyd, prin. Fax 269-4996
Other Schools – See Theresa

Consolidated Catholic S 50/PK-8
705 Milwaukee St 53048 920-269-4326
Dorothy Zitlow, prin. Fax 269-7342
St. John Lutheran S 100/K-8
558 S Water St 53048 920-269-4514
William Vilski, prin. Fax 269-7364

Lone Rock, Richland, Pop. 911
River Valley SD
Supt. — See Spring Green
Lone Rock ES 100/K-5
222 W Pearl St 53556 608-583-2091
Jaime Hegland, prin. Fax 583-2011

Loyal, Clark, Pop. 1,282
Loyal SD 600/PK-12
PO Box 10 54446 715-255-8552
Graeme Williams, supt. Fax 255-8553
www.loyalschools.org
Loyal ES 300/PK-6
PO Box 250 54446 715-255-8561
Chris Thomalla, prin. Fax 255-8553
Loyal JHS 100/7-8
PO Box 10 54446 715-255-8511
Chris Thomalla, prin. Fax 255-8553

St. Anthony S 100/K-6
PO Box 189 54446 715-255-8636
Sr. Carol Schnitzler, prin. Fax 255-8636

Luck, Polk, Pop. 1,209
Luck SD 600/K-12
810 S 7th St 54853 715-472-2151
Rick Palmer, supt. Fax 472-2159
www.lucksd.k12.wi.us
Luck ES 300/K-6
810 S 7th St 54853 715-472-2153
John Nichols, prin. Fax 472-2159

Luxemburg, Kewaunee, Pop. 2,211
Luxemburg-Casco SD 2,000/PK-12
PO Box 70 54217 920-845-2391
Patrick Saunders, supt. Fax 845-5871
www.luxcasco.k12.wi.us/
Luxemburg-Casco IS 500/3-6
PO Box 70 54217 920-845-2371
Jolene Hussong, prin. Fax 845-2232
Luxemburg-Casco PS 400/PK-2
PO Box 220 54217 920-845-2315
Peter Kline, prin. Fax 845-2503
Other Schools – See Casco

Immaculate Conception S 100/K-6
1406 Main St 54217 920-845-2224
Bill Matchefts, prin. Fax 845-5581
St. Paul Lutheran S 50/K-8
N4107 County Road AB 54217 920-845-2095
Kristen Zeitler, prin. Fax 845-9075

Lyndon Station, Juneau, Pop. 465
Mauston SD
Supt. — See Mauston
Lyndon Station ES 100/K-5
PO Box 405 53944 608-666-2341
Tom Reisenauer, prin. Fax 666-2510

Mc Farland, Dane, Pop. 5,724
Mc Farland SD 2,000/PK-12
5101 Farwell St 53558 608-838-3169
Scott Brown, admin. Fax 838-3074
www.mcfarland.k12.wi.us
Elvehjem Early Learning Center 200/PK-K
6009 Johnson St 53558 608-838-3146
Thomas Mooney, prin. Fax 838-4503
Indian Mound MS 500/6-8
6330 Exchange St 53558 608-838-8980
David Witte, prin. Fax 838-4588
Mc Farland PS 300/1-2
6103 Johnson St 53558 608-838-3115
Thomas Mooney, prin. Fax 838-4612
Waubesa IS 500/3-5
5605 Red Oak Trl 53558 608-838-7667
Sue Murphy, prin. Fax 838-4613

Madison, Dane, Pop. 221,551
Madison Metro SD 24,100/PK-12
545 W Dayton St 53703 608-663-1879
Daniel Nerad, supt. Fax 204-0342
www.madison.k12.wi.us
Allis ES 400/K-5
4201 Buckeye Rd 53716 608-204-1056
Julie Frentz, prin. Fax 204-0364
Black Hawk MS 400/6-8
1402 Wyoming Way 53704 608-204-4360
Mary Kelley, prin. Fax 204-0368
Chavez ES 700/K-5
3502 Maple Grove Dr 53719 608-442-2000
Linda Allen, prin. Fax 442-2100
Cherokee Heights MS 500/6-8
4301 Cherokee Dr 53711 608-204-1240
Karen Seno, prin. Fax 204-0378
Crestwood ES 400/K-5
5930 Old Sauk Rd 53705 608-204-1120
Howard Fried, prin. Fax 204-0384
Elvehjem ES 400/PK-5
5106 Academy Dr 53716 608-204-1400
Craig Campbell, prin. Fax 204-0396
Emerson ES 300/PK-5
2421 E Johnson St 53704 608-204-2000
Karen Kepler, prin. Fax 204-0401
Falk ES 300/K-5
6323 Woodington Way 53711 608-204-2180
Lynn Winn, prin. Fax 204-0479
Franklin ES 300/PK-2
305 W Lakeside St 53715 608-204-2292
Catherine McMillan, prin. Fax 204-0405
Glendale ES 400/PK-5
1201 Tompkins Dr 53716 608-204-2400
Mickey Buhl, prin. Fax 204-0409
Gompers ES 200/K-5
1502 Wyoming Way 53704 608-204-4520
Carletta Stanford, prin. Fax 204-0413
Hamilton MS 700/6-8
4801 Waukesha St 53705 608-204-4620
Henry Schmelz, prin. Fax 204-0417
Hawthorne ES 300/PK-5
3344 Concord Ave 53714 608-204-2500
Beth Lehman, prin. Fax 204-0423
Huegel ES 500/K-5
2601 Prairie Rd 53711 608-204-3100
David Bray, prin. Fax 204-0427
Jefferson MS 400/6-8
101 S Gammon Rd 53717 608-663-6403
Anne Fischer, prin. Fax 442-2193
Kennedy ES 500/K-5
221 Meadowlark Dr 53714 608-204-3420
Nancy Caldwell, prin. Fax 204-0431
Lake View ES 300/K-5
1802 Tennyson Ln 53704 608-204-4040
Kristi Kloos, prin. Fax 204-4099
Lapham ES 300/PK-2
1045 E Dayton St 53703 608-204-4140
Michael Hertting, prin. Fax 204-0447
Leopold ES 700/K-5
2602 Post Rd 53713 608-204-4240
John Burkholder, prin. Fax 204-0451
Lincoln ES 400/3-5
909 Sequoia Trl 53713 608-204-4900
Deborah Hoffman, prin. Fax 204-0455
Lindbergh ES 200/K-5
4500 Kennedy Rd 53704 608-204-6500
Mary Hyde, prin. Fax 204-0459
Lowell ES 300/PK-5
401 Maple Ave 53704 608-204-6600
Lisa Kvistad, prin. Fax 204-0463
Marquette ES 200/3-5
1501 Jenifer St 53703 608-204-3220
Andrea Kreft, prin. Fax 204-0467
Mendota ES 300/K-5
4002 School Rd 53704 608-204-7840
Dennis Pauli, prin. Fax 204-0471
Midvale ES 400/PK-2
502 Caromar Dr 53711 608-204-6700
Pam Wilson, prin. Fax 204-0475
Muir ES 500/PK-5
6602 Inner Dr 53705 608-663-8170
Linda Kailin, prin. Fax 442-2200
O'Keeffe MS 400/6-8
510 S Thornton Ave 53703 608-204-6820
Kay Enright, prin. Fax 204-0561
Orchard Ridge ES 200/K-5
5602 Russett Rd 53711 608-204-2320
Barbara Dorn, prin. Fax 204-0483
Randall ES 300/3-5
1802 Regent St 53726 608-204-3300
Fax 204-0487
Sandburg ES 300/K-5
4114 Donald Dr 53704 608-204-7940
Brett Wilfrid, prin. Fax 204-0491
Schenk ES 400/PK-5
230 Schenk St 53714 608-204-1500
Emmett Durtschi, prin. Fax 204-0539
Sennett MS 600/6-8
502 Pflaum Rd 53716 608-204-1920
Colleen Lodholz, prin. Fax 204-0495
Sherman MS 500/6-8
1610 Ruskin St 53704 608-204-2100
Michael Hernandez, prin. Fax 204-0501

Shorewood Hills ES 400/K-5
1105 Shorewood Blvd 53705 608-204-1200
Lynn Berton, prin. Fax 204-0505
Spring Harbor MS 300/6-8
1110 Spring Harbor Dr 53705 608-204-1100
Gail Anderson, prin. Fax 204-0509
Stephens ES 500/K-5
120 S Rosa Rd 53705 608-204-1900
Sarah Galanter-Guziewski, prin. Fax 204-0516
Thoreau ES 400/PK-5
3870 Nakoma Rd 53711 608-204-6940
Elizabeth Fritz, prin. Fax 204-0519
Toki MS 600/6-8
5606 Russett Rd 53711 608-204-4740
Nicole Schaefer, prin. Fax 204-0523
Van Hise ES 300/K-5
4747 Waukesha St 53705 608-204-4800
Peg Keeler, prin. Fax 204-0419
Whitehorse MS 400/6-8
218 Schenk St 53714 608-204-4480
Deborah Ptak, prin. Fax 204-0538
Other Schools – See Verona

Abundant Life Christian S 300/K-12
4901 E Buckeye Rd 53716 608-221-1520
Bill Zehner, admin. Fax 221-8572
Blessed Sacrament S 300/PK-8
2112 Hollister Ave 53726 608-233-6155
Maryann Slater, prin. Fax 238-4220
Eagle S Of Madison 200/K-8
5454 Gunflint Trl 53711 608-273-0309
Elizabeth Conner, admin. Fax 273-0278
Eastside Evangelical Lutheran S 100/K-8
2310 Independence Ln 53704 608-244-3045
Scott Monroe, prin. Fax 244-2168
Edgewood Campus S 300/PK-8
829 Edgewood College Dr 53711 608-663-4100
Sr. Kathleen Malone, prin. Fax 663-4101
High Point Christian S 300/PK-8
7702 Old Sauk Rd 53717 608-836-7170
Ramona Small, prin. Fax 824-9135
Holy Cross Lutheran S 100/PK-8
2670 Milwaukee St 53704 608-249-3101
Timothy Schubkegel, prin. Fax 249-0601
Kids Express Learning Center 100/PK-1
3276 High Point Rd 53719 608-845-3245
Sandra Dahl, prin. Fax 848-3028
Madison Central Montessori S 100/PK-8
4337 W Beltline Hwy 53711 608-274-9549
Mary Lee Gleason, admin. Fax 274-9570
Our Lady Queen of Peace S 500/K-8
418 Holly Ave 53711 608-231-4580
Robert Abshire, prin. Fax 231-4589
Our Redeemer Evangelical Lutheran S 100/PK-8
1701 McKenna Blvd 53711 608-274-2830
David Retzlaff, prin. Fax 274-7606
St. Dennis S 200/K-8
409 Dempsey Rd 53714 608-246-5121
Matt Beisser, prin. Fax 246-5137
St. James S 200/PK-8
1204 Saint James Ct 53715 608-256-3095
Sr. Kathleen Loughrin, prin. Fax 256-6311
St. Maria Goretti S 400/PK-8
5405 Flad Ave 53711 608-271-7551
Elizabeth Adams Young, prin. Fax 275-6625
Three Angels Christian S 50/1-8
900 Femrite Dr 53716 608-222-5775
Wendy Baldwin, admin. Fax 222-2047
Wingra S 100/K-8
3200 Monroe St Ste 3 53711 608-238-2525
Joyce Perkins, admin. Fax 238-6316
Woodland Montessori S 100/PK-K
1124 Colby St 53715 608-256-8076
Jennifer Hoyt, dir. Fax 256-5423

Manawa, Waupaca, Pop. 1,333
Manawa SD 800/PK-12
800 Beech St 54949 920-596-2525
Deborah Watry, supt. Fax 596-5308
www.manawa.k12.wi.us
Manawa ES 300/PK-4
585 E 4th St 54949 920-596-2238
Sondra Reynolds, prin. Fax 596-5339
Manawa MS 200/5-8
800 Beech St 54949 920-596-2551
Steve Gromala, prin. Fax 596-5320

St. Paul Lutheran S 100/K-8
750 Depot St 54949 920-596-2815
Thomas Helpap, prin. Fax 596-2851

Manitowish Waters, Vilas
North Lakeland SD 200/K-8
12686 County Road K 54545 715-543-8417
Richard Vought, supt. Fax 543-8868
www.nles.us
North Lakeland S 200/K-8
12686 County Road K 54545 715-543-8417
Richard Vought, prin. Fax 543-8868

Manitowoc, Manitowoc, Pop. 33,917
Manitowoc SD 5,500/PK-12
PO Box 1657 54221 920-683-4777
Mark Swanson, supt. Fax 686-4780
www.mpsd.k12.wi.us
Franklin ES 400/1-6
800 S 35th St 54220 920-683-4751
Keith Wakeman, prin. Fax 683-5147
Jackson ES 500/1-6
1201 N 18th St 54220 920-683-4752
Steven Kleinfeldt, prin. Fax 683-5148
Jefferson ES 400/1-6
1415 Division St 54220 920-683-4753
Joanne Metzen, prin. Fax 683-5149
Madison ES 300/1-6
701 N 4th St 54220 920-683-4754
Michael Dunlap, prin. Fax 683-5150
Monroe ES 300/1-6
2502 S 14th St 54220 920-683-4755
William Bertsche, prin. Fax 683-5151
Riverview K 500/PK-K
4400 Michigan Ave 54220 920-683-4750
Catherine Burish, prin. Fax 683-5153
Stangel ES 400/1-6
1002 E Cedar Ave 54220 920-683-4756
Deborah Shimanek, prin. Fax 683-5152

Bethany Evangelical Lutheran S 100/K-8
3209 Meadow Ln 54220 920-684-9777
James Wade, prin. Fax 684-9587
First German Evangelical Lutheran S 100/K-8
1025 S 8th St 54220 920-682-7021
Kevin Buch, prin. Fax 682-3538
Immanuel Evangelical Lutheran S 100/K-8
916 Pine St 54220 920-684-3404
James Roecker, prin. Fax 684-6461
St. Francis Cabrini MS 200/6-8
2109 Marshall St 54220 920-683-6884
James Clark, prin. Fax 683-6882
St. Francis De Sales S 200/K-5
1408 Waldo Blvd 54220 920-683-6892
Linda Bender, prin. Fax 683-6889
St. Francis Xavier S 200/PK-5
1418 Grand Ave 54220 920-683-6888
Linda Bender, prin. Fax 683-6881
St. John Evangelical Lutheran S 100/K-8
7531 English Lake Rd Ste A 54220 920-758-2633
Alan Bitter, prin. Fax 758-3418

Maple, Douglas
Maple SD 1,400/K-12
PO Box 188 54854 715-363-2431
Gregg Lundberg, supt. Fax 363-2191
www.maple.k12.wi.us
Other Schools – See Iron River, Poplar

Marathon, Marathon, Pop. 1,642
Marathon City SD 700/PK-12
PO Box 37 54448 715-443-2226
Richard Parks, supt. Fax 443-2611
www.marathon.k12.wi.us
Marathon S 400/PK-8
PO Box 457 54448 715-443-2538
Jeffrey Reiche, prin. Fax 443-2230

St. Mary S 200/K-8
PO Box 102 54448 715-443-3430
Sandra Troyanoski, prin. Fax 443-3045

Maribel, Manitowoc, Pop. 282

St. John Lutheran S 50/K-8
14323 Maribel Rd 54227 920-863-2850
Lance Waege, prin. Fax 863-2850

Marinette, Marinette, Pop. 11,275
Marinette SD 2,100/K-12
2139 Pierce Ave 54143 715-735-1406
Tim Baneck, supt. Fax 732-7930
www.marinette.k12.wi.us
Garfield ES 200/K-4
1615 Carney Blvd 54143 715-732-7915
Robin Ilse, prin. Fax 732-3431
Marinette MS 700/5-8
1011 Water St 54143 715-732-7900
Adam DeWitt, prin. Fax 732-7939
Merryman ES 200/K-4
611 Elizabeth Ave 54143 715-732-7912
Judy Grace, prin. Fax 732-3433
Park ES 200/K-4
1225 Hockridge St 54143 715-732-7913
Dan Malmberg, prin. Fax 732-3434

St. Thomas Aquinas Academy 50/PK-PK, 1-
1200 Main St 54143 715-735-7460
Jennifer Elfering, admin. Fax 735-3375
Trinity Lutheran S 100/PK-8
1216 Colfax St 54143 715-732-2956
Greg Obermiller, prin. Fax 732-2314

Marion, Waupaca, Pop. 1,241
Marion SD 600/PK-12
1001 N Main St 54950 715-754-2511
Sally Peterson, supt. Fax 754-4508
www.marion.k12.wi.us
Marion ES 300/PK-6
1001 N Main St 54950 715-754-4501
Deborah Malueg, prin. Fax 754-4508

Markesan, Green Lake, Pop. 1,349
Markesan SD 600/PK-12
PO Box 248 53946 920-398-2373
Susan Alexander, supt. Fax 398-3281
www.markesan.k12.wi.us
Markesan ES 200/PK-6
PO Box 248 53946 920-398-2373
Connie Hynnek, prin. Fax 398-3281
Markesan MS 100/7-8
PO Box 248 53946 920-398-2373
Pamela Waite, prin. Fax 398-3281

Marshall, Dane, Pop. 3,561
Marshall SD 1,200/PK-12
PO Box 76 53559 608-655-3466
Barb Sramek, supt. Fax 655-4481
www.marshall.k12.wi.us
Marshall Early Learning Center 300/PK-2
PO Box 76 53559 608-655-1588
Robert Opps, prin. Fax 655-1592
Marshall ES 400/3-6
PO Box 76 53559 608-655-4403
Barb Johnson, prin. Fax 655-3425
Marshall MS 200/7-8
PO Box 76 53559 608-655-1571
Mark Mueller, prin. Fax 655-1591

Marshfield, Wood, Pop. 18,796
Marshfield SD 3,900/PK-12
1010 E 4th St 54449 715-387-1101
Bruce King, supt. Fax 387-0133
www.marshfield.k12.wi.us/
Grant ES 600/PK-6
425 W Upham St 54449 715-384-4747
Charmaine Ulrich, prin. Fax 384-2727
Lincoln ES 300/K-6
1621 S Felker Ave 54449 715-387-1296
Todd Felhofer, prin. Fax 389-9402
Madison ES 400/PK-6
510 N Palmetto Ave 54449 715-384-8181
Gregory Kaster, prin. Fax 486-1291
Marshfield MS 600/7-8
900 E 4th St 54449 715-387-1249
David Schoepke, prin. Fax 384-9269
Nasonville ES 300/K-6
11044 US Highway 10 54449 715-676-3611
Barbara Buss, prin. Fax 676-8040
Washington ES 300/PK-6
1112 W 11th St 54449 715-387-1238
James Cain, prin. Fax 389-9302

Columbus MS 100/6-8
710 S Columbus Ave 54449 715-387-1177
Barbara Billings, prin. Fax 384-4535
Immanuel Lutheran S 100/PK-8
604 S Chestnut Ave 54449 715-384-5121
Karen Bahn, admin. Fax 389-2963
MACS Early Childhood Learning Center 50/PK-PK
510 S Columbus Ave 54449 715-459-7188
Jill Jerabek, admin.
Marshfield Children's House Montessori 50/PK-6
1033 S Adams Ave 54449 715-384-7171
Kristin Cuddie, dir. Fax 384-9191
Our Lady of Peace S 100/3-5
1300 W 5th St 54449 715-384-5474
Sr. Mary Ann Wutkowski, prin. Fax 387-8697
St. John the Baptist PS 100/PK-2
307 N Walnut Ave 54449 715-384-4989
Sr. Mary Ann Wutkowski, prin. Fax 384-5131
Trinity Evangelical Lutheran S 50/K-8
9529 State Highway 13 54449 715-676-2121
Todd Dahlke, prin.

Mattoon, Shawano, Pop. 446
Antigo SD
Supt. — See Antigo
Mattoon ES 100/K-5
PO Box 80 54450 715-489-3631
Cindy Fischer, prin. Fax 489-3782

Mauston, Juneau, Pop. 4,291
Mauston SD 1,600/PK-12
510 Grayside Ave 53948 608-847-5451
Steven Smolek, supt. Fax 847-4635
www.mauston.k12.wi.us
Grayside ES 300/3-5
510 Grayside Ave 53948 608-847-5616
Tom Reisenauer, prin. Fax 847-2496
Olson MS 300/6-8
508 Grayside Ave 53948 608-847-6603
Tom Reisenauer, prin. Fax 847-4925
West Side ES 400/PK-2
708 Loomis Dr 53948 608-847-5616
Tom Reisenauer, prin. Fax 847-6342
Other Schools – See Lyndon Station

St. Patrick S 200/PK-8
325 Mansion St 53948 608-847-5844
Mary Kathleen Julian, prin. Fax 847-4103

Mayville, Dodge, Pop. 5,055
Herman SD 22 100/PK-8
N6409 County Road P 53050 920-387-3902
John Mason, supt. Fax 387-3966
www.hermansd.org
Herman S 100/PK-8
N6409 County Road P 53050 920-387-3902
John Mason, prin. Fax 387-3966

Mayville SD 1,100/PK-12
234 N John St 53050 920-387-7963
Ronald Bieri, supt. Fax 387-7979
www.mayville.k12.wi.us
Mayville MS 500/3-8
445 N Henninger St 53050 920-387-7970
Robert Clark, prin. Fax 387-7974
Parkview ES 200/PK-2
259 Oak St 53050 920-387-7973
Therese Fuller, prin. Fax 387-7975

Immanuel Lutheran S 50/PK-8
N8076 County Road AY 53050 920-387-2158
Brian Elmhorst, prin. Fax 387-2158
St. John Lutheran S 200/PK-8
520 Bridge St 53050 920-387-4310
Fax 387-2321
St. Mary S 100/PK-8
28 Naber St 53050 920-387-2920
Wayne Graczyk, prin. Fax 387-4037

Mazomanie, Dane, Pop. 1,528
Wisconsin Heights SD 700/PK-12
10173 US Highway 14 53560 608-767-2595
Mark Elworthy, supt. Fax 767-3579
www.wisheights.k12.wi.us
Mazomanie ES 100/3-5
314 Anne St 53560 608-767-2737
Dale Green, prin. Fax 767-2103
Wisconsin Heights MS 200/6-8
10173 US Highway 14 53560 608-767-2586
Asta Sepetys, prin. Fax 767-2062
Other Schools – See Black Earth

Medford, Taylor, Pop. 4,189
Medford Area SD 2,100/PK-12
124 W State St 54451 715-748-4620
Steve Russ, supt. Fax 748-6839
www.medford.k12.wi.us
Medford ES 600/PK-4
1065 W Broadway Ave 54451 715-748-2316
Dan Miller, prin. Fax 748-2570
Medford MS 600/5-8
509 Clark St 54451 715-748-2516
Al Leonard, prin. Fax 748-1213
Other Schools – See Stetsonville

Holy Rosary S 200/PK-6
215 S Washington Ave 54451 715-748-3336
Daniel Minter, prin. Fax 748-5110
Immanuel Lutheran S 100/PK-8
420 Lincoln St 54451 715-748-2921
Karl Hassler, prin. Fax 748-2948

Mellen, Ashland, Pop. 808
Mellen SD 300/PK-12
PO Box 500 54546 715-274-3601
Jim Schuchardt, supt. Fax 274-3715
www.mellen.k12.wi.us
Mellen S 200/PK-8
PO Box 500 54546 715-274-3601
Melissa Nigh, prin. Fax 274-3715

Melrose, Jackson, Pop. 516
Melrose-Mindoro SD 700/PK-12
N181 State Road 108 54642 608-488-2201
Ron Perry, supt. Fax 488-2805
www.mel-min.k12.wi.us
Melrose S 300/PK-8
805 2nd St 54642 608-488-2311
Tracy Dalton, prin. Fax 488-4015
Other Schools – See Mindoro

Menasha, Winnebago, Pop. 16,306
Menasha JSD 3,700/PK-12
PO Box 360 54952 920-967-1400
Keith Fuchs, supt. Fax 751-5038
www.mjsd.k12.wi.us
Banta Early Learning Center 200/PK-PK
PO Box 360 54952 920-967-1417
Marci Thiry, prin. Fax 751-5038
Butte Des Morts ES 400/K-5
501 Tayco St 54952 920-967-1900
William Gillespie, prin. Fax 751-4645
Clovis Grove ES 500/K-5
974 9th St 54952 920-967-1950
Doug Dahm, prin. Fax 751-5261
Gegan ES 400/K-5
675 W Airport Rd 54952 920-967-1360
Kevin Herrling, prin. Fax 751-4834
Jefferson ES 200/K-5
105 Ice St 54952 920-967-1660
Bridget Kilmer, prin. Fax 751-4831
Maplewood MS 800/6-8
1600 Midway Rd 54952 920-967-1600
Bev Sturke, prin. Fax 832-5837
Nicolet ES 100/K-5
449 Ahnaip St 54952 920-967-1710
Susan Werley, prin. Fax 751-4830

Mt. Calvary Lutheran S 100/K-8
N8728 Coop Rd 54952 920-731-4001
Timothy Zellmer, prin. Fax 731-4041
St. Mary S 100/PK-5
540 2nd St 54952 920-725-5351
Michael Buss, prin. Fax 725-7612
Seton Catholic MS 200/6-8
312 Nicolet Blvd 54952 920-727-0279
Monica Bausom, prin. Fax 727-1215
Trinity Lutheran S 100/PK-8
300 Broad St 54952 920-725-1715
Mike Stapleton, prin. Fax 722-7692

Menomonee Falls, Waukesha, Pop. 34,125
Hamilton SD
Supt. — See Sussex
Marcy ES 500/K-5
W180N4851 Marcy Rd 53051 262-781-8283
Michele Trawicki, prin. Fax 781-6028
Willow Springs Learning Center 300/K-K
W220N6660 Town Line Rd 53051 262-255-6190
Margaret Tackes, prin. Fax 255-4149

Menomonee Falls SD 3,500/K-12
N84W16579 Menomonee Ave 53051 262-255-8440
Dr. Keith Marty, supt. Fax 255-8461
www.sdmf.k12.wi.us
Franklin ES 900/K-5
N81W14701 Franklin Dr 53051 262-255-8470
Kathy Marks, prin. Fax 255-8482
North MS 400/6-8
N88W16750 Garfield Dr 53051 262-255-8450
Tabia Nicholas, prin. Fax 255-8475
Riverside ES 300/K-5
W153N8681 Margaret Rd 53051 262-255-8484
Scott Walter, prin. Fax 255-8393
Shady Lane ES 400/K-5
W172N8959 Shady Ln 53051 262-255-8480
Andrew Heinowski, prin. Fax 255-8448
Valley View ES 300/K-5
W180N8130 Town Hall Rd 53051 262-250-2620
Mary Dohmeier, prin. Fax 255-8476

Bethlehem Lutheran S - South 100/5-8
N84W15252 Menomonee Ave 53051 262-251-3120
Daryl Weber, prin. Fax 257-0407
Calvary Baptist S 200/K-12
N84W19049 Menomonee Ave 53051 262-251-0328
Steven Lafferty, admin. Fax 250-0624
Falls Baptist Academy 100/K-12
N69W12703 Appleton Ave 53051 262-251-7051
Derick Pardee, admin. Fax 251-7043

Grace Evangelical Lutheran S 200/K-8
N87W16173 Kenwood Blvd 53051 262-251-7140
Neal Hinze, prin. Fax 251-3460
Pilgrim Lutheran S 100/PK-8
W156N5429 Bette Dr 53051 262-781-3520
Chris Hopfensperger, prin. Fax 781-8287
St. Anthony S 200/K-8
N74W13646 Appleton Ave 53051 262-251-4390
Ann Schramka, prin. Fax 251-2412
St. Mary S 300/K-8
N89W16215 Cleveland Ave 53051 262-251-1050
Linda Joyner, prin. Fax 502-1671
Zion Lutheran S 100/PK-8
N48W18700 Lisbon Rd 53051 262-781-7437
Rich Maske, lead tchr. Fax 781-4656

Menomonie, Dunn, Pop. 15,244
Menomonie Area SD 2,700/PK-12
215 Pine Ave NE 54751 715-232-1642
Daniel Woll, supt. Fax 232-1317
msd.k12.wi.us
Menomonie MS 700/6-8
920 21st St SE 54751 715-232-1673
Stacey Everson, prin. Fax 232-5486
Oaklawn ES 300/K-5
500 21st St SE 54751 715-232-3798
Lori Smith, prin. Fax 232-1091
River Heights ES 400/PK-5
615 24th Ave W 54751 715-232-3987
Peg Kolden, prin. Fax 232-2321
Wakanda ES K-5
1801 Wakanda St NE 54751 715-232-3898
Nancy Estrem-Fuller, prin. Fax 232-3887
Other Schools – See Downsville, Knapp

St. Joseph S 200/PK-6
910 Wilson Ave 54751 715-232-4920
Renee Cassidy, prin. Fax 232-4923
St. Paul Lutheran S 100/K-8
1100 9th St E 54751 715-235-9622
Peter Wentzel, prin. Fax 235-9625

Mequon, Ozaukee, Pop. 23,820
Mequon-Thiensville SD 3,900/PK-12
5000 W Mequon Rd 53092 262-238-8500
Demond Means, supt. Fax 238-8520
www.mtsd.k12.wi.us
Donges Bay ES 500/PK-5
2401 W Donges Bay Rd 53092 262-238-7925
Robert Dunning, prin. Fax 238-7970
Lake Shore MS 400/6-8
11036 N Range Line Rd 53092 262-238-7613
Carolyn Wilson, prin. Fax 238-7650
Oriole Lane ES 500/K-5
12850 N Oriole Ln 53097 262-238-4261
Mary Jo Tye, prin. Fax 238-4250
Steffen MS 500/6-8
6633 W Steffen Dr 53092 262-238-4706
Deborah Anderson, prin. Fax 238-4740
Wilson ES 500/K-5
11001 N Buntrock Ave 53092 262-238-4601
Fax 238-4662

Lumen Christi MS 300/4-8
11300 N Saint James Ln 53092 262-242-7960
Gloria Markowski, prin. Fax 512-8986
Trinity Lutheran S 100/PK-8
10729 W Freistadt Rd 53097 262-242-2045
Richard Adams, prin. Fax 242-4407

Mercer, Iron
Mercer SD 200/PK-12
2690 W Margaret St 54547 715-476-2154
Jeff Ehrhardt, supt. Fax 476-2587
www.mercer.k12.wi.us
Mercer S 200/PK-12
2690 W Margaret St 54547 715-476-2154
Jody Bognar, prin. Fax 476-2587

Merrill, Lincoln, Pop. 10,145
Merrill Area SD 3,000/PK-12
1111 N Sales St 54452 715-536-4581
Lisa Snyder, supt. Fax 536-1788
www.maps.k12.wi.us
Goodrich ES 400/K-5
505 W 10th St 54452 715-536-5233
Mark Jahnke, prin. Fax 539-3736
Headstart and ECC 100/PK-PK
1111 N Sales St 54452 715-536-2392
Richard Thwaits, contact Fax 536-1788
Jefferson ES 200/K-5
1914 Jackson St 54452 715-536-5432
Jeffrey Damrau, prin. Fax 536-7260
Pine River ES 100/K-5
W4165 State Highway 64 54452 715-536-6101
Rich Thwaits, prin. Fax 536-6328
Prairie River MS 700/6-8
106 N Polk St 54452 715-536-9593
Gerald Beyer, prin. Fax 536-6378
Washington ES 300/K-5
1900 E 6th St 54452 715-536-2373
Paul Klippel, prin. Fax 536-1759
Other Schools – See Hamburg

St. Frances Xavier S 100/PK-8
1708 E 10th St 54452 715-536-6083
Emily Miller, prin. Fax 536-7536
St. John Lutheran S 200/K-8
1104 E 3rd St 54452 715-536-7264
Todd Pehlke, prin. Fax 539-3381
Trinity Lutheran S 200/PK-8
611 W Main St 54452 715-536-7501
Paul Labbus, prin. Fax 539-8531

Merrillan, Jackson, Pop. 586
Alma Center-Humbird-Merrillan SD
Supt. — See Alma Center

Lincoln ES 300/PK-6
207 E Pearl St 54754 715-333-2911
Todd Antony, prin. Fax 333-2914

Merton, Waukesha, Pop. 2,643
Merton Community SD 1,000/PK-8
PO Box 15 53056 262-538-1130
Mark Flynn, supt. Fax 538-4978
www.merton.k12.wi.us
Merton IS 500/4-8
PO Box 15 53056 262-538-1130
Jay Posick, prin. Fax 538-4978
Merton PS 500/PK-3
PO Box 15 53056 262-538-2227
Mike Budisch, prin. Fax 538-3937

Middleton, Dane, Pop. 15,816
Middleton-Cross Plains Area SD 5,500/PK-12
7106 South Ave 53562 608-829-9000
Donald Johnson, supt. Fax 836-1536
www.mcpasd.k12.wi.us
Elm Lawn ES 500/PK-5
6701 Woodgate Rd 53562 608-829-9070
Michael Pisani, prin. Fax 831-4470
Kromrey MS 600/6-8
7009 Donna Dr 53562 608-829-9530
Steve Soeteber, prin. Fax 831-8388
Northside ES 500/K-5
3620 High Rd 53562 608-829-9130
Roz Craney, prin. Fax 831-1355
Sauk Trail ES 400/PK-5
2205 Branch St 53562 608-829-9190
Chris Dahlk, prin. Fax 828-1678
Sunset Ridge ES 500/K-5
8686 Airport Rd 53562 608-829-9300
Todd Mann, prin. Fax 827-1805
Other Schools – See Cross Plains, Verona

St. Peters S 50/K-5
7129 County Road K 53562 608-831-4846
Maria Patt, prin. Fax 831-6095
Westside Christian S 100/PK-8
6815 Schneider Rd 53562 608-831-8540
Henry Hoenecke, prin. Fax 824-6594

Milton, Rock, Pop. 5,464
Milton SD 3,200/PK-12
430 E High St Ste 2 53563 608-868-9200
Bernard Nikolay, supt. Fax 868-9215
www.milton.k12.wi.us
Milton East ES 300/K-3
725 Greenman St 53563 608-868-9380
Theresa Rusch, prin. Fax 868-9256
Milton MS 500/7-8
20 E Madison Ave 53563 608-868-9350
Tim Schigur, prin. Fax 868-9269
Milton West ES 300/PK-3
825 W Madison Ave 53563 608-868-9230
Carol Meland, prin. Fax 868-9225
Northside IS 700/4-6
159 Northside Dr 53563 608-868-9280
Sarah Stuckey, prin. Fax 868-9259
Other Schools – See Janesville

Milwaukee, Milwaukee, Pop. 578,887
Fox Point Bayside SD 900/PK-8
7300 N Lombardy Rd 53217 414-247-4167
Gary Petersen, supt. Fax 351-7164
www.foxbay.k12.wi.us
Bayside MS 400/5-8
601 E Ellsworth Ln 53217 414-247-4201
Don Galster, prin. Fax 247-8963
Stormonth ES 600/PK-4
7301 N Longacre Rd 53217 414-247-4102
Linda Moore, prin. Fax 247-8970

Greenfield SD
Supt. — See Greenfield
Elm Dale ES 500/PK-5
5300 S Honey Creek Dr 53221 414-281-7100
Linda Wandtke, prin. Fax 281-2580

Maple Dale-Indian Hill SD
Supt. — See Fox Point
Indian Hill ES 100/PK-1
1101 W Brown Deer Rd 53217 414-351-7390
Daniel Westfahl, prin. Fax 351-8105
Maple Dale S 300/2-8
8377 N Port Washington Rd 53217 414-351-7380
Mary Dean, prin. Fax 351-8104

Milwaukee SD 73,200/PK-12
PO Box 2181 53201 414-475-8393
William Andrekopoulos, supt. Fax 475-8595
www.milwaukee.k12.wi.us
Academy of Accelerated Learning 600/PK-5
3727 S 78th St 53220 414-604-7300
Susan Miller, prin. Fax 604-7315
Alcott S 300/PK-8
3563 S 97th St 53228 414-604-7400
John Valdes, prin. Fax 604-7415
Allen-Field ES 900/PK-5
730 W Lapham Blvd 53204 414-902-9200
Marybell Harris, prin. Fax 902-9215
Auer Avenue S 500/PK-8
2319 W Auer Ave 53206 414-875-4500
Hattie Knox, prin. Fax 875-4515
Barton ES 500/PK-6
5700 W Green Tree Rd 53223 414-393-3900
Don Wojczulis, prin. Fax 393-3915
Bethune Academy 400/PK-8
1535 N 35th St 53208 414-934-4600
Marion Reiter, prin. Fax 934-4615
Browning ES 500/PK-5
5440 N 64th St 53218 414-393-5200
Sharon McDade, prin. Fax 393-5215
Brown Street Academy 500/PK-5
2029 N 20th St 53205 414-935-3100
Ava Morris, prin. Fax 935-3115

Bruce ES 400/PK-6
6453 N 89th St 53224 414-393-2100
Karen Bradley, prin. Fax 393-2115
Bryant ES 300/PK-5
8718 W Thurston Ave 53225 414-393-6500
Cassandra Brown, prin. Fax 393-6515
Burbank S 600/PK-8
6035 W Adler St 53214 414-256-8400
Angelo Serio, prin. Fax 256-8415
Burdick S 500/PK-8
4348 S Griffin Ave 53207 414-294-1200
Robert Schleck, prin. Fax 294-1215
Burroughs MS 600/6-8
6700 N 80th St 53223 414-393-3500
Darrell Williams, prin. Fax 393-3515
Carleton ES 300/PK-5
4116 W Silver Spring Dr 53209 414-393-5300
Leea Power, prin. Fax 393-5315
Carson Academy of Science 500/PK-8
4920 W Capitol Dr 53216 414-393-4800
Gregory Tolbert, prin. Fax 393-4815
Carver Academy 500/K-8
1900 N 1st St 53212 414-267-0500
Floyd Williams, prin. Fax 267-0515
Cass Street S 500/PK-8
1647 N Cass St 53202 414-212-2700
Ricardo Anderson, prin. Fax 212-2715
Clarke Street S 400/PK-8
2816 W Clarke St 53210 414-267-1000
Betty Laws Blue, prin. Fax 267-1015
Clemens ES 300/PK-5
3600 W Hope Ave 53216 414-875-6300
Jacqueline Richardson, prin. Fax 875-6315
Clement Avenue ES 300/PK-6
3666 S Clement Ave 53207 414-294-1500
April Swick, prin. Fax 294-1515
Congress S 900/PK-8
5225 W Lincoln Creek Dr 53218 414-616-5300
Lorraine Applewhite, prin. Fax 616-5315
Cooper S 400/PK-8
5143 S 21st St 53221 414-304-6300
Jennifer Doucette, prin. Fax 304-6315
Craig Montessori S 400/K-8
7667 W Congress St 53218 414-393-4200
Phillip Dosmann, prin. Fax 393-4214
Curtin S 300/PK-7
3450 S 32nd St 53215 414-902-7700
Virginia Cullun, prin. Fax 902-7715
Doerfler S 700/PK-8
3014 W Scott St 53215 414-902-9500
Clark Addison, prin. Fax 902-9515
Dover Street ES 300/PK-5
619 E Dover St 53207 414-294-1600
Jacklyn Labor, prin. Fax 294-1615
Eighty First Street S 400/PK-8
2964 N 81st St 53222 414-874-5400
James Lindsey, prin. Fax 874-5415
Elm Creative Arts ES 600/PK-5
900 W Walnut St 53205 414-267-1800
Ruth Maegli, prin. Fax 267-1815
Emerson ES 200/PK-5
9025 W Lawrence Ave 53225 414-393-4300
Christlyn Stanley, prin. Fax 393-4315
Engleburg ES 500/PK-5
5100 N 91st St 53225 414-616-5600
Jonathan Leinfelder, prin. Fax 616-5615
Fernwood Montessori S 500/PK-8
3239 S Pennsylvania Ave 53207 414-294-1300
John Sanchez, prin. Fax 294-1315
Fifty Third Street S 400/PK-8
3618 N 53rd St 53216 414-874-5300
Bridgette Hood, prin. Fax 874-5315
Fletcher ES 200/PK-5
9520 W Allyn St 53224 262-236-1600
Carletta Noland, prin. Fax 236-1615
Forest Home Avenue ES 800/PK-5
1516 W Forest Home Ave 53204 414-902-6200
Sara Marquez, prin. Fax 902-6215
Franklin S 400/PK-8
2308 W Nash St 53206 414-875-4400
Michelle Morris, prin. Fax 875-4415
Fratney ES 400/PK-5
3255 N Fratney St 53212 414-267-1100
Rita Tenorio, prin. Fax 267-1115
Gaenslen S 600/PK-8
1250 E Burleigh St 53212 414-267-5700
Ada Rivera, prin. Fax 267-5715
Garden Homes ES 300/PK-5
4456 N Teutonia Ave 53209 414-874-5600
Terry McKissick, prin. Fax 874-5615
Garland ES 300/PK-5
1420 W Goldcrest Ave 53221 414-304-6500
Taimi Parey, prin. Fax 304-6515
Goodrich ES 400/PK-5
8251 N Celina St 53224 262-236-1500
Mary Zimmerman, prin. Fax 236-1515
Grantosa Drive S 700/PK-8
4850 N 82nd St 53218 414-393-4400
Eugene Pitchford, prin. Fax 393-4415
Grant S 700/PK-8
2920 W Grant St 53215 414-902-8000
Ellease Mayo, prin. Fax 902-8015
Green Bay Avenue S 400/PK-7
3872 N 8th St 53206 414-267-4600
Thresessa Childs, prin. Fax 267-4615
Greenfield Bilingual S 600/K-8
1711 S 35th St 53215 414-902-8200
Maria Sanchez, prin. Fax 902-8215
Hampton ES 400/PK-5
5000 N 53rd St 53218 414-393-5400
Bridget Araujo, prin. Fax 393-5415
Hartford Avenue S 700/PK-8
2227 E Hartford Ave 53211 414-906-4700
Cynthia Ellwood, prin. Fax 906-4715
Hawley Road ES 300/PK-5
5610 W Wisconsin Ave 53213 414-256-8500
Glen Stavens, prin. Fax 256-8515

Hawthorne ES 400/PK-5
6945 N 41st St 53209 414-247-7200
Renee Hampton, prin. Fax 247-7215
Hi-Mount Boulevard S 500/PK-8
4921 W Garfield Ave 53208 414-875-2700
Toni Dinkins, prin. Fax 875-2715
Holmes S 400/PK-8
2463 N Buffum St 53212 414-267-1300
Debra Wallace, prin. Fax 267-1315
Hopkins Street S 500/PK-8
1503 W Hopkins St 53206 414-267-0600
Maurice Turner, prin. Fax 267-0615
Kagel ES 400/PK-5
1210 W Mineral St 53204 414-902-7400
Hector LaBoy, prin. Fax 902-7415
Keefe Avenue S 400/PK-8
1618 W Keefe Ave 53206 414-267-4800
Erica Hendricks, prin. Fax 267-4815
Kilbourn ES 300/PK-5
5354 N 68th St 53218 414-393-4500
Lisa Marion-Howard, prin. Fax 393-4515
King S 400/PK-8
3275 N 3rd St 53212 414-267-1500
Shiron Posley, prin. Fax 267-1515
Kluge ES 400/PK-5
5760 N 67th St 53218 414-578-5000
Doris Kennedy, prin. Fax 578-5015
Lafollette S 300/PK-8
3239 N 9th St 53206 414-267-5200
Brenda Sheppard-Nelson, prin. Fax 267-5215
Lancaster S 600/PK-8
4931 N 68th St 53218 414-393-5500
Richard Spates, prin. Fax 393-5515
Lee S 300/PK-8
921 W Meinecke Ave 53206 414-267-1700
James Dawson, prin. Fax 267-1715
Lincoln Avenue ES 600/PK-5
1817 W Lincoln Ave 53215 414-902-9700
Janine Graber, prin. Fax 902-9715
Lincoln MS of the Arts 800/6-8
820 E Knapp St 53202 414-212-3300
Debra Ortiz, prin. Fax 212-3315
Lloyd Street ES 500/PK-5
1228 W Lloyd St 53205 414-267-1600
Clavon Byrd, prin. Fax 267-1615
Longfellow S 800/PK-8
1021 S 21st St 53204 414-902-9800
Wendell Smith, prin. Fax 902-9815
Lowell ES 300/PK-5
4360 S 20th St 53221 414-304-6600
Susan Stoner, prin. Fax 304-6615
MacDowell Montessori S 500/PK-8
1706 W Highland Ave 53233 414-935-1400
Kenneth Wald, prin. Fax 935-1415
Manitoba S 500/PK-8
4040 W Forest Home Ave 53215 414-902-8600
Helen Bugni, prin. Fax 902-8615
Maple Tree ES 400/PK-5
6644 N 107th St 53224 414-578-5100
Jane Behr, prin. Fax 578-5115
Maryland Avenue ES 200/K-5
2418 N Maryland Ave 53211 414-906-4800
Phillip Dosmann, prin. Fax 906-4815
McNair S 300/PK-8
4950 N 24th St 53209 414-616-5200
Willie Fuller, prin. Fax 616-5215
Meir S 400/3-8
1555 N Martin Luther King 53212 414-212-3200
Thomas Hanley, prin. Fax 212-3215
Metcalfe S 300/K-8
3400 W North Ave 53208 414-874-3600
Cynthia Grant, prin. Fax 874-3615
Milwaukee Education Center MS 700/6-8
227 W Pleasant St 53212 414-212-2900
Donna Walker, prin. Fax 212-2967
Milwaukee French Immersion ES 400/PK-5
2360 N 52nd St 53210 414-874-8400
Virginia McFadden, prin. Fax 874-8415
Milwaukee German Immersion ES 600/PK-5
3778 N 82nd St 53222 414-393-5600
Albert Brugger, prin. Fax 393-5615
Milwaukee Sign Language S 600/PK-8
7900 W Acacia St 53223 414-393-3800
Charles Marks, prin. Fax 393-3815
Milwaukee Spanish Immersion ES 500/PK-5
2765 S 55th St 53219 414-604-7600
Yvette Martel, prin. Fax 604-7615
Mitchell Integrated Arts S 700/PK-8
1728 S 23rd St 53204 414-902-8100
Michelle Hagen, prin. Fax 902-8115
Morgandale ES 500/PK-6
3635 S 17th St 53221 414-902-9900
Barbara Luepke, prin. Fax 902-9915
Morse MS for Gifted and Talented 1,100/6-8
4601 N 84th St 53225 414-616-5800
Rogers Onick, prin. Fax 616-5815
Neeskara ES 400/PK-5
1601 N Hawley Rd 53208 414-256-8600
Mary Sandvig, prin. Fax 256-8615
Ninety Fifth Street ES 300/PK-5
3707 N 94th St 53222 414-393-4100
Reginald Lawrence, prin. Fax 393-4115
Parkview ES 400/PK-5
10825 W Villard Ave 53225 414-393-2700
Cheryl Colbert, prin. Fax 393-2715
Pierce ES 400/K-5
2765 N Fratney St 53212 414-267-4400
Alice Somers-Walton, prin. Fax 267-4415
Riley ES 700/PK-5
2424 S 4th St 53207 414-902-7100
Andrew Patterson, prin. Fax 902-7115
River Trail S 500/PK-8
12021 W Florist Ave 53225 414-393-2200
Thyra Handford, prin. Fax 393-2215
Rogers Street Academy 500/PK-8
2430 W Rogers St 53204 414-902-1100
Rosana Mateo, prin. Fax 902-1115

Roosevelt Creative Arts MS 800/6-8
800 W Walnut St 53205 414-267-8800
Linda Roundtree, prin. Fax 267-8815
Sherman Multicultural Arts S 700/PK-8
5110 W Locust St 53210 414-874-5800
Ella Hayes, prin. Fax 874-5815
Siefert ES 300/PK-5
1547 N 14th St 53205 414-935-1500
Janel Howard-Hawkins, prin. Fax 935-1515
Silver Spring ES 300/PK-5
5131 N Green Bay Ave 53209 414-247-7300
Winifred Tidmore, prin. Fax 247-7315
Sixty-Eight Street ECC 200/PK-K
6720 W Moltke Ave 53210 414-874-3070
Jackie Humphrey, prin. Fax 874-3088
Sixty Fifth Street S 400/PK-8
6600 W Melvina St 53216 414-393-6400
Bridgett Hartney, prin. Fax 393-6415
Starms Discovery Learning Center 400/1-8
2035 N 25th St 53205 414-934-4900
Christine Maxwell, prin. Fax 934-4915
Starms ECC 300/PK-K
2616 W Garfield Ave 53205 414-934-4700
Christine Maxwell, prin. Fax 934-4715
Starms Monumental ECC 50/PK-K
2407 W North Ave 53205 414-345-0608
Christine Maxwell, prin. Fax 345-0659
Story S 500/K-8
3815 W Kilbourn Ave 53208 414-934-4800
Portia Ewing, prin. Fax 934-4815
Stuart ES 300/PK-5
7001 N 86th St 53224 414-393-3700
Pamela Bell, prin. Fax 393-3715
Thirty Fifth Street S 400/PK-8
3517 W Courtland Ave 53209 414-465-5200
Sharon Traylor, prin. Fax 874-5215
Thoreau S 600/PK-8
7878 N 60th St 53223 262-236-1800
Ray Collie, prin. Fax 236-1815
Thurston Woods S 500/PK-8
5966 N 35th St 53209 414-393-2800
Ramelann Kalagian, prin. Fax 393-2815
Tippecanoe S 300/K-8
357 E Howard Ave 53207 414-294-1800
Angela Serio, prin. Fax 294-1815
Townsend Street S 400/PK-8
3360 N Sherman Blvd 53216 414-874-5900
Patrick Chatman, prin. Fax 874-5915
Trowbridge Street S 200/PK-8
1943 E Trowbridge St 53207 414-294-1900
Thomas Matthews, prin. Fax 294-1915
Twenty First Street ES 300/PK-5
2121 W Hadley St 53206 414-267-5500
Minnie Novy, prin. Fax 267-5515
Urban Waldorf S 400/PK-8
1312 N 27th St 53208 414-934-8200
Debra Magee, prin. Fax 934-8215
Victory S 500/PK-8
2222 W Henry Ave 53221 414-304-6700
Wanda Katz, prin. Fax 304-6715
Vieau S 700/PK-8
823 S 4th St 53204 414-902-6100
Eduardo Galvan, prin. Fax 902-6115
Wedgewood Park International S 500/6-8
6506 W Warnimont Ave 53220 414-604-7800
Suzanne Kirby, prin. Fax 604-7815
Wheatley ES 200/PK-5
2442 N 20th St 53206 414-267-9000
Edith Bivens, prin. Fax 267-9015
Whitman ES 300/PK-6
4200 S 54th St 53220 414-604-7700
Patricia Cifax, prin. Fax 604-7715
Zablocki ES 600/PK-5
1016 W Oklahoma Ave 53215 414-294-2200
Patricia Walia, prin. Fax 294-2215

Atlas Preparatory Academy 700/K-12
2911 S 32nd St 53215 414-385-0771
Michelle Lukacs, prin. Fax 385-0773
Atonement Lutheran S 200/K-8
4224 W Ruby Ave 53209 414-871-1224
Stephen Schafer, prin. Fax 871-0379
Believers in Christ Christian Academy 300/PK-12
4065 N 25th St 53209 414-444-1146
Candace Covington, prin. Fax 444-5378
Blessed Sacrament S 100/PK-8
3126 S 41st St 53215 414-649-4730
Janet Orlowski, prin. Fax 649-4726
Blessed Savior Catholic S - East 300/PK-8
5140 N 55th St 53218 414-438-2745
Barbara O'Donnell, prin. Fax 438-9330
Blessed Savior Catholic S - North 100/PK-8
5501 N 68th St 53218 414-466-0470
Tom Hage, prin. Fax 466-4177
Blessed Savior Catholic S - South 100/K-8
4059 N 64th St 53216 414-463-3878
Patricia Wilkum, prin. Fax 535-9265
Blessed Savior Catholic S - West 100/K-8
8545 W Villard Ave 53225 414-464-5775
Roger Baehr, prin. Fax 464-5737
Bufkin Christian Academy 100/PK-12
827 N 34th St 53208 414-934-8885
Texas Bufkin, admin. Fax 934-8886
Catholic East S 100/K-8
2491 N Murray Ave 53211 414-964-1770
Julie Ann Robinson, prin. Fax 964-6578
Christian Faith Acad of Higher Learning 100/PK-5
2327 N 52nd St 53210 414-442-9299
Gwen Mallory, prin. Fax 442-9289
Christ Memorial Lutheran S 100/K-8
5719 N Teutonia Ave 53209 414-461-3371
Kenneth Marton, prin. Fax 461-3374
Christ-St. Peter Lutheran S 100/K-8
2229 W Greenfield Ave 53204 414-383-2055
Scott Beyersdorf, prin. Fax 383-2497
Condcordia University S 100/PK-8
8242 N Granville Rd 53224 414-354-6601
Dick Laabs, prin. Fax 354-5586

CrossTrainers Academy | 100/PK-3
830 N 19th St 53233 | 414-935-0500
Jacquelyn Verhulst, admin. | Fax 344-6972
Early View Academy of Excellence | 300/PK-10
7132 W Good Hope Rd 53223 | 414-431-0001
Annie Oliver, admin. | Fax 431-0046
Eastbrook Academy | 300/PK-12
5375 N Green Bay Ave 53209 | 414-228-7905
Julie Loomis, hdmstr. | Fax 228-9854
Emmaus Lutheran S | 300/PK-8
2818 N 23rd St 53206 | 414-444-6090
Milton Mitchell, prin. | Fax 444-3336
Fairview Evangelical Lutheran S | 100/PK-8
137 N 66th St 53213 | 414-258-1534
Kenneth Proeber, prin. | Fax 771-0544
Faith S | 100/PK-8
8444 W Melvina St 53222 | 414-463-5030
Jeffrey Schultz, prin. | Fax 463-5086
Garden Homes Lutheran S | 200/PK-8
2450 W Roosevelt Dr 53209 | 414-444-9050
John Wesenberg, prin. | Fax 444-9105
Gospel Lutheran S | 100/K-8
3965 N 15th St 53206 | 414-372-5159
Susan Boeck, prin. | Fax 372-5179
Harambee Community S | 300/K-8
110 W Burleigh St 53212 | 414-264-4600
Lenora Davis, prin. | Fax 918-4170
Heritage Christian S | 700/PK-12
1300 S 109th St 53214 | 414-259-1231
Thomas Wittkamper, supt. | Fax 257-2548
Hillel Academy | 100/K-8
6401 N Santa Monica Blvd 53217 | 414-962-9545
B. Devorah Shmotkin, prin. | Fax 967-8373
Holy Redeemer Christian Academy | 300/PK-12
3500 W Mother Daniels Way 53209 | 414-466-1800
Alton Townsel, admin. | Fax 466-4930
Holy Wisdom Academy East Campus | 100/PK-3
3329 S 10th St 53215 | 414-744-7188
Richard Mason, prin. | Fax 744-8370
Holy Wisdom Academy West Campus | 100/4-8
3344 S 16th St 53215 | 414-383-3453
Richard Mason, prin. | Fax 672-2645
Hope Christian S | 200/K-8
2345 N 25th St 53206 | 414-931-0350
Jamie Luehring, prin. | Fax 931-0702
Hope MS | 100/5-8
510 E Burleigh St 53212 | 414-264-6284
Patrick Hurley, prin. | Fax 264-6278
Kings Academy Christian S | 200/PK-8
7798 N 60th St 53223 | 414-371-9100
Laurel Nobles, admin. | Fax 371-9200
Loving Shepherd Lutheran S | 100/K-8
3909 W Clinton Ave 53209 | 414-352-2662
Timothy Paschke, prin. | Fax 352-3175
Lutheran Special S | 100/1-8
9700 W Grantosa Dr 53222 | 414-461-8500
Judy Schultz, prin. | Fax 461-4930
Messmer Preparatory S | 400/K-8
3027 N Fratney St 53212 | 414-264-6070
Michelle Paris, prin. | Fax 264-6430
Milwaukee Montessori S | 300/PK-8
345 N 95th St 53226 | 414-259-0370
Monica Van Aken, hdmstr. | Fax 259-0427
Milwaukee SDA S | 100/K-10
10900 W Mill Rd 53225 | 414-353-3520
Alberto Torres, admin. | Fax 353-1451
Mother of Good Counsel S | 200/K-8
3001 N 68th St 53210 | 414-442-7600
Regina Shaw, prin. | Fax 442-0644
Mt. Calvary Lutheran S | 200/PK-8
2862 N 53rd St 53210 | 414-873-3466
Carrie Miller, prin. | Fax 873-0567
Mt. Lebanon Lutheran S | 100/K-8
6100 W Hampton Ave 53218 | 414-464-5410
Roger Kramp, prin. | Fax 464-6210
Mt. Olive Lutheran S | 100/PK-8
5301 W Washington Blvd 53208 | 414-774-2200
Christopher Cody, prin. | Fax 774-2212
Nativity Jesuit MS | 100/6-8
1515 S 29th St 53215 | 414-645-1060
Melodie Hessling, prin. | Fax 645-0505
New Testament Christian Academy | 100/PK-8
10201 W Bradley Rd 53224 | 414-365-1677
Donna Childs, dir. | Fax 365-5611
Noach S | 200/K-12
222 E Burleigh St 53212 | 414-265-5343
Dr. Brenda Noach-Ewing, admin. | Fax 265-2736
Northwest Lutheran S | 200/PK-8
4119 N 81st St 53222 | 414-463-4040
Dennis Wallinger, prin. | Fax 463-0524
Notre Dame MS | 100/5-8
1420 W Scott St 53204 | 414-671-3000
Jean Ellman, prin. | Fax 671-3170
Oklahoma Ave Lutheran S | 50/PK-8
5335 W Oklahoma Ave 53219 | 414-543-3580
Richard Gottschalk, prin. | Fax 543-3610
Our Lady of Good Hope S | 100/K-8
7140 N 41st St 53209 | 414-352-7980
Yolande Lasky, prin. | Fax 352-7258
Our Lady Queen of Peace S | 200/K-8
2733 W Euclid Ave 53215 | 414-672-6660
Janet Orlowski, prin. | Fax 672-2739
Prince of Peace S | 200/1-5
1114 S 25th St 53204 | 414-383-2157
Norbert Smurawa, prin. | Fax 383-7645
Prince of Peace S | 200/PK-K, 6-8
1646 S 22nd St 53204 | 414-645-4922
Judy Birlem, prin. | Fax 645-4940
Risen Savior Lutheran S | 100/K-8
9550 W Brown Deer Rd 53224 | 414-354-7320
Clarence Jenkins, prin. | Fax 354-6815
St. Adalbert S | 400/K-8
1913 W Becher St 53215 | 414-645-5450
Julie Hutchinson, prin. | Fax 645-5510
St. Aemilian Lakeside S | 100/1-10
8901 W Capitol Dr 53222 | 414-463-1880
Tami Trulock, prin. | Fax 463-2770

St. Anthony ES | 700/K-5
1669 S 5th St 53204 | 414-384-1729
Ramon Cruz, prin. | Fax 384-1731
St. Anthony MS | 200/6-8
1747 S 9th St 53204 | 414-384-1730
Ramon Cruz, prin. | Fax 384-1733
St. Bernadette S | 200/K-8
8202 W Denver Ave 53223 | 414-358-4603
Mary Lorusso, prin. | Fax 760-1037
St. Catherine of Alexandria S | 100/PK-8
8660 N 76th Pl 53223 | 414-365-2030
Linda Kuhn, prin. | Fax 365-2021
St. Catherine S | 200/K-8
2647 N 51st St 53210 | 414-445-2846
Deborah Zabinski, prin. | Fax 445-0448
St. Charles Borromeo S | 200/K-8
3100 W Parnell Ave 53221 | 414-282-0767
Ellen Knippel, prin. | Fax 817-9605
St. Gregory the Great S | 300/K-8
3132 S 63rd St 53219 | 414-321-1350
Anne Dunlop, prin. | Fax 328-3881
St. John Evangelical Lutheran S | 100/K-8
4001 S 68th St 53220 | 414-541-5881
Henry Meyer, prin. | Fax 541-7869
St. John Kanty S | 200/K-8
2840 S 10th St 53215 | 414-483-8780
Elizabeth Eichman, prin. | Fax 744-1846
St. Josaphat S | 200/K-8
801 W Lincoln Ave 53215 | 414-645-4378
Carolyn Trawitzki, prin. | Fax 645-1978
St. Leo Catholic Urban Academy | 200/K-8
514 N 31st St 53208 | 414-442-1100
Lewis Lea, prin. | Fax 873-0119
St. Lucas Evangelical Lutheran S | 100/K-8
648 E Dover St 53207 | 414-483-9122
Michael Koestler, prin. | Fax 486-0591
St. Marcus Lutheran S | 300/PK-8
2215 N Palmer St 53212 | 414-562-3163
Jonathan Boche, prin. | Fax 562-3663
St. Margaret Mary S | 200/K-8
3950 N 92nd St 53222 | 414-463-8760
Brenda White, prin. | Fax 463-2373
St. Martini Lutheran S | 200/PK-8
PO Box 04066 53204 | 414-383-7058
Duane Miller, prin. | Fax 383-0637
St. Matthias S | 500/K-8
9300 W Beloit Rd 53227 | 414-321-0894
Dr. Mark Joerres, prin. | Fax 321-9228
St. Peter Immanuel Lutheran S | 200/PK-8
7801 W Acacia St 53223 | 414-353-6800
Amy Puechner, prin. | Fax 353-5510
St. Philips Lutheran S | 100/K-8
3012 N Holton St 53212 | 414-263-7614
Timothy McNeill, prin. | Fax 263-7858
St. Rafael the Archangel S - North | 200/PK-4
2075 S 32nd St 53215 | 414-643-6090
Carolyn Ettlie, prin. | Fax 259-9285
St. Rafael the Archangel S - South | 100/5-8
2251 S 31st St 53215 | 414-645-1300
Carolyn Ettlie, prin. | Fax 645-1415
St. Roman S | 300/K-8
1810 W Bolivar Ave 53221 | 414-282-7970
Cheryl Sanford, prin. | Fax 282-5140
St. Rose S | 200/PK-8
514 N 31st St 53208 | 414-933-6070
Lewis Lea, prin. | Fax 933-3071
St. Sebastian S | 300/K-8
1747 N 54th St 53208 | 414-453-5830
Paul Hohl, prin. | Fax 453-9449
St. Thomas Aquinas Academy | 300/PK-8
341 E Norwich St 53207 | 414-744-1214
Mary Stallmann, prin. | Fax 744-8340
St. Vincent Pallotti S | 100/PK-8
201 N 76th St 53213 | 414-258-4165
Jeffrey Johnson, prin. | Fax 258-9844
Salam S | 400/PK-10
4707 S 13th St 53221 | 414-282-0504
Wanis Shalaby, prin. | Fax 282-6959
Salem Lutheran S | 100/K-8
6844 N 107th St 53224 | 414-353-8190
David Nelson, prin. | Fax 353-5819
Sharon Jr. Academy | 100/1-8
PO Box 06439 53206 | 414-265-9000
Gerthy Desty, prin. | Fax 265-8390
Sherman Park Lutheran S | 100/PK-4
2703 N Sherman Blvd 53210 | 414-447-0266
Chris Couillard, prin. | Fax 445-6556
Siloah Lutheran S | 200/K-8
3721 N 21st St 53206 | 414-873-8240
Terrance Graf, prin. | Fax 873-8250
Tamarack Waldorf S | 200/PK-8
1150 E Brady St 53202 | 414-277-0009
Jean Kacanek, prin. | Fax 277-7799
Travis Academy | 400/K-12
2733 W Wisconsin Ave 53208 | 414-342-4950
Dorothy Travis-Moore, prin. | Fax 342-4957
University S | 1,100/PK-12
2100 W Fairy Chasm Rd 53217 | 414-352-6000
Ward Ghory, hdmstr. | Fax 352-8076
Word of Life Lutheran S | 50/PK-8
3545 S 23rd St 53221 | 414-281-7808
Phillip Krueger, prin. | Fax 281-8823
Yeshiva S | 200/K-8
5115 W Keefe Ave 53216 | 414-871-9376
Rabbi Aryeh Cohen, prin. | Fax 871-9151

Mindoro, LaCrosse
Melrose-Mindoro SD
Supt. — See Melrose
Mindoro ES | 200/K-K, 3-5
N8244 State Road 108 54644 | 608-857-3410
Tracy Dalton, prin. | Fax 857-3421

Mineral Point, Iowa, Pop. 2,495
Mineral Point SD | 800/PK-12
705 Ross St 53565 | 608-987-3924
Terry Hemann, supt. | Fax 987-3766
www.mp.k12.wi.us
Mineral Point ES | 400/PK-5
611 Cothern St 53565 | 608-987-2024
Kelly Seichter, prin. | Fax 987-3904
Mineral Point MS | 200/6-8
705 Ross St 53565 | 608-987-2371
Ted Evans, prin. | Fax 987-3766

Minocqua, Oneida
Minocqua J1 SD | 500/K-8
7450 Titus Dr 54548 | 715-356-5206
Jim Ellis, admin. | Fax 356-1626
www.mhlt.org/
Minocqua S | 500/K-8
7450 Titus Dr 54548 | 715-356-5206
Rob Way, prin. | Fax 356-2649

Trinity Lutheran S | 50/K-8
8781 Brunswick Rd 54548 | 715-356-2255
Peter Micheel, prin. | Fax 356-2132

Minong, Washburn, Pop. 578
Northwood SD | 400/PK-12
N14463 Highway 53 54859 | 715-466-2297
Jean Serum, supt. | Fax 466-5149
northwood.k12.wi.us/
Northwood S | 400/PK-12
N14463 Highway 53 54859 | 715-466-2297
Joshua Tomesh, prin. | Fax 466-5149

Mishicot, Manitowoc, Pop. 1,413
Mishicot SD | 1,000/PK-12
PO Box 280 54228 | 920-755-4633
Colleen Timm, supt. | Fax 755-2390
www.mishicot.k12.wi.us
Mishicot MS | 200/6-8
PO Box 280 54228 | 920-755-4633
Tom Ellenbecker, prin. | Fax 755-2390
Schultz ES | 400/PK-5
PO Box 280 54228 | 920-755-4633
Eric Nelson, prin. | Fax 755-4463

Saint Peter Lutheran S | 50/K-8
325 Randolph St 54228 | 920-755-3857
Eric Lange, prin. | Fax 755-3857

Mondovi, Buffalo, Pop. 2,618
Mondovi SD | 1,000/PK-12
337 N Jackson St 54755 | 715-926-3684
Cheryl Gullicksrud, supt. | Fax 926-3617
www.mondovi.k12.wi.us/
Mondovi ES | 400/PK-5
337 N Jackson St 54755 | 715-926-3645
Paul Franzwa, prin. | Fax 926-3617
Mondovi MS | 200/6-8
337 N Jackson St 54755 | 715-926-3457
Mike Bruning, prin. | Fax 926-3617

Monona, Dane, Pop. 7,716
Monona Grove SD | 1,900/PK-12
5301 Monona Dr 53716 | 608-221-7660
Craig Gerlach, supt. | Fax 221-7688
www.mononagrove.org
Maywood ES | 200/PK-2
902 Nichols Rd 53716 | 608-221-7670
Ann Schroeder, prin. | Fax 223-6504
Winnequah IS | 200/3-6
800 Greenway Rd 53716 | 608-221-7677
Ann Schroeder, prin. | Fax 221-7694
Other Schools – See Cottage Grove

Immaculate Heart of Mary S | 100/PK-8
4913 Schofield St 53716 | 608-222-8831
Sara Latimer, prin. | Fax 221-4492

Monroe, Green, Pop. 10,563
Monroe SD | 2,400/PK-12
925 16th Ave Ste 3 53566 | 608-328-7171
Larry Brown, supt. | Fax 328-7214
www.monroeschools.com
Lincoln Accelerated Learning Academy | 300/PK-5
2625 14th Ave 53566 | 608-328-7172
Tina Van Meer, prin. | Fax 328-7228
Monroe MS | 600/6-8
1510 13th St 53566 | 608-328-7120
Lynn Wheeler, prin. | Fax 328-7224
Northside ES | 400/K-5
3005 8 1/2 St 53566 | 608-328-7134
Amy Timmerman, prin. | Fax 328-7226
Parkside ES | 400/PK-5
920 4th St 53566 | 608-328-7130
Eric Huinker, prin. | Fax 328-7222

St. Victor S | 100/PK-5
1416 20th Ave 53566 | 608-325-3395
Joseph Peters, prin. | Fax 325-3115

Montello, Marquette, Pop. 1,483
Montello SD | 800/PK-12
222 Forest Ln 53949 | 608-297-7617
Jeff Holmes, supt. | Fax 297-7726
www.montello.k12.wi.us
Forest Lane ES | 400/PK-6
222 Forest Ln 53949 | 608-297-2128
Jeff Fimreite, prin. | Fax 297-8075

St. John Lutheran S | 100/K-8
PO Box 190 53949 | 608-297-2866
Richard Janke, prin. | Fax 297-9069

Monticello, Green, Pop. 1,132
Monticello SD | 400/PK-12
334 S Main St 53570 | 608-938-4194
Karen Ballin, supt. | Fax 938-1062
www.monticello.k12.wi.us/
Monticello ES | 200/PK-5
334 S Main St 53570 | 608-938-4194
Karen Ballin, prin. | Fax 938-1062

Monticello MS 100/6-8
334 S Main St 53570 608-938-4194
Allen Brokopp, prin. Fax 938-1062

Morrisonville, Dane
De Forest Area SD
Supt. — See De Forest
Morrisonville ES 100/1-4
4649 Willow St 53571 608-842-6400
Roy Bernards, prin. Fax 846-6549

Mosinee, Marathon, Pop. 3,996
Mosinee SD 2,000/PK-12
591 W State Highway 153 54455 715-693-2530
Jerry Rosso, supt. Fax 693-7272
www.mosineeschools.org
Mosinee ES 600/PK-3
600 12th St 54455 715-693-2810
Davonne Eldredge, prin. Fax 693-1974
Mosinee MS 700/4-8
700 High St 54455 715-693-3660
Ronald Mueller, prin. Fax 693-6655

St. Paul S 100/PK-8
404 High St 54455 715-693-2675
Erin Bailey, prin. Fax 693-1332

Mount Calvary, Fond du Lac, Pop. 935

Consolidated Parochial S 100/K-8
100 Notre Dame St 53057 920-753-4811
Mary Leonard, prin. Fax 753-2411
St. Pauls Lutheran S 100/K-8
N6680 County Rd W 53057 920-922-9056
Dawn Barenz, prin. Fax 922-9149

Mount Horeb, Dane, Pop. 6,188
Mount Horeb Area SD 2,200/PK-12
1304 E Lincoln St 53572 608-437-2400
Wayne Anderson, supt. Fax 437-5597
www.mhasd.k12.wi.us
Early Learning Center 200/PK-K
300 Spellman St 53572 608-437-2400
Rachael Johnson, prin. Fax 437-4027
Mount Horeb Intermediate Center 500/3-5
200 Hanneman Blvd 53572 608-437-2400
Ann Fenley, prin. Fax 437-8483
Mount Horeb MS 500/6-8
900 E Garfield St 53572 608-437-2400
Jeff Rasmussen, prin. Fax 437-6227
Mount Horeb Primary Center 300/1-2
207 Academy St 53572 608-437-2400
Rachael Johnson, prin. Fax 437-4620

Mukwonago, Waukesha, Pop. 6,857
Mukwonago SD 4,900/K-12
423 Division St 53149 262-363-6300
Paul Strobel, supt. Fax 363-6272
www.mukwonago.k12.wi.us
Clarendon Avenue ES 500/K-6
915 Clarendon Ave 53149 262-363-6286
John Shanahan, prin. Fax 363-6289
Park View MS 800/7-8
930 N Rochester St 53149 262-363-6292
Mark Doome, prin. Fax 363-6320
Rolling Hills ES 600/K-6
W322s9230 Beulah Rd 53149 262-363-6318
Shawn McNulty, prin. Fax 363-6343
Section ES 400/K-6
W318S8430 County Road EE 53149 262-363-6260
Robert Slane, prin. Fax 363-6341
Other Schools – See Big Bend, North Prairie

Nature's Classroom Montessori S 50/PK-8
PO Box 660 53149 262-363-6820
Geoffrey Bishop, dir. Fax 363-6821
St. James S 100/PK-8
830 E Highway NN 53149 262-363-8152
Sr. Martha Meyer, prin. Fax 363-2416
St. John Lutheran S 100/PK-8
410 County Road NN 53149 262-363-4999
James Schneck, prin. Fax 363-7383

Muscoda, Grant, Pop. 1,408
Riverdale SD 700/PK-12
PO Box 66 53573 608-739-3832
Bryce Bird, supt. Fax 739-3751
www.riverdale.k12.wi.us/
Riverdale ES 300/PK-5
800 N 6th St 53573 608-739-3101
Sharon Ennis, prin. Fax 739-9118
Riverdale MS 200/6-8
800 N 6th St 53573 608-739-3101
Sharon Ennis, prin. Fax 739-9118

Muskego, Waukesha, Pop. 22,872
Muskego-Norway SD 4,800/PK-12
S87W18763 Woods Rd 53150 262-679-5400
Joe Schroeder, supt. Fax 679-5790
www.mnsd.k12.wi.us
Bay Lane MS 700/5-8
S75W16399 Hilltop Dr 53150 414-422-0430
Erik Olson, prin. Fax 422-2204
Country Meadows ES 300/PK-4
S75W16399 Hilltop Dr 53150 414-422-1607
Gary Goelz, prin. Fax 422-1672
Lake Denoon MS 800/5-8
W216S10586 Crowbar Dr 53150 262-662-1454
Ryan Oertel, prin. Fax 662-1588
Mill Valley ES 300/K-4
W191S6445 Hillendale Dr 53150 262-679-1290
Susan Borden, prin. Fax 679-4087
Muskego ES 200/K-4
S75W17476 Janesville Rd 53150 262-679-1666
Tammy Kapp, prin. Fax 679-4085
Tess Corners ES 400/K-4
W147S6800 Durham Pl 53150 414-422-0660
Ron Rivard, prin. Fax 422-2223
Other Schools – See Wind Lake

St. Leonard S 200/K-8
W173S7777 Westwood Dr 53150 262-679-0451
Sue Watkinson, prin. Fax 679-8519
St. Paul Lutheran S 300/PK-8
S66W14325 Janesville Rd 53150 414-422-0320
Steven Bremer, prin. Fax 422-1711

Nashotah, Waukesha, Pop. 1,378

Country Christian S 200/PK-8
W329N4476 Lakeland Dr 53058 262-367-3756
Bruce Reagan, prin. Fax 367-4045
St. Joan of Arc S 100/PK-8
120 Nashotah Rd 53058 262-646-5821
Mary Ann Rudella, prin. Fax 646-5861

Necedah, Juneau, Pop. 878
Necedah Area SD 700/K-12
1801 S Main St 54646 608-565-2256
Charles Krupa, supt. Fax 565-3201
www.necedah.k12.wi.us
Necedah ES 300/K-6
1801 S Main St 54646 608-565-2256
Larry Gierach, prin. Fax 565-7044

Neenah, Winnebago, Pop. 24,596
Neenah SD 5,300/PK-12
410 S Commercial St 54956 920-751-6800
Mary Pfeiffer, supt. Fax 751-6809
www.neenah.k12.wi.us
Clayton ES 300/PK-5
2916 Fairview Rd 54956 920-751-6950
Kim Benson, prin. Fax 836-2881
Coolidge ES 300/PK-5
321 Alcott Dr 54956 920-751-6955
LeAnn Metzger, prin. Fax 751-6857
Hoover ES 200/PK-5
950 Hunt Ave 54956 920-751-6960
Michael Tauscher, prin. Fax 751-6858
Lakeview ES 400/PK-5
1645 S Commercial St 54956 920-751-6965
Mary Renning, prin. Fax 751-6859
Mann MS 200/6-6
1021 Oak St 54956 920-751-6940
Jon Fleming, prin. Fax 751-7099
Roosevelt ES 100/PK-5
215 E Forest Ave 54956 920-751-6970
Philip Johnson, prin. Fax 751-6861
Shattuck MS 600/7-8
600 Elm St 54956 920-751-6850
Jon Fleming, prin. Fax 751-6899
Spring Road ES 400/PK-5
1191 County Road II 54956 920-751-6975
Michaela Neitzel, prin. Fax 751-6911
Taft Early Learning Center 50/PK-PK
133 S Western Ave 54956 920-751-6980
Michael Tauscher, prin. Fax 751-6912
Tullar ES 400/PK-5
925 Tullar Rd 54956 920-751-6985
Diane Galow, prin. Fax 751-6913
Wilson ES 300/PK-5
920 Higgins Ave 54956 920-751-6995
William Pokel, prin. Fax 751-6984

Fox Valley Christian Academy 200/K-8
PO Box 799 54957 920-725-7985
Denise Pannebaker, prin. Fax 725-3236
Fox Valley SDA S 50/1-8
265 S Green Bay Rd 54956 920-727-9165
Martin Luther Lutheran S 100/PK-8
807 Adams St 54956 920-725-8047
Russ Wilke, prin. Fax 725-3671
New Hope Christian S 200/PK-8
1850 American Dr 54956 920-725-8797
Laurie Prewitt, prin. Fax 886-8729
St. Gabriel S 100/PK-5
900 Geiger St 54956 920-725-4161
Mary Jo Brown, prin. Fax 722-2566
St. Margaret Mary S 300/PK-5
610 Division St 54956 920-729-4565
Eleanor Healy, prin. Fax 729-4567
Trinity Lutheran S 200/PK-8
410 Oak St 54956 920-722-3051
Jason Gibson, prin. Fax 722-8297

Neillsville, Clark, Pop. 2,694
Neillsville SD 600/PK-12
614 E 5th St 54456 715-743-3323
John Gaier, supt. Fax 743-8718
www.neillsville.k12.wi.us
Neillsville S 100/PK-7
504 E 5th St 54456 715-743-8712
Tim Rueth, prin. Fax 743-8715

St. John Lutheran S 100/PK-8
805 W 5th St 54456 715-743-2501
William Tomlin, prin. Fax 743-2501

Nekoosa, Wood, Pop. 2,585
Nekoosa SD 1,400/K-12
600 S Section St 54457 715-886-8000
Wayne Johnson, supt. Fax 886-8012
www.nekoosaschools.org
Alexander MS 500/4-8
540 Birch St 54457 715-886-8040
Barbara Sparish, prin. Fax 886-8097
Humke ES 400/K-3
500 S Section St 54457 715-886-8010
Christopher Sadler, prin. Fax 886-8024

Sacred Heart S 50/PK-6
710 Vilas Ave 54457 715-886-3761
Joan Bond, prin. Fax 886-3745

Neopit, Menominee, Pop. 615
Menominee Indian SD
Supt. — See Keshena
Menominee Indian MS 100/6-8
PO Box 9 54150 715-756-2324
Stephanie Feldner, prin. Fax 756-2496

Neosho, Dodge, Pop. 579
Neosho J3 SD 200/K-8
PO Box 17 53059 920-625-3531
James Rice, supt. Fax 625-3536
www.neoshoschool.com
Neosho S 200/K-8
PO Box 17 53059 920-625-3531
James Rice, prin. Fax 625-3536

Neshkoro, Marquette, Pop. 448
Westfield SD
Supt. — See Westfield
Neshkoro ES 100/PK-6
114 E Park St 54960 920-293-4219
Cory Parman, prin. Fax 293-4400

New Auburn, Chippewa, Pop. 547
New Auburn SD 300/PK-12
PO Box 110 54757 715-237-2202
Thomas Fiedler, supt. Fax 237-2350
www.newauburn.k12.wi.us
New Auburn ES 200/PK-6
PO Box 110 54757 715-237-2505
Brian Henning, prin. Fax 237-2350

New Berlin, Waukesha, Pop. 38,547
New Berlin SD 4,100/PK-12
4333 S Sunnyslope Rd 53151 262-789-6200
Paul Kreutzer, supt. Fax 786-0512
www.nbps.k12.wi.us
Elmwood ES 600/PK-6
5900 S Sunnyslope Rd 53151 262-789-6581
Jo Boardman, prin. Fax 427-7290
Glen Park ES 300/PK-6
3500 S Glen Park Rd 53151 262-789-6570
Tracie Fehrm, prin. Fax 789-6206
Orchard Lane ES 400/K-6
2015 S Sunnyslope Rd 53151 262-789-6500
Cory Whitsell, prin. Fax 789-6286
Poplar Creek ES 500/PK-6
17401 W Cleveland Ave 53146 262-789-6520
Jane Gennerman, prin. Fax 789-6234
Reagan ES PK-6
4225 S Calhoun Rd 53151 262-789-6550
Christine Cody, prin. Fax 789-6205

West Allis SD
Supt. — See West Allis
Hoover ES 400/PK-5
12705 W Euclid Ave 53151 414-604-3810
Ali Hatab, prin. Fax 782-2231

Holy Apostles S 400/K-8
3875 S 159th St 53151 262-786-7331
Greg Dehli-Young, prin. Fax 786-0425
Star of Bethlehem Evangelical Lutheran S 200/PK-8
3700 S Casper Dr 53151 262-786-2901
Michael Wiechmann, prin. Fax 786-2836

Newburg, Washington, Pop. 1,206

St. John Lutheran S 100/K-8
PO Box 169 53060 262-675-6852
Samuel Hunter, prin. Fax 675-0707

New Glarus, Green, Pop. 2,058
New Glarus SD 800/PK-12
PO Box 7 53574 608-527-2410
Barbara Thompson, supt. Fax 527-5101
www.ngsd.k12.wi.us
New Glarus ES 400/PK-5
PO Box 37 53574 608-527-2810
Laura Eicher, prin. Fax 527-6239

New Holstein, Calumet, Pop. 3,200
New Holstein SD 1,200/PK-12
1715 Plymouth St 53061 920-898-5115
Joseph Wieser, supt. Fax 898-4112
www.nhsd.k12.wi.us
New Holstein ES 500/PK-5
2226 Park Ave 53061 920-898-4208
Tammy Richter, prin. Fax 898-9152
New Holstein MS 200/6-8
1717 Plymouth St 53061 920-898-4769
Richard Amundson, prin. Fax 898-4810

Divine Saviour S 100/K-8
1814 Madison St 53061 920-898-4210
Larry Konetzke, prin. Fax 898-4220

New Lisbon, Juneau, Pop. 2,464
New Lisbon SD 600/PK-12
500 S Forest St 53950 608-562-3700
Linda Hanson, supt. Fax 562-5333
www.newlisbon.k12.wi.us
New Lisbon S 400/PK-8
500 S Forest St 53950 608-562-3700
Mark Toelle, prin. Fax 562-3062

New London, Waupaca, Pop. 6,926
New London SD 2,500/PK-12
901 W Washington St 54961 920-982-8530
Bill Fitzpatrick, supt. Fax 982-8551
www.newlondon.k12.wi.us
Lincoln ES 300/PK-5
201 E Washington St 54961 920-982-8540
Pete Schulz, prin. Fax 982-8701
New London MS 600/6-8
1000 W Washington St 54961 920-982-8532
Andy Jones, prin. Fax 982-8605
Parkview ES 300/K-5
1300 Werner Allen Rd 54961 920-982-8538
Jo Collar, prin. Fax 982-8700
Sugar Bush ES 200/K-5
W10736 County Road WW 54961 715-752-4135
Kristin Grable, prin. Fax 752-4010
Other Schools – See Readfield

Emanuel Lutheran S 200/PK-8
200 E Quincy St 54961 920-982-5444
Daniel Aswege, prin. Fax 982-0954
Most Precious Blood S 100/PK-5
120 E Washington St 54961 920-982-2134
James Quinn, prin. Fax 982-1572

New Munster, Kenosha

St. Alphonsus S 100/PK-8
PO Box 922 53152 262-537-4379
Colleen Knapp, prin. Fax 537-3527

New Richmond, Saint Croix, Pop. 7,726
New Richmond SD 2,700/PK-12
701 E 11th St 54017 715-243-7411
Maurice Veilleux, supt. Fax 246-3638
www.newrichmond.k12.wi.us
New Richmond Hillside ES K-5
701 E 11th St 54017 715-243-1400
Frank Norton, prin. Fax 243-1418
New Richmond MS 600/6-8
701 E 11th St 54017 715-243-7471
Doug Hatch, prin. Fax 246-0580
Paperjack ES 500/PK-5
701 E 11th St 54017 715-243-7400
Steve Wojan, prin. Fax 243-8417
Starr ES 700/K-5
701 E 11th St 54017 715-243-7431
Greg Gentle, prin. Fax 246-2898

St. Mary S 200/PK-8
257 S Washington Ave 54017 715-246-2469
Mari Zarcone Patterson, prin. Fax 246-6195

Niagara, Marinette, Pop. 1,805
Niagara SD 200/K-12
700 Jefferson Ave 54151 715-251-1330
Peter Kososki, supt. Fax 251-4544
www.niagara.k12.wi.us
Niagara S 200/K-12
700 Jefferson Ave 54151 715-251-4541
Peter Kososki, prin. Fax 251-3715

North Fond du Lac, Fond du Lac, Pop. 5,024
North Fond Du Lac SD 1,200/PK-12
225 McKinley St 54937 920-929-3750
Aaron Sadoff, supt. Fax 929-3696
www.nfdl.k12.wi.us
Allen MS 300/6-8
305 Mckinley St 54937 920-929-3754
William Paris, prin. Fax 929-3747
Early Learning Center 200/PK-K
923 Minnesota Ave 54937 920-929-3762
Debra Ellingen, prin. Fax 322-9117
Friendship ES 400/1-5
1115 Thurke Ave 54937 920-929-3757
Melanie Cowling, prin. Fax 929-7020

St. Paul Lutheran S 100/K-8
1010 Adams Ave 54937 920-924-9699
Michael Kampman, prin. Fax 922-1080

North Freedom, Sauk, Pop. 627
Baraboo SD
Supt. — See Baraboo
North Freedom ES 200/K-5
S4890 County Road I 53951 608-522-4946
Debra Janke, prin. Fax 522-4506

North Lake, Waukesha
North Lake SD 300/K-8
PO Box 188 53064 262-966-2033
Pete Hirt, supt. Fax 966-3710
www.nlake.k12.wi.us
North Lake S 300/K-8
PO Box 188 53064 262-966-2033
Pete Hirt, prin. Fax 966-3710

North Prairie, Waukesha, Pop. 1,938
Mukwonago SD
Supt. — See Mukwonago
Prairie View ES 400/K-6
W330S6473 County Rd E 53153 262-392-6310
Tracy Hein, prin. Fax 392-6312

Oak Creek, Milwaukee, Pop. 32,312
Oak Creek-Franklin SD 5,600/PK-12
7630 S 10th St 53154 414-768-5886
Sara Larsen, supt. Fax 768-6172
www.oakcreek.k12.wi.us
Carollton ES 400/K-5
8965 S Carollton Dr 53154 414-768-6290
Paul Kenwood, prin. Fax 768-6286
Cedar Hills ES 300/K-5
2225 W Sycamore Ave 53154 414-761-3020
Ed Mittag, prin. Fax 761-6301
Deerfield ES 400/PK-5
3871 E Bluestem Dr 53154 414-768-6220
Christopher Gabrhel, prin. Fax 768-6221
Edgewood ES 400/K-5
8545 S Shepard Ave 53154 414-768-6280
Pamela Ferrill, prin. Fax 768-6287
Meadowview ES 400/K-5
10420 S McGraw Dr 53154 414-768-6240
Jeffrey Peterson, prin. Fax 768-6288
Oak Creek East MS 600/6-8
9330 S Shepard Ave 53154 414-768-6260
Peter DeRubeis, prin. Fax 768-6293
Oak Creek West MS 600/6-8
8401 S 13th St 53154 414-768-6250
Michael Maxson, prin. Fax 768-6296
Shepard Hills ES 500/K-5
9701 S Shepard Hills Dr 53154 414-768-6270
Lois Booth, prin. Fax 768-6289

Grace Lutheran S 100/K-8
8537 S Pennsylvania Ave 53154 414-762-3655
Walter Haas, prin. Fax 762-8869

Parkway Christian Academy 200/K-12
10940 S Nicholson Rd 53154 414-571-2680
Theresa Tamel, admin. Fax 571-2690
St. Matthew S 200/K-8
9329 S Chicago Rd 53154 414-762-6820
Julie Barber, prin. Fax 762-4555

Oakdale, Monroe, Pop. 316
Tomah Area SD
Supt. — See Tomah
Oakdale ES 100/PK-2
217 S Oakwood St 54649 608-374-7081
Patricia Ellsworth, prin. Fax 372-5087

Oakfield, Fond du Lac, Pop. 1,021
Oakfield SD 600/PK-12
PO Box 99 53065 920-583-3146
Joseph Heinzelman, supt. Fax 583-4033
www.oakfield.k12.wi.us/
Oakfield MS 100/6-8
PO Box 69 53065 920-583-4117
Paul Dix, prin. Fax 583-3820
Reynolds ES 200/PK-5
PO Box 99 53065 920-583-3146
Dr. Bruce McMurry, prin. Fax 583-4671

St. Luke Lutheran S 50/K-8
PO Box 277 53065 920-583-3906
Brian Miller, prin.

Oconomowoc, Waukesha, Pop. 13,711
Oconomowoc Area SD 3,000/K-12
W360N7077 Brown St 53066 262-560-1115
Patricia Neudecker, supt. Fax 560-2103
www.oasd.k12.wi.us
Greenland ES 300/K-4
440 Coolidge St 53066 262-560-8100
Dianna Kresovic, prin. Fax 560-8118
Meadow View ES 400/K-4
W360n7077 Brown St 53066 262-560-8000
Jason Schreiber, prin. Fax 560-8018
Nature Hill IS 5-8
850 N Lake Rd 53066 262-569-4945
Ronald Russ, prin. Fax 569-4958
Park Lawn ES 400/K-4
300 Parklawn St 53066 262-560-8200
Joan Marley, prin. Fax 560-8218
Silver Lake IS 5-8
555 Oconomowoc Pkwy 53066 262-560-4305
Ellyn Helberg, prin. Fax 560-4318
Summit ES 400/K-4
1680 E Valley Rd 53066 262-560-8300
Robin Wilson, prin. Fax 560-8318
Other Schools – See Ixonia

Stone Bank SD 300/K-8
N68W33866 County Road K 53066 262-966-2900
Phil Meissen Ph.D., supt. Fax 966-1828
www.stonebank.k12.wi.us
Stone Bank S 300/K-8
N68W33866 County Road K 53066 262-966-2900
Phil Meissen Ph.D., prin. Fax 966-1828

St. Jerome S 300/K-8
1001 S Silver Lake St 53066 262-569-3030
Suzanne Zinda, prin. Fax 569-3023
St. Matthew Lutheran S 200/PK-8
818 W Wisconsin Ave 53066 262-567-5396
Eric Ziel, prin. Fax 567-5865
St. Paul's Lutheran S 200/PK-8
210 E Pleasant St 53066 262-567-5001
Chris Nelson, prin. Fax 567-1207

Oconto, Oconto, Pop. 4,564
Oconto SD 1,200/PK-12
400 Michigan Ave 54153 920-834-7814
Dr. Sara Croney, supt. Fax 834-9884
www.oconto.k12.wi.us
Oconto ES 400/PK-4
810 Scherer Ave 54153 920-834-7808
Barb Blum, prin. Fax 834-9883
Oconto MS 300/5-8
400 Michigan Ave 54153 920-834-7806
Jeffrey Werner, prin. Fax 834-7810

Oconto Falls, Oconto, Pop. 2,729
Oconto Falls SD 1,900/PK-12
200 N Farm Rd 54154 920-848-4471
David Polashek, supt. Fax 848-4474
www.ocontofalls.k12.wi.us
Oconto Falls ES 500/PK-5
415 Maria Volk Dr 54154 920-848-4476
Dan Moore, prin. Fax 848-4454
Washington MS 400/6-8
102 S Washington St 54154 920-846-4463
Tom Menor, prin. Fax 846-4453
Other Schools – See Abrams

St. Anthony S 50/K-5
253 N Franklin St 54154 920-846-2276
Rosemary Marifke, prin. Fax 846-2180

Omro, Winnebago, Pop. 3,282
Omro SD 1,300/PK-12
455 Fox Trl 54963 920-685-5666
Paul Amundson, admin. Fax 685-5757
www.omro.k12.wi.us/
Omro ES 400/2-5
1000 N Webster Ave 54963 920-685-3100
David Wellhoefer, prin. Fax 685-3105
Omro MS, 455 Fox Trl 54963 300/6-8
Paul Williams, prin. 920-685-7403
Patch ES 200/PK-1
607 Tyler Ave 54963 920-685-7400
David Wellhoefer, prin. Fax 685-7042

Onalaska, LaCrosse, Pop. 15,701
Holmen SD
Supt. — See Holmen

Oak Grove Family Learning Center 50/PK-PK
W7908 County Road Z 54650 608-783-9393
Teresa Nuttelman, prin. Fax 783-9299

Onalaska SD 2,800/K-12
1821 E Main St 54650 608-781-9700
John Burnett, supt. Fax 781-9712
www.onalaska.k12.wi.us
Eagle Bluff ES 400/1-5
200 Eagle Bluff Ct 54650 608-783-2453
Todd Saner, prin. Fax 783-2068
Northern Hills ES 300/K-5
511 Spruce St 54650 608-783-4542
Curt Rees, prin. Fax 779-4114
Onalaska K Center S 200/K-K
200 Eagle Bluff Ct 54650 608-783-2453
Todd Saner, prin. Fax 783-2068
Onalaska MS 600/6-8
711 Quincy St 54650 608-783-5366
Roger Fruit, prin. Fax 781-8030
Pertzsch ES 300/K-5
524 Main St 54650 608-783-5644
J. Lyga, prin. Fax 783-1351

St. Patrick S, 127 11th Ave N 54650 200/PK-6
Gregory Wesely, prin. 608-783-5483
St. Paul Evangelical Lutheran S 200/PK-8
PO Box 128 54650 608-783-4822
Robert Wiegman, prin. Fax 779-5942

Oneida, Outagamie, Pop. 808
Pulaski Community SD
Supt. — See Pulaski
Hillcrest ES 200/K-5
4193 Hillcrest Dr 54155 920-272-6900
Jennifer Gracyalny, prin. Fax 272-6905

Ontario, Vernon, Pop. 481
Norwalk-Ontario-Wilton SD 700/PK-12
PO Box 130 54651 608-337-4403
Kelly Burhop, supt. Fax 337-4348
www.now.k12.wi.us/
Norwalk-Ontario-Wilton ES 400/PK-6
PO Box 130 54651 608-337-4420
Kelly Burhop, prin. Fax 337-4348

Oostburg, Sheboygan, Pop. 2,772
Oostburg SD 1,000/PK-12
PO Box 700100 53070 920-564-2346
Brian Hanes, supt. Fax 564-6138
oostburg.k12.wi.us
Oostburg ES 400/PK-5
PO Box 700100 53070 920-564-2392
Kevin Bruggink, prin. Fax 564-6694
Oostburg MS, PO Box 700100 53070 200/6-8
Steve Harder, prin. 920-564-2383

Oostburg Christian S 200/PK-8
PO Box 700319 53070 920-564-2664
Robert Adams, prin. Fax 564-3166

Oregon, Dane, Pop. 8,493
Oregon SD 3,500/K-12
123 E Grove St 53575 608-835-4091
Brian Busler, supt. Fax 835-9509
www.oregonsd.org/
Netherwood Knoll ES 400/K-4
276 Soden Dr 53575 608-835-4100
Daniel Rikli, prin. Fax 835-7827
Oregon MS 600/7-8
601 Pleasant Oak Dr 53575 608-835-4801
Chris Telfer, prin. Fax 835-3849
Prairie View ES 400/K-4
300 Soden Dr 53575 608-835-4201
Heather Sveom, prin. Fax 835-8037
Rome Corners IS 500/5-6
1111 S Perry Pkwy 53575 608-835-4700
Leslie Bergstrom, prin. Fax 835-2704
Other Schools – See Brooklyn

Orfordville, Rock, Pop. 1,336
Parkview SD 1,000/K-12
PO Box 250 53576 608-879-2717
Steve Lutzke, supt. Fax 879-2732
www.parkview.k12.wi.us
Orfordville ES 300/3-6
408 W Beloit St 53576 608-879-2956
JoAnn Wick, prin. Fax 879-9375
Parkview JHS 200/7-8
PO Box 247 53576 608-879-2994
Tracy Elger, prin. Fax 879-2732
Other Schools – See Beloit, Footville

Osceola, Polk, Pop. 2,685
Osceola SD 1,800/PK-12
PO Box 128 54020 715-294-4140
Roger Kumlien, supt. Fax 294-2428
www.osceola.k12.wi.us
Osceola ES 400/PK-2
PO Box 128 54020 715-294-3457
Peggy Weber, prin. Fax 294-2428
Osceola IS 400/3-5
PO Box 128 54020 715-294-2800
Rick Ashley, prin. Fax 294-2428
Osceola MS 400/6-8
PO Box 128 54020 715-294-4180
Rebecca Styles, prin. Fax 294-2428

Oshkosh, Winnebago, Pop. 63,485
Oshkosh Area SD 9,000/PK-12
PO Box 3048 54903 920-424-0160
Bette Lang Ed.D., supt. Fax 424-0466
www.oshkosh.k12.wi.us
Cook ES 200/PK-5
1600 Hazel St 54901 920-424-0152
Philip Marshall, prin. Fax 424-7580
Green Meadow ES 100/PK-5
4304 County Rd N 54904 920-424-0391
Fax 424-7582

Jefferson ES 200/PK-5
244 W 11th Ave 54902 920-424-0165
Jean Stebbins, prin. Fax 424-7583
Lakeside ES 200/PK-5
4991 S US Highway 45 54902 920-424-0131
Fax 424-7584
Lincoln ES 100/PK-5
608 Algoma Blvd 54901 920-424-0167
Erin Kohl, prin. Fax 424-7589
Merrill MS 400/6-8
108 W New York Ave 54901 920-424-0177
Christine Fabian, prin. Fax 424-7512
Oaklawn ES 300/PK-5
112 Viola Ave 54901 920-424-0170
Laura Jackson, prin. Fax 424-7590
Oakwood ES 300/PK-5
1225 N Oakwood Rd 54904 920-424-0315
Kirby Schultz, prin. Fax 424-7591
Read ES 300/PK-5
1120 Algoma Blvd 54901 920-424-0172
Lorie Yaste-Zajicek, prin. Fax 424-7592
Roosevelt ES 200/PK-5
910 N Sawyer St 54902 920-424-0411
Tammy Kielbasa, prin. Fax 424-7593
Smith ES 200/PK-5
1745 Oregon St 54902 920-424-0174
Jean Stebbins, prin. Fax 424-7595
South Park MS 400/6-8
1551 Delaware St 54902 920-424-0431
Lisa McLaughlin, prin. Fax 424-7513
Stanley ES 300/PK-5
915 Hazel St 54901 920-424-0460
Brenna Garrison-Bruden, prin. Fax 424-7598
Stanley MS 400/6-8
915 Hazel St 54901 920-424-0442
Marceline Peters-Felice, prin. Fax 424-7515
Tipler MS 400/6-8
325 S Eagle St 54902 920-424-0320
Ann Schultz, prin. Fax 424-7514
Traeger ES 500/PK-5
3000 W 20th Ave 54904 920-424-0221
Janna Cochrane, prin. Fax 424-7586
Traeger MS 600/6-8
3000 W 20th Ave 54904 920-424-0065
Jeanne Koepke, prin. Fax 424-7511
Washington ES 200/PK-5
929 Winnebago Ave 54901 920-424-0190
Erin Kohl, prin. Fax 424-7597

Grace Lutheran S 100/PK-8
913 Nebraska St 54902 920-231-8957
Peter Iles, prin. Fax 231-8552
Martin Luther Lutheran S 100/PK-8
1526 Algoma Blvd 54901 920-235-1612
Steven Henning, prin. Fax 235-7991
Oshkosh Christian S Valley Christian HS 200/K-12
3450 Vinland St 54901 920-231-9704
Todd Benson, admin. Fax 231-9804
St. Elizabeth Ann Seton S 200/PK-5
1207 Oregon St 54902 920-235-4060
Heidi Potts, prin. Fax 426-6430
St. Francis Cabrini S 200/PK-5
619 Merritt Ave 54901 920-235-0637
Marie Dudenas, prin. Fax 426-6429
St. John Neumann S 200/6-8
110 N Sawyer St 54902 920-426-6421
Nancy Crowley, prin. Fax 235-7453
Trinity Lutheran S 100/K-8
819 School Ave 54901 920-235-1730
Joseph Reinl, admin. Fax 235-1738

Osseo, Trempealeau, Pop. 1,661
Osseo-Fairchild SD 1,000/PK-12
PO Box 130 54758 715-597-3141
Kerry Jacobson, supt. Fax 597-3606
www.ofsd.k12.wi.us
Osseo ES 400/PK-5
13025 15th St 54758 715-597-3196
Mary Kempf, prin. Fax 597-3406
Osseo MS 200/6-8
PO Box 130 54758 715-597-3141
Steve Glocke, prin. Fax 597-3647
Other Schools – See Fairchild

Owen, Clark, Pop. 914
Owen-Withee SD 600/PK-12
PO Box 417 54460 715-229-2151
Robert Houts, supt. Fax 229-4322
www.owen-withee.k12.wi.us
Owen-Withee ES 300/PK-6
PO Box 417 54460 715-229-4488
Lance Batchelor, prin. Fax 229-4981
Owen-Withee JHS 100/7-8
PO Box 417 54460 715-229-2151
Sherry Baker, prin. Fax 229-4322

Oxford, Marquette, Pop. 549
Westfield SD
Supt. — See Westfield
Oxford ES 100/K-6
PO Box 27 53952 608-586-5131
Jennifer Johnson, prin. Fax 586-4521

Palmyra, Jefferson, Pop. 1,763
Palmyra-Eagle Area SD 1,100/PK-12
PO Box 901 53156 262-495-7101
Bruce Gunderson, supt. Fax 495-7151
www.palmyra.k12.wi.us
Palmyra-Eagle MS 200/7-8
PO Box 901 53156 262-495-7101
Tim Kooi, prin. Fax 495-7146
Palmyra ES 300/PK-6
PO Box 901 53156 262-495-7103
Steven Greenquist, prin. Fax 495-7134
Other Schools – See Eagle

Pardeeville, Columbia, Pop. 2,125
Pardeeville Area SD 900/PK-12
120 Oak St 53954 608-429-3666
Gus Knitt, supt. Fax 429-2277
www.pardeeville.k12.wi.us
Marcellon ES 100/K-2
W6150 School Rd 53954 608-429-3412
Mary Kamrath, prin. Fax 429-1562
Pardeeville ES 300/PK-5
503 E Chestnut St 53954 608-429-2151
Mary Kamrath, prin. Fax 429-4807
Pardeeville MS 200/6-8
120 Oak St 53954 608-429-2153
Tonya Broyles-Brouillard, prin. Fax 429-2277

St. John's Lutheran S 50/PK-8
PO Box 367 53954 608-429-3636
Michael Wieting, prin. Fax 429-4876

Park Falls, Price, Pop. 2,464
Park Falls SD 700/PK-12
420 9th St N 54552 715-762-4343
Mark Luoma, admin. Fax 762-5469
cardinalcountry.net
Park Falls ES 300/PK-6
380 9th St N 54552 715-762-3393
Michael Plemon, prin. Fax 762-2428
Park Falls MS 100/7-8
400 9th St N 54552 715-762-3815
Todd Lindstrom, prin. Fax 762-5674

St. Anthony of Padua S 100/PK-8
200 5th Ave S 54552 715-762-4476
Brent Balsavich, prin. Fax 762-0079

Patch Grove, Grant, Pop. 169
River Ridge SD 500/PK-12
PO Box 78 53817 608-994-2715
Dr. Kevin Shetler, supt. Fax 994-2891
www.rrsd.k12.wi.us
River Ridge ES 200/PK-3
PO Box 78 53817 608-994-2715
Rod Lewis, prin. Fax 994-2891
Other Schools – See Bloomington

Pembine, Marinette
Beecher-Dunbar-Pembine SD 300/PK-12
PO Box 247 54156 715-324-5314
Robert Berndt, supt. Fax 324-5282
www.pembine.k12.wi.us/
Pembine ES 100/PK-6
PO Box 247 54156 715-324-5314
Robert Berndt, prin. Fax 324-5282

Pepin, Pepin, Pop. 925
Pepin Area SD 300/PK-12
PO Box 128 54759 715-442-2391
Bruce Quinton, supt. Fax 442-3607
home.centurytel.net/pepinschools
Pepin S 100/PK-8
PO Box 128 54759 715-442-2391
Lydia Gnos, prin. Fax 442-3607

Peshtigo, Marinette, Pop. 3,346
Peshtigo SD 1,200/PK-12
341 N Emery Ave 54157 715-582-3677
Kim Eparvier, supt. Fax 582-3850
www.peshtigo.k12.wi.us
Peshtigo ES 700/PK-6
341 N Emery Ave 54157 715-582-3762
Lisa Peitersen, prin. Fax 582-4106

St. John Lutheran S 50/K-8
N1926 Church Rd 54157 715-582-4565
Jason Rupnow, prin. Fax 582-2836

Pewaukee, Waukesha, Pop. 21,388
Pewaukee SD 2,200/PK-12
404 Lake St 53072 262-691-2100
JoAnn Sternke, supt. Fax 691-1052
www.pewaukee.k12.wi.us
Clark MS 300/7-8
472 Lake St 53072 262-691-2100
Randy Daul, prin. Fax 695-5004
Horizon S 400/4-6
458 Lake St 53072 262-691-2100
Sandra Carter, prin. Fax 695-5033
Pewaukee Lake ES 700/PK-3
436 Lake St 53072 262-691-2100
Debra Ristow, prin. Fax 695-5002

Prairie Hill Waldorf S 200/PK-8
N14W29143 Silvernail Rd 53072 262-646-7497
Jewell Riano, admin. Fax 646-7495
Queen of Apostles S 100/K-8
449 W Wisconsin Ave 53072 262-691-2120
Laurence Patterson, prin. Fax 691-8606
St. Anthony on the Lake S 200/K-7
W280N2101 Prospect Ave 53072 262-691-0460
Barbara Heinle, prin. Fax 691-7376
Trinity Academy 100/K-12
W225N3131 Duplainville Rd 53072 262-695-2933
Robin Mitchell, admin. Fax 695-2934

Phelps, Vilas
Phelps SD 200/K-12
4451 Old School Rd 54554 715-545-2724
Delnice Hill, supt. Fax 545-3728
www.phelps.k12.wi.us
Phelps S 100/K-8
4451 Old School Rd 54554 715-545-2724
Jason Pertile, prin. Fax 545-3728

Phillips, Price, Pop. 1,499
Phillips SD 900/PK-12
PO Box 70 54555 715-339-2419
Wally Leipart, dir. Fax 339-2144
www.phillips.k12.wi.us/
Phillips ES 400/PK-5
400 Turner St 54555 715-339-3864
Dale Houdek, prin. Fax 339-2295
Phillips MS 200/6-8
PO Box 70 54555 715-339-3393
Colin Hoogland, prin. Fax 339-2416

Pigeon Falls, Trempealeau, Pop. 394
Whitehall SD
Supt. — See Whitehall
Pigeon Falls ES 100/PK-1
PO Box 459 54760 715-983-2241
Vickie O'Dell, prin. Fax 983-5722

Pine River, Waushara
Wild Rose SD
Supt. — See Wild Rose
Pleasant View ES 100/K-5
N5275 County Road NN 54965 920-987-5123
Barbara Sobralske, prin. Fax 987-5136

Pittsville, Wood, Pop. 847
Pittsville SD 700/PK-12
5459 Elementary Ave Ste 2 54466 715-884-6694
Terry Reynolds, supt. Fax 884-5218
www.pittsville.k12.wi.us
Pittsville S 500/PK-8
5459 Elementary Ave Ste 1 54466 715-884-2517
JoAnn Sondelski, prin. Fax 884-5218

Plain, Sauk, Pop. 768
River Valley SD
Supt. — See Spring Green
Plain ES 100/K-5
1370 Cherry St 53577 608-546-2228
James Radtke, prin. Fax 546-4028

St. Luke S 100/PK-8
1290 Nachreiner Ave 53577 608-546-2963
Cindy Haag, prin. Fax 546-2616

Plainfield, Waushara, Pop. 899
Tri-County Area SD 500/PK-12
PO Box 67 54966 715-335-6366
Tony Marinack, supt. Fax 335-6365
www.penguin.tricounty.k12.wi.us
Tri-County ES 300/PK-6
PO Box 67 54966 715-335-6366
Shawn Jepson, prin. Fax 335-6322

Platteville, Grant, Pop. 9,854
Platteville SD 1,000/PK-12
780 N 2nd St 53818 608-342-4000
Dean Isaacson, supt. Fax 342-4412
www.platteville.k12.wi.us
Platteville MS 400/4-8
40 E Madison St 53818 608-342-4010
Lisa Finnegan, prin. Fax 342-4497
Westview ES 100/2-3
1205 Camp St 53818 608-342-4050
Don Shaw, prin. Fax 342-4557
Wilkins Early Learning Center 100/PK-1
425 Broadway St 53818 608-342-4040
ReNah Chitwood, prin. Fax 342-4581

St. Marys Parish S 100/K-8
345 N Court St 53818 608-348-5806
Jean Lange, prin. Fax 348-9883

Pleasant Prairie, Kenosha, Pop. 18,551
Kenosha SD
Supt. — See Kenosha
Pleasant Prairie ES 700/PK-5
9208 Wilmot Rd 53158 262-359-2104
Shane Gayle, prin. Fax 359-2157
Prairie Lane ES 500/PK-5
10717 47th Ave 53158 262-359-3600
David Newman, prin. Fax 359-3650
Whittier ES 600/PK-5
8542 Cooper Rd 53158 262-359-2110
Fax 359-2270

Christ Lutheran Academy 50/K-8
8411 Old Green Bay Rd 53158 262-697-6044
Lynnette Frederickson, prin. Fax 697-1720
Good Shepherd Lutheran S 100/PK-4
4311 104th St 53158 262-694-4405
Rev. Donald Hackbarth, prin. Fax 694-0964

Plover, Portage, Pop. 11,256
Stevens Point Area SD
Supt. — See Stevens Point
Plover-Whiting ES 400/K-6
1400 Hoover Ave 54467 715-345-5424
Carl Coffman, prin. Fax 345-7354

St. Bronislava S 200/PK-5
3301 Willow Dr 54467 715-342-2015
Laura Barnett, prin. Fax 342-2016

Plum City, Pierce, Pop. 576
Plum City SD 300/K-12
907 Main St 54761 715-647-2591
Mark Luebker, supt. Fax 647-3015
www.plumcity.k12.wi.us
Plum City ES 100/K-5
621 Main St 54761 715-647-2911
Mark Luebker, prin. Fax 647-4002

Plymouth, Sheboygan, Pop. 8,217
Plymouth SD 2,400/PK-12
125 S Highland Ave 53073 920-892-2661
Clark Reinke, supt. Fax 892-6366
www.plymouth.k12.wi.us
Fairview ES 200/K-5
300 Salem Dr 53073 920-892-2621
Amy Flood, prin. Fax 892-5071
Horizon ES 300/PK-5
411 S Highland Ave 53073 920-892-2225
Todd Hunt, prin. Fax 892-5073

Parkview ES 300/PK-5
500 Parkview Dr 53073 920-892-4076
John Mather, prin. Fax 892-5077
Riverview MS 500/6-8
300 Riverside Cir 53073 920-892-4353
Chris Scudella, prin. Fax 892-5072
Other Schools – See Cascade

St. John Lutheran S 200/PK-8
222 Stafford St 53073 920-893-5114
Sharon Forst, prin. Fax 892-2845
St. John the Baptist S 300/K-8
116 N Pleasant St 53073 920-893-5961
Jeanne Bitkers, prin. Fax 893-3160

Poplar, Douglas, Pop. 591

Maple SD
Supt. — See Maple
Northwestern ES 500/K-5
PO Box 76 54864 715-364-8465
Maija Alexandrov, prin. Fax 364-2270
Northwestern MS 400/6-8
PO Box 46 54864 715-364-2218
Ken Bartelt, prin. Fax 364-2540

Portage, Columbia, Pop. 10,035

Portage Community SD 2,200/PK-12
904 De Witt St 53901 608-742-4879
Charles Poches, supt. Fax 742-4950
www.portage.k12.wi.us
Caledonia ES 100/K-6
N5194 State Road 78 53901 608-742-2601
Robin Kvalo, prin. Fax 742-2521
Fort Winnebago ES 100/K-6
W8349 Dumke Rd 53901 608-742-6016
Robin Kvalo, prin. Fax 742-1171
Lewiston ES 100/K-6
W11195 State Road 127 53901 608-742-2524
Ann Ostrowski, prin. Fax 742-2418
Muir ES 2-6
2600 Woodcrest Dr 53901 608-742-5531
Sue Dietsch, prin. Fax 742-2525
Portage JHS 400/7-8
2505 New Pinery Rd 53901 608-742-2165
Robert Meicher, prin. Fax 742-6987
Rusch ES 400/PK-6
117 W Franklin St 53901 608-742-7376
Robin Kvalo, prin. Fax 742-6987
Woodridge PS 200/PK-1
333 E Slifer St 53901 608-742-3494
Ann Ostrowski, prin. Fax 742-5356
Other Schools – See Endeavor

St. John Lutheran S 100/PK-8
430 W Emmett St 53901 608-742-4222
Rick Schneider, prin. Fax 745-4889
St. Marys Parochial S 100/PK-8
315 W Cook St 53901 608-742-4998
Jamie Hahn, prin. Fax 742-1039

Port Edwards, Wood, Pop. 1,797

Port Edwards SD 500/K-12
801 2nd St 54469 715-887-9000
Pat Sullivan, supt. Fax 887-9040
www.pesd.k12.wi.us
Edwards MS 200/5-8
801 2nd St 54469 715-887-9000
Gus Mancuso, dean Fax 887-9040
Port Edwards ES 100/K-4
801 2nd St 54469 715-887-9000
Pat Sullivan, prin. Fax 887-9095

Port Washington, Ozaukee, Pop. 10,892

Port Washington-Saukville SD 2,600/PK-12
100 W Monroe St 53074 262-268-6000
Michael Weber Ph.D., supt. Fax 268-6020
www.pwssd.k12.wi.us
Dunwiddie ES 300/PK-4
1243 W Lincoln Ave 53074 262-268-5700
Diane Johnson, prin. Fax 268-5720
Jefferson MS 800/5-8
1403 N Holden St 53074 262-268-6100
Arlan Galarowicz, prin. Fax 268-6120
Lincoln ES 400/PK-4
1325 N Theis Ln 53074 262-268-5800
Eric Burke, prin. Fax 268-5820
Other Schools – See Saukville

Port Washington Catholic ES 100/PK-4
1802 N Wisconsin St 53074 262-284-2441
Lee Kaschinska, prin. Fax 284-5408
Port Washington Catholic MS 100/5-8
1802 N Wisconsin St 53074 262-284-2682
Lee Kaschinska, prin. Fax 284-4168
St. Johns Lutheran Academy 100/PK-8
217 N Freeman Dr 53074 262-284-2131
Rev. John Klieve, admin. Fax 268-6558

Port Wing, Bayfield

South Shore SD 200/PK-12
PO Box 40 54865 715-774-3500
Marc Christianson, supt. Fax 774-3569
www.sshore.k12.wi.us
South Shore ES 100/PK-6
PO Box 40 54865 715-774-3817
Marc Christianson, prin. Fax 774-3569

Potosi, Grant, Pop. 728

Potosi SD 400/PK-12
128 US Highway 61 N 53820 608-763-2162
Dr. Steven Lozeau, supt. Fax 763-2035
www.potosisd.k12.wi.us
Potosi ES 200/PK-5
128 US Highway 61 N 53820 608-763-2163
Terry Mengel, prin. Fax 763-2035
Potosi MS 100/6-8
128 US Highway 61 N 53820 608-763-2162
Terry Mengel, prin. Fax 763-2035

SS. Andrew & Thomas S 100/K-8
PO Box 160 53820 608-763-2120
Mary Schneider, prin. Fax 763-4064

Poynette, Columbia, Pop. 2,563

Poynette SD 1,100/PK-12
PO Box 10 53955 608-635-4347
Barbara Wolfe, supt. Fax 635-9200
www.poynette.k12.wi.us
Dekorra ES 100/K-3
W8460 Bilkie Rd 53955 608-635-2386
Brian Sutton, prin. Fax 635-9254
Poynette ES 400/PK-5
PO Box 10 53955 608-635-4347
Brian Sutton, prin. Fax 635-9233
Poynette MS 200/6-8
PO Box 10 53955 608-635-4347
Brian Sutton, prin. Fax 635-9233
Other Schools – See Arlington

Poy Sippi, Waushara, Pop. 1,500

Berlin Area SD
Supt. — See Berlin
Poy Sippi ES, PO Box 406 54967 100/K-4
Scott Bartol, prin. 920-361-2442

Prairie du Chien, Crawford, Pop. 5,880

Prairie du Chien Area SD 1,200/PK-12
420 S Wacouta Ave 53821 608-326-8451
Drew Johnson, supt. Fax 326-0000
www.pdc.k12.wi.us
Bluff View IS 500/3-8
1901 E Wells St 53821 608-326-0503
Aaron Amundson, prin. Fax 326-5364
Kennedy ES 300/PK-2
420 S Wacouta Ave 53821 608-326-8451
Laura Stuckey, prin. Fax 326-7579

St. Gabriel S 200/PK-5
515 N Beaumont Rd 53821 608-326-8624
Kathleen Schwartz, prin. Fax 326-4876
St. John Nepomucene MS 100/6-8
720 S Wacouta Ave 53821 608-326-4400
Kathleen Schwartz, prin. Fax 326-4876

Prairie du Sac, Sauk, Pop. 3,547

Sauk Prairie SD
Supt. — See Sauk City
Grand Avenue ES 400/2-5
225 Grand Ave 53578 608-643-1900
Craig Trautsch, prin. Fax 643-1957
Tower Rock ES 100/3-5
S9033 Denzer Rd 53578 608-544-2581
Laurie Luetscher, lead tchr. Fax 544-5801

Prairie Farm, Barron, Pop. 508

Prairie Farm SD 400/PK-12
630 River Ave S 54762 715-455-1683
Dr. Donald Hauck, supt. Fax 455-1056
www.prairiefarm.k12.wi.us
Prairie Farm ES 200/PK-5
630 River Ave S 54762 715-455-1615
Craig Broeren, prin. Fax 455-1869
Prairie Farm MS 100/6-8
630 River Ave S 54762 715-455-1841
Craig Broeren, prin. Fax 455-1869

Prentice, Price, Pop. 563

Prentice SD 500/PK-12
PO Box 110 54556 715-428-2811
Gregory Krause, supt. Fax 428-2815
www.prentice.k12.wi.us
Ogema ES 100/PK-4
PO Box 110 54556 715-767-5171
Randall Bergman, prin. Fax 428-2815
Prentice S, PO Box 110 54556 300/PK-8
Randall Bergman, prin. 715-428-2812

Prescott, Pierce, Pop. 4,009

Prescott SD 1,100/PK-12
1220 Saint Croix St 54021 715-262-5782
Roger Hulne, supt. Fax 262-5091
www.prescott.k12.wi.us
Malone ES 500/PK-5
505 Campbell St N 54021 715-262-5463
Scott Halverson, prin. Fax 262-0052
Prescott MS 300/6-8
125 Elm St N 54021 715-262-5054
Lyle Nolt, prin. Fax 262-3965

St. Joseph Catholic S 100/PK-6
281 Dakota St S 54021 715-262-5912
Mary Bray, prin. Fax 262-5901

Princeton, Green Lake, Pop. 1,463

Princeton SD 400/K-12
PO Box 147 54968 920-295-6571
Robert Beaver, supt. Fax 295-4778
princeton.wi.schoolwebpages.com
Princeton S 400/K-12
PO Box 147 54968 920-295-6571
Jean Rigden, prin. Fax 295-4778

St. John Lutheran S 50/K-8
227 Harvard St 54968 920-295-3991
Daniel Kell, prin. Fax 295-0119
St. John the Baptist S 100/PK-8
125 Church St 54968 920-295-3541
Fr. Dale Grubba, prin. Fax 295-0178

Pulaski, Brown, Pop. 3,540

Pulaski Community SD 3,600/PK-12
PO Box 36 54162 920-822-6000
Dr. Mel Lightner, supt. Fax 822-6005
connect.pulaski.k12.wi.us
Glenbrook ES 500/K-5
PO Box 825 54162 920-822-6100
Mary Connolly, prin. Fax 822-6105
Pulaski Community MS 900/6-8
911 S Saint Augustine St 54162 920-822-6500
Patrick Fullerton, prin. Fax 822-6505
Other Schools – See Green Bay, Krakow, Oneida, Sobieski

Assumption of the BVM S 200/PK-5
109 E Pulaski St 54162 920-822-5650
Deanne Wilinski, prin. Fax 822-8003

Racine, Racine, Pop. 79,392

Racine USD 20,000/PK-12
2220 Northwestern Ave 53404 262-635-5600
James Shaw, supt. Fax 631-7121
www.racine.k12.wi.us
Brown ES 500/PK-5
5915 Erie St 53402 262-664-6650
Kathleen Jackson, prin. Fax 664-6680
Bull Fine Arts ES 300/K-5
815 De Koven Ave 53403 262-664-6800
Doug Clum, prin. Fax 664-6810
Fratt ES 500/K-5
3501 Kinzie Ave 53405 262-664-8150
Jim Hass, prin. Fax 664-8160
Giese ES 300/PK-5
5120 Byrd Ave 53406 262-664-8250
Anne Swanson, prin. Fax 664-8270
Gifford ES 900/PK-5
8332 Northwestern Ave 53406 262-619-4550
Steven Russo, prin. Fax 619-4595
Gilmore MS 800/6-8
2330 Northwestern Ave 53404 262-619-4260
Kevin Brown, prin. Fax 619-4272
Goodland ES 400/PK-5
4800 Graceland Blvd 53406 262-664-6850
Billie Novick, prin. Fax 664-6870
Janes ES 400/PK-5
1425 N Wisconsin St 53402 262-664-6550
Deborah Coca, prin. Fax 664-6553
Jefferson Lighthouse ES 500/K-5
1722 W 6th St 53404 262-664-6900
Soren Gajewski, prin. Fax 664-6910
Jerstad-Agerholm ES 400/K-5
3535 Lasalle St 53402 262-664-6050
Cecilia Holley-Young, prin. Fax 664-6054
Jerstad-Agerholm MS 800/6-8
3601 Lasalle St 53402 262-664-6075
Cheri Kulland, prin. Fax 664-6120
Johnson ES 500/K-5
2420 Kentucky St 53405 262-664-6950
Kim DeLaO, prin. Fax 664-6960
Jones ES 500/PK-5
3300 Chicory Rd 53403 262-664-8050
Sharon Campbell, prin. Fax 664-8060
Knapp ES 600/PK-5
2701 17th St 53405 262-664-8000
Gayle Titus, prin. Fax 664-8010
Mitchell ES 500/PK-5
2713 Drexel Ave 53403 262-664-6350
Kevin McCormick, prin. Fax 664-6375
Mitchell MS 900/6-8
2701 Drexel Ave 53403 262-664-6400
Robert Wilhelmi, prin. Fax 664-6444
North Park ES 500/PK-5
4748 Elizabeth St 53402 262-664-6450
Mark Zanin, prin. Fax 664-6455
Racine Early Education Center PK-PK
2015 Franklin St 53403 262-664-8200
Charles Leonard, prin. Fax 664-8225
Red Apple ES 500/PK-5
914 Saint Patrick St 53402 262-619-4500
Les Hunt, prin. Fax 619-4505
Roosevelt ES 500/K-5
915 Romayne Ave 53402 262-664-8300
Jeff Rasmussen, prin. Fax 664-8310
Starbuck MS 700/6-8
1516 Ohio St 53405 262-664-6500
Sandra Brand, prin. Fax 664-6510
Thomas ES 400/K-5
930 Martin Luther King Dr 53404 262-664-8400
Staci Kimmons, prin. Fax 664-8444
Wadewitz ES 600/PK-5
2700 Yout St 53404 262-664-6000
Ursula Hamilton-Perry, prin. Fax 664-6005
West Ridge ES 400/K-5
1347 S Emmertsen Rd 53406 262-664-6200
Christopher Thompson, prin. Fax 664-6225
Wind Point ES 400/PK-5
290 Jonsue Ln 53402 262-664-6125
Irene Nahabedian, prin. Fax 664-6141
Other Schools – See Sturtevant

John Paul II Academy 200/K-8
2023 Northwestern Ave 53404 262-637-2012
Tom Siefert, prin. Fax 637-5130
Prairie S 700/PK-12
4050 Lighthouse Dr 53402 262-260-3845
Wm. Mark Murphy, hdmstr. Fax 260-3790
Racine Christian S 200/K-8
912 Virginia St 53405 262-634-0961
David Van Swol, prin. Fax 634-7467
Racine Montessori S 200/PK-8
2317 Howe St 53403 262-637-7892
Rita Lewis, admin.
St. Edward S 300/K-8
1435 Grove Ave 53405 262-636-8044
Vince Kostos, prin. Fax 636-8046
St. John's Lutheran S 200/PK-8
510 Kewaunee St 53402 262-633-2758
Janet Pesch, prin. Fax 637-7089
St. Joseph S 200/K-8
1525 Erie St 53402 262-633-2403
Joe Majowski, prin. Fax 633-4423
St. Lucy S 200/K-8
3035 Drexel Ave 53403 262-554-1801
Rudee Koepke, prin. Fax 554-7618

St. Rita S 300/K-8
4433 Douglas Ave 53402 262-639-3333
Diana Lesnjak, prin. Fax 639-3346
San Juan Diego MS 100/6-8
1101 Douglas Ave 53402 262-619-0402
Br. Mike Kadow, pres. Fax 898-9524
Trinity Lutheran S 300/PK-8
2035 Geneva St 53402 262-632-1766
Gary Marxhausen, prin. Fax 632-3838
Wisconsin Lutheran S 100/PK-8
734 Villa St 53403 262-633-7143
James Boehm, prin. Fax 633-3323

Randolph, Columbia, Pop. 1,820
Randolph SD 500/PK-12
110 Meadowood Dr 53956 920-326-2427
Greg Peyer, supt. Fax 326-2439
www.randolph.k12.wi.us
Randolph S 300/PK-8
265 N High St 53956 920-326-2431
Wayne Vanderploeg, prin. Fax 326-5056

Randolph Christian S 100/PK-8
457 2nd St 53956 920-326-3320
Kyle Heuver, prin. Fax 326-3001

Random Lake, Sheboygan, Pop. 1,585
Random Lake SD 900/PK-12
605 Random Lake Rd 53075 920-994-4342
Thomas Malmstadt, supt. Fax 994-4820
www.randomlake.k12.wi.us
Random Lake ES 300/PK-4
605 Random Lake Rd 53075 920-994-4344
Sandra Mountain, prin. Fax 994-4820
Random Lake MS 300/5-8
605 Random Lake Rd 53075 920-994-2498
David Farnham, prin. Fax 994-4820

Our Lady of the Lakes S 100/PK-6
306 Butler St 53075 920-994-9962
Catherine Pohl, prin. Fax 994-2499
St. John Lutheran S 100/PK-8
W5407 County Road SS 53075 920-994-9190
Richard Wegner, prin. Fax 994-9721

Readfield, Waupaca
New London SD
Supt. — See New London
Readfield ES 200/K-5
PO Box 40 54969 920-667-4265
Kristin Grable, prin. Fax 667-4295

Redgranite, Waushara, Pop. 2,243
Wautoma Area SD
Supt. — See Wautoma
Redgranite ES 100/K-5
PO Box 649 54970 920-566-2357
Clyde Simonson, prin. Fax 566-0490

Reedsburg, Sauk, Pop. 8,497
Reedsburg SD 2,600/PK-12
501 K St 53959 608-524-2401
Thomas Benson, supt. Fax 524-6818
www.rsd.k12.wi.us
Pineview ES 400/PK-5
1121 8th St 53959 608-524-4322
Tammy Hayes, prin. Fax 524-0622
South ES 100/K-5
420 Plum St 53959 608-524-4306
Paul Bierman, prin. Fax 524-3421
Webb MS 600/6-8
707 N Webb Ave 53959 608-524-2328
Casey Campbell, prin. Fax 524-1161
West Side ES 300/K-5
401 Alexander Ave 53959 608-524-4846
Paul Bierman, prin. Fax 524-1835
Other Schools – See La Valle, Loganville, Rock Springs

Sacred Heart S 200/PK-8
545 N Oak St 53959 608-524-3611
Michael Rocha, prin. Fax 524-3831
St. Peter Lutheran S 200/PK-8
346 N Locust St 53959 608-524-4066
Phil Rogers, prin. Fax 524-8821

Reedsville, Manitowoc, Pop. 1,162
Reedsville SD 700/PK-12
PO Box 340 54230 920-754-4341
Robert Scrivner, supt. Fax 754-4344
www.reedsville.k12.wi.us
Reedsville ES 300/PK-6
PO Box 340 54230 920-754-4345
Pat Popp, prin. Fax 754-4577
Reedsville MS 100/7-8
PO Box 340 54230 920-754-4345
Pat Popp, prin. Fax 754-4577

SS. John & James Lutheran S 50/PK-8
223 Manitowoc St 54230 920-754-4432
Mark Hinds, prin. Fax 754-4568

Rhinelander, Oneida, Pop. 7,889
Rhinelander SD 2,600/K-12
665 Coolidge Ave Ste B 54501 715-365-9700
Dr. Roger Erdahl, supt. Fax 365-9719
www.rhinelander.k12.wi.us
Central ES 300/4-5
418 N Pelham St 54501 715-365-9600
Timothy Howell, prin. Fax 365-9612
Crescent ES 300/K-3
3319 Boyce Dr 54501 715-365-9120
Tammy Modic, prin. Fax 365-9124
Pelican ES 300/K-3
3350 V Hickey Rd 54501 715-365-9160
Martha Knudtson, prin. Fax 365-9177
Williams MS 600/6-8
915 Acacia Ln 54501 715-365-9220
Paul Johnson, prin. Fax 369-7562

Three Lakes SD
Supt. — See Three Lakes
Sugar Camp ES 100/PK-6
4066 Camp Four Rd 54501 715-272-1105
James Kuchenbecker, prin. Fax 272-1299

Nativity of Our Lord S 300/PK-8
103 E King St 54501 715-362-5588
Shirley Heise, prin. Fax 362-0952
Zion Lutheran S 100/PK-8
26 W Frederick St 54501 715-365-6300
Steven Brich, prin. Fax 365-6329

Rib Lake, Taylor, Pop. 858
Rib Lake SD 500/PK-12
PO Box 278 54470 715-427-3222
Jeff Tortomasi, supt. Fax 427-3221
www.riblake.k12.wi.us
Rib Lake ES 200/PK-5
PO Box 278 54470 715-427-5818
Angela Woyak, prin. Fax 427-3221
Rib Lake MS 100/6-8
PO Box 278 54470 715-427-5446
Rick Cardey, prin. Fax 427-3221

Rice Lake, Barron, Pop. 8,361
Rice Lake Area SD 2,400/PK-12
700 Augusta St 54868 715-234-9007
Paul Vine, supt. Fax 234-4552
www.ricelake.k12.wi.us
Hilltop DayCare & Preschool 50/PK-PK
104 Cameron Rd 54868 715-234-6671
Paula Christensen, prin. Fax 234-8080
Hilltop ES 300/K-5
202 Cameron Rd 54868 715-234-4998
Randy Drost, prin. Fax 736-0169
Jefferson ES 100/K-5
30 Phipps Ave 54868 715-234-3145
Debra Olson, prin. Fax 736-0909
Kiddie Korner Preschool 50/PK-PK
608 W Marshall St 54868 715-234-5432
Paula Christensen, prin. Fax 234-1642
Lincoln ES 100/K-5
426 N Wilson Ave 54868 715-234-7979
Debra Olson, prin. Fax 236-7657
Rice Lake MS 500/6-8
204 Cameron Rd 54868 715-234-8156
Steve Sirek, prin. Fax 234-9439
Tainter ES 300/PK-5
2201 Carrie Ave 54868 715-234-8065
Lee Pritzl, prin. Fax 234-2081
Other Schools – See Haugen

Meadow Creek Adventist S 50/1-8
1779 20 1/2 St 54868 715-434-7798
Marie Benson, admin.
Redeemer Lutheran S 50/K-8
520 E Orchard Beach Ln 54868 715-234-1423
Jeffrey Seelow, prin. Fax 736-9357
St. Joseph S 200/PK-8
128 W Humbird St 54868 715-234-7721
Sr. Claudine Balio, prin. Fax 234-5062

Richfield, Washington
Richfield J1 SD 400/PK-8
3117 Holy Hill Rd 53076 262-628-1032
Dr. Elliott Moeser, supt. Fax 628-3013
www.richfield.k12.wi.us
Richfield S 300/3-8
3117 Holy Hill Rd 53076 262-628-1032
Dr. Elliott Moeser, prin. Fax 628-3013
Other Schools – See Colgate

Richland Center, Richland, Pop. 5,177
Ithaca SD 400/K-12
24615 State Hwy 58 53581 608-585-2512
Jennifer Vogler, supt. Fax 585-2505
www.ithaca.k12.wi.us/
Ithaca ES 200/K-5
24615 State Hwy 58 53581 608-585-2311
Jennifer Vogler, prin. Fax 585-2505
Ithaca MS 100/6-8
24615 State Hwy 58 53581 608-585-2311
Jennifer Vogler, prin. Fax 585-2505

Richland SD 1,400/PK-12
1996 US Hwy 14 W 53581 608-647-6106
Rachel Schultz, supt. Fax 647-8454
www.richland.k12.wi.us
Doudna ES 400/K-5
1990 Bohmann Dr 53581 608-647-8971
Tom Lambries, prin. Fax 647-7293
Jefferson ES 100/K-5
586 N Main St 53581 608-647-6351
Leslie Lewison, prin. Fax 647-9121
Lincoln ES 50/PK-PK
678 S Park St 53581 608-647-2511
Leslie Lewison, prin. Fax 647-7293
Richland MS 300/6-8
1801 State Hwy 80 S 53581 608-647-6381
David Guy, prin. Fax 647-4735

St. Mary S 100/K-8
155 W 5th St 53581 608-647-2422
Beverly Miller, prin. Fax 647-6029

Ridgeland, Dunn, Pop. 258
Barron Area SD
Supt. — See Barron
Ridgeland-Dallas ES 100/K-4
PO Box 196 54763 715-949-1445
Rachel Waite, prin. Fax 949-1617

Ridgeway, Iowa, Pop. 656
Dodgeville SD
Supt. — See Dodgeville
Ridgeway ES 200/PK-5
208 Jarvis St 53582 608-924-3461
Tom Whitford, prin. Fax 924-1362

Ringle, Marathon
D.C. Everest Area SD
Supt. — See Schofield
Easton ES 100/K-2
E3640 County Road Q 54471 715-446-3600
Julie Fondell, prin. Fax 446-3161
Riverside ES 500/K-5
R12231 River Rd 54471 715-359-2417
Patricia LesStrang, prin. Fax 355-3725

Rio, Columbia, Pop. 998
Rio Community SD 500/PK-12
411 Church St 53960 920-992-3141
Mark McGuire, supt. Fax 992-3157
www.rio.k12.wi.us
Rio ES 300/PK-5
355 Lowville Rd 53960 920-992-3143
Amy Parish, prin. Fax 992-3012

Ripon, Fond du Lac, Pop. 7,268
Ripon Area SD 1,800/PK-12
PO Box 991 54971 920-748-4600
Richard Zimman, supt. Fax 748-2715
www.ripon.k12.wi.us
Barlow Park ES 500/PK-2
PO Box 991 54971 920-748-1550
Myra Misles-Krhin, prin. Fax 748-1552
Murray Park ES 400/3-5
PO Box 991 54971 920-748-4695
Randy Hatlen, prin. Fax 748-4698
Ripon MS 400/6-8
PO Box 991 54971 920-748-4638
Melanie Oppor, prin. Fax 748-4653

River Falls, Pierce, Pop. 13,254
River Falls SD 2,900/PK-12
852 E Division St 54022 715-425-1800
Dr. Tom Westerhaus, supt. Fax 425-1804
www.rfsd.k12.wi.us
Greenwood ES 400/K-5
418 N 8th St 54022 715-425-1810
Nate Schurman, prin. Fax 425-0783
Meyer MS 700/6-8
230 N 9th St 54022 715-425-1820
Michael Johnson, prin. Fax 425-1823
Rocky Branch ES 400/PK-5
1415 Bartosh Ln 54022 715-425-1819
Charles Eaton, prin. Fax 425-0599
Westside ES 500/K-5
1007 W Pine St 54022 715-425-1815
Michael Ballard, prin. Fax 425-1805

Heartland Montessori S 50/PK-6
N8226 945th St 54022 715-426-0350
Patty Borchardt, coord.
St. Bridget S 100/PK-8
135 E Division St 54022 715-425-1872
Susan Steckbauer, prin. Fax 425-1873

Roberts, Saint Croix, Pop. 1,484
St. Croix Central SD
Supt. — See Hammond
St. Croix Central ES 500/PK-4
PO Box 129 54023 715-749-3119
Steve Sanders, prin. Fax 749-3130

Rock Springs, Sauk, Pop. 403
Reedsburg SD
Supt. — See Reedsburg
Rock Springs ES 100/K-5
PO Box 158 53961 608-524-5132
Fax 524-6529

Rosendale, Fond du Lac, Pop. 1,035
Rosendale-Brandon SD 900/PK-12
300 W Wisconsin St 54974 920-872-2851
Gary Hansen, supt. Fax 872-2647
www.rbsd.k12.wi.us
Rosendale IS 200/4-8
200 S Main St 54974 920-872-2126
John Hokenson, prin. Fax 872-2061
Rosendale PS 200/PK-3
300 W Wisconsin St 54974 920-872-2151
John Hokenson, prin. Fax 872-2647
Other Schools – See Brandon

Rosholt, Portage, Pop. 483
Rosholt SD 700/PK-12
PO Box 310 54473 715-677-4542
Kenneth Camlek, supt. Fax 677-3543
www.rosholt.k12.wi.us
Rosholt ES 300/PK-5
PO Box 310 54473 715-677-4543
John Parks, prin. Fax 677-3543
Rosholt MS 200/6-8
PO Box 310 54473 715-677-4541
James Grygleski, prin. Fax 677-6767

St. Adalbert S 50/PK-8
3314 Saint Adalberts Rd 54473 715-677-4517
Patrick Burkhart, prin. Fax 677-4517

Rothschild, Marathon, Pop. 5,096
D.C. Everest Area SD
Supt. — See Schofield
Evergreen ES 400/K-5
1610 Pine Rd 54474 715-359-6591
Richard Koepke, prin. Fax 355-3722
Rothschild ES 300/K-5
810 1st St 54474 715-359-3186
Ronald Foreman, prin. Fax 355-3723

Newman Catholic ES at St. Mark 200/PK-5
602 Military Rd 54474 715-359-9662
Jan Klosinski, prin. Fax 355-8904

Rubicon, Dodge
Rubicon J6 SD 100/K-8
N3501 County Road P 53078 262-673-2920
Daniel Hanrahan, supt. Fax 673-2975
theclasslist.com/saylesville
Saylesville S 100/K-8
N3501 County Road P 53078 262-673-2920
Daniel Hanrahan, prin. Fax 673-2975

Rudolph, Wood, Pop. 422
Wisconsin Rapids SD
Supt. — See Wisconsin Rapids
Rudolph ES 200/K-6
6950 Knowledge Ave 54475 715-435-3340
Terry Whitmore, prin. Fax 435-2070

Saint Croix Falls, Polk, Pop. 2,052
St. Croix Falls SD 1,100/PK-12
PO Box 130 54024 715-483-2507
Glenn Martin, supt. Fax 483-3695
www.scf.k12.wi.us
St. Croix Falls ES 300/1-4
PO Box 130 54024 715-483-9823
Jeff Benoy, prin. Fax 483-3695
St. Croix Falls MS 300/5-8
PO Box 130 54024 715-483-2507
Kathleen Willow, prin. Fax 483-3695
Other Schools – See Dresser

Valley Christian S 100/PK-12
1263 State Road 35 54024 715-483-9126
Ron Brace, admin. Fax 483-5679

Saint Francis, Milwaukee, Pop. 8,809
St. Francis SD 1,400/PK-12
4225 S Lake Dr 53235 414-747-3900
Carol Topinka, supt. Fax 482-7198
www.stfrancisschools.org
Deer Creek IS 400/4-8
3680 S Kinnickinnic Ave 53235 414-482-8400
Mary Garcia-Velez, prin. Fax 482-8406
Willow Glen S 300/PK-3
2600 E Bolivar Ave 53235 414-486-6300
Michelle Mancl, prin. Fax 486-6305

Saint Germain, Vilas
Northland Pines SD
Supt. — See Eagle River
Northand Pines/St Germain ES 100/K-5
8234 State Highway 70 W 54558 715-542-3632
Maggie Peterson, prin. Fax 542-3660

Saint Nazianz, Manitowoc, Pop. 813

St. Gregory S 100/PK-8
PO Box 199 54232 920-773-2530
Rita Steffen, prin. Fax 773-3086

Salem, Kenosha
Salem SD 400/K-8
PO Box 160 53168 262-843-2356
David Milz, supt. Fax 843-4138
www.salem.k12.wi.us
Salem ES K-5
PO Box 160 53168 262-843-2356
Shawn Waller, prin. Fax 843-2506
Salem MS 400/6-8
PO Box 160 53168 262-843-2356
Eileen Bruton, prin. Fax 843-2586

Sauk City, Sauk, Pop. 3,006
Sauk Prairie SD 2,600/PK-12
213 Maple St 53583 608-643-5990
Craig Bender, supt. Fax 643-6216
www.saukpr.k12.wi.us
Black Hawk ES 100/PK-2
E7995 School Rd 53583 608-544-2273
Doug Yost, prin. Fax 544-2114
Sauk Prairie MS 600/6-8
207 Maple St 53583 608-643-5500
Ted Harter, prin. Fax 643-5503
Spruce Street ES 400/PK-2
701 Spruce St 53583 608-643-1838
Cliff Thompson, prin. Fax 643-1849
Other Schools – See Prairie du Sac

St. Aloysius S 100/PK-5
608 Oak St 53583 608-643-6868
John Brennan, prin. Fax 643-3472

Saukville, Ozaukee, Pop. 4,184
Port Washington-Saukville SD
Supt. — See Port Washington
Saukville ES 300/K-4
333 N Mill St 53080 262-268-5900
Kathleen Tubbs, prin. Fax 268-5920

Ozaukee Christian S 100/K-8
341 S Dries St 53080 262-284-6980
Krista Austin, admin. Fax 284-6938

Schofield, Marathon, Pop. 2,160
D.C. Everest Area SD 5,100/K-12
6300 Alderson St 54476 715-359-4221
Kristine Gilmore, supt. Fax 359-2056
www.dce.k12.wi.us
Schofield ES 200/K-5
1310 Grand Ave 54476 715-359-0419
Jeffery Addison, prin. Fax 355-3724
Weston ES 400/K-5
5200 Camp Phillips Rd 54476 715-359-4181
Fritz Lehrke, prin. Fax 355-3726
Other Schools – See Hatley, Ringle, Rothschild, Weston

Newman Catholic CDC at St. Therese PK-PK
112 Kort St W 54476 715-355-5254
Vicki Koeppel, dir. Fax 359-9565
St. Peter Lutheran S 100/PK-8
115 Eau Claire St 54476 715-359-3020
Scott Huebner, prin. Fax 241-6301

Seneca, Crawford
Seneca SD 300/PK-12
PO Box 34 54654 608-734-3411
David Boland, supt. Fax 734-3430
www.seneca.k12.wi.us
Seneca ES 100/PK-4
PO Box 34 54654 608-734-3411
David Boland, prin. Fax 734-3430
Seneca JHS 100/5-8
PO Box 34 54654 608-734-3411
David Boland, prin. Fax 734-3430

Seymour, Outagamie, Pop. 3,432
Seymour Community SD 2,500/PK-12
10 Circle Dr 54165 920-833-2304
Peter Ross, supt. Fax 833-6037
www.seymour.k12.wi.us/
Rock Ledge IS 400/3-5
330 W Hickory St 54165 920-833-7380
Peter Kempen, prin. Fax 833-9684
Rock Ledge PS 400/PK-2
330 W Hickory St 54165 920-833-5155
Christina Heagle, prin. Fax 833-5144
Seymour MS 400/6-8
10 Circle Dr 54165 920-833-7199
Judy Schenk, prin. Fax 833-9376
Other Schools – See Black Creek

Sharon, Walworth, Pop. 1,570
Sharon J11 SD 300/PK-8
104 E School St 53585 262-736-4477
Steven Hubbe, supt. Fax 736-4457
www.sharon.k12.wi.us/
Sharon S 300/PK-8
104 E School St 53585 262-736-4477
Steven Huebbe, prin. Fax 736-4457

Shawano, Shawano, Pop. 8,441
Shawano SD 2,600/PK-12
218 County Road B 54166 715-526-3194
Todd Carlson, supt. Fax 526-3194
www.ssd.k12.wi.us/
Brener ES 700/PK-4
1300 S Union St 54166 715-524-2131
Karen Smith, prin. Fax 524-9899
Lincoln ES 300/K-4
237 S Sawyer St 54166 715-524-2134
Troy Edwards, prin. Fax 526-4372
Shawano Community MS 700/5-8
1050 S Union St 54166 715-526-2192
Daniel Labby, prin. Fax 526-5037

Divine Savior Lutheran S 50/K-8
102 Northridge Dr 54166 715-526-6880
Darrell Dobberpuhl, prin. Fax 524-6618
Sacred Heart S 100/K-8
124 E Center St 54166 715-526-5328
Lois Maczuzak, prin. Fax 526-4107
St. James Lutheran S 200/PK-8
324 S Andrews St 54166 715-524-4213
Susan Longmire, prin. Fax 524-4876

Sheboygan, Sheboygan, Pop. 48,872
Sheboygan Area SD 9,700/PK-12
830 Virginia Ave 53081 920-459-3500
Joseph Sheehan Ph.D., supt. Fax 459-6487
www.sheboygan.k12.wi.us
Cooper ES 300/K-5
2014 Cooper Ave 53083 920-459-3693
Larry Brahan, prin. Fax 459-4033
Early Learning Center 600/PK-PK
1227 Wilson Ave 53081 920-459-4330
David Shoemaker, prin. Fax 459-6708
Farnsworth MS 700/6-8
1017 Union Ave 53081 920-459-3655
Todd DeBruin, prin. Fax 459-3660
Grant ES 400/K-5
1528 N 5th St 53081 920-459-3626
Martha Steinbruecker, prin. Fax 459-3719
Jackson ES 300/K-5
2530 Weeden Creek Rd 53081 920-459-3573
Lynn Walters, prin. Fax 459-6496
Jefferson ES 300/K-5
1538 N 15th St 53081 920-459-3620
Bill Klein, prin. Fax 453-5209
Lincoln-Erdman ES 300/K-5
4101 N 50th St 53083 920-459-3595
John Pfaff, prin. Fax 459-4049
Longfellow ES 400/K-5
819 Kentucky Ave 53081 920-459-3580
Seth Harvatine, prin. Fax 459-0451
Madison ES 300/K-5
2302 David Ave 53081 920-459-3585
Matt Driscoll, prin. Fax 459-3589
Mann MS 700/6-8
2820 Union Ave 53081 920-459-3666
Vicki Ritchie, prin. Fax 459-3669
Pigeon River ES 400/K-5
3508 N 21st St 53083 920-459-3563
Susan Buesing, prin. Fax 459-4002
Sheridan ES 300/K-5
1412 Maryland Ave 53081 920-459-3550
Judy Kapellen, prin. Fax 459-3833
Urban MS 700/6-8
1226 North Ave 53083 920-459-3680
Susan Nennig, prin. Fax 459-4065
Wilson ES 500/K-5
1625 Wilson Ave 53081 920-459-3688
Tom Binder, prin. Fax 803-7760
Other Schools – See Cleveland

Bethlehem Lutheran S 200/PK-8
1121 Georgia Ave 53081 920-452-5071
Patrick Vanic, prin. Fax 452-0209
Christ Child Academy 200/PK-8
2722 Henry St 53081 920-459-2660
Thomas Edson, prin. Fax 459-2665
Ebenezer Christian S 50/K-8
610 N 25th St 53081 920-452-5464
Paula Hause, admin. Fax 803-0478
Holy Family S 200/PK-8
814 Superior Ave 53081 920-452-1571
Kathryn Miller, prin. Fax 208-4371
Immanuel Lutheran S 100/PK-8
1626 Illinois Ave 53081 920-452-9681
Heidi Wallner, prin. Fax 452-0102
St. Dominic S 100/PK-8
2108 N 21st St 53081 920-452-8747
Peggy Henseler, prin. Fax 458-4809
St. Paul Lutheran S 100/K-8
1819 N 13th St 53081 920-452-6882
Wendy Kretschmar, prin. Fax 452-7893
Sheboygan Christian S 200/PK-8
418 Geele Ave 53083 920-457-3060
Corey Navis, admin. Fax 457-6441
Trinity Lutheran S 100/PK-8
824 Wisconsin Ave 53081 920-458-8248
Gregory Becker, prin. Fax 458-8267

Sheboygan Falls, Sheboygan, Pop. 7,527
Sheboygan Falls SD 1,700/PK-12
220 Amherst Ave 53085 920-467-7893
Dave Wessel, supt. Fax 467-7899
www.sheboyganfalls.k12.wi.us
Sheboygan Falls ES 600/PK-4
1 Alfred Miley Ave 53085 920-467-7820
Joseph Mukavitz, prin. Fax 467-7824
Sheboygan Falls MS 500/5-8
101 School St 53085 920-467-7880
Meloney Markofski, prin. Fax 467-7885

St. Mary S 100/PK-6
313 Giddings Ave 53085 920-467-6291
Lisa Oldenburg, prin. Fax 467-4290

Shell Lake, Washburn, Pop. 1,372
Shell Lake SD 600/K-12
271 Highway 63 S 54871 715-468-7816
Brian Nord, supt. Fax 468-7812
www.shelllake.k12.wi.us
Shell Lake ES 200/3-6
271 Highway 63 S 54871 715-468-7815
Michael Werner, prin. Fax 468-7476
Shell Lake PS 100/K-2
271 Highway 63 S 54871 715-468-7889
Michael Werner, prin. Fax 468-4450

Sherwood, Calumet, Pop. 2,290

St. John - Sacred Heart S 200/PK-8
PO Box 78 54169 920-989-1373
Kerry Sievert, prin. Fax 989-1689

Shiocton, Outagamie, Pop. 920
Shiocton SD 800/PK-12
PO Box 68 54170 920-986-3351
Chris VanderHeyden, supt. Fax 986-3291
www.shiocton.k12.wi.us
Shiocton S 500/PK-7
PO Box 68 54170 920-986-3351
Kim Griesbach, prin. Fax 986-3291

Shorewood, Milwaukee, Pop. 13,192
Shorewood SD 2,000/PK-12
1701 E Capitol Dr 53211 414-963-6901
Matthew Joynt, supt. Fax 963-6904
www.shorewoodschools.org
Atwater ES 500/PK-6
2100 E Capitol Dr 53211 414-963-6962
Bonni Haber, prin. Fax 963-6970
Lake Bluff ES 500/PK-6
1600 E Lake Bluff Blvd 53211 414-963-6972
Kirk Juffer, prin. Fax 961-2815
Shorewood IS 300/7-8
3830 N Morris Blvd 53211 414-963-6951
Anthony Strancke, prin. Fax 963-6946

St. Robert S 300/PK-8
2200 E Capitol Dr 53211 414-332-1164
Lauren Beckman, prin. Fax 332-7355

Shullsburg, Lafayette, Pop. 1,198
Shullsburg SD 400/PK-12
444 N Judgement St 53586 608-965-4427
Loras Kruser, admin. Fax 965-3794
www.shullsburg.k12.wi.us
Shullsburg ES 200/PK-5
444 N Judgement St 53586 608-965-4427
Loras Kruser, prin. Fax 965-3794
Shullsburg JHS 100/6-8
444 N Judgement St 53586 608-965-4427
Loras Kruser, prin. Fax 965-3794

Silver Lake, Kenosha, Pop. 2,513
Silver Lake J1 SD 600/K-8
PO Box 69 53170 262-889-4384
Todd Leroy, admin. Fax 889-8450
www.riverview.k12.wi.us
Riverview S 600/K-8
PO Box 69 53170 262-889-4384
Joseph Dawidziak, prin. Fax 889-2083

Siren, Burnett, Pop. 1,015
Siren SD 500/PK-12
24022 4th Ave 54872 715-349-2290
Scott Johnson, supt. Fax 349-7476
www.siren.k12.wi.us
Siren S 400/PK-8
24022 4th Ave 54872 715-349-2278
Jason Wilhelm, prin. Fax 349-2001

Slinger, Washington, Pop. 4,358
Slinger SD 2,900/PK-12
207 Polk St 53086 262-644-9615
Robert Reynolds, supt. Fax 644-7514
www.slinger.k12.wi.us

Slinger ES 500/PK-5
203 Polk St 53086 262-644-6669
Sue Weisse, prin. Fax 644-6550
Slinger MS 600/6-8
521 Olympic Dr 53086 262-644-5226
Dean Goneau, prin. Fax 644-7353
Other Schools – See Allenton, Hartford

St. Peter S 100/PK-5
206 E Washington St 53086 262-644-8083
Virginia Miller, prin. Fax 644-7951

Sobieski, Oconto
Pulaski Community SD
Supt. — See Pulaski
Sunnyside ES 500/K-5
720 County Road C 54171 920-822-6200
Mary King, prin. Fax 822-6205

Soldiers Grove, Crawford, Pop. 614
North Crawford SD 500/PK-12
47050 County Road X 54655 608-735-4318
Daniel Davies, supt. Fax 735-4317
www.northcrawford.com/
North Crawford S 300/PK-8
47050 County Road X 54655 608-624-5201
Brandon Munson, prin. Fax 624-6269

Solon Springs, Douglas, Pop. 577
Solon Springs SD 300/PK-12
8993 E Baldwin Ave 54873 715-378-2263
Fred Schlichting, supt. Fax 378-2073
eyrie.solonk12.net/school/
Solon Springs S 300/PK-12
8993 E Baldwin Ave 54873 715-378-2263
Sue Chandler, prin. Fax 378-2073

Somerset, Saint Croix, Pop. 2,539
Somerset SD 1,500/PK-12
PO Box 100 54025 715-247-3313
Randal Rosburg, supt. Fax 247-5588
www.somerset.k12.wi.us
Somerset ES 600/PK-4
PO Box 100 54025 715-247-3311
Cheryl Wood, prin. Fax 247-3327
Somerset MS 400/5-8
PO Box 100 54025 715-247-4400
Richard Lange, prin. Fax 247-4437

St. Anne S 100/PK-8
140 Church Hill Rd 54025 715-247-3762
Randall Stanke, prin. Fax 247-4335

South Milwaukee, Milwaukee, Pop. 20,849
South Milwaukee SD 3,500/PK-12
901 15th Ave 53172 414-766-5000
David Ewald, supt. Fax 766-5005
www.sdsm.k12.wi.us/
Blakewood ES 400/PK-5
3501 Blakewood Ave 53172 414-766-5900
Daniel Cupertino, prin. Fax 766-5905
Lakeview ES 300/PK-5
711 Marion Ave 53172 414-766-5252
Cynthia Dennis, prin. Fax 766-5253
Luther ES 300/PK-5
718 Hawthorne Ave 53172 414-766-5326
Ann Ecker, prin. Fax 766-5327
Rawson ES 500/PK-5
1410 Rawson Ave 53172 414-766-2904
Colin Jacobs, prin. Fax 766-2905
South Milwaukee MS 700/6-8
1001 15th Ave 53172 414-766-5800
Gregory Fuller, prin. Fax 766-5803

Divine Mercy S 300/K-8
695 College Ave 53172 414-764-4360
Judith Kalinowski, prin. Fax 764-6740
Zion Evangelical Lutheran S 200/K-8
3600 S Chicago Ave 53172 414-762-1258
Fonda Fischer, prin. Fax 762-1258

South Wayne, Lafayette, Pop. 473
Black Hawk SD 500/PK-12
PO Box 303 53587 608-439-5400
Charles McNulty, supt. Fax 439-1022
www.blackhawk.k12.wi.us
Black Hawk ES 100/PK-3
PO Box 303 53587 608-439-5444
Jerry Mortimer, prin. Fax 439-1022
Other Schools – See Gratiot

Sparta, Monroe, Pop. 8,827
Sparta Area SD 2,300/K-12
506 N Black River St 54656 608-269-3151
John Hendricks, supt. Fax 366-3526
www.spartan.org
Cataract ES 100/K-3
506 N Black River St 54656 608-272-3111
Michael Crneckiy, prin.
Lawrence-Lawson ES 200/K-3
506 N Black River St 54656 608-269-3181
Tarry Hall, prin. Fax 366-3437
Maplewood ES 100/K-3
506 N Black River St 54656 608-269-8133
Mike Roddick, prin. Fax 366-3461
Southside ES 200/K-3
506 N Black River St 54656 608-269-8186
Tarry Hall, prin. Fax 366-3446
Sparta Meadowview IS 300/4-5
506 N Black River St 54656 608-269-2187
Paul Fischer, prin. Fax 366-3500
Sparta Meadowview MS 600/6-8
506 N Black River St 54656 608-269-2185
Cheri Kulland, prin. Fax 366-3500

St. Johns Evangelical Lutheran S 100/PK-8
419 Jefferson Ave 54656 608-269-6001
Timothy Mueller, prin. Fax 269-6192

St. Patrick S 100/K-8
318 W Oak St 54656 608-269-4748
Jean Suttie, prin. Fax 269-4748

Spencer, Marathon, Pop. 1,833
Spencer SD 600/PK-12
PO Box 418 54479 715-659-5347
Michael Endreas, supt. Fax 659-5470
www.spencer.k12.wi.us
Spencer ES 400/PK-5
PO Box 418 54479 715-659-4642
Michael Endress, prin. Fax 659-5470

Spooner, Washburn, Pop. 2,670
Spooner Area SD 1,300/PK-12
801 County Highway A 54801 715-635-2171
Dr. Donald Haack, supt. Fax 635-7174
www.spooner.k12.wi.us
Spooner ES 400/PK-4
1821 Scribner St 54801 715-635-2174
Christopher Anderson, prin. Fax 635-7984
Spooner MS 400/5-8
500 College St 54801 715-635-2173
Lynnea Lake, prin. Fax 635-7074

St. Francis De Sales S 100/PK-8
300 Oak St 54801 715-635-2774
Patricia Dougherty, prin. Fax 635-7341

Spring Green, Sauk, Pop. 1,436
River Valley SD 1,400/PK-12
660 W Daley St 53588 608-588-2551
Jamie Benson, supt. Fax 588-2558
www.rvschools.org
River Valley MS 300/6-8
660 W Daley St 53588 608-588-2556
Roger Hoffman, prin. Fax 588-2026
Spring Green ES 300/PK-5
830 W Daley St 53588 608-588-2559
Jaime Hegland, prin. Fax 588-2550
Other Schools – See Arena, Lone Rock, Plain

St. John Evangelist S 100/PK-5
PO Box 129 53588 608-588-2021
Karen Marklein, prin. Fax 588-9372

Spring Valley, Pierce, Pop. 1,283
Spring Valley SD 600/PK-12
PO Box 249 54767 715-778-5551
David Wellington, supt. Fax 778-4761
www.springvalley.k12.wi.us
Spring Valley ES 400/PK-6
PO Box 427 54767 715-778-5602
Kenneth Lasure, prin. Fax 778-5615

Stanley, Chippewa, Pop. 3,304
Stanley-Boyd Area SD 1,000/PK-12
507 E 1st Ave 54768 715-644-5534
James Jones, supt. Fax 644-5584
www.stanleyboyd.k12.wi.us
Stanley-Boyd MS 200/6-8
507 E 1st Ave 54768 715-644-5715
Dave Ludy, prin. Fax 644-5584
Stanley ES 400/PK-5
507 E 1st Ave 54768 715-644-5810
Judy Gulcynski, prin. Fax 644-5584
Other Schools – See Boyd

Stetsonville, Taylor, Pop. 542
Medford Area SD
Supt. — See Medford
Stetsonville ES 200/PK-4
W5338 County Road A 54480 715-678-2600
Don Everhard, prin. Fax 678-2162

Stevens Point, Portage, Pop. 24,298
Stevens Point Area SD 5,000/PK-12
1900 Polk St 54481 715-345-5444
Steven Johnson Ed.D., supt. Fax 345-7302
www.wisp.k12.wi.us
Bannach ES 500/PK-6
5400 Walter St, 715-345-5668
John Zellmer, prin. Fax 345-7346
Madison ES 400/K-6
600 Maria Dr 54481 715-345-5419
Mary Jo Lechner, prin. Fax 345-7349
Other Schools – See Junction City, Plover

St. Joseph ECC 100/PK-PK
1901 Lincoln Ave 54481 715-341-2878
Jane Cotter, dir. Fax 342-2013
St. Paul Lutheran S 200/PK-8
1919 Wyatt Ave 54481 715-344-5660
Bill Zuelsdorff, prin. Fax 344-5240
St. Peter MS 200/6-8
708 1st St 54481 715-344-1890
Ellen Lopas, prin. Fax 342-2005
St. Stanislaus S 100/K-2
2150 High St 54481 715-344-3086
Gregg Hansel, prin. Fax 342-2014
St. Stephen S 100/3-5
1335 Clark St 54481 715-344-3751
Gregg Hansel, prin. Fax 344-3766
Stevens Point Christian Academy 50/K-8
801 US Highway 10 W 54481 715-341-3275
Heidi Uitenbroek, admin. Fax 341-3023

Stockbridge, Calumet, Pop. 676
Stockbridge SD 200/PK-12
PO Box 188 53088 920-439-1782
David Moscinski, supt. Fax 439-1150
www.stockbridge.k12.wi.us/
Stockbridge ES 100/PK-5
PO Box 188 53088 920-439-1158
Chad Marx, prin. Fax 439-1150
Stockbridge MS 100/6-8
PO Box 188 53088 920-439-1158
Chad Marx, prin. Fax 439-1150

Stoddard, Vernon, Pop. 817
De Soto Area SD
Supt. — See De Soto
Stoddard ES 100/PK-5
300 N Cottage St 54658 608-457-2101
George Andrews, prin. Fax 457-2007

St. Matthew Evangelical Lutheran S 50/K-8
PO Box 208 54658 608-457-2700
Christopher Avila, prin. Fax 457-2700

Stone Lake, Sawyer
Hayward Community SD
Supt. — See Hayward
Stone Lake ES 100/K-5
16808W 1st St S 54876 715-865-2101
John Becker, prin. Fax 865-2106

St. Francis Solanus S 50/PK-8
13885 W Mission Rd 54876 715-865-3662
Sr. Felissa Zander, prin. Fax 865-4055

Stoughton, Dane, Pop. 12,646
Stoughton Area SD 2,800/K-12
320 North St 53589 608-877-5001
Mary Gavigan, supt. Fax 877-5028
www.stoughton.k12.wi.us
Fox Prairie ES 400/K-5
1601 W South St 53589 608-877-5101
Michael Jamison, prin. Fax 877-5184
Kegonsa ES 400/K-5
1400 Vernon St 53589 608-877-5201
Fred Trotter, prin. Fax 877-5278
River Bluff MS 500/6-8
235 N Forrest St 53589 608-877-5501
Trish Gates, prin. Fax 877-5508
Sandhill ES 200/K-5
1920 Lincoln Ave 53589 608-877-5401
Cheryl Price, prin. Fax 877-5408

Martin Luther Christian Day S 100/PK-5
PO Box 485 53589 608-873-8073
Ken Kluever, prin.
St. Ann S 100/PK-6
324 N Harrison St 53589 608-873-3343
Joan Leonard, prin. Fax 873-6425

Stratford, Marathon, Pop. 1,515
Stratford SD 800/PK-12
PO Box 7 54484 715-687-3130
Scott Winch, supt. Fax 687-4074
www.stratford.k12.wi.us
Stratford ES 400/PK-6
PO Box 7 54484 715-687-3535
Amy Schmitt, prin. Fax 687-4881

St. Joseph S 200/PK-8
PO Box 6 54484 715-687-4145
Debra Johnston, lead tchr. Fax 687-4343

Strum, Trempealeau, Pop. 971
Eleva-Strum SD 700/PK-12
W23597 US Highway 10 54770 715-695-2696
Mark Gruen, admin. Fax 695-3519
www.esschools.k12.wi.us/
Strum PS 200/PK-3
409 8th Ave S 54770 715-695-2916
Craig Semingson, prin. Fax 695-2690
Other Schools – See Eleva

Sturgeon Bay, Door, Pop. 9,180
Sevastopol SD 600/PK-12
4550 State Highway 57 54235 920-743-6282
Steve Cromell, supt. Fax 743-4009
www.sevastopol.k12.wi.us
Sevastopol ES 200/PK-6
4550 State Highway 57 54235 920-743-6282
Joseph Majeski, prin. Fax 743-4009
Sevastopol JHS 100/7-8
4550 State Highway 57 54235 920-743-6282
Adam Baier, prin. Fax 743-4009

Sturgeon Bay SD 1,200/PK-12
1230 Michigan St 54235 920-746-2800
Joe Stutting, supt. Fax 746-3888
www.sturbay.k12.wi.us
Sawyer ES 100/1-2
60 Willow Dr 54235 920-746-2818
Ann Smejkal, prin. Fax 743-5493
Sunrise ES 200/3-5
1414 Rhode Island St 54235 920-746-2815
Ann Smejkal, prin. Fax 743-5823
Sunset ES 100/PK-K
827 N 8th Ave 54235 920-746-2812
Ann Smejkal, prin. Fax 743-6195
Walker MS 300/6-8
19 N 14th Ave 54235 920-746-2810
Randy Watermolen, prin. Fax 746-3885

St. John Bosco S 100/K-8
15 N Elgin Ave 54235 920-743-4144
James Tabaska, prin. Fax 743-3711
St. Peter Evangelical Lutheran S 100/PK-8
108 W Maple St 54235 920-743-4432
Paul Lutze, prin. Fax 743-5388

Sturtevant, Racine, Pop. 6,190
Racine USD
Supt. — See Racine
Schulte ES 400/K-5
8515 Westminster Dr 53177 262-664-6300
Shelley Kritek, prin. Fax 664-6310

Concordia Lutheran S 200/PK-8
8500 Durand Ave 53177 262-884-0991
Jeannine Fuerstenau, prin. Fax 833-0322

St. Sebastian S 100/K-8
3030 95th St 53177 262-886-2806
Ray Henderson, prin. Fax 886-2055

Suamico, Brown
Howard-Suamico SD
Supt. — See Green Bay
Bay Harbor ES K-4
1590 Harbor Lights Rd 54173 920-662-8800
Kyle Siech, prin. Fax 662-8899

Sullivan, Jefferson, Pop. 667
Jefferson SD
Supt. — See Jefferson
Sullivan ES 200/PK-5
618 Bakertown Rd 53178 920-675-1500
John Orcutt, prin. Fax 675-1520

Sun Prairie, Dane, Pop. 25,392
Sun Prairie Area SD 5,900/PK-12
501 S Bird St 53590 608-834-6500
Tim Culver, supt. Fax 834-6555
www.spasd.k12.wi.us
Bird ES 500/PK-5
1170 N Bird St 53590 608-834-7300
Chad Wiedmeyer, prin. Fax 834-7392
Creekside ES PK-5
1251 Okeeffe Ave 53590 608-834-7700
Evelyn Smojver, prin. Fax 834-7792
Eastside ES 600/PK-5
661 Elizabeth Ln 53590 608-834-7400
Craig Coulthart, prin. Fax 834-7492
Horizon ES 400/PK-5
625 N Heatherstone Dr 53590 608-834-7900
Kathi Klaas, prin. Fax 834-7992
Marsh MS 600/6-8
1351 Columbus St 53590 608-834-7600
Clark Luessman, prin. Fax 834-7692
Northside ES 500/PK-5
230 W Klubertanz Dr 53590 608-834-7100
Tony Dugas, prin. Fax 834-7192
Prairie View MS 600/6-8
400 N Thompson Rd 53590 608-834-7800
Nancy Hery, prin. Fax 834-7892
Royal Oaks ES 500/PK-5
2215 Pennsylvania Ave 53590 608-834-7200
Lori Schultz, prin. Fax 834-7292
Westside ES 400/PK-5
1320 Buena Vista Dr 53590 608-834-7500
Richard Mueller, prin. Fax 834-7592

Peace Lutheran S 100/PK-8
1007 Stonehaven Dr 53590 608-834-1200
Paul Patterson, prin. Fax 825-7754
Sacred Hearts Jesus and Mary S 500/PK-8
221 Columbus St 53590 608-837-8508
Kimberlee Frederick, prin. Fax 825-9585

Superior, Douglas, Pop. 26,779
Superior SD 4,800/PK-12
3025 Tower Ave 54880 715-394-8700
Jay Mitchell, supt. Fax 394-8708
www.superior.k12.wi.us
Bryant ES 400/PK-5
1423 Central Ave 54880 715-394-8785
Kate Tesch, prin. Fax 394-8735
Cooper ES 300/PK-5
1807 Missouri Ave 54880 715-394-8790
Brett Brodeen, prin. Fax 394-8793
Four Corners ES 200/K-5
4465 E County Road B 54880 715-399-8911
Patti Lindelof, prin. Fax 399-0119
Great Lakes ES 400/PK-5
129 N 28th St E 54880 715-395-8500
Cindy Magnuson, prin. Fax 395-8505
Lake Superior ES 200/K-5
6200 E 3rd St 54880 715-398-7672
Mark Howard, prin. Fax 398-3131
Northern Lights ES 600/K-5
1201 N 28th St 54880 715-395-3405
Robyn Deshayes, prin. Fax 395-6072
Superior MS 1,000/6-8
3626 Hammond Ave 54880 715-394-8740
Richard Flaherty, prin. Fax 395-8483

Cathedral S 300/PK-8
1419 Baxter Ave 54880 715-392-2976
Tim Johnson, prin. Fax 392-2977

Suring, Oconto, Pop. 563
Suring SD 500/PK-12
PO Box 158 54174 920-842-2178
Robert Ray, supt. Fax 842-4570
www.suring.k12.wi.us
Suring S 300/PK-8
PO Box 158 54174 920-842-2181
Karl Morrin, prin. Fax 842-4570

St. John Lutheran S 50/PK-8
8905 Saint Johns Rd 54174 920-842-4443
Ruben Rakow, prin. Fax 842-4964

Sussex, Waukesha, Pop. 9,812
Hamilton SD 4,400/K-12
W220N6151 Town Line Rd 53089 262-246-1973
Dr. Kathleen Cooke, supt. Fax 246-6552
www.hamiltondist.k12.wi.us/
Maple Avenue ES 500/K-5
W240N6059 Maple Ave 53089 262-246-4220
Kristin Koeper-Hamblin, prin. Fax 246-3914
Templeton MS 1,000/6-8
N59W22490 Silver Spring Dr 53089 262-246-6477
Patricia Polczynski, prin. Fax 246-0465
Woodside ES 700/K-5
W236N7465 Woodside Rd 53089 262-820-1530
James Edmond, prin. Fax 820-0314
Other Schools – See Lannon, Menomonee Falls

Richmond SD 200/PK-8
N56W26530 Richmond Rd 53089 262-538-1360
George Zimmer, supt. Fax 538-1572
www.richmond.k12.wi.us
Richmond ES 200/PK-4
N56W26530 Richmond Rd 53089 262-538-1360
Patricia Antony, prin. Fax 538-1572
Richmond MS 5-8
N56W26530 Richmond Rd 53089 262-538-1360
George Zimmer, prin. Fax 538-1572

Peace Lutheran Academy 50/PK-8
W240N6145 Maple Ave 53089 262-246-3200
Kimberly Hughes, hdmstr. Fax 246-8455

Theresa, Dodge, Pop. 1,265
Lomira SD
Supt. — See Lomira
Theresa ES 200/K-5
PO Box 157 53091 920-488-2181
Lori Loehr, prin. Fax 488-2722

Thiensville, Ozaukee, Pop. 3,123

Calvary Lutheran S 100/PK-8
110 Division St 53092 262-242-3870
Neil Schliewe, prin. Fax 242-5737
Lumen Christi ES 300/PK-5
116 N Orchard St 53092 262-242-7965
Gloria Markowski, prin. Fax 242-7976

Thorp, Clark, Pop. 1,554
Thorp SD 500/PK-12
PO Box 429 54771 715-669-5548
James Montgomery, admin. Fax 669-5403
www.thorp.k12.wi.us/
Thorp ES 300/PK-5
PO Box 449 54771 715-669-5548
James Montgomery, prin. Fax 669-5403

Thorp Catholic S 100/1-8
411 E School St 54771 715-669-5530
Karen Lipinski, lead tchr. Fax 669-5474

Three Lakes, Oneida
Three Lakes SD 600/PK-12
6930 W School St 54562 715-546-3496
George Karling, supt. Fax 546-8125
www.threelakessd.k12.wi.us
Three Lakes ES 200/PK-6
6930 W School St 54562 715-546-3323
William Greb, prin. Fax 546-4351
Three Lakes JHS 100/7-8
6930 W School St 54562 715-546-3321
William Greb, prin. Fax 546-2828
Other Schools – See Rhinelander

Tigerton, Shawano, Pop. 744
Tigerton SD 300/PK-12
PO Box 10 54486 715-535-4000
Nicholas Alioto, admin. Fax 535-3215
www.tigerton.k12.wi.us
Tigerton ES 200/PK-5
PO Box 370 54486 715-535-4000
Donald Aanonsen, prin. Fax 535-1301

Tomah, Monroe, Pop. 8,620
Tomah Area SD 3,000/PK-12
129 W Clifton St 54660 608-374-7004
Robert Fasbender, supt. Fax 372-5087
www.tomah.k12.wi.us
La Grange ES 300/K-5
600 Straw St 54660 608-374-7057
Paul Wiese, prin. Fax 372-5087
Lemonweir ES 300/K-5
711 N Glendale Ave 54660 608-374-7847
Sandra Murray, prin. Fax 372-5087
Miller ES 300/K-5
813 Oak Ave 54660 608-374-7026
Patricia Ellsworth, prin. Fax 372-5087
Timber PUPS Learning Center PK-PK
26232 County Highway CA 54660 608-374-5622
Deb Granger, coord. Fax 372-5087
Tomah MS 600/6-8
612 Hollister Ave 54660 608-374-7882
Cindy Zahrte, prin. Fax 374-7303
Other Schools – See Camp Douglas, Oakdale, Warrens, Wyeville

St. Mary S 200/K-8
315 W Monroe St 54660 608-372-5765
Dannie Francis, prin. Fax 372-4440
St. Paul Lutheran S 100/K-8
505 Superior Ave 54660 608-372-4542
Richard Bakken, prin. Fax 372-2335

Tomahawk, Lincoln, Pop. 3,829
Tomahawk SD 1,600/PK-12
1048 E King Rd 54487 715-453-5551
Roger Rindo, supt. Fax 453-1855
www.tomahawk.k12.wi.us
Tomahawk ES 600/PK-5
1048 E King Rd 54487 715-453-2126
Dan McGuire, prin. Fax 453-5903
Tomahawk MS 400/6-8
1048 E King Rd 54487 715-453-5371
Mitch Hamm, prin. Fax 453-9630

St. Mary S 100/PK-5
110 N 7th St 54487 715-453-3542
Sonja Doughty, prin. Fax 453-6678

Tony, Rusk, Pop. 97
Flambeau SD 300/PK-12
PO Box 86 54563 715-532-3183
William Pfalzgraf, supt. Fax 532-5405
www.flambeau.k12.wi.us
Flambeau S 300/PK-12
PO Box 86 54563 715-532-3183
Connie Gasior, prin. Fax 532-5405

Trempealeau, Trempealeau, Pop. 1,459
Gale-Ettrick-Trempealeau SD
Supt. — See Galesville
Trempealeau ES 200/PK-5
PO Box 277 54661 608-534-6394
Ron Jones, prin. Fax 534-6395

Trevor, Kenosha
Trevor-Wilmot Consolidated SD 300/K-8
26325 Wilmot Rd 53179 262-862-2356
George Steffen, supt. Fax 862-9226
www.trevor-wilmot.net/
Trevor S 200/3-8
26325 Wilmot Rd 53179 262-862-2356
Ted Gavlin, prin. Fax 862-9226
Other Schools – See Wilmot

Turtle Lake, Barron, Pop. 1,008
Turtle Lake SD 500/PK-12
205 Oak St 54889 715-986-2597
Charles Dunlop, supt. Fax 986-2444
www.cesa11.k12.wi.us/turtle-lake
Turtle Lake S 400/PK-8
205 Oak St 54889 715-986-4470
James Connell, prin. Fax 986-2444

Twin Lakes, Kenosha, Pop. 5,513
Twin Lakes SD 4 400/K-8
1218 Wilmot Ave 53181 262-877-2148
Rebecca Vail, supt. Fax 877-4507
www.twinlakes.k12.wi.us/
Lakewood S 400/K-8
1218 Wilmot Ave 53181 262-877-2148
Joseph Price, prin. Fax 877-4507

Two Rivers, Manitowoc, Pop. 12,144
Two Rivers SD 1,900/K-12
4521 Lincoln Ave 54241 920-793-4560
Randy Fredrikson, supt. Fax 793-4014
www.trschools.k12.wi.us
Clarke MS 600/5-8
4608 Bellevue Pl 54241 920-794-1614
Stanley Phelps, prin. Fax 793-1819
Koenig ES 200/K-4
1114 Lowell St 54241 920-794-7522
Lisa Quistorf, prin. Fax 794-6120
Magee ES 400/K-4
3502 Glenwood St 54241 920-793-1118
Lisa Quistorf, prin. Fax 794-7449

St. John's Lutheran S 100/K-8
3607 45th St 54241 920-793-5001
James Hahn, prin. Fax 793-8669
St. Peter the Fisherman S 200/PK-8
1322 33rd St 54241 920-794-7622
Sr. Mary Lee Schommer, prin. Fax 553-7625

Union Grove, Racine, Pop. 4,614
Union Grove J1 SD 700/K-8
1745 Milldrum St 53182 262-878-2015
Gary Damaschke, supt. Fax 878-3133
www.uges.k12.wi.us
Union Grove S 700/K-8
1745 Milldrum St 53182 262-878-2015
Brenda Stevenson, prin. Fax 878-3133

Yorkville J2 SD 400/K-8
18621 Washington Ave 53182 262-878-3759
Dave Alexander, admin. Fax 878-3794
www.yorkville.elementary.k12.wi.us
Yorkville S 400/K-8
18621 Washington Ave 53182 262-878-3759
Eileen Graf, admin. Fax 878-3794

Providence Catholic S - East Campus 100/K-5
1481 172nd Ave 53182 262-859-2007
Wilson Shierk, prin. Fax 859-2604
Union Grove Christian S 100/PK-12
PO Box 87 53182 262-878-1264
Lee Morey, prin. Fax 878-2085

Valders, Manitowoc, Pop. 995
Valders Area SD 1,100/PK-12
138 Wilson St 54245 920-775-9500
Thomas Hughes, supt. Fax 775-9509
www.valders.k12.wi.us
Valders ES 400/PK-4
331 W Wilson St 54245 920-775-9510
Jason Procknow, prin. Fax 775-9509
Valders MS 300/5-8
138 Jefferson St 54245 920-775-9520
Derrick Krey, prin. Fax 775-9509

Verona, Dane, Pop. 10,166
Madison Metro SD
Supt. — See Madison
Olson ES K-5
801 Redan Dr 53593 608-442-2600
Pam Emmerich, prin. Fax 442-2699

Middleton-Cross Plains Area SD
Supt. — See Middleton
West Middleton ES 300/K-5
7627 W Mineral Point Rd 53593 608-829-9360
Doug Rykal, prin. Fax 829-1147

Verona Area SD 3,700/PK-12
700 N Main St 53593 608-845-4300
Dean Gorrell, supt. Fax 845-4321
www.verona.k12.wi.us
Badger Ridge MS 400/6-8
740 N Main St 53593 608-845-4100
David Jennings, prin. Fax 845-4120
Country View ES 500/K-5
710 Lone Pine Way 53593 608-845-4800
Michelle Nummerdor, prin. Fax 845-4820

Early Learning Center 50/PK-PK
300 Richard St 53593 608-845-4400
Lynette Fassbender, prin. Fax 845-4420
Glacier Edge ES K-5
800 Kimball Ln 53593 608-497-2100
Theresa Taylor, prin. Fax 497-2120
Sugar Creek ES 300/K-5
420 Church Ave 53593 608-845-4700
Todd Brunner, prin. Fax 845-4720
Other Schools – See Fitchburg

Vesper, Wood, Pop. 529
Wisconsin Rapids SD
Supt. — See Wisconsin Rapids
Vesper Community Academy 100/PK-6
6443 Virginia St 54489 715-569-4115
Terry Whitmore, prin. Fax 569-5300

Viola, Vernon, Pop. 659
Kickapoo Area SD 500/PK-12
S6520 State Highway 131 54664 608-627-0102
Thomas Simonson, supt. Fax 627-0118
www.kickapoo.k12.wi.us
Kickapoo ES 200/PK-5
S6520 State Highway 131 54664 608-627-0107
Thomas Simonson, prin. Fax 627-0118

Viroqua, Vernon, Pop. 4,424
Viroqua Area SD 1,100/PK-12
115 N Education Ave 54665 608-637-1186
Dr. Robert Knadle, supt. Fax 637-8554
www.viroqua.k12.wi.us
Viroqua ES 500/PK-4
115 N Education Ave 54665 608-637-7071
William Huebsch, prin. Fax 637-1211
Viroqua MS 300/5-8
100 Blackhawk Dr 54665 608-637-3171
John Schneider, prin. Fax 637-8034

Cornerstone Christian Academy 100/PK-12
S3656 US Highway 14 54665 608-634-4102
Wyman Felde, admin. Fax 634-4162
English Lutheran S 50/K-8
741 N East Ave 54665 608-637-7218
Mark Thiesfeldt, prin.
Pleasant Ridge Waldorf S 200/PK-8
431 E Court St 54665 608-637-7828
Anne-Marie Fryer, admin. Fax 637-3952

Wabeno, Forest
Wabeno Area SD 600/PK-12
PO Box 460 54566 715-473-2592
Kimberly Odekirk, supt. Fax 473-5201
www.wabeno.k12.wi.us
Wabeno ES 300/PK-6
PO Box 460 54566 715-473-3633
Jay Weckler, prin. Fax 473-5201

Wales, Waukesha, Pop. 2,610
Kettle Moraine SD 4,400/PK-12
563 A J Allen Cir 53183 262-968-6300
Patricia Deklotz, supt. Fax 968-6391
www.kmsd.edu/
Wales ES 500/PK-5
219 N Oak Crest Dr 53183 262-968-6400
Rick Grothaus, prin. Fax 968-6405
Other Schools – See Delafield, Dousman, Genesee Depot

Walworth, Walworth, Pop. 2,682
Walworth J1 SD 600/PK-8
PO Box 220 53184 262-275-6896
Pamela Knorr, supt. Fax 275-2272
www.walworth.k12.wi.us
Walworth S 600/PK-8
PO Box 220 53184 262-275-6896
Pamela Knorr, prin. Fax 275-2272

Warrens, Monroe, Pop. 291
Tomah Area SD
Supt. — See Tomah
Warrens ES 100/PK-5
PO Box 8 54666 608-374-7800
Sandra Murray, prin. Fax 372-5087

Washburn, Bayfield, Pop. 2,281
Washburn SD 600/PK-12
PO Box 730 54891 715-373-6199
Susan Masterson, supt. Fax 373-0586
www.washburn.k12.wi.us
Washburn ES 200/PK-5
PO Box 730 54891 715-373-6199
Susan Masterson, prin. Fax 373-0586
Washburn MS 100/6-8
PO Box 730 54891 715-373-6199
Susan Masterson, prin. Fax 373-0586

St. Louis S 100/PK-6
713 Washington Ave 54891 715-373-5322
Betty Swiston, prin. Fax 373-0365

Washington Island, Door
Washington SD 100/K-12
888 Main Rd 54246 920-847-2507
Susan Churchill-Chastan, supt. Fax 847-2865
www.island.k12.wi.us
Washington Island S 100/K-8
888 Main Rd 54246 920-847-2507
Susan Churchill-Chastan, prin. Fax 847-2865

Waterford, Racine, Pop. 4,828
Washington-Caldwell SD 200/K-8
8937 Big Bend Rd 53185 262-662-3466
Mark Pienkos, supt. Fax 662-9888
www.washcald.com
Washington S 200/K-8
8937 Big Bend Rd 53185 262-662-3466
Mark Pienkos, prin. Fax 662-9888

Waterford Graded JSD 1 1,600/K-8
819 W Main St 53185 262-514-8250
Sally Jo Nelson, supt. Fax 514-8251
www.waterford.k12.wi.us
Evergreen ES 400/K-6
817 W Main St 53185 262-514-8210
Chris Multhauf, prin. Fax 514-8211
Fox River MS 400/7-8
921 W Main St 53185 262-514-8240
Darlene Markle, prin. Fax 514-8241
Trailside ES 400/K-6
615 N Milwaukee St 53185 262-514-8220
Jeffrey Worgull, prin. Fax 514-8221
Woodfield ES 400/K-6
905 Barnes Dr 53185 262-514-8230
Shirley Guelig, prin. Fax 514-8231

St. Peters Lutheran S 100/PK-8
145 S 6th St 53185 262-534-6066
Tiffany van Sliedrecht, prin. Fax 534-2571
St. Thomas Aquinas S 200/K-8
302 S 2nd St 53185 262-534-2265
Pamela Kramer, prin. Fax 534-5549

Waterloo, Jefferson, Pop. 3,282
Waterloo SD 800/PK-12
813 N Monroe St 53594 920-478-3633
Connie Schiestl, supt. Fax 478-3821
www.waterloo.k12.wi.us
Waterloo ES 300/PK-4
785 N Monroe St 53594 920-478-2168
Maureen Adams, prin. Fax 478-9589
Waterloo MS 100/5-8
865 N Monroe St 53594 920-478-2696
Ann Kox, prin. Fax 478-3987

St. John Lutheran S 100/PK-8
413 E Madison St 53594 920-478-2707
Mark Eternick, prin. Fax 478-3745
St. Joseph S 100/PK-6
387 S Monroe St 53594 920-478-3221

Watertown, Jefferson, Pop. 22,816
Watertown Unified SD 3,600/PK-12
111 Dodge St 53094 920-262-1460
Douglas Keiser Ph.D., supt. Fax 262-1469
www.watertown.k12.wi.us
Douglas ES 400/PK-5
1120 Center St 53098 920-262-1495
Jennifer Borst, prin. Fax 262-7596
Lebanon ES 100/K-5
W4712 County Road O 53098 920-925-3712
Erin Meyer, prin.
Lincoln ES 200/PK-3
210 N Montgomery St 53094 920-262-1465
Erin Meyer, prin. Fax 262-7581
Riverside MS 800/6-8
131 Hall St 53094 920-262-1480
Kent Jacobson, prin. Fax 262-1468
Schurz ES 300/K-5
1508 Neenah St 53094 920-262-1485
Andrew Bare, prin. Fax 206-7438
Watertown 4 Kids Preschool PK-PK
111 Dodge St 53094 920-262-1460
Ivan Thompson, dir. Fax 262-1469
Webster ES 500/PK-5
634 S 12th St 53094 920-262-1490
Brad Clark, prin. Fax 262-1493

Calvary Baptist Christian S 100/K-8
792 Milford St 53094 920-262-0612
Douglas Stein, admin. Fax 262-1822
Faith Lutheran S 50/PK-5
626 Milford St 53094 920-261-8060
Judi Hoeppner, prin. Fax 261-8060
Good Shepherd Lutheran S 100/PK-8
1611 E Main St 53094 920-261-2579
Gene Ladendorf, prin. Fax 261-2574
Lebanon Lutheran S 100/PK-8
N534 County Road R 53098 920-925-3791
Donna Gerndt, prin. Fax 925-3799
St. Bernard S 100/PK-5
111 S Montgomery St 53094 920-261-7204
Jeffrey Allen, prin. Fax 261-7215
St. Henry S 200/PK-8
300 E Cady St 53094 920-261-2586
Francine Butzine, prin. Fax 261-3681
St. John Lutheran S 200/PK-8
317 N 6th St 53094 920-261-3756
Larry Parker, admin. Fax 261-5147
St. Mark's Lutheran S 300/PK-8
705 E Cady St 53094 920-262-8501
Frederick Uttech, prin. Fax 262-8517
Trinity-St. Luke's Lutheran S 100/PK-4
801 S 5th St 53094 920-261-3615
James Moeller, prin. Fax 261-5840
Trinity-St. Luke's Lutheran S 100/5-8
303 Clark St 53094 920-206-1844
James Moeller, prin. Fax 206-1750

Waukesha, Waukesha, Pop. 67,658
Waukesha SD 12,400/PK-12
222 Maple Ave 53186 262-970-1000
Todd Gray, supt. Fax 970-1021
www.waukesha.k12.wi.us
Banting ES 500/K-6
2019 Butler Dr 53186 262-970-1200
Cynthia Gannon, prin. Fax 970-1220
Bethesda ES 500/PK-6
730 S University Dr 53188 262-970-1300
Randall Kunkel, prin. Fax 970-1320
Blair ES 300/K-6
301 Hyde Park Ave 53188 262-970-1400
Janice Kirkel, prin. Fax 970-1420
Butler MS 600/7-8
310 N Hine Ave 53188 262-970-2900
Sara Behrendt, prin. Fax 970-2920

Central MS 700/7-8
400 N Grand Ave 53186 262-970-3100
Jeff Copson, prin. Fax 970-3120
Hadfield ES 300/K-6
733 Linden St 53186 262-970-1500
Stacy McCoy, prin. Fax 970-1520
Hawthorne ES 300/PK-6
1111 Maitland Dr 53188 262-970-1600
Joseph Russell, prin. Fax 970-1620
Heyer ES 500/PK-6
1209 Heyer Dr 53186 262-970-1700
Greg Deets, prin. Fax 970-1720
Hillcrest ES 200/PK-3
2200 Davidson Rd 53186 262-970-1800
Michael Sukawaty, prin. Fax 970-1820
Horning MS 600/7-8
2000 Wolf Rd 53186 262-970-3300
Mark Wegner, prin. Fax 970-3320
Lowell ES 400/PK-6
140 N Grandview Blvd 53188 262-970-1900
Joe Beine, prin. Fax 970-1920
Meadowbrook ES 400/PK-6
3130 Rolling Ridge Dr 53188 262-970-2000
Don Charpentier, prin. Fax 970-2020
Prairie ES 400/PK-6
1801 Center Rd 53189 262-970-2200
Ryan Krohn, prin. Fax 970-2220
Randall ES 400/PK-6
114 S Charles St 53186 262-970-2300
Bonnie Schlais, prin. Fax 970-2320
Rose Glen ES 600/PK-6
W273S3845 Brookhill Dr 53189 262-970-2400
Christopher Kluck, prin. Fax 970-2420
Saratoga ES 200/K-6
130 Walton Ave 53186 262-970-2500
Jill Ries, prin. Fax 970-2520
Summit View ES 600/PK-6
2100 Summit Ave 53188 262-970-2600
Jeff Peterson, prin. Fax 970-2620
White Rock ES 300/K-6
1150 Whiterock Ave 53186 262-970-2700
Dorothy Smith, prin. Fax 970-2720
Whittier ES 400/PK-6
1103 S East Ave 53186 262-970-2800
William White, prin. Fax 970-2820
Other Schools – See Brookfield

Beautiful Savior Lutheran S 100/PK-8
1205 S East Ave 53186 262-542-6558
Yvonne Gerth, prin. Fax 542-8574
Montessori S of Waukesha 200/PK-7
2600 Summit Ave 53188 262-547-2545
William Walsh, prin. Fax 547-2715
Mount Calvary Lutheran S 200/K-8
1941 Madison St 53188 262-547-6740
Timothy Kassulke, prin. Fax 522-3234
St. Joseph MS 200/6-8
818 N East Ave 53186 262-896-2930
Kathy Rempe, prin. Fax 896-2935
St. Mary S 300/PK-5
520 E Newhall Ave 53186 262-896-2932
Lisa Kovaleski, prin. Fax 896-2931
St. William S 200/PK-5
444 N Moreland Blvd 53188 262-896-2920
Robert Radomski, prin. Fax 896-2931
Trinity Lutheran S 300/PK-8
1060 Whiterock Ave 53186 262-547-8020
David Schroeder, prin. Fax 547-7331
West Suburban Christian Academy 300/PK-8
1721 Northview Rd 53188 262-650-7777
Lynda Meleski, prin. Fax 995-7771

Waumandee, Buffalo

St. Boniface S 50/PK-8
S2026 County Road U 54622 608-626-2611
Christine Pyka, lead tchr.

Waunakee, Dane, Pop. 10,360
Waunakee Community SD 2,900/PK-12
905 Bethel Cir 53597 608-849-2000
Randy Guttenberg, supt. Fax 849-2350
www.waunakee.k12.wi.us
Arboretum ES K-4
1350 Arboretum Dr 53597 608-849-1800
Sheila Weihert, prin. Fax 849-1810
Waunakee Heritage ES 300/PK-4
501 South St 53597 608-849-2030
Dan Carter, prin. Fax 849-2265
Waunakee IS 500/5-6
303 South St 53597 608-849-2176
Christine Hetzel, prin. Fax 849-2198
Waunakee MS 600/7-8
1001 South St 53597 608-849-2060
Shelley Weiss, prin. Fax 849-2088
Waunakee Prairie ES 400/K-5
700 N Madison St 53597 608-849-2200
Lee DePas, prin. Fax 849-2255

Madison Country Day S 300/PK-12
5606 River Rd 53597 608-850-6000
Luke Felker, hdmstr. Fax 850-6006
St. John the Baptist S 300/PK-6
114 E 3rd St 53597 608-849-5325
Conni Stark, prin. Fax 849-5342

Waupaca, Waupaca, Pop. 5,877
Waupaca SD 2,400/K-12
515 School St 54981 715-258-4121
David Poeschl, supt. Fax 258-4125
www.waupaca.k12.wi.us/
Chain O'Lakes ES 200/K-2
N3160 Silver Lake Dr 54981 715-258-4151
Susan Davenport, prin. Fax 258-4512
Waupaca Learning Center ES 800/K-5
1515 Shoemaker Rd 54981 715-258-4141
Boyd Simonson, prin. Fax 258-4138

Waupaca MS 600/6-8
1149 Shoemaker Rd 54981 715-258-4140
Wayne Verdon, prin. Fax 256-5681

Immanuel Evangelical Lutheran S 50/K-8
1120 Evans St 54981 715-258-2769
Aaron Winkelman, prin. Fax 256-2660

Waupun, Dodge, Pop. 10,558
Waupun SD 1,100/PK-12
950 Wilcox St 53963 920-324-9341
Randall Refsland, supt. Fax 324-2630
www.waupun.k12.wi.us
Meadow View PS 200/PK-2
101 Young St 53963 920-324-3361
James Docter, prin. Fax 324-0490
Rock River IS 200/3-6
451 E Spring St 53963 920-324-9322
Steven Buss, prin. Fax 324-2929

Central Wisconsin Christian S 100/PK-5
520 McKinley St 53963 920-324-2721
Mark Buteyn, prin. Fax 324-0252

Wausau, Marathon, Pop. 37,292
Wausau SD 8,600/PK-12
PO Box 359 54402 715-261-0500
Stephen Murley, supt. Fax 261-2503
www.wausau.k12.wi.us
Franklin ES 300/K-5
1509 5th St 54403 715-261-0000
Jon Euting, prin. Fax 261-2144
Grant ES 200/K-5
500 N 4th Ave 54401 715-261-0190
Andrea Sheridan, prin. Fax 261-2223
Hawthorn Hills ES 300/K-5
1600 Kickbusch St 54403 715-261-0045
Christine Budnik, prin. Fax 261-2291
Hewitt-Texas ES 100/K-5
T10331 Quarry Rd 54403 715-261-0015
Dan Sullivan, prin. Fax 261-2305
Jefferson ES 300/K-5
500 W Randolph St 54401 715-261-0175
Marla Berg, prin. Fax 261-3100
Jones ES 300/K-5
1018 S 12th Ave 54401 715-261-0950
Steve Wermund, prin. Fax 261-2157
Kiefer Educational Center 400/PK-K
700 W Strowbridge St 54401 715-261-0265
Julie Burmesch, prin. Fax 261-3499
Lincoln ES 200/K-5
720 S 6th Ave 54401 715-261-0965
Alice Kuether, prin. Fax 261-2690
Maine ES 200/K-5
5901 N 44th Ave 54401 715-261-0250
Dan Sullivan, prin. Fax 675-6852
Mann MS 900/6-8
3101 N 13th St 54403 715-261-0725
Ty Becker, prin. Fax 261-2035
Marshall ES 300/K-5
1918 Lamont St 54403 715-261-0060
Shawn Sullivan, prin. Fax 261-2355
Muir MS 1,000/6-8
1400 Stewart Ave 54401 715-261-0100
Dean Hess, prin. Fax 261-2461
Rib Mountain ES 300/K-5
2701 Robin Ln 54401 715-261-0220
Julie Schell, prin. Fax 261-2752
Riverview ES 400/K-5
4303 Troy St 54403 715-261-0030
Steve Miller, prin. Fax 261-3905
South Mountain ES 300/K-5
5400 Bittersweet Rd 54401 715-261-0235
Julie Sprague, prin. Fax 261-3930
Stettin ES 300/K-5
109 N 56th Ave 54401 715-261-0205
Paul Seiser, prin. Fax 261-2801

Faith Christian Academy 100/K-12
E1045 County Road J 54403 715-842-0797
Joann Korns, admin. Fax 842-0797
Hillside Christian S 50/1-8
6300 Bittersweet Rd 54401 715-241-7722
Jody Marsh, admin. Fax 241-7723
Montessori Children's Village 50/PK-5
214 Sherman St 54401 715-842-9540
Patricia Filak, prin. Fax 842-0534
Newman Catholic ES at St. Anne 300/PK-5
604 N 6th Ave 54401 715-845-5754
Sandra Gilge, prin. Fax 842-4021
Newman Catholic ES at St. Michael 100/PK-5
615 Stark St 54403 715-848-0206
Jeanne Lang, prin. Fax 845-6852
Newman Catholic MS at St. Matthew 100/6-8
225 S 28th Ave 54401 715-842-4857
Tina Meyer, prin. Fax 845-2937
Newman CDC at Holy Name Parish PK-PK
1122 S 9th Ave 54401 715-848-3281
Vicki Koeppel, dir. Fax 849-2881
Our Savior's Evangelical Lutheran S 50/K-8
703 Flieth St 54401 715-845-3253
Beth Krohn, prin. Fax 849-8139
St. John Lutheran S 50/PK-8
E10723 County Road Z 54403 715-845-7031
Paul Belmas, prin. Fax 849-9558
Trinity Lutheran S 200/K-8
501 Stewart Ave 54401 715-848-0166
D.J. Schult, admin. Fax 843-7278

Wausaukee, Marinette, Pop. 551
Wausaukee SD 600/PK-12
PO Box 258 54177 715-856-5153
Jan Dooley, supt. Fax 856-6592
www.wausaukee.k12.wi.us
Wausaukee ES 300/PK-6
PO Box 258 54177 715-856-5152
Jan Dooley, prin. Fax 856-6592
Wausaukee JHS 100/7-8
PO Box 258 54177 715-856-5151
Jan Dooley, prin. Fax 856-6592

Wautoma, Waushara, Pop. 2,103
Wautoma Area SD 1,500/PK-12
PO Box 870 54982 920-787-7112
Jeff Kasuboski, supt. Fax 787-1389
www.wautoma.k12.wi.us
Parkside MS 500/4-8
PO Box 870 54982 920-787-4577
Tom Rheinheimer, prin. Fax 787-7336
Riverview ES 400/PK-3
PO Box 870 54982 920-787-4590
Ann Fajfer, prin. Fax 787-1556
Other Schools – See Redgranite

Wauwatosa, Milwaukee, Pop. 45,014
Wauwatosa SD 6,700/PK-12
12121 W North Ave 53226 414-773-1000
Phil Ertl, supt. Fax 773-1019
www.wauwatosaschools.org
Eisenhower ES 400/PK-5
11600 W Center St 53222 414-773-1100
Kristin Bowers, prin. Fax 773-1120
Jefferson ES 300/PK-5
6927 Maple Ter 53213 414-773-1200
Tom Seidl, prin. Fax 773-1220
Lincoln ES 300/PK-5
1741 N Wauwatosa Ave 53213 414-773-1300
Dean Nemoir, prin. Fax 773-1320
Longfellow MS 800/6-8
7600 W North Ave 53213 414-773-2400
Jason Galien, prin. Fax 773-2420
Madison ES 300/PK-5
9925 W Glendale Ave, 414-773-1400
Lori Lester, prin. Fax 773-1420
McKinley ES 400/PK-5
2435 N 89th St 53226 414-773-1500
Mark Carter, prin. Fax 773-1520
Roosevelt ES 500/PK-5
2535 N 73rd St 53213 414-773-1600
Frank Calarco, prin. Fax 773-1620
Underwood ES 300/PK-5
11132 W Potter Rd 53226 414-773-1700
Mike Leach, prin. Fax 773-1720
Washington ES 400/PK-5
2166 N 68th St 53213 414-773-1800
Anthony Bonds, prin. Fax 773-1820
Whitman MS 600/6-8
11100 W Center St 53222 414-773-2600
Jeff Keranen, prin. Fax 773-2620
Wilson ES 300/PK-5
1060 Glenview Ave 53213 414-773-1900
Jenny Keats, prin. Fax 773-1920

Christ King S 400/K-8
2646 N Swan Blvd 53226 414-258-4160
Sr. Janet Neureuther, prin. Fax 258-1993
Our Redeemer Lutheran S 400/PK-8
10025 W North Ave 53226 414-258-4558
Mary Irish, prin. Fax 258-5775
St. Bernard S 100/K-8
1500 N Wauwatosa Ave 53213 414-258-9977
William Strube, prin. Fax 258-9972
St. John's Evangelical Lutheran S 200/K-8
1278 Dewey Ave 53213 414-258-4214
Scott Uecker, prin. Fax 453-9322
St. Joseph S 200/K-8
2750 N 122nd St 53222 414-771-4626
Patrice Wadzinski, prin. Fax 771-9826
St. Jude the Apostle S 400/K-8
800 Glenview Ave 53213 414-771-1520
Catherine LaDien, prin. Fax 771-3748
St. Pius X S 100/PK-8
2520 N Wauwatosa Ave 53213 414-778-0880
Bruce Varick, prin. Fax 257-1256

Wauzeka, Crawford, Pop. 765
Wauzeka-Steuben SD 200/PK-12
301 E Main St 53826 608-875-5311
Roger Kordus, supt. Fax 875-5100
www.wauzeka.k12.wi.us
Wauzeka-Steuben S 200/PK-12
301 E Main St 53826 608-875-5311
John Luster, prin. Fax 875-5100

Webster, Burnett, Pop. 683
Webster SD 600/PK-12
PO Box 9 54893 715-866-4391
Jim Erickson, supt. Fax 866-4283
www.webster.k12.wi.us
Webster ES 200/PK-4
PO Box 9 54893 715-866-8211
Martha Anderson, prin. Fax 866-8262
Webster MS 100/5-6
PO Box 9 54893 715-866-4282
Martha Anderson, prin. Fax 866-4377

West Allis, Milwaukee, Pop. 58,798
West Allis SD 7,800/PK-12
9333 W Lincoln Ave 53227 414-604-3000
Kurt Wachholz, supt. Fax 546-5795
www.wawm.k12.wi.us
Franklin ES 300/PK-5
2060 S 86th St 53227 414-604-3710
Michelle Weisrock, prin. Fax 546-5682
Irving ES 300/PK-5
10230 W Grant St 53227 414-604-4010
Margaret Crowley, prin. Fax 546-5641
Jefferson ES 400/PK-5
7229 W Becher St 53219 414-604-4110
Lynn Herbst, prin. Fax 546-5683
Lincoln IS 100/5-8
7815 W Lapham St 53214 414-604-4210
Diane Ulezelski, prin. Fax 777-7256
Longfellow ES 200/PK-5
2211 S 60th St 53219 414-604-4310
Peter Gull, prin. Fax 546-5540
Madison ES 200/PK-5
1117 S 104th St 53214 414-604-4410
Joanne Butler, prin. Fax 256-6782
Mann ES 300/PK-5
6213 W Lapham St 53214 414-604-3910
Jeff Thomson, prin. Fax 546-5554
Mitchell ES 300/PK-5
10125 W Montana Ave 53227 414-604-4510
Joseph Hill, prin. Fax 546-5684
Walker ES 200/PK-5
900 S 119th St 53214 414-604-4710
Johnna Noll, prin. Fax 479-3481
Wilson ES 300/PK-5
8710 W Orchard St 53214 414-604-4810
Daniel Hester, prin. Fax 256-6781
Wright IS 700/6-8
9501 W Cleveland Ave 53227 414-604-3410
Jeff Taylor, prin. Fax 546-5785
Other Schools – See New Berlin, West Milwaukee

Good Shepherds Evangelical Lutheran S 100/K-8
1337 S 100th St 53214 414-774-8520
Douglas Needham, prin. Fax 443-9947
Grace Christian Academy 200/PK-12
8420 W Beloit Rd 53227 414-327-4200
Cynthia Hummitzsch, admin. Fax 327-4386
Lamb of God Lutheran S 50/K-8
2217 S 99th St 53227 414-321-8780
Jay Schwall, prin. Fax 321-4184
Mary Queen of Saints Academy 100/PK-8
1435 S 92nd St 53214 414-476-0751
Gail Kraig, prin. Fax 259-9285
Mary Queen of Saints Academy - Lincoln 100/K-8
6021 W Lincoln Ave 53219 414-327-5020
Donna Larson, prin. Fax 327-7308
St. Paul Lutheran S 200/PK-8
7821 W Lincoln Ave 53219 414-541-6251
Duane Graf, prin. Fax 541-2205
Trinity Lutheran ECC 50/PK-K
2500 S 68th St 53219 414-321-6470
S. Durham, dir. Fax 321-6470

West Baraboo, Sauk, Pop. 1,373
Baraboo SD
Supt. — See Baraboo
Willson ES 300/K-5
146 Berkley Blvd 53913 608-355-3925
Molly Fitzgerald, prin. Fax 355-4678

West Bend, Washington, Pop. 29,549
West Bend SD 6,800/K-12
735 S Main St 53095 262-335-5435
Dr. Patricia Herdrich, supt. Fax 335-5470
www.west-bend.k12.wi.us
Badger MS 800/6-8
710 S Main St 53095 262-335-5456
Ted Neitzke, prin. Fax 335-6187
Barton ES 400/K-5
614 School Pl 53090 262-335-5511
James Curler, prin. Fax 335-6191
Decorah ES 400/K-5
1225 Sylvan Way 53095 262-335-5476
Nan Lustig, prin. Fax 335-5192
Fair Park ES 500/K-5
519 N Indiana Ave 53090 262-335-5516
Michael Murphy, prin. Fax 335-6196
Green Tree ES 500/K-5
1330 Green Tree Rd 53090 262-335-5521
Allen Fritschel, prin. Fax 335-8243
McLane ES 600/K-5
833 Chestnut St 53095 262-335-5487
Andy Kasik, prin. Fax 335-8245
Silverbrook MS 600/6-8
120 N Silverbrook Dr 53095 262-335-5499
Jean Broadwater, prin. Fax 335-5610
Other Schools – See Jackson

Good Shepherd Lutheran S 200/PK-8
777 S Indiana Ave 53095 262-334-7881
James Sievert, prin. Fax 334-8039
Holy Angels S 400/PK-8
230 N 8th Ave 53095 262-338-1148
Michael Sternig, prin. Fax 334-6116
St. Frances Cabrini S 400/K-8
529 Hawthorn Dr 53095 262-334-7142
Mark Quinn, prin. Fax 334-8168
St. John Lutheran S 200/PK-8
809 S 6th Ave 53095 262-334-3077
David Kellerman, prin. Fax 334-3591
St. Mary Immaculate Conception S 100/PK-8
415 Roosevelt Dr 53090 262-338-5602
Gail Kraig, prin. Fax 335-2475

Westby, Vernon, Pop. 2,142
Westby Area SD 1,200/PK-12
206 West Ave S 54667 608-634-0101
Michael Murphy, supt. Fax 634-0118
westby.k12.wi.us
Westby ES 300/PK-4
122 Nelson St 54667 608-634-0500
Mark Anderson, prin. Fax 634-0518
Westby MS 300/5-8
206 West Ave S 54667 608-634-0200
Clarice Nestingen, prin. Fax 634-0218
Other Schools – See Coon Valley

Westfield, Marquette, Pop. 1,211
Westfield SD 1,200/PK-12
N7046 County Road CH 53964 608-296-2107
Roger Schmidt, supt. Fax 296-2938
www.westfield.k12.wi.us
Pioneer Westfield MS 200/7-8
N7046 County Road CH 53964 608-296-2141
Julia Ferris, prin. Fax 296-2293
Westfield ES 300/K-6
329 Hawk Ln 53964 608-296-2224
Cory Parman, prin. Fax 296-4001
Other Schools – See Coloma, Neshkoro, Oxford

West Milwaukee, Milwaukee, Pop. 4,012
West Allis SD
Supt. — See West Allis
Pershing ES 300/PK-5
1330 S 47th St 53214 414-604-4610
Chvala Brown, prin. Fax 649-4981
West Milwaukee IS 500/6-8
5104 W Greenfield Ave 53214 414-604-3310
Jeffrey Borland, prin. Fax 389-3815

Weston, Marathon, Pop. 12,921
D.C. Everest Area SD
Supt. — See Schofield
D.C. Everest MS 900/6-7
9302 Schofield Ave 54476 715-241-9700
Casey Nye, prin. Fax 241-9697
Mountain Bay ES K-5
8602 Schofield Ave 54476 715-355-0302
Patrick Phalen, prin. Fax 355-0307

West Salem, LaCrosse, Pop. 4,709
West Salem SD 1,700/PK-12
405 E Hamlin St 54669 608-786-0700
Nancy Burns, supt. Fax 786-2960
www.wsalem.k12.wi.us
West Salem ES 800/PK-5
475 N Mark St 54669 608-786-1662
Barbara Buswell, prin. Fax 786-3415
West Salem MS 400/6-8
450 N Mark St 54669 608-786-2090
Dean Buchanan, prin. Fax 786-1081

Christ-St. John's Lutheran S 100/PK-8
500 Park St 54669 608-786-1250
Robert Makinen, prin. Fax 786-1105
Coulee Region Christian S 100/PK-12
230 W Garland St 54669 608-786-3004
Daniel Odenbach, prin. Fax 786-3005

Weyauwega, Waupaca, Pop. 1,772
Weyauwega-Fremont SD 1,000/PK-12
PO Box 580 54983 920-867-2148
F. James Harlan, supt. Fax 867-2510
www.wegafremont.k12.wi.us
Weyauwega ES 300/K-5
PO Box 580 54983 920-867-2148
Kirk Delwiche, prin. Fax 867-2510
Weyauwega MS 200/6-8
PO Box 580 54983 920-867-2148
Scott Bleck, prin. Fax 867-2510
Other Schools – See Fremont

Christ Lutheran S 50/PK-8
N6412 State Road 49 54983 920-867-3263
Ila Robbert, prin. Fax 867-3263
St. Peter Lutheran S 100/K-8
312 W Main St 54983 920-867-2200
Jeff Miller, prin. Fax 867-4464

Weyerhaeuser, Rusk, Pop. 331
Weyerhaeuser Area SD 200/K-12
402 N 2nd St 54895 715-353-2254
Christopher Nelson, supt. Fax 353-2288
www.fwsd.k12.wi.us
Weyerhaeuser S 100/K-8
402 N 2nd St 54895 715-353-2254
Rhonda Coggins, prin. Fax 353-2288

Whitefish Bay, Milwaukee, Pop. 13,508
Whitefish Bay SD 2,900/PK-12
1200 E Fairmount Ave 53217 414-963-3921
James Rickabaugh, supt. Fax 963-3959
www.wfbschools.com
Cumberland ES 600/PK-5
4780 N Marlborough Dr 53211 414-963-3943
Jayne Heffron, prin. Fax 963-3945
Richards ES 700/PK-5
5812 N Santa Monica Blvd 53217 414-963-3951
Mark Tenorio, prin. Fax 963-3946
Whitefish Bay MS 600/6-8
1144 E Henry Clay St 53217 414-963-6800
Lisa Gies, prin. Fax 963-6808

Holy Family S 200/PK-8
4849 N Wildwood Ave 53217 414-332-8175
Angela Little, prin. Fax 961-7396
St. Monica S 400/K-8
5635 N Santa Monica Blvd 53217 414-332-3660
Maria Schram, prin. Fax 332-8649

Whitehall, Trempealeau, Pop. 1,628
Whitehall SD 800/PK-12
PO Box 37 54773 715-538-4374
Michael Beighley, supt. Fax 538-4639
www.whitehallsd.k12.wi.us
Sunset ES 200/2-5
PO Box 37 54773 715-538-4316
Vickie O'Dell, prin. Fax 538-2350
Whitehall MS 200/6-8
PO Box 37 54773 715-538-4364
Damon Lisowski, prin. Fax 538-4639
Other Schools – See Pigeon Falls

White Lake, Langlade, Pop. 335
White Lake SD 200/K-12
PO Box 67 54491 715-882-8421
William Fisher, supt. Fax 882-2914
www.whitelake.k12.wi.us
White Lake ES 100/K-6
PO Box 67 54491 715-882-2361
Fax 882-2914

Whitewater, Walworth, Pop. 14,311
Whitewater USD 2,000/K-12
419 S Elizabeth St 53190 262-472-8700
Dr. Suzanne Zentner, supt. Fax 472-8710
www.wwusd.org
Lakeview ES 200/K-5
W8363 R and W Townline Rd 53190 262-472-8400
Randall Holschbach, prin. Fax 472-8410
Lincoln ES 400/K-5
242 S Prince St 53190 262-472-8500
Mary Jo Bernhardt, prin. Fax 472-8510
Washington ES 300/K-5
506 E Main St 53190 262-472-8600
Tom Grosinske, prin. Fax 472-8610
Whitewater MS 500/6-8
401 S Elizabeth St 53190 262-472-8300
Eric Runez, prin. Fax 472-8310

Wild Rose, Waushara, Pop. 756
Wild Rose SD 700/PK-12
PO Box 276 54984 920-622-4203
Claude Olson, supt. Fax 622-4604
www.wildrose.k12.wi.us
Wild Rose ES 200/PK-5
PO Box 119 54984 920-622-4204
Barbara Sobralske, prin. Fax 622-4601
Other Schools – See Pine River

Williams Bay, Walworth, Pop. 2,668
Williams Bay SD 500/K-12
PO Box 1410 53191 262-245-1575
Frederic Vorlop, supt. Fax 245-5877
www.williamsbay.k12.wi.us
Williams Bay ES 200/K-6
139 Congress St 53191 262-245-5571
Barbara Isaacson, prin. Fax 245-1839
Williams Bay JHS 100/7-8
PO Box 1410 53191 262-245-6224
Dan Bice, prin. Fax 245-5877

Faith Christian S 200/PK-12
PO Box 1230 53191 262-245-9404
Craig Skrede, admin. Fax 245-0128

Wilmot, Kenosha
Trevor-Wilmot Consolidated SD
Supt. — See Trevor
Wilmot ES 50/K-2
PO Box 68 53192 262-862-1941
Teresa Curley, prin. Fax 862-7301

Wind Lake, Racine, Pop. 3,748
Muskego-Norway SD
Supt. — See Muskego
Lakeview ES 400/K-4
26335 Fries Ln 53185 262-895-7540
Dawn Marisch, prin. Fax 895-7631

Windsor, Dane, Pop. 2,182
De Forest Area SD
Supt. — See De Forest
Windsor ES 400/K-4
4352 Windsor Rd 53598 608-842-6300
Mike Finke, prin. Fax 842-6315

Winneconne, Winnebago, Pop. 2,445
Winneconne Community SD 1,500/PK-12
PO Box 5000 54986 920-582-5802
Dr. Robert Lehman, supt. Fax 582-5816
www.winneconne.k12.wi.us
Winneconne ES 600/PK-5
PO Box 5000 54986 920-582-5803
Lisa Hughes, prin. Fax 582-5816
Winneconne MS 400/6-8
PO Box 5000 54986 920-582-5800
Peggy Larson, prin. Fax 582-5812
Other Schools – See Larsen

Winter, Sawyer, Pop. 352
Winter SD 400/PK-12
PO Box 310 54896 715-266-3301
Dr. Penny Boileau, admin. Fax 266-2216
www.winter.k12.wi.us/
Winter ES 100/PK-5
PO Box 310 54896 715-266-6701
Adam Zopp, prin. Fax 266-2216
Winter MS 100/6-8
PO Box 310 54896 715-266-6701
Adam Zopp, prin. Fax 266-2216

Wisconsin Dells, Columbia, Pop. 2,559
Wisconsin Dells SD 1,700/PK-12
811 County Road H 53965 608-254-7769
Charles Whitsell, supt. Fax 254-8058
www.sdwd.k12.wi.us
Spring Hill ES 400/PK-5
300 Vine St 53965 608-253-2468
Carol Coughlin, prin. Fax 254-6397
Spring Hill MS 400/6-8
300 Vine St 53965 608-253-2468
Brian Grove, prin. Fax 254-6397
Other Schools – See Briggsville, Lake Delton

Trinity Lutheran S 100/PK-6
728 Church St 53965 608-253-3241
David Sellmeyer, prin. Fax 254-7585

Wisconsin Rapids, Wood, Pop. 17,621
Wisconsin Rapids SD 5,300/PK-12
510 Peach St 54494 715-422-6000
Robert Crist, supt. Fax 422-6070
www.wrps.org
Grant ES 400/PK-6
8511 County Road WW 54494 715-422-6175
Timothy Bruns, prin. Fax 422-6384
Grove ES 300/PK-6
471 Grove Ave 54494 715-422-6136
Lee Ann Schmidmayr, prin. Fax 422-6325
Howe ES 400/K-6
221 8th St N 54494 715-422-6166
Scott Kellogg, prin. Fax 422-6385
Pitsch ES 100/PK-6
501 17th St S 54494 715-422-6171
Shannon Matott, prin. Fax 422-6310
Washington ES 300/PK-6
2911 Washington St 54494 715-422-6130
J. L. Gray, prin. Fax 422-6315
Woodside ES 500/PK-6
611 Two Mile Ave 54494 715-422-6145
Paul Mann, prin. Fax 422-6338
WRPS Four-year-old Kindergarten 200/K-K
510 Peach St 54494 715-422-6031
Terry Whitmore, prin. Fax 422-6070
Other Schools – See Rudolph, Vesper

Assumption MS 100/7-8
440 Mead St 54494 715-422-0950
Joan Bond, prin. Fax 422-0955
Good Shepherd Lutheran S 50/K-8
10611 State Highway 13 S 54494 715-325-3355
Donna Tullberg, prin.
Immanuel Lutheran S 100/K-8
111 11th St N 54494 715-423-0272
Brian Betts, prin. Fax 423-2853
Our Lady Queen of Heaven S 100/1-3
750 10th Ave S 54495 715-422-0980
Pam Fochs, prin. Fax 424-2972
St. Lawrence ECC 100/PK-K
551 10th Ave N 54495 715-422-0990
Tara Biebl, lead tchr. Fax 422-0993
St. Paul's Evangelical Lutheran S 100/PK-8
311 14th Ave S 54495 715-421-3634
Jon Engelbrecht, prin. Fax 421-3643
St. Vincent De Paul S 100/4-6
831 12th St S 54494 715-422-0960
Brenda Walczak, prin. Fax 422-0963

Wittenberg, Shawano, Pop. 1,123
Wittenberg-Birnamwood SD 1,300/K-12
400 W Grand Ave 54499 715-253-2213
Garrett Rogowski, supt. Fax 253-3588
www.wittbirn.k12.wi.us/
Wittenberg S 400/K-8
300 S Prouty St 54499 715-253-2221
Nancy Resch, prin. Fax 253-3002
Other Schools – See Birnamwood, Elderon

Wonewoc, Juneau, Pop. 802
Wonewoc-Union Center SD 400/PK-12
101 School Rd 53968 608-464-3165
Arthur Keenan, supt. Fax 464-3325
www.theclasslist.com/wcschools
Wonewoc ES 200/PK-6
101 School Rd 53968 608-464-3165
Michelle Noll, prin. Fax 464-3325
Wonewoc JHS 50/7-8
101 School Rd 53968 608-464-3165
Michelle Noll, prin. Fax 464-3325

St. Paul's Evangelical Lutheran S 100/K-8
PO Box 325 53968 608-464-3212
David Fulton, prin. Fax 464-3258

Woodruff, Oneida
Woodruff J1 SD 600/PK-8
11065 Old 51 N 54568 715-356-3282
Rick Morgan, supt. Fax 358-2933
www.avw.k12.wi.us/
Arbor Vitae-Woodruff S 600/PK-8
11065 Old 51 N 54568 715-356-3282
Steve Holt, prin. Fax 358-2933

Woodville, Saint Croix, Pop. 1,276
Baldwin-Woodville Area SD
Supt. — See Baldwin
Viking MS 500/5-8
500 Southside Dr 54028 715-698-2456
Henry Dupuis, prin. Fax 698-3315

Wrightstown, Brown, Pop. 2,248
Wrightstown Community SD 1,200/K-12
PO Box 128 54180 920-532-5551
Carla Buboltz, supt. Fax 532-4664
www.wrightstown.k12.wi.us
Wrightstown ES 400/K-4
PO Box 128 54180 920-532-4818
Lee Mierow, prin. Fax 532-0171
Wrightstown MS 300/5-8
PO Box 128 54180 920-532-5553
Rich Schenkus, prin. Fax 532-3869

St. John Lutheran S 100/PK-8
261 Clay St 54180 920-532-4361
Jason Williams, prin. Fax 532-4413
St. Paul S 100/PK-8
PO Box 177 54180 920-532-4833
Carol Hoard, prin. Fax 532-0458

Wyeville, Monroe, Pop. 141
Tomah Area SD
Supt. — See Tomah
Wyeville ES 100/K-5
225 W Tomah Rd 54660 608-374-7826
Sandra Murray, prin. Fax 372-5087

WYOMING

WYOMING DEPARTMENT OF EDUCATION
2300 Capitol Ave, Cheyenne 82001-3644
Telephone 307-777-7673
Fax 307-777-6234
Website http://www.k12.wy.us

Superintendent of Public Instruction Jim McBride

WYOMING BOARD OF EDUCATION
2300 Capitol Ave, Cheyenne 82001-3644

Chairperson Bill Anthony

BOARDS OF COOPERATIVE EDUCATIONAL SERVICES (BOCES)

Carbon Co. Higher Education Center BOCES
David Throgmorton, dir. 307-328-9204
705 Rodeo St, Rawlins 82301 Fax 324-3338
www.cchec.org
Central Wyoming BOCES 307-268-3309
, 970 N Glenn Rd, Casper 82601 Fax 268-2611
Douglas BOCES
Connie Woehl, dir. 307-358-5622
203 N 6th St, Douglas 82633 Fax 358-5629
Fremont County BOCES
Sandy Barton, dir. 307-856-2028
320 W Main St, Riverton 82501 Fax 856-4058
www.fcboces.org
Mountain View & Lyman BOCES
Lana Hillstead, dir. 307-782-6401
PO Box 130, Mountain View 82939 Fax 782-7410
Northeast Wyoming BOCES
Julie Cudmore, dir. 307-682-0231
410 N Miller Ave, Gillette 82716 Fax 686-7628
www.newboces.com/
Northwest Wyoming BOCES
Carolyn Connor, dir. 307-864-2171
PO Box 112, Thermopolis 82443 Fax 864-9463
www.nwboces.com/
Oyster Ridge BOCES
Heidi Lively, dir. 307-877-6958
PO Box 423, Kemmerer 83101 Fax 828-9040
www.kemmereroutreach.com
Region V BOCES
Dr. Dennis Donohue, dir. 307-733-8210
PO Box 240, Wilson 83014 Fax 733-8462
Sublette BOCES
Donna Lozier, dir. 307-367-6873
PO Box 977, Pinedale 82941 Fax 367-6634
www.subletteboces.com/
Sweetwater BOCES
Bernadine Craft Ph.D., dir. 307-382-1607
PO Box 428, Rock Springs 82902 Fax 382-1875
www.wwcc.wy.edu/boces/
Uinta BOCES
Michael Williams, dir. 307-789-5742
1013 W Cheyenne Dr Unit A Fax 789-7975
Evanston 82930

PUBLIC, PRIVATE AND CATHOLIC ELEMENTARY SCHOOLS

Afton, Lincoln, Pop. 1,831
Lincoln County SD 2 2,500/K-12
PO Box 219 83110 307-885-3811
Jon Abrams, supt. Fax 885-9562
www.lcsd2.org
Afton ES 400/K-3
PO Box 8002 83110 307-885-8002
Alan Allred, prin. Fax 885-8010
Osmond ES 300/4-6
3120 State Highway 241 83110 307-885-9457
Kelly Tolman, prin. Fax 886-5789
Star Valley MS 400/7-8
PO Box 8001 83110 307-885-5208
Kem Cazier, prin. Fax 885-0472
Other Schools – See Cokeville, Etna, Thayne

Albin, Laramie, Pop. 117
Laramie County SD 2
Supt. — See Pine Bluffs
Albin S 50/K-6
PO Box 38 82050 307-245-4090
Sue Stevens, prin. Fax 246-3261

Alcova, Natrona
Natrona County SD 1
Supt. — See Casper
Alcova ES 50/K-6
PO Box 106 82620 307-472-2079
Tom Rodabaugh, prin. Fax 472-3105

Alta, Teton
Teton County SD 1
Supt. — See Jackson
Alta ES 100/K-6
15 School Rd, 307-353-2472
Bill Hunt, prin. Fax 353-2473

Arapahoe, Fremont, Pop. 393
Fremont County ESD 38 300/PK-8
445 Little Wind Rvr Bottom 82510 307-856-9333
Roger Clark, supt. Fax 857-4327
www.arapahoeschool.com/
Arapahoe S 300/PK-8
445 Little Wind Rvr Bottom 82510 307-856-9333
Sharei Mousseaux, prin. Fax 856-2440

Arvada, Sheridan
Sheridan County SD 3
Supt. — See Clearmont
Arvada ES, 127 Main 82831 50/K-6
Charles Auzqui, prin. 307-736-2219

Baggs, Carbon, Pop. 354
Carbon County SD 1
Supt. — See Rawlins
Little Snake River Valley S 200/K-12
PO Box 9 82321 307-383-2185
Joel Thomas, prin. Fax 383-2184

Bairoil, Sweetwater, Pop. 96
Carbon County SD 1
Supt. — See Rawlins
Bairoil ES 50/K-5
PO Box 27 82322 307-328-9215
Darrin Jennings, prin. Fax 328-9216

Banner, Sheridan
Sheridan County SD 2
Supt. — See Sheridan
Story ES, 103 Fish Hatchery Rd 82832 50/K-5
Janet Marshall, prin. 307-683-2316

Bar Nunn, Natrona, Pop. 1,292
Natrona County SD 1
Supt. — See Casper
Bar Nunn ES 200/PK-5
2050 Siebke Dr 82601 307-577-4507
Rene Rickabaugh, prin. Fax 577-4511

Basin, Big Horn, Pop. 1,224
Big Horn County SD 4 300/PK-12
PO Box 151 82410 307-568-2684
Mary Fisher, supt. Fax 568-2654
www.bgh4.k12.wy.us/
Irwin ES 100/PK-4
PO Box 151 82410 307-568-2488
Jared Moretti, prin. Fax 568-9307
Other Schools – See Manderson

Big Horn, Sheridan
Sheridan County SD 1
Supt. — See Ranchester
Big Horn ES 200/K-5
PO Box 490 82833 307-672-3497
Brent Caldwell, prin. Fax 672-5396
Big Horn MS 100/6-8
PO Box 490 82833 307-674-8190
George Mirich, prin. Fax 672-5306

Big Piney, Sublette, Pop. 455
Sublette County SD 9 600/K-12
PO Box 769 83113 307-276-3322
Gerry Chase, supt. Fax 276-3731
Big Piney ES 200/K-5
PO Box 769 83113 307-276-3313
Christine Meiring, prin. Fax 276-3503
Big Piney MS 100/6-8
PO Box 769 83113 307-276-3315
Scott Gion, prin. Fax 276-5209
Other Schools – See La Barge

Bondurant, Sublette
Sublette County SD 1
Supt. — See Pinedale
Bondurant ES 50/K-4
14224 US Highway 189/191 82922 307-367-2828
Greg Legerski, prin. Fax 367-4706

Buffalo, Johnson, Pop. 4,290
Johnson County SD 1 1,100/K-12
601 W Lott St 82834 307-684-9571
Rod Kessler, supt. Fax 684-5182
www.jcsd1.k12.wy.us
Clear Creek ES 4-5
63 N Burritt Ave 82834 307-684-0153
Craig Anderson, prin. Fax 684-0156
Clear Creek MS 300/6-8
361 W Gatchell St 82834 307-684-5594
Teresa Staab, prin. Fax 684-9096
Meadowlark ES 300/K-3
550 S Burritt Ave 82834 307-684-9518
Kathy Camino, prin. Fax 684-5386

Other Schools – See Kaycee

Burlington, Big Horn, Pop. 248
Big Horn County SD 1
Supt. — See Cowley
Burlington ES 100/PK-6
PO Box 9 82411 307-762-3334
Matt Davidson, prin. Fax 762-3604
Burlington JHS 50/7-8
PO Box 9 82411 307-762-3334
Matt Davidson, prin. Fax 762-3604

Burns, Laramie, Pop. 310
Laramie County SD 2
Supt. — See Pine Bluffs
West ES 200/K-6
PO Box 10 82053 307-245-4150
Jerry Burkett, prin. Fax 547-3721

Carpenter, Laramie
Laramie County SD 2
Supt. — See Pine Bluffs
Carpenter ES 100/K-6
PO Box L 82054 307-245-4180
Laurie Bahl, prin. Fax 649-2247

Casper, Natrona, Pop. 51,738
Natrona County SD 1 11,500/PK-12
970 N Glenn Rd 82601 307-577-0200
Joel Dvorak, supt. Fax 577-4422
www.natronaschools.org/
Cottonwood ES 200/PK-6
1230 W 15th St 82604 307-577-6735
Mari Stoll, prin. Fax 577-6751
Crest Hill ES 300/K-6
4445 S Poplar St 82601 307-577-4512
Jim Stark, prin. Fax 577-4513
Ft. Caspar Academy 400/K-6
2323 Wyoming Blvd SW 82604 307-577-4531
Janelle Ehrich, prin. Fax 577-4534
Frontier MS 500/6-8
900 S Beverly St 82609 307-577-4400
Verba Echols, prin. Fax 233-2274
Grant ES 200/PK-5
1536 S Oakcrest Ave 82601 307-577-4538
Tom Mesecher, prin. Fax 577-4424
James ES 500/K-6
701 Carriage Ln 82609 307-577-6727
Steve Ellbogen, prin. Fax 577-6760
Manor Heights ES 300/K-6
3201 E 15th St 82609 307-577-4545
Kent Thompson, prin. Fax 577-4551
Mountain View ES 200/PK-5
400 N 3rd Ave 82604 307-577-4565
Tom Rodabaugh, prin. Fax 577-4569
North Casper ES 200/PK-5
1014 Glenarm St 82601 307-577-4575
Phil Hubert, prin. Fax 577-6759
Oregon Trail ES 300/K-6
6332 Buckboard Rd 82604 307-577-4578
Randall Harris, prin. Fax 577-4579
Paradise Valley ES 500/PK-6
22 Magnolia St 82604 307-577-4584
Christine Frude, prin. Fax 577-4589

Park ES 300/K-6
140 W 9th St 82601 307-577-4593
Doris Waddell, prin. Fax 577-4597
Pineview ES 200/K-6
639 Payne Ave 82609 307-577-6700
Chris Carruth, prin. Fax 577-6702
Poison Spider S 200/K-8
6150 Raderville Rte 82604 307-577-4555
Tammy Kelly, prin. Fax 261-6891
Red Creek ES 50/K-6
15651 State Highway 487 82604 307-473-1224
Tom Rodabaugh, prin. Fax 473-2475
Sagewood ES 300/PK-6
2451 Shattuck Ave 82601 307-577-4500
Michael Bond, prin. Fax 261-6843
Southridge ES 300/K-6
1600 W 29th St 82604 307-577-6710
Rick Skatula, prin. Fax 577-6711
University Park ES 200/PK-6
600 N Huber Dr 82609 307-577-6715
Sally Huber, prin. Fax 577-6716
Willard ES 300/PK-5
129 N Elk St 82601 307-577-6740
Dr. Leslie Madden, prin. Fax 577-6746
Woods Learning Center 200/K-8
500 S Walsh Dr 82609 307-577-0315
Pam Crabb, contact Fax 577-0316
Other Schools – See Alcova, Bar Nunn, Evansville, Kaycee, Midwest, Mills, Powder River

---

Mountain Road Christian Academy 50/K-8
2657 Casper Mountain Rd 82601 307-235-2859
Mount Hope Lutheran S 100/PK-8
2300 S Hickory St 82604 307-234-6865
Rev. John Hill, prin.
Paradise Valley Christian S 100/PK-12
3041 Paradise Dr 82604 307-234-2450
C. Jeanne Boyd, admin. Fax 577-0763
St. Anthony's S 200/PK-9
218 E 7th St 82601 307-234-2873
Cyndy Novotny, prin. Fax 235-4946

Centennial, Albany
Albany County SD 1
Supt. — See Laramie
Centennial ES 50/K-6
PO Box 326 82055 307-745-9585
Robin Devine, prin. Fax 721-4498

Cheyenne, Laramie, Pop. 55,731
Laramie County SD 1 12,800/K-12
2810 House Ave 82001 307-771-2100
Ted Adams, supt. Fax 771-2364
www.laramie1.org/
Afflerbach ES 400/K-6
400 W Wallick Rd 82007 307-771-2300
Carol Clarke, prin. Fax 771-2304
Alta Vista ES 300/K-6
1514 E 16th St 82001 307-771-2310
Martin McGuffy, prin. Fax 771-2212
Anderson ES 400/K-6
2204 Plain View Rd 82009 307-771-2606
Jim Fraley, prin. Fax 771-2609
Arp ES 300/K-6
1216 E Reiner Ct 82007 307-771-2365
Don Brantz, prin. Fax 771-2368
Baggs ES 300/K-6
3705 Cheyenne St 82001 307-771-2385
Larry Bowman, prin. Fax 771-2388
Bain ES 400/K-6
903 Adams Ave 82001 307-771-2525
Brenda Creel, prin. Fax 771-2540
Buffalo Ridge ES 300/K-6
5331 Pineridge Ave 82009 307-771-2595
Greg Garman, prin. Fax 771-2429
Cole ES 200/K-6
615 W 9th St 82007 307-771-2480
Matt Schlagel, prin. Fax 771-2483
Davis ES 300/K-6
6309 Yellowstone Rd 82009 307-771-2600
Mike Fullmer, prin. Fax 771-2599
Deming ES 100/K-3
715 W 5th Ave 82001 307-771-2400
Tony Crecelius, prin. Fax 771-2402
Dildine ES 500/K-6
4312 Van Buren Ave 82001 307-771-2320
Mike Wortman, prin. Fax 771-2521
Fairview ES 200/3-6
2801 E 10th St 82001 307-771-2610
Susan Barnett, prin. Fax 771-2478
Freedom ES 300/K-6
4500 Happy Jack Rd 82009 307-771-2305
Cindy Farwell, prin. Fax 771-2306
Gilchrist ES 100/K-6
1108 Happy Jack Rd 82009 307-771-2285
Harry Petty, prin. Fax 771-2287
Goins ES 300/K-6
201 Cribbon Ave 82007 307-771-2620
Joyce Chalstrom, prin. Fax 771-2623
Hebard ES 200/K-6
413 Seymour Ave 82007 307-771-2450
Carla Gregorio, prin. Fax 771-2453
Henderson ES 300/K-6
2820 Henderson Dr 82001 307-771-2550
Karen Brooks-Lyons, prin. Fax 771-2554
Hobbs ES 500/K-6
5710 Syracuse Rd 82009 307-771-2560
Randy Hurd, prin. Fax 771-2568
Jessup ES 300/K-6
6113 Evers Blvd 82009 307-771-2570
Sharon Knudson, prin. Fax 771-2574
Lebhart ES 200/K-2
807 Coolidge St 82001 307-771-2614
Susan Barnett, prin. Fax 771-2393
Miller ES 100/4-6
3501 Evans Ave 82001 307-771-2376
Tony Crecelius, prin. Fax 771-2378

Pioneer Park ES 400/K-6
1407 Cosgriff Ct 82001 307-771-2316
April Gates, prin. Fax 771-2319
Rossman ES 200/K-6
916 W College Dr 82007 307-771-2544
Dennis Dix, prin. Fax 771-2549
Saddle Ridge ES K-6
6815 Wilderness Trl 82001 307-771-2360
Eric Jackson, prin.
Sunrise ES K-6
5021 E 13th St 82001 307-771-2280
Larry Sturgeon, prin. Fax 771-2281
Other Schools – See Granite Canon, Horse Creek

St. Mary S 200/PK-12
2200 ONeil Ave 82001 307-638-9268
Carol Ricken, prin. Fax 635-2847
Trinity Lutheran S 100/PK-6
1111 E 22nd St 82001 307-635-2802
Christian Boehlke, prin. Fax 778-0799
Webster Christian S 100/K-12
PO Box 21239 82003 307-635-2175
Shirley Falk, admin. Fax 773-8523

Chugwater, Platte, Pop. 231
Platte County SD 1
Supt. — See Wheatland
Chugwater ES 50/K-6
406 5th St 82210 307-422-3501
George Kopf, prin. Fax 422-3433
Chugwater JHS 50/7-8
406 5th St 82210 307-422-3501
George Kopf, prin. Fax 422-3433

Clearmont, Sheridan, Pop. 117
Sheridan County SD 3 100/PK-12
PO Box 125 82835 307-758-4412
John Baule, supt. Fax 758-4444
Arvada-Clearmont JHS 50/7-8
PO Box 125 82835 307-758-4412
Charles Auzqui, prin. Fax 758-4444
Clearmont ES 50/PK-6
PO Box 125 82835 307-758-4412
Charles Auzqui, prin. Fax 758-4444
Other Schools – See Arvada

Cody, Park, Pop. 9,100
Park County SD 6 2,200/K-12
919 Cody Ave 82414 307-587-4253
Bryan Monteith, supt. Fax 527-5762
www.park6.org/
Cody MS 500/6-8
919 Cody Ave 82414 307-587-4273
Larry Gerber, prin. Fax 587-3547
Eastside ES 300/K-5
919 Cody Ave 82414 307-587-4275
Dr. Kip Hanich, prin. Fax 587-9464
Livingston ES 300/K-5
919 Cody Ave 82414 307-587-4271
Tom Cook, prin. Fax 587-9742
Sunset ES 300/K-5
919 Cody Ave 82414 307-587-4279
Brenda Farmer, prin. Fax 587-6405
Valley ES 50/K-5
919 Cody Ave 82414 307-587-3287
Kelly Merager, prin. Fax 587-9742
Other Schools – See Wapiti

Cokeville, Lincoln, Pop. 492
Lincoln County SD 2
Supt. — See Afton
Cokeville ES 100/K-6
PO Box 400 83114 307-279-3233
Keith Harris, prin. Fax 279-3280

Cowley, Big Horn, Pop. 582
Big Horn County SD 1 600/PK-12
PO Box 688 82420 307-548-2254
Shon Hocker, supt. Fax 548-7610
bighorn1.com
Rocky Mountain ES 200/K-5
PO Box 38 82420 307-548-2211
Karma Sanders, prin. Fax 548-2212
Other Schools – See Burlington, Deaver

Deaver, Big Horn, Pop. 177
Big Horn County SD 1
Supt. — See Cowley
Rocky Mountain MS 100/6-8
PO Box 185 82421 307-664-2252
Wes Townsend, prin. Fax 664-2314

Diamondville, Lincoln, Pop. 695
Lincoln County SD 1 600/K-12
PO Box 335 83116 307-877-9095
Teresa Chaulk, supt. Fax 877-9638
www.lcsd1.k12.wy.us
Other Schools – See Kemmerer

Douglas, Converse, Pop. 5,581
Converse County SD 1 1,600/K-12
615 Hamilton St 82633 307-358-2942
Dan Espeland, supt. Fax 358-3934
www.ccsd1.k12.wy.us
Douglas IS 300/3-5
615 Hamilton St 82633 307-358-5250
Lisa Weigel, prin. Fax 358-2528
Douglas MS 400/6-8
615 Hamilton St 82633 307-358-9771
Fred George, prin. Fax 358-5315
Douglas PS 400/K-2
615 Hamilton St 82633 307-358-3502
Brent Notman, prin. Fax 358-3552
Dry Creek S 50/K-8
615 Hamilton St 82633 307-358-2351
Lisa Weigel, prin. Fax 358-3188
Moss Agate S 50/K-8
615 Hamilton St 82633 307-358-3221
Lisa Weigel, prin. Fax 358-3188

Shawnee S 50/K-8
615 Hamilton St 82633 307-358-3278
Lisa Weigel, prin. Fax 358-3188
White S 50/K-8
615 Hamilton St 82633 307-358-0842
Lisa Weigel, prin. Fax 358-3188

Dubois, Fremont, Pop. 991
Fremont County SD 2 200/K-12
PO Box 188 82513 307-455-2323
Richard Barton, supt. Fax 455-2178
Dubois ES 100/K-5
PO Box 188 82513 307-455-2488
Larry Lewis, prin. Fax 455-2178
Dubois MS 6-8
PO Box 188 82513 307-455-2488
Larry Lewis, prin. Fax 455-2654

Elk Mountain, Carbon, Pop. 192
Carbon County SD 2
Supt. — See Saratoga
Elk Mountain ES 50/K-6
PO Box 20 82324 307-348-7731
Monty Talkington, prin. Fax 348-7321

Encampment, Carbon, Pop. 462
Carbon County SD 2
Supt. — See Saratoga
Encampment S 100/K-12
PO Box 277 82325 307-327-5442
Mike Erickson, prin. Fax 327-5142

Ethete, Fremont, Pop. 1,059
Fremont County SD 14 500/PK-12
638 Blue Sky Hwy 82520 307-332-3904
Michelle Hoffman, supt. Fax 332-7567
www.fremont14.k12.wy.us
Wyoming Indian ES 200/PK-5
23 Coolidge Dr 82520 307-332-2053
Owen St. Clair, prin. Fax 332-6739
Wyoming Indian MS 100/6-8
535 Ethete Rd 82520 307-332-2992
Pam Frederick, prin. Fax 335-7318

Etna, Lincoln
Lincoln County SD 2
Supt. — See Afton
Etna ES 200/4-6
PO Box 5068 83118 307-885-2472
Justin Pierantoni, prin. Fax 883-3050

Evanston, Uinta, Pop. 11,459
Uinta County SD 1 2,900/K-12
PO Box 6002 82931 307-789-7571
James Bailey, supt. Fax 789-6225
www.uinta1.k12.wy.us
Aspen ES 300/K-5
PO Box 6002 82931 307-789-3106
Vesta Demester, prin. Fax 789-6338
Clark ES 200/K-5
PO Box 6002 82931 307-789-2833
Alayne Matthews, prin. Fax 789-7759
Davis MS 400/6-8
PO Box 6002 82931 307-789-8096
Jim Harrell, prin. Fax 789-3386
Evanston MS 300/6-8
PO Box 6002 82931 307-789-5499
Eric Christenot, prin. Fax 789-7972
North Evanston ES 400/K-5
PO Box 6002 82931 307-789-7658
Joseph Ingalls, prin. Fax 789-2046
Uinta Meadows ES 400/K-5
PO Box 6002 82931 307-789-8098
Chris Brown, prin. Fax 789-3426

Evansville, Natrona, Pop. 2,328
Natrona County SD 1
Supt. — See Casper
Evansville ES 200/PK-5
PO Box E 82636 307-577-4518
Donna Mathern, prin. Fax 577-4449

Farson, Sweetwater
Sweetwater County SD 1
Supt. — See Rock Springs
Farson-Eden ES 100/K-5
PO Box 400 82932 307-273-9301
Gregory Lasley, prin. Fax 273-9313
Farson-Eden MS 50/6-8
PO Box 400 82932 307-273-9301
Gregory Lasley, prin. Fax 273-9313

Fort Washakie, Fremont, Pop. 1,334
Fremont County SD 21 300/PK-8
90 Ethete Rd 82514 307-332-5983
Gregory Cox, supt. Fax 332-7267
www.fortwashakieschool.com
Fort Washakie ES 300/PK-6
90 Ethete Rd 82514 307-332-2380
Mike Helenbolt, prin. Fax 332-3597
Fort Washakie MS 100/7-8
90 Ethete Rd 82514 307-332-2380
Randon Lawrence, prin. Fax 332-3597

Gillette, Campbell, Pop. 22,685
Campbell County SD 1 7,600/K-12
PO Box 3033 82717 307-682-5171
Dr. Richard Strahorn, supt. Fax 682-6619
www.ccsd.k12.wy.us
Conestoga ES 400/K-6
4901 Sleepy Hollow Blvd 82718 307-686-2373
Steve Anderson, prin. Fax 687-0350
4-J ES 50/K-6
2830 State Highway 50 82718 307-682-3076
Coi Morehead, prin. Fax 687-5032
Hillcrest ES 300/K-6
800 Butler Spaeth Rd 82716 307-682-7291
Brad Winter, prin. Fax 682-5843
Lakeview ES 300/K-6
410 Lakeside Dr 82716 307-682-7293
Mike Delancey, prin. Fax 682-5843

Meadowlark ES 300/K-6
816 E 7th St 82716 307-682-4740
Barry Jankord, prin. Fax 682-4649
Paintbrush ES 400/K-6
1001 W Lakeway Rd 82718 307-686-1778
David Olsen, prin. Fax 686-2767
Pronghorn ES 400/K-6
3005 Oakcrest Dr 82718 307-682-1676
Steve Fenton, prin. Fax 682-0061
Rawhide ES 100/K-6
200 Prospector Pkwy 82716 307-682-0774
Tana Larsen, prin. Fax 682-7301
Stocktrail ES 300/K-6
800 Stocktrail Ave 82716 307-682-7289
Kathy Quinn, prin. Fax 682-6236
Sunflower ES 400/K-6
2500 Dogwood Ave 82718 307-686-0631
Kevin Sinclair, prin. Fax 682-0351
Wagonwheel ES 400/K-6
800 Hemlock Ave 82716 307-686-1060
Eric Stremcha, prin. Fax 686-4045
Other Schools – See Recluse, Rozet, Weston, Wright

Heritage Christian S 100/PK-12
510 Wall Street Ct 82718 307-686-1392
Brent Potthoff, admin. Fax 682-6515
John Paul II S 100/PK-8
1000 Butler Spaeth Rd 82716 307-682-3319
Lynn Grassel, prin. Fax 682-6386

Glendo, Platte, Pop. 229
Platte County SD 1
Supt. — See Wheatland
Glendo JHS 50/7-8
305 N Paige St 82213 307-735-4471
Stanetta Twiford, prin. Fax 735-4220
Glendo S 50/K-6
305 N Paige St 82213 307-735-4471
Stanetta Twiford, prin. Fax 735-4220

Glenrock, Converse, Pop. 2,351
Converse County SD 2 600/K-12
PO Box 1300 82637 307-436-5331
Kirk Hughes, supt. Fax 436-8235
www.cnv2.k12.wy.us/
Glenrock MS 100/5-8
PO Box 1300 82637 307-436-9258
Kenny Smith, prin. Fax 436-7507
Grant ES 200/K-4
PO Box 1300 82637 307-436-2774
Christine Hendricks, prin. Fax 436-7589

Granger, Sweetwater, Pop. 146
Sweetwater County SD 2
Supt. — See Green River
Granger ES 50/K-4
PO Box 25 82934 307-875-4840
Alan Demaret, prin. Fax 875-9313

Granite Canon, Laramie
Laramie County SD 1
Supt. — See Cheyenne
Willadsen ES 50/K-6
645 Harriman Rd 82059 307-771-2295
Harry Petty, prin. Fax 771-2296

Green River, Sweetwater, Pop. 11,787
Sweetwater County SD 2 2,800/K-12
320 Monroe Ave 82935 307-872-5500
Craig Sorensen, supt. Fax 872-5518
www.sw2.k12.wy.us
Harrison ES 200/K-4
1825 Alabama St 82935 307-872-1700
Lu Kasper, prin. Fax 872-1888
Jackson ES 400/K-4
2200 E Teton Blvd 82935 307-872-1800
Stacy Court, prin. Fax 872-5532
Lincoln MS 400/7-8
350 Monroe Ave 82935 307-872-4400
Clay Cates, prin. Fax 872-4477
Monroe IS 300/5-6
250 Monroe Ave 82935 307-872-4000
Jason Fuss, prin. Fax 872-5542
Truman ES 300/K-4
1055 W Teton Blvd 82935 307-872-1900
Justin Shadrick, prin. Fax 872-5579
Washington ES 300/K-4
750 W 5th North St 82935 307-872-2000
Anne Marie Covey, prin. Fax 872-5578
Other Schools – See Granger, Kemmerer, Mc Kinnon

Greybull, Big Horn, Pop. 1,752
Big Horn County SD 3 500/PK-12
636 14th Ave N 82426 307-765-4756
Martha Young, supt. Fax 765-4617
gps.bgh3.k12.wy.us/
Greybull ES 200/PK-5
636 14th Ave N 82426 307-765-2311
Brenda Jinks, prin. Fax 765-9477
Greybull MS 100/6-8
636 14th Ave N 82426 307-765-4492
Kris Cundall, prin. Fax 765-2833

Guernsey, Platte, Pop. 1,118
Platte County SD 2 200/K-12
PO Box 189 82214 307-836-2735
Dave Barker, supt. Fax 836-2450
www.plt2.k12.wy.us
Guernsey-Sunrise ES 100/K-6
PO Box 189 82214 307-836-2733
Ken Griffith, prin. Fax 836-2450
Guernsey-Sunrise JHS 50/7-8
PO Box 189 82214 307-836-2745
Ken Griffith, prin. Fax 836-2729

Hanna, Carbon, Pop. 863
Carbon County SD 2
Supt. — See Saratoga
Hanna ES 100/K-6
PO Box 1000 82327 307-325-6523
Monty Talkington, prin. Fax 325-9811

Horse Creek, Laramie
Laramie County SD 1
Supt. — See Cheyenne
Clawson ES 50/K-6
376 Road 228A 82061 307-771-2291
Harry Petty, prin. Fax 771-2292

Hudson, Fremont, Pop. 416
Fremont County SD 1
Supt. — See Lander
Hudson ES 50/K-3
PO Box 60 82515 307-335-8881
John Gores, prin. Fax 335-8882

Hulett, Crook, Pop. 429
Crook County SD 1
Supt. — See Sundance
Hulett S 100/K-12
PO Box 127 82720 307-467-5231
Kirby Baier, prin. Fax 467-5280

Jackson, Teton, Pop. 9,038
Teton County SD 1 2,200/K-12
PO Box 568 83001 307-733-2704
Pam Shea, supt. Fax 733-6443
www.tcsd.org/
Colter ES 300/3-5
PO Box 568 83001 307-733-9651
Tom Radkey, prin. Fax 739-1452
Jackson ES 400/K-2
PO Box 568 83001 307-733-5302
Deb Roehrkasse, prin. Fax 739-2116
Jackson Hole MS 500/6-8
PO Box 568 83001 307-733-4234
Jean Coldsmith, prin. Fax 733-4254
Other Schools – See Alta, Kelly, Moran, Wilson

Journeys S 200/PK-12
700 Coyote Canyon Rd 83001 307-733-1313
Nate McClennen, hdmstr. Fax 733-7560

Jeffrey City, Fremont
Fremont County SD 1
Supt. — See Lander
Jeffrey City ES 50/K-6
375 Bob Adams Ave 82310 307-544-2254
Dennis Oman, prin. Fax 544-2346

Kaycee, Johnson, Pop. 273
Johnson County SD 1
Supt. — See Buffalo
Kaycee ES 100/K-6
PO Box 6 82639 307-738-2573
Dale Maynard, prin. Fax 738-2495

Natrona County SD 1
Supt. — See Casper
Willow Creek ES 50/K-6
24135 Willow Creek Rd 82639 307-738-2542
Bruce Youngquist, prin. Fax 738-2542

Kelly, Teton
Teton County SD 1
Supt. — See Jackson
Kelly ES 50/K-5
PO Box 128 83011 307-733-2955
Tom Radkey, prin. Fax 733-7845

Kemmerer, Lincoln, Pop. 2,560
Lincoln County SD 1
Supt. — See Diamondville
Kemmerer ES 200/K-4
1401 Lincoln Heights Dr 83101 307-877-5584
Mike Sharum, prin. Fax 877-9522
Kemmerer MS 200/5-8
1310 Antelope St 83101 307-877-2286
Chris Leathers, prin. Fax 877-3365

Sweetwater County SD 2
Supt. — See Green River
Thoman Ranch S 50/K-8
Fontennelle Route 83101 307-877-3426
Alan Demaret, prin. Fax 877-3426

La Barge, Lincoln, Pop. 421
Sublette County SD 9
Supt. — See Big Piney
Labarge ES 100/K-5
PO Box 36 83123 307-386-2227
Charles Hull, prin. Fax 386-2384

La Grange, Goshen, Pop. 332
Goshen County SD 1
Supt. — See Torrington
La Grange ES 50/K-6
PO Box 188, 307-834-2311
Brian Grasmick, prin. Fax 834-2312

Lance Creek, Niobrara
Niobrara County SD 1
Supt. — See Lusk
Lance Creek S, PO Box 334 82222 50/K-8
Mike Estes, prin. 307-334-3403

Lander, Fremont, Pop. 6,898
Fremont County SD 1 1,800/K-12
400 Baldwin Creek Rd 82520 307-332-4711
Paige Fenton-Hughes, supt. Fax 332-6671
www.fcsd1.com
North ES 300/K-6
626 Washington St 82520 307-332-5943
Dennis Oman, prin. Fax 332-9953
South ES 300/K-6
615 Popo Agie St 82520 307-332-6690
William Alley, prin. Fax 332-5878
Starrett JHS 300/7-8
863 Sweetwater St 82520 307-332-4040
Brian Janish, prin. Fax 332-0435
West ES 300/K-6
350 Smith St 82520 307-332-6967
Leslie Voxland, prin. Fax 332-3475
Other Schools – See Hudson, Jeffrey City

Lander Christian Academy 50/K-8
875 Fremont St 82520 307-332-5598
Gail MacNaughton, admin. Fax 332-1650

Laramie, Albany, Pop. 26,050
Albany County SD 1 3,400/PK-12
1948 E Grand Ave 82070 307-721-4400
Dr. Brian Recht, supt. Fax 721-4408
www.ac1.k12.wy.us
Beitel ES 200/K-6
811 S 17th St 82070 307-721-4436
Robin Devine, prin. Fax 721-4498
Harmony ES, 20 Lewis Rd 82070 50/K-6
Barb Farley, prin. 307-745-5720
Indian Paintbrush ES 300/K-6
1653 N 28th St 82072 307-721-4490
Steve Slyman, prin. Fax 721-4468
Linford ES 300/K-6
120 S Johnson St 82070 307-721-4439
Kelly Carroll, prin. Fax 721-4443
Slade ES 300/K-6
1212 E Baker St 82072 307-721-4446
Heather Moro, prin. Fax 721-4497
Snowy Range Academy 100/K-6
4037 E Grand Ave Ste A 82070 307-745-9930
Lyn Tausan, prin. Fax 745-9931
Spring Creek ES 300/K-6
1203 Russell St 82070 307-721-4410
Liann Brenneman, prin. Fax 721-4418
UW Laboratory S 200/PK-9
PO Box 3374 82071 307-766-2155
Margaret Hudson, prin. Fax 766-6668
Other Schools – See Centennial, Rock River

St. Laurence S 100/K-6
608 S 4th St 82070 307-742-6363
Blake Hunkins, prin. Fax 745-3131

Lingle, Goshen, Pop. 490
Goshen County SD 1
Supt. — See Torrington
Lingle-Ft. Laramie ES 100/K-5
PO Box 379 82223 307-837-2254
Sally Crowser, prin. Fax 837-3025
Lingle-Fort Laramie MS 100/6-8
PO Box 379 82223 307-837-2283
Sally Crowser, prin. Fax 837-2057

Lovell, Big Horn, Pop. 2,277
Big Horn County SD 2 600/K-12
502 Hampshire Ave 82431 307-548-2259
Dan Coe, supt. Fax 548-7555
www.bgh2.k12.wy.us/
Lovell ES 300/K-5
520 Shoshone Ave 82431 307-548-2247
Cheri Hoffman, prin. Fax 548-2593
Lovell MS 100/6-8
325 W 9th St 82431 307-548-6553
Sherie Monk, prin. Fax 548-6136

Lusk, Niobrara, Pop. 1,348
Niobrara County SD 1 300/K-12
PO Box 629 82225 307-334-3793
Richard Luchsinger, supt. Fax 334-0126
www.lusk.k12.wy.us/
Lusk S 100/K-8
PO Box 1239 82225 307-334-2224
Mike Estes, prin. Fax 334-2400
Other Schools – See Lance Creek

Lyman, Uinta, Pop. 1,937
Uinta County SD 6 700/K-12
PO Box 1090 82937 307-786-4100
Randy Hillstead, supt. Fax 787-3241
www.uinta6.k12.wy.us/
Lyman MS, PO Box 1090 82937 200/5-8
Christy Campbell, prin. 307-786-4608
Urie ES 200/K-4
PO Box 1090 82937 307-782-6429
Layne Parmenter, prin. Fax 786-2129

Mc Kinnon, Sweetwater
Sweetwater County SD 2
Supt. — See Green River
Mc Kinnon S 50/K-8
PO Box 1001 82938 307-874-6199
Alan Demaret, prin. Fax 874-6190

Manderson, Big Horn, Pop. 101
Big Horn County SD 4
Supt. — See Basin
Cloud Peak MS 100/6-8
PO Box 97 82432 307-568-2846
Kyle Gunderson, prin. Fax 568-3885
Manderson ES 50/5-5
PO Box 97 82432 307-568-2846
Kyle Gunderson, prin. Fax 568-3885

Medicine Bow, Carbon, Pop. 265
Carbon County SD 2
Supt. — See Saratoga
Medicine Bow ES 50/K-6
PO Box 185 82329 307-379-2345
Monty Talkington, prin. Fax 379-2283

Meeteetse, Park, Pop. 347
Park County SD 16 100/K-12
PO Box 218 82433 307-868-2501
Robert Lewandowski, supt. Fax 868-9264
www.park16.k12.wy.us/
Meeteetse S 100/K-12
PO Box 218 82433 307-868-2501
Jay Curtis, prin. Fax 868-9264

Midwest, Natrona, Pop. 431
Natrona County SD 1
Supt. — See Casper
Midwest S 200/PK-12
PO Box 368 82643 307-437-6545
Bruce Youngquist, prin. Fax 437-6820

Mills, Natrona, Pop. 2,898
Natrona County SD 1
Supt. — See Casper
Mills ES 200/PK-6
PO Box 268 82644 307-577-4558
Cobie Taylor-Logan, prin. Fax 261-6827

Moorcroft, Crook, Pop. 845
Crook County SD 1
Supt. — See Sundance
Moorcroft ES 200/K-6
PO Box 40 82721 307-756-3781
Linda Wolfskill, prin. Fax 756-3681

Moran, Teton
Teton County SD 1
Supt. — See Jackson
Moran ES 50/K-5
PO Box 130 83013 307-543-2438
Tom Radkey, prin. Fax 543-2809

Mountain View, Uinta, Pop. 1,163
Uinta County SD 4 600/K-12
PO Box 130 82939 307-782-3377
Jack Cozort, supt. Fax 782-6879
www.uinta4.k12.wy.us/
Ft. Bridger ES 100/3-4
PO Box 130 82939 307-782-3422
Al Fisher, prin. Fax 782-6879
Mountain View ES 200/K-2
PO Box 130 82939 307-782-6202
Al Fisher, prin. Fax 782-6422
Mountain View MS 200/5-8
PO Box 130 82939 307-782-6338
Kim Dolezal, prin. Fax 782-6876

Newcastle, Weston, Pop. 3,221
Weston County SD 1 800/K-12
116 Casper Ave 82701 307-746-4451
Brad LaCroix, supt. Fax 746-3289
www.weston1.k12.wy.us
Newcastle 3-5 ES 200/3-5
116 Casper Ave 82701 307-746-2717
Tobey Cass, prin. Fax 746-2718
Newcastle K-2 ES 200/K-2
116 Casper Ave 82701 307-746-2717
Tobey Cass, prin. Fax 746-2718
Newcastle MS 200/6-8
116 Casper Ave 82701 307-746-2746
Scott Shoop, prin. Fax 746-4983
Other Schools – See Osage

Osage, Weston
Weston County SD 1
Supt. — See Newcastle
Moats ES 50/K-5
551 Metz 82723 307-465-2253
Fax 465-2398

Parkman, Sheridan
Sheridan County SD 1
Supt. — See Ranchester
Slack ES 50/K-4
562 County Road 144 82838 307-655-2460
Deb Hofmeier, prin. Fax 655-2447

Pavillion, Fremont, Pop. 164
Fremont County SD 6 400/PK-12
PO Box 10 82523 307-856-7970
Diana Clapp, supt. Fax 856-3385
www.fre6.k12.wy.us/
Crowheart ES 50/K-3
PO Box 10 82523 307-486-2202
Paul Lundberg, prin. Fax 486-2372
Wind River ES 100/PK-5
PO Box 10 82523 307-856-6372
Paul Lundberg, prin. Fax 856-7745

Pine Bluffs, Laramie, Pop. 1,162
Laramie County SD 2 900/K-12
PO Box 489 82082 307-245-4050
Jack Cozort, supt. Fax 245-3561
laramie2.org
Pine Bluffs ES 200/K-6
PO Box 430 82082 307-245-4070
Sue Stevens, prin. Fax 245-3091
Other Schools – See Albin, Burns, Carpenter

Pinedale, Sublette, Pop. 1,658
Sublette County SD 1 800/K-12
PO Box 549 82941 307-367-2139
Doris Woodbury, supt. Fax 367-4626
www.pinedaleschools.org/
Pinedale ES 300/K-4
PO Box 549 82941 307-367-2828
Greg Legerski, prin. Fax 367-4706
Pinedale MS 200/5-8
PO Box 549 82941 307-367-2821
Kevan Kennington, prin. Fax 367-4217
Other Schools – See Bondurant

Powder River, Natrona
Natrona County SD 1
Supt. — See Casper
Powder River ES 50/K-6
PO Box 76 82648 307-472-3939
Tammy Kelly, prin. Fax 472-5882

Powell, Park, Pop. 5,288
Park County SD 1 1,600/K-12
160 N Evarts St 82435 307-754-2215
Kevin Mitchell, supt. Fax 764-6156
www.park1.k12.wy.us/
Clark ES 50/K-5
160 N Evarts St 82435 307-645-3241
Brent Walker, prin. Fax 645-3340
Parkside ES 200/K-5
160 N Evarts St 82435 307-754-5187
Kenny Jones, prin. Fax 764-6152
Powell MS 400/6-8
160 N Evarts St 82435 307-754-5716
Jason Sleep, prin. Fax 764-6155
Southside ES 200/K-5
160 N Evarts St 82435 307-754-5189
Ginger Sleep, prin. Fax 764-6153
Westside ES 200/K-5
160 N Evarts St 82435 307-754-5181
Brent Walker, prin. Fax 764-6154

Ranchester, Sheridan, Pop. 717
Sheridan County SD 1 900/K-12
PO Box 819 82839 307-655-9541
Sue Belish, supt. Fax 655-9477
www.sheridan.k12.wy.us/
Tongue River ES 200/K-5
PO Box 849 82839 307-655-2206
Deb Hofmeier, prin. Fax 655-2447
Tongue River MS 100/6-8
PO Box 879 82839 307-655-9533
Terry Myers, prin. Fax 655-9894
Other Schools – See Big Horn, Parkman

Rawlins, Carbon, Pop. 8,658
Carbon County SD 1 1,800/K-12
PO Box 160 82301 307-328-9200
M. Neil Terhune, supt. Fax 328-9258
www.crb1.k12.wy.us/
Highland Hills ES 300/K-5
1525 Darnley Rd 82301 307-328-9299
Bev Miller, prin. Fax 328-9290
Mountain View ES 200/K-5
1002 11th St 82301 307-328-9291
Benita Allard, prin. Fax 328-9218
Pershing ES 200/K-5
302 W Davis St 82301 307-328-9240
Darrin Jennings, prin. Fax 328-9241
Rawlins MS 300/6-8
1001 Brooks St 82301 307-328-9205
Traci Blaize, prin. Fax 328-9226
Other Schools – See Baggs, Bairoil, Sinclair

Recluse, Campbell
Campbell County SD 1
Supt. — See Gillette
Recluse S 50/K-8
31 Greenough Rd 82725 307-682-9612
Laurie Davis, prin. Fax 682-9619

Riverton, Fremont, Pop. 9,430
Fremont County SD 25 2,500/K-12
121 N 5th St W 82501 307-856-9407
Craig Beck, supt. Fax 856-3390
www.fremont25.k12.wy.us
Ashgrove ES 300/K-3
121 N 5th St W 82501 307-856-2626
Alleta Baltes, prin. Fax 856-4318
Jackson ES 200/K-3
121 N 5th St W 82501 307-856-9495
Owen Lampert, prin. Fax 857-1825
Lincoln ES 300/K-3
121 N 5th St W 82501 307-856-2625
Patricia Hardt, prin. Fax 856-7164
Rendezvous ES 400/4-5
121 N 5th St W 82501 307-857-7070
Mary Jo Chouinard, prin. Fax 857-6124
Riverton MS 500/6-8
121 N 5th St W 82501 307-856-9443
Cheryl Mowry, prin. Fax 857-1695

St. Margaret S 100/PK-5
220 N 7th St E 82501 307-856-5922
Sr. Florence McManamen, prin. Fax 857-5892
Trinity Lutheran S 100/K-8
419 E Park Ave 82501 307-857-5710
Susan Tucker, lead tchr. Fax 857-5710

Rock River, Albany, Pop. 214
Albany County SD 1
Supt. — See Laramie
Cozy Hollow S 50/K-8
15 Dodge Creek Ranch Rd 82058 307-322-5448
Ron Leathers, prin. Fax 322-9344
River Bridge S 50/K-8
74 River Bridge Rd 82058 307-378-2271
Ron Leathers, prin.
Rock River S 50/K-12
PO Box 128 82083 307-378-2271
Ron Leathers, prin. Fax 378-2505

Rock Springs, Sweetwater, Pop. 18,772
Sweetwater County SD 1 4,400/K-12
PO Box 1089 82902 307-352-3400
Paul Grube, supt. Fax 352-3411
www.sweetwater1.org/
Desert View ES 400/K-4
PO Box 1089 82902 307-352-3200
James Etherington, prin. Fax 352-3204
Northpark ES 300/K-4
PO Box 1089 82902 307-352-3235
Kelly McGovern, prin. Fax 352-3241
Overland ES 300/K-4
PO Box 1089 82902 307-352-3260
Dr. David Hvidston, prin. Fax 352-3268
Rock Springs East JHS 600/7-8
PO Box 1089 82902 307-352-3474
Kelly Boren, prin. Fax 352-3482
Walnut ES 400/K-4
PO Box 1089 82902 307-352-3225
Tina Johnson, prin. Fax 352-3224
Westridge ES 400/K-4
PO Box 1089 82902 307-352-3250
Richard Edwards, prin. Fax 352-3297
White Mountain ES 600/5-6
PO Box 1089 82902 307-352-3464
Wanda Heiser, prin. Fax 352-3471
Other Schools – See Farson, Wamsutter

Holy Spirit Catholic S 100/PK-6
210 A St 82901 307-362-6077
Iris Bonsell, prin. Fax 362-2177

Rozet, Campbell
Campbell County SD 1
Supt. — See Gillette
Rozet ES 300/K-6
PO Box 200 82727 307-682-3133
Dave Freeland, prin. Fax 682-7850

Saratoga, Carbon, Pop. 1,714
Carbon County SD 2 500/K-12
PO Box 1530 82331 307-326-5271
Robert Gates, supt. Fax 326-8089
www.crb2.k12.wy.us
Saratoga ES 200/K-6
PO Box 1590 82331 307-326-8365
David Rangitsch, prin. Fax 326-5720
Other Schools – See Elk Mountain, Encampment, Hanna, Medicine Bow

Sheridan, Sheridan, Pop. 16,333
Sheridan County SD 2 3,000/K-12
PO Box 919 82801 307-674-7405
Craig Dougherty, supt. Fax 674-5041
www.scsd2.com/
Coffeen ES 200/K-5
1053 S Sheridan Ave 82801 307-674-9333
Nicole Trahan, prin. Fax 674-9570
Highland Park ES 300/K-5
2 Mydland Rd 82801 307-672-2113
Brent Leibach, prin. Fax 673-1227
Meadowlark ES 300/K-5
1410 Desmet Ave 82801 307-672-3786
Jason Hillman, prin. Fax 674-9810
Sagebrush ES 400/K-5
1685 Hillpond Dr 82801 307-672-9059
Mike Wood, prin. Fax 674-6138
Sheridan JHS 700/6-8
500 Lewis St 82801 307-674-9745
Mitch Craft, prin. Fax 672-5311
Woodland Park ES 200/K-5
5135 Coffeen Ave 82801 307-674-7937
Janet Marshall, prin. Fax 673-1009
Other Schools – See Banner

Holy Name S 100/PK-8
121 S Connor St 82801 307-672-2021
Colleen Model, prin. Fax 672-2021
Luther S, 1325 Burton St 82801 50/K-6
Rev. William Heine, prin. 307-672-2766

Shoshoni, Fremont, Pop. 659
Fremont County SD 24 300/PK-12
112 W 3rd St 82649 307-876-2583
Tammy Cox, supt. Fax 876-2469
www.fremont24.com/
Shoshoni ES 200/PK-6
112 W 3rd St 82649 307-876-2563
Garry Smith, prin. Fax 876-2469
Shoshoni JHS 100/7-8
112 W 3rd St 82649 307-876-2576
Dan Martin, prin. Fax 876-9325

Sinclair, Carbon, Pop. 406
Carbon County SD 1
Supt. — See Rawlins
Sinclair ES 50/K-5
PO Box 307 82334 307-328-9293
Nancy Torstenbo, prin. Fax 328-9252

Sundance, Crook, Pop. 1,184
Crook County SD 1 800/K-12
PO Box 830 82729 307-283-2299
Lon Streib, supt. Fax 283-1810
www.crook1.com/
Sundance ES 200/K-6
PO Box 870 82729 307-283-1227
Kathleen Hood, prin. Fax 283-1717
Other Schools – See Hulett, Moorcroft

Ten Sleep, Washakie, Pop. 315
Washakie County SD 2 100/K-12
PO Box 105 82442 307-366-2223
Jerry Erdahl, supt. Fax 366-2304
www.wsh2.k12.wy.us
Ten Sleep ES 50/K-6
PO Box 105 82442 307-366-2233
Jerry Erdahl, prin. Fax 366-2304
Ten Sleep MS 50/7-8
PO Box 105 82442 307-366-2233
Jerry Erdahl, prin. Fax 366-2304

Thayne, Lincoln, Pop. 357
Lincoln County SD 2
Supt. — See Afton
Thayne ES 300/K-3
PO Box 520 83127 307-885-2380
Chad Jenkins, prin. Fax 883-3900

Thermopolis, Hot Springs, Pop. 2,905
Hot Springs County SD 1 500/K-12
415 Springview St 82443 307-864-6515
Marty Kobza, supt. Fax 864-6615
www.hotsprings.k12.wy.us
Thermopolis MS 100/6-8
415 Springview St 82443 307-864-6551
Jodie Cameron, prin. Fax 864-6508
Witters ES 200/K-5
415 Springview St 82443 307-864-6561
Matt Spring, prin. Fax 864-6605

Torrington, Goshen, Pop. 5,533
Goshen County SD 1 — 1,800/K-12
2602 W E St 82240 — 307-532-2171
Ray Schulte, supt. — Fax 532-7085
www.goshen.k12.wy.us
Lincoln ES — 300/K-2
1402 E P St 82240 — 307-532-4003
Steve Zimmerman, prin. — Fax 532-2669
Torrington MS — 300/6-8
2742 W E St 82240 — 307-532-7014
Marvin Haiman, prin. — Fax 532-8402
Trail ES — 300/3-5
1601 E M St 82240 — 307-532-5429
John Riddle, prin. — Fax 532-3451
Other Schools – See La Grange, Lingle, Yoder

Valley Christian S — 100/PK-5
2980 E D St 82240 — 307-532-3133
Cheryl Stoeger, admin. — Fax 532-2874

Upton, Weston, Pop. 857
Weston County SD 7 — 300/K-12
PO Box 470 82730 — 307-468-2461
Troy Claycomb, supt. — Fax 468-2797
bobcat.weston7.k12.wy.us
Upton ES — 100/K-5
PO Box 470 82730 — 307-468-9331
Clark Coberly, prin. — Fax 468-2832
Upton MS — 100/6-8
PO Box 470 82730 — 307-468-9331
Clark Coberly, prin. — Fax 468-2832

Wamsutter, Sweetwater, Pop. 265
Sweetwater County SD 1
Supt. — See Rock Springs
Desert ES — 50/K-5
PO Box 10 82336 — 307-324-7811
Richard Freudenberg, prin. — Fax 324-4824
Desert MS — 50/6-8
PO Box 10 82336 — 307-324-7811
Richard Freudenberg, prin. — Fax 324-4824

Wapiti, Park
Park County SD 6
Supt. — See Cody
Wapiti ES — 50/K-5
3167 Northfork Hwy 82450 — 307-587-3947
Kelly Merager, prin. — Fax 587-4428

Weston, Campbell
Campbell County SD 1
Supt. — See Gillette
Little Powder S — 50/K-8
15902 State Highway 59 N 82731 — 307-682-2725
Laurie Davis, prin. — Fax 682-7096

Wheatland, Platte, Pop. 3,464
Platte County SD 1 — 1,200/K-12
1350 Oak St 82201 — 307-322-5480
Stuart Nelson, supt. — Fax 322-2084
platte.schoolfusion.us/
Libbey ES — 200/K-2
1350 Oak St 82201 — 307-322-3836
Jill Bramlet, prin. — Fax 322-2517
West ES — 200/3-5
1350 Oak St 82201 — 307-322-4180
Valerie Calvert, prin. — Fax 322-4606
Wheatland MS — 200/6-8
1350 Oak St 82201 — 307-322-1550
Steven Loyd, prin. — Fax 322-1560
Other Schools – See Chugwater, Glendo

Wilson, Teton
Teton County SD 1
Supt. — See Jackson
Wilson ES — 200/K-5
PO Box 729 83014 — 307-733-3077
Tracy Poduska, prin. — Fax 733-8431

Worland, Washakie, Pop. 4,967
Washakie County SD 1 — 1,300/K-12
1900 Howell Ave 82401 — 307-347-9286
Mike Hejtmanek, supt. — Fax 347-8116
www.worlandhs.com/
East Side ES — 200/K-5
203 N 15th St 82401 — 307-347-4662
Linda Anderson, prin. — Fax 347-3783
South Side ES — 100/K-5
1229 Howell Ave 82401 — 307-347-3306
Joe Bishop, prin. — Fax 347-6150
West Side ES — 200/K-5
810 S 6th St 82401 — 307-347-4298
Joe Bishop, prin. — Fax 347-4927
Worland MS — 300/6-8
2150 Howell Ave 82401 — 307-347-3233
Richard Schaal, prin. — Fax 347-3710

Worland Adventist Christian S — 50/K-8
660 S 17th St 82401 — 307-347-2026
Claire James, prin.

Wright, Campbell, Pop. 1,425
Campbell County SD 1
Supt. — See Gillette
Cottonwood ES — 300/K-6
PO Box 330 82732 — 307-939-1381
Allan Burke, prin. — Fax 464-1304

Yoder, Goshen, Pop. 163
Goshen County SD 1
Supt. — See Torrington
Southeast ES — 100/K-6
PO Box 160 82244 — 307-532-3679
Brian Grasmick, prin. — Fax 532-5771
Southeast JHS — 100/7-8
PO Box 160 82244 — 307-532-7176
Brian Grasmick, prin. — Fax 532-5771

CHARTER SCHOOLS

Alaska

School	Address	City,State	Zip code	Telephone	Fax	Grade	Contact
Academy Charter S	801 E Arctic Ave	Palmer, AK	99645-6179	907-746-2358	746-2368	K-8	Barbara Gerard
Alaska Native Cultural S	110 Muldoon Rd	Anchorage, AK	99504-1403	907-575-6206		K-6	Timothy Godfrey
Anvil City Science Academy	PO Box 931	Nome, AK	99762-0931	907-443-6207	443-5144	5-8	Todd Hindman
Aquarian Charter S	1705 W 32nd Ave	Anchorage, AK	99517-2002	907-742-4900	742-4919	K-6	Susan Forbes
Aurora Borealis Charter S	705 Frontage Rd Ste A	Kenai, AK	99611-7740	907-283-0292	283-0293	K-8	Larry Nauta
Ayaprun Elitnaurvik Yup'ik Immersion ES	PO Box 1468	Bethel, AK	99559-1468	907-543-1645	543-1647	K-6	Agatha John-Shields
Career Education Center	724 27th Ave	Fairbanks, AK	99701-7037	907-479-4061	479-0230	7-12	Mark Rippy
Chinook Charter S	3002 International St	Fairbanks, AK	99701-7391	907-452-5020	452-5048	K-8	Michele Halbrooks
Eagle Academy Charter S	10901 Mausel St Ste 101	Eagle River, AK	99577-8065	907-742-3025	742-3035	K-6	Mary Meade
Family Partnership Charter S	401 E Fireweed Ln Ste 101	Anchorage, AK	99503-2100	907-742-3700	742-3710	K-12	Reed Whitmore
Fireweed Academy	PO Box 474	Homer, AK	99603-0474	907-235-9728	235-8561	3-6	Kiki Abrahamson
Fronteras Spanish Immersion S	PO Box 871433	Wasilla, AK	99687-1433	907-745-2223	745-6132	K-8	Casey Bowen
Frontier Charter S	400 W Northern Lights Blvd	Anchorage, AK	99503	907-742-1180	742-1188	K-12	Tim Scott
Highland Tech Charter S	5530 E Northern Lights Blvd	Anchorage, AK	99504-3135	907-742-1700	742-1711	7-12	Mark Standley
Juneau Community Charter S	10014 Crazy Horse Dr	Juneau, AK	99801-8529	907-586-2526	586-3543	K-6	Marjorie Hamburger
Kaleidoscope S	549 N Forest Dr	Kenai, AK	99611-7410	907-283-0804	283-3786	K-6	Mick Wykis
Ketchikan Charter S	410 Schoenbar Rd	Ketchikan, AK	99901-6218	907-225-8568	247-8568	K-8	Harry Martin
Kokrine Charter S	601 Loftus Rd	Fairbanks, AK	99709-3430	907-474-0958	479-2104	7-12	Linda Evans
Midnight Sun Family Learning Center	7275 W Midnight Sun Cir	Wasilla, AK	99654	907-357-6786	373-6786	K-8	Jeanne Troshynski
Rilke Schule German Schl of Arts & Sci	PO Box 243594	Anchorage, AK	99524-3594	907-742-7455	742-7456	K-8	Crystal Wrabetz
Soldotna Montessori Charter S	162 E Park Ave	Soldotna, AK	99669-7552	907-260-9221	260-9032	K-6	Mary Jo Sanders
Star of the North Secondary S	2945 Monk Ct	North Pole, AK	99705-6129	907-490-9025	490-9021	7-12	Annie Keep-Barnes
Tongass S of Arts & Sciences	410 Schoenbar Rd	Ketchikan, AK	99901-6218	907-225-5720	225-8822	PK-6	Janet Jackson
Twindly-Bridge Charter S	141 E Seldon Rd Ste C	Wasilla, AK	99654-3358	907-376-6680	746-6683	K-12	Greg Miller
Winterberry Charter S	508 W 2nd Ave	Anchorage, AK	99501-2208	907-742-4980	742-4985	K-6	Shanna Mall

Arizona

School	Address	City,State	Zip code	Telephone	Fax	Grade	Contact
AAEC - Paradise Valley	17811 N 32nd St	Phoenix, AZ	85032-1201	602-243-8004	243-8001	9-12	Dennis Gray
AAEC - Red Mountain	2165 N Power Rd	Mesa, AZ	85215-2971	480-854-1504	854-3564	9-12	Laura Metcalfe
AAEC - SMCC Campus	7050 S 24th St	Phoenix, AZ	85042-5806	602-243-8004	297-8540	9-12	Dr. William R. Conley
Academy Adventures PS	3902 N Flowing Wells Rd	Tucson, AZ	85705-2403	520-407-1200	407-1201	K-5	
Academy of Arizona - Main	2100 W Indian School Rd	Phoenix, AZ	85015-4907	602-274-0422	274-0543	K-8	Angelita Munoz
Academy of Arizona North Campus	13002 N 33rd Ave	Phoenix, AZ	85029-1208	602-843-0681	843-2092	K-8	Diana Likes
Academy of Building Industries	1547 E Lipan Blvd	Fort Mohave, AZ	86426-6031	928-788-2601	788-2610	9-12	Jean Thomas
Academy of Excellence	425 N 36th St	Phoenix, AZ	85008-6303	602-389-4271	389-4278	K-8	Eula Dean
Academy of Excellence - Central AZ	340 W Vah Ki Inn Rd	Coolidge, AZ	85128-3734	520-723-4773	723-4773	K-8	Zedna Grubbs
Academy of Math & Science	1557 W Prince Rd	Tucson, AZ	85705-3023	520-293-2676	888-1732	K-12	Tatyana Chayka
Academy of Tucson ES	9209 E Wrightstown Rd	Tucson, AZ	85715-5514	520-886-6076	886-6575	K-5	Clayton Connor
Academy of Tucson HS	10720 E 22nd St	Tucson, AZ	85748-7029	520-733-0096	733-0097	9-12	Susan Pearson
Academy of Tucson MS	2300 N Tanque Verde Loop Rd	Tucson, AZ	85749-9786	520-749-1413	749-2824	6-8	David Allardice
Academy With Community Partners	433 N Hall	Mesa, AZ	85203-7407	480-833-0068	833-8966	9-12	Margaret Williamson
Accelerated Learning Center	4105 E Shea Blvd	Phoenix, AZ	85028-3525	602-485-0309	485-9356	9-12	Frank Canady
Accelerated Learning Center Laboratory	5245 N Camino De Oeste	Tucson, AZ	85745-8925	520-743-2256	743-2417	K-12	David Jones
Accelerated Learning Charter S	320 S Main St	Cottonwood, AZ	86326-3905	928-634-0650	634-0672	K-8	Susan Pluff
ACCLAIM Academy	7624 W Indian School Rd	Phoenix, AZ	85033-3009	623-691-0919	691-6091	K-8	Melanie Powers
ACE Charter HS	1929 N Stone Ave	Tucson, AZ	85705-5642	520-628-8316	791-9893	9-12	Arnold Palacios
A Child's View S	2846 W Drexel Rd Ste 100	Tucson, AZ	85746	520-578-2075	578-2076	K-5	Morris Shaw
Acorn Montessori Charter S	8556 E Loos Dr	Prescott Valley, AZ	86314-6455	928-772-5778	775-8654	2-7	Cynthia Johnson
Acorn Montessori Charter S - West	7555 E Long Look Dr	Prescott Valley, AZ	86314-5507	928-772-5778	775-8654	K-1	Cynthia Johnson
Adventure S	1950 E Placita Sin Nombre	Tucson, AZ	85718-2092	520-296-0656	721-4472	K-4	Maryann Penczar
Ahwatukee Foothills Prep S	10210 S 50th Pl	Phoenix, AZ	85044-5209	480-763-5101	763-5107	K-6	Howard Brown
All Aboard Charter S	5827 N 35th Ave	Phoenix, AZ	85017-1915	602-433-0500	973-8208	K-4	Rhonda Newton
Allsports Academy	6211 E Speedway Blvd	Tucson, AZ	85712-5128	520-731-2150	731-2160	5-9	Moses Montoya
Alta Vista Charter HS	5040 S Campbell Ave	Tucson, AZ	85706-1510	520-294-4922	294-4933	9-12	Alicia Alvarez
Ambassador Academy	10841 S 48th St	Phoenix, AZ	85044-1716	480-961-2214		K-2	Elba Reyes
American Heritage Academy	2030 E Cherry St	Cottonwood, AZ	86326-6963	928-634-2144	634-9053	K-12	Steve Anderson
American Heritage Academy	675 W Sunland Dr	Camp Verde, AZ	86322-7059	928-634-2144	634-9053	K-8	Steve Anderson
Amerischools Academy	1333 W Camelback Rd	Phoenix, AZ	85013-2106	602-532-0100	532-9964	K-12	Deann Chan
Amerischools Academy	1150 N Country Club Rd	Tucson, AZ	85716-3942	520-620-1100	322-5351	K-12	Courtney Braren
Amerischools Academy - Yuma	2098 S 3rd Ave	Yuma, AZ	85364-6425	928-329-1100	329-9177	K-8	Dea Bermudez
Amerischools College Prep Academy	7444 E Broadway Blvd	Tucson, AZ	85710-1411	520-722-1200	624-4376	K-12	Charlene Mendoza
Apache Trail HS	945 W Apache Trl	Apache Junction, AZ	85120-5409	480-288-0337	288-0340	9-12	Giles Glithero
Apex Academy	945 W Apache Trl	Apache Junction, AZ	85120-5409	480-288-0337	288-0340	K-8	Bill Coats
Arizona Academy of Leadership	PO Box 22046	Tucson, AZ	85734-2046	520-887-5863	887-5869	K-7	Kelvin Strozier
Arizona Academy of Science & Technology	PO Box 13606	Phoenix, AZ	85002-3606	602-253-1199	595-8693	K-12	Joan Miller
AZ Call-A-Teen Center of Excellence	649 N 6th Ave	Phoenix, AZ	85003-1659	602-252-6721	252-2952	9-12	Pam Smith
Arizona Charter Academy	PO Box 1929	Surprise, AZ	85378-1929	623-974-4959	974-4931	K-12	Heather Henderson
AZ Conservatory for Arts & Academics	2820 W Kelton Ln	Phoenix, AZ	85053-3028	602-266-4278	978-2764	6-12	Joann Garrett
Arizona School for the Arts	1313 N 2nd St	Phoenix, AZ	85004-1715	602-257-1444	252-7795	6-12	Dr. Leah Roberts
Arizona Upgrade Academy	327 S 15th St	Cottonwood, AZ	86326-3432	928-634-3722	634-3695	5-12	Allen Smithson
Arizona Virtual Academy	4495 S Palo Verde Rd	Tucson, AZ	85714	520-623-1483	623-1803	K-12	Julie Frein
Arts Academy at Estrella Mountain	2504 S 91st Ave	Tolleson, AZ	85353-8921	623-474-2120	936-5337	PK-8	Veronica Wimberly
Arts Academy at South Mountain	4039 E Raymond St	Phoenix, AZ	85040-1930	602-725-7615		K-8	Verocica Wimberly
Arts Academy of Mesa	2929 E McKellips Rd	Mesa, AZ	85213-3128	480-924-1500	924-0552	K-8	Bob Meko
Ascending Roots Charter S	7310 N 27th Ave	Phoenix, AZ	85051-7505	602-424-1830	424-1831	K-8	Kisha Spellman-White
Avalon S at San Marcos	1045 S San Marcos Dr	Apache Junction, AZ	85120-6337	480-373-9575	373-9600	K-8	Mathew Reese
Az-Tec HS	2330 W 28th St	Yuma, AZ	85364-6954	928-314-1900	726-2826	9-12	Linda Munk
Aztlan Academy	802 W Silverlake Rd	Tucson, AZ	85713-1455	520-573-1500	573-1600	6-12	Judy Bisignano
BASIS S - Tucson	3825 E 2nd St	Tucson, AZ	85716-4368	520-326-3444	326-6359	5-12	Carolyn McGarvey
Basis Scottsdale	11440 N 136th St	Scottsdale, AZ	85259-3812	480-451-7500	451-4555	5-12	Diane Moser
Beginning Academy	5061 N Camino Sumo	Tucson, AZ	85718-6053	520-299-6259	299-6880	K-5	Betsy Sales
Benchmark ES	4120 E Acoma Dr	Phoenix, AZ	85032-4753	602-765-3582	765-1932	K-6	Barbara Darroch
Bennett Academy	2930 W Bethany Home Rd	Phoenix, AZ	85017-1615	602-943-1317		K-8	Nancy Bennett
Berean Academy	4699 E Highway 90	Sierra Vista, AZ	85635-2437	520-459-4113	459-4121	K-12	Mark Bennett
Bradley Academy of Excellence	200 N Dysart Rd	Avondale, AZ	85323-2418	623-932-9902	932-9904	K-8	Tanya Burston
Bright Beginnings S	400 N Andersen Blvd	Chandler, AZ	85224-8273	480-821-1404	821-1463	K-8	Karen Edris
Burke Basic S	131 E Southern Ave	Mesa, AZ	85210-5355	480-964-4602	964-6566	K-8	Glen Gaddie
Calli Olin Academy	4747 W Calle Vicam	Tucson, AZ	85757-8860	520-883-5051		9-12	Theresa Carino
Calli Ollin Academy	200 N Stone Ave Fl 3	Tucson, AZ	85701	520-882-3029	882-3041	9-12	Elizabeth Tridico
Cambridge Academy East	9412 E Brown Rd	Mesa, AZ	85207-4338	480-641-2828	325-2365	K-6	Linda Gonzalez
Camelback Academy	7634 W Camelback Rd	Glendale, AZ	85303-5627	623-247-2204	247-1113	K-6	Karen Kordon
Candeo Schools	PO Box 12384	Glendale, AZ	85318-2384	623-979-6500	942-2710	K-6	
Canyon Pointe Academy	4941 W Union Hills Dr	Glendale, AZ	85308-1486	602-896-1166	896-1164	K-6	Amy Rhone
Canyon Rose Academy	3686 W Orange Grove Rd	Tucson, AZ	85741	520-514-5112	797-8868	9-12	Lisa Cothrun
Carden of Tucson S	5260 N Royal Palm Dr	Tucson, AZ	85705-1148	520-293-6661	408-7366	K-8	Bette Jeppson
Carden Traditional S of Glendale	4744 W Grovers Ave	Glendale, AZ	85308-3453	602-439-5026	547-2841	K-8	Rebeca Venegas
Carden Traditional S of Surprise	15688 W Acoma Dr	Surprise, AZ	85379-5652	623-556-2179	547-2806	K-8	Kristy Faux
Career Success HS	3816 N 27th Ave	Phoenix, AZ	85017-4703	602-285-5525	285-0026	9-12	Robert Duffy
Career Success HS - Cave Creek	PO Box 7010	Cave Creek, AZ	85327-7010	480-575-0075	575-0061	9-12	Maureen Racz
Career Success HS - Copper Square	301 W Roosevelt St	Phoenix, AZ	85003-1324	602-393-4200	393-4205	9-12	Kathy Scott
Career Success S - Sage Campus	3120 N 32nd St	Phoenix, AZ	85018-6202	602-955-0355	508-0682	K-8	Hector Placencia
Carpe Diem Collegiate HS	PO Box 6502	Yuma, AZ	85366-6502	928-317-3113	317-0828	6-12	Rick Ogston
Casa Verde Charter HS	1362 N Casa Grande Ave	Casa Grande, AZ	85122-2648	520-876-1163	876-0667	9-12	Anna McCauley
CASY Country Day S 1	7214 E Jenan Dr	Scottsdale, AZ	85260-5416	480-951-3190	998-4029	K-5	Bill Thompson
Center for Academic Success #1	900 Carmelita Dr	Sierra Vista, AZ	85635-1927	520-458-4200	458-6396	9-12	Stephen Huff
Center for Academic Success #2	510 N G Ave	Douglas, AZ	85607-2822	520-364-2616	417-0973	9-12	Stephen Huff
Center for Academic Success #3	1415 F Ave	Douglas, AZ	85607-1655	520-805-1558	458-1409	K-4	Stephen Huff
Center for Academic Success #4	1415 F Ave	Douglas, AZ	85607-1655	520-805-1558	805-1549	5-8	Marcela Munguia
Center for Academic Success #5	900 Carmelita Dr	Sierra Vista, AZ	85635-1927	520-458-4200	458-1409	K-6	Linda Denno
Center for Creative Education Charter S	215 S Main St	Cottonwood, AZ	86326-3908	928-634-3288	634-9781	K-6	Mary Ann Green
Center for Educational Excellence	1700 E Elliot Rd Ste 9	Tempe, AZ	85284-1631	480-632-1940	632-1398	K-8	Stacey Cochran
Challenge Charter S	5801 W Greenbriar Dr	Glendale, AZ	85308-3847	602-938-5411	938-5393	K-6	Gregory Miller
Challenger Basic S	1315 N Greenfield Rd	Gilbert, AZ	85234-2813	480-830-1750	830-1763	K-6	Brad Tobin
Chandler Preparatory Academy	2020 N Arizona Ave	Chandler, AZ	85225	480-855-5410	855-7789	7-8	Helen Hayes
Chandler Scholastic Academy	2716 N Dobson Rd	Chandler, AZ	85224-1803	480-782-1082	782-1089	K-6	Paul Hudson
Chavez MS	802 W Silverlake Rd	Tucson, AZ	85713-1455	520-573-1500	573-1600	6-12	Sr. Judy Bisignano
Children Reaching for the Sky Prep	1844 S Alvernon Way	Tucson, AZ	85711-5607	520-790-8400	620-6570	K-8	Lee Griffin

School	Address	City,State	Zip code	Telephone	Fax	Grade	Contact
Childrens Success Academy	PO Box 11368	Tucson, AZ	85734-1368	520-799-8403	799-8427	K-8	Nanci Aiken
City HS	PO Box 2608	Tucson, AZ	85702-2608	520-623-7223	547-0680	9-12	Carolyn Brennan
Civano Charter S	10673 E Mira Ln	Tucson, AZ	85747-5983	520-731-3466	731-3477	K-8	Connie Erickson
Compass HS	PO Box 17810	Tucson, AZ	85731-7810	520-296-4070	296-4103	9-12	John Ferguson
Concordia Charter S	142 N Date	Mesa, AZ	85201-6419	602-461-0555	461-0556	K-2	
Copper Canyon Academy	7785 W Peoria Ave	Peoria, AZ	85345-5922	623-930-1734	930-8709	K-8	Jinny Ludwig
Cornerstone Charter S	7107 N Black Canyon Hwy	Phoenix, AZ	85021-7619	602-595-2198	242-2398	9-12	George Smith
Country Gardens Charter S	6301 W Alta Vista Rd	Laveen, AZ	85339	602-237-3741	237-3892	K-12	Goldie Burge
Crestview College Prep HS	2616 E Greenway Rd	Phoenix, AZ	85032-4320	602-765-8470	765-8471	9-12	Donnie Houston
Crittenton Youth Academy	715 W Mariposa St	Phoenix, AZ	85013-2449	602-274-7318	274-7549	6-12	Cheri Rostan
Crown Charter S	PO Box 363	Litchfield Park, AZ	85340-0363	623-535-9300	535-5410	K-6	James Shade
Deer Valley Academy	3050 W Agua Fria Fwy	Phoenix, AZ	85027	623-467-6874	467-6955	9-12	Barbara Daggett
Desert Heights Charter S	5821 W Beverly Ln	Glendale, AZ	85306-1801	602-896-2900	467-9540	K-8	Mark Giles
Desert Hills HS	1515 S Val Vista Dr	Gilbert, AZ	85296-3854	480-813-1151	813-1161	9-12	Art Madden
Desert Marigold S	6210 S 28th St	Phoenix, AZ	85042-4715	602-243-6909	243-6933	K-8	Amy Bird
Desert Mosaic S	5757 W Ajo Hwy	Tucson, AZ	85735-9334	520-578-2022	578-0834	K-12	Lynn Spoon
Desert Pointe Academy	7785 W Peoria Ave	Peoria, AZ	85345-5922	623-930-1734	930-8709	5-12	Jinny Ludwig
Desert Rose Academy	326 W Fort Lowell Rd	Tucson, AZ	85705-3816	520-797-4884	797-8868	9-12	
Desert Sky Community S	122 N Craycroft Rd	Tucson, AZ	85711-3238	520-745-3888	745-5110	K-5	Shelly Adrian
Desert Springs Academy	3833 E 2nd St	Tucson, AZ	85716-4368	520-321-1709	321-9316	K-8	Lydia Capara
Desert Star Community S	1240 S Recycler Rd	Cornville, AZ	86325-5224	928-282-0171	284-9565	K-6	Susan Simon
Desert View Academy	2363 S Kennedy Ln	Yuma, AZ	85365-2416	928-314-1102	314-1086	K-6	Rick Ogston
Destiny Community S	4710 E Baseline Rd	Mesa, AZ	85206-4602	480-325-8950	539-0147	K-8	Wendy Noble
Destiny S	798 E Prickly Pear Dr	Globe, AZ	85501-2395	928-425-0925	425-0927	K-8	Nancy McLendon
DINE Southwest HS	HC 63 Box 303	Winslow, AZ	86047-9424	928-657-3272	657-3272	9-12	Cheryl Chischillie
Discovery Plus Academy	PO Box 549	Pima, AZ	85543-0549	928-485-2498	485-2508	K-6	Donna Bolinger
Dobson Academy	PO Box 6070	Chandler, AZ	85246-6070	480-855-6325	855-6323	K-8	George Ellis
Doby MS	17505 N 79th Ave Ste 112	Glendale, AZ	85308-8724	623-878-8059	878-8175	5-8	Jimmie Daniels
E.A.G.L.E. Academy	423 S Colorado Rd	Golden Valley, AZ	86413-9203	928-565-3400	565-3454	K-12	Karry Whitten
EAGLE College Prep S	2450 W South Mountain Ave	Phoenix, AZ	85041-7601	602-323-5400	323-5401	K-3	
Eagle's Aerie S	17019 S Greenfield Rd	Gilbert, AZ	85295-1918	480-988-3212	988-3280	K-12	Tim Peak
Eastpointe HS	8495 E Broadway Blvd	Tucson, AZ	85710-4009	520-731-8180	731-8179	9-12	Andrew Singleton
East Valley Academy	910 N 85th Pl	Scottsdale, AZ	85257-4561	480-610-1711	421-0183	K-6	Janet Stoeppelman
East Valley HS	7420 E Main St	Mesa, AZ	85207-8306	480-981-2008	641-4473	9-12	Kathy Tolman
E-cademie	417 N 16th St	Phoenix, AZ	85006-3710	602-416-6400	416-6393	9-12	Kristen Smith
E-cademie a Charter HS - Woods	3160 N 33rd Ave	Phoenix, AZ	85017-4817	602-278-5552	385-4495	9-12	
Edge Charter S-Child & Family Resources	2555 E 1st St	Tucson, AZ	85716-4152	520-881-8940	325-8780	9-12	Reese Millen
Edge Charter S - Himmel Park	2555 E 1st St	Tucson, AZ	85716-4152	520-881-1389	881-0852	9-12	Robert Barrette
Edge Charter S - Northwest	2555 E 1st St	Tucson, AZ	85716-4152	520-881-1389	881-0852	9-12	Robert Barrette
Edge Charter S - Sahuarita	2555 E 1st St	Tucson, AZ	85716-4152	520-393-1690	881-1689	9-12	Robert Lopez
Educational Opportunity Center	3834 W 16th St	Yuma, AZ	85364-4107	928-329-0990	783-0886	9-12	Brian Grossenburg
EduPreneurship Student Center	2632 W Augusta Ave	Phoenix, AZ	85051-6732	602-973-8998	973-5510	K-8	Carol Ann Sammans
Edu-Prize S	580 W Melody Ave	Gilbert, AZ	85233-1418	480-813-9537	813-6742	K-8	Lynn Robershotte
Eduprize S	4567 W Roberts Rd	Queen Creek, AZ	85142-7511	480-888-1610	888-1655	K-8	
E-Institute at Acoma	16578 W Greenway Rd Ste 204	Surprise, AZ	85388-2184	623-556-2179	547-2841	9-12	Ken Turer
E-Institute at Union Hills	3515 W Union Hills Dr	Glendale, AZ	85308	602-843-3891	843-4375	9-12	Crispin Zamudio
El Dorado HS	2200 N Arizona Ave Ste 17	Chandler, AZ	85225-3452	480-726-9536	726-9543	9-12	Ramona Gonzales
Esperanza Community Collegial Academy	2507 E Bell Rd	Phoenix, AZ	85032-2413	602-996-1125	996-4238	9-12	Pamela Cullen
Estrella HS	510 N Central Ave	Avondale, AZ	85323-1909	623-932-6561	932-1263	9-12	William Horton
Excalibur Charter S	10839 E Apache Trl Ste 113	Apache Junction, AZ	85120-3415	480-373-9575	373-9600	9-12	Jeffrey Parker
Flagstaff Arts and Leadership Academy	3100 N Fort Valley Rd	Flagstaff, AZ	86001	928-779-7223	779-7041	9-12	Kirk Quitter
Flagstaff Junior Academy	306 W Cedar Ave	Flagstaff, AZ	86001-1413	928-774-6007	774-7268	PK-8	Dulcie Ambrose
Foothills Academy	7191 E Ashler Hills Dr	Scottsdale, AZ	85266-9300	480-488-5583	488-6902	6-12	Donald Senneville
Fountain Hills Charter S	PO Box 18419	Fountain Hills, AZ	85269-8419	480-837-0046	837-0024	K-8	Michael Bashaw
4 Winds Academy	PO Box 1210	Eagar, AZ	85925-1210	928-333-1060	333-2926	K-8	Steve Chavez
Franklin Charter S	320 E Warner Rd	Gilbert, AZ	85296-2976	480-632-0722	632-8716	K-6	Terry Nicoll
Franklin Charter S	21151 S Crismon Rd	Queen Creek, AZ	85142-8957	480-987-0722	987-3517	K-8	Chad McLeod
Franklin Charter S	2345 N Horne	Mesa, AZ	85203-1823	480-649-0712	649-8716	K-6	Rebekah Baker
Franklin Charter S	22951 S Power Rd	Gilbert, AZ	85297	480-632-0722	632-8716	K-8	Thomas Lee
Franklin Phonetic S	6116 E State Route 69	Prescott Valley, AZ	86314-2806	928-775-6747	775-6740	K-8	Cindy Franklin
Freedom Academy	15014 N 56th St Ste 1	Scottsdale, AZ	85254-2407	602-424-0771	424-0773	K-8	Linda Hoffman
Freire Freedom S	300 E University Blvd	Tucson, AZ	85705	520-624-7552	624-7518	6-8	JoAnn Groh
Friendly House Academia Del Pueblo S	201 E Durango St	Phoenix, AZ	85004-2913	602-258-4353	416-7375	K-8	Ximena Doyle
GateWay Early College HS	108 N 40th St	Phoenix, AZ	85034-1795	602-286-8762	286-8752	9-12	
GEM Charter S	1704 N Center St	Mesa, AZ	85201-2223	480-833-2622	833-2655	K-6	Nelleke van Savooyen
Genesis Academy	525 E McDowell Rd	Phoenix, AZ	85004-1537	602-254-8050	254-8094	9-12	Karen Callahan
Gila Preparatory Academy	1976 W Thatcher Blvd	Safford, AZ	85546-3318	928-348-8688	348-8877	6-12	Kathy Maxwell
Gilbert Arts Academy	862 E Elliot Rd	Gilbert, AZ	85234-6912	480-325-6100	953-0831	K-6	Nanette Allen
Glendale Preparatory Academy	7201 W Beardsley Rd	Glendale, AZ	85308-5673	602-889-0822	889-0825	6-12	David Williams
Grand Canyon College Prep Charter S	7541 S Willow Dr	Tempe, AZ	85283-5032	480-233-3622	491-7096	6-12	David Gordon
Great Expectations Academy	1466 W Camino Antigua	Sahuarita, AZ	85629-9720	520-399-2121	399-2123	K-8	Beth Phillips
Guerrero MS	2797 N Introspect Dr	Tucson, AZ	85745-9454	520-807-2836	623-9679	3-8	Carmen Campuzano
Ha:san MS	667 N 7th Ave	Tucson, AZ	85705-8336	520-622-4621		6-8	William Rosenberg
Ha:San Prep & Leadership Charter S	1333 E 10th St	Tucson, AZ	85719-5808	520-882-8826	882-8651	9-12	William Rosenberg
Happy Valley S	7140 W Happy Valley Rd	Peoria, AZ	85383-3255	623-376-2900	376-9030	K-6	Glen Gaddie
Harvest Preparatory Academy	350 E 18th St	Yuma, AZ	85364-5723	928-782-2052		K-12	Deborah Ybarra
Hayes HS	PO Box 10899	Bapchule, AZ	85121-0105	520-315-5100	315-5115	9-12	Richard Stoner
Hearn Academy	17606 N 7th Ave	Phoenix, AZ	85023-1567	602-896-9160	896-1997	K-8	Jane Vert
Heritage Academy	32 S Center St	Mesa, AZ	85210-1306	480-969-5641	969-6972	7-12	Earl Taylor
Heritage ES	13419 W Ocotillo Rd	Glendale, AZ	85307-3220	623-935-1931	935-1931	K-8	Aaron Robinson
Heritage ES - Williams Campus	790 E Rodeo Rd	Williams, AZ	86046-9653	928-635-3998	635-3999	K-3	
Hermosa Montessori Charter S	12051 E Fort Lowell Rd	Tucson, AZ	85749-9702	520-749-5518	749-6087	K-8	Sheila Stolov
Higgins Institute	1805 E Elliot Rd Ste 112	Tempe, AZ	85284-1746	480-413-0829	413-9365	K-8	Martha Wallace
Highland Free S	510 S Highland Ave	Tucson, AZ	85719-6427	520-623-0104	903-1318	K-6	Nicholas Sofka
Hope HS	9040 W Campbell Ave	Phoenix, AZ	85037-1408	623-772-8013		9-12	Richard Clawson
Hope HS Online	5651 W Talavi Blvd	Glendale, AZ	85306	602-674-5555	943-9700	9-12	Beth Collins
Horizon Community Learning Center	16233 S 48th St	Phoenix, AZ	85048-0801	480-659-3000	659-3022	K-12	Jan Gleeson
Horizons Back-to-Basics S	PO Box 2208	Peoria, AZ	85380-2208	602-253-8799	253-8824	K-8	Jorge Vega
Humanities & Science Institute	1105 E Broadway Rd	Tempe, AZ	85282-1505	480-317-5900	529-4999	9-12	Ana Kennedy
Humanities & Sciences Institute	5201 N 7th St	Phoenix, AZ	85014-2802	602-650-1333	650-1881	9-12	Sue Durkin
Imagine Charter S at Avondale	950 N Elisio C Felix Jr Way	Avondale, AZ	85323	602-344-1730	344-1740	PK-5	Joshua Jordan
Imagine Charter S at Bell Canyon	18052 N Black Canyon Hwy	Phoenix, AZ	85053-1715	602-547-7920	547-7923	K-8	Loretta Newell
Imagine Charter S at Camelback	5050 N 19th Ave	Phoenix, AZ	85015	602-344-4620	344-4630	K-5	Carolyn Birney
Imagine Charter S at Coolidge	1290 W Vah Ki Inn Rd	Coolidge, AZ	85128-9314	520-723-5391	723-5491	K-5	Darrin Anderson
Imagine Charter S at Cortez Park	3535 W Dunlap Ave	Phoenix, AZ	85051-5303	602-589-9840	589-9841	K-8	Heidi Schloesser
Imagine Charter S at Desert West	6738 W McDowell Rd	Phoenix, AZ	85035-4642	602-344-7150	344-7160	K-5	Freddie Villalon
Imagine Charter S at East Mesa	9701 E Southern Ave	Mesa, AZ	85209-3769	480-355-6830	355-6840	K-9	Sheri Ruttinger
Imagine Charter S at Rosefield	12050 N Bullard Ave	Surprise, AZ	85379-6325	623-344-4300	344-4310	K-8	Bruce Hannah
Imagine Charter S at Sierra Vista	1000 E Wilcox Dr	Sierra Vista, AZ	85635-2622	520-224-2500	224-2511	K-8	Deborah Summers
Imagine Charter S at Tempe	1538 E Southern Ave	Tempe, AZ	85282-5687	480-355-1640	355-1650	K-6	Sonia Gonzales
Imagine Charter S at West Gilbert	2061 S Gilbert Rd	Gilbert, AZ	85295-4620	480-855-2700	855-2701	K-8	Linda Horner
Imagine Prep at Apache Junction	1843 W 16th Ave	Apache Junction, AZ	85120-6967	480-355-0530	355-0540	9-12	Bridget Carrington
Imagine Prep at Surprise	14850 N 156th Ave	Surprise, AZ	85379-5653	623-344-1770	344-1780	7-12	Sheri Kisselbach
Integrity Education Centre	PO Box 10247	Scottsdale, AZ	85271-0247	480-731-4829	394-0711	K-12	Holly Mullan
Intelli School - Glendale	13806 N 51st Ave	Glendale, AZ	85306-4834	602-564-7300	564-7301	9-12	Janet Jorgensen
Intelli School - Main	1727 N Arizona Ave	Chandler, AZ	85225	602-564-7300	564-7301	9-12	Jonathan Owen
Intelli School - Metro Center	3101 W Peoria Ave Ste B305	Phoenix, AZ	85029-5210	602-564-7240	564-7241	9-12	Jennifer Lowing
Intelli School - Paradise Valley	1107 E Bell Rd Ste 109A	Phoenix, AZ	85022	602-564-7280	564-7281	9-12	Timothy Howard
International Commerce Institute	5201 N 7th St	Phoenix, AZ	85014-2802	602-650-1116	650-1881	9-12	
International Commerce Institute - Tempe	1105 E Broadway Rd	Tempe, AZ	85282-1505	480-317-5900	829-4999	9-12	Ana Kennedy
International Commerce Institute-Tsaile	Dine College - Bldg AJ	Tsaile, AZ	86556	800-762-0010	650-1777	9-12	Arthur Ben
Jefferson Academy of Advanced Learning	40 S 11th St	Show Low, AZ	85901-6001	928-537-5432	537-0440	K-12	Sandy Stewart
Kachina Country Day S - North Campus	10460 N 56th St	Scottsdale, AZ	85253-1133	480-951-0745	951-1267	K-8	Steve Prahcharov
Kestrel HS	PO Box 11028	Prescott, AZ	86304-1028	928-541-1090	541-9939	9-12	W. Sue Foglia
Keystone Montessori Charter S	1025 E Liberty Ln	Phoenix, AZ	85048-8462	480-460-7312	283-0225	K-9	Sherri Sampson
Khalsa Montessori S	2536 N 3rd St	Phoenix, AZ	85004-1308	602-252-3799	252-5224	K-8	Satwant Khalsa
Khalsa Montessori S	3701 E River Rd	Tucson, AZ	85718-6633	520-529-3611	615-0625	K-8	Nirvair Khalsa
Kingman Academy of Learning HS	3420 N Burbank St	Kingman, AZ	86409-3105	928-681-2900	681-2424	9-12	Jeff Martin
Kingman Academy of Learning IS	3419 Harrison St	Kingman, AZ	86409-3604	928-681-3200	681-2424	3-5	Debbie Padilla
Kingman Academy of Learning MS	3269 Harrison St	Kingman, AZ	86409-3679	928-692-5265	681-2424	6-8	Dawn Day
Kingman Academy of Learning PS	3400 N Burbank St	Kingman, AZ	86409-3105	928-692-2500	692-2505	K-2	Trudi Bradley
Lake Havasu Charter S	2700 Jamaica Blvd S	Lk Havasu Cty, AZ	86406-7711	928-505-5427	505-3533	K-12	Patty Hauchrog
La Paloma Academy	2050 N Wilmot Rd	Tucson, AZ	85712-3039	520-721-4205	721-4263	K-8	Jackie Trujillo
La Paloma Academy - Lakeside	8140 E Golflinks Rd	Tucson, AZ	85730-1229	520-733-7373	733-7392	K-8	Randy Musgrove
La Paloma Academy - Midtown	225 N Country Club Rd	Tucson, AZ	85716-5233	520-325-5566	325-6622	K-6	Jason Riegert
La Puerta HS	5757 W McDowell Rd	Phoenix, AZ	85035-4947	623-878-8059	878-8175	9-12	Jimmie Daniels
Leading Edge Academy	415 N Gilbert Rd	Gilbert, AZ	85234	480-545-8011		K-12	

School	Address	City,State	Zip code	Telephone	Fax	Grade	Contact
Leading Edge Academy	4815 W Hunt Hwy	Queen Creek, AZ	85142-3271	480-655-6787	655-6788	K-8	Matt Reese
Leading Edge Academy at East Mesa	1010 S Ellsworth Rd	Mesa, AZ	85208-2957	480-984-5645	627-3634	K-6	Jill Gaitens
Learning Crossroads Basic Academy	1460 S Horne	Mesa, AZ	85204-5760	480-446-9288	449-9565	K-12	Robin Cubley
Learning Foundation & Performing Arts	5761 E Brown Rd	Mesa, AZ	85205	480-807-1100	834-6210	K-12	Nicki Triggs
Learning Foundation & Performing Arts S	1120 S Gilbert Rd	Gilbert, AZ	85296-3465	480-635-1900	635-1906	K-12	Theresa Flynn
Learning Foundation Performing Arts S	851 N Stapley Dr	Mesa, AZ	85203	480-834-6202	834-3991	K-12	Jeannine Rucker
Learning Institute	5312 N 12th St	Phoenix, AZ	85014-2926	602-241-7876	241-7886	7-12	Adele Ferrini
Legacy S	7464 E Main St	Mesa, AZ	85207-8306	480-981-1500	641-4473	K-10	Kathy Tolman
Legacy Traditional S	PO Box 692	Maricopa, AZ	85139-0287	520-423-9999	423-9997	K-6	Aaron Hale
Liberty Arts Academy	3015 S Power Rd	Mesa, AZ	85212-3000	480-830-3444	830-4335	K-6	Debra Coleman
Liberty HS	PO Box 2343	Globe, AZ	85502-2343	928-402-8024	402-8358	9-12	Sara Macdonald Ph.D.
Liberty Traditional Charter S	4027 N 45th Ave	Phoenix, AZ	85031-2840	602-442-8791	353-9270	K-8	Bonnie Knauel
Lifelong Learning Academy	3295 W Orange Grove Rd	Tucson, AZ	85741-2937	520-219-4383	544-0220	K-8	Mary Lou Klem
Life Skills Center of Arizona	8123 N 35th Ave	Phoenix, AZ	85051-9403	602-242-6400	242-6823	9-12	William Flake
Luz Academy of Tucson	2797 N Introspect Dr	Tucson, AZ	85745-9454	520-882-6216	623-9291	9-12	Carmen Campuzano
Madison Preparatory S	5815 S Mcclintock Dr	Tempe, AZ	85283-3227	480-345-2306	345-0059	7-12	David Batchelder
Masada Charter S	PO Box 2277	Colorado City, AZ	86021-2277	928-875-2525	875-2526	K-9	Le Anne Timpson
Math & Science Success Academy	434 W Lerdo Rd	Tucson, AZ	85756-6655	520-751-2783	888-1732	K-5	Adriana Rodriguez
Maya HS	3660 W Glendale Ave	Phoenix, AZ	85051-8335	602-242-3442	242-5255	9-12	George Vallejous
Mesa Arts Academy	221 W 6th Ave	Mesa, AZ	85210-2446	480-844-3965	844-0205	K-8	Susan Douglas
Mesa Preparatory Academy	6659 E University Dr	Mesa, AZ	85205-7605	480-222-4233	222-4234	6-12	Robert Wagner
Metropolitan Arts Institute	1700 N 7th Ave	Phoenix, AZ	85007-1760	602-258-9500	258-9504	9-12	Matthew Baker
Mexicayotl Charter S	850 N Morley Ave	Nogales, AZ	85621-2924	520-287-6790	287-0037	K-12	Baltizar Garcia
Midtown HS	7318 W Lynwood St	Phoenix, AZ	85035-4542	623-936-8682	936-8559	9-12	John White
Midtown PS	4735 N 19th Ave	Phoenix, AZ	85015-3725	602-265-5133	604-2337	K-5	Judy White
Milestones Charter S	4707 E Robert E Lee St	Phoenix, AZ	85032-9529	602-404-1009	404-5456	K-8	Tara Cabardo
Mingus Springs Charter S	PO Box 827	Chino Valley, AZ	86323-0827	928-636-4766	636-5149	K-8	Dawn Gonzales
Mission Academy HS	8910 N Central Ave	Phoenix, AZ	85020-2819	602-944-2097	944-0252	9-12	Jayne Shaw
Mission Charter S	1118 W Glendale Ave	Phoenix, AZ	85021-8635	602-943-4986	943-5936	1-8	Jayne Shaw
Mission Montessori Academy	12990 E Shea Blvd	Scottsdale, AZ	85259-5305	480-860-4330	657-3715	K-7	Betty Matthews
Mohave Accelerated ES East	2850 Silver Creek Rd	Bullhead City, AZ	86442-8309	928-704-9345	704-4977	K-3	
Mohave Accelerated Learning Center	PO Box 21288	Bullhead City, AZ	86439-1288	928-704-9345	704-4977	K-12	Vickie Christensen
Montage Academy	32619 N Scottsdale Rd	Scottsdale, AZ	85266	480-488-0215	488-0241	K-8	Esperanza Vega
Montessori Academy	2928 N 67th Pl	Scottsdale, AZ	85251-6002	480-945-1121	874-2928	K-8	Julianne Lewis
Montessori Charter S of Flagstaff	850 N Locust St	Flagstaff, AZ	86001-3343	928-226-1212	774-0337	K-8	Marina Smith
Montessori Childrens House	2400 W Datsi St	Camp Verde, AZ	86322-8412	928-567-1878	567-2107	K-K	Janet Taylor
Montessori Day Charter S - Mountainside	9215 N 14th St	Phoenix, AZ	85020-2713	602-943-7672	395-0271	K-8	Pat Freeman
Montessori Day Charter S - Tempe	1700 W Warner Rd	Chandler, AZ	85224-2676	480-730-8886	730-9072	K-8	Colleen Ortega
Montessori de Santa Cruz Charter S	PO Box 4706	Tubac, AZ	85646-4706	520-398-0536	398-0776	K-8	Lisa Harrison
Montessori Education Centre Charter S	2834 E Southern Ave	Mesa, AZ	85204-5517	480-926-8375	503-0515	PK-6	Tamara Whiting
Montessori Education Ctr - Charter S N	815 N Gilbert Rd	Mesa, AZ	85203-5805	480-964-1381	668-5457	PK-9	Lisa Wakefield
Montessori House Charter S	2415 N Terrace Cir	Mesa, AZ	85203-1220	480-464-2800	464-2836	K-6	Sheryl Richardson
Montessori S at Anthem	42302 N Vision Way Ste 110	Anthem, AZ	85086-1467	623-551-5083	551-5679	K-8	Debra Slagle
Montessori Schoolhouse	1301 E Fort Lowell Rd	Tucson, AZ	85719-2239	520-319-8668	881-4096	K-5	Michael Ebner
Montezuma MS	5040 S Price Rd	Tempe, AZ	85282-7445	480-831-6057	831-6095	6-8	Abelardo Batista
Mountain English Spanish Academy	2300 E 6th Ave	Flagstaff, AZ	86004-4247	928-773-4088	773-4086	6-8	Ana Archuleta
Mountain Oak Charter S	124 N Virginia St	Prescott, AZ	86301-3224	928-541-7700	445-1301	K-8	Cynthia Roe
Mountain Rose Academy	3686 W Orange Grove Rd	Tucson, AZ	85741	520-930-9373	797-8868	9-12	
Mountain S	311 W Cattle Drive Trl	Flagstaff, AZ	86001-7060	928-779-2392	773-3246	K-6	Renee Fauset
Mt. Turnbull Academy	Hwy 70	Bylas, AZ	85530	928-475-3050	475-3051	9-12	
New Destiny Leadership Charter S	1923 E Broadway Rd	Phoenix, AZ	85040-2411	602-268-2234	268-1622	K-5	
New Horizon S for the Performing Arts	446 E Broadway Rd	Mesa, AZ	85204-2020	480-655-7444	655-8220	K-6	Jim Wyler
New Samaritan HS	1455 S Stapley Dr	Mesa, AZ	85204-5882	480-833-7470	833-7480	9-12	Robert Duffy
New School for the Arts	1216 E Apache Blvd	Tempe, AZ	85281-6005	480-481-9235	970-6625	9-12	Katy Cardenas
New School for the Arts MS	1112 E Apache Blvd	Tempe, AZ	85281-5822	480-481-9235	970-6625	7-8	Katy Cardenas
Newton Montessori & Charter S	PO Box 2166	Camp Verde, AZ	86322-2166	928-567-2363	567-5374	PK-5	Shirley Sullivan
New Visions Academy	PO Box 1539	Cottonwood, AZ	86326-1539	928-634-7320	634-7494	9-12	Ann Jenkins
New Visions Academy - St. John's Campus	PO Box 791	Saint Johns, AZ	85936-0791	928-337-3268	337-3383	9-12	Joey Grant
New Visions Academy - Star Valley S	198 E Ezell Ln	Payson, AZ	85541-2499	928-468-1401	468-1402	9-12	Gary Hampsch
New West S	98 N Oak Dr	Benson, AZ	85602-7732	520-586-1976	586-1655	K-8	Hank Payton
New West S	98 N Oak Dr	Benson, AZ	85602-7732	520-586-1976	586-1655	9-12	Hank Payton
New World Educational Center Charter S	1313 N 2nd St Ste 200	Phoenix, AZ	85004-1701	602-238-9577	238-9210	K-12	Gordon Ilstrup
NFL YET College Prep Academy	4848 S 2nd St	Phoenix, AZ	85040-2122	602-243-7788		K-12	Raul Ruiz
Northern AZ Academy for Career Dev.	PO Box 125	Taylor, AZ	85939-0125	928-536-4222	536-4441	9-12	Kathy Doucette-Edwards
Northern AZ Academy for Career Dev.	502 Airport Rd	Winslow, AZ	86047-5400	928-289-3329	289-4485	9-12	Kathy Doucette-Edwards
Northland Preparatory Academy	3300 E Sparrow Ave	Flagstaff, AZ	86004-6703	928-214-8776	214-8778	7-12	Bob Lombardi
North Pointe Preparatory S	10215 N 43rd Ave	Phoenix, AZ	85051-1025	623-209-0017	209-0021	7-12	Richard Gow
North Star Charter S	10720 W Indian School Rd	Phoenix, AZ	85037	623-907-2661	907-2501	9-12	Christine Ahearn
Nosotros Academy	440 N Grande Ave	Tucson, AZ	85745-2703	520-624-1023	624-7999	9-12	Paul Felix
Oasis HS	8632 W Northern Ave	Glendale, AZ	85305-1308	623-878-8059	878-8175	9-12	Jimmie Daniels
Old Pueblo Children's Academy	165 N Sarnoff Dr	Tucson, AZ	85710-2933	520-296-1600	298-0558	K-8	Ronda McCarthy
Ombudsman Charter S - Central	1525 N Oracle Rd	Tucson, AZ	85705	520-624-2260	882-2160	6-12	Emily Langfeldt
Ombudsman Charter S - East	3943 E Thomas Rd	Phoenix, AZ	85018-7511	602-840-2997	840-1402	6-12	
Ombudsman Charter S - East II	4041 E Thomas Rd	Phoenix, AZ	85018	602-667-7759	667-7793	9-12	
Ombudsman Charter S - Metro	4220 W Northern Ave	Phoenix, AZ	85051-5756	602-840-2997	842-6157	6-12	
Ombudsman Charter S - Northeast	3242 E Bell Rd	Phoenix, AZ	85032-2727	602-485-9872	367-0367	6-12	
Ombudsman Charter S - Northwest	9516 W Peoria Ave	Peoria, AZ	85345-6139	602-840-2997	840-1402	6-12	
Ombudsman Charter S - Pantano	150 N Pantano Rd	Tucson, AZ	85710	520-290-3062	290-3083	6-12	
Ombudsman Charter S - Valencia	1686 W Valencia Rd	Tucson, AZ	85746	520-573-5858	807-9333	6-12	Emily Langfeldt
Ombudsman Charter S - West	3618 W Bell Rd	Glendale, AZ	85308	602-840-2997	840-1402	6-12	
Omega Academy	5757 W McDowell Rd	Phoenix, AZ	85035-4947	602-269-1007	269-1073	K-4	Carmen Gulley
Omega Alpha Academy	1402 N San Antonio Ave	Douglas, AZ	85607-2434	520-805-1261	805-1272	K-12	Dennis Gordon
PACE Preparatory Academy	155 S Montezuma Castle Hwy	Camp Verde, AZ	86322	928-567-1805		9-12	Richard Thelander
PACE Preparatory Academy	6287 E Copper Hill Dr	Prescott Valley, AZ	86314-2906	928-775-9675	775-9673	9-12	Richard Thelander
Pan-American Charter ES	3001 W Indian School Rd	Phoenix, AZ	85017	602-266-3989	266-3979	K-8	Marta Pasos
Paradise Education Center	15533 W Paradise Ln	Surprise, AZ	85374-5851	623-975-2646	975-2841	K-8	Patrick Schrader
Paradise Honors HS	15531 N Reems Rd	Surprise, AZ	85374	623-546-7215	975-4380	9-12	
Paragon Science Academy ES	2975 W Linda Ln	Chandler, AZ	85224-7340	480-814-1600	814-1661	6-8	Nehmet Argin
Paramount Academy	11039 W Olive Ave	Peoria, AZ	85345-9200	623-977-0614	977-0615	K-8	Douglas Williams
Park View MS	8300 E Dana Dr	Prescott Valley, AZ	86314-8183	928-775-5115	775-6253	6-8	Mary Bruhn
Patagonia Community Montessori S	PO Box 1008	Patagonia, AZ	85624-1008	520-394-9530	394-2864	PK-8	Marilyn Cooper
Pathfinder Academy	2542 N 76th Pl	Mesa, AZ	85207-1252	480-986-7071	986-9858	K-8	Susan Stradling
Patriot Academy	19011 E San Tan Blvd	Queen Creek, AZ	85142	480-279-4780	807-1209	K-8	Jay Brown
Paulden Community S	24850 N Naples St	Paulden, AZ	86334	928-636-1430	636-3087	K-8	
Payson Center for Success	PO Box 919	Payson, AZ	85547-0919	928-472-2011	472-2039	9-12	Kathe Ketchem
Peak S	2016 N 1st St Ste A	Flagstaff, AZ	86004-4201	928-779-0771	779-0774	K-8	Paula Drossman
Peoria Accelerated HS	8885 W Peoria Ave	Peoria, AZ	85345-6442	623-979-0031	979-0113	9-12	Marcus Englund
Peoria Horizons Charter S	11820 N 81st Ave	Peoria, AZ	85345-5736	623-979-3559	488-0241	K-8	Karen Martinez
Phoenix Advantage Charter S	3738 N 16th St	Phoenix, AZ	85016-5915	602-263-8777	263-8822	K-8	Jack Rowe
Phoenix Collegiate Academy	5610 S Central Ave	Phoenix, AZ	85040	602-268-9900		6-12	
Pillar Academy of Business & Finance	PO Box 6095	Mohave Valley, AZ	86446-6095	602-944-5111	944-4533	9-12	Richard Hay
Pima Partnership S	1346 N Stone Ave	Tucson, AZ	85705-7338	520-791-2711	791-2202	7-12	Heidi Bacon
Pima Vocational HS	97 E Congress St	Tucson, AZ	85701-1732	520-243-1740	903-0753	9-12	Gloria Proo
Pine Forest Charter S	1120 W Kaibab Ln	Flagstaff, AZ	86001-6217	928-779-9880	779-9792	K-8	Michael Heffernan
Pinnacle HS - Casa Grande	409 W McMurray Blvd	Casa Grande, AZ	85122-2314	520-423-2380	423-2383	9-12	Stacey Boyd
Pinnacle HS - Mesa	151 N Centennial Way	Mesa, AZ	85201-6734	480-668-5003	668-5005	9-12	Shaela Offord
Pinnacle HS - Nogales	2055 N Grand Ave	Nogales, AZ	85621-1038	520-281-5109	281-5132	9-12	Locha Partida
Pinnacle HS - Tempe E	1712 E Guadalupe Rd Ste 101	Tempe, AZ	85283-3983	480-785-7776	785-7778	9-12	Michael Williams
Pinnacle HS - Tempe W	2224 W Southern Ave Ste 2	Tempe, AZ	85282-4345	602-414-0950	414-0927	9-12	Michael Matwick
Pinnacle Pointe Academy	6753 W Pinnacle Peak Rd	Glendale, AZ	85310-5301	623-537-3535	537-4433	K-6	
Pinnacle Virtual HS	4700 S McClintock Dr	Tempe, AZ	85282	480-755-8222	755-8111	7-12	Beth Cirulis
Pioneer Preparatory S	6629 W Clarendon Ave	Phoenix, AZ	85033-4027			K-2	
Polytechnic ES	6859 E Rembrandt Way	Mesa, AZ	85212	480-727-1612	727-1725	K-6	
PPEP TEC - Arnold Learning Center	4140 W Ina Rd Ste 118	Tucson, AZ	85741-2236	520-579-8560	579-8566	9-12	Rebecca Edmonds
PPEP TEC - Borjorquez Learning Center	203 Bisbee Rd	Bisbee, AZ	85603-1122	520-432-5445	432-5414	9-12	Rebecca Edmonds
PPEP TEC - Chavez Learning Center	1233 N Main St Ste B	San Luis, AZ	85349	928-627-8550	627-8980	9-12	Rebecca Edmonds
PPEP TEC - Eugene Lopez Learning Center	158 W Maley St	Willcox, AZ	85643-2130	520-384-2050	384-2112	9-12	Rebecca Edmonds
PPEP TEC - Fernandez Learning Center	1840 E Benson Hwy	Tucson, AZ	85714-1770	520-889-8276	741-4369	9-12	Rebecca Edmonds
PPEP TEC - Paul Learning Center	220 E Florence Blvd	Casa Grande, AZ	85122-4031	520-836-6549	836-0290	9-12	Rebecca Edmonds
PPEP TEC - Pena Learning Center	725 N Central Ave Ste 113	Avondale, AZ	85323-1660	623-925-2161	925-1035	9-12	Rebecca Edmonds
PPEP TEC - Powell Learning Center	4116 Avenida Cochise Ste F	Sierra Vista, AZ	85635-5843	520-458-8205	458-8293	9-12	Rebecca Edmonds
PPEP TEC - Raul H. Castro Learning Ctr	530 E 12th St	Douglas, AZ	85607-1925	520-364-4405	364-1405	9-12	Rebecca Edmonds
PPEP TEC - Robles Junction	10451 S Sasabe Hwy	Tucson, AZ	85736-1254	520-822-3064	822-5070	9-12	Rebecca Edmonds
PPEP TEC - Soltero Learning Center	8677 E Golf Links Rd	Tucson, AZ	85730-1315	520-290-9167	290-9220	9-12	Rebecca Edmonds
PPEP TEC - Yepez Learning Center	115 N Columbia Ave	Somerton, AZ	85350	928-627-9648	627-9197	9-12	Rebecca Edmonds
Precision Academy	7318 W Lynwood St	Phoenix, AZ	85035-4542	623-936-8682	936-8559	9-12	Dr. Caroline White
Precision Academy System Charter S	3906 E Broadway Rd	Phoenix, AZ	85040	602-453-3661	453-3667	9-12	Daniel Martinez

School	Address	City,State	Zip code	Telephone	Fax	Grade	Contact
Premier Charter HS	7544 W Indian School Rd	Phoenix, AZ	85033	623-245-1500	245-1506	9-12	Elisha Madden
Prescott Valley S	9500 E Lorna Ln	Prescott Valley, AZ	86314-2324	928-772-8744	775-4457	K-12	Connie Ruveile
Presidio S	1695 E Fort Lowell Rd	Tucson, AZ	85719-2319	520-881-5222	881-5522	K-12	Terry Garza
Primavera Technical Learning Center	3029 N Alma School Rd	Chandler, AZ	85224	480-456-6678	820-2168	9-12	Damian Creamer
RCB HS - Phoenix	6049 N 43rd Ave	Phoenix, AZ	85019-1641	602-973-6018	589-1349	9-12	Mark Hebert
Redwood Elementary Academy	6810 W Thunderbird Rd	Peoria, AZ	85381-5025	623-878-0986	776-7956	K-8	Ronald Palmer
Rimrock Public HS	PO Box 248	Rimrock, AZ	86335-0248	928-567-9213	567-9304	9-12	Kathleen McCabe
Riverbend Preparatory S	5625 S 51st Ave	Laveen, AZ	85339-6300	602-285-3003	285-5560	K-6	
Romero HS	3005 E Fillmore St	Phoenix, AZ	85008-6120	602-850-2600	850-2615	9-12	Dr. Jane Juliano
RSD Charter HS	12814 N 28th Dr	Phoenix, AZ	85029-1385	602-564-7342	564-7361	9-12	
SABIS International	1903 E Roeser Rd	Phoenix, AZ	85040-3341	602-305-8865	323-5526	K-8	Willie Henry
Sage Academy	5334 E Thunderbird Rd	Scottsdale, AZ	85254-3655	602-485-3402		K-8	Deborah Boehm
Sandoval Preparatory HS	3830 N 67th Ave	Phoenix, AZ	85033-4036	623-845-0781	849-2840	9-12	Robert Wilson
San Pedro Valley HS	360 S Patagonia St	Benson, AZ	85602-6533	520-586-8901	586-6189	9-12	Angela Carreira
San Tan Learning Center	4450 E Elliot Rd	Gilbert, AZ	85234-7901	480-222-0811	539-1028	K-4	
Satori Charter S	3727 N 1st Ave	Tucson, AZ	85719-1609	520-293-7555	293-7020	2-8	Phyllis Gold
Scholars' Academy	PO Box 3475	Quartzsite, AZ	85359-3475	928-927-9420	927-9425	7-12	Steve McClenning
School for Integrated Academics & Tech	518 S 3rd St	Phoenix, AZ	85004-2506	602-258-3927	340-1965	9-12	Geraldine Baumann
School for Integrated Academics & Tech	901 S Campbell Ave	Tucson, AZ	85719-6519	520-791-3016	791-3582	9-12	David Gerber
Scottsdale Preparatory Academy	7496 E Tierra Buena Ln	Scottsdale, AZ	85260-1613	480-703-8510		6-12	Diane Bishop
Sedona Charter S	165 Kachina Dr	Sedona, AZ	86336-4303	928-204-6464	204-6486	K-8	Alice Madar
Self Development Charter S	1709 N Greenfield Rd	Mesa, AZ	85205-3103	480-641-2640	641-2678	K-8	Anjum Majeed
Sequoia Charter S	1460 S Horne	Mesa, AZ	85204-5760	480-649-7737	649-0711	K-12	Ryan LoMonaco
Sequoia Choice S - AZ Distance Learning	1460 S Horne	Mesa, AZ	85204-5760	480-655-7005	655-7911	K-12	Ron Neil
Sequoia Ranch S	PO Box 399	Mayer, AZ	86333-0399	928-632-9851	632-9852	K-12	Michael Pospisil
Sequoia S for Deaf & Hard of Hearing	1460 S Horne	Mesa, AZ	85204-5760	480-649-7737	649-0711	K-12	Curt Radford
Sequoia School - Sequoia Village S	982 Full House Ln	Show Low, AZ	85901-4042	928-537-1208	537-4275	K-12	Tony Rhineheart
Shelby S	PO Box 31570	Mesa, AZ	85275-1570	480-478-4706	478-0861	K-10	Nicole Kamp
Sierra Oaks S	650 W Linda Vista Rd	Oracle, AZ	85623-6039	520-896-3100	896-3101	K-8	Paula Jensen
Sierra Summit Academy	PO Box 1360	Hereford, AZ	85615-1360	520-803-0508	803-0877	8-12	Siamak Khadjenoury
Sky Islands S	201 S Wilmot Rd	Tucson, AZ	85711-4002	520-382-9210		9-12	Shari Popen
Skyline Prep and Arts Academy	550 W Warner Rd	Chandler, AZ	85225-4364	480-287-5588	287-5599	K-8	Ronda Owens
Skyline Ranch S	1084 San Tan Hills Dr	Queen Creek, AZ	85143-3489	480-888-7520	665-6137	K-8	Maribel Lopez
Skyline Technical HS	15220 S 50th St Ste 109	Phoenix, AZ	85044-9132	480-763-8425	763-8427	9-12	Molly Ryan
Skyline West HS	17667 N 91st Ave	Peoria, AZ	85382-3019	623-875-3175	875-9261	7-12	Brian Shipman
Skyview S	125 S Rush St	Prescott, AZ	86303-4432	928-776-1730	776-1742	K-8	John Hurley
Sonoran Desert S	4448 E Main St Ste 7	Mesa, AZ	85205-7916	480-396-5463	396-4980	9-12	Patricia Dalman
Sonoran Science Academy	2325 W Sunset Rd	Tucson, AZ	85741-3809	520-665-3400	665-3420	K-12	Fatih Kartas
Sonoran Science Academy - Broadway	6880 E Broadway Blvd	Tucson, AZ	85710-2818	520-751-2401	751-2451	K-8	Ercan Aydogdu
Sonoran Science Academy - Phoenix	4837 E McDowell Rd	Phoenix, AZ	85008-4225	602-244-9855	244-9856	K-9	Mehmet Argin
Southern Arizona Community HS	2470 N Tucson Blvd	Tucson, AZ	85716-2469	520-319-6113	319-6115	9-12	Abelardo Cubillas
Southgate Academy	850 W Valencia Rd	Tucson, AZ	85706-7619	520-741-7900	741-7901	K-12	Sherry Matyjasik
South Pointe Charter ES	2033 E Southern Ave	Phoenix, AZ	85040-3344	602-953-2933	953-0831	K-6	Tonya Bridges-Brown
South Pointe HS	8325 S Central Ave	Phoenix, AZ	85042-6576	602-243-0600	243-0800	9-12	Larry McGill
South Ridge HS	1122 S 67th Ave	Phoenix, AZ	85043-4417	602-953-2933	953-0831	9-12	Kerry Clark
Southside Community S	2701 S Campbell Ave	Tucson, AZ	85713-5080	520-623-7102	623-7125	K-8	Janet Dougherty
South Verde Technology Magnet S	462 S Main St	Camp Verde, AZ	86322	928-567-8076	567-8093	9-12	
STAR Charter S	145 Leupp Rd	Flagstaff, AZ	86004-8501	928-415-3533	606-9965	K-8	Mark Sorenson
Starshine Academy	2801 N 31st St	Phoenix, AZ	85008-1126	602-957-9557	956-0065	K-12	Patricia McCarty
Starshine St. Johns S	4102 W Union Hills Dr	Glendale, AZ	85308-1702	602-957-9557	956-0065	K-12	Jan Shoop
Stellar Prep	8632 W Northern Ave	Glendale, AZ	85305-1308	623-878-8059	878-8175	K-4	Jimmie Daniels
Stepping Stones Academy	35812 N 7th St	Phoenix, AZ	85086-7410	623-465-4910	587-8514	K-8	Ann Marie Short
Student Choice HS	1833 N Scottsdale Rd	Tempe, AZ	85281-1563	480-947-9511	947-9624	9-12	Peggy Lynam
Sturgeon MS	5757 W McDowell Rd	Phoenix, AZ	85035-4947	602-269-1007	269-1073	5-8	Carmen Gulley
Successful Beginnings Charter S	841 E McNeil	Show Low, AZ	85901-6006	928-537-2365	537-2365	K-5	
Summit ES	1313 N 2nd St	Phoenix, AZ	85004-1733	602-252-7727	252-7729	K-6	Carolyn Sawyer
Summit HS	728 E Mcdowell Rd	Phoenix, AZ	85006-2592	602-258-8959	258-8953	9-12	Christine Enriquez
Sunnyside Charter & Montessori S	PO Box 2166	Camp Verde, AZ	86322-2166	928-567-2363	567-5374	6-9	Dr. Betty Chester
Sun Valley Charter S	5806 S 35th Pl	Phoenix, AZ	85040	602-692-4914	612-2196	K-6	
Sun Valley HS	1143 S Lindsay Rd	Mesa, AZ	85204-6298	480-497-4800	497-1314	9-12	Joe Procopio
Superior S	16025 N Dysart Rd	Surprise, AZ	85374-4062	623-875-5975	875-5985	9-12	Tina Davis
TAG S	10129 E Speedway Blvd	Tucson, AZ	85748-1921	520-296-0006	296-0046	K-8	Ron Hom
Telesis Preparatory Academy	2598 Starlite Ln	Lk Havasu Cty, AZ	86403-4946	928-855-8661	855-9302	K-12	Sandra Breece
Tempe Accelerated HS	5040 S Price Rd	Tempe, AZ	85282-7445	480-831-6057	831-6095	9-12	Abelardo Batista
Tempe Preparatory Academy	1251 E Southern Ave	Tempe, AZ	85282-5605	480-839-3402	755-0546	6-12	Julie Boles
Tertulia Pre-College Community IS	812 S 6th Ave	Phoenix, AZ	85003-2528	602-262-2200	262-2570	5-8	Miriam Zamora
Tertulia Pre-College Community Private S	812 S 6th Ave	Phoenix, AZ	85003-2528	602-262-2200	262-2570	K-4	Miriam Zamora
Toltecali Academy	200 N Stone Ave	Tucson, AZ	85701-1208	520-882-3029	882-3041	9-12	Natalie Carrillo
Transformational Learning Centers	PO Box 5310	Tucson, AZ	85703-0310	520-628-1404	628-1394	K-12	Tina Giberti
Tri-City College Prep HS	5522 Side Rd	Prescott, AZ	86301-8483	928-777-0403	777-0402	9-12	Dr. Mary Ellen Halvorson
Triumphant Learning Center	201 E Main St	Safford, AZ	85546-2051	928-348-8422	348-8423	K-8	Robin Dutt
Tucson Academy of Leadership & Arts	210 E Broadway Blvd	Tucson, AZ	85701-2014	520-882-9144	792-0668	K-9	Leon Buttler
Tucson Accelerated HS	7820 E Wrightstown Rd	Tucson, AZ	85715-4339	520-722-4721	722-4785	9-12	Hanz Raymond
Tucson Country Day S	9239 E Wrightstown Rd	Tucson, AZ	85715-5514	520-296-0883	290-1521	K-8	Richard Cooper
Tucson International Academy	1625 W Valencia Rd Ste 109	Tucson, AZ	85746-6022	520-792-3255	792-3245	K-10	Miguel Montemayor
Tucson International Academy	1230 E Broadway Blvd	Tucson, AZ	85719-5821	520-792-3255	792-3245	K-10	Brian Henderson
Tucson International Academy East Campus	450 N Pantano Rd	Tucson, AZ	85710-2309	520-792-3255		K-8	
Tucson International Academy West Campus	2700 W Broadway Blvd	Tucson, AZ	85745-1715	520-792-3255		K-11	
Tucson Preparatory S	1010 W Lind St	Tucson, AZ	85705-3466	520-622-4185	622-4755	9-12	Jody Sullivan
Tucson Urban League Academy	2305 S Park Ave	Tucson, AZ	85713-3644	520-622-3651	622-4767	6-12	Lorraine Richardson
University Public S	735 E Fillmore St	Phoenix, AZ	85006-3324	480-727-1612	727-1725	K-12	
Vah-ki MS	PO Box 10885	Bapchule, AZ	85121-0104	480-403-8580	315-2017	5-8	Beverly Crawford
Vail HS	9040 S Rita Rd Ste 1270	Tucson, AZ	85747-9192	520-879-1900	879-1901	9-12	Dennis Barger
Valley Academy - Charter S	1520 W Rose Garden Ln	Phoenix, AZ	85027-3529	623-516-7747	516-2703	K-8	Leslie Szotak
Ventana Academic S	6424 E Cave Creek Rd	Cave Creek, AZ	85331	480-488-9362	488-2079	K-8	Helen Shoulders
Venture Academy	1535 W Dunlap Ave	Phoenix, AZ	85021-2953	602-242-4220		K-10	Fred Bennett
Veritas Preparatory Academy	2131 E Lincoln Dr	Phoenix, AZ	85016-1122	602-263-1128	263-7997	6-12	Andrew Ellison
Victory HS	PO Box 8374	Phoenix, AZ	85066-8374	602-243-7583	243-7563	9-12	Shirley Branham
Villa Montessori - Phoenix	4535 N 28th St	Phoenix, AZ	85016-4998	602-955-2210	381-4017	K-8	Margo O'Neill
Vision Charter S	PO Box 23455	Tucson, AZ	85734-3455	520-444-0241	741-8123	9-12	Dr. Wilma Soroosh
Visions Unlimited Academy	1275 E Barney Ln	Benson, AZ	85602-7955	520-586-8691	586-3074	K-8	Richard Valentine
Webster Basic S	7301 E Baseline Rd	Mesa, AZ	85209-4907	480-986-2335	354-3490	K-6	Kelly Wade
Westland S	4141 N 67th Ave	Phoenix, AZ	85033-3314	623-247-6456	247-6520	K-12	Kathryn Couch
West Phoenix HS	3835 W Thomas Rd	Phoenix, AZ	85019-4434	602-269-1110	269-1110	9-12	Robert Villa
Westwind Preparatory Academy	2045 W Northern Ave	Phoenix, AZ	85021-5157	602-864-7731	864-7720	6-12	Debra Slagle
Wildcat S	5660 S 12th Ave	Tucson, AZ	85706-3102	520-294-5473	294-5475	6-9	Scott Mundell
Willow Creek Charter S	2100 Willow Creek Rd	Prescott, AZ	86301-5391	928-776-1212	776-0009	K-8	Terese Soto
YCFA Achieve Academy	10401 Highway 89A	Prescott Valley, AZ	86314	928-775-8005	775-8064	4-12	
Young Leaders PS	PO Box 22046	Tucson, AZ	85734-2046	520-940-3784		K-3	Tonya Strozier
Young Scholars Academy	1501 Valencia Rd	Bullhead City, AZ	86426-5218	928-704-1100	704-1177	K-8	Tonnie Smith
Youngtown Charter S	13226 N 113th Ave	Youngtown, AZ	85363-1026	623-974-0355	815-8902	K-8	Jacob Duran

Arkansas

School	Address	City,State	Zip code	Telephone	Fax	Grade	Contact
Academic Center of Excellence	112 N School St	Osceola, AR	72370-2413	870-563-2150	622-1025	1-10	Ellouise Tubbs
Academics Plus Charter S	900 Edgewood Dr	Maumelle, AR	72113-6275	501-851-3333	851-2599	K-12	Jake Honea
Academy of Technology	PO Box 160	Vilonia, AR	72173-0160	501-796-2018	796-4322	2-4	Brian Ratliff
Arkansas Virtual Academy	10802 Executive Center Dr	Little Rock, AR	72211-4354	501-664-4225	664-4226	K-8	Karen Ghidotti
Benton County School of the Arts	2005 S 12th St	Rogers, AR	72758-6307	479-636-2272	636-5447	K-8	Dr. Paul Hines
Covenant Keepers College Preparatory S	8300 Geyer Springs Rd	Little Rock, AR	72209-4946	501-584-6440		6-8	Dr. Valerie Tatum
Dreamland Academy of Performing Arts	5615 Geyer Springs Rd	Little Rock, AR	72209-1812	501-562-9278	562-9279	K-5	Dr. Carolyn Carter
E-Stem Charter ES	112 W 3rd St	Little Rock, AR	72201-2702	501-552-9000	975-4090	K-4	Cindy Barton
E-Stem Charter HS	112 W 3rd St	Little Rock, AR	72201-2702	501-552-9080	975-4092	9-12	John Bacon
E-Stem Charter MS	112 W 3rd St Ste 200	Little Rock, AR	72201-2709	501-552-9040	975-4091	5-8	Katrina Jones
Haas Hall Academy	3155 N College Ave Ste 108	Fayetteville, AR	72703-3500	479-267-4805	267-4862	9-12	Dr. Martin Schoppmeyer
Hope Academy	1021 E 2nd Ave	Pine Bluff, AR	71601-4571	870-540-0900	540-0905	5-8	Earl Glass
Imboden Area Charter S	PO Box 297	Imboden, AR	72434-0297	870-869-3015	869-3016	K-8	Judy Warren
KIPP: Delta College Preparatory S	215 Cherry St	Helena, AR	72342-3502	870-753-9444	753-9450	5-12	Scott Shirey
Lisa Academy	21 Corporate Hill Dr	Little Rock, AR	72205-4537	501-227-4942	227-4952	K-12	Omer Ozmeral
Lisa Academy-North Little Rock	5410 Landers Rd	No Little Rock, AR	72117-1935	501-945-2727	945-2728	K-8	Emin Cavusoglu
Northwest Arkansas Academy of Fine Arts	506 W Poplar St	Rogers, AR	72756-4440	479-631-2787	899-6479	9-12	Barbara Padgett
Osceola Communication/Arts & Business S	1425 Ohlendorf Rd	Osceola, AR	72370-3688	870-622-0550	622-0550	K-12	Sally Wilson
Raider Open Door Academy	4109 Race St	Jonesboro, AR	72401-7650	870-910-7800	910-7852	5-8	Marilyn Sawyer
Ridgeroad Charter MS	4601 Ridge Rd	No Little Rock, AR	72116-7264	501-771-8155	771-8159	7-8	Lenisha Broadway
School of Excellence	PO Box 148	Humphrey, AR	72073-0148	870-873-2008	873-2008	6-9	Dr. James Young
Vilonia Academy of Service & Technology	49 Eagle St	Vilonia, AR	72173-9215	501-796-2940		5-6	Cathy Riggins

School	Address	City,State	Zip code	Telephone	Fax	Grade	Contact
		California					
Abraxis Charter HS	PO Box 2587	Santa Rosa, CA	95405-0587	707-568-4492	568-3762	9-12	Carley Moore
Academia Avance	PO Box 42095	Los Angeles, CA	90042-0095	213-447-4561	652-0994	6-12	Ricardo Mireles
Academia Semillas del Pueblo	4736 Huntington Dr S	Los Angeles, CA	90032-1942	323-225-4549	987-1240	K-8	Marcos Aguilar
Academic/Vocational Charter Institute	112 Diamond Dr	Watsonville, CA	95076-3184	831-728-6225	728-6233	11-12	Lee Takemoto
Academy Charter S	1285 S Chestnut Ave	Fresno, CA	93702-3909	559-452-0881	452-8038	7-12	Michael Jimenez
Academy for Academic Excellence	17500 Mana Rd	Apple Valley, CA	92307-2181	760-946-5414	946-5343	K-12	Chip Kling
Academy for Career Education Charter S	801 Olive St	Wheatland, CA	95692-9787	530-633-3113	633-3106	9-12	Sharon DiSimone
Academy for Recording Arts	14115 Chadron Ave	Hawthorne, CA	90250-8208	310-263-1022	263-1662	9-12	Jennifer Murphy
Academy of Careers & Exploration	PO Box 249	Helendale, CA	92342-0249	760-952-2396	952-1178	K-12	Heather Lewis
Accelerated Achievement Academy	1059 N State St	Ukiah, CA	95482-3413	707-463-7080	463-7085	4-12	Selah Sawyer
Accelerated Charter S	119 E 37th St	Los Angeles, CA	90011-2603	323-235-6343	235-6346	K-5	Jonathan Williams
Accelerated S	4000 S Main St	Los Angeles, CA	90037-1022	323-235-6343	235-6346	K-8	Kevin Sved
Achieve Academy	1700 28th Ave	Oakland, CA	94601-2455	510-904-6440	904-6761	4-5	Lissa Hines
Achieve Charter S of Paradise	771 Elliott Rd	Paradise, CA	95969-3913	530-872-4100	872-4105	K-6	Casey Taylor
Alameda Community Learning Center	210 Central Ave	Alameda, CA	94501-3246	510-521-7123	521-7350	7-12	Lora Lewis
Alder Grove Charter S	1615 Highland Ave	Eureka, CA	95503-3826	707-268-0854	268-0813	K-12	J. Allen-San Giovanni
Alexander Science Center	3737 S Figueroa St	Los Angeles, CA	90007-4366	213-746-1995	746-7443	K-5	Paula Denen
Alianza Charter S	115 Casserly Rd	Watsonville, CA	95076-9740	831-728-6333	728-6947	K-8	Michael Jones
All Tribes American Indian Charter S	PO Box 1432	Valley Center, CA	92082-1432	760-749-5982	749-4153	6-12	Mary Ann Donohue
Alpaugh Achievement Academy	PO Box 9	Alpaugh, CA	93201-0009	559-949-8644	949-8173	K-12	Robert Hudson
Alvarado Academy	26247 Ellis St	Madera, CA	93638-0813	559-675-2070	675-2074	K-6	Dr. Nicolas Retana
Alvina S	295 W Saginaw Ave	Caruthers, CA	93609-9710	559-864-9411	864-1808	K-8	Mike Iribarren
American Indian Charter HS	3626 35th Ave	Oakland, CA	94619-1402	510-482-6000	482-6002	9-12	Janet Roberts
American Indian Charter S	3637 Magee Ave	Oakland, CA	94619-1427	510-482-6000	482-6002	5-8	Isaac Berniker
American Indian Charter S II	171 12th St	Oakland, CA	94607	510-893-8701	893-0345	6-8	Janet Roberts
Americas Choice HS	10101 Systems Pkwy	Sacramento, CA	95827-3007	916-228-5751	228-5750	9-12	Beate Martinez
Anahuacalmecac University Prep HS	4736 Huntington Dr S	Los Angeles, CA	90032-1942	323-225-4549	987-1240	9-12	Marcos Aguilar
Anderson New Technology HS	2098 North St	Anderson, CA	96007-3477	530-365-3100	365-2957	9-12	Pat Allison
Animo-De La Hoya S	350 S Figueroa St Ste 100	Los Angeles, CA	90071-1115	213-473-0000	473-0041	9-12	Harris Luu
Animo Film & Theatre Arts Charter HS	350 S Figueroa St Ste 213	Los Angeles, CA	90071-1203	213-748-8830	712-2620	9-12	Steve Bachrach
Animo Inglewood Charter HS	3425 W Manchester Blvd	Inglewood, CA	90305-2101	323-565-2100	565-2109	9-12	Leilani Abulon
Animo Jackie Robinson Charter HS	350 S Figueroa St Ste 213	Los Angeles, CA	90071-1203	323-235-7240	235-7250	9-12	Lori Pawinski
Animo Justice Charter HS	350 S Figueroa St Ste 213	Los Angeles, CA	90071-1203	310-235-7241	235-7250	9-12	Will Herrera
Animo Leadership Charter HS	1155 W Arbor Vitae St	Inglewood, CA	90301-2902	310-216-3277	216-7934	9-12	Julio Murcia
Animo Locke HS #1	325 E 111th St	Los Angeles, CA	90061-3093			9-12	Peggy Gutierrez
Animo Locke HS #2	325 E 111th St	Los Angeles, CA	90061-3093			9-12	Rachelle Alexander
Animo Locke HS #3	325 E 111th St	Los Angeles, CA	90061-3093			9-12	Taquan Stewart
Animo Locke Technology HS	350 S Figueroa St Ste 213	Los Angeles, CA	90071-1203	323-568-8613	621-4419	9-12	Angela Beck
Animo Pat Brown Charter HS	2400 S Western Ave	Los Angeles, CA	90018-2607	323-232-9450	232-9458	9-12	Chad Soleo
Animo Ralph Bunche Charter HS	892 E 48th St	Los Angeles, CA	90011-5451	323-232-9436	232-9440	9-12	Xochitl Avellán
Animo South L.A. HS	11100 S Western Ave	Los Angeles, CA	90047-4845	323-779-0544	392-8752	9-12	Gordon Gibbings
Animo Venice HS	5431 W 98th St	Los Angeles, CA	90045-5715	310-392-8751	392-8752	9-12	Tommy Chang
Animo Watts 2 Charter HS	350 S Figueroa St Ste 213	Los Angeles, CA	90071-1203	323-249-4037	621-4419	9-12	Sue Foulkes
Annenberg HS	4000 S Main St	Los Angeles, CA	90037-1022	323-235-6343	235-6346	9-12	Manuel Arellano
Antelope Valley Desert Montessori S	44514 20th St W	Lancaster, CA	93534-2715	661-949-0691	949-0387	K-8	Leslie Barrett
Antelope Valley Learning Academy	701 W Avenue K Ste 126	Lancaster, CA	93534-1137	661-942-2550	940-4427	K-8	Maria Meneses-Trejo Ph.D.
Antelope View Charter S	3243 Center Court Ln	Antelope, CA	95843-9111	916-339-4690	339-4693	6-12	Richard Simas
Antioch Charter Academy	3325 Hacienda Way	Antioch, CA	94509	925-755-7311	755-7313	K-8	Debbie Hobin
Antioch Charter Academy II	1201 W 10th St	Antioch, CA	94509-1406	925-755-1252	755-7527	K-8	Jeannie Dubitsky
Arise HS	3301 E 12th St	Oakland, CA	94601-3424	510-436-5487	436-5493	9-12	Laura Flaxman
Arroyo Paseo Charter HS	4001 El Cajon Blvd Ste 205	San Diego, CA	92105	619-677-3017		9-12	William Wellhouse
Arroyo Vista Charter S	2491 School House Rd	Chula Vista, CA	91915-2534	619-656-9676	656-1858	K-6	Patricia Roth
Arts & Ethics Academy	3360 Coffey Ln Ste A2	Santa Rosa, CA	95403-1995	707-527-6810	546-2882	9-12	Dyan Foster
Arundel ES	200 Arundel Rd	San Carlos, CA	94070-1999	650-508-7311	508-7314	K-4	Steve Kaufman
ASA Charter S	2050 Pacific St	San Bernardino, CA	92404-6179	909-388-1255	388-1257	K-12	Patricia Campbell
Aspire Clarendon Charter S	2665 Clarendon Ave	Huntington Park, CA	90255-4138	323-583-5421		K-5	Rachel Cross
Aspire Huntington Park Charter S	6005 Stafford Ave	Huntington Park, CA	90255-3006	323-584-9033	584-0735	K-5	Stephanie Schulman
Aspire Langston Hughes Academy	612 E Magnolia St	Stockton, CA	95202-1846	209-465-4100		6-12	Alex Hernandez
Aspire Port City Academy	444 N American St	Stockton, CA	95202-2129	209-466-3861	466-4290	K-5	Anthony Solina
Audeo Charter S	10170 Huennekens St	San Diego, CA	92121-2964	858-678-2050	552-9394	6-12	Tim Tuter
Aveson Global Leadership Acadmey	PO Box 434	Pasadena, CA	91102-0434	626-797-1440	797-1918	6-12	Kate Bean
Aveson School of Leaders	PO Box 434	Pasadena, CA	91102-0434	626-797-1440	797-1918	K-5	Kate Bean
Banks Charter S	PO Box 80	Pala, CA	92059-0080	760-742-3300	742-3102	K-5	Bill Rash
Barona Indian Charter S	1095 Barona Rd	Lakeside, CA	92040-1541	619-443-0948	443-7280	K-8	Bill Adams
Bay Area S of Enterprise	2750 Todd St	Alameda, CA	94501-7250	510-748-4314	748-4326	9-12	Patricia Murillo
Bay Area Technology S	4521 Webster St	Oakland, CA	94609-2140	510-645-9932	645-9934	6-9	Matt Demir
Bayshore Prep Charter S	100 N Rancho Santa Fe Rd	San Marcos, CA	92069	760-597-0847	597-0275	K-12	Nancy Spencer
Bellevue-Sante Fe Charter S	1401 San Luis Bay Dr	San Luis Obispo, CA	93405-8007	805-595-7169	595-9013	K-6	Brian Getz
Berkley Maynard Academy	6200 San Pablo Ave	Oakland, CA	94608-2228	510-658-2900	658-1013	K-8	Kristyn Klei
Bert Corona Charter S	9400 Remick Ave	Pacoima, CA	91331-4223	818-834-5805	834-8075	6-8	Rueben Duenas
Big Sur Charter S	47540 Highway 1	Big Sur, CA	93920-9632	805-667-0203	667-0203	K-12	Shawna Garritson
Bitney Springs College Prep HS	11763 Ridge Rd	Grass Valley, CA	95945-5025	530-477-1235	272-1091	9-12	Marshall Goldberg
Blue Oak Charter Montessori ES	2391 Merrychase Dr	Cameron Park, CA	95682-9094	530-676-0164	933-5149	K-3	Sally Traub
Blue Oak Charter S	PO Box 6220	Chico, CA	95927-6220	530-879-7483	879-7490	K-8	Stephen Work-Montana
Bowling Green Charter ES	4211 Turnbridge Dr	Sacramento, CA	95823-1999	916-433-5426	433-5429	K-6	Elizabeth Aguirre
Bowman S	13777 Bowman Rd	Auburn, CA	95603-3196	530-885-1974	888-8175	K-8	Marilyn Gilbert
Bright Star Secondary Academy	2636 S Mansfield Ave	Los Angeles, CA	90016-3512	323-954-9957	954-6415	9-12	Eliza Kim
Brittan Acres S	2000 Belle Ave	San Carlos, CA	94070-3798	650-508-7307	508-7310	K-4	John Triska
Buckingham Magnet Charter S	188 Bella Vista Rd Ste B	Vacaville, CA	95687-3719	707-453-7300	453-7303	9-12	Bob Hampton
Bullis Charter S	102 W Portola Ave	Los Altos, CA	94022-1210	650-947-4939	947-4989	K-6	Wanny Hersey
Butterfield Charter HS	600 W Grand Ave	Porterville, CA	93257-2029	559-782-7057	782-7090	9-12	Linda Gill
Cali Calmecac Language Academy	9491 Starr Rd	Windsor, CA	95492-9460	707-837-7747	837-7752	K-8	Chris Vanden Heuvel
California Academy for Liberal Studies	700 Wilshire Blvd	Los Angeles, CA	90017	213-239-0063	239-9008	9-12	Connie Rivas
California Academy for Liberal Studies	3838 Eagle Rock Blvd	Los Angeles, CA	90065-3638	323-254-4427	254-4099	6-8	Nick Orlando
California Aerospace Academy	5727 Perrin Ave	Mc Clellan, CA	95652-2403	916-286-5101	643-0803	7-12	Willie Thomas
California College Prep Academy	2125 Jefferson Ave	Berkeley, CA	94703-1414	510-658-2900	251-1670	6-12	Megan Reed
California Military Institute	755 N A St	Perris, CA	92570-1958	951-443-2731	657-3085	7-12	Richard Wallis
California Montessori Project-Amer Rvr	4718 Engle Rd	Carmichael, CA	95608-2224	916-864-0081	864-0084	K-8	Deanna Gardner
California Montessori Project-Capitol	4718 Engle Rd	Carmichael, CA	95608-2224	916-325-0910	325-0912	K-8	Bernie Evangelista
California Montessori Project-Elk Grove	4718 Engle Rd	Carmichael, CA	95608-2224	916-714-9699	714-9703	K-8	Deirdre Slamkowski
California Montessori Project-Shingl Spr	4718 Engle Rd	Carmichael, CA	95608-2224	530-672-3095	672-3097	K-8	Kim Zawilski
California Virtual Academy	2360 Shasta Way Ste A	Simi Valley, CA	93065-1800	805-581-0202	581-0330	K-12	Katrina Abston
Camarillo Academy of Progressive Educ	777 Aileen St	Camarillo, CA	93010-2959	805-384-1415		K-12	Janet Kanongata'a
Camino Nuevo Charter Academy	635 S Harvard Blvd	Los Angeles, CA	90005-2511	213-736-5542	736-5664	PK-8	Kate Sobel
Camino Nuevo Charter HS	3500 W Temple St	Los Angeles, CA	90004-3620	213-736-5542	736-5664	9-12	Luz Padua
Camino Nuevo Charter S Burlington Campu	697 S Burlington Ave	Los Angeles, CA	90057-3743	213-413-4245		K-5	Atyani Howard
Camino Real Community Partnership Acad	PO Box 8000	Lompoc, CA	93438-8000	805-742-2770	742-2778	9-12	Kristen Lewis
Camptonville Academy	848 Gold Flat Rd Ste 3	Nevada City, CA	95959-3201	530-478-9458	478-9629	K-12	Janis Jablecki
Canyon ES	421 Entrada Dr	Santa Monica, CA	90402-1303	310-454-7510	454-7543	K-5	Carol Henderson
Capistrano Connections Academy	1211 Puerta Del Sol Ste 220	San Clemente, CA	92673-6357	949-492-9131	492-9140	K-12	Jonathan Horowitz
Capitol Heights Academy	2520 33rd St	Sacramento, CA	95817-1943	916-739-8520	739-8529	K-8	Robert Spencer
Capri ES	850 Chapman Dr	Campbell, CA	95008-6807	408-364-4260	341-7120	K-5	David Wilce
Carver S of Arts & Sciences	10101 Systems Pkwy	Sacramento, CA	95827-3007	916-228-5751	228-5760	9-12	
Casa Ramona Academy for Technology	1524 W 7th St	San Bernardino, CA	92411-2599	909-889-0011	381-2871	K-12	Esther Ramos Estrada
Castlemont ES	3040 Payne Ave	Campbell, CA	95008-0136	408-364-4233	341-7050	K-5	Ivy Sarratt
Castle Rock Charter S	301 W Washington Blvd	Crescent City, CA	95531-8340	707-464-0390	464-9606	K-12	Dennis Burns
Celerity Dyad Charter S	4501 Wadsworth Ave	Los Angeles, CA	90011-3637	310-486-6620		K-8	Craig Knotts
Celerity Nascent Charter	3417 W Jefferson Blvd	Los Angeles, CA	90018-3235	323-732-6613	733-2977	K-8	Grace Canada
Celerity Troika Charter S	7901 S Broadway	Los Angeles, CA	90003	310-486-6620		K-8	Megan McNamara
Centennial College Preparatory Academy	2079 Saturn Ave	Huntington Park, CA	90255-3635	323-826-9616	588-7342	4-12	Diane Garcia
Center for Advanced Learning	4016 S Central Ave	Los Angeles, CA	90011-2708	310-674-2034	735-2654	K-5	
Center for Advanced Research Technology	2555 Clovis Ave	Clovis, CA	93612-3901	559-248-7400	248-7423	11-12	Susan Fisher
Central California Connections Academy	916 W Oak Ave Ste B	Visalia, CA	93291-4716	559-713-1324	713-1330	K-12	Jonathan Horowitz
Central City Value S	221 N Westmoreland Ave	Los Angeles, CA	90004-4815	323-981-7149	981-0162	9-12	Dr. Marie Collins
Century Academy for Excellence	1000 Corporate Pointe # 200	Culver City, CA	90230	310-642-2000	258-0740	6-8	Dr. Giselle Wilson Edman
Century Community Charter S	901 Maple St	Inglewood, CA	90301-3823	310-412-2286	412-4085	6-8	Teri Delahousie-Norris
Challenge Charter High S	2750 Mitchell Ave	Oroville, CA	95966-5414	530-538-2359	538-2374	9-12	Walt Gess
Charter Alternatives Academy	28050 Road 148	Visalia, CA	93292-9297	559-730-7491	730-7490	7-12	Rudy Soleno
Charter Community S and Home Study Acad	6767 Green Valley Rd	Placerville, CA	95667-8984	530-295-2259	642-0492	K-12	Cara Prentiss
Charter HS of Arts Multimedia/Performing	6952 Van Nuys Blvd	Van Nuys, CA	91405-3984	818-994-4744	994-0099	9-12	Dr. Norman Isaacs
Charter Home School Academy	31411 Road 160	Visalia, CA	93292-9019	559-730-7916	735-8060	K-8	Christine Fischer
Charter S of Morgan Hill	9530 Monterey Rd	Morgan Hill, CA	95037-9356	408-463-0618	462-0267	K-8	Paige Ciseswki
Charter S of San Diego	10170 Huennekens St	San Diego, CA	92121-2964	858-678-2020	552-6660	7-12	Mary Bixby
Chavez Dual Language Immersion Charter S	1102 E Yanonali St	Santa Barbara, CA	93103-2704	805-966-7392	966-7243	K-6	Eva Neuer
Chico Country Day S	102 W 11th St	Chico, CA	95928-6006	530-895-2650	895-9159	K-8	Paul Weber

School	Address	City,State	Zip code	Telephone	Fax	Grade	Contact
Childrens Community Charter S	6830 Pentz Rd	Paradise, CA	95969-2902	530-877-2227	872-1396	K-8	Bruce Crist
CHIME Charter MS	22280 Devonshire St	Chatsworth, CA	91311-2736	818-998-6794	998-0121	6-8	Jennifer Lockwood
CHIME Charter S	19722 Collier St	Woodland Hills, CA	91364-3618	818-346-5100	346-5120	K-5	
Choice 2000 On-Line S	11 S D St	Perris, CA	92570-2126	951-940-5700	940-5706	7-12	Chris Cooper
Choices Charter S	4425 Laurelwood Way	Sacramento, CA	95864-0881	916-979-8378		7-12	Marie Pflugrath
Chrysalis Charter S	PO Box 709	Palo Cedro, CA	96073-0709	530-547-9726	547-9734	K-8	Paul Krafel
Chula Vista Learning Community Charter S	590 K St	Chula Vista, CA	91911-1118	619-426-2885	426-3048	K-6	Dr. Jorge Ramirez
Circle of Independent Learning	4700 Calaveras Ave	Fremont, CA	94538-1124	510-797-0100	797-0118	K-12	Mary Musgrove
City Arts & Technology HS	325 La Grande Ave	San Francisco, CA	94112-2866	415-841-2200	585-3009	9-12	Allison Rowland
Civicorps Academy	101 Myrtle St	Oakland, CA	94607-2543	510-992-7819	992-7950	9-12	
Civicorps ES	101 Myrtle St	Oakland, CA	94607-2543	510-420-3701	420-3703	K-5	Kathryn Nicol
Classical Academy	2950 Bear Valley Pkwy S	Escondido, CA	92025-7446	760-546-0101	739-8289	K-8	Jonelle Godfrey
Classical Academy HS	144 Woodward Ave	Escondido, CA	92025-2637	760-480-9845	520-8118	9-12	Cameron Curry
Clear View Charter S	455 Windrose Way	Chula Vista, CA	91910-7400	619-498-3000	498-3007	K-6	Christopher Carroll
Coastal Academy Charter	4183 Avenida de la Plata	Oceanside, CA	92056	760-631-4020	739-4027	K-8	Lori Perez
Coastal Grove Charter S	PO Box 510	Arcata, CA	95518-0510	707-825-8804		K-8	Bettina Eipper
Cole Academy	333 E Walnut St	Santa Ana, CA	92701-5928	714-836-9023	836-9041	K-5	Kitty Fortner
Colegio New City	1633 Long Beach Blvd	Long Beach, CA	90813-1929	562-599-7405	599-7400	9-12	Brookes Marindin
Colfax Charter ES	11724 Addison St	North Hollywood, CA	91607-3202	818-761-5115	985-6017	K-5	Susana Gomez-Judkins
College Ready Academy HS #4	644 W 17th St	Los Angeles, CA	90015-3400	323-342-2870	342-2871	9-12	Janette Rodriguez
College Ready Academy HS #5	644 W 17th St	Los Angeles, CA	90015-3400	323-342-2874	342-2875	9-12	Dean Marolla
College Ready Academy HS #7	1265 E 112th St	Los Angeles, CA	90059-1137	213-804-2548	403-5954	9-12	Raul Carranza Ed.D.
College Ready Middle Academy #3	2621 W 54th St	Los Angeles, CA	90043-2614	323-943-4933	943-4931	6-8	James Waller
Collins School at Cherry Valley	1001 Cherry St	Petaluma, CA	94952-2065	707-778-4740	778-4839	K-8	Karen McGahey
Community Charter MS	11500 Eldridge Ave	Lake View Ter, CA	91342-6505	818-485-0933	485-0940	6-8	Ingrid Anderson
Community Charter S	11500 Eldridge Ave	Sylmar, CA	91342-6505	818-485-0951		9-12	Daniele Assael
Community Collaborative Charter S	9880 Jackson Rd	Sacramento, CA	95827-9706	916-369-5533	369-3959	K-12	Jon Campbell
Community Collaborative Charter S	5129 Arnold Ave	Mc Clellan, CA	95652-1017	916-286-5161	643-2031	K-12	Jon Campbell
Community Harvest Charter S	5300 Sepulveda Blvd	Sherman Oaks, CA	91411-3440	323-373-2000	373-9922	6-12	Charletta Johnson
Community Magnet ES	11301 Bellagio Rd	Los Angeles, CA	90049-1705	310-476-2281	472-6391	K-5	Pamela Marton
Connecting Waters Charter S	12420 Bentley St	Waterford, CA	95386-9158	209-874-9463	874-9531	K-12	Sherri Nelson
Connections Visual and Performing Arts S	17555 Tuolumne Rd	Tuolumne, CA	95379-9701	209-928-4228	928-1422	7-12	Michael Gibson
Conservatory of Vocal/Instrumental Arts	3800 Mountain Blvd	Oakland, CA	94619-1630	510-285-7511		K-8	Dr. Valerie Abad
Constellation Community Charter MS	PO Box 2130	Long Beach, CA	90801-2130	562-435-7181	437-7532	6-8	Daphne Ching-Jackson
CORE Butte Charter S	260 Cohasset Rd Ste 120	Chico, CA	95926-2282	530-894-3952	566-9819	K-8	Jonelle Pena
CORE Butte Charter S	848 Gold Flat Rd Ste 3	Nevada City, CA	95959-3201	530-478-9458	487-9629	K-12	Janis Jablecki
Cornerstone Prep S	7651 S Central Ave	Los Angeles, CA	90001-2945	323-581-4495	581-4214	K-8	Stephan Bean
Creative Arts Charter S	1601 Turk St	San Francisco, CA	94115-4527	415-749-3509	749-3437	K-8	Liz Jaroslow
Creative Connections Arts Academy	7201 Arutas Dr	North Highlands, CA	95660-2809	916-566-1870	331-2959	K-8	Joe Breault
Crenshaw Arts-Tech Charter HS	2941 W 70th St	Los Angeles, CA	90043-4420	323-778-7700	778-7712	9-12	Patricia Smith
Crescendo Charter Academy	13000 Van Ness Ave	Gardena, CA	90249-1726	323-329-1300	329-9300	K-5	Anne Rinaldi
Crescendo Charter ES	4900 S Western Ave	Los Angeles, CA	90062-2326	323-295-9495	295-0845	K-5	Anne Rinaldi
Crescendo Charter Preparatory Central S	8715 LaSalle Ave	Los Angeles, CA	90047-3320	323-945-3906		K-3	John Allen
Crescendo Charter Preparatory South S	8477 S Normandie Ave	Los Angeles, CA	90044-2246	310-532-8680		K-3	John Allen
Crescendo Charter Preparatory West S	1004 W 120th St	Los Angeles, CA	90044-2916	323-945-3906		K-3	John Allen
Crescent View Charter HS	900 S Newmark Ave	Parlier, CA	93648-2034	559-222-8439	222-8430	9-12	Demitri Gonos
Crossroads Charter S	PO Box 368	Armona, CA	93202-0368	559-585-7295	585-7298	K-12	Laurie Blue
Crosswalk Charter S	12061 Jacaranda Ave Ste 5	Hesperia, CA	92345-4962	760-949-2327	949-2378	5-12	Chala Salisbury
Culture & Language Academy of Success	2930 W Imperial Hwy Ste 514	Inglewood, CA	90303-3188	310-777-8400	777-8403	K-8	Janis Bucknor
Cypress Charter HS	2039 Merrill St	Santa Cruz, CA	95062-4176	831-477-0302	477-7659	9-12	Les Forster
Dantzler Preparatory Charter ES	944 W 53rd St	Los Angeles, CA	90037-3643	323-750-3172	294-7115	K-5	Glenetta Pope
Dantzler Preparatory Charter HS	5029 S Vermont Ave	Los Angeles, CA	90037-2907	323-290-6935	932-0143	9-12	Elaine Gills
Dantzler Preparatory Charter MS	5029 S Vermont Ave	Los Angeles, CA	90037-2907	323-290-6930	752-9610	6-8	Carla Chambers
Darnall E-Charter S	6020 Hughes St	San Diego, CA	92115-6520	619-582-1822	287-4732	K-6	Cinda Doughty
Dehesa Charter S	1441 Montiel Rd Ste 143	Escondido, CA	92026-2242	760-743-7880	743-7919	K-12	Terri Novacek
Delta Charter ES	PO Box 127	Clarksburg, CA	95612-0127	916-744-1200	744-1246	K-6	Gary Hexom
Delta Charter S	343 Soquel Ave	Santa Cruz, CA	95062	831-477-5213	479-6173	9-12	Mary Forster
Delta Charter S	31400 S Koster Rd	Tracy, CA	95304-8824	209-830-6363	830-9324	K-12	Stephanie Lytle
Denair Charter Academy	3460 Lester Rd	Denair, CA	95316-9502	209-634-0917	669-9282	K-12	Karla Paul
Desert Sands Charter HS	42455 10th St W Ste 105	Lancaster, CA	93534-7060	661-272-0044	944-4857	9-12	Marcello Palacios
Design HS	6338 N Figueroa St	Los Angeles, CA	90042-2733	323-255-5277		9-12	Susan Mas
Diamond Mountain Charter HS	55 S Weatherlow St	Susanville, CA	96130-4409	530-257-5566	257-5851	9-12	Brett Mitchell
Discovery Charter Preparatory S	12550 Van Nuys Blvd	Pacoima, CA	91331-1354	818-897-1187	897-1295	9-12	Matthew Macarah
Discovery Charter S	1100 Camino Biscay	Chula Vista, CA	91910-7737	619-656-0797	656-3899	K-6	Michael Cole
Discovery Charter S	51 E Beverly Pl	Tracy, CA	95376-3191	209-831-5240	831-5243	5-8	Virginia Stewart
Discovery Charter S	4021 Teale Ave	San Jose, CA	95117-3433	408-243-9800	243-9812	K-8	Stephen Fiss
Dixon Montessori Charter S	180 S 1st St Ste 6	Dixon, CA	95620-3447	707-678-8953	678-4285	K-6	Jen Stevens
Douglas Academy MS	5125 Crenshaw Blvd	Los Angeles, CA	90043-1853	323-290-6982		6-8	Karen Anderson
Douglass Academy ES	2320 W Martin Luther King	Los Angeles, CA	90008	323-290-6900	294-9115	K-5	Michael Piscal
Douglass Academy HS	3200 W Adams Blvd	Los Angeles, CA	90018-1832	323-290-6900	934-7682	9-12	Greg Hill
Downtown College Preparatory	1460 The Alameda	San Jose, CA	95126-2652	408-271-1730	271-1734	9-12	Jennifer Andaluz
Downtown Value S	950 W Washington Blvd	Los Angeles, CA	90015-3312	213-748-8868	748-8062	K-8	Gerry Jacoby
Dunlap Leadership Academy	39500 Dunlap Rd	Dunlap, CA	93621	559-305-7320	338-2026	9-12	Paul Colagiovanni
Eagle Peak Montessori S	800 Hutchinson Rd	Walnut Creek, CA	94598-4505	925-946-0994	946-9409	K-6	Michelle Hammons
East Oakland Leadership Academy	2614 Seminary Ave	Oakland, CA	94605-1570	510-562-5238	562-5239	K-9	Dr. Laura Armstrong
East Palo Alto Academy	2037 Pulgas Ave	East Palo Alto, CA	94303-2025	650-462-8450	462-8452	K-8	Nicki Smith
East Palo Alto Charter S	1286 Runnymede St	East Palo Alto, CA	94303-1332	650-614-9100	614-9183	K-8	Laura Ramirez
East Palo Alto HS	475 Pope St	Menlo Park, CA	94025-2800	650-329-2828	321-6628	9-12	Bonnie Billings
Eastside Campus Westside Prep Charter S	6469 Guthrie St	North Highlands, CA	95660-3944	916-566-1860	339-2033	7-8	
Edison-Bethune Charter Academy	1616 S Fruit Ave	Fresno, CA	93706-2819	559-457-2530	498-0711	K-6	Felicia Quarles
Edison-Brentwood Academy	2086 Clarke Ave	East Palo Alto, CA	94303-1916	650-329-2881	329-2877	K-4	Dianne Witwer
Edison Charter Academy	3531 22nd St	San Francisco, CA	94114-3405	415-970-3330	285-0527	K-8	Gloria Galindo
Education for Change	9860 Sunnyside St	Oakland, CA	94603-2750	510-904-6300	904-6730	K-5	Fernando Yanez
Eel River Charter S	PO Box 218	Covelo, CA	95428-0218	707-983-6946	983-6197	K-8	Betty Tuttle
Einstein Academy	3035 Ash St	San Diego, CA	92102-1718	619-795-1190	795-1180	K-8	David Sciarretta
EJE Academy Charter ES	191 E Chase Ave	El Cajon, CA	92020-6201	619-401-4150	401-4151	K-5	Delia Pacheco
Elk Grove Charter S	9075 Elk Grove Blvd	Elk Grove, CA	95624	916-714-1653	714-1721	1-12	Christy Moustris
El Rancho Charter MS	181 S Del Giorgio Rd	Anaheim, CA	92808-1399	714-997-6238	281-8791	7-8	John Besta
El Sol Science & Arts Charter Academy	1010 N Broadway	Santa Ana, CA	92701-3408	714-543-0023	543-0026	K-8	Alberto Hananel
Emerson Parkside Academy	2625 Josie Ave	Long Beach, CA	90815-1511	562-420-2631	420-7642	K-5	Mark Andreatta
Encore HS for Performing & Visual Arts	16955 Lemon St	Hesperia, CA	92345-5139	760-948-1823		7-12	Denise Griffin
Environmental Charter HS	16315 Grevillea Ave	Lawndale, CA	90260-2858	310-214-3400	214-3410	9-12	Kennedy Hilario
Envision Academy for Arts & Technology	1515 Webster St	Oakland, CA	94612-3355	510-596-8901	596-8905	9-12	Rick Gaston
eScholar Academy	715 Jackson St Ste B	Red Bluff, CA	96080-3771	530-527-0188	527-0273	K-12	Harold Vietti
e-Scholar Charter S	PO Box 130	Mineral, CA	96063-0130	530-527-0188	527-0273	K-12	Dr. Harold Vietti
Escondido Charter HS	1868 E Valley Pkwy	Escondido, CA	92027-2525	760-737-3154	738-8996	9-12	Denny Snyder
Escuela Popular Accelerated Family Lrng	355 W San Fernando St	San Jose, CA	95110-2524	408-275-7190	275-7192	K-12	Patricia Lidia Reguerin
Escuela Popular/Ctr Training & Careers	467 N White Rd	San Jose, CA	95127-1441	408-275-7193	259-7473	9-12	Patricia Reguerin
Excel Charter Academy	1855 N Main St	Los Angeles, CA	90031-3227	323-222-5010	223-8593	6-8	Suzanne Edwards-Acton
Excelsior Education Center Charter S	7151 SVL Box	Victorville, CA	92395-5153	760-245-4448	245-4009	7-12	Ron Newbold
Explorer ES	2230 Truxtun Rd	San Diego, CA	92106-6128	619-398-8600	398-8601	K-5	Jill Green
Fairmont ES	1355 Marshall Rd	Vacaville, CA	95687-5519	707-453-6240	447-0759	K-6	Rochelle Sklansky
FAME Public Charter S	39899 Balentine Dr Ste 335	Newark, CA	94560-5359	510-687-9111	687-9145	K-12	Maram Alaiwat
Family Partnership Home Study Charter S	4949 Foxen Canyon Rd	Santa Maria, CA	93454-9145	805-686-5339		K-12	Tom Goodman
Fammatre Charter ES	2800 New Jersey Ave	San Jose, CA	95124-1556	408-377-5480	377-8751	K-5	Midge Jambor
Farnham Charter ES	15711 Woodard Rd	San Jose, CA	95124-2668	408-377-3321	377-7237	K-5	John Hayes
Feaster Charter S	670 Flower St	Chula Vista, CA	91910-1399	619-422-8397	422-4780	K-6	Marilyn Prall
Fenton Avenue Charter S	11828 Gain St	Sylmar, CA	91342-7132	818-896-7482	890-9986	PK-5	Irene Sumida
Finch S	451 S Villa Ave	Willows, CA	95988-2964	530-934-6320	934-6325	K-12	Susan Domenighini
Five Keys Charter S	70 Oak Grove St	San Francisco, CA	94107-1019	415-734-3310	734-3314	9-12	Steve Good
Folsom Cordova Community Charter S	101 Dean Way	Folsom, CA	95630-2801	916-817-8499	987-1167	K-8	Wayne Edney
Forest Charter S	224 Church St	Nevada City, CA	95959-2505	530-265-4823	265-5037	K-12	Sandy McDivitt
Forest Ranch Charter S	15815 Cedar Creek Rd	Forest Ranch, CA	95942	530-891-3154	891-3155	K-6	
Forestville Academy	6321 Hwy 116	Forestville, CA	95436-9606	707-887-2279	887-2185	K-8	Talin Tamzarian
Four Winds Charter S	2345 Fair St	Chico, CA	95928-6749	530-879-7411	879-7414	K-12	Terri Tozier
Fremont Charter S	1120 W 22nd St	Merced, CA	95340-3540	209-385-6627	385-6301	K-5	Dalinda Saich
Freshwater Charter MS	75 Greenwood Heights Dr	Eureka, CA	95503-9441	707-442-2969	442-9527	6-8	Thom McMahon
Freshwater ES	75 Greenwood Heights Dr	Eureka, CA	95503-9441	707-442-2969	442-9527	K-6	Thom McMahon
Fresno Preparatory Academy	3355 E Shields Ave	Fresno, CA	93726-6906	559-222-3840	222-3540	9-12	Bud Vickers
Frontier Campus Westside Charter S	6691 Silverthorne Cir	Sacramento, CA	95842-2654	916-566-1840	344-8932	7-8	Ellen Giffin
Frontier ES	1854 Mustang Dr	Hanford, CA	93230	559-585-2430	585-2440	K-5	John Raven
Fuenta Nueva Charter S	1435 Buttermilk Ln	Arcata, CA	95521-6909	707-822-3348	822-5862	K-5	Beth Wylie
Full Circle Learning Academy	19609 Vision Dr	Topanga, CA	90290-3116	310-455-3909		K-8	Teresa Langness
Futures HS	3701 Stephen Dr	North Highlands, CA	95660-4532	916-286-1900	263-6059	7-8	Dawn Contreras
Gabriela Charter S	631 S Commonwealth Ave	Los Angeles, CA	90005-4003	213-487-0839	487-0894	K-5	Susan Gurman
Garfield Charter S	3600 Middlefield Rd	Menlo Park, CA	94025-3010	650-369-3759	367-4358	K-8	Alex Hunt
GARR Academy of Math & Entrepreneurial	5101 S Western Ave	Los Angeles, CA	90062-2333	323-294-2008	295-3936	K-5	Doris Sims Ph.D.

School	Address	City,State	Zip code	Telephone	Fax	Grade	Contact
Gates ES	23882 Landisview Ave	Lake Forest, CA	92630-5199	949-837-2260	837-5013	K-6	Yvonne Estling
Gateway HS	1430 Scott St	San Francisco, CA	94115-3510	415-749-3600	749-2716	9-12	Sharon Olken
Gateway to College	4800 Magnolia Ave	Riverside, CA	92506	951-222-8931	222-8975	9-12	Jill Marks
Gertz-Ressler HS-College Ready HS 1	2023 S Union Ave	Los Angeles, CA	90007-1326	213-745-8141	745-8142	9-12	Howard Lappin
Glacier Charter HS	41267 Highway 41	Oakhurst, CA	93644-9403	559-642-1422	642-1592	9-12	Michael Cox
Global Education Academy	4141 S Figueroa St	Los Angeles, CA	90037-2038	310-232-9588	232-9587	K-5	Alfonso Flores
Global Youth Charter HS	3243 Center Court Ln	Antelope, CA	95843-9111	916-339-4680	339-4684	9-12	Addie Ellis
Golden Eagle Charter S	216 N Mount Shasta Blvd	Mount Shasta, CA	96067-2239	530-926-5800	926-5826	K-12	Shelly Adams
Golden Oak Montessori S of Hayward	26036 Clover Rd	Hayward, CA	94542-1308			1-8	Aneema VanGroenou
Golden Valley Charter	2421 Portola Rd Ste C	Ventura, CA	93003-8048	805-642-3435	642-3468	K-12	Terri Adams
Golden Valley Charter S	9601 Lake Natoma Dr	Orangevale, CA	95662-5099	916-987-6141	987-6141	K-8	Debi Lenny
Gold Oak Arts Charter S	3171 Pleasant Valley Rd	Placerville, CA	95667-9299	530-626-3157	626-3159	4-8	Sylvia Shannon
Gold Rush Charter S	14673 Mono Way	Sonora, CA	95370-9220	209-533-8644	588-9988	K-12	Kathleen Hanson
Gompers Charter S	1005 47th St	San Diego, CA	92102-3699	619-263-2171		6-9	Vince Riveroll
Gorman Learning Center	49847 Gorman School Rd	Gorman, CA	93243	909-307-6312	793-5964	K-12	Jean Cummings
Gorman Learning Center	1826 Orange Tree Ln	Redlands, CA	92374-2821	909-307-6312	793-5964	K-12	Denice Burchett
Granada Hills HS	10535 Zelzah Ave	Granada Hills, CA	91344-5999	818-360-2361	363-9504	9-12	Brian Bauer
Grant Community Outreach Academy	5637 Skvarla Ave	Mc Clellan, CA	95652-2439	916-286-5170	640-0227	K-2	Larissa Gonchar
Grant Community Outreach Academy	3337 James Way	Mc Clellan, CA	95652	916-286-5170	640-0227	3-4	Larissa Gonchar
Grant Community Outreach Academy	5800 Skvarla Ave	Mc Clellan, CA	95652-2418	916-640-1431	640-1438	4-5	Larissa Gonchar
Grass Valley Charter S at Bell Hill	342 S School St	Grass Valley, CA	95945-6699	530-273-8723	271-0557	K-8	Brian Martinez
Grayson Charter S	PO Box 7	Westley, CA	95387-0007	209-894-3762	894-3393	K-5	Arturo Duran
Greater San Diego Academy	13881 Campo Rd	Jamul, CA	91935-3208	619-669-3050	669-3066	K-12	Gail Levine
Grizzly ChalleNGe Charter S	PO Box 3209	San Luis Obispo, CA	93403-3209	805-782-6882	594-6341	10-12	Paul Piette
Grove S	200 Nevada St	Redlands, CA	92373-5385	909-798-7831	307-6464	7-12	Tina Booth
Guajome Park Academy	2000 N Santa Fe Ave	Vista, CA	92083-1534	760-631-8500	631-8501	6-12	
Guidance Charter S	1125 E Palmdale Blvd Ste B	Palmdale, CA	93550	661-272-1701	272-1728	K-8	Kamal Al-Khatib
HAAAT	831 E Devonshire Ave	Hemet, CA	92543-3052	951-925-5155	929-9017	9-12	Frank Green
Hallmark Charter S	2445 9th St	Sanger, CA	93657-2780	559-875-1372	875-3573	K-12	Alfred Sanchez
Harmony Magnet Academy	600 W Grand Ave	Porterville, CA	93257-2029	559-568-0347	568-1929	9-12	Jeff Bottoms
Hart-Ransom Academic Charter S	3920 Shoemake Ave	Modesto, CA	95358-8577	209-523-0401	523-1064	K-8	Sherry Smith
Hawthorne Math Science & Tech S	4467 W Broadway	Hawthorne, CA	90250-3819	310-973-8620	973-8167	9-12	Joaquin Hernandez
Health Sciences HS & Middle College	3910 University Ave Ste 100	San Diego, CA	92105-7302	619-528-9070	528-9084	9-12	Sheri North
Hearthstone Charter S	205 Mira Loma Dr Ste 16	Oroville, CA	95965-3582	530-532-5848	532-5847	K-12	Kim Guzzetti
Heather S	2757 Melendy Dr	San Carlos, CA	94070-3604	650-508-7303	508-7306	K-4	Pam Jasso
Helix HS	7323 University Ave	La Mesa, CA	91942-0592	619-466-4194	462-9257	9-12	Dr. Douglas Smith
Heritage Charter S	1855 E Valley Pkwy	Escondido, CA	92027-2517	760-737-3154	738-8996	K-8	Dennis Snyder
Heritage College Ready HS	9719 S Main St	Los Angeles, CA	90003-4135	323-754-2364	755-9501	9-12	Robert Pambello
Heritage Peak Charter S	3600 Madison Ave	North Highlands, CA	95660-5077	866-992-9033	348-4325	K-12	Dr. Paul Keefer
Heritage S	PO Box 296000	Phelan, CA	92329-6000	760-868-2422	868-0589	K-8	John Garner
Hickman Charter S	13306 4th St	Hickman, CA	95323-9634	209-874-9070	874-1457	K-8	Patricia Golding
Hickman ES	13306 4th St	Hickman, CA	95323-9634	209-874-1816	874-3721	K-5	Rusty Wynn
Hickman MS	13306 4th St	Hickman, CA	95323-9634	209-874-1816	874-3721	6-8	Rusty Wynn
High Desert Academy	15411 Village Dr	Victorville, CA	92394-1912	760-843-7445	245-9541	7-12	Marjori Chambers
Higher Learning Academy	4039 Balsam St	Sacramento, CA	95838-3705	916-648-1336	643-9893	K-4	Ana Gutierrez
High Tech High Media Arts	2230 Truxtun Rd	San Diego, CA	92106-6128	619-398-8620	224-1198	9-12	Robert Kuhl
High Tech HS Chula Vista	1945 Discovery Falls Dr	Chula Vista, CA	91915-2037	619-838-2308	243-5050	9-12	Colleen Green
High Tech HS - LA	17111 Victory Blvd	Van Nuys, CA	91406-5455	818-881-2640	881-1754	9-12	Marsha Rybin
High Tech HS North County	1420 W San Marcos Blvd	San Marcos, CA	92078-4017	760-560-6249	243-5050	9-12	Nicole Hinostro
High Tech International HS	2855 Farragut Rd	San Diego, CA	92106-6029	619-398-4900	758-1960	9-12	Kelly Wilson
High Tech Middle Media Arts	2230 Truxtun Rd	San Diego, CA	92106-6128	619-398-8640	758-9568	6-8	Azul Terronez
High Tech MS	2359 Truxtun Rd	San Diego, CA	92106-6049	619-814-5060	814-5088	6-8	Janie Griswold
Holly Drive Leadership Academy	4999 Holly Dr	San Diego, CA	92113-2046	619-266-7333	266-7330	K-8	Alysia Shaw
Holt College Prep Academy	3201 Morada Ln	Stockton, CA	95212-3110	209-955-1477	955-1472	6-12	Scott Traub
HomeTech Charter S	7126 Skyway	Paradise, CA	95969-3271	530-872-1171	872-1172	K-12	Sue Gioia
Horizon Charter S	PO Box 489000	Lincoln, CA	95648-9000	916-408-5200	408-5223	K-12	LuAnn Boone
Huerta Learning Academy	1936 Courtland Ave	Oakland, CA	94601-4614	510-533-9790	533-9794	K-8	Kenneth Reed
Hume Lake Charter S	5545 E Hedges Ave	Fresno, CA	93727-2223	559-335-2000	335-4003	K-12	Mark Zasso
Huntington Park College Ready Academy	2071 Saturn Ave	Huntington Park, CA	90255-3635	323-923-1588	923-1589	9-12	Laura Galvan
ICEF Vista Elementary Academy	4471 Inglewood Blvd	Los Angeles, CA	90066-6209	310-298-6400		K-5	Matt Harris
ICEF Vista Middle Academy	4471 Inglewood Blvd	Los Angeles, CA	90066-6209	310-298-6400		6-8	Sean Nealy
IFTIN Charter S	5465 El Cajon Bl;vd	San Diego, CA	92115	619-265-2411		K-6	Abdulkadir Mohamed
Impact Academy of Arts & Technology	16292 Foothill Blvd	San Leandro, CA	94578-2105	510-300-1560	300-1565	9-12	Jennifer Davis Wickens
Inland Leaders Charter S	13456 Bryant St	Yucaipa, CA	92399-5441	909-446-1100	446-1125	K-6	Michael Gordon Ed.D.
Innovations Academy	123 Camino de La Reina	San Diego, CA	92108	619-550-2416		K-8	Danielle Strachman
Institute of Business Management & Law	6650 Inglewood Ave	Stockton, CA	95207-3861	209-933-7475	472-7841	9-12	Bill Parks
Integrity Charter S	125 Palm Ave	National City, CA	91950-1719	619-474-5643	474-5643	K-6	Sandra Dominguez
International S of Monterey	PO Box 711	Monterey, CA	93942-0711	831-583-2165	899-7653	K-7	Eric Pearlstein
Island Community Day S	1776 6th Avenue Dr	Kingsburg, CA	93631-1701	559-897-6740	897-6872	K-8	Stephen Powers Ph.D.
Island S	7799 21st Ave	Lemoore, CA	93245-9694	559-924-6424	924-0247	K-8	Tom Bates
Ivy Academia	6221 Fallbrook Ave	Woodland Hills, CA	91367-1602	818-348-8190	332-4136	K-12	Tatyana Berkovich
Ivy Bound Academy	15355 Morrison St	Sherman Oaks, CA	91403-1514	818-625-0319	633-0949	5-8	Arzani Kiumars
Jacobs High Tech HS	2861 Womble Rd	San Diego, CA	92106-6025	619-243-5000	243-5050	9-12	Brett Peterson
Jacoby Creek S	1617 Old Arcata Rd	Bayside, CA	95524-9324	707-822-4896	822-4898	K-8	Eric Grantz
Jardin De la Infancia	307 E 7th St	Los Angeles, CA	90014-2209	213-614-1745	614-2046	K-1	Alice Callaghan
Johnson JHS	1300 Stroud Ave	Kingsburg, CA	93631-1000	559-897-1091	897-6867	7-8	Ruben Diaz
Jordan MS	20040 Parthenia St	Northridge, CA	91324-3222	818-882-2496	882-7198	6-8	Myranda Marsh
Journey S	27102 Foxborough	Aliso Viejo, CA	92656-3377	949-448-7232	448-7256	K-5	Tim Connolly
Juan Bautista de Anza S	302 Palm Canyon Dr	Borrego Springs, CA	92004	760-767-5850		7-12	Dr. Sandra Thorpe
Julian Charter S	PO Box 1780	Julian, CA	92036-1780	866-853-0003	765-3849	K-12	Jennifer Cauzza
Kaplan Academy of Southern CA	3737 Martin Luther King Jr	Lynwood, CA	90262	310-770-8920		K-12	Amy Gross
Keiller Leadership Academy MS	7270 Lisbon St	San Diego, CA	92114-3007	619-263-9266	262-2217	6-8	Joel Christman
Kenny Charter S	3525 M L King Blvd	Sacramento, CA	95817-3654	916-277-6500	277-6513	K-6	Charles Bush
Kenter Canyon Charter S	645 N Kenter Ave	Los Angeles, CA	90049-1999	310-472-5918	472-9738	K-5	Terry Moren
Kern Workforce 2000 Academy	5801 Sundale Ave	Bakersfield, CA	93309-2924	661-827-3224	827-3320	9-12	Fuchsia Ward
Keyes To Learning Charter S	PO Box 519	Keyes, CA	95328-0519	209-634-6467	669-7121	K-9	Lee Ann Stangl
Kid Street Learning Center	PO Box 6784	Santa Rosa, CA	95406-0784	707-525-9223	525-9432	K-6	Linda Conklin
King Chavez Academy of Excellence	PO Box 13070	San Diego, CA	92170-3070	619-232-2825	232-2943	K-8	Adriana Diaz
King/Chavez Arts Academy	415 31st St	San Diego, CA	92102-4236	619-525-7320		3-5	Scott Worthing
King/Chavez Athletics Academy	415 31st St	San Diego, CA	92102-4236	619-525-7320		3-5	Dr. Brian French
King/Chavez Preparatory Academy	415 31st St	San Diego, CA	92102-4236	619-525-7320		6-7	Elena Bolanos
King/Chavez Primary Academy	415 31st St	San Diego, CA	92102-4236	619-525-7320		K-2	Irisbelle Rodriguez
King City Arts Charter S	415 Pearl St	King City, CA	93930-2919	831-385-5473	385-1016	K-6	Brad Smith
Kings River-Hardwick S	10300 Excelsior Ave	Hanford, CA	93230-9794	559-584-4475	585-1422	K-8	Jean Fetterhoff
KIPP Academy Fresno	2445 W Dakota Ave	Fresno, CA	93705-2611	559-266-1766	233-5477	5-8	Chi Tschang
KIPP Academy of Opportunity	7019 S Van Ness Ave	Los Angeles, CA	90047-1659	323-778-0125	778-0162	5-8	Ian Guidera
KIPP Adelante Preparatory S	1475 6th Ave Fl 2	San Diego, CA	92101	619-233-3242	233-3212	5-8	Elena Luna
KIPP Bayview Academy	1060 Key Ave	San Francisco, CA	94124-3563	415-467-2522	467-9522	5-8	Molly Wood
KIPP Bridge College Prep S	991 14th St	Oakland, CA	94607-3230	510-879-2421	879-3182	5-8	David Ling
KIPP Heartwood Academy	1250 S King Rd	San Jose, CA	95122-2146	408-928-2400	928-2401	5-8	Lolita Jackson
KIPP King Collegiate HS	2005 Via Barrett	San Lorenzo, CA	94580-1315	510-828-9509	258-0097	9-12	Jason Singer
KIPP LA College Prep S	2810 Whittier Blvd	Los Angeles, CA	90023-1527	323-223-5477	223-5410	5-8	Robert Pombello
KIPP Raices Academy	4545 Dozier Ave	Los Angeles, CA	90022-1118	323-780-3900	780-3939	K-4	Amber Young
KIPP San Francisco Bay Academy	1430 Scott St	San Francisco, CA	94115-3510	415-440-4306	440-4308	5-8	Lydia Glassie
KIPP San Jose Collegiate Charter S	1250 S King Rd	San Jose, CA	95122-2146	408-728-2688	928-2401	9-12	Melissa Gonzales
KIPP Summit Academy	2005 Via Barrett	San Lorenzo, CA	94580-1315	510-258-0106	258-0097	5-8	Cathy Cowan
Klamath River Early College of Redwoods	PO Box 849	Klamath, CA	95548-0849	707-482-1737	482-1738	9-12	Geneva Wiki
LACC Charter HS - East	1020 S Fickett St	Los Angeles, CA	90023-1410	323-526-1460	526-1453	9-12	
LACC Charter HS - South Central	2824 S Main St	Los Angeles, CA	90007-3334	213-749-3601	745-8890	9-12	Noel Trout
LA International Charter S	625 Coleman Ave	Los Angeles, CA	90042-4903	323-257-1499	728-9684	9-12	Clifford Mosely
Lake County International Charter S	PO Box 984	Middletown, CA	95461-0984	707-987-3063	825-9344	K-8	Karl Reichman
Lakeview Charter Academy	11465 Kagel Canyon St	Lake View Ter, CA	91342	818-485-0340	837-0508	6-8	Manuel Ponce
Language Academy	4500 Roosevelt Ave	Sacramento, CA	95820-4546	916-277-7137	277-7141	K-8	Martha Quadros
Larchmont Charter S	1265 N Fairfax Ave	West Hollywood, CA	90046-5205	323-656-6407		K-1	
Larchmont Charter S	815 N El Centro Ave	Los Angeles, CA	90038-3805	323-836-0860	656-1467	2-5	Wendy Zacuto
La Sierra HS	1414 W Olive Ave	Porterville, CA	93257-3062	559-782-4748	782-4708	9-12	Jan Mekeel
La Sierra Jr Academy	1735 E Houston Ave	Visalia, CA	93292-2349	559-733-6963	733-6845	7-8	Rene Moncada
La Sierra Military Academy	1735 E Houston Ave	Visalia, CA	93292-2349	559-733-6963	733-6845	9-12	Rene Moncada
Latino College Preparatory Academy	14271 Story Rd	San Jose, CA	95127-3823	408-729-2283	285-5324	9-12	Jess Barajas
Laverne Elementary Preparatory Academy	PO Box 400880	Hesperia, CA	92340-0880	760-843-9005		K-6	Devra Tarver
La Vida Charter S	PO Box 1461	Ukiah, CA	95482-1461	707-459-6344	459-6377	K-12	Ann Kelly
Leadership HS	241 Oneida Ave Ste 301	San Francisco, CA	94112	415-841-8910	841-8925	9-12	Elizabeth Rood
Leadership Public S - Hayward	28000 Calaroga Ave	Hayward, CA	94545-4600	510-300-1340	372-0396	9-12	Brian Greenberg
Leadership Public S - Richmond	715 Chanslor Ave	Richmond, CA	94801-3533	510-235-4522	588-4593	9-12	Shawn Benjamin
Leadership Public S - San Jose	1881 Cunningham Ave	San Jose, CA	95122-1712	408-937-2700	937-2705	9-12	Larry Vilaubi
Learning Choice Academy	9950 Scripps Lake Dr	San Diego, CA	92131	858-536-8388		K-12	Kathy Bass
Learning Community Charter S	1859 Bird St	Oroville, CA	95965-4854	530-532-5644	532-5794	K-12	

School	Address	City,State	Zip code	Telephone	Fax	Grade	Contact
Learning for Life Charter S	330 Reservation Rd Ste F	Marina, CA	93933-3286	831-582-9820	582-9825	7-12	Cindy Dotson
Learning Works!	88 N Daisy Ave	Pasadena, CA	91107-3704	626-564-2871	564-2870	7-12	Mikala Rahn
Lemoore Middle College HS	351 E Bush St	Lemoore, CA	93245-3651	559-925-3428	925-6057	9-12	Victor Rosa
Lemoore University Charter S	450 Marsh Dr	Lemoore, CA	93245	559-924-6890	924-6839	5-8	Crescenciano Camarena
Lennox Academy	10319 Firmona Ave	Lennox, CA	90304-1419	310-680-5600	671-5029	9-12	Armando Mena
Liberty Charter S	1012 E Bradley Ave	El Cajon, CA	92021-1231	619-579-7232	579-5730	K-12	Jerry Keough
Life Learning Academy	651 8th St Bldg 229	San Francisco, CA	94130-1901	415-397-8957	397-9274	9-12	Teri Delane
Lifeline Education Charter S	357 E Palmer St	Compton, CA	90221-2610	310-605-2510	764-4890	6-12	Paula DeGroat
Lighthouse Community Charter S	444 Hegenberger Rd	Oakland, CA	94621-1418	510-271-8801	271-8803	K-12	Stephen Sexton
Lincoln ES	1900 Mariposa St	Kingsburg, CA	93631-2044	559-897-5141	897-3537	2-3	Jennifer DuPras
Linscott Charter S	220 Elm St	Watsonville, CA	95076-5025	831-728-6301	761-5478	K-8	Robin Higbee
Literacy First Charter S	799 E Washington Ave	El Cajon, CA	92020-5327	619-579-7232	579-5730	K-8	Debbie Beyer
Live Oak Charter S	100 Gnoss Concourse	Petaluma, CA	94952-3395	707-762-9020	762-9019	K-8	Will Stapp
Livermore Valley Charter S	543 Sonoma Ave	Livermore, CA	94550-4045	925-443-1690	443-1692	K-8	Tara Alderman
Locke HS	325 E 111th St	Los Angeles, CA	90061-3093	323-420-2100	420-2128	9-12	Nerine Vernon-Burnside
Long Valley Charter S	PO Box 7	Doyle, CA	96109-0007	530-827-2395	827-3562	K-12	J. D. Lietaker
Loomis Basin Charter S	5438 Laird Rd	Loomis, CA	95650-8916	916-652-2642	652-1822	K-4	Cindy Uptain
Los Angeles Academy of Arts & Enterprise	600 S La Fayette Park Pl	Los Angeles, CA	90057-3243	213-487-0600	487-0500	6-12	Leslie Stoltz
Los Angeles County Online HS	1202 W Avenue J	Lancaster, CA	93534-2902	661-802-4015	884-9671	9-12	Linda Rosson
Los Angeles Leadership Academy	668 S Catalina St	Los Angeles, CA	90005-1708	213-381-8484	381-8489	6-12	Roger Lowenstein
Los Feliz Charter S for the Arts	1265 N Fairfax Ave	West Hollywood, CA	90046-5205	323-656-2810	656-2812	K-6	Karin Newlin
LPS College Park Charter S	8801 MacArthur Blvd	Oakland, CA	94605	510-633-0750	291-9783	9-12	Lisa Haynes
Lucerne Valley Career Academy	8560 Aliento Rd	Lucerne Valley, CA	92356	760-248-6800	248-3330	9-12	Michael Talerico
Lugo Academy	6410 Rita Ave	Huntington Park, CA	90255-4126	323-585-1153	585-1283	K-5	Vicki Perez
Lynhaven ES	881 Cypress Ave	San Jose, CA	95117-2599	408-556-0368	341-7170	K-5	Lesa Nieri
MAAC Community Charter S	1385 3rd Ave	Chula Vista, CA	91911-4302	619-476-0749	476-0913	9-12	Terri Lapinski
MACSA Academica Calmecac	130 N Jackson Ave	San Jose, CA	95116-1907	408-937-3702	937-3705	9-12	Juan Guel
MACSA El Portal Leadership Academy	240 Swanston Ln	Gilroy, CA	95020-4548	408-846-1715	846-1815	9-12	Graciela Valladares
Madera Independent Study Academy	28198 Avenue 14	Madera, CA	93638-4905	559-674-7783	675-8313	K-12	Steve Carney
Magnolia Science Academy	18238 Sherman Way	Reseda, CA	91335-4550	818-609-0507	609-0534	6-12	Engin Eryilmaz
Magnolia Science Academy 2	18425 Kittridge St	Reseda, CA	91335-6138	818-708-0200	708-7472	6-12	Suleyman Karaman
Magnolia Science Academy 3	1254 E Helmick St	Carson, CA	90746-3164	310-327-2841		6-11	Hakki Karaman
Magnolia Science Academy 4	11330 Graham Pl	Los Angeles, CA	90064-3725	310-664-8811	664-8866	6-11	Joseph Hurmali
Magnolia Science Academy 5	PO Box 2470	Los Angeles, CA	90078-2470	323-871-4258	871-8658	6-8	
Magnolia Science Academy - San Diego	6365 Lake Atlin Ave	San Diego, CA	92119-3206	619-644-1300	644-1600	6-8	David Yilmaz
Making Waves Academy	2925 Technology Ct	San Pablo, CA	94806-1952	510-262-1511	262-1518	5-8	Dr. Jeeva Roche-Smith
Mammoth Olympic Academy	PO Box 3509	Mammoth Lakes, CA	93546-3509	760-934-7636	934-7510	9-12	Jim Barnes
Manzanita Charter MS	3200 Barrett Ave	Richmond, CA	94804-1718	510-232-3300	232-0009	6-8	Tara Denison
Mare Island Technology Academy HS	2 Positive Pl	Vallejo, CA	94589-1825	707-552-6482	552-0288	6-12	Rick van Adelsberg
Maria Montessori Charter Academy	1850 Wildcat Blvd	Rocklin, CA	95765-5471	916-630-1510	624-7305	PK-8	Brent Boothby
Marquez Charter S	16821 Marquez Ave	Pacific Plsds, CA	90272-3294	310-454-4019	573-1532	K-5	Phillip Hollis
Marshall Charter MS	5150 W Goldleaf Cir Ste 401	Los Angeles, CA	90056-1663	323-290-6900	294-9115	K-6	Peter Watts
Marshall HS	5946 S Figueroa St	Los Angeles, CA	90003-1018	323-266-1649		9-12	David Morrow
Marysville Charter Academy for the Arts	1917 B St	Marysville, CA	95901	530-749-6157	741-7892	7-12	John Pimentel
MATTIE Academy	1119 E Rhea St	Long Beach, CA	90806-5125	888-449-0997		6-12	Dr. Denice Price
Mattole Valley Charter S	210 Lindley Rd	Petrolia, CA	95558-9534	707-629-3634	629-3649	K-12	Richard Graey
McGill School of Success	3025 Fir St	San Diego, CA	92102-1123	619-239-0632	239-1318	K-2	Deborah Huggins
Memorial Academy Charter S	2850 Logan Ave	San Diego, CA	92113-2412	619-525-7400	525-7498	6-8	Julie Espinosa
Merced Scholars Charter S	808 W 16th St	Merced, CA	95340-4600	209-385-5361	385-5365	6-12	Lori Gomes
Merkin MS	2023 S Union Ave	Los Angeles, CA	90007-1326	213-748-0141	748-0142	6-8	Donna Jacobson
Metropolitan Arts & Tech HS	400 Mansell St	San Francisco, CA	94134-1829	415-550-5920	206-1444	9-12	Glenn Dennis
Met Sacramento Charter HS	810 V St	Sacramento, CA	95818-1330	916-264-4700	264-4701	9-12	Allen Young
Micro Enterprise Charter Academy	5951 Downey Ave	Long Beach, CA	90805-4518	562-630-6096	630-6038	6-7	Marylouise Lau
Mid Valley Alternative Charter S	9895 7th Ave	Hanford, CA	93230-8802	559-583-1149	582-7565	K-8	Charlotte Meade
Milagro Charter ES	1855 N Main St	Los Angeles, CA	90031-3227	323-223-1786	223-8593	K-5	Sacsha Robinett
Millennium Charter HS	51 E Beverly Pl	Tracy, CA	95376-3191	209-831-5240	831-5243	9-12	Virginia Stewart
Millsmont Academy	3200 62nd Ave	Oakland, CA	94605-1614	510-638-9445	638-0744	K-12	Kristin Gallagher
Millsmont Academy Secondary	8030 Atherton St	Oakland, CA	94605-3430	510-562-8030	562-8013	6-10	Diana Adams
Mirus Charter S	14073 Main St Ste 103	Hesperia, CA	92345-4675	760-244-3764	244-3879	7-12	Mary Bixby
Mission View Charter S	20655 Soledad Canyon Rd #12	Santa Clarita, CA	91351	661-299-6759		7-12	Dr. Maria Meneses-Trejo
Mission Vista HS	1306 Melrose Dr	Oceanside, CA	92057	760-758-6800		9-12	Rodney Goldenberg
Modoc Charter S	214 W 1st St	Alturas, CA	96101-3903	530-233-3861	233-3864	K-12	Greg Beale
Mojave River Academy	PO Box 386	Oro Grande, CA	92368-0386	760-245-9260	245-1339	K-12	Joseph Andreasen
Monarch Academy	1445 101st Ave	Oakland, CA	94603-3207	510-568-3101	568-3521	K-5	Tatiana Epanchin-Troyan
Monarch Learning Center	PO Box 992418	Redding, CA	96099-2418	530-247-7307	243-4819	K-8	Chris Johnson
Monroe MS	1055 S Monroe St	San Jose, CA	95128-3199	408-556-0360	341-7020	5-8	Dawnel Sonntag
Montague Charter Academy	13000 Montague St	Pacoima, CA	91331-4146	818-899-0215	834-9782	PK-5	Rebeca Rodriguez
Monterey Bay Charter S	1004B David Ave	Pacific Grove, CA	93950-5443	831-655-4638	655-4815	K-8	Cassandra Gallup-Bridge
Monterey County Home Charter S	PO Box 80851	Salinas, CA	93912-0851	831-755-0331	755-0837	K-12	Mary Sgheiza
Moreno Valley Community Learning Center	13911 Perris Blvd	Moreno Valley, CA	92553-4306	951-485-5771	485-5772	6-12	Robert Byers
Mountain Home Charter S	41267 Highway 41	Oakhurst, CA	93644-9403	559-642-1422	642-1592	K-8	Michael Cox
Mountain Oaks S	PO Box 1209	San Andreas, CA	95249-1209	209-754-0532	754-3556	K-12	
Mountain View Montessori Charter S	12900 Amethyst Rd	Victorville, CA	92395-6393	760-843-3303	843-1074	K-6	Geraldine Terranova
Mueller Charter S	715 I St	Chula Vista, CA	91910-5199	619-422-6192	422-0356	K-8	Dr. Kevin Riley
Muir Charter S	9845 Horn Rd Ste 150	Sacramento, CA	95827-1948	916-366-7319		9-12	Buzz Breedlove
Multicultural Learning Center	7510 DeSoto Ave	Canoga Park, CA	91303-1430	818-716-5783	716-1085	K-6	Toby Bornstein
Museum Charter S	211 Maple St	San Diego, CA	92103-6527	619-236-8712	236-8906	3-9	Phil Beaumont
Napa Valley Language Academy	2700 Kilburn Ave	Napa, CA	94558-5623	707-253-3678	259-8427	K-5	Deborah Wallace
National University Academy	11833 Woodside Ave	Lakeside, CA	92040-2911	619-252-7786		9-12	Bernard Hanlon
Natomas Charter S	4600 Blackrock Dr	Sacramento, CA	95835-1250	916-928-5353	928-5333	K-12	Charlie Leo
Natomas-Pacific Pathways Prep	4400 E Commerce Way	Sacramento, CA	95834-9626	916-928-5300	928-5299	9-12	Tom Rutten
Nevada City Charter S	750 Hoover Ln	Nevada City, CA	95959-2910	530-265-1885	265-1889	K-8	
Nevada City S for the Arts	13032 Bitney Springs Rd # 8	Nevada City, CA	95959	530-273-7736	273-1378	K-8	Holly Pettitt
NEW Academy Canoga Park	21425 Cohasset St	Canoga Park, CA	91303-1450	818-710-2640	710-2654	K-5	Edward Fiszer
NEW Academy of Science & Arts	379 Loma Dr	Los Angeles, CA	90017-1142	213-413-9183	413-9187	K-5	Fausto Barragan
Newcastle Charter S	8951 Valley View Dr	Newcastle, CA	95658-9723	916-663-3307	663-3524	K-8	Kathleen Daugherty
New City S	1230 Pine Ave	Long Beach, CA	90813-3123	562-436-0689	436-7475	K-8	Ted Hamory
New Day Charter Academy	1919 B St	Marysville, CA	95901-3731	530-749-6118	741-7850	K-8	Jill Segner
New Designs Charter S	3756 Santa Rosalia Dr # 523	Los Angeles, CA	90008	323-293-7009	293-7130	6-12	Yaw Audtwun
New Heights Charter S	4126 Arlington Ave	Los Angeles, CA	90008-4028	323-508-0155	508-0156	K-8	Amy Berfield
New Los Angeles Charter S	5100 Wilshire Blvd	Los Angeles, CA	90036-4313	323-939-6400	939-6411	6-8	Matthew Albert
New Millenium Secondary S	20700 Avalon Blvd Ste 285	Carson, CA	90746	310-999-6162	999-6163	9-12	Anthony Kline
New Millennium Charter S	830 Fresno St	Fresno, CA	93706-3117	559-497-9331	497-9109	7-12	Maureen Moore
New Technology HS	1400 Dickson St	Sacramento, CA	95822-3437	916-433-2839	433-2840	9-12	Paula Hanzel
New Village Charter HS	147 N Occidental Blvd	Los Angeles, CA	90026-4601	213-385-4015	385-4020	9-12	Joe Bennett
New West Charter MS	11625 W Pico Blvd	Los Angeles, CA	90064-2908	310-943-5444	231-3399	6-8	Dr. Sharon Weir
Nord Country Charter S	5554 California St	Chico, CA	95973-9795	530-891-3138	891-3273	K-6	Kathleen Dahlgren
Northcoast Prep and Performing Arts Acad	PO Box 276	Arcata, CA	95518-0276	707-822-0861	822-0878	9-12	Dr. Jean Bazemore
North County Trade Tech HS	2585 Business Park Dr	Vista, CA	92081-8831	760-598-0782	598-0895	9-12	
North Oakland Community Charter S	1000 42nd St	Emeryville, CA	94608-3621	510-655-0540	655-1222	K-5	Carolyn Gramstorff
North Valley Charter Academy	16551 Rinaldi St Ste A	Granada Hills, CA	91344	818-368-1557	368-1935	6-12	Diane French
Northwest Prep at Piner-Olivet	2590 Piner Rd Ste B	Santa Rosa, CA	95401	707-522-3320	522-3101	7-12	Keith Muelrath
North Woods Discovery S	14732 Bass Dr	Redding, CA	96003-7303	530-275-5480	275-5416	K-8	John Husome
Norton Space and Aeronautics Academy	503 E Central Ave	San Bernardino, CA	92408-2313	760-946-5414		K-12	Robert Barksdale
Nova Academy Early College HS	2609 W 5th St	Santa Ana, CA	92703-1818	714-569-0948	569-1693	9-12	Dennis Eastman
Nova Meridian Academy	850 Via Lata Ste 105	Colton, CA	92324-3985	909-370-2055		9-12	David Tellyer
Novato Charter S	940 C St	Novato, CA	94949-5060	415-883-4254	883-1859	K-8	Rachel Bishop
Nubia Leadership Academy	6134 Benson Ave	San Diego, CA	92114-4204	619-262-0050	262-4215	K-6	Rosalind Jackson
Nueva Vision Academy Charter	250 Harris Ave Ste 6	Sacramento, CA	95838-3279	916-567-5220	567-5208	9-12	Rosendo Garcia
Nuevo Sol Charter S	1218 4th St	San Fernando, CA	91340-2314	213-446-6488	837-2271	K-5	Ronald Polacios
Nuview Bridge Early College HS	30401 Reservoir Ave	Nuevo, CA	92567-9361	951-928-8498	928-0186	9-12	Rebecca Mashatt
Oakdale Charter S	1235 E D St	Oakdale, CA	95361-3223	209-848-4361	848-4363	9-12	Mike Riley
Oakland Aviation HS	PO Box 14152	Oakland, CA	94614-2152	510-633-6375	633-6351	9-12	John Sulton Ed.D.
Oakland Charter Academy	3001 International Blvd	Oakland, CA	94601-2203	510-532-6751	532-6753	6-8	George Lopez
Oakland Charter HS	171 12th St	Oakland, CA	94607	510-532-6751	532-6753	9-12	John Granucci
Oakland Military Institute	3877 Lusk St	Oakland, CA	94608-3822	510-594-3900	597-9886	6-12	Mark Ryan
Oakland S for the Arts	1970 Broadway	Oakland, CA	94612-2206	510-873-8800	873-8816	6-12	Donn Harris
Oakland Unity HS	6038 Brann St	Oakland, CA	94605-1544	510-635-7170	635-3830	9-12	David Castillo
Oasis Charter HS	285 17th St	Oakland, CA	94612-4123	510-251-8103	251-8115	9-12	Hugo Arabia
Oasis Charter S	PO Box 720	Salinas, CA	93902-0720	831-424-9003	424-9005	K-8	Jane Roberts
Ocean Charter School	12606 Culver Blvd	Los Angeles, CA	90066-6506	310-827-5511	827-2012	K-8	Stephanie Edwards
Ocean Grove Charter S	1166 Broadway Ste Q	Placerville, CA	95667-5745	800-979-4436	295-3583	K-12	Randy Gaschler
Odyssey Charter S	725 W Altadena Dr	Altadena, CA	91001-4103	626-229-0993	229-0586	K-8	Lauren O'Neill
O'Farrell Community S	6130 Skyline Dr	San Diego, CA	92114-5620	619-263-3009	263-4339	6-8	Byron King
Olive Grove Charter S	PO Box 208	Los Olivos, CA	93441-0208	805-693-5933	688-4218	K-12	Jesse Leyva
Open Charter Magnet S	5540 W 77th St	Los Angeles, CA	90045-3214	310-568-0735	568-0904	K-5	Robert Burke
Opportunities for Learning	12731 Ramona Blvd	Baldwin Park, CA	91706	626-814-0161	814-0686	K-12	John Hall

School	Address	City,State	Zip code	Telephone	Fax	Grade	Contact
Opportunities for Learning Charter S	18259 Soledad Canyon Rd	Santa Clarita, CA	91387-3532	661-424-1337	424-1129	7-12	Bill Toomey
Opportunities for Learning S	33621 Del Obispo St	Dana Point, CA	92629	949-248-1282	248-2450	K-12	Judah Marago
Opportunities Unlimited	10513 S Vermont Ave	Los Angeles, CA	90044-3021	323-241-1100	789-6518	9-12	A. Marcoulas
Options for Youth	2627 Alta Arden Expy	Sacramento, CA	95825-1306	916-971-3175	971-3186	K-12	Christopher Timpson
Options for Youth	5720 Watt Ave	North Highlands, CA	95660-4752	916-338-2375	338-2417	7-12	Christopher Timpson
Options for Youth	11088 Olson Dr	Rancho Cordova, CA	95670	916-631-8113	631-8121	K-12	Christopher Timpson
Options for Youth Charter S	609 W Las Tunas Dr	San Gabriel, CA	91776-1112	626-282-0390		K-12	Cheryl Portillo
Options for Youth Charter S	1610 W Burbank Blvd	Burbank, CA	91506-1311	818-566-7525	566-7712	K-12	Francisco Ayala
Options for Youth Charter S	6110 Fair Oaks Blvd Ste E	Carmichael, CA	95608-4826	916-485-5155	485-5484	K-12	Christopher Timpson
Options for Youth - Upland	310 N Mountain Ave	Upland, CA	91786-5115	909-946-0500		K-12	Brian Albright
Options for Youth Victor Valley Charter	15048 Bear Valley Rd	Victorville, CA	92395-9235	626-685-9300	685-9316	7-12	Kathy Lento
Orange County Arts Academy	825 N Broadway	Santa Ana, CA	92701-3423	714-558-2787	558-2775	K-8	Linda Hardman-Greene
Orange County HS of the Arts	1010 N Main St	Santa Ana, CA	92701-3602	714-560-0900	664-0463	7-12	Sue Vaughn
Orchard View Charter S	700 Watertrough Rd	Sebastopol, CA	95472-3917	707-823-4709	823-6187	K-12	Carol Rogers
Orcutt Academy Charter	PO Box 2310	Orcutt, CA	93457-2310	805-938-8929	938-8941	K-12	Alan Majewski
Ouchi HS	2621 W 54th St	Los Angeles, CA	90043-2614	323-293-9169	293-0427	9-12	Ena Lavan
Our Community S	16514 Nordhoff St	North Hills, CA	91343-3728	818-920-5285	920-5383	K-6	Chris Ferris
Pacifica Community Charter S	3754 Dunn Dr	Los Angeles, CA	90034-5805	310-845-9405	845-9402	K-8	Gary Winning
Pacific Coast Charter S	294 Green Valley Rd	Watsonville, CA	95076	831-786-2180	761-6166	K-12	Vicki Carr
Pacific Collegiate Charter S	PO Box 1701	Santa Cruz, CA	95061-1701	831-479-7785	427-5254	7-12	Chris Mercer
Pacific Community Charter S	PO Box 984	Point Arena, CA	95468-0984	707-882-4131	882-4132	K-12	Yolanda Highhouse
Pacific View Charter S	3670 Ocean Ranch Blvd	Oceanside, CA	92056-2669	760-757-0161	435-2666	K-12	Gina Campbell
Pacific View Charter S	2937 Moore Ave	Eureka, CA	95501-3316	707-269-9490	269-9491	K-12	James Malloy
Pacoima Charter S	11016 Norris Ave	Pacoima, CA	91331-2598	818-899-0201	890-3812	PK-5	Irene Smerigan
Palisades Charter ES	800 Via De La Paz	Pacific Plsds, CA	90272-3617	310-454-3700	459-5627	K-5	Tami Weiser
Palisades Charter HS	15777 Bowdoin St	Pacific Plsds, CA	90272-3586	310-454-0611	454-6076	9-12	Martin Griffin
Palm Desert MS	74200 Rutledge Way	Palm Desert, CA	92260-2646	760-862-4320	862-4327	6-8	Sallie Fraser
Paradise Charter MS	6473 Clark Rd	Paradise, CA	95969-3501	530-872-7277	872-2924	6-8	Chris Reid
Paradise Charter S	3361 California Ave	Modesto, CA	95358-9213	209-524-0184	524-0363	K-8	Douglas Fraser
Para Los Ninos Charter S	1617 E 7th St	Los Angeles, CA	90021-1207	213-239-6605	239-9821	K-5	Norma Silva
Para Los Ninos MS	1627 E 7th St	Los Angeles, CA	90021	213-250-4800	250-4900	6-8	Gisselle Acevedo
Pasadena Rosebud Academy	2561 Fair Oaks Ave	Altadena, CA	91001-5074	626-797-7704		K-1	Shawn Brumfield Ed.D.
Pathways Charter S	607 Bobelaine Dr	Santa Rosa, CA	95405-6604	707-573-6117	573-6122	K-12	Dr. Robert Tavonatti
Pathways to College Charter S	PO Box 402672	Hesperia, CA	92340-2672	760-948-9175	947-9648	K-4	Clara Brumfield
Peabody Charter S	3018 Calle Noguera	Santa Barbara, CA	93105-2899	805-563-1172	569-7042	K-6	Kate Ford
Phillips Charter S	1210 Shetler Ave	Napa, CA	94559-4205	707-253-3481	259-8425	K-6	Matthew Manning
Phoenix Academy	PO Box 4925	San Rafael, CA	94913-4925	415-491-0581	491-0981	9-12	Deborah Hemphill
Pine Mountain Learning Center	PO Box 6810	Frazier Park, CA	93222-6810	661-364-3811	242-1985	K-6	Shelly Mason
Piner-Olivet Charter S	2707 Francisco Ave	Santa Rosa, CA	95403-1869	707-522-3310	522-3317	6-8	Diana Drew-Ingham
Pioneer MS	101 W Pioneer Way	Hanford, CA	93230-9489	559-584-0112	584-0118	6-8	Greg Henry
Pioneer Technical Center	28123 Avenue 14	Madera, CA	93638-4905	559-664-1600	673-5569	9-12	Alyson Crafton
Pioneer Union ES	8810 14th Ave	Hanford, CA	93230-9680	559-584-8831	584-7049	K-5	Lisa Horne
Plumas Charter S	424 N Mill Creek Rd	Quincy, CA	95971-9678	530-283-3851	283-3841	K-12	Janet Wolcott
Plumas Lake Charter S	2743 Plumas School Rd	Marysville, CA	95961-8827	530-743-4428	743-1408	K-12	Joe Hendrix
Port of Los Angeles HS	250 W 5th St	San Pedro, CA	90731-3304	310-832-9201	832-1605	9-12	Dr. Marie Collins
Preuss S	9500 Gilman Dr	La Jolla, CA	92093-5004	858-658-7400	658-0988	6-12	Scott Barton
Price Charter MS	2650 New Jersey Ave	San Jose, CA	95124-1520	408-377-2532	377-7406	6-8	Debra Negrete
Primary Charter S	51 E Beverly Pl	Tracy, CA	95376-3191	209-831-5240	831-5243	K-4	Virginia Stewart
Promise Charter S	730 45th St	San Diego, CA	92102-3619	619-262-5083		K-8	Maria Garcia
Provisional Accelerated Learning Academy	PO Box 7100	San Bernardino, CA	92411-0100	909-887-7002	887-8942	9-12	Dr. Mildred Henry
Public Safety Academy	1494 E Art Townsend Dr	San Bernardino, CA	92408-0114	909-382-2211	382-2202	6-12	Michael Dickinson
Puente Charter S	501 S Boyle Ave	Los Angeles, CA	90033-3816	323-780-0076	780-0359	K-K	Jerome Greening
Quail Lake Environmental Charter S	4087 N Quail Lake Dr	Clovis, CA	93619-4646	559-292-1273	292-1276	K-8	Brad Huebert
Rainbow Advanced Institute for Learning	5253 5th St	Fallbrook, CA	92028-9795	760-728-4305	728-7712	6-12	Jerry Ostrove
Ravendale-Termo Charter S	709 Termo Grasshopper Rd	Ravendale, CA	96123	530-234-2010	234-2132	K-12	Merry Lynne Hislop
Reagan ES	1180 Diane Ave	Kingsburg, CA	93631-2830	559-897-6986	897-6987	4-6	Melanie Sembritzki
Redding School of the Arts	2200 Eureka Way	Redding, CA	96001-0337	530-247-6933	245-2633	K-8	Jean Hatch
Redding School of the Arts II	2828 Eureka Way	Redding, CA	96001-0221	530-243-7145		K-2	Margaret Johnson
Redwood Academy of Ukiah	PO Box 1383	Ukiah, CA	95482-1383	707-467-0500	467-4942	7-12	Elna Gordon
Reems Academy of Technology & Art	8425 MacArthur Blvd	Oakland, CA	94605-3553	510-729-6635	562-9539	K-8	Lisa Blair
Renaissance Arts Academy	1800 Colorado Blvd	Los Angeles, CA	90041-1340	323-259-5700	259-5718	6-12	P. K. Candaux
Revere Charter MS	1450 Allenford Ave	Los Angeles, CA	90049-3614	310-451-5789	576-7957	6-8	Fern Somoza
Richmond College Prep S	PO Box 2814	Richmond, CA	94802-2814	510-235-2066	235-2009	K-5	Fernando Johnson
Ridgecrest Charter S	325 S Downs St	Ridgecrest, CA	93555-4531	760-375-1010	375-7766	K-8	Tina Ellingsworth
Rincon Valley Charter S	1000 Yulupa Ave	Santa Rosa, CA	95405-7098	707-539-3410	537-1791	7-8	Matt Reno
Riverbank Language Academy Charter S	2400 Stanislaus St	Riverbank, CA	95367-2233	209-869-8093		K-5	William Redford
River Charter MS	2447 Old Sonoma Rd	Napa, CA	94558-6006	707-253-6813	258-2800	6-8	Linda Inlay
River Oak Charter S	555 Leslie St	Ukiah, CA	95482-5507	707-467-1855	467-1857	K-8	Kathleen Thompson
River Oaks Charter S	1801 Pyrenees Ave	Stockton, CA	95210-5207	209-956-8100	956-8102	K-8	Kat Mathers
Riverside Preparatory S	PO Box 455	Oro Grande, CA	92368-0455	760-245-9260	245-1339	K-12	Joseph Andreasen
River Springs Charter S	43466 Business Park Dr	Temecula, CA	92590-5526	951-252-8800	252-8801	K-12	Dr. Kathleen Hermsmeyer
River Valley Charter HS	9707 1/2 Marilla Dr	Lakeside, CA	92040-2807	619-390-2579	390-2581	7-12	Cheryl Bloom
Rocketship Mateo Sheedy ES	788 Locust St	San Jose, CA	95110-2954	408-286-3330	286-3331	K-5	Maricela Guerrero
Rocketship Two ES	2249 Dobern Ave	San Jose, CA	95116	408-286-3344	286-3331	K-12	Melissa McGonegle
Rocklin Academy	6532 Turnstone Way	Rocklin, CA	95765-5865	916-632-6580	784-3034	K-6	Patricia Teilh
Rocklin Academy at Meyers Street	5035 Meyers St	Rocklin, CA	95677-2811	916-632-6580	784-3034	K-6	Pat Teilh
Rocky Point Charter S	3500 Tamarack Dr	Redding, CA	96003-1747	530-225-0456	225-0499	K-8	Debbie Stierli
Rolling Hills MS	1585 More Ave	Los Gatos, CA	95032-1094	408-364-4235	341-7070	5-8	Kathleen Gibbs
Romero Charter MS	440 Shatto Pl	Los Angeles, CA	90020	213-381-0880	381-0884	6-8	Ana Cubas
Roosevelt Community Learning Center	31191 Road 180	Visalia, CA	93292-9585	559-592-9160	592-2927	K-12	Klara East
Roosevelt ES	1185 10th Ave	Kingsburg, CA	93631-2100	559-897-5193	897-6865	1-1	Laurie Goodman
Rosa Parks Academy	1930 S D St	Stockton, CA	95206-2489	209-944-5590	465-2690	K-5	Dr. Mary Welch
Roseland Accelerated MS	1777 West Ave	Santa Rosa, CA	95407-7449	707-546-7050	546-0434	7-8	Jenny Young
Roseland University Preparatory S	100 Sebastopol Rd	Santa Rosa, CA	95407-6928	707-566-9990	566-9992	9-12	Amy Jones-Kerr
Rosie the Riveter Charter HS	690 N Studebaker Rd	Long Beach, CA	90803-2221	562-431-0302			Alexandra Torres
Russian River Charter S	PO Box 139	Guerneville, CA	95446-0139	707-887-8790	887-8759	7-12	Carol Miller
Sacramento HS	PO Box 5038	Sacramento, CA	95817-0038	916-277-6200	277-6370	9-12	Aaron Thornsberry
Sacramento River Discovery Center	1660 Monroe St	Red Bluff, CA	96080-2694	530-529-1650	529-1694	6-12	Larry Newman
St. Hope Public School 7	5201 Strawberry Ln	Sacramento, CA	95820-4815	916-649-7850	277-7039	K-8	Herinder Pegany
Salmon Creek S	1935 Bohemian Hwy	Occidental, CA	95465-9100	707-874-1205	874-1226	4-8	Dave Miller
San Carlos Charter Learning Center	750 Dartmouth Ave Ste 1	San Carlos, CA	94070	650-508-7343	508-7341	K-8	Chris Mahoney
San Diego Cooperative Charter S	7260 Linda Vista Rd	San Diego, CA	92111-6128	858-496-1613	467-9741	K-8	Dr. Wendy Ranck-Buhr
Sanger Academy Charter S	2207 9th St	Sanger, CA	93657-2711	559-875-5562	875-8045	K-8	Ken Garcia
San Jacinto Valley Academy	480 N San Jacinto Ave	San Jacinto, CA	92583-2729	951-654-6113	644-5083	K-9	Douglas Ferber
San Jose Conservation Corps Charter S	1534 Berger Dr	San Jose, CA	95112-2703	408-283-6521	288-6521	9-12	Joe Frausto
San Jose-Edison Charter S	2021 W Alwood St	West Covina, CA	91790-3259	626-856-1693		K-8	Dr. Denise Patton
San Lorenzo Valley USD Charter S	325 Marion Ave	Ben Lomond, CA	95005-9403	831-336-1827	336-9657	K-12	Jay Dunlap
Santa Barbara Charter S	6100 Stow Canyon Rd	Goleta, CA	93117-1705	805-967-6522	967-6382	K-8	Bev Abrams
Santa Clarita Valley International S	25876 the Old Rd Ste 102	Stevenson Ranch, CA	91381	661-362-8066	255-6078	K-12	Dawn Evenson
Santa Monica Blvd Community Charter S	1022 N Van Ness Ave	Los Angeles, CA	90038-3252	323-469-0971	462-4093	K-5	Linda Lee
Santa Rosa Academy	34878 Monte Vista Dr # 120	Wildomar, CA	92595	951-678-5300	678-1840	K-12	Laura Badillo
Santa Rosa Accelerated Charter	4650 Badger Rd	Santa Rosa, CA	95409-2633	707-528-5319	528-5644	5-6	Matt Marshall
Santa Rosa Charter S	2760 W Steele Ln	Santa Rosa, CA	95403-3236	707-547-2480	547-2482	K-8	LaDonna Moore
Santa Rosa Charter S for the Arts	756 Humboldt St	Santa Rosa, CA	95404-3717	707-522-3170	522-3172	K-8	Anna-Maria Guzman
Santa Ynez Valley Charter S	PO Box 188	Santa Ynez, CA	93460-0188	805-686-7360	686-7383	K-8	Mariann Cooley
Santiago Charter MS	515 N Rancho Santiago Blvd	Orange, CA	92869-2724	714-997-6366	532-4758	7-8	Mary Henry
Sartorette Charter ES	3850 Woodford Dr	San Jose, CA	95124-3799	408-264-4380	264-1758	K-5	Scott Johnson
SAVA: Sacramento Academic and Vocational	3141 Dwight Rd Ste 400	Elk Grove, CA	95758-6473	916-428-3200	428-3232	7-12	Michael O'Leary
SAVA: Sacramento Academic and Vocational	5330 Power Inn Rd Ste D	Sacramento, CA	95820-6757	916-387-8063	387-0139	7-12	Michael O'Leary
School of Arts and Enterprise	295 N Garey Ave	Pomona, CA	91767-5429	909-622-0699	620-1018	9-12	Lucille Berger
School of Extended Educational Options	1460 E Holt Ave Ste 208	Pomona, CA	91767	909-620-5470	629-5029	7-12	Michael Hernandez
School of Unlimited Learning	2336 Calaveras St	Fresno, CA	93721-1104	559-498-8543	642-1592	7-12	Mark Wilson
Sebastopol Independent Charter S	PO Box 1170	Sebastopol, CA	95473-1170	707-824-9700	824-1432	K-8	Susan Olson
Sedona Charter Academy	16519 Victor St	Victorville, CA	92395	760-245-3222	245-3774	K-12	Joseph Andreasen
Sequoia Charter S	21445 Centre Pointe Pkwy	Santa Clarita, CA	91350-2684	661-259-0033	254-8653	7-12	Jill Shenberger
Serna Charter S	19 S Central Ave	Lodi, CA	95240-2901	209-331-7809	331-7997	K-6	Michael Gillespie
Shasta Secondary Home S	1401 Gold St	Redding, CA	96001-1937	530-245-2600	245-2611	6-12	Lynn Peebles
Shasta Trades Academy	1644 Magnolia Ave	Redding, CA	96001-1513	530-245-7838	225-0239	9-12	Robert Shemwell
Shearer Charter S	1590 Elm St	Napa, CA	94559-3924	707-253-3508	253-3847	K-5	Olivia McCormick
Shenandoah HS	6540 Koki Ln	El Dorado, CA	95623-4328	530-622-6212	622-1071	9-12	
Sherman Oaks Community Charter S	1800 Fruitdale Ave Ste C	San Jose, CA	95128-4976	408-795-1140	341-7180	K-6	Irene Preciado
SIATech Charter S	217 Escondido Ave Ste 7	Vista, CA	92084-6170	760-945-1227	631-3412	9-12	Dr. Linda Dawson
Sierra Charter S	1931 N Fine Ave	Fresno, CA	93727-1510	559-490-4290	490-4292	K-12	Lisa Marasco
Sierra Montessori Academy	10911 Wolf Rd	Grass Valley, CA	95949-8179	530-268-9990	268-0613	K-8	Daniel Elkin
Six Rivers Charter HS	1720 M St	Arcata, CA	95521-5741	707-825-2428	825-2034	9-12	Chris Hartley
Sixth Street Prep S	15579 8th St	Victorville, CA	92395-3399	760-241-0962	241-0967	K-6	Linda Mikels
Skirball MS	603 E 115th St	Los Angeles, CA	90059-2322	323-905-1377	905-1378	6-8	Joy May-Harris

School	Address	City,State	Zip code	Telephone	Fax	Grade	Contact
Sky Mountain Charter S	1166 Broadway Ste Q	Placerville, CA	95667-5745	530-295-3566	295-3583	K-12	Susan Clark
Smythe Academy of Arts & Sciences	2781 Northgate Blvd	Sacramento, CA	95833-2208	916-263-8466	263-8465	K-8	Kirk Fujikawa
SOAR Charter Academy	985 Kendall Dr Ste A-353	San Bernardino, CA	92407	909-957-0491		K-6	Trisha Lancaster
Sol Aureus College Prep Charter S	2801 Meadowview Rd	Sacramento, CA	95832-1442	916-421-0600	421-0601	5-8	Alton Nelson
Soledad Enrichment Action Charter S	222 N Virgil Ave	Los Angeles, CA	90004-3622	213-480-4200	555-1212	9-12	Cesar Calderon
Somis Academy	950 Flynn Rd	Camarillo, CA	93012-8764	805-987-1188	987-1108	9-12	Carol Andersen
Sonoma Charter S	17202 Sonoma Hwy	Sonoma, CA	95476-3667	707-935-4232	935-4207	K-8	Paula Hunter
South Bay Preparatory Charter S	1290 Ridder Park Dr	San Jose, CA	95131-2304	408-391-1259	779-0519	6-12	Daniel Ordaz
South Sutter Charter S	2452 El Centro Blvd	East Nicolaus, CA	95659-9748	800-979-4436	295-3583	K-12	Becky Cote
Stallworth Charter S	1610 E Main St	Stockton, CA	95205-5521	209-943-0353	943-5218	K-12	Mary Williams
Steele Canyon HS	12440 Campo Rd	Spring Valley, CA	91978-2331	619-660-3500	660-7198	9-12	Dr. Craig Rocha
Stella Middle Charter Academy	2636 S Mansfield Ave	Los Angeles, CA	90016-3512	323-954-9957	954-6415	5-8	Jeff Hilger
Stellar Charter School	5885 E Bonnyview Rd	Redding, CA	96001-4535	530-245-7730	225-2249	K-12	Cindy Anderson
Stern Math and Science S	5151 State Univ Dr Lot 7	Los Angeles, CA	90032	323-859-2920	859-2924	9-12	Derrick Chau Ph.D.
Stone Bridge S	1870 Salvador Ave	Napa, CA	94558-1633	707-252-5522	251-9767	K-8	William Bindewald
Summit Charter Academy	175 S Mathew St	Porterville, CA	93257-2710	559-782-5902	782-5907	K-6	Cheyenne Ruffa
Summit Charter Academy	2036 E Hatch Rd	Modesto, CA	95351-5142	209-538-8082	538-1620	K-8	Kara Backman
Summit Charter Academy Redwood Campus	15550 Redwood St	Porterville, CA	93257-2530	559-782-5902		7-12	David Huchingson
Summit Leadership Academy	PO Box 401606	Hesperia, CA	92340-1606	760-949-9202	949-9257	9-12	
Summit Preparatory HS	890 Broadway St	Redwood City, CA	94063-3105	650-556-1110	556-1121	9-12	Todd Dickson
SunRidge Charter S	487 Watertrough Rd	Sebastopol, CA	95472-3911	707-824-2844	824-0861	K-8	Mark Rice
Sunset Charter S	1755 S Crystal Ave	Fresno, CA	93706-2797	559-457-3310	495-1334	K-8	Alicia Estigoy
Synergy Charter S	PO Box 78638	Los Angeles, CA	90016-0638	323-233-8559	931-3298	K-5	Randy Palisoc
Synergy Kinetic Academy	980 S Hobart Blvd	Los Angeles, CA	90006-1220	323-459-5469	931-3298	6-8	Meg Palisoc
Temecula Preparatory S	35777 Abelia St	Winchester, CA	92596-8450	951-926-6776	926-6797	K-12	Scott Phillips
Temecula Valley Charter S	35755 Abelia St	Winchester, CA	92596-8450	951-294-6775	294-6780	K-8	JoAnne Burnett
Thomas Charter S	1902 Howard Rd	Madera, CA	93637-5123	559-674-8922	674-8955	K-6	Roger Leach
Tierra Linda MS	750 Dartmouth Ave	San Carlos, CA	94070-1768	650-508-7370	508-7374	5-8	Lesley Martin
Tierra Pacifica Charter S	986 Bostwick Ln	Santa Cruz, CA	95062-1756	831-462-9404	477-0936	K-8	Linda Lambdin
Todays Fresh Start Charter S	4514 Crenshaw Blvd	Los Angeles, CA	90043-1221	323-293-9826	293-9202	K-5	Dr. Jeanette Parker
Topanga Learn Charter S	141 N Topanga Canyon Blvd	Topanga, CA	90290-3831	310-455-3711	455-3517	K-6	Liam Joyce
Tree of Life Montessori S	PO Box 966	Ukiah, CA	95482-0966	707-462-0913	462-0914	1-8	Celeste Beck
Trillium Charter S	1464 Spear Ave	Arcata, CA	95521-4882	707-822-4721	822-7054	K-5	Marianne Keller
Triumph Academy	919 8th St	San Fernando, CA	91340-1312	818-559-7699		6-8	Lonnie Yancsurak
Tubman Village S	6880 Mohawk St	San Diego, CA	92115-1728	619-668-8635	668-2480	K-8	Catherine Pope
Twin Hills MS	1685 Watertrough Rd	Sebastopol, CA	95472-4647	707-823-7446	823-6470	6-8	Catherine Bosch
Twin Ridges Home Study Charter S	111 New Mohawk Rd	Nevada City, CA	95959-3270	530-478-1815	478-0266	K-8	Jenny Travers
Twin Rivers Charter S	840 Cooper Ave	Yuba City, CA	95991-3849	530-755-2872	673-1847	K-8	Bob Loretelli
Uncharted Shores Academy	1545 California St	Crescent City, CA	95531-8330	707-464-9828	464-1428	K-8	Margie Rouge
Union Hill Charter S	11638 Colfax Hwy	Grass Valley, CA	95945-8899	530-273-0647	273-5626	K-8	Debra Young
Union Street Charter S	470 Union St	Arcata, CA	95521-6429	707-822-4845	825-9025	K-5	John Schmidt
University Charter MS at Channel Islands	550 Temple Ave	Camarillo, CA	93010-4833	805-482-4608	388-5814	K-8	Linda Ngarupe
University Charter S	3313 Coffee Rd	Modesto, CA	95355-1534	209-544-8722	544-8864	K-6	Laura Mifflin
University HS	2355 E Keats MS UH134	Fresno, CA	93740-0001	559-278-8263	278-0447	9-12	Dr. James Bushman
University Preparatory Academy	2315 Canoas Garden Ave	San Jose, CA	95125-2005	408-723-1839	779-0519	7-12	Phil Hophan
University Preparatory S	2200 Eureka Way	Redding, CA	96001-0337	530-245-2790	245-2791	6-12	Erin Stuart
University Public S	10038 N Highway 99	Stockton, CA	95212-2127	209-931-5399	931-5185	K-6	Karla Fachner
Urban Academy Charter HS	5150 W Goldleaf Cir Ste 401	Los Angeles, CA	90056-1663	323-290-6900	294-9115	9-12	Michael Piscal
Urban Academy Charter MS	5150 W Goldleaf Cir Ste 401	Los Angeles, CA	90056-1663	323-290-6900	294-9115	6-8	Michael Piscal
Urban Discovery Academy	2850 6th Ave	San Diego, CA	92103	619-788-4668		K-8	Cindy Moser
Vallejo Charter S	436 Del Sur St	Vallejo, CA	94591-8226	707-556-8850	556-8859	K-7	Dr. Katherine Barr
Valley Arts & Science Academy	770 N San Pablo Ave	Fresno, CA	93728-3640	559-497-8272	438-1260	K-6	Karen Eten
Valley Charter HS	108 Campus Way	Modesto, CA	95350-5803	209-558-4415	558-4453	9-12	Bob Vizzolini
Valley Oak Charter S	PO Box 878	Ojai, CA	93024-0878	805-640-4421	646-4700	K-10	Laura Fulmer
Valley Oaks Charter S	3501 Chester Ave	Bakersfield, CA	93301-1629	661-633-5288	633-5287	K-12	John Lindsay
Valley Preparatory Academy	4221 N Hughes Ave	Fresno, CA	93705-1611	559-225-7737	225-0976	K-12	Shelley Melton
Vantage Point Charter S	10862 Spenceville Rd	Penn Valley, CA	95946-9625	530-432-5312	432-8744	K-12	Thomas Bivens
Vaughn Next Century Learning Center	13330 Vaughn St	San Fernando, CA	91340-2216	818-896-7461	834-9036	PK-12	Yvonne Chan
Ventura S of Arts & Global Education	PO Box 392	Ventura, CA	93002-0392	805-648-5503	648-5539	K-8	Mary Galvin
Venture Academy	PO Box 213030	Stockton, CA	95213-9030	209-468-5940	468-9000	K-12	Kathleen Focacci
View Park Accelerated MS	5749 Crenshaw Blvd	Los Angeles, CA	90043-2409	323-290-6970	290-9271	6-8	Dwight Sanders
View Park Prep Accelerated Charter S	3751 W 54th St	Los Angeles, CA	90043-2356	323-290-6950	245-2660	K-5	Robin Harris
View Park Prep Accelerated HS	5701 Crenshaw Blvd	Los Angeles, CA	90043-2409	323-290-6975	290-9487	9-12	Darnice Williams
Village Charter S	4614 Old Redwood Hwy	Santa Rosa, CA	95403-1412	707-591-9262	591-9275	K-8	Rebecca Ivanoff
Village S	825 W Parr Ave	Campbell, CA	95008-6803	408-341-7042	341-7040	K-5	Katie Middlebrook
Visalia Charter Independent Study	909 W Murray Ave	Visalia, CA	93291-4825	559-735-8055	622-3170	9-12	Heather Rocha
Visions in Education Charter S	4800 Manzanita Ave	Carmichael, CA	95608-0825	916-971-7037	971-5590	K-12	Jody Graf
Vista Real Charter HS	401 S A St Ste 3	Oxnard, CA	93030-5278	805-486-5449	486-5455	9-12	Corrine Manley
Voices College-Bound Language Academy	4075 Sacramento Ave	San Jose, CA	95111-1584	408-361-1960		K-8	Frances Teso
Washington Charter S	45768 Portola Ave	Palm Desert, CA	92260-4861	760-862-4350	862-4356	K-5	Allan Lehmann
Washington K	1501 Ellis St	Kingsburg, CA	93631-1826	559-897-2955	897-6863	K-K	Shirley Esau
Watsonville Charter S of the Arts	115 Casserly Rd	Watsonville, CA	95076-8645	831-728-8123	728-6286	K-8	Trish Hucklebridge
Watts Learning Center	310 W 95th St	Los Angeles, CA	90003-4012	323-754-9900	754-0935	K-5	Katherine Nelson
W.E.B. DuBois Charter S	2604 Martin Luther King Blv	Fresno, CA	93706	559-486-1166	486-1199	K-12	Linda Washington
West Charter S	5350 Faught Rd	Santa Rosa, CA	95403-1205	707-524-2741	524-2782	K-8	
West County Community HS	1615 Carlson Blvd	Richmond, CA	94804-5030	510-898-1495	527-1013	9-12	Kristin Kirkman
Westlake Charter S	3800 Del Paso Rd	Sacramento, CA	95834-2599	916-567-5760	567-5769	K-4	Steve Liles
West Park Charter Academy	2695 S Valentine Ave	Fresno, CA	93706-9042	559-485-0727	485-0682	K-12	Liz Hammond
West Sacramento Early College Prep S	919 Westacre Rd	West Sacramento, CA	95691-3223	916-375-7680		6-7	Yolanda Falkenberg
Westside Preparatory Charter S	6537 W 2nd St	Rio Linda, CA	95673-3231	916-566-1980	991-5842	7-8	Janelle Scheftner
Westwood Charter ES	2050 Selby Ave	Los Angeles, CA	90025-6397	310-474-7788	475-1295	K-5	Judy Utvich
Westwood Charter S	PO Box 56	Westwood, CA	96137-0056	877-256-2994	256-2964	K-12	Henry Bietz
Wheatland Charter Academy	123 Beale Hwy Ste 34	Beale Afb, CA	95903	530-788-2097	788-2631	K-12	Jodie Jacklett
White Oaks ES	1901 White Oak Way	San Carlos, CA	94070-4799	650-508-7317	508-7320	K-4	Elizabeth Veal
Whitmore Charter HS	PO Box 307	Ceres, CA	95307-0307	209-556-1073	538-7931	9-12	Paula Smith
Whitmore Charter S	PO Box 307	Ceres, CA	95307-0307	209-556-1073	541-0947	K-8	Paula Smith
Wilder's Preparatory Academy Charter S	830 N La Brea Ave	Inglewood, CA	90302-2206	310-671-5578	671-2424	K-8	Raymond Wilder
Willits Charter S	7 S Marin St	Willits, CA	95490-3114	707-459-5506	459-5576	6-12	Sally Rulison
Willow Creek Academy	630 Nevada St	Sausalito, CA	94965-1654	415-331-7530	331-5524	K-8	Carol Cooper
Wilson College Prep S	400 105th Ave	Oakland, CA	94603-2968	510-635-7737	635-7727	6-12	Thomas Kadelbach
Woodland Star Charter S	17811 Arnold Dr	Sonoma, CA	95476-4019	707-996-3849	996-4369	K-8	Sheila Reilly
Woodson Charter S	3333 N Bond Ave	Fresno, CA	93726-5712	559-229-3529	229-0459	7-12	Antoine Holley
World Academy	1700 28th Ave	Oakland, CA	94601-2455	510-904-6400	904-6763	K-3	Susan Sperber
Youth Build Charter S	22425 Ventura Blvd Ste 399	Woodland Hills, CA	91364	818-939-7545	888-5760	9-12	Phil Matero
Youth Opportunities HS - Watts	1827 E 103rd St	Los Angeles, CA	90002-2928	323-249-7845	249-1170	9-12	
Yuba City Charter S	613A Bogue Rd	Yuba City, CA	95991-9223	530-822-9667	822-9629	K-12	Paul Tice
Yuba County Career Prep Charter S	1104 E St	Marysville, CA	95901-4825	530-741-6025	741-6032	K-12	Carol Holtz
Yuba Environmental Science Charter Acad	PO Box 420	Dobbins, CA	95935-0420	530-692-2210	692-9549	K-8	Bruce Helft
Yuba River Charter S	13026 Bitney Springs Rd # 3	Nevada City, CA	95959	530-272-8078	272-1952	K-8	Caleb Buckley

Colorado

School	Address	City,State	Zip code	Telephone	Fax	Grade	Contact
Academy at High Point	PO Box 440245	Aurora, CO	80044-0245	303-217-5152	217-5153	PK-8	Dr. Terry Lewis
Academy Charter S	1551 Prairie Hawk Dr	Castle Rock, CO	80109-7900	303-660-4881	660-6385	K-8	Yvette Brown
Academy of Charter S	11800 Lowell Blvd	Westminster, CO	80031-5097	303-289-8088	289-8087	K-12	John Kaufman
Academy of Urban Learning Charter S	835 E 18th Ave	Denver, CO	80218-1024	303-282-0900	282-0902	9-12	David Brown
Alta Vista Charter ES	PO Box 449	Lamar, CO	81052-0449	719-336-2154	336-0170	K-6	Talara Coen
American Academy	8600 Park Meadows Dr	Lonetree, CO	80124	303-873-7395	873-7398	K-8	Roberta Harrell
Aspen Community Charter S	PO Box 336	Woody Creek, CO	81656-0336	970-923-4080	923-7380	K-8	Jim Gilchrist
Aurora Academy Charter S	10251 E 1st Ave	Aurora, CO	80010-4308	303-367-5983	367-5820	K-8	Stephen Garretson
Axl Academy	PO Box 460296	Aurora, CO	80046-0296	303-377-0758	579-1858	K-5	Audria Philippon
Banning Lewis Ranch Academy	7094 Cottonwood Tree Dr	Colorado Spgs, CO	80927-5000	719-570-0075		K-8	Eric Dinnell
Battle Rock Charter S	11247 Road G	Cortez, CO	81321-9546	970-565-3237	564-1140	K-6	Matt Linsey-Paek
Belle Creek Charter S	9290 E 107th Ave	Henderson, CO	80640-8964	303-468-0160	468-0164	K-8	Irene German
Blair Edison Charter S	4905 Cathay St	Denver, CO	80249-8376	303-371-9570	371-8348	K-8	Deborah Blair-Minter
Boulder Prep Charter HS	5075 Chaparral Ct	Boulder, CO	80301-3591	303-545-6186	545-6187	9-12	Andre Adeli
Brighton Collegiate HS	3551 E Southern St	Brighton, CO	80601-0015	303-655-0773	655-9155	9-12	Kirk Salmela
Bromley East Charter S	356 Longspur Dr	Brighton, CO	80601-8700	720-685-3297	685-9513	K-8	Bob Bair
Caprock Academy	PO Box 4237	Grand Junction, CO	81502-4237	970-243-1771	243-3612	K-9	Kristin Trezise
Carbondale Community Charter S	PO Box 365	Carbondale, CO	81623-0365	970-963-9647	704-0501	K-8	Tom Penzel
Carbon Valley Charter S	4040 Coriolis Way	Frederick, CO	80504-5449	303-774-9555	774-9592	PK-12	Tony Carey
Cardinal Community Academy	3101 County Road 65	Keenesburg, CO	80643-8604	303-732-9312	732-9314	K-8	Harry Ewing
Challenges Choices & Images Charter S	11200 E 45th Ave	Denver, CO	80239-3018	720-746-2120	746-2123	K-12	Oscar Joseph
Challenge to Excellence Charter S	16995 Carlson Dr	Parker, CO	80134-8000	303-841-9816	840-3246	K-8	Linda Parker
Chavez Academy - Central	1131 N Union Blvd	Colorado Spgs, CO	80909-3862	719-227-7152	227-7153	K-7	Carolyn Gery
Chavez Academy	2500 W 18th St	Pueblo, CO	81003-1152	719-295-1623	295-1625	K-8	Dr. Lawrence Hernandez
Chavez Academy - North	3115 Larkspur Dr	Colorado Spgs, CO	80907-5719	719-227-7152		K-8	Carolyn Gery

School	Address	City,State	Zip code	Telephone	Fax	Grade	Contact
Cherry Creek Charter Academy	6260 S Dayton St	Englewood, CO	80111-5203	303-779-8988	779-8817	K-8	Patricia Leger
Cheyenne Mountain Charter Academy	1832 S Wahsatch Ave	Colorado Spgs, CO	80905-2341	719-471-1999	471-4949	K-12	Colin Mullaney
CIVA Charter S	4635 Northpark Dr	Colorado Spgs, CO	80918-3813	719-633-1306	633-1692	9-12	Randy Zimmerman
Classical Academy Central	1655 Springcrest Rd	Colorado Spgs, CO	80920-1545	719-265-9766	265-1751	K-6	Don Stump
Classical Academy East	8650 Scarborough Dr	Colorado Spgs, CO	80920-7566	719-234-2941	499-4057	K-6	Diana Burditt
Classical Academy HS	975 Stout Rd	Colorado Spgs, CO	80921-3801	719-484-0091	484-0085	9-12	Peter Hilts
Classical Academy MS	975 Stout Rd	Colorado Spgs, CO	80921-3801	719-484-0091	487-2339	7-8	Russ Sojourner
Classical Academy North	975 Stout Rd	Colorado Spgs, CO	80921-3801	719-484-0081	484-0078	K-6	Veronica Wolken
Collegiate Academy of Colorado	8420 Sangre De Cristo Rd	Littleton, CO	80127-4201	303-972-7433	932-0695	K-12	Michael Prosser
Colorado Charter HS	1175 Osage St Ste 100	Denver, CO	80204-3445	303-892-8475	825-3011	10-12	Cyndi Bush-Luna
Colorado Distance & Electronic Learning	4700 E Bromley Ln Ste 205	Brighton, CO	80601-7821	303-637-9234	637-9273	K-12	Tim Spencer
Colorado Springs Charter Academy	2577 N Chelton Rd	Colorado Spgs, CO	80909-1302	719-636-2722	636-2726	K-8	Martha Kasper
Colorado Springs Early College	4435 N Chestnut St	Colorado Spgs, CO	80907-3812	719-955-4675	528-7006	9-12	Keith King
Colorado Virtual Academy	11990 Grant St Ste 402	Northglenn, CO	80233-1136	303-255-4650	255-7044	K-12	Dr. Cassandra Baker-Carr
Community Challenge Charter S	948 Santa Fe Dr	Denver, CO	80204-3937	303-436-9588	436-0919	8-10	Eloy Chavez
Community Leadership Academy	6880 Holly St	Commerce City, CO	80022-2536	303-288-2711	288-2714	K-8	
Community Prep Charter S	332 E Willamette Ave	Colorado Spgs, CO	80903-1116	719-227-8836	636-3407	9-12	Vicki Leaf
Compass Montessori Charter S	10399 W 44th Ave	Wheat Ridge, CO	80033-2701	303-420-8288	420-0139	PK-6	Katy Myers
Compass Montessori Charter S	4441 Salvia St	Golden, CO	80403-1698	303-271-1977	271-1984	PK-12	Katy Myers
Connect Charter S	104 W 7th St	Pueblo, CO	81003-3016	719-542-0224	583-9799	6-8	Judy Mikulas
Core Knowledge Charter S	11661 N Pine Dr	Parker, CO	80138-8022	303-840-7070	840-9785	K-8	Teri Aplin
Corridor Community Academy	420 7th St	Bennett, CO	80102-8124	303-644-5180	644-4918	K-8	Sondra Doolin
Crestone Charter S	PO Box 400	Crestone, CO	81131-0400	719-256-4907	256-4908	K-12	Kathryn Brady
Crown Pointe Academy	7281 Irving St	Westminster, CO	80030-4907	303-428-1882	428-1938	K-8	Barbara Ridenour
DCS Montessori Charter S	311 Castle Pines Pkwy	Castle Rock, CO	80108-8101	303-387-5625	387-5626	PK-6	Paul Dougherty
Denver Arts & Technology Academy	3752 Tennyson St	Denver, CO	80212-1914	720-855-7504	855-7529	K-8	Ray Griffin
Denver S of Science and Technology	2000 Valentia St	Denver, CO	80238-2785	303-320-5570	377-5101	9-12	Bill Kurtz
Denver Venture Charter S	2409 Arapahoe St	Denver, CO	80205-2614	303-292-0430		9-12	Ami Desai
Eagle County Charter Academy	PO Box 169	Wolcott, CO	81655-0169	970-926-0656	926-0786	K-8	Jay Cerny
Early College HS at Arvada	4905 W 60th Ave	Arvada, CO	80003-6916	303-479-3475	308-4701	9-12	Sarah Brock
Excel Academy	11500 W 84th Ave	Arvada, CO	80005-5272	303-467-2295	467-2291	K-8	Dr. Holly Hensey
Flagstaff Academy	2040 Miller Dr	Longmont, CO	80501-6748	303-651-7900	651-7922	K-8	Andrew Moore
Free Horizon Montessori S	581 Conference Pl	Golden, CO	80401-5615	303-231-9801	231-9983	PK-6	Jami Boarman
Frontier Academy Charter S	2560 W 29th St	Greeley, CO	80631-8507	970-330-1780	330-4334	K-6	Rebecca Dougherty
Frontier Academy Charter S	6530 W 16th St	Greeley, CO	80634-8675	970-339-9153	339-5631	7-12	Mary Meersman
Frontier Charter Academy	PO Box 418	Calhan, CO	80808-0418	719-347-3156	347-3054	K-8	
Georgetown Community S	PO Box 74	Georgetown, CO	80444-0074	303-569-3277	569-2761	PK-6	Richard Winter
Global Village Academy	403 S Airport Blvd Unit A	Aurora, CO	80017-3900	303-309-6657	317-6538	K-8	Christina Burton
GLOBE Charter S	1749 N Academy Blvd	Colorado Spgs, CO	80909-2721	719-630-0577	630-0395	K-9	Douglas Miller
GOAL Academy	277 W 18th St	Pueblo, CO	81003	719-671-0483		9-12	Ken Crowell
Guffey Community Charter S	PO Box 147	Guffey, CO	80820-0147	719-689-2093	689-3407	K-8	Pam Moore
Highline Academy	7808 Cherry Creek South Dr	Denver, CO	80231	720-449-0317	449-0328	K-8	Alyssa Whitehead-Bust
Hope Co-Op Online Learning Academy	2001 E Easter Ave Ste 202	Centennial, CO	80122-1661	303-989-3539		K-12	Heather O'Mara
Horizons K-8 School	4545 Sioux Dr	Boulder, CO	80303-3732	303-447-5580	499-9680	K-8	Sonny Zinn
Huerta Preparatory HS	2500 W 18th St	Pueblo, CO	81003-1152	719-583-1030	583-1031	9-12	Richard Mestas
Imagine Charter S at Firestone	5753 Twilight Ave	Firestone, CO	80504-6481	303-772-3711	772-3977	K-8	Ralph Garbart
Imagine Classical Academy	6050 Stetson Hills Blvd	Colorado Spgs, CO	80923-3562	719-306-2966		K-8	Tina Leone
Independence Academy	600 N 14th St	Grand Junction, CO	81501-4416	970-255-8565	255-8504	K-12	Damon Lockhart
Indian Peaks Charter S	PO Box 1819	Granby, CO	80446-1819	970-887-3805	887-3829	K-8	Stephanie Beckler
Irwin Charter ES	5525 Astrozon Blvd	Colorado Spgs, CO	80916-4226	719-884-0987	884-0992	K-5	Elizabeth Berg
Irwin Charter HS	5525 Astrozon Blvd	Colorado Spgs, CO	80916-4226	719-591-2122	576-8071	9-12	Alex Marquez
Irwin Charter MS	5525 Astrozon Blvd	Colorado Spgs, CO	80916-4226	719-591-2122	576-8071	6-8	Holly Varnum
Jefferson Academy	9955 Yarrow St	Broomfield, CO	80021-4048	303-887-1992	887-2435	7-12	Tammy Stringari
Jefferson Academy	9955 Yarrow St	Broomfield, CO	80021-4048	303-438-1011	438-1046	K-6	Mike Munier
Justice HS	1777 6th St	Boulder, CO	80302-5814	303-441-4862	441-1695	9-12	Tijani Cole Ph.D.
KIPP Sunshine Peak Academy	375 S Tejon St	Denver, CO	80223-1961	303-623-5772	623-0410	5-8	Kurt Pusch
Knowledge Quest Academy	705 School House Dr	Milliken, CO	80543-3154	970-587-5742	587-5750	K-8	Conchetta Robinson
Lake George Charter S	PO Box 420	Lake George, CO	80827-0420	719-748-3911	748-8151	PK-6	Pat Walker
Landmark Academy at Reunion	10566 Memphis St	Commerce City, CO	80022-6236	303-287-2901	287-4196	K-6	Catherine Witt
Legacy Academy	1975 Legacy Cir	Elizabeth, CO	80107	303-646-2636	646-2635	K-12	Charla Hannigan
Liberty Common S	1725 Sharp Point Dr	Fort Collins, CO	80525-4424	970-482-9800	482-8007	K-9	Russ Spicer
Life Skills Center of Colorado Springs	1810 Eastlake Blvd	Colorado Spgs, CO	80910-3422	719-471-0684	471-4392	9-12	Charles Holt
Life Skills Center of Denver	1000 Cherokee St	Denver, CO	80204-4039	720-889-2898	889-2897	9-12	Santiago Lopez
Lincoln Academy	6980 Pierce St	Arvada, CO	80003-3646	303-467-5363	467-5367	PK-8	Mary Ann Mahoney
Littleton Charter Academy	1200 W Mineral Ave	Littleton, CO	80120-4536	303-798-5252	798-0298	K-8	Jan Johnson-Pote
Littleton Prep Charter S	5151 S Federal Blvd	Littleton, CO	80123-2975	303-734-1995	734-3620	K-8	Kim Ash
Lotus S for Excellence	11001 E Alameda Ave Ste A	Aurora, CO	80012	303-360-0052	360-0071	6-12	Dr. Adnan Doyuran
Madison Charter Academy	660 Syracuse St	Colorado Spgs, CO	80911-2546	719-391-3977	391-1744	K-8	Dr. Anne Shineman
Magon Academy	7255 Irving St	Westminster, CO	80030-4907	303-412-7610	412-7658	K-3	Marcos Martinez
Marble Charter S	412 W Main St	Marble, CO	81623-9396	970-963-9550	963-8435	K-10	Wendy Boland
Montessori Peaks Academy	9904 W Capri Ave	Littleton, CO	80123-3535	303-972-2627	933-4182	PK-6	Char Weaver
Monument Academy	1150 Village Ridge Pt	Monument, CO	80132-8992	719-481-1950	481-1948	PK-8	Jane Lundeen
Mountain Phoenix Community S	11398 Ranch Elsie Rd	Golden, CO	80403-7309	303-642-7634		K-8	Asia Golden
Mountain View Core Knowledge S	890 Field Ave	Canon City, CO	81212-9250	719-275-1980	275-1998	K-8	Karen Sartori
New America S - Aurora	9125 E 7th Pl	Denver, CO	80230-7111	303-320-9854	363-8083	9-12	Annie Trujillo
New America S - Eagle Valley	500 Red Table Dr	Gypsum, CO	81637	888-304-9943		9-12	Kathleen Brendza
New America S - Jeffco	1005 Wadsworth Blvd	Lakewood, CO	80214-4201	303-894-3171		9-12	Jon Berninzoni
New America S - Northglenn	11700 Irma Dr	Northglenn, CO	80233-2196	303-991-0130	991-0135	9-12	Rhett Parham
New Vision Charter S	2366 E 1st St	Loveland, CO	80537-5906	970-593-6827	461-1947	K-8	Chris Cockrill
Northeast Academy	4895 Peoria St	Denver, CO	80239-2847	303-307-8837	307-8867	K-8	Thomas Bouknight
Northern CO Academy of Arts & Knowledge	4512 McMurry Ave	Fort Collins, CO	80525-3400	970-226-2800	226-2806	K-8	Laura Szech
North Routt Charter S	PO Box 1002	Steamboat Spr, CO	80428-1002	970-871-6062	871-6067	K-8	Colleen Poole
North Star Academy	16700 Keystone Blvd	Parker, CO	80134-3544	720-851-7827	851-0976	K-6	Cynthia Haws
Odyssey Charter S	8750 E 28th Ave	Denver, CO	80238-2609	303-316-3944	316-4016	K-8	Marcia Fulton
Paradox Valley Charter S	PO Box 420	Paradox, CO	81429-0420	970-859-7236	859-7235	PK-8	Jon Orris
Passage Charter S	703 S 9th St	Montrose, CO	81401-4409	970-249-8066	249-3497	9-12	Corinne Vogenthaler
Peak to Peak Charter S	800 Merlin Dr	Lafayette, CO	80026-2146	303-453-4600	453-4613	K-12	Tony Fontana
Pikes Peak S of Expeditionary Learning	11925 Antlers Ridge Dr	Falcon, CO	80831-8658	719-683-9544	683-3475	K-8	Don Knapp
Pinnacle Charter S	1001 W 84th Ave	Federal Heights, CO	80260-4717	303-450-3985	255-6305	K-12	Dr. William Wiener
Pioneer Charter S	3230 E 38th Ave	Denver, CO	80205-3726	303-329-8412	424-4785	PK-6	Dorothy Ward
Platte River Academy	4085 Lark Sparrow St	Highlands Ranch, CO	80126-5209	303-221-1070	221-1069	K-8	Dr. Gary Stueven
Prairie Creeks Charter S	PO Box 889	Strasburg, CO	80136-0889	303-622-6328	622-6327	9-12	Jeffrey Rasp
PS 1 Charter S	1062 Delaware St	Denver, CO	80204-4033	303-575-6690	575-6661	6-12	Laura Laffoon
Pueblo S for the Arts & Sciences	1745 Acero Ave	Pueblo, CO	81004-2645	719-549-2737	549-2659	K-8	Cheryl Gomez
Ridge View Academy	28101 E Quincy Ave	Watkins, CO	80137-9502	303-766-3000	766-3111	9-12	John Fry
Ridgeview Classical S	1800 S Lemay Ave	Fort Collins, CO	80525-1240	970-494-4620	494-4625	K-12	Florian Hild
Rocky Mountain Academy of Evergreen	PO Box 3162	Evergreen, CO	80437-3162	303-670-1070	670-1253	K-8	Ryan Lucas
Rocky Mountain Classical Academy	1710 Piros Dr	Colorado Spgs, CO	80915-4307	719-622-8000	622-8004	K-9	Linda Stahnke
Rocky Mountain Deaf S	1921 Youngfield St	Golden, CO	80401-6302	303-984-5749	984-7290	PK-8	Dr. Janet Dickinson
Roosevelt-Edison Charter S	205 Byron Dr	Colorado Spgs, CO	80910-2599	719-637-0311	380-0176	K-5	Dr. Precious Broadnax
Ross Montessori Charter S	407 Merrill Ave	Carbondale, CO	81623-1643	970-963-7199	963-7342	K-8	Mark Grice
St. Vrain Montessori Charter S	1055 Delaware Ave	Longmont, CO	80501-6143			K-2	Katie Torres
Skyland Community HS	3532 Franklin St	Denver, CO	80205-3961	303-388-4759	388-2470	9-12	Lisa Martin
Southern Colorado Academy	278 S McCulloch Blvd	Pueblo West, CO	81007-2844	719-547-1627		9-12	Chris Beltran
Southwest Early College Charter S	3001 S Federal Blvd	Denver, CO	80236-2711	303-935-5473	935-5591	9-12	Scott Rubin
Southwest Open Charter S	PO Box DD	Cortez, CO	81321-0870	970-565-1150	565-8770	9-12	Judy Hite
STAR Academy	2520 Airport Rd	Colorado Spgs, CO	80910-3120	719-638-5554	638-2246	K-6	Barbara Hyne
Stargate Charter S	3951 Cottonwood Lakes Blvd	Thornton, CO	80241-2187	303-450-3936	450-3941	K-8	Patricia Crone
Stone Creek Charter S	PO Box 5670	Avon, CO	81620-5670	970-748-4535	748-4175	K-8	Katherine Lange
Summit MS	4655 Hanover Ave	Boulder, CO	80305-6036	303-499-9511	499-0215	6-8	David Finell
Swallows Charter Academy	278 S McCulloch Blvd	Pueblo West, CO	81007-2844	719-547-1627	547-2509	K-8	Dana Lambert
21st Century Charter S	525 E Costilla St	Colorado Spgs, CO	80903-3764	719-570-7575	475-0831	K-12	Dr. Patricia Arnold
Twin Peaks Charter Academy	340 S Sunset St	Longmont, CO	80501	720-652-8201	774-9855	K-8	B.J. Buchmann
Union Colony Prep S	2000 Clubhouse Dr	Greeley, CO	80634-3643	970-673-4546	330-7604	6-12	Pat Gilliam
University Schools	6525 W 18th St	Greeley, CO	80634-8674	970-330-2221	506-7070	K-12	Sherry Gerner
Vanguard Classical S	801 Yosemite St	Denver, CO	80230-6087	303-691-2384		K-7	Todd Slechta
Vanguard S	1605 S Corona Ave	Colorado Spgs, CO	80905-2571	719-471-1999	799-6149	7-12	Colin Mullaney
Vista Charter S	PO Box 10000	Montrose, CO	81402-9701	970-249-4470	252-3354	9-12	Coni Wilson
West Denver Preparatory Charter S	1825 S Federal Blvd	Denver, CO	80219-4905	303-573-2017	935-5004	6-8	Chris Gibbons
Wilson Academy	8300 W 94th Ave	Westminster, CO	80021-4590	303-431-3694	423-4388	K-8	Tim Matlick
Windsor Charter Academy	680 Academy Ct	Windsor, CO	80550-3101	970-674-5020	674-5017	K-8	Tracy Stanford
Wyatt-Edison Charter S	3620 Franklin St	Denver, CO	80205-3325	303-292-5515	292-5111	K-8	Helen Hargis
Youth & Family Academy Charter S	1920 Valley Dr	Pueblo, CO	81008-1764	719-546-1740	542-1335	7-12	Michael Baca

Connecticut

School	Address	City,State	Zip code	Telephone	Fax	Grade	Contact
Achievement First Bridgeport Academy	391 E Washington Ave	Bridgeport, CT	06608-2127	203-333-9128	333-9142	K-8	Debon Lewis

School	Address	City,State	Zip code	Telephone	Fax	Grade	Contact
Achievement First Hartford Academy	395 Lyme St	Hartford, CT	06112-1028	860-695-5280	242-6457	K-1	Claire Shin
Achievement First Hartford MS	395 Lyme St	Hartford, CT	06112-1028	860-695-5281	242-6457	5-5	Jeff House
Amistad Academy	407 James St	New Haven, CT	06513-3016	203-773-0390	773-0364	5-8	Matt Taylor
Amistad Academy HS	49 Prince St	New Haven, CT	06519-1603	203-772-1092	772-1784	9-12	Jeff Sudmeyer
Amistad ES	540 Ella T Grasso Blvd	New Haven, CT	06519	203-772-2166	772-2520	K-4	Tisha Markette
Bridge Academy	PO Box 2267	Bridgeport, CT	06608-0267	203-336-9999	336-9852	7-12	
Charter S for Young Children on Asylum	1265 Asylum Ave	Hartford, CT	06105-2206	860-244-3111		PK-3	Andrea Einhorn
Common Ground HS	358 Springside Ave	New Haven, CT	06515-1024	203-389-0823	389-7458	9-12	Oliver Barton
Elm City College Preparatory MS	794 Dixwell Ave	New Haven, CT	06511-1035	203-772-5332	772-3641	5-8	Marc Michaelson
Elm City College Preparatory S	240 Greene St	New Haven, CT	06511-6934	203-498-0702	498-0712	K-4	Morgan Barth
Explorations Charter S	71 Spencer St	Winsted, CT	06098	860-738-9070	738-9092	10-12	Gail Srebnik
Highville Mustard Seed Charter S	130 Leeder Hill Dr	Hamden, CT	06517-2730	203-287-0528	287-0693	PK-8	
Integrated Day Charter S	68 Thermos Ave	Norwich, CT	06360-6957	860-892-1900	892-1902	PK-8	
Interdistrict S for Arts & Communication	190 Governor Winthrop Blvd	New London, CT	06320	860-447-1003	447-0470	6-8	Ruth Cole-Chu
Jumoke Academy	250 Blue Hills Ave	Hartford, CT	06112-1836	860-527-0575	525-7758	6-8	
New Beginnings Family Academy	184 Garden St	Bridgeport, CT	06605-1213	203-384-2897	384-2898	K-8	Paul Whyte
Odyssey Community S	579 Middle Tpke W	Manchester, CT	06040-2728	860-645-1234	533-0324	4-8	Elaine Stancliffe
Park City Prep Charter S	510 Barnum Ave	Bridgeport, CT	06608-2400	203-953-3766	953-3771	6-8	Bruce Ravage
Side by Side Community S	10 Chestnut St	Norwalk, CT	06854-2928	203-857-0306	838-2666	PK-8	Matthew Nittoly
Stamford Academy	229 North St	Stamford, CT	06901-1112	203-324-6300	324-6310	9-12	Michael McGuire
Trailblazers Academy	PO Box 359	Stamford, CT	06904-0359	203-977-5690	977-5688	6-8	Craig Baker

Delaware

School	Address	City,State	Zip code	Telephone	Fax	Grade	Contact
Academy of Dover Charter S	104 Saulsbury Rd	Dover, DE	19904-2705	302-674-0684	674-3894	K-4	Noel Rodriguez
Campus Community HS	350 Pear St	Dover, DE	19904-3016	302-736-0403	736-5330	9-12	Heidi Greene
Campus Community S	21 N Bradford St	Dover, DE	19904-3101	302-736-3300	736-5330	K-8	Trish Hermance
Charter S of Wilmington	100 N DuPont Rd	Wilmington, DE	19807-3199	302-651-2727	652-1246	9-12	Kurt Hollstein
Delaware College Preparatory Academy	510 W 28th St	Wilmington, DE	19802-3022	302-762-7424	792-7172	K-4	Anita Roberson
Delaware Military Academy	112 Middleboro Rd	Wilmington, DE	19804-1621	302-998-0745	998-3521	9-12	Charles Baldwin
East Side Charter S	3000 N Claymont St	Wilmington, DE	19802-2807	302-762-5834	762-3864	K-8	Dominique Taylor
Edison Charter S	2200 N Locust St	Wilmington, DE	19802-4429	302-778-1101	778-2232	K-8	Alina Columbus
Family Foundations Academy	1101 Delaware St	New Castle, DE	19720-6033	302-324-8901	324-8908	1-5	Dr. Tennell Brewington
Kuumba Academy Charter S	519 N Market St	Wilmington, DE	19801-3004	302-472-6450	472-6452	K-5	Dr. Sondra Shippen
MOT Charter S	1156 Levels Rd	Middletown, DE	19709-7700	302-376-5125	376-5120	K-8	Linda Jennings
Moyer Academy	97 Vandever Ave	Wilmington, DE	19802-4219	302-428-9500	428-9506	6-12	Theopalis Gregory
Newark Charter S	2001 Patriot Way	Newark, DE	19711-1809	302-369-2001	368-3460	K-8	Greg Meece
Odyssey Charter S	3821 Lancaster Pike	Wilmington, DE	19805-1512	302-994-6490	994-6915	K-5	Anthony Skoutelas
Pencader Business & Finance Charter HS	170 Lukens Dr	New Castle, DE	19720-2727	302-472-0794	472-0796	9-12	Brad Catts
Positive Outcomes Charter S	3337 S Dupont Hwy	Camden, DE	19934-1378	302-697-8805	697-8813	7-12	Edward Emmett
Prestige Academy	3707 N Market St Fl 2	Wilmington, DE	19802	302-762-3240	762-4782	5-8	
Providence Creek Academy Charter S	PO Box 265	Clayton, DE	19938-0265	302-653-6276	653-7850	K-8	Charles Taylor
Sussex Academy of Arts and Sciences	21777 Sussex Pines Rd	Georgetown, DE	19947-3901	302-856-3636	856-3376	6-8	Patricia Oliphant Ed.D.

District Of Columbia

School	Address	City,State	Zip code	Telephone	Fax	Grade	Contact
Academia Bilingue de la Comunidad S	209 Upshur St NW	Washington, DC	20011-4847	202-822-6301	822-6303	6-8	Peter Martin
Academy for Learning through the Arts	1600 Taylor St NE	Washington, DC	20017-3035	202-526-7280	526-7285	PK-6	Carla Toliver M.Ed.
Achievement Preparatory Academy	908 Wahler Pl SE	Washington, DC	20032	202-441-7000	457-1980	4-8	Shantelle Wright
Angelou Charter HS-Evans Campus	5600 E Capitol St NE	Washington, DC	20019-6739	202-379-4335	727-5548	6-12	Dr. Marian White-Hood
Angelou Charter HS-Shaw Campus	1851 9th St NW	Washington, DC	20001-4133	202-939-9080	939-9084	9-12	Eugene Pinkard
Angelou Charter MS	5600 E Capitol St NE	Washington, DC	20019-6739	202-232-2885	315-3995	6-8	Rashida Waters
Apple Tree Early Learning S - Amidon	401 I St SW	Washington, DC	20024-4438	202-646-0094	646-0095	PK-PK	Anna Busbee
Apple Tree Early Learning S - Girard	2501 14th St NW	Washington, DC	20009	202-667-9490	667-9493	PK-PK	Anne Zummo
Apple Tree Early Learning S - Riverside	680 I St SW	Washington, DC	20024-2432	202-646-0500	646-0510	PK-K	Anna Busbee
Arts & Technology Academy	5300 Blaine St NE	Washington, DC	20019-6665	202-398-6811	388-8467	PK-6	Errick Greene
Bethune Charter S	5413 16th St NW	Washington, DC	20011-3618	202-723-5800	536-2670	PK-8	Dr. Linda McKay
Bethune Day Academy	1404 Jackson St NE	Washington, DC	20017-2951	202-459-4710	536-2670	PK-8	Dr. Linda McKay
Bowman Prep Academy	330 21st St NE	Washington, DC	20002-6713	202-543-8432	543-8438	5-6	Mark Cosenza
Bridges Public Charter S	1250 Taylor St NW	Washington, DC	20011-5624	202-545-0515	545-0517	PK-PK	Olivia Smith
Capital City Public Charter S-Lower	3047 15th St NW	Washington, DC	20009-4211	202-387-0309	387-7074	PK-8	Janine Gomez
Capital City Public Charter S-Upper	3029 14th St NW	Washington, DC	20009-6820	202-387-1102	387-1104	6-9	Kathryn Byrd
Center City Pub Charter S - Capitol Hill	1503 E Capitol St SE	Washington, DC	20003-1508	202-547-7556		PK-8	Christian White
Center City Public Charter - Petworth	510 Webster St NW	Washington, DC	20011-4758	202-726-9212		PK-8	Sr. Maria Faina
Center City Public Charter S - Brentwood	2019 Rhode Island Ave NE	Washington, DC	20018-2834	202-529-5394		PK-5	Robin Toogood
Center City Public Charter - Shaw	711 N St NW	Washington, DC	20001-3505	202-234-1093		PK-8	Jason Lody
Center City Public Charter - Trinidad	1217 W Virginia Ave NE	Washington, DC	20002-3817	202-397-1614		PK-8	Monica Evans
Center City Public Chrtr - Congress Hts	220 Highview Pl SE	Washington, DC	20032-1581	202-562-7070		PK-8	Wallace Henry
Center City Public Chrtr S - Brightwood	6008 Georgia Ave NW	Washington, DC	20011-5104	202-723-3322		PK-8	Nicole Peltier-Lewis
Chavez HS for Public Policy	709 12th St SE	Washington, DC	20003-2962	202-547-3424	387-7808	9-12	Garrett Phelan
Chavez Prep Academy	4115 16th St NW	Washington, DC	20011-7003	202-547-3975	723-3976	6-8	Andrew Touchette
Chavez Public Policy Charter MSHS	3701 Hayes St NE	Washington, DC	20019-1702	202-398-2230	398-1966	6-12	Dr. Marco Clark
Childrens Studio Public Charter S	1301 V St NW	Washington, DC	20009-4413	202-387-6148	986-0792	PK-6	Rashid Johnson
City Collegiate Public Charter S	2001 S St NW Fl 2	Washington, DC	20009	202-339-9494	339-9784	6-12	Dr. Mark Reford
City Lights Charter S	3333 14th St NW Ste 210	Washington, DC	20010-2319	202-832-4366	832-3654	9-12	Brenda Richards
Clark Public Charter S	425 Chesapeake St SE	Washington, DC	20032-3602	202-563-6556	583-1709	PK-8	Keniq Coney
Community Academy Chrtr - Butler Biling	5 Thomas Cir NW	Washington, DC	20005-4177	202-332-6565	332-1073	PK-5	Francis Yasharian
Community Academy Pub Charter - Amos I	1300 Allison St NW	Washington, DC	20011-4441	202-723-4100	723-6867	PK-5	Dr. Janette Johns-Gibson
Community Academy Pub Charter - Amos II	1351 Nicholson St NW	Washington, DC	20011-2813	202-723-5136	723-5139	PK-K	Tanya Clark
Community Academy Pub Charter - Amos III	1400 1st St NW	Washington, DC	20001	202-234-2122	234-2166	PK-5	Toosdhi Tucker
Community Academy Pub Charter S - Rand	33 Riggs Rd NE	Washington, DC	20011-2463	202-723-4010	723-4013	PK-8	Charles Harden
DC Bilingual Public Charter S	1420 Columbia Rd NW	Washington, DC	20009-4794	202-332-4200	745-2562	PK-5	Wanda Perez
DC Prep Charter ES - Edgewood	707 Edgewood St NE	Washington, DC	20017-3341	202-635-4411	635-4412	PK-3	Doreen Land
DC Prep Charter ES - Benning	100 41st St NE	Washington, DC	20019-3310	202-398-2838	635-4591	PK-8	Maurice Porter
DC Prep Charter MS - Edgewood	701 Edgewood St NE	Washington, DC	20017-3341	202-832-5700	832-5701	4-8	Katie Severn
Doar Charter S for Performing Arts	705 Edgewood St NE Fl 2	Washington, DC	20017	202-269-4646	269-4155	PK-12	Julie Doar-Sinkfield
Doar Public Charter S for Performing Art	3700 N Capitol St NW	Washington, DC	20011-8400	202-882-1930	882-1936	PK-5	Craig Barnes
Eagle Academy Public Charter S	770 M St SE	Washington, DC	20003-3621	202-544-2646	544-0187	PK-K	Cassandra Pinkney
Early Childhood Academy	4025 9th St SE	Washington, DC	20032-6051	202-373-5500	399-2666	PK-1	Wendy Edwards
Education Strengthens Families Charter S	2355 Ontario Rd NW	Washington, DC	20009	202-797-7337	797-8470	PK-Ad	Christy McKay
Excel Academy Public Charter S	3845 S Capitol St SW	Washington, DC	20032-1419	202-373-0097	373-0477	PK-8	Caroline John
Friendship Charter S - Blow-Pierce	725 19th St NE	Washington, DC	20002-4713	202-572-1070	399-6157	4-8	Ralph Neal
Friendship Charter S - Chamberlain	1345 Potomac Ave SE	Washington, DC	20003-4411	202-547-5800	547-4554	PK-7	Carolyne Albert-Garvey
Friendship Charter S - Southeast Academy	645 Milwaukee Pl SE	Washington, DC	20032-2606	202-562-1980	562-0726	K-6	Michelle Pierre-Farid
Friendship Collegiate Academy	4095 Minnesota Ave NE	Washington, DC	20019-3541	202-396-5500	399-6957	9-12	Peggy Pendergrass
Friendship Public Charter S - Woodridge	2959 Carlton Ave NE	Washington, DC	20018-2615	202-635-6500	635-6481	PK-8	Crystal Clark
Haynes Public Charter S	3029 14th St NW	Washington, DC	20009-6820	202-667-4446	667-8811	PK-12	Jennifer Niles
Hope Community Charter - Lamond	6200 Kansas Ave NE	Washington, DC	20011-1508	202-722-4421	722-4431	PK-6	Niyeka Wilson
Hope Community Charter - Tolson	2917 8th St NE	Washington, DC	20017-1669	202-832-7370	722-4421	PK-8	Erika Thomas
Hospitality Public Charter HS	4301 13th St NW Fl 3	Washington, DC	20011	202-737-4150	737-4151	9-12	Debra Knight
Howard Road Academy	701 Howard Rd SE	Washington, DC	20020-7101	202-610-4193	610-2845	K-7	Valorie Powell
Howard Road Academy	3000 Pennsylvania Ave SE	Washington, DC	20020-3718	202-582-3322	528-3340	PK-3	Nicole Richardson
Howard Road Academy	4625 G St SE	Washington, DC	20019-7834	202-583-2828	583-2270	3-6	Nicole Richardson
Howard University MS of Math & Science	405 Howard Pl NW	Washington, DC	20059-0001	202-806-7725	667-5964	6-8	Sue White
Hyde Leadership Public Charter S	101 T St NE	Washington, DC	20002-1519	202-529-4400	529-4500	K-12	Dr. JoAnn Cason
Ideal Academy Charter S	100 Peabody St NW Fl 2	Washington, DC	20011-2219	202-723-6798	723-6799	9-12	George Rutherford Ph.D.
Ideal Academy Public Charter S	6130 N Capitol St NW	Washington, DC	20011-1405	202-729-6660	729-6677	PK-8	George Rutherford Ph.D.
IDEA Public Charter HS	1027 45th St NE	Washington, DC	20019-3802	202-399-4750	399-4387	7-12	Charlotte Blount
Imagine Southeast Public Charter S	421 Alabama Ave SE	Washington, DC	20032	202-561-1622	561-1644	PK-8	Stacey Scott
Jordan Public Charter S	100 Peabody St NW	Washington, DC	20011-2212	202-545-0922	545-0923	5-8	Barbara Tobelmann Ph.D.
Kamit Institute Magnificent Achievers	100 Peabody St NW	Washington, DC	20011-2212	202-723-7886	723-0239	7-12	Saungktakhu Richey
KIPP DC/Aim Academy	2600 Douglas St NE	Washington, DC	20018	202-678-5477	678-4383	5-8	Khala Johnson
KIPP DC/KEY Academy	4801 Benning Rd SE	Washington, DC	20019-6145	202-582-5477	582-4678	5-8	Sarah Hayes
KIPP DC/Leap Academy	4801 Benning Rd SE	Washington, DC	20019-6145	202-582-5327	582-4680	PK-4	Laura Bowen
KIPP DC/Will Academy	421 P St NW	Washington, DC	20001-2417	202-328-9455	328-9457	5-8	Susan Schaeffler
Latin American Montessori Bilingual S	1375 Missouri Ave NW	Washington, DC	20011-1807	202-726-6200	722-4125	PK-6	Cristina Encinas
LAYC-Youth Build Pub Charter S	3014 14th St NW	Washington, DC	20009-6819	202-319-0141	518-0618	9-Adu	Andrea Henson
Marshall Academy	2427 M L K Jr Ave SE	Washington, DC	20020	202-563-6862	563-6946	9-12	Alexandra Pardo
MEI Futures Academy	6000 New Hampshire Ave NE	Washington, DC	20011-1536	202-349-4054	832-6353	9-12	Michelle Ireland-Banks
Meridian Public Charter S	1328 Florida Ave NW	Washington, DC	20009-4827	202-387-9830	387-7605	PK-8	Robinette Breedlove
Next Step Public Charter S	1419 Columbia Rd NW	Washington, DC	20009-4705	202-319-2249	332-0398	9-12	Susan Evans
Nia Community Public Charter S	3845 S Capitol St SW	Washington, DC	20032-1419	202-562-5440	562-0569	PK-8	Vernard Howard
Options Public Charter S	1375 E St NE	Washington, DC	20002-5429	202-547-1028	547-1272	5-9	Dr. Donna Montgomery
Paul Charter S	5800 8th St NW	Washington, DC	20011	202-291-7499	291-7495	6-8	Barbara Nophlin
Potomac Lighthouse Public Charter S	1600 Taylor St NE	Washington, DC	20017-3035	202-526-6003	526-6005	PK-5	Cheryl James
Roots Public Charter S	6222 N Capitol St NW	Washington, DC	20011-1408	202-882-5155	882-5157	PK-8	Dr. Bernida Thompson
Roots Public Charter S	115 Kennedy St NW	Washington, DC	20011-5260	202-882-8073	882-8075	K-8	Dr. Bernida Thompson

School	Address	City,State	Zip code	Telephone	Fax	Grade	Contact
Rosario International Public Charter S	1100 Harvard St NW	Washington, DC	20009-5356	202-797-4700	232-6442	10-12	Sonia Gutierrez
St. Coletta of Greater Washington	1901 Independence Ave SE	Washington, DC	20003-1733	202-350-8680	350-8699	PK-12	Janice Corazza
School for Arts in Learning	1100 16th St NW	Washington, DC	20036-4802	202-296-9100	261-0200	PK-6	Terry Bunton
SEED Public Charter S	4300 C St SE	Washington, DC	20019-4100	202-248-7773	248-3021	7-12	Charles Adams
Stokes Charter S	3700 Oakview Ter NE	Washington, DC	20017-2521	202-265-7237	265-4656	K-6	Linda Moore
Tree of Life Community Charter S	2315 18th Pl NE	Washington, DC	20018-3610	202-832-1108	832-1113	PK-8	Patricia Williams-Ofori
Two Rivers Public Charter S	1227 4th St NE	Washington, DC	20002-3431	202-546-4477	546-0869	PK-7	Jessica Wodatch
Washington Charter S for Technical Arts	1346 Florida Ave NW	Washington, DC	20009-4839	202-232-6090	232-6382	9-12	Edward Pinkard
Washington Latin Public Charter S	3855 Massachusetts Ave NW	Washington, DC	20016-5102	202-223-1111	223-6311	5-12	Thomas Soule
Washington MST Public Charter HS	1920 Bladensburg Rd NE	Washington, DC	20002-1812	202-636-8011	636-3495	9-12	Mark Holbrook
Washington Yu Ying Public Charter S	PO Box 21111	Washington, DC	20009-0611	202-536-2503	536-2604	PK-8	Sarah Harris
Young America Works Charter S	6015 Chillum Pl NE	Washington, DC	20011-1501	202-722-9295	722-9293	9-12	Brenda Williams
Florida							
Academy at the Farm	9500 Alex Lange Way	Dade City, FL	33525-8213	352-588-9737	588-0508	K-8	Dr. Michael Rom
Academy Da Vinci	1380 Pinehurst Rd	Dunedin, FL	34698-5407	727-298-2778	298-2780	K-5	Dawn Wilson
Academy for International Studies	717 Prosperity Farms Rd	No Palm Beach, FL	33408-4198	561-776-1130	776-0975	6-6	Kendall Artusi
Academy for Positive Learning Charter S	128 N C St	Lake Worth, FL	33460-3232	561-585-6104	585-7849	K-8	Renatta Adan-Espinoza
Academy of Arts & Minds	3138 Commodore Plz	Miami, FL	33133-5814	305-448-1100	448-9737	9-12	William Machado
Academy of Business & Leadership Ed	7 Williams St	Saint Augustine, FL	32084-2878	904-826-1606	794-4119	5-8	Scott Beebe
Academy of Environmental Science	12695 W Fort Island Trl	Crystal River, FL	34429-5290	352-795-8793	794-0065	10-12	Ben Stofcheck
ACE Charter S - Cntrl FL Speech & Hearng	710 E Bella Vista St	Lakeland, FL	33805-3009	863-686-3189	682-1348	PK-PK	Susan Snover
Achievement Academy - Bartow	695 E Summerlin St	Bartow, FL	33830-4848	863-533-0690	534-0798	PK-PK	Paula Sullivan
Achievement Academy - Lakeland	716 E Bella Vista St	Lakeland, FL	33805-3009	863-683-6504	688-9292	PK-PK	Paula Sullivan
Achievement Academy - Winter Haven	2211 28th St NW	Winter Haven, FL	33881-1807	863-965-7586	968-5016	PK-PK	Paula Sullivan
Advanced Technology Center	1770 Technology Blvd	Daytona Beach, FL	32117-7149	386-506-4100		11-12	Dr. Michelle McCraney
Advantage Academy	100072 W McNab	Tamarac, FL	33321	954-726-5227	726-5228	K-5	Raul Baez
Alachua Learning Center	PO Box 1389	Alachua, FL	32616-1389	386-418-2080	418-4116	1-8	Tom Allin
Alee Academy Charter S	755 S Central Ave	Umatilla, FL	32784-9504	352-669-1280	669-1282	9-12	Jennings Neeld
Alee Academy Charter S	1705 E County Road 44	Eustis, FL	32736-2500	352-357-9426	357-8426	9-12	Jennings Neeld
Allen Leadership Academy	17800 NW 25th Ave	Miami Gardens, FL	33056-3656	305-623-3174	624-1668	K-5	Frances Young
Aloma Charter HS	495 N Semoran Blvd	Winter Park, FL	32792	407-657-4343		9-12	Charles Finch
Altoona S	42630 State Road 19	Altoona, FL	32702-9638	352-669-3444	669-3407	K-3	Jerry Hatfield
Anderson Academy	3304 Sanchez St	Tampa, FL	33605-1853	813-242-4138	242-4175	K-4	Jeanette Anderson
Apalachicola Bay Charter S	350 Fred Meyer St	Apalachicola, FL	32320-2502	850-653-1222	653-1857	K-8	Don Hungerford
Archimedean Academy	12425 SW 72nd St	Miami, FL	33183-2513	305-279-6572	675-8448	K-5	Susan Simpson
Archimedean Middle Conservatory	12425 SW 72nd St	Miami, FL	33183-2513	305-279-6572	675-8448	6-8	Vasiliki Moysidis
Archimedean Upper Conservatory	12425 SW 72nd St	Miami, FL	33183-2513	305-279-6572	675-8448	9-12	Demetrios Demopoulos
ASPIRA De Hostos Charter S	1 NE 19th St	Miami, FL	33132-1030	305-576-1512	576-0810	6-8	Fernando Lopez
ASPIRA South Youth Leadership	14112 SW 288th St	Leisure City, FL	33033-1864	305-246-1111	246-1433	6-8	Jason Trinidad
ASPIRA Youth Leadership	13300 Memorial Hwy	North Miami, FL	33161-3940	305-893-8050	891-6055	6-8	Iliana Pena
Athenian Academy of Pasco	3118 Seven Springs Blvd	New Port Richey, FL	34655-3340	727-372-0200	376-1916	K-7	Manuel Goncalves
Athenian Academy	2817 Saint Marks Dr	Dunedin, FL	34698-1920	727-298-2718	298-2719	K-7	Kathy Manrique
Aventura City of Excellence Charter S	3333 NE 188th St	Aventura, FL	33180-2933	305-466-1499	466-1339	K-8	Julie Alm
Balere Language Academy	10875 Quail Roost Dr	Cutler Bay, FL	33157-6740	305-232-9797	232-4535	K-8	Rocka Malik
Bay Haven Charter Academy	2501 Hawks Landing Blvd	Panama City, FL	32405-6658	850-248-3500	248-3514	K-8	Dr. Tim Kitts
Believers Academy	5840 Corporate Way Ste 100	West Palm Beach, FL	33407-2040	561-340-2507	340-2510	9-12	Lori Dyer
Bellalago Charter Academy	3651 Pleasant Hill Rd	Kissimmee, FL	34746-2935	407-933-1690	933-2143	K-8	Cecile Diez
Berkley Accelerated MS	5316 Berkley Rd	Auburndale, FL	33823-8493	863-968-2400	968-2411	6-8	Jill Bolender
Berkley ES	5240 Berkley Rd	Auburndale, FL	33823-8491	863-968-5024	968-5026	PK-5	Randy Borland
Beulah Academy	8633 Beulah Rd	Pensacola, FL	32526-5203	850-944-2822		6-8	
Big Pine Academy	30220 Overseas Hwy	Big Pine Key, FL	33043-3357	305-872-1266	872-1265	PK-4	Cathy Hoffman
Boca Raton Charter S	269 NE 14th St	Boca Raton, FL	33432-1821	561-750-0437	750-7880	PK-6	Deborah Nash-Utterback
Bok Academy	13895 Hwy 27	Lake Wales, FL	33859-2549	863-638-1010	638-1212	6-8	Donna Dunson
Bonita Springs Charter S	25380 Bernwood Dr	Bonita Springs, FL	34135-7800	239-992-6932	992-7359	K-8	Deborah Tracy
Boston Avenue Charter S	340 N Boston Ave	DeLand, FL	32724-4441	386-586-1328	206-8503	PK-5	Douglas Jackson
Bradenton Charter S	2615 26th St W	Bradenton, FL	34205-3731	941-739-6100	752-3250	3-8	Richard Donnelly
Bright Futures International	757 Lighthouse Dr	No Palm Beach, FL	33408-4741	561-776-3794	776-0975	K-5	Kendall Artusi
Bright Scholars Academy	940 Tarpon St Bldg F	Fort Myers, FL	33916	239-461-5001	461-0046	K-8	Scott Persing
Brooks-DeBartolo Collegiate HS	11602 N 15th St	Tampa, FL	33612-6086	813-971-5600	971-5656	9-12	Dr. Phildra Swagger
Broward Community Charter S	201 N University Dr	Coral Springs, FL	33071-7323	954-341-0082	341-0024	K-8	James Pruitt
Broward Community Charter S West	11401 NW 56th Dr	Coral Springs, FL	33076-3122	954-227-5133	227-0433	K-5	Chana Pommels
Byrneville Charter S	1600 Byrneville Rd	Century, FL	32535-3640	850-256-6350	256-6357	K-5	Dee Wolfe-Sullivan
Campus Charter S	3805 Curtis Blvd	Port Saint John, FL	32927-3942	321-633-8234	633-8234	K-4	Dr. Elaine Clifford
Canoe Creek Charter S	3600 Canoe Creek Rd	Saint Cloud, FL	34772-9132	407-891-7320	891-7730	PK-8	Lori McCarley
Cape Coral Charter S	76 Mid Cape Ter	Cape Coral, FL	33991-2008	239-995-0904	995-0369	K-8	Dr. Deborah Nauss
Capstone Academy	4901 W Fairfield Dr	Pensacola, FL	32506-4111	850-458-7735	455-7754	PK-K	Charles Thomas
Care Charter S of Excellence	1145 Second St	Monticello, FL	32344-2845	850-997-0700	997-2186	K-5	Harriet Cuyler
Caring & Sharing Charter S	PO Box 5936	Gainesville, FL	32627-5936	352-372-1004	372-0894	K-5	Dr. Simon Johnson
Central Charter S	4525 N State Road 7	Laud Lakes, FL	33319-5855	954-735-6295	735-6232	K-5	Tonya Dix-Taylor
Chain of Lakes Collegiate HS	999 Avenue H NE	Winter Haven, FL	33881-4256	863-298-6800	298-6801	11-12	Bridget Fetter
Chancellor Charter S at Lantana	600 S East Coast Ave	Lantana, FL	33462-4577	561-585-1189	585-1166	K-5	Laura Mardyks
Chancery High Charter	7001 S Orange Blossom Trl	Orlando, FL	32809-5714	407-850-9791		9-12	Angela Narine
Charter on the Beach MS	910 Bay Dr Apt 17	Miami Beach, FL	33141-5637	786-258-2505	866-2113	7-8	Gladys Palacio
Charter S at National Deaf Academy	19650 US Highway 441	Mount Dora, FL	32757-6959	352-735-9500	735-4939	PK-12	Rebecca Hilding
Charter S at Waterstone	855 Waterstone Way	Homestead, FL	33033-5941	305-248-6206	248-6208	K-8	Melissa Aguilar
Charter S Institute Annex	5420 N State Road 7	Fort Lauderdale, FL	33319-2922	954-486-1640	486-4549	K-6	Dr. Joseph Valbrun
Charter S Institute Training	520 NW 5th St	Hallandale, FL	33009-3314	954-454-5348	454-2463	K-6	Dr. Joseph Valbrun
Charter S of Boynton Beach	1425 Gateway Blvd	Boynton Beach, FL	33426-8313	866-995-4880	995-4090	K-8	Wayne Owens
Charter S of Excellence - Davie	2801 N University Dr	Pembroke Pines, FL	33024-2547	954-522-2997	522-3159	K-5	Lisa Castro
Charter S of Excellence - Ft Lauderdale	1217 SE 3rd Ave	Fort Lauderdale, FL	33316-1905	954-522-2997	522-3159	K-5	Lisa Castro
Charter S of Fort Pierce	777 E Atlantic Ave Ste 242	Delray Beach, FL	33483	772-219-0949	266-0176	6-12	Dr. Diane Allerdyce
Chautauqua Learn & Serve Charter S	1118 Magnolia Ave	Panama City, FL	32401-2815	850-785-5056	785-5071	Adult	Cynthia McCauley
Children's Reading Center	7901 Saint Johns Ave	Palatka, FL	32177-1730	386-328-9990	328-2747	K-5	Dr. Geri Melosh
Chiles Academy	868 George W Engram Blvd	Daytona Beach, FL	32114-1859	386-322-6102		6-12	Anne Ferguson
Choices in Learning Charter S	893 E State Road 434	Longwood, FL	32750-5306	407-331-8477	331-5075	K-6	Shannon McCutcheon
City of Coral Springs Charter S	3205 N University Dr	Coral Springs, FL	33065-4115	954-340-4100	340-4111	6-12	Billie Miller
City of Hialeah Education Academy	2590 W 24th Ave	Hialeah, FL	33016	305-362-4006	362-7006	9-12	Carlos Alvarez
City of Pembroke Pines Charter HS	17189 Sheridan St	Pembroke Pines, FL	33331-1934	954-538-3700	538-3714	9-12	Peter Bayer
City of Pembroke Pines Charter MS West	18500 Pembroke Rd	Pembroke Pines, FL	33029-6108	954-443-4847	447-1691	6-8	Devarn Flowers
City of Pembroke Pines Charter S East	10801 Pembroke Rd	Pembroke Pines, FL	33025-1707	954-443-4800	443-4811	K-5	Sean Chance
City of Pembroke Pines Charter S West	1680 SW 184th Ave	Pembroke Pines, FL	33029-6120	954-450-6990	443-4820	K-5	Devarn Flowers
City of Pembroke Pines ES - Central	12350 Sheridan St	Pembroke Pines, FL	33026-3813	954-322-3330	322-3383	K-5	Kenneth Bass
City of Pembroke Pines MS - Central	12350 Sheridan St	Pembroke Pines, FL	33026-3813	954-322-3300	322-3383	6-8	Kenneth Bass
Clark Advanced Learning Center	2400 SE Salerno Rd	Stuart, FL	34997-6505	772-419-5751		10-12	Maria Mosley
C.O.A.S.T. Charter S	PO Box 338	Saint Marks, FL	32355-0338	850-925-6344	925-6396	K-8	Susan Flournoy
Collegiate HS at NW FL State College	100 College Blvd E	Niceville, FL	32578-1347	850-729-4949	729-4950	10-12	Charla Cotton
Community Charter S of Excellence	10948 N Central Ave	Tampa, FL	33612-6604	813-931-5100	931-1333	K-6	Charles Malatesta
Compass Middle Charter S	550 E Clower St	Bartow, FL	33830-6403	863-519-8701	519-8704	6-8	Harry Williams
Coral Reef Montessori Academy	10853 SW 216th St	Miami, FL	33170-3146	305-255-0064	255-4085	K-8	Juliet King
Cornerstone ES	303 W Moody Blvd	Bunnell, FL	32110-6047	386-586-7500	845-9292	K-5	Douglas Jackson
Coronado HS	2976 Cleveland Ave	Fort Myers, FL	33901	239-337-9140	337-9141	9-12	Pam Franco
Countryside Montessori Academy	5906 Ehren Cutoff	Land O Lakes, FL	34639-3430	813-996-0991	996-0993	1-6	Elaine Padron
Crossroad Academy Charter S	635 Strong Rd	Quincy, FL	32351	850-875-9626	875-1403	PK-8	Kevin Forehand
Daniels Charter S	2201 SW 42nd Ave	West Park, FL	33023-3456	954-894-2826	985-6673	K-5	Cinderella Ashley-Hill
Dayspring Academy ES	8911 Timber Oaks Ave	Port Richey, FL	34668-2426	727-862-8600	868-5175	K-5	John Legg
Dayspring Academy MS	9509 Palm Ave	Port Richey, FL	34668-4647	727-847-9003	848-8774	6-8	John Legg
Dayspring Charter ES	3550 Davie Blvd	Fort Lauderdale, FL	33312-3438	954-797-1400	797-1405	K-5	Lacresha Blue
DayStar Academy of Excellence	970 N Seacrest Blvd	Boynton Beach, FL	33435-4702	561-369-2323	369-2642	K-5	Doris Bennett
Delray Youth Vocational Charter S	601 N Congress Ave Ste 110	Delray Beach, FL	33445-4625	561-266-2206	266-2208	9-12	Marjorie Waldo
DeSoto HS	PO Box 358604	Gainesville, FL	32635-8604	352-495-3326	495-3327	9-12	Dr. Kay Gonsoulin
Discovery Academy at Lake Alfred	1000 N Buena Vista Dr	Lake Alfred, FL	33850-2031	863-295-5955	295-5978	6-8	Kevin Warren
Discovery MS	11401 NW 56th Dr	Coral Springs, FL	33076-3122	954-227-5133	227-0433	6-8	Chana Pommels
Doctors Charter S of Miami Shores	11301 NW 5th Ave	Miami Shores, FL	33168-3343	305-754-2381	751-5833	6-12	Gary Meredith
Doral Academy	2450 NW 97th Ave	Miami, FL	33172-2308	305-597-9999	591-2669	K-5	Eleonora Cuesta
Doral Academy HS	11100 NW 27th St	Miami, FL	33172-5001	305-597-9950	477-6762	9-12	Francisco Jimenez
Doral Academy MS	2601 NW 112th Ave	Miami, FL	33172-1804	305-591-0020	591-9251	6-8	
Downtown Miami Charter S	305 NW 3rd Ave	Miami, FL	33128-1606	305-579-2112	579-2115	K-6	Candace Chewning
Eagle Academy	3020 NW 33rd Ave	Laud Lakes, FL	33311-1106	954-343-9960	343-9970	6-12	Janet Ward
Eagles Nest ES	1840 NE 41st St	Pompano Beach, FL	33064-6071	954-942-3318	942-3179	K-5	John Foster-Grant
Eagles Nest MS	1840 NE 41st St	Pompano Beach, FL	33064-6071	954-942-3188	942-3179	6-8	John Foster-Grant
Early Beginnings Academy-Civic Center	1411 NW 14th Ave	Miami, FL	33125-1616	305-325-1080	325-1044	PK-K	Carol Byrd
Early Beginnings Academy-North Shore	985 NW 91st St	Miami, FL	33150-2350	305-325-1080	325-1044	PK-K	
Easter Seals Charter S	1219 Dunn Ave	Daytona Beach, FL	32114-2405	386-255-4568		PK-K	Krista Barringer
Educational Horizons Charter S	1281 S Wickham Rd	West Melbourne, FL	32904-2450	321-729-0786	729-8403	1-5	Aileen Tapp
Ed Venture Charter S	117 E Coast Ave	Lantana, FL	33462-5316	561-582-1454	547-9682	10-12	Barbara Fitz

School	Address	City,State	Zip code	Telephone	Fax	Grade	Contact
Einstein Montessori S	5930 SW Archer Rd	Gainesville, FL	32608-4702	352-335-4321	335-1575	2-8	Zach Osbrach
Escambia Charter S	PO Box 1147	Gonzalez, FL	32560-1147	850-937-0500	968-5605	9-12	Jerome Chisholm
Everglades Preparatory Academy	183 S Lake Ave	Pahokee, FL	33476-1803	561-924-3002	924-3013	9-12	Alma Horne
Excel Academy Charter S	3650 N Miami Ave	Miami, FL	33127-3114	305-572-1414	572-1411	K-5	
Excel Academy Charter S North	780 Fisherman St Fl 2	Opa Locka, FL	33054	305-953-8401	953-8486	K-3	Dennis McMillon
Excel Academy Middle Charter S	3650 N Miami Ave	Miami, FL	33127-3114	305-572-1414	572-1411	6-8	Ralph Brantley
Excelsior Charter S of Broward	10046 W McNab Rd	Tamarac, FL	33321-1894	954-726-5227	726-5228	K-5	Raul Biez
Excelsior Language Academy of Hialeah	600 W 20th St	Hialeah, FL	33010-2428	305-883-8359	667-2744	K-8	Yudit Silva
Expressions Learning Arts Academy	5408 SW 13th St	Gainesville, FL	32608-5038	352-373-5223	373-6327	K-5	Cheryl Valantis
Fair Babson Park ES	815 N Scenic Hwy	Babson Park, FL	33827-9795	863-678-4664	678-4669	K-5	Ken Hensen
First Coast Technical Institute	2980 Collins Ave	Saint Augustine, FL	32084-1919	904-824-4401	824-6750		Dr. Christine Cothron
Florida Autism Center of Excellence	6400 E Chelsea St	Tampa, FL	33610-5628	813-621-3223	621-7139	PK-12	Shannon Moss
Florida HS for Accelerated Learners	4131 NW 16th St	Lauderhill, FL	33313-5810	954-731-2585	731-2587	9-12	Laurel Suarez
Florida HS for Accelerated Learners	4800 N University Dr	Sunrise, FL	33351-5746	954-746-4483	746-5031	9-12	Laurel Suarez
Florida HS for Accelerated Learning	3206 S University Dr	Miramar, FL	33025-3007	954-433-1573	433-1589	9-12	Laurel Suarez
Florida Intercultural Academy	1704 Buchanan St	Hollywood, FL	33020-4030	954-924-8006	924-8044	K-8	Evangeline Belano
Florida International Academy	7630 Biscayne Blvd	Miami, FL	33138-5136	305-758-6912	758-6985	6-8	Sonia Mitchell
Florida SIA Tech at Gainesville	5301 NE 40th Ter	Gainesville, FL	32609-1670	352-371-4424	371-4426	9-12	Joy Baldree
Florida State University School	3000 School House Rd	Tallahassee, FL	32311-7855	850-245-3700	245-3997	K-12	Dr. Lynn Wicker
Fort Myers Preparatory & Fitness Academy	3210 Dr M L King Blvd	Fort Myers, FL	33916	239-333-0766	333-0768	K-8	Lisa Hay
Foundation Charter S	1325 George Jenkins Blvd	Lakeland, FL	33815-1367	863-682-8111	687-8205	6-12	Emory Welch
Four Corners Charter S	9100 Teacher Ln	Davenport, FL	33897-6212	407-787-4300	787-4331	K-8	John Bushey
Gainer S	1600 E Moreno St	Pensacola, FL	32503-6163	850-439-3888	439-3898	9-12	Lynn Baldwin
Gamla Charter S	2620 Hollywood Blvd	Hollywood, FL	33020-4807	954-342-4064	342-4107	K-8	Sharon Miller
Gateway Charter HS	12770 Gateway Blvd	Fort Myers, FL	33913-8654	239-768-3350	768-3874	9-12	Joseph Roles
Gateway Charter S	12850 Commonwealth Dr	Fort Myers, FL	33913-8039	239-768-5048	768-5710	K-8	John O'Brien
Genesis Preparatory S	207 NW 23rd Ave	Gainesville, FL	32609-3604	352-379-1188	379-1142	K-3	Charmaine Henry
Gibson Charter S	450 SW 4th St	Miami, FL	33130-1410	305-324-1335	324-1343	K-8	Olga Camarena
Glades Academy	1200 E Main St	Pahokee, FL	33476-1102	561-924-9402	924-9279	K-5	Dr. Don Zumpano
Goodwill L.I.F.E. Academy	3365D Seminole Ave	Fort Myers, FL	33916	239-334-4434	334-4439	6-12	Lynn Pottorf
G-STAR School of the Arts	2065 Prairie Rd Bldg J	West Palm Beach, FL	33406-7700	561-967-2023	963-8975	9-10	Reno Boffice
Guided Path Academy	1199 Lantana Rd	Lantana, FL	33462-1514	561-588-2800	588-0870	K-5	Evelyn Francis
Gulf Coast Academy of Science & Technlgy	10444 Tillery Rd	Spring Hill, FL	34608-3706	352-688-5092	688-5095	6-8	Nevin Siefert
Gulfstream Goodwill LIFE Academy	3800 S Congress Ave	Boynton Beach, FL	33426-8424	561-259-1000	259-1004	9-12	Larry McNutt
Gulfstream Goodwill Transition Academy	950 N Congress Ave	Riviera Beach, FL	33404-6400	561-863-1297	863-1373	10-12	Larry McNutt
Harris Preparatory Academy	1408 E Blount St	Pensacola, FL	32503-5620	850-432-2273	432-4624	K-5	Celestine Lewis
Hartridge Academy	1400 US Highway 92	Winter Haven, FL	33881-8137	863-956-4434	956-3267	K-5	Debra Richards
Healthy Learning Academy	2101 NW 39th Ave	Gainesville, FL	32609	352-372-2573		K-2	Ann Egan
Heritage HS	303 W Moody Blvd	Bunnell, FL	32110-6047	386-586-7500	586-7510	9-12	Doug Jackson
Hillcrest ES	1051 State Road 60 E	Lake Wales, FL	33853-4258	863-678-4216	678-4086	PK-5	Damien Moses
Hoggetowne MS	3930 NE 15th St	Gainesville, FL	32609-2007	352-367-4369	376-3345	6-8	Kristine Santos
Hollywood Academy of Arts & Science	1720 Harrison St	Hollywood, FL	33020-6839	954-925-6404	925-8123	K-8	Dante Fulton
Hope Charter Center	1400 NE Jensen Beach Blvd	Jensen Beach, FL	34957-7226	772-334-3288	334-2203	K-2	Staci Routt
Hope Charter S	1550 E Crown Point Rd	Ocoee, FL	34761-3722	407-656-4673	264-6960	K-8	Crystal Yoakum
Hope Preparatory Academy	3916 E Hillsborough Ave	Tampa, FL	33610-4542	813-236-1462	232-9680	K-5	Celeste Kellar
Imagine Charter S at Broward	9001 Westview Dr	Coral Springs, FL	33067-2869	954-255-0020	255-1336	K-5	Kevin Sawyer
Imagine Charter S at Evening Rose	3611 Austin Davis Ave	Tallahassee, FL	32308-7402	850-877-5187	877-6463	K-8	Suezan Turknett
Imagine Charter School at Lakewood Ranch	PO Box 110135	Bradenton, FL	34211-0002	941-750-0900	750-0966	PK-5	Stephen Sajewski
Imagine Charter S at North Lauderdale	1395 S State Rd 7	N Lauderdale, FL	33068-4023	954-973-8900	974-5588	K-8	Sharonda Feby
Imagine Charter School at North Manatee	5309 29th St E	Ellenton, FL	34222-4116	941-723-1205	723-1207	K-5	Christy Catlin
Imagine Charter S at St. Petersburg	1950 1st Ave N	St Petersburg, FL	33713	727-821-7100	821-7171	PK-5	Bob Connor
Imagine Charter S at West Melbourne	4400 Dixie Hwy NE	Palm Bay, FL	32905-4334	321-729-0500	729-0500	K-12	Thomas Cole
Imagine Charter S at Weston	2500 Glades Cir	Weston, FL	33327-2253	954-659-3600	659-3620	K-5	Jacquelyn Vernon
Imagine S at Land O' Lakes	17901 Hunting Bow Circle	Lutz, FL	33558	813-909-4501	909-4515	K-6	John Selover
Imagine School at North Port	100 Innovation Ave	North Port, FL	34289	941-426-2050	423-8252	K-6	Justin Matthews
Imagine S at Town Center	775 Town Center Blvd	Palm Coast, FL	32164-2520	386-586-0100	586-2784	PK-8	Lisa O'Grady
Imagine Schools at South Vero	6000 4th St	Vero Beach, FL	32968-9563	772-567-2728	562-4804	K-5	Joe Mills
Immokalee Charter S	402 W Main St	Immokalee, FL	34142-3933	239-658-3560		K-4	
Immokalee Community S	123 N 4th St	Immokalee, FL	34142-3721	239-867-3223	867-3224	K-5	Armando Touron
Indian River Charter HS	6055 College Ln	Vero Beach, FL	32966-1285	772-567-6600	567-2288	9-12	Cynthia Trevino-Aversa
Inlet Grove Community HS	7071 Garden Rd	Riviera Beach, FL	33404-4906	561-881-4600	881-4668	9-12	Emma Banks
International S of Broward	3100 NW 75th Ave	Hollywood, FL	33024-2355	954-987-2026	987-7261	6-12	Dr. Jacquelyne Hoy
International Studies Charter HS	396 Alhambra Cir	Coral Gables, FL	33134-5007	305-442-7449	442-7729	9-12	Victoriano Rodriguez
Island S	PO Box 1090	Boca Grande, FL	33921-1090	941-964-8016	964-8017	K-5	Rosa Ramos
Island Village Montessori North S	3975 Fruitville Rd	Sarasota, FL	34232-1614	941-954-4999	342-6502	K-5	Kym Elder
Island Village Montessori S	2001 Pinebrook Rd	Venice, FL	34292-1560	941-484-4999	484-2150	K-6	Kym Elder
Jackson Preparatory S	546 Mary Esther Cut Off NW	Ft Walton Bch, FL	32548	850-833-3321	833-3292	K-8	Mary Gunter
JFK Medical Center Charter S	4696 Davis Rd	Lake Worth, FL	33461-5204	561-868-6100	963-4697	K-5	Chuck Shaw
Keys Gate Charter S	2000 SE 28th Ave	Homestead, FL	33035-2102	305-230-1616	230-1347	K-8	Robin Sandler
Kids Community College	10530 Lake St Charles Blvd	Riverview, FL	33578	813-671-1440	671-1245	K-5	Nicole Williams
Kidz Choice Charter S	9063 Taft St	Pembroke Pines, FL	33024-4650	954-641-9386	704-8404	K-5	Lilly Swanson
Kissimmee Charter Academy	2850 Bill Beck Blvd	Kissimmee, FL	34744-4073	407-847-1400	847-1401	PK-8	Tiffany Ward
Lake Eola Charter S	135 N Magnolia Ave	Orlando, FL	32801-2301	407-246-0900	246-6334	K-8	
Lakeland Montessori Schoolhouse	PO Box 7521	Lakeland, FL	33807-7521	863-413-0003	413-0006	PK-3	Josie Zinninger
Lakeside Academy	716 S Main St	Belle Glade, FL	33430-4202	561-993-5000	993-5001	K-5	Barbara Litinski
Lake Technical Center	2001 Kurt St	Eustis, FL	32726-6199	352-589-2250	357-4776		Terry Miller
Lake Wales HS	1 Highlander Way	Lake Wales, FL	33853-8517	863-678-4222	678-4064	9-12	Clark Berry
Lawrence Academy	777 W Palm Dr	Florida City, FL	33034-3223	305-247-4800	247-4895	K-12	Dr. Keitha Burnett
Leadership Academy West	2030 S Congress Ave	West Palm Beach, FL	33406-7602	561-434-0996	434-0575	9-12	Faith Morrison
Learning Academy	5880 Stewart St	Milton, FL	32570-3632	850-983-3495	983-8098	6-12	Chad White
Learning Gate Charter S	16215 Hanna Rd	Lutz, FL	33549-5701	813-948-4190	948-7587	K-8	Patricia Girard
Lee Alternative Charter HS	1201 Taylor Lane Ext	Lehigh Acres, FL	33936-6151	239-303-2834	303-1373	9-12	Jodie Goebel
Lee Charter Academy	3637 Dr M L King Blvd	Fort Myers, FL	33916	239-334-2235	334-2241	K-8	Dr. Shirley Chapman
Legacy HS	1550 E Crown Point Rd	Ocoee, FL	34761-3722	407-656-4673	656-6094	9-12	Crystal Yoakum
Life Skills Center	407 E Memorial Blvd	Lakeland, FL	33801-1768	863-683-6279	802-3547	9-12	Viesta Skipper
Life Skills Center	2360 W Oakland Park Blvd	Oakland Park, FL	33311-1410	954-735-6970	735-6022	9-12	Derek Stein
Life Skills Center	4901 Central Ave	St Petersburg, FL	33710-8239	727-322-1758	322-2753	9-12	Phynedra Franklin
Life Skills Center	3637 Dr Martin Luther King	Fort Myers, FL	33916	239-332-3484	332-3446	9-12	Sarah White
Life Skills Center Charter S	4526 S Orange Blossom Trl	Orlando, FL	32839-1704	407-271-9422		9-12	
Life Skills Center Miami-Dade County	3555 NW 7th St	Miami, FL	33125-4015	305-643-9111	643-9141	9-12	Stacy London
Life Skills Center of Leon County	324 N Adams St	Tallahassee, FL	32301-1308	850-599-9190	599-9170		Shellonda Ruckers
Life Skills Center of Palm Beach County	600 N Congress Ave Ste 560	Delray Beach, FL	33445-3463	561-279-1354	266-9274	9-12	Mary Delsignore
Life Skills Center of Pinellas North	2471 N McMullen Booth Rd	Clearwater, FL	33759	727-724-9709	724-9703	9-12	Patricia O'Neil
Life Skills Center Opa Locka	3400 NW 135th St	Opa Locka, FL	33054-4708	305-685-1415	685-1614	9-12	Daniel Stanislawczyk
Life Skills Center - Polk East	7500 Cypress Gardens Blvd	Winter Haven, FL	33884-3200	863-439-2242	439-5544	9-12	Ashlee Wright
Literacy/Leadership Technology Academy	6771 Madison Ave	Tampa, FL	33619-6836	813-234-0940	234-0946	9-12	Lesley Logan
Literacy/Leadership Technology Academy	6771 Madison Ave	Tampa, FL	33619-6836	813-234-0940	234-0946	6-8	Sharon Green
Littles-Nguzo Saba Charter S	5829 Corporate Way	West Palm Beach, FL	33407	561-689-9970	682-1342	K-8	Rev. Richard Scott
Manatee S for the Arts	700 Haben Blvd	Palmetto, FL	34221-4173	941-721-6800	721-6805	6-12	Bill Jones
Manatee S of Arts/Science	3700 32nd St W	Bradenton, FL	34205-2708	941-755-5012	755-7934	PK-5	Miriam Jolly
Marco Island Charter MS	1401 Trinidad Ave	Marco Island, FL	34145-3949	239-377-3200	377-3201	6-8	George Abounader
Marion Charter S	39 Cedar Rd	Ocala, FL	34472-8331	352-687-2100	687-2700	K-5	Gina Evers
Marion Military Academy	2091 NE 35th St	Ocala, FL	34479-2909	352-291-6600	291-6601	9-12	Martha Cieplinski
Mascotte Charter ES	460 Midway Ave	Mascotte, FL	34753-8800	352-429-2294	429-5166	PK-5	Wayne Cockcroft
Mater Academy	7700 NW 98th St	Hialeah Gardens, FL	33016-2403	305-698-9900	698-3822	K-5	Kim Guilarte
Mater Academy Charter HS	7901 NW 103rd St	Hialeah Gardens, FL	33016-2419	305-828-1886	828-6175	9-12	Judith Marty
Mater Academy Charter MS	7901 NW 103rd St	Hialeah Gardens, FL	33016-2419	305-828-1886	828-6175	6-8	Judith Marty
Mater Academy East Charter HS	998 SW 1st St	Miami, FL	33130-1112	305-324-6963	324-6966	9-12	Alex Tamargo
Mater Academy East Charter MS	998 SW 1st St	Miami, FL	33130-1112	305-324-4667	324-6966	6-8	Alina Lopez
Mater Academy East Charter S	450 SW 4th St	Miami, FL	33130-1410	305-324-4667	324-6580	K-5	Beatrice Riera
Mater Academy HS International Studies	998 SW 1st St	Miami, FL	33130-1112	305-324-6963	324-6966	9-12	Alex Tamargo
Mater Academy Lakes HS	9010 NW 178th Ln	Hialeah, FL	33018-6548	305-512-3917	512-3708	9-12	Rene Rovirosa
Mater Academy Lakes MS	9010 NW 178th Ln	Hialeah, FL	33018-6548	305-512-3917	512-3708	6-8	Rene Rovirosa
Mater Academy MS International Studies	998 SW 1st St	Miami, FL	33130-1112	305-324-6963	324-6580	6-8	Alejandro Tamargo
Mater Academy of International Studies	450 SW 4th St	Miami, FL	33130-1410	305-324-4667	324-6580	K-5	Beatrice Riera
Mater Gardens Academy	9010 NW 178th Ln	Hialeah, FL	33018-6548	305-512-9775	512-3708	K-8	Lourdes Isla-Marrero
Mater Performing Arts Academy	7901 NW 103rd St	Hialeah Gardens, FL	33016-2419	305-828-1886	828-6175	9-12	Judith Marty
McAuliffe Charter ES	2817 SW 3rd Ln	Cape Coral, FL	33991-1151	239-283-4511	282-0376	PK-5	Dr. Lee Bush
Mc Intosh Area Charter S	PO Box 769	Mc Intosh, FL	32664-0769	352-591-9797	591-9747	K-3	Shirley Lane
McKeel Academy of Applied Tech	1810 W Parker St	Lakeland, FL	33815-1243	863-499-2818	284-4383	6-12	Andrea Whiteley
McKeel ES	411 N Florida Ave	Lakeland, FL	33801-4803	863-499-1287	688-1607	K-5	Steve Viers
Metropolitan Ministries Charter S	110 E Palm Ave	Tampa, FL	33602-2214	813-228-7406	228-7471	K-5	Thom Laux
Miami Childrens Museum Charter S	980 MacArthur Cswy	Miami, FL	33132-1604	305-329-3758	329-3767	K-5	Nina Cortina
Miami Community Charter S	101 S Redland Rd	Florida City, FL	33034-4630	305-245-2552	245-2527	K-8	Jila Rezaie
Micanopy Area Cooperative S	PO Box 386	Micanopy, FL	32667-0386	352-466-0990	466-4090	K-5	Anne Thompson
Micanopy MS	PO Box 109	Micanopy, FL	32667-0109	352-466-1090	466-1030	6-8	Bobby Johnson
Milburn Academy	2400 S Ridgewood Ave Ste 20	South Daytona, FL	32119-3073	386-304-0086		9-12	Sam Smith

School	Address	City,State	Zip code	Telephone	Fax	Grade	Contact
Milburn Academy	3800 Evans Ave	Fort Myers, FL	33901	239-278-4774	278-0470	9-12	Irma Miller
Milburn Academy	6210 17th Ave W	Bradenton, FL	34209-7838	941-761-4393	761-2992	9-12	Krista Morton
Milestones Community School of Lake Co.	10516 Treadway School Rd	Leesburg, FL	34788-4669	352-742-7007	383-0744	K-8	Mike Stewart
Minneola Charter ES	300 E Pearl St	Minneola, FL	34715-9001	352-394-2600	394-2079	K-5	Sandra Reaves
Montessori Academy of Early Enrichment	6201 S Military Trl	Lake Worth, FL	33463-7288	561-649-0004	649-0964	PK-3	Jean Ranck
Montessori Charter ES	1127 United St	Key West, FL	33040-3330	305-294-4910	294-1404	1-5	Judi Dunlap
Mount Pleasant MS	1906 N Rome Ave	Tampa, FL	33607-4424	813-253-0053	253-0182	6-8	Yolanda Waitress
Nap Ford Community Charter S	648 W Livingston St	Orlando, FL	32801-1418	407-245-8711	245-8712	PK-5	
Nature Coast MS	6830 NW 140th St	Chiefland, FL	32626-8271	352-490-0700	490-0702	6-8	Allison Hord
New Dimensions HS	4900 Old Pleasant Hill Rd	Kissimmee, FL	34759-3430	407-870-9949	870-8976	9-12	Tina Cafiero Ed.D.
Newpoint Bay Academy	700 W 23rd St Bldg H	Panama City, FL	32405	850-215-0770	542-0770	9-12	Carla Lovett
Noahs Ark International Charter S	21 W 22nd St	Riviera Beach, FL	33404-5509	561-848-7575	881-4668	K-5	Erika Hadden
North Broward Academy of Excellence	8200 SW 17th St	N Lauderdale, FL	33068-4101	954-718-5032	718-2215	K-5	David McKnight
North Broward Academy of Excellence MS	8200 SW 17th St	N Lauderdale, FL	33068-4101	954-718-2211	718-2215	6-8	David McKnight
North County Charter S	11 N Willow St	Fellsmere, FL	32948-5330	772-571-0153	571-8489	K-5	Dorie Miller
North Nicholas HS	428 SW Pine Island Rd	Cape Coral, FL	33991-1916	239-242-4230		9-12	Michael D'Angelo
North Semoran Charter HS	875 E Semoran Blvd	Apopka, FL	32703-5518	407-886-1825		9-12	Lovely Tinsley
NorthStar Charter HS	8291 Curry Ford Rd	Orlando, FL	32822-7890	407-273-1188	277-3340	8-12	Kelly Young
Oakland Avenue Charter S	456 E Oakland Ave	Oakland, FL	34787	407-877-2039	877-6222	K-5	
Oasis Charter ES	3415 Oasis Blvd	Cape Coral, FL	33914-4924	239-542-1577	549-7662	K-5	Steven Hook
Oasis Charter HS	3519 Oasis Blvd	Cape Coral, FL	33914	239-541-1167	541-1590	9-12	Chris Terrill
Oasis Charter MS	3507 Oasis Blvd	Cape Coral, FL	33914-4914	239-945-1999	540-7677	6-8	Chris Terrill
Oasis MS	202 13th Ave E	Bradenton, FL	34208-3246	941-749-1979		6-8	Edna Bailey
Odyssey Charter S	1755 Eldron Blvd SE	Palm Bay, FL	32909-6832	321-733-0442	733-1178	K-6	Reggie Revis
Okaloosa Academy	81 Roberts Blvd	Ft Walton Bch, FL	32547-5118	850-864-3133	864-4305	6-12	Margaret Walton
One Room S House Project	4180 NE 15th St	Gainesville, FL	32609-2011	352-376-4014	376-3345	K-5	Brett Beckett
Orlando Science Charter S	2427 Lynx Ln	Orlando, FL	32804-4720	407-928-3790	253-7305	6-12	Yalcin Akin
Our Children's Academy	555 Burns Ave	Lake Wales, FL	33853-3335	863-679-3338	679-3944	PK-2	Sharon McManus
Oxford Academy of Miami	10870 SW 113th Pl	Miami, FL	33176-3227	305-598-4494	598-4475	K-5	Angela Klinedirst
PAL Academy Charter S	202 13th Ave E	Bradenton, FL	34208-3246	941-714-7260	714-7333	K-12	Harry Reif
Palm Bay Academy	2112 Palm Bay Rd NE	Palm Bay, FL	32905-2915	321-984-2710	984-0799	K-8	Madhu Longani
Palm Bay Community Charter S	1350 Wyoming Dr SE	Palm Bay, FL	32909-5757	321-409-4500	409-4501	K-8	Eric Lewis
Palm Beach Academy for Learning	1199 Lantana Rd	Lantana, FL	33462-1514	561-649-7505	533-9918	K-2	Olive Balbosa
Palm Beach Maritime Academy	7719 S Dixie Hwy	West Palm Beach, FL	33405-4817	561-547-3775	540-5177	K-8	Marie Turchiaro
Paragon Academy of Technology	2210 Pierce St	Hollywood, FL	33020-4414	954-925-0155	925-0209	6-8	Dr. Steven Montes
Paragon ES	3311 N Andrews Ave	Pompano Beach, FL	33064	954-943-0471	943-0473	K-5	Ardonnis Lumpkin
Parkway Academy	7451 Riviera Blvd	Miramar, FL	33023-6530	954-961-2911	961-2451	9-12	Dr. Clarissa Wright
Passport S	5221 Curry Ford Rd	Orlando, FL	32812-8741	407-658-9900	658-9911	K-8	
Pathways Academy	101 State St W	Jacksonville, FL	32202-3099	904-633-8125		9-12	Maureen Martin
Pemayetv Emahakv Charter S	100 E Harney Pond Rd NE	Okeechobee, FL	34974	863-467-2501	467-8510	K-5	Russell Brown
Pembroke Pines FSU Charter ES	601 SW 172nd Ave	Pembroke Pines, FL	33029-4003	954-499-4244	499-3016	K-5	Lisa Libidinsky
Pensacola Beach ES	900 Via De Luna Dr	Pensacola Beach, FL	32561-2262	850-934-4020	934-4040	K-5	Jeff Castleberry
Pepin Academy	3916 E Hillsborough Ave	Tampa, FL	33610-4542	813-237-1239	236-1195	9-12	Monica Patton
Pinecrest Academy MS	14301 SW 42nd St	Miami, FL	33175-7832	305-207-1027	207-1897	6-8	Maria Nunez
Pinecrest Academy - South	15130 SW 80th St	Miami, FL	33193-1302	305-386-0800	386-6298	K-5	Maria Nunez
Pinecrest Preparatory Academy	14301 SW 42nd St	Miami, FL	33175-7832	305-207-1027	207-1897	K-5	Susie Dopico
Pinecrest Preparatory Academy HS	11100 NW 27th St	Miami, FL	33172-5001	305-597-9950	591-9251	9-12	Athena Guillen
Pinellas Preparatory Academy	2300 Belcher Rd S Ste 100	Largo, FL	33771-4010	727-536-3600	536-3661	4-8	Curtis Fuller
Plato Academy	401 S Old Coachman Rd	Clearwater, FL	33765-4410	727-793-2400	793-2405	PK-6	Steve Christopoulos
Polk Avenue ES	110 E Polk Ave	Lake Wales, FL	33853-4199	863-678-4244	678-4680	PK-5	Gail Quam
Polk Community College Collegiate HS	999 Avenue H NE	Winter Haven, FL	33881-4256	863-669-2322	298-6800	11-12	Sallie Brisbane
Pompano Charter MS	3311 N Andrews Ave	Pompano Beach, FL	33064	954-943-0471	943-0473	6-8	Ardonnis Lumpkin
Potentials Charter S	1201 Australian Ave	Riviera Beach, FL	33404-6635	561-842-3213	863-4352	PK-5	Rosie Portera
Potentials South Charter S	701 NW 35th St	Boca Raton, FL	33431	561-395-2012	395-4607	PK-5	Rosie Portera
Princeton House Charter S	1166 Lee Rd	Orlando, FL	32810-5847	407-523-7121	523-7187	K-12	Carol Tucker
Quest MS	3916 E Hillsborough Ave	Tampa, FL	33610-4542	813-239-2092	232-9680	6-8	George Shaw
Rays of Hope Charter S	1780 W Airport Blvd	Sanford, FL	32771-4091	407-322-5010	322-8003	6-8	Carolyn Flanagan
RCMA Wimauma Academy	18240 US Highway 301 S	Wimauma, FL	33598-4307	813-672-5159	633-6119	K-5	Mark Haggett
Reading Edge Academy	2975 Enterprise Rd	De Bary, FL	32713-2708	386-668-8911		K-5	Margaret Comardo
ReBirth Academy Charter S	1924 E Comanche Ave	Tampa, FL	33610-8226	813-239-1321	239-2702	K-5	K.C. Williams
Renaissance Elementary Charter S	8360 NW 33rd St	Miami, FL	33122-1938	305-591-2225	591-2984	K-8	Ana Cordal
Renaissance Learning Center	5800 Corporate Way	West Palm Beach, FL	33407-2004	561-640-0270	640-0272	K-5	Debra Johnson
Richardson Montessori S	6815 N Rome Ave	Tampa, FL	33604-5839	813-930-2988	930-2929	K-6	Tommie Lee Brumfield
Ridgeview Global Studies Academy	1000 Dunson Rd	Davenport, FL	33896-8383	863-419-3171	419-3172	PK-5	Ralph Frier
Rio Grande Charter S	2210 S Rio Grande Ave	Orlando, FL	32805-5262	407-649-9122	649-8151	PK-5	Dr. Barbara McLean-Smith
Rise Academy	3698 NW 15th St	Lauderhill, FL	33311-4133	954-585-4671	585-4871	K-8	Dawna Thornton
Rise Academy-South Dade Charter S	30960 SW 191st Ave	Homestead, FL	33030-3716	305-677-3779		K-8	Gemma Torcivia
River Cities Community Charter S	1211 Marseille Dr	Miami Beach, FL	33141-2815	786-970-7005	879-7488	6-8	Connie Rodriguez
River City Science Academy	3266 Southside Blvd	Jacksonville, FL	32216-3538	904-312-2038	212-0337	6-8	Dogan Tozoglu
Riviera Beach Maritime Academy	251 W 11th St	Riviera Beach, FL	33404-7534	561-841-7600	841-7626	9-12	Dexter Orange
Round Lake Charter ES	31333 Round Lake Rd	Mount Dora, FL	32757-9599	352-385-4399	735-1860	K-5	Dale Moxley
Royal Palm Charter S	7145 Babcock St SE	Palm Bay, FL	32909-5462	321-723-0650	722-1117	K-2	Tresa Vernon
Sagan Academy	4610 E Hanna Ave	Tampa, FL	33610-2521	813-740-7747	740-7749	6-8	Felita Lott
Saint Peter's Academy	4250 38th Ave	Vero Beach, FL	32967-1711	772-562-1963	562-8920	K-6	Ruth Jefferson
St. Petersburg Collegiate HS	PO Box 13489	St Petersburg, FL	33733-3489	727-341-4610	341-4226	10-12	Starla Metz
Samsula Academy	248 N Samsula Dr	New Smyrna, FL	32168-8762	386-423-6650		K-5	Peggy Comardo
Sarasota Military Academy	801 Orange Ave	Sarasota, FL	34236-4116	941-926-1700	926-1701	9-12	Daniel Kennedy
Sarasota S of Arts/Sciences	645 Central Ave	Sarasota, FL	34236-4016	941-330-1855	330-1835	6-8	Pepar Anspaugh
Sarasota Suncoast Academy	8084 Hawkins Rd	Sarasota, FL	34241-9300	941-924-4242	924-8282	K-5	Steve Crump
School of Arts & Sciences	3208 Thomasville Rd	Tallahassee, FL	32308-7904	850-386-6566	386-8183	K-8	Deborah Powers
School of Success Academy	6974 Wilson Blvd	Jacksonville, FL	32210-3663	904-573-0880	573-0889	6-8	Genell Mills
Sculptor Charter S	1301 Armstrong Dr	Titusville, FL	32780-7907	321-264-9991	264-9995	PK-8	Pat O'Sullivan
Seagull Academy for Independent Living	1801 12th Ave S	Lake Worth, FL	33461-5771	561-540-8110	540-8331	9-Adu	Bob Estreicher
Seaside Neighborhood S	PO Box 4610	Santa Rsa Bch, FL	32459-4610	850-231-0396	231-4725	6-8	Cathy Brubaker
Sebastian Charter JHS	782 Wave St	Sebastian, FL	32958-5049	772-388-8838	388-8815	6-8	Martha McAdams
Shiloh Charter S	905 W Terrace Dr	Plant City, FL	33563-8903	813-707-1060	707-8060	K-5	Danny Pickern
SIA Tech	4811 Payne Stewart Dr	Jacksonville, FL	32209-9208	904-360-8200	768-8618	9-12	Michael LaRoche
SIATech - North	3050 NW 183rd St	Miami Gardens, FL	33056-3536	305-624-1144	624-9172	9-12	Catherine Bonnewell
SIATech - South	12350 SW 285th St	Homestead, FL	33033-1251	305-258-9477	258-9584	9-12	Marjorie Lopez
Six Mile Charter Academy	6851 Lancer Ave	Fort Myers, FL	33912-4334	239-768-9375	225-2477	K-8	Sara Abraham
Smart School Charter MS	3698 NW 15th St	Lauderhill, FL	33311-4133	954-321-6777	321-7760	6-8	Chandra Glen-Phillips
Smart S Institute of Technlgy & Commerce	3020 NW 33rd Ave	Laud Lakes, FL	33311-1106	954-343-9965	343-9970	9-12	
Somerset Academy	12425 SW 53rd St	Miramar, FL	33027-5493	305-829-2406	829-4477	PK-8	Shannine Sadesky-Hunt
Somerset Academy	20803 Johnson St	Pembroke Pines, FL	33029-1916	954-442-0233	442-0813	K-5	Bernardo Montero
Somerset Academy	18491 SW 134th Ave	Miami, FL	33177-2923	305-969-6074	969-6077	K-8	Suzette Ruiz
Somerset Academy Charter HS	23255 SW 115th Ave	Homestead, FL	33032-4505	305-257-3737	257-3751	9-12	Ofelia Alvarez
Somerset Academy Davie	3788 SW 64th Ave	Davie, FL	33314-2417	954-584-5528	584-5598	K-5	Dina Miller
Somerset Academy MS	18491 SW 134th Ave	Miami, FL	33177-2923	305-969-6074	969-6077	6-8	Sandra Grau
Somerset Academy MS - Country Palms	12425 SW 248th St	Homestead, FL	33032	305-969-6074	969-6077	6-8	Suzette Ruiz
Somerset Academy MS - South	23255 SW 115th Ave	Homestead, FL	33032-4505	305-257-3737	257-3751	6-8	Ofelia Alvarez
Somerset Academy MSHS	20803 Johnson St	Pembroke Pines, FL	33029-1916	954-442-0233	442-0813	6-12	Bernardo Montero
Somerset Academy Silver Palms	23255 SW 115th Ave	Homestead, FL	33032-4505	305-257-3737	257-2751	PK-8	Ofelia Alvarez
Somerset Arts Academy	1700 N Krome Ave	Homestead, FL	33030	305-246-4949	249-4919	K-8	Idalia Suarez
South Lake Charter ES	2750 Hartwood Marsh Rd	Clermont, FL	34711	352-243-2960	243-2697	K-5	Christine Watson
South McKeel Elementary Academy	2222 Edgewood Dr S	Lakeland, FL	33803-3631	863-510-0044	510-0021	K-5	Judith Morris
South Tech Academy	1300 SW 30th Ave	Boynton Beach, FL	33426-9099	561-369-7004	369-7024	9-12	James Kidd
Spring Creek ES	44440 Spring Creek Rd	Paisley, FL	32767-9063	352-669-3275	669-3762	PK-6	Robert Curry
Stars MS	1234 Blountstown Hwy	Tallahassee, FL	32304-2715	850-681-7827	827-1263	6-8	A. Samet Kul
Steele/Collins Charter MS	428 W Tennessee St	Tallahassee, FL	32301-1026	850-681-1929	224-1663	6-8	Kim Ardley
Student Leadership Academy	200 Field Ave E	Venice, FL	34285-3936	941-485-5551	485-2694	6-8	Vickie Marble
Summerville Advantage Charter S	11575 SW 243rd St	Homestead, FL	33032-7163	305-253-2123	253-4304	K-5	Minelli Duclerc
Summit Academy	303 W Moody Blvd	Bunnell, FL	32110-6047	386-586-7500	586-7510	6-8	Shawn Viecelli
Summit Charter Central S	720 W Princeton St	Orlando, FL	32804-5214	407-244-5920	244-5923	3-8	
Summit Charter S	1250 N Maitland Ave	Maitland, FL	32751-4305	407-599-4001	599-4004	K-8	Steve Palmer
Suncoast S for Innovative Studies	1300 S Tuttle Ave	Sarasota, FL	34239-2603	941-952-5277	952-5087	K-8	Phil Blankenship
Sunrise Community Charter S	7100 W Oakland Park Blvd	Sunrise, FL	33313-1015	954-747-1550	747-1650	K-5	Erica Whitmoyer
Sunshine ES	2210 Pierce St	Hollywood, FL	33020-4414	954-925-0155	925-0209	K-5	Dr. Steven Montes
Sweetwater Branch Academy	1000 NE Ave Bldg C	Gainesville, FL	32601	352-375-8838	241-5125	6-7	Murat Cetin
Tampa Bay Academy	12012 Boyette Rd	Riverview, FL	33569-5631	813-677-6700	677-5467	K-12	Joanie Rutherford
Tampa Charter S	5429 Beaumont Center # 800	Tampa, FL	33634	813-887-3800	885-9626	3-8	Sheila Thomley
Tampa Transitional School of Excellence	3916 E Hillsborough Ave	Tampa, FL	33610-4542	813-231-4893	232-9680		George Shaw
Terrace Community Charter S	11734 Jefferson Rd	Thonotosassa, FL	33592-2101	813-987-6555	987-6565	6-8	Gary Hocevar
Therapeutic Learning Center	1955 US Highway 1 S	Saint Augustine, FL	32086	904-824-8932	824-8063	PK-PK	Paulette Hudson
Touchdowns4Life Charter S	10044 W McNab Rd	Tamarac, FL	33321-1894	954-726-8785	726-9590	6-8	Wayne Neunie
Treasure Village Montessori Charter S	86731 Old Hwy	Islamorada, FL	33036-3129	305-522-3611	852-3482	K-5	Kelly Astin
Tree of Knowledge Learning Academy	1145 NW 14th Ter	Miami, FL	33136-1050	877-865-5235	470-7490	K-12	Mordechai Salfer
Trinity S for Children	2402 W Osborne Ave	Tampa, FL	33603-1434	813-874-2402	874-2412	K-5	Madeline O'Dea

School	Address	City,State	Zip code	Telephone	Fax	Grade	Contact
Trinity Upper S	4807 N Armenia Ave	Tampa, FL	33603-1427	813-874-2402	874-2412	6-8	
UCP Charter S	3305 S Orange Ave	Orlando, FL	32806-6125	407-852-3333	852-3301	PK-K	Madeline O'Dea
UCP Child Development Center	448 W Donegan Ave	Kissimmee, FL	34741-2335	407-932-3445	932-3480	PK-PK	Ilene Wilkins
UCP East Charter S	2201 Crown Hill Blvd	Orlando, FL	32828-6872	407-281-5100	281-5127	PK-K	Sue Torres-Reyes
UCP East Orange Charter S	12046 Collegiate Way	Orlando, FL	32817-2157	407-281-0441	281-0442	PK-K	Ilene Wilkins
UCP Pine Hills Charter S	5800 Golf Club Pkwy	Orlando, FL	32808-4800	407-299-5553	299-5520	PK-1	Jennifer Park
UCP Seminole Child Development	3590 N US Highway 17/92	Lake Mary, FL	32746	407-322-6222	322-5596	PK-K	Ilene Wilkins
UCP Transitional Learning Academy	3305 S Orange Ave	Orlando, FL	32806-6125	407-852-3333	852-3301	6-8	Marife Gomez
USF/Patel Charter S	11801 USF Bull Run St	Tampa, FL	33617-5103	813-974-3831	974-1280	K-5	Ilene Wilkins
Village of Excellence Academy	8718 N 46th St	Temple Terrace, FL	33617-6002	813-988-8632	983-0683	K-5	L. Rylene Stein
Villages Charter HS	251 Buffalo Trl	Lady Lake, FL	32162-7176	352-259-2350	259-3850	9-12	Cametra Edwards
Villages Charter Intermediate Center	521 Old School Rd	Lady Lake, FL	32162-7170	352-259-2300	259-2056	2-4	Dr. Bill Zwick
Villages Charter MS	450 Village Campus Cir	Lady Lake, FL	32162-7169	352-259-0044	753-1113	5-8	Leanne Yerk
Villages Charter Primary Center	420 Village Campus Cir	Lady Lake, FL	32162-7169	352-259-7700	259-7707	PK-1	Dr. Peggy Irwin
Walton Academy	389 Dorsey Ave	Defuniak Spgs, FL	32435-3013	850-892-3999	892-7854	6-12	Leanne Yerk
Walton Academy of the Performing Arts	PO Box 7578	Tampa, FL	33673-7578	813-231-9272	231-9271	K-5	Bill Eddins
Wayman Academy of the Arts	1176 Labelle St	Jacksonville, FL	32205-6487	904-695-9995	695-9992	K-5	Tanika Walton
Wells Charter S	2426 Remington Blvd	Kissimmee, FL	34744-8467	407-697-1020	697-1021	K-8	Dr. Jim Williams
Western Academy Charter S	500 Royal Plaza Rd Ste F	Ryl Palm Bch, FL	33411-7688	561-792-4123	792-9905	K-8	Walter Thomas
Westminster Academy	830 29th St	Orlando, FL	32805-6219	407-841-6560	841-7311	K-12	Linda Terranova
Whispering Winds Charter S	PO Box 506	Chiefland, FL	32644-0506	352-490-5799	490-7242	K-8	
Wiener S of Opportunity	20000 NW 47th Ave Bldg 7	Miami Gardens, FL	33017	305-623-9631	623-9621	PK-8	Dr. J. Suzann Cornell
Wiener S of Opportunity South	11025 SW 84th St	Miami, FL	33173-3804	305-279-3064	279-2922	K-5	Elizabeth McGettigan
Wilson ES	306 Florida Ave	Lake Wales, FL	33853-3121	863-678-4211	678-4217	PK-5	Jenesa Lamons
Workforce Advantage Academy	2113 E South St	Orlando, FL	32803-6502	407-898-7228	898-6448	11-12	Beverly Lynne
Youth Co-Op Charter S	12051 W Okeechobee Rd	Hialeah Gardens, FL	33018-2933	305-819-8855	819-8455	K-8	Maritza Aragon

Georgia

School	Address	City,State	Zip code	Telephone	Fax	Grade	Contact
Academy of Lithonia	3235 Evans Mill Rd	Lithonia, GA	30038-3012	678-526-9655	526-9758	K-7	Paulette Bolton
Addison ES	3055 Ebenezer Rd	Marietta, GA	30066-4542	770-578-2700	578-2702	PK-5	Genie Byrd
Amana Academy	285 S Main St	Alpharetta, GA	30009-1937	678-624-0989	624-0892	K-6	Amaris Mohler
Atlanta Charter MS	820 Essie Ave SE	Atlanta, GA	30316-2425	678-904-0051	904-0052	6-8	Matt Underwood
Baconton Community Charter S	260 E Walton St	Baconton, GA	31716-7782	229-787-9999	787-0077	PK-12	Lynn Pinson
Berrien Academy Performance Lrng Ctr	1015 Exum Rd	Nashville, GA	31639-2730	229-686-6576	686-6580	9-12	Chris Huckans
Bishop Hall Charter S	1819 E Clay St	Thomasville, GA	31792-4736	229-227-1397	558-9420	9-12	Rich Johnson
Brighten Academy	3264 Brookmont Pkwy	Douglasville, GA	30135-2108	770-615-3680	615-3677	K-8	Soundra Pollocks
Central Educational Center	PO Box 280	Newnan, GA	30264-0280	678-423-2000	423-2008	9-12	Mark Whitlock
Challenge Charter Academy	8134 Geiger St NW Ste 12	Covington, GA	30014-1288	678-625-3975	625-6111	6-12	Ernetta Worthy
Chamblee Charter HS	3688 Chamblee Dunwoody Rd	Chamblee, GA	30341-2185	678-676-6902	676-6910	9-12	Rochelle Lowery
Charter Conservatory Liberal Arts/Tech.	149 Northside Dr E	Statesboro, GA	30458-1089	912-764-5888	489-8493	6-12	Dr. Kathy Harwood
Chesnut Charter ES	4576 N Peachtree Rd	Dunwoody, GA	30338-5892	678-676-7102	676-7110	PK-5	Dr. Richard Reid
Clubview ES	2836 Edgewood Rd	Columbus, GA	31906-1298	706-565-3017	565-3022	PK-5	Adele Lindsey
Coastal Empire Montessori Charter S	301 Buckhalter Rd	Savannah, GA	31405-6111	912-238-1973	238-1974	PK-K	
Connected Academy	86 School Dr	Alpharetta, GA	30009	770-667-2921	667-2926	11-12	Cynthia Burgess
Dekalb Academy of Tech & Environment	1833 Stone Mountain Lith Rd	Lithonia, GA	30058	770-484-5865	484-7785	K-8	Dr. Maury Wills
DeKalb PATH Academy	3007 Hermance Dr NE	Atlanta, GA	30319-2627	404-846-3242	846-3243	5-8	Suttiwan Cox
Destiny Academy of Excellence	3595 Linecrest Rd	Ellenwood, GA	30294-1839	404-328-0898	328-1294	9-12	Ben Jakes
Dooly County HS	712 N 3rd St	Vienna, GA	31092-1111	229-268-8181	268-1916	9-12	Randy Ford
Douglas Co. College & Career Institute	4600 Timber Ridge Dr	Douglasville, GA	30135-1225	770-651-2081	920-4158	9-12	Mandy Johnson
Drew Charter S	301 E Lake Blvd SE	Atlanta, GA	30317-3152	404-687-0001	687-0480	PK-8	Dr. Nicholas Stapleton
Dunwoody Springs Charter S	8100 Roberts Dr	Atlanta, GA	30350-4120	770-673-4060	673-4064	PK-5	Ivy Gainey
Fargo Charter S	PO Box 267	Fargo, GA	31631-0267	912-637-5242	637-5466	K-3	Danny Ellis
Floyd County College and Career Academy	100 Tom Poe Dr	Rome, GA	30161	706-236-1860	236-1862	9-12	Eric Waters
Forsyth County Academy	7745 Majors Rd	Cumming, GA	30041-7050	770-781-3141	455-7133	9-12	Brad Smith
Fulton Science Academy	1675 Hembree Rd	Alpharetta, GA	30009-2083	770-753-4141	753-4948	6-8	Kenan Sener
Futral Road ES	180 Futral Rd	Griffin, GA	30224-7454	770-229-3735	233-6001	PK-5	Larry Jones
Gateway to College Academy	555 N Indian Creek Dr	Clarkston, GA	30021-2361	678-891-3220	891-3610	9-12	Robert Wigfall
Green Acres ES	2000 Gober Ave SE	Smyrna, GA	30080-1111	678-842-6905	842-6907	PK-5	Mike Bivens
Gwinnett S of Math Science and Tech	3737 Brock Rd Bldg 100	Duluth, GA	30096	678-473-6292	542-2385	9-12	Dr. Jeff Mathews
Hapeville Charter MS	3535 S Fulton Ave	Hapeville, GA	30354-1701	404-767-7730	767-7706	6-8	Jannard Rainey
Imagine International Academy - Mableton	6688 Mableton Pkwy SE	Mableton, GA	30126-5302	678-384-8920		K-8	Michael Rossano
Imagine International Academy of Smyrna	4451 Atlanta Rd SE Ste 200	Smyrna, GA	30080-6557	678-370-0980	370-0981	K-8	Gloria Clarke
Imagine Wesley International Academy	1049 Custer Ave SE	Atlanta, GA	30316-3100	678-904-9137	904-9138	K-8	James Taylor
International Community S	3260 Covington Hwy	Decatur, GA	30032-1121	404-499-8969	499-8968	K-6	Laurent Ditmann
International Studies Magnet ES	2237 Cutts Dr	Albany, GA	31705-3899	229-431-3384	431-3381	PK-5	George Zeda
Jenkins-White Charter ES	800 15th Ave	Augusta, GA	30901-4145	706-737-7320	731-7651	PK-5	Janie Norris
Kennesaw Charter S	1370 Lockhart Dr NW	Kennesaw, GA	30144-7047	678-290-9628	290-9638	K-5	Mridula Hormes
KidsPeace S of Georgia	101 Kidspeace Dr	Bowdon, GA	30108-3447	770-437-7200	258-9128	4-12	William Isemann
Kingsley ES	2051 Brendon Dr	Dunwoody, GA	30338-4599	678-874-8902	874-8910	PK-5	Karen Graham
KIPP South Fulton	1286 Washington Ave	East Point, GA	30344-3537	678-278-0160	278-0165	5-8	Jondre Pryor
KIPP WAYS Academy	80 Joseph E Lowery Blvd NW	Atlanta, GA	30314-3421	404-475-1941	475-1946	5-8	Kimberly Karacalidis
Lake Oconee Academy	6350 Lake Oconee Pkwy	Greensboro, GA	30642	919-454-1562	453-1773	K-12	Otho Tucker Ph.D.
Lewis Academy of Excellence	8009 Carlton Rd	Riverdale, GA	30296-1208	770-909-6697	909-6699	K-5	Dr. Patricia Lewis
Marietta Charter S	368 Wright St SW	Marietta, GA	30064-3256	770-590-4430	590-4431	K-5	Christy Tureta
Mercer MS	201 Rommel Ave	Savannah, GA	31408-1636	912-965-6700	965-6719	6-8	Gloria Dukes
Mountain Education Center	218 School St	Blairsville, GA	30512	706-745-9575	745-3588	9-12	Judy Waldroup
Mountain Education Center	136 North Ave	Ellijay, GA	30540-3342	706-276-5002	276-5008	9-12	Julie Martin
Mountain Education Center	123 Mountain View Dr	Dahlonega, GA	30533-0307	706-864-0229	864-9391	9-12	Linda Gilreath
Mountain Education Center	191 Old Big A School Rd	Toccoa, GA	30577	706-886-3114	886-3127	9-12	Shirley Dillard
Mountain Education Center	328 Old Blairsville Rd	Cleveland, GA	30528	706-865-0727	865-0737	9-12	Stephen Gill
Murphey Charter MS	2610 Milledgeville Rd	Augusta, GA	30904-5181	706-737-7350	737-7353	6-8	Veronica Bolton
Neighborhood Charter S	688 Grant St SE	Atlanta, GA	30315-1420	404-624-6226	624-9093	K-5	Jill Kaechele
New Life Academy of Excellence	3159 Campus Dr Ste 100	Norcross, GA	30071-1492	770-248-3032	248-3033	K-8	Alphonsa Forward
North Springs HS of Arts & Sciences	7447 Roswell Rd NE	Atlanta, GA	30328-1026	770-551-2490	551-2498	9-12	Lisa Stueve
Odyssey Charter S	1485 Highway 34 E Ste B1	Newnan, GA	30265-6409	678-423-5155	423-5154	K-6	Andy Geeter
Oglethorpe Charter S	707 Stiles Ave	Savannah, GA	31415-5324	912-201-5075	201-5077	6-8	Kevin Wall
Peachtree Charter MS	4664 N Peachtree Rd	Atlanta, GA	30338-5898	678-676-7702	676-7710	6-8	Steve Donahue
Rainbow ES	2801 Kelley Chapel Rd	Decatur, GA	30034-2299	678-874-1702	874-1710	PK-5	Dr. Annette Roberts
Ridgeview Charter MS	5340 Trimble Rd NE	Atlanta, GA	30342-1413	404-843-7710	847-3292	6-8	Karen Cox
Sawyer Road ES	840 Sawyer Rd	Marietta, GA	30062-2263	770-429-9923	429-9936	K-5	Jill Sims
Sedalia Park ES	2230 Lower Roswell Rd	Marietta, GA	30068-3359	770-509-5162	509-5342	K-5	Dr. Patricia Thomas
Spalding Drive ES	130 W Spalding Dr NE	Atlanta, GA	30328-1999	770-551-5880	673-4090	PK-5	Christine Young
Talbot Co. Charter Alternative Academy	PO Box 515	Talbotton, GA	31827-0515	706-665-8098	665-8099	9-12	Jerome Harris
Taliaferro County S	557 Broad St NW	Crawfordville, GA	30631-2918	706-456-2575	456-2689	PK-12	Jemessyn Foster
TEACH Charter HS	4100 Old Milton Pkwy Ste 10	Alpharetta, GA	30005	770-475-7824	475-8870	9-12	Avni Cokavci
Tech HS	1043 Memorial Dr SE	Atlanta, GA	30316-1473	678-904-5091	904-5095	9-12	Elisa Falco
Unidos Dual Language Charter S	4475 Hendrix Dr	Forest Park, GA	30297-1244	404-361-3494	362-2498	PK-3	Nancy Said
University Community Academy	2050 Tiger Flowers Dr NW	Atlanta, GA	30314-1326	404-753-4050	753-0290	K-8	Dr. James Harris
Walton Career Academy	212 Bryant Rd	Monroe, GA	30655-2408	770-207-3150	266-4485	10-12	Mark Peevy
Walton HS	1590 Bill Murdock Rd	Marietta, GA	30062-5999	770-578-3225	578-3227	9-12	Judith McNeill
Woodland Charter ES	1130 Spalding Dr	Atlanta, GA	30350-5013	770-551-5890	673-4091	PK-5	Ruth Baskerville
World Language Academy	4670 Winder Hwy	Flowery Branch, GA	30542-3611	770-534-1080		K-5	

Hawaii

School	Address	City,State	Zip code	Telephone	Fax	Grade	Contact
Connections New Century Charter S	174 Kamehameha Ave	Hilo, HI	96720	808-961-3664	961-2665	K-12	John Thatcher
Education Laboratory	1776 University Ave	Honolulu, HI	96822	808-956-7833	956-7260	K-12	Fred Birkett
Hakipuu Learning Center	PO Box 1159	Kaneohe, HI	96744-1159	808-235-9155	235-9160	7-12	Charlene Hoe
Halau Ku Mana Charter S	2101 Makiki Heights Dr	Honolulu, HI	96822-2520	808-945-1600	945-1604	K-12	Deenie Music
Halau Lokahi Charter S	401 Waiakamilo Rd Unit 1A	Honolulu, HI	96817	808-832-3594	842-9800	K-12	Laara Allbrett
Hawaii Academy of Arts & Science	PO Box 1494	Pahoa, HI	96778-1494	808-965-3730	965-3733	K-12	Steve Hirakami
Hawai'i Technology Academy	94-810 Moloalo St	Waipahu, HI	96797	808-676-5444	676-5470	K-12	Jeff Piontek
Innovations Public Charter S	75-5815 Queen Kaahumanu Hwy	Kailua Kona, HI	96740-2013	808-327-6205	327-6209	1-7	Barbara Woerner
Kamaile ES	85-180 Ala Akau St	Waianae, HI	96792-2375	808-697-7110	697-7115	PK-6	Glen Kila
Kanuikapono Charter S	PO Box 12	Anahola, HI	96703-0012	808-823-9160	823-9140	4-8	Ipo Torio
Kanu O Ka 'Aina New Century Charter S	PO Box 398	Kamuela, HI	96743-0398	808-887-8144	887-8146	K-12	Dr. Ku Kahakalau
Ka 'Umeke Ka'eo Public Charter S	222 Desha Ave	Hilo, HI	96720-4815	808-933-3482	933-3488	K-6	Albert Nahale'a
Ka Waihona O Ka Na'auao Charter S	89-195 Farrington Hwy	Waianae, HI	96792-4102	808-620-9030	620-9036	K-8	Alvin Parker
Kawaikini Charter S	PO Box 662014	Lihue, HI	96766-7014	808-632-2032	246-4835	K-12	Chris Town
Ke Ana La'ahana Public Charter S	1500 Kalanianaole Ave	Hilo, HI	96720-4914	808-961-6228	961-6229	7-12	Carol Wilhelm
Ke Kula Ni'ihau Kekaha Public Charter S	PO Box 129	Kekaha, HI	96752-0129	808-337-0481	337-1289	PK-12	Haunani Seward
Ke Kula 'O Nawahiokalani'opu'u Charter S	PO Box 506	Keaau, HI	96749-0506	808-982-4260	966-7821	K-6	Kauanoe Kamana
Ke Kula O Samuel Kamakau Lab S	45-037 Kaneohe Bay Dr	Kaneohe, HI	96744-2417	808-235-9174	235-9173	K-12	Marci Sarsona
Kihei Charter S	300 Ohukai Rd Unit 214	Kihei, HI	96753	808-875-0700	874-6745	K-12	Mark Christiano
Kona Pacific Charter S	PO Box 115	Kealakekua, HI	96750-0115	808-322-4900	322-4906	K-4	Usha Kotner
Kualapu'u Charter ES	PO Box 260	Kualapuu, HI	96757-0260	808-567-6900	567-6906	K-6	Lydia Trinidad

School	Address	City,State	Zip code	Telephone	Fax	Grade	Contact
Kua O Ka La Public Charter S	PO Box 1413	Pahoa, HI	96778-1413	808-965-5098	965-9618	6-12	Susan Osborne
Kula Aupuni Niihau A Kahelelani Aloha	PO Box 690390	Makaweli, HI	96769-0390	808-337-2022	337-2033	K-12	Hedy Sullivan
Lanikai ES	140 Alala Rd	Kailua, HI	96734-3199	808-266-7844	266-7848	PK-6	David Sauceda
Thompson Academy	629 Pohukaina St Ste 3	Honolulu, HI	96813-5004	808-441-8001	586-3640	K-12	Diana Oshiro
Volcano S of Arts & Sciences	PO Box 845	Volcano, HI	96785-0845	808-985-9800	985-9898	K-8	Dr. David Rizor
Voyager Charter S	670 Auahi St Ste A5	Honolulu, HI	96813-5166	808-521-9770	521-9772	K-8	Susan Lee Deuber
Wai'alae ES	1045 19th Ave	Honolulu, HI	96816-4699	808-733-4880	733-4886	K-5	Wendy Lagareta
Waimea Charter MS	67-1229 Mamalahoa Hwy	Kamuela, HI	96743-8429	808-887-6090	887-6087	6-8	John Colson
Waters of Life Charter S	PO Box 1012	Kurtistown, HI	96760-1012	808-966-6175	982-7863	K-12	Katheryn Shay
West Hawaii Explorations Academy	73-4460 Queen Kaahumanu Hwy	Kailua Kona, HI	96740	808-327-4751	327-4750	7-12	Heather Nakakura

Idaho

School	Address	City,State	Zip code	Telephone	Fax	Grade	Contact
Academy	240 E Maple St	Pocatello, ID	83201-4647	208-232-1447	232-1448	K-8	Rafael Baca
ANSER Charter S	1187 W River St	Boise, ID	83702-7048	208-426-9840	426-9863	K-7	Dr. Suzanne Gregg
Blackfoot Charter Community Learning Ctr	2801 Hunters Loop	Blackfoot, ID	83221-6206	208-782-0744	782-1338	K-6	Fred Ball
Coeur D'Alene Charter Academy	4904 N Duncan Dr	Coeur d Alene, ID	83815-8329	208-676-1667	676-8667	6-12	Dan Nicklay
Compass Charter S	2511 W Cherry Ln	Meridian, ID	83642-1135	208-855-2802	895-0197	K-9	Kelly Trudeau
Falcon Ridge Charter S	278 S Ten Mile Rd	Kuna, ID	83634-1768	208-922-9228	922-4198	K-8	Julie Vermillion
Garden City Community Charter S	9165 W Chinden Blvd Ste 101	Garden City, ID	83714-1902	208-377-0011	377-0502	K-8	Cindy Hoovel
Idaho Arts Charter S	1220 5th St N	Nampa, ID	83687-3416	208-463-4324	468-0572	K-12	Jackie Collins
Idaho Distance Education Academy	PO Box 338	Deary, ID	83823-0338	208-877-1513	877-1713	K-12	Linda Sterk
Idaho Virtual Academy	1965 S Eagle Rd Ste 190	Meridian, ID	83642-9246	208-332-3559	322-3688	K-9	Cody Claver
Inspire Virtual Charter S	6128 W Fairview Ave Ste 1A	Boise, ID	83704-5000	208-332-4002	332-4008	K-12	Dr. Dallas Taylor
iSUCCEED Virtual HS	8950 W Emerald St Ste 150	Boise, ID	83704-8296	208-375-3116	375-3117	9-12	Dr. Clifford Green
Jefferson Charter S	1209 Adam Smith Ave	Caldwell, ID	83605-5487	208-455-8772	455-8713	K-12	Chuck Ward
Liberty Charter S	1063 E Lewis Ln	Nampa, ID	83686-8843	208-466-7952	466-7961	K-12	Becky Stallcop
McKenna Charter HS	675 S Haskett St	Mountain Home, ID	83647-3375	208-580-2449	580-2450	9-12	Larry Slade
Meridian Medical Arts Charter HS	1789 E Leighfield Dr	Meridian, ID	83646-2692	208-855-4075	855-4081	9-12	Scott Hill
Meridian Technical Charter HS	3800 N Locust Grove Rd	Meridian, ID	83646-5510	208-288-2928	288-5685	9-12	Christian Housel
Moscow Charter S	1723 E F St	Moscow, ID	83843-9571	208-883-3195	892-3855	K-6	Gordon Steinbis
North Star Charter S	1400 Park Ln	Eagle, ID	83616-3322	208-939-9600	939-6090	K-9	Phyllis Smith
North Valley Academy	202 14th Ave E	Gooding, ID	83330-1829	208-934-4567	934-4522	K-12	Judy Studebaker
Pocatello Community Charter S	995 S Arthur Ave	Pocatello, ID	83204-3400	208-478-2522	478-2622	K-8	Vern Anderson
Rolling Hills Charter S	8900 Horseshoe Bend Rd	Boise, ID	83714-3859	208-939-5400	939-5401	K-8	Vickie Scheuffele
Sandpoint Charter S	614 S Madison Ave	Sandpoint, ID	83864-8724	208-255-7771	263-9441	6-8	Alan Millar
Taylors Crossing Charter S	1445 Wood River Rd	Idaho Falls, ID	83401-5095	208-552-0397	529-2755	K-12	Gail Harding-Thomas
Upper Carmen Charter S	PO Box 33	Carmen, ID	83462-0033	208-756-4590	756-1594	K-6	Sue Smith
Victory Charter S	1081 E Lewis Ln	Nampa, ID	83686-8843	208-442-9400	442-9401	K-7	Dr. Marianne Saunders
Vision Charter S	20185 Lolo Ave	Caldwell, ID	83605-8088	208-455-9220	455-9121	K-8	Wendy OldenKamp
White Pine Charter S	PO Box 2825	Idaho Falls, ID	83403-2825	208-522-4432	522-4452	K-8	Charlotte Arnold
Xavier Charter S	771 N College Rd	Twin Falls, ID	83301-3382	208-933-9287	933-9289	K-8	Cindy Fulcher

Illinois

School	Address	City,State	Zip code	Telephone	Fax	Grade	Contact
ACE Technical Charter HS	5410 S State St	Chicago, IL	60609-6382	773-548-8705	548-8706	9-12	Geri Harston
ACT Charter S	4319 W Washington Blvd	Chicago, IL	60624-2232	773-626-4200	626-4268	6-12	Judy Vojta
Addams Alternative HS	1814 S Union Ave	Chicago, IL	60616-1045	312-563-1748	563-1756	9-12	
Amandla Charter S	6800 S Stewart Ave	Chicago, IL	60621-2441	773-396-8022		5-6	Erin Ferguson
Aspira - Antonia Pantoja Alternative HS	3121 N Pulaski Rd	Chicago, IL	60641-5447	773-427-0759	427-0872	9-12	Gabriela Reyes
ASPIRA at Haugan MS	3729 W Leland Ave	Chicago, IL	60625-5706	773-252-0970	267-3568	6-8	Norma Quintano
Aspira Early College S	3986 W Barry Ave	Chicago, IL	60618-6524	773-252-0970	267-3568	9-12	Abigail Ortiz
ASPIRA - Mirta Ramirez	1711 N California Ave	Chicago, IL	60647-5103	773-252-0970	342-8615	9-12	Karime Asaf
Austin Business & Entrepreneurship S	231 N Pine Ave	Chicago, IL	60644-2333	773-534-6316	534-6313	9-12	Dionelle Gary-Burton
Austin Career Education Center	5352 W Chicago Ave	Chicago, IL	60651-2857	773-626-6988	626-2641	9-12	Debra Williams
Beardstown Charter School Learning Acad	515 Canal St	Beardstown, IL	62618-2150	217-323-4529	323-4918	9-12	Carrie Martin
Bronzeville Academic Center	220 W 45th Pl	Chicago, IL	60609-3903	773-538-0059	995-4108	9-12	
Bronzeville Lighthouse Charter S	8 W Root St	Chicago, IL	60609-2931	773-535-1757	535-1459	PK-7	April Knox
Cambridge Lakes S	900 Wester Blvd	Pingree Grove, IL	60140-2050	847-464-4300	464-1872	PK-8	Karen Behrns
Catalyst Charter S	1616 S Spaulding Ave	Chicago, IL	60623-2653	773-534-1753		K-7	Michael Neis
Chicago International Charter S - Avalon	1501 E 83rd Pl	Chicago, IL	60619-6501	773-721-0858	731-0142	K-7	Anthony Chalmers
Chicago International Charter S Basil	1816 W Garfield Blvd	Chicago, IL	60609-5606	773-778-9455	778-9456	PK-8	Chenita Hardy
Chicago International Charter S Bucktown	2235 N Hamilton Ave	Chicago, IL	60647-3360	773-645-3321	645-3327	K-8	Turon Ivy
Chicago International Charter S - Irving	3820 N Spaulding Ave	Chicago, IL	60618-4413	773-433-5000	433-5009	K-5	Amy Torres
Chicago International Charter S Longwood	1309 W 95th St	Chicago, IL	60643	773-238-5330	238-5350	K-12	Robert Lang
Chicago International Charter S - Loomis	9535 S Loomis St	Chicago, IL	60643-1374	773-429-8955	429-8441	K-3	April Shaw
Chicago International Charter S Prairie	11530 S Prairie Ave	Chicago, IL	60628-5691	773-928-0480	928-6971	K-8	Aisha Strong
Chicago International Charter S W Belden	2245 N McVicker Ave	Chicago, IL	60639	773-637-9430	637-9791	K-8	Kristin Baldino
Chicago Intl Charter S Northtown	3900 W Peterson Ave Ste 1	Chicago, IL	60659-3162	773-478-3655	478-6029	9-12	Cheryl Kalkirtz
Chicago Intl Charter S Ralph Ellison	1817 W 80th St	Chicago, IL	60620-4557	312-478-4434	478-4494	9-10	Dr. Eboni Wilson
Chicago Intl Charter S Washington Park	6105 S Michigan Ave	Chicago, IL	60637-2119	773-324-3300	324-3302	K-8	Pamela Creed
Chicago Intl Charter S Wrightwood	8130 S California Ave	Chicago, IL	60652-2716	773-434-4575	434-2026	K-8	Dr. David Lewis
Chicago Math and Science Academy	1709 W Lunt Ave	Chicago, IL	60626-3212	773-761-8960	761-8961	6-12	Salim Ucan
Chicago Virtual Charter S	38 S Peoria St	Chicago, IL	60607-2628	866-612-1450	267-4489	K-8	Dr. Bruce Law
Community Services West - ASA	4651 W Madison St	Chicago, IL	60644-3646	773-921-1315	921-8324	9-12	
Community Youth Development Institute	7836 S Union Ave	Chicago, IL	60620-2409	773-224-2273	224-2214	9-12	
Dr. Pedro Albizu Campos HS	2739 W Division St	Chicago, IL	60622-2854	773-342-8022	342-6609	9-12	Lourdes Lugo
DuSable Leadership Academy	4934 S Wabash Ave	Chicago, IL	60615	773-535-1170	535-1912	9-12	Dr. Loretta Young-Wright
El Quarto Ano - Association House	1116 N Kedzie Ave	Chicago, IL	60651-4152	773-772-7170	772-8617	9-12	
Erie Charter S	2510 W Cortez St	Chicago, IL	60622-3422	773-486-7161	486-7234	K-2	Dr. Jane Montes
Field S	7019 N Ashland Blvd	Chicago, IL	60626-9817	773-534-2030	534-2189	4-8	Sunday Uwumarogie
Ford Academy: Power House Charter HS	3415 W Arthington St Fl 3	Chicago, IL	60624	773-533-7600		9-12	Sabrena Davis
Fort Bowman Academy Charter S	2734 Calvin Blvd	Cahokia, IL	62206-2707	618-332-7404	332-7561	K-12	Beth Peeples
Frazier Preparatory Academy	4027 W Grenshaw St	Chicago, IL	60624-3930	773-534-6776	534-6678	PK-6	Lakita Little
Galapagos Charter S	3814 W Iowa St	Chicago, IL	60651-3708	773-384-9400	384-4866	K-5	Michael Lane
Golder College Prep S	1454 W Superior St	Chicago, IL	60642	312-265-9925	243-8402	9-12	Stephanie Stewart
Houston HS	1231 S Pulaski Rd	Chicago, IL	60623-1234	773-762-2272	762-2065	9-12	
Howard Area Alternative HS	7647 N Paulina St	Chicago, IL	60626-1017	773-381-0366	338-7693	9-12	Benjamin Churchill
KIPP Ascend Charter S	715 S Kildare Ave	Chicago, IL	60624-3564	773-533-1770	533-1784	5-8	Jim O'Conner
Latino Youth Alternative HS	2001 S California Ave	Chicago, IL	60608	773-648-2130	648-2098	9-12	Guadalupe Martinez
LEARN Charter S	1132 S Homan Ave	Chicago, IL	60624-4344	773-826-6330	826-0015	PK-8	Courtney Francis
Legacy Charter S	4217 W 18th St	Chicago, IL	60623-2325	773-542-1640	542-1699	PK-3	Lisa Kenner
Locke Charter Academy	3141 W Jackson Blvd	Chicago, IL	60612-2729	773-265-7230	265-7258	PK-8	Lennie Jones
Lozano Leadership Academy	2570 S Blue Island Ave	Chicago, IL	60608-4817	773-890-0055	890-1537	9-12	
McKinley Lakeside Campus	2929 S Wabash Ave	Chicago, IL	60616	773-375-1999	375-6334	9-12	
Namaste S	3737 S Paulina St	Chicago, IL	60609-2047	773-715-9558	376-6495	K-3	Allison Slade
Noble Street Charter S	1010 N Noble St	Chicago, IL	60642-4011	773-862-1449	278-0421	9-12	William Olsen
North Lawndale College Prep at Collins	1313 S Sacramento Dr	Chicago, IL	60623-2218	773-542-1490	542-6955	9-12	Evelyn Murdock
North Lawndale College Prep Charter HS	1616 S Spaulding Ave	Chicago, IL	60623-2653	773-542-1490	542-1492	9-12	Robert Karpinski
Olive Harvey Middle College S	10001 S Woodlawn Ave	Chicago, IL	60628-1696	773-291-6517	291-6199	9-12	Stefan Fisher
Passages Charter S	1643 W Bryn Mawr Ave	Chicago, IL	60660-4106	773-433-3530	769-3229	PK-5	Shawnee Newsome
Perspectives - Calumet HS of Technology	8131 S May St	Chicago, IL	60620-3007	773-358-6120	358-6129	9-12	Christina Page
Perspectives Charter S	1930 S Archer Ave	Chicago, IL	60616-6505	312-225-7400	225-7411	6-12	Traci Wright
Perspectives Charter S Calumet Campus	8131 S May St	Chicago, IL	60620-3007	773-358-6100	358-6199	9-12	Glennese Ray
Perspectives Charter S - Calumet MS	8131 S May St	Chicago, IL	60620-3007	773-358-6300	358-6399	7-8	Tamara Davis
Perspectives/IIT Math & Science Academy	3663 S Wabash Ave	Chicago, IL	60653-1032	773-358-6800	358-6055	6-12	Mary Cummane
Plato Learning Academy	5545 W Harrison St	Chicago, IL	60644-5367	773-413-3090	413-3095	K-5	Reesheda Graham
Polaris Charter Academy	620 N Sawyer Ave	Chicago, IL	60624-1598	773-535-8652	534-6645	K-8	Tracy Kwock
Prairie Crossing Charter S	1571 Jones Point Rd	Grayslake, IL	60030-3536	847-543-9722	543-9744	K-8	Myron Dagley
Pritzker College Prep Campus	4131 W Cortland St	Chicago, IL	60639-4923	773-862-1449	278-0421	9-12	Pablo Sierra
Prologue Alternative HS	640 W Irving Park Rd	Chicago, IL	60613-3106	773-935-9925	665-8357	9-12	Baboucarr Joof
Providence Englewood Charter S	6515 S Ashland Ave	Chicago, IL	60636-3003	773-434-0202	434-0196	K-7	Angela Johnson-Williams
Rauner College Prep Campus	1337 W Ohio St	Chicago, IL	60642-6430	773-862-1449	278-0421	9-12	Eric Thomas
Robertson Charter S	2240 E Geddes Ave	Decatur, IL	62526-5127	217-428-7072	428-9214	K-8	Cordell Ingram
Rowe - Clark Math & Science Academy	3645 W Chicago Ave	Chicago, IL	60651-3934	773-242-2212	826-6936	9-12	
Shabazz International Charter S	7823 S Ellis Ave	Chicago, IL	60619-3213	773-651-1221	651-0302	K-8	Makita Kheperu
Simon Academy	3348 S Kedzie Ave	Chicago, IL	60623-5114	773-890-3129	847-2855	9-12	
SIU Charter S of East St. Louis	601 James R Thompson Blvd	E Saint Louis, IL	62201-1129	618-482-8370	482-8372	9-12	Anthony Neal
Sizemore Academy of B Shabazz	1540 W 84th St	Chicago, IL	60620-3918	773-779-5666	779-5668	K-8	Soyini Walton
Springfield Ball Charter S	2530 E Ash St	Springfield, IL	62703-5600	217-525-3275	525-3316	PK-8	Nicole Gales
Sullivan House Alt HS	8164 S South Chicago Ave	Chicago, IL	60617-1041	773-978-8680	375-1482	9-12	
Tomorrows Builders Charter S	PO Box 6126	E Saint Louis, IL	62202-6126	618-874-1671	874-8451	9-12	Vickie Kimmel Forby
Truman Middle College HS	1145 W Wilson Ave	Chicago, IL	60640-5691	773-907-4840	907-4844	9-12	
UCCS - Donoghue Campus	707 E 37th St	Chicago, IL	60653-1406	773-729-5300	729-5290	PK-5	Nicole Woodard-Iliev
UCCS - North Kenwood/Oakland Campus	1119 E 46th St	Chicago, IL	60653-4403	773-536-2399	536-2435	K-8	Tanika Island-Smith
UCCS - Woodlawn Campus	6420 S University Ave	Chicago, IL	60637-3608	773-752-8101	324-0653	6-12	Barbara Crock
UCCS - Woodson Campus	4444 S Evans Ave	Chicago, IL	60653-3519	773-624-0700	624-0707	6-8	Jared Washington

School	Address	City,State	Zip code	Telephone	Fax	Grade	Contact
UNO Charter S - Archer Heights Campus I	4248 W 47th St	Chicago, IL	60632-4402	773-579-3470	376-5605	K-8	Christopher Allen
UNO Charter S - Archer Heights Campus II	4248 W 47th St	Chicago, IL	60632-4402	773-579-3470	376-5605	K-8	Sussan Oladipo
UNO Charter S - Bartolome De Las Casas	1641 W 16th St	Chicago, IL	60608-2039	312-432-3224	432-1066	K-8	Catherine Rich
UNO Charter S - Carlos Fuentes Campus	2845 W Barry Ave	Chicago, IL	60618-7015	312-279-9826	279-9852	K-8	Thomas Denneen
UNO Charter S - Octavio Paz Campus	2401 W Congress Pkwy	Chicago, IL	60612-3534	312-432-1170	432-1180	4-8	Dan Goodwin
UNO Charter S - Octavio Paz Campus	2651 W 23rd St	Chicago, IL	60608-3609	773-890-1054		K-3	Vanessa McNorton
UNO Charter S - Officer Donald Marquez	2916 W 47th St	Chicago, IL	60632-1907	773-321-2200	321-2250	K-8	Anik Zampini
UNO Charter S - Rufino Tamayo Campus	5135 S California Ave	Chicago, IL	60632-2124	773-434-6355	434-5036	K-8	Lori Sweeney
UNO Veterans Memorial HS	4248 W 47th St Fl 3	Chicago, IL	60632	773-579-3480	376-5785	9-12	Josephine Gomez
Urban Prep Academy Charter S	6130 S Wolcott Ave	Chicago, IL	60636-2100	773-535-9678	755-1050	9-12	Tim King
Urban Prep Academy Charter S	6201 S Stewart Ave	Chicago, IL	60621-3247	773-535-9724	535-0012	9-10	Dennis Lacewell
Westside Holistic Alternative HS	4909 W Division St	Chicago, IL	60651-3108	773-265-8651		9-12	Daisy Lopez
West Town Academy Alternative HS	2039 W Fulton St	Chicago, IL	60612	312-563-9044	563-9672	9-12	
Young Womens Leadership S	2641 S Calumet Ave	Chicago, IL	60616-2901	312-949-9400	949-9142	7-12	Margaret Small
YouthBuild McLean County Charter S	502 S Morris Ave Unit D	Bloomington, IL	61701-4891	309-827-7507	827-9035	9-12	Tory Kleinhans
Youth Connection Charter S	10 W 35th St Ste 11F4-2	Chicago, IL	60616	312-328-0799	328-0971	9-12	Madeline Matthews
Youth Connection Leadership Academy	3424 S State St Fl 2	Chicago, IL	60616-5000	312-225-4668	225-4862	9-12	

Indiana

School	Address	City,State	Zip code	Telephone	Fax	Grade	Contact
Bowman Leadership Academy	975 W 6th Ave	Gary, IN	46402-1708	219-883-4826	883-1331	K-9	
Brown Charter Academy	3600 N German Church Rd	Indianapolis, IN	46235-8504	317-891-0730	891-0908	K-8	Thelma Wyatt
Campagna Academy Charter S	7403 Cline Ave	Schererville, IN	46375-2645	219-322-8614	322-8436	9-12	Bruce Hillman
Challenge Foundation Academy	3980 Meadows Dr	Indianapolis, IN	46205-3114	317-803-3182		K-12	Dr. Charles Schlegel
Charter School of the Dunes	860 N Lake St	Gary, IN	46403-1070	219-939-9690	939-9031	K-8	Deborah Conkle
Christel House Academy	2717 S East St	Indianapolis, IN	46225-2104	317-783-4690	783-4693	K-8	Carey Dahncke
Community Montessori S	4102 Saint Joseph Rd	New Albany, IN	47150-9750	812-948-1000	948-0441	PK-9	Barbara Burke-Fondren
Decatur Discovery Academy	5125 Decatur Blvd	Indianapolis, IN	46241-7511	317-856-0900		9-12	
East Chicago Lighthouse Charter S	3916 Pulaski St	East Chicago, IN	46312-2420	219-378-7450	378-7460	K-6	Tess Mitchner
East Chicago Urban Enterprise Academy	1402 E Chicago Ave	East Chicago, IN	46312-3587	219-392-3650	392-3652	K-7	
Flanner House ES	2424 Dr Mrtn Lthr Kng Jr St	Indianapolis, IN	46208	317-925-4231	923-9632	K-7	Myron Richardson
Galileo Charter S	777 N 12th St	Richmond, IN	47374-2476	765-983-3709		K-5	Kevin Handley
Gary Lighthouse Charter S	3201 Pierce St	Gary, IN	46408-1100	219-884-2407	884-2420	K-8	Chrissy Hart
Geist Montessori S	6633 W 900 N	Mc Cordsville, IN	46055-9761	317-335-1158	335-3457	K-8	Cynthia Thompson
Herron Charter S	110 E 16th St	Indianapolis, IN	46202-2404	317-231-0010	231-3759	9-12	Janet Harmon McNeal
Hope Academy	8102 Clearvista Pkwy	Indianapolis, IN	46256-1661	317-572-9356	849-1455	K-12	Gale Stone
Imagine Indiana Life Sciences Academy E	4352 N Mitthoefer Rd	Indianapolis, IN	46235-1224	317-890-9100		K-5	
Imagine MASTer Academy	2000 N Wells St Bldg 6	Fort Wayne, IN	46808	260-420-8395	423-3508	K-6	
Imagine Schools on Broadway	2320 Broadway	Fort Wayne, IN	46807-1104	260-458-8395	458-8355	K-5	Ron DelaCuesta
Indiana Math and Science Academy	4575 W 38th St	Indianapolis, IN	46254-3313	317-298-0025	298-0038	6-12	John Aytekin
Indianapolis Lighthouse Charter S	1780 Sloan Ave	Indianapolis, IN	46203-3640	317-351-1534	351-1804	K-8	Kelli Marshall
Indianapolis Metropolitan HS	1635 W Michigan St	Indianapolis, IN	46222-3852	317-524-4262	524-4001	9-12	Scott Bess
Irvington Community S	6705 Julian Ave	Indianapolis, IN	46219-6642	317-357-5359	357-9752	K-12	Timothy Ehrgott
Johnson Academy	7908 S Anthony Blvd	Fort Wayne, IN	46816-2504	260-441-8727	441-9357	K-8	Steve Bollier
Joshua Academy	867 E Walnut St	Evansville, IN	47713-2512	812-401-6300	401-6307	K-5	
KIPP Indianapolis College Prep	1740 E 30th St	Indianapolis, IN	46218-2605	317-637-9780	637-9784	5-8	Shani Ratcliff
KIPP Lead College Prep Charter	150 W 15th Ave	Gary, IN	46407-1219	219-979-9236	979-2611	5-7	April Goble
Lawrence Early College HS	7250 E 75th St	Indianapolis, IN	46256-1914	317-964-8080	964-8089	9-12	Dr. Scott Syverson
Monument Lighthouse Charter S	4002 N Franklin Rd	Indianapolis, IN	46226-5297	317-897-2472	897-2460	K-7	Jamie Brady
New Community S	710 North St	Lafayette, IN	47901-1158	765-420-9617	420-9672	K-7	Daniel Beaver
Options Charter S	PO Box 3790	Carmel, IN	46082-3790	317-815-2098	846-3806	9-12	Barbara Maschino
Options Charter S - Noblesville	9945 Cumberland Pointe Blvd	Noblesville, IN	46060	317-773-8659		9-12	Mike Gustin
Renaissance Academy	4093 W US Highway 20	La Porte, IN	46350-8269	219-878-8711	311-6038	PK-8	Kieran McHugh
Rural Community S	PO Box 85	Graysville, IN	47852-0085	812-382-4500	382-4055	K-8	
Signature S	610 Main St	Evansville, IN	47708-1618	812-421-1820	421-9189	9-12	Vicki Snyder
Southeast Neighborhood S of Excellence	1601 Barth Ave	Indianapolis, IN	46203-2743	317-423-0204	631-4401	K-12	Dr. J.C. Lasmanis
Tindley Accelerated S	3960 Meadows Dr	Indianapolis, IN	46205-3114	317-545-1745	547-4415	6-12	Marcus Robinson
21st Century Charter S	556 Washington St	Gary, IN	46402-1915	219-886-9339	886-9333	K-12	Angela West
Veritas Academy	530 E Ireland Rd	South Bend, IN	46614-2660	574-287-3230	287-2643	K-8	Angela Piazza
West Gary Lighthouse Charter S	725 Clark Rd	Gary, IN	46406-1822	219-977-9583	977-9725	K-6	Hilary Lewis

Iowa

School	Address	City,State	Zip code	Telephone	Fax	Grade	Contact
Elma ES	PO Box 298	Elma, IA	50628-0298	641-393-2280		PK-6	Robert Hughes
eSigourney Entrepreneurial Academy	107 W Marion St	Sigourney, IA	52591-1312	641-622-2025		7-12	Jason Munn
Iowa Central Charter HS	PO Box 49	Burnside, IA	50521-0049	515-359-2235	359-2236	9-12	Mike Jorgensen
Lincoln Academy of Fine Arts	318 E 7th St	Davenport, IA	52803-5507	563-324-0497	322-7503	PK-5	Jeff Womack
Northeast Iowa Charter HS	PO Box 54	Maynard, IA	50655-0054	563-637-2283	637-2294	11-12	John Johnson
NW Iowa Charter HS	300 N 8th Ave W	Hartley, IA	51346-1050	712-928-3406	928-2152	9-12	Mark Petersen
Prescott ES	1151 White St	Dubuque, IA	52001-5005	563-552-4200	552-4201	PK-5	Christine McCarron
Storm Lake/Iowa Central/Buena Vista HS	621 Tornado Dr	Storm Lake, IA	50588-2277	712-732-8065	732-8068	9-12	Michael Hanna

Kansas

School	Address	City,State	Zip code	Telephone	Fax	Grade	Contact
Basehor-Linwood Virtual Charter S	2108 N 155th St	Basehor, KS	66007-9395	913-724-1727	724-4518	K-12	Brenda DeGroot
Career Academy of McPherson County	801 E 1st St	Mc Pherson, KS	67460-3613	620-241-9350		9-12	Kent Nye
Cornerstone Alternative HS	720 E 7th St	Galena, KS	66739-1704	620-783-4499	783-1718	9-12	Jeff Eberhart
Delia Charter S	PO Box 99	Delia, KS	66418-0099	785-771-3470	771-3461	PK-8	Pam Sumner
Dickinson County Learning Center	108 N Factory	Enterprise, KS	67441-9104	785-263-8330	493-0770	9-12	Larry Patrick
Erie HS	410 W 3rd St	Erie, KS	66733-1323	620-244-3287	244-3290	9-12	Ted Hill
Extend HS	124 W Central Ave	El Dorado, KS	67042-2138	316-322-4892	322-4893	9-12	Tammy Fellers
Galesburg S	PO Box 147	Galesburg, KS	66740-0147	620-763-2470	763-2224	K-8	Doug Reed
Holman Academy of Excellence	3334 Haskell Ave	Kansas City, KS	66104-4225	913-627-4200	627-4201	K-5	Earl Williams
Hope Street Academy	1900 SW Hope St	Topeka, KS	66604	785-438-4280	271-3684	8-12	Dale Noll
Insight S of Kansas	16740 W 175th St	Olathe, KS	66062-8984	913-686-5600	664-2796	9-12	
Kinsley-Offerle JSHS	716 Colony Ave	Kinsley, KS	67547-1155	620-659-2126	659-2180	7-12	William King
Lawrence Virtual S	2145 Louisiana St	Lawrence, KS	66046-3001	785-832-5620	832-5622	K-12	Gary Lewis
Learning By Design Charter S	150 Stewart Ave	Haysville, KS	67060-1602	316-554-2331			Terry Eis
Mulvane Academy	PO Box 130	Mulvane, KS	67110-0130	316-777-3070	777-3072	9-12	Barbie Hamlin
Parsons Health Careers Academy	2900 Southern Ave	Parsons, KS	67357-4652	620-421-5950		10-12	Linda Proehl
Peoria Street Learning Center	PO Box 1270	Louisburg, KS	66053-1270	913-837-3458	837-3458	9-12	John Brooks
Pleasantview Academy	5013 S Dean Rd	Hutchinson, KS	67501-9123	620-662-5516	662-5031	PK-12	Terry Fehrenbach
St. Marks S	19001 W 29th St N	Colwich, KS	67030-9753	316-796-1466	796-2548	K-8	Mindy Bruce
Service Valley Charter Academy	21101 Wallace Rd	Parsons, KS	67357	620-421-3449	421-3640	K-8	Mike Ward
Smoky Valley Virtual Charter S	1/2 Viking Blvd	Lindsborg, KS	67456-1914	785-227-4254	227-4292	4-12	Marla Elmquist
Stafford Economic Development Charter S	PO Box 370	Stafford, KS	67578-0370	620-234-5248	234-6041	12-12	Jim Cox
Sterling Academy	125 W Cooper St	Sterling, KS	67579-2500	620-278-4215	278-3882	K-6	Judith Best
Thomas County Academy	710 W 3rd St	Colby, KS	67701-1901	785-460-5000	460-5050	5-8	Diana Wieland
Turning Point Learning Center	315 S Market St	Emporia, KS	66801-4731	620-341-2455	341-2456		Terri Peckham
21st Century Learning Academy	PO Box 6	Mullinville, KS	67109-0006	620-548-2289	548-2389	K-12	Darrel Kohlman
Ulysses Career Learning Academy	111 S Baughman St	Ulysses, KS	67880-2402	620-356-3644		9-12	Sheila Koop
Walden Center Charter S	401 S Hamilton St	Pratt, KS	67124-2534	620-672-4555	672-4558	8-12	Mike Shklar
Walton 21st Century Rural Life ES	PO Box 140	Walton, KS	67151-0140	620-837-3161	837-5669	K-8	Natise Vogt
West Franklin Charter S	PO Box 409	Williamsburg, KS	66095-0409	785-746-5766	746-5748	K-12	Robert Allen
White City Charter JHS	PO Box 8	White City, KS	66872-0008	785-349-2211	349-2138	6-8	Adam McDaniel
Yoder Charter S	PO Box 78	Yoder, KS	67585-0078	620-465-2605	465-2307	K-8	Delon Martens

Kentucky

School	Address	City,State	Zip code	Telephone	Fax	Grade	Contact
Fayette Regional S	3475 Spurr Rd	Lexington, KY	40511-8971	859-246-2806	246-2817	6-12	Ann Burns

Louisiana

School	Address	City,State	Zip code	Telephone	Fax	Grade	Contact
Abramson Science and Tech Charter S	5552 Read Blvd	New Orleans, LA	70127-3104	504-244-4416	244-4417	K-10	Cuneyt Dokmen
Akili Academy of New Orleans	1700 Pratt Dr	New Orleans, LA	70122-2408	504-274-3642		K-1	Sean Gallagher
Algiers Technology Academy	6501 Berkley Dr	New Orleans, LA	70131-5513	504-373-6282	433-7986	9-12	Dr. Henderson Lewis
Ashe Charter S	401 Nashville Ave	New Orleans, LA	70115-2142	504-486-0804	486-0540	K-7	Aqua Stovall
Audubon Charter S	428 Broadway St	New Orleans, LA	70118-3514	504-862-5135	866-1691	PK-8	Janice Dupuy
Avoyelles Charter S	201 Longfellow Rd	Mansura, LA	71350-4292	318-240-8285	253-8453	K-12	Julie Durand
Behrman S	715 Opelousas Ave	New Orleans, LA	70114-2499	504-324-7030	309-8174	PK-8	Rene Lewis-Carter
Belle Chase Academy	100 5th St	Belle Chasse, LA	70037-1002	504-433-5850	433-5590	K-8	Jane Dye
Capdau Charter S	3821 Franklin Ave	New Orleans, LA	70122-6099	504-872-9257	872-0393	PK-8	Heidi Sargent
Capdau-UNO Early College HS	4621 Canal St	New Orleans, LA	70119-5807	504-373-6297	484-3487	9-12	Michael Booker Ed.D.
Capitol PreCollege Academy for Boys	1000 N 23rd St	Baton Rouge, LA	70802-3337	225-343-0745	343-0761	9-12	Vincent Perry
Capitol PreCollege Academy for Girls	1000 N 23rd St	Baton Rouge, LA	70802-3337	225-383-0353	387-1635	9-12	Linda Lewis
Children's Charter S	1143 North St	Baton Rouge, LA	70802-4547	225-387-9273	387-9272	PK-5	Michael Eskridge
City Park Academy	2733 Esplanade Ave	New Orleans, LA	70119-3332	504-940-1740	948-8688	K-8	Christine Mitchell
Community S for Apprenticeship Learning	1555 Madison Ave	Baton Rouge, LA	70802-3460	225-336-1410	336-1414	6-8	Dujan Johnson

School	Address	City,State	Zip code	Telephone	Fax	Grade	Contact
Delhi Charter S	6940 Highway 17	Delhi, LA	71232-7021	318-878-0433	878-0434	K-12	Phillip Gaharan
Easton HS	3019 Canal St	New Orleans, LA	70119-6305	504-324-7400	324-7946	9-12	Alexina Medley
Einstein Charter S	5100 Cannes St	New Orleans, LA	70129-1203	504-324-7450	254-4121	K-8	Shawn Toranto
Eisenhower S	3700 Tall Pines Dr	New Orleans, LA	70131-8499	504-398-7125	398-7129	K-8	Monica Boudouin
Esperanza Charter S	4407 S Carrollton Ave	New Orleans, LA	70119-6823	504-373-6272	432-6301	K-8	Melinda Martinez
Fischer S	1801 L B Landry Ave	New Orleans, LA	70114-6166	504-304-3976	363-1013	PK-8	Dahme Bolden
Franklin HS	2001 Leon C Simon Dr	New Orleans, LA	70122-3525	504-286-2600	286-2642	9-12	Tim Rusnak
Glencoe Charter S	4491 Highway 83	Franklin, LA	70538-7500	337-923-6900	923-0982	K-8	Michael Toney Parrie
Glen Oaks MS	5300 Monarch Ave	Baton Rouge, LA	70811-5628	225-357-3790	357-1841	6-8	John McCain
Green Charter S	2319 Valence St	New Orleans, LA	70115-5959	504-304-3532		K-8	Jay Altman
Harte ES	5300 Berkley Dr	New Orleans, LA	70131-7204	504-373-6281	398-7103	PK-8	Jamar McKneely
Haynes Charter ES	356 East Blvd	Baton Rouge, LA	70802-5914	225-774-1311	774-1323	PK-5	Diana Haynes
Hughes Academy	3519 Trafalgar St	New Orleans, LA	70119-2041	504-352-4453	910-3065	PK-6	John Alford
Hynes Charter S	3774 Gentilly Blvd	New Orleans, LA	70122-6128	504-324-7160	948-1750	PK-8	Michelle Douglas
Intercultural Charter S	5075 Willowbrook Dr	New Orleans, LA	70129	504-255-9170	255-9001	PK-5	Peta LeBlanc
International School	1400 Camp St	New Orleans, LA	70130-4208	504-654-1088	654-1086	K-8	Melanie Tennyson
Jefferson Community Charter S	3528 Montford St	Jefferson, LA	70121-1824	504-836-0808	828-6888	6-8	Glenn Gennaro
Karr HS	3332 Huntlee Dr	New Orleans, LA	70131-7046	504-373-6268	398-7118	9-12	John Hiser
King Charter S for Science & Tech	PO Box 742417	New Orleans, LA	70174-2417	504-940-2243	940-2276	PK-9	Doris Hicks
KIPP Believe College Prep S	1607 S Carrollton Ave	New Orleans, LA	70118-2825	504-304-8857	304-8862	4-7	Adam Meinig
KIPP Central City Academy	PO Box 13567	New Orleans, LA	70185-3567	504-373-6290	302-9737	5-8	Todd Purvis
KIPP Central City PS	PO Box 13567	New Orleans, LA	70185-3567	504-373-6290	302-9737	K-1	Korbin Johnson
Kipp McDonogh 15 S	721 Saint Philip St	New Orleans, LA	70116-2795	504-566-1706	592-8515	PK-8	Heidi Campbell
Lafayette Academy	2727 S Carrollton Ave	New Orleans, LA	70118-4387	504-861-8370		K-7	Mickey Landry
Lafayette Charter HS	516 E Pinhook Rd	Lafayette, LA	70501-8610	337-261-8981	235-6187	9-12	Jody Slaughter-Duhon
Lake Forest Charter S	12000 Hayne Blvd	New Orleans, LA	70128-1127	504-826-7140	248-7020	K-8	Mardele Early
Louisiana S for Agricultural Sciences	5303 Highway 115	Bunkie, LA	71322-4301	318-346-2762	346-4479	8-12	Debbie Bain
Lusher Charter S	5624 Freret St	New Orleans, LA	70115-6547	504-304-3960	861-1839	6-12	Kathleen Riedlinger
Lusher Charter S	7315 Willow St	New Orleans, LA	70118-5232	504-862-5110	309-4171	K-5	Kathy Reidlinger
MAX Charter S	PO Box 2072	Thibodaux, LA	70310-0001	985-227-9500	227-9515	1-8	Cleveland Hill Ph.D.
McDonogh 32 S	800 De Armas St	New Orleans, LA	70114-4414	504-373-6285	361-7957	K-8	Lee Green
McDonogh 42 S	1651 N Tonti St	New Orleans, LA	70119-2540	504-942-3660	309-8031	K-8	Marion Johnson
Milestone/Sabis Charter S	5951 Patton St	New Orleans, LA	70115-3232	504-894-0557	894-0235	K-8	Catherine Boozer
Miller-McCoy Academy for Math & Business	7301 Dwyer Rd	New Orleans, LA	70126-4215	504-303-2084		6-9	Tiffany Hardrick
Moton ES	6820 Chef Menteur Hwy	New Orleans, LA	70126	504-245-1400	248-7300	PK-7	Paulette Bruno
Nelson Charter S	3121 Saint Bernard Ave	New Orleans, LA	70119-1916	504-943-1311	943-1311	PK-8	Edward Brown
New Orleans Charter Science & Math Acdmy	5625 Loyola Ave	New Orleans, LA	70115-5014	504-324-7061	309-4178	9-12	Bridget Ramsey
New Orleans Charter Sci/Math Academy	7301 Dwyer Rd	New Orleans, LA	70126-4215	504-274-3666		9-12	Ben Marcovitz
New Orleans College Prep S	3127 Martin Luther King Jr	New Orleans, LA	70125	504-373-6271		6-12	Ben Kleban
New Orleans Free Academy	3601 Camp St	New Orleans, LA	70115-2537	504-891-1353	891-6915	K-8	Linda Comer
New Orleans Science and Math HS	5625 Loyola Ave	New Orleans, LA	70115-5014	504-324-7061	309-4178	9-12	Bridget Ramsey
New Vision Learning Academy	507 Swayze St	Monroe, LA	71201-8130	318-338-9995	338-9987	PK-6	Rev. Andrew Mansfield
Pointe Coupee Central HS	8434 Pointe Coupee Rd	Morganza, LA	70759-3320	225-638-3085	638-9595	6-12	Harry Wright
Prescott MS	4055 Prescott Rd	Baton Rouge, LA	70805-5199	225-357-6481	355-2672	6-8	Charles Moffatt
Priestley Charter S	2009 Palmyra St	New Orleans, LA	70112-2213	504-324-7200	304-8862	9-12	Michelle Biagas
Singleton Charter S	2220 Oretha C Haley Blvd	New Orleans, LA	70113-1508	504-568-3466	569-3378	PK-8	Melrose Biagas
Sojourner Truth Academy	2437 Jena St	New Orleans, LA	70115-5907	504-274-3622		9-12	Channa Cook
Tubman S	2013 General Meyer Ave	New Orleans, LA	70114-1533	504-363-1064	363-2184	PK-8	Jonathan Williams
Tureaud ES	2021 Pauger St	New Orleans, LA	70116-1533	504-373-1469	942-8670	PK-6	Perretta Mitchell
Walker HS	2832 General Meyer Ave	New Orleans, LA	70114-3097	504-324-7550	309-2960	9-12	Mary Laurie
Wicker S	2011 Bienville St	New Orleans, LA	70112-3397	504-373-6220	571-6317	K-8	Ella Lewis
Wilson Charter S	1111 Milan St	New Orleans, LA	70115-2760	504-373-6274		K-6	Sheila Thomas
Wright Charter S	1426 Napoleon Ave	New Orleans, LA	70115-3980	504-304-3915	896-4095	4-8	Sharon Clark
Maryland							
Academy for College & Career Exploration	1300 W 36th St	Baltimore, MD	21211-2303	410-396-7607	396-0432	9-12	Ivor Mitchell
AFYA Charter MS	2800 Brendan Ave	Baltimore, MD	21213-1213	410-485-2103		6-8	William McKenna
Baltimore Freedom Academy	101 S Caroline St	Baltimore, MD	21231-1723	443-984-2737	675-5205	6-12	Dana Hunter
Baltimore International Academy	3515 Taylor Ave	Baltimore, MD	21236-4406	410-426-3650	426-3651	K-8	Elena Lokounia
Baltimore Montessori Charter ES	1600 Guilford Ave	Baltimore, MD	21202-2823	410-528-5393		K-6	Allison Shecter
Baltimore Talent Development HS	1500 Harlem Ave	Baltimore, MD	21217-2103	443-984-2744	669-7519	9-12	Jeffrey Robinson
Browne S	1000 N Montford Ave	Baltimore, MD	21213-3542	410-396-9239	396-9328	PK-8	Lisa Eason
Chesapeake Science Point Charter S	1321 Mercedes Dr	Hanover, MD	21076	410-684-2886	684-2883	6-8	Fatih Kandil
City Neighbors Charter S	4301 Raspe Ave	Baltimore, MD	21206-1913	410-325-2627	325-2489	K-8	Michael Chalupa
City Springs S	100 S Caroline St	Baltimore, MD	21231-1798	410-396-9165	396-9113	PK-8	Rhonda Richetta
Collington Square S	1409 N Collington Ave	Baltimore, MD	21213-3418	410-396-9198	396-8632	PK-8	D'Andrea Chapman
ConneXions Leadership Academy	2801 N Dukeland St	Baltimore, MD	21216	410-984-1418	669-4418	6-12	Dana Polson
Coppin Academy	2500 W North Ave	Baltimore, MD	21216-3633	410-951-2600	951-2610	9-12	
Crossroads S	802 S Caroline St	Baltimore, MD	21231-3332	410-685-0295	752-8433	PK-8	Marc Martin
Empowerment Academy	851 Braddish Ave	Baltimore, MD	21216-4723	443-984-2381	362-2454	PK-8	Carolyn Smith
Excel Academy	5811 Riverdale Rd	Riverdale, MD	20737-2141	301-277-5320		K-8	Deborah Moore
Green S	335 W 27th St	Baltimore, MD	21211-3004	410-366-2152	366-2154	K-5	Kate Primm
Hampstead Hill Academy	500 S Linwood Ave	Baltimore, MD	21224-3800	410-396-9146	396-3637	PK-8	Matthew Hornbeck
Imagine Discovery Charter S	1726 Whitehead Rd	Baltimore, MD	21207-4003	410-277-0087	277-0085	K-8	Sharon Harris
Imagine - Foundations Public Charter S	4605 Brown Station Rd	Upper Marlboro, MD	20772-9125	301-952-8707	952-8708	K-8	William Hill
Imagine - Lincoln Public Charter S	3120 Branch Ave	Marlow Heights, MD	20748-1004	301-505-6020	505-6021	K-8	William Dooley
Independence S Local I	1250 W 36th St	Baltimore, MD	21211-2301	410-467-1090	467-1091	9-12	Cranston Dize
Inner Harbor East Academy	200 N Central Ave	Baltimore, MD	21202-5005	410-537-5890		PK-12	Beverly Manigo
Jemison MST Academy	1130 N Caroline St	Baltimore, MD	21213-2844	410-276-3095	276-3096	6-8	Kevin Parson
KIPP Ujima Village Academy	4701 Greenspring Ave	Baltimore, MD	21209-4704	410-545-3669	664-6865	5-8	Shayna Hammond
Maryland Acad of Technology & Health Sci	4701 Greenspring Ave	Baltimore, MD	21209-4704	410-545-0955	396-0338	6-12	Rebekah Ghosh
Midtown Academy	1398 W Mount Royal Ave	Baltimore, MD	21217-4134	410-225-3257	225-3514	K-8	Kathleen O'Hanlon
Monocacy Valley Montessori S	217 Dill Ave	Frederick, MD	21701-4905	301-668-5013	668-5015	K-8	Meg Bowen
New Era Academy	2700 Seamon Ave	Baltimore, MD	21225-1117	443-984-2415	355-1130	9-12	Paul Covington
New Song Academy	1530 Presstman St	Baltimore, MD	21217-2312	410-728-2091	728-0829	K-8	Susan Tibbels
Northwood Appold S	4417 Loch Raven Blvd	Baltimore, MD	21218-1554	410-323-9546	323-1836	K-12	Virginia Richardson
Patterson Park S	27 N Lakewood Ave	Baltimore, MD	21224-1155	410-558-1230		K-8	Chad Kramer
REACH MSHS	6820 Fait Ave	Baltimore, MD	21224-3005	443-366-8533		6-12	Michael Frederick
Renaissance Academy	1301 McCulloh St	Baltimore, MD	21217-3044	443-984-3164	947-2968	9-12	Karl Perry
Restoration Academy	253 Paradise Rd	Aberdeen, MD	21001-2324	410-273-5560	273-5556	7-12	Louis Gordon
Rosemont S	2777 Presstman St	Baltimore, MD	21216-4025	410-396-0574	545-3298	PK-8	Charles Shockney
Southwest Baltimore Charter S	31 S Schroeder St	Baltimore, MD	21223-2559	443-984-3385	685-3492	K-5	Turi Nillson
Turning Point Academy	7800 Good Luck Rd	Lanham Seabrook, MD	20706-3505	301-552-0164	552-7307	K-6	Dr. Kenneth Jones
Wolfe Street Academy	245 S Wolfe St	Baltimore, MD	21231-2622	410-396-9140	396-8064	PK-5	Mark Gaither
Massachusetts							
Academy of Pacific Rim Charter S	1 Westinghouse Plz	Hyde Park, MA	02136-2059	617-361-0050	361-0045	5-12	Jenne Colasacco
Academy of Strategic Learning	9 Water St	Amesbury, MA	01913-2936	978-388-8037	388-8073	7-12	Donna Georges
Advanced Math & Science Academy	201 Forest St	Marlborough, MA	01752-3012	508-597-2400	597-2499	6-10	Barbara McGann
Atlantis Charter S	37 Park St	Fall River, MA	02721-1712	508-672-3537	672-2474	K-8	Fernando Goulart
Banneker Charter S	21 Notre Dame Ave	Cambridge, MA	02140-2505	617-497-7771	497-4223	K-6	Marlon Davis
Barnstable Horace Mann Charter S	730 W Barnstable Rd	Marstons Mills, MA	02648-1549	508-420-2272	420-0185	5-6	Kara Peterson
Berkshire Arts & Technology Charter S	PO Box 267	Adams, MA	01220-0267	413-743-7311	743-7327	6-12	Ben Klompus
Boston Collegiate Charter S	11 Mayhew St	Dorchester, MA	02125-1628	617-265-1172	265-1176	5-12	Tobey Jackson
Boston Day & Evening Academy	20 Kearsarge Ave	Roxbury, MA	02119-2318	617-635-6789	635-6380	9-12	Beatriz Zapater
Boston Preparatory Charter S	1286 Hyde Park Ave	Hyde Park, MA	02136-2714	617-333-6688	333-6689	6-10	Amanda Colley
Boston Renaissance Charter S	250 Stuart St	Boston, MA	02116-5435	617-357-0900	357-0949	K-6	Roger Harris
Brooke Charter S	190 Cummins Hwy	Roslindale, MA	02131-3722	617-325-7977	325-2260	K-8	Jon C. Clark
Cape Cod Lighthouse Charter S	225 Route 6A	Orleans, MA	02653	508-240-2800	240-3583	6-8	Katherine McNamara
City on a Hill Charter S	58 Circuit St	Roxbury, MA	02119-1925	617-445-1515	445-9153	9-12	Erica Jamison
Codman Academy	637 Washington St	Dorchester, MA	02124-3510	617-287-0700	287-9064	9-12	Thabiti Brown
Community Charter S of Cambridge	245 Bent St	Cambridge, MA	02141-2001	617-354-0047	354-3624	7-12	Paula Evans
Community Day Charter S	190 Hampshire St	Lawrence, MA	01840	978-682-6628	681-5838	K-8	Sheila Balboni
Conservatory Lab Charter S	25 Arlington St	Brighton, MA	02135-2124	617-254-8904	254-8909	K-5	Diana Lam
Excel Academy Charter S	1150 Saratoga St	East Boston, MA	02128-1228	617-561-1371	561-1378	5-8	Komal Bhasin
Foster Charter S	10 New Bond St	Worcester, MA	01606-2699	508-854-8400	854-8484	K-12	Kathleen Greenwood
Four Rivers Charter S	248 Colrain Rd	Greenfield, MA	01301-9701	413-775-4577	775-4578	7-12	Peter Garbus
Foxboro Regional Charter S	131 Central St	Foxboro, MA	02035-2458	508-543-2508	543-7982	K-12	Mark Logan
Franklin Classical Charter S	201 Main St	Franklin, MA	02038-1933	508-541-3434	541-5396	K-8	Kevin O'Malley
Global Learning Charter S	190 Ashley Blvd	New Bedford, MA	02746-1752	508-991-7000	991-4127	5-12	James Cobbs
Health Careers Academy	110 Fenway	Boston, MA	02115-3782	617-373-8576	373-7850	9-12	Caren Walker-Gregory
Hilltown Cooperative Charter S	PO Box 147	Haydenville, MA	01039-0147	413-268-3421	268-3185	K-8	Amy Aaron
Hill View Montessori S	PO Box 1545	Haverhill, MA	01831-2145	978-521-2616	521-2656	K-6	Katherine Coltin
Holyoke Community Charter S	2200 Northampton St	Holyoke, MA	01040-3430	413-533-0111	536-5444	K-8	Zandrina Atherley
Hughes Academy	91 School St	Springfield, MA	01105-1316	413-747-5200	747-4528	K-8	Joseph Seay

School	Address	City,State	Zip code	Telephone	Fax	Grade	Contact
Innovation Academy Charter S	72 Tyng Rd	Tyngsboro, MA	01879-2044	978-970-0100	970-3522	5-9	Walter Landberg
King Charter S of Excellence	649 State St	Springfield, MA	01109-4105	413-214-7806	214-7838	K-4	Allan Katz
Kipp Academy Lynn Charter S	25 Bessom St	Lynn, MA	01902-1204	781-598-1609	598-1639	5-8	Joshua Zoia
Lawrence Family Development Charter S	34 West St	Lawrence, MA	01841-3426	978-689-9863	689-8133	K-8	Ralph Carrero
Lowell Community Charter S	206 Jackson St	Lowell, MA	01852-2106	978-323-0800	323-4600	K-8	Elizabeth Torosian
Lowell Middlesex Academy Charter S	67 Middle St	Lowell, MA	01852	978-656-3165	459-0456	9-12	Margaret McDevitt
Marblehead Community Charter S	17 Lime St	Marblehead, MA	01945	781-631-0777	631-0500	4-8	Albert Argenziano
Marstons Mills East Horace Mann Charter	760 W Barnstable Rd	Marstons Mills, MA	02648-1549	508-420-1100	420-1486	K-4	Kenneth Keenan
Martha's Vineyard Charter S	PO Box 1150	West Tisbury, MA	02575-1150	508-693-9900	696-9008	K-12	Robert Moore
Massachusetts Academy for Math\Science S	85 Prescott St	Worcester, MA	01605-2610	508-831-5859	831-5880	11-12	Robert Traver
MATCH Charter HS	1001 Commonwealth Ave	Boston, MA	02215-1308	617-232-0300	232-2838	9-12	Alan Safran
McAuliffe Regional Charter S	25 Clinton St	Framingham, MA	01702-6702	508-879-9000	879-1066	6-8	Thomas O'Neill
Mystic Valley Regional Charter S	770 Salem St	Malden, MA	02148-4415	781-388-0222	321-5688	K-12	Christopher Finn
Neighborhood House Charter S	21 Queen St	Dorchester, MA	02122-2509	617-825-0703	825-1829	PK-8	Kevin Andrews
New Leadership Charter S	180 Ashland Ave	Springfield, MA	01119-2704	413-782-9111	782-9991	6-12	Nancy Tromblay
North Central Essential Charter S	1 Oak Hill Rd Ste 100	Fitchburg, MA	01420-3986	978-345-2701	345-9127	7-12	Stephanie Harden
Parker Charter Essential S	49 Antietam St	Ayer, MA	01434-5230	978-772-3293	772-3295	7-12	Teriann Schrader
Phoenix Charter Academy	59 Nichols St	Chelsea, MA	02150-1225	617-889-3100	889-3144	9-12	Beth Anderson
Pioneer Charter S of Science	51 Summer St	Everett, MA	02149-3741	617-389-7277	389-7278	7-8	Ugur Kocak
Pioneer Valley Chinese Immrsn Charter S	317 Russell St	Hadley, MA	01035-3535	413-582-7040	582-7068	K-1	Kathleen Wang
Pioneer Valley Performing Arts Charter S	15 Mulligan Dr	South Hadley, MA	01075-7511	413-552-1580	552-1594	7-12	Robert Brick
Prospect Hill Academy Charter S	15 Webster Ave	Somerville, MA	02143-3311	617-284-7800	284-7840	K-12	Jed Lippard
Rising Tide Charter S	6 Resnik Rd	Plymouth, MA	02360-4873	508-747-2620	830-9441	5-8	Jill Crafts
River Valley Charter S	2 Perry Way	Newburyport, MA	01950-4001	978-465-0065	465-0119	K-8	Dr. Dale Bishop
Roxbury Preparatory Charter S	120 Fisher Ave	Roxbury, MA	02120-3320	617-566-2361	566-2373	6-8	Dana Lehman
SABIS International Charter S	160 Joan St	Springfield, MA	01129-1530	413-783-2600	783-2555	K-12	Maretta Thomsen
Salem Academy Charter S	45 Congress St	Salem, MA	01970-7301	978-744-2105	744-7246	6-12	Rachel Hunt
Seven Hills Charter S	51 Gage St	Worcester, MA	01605-3014	508-799-7500	753-7318	K-8	Gerald Yung
Silver Hill Horace Mann Charter S	675 Washington St	Haverhill, MA	01832-4500	978-374-3448	374-3461	K-5	Euthemia Gillman
Smith Leadership Academy Charter S	23 Leonard St	Boston, MA	02122-2718	617-474-7950	474-7957	6-8	Karmala Sherwood
South Shore Charter S	100 Longwater Cir	Norwell, MA	02061-1650	781-982-4202	982-4201	K-12	Prudence Goodale
Sturgis Charter S	427 Main St	Hyannis, MA	02601-3905	508-778-1782	771-6785	9-12	Eric Hieser
Uphams Corner Charter S	320 Huntington Ave	Boston, MA	02115-5018	617-266-2007	266-2008	5-8	Francois Fils-Aime

Michigan

School	Address	City,State	Zip code	Telephone	Fax	Grade	Contact
Abney Academy	1435 Fulton St E	Grand Rapids, MI	49503-3853	616-454-5541	454-5598	K-5	Lacey James
Academic and Career Education Academy	884 E Isabella Rd	Midland, MI	48640-8326	989-631-5202	631-4541	9-12	Michelle Zielinski
Academic Transitional Academy	1520 Michigan Rd	Port Huron, MI	48060-4750	810-364-3449	364-3347	9-10	Pete Spencer
Academy for Technology & Enterprise	2102 Weiss St	Saginaw, MI	48602-5049	989-399-6150	399-6165	10-12	Julie Walker
Academy of Business and Technology	19625 Wood St	Melvindale, MI	48122-2201	313-382-3422	382-3906	6-12	John Kirk
Academy of Business and Technology ES	5277 Calhoun St	Dearborn, MI	48126-3203	313-581-2223	581-2247	K-5	Dr. Paul Merritt
Academy of Detroit - West	16418 W Mcnichols Rd	Detroit, MI	48235-3354	313-272-5473	272-4823	K-1	Mae Alexander
Academy of Detroit West - Redford	23749 Elmira	Redford, MI	48239-1405	313-387-9238	387-9261	2-6	Geraldine Sumpter
Academy of Flint	4100 W Coldwater Rd	Flint, MI	48504-1102	810-789-9484	789-9483	K-8	Verdell Duncan
Academy of Inkster	28612 Avondale St	Inkster, MI	48141-1642	734-641-1312	641-1317	9-12	Raymond Alvarado
Academy of Lathrup Village	27700 Southfield Rd	Southfield, MI	48076-7901	248-569-0089	569-4944	K-8	Shawn Hurt
Academy of Oak Park - Marlow	21700 Marlow St	Oak Park, MI	48237-2604	248-547-2323	547-2515	K-5	Rashid Fai'Sal
Academy of Oak Park - Mendota	21300 Mendota Ave	Ferndale, MI	48220-2164	248-586-9358	586-9362	9-12	Joe Moody
Academy of Oak Park - Whitcomb	14213 Whitcomb St	Detroit, MI	48227-2126	313-272-8333	272-7554	6-8	Larry Lattimore
Academy of Southfield	18330 George Washington Dr	Southfield, MI	48075-2785	248-557-6121	557-2915	K-8	Carolyn Mosley
Academy of Warren	13943 E 8 Mile Rd	Warren, MI	48089-3351	586-552-8010	552-8014	K-8	Jerry Parker
Academy of Waterford	3000 Sashabaw Rd	Waterford, MI	48329-4040	248-674-1649	674-3173	K-8	Carolyn Edwards
Academy of Westland	300 S Henry Ruff Rd	Westland, MI	48186-5087	734-722-1465	722-8025	K-8	Christopher Lindsay
ACE Academy	1961 Lincoln St	Highland Park, MI	48203	313-868-8368	865-2937	6-12	Craig Bartholomew
Advanced Technology Academy	7265 Calhoun St	Dearborn, MI	48126-1430	313-582-4500	582-3499	K-5	Barry Hawthorne
Advanced Technology Academy	4801 Oakman Blvd	Dearborn, MI	48126-3755	313-582-4500	582-3499	6-12	Barry Hawthorne
A.G.B.U. Alex & Marie Manoogian S	22001 Northwestern Hwy	Southfield, MI	48075-4001	248-569-2988	569-1346	K-12	Dr. Hosep Torossian
Aisha Shule/W.E.B. Dubois Prep Academy	20119 Wisconsin St	Detroit, MI	48221-1132	313-345-6050	345-1059	K-12	Imani Humphrey
Allen Academy	8666 Quincy St	Detroit, MI	48204-2306	313-898-6444	898-6555	K-12	Tim Green
American Montessori Academy	14800 Middlebelt Rd	Livonia, MI	48154-4031	734-525-7100	525-8952	K-6	Amy Pogorzelski
Ann Arbor Learning Community	3980 Research Park Dr	Ann Arbor, MI	48108-2220	734-477-0340	929-6505	K-8	Ticheal Jones
Arbor Academy	55 Arbor St	Battle Creek, MI	49015-2903	269-963-5851	964-2643	K-6	Paul Doersam
Arts Academy in the Woods	32101 Caroline	Fraser, MI	48026-3209	586-294-0391	294-0617	9-12	Maxwell Spayde
Arts & Technology Academy of Pontiac	48980 Woodward Ave	Pontiac, MI	48342-5034	248-452-9309	452-9312	K-8	Patty Woods
Bahweting Charter S	1301 Marquette Ave	Sault S Marie, MI	49783-9533	906-635-5055	635-3805	K-8	Susan Palmer
Battle Creek Area Learning Center	15 Arbor St	Battle Creek, MI	49015-2903	269-565-4782	565-4784	10-12	Charles Crider
Bay-Arenac Community HS	1608 Hudson St	Essexville, MI	48732-1387	989-893-8811	895-7749	9-12	Ryan Donlan
Bay County Public School Academy	1110 State St	Bay City, MI	48706-3699	989-684-6484	684-6202	PK-6	David Smith
Benton Harbor Charter S	455 Riverview Dr	Benton Harbor, MI	49022-5080	269-925-3807	927-3673	PK-8	Tim Harris
Bingham Arts Academy	555 S 5th Ave	Alpena, MI	49707-2744	989-358-2500	358-2503	PK-6	Sarah Prevo
Black River Public S	491 Columbia Ave	Holland, MI	49423-4838	616-355-0055	355-0057	K-12	Shannon Brunink
Blue Water Learning Academy	5202 Taft Rd	Algonac, MI	48001-4701	810-794-8067	794-8888	7-12	James Lenore
Bradford Academy	24218 Garner St	Southfield, MI	48033-2900	248-351-0000	356-4770	K-12	Fred Borowski
Bridge Academy	9600 Buffalo St	Hamtramck, MI	48212-3323	313-887-8100	887-8101	K-8	Dr. Nagi Jaber
Burton Glen Charter Academy	4171 E Atherton Rd	Burton, MI	48519-1435	810-744-2300	744-2400	PK-8	Linda Cainsmith
Business Entrepreneurship Sci & Tech S	200 Highland St	Highland Park, MI	48203-3405	313-869-1000	868-1741	K-8	Delria Crippen
Byron Center Charter S	9930 Burlingame Ave SW	Byron Center, MI	49315-8631	616-878-4852	878-7196	PK-12	Tom Kruzel
Canton Charter Academy	49100 Ford Rd	Canton, MI	48187-5415	734-453-9517	453-9551	K-8	Claudia Williamson
Capitol Area Academy	5525 S Pennsylvania Ave	Lansing, MI	48911-4091	517-882-1400	882-0400	PK-8	Dan Laabs
Carleton Academy	PO Box 712	Hillsdale, MI	49242-0712	517-437-2000	437-2919	K-12	Colleen Gadwood
Carver Academy	14510 2nd Ave	Highland Park, MI	48203-5715	313-865-6024	865-6658	K-8	Jessie Kilgore
Casa Richard Academy	2635 Howard St	Detroit, MI	48216-2058	313-963-7757	963-7768	9-12	Angela Johnson
CASMAN Alternative Academy	225 9th St	Manistee, MI	49660-3109	231-723-4981	723-1555	7-12	Cameron Clark
Center Academy	310 W Oakley St	Flint, MI	48503-3915	810-341-6944	341-6949	K-8	Ronald Newton
Center for Literacy & Creativity	18401 W McNichols Rd	Detroit, MI	48219-4113	313-537-9400	537-9410	K-8	Deborah Holt-Foster
Central Academy	2459 S Industrial Hwy	Ann Arbor, MI	48104-6129	734-822-1100	822-1101	PK-12	Luay Shalabi
Chandler Park Academy	20100 Kelly Rd	Harper Woods, MI	48225-1201	313-839-9886	839-3221	7-12	Ronald Williams
Chandler Park Academy	20200 Kelly Rd	Harper Woods, MI	48225-1203	313-884-8830	884-9130	K-6	Vivian Jackson
Chandler Woods Charter Academy	6895 Samrick Ave NE	Belmont, MI	49306-8844	616-866-6000	866-6001	K-8	Barb Lindquist
Chatfield S	231 Lake Dr	Lapeer, MI	48446-1661	810-667-8970	667-8983	K-8	Betty McCauley
Chavez Academy	8126 W Vernor Hwy	Detroit, MI	48209-1524	313-843-9440	297-6948	K-5	Cheri Wasiel
Chavez HS	1761 Waterman St	Detroit, MI	48209-2194	313-551-0611	551-0552	9-12	Juan Martinez
Chavez MS	6782 Goldsmith St	Detroit, MI	48209-2089	313-842-0006	842-0167	6-8	Rick Guerra
Cherry Hill School of Performing Arts	28500 Avondale St	Inkster, MI	48141	734-722-2811	641-9439	K-12	Steven Mostyn
Cole Academy	1915 W Mount Hope Ave	Lansing, MI	48910-2434	517-372-0038	372-1446	K-5	James Henderson
Commonwealth Cmmnty Development Acad.	13477 Eureka St	Detroit, MI	48212-1754	313-366-9470	366-9471	K-8	Angela Moore
Concord Academy - Antrim	5055 Corey Rd	Mancelona, MI	49659-9467	231-584-2080	584-2082	K-12	Stephen Overton
Concord Academy - Boyne	401 E Dietz Rd	Boyne City, MI	49712-9653	231-582-0194	582-4214	K-12	Larry Kubovchick
Concord Academy-Petoskey	2468 Atkins Rd	Petoskey, MI	49770-9003	231-439-6800	439-6803	K-12	Nick Oshelski
Conner Creek Academy	28111 Imperial Dr	Warren, MI	48093-4281	586-575-9500	575-9483	K-12	Demetria Wesley
Conner Creek Academy East	31300 Ryan Rd	Warren, MI	48092-1354	586-777-5792	698-0392	9-12	Karen Kliewer
Conner Creek Academy East	31300 Ryan Rd	Warren, MI	48092-1354	586-777-3190	698-0392	7-8	Kay Newhouse
Conner Creek Academy East	16911 Eastland St	Roseville, MI	48066-2078	586-779-8055	498-8734	K-6	Karen Smith
Consortium College Preparatory HS	1250 Rosa Parks Blvd	Detroit, MI	48216-1950	313-964-2339	964-3922	7-12	Rod Atkins
Countryside Academy	4800 Meadowbrook Rd	Benton Harbor, MI	49022-9629	269-944-3319	944-3724	K-12	Paul Marazita
Covenant House Life Skills Ctr Central	2959 Martin Luther King Jr	Detroit, MI	48208	313-898-8816	898-8861	9-12	Antoinette Cunningham
Covenant House Life Skills Ctr East	7600 Goethe St	Detroit, MI	48214-1762	313-922-8901	922-8903	9-12	Derrick Bryant
Covenant House Life Skills Ctr West	5668 Baker St	Detroit, MI	48209-2169	313-554-8130	554-8140	9-12	Jose Vera
Creative Learning Academy of Science	540 Lang Rd	Beaverton, MI	48612-8101	989-435-8252	435-4187	K-8	Laura Olson
Creative Montessori Academy	15100 Northline Rd	Southgate, MI	48195-2408	734-284-5600	281-2637	PK-8	Rochelle Cochran
Creative Technologies Academy	350 Pine St	Cedar Springs, MI	49319-8680	616-696-4905	696-4920	K-12	Matthew Nausadis
Crescent Academy	17570 W 12 Mile Rd	Southfield, MI	48076-1905	248-423-4581	423-1027	K-8	Cherise Cupidore
Crockett Academy	4851 14th St	Detroit, MI	48208-2204	313-896-6078	896-1363	K-12	Robert Warmack
Cross Creek Charter Academy	7701 Kalamazoo Ave SE	Byron Center, MI	49315-9320	616-656-4000	656-4001	PK-8	Joe Nieuwkoop
Crossroads Charter Academy	215 N State St	Big Rapids, MI	49307-1444	231-796-6589	796-9874	K-6	Kendall Schroeder
Crossroads Charter Academy	215 Spruce St W	Big Rapids, MI	49307-1471	231-796-9041	796-9790	7-12	Thomas Saporito
da Vinci Institute	559 Murphy Dr	Jackson, MI	49202-1622	517-780-9980	780-9747	K-8	Kristi Rydjord
da Vinci Institute	PO Box 141	Horton, MI	49246-0141	517-796-0031	796-0320	9-12	Sandy Maxson
Dearborn Academy	19310 Ford Rd Ste 2	Dearborn, MI	48128-2403	313-982-1300	982-9087	K-8	Caterina Berry
Detroit Academy of Arts & Sciences	2985 E Jefferson Ave	Detroit, MI	48207-4288	313-259-1744	259-8393	K-6	Stan Bowman
Detroit Academy of Arts & Sciences	2260 Medbury St	Detroit, MI	48211-2718	313-923-0281	923-0437	7-12	Thomas Goodley
Detroit Community ES	12675 Burt Rd	Detroit, MI	48223-3314	313-537-6717	537-0558	K-8	Nicolle Huff
Detroit Community HS	12675 Burt Rd	Detroit, MI	48223-3314	313-537-3570	537-6904	9-12	Carolyn Printup
Detroit Edison Academy	1903 Wilkins St	Detroit, MI	48207-2112	313-833-1100	833-8653	K-8	Ralph Bland
Detroit Enterprise Academy	11224 Kercheval St	Detroit, MI	48214-3323	313-823-5799	823-0342	K-8	Candace Rogers
Detroit Merit Academy	1091 Alter Rd	Detroit, MI	48215-2861	313-331-3328	331-3278	PK-8	Heidi Benser

School	Address	City,State	Zip code	Telephone	Fax	Grade	Contact
Detroit Midtown Academy	950 Selden St	Detroit, MI	48201-2234	313-831-4961	831-4964	7-12	Jennifer Joubert
Detroit Premier Academy	7781 Asbury Park	Detroit, MI	48228-3685	313-945-1472	945-1744	K-8	Von Glass
Detroit Service Learning Academy	21605 W 7 Mile Rd	Detroit, MI	48219-1810	313-541-7619	541-7656	K-8	Eylastine Green-Roberts
Discovery Arts & Technology Academy	27355 Woodsfield St	Inkster, MI	48141-1242	313-827-0762	827-0763	PK-7	Cheralyn Sanford
Discovery S	PO Box 1070	Fennville, MI	49408-1070	269-561-2191	561-2302	K-8	Bruce Foerch
Dove Academy of Detroit	8210 Rolyat St	Detroit, MI	48234-3358	313-366-9110	366-9130	K-6	Frank Nardelli
Dream Academy	248 9th St	Benton Harbor, MI	49022-4723	269-926-1587	926-2371	9-11	Eddie Anderson
Drew Academy	50 W Josephine St	Ecorse, MI	48229-1748	313-383-7501	383-7502	K-8	Sallie Morton
Eagle Crest Charter Academy	11950 Riley St	Holland, MI	49424-8553	616-786-2400	786-4692	K-8	Daniel Harris
Eastern Washtenaw Multicultural Academy	5550 Platt Rd	Ann Arbor, MI	48108-9762	734-677-0732	677-0740	K-12	Mona Berry
Eaton Academy	21450 Universal Ave	Eastpointe, MI	48021-2969	586-777-1519	777-1527	K-12	Thomas White
Edison-Oakland Academy	22111 Woodward Ave	Ferndale, MI	48220-1812	248-582-8191	582-9093	K-8	Gail Georgette Parks
El-Hajj Malik El-Shabazz Academy	1028 W Barnes Ave	Lansing, MI	48910-1377	517-267-8474	484-0095	PK-6	Dr. Eugene Cain
Ellis Academy	18977 Schaefer Hwy	Detroit, MI	48235-1762	313-927-5395	927-5376	K-8	Claude Tiller
Ellis Academy West	19800 Beech Daly Rd	Redford, MI	48240-1348	313-450-0300	450-0305	K-8	Machion Jackson
Endeavor Charter Academy	380 Helmer Rd N	Battle Creek, MI	49037-7776	269-962-9300	962-9393	K-8	Russ Ainslee
Excel Charter Academy	4201 Breton Rd SE	Grand Rapids, MI	49512-3857	616-281-9339	281-6707	K-8	Dr. William Knoester
Flagship Charter Academy	13661 Wisconsin St	Detroit, MI	48238	313-933-7933	933-9061	K-8	Krystal Bell
Ford Academy	20651 W Warren St	Dearborn Hts, MI	48127-2622	313-240-4346	441-9169	4-12	Mary Ellen Fritsch
Ford Academy	PO Box 1148	Dearborn, MI	48121-1148	313-982-6200	982-6195	9-12	Cora Christmas
Fortis Academy	3875 Golfside Dr	Ypsilanti, MI	48197-3726	734-572-3623	572-5792	K-8	Chris Thompson
Frontier International Academy	2619 Florian St	Hamtramck, MI	48212-3452	313-887-7500	887-7501	6-12	Dr. Harun Rashid
Gaudior Academy	27100 Avondale St	Inkster, MI	48141-1816	313-792-9444	792-9445	PK-8	Rosemarie Gonzales
Gist Academy North	4825 Dancy St	Westland, MI	48186-5148	734-728-4813	722-5111	5-8	Celestine Sanders
Gist Academy - South	4825 Dancy St	Westland, MI	48186-5148	734-721-5515	721-9129	K-4	Brendolyn McClain
Grand Blanc Academy	5135 E Hill Rd	Grand Blanc, MI	48439-7637	810-953-3140	953-3165	K-8	Zel Seidenberg
Grand Rapids Child Discovery Center	640 5th St NW	Grand Rapids, MI	49504-5107	616-459-0330	732-4437	K-5	Shel Hiscock
Grand River Prep HS	624 52nd St SE	Kentwood, MI	49548-5837	616-261-1800	261-1853	9-9	David Angerer
Grand Traverse Academy	1245 Hammond Rd E	Traverse City, MI	49686-9000	231-995-0665	995-0880	K-12	Kaye Mentley
Grattan Academy ES	12047 Old Belding Rd NE	Belding, MI	48809-9367	616-691-8999	691-9857	K-5	Michael Devereaux
Grattan Academy HS	9481 Jordan Rd	Greenville, MI	48838-9437	616-754-9360	754-9363	6-12	Michael Devereaux
Great Lakes Academy	46312 Woodward Ave	Pontiac, MI	48342-5006	248-334-6434	334-6457	K-8	Vivian Terry
Great Oaks Academy	4257 Bart Ave	Warren, MI	48091-1977	586-427-4540	427-4541	K-8	Andy Cook
Hamtramck Academy	11420 Conant St	Hamtramck, MI	48212-3134	313-368-7312	368-7376	K-8	Stephanie Glenn
Hanley International Academy	3056 Hanley St	Hamtramck, MI	48212-3572	313-872-9080	872-9113	K-7	Carolyn Glover
Health Careers Academy of St. Clair Co.	PO Box 1500	Marysville, MI	48040-8000	810-455-1010	364-8139	11-12	Patrick Yanik
HEART Academy	19800 Anita St	Harper Woods, MI	48225-1109	313-882-4631	882-4761	9-12	Rosalind Brathwaite
Hillsdale Preparatory S	160 Mechanic Rd	Hillsdale, MI	49242-1053	517-437-4625	437-3830	K-8	James Rowen
Holly Academy	820 Academy Rd	Holly, MI	48442-1546	248-634-5554	634-5564	K-8	Julie Kildee
Honey Creek Community S	PO Box 1406	Ann Arbor, MI	48106-1406	734-994-2636	994-2341	K-8	Al Waters
Hope Academy	10100 Grand River Ave	Detroit, MI	48204-2042	313-934-0054	934-0074	K-6	Veneda Fox Sanders
Hope of Detroit Academy	4443 N Campbell St	Detroit, MI	48210-2520	313-897-8720	897-5142	K-8	Bernadino Cruz
Hospitality Academy of St. Clair County	PO Box 1500	Marysville, MI	48040-8000	810-455-1010	364-8139	11-12	Patrick Yanik
Huron Academy	11401 Metropolitan Pkwy	Sterling Hts, MI	48312-2937	586-446-9170	446-9173	K-6	Rhonda Filippi
Industrial Technology Academy	PO Box 1500	Marysville, MI	48040-8000	810-364-8990	364-8139	11-12	Patrick Yanick
Information Technology Academy	PO Box 1500	Marysville, MI	48040-8000	810-364-8990	364-8139	11-12	Charles Andrews
International Academy of Flint	2820 S Saginaw St	Flint, MI	48503-5708	810-600-5000	600-5300	K-12	Traci Cormier
International Academy of Saginaw	1944 Iowa Ave	Saginaw, MI	48601-5213	989-921-1000	921-1001	K-3	Christi Seiple-Cole
Island City Academy	6421 S Clinton Trl	Eaton Rapids, MI	48827-9698	517-663-0111	663-0167	K-8	Thomas Ackerson
Jackson Arts & Technology Academy	500 Griswold St	Jackson, MI	49203-4062	517-796-0080	796-0104	K-6	Septembra Williams
Joy Preparatory Academy	1129 Oakman Blvd	Detroit, MI	48238-2950	313-867-7828	867-7831	K-2	Frances Gardulescu
Joy Preparatory Academy	15055 Dexter Ave	Detroit, MI	48238-2124	313-340-0023	340-0678	3-8	Frances Gardulescu
Kensington Woods HS	3700 Cleary Dr	Howell, MI	48843-6614	517-545-0828	545-7588	9-12	James Perry
Keystone Academy	47925 Bemis Rd	Belleville, MI	48111-9760	734-697-9470	697-9471	K-8	Kay Blaesser
King Education Center	16827 Appoline St	Detroit, MI	48235-4205	313-341-4944	341-7014	K-7	Dr. Constance Price
Knapp Charter Academy	1759 Leffingwell Ave NE	Grand Rapids, MI	49525-4531	616-364-1100	364-9780	K-8	Jamie Hoeksema
Landmark Academy	4800 Lapeer Rd	Kimball, MI	48074-1517	810-982-7210	982-0679	K-10	Nancy Gardner
Laurus Academy	24590 Lahser Rd	Southfield, MI	48033-6040	248-799-8401	799-8404	K-8	Raul Calderon
Life Skills Center	3100 E Jefferson Ave	Detroit, MI	48207-4221	313-567-3235	567-8554	9-12	Nathaniel King
Life Skills Center of Pontiac	142 Auburn Ave	Pontiac, MI	48342-3008	248-322-1163	322-1164	9-12	Carlotta Quince
Linden Charter Academy	3244 N Linden Rd	Flint, MI	48504-1753	810-720-0515	720-0626	K-8	Linda Cain-Smith
Macomb Academy	39092 Garfield Rd	Clinton Twp, MI	48038-4094	586-228-2201	228-2210	12-12	Dr. Betty Yee
Madison Academy	6170 Torrey Rd	Flint, MI	48507-5954	810-744-9100	744-9101	K-8	Kenneth Maurey
Marshall Academy	18203 Homer Rd	Marshall, MI	49068-8718	269-781-6330	781-8749	K-11	Brent Swan
Merritt Academy	59900 Havenridge Rd	New Haven, MI	48048-1915	586-749-6000	749-8582	K-11	Dan Schluckbier
Metro Charter Academy	34800 Ecorse Rd	Romulus, MI	48174-1642	734-641-3200	641-6530	K-8	Ricky Fountain
Michigan Health Academy	5845 Auburn St	Detroit, MI	48228-3905	313-982-9422	982-9415	9-12	Comerlynn Trout
Michigan Technical Academy	19940 Mansfield St	Detroit, MI	48235-2332	313-272-1649	272-1849	3-5	Susan Williams
Michigan Technical Academy	19900 Evergreen Rd	Detroit, MI	48219-2044	313-538-4927	538-8396	K-2	Sue Soborowski
Michigan Technical Academy	19780 Meyers Rd	Detroit, MI	48235-1229	313-864-0595	864-2271	6-8	James Abercrombie
Michigan Technical Academy HS	23750 Elmira	Redford, MI	48239-1485	313-537-9311	537-9312	9-12	Mel Anglin
Midland Acad Advanced & Creative Studies	4653 E Bailey Bridge Rd	Midland, MI	48640-8542	989-496-2404	496-2466	K-12	Betsy Haigh
Mid-Michigan Leadership Academy	730 W Maple St	Lansing, MI	48906-5086	517-485-5379	485-5892	K-8	Mark Eitrem
Morey Charter S	380 W Blanchard Rd	Shepherd, MI	48883-9552	989-866-6739	866-6737	PK-12	Michael Kennealy
Mt. Clemens Montessori Academy	1070 Hampton Rd	Mount Clemens, MI	48043-2955	586-465-5545	465-2283	PK-5	Genie P'Sachoulias
Nataki Talibah S of Detroit	19176 Northrop St	Detroit, MI	48219-1857	313-531-3720	531-3779	K-8	Melita Smith
New Bedford Academy	6315 Secor Rd	Lambertville, MI	48144-9411	734-854-5437	854-1573	K-8	Greg Sauter
New Beginnings Academy	211 E Michigan Ave	Ypsilanti, MI	48198-5677	734-481-9001	544-2706	K-5	Dr. Wayne Millette
New Branches S	256 Alger St SE	Grand Rapids, MI	49507-3409	616-243-6221	243-0305	K-6	Pamela Duffy
New City Academy	2130 W Holmes Rd	Lansing, MI	48910	517-272-3000	272-3544	K-8	James Woods
Northpointe Academy	53 Candler St	Highland Park, MI	48203-2827	313-868-2916	868-0443	K-8	Deborah Manley
Northridge Academy	5306 North St	Flint, MI	48505-2927	810-785-8811	785-9844	K-8	Dr. Nat Burtley
North Saginaw Charter Academy	2332 Trautner Dr	Saginaw, MI	48604-9593	989-249-5400	249-5800	K-8	Tonya Reed
North Star Academy	3030 Wright St	Marquette, MI	49855-9649	906-226-0156	226-0167	6-12	Karen Anderson
Northwest Academy	115 W Hurlbut St	Charlevoix, MI	49720-1510	231-547-9000	547-9464	K-12	Gary Stutzman
Nsoroma Institute	20045 Joann St	Detroit, MI	48205-1136	248-521-0400	521-0401	K-8	Malik Yakini
Oakland Academy	6325 Oakland Dr	Portage, MI	49024-2589	269-324-8951	324-8974	PK-6	Henry Winter
Oakland International Academy	8228 Conant St	Detroit, MI	48211-1407	313-925-1000	925-1133	4-6	Russell Robinson
Oakland International Academy	6111 Miller St	Detroit, MI	48211-1552	313-347-0249	347-0250	7-12	Dr. Adnan Aabed
Oakland International Academy	4001 Miller St	Detroit, MI	48211-1554	313-923-0790	923-0927	K-3	Karen Abbas
Ojibwe Charter S	11507 W Industrial Dr	Brimley, MI	49715-9087	906-248-2530	248-2532	K-12	Stephanie Vittitow
Old Redford Academy ES	17195 Redford St	Detroit, MI	48219-3259	313-532-7510	543-2055	PK-5	Jennifer Wilkins
Old Redford Academy MS	7000 W Outer Dr	Detroit, MI	48235-3166	313-653-3888	653-4855	6-8	Amelia Norwood
Old Redford Academy Prep HS	8001 W Outer Dr	Detroit, MI	48235-3293	313-543-3080	543-3129	9-12	Shantel Ross
Outlook Academy	310 Thomas St	Allegan, MI	49010-9158	269-686-8227	686-7036	5-10	Mark Dobias
Pansophia Academy	52 Abbott Ave	Coldwater, MI	49036-1430	517-279-4686	279-0089	K-12	Tom Dove
Paragon Charter Academy	3750 McCain Rd	Jackson, MI	49201-7675	517-750-9500	750-9501	K-8	Kathy Watson
Paramount Charter Academy	3624 S Westnedge Ave	Kalamazoo, MI	49008-2969	269-553-6400	553-6401	K-8	Dr. Sharon Lockett-Gibson
Plymouth Educational Center S	1460 E Forest Ave	Detroit, MI	48207-1000	313-831-3280	831-5766	PK-8	Phyllis Ross
Pontiac Academy for Excellence	196 Cesar E Chavez Ave	Pontiac, MI	48342	248-745-9420	745-1275	K-12	Jacqueline Cassell
Powell Academy	4800 Coplin St	Detroit, MI	48215-2109	313-823-5791	823-3410	K-8	Dr. David Badger
Presque Isle Academy	PO Box 731	Onaway, MI	49765-0731	989-733-6708	733-6701	9-12	Rick Bongard
Prevail Academy	353 Cass Ave	Mount Clemens, MI	48043-2112	586-783-0173	783-0179	K-8	Jodi Donkin
Public Safety Academy	PO Box 1500	Marysville, MI	48040-8000	810-455-1010	364-8139	11-12	Patrick Yanik
Reach Academy	25275 Chippendale St	Roseville, MI	48066-3960	586-498-9171	498-9173	PK-5	Paula Dowker
Reh Academy	2201 Owen St	Saginaw, MI	48601-3466	989-753-2349	753-1819	K-8	Diane Hofman
Renaissance Public S Academy	2797 S Isabella Rd	Mount Pleasant, MI	48858-2067	989-773-9889	772-4503	K-8	David Krause
Richfield Public School Academy	3807 N Center Rd	Flint, MI	48506-2642	810-736-1281	736-2326	K-8	Gareth Volz
Ridge Park Charter Academy	4120 Camelot Ridge Dr SE	Grand Rapids, MI	49546-2432	616-222-0093	222-0138	K-8	David King
Riverside Academy East	7124 Miller Rd	Dearborn, MI	48126-1918	313-586-0200	586-0201	K-5	Eman Radha
Riverside Academy West	6409 Schaefer Rd	Dearborn, MI	48126-2212	313-945-6504	945-1976	6-12	Ramzi Saab
Ross Charter Academy	8525 Cole Dr	Warren, MI	48093-5239	586-575-9418	575-9876	K-8	Roy Harris
Ross Hill Academy - Elmwood	3111 Elmwood St	Detroit, MI	48207-2418	313-922-8088	922-2015	K-5	Nellie Williams
Ross Hill Academy - Harper	317 Harper Ave	Detroit, MI	48202-3500	313-875-2207	875-9462	9-12	Nellie Williams
Saginaw County Transition Academy	1000 Tuscola St	Saginaw, MI	48607-1421	989-399-8775	399-9801	7-12	William Pagel
Saginaw Learn to Earn Academy	PO Box 5679	Saginaw, MI	48603-0679	989-399-7400	399-7484	10-12	Richard Beck
Saginaw Preparatory Academy	5173 Lodge St	Saginaw, MI	48601-6829	989-752-9600	752-9618	PK-8	Pamela Williams
St. Clair County Academy of Style	PO Box 1500	Marysville, MI	48040-8000	810-364-8990	364-8139	11-12	Patrick Yanik
St. Clair County Intervention Academy	PO Box 1500	Marysville, MI	48040-8000	810-364-8990	364-7474	6-12	Denice Lapish
St. Clair County Learning Academy	PO Box 1500	Marysville, MI	48040-8000	810-364-8990	364-7474	6-12	Denice Lapish
South Arbor Charter Academy	8200 Carpenter Rd	Ypsilanti, MI	48197-9800	734-528-2821	528-2829	K-8	Timothy DiLaura
Star International Academy	24425 Hass St	Dearborn Hts, MI	48127-3275	313-724-8990	724-8994	K-12	Anita Hassan
Stockwell Academy	9758 E Highland Rd	Howell, MI	48843-9098	810-632-2200	632-2201	K-9	Shelley Stockwell
Summit Academy	PO Box 310	Flat Rock, MI	48134-0310	734-379-6810	379-6745	K-8	Erin Avery
Summit Academy HS	PO Box 190	Flat Rock, MI	48134-0190	734-955-1730	955-1737	9-12	Jason Hamstra
Summit Academy MS	PO Box 190	Flat Rock, MI	48134-0190	734-955-1712	955-1729	6-8	Sally Emerson
Summit Academy North ES	28697 Sibley Rd	Romulus, MI	48174-9736	734-789-1428	789-1431	K-5	Marie Maci

School	Address	City,State	Zip code	Telephone	Fax	Grade	Contact
Sunrise Education Center	686 Aulerich Rd	East Tawas, MI	48730-9339	989-362-2945	362-7968	PK-8	Julie Bather
Taylor Exemplar Academy	26727 Goddard Rd	Taylor, MI	48180-3912	734-941-7742	941-9641	K-7	Phil Price
Three Oaks Public School Academy	1212 Kingsley St	Muskegon, MI	49442-4025	231-767-3365	777-9815	PK-10	Robert Hurd
Threshold Academy	PO Box 113	Greenville, MI	48838-0113	616-761-2296	761-2298	K-6	Victoria Simon
Timberland Charter Academy	2574 McLaughlin Ave	Muskegon, MI	49442-4439	231-767-9700	767-9710	K-8	Andre Johnson
Timbuktu Academy of Science & Technology	10800 E Canfield St	Detroit, MI	48214-1601	313-823-6000	823-9748	K-8	Dr. Ife Kilimanjaro
Toussaint Academy	2450 S Beatrice St	Detroit, MI	48217-1631	313-383-1485	383-6532	K-8	Stephen Turk
Traverse City College Prep Academy	1402 Carlisle Rd	Traverse City, MI	49686-8375	231-929-4539	929-4763	9-12	Cameron Owens
Trillium Academy	15740 Racho Blvd	Taylor, MI	48180-5211	734-374-8222	374-5025	K-12	Angela Romanowski
Triumph Academy	3000 Vivian Rd	Monroe, MI	48162-8600	734-240-2610	240-2785	K-8	Tim Lenahan
Universal Academy	4612 Lonyo St	Detroit, MI	48210-2105	313-581-5006	581-5514	K-12	Nawal Hamadeh
Universal Learning Academy	24480 George St	Dearborn Hts, MI	48127-3278	313-724-8060	724-8082	PK-5	Halim Ahmed
University Prep Academy Murray ES	435 Amsterdam St	Detroit, MI	48202-3407	313-309-0552	309-0555	PK-5	Kimberly Llorens
University Preparatory Academy ES	957 Holden St	Detroit, MI	48202-3443	313-874-9800	874-9822	K-5	Chalita Middleton
University Preparatory Academy HS	600 Antoinette St	Detroit, MI	48202-3457	313-874-4340	874-4510	9-12	Nanette Gill
University Preparatory Academy MS	5310 Saint Antoine St	Detroit, MI	48202-4131	313-831-0100	831-4197	6-8	Matt Marks
University Prep Science & Math MS	1 Campus Martius Fl 11	Detroit, MI	48226	313-309-1960	324-0115	6-7	Margaret Trimer-Hartley
Vanderbilt Charter Academy	301 W 16th St	Holland, MI	49423-3329	616-820-5050	820-5051	K-8	Ivan Kraker
Vanguard Charter Academy	1620 52nd St SW	Wyoming, MI	49519-9629	616-538-3630	538-3646	K-8	Daryl Vriesenga
Victory Academy Charter S	855 Jefferson St	Ypsilanti, MI	48197-5209	734-485-9100	485-9102	K-6	Kevin Whelan
Vista Charter Academy	711 32nd St SE	Grand Rapids, MI	49548-2307	616-246-6920	246-6930	K-8	Joe Grandy
Vista Meadows Academy	20651 W Warren St	Dearborn Hts, MI	48127-2698	313-240-4347	240-4347	9-12	Cathy Nowosatko
Voyageur Academy	4321 Military St	Detroit, MI	48210-2451	313-361-4180	361-4770	K-6	Rod Adkins
Walden Green Montessori S	17339 Roosevelt Rd	Spring Lake, MI	49456-1253	616-842-4523	842-4522	K-8	Tom Hicks
Walker Charter Academy	1801 3 Mile Rd NW	Grand Rapids, MI	49544-1445	616-785-2700	785-0894	K-8	Steve Bagley
Walton Charter Academy	744 E Walton Blvd	Pontiac, MI	48340-1361	248-371-9300	371-1642	K-8	John Brillhart
Warrendale Charter Academy	19400 Sawyer St	Detroit, MI	48228-3330	313-240-4200	240-4203	K-8	Brigitte Brown
Washtenaw Technical Middle College	PO Box D-1	Ann Arbor, MI	48106-1610	734-973-3410	973-3464	10-12	Deborah Trapp
Wavecrest Career Academy	633 Apple Ave	Holland, MI	49423-5434	616-393-7662	393-7633	9-12	Anthony Peterson
WayPoint Academy	2900 E Apple Ave	Muskegon, MI	49442-4504	231-777-4972	767-8488	5-12	Barbara Stellard
Wells Academy	281 S Fair Ave	Benton Harbor, MI	49022-7219	269-926-2885	926-2923	K-6	P. Renene Price
West MI Academy Environmental Science	4463 Leonard St NW	Grand Rapids, MI	49534-2138	616-791-7454	791-7453	PK-12	Josh Hahn
West Michigan Acad of Arts & Academics	17350 Hazel St	Spring Lake, MI	49456-1222	616-844-9961	844-9941	PK-8	Tom Stout
Weston Preparatory Academy	22930 Chippewa St	Detroit, MI	48219-1161	313-387-6038	387-6180	K-12	Holly Davis-Webster
West Village Academy - South Campus	3530 Westwood St	Dearborn, MI	48124-3100	313-274-9200	274-0062	K-8	Donita White
White Pine Academy	510 Russell St	Leslie, MI	49251-9478	517-589-8961	589-9194	K-8	Jared Vickers
Winans Academy of Performing Arts ES	9740 McKinney St	Detroit, MI	48224-2503	313-640-4610	640-4601	K-5	Shelley McIntosh
Winans Academy Performing Arts HS	7616 E Nevada St	Detroit, MI	48234-3284	313-365-5578	365-5684	6-12	Dr. Kirk Goodlow
Windemere Park Charter Academy	3100 W Saginaw St	Lansing, MI	48917-2307	517-327-0700	327-0800	K-8	Jeffrey Whipple
Windover HS	32 S Homer Rd	Midland, MI	48640-8383	989-832-0852	839-7699	9-12	Greg Armstead
Woodland Park Academy	2083 E Grand Blanc Rd	Grand Blanc, MI	48439-8112	810-695-4710	695-1658	K-8	Michele Baskin
Woodland S	7224 Supply Rd	Traverse City, MI	49686-9416	231-947-7474	947-7667	K-8	Nathan Tarsa
Woodmont Academy	25175 Code Rd	Southfield, MI	48033-5805	248-352-1805	352-1810	K-5	Shawn Leonard
Woodward Academy	951 E Lafayette St	Detroit, MI	48207-2999	313-961-2108	963-3501	K-8	Layne Hunt

Minnesota

School	Address	City,State	Zip code	Telephone	Fax	Grade	Contact
Abdulle Academy	415 16th St SW	Rochester, MN	55902-2125	507-252-5995		K-8	Abdulkadir Abdulle
Academia Cesar Chavez	1800 Ames Ave	Saint Paul, MN	55119-4898	651-778-2940	778-2942	K-12	Ramona deRosales
Academy of Biosciences	400 10th St NW	New Brighton, MN	55112-6806	763-571-5039	788-0817	5-12	Lela Olson
Achieve Language Academy	2169 Stillwater Ave E	Saint Paul, MN	55119-3552	651-738-4875	738-8268	K-5	Mary Apuli
Agricultural & Food Sciences Academy	100 Vadnais Blvd	Saint Paul, MN	55127-4036	651-209-3910	209-3911	9-12	Becky Meyer
Artech Charter S	1719 Cannon Rd	Northfield, MN	55057-1680	507-663-8806	663-8802	6-12	Simon Tyler
Aspen Academy	15033 Highway 13 S	Prior Lake, MN	55372-2144	952-226-5940		K-8	Cynthia Sherar
Augsburg Fairview Academy /Health Career	730 Hennepin Ave	Minneapolis, MN	55403-1813	612-333-1614	339-2229	9-12	Dr. William Spira
Aurora Charter S	2520 Minnehaha Ave	Minneapolis, MN	55404-4118	612-870-3891	870-4287	K-3	Cheryl Avina
Avalon Charter S	1745 University Ave W	Saint Paul, MN	55104	651-649-5495	649-5462	9-12	Carrie Bakken
Beacon Academy	12325 Highway 55	Plymouth, MN	55441-4750	763-546-9999	593-9382	K-5	Jordan Ford
Beacon Preparatory S	12325 Highway 55	Plymouth, MN	55441-4750	763-546-9999	593-9382	6-8	Jordan Ford
Best Academy	1300 Olson Memorial Hwy	Minneapolis, MN	55411	612-221-8901		K-6	Eric Mahmoud
Birch Grove Community S	PO Box 2242	Tofte, MN	55615-2242	218-663-0170	663-0160	K-5	Lisa Hoff
Bluesky Online Charter S	33 Wentworth Ave E Ste 300	Saint Paul, MN	55118-3482	651-642-0888	642-0435	7-12	Tom Ellis
Bluffview Montessori S	1321 Gilmore Ave	Winona, MN	55987-2459	507-452-2807	452-6869	K-8	Leslie Hittner
Bright Water ES	2410 Girard Ave N	Minneapolis, MN	55411-2057	612-602-6410		K-6	Ann Luce
Cedar Riverside Community Charter S	1610 S 6th St Ste 100	Minneapolis, MN	55454-1102	612-664-1381	339-2951	K-8	Shelton Rucker
City Academy	1109 Margaret St	Saint Paul, MN	55106-4651	651-298-4624	292-6511	9-12	Milo Cutter
Clarkfield Charter S	301 13th St	Clarkfield, MN	56223-1218	320-669-1995	669-7997	K-8	Wade McKittrick
Cologne Academy	1211 S Village Pkwy	Cologne, MN	55322	952-466-2276		K-8	Lori Magstadt
Community of Peace Academy	471 Magnolia Ave E	Saint Paul, MN	55130-3849	651-776-5151	771-4841	K-12	Karen Rusthoven
Community School of Excellence	1330 Blair Ave	Saint Paul, MN	55104-2007	651-917-0073	917-3717	K-8	Mo Chang
Concordia Creative Learning Academy	930 Geranium Ave E	Saint Paul, MN	55106-2610	651-793-6624	793-6633	K-6	Mary Donaldson
Crosslake Community S	36974 County Road 66	Crosslake, MN	56442-2527	218-692-5437	692-5437	K-6	Tami Martin
Cyber Village Academy	1336 Energy Park Dr Ste 2	Saint Paul, MN	55108-6110	651-523-7170	523-7113	4-8	David Alley
Cygnus Academy	440 Pierce St	Anoka, MN	55303-1604	763-323-0166	323-0165	6-12	Diane Conter
Dakota Area Community Charter S	220 Golden Rule Rd	Dakota, MN	55925-7103	507-643-6869	643-6953	K-5	Darin Shepardson
DaVinci Academy	13001 Central Ave NE	Blaine, MN	55434-4150	763-754-6577	754-6578	K-12	Mari Bergerson
Discovery Public S	126 8th St NW	Faribault, MN	55021-4241	507-331-5423	331-2618	7-12	Steven Darkow
Dugsi Academy	1821 University Ave W	Saint Paul, MN	55104	651-642-0667	642-0668	K-5	Mohamed Osman
Duluth Edison Charter S	1750 Kenwood Ave	Duluth, MN	55811-2224	218-728-9556	728-2075	K-12	Bonnie Jorgenson
Dunwoody Academy	3124 Dean Ct	Minneapolis, MN	55416-4386	612-490-4771		9-12	Benito Matias
Eagle Ridge Academy Charter S	7255 Flying Cloud Dr	Eden Prairie, MN	55344-3549	952-746-7760	746-7765	6-12	John Howitz
East Range Academy of Tech & Science	2000 Siegel Blvd	Eveleth, MN	55734-8642	218-744-7965	744-2349	10-12	Amy Hendrickson
E.C.H.O. Charter S	PO Box 158	Echo, MN	56237-0158	507-925-4143	925-4165	K-8	Larry Schueler
Eci' Nompa Woonspe' Charter S	PO Box 10	Morton, MN	56270-0010	507-697-9055	697-9065	K-12	Tim Blue
Edvisions Off Campus S	PO Box 307	Henderson, MN	56044-0307	507-248-3101	665-2752	9-12	Keven Kroehler
El Colegio Charter S	4137 Bloomington Ave	Minneapolis, MN	55407-3332	612-728-5728	728-5790	9-12	David Greenberg
Emily Charter S	PO Box 40	Emily, MN	56447-0040	218-763-3401	763-4401	K-6	Virginia Brannan
Excell Academy for Higher Learning	6510 Zane Ave N	Brooklyn Park, MN	55429-1571	763-533-0500	533-0508	PK-3	Sabrina Williams
Face to Face Academy	1165 Arcade St	Saint Paul, MN	55106-2615	651-772-5621	772-5566	8-12	Jennifer Plum
Four Directions Charter S	1113 W Broadway Ave	Minneapolis, MN	55411-2505	612-588-0183	588-1844	9-12	Ronald Buckanaga
Fraser Academy	4530 Lyndale Ave S	Minneapolis, MN	55419	612-465-8600	465-8603	K-5	Linda Silrum
Friendship Acad of Fine Arts Charter S	310 E 38th St	Minneapolis, MN	55409	612-879-6703	879-6707	K-4	Ethel Norwood
Frome Academy	8500 Woodbury Xing	Woodbury, MN	55125-9433	651-925-5050		K-5	James Foster
Glacial Hills ES	PO Box 189	Starbuck, MN	56381-0189	320-239-3840	239-2803	K-6	Dyanne Parsons
Global Academy	4065 Central Ave NE	Columbia Hts, MN	55421-2917	763-404-8200	781-5260	K-6	Melissa Storbakken
Goodridge-Grey Accelerated S	3400 Dupont Ave S	Minneapolis, MN	55408	612-238-0788	238-0795	K-6	Dimitri Russell
Great Expectations S	PO Box 310	Grand Marais, MN	55604-0310	218-387-9322	387-9344	K-8	Peter James
Great River Education Center	PO Box 684	Waite Park, MN	56387-0684	320-258-3117	258-3118	7-12	Alonzo Symalla
Great River S	1326 Energy Park Dr	Saint Paul, MN	55108-5202	651-305-2780	305-2781	7-12	Andrea Martin
Green Isle Community S	PO Box 277	Green Isle, MN	55338-0277	507-326-7144	326-5434	K-6	Kristen Kinzler
Harbor City International S	332 W Michigan St Ste 300	Duluth, MN	55802-1644	218-722-7574	625-6068	9-12	Chris Hazleton
Hiawatha Leadership Academy	5033 43rd Ave S	Minneapolis, MN	55417-1616	612-812-4198		PK-2	Jon Bacal
Higher Ground Academy	1381 Marshall Ave	Saint Paul, MN	55104-6353	651-645-1000	645-2100	K-12	Bill Wilson
High School for Recording Arts	550 Vandalia St	Saint Paul, MN	55114-1856	651-287-0890	287-0891	9-12	David Ellis
Hmong Academy	1515 Brewster St	Saint Paul, MN	55108-2612	612-209-8002	209-8003	9-12	Christianna Hang
Hope Community Academy	720 Payne Ave	Saint Paul, MN	55130-4127	651-796-4500	796-4599	K-6	MayChy Vu
International Spanish Language Academy	12007 Excelsior Blvd	Hopkins, MN	55343-8753	952-746-6020	746-6023	K-4	Karen Terhaar
Jeffrey Academy	550 Rice St	Saint Paul, MN	55103-2116	651-290-7683		5-8	Cindy Reuther
Jennings Community Learning Center	2455 University Ave W	Saint Paul, MN	55114-1507	651-649-5403	649-5490	9-12	Bill Zimneiwicz
Kaleidoscope Charter S	7525 Kalland Ave NE	Albertville, MN	55301-9690	763-428-1890	428-1691	K-8	Michelle Strait
KIPP Minnesota Charter S	1601 Laurel Ave	Minneapolis, MN	55403-1205	612-859-7772		K-12	Daisy Mitchell
La Crescent Montessori Academy	28 S Oak St	La Crescent, MN	55947-1332	507-895-4054	895-4064	K-7	Denny Hartman
Lafayette Public Charter S	PO Box 125	Lafayette, MN	56054-0125	507-228-8943	228-2509	K-8	Andrea Harder
Lakes Area Charter S	601 W Nokomis St	Osakis, MN	56360-8203	320-859-5302	859-5342	7-12	Dennis Johnson
Lakes International Language Academy	246 11th Ave SE	Forest Lake, MN	55025	651-464-0771	464-4429	K-4	Cameron Hedlund
Lake Superior HS	5215 Rice Lake Rd	Duluth, MN	55803-8422	218-529-2468	279-3628	7-12	Mike Degen
Learning for Leadership Charter	3300 5th St NE	Minneapolis, MN	55418-1117	612-789-9598		K-12	Stephanie Dess
Liberty HS	308 Northtown Dr NE	Blaine, MN	55434-1039	763-786-4799		9-12	Kathleen Mortensen
Lighthouse Academy of Nations	2600 E 26th St	Minneapolis, MN	55406-1201	612-722-2555	729-2274	9-12	Farhan Hussein
Lincoln International S	730 Hennepin Ave	Minneapolis, MN	55403	612-522-7027		9-12	Nata Samb
Lionsgate Academy	3420 Nevada Ave N	Crystal, MN	55427	763-486-5359		7-12	Jody Van Ness
Long Tieng Academy	4455 16th Ave S	Minneapolis, MN	55407-3601	612-729-1142		9-11	Joe Burniece
Loveworks Academy for Arts	2225 Zenith Ave N	Golden Valley, MN	55422-3852	952-522-6830	522-6840	K-8	April Harrison
Main Street S of Performing Arts	1320 Mainstreet	Hopkins, MN	55343-7497	952-224-1342	224-2955	9-12	Karen Charles
Math & Science Academy	8430 Woodbury Xing	Woodbury, MN	55125-9433	651-353-2317	578-7532	6-12	Paul Simone
Metro Deaf Charter S	1471 Brewster St	Saint Paul, MN	55108-2612	651-224-3995	222-0939	K-8	Dyan Sherwood
Milroy Area Charter S	PO Box 129	Milroy, MN	56263-0129	507-336-2563	336-2568	K-4	William Delaney

School	Address	City,State	Zip code	Telephone	Fax	Grade	Contact
Minisinaakwaang Leadership Academy	20930 367th Ln	Mc Gregor, MN	55760-5968	218-768-5301	768-3357		Henry Flocken
Minneapolis Academy Charter S	5011 31st Ave S	Minneapolis, MN	55417-1405	612-455-1340	455-1345	5-8	Leon Cooper
Minnesota International MS	277 12th Ave N	Minneapolis, MN	55401-1026	612-821-6470	821-6477	5-8	Abdirashid Warsame
Minnesota Internship Center	300 Industrial Blvd NE	Minneapolis, MN	55413-2929	612-722-5416	722-1503	9-12	Kevin Byrne
Minnesota New Country S	PO Box 488	Henderson, MN	56044-0488	507-248-3353	248-3604	7-12	Dee Grover Thomas
Minnesota North Star Academy	1669 Arcade St	Saint Paul, MN	55106-1041	651-771-2000	771-2200	9-12	Kimberly Kause
Minnesota Online HS	1313 5th St SE	Minneapolis, MN	55414-4513	612-227-8499		9-12	Chris Brucker
Minnesota Transitions Charter S	2872 26th Ave S	Minneapolis, MN	55406-1529	612-722-9013	722-0013	K-12	Patty Brostrom
Naytahwaush Community S	PO Box 8	Naytahwaush, MN	56566-0008	218-935-5025	935-5263	K-6	Gayle Gish
Nerstrand Charter S	PO Box 156	Nerstrand, MN	55053-0156	507-333-6850	333-6870	K-5	Lauren Satrom
New Century Charter S	PO Box 484	Hutchinson, MN	55350-0484	320-234-3660	234-3668	7-12	Allen Hoffman
New City S	229 13th Ave NE	Minneapolis, MN	55413-1117	612-623-3309	623-3319	K-6	Terrance Russ
New Discoveries Montessori Academy	PO Box 305	Hutchinson, MN	55350-0305	320-234-6362	234-6300	K-6	Dave Conrad
New Heights Charter S	614 Mulberry St W	Stillwater, MN	55082-4858	651-439-1962	439-0716	K-12	Thomas Kearney
New Millenium Academy	1203 Bryant Ave N	Minneapolis, MN	55411-4087	612-377-6260	377-6261	K-8	Neng Heur
New Spirit S	260 Edmund Ave	Saint Paul, MN	55103-1783	651-225-9177	225-2990	K-8	Walter Stull
New Visions Charter S	1800 2nd St NE	Minneapolis, MN	55418-4306	612-706-5566	706-5599	K-8	Jennifer Geraghty
Noble Academy	6717 85th Ave N	Brooklyn Park, MN	55445-2255	763-255-2460	255-2465	K-5	Neal Thao
Northern Lights Community S	PO Box 2829	Warba, MN	55793-2829	218-492-4400	492-4402	6-12	David Hagman
North Lakes Academy	255b 7th Ave NW	Forest Lake, MN	55025-1157	651-982-2773	464-6409	6-9	Jackie Saunders
North Shore Community S	5926 Ryan Rd	Duluth, MN	55804-9672	218-525-0663	525-0024	K-6	Susan Rose
Northwest Passage HS	11345 Robinson Dr NW	Coon Rapids, MN	55433-3777	763-862-9223	862-9250	9-12	James Steckart
Nova Classical Academy	1668 Montreal Ave	Saint Paul, MN	55116-2469	651-227-8622	699-5959	K-12	Miranda Morton
Odyssey Academy	6201 Noble Ave N	Brooklyn Park, MN	55429-2483	763-971-8200	549-2380	K-9	Kari Mitchell
PACT Charter S	7250 E Ramsey Pkwy	Ramsey, MN	55303-6902	763-712-4200	712-4201	K-12	Daniel DeBruyn
Paideia Academy Charter S	7200 147th St W	Apple Valley, MN	55124-9008	952-953-6200	432-2130	K-8	Chris Pellant
Partnership Academy	305 E 77th St Ste B	Minneapolis, MN	55423	612-866-3630	866-3640	K-7	Lisa Ladue
Pillager Area Charter S	PO Box 130	Pillager, MN	56473-0130	218-746-3875	746-3876	9-12	Mark Wolhart
Pine Grove Leadership Academy	63842 Ojibwe Rd	Sandstone, MN	55072-3342	320-384-7598	384-7485	K-8	Terry Moffatt
Prairie Creek Community S	27695 Denmark Ave	Northfield, MN	55057-5333	507-645-9640	645-8234	K-5	Caroline Jones
Prairie Seeds Academy	6200 W Broadway Ave	Minneapolis, MN	55428-2826	763-450-1388	450-1389	K-8	Choua Yang
Prestige Academy Charter S	1704 Dupont Ave N	Minneapolis, MN	55411-3219	612-465-8121	465-8125	9-12	Inez Grace
Quest Academy	3946 Wooddale Ave S	St Louis Park, MN	55416-2915	952-285-4100	285-4114	5-12	Sue Valdes
Recovery S of Southern MN	1225 Lincoln Ave	Owatonna, MN	55060-4029	507-214-2057		9-12	Gary Braun
Ridgeway Community S	35564 County Road 12	Houston, MN	55943-4006	507-454-9566	454-9567	K-6	Jodi Dansingburg
RiverBend Academy	110 N 6th St	Mankato, MN	56001-4443	507-387-5524	387-5680	7-12	Don Johannsen
River Heights Charter S	60 Marie Ave E	West Saint Paul, MN	55118-5932	651-457-7427	554-7611	9-12	Jane Davin
Riverway Learning Community Charter S	PO Box 43	Minnesota City, MN	55959-0043	507-689-2844	689-2834	PK-12	Laura Krause
Rochester Off Campus Charter HS	2364 Valleyhigh Dr NW	Rochester, MN	55901-7641	507-282-3325	282-0976	9-12	Jay Martini
Sage Academy Charter S	3900 85th Ave N	Brooklyn Park, MN	55443-1908	763-315-4020	315-4028	9-12	Diane Scholten
Saint Croix Preparatory Academy	4260 Stagecoach Trl N	Stillwater, MN	55082	651-395-5900		K-9	Jon Gutierrez
Saint Paul Conservatory Performing Art	75 5th St W Ste 522	Saint Paul, MN	55102-1439	651-290-2225	290-9000	9-12	Terry Tofte
Schoolcraft Learning Community S	PO Box 1685	Bemidji, MN	56619-1685	218-586-3284	586-3285	K-8	Scott Anderson
Seed Academy/Harvest Prep S	1300 Olson Memorial Hwy	Minneapolis, MN	55411	612-381-9743	377-2999	PK-6	Eric Mahmoud
Seven Hills Classical Academy	8600 Bloomington Ave	Bloomington, MN	55425-1920	952-426-6000	426-6020	K-8	Margaret O'Brien
Skills for Tomorrow HS	547 Wheeler St N	Saint Paul, MN	55104-3078	651-647-6000	645-2388	9-12	Claude Maddox
Sobriety HS	2233 University Ave W	Saint Paul, MN	55114	651-773-8378	748-5290	9-12	Jim Czarniecki
Sojourner Truth Academy	3820 Emerson Ave N	Minneapolis, MN	55412-2039	612-588-3599	588-0217	K-8	Julie Guy
Southside Family Charter S	2123 Clinton Ave	Minneapolis, MN	55404-2650	612-872-8322	872-0612	K-8	Eliza Goodwin
Spectrum HS	10129 181st Ave NW	Elk River, MN	55330-3305	763-241-8703		9-12	Vanessa Spark
Stonebridge Community S	4 W Franklin Ave	Minneapolis, MN	55404-2448	612-877-7400	877-7444	K-6	Barbara Novy
Stride Academy	1025 18th St N	Saint Cloud, MN	56303-1205	320-230-5340	253-0006	K-6	Dale Beutel
Studio Academy	415 16th St SW	Rochester, MN	55902-2125	507-529-1662	529-1643	10-12	Kandice Mascotti
Swan River Montessori Charter S	500 Maple St	Monticello, MN	55362-8878	763-271-7926	295-0075	K-6	Sandra Morrow
Tarek Ibn Ziyad Academy	4100 66th St E	Inver Grove, MN	55076-2203	651-457-7072	457-7190	K-5	Asad Zaman
TEAM Academy	501 Elm Ave E	Waseca, MN	56093-3360	507-837-5149	837-5493	K-6	Jody Allen Crowe
Treknorth HS	2518 Hannah Ave NW	Bemidji, MN	56601-2110	218-444-1888	444-1893	7-12	Dan McKeon
Trio Wolf Creek Distance Learning	13750 Lake Blvd	Lindstrom, MN	55045-9361	651-213-2017	257-0576	4-12	Tracy Quarnstrom
Twin Cities Academy Charter S	426 Osceola Ave S	Saint Paul, MN	55102-3535	651-205-4797	205-4799	6-12	Liz Wynne
Twin Cities German Immersion S	1745 University Ave W	Saint Paul, MN	55104	651-492-7106	789-0117	K-8	Judy Ingison
Twin Cities International ES	277 12th Ave N	Minneapolis, MN	55401-1026	612-821-6470	821-6477	K-4	Randal Eckart
Ubah Medical Academy Charter S	1600 Mainstreet	Hopkins, MN	55343-7409	952-988-4940	988-4941	9-12	Heather Mansour
Urban Academy Charter S	133 7th St E	Saint Paul, MN	55101-3460	651-215-9419	215-9571	K-6	Mongsher Ly
Vessey Leadership S	33 Wentworth Ave E Ste 100	Saint Paul, MN	55118-3432	651-776-8776		9-12	Don Vance
Voyageurs Expeditionary HS	102 1st St W	Bemidji, MN	56601-4002	218-444-3130	444-3126	9-12	Julie Johnson-Willborg
Watershed HS	2344 Nicollet Ave Ste 200	Minneapolis, MN	55404-3373	612-871-4363	871-1004	9-12	Phil Grant
Waynewood School of Hope	1000 University Ave W	Saint Paul, MN	55104-4706	651-917-3085		6-8	Beverly Waynewood
Woodson Institute for Excellence	2620 Russell Ave N	Minneapolis, MN	55411-1725	612-455-1611	455-1612	K-6	LaTanya Washington
World Learner Charter S	112050 Hundertmark Rd	Chaska, MN	55318-2817	952-368-7398	368-6094	K-6	Randi Shapiro
Worthington Area Language Academy	PO Box 185	Bigelow, MN	56117-0185	507-683-2004	683-2013	K-6	Randy Haley
Yankton Country S	PO Box 406	Balaton, MN	56115-0406	507-734-2677	734-2678	9-12	Cynthia Duus
Yinghua Academy	1355 Pierce Butler Rte	Saint Paul, MN	55104-1359	651-379-4112	379-4115	K-4	Betsy Lueth

Mississippi

School	Address	City,State	Zip code	Telephone	Fax	Grade	Contact
Hayes Cooper Center for Math & Science	500 N M L K	Merigold, MS	38759	662-748-2734	748-2735	PK-6	Beverly Hardy

Missouri

School	Address	City,State	Zip code	Telephone	Fax	Grade	Contact
Academie Lafayette S	6903 Oak St	Kansas City, MO	64113-2530	816-361-7735	361-5788	K-8	Eric Nelis
Academy of Kansas City	2015 E 72nd St	Kansas City, MO	64132-1756	816-523-4707	523-5449	K-8	Vonnelle Middleton
Allen Village S	706 W 42nd St	Kansas City, MO	64111-3120	816-931-0177	561-4640	K-8	Phyllis Washington
Alta Vista Charter S	1722 Holly St	Kansas City, MO	64108-2217	816-471-2582	471-2139	9-12	Eduardo Mendez
Banneker Charter Academy Technology	8310 Holmes Rd	Kansas City, MO	64131-2254	816-926-9110	926-0115	K-8	Dr. Marion Brown
Bosco Charter HS	548 Brooklyn Ave	Kansas City, MO	64124-1710	816-691-2937	691-6927	9-12	Bernadette Barber
Brookside Charter Academy	5220 Troost Ave	Kansas City, MO	64110-2546	816-531-2192	756-3055	K-5	Millie Krna
Brookside Frontier Math & Science	5605 Troost Ave	Kansas City, MO	64110-2823	816-822-1331	822-1332	6-10	Bilgehan Yasar
City Garden Montessori Charter S	2109 S Spring Ave	Saint Louis, MO	63110-3715	314-664-7646		K-3	Trish Curtis
Confluence Academy-Old North St. Louis	3017 N 13th St	Saint Louis, MO	63107-3924	314-241-1110	241-1115	K-8	Deniece Fields
Confluence Academy-South City Campus	4235 S Compton Ave	Saint Louis, MO	63111-1129	314-481-4700		K-8	Pam Davenport
Confluence Academy-Walnut Park Campus	5421 Thekla Ave	Saint Louis, MO	63120-2513	314-383-8900		K-8	Denean Vaughn
Confluence Prep Academy	3112 Meramec St	Saint Louis, MO	63118-4339	314-752-8700		9-9	John Diehl
Construction Careers Center	1224 Grattan St	Saint Louis, MO	63104-2922	314-588-9991	588-1982	9-12	Gina Washington
Genesis S	3800 E 44th St	Kansas City, MO	64130-2183	816-921-0775	921-4268	5-9	Pamela Pearson
Hedgeman Lyle Academy	1509 Washington Ave Ste 800	Saint Louis, MO	63103-1821	314-322-5517		K-5	Janis Wiley
Hedgeman Lyle MSHS	1881 Pine St	Saint Louis, MO	63103-2264	314-621-0402		6-12	Louis Cross
Hogan Preparatory Academy	1221 E Meyer Blvd	Kansas City, MO	64131-1207	816-444-3464	363-0473	9-12	Danny Tipton
Imagine Academy of Academic Success	1409 E Linton Ave	Saint Louis, MO	63107-1116	314-652-1600	652-1601	K-8	Angela Howard
Imagine Academy of Careers ES	3740 Marine Ave	Saint Louis, MO	63118-4175	314-776-6300	776-1630	K-5	Carmen Jansen
Imagine Academy of Careers MS	1901 N Kingshighway Blvd	Saint Louis, MO	63113-1123	314-361-4940	361-4942	6-8	Kwame Simmons
Imagine Academy of Envrnmntl Sci & Math	1008 S Spring Ave	Saint Louis, MO	63110-2520	314-773-4400	652-8772	K-8	Dr. Angele Burns
Imagine Renaissance Academy	5000 E 17th St	Kansas City, MO	64127-2833	816-241-3465		K-5	Jamie Draper-Griffin
Imagine Renaissance Academy	414 Wallace Ave	Kansas City, MO	64125-1132	816-363-1694		6-12	Geoff Alderman
KIPP Endeavor Academy	PO Box 22624	Kansas City, MO	64113-0624	816-241-3994	241-3339	5-8	Jon Richard
Lamb ES	1000 Charlotte St	Kansas City, MO	64106-3051	816-221-0043	221-0937	K-6	Judy Akers
Lift for Life Academy	1731 S Broadway	Saint Louis, MO	63104-4050	314-436-2337	231-1299	6-10	Katrice Noble
Paideia Academy-College Hill Campus	2017 E Linton Ave	Saint Louis, MO	63107-1134	314-534-9628	534-0815	K-8	Wendy Irving
Paideia Acadmey-Carondelet Campus	7604 Michigan Ave	Saint Louis, MO	63111-3332	314-631-5484	534-1085	K-8	Patrice Coffin
Parks ES	3715 Wyoming St	Kansas City, MO	64111-3945	816-753-6700	753-3436	K-5	Kajuan Cummings
St. Louis Charter S	5279 Fyler Ave	Saint Louis, MO	63139-1300	314-645-9600	645-9700	K-8	Tracy Garrett
Scuola Vita Nuova	544 Wabash Ave	Kansas City, MO	64124-1747	816-231-5788	231-5181	K-8	Nicole King
Thomas Academy	201 E Armour Blvd	Kansas City, MO	64111-1205	816-531-7144	753-8856	K-8	Shane Knight
Tolbert Community Academy	3400 Paseo Blvd	Kansas City, MO	64109-2429	816-561-0114	561-1015	K-8	Dr. Vivian Roper
Tolbert Preparatory Academy	5809 Michigan Ave	Kansas City, MO	64130-3349	816-977-7539		9-12	Tammy Combs
University Academy	6801 Holmes Rd	Kansas City, MO	64131-1382	816-412-5900	412-0322	K-12	Cheri Shannon
Urban Community Leadership Academy	1524 Paseo Blvd	Kansas City, MO	64108-1622	816-483-8035	483-8998	5-9	Joyce McGautha

Nevada

School	Address	City,State	Zip code	Telephone	Fax	Grade	Contact
Academy for Career Education	2800 Vassar St	Reno, NV	89502-3214	775-324-3900	324-3901	10-12	Silvia Marin
Agassi Academy	1201 W Lake Mead Blvd	Las Vegas, NV	89106-2411	702-948-6000	948-6002	K-12	Roy Parker
Bailey Charter ES	1090 Bresson Ave	Reno, NV	89502-2625	775-323-6767	323-6799	K-6	Carl Meibergen
Carson Montessori S	2263 Mouton Dr	Carson City, NV	89706-0446	775-887-9500	887-9502	K-6	Jessica Daniels
Coral Academy of Science Charter S	1350 E 9th St	Reno, NV	89512-2904	775-323-2332	323-2366	K-12	Erdinc Acar
Coral Academy of Science - Las Vegas	8185 Tamarus St	Las Vegas, NV	89123-2464	702-269-8512	269-3258	K-12	Feyzi Tandogan
Davidson Academy of Nevada	PO Box 9119	Reno, NV	89507-9119	775-682-5800	682-5801	6-12	Colleen Harsin
Delta Academy	4075 N Rancho Dr	Las Vegas, NV	89130-3413	702-396-2252	396-0848	K-12	Wayne Tanaka
Explore Knowledge Academy	4801 S Sandhill Rd	Las Vegas, NV	89121-6020	702-870-5032	870-5032	K-12	Sean McManus

School	Address	City,State	Zip code	Telephone	Fax	Grade	Contact
High Desert Montessori Charter S	2590 Orovada St	Reno, NV	89512-2119	775-624-2800	624-2801	PK-8	Carol Andrew
I Can Do Anything Charter HS	1195 Corporate Blvd Ste C	Reno, NV	89502-2363	775-857-1544	857-6825	9-12	Allen Beebe
Imagine S in the Valle	3521 N Durango Dr	Las Vegas, NV	89129-7277	702-631-4751	631-1125	K-5	Connie Burch
Innovations International Charter S	1600 E Oakey Blvd	Las Vegas, NV	89104-3334	702-216-4337	216-4353	K-12	Dr. Connie Malin
Insight S of Nevada	8960 W Tropicana Ave # 500	Las Vegas, NV	89147	702-951-4520	951-4545	9-12	Gary Waters
Las Vegas Charter S for the Deaf	10094 Catalina Canyon Ave	Las Vegas, NV	89147-8047	702-385-3323		K-3	Elaine Haines
Mariposa Academy of Language & Learning	3875 Glen St	Reno, NV	89502-4803	775-826-4040	826-4030	K-6	Maria Jimenez
Nevada Connections Academy	5690 Riggins Ct Ste B	Reno, NV	89502-6278	775-826-4200	826-4288	K-12	Jerry Krummel
Nevada State HS	303 S Water St Ste 120	Henderson, NV	89015-7305	702-953-2600	953-2608	11-12	Dr. John Hawk
Nevada Virtual Academy	187 E Warm Springs Rd Ste C	Las Vegas, NV	89119-4112	702-407-1825	407-5055	K-12	Mike Kazek
Odyssey Charter S	2251 S Jones Blvd	Las Vegas, NV	89146-3161	702-257-0578	259-7793	K-12	Dr. Michelle Robinson
One Hundred Academy of Excellence	2341 Comstock Dr	North Las Vegas, NV	89032-3512	702-636-2551	636-9475	K-8	Hugh Wallace
Rainbow Dreams Academy	950 W Lake Mead Blvd	Las Vegas, NV	89106-2339	702-638-0222	638-0220	K-3	Carol Threats
Rainshadow Community Charter HS	434 Washington St	Reno, NV	89503-4323	775-322-5566	322-5509	9-12	Steve West Ed.D.
Sierra Crest Academy	PO Box 2439	Minden, NV	89423-2439	775-783-9002	552-9815	K-12	David Brackett
Sierra Nevada Academy	13880 Stead Blvd	Reno, NV	89506-1579	775-677-4500	677-4441	K-8	Kim Regan
Silver State HS	3719 N Carson St	Carson City, NV	89706-1934	775-883-7900	883-9130	9-12	Steve Knight
New Hampshire							
Academy for Science & Design	316 Daniel Webster Hwy	Merrimack, NH	03054-4115	603-262-9162	262-9163	7-12	Chris Franklin
Cocheco Arts and Technology Academy	1 Washington St Ste 555	Dover, NH	03820-3851	603-664-9671	664-9679	9-12	Deborah Byrne
CSI Charter S	26 Washington St	Penacook, NH	03303-1519	603-753-0199	753-6429	9-12	Paulette Fitzgerald
Equestrian Academy Charter S	PO Box 808	Rochester, NH	03866-0808	603-335-6900	224-8366	9-12	Meredith Wiles
Great Bay eLearning Charter S	30 Linden St	Exeter, NH	03833-2622	603-775-8935	775-8606	8-12	Cheryl McDonough
North Country Charter Academy	260 Cottage St Ste A	Littleton, NH	03561-4137	603-444-1535	444-9843	7-12	Lisa Lavoie
Seacoast Charter S	PO Box 892	Exeter, NH	03833-0892	603-642-8400	642-8404	1-8	Bill Wilmot
Strong Foundations Charter S	715 Riverwood Dr	Pembroke, NH	03275-3701	603-225-2715	225-2738	K-4	Beth McClure
Surry Village Charter S	11 Village Rd	Surry, NH	03431-8311	603-357-9700	357-9701	K-6	Matora Fiorey
Virtual Learning Academy	30 Linden St	Exeter, NH	03833-2622	603-778-2500	651-5038	9-12	Gary Tirone
New Jersey							
Academy Charter HS	1725 Main St	South Belmar, NJ	07719-3051	732-681-8377	681-8375	9-12	Mary Jo McKinley
Bergen Arts and Science Charter S	200 MacArthur Ave	Garfield, NJ	07026-1214	201-253-0002	253-0110	K-5	Nihat Guvercin
Burch Charter S of Excellence	100 Linden Ave	Irvington, NJ	07111-2560	973-373-3323	373-3228	PK-2	Dorian Dorsey
Camden Academy Charter HS	879 Beideman Ave	Camden, NJ	08105-4227	856-365-1000	365-8179	9-12	Dr. Joseph Conway
Camden's Pride Charter S	820 Lois Ave	Camden, NJ	08105-4124	856-365-1000	365-1005	K-4	Rebecca Brinkman
Camden's Promise Charter S	879 Beideman Ave	Camden, NJ	08105-4227	856-365-1000	365-1005	5-8	Dr. Joe Conway
Capital Prep Charter HS	22 Grand St	Trenton, NJ	08611-2416	609-393-9060	393-9047	9-10	Shenette Gray
Central Jersey Arts Charter S	35 Watchung Ave	Plainfield, NJ	07060-1207	908-753-0030	753-0032	K-6	Ben Fox
Central Jersey College Prep Charter S	17 Schoolhouse Rd	Somerset, NJ	08873-1235	732-302-9991	302-9992	7-12	Bekir Duz
ChARTer-TECHnical HS	413 New Rd	Somers Point, NJ	08244-2143	609-926-7694	926-8472	9-12	Janice Strigh
Classical Academy Charter S of Clifton	20 Valley Rd	Clifton, NJ	07013-1030	973-278-7707	278-7720	6-8	Vincent DeRosa
Community Charter S of Paterson	75 Spruce St	Paterson, NJ	07501-1720	973-413-2057	345-7623	K-3	Christina Hernandez
CREATE Charter S	164 Lembeck Ave	Jersey City, NJ	07305-3803	201-413-1500	413-1800	9-12	Stephen Lipski
Discovery Charter S	303 Washington St	Newark, NJ	07102-2750	973-623-0222	623-0024	4-8	Irene Hall
D.U.E. Season Charter S	1000 Atlantic Ave Ste 524	Camden, NJ	08104	856-225-0511	668-2196	K-8	Dr. Doris Carpenter
East Orange Community Charter S	99 Washington St	East Orange, NJ	07017-1006	973-996-0400	996-0398	K-4	Harvin Dash
Elysian Charter S	301 Garden St Ste 5	Hoboken, NJ	07030-5895	201-876-0102	876-9576	K-8	Carol Stock
Englewood on the Palisades Charter S	65 W Demarest Ave	Englewood, NJ	07631-2316	201-569-9765	568-9576	K-6	Anthony Barckett
Environment Comm Opportunity Charter S	817 Carpenter St	Camden, NJ	08102-1132	856-963-2627	963-2628	K-4	Antoinette Dendtler
Ethical Community Charter S-Jersey City	PO Box 239	Jersey City, NJ	07303-0239	201-606-8108	606-8108	K-1	Dr. Judith Wallach
Fisher S of Advanced Studies	31 Chancery Ln	Trenton, NJ	08618-4805	609-656-1444	656-0999	6-12	G. Dallas Dixon
Foundation Academy Charter S	333 S Broad St	Trenton, NJ	08608-2501	609-920-9200	920-9205	5-8	Ronald Brady
Freedom Academy Charter S	1400 Collings Rd	Camden, NJ	08104-3113	856-962-0766	962-0769	5-8	Ernest Harper
Galloway Community Charter S	112 S New York Rd	Galloway, NJ	08205-9608	609-652-7118	652-3640	K-6	Deborah Nataloni
Golden Door Charter S	180 9th St	Jersey City, NJ	07302-1703	201-795-4400	795-3308	K-8	Brian Stiles
Gray Charter S	55 Liberty St	Newark, NJ	07102-4815	973-824-6661	824-2296	K-8	Verna Gray
Greater Brunswick Charter S	429B Joyce Kilmer Ave	New Brunswick, NJ	08901-3322	732-448-1052	448-1055	K-9	Robert Agree
Greater Newark Charter S	72 Central Ave	Newark, NJ	07102-1905	973-242-3543	242-5792	5-8	Peter Turnamian
Hoboken Charter S	4th and Garden St 3rd Floor	Hoboken, NJ	07030	201-963-0222	963-0880	PK-12	Alfredo Huereca
Hope Academy Charter S	601 Grand Ave	Asbury Park, NJ	07712	732-988-4227	988-9218	K-8	Alexis Harris
Institute of Excellence Charter S	20 E Taunton Rd Ste 540	Berlin, NJ	08009-2625	856-767-6755	767-6754	K-5	Clifton Matthew
International Charter S of Trenton	105 Grand St	Trenton, NJ	08611-2417	609-394-3111	394-3116	K-5	Melissa Benford
Jersey City Community Charter S	128 Danforth Ave	Jersey City, NJ	07305-2626	201-433-2288	433-5803	K-8	Carletta Martin-Goldston
Lady Liberty Academy Charter S	PO Box 180	Newark, NJ	07101-0180	973-623-9005	623-4088	K-8	Charles Mugambe
LEAP Academy University Charter S	549 Cooper St	Camden, NJ	08102-1210	856-614-0400	342-7900	K-12	Dr. Deanna Burney
Learning Community Charter S	1 Canal St	Jersey City, NJ	07302-4330	201-332-0900	332-4981	K-8	Susan Grierson
Liberty Academy Charter S	211 Sherman Ave	Jersey City, NJ	07307-2040	201-217-6771	217-6772	K-8	William Thomas
New Horizons Community Charter S	45 Hayes St	Newark, NJ	07103-3019	973-848-0400	596-0984	K-5	Andre Hollis
North Star Academy Charter S	10 Washington Pl	Newark, NJ	07102-3106	973-642-0101	642-5800	K-12	Michael Ambriz
Oceanside Charter S	1750 Bacharach Blvd	Atlantic City, NJ	08401-4308	609-348-3485	348-5951	PK-8	Jeanine Middleton
PACE Charter School of Hamilton	1949 Hamilton Ave	Hamilton, NJ	08619-3736	609-587-2288	587-8483	K-3	Michael Mikitish
Paterson Charter S Science & Tech	276 Wabash Ave	Paterson, NJ	07503-1612	973-247-0600	247-9924	6-11	Emrah Ayhan
PleasanTech Academy Charter S	535 Mrtn Luther King Jr Ave	Pleasantville, NJ	08232	609-383-1717	484-1085	K-8	Michael Carr
Pressman Charter S	PO Box 71	Plainfield, NJ	07061-0071	908-668-7770		6-7	Dr. Norman Pressman
Pride Academy Charter S	117 Elmwood Ave	East Orange, NJ	07018-2420	973-672-3200	672-3207	5-8	
Princeton Charter S	100 Bunn Dr	Princeton, NJ	08540-2821	609-924-0575	924-0282	K-8	Dr. Broderick Boxley
Queen City Academy Charter S	815 W 7th St	Plainfield, NJ	07063-1449	908-753-4700	753-4816	K-8	RaShawn Adams
Red Bank Charter S	58 Oakland St	Red Bank, NJ	07701-1104	732-450-2092	936-1923	K-8	Meredith Pennotti
Ridge & Valley Charter S	1234 State Route 94	Blairstown, NJ	07825-4115	908-362-1114	362-6680	K-8	Nanci Dvorsky
Riverbank Charter S of Excellence	1238 Hornberger Ave	Roebling, NJ	08554-1606	609-499-4321	278-0363	K-3	Beth Kelley
Robeson Charter S for the Humanities	643 Indiana Ave	Trenton, NJ	08638-3821	609-394-7727	394-7720	9-12	Barbara Gaeta
Sanford Charter S	53 Lincoln Park	Newark, NJ	07102-2390	973-297-1275	297-1120	K-8	Fredrica Bey
Schomburg Charter S	508 Grand St	Jersey City, NJ	07302-4103	201-451-7770	451-1770	K-5	Emma Sheffield
Soaring Heights Charter S	1 Romar Ave	Jersey City, NJ	07305-1713	201-434-4800	434-7474	K-8	Claudia Zuorick
Sussex Co. Charter S for Technology	105 N Church Rd	Sparta, NJ	07871-3203	973-383-6700	383-2901	7-8	Jill Ekel
TEAM Academy Charter S	85 Custer Ave	Newark, NJ	07112-2511	973-705-8326	556-1238	5-8	Ryan Hill
Teaneck Community Charter S	1650 Palisade Ave	Teaneck, NJ	07666-3603	201-833-9600	833-9225	K-8	Dr. Rex Shaw
Thomas Charter S	370 S 7th St	Newark, NJ	07103-2047	973-621-0060	621-0061	K-8	Lynette Tanis
Treat Academy Charter S	443 Clifton Ave	Newark, NJ	07104-1339	973-482-8811	482-7681	K-8	Michael Pallante
Trenton Community Charter S	349 W State St	Trenton, NJ	08618-5705	609-394-0068	695-0193	K-8	Jerri Morrison
Union County TEAMS Charter S	515 W 4th St	Plainfield, NJ	07060-4225	908-754-9043	754-7790	K-8	Sondra Harrison
Unity Charter S	340 Speedwell Ave	Morristown, NJ	07960-2988	973-292-1808	267-9288	K-8	Dr. Char Stanko
University Academy Charter HS	275 W Side Ave	Jersey City, NJ	07305-1130	201-200-3200	200-3262	9-12	Erie Lugo
University Heights Charter S	74 Hartford St	Newark, NJ	07103-2832	973-623-1965	623-8511	K-5	Misha Simmonds Ed.D.
Varisco-Rogers Charter S	233 Woodside Ave	Newark, NJ	07104-3113	973-481-9001	481-9009	2-8	Teresa Segarra
Village Charter S	101 Sullivan Way	Trenton, NJ	08628-3425	609-695-0110	695-1880	K-8	Aisha Thomas-Johnson
Vineland Public Charter S	1155 E Landis Ave	Vineland, NJ	08360-4220	856-985-4782	327-2580	K-2	Dr. Ann Garcia
New Mexico							
Academia De Lengua Y Cultura	PO Box 9087	Albuquerque, NM	87119-9087	505-563-4242	563-4260	6-8	Colleen Adolph
Academy for Tech & Classics	74 Avan Nu PO	Santa Fe, NM	87508-1465	505-473-4282	362-8106	7-12	Ruth Le Blanc
Albuquerque Institute of Math & Science	933 Bradbury Dr SE	Albuquerque, NM	87106-4301	505-559-4249	994-3394	6-12	Kathy Sandoval-Snider
Albuquerque Talent Development Charter S	1800 Atrisco Dr NW	Albuquerque, NM	87105	505-850-9188	821-2554	9-12	Robert Chavez
Alma D Arte Charter HS	PO Box 10	Las Cruces, NM	88004-0010	575-541-0145	541-0146	9-12	Catherine Martinez
Anansi Charter S	PO Box 1709	El Prado, NM	87529-1709	575-776-2256	776-5561	K-3	Michele Hunt
Bataan Military Academy	8001 Mountain Road Pl NE	Albuquerque, NM	87110-7808	505-292-5588	232-3230	9-12	Shelby Tallchief
Bernell Charter S	401 Roma Ave NW Fl 3	Albuquerque, NM	87102	505-468-7701		9-12	Greta Roskom
Biehl Charter HS	123 4th St SW	Albuquerque, NM	87102-3201	505-299-9409	299-9493	9-12	Sandy Beery
Bridge Academy	PO Box 1119	Las Vegas, NM	87701-1119	505-425-3302	454-8688	9-12	Ruben Cordova
Bunche Academy	1718 Yale Blvd SE	Albuquerque, NM	87106-4136	505-292-0100	292-0109	K-5	Jasper Matthews
Career Academic Technical Academy	6805 Academy Pkwy West NE	Albuquerque, NM	87109	505-345-1514	962-2920	10-12	Glee Hare
Carinos De Los Ninos S	PO Box 1097	San Juan Pueblo, NM	87566-1097	505-852-3119	852-3189	K-2	Victoria Garcia
Charter S 37	1501 Cerrillos Rd Bldg 2	Santa Fe, NM	87505	505-983-3337	983-6637	9-12	Ron Lolordo
Chavez Community S	1718 Yale Blvd SE	Albuquerque, NM	87106-4136	505-877-0558	242-1466	9-12	Caryl Thomas
Corrales International S	3821 Singer Blvd NE	Albuquerque, NM	87109-5804	505-344-9733	338-1409	K-8	Carlos Pagan
Cottonwood Classical Preparatory S	1776 Montano Rd NW Bldg 3	Los Ranchos, NM	87107-3248	505-998-1021	345-6397	6-12	Dr. Chad Redwing
Cottonwood Valley Charter S	PO Box 1829	Socorro, NM	87801-1829	575-838-2026	838-2420	K-8	Karin Williams
Creative Education Prep Institute #1	PO Box 50880	Albuquerque, NM	87181-0880	505-314-2374	314-2377	9-12	Tom Crespin
Creative Education Prep Institute #2	69 Hotel Cir NE	Albuquerque, NM	87123-1202	505-237-2373	237-2380	9-12	Nancy Romero
Deming Cesar Chavez Charter HS	PO Box 1658	Deming, NM	88031-1658	575-544-8404	544-8755	9-12	Arlene Trujillo
Digital Arts and Technology Academy	1011 Lamberton Pl NE	Albuquerque, NM	87107-1641	505-341-0888	341-0749	9-12	Lisa Myhre
Duncan Charter S	5201 Central Ave NW	Albuquerque, NM	87105	505-839-4971	831-9027	K-5	Jesus Moncada
East Mountain HS	PO Box 340	Sandia Park, NM	87047-0340	505-281-7400	281-4173	9-12	Doug Wine
El Camino Real Charter S	3713 Isleta Blvd SW	Albuquerque, NM	87105	505-314-2212	314-2216	K-12	Jennifer Mercer

School	Address	City,State	Zip code	Telephone	Fax	Grade	Contact
Espanola Military Academy	PO Box 100	Espanola, NM	87532-0100	505-747-3317	747-0046	6-12	Steve Baca
Gutierrez MS	PO Box 1437	Roswell, NM	88202-1437	575-347-9703	347-9707	6-8	Joe Andreis
Horizon Academy - West	1900 Atrisco Dr NW	Albuquerque, NM	87120-1146	505-998-0459	998-0463	K-6	Amie Duran
Jefferson Montessori Academy	500 W Church St	Carlsbad, NM	88220-5135	575-234-1703	887-9391	K-12	Cindy Holguin
Kennedy HS	1511 Central Ave NE	Albuquerque, NM	87106-4408	505-243-1118	242-7444	9-12	Robert Baade
La Academia de Esperanza	5200 Sequoia Rd NW	Albuquerque, NM	87120-1208	505-764-5500	764-5501	6-12	Steve Woods
La Academia Dolores Huerta	1480 N Main St	Las Cruces, NM	88001-1106	575-526-2984	523-2924	6-8	Gilbert Gutierrez
La Luz del Monte Learning Center	10301 Candelaria Rd NE	Albuquerque, NM	87112-1504	505-296-7677	296-0510	7-8	Al Baysinger
La Promesa Early Learning Center	5201 Central Ave NW	Albuquerque, NM	87105	505-268-3274	268-3276	K-3	Bernadette Maes
La Resolana Learning Academy	1718 Yale Blvd SE	Albuquerque, NM	87106-4136	505-292-0100	292-0109	6-8	Justina Montoya
Las Montanas Charter S	201 E Lohman Ave	Las Cruces, NM	88001-3659	575-636-2100	527-7686	9-10	Joyce Aranda
Learning Community Charter S	5555 McLeod Rd NE	Albuquerque, NM	87109-2408	505-332-3200	332-8780	6-12	Viola Martinez
Leopold Charter S	PO Box 770	Silver City, NM	88062-0770	575-538-2547	388-4970	9-12	Michael May
Lindrith Area Heritage Charter S	PO Box 119	Lindrith, NM	87029-0119	575-774-6669	774-6669	K-8	Rebecca Gibson
Los Puentes Charter S	1106 Griegos Rd NW	Albuquerque, NM	87107-3751	505-342-5959	341-0836	8-12	Ellen Moore
Media Arts Collaborative S	4401 Central Ave NE	Albuquerque, NM	87108-1209	505-243-1957		9-12	Glenna Voigt
Middle College HS	200 College Rd Ste 9	Gallup, NM	87301	505-863-7551	863-7627	10-12	Wally Feldman
Monte Del Sol Charter S	PO Box 4068	Santa Fe, NM	87502-4068	505-982-5225	982-5321	7-12	Ann Salzmann
Montessori ES	3831 Midway Pl NE	Albuquerque, NM	87109	505-796-0149	796-0147	K-6	Mary Jane Besante
Montessori of the Rio Grande Charter S	1650 Gabaldon Dr NW	Albuquerque, NM	87104-2761	505-842-5993	242-2907	K-5	Dr. Bonnie Dodge
Moreno Valley HS	PO Box 1037	Angel Fire, NM	87710-1037	575-377-3100	377-7263	9-12	Jacque Boyd
Mosaic Academy	101 Ute Ave	Aztec, NM	87410-2381	505-334-6364		K-8	Bonnie Braden
Mountain Mahogany Community S	5014 4th St NW	Albuquerque, NM	87107-3908	505-341-1424	341-1428	K-3	Nancy Kent
Native American Community Academy	1100 Cardenas Dr SE	Albuquerque, NM	87108-4809	505-266-0992	266-2905	6-8	Kara Bobroff
North Albuquerque Coop Community ES	4261 Balloon Park Rd NE	Albuquerque, NM	87109-5802	505-344-0746	344-0789	K-6	Shelly Cherrin
North Valley Academy	7939 4th St NW	Albuquerque, NM	87114-1008	505-998-0501	998-0505	K-8	Jerald Snider
Nuestros Valores Charter S	1021 Isleta Blvd SW	Albuquerque, NM	87105-3934	505-873-7758	873-3567	9-12	Monica Aguilar
Public Academy for Performing Arts	4665 Indian School Rd NE	Albuquerque, NM	87110-3918	505-262-4888	262-4893	6-12	Katy Harvey
Red River Valley Charter S	PO Box 742	Red River, NM	87558-0742	575-754-6117	754-3258	K-8	Karen Phillips
Rio Gallinas S	301 Socorro St	Las Vegas, NM	87701-3353	505-454-8687	454-8688	2-8	Cindy McLeod
Roots & Wings Community S	PO Box 1152	El Prado, NM	87529-1152	575-586-2076	586-2087	5-8	Margaret Bartlett
San Diego Riverside S	PO Box 99	Jemez Pueblo, NM	87024-0099	575-834-7419	834-9167	K-8	Eugene Johnson
School for Integrated Academics & Tech	1500 Indian School Rd NW	Albuquerque, NM	87104-2306	505-242-6640	242-6872	9-12	Kelly Callahan
South Valley Academy	3426 Blake Rd SW	Albuquerque, NM	87105-5009	505-452-3132	452-3133	9-12	Alan Marks
Southwest Primary Learning Center	10301 Candelaria Rd NE	Albuquerque, NM	87112-1504	505-296-7677	296-0510	4-6	Deb Young
Southwest Secondary Learning Center	10301 Candelaria Rd NE	Albuquerque, NM	87112-1504	505-296-7677	296-0510	7-12	Scott Glasrud
Taos Municipal Charter S	PO Box 3009	Ranchos de Taos, NM	87557-3009	575-751-7222	751-7546	K-8	Nancy O'Bryan
Turqoise Trail ES	13a San Marcos Loop	Santa Fe, NM	87508-8627	505-467-1700	474-7862	K-6	Sandra Davis
Twenty-First Century Public Academy	3100 Menaul Blvd NE	Albuquerque, NM	87107-1835	505-254-0280	254-8507	6-8	Donna Eldredge
Village Academy	301 S Camino Del Pueblo	Bernalillo, NM	87004-6276	505-867-9094	832-9094	6-8	Pamela Engstrom
Vista Grande HS	PO Box 850	Taos, NM	87571-0850	575-758-5100	770-8681	9-12	Greg Perry
Walatowa Charter HS	PO Box 60	Jemez Pueblo, NM	87024-0060	575-834-0443	834-0449	9-12	Tony Archuleta
YouthBuild Trade & Technology HS	1718 Yale Blvd SE	Albuquerque, NM	87106-4136	505-765-5517	765-5925	9-12	Kay Birukoff
New York							
Achievement Academy Charter S	42 S Dove St	Albany, NY	12202-1253	518-533-1601	694-3666	5-8	O'Rita Swan
Achievement First Brownsville Charter S	2021 Bergen St	Brooklyn, NY	11233-4801	718-342-4302	346-3270	K-1	Gina Musumeci
Achievement First Bushwick Charter S	1300 Greene Ave	Brooklyn, NY	11237-4502	718-922-1581	922-1586	K-6	Lizette Suxo
Achievement First Bushwick ES	1137 Herkimer St	Brooklyn, NY	11233-3109	718-922-1581	922-1586	K-4	Lizette Suxo
Achievement First Bushwick MS	1300 Greene Ave	Brooklyn, NY	11237-4502	718-453-0425	453-0428	5-8	Amy D'Angelo
Achievement First Crown Heights Charter	790 E New York Ave	Brooklyn, NY	11203-1212	718-774-0762	774-0830	K-8	Orpheus Williams
Achievement First East New York ES	557 Pennsylvania Ave	Brooklyn, NY	11207-5727	718-485-4924	342-5194	K-4	Denniston Reid
Achievement First Endeavor MS	850 Kent Ave	Brooklyn, NY	11205-2702	718-622-4786	789-1649	5-8	Eric Redwine
Albany Community Charter S	65 Krank St	Albany, NY	12202-1150	518-433-1500	433-1501	K-4	S. Neal Currie
Albany Prep Charter S	50 Summit Ave	Albany, NY	12209-1617	518-694-5005	694-5012	5-8	Carol Lennon
Amber Charter S	220 E 106th St	New York, NY	10029-4007	212-534-9667	534-6225	K-6	Basthi Acosta
Ark Community Charter S	762 River St	Troy, NY	12180-1231	518-274-6312	274-3615	K-6	Mary Streck
Bedford Stuyvesant Collegiate Charter S	800 Gates Ave	Brooklyn, NY	11221-2203			5-12	Mabel Lajes-Guiteras
Beginning With Children Charter S	11 Bartlett St	Brooklyn, NY	11206-5001	718-388-8847	388-8936	K-8	Timothy Gembka
Brighter Choice Charter S for Boys	116 N Lake Ave	Albany, NY	12206-2710	518-694-8200	694-4123	K-4	Darryl Williams
Brighter Choice Charter S for Girls	250 Central Ave	Albany, NY	12206-2639	518-694-4100	694-4123	K-4	Melissa Jarvis-Cedeno
Bronx Academy of Promise Charter S	1166 River Ave	Bronx, NY	10452-8305			K-8	Jennifer Ciavirella
Bronx Charter for Better Learning	3740 Baychester Ave	Bronx, NY	10466-5031	718-655-6660	655-5555	1-4	Richard Burke
Bronx Charter S for Children	388 Willis Ave	Bronx, NY	10454-1303	718-402-3300	402-3258	K-5	Karen Drezner
Bronx Charter S for Excellence	1960 Benedict Ave	Bronx, NY	10462-4402	718-828-7301	828-7302	K-3	Charlene Reid
Bronx Charter S for the Arts	950 Longfellow Ave	Bronx, NY	10474-4809	718-893-1042	893-7910	K-6	Xanthe Jory
Bronx Community Charter S	2348 Webster Ave	Bronx, NY	10458	718-584-1400		K-8	Martha Andrews
Bronx Global Learning Institute	750 Concourse Vlg W	Bronx, NY	10451-3865	718-993-1740	993-1965	K-5	Celia Domenich
Bronx Lighthouse Charter S	1001 Intervale Ave	Bronx, NY	10459-3151	646-915-0025	915-0037	K-4	Jeffrey Tsang
Bronx Preparatory Charter S	3872 3rd Ave	Bronx, NY	10457-8222	718-294-0841	294-2381	5-12	Dr. Samona Tait
Brooklyn Ascend Charter S	205 Rockaway Pkwy	Brooklyn, NY	11212-3444	718-240-9162		K-12	Nikki Kholsa
Brooklyn Charter S	545 Willoughby Ave	Brooklyn, NY	11206-6815	718-302-2085	302-2426	K-5	Omigbade Escayg
Brooklyn Excelsior Charter S	856 Quincy St	Brooklyn, NY	11221-3612	718-246-5681	246-5864	K-8	Dr. Tom Demarco
Buffalo Academy of Science Charter S	15 Jewett Pkwy	Buffalo, NY	14214-2319	716-446-5681	446-5682	7-12	Levent Kaya
Buffalo United Charter S	325 Manhattan Ave	Buffalo, NY	14214-1809	716-835-9862	835-6272	K-8	Tammy Messmer
Charter S for Applied Technologies	2303 Kenmore Ave	Buffalo, NY	14207-1311	716-876-7505	447-9922	K-12	J. Efrain Martinez
Charter S of Educational Excellence	260 Warburton Ave	Yonkers, NY	10701-2226	914-476-5070	476-2858	K-5	Catalina Castillo
Child Dev. Center / Hamptons Charter S	PO Box 404	Wainscott, NY	11975-0404	631-324-0207	324-4112	K-8	Richard Malone
Community Charter S	404 Edison Ave	Buffalo, NY	14215-2936	716-833-5967	833-5985	K-8	Carol Smith
Community Partnership Charter S	241 Emerson Pl	Brooklyn, NY	11205-3808	718-399-3824	399-2149	K-5	Melanie Bryon
Community Roots Charter S	51 Saint Edwards St	Brooklyn, NY	11205-2932	718-858-1629	858-1754	K-3	Allison Keil
Democracy Prep Charter S	207 W 133rd St	New York, NY	10030-3201	212-281-1248	283-4202	6-12	Seth Andrew
DREAM Charter S	232 E 103rd St	New York, NY	10029-5458	212-289-2594	348-5979	K-8	Josh Klaris
East NY Preparatory Charter S	210 Chester St	Brooklyn, NY	11212-5623	718-485-8591	227-2763	K-5	Sheila Joseph
Elmwood Village Charter S	124 Elmwood Ave	Buffalo, NY	14201	716-886-4581	348-3707	K-6	John Sheffield
Enterprise Charter S	275 Oak St	Buffalo, NY	14203-1643	716-855-2114	855-2967	K-12	Jill Norton
Excellence Charter S	225 Patchen Ave	Brooklyn, NY	11233-1529	718-638-1830	638-2548	K-5	Jabali Sawicki
Explore Charter S	15 Snyder Ave	Brooklyn, NY	11226-4020	718-703-4484	703-8550	K-8	Morton Ballen
Family Life Academy Charter S	14 W 170th St	Bronx, NY	10452-3227	718-410-8100	410-8800	K-5	Marilyn Calo
Future Leaders Institute	134 W 122nd St	New York, NY	10027-5501	212-678-2868	666-2749	K-8	Peter Anderson
Genesee Community Charter S	657 East Ave	Rochester, NY	14607-2101	585-697-1960	271-5904	K-6	Lisa Wing
Girls Preparatory Charter S	442 E Houston St	New York, NY	10002-1122	212-388-0241	388-1086	K-4	Anne Lackritz
Global Concepts Charter S	1001 Ridge Rd	Lackawanna, NY	14218-1755	716-821-1903	821-9563	K-8	Richard Fill
Grand Concourse Charter S	116 E 169th St	Bronx, NY	10452-7704	718-590-1300	590-1065	K-4	Ira Victor
Green Dot NY Charter S	600 Saint Anns Ave	Bronx, NY	10455-2800	718-585-0560	585-0563	9-12	Ashish Kapadia
Green Tech High Charter S	1 Dudley Hts	Albany, NY	12210-2601	518-694-3400	694-3401	9-12	John Taylor
Harbor Science & Arts Charter S	1 E 104th St	New York, NY	10029-4419	212-427-2244	360-7429	K-8	Joanne Hunt
Harlem Childrens Zone Promise Academy I	175 W 134th St	New York, NY	10030-3101	212-368-3470	289-0661	K-2	Dennis McKesey
Harlem Childrens Zone Promise Academy II	2005 Madison Ave	New York, NY	10035-1215	917-492-1481	492-1576	K-12	Kathy Fernald
Harlem Day Charter S	240 E 123rd St	New York, NY	10035-2068	212-876-9953	876-9926	K-5	Anne Burns
Harlem Link Charter S	134 W 122nd St	New York, NY	10027-5501	646-283-2501	666-4248	K-2	Steven Evangelista
Harlem Success Academy 2	301 W 140th St	New York, NY	10030-1406	646-442-6600	281-4638	K-8	Jim Manly
Harlem Success Academy 3	141 E 111th St	New York, NY	10029-2641	646-747-6700		K-5	Emily Gould
Harlem Success Academy 4	160 E 120th St	New York, NY	10035-3508	646-442-6500		K-5	Mitch Center
Harlem Success Charter S	34 W 118th St	New York, NY	10026-1937	212-277-7170	457-5659	K-3	Dan Wood
Harlem Village Academy Charter S	244 W 144th St	New York, NY	10030-1202	646-548-9570	548-9576	5-12	Laurie Warner
Hellenic Classical Charter S	646 5th Ave	Brooklyn, NY	11215-5401	718-499-0957	499-0959	K-5	Christine Tetonis
Hyde Leadership Charter S	730 Bryant Ave	Bronx, NY	10474-6006	718-991-5500	842-8617	K-6	Joanne Goubourn
Icahn Charter S Bronx N	1535 Story Ave	Bronx, NY	10473-4555	212-861-4606	861-4603	K-5	Brenda Carrasquillo
Icahn Charter S	1525 Brook Ave	Bronx, NY	10457-8005	718-716-8105	716-6716	K-8	Jeffrey Litt
Icahn South Bronx Charter S	968 Cauldwell Ave	Bronx, NY	10456-6804	718-991-5157	991-5189	K-5	Midga Agosto
International Leadership Charter S	2900 Exterior St	Bronx, NY	10463-7103	212-437-8361	562-2335	9-12	Elaine Lopez
Johnson Charter S	30 Watervliet Ave	Albany, NY	12206-1983	518-432-4300	432-4311	K-4	Lillian Turner
Johnson Fruit Belt Community Charter S	833 Michigan Ave	Buffalo, NY	14203-1207	716-857-0586		K-4	Kristen Hyland
King Center Charter S	938 Genesee St	Buffalo, NY	14211-3025	716-891-7912	895-2058	K-4	Dr. Clairty Massey
King's Collegiate Charter S	1084 Lenox Rd	Brooklyn, NY	11212-1930	718-342-6047	342-6727	5-8	Lauren Harris
KIPP Academy Charter S	250 E 156th St	Bronx, NY	10451-4796	718-665-3555	585-7982	5-8	Blanca Ruiz
KIPP A.M.P. Charter S	1224 Park Pl	Brooklyn, NY	11213-2703	718-943-3710	774-3673	5-6	Jeff Li
KIPP Infinity Charter S	625 W 133rd St	New York, NY	10027-7303	212-991-2600	234-8396	5-6	Joseph Negron
KIPP Sankofa Charter S	140 Central Park Plz	Buffalo, NY	14214-2235	716-446-5708	446-5709	5-8	Josephine Mayfield
KIPP S.T.A.R College Prep Charter S	433 W 123rd St	New York, NY	10027-5002	212-991-2650	666-4723	5-8	Amber Williams
KIPP Tech Valley Charter S	1 Dudley Hts	Albany, NY	12210-2601	518-694-9494	694-9411	5-8	Dan Ceaser
La Cima Charter S	800 Gates Ave	Brooklyn, NY	11221-2203	718-443-2136	443-7291	K-5	Andrea Zayas
Leadership Preparatory Charter S	600 Lafayette Ave	Brooklyn, NY	11216-1020	718-636-0360	636-0747	K-4	Max Koltuv
Leadership Village Academy Charter S	2351 1st Ave	New York, NY	10035-3422	646-812-9400	996-1626	5-12	Sam Fragomeni
Lindsay Wildcat Academy Charter S	17 Battery Pl	New York, NY	10004-1186	212-209-6037	635-3874	8-12	Ronald Tabano

School	Address	City,State	Zip code	Telephone	Fax	Grade	Contact
Manhattan Charter S	100 Attorney St	New York, NY	10002-3405	212-533-2743	533-2820	K-3	Genie Depolo
Maria de Hostos Charter S	938 Clifford Ave	Rochester, NY	14621-4808	585-544-6170	544-3848	K-6	Miriam Vazquez
Merrick Academy-Queens Public Charter S	20701 Jamaica Ave	Queens Village, NY	11428-1544	718-479-3753	479-8108	K-6	Alma Alston
Mott Haven Academy Charter S	165 Brown Pl	Bronx, NY	10454-4110	718-292-7015	292-7823	K-8	Jessica Nauiokas
New Covenant Charter S	50 Lark St	Albany, NY	12210-1518	518-463-3912	626-9916	K-6	Jecrois Jean-Baptiste
New Heights Academy Charter S	1818 Amsterdam Ave	New York, NY	10031-1715	212-283-5400	283-9999	5-12	Stacy Winitt
NY Center for Autism Charter S	433 E 100th St	New York, NY	10029-6606	212-860-2580	860-2960	K-4	Jamie Pagliaro
Niagara Charter S	2077 Lockport Rd	Niagara Falls, NY	14304-1109	716-297-4520	297-4617	K-6	Karen Marchioli
NYC Charter HS for AECI	300 E 140th St	Bronx, NY	10454-1137	646-400-5566		9-12	Ana Delgado
Opportunity Charter S	240 W 113th St	New York, NY	10026-3306	212-866-6137		6-12	Betty Marsella
Oracle Charter S	888 Delaware Ave	Buffalo, NY	14209-2008	716-362-3188	362-3187	7-12	Julie Forsberg
Our World Neighborhood Charter S	3612 35th Ave	Astoria, NY	11106-1227	718-392-3405	392-2840	K-8	Brian Ferguson
PAVE Academy	71 Sullivan St	Brooklyn, NY	11231-1600	718-858-7813	858-7814	K-8	Robertson Spencer
Peninsula Prep Academy Charter S	155 Beach 67th St	Arverne, NY	11692	347-403-9234	318-4561	K-4	Judith Tyler
Pinnacle Charter S	115 Ash St	Buffalo, NY	14204-1452	716-842-1244	842-1242	K-8	Heidi Rotella
Renaissance Charter S	3559 81st St	Jackson Heights, NY	11372-5033	718-803-0060	803-3785	K-12	Stacey Gauthier
Riverhead Charter S	3685 Middle Country Rd	Calverton, NY	11933-1807	631-369-5252	369-6687	K-6	Dorothy Porteus
Rochester Academy Charter S	841 Genesee St	Rochester, NY	14611-3817	585-424-2251		7-12	Ercan Tozan
Roosevelt Childrens Academy Charter S	105 Pleasant Ave	Roosevelt, NY	11575-2126	516-867-6202	867-6206	K-8	Roxanne Ashley
Ross Global Academy Charter S	52 Chambers St	New York, NY	10007-1259	212-374-3884	889-1760	K-6	Julie Johnson
St. Hope Leadership Academy	222 W 134th St	New York, NY	10030-3002	212-283-1204	283-1207	5-7	Ventura Rodriguez
Sisulu-Walker Charter S	125 W 115th St	New York, NY	10026-2908	212-663-8217	866-5793	K-3	Karen Jones
South Bronx Charter S	300 E 140th St	Bronx, NY	10454-1137	718-401-9216	401-9219	K-2	Evelyn Hey
South Bronx Classical Charter S	977 Fox St	Bronx, NY	10459-3320	718-860-4340	860-4125	K-1	Lester Long
South Buffalo Charter S	2219 S Park Ave	Buffalo, NY	14220	716-826-7213	826-7168	K-8	Carrie Dzierba
Southside Academy Charter S	2200 Onondaga Creek Blvd	Syracuse, NY	13207-2300	315-476-3019	476-6639	K-8	Greg Speranza
Syracuse Academy of Science Charter S	1001 Park Ave	Syracuse, NY	13204-2125	315-428-8997	428-9109	7-12	Tolga Hayali
Tapestry Charter S	40 North St	Buffalo, NY	14202-1106	716-332-0754	332-0758	K-12	Joy Pepper
True North Rochester Prep Charter S	630 Brooks Ave	Rochester, NY	14619-2255	585-436-8629	436-5985	5-8	Stacey Shells
Tubman Charter S	3565 3rd Ave	Bronx, NY	10456-3403	718-537-9912	537-9858	K-8	Cleveland Person
UFT Elementary Charter S	300 Wyona St	Brooklyn, NY	11207-3522	718-922-0538	922-0543	K-8	Michelle Bodden
Urban Choice Charter S	545 Humboldt St	Rochester, NY	14610-1221	585-288-5702	654-9882	K-8	John Bliss
VOICE Charter S of NY	3715 13th St	Long Is City, NY	11101-6024	718-786-6206	786-6421	K-8	Frank Headley
Western NY Maritime Charter S	266 Genesee St	Buffalo, NY	14204-1453	716-842-4240	842-4241	9-12	Lawrence Astyk
Westminster Community Charter S	24 Westminster Ave	Buffalo, NY	14215-1614	716-816-3450	838-7458	K-8	Dr. Yvonne Ragan
Williamsburg Charter S	424 Leonard St	Brooklyn, NY	11222-3908	718-782-9830	782-9834	9-12	Ethan Mitnick
Williamsburg Collegiate Charter S	157 Wilson St	Brooklyn, NY	11211-7706	718-302-4018	302-4641	5-6	Julie Kennedy
North Carolina							
Academy of Moore County	105 Turner St	Southern Pines, NC	28387-7054	910-693-7924	693-7925	K-8	Bill Moore
Alpha Academy	PO Box 35476	Fayetteville, NC	28303-0476	910-223-7711	678-9011	K-8	Eugene Slocum
American Renaissance Charter S	126 E Broad St	Statesville, NC	28677-5852	704-924-8870	873-1398	K-5	Sharon Molleur
American Renaissance MS	217 S Center St	Statesville, NC	28677-5806	704-878-6009	878-9350	6-8	Stephen Gay
Arapahoe Charter S	9005 NC Highway 306 S	Arapahoe, NC	28510-9699	252-249-2599	249-1316	K-8	Tom McCarthy
Arts Based ES	1380 N Martin Luther King	Winston Salem, NC	27101	336-748-4116	748-4117	K-5	Robin Hollis
ArtSpace Charter S	2030 US 70 Hwy	Swannanoa, NC	28778-8211	828-298-2787	298-6221	K-8	Lori Cozzi
Bethany Community MS	181 Bethany Rd	Reidsville, NC	27320-7464	336-951-2500	951-0087	6-8	Vicky Bethel
Bethel Hill Charter S	401 Bethel Hill School Rd	Roxboro, NC	27574-7503	336-599-2823	599-9299	K-6	John Betterton
Brevard Academy	299 Andante Ln	Brevard, NC	28712-9125	828-885-2665	862-3497	K-8	Dr. Janet Walsh
Bridges Charter S	2587 Pleasant Ridge Rd	State Road, NC	28676-9318	336-874-2721	874-3804	K-8	Paul Welborn
Cape Fear Center for Inquiry	3131B Randall Pkwy	Wilmington, NC	28403	910-362-0000	362-0048	K-8	Brian Corrigan
Cape Lookout Marine Science HS	1108 Bridges St	Morehead City, NC	28557-3799	252-726-1601	726-5245	9-12	Susan Smith
Carolina International S	8810 Hickory Ridge Rd	Harrisburg, NC	28075-7659	704-455-3847	455-7247	K-10	Carole Forbes
Carter Community S	1305 W Club Blvd	Durham, NC	27705-3513	919-416-9025	416-9815	K-8	Gail Taylor
Casa Esperanza Montessori S	2600 Sumner Blvd Ste 130	Raleigh, NC	27616-5146	919-855-9811	855-9813	PK-6	Janice Bonham West
Central Park S for Children	724 Foster St	Durham, NC	27701-2111	919-682-1200	683-1261	K-5	Carolyn Kirkland
Charlotte Secondary S	8310 McAlpine Park Dr	Charlotte, NC	28211-6247	704-295-0137	295-0156	6-12	Jeremy Spielman
Charter Day S	7055 Bacons Way NE	Leland, NC	28451-7960	910-655-1214	655-1549	K-8	Mark Cramer
Chatham Charter	PO Box 245	Siler City, NC	27344-0245	919-742-4550	742-2518	K-8	Ronald Joyce
Children's Community S	565 Griffith St	Davidson, NC	28036-9396	704-896-6262	896-2025	K-5	Joy Warner
Childrens Village Academy	PO Box 2206	Kinston, NC	28502-2206	252-939-1958	939-1242	K-6	Gloria Carr-Battle
CIS Academy	PO Box 706	Lumberton, NC	28359-0706	910-521-1669	521-1670	6-8	Ronald Bryant
Clover Garden S	2454 Altmhaw Union Ridge Rd	Burlington, NC	27217	336-586-9440	586-9477	K-12	Linda Humble
Columbus Charter S	35 Bacons Way	Whiteville, NC	28472-6225	910-641-4042	641-4043	K-3	Steven Smith
Community Charter S	510 S Torrence St	Charlotte, NC	28204-3160	704-377-3180	377-3182	K-5	Kristi Dahlstrom
Community Partners Charter HS	PO Box 100	Holly Springs, NC	27540-0100	919-567-9955	567-9956	9-12	Caroll Reed
Crosscreek Charter S	PO Box 1075	Louisburg, NC	27549-1075	919-497-3198	497-0232	K-8	Robin Jackson
Crossnore Academy	PO Box 309	Crossnore, NC	28616-0309	828-733-5241	737-7915	K-12	Sharon Wise
Crossroads Charter HS	5500 N Tryon St	Charlotte, NC	28213-7120	704-597-5100	597-3941	9-12	Gentry Campbell
Delany New S	PO Box 16161	Asheville, NC	28816-0161	828-236-9441	236-9442	K-8	Buffy Fowler
Dillard Academy	PO Box 1188	Goldsboro, NC	27533-1188	919-581-0166	581-0122	K-4	Hilda Hicks
Downtown MS	280 S Liberty St	Winston Salem, NC	27101-5211	336-748-3838	748-3359	5-8	Annie Fleming-Weaver
East Wake Academy	400 NMC Dr	Zebulon, NC	27597-2759	919-404-0444	404-2377	K-12	Brandon Smith
Endeavor Charter S	9400 Forum Dr	Raleigh, NC	27615-2971	919-848-0333	392-1080	K-8	Steve McAdams
Evergreen Community Charter S	50 Bell Rd	Asheville, NC	28805-1538	828-298-2173	298-2269	K-8	Dr. Susan Gottfried
Exploris MS	207 E Hargett St	Raleigh, NC	27601-1437	919-821-3168	836-9768	6-8	Kevin Piacenza
Forsyth Academy	5426 Shattalon Dr	Winston Salem, NC	27106-1919	336-922-1121	922-1033	K-8	Lori Hill
Franklin Academy	604 S Franklin St	Wake Forest, NC	27587-2276	919-554-4911	554-2340	K-12	Denise Kent
Gaston College Preparatory S	320 Pleasant Hill Rd	Gaston, NC	27832-9511	252-308-6932	308-6936	5-12	Caleb Dolan
Grandfather Academy	PO Box 98	Banner Elk, NC	28604-0098	828-898-3868	898-3849	K-12	Doug Herman
Gray Stone Day S	PO Box 960	Misenheimer, NC	28109-0960	704-463-3309	463-0569	9-12	Helen Nance
Greensboro Academy	4049 Battleground Ave	Greensboro, NC	27410-8410	336-286-8404	286-8403	K-8	Rudy Swofford
Guilford Preparatory Charter S	2207A E Cone Blvd	Greensboro, NC	27405	336-954-1344	954-1965	K-8	Robin Buckrham
Haliwa-Saponi Tribal S	130 Haliwa Saponi Trl	Hollister, NC	27844-9390	252-257-5853	257-1093	K-12	Thomas Buchanan
Hawbridge S	PO Box 162	Saxapahaw, NC	27340-0162	336-376-1122	376-6996	9-12	Dr. Marcia Hugh
Healthy Start Academy	807 W Chapel Hill St	Durham, NC	27701-3112	919-956-5599	688-9027	K-8	Dietrich Danner
Highland Charter S	PO Box 1653	Gastonia, NC	28053-1653	704-866-6342	866-8725	K-3	Sherida Lewis Stevens
Hope Elementary Charter S	1116 N Blount St	Raleigh, NC	27604-1302	919-834-0941	834-9338	K-5	Richard Rubin
Howard S	1004 Herring Ave E	Wilson, NC	27893-3311	252-293-4150	293-4151	K-8	Dr. Jo Anne Woodard
Jefferson Classical Academy	2527 US 221A Hwy	Mooresboro, NC	28114-7698	828-657-9998	657-9012	K-12	Joseph Maimone
Joy Charter S	1955 W Cornwallis Rd	Durham, NC	27705-5707	919-493-6056	402-4263	K-8	Dr. Les Stein
Kennedy Charter S	1717 Sharon Rd W	Charlotte, NC	28210-5663	704-688-2939	688-2960	6-12	Stacey Rose
Kestrel Heights S	4700 S Alston Ave	Durham, NC	27713-4419	919-484-1300	484-1355	6-12	Tim Dugan
Kinston Charter Academy	2000 Martin L King Jr Blvd	Kinston, NC	28501	252-522-0210	527-7785	K-8	
KIPP Academy Charlotte	931 Wilann Dr	Charlotte, NC	28215-2147	704-537-2044		5-8	Keith Burnam
Lake Norman Charter S	12820 Church St	Huntersville, NC	28078-4223	704-948-8600	948-8778	5-8	Mike McAlpin
Learning Center	945 Connahetta St	Murphy, NC	28906-3524	828-835-7240	835-9471	K-8	Mary Jo Dyre
Lincoln Charter S Denver	7834 Galway Ln	Denver, NC	28037-8600	704-483-6611	948-8778	K-12	Dave Machado
Lincoln Charter S Lincolnton	133 Eagle Nest Rd	Lincolnton, NC	28092-7383	704-736-9888	736-1166	K-8	Judy Smith
Magellan Charter S	9324 Baileywick Rd	Raleigh, NC	27615-1909	919-844-0277	844-3882	3-8	Mary Griffin
Metrolina Regional Scholars Academy	7000 Endhaven Ln	Charlotte, NC	28277-2370	704-503-1112	503-1183	K-8	Dr. Marie Peine
Millennium Charter Academy	500 Old Springs Rd	Mount Airy, NC	27030-3034	336-789-7570	789-8445	K-8	Kirby McCrary
Mountain Community S	613 Glover St	Hendersonville, NC	28792-5451	828-696-8480	696-8451	K-8	Chadwick Hamby
Mountain Discovery Charter S	890 Jenkins Branch Rd N	Bryson City, NC	28713-4514	828-488-1222	488-0526	K-8	Chantelle Carroll
Neuse Charter S	605 W Noble St	Selma, NC	27576-2723	919-965-8088	965-5599	K-5	Patricia Harris
New Dimensions S	501 E Concord St	Morganton, NC	28655-3413	828-437-5753	437-2980	K-5	Larry Wilkerson
Orange Charter S	920 Corporate Dr	Hillsborough, NC	27278-8557	919-644-6272	644-6275	K-8	David Temple
PACE Academy	1713 Legion Rd	Chapel Hill, NC	27517-2359	919-933-7699	967-9905	9-12	Rhonda R. Franklin
Phoenix Academy	4020 Meeting Way St	High Point, NC	27265-8233	336-869-0079	869-3399	K-9	Kim Norcross
Piedmont Community S	PO Box 3706	Gastonia, NC	28054-0038	704-853-2428	853-3689	K-12	Courtney Madden
Pine Lake Preparatory S	PO Box 5185	Mooresville, NC	28117-5185	704-677-5789		K-12	Kate Dunaway
PreEminent Charter S	3815 Rock Quarry Rd	Raleigh, NC	27610-5123	919-235-0511	235-0514	K-8	Michael Stack
Provisions Academy	PO Box 5437	Sanford, NC	27331-5437	919-499-0945	499-1032	6-12	Dr. Sadie Jordan
Quality Education Academy	5012 Lansing Dr Ste C	Winston Salem, NC	27105	336-744-7138	744-1538	K-12	Simon Johnson
Queens Grant Community S	6400 Matthews Mint Hill Rd	Mint Hill, NC	28227-9323	704-573-6611	573-6995	K-10	Christy Morrin
Quest Academy	9650 Strickland Rd Ste 175	Raleigh, NC	27615-2082	919-841-0441	841-0443	K-8	Dr. Charles Watson
Raleigh Charter HS	1111 Haynes St	Raleigh, NC	27604-1454	919-715-1155	839-1766	9-12	Dr. Thomas Humble
Research Triangle Academy	2013 Ellis Rd	Durham, NC	27703-6127	919-957-7108	957-9698	K-8	Terri Gullick
River Mill Academy	PO Box 1450	Graham, NC	27253-1450	336-229-0909	229-9975	K-12	Tonyan Hunter
Rocky Mount Prep S	3334 Bishop Rd	Battleboro, NC	27804-7639	252-443-9923	443-9932	K-12	Michael Pratt
Roxboro Community S	115 Lake Dr	Roxboro, NC	27573-5672	336-597-0020	597-3152	7-12	Walter Finnigan
Sandhills Theatre Arts Renaissance S	140 Southern Dunes Dr	Vass, NC	28394-9218	910-695-1004	695-7322	K-8	David Jackson
Socrates Academy	3909 Weddington Rd	Matthews, NC	28105-6673	704-321-1711	321-1714	K-3	Janis Dellinger-Holton
Sterling Montessori Academy	202 Treybrooke Dr	Morrisville, NC	27560-9300	919-462-8889	462-8890	K-8	Bill Zajie
Success Institute	1424 Rickert St	Statesville, NC	28677-6856	704-881-0441	881-0870	K-8	Tenna Williams
Sugar Creek Charter S	4101 N Tryon St	Charlotte, NC	28206-2066	704-509-5470	921-1004	K-8	Cheryl Ellis

School	Address	City,State	Zip code	Telephone	Fax	Grade	Contact
Summit Charter S	PO Box 1339	Cashiers, NC	28717-1339	828-743-5755	743-9157	K-8	Dr. Jack Talmadge
Tiller S	1950 US Highway 70 E	Beaufort, NC	28516-7836	252-728-1995	728-3711	K-5	Lynsey Plume
Torchlight Academy	3211 Bramer Dr	Raleigh, NC	27604	919-829-9500	829-0820	K-5	Dr. Cynthia McQueen
Triad Math & Science S	900 16th St	Greensboro, NC	27405-4810	336-621-0061	621-0072	K-7	Hakan Orak
Two Rivers Community S	1018 Archie Carroll Rd	Boone, NC	28607-8506	828-262-5411	262-5412	K-8	June Gilch
Union Academy	675 N M L King Jr Blvd	Monroe, NC	28110-8119	704-283-8883	283-8823	K-12	Ken Templeton
Vance Charter S	1227 Dabney Dr	Henderson, NC	27536-3558	252-431-0641	436-0688	K-12	Dr. John von Rohr
Voyager Academy	4238 Technology Dr	Durham, NC	27704-2128	919-433-3301	433-3305	4-8	Carl Forsyth
Washington Montessori S	500 Avon Ctr	Washington, NC	27889-3851	252-946-1977	946-5938	K-8	Stacey Shepherd
Wilmington Preparatory Academy	3600 S College Rd Ste E	Wilmington, NC	28412-5107	910-254-2010	254-2013	K-4	Margaret Franklin
Woods Charter S	PO Box 5008	Chapel Hill, NC	27514-5001	919-960-8353	960-0133	K-12	Harrell Rentz
Woodson S of Challenge	437 Goldfloss St	Winston Salem, NC	27127-3125	336-723-6838	723-6425	K-12	Ruth Hopkins

Ohio

School	Address	City,State	Zip code	Telephone	Fax	Grade	Contact
A+ Arts Academy	270 S Napoleon Ave	Columbus, OH	43213-4235	614-338-0767	338-0787	6-8	Carolyn Berkley
Academic Acceleration Academy	1990 Jefferson Ave	Columbus, OH	43211-2175	614-298-4742	298-9107	10-12	Brian Terrell
Academy of Arts & Humanities	261 Elm Rd NE	Warren, OH	44483-5003	330-399-6882	399-6884	K-12	Lisa Burgess
Academy of Arts & Sciences	201 W Erie Ave	Lorain, OH	44052-1641	440-244-0156	244-3935	K-3	Joell Mullen-Liscano
Academy of Business & Technology	2436 Parkwood Ave	Toledo, OH	43620-1134	419-242-7508	242-7550	K-8	Linda Ransey
Academy of Columbus	4656 Heaton Rd	Columbus, OH	43229-6612	614-433-7510	433-7515	K-8	Jamie Christman
Academy of Dayton	4095 Little Richmond Rd	Dayton, OH	45417	937-567-1072	567-1075	K-8	Daisy Edwards
Akron Digital Academy	335 S Main St	Akron, OH	44308-1203	330-237-2200	237-2204	K-12	William Romano
Allen Academy III	299 Knightsbridge Dr	Hamilton, OH	45011-3166	513-868-2900	868-0498	K-8	Aleta Benson
Allen Academy II	400 E 2nd St	Dayton, OH	45402-1724	937-586-9756	586-9764	K-8	Novea Jackson
Allen Academy	700 Heck Ave	Dayton, OH	45417	937-586-9815	586-0271	K-8	Brandy Flack
Allen Preparatory S	627 Salem Ave	Dayton, OH	45406-5822	937-278-4201	278-4229	PK-K	Yolanda Clark
Alliance Academy of Cincinnati	1712 Duck Creek Rd	Cincinnati, OH	45207-1644	513-751-5555	751-5072	K-8	Juanita Preston
Alliance Academy of Toledo	1501 Monroe St Ste 2	Toledo, OH	43604-5752	419-418-5150	418-5160	K-12	Kerry Keese
Alternative Education Academy	121 S Main St Ste 102	Akron, OH	44308-1436	800-493-8680	335-2329	K-12	Dr. Maryann Schneider
Amanda-Clearcreek Community S	414 N School St	Amanda, OH	43102-9613	740-969-7254	969-7620	K-K	James Dick
Apex Academy	16005 Terrace Rd	East Cleveland, OH	44112-2001	216-451-1725	451-1765	K-8	Michael Ward
Arise Academy	1 Elizabeth Pl	Dayton, OH	45417	937-853-0560	853-0623	K-12	Carlos Blair
Arts Academy	4125 Leavitt Rd	Lorain, OH	44053-2341	440-960-0470	960-0475	K-12	Alexis Rainbow
Arts & College Preparatory Academy	2202 S Hamilton Rd	Columbus, OH	43232-4304	614-986-9974	986-9976	9-12	Paula Lasley
Arts and Science Prep Academy	2711 Church Ave	Cleveland, OH	44113-2909	216-357-2953	344-2312	K-12	Christopher Terec
Ashland County Community Academy	2011 Baney Rd S	Ashland, OH	44805-4504	419-903-0295	903-0341	9-12	Samuel Wilson
Auglaize County Educational Academy	1130A E Albert St	Lima, OH	45804	419-738-4572	738-4591	K-12	
Aurora Academy	541 Utah St	Toledo, OH	43605-2299	419-693-6841	693-4799	K-8	Cindy Wilson
Autism Academy of Learning	219 Page St	Toledo, OH	43620-1430	419-865-7487	865-8360	K-12	Matthew Bigelow
Bennett Venture Academy	5130 Bennett Rd	Toledo, OH	43612-3422	419-269-2247	269-2257	K-8	Judith Carnivale
Bridge Academy of Ohio	4404 Secor Rd	Toledo, OH	43623-4236	419-475-6620	475-6640	K-5	Mohamad Issa
Bridges Community Academy	190 Saint Francis Ave	Tiffin, OH	44883	419-455-9295	455-9296	K-12	Dona Kaufman
Buckeye On-Line School for Success	119 E 5th St	East Liverpool, OH	43920-3030	330-385-1987	385-4535	K-12	Randall Calhoun
Canton Digital Academy	401 14th St SE	Canton, OH	44707-3819	330-484-8010	484-8032	4-12	
Cardington Lincoln Digital Academy	121 Nichols St	Cardington, OH	43315-1121	419-864-3691	864-0946	K-12	Jennifer Zierden
Carver Preparatory S	2283 Sunbury Rd	Columbus, OH	43219-3528	614-509-2440	509-2460	K-8	William Fowles
CASTLE	1729 Superior Ave E	Cleveland, OH	44114-2925	216-443-5400	443-9017	9-12	Rolando Peterson
Center for Student Achievement	450 Vaughn St	Jackson, OH	45640-1944	740-286-6442		K-12	Philip Karl
Central Academy of Ohio	4346 Secor Rd	Toledo, OH	43623-4234	419-475-6620	475-6640	K-12	
Charles S at Ohio Dominican	3950 Indianola Ave	Columbus, OH	43214-3158	614-258-8588	258-8288	9-12	Gregory Brown
Chase Academy for Communication Arts	1565 Integrity Dr E	Columbus, OH	43209-2707	614-433-3390	443-3454	3-12	Celia Jones
Chavez College Prep ES	1132 Windsor Ave	Columbus, OH	43211-2836	614-743-3445		K-5	
Cincinnati Academy of Excellence	6760 Belkenton Ave	Cincinnati, OH	45236-3870	513-351-8034	366-3395	K-8	Caroline Baker
Cincinnati College Prep Academy	1425 Linn St	Cincinnati, OH	45214-2605	513-684-0777	684-8888	K-12	Guyton Mathews
Cincinnati Leadership Academy	7243 Eastlawn Dr	Cincinnati, OH	45237-3515	513-351-5737		K-8	Derrick Shelton
Cincinnati Prep & Fitness Academy	7601 Harrison Ave	Cincinnati, OH	45231-3107	513-587-6280	587-6299	K-8	Myrrha Satow
Cincinnati Speech & Reading Center	1812 Central Pkwy	Cincinnati, OH	45214-2304	513-651-9624	618-0272	K-3	
Citizens' Academy	1827 Ansel Rd	Cleveland, OH	44106-4107	216-791-4195	791-3013	K-8	Marcellus Gray
City Day Community S	318 S Main St	Dayton, OH	45402-2716	937-223-8130	223-8136	K-8	Shonise Carr
Clay Avenue Community S	1030 Clay Ave	Toledo, OH	43608-2167			K-12	
Cleveland Art & Social Science Academy	10701 Shaker Blvd	Cleveland, OH	44104-3752	216-357-2953	589-0583	K-6	Debroah Mays
Cleveland Entrepreneurship S	540 E 105th St	Cleveland, OH	44108-1397	216-456-2080		6-12	Marshall Emerson
Cleveland Lighthouse Charter S	1701 E 12th St	Cleveland, OH	44114-3237	216-523-1133	523-1134	K-12	Nigena Livingston
Columbus Arts & Tech Academy	2255 Kimberly Pkwy E	Columbus, OH	43232-7210	614-577-0900	888-0300	K-12	Mindy Waronker
Columbus Bilingual Academy	35 Midland Ave	Columbus, OH	43223-1064	614-324-1492	324-1060	K-12	Roy Moore
Columbus Humanities	1333 Morse Rd	Columbus, OH	43229-6322	614-261-7200	261-7612	K-12	
Columbus Prep & Fitness Academy	1160 Watkins Rd	Columbus, OH	43207-2606	614-301-4856	491-4180	K-8	Lynn Hursey
Columbus Preparatory Academy	3330 Chippewa St	Columbus, OH	43204-1653	614-275-3600	275-3601	K-8	Chad Carr
Cornerstone Academy	6023 E Walnut St	Westerville, OH	43081-9620	614-775-0615	775-0633	K-12	Jaime Scott
Coshocton Opportunity S	1205 Cambridge Rd	Coshocton, OH	43812-2741	740-622-5547	622-6573	9-12	John Lear
Crittenton Community S	1418 E Broad St	Columbus, OH	43205-1505	614-372-2401	372-2416	6-9	Anthony Huffman
Cupe Community S	1132 Windsor Ave	Columbus, OH	43211-2836	614-294-3020	299-3680	K-12	Estella Stephens
Dayton Academy	4401 Dayton Liberty Rd	Dayton, OH	45417	937-262-4080	262-4091	K-8	Emory Wyckoff
Dayton Early College Academy	300 College Park Ave	Dayton, OH	45469-0001	937-542-5630	542-5631	7-12	Judy Hennessey Ph.D.
Dayton Technology Design HS	348 W 1st St	Dayton, OH	45402-3006	937-225-3989	268-7522	10-12	David White
Dayton View Academy	1416 W Riverview Ave	Dayton, OH	45402-6217	937-567-9426	567-9446	K-8	Amy Doerman
Dixon Early Learning Center	333 N Middle St	Columbiana, OH	44408-1001	330-482-5358		PK-K	Kimberly Sharshan
Dohn Community HS	608 E McMillan St	Cincinnati, OH	45206-1926	513-281-6100	281-6103	9-12	Pieter Elmendorf
Dunbar Academy	331 14th St	Toledo, OH	43604-5402	419-244-4202	244-4205	K-6	Andre Fox
Eagle Academy	2014 Consaul St	Toledo, OH	43605-1412	419-691-4876	691-5184	K-6	Mitchel Bean
Eagle Heights Academy	1833 Market St	Youngstown, OH	44507-1137	330-742-9090	742-9595	K-8	Hollis Batista
Eagle Learning Center HS	5721 Seaman Rd	Oregon, OH	43616-2631	419-693-0661		9-12	James Kanable
East End Community Heritage S	2569 Saint Leo Pl	Cincinnati, OH	45225-1960	513-281-3900	281-0818	K-12	Janice Glaspie
Edge Academy	92 N Union St	Akron, OH	44304-1347	330-535-4581	535-5074	K-5	
Educational Academy at Linden	1132 Windsor Ave	Columbus, OH	43211-2836	614-291-0235	291-0153	6-8	Estella Stephens
Educational Academy for Boys & Girls	1132 Windsor Ave	Columbus, OH	43211-2836	614-294-3020	299-3680	K-12	
Education Alternatives Community S	21100 Southgate Park Blvd	Maple Heights, OH	44137	216-332-9360	332-9375	K-12	Angela Stanley
Electronic Classroom of Tomorrow	3700 S High St Ste 95	Columbus, OH	43207-4083	614-492-8884	492-8894	K-12	Jeffrey Forster
Elite Academy of the Arts	3443 E 93rd St	Cleveland, OH	44104-5252	216-432-9515	341-8386	K-8	
Elyria Community S	300 Abbe Rd N	Elyria, OH	44035-3724	440-366-5225	366-6280	K-9	Tracey Frierson
Emerson Academy of Dayton	501 Hickory St	Dayton, OH	45410-1232	937-223-2889	223-3757	K-8	Ronald Albino
Englewood Peace Academy	1120 Horace St	Toledo, OH	43606-4737	419-243-7260	243-7268	K-8	Ward Barnett
Fairborn Digital Academy	306 E Whittier Ave	Fairborn, OH	45324-5313	937-879-0511	879-8160	K-12	Robert Grimshaw
FCI Academy	2177 Mock Rd	Columbus, OH	43219-1258	614-471-4527	471-4943	K-12	Eugene Greenfield
Findlay Digital Academy	1219 W Main Cross St # 206	Findlay, OH	45840	419-425-3598	425-3588	9-12	Lawrence Grove
Five R's Academy	4526 Ridge Ave SE	Canton, OH	44707-1118	330-484-8010		9-12	
Focus Learning Academy North	4807 Evanswood Dr	Columbus, OH	43229-6294	614-310-0430	310-0469	9-12	Tiffany Delong
Focus Learning Academy Southeast	4480 Refugee Rd	Columbus, OH	43232-4459	614-269-0150	269-0151	9-12	Rashaun Holliman
Focus Learning Academy Southwest	190 Southwood Ave	Columbus, OH	43207-1133	614-545-2000	545-1995	9-12	Robert Ater
Foundation Academy	75 N Walnut St	Mansfield, OH	44902-1211	419-526-9540	526-9542	K-12	
Fox Academy	2238 Jefferson Ave	Toledo, OH	43604-7120	419-720-4500	720-4502	7-12	Raymond Russell
Foxfire Center for Student Success	PO Box 1818	Zanesville, OH	43702-1818	740-453-4509	455-4084	9-12	
Franklin Local Community S	PO Box 95	Roseville, OH	43777-0095	740-697-7317	697-7186	7-12	Sharon McDermott
Garvey Academy	16200 Euclid Ave	Cleveland, OH	44112-1607	216-451-7995	451-7998	6-9	Ross Cockfield
Glass City Academy	2275 Collingwood Blvd	Toledo, OH	43620	419-720-6311	720-6315	11-12	
Goal Digital Academy	890 W 4th St Ste 400	Mansfield, OH	44906-2561	419-946-1903	529-2976	K-12	Laura Chervenak
Graham Digital Academy	370 E Main St	Saint Paris, OH	43072-9200	937-663-4123	663-4670	K-12	Marcia Ward
Graham S	3950 Indianola Ave	Columbus, OH	43214-3158	614-262-1111	262-5878	9-12	Eileen Meers
Great Leadership Academy	2030 Leonard Ave	Columbus, OH	43219-2105	614-252-2087	252-2311	K-6	Naim Sanders
Great Lakes Environmental Academy	2913 S Republic Blvd	Toledo, OH	43615-1911			6-12	Elizabeth Lewis
Great Western Academy	310 N Wilson Rd	Columbus, OH	43204-6221	614-276-1028	276-1049	K-8	Mona Milner
Groveport Community S	4485 S Hamilton Rd	Groveport, OH	43125-9334	614-574-4100	574-4107	K-8	Todd Baringer
Hamilton County Math & Science S	2675 Civic Center Dr	Cincinnati, OH	45231-1311	513-728-8620	728-8623	K-5	Dwan Moore
Hamilton Local Digital Academy	775 Rathmell Rd	Columbus, OH	43207-4737	614-491-5546	491-8323	K-12	Allyson Price
Harvard Avenue Community S	12000 Harvard Ave	Cleveland, OH	44105-5444	216-283-5100	283-5762	K-8	Belinda Stephens
Heir Force Community S	PO Box 180	Lima, OH	45802-0180	419-228-9241	228-1555	K-8	Darwin Lofton
Hope Academy Broadway Campus	3398 E 55th St	Cleveland, OH	44127-1691	216-271-7747	271-6438	K-8	Victoria Dorsey
Hope Academy Brown Street Campus E	1035 Clay St	Akron, OH	44301-1517	330-785-0180	785-0681	K-8	Darrin Beconder
Hope Academy Canton Campus	1379 Garfield Ave SW	Canton, OH	44706-5200	330-454-3128	454-3145	K-8	Tony Townsend
Hope Academy Cathedral Campus	10615 Lamontier Ave	Cleveland, OH	44104-4847	216-721-6909	721-1565	K-8	Darryl Allen
Hope Academy Chapelside Campus	3845 E 131st St	Cleveland, OH	44120-4661	216-283-6589	283-3087	K-8	Sharon Durant
Hope Academy Cuyahoga Campus	12913 Bennington Ave	Cleveland, OH	44135-3761	216-251-5450	251-6410	K-8	Raymond Terry
Hope Academy East Campus	15720 Kipling Ave	Cleveland, OH	44110-3105	216-383-1214		K-12	Leon Rallings
Hope Academy Lincoln Park	2421 W 11th St	Cleveland, OH	44113-4401	216-263-7008	263-7007	K-8	Holly Williams
Hope Academy Northcoast Campus	4310 E 71st St	Cleveland, OH	44105-5759	216-429-0232	429-0249	K-8	Gretchen Beasley
Hope Academy Northwest	1441 W 116th St	Cleveland, OH	44102-2301	216-226-6800	226-6805	K-12	Kristen Clotworthy

School	Address	City,State	Zip code	Telephone	Fax	Grade	Contact
Hope Academy University Campus	107 S Arlington St	Akron, OH	44306-1328	330-535-7728	535-7864	K-8	Kenan Bishop
Horizon Science Academy	6150 S Marginal Rd	Cleveland, OH	44103-1043	216-432-9576	432-9801	K-5	
Horizon Science Academy	6000 S Marginal Rd	Cleveland, OH	44103-1078	216-432-3660	432-3670	6-12	Cengiz Karatas
Horizon Science Academy Cincinnati	1055 Laidlaw Ave	Cincinnati, OH	45237-5005	513-242-0099	275-4597	K-12	Cafer Cengiz
Horizon Science Academy Cleveland MS	6100 S Marginal Rd	Cleveland, OH	44103-1043	216-432-9940	432-9941	5-8	Hakan Bagcioglu
Horizon Science Academy Columbus	1070 Morse Rd	Columbus, OH	43229-6290	614-846-7616	846-7696	9-12	Hizir Disli
Horizon Science Academy Dayton	545 Odlin Ave	Dayton, OH	45405-2743	937-277-1177	277-3090	K-12	Sedat Duman
Horizon Science Academy - Denison	1700 Denison Ave	Cleveland, OH	44109-2945	216-739-9911	739-9913	K-8	Angela Ross
Horizon Science Academy MS	1341 Bethel Rd	Columbus, OH	43220-2611	614-457-2231	457-5064	6-8	Harun Karan
Horizon Science Academy Springfield	630 S Reynolds Rd	Toledo, OH	43615-6314	419-535-0524	535-0525	5-8	Mustafa Arslan
Horizon Science Academy Toledo	425 Jefferson Ave	Toledo, OH	43604-1060	419-244-5710	244-5721	K-12	Engin Blackstone Ph.D.
IMAC HS	856 W Cook Rd	Mansfield, OH	44907-5012	419-525-6411	525-0082	9-12	Harold Dean
Imani Learning Academy	728 Parkside Blvd	Toledo, OH	43607-3858	419-824-8615		K-8	
Intergenerational S	12200 Fairhill Rd	Cleveland, OH	44120-1070	216-721-0120	721-0126	K-8	Dr. Cathy Whitehouse
International Academy of Columbus	1201 Schrock Rd	Columbus, OH	43229-1117	614-844-5539	844-5857	K-10	Mouhamed Tarazi
ISUS HS	140 N Keowee St	Dayton, OH	45402-1309	937-223-2323	223-9303	9-12	Barbara Wagner
James Leadership Academy	120 Knox Ave	Dayton, OH	45417	937-835-3580	835-3576	9-12	Kecia Williams
Kent Digital Academy	321 N Depeyster St	Kent, OH	44240-2514	330-676-7610	676-7686	K-12	Joseph Clark
Kessler S	118 E Wood St	Youngstown, OH	44503-1625	330-746-3095	746-4272	K-8	Lydia Brown-Payton
King Academy Community S	933 Bank St	Cincinnati, OH	45214-2103	513-421-7519	421-5768	K-8	Andrea Martinez
Klepinger Community S	3650 Klepinger Rd	Dayton, OH	45416-1919	937-610-1710	610-1730	K-8	Roy Swanson
Lake Erie Academy	2740 W Central Ave	Toledo, OH	43606-3452	419-475-3786	475-6048	K-8	Barbara Baker
Lakeside College Preparatory Academy	2459 Washington Ave	Cleveland, OH	44113-2322	216-861-5902		K-4	Kenneth Fraelich
Lakewood City Academy	1470 Warren Rd	Lakewood, OH	44107-3918	216-529-4037	227-5975	K-12	Terrilynn Bornino-Elwell
Lakewood Digital Academy	PO Box 70	Hebron, OH	43025-0070	740-928-5878	928-3152	K-12	Jay Gault
Lancaster Digital Academy	345 E Mulberry St	Lancaster, OH	43130-3166	740-687-7364	687-7303	K-12	Steven Scott
Lancaster Fairfield Community S	320 E Locust St	Lancaster, OH	43130-4437	740-687-7177	687-7178	7-12	Jeffrey Graf
Legacy Academy for Leaders & Arts	1812 Oak Hill Ave	Youngstown, OH	44507-1053	330-747-1620	747-1753	K-8	Joyce Baldwin
Life Skills Center Middleton	631 S Breiel Blvd	Middletown, OH	45042	513-423-1800	423-1818	9-12	Charles Hall
Life Skills Center of Akron	80 W Bowery St	Akron, OH	44308-1109	330-376-8700	376-6700	9-12	John Stack
Life Skills Center of Canton	1100 Cleveland Ave NW	Canton, OH	44702-1816	330-456-4490		9-12	Scott McClain
Life Skills Center of Cincinnati	2612 Gilbert Ave	Cincinnati, OH	45206-1205	513-475-0222	475-0444	9-12	Leisan Smith
Life Skills Center of Cleveland	4600 Carnegie Ave	Cleveland, OH	44103	216-431-7571	431-7652	9-12	Yolanda Eiland
Life Skills Center of Dayton	1721 N Main St	Dayton, OH	45405-4143	937-274-2841	274-2873	9-12	James Brown
Life Skills Center of Elyria	2015 W River Rd N	Elyria, OH	44035-2309	440-324-1755	324-1723	9-12	Kimberly Sweigart
Life Skills Center of Hamilton County	7710 Reading Rd	Cincinnati, OH	45237-2813	513-821-6695	821-8755	9-12	Arnez Booker
Life Skills Center of Lake Erie	9200 Madison Ave	Cleveland, OH	44102-2719	216-631-1090		9-12	Joseph Czerwien
Life Skills Center of North Akron	1458 Brittain Rd	Akron, OH	44310-3641	330-633-5990	633-7005	9-12	Beth Ferguson
Life Skills Center of Northeast OH	12201 Larchmere Blvd	Shaker Heights, OH	44120-1101	216-421-7587	421-8189	9-12	David Pannell
Life Skills Center of Northern Columbus	1900 E Dublin Granville Rd	Columbus, OH	43229	614-891-9041		9-12	Joseph Buckalew
Life Skills Center of SE Columbus	2400 S Hamilton Rd	Columbus, OH	43232-4963	614-863-9175	863-9185	9-12	Andrew Pasquinilli
Life Skills Center of Springfield	1637 Selma Rd	Springfield, OH	45505-4245	937-322-2940	322-2944	9-12	Edward Haskins
Life Skills Center of Summit County	2168 Romig Rd	Akron, OH	44320-3879	330-745-3678	753-1506	9-12	Jennifer Ciptak
Life Skills Center of Toledo	1830 Adams St	Toledo, OH	43604-4428	419-241-5504	241-9176	9-12	Amy Crawford
Life Skills Center of Trumbull County	458 Franklin St SE	Warren, OH	44483-5715	330-392-0231	392-0253	9-12	Kerry Jupina
Life Skills Center of Youngstown	3405 Market St	Youngstown, OH	44507-2009	330-743-6698	743-6702	9-12	Ruthann Smith-Harris
Lighthouse Academy ES	1585 Frederick Blvd Ste 100	Akron, OH	44320-4000	330-836-6370	836-6321	K-5	
Lighthouse Community S	6100 Desmond St	Cincinnati, OH	45227-1897	513-561-7888	561-7818	6-12	Daniel Trujillo
Lion of Judah Academy	1468 E 55th St	Cleveland, OH	44103-1307	216-881-9200	881-9201	K-8	Chester Starks
London Academy	60 S Walnut St	London, OH	43140-1246	740-852-5700	852-3078	K-12	Donald Allen
Lorain Community MS	201 W Erie Ave	Lorain, OH	44052-1641	440-242-2023	204-2134	5-9	Deborah Thoren
Lorain Community S	201 W Erie Ave	Lorain, OH	44052-1641	440-204-2130	204-2134	K-9	Melisa Shady
Madison Ave School of the Arts	1511 Madison Ave	Toledo, OH	43604-4433	419-259-4000	243-1513	K-5	
Madison Community S	2015 W 95th St	Cleveland, OH	44102-3727	216-651-5212	651-9040	K-8	Gregory Cek
Mahoning Unlimited S	100 Debartolo Pl Ste 170	Youngstown, OH	44512-6066	330-965-7828	965-7902	4-12	
Mahoning Valley Opportunity S	496 Glenwood Ave Ste 112	Youngstown, OH	44502	330-744-7656	743-9757	9-12	
Mansfield Community S	215 N Trimble Rd	Mansfield, OH	44906-2630	419-522-4578	522-3563	K-8	Bethany Young
Mansfield Elective Academy	445 Bowman St	Mansfield, OH	44903-1201	419-247-4475	247-3392	K-8	Deborah Franklin
Mansfield Enhancement Academy	445 Bowman St	Mansfield, OH	44903-1201	419-525-0105	525-0106	9-12	Harold Dean
Mansfield Preparatory Academy	3038 Leavitt Rd	Lorain, OH	44052-4112	440-244-0156	244-3935	K-12	
Mansfield Visual & Performing Arts	455 Park Ave W	Mansfield, OH	44906-3117	419-522-3563	522-2705	K-8	Timothy Parsons
Marion City Digital Academy	910 E Church St	Marion, OH	43302-4396	740-223-4417	223-4569	K-12	Raymond Haines
Maritime Academy of Toledo	1000 Monroe St Ste 1	Toledo, OH	43604-5954	419-244-9999	244-9898	5-12	Lisa Zoltowski
Massillon Digital Academy	207 Oak Ave SE	Massillon, OH	44646-6790	330-830-3900	830-0953	K-12	Mark Fortner
Meadows Choice Community S	1853 South Ave	Toledo, OH	43609-2086	419-385-5730	385-5781	K-9	Ellin Bick
Menlo Park Academy	760 Tower Blvd	Lorain, OH	44052-5223	440-925-6365		K-9	Richard Hronek
Miamisburg Digital HS	540 Park Ave	Miamisburg, OH	45342-2854	937-866-3381	865-5250	9-12	Patricia Ward
Miami Valley Academies	5656 Springboro Pike	Dayton, OH	45449-2806	937-294-4522	294-4545	K-12	Jennifer Claypool
Middletown Fitness & Prep Academy	816 2nd Ave	Middletown, OH	45044-4201	513-424-6110	424-6121	K-8	John Rothwell
Midnimo Cross Cultural Community S	1465 Oakland Park Ave	Columbus, OH	43224-3509	614-294-3020	299-3680	K-12	Estella Stephens
Millenium Community ES	PO Box 27369	Columbus, OH	43227-0369	614-255-5585	255-5580	K-6	
MODEL Community S	1615 Holland Rd	Maumee, OH	43537-1622	419-897-4400	897-4403	K-12	Mary Walters
Montessori Renaissance Experience	PO Box 24249	Columbus, OH	43224-0249	614-262-6510	262-5097	K-6	Cynthia Frazier
Mound Street Health Careers Academy	354 Mound St	Dayton, OH	45402-8325	937-223-3041	223-5867	9-12	Anne Beane
Mound Street IT Careers Academy	354 Mound St	Dayton, OH	45402-8325	937-223-3041	223-5867	9-12	Anne Beane
Mound Street Military Careers Academy	354 Mound St	Dayton, OH	45402-8325	937-223-3041	223-5867	9-12	Anne Beane
Mt. Auburn International Academy	244 Southern Ave	Cincinnati, OH	45219-3023	513-241-5500	241-5501	K-12	Aaron Butler
Newark Digital Academy	255 Woods Ave	Newark, OH	43055-4436	740-328-2022	328-2270	K-12	Keith Richards
New Choices Community S	601 S Keowee St	Dayton, OH	45410-1168	937-224-8201	224-8209	7-12	James Dock
New City S	1516 Salem Ave	Dayton, OH	45406-4943	937-277-7155	277-7017	K-12	Robert Burns
New Day Academy	8566 Barbara Dr	Mentor, OH	44060-1917	216-797-1602	797-1604	K-12	Terrance Walton
NIA University Community S	3556 Reading Rd	Cincinnati, OH	45229-2624	513-373-9337	631-1615	7-12	
Noble Academy - Cleveland	1200 E 200th St	Euclid, OH	44117-1172	216-486-8866	486-2846	K-7	Hasan Kose
Noble Academy - Columbus	1329 Bethel Rd	Upper Arlington, OH	43220-2611	614-329-0687	329-0691	K-12	Murat Efe
North Dayton S of Science & Discovery	3901 Turner Rd	Dayton, OH	45415-3654	937-278-6671	278-6964	K-8	Michael Ward
Northland Prep & Fitness ES	1875 Morse Rd	Columbus, OH	43229-6603	614-318-0600	262-9111	K-8	Myrrha Satow
Nu Bethel Center of Excellence	3560 W Siebenthaler Ave	Dayton, OH	45406-1534	937-275-0433	275-0890	K-6	Johnnye Willis
Oakstone Community S	5747 Cleveland Ave	Columbus, OH	43231-2831	614-865-9643	865-9649	K-12	Susan Bone
Ohio Connections Academy	2727 Madison Rd	Cincinnati, OH	45209-2273	513-533-3230	533-3260	K-12	Raymond Lambert
Ohio Virtual Academy	1655 Holland Rd Ste F	Maumee, OH	43537-1656	419-482-0948	482-0954	K-12	Jeffrey Shaw
Old Brooklyn Community MS	4430 State Rd	Cleveland, OH	44109	216-351-0280	661-5975	5-9	Amy Mobley
Old Brooklyn Community S	5983 W 54th St	Parma, OH	44129	216-661-7888	661-5975	K-4	Cherie Kaiser
Orion Academy	1798 Queen City Ave	Cincinnati, OH	45214-1427	513-251-6000	251-3851	K-8	Stephanie Glenn
Outreach Academy for Children	3326 Broadview Rd	Cleveland, OH	44109-3316	216-661-6655	635-1883	K-12	Mary Wideman-Blake
P.A.C.E. S	1601 California Ave	Cincinnati, OH	45237-5603	513-751-7223	482-3322	9-12	Dr. Steven Hawley
Par - Excellence Academy	96 Maholm St	Newark, OH	43055-3994	740-344-7279	344-7272	PK-6	Sharice Martin
Parma Community S	7667 Day Dr Fl 1	Parma, OH	44129	440-888-5490	888-5890	K-8	Linda Geyer
Pathway S of Discovery	173 Avondale Dr	Dayton, OH	45404-2123	937-235-5498	235-5569	K-8	Keith Colbert
Phillips Academy	3648 Victory Ave	Toledo, OH	43607-2564	419-534-4272	534-4276	K-8	Karyn Benner
Phoenix Academy Community S	2238 Jefferson Ave	Toledo, OH	43604-7120	419-720-4500		7-12	Raymond Russell
Phoenix Community Learning Center	7030 Reading Rd Ste 350	Cincinnati, OH	45237-1756	513-351-5801	351-5809	K-8	Elaine Wilson
Phoenix Village Academy Primary 2	3120 Euclid Ave	Cleveland, OH	44115-2508	216-426-8601	426-9528	K-12	DeShawn Adams
Phoenix Village Academy Secondary 1	3120 Euclid Ave	Cleveland, OH	44115-2508			K-12	
Pinnacle Academy	840 E 222nd St	Euclid, OH	44123-3317	216-731-0127	731-0688	K-8	Virginia Schemrich
Pleasant Community Digital S	1107 Owens Rd W	Marion, OH	43302-8421	740-389-4476	389-6985	K-12	Stephen Larcomb
Premier Academy of Ohio	1555 Elaine Rd	Columbus, OH	43227-2347	614-501-3820		7-12	Michael Aldrink
Project Rebuild Community HS	PO Box 8361	Canton, OH	44711-8361	330-452-8414	452-8452	9-12	Joseph Cole
Promise Academy	1701 E 13th St	Cleveland, OH	44114-3227	216-443-0500		9-12	Kamal Chatman
Pschtecin S	985 Mediterranean Ave	Columbus, OH	43229-2541	614-985-3428	985-3115	8-12	Cynthia Bronson
Puritas Community S	15204 Puritas Ave	Cleveland, OH	44135-2716	216-688-0680	688-0609	K-9	Margaret Paulus
Quaker Digital Academy	400 Mill Ave SE Ste 901	New Phila, OH	44663-3878	330-364-0600	364-9310	K-12	Steve Eckert
Quest Academy Community S	190 E 8th St	Lima, OH	45804-2302	419-227-7730	227-7515	K-7	Oscar Marshall
Ridgedale Community S	3103 Hillman Ford Rd	Morral, OH	43337-9302	740-382-6065	383-6538	K-12	
Rittman Academy	75 N Main St	Rittman, OH	44270-1440	330-927-7401		K-12	
Riverside Academy	3280 River Rd	Cincinnati, OH	45204-1214	513-921-7777	921-7704	K-9	Roger Conners
River Valley Digital Academy	197 Brocklesby Rd	Caledonia, OH	43314-9501	740-725-5451	725-5499	K-12	
Romig Road Community S	2405 Romig Rd	Akron, OH	44320-3826	330-848-1100	848-1130	K-4	Karen Shepherd
Schnee Learning Center	2222 Issaquah St	Cuyahoga Falls, OH	44221-3704	330-922-1966		9-12	Dona Cardone
Scholarts Preparatory S	PO Box 360896	Columbus, OH	43236-0896	614-224-1610	224-1647	K-12	Dr. Cheryl Parchia
School for Arts Integrated Learning	55 N High St	New Albany, OH	43054	614-855-2040		2-5	
Sciotoville Elementary Academy	5540 3rd St	Sciotoville, OH	45662	740-776-2920		K-4	
Sciotoville HS	224 Marshall St	Sciotoville, OH	45662-5549	740-776-6777	776-6812	5-12	Rodney Walker
South Scioto Academy	707 E Jenkins Ave	Columbus, OH	43207-1318	614-445-7684		K-6	Michelle Johnson
Southwest Licking Digital Academy	927 South St Unit A	Pataskala, OH	43062-6014	740-927-3941	927-4648	K-12	Jeffrey Severino
Springfield Academy of Excellence	623 S Center St	Springfield, OH	45506-2209	937-325-0933	325-0962	K-6	Edna Chapman
Springfield Prep & Fitness S	1615 Selma Rd	Springfield, OH	45505-4245	937-323-6250	323-6252	K-8	Thomas Zaboski
Stambaugh Charter Academy	2420 Donald Ave	Youngstown, OH	44509-1306	330-792-4806		K-6	Kathleen Grinwis

School	Address	City,State	Zip code	Telephone	Fax	Grade	Contact
Star Academy of Toledo	1850 Airport Hwy	Toledo, OH	43609-2069	419-720-6330	385-1083	K-12	
Stockyard Community ES	3200 W 65th St	Cleveland, OH	44102-5510	216-651-5209		K-6	Audrey Sims
Sullivant Avenue Community S	3435 Sullivant Ave	Columbus, OH	43204-1103	614-308-5991	308-5622	K-5	Lance Weber
Summit Academy Akron	864 E Market St	Akron, OH	44305-2424	330-434-2343	434-5295	8-12	Chuck Rickard
Summit Academy Akron	88 Kent St	Akron, OH	44305-2544	330-253-7441	253-7457	1-8	Dawn Presley
Summit Academy Canton	1620 Market Ave S	Canton, OH	44707	330-458-0393	458-0518	1-7	Shelly Curcic
Summit Academy - Canton	2400 Cleveland Ave NW	Canton, OH	44709-3613	330-453-8547	453-8924	8-12	Rachel Murphy
Summit Academy Cincinnati	745 Derby Ave	Cincinnati, OH	45232-1836	513-321-0561	321-0795	1-12	Dwight Barnett
Summit Academy Columbus	1855 E Dublin Granville Rd	Columbus, OH	43229	614-880-0714	880-0732	1-8	Trina Moore
Summit Academy Columbus HS	1850 Bostwick Rd	Columbus, OH	43227-3301	614-237-5497	237-6519	7-12	Trina Moore
Summit Academy Dayton	1407 E 3rd St	Dayton, OH	45403-1818	937-223-3154	223-3229	K-12	Mark Sebastian
Summit Academy Lorain	760 Tower Blvd	Lorain, OH	44052-5223	440-960-5440	960-5444	5-12	Joshua Preece
Summit Academy Lorain	2140 E 36th St	Lorain, OH	44055-2756	440-277-4110	277-4112	1-8	Greg Plantner
Summit Academy MS Youngstown	810 Oak St	Youngstown, OH	44506-1233	330-743-9235	743-9260	6-9	Jessica Kohler
Summit Academy - Middletown	7 S Marshall Rd	Middletown, OH	45044-5375	513-420-9767	727-1520	1-8	Edward Lemmert
Summit Academy Middletown	4700 Central Ave	Middletown, OH	45044-5354	513-420-9767	727-1520	7-12	Edward Lemmert
Summit Academy Painesville	301 E Erie St	Painesville, OH	44077-3913	440-358-0877	358-0397	1-8	Brian Knight
Summit Academy Parma	5868 Stumph Rd	Parma, OH	44130-1736	440-888-5407	888-5410	K-12	Frank Cheraso
Summit Academy Secondary S Toledo	703 Phillips Ave	Toledo, OH	43612-1332	419-476-0784	476-0763	7-12	Johna McClure
Summit Academy Toledo	3891 Martha Ave	Toledo, OH	43612-1250	419-476-7859	476-7763	1-8	Kurt Aey
Summit Academy Warren	2106 Arbor Ave SE	Warren, OH	44484-5296	330-369-4233	369-4299	K-9	Deanna Hardwick
Summit Academy - Xenia	870 S Detroit St	Xenia, OH	45385-5510	937-372-5210	372-5250	1-8	Michael Harty
Summit Academy - Youngstown	1400 Oak Hill Ave	Youngstown, OH	44507-1018	330-747-0950	747-0957	8-12	Ray Pallante
Summit Academy Youngstown	144 N Schenley Ave	Youngstown, OH	44509-2041	330-259-0421	259-0424	K-5	Eric Ritz
T.C.P. World Academy	6000 Ridge Ave	Cincinnati, OH	45213-1624	513-531-9500	531-2406	K-6	Karen French
Tech Con Institute HS	2075 Shiloh Springs Rd	Dayton, OH	45426	937-854-4000	854-4004	9-12	Demetrius Maddox
Tiffin City Digital Academy	244 S Monroe St	Tiffin, OH	44883-2906	419-447-2515	448-5202	K-12	Jane Tomaszewski
Toledo Academy of Learning	3001A Hill Ave	Toledo, OH	43607	419-255-0253	255-0279	K-12	James Danner
Toledo Preparatory Academy	540 Independence Rd	Toledo, OH	43607-2650	419-539-7173	539-7174	8-12	Bernard Crawford
Toledo S for the Arts	333 14th St	Toledo, OH	43604-7713	419-246-8732	244-3979	6-12	Howard Walters
Tomorrow Center	PO Box 216	Edison, OH	43320-0216	419-946-1903	947-9551	K-12	
TRECA Digital Academy	100 Executive Dr	Marion, OH	43302-6306	740-389-4798	389-6695	K-12	Mike Carder
Trotwood Fitness & Prep Academy	3100 Shiloh Springs Rd	Trotwood, OH	45426-2247	937-854-4100	854-1177	K-8	Jeffrey Neely
Upper Arlington Community S	1950 N Mallway Dr	Upper Arlington, OH	43221-4326	614-487-5200	487-5238	11-12	Kip Greenhill
Upper Arlington IB HS	1650 Ridgeview Rd	Upper Arlington, OH	43221-2997	614-487-5200	487-5238	11-12	Kip Greenhill
Urbana Community S	711 Wood St	Urbana, OH	43078-1498	937-653-1478	652-3845	K-12	Larry Nickels
Victory Academy of Toledo	3319 Nebraska Ave	Toledo, OH	43607-2819	419-534-2304	534-2379	K-8	John Fernbaugh
Villaview Lighthouse Community S	1701 E 12th St	Cleveland, OH	44114	216-486-1147	486-1149	K-12	Nigena Livingston
Virtual Community S of Ohio	6100 Channingway Blvd	Columbus, OH	43232	614-501-9473	501-9470	K-12	Jim McCord
Virtual Schoolhouse	736 Lakeview Rd	Cleveland, OH	44108-2608	216-541-2048	541-2018	K-12	
V L T Academy	1100 Sycamore St	Cincinnati, OH	45202-1321	513-421-1129		K-12	Pia Spaulding
Warren County Virtual Community S	320 E Silver St	Lebanon, OH	45036-1887	513-695-2567	695-2961	9-12	Brian Barot
Washington Park Community S	4000 Washington Park Blvd	Newburgh Hts, OH	44105	216-271-6055	271-6099	K-8	Robert Horrocks
W.E.B. DuBois Academy	1812 Central Pkwy	Cincinnati, OH	45214-2304	513-651-9624	618-0272	K-8	Carlos Blair
Weems S	2280 Professor Ave	Cleveland, OH	44113-4467	216-771-6799	771-6884	K-8	Loren Antolino
West Central Learning Academy	650 E Edwards St	Lima, OH	45801-3724	419-227-9252	227-2511	7-12	
Western Reserve Kindergarten	6194 S Salem Warren Rd	Ellsworth, OH	44416	330-547-4100	547-9302	K-K	
Westpark Community MS	3326 Broadview Rd	Cleveland, OH	44109-3316	216-688-0271	688-0273	5-9	Karil Sako
Westpark Community S	16210 Lorain Ave	Cleveland, OH	44111-5521	216-688-0271	688-0273	K-4	Macey Baldizzi
Westside Academy	4330 Clime Rd N	Columbus, OH	43228-3439	614-272-9392		K-8	Heather O'Bannon
Westside Community S of the Arts	3727 Bosworth Rd	Cleveland, OH	44111-6037	216-635-1882	635-1363	K-9	Deborah Kilbane
Whitehall Prep & Fitness S	3474 E Livingston Ave	Columbus, OH	43227-2219	614-324-4585	238-3184	K-8	Drake Donnell
Wickliffe Progressive Community S	1950 N Mallway Dr	Upper Arlington, OH	43221-4326	614-487-5007		K-5	Chris Collaros
Wildwood Environmental Academy	1546 Dartford Rd	Maumee, OH	43537-1374	419-868-9885	868-9981	K-8	Elizabeth Lewin
Winterfield Venture Academy	305 Wenz Rd	Toledo, OH	43615-6244	419-531-3285	531-3637	K-7	Amy Kramer
Woods Community S	720 Mount Vernon Ave	Columbus, OH	43203-1403	614-252-3630	252-3649	K-8	James Devers
Youngstown Academy of Excellence	1408 Rigby St	Youngstown, OH	44506-1617	330-746-3970	746-3965	K-12	
Youngstown Community ES	50 Essex St	Youngstown, OH	44502-1838	330-746-2240	746-6618	K-6	Sr. Mary Dunn
YouthBuild Columbus Comm S	1183 Essex Ave	Columbus, OH	43201-2925	614-291-0805	291-0890	9-12	Derek Steward
Zanesville Community S	920 Moxahala Ave	Zanesville, OH	43701-5533			9-12	
Zenith Academy	8210 Havens Rd	Blacklick, OH	43004-8630	614-419-6753	888-3290	K-9	

Oklahoma

School	Address	City,State	Zip code	Telephone	Fax	Grade	Contact
ASTEC Charter S	2401 NW 23rd St Ste 3B	Oklahoma City, OK	73107-2431	405-947-6274	947-0035	6-12	Dr. Freda Deskin
Brown Community S	3 S Cincinnati Ave	Tulsa, OK	74103	918-425-1407	425-6693	K-5	Deborah Brown
Dove Science Academy	919 NW 23rd St	Oklahoma City, OK	73106-5691	405-524-9762	524-9471	6-12	Barbaros Aslan
Dove Science Academy	280 S Memorial Dr	Tulsa, OK	74112-2202	918-834-3936	834-3352	6-12	Zekeruya Yuksel
Dove Science Academy	4901 N Lincoln Blvd	Oklahoma City, OK	73105-3322	405-605-5566	605-5578	K-5	Hasan Suzuk
Garvey S	1537 NE 24th St	Oklahoma City, OK	73111-3212	405-427-7616	425-4632	K-6	Dr. Kevin McPherson
Harding Charter Preparatory HS	3333 N Shartel Ave	Oklahoma City, OK	73118-7277	405-528-0562	556-5063	9-12	Richard Caram
Harding Fine Arts Center	PO Box 18895	Oklahoma City, OK	73154-0895	405-702-4322	601-0904	9-12	Sherry Rowan Ph.D.
Independence Charter MS	3232 NW 65th St	Oklahoma City, OK	73116-3512	405-841-3132	841-3134	6-8	Vana Baker
KIPP S	PO Box 776	Oklahoma City, OK	73101-0776	405-425-4622	425-4624	5-8	Tracy McDaniel
KIPP Tulsa Academy	1661 E Virgin St	Tulsa, OK	74106-5552	918-925-1580	925-1590	5-8	Millard House
Santa Fe South HS	301 SE 38th St	Oklahoma City, OK	73129-3099	405-631-6100	681-6993	9-12	Chris Brewster
Santa Fe South MS	4712 S Santa Fe Ave	Oklahoma City, OK	73109-7545	405-631-6100	681-6993	6-8	Chris Brewster
SeeWorth Academy	12600 N Kelley Ave	Oklahoma City, OK	73131-1869	405-475-6400	475-8566	3-12	Janet Grigg
Tulsa S of Arts and Sciences	5155 E 51st St Ste 200	Tulsa, OK	74135-7458	918-828-7727	828-7747	9-12	Pat Lubas
Western Village Academy	1508 NW 106th St	Oklahoma City, OK	73114-5214	405-751-1774	752-6833	PK-5	Margaret Brinson

Oregon

School	Address	City,State	Zip code	Telephone	Fax	Grade	Contact
Acad for Character Education Charter S	PO Box 1652	Cottage Grove, OR	97424-0067	541-942-9707	942-7884	K-12	Starr Sannow
ACE Academy	4222 NE 158th Ave	Portland, OR	97230-5084	503-546-9928		11-12	Michael Taylor
Alliance Charter Academy	1404 7th St	Oregon City, OR	97045-2031	503-593-9337		K-12	Lara Fabrycki
Armadillo Technical Institute	PO Box 1560	Phoenix, OR	97535-1560	541-535-3287		4-12	Mike Warner
Arthur Academy	13717 SE Division St	Portland, OR	97236-2841	503-252-3753	761-4143	K-5	Michelle Duhon
Azbuka Academy	PO Box 16638	Portland, OR	97292-0638	503-737-7627		K-8	Eric Kaganov
Baker Charter S	999 Locust St NE	Salem, OR	97301-0954	503-364-4042	364-4050	K-3	Karl Paulson
Ballston Community Charter S	7575 Zena Rd	Rickreall, OR	97371	503-843-2537		K-12	Jeff Clabaugh
Bethany Charter S	11824 Hazelgreen Rd NE	Silverton, OR	97381-9611	503-873-4300	873-0143	K-8	Kathy Frank
Blue Mountain Charter S	76132 Blue Mountain School	Cottage Grove, OR	97424	541-942-7764	942-7597	K-12	Demian Schwartz
Camas Valley S	PO Box 57	Camas Valley, OR	97416-0057	541-445-2131	445-2041	K-12	Paul Young
Cascade Heights Charter S	13515 SE Rusk Rd	Milwaukie, OR	97222-3243	503-701-0009		K-6	Holly Denman
Center for Advanced Learning	1484 NW Civic Dr	Gresham, OR	97030-5564	503-667-4978		11-12	Bill Lesh
Childs Way Charter S	37895 Row River Rd	Culp Creek, OR	97434-9610	541-946-1821	946-2007	6-12	Mike Kerns
City View Charter S	PO Box 1808	Hillsboro, OR	97123-1808	503-844-9424	844-9425	K-8	Katye Atwood
Clackamas Middle College HS	19729 Highway 213	Oregon City, OR	97045-4190	503-518-5900	518-5928	9-12	Brian Sien
Clackamas Web Academy	8740 SE Sunnybrook Ste 350	Clackamas, OR	97015	503-659-4664	659-4994	1-12	Brad Linn
CM2 Opal S	4015 SW Canyon Rd	Portland, OR	97221-2759	503-417-9917	223-6600	PK-5	Suzanna Lindeman
Columbia County Education Campus	474 N 16th St	Saint Helens, OR	97051-1340	503-366-3207	397-2723	7-12	Colleen Grogan
Corbett Charter S	35800 E Historic Columbia	Corbett, OR	97019	503-695-3621	695-3641	K-12	Robert Dunton
Days Creek Charter S	PO Box 10	Days Creek, OR	97429-0010	541-825-3296	825-3052	6-12	Laurie Newton
Deschutes Edge Charter S	1220 NW Upas Ave	Redmond, OR	97756-1253	541-526-6440	526-6441	6-8	Carrie Carpenter
Dos Mundos Charter S at Westside	3685 Belmont Dr	Hood River, OR	97031-8763	541-386-1535	387-5059	K-5	Dan Patton
EagleRidge HS	422 N 9th St	Klamath Falls, OR	97601-2805	541-850-9949	205-4806	9-12	Tiffany Davis
Eddyville Charter S	PO Box 68	Eddyville, OR	97343-0068	541-875-2942	875-2491	K-12	Don McDonald
Emerson Charter S	105 NW Park Ave	Portland, OR	97209-3315	503-525-6124	223-4875	K-5	Tara O'Neil
Estacada Web Academy	8740 SE Sunnybrook Ste 340	Clackamas, OR	97015	503-867-1696		1-12	Jonica Tabler
Forest Grove Community Charter S	2417 15th Ave	Forest Grove, OR	97116-2815	503-359-4600	359-4622	1-9	Vanessa Gray
Fossil S	PO Box 287	Fossil, OR	97830-0287	541-763-4155		K-8	Brad Sperry
Four Rivers Community S	2449 SW 4th Ave	Ontario, OR	97914-1829	541-889-3715		K-5	Chelle Robins
Goodall Environmental MS	2805 Lansing Ave NE	Salem, OR	97301-8555	503-399-3215	399-4070	6-8	Joe LaFountaine
Gresham Arthur Academy	1890 NE Cleveland Ave	Gresham, OR	97030-4210	503-667-4900	667-4933	K-3	Ryan Hull
Howard Street Charter S	710 Howard St SE	Salem, OR	97302-3098	503-399-3408	375-7861	6-8	Cathy Mink
International S of the Cascades	2105 W Antler Ave	Redmond, OR	97756-9398	541-923-4840	923-4846	9-12	Shay Mikalson
Ione S	PO Box 167	Ione, OR	97843-0167	541-422-7131	422-7555	K-12	Karl Ostheller
Kings Valley Charter S	38840 Kings Valley Hwy	Philomath, OR	97370-9750	541-929-2134	929-8179	K-8	Mark Hazelton
Leadership & Entrepreneurship Charter HS	2044 E Burnside St	Portland, OR	97214	503-254-2537	252-9560	9-12	Lorna Fast Buffalo Horse
Lewis & Clark Montessori Charter S	3445 SE Hillyard Rd	Gresham, OR	97080-9264	503-912-1367	912-1374	K-3	Michael Harris
Lighthouse S	93670 Viking Ln	North Bend, OR	97459-8651	541-751-1649		K-7	Bill Anderson
Lincoln City Career Tech HS	801 SW Highway 101 Ste 404	Lincoln City, OR	97367-2752	541-996-5534	265-8507	9-12	Marie Jones
Lourdes Charter S	39059 Jordan Rd	Scio, OR	97374-9330	503-394-3340		K-8	Linda Duman
Luckiamute Valley Charter S	12975 Kings Valley Hwy	Monmouth, OR	97361-9525	503-838-1933		K-8	Dan Austin
Madrone Trail S	PO Box 579	Medford, OR	97501-0213	541-245-6787	245-0583	K-3	Corinne Brion
Marcola Early College S	38300 Wendling Rd	Marcola, OR	97454-9732	541-867-1696		9-12	Sean Gallagher

School	Address	City,State	Zip code	Telephone	Fax	Grade	Contact
Marcola Web Academy	38300 Wendling Rd	Marcola, OR	97454-9732	541-867-1696		1-12	Sean Gallagher
Milwaukie Academy of the Arts	11300 SE 23rd Ave	Milwaukie, OR	97222-7753	503-353-5851	353-5845	9-12	Tim Taylor
MITCH Charter S	PO Box 230575	Tigard, OR	97281-0575	503-639-5757		K-8	Debi Lorence
MITCH Sherwood Charter S	PO Box 1342	Sherwood, OR	97140-1342	503-925-8007		K-3	Fred Puhl
Mosier Community S	PO Box 307	Mosier, OR	97040-0307	541-478-3321	478-2536	K-6	Carole Schmidt
Muddy Creek Charter S	30252 Bellfountain Rd	Corvallis, OR	97333-9524	541-602-9508		K-5	Jen Renee
Multisensory Learning Academy	22565 NE Halsey St	Fairview, OR	97024-2642	503-261-0202	261-9099	K-5	Terri Amacher
Network Charter S	45 W Broadway Ste 201	Eugene, OR	97401-3046	541-344-1229		7-12	Mary Leighton
Nixyaawi Community S	PO Box 638	Pendleton, OR	97801-0638	541-966-2680		9-12	Fjell Ley
North Columbia Academy	28168 Old Rainier Rd	Rainier, OR	97048-3017	503-556-5041	556-2203	9-12	Kristin Carrico
Optimum Learning Environments Charter S	7905 June Reid Pl NE	Keizer, OR	97303-2559	503-399-5548	399-2647	1-5	Gary Etchemendy
Oregon City Service Learning Academy	PO Box 2110	Oregon City, OR	97045-5010	503-785-8445		9-12	Melanie Marrone
Oregon Coast Technology S	1913 Meade St	North Bend, OR	97459-3432	541-756-8307	756-1313	6-12	James Moyer
Oregon Connections Academy	PO Box 1160	Scio, OR	97374-1160	503-394-4315		K-12	Jerry Wilks
Oregon Virtual Academy	1810 Monroe St	North Bend, OR	97459-3447	541-751-8060	751-8016	K-12	Todd Thorpe
Paisley S	PO Box 97	Paisley, OR	97636-0097	541-943-3111	943-3129	K-12	Mark Jeffery
Phoenix S of Roseburg	3131 NE Diamond Lake Blvd	Roseburg, OR	97470-3632	541-673-3036	957-5906	8-12	Ron Breyne
Portland Arthur Academy	7507 SE Yamhill St	Portland, OR	97215-2284	503-257-3936	257-3929	K-2	Christina Loug
Portland Village S	7654 N Delaware Ave	Portland, OR	97217-6417	503-445-0056	445-0058	K-4	Tom Klein
REALMS	1501 NE Neff Rd	Bend, OR	97701-6149	541-322-5323	322-5473	6-8	Roger White
Resource Link Charter S	PO Box 509	Coos Bay, OR	97420-0102	541-267-1499	266-7314	5-12	Lesli Gieselman
Reynolds Arthur Academy	123 SE 21st St	Troutdale, OR	97060-3300	503-465-8882	465-8883	K-5	Chris Arnold
Riddle Education Center	PO Box 300	Riddle, OR	97469-0300	541-874-3202		7-12	Al Springer
Ridgeline Montessori	2855 Lincoln St	Eugene, OR	97405-2737	541-681-9662	681-4394	K-8	Cindy Bass
Sage Community S	PO Box 655	Chiloquin, OR	97624-0655	541-783-2533	783-2544	K-6	Faith Wilkins
Saint Helens Arthur Academy	33035 Pittsburg Rd	Saint Helens, OR	97051-3305	503-366-7030		K-4	Michael Arthur
Sand Ridge Charter S	30581 Sodaville Mtn Home Rd	Lebanon, OR	97355-9008	541-258-2416		K-12	Mary Northern
SEI Academy Charter S	3920 N Kerby Ave	Portland, OR	97227-1255	503-249-1721	249-1955	6-8	Linda Harris
Sheridan Japanese S	PO Box 446	Sheridan, OR	97378-0446	503-843-3400	843-7438	4-12	Kim Miller
Siletz Valley S	PO Box 247	Siletz, OR	97380-0247	541-444-1100	444-2368	K-12	Robert Line
Sisters Charter Academy of Fine Arts	PO Box 1176	Sisters, OR	97759-1176	541-549-8120	549-1173	K-6	Teresa Schneiderman
Sisters Early College Charter S	8800 SE Sunnyside Rd # 300N	Clackamas, OR	97015	503-654-1642	353-1480	9-12	Teresa Schneiderman
Sisters Web Academy	8800 SE Sunnyside Rd # 300N	Clackamas, OR	97015	503-654-1642	353-1480	K-12	Teresa Schneiderman
South Columbia Family S	34555 Berg Rd	Warren, OR	97053-9611	503-366-9009	366-9010	1-8	Anita Ott
Southwest Charter S	5839 SW Hood Ave	Portland, OR	97239-3716	503-244-1697		K-6	Anne Gurnee
Springwater Environmental Sciences S	PO Box 3010	Oregon City, OR	97045-0301	503-631-7700	631-7720	K-5	Deb Odell
Sweet Home Charter S	1805 Long St	Sweet Home, OR	97386-2322	541-367-1833	367-1898	K-5	Scott Richards
Three Rivers Charter S	4975 Willamette Falls Dr	West Linn, OR	97068-3348	503-723-6019	723-6407	4-8	Katherine Holtgraves
Trillium Charter S	5420 N Interstate Ave	Portland, OR	97217-4569	503-285-3833	281-3937	K-12	Stephanie Hinkle
Upper Chetco Charter S	99603 N Bank Chetco River	Brookings, OR	97415	541-412-9072	412-9047	2-6	Karen Johnson
Village S	2855 Lincoln St	Eugene, OR	97405-2737	541-345-7285	242-6874	K-8	Martha Collins
West Lane Technology Learning Center	24936 Fir Grove Ln	Elmira, OR	97437-9751	541-935-2101		9-12	Donna Garner
Wheeler HS	PO Box 266	Fossil, OR	97830-0266	541-763-4146	763-4010	9-12	Brad Sperry
Willamette Leadership Academy	87230 Central Rd	Eugene, OR	97402-9208	541-935-6815		6-12	Roger McClelland
Woodburn Arthur Academy	575 Gatch St	Woodburn, OR	97071-4927	503-981-5746	761-4143	K-2	Jennifer Hale
		Pennsylvania					
Academy Charter S	900 Agnew Rd	Pittsburgh, PA	15227-3902	412-885-5200		8-12	William Styche
Achievement House Charter S	1021 W Lancaster Ave # 207	Bryn Mawr, PA	19010	610-527-0143	520-1547	9-12	Dr. Alexander Grandee
Ad Prima Charter S	124 Bryn Mawr Ave	Bala Cynwyd, PA	19004-3013	610-617-9121		K-8	Dr. June Brown
Agora Cyber Charter S	60 Chestnut Ave	Devon, PA	19333	866-548-9452		K-12	Kathleen Suloft
Allen Preparatory Charter S	2601 S 58th St	Philadelphia, PA	19143-6146	215-878-1544	878-8171	5-8	Lawrence Jones
Alliance For Progress Charter S	1821 Cecil B Moore Ave	Philadelphia, PA	19121-3135	215-232-4892	232-4893	K-5	Stacey Hill
Architecture & Design Charter HS	675 Sansom St	Philadelphia, PA	19106-3300	215-351-2900	351-9458	9-12	Dr. Peter Kountz
Attucks Youth Build Charter S	605 S Duke St	York, PA	17401-3111	717-848-3610	843-3914	K-6	Jaquie Martino
Avon Grove Charter S	110 State Rd	West Grove, PA	19390-8908	484-667-5000		K-6	Dr. Kevin Brady
Bear Creek Community Charter S	2000 Bear Creek Blvd	Wilkes Barre, PA	18702-9684	570-820-4070		K-6	Margaret Foster
Beaver Area Academic Charter S	Gypsy Glen Rd	Beaver, PA	15009	724-774-0250		9-12	Brian White
Belmont Academy Charter S	907 N 41st St	Philadelphia, PA	19104-1278	215-381-5786		K-4	Jennifer Faustman
Belmont Charter S	4030 Brown St	Philadelphia, PA	19104-4899	215-823-8208		K-7	Jennifer Faustman
Boys Latin of Philadelphia Charter S	4212 Chestnut St Ste 120	Philadelphia, PA	19104	215-972-0841		9-12	David Hardy
Bracetti Academy Charter S	2501 Kensington Ave	Philadelphia, PA	19125-1321	215-291-4436	291-4985	6-12	Angela Villani
Bucks County Montessori Charter S	219 Tyburn Rd	Fairless Hills, PA	19030-4403	215-547-5230	547-5032	K-6	John Funston
Byers Charter S	1911 Arch St	Philadelphia, PA	19103-1403	215-972-1700	972-1701	K-5	Salome Thomas-EL
Career Connections Charter HS	4412 Butler St	Pittsburgh, PA	15201-3012	412-682-1816	682-6559	9-12	Brian White
Center for Student Learning Charter S	134 Yardley Ave	Fallsington, PA	19054-1119	215-428-4100		6-12	Heather Humienny
Central Pennsylvania Digital Charter S	1500 4th Ave	Altoona, PA	16602-3616	814-946-6989		K-12	Norman Miller
Centre Learning Community Charter S	2643 W College Ave	State College, PA	16801-2604	814-861-7980	861-8030	5-8	Kosta Dussias
Chester Community Charter S	214 E 5th St	Chester, PA	19013-4510	610-447-0400	876-5716	K-6	Steven Lee
Chester Co. Family Academy	323 E Gay St Ste B7	West Chester, PA	19380	610-696-5910	696-6324	K-2	Lorraine Anderson
City Charter HS	717 Liberty Ave	Pittsburgh, PA	15222-3510	412-690-2489		9-12	Richard Wertheimer
Clemente Charter S	136 S 4th St	Allentown, PA	18102-5410	610-439-5181	435-4731	6-12	Dr. Maritza Robert
Collegium Charter S	535 James Hance Ct	Exton, PA	19341-2560	610-903-1300	903-1317	K-12	Bill Winters
Columbus Charter S	916 Christian St	Philadelphia, PA	19147-3808	215-925-7400	925-7491	K-8	Rosemary Dougherty
Commonwealth Connections Charter S	5010 E Trindle Rd	Mechanicsburg, PA	17050	717-605-8900		K-9	Dennis Tulli
Community Academy of Philadelphia	1100 E Erie Ave	Philadelphia, PA	19124-5424	215-533-6700		K-12	Joe Proietta
DeHostos Charter S	4322 N 5th St	Philadelphia, PA	19140-2302	215-455-2300	455-6312	K-K,	Evelyn Lebron
Delaware Valley Charter HS	5201 Old York Rd	Philadelphia, PA	19141-2995	215-455-2550		9-12	Ava Greene Bedden
Discovery Charter S	5070 Parkside Ave Unit 6200	Philadelphia, PA	19131-4750	215-879-8182		K-6	Jacquelyn Kelley
Environmental Charter S at Frick Park	829 Milton St	Pittsburgh, PA	15218-1005	412-247-7970		K-3	Jon McCann
Evergreen Community Charter S	PO Box 523	Mountainhome, PA	18342-0523	570-595-6355	595-6038	6-12	Jill Shoesmith
Fell Charter S	777 Main St	Simpson, PA	18407-1236	570-282-5199		K-8	MaryJo Walsh
First Philadelphia Charter S	4300 Tacony St	Philadelphia, PA	19124-4134	215-743-3100		K-3	Stacy Cruise-Clark
Folk Arts-Cultural Treasures Charter S	1023 Callowhill St	Philadelphia, PA	19123-3704	215-569-2600		K-8	Deborah Wei
Forbes Charter S	225 Barnsley Rd	Oxford, PA	19363-4102	610-932-8998		K-6	Dr. Lenetta Lee
Franklin Towne Charter HS	PO Box 310	Philadelphia, PA	19105-0310	215-289-5000	535-8910	9-12	Joseph Venditti
Freire Charter S	2027 Chestnut St	Philadelphia, PA	19103	215-557-8555	557-9051	8-12	Dr. Kelly Davenport
Germantown Settlement Charter S	4811 Germantown Ave	Philadelphia, PA	19144-3014	215-713-0855	713-0553	5-8	Ron Rhodes
Global Leadership Academy	5151 Warren St	Philadelphia, PA	19131-4441	215-477-6672	477-6674	K-8	Dr. Naomi Johnson-Booker
Graystone Academy Charter S	139 Modena Rd	Coatesville, PA	19320-4036	610-383-4311		K-6	Anne Humphrey
Green Woods Charter S	8480 Hagys Mill Rd	Philadelphia, PA	19128-1938	215-482-6337	482-9135	K-8	Jean Wallace
Hope Charter S	2116 E Haines St	Philadelphia, PA	19138-2600	215-336-2730		9-12	Richard L. Chapman
Imani Education Circle Charter S	5612 Greene St Fl 2	Philadelphia, PA	19144	215-713-9240		K-8	Dr. Francine Fulton
Imhotep Institute Charter HS	2101 W Godfrey Ave	Philadelphia, PA	19138-2597	215-438-4140	438-4160	9-12	Christine Wiggins
Independence Charter S	1600 Lombard St	Philadelphia, PA	19146-1507	215-238-8000	238-1998	K-5	Jurate Krokys
Infinity Charter S	51 Banks St Ste 1	Penbrook, PA	17103-2067	717-238-1880		K-6	Nancy Hall
Ketterer Charter S	1133 Village Way	Latrobe, PA	15650-5201	724-537-9110	537-9114	1-12	Sherri Holler
Keystone Education Center Charter S	425 S Good Hope Rd	Greenville, PA	16125-8629	724-588-2511	588-2545	6-12	Mike Gentile
Khepera Charter S	144 Carpenter Ln	Philadelphia, PA	19119-2563	215-843-1700	843-3530	K-8	Dr. Ayesha Imani
KIPP Academy Charter S	2709 N Broad St	Philadelphia, PA	19132-2722	215-227-1728		5-5	Marc Mannella
La Academia Charter S	30 N Ann St	Lancaster, PA	17602-3063	717-295-7763	399-6456	6-12	Evelyn Antonsen
Laboratory Charter S	124 Bryn Mawr Ave	Bala Cynwyd, PA	19004-3013	610-617-9121	660-8416	K-8	Dr. June Hairston-Brown
Lehigh Valley Academy	1560 Valley Center Pkwy	Bethlehem, PA	18017	610-866-9660		K-10	Dr. Barry Cohen
Lehigh Valley Charter HS	675 E Broad St	Bethlehem, PA	18018-6332	610-868-2971		9-12	Dr. Thomas Lubben
Lincoln Charter S	559 W King St	York, PA	17401-3776	717-699-1573	846-4031	K-5	Erin Holman
Lincoln Park Performing Arts Charter S	1 Lincoln Park	Midland, PA	15059-1535	724-643-9004	643-0769	K-12	Rebecca Manning
Manchester Academic Charter S	1214 Liverpool St	Pittsburgh, PA	15233-1309	412-322-0585	322-2176	K-8	Vasilios A. Scoumis
Maritime Academy Charter S	2275 Bridge St	Philadelphia, PA	19137	215-535-4555	535-4398	5-12	Dr. Ann Gillis Waiters
MAST Community Charter S	1800 Byberry Rd	Philadelphia, PA	19116-3012	215-348-1100		K-12	Richard Trzaska
Mastery Charter S - Lenfest	35 S 4th St	Philadelphia, PA	19106-2710	215-922-1902	922-1903	7-12	Scott Gordon
Mastery Charter S - Pickett	5700 Wayne Ave	Philadelphia, PA	19144-3314	215-866-9000		7-12	Scott Gordon
Mastery Charter S - Shoemaker Campus	5301 Media St	Philadelphia, PA	19131-4035	215-922-1902		7-12	Scott Gordon
Mastery Charter S - Thomas Campus	927 Johnston St	Philadelphia, PA	19148-5016	215-922-1902		7-9	Scott Gordon
Math Civics & Sciences Charter S	447 N Broad St	Philadelphia, PA	19123-3643	215-923-4880	923-4859	1-12	Veronica Joyner
Montessori Regional Charter S	2910 Sterrettania Rd	Erie, PA	16506-2646	814-833-7771	833-1838	K-6	Anthony Pirrello
Multi-Cultural Academy Charter S	4666 N 15th St	Philadelphia, PA	19140-1109	215-457-6666	457-2982	9-12	Dr. Vuong Thuy
New Foundations Charter S	8001 Torresdale Ave	Philadelphia, PA	19136-2917	215-624-8100		K-8	Paul Stadelberger
New Hope Academy	459 W King St	York, PA	17401-3801	717-845-4046		7-8	Isiah Anderson
New Media Technology Charter S	8034 Thouron Ave	Philadelphia, PA	19150-2423	267-286-6900		9-12	Dr. Ina Walker
Nittany Valley Charter S	1612 Norma St	State College, PA	16801-6228	814-867-3842	231-0795	1-8	Carolyn Maroncelli
Northside Urban Pathways Charter S	914 Penn Ave	Pittsburgh, PA	15222-3713	412-392-4601	392-4602	6-12	Linda Clautti
Northwood Academy	4621 Castor Ave	Philadelphia, PA	19124-3097	215-289-5606	676-8340	K-6	Brien Gardiner
Nueva Esperanza Academy Charter HS	301 W Hunting Park Ave	Philadelphia, PA	19140-2625	215-457-3667	457-4381	9-12	David Rossi
Palmer Leadership Learning Partners S	910 N 6th St	Philadelphia, PA	19123-1496	215-627-7434	739-2606	PK-8	Yancy Bright
Pan American Community Charter S	126 W Dauphin St	Philadelphia, PA	19133	215-763-8870		K-8	Nicholas Torres
Pantoja Community Charter S	4322 N 5th St	Philadelphia, PA	19140-2302	215-455-1300		K-8	Alfredo Calderon

School	Address	City,State	Zip code	Telephone	Fax	Grade	Contact
Penn Charter S	3000 W School House Ln	Philadelphia, PA	19144-5412	215-844-3460	843-3939	K-12	Darryl Ford
Pennsylvania Cyber Charter S	1 Lincoln Park Ste 3	Midland, PA	15059	724-643-1180	643-1181	K-12	Dr. Nick Trombetta
Pennsylvania Distance Learning Charter S	2200 Georgetown Dr Ste 300	Sewickley, PA	15143-8752	724-933-7300	933-7655	K-12	Dr. James Hoover
Pennsylvania Leadership Charter S	1332 Enterprise Dr	West Chester, PA	19380	610-701-3333		K-12	Dr. James Hanak
PA Learners Online Regional S	475 Waterfront Dr E	Homestead, PA	15120-1144	412-394-5733		K-12	Dr. David Martin
Pennsylvania Virtual Charter S	1 W Main St Ste 400	Norristown, PA	19401-4766	610-275-8501	275-1719	K-12	Joanne Jones Barnett
People for People Charter S	800 N Broad St	Philadelphia, PA	19130-2202	215-763-7060	235-6435	K-5	Andre Williams
Perseus House Charter S of Excellence	2931 Harvard Rd	Erie, PA	16508-1220	814-459-3954		7-12	Dr. John Linden
Philadelphia Academy Charter S	11000 Roosevelt Blvd	Philadelphia, PA	19116-3903	215-676-8320	676-8340	K-8	Brien Gardner
Philadelphia Electrical & Tech Charter S	1420 Chestnut St	Philadelphia, PA	19102-2505	267-514-1823	514-1834	9-12	Michael Nemitz
Philadelphia Harambee Inst Charter S	640 N 66th St	Philadelphia, PA	19151-3606	215-472-8770	472-9611	K-8	Masai Skief
Philadelphia Montessori Charter S	2227 Island Rd	Philadelphia, PA	19142-1009	215-365-4011	365-4367	PK-3	Kathleen Dzura
Philadelphia Performing Arts Charter S	2600 S Broad St	Philadelphia, PA	19145-4616	215-551-4000	551-1113	K-8	Angela Corosanite
Planet Abacus Charter S	6660 Keystone St	Philadelphia, PA	19135-2816	215-332-2111	332-2840	K-5	Dr. June Brown
Pocono Mountain Charter S	16 Carriage Sq	Tobyhanna, PA	18466-8979	570-894-5108		K-12	Dennis Bloom
Preparatory Charter S	1928 Point Breeze Ave	Philadelphia, PA	19145-2612	215-334-6144	334-6147	9-12	John Badagliacco
Propel Charter S - East	1611 Monroeville Ave	Turtle Creek, PA	15145-1652	412-823-0347		K-8	Jeremy Resnick
Propel Charter S - Homestead	129 E 10th Ave	Homestead, PA	15120-1608	412-464-2604		K-8	George Fitch
Propel Charter S - Mc Keesport	413 Shaw Ave	Mc Keesport, PA	15132-3036	412-678-7215		K-6	
Propel Charter S - Montour	24 S 18th St	Pittsburgh, PA	15203-1767	412-325-7305		K-8	Jeremy Resnick
Renaissance Academy - Edison Charter S	40 Pine Crest Ave	Phoenixville, PA	19460-2955	610-983-4080	983-4096	K-12	Gina Guarino-Buli
Renaissance Advantage Charter S	1712 S 56th St	Philadelphia, PA	19143-5308	215-724-2343	724-2374	K-8	Michael Rosenberg
Renaissance Charter S	7500 Germantown Ave Ste I	Philadelphia, PA	19119-1678	215-753-0390	753-0615	6-8	A. Donald Lepore
Sankofa Academy	446 W Gay St	West Chester, PA	19380-2851	610-696-0333		5-12	Dr. LaMont McKim
School Lane Charter S	2400 Bristol Pike	Bensalem, PA	19020-5293	215-245-6055	245-6058	K-8	Karen Schade
Souderton Charter S Collaborative	110 E Broad St	Souderton, PA	18964-1276	215-721-4560	721-4071	K-8	Jennifer Arevalo
Southwest Leadership Academy	7101 Paschall Ave	Philadelphia, PA	19142	215-729-1939	729-1976	K-8	Paulette Royster
Spectrum Charter S	4369 Northern Pike	Monroeville, PA	15146-2807	412-374-8130	374-9629	9-12	Michelle Johnson
Sugar Valley Rural Charter S	PO Box 104	Loganton, PA	17747-0104	570-725-7822	725-7825	K-12	Logan Coney
SUSQ-Cyber Charter S	240 Market St	Bloomsburg, PA	17815	570-523-1155	523-0674	9-12	James Street
Sylvan Heights Science Charter S	915 S 13th St	Harrisburg, PA	17104-3402	717-232-9220	232-9221	K-4	Dr. Kevin Moran
Tidioute Community Charter S	241 Main St	Tidioute, PA	16351-1299	814-484-3550	484-3977	K-12	David Craig
Truebright Science Academy	3821 N Broad St	Philadelphia, PA	19140-3609	215-255-8539		7-12	Ismail Kul
Tuscarora Blended Learning Charter S	101 S 5th St	Huntingdon, PA	16652-1265	814-542-2501		K-12	Tony Payne
21st Century Cyber Charter S	805 Springdale Dr	Exton, PA	19341-2843	484-875-5400	875-5404	6-12	Jon Marsh
Universal Institute Charter S	801 S 15th St	Philadelphia, PA	19146-2215	215-732-7988	732-8066	K-5	John Walker
Urban League of Pittsburgh Charter S	327 N Negley Ave	Pittsburgh, PA	15206-2851	412-361-1008	361-1042	K-5	Dr. Gail Edwards
Vitalistic Therapeutic Charter S	902 4th Ave	Bethlehem, PA	18018-3702	610-861-7570		K-3	Naomi H. Grossman
Wakisha Charter S	1209 Vine St	Philadelphia, PA	19107-1111	267-256-0950	256-0953	6-8	Elbert Sampson
West Oak Lane Charter S	7115 Stenton Ave	Philadelphia, PA	19138-1136	215-927-7995	927-7980	K-5	Robin Conboy
West Philadelphia Achievement Charter S	111 N 49th St	Philadelphia, PA	19139-2718	215-476-6471	476-6470	K-5	Stacey Gill-Phillips
Widener Partnership Charter S	1 University Pl	Chester, PA	19013-5700	610-497-7399		K-5	Dr. Annette Anderson
Wiley Community Charter S	1446 E Lake Rd	Erie, PA	16507-1936	814-461-9600	461-0226	K-8	Theo Overton
Wissahickon Charter S	4700 Wissahickon Ave	Philadelphia, PA	19144	267-338-1020		K-5	Kristi Littell
Wonderland Charter S	2112 Sandy Dr	State College, PA	16803-2282	814-234-5886		K-K	Harold Ohnmeis
World Communications Charter S	512 S Broad St	Philadelphia, PA	19146-1695	215-735-3197	735-3824	6-12	Dr. Martin Ryder
Young Scholars Charter S	1415 N Broad St	Philadelphia, PA	19122-3323	215-232-9727	232-4542	6-8	C. Lars Beck
Young Scholars of Central PA Charter S	1530 Westerly Pkwy	State College, PA	16801-2848	814-237-9727		K-5	Dr. Bulent Tarman
Youth Build Charter S	1231 N Broad St	Philadelphia, PA	19122-4023	215-627-8671	763-5774	9-12	Simran Sidhu

Rhode Island

School	Address	City,State	Zip code	Telephone	Fax	Grade	Contact
BEACON Charter S	320 Main St	Woonsocket, RI	02895-3138	401-671-6261	671-6264	9-12	Robert Pilkington
Blackstone Academy	334 Pleasant St	Pawtucket, RI	02860-5273	401-726-1750	726-1753	9-12	Carolyn Sheehan
Compass S	537 Old North Rd	Kingston, RI	02881-1220	401-788-8322	788-8326	K-8	Allen Zipke
Cuffee S	459 Promenade St	Providence, RI	02908-5601	401-453-2626	453-4964	K-8	David Bourns
CVS Highlander Charter S	42 Lexington Ave	Providence, RI	02907-1716	401-277-2600	277-2603	K-8	Rose Grant
International Charter S	334 Pleasant St	Pawtucket, RI	02860-5273	401-721-0824	721-0976	K-5	Julie Nora Ph.D.
Kingston Hill Academy	850 Stony Fort Rd	Saunderstown, RI	02874-1003	401-783-8282	783-5656	K-8	Stephen Panikoff
Learning Community S	21 Lincoln Ave	Central Falls, RI	02863-2012	401-722-9998	722-0990	K-5	Sarah Friedman
NEL/CPS Construction Career Academy	4 Sharpe Dr	Cranston, RI	02920-4410	401-270-8692	270-8697	9-12	Dr. Michael Silvia
Textron/Chamber of Commerce Academy	130 Broadway	Providence, RI	02903-3003	401-456-1738	521-0653	9-12	Dr. Lawrence DeSalvatore
Times 2 Academy	50 Fillmore St	Providence, RI	02908-3105	401-272-5094	272-0555	K-12	Dr. Lawrence Davenport

South Carolina

School	Address	City,State	Zip code	Telephone	Fax	Grade	Contact
Academy for Teaching and Learning	109 Hinton St	Chester, SC	29706-2022	803-385-6334	385-6335	PK-8	Robyn Welborn
Aiken Academy	10612 Augusta Rd	Belton, SC	29627-9246	864-243-3443	243-5743	1-8	Glynda Caddell
Aiken Performing Arts Academy	130 Avery Ln	Aiken, SC	29801-1902	803-644-4824	641-1155	9-12	Keisha Lloyd-Kennedy
Boykin Academy	4951 Rivers Ave	N Charleston, SC	29406-6301	843-744-8882	744-8885	K-6	Dee Miller
Brashier Middle College HS	PO Box 5616	Greenville, SC	29606-5616	864-963-0171	963-0176	9-12	Michael Sinclair
Bridgewater Academy	316 Bush Dr	Myrtle Beach, SC	29579-7314	843-236-3689	236-4921	K-8	Carol Merrill
Calhoun Falls Charter S	205 Edgefield St	Calhoun Falls, SC	29628-1018	864-418-8014	418-0379	6-12	Deirdre McCullough
Carolina School for Inquiry	7405 Fairfield Rd Ste A	Columbia, SC	29203-9543	803-691-1250	691-1247	K-5	Victoria Dixon-Mokeba
Charleston Charter S for Math & Science	PO Box 21406	Charleston, SC	29413-1406	843-628-1200	720-3085	6-9	Peter Smyth
Charleston Development Academy	233 Line St	Charleston, SC	29403-8100	843-722-2689	722-2694	K-6	Cecelia Gordon Rogers
Children's Attention Home	PO Box 2912	Rock Hill, SC	29732-4912	803-328-8871	324-0437	K-8	Libby Sweatt-Lambert
CHOiCES	PO Box 15386	Florence, SC	29506-0386	843-664-8993	664-8881	5-8	Ralph Porter
Discovery S	PO Box 130	Lancaster, SC	29721-0130	803-285-8430	416-8907	K-5	Tom McDuffie
East Cooper Montessori Charter S	250 Ponsbury Rd	Mount Pleasant, SC	29464-6601	843-216-2883	216-8880	1-8	Jody Swanigan
Fox Creek HS	1297 W Martintown Rd	North Augusta, SC	29841-2062	803-613-9435	613-1533	9-12	Dr. Tim Murph
Fuller Normal Charter S	PO Box 1832	Greenville, SC	29602-1832	864-271-3698	272-0241	K-6	Brenda Humbert
Greenville Technical Charter HS	PO Box 5616	Greenville, SC	29606-5616	864-250-8844	250-8846	9-12	W. Fred Crawford
Greer Middle College	404 Vardry St	Greenville, SC	29601-3308	864-239-2000	271-0207	9-12	Jean Williams
Insight School of South Carolina	7 Technology Cir	Columbia, SC	29203-9591	803-935-0129	935-4508	9-12	Dr. Barbara Stoops
James Island Charter HS	1000 Fort Johnson Rd	Charleston, SC	29412-8898	843-762-2754	762-5228	9-12	Robert Bohnstengel
Langston Charter MS	212 Roper Mountain Road Ext	Greenville, SC	29615-4825	864-286-9700	286-9699	6-8	Gregory Abel
Lloyd Kennedy Charter S	PO Box 418	Aiken, SC	29802-0418	803-644-4824	641-1155	5-8	Keisha Lloyd-Kennedy
Mathis HS	7555 Spartan Blvd N	N Charleston, SC	29420-8820	843-207-8308	207-8309	9-12	Kenneth Sellers
Meyer Center for Special Children	1132 Rutherford Rd	Greenville, SC	29609-3927	864-250-0005	250-0028	PK-K	Louise Anthony
Midlands Math & Business Academy	PO Box 4487	Columbia, SC	29240-4487	803-799-5101	799-5318	4-8	Reginald Flenory
Midland Valley Preparatory S	2432 Jefferson Davis Hwy	Graniteville, SC	29829-3828	803-594-1028	594-0511	PK-8	Lilian Thomas-Wilson
MLD Learning Academy	PO Box 136	Bishopville, SC	29010-0136	803-483-3000	483-3002	PK-9	Benita Robinson
Orange Grove ES	3795 Spruill Ave	Charleston, SC	29405-7149	843-763-1520	769-2245	K-5	Larry Dicenzo
Palmetto Youth Academy	1209 N Douglas St	Florence, SC	29501-0600	843-679-7070	679-7046	3-6	Yvonne Burgess
Phoenix Charter HS	PO Box 170	Alcolu, SC	29001-0170	803-505-6800	505-6801	9-12	Nancy Roberson
Richland One Middle College S	316 Beltline Blvd	Columbia, SC	29205-3624	803-738-7114	738-7117	11-12	Audrey Breland
Sea Islands Youthbuild Charter HS	3483 Maybank Hwy	Johns Island, SC	29455-4821	843-557-1611	557-1788	9-12	Edward Leary
SC Connections Academy	220 Stoneridge Dr	Columbia, SC	29210	803-212-4712	212-4946	K-12	Don Brown
SC Virtual Charter School	140 Stoneridge Dr	Columbia, SC	29210	803-253-6222	253-6279	K-12	Dr. Cherry Daniel
Wohali Academy	PO Box 1005	Travelers Rest, SC	29690-1005	864-834-8013	834-6977	K-12	Laura Blackmore
Young Entrepreneurial Vocational Academy	PO Box 82	Summerton, SC	29148-0082	803-485-4800	485-4802	7-12	Veronica Thomas
Youth Academy Charter S	PO Box 174	Kingstree, SC	29556-0174	843-355-5424	382-5753	7-12	Cheryl West

Tennessee

School	Address	City,State	Zip code	Telephone	Fax	Grade	Contact
Circles of Success Learning Academy	867 S Parkway E	Memphis, TN	38106-5605	901-322-7978	322-7993	K-5	Sheri Catron
City University S of Liberal Arts	1500 Dunn Ave	Memphis, TN	38106-7318	901-775-2219	775-2228	9-12	Dr. T.J. Graham
KIPP Academy	123 Douglas Ave	Nashville, TN	37207-5155	615-226-4484	226-4401	5-8	Randy Dowell
KIPP Diamond Academy	2110 Howell Ave	Memphis, TN	38108-2268	901-416-4615	416-0383	5-8	Sylvia Mitchell
LEAD Academy	1704 Heiman St	Nashville, TN	37208-2406	615-327-5422	327-5425	5-12	Jeremy Kane
Memphis Academy of Health Sciences	3925 Chelsea Avenue Ext	Memphis, TN	38108-2612	901-382-1441	382-1944	6-12	Curtis Weathers
Memphis Academy of Science & Engineering	20 Dudley St	Memphis, TN	38103	901-333-1580	333-1582	6-12	Tommie Henderson
Memphis Business Academy	3333 Old Brownsville Rd	Memphis, TN	38134-8419	901-380-8176	380-8179	6-8	Anthony Anderson
Memphis Business HS	2450 Frayser Blvd	Memphis, TN	38127-5823	901-357-8680	380-8179	9-12	Anthony Anderson
Power Center Academy	6120 Winchester Rd	Memphis, TN	38115-4014	901-333-1940	333-1945	6-8	Derwin Sisnett
Promise Academy	1346 Bryan St	Memphis, TN	38108-2401	901-324-4456	324-4457	K-4	Dr. Blakely Wallace
Smithson-Craighead Academy	3307 Brick Church Pike	Nashville, TN	37207-2301	615-228-9886	228-9799	PK-4	Janelle Glover
Soulsville Charter S	926 E McLemore Ave	Memphis, TN	38106-3338	901-946-2535	507-1460	6-12	NeShante Brown
Southern Avenue Charter S	3310 Kimball Ave	Memphis, TN	38111	901-743-7335	743-7677	K-3	Van Snyder
STAR Academy Charter S	3240 James Rd	Memphis, TN	38128-5311	901-387-5050	387-0798	K-5	Dr. Kia Young

Texas

School	Address	City,State	Zip code	Telephone	Fax	Grade	Contact
A+ Academy	10327 Rylie Rd	Dallas, TX	75217-8240	972-557-5578	557-6130	PK-12	Dr. Shala White-Flowers
Academy of Accelerated Learning	6711 Bellfort St	Houston, TX	77087-6411	713-645-0336	640-2435	PK-5	Gwendolyn Nicks
Academy of Accelerated Learning	6025 Chimney Rock Rd	Houston, TX	77081-4011	713-773-4766	666-2532	PK-5	Donyale Reynolds
Academy of Beaumont	2600 Girolamo St	Beaumont, TX	77703-4800	409-833-1600	838-7512	PK-8	Cynthia Solomon

School	Address	City,State	Zip code	Telephone	Fax	Grade	Contact
Academy of Careers & Technologies	6812 Bandera Rd Ste 102	San Antonio, TX	78238-1378	210-226-7568	226-8548	9-12	Rickey Harrell M.Ed.
Academy of Dallas	1030 Oak Park Dr	Dallas, TX	75232-1238	214-371-9600	371-1053	PK-8	Conrad Hargest
Accelerated Interdisciplinary Academy	PO Box 20589	Houston, TX	77225-0589	713-283-6298	283-6190	PK-5	LaShawn Hawkins
Accelerated Interdisciplinary Academy	PO Box 20589	Houston, TX	77225-0589	903-526-1730	526-3334	PK-5	Kevin Hicks
Accelerated Intermediate Academy	PO Box 20589	Houston, TX	77225-0589	713-283-6298	283-6190	6-8	Dr. David Fuller
Accelerated Intermediate Academy	PO Box 20589	Houston, TX	77225-0589	713-667-1184	667-9181	PK-8	Kevin Hicks
Accelerated Learning Center	721 Omaha Dr	Corpus Christi, TX	78408-2839	361-887-7766	887-6035	PK-12	Maria Garza
Achieve Early College HS	3201 Pecan Blvd Bldg K 2912	Mc Allen, TX	78501	956-872-1653		9-12	Yvette Cavazos
Advantage Academy - Grand Prairie	300 W Pioneer Pkwy	Grand Prairie, TX	75051-4803	972-262-6944		K-12	Betty Sims
Advantage Academy - North Duncanville	4009 Joseph Hardin Dr	Dallas, TX	75236-1507	214-276-5842		K-8	Tonya Williams
Advantage Academy - Rowlett	8200 Schrade Rd	Rowlett, TX	75088-4716	972-412-7761		PK-8	Lisa Hiatt
Advantage Academy - Waxahachie	701 W Highway 287 Byp	Waxahachie, TX	75165-5163	972-937-9851	937-9876	K-12	Michael Partain
Advantage East End HS	7135 Office City Dr Bldg 3	Houston, TX	77087	713-644-0888	644-1833	9-12	Christopher Kaio
Alief Montessori Community S	4215 H St	Houston, TX	77072-5380	281-530-9406	530-2233	PK-5	Nancy Chieu
Allen Charter S	5220 Nomas St	Dallas, TX	75212-3229	972-794-5100	794-5101	PK-5	Connie Hovseth
Alpha Charter Secondary S	701 W State St	Garland, TX	75040-6310	972-272-2173	205-9050	PK-12	
ALTA Academy	8329 Lawndale St	Houston, TX	77012-3707	713-923-8801	926-8255	9-12	Jaime De La Isla
Ambassadors Preparatory Academy	2921 Avenue M	Galveston, TX	77550-4337	409-762-1115	762-1114	K-5	Dr. Patricia Williams
American Youth Works Charter S	216 E 4th St	Austin, TX	78701-3610	512-236-6100	472-1189	9-12	Dr. Carole Lewis
American Youth Works Charter S	1901 E Ben White Blvd	Austin, TX	78741-7840	512-744-1900	916-4708	9-12	Kim Bookman
Amigos Por Vida-Friends for Life Charter	5500 El Camino Del Rey St	Houston, TX	77081	713-399-9945	349-0671	PK-8	Carlos Villagrana
Annunciation Home	PO Box 7667	Austin, TX	78713-7667	512-751-4596	931-2406	6-12	Wendy Rollins
Arlington Classics Academy	2800 W Arkansas Ln	Arlington, TX	76016-5819	817-274-2008	274-8768	K-8	Ken Simon
Austin Academy	621 W Euclid Ave	San Antonio, TX	78212-5128	210-226-5441	226-6192	PK-8	Maribel Rodriguez
Austin Can! Academy Charter S	2406 Rosewood Ave	Austin, TX	78702-2408	512-477-4226	931-8034	9-12	Dr. Joe Gonzales
Austin Discovery S	8509 FM 969 Ste 200	Austin, TX	78724-5771	512-674-0700	674-3133	K-5	Cinnamon Henley
Austin State University Charter S	PO Box 6072	Nacogdoches, TX	75962-0001	936-468-5899	468-7015	K-5	Lysa Hagan
Azleway Charter S	15892 County Road 26	Tyler, TX	75707-2728	903-566-8444	566-2053	K-12	Lacey Hogue
Azleway Charter S Pine Mountain	15892 County Road 26	Tyler, TX	75707-2728	903-549-3194	549-2227	7-12	Bruce Hand
Baker-Ripley Charter S	6500 Rookin St	Houston, TX	77074-5014	713-779-4856		K-5	Pamela Sailors
Barkley/Ruiz ES	1111 S Navidad St	San Antonio, TX	78207-5813	210-227-4022	227-4029	PK-5	Carol Fairman
Bay Area Charter ES	2600 Humble Dr	El Lago, TX	77586-5900	281-326-4555	326-4888	PK-5	Kris Wessale
Bay Area Charter MS	PO Box 2126	League City, TX	77574-2126	281-316-0001	316-0018	6-8	Dr. Rosalind Perez
Benji's Special Education Academy	2903 Jensen Dr	Houston, TX	77026-6019	713-229-0560	224-6724	PK-12	Theaola Robinson
Bexar County Academy	1485 Hillcrest Dr	San Antonio, TX	78228-3900	210-432-8600	432-1195	PK-8	Keyshar Breedlove
Big Springs Charter S	PO Box 399	Leakey, TX	78873-0399	830-232-7101	232-4279	1-12	Deanna Kilpatrick
Bonham Academy	925 S Saint Marys St	San Antonio, TX	78205-3410	210-223-3741	223-3899	PK-6	Dora Espiritu
Boys and Girls Harbor Academy	514 Bayridge Rd	La Porte, TX	77571-3511	281-471-9622	471-4396	K-8	Christina Breland
Brazos River Charter S	PO Box 949	Nemo, TX	76070-0949	254-898-9226	898-2297	9-12	Mike Thames
Brazos S for Inquiry & Creativity	8787 N Houston Rosslyn Rd	Houston, TX	77088-6430	713-983-6877	983-7036	PK-8	Destra Tolliver
Brazos S for Inquiry & Creativity	6210 Rookin St	Houston, TX	77074-3718	713-270-4500	270-4510	6-12	Tiffany Rock
Brazos S for Inquiry & Creativity	1673 Briarcrest Dr Ste A108	Bryan, TX	77802-2749	979-774-5032	774-5039	PK-12	Christopher Osgood
Brazos S for Inquiry & Creativity	4637 Gano St	Houston, TX	77009-3457	713-691-9500	691-9502	PK-8	Mattye Johnson
Briarmeadow Charter S	3601 Dunvale Rd	Houston, TX	77063-5707	713-458-5500	458-5506	PK-8	Peter Heinze
Bright Ideas Charter S	2507 Central Fwy E	Wichita Falls, TX	76302-5802	940-767-1561	767-1904	K-12	Lynda Plummer
Briscoe ES	2015 S Flores St	San Antonio, TX	78204-1990	210-222-8782	222-0822	PK-6	Julie Benavides
Brooks Academy of Science & Engineering	3803 Lyster Rd	San Antonio, TX	78235-5152	210-633-9006	633-9990	6-12	Rufus Samkin
Brown-Fellowship Charter Preschool	6901 S Westmoreland Rd	Dallas, TX	75237-2431	972-709-4700	709-6605	PK-PK	Paula Brown
Brown-Fellowship Charter School	5701 Red Bird Center Dr	Dallas, TX	75237-1917	972-709-4700	709-6605	K-6	Paula Brown
Burch Charter S	5703 Blanco Rd	San Antonio, TX	78216-6616	210-431-9881	432-8467	4-6	Delores Sendejo
Burnham ES	7310 Bishop Flores Dr	El Paso, TX	79912-1429	915-584-9499	585-8814	K-4	Norm Garrett
Cage ES	4528 Leeland St	Houston, TX	77023-3095	713-924-1700	924-1704	PK-5	Jose Covarrubia
Canyon Lakes S	2402 Canyon Lake Dr	Lubbock, TX	79415-2000	806-762-5782	762-0838	6-12	Mark Martin
Cedar Crest Charter S	3500 S Interstate 35	Belton, TX	76513-9498	254-939-4071	605-5886	K-12	Tonya Woods
Cedar Hill Collegiate HS	1515 W Belt Line Rd	Cedar Hill, TX	75104-1603	469-272-2021	293-2652	9-12	Usamah Rodgers
Cedars International Academy	8416 N Interstate 35	Austin, TX	78753-6438	512-419-1551	419-1581	K-7	Sam Greer
Chadwick Charter S	2402 Alpine Rd	Longview, TX	75601-3407	903-753-9400	753-0285	9-12	Terry Lapic
Challenge Early College HS	5601 West Loop S	Houston, TX	77081-2221	713-664-9712	664-9780	9-12	Justin Fuentes
Chapel Hill Academy	4640 Sycamore School Rd	Fort Worth, TX	76133-7356	817-255-2570	255-2559	PK-5	Rhonda Greer
Chavez Academy	3701 Mueller St	Corpus Christi, TX	78408-3139	361-561-5651	561-5654	9-12	Tracy Saenz
Children First Academy of Dallas	1638 E Ann Arbor Ave	Dallas, TX	75216-6335	214-371-2545	371-0283	PK-7	
Children First Academy of Houston	7803 Little York Rd	Houston, TX	77016-2436	713-491-9030	491-9032	PK-7	Sherwin Allen
Children of the Sun Charter S	PO Box 164	Mc Allen, TX	78505-0164	956-488-8883	488-0889	PK-12	Victor Benavidez
Children of the Sun Charter S	PO Box 164	Mc Allen, TX	78505-0164	956-689-3300	292-0371	PK-12	Alejandro Perez
Children's Hope Academy	1313 W Washington St	Levelland, TX	79336-3921	806-897-9735	894-4712	K-12	
Comquest Academy	207 Peach St	Tomball, TX	77375-4733	281-516-0611	290-6524	6-12	Tanis Stanfield
Copeland ES	1826 Basse Rd	San Antonio, TX	78213-4606	210-431-9881	253-2198	K-3	Frank Williams
Cornerstone Academy	9016 Westview Dr	Houston, TX	77055-4602	713-365-5766	365-5787	6-8	Jill Wright
Corpus Christi Academy	3875 S Staples St	Corpus Christi, TX	78411-2347	361-225-4240	225-4021	9-12	Jason Curlee
Corpus Christi Montessori Charter S	3530 Gollihar Rd	Corpus Christi, TX	78415-2759	361-852-0707	852-0640	PK-8	Sylvia Gaertner
Crockett ES	2112 Crockett St	Houston, TX	77007-3923	713-802-4780	802-4783	PK-5	Elida Troutman
Crosstimbers Academy	PO Box 1327	Weatherford, TX	76086-1327	817-594-6220	594-6227	9-12	
Crutch's - Life Support Center	7115 Clarewood Dr	Houston, TX	77036-4401	713-779-9990	779-3047	6-12	Debra Gaddis
Cumberland Academy	8225 S Broadway Ave	Tyler, TX	75703-5494	903-581-2890	581-1476	K-6	James Moyers
Dallas Can! Academy	325 W 12th St Ste 175	Dallas, TX	75208	214-943-2244	946-4427	9-12	Esther Contreras
Dallas Can! Academy Charter S	4621 Ross Ave	Dallas, TX	75204-4994	214-824-4226	841-7951	9-12	Verna Mitchell
DaVinci S for Science and the Arts	7310 Bishop Flores Dr	El Paso, TX	79912-1429	915-584-4024	581-9840	5-9	Antonio Morales
Deja Discovery Learning Center	12995 N Interstate 35	Live Oak, TX	78233	210-637-1331	637-1331	PK-6	
DePelchin - Elkins Campus	PO Box 7667	Austin, TX	78713-7667	713-802-6256	802-6261	K-12	John Merriwether
DePelchin - Richmond Campus	PO Box 7667	Austin, TX	78713-7667	713-558-3984	558-3985	PK-12	John Merriwether
Destiny Honors Academy	1001 E Veterans Mem Ste 301	Killeen, TX	76541	254-200-2465	519-7672	K-8	Mike Anderson
Dominion Academy	1102 Pinemont Dr	Houston, TX	77018-1323	713-476-9800	476-9707	6-8	Shinell Terrance-Clark
Draw Academy	3920 Stoney Brook Dr	Houston, TX	77063-6406	713-706-3729	706-3711	PK-8	Lisa Newton
Eagle Advantage Charter S	4011 Joseph Hardin Dr	Dallas, TX	75236-1507	214-276-5800	467-9131	PK-12	Sam Cooper
East Austin College Prep Academy	6002 Jain Ln	Austin, TX	78721-3104	512-462-2181	462-2028	6-12	Dr. Magali Lopez
East Early College HS	2524 Garland St	Houston, TX	77087-2708	713-847-4809	847-4813	9-12	Joel Castro
East Fort Worth Montessori Academy	501 Oakland Blvd	Fort Worth, TX	76103-1014	817-496-3003	496-3004	PK-5	Joyce Brown
East Texas Charter HS	2402 Alpine Rd	Longview, TX	75601-3407	903-753-9400	753-0285	9-12	Terry Lapic
Eastwood Academy	1315 Dumble St	Houston, TX	77023-1902	713-924-1697	924-1715	9-12	Rebecca Becnel
Eden Park Academy	6215 Manchaca Rd Bldg D	Austin, TX	78745-4927	512-383-0613	383-0665	K-8	Lisa Robinson
Education Center at Denton	4420 Country Club Rd	Denton, TX	76210-3222	940-383-1972	292-2373	PK-12	Sheila Farley
Education Center at Little Elm	5901 Crestwood Pl	Little Elm, TX	75068-3754	972-292-3562	292-3563	K-12	Lisa Ashmore
Education Center at The Colony	5201 S Colony Blvd Ste 575	The Colony, TX	75056-2384	972-370-0108	370-3563	K-12	Donica Hill
Education Center in Aubrey	5411 US Highway 377 S	Aubrey, TX	76227-6212	940-440-9580	440-9581	K-12	Samie Shelby
Education Center in Lewisville	968 Raldon St	Lewisville, TX	75067-5229	972-221-3564	292-2373	PK-12	Gary Stalcup
Education Center International Academy	2422 N Jupiter Rd	Garland, TX	75044-7347	972-530-6157	530-8635	K-12	Julia Edwards
Ehrhart S of Fine Arts & Athletics	PO Box 7733	Beaumont, TX	77726-7733	409-839-8200	839-8242	PK-8	T. Chris Comick
El Paso Academy	11000 Argal Ct	El Paso, TX	79935-3712	915-590-8589	590-0052	9-12	Charles Gonzalez
El Paso Academy West	1065A Doniphan Park Cir	El Paso, TX	79922-1353	915-845-7997	845-7522	9-12	Barbara Duggar
El Paso School of Excellence	1599 George Dieter Dr # 501	El Paso, TX	79936	915-595-1599	595-3100	PK-5	Judy Jimenez
El Paso School of Excellence MS	1605 George Dieter Dr # 501	El Paso, TX	79936	915-598-1755	598-8188	6-8	Alicia Ochoa
Empowerment College Preparatory HS	5655 Selinsky Rd	Houston, TX	77048-1864	713-732-9231	732-9233	9-12	Traci Stewart-Jones
Encino S	PO Box 106	Encino, TX	78353-0106	361-568-3375	568-3625	PK-8	Roberto Gonzalez
Energized for Excellence Academy	6201 Bissonnet St	Houston, TX	77081-6809	713-773-3600	773-3630	PK-8	Lois Bullock
Energized for STEM Academy	3703 Sampson St	Houston, TX	77004-4741	713-749-8876	773-3630	9-12	Lois Bullock
Erath Excels! Academy	6532 S US Highway 377	Stephenville, TX	76401-6189	254-965-8883	965-8654	7-12	Debra Miller
Evolution Academy Charter S	1101 S Sherman St	Richardson, TX	75081-4852	972-907-3755	907-3765	9-12	Cynthia Jones Trigg
Excel Center - Fort Worth	1220 W Presidio St	Fort Worth, TX	76102-4512	817-335-6429	335-7927	PK-12	Janice Hobbs
Excel Center - Lewisville	190 Civic Cir Ste 170	Lewisville, TX	75067-3641	972-906-5522	906-5744	PK-12	Janice Hobbs
Faith Family Academy of Oak Cliff	1620 Falcon Dr	De Soto, TX	75115-2418	214-375-7682	375-7681	PK-12	Sonja Jackson
First Family S	10715 Garland Rd	Dallas, TX	75218-2608	210-658-7071		K-6	
Focus Learning Academy	2524 W Ledbetter Dr	Dallas, TX	75233-4018	214-467-7751	572-9610	PK-8	Linus Walton
Fort Worth Academy of Fine Arts	3901 S Hulen St	Fort Worth, TX	76109-3321	817-924-1482	926-9932	K-12	Craig Schreckengast
Fort Worth Can! Academy	4301 Campus Dr	Fort Worth, TX	76119-5535	817-431-4226	531-0443	9-12	Ku-Masi Lewis
Fort Worth Can! Academy	5508 Black Oak Ln	River Oaks, TX	76114	817-735-1515	735-1465	9-12	Tony Swafford
Fruit of Excellence	PO Box 2047	Bastrop, TX	78602-9047	512-303-5550	303-7028	PK-12	Roslyn Martin
Galaviz Academy	1507 Little York Rd	Houston, TX	77093-3223	832-300-6010	300-6013	9-12	Luis Cano
Garza-Gonzales Charter S	4129 Greenwood Dr	Corpus Christi, TX	78416-1841	361-881-9988	881-9994	PK-12	Adolfo Chapa
Gates Academy	510 Morningview Dr	San Antonio, TX	78220-3220	210-333-3621	333-3644	PK-8	Dr. Derrick Thomas
Gateway Academy	4620 S Lucy	Laredo, TX	78046-7786	956-723-0345	712-1112	9-12	Ernesto Alvarado
Gateway Academy	1230 Townlake Dr	Laredo, TX	78041	956-722-0747	722-0767	9-12	Frances Johnson
Gateway Charter Academy	6103 Houston School Rd	Dallas, TX	75241-2516	214-375-2039	375-1842	PK-12	Lester Singleton
Gateway HS	2951 Williams Dr	Georgetown, TX	78628-2701	512-869-3020	869-3030	9-12	
GCCLR Institute of Technology	4129 Greenwood Dr	Corpus Christi, TX	78416-1841	361-881-9988	881-9994	PK-12	Adolfo Chapa
Gervin Academy	6944 S Sunbelt Dr	San Antonio, TX	78218-3335	210-568-8800	568-8892	PK-12	Barbara Hawkins
Gervin Technology Center	3030 E Commerce St	San Antonio, TX	78220-1013	210-587-3576	587-3587	9-12	Chuck Landy
Girls & Boys Prep Academy	8415 W Bellfort St	Houston, TX	77071-2205	713-270-5994	270-1302	5-8	Tyra Ross

School	Address	City,State	Zip code	Telephone	Fax	Grade	Contact
Girls & Boys Prep Academy	8282 Bissonnet St Ste 400	Houston, TX	77074-3904	713-270-2006		PK-4	Vonda Oliver
Girls & Boys Prep Academy	8415 W Bellfort St	Houston, TX	77071-2205	713-270-5994		9-12	Kimya McKinney
Golden Rule Charter S	2602 W Illinois Ave	Dallas, TX	75233-1002	214-333-9330	333-9325	PK-2	Will Ramos
Golden Rule Charter S	2602 W Illinois Ave	Dallas, TX	75233-1002	214-333-9330	333-9325	PK-2	Will Ramos
Golden Rule Charter S	2602 W Illinois Ave	Dallas, TX	75233-1002	214-333-9330	333-9325	PK-2	Will Ramos
Golden Rule Charter S	2602 W Illinois Ave	Dallas, TX	75233-1002	214-333-9330	333-9325	PK-12	Will Ramos
Guardian Angel Performance Academy	107 Blue Star	San Antonio, TX	78204-1773	210-253-9064		K-8	Jacquelyn Darby
Hampton Preparatory S	8915 S Hampton Rd	Dallas, TX	75232-6002	972-421-1982	421-1986	5-10	Keith Lott
Harbach-Ripley Charter S	6225 Northdale St	Houston, TX	77087-5821	713-640-7150		K-5	Pamela Sailors
Harmony School of Excellence	7340 Gessner Dr	Houston, TX	77040-3144	713-983-8668	983-8667	K-12	Ugur Demircan
Harmony School of Innovation	9421 W Sam Houston Pkwy S	Houston, TX	77099-1849	713-541-3030	541-3032	PK-8	Gurol Duman
Harmony S of Science	13415 W Bellfort Ave	Sugar Land, TX	77478-3184	713-265-2525	265-2565	PK-12	Huseyin Sari
Harmony Science Academy	8505 Lakeside Pkwy	San Antonio, TX	78245-2481	210-674-7788	674-7766	K-12	Irfan Turk
Harmony Science Academy	5651 Westcreek Dr	Fort Worth, TX	76133-2248	817-263-0700	263-0705	K-12	Tevfik Eski
Harmony Science Academy	2031 S Texas Ave	Bryan, TX	77802-1834	979-779-2100	779-2110	PK-12	Ali Tekin
Harmony Science Academy	5435 S Braeswood Blvd	Houston, TX	77096-4001	713-729-4400	729-6600	6-12	Edib Ercetin
Harmony Science Academy	11995 Forestgate Dr	Dallas, TX	75243-5412	972-234-9993	234-9994	PK-12	Fatih Ay
Harmony Science Academy - Austin	930 E Rundberg Ln	Austin, TX	78753-4826	512-835-7900	835-7901	6-12	Ramazan Coskuner
Harmony Science Academy - Austin	11800 Stonehollow Dr # 100	Austin, TX	78758	512-821-1700	821-1702	K-8	Erdal Caglar
Harmony Science Academy - Beaumont	4055 Calder Ave	Beaumont, TX	77706-4925	409-838-4000	838-4009	PK-12	Ahmet Cetinkaya
Harmony Science Academy - Brownsville	1124 Central Blvd	Brownsville, TX	78520-7513	956-574-9555	574-9558	PK-12	Emrah Oral
Harmony Science Academy - El Paso	9405 Betel Dr	El Paso, TX	79907-3457	915-859-4620	859-4630	K-12	Fatih Ay
Harmony Science Academy - Grand Prairie	1102 NW 7th St	Grand Prairie, TX	75050-3468	972-642-9911	642-9922	K-12	Hakan Yagci
Harmony Science Academy - Houston NW	16200 State Highway 249	Houston, TX	77086-1014	281-444-1555	444-1015	PK-12	Atnan Ekin
Harmony Science Academy - Lubbock	1516 53rd St	Lubbock, TX	79412-2916	806-747-1000	747-1005	K-12	Gultekin Kaya
Harmony Science Academy - North Austin	1421 Wells Branch Pkwy #200	Pflugerville, TX	78660	512-251-5000	251-5001	6-12	Mehmet Bayar
Harmony Science Academy - Waco	1900 N Valley Mills Dr	Waco, TX	76710-2559	254-751-7878	751-7877	PK-12	Umit Alpaslan
Harris MS	325 Pruitt Ave	San Antonio, TX	78204-2598	210-226-4952	226-9448	6-8	Moises Ortiz
Hawkins HS	1826 Basse Rd	San Antonio, TX	78213-4606	210-431-9881	435-0896	9-12	Jeff Gaffney
Hawthorne S	115 W Josephine St	San Antonio, TX	78212-4125	210-733-1321	733-1495	PK-8	G. Rodriguez-Pollock
Helping Hands Charter S	PO Box 7667	Austin, TX	78713-7667	512-471-4798	232-9177	K-12	Wendy Riney
Heritage Champions Academy of Huntsville	2407 Sam Houston Ave	Huntsville, TX	77340-5862	936-291-0203	293-8096	K-12	Rodney Brown
Higgs Carter King Gifted & Talented S	PO Box 18854	San Antonio, TX	78218-0854	210-735-2341	733-6434	PK-12	Claudette Yarbrough
Highland Heights ES	865 Paul Quinn St	Houston, TX	77091-4154	713-696-2920	696-2922	PK-5	Kettisha Jones
Hill Country Youth Ranch	PO Box 609	Leakey, TX	78873-0609	830-367-2611	367-2626	1-12	Maria De La Cruz
Hope S	2849 9th Ave	Port Arthur, TX	77642-3961	409-983-6659	983-6408	6-12	
Horizon Montessori III - Harlingen	801 N 13th St Ste 5	Harlingen, TX	78550-5073	956-423-8200	423-8207	PK-6	Felipe Martinez
Horizon Montessori II - Weslaco	1222 W Sugar Cane Dr	Weslaco, TX	78596-3892	956-969-0044	969-0065	PK-6	Patricia Martin
Horizon Montessori I - Mc Allen	221 N Main St	Mc Allen, TX	78501-4630	956-668-1400	668-1404	PK-5	Carol Campos
Houston Acad for International Studies	1515 Winbern St	Houston, TX	77004-3942	713-942-3340	942-3346	9-12	Melissa Jacobs
Houston Can! Academy - Hobby	9020 Gulf Fwy	Houston, TX	77017-7007	832-379-4226	944-6736	9-12	Janie Vega
Houston Can! Academy - Main	2301 Main St	Houston, TX	77002-9101	713-659-4226	651-1493	9-12	Joyce Phillips
Houston Gateway Academy	1020 Coral St	Houston, TX	77012-2906	713-923-5060	923-9070	9-12	
Houston Gateway Academy	3400 Evergreen Dr	Houston, TX	77087-3715	713-649-3092	649-8165	K-8	Fransico Penning
Houston Heights HS	1125 Lawrence St	Houston, TX	77008-6651	713-868-9797	868-9750	8-12	Richard Mik
Houston Heights Learning Academy	902 W 8th St	Houston, TX	77007-1408	713-869-9453	869-0785	PK-5	Yvette East
IDEA Academy Donna	401 S 1st St	Donna, TX	78537-3055	956-464-0203	464-4137	PK-5	Paula Garcia
IDEA Academy Mission	1600 S Schuerbach Rd	Mission, TX	78572-1217	956-583-8315	583-8308	PK-9	Bethany Solis
IDEA Academy San Benito	2151 Russell Ln	San Benito, TX	78586-8969	956-399-5252	399-1959	K-K,	Carrie Sauceda
IDEA Academy San Juan	400 Virgen De San Juan	San Juan, TX	78589-3029	956-702-5150		K-K,	Sam Goessling
IDEA College Prep S Donna	401 S 1st St	Donna, TX	78537-3055	956-464-0203	464-8532	6-12	Jeremy Beard
IDEA Frontier Academy	2800 S Dakota Ave	Brownsville, TX	78521-6133	956-541-2002	544-2004	K-2	Roberta Harris
IDEA Frontier College Prep S	2800 S Dakota Ave	Brownsville, TX	78521-6133	956-541-2002	544-2004	6-12	Rolando Posada
IDEA Quest Academy	14001 N Rooth Rd	Edinburg, TX	78541-4194	956-287-1003	287-2737	K-2	Sharon Chapman
IDEA Quest College Prep S	14001 N Rooth Rd	Edinburg, TX	78541-4194	956-287-1003	287-2737	6-12	Scott Hollinger
Inspired for Excellence Academy North	5426 Cavalcade St	Houston, TX	77026-4023	713-671-4185	773-3630	5-6	Lois Bullock
Inspired for Excellence Academy West	6333 S Braeswood Blvd	Houston, TX	77096-3605	713-772-2200	773-3630	5-6	Lois Bullock
Inspired Vision Academy I	8421 Bohannon Dr	Dallas, TX	75217-1917	214-391-7964	391-7954	PK-4	Lana Sprayberry-King
Inspired Vision Academy II	8501 Bruton Rd	Dallas, TX	75217-1909	972-285-5758	285-0061	5-8	Walter Clinton
Irving MS	1300 Delgado St	San Antonio, TX	78207-1467	210-734-2937	734-0941	6-8	Anita Chavera
iSchool	1800 Lakeway Dr Ste 100	Lewisville, TX	75057-6438	972-317-2470	315-9506	9-12	Kaye Rogers
Jackson Academy	5400 Griggs Rd	Houston, TX	77021-3757	713-845-2451	643-9850	9-12	Ms. A. Jackson
Jamie's House Charter S	PO Box 681183	Houston, TX	77268-1183	281-866-9777	880-9919	6-12	Jewel Teagle
Jubilee Academy	4434 Roland Rd	San Antonio, TX	78222-2830	210-333-6227	337-2357	PK-12	Daniel Amador
Kaleidoscope Charter S	6501 Bellaire Blvd	Houston, TX	77074-6428	713-773-5300	773-5303	6-8	Marie Moreno
Kandy Stripe Academy	8701 Delilah St	Houston, TX	77033-3827	713-734-4909	731-7890	PK-8	Cassandra Anderson
Kelley Charter S	802 Oblate Dr	San Antonio, TX	78216-7330	210-431-9881	432-8467	K-3	Alma Garza
King S	3501 Martin Luther King Dr	San Antonio, TX	78220-2325	210-223-8621	223-6907	PK-8	Nikki Foley-Demby
KIPP 3D Academy	4610 E Crosstimbers St	Houston, TX	77016-6337	713-636-6082	636-6084	5-8	Dan Caesar
KIPP Academy MS	10711 Kipp Way	Houston, TX	77099-2675	832-328-1051	879-1308	5-8	Elliott Witney
KIPP Aspire Academy	735 Fredericksburg Rd	San Antonio, TX	78201-6348	210-735-7300	735-7305	5-8	Joyce Boubel
KIPP Austin Academy of Arts & Letters	8509 FM 969 Bldg A	Austin, TX	78724	512-501-3640		5-8	Kevin Newman
KIPP Austin College Prep S	8509 FM 969 Ste C	Austin, TX	78724-5770	512-637-6870	637-6899	5-8	Freddy Gonzalez
KIPP Austin Collegiate	8509 FM 969 Ste C	Austin, TX	78724-5770	512-637-6870	637-6899	9-12	Carrie Donovan
KIPP Coastal Village	10711 Kipp Way	Houston, TX	77099-2675	832-731-7976		PK-8	Lynn Barnes
KIPP Dream Prep	4610 E Crosstimbers St	Houston, TX	77016-6337	713-636-6082	636-6084	PK-4	Lori Morrison
KIPP Explore Academy	5402 Lawndale St	Houston, TX	77023-3743	832-879-3100		K-4	Frank Cush
KIPP Houston HS	10711 Kipp Way	Houston, TX	77099-2675	832-328-1051	838-4293	9-12	Ken Estrella
KIPP Intrepid Preparatory S	5402 Lawndale St	Houston, TX	77023-3743	281-879-3100	463-7318	5-8	Carie-Anne Simmons
KIPP Liberation College Preparatory S	3150 Yellowstone Blvd	Houston, TX	77054-2306	713-842-1695	842-6689	5-8	Tori Dugar
KIPP Polaris Academy for Boys	9636 Mesa Dr	Houston, TX	77078-3024	713-633-4646	633-4783	5-8	
KIPP SHARP College Preparatory Lower S	8430 Westglen Dr	Houston, TX	77063-6312	281-879-3000		PK-4	Alma Salman
KIPP Sharpstown College Prep	8430 Westglen Dr	Houston, TX	77063-6312	281-879-3000	915-0074	5-8	Chong-Hao Fu
KIPP Shine Prep	10711 Kipp Way	Houston, TX	77099-2675	832-230-0548	230-0579	K-4	Deborah Shifrine
KIPP Spirit College Preparatory S	3730 S Acres Dr	Houston, TX	77047-1020	713-731-1235	731-0386	5-8	Aaron Boudreaux
KIPP Truth Academy	3200 S Lancaster Rd # 230A	Dallas, TX	75216	214-375-8326	375-2990	5-8	Steven Colmus
KIPP University Prep HS	735 Fredericksburg Rd	San Antonio, TX	78201-6348	210-392-5599	579-1039	9-12	Joel Harris
KIPP Voyage Academy for Girls	9636 Mesa Dr	Houston, TX	77078-3024	832-971-0128		5-8	Tasha Ginn
KIPP ZENITH Academy	3730 S Acres Dr	Houston, TX	77047-1020	281-773-3998		K-4	Tiffany George
Kometzky S	PO Box 7667	Austin, TX	78713-7667	512-695-6596	369-5915	PK-12	May Toliver
La Academia de Estrellas	125 Sunset Ave	Dallas, TX	75208-4516	214-946-8908		K-5	Lorraine Mantei
La Amistad Love & Learning Academy	8515 Brookwulf Dr	Houston, TX	77072-3838	281-498-2477	498-2477	PK-4	Frederick Nixon
La Amistad Love & Learning Academy	7860 W Fuqua Dr	Missouri City, TX	77489-2465	281-988-9201	988-9201	PK-4	Frederick Nixon
La Amistad Love & Learning Academy	6600 Sanford Rd	Houston, TX	77096-5548	713-988-9201	988-9201	PK-4	Frederick Nixon
La Escuela de las Americas	2300 W Commerce St Ste 200	San Antonio, TX	78207-3840	210-978-0562	978-0547	PK-5	Anna Marie Lira
La Fe Preparatory S	616 E Father Rahm Ave	El Paso, TX	79901-2912	915-533-4560	533-4175	PK-3	Amy O'Rourke
Landmark S	101 Brushy Creek Rd	Palestine, TX	75803-8619	903-729-4208	729-1389	9-12	Mike Anderson
Lanier MS	2600 Woodhead St	Houston, TX	77098-1615	713-942-1900	942-1907	6-8	William Shell
Laurel Ridge	PO Box 7667	Austin, TX	78713-7667	210-491-3566	491-3552	PK-12	Sally Arnold
Lawson Institute	3100 Cleburne St	Houston, TX	77004-4501	713-225-1551	225-1561	6-8	Sean Porter
Leaders Academy	6011 W Orem Dr	Houston, TX	77085-1273	713-551-8777	556-6005	9-12	Willard York
Lee Academy of Science and Engineering	1826 Basse Rd	San Antonio, TX	78213-4606	210-431-9881	582-2587	9-12	Valarie Walker
Lee Academy	4327 E Lancaster Ave	Fort Worth, TX	76103-3224	817-534-5595	534-3813	9-12	Elmo Jackson
Legacy HS	601 S Washington St	Kaufman, TX	75142-2407	972-962-0306	962-2265	7-12	Mike Anderson
Liberty HS	6400 Southwest Fwy Ste A	Houston, TX	77074-2213	713-458-5555	458-5567	9-12	Monico Rivas
Life S - Lancaster	954 S Interstate 35 E	Lancaster, TX	75146-3304	972-274-7950		K-5	DeWayne Parker
Life S - McKinney	4045 W Eldorado Pkwy	Mc Kinney, TX	75070-4421	972-529-8125	504-0855	K-4	Steven Bazan
Life S - Oak Cliff	4400 S R L Thornton Fwy	Dallas, TX	75224-5110	214-376-8208	376-8209	K-12	Keith Shull
Life S - Red Oak	777 S Interstate 35 E	Red Oak, TX	75154	214-376-8200	617-5767	K-10	Joseph Mena
Lighthouse Charter S	2718 Frontier Dr	San Antonio, TX	78227-4069	210-674-4100	674-4108	PK-7	Deborah Murphy
Lindsley Park Community S	722 Tenison Memorial Dr	Dallas, TX	75223-1138	214-321-9155	321-0702	PK-3	Tom Loew
Little Lions Learning Academy	1127 Mindie Ln	San Antonio, TX	78253-5143	210-658-7071		K-1	
Lowell MS	919 Thompson Pl	San Antonio, TX	78226-1494	210-223-4741	223-6248	6-8	Armando Gutierrez
Mainland Preparatory Academy	319 Newman Rd	La Marque, TX	77568-3440	409-934-9100	934-9130	PK-8	Wilma Green
Manara Academy	PO Box 271119	Flower Mound, TX	75027-1119	972-739-6036		K-8	
Massieu Academy	823 N Center St	Arlington, TX	76011-5859	817-460-0396	460-4762	PK-12	Bobby Dunivan
Mayes Institute	5807 Calhoun Rd	Houston, TX	77021-3301	713-747-5629	747-5683	K-8	Beatrice Mayes
MeadowLand Charter S	PO Box 2266	Boerne, TX	78006-3603	830-331-4094		7-12	Laura Garza
Medical Center Charter S	1920 N Braeswood Blvd	Houston, TX	77030-3711	713-791-9980	791-9594	PK-8	Monica Jolivet
Medical Center Charter S Southwest	10420 Mullins Dr	Houston, TX	77096-4927	713-726-0223		PK-6	Monica Jolivet
Meridell Achievement Center	PO Box 7667	Austin, TX	78713-7667	512-528-2462	515-5875	K-12	Wendy Rollins
Methodist Children's Home	PO Box 7667	Austin, TX	78713-7667	254-750-1265	750-1307	PK-12	Judy Green
Metro Academy of Math & Science	500 Houston St	Arlington, TX	76011-7429	817-226-1261	226-1758	PK-12	Janice Hobbs
Meyerpark Charter S	PO Box 35616	Houston, TX	77235-5616	713-729-9712	729-9720	K-5	Julia Hutcherson
Midland Academy Charter S	500 N Baird St	Midland, TX	79701-4704	432-686-0003	686-0845	K-12	Sam Martinez
Mid-Valley Academy	1785 W US Highway 77	San Benito, TX	78586-4153	956-276-9906	276-9943	9-12	Dr. Daniel Garcia
Mid-Valley Academy	200 N 17th St	Mc Allen, TX	78501-4743	956-618-2303	618-2323	9-12	Dr. Daniel Garcia

School	Address	City,State	Zip code	Telephone	Fax	Grade	Contact
Mid-Valley Academy	103 E 2nd St	Mercedes, TX	78570-2701	956-565-5417	565-8439	9-12	Dr. Daniel Garcia
Milburn Academy - Amarillo	4106 SW 51st Ave	Amarillo, TX	79109-6132	806-463-2284	463-2231	9-12	Mark Peters
Milburn Academy - Beaumont	1310 Pennsylvania St Ste C	Beaumont, TX	77701-5652	409-833-7757	833-7767	9-12	Luther Thompson
Milburn Academy-Corpus Christi	5333 Everhart Rd Bldg C	Corpus Christi, TX	78411-4835	361-225-4424	225-4945	9-12	Sally Irvine
Milburn Academy - Ector County	2525 N Grandview Ave # 600	Odessa, TX	79761	432-550-7833	550-7884	9-12	Deloris Hittinger
Milburn Academy - Fort Worth	6785 Camp Bowie Blvd	Fort Worth, TX	76116	817-731-7627	731-7628	9-12	Armard Anderson
Milburn Academy - Houston	713 E Airtex Dr	Houston, TX	77073	281-209-3505		9-12	G. Lopez
Milburn Academy - Killeen	1001 E Veterans Mem # 301C	Killeen, TX	76541	254-634-4444	634-4044	9-12	Rose Thompson
Milburn Academy - Lubbock	4902 34th St Ste 10	Lubbock, TX	79410-2342	806-740-0811	740-0804	9-12	Starlette Gill
Milburn Academy - Midland	3303 W Illinois Ave	Midland, TX	79703	432-522-7200	522-5201	9-12	Teffanie White
Miller ES	207 Lincolnshire Dr	San Antonio, TX	78220-3114	210-333-0521	333-0563	PK-5	Sandra Booker
Mount Carmel Academy	7155 Ashburn St	Houston, TX	77061-2611	713-643-2008	645-0078	9-12	Maureen Giacchino
National Elite Gymnastics	PO Box 7667	Austin, TX	78713-7667	512-750-8567	288-6644	K-12	Angela Frey
Nelms Charter HS	20625 Clay Rd	Katy, TX	77449-5593	281-398-8031	398-8032	9-12	Vincente Fuentez
Nelms Charter MS	20625 Clay Rd	Katy, TX	77449-5593	281-398-8031	398-8032	5-8	Wendy Wolski
Nelms Charter S - Northeast	20625 Clay Rd	Katy, TX	77449-5593	281-398-8031	398-8032	K-12	Joey Beckham
Nelms Charter S - Northwest	20625 Clay Rd	Katy, TX	77449-5593	979-826-8302	826-2135	K-12	Robert Guercio
New Aspirations	7055 Beechnut St	Houston, TX	77074-6003	713-394-3577	556-6005	9-12	Linda Barnes
New Directions Charter S	1258 Austin Hwy Bldg 2	San Antonio, TX	78209-4891	210-828-2161	826-9962	9-12	Sue Eakle
New Frontiers Charter	1313 SE Military Dr Ste 117	San Antonio, TX	78214-2850	210-533-3655	533-5077	K-8	Ernest Moreno
New Horizons S	850 Highway 574 W	Goldthwaite, TX	76844	325-938-5513	935-5512	1-12	Amy Dickson
North Hills S	606 E Royal Ln	Irving, TX	75039-3503	972-501-0645	501-9439	K-12	Cheryl Huisman
North Houston HS for Business	1126 W Tidwell Rd	Houston, TX	77091-5500	713-686-6900	686-6920	9-12	Timothy Williams
North Houston Multi-Language Academy	1126 W Tidwell Rd	Houston, TX	77091-5500	713-686-6900	686-6920	1-5	Timothy Williams
Northwest Preparatory S	4705 Lyons Ave	Houston, TX	77020-4306	713-672-1959	676-1940	PK-5	Erik Singleton
Northwest Preparatory S	11500 Northwest Fwy Ste 490	Houston, TX	77092-6593	713-491-9220	491-9223	6-8	Steve Roberts
Nova Academy	PO Box 170127	Dallas, TX	75217-0127	214-381-3422	381-3499	K-6	Donna Houston-Woods
Nova Charter S Southeast	PO Box 170127	Dallas, TX	75217-0127	214-309-9030	398-6363	PK-6	Cynthia Peters
NYOS Charter S	1605 Kramer Ln	Austin, TX	78758	512-275-1593	287-5258	PK-5	Terry Berkenhoff
NYOS Charter S	12301 N Lamar Blvd	Austin, TX	78753-1320	512-583-6967	583-6973	6-12	Julie Atchley
Oaks Treatment Center	PO Box 7667	Austin, TX	78713-7667	512-751-4534	464-0277	K-12	Holly Engleman
Odyssey Academy	2803 53rd St	Galveston, TX	77551-5914	409-750-9289	744-0508	PK-8	Jennifer Goodman
Olympic Hills Charter S	PO Box 7667	Austin, TX	78713-7667	512-750-8567	295-4936	K-12	Angela Frey
Omega Academic Center	4434 Roland Rd	San Antonio, TX	78222-2830	210-922-0132	923-2788	6-12	Thomas Baldwin
One Stop Multiservice Charter S	PO Box 164	Mc Allen, TX	78505-0164	956-380-6616	292-0371	PK-12	Alfredo Moreno
One Stop Multiservice Charter S	PO Box 164	Mc Allen, TX	78505-0164	956-969-2600	969-1191	PK-12	Robert Rivera
One-Stop Multiservice Charter S	PO Box 164	Mc Allen, TX	78505-0164	956-519-2227	687-6062	PK-12	Orphelinda Jimenez
Osborne ES	800 Ringold St	Houston, TX	77088-6337	281-405-2525	405-2528	PK-5	Jacqueline Parnell
Outreach Word Academy	PO Box 4873	Victoria, TX	77903-4873	361-579-6922	573-5788	PK-12	Oliver Burbridge
Panola Charter S	448 W Panola St	Carthage, TX	75633-2520	903-693-6355	693-6391	8-12	Mark Thornton
Paradigm Accelerated Charter S	1120 Belle Plain St	Brownwood, TX	76801-1708	325-643-3735	643-9028	7-12	
Paradigm Accelerated Charter S	PO Box 368	Comanche, TX	76442-0368	325-356-9673		7-12	Vicky Cavitt
Paradigm Accelerated Charter S	6810 Guyler St	Wallis, TX	77485	979-478-6116	478-6118	7-12	
Paradigm Accelerated Charter S	PO Box 3159	Early, TX	76802	325-649-0976		7-12	Ronald Johnson
Paradigm Accelerated Charter S	PO Box 160	Dublin, TX	76446-0160	254-445-4844	445-4907	7-12	
Paso Del Norte Academy	400 S Zaragoza Rd Ste 230	El Paso, TX	79907	915-298-3637	298-3644	9-12	Lee Clay
Paso Del Norte Academy - Ysleta	711 N Mesa St	El Paso, TX	79902-3925	915-532-7216	298-3644	9-12	Maria Baquera
Pathfinder Camp	PO Box 7667	Austin, TX	78713-7667	512-695-6596	858-2329	K-12	Mayola Tolliver
Pathways 3H Ranch	PO Box 7667	Austin, TX	78713-7667	830-406-1644	866-3705	6-12	Cathy Berryhill
Peak Academy	4600 Bryan St	Dallas, TX	75204	214-276-0879	276-0856	PK-5	Jacqueline Ray
Peak Advantage	4536 Bryan St	Dallas, TX	75204-8312	214-276-0879	276-0856	6-12	Jacqueline Ray
Pegasus Campus	5299 South Highway 183	Lockhart, TX	78644	512-376-3281	398-3835	K-12	Margaret Riddle
Pegasus Charter HS	601 N Akard St Ste 203	Dallas, TX	75201	214-740-9991	740-9799	4-12	Virginia Hart
Phoenix Charter S	8501 Jack Finney Blvd	Greenville, TX	75402-3018	903-454-7153	454-7806	PK-12	Vickie Glasscock
Pineywoods Community Academy	602 S Raguet St	Lufkin, TX	75904-3936	936-634-5515	634-5518	K-5	David Greak
Pineywoods Community Academy	602 S Raguet St	Lufkin, TX	75904-3936	936-634-5515	634-5518	6-12	Lynette Cheek
Pinnacle S	6550 Camp Bowie Blvd	Fort Worth, TX	76116	817-735-8527	735-1910	K-8	Lori Manning
Porter S	PO Box 2053	Wimberley, TX	78676-6953	512-847-6867	847-0737	9-12	Dr. Yana Bland
Por Vida Academy	1135 Mission Rd	San Antonio, TX	78210-4505	210-532-8816	533-5612	9-12	Steve Langseth
Positive Solutions Charter S	1325 N Flores St	San Antonio, TX	78212	210-299-1025	299-1052	9-12	Bess Farr
Premier HS of Abilene	3161 S 23rd St Ste 4	Abilene, TX	79605-5861	325-698-8111	695-5620	6-12	Sue Pond
Premier HS of Austin	1701 W Ben White Blvd #100A	Austin, TX	78704	512-444-8442	444-1266	6-12	Elizabeth Camarena
Premier HS of Beaumont	209 N 11th St	Beaumont, TX	77702-2213	409-835-4303	835-2882	6-12	Tony Hadnot
Premier HS of Brownsville	955 Paredes Line Rd	Brownsville, TX	78521-2659	956-550-0084	554-0890	6-12	Norma Sorola
Premier HS of Del Rio	4300 E Highway 90	Del Rio, TX	78840-8878	830-298-2100	298-2122	6-12	Sally Buretta
Premier HS of El Paso	1035 Belvidere St	El Paso, TX	79912	915-581-4300		6-12	Lionel Rubio
Premier HS of Fort Worth	6411 Camp Bowie Blvd Ste B	Fort Worth, TX	76116-5449	817-731-2028	731-2129	6-12	Butch Jackson
Premier HS of Laredo	1720 E Hillside Rd	Laredo, TX	78041-3336	956-723-7788	753-6101	6-12	Dr. Amira Mejia
Premier HS of Lindale	17141 State Highway 110 N	Lindale, TX	75771-5933	903-881-9940	882-0183	6-12	Brad Crain
Premier HS of Lubbock	3501 50th St Ste 200	Lubbock, TX	79413-4043	806-763-1518	763-9310	6-12	Dawn Dockter
Premier HS of Midland	2500 W Illinois Ave	Midland, TX	79701-6339	432-682-0384	682-0897	6-12	Molly Jasso
Premier HS of Miracle Farm	10802 FM 2621	Brenham, TX	77833-0164	979-836-0901	277-0939	9-12	Jack Meeker
Premier HS of Mission	1203 St Claire Blvd	Mission, TX	78572-6601	956-424-9290	424-7661	6-12	Cleo Hinojosa
Premier HS of North Austin	1835A Kramer Ln	Austin, TX	78758	512-832-0965		6-12	Amanda Zamora
Premier HS of Palmview	406 W Veterans Blvd	Palmview, TX	78572-8327	956-432-0850	432-0851	6-12	Selma Femat
Premier HS of Pharr	200 E Expressway 83 Ste E	Pharr, TX	78577-6506	956-781-8800	781-7464	6-12	Rosie Zamora
Premier HS of San Antonio	3622 Fredericksburg Rd	San Antonio, TX	78201-3841	210-434-6090	434-7578	6-12	Kathryn Jackson
Premier HS of San Juan	1200 E Business 83	San Juan, TX	78589-4758	956-961-4721		6-12	Alma Prado
Premier HS of Tyler	1106 N Glenwood Blvd	Tyler, TX	75702-5059	903-592-5222	592-0324	6-12	Laqueta Timmons
Premier HS of Waco	4720 N 19th St	Waco, TX	76708-1213	254-752-0441	752-0445	6-12	Lisa Linton
Preparatory Academy of Houston	12525 Fondren Rd Ste M	Houston, TX	77035-5226	713-721-6905	524-6344	PK-12	Linda Ware
Preschool Academy	1826 Basse Rd	San Antonio, TX	78213-4606	210-431-9881	432-8467	PK-PK	Susan Norris
Project Chrysalis MS	4528 Leeland St	Houston, TX	77023-3047	713-924-1700	924-1704	6-8	Deborah Silber
Pro-Vision Charter S	4422 Balkin St	Houston, TX	77021-4104	713-748-0031	748-0037	5-8	Cornelius Wright
Quest Academy	111 S Beckley Ave	Dallas, TX	75203-2610	214-946-5157	946-5150	6-12	Rosanna Wheeler
Quest MS	1511 FM 407 Bldg B	Lewisville, TX	75067	972-316-6700		7-8	Glenda Simons
Radiance Academy of Learning	2845 Thousand Oaks Dr	San Antonio, TX	78232-4107	210-545-4415	545-4478	9-12	
Radiance Academy of Learning - Daystar	413 Kitty Hawk Rd	Universal City, TX	78148-3826	210-659-1210	659-2209	K-2	
Radiance Academy of Learning - Del Rio	709 Kings Way	Del Rio, TX	78840-2029	830-774-6230	774-6235	6-9	
Radiance Academy of Learning - Intrntl	4151 Culebra Rd	San Antonio, TX	78228-4557	210-433-1673	434-8667	K-8	
Radiance Academy of Learning - Main	2235 Thousand Oaks Dr # 130	San Antonio, TX	78232	210-404-9650	404-1271	PK-8	
Radiance Academy of Learning - Westlake	1305 SW Loop 410 Ste 120	San Antonio, TX	78227	210-670-8800	670-0903	PK-12	
Radiance Academy of Lrn - Mission Jordan	5939 Padre Dr	San Antonio, TX	78214-2332	210-595-6604	595-7263	K-2	
Ramirez Charter S	702 Avenue T	Lubbock, TX	79401-2303	806-766-1833	766-1825	K-6	Stace McEwin
Ranch Academy	3120 VZ County Road 2318	Canton, TX	75103-4671	903-479-3601	479-1161	6-12	Richard Boardman
Ranch Academy - Tyler Campus	3120 VZ County Road 2318	Canton, TX	75103-4671	903-479-3601	479-1161	1-12	Scott Moss
Rapoport Academy	1020 Elm St	Waco, TX	76704	254-799-4191		PK-4	
Rapoport Academy Preparatory S	1020 Elm St	Waco, TX	76704	254-754-2288	754-8002	9-12	
Rapoport Academy - Quinn Campus	1020 Elm St	Waco, TX	76704-2278	254-754-8000	754-8009	5-8	
Raven S	PO Box 515	New Waverly, TX	77358-0515	936-344-6677	344-7236	9-12	Greg Shipp
Reach Charter S	520 Mercury Dr	Houston, TX	77013-5217	713-675-1118	675-1118	11-12	Bertie Simmons
Reconciliation Academy	4311 Bryan St	Dallas, TX	75204-6738	214-821-9192	887-0806	PK-12	Leonard Brannon
Rhodes S	12822 Robert E Lee Rd	Houston, TX	77044-2411	281-458-4334	458-7595	PK-5	Michelle Bonton
Richland Collegiate HS	12800 Abrams Rd	Dallas, TX	75243-2199	972-761-6888	761-6890	11-12	Kristyn Edney
Ripley House Charter S	4410 Navigation Blvd	Houston, TX	77011-1036	713-315-6480	547-8201	K-5	Karen Elsen
Rise Academy	PO Box 2837	Lubbock, TX	79408-2837	806-744-0430	201-7088	PK-8	Richard Baumgartner
Riverside Park ES	202 School St	San Antonio, TX	78210-3940	210-534-6951	534-6987	PK-5	Kristin Willmann
Saenz Charter JHS	1830 Basse Rd	San Antonio, TX	78213	210-431-9881	435-8096	7-8	Jeff Gaffney
SAILL Charter S	PO Box 141909	Austin, TX	78714-1909	512-579-4084	579-4087	K-12	Christina Blair
St. Anthony Academy	3732 Myrtle St	Dallas, TX	75215-3849	214-421-3645	421-7416	PK-8	David Ray
St. Johns Academy	2019 Crawford St	Houston, TX	77002-9002	713-659-3237	659-5673	PK-K	Shundra Cannon
St. Mary's Academy Charter S	507 N Filmore St	Beeville, TX	78102-5000	361-358-5601	358-5704	K-8	Stan Simonson
San Antonio Can! HS	1807 Centennial Blvd	San Antonio, TX	78211-1205	210-923-1226	928-3366	9-12	Mark Peters
San Antonio Preparatory Academy	8308 Fredericksburg Rd	San Antonio, TX	78229-3316	210-614-7199	614-7199	PK-8	Raul Garcia
San Antonio S for Inquiry & Creativity	4618 San Pedro Ave	San Antonio, TX	78212-1411	210-738-0020	738-0033	K-12	Dr. Debbie De Leon
San Antonio Technology Academy	6655 First Park Ten Ste 110	San Antonio, TX	78213	210-527-9250	225-7282	9-12	Earl Costley
Sanchez HS	6001 Gulf Fwy	Houston, TX	77023	713-926-1112	926-1346	7-12	Eduardo Lopez
Sanchez HS	201 Meredith Dr	San Antonio, TX	78228-3231	210-270-8567	886-0816	8-12	Diana Perez
San Marcos Treatment Center	PO Box 7667	Austin, TX	78713-7667	512-805-3708	805-3719	K-12	Charles James
School of Liberal Arts & Science	PO Box 5129	Dallas, TX	75208-9129	214-941-4881	941-4866	PK-10	Linda Gromowsky
School of Science and Technology	1450 NE Loop 410	San Antonio, TX	78209-1513	210-804-0222	822-3422	6-12	Mark Namver
School of Science and Technology	4737 Saratoga Blvd	Corpus Christi, TX	78413-2117	361-851-2450	851-2475	K-8	
School of Science and Technology	5707 Bandera Rd	Leon Valley, TX	78238-1918	210-543-1111	543-1112	K-9	
School of Science and Technology	12200 Crownpoint Dr	San Antonio, TX	78233	210-888-1218	888-1219	K-8	
Seashore Learning Center	14493 S Padre Isl A PMB 307	Corpus Christi, TX	78418	361-949-1222	949-6762	PK-4	Dr. Kim Fuller
Seashore Middle Academy	14493 S Padre Islnd PMB385	Corpus Christi, TX	78418	361-654-1134	654-1139	5-8	Barbara Beeler
Sentry Technology Prep S	PO Box 164	Mc Allen, TX	78505-0164	956-542-3363	292-0371	PK-12	Carlos Verduzco

School	Address	City,State	Zip code	Telephone	Fax	Grade	Contact
SER-Ninos Charter S	5815 Alder Dr	Houston, TX	77081-2708	713-667-6145	667-0645	PK-8	Charmaine Constantine
Settlement Home	PO Box 7667	Austin, TX	78713-7667	512-695-6596	836-2159	K-12	Mayola Toliver
Shekinah Radiance Academy - Abundnt Life	5130 Casey St	La Marque, TX	77568-2707	409-935-8773	935-6206	K-12	
Shekinah Radiance Academy - Dallas Ctr	2427 N Highway 175	Seagoville, TX	75159-2141	972-287-5879	287-8119	K-6	
Shekinah Radiance Academy - Live Oak	13069 N Interstate 35	San Antonio, TX	78233-2615	210-590-0838	590-0856	PK-5	
Shekinah Radiance Academy - Pearsall	5203 Old Pearsall Rd	San Antonio, TX	78242-1918	210-623-3030	623-3046	PK-6	
Shekinah Radiance Academy - Walzem	6663 Walzem Rd	San Antonio, TX	78239-3612	210-967-6933	967-6280	PK-12	
Shekinah Radiance Academy - W Columbia	725 W Brazos Ave	West Columbia, TX	77486-2617	979-345-2434	345-5134	K-12	Deann Phillips
Shoreline Academy	1220 Gregory St	Taft, TX	78390-3044	361-528-3959	528-2143	7-12	Leticia Flores
South Plains Academy	4008 Avenue R	Lubbock, TX	79412-1603	806-744-0330	741-1089	9-12	Sarah Castro
Southwest ES	8440 Bissonnet St	Houston, TX	77074-3908	713-988-5839	270-0076	PK-4	Tyrone Davis
Southwest HS	6400 Southwest Fwy Ste S	Houston, TX	77074-2213	713-954-9528	953-0119	9-12	Tyrone Davis
Southwest MS	6400 Southwest Fwy Ste S	Houston, TX	77074-2213	713-954-9528	953-0119	6-8	Elizabeth Perez
Southwest Preparatory S NE Campus	1258 Austin Hwy Ste 220	San Antonio, TX	78209	210-829-8017	829-8514	9-12	Joe Inman
Southwest Preparatory S NW Campus	6535 Culebra Rd	San Antonio, TX	78238-4910	210-432-2634	432-5482	9-12	Otis Spears
Southwest Preparatory S SE Campus	735 S WW White Rd	San Antonio, TX	78220-2524	210-333-1403	333-3024	9-12	Marsha Hagin
Star Charter S	1901 Fleischer Dr	Austin, TX	78728-5704	512-989-2672	989-3150	K-12	William Clark
Stepping Stones Charter S	11250 S Wilcrest Dr	Houston, TX	77099-4313	281-988-7797	988-7736	K-6	Jackie Ibarra-Lanford
Storm ES	435 Brady Blvd	San Antonio, TX	78207-8099	210-224-7321	224-1998	PK-5	Lori Manning
Summit Academy	6550 Camp Bowie Blvd	Fort Worth, TX	76116	817-336-5134	336-2573	9-12	Wanda Huckaby
Summit International Preparatory S	1100 Roosevelt St	Arlington, TX	76011-4837	817-287-5121	287-5132	K-12	Jorge Botello
Tafolla Charter S	PO Box 1709	Uvalde, TX	78802-1709	830-278-1297	591-1465	PK-12	
Tekoa Academy	326 Thomas Blvd	Port Arthur, TX	77640-5242	409-982-5400	982-8498	PK-12	Rick Haley
Temple Education Center	1400 E Avenue B	Temple, TX	76501-4710	254-778-8682	778-8690	PK-12	Melissa Greotsch
Texans Can! Academy Carrollton/Farmers	2720 Hollandale Ln	Farmers Branch, TX	75234-2035	972-243-2178	243-2669	9-12	Mene Khepera
Texans Can! Academy-Dallas South Campus	6605 Sebring Dr	Dallas, TX	75241-6722	214-225-1194	372-2294	9-12	David Nowlin
Texas Empowerment Academy	3613 Bluestein Dr	Austin, TX	78721-2900	512-494-1076	494-0199	5-12	Angela Frey
Texas NeuroRehabilitation Center	PO Box 7667	Austin, TX	78713-7667	512-750-8567	462-6665	K-12	Mark Terry
Texas Preparatory S	PO Box 1643	San Marcos, TX	78667-1643	512-805-3000	805-7739	PK-8	M. Foreman
Texas Serenity Academy	530 N Sam Houston Pkwy E	Houston, TX	77060	281-820-8540		K-12	David Fuller
Texas Virtual Academy at Southwest	104 Industrial Blvd Ste B-2	Sugar Land, TX	77478	866-360-0161	313-1240	3-8	Teri Johnson
TLC Academy	5687 Melrose Ave	San Angelo, TX	76901-5100	325-224-2900	942-6795	PK-12	Claudette Morgan-Scott
Transformative Charter Academy	807 N 8th St	Killeen, TX	76541-4818	254-628-8989	628-8981	9-12	Lou Blanchard
Treetops School International	12500 S Pipeline Rd	Euless, TX	76040-5853	817-283-1771	684-0892	K-12	Janice Chancelor
Trinity Basin Preparatory S	PO Box 5129	Dallas, TX	75208-9129	214-942-6501	942-8864	PK-8	Tonya Woods
Trinity Charter - Krause Center Campus	25752 Kingsland Blvd	Katy, TX	77494-2086	281-392-7505	392-6887	6-12	Tanna Lazaroff
Trinity Charter - Nelson Center Campus	4601 N Interstate 35	Denton, TX	76207-3419	940-484-8232	484-1385	1-10	Wade Cherry
Trinity Charter - New Life Campus	650 Scarbourough	Canyon Lake, TX	78133-4529	830-964-4390	964-4376	4-12	Louis Bullock
TSU Charter Lab S	3805 Burkett St	Houston, TX	77004-4621	713-807-5181	741-1220	K-5	Shirley Harris
Two Dimensions Preparatory Academy	12121 Veterans Memorial Dr	Houston, TX	77067	281-440-8853	440-4233	PK-5	Shirley Harris
Two Dimensions Preparatory Academy	12121 Veterans Memorial Dr	Houston, TX	77067	281-872-0988	872-2858	PK-2	Shirley Harris
Two Dimensions Preparatory Academy	12121 Veterans Memorial Dr	Houston, TX	77067	281-987-7300	987-7306	PK-4	
Universal Academy	2616 N MacArthur Blvd	Irving, TX	75062-5401	972-255-1800	255-6122	PK-12	Janice Blackmon
Universal Academy - Flower Mound	1001 E Sandy Lake Rd	Coppell, TX	75019-3112	972-393-5834	393-5657	PK-12	Melissa Chavez
University Charter S	2200 E 6th St	Austin, TX	78702-3457	512-495-9705	495-9631	PK-5	Dr. Carolyn Black
University of Houston Charter S of Tech	3855 Holman St	Houston, TX	77204-6056	713-743-9111	743-9121	K-5	Michael Sandoval
University S	1404 W Walnut Hill Ln	Irving, TX	75038-3009	972-753-6165	550-1425	6-12	Narciso Garcia
Vanguard Academy	1200 E Kelly Ave	Pharr, TX	78577-5033	956-283-1700	702-2180	PK-9	Twilet Alexander
Varnett Charter S - East	PO Box 1457	Houston, TX	77251-1457	713-637-6574	637-8319	PK-5	Dora Morrow
Varnett Charter S - Northeast	PO Box 1457	Houston, TX	77251-1457	713-631-4396	491-3597	PK-5	M. Annette Cluff
Varnett Charter S - Southwest	PO Box 1457	Houston, TX	77251-1457	713-723-4699	283-1728	PK-5	
Village at South Park S	5874 Bellfort St	Houston, TX	77033-2144	210-658-7071		K-2	Michael Griffin
Vista Academy of Amarillo	3242 Hobbs Rd Ste F	Amarillo, TX	79109-3213	806-367-5447	367-5449	K-8	Stephanie Scott
Vista Academy of Carrollton	1615 W Belt Line Rd	Carrollton, TX	75006-6633	972-242-5864	245-2820	K-6	Chris Sisk
Vista Academy of Coppell	2400 N Josey Ln	Carrollton, TX	75006-1617	972-242-5864		K-6	Fernando Natividad
Vista Academy of Dallas	7300 Bruton Rd	Dallas, TX	75217-1447	214-792-9331		K-6	Debbie Foster
Vista Academy of Garland	3024 Anita Dr	Garland, TX	75041-2708	972-840-1100		K-6	Andrea Benedict
Vista Academy of Hickory Creek	800 Point Vista Dr Ste 518	Hickory Creek, TX	75065-7639	940-321-1144	321-1116	K-6	Gwen Abshire
Vista Academy of Jasper	1501 S Wheeler St	Jasper, TX	75951-5103	409-384-1228		K-6	Camille Penny
Vista Academy of Lancaster	634 W Wintergreen Rd	Lancaster, TX	75134	972-275-1541		K-6	Kim Young
Vista Academy of Willis	202 S Thomason St	Willis, TX	77378-8987	936-890-0100		K-12	Valerie Ovalle
Waco Charter S	615 N 25th St	Waco, TX	76707-3443	254-754-8169	754-7389	K-5	Pamela Tankerson
Walker IS	1826 Basse Rd	San Antonio, TX	78213-4606	210-654-4411	599-3546	4-6	Melinda Alexander
Wallace Accelerated HS	149 S State Highway 208	Colorado City, TX	79512-6603	325-728-2392	728-1025	8-12	Mary Ozuna
Waxahachie Faith Family Academy	1620 Falcon Dr	De Soto, TX	75115-2418	972-938-3996	937-5806	PK-12	Dr. Kimberly Agnew
Wesley ES	800 Dillard St	Houston, TX	77091-2301	713-696-2860	696-2866	PK-5	Natalie Blasingame
Westchester Academy International Study	901 Yorkchester Dr	Houston, TX	77079-3446	713-365-5678	365-5686	6-12	Jean Pickering
West Houston Charter S	5618 11th St	Katy, TX	77493-1971	281-391-5003	391-5010	K-8	Mark Rosevear
Westlake Academy	2600 Ottinger Rd	Westlake, TX	76262	817-490-5757	490-5758	K-12	Dr. Rosalind Perez
White Memorial HS	PO Box 2126	League City, TX	77574-2126	281-316-0001	316-0018	9-12	Linda Sanchez
Whittier MS	2101 Edison Dr	San Antonio, TX	78201-3499	210-735-7181	735-0704	6-8	Delesa O'Dell-Thomas
Williams Charter MS	6100 Knox St	Houston, TX	77091-4143	713-696-2600	696-2604	6-8	Kathleen Moore
Williams House S	108 E Main St	Lometa, TX	76853-2105	512-752-7501	752-7503	K-12	Mauricio Dominguez
Williams Preparatory S	1750 Viceroy Dr	Dallas, TX	75235-2308	214-276-0352	637-6393	K-12	Emily McClarnon
Winfree Academy Charter S	6221 Riverside Dr Ste 110	Irving, TX	75039-3529	940-243-0480	243-0219	9-12	Tommy Thomas
Winfree Academy Charter S	6221 Riverside Dr Ste 110	Irving, TX	75039-3529	972-234-9855	234-9975	9-12	Paulette Gillespie
Winfree Academy Charter S	6221 Riverside Dr Ste 110	Irving, TX	75039-3529	817-481-5803	329-6307	9-12	Eddie Vernon
Winfree Academy Charter S	6221 Riverside Dr Ste 110	Irving, TX	75039-3529	972-251-2010	251-4301	9-12	Mike Quinlan
Winfree Academy Charter S	6221 Riverside Dr Ste 110	Irving, TX	75039-3529	214-222-2200	222-0201	9-12	Chuck Jaecks
Winfree Academy Charter S	6221 Riverside Dr Ste 110	Irving, TX	75039-3529	817-590-2240	590-8724	9-12	Debi Christensen
Wood Charter S at Afton Oaks	3201 Cherry Ridge Ste C315	San Antonio, TX	78230	210-499-0351	403-3058	6-12	Jessica Raney
Wood Charter S at Hays County	3201 Cherry Ridge Ste C315	San Antonio, TX	78230	512-393-5220		6-12	Alberto Ibarra
Wood Charter S at Huebner Road	3201 Cherry Ridge Ste C315	San Antonio, TX	78230	210-798-0350	690-4139	6-12	Luz Navarro
Yes Prep S - East End	3401 Hardy St	Houston, TX	77009-5928	713-333-2931	333-2935	6-12	Bill Durbin
Yes Prep S - Lee	6529 Beverlyhill St	Houston, TX	77057-6406	713-574-9535	787-1736	6-6	Mark DiBella
Yes Prep S - North Central	13703 Aldine Westfield Rd	Houston, TX	77039-2001	281-227-2044	227-0696	6-10	Keith Desrosiers
Yes Prep S - Southeast	353 Crenshaw Rd	Houston, TX	77034-1543	713-910-2510	910-2350	6-12	Jason Bernal
Yes Prep S - Southwest	4411 Anderson Rd	Houston, TX	77053-2307	281-413-0001	413-0003	6-9	Dr. Sara Gallo
Young Learners Charter S	3333 Bering Dr Ste 200	Houston, TX	77057-6727	713-784-6345	974-3137	PK-PK	Anella Coleman
Young Scholars Academy of Excellence	1809 Louisiana St	Houston, TX	77002-8013	713-654-1404	654-1401	PK-4	Carlos Rodriguez
Yzaguirre S for Success	2950 Broadway St	Houston, TX	77017-1706	713-640-3700	641-1853	PK-12	Raul Yzaguirre
Yzaguirre S for Success	2255 N Coria St	Brownsville, TX	78520-8731	956-542-2404	542-2667	PK-5	Charles Polk
Zoe Learning Academy	515 W Center St	Duncanville, TX	75116-3211	972-296-3335		PK-6	Martina Edebor
Zoe Learning Academy	3505 Alice St	Houston, TX	77021-4867	713-748-4228	748-7833	PK-6	
Utah							
Academy for Math Engineering & Science	5715 S 1300 E	Salt Lake City, UT	84121-1023	801-278-9460	277-3527	9-12	Al Church
American Leadership Academy	898 W 1100 S	Spanish Fork, UT	84660-5654	801-794-2226	794-2130	K-12	Rob Muhlestein
American Preparatory Academy	12892 Pony Express Rd	Draper, UT	84020-9273	801-553-8500	576-9300	K-9	Carolyn Sharette
Beehive Science & Tech Academy	1011 Murray Holladay Rd	Salt Lake City, UT	84117	801-265-2782	618-4115	7-12	Frank Erdogan
Bowen Laboratory ES	6700 Old Main Hl	Logan, UT	84322-6700	435-797-3088	797-3668	K-5	Mark Peterson
Canyon Rim Academy	3005 S 2900 E	Salt Lake City, UT	84109-2108	801-474-2066	415-3500	K-6	Merry Fusselman
CBA Center	305 E 200 N	Delta, UT	84624-8405	435-864-5695	864-5711	9-12	Mike Louder
Channing Hall Charter S	13515 S 150 E	Draper, UT	84020-8602	801-572-2709	571-8786	K-8	Heather Shepherd
City Academy	555 E 200 S	Salt Lake City, UT	84102-2007	801-596-8489	521-4181	7-12	Sonja Woodbury
C.S. Lewis Academy	364 N State Road 198	Santaquin, UT	84655-5537	801-754-3376	754-3102	K-7	Jason Finch
DaVinci Academy of Science and the Arts	2033 Grant Ave	Ogden, UT	84401-0409	801-409-0700	866-1311	9-12	Jessie Kidd
Dual Immersion Academy	PO Box 58308	Salt Lake City, UT	84158-0308	801-347-1750	972-9482	K-6	Julia Barrientos
East Hollywood HS	2185 S 3600 W	West Valley, UT	84119-1121	801-886-8181	972-9585	9-12	Eric Lindsay
Edison Charter S - North	180 E 2600 N	North Logan, UT	84341-1551	435-787-2820	787-0299	K-8	Scott Jackson
Edison Charter S - South	1275 W 2350 S	Logan, UT	84321-6181	435-752-0123	787-4350	K-8	Eldon Budge
Emerson Alcott Academy	PO Box 373	Roosevelt, UT	84066-0373	435-724-4300	722-5044	K-8	Bobby Drake
Entheos Academy	4702 W 6200 S	Kearns, UT	84118-6702	801-417-5444	417-5448	K-8	Craig Pace
Fast Forward Charter S	875 W 1400 N	Logan, UT	84321-6804	435-713-4255	753-9615	9-12	Stephanie Sorenson
Freedom Academy	1190 W 900 N	Provo, UT	84604-3171	801-437-3100	437-3149	K-8	Lynne Herring
Gateway Preparatory Academy	201 E Thoroughbred Way	Enoch, UT	84721-7217	866-433-1388	433-1388	K-8	Rob Lee
Guadalupe S	340 Goshen St	Salt Lake City, UT	84104-1216	801-531-6100	531-6160	K-3	Vicki Mori
Hancock Charter S	125 N 100 E	Pleasant Grove, UT	84062-2355	801-796-5646	785-4934	K-8	Julie Adamic
Intech Collegiate HS	1787 Research Park Way	North Logan, UT	84341-5600	435-753-7377	753-3775	9-12	Jason Stanger
Itineris Early College HS	9301 Wights Fort Rd	West Jordan, UT	84088-8850	801-256-5970	256-5992	11-12	Stephen Jolley
Lakeview Academy	527 W 400 N	Saratoga Sprngs, UT	84045-3101	801-331-6788	331-6792	K-9	Harold Stone
Legacy Preparatory Academy	PO Box 1253	Bountiful, UT	84011-1253	801-936-0555	936-1038	K-9	Elizabeth Hatch
Liberty Academy	1195 Elk Ridge Dr	Salem, UT	84653-5521	801-465-4434	465-7808	K-12	Rob Muhlestein
Lincoln Academy	1582 W 3300 N	Pleasant Grove, UT	84062-9041	801-756-2039	785-2109	K-9	Jake Hunt
Maeser Prep Academy	531 N State St	Lindon, UT	84042-1339	801-785-4687	785-2562	9-12	Justin Kennington
Merit College Prep Academy	PO Box 1059	Springville, UT	84663-7059	801-491-7600		9-12	Paul Baltes

School	Address	City,State	Zip code	Telephone	Fax	Grade	Contact
Moab Charter S	358 E 300 S	Moab, UT	84532-2624	435-259-2277	259-6652	K-6	Joe Heywood
Monticello Academy	2782 Corporate Park Dr	Salt Lake City, UT	84120-5549	801-417-8040	417-8041	K-9	Kim Coleman
Mountainville Academy	195 S Main St	Alpine, UT	84004-1630	801-756-9805	763-9823	K-8	Wade Glathar
Navigator Pointe Academy	6844 Navigator Dr	West Jordan, UT	84084-4405	801-840-1210	840-1236	K-8	Judy Farris
North Davis Preparatory Academy	1765 W Hill Field Rd	Layton, UT	84041-7323	801-547-1809	547-1649	K-9	Deborah Gomberg
Northern Utah Acad for Math Engnrg & Sci	2750 University Park Blvd	Layton, UT	84041-9099	801-402-5922	402-5921	9-12	Rob Stillwell
North Star Academy	2920 W 14010 S	Bluffdale, UT	84065-5331	801-302-9579	302-9578	K-9	Mike Bennett
Odyssey Charter S	738 Quality Dr	American Fork, UT	84003-3309	801-492-8105	763-8743	K-8	Wendy Rapier
Ogden Preparatory Academy	2221 Grant Ave	Ogden, UT	84401-1405	801-627-2066	394-2267	K-4	Kathleen Thornburg
Ogden Preparatory Academy	215 E 22nd St	Ogden, UT	84401-2646	801-627-3066	395-2267	5-9	Kathleen Thornburg
Open Classroom	134 D St	Salt Lake City, UT	84103-2640	801-578-8144	578-8147	K-8	Dellis Hatch
Paradigm HS	8683 S 700 W	Sandy, UT	84070-2562	801-676-1018	676-1036	9-12	Scott Jones
Pinnacle Canyon Academy	210 N 600 E	Price, UT	84501-2613	435-613-8102	613-8105	K-12	Roberta Hardy
Providence Hall	4795 Mount Ogden Peak Dr	Herriman, UT	84096-3497	801-432-7866	446-3951	K-6	Mark Johnson
Quest Academy	4862 W 4000 S	West Haven, UT	84401-9633	801-731-9859		K-6	Catherine Montgomery
Ranches Academy	7789 Tawny Owl Cir	Eagle Mountain, UT	84005-4308	801-789-4000	789-4001	K-8	Susie Scherer
Reagan Academy	1143 W Center St	Springville, UT	84663-3028	801-489-7828	491-2829	K-8	Brian Myrup
Renaissance Academy	3435 N 1120 E	Lehi, UT	84043-6538	801-768-4202	768-4295	K-8	Kyle Young
Rockwell Charter HS	3435 Stonebridge Ln	Eagle Mountain, UT	84005-5807	801-768-2903	789-4001	9-12	Darren Beck
Salt Lake Arts Academy	844 S 200 E	Salt Lake City, UT	84111-4203	801-531-1173	531-7726	5-8	Amy Wadsworth
Salt Lake Center for Science Education	1400 Goodwin Ave	Salt Lake City, UT	84116-1629	801-578-8226	578-8677	9-12	Larry Madden
Salt Lake School for the Performing Arts	2166 S 1700 E Ste A103B	Salt Lake City, UT	84106	801-466-6700	485-1707	9-12	Shalee Schmidt
Soldier Hollow S	PO Box 779	Midway, UT	84049-0779	435-654-1347	654-1349	K-8	Charles Weber
Spectrum Academy	575 Cutler Dr	North Salt Lake, UT	84054-2953	801-936-0318	936-0568	K-8	Jaime Christensen
Success Academy at Dixie	225 S 700 E	Saint George, UT	84770-3875	435-652-7830	656-4149	10-12	Vickie Wilson
Success Academy at SUU	351 W Center St	Cedar City, UT	84720-2470	435-865-8790	865-8795	9-12	Vickie Wilson
Success S	4122 Carriage Sq Ste 2B	Taylorsville, UT	84119-5569	801-964-4258	964-4259	7-12	Diane Austin
Summit Academy	PO Box 401	Sandy, UT	84091-0401	801-572-4166	572-4169	K-8	Steve Crandall
Syracuse Arts Academy	2893 W 1700 S	Syracuse, UT	84075-9838	801-779-2066	779-2087	K-6	Jan Whimpey
Timpanogos Academy	55 S 100 E	Lindon, UT	84042-2058	801-785-4979	785-9690	K-8	Errol Porter
Tuacahn HS for the Performing Arts	1100 Tuacahn	Ivins, UT	84738-6088	435-652-3201	652-3306	9-12	Bill Fowler
Uintah River HS	PO Box 235	Fort Duchesne, UT	84026-0235	435-725-4088	722-0811	9-12	Byron Richardson
Utah County Academy of Sciences	940 W 800 S	Orem, UT	84058-5915	801-863-2222	225-2214	10-12	Clark Baron
Venture Academy	2590 Washington Blvd #300	Ogden, UT	84401	801-644-0341	622-7251	K-8	Mark Child
Walden S of Liberal Arts	4232 N University Ave	Provo, UT	84604	801-374-1545	374-3397	K-12	Diana West
Wasatch Peak Academy	414 Cutler Dr	North Salt Lake, UT	84054-2951	801-936-3066	936-0887	K-6	Sandra Shepard
Washington Academy	2277 S 3000 E	Saint George, UT	84790-8510	435-673-2232	673-0142	K-8	Amy Trombetti
Webster Academy	205 E 400 S	Orem, UT	84058-6311	801-426-6624	426-6645	K-8	Rick Kempton

Virginia

School	Address	City,State	Zip code	Telephone	Fax	Grade	Contact
Community Public Charter S	901 Rose Hill Dr	Charlottesville, VA	22903-5239	434-972-1607		6-8	Chad Sansing
Hampton Harbour Academy	23 Semple Farm Rd	Hampton, VA	23666-1456	757-766-5313	766-5319	6-8	Andrea James
Murray Charter HS	1200 Forest St	Charlottesville, VA	22903-5264	434-296-3090	979-6479	9-12	Dr. Vicki Crews-Miller
York River Academy	9300 George Washington Mem	Yorktown, VA	23692	757-898-0516	890-1045	9-12	Walter Cross

Wisconsin

School	Address	City,State	Zip code	Telephone	Fax	Grade	Contact
A2 Charter S	2530 Weeden Creek Rd	Sheboygan, WI	53081-7499	920-459-3573	459-6496	4-5	Lynn Walters
Academic Center HS	601 University Ave	Colfax, WI	54730-9773	715-962-3676	962-4024	9-12	John Dachel
Academy of Learning-21st Century Skills	2450 S 68th St	West Allis, WI	53219-1904	414-604-3520		9-12	Allison Ender
Academy of Learning & Leadership	1530 W Center St	Milwaukee, WI	53206-2101	414-372-3942	372-8260	K-8	Dr. M. Camille Mortimore
A L A S	971 W Windlake Ave	Milwaukee, WI	53204-3822	414-902-7300	902-7315	9-12	Maria Zuniga
A L B A	1712 S 32nd St	Milwaukee, WI	53215-2104	414-902-7525		K-5	Brenda Martinez
Alliance Charter S	215 E Forest Ave	Neenah, WI	54956-2765	920-751-6970	751-6861	K-5	Philip Johnson
Alliance S	234 W Galena St	Milwaukee, WI	53212-3955	414-227-2550		9-12	Tina Owen
ALPS Charter S	108 W New York Ave	Oshkosh, WI	54901-3760	920-424-0349	424-7596	3-8	Shelly Muza
Andrews Academy	26 Eclipse Ctr	Beloit, WI	53511-3550	608-361-3335	361-3350	9-12	Mark Dax
Appleton Career Academy	5000 N Ballard Rd	Appleton, WI	54913-8942	920-832-4300		10-12	Dave Mueller
Appleton Central Alternative HS	PO Box 2019	Appleton, WI	54912-2019	920-832-6136	993-7074	9-12	Katherine Peckham
Appleton Community Learning Center	PO Box 2019	Appleton, WI	54912-2019	920-832-6136		7-8	Katherine Peckham
Appleton eSchool	2121 E Emmers Dr	Appleton, WI	54915-3802	920-832-6212	832-1741	9-12	Ben Vogel
Appleton Montessori Charter S	2725 E Forest St	Appleton, WI	54915-3332	920-832-6265	832-6199	1-6	Dom Ferrito
Argyle Land Ethic Academy	PO Box 256	Argyle, WI	53504-0256	608-543-3318	543-3868	11-12	Jeff Eastlick
Audubon Technology & Communication Ctr	3300 S 39th St	Milwaukee, WI	53215-4019	414-902-7800	902-7815	6-12	Barbara Goss
Barron Area Montessori S	808 E Woodland Ave	Barron, WI	54812-1759	715-537-5612		PK-2	Lu Karl
Barron County Alternative S	1107 Heart Island Pkwy	Rice Lake, WI	54868-3900	715-736-3464	234-4552	9-12	Chris Crowe
Beaver Dam Charter S	400 E Burnett St	Beaver Dam, WI	53916-1902	920-885-7420	885-7429	6-12	Jesse Peters
Birchwood Discovery Center	201 E Birch Ave	Birchwood, WI	54817-8800	715-354-3471		K-8	Jeffrey Stanley
Bright Horizons Charter S	PO Box 68	Wilmot, WI	53192-0068	262-862-6461	862-7301	K-K	Teresa Curley
Brompton S	7951 36th Ave	Kenosha, WI	53142-2119	262-942-2191	942-2194	K-5	Patricia Jones
Bruce - Guadalupe Community S	1028 S 9th St	Milwaukee, WI	53204-1335	414-643-6441	649-9022	K-8	Mary Beth Kuxhause
Business & Economics Acad of Milwaukee	3814 W North Ave	Milwaukee, WI	53208-1351	414-615-3915	444-2291	PK-8	Willie Jude
Capitol West Academy	3939 N 88th St	Milwaukee, WI	53222-2748	414-465-1302	465-1319	PK-7	Donna Niccolai-Weber
C.A.R.E. Charter S	2000 Polk St	Stevens Point, WI	54481-5876	715-345-5413	345-5696	7-9	Connie Negaard
Carmen HS of Science and Technology	1712 S 32nd St	Milwaukee, WI	53215-2104	414-384-4444	384-4455	9-12	Dr. Patricia Hoben
Carter S of Excellence	2001 W Vliet St	Milwaukee, WI	53205-1943	414-933-4044	933-4958	PK-5	Shirley McCarty
Central Cities Health Institute	1801 16th St S	Wisc Rapids, WI	54494-5413	715-423-1520		11-12	Kathy Jarosinski
Central City Cyberschool	4301 N 44th St	Milwaukee, WI	53216-1473	414-444-2330	444-2435	K-8	Christine Faltz
Chippewa Valley Montessori Charter S	400 Cameron St	Eau Claire, WI	54703-5101	715-852-6950	852-3504	K-6	Todd Johnson
Chippewa Valley Technology Charter S	400 Cameron St	Eau Claire, WI	54703-5101	715-852-3101	852-6304	9-12	Robert Scidmore
CITIES - Project HS	700 W Michigan St Ste 200	Milwaukee, WI	53233-2415	414-344-8480	347-0110	9-12	Joseph O'Shea
Classical Charter S	3310 N Durkee St	Appleton, WI	54911-1215	920-832-4968	997-1390	K-8	Constance Ford
Community HS	1017 N 12th St	Milwaukee, WI	53233-1307	414-934-4057	934-4067	9-10	Jason O'Brien
Comprehensive Learning Center	258 E Gage St	Richland Center, WI	53581	608-647-6106	647-7293	9-12	Terry McGraw
Connects Learning Center	6201 S Barland Ave	Cudahy, WI	53110-2951	414-766-5090	766-5095	9-12	Stacey Adamczyk
CORE Charter S	W2662 Kennedy Ave	Kimberly, WI	54136-2339	920-687-3024	687-3029	9-12	David Lamers
Coulee Montessori Charter S	1307 Hayes St	La Crosse, WI	54603-1949	608-789-7685	789-7080	K-8	Harvey Witzenburg
Crandon Alternative Resource S	9750 US Highway 8 W	Crandon, WI	54520-8499	715-478-3713	478-5570	9-12	Cheri Collins
CRES Academy	527 S Franklin St	Janesville, WI	53548-4779	608-314-8718		9-12	Karen Schulte
Crossroads Charter S	220 Ransom St	Ripon, WI	54971-1444	920-748-4616		6-12	Rick Bunge
Denmark Empowerment Charter S	450 N Wall St	Denmark, WI	54208-9416	920-863-4031	863-5526	7-12	Kevin Kilstofe
Dimensions of Learning Academy	6218 25th Ave	Kenosha, WI	53143-4370	262-605-6849	605-1234	K-8	Diana Pearson
Discovery Charter S	200 Fuller St	Columbus, WI	53925-1647	920-623-5952	623-6026	K-2	Sue Sewell
Downtown Institute of Arts and Letters	227 W Pleasant St	Milwaukee, WI	53212-3941	414-212-3001		9-12	Donna Walker
Downtown Montessori Academy	2507 S Graham St	Milwaukee, WI	53207-1609	414-774-6005	774-6007	K-8	Virginia Flynn
Eagleville Charter S	S101W34511 County Road LO	Eagle, WI	53119-1860	262-363-6258	594-5495	1-6	Jodi Kujawa
Eclipse Center Charter S	26 Eclipse Ctr	Beloit, WI	53511-3550	608-361-3340	361-3350	9-12	Mark Dax
ES for the Arts and Academics	1528 N 5th St	Sheboygan, WI	53081-2834	920-459-3626		K-5	Marty Steinbruecker
Enrich Excel Achieve Learning Academy	120 S 14th Ave	Wausau, WI	54401-4217	715-261-0100	261-2350	9-12	Jason McFarlane
Etude S of the Arts and Academics	721 N 6th St	Sheboygan, WI	53081-4112	920-459-3504		9-12	Ted Hamm
Fairview S	6500 W Kinnickinnic River	Milwaukee, WI	53219	414-546-7700	546-7715	PK-8	Richard Cohn
Flambeau Charter S	PO Box 86	Tony, WI	54563-0086	715-532-5559	532-9040	11-12	Linda Michek
Foster and Williams HS	6700 N 80th St	Milwaukee, WI	53223-5506	414-393-3898	393-3802	9-12	Mark Fennema
Foster ES	305 W Foster St	Appleton, WI	54915-1515	920-832-6288	832-4831	PK-6	Nichole Schweitzer
Fox River Academy	1000 S Mason St	Appleton, WI	54914-5457	920-832-6260	993-7060	3-6	Sandy Vander Velden
Franklin ES	1401 W 5th Ave	Oshkosh, WI	54902-5697	920-424-0078	424-7581	PK-5	Jami Kohl
Fritsche MS	2969 S Howell Ave	Milwaukee, WI	53207-2083	414-294-1000	294-1015	6-8	Karen Nastulski
Genesis HS	1011 W Center St	Milwaukee, WI	53206-3299	414-267-4900	267-4915	9-12	Kathelyne Dye
Gibraltar Charter S	1100 Sauk St	Lodi, WI	53555-1446	608-592-3853	592-1045	9-12	Kim Amidon
Glidden Class ACT Charter S	370 Grant St	Glidden, WI	54527-9200	715-264-2141		11-12	Charles Pouba
Green Lake Global & Environmental Acad	PO Box 369	Green Lake, WI	54941-0369	920-294-6411	294-6411	7-8	E. Jon Tracy
HACIL	PO Box 860	Hayward, WI	54843-0860	715-934-2112		K-12	Bill Turner
Harborside Academy	714 49th St	Kenosha, WI	53140-3353	262-925-1400	925-1450	9-12	William Haithcock
Health Care Academy	1700 Edgewood Ave E	Ladysmith, WI	54848-3003	715-532-5531		7-12	Matt Bunton
Highland Community S	3030 W Highland Blvd	Milwaukee, WI	53208-3246	414-342-1412	342-1408	PK-3	Kathy Ronco
Hines Academy	7151 N 86th St	Milwaukee, WI	53224-4861	414-358-3542	760-4364	PK-8	Barbara Horton
Hmong American Peace Academy	1418 S Layton Blvd	Milwaukee, WI	53215-1923	414-383-4944	383-4950	PK-8	Chris Her-Xiong
Honey Creek Continuous Progess ES	6701 W Eden Pl	Milwaukee, WI	53220-1335	414-604-7900	604-7915	PK-5	Gitanjali Chawla
Honors High Online S	401 Highland Dr	Fredonia, WI	53021-9491	262-692-3988	692-3952	9-12	Kurt Bergland
Humboldt Park ES	3230 S Adams Ave	Milwaukee, WI	53207-2700	414-294-1700	294-1715	PK-8	Eugene Vlies
IDEAL Charter S	4965 S 20th St	Milwaukee, WI	53221-2860	414-304-6200	304-6215	K-8	Barbara Ernest
Inland Seas S of Expedition	2156 S 4th St Stop 4	Milwaukee, WI	53207-1146	414-933-9713	431-0018	9-12	Berlean Henderson
Insight S of Wisconsin	445 State Road 70	Grantsburg, WI	54840-7837	866-800-0027	418-8023	9-12	Jeff Bush
International Peace Academy	1418 S Layton Blvd	Milwaukee, WI	53215-1923	414-383-4944	383-4950	9-12	Chris Her-Xiong
iQ Academy of Wisconsin	222 Maple Ave	Waukesha, WI	53186-4725	262-970-1074		6-12	Rick Nettesheim
Island City Research Academy	980 8th Ave	Cumberland, WI	54829-9188	715-822-5122		7-8	Jim Sciacca

School	Address	City,State	Zip code	Telephone	Fax	Grade	Contact
Janesville Academy for Intl Studies	31 W Milwaukee St	Janesville, WI	53548-2911	608-314-1180	314-1180	9-12	Donna Behn
Janesville Virtual Academy	1831 Mount Zion Ave	Janesville, WI	53545-1236	608-743-5146		9-12	Donna Behn
JEDI Virtual HS	448 E High St	Milton, WI	53563-1502	608-758-6232	868-4864	9-12	Ronald Dayton
Jefferson S for the Arts	1800 East Ave	Stevens Point, WI	54481-3799	715-345-5418	345-7352	K-6	Dave Lockett
Juneau County Charter S	N11003 17th Ave	Necedah, WI	54646-7618	608-742-8811		7-12	Michele Yates-Wickus
Kaleidoscope Academy	318 E Brewster St	Appleton, WI	54911-3702	920-832-6294		6-8	Al Brant
Kenosha e-School	6729 18th Ave	Kenosha, WI	53143-4918	262-653-6300		9-12	William Hittman
Kenosha Schl of Enhanced Tech/Curriculum	6811 18th Ave	Kenosha, WI	53143-4932	262-925-1400	925-1450	K-8	Angela Andersson
Kiel eSchool	PO Box 201	Kiel, WI	53042-0201	920-894-2266	894-5100	7-12	Heidi Smith
Kosciuszko Montessori S	971 W Windlake Ave	Milwaukee, WI	53204-3822	414-902-7200	902-7215	PK-8	
La Causa S	PO Box 04188	Milwaukee, WI	53204-0188	414-647-8750	647-8797	K-8	Wendy Bahr
LaCrossroads Charter HS	1500 Ranger Dr	La Crosse, WI	54603-2713	608-789-7700	789-7711	9-12	Doug Leclair
Lake Country Academy	4101 Technology Pkwy	Sheboygan, WI	53083-6049	920-208-3021		PK-8	Carla Koepp
Lakeview Montessori S	506 N Black River St	Sparta, WI	54656-1548	608-366-3468	366-3473	PK-3	Mike Roddick
Lalich Charter S	5503 W Range View Dr	Hurley, WI	54534-9000	715-561-4900	561-4157	6-12	Jeffrey Gulan
Laurel HS	100 Blackhawk Dr	Viroqua, WI	54665-1399	608-637-1605		9-12	Renee Baker
LEAN Alternative Charter S	304 E Main St	Lena, WI	54139-9488	920-829-5703		9-12	Jann Sharpe
LEAPP Charter HS	300 Simonson Blvd	Deerfield, WI	53531-9543	608-764-8682	764-5433	10-12	Barb Callahan
Lucas Charter S	N5639 200th St	Menomonie, WI	54751-5256	715-232-1790	232-2026	9-12	James Swanson
Madison Academic Campus	8135 W Florist Ave	Milwaukee, WI	53218-1745	414-393-6100		9-12	Zanetta Cistrunk
Magellan Charter S	225 N Badger Ave	Appleton, WI	54914-3832	920-832-6226	832-4857	7-8	Paula Sween
Manitowoc County Comprehensive Charter S	1010 Huron St	Manitowoc, WI	54220-3314	920-683-4780		1-8	Kristen Lee
Marshall Charter S	PO Box 76	Marshall, WI	53559-0076	608-655-1310	655-3046	11-12	Rick Waski
Marshall Montessori IB Charter HS	4141 N 64th St	Milwaukee, WI	53216-1198	414-393-2566	393-2568	6-12	Sara Hmielewski
Marshall Montessori IB HS	4141 N 64th St	Milwaukee, WI	53216-1198	414-393-2566	393-2568	9-12	Sara Hmielewski
McDill Academies	2516 School St	Stevens Point, WI	54481-6100	715-345-5420	345-7345	K-6	Dennis Raabe
McKinley Academy	1010 Huron St	Manitowoc, WI	54220-3314	920-683-4780	683-4782	9-12	Kristin Lee
McKinley Center	2926 Blaine St	Stevens Point, WI	54481-4799	715-345-5421	345-7350	PK-6	John Blader
McKinley Charter MS	2340 Mohr Ave	Racine, WI	53405-2645	262-664-6150	664-6196	6-8	Lori Sue Pelk
McKinley Charter S	1266 McKinley Rd	Eau Claire, WI	54703-2220	715-852-6900	852-6904	6-12	Peter Riley
Mead Charter S	241 17th Ave S	Wisc Rapids, WI	54495-2401	715-422-6150	422-6333	PK-6	Margie Dorshorst
Meeme LEADS Charter S	12121 County Road XX	Newton, WI	53063-9732	920-693-8255	693-8730	PK-4	Heidi Smith
Mellen Technology Charter S	PO Box 500	Mellen, WI	54546-0500	715-274-3601	274-3715	11-12	Melissa Nigh
Mercer Environmental Tourism S	2690 W Margaret St	Mercer, WI	54547-9181	715-476-2154	476-2587	10-12	Lori Boltz
Merrill Adult Diploma Academy	1101A N Mill St	Merrill, WI	54452-1170	715-536-4594		9-12	Shannon Murray
Merrill Healthy Living Charter S	108 W New York Ave	Oshkosh, WI	54901-3760	920-424-0420	424-7504	PK-5	Julie Brilli
Merrimac Community Charter S	360 School St	Merrimac, WI	53561-9584	608-493-2217	493-2895	K-5	Sid Malek
Middleton Alternative HS	2429 Clark St	Middleton, WI	53562-2619	608-829-9640	831-5160	9-12	Jill Gurtner
Milwaukee Academy of Chinese Language	2430 W Wisconsin Ave	Milwaukee, WI	53233-1828	414-934-4340	934-4345	PK-6	James Sayavong
Milwaukee Academy of Science	2000 W Kilbourn Ave	Milwaukee, WI	53233-1625	414-933-0302	933-1914	PK-12	Judy Merryfield
Milwaukee African American Immersion	1011 W Center St	Milwaukee, WI	53206-3262	414-267-5000	267-4915	9-12	Lonnie Anderson
Milwaukee Business HS	1017 N 12th St	Milwaukee, WI	53233-1307	414-934-4005	934-4115	9-12	Eric Radomski
Milwaukee College Prep S	2449 N 36th St	Milwaukee, WI	53210-3040	414-445-8020	445-8167	K-8	Robert Rauh
Milwaukee Leadership Training Center	2360 N 52nd St	Milwaukee, WI	53210-2701	414-874-8588	874-8515	5-8	Shirley McCarty
Milwaukee Learning Lab	6506 W Warnimont Ave	Milwaukee, WI	53220-1344	414-604-7940		9-12	David Coyle
Milwaukee Renaissance Academy	2212 N 12th St	Milwaukee, WI	53205-1320	414-431-0114	372-9113	6-12	Deanna Singh
Milwaukee S of Entrepreneurship	6914 W Appleton Ave	Milwaukee, WI	53216-2732	414-438-5200	438-5208	11-12	John Polczynski
Monona Grove Alternative HS	4400 Monona Dr	Monona, WI	53716-1097	608-221-7666		10-12	Paul Brost
Monroe Alternative Charter S	1220 16th Ave	Monroe, WI	53566-2047	608-328-7270	328-7826	7-12	Lynne Wheeler
Monroe Independent Virtual Charter S	801 32nd Ave	Monroe, WI	53566-1900	608-328-7299	328-7288	9-12	
Monroe Virtual Charter MS	801 32nd Ave	Monroe, WI	53566-1900	608-328-7135		6-8	Cory Hirsbrunner
NE Wisconsin Online Charter S	595 Baeten Rd	Green Bay, WI	54304-5763	920-492-5960		6-12	Carol Conway-Gerhardt
New Century Charter S	401 W Verona Ave	Verona, WI	53593-1318	608-845-4900	845-4961	K-5	Lynn Berge
New Horizons Charter S	709 Weston Ave	Wausau, WI	54403-6765	715-261-0060	261-2461	6-8	Shawn Sullivan
New Horizons for Learning	1701 E Capitol Dr	Shorewood, WI	53211-1911	414-963-6922	961-2819	9-12	Timothy Kenney
New Path Charter S	320 E Central Ave	Oconto Falls, WI	54154-1456	920-848-4455		7-12	Michelle Bloedorn
Next Door Charter S	2545 N 29th St	Milwaukee, WI	53210-3155	414-562-2929	562-1979	PK-K	Sharon Schulz
Niikuusara Community S	540 Birch St	Nekoosa, WI	54457-1318	715-886-8100		5-7	Jon Sprehn
Northeast Wisconsin Montessori S	411 E Washington Ave	Cleveland, WI	53015-1517	920-693-8241		1-6	Deb Streblow
Northern Star S	5075 N Sherman Blvd	Milwaukee, WI	53209-5246	414-393-5000	393-5015	6-8	Valerie Benton-Davis
Northwoods Community ES	9086 County K	Harshaw, WI	54529-9731	715-282-8200	282-8218	K-5	Janet Bontz
Northwoods Community Secondary S	511 S Pelham St	Rhinelander, WI	54501-3316	715-365-9660	365-9774	6-12	Dr. Janet Bontz
NR4Kids Charter S	701 E 11th St	New Richmond, WI	54017-2399	715-243-1289		PK-K	Steve Wojan
Nuestro Mundo Community S	4201 Buckeye Rd	Madison, WI	53716-1648	608-663-1079	204-0364	K-5	Javier Bolivar
Oakwood Environmental Educ Charter S	1225 N Oakwood Rd	Oshkosh, WI	54904-8456	920-424-0315	424-7591	K-5	Kirby Schultz
Oconto Early Literacy Charter S	810 Scherer Ave	Oconto, WI	54153-1110	920-834-7808	834-9883	PK-PK	Barbara Blum
Oconto Falls Alternative Learning Site	320 E Central Ave	Oconto Falls, WI	54154-1456	920-848-4455	848-3899	10-12	Becky Spengler
Odyssey Charter S	2037 N Elinor St	Appleton, WI	54914-2255	920-832-6252	832-4389	3-6	Val Dreier
Oshkosh East HS	405 Washington Ave	Oshkosh, WI	54901-5043	920-232-0698	232-0676	9-12	Guy Powell
Paideia Academy	5821 10th Ave	Kenosha, WI	53140-4008	262-658-4540	658-4583	6-8	Ellen Becker
Parkside ES-Seeds of Health	2552 S 19th St	Milwaukee, WI	53215-3010	414-672-8296	672-9165	K-K	Karen Rutt
Pathways Charter S	PO Box 310	Winter, WI	54896-0310	715-266-3301		11-12	Adam Zopp
Phantom Knight S of Opportunity	300 S 6th St	De Pere, WI	54115-1214	920-425-1915	429-1919	7-12	Dr. Jason Lau
Philip Alternative Charter S	621 W College Ave	Waukesha, WI	53186	262-970-4355	970-4380	9-12	Jim Haessly
Portage Academy of Achievement	117 W Franklin St	Portage, WI	53901-1755	608-742-7376		9-12	Brian Seguin
Preparatory School for Global Leadership	1916 N 4th St	Milwaukee, WI	53212-3612	414-264-3380	264-4450	6-12	Angela Dye M.Ed.
Professional Learning Institute	2430 W Wisconsin Ave	Milwaukee, WI	53233-1828	414-304-6180	304-6188	9-12	Theresa Erbe
Project Change Alt Recovery Charter Schl	111 E Main St	Waukesha, WI	53186-5016	262-970-1102		9-12	James Haessly
Promethean Charter S	PO Box 247	Butternut, WI	54514-0247	715-769-3434	769-3712	9-12	Joni Weinert
REACH	850 Tiger Dr	Ripon, WI	54971	920-748-4618		9-12	Dan Tjernagel
REAL Charter S	5915 Erie St	Racine, WI	53402-1925	262-664-8100	664-8110	6-12	Robert Holzem
Renaissance Charter Alternative Academy	211 N Fremont St	River Falls, WI	54022-2148	715-425-7687	425-7671	9-12	Dr. Elaine Baumann
Renaissance S for the Arts	610 N Badger Ave	Appleton, WI	54914-3405	920-832-5708	832-4198	9-12	Michael Pekarske
Rhinelander Environmental Steward Acad	915 Acacia Ln	Rhinelander, WI	54501-2806	715-365-9220		7-12	Kirby Kohler
River Crossings Charter S	191 E Slifer St	Portage, WI	53901-1297	608-742-3764		7-8	Bob Meicher
River Falls Public Montessori Academy	211 N Fremont St	River Falls, WI	54022-2148	715-425-7645	425-7671	K-6	Nate Schurman
Riverview Academy	830 Virginia Ave	Sheboygan, WI	53081-4427	920-459-6746		10-12	Rich Miesfeld
Rock River Charter S	31 W Milwaukee St	Janesville, WI	53548-2911	608-752-8273	752-8430	9-12	Marge Hallenbeck
Roosevelt IDEA	2200 Wisconsin Ave	Plover, WI	54467-2981	715-345-5425	345-7347	K-6	Pam Bork
Rural Virtual Academy	124 W State St	Medford, WI	54451-1760	715-748-4620	748-6839	K-8	Charlie Heckel
School for Early Develpmnt & Achievmnt	2020 W Wells St	Milwaukee, WI	53233-2720	414-937-2024	937-2021	K-2	Joan Kuehl
School for Urban Planning & Architecture	1712 S 32nd St	Milwaukee, WI	53215-2104	414-902-7566	902-7570	9-12	Cris Parr
School of Enterprise Marketing	1700 Klatt Rd	New London, WI	54961-8603	920-982-8420		10-12	Joseph Pomrening
School of Sci Engineering & Technology	PO Box 125	Blair, WI	54616-0125	608-989-9835	989-2451	K-6	Connie Biedron
School of Technology & Arts I	1111 7th St S	La Crosse, WI	54601-5474	608-789-7695	789-7030	K-5	Nancy Matchett
School of Technology & Arts II	1900 Denton St	La Crosse, WI	54601-5816	608-789-7672	789-7030	6-8	Penny Reedy
Shapiro ES	1050 W 18th Ave	Oshkosh, WI	54902-6688	920-424-0164	424-7594	PK-5	Lynn Brown
Sparta Area Independent Learning S	506 N Black River St	Sparta, WI	54656-1548	608-366-3430	366-3526	9-12	Dale Stafslien
Sparta Charter Preschool	506 N Black River St	Sparta, WI	54656-1548	608-269-3151	366-3525	PK-PK	Jacob Dodge
Sparta High Point S	506 N Black River St	Sparta, WI	54656-1548	608-366-3443	366-3525	6-12	Mathew Toetz
Spruce ES	7904 County Road A	Lena, WI	54139-9738	920-848-4476		1-5	Thomas Menor
Success Academy	721 N 6th St	Sheboygan, WI	53081-4112	920-459-0950		9-12	Diane Wilcenski
Synectics Charter S	26 Eclipse Ctr	Beloit, WI	53511-3550	608-361-3335	361-3620	6-8	Deborah Williams
TAGOS Leadership Academy	1350 N Parker Dr	Janesville, WI	53545-0724	608-931-8434		7-12	Al Lindau
Tenor High S	840 N Jackson St	Milwaukee, WI	53202-3807	414-431-4371	431-4376	9-12	Jodi Weber
Tesla Engineering Charter S	2121 E Emmers Dr	Appleton, WI	54915-3802	920-997-1399	832-4880	9-12	Matt Mineau
Time 4 Learning Charter S	5900 S 51st St	Greendale, WI	53129-2634	414-423-2750	423-0592	PK-PK	Theresa West
Tosa S of Health Science & Technology	1060 Glenview Ave	Wauwatosa, WI	53213-3034	414-773-1900	773-1920	1-5	Jenny Keats
Transitional Skills Center	850 Maple St	Glenwood City, WI	54013-4346	715-265-4266	265-7129	10-12	Elizabeth Haltimer
Truth Institute	1011 W Center St	Milwaukee, WI	53206-3262	414-267-4978	267-4915	9-12	Cheryl Hunter
21st Century Prep S	1220 Mound Ave	Racine, WI	53404-3350	262-598-0026	598-0031	PK-8	Dr. Robert Morelan
Valley New S	10 E College Ave Ste 228	Appleton, WI	54911	920-993-7037	832-1725	7-12	David Debbink
Ventures Charter S	502 N Main St	Holmen, WI	54636-9313	608-526-3391	526-6716	6-8	Keri Holter
Veritas HS	3025 W Oklahoma Ave	Milwaukee, WI	53215-4347	414-389-5574	389-5576	9-12	Sherry Tolkan
Vernon County Area Better Futures HS	103 N Education Ave	Viroqua, WI	54665-1318	608-637-1192		9-12	Fritz Cushing
Verona Area Core Knowledge Charter S	740 N Main St	Verona, WI	53593-1153	608-845-4130	845-4961	K-8	Robert McNallie
Waadookodaading Charter S	PO Box 860	Hayward, WI	54843-0860	715-634-2619	934-2246	PK-4	Monica White
Walworth County Education Alternative HS	400 County Road H	Elkhorn, WI	53121-2035	262-741-8352		9-12	Jerry Hawver
Warriner HS for Personalized Learning	721 N 6th St	Sheboygan, WI	53081-4112	920-459-3504		9-12	Ted Hamm
Washington S for Comprehensive Literacy	1238 Geele Ave	Sheboygan, WI	53083-4797	920-459-3661	459-3197	K-5	Karl Bekkum
Washington Service Learning Center	3500 Prais St	Stevens Point, WI	54481-2298	715-345-5426	345-7353	K-6	William Carlson
Waukesha Academy of Health Professions	401 E Roberta Ave	Waukesha, WI	53186-6637	262-970-3710	970-3720	9-12	Mike Nowak
Waukesha Engineering Preparatory Academy	401 E Roberta Ave	Waukesha, WI	53186-6637	262-970-3710	970-3720	9-12	Michael Nowak
Waupaca County Charter S	PO Box 457	Weyauwega, WI	54983-0457	920-867-4744		6-12	Wendy Cartledge
Wausau Area Montessori Charter S	3101 N 13th St	Wausau, WI	54403-2317	715-261-0795	261-2035	1-5	Barry Wolff
W.E.B. DuBois HS	4141 N 64th St	Milwaukee, WI	53216-1198	414-393-2580	393-2585	9-12	Willie Hickman
Westside Academy I	1945 N 31st St	Milwaukee, WI	53208-1902	414-934-5000	934-5015	PK-3	James Sonnenberg

School	Address	City,State	Zip code	Telephone	Fax	Grade	Contact
Westside Academy II	1940 N 36th St	Milwaukee, WI	53208-1927	414-934-4400	934-4415	4-8	James Sonnenberg
Whitetail Academy Charter S	PO Box 86	Tony, WI	54563-0086	715-532-5559	532-5405	9-12	John Kopacz
Whittier ES	4382 S 3rd St	Milwaukee, WI	53207-4999	414-294-1400	294-1415	PK-5	Peggy Mystrow
Wildlands Research Charter S	E19320 Bartig Rd	Augusta, WI	54722-7501	715-877-2292	877-2234	7-12	Paul Tweed
WindlakeES-Seeds of Health	2433 S 15th St	Milwaukee, WI	53215-3132	414-643-9052	643-0162	1-8	Karen Rutt
Wings Academy	1501 S Layton Blvd	Milwaukee, WI	53215-1924	414-431-1356	431-1358	1-12	Dani LaPorte
Wisconsin Career Academy	4801 S 2nd St	Milwaukee, WI	53207-5919	414-483-2117	483-2152	6-12	Yasar Bora
Wisconsin Connections Academy	PO Box 2019	Appleton, WI	54912-2019	920-832-4800	832-6284	K-8	Michelle Mueller
Wisconsin River Academy	1201 Northpoint Dr	Stevens Point, WI	54481-1114	715-345-5401		11-12	Mike Devine
Wisconsin Virtual Academy	401 Highland Dr	Fredonia, WI	53021-9491	262-692-3988	692-3952	K-12	Kurt Bergland
Woodlands S	5510 W Blue Mound Rd	Milwaukee, WI	53208-3012	414-475-1600	475-9575	PK-8	Maureen Sullivan
WORK Institute	1017 N 12th St	Milwaukee, WI	53233-1307	414-934-4044	934-4016	9-12	Nebritt Herring
Wright Charter MS	1717 Fish Hatchery Rd	Madison, WI	53713-1244	608-204-1340	204-0547	6-8	Nancy Evans
YMCA Young Leaders Academy	1350 W North Ave	Milwaukee, WI	53205-1264	414-374-9400	374-9459	K-8	Ronn Johnson
Wyoming							
Arapaho Charter HS	445 Little Wind Rvr Bottom	Arapahoe, WY	82510	307-856-3862	856-3946	9-12	Mel Miller
Fort Washakie Charter HS	90 Ethete Rd	Fort Washakie, WY	82514	307-332-2380	332-7267	9-12	Shad Hamilton

BUREAU OF INDIAN AFFAIRS SCHOOLS

BUREAU OF INDIAN AFFAIRS
1849 C St NW, Washington, DC 20240-0001
Telephone 202-208-6123
Fax 208-3312
Website enan.bia.edu/home.aspx

BUREAU OF INDIAN AFFAIRS SCHOOLS

Agency/School	Address	City,State	Zip code	Telephone	Fax	Grade	Enr	Superintendent/Principal
Billings Area Office	**316 N 26th St Ste 3051**	**Billings, MT**	**59101-1373**	**406-247-7953**	**247-7965**	**K-12**		**Barb Parisian**
Blackfeet Dormitory	PO Box 880	Browning, MT	59417-0880	406-338-7441	338-5725	1-12		Lyle MacDonald
Northern Cheyenne Tribal S of Busby	PO Box 150	Busby, MT	59016-0150	406-592-3646	592-3645	K-12		Wanda Belgarde
St. Stephens Indian S	PO Box 345	Saint Stephens, WY	82524-0345	307-856-4147	856-3742	K-12		Marilyn Groesbeck
Shoshone Bannock S	17400 N Hiline Rd	Pocatello, ID	83202-1669	208-238-4200	238-2628	7-12		Dr. Phillip Shortman
Two Eagle River S	PO Box 160	Pablo, MT	59855-0160	406-675-0292	675-0294	7-12		Clarice King
Bureau of Indian Education Arizona South	**2901 N Central Ave Ste 970**	**Phoenix, AZ**	**85012-2729**	**602-265-1592**	**263-0293**	**K-12**		**Luvette Russell**
Blackwater Community S	3652 E Blackwater School Rd	Coolidge, AZ	85128-6609	520-215-5859	215-5862	K-2		Jacquelyn Power
Casa Blanca S	PO Box 10940	Bapchule, AZ	85121-0105	520-315-3489	315-3504	K-4		Patty Cook
Cibecue Community S	PO Box 80068	Cibecue, AZ	85911-0068	928-332-2480	332-2341	K-12		Juan Aragon
Gila Crossing S	RR 2 Box 809	Laveen, AZ	85339-9711	520-550-4834	550-4252	K-8		Ames Singley
Kennedy S, John F.	PO Box 130	Whiteriver, AZ	85941-0130	928-338-4593	338-4592	K-8		Dr. Rea Goklish
Roosevelt JHS, Theodore	PO Box 567	Fort Apache, AZ	85926-0567	928-338-4464	338-1009	6-8		Mike Brock
Salt River ES	10005 E Osborn Rd	Scottsdale, AZ	85256-4019	480-362-2400	362-2467	K-6		Jacque Bradley
Salt River HS	10005 E Osborn Rd	Scottsdale, AZ	85256-4019	480-362-2000	362-2090	7-12		Mike McCarthy
San Simon S	HC 1 Box 8292	Sells, AZ	85634-9711	520-362-2231	362-2405	K-8		Frank Rogers
Santa Rosa Boarding S	HC 1 Box 8400	Sells, AZ	85634-9713	520-361-2276	361-2511	K-8		Keith Seaman
Santa Rosa Ranch S	HC 2 Box 7570	Sells, AZ	85634-9741	520-383-2359	383-3960	K-8		Delbert Ortiz
Tohono O'Odham HS	HC 1 Box 8513	Sells, AZ	85634-9735	520-362-2400	362-2256	9-12		Leon Oo-Sah-We
Cheyenne River Agency	**PO Box 2020**	**Eagle Butte, SD**	**57625-2020**	**605-964-8722**	**964-1155**	**K-12**		**Dr. Cherie Farlee**
Cheyenne-Eagle Butte S	PO Box 672	Eagle Butte, SD	57625-0672	605-964-8777	964-8776	K-12		Dr. Nadine Eastman
Pierre Indian Learning Center	3001 E Sully Ave	Pierre, SD	57501	605-224-8661	224-8465	K-8		Darrell Jeanotte
Takini S	HC 77 Box 537	Howes, SD	57748-9511	605-538-4399	538-4315	K-12		Ted Rowland
Tiospaye Topa S	PO Box 300	Ridgeview, SD	57652-0300	605-733-2290	733-2299	K-12		Don Farlee
Chinle Agency	**PO Box 6003**	**Chinle, AZ**	**86503-6003**	**928-674-5131**	**674-5134**	**K-12**		**Dr. Rena Yazzie**
Black Mesa Community S	PO Box 97	Pinon, AZ	86510-0097	928-674-3632	659-8187	K-8		Marie Rose
Chinle Boarding S	PO Box 70	Many Farms, AZ	86538-3070	928-781-6221	781-6376	K-8		Gregory Morring
Cottonwood Day S	Navajo Route 4	Chinle, AZ	86503	928-725-3256	725-3255	K-8		Rachel Maho
Jeehdeez'a Academy	PO Box 1073	Pinon, AZ	86510-1073	928-725-3308	725-3306	K-5		Roberta Tayah-Yazzie
Lukachukai Community S	Navajo Route 13	Lukachukai, AZ	86507	928-787-4400	787-2311	K-8		Stanley Kedelty
Many Farms HS	PO Box 307	Many Farms, AZ	86538-3307	928-781-6226	781-6355	9-12		Brian Dillon
Nazlini Community S	HC 58 Box 35	Ganado, AZ	86505-9704	928-755-6125	755-3729	K-8		Ronald Arias
Pinon Community S	PO Box 159	Pinon, AZ	86510-0159	928-725-3234	725-3232	K-12		Phyllis Tachine
Rock Point Community S	Highway 191	Rock Point, AZ	86545	928-659-4221	659-4235	K-12		Gloria Johnson
Rough Rock Community S	HC 61 Box 5050PTT	Chinle, AZ	86503	928-728-3501	728-3564	K-12		Dr. Charles Monty Roessel
Crow Creek/Lower Brule Agency	**190 Oyate Cir**	**Lower Brule, SD**	**57548-8501**	**605-473-5531**	**473-9217**	**K-12**		**Dan Shroyer**
Crow Creek Reservation HS	PO Box 12	Stephan, SD	57346-0012	605-852-2455	852-2140	6-12		Joe Ashley
Crow Creek Sioux Tribal ES	PO Box 469	Fort Thompson, SD	57339-0469	605-245-2373	245-2310	K-5		Silas Blaine
Enemy Swim S	13525 446th Ave	Waubay, SD	57273-5715	605-947-4605	947-4188	K-8		Virginia Donley
Lower Brule Day S	PO Box 245	Lower Brule, SD	57548-0245	605-473-0216	473-0217	PK-6		Bill Williams
Lower Brule HS	PO Box 245	Lower Brule, SD	57548-0245	605-473-0216	473-0217	7-12		Cody Russell
Tiospa Zina Tribal S	PO Box 719	Agency Village, SD	57262-0719	605-698-3954	698-7766	K-12		Robin Cook
Fort Defiance Agency	**PO Box 110**	**Fort Defiance, AZ**	**86504-0110**	**928-729-7255**	**729-7286**	**K-12**		**Jacqueline Wade**
Ch'ooshgai Community S	PO Box 321	Tohatchi, NM	87325-0321	505-733-2719	733-2703	K-8		Lena Draper
Crystal Boarding S	Navajo Route 12	Navajo, NM	87328	505-777-2385	777-2648	K-6		Lorraine Dodge
Dilcon Community S	HC 63 Box G	Winslow, AZ	86047-9414	928-657-3485	657-3213	K-8		Dr. Tommy Lewis
Greasewood Springs Community S	HC 58 Box 60	Ganado, AZ	86505-9706	928-654-3383	654-3384	K-8		Johanson Phillips
Hunters Point Boarding S	PO Box 99	Saint Michaels, AZ	86511-0099	928-871-4439	871-4435	K-5		Theresa Kedelty
Kin Dah Lichi'i Olta	PO Box 800	Ganado, AZ	86505-0800	928-755-3439	755-3448	K-6		Ora James
Pine Springs Day S	PO Box 4198	Houck, AZ	86506-4198	928-871-4311	871-4341	K-4		Lou Ann Jones
Seba Dalkai Boarding S	HC 63 Box H	Winslow, AZ	86047-9415	928-657-3208	657-3224	K-8		Esther Frejo
Tiiyaatin Residential Hall	1100 W Buffalo St	Holbrook, AZ	86025-2330	928-524-6222	524-2231	9-12		Maye Bigboy
Wide Ruins Community S	PO Box 309	Chambers, AZ	86502-0309	928-652-3251	652-3252	K-6		Teresa Lang-Tsinagine
Winslow Residential Hall	600 N Alfred Ave	Winslow, AZ	86047-3130	928-289-4483	289-2821	7-12		Helena Botone
Hopi Agency	**PO Box 568**	**Keams Canyon, AZ**	**86034-0568**	**928-738-2262**	**738-5139**	**K-12**	500	**Jimmy Hastings**
First Mesa ES	PO Box 750	Polacca, AZ	86042-0750	928-737-2581	738-5139	K-6		K. Wiggins
Havasupai S	PO Box 40	Supai, AZ	86435-0040	928-448-2901	448-2551	K-8		
Hopi Day S	PO Box 42	Kykotsmovi, AZ	86039-0042	928-734-2468	734-2470	K-6		Dr. John Thomas
Hopi JSHS	PO Box 337	Keams Canyon, AZ	86034-0337	928-738-5111	738-5333	7-12	500	Dr. Paul Reynolds
Hotevilla-Bacavi Community S	PO Box 48	Hotevilla, AZ	86030-0048	928-734-2462	734-2225	K-8		Alma Sinquah
Keams Canyon ES	PO Box 397	Keams Canyon, AZ	86034-0397	928-738-2385	738-5519	K-6		Michael Krug
Moencopi Day S	PO Box 185	Tuba City, AZ	86045-0185	928-283-5361	283-4662	K-6		Leroy Shingortewa
Second Mesa Day S	PO Box 98	Second Mesa, AZ	86043-0098	928-737-2571	737-2565	K-6		Gary Polacca
Minneapolis Agency	**1 Federal Dr Rm 550**	**Fort Snelling, MN**	**55111-4008**	**612-725-4591**	**713-4438**	**K-12**	600	**Lynn Lafferty**
Bug-O-Nay-Ge-Shig S	15353 Silver Eagle Dr NW	Bena, MN	56626-1012	218-665-3000	665-3024	K-12		Rochelle Johnson
Circle of Life S	PO Box 447	White Earth, MN	56591-0447	218-983-4180	983-3767	K-12		Mitch Vogt
Circle of Nations Indian Boarding S	832 8th St N	Wahpeton, ND	58075-3642	701-642-3796	642-5880	4-8		David Keehn
Fond du Lac Ojibwe S	105 University Rd	Cloquet, MN	55720-8520	218-878-7571	878-7573	K-12		Mike Rabideaux
Lac Courte Oreilles Ojibwa S	8875 N Round Lake School Rd	Hayward, WI	54843	715-634-8924	634-6058	K-12		Dennis White
Lumsden Bahweting Anishinabe S, J.K.	1301 Marquette Ave	Sault S Marie, MI	49783-9533	906-635-5055	635-3805	K-8	400	Susan Palmer
Menominee Tribal S	PO Box 39	Neopit, WI	54150-0039	715-756-2354	756-2364	K-8		Robert Tucker
Meskwaki Settlement S	1605 305th St	Tama, IA	52339	641-484-4990	484-3264	K-12		Jerry Stephens
Nah Tah Wahsh Public S Academy	N14911 Hannahville Road B 1	Wilson, MI	49896-9612	906-466-2952	466-2556	K-12	200	Tom Miller
Nay Ah Shing S	43651 Oodena Dr	Onamia, MN	56359-2320	320-532-4695	532-4675	K-12		Eric North
Oneida Nation ES	PO Box 365	Oneida, WI	54155-0365	920-869-1676	869-1684	K-12		Sharon Mousseau
New Mexico Navajo Central Agency	**PO Box 328**	**Crownpoint, NM**	**87313-0328**	**505-786-6152**	**786-6112**	**K-12**	4,500	**Charlotte Garcia**
Dibe Yazhi Habitiin Olta S	PO Box 679	Crownpoint, NM	87313-0679	505-786-5237	786-7078	K-8		Dr. Glenn Whiteeagle
Dzilth-Na-O-Dith-Hle Comm. S	35 Road 7585 Ste 5003	Bloomfield, NM	87413	505-632-1697	632-8563	K-12		Freda Nells

Agency/School	Address	City,State	Zip code	Telephone	Fax	Grade	Enr	Superintendent/Principal
Lake Valley Navajo S	PO Box 748	Crownpoint, NM	87313-0748	505-786-5392	786-5956	K-8		Geraldine Thomason
Mariano Lake Community S	PO Box 787	Crownpoint, NM	87313-0787	505-786-5265	786-5203	K-6		Delores Bitsilly
NaNeel Zhiin Ji'olta S	HC 79 Box 9	Cuba, NM	87013-9701	575-731-2272	731-2252	K-8		Kenneth Toledo
Ojo Encino S	HC 79 Box 7	Cuba, NM	87013-9701	505-731-2333	731-2361	K-8		Daniel Martin
Pueblo Pintado Community S	HC 79 Box 80	Cuba, NM	87013-9600	575-655-3341	655-3342	K-8		Notah Benally
T'iists'oozi Bi'olta S	PO Box 178	Crownpoint, NM	87313-0178	505-786-6159	786-6163	K-8		Virginia Jumbo
Tse'ii'ahi' Community S	PO Box 828	Crownpoint, NM	87313-0828	505-786-5389	726-5635	K-4		Rebecca Vesely
New Mexico Navajo South Agency	**PO Box 26567**	**Albuquerque, NM**	**87125-6567**	**505-563-3690**	**563-3078**	**K-12**	2,800	**William Nuttle**
Alamo S	PO Box 907	Magdalena, NM	87825-0907	575-854-2635	854-2545	K-12		Alfonso Garcia
Baca Community S	PO Box 509	Prewitt, NM	87045-0509	505-876-2769	876-2310	K-4		Timothy Nelson
Bread Springs Day S	PO Box 1117	Gallup, NM	87305-1117	505-778-5665	778-5692	K-3		Carl Granfors
Chi-Chil Tah/Jones Ranch S	PO Box 278	Vanderwagen, NM	87326-0278	505-778-5574	778-5575	K-8		George Waybenais
Isleta ES	PO Box 550	Isleta, NM	87022-0550	505-869-2321	869-1625	K-6		
Jemez Day S	PO Box 139	Jemez Pueblo, NM	87024-0139	575-834-7304	834-7081	K-6		Freddie Cardenas
Laguna ES	PO Box 191	Laguna, NM	87026-0191	505-552-9200	552-7294	K-5		Rebecca McKie
Laguna MS	PO Box 268	Laguna, NM	87026-0268	505-552-9091	552-6466	6-8		Yolanda Batrez
Mescalero Apache S	PO Box 230	Mescalero, NM	88340-0230	575-464-4431	464-4822	K-12		Charles Harrison
Pine Hill S	PO Box 220	Pinehill, NM	87357-0220	505-775-3243	775-3241	K-12		Sam Alonzo
San Felipe Pueblo S	PO Box 4343	San Felipe Pb, NM	87001-4343	505-867-3364	867-6253	K-7		Marian Sema
Sky City Community S	PO Box 349	Pueblo of Acoma, NM	87034-0349	505-552-6671	552-6672	K-8		Pauline Villegas
To'Hajiilee'He S	PO Box 3438	Canoncito, NM	87026-3438	505-831-6426	836-4914	K-12		Jane Pitts
T'siya S, Zia	1000 Borrego Canyon Rd	Zia Pueblo, NM	87053-6104	505-867-3553	867-5079	K-8		Joe Robledo
Wingate HS	PO Box 2	Fort Wingate, NM	87316-0002	505-488-6400	488-6444	9-12		Mary Ann Sherman
Wingate S	PO Box 1	Fort Wingate, NM	87316-0001	505-488-6300	488-6312	K-8		Dianne Owens
New Mexico North Agency	**PO Box 4269**	**Espanola, NM**	**87533-4269**	**505-753-1466**	**753-1475**	**K-12**	200	**Dr. Benjamin Atencio**
Ohkay Owingeh Community S	PO Box 1077	San Juan Pueblo, NM	87566-1077	505-852-2154	852-4305	K-8		Rudy Bentz
San Ildefonso S	36 Tunyo Po	Santa Fe, NM	87506-7258	505-455-2366	455-7194	K-6		Dolly Neikrug
Santa Clara Day S	PO Box 2183	Espanola, NM	87532-2183	505-753-4406	753-8866	K-6		Robin Rodar
Santa Fe Indian S	PO Box 5340	Santa Fe, NM	87502-5340	505-989-6300	989-6317	7-12		Joe Abeyta
Taos Day S	PO Box X	Taos, NM	87571-1850	575-758-3652	758-1566	K-8	200	Patricia Kessler
Te Tsu Geh Oweenge S	RR 42 Box 2	Santa Fe, NM	87506-8368	505-982-1516	982-2331	K-6		Ralph Paiz
Northern Navajo Agency	**PO Box 3239**	**Shiprock, NM**	**87420-3239**	**505-368-3400**	**368-3409**	**K-12**		**Dr. Joel Longie**
Aneth Community S	PO Box 600	Montezuma Creek, UT	84534-0600	435-651-3271	651-3272	K-6		Clayton Michael Aaron
Atsa'biya'a'zh Community S	PO Box 1809	Shiprock, NM	87420-1809	505-368-2100	368-2076	K-6		Dean Cunningham
Beclabito Day S	PO Box 1200	Shiprock, NM	87420-1200	928-656-3555	656-3557	K-4		Daniel Sosnowski
Cove Day S	PO Box 2000	Red Valley, AZ	86544-2000	928-653-4457	653-4415	K-6		Perfilliea Charlie
Navajo Prep S	1220 W Apache St	Farmington, NM	87401-3886	505-326-6571	326-2155	9-12		John Tohtsoni
Nenahnezad Community S	PO Box 337	Fruitland, NM	87416-0337	505-598-6922	598-0970	K-6		Sylvia Ashley
Red Rock Day S	PO Box 2007	Red Valley, AZ	86544-2007	928-653-4456	653-5711	K-8		Susanna Gaddy
Sanostee Day S	PO Box 159	Sanostee, NM	87461-0159	505-723-2476	723-2425	K-3		Jeannie Haskie
Shiprock Alternative Dormitory Program	PO Box 1809	Shiprock, NM	87420-1809	505-368-2100	368-2076	9-12		Rick Hover
T'iisNazbas Community S	PO Box 102	Teec Nos Pos, AZ	86514-0102	928-656-3252	656-3486	K-8		Delphina John
Tohaali' Community S	PO Box 9857	Newcomb, NM	87455-9857	505-789-3201	789-3202	K-8		Delores Bitsilly
Oklahoma Education Office	**200 NW 4th St Ste 4049**	**Oklahoma City, OK**	**73102-3072**	**405-605-6051**	**605-6057**	**K-12**		**Joy Martin**
Chickasaw Children's Village	1185 Village Rd	Kingston, OK	73439	580-564-3060		1-12		Sallie Wallace
Eufaula Dormitory	Swadley Dr	Eufaula, OK	74432	918-689-2522	689-2438	1-12		Greg Anderson
Jones Academy	HC 74 Box 102-5	Hartshorne, OK	74547-9717	918-297-2518	297-2364	1-12		Brad Spears
Kickapoo Nation S	PO Box 106	Powhattan, KS	66527-0106	785-474-3550	474-3530	K-12		Don Barta
Riverside Indian S	RR 1	Anadarko, OK	73005	405-247-6673	247-5529	4-12		Tony Dearman
Sequoyah HS	PO Box 948	Tahlequah, OK	74465-0948	918-453-5400	456-0634	9-12		Gina Stanley
Pacific Regional Office	**2800 Cottage Way Ste W2820**	**Sacramento, CA**	**95825-1886**	**916-978-6057**	**978-6056**	**K-12**	1,100	
Duckwater Shoshone S	PO Box 140068	Duckwater, NV	89314-0068	775-863-0180	863-0199	K-8		Keith Honnaker
Noli S	PO Box 700	San Jacinto, CA	92581-0700	951-654-5596	654-7198	6-12		Donovan Post
Pyramid Lake HS	PO Box 256	Nixon, NV	89424-0256	775-574-1016	574-1037	7-12		Randy Melendez
Sherman Indian HS	9010 Magnolia Ave	Riverside, CA	92503-3972	951-276-6332	276-6336	9-12		Roland Doepner
Pine Ridge Agency	**PO Box 333**	**Pine Ridge, SD**	**57770-0333**	**605-867-1306**	**867-5610**	**K-12**		**Norma Tibbitts**
American Horse S	PO Box 660	Allen, SD	57714-0660	605-455-6750	455-2249	K-8		Gloria Kitsopoulas
Crazy Horse S	PO Box 260	Wanblee, SD	57577-0260	605-455-6800	462-6510	K-12		Dena Bogay
Little Wound S	PO Box 500	Kyle, SD	57752-0500	605-455-6175	455-2703	K-12		Linda Hunter
Loneman S	PO Box 50	Oglala, SD	57764-0050	605-455-6882	867-5109	K-8		Deborah Bordeaux
Pine Ridge S	PO Box 1202	Pine Ridge, SD	57770-1202	605-867-5198	867-5482	K-12		Victoria Sherman
Porcupine S	PO Box 180	Porcupine, SD	57772-0180	605-455-6450	867-5480	K-8		Jerry Lessert
Wounded Knee S	PO Box 350	Manderson, SD	57756-0350	605-455-6363	867-2051	K-8		Marnee White Wolf
Portland Area Office	**911 NE 11th Ave**	**Portland, OR**	**97232**	**503-872-2743**	**231-6219**	**PK-12**		
Chemawa Indian S	3700 Chemawa Rd NE	Salem, OR	97305-1199	503-399-5721	399-5870	9-12		Jon Claymore
Chief Leschi S	5625 52nd St E	Puyallup, WA	98371-3610	253-445-6000	445-2350	K-12		
Couer D'Alene Tribal S	PO Box 338	Desmet, ID	83824-0338	208-686-5808	686-5080	K-8		Bob Sobotta
Lummi HS	2334 Lummi View Dr	Bellingham, WA	98226-9277	360-758-4300		9-12		
Lummi Tribal S	2334 Lummi View Dr	Bellingham, WA	98226-9277	360-758-4300		K-8		
Muckleshoot Tribal S	39015 172nd Ave SE	Auburn, WA	98092-9763	253-931-6709	939-2922	K-12		
Paschal Sherman Indian S	25A Mission Rd	Omak, WA	98841-9455	509-422-7590	826-3855	K-9		Ryan Christoph
Quileute Tribal S	40 Ocean Dr	La Push, WA	98350	360-374-5700		K-12		Leon Strom
Wa He Lut Indian S	11110 Conine Ave SE	Olympia, WA	98513-9603	360-456-1311	456-1319	K-8		Harvey Whitford
Yakima Tribal S	PO Box 151	Toppenish, WA	98948-0151	509-865-5121	865-6092	9-12		
Rosebud Agency	**PO Box 669**	**Mission, SD**	**57555-0669**	**605-856-4478**	**856-4487**	**K-12**		**Neva Sherwood**
Marty Indian S	PO Box 187	Marty, SD	57361-0187	605-384-2212	384-5933	K-12		Tony Garcia
St. Francis Indian S	PO Box 379	Saint Francis, SD	57572-0379	605-747-2299	747-2379	K-12		Larry Parker
Sicangu Owaye Oti	PO Box 669	Mission, SD	57555-0669	605-856-4486	856-4490	1-12		Nancy Hernandez
South & Eastern States Agency	**545 Marriott Dr Ste 720**	**Nashville, TN**	**37214-5081**	**615-564-6630**	**564-6631**	**PK-12**		
Ahafachkee S	HC 61 Box 40	Clewiston, FL	33440-9772	863-983-6348	983-6535	K-12		Terry Porter
Bogue Chitto S	13241 Highway 491 N	Philadelphia, MS	39350-5463	601-389-1000	389-1002	K-8		Evelyn Terrell
Cherokee Central JSHS	PO Box 134	Cherokee, NC	28719-0134	828-497-5511	497-4372	7-12		Arlin Middleton
Cherokee Central S	PO Box 134	Cherokee, NC	28719-0134	828-497-9130	497-4351	K-8		Charlee Easton
Chitimacha Day S	3613 Chitimacha Trl	Jeanerette, LA	70544-8317	337-923-9960	923-7346	K-8		Tanya Rosamond
Choctaw Central HS	150 Recreation Rd	Choctaw, MS	39350-7180	601-663-7777	656-7077	9-12		Greg Carlyle
Choctaw Central MS	150 Recreation Rd	Choctaw, MS	39350-7180	601-656-8938	656-1558	7-8		Roger McLeod
Conehatta S	851 Tushka Rd	Conehatta, MS	39057-2804	601-775-8254	775-9229	K-8		Charles Hull
Indian Island S	10 Wabanaki Way	Indian Island, ME	04468-1254	207-827-4285	827-3599	PK-8		Linda McLeod
Indian Township S	13 School Dr	Princeton, ME	04668-5000	207-796-2362	796-2726	PK-8		Ralph Shannon
Miccosukee Indian S	PO Box 440021	Miami, FL	33144-0021	305-894-2364	894-2365	K-12		Tom Albano
Pearl River ES	470 Industrial Rd	Choctaw, MS	39350-4256	601-656-9051	656-9054	K-6		David McCullom
Rafferty S, Beatrice	22 Bayview Dr	Pleasant Point, ME	04667-4111	207-853-6085	853-2483	PK-8		Mike Chadwick
Red Water S	555 Red Water Rd	Carthage, MS	39051-9103	601-267-8500	267-5193	K-8		Bobbie Boone
Standing Pine ES	538 Highway 487 E	Carthage, MS	39051-6031	601-267-9225	267-9129	K-6		Jackie Harpole
Tucker S	126 E Tucker Cir	Philadelphia, MS	39350-8351	601-656-8775	656-9341	K-8		Joe Wood
Standing Rock Agency	**PO Box E**	**Fort Yates, ND**	**58538-0523**	**701-854-3497**	**854-7280**	**K-12**	200	**Emma Blue Earth**
Jamerson S, Theodore	3315 University Dr	Bismarck, ND	58504-7565	701-255-3285	530-0601	K-8		Francis Azure
Little Eagle S	PO Box 26	Little Eagle, SD	57639-0026	605-823-4235	823-2292	K-8		Charmaine Weston
Rock Creek Grant S	PO Box 127	Bullhead, SD	57621-0127	605-823-4971	823-4350	K-8		Linda Lawrence
Standing Rock Community S	PO Box 377	Fort Yates, ND	58538-0377	701-854-2142	854-2145	K-12	200	Dr. Harold Larson
Tate Topa Tribal S	PO Box 199	Fort Totten, ND	58335-0199	701-766-1439	766-1471	K-8		Dean Dauphinais
Turtle Mountain Education Line Office	**PO Box 30**	**Belcourt, ND**	**58316-0030**	**701-477-3463**	**477-9364**	**PK-12**	200	**Rose-Marie Davis**
Dunseith Day S	PO Box 759	Dunseith, ND	58329-0759	701-263-4636	263-4200	K-8		Yvonne St. Claire
Mandaree S	PO Box 488	Mandaree, ND	58757-0488	701-759-3311	759-3493	K-12		Peggy Herz
Ojibwa Indian S	PO Box 600	Belcourt, ND	58316-0600	701-477-3108	477-3760	K-8		Michael Blue
Trenton S	PO Box 239	Trenton, ND	58853-0239	701-774-8221	774-8040	PK-12	100	Michael O'Brien
Turtle Mountain ES	PO Box 440	Belcourt, ND	58316-0440	701-477-6471	477-8835	K-5		Dave Gourneau
Turtle Mountain HS	PO Box 440	Belcourt, ND	58316-0440	701-477-6471	477-8821	9-12		Kellie Hall
Turtle Mountain MS	PO Box 440	Belcourt, ND	58316-0440	701-477-6471	477-3973	6-8		Louis Dauphinais
Twin Buttes S	7997 7A St NW	Halliday, ND	58636-4004	701-938-4396	938-4398	K-8	50	Chad Dahlen
White Shield S	2 2nd Ave W	Roseglen, ND	58775-6009	701-743-4355	743-4501	K-12		Ioane Schmidt
Western Navajo Agency	**PO Box 746**	**Tuba City, AZ**	**86045-0746**	**928-283-2218**	**283-2286**	**K-12**	400	**Lemual Adson**
Chilchinbeto Community S	PO Box 740	Kayenta, AZ	86033-0740	928-697-3800	697-3448	K-8		Don Stryker
Dennehotso Boarding S	PO Box 2570	Dennehotso, AZ	86535-2570	928-658-3201	658-3221	K-8		James Brown
Greyhills Academy HS	PO Box 160	Tuba City, AZ	86045-0160	928-283-6271	283-6604	9-12		Dewight Witherspoon
Kaibeto Boarding S	PO Box 1420	Kaibito, AZ	86053-1420	928-673-3480	673-3489	K-8		Ronald Thompson
Kayenta Community S	PO Box 188	Kayenta, AZ	86033-0188	928-697-3439	697-3490	K-8		Velma Eisenberger
KinLani Bordertown Dormitory	901 N Kinlani Dr	Flagstaff, AZ	86001-1585	928-774-5270	774-5270	9-12		Perfillea Charley
Leupp S	HC 61 Box D	Winslow, AZ	86047-9313	928-686-6211	686-6216	K-12		Renee White-Alcott
Little Singer Community S	HC 61 Box 310	Winslow, AZ	86047	928-526-6680	526-8894	K-6		Etta Shirley
Naa Tsis 'Aan Community S	PO Box 10010	Tonalea, AZ	86044-5010	928-672-2335	672-2609	K-8		Tim Clashin
Richfield Residential Hall	PO Box 638	Richfield, UT	84701-0638	435-896-5101	896-6157	9-12		Cody Workman
Rocky Ridge Boarding S	PO Box 299	Kykotsmovi, AZ	86039-0299	928-725-3650	725-3655	K-8		David Moore

Agency/School	Address	City,State	Zip code	Telephone	Fax	Grade	Enr	Superintendent/Principal
Shonto Preparatory S	PO Box 7900	Shonto, AZ	86054-7900	928-672-2652	672-3504	K-12	400	Fannie Spain
Tonalea Day S	PO Box 39	Tonalea, AZ	86044-0039	928-283-6325	283-6326	K-8		Charles Fike
Tuba City Boarding S	PO Box 187	Tuba City, AZ	86045-0187	928-283-2330	283-2348	K-8		Don Coffland

DEPARTMENT OF DEFENSE DEPENDENT SCHOOLS

DEPT. OF DEFENSE DEPENDENT SCHOOLS
4040 Fairfax Dr Fl 9, Arlington, VA 22203
Telephone 703-588-3104
Website http://www.dodea.edu

DEPARTMENT OF DEFENSE DEPENDENT SCHOOLS

District/School	Address	City,State	Zip code	Telephone	Fax	Grade	Enr	Superintendent/Principal
Fort Campbell Dependent SD	**77 Texas Ave**	**Fort Campbell, KY**	**42223-5127**	**270-439-1927**	**439-3179**	**PK-12**	**4,300**	**Jo Blease**
Barkley ES	4720 Polk Rd	Fort Campbell, KY	42223-1900	270-439-3795	439-1901	PK-5	600	Madeline Haller
Fort Campbell HS	1101 Bastogne Ave	Fort Campbell, KY	42223-5133	931-431-5056	431-9386	9-12	600	Dave Witte
Jackson ES	675 Mississippi Ave	Fort Campbell, KY	42223-5353	931-431-6211	431-4453	PK-5	700	Susan Ahart
Lincoln ES	4718 Polk Rd	Fort Campbell, KY	42223-1400	270-439-3794	439-2335	PK-5	600	Sandy Meacham
Lucas ES, Andre	2115 Airborne St	Fort Campbell, KY	42223-5333	931-431-7711	431-5842	PK-5	500	Ted Turnipseed
Mahaffey MS	585 S Carolina Ave	Fort Campbell, KY	42223-5134	270-439-3792	439-3472	6-8	400	Hugh McKinnon
Marshall ES	75 Texas Ave	Fort Campbell, KY	42223-5135	270-439-3793	439-4382	PK-5	500	Dr. Suzanne Jones
Wassom MS	3066 Forest Rd	Fort Campbell, KY	42223-5272	270-439-3791	439-0671	6-8	300	Walt Coulter
Fort Knox Community SD	**281 Fayette Ave**	**Fort Knox, KY**	**40121-6201**	**502-624-2345**	**624-4256**	**PK-12**	**2,000**	**Todd Curkendall**
Fort Knox HS	107 Missouri St	Fort Knox, KY	40121-6812	502-624-3697	624-6171	9-12	400	Sarah Turner
Kingsolver ES	427 3rd Ave	Fort Knox, KY	40121	502-624-8650	624-3969	PK-3	200	Dr. Andrea McClain
Macdonald IS	128 McCracken St	Fort Knox, KY	40121-2706	502-624-5650	624-2108	4-6	200	Dr. Youlanda Washington
Mudge ES	190 S Paquette St	Fort Knox, KY	40121-2278	502-624-8345	624-3969	PK-3	100	Dr. Gregg Mowen
Pierce ES	174 Maine St	Fort Knox, KY	40121-2290	502-624-7449	624-5274	PK-3	200	Dr. Wanda Bradley
Scott MS	266 Mississippi St	Fort Knox, KY	40121-6814	502-624-2236	624-5433	7-8	300	Linda Haberman
Van Voorhis ES	120 Folger St	Fort Knox, KY	40121-6086	502-624-5854	624-7267	PK-3	400	Laura Gibson
Walker IS	114 Conroy Ave	Fort Knox, KY	40121-2276	502-624-7835	624-6759	4-6	200	Todd Kreider
Georgia / Alabama Dependent SD	**7441 Custer Rd Bldg 2670**	**Fort Benning, GA**	**31905**	**706-545-7276**	**545-8227**	**PK-8**	**2,600**	**Dr. Dell McMullen**
Dexter ES, Herbert J.	99 Yeager Ave	Fort Benning, GA	31905-9699	706-545-3424	545-9106	PK-5		Dr. Renee Mallory
Faith MS, Don C.	1375 Ingersoll St	Fort Benning, GA	31905-7200	706-545-5524	545-0301	6-8		Dr. Julio Gonzalez
Fort Rucker ES	PO Box 620279	Fort Rucker, AL	36362-0279	334-598-4408	598-6784	2-6		Barbara Doherty
Fort Rucker PS	PO Box 620279	Fort Rucker, AL	36362-0279	334-598-4473	598-5534	PK-1		Deborah Patton
Loyd ES, Frank R.	5701 Santa Fe Rd	Fort Benning, GA	31905-2724	706-544-8964	544-8972	PK-5		Julita Martinez
Maxwell AFB ES	800 Magnolia Blvd	Maxwell AFB, AL	36112-5922	334-953-7804	953-5302	PK-6		Melissa Hayes
McBride ES, Morris R.	700 Custer Rd	Fort Benning, GA	31905-7402	706-544-9411	544-9299	PK-5		Phyllis Parker
Robins AFB ES	895 11th St	Robins AFB, GA	31098	478-926-5003	926-5745	PK-6		Melissa Hayes
Stowers ES, Freddie	7791 Stowers Dr	Fort Benning, GA	31905-3130	706-544-2312	544-2349	PK-5		Angie McPherson
White ES, Edward A.	300 1st Division Rd	Fort Benning, GA	31905-6627	706-545-4623	545-5469	PK-5		Dr. Tommy Lee
Wilson ES, Richard G.	112 Lavoie Ave	Fort Benning, GA	31905-7523	706-545-5723	545-9505	PK-5		Dr. Renee Mallory
NY/VA Domestic Dependent School System	**3308 John Quick Rd Ste 201**	**Quantico, VA**	**22134-1752**	**703-784-2319**	**784-3100**	**PK-12**	**1,200**	**Michael Gould**
Ashurst ES	4320 Dulaney Rd	Quantico, VA	22134-2248	703-221-4108	784-2694	PK-3		Janice Weiss
Burrows ES, W.W.	3308 John Quick Rd	Quantico, VA	22134-1702	703-640-6118	784-1353	4-5		Randy Ekanger
Dahlgren S	6117 Sampson Rd Ste 206	Dahlgren, VA	22448	540-653-8822	653-4591	PK-8		Alice Herring
Quantico MSHS	3307 Purvis Rd	Quantico, VA	22134-2198	703-784-0303	784-4851	6-12		Michael Hollier
Russell ES, John H.	3301 Purvis Rd	Quantico, VA	22134-2199	703-221-4161	784-4870	PK-3		Donna Kacmarski
West Point ES	705A Barry Rd	West Point, NY	10996-1196	845-938-2313	938-3352	PK-4		Shawne Cryderman
West Point MS	705 Barry Rd	West Point, NY	10996-1110	845-938-2923	938-2568	5-8		David Rudy
North Carolina Dependent SD	**PO Box 70089**	**Fort Bragg, NC**	**28307-0089**	**910-907-0200**	**907-1405**	**PK-9**		**Thomas Hager**
Albritton JHS	PO Box 70089	Fort Bragg, NC	28307-0089	910-907-0201	432-4072	7-9		Mike Thornburg
Bitz IS	2028 Bevin St	Camp Lejeune, NC	28547-1436	910-451-2575	451-1475	3-5		Daniel Osgood
Bowley ES	PO Box 70089	Fort Bragg, NC	28307-0089	910-907-0202	907-3513	PK-4		Dr. Susan Walters
Brewster MS	1290 Stone St Bldg 883	Camp Lejeune, NC	28547	910-451-2561	451-2600	6-8		Dewarda Sholar
Butner ES	PO Box 70089	Fort Bragg, NC	28307-0089	910-907-0203	432-8400	PK-4		
Delalio ES	1500 Curtis Rd	Jacksonville, NC	28540-3406	910-449-0601	449-0677	PK-5		Cassandra White
Devers ES	PO Box 70089	Fort Bragg, NC	28307-0089	910-907-0204	396-7374	PK-4		Ginny Breece
Holbrook ES	PO Box 70089	Fort Bragg, NC	28307-0089	910-907-0205	432-8385	PK-4		Priscilla Joiner
Irwin IS	PO Box 70089	Fort Bragg, NC	28307-0089	910-907-0206	907-1247	5-6		
Johnson PS	2027 Stone St	Camp Lejeune, NC	28547-2506	910-451-2431	451-2433	PK-2		Carol Perry
Lejeune HS	835 Stone St	Camp Lejeune, NC	28547-2520	910-451-2451	451-3130	9-12		Wyonia Chevis
McNair ES	PO Box 70089	Fort Bragg, NC	28307-0089	910-907-0207	432-8386	PK-4		Timothy Howle
Murray ES	PO Box 70089	Fort Bragg, NC	28307-0089	910-907-0208	907-0506	PK-4		Charles Council
Pope ES	PO Box 70089	Fort Bragg, NC	28307-0089	910-907-0209	907-0901	PK-4		Dr. Bob Kirkpatrick
Tarawa Terrace II ES	84 Iwo Jima Blvd	Tarawa Terrace, NC	28543-1231	910-450-1635	450-1637	PK-5		Andrew Starrett
Tarawa Terrace I PS	60 Tarawa Blvd	Jacksonville, NC	28543-1153	910-450-1658	450-1661	PK-1		Linda Hawes
South Carolina / Fort Stewart SD	**376 Davis Ave**	**Fort Stewart, GA**	**31315-1033**	**912-408-3080**	**876-4339**	**PK-6**	**5,100**	**Dr. Joseph Guiendon**
Bolden ES, Charles Frank	1523 Laurel Bay Blvd	Beaufort, SC	29906-3675	843-846-6112	846-9283	3-8	4,000	Dr. Jacque Taton-Saunders
Brittin ES	2772 Hero Rd	Fort Stewart, GA	31315-1713	912-368-3324	368-3412	K-6		Joseph Motolenich
Diamond ES	482 Davis Ave	Fort Stewart, GA	31315-1015	912-876-5797	876-8350	PK-6		Linda Kidd
Elliott ES, Middleton Stuart	1635 Albacore St	Beaufort, SC	29906-3570	843-846-6982	846-6720	PK-2	300	Barbara Hazzard
Galer ES, Robert Edward	1516 Cardinal Ln	Beaufort, SC	29906-3486	843-846-6100	846-1860	PK-2	300	Noel Tillman
Kessler ES	1127 Austin Rd	Fort Stewart, GA	31315-5792	912-368-3958	368-5048	PK-6	200	Carol Lee Kipp Caldwell
Pierce Terrace ES	5715 Adams Ct	Columbia, SC	29206-5379	803-782-1772	738-8895	PK-1	300	Carol Kress
Pinckney ES, Charles C.	5900 Chesnut Rd	Columbia, SC	29206-5365	803-787-6815	790-2169	4-6		Carol Kress

CATHOLIC SCHOOL SUPERINTENDENTS

NATIONAL CATHOLIC EDUCATIONAL ASSOC.
1077 30th St NW Ste 100, Washington, DC 20007-3816
Telephone 202-337-6232
Fax 333-6706
Website ncea.org

CATHOLIC SCHOOL SUPERINTENDENTS

Archdiocese/Diocese	Address	City,State	Zip code	Telephone	Fax	Grade	Enr	Superintendent
Diocese of Albany	40 N Main Ave	Albany, NY	12203-1481	518-453-6666	453-6667	PK-12	8,400	Sr. Mary Jane Herb
Diocese of Alexandria	PO Box 7417	Alexandria, LA	71306-0417	318-445-2401	448-6121	PK-12	2,800	Sr. Ann Lacour
Diocese of Allentown	2145 Madison Ave	Bethlehem, PA	18017-4698	610-866-0581	867-8702	PK-12	15,000	Philip Fromuth
Diocese of Altoona-Johnstown	126A Logan Blvd	Hollidaysburg, PA	16648-2698	814-693-1401	695-8894	PK-12	4,300	Sr. Donna Leiden
Diocese of Amarillo	1800 N Spring St	Amarillo, TX	79107-7252	806-383-2243	383-8452	PK-12	800	Bernice Noggler

Archdiocese/Diocese	Address	City,State	Zip code	Telephone	Fax	Grade	Enr	Superintendent
Archdiocese of Anchorage	225 Cordova St	Anchorage, AK	99501-2409	907-297-7790	297-7758	PK-12	300	Sr. Ann Fallon
Diocese of Arlington	200 N Glebe Rd Ste 503	Arlington, VA	22203	703-841-2519	524-8670	PK-12	17,400	Sr. Bernadette McManigal
Archdiocese of Atlanta	680 W Peachtree St NW	Atlanta, GA	30308-1931	404-888-7833	885-7430	PK-12	11,400	Diane Starkovich
Diocese of Austin	PO Box 15405	Austin, TX	78761-5405	512-873-7771	873-8338	PK-12	5,100	Dr. Ned Vanders
Diocese of Baker	PO Box 5999	Bend, OR	97708-5999	541-388-4004	388-2566	PK-8	500	Roger Richmond
Archdiocese of Baltimore	320 Cathedral St	Baltimore, MD	21201-4421	410-547-5393	539-5566	PK-12	35,200	Dr. Ronald Valenti
Diocese of Baton Rouge	PO Box 2028	Baton Rouge, LA	70821-2028	225-336-8735	336-8711	PK-12	16,200	Dr. Melanie Verges
Diocese of Beaumont	PO Box 3948	Beaumont, TX	77704-3948	409-838-0451	838-4511	PK-12	1,700	Nancy Collins
Diocese of Belleville	2620 Lebanon Ave	Belleville, IL	62221	618-235-9601	235-7115	PK-12	6,400	Thomas Posnanski
Diocese of Biloxi	1790 Popps Ferry Rd	Biloxi, MS	39532-2118	228-702-2130	702-2178	PK-12	3,700	Dr. Mike Ladner
Diocese of Birmingham	PO Box 12047	Birmingham, AL	35202-2047	205-838-8303	838-8330	PK-12	6,600	Frances Lawlor
Diocese of Bismarck	PO Box 1137	Bismarck, ND	58502-1137	701-222-3035	222-0269	PK-12	2,500	Betty Greff
Diocese of Boise	1501 S Federal Way Ste 400	Boise, ID	83705-2591	208-342-1311	342-0224	PK-12	3,100	Dan Makley
Archdiocese of Boston	66 Brooks Dr	Braintree, MA	02184-3839	617-779-3601	746-5702	PK-12	45,100	Dr. Mary Grassa O'Neill
Diocese of Bridgeport	238 Jewett Ave	Bridgeport, CT	06606-2892	203-416-1375	372-1961	PK-12	12,500	Dr. Margaret Dames
Diocese of Brooklyn	PO Box 159013	Brooklyn, NY	11215-9013	718-965-7300	965-7323	PK-12	53,800	Dr. Thomas Chadzutko
Diocese of Brownsville	700 Virgen de San Juan	San Juan, TX	78589-3030	956-787-8571	784-5081	PK-12	3,900	Lisette Allen
Diocese of Buffalo	795 Main St	Buffalo, NY	14203-1250	716-847-5501	847-5593	PK-12	19,800	Dr. Rosemary Henry
Diocese of Burlington	PO Box 489	Burlington, VT	05402-0489	802-658-6110	658-6112	PK-12	2,400	Mona Faulkner
Diocese of Camden	631 Market St	Camden, NJ	08102-1103	856-756-7900	756-0225	PK-12	16,100	Mary Boyle
Diocese of Charleston	1662 Ingram Rd	Charleston, SC	29407-4242	843-402-9115	402-7724	PK-12	7,400	Sr. Julia Hutchison
Diocese of Charlotte	1123 S Church St	Charlotte, NC	28203-4003	704-370-3270	370-3292	PK-12	7,800	Linda Cherry
Diocese of Cheyenne	2121 Capitol Ave	Cheyenne, WY	82001-3619	307-638-1530	637-7936	PK-12	900	Gary Catalano
Archdiocese of Chicago	PO Box 1979	Chicago, IL	60690-1979	312-751-5200	751-5295	PK-12	95,900	Sr. Mary McCaughey
Archdiocese of Cincinnati	100 E 8th St	Cincinnati, OH	45202	513-421-3131	421-6271	PK-12	48,000	Br. Joseph Kamis
Diocese of Cleveland	1404 E 9th St	Cleveland, OH	44114-1735	216-696-6525	579-9655	PK-12	52,300	Margaret Lyons
Diocese of Colorado Springs	228 N Cascade Ave	Colorado Spgs, CO	80903-1324	719-636-2345	866-6453	PK-12	2,100	Michelle Maher
Diocese of Columbus	197 E Gay St Fl 3	Columbus, OH	43215	614-221-5829	241-2563	PK-12	17,800	Lucia McQuaide
Diocese of Corpus Christi	PO Box 2620	Corpus Christi, TX	78403-2620	361-882-6191	693-6798	PK-12	3,300	Rene Gonzalez
Diocese of Covington	PO Box 15550	Covington, KY	41015-0550	859-392-1500	392-1537	K-12	11,400	Dr. Lawrence Bowman
Diocese of Crookston	PO Box 610	Crookston, MN	56716-0610	218-281-4533	281-5991	PK-12	1,500	Al Foley
Diocese of Dallas	PO Box 190507	Dallas, TX	75219-0507	214-528-2360	522-1753	PK-12	14,700	Sr. Gloria Cain
Diocese of Davenport	2706 N Gaines St	Davenport, IA	52804-1914	563-324-1911	324-5811	PK-12	4,900	Mary Wieser
Archdiocese of Denver	1300 S Steele St	Denver, CO	80210-2599	303-715-3200	715-2042	PK-12	14,500	Richard Thompson
Diocese of Des Moines	601 Grand Ave	Des Moines, IA	50309-2501	515-237-5013	237-5070	PK-12	6,100	Luvern Gubbels Ed.D.
Archdiocese of Detroit	305 Michigan Ave Ste 600	Detroit, MI	48226-2625	313-237-5775	237-5857	PK-12	36,700	Sr. Mary Gehringer
Diocese of Dodge City	PO Box 137	Dodge City, KS	67801-0137	620-227-1513	227-1570	PK-8	1,000	Ann Depperschmidt
Archdiocese of Dubuque	1229 Mount Loretta Ave	Dubuque, IA	52003-8787	563-556-2580	556-5464	PK-12	13,000	Dr. Jeff Henderson
Diocese of Duluth	2830 E 4th St	Duluth, MN	55812-1501	218-724-9111	724-1056	PK-8	1,700	Cynthia Zook
Diocese of El Paso	499 Saint Matthews St	El Paso, TX	79907-4214	915-872-8426	872-8434	PK-12	4,500	Sr. Elizabeth Swartz
Diocese of Erie	PO Box 10397	Erie, PA	16514-0397	814-824-1241	824-1239	PK-12	10,200	Patricia McLaughlin
Diocese of Evansville	PO Box 4169	Evansville, IN	47724-0169	812-424-5536	421-1334	PK-12	7,800	Donna Halverson
Diocese of Fairbanks	615 Monroe St	Fairbanks, AK	99701-2936	907-456-4574	456-7481	K-12	500	
Diocese of Fall River	423 Highland Ave	Fall River, MA	02720-3718	508-678-2828	674-4218	PK-12	7,700	Dr. George Milot
Diocese of Fargo	5201 Bishops Blvd S Ste A	Fargo, ND	58104-7605	701-356-7900	356-7994	PK-12	2,100	Thomas Frei
Diocese of Fort Worth	800 W Loop 820 S	Fort Worth, TX	76108-2936	817-560-3300	244-8839	PK-12	6,600	Donald Miller
Diocese of Fresno	1510 N Fresno St	Fresno, CA	93703-3711	559-488-7420	488-7422	PK-12	6,800	Richard Sexton
Diocese of Ft. Wayne-South Bend	PO Box 390	Fort Wayne, IN	46801-0390	260-422-4611	426-3077	PK-12	13,400	Michelle Hittie
Diocese of Gallup	PO Box 1338	Gallup, NM	87305-1338	505-863-4406	863-2269	PK-12	1,500	Sr. Rene Backe
Diocese of Galveston-Houston	2403 Holcombe Blvd	Houston, TX	77021-2023	713-741-8704	741-7379	PK-12	18,100	Sr. Kevina Keating
Diocese of Gary	9292 Broadway	Merrillville, IN	46410-7088	219-769-9292	738-9034	K-12	7,400	Barbara O'Block Ed.D.
Diocese of Gaylord	611 W North St	Gaylord, MI	49735-8349	989-732-5147	705-3589	PK-12	3,200	Charles Taylor
Diocese of Grand Island	PO Box 996	Grand Island, NE	68802-0996	308-382-6565	382-6569	PK-12	1,500	Rev. Thomas Ryan
Diocese of Grand Rapids	360 Division Ave S Ste 3	Grand Rapids, MI	49503	616-243-0491	243-1442	PK-12	7,000	Bernard Stanko Ed.D.
Diocese of Great Falls-Billings	PO Box 1399	Great Falls, MT	59403-1399	406-727-6683	252-9875	PK-12	2,600	Harry Plummer
Diocese of Green Bay	PO Box 23825	Green Bay, WI	54305-3825	920-437-7531	437-0694	PK-12	11,800	Mark Salisbury
Diocese of Greensburg	723 E Pittsburgh St	Greensburg, PA	15601-2697	724-837-0901	837-0857	PK-12	4,600	Trent Bocan
Diocese of Harrisburg	PO Box 3553	Harrisburg, PA	17105-3553	717-657-4804	657-3790	PK-12	13,200	Livia Riley
Archdiocese of Hartford	467 Bloomfield Ave	Bloomfield, CT	06002-2903	860-242-4362	242-8683	PK-12	18,300	Dr. Dale Hoyt
Diocese of Helena	PO Box 1729	Helena, MT	59624-1729	406-442-5820	442-5191	PK-12	1,400	Patrick Haggarty
Diocese of Honolulu	6301 Pali Hwy	Kaneohe, HI	96744-5224	808-263-8844	262-6126	PK-12	11,200	Carmen Himenes Ed.D.
Diocese of Houma-Thibodaux	PO Box 505	Schriever, LA	70395-0505	985-850-3113	850-3225	PK-12	5,900	Sr. Immaculata Paisant
Archdiocese of Indianapolis	PO Box 1410	Indianapolis, IN	46206-1410	317-236-1430	261-3364	PK-12	22,600	Ron Costello Ed.D.
Diocese of Jackson	PO Box 2248	Jackson, MS	39225-2248	601-969-2742	960-8469	PK-12	4,400	Sr. Deborah Hughes
Diocese of Jefferson City	PO Box 104900	Jefferson City, MO	65110-4900	573-635-9127	635-2286	PK-12	6,800	Donald Novotney
Diocese of Joliet	402 S Independence Blvd	Romeoville, IL	60446-2264	815-838-2181	838-2182	PK-12	23,900	Sr. Helen Kormelink
Diocese of Juneau	415 6th St Ste 300	Juneau, AK	99801-1091	907-225-7400	463-3237	PK-6	100	
Diocese of Kalamazoo	215 N Westnedge Ave	Kalamazoo, MI	49007-3718	269-349-8714	349-6440	PK-12	3,600	Margaret Erich
Archdiocese of Kansas City	12615 Parallel Pkwy	Kansas City, KS	66109-3748	913-721-1570	721-5598	PK-12	15,600	Dr. Kathleen O'Hara
Diocese of Kansas City-Saint Joseph	PO Box 419037	Kansas City, MO	64141-6037	816-756-1850	756-1571	PK-12	12,500	Marlon De La Torre
Diocese of Knoxville	PO Box 11127	Knoxville, TN	37939-1127	865-584-3307	584-4319	PK-12	3,600	Dr. Sherry Morgan
Diocese of La Crosse	PO Box 4004	La Crosse, WI	54602-4004	608-788-7707	788-7709	PK-12	8,800	Diana Roberts
Diocese of Lafayette	2300 S 9th St	Lafayette, IN	47909-2400	765-474-6644	474-3403	PK-12	4,800	Marie Williams
Diocese of Lafayette	1408 Carmel Dr	Lafayette, LA	70501-5215	337-261-5529	261-5572	PK-12	15,300	Anna Larriviere
Diocese of Lake Charles	1112 Bilbo St	Lake Charles, LA	70601-5226	337-433-9640	433-9685	PK-12	2,700	Kimberlee Gazzolo
Diocese of Lansing	300 W Ottawa St	Lansing, MI	48933-1577	517-342-2482	342-2515	PK-12	10,300	Rev. Steven Mattson
Diocese of Laredo	1201 Corpus Christi St	Laredo, TX	78040-5354	956-753-5208	753-5203	K-12	2,100	Dr. Rosa Maria Vida
Diocese of Las Cruces	1280 Med Park Dr	Las Cruces, NM	88005-3239	575-523-7577	524-3874	PK-8	500	Ben Trujillo
Diocese of Las Vegas	PO Box 18316	Las Vegas, NV	89114-8316	702-697-3903	735-8941	K-12	3,800	
Diocese of Lexington	1310 W Main St	Lexington, KY	40508-2048	859-253-1993	255-1134	K-12	4,500	William Farnau
Diocese of Lincoln	PO Box 80328	Lincoln, NE	68501-0328	402-488-2040	488-6525	K-12	7,200	Rev. John Perkinton
Diocese of Little Rock	PO Box 7565	Little Rock, AR	72217-7565	501-664-0340	603-0518	K-12	7,500	Vernell Bowen M.Ed.
Archdiocese of Los Angeles	3424 Wilshire Blvd	Los Angeles, CA	90010-2241	213-637-7300	637-6140	PK-12	87,000	Nancy Coonis
Archdiocese of Louisville	1935 Lewiston Dr	Louisville, KY	40216-2523	502-448-8581	448-5518	PK-12	22,100	Leisa Schulz
Diocese of Lubbock	PO Box 98700	Lubbock, TX	79499-8700	806-792-3943	792-8109	PK-12	400	Leo Cottenoir
Diocese of Madison	PO Box 44983	Madison, WI	53744-4983	608-821-3180	821-3181	PK-12	8,000	Michael Lancaster
Diocese of Manchester	PO Box 310	Manchester, NH	03105-0310	603-669-3100	669-0377	PK-12	7,900	Mary Moran
Diocese of Marquette	PO Box 1000	Marquette, MI	49855-1000	906-227-9127	225-0437	PK-8	1,400	Joseph Steepleton
Diocese of Memphis	5825 Shelby Oaks Dr	Memphis, TN	38134-7316	901-373-1219	373-1223	PK-12	8,200	Dr. Mary McDonald
Diocese of Metuchen	PO Box 191	Metuchen, NJ	08840-0191	732-562-1990	562-1016	PK-12	14,300	Ellen Ayoub
Archdiocese of Miami	9401 Biscayne Blvd	Miami Shores, FL	33138-2970	305-762-1070	762-1115	PK-12	36,500	Br. Richard DeMaria Ph.D.
Archdiocese of Milwaukee	PO Box 3087	Milwaukee, WI	53201-3087	414-758-2253	769-3408	PK-12	32,400	David Lodes
Archdiocese of Mobile	PO Box 129	Mobile, AL	36601-0129	251-438-4611	438-4612	PK-12	6,100	Gwen Byrd
Diocese of Monterey	485 Church St	Monterey, CA	93940-3207	831-373-1608	373-0173	PK-12	5,300	Kim Pryzbylski Ph.D.
Diocese of Nashville	30 White Bridge Rd	Nashville, TN	37205-1401	615-352-7218	353-7972	PK-12	6,300	Dr. Therese Williams
Archdiocese of Newark	PO Box 9500	Newark, NJ	07104-0500	973-497-4260	497-4249	PK-12	41,200	Rev. Kevin Hanbury Ed.D.
Archdiocese of New Orleans	7887 Walmsley Ave	New Orleans, LA	70125-3496	504-866-7916	861-6260	PK-12	41,700	Sr. Kathleen Finnerty
Diocese of New Ulm	1400 6th St N	New Ulm, MN	56073-2057	507-359-2966	354-3667	PK-12	2,700	Karla Cross
Archdiocese of New York	1011 1st Ave Fl 18	New York, NY	10022	212-371-1000	317-9236	PK-12	91,900	Dr. Timothy McNiff
Diocese of Norwich	43 Perkins Ave	Norwich, CT	06360-3643	860-887-4086	887-9371	PK-12	5,600	Sr. Joan O'Connor
Diocese of Oakland	2121 Harrison St	Oakland, CA	94612	510-628-2154	451-5331	PK-12	18,500	Sr. Barbara Bray
Diocese of Ogdensburg	PO Box 369	Ogdensburg, NY	13669-0369	315-393-2920	393-8977	PK-12	2,600	Sr. Ellen Coughlin
Archdiocese of Oklahoma City	PO Box 32180	Oklahoma City, OK	73123-0380	405-721-5651	709-2811	PK-12	5,100	Sr. Catherine Powers
Archdiocese of Omaha	PO Box 4130	Omaha, NE	68104-0130	402-554-8493	827-3792	PK-12	20,000	Msgr. James Gilg
Diocese of Orange	PO Box 14195	Orange, CA	92863-1595	714-282-3055	282-5059	PK-12	19,600	Rev. Gerald Horan
Diocese of Orlando	PO Box 1800	Orlando, FL	32802-1800	407-246-4900	246-4940	PK-12	14,800	Dr. Nicholas Wolsonovich
Diocese of Owensboro	600 Locust St	Owensboro, KY	42301-2130	270-683-1545	683-6883	K-12	4,100	Jim Mattingly
Diocese of Palm Beach	PO Box 109650	Palm Bch Gdns, FL	33410-9650	561-775-9547	775-9545	PK-12	8,000	Sr. Joan Dawson
Diocese of Paterson	777 Valley Rd	Clifton, NJ	07013-2297	973-777-8818	779-0083	PK-12	14,700	John Eriksen
Diocese of Pensacola-Tallahassee	11 N B St	Pensacola, FL	32502-4601	850-435-3500	436-6424	PK-12	3,000	Kevin Vickery
Diocese of Peoria	412 NE Madison Ave	Peoria, IL	61603-3720	309-671-1579	671-1595	PK-12	12,900	Br. William Dygert
Archdiocese of Philadelphia	222 N 17th St	Philadelphia, PA	19103-1295	215-587-3700	587-5644	PK-12	91,800	Dr. Richard McCarron
Diocese of Phoenix	400 E Monroe St	Phoenix, AZ	85004-2336	602-354-2345	354-2436	PK-12	15,100	MaryBeth Mueller
Diocese of Pittsburgh	111 Blvd of the Allies	Pittsburgh, PA	15222-1618	412-456-3090	456-3098	PK-12	22,800	Dr. Robert Paserba
Archdiocese of Portland	2838 E Burnside St	Portland, OR	97214-1895	503-233-8300	236-3683	PK-12	14,400	Robert Mizia
Diocese of Portland	PO Box 11559	Portland, ME	04104-7559	207-773-6471	773-0182	PK-12	4,200	Sr. Rosemary Donohue
Diocese of Providence	1 Cathedral Sq	Providence, RI	02903-3695	401-278-4550	278-4596	PK-12	15,300	David Beaudoin
Diocese of Pueblo	1001 N Grand Ave	Pueblo, CO	81003-2979	719-544-9861	544-5202	PK-8	1,000	Sr. Betty Werner
Diocese of Raleigh	715 Nazareth St	Raleigh, NC	27606-2187	919-821-9749	821-8140	PK-12	8,800	Dr. Michael Fedewa
Diocese of Rapid City	300 Fairmont Blvd	Rapid City, SD	57701-5423	605-343-8484	343-1315	K-12	1,400	Barb Honeycutt
Diocese of Reno	290 S Arlington Ave Ste 200	Reno, NV	89501-1713	775-326-9430	348-8619	PK-12	1,700	Kitty Bergin
Diocese of Richmond	7800 Carousel Ln	Richmond, VA	23294-4201	804-359-5661	358-9159	PK-12	9,800	Francine Conway
Diocese of Rochester	1150 Buffalo Rd	Rochester, NY	14624-1890	585-328-3228	328-3149	PK-12	8,900	Sr. Janice Morgan
Diocese of Rockford	PO Box 7044	Rockford, IL	61125-7044	815-399-4300	399-6278	PK-12	15,100	Sr. Patricia Downey
Diocese of Rockville Center	PO Box 9023	Rockville Ctr, NY	11571-9023	516-678-5800	678-7362	PK-12	34,000	Sr. Joanne Callahan
Diocese of Sacramento	2110 Broadway	Sacramento, CA	95818-2518	916-733-0110	733-0120	PK-12	14,800	Domenic Puglisi
Diocese of Saginaw	5800 Weiss St	Saginaw, MI	48603-2762	989-799-7910	797-6645	PK-12	3,800	Barbara Davis

Archdiocese/Diocese	Address	City,State	Zip code	Telephone	Fax	Grade	Enr	Superintendent
Diocese of St. Augustine	11625 Old St Augustine Rd	Jacksonville, FL	32258	904-262-3200	596-1042	PK-12	10,900	Patricia Tierney
Diocese of St. Cloud	305 7th Ave N Ste 201	Saint Cloud, MN	56303-3633	320-251-0111	251-0259	PK-12	5,700	Linda Kaiser
Archdiocese of St. Louis	20 Archbishop May Dr	Saint Louis, MO	63119-5738	314-792-7300	792-7350	PK-12	48,400	George Henry
Archdiocese of St. Paul	328 Kellogg Blvd W	Saint Paul, MN	55102-1900	651-291-4500	290-1628	PK-12	35,400	Martha Frauenheim
Diocese of St. Petersburg	PO Box 40200	St Petersburg, FL	33743-0200	727-347-5539	374-0209	PK-12	14,300	Dr. John Cummings
Diocese of Salina	PO Box 825	Salina, KS	67402-0825	785-827-8746	827-6133	PK-12	2,400	Dr. Nick Compagnone
Diocese of Salt Lake City	27 C St	Salt Lake City, UT	84103-2302	801-328-8641	328-8643	PK-12	5,400	Sr. Catherine Kamphaus
Diocese of San Angelo	PO Box 1829	San Angelo, TX	76902-1829	325-651-7500	651-6688	PK-8	700	Sr. Elizabeth Ann Swartz
Archdiocese of San Antonio	2718 W Woodlawn Ave	San Antonio, TX	78228-5195	210-734-2620	734-9112	PK-12	14,100	Sr. Carla Lusch
Diocese of San Bernardino	1201 E Highland Ave	San Bernardino, CA	92404-4607	909-475-5437	475-5477	PK-12	8,000	Patricia Vesely
Diocese of San Diego	PO Box 85728	San Diego, CA	92186-5728	858-490-8241	490-8272	PK-12	15,400	Stevan Laaperi
Archdiocese of San Francisco	1 Peter Yorke Way	San Francisco, CA	94109-6602	415-614-5660	614-5664	PK-12	26,200	Maureen Huntington
Diocese of San Jose	1150 N 1st St Ste 100	San Jose, CA	95112-4966	408-983-0185	983-0192	PK-12	16,500	Kathy Almazol
Archdiocese of Santa Fe	4000 Saint Josephs Pl NW	Albuquerque, NM	87120-1714	505-831-8173	831-8107	PK-12	5,500	Sr. Mary Klersey M.P.
Diocese of Santa Rosa	PO Box 6654	Santa Rosa, CA	95406-0654	707-566-3311	566-3382	PK-12	4,600	Dr. John Collins
Diocese of Savannah	601 E Liberty St	Savannah, GA	31401-5118	912-201-4121	201-4101	K-12	5,600	Sr. Rose Mary Collins
Diocese of Scranton	300 Wyoming Ave	Scranton, PA	18503-1243	570-207-2251	207-2261	PK-12	8,000	Joseph Casciano
Archdiocese of Seattle	710 9th Ave	Seattle, WA	98104-2017	206-382-4861	654-4651	PK-12	22,600	Joseph Tyson
Diocese of Shreveport	3500 Fairfield Ave	Shreveport, LA	71104-4108	318-219-7253	868-5057	PK-12	1,700	Sr. Carol Shively
Diocese of Sioux City	PO Box 3379	Sioux City, IA	51102-3379	712-255-7933	233-7598	PK-12	6,200	Dan Ryan
Diocese of Sioux Falls	523 N Duluth Ave	Sioux Falls, SD	57104-2714	605-988-3766	988-3795	PK-12	5,000	Matt Althoff
Diocese of Spokane	PO Box 1453	Spokane, WA	99210-1453	509-358-7330	358-7302	PK-12	4,300	Duane Schafer Ph.D.
Diocese of Springfield-Cape Girardeau	601 S Jefferson Ave	Springfield, MO	65806-3107	417-866-0841	866-1140	PK-12	4,400	Leon Witt
Diocese of Springfield	PO Box 3187	Springfield, IL	62708-3187	217-698-8500	698-8620	PK-12	11,300	Jean Johnson
Diocese of Springfield	PO Box 1730	Springfield, MA	01102-1730	413-452-0830	452-0555	PK-12	5,100	Sr. M. Andrea Ciszewski
Diocese of Steubenville	PO Box 969	Steubenville, OH	43952-5969	740-282-3631	282-3327	PK-12	2,300	Paul Ward
Diocese of Stockton	1105 N Lincoln St	Stockton, CA	95203-2410	209-466-0636	941-9722	PK-12	4,600	Sr. Marian Clare Valenteen
Diocese of Superior	PO Box 280	Haugen, WI	54841-0280	715-234-5044	234-5241	PK-8	2,500	Peggy Schoenfuss
Diocese of Syracuse	PO Box 511	Syracuse, NY	13202	315-470-1450	470-1470	PK-12	7,400	Christopher Mominey
Diocese of Toledo	PO Box 985	Toledo, OH	43697-0985	419-244-6711	244-4791	PK-12	22,400	Jack Altenburger
Diocese of Trenton	PO Box 5147	Trenton, NJ	08638-0147	609-406-7400	406-7416	PK-12	22,200	
Diocese of Tucson	PO Box 31	Tucson, AZ	85702-0031	520-792-3410	838-2589	PK-12	7,600	Sr. Rosa Maria Ruiz
Diocese of Tulsa	820 S Boulder Ave	Tulsa, OK	74119-1624	918-582-9177	582-1851	PK-12	4,500	Todd Goldsmith
Diocese of Tyler	1015 E Southeast Loop 323	Tyler, TX	75701-9656	903-534-1077	534-1370	PK-12	1,000	Dr. C. Charles LeBlanc
Diocese of Venice	1000 Pinebrook Rd	Venice, FL	34285-6426	941-484-9543	484-1121	PK-12	4,700	Dr. Kathleen Schwartz
Diocese of Victoria	PO Box 4070	Victoria, TX	77903-4070	361-573-0828	573-5725	PK-12	2,800	John Quary
Archdiocese of Washington DC	PO Box 29260	Washington, DC	20017-0260	301-853-4518	853-7670	PK-12	29,400	Dr. Patricia Weitzel-O'Neill
Diocese of Wheeling-Charleston	PO Box 230	Wheeling, WV	26003-0010	304-232-0444	233-8551	PK-12	6,500	Sr. Elaine Poitras Ph.D.
Diocese of Wichita	424 N Broadway St	Wichita, KS	67202-2310	316-269-3950	269-2486	PK-12	10,500	Bob Voboril
Diocese of Wilmington	1626 N Union St	Wilmington, DE	19806-2540	302-573-3133	573-6945	PK-12	14,000	Catherine Weaver
Diocese of Winona	PO Box 588	Winona, MN	55987-0588	507-454-4643	454-8106	PK-12	5,600	P.J. Thompson
Diocese of Worcester	49 Elm St	Worcester, MA	01609-2514	508-929-4317	929-4386	PK-12	8,600	
Diocese of Yakima	5301 Tieton Dr Ste B	Yakima, WA	98908-3479	509-965-7110	966-8334	PK-12	1,900	Rev. Thomas Kuykendall
Diocese of Youngstown	144 W Wood St	Youngstown, OH	44503-1081	330-744-8451	744-5099	K-12	9,500	Dr. Michael Skube

LUTHERAN SCHOOL SUPERINTENDENTS

LUTHERAN CHURCH MISSOURI SYNOD

1333 S Kirkwood Rd, Saint Louis, MO 63122-7295
Telephone 314-965-9000
Fax 996-1016
Website http://www.lcms.org

LUTHERAN SCHOOL SUPERINTENDENTS

Region	Address	City,State	Zip code	Telephone	Fax	Superintendent
Atlantic	171 White Plains Rd	Bronxville, NY	10708-1923	914-337-5700	337-7471	Dr. David Benke
California-Nevada-Hawaii	2772 Constitution Dr Ste A	Livermore, CA	94551-7571	925-245-4000	245-1107	Dr. Robert Newton
Central Illinois	1850 N Grand Ave W	Springfield, IL	62702-1626	217-793-1802	793-1822	Rev. David Bueltmann
Eastern	5111 Main St	Williamsville, NY	14221-5203	716-634-5111	634-5452	Robert Foerster
English	33100 Freedom Rd	Farmington, MI	48336-4030	248-476-0039	476-0188	Rev. David Stechholz
Florida-Georgia	7207 Monetary Dr	Orlando, FL	32809-5753	407-857-5556	857-5665	Mark Brink
Indiana	1145 Barr St	Fort Wayne, IN	46802-3135	260-423-1511	423-1514	Daniel May
Iowa East	1100 Blairs Ferry Rd	Marion, IA	52302-3093	319-373-2112	373-9827	Dr. Gary Arp
Iowa West	PO Box 1155	Fort Dodge, IA	50501-1155	515-576-7666	576-2323	Bob Riggert
Kansas	1000 SW 10th Ave	Topeka, KS	66604-1104	785-357-4441	357-5071	Jim Bradshaw
Michigan	3773 Geddes Rd	Ann Arbor, MI	48105-3028	734-665-3791	665-0255	
Mid-South	1675 Wynne Rd	Cordova, TN	38016-4905	901-373-1343	373-4826	Rev. Kenneth Lampe
Minnesota North	PO Box 604	Brainerd, MN	56401-0604	218-829-1781	829-0037	Rev. Donald Fondow
Minnesota South	14301 Grand Ave	Burnsville, MN	55306-5790	952-435-2550	435-2581	Dr. Lane Seitz
Missouri	660 Mason Ridge Center Dr	Saint Louis, MO	63141-8557	314-317-4550	317-4574	Dennis Gehrke
Montana	30 Broadwater Ave	Billings, MT	59101-1826	406-259-2908	259-1305	Rev. Terry Forke
Nebraska	PO Box 407	Seward, NE	68434-0407	888-643-2961	643-2990	Rev. Russ Sommerfeld
New England	400 Wilbraham Rd	Springfield, MA	01109-2723	413-783-0131	783-0909	Rev. James Keurulainen
New Jersey	1168 Springfield Ave	Mountainside, NJ	07092-2906	908-233-8111	233-3883	Rev. William Klettke
North Dakota	PO Box 9029	Fargo, ND	58106-9029	877-526-7633	293-9022	Dr. James Baneck
Northern Illinois	2301 S Wolf Rd	Hillside, IL	60162-2211	708-449-3020	449-3026	Rev. Dan Gilbert
Northwest	1700 NE Knott St	Portland, OR	97212-3301	503-288-8383	284-2785	Dr. Warren Schumacher
North Wisconsin	PO Box 8064	Wausau, WI	54402-8064	715-845-8241	845-3836	Rev. Joel Hoelter
Ohio	PO Box 38277	Olmsted Falls, OH	44138-0277	440-235-2297	235-1970	Rev. Terry Cripe
Oklahoma	308 NW 164th St	Edmond, OK	73013-2006	405-348-7600	384-7601	Rev. Barrie Henke
Pacific Southwest	1540 Concordia	Irvine, CA	92612-3203	949-854-3232	854-8140	Rachel Klitzing
Rocky Mountain	14334 E Evans Ave	Aurora, CO	80014-1408	303-695-8001	695-4047	Rev. Randall Golter
SELC	4850 S Lake Dr	Cudahy, WI	53110-1743	414-481-8286	481-0736	Rev. Carl Krueger
South Dakota	PO Box 89110	Sioux Falls, SD	57109-9110	605-361-1514	361-7959	Rev. Dale Sattgast
Southeastern	6315 Grovedale Dr	Alexandria, VA	22310-2501	703-971-9371	922-6047	Dr. Jon Diefenthaler
Southern	68446 Tammany Trace Dr Ste	Mandeville, LA	70471	504-282-2632	871-9696	Rev. Kurtis Schultz
Southern Illinois	2408 Lebanon Ave	Belleville, IL	62221-2529	618-234-4767	234-4830	Roger Sprengel
South Wisconsin	8100 W Capitol Dr	Milwaukee, WI	53222-1981	414-464-8100	464-0602	Gary Janetzke
Texas	7900 E Highway 290	Austin, TX	78724-2402	512-926-4272	926-1006	Dr. William Hinz
Wyoming	2400 S Hickory St	Casper, WY	82604-3471	307-265-9000	234-6629	Rev. Richard Boche

GENERAL CONFERENCE OF SEVENTH-DAY ADVENTISTS SUPERINTENDENTS

NORTH AMERICAN DIV. OFFICE OF EDUCATION
12501 Old Columbia Pike, Silver Spring, MD 20904-6601
Telephone 301-680-6440
Fax 680-6463
Website http://www.nadeducation.adventist.org

GENERAL CONFERENCE OF SEVENTH-DAY ADVENTISTS SUPERINTENDENTS

Conference	Address	City,State	Zip code	Telephone	Fax	Superintendent
Atlantic Union	**PO Box 1189**	**South Lancaster, MA**	**01561-1189**	**978-368-8333**	**368-7948**	**Astrid Thomassian**
Greater New York Conference	PO Box 5029	Manhasset, NY	11030-5029	516-627-9350	627-9272	David Cadavero
New York Conference	4930 W Seneca Tpke	Syracuse, NY	13215-2225	315-469-6921	469-6924	Stan Rouse M.A.
Northeastern Conference	11550 Merrick Blvd	Jamaica, NY	11434-1852	718-291-8006	739-5133	Pollyanna Barnes Ph.D.
Northern New England Conference	91 Allen Ave	Portland, ME	04103-3710	207-797-3760	797-2851	Trudy Wright M.A.
Southern New England Conference	PO Box 1169	South Lancaster, MA	01561-1169	978-365-4551	365-3838	Gary Swinyar
Columbia Union Conference	**5427 Twin Knolls Rd**	**Columbia, MD**	**21045-3200**	**410-997-3414**	**997-7420**	**Hamlet Canosa**
Allegheny East Conference	PO Box 266	Pine Forge, PA	19548-0266	610-326-4610	326-3946	James Willis M.Ed.
Allegheny West Conference	1339 E Broad St	Columbus, OH	43205-1588	614-252-5271	252-3246	
Chesapeake Conference	6600 Martin Rd	Columbia, MD	21044-3999	410-995-1910	995-1434	Carole Smith Ed.D.
Mountain View Conference	1400 Liberty St	Parkersburg, WV	26101-4124	304-422-4581	422-4582	Larry Boggess
New Jersey Conference	2160 US Highway 1	Trenton, NJ	08648-4447	609-392-7131	396-9273	Wayne Hancock Ed.D.
Ohio Conference	PO Box 1230	Mount Vernon, OH	43050-8230	740-397-4665	397-1648	E. Jay Colburn
Pennsylvania Conference	720 Museum Rd	Reading, PA	19611-1429	610-374-8331	374-9331	David Morgan
Potomac Conference	606 Greenville Ave	Staunton, VA	24401-4881	540-886-0771	886-5734	
Lake Union Conference	**PO Box 287**	**Berrien Springs, MI**	**49103-0287**	**269-473-8200**	**473-8209**	**Don Livesay**
Illinois Conference	619 Plainfield Rd Ste 200	Willowbrook, IL	60527-8438	630-734-0920	734-0929	James Martz
Indiana Conference	PO Box 1950	Carmel, IN	46082-1950	317-844-6201	571-9281	Mark Haynal M.A.
Lake Region Conference	8517 S State St	Chicago, IL	60619-5697	773-846-2661	846-5309	Ruth Horton
Michigan Conference	PO Box 19009	Lansing, MI	48901-9009	517-316-1500	316-1501	Linda Fuchs
Wisconsin Conference	PO Box 7310	Madison, WI	53707-7310	608-241-5235	837-9421	Kenneth Kirkham M.A.
Mid-America Union Conference	**PO Box 6128**	**Lincoln, NE**	**68506-0128**	**402-484-3000**	**483-4453**	**John Kriegelstein**
Central States Conference	3301 Parallel Pkwy	Kansas City, KS	66104-4354	913-371-1071	371-1609	Desiree Bryant M.A.
Dakota Conference	PO Box 520	Pierre, SD	57501-0520	605-224-8868	224-7886	Leonard Quaile
Iowa-Missouri Conference	PO Box 65665	West Des Moines, IA	50265-0665	515-223-1197	223-5692	Gary Rouse M.A.
Kansas-Nebraska Conference	3440 SW Urish Rd	Topeka, KS	66614-4601	785-478-4726	478-1000	Gary Kruger
Minnesota Conference	7384 Kirkwood Ct	Maple Grove, MN	55369-5200	763-424-8923	424-9576	Pamela Consuegra M.S.
Rocky Mountain Conference	2520 S Downing St	Denver, CO	80210-5818	303-282-3650	733-1843	Pat Chapman
North Pacific Union Conference	**5709 N 20th St**	**Ridgefield, WA**	**98642-7724**	**360-857-7000**	**857-7001**	**Alan Hurlbert M.Ed.**
Alaska Conference	6100 OMalley Rd	Anchorage, AK	99507-6958	907-346-1004	346-3279	John Kriegelstein M.Ed.
Idaho Conference	7777 W Fairview Ave	Boise, ID	83704-8418	208-375-7524	375-7526	Paulette Jackson
Montana Conference	175 Canyon View Rd	Bozeman, MT	59715-0607	406-587-3101	587-1598	Archie Harris
Oregon Conference	13455 SE 97th Ave	Clackamas, OR	97015-8662	503-652-2225	794-4286	John Gatchet
Upper Columbia Conference	PO Box 19039	Spokane, WA	99219-9039	509-838-2761	838-4882	
Washington Conference	3450 S 344th Way Ste 200	Federal Way, WA	98001-9540	253-681-6008	681-6009	Lon Gruesbeck M.A.
Pacific Union Conference	**PO Box 5005**	**Westlake Vlg, CA**	**91359-5005**	**805-413-7314**	**413-7319**	**Dr. Kelly Bock**
Arizona Conference	PO Box 12340	Scottsdale, AZ	85267-2340	480-991-6777	991-4833	Ivan Weiss M.A.
Central California Conference	PO Box 770	Clovis, CA	93613-0770	559-347-3000	347-3120	Vern Biloff M.A.
Hawaii Conference	2728 Pali Hwy	Honolulu, HI	96817	808-595-7591	595-2345	Teryl Loeffler M.Ed.
Nevada-Utah Conference	PO Box 10730	Reno, NV	89510-0730	775-322-6929	954-0005	Larry Unterseher
Northern California Conference	PO Box 23165	Pleasant Hill, CA	94523-0165	925-685-4300	685-4380	Berit VonPohle
Southeastern California Conference	PO Box 8050	Riverside, CA	92515-8050	951-509-2200	509-2390	Donald Dudley
Southern California Conference	PO Box 969	Glendale, CA	91209-0969	818-546-8400	546-8454	Richard Carey
Southern Union Conference	**PO Box 849**	**Decatur, GA**	**30031-0849**	**404-299-1832**	**299-9726**	**Conrad Gill M.A.**
Carolina Conference	PO Box 560339	Charlotte, NC	28256-0339	704-596-3200	596-5775	Jim Davidson
Florida Conference	PO Box 2626	Winter Park, FL	32790-2626	407-644-5000	644-7550	Jim Epperson Ed.D.
Georgia-Cumberland Conference	PO Box 12000	Calhoun, GA	30703-7001	706-629-7951	526-3684	Cynthia Gettys Ph.D.
Gulf States Conference	PO Box 240249	Montgomery, AL	36124-0249	334-272-7493	272-7987	Dr. Rita Henriguez-Green
Kentucky-Tennessee Conference	PO Box 1088	Goodlettsville, TN	37070-1088	615-859-1391	859-2120	Larry Boughman Ph.D.
South Atlantic Conference	PO Box 92447	Atlanta, GA	30314-0447	404-792-0535	792-7817	Pennie Lister-Smith
South Central Conference	PO Box 78767	Nashville, TN	37207-8767	615-226-6500	262-9141	Erma Lee
Southeastern Conference	1701 Robie Ave	Mount Dora, FL	32757-6339	352-735-3142	735-3562	Elisa Young
Southwestern Union Conference	**PO Box 4000**	**Burleson, TX**	**76097-1630**	**817-295-0476**	**447-2443**	**Doug Walker M.A.**
Arkansas-Louisiana Conference	PO Box 31000	Shreveport, LA	71130-1000	318-631-6240	631-6247	Don Hevener M.A.
Oklahoma Conference	PO Box 32098	Oklahoma City, OK	73123-0298	405-721-6110	721-7594	Jack Francisco
Southwest Region Conference	PO Box 226289	Dallas, TX	75222-6289	214-943-4491	946-2528	Shakuntala Ramsarran
Texas Conference	PO Box 800	Alvarado, TX	76009-0800	817-790-2255	783-5266	Bonnie Eder Ed.D.
Texico Conference	PO Box 1366	Corrales, NM	87048-1366	505-244-1611	244-1811